66

A LOVE SUPREME · JOHN COLTRANE
stereo

SYMPHONICA | GEORGE MICHÆL

HI
MIRACLES

SENSATIONAL
AMERICAN
HIT-MAKERS

INTROSPECTIVE/PET SHOP BOYS/LIMITED EDITION

RECORD COLLECTOR'S
RARE RECORD PRICE GUIDE

Mötörhead

HEX ENDUCTION HOUR
BY THE FALL

Beyoncé

SABBATH

Blade

ELVIS

RCA VICTOR

FLAMING STAR &
SUMMER KISSES

TIME OF THE LAST PERSECUTION

BILL FAY

DAVID BOWIE STARMAN LYRICS
SOLD £204,000

SIGNED BEATLES PROGRAMME & BAG
SOLD £44,600

SOLD £34,700

SOLD £29,700

SOLD £20,400

SOLD £27,200

SOLD £23.430

SOLD £13,560

SOLD £13,070

SOLD £8,015

SOLD £4,680

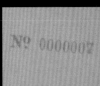

SOLD £23,000

THE ROLLING STONES - 'SATANIC MAJESTIES' ACETATE
SOLD £11,600

T-Rex RIDE A WHITE SWAN / JEWEL / SUMMERTIME BLUES ACETATE
SOLD £9,900

QUEEN BOHEMIAN RHAPSODY - 1978 BLUE VINYL
SOLD £6,800

PlasticWax**Records**

222 Cheltenham Rd, Bristol BS6 5QU

Serving music lovers since 1978

Plastic Wax Records is Bristol's longest established independent record shop with the largest range of used vinyl and CDs in the South West, including rare collector editions. We cover most genres: Rock, Reggae, Soul, Punk, Hip Hop, Prog, Indie, Electronica, Ska, Funk, African, Country, Jazz, Classical and Soundtracks.

We offer special discounts for bulk purchases so please enquire for details.

Looking to sell? We are constantly looking to purchase good quality stock so if you are looking to sell your collection or even rare single records or CDs, please contact us.

FLASHBACK RECORDS

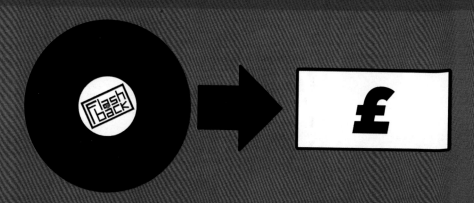

RCRRPG CONTENTS

The handover, August 30, 2022.
Editor Emeritus Ian Shirley (L)
— the longest serving chief of
the tome — pictured here at the
weigh-in with new incumbent,
Daryl Easlea.

EDITOR
Daryl Easlea

DESIGN & PRODUCTION
Val Cutts
Yura Surkov

ADVERTISING MANAGER
Bill Edwards

MARKETING MANAGER
Kiran Summan

RECORD COLLECTOR EDITOR
Paul Lester

PUBLISHER
David Saunders

SINCERE THANKS
Tim Jones/Sue Maritz/Peter Barry/Bruno Irace/
Brenda Cobb/Aabha Barve/Daniel Rodrigues/
Johnny Sharp/Rebecca Marsh

Published in the United Kingdom 2024 by Diamond Publishing Ltd.
4th Floor, Harmsworth House, 13-15, Bouverie Street, London EC4Y 8DP

Copyright © 2024 Diamond Publishing Ltd.

All rights reserved

Founded by Sean O'Mahony in 1986.

diamondpublishing
PART OF THE METROPOLIS GROUP

ISBN 978-1-916421-97-4

WELCOME TO *RECORD COLLECTOR'S RARE RECORD PRICE GUIDE*

Hello and welcome to the 18th edition of *Record Collector's Rare Record Price Guide*, the largest and most comprehensive book of its kind. Its publication coincides with the 45th anniversary of *Record Collector*, the UK's longest running popular music magazine and the world's leading periodical in its field. Whether you have been with us since the beginning, or this is your first time, it's a great pleasure to have you along, we hope the book gives you many happy hours of discovery and reconnection with your music collection.

Record Collector's Rare Record Price Guide – established by *Beatles Book* and *Record Collector* founder Sean 'Johnny Dean' O'Mahony – grew out of the discographies that the original A5 magazine contained. An experienced and inventive publisher, O'Mahony had been instrumental in the success of *Parker's Car Price Guide*, and he ascertained that buying a record was similar to purchasing a motor. It wasn't simply a question of how well it drove, but its condition, year of make and the quality of its upholstery all affected its value. If even the swankiest Bentley had an enormous prang, its value would plummet – just as if that stereo first pressing of *Please Please Me* had a scratch running right through it.

After the tentative first edition of RCRRPG (dated 1987, but published in 1986), the book started its once-every-24-month cycle in 1993. Compiled by the expert research team of *Record Collector*, and edited by a list of names that have since gone onto music writing legend (see p.1231), the goal of this book is simple, and like the song, remains the same: to attempt to list and value every collectable pop and rock record issued in the UK since 1950.

The early editions of the book were a positive boon to dealers and collectors alike; wool could not be pulled over eyes as the detailed grading system identified a record's worth – based on meticulous research and conversations with many respected heads. As regular readers will already know, *Record Collector's Rare Record Price Guide* doesn't just include vinyl singles, EPs and LPs, it also provides information about every other way in which recorded music has been sold over the last 70 years or more, from the shellac 1950s to the digital 2020s. Although most items listed in this book could be broadly described as 'rock' or 'pop', every aspect of recorded music outside of the specialist classical field is covered.

This, the 18th edition, is my first Guide as editor, and in many ways, I see this as a transitional volume, incorporating the very best of all the things people have loved over the past 30 years, while beginning the process of fundamental change. Like all 18-year-olds, it's full of ambition and dreams. Think of it as an historic building, say, a hotel, undergoing renovation: the exterior, foyer and premium rooms have been renovated – work is underway on the ballroom, yet some of the bedrooms at the back are just being started.

My intention, as a life-long music fan as much as anything else, is to appreciate and embrace the book's natural limitations. When completed in August 2024, it should be the best snapshot there can be of the market as it stands. My long term aim is to make the book and website as one, evolving with the mores of the day. No matter how obscure your tastes, you'll find the most sought-after items here whether your passion is MOR, freakbeat, soul, blues, soundtracks, post-punk, disco, house, lovers rock, psychedelia, hip hop, reggae, NWOBHM, Northern, British jazz, folk, shoegaze, prog or indie. If it's collectable, and it was released in the UK, then you'll find it in *Record Collector's Rare Record Price Guide*.

HOW MUCH?

The question we're often asked about the prices listed in this book is how we arrive at them. The answer is: a mix of our 45 years of experience in the field; our ongoing research into the latest prices at record fairs, shops, and sales both via auction and online; and the invaluable help of a dedicated and extremely knowledgeable team of consultants and experts, who themselves regularly buy and sell items in their specialist areas.

Of course, there is no *fixed* value for a second-hand record, no matter how rare it may be. In some ways, editing *Record Collector's Rare Record Price Guide* is the poisoned chalice that people repeatedly inform me it is – how can a price be **THE** price? Many people have blamed the *RCRRPG* over the years for taking the fun out of dipping into the charity shop and bagging a genuine bargain. Well, there are still bargains to be found out there, while in other situations like a feverishly competitive online auction, particularly sought-after items can fetch prices way above their 'book' value. The price of a rare record is purely determined by what people are prepared to pay for it. I, like many of you, have sat in auctions or watched online in wonder as £100 albums sell for 10 times that price.

Our scrutiny of the collecting market since the start of the 1980s allows us to make the best possible judgement about the records in this book. Prices may vary from one part of the country to another, or depending whether a disc is being sold in a shop, an auction house, via an advert in *Record Collector*, at a major international fair, or on internet sites like 991.com, Discogs, Popsike, Raresoulman or eBay. But we believe that the guide values we list are the most realistic you'll find anywhere.

The other important point, which can't be repeated often enough, is that anyone selling records to a professional dealer can't expect to raise more than 50 per cent of the price listed here, except in very unusual cases. It doesn't matter whether you're selling rock'n'roll or jewellery, the same basic mark-up applies right across the collecting field, to cover the dealer's costs and profit margin. If you're selling directly to another collector, however, face-to-face or over the internet, you can hope to obtain the prices we list or more, though please remember that all the values in this book are for records in perfect 'Mint' condition. To find out what you should be paying or charging, for a record in less than perfect condition, check in our legendary Ready Reckoner.

WHAT'S IN?

Although many of the most valuable items listed in *Record Collector's Rare Record Price Guide* cover the past six decades, record collecting is not all about the distant past. As you turn the pages, you'll find plenty of releases from the last two decades and collectables by major artists like Taylor Swift, for example, alongside albums by Paul Weller or new rarities which were on sale one day (especially Record Store Day) and became fiendishly hard to track down even a few weeks later. A great amount of the vinyl pressings of the past decade have been, although not stated, limited editions, as the demand may have only meant a few thousand copies of a new album or reissue would have been made. Hence, there are some occasions where the reissue from the 2010s will be listed higher than a first pressing. Also, the sharp decline in vinyl demand in the 00s has led to some deeply surprising collectables – LPs made in strictly limited numbers are well into three figures, while the CDs that were then omnipresent are worth pence.

But there are some things you can't predict, like the next old 7" worth £15 today, which will be worth £60 in three months time. Or bands who were sizzlingly collectable one year and saw their prices tumbling the next. Also, don't forget that virtually every record listed in this book, even the ones worth thousands of pounds, were once available for a few pounds. For all those thousands of releases which have already become collector's items, however, *Record Collector's Rare Record Price Guide* tells you what they are, what they look like, and how much they're going to cost. In the past, there has been a policy of waiting a number of years before adding releases into the book. I have taken a far broader view with this, as I think the beauty of the *RCRRPG* should be, that, like a football league, a team can rise from nowhere, top the league one year, and be back in non-league several years later. Will Taylor turn out to be Brighton & Hove Albion or Southend United?

THE STATE OF THE MARKET

According to the *Official Charts Company*, 6.1 million new records were purchased in 2023, up 11.8 per cent on the previous year. To underline how deeply the 'vinyl revival' has penetrated the popular psyche in the UK, in March 2024, the Consumer Price Index (CPI) added, as well as air fryers, 'vinyl records' to its basket – alongside gluten-free bread and sunflower seeds to monitor inflation. In the final days of a political administration that few relished, out from the list tumbled hand sanitiser and blow-up beds, and in came our beloved long-player.

LOOK WHAT YOU MADE ME DO

Part of that is undoubtedly the so-called 'Taylor Swift effect' which turned a lot of non-traditional buyers onto the album – a format the all-conquering songstress champions – but now, Tay-Tay or no Tay-Tay, sales of vinyl, whether it be brand new or via a record/boot fair/charity shop, are strong. It is easy for the old school to scoff at the joy of younger collectors holding a re-press of a Beatles album, but, how lovely, we say – the more the merrier. Albums that were once strictly fodder are now climbing in price, as new generations, free from the shackles of what a journalist once wrote in 1974, dip in and show little fear. Fleetwood Mac's *Rumours* is an obvious example; new copies in the shops are priced to sell at around £20, while a good nick first press is around £35. A couple of decades ago, it was a charity shop special. If you picked one up for more than a fiver, you'd gone to the posh part of town. And so it goes .

So, what a beautiful place to be. For many readers, for whom the joy and mystique of albums has never dimmed, the pleasure of seeing new listeners joining the fray is extremely heartening. In this, my first *RCRRPG* as editor, I am very aware in my role that I am standing on the shoulders of giants. Back then, verifying a catalogue number meant a true leap of faith in dealer knowledge, or a consultation of the *Music Master*, the other 'Big Red Book' of our childhoods (Eamonn Andrews, of course – one of the very few TV presenters to be immortalised by Soft Machine – brandished the other one); not today's procession of clicks where information can both be ascertained and corroborated.

IT'S LIKE THE 70s, MAN

Any vinyl revival though, means a proliferation of formats and just like it was in the late 70s, the market is now awash with all the gimmicks to maintain a record's sales. However, whereas then it was one thing to stick out limited picture discs, now, discrete versions of releases are targeted to different parts of a fanbase. Multiple releases cater to official artist sites, and then to Amazon, HMV and indies all have different limited versions. To return to Tay-Tay (and this editor is resolutely onside), her album *The Tortured Poets Department* came in 34 different versions. *34*. That's at least 31 more than *Sgt. Pepper* had in 1967. Multi-formatting can lead to completist overload, but then, in some respects, 'twas ever thus. It's like the 70s, man.

Another fascinating development in the realm of collecting has been the popularity of the White Label Auction, which began in 2019 in aid of the BRIT Trust. Test-pressings, as many will know through the Guide across the years, were once the preserve of industry insiders, sent out to approve final pressings of an album. These first-off-the-press copies were typically sent to the artists, managers, mastering engineers and A&Rs to check over. Once approved, copies were archived, and with only five or 10 usually being produced, inevitably they were highly prized by superfans and collectors. By the time the first wave of the LP's comeback was complete, Johnny Chandler, industry veteran, A&R and Cultural Projects Director at Universal Music Recordings, saw an opportunity to make these largely overlooked artefacts come to life. Chandler, who ran his own record shop, Division One, in London in the 90s was a frequent contributor to *RC* back in the day, spearheaded the auction, and demonstrated how easily collecting could go down new routes. Over four auctions to date, more than £150,000 has been raised for charity, which has truly shone a light on collecting and the importance of vinyl to people's lives. Look out for these tags: @WhiteLabelAuct #WhiteLabelAuction. All of this stimulates interest and longevity in the collecting market.

HAVE GAVEL, WILL TRAVEL

One of the most heartening things as a new editor was looking at the existing prices in the book. There are, of course, many fluctuations, but, thanks to the skill and judgement of my delightful predecessor, Ian Shirley, and his team, there are few seismic changes, and a good proportion of previous prices remain in the right ballpark. RC watched the online auction which sold off the collection of writer, DJ and tremendous egg, Danny Baker. RC was heartened to see the big hitters all falling not far from the prices RCRRPG has suggested.

Danny's actions – met with some incredulity by Bob Stanley in RC earlier in 2024 – have chimed with many fervent collectors. People are getting older, and the thought of what may happen to their collection in future years has led to a spate of sales. In fact, the very subject of collecting had inspired several university dissertations in recent years: As academic Holly Lippold writes in her MA thesis, As Long As It Doesn't End Up In The Charity Shop: Thematic Analysis Exploring The Vinyl Record Collection As An Extension Of Self-Identity In Male Mid-Life, "the vinyl record collection may ground owner memories, evoke nostalgia and provide a link between past and current identity." Music is, of course, all about identity and memory, and frankly, that is why we do what we do. Billy Edwards, a 21-year-old Graduate from Cardiff University wrote A World Before I Was Born: How Can We Explain The Resurgence Behind Vinyl Records As A Music Format In The Last Decade And Its Long-Time Avid Collector Fandom? Edwards says there needs to be a greater recognition for "the younger and more casual portion of music fandom", which will "demonstrate that the format's audience has evolved beyond the 'audiophile' phenomenon". All are welcome at RCRRPG, and the fact that collections are being shown and shared is fabulous for the love of music, no matter what you may be into. Collectors are a diverse bunch, and now collecting feels more mainstream than ever. The vinyl revival of the past decade has made LPs respectable again, especially when there was a time that the Compact Disc looked as if would win out.

And yet... CDs are not completely over. Many who made the wholesale switch from vinyl in the 90s are reluctant to part or change again. These listeners use streaming services as an all-you-can-eat buffet, but then, if they really want to savour a dish, they will go to a specialist restaurant and enjoy it there – the record or CD shop. As vinyl prices, old and new, continue to accelerate, CDs seem attractively inexpensive, especially some of the beautifully packaged collections that were released in the early 2000s.

OLD WARHORSES HOLDING VALUE

This RCRRPG will be a transitional volume, offering a 'safe space' (to use the current parlance), a sense check, a voice of reason away from the big shouty excitement of paying over the odds for things online leading to inflated prices that people hold as gospel.

In summary, it seems that the old warhorses seem to be holding their value, with something of a decline in 50s prices; the demand and values for scarce 90s/00s and current limited vinyl is sky high. The key original pressings of Britpop, and the catalogue of Oasis especially, have increased significantly in value; metal has remained strong, and the demand for punk and post-punk is shown in strong figures. Soul, Northern and reggae are all buoyant. Bolstered by creating the instant collectible of Now And Then (HOW much will the 10" be worth when the dust has settled?), The Beatles remain, um, fab. Vinyl champion Jack White is creating instant collectables, too. All is well.

HOW GET THE MOST FROM THE GUIDE

PRICING YOUR RECORDS

Although *Record Collector's Rare Record Price Guide* contains a comprehensive listing of collectable UK releases, it does NOT list all the recordings made by the artists we've included. More detailed discographies of important artists can be found every month in *Record Collector* magazine or at www.rarerecordpriceguide.com

MINIMUM VALUES FOR INCLUSION

Only those releases which are currently sold at the minimum values listed below have been included. Any other releases sell for less than these prices.

7" SINGLES, MAXI-SINGLES, CASSETTE SINGLES, DOUBLE PACKS, 78s, 10" SINGLES, EPs & 12" SINGLES, BLU-RAYS, LPs & PICTURE DISCS: £15

CD SINGLES & CD ALBUMS: £30

CURRENT MINT VALUES

The prices listed in this book are for the original issues of records, cassettes and CDs in MINT condition. Bear in mind that most records which turn up will not be in Mint condition and their value will be affected accordingly. To find out the value of any item which is in less than Mint condition, consult our Grading System and the Ready Reckoner.

ALPHABETICAL ORDER

The artists in this Guide are listed in alphabetical order, from A to Z. After the alphabetical listings, there is a section of Various Artists compilation releases, divided into several sections covering singles and 50s & 60s EPs, 70s, 80s & 90s EPs, LPs, film soundtrack LPs, library music and tax dodge records. The alphabetical order within the Guide has been determined by the first letter of a group name or an artist's surname. The order follows the usual alphabetical principle of 'reading through' an artist's name or title, so that (for example) 'Peter Gabriel' is listed before 'Gabriel's Angels', and 'Generation X' is listed before 'Gen X'. Names and titles which include numbers appear as if the number was spelt out in full; e.g. the band '23 Skidoo' are listed as if their name was styled 'Twenty Three Skidoo'.

CHRONOLOGICAL ORDER

Within each artist entry, records are listed in chronological order of release. Singles are listed first; then EPs; and then, LPs (including cassette and CD albums). In the case of long entries, different formats of releases have also been grouped together under separate headers to make them easier to find.

PACKAGING AND INSERTS

All prices refer to records with all their original packaging and inserts (where applicable) intact. Wherever possible, we have provided details of inserts and special items of packaging for each entry – pointing out gatefold sleeves, lyric inserts and general ephemera like posters. Any record with some or all of these additional items missing will obviously be worth less than the values listed here. The level of depreciation depends on the missing items: in some cases, the value of an album can be dramatically reduced without its collectable insert while in others, it is the record itself that is desirable, and the insert is only of secondary importance.

PICTURE SLEEVES

Since 1978, most singles have been issued in picture sleeves. Before 1978, however, picture covers were the exception in the UK rather than the rule. All those singles which originally appeared in a picture sleeve are listed with the abbreviation (p/s). Most singles from the 1950s, 1960s and early 1970s were issued in 'company' sleeves, carrying the name and logo of the label which issued the record. Unless a picture sleeve is indicated, the prices listed in this guide are for singles with their company sleeves intact and, like the records themselves, in Mint condition. Many collectors are not too concerned about company sleeves – although in isolated cases (like the cult 60s label Planet), the company sleeves can be harder to find than the records themselves.

Company sleeves don't usually have much effect on a record's value. For example, an original Creation single from 1966, valued at £45, may only be worth £35 without its Planet company sleeve. At the other extreme, no 60s collector is going to be bothered if a copy of a rarity like Searchin' In The Wilderness by Allen Pound's Get Rich comes in a plain sleeve, or indeed, no sleeve at all – what matters here is that the record is in Mint condition.

FREEBIES & INSERTS

Two prices have been listed for those items which were available in more than one form. 'Freebie' singles given away with newspapers and magazines have two values: the first for the record with the publication, the second for the disc itself. Records which were issued only briefly with an insert, like a poster or lyric sheet, are often priced both with and without the extra packaging.

CHANGES IN DESIGN

Two or more prices have been given for records which were released more than once with the same catalogue number, but in slightly different form – with a change of label colour or sleeve design (for instance, the substitution of triangular centres by round centres on late 1950s singles), or the manufacture of more recent singles in a variety of different coloured vinyl. These variations of packaging and presentation can make an enormous difference to the value of a record, which is why we have documented them here. They help collectors identify the first pressing or edition of each release, which is almost always more sought-after than later issues of the same record. One notable example is the first edition of the Beatles' *Please Please Me* LP, which featured the black-and-gold Parlophone label for a few weeks, before the introduction of the more modern-looking yellow-and-black label. Black-and-gold copies of the stereo version of this LP are worth up to £6,000, while standard yellow and black label later pressings are worth between £3,000 and £500. Occasionally, second pressings can be worth more than the originals, as was the case with early Shadows and Cliff Richard singles. Green label copies of these 45s sold in their millions, while later re-pressings on black labels are much scarcer. So always check which pressing of any record you are buying before parting with your money.

MONO AND STEREO

In the case of EPs and LPs from the 1950s and 1960s, mono and stereo releases often have different values – and different catalogue numbers. Both prices are listed with the separate catalogue numbers for the two versions of each release (mono first, then stereo). Where the mono and stereo editions are worth the same amount, only one price has been listed. The last few years have seen a polarisation in the prices between mono and stereo pressings – increasingly so for those late mono releases from 1968 to 1970, when the single-channelled format was being phased out in favour of the twin-tracked stereo. Similarly, early stereo copies have proved to be sound investments.

UK RELEASES AND EXPORT ISSUES

Only UK releases are included in *Record Collector's Rare Record Price Guide*, not overseas issues. The exceptions to this rule are a handful of folk releases and U2 singles, all from the Irish Republic, which were heavily imported into Britain, but not officially issued here. The other exceptions are 'Export Releases'. These were manufactured in the UK in the 1950s and 1960s by companies like EMI and Decca for distribution to countries which didn't have their own pressing plants. Because they were pressed in very small quantities, and then distributed to the furthest corners of the globe, export records by artists like the Beatles, Pink Floyd and the Rolling Stones are often worth many times the values of similar items pressed for the UK.

UK RELEASES PRESSED OVERSEAS

Although the great majority of the records we've listed were manufactured in the UK, not all UK releases were made in this country – or vice versa. For example, a large proportion of The Rolling Stones' US singles on the London label in the 1960s were actually manufactured in Britain. More recently, many British releases by major labels – notably Warner – have been made in Europe and sent in identical form to Britain and many other countries. In these cases, the record sleeves often carry many different catalogue numbers, to cater for every country where the records are being distributed. The problem of identifying the country where a particular record has been issued has grown more difficult with the advent of CDs. In these cases, it is the packaging that helps you identify the origin of a particular CD, rather than the disc itself.

78 rpm RELEASES

The common misconception about 78s is that they are more valuable than 7" singles. In fact, the opposite is true in most cases, as far more 78s were sold in the 1950s than 45 rpm 7" singles. The last batches of 78s issued from 1958 to 1960 are the main exception to this rule (see Eddie Cochran's entry, for example). As these were often only available in small quantities, as the public switched to 45s, or even by special order, they can prove to be much harder to find than their 45rpm equivalents.

COMMERCIAL RELEASES, NOT PROMOS

In general, this Guide only includes records which were manufactured for commercial release, or for distribution in some way to the public – as a freebie with a magazine, for example. Promotional records, demos, acetates and test-pressings have not usually been included, apart from exceptional cases where these items actually reached the public, or where (as with artists like the pre-Iron Maiden act, Urchin) one promo single has become so famous among collectors that it would have been misleading for it not to be mentioned. The major exceptions to this rule are artists like The Beatles, and acts like Pet Shop Boys, Depeche Mode and Madonna, whose promos – often with extended and hard to find remixes – are sometimes more valuable than their commercial releases and highly sought after by their fans. Also, although we have included some CDR promo releases this market is no longer vibrant. Some collectors still want them – especially completists – in theory, watermarked and numbered CDRs should not be sold commercially. Full details of the values of non-commercial rarities like promos, demos, acetates and test pressings can be found in the articles and discographies in *Record Collector* every month.

IMPORTANT NOTE

Every effort has been taken to ensure that the information contained in *Record Collector's Rare Record Price Guide* is as accurate and up to date as possible. However, the publishers cannot take any responsibility for any errors or omissions; nor can they be held responsible or liable for any loss or damage to any person acting on the information in this Guide. The publishers welcome any corrections or additions to the Guide, which will be considered for future editions; mail me: daryl.easlea@emap.com

A BRIEF SUMMARY

ALL PRICES REFER TO RECORDS AND PACKAGING IN MINT CONDITION
(See Grading System and Ready Reckoner)

ARTISTS AND GROUPS are listed in alphabetical order. Numerical names (e.g. 10cc are listed as if the numbers are spelt in full).

ALL RECORDS LISTED ARE UK COMMERCIAL RELEASES
with the following exceptions:
(1) Records pressed in the UK for export overseas.
(2) Important demo or promo releases.
(3) Records or flexidiscs included as freebies with magazines, books and other records.

In general, promo and demo editions are not included, except when these records contain unique material and/or packaging or are by major collectable artists.

EACH ENTRY includes:

LPS & SINGLES 7", 45s & cassettes, 10" singles & flexidiscs, EPs & 12"s, picture discs valued at £15 or more

CD SINGLES AND ALBUMS valued at £30 or more

Records worth less than these prices have not been included, but can be found on www.rarerecordpriceguide.com

WITHIN EACH ENTRY records are listed in chronological order of release, within each of the following categories (where applicable): 78s, SINGLES, EPs, LPs, CDs, PROMOS. The exceptions are major artists like ABBA, The Beatles, The Rolling Stones and Elvis Presley, where the entry is further divided into originals, reissues and label variations.

ABBREVIATIONS

alt	alternative	vers	version
BD	blu-ray disc	EP	extended-play record
cass.	cassette	vol	volume
p/s	picture sleeve	ext	extended
cat. no.	catalogue number	w/	with
pic disc	picture disc	flexi	flexidisc
CD	compact disc	w/l	white label
pt(s)	part(s)	g/f(old)	gatefold sleeve
co.	company	2CD	double CD
RSD.	Record Store Day	inst	instrumental
sl	sleeve	2LP	double LP
SDE	Super Deluxe Edition	intl.	international
d/pack	double pack	2 x 45	two 45rpm singles
st	stereo	LP	long-playing record
stkr	sticker	3LP	triple LP
t/p	test pressing	m/s	mono/stereo
edn	edition	78	78rpm single

IMPORTANT RECORD COMPANY ABBREVIATIONS

Amalgam	Amalgamated
B. Banquet	Beggars Banquet
B'full/Brains	Bucketfull Of Brains
Ch' Herring	Chopped Herring
Col	Columbia
DGM	Discipline Global Mobile
E. Antenna	Esoteric Antenna
Elek	Elektra
Font	Fontana
L.T.E.Vinyl	Let Them Eat Vinyl
L.T.T. Slaughter	Lambs To The Slaughter
M.F.N	Music For Nations
MFP	Music For Pleasure
M. Minor	Major Minor
M.O.Vinyl	Music On Vinyl
Parl	Parlophone
PSI	Phil Spector International
Pye Intl	Pye International
R. Digest	Readers Digest
Regal Zono	Regal Zonophone
R. Stones	Rolling Stones
S'side	Stateside
St.Tones	Street Tones
T. Motown	Tamla Motown
UA	United Artists
Warner(s)	Warner Brothers
WRC	World Record Club

TERMS USED IN *RCRRPG*

acetate	One-off disc cut by hand in a mastering studio, used for demonstration
adaptor	Plastic outer disc clipped onto 3" CDs to make them compatible with 5" CD players
art sleeve	Pictorial cover using graphics rather than photographs or drawings
artwork	Original design for sleeves or labels
audiophile pressing	High quality pressing for hi-fi enthusiasts
Black Friday	A mini-version of Record Store Day (RSD), the last Friday in November; has yet to really take off in UK
blister pack	Shaped outer PVC packaging, usually for 3" CDs
blu-ray disc (BD)	Highest quality physical method (bar SACD) of delivery of specialist hi-fi releases such as in Dolby Atmos
bonus disc	Disc given away free with another disc
bootleg	Illegal pressing of unissued material
box set	Records or CDs in presentation case
budget release	Pressing which retailed below full-price
catalogue number	Manufacturer's reference number on record labels and sleeves
CDR	One-off CD, digital equivalent of acetate
CDROM	Audio/visual computer-compatible CD
CD Video	5" CD containing several audio tracks and (usually) one video track; now obsolete
company sleeve	Standard non-picture sleeve for singles, printed with name or logo of label
counterfeit	Illegal reproduction of official release (unlike pirating which is an illegal REPACKAGE of material)
DAT	Digital audio tape
deleted	No longer commercially available
dead wax	US term for run-out groove
demo	Record issued for demonstration purposes
die-cut sleeve	Sleeve with circular hole cut into the centre
digipak	Gatefold CD sleeve with plastic inner tray
dink	Colloquial term for 7"s with large centre hole. Also can mean the adapter itself.
DJ-only	Record issued for radio airplay only
(Dolby) Atmos	Spatial surround sound format, often sold physically on Blu-Ray
double groove	Record with two grooves pressed concentrically on same side
double-pack	Two singles issued together as one package
DVDA	Digital versatile disc – Audio
DVD	Digital versatile disc
8-track cartridge	1970s tape format, popular for in-car entertainment; now obsolete
EP	Extended play disc, with four or more tracks, usually in a picture sleeve
EPK	Electronic press kit; i.e. short promo-only documentary available on video
ephemera	Replica documents such as lanyards, badges, stuff, often inside 21st-century box sets
envelope p/s	Large mailing-type cover with envelope-style foldover flap
etched disc	One-sided vinyl record with laser-etched graphics (eg group's signatures) on other side
export issue	Record or CD pressed in the UK for sale exclusively overseas
factory custom pressing	Unofficial record pressed after hours (usually on coloured vinyl) at official pressing plant
flexidisc	Thin, flexible record, usually issued free with magazine, etc.
flipback sleeve	LP or EP cover glued together with card flaps from the front folded over onto the back
foldaround/foldout/ foldover sleeve	Sleeve which opens out as a poster, etc.
freebie	Record given away free of charge
gatefold sleeve	Double-size sleeve opening out like a book
half-speed	21st vogue for mastering an LP at half speed, thus enhancing sound quality
hype sticker	US term for marketing sticker, often attached to shrink wrap to 'hype' the product therein.
import	Record or CD pressed abroad but sold in the UK

inlay	Printed paper booklet with CD packaging
insert	Loose item included as part of a record's packaging
interview album	Spoken-word record, often used as promo
jewel case	Standard clear plastic case for cassettes and CDs
jukebox centre	Plastic centre inserted into record with large centre hole, also known as dink or spider
jukebox issue	Record issued exclusively to jukebox franchise holders
laminated sleeve	Cover with high-gloss plastic coating
large centre hole	1.5 inch (3.8 cm) hole in singles
LP	Long-playing vinyl record; standard album format superseded by CDs, but now BACK!!
matrix number	Mastertape number, scratched into the 'land' or run-off groove area; sometimes also found on the record label
maxi-single	Early 70s term for an EP, featuring more than two tracks, often in a picture sleeve
mid-price release	Record which retails at a discount
mispressing	Record or CD pressed with incorrect material
mono	One-channelled playback system
National Album Day (NAD)	Special editions are released on October 14th every year, around a theme - for example, 2024's will be 'Great British groups'
numbered (no'd)	Individually numbered, limited edition release
obi (strip)	Sealed paper strip wrapped around sleeve of disc; originated in Japan where obis were printed with Japanese translations of foreign titles
one-sided	Vinyl record which plays on one side only
onsert	That loose bit of card at the back of a boxset you're not sure what to do with when the shrink wrap comes off
picture disc	Novelty record made by sealing a picture within clear vinyl
picture sleeve	Pictorial paper or card sleeve, used specifically for one particular record
plain sleeve	Single sleeve without special printing or artwork
premium	Record available via a special offer with another product, eg food or drink
press kit	Information pack with photos and biography, used by record companies to promote new releases
printed inner	Printed protective sleeve inside main cover
private pressing	Record issued and distributed by private individuals rather than a company
promo	Promotional record or item sent out to the media for publicity purposes
push-out centre	Centre of a single connected to the rest of the disc at 3 or 4 points, so it can be pushed out for use on jukeboxes, etc.
quadrophonic	1970s four-channelled playback system, returning to vogue
reel-to-reel	1960s tape format, superseded by cassette
Record Store Day (RSD)	Began in the US in 2007, limited releases are made available on the third Saturday of April at UK independent record shops
reissue	Re-release of a deleted disc, second run of a record or CD which hasn't been deleted
remix	Different version of existing track created by rearranging its component parts
replaceable/removeable	Centre which can be removed from a record without damage and later replaced (not to be confused with jukebox or 'spider' centres)
run-off groove	groove between end of playing surface and record label, also known as deadwax or 'land'
sampler	Compilation showcasing an artist or label
sealed/shrinkwrapped	Machine-wrapped in cellophane
shaped disc	Any non-circular record
shellac	Brittle material used for 78s
slipcase	Small card cover used for some CDs and cassette singles
solid centre	Centre of record which cannot be removed, as on LPs
stickered sleeve	Sleeve with sticker as an integral part of its packaging
stereo	Two-channelled playback system
test-pressing	Manufacturer's sample record, pressed for quality control
tri-centre	Push-out triangular centre on some 1950s singles/EPs
tri-fold	Triple fold-out sleeve
uncut picture disc	Shaped disc not yet trimmed to proper shape
unissued/unreleased	Disc not made commercially available; may or may not have been pressed
vinyl	Material from which records are made
warp	Buckle in vinyl caused by heat
white label	Term for promos or test pressings without artwork for quality control
withdrawn	Record deliberately removed from sale by its manufacturer

RECORD COLLECTOR'S GRADING SYSTEM: THE MAGNIFICENT SEVEN

Record Collector introduced a set of standards for the condition of second-hand records, cassettes and CDs back in the 1980s. It was designed for those selling their wares in the magazine (in the fabled 'Set Sales', which are still here 45 years later) to assess the amount of wear and tear of the disc, sleeve and contents.

Although, of course, subject to much debate and argument – one person's VG is another's E – the seven standard condition categories, and a description of what each one means, are listed here:

MINT: The record itself is in brand new condition with no surface marks or deterioration in sound quality. The cover and any extra items such as lyric sheets, booklets or posters are in perfect condition. Records advertised as Sealed or Unplayed should be Mint.

EXCELLENT: The record shows some signs of having been played, but there is very little lessening in sound quality. The cover and packaging might have slight wear and/or creasing.

VERY GOOD: The record has obviously been played many times, but displays no major deterioration in sound quality, despite noticeable surface marks and the occasional light scratch. Normal wear and tear on the cover or extra items, without any major defects, is acceptable.

GOOD: The record has been played so much that the sound quality has noticeably deteriorated, perhaps with some distortion and mild scratches. The cover and contents suffer from folding, scuffing of edges, spine splits, discolouration, etc.

FAIR: The record is still just playable but has not been cared for properly and displays considerable surface noise; it may jump or skip. The cover and contents could well be torn, stained and/or defaced.

POOR: The record will not play properly due to scratches, bad surface noise, etc. The cover and contents will be badly damaged or partly missing.

BAD: The record is unplayable or might even be broken, and is only of use as a collection-filler.

CDs & CASSETTES: CDs and cassettes should either play perfectly, or they don't. Tape is liable to deteriorate with age, even if it remains unplayed, so care should be taken when buying old cassettes. CDs are difficult to grade visually: they can look perfect but actually be faulty and vice versa. Cassette and CD inlays and booklets should be graded in the same way as record covers and sleeves. Generally speaking, plastic cases for cassettes and CDs can easily be replaced if they are broken or scratched, but card covers and digipaks are subject to the same wear as record sleeves.

GRADING READY RECKONER

Introduced in the 80s, and now agreeably vintage in the internet age, *RC*'s legendary Ready Reckoner assists in assessing values across the 'Magnificent Seven' conditions. For example, if a record is valued at £50 Mint, but is considered only to be Very Good, the Ready Reckoner will suggest the appropriate price — in this case, £25. As very few collectors are interested in Poor or Bad condition, we consider that anything worth less than £15 Mint is effectively worthless when Poor or Bad.

MINT	EX	VG	Good	Fair	Poor	Bad
1,000	800	500	300	150	80	25
500	400	250	150	75	40	12
300	240	150	90	45	25	8
250	200	125	75	38	20	6
200	160	100	60	30	15	5
150	120	75	45	25	13	4
125	100	60	38	18	12	3
100	80	50	30	15	8	2.50
75	60	35	22	10	6	2
50	40	25	15	8	4	1.50
40	32	20	12	6	3	1
30	25	15	9	4.50	2.50	—
25	20	12	7.50	3.50	2	—
22	18	11	6.50	3	1.75	—
20	16	10	6	2.50	1.50	—
15	12	8	4.50	2	1	—

A

96	Tycoon TY2 PY102	House Under The Ground/40 (p/s)	£25
98	Tycoon 556 022-1	HOW ACE ARE BUILDINGS (2LP, gatefold, printed inners)	£50
18	London LMS 5521251	HI-FI SERIOUS (LP, 2CD, reissue, red vinyl)	£25

AAAH!

| 81 | Flesh Logic EJSP 9863 | Slip Away/Duty Calls (p/s) | £90 |
| 82 | Dangerous DRC 8401 | Input/Output (p/s) | £40 |

AALIYAH

94	Jive JIVE 357	Back & Forth (LP Version)/(MR Lee & R Kelly's Remix)	£30
94	Jive HIP 149	AGE AIN'T NOTHING BUT A NUMBER (2-LP)	£100
96	Atlantic 7567 92715-1	ONE IN A MILLION (2-LP)	£200
01	Background 724381076712	AALIYAH (2-LP, gatefold sleeve)	£200
02	Edel 0146091 ERE	I CARE 4 U (2-LP, gatefold)	£100

AARDVARK (1)

70	Deram Nova DN 17	AARDVARK (LP, mono)	£325
70	Deram Nova SDN 17	AARDVARK (LP, stereo)	£250
85	See For Miles SEE 43	PUT THAT IN YOUR PIPE AND SMOKE IT (LP, reissue of 1970 LP)	£30
(see also Home)			

AARDVARK (2)

| 74 | Ra 5019 | Lonely Sea/Hawaii Five-O | £18 |

AARDVARKS

| 99 | Detour DR 070 | Buttermilk Boy/Bad Clothes (p/s, 40 only, light blue vinyl) | £30 |
| 95 | Delerium DELEC LP 029 | BARGAIN (LP) | £18 |

A TO AUSTR

70	Holy Ground HG 113	A TO AUSTR - MUSICS FROM HOLY GROUND (LP, with booklet, 99 only)	£1000
89	Magic Mixture MM 1	A TO AUSTR (LP, reissue, 450 only, signed)	£40
95	Holy Ground 010101LP	A TO AUSTR (LP, second reissue, foldover gatefold sleeve)	£25

ABACUS (1)

| 71 | Polydor 2371 215 | ABACUS (LP) | £100 |

ABACUS (2)

| 74 | York YR 207 | Indian Dancer/Be That Way | £25 |

ABA SHANTI

94	Aba Shanti ABA 002	Zulu Warrior/Verse II/Verse III/Verse IV (10")	£35
95	Aba Shanti ABA12001	Positive Vibration/Verse II/Love & Unity/Verse II (12")	£35
13	Sufferahs Choice DUBK 022	Jah Bible/(Dubwise)/(Falasha Style)/(Raw Mix) (12", as Dubkasm meets Aba Shanti)	£20
96	Jalasha ABA LP 001	THE WRATH OF JAH (LP)	£40
96	Jalasha ABA LP 003	JAH LIGHTNING & THUNDER VERSE II (LP)	£60
99	Jalasha ABA LP 004	JERICHO WALLS VERSE THREE HORNS OF JAH (LP)	£50
15	Falasha ABA LP 01	THE WRATH OF JAH (LP, reissue)	£25

ABBA

SINGLES : ORIGINAL SINGLES

73	Epic EPC 1793	Ring Ring/Rock'N'Roll Band (yellow label)	£70
74	Epic EPC 2848	So Long/I've Been Waiting For You (yellow label)	£15
79	Epic EPC 7499	Angeleyes/Voulez-Vous (orange or yellow vinyl, p/s)	£300
80	Epic EPC 12-8835	The Winner Takes It All/Elaine (12", gatefold pop-up p/s)	£25
81	Epic EPCA 13-1456	Lay All Your Love On Me/On And On And On (12" p/s)	£15
82	Epic EPCA 11-2971	Under Attack/You Owe Me One (picture disc)	£40
83	Epic WA 3894	Thank You For The Music/Our Last Summer (shaped picture disc)	£25
21	Polar 00602567807513	I Still Have Faith In You (7", single-sided, etched, 00602567807513, p/s, printed inner)	£15

SINGLES : REISSUES AND BOX SETS

84	Epic ABBA 26	ANNIVERSARY BOXED SET (26 x 7" box set, blue vinyl, numbered edition of 2000, certificate)	£500
84	Epic ABBA 26	ANNIVERSARY BOXED SET (26 x black vinyl 7")	£100
99	Polydor 563 286-2	ABBA Singles Collection 1974-1982 (29CD singles in card sleeves, 1-track CD picture disc, booklet, silver tin, 20,000 only)	£60
04	Polydor 982054-1	Waterloo/Watch Out (picture disc, 2000 only, PVS sleeve, numbered hype sticker)	£30
14	Polar 00602537649594	THE SINGLES (40x7" box set, download card)	£200
19	Polar 00602577309182	VOULEZ-VOUS (7x7" box set, coloured vinyl, stamped numbered edition)	£60
23	Polar 00602448432223	RING RING - THE SINGLES (5x7" box set, coloured vinyl, stamped numbered edition)	£50
23	Polar 00602455075352	THE VISITORS - THE SINGLES (4x7" box set, coloured vinyl, stamped numbered edition)	£100

ALBUMS : ORIGINAL ALBUMS

74	Epic EPC 80179	WATERLOO (LP, yellow label)	£20
75	Epic EPC 80835	ABBA (LP, yellow label)	£15
76	Epic S EPC 86018	ARRIVAL (LP, printed inner)	£15
79	Epic EPC 11-86086	VOULEZ-VOUS (LP, picture disc)	£80
80	Epic ABBOX 1	SUPER TROUPER (LP, box set, book, poster, fan club flyer)	£60
99	Simply Vinyl SVLP 103	ABBA (LP, 180g, PVC outer)	£35

14	Polar 00602537716074	**LIVE AT WEMBLEY ARENA** (3LP, trifold sleeve, printed inners)	£50
21	Polar 00602438690695	**VOYAGE** (LP, gatefold, printed inner)	£30
21	Polar 00602438690701	**VOYAGE** (LP, gatefold, printed inner, white vinyl)	£20
21	Polar 00602438690671	**VOYAGE** (LP, gatefold, printed inner, solid blue vinyl)	£20
21	Polar 00602438690657	**VOYAGE** (LP, gatefold, printed inner, orange translucent vinyl)	£20
21	Polar 00602438690725	**VOYAGE** (LP, picture disc, die-cut sleeve)	£20
21	Polar 00602438690770	**VOYAGE** (LP, picture disc, die-cut sleeve, alternative artwork)	£30

ALBUMS : COMPILATIONS/BOX SETS

76	Epic EPC 69218	**GREATEST HITS** (LP, gatefold, yellow label, some with "Fernando" sticker)	£15
79	Epic EPC 10017	**GREATEST HITS VOL. 2** (LP, gatefold, printed inner)	£15
83	Epic ABBOX 2	**THE SINGLES - THE FIRST TEN YEARS** (2LP box set, picture discs, poster, ticket & book)	£75
92	Polydor 517007	**GOLD** (2LP, printed inners)	£30
05	Polar POLS 252	**THE COMPLETE STUDIO RECORDINGS** (12CD box set, 2 booklets)	£200
14	Polar 0600753538012	**THE STUDIO ALBUMS** (8LP, box set)	£120
20	Polar 00602508378997	**THE STUDIO ALBUMS** (8LP, box set, ltd ed, red/orange/silver/white/green/blue/gold/ yellow vinyl)	£120
22	Polar 0602445149476	**VINYL ALBUM BOX SET** (10LP box set, 180g, some copies with 140g Voyage)	£80

(see also Hep Stars, Hootenanny Singers, Agnetha Faltskog, Frida, Northern Lights)

ABBASANI

| 91 | Roots Rock RR 001 | **Revelation Time/Version** | £40 |
| 91 | Roots Rock RR 009 | **REVELATION TIME** (LP) | £30 |

ABC

82	Neutron NTRS 1	**THE LEXICON OF LOVE** (LP, printed inner)	£15
91	Parlophone PCS 7355	**ABRACADABRA** (LP, printed inner)	£15
16	Virgin EMI ABCBOX 1	**THE BOX INSIDE THE BOX** (2LP/3DVD box set, booklet, laminate, print signed by Martin Fry)	£150
23	Neutron NTRS 40X1	**THE LEXICON OF LOVE** (40th Anniversary Edition) (4LP/1BD box set, double gatefold, printed inners)	£100

(see also Vice Versa)

ABERDEEN

| 94 | Sarah SARAH 93 | **Bryon/Toy Tambourine** (p/s, insert) | £45 |
| 95 | Sarah SARAH 97 | **Fireworks/When It Doesn't Matter/Sunny Summer** (p/s, insert) | £45 |

A.B.H.

| 78 | Music Bank BECK 694 | **Geoffrey**(Who Wants To Listen To Punk Rock)/**Colt 45 Rock** (no p/s) | £200 |

A BIGGER SPLASH

| 82 | Mean BIGGER 1 | **INNOCENT BYSTANDERS EP** | £15 |

ABILITY II

| 90 | Bassic BASS 4T | **Pressure/Dub Version** (12") | £70 |
| 91 | Outer Rhythm FOOT 12 | **Pressure/Dub Version** (12", p/s reissue) | £30 |

ABOVE & BEYOND

04	Anjunabeats ANJ 034	**Surrender** (Original Mix)/(Filterheadz Remix) (12", p/s as Presents Tranquility Base)	£20
05	Anjunabeats ANJ 049	**Air For Life** (Original Mix)/(Airwave Remix)/(Mirco De Govia Remix) (12", p/ as Above & Beyond VS Andy Moor)	£35
06	Anjunabeats ANJ-059	**Alone Tonight** (Club Mix)/(Nasty Dub) (12", p/s)	£25
07	Anjunabeats ANJ-080	**Tri State Remixes - Stealing Time** (Deep Club Mix)/(Robert Nickson Mix) (12", p/s)	£30
09	Anjunabeats ANJ-138	**Anjunabeach** (Original Mix)/(Jerome Isma Ae Remix) (12", p/s)	£35
14	Anjunabeats ANJLP037	**ACOUSTIC** (2-LP, 1st pressing)	£70
18	Anjunabeats ANJUNLP 024	**GROUP THERAPY** (2-LP, 1st reissue, gatefold)	£50
18	Anjunabeats ANJLP053	**ACOUSTIC - LIVE AT THE HOLLYWOOD BOWL** (3-LP)	£60
19	Anjunabeats ANJLP037	**ACOUSTIC** (2-LP, repressing, 180gm vinyl)	£50
20	Anjunabeats ANJLP096	**2000 - 2020** (8-LP)	£250

(see also Oceanlab)

MICK ABRAHAMS (BAND)

71	Chrysalis ILPS 9147	**(A MUSICAL EVENING WITH) THE MICK ABRAHAMS BAND** (LP, g/fold sleeve)	£40
72	Chrysalis CHR 1005	**AT LAST** (LP, first pressing, circular foldout sleeve, Island logo and address in white on green label)	£100
91	Edsel ED 335	**AT LAST** (LP, repressing with standard sleeve)	£25

(see also Blodwyn Pig, Jethro Tull, Mighty Flyers)

ABRASIVE WHEELS

81	Abrasive ABW 1	**Army Song/Juvenile/So Low** (p/s, 3000 copies)	£15
81	Riot City RIOT 4	**Vicious Circles/Attack/Voice Of Youth** (p/s)	£15
82	Riot City CITY 001	**WHEN THE PUNKS GO MARCHING IN** (LP)	£20
84	Clay CLAY 9	**BLACK LEATHER GIRL** (LP)	£18
95	Captain Oi! AHOY LP 5	**WHEN THE PUNKS GO MARCHING IN** (LP, reissue, green vinyl)	£15
96	Captain Oi! AHOY LP 51	**THE PUNK SINGLES COLLECTION** (LP)	£15

ABS

| 89 | Link MLP 100 | **MENTAL ENENA** (LP) | £15 |
| 90 | Blasting Youth | **NAIL IT DOWN** (LP, with insert) | £15 |

MIKE ABSALOM

65	Sportsdisc ILP 1081	**THE MIGHTY ABSALOM SINGS BATHROOM BALLADS** (LP)	£20
69	Saydisc SDL 162	**SAVE THE LAST GHERKIN FOR ME** (LP)	£90
71	Vertigo 6360 053	**MIKE ABSALOM** (LP, swirl label, poster sleeve)	£400
72	Philips 6308 131	**HECTOR AND OTHER PECCADILLOS** (LP)	£60
74	Sportsdisc ILP 1081	**MIKE ABSALOM SINGS BATHROOM BALLADS** (LP)	£20

ABSENT FRIENDS

| 85 | Zebra 1 | **Stand Up And Fight/Drift Apart** (p/s) | £30 |

MINT VALUE £

ABSENTEES
83   Awol AWOL 1   **If You Don't Want Me/AWOL** (no p/s) **£25**

ABSOLUTE
85   Reset 12 REST 5   **TV Glare/At The Third Stroke** (12", p/s) **£20**
87   Reset 7 REST 8   **Can't You See/Love In My Heart** (release cancelled) **£60**
(see also Erasure)

ABSOLUTE ALBERT
82   Completely A MAD 1   **Noises/In Flight** (p/s) **£20**

ABSOLUTE BEGINNERS
84   Roundabout RDA BS 1   **Dream In A Haze/Southern Beat** (hand-made p/s) **£25**

ABSOLUTE ELSEWHERE
76   Warner Bros K 256192   **IN SEARCH OF ANCIENT GODS** (LP, gatefold, die-cut, with booklet, quadrophonic) **£18**
(see also Bill Bruford)

ABSTRAC & LADY PENELOPE
97   Confetti Records COEP 03   **Love In Dub/Dub In Love/Deeper** (Part 1) (12") (as Abstrac and Lady P) **£30**
97   Confetti Records COEP 04   **Love Devotion/Feel The Sunshine/Mind Games** (12") **£30**
(see also Lady Penelope)

ABYSSINIANS
73   Harry J. HJ 6652   **Yim Mas Gan/JOHN CROW GENERATION: Crank Shaft** **£30**
75   Grounation GR 2029   **Love Comes And Goes/**(Version) **£20**
75   2nd Tracs SK1   **Tenayistillin Wandimae/Tenayistillin** **£15**
76   Tropical S'tracks TST 109   **African Race/Satta A Massagana** **£15**
76   Nationwide NW009   **Sweet Feelings/Version** (actually by Carlton & The Shoes) **£15**
77   Klik KL 631   **Forward On To Zion/Satta A Massagana** **£15**
78   Different HAVED 7   **Satte A Massagana/I & I** (12") **£30**
78   Different GETL 100   **FORWARD ON TO ZION** (LP) **£50**
78   Virgin Front Line FL1019   **ARISE** (LP, with lyric sheet) **£25**
16   UMC 00602547512222   **THE CLINCH SINGLES COLLECTION** (7x7" box set) **£50**

ACADEMY
69   Morgan Bluetown BTS 2   **Rachel's Dream/Munching The Candy** (as Academy featuring Polly Perkins) **£30**
69   Morgan Bluetown BT 5001   **POP-LORE ACCORDING TO THE ACADEMY** (LP) **£200**
(see also Polly Perkins)

ACANTHUS
10   Finders Keepers FKR 038LP   **LE FRISSON DES VAMPIRES** (OST) (LP, insert) **£20**

ACCENT (1)
67   Decca F 12679   **Red Sky At Night/Wind Of Change** **£225**
(see also Rick Hayward)

ACCENT (2)
84   Motion 1111   **We Are Lost/Blue And Royal Line** (p/s with insert) **£30**

ACCESS
81   Ellie Jay EJSP 9674 STA001-7   **AUDACITY EP** (EP, p/s) **£25**

ACCIDENT
84   Flicknife SHARP 016   **A CLOCKWORK LEGION** (LP) **£25**
87   Link LP 12   **CRAZY!** (LP) **£20**
(see also Major Accident)

ACCIDENT ON THE EAST LANCS.
80   Roach RR 1   **The Back End Of Nowhere/Rat Race** (p/s) **£75**
80   Roach SPLIFF 001   **We Want It Legalised/Tell Me What Ya Mean** (no p/s) **£50**
81   Cargo 001   **SHOTGUNS AND HOTSHOTS** (cassette) **£30**
14   Ozit Dandelion   **RAINY CITY PUNK VOLUME 2: ACCIDENT ON THE EAST LANCS** (2-LP, purple vinyl, 500 only, numbered) **£20**

ACCIDENTS
80   H. Line 'n' Sinker HOOK 1   **Blood Spattered With Guitars/Curtains For You** (p/s) **£20**
80   H. Line 'n' Sinker   **KISS ME ON THE APOCALYPSE** (LP, unreleased; test pressings only) **£150**
96   Detour DRLP04   **KISS ME ON THE APOCALYPSE** (LP reissue of unissued album) **£20**

ACCOLADE
70   Columbia DB 8688   **Natural Day/Prelude To A Dawn** **£35**
70   Columbia SCX 6405   **ACCOLADE** (LP) **£100**
72   Regal Zono. SLRZ 1024   **ACCOLADE 2** (LP) **£150**
(see also Gordon Giltrap, Wizz Jones, Pauline Filby, Don Partridge)

ACCURSED
83   Wrek 'EM ACC 1   **AGGRESSIVE PUNK** (LP) **£20**
83   Wrek 'EM ACC 3   **UP WITH THE PUNKS** (LP) **£15**
84   Wrek 'EM ACC 4   **LAUGHING AT YOU** (LP) **£15**

ACCUSED
87   Children Of The Revolution/
     Earache GURT 17/MOSH 1   **THE RETURN OF MARTHA SPLATTERHEAD** (LP, insert) **£25**

AC/DC
SINGLES
76   Atlantic K 10745   **It's A Long Way To The Top** (If You Wanna Rock'N'Roll)/**Can I Sit Next To You, Girl?** (no p/s) **£22**
76   Atlantic K 10805   **Jailbreak/Fling Thing** (original issue, running times on dark label, heavy print, no p/s) **£22**
76   Atlantic K 10860   **High Voltage/Live Wire** (in p/s) **£150**
76   Atlantic K 10860   **High Voltage/Live Wire** (no p/s) **£15**

77	Atlantic K 10899	**Dirty Deeds Done Dirt Cheap/Big Balls/The Jack** (maxi-single, 'schoolboy' p/s)	£120
78	Atlantic K 11142T	**Rock'N'Roll Damnation/Sin City** (12", p/s)	£18
78	Atlantic K 11207T	**Whole Lotta Rosie** (live)**/Hell Ain't A Bad Place To Be** (live) (12", no p/s)	£15
80	Atlantic K 11435	**Touch Too Much/Live Wire** (live)**/Shot Down In Flames** (live) (p/s, misprinted back-to-front)	£15
80	Atlantic K 10805	**Jailbreak/Fling Thing** (reissue, light label, fine print; first pressing initially without 'Elephant Head' motif on p/s)	£15
80	Atlantic K 11142	**Rock'N'Roll Damnation/Sin City** (reissue, without 'Elephant Head' motif on p/s)	£15
80	Atlantic K 11600	**You Shook Me All Night Long/Have A Drink With Me** (p/s, mispressing, A-side plays "Shake A Leg")	£100
82	Atlantic SAM 143	**For Those About To Rock** (We Salute You)**/C.O.D.** (12", p/s, promo only)	£40
84	Atlantic A 9651P	**Nervous Shakedown/Rock'N'Roll Ain't Noise Pollution** (live) (shaped picture disc)	£15
85	Atlantic A 9532P	**Danger/Back In Business** (fly-shaped picture disc)	£20
86	Atlantic A 9474P	**Shake Your Foundations/Stand Up** (Angus-shaped picture disc)	£20
86	Atlantic A 9425P	**Who Made Who/Guns For Hire** (live) (shaped picture disc)	£20
86	Atlantic A 9425TW	**Who Made Who** (remix)**/Guns For Hire** (live) (12", stickered p/s & poster)	£15
86	Atlantic A 9377P	**You Shook Me All Night Long/She's Got Balls** (live) (shaped picture disc)	£20
88	Atlantic A 9136TP	**Heatseeker/Go Zone/Snake Eye** (12", picture disc)	£15
90	Atco B8907T	**Thunderstruck/Fire Your Guns/DT/Chase The Ace** (12" coloured test pressings, white, blue, red, clear, yellow, green & marbled swirl pattern)	£300
91	Atco B8886T	**Money Talks/Mistress For Christmas/Borrowed Time** (12" poster p/s)	£20

ALBUMS

76	Atlantic K50257	**HIGH VOLTAGE** (LP, 1st pressing, cartoon sleeve, reissues have barcode)	£30
76	Atlantic K50323	**DIRTY DEEDS DONE CHEAP** (LP)	£15
77	Atlantic K50483	**LET THERE BE ROCK** (LP, etched matrix numbers K50366 A-1/B-2)	£30
77	Atlantic K50366	**LET THERE BE ROCK** (LP, mispressing, both sides play Side 1)	£200
78	Atlantic K50483	**POWERAGE** (LP)	£30
78	Atlantic K50366	**IF YOU WANT BLOOD YOU'VE GOT IT** (LP)	£20
79	Atlantic K50625	**HIGHWAY TO HELL** (LP)	£30
79	Atlantic K50628	**HIGHWAY TO HELL** (LP, test pressing in alternative "live" proof sleeve)	£300
80	Atlantic K50735	**BACK IN BLACK** (LP, embossed sleeve, with inner, A1/B1 Matrixes)	£35
81	Atlantic K50851	**FOR THOSE ABOUT TO ROCK** (LP, gatefold)	£20
81	Atlantic SAM 155	**JAPAN TOUR ' 81** (LP, picture disc, promo only, clear rim)	£150
81	Atlantic SAM 155	**JAPAN TOUR ' 81** (LP, picture disc, promo only, black rim)	£120
81	Atlantic 60149	**BOX SET** (3-LP, including "High Voltage", "Dirty Deeds Done Cheap" & Powerage, promo 7" & poster; export issue)	£45
83	Atlantic 780100-1	**FLICK OF THE SWITCH** (LP)	£20
88	Atlantic WX 144	**BLOW UP YOUR VIDEO** (LP, black inner sleeve)	£15
91	Atco WX 364P	**THE RAZOR'S EDGE** (LP, picture disc with inlay card)	£15
95	East West 7559 61780-1	**BALLBREAKER** (LP)	£60
00	Elektra 7559-62494-1	**STIFF UPPER LIP** (LP)	£60
03	Epic 509298-7	**ACDCROCKS.com BOX** (15 x CD box set)	£150
09	Columbia 38377	**BLACK ICE** (2-LP, gatefold, inner sleeves)	£20
14	Columbia 88875034841	**ROCK OR BUST** (LP, gatefold, lenticular sleeve)	£20

(see also Geordie, A II Z, Home)

BUDDY ACE

68	Action ACT 4504	**Got To Get Myself Together/Darling Depend On Me**	£30
64	Vocalion VEP 1-70164	**BUDDY ACE** (EP)	£80

CHARLIE ACE

70	High Note HS 051	**Creation** (Version)**/GAYTONES: Creation** (Version Three)	£20
70	Punch PH 49	**Silver And Gold/PHILL PRATT ALLSTARS: Bump And Bore**	£30
70	Punch PH 67	**Do Something/MAYTONES: Run Babylon**	£15
71	Upsetter US 359	**The Creeper/UPSETTERS: The Creeper** (Version)	£30
72	Camel CA 92	**The Commandments Of Joshua/GABY AND WILTON: Only Love**	£15
74	Tropical AL 026	**Hot Butter Dub/Pits And Pieces**	£25

(see also Charles, Gaytones, Phil Pratt Allstars, Maytones, G.G. Allstars, Upsetters)

JOHNNY ACE

61	Vogue V 9180	**Pledging My Love/Anymore**	£50
62	Vogue VE 1-70150	**JOHNNY ACE** (EP)	£60
61	Vocalion VA 160177	**THE MEMORIAL ALBUM** (LP)	£150

RICHARD ACE (& SOUND DIMENSIONS)

67	Coxsone CS 7031	**Don't Let The Sun Catch You Crying/VICEROYS: Maga Down**	£130
67	Studio One SO 2022	**I Need You/SOUL VENDORS: Cool Shade**	£120
69	Studio One SO 2072	**More Reggae** (with Sound Dimensions)**/GLADIATORS: Hello Carol**	£100
69	Trojan TR 654	**Hang 'Em High/BLACK & GEORGE: Candy Lady**	£150
70	Sugar SU 104	**Sound Of The Reggae/Got To Build A Wall**	£50

(see also Viceroys, Soul Vendors, Gladiators, Ken Boothe)

ACE LANE

83	Expulsion EXIT3	**SEE YOU IN HEAVEN** (LP)	£15

ACEN

92	Production House PNT 034	**Close Your Eyes** (XXX Mix)**/Close Your Eyes** (Vitamin 'E' Mix) (12")	£20
92	Production House PNT 034R	**Close Your Eyes** (Remix I: Optikonfusion!)**/Close Your Eyes** (Remix II: The Sequel) (12")	£30
93	Production House PNT 034 R-A, PNT 051 A-2	**Close Your Eyes** (Non Beatles Version Mispress) (12")	£90
92	Production House PNT 042	**Trip II The Moon** (Part 1)**/Obsessed** (12", die-cut p/s)	£25
92	Production House PNT 042R	**Trip II The Moon** (Part 2) (12", Promo 100 copies)	£60
92	Production House PNT 042R	**Trip II The Moon** (Part 2, The Darkside)**/The Life And Crimes Of A Ruffneck** (12", die-cut p/s)	£25

92	Production House PNT 042 RX	**Trip II The Moon** (Part 3, Kaleidoscopiklimax)/**Obsessed** (Part 2, Pictures Of Silence) (12", die-cut p/s) £25
93	Production House PNT 051R	**Window In The Sky** (DMS Remix)/**Window In The Sky** (Nino's Night Remix) (white label 12") £15
93	Production House PNT 051	**Krystal Fairground** (12", Promo, one-sided) £50
94	FFRR PROXDJ 1	**Trip To The Moon** (Omar Santana Mix) (10" 1-sided) £200

A CERTAIN RATIO

79	Factory FAC 5	**All Night Party/The Thin Boys** (p/s, 5,000 only, 1,000 with sticker stating ltd. edition on poor quality vinyl) £25
79	Factory FAC 5	**All Night Party/The Thin Boys** (p/s, 5,000 only, 4,000 without sticker stating ltd. edition on poor quality vinyl) £20
80	Factory FACT 16C	**THE GRAVEYARD & THE BALLROOM** (cassette in plastic wallet, first 400 in orange, then later blue, green, brown, red and grey. 1000 only) £30
81	Factory FACT 35	**TO EACH** (LP, gatefold) £20
82	Factory FACT 55	**SEXTET** (LP, textured sleeve with insert) £20
82	Factory FACT 65	**I'D LIKE TO SEE YOU AGAIN** (LP) £15
85	private label	**A CERTAIN RATIO LIVE IN AMERICA** (cassette, sold at gigs) £15
85	Factory FACT 16C	**THE GRAVEYARD AND THE BALLROOM** (reissue, cassette, in box with insert) £25
86	Factory FACT 135c	**THE OLD AND THE NEW** (cassette, in box with insert) £25
86	Factory FACT 166	**FORCE** (LP, inner and insert) £15
86	Factory FACT 166c	**FORCE** (cassette, in box with insert) £25
92	Robs LPROB 20	**UP IN DOWNVILLE** (LP) £25
94	Creation CRELP 159	**LOOKING FOR A CERTAIN RATIO** (LP, also as 2 x 12") £25
02	Soul Jazz SJRLP60	**EARLY** (2-LP) £18
02	Soul Jazz SJR 65 10	**B-SIDES, SESSIONS AND RARITIES** (2 x 10") £20
04	Universal Sound US LP 70	**THE GRAVEYARD AND THE BALLROOM** (LP, reissue with free 12") £20
19	Mute ACRBOX1	**ACR:BOX** (7-LP box set) £60

(see also Sir Horatio)

ACES (2)

81	Etc ETC 01	**One Way Street/Why Should It Be Mine** (p/s) £18

(see also Menace)

A CHOCOLATE MORNING

91	Still CM 001	**WASTED EP** (12" p/s) £70
92	What's Happening? WHAT 001	**If You Want Me/This Isn't Mine** (p/s) £25

ACID GALLERY

69	CBS 4608	**Dance Around The Maypole/Right Toe Blues** £100

(see also Christie, Epics, Carl Wayne & Vikings, Roy Wood)

ACID MOTHERS TEMPLE AND THE MELTING PARAISO UFO

01	Staticresonance 2	**MONSTER OF THE UNIVERSE** (Monster Of The Universe/Wholly Weary Flashback/Surfin' Paris-Texas/Midnight Mountain Dew (EP, 500 only, p/s 2 x 7" sold on tour, 500 only) £15
01	Staticresonance 1	**ABSOLUTELY FREAKOUT, (ZAP YOUR MIND)** (LP, 1000 only) £50

(See also Cotton Casino)

ACIDULANT

18	Balkan BV 23	**BORING KINGDOM EP** (12", 200 only) £15

JEWEL ACKAH

84	Jetacks JA 001	**AKARA - CHI SPECIAL** (LP) £20
84	Dassi DRS 1	**LONDON CONNECTION** (LP) £20
86	Highlife HW2016	**ELECTRIC HI-LIFE** (LP) £20
86	Asona ASR 4010	**ELECTRIC HI-LIFE** (LP, different cover) £18

ACKEE

86	Heavyweight HW 003	**Call Me Rambo/CHESSE ROOTS: Rambo Gun Salute** (12", as Ackie) £25
87	Route One RO 004	**Ragamuffin Boogie Rock/Lick Them** (Dance Hall Style) (12") £150
87	Route One RO 005	**Roughneck Time/Version** (12") £100

DAVID ACKLES

68	Elektra EKL 4022	**DAVID ACKLES** (LP, orange label, mono) £35
68	Electra EKS 74022	**DAVID ACKLES** (LP, orange label, stereo) £25
70	Elektra EKS 74060	**SUBWAY TO THE COUNTRY** (LP, orange label) £15
72	Elektra K 42112	**AMERICAN GOTHIC** (LP) £15
73	CBS 32466	**FIVE AND DIME** (LP) £15

BARBARA ACKLIN

68	MCA MU 1038	**Love Makes A Woman/Come And See Me Baby** £20
69	MCA MU 1071	**Am I The Same Girl/Be By My Side** (DJ Copy) £50
87	Debut DEBTX 3024	**Am I The Same Girl/Love Makes A Woman/From The Preacher To The Teacher** (12") £15
69	MCA MUP(S) 366	**LOVE MAKES A WOMAN** (LP) £25
71	MCA MUPS 410	**SEVEN DAYS OF NIGHT** (LP) £20
71	MCA MUPS 416	**SOMEONE ELSE'S ARMS** (LP) £20
75	Capitol E-ST 11377	**A PLACE IN THE SUN** (LP) £15
87	Kent 072	**GROOVY IDEAS** (LP) £18

ACME ATTRACTIONS

80	A Trax KICK 007	**Anyway/Never Again** (p/s) £40
81	Orchid OR1	**Eve Of Destruction/It's OK** (p/s, with Bonnie Parker) £20

ACOUSTIC LADYLAND

06	V2 VVR1043681	**SKINNY GRIN** (LP) £18

ACRO

95	Lucky Spin STU 10	**Superpod/Skylab** (12" 1-sided white label) £25

ACROSS THE WATER

75	John Hassell Recordings MCW 001	ACROSS THE WATER (LP, two known acetate copies in finished hand-made sleeves)	£3000
20	Seelie Court SCLP 001	ACROSS THE WATER (LP, reissue, gatefold)	£20

ACRYLIC TONES

95	Detour DRLP002	THE ACRYLIC TONES (LP)	£15

ACT (1)

67	Columbia DB 8179	Cobbled Streets/One Heart	£25
67	Columbia DB 8261	Here Come Those Tears Again/Without You	£15
68	Columbia DB 8331	Just A Little Bit/The Remedies Of Doctor Brohnicoy	£70

ACT (3)

87	ZTT CT 01	Snobbery And Decay (Moonlighting Mix)/Instant 1/Instant 2 (12" promo, plain black die-cut sleeve)	£30
88	ZTT BET 1	Chance/Winner '88 (p/s, withdrawn)	£30
88	ZTT BETT 1	Chance (12 To 1 Mix)/Winner '88/Chance (We Give You Another Chance) (12", p/s, withdrawn)	£150

(see also Propaganda, Claudia Brucken, Glenn Gregory & Claudia Brucken, Thomas Leer)

ACTION

65	Parlophone R 5354	Land Of 1000 Dances/In My Lonely Room	£100
66	Parlophone R 5410	I'll Keep Holding On/Hey Sah-Lo-Ney	£150
66	Parlophone R 5474	Baby You've Got It/Since I Lost My Baby	£100
67	Parlophone R 5572	Never Ever/Twenty Fourth Hour	£100
67	Parlophone R 5610	Shadows And Reflections/Something Has Hit Me	£150
67	Parlophone R 5410	Shadows And Reflections/Something Has Hit Me (p/s for export to Holland)	£150
80	Edsel ED 101	THE ULTIMATE ACTION (LP, with inner sleeve, first pressing with extra tracks)	£25
85	Castle DOJO LP 3	ACTION SPEAK LOUDER THAN... (mini-LP)	£15
95	Dig The Fuzz DIG 005	BRAIN - THE LOST RECORDINGS (LP, insert, booklet)	£20
98	Dig The Fuzz DIG 025	ROLLED GOLD (LP)	£15
14	Demon ACTIONBOXRSD	THE SINGLES BOXSET (8 x 7", booklet)	£60

(see also Boys, Sandra Barry & Boys, Mighty Baby, Reg King, Stone's Masonry)

ACTION PACT

81	Subversive ANARCHO 1	HEATHROW TOUCHDOWN (EP, 1 side by Dead Man's Shadow)	£20
82	Fallout FALL 003	Suicide Bag/Stanwell/Blue Blood (p/s)	£15
83	Fallout FALL 013	MERCURY THEATRE ON THE AIR (LP)	£15
84	Fallout FALL 030	SURVIVAL OF THE FATTEST (LP)	£20

ACTION PAINTING!

90	Sarah SARAH 028	These Things Happen/Boy Meets World (wraparound p/s, with insert)	£25
93	Sarah SARAH 73	Classical Music/Sensation No. 5/Hip To Hate (p/s, insert)	£25
93	Sarah SARAH 87	Mustard Gas/Art Student/Collapsing Cloud (p/s, insert)	£25

ACTION REPLAY

79	Rok ROK XV/XVI	Decisions/ZEROS: What's Wrong With Pop Group (die-cut company sleeve)	£30

ACTIVE MINDS

98	HC 001	Hobson's Choice/Hobson's Choice (stickered white labels, 500 only)	£30
02	VELSH 001	Hobson's Choice (Original Mix)/(Dark Side Remix) (12" reissue, white label)	£25

ACTIVE RESTRAINT

82	Sticky PEEL OFF 3	Terror In My Home/Turns Out Roses (p/s)	£25

ACTIVES

83	Quiet Records QS 001	RIOT (EP)	£80
84	Quiet Records QS 004	WAIT & SEE (EP" 12")	£60
83	Quiet Records QLP 4	KICK IT DOWN (LP, with insert)	£70
03	Intimidation INT 8	REACTIVATED (LP, splatter vinyl)	£25

ACTRESS (1)

69	CBS 4016	It's What You Give/Good Job With Prospects	£200

ACTRESS (2)

10	Honest Jons HJRLP 49	SPLAZSH (LP, as 2 x 12", embossed sleeve)	£20
12	Honest Jons HJRLP 60	R.I.P. (2-LP, embossed sleeve)	£20
14	Ninja Tune WDNT 006	GHETTOVILLE (2-LP)	£20
17	Ninja Tune ZEN 241X	AZD (2-LP)	£20

ACUTE LOGIC

81	Illogical EJSP 9589	Morroccan Nights/The Obsession/The Balcony (p/s, insert)	£30

ADAM & THE ANTS

79	Want 1	Cartrouble Part 1/Cartrouble Part 2/Kick (1-sided promo)	£15
88	Damaged Goods FNARR 7	Young Parisians/Lady/Interviews (12" reissue with fanzine)	£20
79	Do It RIDE 3	DIRK WEARS WHITE SOX (LP, 1st pressing with 'Do It' labels)	£20
80	CBS 84549	KINGS OF THE WILD FRONTIER (LP, inner with booklet)	£15
79	Do It RIDE 3M	DIRK WEARS WHITE SOX (cassette with insert)	£15
80	CBS 4025361	DIRK WEARS WHITE SOX (cassette reissue)	£20
83	CBS 25361	DIRK WEARS WHITE SOX (LP, reissue with different cover, modified track listing)	£15
90	Strange Fruit SFRLP 115	PEEL SESSIONS (LP)	£15
00	Sony ANTBOX 5007822	ANTBOX (3-CD with book in 7" sized box)	£35
06	Sony 88697009032	ADAM & THE ANTS - REMASTERED (7-CD, box set)	£40
14	Blue Back Hussar BBH003LP	DIRK WEARS WHITE SOX (LP, reissue, white vinyl)	£25

(see also Adam Ant, Maneaters, Models)

ADAM AND DEE

69	Tangerine DP 0002	Question Of Childhood/Run To Her	£120

ADAM F

MINT VALUE £

ADAM F
93	Lucky Spin ADM04	STRONGER THAN EVER: Light Years/Sea Of Destiny (12")	£15
93	Lucky Spin ADM01	Pressure (Mix 1)/Pressure (Mix 2) (12")	£100
94	Lucky Spin LSR 015	Eclipse/Whiplash (12")	£30
01	EMI 7243 5 34250 1 2	KAOS ANTI ACOUSTIC WARFARE (3LP, printed inners)	£20

ADAM, MIKE & TIM
64	Decca F 12040	Little Baby/You're The Reason Why	£25

ARTHUR K. ADAMS
68	Blue Horizon 57-3136	She Drives Me Out Of My Mind/Gimme Some Of Your Lovin'	£25

BILLY ADAMS (2)
69	London 10258	I Need Your Love/Why Don't You Believe Me (DJ Copy)	£20

BRYAN ADAMS
91	A&M 397 164-1	WAKING UP THE NEIGHBOURS (2LP, printed inners, insert)	£25
96	A&M 540 551-1	18 TIL I DIE (LP, printed inner)	£100

DERROLL ADAMS
67	Ace Of Clubs ACL 1227	PORTLAND TOWN (LP)	£60
72	Village Thing VTS 17	FEELIN' FINE (LP, with inner sleeve)	£70
72	Village Thing VTS 17	FEELIN' FINE (LP, without inner sleeve)	£40

(see also Ramblin' Jack Elliott)

FAYE ADAMS
56	London HLU 8339	I'll Be True/Happiness To My Soul (Gold Tri label)	£400
56	London HLU 8339	I'll Be True/Happiness To My Soul (78)	£25

GAYLE ADAMS
82	Epic A13 2167	Baby I Need Your Loving/Don't Jump To Conclusions (12")	£15
80	Epic EPC 84435	GAYLE ADAMS (LP)	£15
82	Epic EPC 85687	LOVE FEVER (LP)	£15

GLADSTON ADAMS
69	Trojan TR 659	Dollars And Cents/TOMMY McCOOK: Popcorn Reggay	£50

(see also Gladstone Anderson)

GLEN ADAMS
67	Island WI 3072	Silent Lover/I Remember	£60
67	Island WI 3083	She (actually titled "I'm Shocking")/SONNY BURKE: Some Other Time	£80
67	Island WI 3099	Grab A Girl/DELROY WILSON: This Heart Of Mine	£70
67	Island WI 3100	Hold Down Miss Winey/VINCENT GORDON: Sounds And Soul	£70
67	Island WI 3120	She's So Fine/ROY SHIRLEY: Girlie	£80
68	Trojan TR 621	Rent Too High/Every Time	£60
68	Duke DU 58	My Girl/GLADIATORS: You Were To Be	£45
68	Bullet BU 414	Cat Woman/PETER TOUCH (Peter Tosh):Selassie Serenade	£20
68	Collins Downbeat CR 006	Cool Cool Rock Steady (as Glen Addams & Collins Band)/OWEN GRAY & COLLINS BAND: Girl I Will Be Leaving	£125
68	Collins Downbeat CR 010	King Sized/I'm Gonna Take You Back (B-side actually by Owen Gray)	£90
68	Giant GN 33	Lonely Girl/ROY SHIRLEY: Warming Up The Scene	£180
69	Amalgamated AMG 837	She's So Fine/ERNEST WILSON: Private Number	£50
69	Crab CRAB 21	Mighty Organ/ERNEST WILSON: Just Once	£75
69	Sound Systems SS 105	Down To Earth Reggae/Reggae From Mankind	£30
70	Gas GAS 141	Leaving On A Jet Plane/REGGAE BOYS: Phrases	£50
70	Junior JR 110	Sound In/Sound & Pleasure	£20
71	Big BG 321	Weary Version 3/TONY BREVETT: Hills And Valleys	£20
71	Explosion EX 2048	Never Fall In Love/JET SCENE: Jet 747	£20
71	Upsetter US 367	Never Had A Dream/UPSETTERS: Version	£50

(see also Glen Adams, Reggae Boys, Roy Shirley, Maxie & Glen, Delroy Wilson, Derrick Morgan, Owen Gray, Paul Sinclair)

JUNE ADAMS
66	King KG 1038	River Keep Movin'/Heavenly Father	£15

LLOYD ADAMS
62	Wasp W001	I Wish Your Picture Was You/Pleading For Love (Possibly unreleased)	£35
62	Wasp W009	I Wish Your Picture Was You/Pleading For Love	£30

MARIE ADAMS
59	Capitol CL 14963	A Fool In Love/What Do You Want To Make Those Eyes At Me For	£40
59	Capitol CL 14964	A Fool In Love/What Do You Want To Make Those Eyes At Me For (promo copy in picture sleeve)	£60

(see also Johnny Otis)

PEPPER ADAMS
58	Vogue LAE 12134	CRITICS CHOICE (LP)	£40
59	Pye NLP 28007	COOL SOUND (LP)	£35
74	Spotlite SPJ PA6	EPHEMERA (LP)	£20

RITCHIE ADAMS
60	London HLU 9200	Back To School/Don't Go My Love, Don't Go	£20

RYAN ADAMS
04	Lost Highway 602498630990	Wonderwall/One By One (p/s)	£20
00	Cooking Vinyl COOK 205	HEARTBREAKER (LP, with inner)	£70
03	Lost Highway 986 100 1	ROCK N ROLL (LP)	£35
03	Lost Highway 986 100-1	ROCK N ROLL (LP, 'blood' cover)	£100
03	Lost Highway 986 136-1	LOVE IS HELL PARTS 1 & 2 (LP, as 2x10")	£25
05	Lost Highway B0004707-01	JACKSONVILLE CITY NIGHTS (2-LP as Ryan Adams And The Cardinals)	£20

08	Lost Highway 02517872608	CARDINOLOGY (2-LP)	£25
05	Lost Highway B0004343-01	COLD ROSES (2-LP, embossed cover, as Ryan Adams And The Cardinals)	£50
11	Columbia 88697973101	ASHES AND FIRE (LP)	£18
13	Pax Americana 039	RYAN ADAMS (LP)	£20
16	Pax Americana 056	HEARTBREAKER (4-LP, DVD, reissue)	£40
17	Pax Americana PAX 059	LIVE AT ROUGH TRADE (LP)	£30

STEVE ADAMS
| 77 | Mind's Ear MER 2010 | STEVE ADAMS (LP) | £15 |

WOODROW ADAMS
| 65 | Blue Horizon BH 1001 | Baby You Just Don't Know/Wine Head Woman (99 copies only) | £400 |

ZAYNE ADAMS
| 69 | NEMS 56 4473 | Can't You See Me/If You Were My Woman | £15 |
| 69 | NEMS 56-4697 | Today/Don't Take My World Away (Demo only) | £15 |

ADAM'S APPLES
| 77 | Brunswick BR 42 | Don't Take It Out On This World/Don't You Want To Take Me Home | £18 |

BARRY ADAMSON
89	Mute STUMM 53	MOSS SIDE STORY (LP, inner)	£15
92	Mute STUMM 105	SOUL MURDER (LP, inner)	£15
93	Mute STUMM 120	THE NEGRO INSIDE ME (LP, inner)	£15
96	Mute STUMM 134	OEDIPUS SCHMOEDIPUS (LP, inner)	£25
98	Mute STUMM 161	AS ABOVE SO BELOW (LP)	£25
02	Mute STUMM 176	THE KING OF NOTTING HILL (2-LP)	£25
08	Central Control CC1007LP	BACK TO THE CAT (LP)	£20

A DANCING MIRAGE
| 82 | Wide WIDE 001 | BOYS IN COLOUR EP | £25 |

AD ASTRA
| 83 | Sane 45001 | Give Me The Girl/Find The Time | £25 |

AD CONSPIRACY
| 79 | Diamond Age AD 22957 | AD CONSPIRACY (LP) | £70 |

CANNONBALL ADDERLEY
58	Riverside RLP12 286	THINGS ARE GETTING BETTER (LP, with Milt Jackson)	£25
59	Riverside RLP12 303	CANNONBALL TAKES CHARGE (LP)	£25
60	Riverside RLP12 322	THEM DIRTY BLUES (LP)	£25
61	Riverside RLP 433	KNOW WHAT I MEAN (LP, with BILL EVANS)	£25
61	Riverside RLP 377	AFRICAN WALTZ (LP)	£25
61	Riverside RLP 388	PLUS (LP)	£25
62	Riverside RLP 311	THE CANNONBALL ADDERLEY QUINTET IN SAN FRANCISCO (LP)	£25
63	Riverside RLP 444	JAZZ WORKSHOP REVISITED (LP)	£20
64	Riverside RLP 477	NIPPON SOUL (LP)	£20
67	Capitol ST 2663	MERCY! MERCY! MERCY! (LP)	£20
67	Capitol T2617	WHY AM I TREATED SO BAD? (LP)	£20
68	Mercury LML/SLML 4022	THEM ADDERLEYS (LP, mono/stereo)	£20
73	Fantasy FT 517	INSIDE STRAIGHT (LP)	£15
79	Blue Note BNS 540036	SOMETHIN' ELSE (LP, reissue)	£18
84	Blue Note BST 81595	SOMETHIN' ELSE (LP, reissue)	£20

(see also Nancy Wilson, Miles Davis, John Coltrane)

NAT ADDERLEY
56	London LTZC 15018	THAT'S NAT (LP)	£20
62	Riverside RLP 12-318	WORK SONG (LP)	£25
62	Riverside RLP 12-330	THAT'S RIGHT! (LP, as Nat Adderley and the Big Sax Section)	£25
65	Fontana FJL 118	NATURALLY (LP)	£20
65	Atlantic ATL 5032	AUTOBIOGRAPHY (LP)	£20
66	Atlantic 587 023/588 023	SAYIN' SOMETHIN' (LP, Mono/Stereo)	£20
68	Mercury LML/SLML 4022	THEM ADDERLEYS (LP, mono/stereo)	£20
69	A&M AMLS 947	CALLING OUT LOUD (LP)	£18

ADDICTION
92	Vicious Pumpin' OBS 002	ADDICTION EP (12", stamped white label)	£20
92	Vicious Pumpin' VIC 003	MIND PENETRATION EP (12", stamped white label)	£25
92	Vicious Pumpin' VIC 003R	MIND PENETRATION (THE REMIXES) EP (12", stamped white label)	£40
92	Vicious Vinyl VIC 001	THE CREATIVE DUB EP (12")	£15

ADDICTS
| 64 | Decca F 11902 | That's My Girl/Here She Comes | £40 |

ADDIS POSSE
| 90 | Warriors Dance WAFT 14 | Let The Warriors Dance (Charge Mix)/(Addis Acid Mix)/(Funky Funky Drum Drum Mix)/(Live & Def Mix) (12") | £15 |

ADDIS ROCKERS
| 85 | Warrior WAR 2 | ENTER ADDIS ABABA (LP) | £20 |

ADDIX
| 79 | Zig Zag ZZ 22002 | Too Blind To See/(No Such Thing As A) Bad Boy (p/s) | £15 |

ADD N TO X
95	Blow Up 004LP	VERO ELECTRONICS (LP)	£18
98	Satellite STL010	ON THE WIRES OF OUR NERVES (2-LP, inners)	£20
99	Mute STUMM 170	AVANT HARD (2-LP, gatefold)	£30
00	Mute STUMM 187	ADD INSULT TO INJURY (2-LP)	£20

MINT VALUE £

02	Mute STUMM 204	LOUD LIKE NATURE (2-LP)	£20

ADDRISSI BROTHERS
| 59 | Columbia DB 4370 | Back To The Old Salt Mine/It's Love | £20 |

JEAN ADEBAMBO
79	Ade J AJ 101	Say That You Love Me/(Instrumental)/Dance Of Love/(Instrumental) (12")	£80
84	Ade J AJ 106	Never Before/This Will Be (12", p/s)	£30
83	Ade J AJ 0123	FEELINGS (LP)	£50
85	Ade J AJ 0124	OFF KEY LOVING (LP)	£50

ADELE
07	Pacemaker 1	Hometown Glory/Best For Last (7", 500 only)	£15
08	XL XLS S321	Chasing Pavements/That's It I Quit...	£30
08	XL XLS 393	Make You Feel My Love/Painting Pictures (p/s, 500 only)	£15
12	XL XLS 593	Skyfall/Instrumental (p/s)	£40
08	XL XLLP 313	19 (LP, printed inner)	£25
11	XL XLLP 520	21 (LP, printed inner)	£20
21	Columbia/Sony 19439937971	30 (2LP, printed inners)	£18
21	Columbia/Sony 19439943231	30 (2LP, printed inners, white vinyl, Amazon exclusive)	£25
21	Columbia/Sony 19439949071	30 (2LP, printed inners, clear vinyl, HMV exclusive)	£20

ADEM
| 04 | Domino WIGLP 129 | HOMESONGS (LP) | £25 |
| 06 | Domino WIGLP 160 | LOVE AND OTHER PLANETS (LP) | £15 |

BOBBY ADENO
| 66 | Vocalion V 9279 | The Hands Of Time/It's A Sad World (DJ copy) | £40 |
| 66 | Vocalion V 9279 | The Hands Of Time/It's A Sad World | £25 |

SEGUN ADEWALE
| 85 | Stern's Africa STERNS1009 | OJO JE (LP) | £15 |

ADICTS
81	Dining Out TUX 1	LUNCH WITH THE ADICTS (EP, 1st variation with 'brown' bricks with insert & screen-printed p/s)	£125
81	Dining Out TUX 1	LUNCH WITH THE ADICTS (EP, 2nd variation with 'white' bricks with insert & screen-printed p/s)	£80
82	Fall Out FALL 002	Viva La Revolution/Steamroller (p/s)	£20
82	Razor RZS 101	Chinese Takeaway/You'll Never Walk Alone (p/s)	£15
81	Dwed SMT 008	SONGS OF PRAISE (LP)	£75
81	Fall Out FALL LP 006	SONGS OF PRAISE (LP, reissue, yellow vinyl, 2,000 only)	£60
81	Fall Out FALL LP 006P	SONGS OF PRAISE (LP, reissue, picture disc)	£20
82	Razor RAZ 2	SOUND OF MUSIC (LP)	£35
85	Razor RAZ 15	SMART ALEX (LP)	£20
87	Fall Out FALL LP 021	THIS IS YOUR LIFE (LP)	£18
87	Fall Out FALL LP 042	FIFTH OVERTURE (LP)	£20
90	Fall Out FALL LP 046	ROCKERS INTO ORBIT (LP, green vinyl, stickered sleeve)	£18
17	Razor RAZ 2	AND SO IT WAS! (LP)	£15

PETER ADLER
| 66 | Decca 12394 | I'm Gonna Turn My Life Around/But I Was Cool | £15 |

ADLIBS (U.K.)
| 65 | Fontana TF 584 | Neighbour Neighbour/Lovely Ladies | £50 |

AD-LIBS (U.S.)
66	Red Bird RB 10-102	The Boy From New York City/Kicked Around (DJ Copy)	£50
66	Red Bird RB 10-102	The Boy From New York City/Kicked Around	£35
69	Deep Soul DS 9102	Giving Up/Appreciation	£35

ADMINISTRATORS
| 81 | Cha Cha CHAD 36 | Say You Love Me/So I Can Love You (12") | £70 |

ADMIRAL
| 85 | Jah Tubby's JT 101 | General Governor/(Version)//Black Is My Beauty/(Version) (12", with the Offbeat Posse) | £50 |

ADMIRAL SIR CLOUDESLEY SHOVELL
13	Rise Above RISE7/175FREE	SHARON TATE EXPERIENCE:Christmas Killer/ADMIRAL SIR CLOUDESLEY SHOVEL: Blow Up The Xmas Tree 300 only: 100 white vinyl, 100 red vinyl and 100 green vinyl	£80
12	Rise Above RISELP142	DON'T HEAR IT...FEAR IT! (LP, with 7", both on clear vinyl, limited edition)	£40
12	Rise Above RISELP142	DON'T HEAR IT...FEAR IT! (LP, red, green or purple vinyl)	£20
14	Rise Above RISELP179	CHECK EM BEFORE YOU WRECK EM (LP, with 7", clear vinyl with poster)	£25
16	Rise Above RISELP205	KEEP IT GREASY (LP, with 7", clear vinyl)	£25
19	Rise Above RISELP235	VERY UNCERTAIN TIMES (LP, with 7")	£20

ADMIRALS (1)
| 65 | Fontana TF 597 | Promised Land/Palisades Park | £30 |

ADMIRAL TIBET
86	Redman Intl. RED 4	New Tactics/RED DRAGON: Ease Off (12")	£20
92	Rix RIZ 006	Permission/Sixth Commandment Dub/Version (12")	£50
80s	Live & Love LLD301	Victim of Babylon/GREGORY PECK: Wah Do You (12")	£15
(see also Red Dragon)

ADMIT YOU'RE SHIT
| 85 | Mortahate MORT 17 | EXPECT NO MERCY . . . IF YOU CROSS YOUR REAL FRIENDS (EP) | £25 |

MINT VALUE £

| 86 | Mortarhate MORT 27 | 12 INCHES OF AYS? ARE YOU SURE (LP, insert) .... £15 |

AD NAUSEUM
| 87 | No label or cat no | THE GREATEST SHOW ON EARTH (Mini-LP) .... £20 |

A.D. 1984
79	Voyage Intl. VOY 005	The Russians Are Coming/New Moon Falling (p/s) £20
80	Grand Prix 001/002	Race To Nowhere/Leisure Crime (with lyric sheet) £15
83	Grand Prix GP 011	Mushroom Music (& Mayhem)/1984 .... £15

ADOLESCENTS
| 90 | Overground OVER 07 | ADOLESCENTS (LP, reissue of original US pressing) .... £15 |

ADRENALIN
| 79 | Hithouse 12 HIT 2 | Feel The Real/Feel The Real (Instrumental) (12" stamped white label) .... £30 |

AD2000
| 84 | Disco Funk Music DF 001B | Love Time Machine/Love Time Machine (Instrumental) (12") .... £300 |

ADULT JAZZ
| 14 | Spare Thought SPTHLP 002 | GIST IS (LP, as 2 x 12") .... £60 |

ADVENTURES
| 61 | Philips BBL 7548 | CAN'T STOP TWISTIN' (LP) .... £30 |

ANTHONY ADVERSE
| 85 | El ACME 11 | RED SHOES (LP) .... £30 |
| 80 | ÈL ACME 22 | SPIN (LP) .... £15 |

ADVERTISING
| 78 | EMI EMC 3253 | ADVERTISING JINGLES (LP) .... £18 |
(see also Secret Affair, Innocents, Simon Boswell)

ADVERTS
77	Stiff BUY 13	One Chord Wonders/Quickstep (p/s, 1st pressing with push-out centre) £40
77	Stiff BUY 13	One Chord Wonders/Quickstep (p/s, re-pressing with solid centre) £15
78	Bright BRL 201	CROSSING THE RED SEA WITH THE ADVERTS (LP, red vinyl, 5,000 only) £80
78	Bright BULB 1	CROSSING THE RED SEA WITH THE ADVERTS (LP, black vinyl second pressing) £20
79	RCA PL 25246	CAST OF THOUSANDS (LP) £30
81	Butt/Bright ALSO 002	CROSSING THE RED SEA WITH THE ADVERTS (LP, reissue, red vinyl) £15
90	Receiver RRLP 136	LIVE AT THE ROXY CLUB (LP) £15

ADVOCATES
| 73 | Dovetail DOVE 1 | ADVOCATES (LP) .... £30 |
| 75 | Dovetail DOVE 7 | HERE I REST MY CASE (LP) .... £30 |

AERIAL FX
| 82 | Kamera ERA 012 | Instant Feelings/5:15 (p/s, pressed in France but issued in U.K.) .... £15 |
| 82 | Kamera KAM 008 | WATCHING THE DANCE (LP, pressed in France but issued in U.K.) .... £30 |

AEROPHONE
| 71 | RPM 357 | Sweet Sweet Suzie/Of Tomorrow .... £15 |

AEROSMITH
73	CBS 32005	AEROSMITH (LP) £20
74	CBS 80015	GET YOUR WINGS (LP) £15
89	Geffen WX 304	PUMP (LP, inner) £18
93	Geffen GEF 24444	GET A GRIP (2-LP, inners) £40
(see also Run DMC)

AEROVONS
| 69 | Parlophone R 5790 | The Train/A Song For Jane .... £70 |
| 69 | Parlophone R 5804 | World Of You/Say Georgia .... £150 |

A FAIR SET
| 65 | Decca F 12168 | Honey And Wine/Run Around .... £20 |

PETER AFENDOULIS
| 78 | Folkland FL 1018 | THERE'S ONLY ONE F IN AFENDOULIS (LP, mail-order only) .... £30 |

AFEX
| 67 | King KG 1058 | She Got The Time/I Never Knew Love Was Like This .... £250 |

AFFINITY
| 70 | Vertigo 6059 007 | I Wonder If I Care As Much/Three Sisters .... £35 |
| 70 | Vertigo 6360 004 | AFFINITY (LP, gatefold sleeve, large swirl label) .... £700 |
(see also Linda Hoyle, Jeff Beck Group, Queen, Ice)

AFFLECKS PALACE
| 19 | Spirit Of Spike Island | HELLO. IS ANYONE AWAKE? (12", p/s, 300 only) .... £40 |
| 20 | Spirit Of Spike Island SOS12 | EVERYTHING IS AN ATTEMPT TO BE HUMAN (12", p/s) .... £40 |

AFFLICTED (1)
| 71 | Scott SC 02 | Miranda/Stolen Dreams .... £100 |

AFFLICTED (2)
81	Bonk AFF 1	I'm Afflicted/Be Aware (rubber-stamped white labels, p/s, with insert) £70
81	Bonk AFF 1	I'm Afflicted/Be Aware (rubber-stamped white labels, p/s, without insert) £30
82	Bonk AFF 2	All Right Boy/Who Can Tell (with p/s, stamped white labels) £60
82	Bonk AFF 4	One Forty Two/Senseless Whale Stalker (untitled single in stamped striped bag) £20
82	Bonk AFF 3	THE AFFLICTED MAN'S MUSICAL BAG (LP, stamped white label in stamped bag sleeve) .. £25

AFFLICTED MAN
| 80 | Human HUM1 | I'M OFF MI HEAD (LP) .... £20 |

AFGHAN WHIGS
93	Blast First BFFP 90	GENTLEMEN (LP, with free 12")	£30
96	Mute STUMM 143	BLACK LOVE (LP)	£40
98	Columbia 491486	1965 (LP)	£30
10	Music On Vinyl MOVLP 149	1965 (2-LP, reissue)	£30
14	Music On VInyl MOVLP 821	BLACK LOVE (LP, reissue)	£18
14	Sub Pop SP 1061	DO TO THE BEAST (LP, 2 x 12", white vinyl, mispressing, skips on first track on side D (Royal Cream))	£15

AFI
| 03 | Nitro 65522300261 | SING THE SORROW (2-LP, red vinyl, inner sleeves) | £50 |

A FINAL DISCIPLINE
| 82 | Clock House CH 0504 | Empty Pictures/And Still I Miss You | £20 |

A FLEETING GLANCE
| 70 | Private Pressing AS 2324 | A FLEETING GLANCE (LP) | £3000 |

AFRICAN
| 72 | Sioux SI 006 | Cock Mouth Kill Cock/ERROL T: I Need You Now | £30 |

AFRICAN BEAVERS
| 65 | RCA RCA 1447 | Find My Baby/Jungle Fever | £20 |

AFRICAN BROTHERS (ACTUALLY MATUMBI)
| 77 | Mainline ML 1 | Gimme Gimme African Love/PURE ROOTS: African Love Dub | £15 |

AFRICAN BROTHERS BAND
70	Afribros PAB 001	AFRICAN DANCE BAND INTERNATIONAL (LP)	£50
73	Afribros PAB 003	HIGHLIFE TIME (LP)	£50
73	Leo Mensah PN 06	HIGHLIFE TIME (LP)	£35
74	Afribros PAB 003	HIGHLIFE TIME (LP, reissue, different cover)	£35

AFRICAN CONNEXION
| 84 | Oval OVALT 28/12 | MIDNIGHT PRESSURE (12", p/s) | £30 |

AFRICAN HEAD CHARGE
81	ON-U LP 13	MY LIFE IN A HOLE IN THE GROUND (LP)	£35
82	ON-U LP 19	ENVIRONMENTAL STUDIES (LP)	£35
83	ON-U LP 27	DRASTIC SEASON (LP)	£35
86	ON-U LP 40	OFF THE BEATEN TRACK (LP)	£35
90	ON-U LP 50	SONGS OF PRAISE (LP)	£35
93	ON-U LP 65	IN PURSUIT OF SHASHAMANE LAND (LP, with free 7")	£30

AFRICAN MUSIC MACHINE
| 72 | Mojo 2092 046 | Black Water Gold (Pearl)/Making Nassau Fruit Drink | £15 |

AFRICAN PRINCESS
| 81 | Jah Shaka SHAKA 809 | Jah Jah Children Cry/Jah Jah Dub (12") | £75 |

AFRICAN STONE
76	Concrete Jungle CJ 600	How Long Must I Wait/4TH STREET ORCHESTRA: Long Wait	£25
76	Concrete Jungle CJ 604	Singer Man/Song (as African Stones)	£15
76	K & B	Run Rasta Run/Run Rasta Run	£25

AFRICANS
| 81 | Lord Koos KLP 2 | HAVE A GRAND TIME (LP, compilation) | £40 |

AFRIKA
| 82 | L 100 | I Want You Tonight/I Want You Tonight (Remix) (p/s) | £200 |

AFRIKAN STAR
| 80 | Black Vinyl BV0 77 | Livin' In The System/Run & Hide (DIY p/s) | £25 |

AFRIQUE
| 74 | Mainstream MSL 1018 | SOUL MAKOSSA (LP) | £20 |

AFRO
| 71 | Punch PH 89 | Lonely World/ALTON ELLIS ALL STARS: Put It On | £15 |

AFRO DIMENSIONS
| 72 | Ackee 535 | Dance With Me/Lonely Nights | £25 |
| 72 | Jay Boy BOY 84 | If You Don't Want My Love/Just Because | £20 |

AFRO ENCHANTERS
| 63 | Island WI 071 | Peace And Love/Wayward African | £30 |

AFRO FUNK
| 75 | Kabana KAB 1 | Obanya Special/Try And Try | £15 |
| 75 | Kabana BSC 01 | BODY MUSIC (LP) | £50 |

AFRO NATIONAL
| 75 | Afro National NO 100 | Push Am Forward/Salenotu | £20 |

AFROTONES
69	Duke DU 19	Freedom Sound/BOYS: Easy Sound (4-prong centre)	£100
69	High Note HS 023	I'm In A Corner/BELTONES: Broken Heart	£50
17	Duke DU 19	Freedom Sound/BOYS: Easy Sound (reissue, solid centre)	£50
(see also Delroy Wilson)			

AFTER DARK
81	After Dark AD 001	Evil Woman/Johnny/Lucy (p/s)	£40
83	Lazer PROMO 1	Deathbringer/Call Of The Wild (picture disc, promo only)	£30
83	Lazer PROMO 1	Deathbringer/Call Of The Wild (white label test pressing)	£60

AFTER EIGHT
81 Airship AP 346   JUST THE WAY WE ARE (LP)..£20

AFTERMATH (U.K.)
81 Red Star AFTERMATH 0001 The Freedom Fighter/All The Others/1980 (p/s)...£15

AFTERMATH (1)
80 S Records AM 001   For You/Mixed Up Kid £50

AFTERSHAVE
73 Splendid SPS 401   Warmaker/One Of The Best...£175

AFTER TEA
68 Ace Of Clubs SCL-R 1251 AFTER TEA (LP)...£50
(see also Ray Fenwick)

AFTER THE FIRE
75 Rapid RR 001   SIGNS OF CHANGE (LP, with insert) £25
(see also Narnia, Waiting For The Sun)

AGATHOCLES
90 Deaf DEAF 01   SUPPOSE IT WAS YOU (split LP with DRUDGE)..£20

YASUKO AGAWA
86 Blue Bird BRT 26   L.A. Nights/New York Afternoon (12")...£35

AGED IN HARMONY
16 Melodies Int. MEL 002/3/4 YOU'RE A MELODY (box set of 3 x 7") £25

AGENT ORANGE
92 Dog Tag AO 001   Sounds Flakey To Me (Jungle Mix)/Only You Have The Bass/Sounds Flakey To Me
                            (Original Mix) (12")..£18
93 Dog Tag AO 002   TECNOSKA EP: The Nuttiest Ska/Gettin' Rougher (Ska Mix)/Gettin' Rougher (Kaos
                            Remix) (12")..£15

AGENTS
79 Grapevine GRP 142   Trouble/The Love I Hold £15

AGGRESSORS
70 Pye 7N 17889   Whisky And Soda/Soul Of The Jungle £15
70 Marble Arch 1260   REGGAE STEADAE GO (LP)...£15

AGGROVATORS
70 Jackpot JP 751   Sex Machine/You Left Me And Gone (both act. by Dave Barker & Aggrovators)..............£30
70 Smash SMA 2302   Big Red Ball Parts 1 & 2 (A-side actually "Big Red Bumble" by Lloyd Tyrell; B-side
                            actually "Big Bumble Version" by Lloyd & Devon)......................................£25
71 Smash SMA 2312   One More Bottle Of Beer/Beer Version £15
73 Smash SMA 2339   Straight To Jackson Head/HORACE ANDY: You Are My Angel £20
73 Downtown DT 500   Dreadlocks Man/Rasta Want Peace (both actually by Rasta Twins).............£15
76 Grounation GROL 507   RASTA DUB '76 (LP)...£40
78 Live & Love LAP 04   JAMMIES IN A LION STYLE DUB (LP) £35
78 Third World TWS 939   KAYA DUB (LP)..£50
78 Conflict COLP 2006   RASTA DUB 2000 (LP) £50
90 Attack ATLP 111   DUB JACKPOT (LP, with King Tubby) £25
(see also Dave Barker, Dennis Alcapone, Jerry Lewis [Jamaica], Delroy Wilson, John Holt, Alton Ellis, Cornell Campbell)

AGGROVATORS AND THE REVOLUTIONARIES
77 Third World TWS 900   THE AGGROVATORS MEET THE REVOLUTIONARIES AT CHANNEL ONE (LP)....................£30
78 Burning Sounds BS 1028 GUERILLA DUB (LP)..£35

AGINCOURT
70 Merlin HF 3   FLY AWAY (LP, lyric insert) £2000
11 Merlin HF3   FLY AWAY (reissue, lyric insert, with or without certificate, RCLP 001 matrix) £70
21 Trading Places TDP 54056 FLY AWAY (LP, reissue) £20
(see also Friends, Ithaca, Alice Through The Looking Glass, Tomorrow Come Someday)

AGITATORS
79 Redball RR 028   BOUND AND GAGGED WITH RUBBER TUBING EP £40
80 Rasclaat CLAAT 2   NOT QUITE RIGHT IN THE HEAD (LP)..£80

AGNES STRANGE
75 Birdsnest BRL 9000   STRANGE FLAVOUR (LP)...£150
00 Thorns 7788   DUST IN THE SUNLIGHT (LP)..£15

AGNOSTIC FRONT
85 Rough Justice JUST 3   CAUSE FOR ALARM (LP)...£15

AGONY COLUMN
79 Tyger TYG 2   (I Had It) All Worked Out/Good Grief (p/s) £15

AGRO
95 Epsilon 001   THE ASSOCIATION OF AUTONOMOUS ASTRONAUTS EP (12")...................£20

AGROS
71 Punch PH 56   What Do You Fall In Love For/SLICKERS: Too Much.................................£20

CHRISTINA AGUILERA
06 RCA 82876 82639   BACK TO BASICS (3LP, numbered, book sleeve, printed inners) £350
10 RCA 88697 60867 1   BIONIC (3LP, two lyric inserts)..£100
23 Sony Music Latin
    CI880825.1   AGUILERA (2LP, fourth side etched, red vinyl, gatefold, printed inners)......£30

A GUY CALLED GERALD
88 Rham RS8804   Voodoo Ray/Escape/Rhapsody In Acid/Blow Your House Down (12", p/s) £25
89 Avernus AVERNUS 1   Trip City Mambo/Valentines Theme (12", stamped white labels)................£250

MINT VALUE £

90	Columbia XPR 1535	**Emotions Electric** (Frankie Foncett Remix 1)/**Emotions Electric** (Frankie Foncett Remix 2) (12", promo in stickered plain sleeve)	£15
92	Juice Box JBOX 003	**Cops/The Trak/28 Gun Bad Boy/Paranoia** (12")	£40
92	Juice Box JBOX 004	**Ses Makes You Wise/Sunshine/King Of The Jungle/Boase up** (12")	£15
92	Juice Box JBOX 005	**The Musical Magical Midi Machine/Let It Go/Like A Drug/Free Africa** (12")	£15
92	Columbia XPR 1684	**Cops/The Track/Paranoia/28 Gun Bad Boy** (12" white label promo)	£40
93	Juice Box JBOX 009	**Too Fucked To Dance/Darker Than I Should Be/Anything v2.1/Is The Right Time** (12")	£20
93	Juice Box JBOX 014	**The Glok Track/Gerald's Bassline/Ease The Pressure/Take Me** (12")	£15
89	Rham! RA 1	**HOT LEMONADE** (LP)	£20
89	Rham! RA 1	**HOT LEMONADE** (LP, repressing, pink sleeve with Voodoo Ray as 1st track on Side 2)	£20
90	CBS 4664820	**AUTOMANIKK** (LP, with free 12")	£20
94	Juice Box JBOX 12	**28 GUN BAD BOY** (LP, promo)	£70
95	Juice Box JBLP 25	**BLACK SECRET TECHNOLOGY** (2-LP, 1st pressing, black and blue sleeve)	£30
96	Juice Box JBLP 30	**BLACK SECRET TECHNOLOGY** (2-LP, 2nd pressing, full colour sleeve, new design)	£25

ERIC AGYEMANG
78	Apogee BEBLOP 013	**HIGHLIFE SAFARI** (LP)	£50
85	Thornhill TR- LP 01	**METE AWO YI MU** (LIVING IN THE COLD) (LP, with Thomas Frimpong)	£40
87	Asona ASR 6010EX	**NANANOM** (LP)	£20

A-HA
84	Warner Bros W 9146	**Take On Me/And You Tell Me** (silver/blue p/s)	£40
84	Warner Bros W 9146T	**Take On Me** (Extended)/**And You Tell Me/Stop And Make Your Mind Up** (12", silver/blue p/s, with poster & stickers)	£150
84	Warner Bros W 9146T	**Take On Me** (Extended)/**And You Tell Me/Stop And Make Your Mind Up** (12", silver/blue p/s, without poster & stickers)	£80
88	Warner Bros W7749W	**Touchy!/Hurry Home** ('felt' p/s)	£15

AHAB & WAILERS
63	Pye 7N 15553	**Cleopatra's Needle/Neb's Tune**	£40

A HEADS
82	TW Records HIT 107	**Dying Man/Hell Cell/Changing Places** (p/s)	£18

AIKEN'S DRUM
81	Private Pressing SRTX/CUS 1134	**AIKEN'S DRUM** (LP)	£40

JOSS AIKINS AND THE ENVOYS
65	Volta NO 1	**The Founder/The Unity Highlife** (with Teddy Osei)	£60

(see also Osibisa)

AIM (2)
99	Grand Central GCLP 105	**COLD WATER MUSIC** (2-LP)	£40
02	Grand Central GCLP 112	**HINTERLAND** (2-LP)	£30

AIR (1)
71	Atlantic 2400 148	**AIR** (LP)	£20

AIR (2)
98	Source V 2848	**MOON SAFARI** (LP, with inner)	£40
00	Record Makers V2910	**VIRGIN SUICIDES** (LP)	£60
01	Virgin V 2945	**10,000 HZ LEGEND** (LP)	£30
03	Record Makers REC 09	**CITY READING** (2-LP, with Alessandro Baricco)	£25
05	Virgin 72435 966322 7	**TALKIE WALKIE** (LP)	£20
07	EMI V 3032	**POCKET SYMPHONY** (LP, white vinyl)	£15
10	Vinyl Factory VF 007	**LOVE 2** (2-LP, 300 only in box with print, booklet and certificate)	£150
12	Vinyl Factory VF 042	**LA VOYAGE DANS LA LUNE** (2-LP, gatefold with DVD)	£30
12	Vinyl Factory VF 043	**LA VOYAGE DANS LA LUNE** (4-LP, art print, DVD, cloth box)	£80
14	Vinyl Factory VF 112	**MUSIC FOR MUSEUM** (2-LP, clear vinyl, poster)	£75
16	Parlophone 0190295990121	**TWENTYEARS** (2-LP, box set, random coloured LPs, 3-CD and poster)	£30

AIRBRIDGE
83	Rattees RATT 001	**Words And Pictures/Zero Minus One**	£15

AIRHEAD
92	Korova 9030 74679 2	**BOING!** (LP)	£20

AIRKRAFT
79	Lathe TSR1	**Here Comes That Sound/Video Romance/White Boys**	£25

AIR LIQUIDE
94	Rising High RSN 79	**If There Was No Gravity/Auroral Belt/Stratus Static/THX Is On** (12", black or blue vinyl)	£15
94	Rising High RSN LP 15	**NEPHOLOGY - THE NEW RELIGION** (2-LP)	£40
95	Rising High RSN LP 38	**SONIC WEATHER MACHINE** (2-LP, black or blue vinyl)	£30

AIR MIAMI
95	4AD CAD 5011	**ME. ME. ME.** (LP)	£30

AIRPEOPLE
95	Malawi COB 139906	**7 Deadlines/**(Flaw Mix) (12")	£50

AIRSHIP
79	Decca FR 13856	**Get Out, Take Your Mother With You/Gimme A Can Of Spray Paint**	£40

AIRTO
71	Buddah 2318 040	**SEEDS ON THE GROUND - THE NATURAL SOUNDS OF AIRTO** (LP, gatefold)	£20
73	CTI CTL 18	**FINGERS** (LP)	£15
74	CTI CTL 21	**IN CONCERT** (LP, with Deodato)	£15
74	CTI CTL 23	**VIRGIN LAND** (LP)	£15

AISHA

86	Ariwa ARI 48	Dancing Time/The Creator (12")	£35
86	Ariwa ARI 52	That's How Heartaches Are Made/AISHA & BLACKSTEEL: Prophecy Dub (12")	£15
86	Ariwa ARI 060	Prophecy/THE ROBOTICS: Dub (12")	£25
94	Ariwa ARI 153	Only Jah Works/Crisis (12")	£18
87	Ariwa ARILP 029	HIGH PRIESTESS (LP)	£40
93	Twinkle NG 538	DAUGHTERS OF ZION (LP)	£20
94	Ariwa ARLP 084	TRUE ROOTS (LP)	£15
96	Twinkle NG 550	RAISE YOUR VOICE (LP)	£20

BOBBY AITKEN (& CARIBBEATS)

62	Island WI 028	Baby Baby (actually with Patsy)/Lonely Boy	£25
62	Blue Beat BB 93	Never Never (South Virginia)/Isabella (as Bobby Aitken & Buster's Group)	£25
63	Blue Beat BB 146	Don't Leave Me/Mom And Dad (as Bobby Aitken & Tinse)	£25
63	Rio R 14	I've Told You/Please Go Back	£25
63	Rio R 15	It Takes A Friend/LAUREL AITKEN: Sunshine	£25
64	Rio R 34	Rolling Stone/LESTER STERLING'S GROUP: Man About Town	£50
64	Rio R 40	Garden Of Eden/Whiplash	£40
64	Rio R 50	Little Girl/Together	£40
65	Rio R 52	Rain Came Tumbling Down/SHENLEY & LUNAN: Something Is On Your Mind	£30
65	Rio R 64	Mr Judge/BINZ: Times Have Changed	£25
65	Black Swan WI 441	Jerico/LESTER STERLING: Lunch Time	£40
66	Ska Beat JB 252	Thunderball/ORIGINATORS: Chelip Chelip	£200
67	Doctor Bird DB 1071	Keep On Pushing/You Won't Regret It	£80
67	Doctor Bird DB 1072	Let Them Have A Home/Temptation (with Caribbeats)	£60
67	Doctor Bird DB 1077	Sweets For My Sweet/How Sweet It Is (with Caribbeats)	£60
67	Island WI 3028	Kiss Bam Bam (El Bang Bang)/CYNTHIA RICHARDS: How Could I	£130
67	Giant GN 11	What A Fool/Curfew (with Caribbeats)	£50

(see also Caribbeats, Laurel Aitken, Frank Cosmo, Lloyd & Glen)

LAUREL AITKEN (& BLUE BEATS)

59	Kalypso XX 15	Sweet Chariot/Nebuchnezer	£50
59	Kalypso XX 16	Aitken's Boogie/Cherrie	£50
60	Kalypso XX 19	Baba Kill Me Goat/Tribute To Collie Smith	£40
60	Starlite ST45 011	Boogie In My Bones/Little Sheila	£40
60	Starlite ST45 014	Honey Girl (with Caribs)/Drinkin' Whisky (with Bluebeats)	£50
60	Melodisc M 1570	Mary Lee/Lonesome Lover (with Bluebeats)	£40
60	Blue Beat B 1	Boogie Rock/Heavenly Angel (with the BOOGIE CATS) (white label)	£50
60	Blue Beat BB 1	Boogie Rock/Heavenly Angel (with the BOOGIE CATS) (blue label)	£40
60	Blue Beat BB 10	Jeannie Is Back/If It's Money You Need	£30
60	Blue Beat BB 14	Judgment Day/Yea Yea Baby	£30
60	Blue Beat BB 22	Railroad Track/Tell Me Darling (with the Blue Beats)	£35
60	Blue Beat BB 25	More Whisky/LLOYD CLARKE: Parapinto Boogie	£35
61	Starlite ST45 034	Love Me Baby/Stars Were Made	£50
61	Blue Beat BB 40	Bar Tender/Mash Potato Boogie	£45
61	Blue Beat BB 52	Bouncing Woman/Nursery Rhyme Boogie (with Blue Beats)	£45
61	Blue Beat BB 70	Mighty Redeemer/Please Don't Leave Me	£40
62	Blue Beat BB 84	Brother David/Back To New Orleans (with Blue Beats)	£40
62	Blue Beat BB 109	Lucille/I Love You More Everyday	£40
62	Blue Beat BB 120	Sixty Days And Sixty Nights/Going To Kansas City (with Les Dawson Trio)	£40
62	Blue Beat BB 142	Jenny Jenny/Weary Wanderer (with Bandits and Ruddy & Sketto)	£50
62	Dice CC 1	Mabel/You Got Me Rocking (with Hyacinth)	£40
63	Dice CC 13	Sweet Jamaica/Bossa Nova Hop	£40
63	Blue Beat BB 164	Zion/Swing Low Sweet Chariot	£50
63	Blue Beat BB 194	Little Girl/Daniel Saw The Stone (with Ruddy and Sketto)	£50
63	Duke DK 1002	Low Down Dirty Girl/Pink Lane Shuffle	£45
63	Island WI 092	I Shall Remove/We Got To Move	£60
63	Island WI 095	What A Weeping/Zion City Wall	£60
63	Island WI 099	In My Soul/One More River To Cross	£60
63	Rio R 11	Adam & Eve/BOBBY AITKEN: Devil Woman	£50
63	Rio R 12	Mary/Hometown	£50
63	Rio R 13	Bad Minded Woman/Life	£50
63	Rio R 17	Devil Or Angel/Fire	£50
63	Rio R 18	Freedom Train/Peace Perfect Peace	£50
64	Rio R 35	Rock Of Ages/The Mule	£55
64	Rio R 36	Leave Me Standing/Bagaboo (Bug-A-Boo)	£45
64	Rio R 37	John Saw Them Coming/Jericho	£55
64	R&B JB 167	Yes Indeed/You Can't Stop Me From Loving You	£60
64	R&B JB 170	Pick Up Your Bundle And Go/Let My People Go	£60
64	R&B JB 171	Bachelor Life/You Was Up	£60
64	Columbia DB 7280	Be Mine/Don't Stay Out Late	£20
64	Blue Beat BB 249	This Great Day/I May Never See My Baby	£50
64	J.N.A.C. 1	West Indian Cricket Test/3 Cheers For Worrell	£30
64	Black Swan WI 401	Lion Of Judah/Remember My Darling (B-side with Cynthia Richards)	£60
64	Black Swan WI 411	The Saint/Go Gal Go	£45
64	Dice CC 28	Jamaica/I Don't Want No More	£45
65	Dice CC 31	We Shall Overcome/You Left Me Standing	£45
65	Rio R 53	Mary Don't You Weep/I Believe	£50
65	Rio R 54	Mary Lou/Jump And Shout	£50

MINT VALUE £

65	Rio R 56	One More Time/Ring Don't Mean A Thing	£50
65	Rio R 60	Come And Let Us Go/Lonely Nights	£50
65	Rio R 65	Let's Be Lovers/I Need You	£50
65	Venus VE 4	How Can I Forget You?/Weeping And Crying	£45
65	Island WI 198	Boogie In My Bones/Little Sheila	£45
66	Blue Beat BB 340	Clementine/Bongo Jerk	£55
66	Blue Beat BB 369	Shame And Scandal/Coconut Woman	£55
66	Ska Beat JB 232	Jamboree/Looking For My Baby	£55
66	Ska Beat JB 236	Propaganda/Shake	£45
66	Ska Beat JB 239	Green Banana/Darling	£45
66	Rio R 91	How Can I Forget You/I've Been Weeping And Crying	£45
66	Rio R 92	Baby Don't Do It/That Girl	£45
66	Rio R 97	We Shall Overcome/Street Of Glory	£45
66	Rio R 99	Clap Your Hands/Revival	£45
66	Rainbow RAI 101	Don't Break Your Promises/Last Night (with Soulmen)	£45
66	Rainbow RAI 106	Voodoo Woman/Bewildered And Blue (B-side with Carols)	£50
67	Rainbow RAI 111	Sweet Precious Love/I Want To Love You Forever (with Carols)	£50
67	Columbia Blue Beat DB 102	Rock Steady/Blowin' In The Wind	£35
67	Columbia Blue Beat DB 106	I'm Still In Love With You Girl/Blue Rhythm	£35
67	Fab FAB 5	Never You Hurt/I Need You (as Laurel Aitken & Soulmen)	£50
68	Fab FAB 45	For Sentimental Reasons/Last Waltz (as Laurel Aitken & Rainbows)	£40
68	Doctor Bird DB 1160	Mr Lee/Birmingham Girl	£60
68	Doctor Bird DB 1161	La La La (Means I Love You)/DETOURS: Sunnyside	£60
69	Ackee ACK 105	Sin City/Skinhead A Wreck The Town(credited to Winston Groovy)(white label only, unissued)	£250
69	Doctor Bird DB 1187	Fire In Your Wire/Quando Quando	£50
69	Doctor Bird DB 1190	Rice And Peas/CLASSICS: Worried Over Me	£50
69	Doctor Bird DB 1196	Reggae Prayer/Deliverance Will Come	£50
69	Doctor Bird/J.J. DB 1197	The Rise And Fall (Of Laurel)/If You're Not Black	£50
69	Doctor Bird DB 1202	Haile Haile (The Lion)/SEVEN LETTERS: Call Collect	£50
69	Doctor Bird DB 1203	Carolina/Kingston Town	£50
69	Junior JR 105	Think Me No Know/RICO: Trombone Man	£50
69	Nu Beat NB 024	Woppi King/Mr Soul	£50
69	Nu Beat NB 025	Suffering Still (with Girlie)/Reggae '69	£50
69	Nu Beat NB 032	Haile Selassie/Blues Dance	£50
69	Nu Beat NB 033	Lawd Doctor (with Girlie)/Big Fight In Hell Stadium	£50
69	Nu Beat NB 035	Run Powell Run/RICO RODRIGUEZ: A Message To You	£50
69	Nu Beat NB 039	Save The Last Dance/Walk Right Back	£50
69	Nu Beat NB 040	Don't Be Cruel/John B.	£30
69	Nu Beat NB 043	Shoo Be Doo/Babylon Gone	£30
69	Nu Beat NB 044	Landlords And Tenants/Everybody Sufferin'	£30
69	Nu Beat NB 045	Jesse James/Freedom	£40
69	Nu Beat NB 046	Pussy Price Gone Up/Gimme Back Me Dollar	£40
69	Junior JR 106	River Nile (existence unconfirmed, white labels only)	£40
69	Nu Beat NB 047	Skinhead Train/GRUVY BEATS: Kent People	£70
70	Nu Beat NB 048	Skinhead Invasion/Benwood Dick (unissued, blank white label demos only)	£125
70	Nu Beat NB 048	Mr Popcorn/GRUVY BEATS: Share Your Popcorn	£18
70	Nu Beat NB 049	I've Got Your Love/GRUVY BEATS: Blue Mink	£20
70	Nu Beat NB 050	Scandal In Brixton Market/Soul Grinder (both sides with Girlie)	£20
70	New Beat NB 054	Nobody But Me/Baby Please Don't Go	£15
70	New Beat NB 056	I'll Never Love Any Girl/The Best I Can	£15
70	New Beat NB 057	Reggae Popcorn/Take Me Back	£20
70	New Beat NB 063	Baby I Need Your Loving/Think It Over	£20
70	New Beat NB 065	Sex Machine/Since You Left	£20
70	New Beat NB 072	Pachanga/Version	£20
70	Ackee ACK 104	Pussy Got Thirteen Life/Single Man	£25
70	Ackee ACK 106	Sin Pon You/Everynight	£80
70	Bamboo BAM 16	Moon Rock/Cut Up Munno (apparantly, white labels only)	£80
70	Pama Supreme PS 300	Why Can't I Touch You/Can't Turn Your Back On Me	£15
71	Trojan TR 7826	It's Too Late/AITKEN'S BAND: Slow Rock	£15
71	Black Swan BW 1408	If It's Hell Below/Just A Little Bit Of Love	£40
71	Big Shot BI 595	Dancing With My Baby/Do The Boogaloo	£20
72	Camel CA 90	Africa Arise/GI GINGRI: Holy Mount Zion	£15
77	Dip DL 5012	For Ever And Ever/None Sweeter Than You	£20
78	Ultra PFUL 2005	Hoocihe Coochie Man/Sexy Boogie (12")	£60
66	Rio LR 1	SKA WITH LAUREL (LP)	£300
67	Doctor Bird DLM 5012	SAYS FIRE (LP)	£150
69	Pama PSP 1012	THE HIGH PRIEST OF REGGAE (LP)	£100
69	Pama ECO 8	SCANDAL IN BRIXTON MARKET (LP, with Girlie)	£100
69	J.J.	RISE AND FALL (LP)	£120
73	Count Shelly CSLP 01	SOPHIA (LP, SOPHIA on cover, 'MARIA SOFIA' on label)	£45
93	GAZ 009	GODFATHER OF SKA (LP)	£18

(see also Laurel & Owen, Girlie, King Horror, Ruts, Bobby Aitken, Classics, Beresford Ricketts, Duke Reid, Tommy McCook)

A-JAES

| 64 | Oak RGJ 132 | I'm Leaving You/Kansas City | £700 |

AJAX PROJECT

| 92 | MACH III | MACH III EP (12" white labels only) | £15 |

JEWEL AKENS
65	London HA-N 8234	THE BIRDS AND THE BEES (LP) £25

AKERCOCKE
05	Earache 7MOSH 322	Eyes Of The Dawn (Demo)/The Fulcrum (transluscent red vinyl, no p/s) £15

AK 47
81	Output ORR 202	Stop! Dance!/Autobiography/Hilversum-Ao (p/s) £50
91	Rugger Bugger SEEP 004	DON'T CALL ME VANILLA (LP, with lyric sheet) £30

(see also AK Process)

TOSHIKO AKIYOSHI
58	Columbia 33CX 101101	NEWPORT JAZZ FESTIVAL 1957 (LP) £15

JAN AKKERMAN
72	Harvest SHSP 4026	PROFILE (LP) £20
73	Atlantic K40522	TABERNAKEL (LP, gatefold) £15

(see also Hunters.[Holland], Brainbox, Focus)

AK PROCESS
79	Output OPR 101	Electronic Music: After All Love/Post Town (p/s, white labels) £15

(see also AK 47)

AL ET ALL
80	Arny's Shack As 047	STRANGE AFFAIR (LP) £200

AL & THE VIBRATORS
67	Doctor Bird DB 1062	Cool Water/BABA BROOKS: Roll Call £70
67	Doctor Bird DB 1085	Move Up/Lonesome Lover £40
69	High Note HS 005	Check Up/I'll Come Back (featuring Byron Lee & The Dragonaires) £40
69	High Note HS 007	Move Up Calypso/PATSY: Fire In Your Wire £30

(see also Vibrators, Patsy Todd, Lord Power)

STEVE ALAIMO
63	Pye International 7N 25174	Every Day I Have To Cry/(Please Take A Chance On Me) Little Girl (DJ Copy) £50
63	Pye International 7N 25174	Every Day I Have To Cry/(Please Take A Chance On Me) Little Girl £30
66	HMV POP 1531	So Much Love/Truer Than True (DJ Copy) £30
66	HMV POP 1531	So Much Love/Truer Than True. £20

ALAN PARSONS
14	MOVLP1010	THE TIME MACHINE (2-LP, 180gm, translucent) £70

(see also Alan Parsons Project, Andrew Powell & Philharmonic Orchestra)

ALARM
81	White Cross W3/4	Unsafe Building/Up For Murder (wraparound p/s) £100
84	I.R.S. IRS 103	The Deceiver/Reason 41 (p/s, mispress on mustard vinyl) £400
91	I.R.S. EIRSA 1055	RAW (LP, printed inner) £20
02	Vinyl Japan ASK LP 135	A FLASHING BLUR OF STRIPPED DOWN EXCITEMENT (LP) £30

(see also Seventeen)

DAMON ALBARN
02	Honest Jons HJRLP1	MALI MUSIC (2-LP) £25
03	Honest Jons HJP10	DEMOCRAZY (2x10" white vinyl, picture disc, 5,000 only) £15
08	Vinyl Factory VF 001	MONKEY: JOURNEY TO THE WEST (2-LP, signed print, programme, tone generator) £60
14	Parlophone 825646331291	EVERYDAY ROBOTS ((2-LP, with CD) £20

(see also Blur, Gorillaz, Monkey, GB & TQ)

EDDIE ALBERT
55	London HL 8136	I'm In Favour Of Friendship/Come Pretty Little Girl £15
56	London HLU 8241	Little Child (Daddy Dear) (with Sondra Lee)/Jenny Kissed Me £15

VIV ALBERTINE
13	Cadiz CADIZLP 120	THE VERMILION BORDER (2-LP, red vinyl) £18

(see also the Slits)

ALBERTO Y LOST TRIOS PARANOIAS
77	Stiff LAST 2	SNUFF ROCK EP (12" promo, only 50-100 pressed) £200
76	Transatlantic TRA 316	ALBERTO Y LOST TRIOS PARANOIAS (LP, with insert) £15
77	Transatlantic TRA 349	ITALIANS FROM OUTER SPACE (LP) £15
78	Logo LOGO 1009	SKITE (LP) £15
80	Logo MOGO 4008	THE WORST OF THE BERTS (LP) £15

(see also Mothmen, Charlie Parkas)

ALBIANS
80	K & K KK 0012	Who Is Going To Love Me/VIN GORDON: Who Is Going To Rock Me Tonight (12") £20

(See also N. McCoy & Albians)

ALBION
09	Ambassador's Reception ABR005	Space Time Continuum/Milky Way/Thunder Strikes/Voodoo Safari (12") £15

ALBION BAND
73	Island HELP 25	BATTLE OF THE FIELD (LP, as Albion Country Band) £20
77	Harvest SHSP 4059	THE PROSPECT BEFORE US (LP, as Albion Dance Band) £15
78	Harvest SHSP 4092	RISE UP LIKE THE SUN (LP, textured sleeve) £15

(see also Shirley Collins, Fairport Convention)

DENNIS ALCAPONE
70	Explosion EX 2039	Revelation Version/Marka Version £30
70	Supreme SUP 214	You Must Believe Me (with Niney)/RUPIE EDWARDS ALLSTARS: Funk The Funk £20
70	Big Shot BI 565	Shades Of Hudson/Spanish Amigo £30
71	Treasure Isle TI 7069	The Great Woggie/TOMMY McCOOK & SUPERSONICS: Buttercup Version £20

MINT VALUE £

71	Banana BA 328	Duppy Serenade (as Innkeeper)/Sunshine Version	£20
71	Banana BA 341	(Love Me) Forever Version/I Don't Want To See You Cry	£30
71	Upsetter US 373	Well Dread/UPSETTERS: Dread Version	£20
71	Upsetter US 377	Alpha And Omega/JUNIOR BYLES: Beat Down Babylon	£25
71	Duke DU 125	Medley Version/Version Two	£15
71	Prince Buster PB 8	Sons Of Zion/ANSELL COLLINS: Short Circuit	£25
71	Prince Buster PB 12	Let It Roll (with Max Romeo)/ANSELL COLLINS: Clear Blue	£25
71	Dynamic DYN 421	Horse And Buggy/ROLAND ALPHONSO & DENZIL LAING: Buggy And Horse	£15
71	Dynamic DYN 422	Ripe Cherry/INNER CIRCLE: Red Cherry	£15
71	Dynamic DYN 427	Alcapones Guns Don't Bark/Alcapones Guns Don't Bark Version	£15
71	Camel CA 74	This A Butter/PHIL PRATT ALLSTARS: Version	£15
71	Tropical AL 003	False Prophet/MAX ROMEO: Rude Medley	£15
72	Downtown DT 496	Swinging along/DELROY WILSON: My Baby Is Gone	£20
72	Tropical AL 019	Worldwide Love (with Twinkle Brothers)/CARL MASTERS: Gable Up	£15
72	Ackee ACK 146	Power Version/BLUESBLASTERS: Martie (B-side actually titled "Margie")	£40
72	Prince Buster PB 24	Giant/PRINCE BUSTER: Science	£35
72	Upsetter US 381	Wonderman (with Dave Barker, actually by Dave Barker)/ Place Called Africa (with Dave Barker & Junior Byles)	£30
72	Upsetter US 388	Master Key/UPSETTERS: Keyhole	£30
72	Grape GR 3035	Rasta Dub/UPSETTERS: Rasta Version	£30
72	Attack ATT 8027	Fine Style/WINSTON SCOTLAND: On The Track	£15
72	Duke DU 131	The Sky's The Limit/HUDSON'S ALLSTARS: Limit Version	£25
72	Duke DU 147	Get In The Groove (with Dennis Brown)/DYNAMITES: Version	£20
72	Techniques TE 918	Look Into Yourself/TECHNIQUES ALLSTARS: Yourself Version	£15
72	Green Door GD 4041	Rub Up A Daughter/TONY'S ALLSTARS: Daughter Version	£15
72	Bullet BU 509	Dub Up A Daughter/PRINCE TONY ALL STARS: Version	£15
72	Treasure Isle TI 7069	Great Woogie/Buttercup	£25
73	Prince Buster PB51	Kings And Castles/Version	£20
73	Downtown DT 508	You Don't Say/TONY'S ALLSTARS: Version	£20
73	Treasure Isle TI 7074	Wake Up Jamaica/Version (with Tommy McCook)	£30
73	Jackpot JP 808	Cassius Clay/SLIM SMITH: Love And Affection	£20
73	Bread BR 1121	Musical Liquidator/Lorna Banana (B-side with Prince Jazzbo)	£40
71	Trojan TBL 187	GUNS DON'T ARGUE (LP)	£40
73	Magnet MGT 001	KING OF THE TRACK (LP)	£50
74	Attack ATLP 1005	BELCH IT OFF (LP)	£40
75	Live And Love LALP 104	DREAD CAPONE (LP)	£40
77	Third World TWS 801	SIX MILLION DOLLAR MAN (LP)	£15
77	Third World TWS 911	INVESTIGATOR ROCK (LP)	£30
89	Trojan TRLPS 272	MY VOICE IS INSURED FOR HALF A MILLION DOLLARS (LP)	£15

(see also El Paso, Dennis & Lizzy, Mad Roy, D. Smith, Wailing Souls, Innkeepers, GG Allstars, Stranger Cole, Lizzy & Dennis, Lee)

CRAIG ALDEN
| 60 | London HLW 9224 | Crazy Little Horn/Goggle-Eye'd | £15 |

STEVE ALDO (& CHALLENGERS)
64	Decca F 12041	Can I Get A Witness/Baby What You Want Me To Do (with Challengers)	£50
66	Parlophone R 5432	Everybody Has To Cry/You're Absolutely Right (solo)	£200
66	Parlophone R 5432	Everybody Has To Cry/You're Absolutely Right (solo) (DJ Copy)	£150

URIE ALDRIDGE
| 71 | Harry J. HJ 6634 | Set Me Free/LLOYD WILLIS: Free Version | £15 |

(see also John Holt)

ALEANNA
| 78 | Inchecronin INC 7421 | ALEANNA (LP) | £40 |

ALEEM
| 84 | Streetwave MKHAN 26 | Release Yourself/Dub (12") | £20 |
| 84 | Streetwave MKHAN 61 | Get Loose/Release Yourself (12") | £15 |

ALESSI
| 76 | A&M AMLH 64608 | ALESSI (LP, inner) | £20 |

ALETHIANS
| 72 | Myrrh MST 6506 | ONE WAY (LP, David Pope and the Right Angle on side 2) | £30 |
| 73 | Myrrh Gold MYR 1002 | R.S.V.P. (LP) | £40 |

ALEX G
14	Lucky Number LUCKY071LP	DSU (LP, with CD)	£20
15	Lucky Number LUCKY076LP	TRICK (LP. with CD)	£30
15	Lucky Number LUCKY076LP	TRICK (LP. with CD, blue vinyl, 300 only)	£50
15	Lucky Number LUCKY077LP	RULES (LP, with free CD, 1000 only)	£30
15	Domino WIGLP350	BEACH MUSIC (LP, blue vinyl with free 12")	£60
17	Domino WIGLP398X	ROCKET (LP. red vinyl)	£40
19	Domino WIGLP451	HOUSE OF SUGAR LP, purple vinyl, glitter sleeve)	£30
19	Domino WIGLP451	HOUSE OF SUGAR LP, purple vinyl with free 7", glitter sleeve)	£40

ARTHUR ALEXANDER
62	London HLD 9523	You Better Move On/A Shot Of Rhythm And Blues	£40
63	London HLD 9566	Where Have You Been/Soldier Of Love	£30
63	London HLD 9641	Anna/I Hang My Head And Cry	£35
63	London HLD 9667	Go Home Girl/You're The Reason	£20
64	London HLD 9899	Black Night/Ole John Amos	£20
66	London HLU 10023	(Baby) For You/The Other Woman	£20
63	London RE-D 1364	ALEXANDER THE GREAT (EP)	£40

63	London RE-D 1401	ARTHUR ALEXANDER (EP)	£40
62	London HA-D 2457	YOU BETTER MOVE ON (LP)	£80
82	Ace CH 66	A SHOT OF RHYTHM AND SOUL (LP)	£18
87	Ace CH 207	SOLDIER OF LOVE (LP)	£15

JEFF ALEXANDER & HIS ORCHESTRA

58	London HA-P 2130	ALFRED HITCHCOCK PRESENTS - MUSIC TO BE MURDERED BY (LP, mono)	£20
58	London SH-P 6012	ALFRED HITCHCOCK PRESENTS - MUSIC TO BE MURDERED BY (LP, stereo)	£20

LLOYD ALEXANDER REAL ESTATE

68	President PT 157	Gonna Live Again/Watcha Gonna Do	£80

LUCIEN ALEXANDER

67	Polydor 56205	Baby, You've Been On My Mind/Play Along (Miss R)	£20

ALEXISONFIRE

06	Hassle HOFF016LP	CRISIS (LP, die-cut sleeve, 500 only)	£60

ALFA MIST

17	Pink Bird 002	ANTIPHON (2-LP, 1st pressing, numbered white labels in finished sleeve)	£250
17	Pink Bird 002	ANTIPHON (2-LP, 2nd pressing, orange label, 350 copies in sleeve)	£100
18	Black Acre ACRELP011	ANTIPHON (2-LP, 3rd pressing, gatefold sleeve, printed labels)	£60
18	Black Acre ACRELP011	ANTIPHON (2-LP, 4th pressing, gatefold sleeve, orange vinyl, printed labels)	£50
19	Seiko SEKIT 002	STRUCTURALISM (2-LP)	£35

ALF AND TEEP

71	Fab FAB 16	Freedom, Justice and Equality/THREE TOPS: Down At The Boneyard (promo only, black label)	£100

ALFI & HARRY

56	London HLU 8242	Trouble With Harry/A Little Beauty (triangular centre, gold lettering on label)	£15

(see also David Seville)

CLEM ALFORD

74	Columbia SCX 6571	MIRROR IMAGE - THE ELECTRONIC SITAR OF CLEM ALFORD (LP)	£40
75	KPM KPM 1183	INDIA (LP, music library issue, side 2 only)	£40

(see also Magic Carpet)

ALFRED & MELMOTH

68	Island WI 3130	I Want Someone/ALFRED BROWN: One Scotch One Bourbon One Beer	£20

SANDRA ALFRED

58	Oriole CB 1408	Rocket And Roll/Six Day Rock	£50
58	Oriole CB 1408	Rocket And Roll/Six Day Rock (78)	£15

(see also Sandra Barry, Slack Alice)

ALIAS

98	V.I.P. 005	WHO'S STORY (12", EP)	£25

ALICE THROUGH THE LOOKING GLASS

69	H&F Recording/SNP (no cat. no.)	ALICE THROUGH THE LOOKING GLASS (LP, private pressing, handmade sleeve, actually by Peter Howell & John Ferdinando)	£1000
97	Tenth Planet TP 032	ALICE THROUGH THE LOOKING GLASS (LP, reissue, no'd, 1,000 only)	£20

(see also Ithaca, Friends, Agincourt, Tomorrow Come Someday, BBC Radiophonic Workshop/Peter Howell)

ALICE IN CHAINS

93	Columbia 659 090-6	Them Bones/We Die Young/Got Me Wrong/Am I Inside (12", no'd, blue vinyl)	£40
91	Columbia 467201-1	FACELIFT (LP)	£200
92	Columbia 472330-1	DIRT (LP, inner)	£200
94	Columbia 475713-1	JAR OF FLIES/SAP (LP, yellow vinyl with blue flies, 1-sided, etched 12" EP)	£150
95	Columbia 481114-1	ALICE IN CHAINS (2-LP, gatefold sleeve, inners)	£150
96	Columbia 4843001	MTV UNPLUGGED (2-LP)	£150
01	Simply Vinyl SVLP 0025	DIRT (LP, reissue 180gm vinyl)	£40
10	Virgin 50999 9 67159 1 8	BLACK GIVES WAY TO BLUE (2-LP)	£18
10	Music On Vinyl MOVLP 086	JAR OF FLIES/SAP (2-LP, reissue, gatefold, orange and blue vinyl)	£25
10	Music On Vinyl MOVLP 138	MTV UNPLUGGED (2-LP, reissue, 180gm)	£18

(see also Mad Season)

ALICE ISLAND BAND

74	Warren WAR 341	SPLENDID ISOLATION (LP, with insert, allegedly 50 only)	£500

ALIEN

92	Alien And Monster MDF15	How'd Ya Feel/Ruff House (12")	£20

ALIEN KULTURE

81	RAR LRAR 1	Asian Youth/Culture Crossover (p/s)	£40

ALIEN SEX FIEND

83	Anagram GRAM 10	WHO'S BEEN SLEEPING IN MY BRAIN (LP)	£15
90	Windsong 02	ASF BOX (box set, export issue, 4,000 only, with 3 coloured vinyl singles [12", 11" & 10"], poster, T-shirt & imitation dog turd)	£35
93	Anagram GRAM 69	LEGENDARY BATCAVE TAPES (LP)	£15
94	Anagram GRAM 80	INFERNO - THE ODYSSEY CONTINUES (2-LP)	£25

(see also Demon Preacher, Demons)

ALIENS (1)

78	Alien ALI 001	When The River Runs Dry/Winds Of Time (no p/s)	£40

ALIENS (2)

07	EMI 9463868181	ASTRONOMY FOR DOGS (2-LP)	£40
08	Petrock LP 002	LUNA (2-LP)	£35

(see also Beta Band)

MINT VALUE £

NUSRAT FATEH ALI KHAN
86	Womad 004	BEST OF QAWWAL AND PARTY VOLUME ONE (LP)	£30
88	Womad 008	QAWWAL AND PARTY VOLUME TWO (LP)	£30
89	Real World RWLP3	SHAHEN-SHAH (LP)	£30
90	Real World RWLP15	MUSTT MUSTT (LP)	£25
91	Star SRLP5130	MAGIC TOUCH (LP)	£70

ALKALINE TRIO
03	Vagrant 980 123-9	GOOD MOURNING (LP)	£60
05	Vagrant VRUK 012LP	CRIMSON (LP, red vinyl, stickered sleeve, inner)	£15
08	V2 VVR1051181	AGONY & IRONY (LP)	£25
10	Heart & Skull HOFF092LP	THIS ADDICTION (LP, white vinyl)	£20
11	Vagrant VR 353	FROM HERE TO INFIRMARY (LP, reissue, green vinyl)	£20
11	Vagrant VR 353	FROM HERE TO INFIRMARY (LP, reissue, blue vinyl, 300 only)	£25

ALKATRAZ
76	Rockfield UAS 30001	DOING A MOONLIGHT (LP)	£20

(see also Man, Quicksand)

ALL ABOUT EVE
85	Eden EDEN 1	D For Desire/Don't Follow Me (12", p/s)	£20
92	MCA 10712	ULTRAVIOLET (LP, printed inner)	£40

(see also Ghost Dance, Gene Loves Jezebel)

ALL SORTS OF FOLK
72	Private Pressing CH 101	ALL SORTS OF FOLK (LP)	£175

ALL SOUNDBWOY OUT
07	ASBO 001	ASBO (1-sided white label 12")	£30

(see also Loefa)

RICHARD ALLAN
60	Parlophone R 4634	As Time Goes By/Only One	£20

ALL DAY
73	Private pressing	YORK POP MUSIC PROJECT (LP)	£150

ANNISTEEN ALLEN
55	Capitol CL 14264	Fujiyama Mama/Wheels Of Love	£200
57	Brunswick 05639	Don't Nobody Move/The Money Tree	£40

DAEVID ALLEN
75	Caroline C 1512	BANANA MOON (LP, black and white 'Twins' label, ends in a continuous loop)	£40
76	Virgin V 5024	GOOD MORNING! (LP, by Daevid Allen & Euterpe)	£30
77	Affinity AFF3	NOW IS THE HAPPIEST TIME OF YOUR LIFE (LP)	£20
79	Charly CRL 5015	N'EXISTE PAS! (LP, with lyric insert)	£20
79	Charly CR 30165	BANANA MOON (LP, reissue, gatefold)	£20
82	Charly CR 30218	DIVIDED ALIEN PLAYBAX 80 (LP)	£15
82	Shanghai HAI 201	THE DEATH OF ROCK AND OTHER ENTRANCES (LP)	£15
89	Demi Monde DMLP 1019	THE OWL AND THE TREE (LP)	£25
90	Demi Monde DMLP 1025	AUSTRALIA AQUIARIA (LP)	£25
90	Voiceprint VP 101	THE AUSTRALIAN YEARS (LP)	£25
13	Vinyl Lovers 901462	STROKING THE TAIL OF THE BIRD (LP, with free 7", reissue, with Gilli Smythe and Harry Williamson)	£20

(see also Gong, Planet Gong, Soft Machine)

DEAN ALLEN
58	London HLM 8698	Rock Me To Sleep/Ooh-Ooh Baby Baby	£18

JEFF ALLEN
57	HMV JO 477	That'll Be The Day/Guilty Mind (export issue)	£25

LEE ALLEN (& HIS BAND)
58	HMV POP 452	Walkin' With Mr. Lee/Promenade	£20
59	Top Rank JKR 8020	WALKIN' WITH MR LEE (EP)	£20
62	Ember ELR 3312	MOOD MUSIC LIBRARY (LP, uncredited library issue, generic sleeve)	£30

(see also Huey 'Piano' Smith & Clowns)

LILY ALLEN
06	Regal LILY 001	LDN/Knock Em Down (500 only, jukebox centre)	£15
06	Regal 7REG 135	Smile/Smile (Gutter Mix) (stickered, black, die-cut sleeve)	£25
06	Regal REG 137	LDN/Nan,You're A Window Shopper (stickered, black die-cut sleeve)	£15
09	Regal REG 150	The Fear/Kabul Shit (7", picture disc, PVC sleeve, hype sticker)	£15
06	Regal 3694931	ALRIGHT, STILL (LP, approx 200 pressed, black die cut sleeve, stickered)	£70
09	Regal REG 151LP	IT'S NOT ME IT'S YOU (LP, printed inners)	£30
14	Regal REG 183	Air Balloon/Hard Out Here (7", ltd. ed., white vinyl, die-cut sleeve, sticker)	£15
14	Regal REG 184LP	SHEEZUS (LP/CD, printed inner)	£30
18	Parlophone 0190295673680	NO SHAME (LP, printed inner)	£20

MAURICE ALLEN
58	Pye Nixa 7N 15128	Ooh Baby/Rockhearted	£15

PATRICK ALLEN
77	Kab KB 5540	Groovy Feeling/Instrumental	£20

PETER ALLEN
77	A&M AMLH 63706	IT IS TIME FOR (2 x LP)	£15

REX ALLEN
54	Brunswick 05341	This Ole House/They Were Doin' The Mambo (with Tex Williams)	£20

(see also Patti Page)

RODNEY ALLEN
88	Subway 18T	CIRCLE LINE EP (12" p/s)	£15
87	Subway SUBORG 2	HAPPYSAD (LP)	£15

(Blue Aeroplanes)

STEVE ALLEN
72	M&M FFMS 10021	Life On Mars/Baby I'm A Want You/Everything I Own/Diary (Medley) (demo)	£20

TONY ALLEN (1)
00	Strut STRUTAALP001	JEALOUSY (LP, reissue with Africa 70)	£25
00	Strut STRUTAALP002	NO DISCRIMINATION (LP, reissue with Afro Messengers)	£25
00	Strut STRUTAALP003	NO ACCOMODATION FOR LAGOS (LP, reissue with Africa 70)	£25

TONY ALLEN (2)
84	Earthworks MWKS 3001	N.E.P.A. (Never Expect Power Always)/N.E.P.A. Dance Dub/When One Road Close (Another One Go Open)/Road Close Dance Dub (12", p/s)	£15

VERNON ALLEN
64	R&B JB 169	Far I Come/Babylon	£1250

(VERNON) ALLEN & (MILTON) HAMILTON
66	Blue Beat BB 348	It Is I/Baby What's More	£15
66	Blue Beat BB 353	You're The Angel/Someone Like You	£15

ALL FALL DOWN
83	Confidential KIS 1	Arechibo/A Changing Face (12")	£45

ALLISON
94	Twinkle NG 544	WAILING (LP)	£15

GENE ALLISON
58	London HLU 8605	Hey, Hey, I Love You/You Can Make It If You Try	£125

GEORGE ALLISON
80	Cartridge CR-D 107	Ten To One/Hard Times (12")	£150
85	Gibbous GBM 15	EXCLUSIVE (LP)	£20

JERRY ALLISON & CRICKETS
65	Liberty LIB 10196	Now Hear This/Everybody's Got A Little Problem	£20

(see also Crickets, Ivan)

LUTHER ALLISON
71	Delmark DS 625	LOVE ME MAMA (LP, blue label)	£25

MOSE ALLISON
61	Fontana H 292	Baby Please Don't Go/Deed I Do	£20
59	Esquire EP 214	PARCHMAN FARM (EP)	£15
64	Columbia SEG 8353	ALLISON SINGS THE BLUES (EP)	£20
59	Esquire 32-051	BACK COUNTRY SUITE (LP)	£25
59	Esquire 32-071	LOCAL COLOUR (LP)	£25
59	Esquire 32-083	YOUNG MAN MOSE (LP)	£25
60	Esquire 32-094	CREEK BANK (LP)	£20
61	Esquire 32-131	AUTUMN SONG (LP)	£20
62	Esquire 32-171	RAMBLIN' WITH MOSE (LP)	£15
63	London HA-K 8083	SWINGIN' MACHINE (LP, as Mose Allison Jazz Group)	£15
64	Columbia SX 6058	V-8 FORD (LP)	£15

ALLISONS (U.K.)
61	Fontana TFL 5135	ARE YOU SURE (LP, mono)	£20
61	Fontana STFL 558	ARE YOU SURE (LP, stereo)	£30

ALLISONS (U.S.)
64	Stateside SS 289	Surfer Street/Money (vocal: Darlene Love)	£35

(see also Blossoms, Darlene Love)

ALLMAN BROTHERS BAND
69	Atco 228 033	THE ALLMAN BROTHERS BAND (LP, gatefold sleeve)	£100
71	Atco 2400 032	IDLEWILD SOUTH (LP)	£80
71	Atlantic 2402 035	AT FILLMORE EAST (2-LP, 1st pressing, plum/orange labels, gatefold sleeve)	£50
71	Atlantic K60011	AT FILLMORE EAST (2-LP, 2nd pressing, green/orange labels, gatefold sleeve)	£20
72	Capricorn K67501	EAT A PEACH (2-LP, gatefold sleeve with insert)	£30
73	Capricorn K47507	BROTHERS AND SISTERS (LP, gatefold sleeve with insert)	£15
75	Warner Bros. 2659 034	EAT A PEACH (LP, reissue, gatefold)	£15

(see also Gregg Allman, Duane & Gregg Allman, Allman Joys, Hour Glass)

DUANE & GREGG ALLMAN
73	Polydor 2310 235	DUANE & GREGG ALLMAN (LP, laminated sleeve)	£15

(see also Allman Brothers, Gregg Allman)

GREGG ALLMAN
73	Capricorn K 47508/CP0116	LAID BACK (LP)	£15

(see also Allman Brothers, Duane & Gregg Allman)

ALLMAN JOYS
73	Mercury 6398 005	ALLMAN JOYS (LP)	£20

ALL NATION ROCKERS
93	Sound N Presuure SNP 002	Rockers Arise/Rockers Version/Travelling Version (12")	£25
95	Sound N Presuure SNP 004	Once Inna Dubtime/Talking Dread Version/Ruud Boy Sweeps The Rebound Version (12", as A.N.R.)	£20

ALL NIGHT BAND
79	Contact CON 5	Lovely Ladies/It's My Life	£15

ALL THE RAGE
82	Rage RR 001	Concrete City/Emergency (p/s)	£150

JOHNNY ALMOND MUSIC MACHINE
69	Deram DM 266	Solar Level/To R.K.	£35
69	Deram DML/SML 1043	PATENT PENDING (LP)	£70
70	Deram DML 1057	HOLLYWOOD BLUES (LP, mono)	£80
70	Deram SML 1057	HOLLYWOOD BLUES (LP, stereo)	£60

(see also Alan Price Set, Zoot Money, Paul Williams Set, John Mayall & Bluesbreakers, Mark-Almond)

MARC ALMOND
82	Lyntone LYN 12505	Discipline (as 'Marc Almond & Friends', pink flexidisc with Flexipop issue 23. Friends are Throbbing Gristle)	£20
84	Gutter Hearts GH 1	BITE BACK + BLUES (fan club-only LP, credited to "Raoul & The Ruined")	£30
88	Parlophone PSR 500	Kept Boy (1-sided 7" with etched reverse - intended to be free with THE STARS WE ARE LP - but plans scrapped)	£30
16	UMC 570 582-6	TRIALS OF EYELINER (ANTHOLOGY 1979/2016) (10CD/1CD EP, 64-page book) box,	£100

(see also Soft Cell, Marc & Mambas, Burmoe Brothers, Vicious Pink Phenomena, Annie Hogan, Sally Timms, Gene Pitney)

ALMOND MARZIPAN
70	Trend TNT 53	Open Up Your Heart/Summer Love	£15

ALMOST A DREAM
73	Box BX1	Something's Moving/The Undead	£30

ALMOST ALONE
84	Family FAM 001	Blue City/It's So Sad (p/s)	£20

ALPHA & OMEGA
88	Roaring Lion RL 001	Gather Together/On It's Way	£80
92	Alpha & Omega A&O 501	Watch And Pray/Yemenite Chant	£35
96	Alpha & Omega A&O 1002	Rastafari/Version/Words Of Thy Mouth/Version (10")	£25
96	A&O 1201	Ancient African Civilisation/DISCIPLES & ALPHA & OMEGA: Eternal Dub (12")	£25
90	A&O 001	DANIEL IN THE LIONS DEN (LP)	£60
92	A&O 009	KING & QUEEN (LP)	£70
92	A&O 027	WATCH AND PRAY (LP)	£70
92	A&O 077	ALMIGHTY JAH (LP, listed as Alpha & Omega Meets Dub Judah)	£40
93	A&O 093	EVERYDAY LIFE (LP)	£50
94	A&O 094	SAFE IN THE ARK (LP)	£40
96	A&O 096	TREE OF LIFE (LP)	£30
96	A&O 097	VOICE IN THE WILDERNESS (LP)	£35

ALPHABET
81	No Label or Cat. No	This Strange Love/The Handsome Beast (p/s)	£15

ORVILLE ALPHANSO
65	Caribou CRC 1	Bellylick/Inspiration	£40

ALPHASTONE
98	Enraptured RAPTLP 18	ELASTICATED WAVEBAND (LP, clear vinyl, 100 only)	£15
01	Enraptured RAPTLP 33	LIFE IS A MOTORWAY EP (2LP, gatefold sleeve, limited issue)	£15

CARLTON ALPHONSO
67	Pama PM 700	Where In This World/Peace Makers	£50
69	Grape GR 3000	Belittle Me/Keep Your Love	£50

CLYDE ALPHONSO
69	Studio One SO 2076	Good Enough/Let The Music Play	£130

PANCHO ALPHONSO AND THE REVOLUTIONARIES
79	Attack ATT TACK 8	Never Give Up In A Babylon/Love Is A Pleasure (12")	£25
78	Trojan TRLS 165	NEVER GET TO ZION (LP)	£25

(see also Alphonso Pancho)

ROLAND ALPHONSO (ALIAS ROLAND AL)
61	Blue Beat BB 58	Blackberry Brandy/ALVIN & CECIL: Marjorie	£25
62	Blue Beat BB 112	Four Corners Of The World (with Alley Cats)/SHINERS: Romantic Shuffle	£30
64	R&B JB 161	Mr President/The MAYTALS: A Man Who Knows	£25
64	R&B JB 164	Crime Wave/MAYTALS: Hello Honey	£60
65	Island WI 217	El Pussy Cat/LORD BRYNNER: Tiger In Your Tank	£50
65	Ska Beat JB 210	Nimble Foot/ANDY & JOEY: Love Is Stronger	£70
65	Ska Beat JB 216	Nuclear Weapon (with Baba Brooks)/STRANGER COLE: Love Thy Neighbour	£60
65	Rio R 5804	Jazz Ska/HYACINTH: Oh Gee	£60
66	Blue Beat BB 356	Just A Closer Walk/Jericho Train	£500
66	Island WI 259	James Bond/LEE PERRY: Just Keep It Up	£350
66	Doctor Bird DB 1010	From Russia With Love/Cleopatra (with Soul Brothers)	£130
66	Doctor Bird DB 1011	Sufferer's Choice (with Soul Brothers)/SOULETTES: I Want To Be	£80
66	Doctor Bird DB 1013	WAILERS: Rude Boy/ROLANDO AL & SOUL BROTHERS: Ringo's Theme (This Boy)	£90
66	Doctor Bird DB 1017	Sugar And Spice/Get Out Of My Life (with Soul Brothers)	£50
66	Doctor Bird DB 1020	Phoenix City (with Soul Brothers)/DEACONS: Men Alone	£50
66	Doctor Bird DB 1023	Doctor Ring-A-Ding/FREDDIE & HEARTACHES: Here Is My Heart	£80
66	Doctor Bird DB 1035	I Love You/Song Of Love	£50
66	Doctor Bird DB 1039	WAILERS: Rasta Put It On/ROLAND AL & SOUL BROTHERS: Ska With Ringo	£150
66	Ska Beat JB 231	Rinky Dink (So Good) (with Studio One Orchestra)/ SCRATCH & DYNAMITES: Deacon Johnson	£45
67	Pyramid PYR 6003	Middle East/Wise Man	£50
67	Pyramid PYR 6005	Women Of The World (& Beverley's Allstars)/SPANISHTONIANS: The Kisses	£50
67	Pyramid PYR 6006	On The Move (& Beverley's Allstars)/DESMOND DEKKER & ACES: It's A Shame	£50

67	Pyramid PYR 6007	Jungle Bit (& Beverley's Allstars)/**NORMAN GRANT: Somebody Please Help Me**	£50
67	Pyramid PYR 6008	The Cat/**DESMOND DEKKER & ACES: Rudy Got Soul**	£50
67	Pyramid PYR 6009	Guantanamera Ska (& Beverley's Allstars)/**SPANISHTONIANS: Suffer Me Not**	£30
67	Pyramid PYR 6011	Nothing For Nothing/**DESMOND DEKKER & ACES: Rude Boy Train**	£50
67	Pyramid PYR 6018	Sock It To Me (& Beverley's Allstars)/**SPANISHTONIANS: Rudie Gets Plenty**	£100
68	Pyramid PYR 6022	Whiter Shade Of Pale/On The Move	£80
68	Pyramid PYR 6030	Dreamland/**MAYTALS: 54-46, That's My Number**	£50
68	Pyramid PYR 6043	Stream Of Life/**MAYTALS: Struggle**	£50
68	Coxsone CS 7077	Reggae In The Grass/**ROY RICHARDS: Get Smart**	£60
69	Gas GAS 112	A Thousand Tons Of Megaton (actually by Derrick Morgan)/**Musical Resurrection**	£40
70	Punch PH 39	Roll On (& Upsetters)/**CARL DAWKINS: True Love**	£65
71	Banana BA 340	Mellow Mood (Way To My Heart)/**MAYTALS: Marching On**	£60
12	Duke Reid's THB 7017	Easter Bonnet/**STRANGER AND KEN: Feeling Of Love**	£20
68	Hi Note BSLP 5001	ABC ROCK STEADY (with the Originals Orchestra)	£150

ALPHORAS
78	Junior JR 107	Running Out Of Love/It Pains Me (actually by LEROY SMART)	£15

ALPINES
68	Double D DD 110	Get Ready/**CARIBBEATS: Come Back Charlie**	£30

ALQUIN
73	Polydor 2480 152	MARKS (LP)	£15

ALSATIANS
80	SRT SRTS/80/CUS-629	Teen Romance/Our Man In Marrakesh (no p/s, 1000 only)	£40

RITA ALSTON
70	Trojan TR 7751	Popcorn Funky Reggae/**NAT COLE: My Love**	£30
(see also Rita, Nat Cole)			

SHIRLEY ALSTON
75	London HLA 10506	I'd Rather Not Be Loving You/Can't Stop Singin' (Bout The Boy I Love)	£25
75	London SHA 8491	WITH A LITTLE HELP FROM MY FRIENDS (LP)	£25
(see also Shirelles)			

ALTECS
61	London HLU 9387	Easy/Recess	£15
(see also The Black Dog)			

ALTERATIONS
78	Bead Records BEAD 9	CUSACK/BERESFORD/DAY/TOOP (LP)	£30

ALTERED STATES
88	Red Rhino CALC 31	IS ANYONE OUT THERE? (LP)	£60

ALTERN 8
92	Network A8 PIC 1	FULL ON...MASK HYSTERIA (LP)	£15
92	Network TOP LP1	FULL ON...MASK HYSTERIA (LP & 12")	£20
(see also Progressive Logic, Mark Archer)			

ALTERNATIVE
83	Corpus Christi CHRIST 13	IF THEY TREAT YOU LIKE SHIT - ACT LIKE MANURE (LP, insert)	£50

ALTERNATIVE TV
77	Sniffing Glue SG 75 RPS	Love Lies Limp (1-sided flexidisc with Sniffing Glue fanzine issue 12)	£20
77	Deptford Fun City DFC 002	How Much Longer/You Bastard (p/s)	£15
77	Deptford Fun City DFC 02	How Much Longer/You Bastard (p/s, labelled 'alternate versions')	£15
78	Deptford Fun City DFC 04	Life After Life/Life After Dub (p/s)	£15
78	Deptford Fun City DFC 05	Life/Love Lies Limp (p/s)	£15
78	Deptford Fun City DFC 07	Action Time Vision/Another Coke (live p/s)	£15
78	Deptford Fun City DLP 01	THE IMAGE HAS CRACKED (LP)	£40
78	Deptford Fun City DFC 02	WHAT YOU SEE IS ... WHAT YOU ARE (LP, 1 side by Here & Now)	£20
78	Deptford Fun City DFC 3	VIBING UP THE SENILE MAN (LP)	£20
79	Crystal CLP 01	LIVE AT THE RAT CLUB (LP)	£18
80	Deptford Fun City DLP 05	ACTION TIME VISION (LP, with inner sleeve)	£20
90	Chapter 22 CHAP LP 51	DRAGON LOVE (LP)	£15
(see also Mark Perry, Good Missionaries, The Door & The Window, Reflections, Jools Holland, Alex Fergusson, Rat & Whale)			

ALTERNATORS
78	Energy NRG 001	No Answers/The Kid Don't Know (no p/s)	£60

ALTHEA & DONNA
78	Virgin Frontline FL1012	UPTOWN TOP RANKING (LP)	£25
01	Front Line LPFL 2023	UPTOWN TOP RANKING (LP, reissue)	£20

ALTON (ELLIS) & EDDY
60	Blue Beat BB 17	Muriel/**CLUE J. & HIS BLUES BLASTERS: Silky**	£20
62	Island WI 009	My Love Divine/Let Me Dream	£30
(see also Alton Ellis)			

ALVARO
77	Squeaky Shoes SSRM 1	DRINKING MY OWN SPERM (LP)	£20
79	Squeaky Shoes SSRM 2	MUMS MILK NOT POWDER (LP)	£15
(see also 101'ers)			

ALVYN
69	Morgan MR 18S	You've Gotta Have An Image/Mind The Gap	£15

ALWAYS
86	El GPO 16T	ARIEL (12", p/s)	£15
87	El GPO 27T	METROLAND (12", p/s)	£15

MINT VALUE £

88	El GPOT 34	Thames Valley Leather Club/Amateur (10", p/s)	£15
88	El ACME 12	THAMES VALLEY LEATHER CLUB (LP)	£20

AMALGAM (1)
69	Transatlantic TRA 196	A PRAYER FOR PEACE (LP)	£70
73	A Records A 002	PLAY BLACKWELL & HIGGINS (LP)	£50

AMALGAM (2)
80	Impetus IMPLP 47901	WIPE OUT (4-LP box set with booklet)	£50

GLEN AMAMS
69	Escort ES 804	Rich In Love/WOODPECKERS: Zumbelly	£50

(see also Glen Adams)

AMAZIAH
79	Sonrise SR 001	STRAIGHT TALKER (LP, private pressing with insert)	£75

AMAZING BLONDEL
70	Bell SBLL 131	THE AMAZING BLONDEL AND A FEW FACES (LP, blue/silver label)	£250
70	Island ILPS 9136	EVENSONG (LP, gatefold sleeve)	£40
71	Island ILPS 9156	FANTASIA LINDUM (LP, with inner lyric sleeve)	£30
71	Island ILPS 9156	FANTASIA LINDUM (LP, without inner lyric sleeve)	£20
72	Island ILPS 9205	ENGLAND (LP, gatefold)	£25
73	Island ILPS 9257	BLONDEL (LP, gatefold sleeve)	£20
74	DJM DJF 20442	MULGRAVE STREET (LP)	£15
75	DJM DJF 20446	INSPIRATION (LP)	£15
13	Prog Temple PTLP 8008	THE AMAZING BLONDEL AND A FEW FACES (LP, reissue)	£15

(see also Dimples, Gospel Garden, Methusilah)

AMAZING DANCING BAND
67	Verve VLP/SVLP 9214	AMAZING DANCING BAND (LP, mono/stereo)	£20
68	Verve VLP 9234	VOLUME TWO - THESE BOOTS ARE MADE FOR DANCIN' (LP, mono)	£18
68	Verve SVLP 9234	VOLUME TWO - THESE BOOTS ARE MADE FOR DANCIN' (LP, stereo)	£15

AMAZING FRIENDLY APPLE
69	Decca F 12887	Water Woman/Magician	£100

AMAZING SPACE FROGS
79	Ribbett RIB 1	THE DIRTY HABITS EP	£300

(see also Basczax, Blitzkrieg Bop, No Way)

AMAZON
81	Megamusic MEGA 1	Fallen Angel/Hypnotising You (p/s)	£20

AMAZON TRUST
70	Polydor 2058065	Run Baby Run/Sheila Lee	£50
71	Jade JD 03	Seeing What I See/Night Of Fear	£100

AMAZONS
15	Goth Cruise (No Cat. No.)	Junk Food Forever/Something In The Water (p/s)	£20

AMBER ASYLUM
96	Elfenblut SAG 1	FROZEN IN AMBER (LP, inner)	£15

AMBERGRIS
70	Paramount SPFL 262	AMBERGRIS (LP)	£15

AMBER RUN
15	RCA 88875069521	5AM (LP)	£30

AMBER SQUAD
80	Sound Of Leicester ST 1	(I Can't) Put My Finger On You/Tell You A Lie (p/s)	£25
80	Dead Good DEAD 17	Can We Go Dancing?/You Should See (What I Do To You In My Dreams) (p/s)	£20

(AMERICAN) AMBOY DUKES
68	Fontana TF 971	Let's Go Get Stoned/It's Not True	£20
67	Fontana (S)TL 5468	THE AMBOY DUKES (LP)	£75
69	London HA-T/SH-T 8378	JOURNEY TO THE CENTER OF THE MIND (LP, as American Amboy Dukes)	£80
69	London HA-T/SH-T 8392	MIGRATION (LP, as American Amboy Dukes)	£45
74	Discreet DS 2203	TOOTH, FANG AND CLAW (LP)	£15

(see also Ted Nugent)

SAMMY AMBROSE
65	Stateside SS 385	This Diamond Ring/Bad Night	£100
65	Stateside SS 399	Monkey See Monkey Do/Welcome To Dreamsville (DJ Copy)	£400
65	Stateside SS 399	Monkey See Monkey Do/Welcome To Dreamsville	£250
87	Kent 6T3	Welcome To Dreamsville/PLATTERS: Not My Girl	£25

AMBROSE SLADE
69	Fontana TF 1015	Genesis/Roach Daddy	£300
69	Fontana STL 5492	BEGINNINGS (LP, laminated sleeve, black label with silver print; beware of counterfeits with matt sleeve & black & white label)	£1000
75	Contour 6870 678	BEGINNINGS OF SLADE (LP, reissue, different cover & running order, withdrawn)	£100
10	Morgan Blue Town BT5006	BEGINNINGS (LP, reissue, 750 only with insert & signed certificate)	£70
22	BMG BMGCAT 657LP	BALLZY (LP, turquoise vinyl, RSD)	£30

(see also Slade, 'NBetweens)

AMEBIX
82	Spiderleg SDL 6	Who's The Enemy/Carnage/No Gods No Masters/Enemies (p/s)	£30
83	Spiderleg SDL 10	Winter/Beginning Of The End (p/s)	£25
82	Spiderleg SDLP 14	NO SANCTUARY (LP)	£30
85	Alternative Tentacles VIRUS46	ARISE (LP)	£50

| 87 | Heavy Metal HMRLP 99 | MONOLITH (LP) | £25 |
| 10 | Back On Black BOBV217LP | MONOLITH (LP, clear vinyl reissue) | £18 |

AMEN CORNER
69	Immediate AS 3	So Fine (promo only 'single sampler' for IMSP 023)	£20
68	Deram DML/SML 1021	ROUND AMEN CORNER (LP)	£30
69	Immediate IMSP 023	THE NATIONAL WELSH COAST LIVE EXPLOSION COMPANY (LP, g/fold sleeve, pink label)	£30
69	Immediate IMSP 028	FAREWELL TO THE REAL MAGNIFICENT SEVEN (LP, gatefold sleeve)	£30

(see also Fairweather, Mayfield's Mule, Judas Jump)

AMERICAN BREED
68	Dot DOT 101	Green Light/Don't It Make You Cry	£15
67	Dot DOLP 255	AMERICAN BREED (LP)	£15
68	Dot (S)LPD 502	BEND ME, SHAPE ME (LP)	£15
68	Dot (S)LPD 507	NO WAY TO TREAT A LADY (LP, soundtrack)	£20
68	Dot (S)LPD 518	PUMPKIN, POWDER, SCARLET AND GREEN (LP)	£20

AMERICAN GYPSY
| 70 | CBS 64276 | AMERICAN GYPSY (2-LP) | £30 |

AMERICAN JAM (BAND)
| 72 | Parlophone R5971 | American Jam/Natures Child | £20 |
| 74 | Young Blood YB 1056 | Jam Jam/Back On The Road | £18 |

(see also Kansas Hook)

AMERICAN MUSIC CLUB
87	Zippo ZONG 0202	ENGINE (LP, with inner sleeve)	£15
88	Demon FIEND 134	CALIFORNIA (LP)	£15
89	Demon FIEND 151	UNITED KINGDOM (LP)	£15
93	Virgin V2708	MERCURY (LP)	£20

AMERICAN POETS
66	London HLC 10037	She Blew A Good Thing/Out To Lunch (as American Poets) (DJ copy)	£200
66	London HLC 10037	She Blew A Good Thing/Out To Lunch (as American Poets)	£100
71	United Artists UP 35308	She Blew A Good Thing/Out To Lunch (reissue, as Poets)	£20

AMERICAN SPRING
72	United Artists UP 35376	Good Time/Sweet Mountain	£15
72	United Artists UP 35421	Mama Said/Tennessee Waltz	£15
73	CBS CBS 1590	Shyin' Away/Falling In Love	£20
72	United Artists UAG 29363	AMERICAN SPRING (LP, "Tree" cover)	£50
72	United Artists UAG 29363	AMERICAN SPRING (LP, "Tree" gatefold cover with picture of group)	£60

(see also Beach Boys, Honeys)

AMERICAN YOUTH CHOIR
| 71 | Polydor 2066 013 | Together We Can Make It/Keep Your Fine Self Near Me | £30 |

AMES BROTHERS
| 54 | HMV 7M 179 | I Can't Believe That You're In Love/Boogie Woogie Maxixe | £20 |

NANCY AMES
66	Columbia DB 7809	Friends And Lovers Forever/I've Got A Lot Of Love (Left In Me)	£30
66	Columbia DB 8039	Cry Softly/I Don't Want To Talk About It (DJ copy)	£200
66	Columbia DB 8039	Cry Softly/I Don't Want To Talk About It	£100

AMIGO
| 76 | Lucky LY 6015 | Judas A No Rasta/Version | £70 |

AMIN-PECK
| 82 | Connection CON 8201 | Love Disgrace/Singing In The Wind (p/s) | £40 |
| 82 | Connection CONT 8204 | Girls On Me/Anxiety/Coda (12") | £15 |

AMITY
| 76 | Red Rag RRR 001 | AMITY (LP) | £150 |

AMM
66	Incus EP 1	AT THE ROUNDHOUSE (EP)	£80
67	EUK 7256	AMMMUSIC (LP, mono)	£300
67	Elektra EUKS 7256	AMMMUSIC (LP, stereo)	£200
78	Matchless MR 03	TO HEAR AND BACK AGAIN (LP)	£40
81	Matchless MR 5	THE CRYPT (2LP first pressing, box set, inserts, no text on front cover)	£100
83	Matchless MR 6	GENERATIVE THEMES (LP)	£40
87	Matchless MR13	INEXHAUSTABLE DOCUMENT (LP)	£30
88	Matchless MR 5	THE CRYPT (2LP reissue box set, with rotated radio and text, inserts)	£80
90	Pogus O201-4	COMBINE AND LAMINATES (LP)	£20

(see also Eddie Provost Band)

ALBERT AMMONS
| 54 | Mercury MG 25012 | ALBERT AMMONS (10" LP) | £20 |

(see also [Big] Joe Turner)

GENE AMMONS (BAND)
60	Starlite ST45 017	Echo Chamber Blues/Ammons' Boogie	£40
58	Esquire 32-047	HI FI JAM SESSION (LP)	£20
59	Esquire 32-077	FUNKY (LP)	£30
60	Esquire 32-097	JAMMIN' WITH GENE (LP)	£25
62	Esquire 32-147	BLUE GENE (LP)	£20
63	Esquire 32-177	BOSS TENOR (LP)	£25
63	Esquire 32-178	BAD! BOSSA NOVA (LP)	£25

			MINT VALUE £
72	Prestige PR 24021	JUG & DODO (LP, with Dodo Marmarosa)	£15
73	Prestige PR 10019	YOU TALK THAT TALK (LP)	£15
73	Prestige PR 10021	BROTHER JUG (LP)	£20

AMON DÜÜL

81	Illuminated JAMS 24	HAWK MEETS PENGUIN (LP)	£20

AMON DÜÜL II

70	Liberty LBF 15355	Archangel's Thunderbird/Burning Sister	£25
69	Liberty LBS 83279	PHALLUS DEI (LP)	£400
70	Liberty LSP 101/LBS 83359	YETI (2LP, 1st pressing, textured gatefold)	£125
71	United Artists UAD 60003/4	DANCE OF THE LEMMINGS (2LP, laminated gatefold)	£70
72	United Artists LSP 101	YETI (2LP, 2nd pressing, matt gatefold)	£80
72	Sunset SLS 50257	PHALLUS DEI (LP, reissue)	£25
72	United Artists UAG 23937	CARNIVAL IN BABYLON (LP, gatefold)	£35
72	United Artists UAG 29406	WOLF CITY (LP, gatefold sleeve)	£30
73	United Artists USP 102	LIVE IN LONDON (LP)	£25
73	United Artists UAS 29504	VIVE LA TRANCE (LP, with inner sleeve)	£20
75	United Artists UA 29723 G	LEMMINGMANIA (LP)	£20
74	Atlantic K 50136	HIJACK (LP)	£20

(see also Utopia)

AMORPHOUS ANDROGYNOUS

93	Quigley LPEBV 1	TALES OF EPHIDRINA (LP, gatefold)	£60
02	FSOL FSOLLP101	THE ISNESS (2LP, gatefold, printed inners)	£60
05	Harvest 0946 3 33994 1 9	ALICE IN ULTRALAND (2LP, gatefold, stamped numbered edition)	£150
18	EBV LPRSDTOT74	THE ISNESS (2LP reissue, numbered, PVC outer, RSD)	£30
20	fsoldigital.com LP TOT 79	WE PERSUADE OURSELVES WE ARE IMMORTAL (with Peter Hammill) (LP, printed inner)	£25
23	Quigley/UMR 00602448888907	TALES OF EPHIDRENA (2LP augmented reissue, gatefold, RSD)	£35

(see also Future Sound Of London, Peter Hammill)

AMOS & SARA

82	It's War Boys	Go Home Soldier/Enough Is Enough/Surveillance O.H.M.S. (12", screenprint p/s)	£20

(see also Homosexuals)

TORI AMOS

91	East West YZ 618T	ME AND A GUN EP: Silent All These Years/Upside Down/Me & A Gun(12", p/s)	£18
91	East West YZ 618DJ	Silent All These Years/Upside Down (p/s, promo, DJ Edit)	£20
92	East West A 7531DJ	China (radio edit)/China (7", p/s, promo)	£20
92	East West A 7504DJ	Winter (radio edit)/The Pool (promo 7" in p/s)	£20
92	Atlantic A 7479	Crucify/Here In My Head (7" misprint b-side 'Here In My Hand', p/s)	£15
92	East West A7479	Crucify/Here In My Head (7", injection moulded label, p/s)	£15
94	East West A 7257	Past The Mission (LP Version)/ Past The Mission (Live) (7", p/s)	£20
96	Atlantic A 5450LC	Professional Widow (Mr Roy's 7" Edit)/ Professional Widow (Armand's Star Trunk Funkin' Mix) (Radio Edit) (7", promo, jukebox issue)	£35
00	6am n' Rockin 6 AMR 001	Let's Do It Again (Mix 1)/ Let's Do It Again (Mix 2) (12", white label, green p/s, Tori Amos vs Andy Gray)	£30
20	Decca 350 412-3	CHRISTMASTIDE EP: Christmastide/Circle Of Seasons/Holly/Better Angels (12", p/s, Christmas card,12"x12" signed print)	£65
20	Decca 350 412-3	CHRISTMASTIDE EP: Christmastide/Circle Of Seasons/Holly/Better Angels (12", p/s, Christmas card)	£25
23	Universal/Deutsche Grammophon 486 4883	Swimming Pools (Drank)/Instrumental Version (10", with Trevor Horn, clear vinyl, 10"x10" signed art card)	£70
23	Universal/Deutsche Grammophon 486 4883	Swimming Pools (Drank)/Instrumental Version (10", with Trevor Horn, clear vinyl)	£35
92	East West 7567 82358-1	LITTLE EARTHQUAKES (LP)	£50
94	East West 7567-82567-1	UNDER THE PINK (LP)	£35
96	East West 7567 82862-1	BOYS FOR PELE (2LP, clear vinyl, lyric insert)	£50
98	East West 7567 83095-1	FROM THE CHOIRGIRL HOTEL (LP)	£150
99	East West 7567-82358-1	LITTLE EARTHQUAKES (LP, 180g 'high quality' UK reissue, Obi strip)	£50
05	Epic 8 2796 97780 2	THE ORIGINAL BOOTLEGS (12CD box set, 6 stickers, website exclusive)	£65
07	Epic 82876 86140 1	AMERICAN DOLL POSSE (2LP, gatefold, printed inners, 180g)	£60
11	Deutsche Grammophon 477 9858	NIGHT OF HUNTERS (2LP, gatefold, printed)	£70
13	Atlantic/Music On Vinyl MOVLP 830	UNDER THE PINK (LP, reissue, 180g vinyl)	£30
13	Atlantic/Music On Vinyl MOVLP 830	UNDER THE PINK (LP, 180g pink vinyl, numbered)	£40
14	Mercury Classics 28948109036	UNREPENTANT GERALDINES (2LP, 180g, printed inners)	£45
16	Atlantic 081227947774	BOYS FOR PELE (2LP, 180g vinyl, lyric insert)	£25
17	Decca 28948155880	NATIVE INVADER (2LP, gatefold, 180g, printed inners)	£30
22	Decca 357 390-4	OCEAN TO OCEAN (2LP,gatefold, printed inners, blue translucent vinyl, signed art card)	£70
22	East West 7567-82358-1	LITTLE EARTHQUAKES (2LP, 140g clear vinyl, 30th anniversary issue)	£40
23	Epic 19658800991	SCARLET'S WALK (2LP, half-speed remaster, lyric inserts)	£25
24	Decca 168768542	UNREPENTANT GERALDINES (2LP, 10th Anniversary, deluxe edition, red swirl vinyl, signed print)	£65
24	Decca 168768542	UNREPENTANT GERALDINES (2LP, 10th Anniversary, deluxe edition, signed print)	£45

(see also Y Kant Tori Read, Armand Van Helden, Trevor Horn)

CURTIS AMY

60	Vogue LAE 12277	THE BLUES MESSAGE (LP, with Paul Bryant)	£15
61	Vogue LA 12287	GROOVIN' BLUE (LP, with Frank Butler)	£30
62	Vogue LAE 12298	MEETIN' HERE (LP, with Paul Bryant)	£15

63	Fontana 688136ZL	KATANGA (LP)	£30

ANABAS
83	Flame On FLAME 003	Barricades/Dream Dance (p/s)	£15

ANACONDA
20	Seelie Court SCLP 003	SYMPATHY FOR THE MADMAN (LP, issue of acetate originally recorded in 1969)	£18

ANACRUSIS
91	Metal Blade ZORRO 23	MANIC IMPRESSIONS (LP)	£18

ANAL FLEAS
82	Rectal FLEA 45	Psych/Over the Edge/Landlord/Go Down (p/s, with insert)	£100

ANALYSIS
81	Survival SUR 003	Surface Tension/Connections (p/s)	£30

ANAN
68	Pye 7N 17571	Haze Woman/I Wonder Where My Sister's Gone	£50
68	Pye 7N 17642	Madena/Standing Still	£20

ANATHEMA
90	Private Pressing	AN ILLIAD OF WOES EP (4 track demo cassette)	£30
91	Private Pressing	ALL FAITH IS LOST EP (4 track demo cassette)	£30
92	Peaceville VILE 36T	THE CRESTFALLEN EP (12", p/s)	£30
94	Peaceville CC 6	WE ARE THE BIBLE EP (purple vinyl, p/s)	£25
93	Peaceville VILE 34	SERENADES (LP)	£30
95	Peaceville VILE 52	THE SILENT ENIGMA (LP)	£25
96	Peaceville VILE 64	ETERNITY (LP)	£25
99	Music For Nations MFN 250	JUDGEMENT (LP)	£35
01	Music For Nations MFN 260	A FINE DAY TO EXIT (LP)	£25
02	Peaceville VILELP 73	ALTERNATIVE 4 (LP, first issued on CD in 1998)	£30
10	Peaceville VILELP 305	A NATURAL DISASTER (2-LP, first issued on CD in 2003)	£20
10	K-Scope 812	WE'RE HERE BECAUSE WE'RE HERE (2-LP, 2000 only)	£20

THE ANCHORESS
16	K Scope KSCOPE 920	CONFESSIONS OF A ROMANCE NOVELIST (2LP, gatefold,	£25
21	K Scope KSCOPE 1110	THE ART OF LOSING (2LP/7", gatefold, printed inners)	£30
21	K Scope KSCOPE 1111	THE ART OF LOSING (2LP, gatefold, printed inners, gold vinyl)	£40
23	Drowned In Sound DIS 2004	VERSIONS (LP, printed inner, eco-vinyl, 1000 limited)	£20

(see also Catherine Anne Davies & Bernard Butler)

ANCIENT GREASE
71	Mercury 6338 033	WOMAN AND CHILDREN FIRST (LP, black/silver labels)	£250

(see also Eyes Of Blue, Big Sleep, Man, Gary Pickford-Hopkins, Gentle Giant)

ANCIENT GREEKS
81	Slam! SSM 027	I Am An Island/Yap (no p/s)	£30

AND ALSO THE TREES
83	Reflex (no cat. no.)	AND ALSO THE TREES (EP, cassette only)	£15
84	Reflex LEX 1	AND ALSO THE TREES (LP)	£18

ERIC ANDERSEN
65	Fontana TFL 6061	TODAY IS THE HIGHWAY (LP)	£60
68	Fontana TFL/STFL 6068	'BOUT CHANGES AND THINGS TAKE 2 (LP, black/silver label, mono/stereo)	£40
68	Vanguard SVRL 19003	MORE HITS FROM TIN CAN ALLEY (LP)	£20
72	CBS 65145	BLUE RIVER (LP)	£15

CAROL ANDERSON
79	Grapevine GRP 133	Sad Girl/I'll Get Off At The Next Stop	£30
99	Goldmine GSS GS 035	Sad Girl/VELVET HAMMER: Happy	£20

CHRISTIAN ANDERSON
74	DJM DJS 330	Supergirl/My Imagination (DJ Copy)	£15

ERNESTINE ANDERSON
61	Mercury AMT 1137	A Lover's Question/That's All I Want From You	£15
64	Sue WI 309	Keep An Eye On Love/Continental Mind	£70
65	Mercury MF 912	Jerk & Twine/You Can't Buy Love	£20
64	Sue ILP 911	THE NEW SOUND OF ERNESTINE ANDERSON (LP, unissued)	£150

GLADSTONE ANDERSON (& FOLLOWERS)
69	Blue Cat BS 172	Judas/The World Come To An End (with Followers)	£50
74	Ashanti ASH 413	It May Sound Silly/Gladdy's Workshop	£15
79	Love & Inity VG 006	Holly Children/Black Music (12")	£30
73	Ashanti SHAN 103	IT MAY SOUND SILLY (LP)	£25
83	Seven Leaves SLLP 4	PEACE PIPE (LP)	£25
94	Roots RRLP 009	FOREVER DUB (LP)	£25

(see also Stranger & Gladdy, Tommy McCook)

HALEY ANDERSON
83	Magnet 12 MID 5	All To Myself (Dance Mix)/(7" Version)/(Instrumental) (12")	£40

IAN (A.) ANDERSON
71	Village Thing VTSX 1002	One More Chance/Policeman's Ball	£18
69	Saydisc EP SD 134	ALMOST THE COUNTRY BLUES (EP, with Elliot Jackson)	£50
68	Saydisc Matchbox SDM 159	THE INVERTED WORLD (LP, with Mike Cooper)	£70
69	Liberty LBS 83242E	STEREO DEATH BREAKDOWN (LP, blue label, as Ian Anderson Country Blues Band)	£60
70	Fontana STL 5542	BOOK OF CHANGES (LP, black/silver labels)	£120
70	Village Thing VTS 3	ROYAL YORK CRESCENT (LP, with lyric insert)	£35

MINT VALUE £

72	Village Thing VTS 9	**A VULTURE IS NOT A BIRD YOU CAN TRUST** (LP, laminated front cover)	£40
72	Village Thing VTS 18	**SINGER SLEEPS ON AS BLAZE RAGES** (LP)	£60

(see also Mike Cooper, Anderson Jones Jackson)

JAMES ANDERSON
71	Atlantic 2091-055	**Mama Mama/Muskatel Muskatel**	£20

JON ANDERSON
76	Atlantic K50261	**OLIAS OF SUNHILLOW** (LP, gatefold, insert)	£30

(see also Hans Christian, Warriors, Yes, Mike Oldfield)

KIP ANDERSON
67	President PT 163	**You'll Lose A Good Thing/I'm Out Of Love**	£15

LAURIE ANDERSON
82	Warner Bros.WB K 57 002	**BIG SCIENCE** (LP)	£15

MILLER ANDERSON
71	Deram DM 337	**Bright City/Another Time, Another Place**	£15
71	Deram SDL 3	**BRIGHT CITY** (LP, gatefold sleeve)	£175

(see also Voice, At Last The 1958 Rock'n'Roll Show, Keef Hartley Band, Hemlock, Dog Soldier, Lyn Dobson)

REUBEN ANDERSON
66	Doctor Bird DB 1045	**Christmas Time Again/DESMOND TUCKER: Oh Holy Night**	£40

SONNY ANDERSON
60	London HLP 9036	**Lonely Lonely Train/Yes, I'm Gonna Love You**	£40

UDELL T. ANDERSON
69	Direction 58-4212	**Love Ain't Love/Funky Walk**	£15
69	Direction 58-4459	**Keep On Loving Me/Rainmaker**	£15

VICKI ANDERSON
73	Mojo 2093 005	**I'm Too Tough For Mr Big Stuff** (Hot Pants)/**Sound Funky**	£20
04	Soul Brother LP SBPJ 24	**MOTHER POPCORN** (2-LP)	£40

(see also Bobby Byrd, James Brown)

ANDERSON, JONES, JACKSON
68	Saydisc 33 SD 125	**ANDERSON, JONES, JACKSON** (EP)	£35

(see also Ian A. Anderson)

ANDERSON'S ALLSTARS
68	Blue Cat BS 133	**Intensified Girls/Jump And Shout**	£150

BARBARA ANDREWS
70	Escort ERT 838	**Lonesome Feeling/RAINY BOP: Hop Scotch**	£20

CATHERINE ANDREWS
80	Cat Tracks PURR LP 2	**FRUITS** (LP, with lyric sheet & poster sleeve)	£50

(see also Gordon Giltrap, Inner City Unit)

CHRIS ANDREWS
67	Decca F 22668	**Hold On/Easy**	£25

(see also Chris Ravel & Ravers)

DAVE ANDREWS & SUGAR
68	Jewel JL 04	**I'm On My Way/Beatin' Of My Heart**	£60

(see also Heinz)

ERNIE ANDREWS
65	Capitol CL 15407	**Where Were You/What Do I See In The Girl**	£25

HARVEY ANDREWS
65	Transatlantic TRAEP 133	**HARVEY ANDREWS** (EP)	£35
70	Decca Nova SDN 9	**PLACES AND FACES** (LP)	£50
73	Fly HIFLY 15	**FRIENDS OF MINE** (LP, gatefold sleeve)	£15

INEZ ANDREWS & ANDREWETTES
65	Vogue EDVP 1283	**INEZ ANDREWS & ANDREWETTES** (EP)	£40

JOHN ANDREWS & LONELY ONES
66	Parlophone R 5455	**A Rose Growing In The Ruins/It's Just Love** (DJ copy)	£350
66	Parlophone R 5455	**A Rose Growing In The Ruins/It's Just Love**	£250

LEE ANDREWS (& HEARTS)
57	London HL 7031	**Teardrops/Girl Around The Corner** (solo, export issue)	£100
58	London HLM 8546	**Teardrops/Girl Around The Corner** (solo)	£100
58	London HLU 8661	**Try The Impossible/Nobody's Home** (as Lee Andrews & Hearts)	£150
58	London HLU 8661	**Try The Impossible/Nobody's Home** (as Lee Andrews & Hearts) (78)	£15

RUBY ANDREWS
76	ABC 4156	**I Got A Bone To Pick With You/I Don't Know How To Love You**	£20

TIM ANDREWS
67	Parlophone R 5656	**Sad Simon Lives Again/You Won't Be Seeing Me Anymore**	£20
68	Parlophone R 5695	**(Something About) Suburbia/Your Tea Is Strong**	£20
70	Parlophone R 5824	**Tiny Goddess/Josephine**	£40

(see also Fleur De Lys, Rupert's People)

ANDREWS SISTERS
53	Brunswick LA 8599	**SING SING SING** (10" LP)	£15

ANDROIDS
79	Android AND 001	**Robot Riot/Andwellas Dream** (p/s)	£15

ANDROIDS OF MU
80	Fuck Off FLP 01	**BLOOD ROBOTS** (LP)	£50

ANDROMEDA (1)
69	RCA RCA 1854	Go Your Way/Keep Out 'Cos I'm Dying	£30
69	RCA SF 8031	ANDROMEDA (LP)	£800
90	Reflection MM 06	SEVEN, LONELY STREET (LP, with numbered & signed booklet, 500 only)	£25
95	Kissing Spell KSLP 9497	LIVE 1967 (LP)	£15
17	Repertoire V 246	ANDROMEDA (LP, reissue)	£15

(see Attack, Five Day Week Straw People, Hard Stuff, Atomic Rooster, John Du Cann, Fuzzy Duck)

ANDROMEDA (2)
91	Intrigue IGE15T	Survival (Urban Mix)/(City Mix)/Savage (12")	£15
91	Intrigue IGE AD1	CONTROL OF THE DANCEFLOOR (LP)	£40

AND THE NATIVE HIPSTERS
79	Heater Volume HVR 003	There Goes Concorde Again.../Stands, Still The Building.../I Wanna Be Around (several different coloured photocopied foldaround sleeves with insert in polythene bag)	£30
82	Illuminated/Glass HIP 1	TENDERLY HURT ME (Poor Prince/Hang Ten/Tenderly Hurt Me/Stuck) (12" EP, p/s)	£15

ANDWELLA('S DREAM)
69	CBS 4301	Sunday/Midday Sun (as Andwella's Dream)	£35
69	CBS 4469	Mrs. Man/Felix (as Andwella's Dream)	£80
69	CBS 4634	Mr. Sunshine/Shades Of Grey (as Andwella's Dream)	£50
70	Reflection RS 1	Every Little Minute/Michael Fitzhenry (as Andwellas Dream)	£15
70	Reflection RS 3	Hold Onto Your Mind/Shadow Of The Night (as Andwella)	£30
69	CBS 63673	LOVE AND POETRY (LP, as Andwella's Dream)	£1000
70	Reflection REFL 10	WORLD'S END (LP, as Andwella, stickered sleeve with poster)	£150
70	Reflection REFL 10	WORLD'S END (LP, without poster)	£80
71	Reflection REF 1010	PEOPLE'S PEOPLE (LP, as Andwella)	£100
09	Sunbeam SDR2LP 5063	LOVE & POETRY (2-LP, reissue)	£20

(see also David Lewis, David Baxter)

BOB ANDY
67	Island WI 3040	I've Got To Go Back Home/SONNY BURKE: Rudy Girl	£70
68	Studio One SO 2063	Too Experienced/Let Them Stay	£70
68	Coxsone CS 7074	My Time (miscredited to Alton Ellis)/MARCIA GRIFFITHS: Mark My Word	£200
69	Doctor Bird DB 1183	The Way I Feel/ETHIOPIANS: Long Time Now	£100
69	Doctor Bird DB 1191	Games People Play/The Sun Shines For Me	£25
69	Studio One SO 2075	I'm Going Home/SOUND DIMENSION: Straight Flush	£50
71	London HLJ 7127	Games People Play/GAYLETTES: Son Of A Preacher Man (export issue)	£15
72	Sioux SI 019	Baby I Need Your Loving/CIRCLES: Mammy Blue	£15
72	Sioux SI 020	Everyday People/HONG GANG: Smoking Wild	£15
72	Green Door GD 4047	Life/HARRY J. ALL STARS: Version	£20
73	Green Door GD 4059	You Don't Know/The Border Song	£100
75	Fab FAB 241	Feeling Soul/SOUND DIMENSION: Part 2	£40
76	DEB	War In The City/Version	£30
77	Sky Note SKY 1011	The Ghetto Stay In The Mind/Ghetto Dub	£25
78	Sky Note SKYLP 15	LOTS OF LOVE AND I (LP)	£25

(see also Bob & Marcia, Ethiopians, Larry & Alvin)

HORACE ANDY
72	Song Bird SB 1085	Lonely Woman/Lonely Version	£20
73	Randy's RAN 533	Don't Think About Me (with Earl Flute)/DINO PERKINS: Skin Him Alive	£20
73	RCA TCA 2401	I Stand Before You/Unity Strength And Love	£70
74	Harry J HJ 6699	Lonely Woman/Lonely Woman (Instrumental)	£15
75	Fab FAB 260	Oh Lord Why Lord/SOUND DIMENSION: Part 2	£25
77	Serious Business SB 02	Rock To Sleep/Version	£35
78	Carib Gems CGDD110	Guiding Star (with Tapper Zukie)/Zion Gate (12")	£20
79	Sufferer's Height SUFF 005	Pure Ranking/The Return Of Jammy's Hi-Fi (Round One)/TREVOR RANKING: Whip Them Jah Jah (12")	£30
79	Star PTP 1024	Tonight/Don't Let Problems Get You Down (12")	£35
70s	Terminal TM 101	Roots Of All Evil/I Will Forgive You	£15
80	Unity UN 002	This Must Be Hell/If I Wasn't A Man (12", with DEADLY HEADLEY)	£15
82	Wackie's WR 5252	Money Money/AL MOODIE: Bull Bay Jumping (12")	£25
84	Music Hawk MHD 13	Confusion/Version (12")	£40
84	Blacker Dread BD 009	Cus-Cus/S.C.O.M RHYTHM SECTION: Watch Your Step	£15
84	Blacker Dread BD 012	Money Money/Evil Money (no centre)	£15
85	Rough Trade RTT 172	Get Down/RHYTHM POSSE : Get Down Deeper (12")	£50
86	Music Hawk MF 16	User/Dub (12")	£20
89	Highest Grade HGR 002	Right Saloon/LECTURER: Weapon (12")	£30
95	Blood & Fire BAFT 01	Problems/Problems Dub (12" reissue)	£15
72	Trojan TBL 197	YOU ARE MY ANGEL (LP)	£45
78	Solid Groove SGL 107	EXCLUSIVELY (LP)	£40
84	Music Hawk MHLP001	CONFUSION (LP)	£20
87	Tachyon WR 2740	EVERYDAY PEOPLE (LP)	£20
95	Blood & Fire BAFLP 007	IN THE LIGHT DUB (LP, reissue)	£20
96	Trojan TBL 197	YOU ARE MY ANGEL (LP, reissue)	£15
99	Virgin SADLP 9	LIVING IN THE FLOOD (LP)	£15

(see also Jon Cuno, Big Youth)

PATRICK ANDY
78	Grove Music GMDM 3	Woman, Woman, Woman/TOMMY MCCOOK: Lamb's Bread (12")	£35

ANDY & CLYDE
65	Rio R 62	Never Be A Slave/Magic Is Love	£20
65	Rio R 71	We All Have To Part/UPSETTERS: Scandalizing	£80

ANDY & JOEY
62	Island WI 056	Have You Ever/Cross My Heart	£40
64	Port-O-Jam PJ 4009	I Want To Know/My Love Has Gone	£50
64	Ska Beat JB 162	You're Wondering Now/You'll Never (copies also exist on R&B label)	£60

(see also Roland Alphonso)

JOHNNY ANGEL
| 60 | Parlophone R 4679 | Too Young To Go Steady/You're Thrilling | £20 |
| 63 | Parlophone R 5026 | A Touch Of Venus/The Two Together | £70 |

MARIAN ANGEL
65	Columbia DB 7537	It's Gonna Be Alright/Tomorrow's Fool	£30
65	Columbia DB 7705	You Can't Buy My Love/One Way Only	£25
66	CBS 202391	A Little Bit Of Sunshine/All The Time In The World	£20

ANGEL PAVEMENT
| 69 | Fontana TF 1059 | Baby You've Gotta Stay/Green Mello Hill | £20 |
| 70 | Fontana TF 1072 | Tell Me What I've Got To Do/When Will I See June Again | £25 |

(see also Fortes Mentum, Pussy)

ANGEL STREET
| 79 | Ellie Jay EJSP 9290 | Done It Again/Song For You (500 only) | £200 |

ANGEL WITCH
80	EMI 12EMI 5064	Sweet Danger/Hades Paradise/Flight Nineteen (12", p/s)	£20
85	Killerwatt KIL 3001	Goodbye/Reawakening (no p/s)	£15
80	Bronze BRON 532	ANGELWITCH (LP)	£20
85	Killerwatt KILP 4001	SCREAMIN' N' BLEEDIN' (LP)	£15
86	Killerwatt KILP 4003	FRONTAL ASSAULT (LP)	£18
12	Rise Above RISELP145	AS ABOVE, SO BELOW (2-LP, clear vinyl, 1-sided 7", A2 poster, 100 only)	£70
12	Rise Above RISELP145	AS ABOVE, SO BELOW (LP, 2 x white vinyl 12", inners, insert)	£30

(see also Tytan)

ANGEL (2)
| 76 | Casablanca CBC 4007 | ANGEL (LP, with insert) | £15 |

ANGELA & HER FANS
| 66 | Pye 7N 17108 | Love Ya Illya/I Know You | £15 |

(see also Alma Cogan)

ANGELIC UPSTARTS
78	Dead IS/AU/1024	Murder Of Liddle Towers/Police Oppression (p/s, 1,000 only)	£300
78	Rough Trade RT/SW 001	Murder Of Liddle Towers/Police Oppression (reissue, p/s)	£15
81	Zonophone Z 12	England/Stick's Diary (p/s)	£15
83	Anagram ANA 12	The Burglar (p/s, unissued)	£0
85	Gas GM 3010	Brighton Bomb/Thin Red Line/Soldier (12", banned 'Maggie Thatcher' p/s)	£15
79	Warner Bros K 56717	TEENAGE WARNING (LP)	£25
80	Warner Bros K 56806	WE GOTTA GET OUT OF THIS PLACE (LP)	£15
81	Zonophone ZEM 102	LIVE (LP, with free live flexidisc: "We're Gonna Take The World"/Leave Me Alone/"The Young Ones"/"White Riot" [no cat. no.])	£15
81	Zonophone ZEM 102	LIVE (LP)	£15
81	EMI ZONO 104	2,000,000 VOICE (LP)	£20
83	Anagram GRAM 007	ANGEL DUST (LP)	£15
85	Gas GLP 4012	THE POWER OF THE PRESS (LP)	£15
85	Razor RAZM 32	LIVE IN YUGOSLAVIA (LP)	£15
85	Anagram GRAM004	REASONS WHY (LP, with inner sleeve)	£15
90	Link LP 140	LOST & FOUND (LP)	£15

BOBBY ANGELO & TUXEDOS
| 61 | HMV POP 892 | Baby Sittin'/Skinny Lizzie | £20 |
| 61 | HMV POP 982 | I Gotta Have You/Don't Stop | £30 |

(see also Innocents [UK])

ANGELS AND EIGHTEEN
| 72 | RAK 137 | Midnight Flight/Flight 2 | £80 |

GUY ANGIER
| 70 | (No label or cat no) | GUITAR AND BANANAS (LP, with insert) | £80 |

ANGLIANS
| 67 | CBS 202489 | A Friend Of Mine/Daytime Lover | £15 |

(see also Moving Finger)

ANGLOS
65	Brit WI 004	Incense/You're Fooling Me	£60
65	Fontana 561	Incense/You're Fooling Me (unissued)	£200
65	Fontana TF 589	Incense/You're Fooling Me (reissue)	£25
67	Sue WI 4033	Incense/You're Fooling Me (unissued)	£200

(see also Spencer Davis Group, Stevie Winwood)

ANGOR WAT
| 85 | Children Of The Revolution GURT8 | GENERAL STRIKE (LP) | £15 |

ANIKA
| 10 | Invada INV099LP | ANIKA (LP, blue vinyl) | £15 |

ANIMAL COLLECTIVE
| 06 | No label or Cat. No.) | Purple Bottle/Polly (tour 7", white label, plain white die-cut sleeve. Later pressings have track info on sleeve) | £15 |
| 07 | Domino RUG 270T | Fireworks (1-sided pink vinyl other side etched 10", stickered, die-cut pink sleeve) | £15 |

04	Fat Cat FATSPLP 08	**SUNG TONGS** (2-LP, gatefold)	£20
05	Fat Cat FATSPLP 11	**FEELS** (2-LP)	£40
06	Domino WIGLP 199	**STRAWBERRY JAM** (2-LP, gatefold with inners)	£30
09	Fat Cat FATSP08LPX	**SUNG TONGS** (2-LP, reissue, 180 gm vinyl)	£30
09	Fat Cat FATSP11LPX	**FEELS** (2-LP, gatefold, reissue 180gm vinyl)	£15
09	Domino WIGLP 216	**MERRIWEATHER POST PAVILION** (2-LP, gatefold, inners)	£25
09	Fat Cat FATSP17LPX	**SPIRIT THEY'VE GONE, SPIRIT THEY'VE VANISHED** (2-LP)	£40
09	Fat Cat FATSP18LPX	**DANSE MANATEE** (LP)	£20
15	Domino WIGLP 364	**LIVE AT 9.30** (3-LP boxset, poster, hand numbered with screenprint)	£35
15	Domino WIGLP 364	**LIVE AT 9.30** (3-LP boxset, poster, hand numbered without screenprint)	£25
16	Domino WIGLP 362	**PAINTING WITH** (LP, 4 different covers)	£18
(see also Avey Tare)			

ANIMAL FARM

84	Rot Records ASS 7	**Model Soldier/John And Julie** (p/s)	£15

ANIMALS

63	Graphic Sound ALO 10867	**THE ANIMALS** (12" EP, 1-sided, 99 only, private pressing, blank white cover, printed label. Some credited to the Animals or The Alan Price Rhythm and Blues Group)	£500
64	Columbia SEG 8374	**THE ANIMALS IS HERE** (EP)	£20
65	Columbia SEG 8400	**THE ANIMALS** (EP)	£20
65	Columbia SEG 8439	**THE ANIMALS** (EP)	£20
65	Columbia SEG 8452	**THE ANIMALS ARE BACK** (EP)	£35
66	Decca DFE 8643	**IN THE BEGINNING THERE WAS EARLY ANIMALS** (EP)	£30
66	Columbia SEG 8499	**ANIMAL TRACKS** (EP)	£45
64	Columbia 33SX 1669	**THE ANIMALS** (LP, blue/black label with "sold in the U.K..." label text)	£100
64	Regal SREG 1104	**THE ANIMALS** (LP, export only. 'stereo' blue labels)	£45
65	Columbia 33SX 1708	**ANIMAL TRACKS** (LP, 1st pressing with 33SX on labels)	£120
66	Columbia SX 1708	**ANIMAL TRACKS** (LP, 2nd pressing, SX 1708 on labels)	£75
66	Columbia SX 6035	**THE MOST OF THE ANIMALS** (LP, 1st pressing, blue/black labels, flipback sleeve)	£30
66	Decca LK 4797	**ANIMALISMS** (LP)	£150
68	Regal SREG 1104	**THE ANIMALS** (LP, export only. 'mono' black labels)	£65
69	Regal Starline SR5 5006	**THE ANIMALS** (LP, 'stereo' reissue of 33SX 1669, flipback sleeve)	£25
69	Columbia SX 6035	**THE MOST OF THE ANIMALS** (LP, 2nd pressing, black/silver labels, flipback sleeve)	£25
88	See For Miles SEE 244	**THE EP COLLECTION** (LP)	£15
(see also Eric Burdon & Animals, Alan Price, Danny McCullough)			

ANIMATED EGG

69	Marble Arch MAL 890	**ANIMATED EGG** (LP)	£25

ANIMATION

82	Dance Fools Dance DF 2 2	**FRAME ON EP**	£20

PAUL ANKA

SINGLES

59	Columbia DB 4324	**Lonely Boy/Your Love** (78)	£30
59	Columbia DB 4355	**Put Your Head On My Shoulder/Don't Ever Leave Me** (78)	£70
68	RCA RCA 1676	**Can't Get You Out Of My Mind/When We Get There**	£40
68	RCA RCA 1676	**Can't Get You Out Of My Mind/When We Get There** (DJ copy)	£60
77	RCA PB 9394	**When We Get There/I Can't Help Loving You**	£40
(see also Micki Marlo & Paul Anka, Neil Sedaka)			

ANNA

82	RCA RCAT 213	**Systems Breaking Down/Dance Version** (12", p/s)	£25

ANNABEL DREAM

60s	Oak (no cat no)	**My Last Date With You/Gary, Won't You Marry Me** (Unreleased - acetate only)	£50

ANNETTE

88	Deconstruction PT 42562	**Dream 17/Nightmare On Dream Street/Dream Slumber** (12", p/s)	£18

ANNETTE (& AFTERBEATS)

65	HMV POP 1447	**The Monkey's Uncle** (with The Beach Boys)/**How Will I Know My Love**	£15

ANNIE AND THE AEROPLANES

88	Pipedream PIPE 1	**A Million Zillion Miles/Travelling Song**	£15

ANNIS

79	GTO GT 266	**Don't Play Your Games/After Me**	£15

ANNIVERSARY

78	Aerco AERE 102	**GIVE ME A SMILE** (EP)	£25

ANNO DOMINI

71	Deram SML-R 1085	**ON THIS NEW DAY** (LP)	£400

ANON

93	Nucleus NUKE 006	**Alright/OK Armando** (12")	£20

ANONYMOUSLY YOURS

69	Trojan TR 680	**Get Back/ERNIE SMITH : Not For Sale**	£15
69	Trojan TR 681	**It's Your Thing/69** (B-side actually by Wallace Wilson)	£50
69	Duke DU 38	**Dream Baby/Staggerlee**	£15
69	Duke DU 40	**Organism/Itch**	£30

ANOREXIA

80	Slim SJP 812	**Rapist In The Park/I'm A Square/Pets**	£35
82	Slim BRS 011	**Softly Quietly Or Shout/Steven/Inanimate Objects/Marching Song** (p/s)	£25

MINT VALUE £

ANOTHER PRETTY FACE
79	New Pleasure Z1	All The Boys Love Carrie/That's Not Enough (green and white foldout p/s) £25
79	New Pleasure Z2	All The Boys Love Carrie/That's Not Enough (red and white p/s) £15
80	Chicken Jazz JAZZ 2	I'M SORRY THAT I BEAT YOU, I'M SORRY THAT I SCREAMED, FOR A MOMENT THERE I REALLY LOST CONTROL (8-track cassette with fanzine and badge. Some copies exist with tracks of DNV single taped onto the end) £30
81	Chicken Jazz JAZZ 3	Soul To Soul/A Woman's Place/God On The Screen (foldout p/s) £15

ANOTHER SUNNY DAY
88	Sarah SARAH 003	Anorak City (flexidisc free with Are You Scared To Get Happy fanzine (SARAH 004, 1,500 only – must be together) £200
88	Sarah SARAH 007	I'm In Love With A Girl Who Doesn't Know I Exist/Things Will Be Nice/The Centre Of My Little World (14" x 10" foldout poster p/s) £60
89	Caff CAFF 7	Genetic Engineering/Kilburn Towers (p/s, with inner) £30
89	Sarah SARAH 016	What's happened?/Can't You Tell It's True?/Impossible (foldover p/s in poly bag, insert) £25
89	Sarah SARAH 022	You Should All Be Murdered/Horseriding/Green (foldover p/s in poly bag, insert) £30
90	Sarah SARAH 035	Rio/The Very Beginning (p/s, insert) £25
92	Sarah SARAH 060	New Year's Honours/I Don't Suppose I'll Get A Second Chance (p/s, insert) £25
92	Sarah SARAH 613	LONDON WEEKEND (LP) £75

BRETT ANSELL
| 62 | Oriole CB 1701 | That's Where Lonesome Lives/The Door Is Open ....£25 |

ANSELL (COLLINS) & ELAINE
| 72 | Camel CA 98 | Presenting Cheater/RON WILSON: Official Trombone ....£15 |

MARK ANSLEY
| 70 | Mother MOT 2 | 909/Venus ....£50 |

ANSWERS (1)
| 66 | Columbia DB 7847 | It's Just A Fear/You've Gotta Believe Me ....£200 |
| 66 | Columbia DB 7953 | That's What You're Doing To Me/Got A Letter From My Baby ....£70 |

(see also Misunderstood, High Tide)

ANSWERS (2)
| 71 | Spark SRL 1058 | Give Me All That I Need/Tawny Wood ....£20 |

ANT
| 74 | Pye 7N 45332 | Banana Pie/No Road Goes Your Way ....£15 |

ADAM ANT
| 95 | EMI CDEMS370 | Beautiful Dream (single version)/Let's Have A Fight/Billy Boy/Wonderful (acoustic) (CD withdrawn, 7 known copies) ....£75 |
| 95 | EMI CDEM370 | Beautiful Dream (single version)/Shake Your Hips/Antmusic (Acoustic)/Beautiful Dream (Lucas Full Length Mix) (CD, withdrawn, 2 known copies) ....£100 |

(see also Adam & The Ants, Maneaters)

ANTEEEKS
| 66 | Philips BF 1471 | I Don't Want You/Ball And Chain ....£200 |

ANTHEM (1)
| 71 | Buddah 2359017 | ANTHEM (LP) ....£40 |

ANTHEM (2)
| 81 | EJSP9576 | England/Some Like It Hot/Do You Mind (EP, p/s, 500 only) ....£140 |

ANTHILL MOB (1)
92	Anthill ANT 1T	Penelope's Theme (12" white label) £35
93	Anthill ANT 2T	Antology/Black Rushin'/The Hooded Claw (Tango Mix) (12") £30
93	Anthill ANT 3T	Antology (The Top Buzz Stonehenge Remix)/Black Rushin' (Anthill Remix) (12") £20

ANTHILL MOB (2)
95	Confetti MK 01	Feel It/Deep Down/Untitled/Untitled (white label 12") £30
95	Confetti MK001	MAKESHIFT EP (12") £90
96	Confetti COEP 01	Promise Of... /Was She Ever Mine?/So In Love/Got To Do It (12") £35
96	Confetti COEP 02	Feel The Groove/ANTHILL MOB FEATURING P. PITSTOP - Do You Know?/P. PITSTOP - I Know How To Love! (12") £25
97	Confetti COEP 05	Why (Inside The Rise)/Things Just Started (12") £25
97	Confetti COEP 06	Cloudy Day/Agitator (12") £15
97	Confetti CODP 0197/0187	Missing/Player/X2C/Flava/Sound/Cuts (2 x 12") £200
97	Confetti COEP 08	Higher/How Ya Feeling (12") £15
97	Love Peace & Unity LOVE 03	Burning (The Original Mix) (10" picture disc, 500 only, same track both sides) £35
97	Makeshift MR 001	Set You Free/In The Name/Shake The House/Heaven Knows (12") £15
98	Makeshift MR 002	Never Ever Time/Time To Move/Don't Know/Give Me (12") £20
98	Quench QUE 14	Don't Leave Me/Listen (12") £30
00	Confetti COEP 19	ANTHILL MOB EP (12") £25
97	Love Peace & Unity LOVE 04	A SPECIAL COLLECTION OF ENCHANTED RHYTHMS (2 x LP) £250

(see also Mystic matt And The Anthill Mob)

BILLIE ANTHONY
| 54 | Columbia SCM 5143 | This Ole House/Oh, What A Dream ....£20 |

(see also Big Ben Banjo Band)

DAVID ANTHONY
| 68 | Island WI 3148 | All Night/Get Out Of My Mind ....£40 |

(see also Dave Anthony's Moods)

MALCOLM ANTHONY
| 70 | Nashville 6076 004 | Memories/Traces Of Tomorrow (demo) ....£15 |
| 70 | Vertigo 6076 004 | Memories/Traces Of Tomorrow ....£50 |

RAY ANTHONY (2)
79	Mango Media 23	The Arabian Funk/Time	£25

RAYBURN ANTHONY
60	London HLS 9167	Who's Gonna Shoe Your Pretty Little Feet/There's No Tomorrow	£15

DAVE ANTHONY'S MOODS
66	Parlophone R 5438	New Directions/Give It A Chance	£60

(see also David Anthony)

ANTHRAX (U.K.)
83	Crass 221984/9	CAPITALISM IS CANNIBALISM (EP, foldout p/s)	£20

ANTHRAX (U.S.)
86	Island 12ISP 285	Madhouse/Air/God Save The Queen (12", picture disc)	£20
86	Island 12IS 285	Madhouse/Air/God Save The Queen (12", p/s with patch)	£15
87	Island ISX 316	I Am The Law (live)/Bud E.Luvbomm And Satan's Lounge Band/Madhouse (live) (red vinyl, p/s)	£20
86	Music For Nations MFN62	SPREADING THE DISEASE (LP)	£20
86	Music For Nations MFN62P	SPREADING THE DISEASE (LP, picture disc)	£20
87	Music For Nations MFN14	FISTFUL OF METAL (LP)	£15
87	Music For Nations MFN14P	FISTFUL OF METAL (LP, picture disc)	£20
87	Island ILPS 9865	AMONG THE LIVING (LP)	£20
87	Island PILPS 9865	AMONG THE LIVING (LP, picture disc)	£20
90	Island ILPSP 9967	PERSISTENCE OF TIME (LP, picture disc)	£15
94	BMG 74321 19059 1	LIVE - THE ISLAND YEARS (LP)	£20

ANTILLES
83	Creole CR 51	I've Got To Have You/Latin Dream	£40
83	Creole CR 12-51	I've Got To Have You/Latin Dream (12")	£60

ANTI NOWHERE LEAGUE
81	WXYZ ABCD 1	Streets Of London (1-sided test pressing)	£35
87	GWR A1	Crime/Working For The Company (Unreleased Test Pressing)	£20
82	WXYZ LMNOP1	WE ARE...THE LEAGUE (LP, 1st pressing, uncensored lyrics)	£25
82	WXYZ LMNOP1	WE ARE...THE LEAGUE (LP, 2nd pressing, censored lyrics)	£15

ANTI PASTI
80	Dose DOSE1	FORE SORE POINTS (EP, 500 only, clear and black vinyl)	£18

ANTI SECT
84	Endangered Music EDR 4	Out From The Void/Hope Future Poisoned By Fear	£25
83	Spiderleg SDL 16	IN DARKNESS THERE IS NO CHOICE (LP)	£30
84	Clown Disc Big Top 1/2	LIVE IN THE DARKNESS (LP, splattered grey vinyl with insert, 1,000 only)	£20
94	Discipline DISCLP 03	PEACE IS BETTER THAN A PLACE IN HISTORY (LP)	£20
17	Rise Above RISELP 216	THE RISING OF THE LIGHTS (LP, clear vinyl, 100 only)	£20

ANTI-SOCIAL WORKERS & MAD PROFESSOR
83	Ariwa ARI008LP	POSITIVE STYLE PUNKY REGGAE PARTY (LP)	£20

ANTI SOCIAL (1)
77	Dynamite DRO 1	Traffic Lights/Teacher Teacher (no p/s)	£500
82	Beat The System BTS 2	Battle Scarred Skinheads/Sewer Rat/Official Hooligan (p/s)	£18

ANTI SOCIAL (2)
82	Lightbeat SOCIAL 1	MADE IN ENGLAND (EP)	£20

ANTI STATE CONTROL
83	Asc Records ASC1	Glue Sniffing Blues/M.U.S.E/Third World Bomb (p/s)	£800

ANTI SYSTEM
83	Reconcilliation RECONCILE 3	Strangelove/So Long As/MORBID HUMOUR: Oh My God (Parts 1 and 2)	£30
83	Paragon/Pax PAX 11	DEFENCE OF THE REALM (EP)	£25
86	Reconcilliation RECONCILE 4	A LOOK AT LIFE (12" EP)	£20
85	Reconcilliation RECONCILE 1	NO LAUGHING MATTER (LP)	£30
17	Boss Tunage BTRC12-110	AT WHAT PRICE IS FREEDOM? (LP with CD, white vinyl 100 only)	£18

ANTOINE
66	Vogue VRL 3024	ANTOINE (LP)	£20
67	Vogue VRL 3032	ANTOINE (LP)	£15

ANTOINETTE
64	Piccadilly 7N 35201	There He Goes (The Boy I Love)/Little Things Mean A Lot	£15
66	Piccadilly 7N 35293	Why Don't I Run Away From You/There's No-One In The Whole Wide World	£20

REY ANTON
64	Parlophone R 5132	You Can't Judge A Book By The Cover/It's Cold Outside (with Peppermint Men)	£20
64	Parlophone R 5172	Heard It All Before/I Want You (with Peppermint Men)	£15
65	Parlophone R 5274	Girl You Don't Know Me/Don't Treat Me Bad (with Peppermint Men)	£50
65	Parlophone R 5358	Premeditation/Now That It's Over (with Pro Form)	£30

ANTONIO
98	Locked On LOCKED009	Hyperfunk (New Horizons Mix)/(Vocal Mix)/(Original Mix) (12")	£30

ANTONIOU
82	Elite DAZZ 17	Sound On Sound/Street Sound (12" stickered plain sleeve)	£15

(see also Atmosfear)

TONY ANTONIU
84	Spartan 12 SP 12	Send In The Night/(Extended Version) (12")	£30

ANTONY
67	Westleigh WSC 1	No Ones Caring/Be Aware Of The Dark	£30

DAVE ANTONY
68   Mercury MF 1031   Race With The Wind/Playin' Hide And Seek £20
(see also Dave Anthony['s Moods])

MARK ANTONY & AVENGERS
60s Malconi MCD LP 17   MARK ANTONY & THE AVENGERS (LP, private pressing, plain sleeve)...............£100

MIKI ANTONY
78   EMI EMC 3259   CITY OF THE ANGELS (LP) £15

ANNIE ANXIETY
81   Crass Records 32984/3   BARBED WIRE HALO: Cyanide Tears/Hello Horror (gatefold sleeve)...................£15
(see also Crass, Little Annie)

ANY TROUBLE
79   Pennine PSS 7165   Yesterdays Love/Nice Girls, (1000 only, 100 with 'sewn' p/s) £20
79   Pennine PSS 7165   Yesterdays Love/Nice Girls, (1000 only, p/s) £15

ANYWAYS/SHAKE APPEAL
88   Jericho JR 001   Wall of Hurt/Amphetamine (no sleeve)..£15

AOA
85   COR COR 4   WHO ARE THEY TRYING TO CON (EP, 12", comes with 7" sleeve with lyrics) £20
86   COR GURT 12   UNLIMITED GENOCIDE (Split LP with OI POLLOI, insert) £20
88   ENDANGERED EDR LP 2   SATISFACTORY ARRANGEMENT (LP) £30

AOS3
94   Words Of Warning   GODS SECRET AGENT (LP) £30
     WOWLP28
95   Inna State ANOKLP001   DIVERSIONARY TACTICS (LP) £15

APARTMENT
80   Heartbeat PULSE 7   The Car/Winter (p/s) £20

APATCHI BAND
73   President PT 392   Issmak/Crashpad £30

APB
81   Oily SLICK 6   Chain Reaction/Power Crisis (p/s) £15
81   Oily SLICK 7   Shoot You Down/Talk To Me (blue or black p/s)...£15

APES
72   Leicester Rec. Co LRS LS 1   APES (LP) £50

APEX RHYTHM & BLUES ALLSTARS
59   John Lever AP 100   Yorkshire Relish/Caravan £40
60s John Lever JLEP 1   APEX RHYTHM & BLUES ALLSTARS (EP, no p/s)..£350
(see also Ian Hunter)

APHEX TWIN
16   Warp WAP 391   CHEETAH (12" EP, printed inner) £15

SINGLES : SINGLES AND EPS
91   Mighty Force 01   ANALOGUE BUBBLEBATH VOL. 1 (12" EP, label on 1 side only, other side has white label, some stamped)...........£80
91   Rabbit City CUT 002   ANALOGUE BUBBLEBATH VOL. 2 (12" EP, stamped white label).........................£70
92   R&S RSUK 12   Didgeridoo/Analogue Bubblebath 1/Flaphead/Isoprophlex (12", stickered R&S sleeve, 'Isoprophlex' is actually 'Phloam').....£40
93   Mighty Force MF 201   ANALOGUE BUBBLEBATH VOL. 1 (12", repressing of 1000 copies, MF201 on label, other side has plain white label).....£50
93   Rephlex CAT 008   ANALOGUE BUBBLEBATH VOL. 3 (12" EP, paper bag sleeve, Cornwall map, as AFX)...£60
93   Warp WAP 39   On/73-Yips/D-Scape/Xepha (12", gatefold p/s) £50
93   Warp WAP 39R   On (D-Scape Mix)/On (Reload Mix)/On (µ-Ziq Mix)/On (28 Mix) (12", p/s)..........£40
93   Warp WAP 60   VENTOLIN EP (12", p/s) £20
93   Warp WAP 60R   VENTOLIN EP (THE REMIXES) (12", p/s)...£20
93   Warp WAP 60/WAP 60R   VENTOLIN EP (2 x 12", includes both above 12"s, stickered gatefold p/s) £60
94   Rephlex CAT 019 EP   ANALOGUE BUBBLEBATH VOL. 4 (12" EP, p/s with insert, as AFX).....................£40
95   Rephlex CAT 034   ANALOGUE BUBBLEBATH VOL. 5 (as AFX, 12" white label only)........................£700
95   Warp WAP 63   Donkey Rhubarb/Vaz Deferenz/Icct Hedral (Philip Glass Orchestration)/Pancake Lizard (12", p/s)....£30
95   Warp WAP 67   HANGABLE AUTO BULB EP (12",as AFX)...£80
95   Warp WAP 69   HANGABLE AUTO BULB 2 EP (12", as AFX)...£100
96   Warp WAP 78   Boy/Girl EP (12", p/s) £40
97   Warp WAP 94P/WAP 94RP   Come To Daddy(Pappy Mix)/Flim/Come To Daddy (Little Lord Faulteroy Mix)/Bucephalus Bouncing Ball/To Cure A Weakling Child (Contour Regard)/Funny Little Man/Come To Daddy (Mummy Mix)/IZ-US (2 x promo 12", 500 only) £150
99   Warp WAP105   Windowlicker/Formula $(\Delta M_i^{-1}=-\alpha \sum D_i [\eta] [\sum Fj_i [\eta-1]+Fext_i [\eta^{-1}]]))$/Nanno (12", printed inner)........£30
01   Warp DRUKQS 01 54   Cymru Beats (Argonaut Mix)/Cock 10 (Delco Freedom Mix) (12", stickered black sleeve, promo)......£30
05   Warp WAP 195   46 Analord-Masplid/Naks 11 (Mono) (as AFX)/LFO: Flue Shot (Kringlan)/Pathfinder (12")......£50
05   Rephlex ANALORD 10   ANALORD 10: Fenix Funk 5/XMD 5a (12" in PVC binder with 12 sleeves for the Analord series, website exclusive)......£400
05   Rephlex ANALORD 01   ANALORD 01 (12" EP, stickered plastic sleeve as AFX)......................................£45
05   Rephlex ANALORD 02   ANALORD 02 (12" EP as AFX)...£45
05   Rephlex ANALORD 03   ANALORD 03 (12" EP as AFX)...£45
05   Rephlex ANALORD 04   ANALORD 04 (12" EP as AFX)...£50
05   Rephlex ANALORD 05   ANALORD 05 (12" EP as AFX)...£45
05   Rephlex ANALORD 06   ANALORD 06 (12" EP as AFX)...£45
05   Rephlex ANALORD 07   ANALORD 07 (12" EP as AFX)...£50

06	Rephlex ANALORD 08	ANALORD 08 (12" EP as AFX)	£45
05	Rephlex ANALORD 09	ANALORD 09 (12" EP as AFX)	£50
05	Rephlex ANALORD10PIC	ANALORD 10 (12" EP as AFX, picture disc)	£45
05	Rephlex ANALORD 11	ANALORD 11 (12" EP as AFX)	£60
12	Warp WAP 105	Windowlicker/Formula ($\Delta M_i^{-1} = -\alpha \sum D_i [\eta] [\sum Fj_i [\eta-1]+Fext_i [\eta^{-1}]])$/Nanno (12" reissue)	£15
15	Warp WAP 381	MARCHROMT30a Edit 2b/XMAS_EVET1 N/MARCHROMT38 Fast (12" white label, hand-stamped)	£15
15	Warp WAP 384	ORPHANED DEEJAY SELEK 2006-8 (12" EP, p/s, as A.F.X.)	£15
15	Warp WAP 375	COMPUTER CONTROLLED ACOUSTIC INSTRUMENTS PT. 2 (12" EP, printed inner)	£15
17	Warp WAP 400	LONDON 03.06.17 (12", as AFX, stamped white labels in plain lime green sleeve, sold at Field Day Festival 2017)	£300
18	Warp Warp WAP 423X	COLLAPSE (12" EP, silver foil sleeve, stickers ,ltd. ed. website exclusive)	£20
18	Warp WAP 423	COLLAPSE (12" EP, download card)	£15
19	Warp WAP 105	Windowlicker/Formula ($\Delta M_i^{-1} = -\alpha \sum D_i [\eta] [\sum Fj_i [\eta-1]+Fext_i [\eta^{-1}]])$/Nanno (12" repress)	£20
19	Warp WAP 436	LONDON 14.09.2019 (12" EP, available via card at London show)	£150
19	Warp WAP 437	MANCHESTER 20.09.2019 (12" EP, Warehouse Project 19 exclusive, address card/instructions)	£90
19	Warp WARPLP300-1	PEEL SESSIONS 2 TX 10/04/95 (12" EP, printed inner)	£15
23	Warp WAP 483	BARCELONA 16.06.2023 (10" EP, limited edition, via cards from Sonar show)	£150
23	Warp WAP 480C	Blackbox Life Recorder 21f / In A Room7 F760 (12" EP, clear vinyl, fold-out sleeve, website exclusive)	£30
23	Warp WAP 480	Blackbox Life Recorder 21f / In A Room7 F760 (12" EP, fold-out sleeve)	£20
23	Warp WAP 482	LONDON 19.08.2023 (12" EP, 100 copies with screen printed sleeve, Field Day exclusive)	£300
23	Warp WAP 482	LONDON 19.8.2023 (12" EP, Field Day exclusive)	£150

ALBUMS

93	Rephlex CAT 008	ANALOGUE BUBBLEBATH VOL. 3 (CD, bubble wrap sleeve)	£30
92	R&S/Apollo AMBLP 3922	SELECTED AMBIENT WORKS 85-92 (2LP, 1st issue without barcode)	£150
94	Warp WARPLP 21LTD	SELECTED AMBIENT WORKS VOL. 2 (3LP, brown vinyl, black and white sleeve with numbered sticker)	£300
94	Warp WARPLP 21	SELECTED AMBIENT WORKS VOL. 2 (3LP, black vinyl, stickered colour sleeve)	£350
95	Warp WARPLP 30	I CARE BECAUSE YOU DO (2LP, stickered sleeve, some with poster)	£50
96	Warp WARPLP 43	RICHARD D. JAMES ALBUM (2LP, orange sticker)	£50
02	Warp WARPLP 92	DRUKQS (2LP, 2x12", oversize box,180g)	£500
02	Warp WARPLP 92	DRUKQS (2LP 2x12", 1st pressing with mispressed side B containing 2 tracks by unknown artist)	£150
02	Warp WARPLP 92X	DRUKQS (2LP 2x 12",oversized numbered box, 1,000 only, audiophile edition)	£500
02	Rephlex CAT 008	ANALOGUE BUBBLEBATH VOL 3 (2LP, as AFX, reissue)	£30
06	Rephlex CAT 173 CD	CHOSEN LORDS (CD, compilation of ANALORD series, card digipak)	£30
12	Warp WARPLP 30	I CARE BECAUSE YOU DO (2LP, reissue, 180g)	£25
12	Warp WARPLP 43	RICHARD D. JAMES ALBUM (LP, reissue, 180g)	£20
13	Apollo AMBLP 3922	SELECTED AMBIENT WORKS 85-92 (2-LP, reissue)	£40
14	Warp WARPLP 247X	SYRO (3LP special 'ballot' edition of 200 copies in box with additional track on playable print)	£600
14	Warp WARPLP 247	SYRO (3LP, printed inners, booklet)	£30

(see also Caustic Window, Polygon Window, Q-Chastic, Kosmic Kommando, Tuss, Mike & Rich)

APHRODITE'S CHILD

68	Mercury MF 1039	Rain & Tears/Don't Try To Catch A River	£15
69	Mercury MF 1079	End Of The World/You Always Stand In My Way	£15
69	Polydor 56769	I Want To Live/Magic Mirror	£20
72	Vertigo 6032 900	Break/Babylon	£15
68	Mercury SMCL 20140	END OF THE WORLD/RAIN AND TEARS (LP, black/silver label, laminated sleeve)	£35
69	Polydor 2384 005	IT'S FIVE O'CLOCK (LP, gatefold sleeve)	£40
72	Vertigo 6673 001	666 - THE APOCALYPSE OF JOHN (2-LP, swirl labels, gatefold, red laminated sleeve. Sleeve has cat number 6673 001, albums have 6333500/6333501 on labels)	£1000
75	Philips 6483025	RAIN & TEARS (LP)	£15
77	Vertigo 6641 581	666 (2-LP, reissue, as Aphrodite's Child with Demis Roussos & Vangelis, different sleeve, 'spaceship' labels)	£60

(see also Vangelis, Forminx)

APOCALYPSE
82	Gate GATE 2	Storm Child/Chosen Few (p/s)	£125

APOLLO FOUR FORTY
97	Stealth Sonic Recordings SSX2440LP	ELECTRO GLIDE IN BLUE (2-LP)	£20

APOLLO TWO
93	Good Looking GLR 003	VOLUME 1 (12", EP)	£25

A POPULAR HISTORY OF SIGNS
82	Melodia M4	Dancing with Ideas/The Traveller (p/s)	£15

APOSTLES
82	No Label	BLOW IT UP BURN IT DOWN KICK IT TILL IT BREAKS EP (fold out p/s)	£15
82	BBP	THE 2ND DARK AGE (Cassette LP)	£15
83	Cause For Concern CFC 2	LIVE AT THE LMC (LP, one side by THE MOB)	£25
83	BBP BBP 005	SWIMMERS IN THE SEA OF LIFE (cassette album)	£15
86	Acid Strings 001	HOW MUCH LONGER? (LP, with inserts)	£20
86	Mortarhate MORT 23	PUNK OBITUARY (LP, gatefold, insert, lyric sheet)	£15
86	Children Of The Revolution GURT 11	THE LIVES AND TIMES OF THE APOSTLES (LP, inserts)	£20
87	No Label or Cat No	CARTOGRAPHY (Cassette LP one side by THE DEMOLITION COMPANY)	£15

MINT VALUE £

87	Active Sounds AB 001	EQUINOX SCREAMS (LP)	£18
88	Acid Strings ASR 002	THE ACTS OF THE APOSTLES IN THE THEATRE OF FEAR (LP)	£25
88	Active Sounds ASP 20	SPLIT (LP, with booklet/inserts, one side by STATEMENT)	£30
88	Big Banana BBP 068	HYMN TO PAN (Cassette LP)	£15

APOSTOLIC INTERVENTION
67	Immediate IM 043	(Tell Me) Have You Ever Seen Me/Madame Garcia	£250

(see also Small Faces, Humble Pie)

APPALOOSA
94	Recoil RCL 003	UNPLUGGED EP (12", 3-track, die-cut sleeve)	£15

(see also Global Communications)

APPLE
68	Page One POF 101	Let's Take A Trip Down The Rhine/Buffalo Billy Can	£100
68	Page One POF 110	Doctor Rock/The Other Side	£90
69	Page One POLS 016	AN APPLE A DAY (LP, textured sleeve, blue/silver labels with 'apple' insert)	£1500
69	Page One POLS 016	AN APPLE A DAY (LP, without 'apple' insert)	£1000

APPLE BOUTIQUE
87	Creation CRE052T	Love Resistance/Don't Even Believe In You/The Ballad Of Jet Harris (12")	£60
18	Option Nerve ON 1	Love Resistance/Don't Even Believe In You/The Ballad Of Jet Harris (reissue, red orange swirl vinyl, postcard, poster and badge p/s)	£20

APPLEJACKS (U.K.)
65	Decca F 12050	Chim Chim Chiree/It's Not A Game Anymore (export, unissued)	£25
65	Decca F 12216	I Go To Sleep/Make Up Or Break Up	£20
67	CBS 202615	You've Been Cheating/Love Was In My Eyes	£40
64	Decca LK 4635	THE APPLEJACKS (LP)	£100

APPLETREE THEATRE
68	Verve (S)VLP 6018	PLAYBACK (LP)	£70

APPOLINAIRES
82	Two Tone CHS TT 12 20	The Feelings Gone (Dance Mix)/The Feelings Back/The Bongo Medley (Extremely Long Version) (12", p/s)	£15
82	Two Tone CHS TT 12 22	Envy The Love/Give It Up (12", p/s)	£25

APPRECIATIONS
77	Destiny 1016	I Can't Hide It/Instrumental Version (2 acetates only)	£175
80s	Soul City 157	I Can't Hide It/No No No (reissue)	£15

APPROACHING FOOTSTEPS
82	Sanctuary HEH 001	Autumn/Fire And Ashes	£25

APRIL & THE PENNIES
80	Rockelly RKR 10780	Light Of Love/Paradise Walk (no p/s, some with postcard)	£75
80	Rockelly RKR 10381	Love And Inspiration/You're So Different From The Rest	£50
81	Rockelly RKR 10781	Heroes Of The Night/Comes The Dawn	£75

APRIL SHOWERS (1)
73	Ritual RT2	Nowhere To Hide/Suzy Q	£15

APRIL SHOWERS (2)
84	Chrysalis CHS 2787	Abandon Ship/Everytime We Say Goodbye	£50
84	Chrysalis CHS 122787	Abandon Ship/Everytime We Say Goodbye (12", p/s)	£120

APRIL WINE
72	Pye 7N 45145	You Could Have Been A Lady/Teacher	£25

AQUA LEVI & THE ROOTS IMENSION
91	Roots RI 001	His Foundation/His Dub (12")	£60
92	Roots RI 003	Gather My Children/Gather My Dub (12")	£50
92	Roots RI 7002	Babylon Mus Set Me Free/Freedom Dub	£35

AQUA REGIA
88	Irdial Discs AQR 1	HOT LOVE 3 & 5 (12", p/s)	£120
88	Irdial Discs AQR 2	Pump Up The LEDS to Red, Take Some Drugs And Shake Your Head!/Version (12")	£50
89	Irdial 12 IRD AQR 6 R1	New York City Smile On Me!/Untitled/(George Kelly Baron Remix 1)/(George Kelly Baron Remix II) (12", with free 7")	£18
89	Irdial Discs 11 IRD AQR 4	THE AGE OF AQUEOUS (2-LP)	£18

AQUARIAN AGE
68	Parlophone R 5700	10,000 Words In A Cardboard Box/Good Wizard Meets Naughty Wizard	£600

(see also Twink, Tomorrow, Clem Cattini Ork, Nicky Hopkins)

AQUARIAN DREAM
79	Buddah BDSL 488	Phoenix/East 6th Street (12")	£20
76	Buddah DISC 008	NORMAN CONNORS PRESENTS AQUARIAN DREAM (LP)	£50
78	Elektra K 52109	FANTASY (LP)	£15

(see also Norman Connors)

AQUARIANS
71	Ackee ACK 137	Rebel/Invasion Version	£35

(see also Augustus Pablo, Herman)

AQUATONES
58	London HLO 8631	You/She's The One For Me	£25

AQUILA (1)
70	RCA SF 8126	THE AQUILA SUITE (LP, gatefold sleeve, orange labels)	£150

(see also Patrick Campbell-Lyons)

AQUILA (2)
83	Graphic S82 CUS 1486 1982	**Fall/Threatened** (p/s)	£20

(see also 101ers)

AQUIZIM
80	Ariwa ARI 1007	**Time Of My Life/Sheila** (12")	£15
80	Ariwa ARI 1011	**GARRET PEPER CROSS: Magnet/AQUIZIM: Electromatic Magnet** (12")	£15
81	Ariwa ARI 1015	**Kunte Kinte/Version** (10", stamped white labels)	£30
82	Ariwa ARI 1005	**True True Loving/Concrete Slave Ship/RANKING ANN: Liberated Woman** (12")	£20
82	Ariwa ARI 1025	**African Connection/AQUIZIM & MAD PROFESSOR: African Voyage** (12")	£50

ARABIS
69	Doctor Bird DB 1204	**Jump High Jump Low/TONY SHABAZZ: Stool Pigeon**	£18

ARABS
78	Hit Run APLP 9002	**CRY TUFF - DUB ENCOUNTER CHAPTER 1**	£55

(see also Prince Far I)

ARAB STRAP
96	Chemikal U'nd CHEM 007	**The First Big Weekend/Gilded** (700 only)	£20
97	Chemikal U'nd TWEM 017	**THE GIRLS OF SUMMER EP** (12", p/s)	£15
96	Chemikal U'nd CHEM 010	**THE WEEK NEVER STARTS AROUND HERE** (LP)	£35
98	Chemikal U'nd CHEM 021	**PHILOPHOBIA** (2-LP, inners)	£40
99	Go! Beat 547387	**MAD FOR SADNESS** (LP, 1000 only)	£60
99	Go! Beat 5478051	**ELEPHANT SHOE** (LP)	£40
01	Chemikal U'nd CHEM 050	**THE RED THREAD** (LP)	£30
05	Chemikal U'nd CHEM 082	**THE LAST ROMANCE** (LP)	£25
08	Chemikal U'nd CHEM 065	**MONDAY AT THE HUG & PINT** (LP)	£20
10	Chemikal U'nd CHEM 135	**SCENES OF A SEXUAL NATURE** (3-CD, CD Rom, 4-LP & cassette, 1000 only, numbered with certificate)	£150

ARAGORN
81	Neat NEAT 07	**Black Ice/Noonday** (p/s)	£15

A RAINCOAT
75	EMI EMC 3090	**DIGALONGAMACS** (LP)	£15

ARANBEE POP SYMPHONY ORCHESTRA
66	Immediate IMLP/IMSP 003	**TODAY'S POP SYMPHONY** (LP, lilac labels)	£125

(see also Andrew Oldham Orchestra, Keith Richard[s])

ARBITRATER
91	Cyclone CYCLONE 1	**BALANCE OF POWER** (LP)	£25
93	Cyclone CYCLONE 2	**DARKENED REALITY** (CD)	£200

A.R.C. ROCKBAND
79	Rock Records	**Homemade Wine/The Chase** (p/s)	£80

ARC (1)
71	Decca SKL-R 5077	**ARC . . . AT THIS** (LP, blue/silver "boxed" Decca labels)	£200

(see also Heavy Jelly, Skip Bifferty, Bell & Arc)

ARC (2)
80	Orchrist ORC 1	**Tribute To Mike Hailwood/For My Next Kick** (p/s)	£50
81	Slipped Disc SD001	**War Of The Ring/Ice Cream Theme** (p/s)	£150

ARCADE FIRE
05	Rough Trade RTRADLP 219	**FUNERAL** (LP)	£25
06	Universal 1724447	**NEON BIBLE** (2-LP, 4th side etched, stickered sleeve)	£20
10	Universal 2743427	**THE SUBURBS** (2-LP, gatefold, inners)	£20
13	Sonovox 3752119	**REFLEKTOR** (2-LP, metallic gatefold, with inners)	£20
17	Sonovox 88985447851	**EVERYTHING NOW** (LP, 'Day' or 'Night' cover)	£20

ARCADIUM
69	Middle Earth MDS 102	**Sing My Song/Riding Alone**	£200
69	Middle Earth MDLS 302	**BREATHE AWHILE** (LP, laminated sleeve)	£1250
11	Acne ADLP 1077	**BREATHE AWHILE** (LP, reissue with free 7")	£15

(see also Kingdom Come, 'Middle Earth Sampler' in Various Artists)

ARC ANGELS
92	Geffen 24465	**ARC ANGELS** (LP)	£35

ELIZABETH ARCHER & THE EQUATORS
77	Lightning TRO 9011	**Feel Like Making Love/Version**	£30

MARK ARCHER
11	Balkan BV 08	**FREQUENCY REMIXES** (12" yellow vinyl)	£15
14	Balkan BV 11, BV 12 BV 13	**RAVE ARMAGEDDON SURVIVAL KIT** (3 x 12", limited edition of 101, red, green and blue vinyl hand-numbered. Rave SOS flare, filtration unit, eye, hand and dancefloor protection gear, T-shirt and sticker pack)	£75

(see also Altern 8)

YVONNE ARCHER
81	Virgo Stomach VG 003	**Ain't Nobody/Checking Out The Way We Feel** (12")	£80

ARCHIE WHITEWATER
70	Pye Intl. NSPL 28143	**ARCHIE WHITEWATER** (LP)	£100

ARCHITECTURE IN HELSINKI
06	Moshi Moshi MOSHILP07	**IN CASE WE DIE** (LP)	£20

ARCHIVE
96	Island ARKLP 1001	**LONDINIUM** (2-LP)	£100

MINT VALUE £

| 99 | Independiente ISOM 10LP | TAKE MY HEAD (LP, with free 12") | £80 |
| 99 | Independiente ISOM 10LP | TAKE MY HEAD (LP, without free 12") | £60 |

ARCTIC MONKEYS

05	Bang Bang (No Cat no)	FIVE MINUTES WITH EP (7" white label with stickered die-cut sleeve)	£60
05	Bang Bang BANGB 71	FIVE MINUTES WITH EP (500 only, p/s)	£80
05	Bang Bang BANGBCD	FIVE MINUTES WITH EP (CD, 1000 only)	£70
05	Domino RUG 212	I Bet You Look Good On The Dancefloor/Bigger Boys And Stolen Sweethearts (p/s, stickered)	£15
06	Domino RUG 236	Leave Before The Lights Come On/Baby I'm Yours (p/s)	£20
06	Domino RUG 226	WHO THE FUCK ARE ARCTIC MONKEYS? (10" EP, p/s)	£15
07	Domino RUF 279	Death Ramps/Nettles (As DEATH RAMPS, 250 only, stamped labels)	£25
07	Domino RUG 261T	Flourescent Adolescent/The Bakery/Plastic Tramp/Too Much To Ask (10", p/s)	£15
09	Domino RUG 338	Crying Lightning/Red Right Hand (signed 7", 55 only for Oxfam Charity)	£30
09	Domino RUG 349T	Cornerstone/Catapult/Sketchhead/Fright Lined Dining Rooms (10")	£35
10	Domino RUG 359T	My Propeller/Joining The Dots/The Afternoon's Hat/Don't Forget Who's Legs You're On (10")	£15
12	Domino RUG 468	R U MINE/Electricity (7" purple vinyl, white label with stickered die-cut sleeve, 1750 only)	£80
06	Domino WIG 162	WHATEVER PEOPLE SAY I AM THATS WHAT I'M NOT (LP, inner)	£20
07	Domino WIGLP 188	FAVOURITE WORST NIGHTMARE (LP)	£20
08	Domino DOMDVD 005X	AT THE APOLLO/LIVE IN TEXAS 7 JUNE 2006 (LP/DVD box set, stickered sleeve)	£80
09	Domino WIGLP 220	HUMBUG (LP, gatefold, 180gm)	£15
11	Domino WIGLP 258	SUCK IT AND SEE (LP, 180gm, download card)	£18
13	Domino WIGLP 317	AM (LP/7", gatefold, insert, booklet)	£100
18	Domino WIGLP 339X	TRANQUILITY BASE HOTEL & CASINO (LP, gatefold, booklet, clear vinyl, indie store exclusive)	£30
18	Domino WIGLP 339XM	TRANQUILITY BASE HOTEL + CASINO (LP, gatefold, booklet, silver vinyl, website exclusive)	£20
18	Domino WIGLP339PU	TRANQUILITY BASE HOTEL + CASINO (LP, gatefold, booklet, gold vinyl, available at tour/pop-up shops)	£80
20	Domino WIGLP 490XM	LIVE AT THE ROYAL ALBERT HALL (2LP, gatefold, printed inners, clear vinyl, poster)	£30
22	Domino WIGLP 455XM	THE CAR (LP, tip-on sleeve, printed inner, grey vinyl)	£30
22	Domino WIGLP 455X	THE CAR (LP, tip-on sleeve, printed inner, custard yellow vinyl)	£25

ARCTIC STRINGS

| 75 | Black Magic DEMO 2 | Turn Me On/Non Stop | £20 |

ARCTURUS

| 96 | Ancient Lore Creations ALC 002 PLP | ASPERA HIEMS SYMFONIA (LP, picture disc, 1000 only) | £40 |
| 97 | Music For Nations MFN 230 | LA MASQUERADE INFENALE (LP, 1000 only) | £60 |

NEIL ARDLEY

70	Columbia SCX 6414	GREEK VARIATIONS (LP, with Ian Carr & Don Rendell)	£250
72	Regal Zono. SLRZ 1028	A SYMPHONY OF AMARANTHS (LP, red/silver labels)	£200
74	Argo ZDA 164/5	WILL POWER (2-LP, with Ian Carr, Stan Tracey & Mike Gibbs)	£125
75	Gull GULP 1018	KALEIDOSCOPE OF RAINBOWS (LP)	£20
78	Decca TXS-R 133	HARMONY OF THE SPHERES (LP, featuring John Martyn)	£20
09	Gull/Pure Pleasure GULP 1018	KALEIDOSCOPE OF RAINBOWS (2-LP, reissue)	£18

(see also Don Rendell, New Jazz Orchestra, Michael Gibbs)

COLIN AREETY

| 73 | Deram 383 | (If Loving You Is Wrong) I Don't Want To Be Right/One Night Affair | £20 |

ARGENT

70	CBS 63781	ARGENT (LP, gatefold sleeve)	£60
71	Epic EPC 64190	RING OF HANDS (LP, gatefold sleeve)	£30
72	Epic EPC 64962	ALL TOGETHER NOW (LP, gatefold sleeve, with booklet)	£25
74	Epic EQ 32195/Q 65475	IN DEEP (LP, quadrophonic)	£25
74	Epic EPC 88063	ENCORE (2-LP, gatefold)	£15
75	RCA RS 1020	COUNTERPOINTS (LP)	£15

(see also Zombies, Unit 4 + 2, Roulettes, John Verity Band)

ARGONAUTS

| 85 | Lyntone LYN 18249/50 | Apeman/Under My Thumb (signed white label, no p/s) | £60 |

(see also Madness)

ARGOSY

| 69 | DJM DJS 214 | Mr. Boyd/Imagine | £120 |

(see also Elton John, Supertramp)

ARGUS

| 84 | ABS SRT 4KS258 | Holocaust/The Widow (title sleeve) | £100 |

(see also People Like Us)

ARIEL

| 73 | Harvest SHSP 4028 | A STRANGE FANTASTIC DREAM (LP, textured sleeve) | £20 |
| 75 | Harvest SHSP 4039 | ROCK AND ROLL SCARS (LP) | £15 |

ARIEL M

| 97 | Domino WIGLP 37 | ARIEL M (LP) | £20 |

ARIZONA SWAMP COMPANY

| 70 | Parlophone R 5841 | Train Keeps Rollin'/Tennessee Woman | £50 |

(see also Nashville Teens)

ARKITEX

| 79 | Arkitex AKX 1 | Only One/Drivin All Night/Big Brother (no p/s) | £125 |

MINT VALUE £

ARMADA ORCHESTRA/ULTRAFUNK
75	Contempo CLP 528	DISCO ARMADA (LP)	£15
76	Contempo CLP 536	PHILLY ARMADA (LP)	£15

ARMAGEDDON
75	A&M AMLH 64513	ARMAGEDDON (LP, with lyric inner sleeve, silver labels)	£60

(see also Keith Relf, Steamhammer, Captain Beyond)

ARMAGIDEON
93	Armagideon ASLP 001	HORNS ENCOUNTER VOLUME 1 (LP)	£20
94	Armagideon ASLP 002	NATURAL ELEMENTS DUB (LP)	£15

JOAN ARMATRADING
85	A&M AMLH 64588	JOAN ARMATRADING (LP, 'Nimbus' supercuts repressing)	£50

ARMED FORCE
80	Armed Forces AF1	Popstar/Attack (p/s, 500 only)	£20

ARMENTA
83	Savoir Faire FAIT 005	I Wanna Be With You/Part 2/Part 3 (12")	£15

RUSSELL ARMS
57	London HLB 8406	Cinco Robles (Five Oaks)/The World Is Made Of Lisa (gold label)	£20

CHUCK ARMSTRONG
73	Action ACT 4620	God Bless The Children/Black Foxy Woman	£15

FRANKIE ARMSTRONG (& FRIENDS)
79	Action Against Corrie RRFA 001	We Must Choose/RED RINSE: A Woman's Right To Choose (private pressing)	£30
72	Topic 12TS 216	LOVELY ON THE WATER (LP)	£30
75	Topic 12TS 273	SONGS AND BALLADS (LP)	£18

(see also A.L. Lloyd)

LORNA ARMSTRONG
74	Ackee 535	Dance With Me/Lonely Nights	£15

LOUIS ARMSTRONG
SINGLES
69	United Artists UP 35059	We Have All The Time In The World/Pretty Little Missy	£15

BRENDA ARNAU
80	Pye 7P 185	Electra Flash/Dance Electra Flash (p/s)	£45

GINNY ARNELL
63	MGM MGM 1217	Dumb Head/How Many Times Can One Heart Break	£15
63	MGM MGM 1243	I Wish I Knew What Dress To Wear/He's My Little Devil	£15

CALVIN ARNOLD
68	MGM MGM 1378	Funky Way/Snatchin' Back	£20
68	MGM MGM 1449	Mama In Law/Mini Skirt	£20

KOKOMO ARNOLD
69	Saydisc Matchbox SDR 163	KOKOMO ARNOLD (LP)	£30

P.P. ARNOLD
66	Immediate IM 040	Everything's Gonna Be Alright/Life Is But Nothin'	£200
66	Immediate IM 040	Everything's Gonna Be Alright/Life Is But Nothin' (DJ copy)	£300
67	Immediate IM 047	The First Cut Is The Deepest/Speak To Me	£25
67	Immediate IM 055	The Time Has Come/If You See What I Mean	£20
68	Immediate IM 061	(If You Think You're) Groovy/Though It Hurts Me Badly	£20
67	Immediate IMLP/IMSP 011	THE FIRST LADY OF IMMEDIATE (LP, withdrawn)	£400
68	Immediate IMSP 017	KAFUNTA (LP, gatefold sleeve)	£100
83	See For Miles SEE 235	KAFUNTA - THE BEST OF (LP)	£20

(see also Ikettes, Nice, Small Faces, Spectrum, P.P. & Primes)

P.P. ARNOLD & THE JEFF WAYNE SINGERS
60s	Pepsi Lyntone 2498	We've Got Pepsi (1-sided with Pepsi Company sleeve)	£15

ARPADYS
77	Polydor 2933802	ARPADYS (LP)	£25

ARRIVAL
70	Decca SKL 5055	ARRIVAL (LP, blue/silver with 'boxed' Decca logo)	£20

ARS NOVA
68	Elektra EKS 74020	ARS NOVA (LP, orange label, gatefold sleeve)	£40
69	Atlantic 588 196	SUNSHINE AND SHADOWS (LP)	£40

ART
67	Island WIP 6019	What's That Sound (For What It's Worth)/Rome Take Away Three	£20
69	Island WIP 6048	Room With A View/SPOOKY TOOTH: Nobody There At All (promo only)	£50
75	Island WIP 6048	What's That Sound (For What It's Worth)/Flying Anchors (with promo Art sleeve)	£30
67	Island ILP 967	SUPERNATURAL FAIRY TALES (LP, first pressing, pink label with black/orange circle logo, laminated sleeve)	£400
70	Island ILP 967	SUPERNATURAL FAIRY TALES (LP, second pressing, pink label with 'i' logo and factory stamped matrix numbers, those with hand written matrixes are bootlegs, laminated sleeve)	£300
75	Island ILP 967	SUPERNATURAL FAIRY TALES (LP, reissue, matt sleeve, 'palm tree' label)	£35
15	Island 47089803	SUPERNATURAL FAIRY TALES (LP, reissue)	£20

(see also V.I.P.'s, Baron With His Pounding Piano, Spooky Tooth, Luther Grosvenor, Hapshash & Coloured Coat)

ART ATTACKS
78	Albatross TIT 1	I'm A Dalek/Neutron Bomb (p/s)	£20

ART BEARS

79	Fresh FRESH 3	First And Last: Punk Rock Stars/Rat City/First And Last (p/s)	£20
96	Overground OVER 58	OUTRAGE AND HORROR (LP, 600 only, pressed in U.K. for export to Japan)	£30

(see also Monochrome Set, Tagmemics, Kray Cherubs)

ART BEARS

78	Recommended REC 2188	HOPES AND FEARS (LP, gatefold sleeve with poster & booklet)	£35
79	Recommended REC 0618	WINTER SONGS (LP, with booklet)	£30
81	Recommended RE 6622	THE WORLD AS IT IS TODAY (LP, 45rpm, with booklet)	£25
84	Re RE 2188	HOPES AND FEARS (LP, reissue)	£15
10	ReR MegacorpRER VAB1	HOPES AND FEARS (LP, reissue, 180gm)	£15

(see also Henry Cow, Slapp Happy)

ART ENSEMBLE OF CHICAGO

72	Freedom FLP 40108	THE SPIRITUAL (LP)	£40
74	Freedom FLP 40122	TUTANKAMUN (LP)	£35
00	Universal Sound USLP 11	LES STANCES A SOPHIE (LP, reissue)	£20
80	Affinity AFF (D) 46	LIVE (2-LP)	£20

ARTERY

83	Red Flame RF 18	ONE AFTERNOON IN A HOT AIR BALOON (LP)	£18
84	Golden Dawn GDLP 01	SECOND COMING (LP)	£15
85	Golden Dawn GDLP 02	NUMBER FOUR (LP)	£15

(see also Mission)

DAVE & TONI ARTHUR

67	Transatlantic TRA 154	MORNING STANDS ON TIPTOE (LP)	£60
69	Topic 12T 190	THE LARK IN THE MORNING (LP, blue label)	£30
71	Trailer LER 2017	HEARKEN TO THE WITCHES' RUNE (LP, red label)	£20

ARTISTICS

66	Coral Q 72488	I'm Gonna Miss You/Hope We Have	£80
66	Coral Q 72488	I'm Gonna Miss You/Hope We Have (DJ Copy)	£150
67	Coral Q 72492	Girl I Need You/I'm Glad I Met You	£60
67	Coral Q 72492	Girl I Need You/I'm Glad I Met You (DJ Copy)	£150
76	Brunswick BR 39	I'm Gonna Miss You/GENE CHANDLER: There Was A Time	£15
66	Columbia	GET MY HANDS ON SOME LOVIN' (LP, unconfirmed existence)	£250

ART MOVEMENT

67	Livingston LRL/PR 141	Bitter Suite/Here Today/Blame Yourself/She Was Really Saying Something	£30
68	Decca F 12768	I Love Being In Love With You/The Game Of Love	£20
69	Columbia DB 8602	Yes Sir . . . No Sir/Sally Goes Round The Moon	£15
70	Columbia DB 8697	The Sooner I Get To You/Morning Girl	£35

ART NOUVEAU

79	Gimpy Dak DAK 1	Fear Machine/Animal Instincts (p/s)	£50

ART NOUVEAUX

64	Fontana TF 843	Extra Terrestrial Visitations/The Way To Play It	£35

ART OBJECTS

81	Heartbeat HB 5	BAGPIPE MUSIC (LP)	£18

ART OF NOISE

86	China WOKP 9	Paranoimia/Why Me (shaped picture disc)	£15

ARTWOODS

64	Decca F 12015	Sweet Mary/If I Ever Get My Hands On You	£70
65	Decca F 12091	Oh My Love/Big City	£60
65	Decca F 12206	Goodbye Sisters/She Knows What To Do	£60
66	Decca F 12384	I Take What I Want/I'm Looking For A Saxophonist Doubling French Horn Wearing Size 37 Boots	£80
66	Decca F 12465	I Feel Good/Molly Anderson's Cookery Book	£90
67	Parlophone R 5590	What Shall I Do/In The Deep End	£100
66	Decca DFE 8654	JAZZ IN JEANS (EP)	£500
66	Decca LK 4830	ART GALLERY (LP, red/silver label with 'unboxed' Decca logo and 'FFrr' laminated front sleeve)	£700
70	Decca Eclipse ECM 2025	ART GALLERY (LP, reissue in different sleeve, also stereo [ECS 2025])	£125
73	Spark SRLM 2006	THE ARTWOODS (LP)	£60
16	Record Collector RCLP 020	LIVE AT KLOOKS KLEEK (2-LP)	£30

(see also St. Valentine's Day Massacre, Keef Hartley Band, Jon Lord, Dog Soldier, Lucas & Mike Cotton Sound)

ARTWORK

02	Big Apple BAM 001	RED EP (12")	£15
02	Big Apple BAM 001	RED EP (12", red vinyl)	£25

ART ZOYD

82	Recommended RR 14/15	PHASE IV (2-LP with booklet, inserts and free 1-sided 7")	£20

ARZACHEL

69	Evolution Z 1003	ARZACHEL (LP, blue label, laminated front sleeve)	£1000

(see also Egg, Steve Hillage, Khan, Hatfield & the North, National Health, Gong)

ASGARD

72	Threshold THS 6	IN THE REALM OF ASGARD (LP, white/blue label, gatefold sleeve)	£175

DANIEL ASH

90	Beggars Banquet BEGA 114	COMING DOWN (LP)	£20
92	Beggars Banquet BBQLP 129	FOOLISH THING DESIRE (LP)	£50

(see also Bauhaus, Tones On Tail), Love And Rockets)

VIC ASH QUARTET
56	Nixa NJE 1032	VIC ASH & FOUR (EP)	£15
56	Columbia SEG 7634	CLARINET VIRTUOSO (EP)	£15
56	Tempo EXA 44	MODERN JAZZ SCENE (EP)	£50

(see also Maxine Sullivan, Jazz Five)

ASH (1)
83	Criminal CRI MLP 137	Chase The Spotlight/Evermore (no p/s)	£15

ASH (2)
94	Infectious INFECT 13S	Petrol/The Little Pond/A Message From Oscar Wilde And Patrick The Brewer (p/s, 500 only)	£15
95	Infectious INFECT 24S	Girl From Mars/Astral (Conversations With Toulouse Lautrec)/Cantina Band (p/s, numbered)	£20
97	Barbie Records KEN 1	I Only Want To Be With You/Kung Fu (Live) (silver speckled vinyl p/s, fan club 7")	£40
12	Noyes NR 031	LITTLE INFINITY EP (12", hand-numbered)	£15
94	Infectious INFECT 14LP	TRAILER (LP, with yellow vinyl 7", "Silver Surfer"/"Jazz '59" [INFECT 14S])	£40
96	Infectious INFECT 40LP	1977 (LP, gatefold, inner)	£75
98	Infectious INFECT 60LP	NU-CLEAR SOUNDS (LP, gatefold, clear vinyl)	£35
01	Infectious INFECT 100LP	FREE ALL ANGELS (LP, gatefold)	£50
04	Infectious 5050467319714	MELTDOWN (LP, laminated sleeve)	£25

ASHANTIS
77	Red Bus EMC 3109	LET'S STAY TOGETHER (LP)	£20

DOROTHY ASHBY
65	Atlantic ATL 5047	THE FANTASTIC JAZZ HARP OF DOROTHY ASHBY (LP)	£20

HAROLD ASHBY
60	Columbia 33SX 1257	BORN TO SWING (LP)	£600
61	Columbia 33SX 1379	TENOR STUFF (LP, with Paul Gonsalves)	£100

ASH CAN SCHOOL
86	Unit Two TWO 01	She's Only Sleeping/A Day Out Of Paris (p/s)	£30

RICHARD ASHCROFT
00	Hut HUTDLP 63	ALONE WITH EVERYBODY (2-LP)	£40
02	Hut HUTDLP 77	HUMAN CONDITIONS (2-LP)	£40

RAFMRA ASHER
78	Maccabees FG1	Fourth Generation/Version	£20

ASHFORD & SIMPSON
77	Warner Bros. K17679 (T)	Love Don't Make It Right/Bourgie Bourgie (with incorrect mastering) (12")	£20
77	Warner Bros. K17679 (T)	Love Don't Make It Right/Bourgie Bourgie (with correct mastering) (12")	£60
78	Warner Bros. 12K 17096	Don't Cost You Nothing/Let Love Use Me (12")	£15
74	Warner Bros. K46283	GIMME SOMETHING REAL (LP)	£18
74	Warner Bros. K56050	I WANNA BE SELFISH (LP)	£18

ASHKAN
70	Decca Nova DN-R 1	IN FROM THE COLD (LP, mono)	£250
70	Decca Nova SDN-R 1	IN FROM THE COLD (LP, stereo)	£175

(see also Fleetwood Mac)

STEVE ASHLEY
74	Gull GULP 1003	STROLL ON (LP, with lyric inner)	£20

MICKEY ASHMAN
60	Pye Jazz NJL 25	TAKING THE MICKEY (LP)	£20
61	Pye Jazz NJL 29	THROUGH DARKEST ASHMAN (LP)	£50

ASHRA
77	Virgin V 2080	NEW AGE OF EARTH (LP)	£15

ASHTON, GARDNER & DYKE
69	Polydor 56306	Maiden Voyage/See The Sun In My Eyes	£80
69	Polydor 583 081	ASHTON, GARDNER & DYKE (LP)	£25
70	Capitol E-ST 563	THE WORST OF ASHTON, GARDNER AND DYKE (LP)	£18
72	Capitol EA-ST 22862	WHAT A BLOODY LONG DAY IT'S BEEN (LP, gatefold sleeve)	£20

(see also Ashton & Lord, Remo Four, Creation, Birds, Mike Hurst & Method, Badger, Medicine Head)

MARK ASHTON
72	United Artists UP 353390	Get Up And Groove/Barking Dogs	£15

ASHTON ON RIBBLE HIGH SCHOOL MUSIC SOCIETY
74	(No label or cat no)	ASHTON SOUND 74 (LP, with inserts)	£100

(TONY) ASHTON & (JON) LORD
74	Purple TPS 3507	FIRST OF THE BIG BANDS (LP)	£25

(see also Ashton Gardner & Dyke, Paice Ashton & Lord, Jon Lord, Deep Purple, Green Bullfrog, Cozy Powell)

ASIA
92	IRS 951.959	AQUA (LP, gatefold sleeve)	£40

(see also Yes, Emerson Lake & Palmer, Steve Howe)

ASIA FIELDS
90	Frank FRANK 2	Friction/Jack-knifed (12", test pressing only, plain white die-cut sleeve)	£25

ASIAN DUB FOUNDATION
95	Nation NAT 58 LP	FACTS AND FICTIONS (2-LP)	£18
98	FFRR 556 066	RAFI'S REVENGE (2-LP)	£30
00	FFRR 8573 820421	COMMUNITY MUSIC (2-LP)	£18

ED ASKEW
69 Fontana STL 5519   ED ASKEW (LP)..£60
ASLAN
76 Profile GMOR 006   PAWS FOR THOUGHT (LP)...£70
77 Profile GMOR 144   SECOND HELPINGS (LP)..£70
AS ONE
95 New Electronica Elec 23LP REFLECTIONS ON REFLECTIONS (2-LP)......................£35
95 New Electronica Elec 26LP CELESTIAL SOUL (2-LP)...£20
ASPECTS
13 Psycho Boogie BOOGS 002   LEFT HAND PATH (LP)..£15
RON ASPERY
72 Blakey BLP5989   BACK DOOR (LP)...£40
GARY & VERA ASPEY
76 Topic 12TS 299   A TASTE OF HOTPOT (LP)..£25
ASPHALT RIBBONS
88 Tigerlily LILY 002   DOWNSIDE EP (12", p/s)..£25
89 In Tape IT 063   THE ORCHARD EP (p/s)..£30
89 In Tape ITTI 063   THE ORCHARD EP (12", p/s)..£35
89 In Tape ITTI 063   THE ORCHARD EP (12", p/s + T-Shirt insert)..................£50
89 In Tape ITTI 063   THE ORCHARD EP (12", 200 pressed at 48rpm and withdrawn)...£40
89 In Tape IT 068   Good Love/Long Lost Uncle/The Day I Turned Bad (p/s)........£35
89 In Tape ITTI 068   Good Love/Long Lost Uncle/The Day I Turned Bad (12", p/s)...£25
89 In Tape IT 6545 1   Over Again/EVA: Unquenchable (p/s, promo only)...........£25
91 Tiger Lily LILY 001   A Time To Go/LIFE WITH PATRICK: Wrong (7" sampler)......£15
91 Tiger Lily LILY 002   PASSION, COOLNESS, INDIFFERENCE, BOREDOM, MOCKERY, CONTEMPT, DISGUST EP (12")...£30
91 ETT 101-1   OLD HORSE (LP)...£80
(see also Tindersticks, Stuart A. Staples)
MARY ASQUITH
78 Mother Earth MUM 1204   CLOSING TIME (LP)..£30
ASSAGAI
71 Vertigo 6059 034   Telephone Girl/I'll Wait For You...................................£40
71 Vertigo 6360 030   ASSAGAI (LP, gatefold sleeve, large swirl label).............£250
72 Philips 6308 079   ZIMBABWE (LP, black/silver labels)..............................£120
74 Contour 2870 394   ASSAGAI (LP, reissue of Philips 6308 079).....................£20
75 Sounds Superb SPR 90054   AFRO ROCK (LP) (Same as Vertigo 6360030)..................£15
ASSEMBLED MULTITUDE
70 Atlantic 2466 004   THE ASSEMBLED MULTITUDE (LP)...............................£20
ASSOCIATES
79 Double Hip DHR 1   Boys Keep Swinging/Mona Property Girl (no p/s, 500 only)...£100
79 MCA MCA 537   Boys Keep Swinging/Mona Property Girl (no p/s, demos more common, £25)...£40
80 Fiction FIX 05   THE AFFECTIONATE PUNCH (LP)................................£20
82 Beggars Banquet BEGA 43   FOURTH DRAWER DOWN (LP, gatefold sleeve with poster, label credits SITU 2)...£15
ASSOCIATION
67 London HA-T 8305   AND THEN . . . ALONG COMES THE ASSOCIATION (LP)...£40
67 London HA-T 8313   RENAISSANCE (LP)..£35
67 London HA-T/SH-T 8342   INSIGHT OUT (LP)..£35
68 Warner Bros W(S) 1733   BIRTHDAY (LP)...£30
69 Warner Bros W(S) 1767   GREATEST HITS (LP)..£20
69 Warner Bros W(S) 1786   GOODBYE COLUMBUS (LP, soundtrack)........................£18
69 Warner Bros W(S) 1800   THE ASSOCIATION (LP)..£20
72 CBS S 65009   WATERBEDS IN TRINIDAD! (LP).................................£15
A STATE OF MIND
85 Mind Matters NO THOUGHT 4 What's The Difference?/Animal Human Exploitation (fold out p/s)...£15
ASTERIX
70 Decca F 13075   Everybody/If I Could Fly...£20
EDWIN/TED ASTLEY (ORCHESTRA)
65 RCA RCA 1492   Danger Man/The Saint..£40
VIRGINIA ASTLEY
83 Happy Valley HA 001   FROM GARDENS WHERE WE FEEL SECURE (LP)............£35
(see also David Sylvian)
ASTON HALL
80 Tamebeat TAME 001   The Daily Sun/Popular People (p/s)...........................£15
ASTON & YEN
66 Doctor Bird DB 1064   Skillamy/BABA BROOKS & BAND: Party Time..................£30
ASTORS
65 Atlantic AT 4037   Candy/I Found Out..£80
65 Atlantic AT 4037   Candy/I Found Out (DJ Copy).....................................£120
69 Atlantic 584 245   Candy/I Found Out (reissue).....................................£15
ASTRA
08 Rise Above RISELP 120   THE WEIRDING (LP, gatefold with poster)....................£20
12 Rise Above RISELP 137   THE BLACK CHORD (LP, gatefold, booklet, clear vinyl, 100 only)...£25

ASTRAL NAVIGATIONS
71	Holyground HG 114/ NSR 172	ASTRAL NAVIGATIONS (LP, actually by Lightyears Away & Thundermother, poster cover & booklet, 250 copies only, some numbered) £500
89	Magic Mixture MM 2	ASTRAL NAVIGATIONS (LP, reissue with booklet, 425 copies only) £50

(see also David John & Mood)

ASTRAL PROJECTION
96	Tip TIP LP 5	TRUST IN TRANCE (2-LP)..£50
97	Transient TRANR607 LP	THE ASTRAL FILES (2-LP)..£50
97	Transient TRANR612 LP	DANCING GALAXY (2-LP)..£75
99	Transient TRANR621 LP	ANOTHER WORLD (2-LP)..£40

ASTRA NOVA ORCHESTRA
74	Alaska ALA 26	Ev'ry Little Beat Of Your Heart/Soul Sleeper £30

A STREAM
82	SRTS 82 CUS 1294	Hero/Space Invaders £20

ASTROBOTNIA
02	Rephlex CAT 123 LP	PART 01 (LP)...£15
02	Rephlex CAT 125 LP	PART 03 (LP)...£15

ASTRONAUTS (U.K.)
79	Bugle BLAST 1	THE ASTRONAUTS EP (All Night Party/Back Soon/Everything Stops The Baby/Survivors) (p/s)..£15
80	Bugle BLAST 5	PRANKSTERS IN REVOLT (EP)...£20
81	Bugle GENIUS 001	PETER PAN HITS THE SUBURBS (LP) £50
86	All The Madmen MAD 5	IT'S ALL DONE BY MIRRORS (LP) £15
87	All The Madmen MADLP005	THE SEEDY SIDE OF (LP) £15

(see also Syndicate)

ASWAD
76	Island WIP 6312	Back to Africa/Africa £15
78	Grove Music GMDM 9	It's Not Our Wish (That We Should Fight)/Stranger (green vinyl) £20
80	Grove Music 12WIP 6575	Rainbow Culture/Covenant (dub) (12") £18
80	Island 12WIP 6646	Warrior Charge/Dub Charge (12") £15
81	Grove Music IPR 2037	Warrior Charge/Dub Charge (12", with 'Limited Edition' on labels) £60
81	Grove Music 12WIP 6693	Babylon/Behold (12")..£20
76	Island ILPS 9399	ASWAD (LP, inner)..£15
79	Grove Music GMLP 6	HULET (LP) £15
81	Island ASWAD 1	SHOWCASE (LP) £15
82	Island ILPS 9711	NEW CHAPTER OF DUB (LP) £25

ASYLUM CHOIR
68	Mercury SMCL 21041	A LOOK INSIDE THE ASYLUM CHOIR (LP) £30

ASYLUM (1)
74	Wax SR 2073	It's My Destiny - Lazy Love/Suzy's Back (p/s) £100

ASYLUM (2)
79	Peeping Tom HRSL 291/EJSP 9280	COMMERCIAL QUEEN EP (p/s)...£40

ATACAMA
71	Charisma CAS 1039	ATACAMA (LP, pink/white 'scroll' label) £35
72	Charisma CAS 1060	THE SUN BURNS UP ABOVE (LP, large 'mad hatter' label).....................................£30

ATAVISTIC
90	Deaf DEAF 3	VANISHING POINT (LP)...£15

ATHENIANS
64	ESC ESC 1	You Tell Me/Little Queenie (custom sleeve) £50
64	Waverley SLP 532	I've Got Love If You Want It/I'm A Lover Not A Fighter (p/s) £150
64	Waverley SLP 532	I've Got Love If You Want It/I'm A Lover Not A Fighter £80
65	Waverley SLP 533	Thinking Of Our Love/Mercy Mercy (in custom sleeve) £60
65	Waverley SLP 533	Thinking Of Our Love/Mercy Mercy (not in custom sleeve) £40

GLENN ATHENS & TROJANS
65	Spot 7E 1018	GLENN ATHENS & TROJANS (EP) £200

ATHLETE
02	Parlophone 5822 991	VEHICLES AND ANIMALS (LP, stickered sleeve) £20
05	Parlophone 560 7401	TOURIST (2-LP)...£40
07	Parlophone 503 1791	BEYOND THE NEIGHBOURHOOD (LP, with booklet)..£40
09	Fiction 2714837	BLACK SWAN (LP) £18

JUAN ATKINS
91	ULR ULRT 3001	THE FUTURE SOUND EP (12")..£75

PETE ATKIN
67	MJB BEVLP 1009	WHILE THE MUSIC LASTS (LP, 99 copies, with Julie Covington)..............................£400
67	Private pressing	THE PARTY'S MOVING ON (LP, 160 copies, with Julie Covington) £175
70	Fontana 6309 011	BEWARE THE BEAUTIFUL STRANGER (LP, black/silver labels) £30
71	Philips 6308 070	DRIVING THROUGH MYTHICAL AMERICA (LP) £30

DAVE ATKINSON
76	(No label or cat no)	THE BEGGAR & THE SAND (LP) £50

STEVE ATKINSON
81	Ellie Jay EJSP 9779	SMALL BOATS (LP) £200

MINT VALUE £

ATLANTIC BRIDGE
70 Dawn DNLS 3014   **ATLANTIC BRIDGE** (LP, gatefold sleeve, red/black labels) £70

ATLANTICS (1)
64 Windsor WPS 129   **Don't Say No/Send Him To Me** £20

ATLANTIS
72 Fury FY 302   **I Ain't Got Time/Teddy Boyd's Rock 'N' Roll Show** £100
73 Vertigo 6360 609   **ATLANTIS** (LP, small swirl label, sleeve printed in Germany) £40
(see also Rocking Horse)

ATLANTIS PEOPLE
80 Ice GUY 33   **Stormy Weather/No Such Thing** £40
80 Ice GUY 33 12   **Stormy Weather/No Such Thing** (12") £80

ATLANTIS RISING
83 CMI CMI700   **Tightrope/Reverie: A Vision** £20

ATLAS (1)
78 Emerging WIL 001   **AGAINST ALL THE ODDS** (LP, private pressing) £25

ATLAS (2)
94 Dee Jay DJX 021   **Drifting Thru The Galaxy/Second Heaven** (12") £30
94 Dee Jay DJX 021X   **Drifting Thru The Galaxy/Second Heaven** (12", white label test pressing) £25

AT LAST THE 1958 ROCK & ROLL SHOW
68 CBS 3349   **I Can't Drive/Working On The Railroad** £25
(see also Ian Hunter, Mott The Hoople, Freddie 'Fingers' Lee, Miller Anderson, Charles Woolfe)

ATMOSFEAR
79 Elite DAZZ 1   **Dancing In Outer Space/Outer Space** (Version) (12") £20
79 MCA 12 MCA 543   **Dancing In Outer Space/Outer Space** (Version) (12", co. sleeve) £18
80 Elite DAZZ 2   **Motivation/Extract** (12" die-cut cover) £20
80 MCA MCA 580   **Motivation/Extract** (demo only) £20
81 MCA MCAT 580   **Motivation/Extract** (12" repressing, p/s) £15
81 Elite DAZZ 8   **Invasion/Alternative II/Interplay/Untitled/Starburst** (Reach For The Stars) (12") £20
82 Elite DAZZ 12-7   **Xtra Special** (Dry Mix)/(Wet Mix) £20
82 Elite/City Sounds LDAZZ 12 **Xtra Special** (Dry Mix)/(Wet Mix) (12") £15
84 Elite ATM 33-1   **FIRST/FOURMOST** (12") £15
81 Elite MCF 3110   **EN TRANCE** (LP) £40
99 Disorient SUSHI 17   **ALTERED SLATES** (2-LP) £20
05 Discotheque DQFDV013   **EN TRANCE** (2-LP reissue) £20
18 Mr Bongo MRBLP180   **EN TRANCE** (LP, reissue) £15
(see also Antoniou, Norma Lewis)

ATOMIC ROOSTER
70 B&C CB 121   **Friday The 13th/Banstead** (initial copies in p/s) £15
70 B&C CAS 1010   **ATOMIC ROOSTER** (LP, Matrix CAS +1010 + A/CAS + 1010 + B (Flute Mix) £200
70 B&C CAS 1010   **ATOMIC ROOSTER** (LP, Matrix CAS +1010 + A2/CAS + 1010 + B2 (Flute Mix) £150
70 B&C CAS 1010   **ATOMIC ROOSTER** (LP, Matrix CAS +1010 + A1U/CAS + 1010 + B1U (Guitar Mix) £100
70 B&C CAS 1026   **DEATH WALKS BEHIND YOU** (LP, gatefold sleeve) £100
71 Pegasus PEG 1   **IN HEARING OF ATOMIC ROOSTER** (LP, gatefold sleeve) £50
72 Dawn DNLS 3038   **MADE IN ENGLAND** (LP, limited 'denim' cover, gatefold, with poster, lilac label) £100
73 Dawn DNLS 3038   **MADE IN ENGLAND** (LP, re-pressing, standard cover, gatefold insert, lilac label) £30
73 Dawn DNLS 3049   **NICE'N'GREASY** (LP, lilac label) £40
80 EMI EMC3341   **ATOMIC ROOSTER** (LP) £15
83 Towerbell TOW LP 4   **HEADLINE NEWS** (LP) £15
(see also Cactus, Chris Farlowe, Crazy World Of Arthur Brown, Hard Stuff, Leaf Hound, Andromeda, John Du Cann, Bullet. Bernie Torme, David Gilmore)

ATOMS FOR PEACE
13 XL XLT 584SP   **Default** (1-sided 12", hand silk-screened cover, 100 only) £20
13 XL XLT 592SP   **Judge, Jury & Executioner/S.A.D.** (12" hand-printed sleeve, 100 only) £20
13 XL XLT 603SP   **Ingenue** (1-sided 12", hand silk-screened cover, 100 only) £20
13 XL XLT 605SP   **Before Your Very Eyes/Magic Beanz** (12" hand-printed sleeve, 100 only) £20
13 XL XLT 612SP   **Dropped** (1-sided 12", hand silk-screened cover, 100 only) £20
13 XL XLT 613SP   **Unless** (1-sided, hand silk-screened cover, 100 only) £20
13 XL XLT 614SP   **Stuck Together Pieces** (1-sided, 12", hand silk-screened cover, 100 only) £20
13 XL XLT 615SP   **Reverse Running** (1-sided 12", hand silk-screened cover, 100 only) £20
13 XL XLLP 583X   **AMOK** (2-LP, hand-printed cover, 50 only) £100
13 XL (No Cat. No.)   **AMOK** (9 x 1-sided 12" with hand printed sleeves, box set) £70
13 XL XLLP583X   **AMOK** (2-LP, CD) £18
(see also Radiohead, Red Hot Chilli Peppers)

ATORIE
89 Conscious CON001   **It's My Time/Peace Of Mind** (12") £35

A II Z
81 Polydor POSPX 243   **No Fun After Midnight/Treason/Valhalla's Force** (12", p/s, red vinyl) £15
80 Polydor 2383 587   **THE WITCH OF BERKELEY - LIVE** (LP, initially sealed with sew-on patch) £20
80 Polydor 2383 587   **THE WITCH OF BERKELEY - LIVE** (LP) £15
(see also AC/DC)

A TRIBE CALLED QUEST
90 Jive JIVE 256   **Bonita Applebaum** (7" Why? Edit)/**Bonita Applebaum** (Album Version) (p/s) £20
90 Jive JIVE 265   **Can I Kick It?** (Boilerhouse Mix)/(Radio Edit) (p/s, paper or injection moulded labels) £15
90 Jive HIP 96   **PEOPLES INSTINCTIVE TRAVELS AND THE PATH OF RHYTHM** (LP, inner) £40
91 Jive HIP 117   **THE LOW END THEORY** (LP, inner sleeve) £60
93 Jive HIP 143   **MIDNIGHT MARAUDERS** (2-LP, inners) £50

96	Jive HIP 170	BEATS RHYTHM AND LIFE (2-LP, gatefold)	£50
98	Jive 0521031	LOVE MOVEMENT (3-LP, inners)	£50
99	Jive 523841	THE ANTHOLOGY (3-LP)	£30
17	Epic 88985377871	WE GOT IT FROM HERE...THANK YOU 4 YOUR SERVICE (2-LP)	£20

ATTACK (U.K.)

67	Decca F 12550	Try It/We Don't Know	£150
67	Decca F 12578	Any More Than I Do/Hi-Ho Silver Lining	£45
67	Decca F 12631	Created By Clive/Colour Of My Mind	£100
67	Decca F 12631	Created By Clive/Colour Of My Mind (p/s for export to Holland)	£200
68	Decca F 12725	Neville Thumbcatch/Lady Orange Peel	£175
72	Decca F 13353	Hi-Ho Silver Lining/Any More Than I Do (reissue, unissued)	£0
90	Reflection MM 08	MAGIC IN THE AIR (LP)	£25

(see also Andromeda, Five Day Week Straw People, Nice)

ATTACK (U.S.)

67	Philips BF 1585	Washington Square/Please Phil Spector	£18

ATTACK WAVE PESTREPELLER

98	Prescription DRUG 4	NUG YAR (LP, hand-made sleeve, label, with insert 99 copies only)	£18

ATTAK

83	No Future PUNK 6	THEY WILL EAT YOU WHEN THEY MEAT YOU (LP)	£15

ATTENDANTS

80	Black & White BW 2	Happy Families/Deadbeats & Knowones (p/s)	£20

AT THE DRIVE IN

13	Transgressive TRANS 154X	ACROBAT TENEMENT (LP, red vinyl reissue)	£18
13	Transgressive TRANS 155X	RELATIONSHIP OF COMMAND (2-LP, 4000 copies, orange vinyl reissue)	£80
17	Rise RISE 369-2	IN*TER*A*LI*A (LP, half-blue, half splatter, 150 only)	£30

AT THE GATES

94	Peaceville CC 7	Souls Of The Evil Departed/All Life Ends (yellow vinyl, p/s)	£30
92	Deaf DEAF 10	THE RED IN THE SKY IS OURS (LP)	£25
93	Deaf DEAF 14	WITH FEAR I KISS THE BURNING DARKNESS (LP)	£25
94	Peaceville VILE 47	TERMINAL SPIRIT DISEASE (LP, inner)	£50
95	Earache MOSH 143	SLAUGHTER OF THE SOUL (LP, no inner)	£40
02	Earache MOSH 143	SLAUGHTER OF THE SOUL (LP, reissue, inner)	£25
02	Earache MOSH 143	SLAUGHTER OF THE SOUL (LP, orange vinyl reissue)	£25
06	Earache MOSH 143 PD	SLAUGHTER OF THE SOUL (LP, 2nd reissue, picture disc)	£20

AT THE SIGNE OF THE BULL

72	Guildhall/Boston GHS 7	AT THE SIGNE OF THE BULL (LP)	£25

ATTRACTION

66	Columbia DB 7936	Stupid Girl/Please Tell Me	£40
66	Columbia DB 8010	Party Line/She's A Girl	£125

ATTRITION

82	Private AC 001	DEATH HOUSE (cassette)	£25
83	Third Mind TMT 06	ONSLAUGHT (cassette)	£15
83	Adventures In Reality ARR 12	ACTION AND REACTION (Cassette)	£15
83	Adventures in Reality ARR 11	DEATH HOUSE (cassette)	£15
83	Rabbit RR 003	DEUX DEMOS (cassette)	£15
84	Third Mind TMLP 06	THE ATTRITION OF REASON (LP)	£15

ATTRIX

78	Attrix RB 01	Lost Lenore/Hard Times (p/s, stamped white labels)	£15

AU GO-GO SINGERS

64	Columbia 33SX 1696	THEY CALL US AU GO-GO SINGERS (LP)	£25

(see also Buffalo Springfield, Stephen Stills)

AU PAIRS

79	021 OTO 2	You/Domestic Departures/Kerb Crawler (rubber stamped labels)	£20
81	Human HUMAN 1	PLAYING WITH A DIFFERENT SEX (LP, with iron-on transfer)	£30
81	Human HUMAN 1	PLAYING WITH A DIFFERENT SEX (LP, without iron-on transfer)	£25
82	Kamera KAM 010	SENSE AND SENSUALITY (LP, with insert)	£18

AUBREY SMALL

72	Polydor 2058 204	Loser/Oh What A Day It's Been	£15
71	Polydor 2383 048	AUBREY SMALL (LP, with gatefold insert)	£125

(see also Sons Of Man)

AUDIENCE

71	Charisma CB 156	Eye To Eye/Eye To Eye (double B side mispressing)	£25
69	Polydor 583 065	AUDIENCE (LP)	£300
70	Charisma CAS 1012	FRIEND'S FRIEND'S FRIEND (LP, 1st pressing, pink label with 'scroll' logo, matrix A//2-B//2)	£100
70	Charisma CAS 1014	FRIEND'S FRIEND'S FRIEND (LP, 2nd pressing, pink label with 'scroll' logo, matrix A-2u/B-2u)	£40
71	Charisma CAS 1032	THE HOUSE ON THE HILL (LP, pink scroll label, gatefold sleeve with lyric inner sleeve)	£50
72	Charisma CAS 1032	THE HOUSE ON THE HILL (LP, gatefold, 'Mad Hatter' label)	£18
72	Charisma CAS 1054	LUNCH (LP, gatefold sleeve, with lyric inner sleeve)	£50
72	Charisma CAS 1054	LUNCH (LP, 'Mad Hatter' label)	£18

(see also Stackridge, Hot Chocolate)

AUDIO ARTS
87	Audio Arts AA 004	INTERIM ART: The Difference/Head Low (p/s)	£40
89	Audio Arts AA 007	PLACEMENT & RECOGNITION: Vinny/World Service (p/s)	£40
84	Audio Arts AA 002	ORCHARD GALLERY (LP)	£30
87	New Media NMW 004	ACCENT FOR A START (LP)	£50

AUDIO ACTIVE
94	On U Sound ONULP 73	WE ARE AUDIO ACTIVE (TOKYO SPACE COWBOYS) (LP)	£18

AUDREY
69	Downtown DT 414	Love Me Tonight/BROTHER DAN ALLSTARS: Shoot Them Amigo	£30
69	Downtown DT 418	Lover's Concerto/HERBIE GREY & RUDIES Along Came Roy	£30
69	Downtown DT 436	You'll Lose A Good Thing/DESMOND RILEY: If I Had Wings	£100
69	Downtown DT 449	Pop Your Corn/Pledging My Love	£30
70	Downtown DT 452	Sweeter Than Sugar/The Way You Move	£35
70	Downtown DT 454	Oh I Was Wrong/Let's Try It Again (B-side with Dandy)	£30
70	Downtown DT 457	Someday We'll Be Together/MUSIC DOCTORS: Sunset Rock	£30
70	Downtown DT 463	How Glad I Am/DANDY & AUDREY: I'm So Glad	£15
70	Trend 6099 006	Getting Ready For A Heartache/M Y O B: Leave Me Alone	£15
81	Jah Shaka 826	English Girl/African Queen (12")	£25
84	Ariwa ARI 122	English Girl/English Girl (Dub)/English Girl (Riddim) (12", as Sister Audrey)	£15

(see also Dandy)

AUDREY & THE DREAMERS
68	Downtown DT408	I Second That Emotion/THE DREAMERS: Dear Love	£30

MIKE AUDSLEY
72	Sonet SNTF 641	DARK AND DEVIL WATERS (LP, with insert)	£18

LOREN AUERBACH
84	Christabel CRL 001	AFTER THE LONG NIGHT (LP)	£40
85	Christabel CRL 002	PLAYING THE GAME (LP)	£40

BRIAN AUGER (&) TRINITY
65	Columbia DB 7590	Fool Killer/Let's Do It Tonight (as Brian Auger Trinity)	£60
65	Columbia DB 7715	Green Onions '65/Kiko (as Brian Auger Trinity)	£75
67	Columbia DB 8163	Tiger/Oh Baby, Won't You Come Back Home To Croydon, Where Everybody Beedle's And Bo's (solo)	£60
67	Marmalade 598 003	Red Beans And Rice Pts 1 & 2	£45
68	Marmalade 598 006	I Don't Know Where You Are/A Kind Of Love In (with Julie Driscoll, unissued in favour of "This Wheel's On Fire")	£0
69	Marmalade 598 015	What You Gonna Do/Bumpin' On Sunset	£18
68	Marmalade 608 004	DON'T SEND ME NO FLOWERS (LP, with Jimmy Page & Sonny Boy Williamson)	£120
69	Marmalade 607/608 003	DEFINITELY WHAT! (LP)	£100
69	Polydor 2334 004	THE BEST OF BRIAN AUGER, JULIE DRISCOLL & THE TRINITY (LP)	£20
70	RCA SF 8101	BEFOUR (LP)	£35
71	RCA SF 8170	OBLIVION EXPRESS (LP)	£25
71	Polydor 2383 062	BETTER LAND (LP, as Brian Auger's Oblivion Express)	£30
72	Polydor 2383 104	SECOND WIND (LP, as Brian Auger's Oblivion Express)	£30
73	CBS 65625	CLOSER TO IT (LP)	£25
74	CBS 80058	STRAIGHT AHEAD (LP)	£20

(see also Julie Driscoll Brian Auger & Trinity, Shotgun Express, Jimmy Page, Sonny Boy Williamson)

NAT AUGUSTIN
83	Debut DEBT 12 6	All Of My Love/Summer Is Here Again (12")	£60

AUM
69	London HA-K/SH-K 8401	BLUESVIBES (LP)	£45

CLIFF AUNGIER
68	Polydor 56250	Time/Fisherboy	£30
69	Pye NSPL 18294	THE LADY FROM BALTIMORE (LP)	£20

(see also Royd Rivers & Cliff Aungier)

AUNTIE FLO & ESA
15	Highlife HGHLFWS 02	HIGHLIFE IN KENYA (12", p/s)	£30

AUNTIE SOCIAL
83	SRT S83-CUS-2014	Preacher/I Want You Back (p/s)	£50

AURORA
83	Aurora RAM 9	I'll Be Your Fantasy/If I Really Knew Her (no p/s)	£40

(see also AC/DC)

AURORA BOREALIS
97	Kalevala KALA 006	Aurora Borealis (Part 1)/Aurora Borealis (Part 3)	£20

AUSGANG
85	FM WKFM LP 52	MANIPULATE (LP, with booklet)	£15

AUSTIN
93	Suburban Base SUBBASE 18	THE AUSTIN EP (12", stamped white label)	£30

PATTI AUSTIN
71	CBS 7180	Are We Ready For Love/Now That I Know What Loneliness Is	£30
74	Probe PRO 608	Music To My Heart/Love 'Em And Leave 'Em Kind Of Love	£15

PETER AUSTIN
68	Caltone TONE 125	Your Love/Time Is Getting Harder	£120

(see also Little Freddy, Mr. Foundation)

REG AUSTIN
65   Pye 7N 15885 | My Saddest Day/I'll Find Her £40

SIL AUSTIN
58   Mercury MEP 9540 | **THE BAND WITH THE BEAT** (EP) £15
58   Mercury MEP 9541 | **GO SIL GO** (EP) £15
58   Mercury MPL 6534 | **SLOW WALK ROCK** (LP)..£15

AUSTRALIAN PLAYBOYS
67   Immediate IM 054 | Black Sheep R.I.P./Sad £900
(see also Procession, Manfred Mann Earth Band)

AUTECHRE
91   Hardcore HARD 003 | Cavity Job/Accelera 1 + 2 (12", 1,000 only)..................................£40
94   Warp WAP 54 | **ANTI EP** (12", p/s sealed with sticker)....................................£50
94   Warp 10WAP 44 | **BASSCADET EP** (3 x 10" p/s in box) £25
95   Warp WAP64r | **ANVIL VAPRE EP** (12")..£15
95   Warp WAP 58 | **GARBAGE EP** (12")..£20
96   Warp WAP 72 | **We R Are Why/Are Y Are We** (12, p/s, mail order only) £25
99   Warp WAP 124 | **SPLTRMX: Weissensee Against Im Gluck/At Drowning In A Sea Of Independence** (12", 3000 only)...£18
99   Warp WAPEP7.1 | **EP 7.1** (12")..£20
99   Warp WAPE7.2 | **EP 7.2** (12")..£20
99   Warp WAP 112 | **PEEL SESSION** (12")...£15
00   Warp WAP 150 | **PEEL SESSION 2 EP** (12")...£15
10   Warp WAP 505X | **MOVE OF TEN** (PART 1) (12", p/s)...£20
10   Warp WAP 505Y | **MOVE OF TEN** (PART 2) (12", p/s)...£20
93   Warp WARPLP 17 | **INCUNABULA** (2-LP set, silver vinyl, 1000 only)..................£80
93   Warp WARPLP 17 | **INCUNABULA** (2-LP set, standard black vinyl) £50
94   Warp WARPLP 25 | **AMBER** (2-LP, 1st pressing with "FUCK OFF TRAINSPOTTER" on run-out groove of B-side) £100
95   Warp WARPLP 38 | **TRI REPEATE** (2-LP, inners) £80
97   Warp WARPLP 49 | **CHIASTIC SLIDE** (2-LP)...£45
98   Warp WARPLP 66 | **LP5** (2-LP, cardboard sleeve)..£40
01   Warp WARPLP 128 | **CONFIELD** (2-LP)...£60
01   Warp WARPLP 17 | **INCUNABULA** (2-LP, repressing)..£30
01   Warp WARPLP 25 | **AMBER** (2-LP, repressing, without "TRAINSPOTTER" reference on run-out on side B).......£50
01   Warp WARPLP 38 | **TRI REPEATE** (2-LP, reissue, inners, not sticker on front of sleeve) £35
03   Warp WARPLP 111 | **DRAFT 7.30** (2-LP) £40
05   Warp WARPLP 180 | **UNTITLED** (2-LP)..£35
08   Warp WARPLP 337 | **QUARISTICE** (2-LP)..£40
08   Warp WARPCD 333X | **QUARISTICE** (2-CD metal sleeve) £70
10   Warp WARPLP 210 | **OVERSTEPS** (2-LP box set) £35
13   Warp WARPLP 234 | **EXAI** (4-LP box set) £50
18   Warp WARPLP364 | **NTS SESSIONS** (12-LP box set) £150
(see also Gescom)

AUTEURS
91   No Label or cat no | **THE DEMO EP** (cassette, hand-drawn labels, 6 tracks) £50
93   Hut PM 264 | **NEW WAVE** (LP with free 7")..£40
94   Hut Recordings HUTLPX 16 | **NOW I'M A COWBOY** (LP, with free 1-sided 7")...........£60
96   Hut HUT LP33 | **AFTER MURDER PARK** (LP) £70
99   Hut HUT LP53 | **HOW I LEARNED TO LOVE THE BOOTBOYS** (LP) £70

AUTOGRAPHS
78   RAK RAK 281 | **While I'm Still Young/Fabulous** (p/s) £15
78   Strawberry Mastering | **While I'm Still Young** (different version, acetate only) £30

AUTOMATIC DLAMINI
92   Big Intl. BOT 04 | **FROM A DIVA TO A DIVER** (LP) £20

AUTOMATIC FINE TUNING
76   Charisma CAS 1122 | **A.F.T** (LP) £25

AUTOMATICS
78   Island WIP 6433 | **Wakin' With The Radio On/Watch Her Now** (unissued)......£0
78   Island WIP 6439 | **When Tanks Roll Over Poland Again/Watch Her Now** (p/s)......£15

AUTOMATION
84   Jung Rhythm SWE T2 | **Dancing In Outer Space/Outer Space 84 Rap** (featuring Family Quest) (12") £15

AUTOPILOT
79   Merimusic/Ze-La Records JHEPS 2244 | **LOVE IS A PROCESS EP** (oversize card p/s)......£40

AUTOPSY
89   Peaceville VILE 12 | **SEVERED SURVIVAL** (LP, with inner) £25
89   Peaceville VILE 12 | **SEVERED SURVIVAL** (LP, picture disc) £30
91   Peaceville VILE 25 | **MENTAL FUNERAL** (LP, green vinyl, inner) £40
91   Peaceville VILE 25 | **MENTAL FUNERAL** (LP, picture disc) £30
92   Peaceville VILE 33 | **ACTS OF THE UNSPEAKABLE** (LP) £15
11   Peaceville VILELP 317 | **MACABRE ETERNAL** (2-LP, blue vinyl with poster)......£20

AUTOSALVAGE
88   Edsel ED 286 | **AUTOSALVAGE** (LP, reissue) £25

AUTUMN
72   Pye 7N45144 | **Stood Up/Not The Way She Looks** £20

MINT VALUE £

73	Pye 7N 45249	Down Down Down/October £15

AUTUMN VINE
70	Evolution E 2447	He Ain't No Superman/Maxi Baby...£15

AVALANCHE (1)
71	Parlophone R 5890	Finding My Way Home/Rabbits £40

(see also Norman Haines Band)

AVALANCHE (2)
80	Childers AVA 1	The Preacher/Mean Lady (no p/s) £90

AVALANCHES
99	Rex REKD 01T	Undersea Community/Yamaha Superstar/Slow Walking/Thank You Caroline £15
01	XL XLS 128	Since I Left You/Thank You Caroline (Andy Votel Mix) (with tattoo)........£20
01	XL Recordings XLLP 138	SINCE I LEFT YOU (2-LP, gatefold)..£60
16	XL XLLP 755X	WILDFLOWER (2-LP, with CD) £30
12	XL XLLP 138	SINCE I LEFT YOU (LP, gatefold, reissue marbled vinyl) £40

AVALON
82	SRTS 82/CUS/1296	Going Thru'/Gypsy Secret (not released in p/s) £130

FRANKIE AVALON
58	London HL 8636	You Excite Me/Darlin' £25
58	HMV POP 517	Ginger Bread/Blue Betty £15

AVALONS
66	Island WI 263	Everyday/I Love You £15

AVANT-GARDE
68	CBS 3704	Naturally Stoned/Honey And Gall £15

AVENGER
84	Neat NEAT 1018	BLOOD SPORTS (LP)..£15
85	Neat NEAT 1026	KILLER ELITE (LP, with lyric insert) £15

AVENGERS (1)
68	Parlophone R 5661	Everyone's Gonna Wonder/Take My Hand..£15

(see also Vanity Fair)

AVERAGE WHITE BAND
73	MCA MUPS 486	SHOW YOUR HAND (LP, black/silver labels) £25

AVIATOR
80	Harvest SHSP 4107	TURBULENCE (LP) £15

AVOCADOS
81	Choo Choo Train CHUG 3	I Never Knew/Television Brought Me Up £35

ALAN AVON & TOY SHOP
70	Concord CON 005	These Are The Reasons/Night To Remember £150

AWAY FROM THE SAND
73	Beaujangle DV 003	AWAY FROM THE SAND (LP, allegedly only 50 copies) £100

AWESOME 3
92	Entity NTT 12 07	Don't Go/Headstrong (12") £15
92	Citybeat CBE 1271	Don't Go (Kicks Like A Mule Mix)/Don't Go (Second Movement)/(Original Mix)/Headstrong (12". p/s) £15

AXEGRINDER
89	Peaceville VILE 7	RISE OF THE SERPENT MEN (LP) £30

DAVID AXELROD
06	Stateside SS 2230	Holy Thursday/Song Of Innocence (reissue)..£25
06	Stateside SS 2231	London/The Poison Tree (reissue) £15
02	Stateside SS 2227	Holy Thursday/DAVID MCCALLUM: The Edge (reissue) £35
68	Capitol ST 2982	SONG OF INNOCENCE (LP, 'Sold in the U.K...' on label) £70
71	RCA LSP 4636	MESSIAH (LP) £40
73	MCA MUPS 472	THE AUCTION (LP, black/blue hexagon label) £40
99	Stateside 7243 4 99405 12	1968 TO 1970 AN ANTHOLOGY (2-LP) £30
01	Mo Wax MWR 141LP	DAVID AXELROD (LP) £50
01	Mo Wax MWR 141LPX	DAVID AXELROD (LP as 2 x 12") £60
02	Stateside 7243537484 1 8	ANTHOLOGY II (2-LP) £30
06	Capitol 0946 3 11617 11	THE EDGE: DAVID AXELROD AT CAPITOL RECORDS (2-LP) £50

(see also Electric Prunes)

HOYT AXTON
64	Stateside SL 10082	GREENBACK DOLLAR (LP) £15
64	Stateside SL 10096	THUNDER 'N' LIGHTNIN' (LP)..£15
66	London HA-F/SH-F 8276	THE BEST OF HOYT AXTON (LP) £15

AXXESS
83	Lamborghini LMGLP 100	NOVELS FOR THE MOONS (LP) £30

AYERS, CALE, NICO & ENO
74	Island ILPS 9291	JUNE 1ST, 1974 (LP) £18

(see also Kevin Ayers, John Cale, Nico, Brian Eno)

KEVIN AYERS (& WHOLE WORLD)
70	Harvest HAR 5011	Singing A Song In The Morning/Eleanor's Cake Which Ate Her.....................£20
70	Harvest HAR 5027	Butterfly Dance/Puis-Je? (with Whole World) £25
73	Harvest HAR 5071	Caribbean Moon/Take Me To Tahiti (p/s) £20
76	Harvest HAR 5107	Stranger In Blue Suede Shoes/Fake Mexican Tourist Blues (possibly in p/s) £20

76	Harvest HAR 5109	Caribbean Moon/Take Me To Tahiti (reissue, in different p/s)	£20
70	Harvest SHVL 763	JOY OF A TOY (LP, gatefold sleeve, 1st pressing with no EMI box)	£150
70	Harvest SHSP 4005	SHOOTING AT THE MOON (LP, with Whole World)	£80
72	Harvest SHVL 800	WHATEVERSHEBRINGSWESING (LP, textured gatefold sleeve)	£60
73	Harvest SHVL 807	BANANAMOUR (LP, gatefold sleeve, with booklet)	£200
73	Harvest SHVL 807	BANANAMOUR (LP, gatefold sleeve, without booklet)	£30
74	Island ILPS 9263	THE CONFESSIONS OF DR. DREAM AND OTHER STORIES (LP, with inner)	£30
75	Island ILPS 9322	SWEET DECEIVER (LP, with inner sleeve)	£15
75	Harvest SHDW 407	JOY OF A TOY/SHOOTING AT THE MOON (2-LP, reissue, gatefold sleeve)	£25
76	Harvest SHSP 2005	ODD DITTIES (LP)	£18
76	Harvest SHSP 4057	YES WE HAVE NO MAÑANAS (LP, textured sleeve, with inner sleeve)	£20
78	Harvest SHSP 4085	RAINBOW TAKEAWAY (LP)	£15
80	Harvest SHSP 4106	THAT'S WHAT YOU GET BABE (LP)	£15
86	Illuminated AMA 25	AS CLOSE AS YOU THINK (LP)	£25
86	Harvest Black EMS 1124	BANANAMOUR (LP, reissue)	£15
92	Permanent PERM LP 5	STILL LIFE WITH GUITAR (LP)	£15

(see also Soft Machine, Lady June, Lol Coxhill, David Bedford, Mike Oldfield, Bridget St. John)

ROY AYERS (UBIQUITY)

87	Urban URB 6	Can't You See Me/Love Will Bring Us Back Together	£20
87	Urban URBX 6	Can't You See Me/Love Will Bring Us Back Together/Sweet Tears (12", p/s)	£15
72	Polydor PD 5022	HE'S COMING (LP, as Roy Ayers Ubiquity)	£40
75	Polydor PD 6057	MYSTIC VOYAGE (LP)	£20
77	Polydor 2391 246	VIBRATIONS (LP, as Roy Ayers Ubiquity)	£20
81	Polydor 2391 517	AFRICA, CENTRE OF THE WORLD (LP)	£15
83	Uno Melodic UMLP 1	SILVER VIBRATIONS (LP)	£100
83	Uno Melodic UMLP 2	DRIVIN' ON UP (LP)	£30
88	Urban UMID 1	EVERYBODY LOVES THE SUNSHINE (LP, reissue as Roy Ayers Ubiquity)	£50

(see also Jack Wilson Quartet)

ALBERT AYLER

64	Transatlantic TRA 130	SPIRITS (LP)	£40
64	Fontana Jazz SFJL 925	GHOSTS (LP)	£40
64	Fontana Jazz SFJL 927	MY NAME IS (LP)	£45
65	Fontana 933 SFJL	SPIRITUAL UNITY (LP)	£50
65	Fontana SFJL 925	GHOSTS (LP, reissue)	£30
65	Fontana Jazz SFJL 927	MY NAME IS (LP, reissue)	£30
67	Polydor 2383089	WITCHES & DEVILS (LP)	£40
68	Impulse IMPL 8022	NEW GRASS (LP, gatefold sleeve)	£30
69	Impulse SIPL 519	NEW GRASS (LP, reissue, single sleeve)	£20
69	Sonet SNTF 604	FIRST RECORDINGS (LP)	£25
70s	Freedom 41000 FLP	VIBRATIONS (LP)	£15

DENNIS AYLER

| 16 | 22a 010 | Put It On/Ms.Chambers/Smoke | £15 |

AYRSHIRE FOLK

| 74 | Deroy DER 1052 | AYRSHIRE FOLK (LP, private pressing) | £70 |

AYSHEA

65	Fontana TF 627	Eeny Meeny/Peep My Love	£20
68	Polydor 56276	Celebration Of The Year/Only Love Can Save Me Now	£30
70	Polydor 2001 029	Mr White's White Flying Machine/Ship Of The Line	£30
70	Polydor 2384 026	AYSHEA (LP)	£30

(see also Roy Wood)

AZANYAH

| 12 | Jazzman JMANLP 047 | THE ONE (LP, reissue) | £15 |

A-ZONE

| 94 | White House WYHS 028 | Calling The People/Safety Zone (12") | £20 |

AZTEC CAMERA

81	Postcard 81-3	Just Like Gold/We Could Send Letters (die-cut sleeve, with card)	£50
81	Postcard 81-3	Just Like Gold/We Could Send Letters (die-cut sleeve, without card)	£20
81	Postcard 81-8	Mattress Of Wire/Lost Outside The Tunnel (p/s)	£35
83	Rainhill ACFC 1	Oblivious (Langer/Winstanley Remix)/Oblivious (Colin Fairley Remix) (no p/s)	£20
83	Rough Trade ROUGH 47	HIGH LAND HARD RAIN (LP)	£15
12	Domino REWIG LP 92	HIGH LAND, HARD RAIN (LP, reissue with inner and bonus 7" EP)	£25

(see also French Impressionists)

AZYMUTH

| 79 | Milestone MRC 101 | Jazz Carnival/Fly Over The Horizon (12") | £15 |
| 80 | Milestone MRC 102 | Dear Limmertz/Papasong (12") | £15 |

B

FRANKIE 'ALROUNDER' B

| 86 | Ital Stuff IS 001 | Scratch Mi Back/Version (12") | £125 |

MINT VALUE £

IKE B & CRYSTALITES
68   Island WI 3151   **Try A Little Merriness/Patricia** £25

MEHER BABA
70   Univ. Spiritual League 1   **HAPPY BIRTHDAY** (LP, with booklet and lyric sheet 6 Pete Townshend tracks, 100 only) £300
70   Univ. Spiritual League 2   **I AM** (LP, with inserts, features 5 Pete Townshend tracks) £100
76   Univ. Spiritual League 3   **WITH LOVE** (LP, features 3 Pete Townshend tracks) £100
70s MBO MBO 1   **STAR OF THE SILENT SCREEN . . . MEHER BABA** (LP, reissue of "Happy Birthday" without inserts)..£20
70s MBO MBO 2   **I AM** (LP, reissue, without inserts) £20
(see also Pete Townshend)

BABE RUTH
72   Harvest SHSP 4022   **FIRST BASE** (LP, 1st pressing with 'Sympathy Music Ltd' credit for 'Wells Fargo' with lyric insert)..£40
72   Harvest SHSP 4022   **FIRST BASE** (LP, 2nd pressing with 'Tone Music' credit for 'Wells Fargo' with lyric insert)..£20
74   Harvest SHVL 812   **AMAR CABALLERO** (LP, gatefold sleeve) £20
75   Harvest SHSP 4038   **BABE RUTH** (LP, inner lyric sleeve)...£20
(see also Wild Turkey, Elias Hulk, Liquid Gold, Whitesnake)

BABES IN TOYLAND
93   Twin Tone TTR89208   **TO MOTHER** (EP, insert, booklet & green vinyl) £25
93   Southern 18512-1   **PAINKILLERS** (12" EP) £25
92   Southern 18591   **FONTANELLE** (LP) £20

BABLA AND HIS ORCHESTRA
79   Savera SAV 1001   **YESTERDAY ONCE MORE** (LP) £18

BABY
69   Spark SRL 1030   **Heartbreaker/Michael Blues**..£20

BABY BERTHA
72   SRT 72183   **BABY BERTHA** (LP, 50 only) £100

BABY CHARLES
09   Record Kicks RK45 014   **I Bet You Look Good On The Dancefloor/Time Wasting** £30

BABY BIRD
96   Echo ECS026   **You're Gorgeous/You're Gorgeous Too/Bebe Lemonade** (p/s, gold vinyl) £40
96   ECHO LP11   **UGLY BEAUTIFUL** (2-LP) £35
98   Echo ECHLP 24   **THERES SOMETHING GOING ON** (LP)..£30

BABY D
92   Production House PNT 043RX   **Let Me Be Your Fantasy** (Acen In Wonderland)/**Fantasy** (Ray Keith Remix) (12") £15
96   Systematic 828683 1   **DELIVERANCE** (3-LP) £20

BABY HUEY
71   Buddah 2365 001   **LIVING LEGEND - THE BABY HUEY STORY** (LP) £40

BABY JANE & ROCKABYES
63   United Artists UP 1010   **How Much Is That Doggie In The Window/My Boy John**..£15

BABY LAUREL
82   Badger SRTS 82 CUS 1483   **Trouble In The Air/Leavin Home** £50

BABYLON
69   Polydor 56356   **Into The Promised Land/Nobody's Fault But Mine** (p/s)..£40
69   Polydor 56356   **Into The Promised Land/Nobody's Fault But Mine** (no p/s)....................................£25
(see also Carole Grimes)

BABYLON TIMEWARP
93   Subliminal TENSE 001   **Durban Poison/Durban Poison** (-32Hz And Dropping Mix)/ **Durban Poison** (The Kashmir Mix)(12")..£40
93   Subliminal TENSE 003   **I Come In Peace/Durban Poison** (Remix)/**Durban Poison** (Remix) (12") £30
95   Mistermen MR 3   **MISTERMEN VOL. 3: Durban Poison/Changing** (12", p/s) £25

BABYSHAMBLES
04   High Society (no cat no)   **What Katie Did** (Demo) (1,000 numbered copies of clear flexi, with Annelise's Magazine. With magazine) £20
04   High Society HS7IN011   **Babyshambles/At The Flophouse** (p/s, 1000 only) £18
04   High Society (no cat no)   **What Katie Did** (Demo) (1,000 numbered copies of clear flexi, with Annelise's Magazine. Without magazine)..£18
13   Parlophone R 6905   **Nothing Comes To Nothing/Picture Me In A Hospital** (Demo) (pink vinyl, p/s) £15
06   Regal 379 9021   **BLINDING EP** (12") £30
05   Rough Trade RTRADLP240   **DOWN IN ALBION** (2LP, fourth side etched, textured sleeve, printed inners)...................£45
07   Parlophone 508 6201   **SHOTTER'S NATION** (LP, printed inner) £55
13   Parlophone 825646418619   **SEQUEL TO THE PREQUEL** (LP/CD, clear vinyl)..£45
15   Rough Trade RTRADLP240   **DOWN IN ALBION** (2LP, fourth side etched, reissue, non-textured cover)...................£25
18   Parlophone 508 6201   **SHOTTER'S NATION** (LP, reissue, clear/black marbled vinyl, numbered, insert, 180g).......£50
(see also Libertines)

BABY SUNSHINE
75   Deroy DER 1301   **BABY SUNSHINE** (LP, with insert)..£80
(see also Fairy's Moke)

BACCA
73   Grape GR 3048   **George Foreman/Version** £15

BURT BACHARACH
65   London HLR 9983   **What's New Pussycat/My Little Red Book** (B-side with Tony Middleton) £20
67   RCA Victor RD 7874   **CASINO ROYALE** (LP, soundtrack, mono) £40

MINT VALUE £

67	RCA Victor SF 7874	CASINO ROYALE (LP, soundtrack, stereo)	£30

(see also Tony Middleton, Breakaways)

BACHDENKEL
77	Initial IRL 001	LEMMINGS (LP, stickered gatefold sleeve, with bonus EP)	£50
77	Initial IRL 001	LEMMINGS (LP)	£15
77	Initial IRL 002	STALINGRAD (LP, numbered with lyric insert)	£40

JOHNNY BACHELOR
60	London HLN 9074	Mumbles/Arabella Jean	£50

BACHELORS (U.K.)
58	Parlophone R 4454	Platter Party/Love Is A Two Way Street	£20
59	Parlophone R 4547	Please Don't Touch/Ding Dong	£20

BACH TWO BACH
71	Mushroom 100 MR 10	BACH TWO BACH (LP)	£20

BACK ALLEY CHOIR
72	York SYK 517	Smile Born Of Courtesy/Why Are You Here	£40
73	York FYK 406	BACK ALLEY CHOIR (LP, 500 only)	£600

BACK DOOR
72	Blakey BLP 5989	BACK DOOR (LP, sold at gigs)	£80
73	Warner Bros. K46231	BACK DOOR (LP, reissue of Blakey LP)	£20
76	Warner Bros. K56243	ACTIVATE (LP)	£15

(see also Whitesnake)

BACKHOUSE JAMES BLUES BAND
68	private pressing	BACKHOUSE JAMES BLUES BAND (LP, 30 copies only, white labels in sleeve)	£1000
13	RCLP 007	BACKHOUSE JAMES BLUES BAND (LP, reissue with signed and numbered certificate)	£20

MIRIAM BACKHOUSE
77	Mother Earth MUM 1203	GYPSY WITHOUT A ROAD (LP)	£120

BACKLASH
80	Gargoyle GRGL 777	OFF WITH HIS HEAD (EP)	£50

BACKSEAT ROMEOS
80	Future Earth FER 007	Zero Ambition/In The Night (p/s)	£35

BACKTRAX
80	S 80 CUS 842	It's Never Too Late/Be Mine	£25

BACKYARD HEAVIES
73	Action ACT 4616	Just Keep On Truckin'/Never Can Say Goodbye	£30

BACON FAT
70	Blue Horizon 57-3171	Nobody But You/Small's On 53rd	£18
70	Blue Horizon 57-3181	Evil/Blues Feeling	£25
70	Blue Horizon 7-63858	GREASE ONE FOR ME (LP)	£100
71	Blue Horizon 2431 001	TOUGH DUDE (LP)	£100

(see also Dirty Blues Band, George 'Harmonica' Smith)

GAR BACON
59	Fontana H 196	Marshal, Marshal/Too Young To Love	£15

WALLY BADAROU
82	Island Visual Arts WAL 1	ISLAND VISUAL ARTS INTRODUCES WALLY BADAROU (LP, promo)	£40
84	Island ILPS 9822	ECHOES (LP)	£20
89	Island ILPS 9897	WORDS OF A MOUNTAIN (LP, insert)	£20
16	Expansion/Love Vinyl LVLP 01	BACK TO SCALES TO-NIGHT (LP, vinyl issue of 1980 CD)	£15
23	Be With Records BEWITH120LP	COLORS OF SCIENCE (LP)	£25

(see also Level 42, Grace Jones)

BAD BRAINS
82	Alt. Tentacles VIRUS 13	I Luv Jah/Sailin' On/Big Takeover (12", p/s)	£18
83	Food For Thought YUMT101	I And I Survive (An' T'ing)/Destroy Babylon (12", insert, p/s)	£20
83	Abstract ABT 007	ROCK FOR LIGHT (LP)	£30
91	Caroline CARLP 8	ROCK FOR LIGHT (LP, reissue, stickered sleeve with 3 bonus tracks)	£15

BAD COMPANY (1)
74	Island ILPS 9279	BAD COMPANY (LP, first pressing, A-1U TG 2/B-1U HR 2, 'Robor Limited' gatefold sleeve, no "Published by Island Music Ltd")	£40
75	Island ILPS 9304	STRAIGHT SHOOTER (LP)	£20
76	Island ILSP 9346	RUN WITH THE PACK (LP)	£20
77	Island ILPS 9279	BAD COMPANY (LP, later EMI pressing with "Published by Island Music Ltd" credit)	£15

BAD COMPANY (2)
98	BC Recordings BCR 001	The Nine/The Bridge (company p/s)	£20
00	BC R'dings BCRLP 001	INSIDE THE MACHINE (5 x 12")	£35
00	BC R'dings BCRUKLP 001	DIGITAL NATION (5 x 12")	£25

BAD DREAM FANCY DRESS
88	El GOPT T33	Curry Crazy/Up The King Of Lumembourg (10", p/s)	£15
88	El ACME 18	CHOIRBOY GAS (LP)	£20

BADFINGER
70	Apple APPLE 31	No Matter What/Better Days (p/s)	£15
71	Apple APPLE 35	Name Of The Game/Suitcase (unreleased)	£0
72	Apple APPLE 40	Day After Day/Sweet Tuesday Morning (p/s)	£15
72	Apple APPLE 42	Baby Blue/Flying (unreleased in U.K.)	£0

			MINT VALUE £

BADGE

74	Apple APPLE 49	Apple Of My Eye/Blind Owl (Demo)	£80
74	Apple APPLE 49	Apple Of My Eye/Blind Owl	£40
70	Apple SAPCOR 12	MAGIC CHRISTIAN MUSIC (LP)	£70
70	Apple SAPCOR 16	NO DICE (LP, gatefold sleeve)	£70
72	Apple SAPCOR 19	STRAIGHT UP (LP)	£100
73	Warner Bros K 56023	BADFINGER (LP, with insert)	£50
74	Apple SAPCOR 27	ASS (LP, with inner sleeve)	£80
74	Warner Bros K 56076	WISH YOU WERE HERE (LP, withdrawn)	£150
79	Elektra K52129	AIRWAVES (LP, with lyric inner sleeve)	£20
91	Apple SAPCOR 12	MAGIC CHRISTIAN MUSIC (LP, reissue, gatefold sleeve with bonus 12" [Sapcor 121])	£30
92	Apple SAPCOR 16	NO DICE (LP, reissue, gatefold sleeve with bonus 12" [SAPCOR 161])	£30
93	Apple SAPCOR 19	STRAIGHT UP (LP, reissue, gatefold sleeve with bonus 12" [SAPCOR 191])	£30
95	Apple SAPCOR 28	COME AND GET IT - THE BEST OF BADFINGER (2-LP, gatefold sleeve)	£30

(see also Iveys, Masterminds, Gary Walker & Rain, Natural Gas, Blue Goose)

BADGE

81	Metal Minded MM 2	Silver Woman/Something I've Lost (p/s)	£25

BADGER (1)

73	Atlantic K 40473	ONE LIVE BADGER (LP, gatefold pop-up sleeve)	£40
74	Epic EPC 80009	WHITE LADY (LP)	£15

(see also Ashton Gardner & Dyke, Jackie Lomax, Yes, Flash, Jeff Beck)

BADGER (2)

81	Noize Gate NG 02	Over The Wall/Faceless Gang (p/s)	£40

BADGER BELL BAND

85	Noize Gate SETT 001	Nothing Left/Rock The Vicar (no p/s)	£40

(see also Badger (2))

BADGEWEARER

95	Amanita AMA LP 05	A TOY GUN IN SAFE HANDS (LP)	£15

BAD INFLUENCE

92	Bi BIR 01	F.U.B.A.R (12" EP stamped white labels)	£20
92	Bi BIR 02	Never Too Much/Such A Feeling (12")	£20
92	Bi BIR 03	Sudden Impact/Untitled/Untitled (12")	£40
93	Metamoprhasis MORPHO 003	UNFAIR INFLUENCE (12" EP)	£20

HENK BADINGS

60	Philips SABL 206	ELECTRONIC MUSIC (LP, gatefold)	£30

BAD LIEUTENANT

09	Triple Echo BADLP01LP	NEVER CRY ANOTHER TEAR (2-LP)	£40

(see also Joy Division, New Order, Electronic, The Other Two)

BADLY DRAWN BOY

97	Mo Wax (no cat no)	Nursery Rhyme (with UNKLE, 5" promo 150 only)	£40
90s	Twisted Nerve (no cat. no.)	I Love You All (one-track musical box, 150 only)	£100
98	Twisted Nerve TNXMS1	Donna And Blitzen (1 track on 5 track one-sided red vinyl 7", 195 copies, p/s)	£50
97	Twisted Nerve TN 001	EP1 (EP, 500 only)	£50
98	Twisted Nerve TN 002	EP2: I Love You All/The Treeclimber/I Love You All (I Loop You All Andy Votel Mix)/Thinking Of You (EP, 1,000 only)	£30
00	Twisted Nerve TNXLCD 133	THE HOUR OF THE BEWILDERBEAST (LP, 1st pressing, withdrawn, with version of 'Magic In The Air' with the line "Love Is Contagious", and Woody Allen on sleeve)	£30
00	Twisted Nerve TNXLLP133	THE HOUR OF THE BEWILDERBEAST (LP)	£20
10	One Last Fruit OLFCDXX 01	IT'S WHAT I'M THINKING (PART 1 PHOTOGRAPHING SNOWFLAKES) (box set, LP, 2-CD, 4 badges, signed)	£60
15	Twisted Nerve TNXLLP 695X	THE HOUR OF BEWILDERBEAST (3-LP, reissue, leatherette cover)	£30

(see also Doves)

BADOO

80	KG Imperial KG 001	Rocking Of The Five Thousand/BADOO & TOYAN: Reaching To Be Free (12")	£20

BAD TASTE

88	Newgate SRT8KS 1554	Rockin' Girl (p/s, with insert)	£30

JOAN BAEZ

89	Virgin VGC 9	DIAMONDS AND DUST IN THE BULLRING (LP)	£40

(see also Bob Dylan)

BAFFLED

96	Urban Beat URB 002	Going On/Dreams (12")	£25
96	Urban Beat URB 003	Over U (Big Splash Mix)/(Deep Pan Mix)/The Feeling (Rinsing Mix)/(Bonus Roast Mix) (12", as Baffled 2)	£25

BAGGA

77	Matumbi MAT 002	Daughter Of Zion/Version	£50

BAGHDAD FIVE

83	Risky R 2511	Lovin Affection/Lonely Avenue	£25

BAG-O-WIRE

75	Klik KLP 9007	BAG-O-WIRE (LP)	£40
77	Epic 82133	BAG-O-WIRE (LP)	£30

JULIAN BAHULAS JAZZ AFRIKA

82	Tsafrika TSA 001	SON OF THE SOIL (LP)	£30

BAHUMUTSI

87	Sounds From Bahumutsi SFB 001A	BUSANG MEROPA/BRING BACK THE DRUMS (LP)	£100

BURR BAILEY (& SIX SHOOTERS)
63	Decca F 11686	San Francisco Bay/Like A Bird Without Feathers (with Six Shooters) £20
64	Decca F 11846	Chahawki/You Made Me Cry £30

CLIVE BAILEY & RICO'S GROUP
62	Blue Beat BB 92	Evening Train/Take Me Home (as Recko and his Blues Group) £20
68	Double D DD104	Drink & Drive/Oh Oh Sugar (with Double D band) £35

DEREK BAILEY
70	Incus INCUS 2	SOLO GUITAR (LP) £100
71	Incus INCUS 2R	SOLO GUITAR (LP) £70
74	Incus INCUS 12	LOT 74 (LP) £60
80	Incus INCUS 40	AIDA (LP) £70
85	Incus INCUS 48	NOTES (LP) £25
04	Organ Of Corti 10	TAPS (LP, 220gm vinyl, limited issue) £15

(see also Tony Oxley, Springboard, Steve Lacy & Derek Bailey, Anthony Braxton & Derek Bailey, Jamie Muir & Derek Bailey)

DEREK BAILEY, BARRY GUY & PAUL RUTHERFORD
70	Incus INCUS 3/4	ISKRA 1903 (LP) £50

(see also Barry Guy)

DEREK BAILEY & HAN BENNINK
72	Incus INCUS 9	SELECTIONS FROM LIVE PERFORMANCES AT VERITY'S PLACE (LP) £50
76	Incus INCUS 25	COMPANY 3 (LP) £50

DEREK BAILEY, ANTHONY BRAXTON & EVAN PARKER
76	Incus INCUS 23	COMPANY 2 (LP) £50

DEREK BAILEY & TONY COE
79	Incus INCUS 34	TIME (LP) £50

DEREK BAILEY, HUGH DAVIES, JAMIE MUIR, EVAN PARKER
75	Incus INCUS 17	THE MUSIC IMPROVISATION COMPANY 1968-1971 (LP) £40

DEREK BAILEY & TRISTAN HONSINGER
76	Incus INCUS 20	DUO (LP) £50

DEREK BAILEY & EVAN PARKER
75	Incus INCUS 16	THE LONDON CONCERT (LP) £50
85	Incus INCUS 50	COMPATIBLES (LP) £50

(see also Evan Parker)

DEREK BAILEY, EVAN PARKER & HAN BENNINK
70	Incus INCUS 1	THE TOPOGRAPHY OF THE LUNGS (LP) £150
77	Incus INCUS 1	THE TOPOGRAPHY OF THE LUNGS (LP, reissue) £40

PAUL BAILEY SOUND
80	Scott PSB 001	TAKE A WALK IN THE MOONLIGHT (LP) £50

ROY BAILEY (U.K.)
82	Fuse CF 382	HARD TIMES (LP, with insert) £15

(see also Leon Rosselson)

ZEDDIE BAILEY
73	Grape GR 3037	Babylon Gone/TONY KING: Speak No Evil £25

ELROY BAILY
80	Arawak ARK DD 027	24 Hour Love/Wabadab (12") £30
79	Burning Vibrations RRIG 7759	RED HOT DUB (LP) £40

(see also Ras Elroy)

ARTHUR BAIRD SKIFFLE GROUP
56	Beltona BL 2669	Union Train/Union Maid £15

ANITA BAKER
86	Elektra EKT 37	RAPTURE (LP, printed inner) £15
88	Elektra EKT 49	GIVING YOU THE BEST THAT I GOT (LP, printed inner) £15
90	Elektra EKT 72	COMPOSTIONS (LP, printed inner) £15
91	Elektra EKT 100	THE SONGSTRESS (LP, printed inner, UK issue of US 1983 LP) £15
94	Elektra 7559 61555 1	RYHTHM OF LOVE (LP, printed inner) £100

CHET BAKER (QUARTET)
54	Vogue LDE 045	CHET BAKER QUARTET (10" LP) £30
55	Philips BBL 7022	CHET BAKER AND STRINGS (LP) £20
55	Vogue LDE 116	CHET BAKER QUARTET (10" LP) £20
56	Vogue LAE 120	CHET BAKER SINGS (LP) £20
56	Vogue LDE 159	CHET BAKER SEXTET (10" LP) £25
56	Vogue LDE 163	CHET BAKER ENSEMBLE (10" LP) £25
56	Vogue LDE 182	CHET BAKER SINGS (10" LP) £20
56	Felsted PDL 85008	CHET BAKER QUARTET VOL. 1 (LP) £25
56	Felsted PDL 85013	CHET BAKER QUARTET VOL. 2 (LP) £20
57	Felsted PDL 85036	I GET CHET (LP, with Bobby Jaspar) £50
57	Vogue LAE 12044	CHET BAKER QUARTET AT ANN ARBOR (LP) £20
57	Vogue LAE 12076	CHET BAKER AND HIS CREW (LP, mono) £25
58	Vogue LAE 12109	CHET BAKER - PHIL'S BLUES (LP) £20
59	Vogue SEA 5005	CHET BAKER AND HIS CREW (LP, stereo) £20
59	Vogue LAE 12164	CHET BAKER SINGS (LP) £20
59	Vogue LAE 12183	CHET BAKER AND ART PEPPER SEXTET - PLAYBOYS! (LP) £60

(see also Art Pepper, Gerry Mulligan)

MINT VALUE £

DESMOND BAKER & CLAREDONIANS
66 Island WI 295   Rude Boy Gone Jail/SHARKS: Don't Fool Me £50
(see also Claredonians)

ERNEST BAKER
00 Grapevine 2000 110   Alone Again/Do It With Feeling £15

GEORGE BAKER SELECTION
70 Penny Farthing 717   Little Green Bag/Pretty Little Dreamer £15
79 Penny Farthing PELS 503 LITTLE GREEN BAG (LP)..£60

GINGER BAKER('S AIRFORCE)
70 Polydor 2662 001   GINGER BAKER'S AIRFORCE (2-LP, gatefold sleeve)......................................£50
70 Polydor 2383 029   AIRFORCE II (LP, gatefold sleeve, with insert).......................................£30
72 Polydor 2383 133   STRATAVARIOUS (LP) £20
(see also Graham Bond Organisation, Cream, Blind Faith, Fela Ransome-Kuti [& Africa '70], Harold McNair, Griffin, Baker-Gurvitz Army)

GLEN BAKER
85 The Stand THE STAND 3   BRIEF ENCOUNTER (LP) £20
(see also Enid)

JEANETTE BAKER
59 Vogue Pop V 9143   Everything Reminds Me Of You/Crazy With You £150

JOHN BAKER
08 Trunk JBH 030 LP   THE JOHN BAKER TAPES (LP, 500 only)..£20

JULIEN BAKER
17 Matador OLE-1127-7   Funeral Pyre/Distant Solar Systems (p/s)...£25
18 Matador OLE 1129 1   TURN OUT THE LIGHTS (LP, screen printed sleeve, 50 only)...........................£80

KENNY BAKER
55 Jazz Today JTL 1   OPERATION JAM SESSION (10" LP, with The Jazz Today Unit)...........................£60
55 Jazz Today JTL 4   KENNY BAKER QUARTET/AFTER HOURS GROUP (10" LP) £30
55 Jazz Today JTL 5   TRIBUTE TO BENNY CARTER (10" LP, with The Jazz Today Unit, one side by Bertie King Jazz Group)..........£20
59 Columbia 33S1140   BLOWIN' UP A STORM (10" LP) £20
78 77 77S 56   BAKER'S JAM (LP) £20

LAVERN BAKER (& GLIDERS)
55 Columbia SCM 5172   Tweedle Dee/Tomorrow Night (with Gliders) £300
55 Columbia DB 3591   Tweedle Dee/Tomorrow Night (with Gliders) (78).....................................£15
55 London HLA 8199   Play It Fair/That Old Lucky Sun (with Gliders) £150
55 London HLA 8199   Play It Fair/That Old Lucky Sun (with Gliders) (78)................................£15
56 London HLE 8260   My Happiness Forever (with Gliders)/Get Up! Get Up! (You Sleepy Head)...............£100
57 Columbia DB 3879   Jim Dandy/Tra La La (with Gliders)...£150
57 London HLE 8396   I Can't Love You Enough/Still £100
57 London HLE 8442   Game Of Love/Jim Dandy Got Married £100
57 London HLE 8524   Humpty Dumpty Heart/Love Me Right..£50
58 London HLE 8638   Learning To Love/Substitute £50
58 London HLE 8672   Whipper Snapper/Harbour Lights £50
59 London HLE 8790   I Cried A Tear/St. Louis Blues £20
59 London HLE 8871   I Waited Too Long/You're Teasing Me £20
59 London HLE 8945   So High So Low/If You Love Me (I Won't Care) £20
60 London HLE 9023   Tiny Tim/For Love Of You £20
60 London HLE 9252   Bumble Bee/My Turn Will Come £20
61 London HLE 9300   You're The Boss/I'll Never Be Free (with Jimmy Ricks) £20
61 London HLK 9343   Saved/Don Juan £30
61 London HLK 9468   Hey, Memphis/Voodoo Voodoo £50
63 London HLK 9649   See See Rider/The Story Of My Love (I Had A Dream) £15
65 Atlantic AET 6009   THE BEST OF LAVERN BAKER (EP)..£60
58 London HA-E 2107   ROCK 'N' ROLL WITH LAVERN BAKER (LP, with thin card cover) £200
58 London Jazz LTZK 15139   SINGS BESSIE SMITH (LP)..£50
61 London HA-K 2422   SAVED (LP) £30
63 London HA-K 8074   SEE SEE RIDER (LP) £20
64 Atlantic ATL 5002   THE BEST OF LAVERN BAKER (LP, plum label)..£20
68 Atlantic 587/588 133   SEE SEE RIDER (LP, reissue) £30
84 Charly CRB 1072   REAL GONE GAL (LP) £15

MICKEY BAKER
70 Major Minor SMLP 67   IN BLUNDERLAND (LP)..£50
(see also Mighty Flea, Champion Jack Dupree, Mickey & Sylvia)

SALLY BAKER
70s Old Dog PUP 1   IN THE SPOTLIGHT (LP) £50

SAM BAKER
68 Monument MON 1009   I Believe In You/I'm Number One £30

TOM BAKER
79 Argo ZDSW 722/3   THE STRANGE CASE OF DR. JEKYLL & MR. HYDE (2-LP)...................................£20

TWO-TON BAKER
55 London HL 8121   Clink, Clank (In My Piggy Bank)/Mr. Froggie (Went A Courtin') £15

VICKY BAKER
64 London HLU 9856   No More Foolish Stories/Darling Say The Word.......................................£15

BAKER-GURVITZ ARMY
74 Vertigo 9103 201   BAKER-GURVITZ ARMY (LP, with lyric insert) £25

(see also Ginger Baker('s Airforce), Three Man Army, Parrish & Gurvitz, Gun, Sharks)

BAKERLOO
| 69 | Harvest HAR 5004 | Driving Backwards/Once Upon A Time | £25 |
| 69 | Harvest SHVL 762 | BAKERLOO (LP, gatefold, no EMI on label) | £350 |

(see also Colosseum, Uriah Heep, Humble Pie)

BAKER TWINS
| 64 | Pye 7N 15628 | He's No Good/Words Written On Water | £15 |

BALANCE
| 73 | Incus INCUS 11 | BALANCE (LP) | £100 |
| 73 | private pressing | IN FOR THE COUNT (LP) | £30 |

CHRIS BALDO
| 68 | Vogue VRS 7029 | Living For Your Love/Arretez - Vous A Saint Michel | £15 |

LONG JOHN BALDRY
64	United Artists UP 1056	You'll Be Mine (with Rod Stewart)/Up Above My Head (I Hear Music In The Air)	£50
65	United Artists UP 1078	I'm On To You Baby/Goodbye Baby	£20
65	United Artists UP 1107	How Long Will It Last/House Next Door	£30
66	United Artists UP 1136	The Drifter/Only A Fool Breaks His Own Heart	£50
66	United Artists UP 1158	Cuckoo/Bring My Baby Back To Me	£30
67	United Artists UP 1204	Only A Fool Breaks His Own Heart/Let Him Go (And Let Me Love You)	£20
65	United Artists UEP 1013	LONG JOHN'S BLUES (EP, with Hoochie Coochie Men)	£100
64	United Artists ULP 1081	LONG JOHN'S BLUES (LP, with Hoochie Coochie Men)	£50
66	United Artists (S)ULP 1146	LOOKING AT LONG JOHN (LP)	£40
68	Pye N(S)PL 18228	LET THERE BE LONG JOHN (LP, unissued)	£0
69	Pye N(S)PL 18306	WAIT FOR ME (LP)	£15

(see also Rod Stewart, Alexis Korner, Bluesology)

BALDWIN
| 67 | Decca F 22624 | The Land At Rainbows End/Beautiful Butterfly | £60 |

KEITH BALFOUR
| 69 | Studio One SO 2079 | Dreaming/Tired Of Waiting | £20 |

BALIL
| 93 | Rising High RSN 72 | Parasight/Island/Rosary Pilots/Avidya (12") | £20 |

CANNON BALL (CARL BRYAN) & JOHNNY MELODY (MOORE)
| 69 | Big Shot BI 518 | Parapinto/Cool Hand Luke | £100 |

DAVE BALL
| 83 | Some Bizarrre BIZL5 | IN STRICT TEMPO (LP) | £18 |

(see also Soft Cell)

ED BALL
| 95 | Creation CRELP 183 | WELCOME TO THE WONDERFUL WORLD OF (2-LP) | £15 |

(see also Times, O Level, TV Personalities, Teenage Filmstars)

FLORENCE BALLARD
| 68 | Stateside SS 2113 | It Doesn't Matter How I Say It (It's What I Say That Matters)/Goin' Out Of My Head | £75 |
| 68 | Stateside SS 2113 | It Doesn't Matter How I Say It (It's What I Say That Matters)/Goin' Out Of My Head (DJ Copy) | £100 |

(see also Supremes)

HANK BALLARD (& MIDNIGHTERS)
59	Parlophone R 4558	The Twist/Kansas City	£15
60	Parlophone R 4682	Finger Poppin' Time/I Love You, I Love You So-o-o	£15
60	Parlophone R 4688	The Twist/Teardrops On Your Letter	£15
60	Parlophone R 4707	Let's Go, Let's Go, Let's Go/If You'd Forgive Me	£15
61	Parlophone R 4728	The Hoochie Coochie Coo/LITTLE WILLIE JOHN: Walk Slow	£15
61	Parlophone R 4762	Let's Go Again/Deep Blue Sea	£35
61	Parlophone R 4771	The Continental Walk/What Is This I See	£15
61	Parlophone PMC 1158	SPOTLIGHT ON HANK BALLARD (LP)	£75
63	London HA 8101	THE JUMPIN' HANK BALLARD (LP)	£40

BALLOON CORPS
| 69 | Stateside SS8034 | Make It Right/Muddy Water | £20 |

BALLOON FARM
| 68 | London HLP 10185 | A Question Of Temperature/Hurtin' For Your Love | £120 |

BALLOONS
| 78 | Earwacks WAK 001 | Calling All Human Beings/(Love Runs) Through Your Elbow | £20 |

BALLS
| 71 | Wizard WIZ 101 | Fight For My Country/Janie Slow Down | £30 |

(see also Denny Laine, Lemon Tree, Trevor Burton, Uglys, Wizzard)

LORI BALMER
| 68 | Polydor 56293 | Treacle Brown/Four Faces West | £40 |

BALTIMORE & OHIO MARCHING BAND
67	Stateside SS 2065	Lapland/Condition Red	£60
67	Stateside SS 2065	Lapland/Condition Red (DJ copy)	£200
68	Stateside (S)SL 10231	LAPLAND (LP)	£20

BAMA WINDS
| 69 | Island ILPS 9096 | WINDY (LP) | £30 |

BAM BAM (1)
| 81 | Vox Populi VOP 001 | Polka Dot!/Crocodile Tears (p/s) | £20 |

BAM BAM (2)
88	Desire WANTX 7	Where's Your Child/(Suck Mix) (12", p/s)	£15

BAMBI
76	Sol-Doon SDR 019	Lady Of Lies/Somebody Told Me	£15

BAMBIS
64	Oriole CB 1965	Not Wrong/Handle With Care	£40
65	CBS 201778	Baby Blue/If This Is Love	£40

BAMBOO SHOOT
68	Columbia DB 8370	The Fox Has Gone To Ground/There And Back Again Lane	£200

BAMBOO ZOO
81	Phoney Gram PHOG 8101	LOOK! LISTEN! CONSUME! (LP)	£18

BAMBOOS
06	Tru Thoughts TRULP 092	STEP IT UP (LP)	£15
07	Tru Thoughts TRULP 125	RAWVILLE (LP)	£20

BANANA BUNCH
70	Page One POF 183	Tra-La-La Song/Funky Hoe	£15

(see also Nite People)

BANANARAMA
85	London NANPD 9	Do Not Disturb/Ghost (3- shaped picture discs sold separately with plinth to hold all three, PVC sleeve)	£15
86	London NANPD 11	More Than Physical/Venus/Scarlett (picture disc, PVC sleeve)	£30
87	London Records NANPP 13	I Heard A Rumour/Clean Cut Boy (Party Size) (p/s, posterbag)	£20
93	London Records NANPP 3.1	PLEASE YOURSELF (LP)	£15
15	Edsel BANANABOX 01	IN A BUNCH (THE SINGLES 1981-1993) (33-CD box set, poster, 48-page booklet)	£250
19	Strike Force Entertainment SFELP081D	VIVA (2-LP, reissue, g/f, RSD, blue neon vinyl)	£60
19	Strike Force Entertainment SFELP080D	DRAMA (2-LP, reissue, g/f, RSD, burgundy vinyl)	£50
19	In Synk SYNK1V	IN STEREO (LP, printed inner, clear vinyl)	£20
20	In Synk SYNK9LP	ULTRA VIOLET (LP, Reissue, Violet vinyl, some copies signed)	£35
22	In Synk SYNK25V	MASQUERADE (LP, red or blue transparent vinyl, printed inner)	£20
23	In Synk SYNK25VXD	MASQUERADE - THE UNMASKED EDITION (2-LP,1000-only, clear pink vinyl, printed inners)	£50

BANBARRA
76	United Artists UP 36113	Shack Up Part 1/ Shack Up Part 2	£15
85	Stateside 12STATES 1	Shack Up (Extended)/Shack Up (Part 1)/Shack Up (Part II) (12", p/s)	£25

BANCO DE GAIA
94	Planet Dog BARKLP 003	MAYA (2-LP)	£20
94	Planet Dog BARKLP 003	MAYA (3-LP, numbered)	£25
95	Planet Dog BARKLP 011 S	LAST TRAIN TO LHASA (4LP, limited edition)	£50
97	Planet Dog BARKLP 025	BIG MEN CRY (2-LP)	£20

THE BAND
68	Capitol CL 15559	The Weight/I Shall Be Released (artist credit: Jaime Robbie Robertson. Rick Danko, Richard Manuel, Garth Hudson, Levon Helm (the Band)) (demo)	£30
68	Capitol CL 15559	The Weight/I Shall Be Released (artist credit: Jaime Robbie Robertson. Rick Danko, Richard Manuel, Garth Hudson, Levon Helm (the Band))	£25
69	Capitol CL 15613	Up On Cripple Creek/The Night They Drove Old Dixie Down (Demo)	£20
69	Capitol CL 15613	Up On Cripple Creek/The Night They Drove Old Dixie Down	£15
69	Capitol CL 15629	Rag Mama Rag/The Unfaithful Servant (Demo)	£20
69	Capitol CL 15767	Ain't Got No Home/Get Up Jake (Demo)	£20
68	Capitol T 2955	MUSIC FROM BIG PINK (LP, black/rainbow label, mono)	£70
68	Capitol ST 2955	MUSIC FROM BIG PINK (LP, black/rainbow label, stereo)	£40
69	Capitol EST 132	THE BAND (LP, 1st pressing, lemon yellow label, textured sleeve)	£20
70	Capitol EA-SW 425	STAGE FRIGHT (LP, 1st pressing, lemon yellow labels, gatefold sleeve and insert)	£15
71	Capitol EA ST 651	CAHOOTS (LP)	£15
72	Capitol E-ST 2955	MUSIC FROM BIG PINK (LP, reissue, orange labels)	£15
72	Capitol E-ST 132	THE BAND (LP, reissue, orange labels)	£15
97	EMI LPCENT 23	THE BAND (LP, reissue, EMI 100 Centenary, stickered sleeve)	£15

(see also Levon & The Hawks, Bob Dylan, Ronnie Hawkins, Robbie Robertson)

BANDA BLACK RIO
96	Universal Sound US LP3	THE BEST OF BANDA BLACK RIO (LP)	£30

B & THE FAMILY
16	Super Disco Edits SDE 19	A Good Time/You're Gonna Love Me	£20

BANDITS
85	Hosspig HPG1	Treasure Trove/Right In The Head (p/s)	£25

BANDITZ
80	Phaeton SPIN 2	JCB/Damage Your Health (p/s)	£15

BAND OF ANGELS
64	United Artists UP 1049	Not True As Yet/Me	£15
64	United Artists UP 1066	She'll Never Be You/Gonna Make A Woman Of You	£15
66	Piccadilly 7N 35279	Leave It To Me/Too Late My Love	£15
66	Piccadilly 7N 35292	Invitation/Cheat And Lie	£100

(see also Mike D'Abo, Manfred Mann)

BAND OF JOY
78	Poydor 2310588	BAND OF JOY (LP, with lyric insert)	£30

BAND OF MERCY & SALVATION
69   Duke DU 20   Suffering Stink/BOB MELODY: The Break (B-side actually by Winston Francis) £200

BANDOGGS
78   Transatlantic LTRA 504   BANDOGGS (LP, cream label)...£18
(see also Peter & Chris Coe)

BANDULU
93   Infonet INF003LP   GUIDANCE (2-LP) £25
94   Infonet INF006LP   ANTIMATTERS (2-LP) £20

BANDY LEGS
74   WWW WWS 01   Ride Ride/Don't Play Games £20
76   Jet JET 783   Bet You Can't Dance/Circles £20
(see also Quartz)

BANG (1)
72   EST 11015   BANG (LP) £60
(see also Quartz)

BANG (2)
72   Capitol CL15722   Questions/Future Shock £20

ED BANGER
81   Spiv DIV 1   I've Just Had My Car Nicked/P.C. Plod/Sponge (p/s, with photo insert) £20
(see also Nosebleeds, Slaughter & The Dogs)

BANGOR FLYING CIRCUS
70   Stateside-Dunhill SSL 5022 BANGOR FLYING CIRCUS (LP) £40

BANG THE PARTY
87   Warriors Dance WDT 100   I Feel Good All Over/Jacques Theme (Main Mix)/Jacques Theme (Alternative Mix)
                               (12") £18

DEVENDRA BANHART
05   XL XLLP 185   REJOICING IN THE HANDS/NINO ROJO (2-LP) £25
13   Nonesuch 534455-1   MALA (2-LP with poster, CD and 7") £15

BANISHED
93   Peaceville CC 3   Altered Minds/Cast Out The Flesh (blue vinyl, p/s) £15
93   Deaf DEAF 13   DELIVER ME UNTO PAIN (LP)...£25
(see also Baphomet)

BANKRUPT
84   SG 085   Joy Of Love/Acapella Version/Untitled/Untitled (12", stamped white labels) £40

BESSIE BANKS
64   Red Bird BC 106   Go Now/Sounds Like My Baby..£100
64   Red Bird BC 106   Go Now/Sounds Like My Baby(DJ Copy)...£150
67   Verve VS 563   I Can't Make It (Without You Baby)/Need You £120
67   Verve VS 563   I Can't Make It (Without You Baby)/Need You (DJ Copy) £100
68   Soul City SC 105   Go Now/Sounds Like My Baby (reissue)...£25
75   Contempo CS 2070   Baby You Sure Know How To Get To Me/Try To Leave Me If You Can £35

DARRELL BANKS
66   London HL 10070   Open The Door To Your Heart/Our Love (Is In The Pocket) (demo only) £1000
66   London HL 10070   Open The Door To Your Heart/Our Love (Is In The Pocket) (1 known stock copy) £12000
66   Stateside SS 536   Open The Door To Your Heart/Our Love (Is In The Pocket) (1st pressing demo with
                               white/red label) £200
66   Stateside SS 536   Open The Door To Your Heart/Our Love (Is In The Pocket) (1st pressing) £40
66   Stateside SS 536   Open The Door To Your Heart/Our Love (Is In The Pocket) (2st pressing demo with
                               green/white label) £100
66   Stateside SS 536   Open The Door To Your Heart/Our Love (Is In The Pocket) (2nd pressing).................£20
67   Atlantic 584 120   Angel Baby (Don't You Ever Leave Me)/Look Into The Eyes Of A Fool..................£70
69   Stax STAX 124   Just Because Your Love Is Gone/I'm The One Who Loves You (Demo) £150
69   Stax STAX 124   Just Because Your Love Is Gone/I'm The One Who Loves You £125
77   Atlantic K 10879   Angel Baby (Don't You Ever Leave Me)/Look Into The Eyes Of A Fool (reissue) £20
69   Stax SXATS 1011   HERE TO STAY (LP) £50

HOMER BANKS
66   Liberty LIB 12028   A Lot Of Love/Fighting To Win £30
66   Liberty LIB 12028   A Lot Of Love/Fighting To Win (DJ Copy) £60
67   Liberty LIB 12047   60 Minutes Of Your Love/Do You Know What £30
67   Liberty LIB 12047   60 Minutes Of Your Love/Do You Know What (DJ Copy)......................................£60
67   Liberty LIB 12060   Hooked By Love/Lady Of Stone £40
67   Liberty LIB 12060   Hooked By Love/Lady Of Stone (DJ Copy)..£75
68   Minit MLF 11004   Round The Clock Lover Man/Foolish Hearts Break Fast..£15
68   Minit MLF 11007   60 Minutes Of Your Love/A Lot Of Love..£15
70   Liberty LBF 15392   60 Minutes Of Your Love/I Know You Know I Know You Know...............................£15

LARRY BANKS
67   Stateside SS 579   I Don't Wanna Do It/I'm Coming Home £60
67   Stateside SS 579   I Don't Wanna Do It/I'm Coming Home (DJ Copy)...£75
09   Kent 6T 25   My Life Is No Better/JACKIE DAY: Get To Steppin £20

LLOYD BANKS
66   Reaction 591 008   We'll Meet Again/Look Out Girl...£20

PETER BANKS
73   Sovereign SVNA 7256   PETER BANKS (LP, gatefold sleeve) £40
(see also Syndicats, Syn, Neat Change, Yes, Flash, Jan Akkerman)

MINT VALUE £

TONY BANKS
79	Charisma CAS 1148	A CURIOUS FEELING (LP, printed inner)	£15
83	Atlantic 78 00731	THE WICKED LADY (OST) (LP)	£15
91	Virgin 211 638	STILL (LP, printed inner)	£30
15	Esoteric ECLEC 42507	A CHORD TOO FAR (4CD box set, booklet)	£35

(see also Genesis)

BANNED
77	Can't Eat EAT 1 UP	Little Girl/CPGJ's (stamped white labels, in handmade p/s)	£60
77	Can't Eat EAT 1 UP	Little Girl/CPGJ's (stamped white labels)	£25

(see also Gryphon)

BANSHEES
64	Columbia DB 7361	I Got A Woman/Don't Say Goodnight And Mean Goodbye	£25
65	Columbia DB 7530	Big Buildin'/Mockingbird	£20
65	Columbia DB 7752	I'm Gonna Keep On Loving You/Yes Indeed	£15

BANTAM
70	COUN 248	BANTAM (LP, private pressing, white label, hand-made wraparound sleeve)	£175

PATO BANTON
85	Ariwa ARI LP 023	MAD PROFESSOR CAPTURES PATO BANTON (LP)	£15

STARKY BANTON
97	Dub Organiser DOT 101	I And I Saw Dem Coming/I And I Dub/The Herb/Herbal Dub (10")	£15

BAPHOMET
92	Peaceville VILE 31	THE DEAD SHALL INHERIT (LP)	£80

(see also Banished)

BAPTEME DU FEU
17	La VIda Es Un Mus MUS 136	RIXE EP (p/s, clear vinyl with extra wraparound sleeve, lyric sheet and sticker)	£25

DENISE BAPTISTE
80	Gigi G 001	Weak In The Knees/EXILE BAND: Instrumental	£50

SELWYN BAPTISTE
70	Black Swan BW 1402	Mo' Bay/RECO'S ALL STARS: Going West	£20

BARBARA & BRENDA
68	Direction 58-3799	Never Love A Robin/Sally's Party	£15

BARBARA & ERNIE
71	Atlantic 2466 015	PRELUDE TO (LP)	£50

BARBARA & WINSTON
64	Island WI 418	The Dream/I Love You	£30

BARBARELLA
92	Eye Q 4509 90679 1	THE ART OF DANCE (2-LP)	£25

BARBARIANS
65	Stateside SS 449	Are You A Boy Or Are You A Girl/Take It Or Leave It	£25
66	Stateside SS 497	Moulty/I'll Keep On Seeing You	£30

BARBECUE BOB
67	Kokomo K 1002	GEORGIA BLUES NO. 1 (LP, 99 copies only)	£100

BARBED WIRE
86	Oi Records OIR 006	THE AGE THAT DIDN'T CARE (LP)	£20

JOHN HENRY BARBEE
65	Storyville 616 013	I AIN'T GONNA PICK NO MORE COTTON (LP)	£20
65	Storyville 670 171	PORTRAITS IN BLUES VOLUME 9 (LP)	£25

CHRIS BARBER AND HIS BAND
67	Marmalade 598 005	Catcall/Mercy Mercy Mercy	£75
69	Marmalade 558 013	Battersea Rain Dance/Sleepy Joe	£25
69	Marmalade 608 009	BATTERSEA RAIN DANCE (LP, as Chris Barber & His Band)	£50
69	Polydor 2384 020	BATTERSEA RAIN DANCE (LP) (2nd Pressing)	£25

CHRIS BARBER SOUL BAND
65	Columbia DB 7461	Finishing Straight/Morning Train	£30

(see also Louis Jordan & Chris Barber)

EDDIE BARCLAY & QUINCY JONES
58	Felsted PDL 85056	EDDIE AND QUINCY (LP)	£15

RUE BARCLAY & PEGGY DUNCAN
54	London HL 8033	Tongue Tied Boy/River Of Tears	£15

BARCLAY JAMES HARVEST
68	Parlophone R 5693	Early Morning/Mr. Sunshine	£35
69	Harvest HAR 5003	Brother Thrush/Poor Wages	£15
70	Harvest HAR 5025	Taking Some Time On/The Iron Maiden	£15
70	Harvest SHVL 770	BARCLAY JAMES HARVEST (LP, 1st pressing, textured gatefold sleeve, 'The Gramophone Co. Ltd' label text, no EMI box on label)	£50
71	Harvest SHVL 788	ONCE AGAIN (LP, gatefold sleeve, no EMI box on label)	£30
71	Harvest SHVL 794	BARCLAY JAMES HARVEST AND OTHER SHORT STORIES (LP, gatefold sleeve)	£25
72	Harvest Q4SHVL 788	ONCE AGAIN (LP, quadrophonic)	£40
73	Harvest SHSP 4023	BABY JAMES HARVEST (LP, inner)	£25
76	Harvest SHVL 770	BARCLAY JAMES HARVEST (LP, re-pressing, gatefold sleeve, repressing EMI box on label and 'EMI Records Ltd')	£25

(see also John Lees)

PETER BARDENS
70	Transatlantic TRA 222	THE ANSWER (LP, white/lilac label with 't' logo)	£100
71	Transatlantic TRA 243	PETER BARDENS (LP, gatefold sleeve, side one label is multi-coloured)	£50
76	Transatlantic TRASAM 36	VINTAGE '69 (LP, featuring Peter Green, clear vinyl)	£20
76	Transatlantic TRASAM 36	VINTAGE '69 (LP, featuring Peter Green)	£15

(see also Cheynes, Peter B's, Shotgun Express, Them, Village, Camel, Steve Tilston)

BARDO POND
11	Agitated AGIT 009	Fallen/CARLTON MELTON: Slow Growth (12", clear vinyl, 100 only)	£15
14	Fire Blaze 340	LOOKING FOR ANOTHER PLACE (12" EP)	£15
15	Fire Blaze 420	IS THERE A HEAVEN? (12" EP)	£18
01	Matador Ole 459-1	DILATE (2-LP)	£50
03	ATP ATPRLP6	ON THE ELLIPSE (2-LP, gatefold)	£40
12	Latitudes GMT 029V	YNTRA (LP, with insert)	£20
13	Fire FV 291	TICKET CRYSTALS (2-LP, reissue)	£25
13	Fire BLAZE 207	RISE ABOVE IT ALL (2-LP)	£15

BRIGITTE BARDOT
66	Vogue VRS 7018	Mister Sun/Gang Gang (p/s)	£100
66	Vogue VRS 7018	Mister Sun/Gang Gang	£30
68	Pye International 7N 25450	Harley-Davidson/Contact (p/s)	£100
68	Pye International 7N 25450	Harley-Davidson/Contact	£20
63	Philips BL 7561	BRIGITTE BARDOT (LP)	£120
64	Philips B 77 984	'BB'	£100

BARDS (1)
68	Capitol CL 15536	The Owl And The Pussycat/Light Of Love	£15

BARDS (2)
71	Folk Heritage FHR 019M	TIME FOR THE BARDS (LP)	£150

BARDS OF BARLEYCORN
77	Beet Music BMR 101	WHEN GRANDMA USED TO CALL (LP)	£20

BARE FOOT
71	Pye 7N 45110	Frightened/Girl Are You A Woman Now (Promo copies say "Bear Foot")	£20

BAREFOOT BLUES BAND
70	Beacon BEA 163	Can't You See/Sunday Morning Barefoot Blues	£25

JOHN BARHAM & ASHISH KHAN
73	Elektra K 42129	JUGALBANDI (LP)	£15

MARK BARKAN
67	Stateside SS 2064	A Great Day For The Clown/Pity The Woman (DJ copy)	£40

BAR-KAYS
78	Stax 12 STAX 505	Holy Ghost/Monster (12")	£15
69	Atco 228 030	SOUL FINGER (LP)	£20
69	Stax SXATS 1009	GOTTA GROOVE (LP)	£20
71	Stax 2362 003	BLACK ROCK (LP)	£20
73	Stax 2325 087	DO YOU SEE WHAT I SEE? (LP)	£20
76	Stax STX 1033	COLD BLOODED (LP)	£20
77	Mercury 9100 048	FLYING HIGH ON YOUR LOVE (LP)	£15

(see also Otis Redding)

DAVE BARKER
70	Duke DU 74	Funkey Reggae/TOMMY McCOOK & SUPERSONICS: I Love You My Baby (B-side actually by Versatiles)	£40
70	Punch PH 20	Prisoner Of Love/BUSTY & UPSETTERS: Soul Juice	£25
70	Punch PH 22	You Betray Me/Will You Still Love Me Tomorrow?	£30
70	Punch PH 25	Shocks Of Mighty Parts 1 & 2	£15
70	Punch PH 42	Reggae Meeting/MARTIN ALL STARS: Soul Bone	£20
70	Jackpot JP 736	The Fastest Man Alive/NORMAN GRANT: Bloodshot Eyes	£15
70	Jackpot JP 742	Wet Version/I Got To Get Away	£30
70	Jackpot JP 745	Girl Of My Dreams/On Broadway	£20
70	High Note HS 049	She Want It/FIRST GENERATION: Give Him Up	£30
70	Randy's RAN 503	October/RANDY'S ALLSTARS: Time Out	£70
70	Unity UN 567	Blessed Are The Meek (with Slim Smith)/JEFF BARNES & UNIQUES: The People's Voice	£20
70	Techniques TE915	Karatae/Version	£15
70	Upsetter US 331	Shocks Of Mighty/Set Me Free (with Upsetters)	£25
70	Upsetter US 344	Some Sympathy/UNTOUCHABLES: Tender Love	£30
70	Upsetter US 347	Sound Underground/Don't Let The Sun Catch You Crying (features the Wailers)	£50
71	Upsetter US 358	Shocks '71/HURRICANES: You've Got To Be Mine	£20
71	Upsetter US 362	Groove Me/UPSETTERS: Screwdriver	£30
71	Upsetter US 364	What A Confusion/UPSETTERS: Confusion - Version 2	£50
71	Ackee ACK 113	Johnny Dollar/Version	£30
71	Ackee ACK 119	Life Of A Millionaire/Version	£20
71	Trojan TR 7851	Sex Machine/You Left Me And Gone (both sides with Aggrovators)	£20
71	Punch PH 69	What A Confusion/BOB MARLEY: Small Axe	£50
71	Supreme SUP 228	Double Heavy/Johnny Dollar	£30
71	Downtown DT 482	Only The Strong Survive/Only The Strong - Version	£15
72	Fab FAB 25	Green Grow The Lilacs/JIMMY RILEY: Keep An Eye (On Your Closest Friend) (white label)	£15
80	Black Jack BJD 4507	Glow Of Love/Version (12")	£20
76	Trojan TRL 127	PRISONER OF LOVE (LP)	£60

MINT VALUE £

(see also Glen & Dave, Bobby & Dave, Aggrovators, David Crooks, Dennis Alcapone, Don Drummond, Owen Gary, Lizzy & Dennis, Bob Marley, Lester Sterling, Busty Brown)

RONNIE BARKER
69	MGM MGM-C-8107	A PINT OF OLD AND FILTHY (LP)	£20

STAN BARKER
79	Nelson N1001	VOLUME 1 (LP)	£40

BARK PSYCHOSIS
90	Cheree CHEREE 6T	All Different Things/By-Blow (12", p/s)	£15
90	Cheree CHEREE 10T	Nothing Feels/I Know (12", p/s)	£15
91	3rd Stone STONE 004T	Manman/Blood Rush/Tooled Up (12", p/s)	£15
92	3rd Stone STONE 006T	Scum (1-sided etched 12", p/s)	£30
94	Circa YRT 117	Blue/Hex/Big Shot (Alice's Cheshire Cat Mix) (12", p/s, white vinyl)	£15
94	Circa CIRCA 29	HEX (LP, printed inner)	£120
04	Fire FIRELP 90	CODENAME: DUSTSUCKER (LP, printed inner)	£100
17	Fire Records FIRELP 084	HEX (2LP, reissue, 45rpm, 180g, printed inners, hype sticker)	£80
18	Fire Records FIRELP 090	CODENAME: DUSTSUCKER (2LP, reissue, gatefold, printed inners, postcard, 180g)	£30
19	Hidden Art HI-ART 23LP	INDEPENDENCY (2LP, first vinyl issue of 1994 CD, red vinyl, RSD)	£35
23	Rolling Heads Ltd. RH001LP	SCUM (LP, reissue of 1992 12", RSD)	£20

BARLASTON DOWN
73	Decca F13321	Always/Mean Woman Mambo	£15

BARLEY BREE
67	Piccadilly 7N 35393	Sometime In The Morning/Save Your Love	£15

BARNES/ADAMS
60s	Lyntone LYN 1021	When It Comes To The Crunch (It's Smiths Time)/Rhythm And Crunch (flexi, p/s)	£15

BARNEY J. BARNES & INTRO.
67	Decca F 12662	It Must Be Love/Can't Stand The Pain	£100

DENA BARNES
80	Grapevine GRP 141	If You Ever Walked Out Of My Life/Who Am I	£40

JEFF BARNES
70	Unity UN 568	1,000 Tons Of Version/Wake The Nation (B-side with Hugh Roy)	£50
70	Pama PM 802	Jeff Barnes Thing/LENNOX BROWN: Lover's Mood	£30
71	Smash SMA 2313	Wake The Nation (with Hugh Roy)/1,000 Tons Of Version	£40
71	Gas 163	Peoples Version (work Out) (with PAT KELLY)/TONY LEE & PAT KELLY: Too Late	£40

(see also Hugh Roy, Dave Barker, Darker Shade Of Blue, Delroy Wilson)

J.J. BARNES
67	Polydor 56722	Day Tripper/Deeper In Love	£35
69	Stax STAX 130	Baby Please Come Back Home/Easy Living	£35
78	Contempo CLS 2105	She's Mine/Erroll Flynn	£20
75	Contempo CLP 520	THE GROOVESVILLE MASTERS (LP)	£50
77	Contempo CLP 604	SARA SMILE (LP)	£20

J.J. BARNES/STEVE MANCHA
69	Stax SXATS 1012	RARE STAMPS (LP)	£60

LLOYD BARNES
64	Blue Beat BB 235	Time Is Hard/BUSTER'S ALLSTARS: Reincarnation	£60

RICHARD BARNES
70	Philips 630 8027	RICHARD BARNES (LP, black/silver label)	£40

(see also Quiet Five, Tony Hazzard)

SIDNEY BARNES
76	Charly CYS 1007	I Hurt On The Other Side/Good Lovin' (as Sid Barnes)	£18

TOWANDA BARNES
78	Grapevine GRP 116	You Don't Mean It/SAM WILLIAMS: Love Slipped Thru' My Fingers	£25

ERIC BARNET(T)
68	Gas GAS 100	The Horse (actually by Theo Beckford & Group)/Action Line (actually by Versatiles)	£50
69	Gas GAS 106	Te Ta Toe (act. by Theo Beckford & Group)/MILTON BOOTHE: Lonely And Blue	£40
69	Crab CRAB 37	Quaker City/Double Up (both actually by Theo Beckford & Group)	£50
70	Gas GAS 130	Pink Shark/Swing Free (both actually by Theo Beckford & Group, white labels only)	£40
70	Gas GAS 147	Bumper To Bumper/Fat Turkey (both actually by Theo Beckford & Group)	£30

(see also Theo[philus] Beckford)

H.B. BARNUM
61	Fontana H 299	Lost Love/Hallelujah	£15
65	Capitol CL 15391	The Record (Baby I Love You)/I'm A Man	£40
65	Capitol CL 15391	The Record (Baby I Love You)/I'm A Man (DJ Copy)	£80
79	Capitol CL 16067	Heartbreaker/BOBBY PARIS: I Walked Away	£15
64	RCA Victor RCX 7147	THE GREAT H.B. BARNUM (EP)	£150
62	RCA Victor RD/SF 7500	THE BIG VOICE OF BARNUM . . . H.B., THAT IS (LP, mono/stereo)	£15
63	RCA Victor RD/SF 7543	EVERYBODY LOVES H.B. (LP, mono/stereo)	£15

(see also Robins)

CARL BARON & CHEETAHS
63	Columbia DB 7162	This Is Only The Beginning/Beg Borrow Or Steal	£15

BARON WITH HIS POUNDING PIANO
65	Sue WI 398	Is A Blue Bird Blue/In The Mood	£50

(see also V.I.P.'s)

BARONS (U.S.)
57	London HLP 8391	Don't Walk Out/Once In A Lifetime £1000
57	London HLP 8391	Don't Walk Out/Once In A Lifetime (78) £40

BARONS OF SOUL
05	Grapevine 2000 151	You Need Love/You Need Love (unissued, demo copies only) £40

BARRACUDAS
79	Cells CELLOUT 1	I Want My Woody Back/Subway Surfin' (p/s) £20
80	Zonophone Z 5	Summer Fun/Chevy Baby (p/s, with stickers) £15
80	Zonophone ZONO 103	DROP OUT WITH THE BARRACUDAS (LP)..£18
83	Closer CL0001	MEAN TIME (LP) £20

MARTIN BARRE
93	Presshouse MBSBCD 92	A SUMMER BAND (LP, 500 only) £30

(see also Jethro Tull)

DICKIE BARRETT
58	MGM MGM 976	Smoke Gets In Your Eyes/Remember Me £20

RICHARD BARRETT & CHANTELS
59	HMV POP 609	Come Softly To Me/Walking Through Dreamland..£20

(see also Chantels)

RICHIE BARRETT
62	London HLK 9552	Some Other Guy/Tricky Dicky £40

SYD BARRETT

SINGLES
69	Harvest HAR 5009	Octopus/Golden Hair £250
69	Harvest HAR 5009	Octopus/Golden Hair (Promo with mispelt 'Barratt' and release date 14.11.69) £350
88	Strange Fruit SFPS 043	THE PEEL SESSIONS (12", EP) £15

ALBUMS : ORIGINAL HARVEST ALBUMS
70	Harvest SHVL 765	THE MADCAP LAUGHS (LP, laminated sleeve, no EMI box on label) £300
70	Harvest SHVL 765	THE MADCAP LAUGHS (LP, matt gatefold sleeve, no EMI box on label) £150
70	Harvest SHSP 4007	BARRETT (LP, 1st pressing, laminated sleeve, 'Gramophone Co. Ltd' label text with no EMI box on label) £300
70	Harvest SHSP 4007	BARRETT (LP, 1st pressing, textured flipback sleeve, 'Gramophone Co. Ltd' and no EMI logo on label) £150

ALBUMS : REISSUES
71	Harvest SHSP 4007	BARRETT (LP, 2nd pressing, textured flipback sleeve, 'Gramophone Co. Ltd' and one EMI box on label. Some copies with EMI box on label) £100
72	Harvest SHSP 4007	BARRETT (LP, 3rd pressing, textured non-flipback sleeve, 'Gramophone Co. Ltd' and one EMI box on label) £65
73	Harvest SHVL 765	THE MADCAP LAUGHS (2nd pressing, boxed EMI logo) £70
74	Harvest SHSP 4007	BARRETT (LP, 4th pressing, textured non-flipback sleeve, 'EMI Records Ltd' and one EMI box on label. Some copies with EMI box on B-side only)...£50
74	Harvest SHDW 404	SYD BARRETT (2-LP, reissue of "Madcap" & "Barrett", gatefold sleeve)..........................£40
82	Harvest SHVL 765	THE MADCAP LAUGHS (LP, 3rd pressing, boxed EMI logo, with "copying and hiring of this record prohibited" at bottom of label)...£30
82	Harvest SHSP 4007	BARRETT (LP, 5th pressing, textured sleeve, text at top of label begins. 'All Rights Of The Producer...' One EMI box on label'Gramophone Co. Ltd'. One EMI box) £50
87	Harvest SHVL 765	THE MADCAP LAUGHS (LP, black label) £20
86	Harvest SHVL 765	BARRETT (LP, 6th pressing, non-textured sleeve, with or without barcode on back of sleeve with black 'Harvest' label)..£30
88	Harvest SHSP 4126	OPEL (LP, gatefold sleeve, black label) £20
97	Harvest 7423 855663 18	THE MADCAP LAUGHS (LP, 180gm reissue, heavy quality sleeve) £20
97	Harvest 7423 821450 11	BARRETT (LP, 180gm reissue, heavy quality sleeve) £25
99	Simply Vinyl SVLP 153	OPEL (LP, 180gm reissue, heavy quality gatefold sleeve)...£25
00	Simply Vinyl SVLP 281	BARRETT (LP, 180gm reissue, heavy quality gatefold sleeve) £22
00	Simply Vinyl SVLP 289	THE MADCAP LAUGHS (LP, 180gm reissue, heavy quality gatefold sleeve) £20
10	Harvest 985031	AN INTRODUCTION TO (2-LP)..£20

(see also Pink Floyd)

WILD WILLY BARRETT
86	Galvanised DIP 1	ORGANIC BONDAGE (LP, with Stephen Two Names; in wooden sleeve)............................£15

(see also John Otway/Wild Willy Barrett)

RAY BARRETTO
69	London HL 10262	Acid/Mercy Mercy Baby (withdrawn) £100
67	Island ILP 946	EL WATUSI (LP)..£40
69	London HA/SH 8383	ACID (LP)..£50

BARRIER
68	Eyemark EMS 1013	Georgie Brown/Dawn Breaks Through (in handmade p/s) £450
68	Eyemark EMS 1013	Georgie Brown/Dawn Breaks Through £250
68	Philips BF 1692	The Tide Is Turning/Place In Your Heart £15
68	Philips BF 1731	Spot The Lights/Uh..£70

BARRINO BROTHERS
72	Invictus INV 523	I Shall Not Be Moved/When Love Was A Child £15

BARRON KNIGHTS
64	Columbia DB 7188	Comin' Home Baby/Peanut Butter £40
67	Columbia DB 8161	Lazy Fat People/In The Night £15
72	Penny Farthing PEN 786	You're All I Need/Nothin' Doin' £15
66	Columbia SEG 8526	THOSE VERSATILE BARRON KNIGHTS (EP) £15

AL BARRY

70	Doctor Bird DB 1502	Morning Sun/MARKONIANS: Over And Over	£400
71	Creole 1005	Down We Go/It Pays To Do Good	£30
12	Doctor Bird DB 1502	Morning Sun/MARKONIANS: Over And Over (reissue, jukebox centre)	£25

(see also Desmond Dekker & Aces)

DAVE BARRY & SARA BERNER

56	London HLU 8324	Out Of This World With Flying Saucers Parts 1 & 2 (Tri Gold)	£40

JOE BARRY

62	Mercury ZEP 10130	A FOOL TO CARE (EP)	£40

JOHN BARRY (SEVEN)

SINGLES

57	Parlophone R 4363	Zip Zip/Three Little Fishes (as John Barry & The Seven)	£40
58	Parlophone R 4394	Every Which Way/You've Gotta Way (as John Barry Seven)	£15
64	Columbia DB 7414	Twenty-Four Hours Ago/Seven Faces	£20
63	Ember EMB S 181	007/From Russia With Love (in p/s)	£15

EPs

58	Parlophone GEP 8737	THE BIG BEAT (as John Barry Seven)	£40
62	Columbia SEG 8138	BEAT GIRL (as John Barry Seven, with Adam Faith)	£20
63	United Artists UEP 1011	FROM RUSSIA WITH LOVE (soundtrack)	£15
64	United Artists UEP 1012	GOLDFINGER (soundtrack)	£15
65	Ember EMB EP 4551	JAMES BOND IS BACK	£25
65	United Artists UEP 1015	THUNDERBALL: Thunderball/Death Of Fiona/Bond Below Disco Volante/ Mr Kiss Kiss Bang Bang (soundtrack)	£15

ALBUMS

60	Columbia 33SX 1225	BEAT GIRL (soundtrack, with Adam Faith)	£40
61	Columbia 33SX 1358	STRINGBEAT (mono)	£30
61	Columbia SCX 3401	STRINGBEAT (stereo)	£35
63	United Artists (S)ULP 1052	FROM RUSSIA WITH LOVE (soundtrack, mono)	£25
63	United Artists (S)ULP 1052	FROM RUSSIA WITH LOVE (soundtrack, stereo)	£25
63	Colpix PXL 459	ELIZABETH TAYLOR IN LONDON (mono)	£20
63	Colpix PXL 459	ELIZABETH TAYLOR IN LONDON (stereo)	£20
64	Ember NR 5012	ZULU (soundtrack, yellow/orange label, flipback sleeve)	£20
64	Stateside S(S)L 10087	MAN IN THE MIDDLE (soundtrack, with Lionel Bart)	£15
64	United Artists (S)ULP 1076	GOLDFINGER (soundtrack, mono)	£15
64	United Artists (S)ULP 1076	GOLDFINGER (soundtrack, stereo)	£15
65	Ember NR 5025	JOHN BARRY PLAYS 007	£20
65	CBS BPG 62530	THE IPCRESS FILE (soundtrack, mono only)	£150
65	United Artists ULP 1104	THE KNACK (AND HOW TO GET IT) (soundtrack)	£80
65	United Artists (S)ULP 1110	THUNDERBALL (soundtrack, mono)	£15
65	United Artists (S)ULP 1110	THUNDERBALL (soundtrack, stereo)	£15
66	Fontana STL 5387	THE WRONG BOX (soundtrack, release cancelled)	£0
66	CBS (S)BPG 62869	THE QUILLER MEMORANDUM (soundtrack, mono)	£25
66	CBS (S)BPG 62869	THE QUILLER MEMORANDUM (soundtrack, stereo)	£25
67	United Artists (S)ULP 1168	THE WHISPERERS (soundtrack)	£40
67	United Artists (S)ULP 1171	YOU ONLY LIVE TWICE (soundtrack)	£15
68	Stateside S(S)L 10263	DEADFALL (soundtrack, Shirley Bassey on 1 track)	£20
69	United Artists UAS 29020	ON HER MAJESTY'S SECRET SERVICE (soundtrack, foldout sleeve)	£25
69	MCA MUPS 360	BOOM! (soundtrack, with Georgie Fame)	£30
71	United Artists UAS 29216	DIAMONDS ARE FOREVER (LP, soundtrack)	£25
71	Probe SPB 1027	THE LAST VALLEY (soundtrack, with insert)	£15
72	Ember SE 8008	JOHN BARRY REVISITED (foldout sleeve, initial pressing in 'nude' gatefold sleeve)	£30

(see also Alan Bown, Chad & Jeremy, Adam Faith, Elizabeth Taylor, Desmond Lane, Johnny Pearson, Jim Lowe, Lyn Paul, Lance Fortune, Alan Haven,, Marion Ryan, Dick Kallman)

LEN BARRY

65	Cameo Parkway P 969	Hearts Are Trump/Little White House	£30
65	Brunswick 05942	1-2-3/Bullseye (DJ Copy)	£30
66	Brunswick 05949	Like A Baby/Happiness (DJ Copy)	£30
66	Brunswick 05955	Somewhere/It's A Crying Shame (DJ Copy)	£30
66	Brunswick 05962	It's That Time Of The Year/Happily Ever After (DJ Copy)	£30
66	Brunswick 05966	I Struck It Rich/Love Is	£20
66	Brunswick 05966	I Struck It Rich/Love Is (DJ Copy)	£40
67	RCA RCA 1588	The Moving Finger Writes/Our Love	£20
67	RCA RCA 1588	The Moving Finger Writes/Our Love (DJ Copy)	£30
73	Paramount PARA 3031	Heaven And Earth/I'm Marching To The Music	£15
66	Cameo Parkway CPE 556	HAVIN' A GOOD TIME (EP)	£30
65	Brunswick LAT 8637	1-2-3 (LP)	£25
66	Brunswick LAT 8656	IT'S THAT TIME OF YEAR (LP, unreleased, no sleeve)	£750
66	Cameo Parkway C 1082	LEN BARRY AND THE DOVELLS (LP)	£30
69	Bulldog BDL 1013	MORE FROM THE 1-2-3 MAN (LP)	£20

(see also Dovells)

SANDRA BARRY (& THE BOYS)

64	Decca F 11851	Really Gonna Shake/When We Get Married (as Sandra Barry & Boys)	£80

(see also Boys, Sandra Alfred, Slack Alice)

BARRY & THE TAMERLANES

63	Warner Bros WB 116	I Wonder What She's Doing Tonight/Don't Go	£20
64	Warner Bros WM 8145	I WONDER WHAT SHE'S DOING TONIGHT (LP)	£40

(see also Barry De Vorzon)

BARRY SISTERS (U.S.)
56	London HLA 8248	Cha Cha Joe/Baby Come A Little Closer	£20
56	London HLA 8304	Till You Come Back To Me/Intrigue	£70
60	Columbia 33SX 1309	SIDE BY SIDE (LP)	£15

LIONEL BART
| 68 | Deram SML 1028 | ISN'T THIS WHERE WE CAME IN (LP, stereo, gatefold sleeve) | £40 |

CHRIS BARTLEY
67	Cameo Parkway P 101	The Sweetest Thing This Side Of Heaven/Love Me Baby	£70
67	Cameo Parkway P 101	The Sweetest Thing This Side Of Heaven/Love Me Baby (DJ Copy)	£125
68	Bell BLL 1031	I Found A Goodie/Be Mine Forever	£30
86	Move MIS 4	Baby I'm For Real/I've Found A Goodie/Truer Words Were Never Spoken/The Sweetest Thing This Side Of Heaven (12", p/s)	£15

EILEEN BARTON
| 55 | Vogue Coral Q 72075 | Fujiyama Mama/I'd've Baked A Cake | £100 |

MARIA BARTON
| 80 | Airship AP 56 | RAINFUL DAYS (LP) | £100 |

BASCZAX
| 79 | Pipeline ICI ONE | Madison Fallout/Auto Mekanik Destruktor (4 single sided 7" pages as sleeve) | £25 |

(see alsoThe Amazing Space Frogs, Blitzkrieg Bop, The Gynaecologists)

BASE
| 80 | Base BASE001 | Violent Death/Frenchmen/One-Way Girl (hand-made p/s) | £80 |

BASELINE
| 81 | Extrabit EX 1 | Suspended Animation/Truth About The Lies (with p/s) | £125 |
| 81 | Extrabit EX 1 | Suspended Animation/Truth About The Lies (without p/s) | £50 |

BASEMENT 5
| 80 | Island ILPS 9641 | 1965-1980 (LP, printed inner, embossed sleeve, poster) | £25 |
| 17 | Pias PIAS 6580LPX | 1965-1980 (LP, reissue, printed inner, booklet, red vinyl, Rough Trade exclusive) | £20 |

BASEMENT JAXX
99	XL XLLP129	REMEDY (2LP, printed inners, embossed logo)	£20
01	XL XLLP 143	ROOTY (2LP, gayefold, printed inners)	£20
01	XL XLLP 143X	ROOTY (2LP picture discs, gatefold PVC with sticker)	£25
03	XL XLLP174	KISH KASH (2LP, printed inners)	£15
06	XL XLLP 205	CRAZY ITCH RADIO (2LP, printed inners)	£15
09	XL XLLP 453	SCARS (2LP, gatefold, printed inners)	£15
14	Atlantic Jaxx JAXXLP 008	JUNTO (2LP, gatefold, printed inners)	£20

BASEMENT PHIL
| 91 | Basement BRSS 001 | Take Me Up (Part 1)/(Part 2)/(Part 3) (12" promo) | £25 |

BASES/BASSIES
| 66 | Coxsone DIR CS 2001 | Checking Out/NORMA FRASER: Telling Me lies (white labels only) | £250 |
| 67 | Coxsone CS 7030 | River Jordan/SOUL VENDORS: Swing Easy | £150 |

BASH STREET KIDS
| 79 | Agenda GM 480 | C'mon Kids/Travelling Man (p/s) | £40 |

BASHERS
| 76 | Virgin VS 154 | The Womble Bashers/Womble Bashers Wock | £20 |

(see also Mike McGear)

BASHFUL ALLEY
| 82 | Ellie Jay BA 001 | Running Blind/My, My, My (p/s, black-and-white or black-and-yellow sleeve) | £50 |
| 82 | Graffiti BA 001 | Running Blind/My, My, My (p/s, reissue) | £35 |

BASIC BLACK AND PEARL
| 75 | Bus Stop BUS 1030 | There'll Come A Time, There'll Come A Day/Right On Baby | £30 |

BASIC INFLUENCE
| 95 | Hardliners HL 004 | Still Water/Rain Forest (12") | £30 |
| 98 | Hardliners HL 32 | Still Waters (Remix)/ICE MINUS: Zen (12") | £15 |

COUNT BASIE & HIS ORCHESTRA
| 67 | Coral Q 72497 | Green Onions/Hang On Sloopy | £15 |

(see also Joe Williams, Jackie Wilson, Lester Young, Ella Fitzgerald)

BASIL
| 87 | Serpent Sounds CBH 1561 | Come Dance With Me/Instrumental Version (12") | £20 |

BASKING SHARKS
83	Fin FON 01	Diamond Age/New Industry (p/s, insert)	£15
83	SRR SRR 0013	THRILL OF THE GAME EP	£20
83	RS 001	SHARK ISLAND (LP)	£35

BILLY BASS
| 69 | Pama PM 761 | I Need Your Love So Bad/I'm Coming To | £50 |

FONTELLA BASS
65	Chess CRS 8007	Don't Mess Up A Good Thing (with Bobby McClure)/OLIVER SAIN: Jerk Loose	£30
65	Chess CRS 8007	Don't Mess Up A Good Thing/Baby What You Want Me To Do (different B-side, existence unconfirmed)	£0
65	Chess CRS 8023	Rescue Me/Soul Of The Man	£15
65	Chess CRS 8023	Rescue Me/Soul Of The Man (DJ Copy)	£70
66	Chess CRS 8027	Recovery/Leave It In The Hands Of Love	£20
66	Chess CRS 8027	Recovery/Leave It In The Hands Of Love (DJ Copy)	£35

MINT VALUE £

66	Chess CRS 8032	I Can't Rest/Surrender	£30
66	Chess CRS 8032	I Can't Rest/Surrender (DJ Copy)	£80
66	Chess CRS 8042	Safe And Sound/You'll Never Know (DJ Copy)	£40
69	Chess CRS 8090	Rescue Me/I Can't Rest (DJ Copy)	£25
66	Chess CRE 6015	FONTELLA'S HITS (EP)	£25
66	Chess CRE 6020	I CAN'T REST (EP)	£50
66	Chess CRE 6025	FONTELLA BASS AND BOBBY McCLURE (EP)	£40
66	Chess CRL 4517	THE NEW LOOK (LP)	£80
72	Mojo 2916 018	FREE (LP)	£30

JEAN BASSA
15	22a 005	ALL MY PEOPLE (12" EP)	£20

BASS BALLISTICS
92	J4M JFM 6	BASS BALLISTICS EP (12")	£20

BASS SELECTIVE
92	No label or cat no	Life And Loves Of A Ruffneck/Don't Stop (12", white label only)	£25
92	Dj Only Records DJOR 001	Flat Line/Blow Out/Get A Little Stupid/Make Me Rush (12")	£25
92	Dj Only Records DJOR 002	THE EXPANSIONS EP (12")	£40
93	Dj Only Records DJOR 003	Jessica's Jaw/We Need Some Love/Drum Thunder (12")	£35
93	Sour SOUR 003	THE END OF THE BEGINNING EP (12")	£30

BASTILLE
11	Young & Lost Club YALC0059	Flaws/Icarus (p/s)	£100
12	Virgin VS 2037	Overjoyed/Sleepsong (p/s)	£30
12	Virgin VS 2041	Bad Blood/Hunt (Demo) (p/s, lyric insert)	£30
13	Virgin VS 2057	Pompeii/Poet (p/s)	£40
13	Virgin VS 2066	Laura Palmer/Thinkin Bout You (p/s, reissue)	£40
13	Virgin VS 2077	Things We Lost In The Fire/Icarus (Live) (p/s)	£40
13	Virgin VST 2082	Of The Night/(MNEK Remix)/Oblivion (Live)/Of The Night (Icarus Remix) (10" picture disc)	£30
14	Virgin VS 2104	Oblivion/Bad News (p/s)	£30
16	Virgin VS 2130	Hangin/Overload (p/s, white vinyl)	£15
12	Virgin VS 2037	THE SINGLES CLUB (box set 7 x 7")	£200
14	Virgin VX 3133	VS (LP, pink vinyl)	£60
20	Virgin VX 3097	ALL THIS BAD BLOOD (2-LP, reissue)	£35

JOE BATAAN
69	London HA/SH 8386	RIOT! (LP)	£40

JUNE BATEMAN
64	Sue WI 347	I Don't Wanna/NOBLE 'THIN MAN' WATTS & HIS BAND: Noble's Theme	£75

COLLIN BATES TRIO
67	Troubadour No. 265	COLIN BATES TRIO (LP, private pressing)	£500
68	Fontana SFJL 913	BREW (LP)	£200

BAT FOR LASHES
04	No label or Cat. No.	WHO STOLE PETRETSKI'S THUNDER? (CD-R tour only EP, hand-drawn cover)	£35
09	Echo 6930191	TWO SUNS (LP, gatefold, inner)	£45
12	Echo/Parlophone P915 5402	THE HAUNTED MAN (2-LP, with CD)	£20
12	Echo/Parlophone P915 5402	THE HAUNTED MAN (2-LP, white vinyl with CD)	£25
16	Parlophone 0190295983901	THE BRIDE (2-LP, magenta vinyl)	£20
16	Parlophone 0190295983901	THE BRIDE (2-LP, picture discs with CD, prints and air freshner)	£40

(see also Sexwitch, Toy)

BATHORY
84	Under One Flag FLAG 8	BATHORY (LP)	£20
85	Under One Flag FLAG 9	THE RETURN... (LP, inner)	£40
87	Under One Flag FLAG 11	UNDER THE SIGN OF THE BLACK MARK (LP)	£20
88	Under One Flag FLAG 26	BLOOD FIRE DEATH (LP, gatefold sleeve, insert)	£30
88	Under One Flag FLAG 26 P	BLOOD FIRE DEATH (LP, picture disc)	£35

BATMAN THEME
88	Bam Caruso NRIC 107	Batman Theme/Batman Theme (Instrumental Mix) (p/s)	£15

(see also Jan & Dean)

STIV BATORS
79	London/Bomp HLZ 10575	It's Cold Outside/The Last Year (p/s)	£15

(see also Dead Boys, Lords Of The New Church, Wanderers)

BATS
66	Decca F 22534	Listen To My Heart/Stop Don't Do It	£25
67	Decca F 22568	You Will Now, Won't You?/You Look Good Together	£25

MIKE BATT
68	Liberty LBF 15093	Mister Poem/Fading Yellow	£25
68	Liberty LBF 15122	I See Wonderful Things In You/Mary Goes Round	£25
69	Liberty LBF 15210	Your Mother Should Know/Suddenly	£20
70	Penny Farthing PAGS 534	BATT TRACKS (LP)	£15

(see also Farnborough Fireworks Factory, Hapshash & Coloured Coat, Anderson Harley & Batt)

BATTERED ORNAMENTS
70	Harvest HAR 5013	Goodbye We Loved You (Madly)/CHRIS SPEDDING: Rock'n'Roll Band	£25
69	Harvest SHVL 758	MANTLE-PIECE (LP, gatefold sleeve, no EMI box on label)	£500
82	GI WAX 3	MANTLE-PIECE (LP, reissue)	£20

(see also Pete Brown & His Battered Ornaments, Chris Spedding, People Band)

BATTERSEA
78	Rak RK 1013	Born And Bred/Summer Rain (no p/s)	£15

SKIP BATTIN
72	Signpost SG 4255	SKIP (LP)	£18

(see also Skip & Flip, Byrds, Flying Burrito Brothers, Evergreen Blueshoes)

ROSE BATTISTE
11	Outta Sight OSV 036	Hit And Run/I Miss My Baby (reissue)	£15

LUCIO BATTISTI
77	RCA PB 6129	To Feel In Love/Only (demo)	£30
79	RCA PB 9439	Baby It's You/Lady (demo)	£50

BATTLEAXE
82	Guardian GRC 132	Burn This Town/Battleaxe (no p/s)	£40
83	Music For Nations MFN8	BURN THIS TOWN (LP)	£15

BATTLES
07	Warp WARPLP 156	MIRRORED (2-LP)	£20

BAUHAUS
79	Small Wonder TEENY 2	Bela Lugosi's Dead/Boys/Dark Entries (12", p/s, white vinyl, 5000 only)	£70
80	Axis AXIS 3	Dark Entries/Untitled (brown label, p/s)	£40
80	Beggars Banquet BEG 37	Dark Entries/Untitled (p/s, red Beggars Banquet labels)	£15
80	4AD AD 7	Terror Couple Kill Colonel/Scopes/Terror Couple Kill Colonel II (version) (mispressed with 'rejected' version of third track, p/s)	£20
81	Beggars Banquet BEG 54T	Kick In The Eye/Satori (12", white label in stamped plain sleeve)	£15
82	Beggars Banquet BEG 74T	Kick In The Eye/Poison Pen/Harry/Earwax (12" mispressing, p/s, matrix: A1)	£25
82	Beggars Banquet BEG 79	Spirit/Terror Couple Kill Colonel (live) (p/s, mispressed, A-side plays Gary Numan's "We Take Mystery [To Bed]")	£25
82	Lyntone LYN 12106	A God In An Alcove (Early Version) (hard vinyl test pressing)	£15
82	Beggars Banquet BEG 83	Ziggy Stardust/Third Uncle (original glossy card sleeve, signed by band for record company staff)	£30
82	Beggars Banquet BEG 83T	Ziggy Stardust/Party Of The First Part/Third Uncle/Waiting For The Man, 12" glossy card p/s, no poster, signed for record company staff)	£30
83	Lyntone LYN 13777/8	The Sanity Assassin/Spirit In The Sky (fan club freebie, 320 only)	£500
88	Small Wonder TEENY 2P	Bela Lugosi's Dead/Boys/Dark Entries (12", reissue, luminous picture disc in PVC sleeve)	£25
89	Small Wonder TEENY 2	Bela Lugosi's Dead/Boys/Dark Entries (12", reissue, green vinyl, p/s)	£25
89	Small Wonder TEENY 2	Bela Lugosi's Dead/Boys/Dark Entries (12", reissue, blue vinyl, p/s)	£25
90	Beggars Banquet BEG 74T	Kick In The Eye/In Fear Of Dub/Harry/Earwax (Searching For Satori EP) (12", reissue, black sleeve lettering, green/gold labels)	£15
91	Small Wonder TEENY 2	Bela Lugosi's Dead/Boys/Dark Entries (12", reissue, pink, clear or purple vinyl, in corresponding coloured p/s)	£25
80	4AD CAD 13	IN THE FLAT FIELD (LP, inner, 8 Hogarth Road address on rear sleeve)	£30
81	Beggars Banquet BEGA 29	MASK (LP, gatefold, group photo inside, Beggars Banquet labels)	£20
82	Beggars Banquet BEGA 38	PRESS THE EJECT AND GIVE ME THE TAPE (LP, with bonus 45 "Satori In Paris" [BH 1] & poster)	£20
82	Beggars Banquet BEGA 42	THE SKY'S GONE OUT (LP, with bonus LP "Press The Eject And Give Me The Tape" [BEGA 38] inner sleeves & stickered sleeve)	£20
83	Beggars Banquet BEGA 45P	BURNING FROM THE INSIDE (LP, picture disc)	£20
83	Beggars Banquet BEGA 45P	BURNING FROM THE INSIDE (LP, with 5" die cut and BEGA 45P cat number on sleeve)	£20
85	Beggars Banquet BEGA 64	1979-1983 (2-LP, with inserts, 50,000 copies, numbered)	£25
85	Beggars Banquet BEGA 64	1979 - 1983 (2-LP, standard un-numbered edition)	£18
08	Vinyl VIN180LP005	IN THE FLAT FIELD (LP, reissue, with free white vinyl 12")	£20
08	Let Them Eat Vinyl LETV013LP	GO AWAY WHITE (LP, gatefold, white vinyl)	£100
09	Vinyl 180 VIN180LP020	THIS IS FOR WHEN...(2-LP)	£70

(see also Tones On Tail, David J, Peter Murphy, Daniel Ash)

ART BAXTER
57	Philips BBR 8107	ROCK YOU SINNERS (10" LP)	£125

DAVID BAXTER
70	Reflection REFL 9	GOODBYE DAVE (LP, white/brown label)	£100

(see also David Lewis)

LES BAXTER & HIS ORCHESTRA
55	Capitol CL 14239	Earth Angel/Happy Baby (as Les Baxter & Bombers)	£30

TODD BAYTEE
86	The White Label WL1	In Your Eyes (12" Mix)/(7" Mix)/(Jazz Mix) (12")	£250

B.B. BLUNDER
71	United Artists UP 35204	Little Boy/10,000 Miles	£20
71	United Artists UAG 29156	WORKERS' PLAYTIME (LP, gatefold sleeve)	£60

(see also Reg King & B.B. Blunder, Action, Julie Driscoll Brian Auger & Trinity, Kevin Westlake, Mark Charig, Blossom Toes)

BBC RADIOPHONIC WORKSHOP/PETER HOWELL
64	Decca F 11837	Doctor Who/BRENDA & JOHNNY: This Can't Be Love (unboxed Decca logo)	£30
18	Electronic Sound ES 743	Strange Beacons/Mind The Gap (p/s)	£15
68	BBC Enterprises REC 25M	BBC RADIOPHONIC WORKSHOP (LP)	£45
72	BBC REC 93S	TEST CARD MUSIC (LP)	£25
73	BBC REC 93 S	FOURTH DIMENSION (LP)	£15
76	BBC REC 225	OUT OF THIS WORLD (LP)	£15
70	BBC REC 25 M	BBC RADIOPHONIC MUSIC - WORK BY DELIA DERBYSHIRE (LP)	£30
78	BBC REC 307	THROUGH A GLASS DARKLY (LP)	£30
78	BBC REC 316	DOCTOR WHO SOUND EFFECTS No. 19 (LP)	£18

MINT VALUE £

83	BBC REH 462	**DR. WHO - THE MUSIC** (LP)	£15
04	Rephlex 147 LP	**MUSIC FROM THE BBC RADIOPHONIC WORKSHOP** (4 x 10")	£30

(see also Dr. Who, Jon Pertwee, Ray Cathode, Radiophonic Workshop, Ithaca, Alice Through The Looking Glass, Agincourt, Blossom Toes, Dudley Simpson & Brian Hodgson)

BEACH BOYS

SINGLES

62	Capitol CL 15273	**Surfin' Safari/409**	£50
63	Capitol CL 15285	**Ten Little Indians/County Fair**	£100
63	Capitol CL 15305	**Surfin' USA/Shut Down**	£20
64	Capitol CL 15339	**Fun, Fun, Fun/Why Do Fools Fall In Love**	£25
65	Capitol CL 15425	**The Little Girl I Once Knew/There's No Other** (Like My Baby)	£15
76	Reprise K 14411	**Child Of Winter/Susie Cincinnati** (withdrawn)	£125
79	Capitol BBP 26	**SINGLES COLLECTION** (26 x 7" box set)	£50

EPs

63	Capitol EAP 1-20540	**SURFIN' USA**	£30
64	Capitol EAP 1-20603	**FUN, FUN, FUN**	£30
64	Capitol EAP 5267	**FOUR BY THE BEACH BOYS**	£25
64	Capitol EAP 4-2198	**BEACH BOYS CONCERT**	£25
64	Capitol EAP 1-20781	**THE BEACH BOYS HITS**	£15
67	Capitol EAP 6-2458	**GOD ONLY KNOWS**	£30

ALBUMS

62	Capitol T 1808	**SURFIN' SAFARI** (mono only)	£50
63	Capitol T 1890	**SURFIN' USA** (mono)	£35
63	Capitol (S)T 1890	**SURFIN' USA** (stereo)	£50
63	Capitol ST 1981	**SURFER GIRL** (mono)	£35
63	Capitol ST 1981	**SURFER GIRL** (stereo)	£50
63	Capitol ST 1998	**LITTLE DEUCE COUPE** (mono)	£30
63	Capitol ST 1998	**LITTLE DEUCE COUPE** (stereo)	£50
63	Capitol T 2027	**SHUT DOWN VOLUME 2** (mono)	£30
63	Capitol ST 2027	**SHUT DOWN VOLUME 2** (stereo)	£50
64	Capitol T 2110	**ALL SUMMER LONG** (mono)	£30
64	Capitol ST 2110	**ALL SUMMER LONG** (stereo)	£40
64	Capitol T 2164	**THE BEACH BOYS' CHRISTMAS ALBUM** (mono)	£35
64	Capitol ST 2164	**THE BEACH BOYS' CHRISTMAS ALBUM** (stereo)	£40
64	Capitol T 2198	**BEACH BOYS CONCERT** (mono)	£20
64	Capitol ST 2198	**BEACH BOYS CONCERT** (stereo)	£25
65	Capitol T 2269	**BEACH BOYS TODAY!** (mono)	£25
65	Capitol ST 2269	**BEACH BOYS TODAY!** (stereo)	£30
65	Capitol ST 2354	**SUMMER DAYS** (AND SUMMER NIGHTS!!) (mono)	£25
65	Capitol ST 2354	**SUMMER DAYS** (AND SUMMER NIGHTS!!) (stereo)	£30
65	Capitol (S)T 2398	**BEACH BOYS' PARTY!** (mono)	£20
65	Capitol (S)T 2398	**BEACH BOYS' PARTY!** (stereo)	£25
66	Capitol T 2458	**PET SOUNDS** (mono)	£150
66	Capitol ST 2458	**PET SOUNDS** (stereo)	£150
66	Capitol T 20856	**THE BEST OF THE BEACH BOYS** (mono)	£15
66	Capitol ST 20856	**THE BEST OF THE BEACH BOYS** (stererо)	£18
67	Capitol T 9001	**SMILEY SMILE** (mono)	£45
67	Capitol ST 9001	**SMILEY SMILE** (stereo)	£35
67	Capitol ST 20956/T 20956	**THE BEST OF THE BEACH BOYS VOL. 2** (stereo or mono)	£15
68	Capitol T 2859	**WILD HONEY** (mono)	£45
68	Capitol ST 2859	**WILD HONEY** (stereo)	£25
68	Capitol T 2895	**FRIENDS** (mono)	£50
68	Capitol (S)T 2895	**FRIENDS** (stereo)	£40
69	Capitol T 21142	**THE BEST OF THE BEACH BOYS VOL. 3** (mono)	£15
69	Capitol E-T 133	**20/20** (mono, gatefold sleeve)	£20
69	Capitol E-ST 133	**20/20** (stereo, gatefold sleeve)	£18

(The above LPs were originally issued with flipback sleeves & rainbow-rim black labels; later yellow label copies from 1969 and 70s orange label pressings - in stereo - are worth up to half the value.)

70	Stateside SSLA 8251	**SUNFLOWER** (gatefold sleeve)	£22
71	Stateside SSL 10313	**SURF'S UP** (textured sleeve, with gatefold insert)	£20
71	Stateside SSL 10313	**SURF'S UP** (textured sleeve, without gatefold insert)	£15
73	Reprise/Brother K 54008	**HOLLAND** (with insert & bonus EP "Mount Vernon And Fairway" [K 54008/7] in p/s)	£30
75	Capitols ST 2458	**PET SOUNDS** (LP, reissue, orange label, stereo)	£15
79	Caribou CRB 1866081	**L.A. LIGHT** (LP, picture disc)	£18
81	WRC SM 651-657	**THE CAPITOL YEARS** (7-LP box set)	£25
97	EMI LPCENT2	**PET SOUNDS** (LP, reissue, EMI 100 Centenary, stickered sleeve)	£30
99	Simply Vinyl SVLP 149	**PET SOUNDS** (LP, reissue, 180gm vinyl)	£20
00	Simply Vinyl SVLP 219	**SMILEY SMILE** (LP, reissue 180gm vinyl)	£15

(see also Brian Wilson, Dennis Wilson, Legendary Masked Surfers, American Spring, Annette,s, Rutles, Moon, Murry Wilson, Survivors)

BEACH HOUSE

10	Bella Union BELLAV 225	**TEEN DREAM** (2-LP, DVD, CD)	£20
12	Bella Union BELLAV 144	**BEACH HOUSE** (LP, white vinyl, with CD)	£15
12	Bella Union BELLAV 160	**DEVOTION** (LP, blue vinyl with CD)	£15
12	Bella Union BELLAV 334	**BLOOM** (2-LP with CD)	£20
15	Bella Union BELLA 500VX	**DEPRESSION CHERRY** (LP, white vinyl, CD, felt cover)	£20
15	Bella Union BELLA 500V	**DEPRESSION CHERRY** (LP, clear vinyl, 200 only)	£30
15	Bella Union BELLA 512V	**THANK YOUR LUCKY STARS** (LP)	£20

BEACHCOMBERS
63	Columbia DB 7124	Mad Goose/You Can't Sit Down	£20
64	Columbia DB 7200	Night Train/The Keel Row	£30

(see also Pat Wayne)

BEACH-NUTS
65	London HL 9988	Out In The Sun (Hey-O)/Someday Soon	£30

(see also Strangeloves)

BEACON STREET UNION
68	MGM MGM 1416	Blue Suede Shoes/Four Hundred And Five	£25
68	MGM MGM-C(S) 8069	THE EYES OF THE BEACON STREET UNION (LP)	£100

BEADY EYE
10	Beady Eye EYE 1	Bring The Light/Sons Of The Stage (4,000 only)	£15
10	Beady Eye EYE 3	Four Letter Word/World Outside My Room (4,000 only)	£18
13	Columbia PG 1922 001	Flick Of The Finger (Remix)/Soul Love (Remix) (p/s only, sold through Pretty Green shop)	£20
11	Columbia BOX 1	SINGLES BOX SET (5 x 7" in special box)	£40
11	Beady Eye BEADYLP 2	DIFFERENT GEAR, STILL SPEEDING (2-LP)	£18
11	Columbia 88883721371	BE (2-LP, pre-order version with poster, signed)	£50
11	Columbia 88883721371	BE (CD, pre-order version, signed)	£40

(see also Oasis, Liam Gallagher, Ride)

BEAK>
09	Invada INV 100LP	BEAK> (2-LP, white vinyl)	£25
10	Invada INV 100LP	BEAK> (2-LP, blue vinyl repressing)	£20
10	Invada INV (No cat no)	BEAK> (2-CD in 12" pizza box, 250 copies)	£40
12	Invada INV 100LP	BEAK> (2-LP, red vinyl repressing)	£20
12	Invada INV 107LP	>> (2-LP, white signed cover, tour edition, 100 only)	£40
12	Invada INV 107LP	>> (2-LP, orange vinyl repressing)	£20
12	Invada INV 107LP	>> (2-LP)	£20
14	Invada INV 137LPCOL	+ (LP, orange and white swirl vinyl or black and white swirl vinyl)	£18

(see also Portishead)

GEORGE BEAN
63	Decca F 11762	Secret Love/Lonely Weekends	£25
65	Decca F 12228	She Belongs To Me/Why Must They Criticise? (as George Bean & Runners)	£15
67	CBS 2801	The Candy Shop Is Closed/Smile From Sequin	£25
68	CBS 3374	Bring Back Lovin'/Floatin'	£35

(see also Trifle, Bean & Loopy's Lot)

BEAN & LOOPY'S LOT
66	Parlophone R 5458	A Stitch In Time/Haywire	£50

(see also Alan Bown Set)

BEAR
68	Verve FTS 3059	GREETINGS CHILDREN OF PARADISE (LP)	£35

DEAN BEARD & CREW CATS
57	London HLE 8463	Rakin' And Scrapin'/On My Mind Again	£250
57	London HLE 8463	Rakin' And Scrapin'/On My Mind Again (78)	£15

BEARDED LADY
74	Young Blood YB 1018	Rock Star/Country Lady	£15

BEARS
79	Good Vibrations Intl. GVI 1	Insane/Decisions (p/s)	£15
79	Waldo's JS 001	On Me/Wot's Up Mate (p/s, various designs, with insert)	£15
86	Tigerbeat GROWL 001	INSANE!! (LP)	£20

BEARZ
80	Axis AXIS 2	She's My Girl/Girls Will Do (p/s)	£20

BEAS
68	Pama PM 744	Dr. Goldfoot And His Bikini Machine/Where Do I Go From You	£50

BEASTIE BOYS
87	Rat Cage MOTR 26	COOKY PUSS (12", p/s, reissue)	£15
87	Def Jam BEASTP 1	No Sleep Till Brooklyn/Posse In Effect (plane-shaped picture disc)	£25
89	Capitol 12CL 540	HEY LADIES (LOVE AMERICAN STYLE EP) (12", p/s)	£15
92	Capitol 12CLS 665	FROZEN METAL HEADS EP (12", p/s, white vinyl)	£15
94	Capitol 10CL716	Get It Together/(Buck Wild Remix)/(Intrumental)/Sabotage (10" p/s)	£15
87	Def Jam 450 062 1	LICENSED TO ILL (LP, with poster)	£30
89	Capitol EST2102	PAUL'S BOUTIQUE (LP)	£80
92	Grand Royal EST 2171	CHECK YOUR HEAD (2-LP)	£35
94	Grand Royal EST 2229	ILL COMMUNICATION (2-LP, gatefold, numbered)	£60
94	Grand Royal GR006	ILL COMMUNICATION (2-LP, gatefold)	£50
98	Grand Royal GR062	HELLO NASTY (2-LP, orange vinyl)	£40
04	Capitol 7243 4 73397	TO THE 5 BOROUGHS (2-LP)	£30
05	Capitol 0946 344667 1 4	SOLID GOLD HITS (2-LP)	£20

BEAT
80	Go-Feet BEAT 001	JUST CAN'T STOP IT (LP, with inner)	£15

(see also Fine Young Cannibals)

BEAT JUNKIES
96	Ugly UGM 001	THE BEAT JUNKIES EP (12')	£15

MINT VALUE £

NICKY BEAT & THE BEATNICKS
78 Rigid IS/BEAT/1033   **I Can Hear Voices/Split Second Love/Starstruck** (oversized p/s, poster insert)..............**£150**

BEAT BOYS
63 Decca F 11730   **That's My Plan/Third Time Lucky** **£25**

BEAT BROTHERS
63 Polydor NH 52185   **Nick Nack Hully Gully/Lantern Hully Gully** **£25**
(see also Tony Sheridan & Beat Brothers, Bobby Patrick Big Six)

BEAT CHICS
64 Decca F 12016   **Skinny Minnie/Now I Know** **£25**

BEAT HAPPENING
86 Rough Trade ROUGH 105   **BEAT HAPPENING** (LP, reissue) **£40**
87 53rd and 3rd/K AGAS 2   **JAMBOREE** (LP, with free flexi, stickered sleeve) **£35**
89 Rough Trade ROUGH 145   **BLACK CANDY** (LP) **£30**

BEATHOVEN
88 CBS 651 626-7   **Socrates/Socrates** (withdrawn) **£30**

THE BEATLES
SINGLES : 1962
(There is very specific label information for different pressings of Beatles singles and this is given either at the top of each year or in the body of the entry itself. Thus when it comes to these two pressings of their debut single issued in 1962 labels will have "The Parlophone Co. Ltd." in upper or lower case & "Recording first published 1962," label text, without "Sold in UK ...". Also, please note that all Beatles 7" singles issued before 1967 have a 4-prong push-out centre: unless otherwise stated)

62 Parlophone 45-R 4949   **Love Me Do/P.S. I Love You** (First pressing, red label, 'Ringo on drums & no tambourine' version; with or without "Made In Great Britain" credit, Matrix 7XCE 17144-1N/7XCE 17145-1N, in sleeve Type A, B or C) **£150**
62 Parlophone 45-R 4949   **Love Me Do/P.S. I Love You** (First pressing, red label, 'Ringo on drums & no tambourine' version; label variation with "Made In Great Britain" credit on only one side, Matrix 7XCE 17144-1N/7XCE 17145-1N, in sleeve Type A, B, or C) **£130**

SINGLES : 1963
(with "The Parlophone Co. Ltd." in either upper or lower case & "Recording first published 1963" label text without "Sold in the UK..." unless otherwise stated)
63 Parlophone 45-R 4983   **Please Please Me/Ask Me Why** (First pressing, red label; with or without "Made In Great Britain"credit, Matrix 7XCE 17217-1N/&XCE 17218-1N, in sleeve Type A, B or C)..**£200**
63 Parlophone R 5015   **From Me To You/Thank You Girl** (First pressing, Matrixes: 7XCE 17329 - 1N/7XCE 17330 - 1N, in sleeve Type 1 sleeve)..**£15**
63 Parlophone R 5055   **She Loves You/I'll Get You** (First pressing, Matrix numbers: 7XCE 17395-1N/7XCE 17396-1N in Type 1 sleeve)..**£15**
63 Parlophone R 5055   **She Loves You/I'll Get You** (First pressing, label variation, with elongated "Northern Songs Ltd" and different typography for "7XCEE. 17395" and "Recording First Published 1963" Matrix numbers: 7XCE 17395-1N/7XCE 17396-1N, in Type 1 sleeve) **£15**
63 Parlophone R 5055   **She Loves You/I'll Get You** (First pressing, second label variation, smaller "She Love You" typography and "Northern Songs Ltd" on three lines; Matrix numbers: 7XCE 17395-1N/7XCE 17396-1N, in Type 1 sleeve) **£15**
63 Parlophone R 5084   **I Want To Hold Your Hand/This Boy** (First pressing, with "The Parlophone Co. Ltd" in upper-case only, Matrixes: 7XCE 17559-1N/7XCE 17560-1N, in Type 1 sleeve).................**£15**
63 Parlophone R 5084   **I Want To Hold Your Hand/This Boy** (First pressing, label variation with "N.C.B." after "Northern Songs Mus Ltd" with "The Parlophone Co. Ltd" in upper-case only, Matrixes: 7XCE 17559-1N/7XCE 17560-1N) **£15**
63 Parlophone 45-R 4949   **Love Me Do/P.S. I Love You** (Second pressing, black label, with The Parlophone Co. Ltd in upper-lower case, matrix suffixed with '1N' indicating 'Ringo on drums & no tambourine' version)...**£150**
63 Parlophone 45-R 4983   **Please Please Me/Ask Me Why** (Second pressing, black label, with "The Parlophone Co. Ltd" in upper-lower case, with "45" prefix, Matrixes: 7XCE 17217-1N/7XCE 17218-1N)....**£20**
63 Parlophone R 4983   **Please Please Me/Ask Me Why** (Third pressing, black label, with "The Parlophone Co. Ltd" in upper-lower case, without "45" prefix) **£20**

SINGLES : 1964
(with "The Parlophone Co. Ltd." in either upper or lower case & "Recording first published 1964" label text with "Sold in the UK..." unless otherwise stated)
64 Parlophone R 5114   **Can't Buy Me Love/You Can't Do That** (First pressing, with "The Parlophone Co. Ltd" in upper case, in Type 1 sleeve) **£20**
64 Parlophone R 5114   **Can't Buy Me Love/You Can't Do That** (First pressing with label variation, with "The Parlophone Co. Ltd" in upper case but "NCB" added after "Northern Songs") **£20**
64 Parlophone R 5160   **A Hard Day's Night/Things We Said Today** (First pressing in Type 1B sleeve)..............**£20**
64 Parlophone R 5200   **I Feel Fine/She's A Woman** (First pressing, with "The Parlophone Co. Ltd" in upper case, in Type 1B sleeve) **£20**
64 Parlophone R 5200   **I Feel Fine/She's A Woman** (First pressing, label variation, different "Northern Songs NCB" layout and "Recording First Published 1964" below Maxtrix number)......................**£20**
64 Parlophone R 5084   **I Want To Hold Your Hand/This Boy** (Second pressing) **£80**
64 Parlophone R 4949   **Love Me Do/P.S. I Love You** (Third pressing, black label, with "The Parlophone Co. Ltd" in upper case, matrix suffixed with 1N' indicating 'Ringo on drums & no tambourine' version)..**£80**

(with "The Parlophone Co. Ltd.", "Recording first published 1962" & Sold in UK ... label text)
64 Parlophone R 4983   **Please Please Me/Ask Me Why** (Fourth pressing, with "The Parlophone Co. Ltd" in upper/lower case and "Sold in the U.K." label text) **£80**

SINGLES : 1965
(with "The Parlophone Co. Ltd." in upper case & "Sold in the UK...". 2nd and other pressings from 1965 have "The Gramophone Co. Ltd" unless otherwise stated)
65 Parlophone DP 562   **If I Fell/Tell Me Why** (First U.K. pressing of 1964 export single, Matrixes: &XCE 17756-1N/7XCE 17757-1N, in Type 1B sleeve) **£100**
65 Parlophone R 5265   **Ticket To Ride/Yes It Is** (First pressing, in Type 2 sleeve) **£15**
65 Parlophone R 5265   **Ticket To Ride/Yes It Is** (First pressing, label variation, smaller "Sold In U.K..." text, larger "Northern Songs NCB" type and (Lennon-McCartney **credit longer than "Ticket To Ride" song title**) **£15**
65 Parlophone R 5265   **Ticket To Ride/Yes It Is** (First pressing, label variation, smaller "Northern Songs NCB" type, brackets around matrix number, larger "Trade Mark" and "Parlophone"logos and "T" in "Gt Britain" is in upper (T), **not lower case** (t)) **£15**
65 Parlophone R 5305   **Help!/I'm Down** (First pressing, in Type 2 sleeve) **£20**

65	Parlophone R 5305	**Help!/I'm Down** (Second pressing, with "The Gramophone Co Ltd" label text) **£15**
65	Parlophone R 5389	**We Can Work It Out/Day Tripper** (First pressing, in Type 3 sleeve) **£20**
65	Parlophone R 5389	**We Can Work It Out/Day Tripper** (Second pressing, with "The Gramophone Co Ltd" label text) **£15**
65	Parlophone R 5389	**We Can Work It Out/Day Tripper** (Second pressing, label variation with different type for "Sold In U.K...", "Northern Songs NCB", matrix number and date. Comma "," separates "Lennon, McCartney" rather than a dash "-") **£15**
65	Parlophone R 4949	**Love Me Do/P.S. I Love You** (Fourth pressing, black label, with "The Parlophone Co. Ltd" in upper case, "T" in "Gt Britain" now upper case to read "GT. Britain" "Recorded first published" also now in lower case: matrix suffixed with 1N' indicating 'Ringo on drums & no tambourine' version) **£100**

SINGLES : 1966
(with "The Gramophone Co. Ltd." in upper case & "Sold in the UK...". label text, unless otherwise stated)

66	Parlophone R 5452	**Paperback Writer/Rain** (First pressing, in Type 4 or 5 sleeve) **£15**
66	Parlophone R 5452	**Paperback Writer/Rain** (First pressing, label variation, with larger "Northern Songs, NCB" credit and larger "P" before "1966") **£15**
66	Parlophone R 5493	**Yellow Submarine/Eleanor Rigby** (First pressing, in Type 5 or 6 sleeve) **£15**
66	Parlophone R 5493	**Yellow Submarine/Eleanor Rigby** (First pressing, label variation with larger "Northern Songs, NCB", no brackets on Matrix number, larger circled "P" and larger typeface for "Eleanor Rigby") **£15**
66	Parlophone R 5493	**Yellow Submarine/Eleanor Rigby** (First pressing, label variation with mid-size "Northern Songs, NCB", no brackets on Matrix number, with comma "," separating "Lennon, McCartney" rather than a "-" "Lennon-McCartney", larger typeface for "Eleanor Rigby" and "Sold In U.K...") **£15**
66	Parlophone R5493	**Yellow Submarine/Eleanor Rigby** (Second pressing, solid centre, label variation, larger "Northern Songs, NCB" text, smaller "Lennon-McCartney" credit and larger circled "P") **£20**
66	Parlophone R 5493	**Yellow Submarine/Eleanor Rigby** (Second pressing, solid centre label variation, larger "Northern Songs, NCB" text, no brackets on Matrix number and larger typeface on "Eleanor Rigby") **£15**
66	Parlophone R 5084	**I Want To Hold Your Hand/This Boy** (Third pressing, solid centre, "The Parlophone Co" rim text, 'Sold in UK' to centre) **£300**
66	Parlophone R 5114	**Can't Buy Me Love/You Can't Do That** (Second pressing, solid centre, with "The Parlophone Co. Ltd" label text) **£150**
66	Parlophone R 5200	**I Feel Fine/She's A Woman** (Second pressing, solid centre) **£150**

SINGLES : 1967
(All pressings after 1967 have push-out or solid centres with "The Gramophone Co. Ltd." in upper case & "Sold in the UK..." label text, unless otherwise stated)

67	Parlophone R 5570	**Strawberry Fields Forever/Penny Lane** (First pressing, 250,000 only in p/s)...................**£75**
67	Parlophone R 5570	**Strawberry Fields Forever/Penny Lane** (Second pressing, in Type 5,6 or 7 sleeve)...........**£15**
67	Parlophone R 5620	**All You Need Is Love/Baby You're A Rich Man** (First pressing, solid or pushout centre, with no reference to "Live World Television Transmission")...................**£70**
67	Parlophone R 5620	**All You Need Is Love/Baby You're A Rich Man** (Second pressing, with reference to "Live World Television Transmission") **£15**
67	Parlophone R 5620	**All You Need Is Love/Baby You're A Rich Man** (First pressing, label variation, push-out/solid centre with reference to "Live World Television Transmission" and "Northern Songs NCB" on three lines rather than two, brackets around matrix number, "1967" above Matrix number and "Recorded during 'Live;..." text starts after Lennon-McCartney credit rather than beneath it) **£25**
67	Parlophone R 5655	**Hello Goodbye/I Am The Walrus** (First pressing, label variation with "Northern Songs NCB" on three lines not two, different typeface and matrix number appearing beneath date of "1967", smaller typeface for "Hello, Goodbye" and ""Lennon, McCartney" separated by a "," rather than a "-", "Lennon-McCartney") **£15**
67	Parlophone R 5452	**Paperback Writer/Rain** (Second pressing, solid centre only) **£80**
67	Parlophone R 5493	**Yellow Submarine/Eleanor Rigby** (Second pressing, solid centre only) **£15**
67	Parlophone R5305	**Help!/I'm Down** (Third pressing, solid centre, "The Gramophone Co. Ltd" and "Sold in U.K..." label text) **£100**
67	Parlophone R5305	**Help!/I'm Down** (Third pressing, solid centre, "The Parlophone Co. Ltd" and "Sold in U.K..." label text) **£90**

SINGLES : 1968
(All Apple pressings except for early issues of "Let It Be" come in black glossy 'Apple' sleeves)

68	Parlophone R 5675	**Lady Madonna/The Inner Light** (First pressing, with Fan Club insert; sleeve with 7/- to 50/- on reverse) **£60**
68	Parlophone R 5675	**Lady Madonna/The Inner Light** (no fan club insert) **£20**
68	Apple R 5722	**Hey Jude/Revolution** (First pressing, push-out or solid centre) **£20**
68	Parlophone R 5084	**I Want To Hold Your Hand/This Boy** (Fourth pressing, solid centre, with "The Gramophone Co" rim text) **£300**

SINGLES : 1969
(All Apple pressings except for early issues of "Let It Be" come in black gloss "Apple" sleeves)

69	Apple R 5777	**Get Back/Don't Let Me Down** (First pressing, push-out or solid centre, as "The Beatles with Billy Preston") **£20**
69	Apple R 5777	**Get Back/Don't Let Me Down** (First pressing, label variation with "Northern Songs/NCB" rather than "Northern Songs" solid centre or push-out centre, as "The Beatles with Billy Preston") **£20**
69	Apple R 5777	**Get Back/Don't Let Me Down** (Second pressing, solid centre or push-out centre as "The Beatles with Billy Preston", without "Sold In UK..." label text)...................**£25**
69	Apple R 5786	**Ballad Of John And Yoko/Old Brown Shoe** (First pressing, solid or push-out centre) **£25**
69	Apple R 5786	**Ballad Of John And Yoko/Old Brown Shoe** (Second pressing, solid centre or push-out centre without "Sold in UK..." label text)...................**£20**
69	Apple R 5814	**Something/Come Together** (First pressing, solid centre or push-out centre without "Sold in UK..." label text)...................**£45**
69	Apple R 5722	**Hey Jude/Revolution** (Second pressing, without "Sold in UK..." label text)...................**£15**
69	Parlophone R 5305	**Help!/I'm Down** (Fourth pressing, with "The Parlophone Co. Ltd" but no "Sold in U.K..." label text)...................**£40**
69	Parlophone R 5389	**We Can Work It Out/Day Tripper** (Third pressing, solid centre, no "sold in U.K..." label text)...................**£80**
69	Parlophone R 5452	**Paperback Writer/Rain** (Third pressing, no "Sold in U.K...." label text) **£40**
69	Parlophone R 5570	**Strawberry Fields Forever/Penny Lane** (Third pressing, no "Sold in U.K..." label text) **£35**

MINT VALUE £

69	Parlophone R 5493	**Yellow Submarine/Eleanor Rigby** (Third pressing, no "Sold In U.K...." label text) £40
69	Parlophone R 5620	**All You Need Is Love/Baby You're A Rich Man** (Third pressing, no "Sold In U.K..." label text, push-out centre) £40
69	Parlophone R5675	**Lady Madonna/The Inner Light** (Third pressing, no "Sold in U.K..." label text) £35

SINGLES : 1970

70	Apple R 5833	**Let It Be/You Know My Name** (Look Up The Number) (First pressing, scratched-out B-side matrix: APPLES 1002, p/s) £30
70	Apple R 5833	**Let It Be/You Know My Name** (Look Up The Number) (Second pressing, scratched-out B-side matrix: APPLES 1002, no p/s) £15
70	Apple R 5833	**Let It Be/You Know My Name** (Look Up The Number) (Third pressing, B-side matrix: 7YCE 21408, no p/s) £15

SINGLES : 70S, 80S, 90S & 00S SINGLES: REISSUES AND PICTURE DISCS

(Please note that 1970s Parlophone copies of Beatles singles with EMI boxed logos are of nominal value. Add £10 to the value for any single with a red & white 'Factory Sample Not For Sale' sticker.)

82	Parlophone RP 4949	**Love Me Do/P.S. I Love You** (7" picture disc, with/without publishing miscredit) £15
84	Parlophone RP 5160	**A Hard Day's Night/Things We Said Today** (picture disc)....................£15
86	Parlophone RP 5452	**Paperback Writer/Rain** (picture disc)....................£15
	(Issued in PVC sleeve)	
88	Apple 12R 5722	**Hey Jude/Revolution** (12", p/s) £30
96	Apple R 6425	**Real Love/Baby's In Black** (7", p/s) £15
10	Parlophone 5099964163970	**Paperback Writer/Rain** (jukebox centre) £40
12	Parlophone 45-R 4949	**Love Me Do/PS I Love You** (reissue, withdrawn as A side has album version with Andy White on drums and Ringo on tambourine, Matrixes: BC88258-01A1 01740174/ BC88258-01B1 0174017 J G i i and incorrect catalogue number R 47414 on B-side) £20
17	Parlophone 0602557385618	**Strawberry Fields Forever/Penny Lane** (p/s) £20
23	Apple 0602448145864	**Now And Then/Love Me Do** (7", p/s, black vinyl) £15
	all 7"s have same cat no. barcode: 602448145864	
23	Apple 0602448145864	**Now And Then/Love Me Do** (7", p/s, blue vinyl) £20
	all 7s have same cat no: barcode: 602448631084	
23	Apple 0602448145864	**Now And Then/Love Me Do** (7", p/s, clear vinyl) £18
	all 7"s have same catalogue number: barcode - 0602448631077	
23	Apple 0602448145864	**Now And Then/Love Me Do** (7", p/s,blue/white marble vinyl) £15
	All 7s have same cat no. Barcode: 602448631022	
23	Apple 0602455434869	**Now And Then/Love Me Do** (10", p/s)....................£200
23	Apple 0602458451795	**Now And Then/Love Me Do** (cassette single, Ltd. Ed) £50
23	Apple 0602458129526	**Now And Then/Love Me Do** (12", p/s, red vinyl) £20

SINGLES : BOX SETS

76	Parlophone/Apple BS 24	**THE BEATLES' SINGLES COLLECTION 1962-1970** (24 x 7", each in green p/s, green & white stickered box set) £70
76	Parlophone/Apple/World Record Club	**THE BEATLES' COLLECTION** (24 x 7", mail-order black box set; later copies with "Sgt. Pepper's Lonely Hearts Club Band" [R 6022]) £70
78	Parlophone/Apple BSC 1	**THE BEATLES' SINGLES COLLECTION** (26 x 7" blue box set, with insert; some copies include mispressing of "Get Back" [Apple R 5777]) £70
82	Parlophone/Apple BSCP 1	**THE BEATLES' SINGLES COLLECTION** (27 x 7" blue box set, with bonus picture disc "Love Me Do" [RP 4949], export issue) £45
82	Parlophone/Apple BSCP 1	**THE BEATLES' SINGLES COLLECTION** (27 x 7" blue box set, with mispressed picture disc Love Me Do/"Love Me Do" [RP 4949], export issue) £50
89	Parlophone/Apple CDBSC 1	**THE BEATLES' SINGLES COLLECTION** (22 x 3" CD single box set) £75
89	Parlophone/Apple CDBSCP 1	**THE BEATLES' SINGLES COLLECTION** (22 x 5" CD single box set) £65
12	Apple 5099968	**SINGLES BOX SET** (4x7", poster) £25
19	Apple 0602547261717	**THE SINGLES COLLECTION** (23x7" slipcase box set, spined sleeves, polylined inners, booklet)....................£150

SINGLES : CONTRACT PRESSINGS: SINGLES

Records were often pressed by rival companies on behalf of one another under contract to meet spikes in demand. Non-EMI companies frequently pressed batches of Beatles' records for Parlophone. Occasionally demand for a record was so strong that more than one company was contracted to press batches simultaneously. Subtle differences indicating the origin of a contract pressing can be identified. Many collectors like to include examples in their collections. EMI Pressings: Pre-1966 EMI pressings have full push-out and solid centres. Thereafter many records were produced with a mix of push-out and solid centres. EMI always pressed Stamper Letters into the vinyl's run-out area positioned at 3 o'clock to the Matrix Number. Up to three letters from the code 'GRAMOPHLTD' were used, each representing a number from 1 to 0. Mother Plate Numbers using a conventional numbering sequence starting with 1 were pressed into the vinyl at 9 o'clock to the Matrix Number. The edges of EMI pressings are all straight-cut. Non-EMI Pressings: Philips' contract pressings (the 'Hey Jude' single) are the easiest to spot as they alone have three-pronged centres. All the others had four prongs except some ORIOLE pressings of "Can't Buy Me Love" which have solid centres. The centres of Decca and PYE pressings have similar raised sections containing the spindle hole, though PYE's are much less prominent. The outermost edges of records made by CBS, PHILIPS, ORIOLE and PYE are not straight-cut but are slightly tapered-off. The edges of Decca pressings are all straight-cut. EMI Stamper Letters are seldom seen on contract pressings though Mother Plate Numbers almost always appear. Controversy long surrounded one style of Beatles' contract pressing. Previously thought to have been pressed by PYE they are now considered to have been made by ORIOLE before its acquisition by CBS in September 1964. The labels on the essentially flat centres of these pressings are often rough-textured with rough edges. The vinyl is thicker and heavier than other pressings. Some November 1964 pressings of 'I Feel Fine' also have these characteristics and are assumed to have come from this source, CBS by then using the old ORIOLE presses. Some 1968 copies of 'Hey Jude' are identical in appearance but are less heavy. Both are now considered to be CBS contract pressings. PYE is believed to have pressed copies of one Beatles' 45 ('Hey Jude') and one EP ('Million Sellers'). The centres of these two pressings look very similar to those made by Decca but they have a less prominent ridge and the edges of the records are slightly tapered. Beatles fans and collectors worldwide continue to scrutinise the magical mystery tour of Beatles' contract pressings and new information continues to be unearthed. The following details are where we at Record Collector stand at the present time

63	Parlophone R 5055	**She Loves You/I'll Get You** (Decca pressing)....................£30
63	Parlophone R 5055	**She Loves You/I'll Get You** (Decca pressing, variation, "Parlophone Co.Ltd" in upper case, different typography for "Northern Songs" Matrix number and "Recording First Published 1963")....................£25
63	Parlophone R 5084	**I Want To Hold Your Hand/This Boy** (Decca pressing)....................£25
63	Parlophone R 5084	**I Want To Hold Your Hand/This Boy** (Decca pressing, label variation with "N.C.B." after "Northern Songs Mus. Ltd.")....................£25
63	Parlophone R 5084	**I Want To Hold Your Hand/This Boy** (Oriole pressing)....................£30
63	Parlohone R 5084	**I Want To Hold Your Hand/This Boy** (Pye pressing, label variant with differnt typography and "N.C.B." after "Northern Songs Mus Ltd.")....................£25
64	Parlophone R 5114	**Can't Buy Me Love/You Can't Do That** (Oriole pressing) £25

64	Parlophone R 5114	**Can't Buy Me Love/You Can't Do That** (Oriole pressing with solid centre)	£45
64	Parlophone R5114	**Can't Buy Me Love/You Can't Do That** (Pye contract pressing with solid centre, side 1, matrix 7XCE 17657-1N)	£40
64	Parlophone R 5114	**Can't Buy Me Love/You Can't Do That** (Pye pressing label variation with "NCB" out of alignment with the "N" and "S" of "Northern Songs")	£25
64	Parlophone R 5200	**I Feel Fine/She's A Woman** (Pye pressing)	£25
64	Parlophone R 5200	**I Feel Fine/She's A Woman** (CBS pressing)	£25
64	Parlophone R 5200	**I Feel Fine/She's A Woman** (Decca pressing)	£25
65	Parlophone R 5305	**Help!/I'm Down** (Decca contract pressing)	£25
67	Parlophone R 5655	**Hello Goodbye/I Am The Walrus** (Decca pressing)	£25
67	Parlophone R 5655	**Hello Goodbye/I Am The Walrus** (Decca contract pressing, label variation, with "Northern Songs NCB" on three lines not two, "1967" above not below matrix number and "Lennon, McCartney" separated by a comma "," rather than a "-", "Lennon-McCartney")	£25
68	Apple R 5722	**Hey Jude/Revolution** (Decca contract pressing)	£40
68	Apple R 5722	**Hey Jude/Revolution** (Pye contract pressing)	£40
68	Apple R 5722	**Hey Jude/Revolution** (CBS contract pressing)	£40
68	Apple R 5722	**Hey Jude/Revolution** (Philips contract pressing, three-pronged push-out centre)	£70

SINGLES : DEMO SINGLES

(Beatles demo singles between 1962 and 1966 have a red "A" on the A side unless otherwise stated. Demos from All You Need Is Love (1967) to Something (1969) have a white "A" on a green label. Finally, demos with the centre's missing are worth half these values)

62	Parlophone 45-R 4949	**Love Me Do/P.S. I Love You** (Demo copy, McCartney misspelt "McArtney", 250 only)	£6000
63	Parlophone 45-R 4983	**Please Please Me/Ask Me Why** (demo copy)	£2000
63	Parlophone (45-)R 5015	**From Me To You/Thank You Girl** (Demo copy, with or without '45-' prefix)	£1000
63	Parlophone R 5055	**She Loves You/I'll Get You** (Demo copy)	£800
63	Parlophone R 5084	**I Want To Hold Your Hand/This Boy** (Demo copy)	£800
64	Parlophone R 5114	**Can't Buy Me Love/You Can't Do That** (Demo copy)	£800
64	Parlophone R 5160	**A Hard Day's Night/Things We Said Today** (Demo copy, red "A" on both sides)	£800
64	Parlophone R 5200	**I Feel Fine/She's A Woman** (Demo single, existence unconfirmed)	£0
65	Parlophone R 5265	**Ticket To Ride/Yes It Is** (Demo copy)	£700
65	Parlophone R 5305	**Help!/I'm Down** (Demo copy, existence unconfirmed)	£0
65	Parlophone R 5389	**We Can Work It Out/Day Tripper** (Demo copy, red "A" on both sides)	£600
66	Parlophone R 5452	**Paperback Writer/Rain** (Demo copy)	£600
66	Parlophone R 5493	**Yellow Submarine/Eleanor Rigby** (Demo copy, existence unconfirmed)	£0
67	Parlophone R 5570	**Strawberry Fields Forever/Penny Lane** (existence unconfirmed)	£0
67	Parlophone R 5620	**All You Need Is Love/Baby You're A Rich Man** (Demo copy)	£450
67	Parlophone R 5655	**Hello, Goodbye/I Am The Walrus**	£500
68	Apple (no cat. no.)	**Hey Jude/Revolution** (Demo copy, green & white Apple 'custom' label, handwritten details)	£450
69	Apple R 5777	**Get Back/Don't Let Me Down** (Demo copy, green and white Apple 'custom' label test pressing, typed details)	£400
69	Parlophone R 5786	**Ballad Of John And Yoko/Old Brown Shoe** (Demo copy, existence unconfirmed)	£0
68	Parlophone R 5675	**Lady Madonna/The Inner Light** (Demo copy)	£500
69	Parlophone R 5814	**Something/Come Together** (Demo copy)	£600
70	Parlophone R 5833	**Let It Be/You Know My Name** (Look Up The Number) (existence unconfirmed)	£0
76	Parlophone R 6013	**Yesterday/I Should Have Known Better** (Demo, silver/black paper label with a silver "A", green generic p/s)	£25
76	Parlophone R 6016	**Back In The U.S.S.R./Twist And Shout** (silver/black paper label with a silver "A", green generic p/s)	£25
78	Parlophone R 6022	**Sgt. Pepper's Lonely Hearts Club Band/With A Little Help From My Friends/A Day In The Life** (silver/black paper label with a silver "A", p/s)	£25

SINGLES : FRENCH PRESSINGS - SINGLES

67	Parlophone R 5655	**Hello Goodbye/I Am The Walrus** (Pathé Marconi pressing, alleged push-out centre version)	£100
67	Parlophone R 5655	**Hello Goodbye/I Am The Walrus** (Pathé Marconi pressing)	£25

SINGLES : POLYDOR RECORDINGS

(With push-out centres & orange labels)

62	Polydor NH 66833	**My Bonnie/The Saints** (When The Saints Go Marching In) (as Tony Sheridan & The Beatles; 1st pressing, 'broad' title& "Made In England" label text)	£100
63	Polydor NH 66833	**My Bonnie/The Saints** (When The Saints Go Marching In) (as Tony Sheridan & The Beatles; 2nd pressing, push-out or solid centre, 'narrow' title & "Made In England" label text)	£70
64	Polydor NH 52275	**Cry For A Shadow** (A-side credited to 'Beatles')/**TONY SHERIDAN & THE BEATLES: Why** (Can't You Love Me Again) ('scroll' label, with "Made In England" text)	£65
64	Polydor NH 52317	**Ain't She Sweet** (A-side as 'The Beatles, vocal: John Lennon')/**If You Love Me, Baby** (B-side credited to 'The Beatles with Tony Sheridan, vocal'; 1st pressing, 'scroll' label with "Made In England" text)	£65
64	Polydor NH 52317	**Ain't She Sweet/If You Love Me, Baby** (2nd pressing, red label, with "Made In England" text)	£20
64	Polydor NH 52906	**Sweet Georgia Brown/Nobody's Child** (German import only, unissued in U.K.)	£40

SINGLES : UNIQUE PROMO SINGLES

68	Apple (no cat. no.)	**OUR FIRST FOUR** (4 x 7" in presentation pack, including Hey Jude [R 5722] & Those Were The Days by Mary Hopkin [APPLE 2], Sour Milk Sea by Jackie Lomax [APPLE 3] & Thingumybob by Black Dyke Mills Band [APPLE 4]; each mounted in PVC pocket on printed dayglo card insert, in 10" x 12" card in plastic box)	£4000
68	Apple (no cat. no.)	**OUR FIRST FOUR** (4 x 7" in presentation pack, including Hey Jude [R 5722] & Those Were The Days by Mary Hopkin [APPLE 2], Sour Milk Sea by Jackie Lomax [APPLE 3] & Thingumybob by Black Dyke Mills Band [APPLE 4]; each mounted in PVC pocket on printed dayglo card insert, in 10" x 12" card sleeve)	£2500
76	EMI SPSR 401	**Medley Of Songs For "Rock'n'Roll Music"** (excerpts)	£600

EXPORT SINGLES

| 64 | Parlophone DP 562 | **If I Fell/Tell Me Why** (First pressing, export single without "Sold in UK..." label text) | £100 |

MINT VALUE £

65	Parlophone DP 563	**Yesterday/Dizzy Miss Lizzy** (export single)	£100
66	Parlophone DP 564	**Michelle/Drive My Car** (export single)	£175
68	Parlophone DP 570	**Hey Jude/Revolution** (Export copy with Swedish p/s)	£60
68	Parlophone DP 570	**Hey Jude/Revolution** (Export copy without Swedish p/s)	£45
70	Parlophone P-R 5833	**Let It Be/You Know My Name** (Look Up The Number) (Export copy, no p/s)	£60

("Let It Be" was pressed with "Parlophone" label text on one side & "Gramophone" on the other)

| 70 | Apple P-R 5833 | **Let It Be/You Know My Name** (Look Up The Number) (Export copy, no p/s) | £300 |

EPS : 1963

(With "The Parlophone Co. Ltd" and "Recording first published 1963" label text. Unless otherwise stated, all 60s EPs have push-out centres and laminated flipback sleeves.)

63	Parlophone GEP 8882	**TWIST AND SHOUT** (EP, First pressing)	£30
63	Parlophone GEP 8880	**THE BEATLES' HITS** (EP, First pressing, without "Recording first published 1963" label text)	£20
63	Parlophone GEP 8883	**THE BEATLES** (No. 1) (EP, first pressing, without "Recording first published 1963" label text)	£25
63	Parlophone GEP 8880	**THE BEATLES' HITS** (EP, Second pressing)	£20

EPS : 1964

(With "The Parlophone Co. Ltd." & "Recording first published 1964" label text & "Sold in the UK..." unless otherwise stated)

64	Parlophone GEP 8891	**ALL MY LOVING** (EP, First pressing without "Sold in UK" label text)	£35
64	Parlophone GEP 8891	**ALL MY LOVING** (EP, Second pressing, with "Sold in U.K...." label text)	£25
64	Parlophone GEP 8899	**GOLDEN DISCS** (unreleased, 2 x 1-sided test pressings [matrices: 7TCE-1N & 7TCE-1N] & 1 set of label proofs only;price does not include labels)	£2500
64	Parlophone GEP 8913	**LONG TALL SALLY** (EP, First pressing)	£30
64	Parlophone GEP 8920	**EXTRACTS FROM THE FILM "A HARD DAY'S NIGHT"** (EP)	£40
64	Parlophone GEP 8924	**EXTRACTS FROM THE ALBUM "A HARD DAY'S NIGHT"** (EP)	£45

EPS : 1965

(With "The Parlophone Co. Ltd", & "Sold in UK.." label text, unless otherwise stated.)

65	Parlophone GEP 8931	**BEATLES FOR SALE** (EP, First pressing)	£40
65	Parlophone GEP 8938	**BEATLES FOR SALE** (No. 2) (EP, first pressing)	£45
65	Parlophone GEP 8946	**THE BEATLES MILLION SELLERS** (EP, with 'Golden Discs' text on labels)	£25

EPS : 1966

(With "The Gramophone Co. Ltd" & "Sold in UK..." label text unless otherwise stated.)

66	Parlophone GEP 8948	**YESTERDAY** (EP, First pressing)	£120
66	Parlophone GEP 8952	**NOWHERE MAN** (EP, first pressing)	£150
66	Parlophone GEP 8946	**THE BEATLES' MILLION SELLERS** (EP, Second pressing, with "Million Sellers" label text)	£15

EPS : 1967

(With "The Gramophone Co. Ltd" & "Sold in UK..." label text unless otherwise stated. Please note that any EP titles with "The Gramophone Co Ltd" but without "Sold in UK..." are 70s re-pressing with EMI label text & varnished sleeves).

67	Parlophone MMT-1	**MAGICAL MYSTERY TOUR** (2-EP, gatefold sleeve, first pressing with booklet & blue lyric sheet; push-out or solid centre; mono)	£75
67	Parlophone SMMT-1	**MAGICAL MYSTERY TOUR** (2-EP, gatefold sleeve, first pressing with booklet & blue lyric sheet; stereo)	£75
67	Parlophone GEP 8931	**BEATLES FOR SALE** (EP, Second pressing with "The Parlophone Co. Ltd" label text; solid centre)	£25
67	Parlophone GEP 8952	**NOWHERE MAN** (EP, Second pressing solid centre)	£35

EPS : CONTRACT PRESSINGS : EPS

| 66 | GEP 8946 | **THE BEATLES MILLION SELLERS** (EP, Pye contract pressing, with 'Golden Discs' text on labels) | £50 |

EPS : EPS REISSUES AND BOXED SETS

(EPs reissued in the 70s have EMI label text and come in varnished sleeves with flipbacks. Later 80s reissues are housed in cheaper varnished sleeves without flipbacks are are generally worth £8-£10).

73	Parlophone SMMT-1	**MAGICAL MYSTERY TOUR** (2-EP, gatefold sleeve, stereo only, with booklet & yellow lyric sheet)	£15
81	Parlophone BEP 14	**THE BEATLES EP COLLECTION** (14-EP box set, with bonus stereo EP [SGE 1])	£120
76	Parlophone GEP 8882	**TWIST AND SHOUT** (reissue, 'EMI' text on label)	£15
76	Parlophone GEP 8880	**THE BEATLES HITS** (reissue with 'EMI' text)	£15
76	Parlophone GEP 8883	**THE BEATLES NO. 1** (reissue, with 'EMI' text)	£15
76	Parlophone GEP 8913	**LONG TALL SALLY** (reissue with 'EMI' text)	£15
76	Parlophone GEP 8920	**EXTRACTS FROM THE FILM "A HARD DAY'S NIGHT"** (reissue with 'EMI' text)	£18
76	Parlophone GEP 8924	**EXTRACTS FROM THE ALBUM "A HARD DAY'S NIGHT"** (reissue with 'EMI' text)	£18
76	Parlophone GEP 8931	**BEATLES FOR SALE** (reissue with 'EMI' text)	£20
76	Parlophone GEP 8946	**THE BEATLES MILLION SELLERS** (reissue with 'EMI' text)	£15
76	Parlophone GEP 8948	**YESTERDAY** (reissue with 'EMI' text)	£20
76	Parlophone GEP 8952	**NOWHERE MAN** (reissue with 'EMI' text)	£25
76	Parlophone SMMT-1	**MAGICAL MYSTERY TOUR** (reissue with 'EMI' text)	£30
95	Apple R 6406	**BABY IT'S YOU** (7" EP)	£15
12	Apple 5099940490892	**MAGICAL MYSTERY TOUR** (1BD/1DVD/2x7"EP box set, booklet)	£60
14	Parlophone GEP 8913	**LONG TALL SALLY** (reissue for 'Black Friday' RSD, mono, insert for Beatles In Mono box, hype sticker)	£15

EPS : POLYDOR RECORDINGS : EPS

| 64 | Polydor EPH 21 610 | **TONY SHERIDAN WITH THE BEATLES** (1st pressing, German import in U.K. p/s, orange 'scroll' label; Why songwriting credit as 'Sheridan' or 'Sheridan-Crompton') | £125 |
| 64 | Polydor EPH 21 610 | **TONY SHERIDAN WITH THE BEATLES** (2nd pressing, German import in U.K. p/s, red label;Why songwriting credit as 'Sheridan' or 'Sheridan-Crompton') | £50 |

ALBUMS : PLEASE PLEASE ME

(First pressings from 1963 have 'The Parlophone Co Ltd' label text but no 'Sold in UK...' label text unless otherwise stated. 1963 pressings come in polythene-lined 'Use Emitex' die-cut inners with flipback sleeves. All later label and sleeve variations are clearly stated in the entry for each repressing)

| 63 | Parlophone PMC 1202 | **PLEASE PLEASE ME** (First pressing, black & gold label, with "Dick James Mus. Co." publishing credit for "I Saw Her Standing There", "Misery", Do You Want To Know A Secret & "There's A Place"; "Made by Ernest J Day Ltd" sleeve with printers credit on | £1200 |

right hand side rear of sleeve; Front photo credited to "Angus McBean" at bottom far right of front cover of sleeve less than 5mm from edge. "A" of Angus starting under second letter "S" in the word "songs" in the album title: large mono in top right corner. Research estimates that around 25,000 pressed)......................

63　Parlophone PCS 3042　**PLEASE PLEASE ME** (First pressing, black & gold label, with "Dick James Mus. Co."publishing credit for "Please Please Me", "I Saw Her Standing There", "Misery", Do You Want To Know A Secret & "There's A Place"; E. J. Day sleeve; stereo) **£6000**

63　Parlophone PMC 1202　**PLEASE PLEASE ME** (Second pressing, black & gold label, with "Northern Songs" publishing credit for "I Saw Her Standing There", "Misery", Do You Want To Know A Secret & "There's A Place"; Made by Ernest J Day Ltd" sleeve with printers credit on right hand side rear of sleeve; Front photo credited to "Angus McBean" at bottom far right of front cover of sleeve less than 5mm from edge. "A" of Angus starting under second letter "S" in the word "songs" in the album title: large mono in top right corner. Research estimates that around 12,000 pressed)....................**£1200**

63　Parlophone PCS 3042　**PLEASE PLEASE ME** (Second pressing, black & gold label, with "Northern Songs" publishing credit for "Please Please Me", "I Saw Her Standing There", "Misery", Do You Want To Know A Secret & "There's A Place"; E. J. Day sleeve; stereo)....................**£5000**

63　Parlophone PMC 1202　**PLEASE PLEASE ME (Third pressing, black & yellow label with 33 1/3 RPM on label next to matrix number. Many of these records have LOWER stamper numbers than some black and gold second pressings (with Northern Songs credit) suggesting that these records were being pressed at the same time. Made by Ernest J Day Ltd" sleeve with printers credit on right hand side rear of sleeve; Front photo credited to "Angus McBean" at bottom far right of front cover of sleeve less than 5mm from edge. "A" of Angus starting under second letter "S" in the word "songs" in the album title: large mono in top right corner. Research estimates that around 5,000 pressed) £500**

63　Parlophone PCS 3042　**PLEASE PLEASE ME** (Third pressing, black & yellow label with 33 1/3 on label, stereo)......................**£3000**

63　Parlophone PMC 1202　**PLEASE PLEASE ME** (Fourth pressing, black/yellow label Made by Ernest J Day Ltd" sleeve with printers credit on right hand side rear of sleeve; Front photo credited to "Angus McBean" at bottom far right of front cover of sleeve less than 5mm from edge. "A" of Angus starting under second letter "S" in the word "songs" in the album title: large mono in top right corner. Research estimates that around 25,000 pressed. Please note that there are some in sleeves with the Angus McBean credit around 20mm from the edge with the "A" of Angus starting under the letter "G" in "songs".) **£150**

63　Parlophone PCS 3042　**PLEASE PLEASE ME** (Fourth pressing, with large "stereo" on front cover; E. J. Day sleeve; stereo)......................**£250**

63　Parlophone PMC 1202　**PLEASE PLEASE ME** (Fifth pressing, "Recording first published 1963" added below matrix number. Research estimates around 184,000 pressed. E. J. Day sleeve with medium mono and"A" of "Angus" starting under the letter "G" in "Songs" or Garrod & Lofthouse Ltd sleeve with large mono and McBean credit around 20mm from edge with "A" of "Angus" starting under letter "G" in "Songs." Large "mono"on front cover; mono) **£100**

63　Parlophone PCS 3042　**PLEASE PLEASE ME** (Fifth pressing, G & L or E. J. Day sleeve, with large "stereo"on front cover; stereo) **£150**

64　Parlophone PCS 3042　**PLEASE PLEASE ME** (sixth pressing, with 'The Parlophone Co. Ltd', 'Recording first published 1963' & 'Sold in UK...' label text. G & L sleeve, with large "stereo" on front cover; stereo)......................**£80**

65　Parlophone PMC 1202　**PLEASE PLEASE ME** (sixth pressing, from July 1965 until August 1969 "Sold in U.K. subject to resale price conditions, see price lists." printed on centre of all labels. In February 1965 "Recording first published" replaced with (P) **in a circle 1963. Records with (P)** 1963 start with side 2 matrix XEX 422 - 2N: Research suggests that 250,000 **copies pressed. G & L sleeve, with large or small "mono" with** McBean credit around **20mm from edge with "A" of "Angus" starting under letter "G" in "Songs; mono)** **£70**

65　Parlophone PCS 3042　**PLEASE PLEASE ME** (Seventh pressing, with 'The Gramophone Co Ltd' & 'Sold in UK...' label text, stereo, with small "stereo" on front cover)......................**£60**

69　Parlophone PMC 1202　**PLEASE PLEASE ME** (Seventh pressing, pressed between August to December 1969, "Sold in U.K. .." text removed mono, with small "mono" on front cover made by Garrod & Lofthouse Ltd. Angus McBean credit 20mm from the edge with the "A" of "Angus" starting under the letter "G" in "Songs". Research estimates than only 1000 copies pressed) **£400**

69　Parlophone PCS 3042　**PLEASE PLEASE ME** (Eigth pressing, 'The Gramophone Co Ltd' label text, small "stereo" on front cover; stereo)......................**£60**

69　Parlophone PMC 1202　**PLEASE PLEASE ME** (Re-pressing 1969, mono) **£50**

69　Parlophone PCS 3042　**PLEASE PLEASE ME** (1969 re-pressing, stereo, with one boxed EMI logo on label).........**£100**

(with laminated flipback sleeves & silver/black labels with one boxed EMI logo)

70　Parlophone PMC 1202　**PLEASE PLEASE ME** (Eigth pressing, black and silver label, single boxed EMI logo at 6 'o' clock, with G & L sleeve & sepia "LP advertising" inner. Label has "The Gramophone Co. Ltd." but no "Sold in UK ..."small "mono" on front cover made by Garrod & Lofthouse Ltd. Angus McBean credit 20mm from the edge with the "A" of "Angus" starting under the letter "G" in "Songs". Research suggests that around 1000 copies pressed; mono) **£350**

73　Parlophone PCS 3042　**PLEASE PLEASE ME** (French pressing)......................**£15**

82　Parlophone PMC 1202　**PLEASE PLEASE ME** (mono) **£15**

(lightweight vinyl with yellow/black labels listing "mono")

95　Parlophone PMC 1202　**PLEASE PLEASE ME** (LP, mono) **£20**

ALBUMS : WITH THE BEATLES

(First pressings from 1963 have 'The Parlophone Co Ltd' label text but no 'Sold in UK...' label text unless otherwise stated. 1963 pressings come in polythene-lined 'Use Emitex' die-cut inners with flipback sleeves. All later label and sleeve variations are clearly stated in the entry for each repressing)

63　Parlophone PMC 1206　**WITH THE BEATLES** (First pressing, black & yellow label, with "Recording first published", & "Jobete" publishing credit for "Money"; G&L or E.J. Day sleeve, with large "Mono" on front cover, mono)......................**£200**

63　Parlophone PCS 3045　**WITH THE BEATLES** (First pressing black & yellow label, with "Recording first published", & "Jobete" publishing credit for "Money"; G & L or E. J. Day sleeve, with large "stereo" on front cover; stereo) **£250**

63　Parlophone PMC 1206　**WITH THE BEATLES** (Second pressing, black & yellow label, with "Recording first published", & "Dominion, Belinda" publishing credit for "Money"; G & L or E. J. Day sleeve, with large "mono" on front cover; mono) **£125**

63　Parlophone PCS 3045　**WITH THE BEATLES** (Second pressing, black & yellow label, with "Recording first published", & "Dominion, Belinda" publishing credit for "Money"; G & L or E. J. Day sleeve,with large "stereo" on front cover; stereo)......................**£200**

65　Parlophone PCS 3045　**WITH THE BEATLES** (Third pressing, 'The Gramophone Co Ltd' & 'Sold in UK...' label text, small "stereo" on front cover; stereo)......................**£60**

69　Parlophone PCS 3045　**WITH THE BEATLES** (Fourth pressing, with 'The Gramphone Co Ltd' label text but no 'Sold in UK...' label text, G&L sleeve with either plain white or sepia 'LP advertising'　**£60**

MINT VALUE £

		inner, small "stereo" on front cover; stereo)	
69	Parlophone PCS 3045	**WITH THE BEATLES** (silver/black labels with one boxed EMI logo, stereo only)	£30
73	Parlophone PCS 3045	**WITH THE BEATLES** (French pressing, with 'Made In France' on EMI rim copy)	£15
82	Parlophone PMC 1206	**WITH THE BEATLES** (repressing with yellow/black labels on lightweight vinyl, mono)	£15

ALBUMS : A HARD DAY'S NIGHT

(First pressings from 1964 have 'The Parlophone Co Ltd' & 'Sold in UK...' label text. All later label and sleeve variations are clearly stated in the entry for each repressing)

64	Parlophone PMC 1230	**A HARD DAY'S NIGHT** (First pressing, G & L or E. J. Day sleeve, mid-sized "mono" on front cover; mono)	£100
64	Parlophone PCS 3058	**A HARD DAY'S NIGHT** (First pressing, G & L or E. J. Day sleeve, mid-sized "stereo"on front cover; stereo)	£250
65	Parlophone PMC 1230	**A HARD DAY'S NIGHT** (Second pressing, small "mono" on front cover; mono)	£60
65	Parlophone PCS 3058	**A HARD DAY'S NIGHT** (Second pressing, small "stereo" on front cover; stereo)	£75
65	Parlophone PCS 3058	**A HARD DAY'S NIGHT** (Second pressing, outline "stereo" on front cover; stereo)	£200
69	Parlophone PMC 1230	**A HARD DAY'S NIGHT** (Third pressing, with 'The Gramophone Co Ltd' label text but no 'Sold in UK...' label text, G&L sleeve with plain white or sepia 'LP advertising' inners.Small "mono" on front cover; mono)	£60
69	Parlophone PCS 3058	**A HARD DAY'S NIGHT** (Third pressing, with 'The Gramophone Co Ltd' label text but no 'Sold in UK...' label text, G&L sleeve with plain white or sepia 'LP advertising' inners.Small "stereo" on front cover; stereo)	£60
69	Parlophone PCS 3058	**A HARD DAY'S NIGHT** (stereo only, with laminated flipback sleeves & silver/black labels with one boxed EMI logo)	£30
73	Parlophone PCS 3058	**A HARD DAY'S NIGHT** (French pressing, 'Made in France' on EMI rim copy)	£15
82	Parlophone PMC 1230	**A HARD DAY'S NIGHT** (lightweight vinyl with yellow/black labels listing "mono")	£15

ALBUMS : BEATLES FOR SALE

(First pressings from 1964 have 'The Parlophone Co Ltd' & 'Sold in UK...' rim text with flipback sleeves)

64	Parlophone PMC 1240	**BEATLES FOR SALE** (First pressing, G & L gatefold sleeve with visible flaps inside gatefold sleeve, with outline "mono"on front cover; mono)	£100
64	Parlophone PCS 3062	**BEATLES FOR SALE** (First pressing, G & L gatefold sleeve with visible flaps inside gatefold, with outline "stereo" on front cover; stereo)	£200
65	Parlophone PCS 3062	**BEATLES FOR SALE** (Second pressing, with 'The Gramophone Co Ltd' & 'Sold in UK...' label rim text, outline "stereo" on front gatefold sleeve; stereo)	£75
69	Parlophone PCS 3062	**BEATLES FOR SALE** (Third pressing, with The Gramophone Co Ltd' label rim text but no 'Sold in UK...' text, gatefold sleeve; stereo)	£60
69	Parlophone PCS 3062	**BEATLES FOR SALE** (1969 repressing - gatefold sleeve, stereo only, with laminated flipback sleeve & silver/black labels with one boxed EMI logo)	£30
73	Parlophone PCS 3062	**BEATLES FOR SALE** (French pressing with 'Made in France' on EMI rim copy, gatefold sleeve)	£15
98	Parlophone PMC 1240	**BEATLES FOR SALE** (LP, gatefold, mono)	£20

ALBUMS : HELP!

65	Parlophone PMC 1255	**HELP!** (LP, first pressing, G & L sleeve, with outline "mono" on front cover; mono)	£100
65	Parlophone PCS 3071	**HELP!** (LP, first pressing, G & L sleeve, with outline "stereo" on front cover; stereo)	£150
66	Parlophone PMC 1255	**HELP!** (LP, second pressing, G & L sleeve, plain white or sepia "LP advertising" inner sleeves; mono, with small solid black "mono" on front cover)	£70
66	Parlophone PCS 3071	**HELP!** (LP, second pressing, G & L sleeve, plain white or sepia "LP advertising" inner sleeves; stereo, with small solid black "stereo" on front cover)	£80
69	Parlophone PMC 1255	**HELP!** (LP, third pressing, small solid black "mono" on front cover; mono)	£60
69	Parlophone PCS 3071	**HELP!** (LP, third pressing, small solid black "stereo" on front cover; stereo)	£60
69	Parlophone PMC 1255	**HELP!** (LP, 1969 repressing, mono, one EMI boxed logo, with laminated flipback sleeve & silver/black labels with one boxed EMI logo)	£400
69	Parlophone PCS 3071	**HELP!** (LP, 1969 repressing, stereo, with laminated flipback sleeve & silver/black labels with one boxed EMI logo)	£30
73	Parlophone PCS 3071	**HELP!** (French pressing, with 'Made in France' on EMI label rim)	£15

ALBUMS : RUBBER SOUL

(First pressings from 1965 have 'The Gramophone Co Ltd' & 'Sold in UK...' label text.)

65	Parlophone PMC 1267	**RUBBER SOUL** (First pressing, G & L or E. J. Day sleeve; mono, "loud cut" with XEX 579-1 and EXE 580-1 matrixes)	£250
65	Parlophone PCS 3075	**RUBBER SOUL** (First pressing, G & L or E. J. Day sleeve; stereo)	£225
65	Parlophone PMC 1267	**RUBBER SOUL** (Second pressing, matrix: [XEX 579-4 or 5]; mono)	£90
69	Parlophone PCS 3075	**RUBBER SOUL** (Second pressing, with 'The Gramophone Co Ltd' label text but no 'Sold In UK...' label text, some with E. J. Day sleeve; stereo)	£60
69	Parlophone PMC 1267	**RUBBER SOUL** (Third pressing, mono)	£60
69	Parlophone PCS 3075	**RUBBER SOUL** (1969 repressing, with laminated flipback sleeves & silver/black labels with one boxed EMI logo, stereo only)	£60
73	Parlophone PCS 3075	**RUBBER SOUL** (French pressing, with 'Made in France' on EMI rim copy)	£15

ALBUMS : REVOLVER

(First pressings from 1966 have 'The Gramophone Co Ltd' & 'Sold in UK...' label text)

66	Parlophone PMC 7009	**REVOLVER** (First pressing, Side Two matrix [XEX 606-1], (G & L or E. J. Day sleeve; mono)	£500
66	Parlophone PMC 7009	**REVOLVER** (First pressing, G & L or E. J. Day sleeve; mono)	£125
66	Parlophone PCS 7009	**REVOLVER** (First pressing, G & L or E. J. Day sleeve; stereo)	£175
66	Parlophone PMC 7009	**REVOLVER** (Second pressing, G & L or E. J. Day sleeve, plain white or sepia "LP advertising" inner sleeves mono)	£100
69	Parlophone PMC 7009	**REVOLVER** (Third pressing, with 'The Gramophone Co Ltd' label text but no 'Sold in UK...' label text, plain white or sepia 'LP advertising' inners, mono)	£75
69	Parlophone PCS 7009	**REVOLVER** (Second pressing, with 'The Gramophone Co Ltd' label text but no 'Sold in UK...' label text, plain white or sepia 'LP advertising' inners stereo)	£50
69	Parlophone PCS 7009	**REVOLVER** (1969 repressing, with laminated flipback sleeves & silver/black labels with one boxed EMI logo, stereo only)	£50
73	Parlophone PCS 7009	**REVOLVER** (French pressing with 'Made in France' on EMI rim copy)	£15
80	Parlophone PMC 7009	**REVOLVER** (mono, pressed between 1980 and 1982, Black label with two white-black EMI logos and silver print. Matrix numbers: Side 1: YEX 605-3; Side 2: YEX 606-4)	£15
22	Apple 0602445599707	**REVOLVER** (LP, picture disc, die-cut sleeve)	£35
22	Apple 0602445599523	**REVOLVER** (4LP, 7", box set, 100 page book)	£100

22	Apple 4559941	**REVOLVER** (4CD, CD single, 100 page booklet, box set)..	**£60**

ALBUMS : A COLLECTION OF BEATLES OLDIES

(First pressing from 1966 has 'The Gramophone Co Ltd' & 'Sold in UK...' label text.)

66	Parlophone PMC 7016	**A COLLECTION OF BEATLES OLDIES** (First pressing, G & L or E. J. Day sleeve; mono)	**£100**
66	Parlophone PCS 7016	**A COLLECTION OF BEATLES OLDIES** (First pressing, G & L or E. J. Day sleeve; stereo)......	**£100**
69	Parlophone PMC 7016	**A COLLECTION OF BEATLES OLDIES** (Second pressing, with 'The Gramophone Co Ltd' label text but no 'Sold in UK...' label text, plain white or sepia 'LP advertising' inners mono)	**£40**
69	Parlophone PCS 7016	**A COLLECTION OF BEATLES OLDIES** (Second pressing, with 'The Gramophone Co Ltd' label text but no 'Sold in UK...' label text, plain white or sepia 'LP advertising' inners stereo)	**£35**
69	Parlophone PCS 7016	**A COLLECTION OF BEATLES OLDIES** (stereo only, with laminated flipback sleeves & silver/black labels with one boxed EMI logo)	**£25**
73	Parlophone PCS 7016	**A COLLECTION OF BEATLES OLDIES** (LP, French pressing, with 'Made in France' on EMI rim copy)	**£15**

ALBUMS : SGT. PEPPER'S LONELY HEARTS CLUB BAND

(First pressing from 1967 has 'The Gramophone Co Ltd' & 'Sold in UK...' label text)

67	Parlophone PMC 7027	**SGT. PEPPER'S LONELY HEARTS CLUB BAND** (First pressing, G & L laminated gatefold sleeve, visible flaps inside gatefold sleeve, with red & white inner & cut-out insert; mono)	**£150**
67	Parlophone PCS 7027	**SGT. PEPPER'S LONELY HEARTS CLUB BAND** (First pressing, G & L laminated gatefold sleeve, visible flaps inside gatefold sleeve, with red & white inner & cut-out insert; stereo)	**£175**
69	Parlophone PCS 7027	**SGT. PEPPER'S LONELY HEARTS CLUB BAND** (Second pressing, with 'The Gramophone Co Ltd' label text but no 'Sold in UK...' label text, plain white or sepia 'LP advertising' inners gatefold sleeve, with white inner and cut-out insert; stereo)	**£35**
69	Parlophone PMC 7027	**SGT. PEPPER'S LONELY HEARTS CLUB BAND** (Third pressing, with 'The Gramophone Co Ltd' label text but no 'Sold in UK...' label text, plain white or sepia 'LP advertising' inners laminated gatefold sleeve, & cut-out insert; mono)	**£60**
69	Parlophone PMC 7027	**SGT. PEPPER'S LONELY HEARTS CLUB BAND** (1969 repressing, laminated gatefold sleeve, with cut-out insert, mono, with laminated flipback sleeves & silver/black labels with one boxed EMI logo)	**£60**
69	Parlophone PCS 7027	**SGT. PEPPER'S LONELY HEARTS CLUB BAND** (1969 repressing, laminated gatefold sleeve, with cut-out insert, stereo, with laminated flipback sleeves & silver/black labels with one boxed EMI logo)	**£30**
73	Parlophone PCS 7027	**SGT. PEPPER'S LONELY HEARTS CLUB BAND** (French pressing, gatefold sleeve with cut-out insert, some copies with banded vinyl, with 'Made In France' on EMI rim).............	**£18**
84	Parlophone/Nimbus PCS 7027	**SGT. PEPPER'S LONELY HEARTS CLUB BAND** (mail-order only, from Practical Hi-Fi Magazine, Nimbus pressing)	**£2000**
17	Parlophone 0602557455342	**SGT. PEPPER'S LONELY HEARTS CLUB BAND** (2LP, gatefold, 4-page insert, cut-outs)	**£50**
17	Parlophone 0602567098355	**SGT. PEPPER'S LONELY HEARTS CLUB BAND** (LP, picture disc, die-cut sleeve, sticker to bottom left)	**£35**
17	Parlophone 0602557455328	**SGT. PEPPER'S LONELY HEARTS CLUB BAND** (4CD, 1DVD, 1BD, box set, book, lenticular sleeve)	**£70**

ALBUMS : THE BEATLES ('WHITE ALBUM')

68	Apple PMC/PCS 7067/8	**THE BEATLES** (First pressing, mono or stereo, numbered below 0000010).................	**£25000**
68	Apple PMC/PCS 7067/8	**THE BEATLES** (First pressing, 2LP, mono or stereo, numbered between 0000011 & 0001000)..	**£5000**
68	Apple PMC/PCS 7067/8	**THE BEATLES** (First pressing, 2LP, mono or stereo, numbered between 0001001 & 0010000)..	**£1000**
68	Apple PMC 7067/8	**THE BEATLES** (First pressing, 2LP, mono, numbered above 0010000)	**£300**
68	Apple PCS 7067/8	**THE BEATLES** (First pressing, 2LP, stereo, numbered above 0010000)	**£250**
69	Apple PCS 7067/8	**THE BEATLES** (Second pressing, 2LP, side opening, numbered gatefold, prints, lyric poster, stereo)	**£100**
73	Apple PCS 7067/8	**THE BEATLES** (2LP, French pressing, un-numbered, laminated, side-opening gatefold, prints & lyric poster, 'Made in France by Pathe Marconi EMI' rim copy)......................	**£25**
73	Apple PCS 7067/8	**THE BEATLES** (2LP, un-numbered, laminated, side-opening gatefold sleeve, with poster & 4 soft card colour prints, stereo only)	**£35**
82	Apple PMC 7067/8	**THE BEATLES** (2LP, un-numbered, side-opening gatefold, lyric poster, prints, light green Apple label; mono)	**£30**
95	Apple PCS 7067/8	**THE BEATLES** (2LP, side-opening gatefold, lyric poster, prints)	**£25**
18	Apple 0602567572015	**THE BEATLES AND ESHER DEMOS** (4LP half-speed remastered, box set, prints, poster, 4-page insert)..	**£100**
18	Apple 0602567571957	**THE BEATLES** (6CD/1BD box set, prints, poster, transparent printed plastic slipcase, numbered)...	**£140**

ALBUMS : YELLOW SUBMARINE

69	Apple PMC 7070	**YELLOW SUBMARINE** (LP, first pressing with red lines above & below rear sleevenote; mono)	**£300**
69	Apple PCS 7070	**YELLOW SUBMARINE** (LP, first pressing with red lines above & below rear sleevenote; stereo)..	**£150**
69	Apple PCS 7070	**YELLOW SUBMARINE** (LP, second pressing with red lines above & below rear sleevenote; stereo)	**£50**
73	Apple PCS 7070	**YELLOW SUBMARINE** (LP, French pressing, with 'Made in France by Pathe Marconi EMI' on rim)	**£15**
99	Apple 521 4811	**YELLOW SUBMARINE SONGTRACK** (yellow vinyl, gatefold stickered sleeve)...................	**£35**
99	Apple 521 4811	**YELLOW SUBMARINE SONGTRACK** (LP, gatefold stickered sleeve)	**£30**

ALBUMS : ABBEY ROAD

69	Apple PCS 7088	**ABBEY ROAD** (LP, first pressing, black or plain white inner sleeve, with Apple logo aligned to Side 1 track listing on rear sleeve; with "Her Majesty" credit on label).............	**£80**
69	Apple PCS 7088	**ABBEY ROAD** (LP, first pressing Apple logo misaligned to Side 1 track listing on rear sleeve; with or without "Her Majesty" credit on label; black or plain white inner sleeve)...	**£100**
73	Apple PCS 7088	**ABBEY ROAD** (some copies with banded vinyl, French Pressing, with 'Made in France by Pathe Marconi EMI' rim copy)...	**£15**
19	Apple 0602508007446	**ABBEY ROAD** (ANNIVERSARY EDITION) (3LP box set, insert)....................................	**£60**
19	Apple 0602508048883	**ABBEY ROAD** (ANNIVERSARY EDITION) (LP, picture disc, die-cut sleeve)	**£50**
19	Apple 0602508007446	**ABBEY ROAD** (ANNVERSARY EDITION) (3CD/1BD box set, book).................................	**£50**

MINT VALUE £

ALBUMS : LET IT BE

70	Apple PXS 1	**LET IT BE** (LP box set, first pressing dark green label red Apple logo on rear sleeve & white inner, with Get Back book housed in black card tray ['PXS 1' not listed on package], with rare Apple mini poster) £1000
70	Apple PXS 1	**LET IT BE** (LP box set, first pressing dark green label red Apple logo on rear sleeve & white inner, with Get Back book housed in black card tray ['PXS 1' not listed on package], without rare Apple mini poster) £800
70	PCS 7096	**LET IT BE** (LP, 2nd pressing, laminated sleeve, green Apple logo on rear sleeve, white inner) £40
73	Apple PCS 7096	**LET IT BE** (French pressing with 'Made in France by Pathe Marconi EMI' rim text)...........£15
21	Apple 0602507138691	**LET IT BE** (4LP/1x12" box set, die-cut outer, book, sticker)...........................£60
21	Apple 0602507138691	**LET IT BE** (5CD/1BD box set, die cut sleeve, booklet, sticker, promo insert) £40
21	Apple 0602435922416	**LET IT BE** (LP, picture disc, die-cut sleeve, sticker to top left of shrinkwrap) £25

ALBUMS : ALBUM BOX SETS

78	Parlophone BC 13	**THE BEATLES COLLECTION** (13 x LP, stereo, some with poster) £300
80	World Record Club SM 701/ 708	**FROM LIVERPOOL - THE BEATLES BOX** (8LP, mail order exclusive, certificate of authenticity) £100
82	Parlophone BMC 10	**THE BEATLES MONO COLLECTION** (10 x LP, red box)...................................£350
12	Apple 5099963380910	**THE BEATLES - THE ORIGINAL STUDIO RECORDINGS** (16LP box set, hardback book, slipcase, 180g)...£500
14	Apple 5099963379716	**THE BEATLES IN MONO** (14LP, flip-top box, hardback book, slipcase) £1000
23	Apple 0602458396652	**THE BEATLES 1962-1966/1967-1970** (6LP slipcase box set, 3 red/3 blue vinyl, half-speed masters, 180g, sticker to top left shrinkwrap) £150

ALBUMS : CD ALBUMS AND BOX SETS

87	HMV BEACD 25/1	**PLEASE PLEASE ME/WITH THE BEATLES/A HARD DAY'S NIGHT/BEATLES FOR SALE** (4 x CD, numbered 12" black box set withBook Of Beatles Lists paperback book) £100
87	HMV BEACD 25/2	**HELP!/RUBBER SOUL/REVOLVER** (3 x CD, numbered 12" red box set with insert & reprint of Beatles Book Monthly, issue 12) £50
87	HMV BEACD 25/4	**THE BEATLES** (2CD, numbered 12" box set with booklet & badge) £30
87	HMV BEACD 25/5	**YELLOW SUBMARINE** (CD, numbered 12" box set with insert, cut-outs & badge) £50
09	Apple 5099969944901	**THE BEATLES - THE ORIGINAL STUDIO RECORDINGS** (16CD/1DVD box set, slipcase) £100
09	Apple 5099969945120	**THE BEATLES IN MONO** (13CD, box set, booklet) £150
09	Apple 5099969944963	**THE BEATLES STEREO USB** (USB stick of stereo studio masters, green metal apple holder, box set, pamphlet, protective plastic layer)...£300

ALBUMS : CONTRACT PRESSINGS : LPS

(Records were often pressed by non-EMI companies under contract, owing to overwhelming demand for Beatles records. Subtle differences indicating their origin can be detected. Philips pressings (the 'Hey Jude' single only) are the easiest to spot as they alone have three-pronged centres. All the others had four except for the French Pathe-Marconi pressings of 'Hello Goodbye' which have solid centres and 'Made In France' at the foot of the label. The centre of a Decca contract pressing has a ridge 3mm from the perimeter. Pre-1966 EMI pressings have flat push-out centres. Thereafter many records were produced with a mix of push-out and solid centres. EMI always pressed stamper letters into the vinyl, positioned at 3 o' clock to the matrix number. Up to three letters from the code 'GRAMOPHLTD' were used each representing a number. EMI stamper letters are seldom seen on contract pressings. Great controversy has surrounded the origin of the only other known style of pre-1965 Beatles' contract pressings. Previously thought to have been made by Pye they are now believed to have been pressed at the ORIOLE pressing plant before their September 1964 aquisition by CBS. The centres of these pressings have no ridge and are finished with rough edges. They are also thicker and heavier than any of the other pressings. Although released in November 1964 'I Feel Fine' also has these characteristics and is assumed to have come from this source. CBS using the old ORIOLE presses. However, it is thought that PYE actually pressed one Beatles 45 and one EP after 1964. The centres of these two pressings look very similar to those made by DECCA but have a less prominent ridge. The edges of records made by PHILIPS, ORIOLE and PYE are not straight-cut but are tapered off. The edges of EMI, DECCA and Pathe-Marconi pressings are all straight-cut. (Decca contract pressings have no stamper letters (G or D) positioned at 3 o'clock to the matrix number; the label has a circularimpression 15mm from the outer edge. Pye pressings between 1973 and 1979 are a dark, translucent red when held up to a strong light.) Let us hope that the online community of Beatles fans and collectors worldwide will one day solve the magical mystery tour of Beatles contract pressings. Until that day, the following is where we at Record Collector stand at the present time)

63	Parlophone PMC 1202	**PLEASE PLEASE ME** (Decca contract pressing) £200
63	Parlophone PMC 1206	**WITH THE BEATLES** (Pye contract pressing)..£150
63	Parlophone PMC 1206	**WITH THE BEATLES** (Decca contract pressing)...£150
68	Parlophone P-PCS 7067/8	**THE BEATLES** (2LP, Decca contract pressing, yellow & black labels) £3000

(Decca contract pressings have no stamper letters (G or D) positioned at 3 o'clock to the matrix number; the label has a circularimpression 15mm from the outer edge. Pye pressings are a dark, translucent red when held up to a strong light.)

69	Parlophone P-PCS 7088	**ABBEY ROAD** (LP, contract pressing export issue, yellow & black labels, Decca pressing)...£1000
69	Parlophone P-PCS 7099	**ABBEY ROAD** (LP, contract pressing, export issue, silver & black labels, Decca pressing)..£500
70s	Apple PCSP 717	**THE BEATLES 1962-1966** (2-LP, gatefold sleeve with lyric inners, Pye pressing) £50

ALBUMS : EXPORT LPS : ORIGINALS

(with black/yellow labels unless otherwise stated)

68	Parlophone PCS 3075	**RUBBER SOUL** (LP, with "Sold in U.K." label text, but silver 'Stereo' on top right hand corner, small batch pressed for export) £400
68	Parlophone PCS 3075	**RUBBER SOUL** (LP, with "Sold in U.K." label text, but black 'Stereo' on top right hand corner, small batch pressed for export) £150
65	Parlophone CPCS 101	**SOMETHING NEW** (LP, export 2nd pressing, with "Parlophone Co. Ltd." label text, no "sold in the U.K." label text)..£500
65	Parlophone CPCS 101	**SOMETHING NEW** (LP, export 2nd pressing, with "Gramophone Co. Ltd." label text) £350
66	Parlophone CPCS 103	**THE BEATLES' SECOND ALBUM** (LP, export, first pressing with yellow/black labels)........£450
66	Parlophone CPCS 104	**BEATLES VI** (LP, first export pressing with yellow/black labels) £500
68	Parlophone P-PCS 7067/8	**THE BEATLES** (2LP, export pressing, yellow/black labels, numbered, top opening 'mono' gatefold sleeve with "stereo" sticker & black inners, poster & 4 colour prints)....£800
69	Odeon PPCS 7070	**YELLOW SUBMARINE** (LP, export pressing Odeon sticker on rear of Apple sleeve) £2000

(with yellow/black labels)

| 69 | Parlophone P-PCS 7088 | **ABBEY ROAD** (LP, export pressing, Parlophone sticker on rear of Apple sleeve, Apple logo on label) ....£800 |
| 70 | Parlophone P-PCS 7096 | **LET IT BE** (LP, First export pressing with silver/black labels, one EMI boxed logo) ....£1000 |

(with silver/black labels)

| 70 | Parlophone CPCS 106 | **HEY JUDE** (silver/black label, large boxed Parlophone label at top and small EMI boxed logo at bottom, laminated sleeve) ....£600 |

ALBUMS : EXPORT LPS : REISSUES

69	Parlophone P-PCS 7088	**ABBEY ROAD** (LP, export copy reissue, Parlophone sticker on rear of Apple sleeve; one EMI boxed logo) £125
69	Apple CPCS 106	**HEY JUDE** (2nd reissue, dark green label) £75
69	Parlophone CPCS 101	**SOMETHING NEW** (one EMI boxed logo) £150
69	Parlophone CPCS 103	**THE BEATLES' SECOND ALBUM** (LP, export, second pressing with sliver/black labels, one EMI boxed logo) £150
69	Parlophone CPCS 104	**BEATLES VI** (LP, second export pressing with silver/black labels, one EMI boxed logo)....£250
70	Parl./Apple (P-)PCS 7096	**LET IT BE** (LP, export pressing second reissue, Apple label [PCS 7096] in Parlophone sleeve) £35

(with silver/black labels)

70	Parlophone CPCS 103	**THE BEATLES' SECOND ALBUM** (LP, export, 2nd reissue, silver/black labels two EMI boxed logos) £100
73	Apple CPCS 106	**HEY JUDE** (3rd reissue, light green label) £25
78	Apple PCS 7067/8	**THE BEATLES** (2LP, export pressing, white vinyl, gatefold sleeve) £40
78	Parlophone PCTC 255	**MAGICAL MYSTERY TOUR** (LP, transparent yellow vinyl) £50

(with silver/black labels)

78	Apple PCS 7088	**ABBEY ROAD** (LP, green vinyl)...£50
78	Apple PCS 7096	**LET IT BE** (LP white vinyl) £50
70s	Parl./Apple (P-)CPCS 106	**HEY JUDE** (Apple label [CPCS 106] in Parlophone sleeve [P-CPSC 106]) £35

ALBUMS : FRENCH PRESSINGS

(Parlophone label LPs have 'Made in France' on EMI rim copy. Apple label LPs have 'Made in France by Pathe Marconi EMI' rim copy. All albums are in British-printed sleeves bearing 'Made in France' stickers.)

73	Apple PCSP 718	**THE BEATLES 1967-1970** (2-LP, gatefold sleeve with lyric inners) £15

ALBUMS : LPS : 1970S RE-PRESSINGS

(Black and silver labels with 'EMI Records Ltd' on label and 2 EMI boxes. Unless otherwise specified all have front laminated and non-flipback sleeves. Those albums with Apple labels are slightly lighter than those on 60s original pressings)

70s	Parlophone PCS 3042	**PLEASE PLEASE ME** (LP) £25
70s	Parlophone PCS 3045	**WITH THE BEATLES** (LP) £20
70s	Parlophone PCS 3058	**A HARD DAYS NIGHT** (LP) £25
70s	Parlophone PCS 3062	**BEATLES FOR SALE** (LP) £20
70s	Parlophone PCS 3071	**HELP!** (LP) £20
70s	Parlophone PCS 3075	**RUBBER SOUL** (LP) £30
70s	Parlophone PCS 7009	**REVOLVER** (LP) £30
70s	Parlophone PCS 7016	**A COLLECTION OF BEATLES OLDIES** (LP) £20
70s	Parlophone PCS 7027	**SGT. PEPPER'S LONELY HEARTS CLUB BAND** (LP, fully laminated sleeve) £30
70s	Apple PCS 7067/68	**THE BEATLES** (WHITE ALBUM) (2-LP, fully laminated sleeve).....................................£40
76	Parlophone PCTC 255	**MAGICAL MYSTERY TOUR** (LP, with booklet) £25
70s	Apple PCS 7070	**YELLOW SUBMARINE** (LP) £25
70s	Apple PCS 7088	**ABBEY ROAD** (LP, fully laminated sleeve) £35
70s	Apple PCS 7096	**LET IT BE** (LP, fully laminated sleeve) £25

ALBUMS : LPS : 1980S RE-PRESSINGS

(These repressings come in non-laminated 'varnished' sleeves and have black and silver labels. Most sleeves have barcodes)

88	Parlophone PCTC 255	**MAGICAL MYSTERY TOUR** (gatefold, with booklet) £18
80s	Parlophone PMC 1202	**PLEASE PLEASE ME** (LP, mono) £18
80s	Parlophone PMC 1206	**WITH THE BEATLES** (LP, mono) £15
80s	Parlophone PMC 1230	**A HARD DAYS NIGHT** (LP, mono)...£15
80s	Parlophone PMC 1240	**BEATLES FOR SALE** (LP, mono) £15
80s	Parlophone PCS 3071	**HELP!** (LP, stereo) £15
80s	Parlophone PCS 3075	**RUBBER SOUL** (LP, stereo) £20
80s	Parlophone PCS 7009	**REVOLVER** (LP, stereo)..£20
80s	Parlophone PCS 7016	**A COLLECTION OF BEATLES OLDIES** (LP, stereo) £15
80s	Parlophone PCS 7027	**SGT. PEPPER'S LONELY HEARTS CLUB BAND** (LP, stereo) £20
80s	Apple PCS 7067/68	**THE BEATLES** (WHITE ALBUM) (2-LP, stereo) £25
80s	Apple PCS 7070	**YELLOW SUBMARINE** (LP, stereo) £18
80s	Apple PCS 7088	**ABBEY ROAD** (LP, stereo) £20
80s	Apple PCS 7096	**LET IT BE** (LP, stereo) £18

ALBUMS : LPS:RETROSPECTIVES

73	Apple PCSP 717	**THE BEATLES 1962-1966** (2LP, gatefold, printed inners, labels state PCS 7171 and PCS 7172)..£40
73	Apple PCSP 718	**THE BEATLES 1967-1970** (2LP, laminated gatefold, printed inners, labels state 7181 and 7182)..£40
76	Parlophone PCSP 719	**ROCK N ROLL MUSIC** (2LP, gatefold)..£30
76	Parlophone PCTC 255	**MAGICAL MYSTERY TOUR** (LP, gatefold with 24-page stapled insert)...........................£40
76	Polydor 2683 068	**THE BEATLES TAPES** (2LP, gatefold, booklet) £30
77	EMI EMTV 4	**THE BEATLES AT THE HOLLYWOOD BOWL** (gatefold, printed inner) £20
77	Lingasong LNS 1	**LIVE AT THE STAR CLUB 1962** (2LP, gatefold) £30
77	Parlophone PCSP 721	**LOVE SONGS** (2LP, gatefold) £30
77	EMI HRL 026	**HISTORY OF ROCK VOL.26 THE BEATLES** (2LP gatefold) £30
78	Apple PCSPR 717	**THE BEATLES 1962-1966** (2LP, red vinyl, gatefold, hype sticker, printed inners)............£40
78	Apple PCSPB 718	**THE BEATLES 1967-1970** (2LP, blue vinyl, gatefold, hype sticker, printed inners) £40
79	Parlophone PCM 1001	**RARITIES** (LP) £30
82	Parlophone PCS 7218	**REEL MUSIC** (LP. printed inner, 12-page 'Souvenir Program') £25
88	Parlophone BPM 1	**PAST MASTERS VOLUME 1 & 2** (2LP, gatefold)..£60
94	Apple PCSP 726	**LIVE AT THE BBC** (2LP, gatefold, printed inners) £50
95	Apple PCSP 727	**ANTHOLOGY 1** (3LP, trifold sleeve) £60
96	Apple PCSP 728	**ANTHOLOGY 2** (3LP, trifold sleeve) £70
96	Apple PCSP 729	**ANTHOLOGY 3** (3LP, trifold sleeve) £70
00	Apple 529 3251	**THE BEATLES 1** (2LP, gatefold sleeve, with poster & 4 prints).....................................£60

MINT VALUE £

Year	Catalogue	Description	Value
00	Apple 7243 529325 11	**THE BEATLES 1** (2LP, gatefold sleeve, with poster & 4 prints, signed certificate– 5293261 A-100/5293261 B-100/5293261 A-100 and 5293261 B-100 matrixes - 100 only)	£500
03	Apple 595 4380	**LET IT BE...NAKED** (LP/7", gatefold, booklet, Fly On The Wall 7" EP)	£200
07	Apple 379 8081	**LOVE** (2LP, gatefold sleeve, 28-page booklet)	£50
13	Apple 3750506	**ON AIR - LIVE AT THE BBC VOLUME 2** (3LP, trifold, printed inners)	£60
15	Apple 0602547567727	**1+** (CD/2BD, booklet, slipcase)	£30
16	Apple 5705499	**LIVE AT THE HOLLYWOOD BOWL** (LP, gatefold, printed inner)	£25
23	Apple 0602455920539	**THE BEATLES 1962-1966** (3LP, gatefold, printed inners, half-speed mastered, 180g, red vinyl)	£60
23	Apple 0602455920805	**THE BEATLES 1967-1970** (3LP, gatefold, printed inners, half-speed mastered, 180g, blue vinyl)	£50

ALBUMS : POLYDOR RECORDINGS : LPS

Year	Catalogue	Description	Value
64	Polydor Hi-Fi 46 432	**THE BEATLES' FIRST** (purple/black sleeve, Germany only, unissued in U.K.)	£100
67	Polydor Special 236 201	**THE BEATLES' FIRST** (as Tony Sheridan & The Beatles, 1st pressing, without 'stereo' on label or sleeve, 'pop art' sleeve)	£50
67	Polydor Special 236 201	**THE BEATLES' FIRST** (later pressings with 'stereo' on label & sleeve, minor label variations, 'pop art' sleeve)	£30

ALBUMS : REEL-TO-REEL TAPES: ORIGINALS

(All Beatles Reel-to-Reel tapes up to 1967 (from PLEASE PLEASE ME to SGT. PEPPERS LONELY HEARTS CLUB BAND were issued on 4 inch spools with printed leaders and were housed in card trays in card boxes. From THE BEATLES (WHITE ALBUM) to LET IT BE albums were still 4 inch spools but housed in jewel cases with card inlays)

Year	Catalogue	Description	Value
65	Parlophone TA-PMC 1240	**BEATLES FOR SALE** (Mono only)	£20
65	Parlophone TA-PMC 1255	**HELP!** (Mono-only)	£20
65	Parlophone TA-PMC 1267	**RUBBER SOUL** (Mono only, reel-to-reel tape)	£20
66	Parlophone TA-PMC 7009	**REVOLVER** (Mono only)	£25
70	Apple TD-PCS 7088	**ABBEY ROAD** (Stereo, jewel case)	£70
70	Apple TA-PMC 7088	**ABBEY ROAD** (Mono, jewel case)	£100
69	Apple DTD-PCS 7067/8	**THE BEATLES** (WHITE ALBUM) (5 inch spool, Stereo, jewel case)	£100
69	Apple DTA-PMC 7067/8	**THE BEATLES** (WHITE ALBUM) (5 inch spool, Mono, jewel case)	£100
67	Parlophone TA-PMC 7027	**SGT. PEPPER'S LONELY HEARTS CLUB BAND** (Mono only)	£30

(All Beatles Reel-to-Reel tapes up to 1967 (from PLEASE PLEASE ME to SGT. PEPPERS LONELY HEARTS CLUB BAND were issued on 4 inch spools with printed leaders and were housed in card trays in card boxes)

Year	Catalogue	Description	Value
67	Parlophone TA-PMC 7016	**A COLLECTION OF BEATLES OLDIES** (Mono only)	£20
63	Parlophone TA-PMC 1202	**PLEASE PLEASE ME** (Mono only)	£25
64	Parlophone TA-PMC 1206	**WITH THE BEATLES** (Mono only)	£25
64	Parlophone TA-PMC 1230	**A HARD DAYS NIGHT** (Mono only)	£20
70	Apple TA-PMC 7096	**LET IT BE** (Mono, jewel case)	£100
70	Apple TD-PCS 7096	**LET IT BE** (Stereo, jewel case)	£80

ALBUMS : REEL-TO-REEL TAPES: REISSUES

(These albums were all reissued on reel-to-reel tape in 1968 and are all on 4 inch tape inside jewel cases with card inserts)

Year	Catalogue	Description	Value
68	Parlophone TA-PMC 1202	**PLEASE PLEASE ME** (Reissue, Mono, jewel case)	£25
68	Parlophone TD-PCS 3042	**PLEASE PLEASE ME** (Reissue, Stereo, jewel case)	£25
68	Parlophone TA-PMC 1206	**WITH THE BEATLES** (Reissue, Mono, jewel case)	£30
68	Parlophone TD-PCS 3045	**WITH THE BEATLES** (Reissue, Stereo, jewel case)	£25
68	Parlophone TA-PMC 1230	**A HARD DAY'S NIGHT** (Reissue, Mono, jewel case)	£25
68	Parlophone TD-PCS 3058	**A HARD DAY'S NIGHT** (Reissue, Stereo, jewel case)	£25
68	Parlophone TA-PMC 1240	**BEATLES FOR SALE** (Reissue, Mono, jewel case)	£30
68	Parlophone TD-PCS 3062	**BEATLES FOR SALE** (Reissue, Stereo, jewel case)	£25
68	Parlophone TA-PCM 1255	**HELP!** (Reissue, Mono, jewel case)	£25
68	Parlophone TD-PCS 3071	**HELP!** (Reissue, Stereo, jewel case)	£25
68	Parlophone TA-PMC 1267	**RUBBER SOUL** (Reissue, Mono, jewel case)	£30
68	Parlophone TD-PCS 3075	**RUBBER SOUL** (Reissue, Stereo, jewel case)	£25
68	Parlophone TA-PMC 7009	**REVOLVER** (Reissue, Mono, jewel case)	£30
68	Parlophone TD-PCS 7009	**REVOLVER** (Reissue, Stereo, jewel case)	£25
68	Parlophone TA-PMC 7016	**A COLLECTION OF BEATLES OLDIES** (Reissue, Mono, jewel case)	£30
68	Parlophone TD-PCS 7016	**A COLLECTION OF BEATLES OLDIES** (Reissue, Stereo, jewel case)	£25
68	Parlophone TA-PMC 7027	**SGT. PEPPER'S LONELY HEARTS CLUB BAND** (Reissue, Mono, jewel case)	£40
68	Parlophone TD-PCS 7027	**SGT. PEPPER'S LONELY HEARTS CLUB BAND** (Reissue, Stereo, jewel case)	£35

MISPRESSINGS

Year	Catalogue	Description	Value
63	Parlophone R 4983	**Please Please Me/Ask Me Why** (Mispressing, A-side actually plays 'Quiet Morning' by the Brian Fahey Orchestra)	£50
64	Parlophone GEP 8882	**TWIST AND SHOUT** (label error: "Do You Want A Know A Secret")	£20
64	Parlophone PCS 3062	**BEATLES FOR SALE** (label error: "I'm A Losser")	£250
65	Parlophone GEP 8946	**THE BEATLES' MILLION SELLERS** (label error: "Beatles Golden Discs")	£20
65	Parlophone PCS 3075	**RUBBER SOUL** (label error: "Norweigian Wood")	£400
65	Parlophone CPCS 101	**SOMETHING NEW** (LP, 1st pressing, 1G/1G mother stampers, export issue, label misprint error: "Sold in UK")	£500
66	Parlophone PMC 7009	**REVOLVER** (copies with side 2 matrix no.: XEX 606-1 have 'Remix 11' ofTomorrow Never Knows, G & L or E. J. Day version; mono only)	£500
66	Parlophone CPCS 106	**BEATLES VI** (LP, export issue, label error: "Sold in UK")	£500
67	Parlophone PMC 7027	**SGT. PEPPER'S LONELY HEARTS CLUB BAND** (First pressing with label misprint omits "A Day In The Life" credit; G & L laminatedgatefold sleeve, with plain white inner & insert,; mono only)	£200

With "The Gramophone Co Ltd" & "Sold in the UK..." label text

Year	Catalogue	Description	Value
68	Apple PCS 7067/8	**THE BEATLES** (2LP label misprinting error: "Rocky Racoon")	£200
69	Apple PCS 7088	**ABBEY ROAD** (label omits "Her Majesty")	£100
69	Apple CPCS 106	**HEY JUDE** (label misprint error: "Revolutions")	£300
69	Parlophone PCS 7009	**REVOLVER** (1969 repressing, stereo only with misprint "I Got To Get You Into My Life" on side 2)	£70

(with laminated flipback sleeves & silver/black labels with one boxed EMI logo)

69	Parlophone PMC 7027	**SGT. PEPPER'S LONELY HEARTS CLUB BAND** (1969 Misspressing, mono; matrix YEX 637/8; plays stereo) £200
99	Parlophone PCS 3075	**RUBBER SOUL** (label error: pressed on Apple) £100
12	Parlophone 45-R 4949	**Love Me Do/PS I Love You** (reissue, withdrawn as A side has album version with Andy White on drums and Ringo on tambourine, Matrixes: BC88258-01A1 01740174/ BC88258-01B1 0174017 J G i i and incorrect catalogue number R 47414 on B-side) £20

FLEXIDISCS : FESTIVE FLEXIDISCS, LP & COLLECTION
(Fan club flexidiscs are worth around £20 less without newsletters and half the listed values without picture sleeves.)

63	Lyntone LYN 492	**The Beatles' Christmas Record** (Flexidisc, gatefold p/s) £120
64	Lyntone LYN 757	**Another Beatles Christmas Record** (Flexidisc, p/s, with gatefold newsletter insert) £100
65	Lyntone LYN 948	**The Beatles' Third Christmas Record** (Flexidisc, p/s, with gatefold newsletter insert) £100
66	Lyntone LYN 1145	**Pantomime: Everywhere It's Christmas** (Flexidisc, p/s, with 7" x 7" newsletter insert) ..£100
67	Lyntone LYN 1360	**Christmas Time (Is Here Again)** (Flexidisc, p/s, with 7" x 7" newsletter insert) £100
68	Lyntone LYN 1743/4	**The Beatles' Sixth Christmas Record** (Flexidisc, p/s, with 'Superpix' sales insert) £100
68	Lyntone LYN 1743/4	**The Beatles' Sixth Christmas Record** (Flexidisc, p/s, without "Superpix" sales insert) £100
69	Lyntone LYN 1970/1-IL	**The Beatles' Seventh Christmas Record** (Flexidisc, p/s, with 2 x foolscap fan club newsletters) £100
69	Lyntone LYN 1970/1-IL	**The Beatles' Seventh Christmas Record** (p/s) £75
70	Apple/Lyntone LYN 2154	**FROM THEN TO YOU** (The Beatles' Christmas Album) (LP) £500
17	Apple 0602557914856	**HAPPY CHRISTMAS BEATLE PEOPLE! THE CHRISTMAS RECORDS** (7x7" set, white/red/ blue/yellow/green/clear/orange vinyl, booklet, box set) £120

(see also John Lennon, Paul McCartney/Wings, George Harrison, Ringo Starr, Pete Best Four, Quarry Men, Tony Sheridan, George Martin, Billy Preston, Yoko Ono, Fireman, Twin Freaks, Suzy & The Red Stripes)

BEATMEN
| 64 | Pye 7N 15659 | You Can't Sit Down/Come On Pretty Babe ....£20 |
| 65 | Pye 7N 15792 | Now The Sun Has Gone/Please Believe ....£40 |

BEAT MERCHANTS
| 64 | Columbia DB 7367 | Pretty Face/Messin' With The Man ....£80 |
| 65 | Columbia DB 7492 | So Fine/She Said Yeah ....£70 |

BEAT NECESSITY
| 81 | Newtown NTP 2 | Pleasure Pain/VELDT: Ghost Child ....£15 |
| 82 | Newtown NTP 3 | When You're Down On Your Luck/Telephone/Don't Know ....£15 |

BEATPUMP
| 80 | Slow Lorries SLOW 1 | THE FIVE MONTH PLAN EP (p/s) ....£25 |

BEATSTALKERS
65	Decca F 12259	Ev'rybody's Talking 'Bout My Baby/Mr. Disappointed £80
66	Decca F 12352	Left Right Left/You'd Better Get A Better Hold On £60
66	Decca F 12460	A Love Like Yours/Base Line £60
67	CBS 2732	My One Chance To Make It/Ain't No Soul (Left In These Ole Shoes) £80
67	CBS 3105	Silver Treetop School For Boys/Sugar Coated Man £75
68	CBS 3557	Rain Coloured Roses/Everything Is For You £60
69	CBS 3936	Little Boy/When I'm Five £70

PAUL BEATTIE
| 57 | Parlophone R 4385 | I'm Comin' Home/Nothing So Strange ....£30 |
| 68 | Parlophone R 4664 | Slick Chick/The Big Bounce ....£30 |

BEAU
| 69 | Dandelion S 63751 | BEAU (LP, black/red/silver label) ....£50 |
| 71 | Dandelion DAN 8006 | CREATION (LP, with The Way We Live) ....£40 |

(see also Way We Live)

BEAU BRUMMEL
| 82 | Moonlight MNS 004 | Hot George/Oscar ....£15 |

(see also Paul Roland, Andy Ellison)

BEAU BRUMMELS
| 66 | Pye International 7N 25342 | Good Time Music/Sad Little Girl (unissued) ....£0 |
| 65 | Pye International NPL 28062 | INTRODUCING THE BEAU BRUMMELS (LP, mono only) ....£20 |

BEAU-MARKS
| 60 | Top Rank JAR 377 | Clap Your Hands/Daddy Said ....£20 |

(see also Del-Tones)

JIMMY BEAUMONT
| 66 | London HLZ 10059 | You Got Too Much Going For You/I Never Loved Her Anyway.................£100 |
| 66 | London HLZ 10059 | You Got Too Much Going For You/I Never Loved Her Anyway (DJ Copy).......£200 |

BEAUTIFUL SOUTH
92	Go! Discs 828 310-1	0898 BEAUTIFUL SOUTH (LP, inner) £20
94	Go! Discs 828 507-1	MIAOW (LP, withdrawn HMV-style 'dog' sleeve with lyric inner) £80
94	Go! Discs 828 507-1	MIAOW (LP, 'cat' sleeve with lyric inner) £60
94	Go! Discs 828 572-1	CARRY ON UP THE CHARTS (LP) £100
96	Go! Discs 828 845-1	BLUE IS THE COLOUR (LP, with lyric inner) £100
98	Go! Discs 538166	QUENCH (LP, inner) £100
01	Mercury 586 444 1	SOLID BRONZE (2-LP)..£100

BEAZERS
| 64 | Decca F 11827 | Blue Beat/I Wanna Shout...£45 |

(see also Chris Farlowe, Little Joe Cook)

BE-BOP DELUXE
73	Smile LAFS 001	Teenage Archangel/Jets At Dawn (mono, 1,000 only) £25
75	Harvest HAR 5091	Between The Worlds/Lights (withdrawn) £50
74	Harvest SHVL 813	AXE VICTIM (LP, gatefold sleeve) £18

MINT VALUE £

75	Harvest SHSP 4045	**FUTURAMA** (LP)	£15
76	Harvest SHSP 4053	**SUNBURST FINISH** (LP, insert)	£15
77	Harvest SHVL 816	**LIVE! IN THE AIR AGE** (LP, with bonus EP "Live! In The Air Age" [PSR 412])	£20
78	Harvest SHDW 410	**THE BEST AND THE REST OF BE BOP DELUXE** (2-LP)	£15

(see also A-Austr, Axe Victim)

BE-BOP PRESERVATION SOCIETY

71	Dawn DNLS 3027	**THE BE-BOP PRESERVATION SOCIETY** (LP, gatefold sleeve, orange label with insert)	£30

BECK

94	Geffen GFS 73	**Pay No Mind** (Snoozer)/**Special People** (withdrawn)	£80
94	Geffen GFST 73	**Pay No Mind** (Snoozer)/**Special People/Trouble All My Days/Super Golden** (Sunchild) (12", p/s, withdrawn - at least 100 pressed up)	£50
94	Geffen GFS 19235	**Beercan/Spanking Room** (p/s, 1500 copies)	£20
09	Matador OLE 865-7	**Green Light/SONIC YOUTH: Pay No Mind** (green vinyl, very few sold in UK for Record Store Day)	£60
94	Geffen GEF 24634	**MELLOW GOLD** (LP, inner)	£40
98	Simply Vinyl SVLP 0051	**ODELAY** (LP, reissue, 180gm)	£40
05	Interscope 9864087	**GUERO** (2-LP)	£20

BECK, BOGERT & APPICE

75	CBS EQ 32140/Q 65455	**BECK, BOGERT & APPICE** (LP, quadrophonic)	£18

(see also Jeff Beck, Vanilla Fudge, Cactus)

GORDON BECK (QUARTET)

67	Major Minor MM/SMLP 88	**DR. DOOLITTLE LOVES JAZZ** (LP, as Gordon Beck + Two)	£50
68	M. Minor MMLP/SMLP 21	**EXPERIMENTS WITH POPS** (LP, as Gordon Beck Quartet)	£125
68	M. Minor MMLP/SMLP 22	**HALF A JAZZ SIXPENCE** (LP, as Gordon Beck + 2)	£100
68	Morgan MJ 1	**GYROSCOPE** (LP, as Gordon Beck Trio)	£250
72	Dire FO 341	**BECK-MATTHEWSON-HUMAIR TRIO** (LP)	£30

(see also Seven Ages Of Man)

JEFF BECK

69	Columbia DB 8590	**Plinth** (Water Down The Drain)/**Hangman's Knee** (unissued)	£0
68	Columbia S(C)X 6293	**TRUTH** (LP, 1st pressing, blue/black labels, stereo with "sold in U.K." label text)	£150
68	Columbia SX 6293	**TRUTH** (LP, 1st pressing, blue/black labels, mono with "sold in U.K." label text)	£200
68	Columbia SX 6293	**TRUTH** (LP, 2nd pressing, silver/black labels, boxed Columbia logo, with "sold in U.K." label text mono)	£70
69	Columbia SX 6351	**BECK-OLA** (LP, 1st pressing, blue/black labels, mono)	£150
69	Columbia S(C)X 6351	**BECK-OLA** (LP, 1st pressing, blue/black labels, stereo)	£100
69	Columbia SCX 6293	**TRUTH** (LP, 3rd pressing, silver/black labels, stereo)	£15
69	Columbia SX 6351	**BECK-OLA** (LP, 2nd pressing, silver/black labels, mono)	£20
69	Columbia SCX 6351	**BECK-OLA** (LP, 2nd pressing, silver/black labels, stereo)	£15
72	Epic EPC 64619	**ROUGH AND READY** (LP, yellow label)	£30
72	Epic EPC 64899	**JEFF BECK GROUP** (LP, yellow label)	£20
72	Epic EQ 30973	**ROUGH AND READY** (LP, quadrophonic)	£40
74	CBS EQ 31331	**JEFF BECK GROUP** (LP, quadrophonic)	£20
97	EMI LPCENT 3	**BECK-OLA** (LP, reissue, EMI centenary issue, stickered sleeve)	£20

(see also Yardbirds, Beck Bogert Appice, Donovan, Rod Stewart, Cozy Powell, Buddy Guy)

BECKETT

74	Raft RA 48502	**BECKETT** (LP, with lyric insert)	£20

HAROLD BECKETT

71	Philips 6308 026	**FLARE UP** (LP)	£120
72	RCA SF 8225	**WARM SMILES** (LP)	£100
73	RCA SF 8264	**THEME FOR FEGA** (LP)	£60
75	Cadillac SGC 1004	**JOY UNLIMITED** (LP)	£50
76	Ogun OG 800	**MEMORIES OF BACARES** (LP, as Harry Beckett's Joy Unlimited)	£15

(see also Graham Collier, Galliard, Ninesense)

STUART BECKETT

60s	Sherwood SRS 1001	**Kariline/Breakthrough**	£15

(KEE) LYN BECKFORD

68	Island WI 3144	**Combination/Hey Little Girl**	£60
69	Jackpot JP 707	**Kiss Me Quick/MRS. MILLER: Feel It**	£120
69	Big Shot BI 521	**Suzie Wong** (as K. Beckford)/**SWINGING KINGS: Deebo**	£50
71	G.G. GG 4514	**Groove Me/Groove Version** (as Keeling Beckford)	£35

THEO(PHILUS) BECKFORD

61	Blue Beat BB 33	**Jack And Jill Shuffle/Little Lady** (as Theophilus Beckford & Clue J. & His Blues Blasters)	£30
61	Blue Beat BB 50	**Georgie And The Old Shoe/That's Me** (as Theo Beckford & City Slickers)	£30
62	Blue Beat BB 87	**Walking Down King Street/The Clock** (B-side actually by Sir D's Group)	£30
62	Blue Beat BB 132	**Bringing In The Sheep** (song actually "Bringing In The Sheaves")/**Run Away**	£30
62	Island WI 026	**I Don't Want You** (actually by King Edward's All Stars)/**Seven Long Years**	£40
63	Island WI 106	**Daphney/Boiler Man**	£40
63	R & B JB 136	**Bullo Man/Daphney**	£50
64	Blue Beat BB 250	**She's Gone/Old Flame** (as Cotheo Beckford, B-side act. by Frederick Hibbert)	£45
64	Blue Beat BB 257	**Don't Worry To Cry/Love Me Or Leave Me** (as Theophilus Beckford, B-side actually by Lloyd Clarke)	£40
64	Blue Beat BB 256	**Glamour Girl/BUSTER'S ALLSTARS: Down Beat Burial**	£120
64	Blue Beat BB 287	**On Your Knees/Now You're Gone** (with Yvonne Harrison)	£40
65	Blue Beat BB 303	**Dig The Dig** (as Basil Gabbidon)/**Don't Let Me Cry No More**	£40
65	Black Swan WI 452	**Take Your Time/STRANGER COLE: Happy-Go-Lucky**	£40
65	Island WI 238	**Trench Town People/PIONEERS: Sometime**	£40
65	Island WI 243	**You Are The One Girl/Grudgeful People**	£40

65	Island WI 246	**If Life Was A Thing/L. CLARKE: Parro Saw The Light** (B-side actually "Pharaoh Saw The Light" by Lloyd Clarke)..................................£40
65	Island WI 248	**What A Whoe/Bajan Girl** £40
68	Nu Beat NB 009	**Easy Snappin'/ERIC MORRIS: My Lonely Days**..................................£50
69	Crab CRAB 25	**Brother Ram Goat** (as T. Beckford)/**STARLIGHTS: What A Condition** £30

(see also Eric Barnet[t], Maytals, Clue J & His Bluesblasters)

BED BUGS

90	Snake Rattle 01	**Haywire/No Safe Haven** £15

CHUCK BEDFORD

74	Bell 1378	**When I See You Smile/Don't Make Me History** £15

DAVID BEDFORD

75	Virgin VDJ 10	**An Extract From THE RIME OF THE ANCIENT MARINER - Part Two/An Extract From THE RIME OF THE ANCIENT MARINER - Part 2** (B&W girl and dragon logo)..................................£25
70	Argo ZRG 638	**MUSIC FOR ALBION MOONLIGHT** (LP, 1 side by Elizabeth Lutyens) £25
72	Dandelion 2310 165	**NURSE'S SONG WITH ELEPHANTS** (LP, gatefold sleeve) £30
75	Virgin V2020	**STAR'S END** (LP, stickered) £15

(see also Coxhill/Bedford Trio, Kevin Ayers & Whole World, Mike Oldfield, Roy Harper, Edgar Broughton Band)

BEDLAM

73	Chrysalis CHR 1048	**BEDLAM** (LP) £20

(see also Cozy Powell, Ace Kefford Stand, Big Bertha, Youngblood)

BEE BEE CEE

77	Rel RE 48-S	**You Gotta Know Girl/We Ain't Listening** (p/s, 2,000 only)..................................£70

BEECH NUT

70	Pastel PT 1	**Send For The Magician/Shot In The Dark** £30

BEEFEATERS

64	Pye International 7N 25277	**Please Let Me Love You/Don't Be Long** £100
70	Elektra 2101 007	**Please Let Me Love You/Don't Be Long** (reissue)..................................£15

(see also Byrds)

BEE GEES

69	Polydor 56304	**Odessa Parts 1 & 2** (unissued) £0
81	RSO SNF 1	**Night Fever** (promo only 7" with p/s to coincide with ITV showing 'Saturday Night Fever' on Royal Wedding Day) £20
67	Polydor 582/583 012	**BEE GEES 1ST** (LP) £30
68	Polydor 582/583 020	**HORIZONTAL** (LP) £25
68	Polydor 236 221	**RARE PRECIOUS AND BEAUTIFUL** (LP) £15
68	Polydor 236 513	**RARE PRECIOUS AND BEAUTIFUL VOL. 2** (LP) £15
68	Polydor 582/583 036	**IDEA** (LP) £15
69	Polydor 236 556	**RARE PRECIOUS AND BEAUTIFUL VOL. 3** (LP) £15
69	Polydor 582 049/050	**ODESSA** (2-LP, felt cover, gatefold sleeve, mono) £50
69	Polydor 583 049/050	**ODESSA** (2-LP, felt cover, gatefold sleeve, stereo)..................................£50
70	Polydor 2383 010	**CUCUMBER CASTLE** (LP) £20
70	Polydor 2310 069	**TWO YEARS ON** (LP) £15
71	Polydor 2383 052	**TRAFALGAR** (LP)..................................£20
72	Polydor 2383 139	**TO WHOM IT MAY CONCERN** (LP) £15

(see also Barry Gibb, Robin Gibb, Maurice Gibb, Humpy Bong, Fut)

MARK BEER

81	My China TAO 001	**DUST ON THE ROAD** (LP) £15

BEES MAKE HONEY

73	EMI EMC 3013	**MUSIC EVERY NIGHT** (LP) £20

BEES (UK) (1)

67	Columbia Blue Beat DB 101	**Jesse James Rides Again/The Girl In My Dreams** £35
68	Columbia Blue Beat DB 111	**The Prisoner From Alcatraz/The Ska's The Limit** £35

(see also Pyramids)

BEES (UK) (2)

80	Paw THF 003	**Leave Willie Alone/Mr Gaynor** £20

BEES (UK) (3)

04	Virgin BEES 1	**I Love You/I Love You** (Instrumental)..................................£15
01	We Love You AMOUR 6LP	**SUNSHINE HIT ME** (LP, inner sleeve) £30
04	Virgin V 2983	**FREE THE BEES** (2-LP, gatefold, with transfer) £30
07	Virgin V 3024	**OCTOPUS** (LP, with inner sleeve) £18

BILLY BEETHOVEN

75	DJM DJS 10377	**Dreams** (Out In The Forest)/**We're Free** £80

(see also Graham Bonnet)

BEEZ

79	Edible SNACK 001	**Easy/Vagrant** (gatefold p/s) £200
79	Edible SNACK 002	**THE BEEZ EP: Do The Suicide** (no p/s, stickered sleeve) £200

B.E.F. (BRITISH ELECTRIC FOUNDATION)

91	Ten TEN 386	**Free** (Edit)/**Secret Life Of Arabia** (stickered/unstickered p/s, as B.E.F. Featuring Billy MacKenzie, unissued 200 copies only) £40
81	Virgin BEF 1	**MUSIC FOR LISTENING TO** (LP) £30

(see also Heaven 17)

BEGGARS FARM

84	White Rabbit WR 1001	**THE DEPTH OF A DREAM** (LP) £25

BEGGARS HILL

76	Moonshine MS 60	**BEGGARS HILL** (LP, private pressing) £175

MINT VALUE £

BEGGARS OPERA
70	Vertigo 6059 026	Sarabande/Think	£20
72	Vertigo 6059 060	Hobo/Pathfinder	£20
70	Vertigo 6360 018	ACT ONE (LP, large swirl label, gatefold sleeve)	£200
71	Vertigo 6360 054	WATERS OF CHANGE (LP, small swirl label, gatefold sleeve)	£300
72	Vertigo 6360 073	PATHFINDER (LP, small swirl label, foldout poster cover)	£300
73	Vertigo 6360 090	GET YOUR DOG OFF ME! (LP, 'spaceship' label)	£40

BEGINNING OF THE END
71	Atlantic 2091 097	Funky Nassau Parts 1 & 2 (initial pressing on red label)	£15
72	Atlantic 2091 166	Monkey Tamarind/Hey Pretty Girl	£15
76	Warner Bros. WEA K10021	Funky Nassau (Full Length Version)/Funky Nassau Parts 1 & 2 (12")	£40
71	Atlantic K 40304	FUNKY NASSAU (LP)	£40

SVEINBJORN BEINTEINSSON
90	Durtro 005	EDDA (LP, with booklet)	£20

BELBURY POLY
10	Ghost Box GBX 703	Swingalong/Mordant Music: Inn Ohn The Lake (p/s)	£15
11	Ghost Box GBX 003	THE WILLOWS (LP)	£35
12	Ghost Box GBX 016LP	THE BELBURY TAKES (LP)	£25

(see also Daphne Oram)

BEL CANTOS
65	R&B MRB 5003	Feel Aw Right Parts 1 & 2	£20

BELFAST GYPSIES
66	Island WI 3007	Gloria's Dream/Secret Police	£80
77	Sonet SNTF 738	LEGENDARY MASTER RECORDINGS (LP)	£25

(see also Them, Jackie McAuley, Freaks Of Nature)

ALEXANDER BELL
67	CBS 2977	Alexander Bell Believes/Hymn ... With Love	£30

ANDY BELL
19	Sonic Cathedral SCR114	Plastic Bag/The Commune (poster p/s, clear vinyl, 200 only)	£50
20	Sonic Cathedral SCR170LP	THE VIEW FROM HALFWAY DOWN (LP, white/splatter vinyl)	£60

(see also Ride, Beady Eye)

ARCHIE BELL & THE DRELLS
68	Atlantic 584 185	Tighten Up/Dog Eat Dog	£15
68	Atlantic 584 217	I Can't Stop Dancing/You're Such A Beautiful Child	£15
76	Philly Int. 4803	Where Will You Go When The Party's Over?/I Swear You're Beautiful	£15
81	Becket BKS 1	Any Time Is Right/Harder And Harder (as Archie Bell)	£100
86	Nightmare MARE 16	Look Back Over Your Shoulder/Look Back Over Your Shoulder (Dub Mix) (12")	£25
04	UK Atlantic 504676251	A Thousand Wonders/Here I Go Again (promo only)	£15
68	Atlantic	TIGHTEN UP (LP)	£20
72	Atlantic K 40454	HERE I GO AGAIN (LP)	£20

BELINDA BELL
73	Columbia SCXA 9255	STONE VALLEY (LP, gatefold sleeve)	£15

CHARLES BELL & CONTEMPORARY JAZZ QUARTET
63	London HA-K/SH-K 8095	ANOTHER DIMENSION (LP)	£30

ERIC BELL BAND
81	Hobo HOS 016	Lonely Man/Anyone Seen My Baby (p/s)	£30

(see also Thin Lizzy)

FREDDIE BELL & BELLBOYS
56	Mercury MEP 9508	ROCK WITH THE BELL BOYS (EP)	£20
57	Mercury MEP 9512	ROCK WITH THE BELL BOYS VOL. 2 (EP)	£30

FREDRICK BELL
68	Nu Beat NB 004	Rocksteady Cool/CARLTON ALPHONSO: I Have Changed	£50

GARY BELL
67	CBS 202234	Is This What I Get For Loving You?/To Keep You	£15

GRAHAM BELL
72	Charisma CAS 1061	GRAHAM BELL (LP, large 'mad hatter' label)	£20

(see also Heavy Jelly, Griffin, Skip Bifferty, Bell & Arc)

MADELINE BELL
63	HMV POP 1215	I Long For Your Love/Because You Didn't Care	£20
64	Columbia DB 7257	You Don't Love Me No More/Don't Cross Over To My Side Of The Street	£20
65	Philips BF 1448	What The World Needs Now Is Love/I Can't Wait To See My Baby's Face	£30
66	Philips BF 1501	Don't Come Running To Me/I Got Carried Away	£25
67	Philips BF 1611	Picture Me Gone/Go Ahead On	£30
66	Philips BF 1526	One Step At A Time/You Won't See Me	£15
68	Philips BF 1656	I'm Gonna Make You Love Me/I'm Gonna Leave You	£15
67	Philips SBL 7818	BELLS A POPPIN' (LP, stereo)	£60
67	Philips SBL 7818	BELLS A POPPIN' (LP, mono)	£70
68	Philips SBL 7865	DOIN' THINGS (LP)	£60
71	Philips 6308 053	MADELINE BELL (LP)	£20
73	RCA RCA 2240	COMING ATCHA (LP)	£50
76	Pye NSPL 18483	THIS IS ONE GIRL (LP)	£20

(see also Seven Ages Of Man, Underground, Ian Green [Revelation])

WILLIAM BELL
67	Atlantic 584 076	Never Like This Before/Soldier's Goodbye	£15

69	Stax STAX 128	Happy/Johnny I Love You	£50
69	Atco 228 003	A TRIBUTE TO A KING (LP)	£40
69	Stax SXATS 1016	BOUND TO HAPPEN (LP)	£35
71	Stax 2362 009	WOW . . . WILLIAM BELL (LP)	£25
72	Stax 2362 027	PHASES OF REALITY (LP)	£35
76	Mercury 9100038	COMING BACK FOR MORE (LP)	£18
76	Stax STX 1010	RELATING (LP)	£18
76	Stax STX 1050	BOUND TO HAPPEN (LP, reissue)	£20
84	Charly R&B CRB 1076	DO RIGHT MAN (LP)	£15

GEORGE BELLAMY
65	Parlophone R 5282	Where I'm Bound/How Could I Ever	£20

(see also Tornados)

PETER BELLAMY
68	Xtra XTRA 1010	PETER BELLAMY (LP)	£25
68	XTRA XTRA 1060	MAINLY NORFOLK - SONGS AND BALLADS (LP)	£40
69	Xtra XTRA 1075	FAIR ENGLAND'S SHORE (LP)	£40
69	Topic 12T 200	THE FOX JUMPS OVER THE PARSON'S GATE (LP, blue label)	£20
70	Argo ZFB 11	OAK, ASH AND THORN (LP)	£20
72	Argo ZFB 37	WON'T YOU GO MY WAY (LP)	£20
72	Argo ZFB 81	MERLIN'S ISLE OF GRAMARYE (LP)	£20
74	Trailer LER 2089	TELL IT LIKE IT IS (LP)	£15
77	Free Reed 21/22	TRANSPORTS (2-LP, gatefold, booklet)	£20
79	Topic 12TS 400	BOTH SIDES THEN (LP)	£15

(see also Young Tradition)

BELL & ARC
71	Charisma CAS 1053	BELL & ARC (LP, gatefold sleeve, pink scroll label)	£60

(see also Skip Bifferty, Arc, Graham Bell)

BELL BROTHERS
68	Action ACT 4510	Tell Him No/Throw Away The Key	£30

BELLE & SEBASTIAN
97	Jeepster JPR 12 001	Dog On Wheels/The State I Am In/String Bean Jim/Belle & Sebastian (12")	£15
97	Jeepster JPR 12 002	Lazy Line Painter Jane/You Made Me Forget My Dreams/Photo Jenny/A Century Of Elvis (12")	£18
17	Beggars Banquet (No Cat. No.)	THE NATIONAL: England (Live)/BELLE & SEBASTIAN: The State I Am In (12" p/s, splatter vinyl, booklet)	£60
96	Elektric Honey EHRLP 5	TIGERMILK (LP, 1,000 only)	£400
96	Jeepster JPRLP001	IF YOU'RE FEELING SINISTER (LP, 1st pressing, gatefold)	£50
99	Jeepster JPRLP007	TIGERMILK (LP, reissue)	£40
98	Jeepster JPRLP003	THE BOY WITH THE ARAB STRAP (LP, gatefold)	£40
00	Jeepster JPRLP010	FOLD YOUR HANDS CHILD, YOU WALK LIKE A PEASANT (LP, gatefold)	£40
02	Jeepster JPRLP014	STORYTELLING (LP, gatefold)	£40
04	Rough Trade RTRADELP 080	DEAR CATASTROPHE WAITRESS (2-LP)	£35
05	Jeepster JRPLP015	PUSH BARMAN TO OPEN OLD WOUNDS (3-LP)	£60
06	Rough Trade RTRADELP 280	THE LIFE PURSUIT (2-LP)	£30
08	Jeepster JPRLP018	THE BBC SESSIONS (2-LP)	£25
09	Jeepster JPRLP001	IF YOU'RE FEELING SINISTER (LP, reissue, with 'Universal Music' credit, gatefold)	£20
10	Rough Trade RTRADELP 480	WRITE ABOUT LOVE (LP, with free 7")	£25
13	Rough Trade RTRADLP 670	THE THIRD EYE CENTRE (2-LP)	£25
14	Jeepster JPRLP003	THE BOY WITH THE ARAB STRAP (LP, reissue, with 'Universal Music' credit, gatefold)	£25
14	Jeepster JPRLP015	PUSH BARMAN TO OPEN OLD WOUNDS 3-LP, reissue, with download)	£30
15	Matador OLE 1056-8	GIRLS IN PEACETIME WANT TO DANCE (4-LP, with badges and poster)	£30

(see also Isobel Campbell, Gentle Waves)

BELLES
70	President PT 311	Don't Pretend/Words Can't Explain	£15

BELLINO
63	Fontana 267259	Boss Bossa Nova/Bossa Rock	£50

ERROL BELLOT
82	Jet Sounds JS 001	Don't Joke With Love/Wicked Them (with Militant Mikey, 12")	£40
85	Jah Tubbys JT 012	New Kind Of Sound/Version (12", with the Offbeat Posse)	£40
86	Jah Tubbys JT 019	Sound In Fury/Trouble Maker (12", with the Offbeat Posse)	£45
00	Jah Tubbys JT 7002	Glory Hallalujah/DUB TEACHER: Glory Dub	£20
00	Jah Tubbys JT 7004	Jah Creation/DISCIPLES RIDDIM SECTION: Creation Style	£20
01	Jah Tubbys JT 7007	Roots Gone International/OFFBEAT POSSE: International Ridim	£15
03	Jah Tubbys JT 014	It's War/Don't Judge (10", with the Offbeat Posse)	£30
03	Jah Tubbys JT 10016	Praise H.I.M/New Life (10", with the Offbeat Posse)	£30

ERROL BELLOT & DIXIE PEACH
03	Jah Tubbys JT 10011	The Warning/THE OFFBEAT POSSE: Dub Warning (10")	£30

(see also Dixie Peach)

TONY BELLUS
59	London HL 8933	Robbin' The Cradle/Valentine Girl	£40

BELLY
93	4AD CAD 3002	STAR (LP, inner)	£20
95	4AD CAD 5044	KING (LP)	£30

BELMONTS
61	Pye International 7N 25094	Tell Me Why/Smoke From Your Cigarette	£30
62	Stateside SS 128	Come On Little Angel/How About Me?	£35

BELOVED (1)
(see also Dion & Belmonts)

BELOVED (1)
88	WEA SAM 481	ACID LOVE EP (12" stamped white labels only)	£60
93	East West WX 500	CONSCIENCE (LP)	£50
96	East West 0630-13316-1	X (with free 12")	£30

BELOVED ONES
68	CBS 3303	My Year Is A Day/She And I	£15

BELT & BRACES ROADSHOW BAND
75	Belt & Braces Roadshow	BELT & BRACES ROADSHOW BAND (LP, with lyric sheet)	£15

BELTONES
68	Trojan TR 628	No More Heartaches/I'll Follow You	£40
69	Duke DU 17	Home Without You/Why Pretend	£50
69	High Note HS 017	Mary Mary/Going Away	£50
69	High Note HS 023	A Broken Heart/AFROTONES: All For One	£50
72	Ackee ACK 150	Wrapped Up In Love/SOUND DIMENSION: Pasero	£50

(see Bop & Beltones, Trevor Shield)

JOHN BELTRAN
96	Peacefrog PF 049	TEN DAYS OF BLUE (2-LP)	£18

BEN
71	Vertigo 6360 052	BEN (LP, gatefold sleeve, small swirl label)	£1500

(see also Jonathan Kelly)

BENGA
02	Big Apple BAM 002	Skank/Dose (12", blue vinyl)	£25
03	Big Apple BAM 003	The Judgement (with Skream)/SKREAM: The Bug/BENGA: Amber (12", green vinyl)	£30
03	Big Apple BAM 003	The Judgement (with Skream)/SKREAM: The Bug/BENGA: Amber (12")	£30
04	Big Apple BAM 005	Hydro/Walkin' Bass/SKREAM: Elektro/Afrika (12")	£20
04	Benga Beats BBV 01	BENGA BEATS VOLUME 1 EP (12")	£20
08	Tempa TEMPA LP 010	DIARY OF AN AFRO WARRIOR (LP as 3 x 12")	£20

BENNY BENGIMAN
81	Negus Roots NERT 010	Health And Sorrow/Love A Dub Song	£25

JOE BENJAMIN
69	UPC 106	Good Morning Baby/Tell Me Why	£30
70	UPC 111	The Same Old Song And Dance/Let Us Break Bread	£25

TONY BENJAMIN & THE SANE INMATES
82	Ariwa ARI 008	Treasures In The World/Psychological Pen (12")	£40
83	Ariwa ARILP 009	AFRICAN REBEL (LP)	£70

BENJAMIN DELANEY LION
69	Rollick & Taylor	SATORI (LP, 70 only)	£1500

BOBBY BENNETT (U.K.)
69	Columbia DB 8532	Music Mother Made/You're Ready Now	£50

BOYD BENNETT & HIS ROCKETS (WITH BIG MOE)
55	Parlophone MSP 6161	Everlovin'/Boogie At Midnight (with Big Moe)	£100
55	Parlophone MSP 6161	Everlovin'/Boogie At Midnight (with Big Moe) (78)	£15
55	Parlophone MSP 6180	Seventeen/Little Ole You-All (as Boyd Bennett & His Rockets)	£50
56	Parlophone MSP 6203	My Boy - Flat Top/Banjo Rock And Roll (with Big Moe)	£100
56	Parlophone MSP 6233	Blue Suede Shoes/Oo-Oo-Oo (with Big Moe)	£100
56	Parlophone R 4214	The Groovy Age/Hit That Jive, Jack (as Big Moe with Boyd Bennett & His Rockets)	£80
56	Parlophone R 4252	The Most/Rockin' Up A Storm (as Big Moe with Boyd Bennett & His Rockets)	£80
56	Parlophone R 4252	The Most/Rockin' Up A Storm (as Boyd Bennett & His Rockets) (78)	£15
58	Parlophone R 4423	Click Clack/Move (as Boyd Bennett & His Rockets)	£80
58	Parlophone R 4423	Click Clack/Move (as Boyd Bennett & His Rockets) (78)	£15
59	Mercury AMT 1031	Tear It Up/Tight Tights (as Big Moe & His Orchestra)	£30
59	Mercury AMT 1031	Tear It Up/Tight Tights (as Big Moe & His Orchestra) (78)	£15

(see also Moon Mullican)

BRIAN BENNETT
67	Columbia DB 8294	Canvas/Slippery Jim De Grize	£20
74	Fontana 6007 040	Chase Side Shoot-Up/Pegasus	£20
67	Columbia S(C)X 6144	CHANGE OF DIRECTION (LP)	£50
69	Col. Studio Two TWO 268	THE ILLUSTRATED LONDON NOISE (LP)	£60
77	DJM DJF 20499	ROCK DREAMS (LP, with insert, as the Brian Bennett Band)	£20
78	DJM DJF 20532	VOYAGE (LP)	£40

(see also Shadows, Thunder Company, Wasp, Marty Wilde, Krewcats, Collage, Alan Skidmore, Big Jim Sullivan, Heat Exchange, Julian [Scott])

CAROLE BENNETT
57	Capitol CL 14725	Haunted Lover/Let The Chips Fall (Where They May)	£20

CLIFF BENNETT & REBEL ROUSERS
61	Parlophone R 4793	You've Got What I Like/I'm In Love With You	£30
61	Parlophone R 4836	That's What I Said/When I Get Paid	£25
62	Parlophone R 4895	Poor Joe/Hurtin' Inside (Twist)	£15
63	Parlophone R 5080	You Really Got A Hold On Me/Alright	£20
63	Parlophone DP 561	When I Get Paid/That's What I Said (export issue, black label)	£15
65	Parlophone GEP 8923	CLIFF BENNETT AND THE REBEL ROUSERS (EP)	£20
65	Parlophone GEP 8936	TRY IT BABY (EP)	£25
66	Parlophone GEP 8955	WE'RE GONNA MAKE IT (EP)	£30
64	Parlophone PMC 1242	CLIFF BENNETT AND THE REBEL ROUSERS (LP, yellow/black label)	£50

| 66 | EMI Regal REG 1039 | CLIFF BENNETT (LP, export issue) | £20 |
| 67 | Parlophone PMC/PCS 7017 | GOT TO GET YOU INTO OUR LIFE (LP, yellow/black label) | £40 |

CLIFF BENNETT BAND
| 68 | Parlophone PMC/PCS 7054 | BRANCHES OUT (LP, yellow/black label, with "sold in the U.K." label text) | £40 |

CLIFF BENNETT'S REBELLION
| 71 | CBS 64487 | CLIFF BENNETT'S REBELLION (LP) | £20 |

(see also Charles Hodges, Rebel Rousers, Toefat, Screaming Lord Sutch & Savages)

DUSTER BENNETT
68	Blue Horizon 57-3141	It's A Man Down There/Things Are Changing	£25
69	Blue Horizon 57-3148	Raining In My Heart/Jumpin' For Joy	£20
69	Blue Horizon 57-3154	Bright Lights, Big City/Fresh Country Jam (with His House Band)	£25
69	Blue Horizon 57-3164	I'm Gonna Wind Up Endin' Up Or I'm Gonna End Up Windin' Up With You/ Rock Of Ages, Cleft For Me	£25
70	Blue Horizon 57-3173	I Chose To Sing The Blues/If You Could Hang Your Washing Like You Hang Your Lines	£15
68	Blue Horizon 7-63208	SMILING LIKE I'M HAPPY (LP, mono with His House Band, i.e. Fleetwood Mac)	£70
68	Blue Horizon S 7-63208	SMILING LIKE I'M HAPPY (LP, stereo with His House Band, i.e. Fleetwood Mac)	£50
69	Blue Horizon S 7-63221	BRIGHT LIGHTS... (LP, gatefold sleeve)	£100
70	Blue Horizon 7-63868	12 DB's (LP, with lyric sheet)	£50

(see also Fleetwood Mac)

JO JO BENNETT
67	Doctor Bird DB 1097	The Lecture/Cantelope Rock (with Fugitives)	£50
67	Doctor Bird DB 1116	Rocksteady/Real Gone Loser (with Fugitives)	£60
70	Explosion EX 2029	Groovy Jo Jo/Ten Steps To Soul (both actually with Mudie's All Stars)	£30
70	Trojan TR 7774	Leaving Rome/In The Nude (both with Mudie's All Stars)	£15
70	Trojan TBL 133	GROOVY JO JO (LP, with Mudie's Allstars)	£50

(see also Fugitives, I Roy)

JOE BENNETT & SPARKLETONES
| 57 | HMV POP 399 | Black Slacks/Boppin' Rock Boogie | £100 |
| 58 | HMV POP 445 | Rocket/Penny Loafers And Bobby Socks | £100 |

PETER E, BENNETT
| 71 | RCA SF 8190 | THE BALLAD OF GALDWAIN (LP, lyric insert, orange/white label) | £15 |

RAY BENNETT
| 62 | Decca DFE 8516 | INTRODUCING RAY BENNETT (EP, p/s) | £30 |

ROY BENNETT
| 68 | Blue Cat BS 146 | I Dangerous/DEE SET: I Know A Place | £80 |

RUDI BENNETT
| 68 | Decca F12729 | I'm So Proud/You're My Adee | £20 |

VAL BENNETT
68	Island WI 3113	Jumping With Mr. Lee/ROY SHIRLEY: Keep Your Eyes On The Road	£50
68	Island WI 3146	The Russians Are Coming (Take Five)/LESTER STERLING: Sir Lee's Whip	£80
68	Trojan TR 611	Spanish Harlem/ROY SHIRLEY: If I Did Know	£30
69	Trojan TR 640	Baby Baby/Barbara	£30
69	Crab CRAB 6	Reggae City/CANNON KING: Mellow Trumpet (B-side actually by Carl 'King Cannon Ball' Bryan)	£80
69	Camel CA 24	Midnight Spin/SOUL CATS: Money Money	£60

(see also Roy Shirley, Max Romeo, Derrick Morgan, Clancy Eccles, Harry J Allstars, George A Penny, Lloyd Terrell,

JON BENNS
| 80 | Aveda AVA 106 | BENNS MEANS LAFFS (LP) | £15 |

(see also The Enid)

BENNY (AKA B.E.N.N.Y THE BUTCHER)
18	Daupe! DM SP 032	BUTCHER ON STEROIDS (12", p/s, with DJ Green Lantern, 187 copies)	£100
18	Daupe! DM SP 032	BUTCHER ON STEROIDS (12", p/s, with DJ Green Lantern, red vinyl, 187 copies)	£100
18	Daupe! DM SP 032	BUTCHER ON STEROIDS (12", p/s, with DJ Green Lantern, green vinyl, 187 copies)	£100
18	Daupe! DM SP 032	BUTCHER ON STEROIDS (12", p/s, with DJ Green Lantern, cream vinyl, 187 copies)	£100
18	Daupe! DM SP 032	BUTCHER ON STEROIDS (12", p/s, with DJ Green Lantern, with obi strip 20 copies)	£300
19	Daupe! DM SP 041	TANA TALK 3 (2-LP, 500 copies)	£200
19	Daupe! DM SP 041	TANA TALK 3 (2-LP, blue vinyl, 333 copies)	£300
19	Daupe! DM SP 041	TANA TALK 3 (2-LP, splatter vinyl, 333 copies)	£300
19	Daupe! DM SP 041	TANA TALK 3 (2-LP, white vinyl, 333 copies)	£300
19	Daupe! DM SP 041	TANA TALK 3 (2-LP, with obi strip, 20 copies)	£500

BARRY BENSON
66	Parlophone R 5446	Stay A Little While/That's For Sure	£35
66	Parlophone R 5446	Stay A Little While/That's For Sure (DJ Copy)	£50
66	Parlophone R 5484	Not A One Girl Guy/Sunshine Child	£25
67	Parlophone R 5578	Cousin Jane/Meet Jacqueline	£20

GARY BENSON
| 70 | Penny Farthing PELS 506 | THE REUNION (LP) | £50 |
| 73 | Birth RAB 5 | THE CONCERT (LP, gatefold sleeve) | £30 |

GEORGE BENSON (QUARTET)
80	Warner Bros. LV 40	Give Me The Night/The World Is A Ghetto (12")	£15
66	CBS (S)BPG 62817	IT'S UPTOWN (LP, flipback sleeve, as George Benson Quartet)	£25
67	CBS (S)BPG 62971	THE GEORGE BENSON COOKBOOK (LP)	£15
69	A&M AMLS 945	SHAPE OF THINGS TO COME (LP)	£30
72	CTI 6015	WHITE RABBIT (LP)	£15
73	CTI CTL 20	BODY TALK (LP, gatefold)	£15

MINT VALUE £

76	CTI CTI 6063	GOOD KING BAD (LP, gatefold)	£15
76	CTI CTI 6069	BENSON & FARREN (LP, with Joe Farrell)	£15
76	Warner Bros. K56199	BREEZIN' (LP)	£15
77	Warner Bros. K56327	IN FLIGHT (LP)	£15
78	CTI CTI 7085	SPACE (LP)	£15

SHARON BENSON
95	Leap Of Faith LEAP 002	Anything For You (Remake)/(For The People Mix)/(Original)/(Remake)/(80s Old School)/(Rare Mix) (12")	£30
95	Leap Of Faith LEAP 003	Rock Me Down (Full Freddie Mix)/(Sugar Johnson Rare Mix)/(Marvin Gaye Remix)/(Dark Knight Bass Head Remix)/(Lex Mix) (12")	£30
95	Leap Of Faith LEAP 001LP	SHARON BENSON (LP, plain die-cut sleeve)	£30

BENT
| 00 | Sport SPORTLP 01 | PROGRAMMED TO LOVE (2-LP without free 7") | £35 |
| 00 | Sport SPORTLPX 01 | PROGRAMMED TO LOVE (2-LP with free 7") | £45 |

MICHAEL BENTINE
| 62 | Parlophone PMC 1179 | IT'S A SQUARE WORLD (LP, also stereo PCS 3031) | £15 |

ACE BENTLEY
| 81 | Traffic Light TL 181 | Beat Boys/Sometimes In The Night (p/s) | £40 |

BRIAN BENTLEY & THE BACHELORS
| 60 | Philips PB 1085 | Wishing Well/Please Make Up Your Mind | £25 |

ED BENTLEY
| 79 | SB SB 1001 | Bentley Boogie/Hot E/Walk On High (12") | £60 |

BROOK BENTON & DINAH WASHINGTON
| 61 | Mercury SEZ 19022 | A ROCKING GOOD WAY (EP, stereo) | £15 |
| 64 | Mercury 20069 MCL | THE TWO OF US (LP) | £15 |

STEVE BERESFORD
| 75 | Incus INCUS 15 | TEATIME (LP) | £40 |

BERETS
| 70 | Avant Garde AVS 116 | THE MASS FOR PEACE (LP, with insert) | £20 |

BERLIN BLONDES
| 80 | EMI EMC 3346 | BERLIN BLONDES (LP) | £15 |

BERNADETTE
| 67 | Rim RIM 2 | Come Kiss Me Love/Let Me Do The Talking | £20 |

JACKIE BERNARD
71	Fab FAB 16	Torture And Flames/WESTMORELITES: Longing To Hold You (promo only, black label)	£70
72	KSK 001	Tribute To Slim Smith (Soul Dragon)/Version (white label only)	£50
76	Grounation GRO 2061	Fantasy Rock/Roots Music	£15
78	One Stop OSM 001	Keep Rowing/Version (12")	£50
(see also Kingstonians)

KENNY BERNARD (& WRANGLERS)
65	Pye 7N 15920	The Tracker/You Gotta Give (with Wranglers)	£20
65	Pye 7N 15920	The Tracker/You Gotta Give (with Wranglers) (DJ Copy)	£125
66	Pye 7N 17131	Nothing Can Change This Love/What Love Brings	£70
66	Pye 7N 17131	Nothing Can Change This Love/What Love Brings (DJ Copy)	£100
67	Pye 7N 17233	Ain't No Soul (Left In These Old Shoes)/Hey Woman	£40
67	Pye 7N 17284	I Do/Isn't That A Good Idea	£15
67	CBS 2936	Somebody/Pity My Feet	£100
67	CBS 2936	Somebody/Pity My Feet (DJ copy)	£150
68	CBS 3860	Victim Of Perfume And Lace/A Change Is Gonna Come	£25
(see also Kenny & Wranglers, Wranglers, Cat's Pyjamas)

ROD BERNARD
| 59 | London HLM 8849 | This Should Go On Forever/Pardon, Mr. Gordon | £20 |

BERNHARDTS
| 84 | Parlophone 12R 6078 | I Hear You Calling (Extended)/Send Your Heart To Me (Extended) (12" p/s) | £20 |

BERNIE & BUZZ BAND
| 68 | Decca F 22829 | The House That Jack Built/PETE KELLY'S SOULUTION: Midnight Confessions (export issue) | £18 |
| 68 | Deram DM 181 | When Something's Wrong With My Baby/Don't Knock It | £35 |
(see also Pete Kelly's Soulution)

ELMER BERNSTEIN
63	MGM MGM 1238	Rat Race/Saints & Sinners	£20
63	MGM MGM 1238	Rat Race/Saints & Sinners (DJ Copy)	£40
56	Brunswick LAT 8101	THE MAN WITH THE GOLDEN ARM (LP, soundtrack)	£20
57	Brunswick LAT 8195	SWEET SMELL OF SUCCESS (LP, soundtrack)	£20
62	MGM MGM-C 891	WALK ON THE WILD SIDE (LP, soundtrack)	£15
63	MGM MGM-C 934	TO KILL A MOCKINGBIRD (LP, soundtrack)	£15
63	United Artists ULP 1041	THE GREAT ESCAPE (LP, soundtrack, mono/stereo)	£15
67	RCA Victor RD 7792	THE SILENCERS (LP, soundtrack, feat. Vikki Carr)	£30

ROCK BERNTSEN
| 84 | Forest Tracks FT 3017 | KELPERS AFTER ALL (LP, with insert) | £18 |

CHUCK BERRY
78s
| 56 | London HLU 8275 | Down Bound Train/No Money Down | £50 |

57	London HLN 8375	You Can't Catch Me/Havana Moon	£35
57	London HLU 8428	Roll Over Beethoven/Drifting Heart	£25
57	London HLM 8531	Rock And Roll Music/Blue Feeling	£15
58	London HLM 8585	Sweet Little Sixteen/Reelin' And Rockin'	£15
58	London HLM 8629	Johnny B. Goode/Around And Around	£15
58	London HL 8677	Beautiful Delilah/Vacation Time	£20
58	London HL 7055	Carol/Hey Pedro (export single)	£30
58	London HL 8712	Carol/Hey Pedro	£25
58	London HLM 8767	Sweet Little Rock And Roller/Jo Jo Gun	£35
59	London HLM 8853	Almost Grown/Little Queenie	£50
59	London HLM 8921	Back In The U.S.A./Memphis, Tennessee	£50

SINGLES

56	London HLU 8275	No Money Down/Down Bound Train (silver lettering on label, triangular centre)	£400
56	London HLU 8275	No Money Down/Down Bound Train (silver lettering on label, round centre)	£150
57	London HLN 8375	You Can't Catch Me/Havana Moon (gold lettering on label)	£350
57	London HLN 8375	You Can't Catch Me/Havana Moon (silver lettering on label)	£100
57	London HLU 8428	Roll Over Beethoven/Drifting Heart	£50
57	Columbia DB 3951	School Day (Ring! Ring! Goes The Bell)/Deep Feeling	£50
57	London HLM 8531	Rock And Roll Music/Blue Feeling	£30
58	London HLM 8585	Sweet Little Sixteen/Reelin' And Rockin'	£30
58	London HLM 8629	Johnny B. Goode/Around And Around	£25
58	London HL 8677	Beautiful Delilah/Vacation Time	£25
58	London HL 8712	Carol/Hey Pedro	£25
58	London HL 7055	Carol/Hey Pedro (export issue)	£25
58	London HLM 8767	Sweet Little Rock And Roller/Jo Jo Gun	£25
59	London HLM 8853	Almost Grown/Little Queenie	£25
59	London HLM 8921	Back In The U.S.A./Memphis, Tennessee	£25

(Originally issued with triangular centres; later silver top label/round centre pressings are worth half to two-thirds these values.)

60	London HLM 9069	Let It Rock/Too Pooped To Pop	£25
60	London HLM 9159	Bye Bye Johnny/Mad Lad	£25
61	Pye International 7N 25100	I'm Talkin' 'Bout You/Little Star (blue label)	£25

EPs

56	London REU 1053	RHYTHM AND BLUES WITH CHUCK BERRY (maroon/gold label, tri-centre)	£150
56	London REU 1053	RHYTHM AND BLUES WITH CHUCK BERRY (later pressing, maroon/silver label, round centre)	£40
60	London REM 1188	REELIN' AND ROCKIN' (maroon and gold label, tri centre)	£250
60	London REM 1188	REELIN' AND ROCKIN' (round centre)	£100
63	Pye Intl. NEP 44011	CHUCK BERRY	£15
63	Pye Intl. NEP 44013	THIS IS CHUCK BERRY	£15
64	Pye Intl. NEP 44018	THE BEST OF CHUCK BERRY	£15
64	Pye Intl. NEP 44028	CHUCK BERRY HITS	£15
64	Pye Intl. NEP 44033	BLUE MOOD	£15
65	Chess CRE 6002	THE PROMISED LAND	£15
65	Chess CRE 6005	COME ON	£15
66	Chess CRE 6012	I GOT A BOOKING	£15
66	Chess CRE 6016	YOU CAME A LONG WAY FROM ST. LOUIS	£25

ALBUMS

58	London HA-M 2132	ONE DOZEN BERRYS	£150
60	Pye Intl. NPL 28019	NEW JUKE BOX HITS	£30
63	Pye Intl. NPL 28024	CHUCK BERRY	£20
63	Pye Intl. NPL 28027	CHUCK BERRY ON STAGE	£20
63	Pye Intl. NPL 28028	MORE CHUCK BERRY	£20
64	Pye Intl. NPL 28031	THE LATEST AND THE GREATEST	£20
64	Pye Intl. NPL 28039	YOU NEVER CAN TELL	£20
65	Chess CRL 4005	CHUCK BERRY IN LONDON	£20
65	Chess CRL 4506	FRESH BERRYS	£20

CHUCK BERRY/BO DIDDLEY

| 64 | Pye Intl. NEP 44017 | CHUCK AND BO, VOL. 3 (EP) | £15 |

(see also Bo Diddley)

DAVE BERRY (& CRUISERS)

65	Decca DFE 8625	CAN I GET IT FROM YOU (EP)	£15
64	Decca DFE 8601	DAVE BERRY (EP)	£15
64	Decca LK 4653	DAVE BERRY (LP)	£20
66	Ace Of Clubs ACL 1218	ONE DOZEN BERRIES (LP, also stereo SCL 1218)	£15
66	Decca LK 4823	THE SPECIAL SOUND OF DAVE BERRY (LP)	£15
68	Decca LK/SKL 4932	DAVE BERRY '68 (LP)	£20

(see also Cruisers)

HEIDI BERRY

87	Creation CRELP 023	FIREFLY (LP)	£15
89	Creation CRELP 048	BELOW THE WAVES (LP)	£20
91	4AD CAD 1012	LOVE (LP)	£25
93	4AD CAD 3009	HEIDI BERRY (LP)	£30
96	4AD CAD 6011	MIRACLE (LP)	£35

LEN & BARBARA BERRY

| 60s | Greenwich Village GVR 229 | THE PORTWAY PEDDLERS (LP) | £50 |

MINT VALUE £

MIKE BERRY (& THE OUTLAWS)
66	HMV POP 1530	Warm Baby/Just Thought I'd 'Phone	£15
63	HMV 7EG 8808	A TRIBUTE TO BUDDY HOLLY (EP)	£20

(see also Outlaws, Le Roys, Shepperton Flames, Innocents [U.K], UK Jones)

RICHARD BERRY & PHARAOHS
64	Ember EMB EP 4527	RHYTHM AND BLUES VOL. 3 (EP)	£100

BERRY STREET STATION
75	Crystal CR 7024	Chocolate Sugar/All I Want Is You	£15

BERTY B AND DILLINJA
95	Lionheart BERT1	Lionheart/Art Of Control (12")	£15

(see also Dillinja, Cybotron Featuring Dillinja)

BESHARA
82	Home Spun HS 002	Glory Glory/Version (12")	£80
84	Mass Media Music MM121004	Men Cry Too/Version (12", purple vinyl)	£20

ADAM BEST
70	Fontana SFL 13209	WALL OF SOUND (LP)	£20

PETE BEST FOUR
64	Decca F 11929	I'm Gonna Knock On Your Door/Why Did I Fall In Love With You?	£60

(see also Beatles, Lee Curtis & All Stars)

BEST EVER
75	Polydor 2001594	Rope A Dope/People's Choice (with Muhammad Ali)	£20

RICHARD BESWICK & PHILIPP WACHSMANN
81	Bead Records BEAD 18	HELLO BRENDA! (LP)	£25

BETA BAND
97	Regal REG 16	CHAMPION VERSIONS EP: Dry The Rain/I Know/B+A/Dog's Got A Bone (12", p/s, 1,000 only)	£80
98	Regal REG 18	THE PATTY PATTY SOUND EP: Inner Meet Me/The House/The Monolith/ She's The One (2 x 12", p/s, 1,000 only)	£40
98	Regal REG 20	LOS AMIGOS DEL BETA BANDITOS EP: Push It Out/It's Over/Dr Baker/Needles In My Eyes (12", p/s)	£30
13	Regal REGS 16	CHAMPION VERSIONS (12", reissue 750 only)	£25
13	Regal REGS 18	THE PATTY PATTY SOUND (12", reissue, 750 only)	£25
13	Regal REGS 20	LOS AMIGOS DEL BETA BANDITOS (12", reissue, 750 only)	£20
99	Regal REG 30	THE BETA BAND (2-LP)	£50
01	Regal REG 59	HOT SHOTS II (2-LP)	£50
04	Regal REG 101	HEROES TO ZEROS (LP, gatefold sleeve)	£40
18	Because Music BEC 5543698	THE BETA BAND (3LP, reissue, gatefold, plus original third album reinstated with Happiness & Colour/The Hut)	£25

(see also Aliens, Steve Mason, Lone Pigeon)

BETTERDAYS
65	Polydor BM 56024	Don't Want That/Here 'Tis	£175
96	Dig The Fuzz DIG 008	HOWLIN' (LP, with booklet)	£15

HAROLD BETTERS
65	Sue WI 378	Do Anything You Wanna (Parts 1 & 2)	£60

AL BETTS
73	Peer Int. PIL 9018	CONTRASTS IN JAZZ VOLUME 2 (LP)	£15

BETWEEN PICTURES
81	A Side AS 002	Treat Me Like An Equal/Life On Your Own	£15

BEVERLEY
66	Deram DM 101	Happy New Year/Where The Good Times Are	£50
67	Deram DM 137	Museum/DENNY CORDELL TEA TIME ENSEMBLE: A Quick One For Sanity	£35

(see also John & Beverley Martyn, Levee Breakers)

BEVERLEY SISTERS
55	Philips BBR 8052	A DATE WITH THE BEVS (10" LP)	£20

BEVERLEY & DUANE
97	Expansion EXLPM3	BEVERELY & DUANE (LP, reissue)	£15

BEVERLEY'S ALLSTARS
65	Black Swan WI 449	Go Home/THEO BECKFORD: Ungrateful People	£40
69	Trojan TR 683	Double Shot/Gimme Gimme Gal (B-side act. "Banana Water" by Mellotones)	£50
70	Trojan TR 7729	Moon Dust/Fat Cat (both sides actually by Ansell Collins)	£40

(see also Clarendonians, Gaylads, Ken Boothe, Glen Brown, Desmond Dekker, Bob Marley, Maytals, Melodians, Derrick Morgan, Pioneers, Rockstones, Bruce Ruffin, Delroy Wilson)

FRANK BEVERLY & BUTLERS
00	Goldmine Soul Supply GS002	If That's What You Wanted/EDDIE FOSTER: I Never Knew (reissue, as Frankie Beverly)	£30

BEVERLY HILLS BLUES BAND
76	Warner Bros K 16752	Just Because/If I Can Just Get Through Tonight	£15

(see also Four Seasons)

BEVIS FROND
87	Woronzow WOO 3	MIASMA (LP, laminated cover, 500 copies only)	£15
87	Woronzow WOO 5 1/2	BEVIS THROUGH THE LOOKING GLASS - THE GREAT MAGNET DISASTER (2-LP, 500 only, originals all signed, with booklet; counterfeits unsigned)	£40
88	Woronzow WOO 8	TRIPTYCH (LP)	£20
80s	Reckless RECKLP 15	TRIPTYCH (LP, reissue)	£15

91	Woronzow WOO 16	NEW RIVER HEAD (2-LP, 1st 500 with EP & insert)	£18
92	Woronzow WOO 26	SUPERSEEDER (2-LP)	£30
93	Woronzow WOO 22	SPRAWL (2-LP, gatefold sleeve, with insert)	£30
96	Woronzow WOO28	SON OF WALTER (2-LP)	£30
97	Woronzow WOO 406	NORTH CIRCULAR (3-LP, with insert, 750 only, signed & numbered)	£75
99	Woronzow WOO 31	VAVONA BURR (2-LP)	£35
00	Woronzow WOO 42	VALEDICTORY SONGS (2-LP)	£35

(see also Von Trap Family, Room 13)

BEYONCE

03	Columbia 674067 6	Crazy In Love (Album Version)/(Instrumental Album Version)/ Krazy In Luv (Rockwilder Remix)/ (Lego's Poontin Muzik Dub) (12", p/s)	£15
03	Columbia 09395 1	DANGEROUSLY IN LOVE (LP, printed inner)	£100
14	Parkwood Entertainment/ Columbia 88843067251	BEYONCE (2LP, DVD, embossed gatefold, printed inners,booklet)	£200
17	Parkwood Entertainment/ Columbia 88985446751	LEMONADE (2LP, gatefold, yellow vinyl, booklet)	£30
20	Parkwood Entertainment/ Columbia 19075959261	HOMECOMING: THE LIVE ALBUM (4LP, printed inners, booklet)	£50
22	Parkwood Entertainment/ Columbia19658747571	RENAISSANCE (2LP, ltd. alternate cover, slipcase, printed inners, poster booklet)	£100
22	Parkwood Entertainment/ Columbia 19658719671	RENAISSANCE (2LP, slipcase, printed inners, poster, booklet)	£40
24	Parkwood Entertainment/ Columbia 19658899611	ACT II: COWBOY CARTER (2LP, ltd ed red vinyl, gatefold, blonde image to rear)	£30
24	Parkwood Entertainment/ Columbia 19658899601	ACT II: COWBOY CARTER (2LP, ltd ed white vinyl, gatefold, snake spectacles image to rear)	£40
24	Parkwood Entertainment/ Columbia 19658894931	ACT II: COWBOY CARTER (2LP, ltd ed, black vinyl, gatefold, braids and beads image to rear)	£20

BEYOND THE IMPLODE

| 79 | Diverse DIVE 101 | LAST THOUGHTS EP (EP, 250 copies with hand-written labels, numbered, with 'Look Back' Fanzine) | £250 |
| 80 | Diverse DIVE 102 | 11th HOUR BREAKDOWN EP | £75 |

BEYOND THE WIZARD'S SLEEVE

05	3rd Mynd 02	BEYOND THE WIZARD'S SLEEVE (LP)	£15
06	3rd Mynd 03	SPRING (LP)	£18
07	3rd Mynd 04	GEORGE (LP, red vinyl)	£15
07	3rd Mynd 05	WEST (LP, clear vinyl)	£15

BEYOND THE QUARRY

| 92 | Flair (No Cat. No) | Comedown/Disappointment/One Way/Relegate (12", purple vinyl) | £70 |

B-52'S

79	PSR 438	Rock Lobster/52 Girls (p/s, reproduction of original US pressing, given away free with The B-52'S LP)	£15
79	Island ILPS 9580	THE B-52's (LP, insert, with bonus single "Rock Lobster"/"52 Girls" [PSR 438])	£40
79	Island ILPS 9580	THE B-52's (LP, insert, without bonus single "Rock Lobster"/"52 Girls" [PSR 438])	£20
80	Island ILPS 9622	WILD PLANET (LP, in plastic bag with badge)	£20

B FILM

| 80 | Plastic Records BEE 001 | Night Running/Danger Man | £20 |

MAURICIO BIANCHI

| 81 | Sterile SR 2 | SYMPATHY FOR A GENOCIDE (LP, 200 only) | £200 |
| 83 | Broken BV 3 | THE PLAIN TRUTH (LP) | £70 |

GENE BIANCO GROUP

| 60 | Vogue V 9167 | Alarm Clock Rock/Harp Rock Boogie | £30 |

BIBBY

| 65 | Blue Beat BB 289 | Rub It Down/Wicked Man (actually by Harris Seaton) | £30 |

(see also B.B. Seaton, Horace Seaton)

BIBIO

| 09 | Warp WARPLP 177 | AMBIVALANCE AVENUE (2-LP) | £30 |
| 09 | Warp WARPLP 190 | THE APPLE AND THE TOOTH (LP) | £25 |

BIDDU

67	Regal Zonophone RZ 3002	Daughter Of Love/Look Out Here I Come	£15
77	Epic EPC 5416	Soul Coaxing/Nirvana (12", p/s)	£15
78	Epic EPCS 6230	Blacker Than Berry/James Bond Disco Theme (12", white label promo only)	£15

BIFF BANG POW!

84	Creation CRE 003	Fifty Years Of Fun/Then When I Scream (foldaround sprayed p/s in poly bag)	£30
84	Creation CRE 007	There Must Be A Better Life/The Chocolate Elephant Man (foldaway p/s in poly bag)	£30
90	Caff CAFF 13	Sleep/TIMES: Extase (p/s, with insert)	£20
90	Creation CRELP 058	SONGS FOR THE SAD EYED GIRL (LP)	£15
91	Creation CRELP 099	L'AMOUR, DEMURE, STENHOUSEMUIR (LP)	£20

(see also Laughing Apple, Times)

BIFFY CLYRO

99	Babi Yaga YAGA 001	Iname/All The Way Down (Chapter 2)/Travis Perkins (CD)	£100
00	Electric Honey HER 013 CD	Thekidswhopoptodaywillrocktomorrow (CD, 1000 only)	£80
01	Beggars Banquet BBQ 335	Justboy/Unsubtle/Being Gabriel (p/s)	£20
01	Beggars Banquet BBQ 352	27/Breatheher/Instructio4 (p/s)	£20
02	Beggars Banquet BBQ 358	57/Kill The Old, Torture Their Young (Evening Session Version) (p/s)	£20
09	14FLR41	Many Of Horrors/Lonely Revolutions (p/s, blue vinyl, signed)	£25
02	Beggars Banquet BBQLP226	BLACKENED SKY (LP)	£70
03	Beggars Banquet BBQLP233	THE VERTIGO OF BLISS (LP)	£75

			MINT VALUE £
04	Beggars Banquet BBQLP238	**INFINITY LAND** (LP)	£75
09	14th Floor 5051865629702	**ONLY REVOLUTIONS** (LP, 2-CD, DVD box set)	£250
10	14th Floor 825646789566	**LONELY REVOLUTIONS** (2-LP, 300 only)	£300
12	Beggars Banquet BBQLP2089	**BLACKENED SKY** (2-LP, reissue, purple vinyl)	£30
12	Beggars Banquet BBQLP2091	**INFINITY LAND** (2-LP, reissue, grey vinyl)	£30
13	Beggars Banque tBBQLP 2090	**THE VERTIGO OF BLISS** (2-LP, reissue, white vinyl, 300 only)	£50
13	14th Floor 825646550371	**OPPOSITES** (2-LP, 3-CD and DVD box set)	£70

BIG AFRICA
87	Leopard BALMS 2	**I Need You/I Need You Dub**	£25
87	Leopard BALMT 2	**I Need You/I Need You Dub** (12")	£50

BIG AMONGST SHEEP
82	Rock Solid RSR 2001	**TERMINAL VELOCITY** (LP)	£60

(see also Inner City Unit, Silverwing)

BIG AUDIO DYNAMITE
85	CBS CK 40220	**THIS IS BIG AUDIO DYNAMITE** (LP, inner)	£18
90	CBS 4674661	**KOOL-AID** (LP, as Big Audio Dynamite II)	£25
91	Columbia 4677061	**THE GLOBE** (LP, as Big Audio Dynamite II)	£35
94	Columbia C2S 6534	**HIGHER POWER** (2-LP as Big Audio)	£40

(see also The Clash)

BIG BERTHA FEATURING ACE KEFFORD
69	Atlantic 584 298	**This World's An Apple/Gravy Booby Jamm**	£35

(see also Cozy Powell, Ace Kefford Stand, Bedlam, Youngblood)

BIG BIG TRAIN
17	Plane Groovy PLGS 07	**Merry Christmas/Snowfalls** (gatefold p/s, white vinyl)	£15
91	Least Peculiar (no cat no)	**FROM THE RIVER TO THE SEA** (cassette)	£30
92	English Peculiar BBTLPT2	**FROM THE RIVER TO THE SEA** (CD)	£90
93	Least Peculiar BBT LPT3	**THE INFANT HERCULES** (cassette)	£100
94	Giant Electric Pea GEPCD 1007	**GOODBYE TO THE AGE OF STEAM** (CD)	£30
97	Giant Electric Pea GEPCD 1020	**ENGLISH BOY WONDERS** (CD)	£30
02	Treefrog TFCD 001	**BARD** (CD)	£80
04	Treefrog TFCD 002	**GATHERING SPEED** (CD)	£30
12	Plane Groovy PLG 010	**ENGLISH ELECTRIC PART ONE** (2LP, numbered, 500 only)	£200
13	Plane Groovy PLG 017	**ENGLISH ELECTRIC PART TWO** (2LP, gatefold, insert, numbered, 500 only)	£100
16	Plane Groovy PLG 044	**FOLKLORE** (2LP, gatefold)	£100
17	Plane Groovy PLG 050	**GRIMSPOUND** (2LP, gatefold, opaque vinyl)	£60
17	Plane Groovy PLG 044	**FOLKLORE** (2LP, reissue, blue vinyl)	£45
17	Plane Groovy PLG 056	**THE SECOND BRIGHTEST STAR** (2LP, insert, foam green vinyl)	£70
18	Plane Groovy PLG 071	**MERCHANTS OF LIGHT** (3LP box set, booklet, insert)	£50
19	Plane Groovy PLG 074	**GRAND TOUR** (2LP, cream vinyl, booklet)	£60
19	Plane Groovy PLG 078	**ENGLISH ELECTRIC PART ONE** (2LP, reissue, blue vinyl)	£80
19	Plane Groovy PLG 017	**ENGLISH ELECTRIC PART TWO** (2LP, reissue, orange vinyl)	£60
21	Plane Groovy PLG 096	**COMMON GROUND** (2LP, gatefold, Insert, blue vinyl, 180g, 500 only)	£60
21	Plane Groovy PLG 096	**COMMON GROUND** (2LP, gatefold, insert,180g)	£40
22	Plane Groovy PLG 105	**WELCOME TO THE PLANET** (LP, 180g, printed inner, transparent red vinyl, limited)	£30
22	Plane Groovy PLG105	**WELCOME TO THE PLANET** (LP, 180g, printed inner)	£20
24	Inside Out IOM 700	**THE LIKES OF US** (2LP, gatefold, insert, blue vinyl, 300 only)	£30
24	Inside Out IOM 700	**THE LIKES OF US** (2LP, gatefold, insert, green vinyl, Burning Shed exclusive)	£40
24	Inside Out IOM 700	**THE LIKES OF US** (2LP, gatefold, insert)	£25

(see also David Longdon)

BIG BLACK
86	Homestead HMS 044	**HAMMER PARTY** (LP)	£15
86	Blast First BFFP 11	**ATOMIZER** (LP)	£18
87	Blast First BFFP 19	**SONGS ABOUT FUCKING** (LP, usually with sticker over 'Fucking')	£25
87	Blast First CHAT 2	**TALK ABOUT FUCKING** (LP, promo interview disc with question sheet insert)	£15
87	NOT 2 (BUT 1)	**SOUND OF IMPACT** (LP, matt sleeve, numbered up to 1,000, with 8-page booklet)	£30
87	NOT 2 (BUT 1)	**SOUND OF IMPACT** (LP, laminated sleeve, numbered from 1,001-1,500, with 8-page booklet)	£20
92	Touch & Go TG 24	**SONGS ABOUT FUCKING** (LP, reissue)	£15
92	Touch & Go TG 81	**PIGPILE** (LP, boxed set with video & T-shirt with insert)	£30

(see also Rapeman)

BIG BOB
59	Top Rank JAR 185	**Your Line Was Busy/What Am I**	£25

BIG BOPPER
58	Mercury AMT 1002	**Chantilly Lace/The Purple People Eater Meets The Witchdoctor**	£20
59	Mercury AMT 1017	**Big Bopper's Wedding/Little Red Riding Hood**	£25
59	Mercury AMT 1046	**It's The Truth, Ruth/That's What I Am Talking About**	£30
59	Mercury ZEP 10004	**THE BIG BOPPER** (EP)	£100
59	Mercury ZEP 10027	**PINK PETTICOATS** (EP)	£100
58	Mercury MMC 14008	**CHANTILLY LACE** (LP)	£150

BIG BOY PETE
68	Camp 602 005	**Cold Turkey/My Love Is Like A Spaceship**	£80
96	Tenth Planet TP 026	**HOMAGE TO CATATONIA** (LP)	£18

(see also Miller, Pete Miller)

BIG BROTHER & HOLDING COMPANY

67	Fontana TF 881	Bye Bye Baby/All Is Loneliness	£25
68	CBS 3683	Piece Of My Heart/Turtle Blues (p/s)	£25
67	Fontana TL 5457	BIG BROTHER & THE HOLDING COMPANY (LP, with Janis Joplin, mono)	£60
67	Fontana (S)TL 5457	BIG BROTHER & THE HOLDING COMPANY (LP, with Janis Joplin, stereo)	£40
68	CBS 63392	CHEAP THRILLS (LP, 1st pressing, with Janis Joplin, laminated single sleeve with 'Ernest J. Day & Co Ltd' printing credit, mono)	£75
68	CBS (S)63392	CHEAP THRILLS (LP, 1st pressing, with Janis Joplin, laminated single sleeve with 'Ernest J. Day & Co' printer credit stereo)	£50
69	London HA-T/SH-T 8377	BIG BROTHER & THE HOLDING COMPANY (LP, reissue, mono/stereo)	£20
71	CBS S 64118	BE A BROTHER (LP)	£25
73	CBS (S)63392	CHEAP THRILLS (LP, reissue, no printer credit on rear of sleeve)	£20
82	CBS 32004	CHEAP THRILLS (LP, 'Nice Price' reissue)	£15
84	Edsel ED 135	CHEAPER THRILLS (LP)	£15
99	Simply Vinyl SVLP 064	CHEAP THRILLS (LP, reissue)	£20

(see also Janis Joplin, Nick Gravenites)

BIG CARROT

73	EMI EMI 2047	Blackjack/Squint Eye Mangle	£50
73	EMI EMI 2047	Blackjack/Squint Eye Mangle (Demo copy)	£50

(see also Marc Bolan/T. Rex)

BIG CHARLIE

64	Blue Beat BB 241	Red Sea/You May Not Believe	£40

BIG CITY BEAT BAND

88	Big City Beat BCB 001	Can I Be Your Friend (Radio Mix)/Club Mix (12", white label)	£80
88	Big City Beat BCB 001	Can I Be Your Friend (Radio Mix)/(Dub)/(Club Mix) (12")	£80

BIG COMBO

81	Nothing Shaking SHAD 2	The Man In The Desert/Play For Today (p/s)	£20

BIG COUNTRY

83	Mercury COUP 4	Chance/The Tracks Of My Tears/The Crossing (12", picture disc)	£15
83	Phonogram COUNT 313	In A Big Country (Pure Mix)/Heart And Soul/In A Big Country/All Of Us (12")	£15
84	Mercury (no cat no)	THE BIG COUNTRY 12" COLLECTION (boxed set with 5 x 12")	£200
13	Cherry Red CHERRY 505	In A Broken Promise Land/Flower Of Scotland/Strong (Acoustic) (p/s)	£20
91	Vertigo 510230-1	NO PLACE LIKE HOME (LP)	£15
93	Compulsion NOIS 2	THE BUFFALO SKINNERS (LP)	£150
94	Compulsion NOIS 5	WITHOUT THE AID OF A SAFETY NET (LP)	£100
95	Transatlantic TRALP109	WHY THE LONG FACE (LP, 3000 only, numbered)	£100
99	Track Records TRCK TRK1000CDSP	DRIVING TO DAMASCUS (CD, ltd. ed digipak)	£30
11	Track TRALP 1069	DRIVING TO DAMASCUS (2-LP, reissue of LP originally issued on CD in 1999)	£75
12	Universal 278 909 1	THE CROSSING (2-LP, 30th anniversary reissue)	£125
13	Cherry Red CHERRY 505	THE JOURNEY (LP, die-cut cover, orange vinyl, 250 only, numbered)	£150

(see also Skids)

BIG DADDY KANE

88	Cold Chillin' W7676	Set It Off/Get Into It (p/s)	£80
88	Cold Chillin' W7676T	Set It Off (Extended Mix)/Get Into It, Set It Off (12", stickered sleeve)	£20
88	Cold Chillin' W7953	Raw/Word To The Mother (Land) (p/s, original US issue released in 1987)	£40
89	Cold Chillin' W 2973	Wrath Of Kane/Raw (Remix) (p/s)	£20
88	Cold Chillin' 925 731-1	LONG LIVE THE KANE (LP)	£20
89	Cold Chillin' WX 305	IT'S A BIG DADDY THING (LP)	£20
98	Blakjam BJAM 8811	VETERANZ DAY (2LP)	£20
17	Omerta Inc.OMINC010	LONG LIVE THE KANE (LP, reissue, purple/gold vinyl, 180g, ltd.ed of 300))	£60

BIG DAISY

80	Ellie Jay 9428	Fever/Footprints (p/s)	£250

(see also Wishbone Ash)

BIG DAVE (CAVANAUGH) & HIS ORCHESTRA

54	Capitol CL 14195	Loosely With Feeling/The Cat From Coos Bay (triangular centre)	£20
55	Capitol CL 14245	Rock And Roll Party/Your Kind Of Love (triangular centre)	£30

BIG DREAD

75	B&C BC 003	Musically Mad/Musical Excursion (white labels only)	£30

BIG IN JAPAN

77	Eric's ERICS 0001	Big In Japan/CHUDDIE NUDDIES: Do The Chud (p/s)	£20
78	Zoo CAGE 1	FROM Y TO Z AND NEVER AGAIN (EP, foldout p/s)	£40

(see also Pink Industry/Military, Holly, Holly Johnson, Yachts, Bill Drummond, Siouxsie & Banshees, Lightning Raiders, Justified Ancients of Mu Mu/JAMMS, KLF, Teardrop Explodes)

BIG JOE (JOSEPH SPALDING)

73	Atra ATRA 005	Jah Guide/SWEET HARMONY: Student Dub	£15
73	Atra ATRA 010	Down Santic Way/Santic Dub	£20
74	Dip DL 5007	Selassie Skank/Version	£20
74	Dip DL 5008	Weed Specialist/CHERRY & DUB MASTER: Rub A Daughter	£15
74	Dip DL 5027	Hog In A Me Minty/Sweet Melody	£30
76	Bimbo Music BM 4	Zion Dread/D. MORGAN: What A Disturbance	£15
76	Burning Sounds BS 008	Natty Dread Don't Bow/CHANNEL ONE: Natty Dubbing	£15
77	ATA ATA 1001	Set Your Face At Ease/Version	£30
77	Venture VEN7770	Natty Don't Make War/CHANNEL ONE FLYERS: War Dubbing	£15
79	Tribesman TM 013	Respect Jah Word (with Rodney)/The Profit Says (12")	£50
77	Live & Love LAP001	KEEP ROCKING AND SWINGING (LP)	£50

MINT VALUE £

78	Live & Love LAP 010	**AT THE CONTROL** (LP)	£40
78	Trojan TRLS 152	**AFRICAN PRINCESS** (LP)	£30

BIG LUCKY, BIG AMOS & DONALD HINES
72	London SHU 8425	**RIVER TOWN BLUES** (LP)	£25

BIG MAYBELLE
57	London HLC 8447	**I Don't Want To Cry/All Of Me**	£50
59	London HLC 8854	**Baby, Won't You Please Come Home/Say It Isn't So**	£20
67	CBS 2735	**Turn The World Around The Other Way/I Can't Wait Any Longer**	£20
67	CBS 2926	**Mama** (He Treats Your Daughter Mean)**/Keep That Man**	£50
68	Direction 58-3312	**Quittin' Time/I Can't Wait Any Longer**	£30
68	Direction 58-3312	**Quittin' Time/I Can't Wait Any Longer** (DJ Copy)	£40
67	CBS 62999	**THE PURE SOUL OF BIG MAYBELLE** (LP)	£30

BIG MOOSE (WALKER)
68	Python PKM 01	**Ramblin' Woman/Puppy Howl Blues**	£50

BIG OUTDOOR TYPE
84	Havasac SAC 01	**Call You On Sundays/Seventeen** (p/s)	£50

BIG SLEEP
71	Pegasus PEG 4	**BLUEBELL WOOD** (LP, gatefold sleeve)	£150

(see also Eyes Of Blue, Ancient Grease, Gentle Giant, Man, Ritchie Francis, Gary Pickford-Hopkins)

BIG SPENDERS
70	Gemini GMS 010	**Who's Making Love/Cum Ba Ye**	£15

BIG STAR
78	Stax STAX 504	**September Gurls/Mod Lang** (DJ Copy)	£50
78	Stax STAX 504	**September Gurls/Mod Lang**	£50
78	Aura AUS 103	**Kizza Me/Dream Lover** (p/s)	£20
78	Aura AUS 107	**Jesus Christ/Big Black Car**	£20
78	Stax SXSP 302	**RADIO CITY/BIG STAR** (2-LP)	£60
78	Aura AUL 703	**THIRD ALBUM** (LP)	£20
86	Big Beat WIK 53	**NO. 1 RECORD** (LP, reissue)	£30
86	Big Beat WIK 54	**RADIO CITY** (LP, reissue)	£30
11	Omnivore	**BIG STAR III** (replica test pressing in box, inserts, 2000 only)	£35

(see also Box Tops)

BIG T
73	Avalanche AV 67324	**Tea For Two/I Know A Place**	£25

BIG THREE (U.K.)
63	Decca DFE 8552	**AT THE CAVERN** (EP)	£25
73	Polydor 2383 199	**RESURRECTION** (LP)	£15

(see also Escorts, Paddy Klaus & Gibson, Johnny Gustafson, Faron's Flamingos, Johnny & John)

BIG THREE (U.S.)
68	Roulette RCP 5002	**THE BIG THREE FEATURING MAMA CASS** (LP)	£30

(see also Mama Cass [Elliot], Mamas & Papas)

BIG TROUBLE
72	Pye 7N45292	**You Said A Bad Word/Cyclone Blues**	£15

BIG VERN & CHATTERBOX
93	Straight From The Bedroom	**Volume 3** (12")	£35

BIG YOUTH
72	Blue Beat BB 424	**Chi Chi Run/JOHN HOLT: OK Fred**	£25
73	Downtown DT 497	**Dock Of The Bay/CRYSTALITES: Bass And Drums** (Version)	£20
73	Gayfeet CS 206	**Medicine Doctor/Facts Of Life**	£20
73	Prince Buster PB 50	**Cain And Abel/Cain And Abel** (Version)	£20
73	Grape GR 3040	**Foreman Versus Frazier/Foreman Versus Frazier Round Two**	£20
73	Grape GR 3051	**Opportunity Rock/Double Attack**	£25
73	Grape GR 3061	**Concrete Jungle/Screaming Target**	£15
73	Green Door GD 4051	**Cool Breeze/CRYSTALITES: Windstorm**	£25
75	Angem ANG 103	**All Nations/ANSEL COLLINS : Stalag 17**	£20
75	Klik KLP 9001	**Dread Locks Dread/Version**	£15
77	Eji E 011	**Strictly Rockers/AUGUSTUS PABLO : No Entry** (12")	£40
72	Fab MS 8	**CHI CHI RUN** (LP)	£45
73	Trojan TRLS 61	**SCREAMING TARGET** (LP, orange & white label)	£50
75	Klik KLP9001	**DREAD LOCKS DREAD** (LP)	£25
78	Virgin Front Line FL 1011	**ISIAH, FIRST PROPHET OF OLD** (LP)	£18
78	Virgin Front Line FL 1014	**DREAD LOCKS DREAD** (LP, reissue)	£25
76	Trojan TRLS 123	**NATTY CULTURAL DREAD** (LP, orange/white labels)	£30
76	Trojan TRLS 137	**HIT THE ROAD JACK** (LP)	£20
77	Trojan BYD 1	**REGGAE PHENOMENON** (2-LP, blue labels)	£25
80	Trojan TRLS 123	**NATTY CULTURAL DREAD** (LP, reissue, blue labels)	£20
80	Trojan TRLS 189	**EVERYDAY SKANK** (LP)	£15
83	Virgin VX 1009	**DREADLOCKS DREAD** (LP, reissue)	£18
90	Trojan TRLD 411	**REGGAE PHENOMENON** (2-LP, reissue, orange/white labels)	£18

(see also Upsetters)

BIG YOUTH & KEITH HUDSON
73	Pyramid PYR 7055	**Can You Keep A Secret/HORACE ANDY & EARL FLUTE: Peter And Judas**	£35

BIGGA DREAD
02	Chariot Cha 001	**Batty Dread/Closet Bwoy/Truck Inna Garage/Special Request** (10")	£30

BIJOUX TOO
86	Apex APE 002	Shadows In My Heart/Come On Back (oversized p/s, Welsh-only release).......................£30

THEO BIKEL
69	Reprise RS 2344	I Love My Dog/The Great Mandela (The Wheel Of Life)...£15

BIKINIS
58	Columbia DB 4149	Bikini/Boogie Rock And Roll £15

BILBO BAGGINS
74	Polydor 2058 479	Saturday Night/Monday Morning Blues..£15

(MR.) ACKER BILK (& HIS PARAMOUNT JAZZ BAND)
60	Melodisc 1547	Goodnight Sweet Prince/East Coast Trot..£25

BILLIE & EDDIE
59	Top Rank JAR 249	The King Is Coming Back/Come Back, Baby..£20

TREVOR BILLMUSS
70	Charisma CB 130	Whoops Amour/Sunday Afternoon In Belgrave Square £15
70	Charisma CAS 1017	FAMILY APOLOGY (LP)..£30

BILL THE MURDERER
78	SRT/78/CUS192	I'd Find You/Spring Rain (no p/s) £100

BONNIE 'PRINCE' BILLY
07	No label or Cat. No.	BONNY (7" tour EP) £15
12	Spiritual Pyjamas SPIRITUAL 004	Hummingbird/Tribulations/Because Of Your Eyes (10")......................................£20
99	Domino WIGLP 59	I SEE A DARKNESS (LP)...£25
01	Domino WIGLP 89	EASE DOWN THE ROAD (LP)...£15
03	Palace/Domino WIGLP121	MASTER & EVERYONE (LP, insert)...£15
04	Domino WIGLP 140	SINGS GREATEST PALACE MUSIC (LP, 1-sided) £15
08	Domino WIGLP 213	IS IT THE SEA (2-LP with Harum Scarem and Alex Neilson) £20
09	Domino WIGLP 233	BEWARE (LP)..£15
12	Faber And Faber FAB 02EP	WILL OLDHAM ON BONNIE PRINCE BILLY (2 x 10" in box with book, 300 only) £200
17	Domino WIGLP P420	WOLF OF THE COSMOS (LP)...£30

BILLY & ESSENTIALS
63	London HLW 9657	Over The Weekend/Maybe You'll Be There...£30

BILLY & LILLIE (& BILLY FORD & THUNDERBIRDS)
58	London HLU 8564	La Dee Dah/BILLY FORD'S THUNDERBIRDS: The Monster....................................£20
58	London HLU 8630	Creepin', Crawlin', Cryin'/Happiness (with Billy Ford & Thunderbirds) £30
59	London HLU 8795	I Promise You/Lucky Ladybug £20

BILLY BARRY BELLY
87	Sidetrack SIDE 001	Do They Know/Conversations With... (p/s) £25

(see also Chris Sievey, Frank Sidebottom)

BIM & BAM
70	Crab CRAB 48	The Pill (with Clover)/TOMMY McCOOK: Spring Fever £15
70	Crab CRAB 49	Immigrant Plight (w/ Clover)/PETER AUSTIN & HORTENSE: Bang Shangalang...............£15
73	Gayfeet GS 201	Fatty/Landlord £30

BIM, BAM & CLOVER
70	Trojan TR 7754	Party Time Parts 1 & 2...£15

BINGO
79	Polydor 2066365	We Can't Get Enough/Mumblin' Man £20

SONNY BINNS (& RUDIES)
69	Downtown DT 420	The Untouchables/Lazy Boy £40
69	Downtown DT 424	Wheels/Night Train £40
70	Escort ES 818	Boss A Moon (as S. Binns)/BUNNY LEE ALLSTARS: Brotherly Love......................£40

(see also Rudies)

BINO
81	Upper Class CPS 1	Dream (For My Sake)/Tonight (p/s) £15

BINTANGS
70	Decca F22995	Ridin' On The L And N/Down South Blues..£18

BIOME
12	Macabre Unit MUV 001	Persepolis/DCULT: Inner Peace (12")..£15
12	Macabre Unit MUV 003	Incubus/DEMON: Symmetry (12")..£20
13	Macabre Unit MUV 004	Black Widow/Quasar/Mystery (12")..£30

BIONIC ECHO
86	Josiah KJ 003	Digital/Chatty Chatty Mouth (12")..£80

BIOTA
85	Recommended DYS 12 & 13	RACKABONES (LP, with inserts) £30
87	Recommended RRC27	BELLOWING ROOM (LP) £30
88	Recommended RRC31	TINCT (LP) £25

KEV BIRD
91	Basement BRSS 003	Inside Your Mind (Full Length Mix)/En Bass (Original Mix)/En Bass (Crash Mix) (12", promo) £20
92	Basement BRSS 006	THE VISIT TO 14B EP (12", with The Wax Doctor) £15

BIRD LEGS & PAULINE
66	Sue WI 4014	Spring/In So Many Ways £40

MINT VALUE £

BIRD CURTIS
67	Tony Pike TPMLP 144	BIRD CURTIS QUINTET (LP)	£400

BIRDS
64	Decca F 12031	You're On My Mind/You Don't Love Me (You Don't Care)	£100
65	Decca F 12140	Leaving Here/Next In Line	£100
65	Decca F 12257	No Good Without You Baby/How Can It Be	£90
85	Demon WEST 901	THESE BIRDS ARE DANGEROUS (LP)	£15

(see also Birds Birds, Ron Wood, Faces, Creation, Ashton Gardner & Dyke)

BIRDS BIRDS
66	Reaction 591 005	Say Those Magic Words/Daddy Daddy	£500

(see also Birds, Gods)

BIRDS & BRASS
70	Rediffusion ZS 57	SOUNDSATIONAL (LP)	£15
74	Rediffusion 0100 171	... ARE BACK (LP)	£15

BIRDS OF A FEATHER
70	Page One POLS 027	BIRDS OF A FEATHER (LP)	£100

(see also Chanters)

BIRDS WITH EARS
81	Attrix RB12LP	YOUTH IN ASIA (LP)	£15

JANE BIRKIN & SERGE GAINSBOURG
69	Fontana STL 5493	JANE BIRKIN AND SERGE GAINSBOURG (LP)	£15

BIRMINGHAM
71	Grosvenor GRS 1011	BIRMINGHAM (LP)	£80

(see also Dave Peace Quartet)

BIRTH CONTROL
71	Charisma CAS 1036	BIRTH CONTROL (LP, pink/white 'scroll' label)	£150

BIRTHDAY PARTY
80	Missing Link ML-18	Mr. Clarinet/Happy Birthday	£50
81	(no cat. no.)	Mr. Clarinet/Missing Link (sold at gigs only)	£50
82	4AD BAD 301	THE BAD SEED EP	£15
82	4AD JAD 202	DRUNK ON THE POPE'S BLOOD/THE AGONY IS THE ECSTACY (12" EP, with Lydia Lunch)	£15
81	4AD CAD 104	PRAYERS ON FIRE (LP, inner)	£20
82	4AD CAD 207	JUNK YARD (LP, with inner)	£20
83	Mute MUTE 29	MUTINY (LP, insert)	£20
92	4AD DAD 2016	HITS (2-LP)	£50

(see also Nick Cave & Bad Seeds, These Immortal Souls)

DAVE BISHOP
78	Bible COM L	FIRST EP (with The Apostles, fold-out p/s)	£15

BITCH (2)
79	Hurricane FIRE 5	Big City/Wild Kids (p/s)	£20

BITCH (3)
81	Rutland RX 101	First Bite/Maggie (with p/s & promo insert)	£20
81	Rutland RX 101	First Bite/Maggie	£15

BITCHES SIN
83	Quiet QT 001	No More Chances/Overnight/Ice Angels (12", p/s)	£25
82	Heavy Metal HMRLP 4	PREDATOR (LP, textured sleeve)	£20

BITING TONGUES
81	Situation 2 SITU 1	DON'T HEAL (LP)	£15

BITSTREAM
99	Signal SIGNAL 01	MONOLITH EP (12")	£50

BITTERNESS
74	Brent BR 1	She Flies/Have We Seen Tomorrow	£20

BIZ
93	Warp WARP LP 9	ELECTRO SOMA (LP, orange vinyl)	£15

BIZARRE
79	Polydor 2383 553	BIZARRE (LP)	£20

(see also Alan Hawkshaw)

BIZARRE INC
89	Blue Chip BLUE TEC. 1	TECHNOLOGICAL (LP)	£15

BIZARRE UNIT
81	MRS MRS 004	Dancing/Away From The Screaming Car	£20

(see also Paul Nova)

BIZ MARKIE
88	Cold Chillin' W7890	Vapors/The Do Do (p/s)	£25
88	Cold Chillin' W7930	Biz Is Goin' Off/The Doo Doo (p/s)	£20
90	Warners W9823	Just A Friend ('Ard Done By Mix)/Just A Friend (LP version) (p/s)	£20

BJÖRK
96	O. L. Indian 193TP12DM	Enjoy (Beats Mix)/Possibly Maybe (Lucy Mix) (p/s, 1,000 only, numbered)	£15
96	O. L. Indian 193TP12DM	Enjoy/Possibly Maybe (12", 1,000 only, numbered p/s)	£18
08	One L. Indian 805TP12	EARTH INTRUDERS (CD, DVD & 2 x 12")	£20
08	One L. Indian 837TP12	DECLARE INDEPENDENCE (CD, DVD & 2 x 12")	£20

08	One L. Indian 838TP12	**INNOCENCE** (CD, DVD & 2 x 12")...£20
08	One L. Indian 853TP12	**WANDERLUST** (CD, DVD & 2 x 12")...£20
93	One L. Indian TPLP 31L	**DEBUT** (LP, 5,000 with 16-page lyric booklet)..£100
93	One L. Indian TPLP 31L	**DEBUT** (LP)...£70
94	One L. Indian 152TP 12	**THE BEST MIXES FROM THE ALBUM "DEBUT" FOR THOSE PEOPLE WHO DON'T BUY WHITE LABELS** (mini-LP)...£40
95	One L. Indian TPLP 51L	**POST** (LP, pink vinyl, with inner sleeve)...£75
96	One L. Indian TPLPT51	**TELEGRAM** (LP)...£60
97	One L. Indian TPLP71	**HOMOGENIC** (LP, with poster)...£60
00	One L. Indian TPLP151	**SELMA SONGS** (LP)...£50
01	One L. Indian TPLP101	**VESPERTINE** (2 x LP, gatefold) £50
02	One L. Indian TPLP359	**GREATEST HITS** (2 x LP, gatefold) £70
04	One L. Indian TPLP358	**MEDULLA** (2-LP, 33rpm version) £35
04	One L. Indian TPLP358	**MEDULLA** (2-LP, 45rpm version) £35
06	One L. Indian TPLP101SACD	**SURROUNDED** (7 dualdisc box-set of all albums) £60
07	One L. Indian TPLP460H	**VOLTA** (2-LP fold-out cover, stickered sleeve) £35
08	One L. Indian TPLP31DMM	**DEBUT** (2-LP, reissue, DMM mastered, stickered sleeve, numbered, 1000 only)............£100
08	One L. Indian TPLP51DMM	**POST** (2-LP, reissue, DMM mastered, stickered sleeve, numbered, 1000 only)...........£100
08	One L. Indian TPLP71DMM	**HOMOGENIC** (2-LP, reissue, DMM mastered, stickered sleeve, numbered, 1000 only)...£100
08	One L. Indian TPLP151DMM	**SELMASONGS** (2-LP, reissue, DMM mastered, stickered sleeve, numbered, 1000 only) .£100
08	One L. Indian TPLP101DMM	**VESPERTINE** (2-LP, reissue, DMM mastered, stickered sleeve, numbered, 1000 only) £100
08	One L. Indian TPLP358DMM	**MEDULLA** (2-LP, reissue, DMM mastered, stickered sleeve, numbered, 1000 only) £100
09	One L. Indian TPLP916	**VOLTAIC** (2-LP, 2-CD and 2-DVD) £40
11	One L. Indian TPLP1016	**BIOPHILIA** (LP, 2x12")..£35
15	One L. Indian TPLP 1231	**VULNICURA** (2-LP, yellow vinyl, PVC outer, gatefold sleeve, inners)..................£30

(see also Sugarcubes, Kukl)

BLACK
| 81 | Rox ROX 17 | Human Features/Electric Church (p/s)...£20 |
| 82 | Wonderful World WWW3 | More Than The Sun/Jump (no p/s) ....£20 |

BILL BLACK'S COMBO
64	London HLU 9925	Little Queenie/Boo-Ray...£30
64	London HLU 9925	Little Queenie/Boo-Ray (DJ Copy)..£100
64	London HA-U 8187	PLAYS CHUCK BERRY (LP)...£15

(see also Elvis Presley)

CILLA BLACK
| 67 | Parlophone GEP 8967 | TIME FOR CILLA (EP) ....£15 |

FRANK BLACK
93	4AD CADD 3004	FRANK BLACK (LP, die-cut screen-printed sleeve, with lyric inner) £20
96	EPC 481647	THE CULT OF RAY (LP)..£25
99	4AD DAD 4009	TEENAGER OF THE YEAR (2-LP) £25
98	PIAS BIAS 370LP	FRANK BLACK AND THE CATHOLICS (LP) £30
03	Diverse DIV 006LP	SHOW ME YOUR TEARS (LP, as Frank Black And The Catholics) £45
10	Vinyl Lovers 7901295	CHRISTMASS (LP, with free 7") £20

(see also Pixies)

IKA BLACK & THE NATIONS CRK
| 81 | I One I IONE 001 | Human Life/Better Life (12") ....£25 |

MARY BLACK
89	Grapevine GRALP 009	NO FRONTIERS (LP, with lyric inner sleeve) £25
92	Grapevine GRALP 009	NO FRONTIERS (LP, audiophile pressing, white sleeve) £30
92	Grapevine GRALP 009	NO FRONTIERS (LP, audiophile pressing, red sleeve with different design and inner sleeve)...£30
95	Grapevine GRALP 011	THE HOLY GROUND (LP, audiophile pressing)...£20
95	Grapevine GRALP 014	CIRCUS (LP, audiophile pressing with lyric inner).......................................£20

SAM BLACK
| 74 | DJM DJS 334 | I'm Goin' Left/Take Me With You ....£50 |

STEVE BLACK
| 83 | Dudu DAR 001 | HAPPY BIRTHDAY TO U (LP)..£400 |

BLACK ABBOTTS
| 71 | Evolution E 3004 | Love Is Alive/The Painter ....£25 |

BLACK ACE
| 61 | XX MIN 701 | BLACK ACE (EP)..£30 |
| 62 | Heritage HLP 1006 | BLACK ACE (LP, 99 copies only) ....£75 |

BLACKALICIOUS
| 99 | Mo Wax MWR 112LP | NIA (2-LP) ....£25 |

BLACK ARK PLAYERS
| 80 | Black Ark Intl. BALP 4000 | BLACK ARK IN DUB (LP, white label, green vinyl)....................................£45 |
| 80 | Black Ark Intl. BALP 4000 | BLACK ARK IN DUB (LP) ....£40 |

BLACK AXE
| 80 | Metal MELT 1 | Highway Rider/Red Lights (in p/s)...£20 |

BLACKBEARD
| 78 | Ballistic LBR 1013 | STRICTLY DUB WISE (LP)...£30 |
| 80 | More Cut RDC 2002 | I WAH DUB (LP)..£30 |

BLACK BEATLES
| 70 | Pama PM 804 | Reggae And Shout/LENOX BROWN: The Green Hornet ....£30 |

BLACKBIRDS
68	Saga OPP 3	**No Destination/Space** (either p/s or company sleeve, possibly promo only)	£30
68	Saga FID 2113	**NO DESTINATION** (LP, black/silver label)	£40

TONY BLACKBURN
69	Polydor 583 082	**TONY BLACKBURN** (LP)	£15

BLACKBYRDS
78	Fantasy FTCT 194	**Rock Creek Park/Don't Know What To Say** (12")	£20
85	Streetwave SWAVE 3	**Rock Creek Park/Walking In Rhythm** (12")	£15
75	Fantasy FT 9444	**BLACKBYRDS** (LP)	£20
75	Fantasy FT 522	**FLYING START** (LP)	£15
76	Fantasy FTA 3003	**CITY LIFE** (LP)	£15
77	Fantasy FT 534	**ACTION** (LP)	£15
79	Fantasy FT 555	**NIGHT GROOVES - THE BEST OF THE BLACKBYRDS** (LP)	£15

(see also Donald Byrd)

BLACK CAT
81	Gate MS02	**Queen Of The Hop/Let's Rock/Rockin Chair/Black Cat Boogie** (p/s)	£15
83	Underworld BBUW 09	**Dance With The Dolly/She's A Rocker** (p/s)	£40

BLACK CAT BONES
68	Sceptre SALR 1216	**COME ABOARD QE2** (LP, sold on liner, one track by Black Cat Bones)	£25
70	Decca Nova DN 15	**BARBED WIRE SANDWICH** (LP, mono, blue/silver label)	£500
70	Decca Nova SDN 15	**BARBED WIRE SANDWICH** (LP, stereo, blue/silver label)	£600

(see also Leaf Hound, Brian Short, Free, Foghat)

BLACK COCK
94	Black Cock BCOK 069	**ON THE NEST EP** (12", beware of bootlegs)	£70
95	Black Cock BCK 077	**FREE RANGE EP** (12")	£40
97	Black Cock BK 068	**Give It Up/Cosmic** (12")	£25
97	Black Cock BK 068	**Give It Up/Cosmic** (12", repressing)	£25
97	Black Cock BK 076	**Luna Parrrrty/Frog Scene** (12", white label, stickered sleeve)	£25

(see also DH Harvey, Ersatz)

BLACK COUNTRY, NEW ROAD
19	Speedy Wunderground SW026	**Athen's France** (Part 1)/(Part 2) (die-cut p/s, 250 only)	£100
19	Blank Editions BETBC018	**Sunglasses/Sunglasses** (Cont) (1st pressing, unique individual sleeves, certificate of ownership, stickered p/s)	£70
19	Blank Editions BETBC018	**Sunglasses/Sunglasses** (Cont) (2nd pressing, standard p/s, insert)	£40
19	Blank Editions BETBC018	**Sunglasses/Sunglasses** (Cont) (3rd pressing, 'assembly' p/s)	£30

BLACK COUNTRY THREE
66	W.F.C. WS 100	**BLACK COUNTRY SONGS** (EP)	£250
66	Transatlantic TRA 140	**BLACK COUNTRY THREE** (LP)	£50

(see also Jon Raven)

BLACK CROWES
91	Def American 7-17580	**HARD TO HANDLE** (7 x 7" box set, with 2 bonus tracks)	£20
90	Def American 842515	**SHAKE YOUR MONEY MAKER** (LP)	£30
92	Def American 512263	**SOUTHERN HARMONY AND MUSICAL COMPANION** (LP)	£30
94	American 74321 23682 1	**AMORICA** (LP, white vinyl)	£60
99	American 491699 1	**BY YOUR SIDE** (LP)	£60

BLACK DEVIL
04	Rephlex CAT 146EP	**DISCO CLUB** (12", p/s)	£15

BLACK DOG
91	GPR GENP(X) 2	**PARALLEL EP** (12", p/s)	£30
92	Black Dog Prods BDP 001	**VIRTUAL EP** (12", p/s)	£50
92	Black Dog Prods BDP 002	**AGE OF SLACK** (12", p/s)	£50
92	Black Dog Prods BDP 003	**BLACK DOG EP** (12", p/s, 500 only)	£125
92	GPR GENP(X) 3	**VIR 2 L** (12", custom sleeve)	£50
92	GPR GENP(R) 03	**VIR 2 L/Shout** (12" remix with SHIVA)	£30
92	GPR GENP(X) 9	**VANTOOL EP** (12", custom sleeve)	£100
93	GPR GENP(X) 17	**COST II** (12", custom sleeve)	£15
93	Rising High RSN 046	**BLACK DOG PRODUCTIONS** (12", 4-track, p/s)	£20
07	Soma SOMA 214	**VIRTUAL EP** (12" reissue)	£20
91	GPR GPR 004	**PARALLEL SQUELCH** (LP)	£30
92	GPR GPRLP 1	**TEMPLE OF TRANSPARENT BALLS** (2-LP, with poster)	£45
92	GPR GPRLP 1	**TEMPLE OF TRANSPARENT BALLS** (2-LP, without poster)	£30
95	GPR GPRLP 15	**PARALLEL** (2-LP)	£35
95	GPR GPRCD 15	**PARALLEL** (CD)	£30
95	Warp PUP LP1	**SPANNERS** (2-LP)	£40
95	Warp WAP LP 8LTD	**BYTES** (LP, bronze vinyl)	£40
96	Warp PUP LP2	**MUSIC FOR ADVERTS** (AND SHORT FILMS) (2-LP)	£20

(see also Alter Ego, Plaid, Repeat, Unexplored Beats, Shiva)

BLACK DYKE MILLS BAND
68	Apple APPLE 4	**Thingumybob/Yellow Submarine**	£40

BLACK DYNAMITES
60	Top Rank JAR 319	**Brush Those Tears/Lonely Cissy**	£15

BLACK-EDS
80	Acne ACNE 1	**Isn't It Strange/Living Doll/Jimmy 2 Stroke** (p/s)	£20

BLACK FAITH
| 74 | Fresh Air 6121107 | The Vow/Stop The World | £20 |

BLACK FANTASY
| 84 | Dingle TIG 001 | Evil Places/Fade Away From Me (p/s) | £100 |

J.D. BLACKFOOT
| 71 | Mercury 6338 031 | THE ULTIMATE PROPHECY (LP) | £70 |

BLACKFOOT SUE
73	Jam JAL 104	NOTHING TO HIDE (LP, gatefold sleeve with poster)	£50
73	Jam JAL 104	NOTHING TO HIDE (LP, gatefold sleeve without poster)	£20
75	DJM DJLPS 455	GUN RUNNING (LP, withdrawn)	£65

BLACK GRAPE
95	Radioactive RAR 11224	IT'S GREAT WHEN YOU'RE STRAIGHT YEAH (LP)	£50
97	Radioactive RAR 11716	STUPID STUPID STUPID (LP)	£15
17	UMC 5757997	POP VOODOO (LP, yellow vinyl, signed)	£18

(see also Happy Mondays, Ruthless Rap Assassins)

BLACK HARMONY
| 79 | Burning Sounds BS 14 | I'm Still Waiting/Love Marcus | £20 |
| 79 | Laser LAS 9 | Don't Let It Go To Your Head/DEB PLAYERS : Don't Let It Go To Your Brain (12") | £18 |

BLACK HEARTED BROTHER
| 13 | Sonic Cathedrals SCRO70LP | STARS ARE OUR HOME (2-LP) | £18 |

(see also Slowdive)

BLACK HONEY
15	(No label or cat. no.)	Corrine/Mothership (p/s, pink vinyl)	£15
16	Black Honey	HEADSPIN EP (10", p/s, red vinyl)	£30
17	Black Honey	Hello Today/Ghost (heart-shaped red/white 10")	£40
20	Foxfire BHRSD001	Corrine/Mothership (green heart-shaped 10")	£15

BLACK IVORY
| 79 | Buddah BDLP 4060 | HANGIN HEAVY (LP) | £15 |

BLACKJACK
| 80 | Polydor POSP 76 | Without Your Love/Heart Of Mine (p/s) | £18 |
| 79 | Polydor 2391 411 | BLACKJACK (LP) | £18 |

(see also Michael Bolton)

BLACK KEYS
03	Fat Possum 111-7	Hard Row/Evil (p/s)	£15
06	V2 VVR1042541	MAGIC POTION (LP)	£20
09	V2 VVR737199	BROTHERS (2-LP)	£18
12	Fat Possum FP803713	THICKFREAKNESS (LP, picture disc, 300 only)	£15
12	Fat Possum FP80379-3	RUBBER FACTORY (LP, picture disc)	£15
12	Nonesuch 530454-1	EL CAMINO (2-LP, CD, numbered)	£20

BLACK KNIGHTS
| 65 | Columbia DB 7443 | I Gotta Woman/Angel Of Love | £25 |

BLACK LIPS
| 07 | Vice VICE 004LP | GOOD BAD NOT EVIL (LP, gatefold) | £15 |

DON BLACKMAN
| 82 | Arista RIST 30 | Hearts Desire/Let Your Conscience Be Your Guide (12", EP) | £15 |

HONOR BLACKMAN
68	CBS 3896	Before Today/I'll Always Be Loving You (in p/s)	£30
64	Decca LK/SKL 4642	EVERYTHING I'VE GOT (LP, mono/stereo)	£20
80	Deram 844057-1	KINKY BOOTS (LP)	£20

(see also Patrick MacNee & Honor Blackman)

PAUL BLACKMAN
| 79 | Daddy Kool DKR 123 | Earth, Wind & Fire/A. Pablo: Ras-Menlik Congo (12") | £50 |

(see also Augustus Pablo)

BLACK MIDI
| 18 | Speedy Wunderground SW005 | Bmbmbm/Savage Gary's Dbdbdb (1st pressing of 250, numbered) | £35 |
| 18 | Speedy Wunderground SW024 | Bmbmbm/Savage Gary's Dbdbdb (2nd pressing of 250, un-numbered) | £25 |

RITCHIE BLACKMORE (ORCHESTRA)
| 65 | Oriole CB 314 | Getaway/Little Brown Jug (Spelt "Richie" on label) | £600 |

(see also Outlaws, Neil Christian & Crusaders, Deep Purple, [Ritchie Blackmore's] Rainbow, Rally Rounders, Green Bullfrog)

BLACK OAK ARKANSAS
| 71 | Atlantic 2400 180 | BLACK OAK ARKANSAS (LP) | £15 |

BLACK PEACHES
| 15 | 1965 Recordings/PIAS OLIVE 1013V | GET DOWN YOU DIRTY RASCALS (LP, peach coloured vinyl, DL code) | £15 |
| 19 | Hanging Moon HANLP 001 | FIRE IN THE HOLE (LP/7", numbered ltd. 'dinked' edition of 350, teal vinyl) | £20 |

(see also Grovesnor, Hot Chip)

BLACK RADICAL/SIR NOVA
| 88 | Bass Inc B1001 500 | B Boys Be Wise/We Outta Here (12") | £60 |

BLACK REBEL MOTORCYCLE CLUB
| 02 | Virgin VUSLP 224 | BLACK REBEL MOTORCYCLE CLUB (LP) | £50 |
| 03 | Virgin VUSLP 245 | TAKE THEM ON YOUR OWN (2-LP, gatefold, with inner sleeves) | £50 |

05	Echo ECHLP 67	HOWL (2-LP, with inner sleeves)	£50
10	Cobraside CSDLP 1142	BEAT THE DEVIL'S TATTOO (2-LP, white vinyl 400 copies, tour only)	£30
10	Cobraside CSDLP 1142	BEAT THE DEVIL'S TATTOO (2-LP, grey vinyl)	£20

BLACK RIDERS
| 85 | Plastic Head GILP 555 | CHOSEN FEW (LP) | £15 |

BLACK ROD
| 73 | Phoenix NIX 133 | See What You Get Out Of Me/Mad Donkey | £15 |

BLACK ROOTS
81	Nubian NR 0021D	Chanting For Freedom/Confusion/What Them A Do (12")	£15
84	Bullet BOL 9	Boys Will Be Boys/Liar (p/s, some with patch)	£35
84	Nubian NR 001	Bristol Rock/Tribal War/The Father/The System (12")	£25
83	Kick KIC LP 02	BLACK ROOTS (LP)	£30
84	Bullet BULP 3	BOYS WILL BE BOYS (LP)	£15
84	BBC REC 555	THE FRONT LINE (LP)	£30
84	BBC REC 5570	IN SESSION (LP)	£20
11	Bristol Archive ARC219V	REGGAE SINGLES ANTHOLOGY (2-LP)	£18

BLACK ROSE
| 82 | Teesbeat TB 5 | Sucker For Your Love/No Point Runnin' (in p/s) | £125 |
| 82 | Teesbeat TB 5 | Sucker For Your Love/No Point Runnin' | £35 |

BLACK SABBATH
| 13 | Vertigo 3734950 | 13 (2-LP) | £15 |

SINGLES
70	Fontana TF 1067	Evil Woman/Wicked World (A label promo)	£200
70	Fontana TF 1067	Evil Woman/Wicked World	£125
70	Vertigo V2	Evil Woman/Wicked World (A label promo)	£150
70	Vertigo V2	Evil Woman/Wicked World (reissue, Vertigo 'swirl' sleeve)	£35
70	Vertigo V2	Evil Woman/Wicked World (reissue, later silver label)	£15
70	Vertigo 6059010	Paranoid/The Wizard (promo)	£100
70	Vertigo 6059 010	Paranoid/The Wizard (Vertigo 'swirl' sleeve)	£20
72	Vertigo 6059061	Tomorrow's Dream/Laguna Sunrise (promo)	£60
72	Vertigo 6059 061	Tomorrow's Dream/Laguna Sunrise (Vertigo 'swirl' sleeve)	£25
72	Phonogram DJ 005	Children Of The Grave/STATUS QUO: Roadhouse Blues (100 promo copies only)	£500
78	Vertigo SAB 002	Hard Road/Symptom Of The Universe (purple vinyl with 'Sympton' typo on label)	£30
82	NEMS NEP 1	Paranoid/Iron Man (picture disc)	£20
86	Vertigo SABDJ 12	In For The Kill/Turn To Stone/Heart Like A Wheel (12", promo only)	£15
87	Vertigo SABAF 1	4 SONGS FROM THE ETERNAL IDOL (12", p/s, promo only)	£15
89	I.R.S. EIRSB 115	Devil And Daughter (box set, 1-sided disc with stencil, insert & 2 postcards)	£20
10	Vertigo 00602527391199	Paranoid (Alternative Lyric Version)/METALLICA: Frantic (UNKLE Remix) (12", 1000 only)	£20
14	Secret 7" S715	Age Of Reason (100 only, each with unique art sleeve)	£100

ALBUMS
70	Vertigo VO 6	BLACK SABBATH (LP, 1st pressing, with black gatefold inner sleeve, no composers/publishers credits on cross; large swirl label with "A Philips record product" text on label and "Copyright subsists in all Stereo recordings" text)	£500
70	Vertigo VO 6	BLACK SABBATH (LP, 2nd pressing, with Dunbar credit for 'Warning'; swirl label, without "A Philips record product" on label and without composers/publishers credits, with "Copyright subsists in all Vertigo recordings" text)	£300
70	Vertigo 6360 011	PARANOID (LP, 1st pressing with 'Jim Simpson' management credit inside gatefold sleeve, large swirl label)	£350
70	Vertigo 6360 011	PARANOID (LP, 2nd pressing, large swirl label, without Jim Simpson credit inside laminated sleeve)	£200
70	Vertigo 6360 011	PARANOID (LP, 3rd pressing, small swirl label, gatefold sleeve)	£100
70	Vertigo 6360 011	PARANOID (LP, gatefold sleeve, later spaceship label)	£100
71	Vertigo 6360 050	MASTER OF REALITY (LP in box cover, swirl label, with poster)	£500
71	Vertigo 6360 050	MASTER OF REALITY (LP in box cover, swirl label, without poster)	£350
71	Vertigo VO 6	BLACK SABBATH (LP, 3rd pressing, 'Vertigo' lettering beneath small swirl above centre hole, composers/publishers credits in lower case. "Copyright subsists in all Vertigo recordings" credit)	£100
72	Vertigo 6360 071	BLACK SABBATH VOL. 4 (LP, 1st pressing, no "Made in England" beneath 1972 on top right hand side" gatefold sleeve with booklet attached, small swirl label, "PORKY/PECKO" hand etched in run out grooves)	£250
72	Vertigo 6360 071	BLACK SABBATH VOL. 4 (LP, 2nd pressing, with "Made in England" beneath 1972 on top right hand side" gatefold sleeve with booklet attached, small swirl label, no "PORKY/PECKO" hand etching in run out grooves)	£150
72	Vertigo 6360 071	BLACK SABBATH VOL. 4 (LP, gatefold sleeve with booklet attached, 'spaceship' label)	£150
73	Vertigo VO6	BLACK SABBATH (LP, 4th pressing, 'spaceship' label)	£100
73	WWA WWA 05	SABBATH BLOODY SABBATH (LP, 1st pressing, no ridge around rim, 1 Y 1/ 2 Y 1 matrix numbers, silver WWA logo, gatefold with "Manufactured and printed in England" (no "Howard's Printers" reference), inside image extends to edge of sleeve with no border, textured lyric inner)	£60
73	WWA ACB 00166	SABBATH BLOODY SABBATH (LP, reissue, Audio Club of Great Britain pressing)	£30
73	WWA 006	BLACK SABBATH (LP, reissue, in Vertigo sleeves with WWA006 sticker on rear)	£50
73	WWA 006	BLACK SABBATH (LP, reissue)	£20
73	WWA 007	PARANOID (LP, reissue)	£40
73	WWA 009	BLACK SABBATH VOL 4 (LP, reissue, gatefold)	£40
73	Vertigo 6360 050	MASTER OF REALITY (LP, ' spaceship' label, with poster, reissue)	£100
73	WWA WWA 008	MASTER OF REALITY (LP, 'transitional sleeve' with sticker over Vertigo cat no on rear, with poster, reissue)	£80
73	WWA 008	MASTER OF REALITY (LP, label, with poster, reissue)	£30
73	WWA WWA 005	SABBATH BLOODY SABBATH (LP, reissue)	£15
75	NEMS 9119001	SABOTAGE (LP, 1st pressing with "Record and Tapes" logo matrix numbers 1//Y2 S 1 3	£100

		5 & 2 Y2 S 1 1 4 with 'Sterling' stamped into dead wax on both sides, textured sleeve made by 'Robert Stace', "Meglomania" typo)...	
75	NEMS 9119001	**SABOTAGE** (LP, 2nd pressing with no "Record and Tapes" logo matrix numbers 1//Y2 S 1 3 5 & 2 Y2 S 1 1 4 with 'Sterling' stamped into dead wax on both sides, textured sleeve made by 'Robert Stace', "Meglomania" typo)...	£50
75	NEMS 6641 335	**WE SOLD OUR SOUL FOR ROCK N ROLL** (2-LP)	£18
76	Vertigo 9102 750	**TECHNICAL ECSTACY** (LP, insert)	£35
76	NEMS NEL 6003	**PARANOID** (LP, reissue)	£20
76	NEMS NEL 6004	**MASTER OF REALITY** (LP, reissue, stickered sleeve)	£20
76	NEMS NEL 6005	**BLACK SABBATH VOL 4** (LP, reissue, gatefold)	£20
78	Vertigo 9102 751	**NEVER SAY DIE** (LP, laminated sleeve, inner)	£40
80	Vertigo 9102 752	**HEAVEN AND HELL** (LP, A1/B2 matrixes)	£35
80	NEMS NEL 6018	**SABOTAGE** (LP, reissue)	£15
80	NEMS BS 001	**LIVE AT LAST** (LP)	£30
80	NEMS NEL 6017	**SABBATH BLOODY SABBATH** (LP, reissue)	£15
81	Vertigo 6302 119	**MOB RULES** (LP)	£50
83	Vertigo SAB 10	**LIVE EVIL** (2-LP, gatefold, inners orange Vertigo label)	£35
83	Vertigo VER 8	**BORN AGAIN** (LP)	£30
85	Nems BSBLP 001	**THE SABBATH COLLECTION** (7-LP box set)	£50
86	Vertigo VERH 29	**SEVENTH STAR** (LP, as Black Sabbath featuring Tony Iommi)	£30
87	Vertigo VERH 51	**ETERNAL IDOL** (LP, lyric inner)	£30
88	Castle BSBCD 001	**THE BLACK SABBATH CD COLLECTION** (6-CD box set with badge & book, numbered, 3,000 only)	£40
89	IRS METAL 24 1005	**HEADLESS CROSS** (LP, poster)	£75
89	IRS EIRSAPD 1002	**HEADLESS CROSS** (LP, picture disc with extra track)	£35
89	Vertigo 8388181	**BLACKEST SABBATH** (2-LP)	£18
90	IRS EIRSA 1038	**TYR** (LP, inner)	£100
90	IRS EIRSAPD 1038	**TYR** (LP, picture disc with 2 extra tracks)	£35
91	Essential ESBLP 142	**THE OZZY OSBOURNE YEARS** (5LP box set, booklet)	£90
92	IRS 713155 1	**DEHUMANIZER** (LP)	£80
94	IRS 07777132221 1	**CROSS PURPOSES** (LP, with inner)	£300
97	Castle ORRLP 004	**BLACK SABBATH** (LP, reissue, 5000 only with free 7")	£20
00	Metal-is RAWLP 145	**THE BEST OF BLACK SABBATH** (4LP, gatefold, numbered and stickered)	£80
02	Earmark 41045	**PAST LIVES** (2LP, trifold sleeve, poster)	£60
13	Vertigo 602537349593	**13** (2-LP, 2-CD, DVD, box set)	£45

(see also Ozzy Osborne, Dio, Elf, Cozy Powell, Quartz,, Brian May)

BLACK SHEEP
91	Mercury MER 356	**Try Counting Sheep**/(Original Sheep LP Mix) (p/s)	£60
91	Mercury MER 369	**Strobelite Honey** (Maybe We Did Mix)/(The Original) (p/s)	£50

BLACK SLATE
76	Slate KG 04	**Sticks Man/Robber Man In Dub**	£20
78	Ted TCDD 003	**Mind Your Motion/You Can't Make Us** (12")	£35
78	Ted TCDD 008	**Sticks Man/Version** (12")	£25
80	TCD TCDLP1	**AMIGO** (LP)	£15
81	TCD TCDLP 02	**OGIMA** (DUB SLATE) (LP)	£40
82	Top Ranking TRY IT 1	**SIX PLUS ONE** (LP, with free dub LP)	£20

BLACKSTAR
95	Congo Natty RASTA 1	**TRIBUTE TO HAILE SELASSIE I** (2-LP)	£40

BLACK STASH
75	Seville 1004	**Mighty Love Man/Mighty Love Man Part 2**	£15

BLACK STONES
78	Chanah Jah CJ3026	**Punk Rockers/Open The Gates** (12" p/s)	£15

BLACKSTREET
94	Interscope 6544 92351 1	**BLACKSTREET** (2-LP, insert)	£40
96	Interscope INTLP 90071	**ANOTHER LEVEL** (2-LP)	£30

BLACK SWAN
71	Ember EMBS 303	**Echoes And Rainbows/Belong Belong** (with p/s)	£15

BLACK SYMBOL
79	Black Symbol BS 001	**Non A Jah Jah Children Passing/Version** (12")	£50
80	Black Symbol BS 003	**Loving Jah/Everything Has Time** (12")	£70
80	Black Symbol BS 006	**My Heart Reveal Dancer/Dub Piano**	£25
82	Black Symbol BS 008	**Solidarity/Tension** (12")	£30

BLACKTHORN
77	WHM 1921	**BLACKTHORN** (LP)	£60
78	WHM 1922	**BLACKTHORN II** (LP)	£100

BLACK UHURU
77	Carib Gems CG 015	**Sun Is Shining/REVOLUTIONARIES : Version**	£20
77	Third World TWDIS 009	**Natural Mystic/Sorry For The Man** (12")	£20
79	Warrior WAR 140	**Bad Girl/African Love/PRINCE HAMMER - Yogi Bear** (12")	£25
79	DEB DEB 034	**Rent Man/Rent Board/ALTON ELLIS - La La Means I Love You/Version** (12")	£20
79	DEB DEB 036	**Wood For My Fire/EARL CUNNINGHAM/JAH THOMAS - Words Of The Father** (12")	£20
79	D Roy DDR 09	**Plastic Smile/Guess Who's Coming To Dinner** (12")	£25
79	D Roy DRDD 15	**Shine Eye** (featuring Keith Richards)/**D-ROY BAND: Licking Stick** (12")	£25
80	Island 12WIP 6626	**Sinsemilla** (Discomix)/**Guess Who's Coming To Dinner** (Discomix) (12")	£15
85	Taxi BUT 1	**Fit You Haffe Fit/Fitness** (12")	£18
77	Third World TWS 925	**LOVE CRISIS** (LP, as Black Sounds Uhro)	£40

79	D-Roy DRLP 1003	SHOWCASE (LP)	£25
80	Island ILPS 9593	SINSEMILLA (LP)	£25
81	Greensleeves GREL 23	BLACK SOUNDS OF FREEDOM (LP)	£25
82	CSA CSLP 2	UHURU IN DUB (LP)	£15

(See also Don Carlos)

BLACK VELVET

70	Beacon BEA 151	Please Let Me In/Clown	£20
71	Mams MAM 47	Make It Better/Tropicana	£15
70	Beacon BEAS 16	THIS IS BLACK VELVET (LP)	£25
72	Pye NSPL 18392	PEOPLE OF THE WORLD (LP)	£25
73	Seven Sun SUNLP1	CAN YOU FEEL IT? (LP)	£80

BLACKWELL

| 76 | Penny Farthing PELS 559 | BOOGIE DOWN MESS AROUND (LP) | £20 |

CHARLES BLACKWELL ORCHESTRA

| 60 | Triumph TRY 4000 | THOSE PLUCKING STRINGS (LP, unreleased, test pressings only) | £500 |

OTIS BLACKWELL

| 58 | London HLE 8616 | Make Ready For Love/When You're Around | £40 |

RORY BLACKWELL & HIS BLACKJACKS

| 57 | Parlophone R 4326 | Bye Bye Love/Such A Shame | £20 |

SCRAPPER BLACKWELL

| 63 | '77' LA 12/4 | BLUES BEFORE SUNRISE (LP) | £40 |
| 60s | Xtra XTRA 5011 | MR SCRAPPER'S BLUES (LP) | £25 |

BLACKWELLS (U.K.)

| 65 | Columbia DB 7442 | Why Don't You Love Me/All I Want Is Your Love | £15 |

BLACK WIDOW

70	CBS 5031	Come To The Sabbat/Way To Power	£20
71	CBS 7596	Wish You Would/Accident	£20
70	CBS 63948	SACRIFICE (LP, gatefold sleeve)	£100
70	CBS 64133	BLACK WIDOW II (LP, gatefold sleeve)	£100
72	CBS 64562	BLACK WIDOW III (LP, with inner)	£100

(see also Pesky Gee)

BLADE

88	Chart Moves 732-1532	Chart Moves (12", not officially released. Intended to be instructions to game of same name but never used in final version of game)	£25
89	Raw Bass 1202	Lyrical Maniac/The Comin' Is Near/We're Going Independent (12")	£15
89	691 Influential 1203	Mind Of An Ordinary Citizen/Forward (12")	£15
91	691 Influential 1204	Rough It Up/Whatcha Waitin' For?/You Better Get Yours (12")	£15
96	691 Influential SURV 1	Survival Of The Hardest Working (12")	£25
04	691 Influential BLADEDJ 1209	Pop Idol/(Instrumental)/(Accapella)/Scream/(Instrumental)/(Accapella)(12", spray painted promo)	£30
92	691 Influential 1205	SURVIVAL OF THE HARDEST WORKING (LP, inserts)	£15
93	691 Influential 1207	THE LION GOES FROM STRENGTH TO STRENGTH (2LP, gatefold, white vinyl, 20 copies only))	£750
95	691 Influential 1208	PLANNED AND EXECUTED (LP, insert)	£15
95	691 Influential 1208	PLANNED AND EXECUTED (LP, limited edition, red vinyl, insert)	£40
04	691 Influential 08 52760 20 1	STORMS ARE BREWING INSTRUMENTALS (2LP, 500-only, Blade-spraypainted cover)	£50

ANDY BLADE

| 80 | SMS SMS 001 | Break The News/Girl With The Goods (p/s) | £25 |

(see also Eater)

BLADE RUNNER

| 84 | Ebony EBON 21 | HUNTED (LP) | £15 |

BLADES

81	Reekus RKS005	The Bride Wore White/Animation (p/s)	£25
80	Energy NRG 3	Hot For You/The Reunion (p/s; Irish with paper labels)	£20
80	Energy NRG 3	Hot For You/The Reunion (p/s; later UK pressing with plastic labels, in plastic sleeve)	£15
81	Energy NRG 5	Ghost Of A Chance/Real Emotion (p/s; Irish with paper labels)	£20
84	Reekus RKLP 1	THE LAST MAN IN EUROPE (LP)	£20
86	Reekus RKLP 3	RAY TOWN REVISITED (LP)	£20

(see also Partisans)

BLADES OF GRASS

| 67 | Stateside SS 2040 | Happy/That's What A Boy Likes | £15 |

BLAGGER

| 70 | Mount Clifton MCL 002 | Day After Day/The Hunt Is On | £30 |

BLAH BLAH BLAH

| 81 | Some Bizzare | BLAH BLAH BLAH (LP, unreleased, stickered sleeve, white label test pressings only) | £40 |

HAL BLAINE (& YOUNG COUGARS)

| 64 | RCA RD 7624 | DEUCES, T'S, ROADSTERS AND DRUMS (LP, mono) | £15 |
| 64 | RCA SF 7624 | DEUCES, T'S, ROADSTERS AND DRUMS (LP, stereo) | £15 |

BLAIR

| 79 | Miracle M4-12 | Night Life/Virgo Princess (12") | £40 |

ARNOLD BLAIR

| 76 | Curtom NEET 1024 | Trying To Get Next To You/I Won The Big Deal/House Party (12" with Fred Wesley) | £15 |
| 16 | Super Disco Edits SDE 20 | Finally Made It Home/I Won The Big Deal This Time (Alternative Version) | £20 |

JOYCE BLAIR AND OLIVER REED
63	Picadilly 7N 35083	Baby It's Cold Outside/JOYCE BLAIR: Safe In The Arms Of My Darling............£15

VERN BLAIR DEBATE
05	Funk 45 FUNK45 024	Super Funk/Ooh Ah Ee (reissue) £15

KARL BLAKE
83	Glass GLASS 013	THE PREHENSILE TAPES (LP) £20
91	Tak Tak Tak TAK 07	MANDIBLES (cassette, 500 only) £15

(see also Lemon Kittens, Underneath, Gland Shrouds, Sol Invictus)

KEITH BLAKE
68	Blue Cat BS 102	Musically/I'm Moving On............£175

(see also Overtakers, Uniques, Prince Allah)

TIM BLAKE
78	Barclay Towers CLAY 7005	BLAKE'S NEW JERUSALEM (LP)............£15

(see also Gong, Hawkwind)

WINSTON BLAKE & M-SQUAD
69	Crab 40	Big Thing/RUPIE EDWARDS : Exclusively Yours £20

ART BLAKEY JAZZ MESSENGERS
57	Parlophone PMC 1084	HARD DRIVE (LP) £25
58	Parlophone PMC 1099	BIG BAND (LP) £25
59	Vogue LAE 12096	RITUAL (LP) £25
59	London 15157	ART BLAKEY'S JAZZ MESSENGERS WITH THELONIOUS MONK (LP)............£20
61	Fontana TFL 5116	OLYMPIA CONCERT (LP)............£25
62	HMV CLP 1532	ART BLAKEY JAZZ MESSENGERS (LP, also stereo CSD 1423)............£30
62	Fontana TFL 5184	DANGEROUS FRIENDSHIPS (LP, soundtrack) £25
63	RCA Victor RD 7555	A NIGHT IN TUNISIA (LP)............£25
63	United Artists (S)ULP 1017	THREE BLIND MICE (LP, mono/stereo) £20
64	Riverside RLP 438	CARAVAN (LP) £20
64	HMV CLP 1760	A JAZZ MESSAGE (LP)............£30
64	Riverside RLP 464	UGETSU (LP)............£30
65	Limelight (S)LML 4000	'S MAKE IT (LP)............£25
66	Limelight (S)LML 4012	SOUL FINGER (LP) £25
66	Limelight (S)LML 4021	BUTTERCORN LADY (LP) £25
66	Fontana FJL 111	SOUL! (LP)............£25
67	Limelight (S)LML 4023	HOLD ON, I'M COMIN' (LP) £20
67	Atlantic 590 009	BLUE MONK (LP, with Thelonious Monk)............£20
68	Riverside 673013	KYOTO (LP) £25
69	Polydor 545101	DRUM THUNDER (LP) £15

(see also Annie Ross)

ART BLAKEY/MILES DAVIS
66	Fontana FJL 135	L'ASCENSEUR POUR L'ECHAFAUD/FEMME DISPARAISSANTE (LP, soundtrack, 1 side each) £30

(see also Thelonious Monk, Miles Davis)

BLAK TWANG
02	Bad Magic MAGICT 25	SO ROTTEN EP (12", p/s) £20
96	Sound Of Money SNM 008	DETTWORK SOUTH EAST (LP - unissued) £75
02	Bad Magic MAGIC LP 5	KIK OFF (2-LP, artwork by Banksy) £50

BLANCK MASS
11	Rock Action ROCKACT 58LP	BLANCK MASS (2-LP) £20
17	Sacred Bones SBR-174	WORLD EATER (LP, red vinyl, 200 only with print) £50

BLANCMANGE
80	Blaah Music MFT-1	IRENE AND MAVIS (EP, gatefold p/s) £40

BOBBY BLAND
61	Vogue V 9178	Cry Cry Cry/I've Been Wrong So Long £30
61	Vogue V 9182	Lead Me On/Hold Me Tenderly £30
61	Vogue V 9188	Don't Cry No More/St. James Infirmary £30
62	Vogue V 9190	You're The One (That I Need)/Turn On Your Love Light............£30
62	Vogue V 9192	Blue Moon/Who Will The Next Fool Be?............£30
64	Vocalion VP 9222	Ain't Nothing You Can Do/Honey Child £30
64	Vocalion VP 9229	After It's Too Late/Share Your Love With Me £30
65	Vocalion VP 9232	Yield Not To Temptation/How Does A Cheating Woman Feel? £30
65	Vocalion VP 9251	These Hands (Small But Mighty)/Today............£30
66	Vocalion VP 9262	I'm Too Far Gone (To Turn Around)/ If You Could Read My Mind £25
66	Vocalion VP 9273	Good Time Charlie/Good Time Charlie (Working His Groove Bag)............£35
68	Sue WI 4044	That Did It/A Touch Of The Blues £50
69	Action ACT 4524	Rockin' In The Same Old Boat/Wouldn't You Rather Have Me?............£30
69	Action ACT 4538	Gotta Get To Know You/Baby I'm On My Way £30
69	Action ACT 4548	Share Your Love With Me/Honey Child £40
69	Action ACT 4553	Chains Of Love/Ask Me 'Bout Nothing But The Blues £30
63	Vocalion VEP 170153	BOBBY BLAND (EP) £80
64	Vocalion VEP 170157	BOBBY BLAND SINGS (EP) £100
60	Vogue VA 160183	TWO STEPS FROM THE BLUES (LP) £200
61	Vocalion VA 160183	TWO STEPS FROM THE BLUES (LP) £200
61	Vogue VAP 8027	AIN'T NOTHING YOU CAN DO (LP) £75
64	Vocalion VAP 8027	AIN'T NOTHING YOU CAN DO (LP) £40
63	Vogue VAP 8034	CALL ON ME/ THAT'S THE WAY LOVE IS (LP)............£75

MINT VALUE £

64	Vocalion VAP 8034	CALL ON ME/ THAT'S THE WAY LOVE IS (LP)	£40
66	Vocalion VAP 8041	HERE'S THE MAN (LP)	£50
68	Island ILP 974	A TOUCH OF THE BLUES (LP)	£100
69	Action ACLP 6006	A PIECE OF GOLD (LP)	£40
74	ABC ABCL 5053	DREAMER (LP)	£30
74	Polydor 2383 257	BLUES FOR MR. CRUMP (LP, with tracks by Junior Parker & Howlin' Wolf)	£20
85	Kent 044	THE SOULFUL SIDE OF BOBBY BLAND (LP)	£15

MARCIE BLANE
63	London HLU 9787	You Gave My Number To Billy/Told You So	£15
63	London REU 1393	MARCIE BLANE (EP)	£75

BLANKS
79	Void SRTS/79/CUS/560	The Northern Ripper/Understand (p/s)	£70

(see also Destructors)

BLANK STUDENTS
80	Dexter Discs	We Are Natives/I Want To Be Happy (500 only)	£25

BLAPPS POSSE
92	Ruff Lick LIKK 002	SET YOURSELF FREE (12" EP)	£15

BLARNEY SISTERS
67	GO AJ11407	The Greatest Blessing/Golden Band	£15

BLAWAN
11	Down 001	Getting Me Down (1-sided 12")	£25
12	Hinge Finger HINF 8674	HIS HE SHE & SHE (12" EP, p/s)	£25

BLAZE X
80	Fixed Wheel FX 1	Some Hope/Rippy (Irish pressing, gatefold p/s)	£150

BLAZERS
58	Fontana TFR 6010	ROCK AND ROLL (10" LP)	£30

BLEACH BOYS
78	Tramp THF 002	Chloroform/You've Got Nothing (no p/s, 1,000 only)	£60
85	Zombie International ZOMBO 103010	Stocking-Clad Nazi Death Squad Bitches/Death Before Disco/Gimme That Neutron Taste (12", p/s)	£25

BLEAK HOUSE
80s	Buzzard BUZZ 1	Rainbow Warrior/Isandlhwana/Inquisition (in p/s)	£100
80s	Buzzard BUZZ 1	Rainbow Warrior/Isandlhwana/Inquisition	£30
82	Buzzard BUZZ 2	LIONS IN WINTER (Chase The Wind/No Reply/Down To Zero/ Flight Of The Salamander) (EP, p/s with insert)	£90

BLEECHERS
69	Trojan TR 679	Ease Up/You're Gonna Feel It	£30
69	Upsetter US 314	Come Into My Parlour/MELOTONES: Dry Up Your Tears	£120
70	Col. Blue Beat DB 118	Send Me The Pillow (That You Dream On)/Adam And Eve	£30
71	Duke DU 118	Put It Good/J.J. ALLSTARS: Good Good Version	£30

(see also Busty Brown, Upsetters)

BLEEDING HEARTS
80	Crazy Plane SP 003	This Is The Way/OK	£30

PETER BLEGVAD
77	Virgin V 2082	KEW RHONE (LP, with John Greaves)	£15

(see also Slapp Happy)

BLENDELLS
64	Reprise RS 20291	La La La La La La/Huggies Bunnies (DJ Copy)	£20
64	Reprise RS 20340	Dance With Me/Get Your Baby	£50
64	Reprise RS 20340	Dance With Me/Get Your Baby (DJ Copy)	£60

CARLA BLEY
72	JCOA JT 4001	ESCALATOR OVER THE HILL (3xLP, gatefold with Paul Haines & Jack Bruce)	£25
74	Watt WATT 1	TROPIC APPETITES (LP, gatefold sleeve)	£15

(see also Jazz Composers Orchestra, Michael Mantler, Jack Bruce)

PAUL BLEY TRIO
69	Fontana SFJL 929	TOUCHING (LP)	£100

(see also Bley-Peacock Synthesizer Show, Annette Peacock)

BLEY-PEACOCK SYNTHESIZER SHOW
72	Polydor 2425 043	REVENGE (LP)	£250

(see also Annette Peacock, Paul Bley)

BLIND BLAKE
58	Ristic LP 18	THE LEGENDARY BLIND BLAKE (10" LP)	£35

(see also Paramount Allstars)

BLIND BLAKE/CHARLIE JACKSON
50s	Heritage HLP 1011	BLIND BLAKE AND CHARLIE JACKSON (LP, 99 only)	£40

BLIND FAITH
69	Island (no cat. no.)	Change Of Address From June 23rd 1969 (promo issue, 500 only)	£500
69	Polydor 583 059	BLIND FAITH (LP, gatefold sleeve, first pressing with single paper on left gatefold stating distribution by Polydor and Island)	£100
69	Polydor 583 059	BLIND FAITH (LP, gatefold sleeve, later issue without Polydor and Island distribution credit)	£40
77	RSO 2394142	BLIND FAITH (LP, reissue)	£15
83	RSO SPELP 14	BLIND FAITH (LP, reissue)	£15
08	RSO 53167	BLIND FAITH (LP, reissue 180gm vinyl)	£15

(see also Stevie Winwood, Ginger Baker, Eric Clapton)

BLIND LEMON CLEGG
80 Pollen PBM 029   RUN FOR YOUR MONEY EP £50

BLINDERS
17 (No label or Cat. No.)   Swine/Ramona Flowers (p/s) £70
19 Modern Sky   Rat In A Gabe/Nuclear Love (p/s) £30
18 Modern Sky MODERN060LP COLUMBIA (LP) £15

BLINKERS
69 Pye 7N 17752   Original Sin/Dreams Secondhand £60

BLINKY & EDWIN STARR
69 Tamla Motown TMG 720   Oh How Happy/Ooo Baby Baby (unissued, demos only)................£375
70 T. Motown (S)TML 11131   JUST WE TWO (LP, as Edwin Starr & Blinky)..............................£25
(see also Edwin Starr)

BLISS
69 Chapter One CH 107   Courtyards In Castile/Lifetime £15

MELVIN BLISS
77 Contempo CS 2013   Reward/Synthetic Substitution £80

BLITZ
81 No Future OI 1   ALL OUT ATTACK (EP, rubber-stamped labels, 500 only, fold-out sleeve)........£30
81 No Future OI 1   ALL OUT ATTACK (EP, reissue, initially with white labels, fold-out sleeve) £15
82 No Future OI 16   Warriors/Youth (p/s) £15
82 No Future PUNK 1   VOICE OF A GENERATION (LP, with inner sleeve) £35
83 Future FL 1   SECOND EMPIRE JUSTICE (LP) £35
88 Link LINK LP 029   BLITZED - AN ALL OUT ATTACK (LP) £15

BLITZ BOYS
80 Told You So TYS 001   Eddy's New Shoes/Eddie's Friend/She Told My Friends (foldover p/s)........£125

BLITZKREIG (1)
79 Ellie Jay/BRP EJSP 9257 SURVIVAL (LP) £100

BLITZKRIEG (2)
81 Neat NEAT 10   Buried Alive/Blitzkrieg (p/s) £60
85 Neat NEAT 1023   A TIME OF CHANGES (LP) £40

BLITZKRIEG (3)
83 Sexual Phonograph SPH2   Animals In Lipstick/Land Of Failure/No Compromise (p/s, SPH2 on cover but SPH3 on label) £15

BLITZKRIEG BOP
77 Mortonsound MTN 3172/3   Let's Go/Nine Till Five/Bugger Off (p/s, 500 only) £100
77 Lightning GIL 504   Let's Go (re-recorded)/Life Is Just A So-So/Mental Case (p/s)........£30
78 Lightning GIL 543   U.F.O./Bobby Joe (p/s) £20
(see also Basczax, The Gynaecologists, Nicky Beat)

BLIZZARD KING
97 Kalevala KALA 005   Break On Through/Strangers In The Night/In The Ghetto £20

BLO
75 Afrodisia DWAPS 2009   PHASE IV (LP) £40
01 Strut STRUTALP 004   PHASES 1972-1982 (2-LP) £25

BLOC PARTY
04 Trash Aesthetics TA701   She's Hearing Voices/The Marshals Are Dead/The Answer (p/s clear vinyl, 500 only) £50
04 Moshi Moshi MOSHI10   Banquet/Staying Fat (p/s, 500 only)..£15
04 Wichita WEBB 070S   Helicopter/Skeleton (green vinyl) £20
07 Wichita WEBB 118S   The Prayer/England (1st 7" of 2 and comes in box) £15
08 Wichita WEBB 180T   MERCURY EP (2 x 7", CD in box) £15
12 Transgressive TRANS 137 She's Hearing Voices/The Marshals Are Dead/The Answer (red vinyl, 500 only)...........£15
05 Wichita WEBB 075LP   SILENT ALARM (LP) £50
05 Wichita WEBB 075PD   SILENT ALARM (LP, picture disc) £50
05 Wichita WEBB 090LP   SILENT ALARM REMIXED (2-LP) £25
07 Wichita WEBB 120 LP   A WEEKEND IN THE CITY (LP) £15
07 Wichita WEBB 120 PD   A WEEKEND IN THE CITY (LP, picture disc) £30
08 Wichita WEBB 185PD   INTIMACY (LP, picture disc, 500 only) £15
09 Wichita WEBB 210LP   INTIMACY REMIXED (3-LP) £18
15 Wichita WEBB250LPTEN   SILENT ALARM (LP, reissue with free 7", 1000 only).................£50

BLOCKHEAD
04 Ninja Tune ZEN 88   MUSIC BY CAVELIGHT (2xLP) £25

BLODWYN PIG
69 Island WIP 6059   Dear Jill/Sweet Caroline..£15
69 Island WIP 6069   Walk On The Water/Summer Day £15
69 Island ILPS 9101   AHEAD RINGS OUT (LP, 1st pressing, gatefold sleeve, pink label with black/orange circle logo)........£100
69 Island ILPS 9101   AHEAD RINGS OUT (LP, 2nd pressing, gatefold sleeve, with block logo)...........£50
70 Island ILPS 9101   AHEAD RINGS OUT (LP, gatefold sleeve, 3rd pressing with white i' logo)..........£40
70 Chrysalis ILPS 9122   GETTING TO THIS (LP, gatefold sleeve, island logo and address in white on green label) ..£70
70s Island ILPS 9101   AHEAD RINGS OUT (LP, gatefold sleeve, reissue 'pink rim palm tree' label) £15
(see also Mick Abrahams, Jethro Tull)

BLOND
69 Fontana STL 5515   THE LILAC YEARS (LP, gatefold sleeve) £125
(see also Tages)

BLONDE ON BLONDE
69	Pye 7N 17637	All Day All Night/Country Life	£40
70	Ember EMB S 279	Castles In The Sky/Circles (in p/s)	£20
72	Ember EMB S 316	Sad Song For An Easy Lady/Happy Families (p/s)	£15
69	Pye NSPL 18288	CONTRASTS (LP, gatefold sleeve, blue/black label with logo/banner on top)	£175
70	Ember NR 5049	RE-BIRTH (LP, gatefold sleeve)	£100
71	Ember NR 5058	REFLECTIONS ON A LIFE (LP, gatefold sleeve)	£100
70s	Ember LP 7005	BLONDE ON BLONDE (LP, unissued, test pressings only)	£300

BLONDIE
76	Private Stock PVT 90	X Offender/In The Sun (unissued, promos or stock copies, no p/s)	£2000
76	Private Stock PVT 105	In The Flesh/X Offender (demo in promo p/s)	£50
76	Private Stock PVT 105	In The Flesh/X Offender (no p/s)	£20
81	Chrysalis 12-2485	Rapture (Special Disco Mix)/Live It Up (Special Disco Mix) (12", p/s)	£15
98	EMI 12 ATOM 150	ATOMIC 98 (Remixes) (12", p/s, withdrawn)	£15
76	Private Stock PVLP 1017	BLONDIE (LP)	£20
77	Chrysalis CHR 1166	PLASTIC LETTERS (LP)	£20
78	Chrysalis CHR 1166-P	PLASTIC LETTERS (LP, picture disc)	£20
78	Chrysalis CDL1192	PARALLEL LINES (LP, inner)	£20
81	Chrysalis CDL TV1	THE BEST OF BLONDIE (LP, with poster)	£15
82	Chrysalis PCDL 1384	THE HUNTER (LP, picture disc)	£15
89	Chrysalis CHR 1658	THE 12" MIXES (2-LP)	£15
97	Chrysalis 7243821459 1 2	PARALLEL LINES (LP, reissue, part of EMI 100 series, stickered sleeve)	£20

(see also Debbie Harry, Wind In The Willows)

ALPHA BLONDY
86	Sterns STERNS 1017	APARTHEID IS NAZISIM (LP)	£15
87	Stern's STERNS 1019	JESUSALEM (LP, with the Wailers)	£18

BLOOBLO
78	Mother & Son	IS THAT YOU (LP)	£25

BLOOD
83	No Future OI 22	Megalomania/Calling The Shots/Parasite In Paradise (p/s)	£20
83	Noise NOY 1	Stark Raving Normal/Mesrine (p/s)	£18
82	Noise NOYZLP 1	FALSE GESTURES FOR A DEVIOUS PUBLIC (LP, inner)	£35
85	Conquest QUEST 3	SE PARARE NEX (LP)	£15
89	Link Classics CLINK 5	FALSE GESTURES FOR A DEVIOUS PUBLIC (LP, reissue, red vinyl)	£15

BARRY BLOOD
75	Alaska ALA 24	Poor Annie/On The Run	£40
82	Wretchord WOO 1	She's The Queen Of My Rock And Roll/What D'Ya Say?	£40

BLOOD DIVINE
96	Peaceville VILE 62	AWAKEN (LP)	£18

(see also Cradle Of filth, Anathema)

BLOOD RED SHOES
06	Jonson Family	Bless His Heart/Don't Always Say Yes/Victory For The Magpie (p/s, insert, 500 only)	£25
06	Try Harder	Stitch Me Back/Meet Me At Eight (500 only)	£30
17	Jazz Life JAZZLIFE 09	Eye To Eye (gig only red flexi)	£25
08	V2 1763548	BOX OF SECRETS (LP)	£25
10	V2 VVR736628	FIRE LIKE THIS (LP, silkscreened sleeve)	£15
12	V2 VVR795935	IN TIME TO VOICES (LP, silkscreened cover with CD)	£20
14	Jazz Life JAZZLIFE 1 BDL	BLOOD RED SHOES (LP, orange/purple vinyl with 2 CDs)	£20

BLOODROCK
71	Capitol E-ST 491	BLOODROCK 2 (LP)	£15
71	Capitol E-ST 765	BLOODROCK 3 (LP)	£15

BLOOD SHANTI
96	Aba Shanti ABA 12003	Tear Down Babylon/Verse 1/Verse 2/Verse 3/Verse 4 (12")	£35
96	Falasha ABA10002	Children Of The Most High/Verse 1/Verse 2/Verse 3 (12")	£40
00	Falasha AB12004	Jah Liveth (One Love)/Dub/Hail Jah/Dub (12")	£30
02	Aba Shanti ABALP 002	PURE SPIRIT (LP)	£30
02	Aba Shanti ABALP 005	UNDILUTED (LP)	£20

BLOOD SISTERS
79	Ballistic Records BP 314	Ring My Bell/ONE BLOOD: One Blood dub (p/s)	£35
79	Sound City SCD 002	Ring My Bell/Dub (12")	£20
79	Sound City SCD 004	What About Me/I'd Rather Go Blind (12")	£15
80	King & City KCD001	Be Thankful/What About Me (12")	£20
81	Ballistic 12BP314	Don't Say Goodbye Too Loud/Let Me Love You (12", some on clear vinyl)	£20

BLOOD, SWEAT & TEARS
68	CBS 3563	I Can't Quit Her/House In The Country	£20
74	CBS 2462	Tell Me That I'm Wrong/Rock Reprise	£20
68	CBS 63296	CHILD IS THE FATHER TO THE MAN (LP)	£20

(see also Al Kooper)

ROGER BLOOM'S HAMMER
67	CBS 202654	Out Of The Blue/Life's A Gamble	£40
67	CBS 2848	Polly Pan/Fifteen Degree Temperature Rise	£40

MIKE BLOOMFIELD
69	CBS 63652	IT'S NOT KILLING ME (LP)	£20

(see also Barry Goldberg Reunion, Stephen Stills, K.G.B.)

MIKE BLOOMFIELD & AL KOOPER

69	CBS 66216	THE LIVE ADVENTURES OF MIKE BLOOMFIELD AND AL KOOPER (2-LP, mono)	£60
69	CBS 66216	THE LIVE ADVENTURES OF MIKE BLOOMFIELD AND AL KOOPER (2-LP, stereo)	£25

(see also Al Kooper, Paul Butterfield Blues Band, Electric Flag)

BLOOMFIELDS

72	Pye 7N 45114	The Loner/Homing In On The Next Trade Wind	£15

BLOSSOM TOES

67	Marmalade 598 002	What On Earth/Mrs Murphy's Budgerigar/Look At Me I'm You (in p/s)	£70
67	Marmalade 598 002	What On Earth/Mrs Murphy's Budgerigar/Look At Me I'm You	£30
68	Marmalade 598 009	I'll Be Your Baby Tonight/Love Is	£30
68	Marmalade 598 012	Postcard/Everyone's Leaving Me Now	£30
69	Marmalade 598 014	Peace Loving Man/Up Above My Hobby Horse's Head	£30
69	Marmalade 598 022	New Day/Love Bomb (unissued, existence unconfirmed)	£0
67	Marmalade 607 001	WE ARE EVER SO CLEAN (LP, mono)	£700
67	Marmalade 608 001	WE ARE EVER SO CLEAN (LP, stereo)	£800
69	Marmalade 608 010	IF ONLY FOR A MOMENT (LP)	£800
88	Decal LIKD 43	COLLECTION (2-LP)	£15
07	Sunbeam SBR2LP5035	WE ARE EVER SO CLEAN (2-LP, reissue)	£20
07	Sunbeam SBR2LP5036	IF ONLY FOR A MOMENT (2-LP, reissue)	£20

(see also B.B. Blunder, Stud, Kevin Westlake, Solid Gold Cadillac)

BLOSSOMS (1)

58	Capitol CL 14833	Move On/He Promised Me	£50
58	Capitol CL 14856	Little Louie/Have Faith In Me	£40
58	Capitol CL 14947	No Other Love/Baby Daddy-O	£40
68	MGM MGM 1435	Tweedle Dee/You Got Me Hummin'	£20
71	Pama PM 814	Stand By/Soul And Inspiration	£30

(see also Darlene Love, Allisons [U.S.])

BLOSSOMS (2)

14	RIP 0001	BLOOM EP (CD-R, 100 only)	£50
14	Skeleton Key SKL 015	Blow/Winters Kiss (yellow vinyl)	£50
15	Skeleton Key SKL 016	Cut Me And I'll Bleed/The Urge (live) (clear vinyl)	£18
16	Virgin 4771395	You Pulled A Gun On Me/Getting Away With It (live)	£20
16	Virgin V 3156	BLOSSOMS (LP)	£25

MICHAEL BLOUNT

70	CBS 5248	Ryba Jyba/Acorn Street	£15
71	CBS 64230	PATCHWORK (LP)	£20
72	York FYK 401	SOUVENIRS (LP)	£20
73	York FYK 414	FANTASIES (LP)	£20

BLOWZABELLA

82	Plant Life PLR 051	IN COLOUR (LP)	£30
90	Special Delivery SPD 1028	VANILLA (LP)	£40

BLUE

73	RSO 2394 105	BLUE (LP)	£15

(see also Poets, Thunderclap Newman)

BOBBY BLUE

70	Duke DU 86	Going In Circles (actually by Lloyd Charmers)/Doggone Right (actually by Winston Francis)	£20

DAVID BLUE

67	Elektra EKL 4003	DAVID BLUE (LP, red label)	£50
72	Asylum SYL 9001	STORIES (LP)	£20
73	Asylum SYL 9009	NICE BABY AND THE ANGEL (LP)	£20
75	Asylum SYL 9025	COMIN' BACK FOR MORE (LP)	£20
76	Asylum K 53056	CUPID'S ARROW (LP)	£20

PAMELA BLUE

63	Decca F 11761	My Friend Bobby/Hey There Stranger	£70

TIMOTHY BLUE

68	Spark SRL 1014	The Room At The Top Of The Stairs/She Won't See The Light	£20

BLUE ACES

64	Pye 7N 15672	Land Of Love/Love Song Of The Waterfall	£15
64	Pye 7N 15713	I Beat You To It/I Just Can't Help Loving You	£15
65	Pye 7N 15821	Ain't What You Say/You Don't Care	£15
65	Columbia DB 7755	Tell Me What You're Gonna Do/All I Want	£100
66	Columbia DB 7954	That's All Right/Talk About My Baby	£100

(see also Riot Squad)

BLUE ANCHOR

79	Workhouse WHR 6	PLENTY LOVE & BACON (LP)	£15

BLUE ANGEL

80	Polydor 2391 486	BLUE ANGEL (LP)	£25

BLUE AQUARIUS

73	Akashic 998	The Ultimate Train/At The Feet Of The Master	£30

BLUE ARSED FLY

95	Ferox FER 012	IN THE BAG (12")	£15
96	Mosquito MSQ 04	BLUE ARSED FLY EP (12")	£20

(see also Christian Vogel, Neil Landstrumm)

BLUE BEARD
71	Ember EMB S 302	Country Man/Sly Willy (in p/s)	£30
71	Ember EMB S 302	Country Man/Sly Willy (no p/s)	£20
71	Ember LT 7004	BLUE BEARD (LP, unreleased, test pressings only)	£200

BLUEBEATS
64	Ember EMB EP 4525	THE FABULOUS BLUEBEATS VOL. 1 (EP)	£30
64	Ember EMB EP 4526	THE FABULOUS BLUEBEATS VOL. 2 (EP)	£30

BLUE BEATS
60	Blue Beat 45/BB 20	Baby What You Done Me Wrong/Go Pretty Baby Go	£20

BLUE-BELLES
62	HMV POP 1029	I Sold My Heart To The Junkman/Itty Bitty Twist	£15

(see also Patti Labelle)

BLUE BELLS & JAH BERRY
78	Burning Rockers BRD 001	Teacher Teach, Teach The Youth/Golden Rule (12")	£30

BLUEBERRIES
66	Mercury MF 894	It's Gonna Work Out Fine/Please Don't Let Me Know	£75

BLUE BLOOD
70	Sonet SNTF 615	BLUE BLOOD (LP)	£25

BLUE BLUDD
87	Blud Donor no cat. No.	LIQUOR 'N' POKER (EP)	£20

BLUEBOY
91	Sarah SARAH 55	Clearer/Alison (p/s, insert)	£20
93	Sarah SARAH 70	Cloud Babies (6" one-sided flexi with fanzine)	£15
92	Sarah SARAH 65	Popkiss/Chelsea Guitar/Fearon (p/s, insert)	£20
93	Sarah SARAH 74	Meet Johnny Rave/Elle/Air France (p/s)	£60
93	Sarah SARAH 80	SOME GORGEOUS ACCIDENT EP (wraparound p/s in ply bay, insert)	£15
94	Sarah SARAH 88	River/Nimbus/Hit	£15
95	Sarah SARAH 99	Dirty Mags/Loony Tunes/Toulouse (p/s)	£20
92	Sarah SARAH 612	IF WISHES WERE HORSES (LP)	£40
94	Sarah SARAH 620	UNISEX (LP)	£40

BLUE CHEER
68	Philips BF 1646	Summertime Blues/Out Of Focus	£25
69	Philips BF 1778	West Coast Child Of Sunshine/When It All Gets Old	£15
71	Philips 6051 010	Pilot/Babaji (Twilight Raga)	£15
68	Philips BL 7839	VINCEBUS ERUPTUM (LP, mono)	£75
68	Philips (S)BL 7839	VINCEBUS ERUPTUM (LP, stereo)	£50
68	Philips SBL 7860	OUTSIDEINSIDE (LP, gatefold sleeve)	£75
69	Philips SBL 7896	NEW! IMPROVED! (LP)	£60
69	Philips 6336 001	BLUE CHEER (LP)	£60
71	Philips 6336 004	B.C. #5 THE ORIGINAL HUMAN BEING (LP)	£60

(see also Leigh Stephens, Group B)

BLUE CHIPS
65	Pye 7N 15970	I'm On The Right Side/You're Good To Me	£30
66	Pye 7N 17111	Some Kind Of Lovin'/I Know A Boy	£20
66	Pye 7N 17155	Tell Her/Good Lovin' Never Hurt	£20

BLUE EPITAPH
74	Holyground HG 117	ODE (LP, 99 copies only)	£400
91	Holyground HG 117	ODE (LP, reissue, folded gatefold sleeve)	£25

(see also Magus)

BLUE EYES
91	Union Hall 001	Pick Up The Mic On A Soul Tip/The Law (12")	£15

BLUE & FERRIS
68	Blue Cat BS 147	You Stole My Money/Tell Me The Reason	£60

BLUE FLAMES
63	R&B JB 114	J.A. Blues/Orange Street	£60
63	R&B JB 126	Stop Right Here/Rik's Tune	£60

(see also Georgie Fame & Blue Flames)

BLUE GOOSE
75	Anchor ANCL 2005	BLUE GOOSE (LP)	£15

(see also Badfinger, Curtis Knight & Zeus, Motorhead)

BLUE HORIZON
71	Folk Heritage FHR 022S	BLUE HORIZON (LP)	£350

BLUE JEANS
69	Columbia DB 8555	Hey Mrs. Housewife/Sandfly	£50

(see also Swinging Blue Jeans, Ray Ennis & Blue Jeans)

BLUE MEN
60	Triumph RGXST 5000	I HEAR A NEW WORLD (PART ONE) (EP)	£300
60	Triumph RGXST 5001	I HEAR A NEW WORLD (PART TWO) (EP, only sleeves exist, this price is for sleeve)	£25
60	Triumph TRX ST 9000	I HEAR A NEW WORLD (LP, unreleased, white label demos only)	£800
20	Electronic Sound ES 762	I HEAR A NEW WORLD (PART ONE) (p/s, reissue)	£15

(see also Joe Meek, Peter Jay & Blue Men, Rodd-Ken & Cavaliers)

BLUE MINK
70	Philips SBL 7926	MELTING POT (LP)	£15

71	Philips 6308 024	OUR WORLD (LP)	£15
73	EMI EMA 756	ONLY WHEN I LAUGH (LP, gatefold sleeve)	£15
74	EMI EMC3021	FRUITY (LP)	£15

BLUE MIST
74	Ice ICE 1	Riding To The War/Who Are You	£15

BLUE MOVIES
79	ROK ROK 9	Mary Jane/THE NOISE: Criminal (company sleeve)	£15

BLUE NILE
81	RSO RSO 84	I Love This Life/The Second Act (p/s)	£20
83	Linn LKH 001	A WALK ACROSS THE ROOFTOPS (LP)	£40
89	Linn LKH 2	HATS (LP)	£80
12	Virgin LKHR 1	A WALK ACROSS THE ROOFTOPS (LP, reissue, 180g)	£40
13	Virgin LKHR2	HATS (LP, reissue, 180g)	£70
14	Epstein EPL01	PEACE AT LAST (2LP, first UK vinyl issue of 1996 CD, gatefold, numbered)	£100
19	Confetti BLUELP 001	A WALK ACROSS THE ROOFTOPS (LP, second reissue, 180g)	£70
19	Confetti BLUELP 002	HATS (LP, second reissue, 180g)	£60
19	Confetti BLUE LP 003	PEACE AT LAST (LP, reissue, 180g)	£60
20	Confetti Records BLUELP 004	HIGH (LP, printed inner, reissue)	£80

(see also Paul Buchanan)

BLUE NOTES
76	Ogun OGD 001/002	BLUE NOTES FOR MONGEZI (2-LP)	£50
78	OGUN OG 220	BLUE NOTES IN CONCERT VOLUME 1 (LP)	£25
87	OGUN OG 532	BLUE NOTES FOR JOHNNY (LP)	£20

BLUE ORCHIDS
84	Rough Trade ROUGH 36	GREATEST HITS (LP)	£15

(see also Nosebleeds, Fall, Fates)

BLUE OX BABES
88	Go! Discs GOLP 14	APPLES AND ORANGES (LP, unissued, test pressings only)	£50
88	Go! Discs ZGOLP 14	APPLES AND ORANGES (cassette, printed inlay, unreleased)	£20

(see also Dexys midnight Runners)

BLUE ÖYSTER CULT
73	CBS 64904	BLUE ÖYSTER CULT (LP)	£20

BLUE PHANTOM
72	Kaleidoscope KAL 101	DISTORTIONS (LP, laminated front cover, yellow label)	£150

BLUE RIDGE RANGERS
73	Fantasy FT 511	BLUE RIDGE RANGERS (LP)	£18

(see also John Fogerty, Creedence Clearwater Revival)

BLUE RONDOS
64	Pye 7N 15734	Little Baby/Baby I Go For You	£30
65	Pye 7N 15833	Don't Want Your Lovin' No More/What Can I Do	£40

BLUES
81	Precious PRE 1	Aim For The Eyes/Out Of Town	£125

BLUES EXPLOSION
04	Mute STÜMM 236	DAMAGE (LP, gatefold with booklet)	£18

BLUE SAND
67	Saturn HEY 006	Florida Bound/Blue Mama/The Dream/Name Of The Game	£35

BLUES BAND
80	Blues Band BBBP 101	OFFICIAL BOOTLEG ALBUM (LP, numbered, with autographs, 3000 only)	£18

(see also Paul Jones, McGuinness-Flint, Manfred Mann)

BLUE BENDER
66	Rio R93	Girl Next Door/Leave Me Out	£20

BLUES BUSTERS
59	Limbo XL101	Little Vilma/ Early One Morning	£30
61	Starlite ST45 031	The Spiritual/ Lost My Baby	£40
61	Blue Beat BB55	Donna/You're Driving Me Crazy	£25
62	Blue Beat BB73	There's Always Sunshine/ You Had It Wrong	£25
62	Starlite ST45 072	Your Love/You Send Me Crazy	£25
62	Island WI-023	Behold/Oh Baby	£30
62	Blue Beat BB102	Tell Me Why/ I've Done You Wrong	£30
65	Island WI-214	How Sweet It Is/ I Had A Dream	£40
65	Island WI-219	Wide Awake In A Dream (actually by Philip James solo)/ MAYTALS: Tell Me The Reason	£75
65	Island WI-222	Wings Of A Dove/ BYRON LEE & DRAGONAIRES: Dan Is The Man	£40
66	Doctor Bird DB1030	I've Been Trying/ Pretty Girls	£60
67	Doctor Bird DB 1078	There's Always Sunshine/ Lovers' Reward	£60
77	Spank SP 20	The Closer I Get To You/WILLIE LINDO: Midnight (12")	£40
65	Island ILP-923	BEHOLD! (LP)	£60
67	Doctor Bird DLM5008	BEST OF THE BLUES BUSTERS (LP)	£150
76	Dynamic DYLP 3007	PHILLIP & LLOYD (LP)	£25

BLUES BY FIVE
64	Decca F 12029	Boom Boom/I Cried	£120

BLUES COUNCIL
65	Parlophone R 5264	Baby Don't Look Down/What Will I Do	£100

MINT VALUE £

BLUES 5
64	Studio 36 (no cat. no.)	Hey Baby/When You're In Love	£150

BLUE SKIES
70	Pendant PN 004	Nightmares/Marigold	£50

BLUES MAGOOS
66	Mercury MF 954	(We Ain't Got) Nothin' Yet/Gotta Get Away	£30
67	Fontana TF 848	One By One/Love Seems Doomed	£15
66	Fontana TL 5402	BLUES MAGOOS (LP, mono)	£50
66	Fontana (S)TL 5402	BLUES MAGOOS (LP, stereo)	£30
71	Probe SPB 1024	GULF COAST BOUND (LP)	£20

BLUES MASTERS
63	Island WI 078	5 O'Clock Whistle/African Blood (both sides actually by Baba Brooks)	£40

BLUESOLOGY
65	Fontana TF 594	Come Back Baby/Time's Getting Tougher Than Tough	£350
66	Fontana TF 668	Mister Frantic/Everyday (I Have The Blues)	£350

(see also Stu Brown & Bluesology, Elton John, Long John Baldry, Elton Dean, Mark Charig)

BLUES PROJECT
67	Verve Forecast VS 1505	I Can't Keep From Crying/The Way My Baby Walks	£35
67	Verve (S)VLP 6004	PROJECTIONS (LP)	£75

(see also Al Kooper, Tommy Flanders, Seatrain)

BLUE STARS
65	Decca F 12303	Please Be A Little Kind/I Can Take It	£200
94	Dig The Fuzz DIG 020	THE BLUE STARS (LP)	£20

BLUETONES
96	Superior Quality BLUELP 004	EXPECTING TO FLY (LP, booklet, numbered, 5000 only)	£50
96	Superior Quality BLUELP 004	EXPECTING TO FLY (LP)	£30
98	Superior Quality BLUE V008	RETURN TO THE LAST CHANCE SALOON (LP, white vinyl)	£20
03	Superior Quality BLUE 019LP	LUXEMBOURG (LP)	£18

BLUE TRAIN
87	Dreamworld DREAM 007T	LAND OF GOLD (12" EP)	£40

BLUE VELVET BAND
69	Warner Bros WS 1802	SWEET MOMENTS WITH THE BLUE VELVET BAND (LP, gatefold sleeve)	£20

BLUEWATER FOLK
70	Folk Heritage FHJR 013S	BLUEWATER FOLK (LP)	£50

BLUE YOGURT
70	Penny Farthing PEN 732	Lydia/Umbrella Man	£40

COLIN BLUNSTONE
71	Epic EPC 64557	ONE YEAR (LP, textured sleeve)	£15
72	Epic EPC 65278	ENNISMORE (LP, textured sleeve)	£15

(see also Zombies, Neil MacArthur, Mitchell-Coe Mysteries)

BLUNT INSTRUMENT
78	Diesel DCL 01	No Excuse/Interrogation (p/s)	£15

JAMES BLUNT
05	Atlantic ATO 207	You're Beautiful (Edit)/So Long Jimmy (Acoustic)	£30
05	Atlantic ATO 230	Goodbye My Lover(Video Mix)/Where Is My Mind? (Live In Manchester)	£15
07	Atlantic ATO 285	1973/So Happy (pink vinyl, stickered, p/s)	£30
18	Atlantic/Custard 286396-1	ALL THE LOST SOULS (2LP, vinyl issue of 2007 CD, clear vinyl, book, print)	£70
19	Atlantic/Custard 0190295366773	ONCE UPON A MIND (LP, printed inner, green vinyl)	£20
21	Atlantic 0190296614910	THE STARS BENEATH MY FEET (2004-2021) (2LP, gatefold, printed inners, clear vinyl)	£25
23	Atlantic/Custard 5054197707513	WHO WE USED TO BE (LP, recycled, Assai Records Obi Edition, 300 copies, printed inner)	£25

BLUR
94	Food 12 FOOD 53	Parklife (as Blur starring Phil Daniels)/Supa Shoppa/To The End (French Version)/Beard (12", p/s, poster)	£50

SINGLES
91	Food 12FOODX 29	There's No Other Way (The Blur Remix)/Won't Do It/ Day Upon Day (live) (12", p/s lists '12 FOODDX 29')	£20
92	Food FOOD 37	Popscene/Mace (p/s)	£15
92	Food 12FOOD 37	Popscene/I'm Fine/Mace/Garden Central (12", p/s)	£18
92	Food BLUR 6	The Wassailing Song (1-sided gig freebie, as "Gold, Frankinscence and Blur" no p/s, 500 only)	£150
97	Food FOOD 93	Song 2/Get Out Of Cities (p/s. purple vinyl)	£20
99	Food BLURBOX 10	THE 10 YEAR ANNIVERSARY BOX SET (22xCD singles)	£60
03	Parlophone R 6606	Out Of Time/Money Makes Me Crazy (Marrakech Mix) (p/s, Banksy artwork)	£200
03	EMI R 6610	Crazy Beat/The Outsider (p/s, red vinyl 'Banksy' cover)	£200
03	EMI R 6619	Good Song/Morricone (p/s, red vinyl)	£300
05	Fan Club SGLAD 01	Some Glad Morning (CD, card wallet, fan club issue)	£30
10	Parlophone LCO 3098	Fools Day (1-sided 7", jukebox centre, blue Parlophone sleeve, 1000 only)	£30

ALBUMS : LPS
91	Food FOODLP 6	LEISURE (LP, printed inner)	£60
93	Food FOODLP 9	MODERN LIFE IS RUBBISH (LP, printed inner)	£120

94	Food FOODLP 10	**PARKLIFE** (LP, with inner)	£150
95	Food FOODLP 14	**THE GREAT ESCAPE** (LP, printed inner)	£80
95	Food FOODLP 14	**THE GREAT ESCAPE** (LP 12" box, book, print. Produced by Vinyl Experience, 2000 only)	£70
97	Food FOODLP 19	**BLUR** (2LP, gatefold, printed inners)	£140
97	Food FOODLP 19	**BLUR** (1LP version, textured gatefold, printed inner)	£120
99	Food FOODLP 29	**13** (2-LP, stickered, gategold, with inner sleeves)	£50
00	Food FOODLPD 33	**THE BEST OF** (2LP, gatefold, printed inners, PVC printed with 'Blur')	£350
03	Parlophone 07243-582887-1-7	**THINK TANK** (2LP, gatefold sleeve, printed inners)	£200
12	EMI BLURBOXLP 1	**BLUR 21** (12LP box set, download cards)	£300
12	EMI BLURBOX21	**BLUR 21** (18 CD, 3 DVD & 7" box set)	£70
12	Parlophone CDLHN 100X	**PARKLIVE** (4CD/DVD box set)	£50
12	Food FOODLPX 6	**LEISURE** (LP, reissue, 180g)	£25
12	Food FOODLPX 9	**MODERN LIFE IS RUBBISH** (2LP, reissue, gatefold, printed inners, 180g)	£40
12	Food FOODLPX 10	**PARKLIFE** (2LP, reissue, gatefold, printed inners, 180g)	£30
13	Food FOODLPX 14	**THE GREAT ESCAPE** (LP, reissue, 180g, printed inner)	£30
12	Food FOODLPX 19	**BLUR** (2LP, reissue, gatefold, 180g)	£30
12	Food FOODLPX 29	**13** (2LP, reissue, gatefold, 180g, embossed inners)	£35
15	Parlophone 0825646141715	**MAGIC WHIP** (2LP gatefold, printed inner, poster, obi)	£40
23	Parlophone 5054197660160	**BALLAD OF DARREN** (LP, blue vinyl, printed inner)	£25
24	Parlophone 5054197991639	**LIVE AT WEMBLEY STADIUM** (3LP, trifold sleeve, printed inners, insert)	£40

PROMOS

90	no cat. no.	**Bad Day/Bad Day** (version) (white label)	£20
94	Food FOODLP19	**PARKLIFE** (LP, blue vinyl promo)	£40
93	Food BBLUR1	**BASICALLY BLUR** (CD, interview disc with 3 tracks from Modern Life Is Rubbish)	£80
94	Food CD5 BET BET BET	**Girls and Boys/Jubilee/Trouble In The Message Centre/Lot 105** (Live CD promo produced for Mark Radcliffe show)	£30
94	Food FOOD DJ 53	**Parklife** (as Blur starring Phil Daniels) **/Supa Shoppa** (7", p/s, promo)	£150
91	Food 12BLUR 4	**High Cool** (Easy Listening Mix)**/Bad Day** (Leisurely Mix) (12", blue & gold company sleeve, promo, 1,000 only)	£25
99	Food FOOD CDJX 29	**13** (CD in duffelbag with folder, photos, ski-hat and biography, promo only)	£80
99	Food 10FOODDJ 117	**Tender** (10" promo record plays inside to out, foil sealed)	£20
02	The Bombo!	(red label, bearing Arabic writing which translates as "Don't bomb when you are the bomb"; large centre hole; 1,000 7" were pressed, but many were blown up)	£30

(see also Graham Coxon, Gorillaz, Damon Albarn, The Good, The Bad & The Queen)

BLUSH

79	Venal Vinyl PMB 117	**Everyday/Before We Came Together** (no p/s, 200 only)	£150

B-MOVIE

80	Dead Good DEAD 9	**TAKE THREE** (EP)	£20
80	Dead Good BIG DEAD 12	**NOWHERE GIRL** (12" EP, with insert, 800 only)	£20
88	Wax 12 WAX 3	**Nowhere Girl/Remembrance Day** (12", p/s, 250 on orange vinyl, numbered)	£15
88	Wax 12 WAX 3	**Nowhere Girl/Remembrance Day** (12", p/s, pink vinyl, numbered)	£15

EDDIE BO

73	Action ACT 4609	**Check Your Bucket Parts 1 & 2**	£30

BO & PEEP

64	Decca F 11968	**Young Love/The Rise Of The Brighton Surf**	£40

(see also Andrew Oldham Orchestra)

BOARDS OF CANADA

94	Music 70 AOMC43	**PLAY BY NUMBERS EP** (Cassette)	£50
94	Music 70 AOCS43	**PLAY BY NUMBERS EP** (CD)	£60
94	Music 70 THS 012	**HOOPER'S BAY** (12" EP)	£100
94	Music 70 THS 012	**HOOPER'S BAY** (cassette EP)	£30
98	Skam KMAS 1	**Aquarius/Chinook** (p/s, with insert, 500 only)	£60
98	Warp 10WARP LP 55P	**Telephasic Workshop/Roygbiv** (10" promo, 2000 only)	£25
00	Warp Records WAP 144	**In A Beautiful Place Out In The Country** (12", EP)	£40
99	Warp WAP 114	**THE PEEL SESSIONS** (12", p/s)	£15
06	Warp WAP 200	**TRANS CANADA HIGHWAY EP** (12", white vinyl)	£25
13	Warp 37367	**------ / ------ / ------ / XXXXXX / ------ / ------** (12" p/s. 6 known copies)	£1500
95	Music 70 BOARD 1	**TWOISM** (LP, 100 copies only)	£400
95	Music 70 BOARD 1	**TWOISM** (Cassette, 100 copies only)	£100
98	Warp 10 WARP LP 55 P	**MUSIC HAS THE RIGHT TO CHILDREN** (10", Promo)	£40
98	Warp Skam WARP LP 55, SKALP001	**MUSIC HAS THE RIGHT TO CHILDREN** (2-LP)	£65
02	Warp	**GEOGADDI** (LP, blue vinyl test pressing - etched - 10 only)	£200
02	Warp/Music 70 WARLP LP 101	**GEOGADDI** (3-LP)	£60
02	Warp WARPLP 70	**TWOISM** (LP, reissue, die-cut sleeve)	£20
05	Warp WARPLP 123	**CAMPFIRE HEADPHASE** (2-LP)	£30
13	Warp WARPLP 257	**TOMORROW'S HARVEST** (2-LP, gatefold, inners)	£25
13	Warp WARPLP 70R	**TWOISM** (LP, reissue in die-cut sleeve with sticker and download code)	£15
13	Warp WARPLP 55	**MUSIC HAS THE RIGHT TO CHILDREN** (2-LP, reissue, gatefold sleeve, sticker, and download code)	£20
13	Warp WARPLP 101R	**GEOGADDI** (3-LP, reissue, 1 side etched, sticker sheet and download code)	£20

BOARDWALKERS

60s	own label J.C. 1	**A Miracle/Any Man's Girl**	£200

(see also Warren Davis)

BOATMEN

70s	Sweet Folk SFA 018	**STRAIGHT FROM THE TUNNEL'S MOUTH** (LP)	£40

BOBALOUIS
81	WEA K18441	Not A Second Chance/City Boys	£20

BOB (RELF) & EARL (NELSON)
65	Sue WI 374	Harlem Shuffle/I'll Keep Running Back	£20
65	Sue WI 393	Baby I'm Satisfied/The Sissy	£40
67	Sue WI 4030	Don't Ever Leave Me/Fancy Free	£75
69	Warner Bros WB 6059	Everybody Jerk/He's A Playbrother	£40
67	Sue ILP 951	HARLEM SHUFFLE (LP)	£80
69	B & C BCB 1	BOB & EARL (LP)	£15
69	Joy JOYS 199	TOGETHER (LP)	£15

(see also Jackie Lee, Earl Nelson, Hollywood Flames)

BOB (ANDY) & MARCIA (GRIFFITHS)
70	Bamboo BAM 40	Always Together/BOB ANDY: Desperate Lover	£40
70	Escort ES 824	Young, Gifted And Black/BARRINGTON BIGGS: My Cheri Amour (Different version: no strings)	£30
70	Trojan TBL 122	YOUNG, GIFTED & BLACK (LP)	£30
72	Trojan TRLS 26	PIED PIPER (LP)	£25

(see also Bob Andy, Marcia Griffiths)

BOB (ANDY) & TIE (TYRONE EVANS)
69	Coxsone CS 7086	I Don't Care/LASCELLES PERKINS: Little Green Apples	£60

BOB(B)ETTES
57	London HLE 8477	Mr. Lee/Look At The Stars	£40
58	London HLE 8597	Come-A Come-A/Speedy	£40
60	London HLE 9173	I Shot Mr. Lee/Untrue Love	£60
60	London HLE 9248	Have Mercy Baby/Dance With Me Georgie	£40
60	Pye International 7N 25060	I Shot Mr. Lee/Billy (as Bobettes)	£40
72	Action ACT 4603	That's A Bad Thing To Know/All In Your Mind	£18

BOBBSEY TWINS
57	London HLA 8474	A Change Of Heart/Part-Time Gal	£30

BOBBY & DAVE
71	Ackee ACK 116	Build My World Around You/LIZZY & TONY BOP: Sammy Version	£40

(see also Dave Barker, Lizzy & Dennis)

BOBBY & LAURIE
66	Parlophone R 5480	Hitch Hiker/You'll Come 'Round	£15

BOBBY & MIDNITES
84	CBS 26046	WHERE THE BEAT MEETS THE STREET (LP)	£25

(see also Grateful Dead)

BOBBY (ELLIS) & TOMMY (MCCOOK)
74	Attack ATLP 1004	GREEN MANGO (LP)	£35

BOBCATS
67	Pye 7N 17242	Can't See For Looking/Let Me Get By	£25

WILLIE BOBO
66	Verve SVLP9134	ELATION (LP)	£20
71	A&M AMLS 68034	DO WHAT YOU WANT TO DO (LP)	£25

BOCKY & VISIONS
65	Atlantic AT 4049	I Go Crazy/Good Good Lovin'	£40

BODGERS
82	SRTS/82/CUS/1484	Stutter/I Hate Phoning Girls (no p/s)	£100

BODGER'S MATE
78	Cottage COT 521	BRIGHTER THAN USUAL (LP)	£20

BODKIN
72	West CSA 104	BODKIN (LP, private pressing, red label 10-20 in silk screened cover)	£1200
72	West CSA 104	BODKIN (LP, private pressing, red label, in posthumously designed sleeve)	£800
12	Acme ADLP 1085	BODKIN (LP, reissue)	£15

BODY
81	Recession	THE BODY ALBUM (LP, private pressing with booklet)	£50

BODYSNATCHERS (1)
80	2-Tone CHS TT 9	Let's Do Rocksteady/Ruder Than You (paper label, company sleeve)	£20
80	2-Tone CHS TT 12	Easy Life/Too Experienced (paper label, company sleeve)	£20

BODYSNATCHERS (2)
97	Backbone (No Cat. No)	GENOCIDE (EP, 30 test copies)	£100

(see also Icepick)

BOEING DUVEEN & BEAUTIFUL SOUP
68	Parlophone R 5696	Jabberwock/Which Dreamed It (demos without p/s)	£100
68	Parlophone R 5696	Jabberwock/Which Dreamed It (demos with p/s)	£250
68	Parlophone R 5696	Jabberwock/Which Dreamed It	£150

BOFFALONGO
71	United Artists UAG 29130	BEYOND YOUR HEAD (LP)	£15

BOG UGLY AND THE WOOFTERS
78	Toadstool GOOD 2	Disco Veteran/I've Seen It Vomit (p/s)	£25

DIRK BOGARDE
60	Decca LK 4373	LYRICS FOR LOVERS (LP)	£15

BOGAZ
| 83 | AGR 7 AGR 2 | I've Got Love/I've Got Love (Instrumental) | £30 |
| 83 | AGR 12 AGR 2 | I've Got Love/I've Got Love (Instrumental) (12") | £45 |

BOGIES
| 64 | private press (no cat. no.) | THE BOGIES ON CAMPUS (LP) | £40 |
| 64 | private press (no cat. no.) | BYE BYE BOGIES (LP) | £40 |

ERIC BOGLE
77	Autogram ALLP 211	LIVE IN PERSON (LP)	£35
81	Plant Life PLR 033	PLAIN AND SIMPLE (LP)	£15
83	Plant Life PLR 046	SCRAPS OF PAPER (LP)	£15
85	Topic 12TS 437	WHEN THE WIND BLOWS (LP)	£15
88	Plant Life PLR 042	NOW I'M EASY (LP)	£15

LEE BOGLE
| 71 | Black Swan BW 1406 | Tomorrow's Dreams/SWANS: Hot Pants Reggae | £15 |

BOGUS ORDER
| 90 | Ninja Tune ZEN 01 | ZEB BRAKES (LP) | £25 |

BUDDY BOHN
| 71 | Purple TPSA 7503 | A DROP IN THE OCEAN (LP, gatefold sleeve) | £30 |

BOILER SHOP
| 72 | Music Box MB 03 | Seeing Things In Colour/Darkness | £40 |

HOUSTON BOINES
| 66 | Blue Horizon 45 BH 1006 | Superintendent Blues/Monkey Motion (99 copies only, Ike Turner on piano) | £200 |

BOISTEROUS
| 95 | Hammer HR 5 | SKIP RAIDERS (LP) | £15 |

BOLA
95	Skam SKA 5	Forcasa 3/Krak Jakomo/Metalurg 2/Ballom (12", custom sleeve)	£50
98	Skam KMAS002	KS (500 pressed)	£30
00	33 33Shapes	SHAPES (LP, 3x12")	£35

MARC BOLAN
65	Decca F 12288	The Wizard/Beyond The Rising Sun (some as Marc Bölan)	£500
65	Decca F 12288	The Wizard/Beyond The Rising Sun (demo copy)	£350
66	Decca F 12413	The Third Degree/San Francisco Poet	£500
66	Decca F 12413	The Third Degree/San Francisco Poet (demo copy)	£350
66	Parlophone R 5539	Hippy Gumbo/Misfit	£650
66	Parlophone R 5539	Hippy Gumbo/Misfit (demo copy)	£500
72	Track 2094 013	Jasper C. Debussy/Hippy Gumbo/The Perfumed Garden Of Gulliver Smith (p/s, withdrawn)	£50
72	Track 2094 013	Jasper C. Debussy/Hippy Gumbo/The Perfumed Garden Of Gulliver Smith (white label demo)	£70
81	Rarn MBFS 001P	Sing Me A Song/Endless Sleep (Extended Version)/The Lilac Hand Of Menthol Dan (12" picture disc, misprinted with black rim)	£15
81	Rarn MBFS 001P	Sing Me A Song/Endless Sleep (Extended Version)/The Lilac Hand Of Menthol Dan (12", picture disc misprinted back-to-front)	£15
72	Track 2406 101	HARD ON LOVE (LP, unreleased, white label test pressing, 3 known copies)	£1000
72	Track 2406 009	HARD ON LOVE (LP, unreleased, 2-sided EMIdisc acetate with "swearing intro")	£2250
74	Track 2410 201	THE BEGINNING OF DOVES (LP, laminated sleeve, black/silver label)	£35
81	Cherry Red PERED 20	YOU SCARE ME TO DEATH (LP, picture disc)	£15
89	Media Motion MEDIA 2	THE BEGINNING OF DOVES (LP, reissue, 750 only, withdrawn)	£25

(see also Marc Bolan/T. Rex, Marc Bolan & Gloria Jones, Toby Tyler, John's Children, Big Carrot, Dib Cochran & The Earwigs)

MARC BOLAN & GLORIA JONES
| 77 | EMI EMI 2572 | To Know Him Is To Love Him/City Port | £15 |

(see also Gloria Jones)

MARC BOLAN/T. REX
SINGLES
70	Octopus OCTO 1	Ride A White Swan/Summertime Blues/Jewel (unreleased, handwritten white label, 2/3 test pressings only)	£2500
70	Fly BUG 1	Ride A White Swan/Is It Love/Summertime Blues (p/s, purple labels)	£20
71	Fly	Hot Love/Woodland Rock/King Of The Mountain Cometh (IBC Sound Recordings Studios acetate)	£250
71	Fly BUG 10	Get It On/There Was A Time/Raw Ramp (p/s, black label with silver 'fly' logo)	£15
71	Fly GRUB 1	Electric Warrior Preview Single: Jeepster/Life's A Gas (gig freebie, in pink envelope sleeve)	£200
71	Fly GRUB 1	Electric Warrior Preview Single: Jeepster/Life's A Gas (gig freebie, originally in pink envelope sleeve, this price is for later standard paper sleeve)	£145
72	Magni Fly ECHO 102	One Inch Rock/The Woodland Bop/The Throat Of Winter (unreleased, rejected 1-sided test pressing for B-side of "Deborah"/"One Inch Rock", stamped white label)	£150
72	EMI MARC X	Metal Guru (rejected 1-sided test pressing with Marc's annotation 'bad cut')	£300
72	EMI MARC 3	Solid Gold Easy Action/(5th Dimension track) (mispressing)	£15
72	EMI MARC 3	Solid Gold Easy Action/(Partridge Family track) (mispressing)	£15
72	EMI SPRS 346	Chariot Choogle/The Slider (promo only, 'T. Rex' picture label)	£425
72	EMI SPRS 346	Chariot Choogle/The Slider (promo only, white label)	£375
72	Lyntone	Christmas Time/Wanna Spend My Christmas With You/ Christmas/Everybody Knows It's Christmas (fan club flexi, with letter in brown envelope)	£45
72	Lyntone	Christmas Time/Wanna Spend My Christmas With You/ Christmas/Everybody Knows It's Christmas (fan club flexi, without letter in brown envelope)	£30
75	EMI MARC 12	Christmas Bop/Telegram Sam/Metal Guru (unreleased, A- & B-side paper labels exist, 2 sets only this price is for the labels)	£1250

MINT VALUE £

82	Marc ABOLAN 2	**THE CHILDREN OF RARN** (10" EP, p/s, 33rpm, gatefold sleeve with 12-page lyric book) ...£25	
84	Cube BUG 99	**Sailor Of The Highway/Do You Remember** (7" in plain black sleeve).........................£15	
87	Strange Fruit SFPS 031	**PEEL SESSIONS** (12")...£15	
94	Edsel MBPROMO 1	**T. REX** (CD, picture disc, 4-track sampler, tri-fold digipak, promo only)........................£15	
07	Edsel BOLAN 1	**Metal Guru/The Slider** (Acoustic Demo) (Blue vinyl, numbered, 1,000 only) £15	
07	Edsel BOLAN 2	**Children Of The Revolution/The Leopards** (Electric Demo) (Red vinyl, numbered, 1,000 only)..£15	
07	Edsel TREXMAS 1	**Christmas Bop/The Xmas Riff/Xmas Flexi message** (7", promo)...................................£60	
12	Universal 533812-3	**ELECTRIC SEVENS** (4 x 7" box set)..£20	
14	Secret 7" S721	**Get It On** (100 only, each with unique art sleeve) £50	

ALBUMS

70	Fly HIFLY 2	**T. REX** (semi-gatefold sleeve, white label with 'Fly' logo) £50	
71	Fly HIFLY 6	**ELECTRIC WARRIOR** (unreleased version with "Jeepster" on side 2, 1 test pressing copy only, with Marc's annotations on white sleeve) £700	
71	Fly HIFLY 6	**ELECTRIC WARRIOR** (with poster & inner sleeve, stickered sleeve, white label with 'Fly' logo) £150	
71	Fly HIFLY 6	**ELECTRIC WARRIOR** (with poster & inner sleeve, non-stickered sleeve, white label with 'Fly' logo) £60	
72	Fly HIFLY 8	**BOLAN BOOGIE** (1-sided test pressing with "The Visit" instead of "Jewel") £375	
72	Fly HIFLY 8	**BOLAN BOOGIE** £15	
72	EMI BLN 5001	**THE SLIDER** (with lyric inner sleeve, sleeve with 'sniped' spine edges, flipbacks, blue/red T-Rex label)..£40	
73	EMI BLN 5002	**TANX** (with poster & inner sleeve)...£30	
73	EMI BLN 5003	**GREAT HITS** (with poster)..£15	
74	EMI BNLA 7751	**ZINC ALLOY AND THE HIDDEN RIDERS OF TOMORROW** (with 3-way numbered promo fold-out sleeve & inner, given as competition prize with letter from Pink or Mirabelle magazines, 1,000 only) £300	
74	EMI BNLA 7751	**ZINC ALLOY AND THE HIDDEN RIDERS OF TOMORROW** (with 3-way promo fold-out sleeve & inner, without letter; numbered) £300	
74	EMI BNLA 7751	**ZINC ALLOY AND THE HIDDEN RIDERS OF TOMORROW** (with 3-way promo fold-out sleeve & inner, without letter; unnumbered) £250	
74	EMI BLNA 7751	**ZINC ALLOY AND THE HIDDEN RIDERS OF TOMORROW** (commercial gatefold sleeve with lyric inner sleeve)...£20	
75	EMI BNLA 7752	**BOLAN'S ZIP GUN** (diamond-cut laminated sleeve & inner sleeve, blue/red T-Rex label) .£25	
76	EMI BLNA 5004	**FUTURISTIC DRAGON** (with lyric inner sleeve)..£25	
77	EMI BLNA 5005	**DANDY IN THE UNDERWORLD** (with round-cut sleeve & lyric inner sleeve) £25	
78	Cube HIFLD 1	**MARC: THE WORDS AND MUSIC OF MARC BOLAN 1947-1977** (2-LP, gatefold sleeve, with free single [BINT 1])...£20	
81	Marc ABOLAN 1P	**T. REX IN CONCERT** (picture disc, 2 designs)...£20	
82	Cube/Dakota ICSX 1004	**ACROSS THE AIRWAVES** (picture disc)...£20	
82	Marc ABOLAN 3P	**ELECTRIC WARRIOR** (picture disc) £20	
84	Marc ABOLAN 5	**T. REXTASY** (with 12" "Jam (live)"/**Elemental Child** (live) [ABOLAN 5F], Official Fanclub only)...£18	
80	EMI NUT 28	**THE UNOBTAINABLE T-REX** (LP, initial batch with rejected rear sleeve photo of Bolan with tongue out)..£200	
86	Marc On Wax WARRIOR 1/4	**HISTORY OF T. REX** (4-LP, numbered picture disc set, with free fanclub T-shirt) £45	
86	Marc On Wax WARRIOR 1/4	**HISTORY OF T. REX** (4-LP, numbered picture disc set, without free fanclub T-shirt)..........£35	

(see also Marc Bolan, Tyrannosaurus Rex, Dib Cochran & the Earwigs, John's Children, Big Carrot)

FRANCY BOLAND

75	Freedom FLP40176	**PAPILLON NOIR** (LP)..£18	

(see also Kenny Clarke with Francy Boland)

TOMMY BOLIN

75	Atlantic K 50208	**TEASER** (LP, stickered)..£25	
75	Atlantic K 50208	**TEASER** (LP, unstickered)..£15	
76	CBS S 81612	**PRIVATE EYES** (LP)...£15	

(see also James Gang, Deep Purple)

BOLLARDS

70s	Bumkin Records	**BOLLARDS** (LP)..£15	

BOLLWEEVIL

81	Ellie Jay EJSP 9715	**Rock Solid/Sands Of Time** (p/s)...£90	

BOLT THROWER

88	Strange Fruit SFPS 056	**PEEL SESSIONS** (12")...£20	
91	Strange Fruit SFRLP 116	**PEEL SESSIONS 1988-90** (LP)...£20	
88	Vinyl Solution SOL 11	**IN BATTLE THERE IS NO LAW** (LP, with insert) £20	
89	Earache MOSH 12	**REALM OF CHAOS** (LP, with booklet) £20	
89	Earache MOSH 13	**REALM OF CHAOS** (LP, picture disc)..£15	
91	Earache MOSH 29	**WAR MASTER** (LP, booklet)..£25	

MEL BOLTON'S MIGHTY FIRE

16	Super Disco Edits SDE 16	**Love/I Wanna Talk To You About Loving** (reissue) £20	

BOMAR

68	Flesh FH 01	**Suddenly A Dream/Terry O McDonald's Son**..£18	

BOMB AND DAGGER

86	SSR BDSS01	**Wake Up/No Real Place** (p/s) £40	

BOMBAY DUCKS

80s	United Dairies UD 05	**DANCE MUSIC** (LP)..£15	

BON JOVI

84	Vertigo VERX 14	**Runaway/Breakout** (live)/**Runaway** (live) (12", p/s)...£15	
85	Vertigo VERP 19	**In And Out Of Love/Roulette** (live) (picture disc)..£30	
85	Vertigo VERXR 22	**Red Hot And Two Parts Live: The Hardest Part Is The Night/ Tokyo Road** (live)/**In And** £15	

		Out Of Love (live) (12", p/s, red vinyl)	
88	Vertigo VERHP 38	**SLIPPERY WHEN WET** (LP, picture disc with poster)	£15
88	Vertigo VERHP 62	**NEW JERSEY** (LP, picture disc, stickered PVC sleeve)	£15
95	Mercury 528 248-1	**THESE DAYS** (2-LP)	£60

BONA DISH

82	In Phaze	**BONA DISH ON C30** (cassette)	£70
82	In Phase IP 010	**EP** (cassette)	£40
82	In Phaze	**CARDBOARD TUBE** (cassette in cardboard tube packaging)	£50

JOE BONAMASSA

06	Provogue PRD71851	**YOU AND ME** (LP, pressed in Netherlands)	£15

BONA RAYS

81	Mystery EJSP 9614	**Catch 22/We're Never Going To Miss You**	£35

BON-BONS

55	London HL 8139	**That's The Way Love Goes/Make My Dreams Come True**	£20
56	London HLU 8262	**Circle/Frog On A Log**	£20

BRIGITTE BOND

64	Blue Beat BB 212	**Oh Yeah Baby/Blue Beat Baby** (with the Bluebeats)	£45

GRAHAM BOND (ORGANISATION)

64	Decca F 11909	**Long Tall Shorty/Long Legged Baby** (as Graham Bond Organization)	£50
65	Columbia DB 7471	**Wade In The Water/Tammy** (as Graham Bond Organisation)	£50
65	Columbia DB 7528	**Tell Me** (I'm Gonna Love Again)/**Love Come Shining Through** (as Graham Bond Organisation)	£50
65	Columbia DB 7647	**Lease On Love/My Heart's In Little Pieces** (as Graham Bond Organisation)	£35
66	Columbia DB 7838	**St James Infirmary/Soul Tango** (as Graham Bond Organisation)	£40
67	Page One POF 014	**You've Gotta Have Love Babe/I Love You**	£50
70	Warner Bros WB 8004	**Walking In The Park/Springtime In The City** (solo)	£15
71	Vertigo 6059 042	**Twelve Gates To The City/Water Water** (as Graham Bond with Magick)	£30
65	Columbia 33SX 1711	**THE SOUND OF '65** (LP, 1st pressing, with '33SX' on blue/black label and "sold in the U.K." label text)	£400

(N.B, LP has '33SX' on the sleeve, but only the 1st pressings have '33SX' on the label)

65	Columbia 33SX 1750	**THERE'S A BOND BETWEEN US** (LP, 1st pressing, with '33SX' on blue/black label and "sold in the UK" label text)	£400
66	Columbia SX 1711	**THE SOUND OF '65** (LP, 2nd pressing, with 'SX' on blue/black label)	£200
66	Columbia SX 1750	**THERE'S A BOND BETWEEN US** (LP, 2nd pressing, with 'SX' on blue/black label)	£150
69	Columbia SX 1750	**THERE'S A BOND BETWEEN US** (LP, 3rd Pressing, black/silver with boxed EMI logol)	£60
69	Columbia SX 1711	**THE SOUND OF '65** (LP, 3rd pressing, with boxed logo on silver/black label)	£60
71	Warner Bros WS 3001	**SOLID BOND** (2-LP, gatefold sleeve, orange label)	£50
71	Vertigo 6360 021	**HOLY MAGICK** (LP, gatefold sleeve, large swirl label, as Graham Bond & Magick)	£150
71	Vertigo 6360 042	**WE PUT OUR MAGICK ON YOU** (LP, gatefold sleeve, swirl label,	£150
72	Philips 6382 010	**BOND IN AMERICA** (2-LP, solo [individual discs: 6499 200/1], unreleased)	£35
72	Philips 6382 010	**THIS IS GRAHAM BOND** (LP, solo)	£20
88	Edsel DED 254	**THE SOUND OF '65/THERE'S A BOND BETWEEN US** (2-LP, reissue)	£30

(see also Jack Bruce, Dick Heckstall-Smith, Ginger Baker, Duffy Power, Who, Don Rendell, Steve York's Camelo Pardalis)

GRAHAM BOND & PETE BROWN

71	Greenwich GSS 104	**Lost Tribe/Macumbe/Milk Is Turning Sour In My Shoes** (maxi-single)	£25
72	Chapter One CHS-R 813	**TWO HEADS ARE BETTER THAN ONE** (LP)	£250

(see also Pete Brown)

ISABEL BOND

68	Major Minor MM 565	**Cry/When A Woman Loves A Man** (in p/s)	£20
68	Major Minor MMLP 28	**THE HEART AND SOUL OF ISABEL BOND** (LP)	£50

JACKI BOND

65	Columbia DB 7719	**My Sister's Boy/Now I Know**	£20
66	Strike JH 302	**Tell Him To Go Away/Don't You Worry**	£25
66	Strike JH 320	**He Say/Why Can't I Love Him**	£50

JOHNNY BOND

60	London HL 7100	**Hot Rod Lincoln/Five-Minute Love Affair** (export issue)	£15

JOYCE BOND

66	Island WI 3019	**Tell Me What It's All About/Tell Me Right Now**	£50
67	Airborne NBP 0011	**It's Alright/Mrs. Soul**	£125
67	Island WIP 6010	**Do The Teasy/Sugar**	£30
67	Island WIP 6018	**This Train/Not So With Me**	£20
68	Island WIP 6051	**Ob-La-Di, Ob-La-Da/Robin Hood Rides Again** (as Joyce Bond Review)	£20
68	Pama PM 718	**Back To School/They Wish**	£18
69	Pama PM 771	**Mr. Pitiful/Let's Get Married** (as Joyce Bond & Little John)	£18
68	Island ILP 968	**SOUL AND SKA** (LP, mono only)	£175
72	Windmill WMD 121	**SOUL OF CHANGE** (LP)	£35

OLIVER BOND

66	Parlophone R 5476	**I Saw You All Alone/Let Me Love You**	£20

(see also Oliver Bone)

PETER BOND

77	Trailer LER 2108	**IT'S ALL RIGHT FOR SOME** (LP, yellow label)	£15

RONNIE BOND (1)

69	Page One POF 123	**Anything For You/Carolyn**	£20

(see also Troggs)

TONY BOND
66   Decca SKL 4776   PRESENTING TONY BOND (LP) **£20**
(see also Kestrels)

GARY (U.S.) BONDS
61   Top Rank 35/114   DANCE 'TIL QUARTER TO THREE WITH U.S. BONDS (LP) **£25**
62   Stateside SL 10001   TWIST UP CALYPSO (LP) **£20**

OLIVER BONE & SOUNDS MAXIMUM
66   Parlophone R 5527   Knock On Wood/Jugger Tea **£30**
(see also Oliver Bond)

MATTHEW BONES
71   Pye 7N 45100   I Am The Pixi/Two Sugars **£15**

BONESCHI ELECTRONIC COMBO
73   Chappell International CAL SOUNDS ELECTRONIC (LP) **£50**
     4004

BONESHAKER
71   London HLU 10332   Sweetness/Badman Strikes Again **£60**

BONES & NATTY
95   BN 001   Pow/Thunder (12", white label only) **£80**

BONE THUGS-N-HARMONY
95   Ruthless EPC 481038 1   E 1999 ETERNAL (LP, inner) **£60**

BONGO HERMAN (DAVIS)
70   Songbird SB 1018   True Grit/True Grit Version 2 (both credited with Les Crystalites but actually with Les &
                             Crystalites) **£35**
71   Songbird SB 1060   BONGO HERMAN & LES BUNNY: Know For I/CRYSTALITES: Version (B-side actually
                             titled 'Know Fari') **£20**
71   Songbird SB 1066   BONGO HERMAN & LES & BUNNY: Salaam (Peace)/CRYSTALITES: Scraper..................... **£20**
72   Big BG 332   Eternal Drums/ERROL DUNKLEY: Darling Ooh Wee (both actually by Hugh Roy Junior) ..**£20**
72   Green Door GD 4049   African Breakfast/BONGO HERMAN & LES AND BUNNY: Chairman Of The Board **£20**
72   Songbird SB 1069   We Are Praying/CRYSTALITES: Version **£15**

BONGO LES & HERMAN
69   Explosion EX 2002   Dr. Who Part 1/Dr. Who Part II **£25**
71   Songbird SB 1050   Home Sweet Home/Hail I **£30**
(see also Heptones, Meditators)

JUKE BOY BONNER
69   Blue Horizon 57-3163   Runnin' Shoes/Jackin' In My Plans **£40**
60s Jan & Dil JR 451   MORE DOWN HOME BLUES (EP) **£50**
68   Flyright LP 3501   THE ONE MAN TRIO (LP) **£25**
69   Liberty LBS 83319   THINGS AIN'T RIGHT (LP) **£25**

GRAHAM BONNET
72   RCA RCA 2230   Rare Specimen/Whisper In The Night **£25**
73   RCA RCA 2380   Trying To Say Goodbye/Castles In The Air **£15**
77   Ring O' 2017 106   Danny/Rock Island Line (promo p/s) **£18**
77   Ring O' 2320 103   GRAHAM BONNET (LP, with inner sleeve) **£18**
(see also Rainbow, Cozy Powell, Fut, Michael Schenker Group, Jon Lord)

GRAHAM BONNEY
66   Columbia DB 7843   Super Girl/Hill Of Lovin' **£35**
70   Columbia DB 8648   Sign On The Dotted Line/Words We Said **£25**
70   Columbia DB 8687   When Evelyn Was Mine/Sunny Has Gone **£20**
66   Columbia SX/SCX 6052   SUPER GIRL (LP, mono/stereo) **£30**
(see also Riot Squad)

BONNIE
67   Ska Beat JB 270   Do You Get The Message/A Man Called Dan **£30**
69   Jolly JY 014   Loving You/Shoo Be Doo **£15**

BONNIE & SKITTO
63   Island WI 122   Get Ready (actually by Vikings (with Toots Hibbert)/ DON DRUMMOND: The Rocket **£50**
63   R&B JB 110   Hey Mr. Chauffer/DON DRUMMOND: Jet Stream **£60**

BONNIE & TREASURES
65   London HLU 9998   Home Of The Brave/Our Song **£35**

BONOBO
00   Tru Thoughts TRU 004   Terrapin (12") **£15**
13   Ninja Tune ZEN 12357   Cirrus (12" 1-sided picture disc with Zoetrope viewer, PVC sleeve some with art print) ..**£80**
00   Tru Thoughts TRU LP 007 ANIMAL MAGIC (2xLP) **£40**
01   Ninja Tune ZEN 63   ANIMAL MAGIC (2xLP) **£30**
02   Tru Thoughts TRU LP 031 ONE OFFS...REMIXES & B SIDES (2xLP) **£30**
03   Ninja Tune ZEN 80   DIAL M FOR MONKEY (2xLP) **£30**
06   Ninja Tune ZEN 119   DAYS TO COME (2xLP) **£30**
10   Ninja Tune ZEN 140   BLACK SANDS (2xLP) **£20**
13   Ninja Tune ZEN 195X   THE NORTH BORDERS (Box set, 6 x 10", with CD and posters) **£30**
13   Ninja Tune ZEN 195   THE NORTH BORDERS (2-LP, inners) **£20**

BONZO DOG (DOO-DAH) BAND
66   Parlophone R 5430   My Brother Makes The Noises For The Talkies/I'm Gonna Bring A Watermelon To My
                             Gal Tonight **£20**
66   Parlophone R 5499   Alley Oop/Button Up Your Overcoat **£20**
92   China WOK 2021   No Matter Who You Vote For The Government Always Gets In/ NEIL INNES: Them
                             (promo only) **£15**

MINT VALUE £

67	Liberty LBL 83056	GORILLA (LP, mono with booklet)	£80
67	Liberty LBS 83056	GORILLA (LP, stereo with booklet)	£40
67	Liberty LBL/LBS 83056	GORILLA (LP, without booklet, blue label)	£20
71	Liberty LBL/LBS 83158E	THE DOUGHNUT IN GRANNY'S GREENHOUSE (LP, gatefold sleeve, with booklet, blue label)	£70
71	Liberty LBS 83158E	THE DOUGHNUT IN GRANNY'S GREENHOUSE (LP, gatefold sleeve, without booklet, blue label)	£25
69	Liberty LBS 83257	TADPOLES (LP, die-cut sleeve, with insert, blue label)	£50
69	Liberty LBS 83257	TADPOLES (LP, die-cut sleeve, without insert, blue label)	£25
69	Liberty LBS 83290	KEYNSHAM (LP, gatefold sleeve, blue label)	£35
72	United Artists UAS 29288	LET'S MAKE UP AND BE FRIENDLY (LP)	£22
74	United Artists UAD 60071/2	THE HISTORY OF THE BONZOS (2-LP, gatefold sleeve with booklet)	£25

(see also Vivian Stanshall, Neil Innes, Grimms, Roger Ruskin Spear, Topo D. Bill)

BETTY BOO
79	Grapevine GRP 125	Say It Isn't So/Say It Isn't So (Instrumental)	£20

BOOK EM DANNO
89	Splinter SG 1	Brand New Disease/Eighties Hero/Top Of The Agenda/You'd Better Believe It (12")	£80

JAMES BOOKER
61	Vogue V 9177	Cool Turkey/Gonzo	£30
63	Vocalion VEP 170154	GONZO (EP)	£60

BOOKER T (JAMAICA)
75	Ethnic Fight EF 016	Down Presser/Pressure Dub	£25

BOOKER T. & THE M.G.S
62	London HLK 9595	Green Onions/Behave Yourself	£20
63	London REK 1367	R&B WITH BOOKER T (EP)	£20
64	Atlantic AET 6002	R&B WITH BOOKER T VOL. 2 (EP)	£20
64	London HA-K 8182	GREEN ONIONS (LP, plum label)	£35
65	Atlantic ATL 5027	SOUL DRESSING (LP, plum label, 1st pressing with green & white sleeve)	£30
66	Atlantic 587/588 033	GREEN ONIONS (LP, reissue, mono/stereo)	£15
67	Stax 589 002	AND NOW! (LP)	£30
68	Stax 589 013	SOUL CHRISTMAS (LP)	£15
68	Stax 230 002/231 002	DOIN' OUR THING (LP)	£15
68	Stax (S)XATS 1001	SOUL LIMBO (LP)	£15
69	Atco 228 004	GET READY (LP)	£15
69	Stax (S)XATS 1005	UPTIGHT (LP, soundtrack, with Judy Clay)	£15
69	Stax (S)XATS 1015	THE BOOKER T. SET (LP)	£15
69	Atco 228 015	THE BEST OF BOOKER T. AND THE M.G.s (LP)	£15
70	Stax SXATS 1031	McLEMORE AVENUE (LP)	£15
71	Stax 2325 030	MELTING POT (LP)	£15

(see also Mar-Keys, Steve Cropper, Albert King)

BOOMBACK
85	Headphone HP/DC/003	Ghetto Life/Roadblock (12")	£125

BOOMTOWN RATS
13	Mercury RATLIFEDJ1	RATLIFE (10", 100 copies, signed, only available at gigs)	£50

PAT BOONE
SINGLES
55	London HLD 8172	Ain't That A Shame/Tennessee Saturday Night ()gold label)	£35

ALBUMS
63	London SH-D 8109	SINGS ... GUESS WHO? (LP, stereo)	£15

(see also Fontane Sisters)

BOONES FARM
72	CBS 8212	If You Can't Be My Woman/Start Today	£20

BOO RADLEYS
92	Creation CRELP 120	EVERYTHING'S ALRIGHT FOREVER (LP, first 1000 with free Sunfly 7")	£15
93	Creation CRELP 149	GIANT STEPS (2-LP)	£60
95	Creation CRELP 179	WAKE UP! (LP, gatefold sleeve)	£15
96	Creation CRELP 194	C'MON KIDS (2-LP with free 7')	£30
96	Creation CRELP 194	C'MON KIDS (2-LP without free 7')	£20

BILL BOOTH REVIVAL MACHINE
75	HEADSRTM/CUS038	FACE TO FACE (LP)	£18

KEN BOOTHE
66	Island WI 3020	The Train Is Coming/This Is Me	£60
66	Island WI 3035	Don't Want To See You Cry/Baby I Need You (B-side actually by Wailers)	£100
66	Ska Beat JB 248	You're No Good/SOULETTES: Don't Care What The People Say	£100
67	Doctor Bird DB 1110	Say You/LYN TAITT & JETS: Smokey Places	£60
67	Coxsone CS 7006	Lonely Teardrops/Oowee Baby	£70
67	Coxsone CS 7020	Home Home Home/SOUL BROTHERS: Windell	£50
67	Caltone TONE 107	The One I Love/You Left The Water Running	£75
67	Studio One SO 2000	Feel Good/Mustang Sally	£40
67	Studio One SO 2012	Puppet On A String/ROLAND ALPHONSO: Look Away Ska	£40
67	Studio One SO 2014	Fatty Fatty (actually by Heptones)/Mother Word (actually by Delroy Wilson)	£50
67	Studio One SO 2026	Why Did You Leave (actually by Leroy Sibbles)/Don't Try To Reach Me (actually by Gaylads)	£50
68	Studio One SO 2039	When I Fall In Love/HEPTONES: Christmas Time	£60
68	Studio One SO 2041	The Girl I Left Behind/TERMITES: My Last Love	£90

MINT VALUE £

68	Studio One SO 2053	Tomorrow/Movin' Away	£70
68	Fab FAB 63	I Remember Someone/Can't You See?	£150
68	Coxsone CS 7041	Everybody Knows/GAYLADS: I'm Free	£60
69	Coxsone CS 7094	Sherry/I've Got You	£60
69	Studio One SO 2073	You're On My Mind/RICHARD ACE & SOUND DIMENSIONS: Love To Cherish	£60
69	High Note HS 003	Lady With The Starlight/LESLIE BUTLER & COUNT OSSIE: Gay Drums	£40
69	Bamboo BAM 4	Pleading/COUNT MATCHUKI & SOUND DIMENSION: Call 1143	£80
69	Bamboo BAM 8	Be Yourself/SOUND DIMENSION: Rathid	£70
70	Trojan TR 7716	Why, Baby Why/Keep My Love From Fading	£25
70	Trojan TR 7756	Freedom Street/BEVERLEY'S ALLSTARS: Freedom Version	£20
70	Trojan TR 7772	It's Gonna Take A Miracle/Now I Know	£25
70	Trojan TR 7780	Drums Of Freedom/BEVERLEY'S ALLSTARS: Version	£20
70	Gas GAS 169	Give To Me/Why	£20
70	Jackpot JP 748	You Left The Water Running/PHIL PRATT ALL STARS: Cut Throat	£30
70	Punch PH 30	Artibella/PRATT ALLSTARS: Version Of Artibella	£30
70	Punch PH 33	Morning/Morning (Version)	£15
71	Punch PH 70	Stop Your Crying/CONSCIOUS MINDS: Suffering Through The Nation	£15
71	Banana BA 352	Original Six (Parts 1 & 2)	£15
71	Summit SUM 8518	I Wish It Could Be Peaceful Again/BEVERLEY'S ALLSTARS: Peaceful Version	£15
71	Summit SUM 8519	Your Feeling And Mine/BEVERLEY'S ALLSTARS: Your Feeling Version	£15
71	Big Shot BI 590	So Nice/So Nice Version	£20
71	Dynamic DYN 411	Hallelujah/Trying To Reach	£15
72	Camel CA 91	Ain't No Sunshine/LLOYD & HORTENSE: You Are Everything	£25
73	Trojan TR 7893	Is It Because I'm Black/Black, Gold And Green	£15
73	Green Door GD 4053	Silver Words/Rasta God Version	£20
75	Fab FAB 270	Thinking/Moving Away	£30
75	Torpedo TOR 35	Lady With The Starlight/Light Version	£20
79	Attack TACK 6	You're No Good/PRINCE JAMMY: Out Of Order Dub (12")	£30
79	Trojan TRO T 9052	Who Gets Your Love/(Version)/Is It Because I'm Black (12")	£18
02	Trojan TJH10001	Can't You See (1968 Version)/(1971 Version)/Tears From My Eyes/Ain't No Sunshine (10")	£20
67	Studio One SOL 9001	MR. ROCK STEADY (LP)	£200
73	Trojan TRLS 58	BLACK, GOLD AND GREEN (LP)	£40
74	Trojan TRLS 83	LETS GET IT ON (LP)	£25
74	Trojan TRLS 95	EVERYTHING I OWN (LP)	£25
75	Trojan TRLS 120	FREEDOM STREET (LP)	£40
78	Trojan TRLS 148	BLOOD BROTHER (LP)	£20
79	Phil Pratt PP01LP	GOT TO GET AWAY (LP)	£40
87	Trojan TRLS 249	EIGHTEEN CLASSIC SONGS (LP)	£18

(see also Stranger & Ken, Gaylads, Richard Ace)

BOOTLES
64	Vocalion VN 9216	I'll Let You Hold My Hand/Never Till Now	£25

BOOTS
68	CBS 3550	Even The Bad Times Are Good/The Animal In Me	£20
68	CBS 3833	Keep Your Lovelight Burning/Give Me One More Chance	£25
70	Youngblood YB 1018	You Better Run/A To D	£60

DAVE BOOTS
72	Solent SM 013	GREEN SATIN AND GOLD (LP, credited to Maurice King & Dave Boots, private press 99 copies)	£100

BOOTS FOR DANCING
80	Pop Aural POP 002	BOOTS FOR DANCING EP (12")	£15

BOOTSY'S RUBBER BAND
76	Warner Bros K 56200	STRETCHIN' OUT IN BOOTSY'S RUBBER BAND (LP)	£18
77	Warner Bros K 56302	AHH... THE NAME IS BOOTSY, BABY! (LP, gatefold sleeve)	£18
78	Warner Bros K 56424	BOOTSY? PLAYER OF THE YEAR (LP, gatefold sleeve)	£15
79	Warner Bros K 56615	THE BOOT IS MADE FOR FONK-N (LP, with inner sleeve)	£15
81	Warner Bros K 56998	THE ONE GIVETH, THE COUNT TAKETH AWAY (LP)	£15

(see also Parliament, Funkadelic)

BOOVER BOYS
70	Torpedo TOR 22	A.G.G.R.O/Sha La La La Lee	£100

RANNY BOP
70	Escort ERT 837	Crock Iron/Memphis Bop	£28
70	Gas GAS 155	Pipe Dream/Suck Suck	£20

(see aso Ranny Williams)

BORDER
78	Pear PEAR 1	Song For J/Easy/Going Away (p/s, 500 only)	£40

BORE-TOWN BOP
81	Vital VIS001	Try/Surf's Up (p/s)	£15

BORZOI
87	CS 2509	It's Called Rincarnation/I'm At War (p/s)	£20

BOSCH
80	Trific TRIF 1	The Two Tree/Packing Jean (p/s)	£25

BOSS ATTACK
71	Fab FAB 187	Hell-El/TEARDROPS: Let Me Be Free	£20

BOSS COMBO
62   Coral LVA 9205   GOLDEN ROCK AND ROLL INSTRUMENTALS (LP).................................£20

BOSS GUITARS
65   London HA-R/SH-R 8237   PLAY THE WINNERS (LP)...£20

EARL BOSTIC (ORCHESTRA)
SINGLES
66   Island WI 271   Honeymoon Night/PATSY COLE: Disappointed Bride.......................£15
EPs
55   Parlophone GEP 8520   EARL BOSTIC AND HIS ALTO SAX...£15
55   Vogue EPV 1010   EARL BOSTIC..£15
58   Parlophone GEP 8701   BOSTIC BEAT..£20
58   Parlophone GEP 8741   ROCKING WITH BOSTIC..£20
ALBUMS
54   Vogue LDE 100   EARL BOSTIC AND HIS ORCHESTRA (10").................................£30
54   Parlophone PMD 1016   EARL BOSTIC AND HIS ALTO SAX (10" LP)...............................£25
56   Parlophone PMD 1040   EARL BOSTIC AND HIS ALTO SAX NO. 2.................................£25
58   Parlophone PMD 1054   BOSTIC MEETS DOGGETT (10" LP, with Bill Doggett)...................£30
58   Parlophone PMD 1068   BOSTIC ROCKS (10" LP)..£30
(see also Bill Doggett, Sonny Carter)

BOSTON
76   Epic EPCH 81611   BOSTON (LP, audiophile pressing)...................................£20
86   MCA MCGP 6017   THIRD STAGE (LP, picture disc).....................................£15
94   MCA MCGP 6017   WALK ON (LP, picture disc)...£15

BOSTON BOPPERS
74   Penny Farthing PEN 828 Did You Get What You Wanted/Whirlwind Girl..........................£25

BOSTON CRABS
65   Columbia DB 7586   Down In Mexico/Who?..£20
65   Columbia DB 7679   As Long As I Have You/Alley Oop...................................£20
66   Columbia DB 7830   Gin House/You Didn't Have To Be So Nice............................£20

BOSTON DEXTERS
64   Contemporary CR 101   Matchbox/La Bamba..£200
64   Contemporary CR 102   You've Been Talking About Me/Nothing's Gonna Change Me............£150
64   Contemporary CR 103   What Kind Of Girl Are You/I've Got Troubles Of My Own.............£150
65   Columbia DB 7498   I Believe To My Soul/I've Got Something To Tell You................£50
65   Columbia DB 7641   Try Hard/No More Tears..£45
(see also Tam White)

JACK ANGLIN BOSTON AND THE SOULITES
69   Ackee ACK 103   Starvation/Slave..£20

BO STREET RUNNERS
64   Decca F 11986   Bo Street Runner/Tell Me..£50
65   Columbia DB 7488   Tell Me What You're Gonna Do/And I Do Just What I Want............£60
65   Columbia DB 7640   Baby Never Say Goodbye/Get Out Of My Way...........................£60
66   Columbia DB 7901   Drive My Car/So Very Woman (featuring Mike [Too Much] Patto).......£70
64   Oak RGJ 131   BO STREET RUNNERS (EP, 49 copies only)..........................£1000
(see also [Mike] Patto, Timebox, Chicago Line, Cheynes, Fleetwood Mac)

EVE BOSWELL
53   Parlophone MSP 6006   Sugar Bush/Moon Above Malaya (China Nights)........................£15
57   Parlophone GEP 8601   THE ENCHANTING EVE (EP)..£15
56   Parlophone PMD 1039   SUGAR AND SPICE (10" LP)...£75
57   Parlophone PMC 1038   SENTIMENTAL EVE (LP)..£200
59   Parlophone PMC 1105   FOLLOWING THE SUN AROUND (LP).....................................£100

SIMON BOSWELL
75   Transatlantic TRA 307   MIND PARASITES (LP)..£18
(see also Advertising)

BOTH HANDS FREE (1)
76   Kemp/Pegrum KP 001 (J) BOTH HANDS FREE (LP)..£150
20   RCM RCLP 031   BOTH HANDS FREE (LP, reissue)......................................£30

BOTH HANDS FREE (2)
78   Zyzzle ZYZZLE 1   USE FROM THE POCKET (LP, handwritten labels)......................£100

BOTHY BAND
75   Polydor 2383379   THE BOTHY BAND (LP)..£18

RAMON BOUCHE
67   Columbia 8257   I Gotta Be With You/The Real Thing (DJ Copy)......................£200

BOULEVARD
79   Chopper CHOP 5D   MAGIC MAN (12", red vinyl, no p/s).................................£15
81   Boulevard VARD 1   Dawn Raid/Take It Or Leave It (p/s)................................£40

DENNIS BOVELL
78   Tempus TEMLP 001   STRICTLY DUB WIZE (LP, as Black Beard))............................£30
78   Ballistic LBR 1013   STRICTLY DUB WIZE (LP, reissue)....................................£20
81   Fontana 638 1047   BRAIN DAMAGE (2LP)...£40
93   Arawak ARKLP105   DUB DEM SILLY (LP)...£15
(see also Matumbi)

JIMMY BOWEN

57	Columbia DB 3915	I'm Stickin' With You/Ever Lovin' Fingers	£30
57	Columbia DB 3984	Warm Up To Me, Baby/I Trusted You	£30
57	Columbia DB 4027	Cross Over/It's Shameful	£15
58	Columbia DB 4184	The Two Step/By The Light Of The Silvery Moon	£15
65	Reprise RS 23043	The Eagle (demos & some issues list "The Golden Eagle")/Spanish Cricket	£15
58	Columbia SEG 7757	MEET JIMMY BOWEN (EP)	£30
58	Columbia SEG 7793	MEET JIMMY BOWEN NO. 2 (EP)	£30

BOWERY ELECTRIC

| 00 | Beggars Banquet BBQLP 213 | LUSHLIFE (LP) | £40 |

DAVID BOWIE

SINGLES : DEMO SINGLES

66	Pye 7N 17020	Can't Help Thinking About Me/And I Say To Myself (Demo copy, push-out centre)	£1000
66	Pye 7N 17020	Can't Help Thinking About Me/And I Say To Myself (demo copy, solid centre)	£500
66	Pye 7N 17079	Do Anything You Say/Good Morning Girl (Demo copy, push-out centre)	£1000
66	Pye 7N 17079	Do Anything You Say/Good Morning Girl (Demo copy, solid centre)	£500
66	Pye 7N 17157	I Dig Everything/I'm Not Losing Sleep (Demo copy, push-out centre)	£1000
66	Pye 7N 17157	I Dig Everything/I'm Not Losing sleep (Demo copy, solid centre)	£500
66	Deram DM 107	Rubber Band/The London Boys (Demo copy)	£300
67	Deram DM 123	The Laughing Gnome/The Gospel According To Tony Day (Demo copy)	£200
67	Deram DM 135	Love You Till Tuesday/Did You Ever Have A Dream (Demo copy)	£200
70	Mercury MF 1135	The Prettiest Star/Conversation Piece (Demo copy)	£300
70	Mercury 6052 026	Memory Of A Free Festival Parts 1 & 2 (Demo copy, large centre)	£300
70	Mercury 6052 026	Memory Of A Free Festival Parts 1 & 2 (Demo copy, push-out centre)	£175
71	Mercury 6052 049	Holy Holy/Black Country Rock (Demo copy)	£175
72	RCA 2160	Changes/Andy Warhol (Demo copy)	£45
72	RCA 2160	Starman/Suffragette City (Demo copy in p/s)	£75
72	RCA 2199	Starman/Suffragette City (Demo copy, not in p/s)	£25
72	RCA 2302	The Jean Genie/Ziggy Stardust (Demo copy)	£20
72	RCA 2263	John, I'm Only Dancing/Hang Onto Yourself (Demo copy)	£25
73	RCA 2316	Life On Mars?/The Man Who Sold The World (Demo copy in p/s)	£40
73	RCA 2316	Life On Mars?/The Man Who Sold The World (Demo copy without p/s)	£15
73	RCA 2352	Drive-In Saturday/Round And Round (Demo copy)	£30
73	RCA 2424	Sorrow/Amsterdam (Demo copy)	£15
74	RCA LPBO 5009	Rebel Rebel/Queen Bitch (Demo copy, label states "Bowie" not "David Bowie")	£25
74	RCA LPBO 5009	Rock'N'Roll Suicide/Quicksand (Demo copy)	£20
74	RCA APBO 0293	Diamond Dogs/Holy Holy (Demo copy, as "Bowie" not "David Bowie", push-out centre)	£25
74	RCA APBO 0293	Diamond Dogs/Holy Holy (as "Bowie" not "David Bowie", solid centre)	£35
74	RCA 2466	Knock On Wood/Panic In Detroit (Demo copy)	£15
75	RCA 2523	Young Americans (short version)/Young Americans (long version) (Demo copy)	£25
75	RCA 2640	Golden Years/Can You Hear Me (Demo copy, solid centre, as "Bowie" not "David Bowie")	£60
75	RCA 2640	Golden Years/Can You Hear Me (Demo copy, push-out centre, as "Bowie" not "David Bowie")	£15
75	Decca F 13579	The London Boys/Love You Till Tuesday (Demo)	£40
75	RCA 2579	Fame/Right (Demo copy)	£15
75	RCA 2593	Space Oddity/Velvet Goldmine (Demo copy in p/s)	£30
75	RCA 2593	Space Oddity/Velvet Goldmine (Demo copy, no p/s)	£15
76	RCA 2682	TVC15/We Are The Dead (Demo copy)	£15
76	RCA 2726	Suffragette City/Stay (Demo copy in p/s)	£25
76	RCA 2726	Suffragette City/Stay (Demo copy, no p/s)	£15
77	RCA PB 0905	Sound And Vision/A New Career In A New Town (Demo copy)	£15
77	RCA PB 1017	Be My Wife/Speed Of Life (Demo copy in promo sleeve with titles on front)	£500
77	RCA PB 1017	Be My Wife/Speed Of Life (Demo copy not in sleeve)	£15
77	RCA PB 1121	Heroes/V-2 Schneider (Demo copy)	£20
77	RCA PB 1190	Beauty And The Beast/Sense Of Doubt (Demo copy with p/s)	£20
78	RCA BOW 1	Breaking Glass/Art Decade/Ziggy Stardust (Demo copy with p/s)	£20
79	RCA BOW 2	Boys Keep Swinging/Fantastic Voyage (Demo copy)	£15
79	RCA BOW 3	DJ/Repetition (Demo copy)	£15
79	RCA BOW 4	John, I'm Only Dancing (Again)(1975)/John, I'm Only Dancing (1972) (Demo copy p/s)	£15
80	RCA BOW 5	Alabama Song/Space Oddity (Demo copy, poster p/s)	£20

SINGLES : IRISH PRESSINGS

70	Mercury EMF 1135	The Prettiest Star/Conversation Piece (Irish pressing)	£2000
73	RCA 2352	Drive-In Saturday/Round And Round (Irish pressing)	£100
73	RCA 2424	Sorrow/Amsterdam (Irish pressing)	£30
73	Deram DM(1) 123	The Laughing Gnome/The Gospel According To Tony Day (Irish pressing)	£120
73	Deram DM(1) 123	The Laughing Gnome/The Gospel According To Tony Day (Irish pressing)	£120
74	RCA LPBO 5009	Rebel Rebel/Queen Bitch (Irish pressing)	£100
74	RCA LPBO 5021	Rock'N'Roll Suicide/Quicksand (Irish pressing)	£100
75	RCA 2523	Young Americans/Sufragette City (Irish pressing)	£100
79	RCA 2316	Life On Mars?/The Man Who Sold The World (Irish pressing)	£100
82	RCA BOW 11	Wild Is The WInd/Golden Years (Irish pressing, p/s)	£15

SINGLES

66	Pye 7N 17020	Can't Help Thinking About Me/And I Say To Myself (with Lower Third)	£300
66	Pye 7N 17079	Do Anything You Say/Good Morning Girl	£400
66	Pye 7N 17157	I Dig Everything/I'm Not Losing Sleep	£400

MINT VALUE £

66	Deram DM 107	**Rubber Band/The London Boys**	£450
67	Deram DM 123	**The Laughing Gnome/The Gospel According To Tony Day** (with inverted matrix number on label)	£60
67	Deram DM 135	**Love You Till Tuesday/Did You Ever Have A Dream**	£200
69	Philips BF 1801	**Space Oddity/Wild Eyed Boy From Freecloud** (mono, solid centre)	£150
69	Philips BF 1801	**Space Oddity/Wild Eyed Boy From Freecloud** (mono, push-out centre)	£20
69	Philips BF 1801	**Space Oddity/Wild Eyed Boy From Freecloud** (unreleased p/s, only 2 or 3 copies known to exist)	£3000
69	Philips BF 1801	**Space Oddity/Wild Eyed Boy From Freecloud** (UK pressed stereo 45: unconfirmed)	£0

(is this really a UK pressing or a Dutch pressing as is generally acknowledged?)

69	Philips BF 1801	**Space Oddity/Wild Eyed Boy From Freecloud** (mono, large centre)	£15
70	Mercury MF 1135	**The Prettiest Star/Conversation Piece**	£250
70	Mercury 6052 026	**Memory Of A Free Festival Parts 1 & 2** (large centre)	£250
70	Mercury 6052 026	**Memory Of A Free Festival Parts 1 & 2** (push-out centre)	£200
71	Mercury 6052 049	**Holy Holy/Black Country Rock**	£150
72	RCA RCA 2160	**Changes/Andy Warhol**	£25
72	RCA RCA 2199	**Starman/Suffragette City** (in p/s)	£60
72	Pye 7NX 8002	**FOR THE COLLECTOR EP** (Do Anything You Say/I Dig Everything//I Can't Help Thinking About Me/I'm Not Losing Sleep (re-issue, blue label with art sleeve)	£20
72	Pye 7NX 8002	**FOR THE COLLECTOR EP** (Do Anything You Say/I Dig Everything//I Can't Help Thinking About Me/I'm Not Losing Sleep (re-issue, pink label with push-out centre)	£20
73	RCA RCA 2316	**Life On Mars?/The Man Who Sold The World** (in p/s)	£20
74	RCA LPBO 5009	**Rebel Rebel/Queen Bitch** (label states "Bowie" not "David Bowie")	£15
74	RCA APBO 0293	**Diamond Dogs/Holy Holy** ("Bowie" not "David Bowie", solid centre)	£25
74	RCA/Mainman	**Bowie's Greatest Hits** (excerpts from Knock On Wood/ Lyntone LYN 2929 Space Oddity/ The Man Who Sold The World/Life On Mars?/Starman/Jean Genie/Sorrow/Diamond dogs) 33rpm 1-sided flexidisc with Record Mirror/Popswop magazines)	£35
76	RCA RCA 2726	**Suffragette City/Stay** (p/s)	£15
77	RCA PB 1017	**Be My Wife/Speed Of Life** (solid centre)	£20
77	RCA PB 1190	**Beauty And The Beast/Sense Of Doubt** (sold centre centre with p/s)	£20
79	RCA BOW 3	**DJ/Repetition** (p/s, green vinyl)	£50
79	RCA 2316	**Life On Mars?/The Man Who Sold The World** (re-issue, black label, solid centre)	£15
80	RCA BOW 5	**Alabama Song/Space Oddity** (pink vinyl, custom factory pressing, poster p/s)	£500
80	RCA BOW 6	**Ashes To Ashes/Move On** (with 3 different p/s & 4 different sheets of 9 stamps)	£15
82	RCA BOW 11	**IN BERTOLT BRECHT'S "BAAL"** (Baal's Hymn/Remembering Marie A//Ballad Of The Adventureres/The Drowned Girl/Dirty Song, EP, foldout p/s)	£15
82	RCA BOW 100	**FASHIONS** (10 x 7" picture discs in plastic wallet [BOWP 101-110], each £8)	£100
93	BMG Arista 74321 148687	**Black Tie White Noise/You've Been Around** (black moulded label, large centre)	£15
95	RCA 329407	**Strangers When We Meet** (Edit)**/The Man Who Sold The World** (live) (green vinyl, stickered card p/s)	£20
95	RCA 353847	**Hallo Spaceboy** (Remix)**/The Heart's Filthy Lesson** (Radio Edit) (pink vinyl, stickered card p/s)	£20
95	RCA 74321 353847JB	**Hallo Spaceboy** (Remix)**/The Heart's Filthy Lesson** (Radio Edit) (juke box issue, moulded label)	£50
99	Castle ESBO7 765	**I DIG EVERYTHING: THE 1966 PYE SINGLES** (box set)	£20
02	Columbia COL 672744 7/ 6727447000	**Slow Burn/Wood Jackson** (orange vinyl, p/s)	£15
09	Parlophone LCO 299	**DAVID BOWIE : Heroes/TV ON THE RADIO : Heroes**	£40
13	EMI DBSTAR40	**Starman** (original version)**/Top Of The Pops Version** (picture disc, stickered PVC sleeve)	£150
13	EMI DBDRIVE 40	**Drive In Saturday/**(Russell Harty Plus Pop Version) (picture disc in PVC stickered sleeve)	£20
18	Parlophone DBBAAL 2018	**IN BERTOLT BRECHT'S 'BAAL'** (10" p/s, booklet, limited edition)	£20
19	Parlophone 0190295495060	**CLAREVILLE ROAD DEMOS** (with John 'Hutch' Hutchinson) (3x7" box set, insert, photo)	£15
19	Parlophone DBSO 72019	**SPACE ODDITY** (2x7" box set, 50th Anniversary edition, p/s, poster, photo print)	£20
19	Parlophone 0190295495084	**SPYING THROUGH A KEYHOLE - DEMOS & UNRELEASED SONGS** (4x7" box set, 4-page insert, postcard)	£20
21	Parlophone 10WOAC 50	**THE WIDTH OF A CIRCLE EP** (10" EP, p/s, website exclusive)	£30
21	ISO/Parl. DB 80147	**Mother/Tryin' To Get To Heaven** (p/s, numbered, limited, 100 copies cream)	£150
21	ISO/Parl. DB 80147	**Mother/Tryin' To Get To Heaven** (p/s, numbered, limited, black vinyl)	£15
23	Decca 0602448700155	**LAUGHING WITH LIZA - THE VOCALION AND DERAM SINGLES 1964-1967 PLUS** (5x7" box set, booklet)	£50

ALBUMS

67	Deram DML 1007	**DAVID BOWIE** (1st pressing, brown label, mono)	£1000
67	Deram SML 1007	**DAVID BOWIE** (1st pressing, red label, stereo)	£1000
69	Philips SBL 7912	**DAVID BOWIE** (1st pressing, unlaminated gatefold sleeve, black/silver label)	£700
70	Decca PA 58	**THE WORLD OF DAVID BOWIE** (mono)	£40
71	Mercury 6338 041	**THE MAN WHO SOLD THE WORLD** (LP, 1st pressing, with 'Produced by Tonny Viconti' mis-print on label, black/silver labels with 'dress' cover)	£1000
71	Mercury 6338 041	**THE MAN WHO SOLD THE WORLD** (LP, 2nd pressing, without 'Produced by Tonny Viconti' mis-print on label, black/silver labels with 'dress' cover)	£900
71	Mercury 6338 041	**THE MAN WHO SOLD THE WORLD** (cassette, with 'dress' cover)	£50
71	RCA SF 8244	**HUNKY DORY** (LP, 1st pressing, orange label with lyric sheet, 1st pressing with laminated sleeve, no GEM logo on right hand top corner of rear cover and no Mainman reference on sleeve or labels)	£600
71	RCA SF 8244	**HUNKY DORY** (LP, 2nd pressing, non-laminated sleeve, orange label with 'Chrysalis Music Ltd./Titanic Music' credits, lyric sheet)	£75
71	RCA SF 8244	**HUNKY DORY** (LP, 3rd pressing, non-laminated sleeve, orange label with 'Mainman/ Chrysalis' credits, lyric sheet)	£50
72	RCA SF 8287	**THE RISE AND FALL OF ZIGGY STARDUST AND THE SPIDERS FROM MARS** (1st pressing, Stamped matrixes: BGBS 0864 1E/0865 1E (with A4S etched into dead wax on side 1, B2K etched into dead wax on side 2) **with with 'Gem Productions' and no 'Mainman' logo on rear sleeve, "Victor" under RCA label not "International", glossy orange label with "Titanic/Chrysalis" credits on labels, lyric inner sleeve)**	£250

MINT VALUE £

72	RCA SF 8287	THE RISE AND FALL OF ZIGGY STARDUST AND THE SPIDERS FROM MARS (2nd pressing, Gem Production and Mainman on rear of sleeve, 'Mainman/Chrysalis' publishing credits)	£70
72	RCA LSP 4813	SPACE ODDITY (LP, reissue of SBL 7912 in different sleeve, orange label with lyric inner sleeve & poster)	£75
72	RCA LSP 4816	THE MAN WHO SOLD THE WORLD (first reissue, 'Titanic' credit, 'Ziggy' sleeve glossy orange labels with inner sleeve & foldout poster)	£40
73	RCA LSP-486	THE MAN WHO SOLD THE WORLD (second reissue 'Mainman' credit, lyric inner)	£20
73	RCA RS 1001	ALADDIN SANE (gloss orange label with 'Victor' on right side, 'Shorewood' gatefold sleeve & lyric inner sleeve, with fan club membership folder. Matrix numbers: CPRY 4543-3T/4544-3T)	£100
73	RCA RS 1001	ALADDIN SANE (orange label, 'Dynaflex' pressing, gatefold sleeve & lyric inner sleeve)	£35
73	RCA RS 1003	PIN UPS (LP, insert, orange label)	£40
74	RCA APL1 0576	DIAMOND DOGS (LP, 1st pressing, gatefold sleeve, orange label, 'Mainman' logo on rear sleeve, ARL1-0576A-1oly/ARL1-0576B-1oly matrixes)	£80
74	RCA APL 2-0771	DAVID LIVE (2-LP, 1st pressing, gatefold sleeve, orange label, photos on inners. 1st pressing has July 14th and 15th dates on inside cover, later pressings from 1974 have corrected dates of July 12nd and 13th)	£30
75	RCA Victor RS 1006	YOUNG AMERICANS	£40
76	RCA APL 1 1327	STATION TO STATION (LP, 1st pressing, 'Garrodprint Ltd' on sleeve with 'ZZ' in top rear right corner, matt orange label, lyric inner with cat no, Matrix numbers: two sets crossed out before APLI-1327-A-1E/B-1E)	£60
76	RCA RS 1055	CHANGESONEBOWIE (with 'sax' version of "John I'm Only Dancing")	£30
76	RCA APLI 1327	STATION TO STATION (with original colour proof sleeve)	£500
77	RCA INTS 5065	LOW (red vinyl, semi-official 'factory custom pressing')	£500
77	RCA PL12030	LOW (LP, insert, fan club flyer, sticker on front ('Featuring the hit single Sound & Vision') and back of sleeve (tracklisting))	£100
77	RCA PL12030	LOW (LP, insert, sticker on front ('Featuring the hit single Sound & Vision') and back of sleeve (tracklisting)	£70
77	RCA PL 12522	HEROES (LP, with insert, laminated sleeve, orange label)	£80
78	RCA PL 02913	STAGE (2-LP, gatefold sleeve, yellow vinyl)	£35
78	RCA PL 02913	STAGE (2-LP, gatefold sleeve)	£25
78	RCA Red Seal RL 12743	DAVID BOWIE NARRATES PROKOFIEV'S PETER AND THE WOLF	£20
79	RCA BOW 1	LODGER (gatefold sleeve, insert)	£35
80	RCA BOW LP 2	SCARY MONSTERS (AND SUPER CREEPS) (purple vinyl, semi-official 'factory custom pressing')	£600
80	RCA BOWLP2	SCARY MONSTERS AND SUPER CREEPS	£30
80	RCA International INTS 5066	HEROES (LP, repressing, insert, green label)	£25
80	RCA International INS 5063	THE RISE AND FALL OF ZIGGY STARDUST AND THE SPIDERS FROM MARS (LP, reissue, green label)	£25
81	EMI America AML 3029	LET'S DANCE (LP, inner)	£20
81	RCA International INTS 5067	ALADDIN SANE (LP, reissue, single sleeve, green label)	£25
81	RCA Intl. INTS 5068	DIAMOND DOGS (LP, reissue, green label)	£20
81	RCA Intl. INTS 5235	PIN UPS (LP, reissue, green label)	£15
81	RCA BOWLP3	CHANGESTWOBOWIE (LP, inner)	£25
81	RCA Int. RCAPL 12030	LOW (LP, repressing, green label)	£25
83	RCA NL 14654	THE MAN WHO SOLD THE WORLD (third reissue, silver on black labels)	£20
83	RCA INTS 5237	THE MAN WHO SOLD THE WORLD (fourth reissue, black on green labels)	£20
83	RCA International NL 83843	THE RISE AND FALL OF ZIGGY STARDUST AND THE SPIDERS FROM MARS (LP, reissue, black label)	£20
83	RCA PL 84862(2)	ZIGGY STARDUST - THE MOTION PICTURE (2-LP)	£25
84	RCA BOPIC 3	ZIGGY STARDUST (picture disc with numbered insert)	£18
84	RCA BOPIC 5	DIAMOND DOGS (picture disc with numbered insert)	£18
84	RCA BOPIC5	DIAMOND DOGS (LP, reissue, picture disc, numbered)	£50
84	RCA BOPIC 4	PIN-UPS (picture disc with numbered insert)	£18
84	RCA BOPIC 2	HUNKY DORY (picture disc with numbered insert)	£50
84	Deram 800 087-1	DAVID BOWIE (reissue)	£20
84	RCA BOPIC 1	ALADDIN SANE (picture disc with numbered insert)	£18
84	RCA BOPIC 4	PIN UPS (LP, reissue, picture disc, numbered)	£40
84	RCA PL 81327	STATION TO STATION (LP, reissue, black label)	£18
84	RCA Int. INTS 5212	LODGER (LP, reissue, non gatefold sleeve, green label)	£15
90	EMI EMC 3571	SPACE ODDITY (LP, 1990 reissue, gatefold with extra tracks)	£25
90	EMI EMC 3573	THE MAN WHO SOLD THE WORLD (LP, reissue, gatefold, 'dress cover', with four bonus tracks)	£40
90	EMI WMC 3572	HUNKY DORY (LP, reissue, gatefold with bonus tracks)	£20
90	EMI EMC 3577	ZIGGY STARDUST (LP, 1990 reissue, gatefold with unreleased tracks)	£20
90	EMI EMC 3584	DIAMOND DOGS (LP, remastered with 2 bonus tracks - Dodo/Candidate)	£30
90	EMI DBTV1	CHANGESBOWIE (2-LP, gatefold)	£20
91	EMI EMD 1021	YOUNG AMERICANS (remastered with 3 bonus tracks)	£25
91	EMI EMD 1020	STATION TO STATION (remastered with 2 bonus tracks, gatefold sleeve)	£30
93	BMG 74321 13697 1	BLACK TIE WHITE NOISE (LP, inner)	£150
93	EMI EM 1512	THE SINGLES COLLECTION (3-LP)	£50
94	MAINMAN GYLP 002	SANTA MONICA LIVE '72 (2xLP, clear vinyl)	£40
95	RCA 307021	EXCERPTS FROM OUTSIDE (with 12" booklet & lyric sheet)	£50
97	RCA 44949	EARTHLING (gatefold sleeve, stickered sleeve)	£200
97	EMI LPCENT 4	THE RISE AND FALL OF ZIGGY STARDUST AND THE SPIDERS FROM MARS (LP, reissue, EMI 100 Centenary, stickered lseeve)	£50
97	EMI LPCENT 21	HUNKY DORY (LP, reissue, EMI 100 Centenary edition, stickered sleeve)	£30
99	EMI 7243 4 99463 1 6	ALADDIN SANE (LP, reissue, gatefold)	£60
01	Simply Vinyl SVLP 264	THE MAN WHO SOLD THE WORLD (reissue, remaster, 'dress' sleeve)	£25
02	ISO/Columbia 508222 1	HEATHEN (LP, printed inner)	£100
03	EMI 0724359451121	SOUND AND VISION (4CD box set, booklet, printed plastic slip case)	£35
03	EMI 07243 5 41979 1 8	ZIGGY STARDUST - THE MOTION PICTURE SOUNDTRACK (2LP, gatefold, red vinyl,	£50

		reissue)..	
09	EMI DBSOLP 40	DAVID BOWIE (LP, reissue, gatefold with poster)	£20
10	EMI BOWSTSD2010	STATION TO STATION (5CD/DVDA/3LP box set, badges, ephemera)	£150
11	Deram 532760-1	DAVID BOWIE (2LP, reissue of Deram debut, gatefold)	£40
11	Music On Vinyl MOVLP 470	HEATHEN (LP, reissue, standard black vinyl, 180gm)	£40
12	EMI DBZSX 40	ZIGGY STARDUST AND THE SPIDERS FROM MARS (LP, with DVD)................................	£20
13	Music On Vinyl MOVLP 470	HEATHEN (LP, orange vinyl, 500 only, V&A Exhibition exclusive, numbered stickered sleeve)..	£150
13	Music On Vinyl MOVLP 500	OUTSIDE (LP, reissue, green vinyl 500 only, V&A Exhibition exclusive, numbered stickered sleeve)	£150
13	Music On Vinyl MOVLP 815	EARTHLING (LP, reissue, blue vinyl, inner, numbered)...	£100
13	ISO/Columbia 88765 461861	THE NEXT DAY (2LP/CD, gatefold, printed inners,180g)..	£35
14	ISO/M.O.Vinyl MOVLP 875	REALITY (LP, booklet, reissue, Music On Vinyl plastic sleeve & sticker, first edition numbered,180g)..	£50
15	Parlophone DBXL 1	FIVE YEARS 1969-1973 (13LP box set, book)	£600
16	ISO/Columbia 88875173871	BLACKSTAR (LP, clear vinyl, die-cut gatefold, booklet, download, 5000 pressed)	£500
16	ISO/Columbia 88875173871 S1	BLACKSTAR (LP, black vinyl, die-cut gatefold, booklet, download, 1st pressing with '(c) & (p) 2015 ISO Records' on back cover and not 2015, 2016 which is repressing)...............	£40
16	ISO/Columbia 88875173871	BLACKSTAR (LP, black vinyl, die-cut gatefold, booklet, download, 2nd pressing with 2016 copyright info on back)	£25
16	Parlophone DBBBCLP 6872	BOWIE AT THE BEEB (4LP, textured box set with lift-off lid, booklet)	£100
16	Parlophone DBXL 2	WHO CAN I BE NOW? [1974-1976] (13LP box set, book)..	£250
16	Columbia 88985 37455 1	LAZARUS (ORIGINAL CAST RECORDING) (with Enda Walsh) (3LP, sixth side etched, trifold sleeve, booklet)...	£30
17	Parlophone DBRSD 7476	CRACKED ACTOR (LIVE LOS ANGELES '74) (3LP, fourth side etched, trifold sleeve, RSD) ...	£60
17	Parlophone DBXL 3	A NEW CAREER IN A NEW TOWN [1977-1982] (13LP box set, book, onsert)	£200
17	Parlophone DBRSD 6973	BOWPROMO (1-sided LP box set, photos, press release, RSD)	£35
18	Parlophone DBXL4	LOVING THE ALIEN [1983-1988] (15LP box set, book, onsert)	£250
18	Parl. 0190295570453	BOWIE GLASTONBURY 2000 (3LP, trifold sleeve, booklet, printed inners)	£40
19	Decca SPA 5890	THE WORLD OF DAVID BOWIE (LP, printed inner, blue vinyl, Decca 90 edition)........	£20
19	Parlophone DBCP 6869	CONVERSATION PIECE (5CD box set, 120-pg book, onsert)	£70
20	Parlophone DBRSDLP 2020	I'M ONLY DANCING (THE SOUL TOUR 74) (2LP, gatefold, RSD)	£40
20	Parlophone 0190295198787	METROBOLIST (LP, cartoon gatefold with Keef pics, 50 copies on gold vinyl)	£1000
20	Parlophone 0190295198787	METROBOLIST (LP, cartoon gatefold with Keef pics, 1970 copies on white vinyl)	£100
20	Parlophone 0190295198787	METROBOLIST (LP, cartoon gatefold with Keef pics, black vinyl)	£20
21	Parlophone CDWOAC 50	THE WIDTH OF A CIRCLE (2CD box set, booklet)	£30
21	Parlophone DBXL 5	BRILLIANT ADVENTURE [1992-2001] (18LP box set, book, onsert)	£150
21	ISO/Parl. DBBLALP 95993	LIVEANDWELL.COM (2LP, printed inners)...	£40
21	ISO/Parl. DBBLALP 95992	NO TRENDY RÉCHAUFFÉ [LIVE BIRMINGHAM 95] (2LP, gatefold, ltd. ed.)	£40
22	ISO/Parl. LPTOYBOX 1	TOY (6x10" box set, booklet)	£50
22	Parlophone DBDS 71	DIVINE SYMMETRY - THE ROAD TO HUNKY DORY (4CD/1BD box set, 100-pg book, notebook)..	£70
23	ISO/Parlophone DBMDLP 2022	MOONAGE DAYDREAM (A FILM BY BRETT MORGEN) (3LP, trifold, printed inners, booklet)..	£50
23	Parlophone DBLP 377350	ZIGGY STARDUST - THE MOTION PICTURE SOUNDTRACK (2LP, gatefold, gold vinyl, printed inners, 50th anniversary edition)	£30
24	Parlophone DBRNRSLP 722	WAITING IN THE SKY (BEFORE THE STARMAN CAME TO EARTH) (LP, half-speed master, printed inner, RSD)..	£60

ALBUMS : CDS

84	Deram 800 087-2	DAVID BOWIE (withdrawn with white title)	£80
84	RCA PD 84202	CHANGESTWOBOWIE (withdrawn)	£30
84	RCA PD 89002	STAGE (2-CD, withdrawn)..	£40
84	RCA PD 94792	GOLDEN YEARS (withdrawn)...	£30
84	RCA PD 84919	FAME AND FASHION (ALL TIME GREATEST HITS) (withdrawn)	£50
85	RCA PD 81732	CHANGESONEBOWIE (withdrawn)	£35

PROMOS

71	Gem BOWPROMO 1	BOWPROMO (LP, white label only, also known as HUNKY DORY SAMPLER Some with handwritten sleeve or Gem sticker on A-side, B-side features DANA GILLESPIE, 500 only)	£2000
71	None	HUNKY DORY (LP, preview pressing. Green labels with large red G and track listing, Matrixes Side 1: APRS-5947-35-A1A R Side 2: APRS-5948-35-A1A R, white sleeve with typed track listing and handwritten details "David Bowie Hunky Dory Preview Pressing 19 October 1971)...	£3000
77	RCA BOW-1E	From The New Album 'Low' (1-sided promo, excerpts from Speed Of Life, Breaking Glass, What In The World, Sound And Vision)	£1500
83	RCA LIFETIMES 1	LIFETIMES (LP, promo, numbered, with insert)	£100
90	BMG BOW 908	SO FAR (CD, 8-track sampler for "Sound & Vision" box set)	£40
93	EMI BOWIE 1	SELECTIONS FROM THE SINGLES COLLECTION 10-track sampler,card p/s, promo only)..	£18
93	BMG MEAT 1	Pallas Athena (12", white label, no p/s, includes two exclusive Meat Beat Manifesto remixes)	£40
93	Back To Basics HOME 1	Night Flights/(B-side by Moodswings) (12")..	£18
93	BBC MMCD 0072	BBC SESSIONS 1969-1972 (CD, picture disc, promo-only, withdrawn)	£75
95	RCA HALLO 2	Hallo Spaceboy (12" Remix) (12", 1-sided, no p/s)...	£18
95	BMG SOLO 1	EXCLUSIVE TOUR CD: Strangers When We Meet/MORRISSEY: The Boy Racer (Outside Tour CD)	£90
96	RCA SPACE 2	Hallo Spaceboy (12" Remix) (1-sided 12", some copies listed as RCA HALLO 2, no p/s)	£25
96	RCA SPACE 3	Hallo Spaceboy (Double Click Mix)/Hallo Spaceboy (Instrumental)/ Hallo Spaceboy (Lost In Space Mix) (12", no p/s)...	£50
99	EMI QUEENWL 28	Under Pressure (Remixes) (with Queen) (12", white label, unreleased mix, promo only)...	£30

(see also Davie Jones & King Bees, Davy Jones & Lower Third, Manish Boys, Arnold Corns, Mick Ronson, Queen, Bing Crosby, Tin Machine)

MINT VALUE £

DAVID BOWIE AND BING CROSBY
82	RCA BOW 12 (PRO)	Peace On Earth/Little Drummer Boy//Dialogue/Peace On Earth/LDB (Demo copy, p/s)	£20
82	RCA BOW 12	Peace On Earth/Little Drummer Boy/Fantastic Voyage (Irish pressing, p/s)	£15

(see also David Bowie, Bing Crosby)

CANDY BOWMAN
81	RCA RCAT 148	Since I Found You/I Wanna Feel Your Love (12")	£20

BOWMAN-HYDE PLAYERS
61	Parlophone PMC 1155	SING ME A SOUVENIR (LP)	£20

ALAN BOWN (SET)
65	Pye 7N 15934	Can't Let Her Go/I'm The One	£30
66	Pye 7N 17084	Baby Don't Push Me/Everything's Gonna Be Alright	£30
66	Pye 7N 17148	Headline News/Mister Pleasure	£50
66	Pye 7N 17192	Emergency 999/Settle Down	£60
67	Pye 7N 17256	Gonna Fix You Good (Everytime You're Bad)/I Really Really Care	£50
68	MGM MGM 1387	Story Book/Little Lesley	£25
68	Music Factory CUB LS 1	OUTWARD BOWN (LP, stereo)	£100
68	Music Factory LM 1	OUTWARD BOWN (LP, mono)	£100
69	Deram SML 1049	THE ALAN BOWN! (LP, stereo)	£70
69	Deram DML 1049	THE ALAN BOWN! (LP, mono)	£80
70	Island ILPS 9131	LISTEN (LP, with inner sleeve)	£30
71	Island ILPS 9163	STRETCHING OUT (LP, gatefold sleeve)	£30
96	Tenth Planet TP 027	OUTWARD BOWN FIRST ALBUM (LP, reissue)	£20

(see also John Barry Seven, Bronco, Jonesy)

ALAN BOWN SET/JIMMY JAMES & VAGABONDS
68	Pye N(S)PL 18156	LONDON SWINGS - LIVE AT THE MARQUEE CLUB (LP, 1 side each)	£30

(see also Jimmy James & Vagabonds)

ANDREW BOWN
70	Parlophone R 5856	Tarot (Theme From 'Ace Of Wands')/Lulli Rides Again	£75

(see also Andy Bown)

ANDY BOWN
79	EMI EMI 2943	Good Advice/One More Chance (p/s)	£15
72	Mercury 6310 002	GONE TO MY HEAD (LP)	£20
73	GM GML 1001	SWEET WILLIAM (LP)	£20

(see also Andrew Bown, Herd, Judas Jump, Status Quo, Rossi & Frost, Storyteller)

BENDALLS BOX
81	Circus CIRC 004	Nightmares/Games Today (p/s)	£25

DAVID BOX
64	London HLU 9874	If You Can't Say Something Nice/Sweet Sweet Day	£15
64	London HLU 9924	Little Lonely Summer Girl/No One Will Ever Know	£15

(see also Crickets)

BOXER
75	Virgin VDJ 12	All The Time In The World/Don't Wait (12", promo only)	£15
75	Virgin V 2049	BELOW THE BELT (LP, gatefold sleeve with uncensored full-frontal back cover)	£30
76	Virgin V 2049	BELOW THE BELT (LP, censored sleeve)	£15
76	Virgin V 2073	BLOODLETTING (LP, withdrawn)	£100

(see also Patto, Timebox, Koobas, May Blitz)

BOXER REBELLION
13	Absentee TBR012VL	PROMISES (LP)	£50
14	Absentee TBR003VL	EXITS (LP)	£30
15	Absentee TBR12BOX 1	THE BOXER REBELLION (3-LP, box set, signed hand-written lyric sheet, 5 art cards and download card, 500 only	£150

BOX TOPS
68	Stateside (S)SL 10218	THE LETTER/NEON RAINBOW (LP, flipback sleeve)	£20
68	Bell MBLL/SBLL 105	CRY LIKE A BABY (LP)	£15
69	Bell MBLL/SBLL 108	NON-STOP (LP)	£15
69	Bell SBLL 120	DIMENSIONS (LP)	£15

(see also Big Star)

JUNIOR BOYCE (ACTUALLY JR. BYLES)
77	Observer OB 004	Natty Dreadlocks/Sick-More Tree/What Kind Of World/Sic Easy Stepping (12", with Ranking Buckers)	£30

(see also Junior Byles)

TOMMY BOYCE & BOBBY HART
67	A&M AML 907	TEST PATTERNS (LP)	£25

(see also Monkees)

EDDIE BOYD
66	Blue Horizon 45 BH 1009	It's So Miserable To Be Alone/Empty Arms	£150
67	Blue Horizon 57-3137	The Big Boat/Sent For You Yesterday (with Fleetwood Mac) (no Fleetwood Mac credit on label)	£40
68	Blue Horizon 57-3137	The Big Boat/Sent For You Yesterday (with Fleetwood Mac) (Fleetwood Mac credit on label)	£40
62	Esquire EP 247	BOYD'S BLUES (EP, as Eddie Boyd Blues Combo)	£70
65	Fontana SFJL 905	FIVE LONG YEARS (LP)	£60
67	Decca LK/SKL 4872	EDDIE BOYD AND HIS BLUES BAND FEATURING PETER GREEN (LP)	£120
68	Blue Horizon 7-63202	7936 SOUTH RHODES (LP, with Fleetwood Mac)	£100
68	Storyville SLP 4054	IN CONCERT (LP)	£25

(see also Fleetwood Mac)
EDDIE BOYD/BUDDY GUY
66   Chess CRE 6009   WITH THE BLUES (EP, 2 tracks each) £25
(see also Buddy Guy)
MOSES BOYD EXODUS
16   Exodus XODUS 001   Rye Lane Shuffle/Drum Dance (12", p/s) £25
17   Exodus XOEP03   ABSOLUTE ZERO (12" EP, p/s) £15
20   Exodus XOLP001XX   DARK MATTER (2-LP, wrapped in flag, 'dinked' edition, grey vinyl, as Moses Boyd) £40
BOY FRIDAY (& GROOVERS)
70   Downtown DT 470   Version Girl/Grumble Man £20
71   Downtown DT 471   Music So Good/Right Track (both with Groovers) £35
71   Downtown DT 472   Sounds I Remember/JOAN LONG: Reconsider Our Love £18
71   Downtown DT 473   Take A Message Ruby/Second Note £50
71   Downtown DT 476   There'll Always Be Sunshine/Sunshine Track £20
71   Downtown DT 477   Hot Pants Girl/Raunchy £15
71   Downtown DT 481   El Raunchy/Conversation (as Boy Friday & Collins).......................£15
(see also Dandy & Superboys)
BOYFRIENDS
82   Plastic PRES 001   Boyfriend/Give A Little, Take A Little (p/s) £40
BOY HAIRDRESSERS
88   53rd & 3rd AGARR T12   Golden Showers/Tidalwave/The Assumption As An Elevator (12", p/s) £30
(see also Teenage Fanclub, Clouds)
BILLY BOYLE
62   Decca F 11503   My Baby's Crazy 'Bout Elvis/Held For Questioning £15
70   UPC UPC112   Lookin' For Love/Pisces Man £20
(see also Le Roys)
A. BOYNE
70   Punch PH 36   Oh My Darling (actually Audley Rollins)/DENNIS SMITH: Ball Of Confusion £20
BILLY BOYO
82   Greensleeves GRELD 89   Righteousness/Itie Title Girl (12")...£15
BOYRACER
93   Sarah SARAH 76   B IS FOR BOYRACER EP (p/s, insert) £20
93   Sarah SARAH 85   FROM PURITY TO PURGATORY EP (p/s, insert) £30
94   Sarah SARAH 96   PURE HATED EP (p/s, insert) £20
BOYS IN DARKNESS
81   Bid For Freedom BID 1   Back To France/A Man An Island (no p/s) £15
BOYS (JAMAICA)
69   Duke DU 19   Easy Sound/AFROTONES: Freedom Sound £45
(see also Harry J. Allstars)
BOYS BLUE
65   HMV POP 1427   You Got What I Want/Take A Heart £50
(see also Jeff Elroy & Boys Blue)
BOYS (U.K.) (1)
63   Parlophone R 5027   Polaris/Jumpin'..£20
64   Pye 7N 15726   It Ain't Fair/I Want You...£100
BOYS (U.K.) (2)
77   NEMS NES 102   I Don't Care/Soda Pressing (p/s) £15
77   NEMS NES 111   First Time/Whatcha Gonna Do/Turning Grey (p/s) £15
77   NEMS NES 6001   THE BOYS (LP, 1st pressing with 33 and a thrid on labels) £25
78   NEMS NEL 6015   ALTERNATIVE CHARTBUSTERS (LP, 1st pressing, laminated sleeve. inner, 33 and a third on labels) £30
79   Safari 1-2 BOYS   TO HELL WITH THE BOYS (LP, with songbook & stickered sleeve) £25
80   Safari BOYS 4   BOYS ONLY (LP) £15
(see also Yobs, Rowdies, Hollywood Brats)
BOYZ II MEN
91   Motown 53000-1   COOLEYHIGHHARMONY (LP) £20
94   Motown 53043-1   II (LP) £25
BOZ
66   Columbia DB 7832   You're Just The Kind Of Girl I Want/Isn't That So £30
66   Columbia DB 7889   Meeting Time/No (Ah) Body Knows The Blues £30
66   Columbia DB 7972   The Baby Song/Carry On Screaming £20
68   Columbia DB 8406   I Shall Be Released/Dove In The Flood £50
68   Columbia DB 8468   Light My Fire/Back Against The Wall £15
(see also King Crimson, Bad Company)
BOZOS
78   Other BOZ 101   Weekend Girl/Fool Out Of Me..£25
BRACKEN
79   Look LKLP 6438   PRINCE OF THE NORTHLANDS (LP, private pressing, with insert) £60
WILLIE BRACKENRIDGE
79   Burning Vibrations BVD 005   Blood Money/You Are On My Mind (12") £35
BOBBY BRADFORD
73   Emanem 302   LOVE'S DREAM (LP) £25

JAN BRADLEY
63 Pye International 7N 25182 **Mama Didn't Lie/Lovers Like Me** £35

MARTIN BRADLEY
80 Greenwich Village GVR 205 **TIME CAN'T STAND STILL** (LP)..£15

OWEN BRADLEY (ORCHESTRA/QUINTET)
60 Brunswick LAT 8327 **THE BIG GUITAR** (LP)..£20

BRADLEY STRYDER
92 Rephlex CAT 001 **BRADLEY'S BEAT** (12" EP, logo sleeve) £20

SONNY BRADSHAW QUINTET
62 Top TD 106 **This Is Happiness/Island In The Sun** £15

SONNY BRADSHAW (& YOUNG JAMAICA)
61 Duke DK 1003 **Yellow Birds/Festival Jump Up** £15

TINY BRADSHAW & HIS ORCHESTRA
54 Parlophone GEP 8507 **TRAIN KEPT A ROLLING** (EP)..£30
56 Parlophone GEP 8552 **POMPTON TURNPIKE** (EP)..£15

TINY BRADSHAW ORCHESTRA/WYNONIE HARRIS
70 Polydor 623 273 **KINGS OF RHYTHM AND BLUES** (LP, 1 side each) £15
(see also Wynonie Harris)

DON BRADSHAW-LEATHER
72 Distance DIST 101 **DISTANCE BETWEEN US** (2-LP, gatefold sleeve, private pressing)................£400

BOB BRADY & CONCHORDS
68 Bell BLL 1025 **Everybody's Goin' To The Love-In/It's Been A Long Time Between Kisses** £60
70 Bell BLL 1114 **Everybody's Goin' To The Love-In/It's Been A Long Time Between Kisses** (reissue) £20

PHIL BRADY & THE RANCH SET
67 Go AJ 11406 **Lonesome For You/Please Come Back** £18

VICTOR BRADY
70 Polydor 2489010 **BROWN RAIN** (LP) £40

BRADY BUNCH
73 Paramount SPFL 284 **MEET THE BRADY BUNCH** (LP) £15

AL 'TNT' BRAGGS
66 Vocalion VP 9278 **Earthquake/How Long** (Do You Hold On)..................................£20
66 Vocalion VP 9278 **Earthquake/How Long** (Do You Hold On) (DJ Copy)......................£60
68 Action ACT 4506 **Earthquake/How Long** (Do You Hold On) (reissue) £20
69 Action ACT 4526 **I'm A Good Man/I Like What You Do To Me** £15
65 Vocalion VEP 170163 **AL 'TNT' BRAGGS** (EP) £125

ERNEL BRAHAM
66 Rio R 79 **Musical Fight/EDWARDS ALLSTARS: Pipeline** £40

ROY BRAHAM
64 R&B 166 **Believe Me/Red Sea** £40

BRAIN
67 Parlophone R 5595 **Nightmares In Red/Kick The Donkey** £150
(see also Giles Giles & Fripp, Trendsetters Ltd, League Of Gentlemen)

BRAINBOX
69 Parlophone R 5775 **Woman's Gone/Down Man** £20
70 Parlophone R 5842 **So Helpless/To You** £15
70 Parlophone PCS 7094 **BRAINBOX** (LP, black/silver/white boxed Parlophone label) £200
(see also Jan Akkerman, Hunters, Focus)

BRAINCHILD
70 A&M AMLS 979 **HEALING OF THE LUNATIC OWL** (LP, brown label)....................£120

BRAIN DONOR
01 Impressario IMPODDLP001 **LOVE PEACE AND FUCK** (2-LP, green & white vinyl)....................£15

BRAINIAC 5
78 Roach RREP 5001 **MUSHY DOUBT** (EP, 33rpm, p/s) £15

BRAINKILLERS
93 Vibe Alive VALV 36 **Crackhead/Dark Moon/Stupid/This Is Where It Takes Us** (12", with Lewi Cifer)............£50
93 Vibe Alive VALV 76 **On A Different Mission/One Stype/Hurt Me/Girl U Look Good** (12", stickered die-cut paper sleeve, with Lewi Cifer)........£20
94 3rd Party, Kemet KM3RD#1 **BORDER LINE EP** (with FAMILY OF INTELLIGENCE) (12")......£20

BRAIN KILLERS/FAMILY OF INTELLIGENCE
94 3rd Party/Kemet KM3Rd 1 **Screwface/Jungle Love/Champion Of Champions/Bonus Beats 1** (12")..............£30

BRAINSTORM
79 Miracle M5 **Lovin' Is Really My Game/Stormin'** (12", red or black vinyl no p/s) £20

BRAINTAX
92 Low Life Low 2 **FAT HEAD** (EP 12" - 500 pressed) £40
97 Low Life Low 4 **FUTURE YEARS** (EP, 12")..£20
01 Low Life LOW 15 **BIRO FUNK** (2-LP)..£25
06 Low Life LOW 50 **PANORAMA** (LP) £25
08 Low Life LOW 50 **MY LAST AND BEST ALBUM** (LP) £25

BRAKES
80 Magnet MAGL **FOR WHY YOU KICKA MY DONKEY?** (LP) £15

DELANEY BRAMLETT
64	Vocalion VP 9227	Heartbreak Hotel/You Never Looked Sweeter	£15
65	Vocalion VP 9237	Liverpool Lou/You Have No Choice	£30
65	Vocalion VP 9237	Liverpool Lou/You Have No Choice (DJ Copy)	£50

(see also Delaney & Bonnie, King Curtis with Delaney & Friends)

BRAM STOKER
72	Windmill WMD 117	HEAVY ROCK SPECTACULAR (LP)	£30

BRAN
74	Gwawr GWA 104	BRAN EP	£50
75	Sain 1038M	AIL-DDECHRA (LP)	£300
76	Sain 1070M	HEDFAN (LP)	£100
78	Sain 1120M	GWRACH Y NOS (LP)	£40

GLENN BRANCA
89	Blast First BFFP 39	SYMPHONY NO 6 (LP)	£15

BRAND
64	Piccadilly 7N 35216	I'm A Lover Not A Fighter/Zulu Stomp	£100

BRAND NEW
03	Eat Sleep	Jude Law And A Semester Abroad/Am I Wrong (p/s)	£30
03	Sore Point SORE 004S	The Quiet Things That No One Ever Knows/Jude Law And A Session Abroad (live in session) (die-cut sleeve, red vinyl)	£15
04	Sore Point SORE 011S	Sic Transit Gloria...Glory Fades/Jaws Theme Swimming (Demo) (pink vinyl)	£15
07	Interscope 1733030	Jesus/Brothers (picture sleeve, stickered sleeve)	£60

BRAND NEW HEAVIES
91	Acid Jazz JAZID 39P	Never Stop (12", company sleeve, withdrawn)	£20
90	Acid Jazz JAZID LP 23	THE BRAND NEW HEAVIES (LP)	£15
97	FFRR 828 887-1	SHELTER (2-LP)	£30
12	Acid Jazz AJLP 293	THE BRAND NEW HEAVIES (LP, reissue)	£15

JOHNNY BRANDON
56	Parlophone MSP 6238	Rock-A-Bye Baby/Lonely Lips	£40
56	Parlophone R 4207	Shim Sham Shuffle/I Didn't Know	£40
56	Decca F 10778	Glendora/Song For A Summer Night	£15
55	Pye NEP 24003	JOHNNY BRANDON HITS (EP)	£15

VERN BRANDON
62	Decca F 11472	Let Me Be The One/Gotta Know The Reason	£20

BRANDY
94	Atlantic 7567 82610-1	BRANDY (LP)	£30
98	Atlantic 7567 83039-1	NEVER SAY NEVER (2-LP)	£25
02	Atlantic 7567 83110-1	FULL MOON (2-LP)	£25
05	Atlantic 7567 83633-1	AFRODISIAC (2-LP)	£20

BRANDY WINE BRIDGE
77	Cottage COT 311	THE GREY LADY (LP, as Brandywinebridge)	£25
78	Cottage COT 321	AN ENGLISH MEADOW (LP, hand-drawn sleeve with insert)	£25

JOHNNY BRANTLEY'S ALL STARS
58	London HLU 8606	The Place/Pot Luck	£20

BRASS ALLEY
73	Alaska ALA 11	You Better Run/Be My Friend	£20

BRASS BIRD
68	TP TO 024	Simple Life/A Place To Die	£60

BRASS CONSTRUCTION
76	United Artists UAS 29923	BRASS CONSTRUCTION (LP)	£15

BRASS RAIL
70	Hot Pursuit HP 1	Deep In The Woods/Light Up The Sky	£30

ANDRÉ BRASSEUR
67	CBS 202557	The Kid/Holiday	£20
67	CBS 202557	The Kid/Holiday (DJ Copy)	£50
66	CBS 62858	TASTY (LP)	£15

BRASS INCORPORATED
70	Pye International 7N 25520	At The Sign Of The Swinging Cymbal/Just Like That	£25

BRASS MONKEY
71	Philips 6303 025	BRASS MONKEY (LP)	£30
71	Philips 6303 027	NO VISIBLE MEANS OF SUPPORT (LP)	£30

BRASS TACKS
68	Big T BIG 110	I'll Keep On Holding On/Let The Sunshine In	£35
68	Big T BIG 114	Maxwell Ferguson/Sunshine After The Rain	£100

RICHARD BRAUTIGAN
69	Zapple ZAPPLE 03	LISTENING TO RICHARD BRAUTIGAN (LP, unreleased, acetates exist)	£1500

CEDRIC BRAVO
65	Ska Beat JB 229	Merry Christmas/Sugar Baby	£15

LOS BRAVOS
66	Decca F 22529	Going Nowhere/Brand New Baby	£20
66	Decca LK 4822	BLACK IS BLACK (LP)	£15
68	Decca LK/SKL 4905	LOS BRAVOS (LP)	£20

MINT VALUE £

(see also Mike Kennedy)

ANTHONY BRAXTON
85	Leo 414/415/416	QUARTET (2-LP box set with insert)	£35

ANTHONY BRAXTON & DEREK BAILEY
73	Emanem 601	DUO (2-LP)	£30
84	Incus INCUS 43	ROYAL VOLUME 1 (LP)	£20

(see also Derek Bailey)

TONI BRAXTON
93	Arista 74321 16268 1	TONI BRAXTON (LP)	£40
96	La Face 73008-26020-1	SECRETS (LP)	£70
00	La Face 73008-26069-1	THE HEAT (LP)	£70

PRISCILLA BRAZIER
74	Dovetail DOVE 9	PRISCILLA BRAZIER (LP)	£25
76	Key KL 038	SOMETHING BEAUTIFUL (LP)	£35

BREAD
69	Elektra EKS 74044	BREAD (LP)	£25

(see also David Gates, Pleasure Fair)

BREAD & BEER BAND
69	Decca F 12891	Dick Barton Theme (The Devil's Gallop)/Breakdown Blues	£75
72	Decca F 13354	Dick Barton Theme (The Devil's Gallop)/Breakdown Blues (reissue)	£40
69	Rubbish (no cat. no.)	THE BREAD AND BEER BAND (LP, 1 copy known to exist)	£2000

(see also Elton John, Caleb)

BREAD, LOVE & DREAMS
69	Decca F 12958	Virgin Kiss/Switch Out The Sun	£22
69	Decca LK 5008	BREAD, LOVE AND DREAMS (LP, unboxed large Decca on label, mono)	£250
69	Decca SKL 5008	BREAD, LOVE AND DREAMS (LP, unboxed large Decca on label, stereo)	£200
70	Decca LK 5048	THE STRANGE TALE OF CAPTAIN SHANNON AND THE HUNCHBACK FROM GIGHA (LP, small boxed Decca label, mono)	£250
70	Decca SKL 5048	THE STRANGE TALE OF CAPTAIN SHANNON AND THE HUNCHBACK FROM GIGHA (LP, small boxed Decca label, stereo)	£200
71	Decca SKL 5081	AMARYLLIS (LP, small boxed Decca label)	£800
07	Sunbeam SBRLP 5027	AMARYLLIS (LP, reissue)	£15
08	Sunbeam SBRLP 5042	THE STRANGE TALE OF CAPTAIN SHANNON AND THE HUNCHBACK FROM GIGHA (LP, reissue)	£20

(see also Human Beast)

BREAKAWAYS
62	Pye 7N 15471	He's A Rebel/Wishing Star	£15
64	Pye 7N 15618	That's How It Goes/He Doesn't Love Me	£50
67	CBS 2833	Sacred Love/Don't Be A Baby	£20

(see also Vernons Girls, Burt Bacharach Orchestra, Mike Patto, Ken Cope, Sharades,, Dany Chandelle, Nicky James)

BREAKDOWN
77	MCP 001	MEET ME ON THE HIGHWAY (LP, private pressing with insert)	£30

BREAKERS
81	Riot RS 1001	Radio Love/My Momma Told Me (p/s)	£20

BREAKING THE ILLUSION
92	Lowlife LOW 1	WHERE WILL IT END? (EP, 12" p/s, 1000 pressed)	£15

BREAKOUT
81	Guardian GRC 101	Wall Of Solitude/Get Out Fight Back	£100

DANNY BREAKS
93	Droppin Science DS 001	DROPPIN SCIENCE VOLUME 01 (12")	£30
94	Droppin Science DS 002	DROPPIN SCIENCE VOLUME 02 (12")	£25
94	Droppin Science DS 003	DROPPIN SCIENCE VOLUME 03 (12")	£30
95	Droppin Science DS 001R	DROPPIN SCIENCE VOLUME 01 REMIXES (12")	£18
95	Droppin Science DS 003R	DROPPIN SCIENCE VOLUME 03 REMIXES (12")	£20
95	Droppin Science DS 005	DROPPIN SCIENCE VOLUME 05 (12")	£15

BREAKTHRU'
68	Mercury MF 1066	Ice Cream Tree/Julius Caesar	£25

BREAKWATER
86	Arista ARIST 12674	Say You Love Me Girl/Work It Out (12", p/s)	£15

BREATHERS
80	Diversion DIV 1	Living In The Age Age/Counting On Counting	£15

BREATHLESS
81	Magnum Force MFEP 005	SOCK HOP BOPPIN' (EP)	£20

BREEDERS
93	4AD BREED 1	Cannonball (12" promo)	£30
17	4AD 4AD0036S1	Wait In The Car/Archangel's Thunderbird (p/s, orange vinyl tour only)	£20
93	4AD BAD 3011	Cannonball/Cro-Aloha/Lord Of The Thighs/900 (12", p/s)	£15
90	4AD CAD 0006	POD (LP)	£25
93	4AD CAD 3014	LAST SPLASH (LP, with free 7")	£40
02	4AD CAD 2205	TITLE TK (LP, inner)	£40
08	4AD CAD 2803	MOUNTAIN BATTLES (LP, inner sleeve and booklet)	£40
13	4AD DAD 3308	LSXX (3-LP, 4 x 10" box set)	£50
21	4AD CAD 006	POD (LP, reissue, pink vinyl)	£40

JIMMY BREEDLOVE
57	London HLE 8490	Over Somebody Else's Shoulder/That's My Baby	£100
57	London HLE 8490	Over Somebody Else's Shoulder/That's My Baby (78)	£15
62	Pye International 7N 25121	You're Following Me/Fabulous	£30

(see also Cues)

BEVERLEY BREMERS
72	Wand WN 18	Get Smart Girl/Don't Say You Don't Remember	£15

BRENDA & TABULATIONS
67	London HL 10127	Dry Your Eyes/The Wash	£30
67	London HL 10174	When You're Gone/Hey Boy	£25
68	Direction 58-3678	Baby You're So Right For Me/To The One I Love	£15
69	Action ACT 4541	That's In The Past/I Can't Get Over Her	£30
70	London HL 10325	A Child No One Wanted/'Scuse Uz Y'all	£15
71	CBS 7279	Right On The Tip of My Tongue/Always And Forever	£15
69	Action ACLP 6003	DRY YOUR EYES (LP)	£50
77	Casablanca CAL 2016	I KEEP COMING BACK FOR MORE (LP)	£15

ROSE BRENNAN
55	HMV 7M 299	Ding Dong/Sincerely	£15

BRENT FORD & NYLONS
78	Brumbeat	19th Nervous Breakdown/Big Rock Candy Mountain (handmade foldout p/s)	£50

TONY BRENT & JULIE DAWN
53	Columbia SCM 5029	Ding Dong Boogie/When Are We Gonna Get Married?	£15

BRENTFORD ROAD ALLSTARS
70	Bamboo BAM 23	Love At First Sight/MAYTALS: Life Could Be A Dream	£50
70	Bamboo BAM 25	Soul Shake/Moon Ride	£50

PAUL BRETT('S SAGE)
70	Pye 7N 17974	Three D Mona Lisa/Mediterranean Lazy Heat Wave	£15
70	Pye NSPL 18347	PAUL BRETT SAGE (LP, blue/black label with logo banner on top)	£75
71	Dawn DNLS 3021	JUBILATION FOUNDRY (LP, gatefold sleeve, as Paul Brett's Sage, orange label)	£50
72	Dawn DNLS 3032	SCHIZOPHRENIA (LP, foldout sleeve, as Paul Brett's Sage, lilac label)	£50
73	Bradley's BRADL 1001	PAUL BRETT (LP, fully laminate envelope sleeve with inner)	£30
73	Bradley's BRADL 1004	CLOCKS (LP)	£15
75	Private pressing PF 001	PHOENIX FUTURE (LP, 500 only, numbered on rear sleeve)	£30
70s	Private pressing	MUSIC MANIFOLD (LP, library issue)	£25

(see also Elmer Gantry's Velvet Opera, Fire)

STEVE BRETT (& THE MAVERICKS)
65	Columbia DB 7470	Wishing/Anything That's Part Of You	£180
65	Columbia DB 7581	Sad, Lonely And Blue/Candy	£125
65	Columbia DB 7794	Chains On My Heart/Sugar Shack	£100

(see also 'NBetweens, Slade)

TONY BREVETT
71	Supreme SUP 224	Don't Get Weary/BREVETT ALLSTARS: Version	£20
71	Bullet BU 497	So Ashamed (credited to Tony Bravett)/GREGORY ISAACS: My Only Lover	£30
74	Dip DL 5019	From Dusk To Dawn/JAH ALI: Black Snowfall	£20
74	Dip DL 5028	You Don't Love Me/Version	£20

(see also Melodians, Glen Adams)

BREW
60s	Oak LONDON	Crossroads/Play Your Tune (acetate, unreleased, handwritten labels)	£150

(see also Camel)

TERESA BREWER
SINGLES
55	Vogue Coral Q 72066	Tweedlee Dee/Rock Love	£20

ALBUMS
51	London H-APB 1006	SHOWCASE (10")	£15

(see also Snooky Lanson)

BREWER'S DROOP
72	RCA SF 8301	OPENING TIME (LP, gatefold sleeve, orange label)	£25

(see also McGuinness Flint)

BRIAR
87	UK UKALP 002	CROWN OF THORNS (LP)	£15

DICK BRICE
80s	Sylvan SYL 101R	A FEW ON 'IMS OWN (LP)	£50

BRIDGE
85	Atlantic 9565(T)	Baby, Don't Hold Your Love Back/(Instrumental Version) (12")	£20
00	First Direction FER LP1	CRYING FOR LOVE (2-LP, compilation)	£150

BOBBY BRIDGER
70	Beacon BEA 159	Sugar Shaker/You're In Love	£15

PHOEBE BRIDGERS
20	Dead Oceans DOC254	COPYCAT KILLER (12", p/s)	£50
20	Dead Oceans DOC200LP-C3	PUNISHER (LP, blue and green swirly coloured vinyl)	£50
20	Dead Oceans DOC200LP-C8	PUNISHER (LP, green and black galaxy coloured vinyl)	£60
20	Dead Oceans DOC200LP-C9	PUNISHER (LP, galaxy blue and blue vinyl)	£50
21	Dead Oceans DOC200LP-C9	PUNISHER (LP, repressing, red vinyl with booklet)	£50

SLIM BRIDGES & THE WILD FLOWERS
81 Cricus CIRC 0006   **Rocking Goose/Mole At The Circus** (p/s) **£20**

DEE DEE BRIDGEWATER
78 Elektra K 52067   **JUST FAMILY** (LP)... **£15**

BRIEF ENCOUNTER
10 Jazzman JMANLP 038   **THE BRIEF ENCOUNTER** (LP, reissue) **£30**

MARC BRIERLEY
68 CBS 3857   **Hold On, Hold On, The Garden Sure Looks Good Spread On The Floor/Autograph Of Time** **£15**
60s Transatlantic TRAEP 147   **MARC BRIERLEY** (EP) **£50**
68 CBS 63478   **WELCOME TO THE CITADEL** (LP, orange label with textured surface) **£400**
69 CBS 63835   **HELLO** (LP, gatefold sleeve, stickered sleeve, orange label) **£100**
69 CBS 63835   **HELLO** (LP, gatefold sleeve, no sticker, orange label) **£90**
(see also Tractor)

ANNE BRIGGS
63 Topic TOP 94   **THE HAZARDS OF LOVE** (EP, with leaflet) **£150**
71 Topic 12T 207   **ANNE BRIGGS** (LP) **£300**
71 CBS 64612   **THE TIME HAS COME** (LP)... **£500**
15 Topic 12T2207   **ANNE BRIGGS** (LP, reissue) **£18**
17 Earth EARTHLP 019   **THE TIME HAS COME** (LP, reissue with obi) **£15**
(see also A.L. Lloyd)

BRIAN BRIGGS
80 Bearsville ILPS 9644   **BRIAN DAMAGE** (LP)... **£20**
81 Avatar AALP/BRK 6996   **BRIAN DAMAGE** (LP, reissue) **£15**

DUGGIE BRIGGS
78 It ITEP 5   **THE DUGGIE BRIGGS FLASHES ON IT AGAIN** (EP) **£18**

ANNIE BRIGHT
69 Columbia DB 8587   **Concerning Love/Sneakin' Up On You** **£15**

GREGORY BRIGHT
69 Private Pressing   **ROOM BY GREG** (LP) **£400**

LEN BRIGHT COMBO
86 Empire LEN 1   **Someone Must've Nailed Us Together/Mona** (p/s)...................................... **£18**
86 Empire NICE 1   **THE LEN BRIGHT COMBO** (LP) **£20**
86 Ambassador AMBAS 1   **COMBO TIME!** (LP) **£20**
(see also Wreckless Eric, Milkshakes)

BRIGHT LIGHT
73 Warm WM 01   **Hold Out For Love/Inbetween Dreams**.. **£15**

BRIGHTER
89 Sarah SARAH 019   **Around The World In 80 Days** (p/s, with inserts) **£25**
90 Sarah SARAH 27   **Noah's Ark/I Don't Think It Matters/Does Love Last Forever?** (foldover p/s, postcard insert)... **£25**
91 Sarah SARAH 56   **Poppy Day/Half-Hearted/So You Said** (p/s, insert)...................................... **£25**
92 Sarah SARAH 69   **DISNEY EP** (10", p/s) **£30**
91 Sarah SARAH 404   **LAUREL** (LP, 10")... **£40**

BRIGHT EYES (2)
05 Saddle Creek SCE 79V   **First Day Of My Life/When The President Talks To God** (p/s) **£20**
02 Wichita WEBB 034   **LIFTED OR THE STORY IS IN THE SOIL, KEEP YOUR EAR TO THE GROUND** (LP) .. **£15**
05 Saddle Creek SCE 72   **I'M WIDE AWAKE IT'S MORNING** (LP)... **£15**
10 Wichita WEBB 001 LPTEN   **FEVERS AND MIRRORS** (LP, reissue) **£15**

SARAH BRIGHTMAN
83 Polydor POSP 659   **Rhythm Of The Rain/Action Man** (p/s) **£20**

IAN BRIGHTON
77 Bead Records BEAD 3   **MARSH GAS** (LP) **£50**

BRIGHTWINTER
70s Myrrh MYR 1030   **A BAND FOR ALL SEASONS** (LP)... **£25**

BRILLIANT CORNERS
84 SS20 SS21   **She's Got Fever/Black Water** (red p/s) **£15**
84 SS20 SS21   **She's Got Fever/Black Water** (pink p/s) **£30**
86 McQueen MCQLP2   **WHAT'S IN A WORD** (LP)... **£18**
88 McQueen MCQLP   **SOMEBODY UP THERE LIKES ME** (LP, with inner).. **£15**
00 Vinyl Japan ASKLP 117   **THE BBC SESSIONS** (LP) **£15**

CHARLES BRIMMER
80 Hayley HR 001   **Show And Tell** (1-sided white label test pressings only)............................. **£80**

LOS BRINCOS
67 Page One POF 023   **Lola/Passport** (1st 5,000 in p/s) **£40**
67 Page One POF 023   **Lola/Passport** (no p/s) **£15**
67 Page One POF 031   **Nobody Wants You Now/Train** (as Brincos) **£70**

BRINDLEY BRAE
73 Harmony DB 0002   **VILLAGE MUSIC** (LP, 50 copies only, private pressing with insert) **£150**
(see also Bev Pegg, Away From The Sand)

BRING ME THE HORIZON
10 Let Them Eat Vinyl LETV027LP   **THERE IS A HELL BELIEVE ME I'VE SEEN IT, THERE IS A HEAVEN LET'S KEEP IT A SECRET** (LP, translucent vinyl) **£40**

| 11 | Let Them Eat Vinyl LETV026LP | COUNT YOUR BLESSINGS (LP, reissue, blue vinyl, 1000 only) | £40 |
| 11 | Let Them Eat Vinyl LETV028LP | SUICIDE SEASON (LP, reissue, red vinyl) | £40 |

BRINSLEY SCHWARZ

71	Liberty LBY 15419	Country Girl/Funk Angel	£15
74	United Artists UP 35700	(What's So Funny 'Bout) **Peace, Love And Understanding/ Ever Since You're Gone** (4-prong push-out centre)	£20
70	United Artists UAS 29111	BRINSLEY SCHWARZ (LP, gatefold sleeve, orange/pink label)	£50
70	Liberty LBG 83427	DESPITE IT ALL (LP, gatefold sleeve)	£40
72	United Artists UAS 29217	SILVER PISTOL (LP, with poster)	£35
72	United Artists UAS 29374	NERVOUS ON THE ROAD (LP)	£15
73	United Artists UAS 29489	PLEASE DON'T EVER CHANGE (LP)	£20
78	United Artists UAK 30177	FIFTEEN THOUGHTS OF BRINSLEY SCHWARTZ (LP, poster)	£20

(see also Kippington Lodge, Hitters, Limelight, Nick Lowe, Ernie Graham, Chilli Willi & Red Hot Peppers, Ducks Deluxe)

LLOYD BRISCO

| 64 | Rio R42 | Fabulous Eyes/What You See | £40 |
| 64 | Island WI 187 | Jonah The Master/Mr. Cleveland | £40 |

BRITISH LIONS

| 78 | Vertigo 9102 019 | BRITISH LIONS (LP, with inner sleeve) | £15 |
| 80 | Cherry Red ARED 7 | TROUBLE WITH WOMEN (LP) | £15 |

(see also Mott The Hoople, Medicine Head)

BRITISH SEA POWER

12	Golden Chariot GOLDEN CHARIOT 006-011	BSP EP BOX SET (6 x CD box set)	£120
02	Rough Trade RTRADLP 090	THE DECLINE OF BRITISH SEA POWER (2-LP, insert)	£25
05	Rough Trade RTRADLP 200	OPEN SEASON (LP)	£18
08	Rough Trade RTRADLP 300	DO YOU LIKE ROCK MUSIC? (LP)	£18
11	Rough Trade RTRADLP 549	VALHALLA DANCEHALL (2-LP)	£18
13	Rough Trade RTRADLP 666	MACHINERIES OF JOY (LP, with CD EP)	£15

(see also The Wurzels)

BRITISH SHOES

| 79 | NWJ SRTS/79/CUS 542 | Running From Mummy/Where Would We Be Without Shoes (p/s) | £100 |
| 79 | NWJ SRTS/79/CUS 542 | Running From Mummy/Where Would We Be Without Shoes (no p/s) | £50 |

BRITISH WALKERS

| 65 | Pye International 7N 25298 | I Found You/Diddley Daddy | £25 |

BRITT

| 66 | Piccadilly 7N 35273 | You Really Have Started Something/Leave My Baby Alone | £30 |

MEL BRITT

| 00 | Goldmine Soul Supply GS 003 | She'll Come Running Back/ANDERSON BROTHERS: I Can See Him Loving You (reissue) | £20 |

TINA BRITT

| 65 | London HLC 9974 | The Real Thing/Teardrops Fell | £70 |
| 65 | London HLC 9974 | The Real Thing/Teardrops Fell (DJ Copy) | £100 |

BUDDY BRITTEN & REGENTS

62	Piccadilly 7N 35075	My Pride, My Joy/Long Gone Baby	£15
62	Decca F 11435	Don't Spread It Around/The Beat Of My Heart	£15
63	Oriole CB 1827	If You Gotta Make A Fool Of Somebody/Money	£15
63	Oriole CB 1839	Hey There/I'll Cry No More	£15
63	Oriole CB 1889	Money/Sorrow Tomorrow	£20

(see also Regents)

TERRY BRITTEN

| 69 | Columbia DB8580 | 2000 Weeks/Bargain Day | £100 |

CHRIS BRITTON

| 69 | Page One POLS 022 | AS I AM (LP, gatefold sleeve, blue/silver label) | £400 |

(see also Troggs)

JEFF BRITTON & THE SPITFIRES

| 76 | Decca F13643 | Rub Out/Breakwood | £20 |

BRIXTON MARKET

| 69 | Beacon BEA 138 | Children Get Ready/Bangarang | £15 |
| 69 | Beacon SBEAB 8 | BLACK FUNK (LP) | £15 |

JO BROADBERY & THE STANDOUTS

| 80 | Revenge REVLP-1 | JO BROADBERRY AND THE STANDOUTS (LP) | £20 |

BROADCAST

96	Wurlitzer Jukebox WJ 6	Accidentals/We've Got Time (p/s, with sticker)	£40
96	Duophonic DS 45-16	THE BOOK LOVERS EP (12", p/s, 2,000)	£25
99	Warp 7WAP 125	Echo's Answer/Test Area	£15
00	Warp WAP 141	EXTENDED PLAY TWO EP (12", p/s)	£15
03	Warp WAP 162	Pendulum/Small Song IV/One Hour Empore/Still Feel Like Tears/Violent Playground/Minus Two (12" p/s)	£15
09	Warp WARPCD 189T	MOTHER IS THE MILKY WAY (Tour CD in card sleeve)	£35
97	Warp WARPLP 52	WORK & NON WORK (LP)	£40
00	Warp WARPLP 65	THE NOISE MADE BY PEOPLE (LP, gatefold sleeve, insert)	£40
03	Warp WARPLP 106	HAHA SOUND (LP)	£30
05	Warp WARPLP 136	TENDER BUTTONS (LP)	£30
06	Warp WARPLP 146	THE FUTURE CRAYON (2-LP)	£40

MINT VALUE £

09	Warp WARPLP 189	INVESTIGATES WITCH CULTS OF THE RADIO AGE (LP, with the Focus Group)	£30
13	Warp WARPLP 233	BERBERIAN SOUND STUDIO (LP)	£15

BROADSIDE
71	Lincolnshire Ass. LA 4	THE GIPSY'S WEDDING DAY (10" LP)	£50
73	Topic 12TS 228	THE MOON SHONE BRIGHT (As The Broadside From Grimsby) (LP, blue label)	£40
75	Guildhall GHS 5	SONGS FROM THE STOCKS (LP)	£80
75	Guildhall GHS 12	DRIVE THE DARK AWAY (LP)	£50

BROADSIDE OUTCASTS
78	Profile GMOR 154	ABO EP	£20

PETER BROGGS
79	Hit Run HITDD 13	Higher Field Marshall (Feat. Prince Far I)/I And I A The Chosen One/PRINCE FAR I & BRIGADIER JAM DOWN : Loved By Everyone (12")	£50
80	Cha Cha CHAD 25	Never Forget Jah/CORNELL CAMBELL: Rainbow (12")	£70
80	Selena SO 006	Jah Golden Throne/DEXTER MCKINTYRE : 144.00 Saints	£60
79	Shashamane IMF 004	PROGRESSIVE YOUTH (LP)	£50

BROKEN BONES
83	Fall Out FALL LP 028	BROKEN BONES (LP)	£15
84	Stoned Spliff 1	LIVE AT THE 100 CLUB (LP)	£20

(see also Discharge)

BROKEN BOW
87	Sodium	Vagrant/Bite Back	£25

BROKEN GLASS (1)
75	Capitol E-ST 11510	BROKEN GLASS (LP, with insert)	£18

(see also Chicken Shack, Warhorse, Miller Anderson, Bronco)

BROKEN GLASS (2)
84	Streetwave MKHAN 17	Style Of The Street (12")	£20

BROKEN ROSE
86	Exhibit 1 EXL 006	WAR TEARS (LP)	£100

(see also Bizarre Unit, Paul Nova)

JOHN BROMLEY
68	Polydor 56244	What A Woman Does/My My	£30
68	Polydor 56287	And The Feeling Goes/Sweet Little Princess	£20
69	Polydor 56305	Melody Fayre/Sugar Love	£40
69	Polydor 56340	Hold Me Woman/Weather Man	£30
69	Atlantic 584 289	Kick A Tin Can/Wonderland Avenue U.S.A.	£30
69	Polydor 583 048	SING (LP)	£100

(see also Fleur De Lys)

BRONCO
70	Island WIP 6096	Lazy Now/A Matter Of Perspective	£20
70	Island ILPS 9124	COUNTRY HOME (LP, gatefold sleeve, pink 'i' label)	£40
70	Island ILPS 9124	COUNTRY HOME (LP, gatefold sleeve, 'pink rim palm tree' label)	£20
71	Island ILPS 9161	ACE OF SUNLIGHT (LP, gatefold sleeve, 'pink rim palm tree' label)	£25
73	Polydor 2383 215	SMOKIN' MIXTURE (LP, gatefold sleeve)	£20

(see also Alan Bown Set)

BRONX
06	Wichita WEBB 114S	White Guilt/Rockers NYC (red vinyl, p/s)	£15

BRONX CHEER
72	Dawn DNLS 3034	GREATEST HITS VOLUME 3 (LP, gatefold sleeve with insert, lilac label)	£20

MICHAEL BROOK
92	4AD CAD 2007	COBALT BLUE (LP, featuring Brian Eno)	£40

TONY BROOK & BREAKERS
64	Columbia DB 7279	Meanie Genie/Ooh Poo Pah Doo (in p/s)	£200
64	Columbia DB 7279	Meanie Genie/Ooh Poo Pah Doo	£80
65	Columbia DB 7444	Love Dances On/I Won't Hurt You	£15

BROOK BROTHERS
62	Pye NEP 24155	BROOK BROTHERS (EP)	£15
61	Pye NPL 18067	BROOK BROTHERS (LP)	£20

GARY BROOKER
81	Chrysalis CHS 2396	Leave The Candle/Chasing The Chop (Eric Clapton guest appearance)	£100

PAUL BROOKES
78	State ETAT 21	STEPS FROM BEYOND (LP)	£20

HOWARD S BROOKING
82	H.S.B. S82/CUS/1596	In The Autumn Gold/Checkmate (no p/s)	£15

BROOKLYN
80	Rondelet ROUND 3	I Wanna Be A Detective (p/s)	£30
81	Rondelet ROUND 6	Hollywood/Late Again (p/s)	£20
80	Rondelet ABOUT 3	YOU NEVER KNOW WHAT YOU'LL FIND (LP)	£30

BABA BROOKS
63	Island WI 078	5 O'Clock Whistle/African Blood (by Blues Masters)	£50
63	Island WI 096	Bank To Bank (Parts 1 & 2)	£40
63	Island WI 127	Three Blind Mice/BILLY & BOBBY: We Ain't Got Nothing	£30
63	R&B JB 125	Water Melon Man/STRANGER COLE: Things Come To Those Who Wait	£40
64	Black Swan WI 137	Portrait Of My Love/STRANGER COLE: Goodbye Peggy	£40

64	Black Swan WI 412	Jelly Beans/ERIC MORRIS: Sampson	£40
64	Black Swan WI 414	Key To The City/ERIC MORRIS: Solomon Grundie	£40
64	Black Swan WI 434	Spider/Melody Jamboree	£40
64	Black Swan WI 438	Cork Foot/HERSANG COMBO: B.B.C. Channel 2	£40
65	Black Swan WI 442	Musical Workshop/DUKE WHITE: Be Wise	£40
65	Black Swan WI 444	Bus Strike/DUKE WHITE: Sow Good Seeds	£40
65	Black Swan WI 451	Ethiopia/ARCHIBALD TROTT: Promised Land	£40
65	Black Swan WI 456	Dreadnaught/PLAYGIRLS: Looks Are Deceiving	£65
65	Black Swan WI 466	Baby Elephant Walk/DON DRUMMOND: Don's Special	£30
65	Ska Beat JB 189	Dr. Decker/OWEN & LEON SILVERA : Woman	£40
65	Ska Beat JB 220	One Eyed Giant (with His Band)/DYNAMITES: Walk Out On Me	£50
65	Island WI 229	Guns Fever/DOTTY & BONNIE: Don't Do It	£45
65	Island WI 233	Independent Ska/STRANGER & CLAUDETTE: Seven Days	£45
65	Island WI 235	Duck Soup/ZODIACS: Renegade	£150
65	Island WI 239	Vitamin A/ALTON ELLIS: Dance Crasher	£60
65	Island WI 241	Teenage Ska/ALTON ELLIS: You Are Not To Blame	£70
65	Rio R 061	Shenk I Sheck (& Band)/SHENLEY & HIACYNTH: Set Me Free	£50
66	Doctor Bird DB 1042	The Clock (& Band)/LYN TAITT & COMETS & SILVERTONES: Raindrops	£50
66	Doctor Bird DB 1046	Jam Session (with His Band)/CONQUERORS: What A Agony	£60
67	Ska Beat JB 268	One Eyed Giant (with His Band)/DYNAMITES: Walk Out On Me (reissue)	£30

(see also Blues Masters, Eric Brooks, Stranger & Patsy, Riots, Joey Smith, Saints, Richard Brothers, Derrick Morgan, Lord Tanamo, Lord Brisco, Hippy Boys, Roy Panton, Higgs & Wilson, Vinley Gayle, Joe White, Stranger & Patsy)

CEDRIC 'IM' BROOKS
75	Tropical AL046	South African Reggae/Part 2	£15
78	Water Lily ARCO LP 009	UNITED AFRICA (LP)	£25
03	Honest Jon's HJRLP4	THE MAGICAL LIGHT OF SABA (2LP, envelope sleeve, die cut inner)	£70

CHUCK BROOKS
69	Soul City SC 116	Black Sheep/I've Got To Get Myself Together	£20
69	Soul City SC 116	Black Sheep/I've Got To Get Myself Together (DJ Copy)	£75

DALE BROOKS
66	Stateside SS 553	I Wanna Be Your Girl/Like Other Girls Do	£30

DONNIE BROOKS
61	London HA-N 2391	THE HAPPIEST DONNIE BROOKS (LP)	£20

ELKIE BROOKS
64	Decca F 11928	Something's Got A Hold On Me/Hello Stranger	£50
64	Decca F 11983	Nothing Left To Do But Cry/Strange Though It Seems	£40
65	Decca F 12061	The Way You Do The Things You Do/Blue Tonight	£40
65	HMV POP 1431	He's Gotta Love Me/When You Appear	£40
65	HMV POP 1431	He's Gotta Love Me/When You Appear (DJ Copy)	£80
65	HMV POP 1480	All My Life/Can't Stop Thinking Of You	£20
66	HMV POP 1512	Baby Let Me Love You/Stop The Music	£30
66	HMV POP 1512	Baby Let Me Love You/Stop The Music (DJ Copy)	£90
74	Chrysalis CHS 2069	Sacrifice/ALICE COOPER: I'm Flash (p/s, unissued, promo only)	£35
84	A & M SCREEN 1	SCREEN GEMS (CD, beware of copies!)	£50

(see also Dada, Vinegar Joe, Steve York's Camelo Pardalis, Elki & Owen)

JULIAN BROOKS
70	Pye 7N17996	Justine/Lazy Guy	£25

MERLYN BROOKS
76	Jama JAMA 0027	I've Been Down/CONSCIOUS MINDS: I've Been Dubbing	£25
76	Pacific PAC 002	Mechanical Body/Mechanical Dub	£25

MIKE BROOKS
79	Hit Run HIT DD 9	Love Is Like A Password/Feeling Of Reggae (12")	£25
79	Hit Run HIT DD 23	Long Long Time/Dub In Time	£30
76	Burning Sounds BSLP 1026	WHAT A GATHERING (LP)	£15

NORMAN BROOKS & G-BOYS
54	London L 1166	Hello Sunshine/You're My Baby	£15
54	London L 1202	Somebody Wonderful/You Shouldn't Have Kissed Me The First Time	£15
54	London L 1228	A Sky-Blue Shirt And A Rainbow Tie/This Waltz With You	£15
54	London HL 8015	I'm Kinda Crazy/I'd Like To Be In Your Shoes, Baby	£15
54	London HL 8041	I Can't Give You Anything But Love (solo)/GO-BOYS: Johnny's Tune	£15

PAM BROOKS
70	Big BG 307	Oh Me Oh My/ANSELL COLLINS: Staccato	£18

RAY BROOKS
72	Polydor 2001 334	Pictures/On My Own	£15
71	Polydor 2310 140	LEND ME SOME OF YOUR TIME (LP, gatefold)	£30

ROY BROOKS AND THE ARTISTIC TRUTH
10	Jazzman JMANLP 034	ETHNIC EXPRESSIONS (LP, reissue)	£20

WES BROOKS
77	ATA ATA 1003	Lay Down Your Arms/Version	£70

BROOKS & JERRY
68	Direction 58-3267	I Got What It Takes Parts 1 & 2	£15
68	Direction 58-3267	I Got What It Takes Parts 1 & 2 (DJ Copy)	£30

BIG BILL BROONZY/CHICAGO BILL
58	Vogue V 2351	Guitar Shuffle/When Did You Leave Heaven	£30

MINT VALUE £

55	Vogue EPV 1024	HEY BUD BLUES (EP)	£20
56	Vogue EPV 1074	SINGS THE BLUES (EP)	£20
56	Vogue EPV 1107	GUITAR SHUFFLE (EP)	£20
56	Pye Jazz NJE 1005	MISSISSIPPI BLUES VOLUME 1 (EP)	£20
56	Pye Jazz NJE 1015	MISSISSIPPI BLUES VOLUME 2 (EP)	£20
56	Melodisc EPM7 65	KEEP YOUR HANDS OFF (EP)	£15
57	Vogue LAE 12009	BIG BILL BLUES (LP)	£25
57	Philips BBL 7113	BIG BILL BROONZY (LP)	£25
58	Vogue LAE 12063	THE BLUES (LP)	£25
58	Pye Nixa Jazz NJL 16	TRIBUTE TO BIG BILL (LP)	£25
59	Tempo TAP 23	AN EVENING WITH BIG BILL BROONZY (LP)	£25

BIG BILL BROONZY & PETE SEEGER

64	Xtra XTRA 1006	IN CONCERT (LP)	£20
66	Verve Folkways VLP 5006	IN CONCERT (LP, reissue, also stereo SVLP 506)	£15

(see also Pete Seeger)

BIG BILL BROONZY/SONNY BOY WILLIAMSON [I]

65	RCA Victor RD 7685	BIG BILL AND SONNY BOY (LP)	£30

(see also Sonny Boy Williamson [I])

BIG BILL BROONZY, SONNY TERRY & BROWNIE MCGHEE

64	Xtra XTRA 1004	BIG BILL BROONZY/SONNY TERRY/BROWNIE McGHEE (LP)	£30

(see also Sonny Terry & Brownie McGhee, Washboard Sam)

BROTH

71	Mercury 6338 032	BROTH (LP)	£60

BROTHER BUNG

68	Avenue BEV 1054	BLUES CRUSADE (EP)	£15

(see also Bob Pearce)

BROTHER DAN ALLSTARS

68	Trojan TR 601	Donkey Returns/Tribute To Sir K.B.	£40
68	Trojan TR 602	Eastern Organ/JIVERS: Our Love Will Last	£40
68	Trojan TR 603	Hold Pon Them/OWEN GRAY: Answer Me	£30
68	Trojan TR 607	Read Up/Gallop	£30
68	Trojan TR 608	Another Saturday Night/Bee's Knees	£30
68	Trojan TBL 101	LET'S CATCH THE BEAT (LP)	£100
69	Trojan TRL 1	FOLLOW THAT DONKEY (LP)	£100

(see also Pooch Jackson)

BROTHER SUSAN

74	EMI EMI 2117	See My Fingers Fly/Full Blooded Natural Man	£18
74	EMI EMI 2174	Ride Ride Ride/Flash	£18

BROTHER TREVOR & U BROWN

78	Matumbi Music MM005	Skip Away/Selassi I (12")	£25

(see also Matumbi)

BROTHERHOOD (1)

69	Philips BF 1756	Paper Man/Give It To Me Now	£15

BROTHERHOOD (2)

91	Bite It BITE 1	DESCENDANTS OF THE HOLOCAUST (EP)	£30
91	Bite It BITE 2	DESCENDANTS OF THE HOLOCAUST (remix 12")	£15

BROTHERHOOD OF BREATH

74	Ogun OG 100	LIVE AT WILLISAU (LP, with Chris McGregor)	£20

(see also Chris McGregor's Brotherhood Of Breath, Mark Charig)

BROTHERHOOD OF LIZARDS

89	Deltic DELT LP5	LIZARDLAND (LP)	£20

(see also Gypp, Martin Newall, Cleaners From Venus)

BROTHERHOOD OF MAN

71	Deram DM 327	Reach Out Your Hand/Better Tomorrow	£20

(see also Sue & Sunny, Stockingtops)

BROTHERLY LOVE

67	CBS 2978	Ocean Of Tears/Mr Average Man	£15

BROTHERS & SISTERS (U.K.)

68	Private pressing	ARE WATCHING YOU (LP)	£90

BROTHERS & SISTERS (U.S.)

69	CBS 63746	DYLAN'S GOSPEL (LP)	£15

BROTHERS GRIMM

66	Ember EMB 222	A Man Needs Love/Looky Looky	£50

BROTHERS KANE

66	Decca F 12448	Walking In The Sand/Won't You Stay Long	£25

(see also Sarstedt Brothers, Peter Lincoln, Peter Sarstedt, Wes Sands, Eden Kane)

BROTHERS TWO

68	Action ACT 4513	Here I Am, In Love Again/I'm Tired Of You Baby	£30

BROTHERS (2)

89	BASL 007T	Brothers Groove/Funky Paella (12", p/s)	£15

EDGAR BROUGHTON BAND

69	Harvest HAR 5001	Evil/Death Of An Electric Citizen	£15
69	Harvest SHVL 757	WASA WASA (LP, 1st pressing, gatefold sleeve, no EMI box on label with "the	£170

		Gramophone Co" and "sold in U.K." label text)	
69	Harvest SHVL 757	**WASA WASA** (LP, 1st pressing, gatefold sleeve, no EMI box on label without "the Gramophone Co" and "sold in U.K." label text) **£100**	
69	Harvest SHVL 757	**WASA WASA** (LP, 2nd pressing, gatefold sleeve, later issue with EMI box on label) **£50**	
69	Harvest SHVL 757	**WASA WASA** (LP, 2nd pressing variation, gatefold sleeve, no EMI box on label or "the Gramophone Co" and "sold in U.K." label text) **£40**	
70	Harvest SHVL 772	**SING BROTHER SING** (LP, gatefold sleeve, with lyric insert, no EMI on label) **£100**	
71	Harvest SHVL 791	**THE EDGAR BROUGHTON BAND** (LP, 1st pressing, textured gatefold) **£100**	
71	Harvest SHVL 791	**THE EDGAR BROUGHTON BAND** (LP, 2nd pressing with EMI boxed logo on side 1 only, textured gatefold) **£40**	
72	Harvest SHTC 252	**IN SIDE OUT** (LP, multifold gatefold sleeve with lyric sheet, some copies come with Harvest "Letter of introduction".) **£100**	
73	Harvest SHVL 810	**OORA** (LP, wraparound card sleeve in clear artwork plastic bag, inner sleeve).................**£80**	
74	Harvest SHVL 772	**SING BROTHER SING** (LP, reissue gatefold, EMI box on label) **£25**	
74	Harvest SHVL 791	**THE EDGAR BROUGHTON BAND** (LP, reissue, boxed EMI on label)..................................**£25**	
75	Harvest SHSM 2001	**A BUNCH OF 45s** (LP) **£18**	
76	Nems NEL 6006	**BANDAGES** (LP with lyric inner sleeve) **£20**	
88	BGO BBOLP 7	**SING BROTHER SING** (LP, reissue, gatefold sleeve)...**£18**	

AL BROWN (JAMAICA)

71	Banana BA 360	**No Soul Today/RUFFIANS: Where Did I Go Wrong** (B-side actually "Bang Shang Alang" by Peter Austin & Hortense Ellis) **£35**
71	Fab FAB 186	**Ain't Got No Soul/TEARDROPS: I Got A Feeling** **£30**

ARTHUR BROWN (CRAZY WORLD OF)

65	Lyntone LYN 770/1	**You Don't Know** (as Arthur Brown & Diamonds)**/DIAMONDS: You'll Be Mine** (Reading University Rag Week flexidisc) **£60**
68	Track 612 005	**THE CRAZY WORLD OF ARTHUR BROWN** (LP, mono, black/silver label).......................**£120**
68	Track 613 005	**THE CRAZY WORLD OF ARTHUR BROWN** (LP, stereo, black/silver labels) **£80**
74	Gull GULP 1008	**DANCE** (LP)..**£15**
77	Gull GUD 2003/4	**THE LOST EARS** (2-LP, gatefold sleeve, as Arthur Brown's Kingdom Come) **£22**
88	Reckless 2 RECK	**STRANGELANDS** (LP, unreleased) **£0**

(see also Kingdom Come, Nick Greenwood, Atomic Rooster)

BARRY BROWN

78	Justice JUDIS 104	**Step It Up/Youthman Version** (12", with SHORTY THE PRESIDENT).............................**£20**
78	Tribesman TM 008	**Unity Is Strength/DRUMMIE BENJI: Higher Region** (12")..**£35**
79	Justice JUDIS 126	**Big Big Politician/No Wicked Shall Enter** (12") **£30**
79	Justice JUDIS 135	**We Can't Live Like This/From Creation I Man There** (12") **£30**
79	Sufferer's Heights SUFF 003	**I Love Sweet Jah Jah/RANKING JOE : Youthman Promotion** (12").............................**£40**
80	Daddy Kool DKR 124	**Peace And Love** (with Ranking Toyan) **JAH THOMAS & ROOTS RADICS: Adapter Chapter** (12") **£50**
80	Strong Like Sampson SLSD 07	**Natty Dread Nah Run/ANTHONY JOHNSON: Life Is Not Easy** (12") **£40**
80	Strong Like... SLSD 010	**Don't You Try/ANTHONY JOHNSON: Hey Mr Rich Man** (12") **£40**
80	Attack TACK 17	**Mr. CID/SCIENTIST AND ROOTS RADICAL BAND: King Tubby's Rockers** (12") **£35**
80	Black Roots BR 009	**Things And Time/Time Dub** (12") **£25**
80	Attack TACK 21	**Separation/Scientist In A Fine Style** (12")...**£50**
80	Attack TACK 23	**Living As A Brother/SCIENTIST: Second Hand Girl** (12")..**£30**
80	Justice JUDIS 135	**We Can't Live Like This/From Creation I Man Free** (12") **£40**
81	City Sounds CSD 003	**Warmonger/ROOTS RADICS BAND: Radical Style** (12", green vinyl) **£50**
81	Greensleeves GRED 68	**Give Israel Another Try/Sweet Sixteen** (12") **£30**
82	Selena SD004	**Them Ha Fi Get A Beatin'/ROOTS RADICS BAND : Stop The Fighting** (12") **£40**
82	Selena SD008	**Physical Fitness/HEPTONES : Lovers Feeling** (12", blue vinyl) **£35**
83	Downbeat DBD 004	**Belly Full** (with General Saint)**/WAYNE WADE: Little Suzie** (12")..............................**£40**
84	Greensleeves GRED 150	**Belly Move/Why The World Stay So** (12") **£20**
03	Trojan TACK 23	**Living As A Brother/Caring For My Sister** (12") **£15**
79	Paradise PDL 006	**STEP IT UP YOUTHMAN** (LP)...**£25**
80	Trojan TRLS 191	**COOL PON YOUR CORNER** (LP)..**£50**
80	Black Roots BRLP 1000	**I'M NOT SO LUCKY** (LP)...**£18**
80	Third World TWS 937	**SHOWCASE** (LP) **£40**
84	Uptempo UT 003	**ROOTS & CULTURE** (LP) **£35**

BEN BROWN

67	Polydor 56198	**Ask The Lonely/Sidewinder** **£50**

BUSTER BROWN

60	Melodisc 1559	**Fannie Mae/Lost In A Dream** **£70**
65	Sue WI 368	**Fannie Mae/Lost In A Dream** (reissue)...**£40**
67	Island WI 3031	**My Blue Heaven/Two Women** **£20**
69	Blue Horizon 57-3147	**Sugar Babe/I'm Going, But I'll Be Back** **£45**
60s	No Cat No	**B. AND BUSTER BROWN** (EP, with B. Brown) **£20**

BUSTY BROWN

68	Doctor Bird DB 1158	**Here Comes The Night/Don't Look Back** **£50**
69	Upsetter US 304	**What A Price/How Can I Forget?** **£40**
69	Upsetter US 308	**To Love Somebody/BLEECHERS: Farmer's In The Den** **£40**
69	Punch PH 10	**Broken Heart/Tribute To A King** **£40**
70	Punch PH 38	**Greatest Love/I Love You Madly** **£20**
70	Escort ES 822	**Fight For Your Right/MEDITATORS: Soul Fight** (Busty Top A Pop) (B-side actually "Soul Fight" by Busty Brown)...**£25**
70	Escort ES 845	**Man Short** (with Gaytones)**/DAVE BARKER: She Want It**...**£20**
70	Gas GAS 154	**I Love You Madly/Greatest Love** **£15**
70	High Note HS 048	**Man Short** (with Gaytones)**/GAYTONES: Another Version** **£15**
71	Bullet BU 476	**Never Love Another/Version** **£15**

			MINT VALUE £

| 71 | Punch PH 72 | You Inspire Me/UPSETTERS: Version | £35 |
| 71 | Pama Supreme PS 356 | Throw Away Your Gun/TWINKLE BROTHERS: Sad Song | £30 |

CHARLES BROWN (BAND)

56	Vogue V 9061	I'll Always Be In Love With You/Soothe Me	£400
56	Vogue V 9061	I'll Always Be In Love With You/Soothe Me (78)	£15
57	Vogue V 9065	Confidential/Trouble Blues	£300
57	Vogue V 9065	Confidential/Trouble Blues (78 rpm)	£15

(see also Brown Brothers)

CLARENCE 'GATEMOUTH' BROWN

65	Vocalion VE 170161	CLARENCE 'GATEMOUTH' BROWN (EP)	£90
72	Python PLP 26	CLARENCE 'GATEMOUTH' BROWN VOL. 1: 1948-1953 (LP)	£25
72	Python PLP 27	CLARENCE 'GATEMOUTH' BROWN VOL. 2: 1956-1965 (LP)	£25

CLIFFORD BROWN (& HIS GROUP)

54	Vogue LDE 042	CLIFFORD "BROWNIE" BROWN QUARTET (10" LP)	£40
55	Vogue LDE 121	THE CLIFFORD BROWN SEXTET (10" LP)	£40
58	Emarcy EJL 1278	STUDY IN BROWN (LP)	£35

(see also Art Farmer, Sonny Rollins, Max Roach)

DANNY BROWN

| 16 | Warp WARPLP 276X | ATROCITY EXHIBITION (2-LP, electric blue vinyl) | £40 |

DENNIS BROWN

70	Bamboo BAM 56	Love Grows/SOUND DIMENSION: Less Problem	£50
70	Banana BA 309	No Man Is An Island/SOUL SISTERS: Another Night	£50
71	Banana BA 336	Never Fall In Love/Make It With You	£50
71	Ocean OC 001	Little Green Apples/SOUND DIMENSION: Version	£25
72	Duke DU 139	What About The Half/What About The Half Version	£30
72	Explosion EX 2068	Black Magic Woman/PHILL PRATT ALL STARS: Black Magic Woman Pt 2	£25
72	Pressure Beat PR 5513	Money In My Pocket/JOE GIBBS ALLSTARS: Money Love	£25
72	Randy's RAN 526	Cheater/TOMMY McCOOK & IMPACT ALLSTARS: Harvest In The East	£25
72	Randy's RAN 528	Meet Me On The Corner (actually unknown instrumental)/IMPACT ALLSTARS: Version	£20
73	Ashanti ASH 402	It's Too Late/Song My Mother Used To Sing	£18
73	Jackpot JP 813	He Can't Spell/CRYSTALITES: Acid Version	£20
73	Smash SMA 2327	Concentration/Version	£20
77	Observer OBS 999	Jah Is Watching/Hustling/Rock On/Murder Observer Style (12" with DILLINGER)	£40
77	Observer OB 003	Tenement Yard/Kill Landlord/HORACE ANDY: Them Never Tell I/Teacher Gal (12", with Ranking Buckers)	£25
77	DEB 0002	Half/Troubled World (12")	£20
78	DEB DDDEB 010	Oh What A Day/Man Next Door (12")	£20
78	Diamond DM DC 702	Children Of Israel/Version (12", p/s)	£25
79	Laser LAS 20	Slave Driver/Version (12")	£20
79	Laser LAS 20(T)	Slave Driver/Dub Driver (12")	£15
79	Observer OBS 902	Blessed Are The Men (The Pill)/JUNIOR DELGADO : Cry Cry (12")	£20
79	3 in 1 SKLP 001	Tribulation (with Jah Bop)/JUNIOR BYLES: Can You Feel It (12")	£25
80	High Times HT 001	Blood City/FREDDIE McGREGOR : Natural Collie (12")	£35
80	Pratt PP 30	Black Magic Woman/Version (12")	£40
80	DEB DEB 039	I Don't Want To Be No General/General (Version) (12" with Ranking Dread)	£25
83	Tad's TRD 21483	Easy Take It Easy/Easy Version (12")	£25
83	Natty Congo NCDM 020	Breaking Down The Barriers/Dubbing The Barriers (12")	£40
83	Taxi IPR 2059	Revolution/Dub Revolution (12")	£15
84	Blue Moon BMS 1002	Slave Driver/Version (12")	£15
84	Greensleeves GRED 167	It's Magic/PAD ANTHONY: Crazy Love (12")	£25
86	Jakki JM 468	Rebel With A Cause/JACKIE MITTOO: Trade Mark (12")	£25
80s	Live & Love LLD 117	Little Village/Version (12")	£25
73	Trojan TRLS 57	SUPER REGGAE & SOUL HITS (LP)	£30
75	Trojan TRLS 107	JUST DENNIS (LP)	£20
77	DEB DEBLP 01	WOLF AND LEOPARDS (LP)	£25
77	Pioneer PIO LP2	MEETS HARRY HIPPY (LP)	£50
78	Lightning LIP 7	VISIONS OF (LP)	£20
78	Laser LASL 1	WORDS OF WISDOM (LP, stickered sleeve with free 12" Money In My Pocket)	£25
78	Laser LASL 1	WORDS OF WISDOM (LP)	£20
80	Laser LASL 6	JOSEPH'S COAT OF MANY COLOURS (LP)	£18
86	Trojan TRSL 238	THE EXIT (LP)	£15

(see also Big Youth & Dennis Brown, Hugh Roy, Big Youth, Sound Dimension)

DENNIS BROWN & ASWAD

| 80 | Simba SM003 | Promised Land/More Dub (12") | £20 |

DUSTY BROWN

| 61 | Starlite ST45 058 | Please Don't Go/Well You Know | £15 |

FAY BROWN

| 55 | Columbia SCM 5185 | Unchained Melody/I Was Wrong | £15 |

GABRIEL BROWN

| 77 | Policy Wheel PW 4592 | GABRIEL BROWN AND HIS GUITAR (LP, withdrawn) | £15 |

GLEN BROWN

68	Blue Cat BS 131	Way Of Life (with Joe White & Trevor Shield)/ KARL BRYAN & LYN TAITT: I'm So Proud	£175
70	Summit SUM 8502	Collie And Wine/BEVERLEY'S ALLSTARS: Version	£40
70	Songbird SB 1021	Love I/CRYSTALITES: Heavy Load	£25
72	Songbird SB 1081	Smokey Eyes (with Crystalites)/Smokey Eyes (Version)	£20

73	Downtown DT 5072	Wedden Skank/BERRY SIMPSON: Daughter A Whole Lotta Sugar	£25
79	Kingley Sounds REX 4	Marcus Garvey Words/SLYFORD WALKER: Africa (12")	£35
96	Blood & Fire BAFLP 015	TERMINATION DUB (LP, as Glen Brown & King Tubby)	£25

GLENMORE BROWN & HOPETON LEWIS
| 68 | Fab FAB 42 | Girl You're Cold/Soul Man | £130 |

(see also Hopeton Lewis & Glenmore Brown)

GREGG BROWN
| 84 | Beau-Jolly BJ 1004 | Baby Talk/Baby Talk (Edit) (p/s) | £20 |
| 84 | Beau-Jolly 12 BJ 1004 | Baby Talk (Club Mix)/Extended Mix (12", p/s) | £40 |

HENRY BROWN
| 61 | '77' LA 12-5 | HENRY BROWN BLUES (LP) | £30 |

HUX BROWN & SCOTTY
| 71 | High Note HS 056 | Unbelievable Sounds/GAYTONES: Unbelievable Sounds Version | £25 |

IAN BROWN
01	Polydor 5872 847	F.E.A.R/F.E.A.R. (Instrumental) (stickered p/s)	£20
98	Polydor 539 916-1	UNFINISHED MONKEY BUSINESS (LP, gatefold, booklet)	£60
99	Polydor 543 141-1	GOLDEN GREATS (LP, gold vinyl, printed inner)	£60
01	Polydor 589 126-1	MUSIC OF THE SPHERES (LP)	£60
02	Polydor SPHERE2	REMIXES OF THE SPHERES (2x12" Promo Sampler)	£30
02	Polydor 065 927-1	REMIXES OF THE SPHERES (2LP, printed inners)	£50
05	Fiction 987289	THE GREATEST (2LP, printed inners)	£30
07	Fiction 174 341-4	THE WORLD IS YOURS (2LP, gatefold, printed inners)	£90
09	Fiction 2717 470	MY WAY (LP, printed inner)	£150
12	Fiction (No Cat No)	COLLECTED (10CD, LP, DVD boxed set, book, print, certificate of authenticity, 1000 only)	£150
16	Fiction SOLARIZED LP 1	SOLARIZED (LP, vinyl issue of 2004 CD)	£60

(see also Stone Roses)

IRVING BROWN
70	Bamboo BAM 36	Today/SOUND DIMENSION: Young Gifted And Black Version	£40
70	Bamboo BAM 58	I'm Still Around/Run Come	£40
70	Bamboo BAM 61	Let's Make It Up (actually by Larry Marshall)/BURNING SPEAR: Free	£40
71	Bamboo Now BN 1003	Now I'm Alone/Funky Night	£40

(see also Larry Marshall)

JAMES BROWN (& FAMOUS FLAMES)
| 78 | Polydor 2391 384 | TAKE A LOOK AT THOSE CAKES (LP) | £15 |

SINGLES
60	Parlophone R 4667	Think/You've Got The Power (with Famous Flames)	£50
60	Fontana H 273	This Old Heart/Wonder When You're Coming Home	£35
62	Parlophone R 4922	Night Train/Why Does Everything Happen To Me (with Famous Flames)	£40
62	Parlophone R 4952	Shout And Shimmy/Come Over Here (with Famous Flames)	£30
63	London HL 9730	Prisoner Of Love/Choo-Choo (Locomotion) (with Famous Flames)	£20
63	London HL 9775	These Foolish Things/(Can You) Feel It (Part 1) (with Famous Flames)	£20
64	Philips BF 1368	Out Of Sight/Maybe The Last Time (& His Orchestra)	£25
64	Sue WI 360	Night Train/Why Does Everything Happen To Me (with Famous Flames)	£35
65	London HL 9945	Have Mercy Baby/Just Won't Do Right (with Famous Flames)	£18
65	London HL 9990	Papa's Got A Brand New Bag Parts 1 & 2 (with Famous Flames)	£20
65	Ember EMB S 216	Tell Me What You're Gonna Do/Lost Someone (p/s)	£40
65	Ember EMB S 216	Tell Me What You're Gonna Do/Lost Someone	£20
65	Philips BF 1458	Try Me/Papa's Got A Brand New Bag	£20
66	Philips BF 1481	New Breed Parts 1 & 2	£20
66	Pye International 7N 25350	I Got You (I Feel Good)/I Can't Help It (I Just Do-Do-Do) (with Famous Flames)	£15
66	Pye International 7N 25379	Money Won't Change You Parts 1 & 2 (with Famous Flames)	£15
67	Pye International 7N 25441	Get It Together Parts 1 & 2 (with Famous Flames)	£15
68	Polydor 56740	I Can't Stand Myself/There Was A Time	£15
68	Polydor 56540	That's Life/Please, Please, Please (with Famous Flames)	£15
72	Polydor 2066 185	King Heroin/Theme From King Heroin	£20
72	Polydor 2066 283	What My Baby Needs Now Is A Little More Lovin'/ This Guy's In Love With You (with Lyn Collins)	£15

EPs
64	London RE 1410	JAMES BROWN AND THE FAMOUS FLAMES (EP, flip-back p/s, 4-prong push-out centre)	£90
64	Ember EMB EP 4549	I DO JUST WHAT I WANT	£40
66	Pye Intl. NEP 44059	I GOT YOU	£40
66	Pye Intl. NEP 44068	I'LL GO CRAZY	£40
67	Pye Intl. NEP 44072	PRISONER OF LOVE	£40
67	Pye Intl. NEP 44076	HOW LONG DARLING	£40
67	Pye Intl. NEP 44088	BRING IT UP	£45
70	Polydor 580 701	TURN IT LOOSE	£30

ALBUMS
64	London HA 8177	PURE DYNAMITE! (as James Brown & Famous Flames)	£80
64	London HA 8184	LIVE AT THE APOLLO (as James Brown & Famous Flames)	£60
64	Ember EMB 3357	TELL ME WHAT YOU'RE GONNA DO	£45
64	Philips BL 7630	SHOWTIME	£30
65	London HA 8203	UNBEATABLE 16 HITS	£45
65	London HA 8231	PLEASE, PLEASE, PLEASE (as James Brown & Famous Flames)	£80
65	Philips BL 7664	GRITS AND SOUL	£60

MINT VALUE £

65	London HA 8240	JAMES BROWN TOURS THE U.S.A. (with Famous Flames)	£50
66	London HA 8262	PAPA'S GOT A BRAND NEW BAG (as James Brown & Famous Flames)	£50
66	Philips BL 7697	JAMES BROWN PLAYS JAMES BROWN TODAY AND YESTERDAY	£40
66	Pye Intl. NPL 28074	I GOT YOU (I FEEL GOOD)	£50
66	Philips BL 7718	JAMES BROWN PLAYS NEW BREED	£20
66	Pye Intl. NPL 28079	IT'S A MAN'S MAN'S MAN'S WORLD	£30
66	Pye Intl. NPL 28097	THE JAMES BROWN CHRISTMAS ALBUM	£40
67	Pye Intl. NPL 28093	MIGHTY INSTRUMENTALS	£40
67	Philips (S)BL 7761	HANDFUL OF SOUL	£25
67	Pye Intl. NPL 28099	PAPA'S GOT A BRAND NEW BAG (reissue)	£20
67	Pye Intl. NPL 28100	MR. EXCITEMENT	£30
67	Polydor 582 703	THE JAMES BROWN SHOW (live)	£20
67	Pye Intl. NPL 28103	SINGS RAW SOUL	£30
67	Pye Intl. NPL 28104	LIVE AT THE GARDEN	£35
68	Philips (S)BL 7823	JAMES BROWN PLAYS THE REAL THING	£25
68	Polydor 184 136	I CAN'T STAND MYSELF	£20
69	Polydor 184 148	SOUL FIRE	£15
69	Mercury 20133 SMCL	JAMES BROWN SINGS OUT OF SIGHT	£25
69	Polydor 583 729/30	LIVE AT THE APOLLO VOLUME TWO (2-LP)	£18
69	Polydor 583 741	SAY IT LOUD - I'M BLACK AND I'M PROUD	£20
69	Polydor 583 768	IT'S A MOTHER	£20
69	Polydor 643 317	THIS IS ... JAMES BROWN	£15
70	Polydor 583 742	GETTIN' DOWN TO IT	£20
70	Polydor 184 319	THE POPCORN	£20
70	Polydor 2343 010	AIN'T IT FUNKY	£25
71	Polydor 2625 004	SEX MACHINE (2LP)	£20
71	Polydor 2310 022	SOUL ON TOP	£20
71	Polydor 2310 029	IT'S A NEW DAY	£20
71	Polydor 2310 089	SUPER BAD (LP)	£20
72	Polydor 2659 011	REVOLUTION OF THE MIND: RECORDED LIVE AT THE APOLLO VOL. III (2LP, gatefold)	£20
72	Polydor 2391 033	THERE IT IS (LP)	£20
73	Polydor 2659 018	GET ON THE GOOD FOOT (2LP, gatefold)	£25
73	Polydor 2490 117	BLACK CAESAR (LP, OST)	£40
73	Polydor 2391 084	SLAUGHTER'S BIG RIP-OFF (LP, OST)	£30
74	Polydor 2391 116	SOUL CLASSICS VOLUME TWO (LP)	£15
74	Polydor 2659 030	THE PAYBACK (2LP. gatefold. US pressing stickered for Europe)	£40
74	Polydor 2659 036	HELL (2LP, gatefold, labels state title is 'It's Hell')	£40
74	Polydor 2391 164	REALITY (LP)	£15
75	Polydor 2391 166	SOUL CLASSICS VOLUME THREE (LP)	£15
75	Polydor 2391 175	SEX MACHINE TODAY (LP)	£15
75	Polydor 2391 197	EVERYBODY'S DOIN' THE HUSTLE AND DEAD ON THE DOUBLE BUMP (LP)	£15
75	Polydor 2391 214	HOT (LP)	£15
76	Polydor 2391 228	GET UP OFFA THAT THING (LP)	£18
76	Polydor 2391 258	BODYHEAT (LP)	£25
77	Polydor 2391 300	MUTHA'S NATURE (James Brown & the New JBs) (LP)	£20
84	Polydor REVO 1	ROOTS OF A REVOLUTION (2LP, gatefold)	£20
86	Urban URBDP 11	IN THE JUNGLE GROOVE (2LP)	£40
91	Polydor 845 828-1	SEX MACHINE - THE VERY BEST OF JAMES BROWN (LP)	£25
01	Polydor/Simply Vinyl SVLP 314	MOTHERLODE (2LP, vinyl issue of 1988 CD, PVC outer)	£50
05	Polydor 981 472-6	GREATEST BREAKBEATS (3LP, printed inners)	£35

(see also Lyn Collins, JBs, Maceo & All King's Men, Nat Kendrick & Swans)

JAMES BROWN (JAMAICA)

71	Punch PH 76	Don't Say/TRANS AM ALLSTARS: Don't Say Version	£15
72	Ashanti ASH 408	Mama Don't Want To See You/Mama Don't Want To See You Version	£15
75	Mango MAN 1001	Stop The War In Babylon/Dub In Peace	£15

JIM EDWARD (BROWN) & MAXINE BROWN

55	London HL 8123	Itsy Witsy Bitsy Me/Why Am I Falling?	£30
55	London HLU 8166	Your Love Is Wild As The West Wind/Draggin' Mainstreet	£30
55	London HLU 8200	You Thought I Thought/Here Today And Gone Tomorrow (B-side with Bonnie)	£30

JOE BROWN (& BRUVVERS)

59	Decca F 11185	People Gotta Talk/Comes The Day (solo, triangular centre)	£15

(see also Vicki Brown, Browns Homebrew)

KENT BROWN & RAINBOWS

68	Fab FAB 53	When You Going To Show Me How/Come Ya Come Ya	£15

(see also Kent & Jeannie, Sir D's Group)

LAWRENCE BROWN

56	Columbia 33CX 10046	SLIDE TROMBONE (LP)	£35

LEROY BROWN

78	Revue REVD 10	Blood A Go Run/Taxi (12")	£40
79	Jah Lion JL DC 606	Gone Gone/TRISTAN PALMER: Gone Clear (12")	£60

LES BROWN (JR)

60s	Vocalion VA 8011	WILDEST DRUMS YET (LP)	£15

MARION BROWN

69	Polydor 583724	PORTO NOVO (LP)	£60

MAXINE BROWN
61	London HLU 9286	All In My Mind/Harry, Let's Marry	£40
62	HMV POP 1102	Am I Falling In Love/Promise Me Anything (DJ Copy)	£250
62	HMV POP 1102	Am I Falling In Love/Promise Me Anything	£150
63	Stateside SS 188	Ask Me/Yesterday's Kisses	£40
64	Pye International 7N 25272	Oh No Not My Baby/You Upset My Soul	£30
65	Pye International 7N 25299	It's Gonna Be Alright/You Do Something To Me	£30
65	Pye International 7N 25317	One Step At A Time/Anything For A Laugh	£40
67	Pye International 7N 25410	I've Got A Lot Of Love Left In Me/Hold On (I'm Comin') (B-side with Chuck Jackson)	£30
67	Pye International 7N 25434	Since I Found You/Gotta Find A Way	£25
70	Major Minor MM 709	Reason To Believe/I Can't Get Along Without You	£25
85	Kent 047	LIKE NEVER BEFORE (LP)	£15

(see also Chuck Jackson & Maxine Brown)

NAPPY BROWN (& HIS BAND)
55	London HL 8145	Don't Be Angry/It's Really You	£300
55	London HL 8145	Don't Be Angry/It's Really You (78)	£15
55	London HLC 8182	Pitter Patter/There'll Come A Day	£250
55	London HLC 8182	Pitter Patter/There'll Come A Day (78)	£15
57	London HLC 8384	Little By Little/I'm Getting Lonesome (& His Band) (gold lettering on label)	£250
57	London HLC 8384	Little By Little/I'm Getting Lonesome (& His Band) (silver lettering on label)	£100
58	London HLC 8760	It Don't Hurt No More/My Baby	£50
58	London HLC 8760	It Don't Hurt No More/My Baby (78)	£15

NOEL BROWN
68	Island WI 3149	Man's Temptation/Heartbreak Girl	£80
69	Songbird SB 1012	By The Time I Get To Phoenix/Heartbreak Girl	£40
70	Bullet BU 423	Phoenix (actually by "By The Time I Get To Phoenix")/Heartbreak Girl	£30

(see also Bunny Brown)

PAMELA BROWN
70	Joe JRS 8	People Are Running/CRITICS: School Days	£15

PATRICK BROWN
82	Kufe EB 003	Fantasy/On The Right Track (12")	£40

PETE BROWN(& PIBLOKTO)
69	Parlophone R 5767	The Week Looked Good On Paper/Morning Call (as Pete Brown & His Battered Ornaments, promo p/s)	£65
69	Parlophone R 5767	The Week Looked Good On Paper/Morning Call (as Pete Brown & His Battered Ornaments)	£22
69	Harvest HAR 5008	Living Life Backwards/High Flying Electric Bird (as Pete Brown & Piblokto!)	£20
70	Harvest HAR 5023	Can't Get Off The Planet/Broken Magic (with His Battered Ornaments)	£15
70	Harvest HAR 5028	Flying Hero Sandwich/My Last Band (as Pete Brown & Piblokto!)	£25
69	Harvest SHVL 752	A MEAL YOU CAN SHAKE HANDS WITH IN THE DARK (LP, as Pete Brown & His Battered Ornaments, with "Sold in U.K" label text on 4 lines, stereo)	£350
69	Harvest SHVL 752	A MEAL YOU CAN SHAKE HANDS WITH IN THE DARK (LP, as Pete Brown & His Battered Ornaments, without "Sold in U.K" label text on 4 lines, stereo	£100
70	Harvest SHVL 768	THE ART SCHOOL DANCE GOES ON FOREVER (LP, as Pete Brown & Piblokto!, gatefold sleeve, no EMI on label)	£350
70	Harvest SHVL 782	THOUSANDS ON A RAFT (LP, as Pete Brown & Piblokto!, gatefold sleeve, no EMI on label)	£300
73	Deram SML 1103	THE NOT FORGOTTEN ASSOCIATION (LP, with Graham Bond)	£120
77	Harvest SHSM 2017	MY LAST BAND (LP, as Pete Brown & Piblokto)	£20
82	Discs Intl. INTLP 1	PARTY IN THE RAIN (LP, with Ian Lynn, private pressing)	£15
12	Pure Pleasure PPAN SHVL 752	A MEAL YOU CAN SHAKE HANDS WITH IN THE DARK (2-LP, reissue)	£20

(see also Battered Ornaments, Graham Bond & Pete Brown, Deke Leonard, Cream)

PETER BROWN
77	T.K TKR 82514	DO YOU WANNA GET FUNKY WITH ME? (LP)	£15

POLLY BROWN
73	Pye NSPL 18396	POLLY BROWN (LP)	£20

RANDY BROWN
87	Threeway WAYLP 1	WELCOME TO MY ROOM (LP)	£20

ROY BROWN
57	London HLP 8398	I'm Sticking With You/Party Doll (gold label print)	£400
57	London HLP 8398	I'm Sticking With You/Party Doll (later silver print pressing)	£150
57	London HLP 8398	I'm Sticking With You/Party Doll (gold label print, later silver) (78)	£15
57	London HLP 8448	Saturday Night/Everybody	£500
57	London HLP 8448	Saturday Night/Everybody (78)	£15

RUTH BROWN (& HER RHYTHMAKERS)
55	London HL 8153	Mambo Baby/Mama (He Treats Your Daughter Mean) (with Rhythmakers)	£250
55	London HL 8153	Mambo Baby/Mama (He Treats Your Daughter Mean) (with Rhythmakers) (78)	£15
55	London HLE 8210	As Long As I'm Moving/R.B. Blues (with Her Rhythmakers)	£250
55	London HLE 8210	As Long As I'm Moving/R.B. Blues (with Her Rhythmakers) (78)	£15
56	London HLE 8310	I Want To Do More/Sweet Baby Of Mine	£150
56	London HLE 8310	I Want To Do More/Sweet Baby Of Mine (78)	£15
57	London HLE 8401	Mom Oh Mom/I Want To Be Loved (But Only By You)	£150
57	London HLE 8401	Mom Oh Mom/I Want To Be Loved (But Only By You) (78)	£15
57	Columbia DB 3913	Lucky Lips/My Heart Is Breaking Over You	£250
57	Columbia DB 3913	Lucky Lips/My Heart Is Breaking Over You (78)	£15
57	London HLE 8483	When I Get You Baby/One More Time	£80

MINT VALUE £

57	London HLE 8483	When I Get You Baby/One More Time (78)	£15
58	London HLE 8552	A New Love/Look Me Up	£80
58	London HLE 8552	A New Love/Look Me Up (78)	£15
58	London HLE 8645	Just Too Much/Book Of Lies	£80
58	London HLE 8645	Just Too Much/Book Of Lies (78)	£15
58	London HLE 8757	This Little Girl's Gone Rockin'/Why Me	£60
58	London HLE 8757	This Little Girl's Gone Rockin'/Why Me (78)	£15
58	London HL 7061	This Little Girl's Gone Rockin'/Why Me (export issue)	£60
59	London HLE 8887	Jack O' Diamonds/I Can't Hear A Word You Say	£25
59	London HLE 8887	Jack O' Diamonds/I Can't Hear A Word You Say (78)	£15
59	London HLE 8946	I Don't Know/Papa Daddy	£25
59	London HLE 8946	I Don't Know/Papa Daddy (78)	£35
60	London HLE 9093	Don't Deceive Me/I Burned Your Letter	£25
61	London HLK 9304	Sure 'Nuff/Here He Comes	£25
55	London REE 1038	THE QUEEN OF R&B (EP)	£150
63	Philips BE 12537	GOSPEL TIME (EP)	£50
60	London Jazz LTZ-K 15187	LATE DATE WITH RUTH BROWN (LP)	£60
62	Philips 652 012 BL	ALONG COMES RUTH (LP)	£50
63	Philips 652 020 BL	GOSPEL TIME (LP)	£40
64	Atlantic ATL 5007	THE BEST OF RUTH BROWN (LP, plum label)	£100
76	President PTLS 1067	SUGAR BABE (LP)	£20
84	Charly CRB 1069	ROCKIN' WITH RUTH (LP)	£15

RUTH BROWN/JOE TURNER
56	London REE 1047	THE KING AND QUEEN OF R&B (EP, 2 tracks each)	£200

SANDY BROWN('S JAZZ BAND)
53	Esquire 20-022	SANDY BROWN (10" LP, with Bobby Mickleburgh)	£20
56	Tempo TAP 3	SANDY'S SIDEMEN PLAYING COMPOSITIONS BY AL FAIRWEATHER (LP)	£25
57	Nixa Jazz Today NJL 9	McJAZZ (LP)	£15
66	Fontana TE1 7473	SANDY BROWN ALL STARS (LP)	£15
69	Fontana SFJL 921	HAIR AT ITS HAIRIEST (LP, as Sandy Brown & His Gentlemen Friends)	£15

(see also Wally Fawkes)

SHIRLEY BROWN
75	Stax STXS 2032	I Can't Give You Up/It Ain't No Fun	£20
75	Stax STX 1031	WOMAN TO WOMAN (LP)	£20
79	Stax STX 2014	FOR THE REAL FEELING (LP)	£15

(see also Oliver Sain)

STU BROWN & BLUESOLOGY
67	Polydor 56195	Since I Found You Baby/Just A Little Bit	£300

(see also Bluesology, Elton John)

U BROWN
75	Fay FM 606	Jah Jah Whip Them/Skanking in Dub	£30
76	Fay Music FM 608	Wet Up Your Pant/Ringo Don't Take Your Gun To Town (with Little Youth)	£20
77	Klik KLP 9018	SATTA DREAD (LP)	£60
78	Virgin Frontline FL 1003	MR. BROWN SOMETHING (LP)	£18
79	Virgin Frontline FL 1030	CAN'T KEEP A GOOD MAN DOWN (LP)	£15
84	VSLP 5005	SUPERSTAR (LP)	£15

VICKI BROWN
77	Power Exchange PXL 012	FROM THE INSIDE (LP)	£15

VINCENT BROWN
70	Gas GAS 128	Look What You're Going To Do/Hold On To What You Have Got	£20

WILLIAM BROWN
71	Ackee ACK 128	I'm Alone/BELTONES: Soul People	£45

BROWN BROTHERS
59	Vogue V 9131	Let The Good Times Roll/You're Right, I'm Left	£150
59	Vogue V 9131	Let The Good Times Roll/You're Right, I'm Left (78)	£15

(see also Charles Brown)

CHARLEY BROWNE
78	Hurry! LT1113	Feeling Under The Weather/Sez Lez (no p/s)	£15

DUNCAN BROWNE
68	Immediate IM 070	On The Bombsite/Alfred Bell	£25
68	Immediate IMSP 018	GIVE ME, TAKE YOU (LP, insert, lilac label with "sold in U.K." label text)	£500
73	RAK SRKA 6754	DUNCAN BROWNE (LP, gatefold sleeve)	£50

FRIDAY BROWN(E)
66	Parlophone R 5396	Getting Nowhere/And (To Me He Meant Everything) (as Friday Browne)	£25
66	Fontana TF 736	32nd Love Affair/Born A Woman	£150
71	Philips 6308 074	FRIDAY BROWN (LP)	£40

(see also High Society, Manchester Mob, Graham Gouldman)

JACKSON BROWNE
74	Asylum K2 43007	LATE FOR THE SKY (LP, quadrophonic)	£15
85	Asylum K53070	RUNNING ON EMPTY (LP, Nimbus Supercut, mail order only via through Hi Fi Today)	£50

SANDRA BROWNE (& BOYFRIENDS)
63	Columbia DB 4998	By Hook Or By Crook/Johnny Boy (as Sandra Browne & Boyfriends)	£15
63	Columbia DB 7109	You'd Think He Didn't Know Me/Mama Never Told Me	£15
65	Columbia DB 7465	Knock On Any Door/I Want Love	£15

THOMAS F. BROWNE
71   Vertigo 6325 250   WEDNESDAY'S CHILD (LP, gatefold sleeve, small swirl label)................................£400
(see also Gary Wright, The Gladiators)

TOBY BROWNE
64   Parlophone 5192   Play The Music, Keep On Dancing/Child..£15

DUKE BROWNER
79   Grapevine GRP 145   Crying Over You/Crying Over You (Instrumental) £20
(see also Kaddo Strings)

BROWNS
59   RCA RD 27153   SWEET SOUNDS BY THE BROWNS (LP, mono)..£20
59   RCA RD 27153/SF 5052   SWEET SOUNDS BY THE BROWNS (LP, stereo)................................£20
(see also Jim Edward & Maxine Brown)

BROWN'S FERRY FOUR
54   Parlophone CMSP 11   I Need The Prayers/Through The Pearly Gates (with Clyde Moody, export issue) £15
(see also Grandpa Jones, Merle Travis)

BROWNS HOME BREW
72   Bell BELLS 208   BROWN'S HOME BREW (LP)..£100
74   Vertigo 6360 114   TOGETHER (LP, spaceship label)..£15
(see also Joe Brown)

BROWN SUGAR (1)
77   Lovers Rock CJ 613   I'm In Love With A Dreadlocks/Version £30
77   Lovers Rock CJ 614   Hello Stranger/Version £30
77   Lovers Rock CJ 619   Black Pride/Version (p/s) £30
77   Lovers Rock CJ 624   Do You Really Love Me/Version £30
77   Lucky LY 6041   For All Eternity/For All Eternity (Version) £18
78   Lovers Rock LR DIS 07   Forever My Darling/Free/Albatross (12") £100
79   Studio 16 WE 014   You And Your Smiling Face/Version (12") £20
79   Studio 16 WE 017   Our Reggae Music/Dub (12") £15
80   Studio 16 WE 092   Dreaming Of Zion/Version (12") £40
80   Studio 16 WE 106   Confession Hurts/Version (12") £30
80   Studio 16 WE 113   Runaway Love/Version (12") £30
80   Black Roots BRLP 1000   NOT SO LUCKY (LP) £15
(see also Kofi)

ANNETTE (REIS) & VICTOR BROX
74   Sonet SNTF 663   ROLLIN' BACK (LP)..£15
(see also Aynsley Dunbar Retaliation)

DAVE BRUBECK (QUARTET)
54   Vogue LDE 090   DAVE BRUBECK TRIO (10" LP)..£20
54   Vogue LDE 095   DAVE BRUBECK QUARTET (10" LP)..£20
54   Vogue LDE 104   DAVE BRUBECK QUARTET VOL. 2 (10" LP) £20
55   Vogue LDE 114   DAVE BRUBECK QUARTET VOL. 3 (10" LP) £15
57   Fontana TFL 5017   DAVE DIGS DISNEY (LP) £15
59   Vogue LAE 12008   THE FABULOUS DAVE BRUBECK TRIO AND OCTET (LP) £15
59   Fontana STFL 523   TIME OUT (LP, stereo) £60
59   Fontana TFL 5085   TIME OUT (LP, mono) £50
59   CBS BPG 62068   TIME OUT (LP) £40
59   Fontana TFL 5071   GONE WITH THE WIND (LP, also stereo STFL 501) £15
60   Vogue LAE 12114   DAVE BRUBECK QUARTET FEATURING PAUL DESMOND (LP) £15
60   Fontana (S)TFL 532   THE RIDDLE (LP) £18
60   Fontana (S)TFL 530   SOUTHERN SCENE (LP) £15
61   CBS BPG 62078   TIME FURTHER OUT (LP) £20
61   Fontana TFL 5160   TIME FURTHER OUT (LP) £20
62   CBS BDG 62013   COUNTDOWN TIME IN OUTER SPACE (LP) £18
64   CBS SPBG 62431   JAZZ IMPRESSIONS OF JAPAN (LP) £20
(see also Jimmy Rushing, Carmen McRae)

JACK BRUCE
65   Polydor BM 56036   I'm Getting Tired (Of Drinking And Gambling)/Rootin' Tootin' £100
71   Polydor 2058 153   The Consul At Sunset/Letter Of Thanks £15
69   Polydor 583 058   SONGS FOR A TAILOR (LP, laminated gatefold sleeve) £18
70   Polydor 2343 033   THINGS WE LIKE (LP) £18
71   Polydor 2310 070   THINGS WE LIKE (LP, reissue) £15
71   Polydor 2310 107   HARMONY ROW (LP, gatefold sleeve) £20
(see also Alexis Korner's Blues Incorporated, Cream, Manfred Mann, Graham Bond Organisation, John Mayall, West Bruce & Laing, Lifetime, Rocket 88, Carla Bley, Duffy Power, Cozy Powell)

TOMMY BRUCE (& BRUISERS)
64   Columbia DB 7387   Over Suzanne/It's Drivin' Me Wild £15
65   Polydor BM 56006   Boom Boom/Can Your Monkey Do The Dog (with Bruisers) £20
66   RCA RCA 1535   Monster Gonzales/I Hate Getting Up In The Morning £20
61   Columbia SEG 8077   KNOCKOUT (EP) £50

HEIDI BRÜHL
69   Philips BF 1768   The Drifter/Berlin £200
69   Philips BF 1768   The Drifter/Berlin (DJ Copy) £250

BRUMBEATS
64   Decca F 11834   Cry Little Girl, Cry/I Don't Understand £15

MINT VALUE £

BRUNNING (HALL) SUNFLOWER BLUES BAND
68	Saga FID 2118	**BULLEN STREET BLUES** (LP, as Brunning Sunflower Blues Band, with black/silver label)	...£30
69	Saga EROS 8132	**TRACKSIDE BLUES** (LP, black/silver labels)	£45
70	Saga EROS 8150	**I WISH YOU WOULD** (LP, as Brunning Sunflower Blues Band, with black/silver labels)	£75
71	Gemini GM 2010	**THE BRUNNING/HALL SUNFLOWER BLUES BAND** (LP, with white/red labels)	£120

(see also Five's Company, Fleetwood Mac, Leaf Hound)

BRUNO
66	Parlophone R5450	**Wonderboy/Window In My Room**	£20
66	Parlophone R5507	**The English Girl/The Driver**	£20

TONY BRUNO
68	Capitol CL 15534	**What's Yesterday/Small Town, Bring Down**	£50

BRUTE FORCE
69	Apple APPLE 8	**King Of Fuh/Nobody Knows** (unissued)	£2000

TONY BRUTUS
82	Intense INT 013	**Water Pistol/Shooting Water** (12")	£100
13	Intense/Pressure Sounds PST110	**Water Pistol/Water Pistol** (Alt Vocal)/**Water Pistol** (Dub) (12")	£25

CARL BRYAN
69	Trojan TR 673	**Red Ash/SILVERTONES: Bluebirds Flying Over**	£30
69	Duke DU 13	**Soul Pipe/Overproof**	£30
69	Camel CA 22	**Run For Your Life/TWO SPARKS: When We Were Young**	£30
69	Gas GAS 133	**Stagger Back/The Creeper**	£50
69	Gas GAS 134	**Walking The Dead/TREVOR & KEITH: Got What You Want**	£30

(see also Cannon Ball & Johnny Melody, King Cannon, Vincent Foster, Hugh Malcolm, King Cannonball, Glen Brown, Shenley Duffas, Alton Ellis, Kid Gungo, Jackie Mittoo, Johnny Moore, Joe White, Royals)

RAD BRYAN
71	Techniques TE 909	**Jumping Jack/ANSELL COLLINS: Point Blank**	£30
71	Bullet BU 463	**Shock Attack/Cuban Waltz**	£30
71	Big Shot BI 559	**Just Do The Right Things/Corporal Jones**	£20
71	Big Shot BI 591	**I'll Be Right There** (actually by Techniques)/**PLAYBOYS: Hot Pants Rock**	£30
71	Big Shot BI 592	**My Best Girl/My Best Girl Version**	£20
71	Black Swan BW 1410	**Girl You Rock My Soul/Version**	£35

WES BRYAN
58	London HLU 8607	**Lonesome Love/Tiny Spaceman**	£40
59	London HLU 8978	**Honey Baby/So Blue Over You**	£50

BRYAN & BRUNELLES
65	HMV POP 1394	**Jacqueline/Louie Louie**	£45

ANITA BRYANT
66	CBS 202026	**Another Year, Another Love/My Mind's Playing Tricks On Me Again**	£50
61	London HA-L 2381	**IN MY LITTLE CORNER OF THE WORLD** (LP)	£30

DON BRYANT
70	London HA-U/SH-U 8409	**PRECIOUS SOUL** (LP)	£40

JOHN BRYANT (1)
65	Fontana H 625	**Tell Me What You See/Poor Unfortunate Me**	£15
71	Polydor 2383069	**JOHN BRYANT** (LP, gatefold sleeve)	£20

JOHN BRYANT (2)
69	Decca 12894	**She's In Need Of Love**	£25
68	MCA MU 1020	**Columbine/I Bring The Sun**	£20

LAURA K. BRYANT
58	London HLU 8551	**Bobby/Angel Tears**	£20

MARIE/MARGARET BRYANT
61	Kalypso XX 27	**Water Melon/Tomato**	£15
61	Kalypso XX 28	**Don't Touch Me Nylons/Little Boy**	£15
62	Melodisc MLP 12 132	**DON'T TOUCH ME NYLONS** (LP, with sleeve)	£30

RUSTY BRYANT
57	London HB-D 1066	**RUSTY BRYANT** (10" LP)	£30

SANDRA BRYANT
68	Major Minor MM 553	**Out To Get You/There's No Lock Upon My Door**	£30

GAVIN BRYARS
75	Obscure OBS 1	**THE SINKING OF THE TITANIC** (LP, 1st pressing with grey labels)	£70
76	Obscure OBS 1	**THE SINKING OF THE TITANIC** (LP, 2nd pressing with red labels)	£60
78	Obscure OBS 8	**MACHINE MUSIC** (split LP with John White)	£20
87	EG EGED 21	**THE SINKING OF THE TITANIC** (LP, reissue)	£20

(see also Brian Eno)

CALUM BRYCE
68	Condor PS 1001	**Lovemaker/I'm Glad**	£475

BERYL BRYDEN('S BACK-ROOM SKIFFLE)
56	Decca F 10823	**Casey Jones/Kansas City Blues**	£20
57	Decca (no cat. no.)	**Rock Me/This Train** (test pressing, with Alexis Korner & Cyril Davies)	£60

(see also Alexis Korner, Cyril Davies)

BETSY BRYE
59	Columbia DB 4350	**Sleep Walk/Daddy Daddy** (Gotta Get A Phone In My Room)	£25

BRYGADA KRYZYS
82   Fresh Records FRESH 13   BRYGADA KRYZYS (LP) £25

B'S
70s private pressing   IN YOUR BONNET (LP) £35

B SIDE
93   B Promo B Side   Rip Piece Off/Can't Slow Me Down (12") £20

B.T.B.
68   Liberty LBF 15067   Do It To 'Em/Sparrows And Daisies £15

B.T. EXPRESS
75   Pye Intl. NSPL 28207   DO IT (TIL YOU'RE SATISFIED) (LP)..£15
75   EMI International INA 1501   NON-STOP (LP) £15

B.T.P. FOLDERS
80   Future Earth FER 005   Radio/All Of A Sudden (p/s) £50

B TROOP
81   Illuminated JAMS 6   EUROPEANS (LP) £15

B12
94   B12 15   B12 (12", 4-track promo only, 10 copies pressed) £40
93   Warp WAPLP 9LTD   ELECTRO - SOMA (2-LP, orange vinyl) £40
96   Warp WARPLP 37   TIME TOURISTS (2-LP) £20
07   B12 B1215   Practopia (12")...£20
(see also Redcell, Musicology)

BUBA & SHOP ASSISTANTS
85   Villa 21 002   Something To Do/Dreaming Backwards (p/s, with insert in poly bag) £75
(see also Shop Assistants, Pastels)

BUBBLEGUM
68   Philips BF1677   Little Red Bucket/With The Sun In Your Hair...£45

BUBBLES (1)
63   Duke DK 1001   The Wasp/Bopping In The Barnyard (matrix: DK 1001A-1, plays Rocking Crickets by Hot Toddy's)..£18

BUBBLES (2)
75   Decca F 13583   This Is Where The Hurdie Gurdie Heebie Geebie Greenie Meenie Man Came In/Zap N' Cat..£35

BUCCA
82   Plant Life PLR 039   THE HOLE IN THE HARPERS HEAD (LP)..£20

GILLY BUCHANAN
80   Toe TOE 002   Me No Mix/PATRICK ANDY: Ain't No Me (12") £80

PAUL BUCHANAN
12   Newsroom Records ROOMLP01   MID AIR (LP, printed inner, ltd ed, 180g) £100
22   Newsroom Records ROOMLP02   MID AIR (2LP, 10th anniversary edition, gatefold) £25
(see also Blue Nile)

LINDSEY BUCKINGHAM
84   Mercury MERX 168   Go Insane (Extended Remix)/(Go Insane (Dub Mix)/Play In The Rain Part 1 (12" white label promo with 1 on side 1 and 2 on side 2)...£100
13   Back On Black RCV078LP   SEEDS WE SOW (2-LP, reissue, clear red vinyl) £80
(see also Fleetwood Mac)

BUCKINGHAM-NICKS
74   Polydor 2066 398   Don't Let Me Down Again/Races Are Run...£15
73   Polydor 2391 013   BUCKINGHAM-NICKS (LP, with insert, with stickered sleeve) £40
73   Polydor 2391 093   BUCKINGHAM-NICKS (LP, with insert, without stickered sleeve) £35
81   Polydor 2482 378   BUCKINGHAM-NICKS (LP, reissue with insert)..£25
(see also Lindsay Buckingham, Fleetwood Mac)

BUCKINGHAMS (U.S.)
67   CBS 2995   Hey Baby/And Our Love..£15
68   CBS 2640   Don't You Care/Why Don't You Love Me £25

BOB BUCKLE
73   Ash ALP 107 S   COME LISTEN TO (LP)..£50

JEFF BUCKLEY
93   Big Cat ABB 61XCD   LIVE AT SIN-E EP (Mojo Pin/Eternal Life/Je N'en Connais Pas La Fin/The Way Young Lovers Do (CD))...£30
95   Columbia 662042 1   Last Goodbye (Edit)/Lover, You Should've Come Over (Live And Acoustic In Japan)/Tongue (Live) (10", p/s, 5000 only)...£30
95   Columbia 661498   Last Goodbye/Last Goodbye (Full)/So Real (Live)/Dream Brother (Live) (12")...............£30
95   Columbia 88697098847   Hallelujah/I Know It's Over (Live 1995) (p/s, numbered sleeve, 2,700 only, blue/black vinyl)...£20
04   Big Cat ABB 61X   LIVE AT SIN-E (12" reissue) £40
94   Columbia 475928   GRACE (LP, with insert) £60
98   Columbia 3C 67229   SKETCHES FOR MY SWEETHEART THE DRUNK (3-LP) £40
99   Simply Vinyl SVLP 077   GRACE (LP, reissue, insert) £25
07   Columbia 4979721   MYSTERY WHITE BOY LIVE 95-96 (LP) £20

SEAN BUCKLEY & BREADCRUMBS
65   Stateside SS 421   It Hurts Me When I Cry/Everybody Knows..£70

MINT VALUE £

TIM BUCKLEY

67	Elektra EKSN 45008	Aren't You The Girl/Strange Street Affair Under Blue	£15
70	Straight S 4799	Happy Time/So Lonely	£20
66	Elektra EKL 4004	TIM BUCKLEY (LP, dark orange label, black lettering, mono)	£75
67	Elektra EKS 74004	TIM BUCKLEY (LP, dark orange label, black lettering, stereo)	£75
67	Elektra EKL 318	GOODBYE AND HELLO (LP, dark orange label, gatefold sleeve, mono)	£70
67	Elektra EKS 7318	GOODBYE AND HELLO (LP, dark orange label, gatefold sleeve, stereo)	£75
68	Elektra EKS 74045	HAPPY SAD (LP, light orange label, silver lettering)	£70
69	Straight STS 1060	BLUE AFTERNOON (LP)	£80
70	Elektra 2410 005	LORCA (LP)	£50
71	Straight STS 1064	STARSAILOR (LP)	£100
74	Warner Bros K 46176	GREETINGS FROM L.A. (LP, gatefold sleeve, postcard)	£25
74	Elektra K42072	HAPPY SAD (LP, reissue, butterfly label)	£20
74	Discreet K 49201	SEFRONIA (LP)	£25
74	Discreet K 59204	LOOK AT THE FOOL (LP)	£25
76	Elektra K42079	GOODBYE AND HELLO (LP, reissue, inside loading gatefold sleeve, Butterfly label)	£20
84	Elektra ELK 42079	GOODBYE AND HELLO (LP, reissue, red label)	£15
90	Demon DFIEND 200	DREAM LETTER - LIVE IN LONDON 1968 (2-LP)	£25

SID BUCKNOR PRODUCTIONS

76	Lyntone/Tropical Sounds DSR SB1008/1009	DUB SENSATION (LP, 50 copies, promo only in stamped white card sleeve)	£250

BUCKY & STRINGS

62	Salvo SLO 1807	Lolita's On The Loose/Lonely Island (99 copies only)	£20

BILLY BUDD

69	Page One POF 138	Alice Long (You're Still My Favourite Girlfriend)/The Straight Life	£20

HAROLD BUDD

78	Obscure OBS 10	PAVILLION OF DREAMS (LP)	£20

HAROLD BUDD & BRIAN ENO

80	Editions EG EGAMB 002	AMBIENT 2 (THE PLATEAUX OF MIRRORS) (LP)	£40
87	Editions EG EGED 18	AMBIENT 2 (THE PLATEAUX OF MIRRORS) (LP, reissue)	£15

(see also Brian Eno)

ROY BUDD

65	Pye 7N 15807	Birth Of The Budd/M'Ghee M'Ghee	£15
70	Pye 7N 45051	Carter (Theme)/Plaything (in p/s)	£70
70	Pye 7N 45051	Carter (Theme)/Plaything	£50
68	Pye NPL 18212	AT NEWPORT (LP)	£18
71	Pye NSPL 18348	PLAYS SOLDIER BLUE AND OTHER THEMES (LP)	£20
72	Polydor 2383 102	KIDNAPPED (Roy Budd/Mary Hopkin)	£25
72	Pye NSPL 18389	CONCERTO FOR HARRY - SOMETHING TO HIDE (Roy Budd)	£25
73	Pye NSPL 18398	FEAR IS THE KEY (LP, soundtrack)	£50
76	Bradley's BRADS 8002	DIAMONDS (LP, soundtrack)	£50
70s	Pye NSPL 19494	EVERYTHING'S COMING UP (LP)	£15
99	Cinephile CINLP001	GET CARTER (LP, gatefold)	£25
00	Cinephile CINLP004	THE BLACK WINDMILL (LP, gatefold)	£30

BUDDY & SKETTO

62	Dice 45/CC 7	Little Schoolgirl/Hush Baby	£25

BUDGIE

71	MCA MK 5072	Crash Course In Brain Surgery/Nude Disintegrating Parachutist Woman	£20
71	MCA MKPS 2018	BUDGIE (LP, pink/red label, initial pressing with laminated sleeve and poster)	£150
71	MCA MKPS 2018	BUDGIE (LP, pink/red label, with no poster)	£100
71	MCA MKPS 2018	BUDGIE (LP, later pressing with blue/black label)	£15
72	MCA MKPS 2023	SQUAWK (LP, 1st pressing, Matrix numbers: 7-LNMG-216-1I/262-1L, blue/black hexagon label, matt sleeve)	£50
72	MCA MKPS 2023	SQUAWK (LP, 2nd pressing, black label, matt sleeve)	£40
73	MCA MDKS 8010	NEVER TURN YOUR BACK ON A FRIEND (LP, black label, gatefold sleeve)	£100
74	MCA MDKS 8010	NEVER TURN YOUR BACK ON A FRIEND (LP, reissue, rainbow label, gatefold sleev	£40
74	MCA MCF 2546	IN FOR THE KILL (LP, rainbow label, black background)	£40
75	MCA MCF 2723	BANDOLIER (LP)	£30
75	MCA MCF 2766	THE BEST OF BUDGIE (LP)	£15
76	A&M AMLH 68377	IF I WAS BRITANNIA I'D WAIVE THE RULES (LP, silver/green label)	£15
78	A&M AMLH 64675	IMPECKABLE (LP)	£15
80	Active ACTLP 1	POWER SUPPLY (LP, with insert)	£15
80	RCA RCALP 3046	POWER SUPPLY (LP, reissue, with different back sleeve)	£20
81	RCA RCALP 6003	NIGHT FLIGHT (LP)	£15
82	RCA RCALP 6054	DELIVER US FROM EVIL (LP)	£15

(see also Tredegar)

NANA BUDJEI

88	Asona ARLP 015	AFRIKAMAN (LP)	£20
90	KBN 0248	YONKO PA (LP)	£18

DENNIS BUDLIMAR

67	Fontana TL 5307	THE CREEPER (LP)	£20

BUENA VISTAS

66	Stateside SS 525	Hot Shot/T.N.T.	£25

BUFFALO

81	Heavy Metal HEAVY 3	Battle Torn Heroes/Women Of The Night (p/s)	£30

82 Heavy Metal HEAVY 15 | **Mean Machine/The Rumour** (p/s) **£25**

BUFFALO SPRINGFIELD
67	Atlantic 584 077	**For What It's Worth** (Stop Hey What's That Sound)/**Do I Have To Come Right Out And Say It** **£25**
67	Atlantic 584 145	**Rock'n'Roll Woman/A Child's Claim To Fame** **£15**
68	Atlantic 584 165	**Expecting To Fly/Everydays** **£15**
68	Atlantic 584 189	**Uno-Mundo/Merry-Go-Round** **£15**
67	Atlantic 587 070	**BUFFALO SPRINGFIELD** (LP, plum label, mispressing, lists "For What It's Worth" but plays "Baby Don't Scold Me"; matrix no. ends '1' mono) **£120**
67	Atlantic 588 070	**BUFFALO SPRINGFIELD** ((LP, plum label, mispressing, lists "For What It's Worth" but plays "Baby Don't Scold Me"; matrix no. ends '1' stereo) **£70**
67	Atlantic 587 070	**BUFFALO SPRINGFIELD** (LP, plum label, plays "For What It's Worth", mono) **£50**
67	Atlantic 588 070	**BUFFALO SPRINGFIELD** (LP, plum label, plays "For What It's Worth", stereo) **£40**
68	Atlantic 587 091	**BUFFALO SPRINGFIELD AGAIN** (LP, plum label, mono) **£70**
68	Atlantic 588 091	**BUFFALO SPRINGFIELD AGAIN** (LP, plum label, stereo) **£50**
69	Atco 228 024	**LAST TIME AROUND** (LP, plum label, gatefold sleeve) **£40**
69	Atco 228 012	**RETROSPECTIVE** (LP, plum label) **£25**
70	Atlantic 2464 012	**EXPECTING TO FLY** (LP, plum label) **£25**
72	Atlantic K 40014	**BUFFALO SPRINGFIELD AGAIN** (LP, reissue, green & orange label) **£15**
72	Atlantic K 40077	**LAST TIME AROUND** (LP, reissue, green & orange label, gatefold sleeve) **£15**
73	Atlantic K 30028	**BUFFALO SPRINGFIELD - ATLANTIC MASTERS: THE BEGINNNING** (LP) **£15**

(see also Neil Young, Stephen Stills, Au-Go-Go Singers, Crosby Stills Nash & Young)

BUFFALO TOM
89	Caff CAFF 6	**Enemy/Deep In The Ground** (p/s) **£20**
92	Situation 2 SITU 36	**LET ME COME OVER** (LP) **£15**
93	Beggars Banquet BBQLP 142	**BIG RED LETTER DAY** (LP) **£15**

BUFF MEDWAYS
01	Vinyl Japan ASKLP 132	**THIS IS THIS** (LP) **£25**
02	Transcopic TRANLP 016	**STEADY THE BUFFS** (LP) **£25**
03	Transcopic TRANLP 026	**1914** (LP, as the Buffs) **£20**

(see also Billy Childish, Wild Billy Childish & Buff Medways, Nilkshakes, Thee Headcoats)

BUFFOONS
67 Columbia DB 8317 | **My World Fell Down/Tomorrow Is Another Day** **£18**

BUG
08 Ninja Tune ZEN 132 | **LONDON ZOO** (3-LP, gatefold) **£20**

BUG CENTRAL
| 99 | Dole Office/DHSS 1 | **Gotta Get A Real Job/No Free Records** (Unreleased, white label test pressings only) ...... **£35** |
| 99 | Helen Of Oi HOO 48 | **THE MEEK WILL INHERIT NOTHING** (LP, with inserts) .... **£15** |

JAKE BUGG
12	Kitchenware JAKE 01	**Trouble Town/Someone Told Me** (p/s) **£50**
13	EMI (No Cat/ No.)	**What Doesn't Kill You** (1-sided, die-cut sleeve) **£20**
14	Secret 7" S717	**Strange Creatures** (100 only, each in unique art sleeve) **£20**
12	Mercury 3717304	**JAKE BUGG** (LP) **£15**

THE BUGGER ALL STARS
| 81 | Bead Records BEAD 19 | **THE BUGGER ALL STARS** (LP) .... **£20** |
| 83 | Bead Records BEAD 21 | **BONZO BITES BACK** (LP) .... **£20** |

BUGGIS
75 Third World TW 031 | **Buggis Is Mood/GENE RONDO: Declaration Of Rights** **£20**

BUGGY
70 Parlophone R5832 | **The Rolly Pole Coaster/Harry The Keeper** **£15**

SANDY BULL
69 Vanguard 19040 | **E PLURIBUS UNUM** (LP) **£25**

BULLDOG BREED
69	Deram DM 270	**Portcullis Gate/Halo In My Hair** **£150**
70	Deram Nova DN 5	**MADE IN ENGLAND** (LP, mono) **£350**
70	Deram Nova SDN 5	**MADE IN ENGLAND** (LP, stereo) **£300**
02	Acme ADLP 1036	**MADE IN ENGLAND** (LP, reissue with free 7") **£15**

(see also Flies)

BULLDOGS
64 Mercury MF 808 | **John, Paul, George And Ringo/What Do I See** **£20**

BULLET TRAIN
79 Sidewalk 12YSID 109 | **Don't Hold Back My Bullets/Bang Bang** (12") **£39**

BULLET (1)
| 71 | Purple PUR 101 | **Hobo/Sinister Minister** .... **£20** |
| 75 | Contour 2870 437 | **THE HANGED MAN** (LP, TV soundtrack) .... **£40** |

(see also Hard Stuff, Quatermass, Atomic Rooster)

BULLET (2)
78 Pennine PSS 138 | **Don't Go/Streetcrawler** (500 only) **£20**

BULLETS
78 Big Bear BB 16 | **Girl On Page 3/Grammar School Girls** (p/s) **£15**

JOHN BULL BREED
66 Polydor BM 56065 | **Can't Chance A Breakup/I'm A Man** **£375**

BULL MINSTRELS
73 Boston /Guildhall GHS 9 | **HORNCASTLE FAYRE** (LP) **£20**

BULLRING
70   CBS 4881   Birmingham Brass Band/Lady Of The Morning Sun £15

BULLY BOYS BAND
70   Stateside SSL 5032   MOVIE SCENE - HEAVY SOUNDS FROM TODAY'S FILMS (LP)..............................£20

BULLY WEE (BAND)
75   Folksound FS 102   BULLYWEE (LP)..£20
76   Red Rag RRR 007   THE ENCHANTED LADY (LP) £15
78   Red Rag RRR 017   SILVERMINES (LP, as Bullywee Band, with insert)..£15
80   Jigsaw SAW 1   THE MADMAN OF GOTHAM (LP) £20

BUMBLE BEE SLIM
60s   Fontana 688 138ZL   BEE'S BACK IN TOWN (LP) £25

BUMBLEBEE UNLIMITED
79   Sky SKY1004   Love Bug/Disco Version..£15
14   Groove Line GLR12 003   Lady Bug (Disco Mix)/Lady Bug (Disco Remix) (12" reissue) £15

BUMBLES
72   Purple PUR 107   Beep Beep/Buzz Off (promo only p/s)..£25
(see laos Hard Stuff, Atomic Rooster, Curtis Muldoon)

BUNCH (1)
67   CBS 202506   We're Not What We Appear To Be/You Never Came Home £70
67   CBS 2740   Don't Come Back To Me/You Can't Do This £25
67   CBS 3060   Looking Glass Alice/Spare A Shilling..£200
68   CBS 3692   Birthday/Still £30
68   CBS 3709   Birthday/Still (reissue)..£15
(see also Peter & The Wolves, Sounds Around, John Pantry)

BUNCH (2)
72   Island ILPS 9189   ROCK ON (LP, with 1-sided flexi attached to die-cut sleeve: "Let There Be Drums" [WI 4002])..£60
72   Island ILPS 9189   ROCK ON (LP, without 1-sided flexi: "Let There Be Drums" [WI 4002]) £20
(see also Fairport Convention, Sandy Denny, Average White Band, Richard Thompson)

BUNCH OF FIVES
66   Parlophone R 5494   Go Home Baby/At The Station £120
(see also Viv Prince, Egg, Junior's Eyes, Outsiders [U.K.])

BUNDLE
70   Polydor 2058 029   Dirty La Rue/Progressive Underground £15

ROGER BUNN
70   Major Minor SMLP 70   PIECE OF MIND (LP, red/white/black label) £200
(see also Pete Browns Pitlokto, Roxy Music)

BUNNIES (OF LONDON)
68   Decca LK4951   CAUGHT LIVE AT THE PLAYBOY CLUB (LP) £20
69   Decca SKL5026   THE BUNNIES AGAIN SINGIN' AND SWINGIN' AT THE LONDON PLAYBOY CLUB (LP) £20

BUNNY & RICKY
75   Attack ATT 8107   Two Bad Bull (as Bunnie And Rickey)(actually by Pat Simpson)/UPSETTERS: Bad Cow.....£30
75   Attack ATT 8109   Bushwood Contrash/UPSETTERS: Callying Butt £30
75   Locks LOX 11   Freedom Fighter/UPSETTERS: Iron Wolf..£15

BUNNY & RUDDY
68   Nu Beat NB 007   Rhythm & Soul/BOBBY KALPHAT: True Romance £80
68   Nu Beat NB 011   On The Town/MONTY MORRIS: Simple Simon £40

BINGY BUNNY
82   Cha Cha CHAD 46   Keep It In The Family (with MORWELLS)/SCIENTIST : Extended Dub/Me & Jane (with MORWELLS)/SCIENTIST : Extended Dub (12") £40
82   Cha Cha CHAD 48   Street Lover (with MORWELLS)/NICODEMUS : How You Look Girl 'Pon The Street (12")..£30
82   Cha Cha CHALP 015   ME & JANE (LP) £60

BINGY BUNNY & BONGO LES
73   Ackee ACK 506   International Scout/International Scout Version £15
(see also Bongo Les, Mediators)

BUNNY BROWN
72   Songbird SB 1073   Fat Boy/Fat Boy - Version £15
78   JCB JCB 002   I Love The Way You Love/Version £18
(see also Noel Brown, Winston Scotland)

BUNNY LION
77   M&M MM03   Introducing Bunny Lion/REVOLUTIONARIES: Version (12", as Linval Thompson)...........£20
79   Starlight SLP 900   RED (LP) £25

BUNNY MACK
80   Rokel MACK 1   Let Me Love You/Love You Forever (12") £20

BOB BUNTING
68   Transatlantic TRA 166   YOU'VE GOT TO GO DOWN THIS WAY (LP) £50

VASHTI BUNYAN
70   Philips 6308 019   JUST ANOTHER DIAMOND DAY (LP)..£1500
00   Spinney SPINNEY 001   JUST ANOTHER DIAMOND DAY (LP, reissue, gatefold) £20
05   Fat Cat FATLP 38   LOOKAFTERING (LP) £20
07   Fat Cat FATLP 59   SOME THINGS JUST STICK IN YOUR MIND (SINGLES AND DEMOS 1964-1967) (2-LP).......£25
(see also Vashti, Fairport Convention, Dave Swarbrick, Robin Williamson)

BUOYS
70	Wand WN7	Timothy/It Feels Good	£20
71	Wand MSW 8296	Give Up Your Guns/The Prince Of Thieves	£15

VERNON BURCH
75	United Artists UAS 29743	I'LL BE YOUR SUNSHINE (LP)	£15

ERIC BURDON (BAND)
75	Capitol E-ST 11426	STOP (LP, as Eric Burdon Band)	£15
78	Polydor 2302 078	SURVIVOR (LP, with 5 inserts with lyrics and drawings)	£25

ERIC BURDON & THE ANIMALS
66	Decca F 12502	Mama Told Me Not To Come/See See Rider (unreleased)	£0
67	MGM C(S) 8052	WINDS OF CHANGE (LP, yellow/black label with "sold in the U.K." label text)	£80
68	MGM C(S) 8074	THE TWAIN SHALL MEET (LP, yellow black labels with "sold in the U.K." text)	£80
68	MGM C(S) 8105	LOVE IS (LP, blue/gold labels with "sold in the U.K." text)	£100
71	MGM 2619 002	LOVE IS (2-LP; individual LP nos.: 2354 006/7)	£50

(see also Animals, Stud, Zoot Money's Big Roll Band)

ERIC BURDON & WAR
70	Polydor 2310 041	ERIC BURDON DECLARES "WAR" (LP)	£30
70	Liberty LDS 8400 3/4	BLACK MAN'S BURDON (2-LP, gatefold, with banned track "P.C. 3")	£50
70	Liberty LDS 8400	BLACK MAN'S BURDON (2-LP, gatefold, without banned track "P.C. 3")	£20
76	ABC ABCL 5207	LOVE IS ALL AROUND (LP)	£20

(see also War)

ERIC BURDON & JIMMY WITHERSPOON
71	United Artists UAG 29251	GUILTY! (LP, gatefold sleeve)	£18

(see also Jimmy Witherspoon)

DAVID BURGE
69	Vox STGBY 637	AVANT GARDE PIANO MUSIC (LP)	£15

DAVE BURGESS (TRIO)
58	Oriole CB 1413	I'm Available/Who's Gonna Cry?	£20

LEROY BURGESS
01	Soul Brother LP SBPJ 6	ANTHOLOGY 1 - THE VOICE (2-LP)	£35
07	Soul Brother LP SBPJ 34	THROWBACK HARLEM 79-83 (2-LP, compilation)	£25

MARK BURGESS AND THE SONS OF GOD
93	Imaginary ILLUSION 44	ZIMA JUNCTION (LP)	£40

(see also Chameleons)

SONNY BURGESS
60	London HLS 9064	Sadie's Back In Town/A Kiss Goodnight	£200

TIM BURGESS
03	PIAS B099LP	I BELIEVE (LP)	£25

(see also Charlatans (U.K.))

JIM BURGETT
61	Philips PB 1133	Let's Investigate/The Living Dead	£40

BURGUNDY BLOOD
13	Ch' Herring CHBURG 001	THE CORDIAL STANCE EP (12", black vinyl, 200 copies only)	£15
13	Ch' Herring CHBURG 001	THE CORDIAL STANCE EP (12", burgundy vinyl, 75 copies only)	£30
13	Ch' Herring CHBURG 001	THE CORDIAL STANCE EP (12", white vinyl, 75 copies only)	£20
14	Fresh Herring FHBURGLP01	SUEDE COMET (2LP, gatefold, ltd. black/clear/red, clear, purple editions)	£30
20	Ch' Herring CHBURGLP 02	THE FALL OF MAN (LP, white yellow marbled vinyl)	£20

ELPEDO BURKE
75	Black Wax WAX 3	Madgie/MIGHTY CLOUD: Madgie Dub	£15

KEVIN BURKE
78	Rockburgh ROC 105	IF THE CAP FITS (LP)	£15

SOLOMON BURKE
61	London HLK 9454	Just Out Of Reach/Be Bop Grandma	£40
62	London HLK 9512	Cry To Me/I Almost Lost My Mind	£50
62	London HLK 9560	Down In The Valley/I'm Hanging Up My Heart For You	£20
63	London HLK 9715	If You Need Me/You Can Make It If You Try	£20
63	London HLK 9763	Can't Nobody Love You/Stupidity	£40
64	London HLK 9849	He'll Have To Go/Rockin' Soul	£20
64	London HLK 9887	Goodbye Baby (Baby Goodbye)/Someone To Love Me	£20
64	Atlantic AT 4004	Everybody Needs Somebody To Love/Looking For My Baby	£30
64	Atlantic AT 4014	The Price/More Rockin' Soul	£15
65	Atlantic AT 4022	Got To Get You Off My Mind/Peepin'	£20
65	Atlantic AT 4030	Maggie's Farm/Tonight's The Night	£20
65	Atlantic AT 4044	Someone Is Watching/Dance, Dance, Dance	£18
65	Atlantic AT 4061	Only Love (Can Save Me Now)/Little Girl That Loves Me	£22
66	Atlantic AT 4073	Baby Come On Home/No, No, No, I Can't Stop Lovin' You Now	£18
63	London REK 1379	TONIGHT MY HEART SHE IS CRYING (EP)	£70
65	Atlantic AET 6008	ROCK'N'SOUL (EP)	£60
63	London HA-K 8018	SOLOMON BURKE'S GREATEST (LP)	£70
64	Atlantic ATL 5009	ROCK'N'SOUL (LP)	£50
66	Atlantic 587/588 016	THE BEST OF SOLOMON BURKE (LP)	£30
68	Atlantic 587 105	KING SOLOMON (LP)	£35
68	Atlantic 587/588 117	I WISH I KNEW (LP)	£30
69	Bell MBLL/SBLL 118	PROUD MARY (LP)	£20

MINT VALUE £

72 MGM 2315 048   THE ELECTRONIC MAGNETISM (LP) £15
(see also Soul Clan)

SONNY BURKE (U.K.)
62 Island WI 155   Let And Let Live/Our Love Is True £25
64 Black Swan WI 457   I Love You Still/It's Always A Pleasure £25
64 Black Swan WI 458   City In The Sky/Everyday I Love You More £25
65 Black Swan WI 469   Glad/Jeanie £25
65 Black Swan WI 470   Dance With Me/My Girl Can't Cook £25
65 Black Swan WI 471   Wicked People/Good Heaven Knows £25
66 Blue Beat BB 363   Blue Island/You Came And Left................................ £40
67 Blue Beat BB 371   Look In Her Eyes/LLOYD CLARKE: Love Is Strange £40
67 Ska Beat JB272   Have Faith/Guinea Pig £40
68 Island ILP 972   THE SOUNDS OF SONNY BURKE (LP, mono only)............ £125
(see also Bob Andy, Gaylads, Ken Parker, Eddie Thornton Outfit, Glen Adams, Stranger Cole, Gaylads, Sonny & Yvonne)

SONNY BURKE OUTFIT
68 Instant IN 003   Baby Be My Girl/All You £120
(see also Sonny Burke)

DAVE BURLAND
71 Trailer LER 2029   A DALESMAN'S LITANY (LP, red label) £25
72 Trailer LER 2082   DAVE BURLAND (LP) £20
75 Rubber RUB 012   SONGS AND BUTTERED HAYCOCKS (LP)......................... £18
79 Rubber RUB 036   YOU CAN'T FOOL THE FAT MAN (LP) £15
80 Rubber RUB 012/036   DOUBLE TAKE (2-LP, reissue) £18

PETER BURMAN
62 Columbia 33SX 1452   JAZZ TETE A TETE (LP) £200

BURMOE BROTHERS
85 Wild Blue Yonder WBY 121 Skin/Leber Oder Lippenstift/Under The Blanket Of Love (12", p/s) ... £15
(see also Marc Almond, Nick Cave)

BURN
00s Virgin HUTCDP 146   Facing The Music (1-sided, numbered gold-embossed p/s, 1000 only) £20

CHRIS BURN & JOHN BUTCHER
85 Bead Records BEAD 24   FONETIKS (LP) £20

JEAN-JACQUES BURNEL
80 United Artists BP 361   Girl From The Snow Country/Ode To Joy (live)/Do The European (live) (p/s,
                             unissued)... £500
79 United Artists UAG 30214 EUROMAN COMETH (LP, inner) £15

CHARMAINE BURNETT
79 Hawkeye HD 21   Make It With You/Let's Get Started (12") £15
81 Pro PROD 001   (Am I The) Same Girl/Direct Response (12") £25
82 Dread At The Controls DATC Dancing Shoes/Congo Dubba (12").............................. £30
    007

FRANCES BURNETT
59 Coral Q 72374   Please Remember Me/How I Miss You So (triangular centre) £60
59 Coral Q 72374   Please Remember Me/How I Miss You So (round centre) £30

KING BURNETT
75 Dip DL 5056   I Man Free/UPSETTERS: Version £25
75 Dip DL 5073   Key Card/UPSETTERS: Domino Game £25
(see also Congos)

DORSEY BURNETTE
65 Tamla Motown TMG 534   Jimmy Brown/Everybody's Angel £225
65 Tamla Motown TMG 534   Jimmy Brown/Everybody's Angel (DJ copy) £250
63 London RE-D 1402   DORSEY BURNETTE SINGS (EP) £40
63 London HA-D 8050   DORSEY BURNETTE (LP) £70
(see also Johnny & Dorsey Burnette)

HANK C. BURNETTE
74 Southern Sound SSRLP 400 SPINNIN ROCK BOOGIE (LP) £30
76 Sonet SNTF 693   DONT'T MESS WITH MY DUCKTAIL (LP) £15
78 Sonet SNTF 750   ROCKABILLY GASSEROONIE (LP)................................. £15

JOHNNY BURNETTE (TRIO)
SINGLES
56 Vogue Coral Q 72177   Tear It Up/You're Undecided (as Johnny Burnette & Rock'N'Roll Trio) £500
56 Vogue Coral Q 72177   Tear It Up/You're Undecided (as Johnny Burnette & Rock'N'Roll Trio) (78) £60
57 Vogue Coral Q 72227   Honey Hush/Lonesome Train (as Johnny Burnette Trio) £500
57 Vogue Coral Q 72227   Honey Hush/Lonesome Train (as Johnny Burnette Trio) (78) £70
57 Vogue Coral Q 72283   Touch Me/Eager Beaver Baby (as Johnny Burnette Trio) £200
57 Vogue Coral Q 72283   Touch Me/Eager Beaver Baby (as Johnny Burnette Trio) (78) £60
60 London HLG 9172   Dreamin'/Cincinnati Fireball (78)............................ £250
61 London HLG 9453   God Country And My Baby/Honestly I Do (withdrawn) £50
63 Capitol CL 15322   All Week Long/It Isn't There £20
64 Capitol CL 15347   Sweet Suzie/Walking Talking Doll £35
96 Cruisin' The 50s CASB 003 The Train Kept A Rollin'/Sweet Love On My Mind (300 copies only) (78)....... £20

EPs
60 London RE-G 1263   DREAMIN' £25
61 London RE-G 1291   LITTLE BOY SAD £25
61 London RE-G 1309   BIG BIG WORLD £25

61	London RE-G 1327	GIRLS	£25
63	Liberty LEP 2091	HIT AFTER HIT	£25
64	Capitol EAP 20645	FOUR BY BURNETTE	£60

ALBUMS

56	Coral LVC 10041	ROCK AND ROLL TRIO (10", as Johnny Burnette Trio)	£800
61	London HA-G 2306	DREAMIN'	£40
61	London HA-G 2349	YOU'RE SIXTEEN	£40
61	London HA-G 2375	JOHNNY BURNETTE SINGS (mono)	£40
61	London SAH-G 6175	JOHNNY BURNETTE SINGS (stereo)	£60
62	Liberty LBY 1006	BURNETTE'S HITS AND OTHER FAVOURITES	£20
64	Liberty LBY 1231	THE JOHNNY BURNETTE STORY	£20
66	Ace Of Hearts AH 120	ROCK AND ROLL TRIO (reissue, as Johnny Burnette Trio)	£20
68	Coral CP 10	TEAR IT UP (as Johnny Burnette Trio)	£20

(see also Johnny & Dorsey Burnette)

JOHNNY & DORSEY BURNETTE

| 63 | Reprise R 20153 | Hey Sue/It Don't Matter Much | £70 |

(see also Johnny Burnette, Dorsey Burnette)

SMILEY BURNETTE

| 54 | London HL 8071 | Lazy Locomotive/That Long White Line | £25 |
| 54 | London HL 8085 | Chuggin' On Down "66"/Mucho Gusto | £25 |

BURNIN' RED IVANHOE

| 70 | Warner Bros WS 3013 | BURNIN' RED IVANHOE (LP, green label) | £70 |
| 72 | Dandelion 2310 145 | W.W.W. (LP, gatefold sleeve) | £70 |

BURNING BUSH

| 84 | Kongo DP 001 | Go To School/School/Jah Is Coming?Hail The Emperor (12") | £20 |

BURNING SKIES OF ELYSIUM

| 87 | Crisis EL 3 | THE LAST REVOLVING DOOR (LP) | £25 |

BURNING SPEAR

70	Bamboo 50	SOUND DIMENTION: Soul Food/BURNING SPEAR: Door Peeper	£80
71	Fab FAB 18	Creation Rebel/ERROL DUNKLEY: Get Up Now (black label, promo only)	£30
75	Fab FAB 240	Foggy Road/Version	£45
76	Island WIP 6346	Lion/Door Peep	£18
76	Island WIP 6294	Black Wa-Da-Da (Invasion (Dub Version))/I And I Survive (Slavery Days) (Dub Version)	£15
78	Island Pre IPR 2027	Civilised Reggae/Social Living (12")	£20
79	Burning Spear BS 001	Free The Whole Wide World/Jah Jah No Dead (12")	£30
79	Tribesman TM 20	Free The Whole Wide World/Jah Jah No Dead (12")	£60
82	Radic 12RIC 114	Jah Is My Driver/Driver Dub/Distance/Forever	£70
75	Island ILPS 9377	MARCUS GARVEY (LP, 1st pressing has stickered sleeve)	£40
76	Island ILPS 9382	GARVEY'S GHOST (LP)	£40
76	Island ILPS 9412	MAN IN THE HILLS (LP, gatefold)	£25
77	Island MLPS 9431	DRY & HEAVY (LP)	£15
77	Island ILPS 9513	LIVE (LP)	£15
78	1 Stop STOP 1001	SOCIAL LIVING (LP)	£30
79	Island PRELP 3	LIVING DUB VOL 1 (LP)	£30
79	Island ILPS 9567	HARDER THAN THE BEST (LP)	£15
80	Burning Spear RDC 2003	HAIL H.I.M (LP, printed inner)	£30
00	Island/Simply Vinyl SVLP 191	MARCUS GARVEY/GARVEY'S GHOST (2LP, reissue, 180g)	£20
01	Pressure Sounds PSLP 33	SPEAR BURNING (2LP, gatefold)	£60
04	Soul Jazz SJRLP 101	SOUNDS FROM BURNING SPEAR (2LP, printed inners)	£50
15	Island 5360235	SOCIAL LIVING/LIVING DUB (2LP, gatefold)	£35

(see also Irving Brown, King Cry Cry)

JAN BURNNETTE

62	Oriole CB 1716	I Could Have Loved You So Well/The Miracle Of Life	£15
63	Oriole CB 1807	The Boy I Used To Know/Unimportant Things	£15
63	Oriole CB 1841	Till I Hear The Truth From You/Fool In Love	£15
64	Oriole CB 1920	Too Young/The Four Winds And The Seven Seas	£15

CLARKIE BURNS

| 78 | Jungle Beats JBCD 805 | Troubles (with I ROY)/I ROY: Worries (12") | £80 |

EDDIE 'GUITAR' BURNS

| 72 | Action ACMP 100 | BOTTLE UP AND GO (LP) | £30 |
| 75 | Big Bear BEAR 7 | DETROIT BLACKBOTTOM (LP) | £20 |

JACKIE BURNS & BELLES

| 63 | MGM MGM 1226 | He's My Guy/I Do The Best I Can | £100 |

JIMMY BURNS

| 79 | Grapevine GRP 118 | I Really Love You/I Love You Girl | £25 |
| 79 | Grapevine GRP 118 | I Really Love You/I Love You Girl (DJ Copy) | £30 |

LISA BURNS

| 78 | MCA MCF 2849 | LISA BURNS (LP) | £15 |

RANDY BURNS

| 68 | Fontana STL 5520 | EVENING OF THE MAGICIAN (LP) | £50 |

(see also Blue Cheer)

RAY BURNS

| 56 | Columbia DB 3811 | Condemned For Life (With A Rock And Roll Wife)/The Mare Piccola | £35 |

MINT VALUE £

55	Columbia SEG 7594	RAY BURNS (EP)	£20

(see also Ruby Murray, Ronnie Harris, Diana Decker, Ray Martin)

HAROLD BURRAGE
65	Sue WI 353	I'll Take One/A Long Ways Together	£50
81	Flywright FLY 579	SHE KNOCKS ME OUT - ORIGINAL COBRA BLUES (LP)	£15

KENNY BURRELL
61	Esquire 32-140	ALL NIGHT LONG (LP, as Kenny Burrell All Stars)	£40
64	Verve VLP 9058	BLUE BLASH (LP, with Jimmy Smith)	£25
65	Verve VLP 9099	GUITAR FORMS (LP)	£20
67	Transatlantic PR 7315	SOUL CALL (LP)	£15
66	Stateside SL 10163	CRASH! (LP, with Brother Jack McDuff)	£30
68	Verve (S)VLP 9217	BLUES, THE COMMON GROUND (LP)	£20
69	Verve SVLP 9246	NIGHT SONG (LP)	£18
79	Blue Note BNS 40015	MIDNIGHT BLUE (LP, reissue, blue label with black 'b')	£18

(see also Brother Jack McDuff, Jimmy Smith)

ROLAND BURRELL
84	C&E CEDI 105	Rip Off/Version (12")	£80

WILLIAM S. BURROUGHS
80	Industrial IR 0016	NOTHING HERE NOW BUT THE RECORDINGS (LP)	£80

CHINA BURTON
79	Logo GO 354	You Don't Care (About Our Love)/(Instrumental Version)	£100
79	Logo GO 354	You Don't Care (About Our Love)/(Instrumental Version) (DJ Copy)	£100
79	Logo GO(T) 354	You Don't Care (About Our Love) (Long Version)/(Short Version)/(Instrumental Version) (12")	£300

GARY BURTON (QUARTET)
68	RCA Victor SF 7923	LOFTY FAKE ANAGRAM (LP)	£20
69	RCA SF 7980	IN CONCERT (LP)	£15
69	RCA Victor SF 8015	GENUINE TONGUE FUNERAL (LP)	£18
71	Atlantic 2400 107	GOOD VIBES (LP)	£18

(see also Michael Gibbs)

JAMES BURTON
71	A&M AMLS 64293	THE GUITAR SOUNDS OF JAMES BURTON (LP)	£50

(see also Jim & Joe, Shindogs)

JOHNNY BURTON
72	Philips 60006 238	Polevault Man/The Polythene Doll	£25

TOMMY BURTON COMBO
64	Blue Beat BB 237	Lavender Blue/I'm Walking	£25

TREVOR BURTON
71	Wizard WIZ 103	Fight For My Country/Janie Slow Down	£30
85	Bluebar BARLP 1	DOUBLE ZERO (LP)	£20

(see also B,L&G; Uglys, Move, Balls, Denny Laine, Danny King's Mayfair Set, Magic Christians, Idle Race)

BURU
83	CSA CSALP 04	BURO (LP)	£30

BURZUM
93	Misanthropy Amazon 001	HVIS LYSET TAR OSS (LP, marbled vinyl, with poster)	£200
94	Misanthropy Amazon 002	DET SOM ENGANG VAR (LP, with stickered sleeve, inner sleeve and poster)	£200
95	Misanthropy Amazon 003	BURZUM/ASKE (2-LP, gatefold sleeve)	£100
96	Misanthropy Amazon 009	FILOSOFEM (2-LP, 1 side etched, stickered gatefold sleeve, booklet)	£200
97	Misanthropy Amazon 013	DAUOI BALDRS (LP, with postcards and booklet, 1,000 only)	£25
99	Misanthropy Amazon 021	HILOSKJALF (LP, booket and insert, 1,000 only)	£50
08	Back On Black BOBV 087LP	HVIS LYSET TAR OSS (LP, reissue)	£25
08	Back On Black BOBV 089LP	FILOSOFEM (LP, reissue, gatefold)	£25
10	Back On Black BOBV 215LP	BELUS (LP, white vinyl)	£50
10	Back On Black BOBV 215LP	BELUS (LP, black vinyl)	£20
11	Back On Black BOBV 293LP	FALLEN (LP, clear vinyl)	£20

ERNIE BUSH
76	Contempo CX 12	Breakaway/BANZAI: Chinese King Fu	£15

KATE BUSH
78	EMI EMI 2719	Wuthering Heights/Kite (p/s)	£40
78	EMI EMI 2806	The Man With The Child In His Eyes/Moving (p/s)	£15
79	EMI PSR 442/3	KATE BUSH ON STAGE (EP, double pack, gatefold sleeve, promo only)	£60
82	EMI IEMI 9001	Night Of The Swallow/Houdini (pressed in England for export to Ireland, p/s)	£100
84	EMI KBS 1	THE SINGLE FILE (13 x 7" box set with lyric booklet)	£70
93	EMI EM 280	Eat The Music/Big Stripey Lie (p/s, picture labels, release cancelled, 17 copies only)	£1600
93	EMI 12EMPD 280	Eat The Music/Eat The Music (Madagascan Remix)/Big Stripey Lie (12", picture disc, unissued)	£0
93	EMI CDEM 280	Eat The Music/(Madagascan Remix)/Big Stripey Lie (CD, unissued)	£0
93	EMI MUSIC 1	Eat The Music (CD, 1-track promo for unissued single, no inlay, withdrawn)	£150
78	EMI EMA 787	LIONHEART (LP, gatefold with gold embossed titles, inner)	£20
78	EMI EMC 3223	THE KICK INSIDE (LP, laminated sleeve)	£20
79	EMI EM CP 3223	THE KICK INSIDE (LP, picture disc, stickered sleeve)	£150
79	EMI EM CP 3223	THE KICK INSIDE (LP, picture disc, stickered sleeve, second pressing with "manufactured in the U.K. by EMI Records Ltd" wording)	£30
79	EMI EM CP 3223	THE KICK INSIDE (LP, picture disc, mispress with same picture both sides)	£150
80	EMI EMA 794	NEVER FOR EVER (LP, gatefold)	£15

82	EMI EMC 3419	THE DREAMING (LP, inner)	£20
85	EMI KAB 1	THE HOUNDS OF LOVE (LP, with inner and insert)	£25
86	EMI KBTV1	THE WHOLE STORY (LP, gatefold)	£20
89	EMI EMD 1010	THE SENSUAL WORLD (LP)	£20
90	EMI KBBX 1	THIS WOMAN'S WORK (9-LP, box set)	£250
90	EMI CDKBBX 1	THIS WOMAN'S WORK (CD, box set)	£80
93	EMD 1047	THE RED SHOES (LP, lyric inner)	£100
93	EMI (No Cat. No)	THE RED SHOES (CD, video, slide transparency, fountain pen, parchment discography & red ribbon box set, promo)	£200
97	EMI LPCENT5	THE KICK INSIDE (LP, reissue, EMI 100 Centenary, stickered sleeve)	£40
97	EMI CENT 34	THE HOUNDS OF LOVE (LP, reissue, EMI 100 Centenary, stickered sleeve)	£40
05	EMI 343960-1	AERIAL (2-LP, gatefold, booklet, stickered sleeve)	£125
11	Fish People FPLP 001	DIRECTOR'S CUT (2-LP, booklet)	£18
11	Fish People FPLP 007	50 WORDS FOR SNOW (2-LP, booklet, CD)	£40
16	Fish People 0190295920166	BEFORE THE DAWN (4-LP, box set)	£50
21	Fish People 0190296729041	HOUNDS OF LOVE (LP, reissue, obi, recycled vinyl)	£60

(see also Lesley Duncan)

RAY BUSH & AVON CITIES' SKIFFLE

56	Tempo A 146	Hey Hey Daddy Blues/Green Corn	£25
56	Tempo A 149	Fisherman's Blues/This Little Light Of Mine	£25
57	Tempo A 156	How Long, How Long, Blues/Julian Johnson	£25
57	Tempo A 157	Lonesome Day Blues/I Don't Know	£25
57	Tempo EXA 40	RAY BUSH & AVON CITIES' SKIFFLE (EP)	£25
57	Tempo EXA 50	RAY BUSH & AVON CITIES' SKIFFLE NO. 2 (EP)	£25

(see also Avon Cities Jazz Band)

CLEMENT BUSHAY

| 75 | Summertime BUS 10 LP | DREAD IN SESSION (LP) | £85 |
| 23 | Lantern LANR 034 | DREAD IN SESSION (LP, reissue, sticker to shrink) | £20 |

BUSH CHEMISTS

98	Conscious Sounds DNC 1203	Collie Weed/Collie Dub/Earth Rocker/Rocker Dub (12")	£40
06	Jah Tubbys JT10025	Star Dub/Waters Edge (10")	£18
94	JKPD JKPD 001	MEETS THE BUSH CHEMISTS AT CONSCIOUS SOUNDS (LP, with Jonah Dan)	£25
94	Conscious Sounds DNC 003	STRICTLY DUBWISE (LP)	£20
96	Conscious Sounds DNC 005	LIGHT UP YOUR SPLIFF (LP)	£40
98	Dubhead DBHD 009LP	CULTURE FREEMAN MEETS THE BUSH CHEMISTS (LP)	£20
99	Dubhead DBHD 010LP	LIGHT UP YOUR CHALICE (LP)	£18
01	Dubhead DBHD 023LP	DUB FIRE BLAZING (LP)	£20

(see also King General, King General & Bush Chemists)

BUSHKILLER

| 94 | Danger 002 | TROUBLEMAKERS (EP) | £25 |

BUSH TETRAS

| 82 | Fetish FET 16EP | RITUALS (12" EP) | £15 |

BUSINESS

83	Secret SHH 150	OUT OF BUSINESS (12" EP, unissued, white label promo, 10 copies only)	£100
85	Wonderful World Of... 121	Get Out Of My House/All Out Tonight/Foreign Girl/Outlaw (12", p/s)	£25
85	Diamond DIA 001	Drinking N Driving/H-Bomb (live) (p/s)	£15
85	Diamond DIA 001T	Drinking N Driving/H-Bomb (live)/Hurry Up Harry/Drinking 'N' Driving (original version) (12", p/s)	£25
83	Secret SEC 11	SUBURBAN REBELS (LP)	£40
83	Syndicate SYNLP 2	1980-81 OFFICIAL BOOTLEGS (LP)	£15
83	Wonderful WOWDLP 4	OFFICIAL BUSINESS 1980-81 (LP)	£20
84	Syndicate SYNLP 6	LOUD, PROUD 'N' PUNK, LIVE (LP)	£20
85	Harry May SE 13	SATURDAY HEROES (LP)	£20
86	Dojo DOJO LP 35	SINGALONGABUSINESS (LP)	£15
90	Link LRMO 1	IN AND OUT OF BUSINESS (LP, mail-order, 550 only)	£20
91	Wonderful WOWDLP 5	SUBURBAN REBELS/SMASH THE DISCOS - BACK TO BACK VOL 2. (2xLP)	£25

BUSKERS

| 73 | Rubber RUB 007 | LIFE OF A MAN (LP) | £18 |
| 75 | Hawk HALPX 142 | THE BUSKERS (LP) | £15 |

GEORGE HENRY BUSSEY/JIM BUNKLEY

| 71 | Revival RVS 1003 | GEORGE HENRY BUSSEY/JIM BUNKLEY (LP) | £15 |

BUSTA RHYMES

| 98 | Elektra E3847LC | Turn It Up (Remix)/Fire It Up (Clean) | £50 |

BUSTER

| 73 | Bradleys BRAD 310 | Motor Machine/Ring Around | £25 |
| 74 | Bradleys BRAD 7401 | Superstar/Rainbows & Colours | £20 |

BUSTERS

| 63 | Stateside SS 231 | Bust Out/Astronauts | £25 |

BUSTER('S) ALLSTARS

64	Blue Beat BB 244	Prince Royal/COSMO: One God	£50
64	Blue Beat BB 269	The Tickler/COSMO: Rice And Badge	£50
65	Blue Beat BB 294	Eye For Eye/South Virginia	£50
65	Blue Beat BB 322	Happy Independence 65/STRANGER COLE: When The Party Is Over	£50
65	Blue Beat BB 325	Congo Revolution/Little Darlin' - No One	£150
65	Blue Beat BB 333	When The Party Is Over/Matilda (with Stranger Cole)	£50

MINT VALUE £

66	Blue Beat BB 342	Cincinnatti Kid/Sammy Dead	£75
67	Blue Beat BB 372	Sounds And Pressure/My Darling (both actually by Hopeton Lewis)	£50
67	Blue Beat BB 384	Take It Easy/Why Must I Cry (both actually by Hopeton Lewis)	£50
69	Fab FAB 101	Pum Pum A Go Kill You/Oh Lady Oh	£20
70	Fab FAB 124	The Rebel/The Preacher	£20

(see also Prince Buster, Teddy King, Little Darling, Khandars, Higgs & Wilson, Owen Gray, Charmers, Fitzroy D Long, Maytals, Derrick Morgan, Eric Morris, Personalities, Roy & Millie, Zoot Simms, Spanish Boys, Spanish Town Skabeats)

BUSTER'S GROUP

61	Starlite ST45 052	Buster's Shack/ERIC MORRIS: Search The World	£40
65	Blue Beat BB 395	This Gun For Hire/Yes Daddy	£60

(see also Prince Buster, Rico, Owen Gray)

BUSTY & COOL

62	Blue Beat BB 144	Mr Policeman/What A World	£20

TONY BUTALA

62	Salvo SLO 1801	Long Black Stockings/Rumors (99 copies only)	£40

STAN BUTCHER

66	CBS SS62838	HIS BIRDS AND BRASS (LP)	£20
67	CBS 63072	SWING LIKE A BASTARD (LP)	£35

SAM BUTERA (& WITNESSES)

58	HMV POP 476	Good Gracious Baby/It's Better Than Nothing At All	£50
58	Capitol CL 14913	Bim Bam/Twinkle In Your Eye (as Sam Butera & Witnesses)	£250
59	Capitol CL 14988	Handle With Care/French Poodle	£20
64	Prima PR 1003	Skinnie Minnie/Little Liza Jane	£18
56	HMV 7EG 8087	SAX SERENADE (EP)	£15
60	London HA-D 2288	THE RAT RACE (LP, as Sam Butera & Witnesses)	£20

(see also Louis Prima)

BILLY BUTLER (& ENCHANTERS)

69	Soul City SC 113	The Right Track/Boston Monkey	£40
74	Epic S EPC 2508	The Right Track/Can't Live Without Her (Yellow label, solid or push-out centre)	£15

HAROLD BUTLER

77	Charmers 3	GOLD CONNECTION (LP)	£150

JERRY BUTLER

58	London 45-HL 8697	For Your Precious Love/Sweet Was The Wine (as Jerry Butler & the Impressions)	£100
58	London HL 8697	For Your Precious Love/Sweet Was The Wine (as Jerry Butler & the Impressions) (78 rpm)	£100
60	Top Rank JAR 389	I Found A Love/A Lonely Soldier	£45
60	Top Rank JAR 531	He Will Break Your Heart/Thanks To You	£55
61	Top Rank JAR 562	Find Another Girl/When Trouble Calls	£40
61	Columbia DB 4743	Moon River/Aware Of Love	£25
62	Stateside SS 121	Make It Easy On Yourself/It's Too Late	£25
63	Stateside SS 158	You Can Run But You Can't Hide/I'm The One	£30
63	Stateside SS 170	You Go Right Through Me/The Wishing Star	£20
63	Stateside SS 195	Whatever You Want/You Won't Be Sorry	£20
64	Stateside SS 252	Need To Belong/Give Me Your Love	£25
64	Stateside SS 300	Giving Up On Love/I've Been Trying	£20
65	Fontana TF 553	Good Times/I've Grown Accustomed To Her Face	£20
65	Fontana TF 588	I Can't Stand To See You Cry/Nobody Needs Your Love	£15
65	Mercury MF 932	Love (Oh, How Sweet It Is)/Loneliness	£15
66	Sue WI 4003	I Stand Accused/I Don't Want To Hear Anymore	£50
66	Sue WI 4009	Just For You/Believe In Me	£50
69	Mercury MF 1122	Moody Woman/Go Away - Find Yourself	£20
69	Mercury MF 1122	Moody Woman/Go Away - Find Yourself (DJ copy)	£150
72	Mercury 6052 119	Moody Woman/A Brand New Me	£15
62	Stateside SL 10032	HE WILL BREAK YOUR HEART (LP, flipback sleeve)	£80
63	Stateside SL 10050	FOLK SONGS (LP)	£40
68	Fontana (S)TL 5246	LOVE ME (LP)	£45
68	Mercury 20118 (S)MCL	MR. DREAM MERCHANT (LP)	£30
69	Mercury 20144 (S)MCL	SOUL GOES ON (LP)	£35
69	Mercury SMCL 20175	ICE ON ICE (LP)	£20
69	Mercury 20154 (S)MCL	THE ICE MAN COMETH (LP)	£35
70	Joys JOYS 171	MAKE IT EASY ON YOURSELF (LP)	£15
72	Mercury 6338 102	SPICE OF LIFE (LP)	£15
76	Tamla Motown STML 12032	LOVE'S ON THE MENU (LP)	£15
77	Tamla Motown Motown STML 12052	SUITE FOR THE SINGLE GIRL (LP)	£15

(see also Betty Everett & Jerry Butler, Impressions)

LESLIE BUTLER (& FUGITIVES)

67	Island WI 3069	Hornpipe Rock Steady/You Don't Have To Say You Love Me	£45
67	Doctor Bird DB 1083	Winchester Rocksteady (with Fugitives)/ASTON CAMPBELL & CONQUERORS : Ramona	£50
68	High Note HS 008	Top Cat/WEBBER SISTERS: Stars Above	£50
68	High Note HS 009	Revival/GAYLADS: Over The Rainbow's End	£60
75	Trojan TRLS 112	JA-GAN (LP)	£50

(see also Ken Boothe, Fugitives, Gaylads)

BUTTERCUPS

68	Pama PM 742	If I Love You/Loving You	£15
69	Pama PM 760	Come Put My Life In Order/If I Love You	£15

BILLY BUTTERFIELD & HIS ORCHESTRA
55   London HLF 8181   The Magnificent Matador/Sugar Blues Mambo £35

PAUL BUTTERFIELD BLUES BAND
66   London HLZ 10100   Come On In/I Got A Mind To Give Up Living £35
67   Elektra EKSN 45020   Run Out Of Time/One More Heartache £20
65   Elektra EKL/EKS 294   PAUL BUTTERFIELD BLUES BAND (LP, with rare gold 'guitar player' label) £200
65   Elektra EKL/EKS 294   PAUL BUTTERFIELD BLUES BAND (LP, orange label) £50
66   Elektra EKL/EKS 315   EAST - WEST (LP, orange label) £50
67   Elek. EKL 4015/EKS 74015   THE RESURRECTION OF PIGBOY CRABSHAW (LP, orange label) £35
68   Elektra EKL 4025   IN MY OWN DREAM (LP, orange label, also stereo EKS 74025) £40
69   Elektra EKS 74053   KEEP ON MOVIN' (LP) £20
71   Elektra EKD 2001   LIVE (2-LP) £20
72   Elektra K 62011   GOLDEN BUTTER (LP, gatefold sleeve) £18
(see also John Mayall's Bluesbreakers, Mike Bloomfield)

BUTTERFLIES
68   President PT 192   Love Me Forever/He's Got Everything £15

BUTTERFLYS
64   Red Bird RB 10009   Goodnight Baby/The Swim £22

BUTTERSCOTCH
70   RCA LSA 5000   BUTTERSCOTCH (LP, with insert and music book) £20

BUTTHOLE SURFERS
85   Fundamental SAVE 5   PSYCHIC...POWERLESS...ANOTHER MAN'S SAC (LP) £20
86   Red Rhino Europe RRELP 2   REMBRANDT PUSSYHORSE (LP) £20
87   Blast First BFFP 15   LOCUST ABORTION TECHNICIAN (LP) £30
88   Blast First BFFP 29   HAIRWAY TO STEVEN (LP) £20
91   Rough Trade R 2081 2601   PIOUGHD (LP, with bonus white label 12") £30
93   Capitol EST 2192   ELECTRIC LARRYLAND (2LP, one disc etched on one side, poster) £80
96   Capitol EST 2285   ELECTRIC LARRYLAND (2LP, one disc etched on one side, poster) £60

BUTTONDOWN BRASS
67   Fontana LPS 16255   HA HA HA (HEE-HEE-HEE) (LP) £15
76   DJM DJS 22046   FUNK IN HELL (LP) £40
76   DJM DJSLM2023   FIREDOG (LP) £15
77   DJM DJS 22076   COPS N'ROBBERS (LP) £15

BUY OFF THE BAR
88   Bi-Joopiter BIJOOP 023   PARBOILED (LP, screen printed sleeve with insert) £20

BUZZ AND THE FLYERS
80   Hot Rock HR45 007   Go Cat Wild/Dance To The Bop (p/s) £15

BUZZ & BUCKY
65   Stateside SS 428   Tiger A Go Go/Bay City £50
(see also Ronny & The Daytonas)

BUZZ (1)
66   Columbia DB 7887   You're Holding Me Down/I've Gotta Buzz £250
(see also Boston Dexters, Tam White)

BUZZ (2)
79   Redball RR 06   Insanity/Him Not Me/Sick At Heart (p/s) £30

BUZZARD
85   PTO MSPT01   Catch Me Alone/Raven Eyed Queen £45

BUZZCOCKS
77   New Hormones ORG-1   SPIRAL SCRATCH (EP, 1st pressing, plastic labels, p/s doesn't credit Howard Devoto on
                                        front of sleeve beneath band name) £150
77   United Artists UP 36316   Orgasm Addict/Whatever Happened To...? (p/s) £18
77   United Artists UP 36316   Whatever Happened To? (1-sided, promo only) £50
77   United Artists UP 36348   What Do I Get? (1-sided, promo) £60
78   United Artists UP 36348   What Do I Get?/Oh Shit (Mispress, plays Stranglers Peaches) (p/s) £75
78   United Artists UP 36455   Ever Fallen In Love (With Someone You Shouldn't've?)/Just Lust (p/s mispressed with
                                        Gerry Rafferty track Island on B-side) £25
78   United Artists UALP 15   Moving Away From The Pulsebeat (12", 1-sided, die-cut co. sl., promo only) £25
79   New Hormones ORG 1   SPIRAL SCRATCH (EP, reissue, p/s credits Howard Devoto, paper label) £15
80   United Artists BP 365 DJ   Why She's A Girl From The Chainstore/Are Everything (DJ promo) £20
91   Document DPRO-1   SPIRAL SCRATCH (EP, 2nd reissue, promo only 7") £18
95   United Artists ESP001   What Do I Get?/Mad Mad Judy/Raison D'Etre (Demo) (Fan Club only, no p/s) £20
78   United Artists UAG 30159   ANOTHER MUSIC IN A DIFFERENT KITCHEN (LP, black inner sleeve, in printed carrier
                                        bag) £70
78   United Artists UAG 30159   ANOTHER MUSIC IN A DIFFERENT KITCHEN (LP, black inner sleeve) £30
78   United Artists UAG 30159   ANOTHER MUSIC IN A DIFFERENT KITCHEN (LP, black inner, mispressing without "I
                                        Need") £50
78   United Artists UAG 30197   LOVE BITES (LP, embossed sleeve with insert, 'Buzzcocks' logo on labels) £30
78   United Artists UAG 30197   LOVE BITES (LP, mispressing, Side A plays first side of Maxine Nightingale's LOVE LINE
                                        LP, with insert & embossed sleeve) £45
79   United Artists UAG 30260   A DIFFERENT KIND OF TENSION (LP, with inner sleeve) £25
80   United Artists UAK 30279   SINGLES - GOING STEADY (LP, withdrawn at band's request) £200
80   Liberty UAG 30159   ANOTHER MUSIC IN A DIFFERENT KITCHEN (LP, reissue with b/w photo on sleeve, black
                                        inner) £20
81   Liberty LBR 1043   SINGLES - GOING STEADY (LP) £20
85   Liberty UAG 30197   LOVE BITES (LP, reissue, non embossed sleeve, no 'Buzzcocks' logo on label) £15
89   Strange Fruit SFRLP 104   PEEL SESSIONS (LP) £20

MINT VALUE £

89	EMI LP PRODT 1	PRODUCT (5LP box set, booklet)	£80
89	Absolutely Free FREELP 02	LIVE AT THE ROXY (LP)	£15
91	Document DLP 2	TIME'S UP (LP, mock bootleg, with bonus 33rpm interview single [FDLP 2])	£20
93	Castle ESSLP 195	TRADE TEST TRANSMISSIONS (LP)	£50
17	Domino REWIG113X	MK.1 (Box set, LP, 7" 2CD, fanzine, booklet, postcards, photos, badges and posters)	£80

(see also Pete Shelley)

BUZZIN CUZZINS
94	Azuli Records AZNY 024	Let Me Show You Love (12")	£60

JAKI BYARD
67	Transatlantic PR 7419	LIVE! VOL 1 (LP, white purple label)	£20
68	Transatlantic PR 7463	FREEDOM TOGETHER! (LP)	£20
68	Transatlantic PR 7550	SUNSHINE OF MY SOUL (LP)	£20

DON BYAS & HIS RHYTHM
64	Realm RM 230	ON 52ND STREET (LP)	£15

BYE LAWS
69	Pye 7N 17701	Run Baby Run/To Sir With Love	£20

TREVOR BYFIELD
80	Ethnic Fight EF 086	Jah Guide/TREVOR & CLIVE: Sea Of Love (12")	£45

ANTHONY BYGRAVES
74	Pye 7N 45429	Painted Lady/Love Star Ship	£15

JUNIOR BYLES
71	Bullet BU 499	Beat Down Babylon/UPSETTERS: Version	£30
71	Upsetter US 365	Place Called Africa/UPSETTERS: Earthquake	£35
72	Upsetter US 387	Festival Da Da/UPSETTERS: Version	£25
72	Pama PM 857	Fever/GROOVERS: Soul Sister (B-side actually by Heptones)	£60
72	Dynamic DYN 432	Pharaoh Hiding/UPSETTERS: Hail To Power	£25
72	Randy's RAN 523	King Of Babylon/UPSETTERS: Nebuchadnezzer	£25
72	Punch PH 109	Pharaoh Hiding/UPSETTERS: Hail To Power	£20
73	Pama PM 878	Education Rock/KEN McKAY: Nobody Knows	£15
73	Count Shelley CS 31	Break Up To Make Up (with Heptones)/YOUTH MAN (DILLINGER): Plat Skank	£25
74	Magnet MAG 27	Curly Locks/Now Generation	£15
74	Dip DL 5035	Curly Locks/Now Generation	£20
75	Dip DL 5074	Long Way/All The Way	£25
75	Ethnic Fight ETH 26	Mumbling And Grumbling/King Size Mumble	£25
76	Jessus JI 006	Know Where You Are Going/JESSUS EXPERIENCE: Going To Zion	£20
76	Black Wax WAX 17	Pitchy Patchy/THE JA-MAN ALL STARS: 129 Beat Street	£15
72	Trojan TRL 52	BEAT DOWN BABYLON (LP, beware of Canadian imports)	£60
87	Trojan TRLS 253	BEAT DOWN BABYLON: THE UPSETTER YEARS (LP)	£30
88	Trojan TRLS 269	WHEN WILL BETTER COME (LP)	£20
98	Blood & Fire BAFLP 023	129 BEAT STREET - JA-MAN SPECIAL 1975-1978 (as Junior Byles & Friends) (LP, ltd. ed.)	£40

(see also King Chubby, Lloyd Terrell, Dennis Alcapone, Upsetters, Bob Marley, Lee & Junior)

JUNIOR BYLES & RUPERT REID
76	Black Wax WAX 15	Chant Down Babylon/THE JA-MAN ALL STARS: Version	£20

BOBBY BYRD
73	Mojo 2093 028	Saying It And Doing It Are Two Different Things/VICKI ANDERSON: Don't Throw Your Love In Garbage/In The Land Of Milk & Honey	£15
71	Mojo 2918 002	I NEED HELP (LIVE ON STAGE) (LP)	£40

(see also JB's, James Brown, Anna King & Bobby Byrd, Vicki Anderson)

CHARLIE BYRD
84	Riverside RLP 9451	THE GUITAR ARTISTRY OF CHARLIE BYRD (LP, Nimbus Supercut, mail oder only through Practical Hi Fi magazine)	£40

DONALD BYRD
80	Blue Note 12 UP 622	Dominoes/Wind Parade (12")	£30
81	Elektra K 12559	Love Has Come Around/Loving You (12")	£15
55	Esquire 32-013	BYRD'S EYE VIEW (LP)	£50
55	Esquire 32-019	BYRD JAZZ (THE MOTOR CITY SCENES) (LP, as Donald Byrd Sextet)	£100
56	Esquire 32-032	JAZZ FOR THE CARRIAGE TRADE (LP)	£25
60s	Esquire 32-039	INFORMAL JAZZ (LP)	£25
75	Blue Note BN-LA047	BLACK BYRD (LP, reissue)	£25
75	Blue Note UAG 20001	PLACES AND SPACES (LP)	£40
76	Blue Note UAG 20008	CARICATURES (LP)	£15
78	Elektra K52097	THANK YOU FOR F.U.M.L. (FUNKING UP MY LIFE) (LP)	£20
78	Elektra K52199	DONALD BYRD & 125th STREET (LP)	£15
82	Elektra K 52427	WORDS, SOUNDS, COLOURS AND SHAPES (LP)	£20
92	Blue Note 7844661	BLACK BYRD (LP, reissue)	£20
92	Blue Note B1 98638	THE BEST OF DONALD BYRD (2-LP)	£30
95	Blue Note 31875	KOFI (LP)	£40
97	Blue Note 7243 8 53923 1 3	STREET LADY (LP, reissue)	£25
97	Blue Note 72438 54326 1 3	PLACES AND SPACES (LP, reissue)	£20

(see also Blackbyrds, Art Farmer)

RUSSELL BYRD
64	Sue WI 305	Hitch Hike Parts 1 & 2	£50

ESTHER BYRDE
79	Survival SUR 1	Touch Me Take Me/Tracks Of Love	£50

BYRDS

SINGLES

66	CBS 202067	Eight Miles High/Why	£15
66	CBS 202295	Mr Spaceman/What's Happening?!?!	£20
67	CBS 2924	Lady Friend/Don't Make Waves	£20
72	CBS 7712	America's Great National Pastime/Farther Along (unreleased)	£0

EPs

66	CBS EP 6069	THE TIMES THEY ARE A' CHANGIN' (EP)	£25
66	CBS EP 6077	EIGHT MILES HIGH (EP)	£30

ALBUMS

65	CBS BPG 62571	MR TAMBOURINE MAN (LP, mono)	£45
65	CBS (S)BPG 62571	MR TAMBOURINE MAN (LP, stereo)	£35
66	CBS BPG 62652	TURN! TURN! TURN! (LP, mono)	£45
66	CBS (S)BPG 62652	TURN! TURN! TURN! (LP, stereo)	£40
66	CBS BPG 62783	FIFTH DIMENSION (LP, mono)	£45
66	CBS (S)BPG 62783	FIFTH DIMENSION (LP, stereo)	£40

(All of the above LPs originally issued with textured orange labels and front laminated flipback sleeves)

67	CBS BPG 62988	YOUNGER THAN YESTERDAY (LP, mono)	£45
67	CBS (S)BPG 62988	YOUNGER THAN YESTERDAY (LP, stereo, with large white 'stereo' sticker on back sleeve)	£40
68	CBS BPG 63107	THE BYRDS GREATEST HITS (LP, mono)	£25
68	CBS SBPG 63107	THE BYRDS GREATEST HITS (LP, stereo)	£20
68	CBS BPG 63169	THE NOTORIOUS BYRD BROTHERS (LP, mono, 'Ernest J, Day' on rear)	£50
68	CBS (S)BPG 63169	THE NOTORIOUS BYRD BROTHERS (LP, stereo)	£35
68	CBS 63353	SWEETHEART OF THE RODEO (LP, mono, no 'M' or 'mono' on label but lacks 'S' prefix found on stereo copies)	£45
68	CBS 63353	SWEETHEART OF THE RODEO (LP, stereo, large white 'stereo' sticker on black sleeve)	£45

(The above LPs were issued with textured orange labels and front laminated non-flipback sleeves)

69	CBS 63545	DR BYRDS & MR HYDE (LP, mono)	£40
69	CBS S 63545	DR BYRDS & MR HYDE (LP, stereo)	£25
69	CBS S 63795	BALLAD OF EASY RIDER (LP, stereo only)	£25
69	CBS SBPG 62571	MR TAMBOURINE MAN (LP, 2nd stereo issue)	£25
70	CBS SPBG 62783	FIFTH DIMENSION (LP, 2nd stereo issue)	£25
70	CBS SBPG 62988	YOUNGER THAN YESTERDAY (2nd stereo issue, small gold 'stereo' sticker on rear)	£25

(The above LPs were originally issued with smooth orange labels and front laminated non-flipback sleeves)

70	CBS 66253	UNTITLED (LP, discs have S 64094 and S 64095 on labels as well as main cat no.)	£25
71	Bumble GEXP 8001	PRE-FLYTE (LP)	£25
71	CBS S 64389	BYRDMANIAX (LP)	£18
72	CBS 64676	FARTHER ALONG (LP)	£15
72	CBS S 64650	THE BYRDS GREATEST HITS VOL. 2 (LP)	£15
73	Asylum SYLA 8754	THE BYRDS (LP, gatefold sleeve)	£20
73	CBS 63169	NOTORIOUS BYRD BROTHERS LP, 2nd stereo issue)	£25
73	CBS S 63353	SWEETHEART OF THE RADIO (LP, 2nd stereo issue, 'stereo' printed on label)	£25
73	CBS SBPG 63107	THE BYRDS GREATEST HITS (LP, 2nd stereo reissue, slightly altered sleeve design)	£15
73	CBS 68252	HISTORY OF THE BYRDS (2-LP)	£18
75	CBS 63353	SWEETHEARTS OF THE RODEO (LP, reissue)	£15
82	CBS 32284	FIFTH DIMENSION (LP, reissue)	£15
87	Edsel ED 227	YOUNGER THAN YESTERDAY (LP, stereo reissue)	£15
87	Edsel ED 234	SWEETHEART OF THE RODEO (LP, stereo reissue)	£18
88	Edsel ED 262	NOTORIOUS BYRD BROTHERS LP, stereo reissue)	£18
91	BGO BGOLP 106	FIFTH DIMENSION (LP, stereo reissue)	£15
98	Simply Vinyl 0037/492519 1	TURN! TURN! TURN! (LP, stereo reissue)	£18
98	Simply Vinyl SVLP 032/ 62571	MR TAMBOURINE MAN (LP, stereo reissue)	£18
98	Simply Vinyl SVLP 0006/ 63169	NOTORIOUS BYRD BROTHERS (LPs, stereo reissue)	£18
99	Simply Vinyl SVLP 007/ 62988	YOUNGER THAN YESTERDAY (LP, stereo reissue)	£18
00	Simply Vinyl SVLP0057/ 63353	SWEETHEART OF THE RODEO (LP, stereo reissue)	£18
02	Simply Vinyl SVLP 375	THE VERY BEST OF (2-LP)	£18

(see also Beefeaters, David Crosby, Gene Clark, Gram Parsons, Gene Parsons, Skip Battin, Flying Burrito Brothers, Evergreen Blueshoes, Dillard & Clark, Kentucky Colonels)

PACKIE BYRNE (& BONNIE SHALJEAN)

69	EFDSS LP 1009	PACKIE BYRNE (LP)	£20

DAVID BYRNE & BRIAN ENO

08	Todomundo LP TODO 002	EVERYTHING THAT HAPPENS WILL HAPPEN TODAY (LP, printed inner)	£200
08	Todomundo TODO 002	EVERYTHING THAT HAPPENS WILL HAPPEN TODAY (2CD, circular tin with 3D house with sound effect of knocking, dice, pill, booklet)	£100

(see also Brian Eno & David Byrne, Brian Eno, David Byrne, Talking Heads)

MARTIN BYRNES

70	Leader LEA 2004	BYRNES (LP)	£15

DAVID BYRON

75	Bronze ILPS 9342	TAKE NO PRISONERS (LP, lyric inner sleeve)	£15
78	Arista SPART 1077	BABY FACED KILLER (LP)	£25
81	Creole CRX 2	ON THE ROCKS (LP, as BYRON BAND)	£20

(see also Uriah Heep)

SOL BYRON & IMPACTS
60s Flamingo PR 5027   Pride And Joy/Thou Shall Not Steal £15

BYSTANDERS (1)
65 | Pylot WD 501 | That's The End/This Time £150
66 | Piccadilly 7N 35330 | (You're Gonna) **Hurt Yourself/Have I Offended The Girl** £25
66 | Piccadilly 7N 35351 | **My Love - Come Home/If You Walk Away** £30
67 | Piccadilly 7N 35363 | 98.6/Stubborn Kind Of Fellow £20
67 | Piccadilly 7N 35382 | Royal Blue Summer Sunshine Day/Make Up Your Mind £30
67 | Piccadilly 7N 35399 | Pattern People/Green Grass £15
68 | Pye 7N 17476 | When Jezamine Goes/Cave Of Clear Light £50
68 | Pye 7N 17540 | This World Is My World/Painting The Time £15

(see also Man)

BYSTANDERS (2)
81 Uncle Robert UR 001   Nowhere To Hide/Sweet Fanny Adams/True Blue/I Wonder (EP) £20

BYZANTIUM
72 | Private pressing | **LIVE AND STUDIO** ('BLACK AND WHITE') (LP, 100 only with insert) £300
72 | A&M AMLH 68104 | **BYZANTIUM** (LP, with poster, brown label) £100
72 | A&M AMLH 68104 | **BYZANTIUM** (LP, without poster) £50
73 | A&M AMLH 68163 | **SEASONS CHANGING** (LP, poster sleeve, brown labels) £100

(see also Ora)

C

ANDY C
92 | RAM RAMM 001 | **SOUR MASH EP** (12") £50
93 | RAM RAMM 003 | **BASS LOGIC EP** (12") £35
93 | RAM RAMM 006 | Slip 'N' Slide/Bass Constructor (Sonz Of A Loop Da Loop Era Remix) (12") £25
95 | RAM RAMM 012 | Cool Down/Roll On (12") £15

(See also Randall and Andy C.)

ERROL C
76 Concrete Jungle CJ 601   Jah For I/4TH STREET ORCHESTRA: Version £35

FANTASTIC JOHNNY C
67 | London HL 10169 | Boogaloo Down Broadway/Look What Love Can Make You Do £15
68 | London HL 10212 | Hitch It To The Horse/Cool Broadway £15
69 | Action ACT 4543 | Is There Anything Better Than Making Love/New Love £18
69 | Action ACLP 6001 | **BOOGALOO DOWN BROADWAY** (LP) £40

ROY C
66 | Island WI 273 | Shotgun Wedding/I'm Going To Make It £20
67 | Ember EMB S 230 | Twistin' Pneumonia/Tear Avenue £15
66 | Ember NR 5035 | **THE SHOTGUN WEDDING MAN** (LP) £30
75 | Mercury 9100 017 | **SEX AND SOUL** (LP) £15

CABARET VOLTAIRE
78 | Rough Trade RT 003 | **EXTENDED PLAY EP** (paper p/s) £15
79 | Rough Trade RT 018 | **Nag Nag Nag/Is That Me** (p/s) £15
80 | Rough Trade RT 038 | **THREE MANTRAS** (12", p/s) £15
81 | Rough Trade RT 096 | **Eddie's Out/Walls Of Jericho** (12" p/s with free 7" Jazz The Glass/Burnt To The Ground (RT 095) £30
82 | Rough Trade ROUGH 42 | **2 x 45** (2 x 12") £18
83 | Factory FAC 82 | **Yashar** (7.20)/**Yashar** (5.00) (12") £15
85 | Virgin CVDJS1 | **Big Funk/Kino** (white label, 500 only) £18
91 | Plastex EXL 1 | **COLOURS** (12" EP. p/s) £20
79 | Rough Trade ROUGH 4 | **MIX UP** (LP) £25
80 | Rough Trade ROUGH 7 | **LIVE AT THE Y.M.C.A 27.10.79** (LP) £15
80 | Rough Trade ROUGH 11 | **VOICE OF AMERICA** (LP) £25
80 | Industrial IRC 35 | **1974-1976** (LP, cassette) £30
81 | Rough Trade ROUGH 27 | **RED MECCA** (LP) £25
83 | Some Bizarre CV1 | **THE CRACKDOWN** (LP, with free 12") £20
83 | Doublevision DVR 1 | **JOHNNY YESNO** (LP, soundtrack) £15
84 | Some Bizarre CV2 | **MICROPHONIES** (LP) £20
85 | Some Bizzare CV3 | **THE COVENANT, THE SWORD AND THE ARM OF THE LORD** (LP) £20
85 | Some Bizarre CVM 1 | **DRINKING GASOLINE** (LP as 2 x 12") £15
87 | Parlophone PCS 7312 | **CODE** (LP) £15
90 | Parlophone PCSX 7338 | **GROOVY, LAIDBACK AND NASTY** (LP, with free 12") £25
90 | Parlophone PCSX 7338 | **GROOVY, LAIDBACK AND NASTY** (LP, without free 12") £18
90 | Mute CABS 5 | **LISTEN UP WITH CABARET VOLTAIRE** (2-LP) £20
90 | Mute CABS 6 | **THE LIVING LEGENDS** (2-LP) £25
92 | Plasticity EXL LP03 | **PLASTICITY** (2-LP) £80
92 | Virgin CV 4 | **TECHNOLOGY: WESTERN REWORKS 1992** (2-LP) £70

(see also , Chemical Agent, Citrus, Cold Warrior, Richard H. Kirk, Hafler Trio,, Stephen Mallinder, Multiple Transmission, Papadoctrine, Pressure Co, Robot and Humanoids, Wicky Wacky, Sandoz, Sweet Exorcist, Wranger)

CABLES
68 Coxsone CS 7072   What Kind Of World?/My Broken Heart £70

68	Coxsone CS 7082	Soul Power/HEPTONES: Love Me Alway	£125
68	Studio One SO 2060	Baby Why?/Be A Man	£70
68	Studio One SO 2071	Love Is A Pleasure/Cheer Up	£80
69	Studio One SO 2085	Got To Find Someone/ALEXANDER HENRY: Please Be True	£80
69	Bamboo BAM 12	So Long/PRESSURE BOYS: More Love	£60
70	Bamboo BAM 19	How Can I Trust You?/SOUND DIMENSIONS: How Can I Trust You? (Inst.)	£60
70	Trojan TR 7792	Salt Of The Earth/Ring A Bell	£15
70	Harry J. HJ 6614	Didn't I/JAY BOYS: Tilly	£20
70	Harry J. HJ 6620	Feel Alright/Equal Rights	£15
71	Big Shot BI 598	A Sometime Girl/IN CROWD BAND: A Sometime Girl Version	£15
86	Studio One PSOL 002	WHAT KIND OF WORLD (LP, repressing, red and white labels)	£30

(see also Alton Ellis)

CACHE
| 81 | Groove GP 111 T | Where Is My Sunshine/Jazzin' And Crusin' (12") | £30 |

CACTUS
70	Atco 2400 020	CACTUS (LP)	£50
71	Atco 2400 114	ONE WAY ... OR ANOTHER (LP)	£30
72	Atlantic K 40307	RESTRICTIONS (LP)	£20
72	Atlantic K 50013	'OT AND SWEATY (LP)	£18

(see also Vanilla Fudge, Leaf Hound, Beck Bogert Appice, Atomic Rooster)

ALAN CADDY
| 64 | HMV POP 1286 | Tornado/Workout | £35 |

(see also Tornados)

CADETS (U.K.)
| 65 | Pye 7N 15852 | Jealous Heart/Right Or Wrong | £20 |

CADETS (U.S.)
56	London HLU 8313	Stranded In The Jungle/I Want You (gold label lettering)	£500
56	London HLU 8313	Stranded In The Jungle/I Want You (silver label lettering)	£250
56	London HLU 8313	Stranded In The Jungle/I Want You (78)	£20

CADILLACS (1)
| 59 | London HLJ 8786 | Peek-A-Boo/Oh, Oh, Lolita | £40 |

BOBBY CADMAN
| 74 | Regal Zonophone RZ3008 | A Magic Spell/Own Up Time | £25 |

CADO BELLE
| 76 | Anchor 1033 | Got To Love/Paper In The Rain | £15 |

SUSAN CADOGAN
74	Dip DL 5030	Hurt So Good/UPSETTERS: Loving Is Good	£15
75	Lucky LY 5078	Feeling Right/Congratulations	£15
77	Trojan TR9028	Nice And Easy/If You Need Me	£20
75	Upsetter UP 121	SEXY SUZY (LP, white label pre-release, 500 only, 'Upsetter Records Sexy Suzy' in white type, die-cut sleeve)	£70
76	Trojan TRLS 122	SUSAN CADOGAN (LP)	£50

CAEDMON
78	Private pressing	CAEDMON (LP, with insert, with bonus 7": Beyond The Second Mile/Give Me Jesus)	£750
78	Private pressing	CAEDMON (LP, with insert, without bonus 7": Beyond The Second Mile/Give Me Jesus)	£600
97	English Garden ENG 1014	CAEDMON (LP, reissue)	£25

CAESAR & CLEO
| 65 | Reprise R 20419 | Love Is Strange/Let The Good Times Roll (in p/s) | £25 |
| 65 | Reprise R 30056 | CAESAR AND CLEO (EP, 2 tracks each by Caesar & Cleo and Sonny & Cher) | £20 |

(see also Sonny & Cher)

CAESARS
| 65 | Decca F 12251 | On The Outside Looking In/Can You Blame Me? | £15 |

CAFE SOCIETY
| 75 | Konk KONK 102 | CAFE SOCIETY (LP, with inner sleeve) | £20 |

(see also Tom Robinson Band, Claire Hamill)

BUTCH CAGE/MABEL LEE WILLIAMS
| 60s | Storyville SLP 129 | COUNTRY BLUES (LP) | £20 |

AUBREY CAGLE
| 62 | Starlite ST 45 082 | Come Along Little Girl/Blue Lonely World | £75 |

JEREMY CAHILL
| 70s | Solent | September Blues/Yesterday | £15 |

(see also Shide & Acorn)

PATRICIA CAHILL
| 70 | Deram Nova SDN 22 | SUMMER'S DAUGHTER (LP) | £30 |

DAVID CAIN
| 69 | BBC RESR7 | THE SEASONS (LP) | £50 |

CAIN (1)
| 68 | Page One POF 054 | Her Emotion/Take Me Back One Time | £35 |
| 78 | SHP 103 | VISITOR 2035 (2-LP, fold-out lyric sheet) | £20 |

CAIN (2)
| 80s | private pressing | CAIN (2-LP) | £30 |

MINT VALUE £

DAVID CAIN & RONALD DUNCAN
12	Trunk JBH 043 LP	THE SEASONS (LP, 750 only)	£15

MARTI CAINE
82	BBC RESL 113	Can I Speak To The World Please?/Tin Heart And The Rebel (p/s)	£18
79	Pye Records N114	THE LADY'S GONNA SING (LP)	£25
81	BBC REB 408	POINT OF VIEW (LP)	£100

TUBAL CAINE
70	Attack ATT 8023	I'm A Drifter Part 1/CIMARONS: I'm A Drifter Part 2	£30

AL CAIOLA (ORCHESTRA)
56	London HLC 8285	Flamenco Love/From The Heart	£15
66	United Artists (S)ULP 1115	SOUNDS FOR SPIES AND PRIVATE EYES (LP)	£20

(see also Hugo Montenegro)

CAIR PARAVEL
76	Koala KOA PO 16	SOME OTHER MORNING (LP, insert)	£600

CAKE
68	MCA MUPS 303	THE CAKE (LP)	£30
69	MCA MUPS 390	A SLICE OF CAKE (LP)	£30

J.J. CALE
66	Liberty LIB 55881	Outside Lookin' In/In Our Time	£18
72	A&M AMLS 68105	NATURALLY (LP, tan label)	£30
79	Shelter ISA 5018	FIVE (LP, with bonus single "Katy Cool"/"Juan And Maria Juarez Blues" [JJ-1])	£15
92	Silvertone ORE 532	NUMBER TEN (LP)	£20

(see also Leathercoated Minds)

JOHN CALE
74	Island WIP 6202	The Man Who Couldn't Afford To.../Sylvia Said (Demo copy)	£15
77	Illegal IL 006	Jack The Ripper In The Moulin Rouge/Memphis (unissued, test pressings only)	£25
71	CBS 64256	VINTAGE VIOLENCE (LP, dark orange labels)	£35
71	CBS 64259	CHURCH OF ANTHRAX (LP, with Terry Riley, dark orange labels)	£35
73	Reprise K 44239	PARIS 1919 (LP, with lyric insert)	£35
74	Island ILPS 9301	FEAR (LP, pink rim)	£30
75	Island ILPS 9317	SLOW DAZZLE (LP, pink rim with picture inner sleeve)	£15
75	Island ILPS 9350	HELEN OF TROY (LP, orange palm tree label, inner sleeve, withdrawn A1/B1 matrix includes 'Leaving It Up To You')	£30
75	Island ILPS 9350	HELEN OF TROY (LP, orange palm tree label, inner sleeve, A1/B2 matrix includes 'Coral Moon' in place of 'Leaving It Up To You')	£20
77	Island ILPS 9459	GUTS (LP)	£20
77	Island ILPS 9350	HELEN OF TROY (LP, repressing, orange palm tree label, inner sleeve, A1/B3 matrix reinstates 'Leaving It Up To You')	£15
82	Ze ILPS 7019	MUSIC FOR A NEW SOCIETY (LP)	£15
84	Ze ILPS 7026	COMES ALIVE (LP)	£15
89	Land LAND 09	WORDS FOR THE DYING (LP)	£15
07	EMI 377 660 1	CIRCUS LIVE (3LP with free 7", gatefold, poster, sealed)	£90
12	Double Six DS047LPX	SHIFTY ADVENTURES IN NOOKIE WOOD (LP, lyric insert and 1-sided 7")	£22
16	Domino REWIGLP 107X	FRAGMENTS OF A RAINY SEASON (3-LP reissue, inners)	£40

(see also Velvet Underground, Nico, Terry Riley, Ayers Cale Nico & Eno, Judy Nylon, Eno & Cale)

CALEB (QUAYE)
67	Philips BF 1588	Baby Your Phrasing Is Bad/Woman Of Distinction (300-500 pressed)	£950

(see also Mirage, Hookfoot, Bread & Beer Band, Elton John)

CALEDONIANS
69	Fab FAB 103	Funny Way Of Laughing/Don't Please	£60

(see also Clarendonians, Prince Buster)

CALENDAR CROWD
82	Romantic RR002	Perfect Hideaway/Perfect Hideaway Dub (p/s)	£20

CALIBAN
84	Caliban CLB 001	Digital Reggae/Open Mind (no p/s)	£50

CALIBRE
09	Signature SIG 015	Let Me Hold You/Love's Too Tight To Mention (12")	£30
01	Creative Source CRSE002LP	MUSIQUE CONCRETE (LP as 5 x 12")	£25
05	Signature SIGLP001	SECOND SUN (LP as 4 x 12")	£40
07	Signature SIGLP002	SHELFLIFE (LP as 4 x 12")	£30
08	Signature SIGLP003	OVERFLOW (LP as 5 x 12")	£30
09	Signature SIGLP004	SHELFLIFE VOL. 2 (LP as 4 x 12")	£35
10	Signature SIGLP006	EVEN IF... (LP as 3 x 12")	£30
11	Signature SIGLP007	CONDITION (LP as 3 x 12" with CD)	£30
14	Signature SIGLP010	SHELFLIFE VOL. 3 (LP as 3 x 12" with CD)	£35

CALIFORNIA IN-CROWD
66	Fontana TF 779	Questions And Answers/Happiness In My Heart	£70

CALIFORNIANS
67	CBS 2263	Golden Apples/Little Ship With A Red Sail	£75
67	Decca F 12678	Follow Me/What Love Can Do	£20
68	Decca F 12802	Out In The Sun/The Sound	£20
69	Fontana TF 991	Mandy/The Cooks Of Cake And Kindness	£100
69	Fontana TF 1052	Sad Old Song/Weep No More	£15

(see also Warren Zevon)

CALLAN & JOHN
69 CBS 4447 — House Of Delight/Long Shadow Day £40

CALLICOTT, (MISSISSIPPI) JOE
68 Blue Horizon 7-63227 — PRESENTING THE COUNTRY BLUES (LP) £110
71 Revival RVS 1002 — DEAL GONE DOWN (LP, as Joe Callicott) £25

TERRY CALLIER
78 Elektra K 52096 — FIRE ON ICE (LP) £15
79 Elektra K 52140 — TURN YOU TO LOVE (LP) £15
98 Verve/Talkin Loud 539 249 1 — TIMEPEACE (LP) £30

CALLIES
71 Rubber RUB 002 — ON YOUR SIDE (LP, gatefold sleeve) £15

CALLINAN-FLYNN
72 Mushroom 50 MR 17 — We Are The People (The Road To Derry Town)/The Old Man And The Flower £30
72 Mushroom 150 MR 18 — FREEDOM'S LAMENT (LP) £200

CALLING HEARTS
91 Illuminated ILL 6 — Return To Base/In The Jungle (p/s) £15

CALLIOPE
69 Uni UN 514 — Clear Mud/Wiser £15
68 Buddah 203 016 — STEAMED (LP) £25

GEORGE CALSTOCK
78 Hit Run DD2 — The Ungodly (Feat. U Black)/DOCTOR PABLO: Righteous Melody (12") £35

ROBERT CALVERT
72 United Artists UP 35543 — Ejection/Catch A Falling Starfighter (p/s) £25
74 United Artists UAS 29507 — CAPTAIN LOCKHEED AND THE STARFIGHTERS (LP, embossed gatefold sleeve, with attached booklet and inner sleeve) £40
75 United Artists UAS 29852 — LUCKY LIEF AND THE LONGSHIPS (LP, gatefold sleeve) £20
81 A-Side IF 0311 — HYPE (SONGS OF TOM MAHLER) (LP) £15
88 Beat Goes On BGOLP 2 — LUCKY LIEF AND THE LONGSHIPS (LP, gatefold sleeve, reissue) £20
88 Beat Goes On BGOLP 5 — CAPTAIN LOCKHEED AND THE STARFIGHTERS (LP, gatefold sleeve with booklet, reissue) £15
89 Clear BLACK 1 — ROBERT CALVERT AT THE QUEEN ELIZABETH HALL (LP, mail order only, with badge, poster & T-shirt, gatefold sleeve) £40

(see also Hawkwind, Imperial Pompadours, Catapilla, Adrian Wagner, John Stevens Away)

CALYPSO JOE
69 Escort ES 801 — Adults Only/Calalue £50

CAMALEONTI
68 CBS 3968 — Applause/Applausi £20

CAMARQUE
83 Clubland SJP 848 — Howl Of The Pack/Someone Just Like You (in p/s) £75
83 Clubland SJP 848 — Howl Of The Pack/Someone Just Like You £30

CAMBERWELL NOW
83 Duplicate 0011 — MERIDIAN (12", p/s) £20
87 Ink 1224 — GREENFINGERS (12", p/s) £15
86 Ink 19 — GHOST TRADE (LP) £30

(see also This Heat, Camberwell Now)

CAMBODIANS
70 Duke DU 101 — Coolie Man/J.J. ALLSTARS: Coolie Version £35

CAMEL
73 MCA MUPS 473 — CAMEL (LP, 1st pressing, black/blue hexagon label) £175
73 MCA MUPS 473 — CAMEL (LP, 2nd pressing, black label) £50
74 Deram SML 1107 — MIRAGE (LP, with insert, red/white label, small Deram logo) £60
73 MCA MCF 6265 — CAMEL (LP, later rainbow label with black background) £30
75 Decca SKL-R 5207 — THE SNOW GOOSE (LP, laminated sleeve, insert) £40
76 Decca TXS-R 115 — MOON MADNESS (LP, 1st pressing with textured gatefold sleeve and P1 matrixes) £30
77 Decca TXS-R 124 — RAIN DANCES (LP, with inner) £20
78 Decca TXS R 132 — BREATHLESS (LP, insert) £20
78 Decca DBC-R 7/8 — A LIVE RECORD (2-LP, gatefold) £20
79 Decca TXS R 137 — I CAN SEE YOUR HOUSE FROM HERE (LP, insert) £15
06 Tapestry TPT 227 — CAMEL (LP, repressing, 500 only) £18

(see also Pete Bardens, Gong/Camel, Caravan, Hatfield & The North)

CAMEL DRIVERS
68 Pye International 7N 25471 — Sunday Morning 6 O'Clock/Give It A Try £15

CAMEOS (1)
63 Columbia DB 7092 — Powercut/High Low And Lonesomely £30
64 Columbia DB 7201 — My Baby's Coming Home/Where E'er You Walk £30

CAMERA OBSCURA (2)
98 Andmoresounds AND 0945 — Park And Ride/Swimming Pool £25
98 Andmoresounds AND 1145 — Your Sound/Autumn Tides/Annawaltzerpose £25
01 Andmoresounds AND 1733 — BIGGEST BLUEST HI-FI (LP) £35
03 Elefant ER-1104LP — UNDERACHIEVERS PLEASE TRY HARDER (LP, gatefold sleeve) £20
06 Elefant ER-1123LP — LET'S GET OUT OF THIS COUNTRY (LP) £18

CAMERA 3
79 Service SER 001 — Russians In Space/The Solution To All Our Problems (p/s) £20

MINT VALUE £

CAMERAS IN CARS
80	In Cinc CINC 1	Time Room/Avoid A Void/Bright Boy/The Author (p/s) £15

DION CAMERON & THREE TOPS
66	Rio R 111	Lord Have Mercy/Get Ready £60

(see also Dion & Three Tops)

G.C. CAMERON
80	Flamingo FM-11	Live For Love/If I Love You...£50
80	Flamingo FM T-11	Live For Love/If I Love You (12")..£60
89	Ardent ADS 9002	Wait Until Tomorrow/Shadows £18
76	Tamla Motown ATML12029	G.C. CAMERON (LP)...£15

(see also Detroit Spinners)

JOHN CAMERON (QUARTET)
69	Deram DM 256	Troublemaker/Off Centre...£60
67	Columbia SCX 6116	COVER LOVER (LP) £30
68	Columbia Studio Two 197	WARM & GENTLE (LP) £20
69	Deram DML/SML 1044	OFF CENTRE (LP) £100
01	Trunk KES 001 LP	KES (1-sided LP, 500 only) £20
03	Trunk JBH 002	PSYCHOMANIA (LP, 1000 only, as John Cameron & Frog) £60

(see also Frog)

AL CAMPBELL
73	Magnet MA 023	When Spring Is Around/It Wouldn't Be Fair £30
75	Sunshot SS 008	Can't Get No Peace/REVOLUTIONARIES: Peace & Love £20
78	Phil Pratt SS 1009	Gee Baby/Where Were You (12") £20
78	Deb DEB 018	Love The Way It Should Be/Version (12") £40
79	Saferno SOF 004	Gone Down The Drain/One More Chance (12") £30
79	Nigara NADD 103	La-La Means I Love You (12") £40
70s	Ethnic ETH DD 2244	Down In A Babylon/Babylon Dub (12") £30
80	Strong Like Sampson SLSD 14	Jah Shine On Me/SUGAR MINOTT: Hall Of Love (12") £35
80	JB JBD 019	You Jamming/You Jamming (Part 2) (12") £30
80	JB Music JBD 004	Late Night Blues/Shower Me With Blessings (12") £15
81	Greensleeves GRED 51	Unfaithful Children/WAILING SOULS: Who No Waan Come (12")........£60
81	JB JBD 029	Feed Back/Part 2 (12") £30
82	Greensleeves GRED 94	Dance Hall Stylee/Fight I Down (12") £20
82	Silver Camel SC 014	Lambs Bread/I Was Born A Loser (10", p/s) £15
78	Sunshot SS 1002	GEE BABY (LP) £85
78	Terminal TMLP 1002	NO MORE RUNNING (LP) £100
78	ITAL IT001	LOVING MOODS OF (LP)..£50
78	Jamaica Sounds JSLP 015	AIN'T THAT LOVING YOU (LP) £50
78	Manic PFULP 8551	MR. MUSIC MAN (LP) £30
78	D.E.B. DBLP07	SHOWCASE (LP) £100
79	Burning Sounds BS 1036	DIAMONDS (LP) £30
79	Hawkeye HLD 03	RAINY DAYS (LP) £35
80	Ethnic Fight ETH 2236	MORE SHOWCASE (LP) £60
80	JB JBLP 002	LATE NIGHT BLUES (LP) £100
80	JB JBLP 005	WORKING MAN (LP) £60
83	Vista Sounds VSLP 4033	AIN'T THAT LOVING YOU (LP, reissue) £25
84	CSA CSLP 14	BAD BOY (LP) £20

AL CAMPBELL & TRINITY
78	Deb DEB 013	Reggae Dance/Dragon Dance/AL CAMPBELL: Roots Man Style (12") £30

ALEX CAMPBELL
68	Saga OPP 2	Victoria Dines Alone/Pack Up Your Sorrows £30
64	Xtra XTRA 1014	ALEX CAMPBELL (LP, with Martin Carthy)..£25
65	Polydor 623 035	IN COPENHAGEN (LP) £18
67	Saga ERO 8021	ALEX CAMPBELL AND HIS FRIENDS (LP, with Sandy Denny) £15
71	Ad-Rhythm/Tepee ARPS 1	THIS IS ALEX CAMPBELL VOL. 1 (LP) £15
71	Ad-Rhythm/Tepee ARPS 2	THIS IS ALEX CAMPBELL VOL. 2 (LP) £15
87	Sundown SDLP 2048	WITH THE GREATEST RESPECT (2-LP, reissue of "This Is..." Vols. 1 & 2) ...£18

(see also Sandy Denny)

AMBROSE CAMPBELL
66	Columbia SX 6081	HIGH LIFE TODAY (LP) £60

CAT CAMPBELL & NICKY THOMAS
72	Pressure Beat PB 5511	Hammering/PETER TOSH: Medicine Man £20

CHOKER CAMPBELL
65	Tamla Motown TMG 517	Mickey's Monkey/Pride And Joy (as Choker Campbell's Big Band) £140
65	Tamla Motown TMG 517	Mickey's Monkey/Pride And Joy (as Choker Campbell's Big Band) (DJ copy)...£250
65	Tamla Motown TML 11011	HITS OF THE SIXTIES (LP, as Choker Campbell & His 16-Piece Band) £125

CORNELL CAMPBELL (AKA CORNEL CAMPBELL)
63	Island WI 039	Rosabelle/Turndown Date (B-side actually "Under The Old Oak Tree") £45
63	Island WI 083	Each Lonely Night/ROLAND ALPHONSO: Steamline £40
64	Port-O-Jam PJ 4008	Jericho Road (with Dimple Hinds)/DON DRUMMOND & GROUP: Roll On Sweet Don £80
64	Rio R 38	Gloria/I'll Be True £25
72	Dynamic DYN 446	My Confession/AGGROVATORS: Version £25
72	Green Door GD 4042	Dearest Darling/Star Dust £20
72	Jackpot JP 801	Queen And The Minstrel/Put Yourself In My Place......................................£30
72	Bullet BU 515	For Once In My Life/Didn't I? £25

73	Jackpot JP 809	Pity The Children/You're No Good	£35
73	Green Door GD 4057	Give Me Love/Help Them O Lord	£70
73	Duke DU 158	Shotgun Wedding/Girl Of My Dreams	£18
73	Duke DU 159	The Very Best I Can/Heading For The Mountains	£15
73	Gayfeet GS 209	My Baby Just Care For Me/Jah Jah Me Horn Ya	£20
75	Action ACT 102	Natty In A Greenwich Farm/Natty Version	£15
77	Third World TW57	The Investigator/Version	£15
78	Cactus CT 118	My Country/ Part 2	£30
79	Lord Koos EQ 1001	Mash You Down/Sweet Talking (12")	£15
80	Cha Cha CHAD25	Rainbow/PETER BROGGS: Never Forget Jah (12")	£70
70s	Wambesi TW 004	I'm A Man/Jah Jah Give Us Love (12")	£15
80s	Live & Love LLDIS0022	Nothing Don't Come Easy/Version (12")	£20
80	Papa D PD0167	Rasta Come From Jail (with SASSAFRASS)/100 Pounds of Collie (with PAPA TULLO)	£18
87	Live & Love LLDIS0022	Nothing Don't Come Easy/Version/SUPER BLACK: Bad Boys/Version (12")	£25
04	Trojan/Jackpot TJGSE013	You're No Good/Pity The Children (reissue)	£25
72	Trojan TBL 199	CORNELL CAMPBELL (LP)	£50
75	Groundnation GROL 503	DANCE IN A GREENWICH FARM (LP)	£50
76	Angen ANGL 03	GORGON (LP)	£50
76	Third World TWS 301	STALOWATT (LP)	£40
78	Justice JUSLP 09	ROPIN (LP)	£30
79	Striker Lee TSL 104	NATTY DREAD IN A GREENWICH FARM (LP)	£40
79	Burning Sounds BS 1034	SWEET BABY (LP)	£25
82	Starlight SDLP 908	BOXING (LP)	£25
83	Vista Sounds VSLP 4020	FIGHT AGAINST CORRUPTION (LP)	£20
00	Simply Vinyl SVLP 391	I SHALL NOT REMOVE (2-LP)	£20

(see also Eternals, Don Cornel & Eternals, Clarendonians, Charmers, Stranger & Patsy, GG Allstars, Flames)

DAVID CAMPBELL

67	Transatlantic TRA 141	DAVID CAMPBELL (LP)	£30
67	Transatlantic TRA 153	YOUNG BLOOD (LP)	£20
72	Decca SKL 5139	SUN WHEEL (LP)	£25

ERROL CAMPBELL

77	Tempus 103	Jah Man/Jah	£30
76	Shebazz SHE 001	Wolves/Follow	£30

ETHNA CAMPBELL

64	Mercury MF 804	What's Easy For Two Is Hard For One/Again	£20
74	Philips 6382138	FOR THE GOOD TIMES (LP)	£15

IAN CAMPBELL (FOLK) GROUP

65	Transatlantic TRASP 5	The Times They Are A-Changin'/Across The Hills (in p/s)	£15
68	Transatlantic TRA 163	THE CIRCLE GAME (LP)	£15
71	Acorn CF 233	HOPE IS A STAR (LP)	£30
71	Argo ZFB 13	THE SUN IS BURNING (LP)	£15

(see also Dave Swarbrick)

ISOBEL CAMPBELL

03	Snowstorm STORM 024LP	AMORINO (LP, 1500 only)	£50
06	V2 VVR1043451	MILKWHITE SHEETS (LP)	£15

(see also Belle & Sebastian, Gentle Waves, Isobel Campbell & Mark Lanegan)

ISOBEL CAMPBELL & MARK LANEGAN

06	V2 VVR5036037	Ramblin Man/Further Into The Night	£15
08	V2 VVR5050637	Who Built The Road/Wild Is The Night	£15
10	V2 VVR749786	You Won't Let Me Down Again/Hawk (Extended)	£15
06	V2 VVR 1035821	BALLAD OF THE BROKEN SEAS (LP)	£150
08	V2 VVR1050621	SUNDAY AT DEVIL DIRT (LP)	£200
10	V2 VVR745755	HAWK (LP)	£200

(see also Mark Lanegan, Solusavers, Belle & Sebastian)

JIMMY CAMPBELL

69	Fontana TF 1009	On A Monday/Dear Marge (in p/s)	£35
69	Fontana TF 1009	On A Monday/Dear Marge	£21
69	Fontana STL 5508	SON OF ANASTASIA (LP, black/silver label)	£120
70	Vertigo 6360 010	HALF BAKED (LP, gatefold sleeve, large swirl label)	£150
72	Philips 6308 100	JIMMY CAMPBELL'S ALBUM (LP, black/silver label)	£150

(see also Kirkbys, 23rd Turnoff, Rockin' Horse)

JO-ANN CAMPBELL

58	London HLU 8536	Wait A Minute/It's True	£50
60	HMV POP 776	Bobby, Bobby, Bobby/A Kookie Little Paradise	£25
61	HMV POP 873	Motorcycle Michael/Puka Puka Pants	£20
62	HMV POP 1003	You Made Me Love You/I Changed My Mind Jack	£20
62	Cameo Parkway CP 237	Mr Fix It Man/Let Me Do It My Way	£15
63	Cameo Parkway CP 249	Mother Please/Waitin' For Love	£15

JUNIOR CAMPBELL

74	Deram SML 1106	SECOND TIME AROUND (LP)	£18

(see also Marmalade, Clan, Dean Ford & Gaylords)

LLOYD CAMPBELL

76	Love LOV 2	FIGHTING DUB (LP, artist commonly listed as Skin, Flesh & Bone)	£50

MARTIN CAMPBELL

90	Jah Works JW 002T	Who Can We Run To?/SISTER NETIFA: Woman Determined (12")	£20
91	Jah Works JW 015	Got To Pray/Praying Dub (12")	£20

MINT VALUE £

95	Raghga Delic LIC 1	Wicked Rule/Dub/Version/Drums (12")	£25
97	Channel 1 (UK) NXTB 007	Wicked Rule/Remix Next Vs/Wicked Dub/Everywhere/I Walk/Next Version/Dub (12")	£18
98	Channel 1 TBX 010	ROOTSMAN - THE REAL THING (LP)	£25
90	Jah Works JW008P	THE DREAM IS OVER (LP)	£30
02	Channel 1 LOGLP 015	HISTORICAL TRACKS (1978-1981) THE FOUNDATION (LP)	£15

PETE CAMPBELL

79	Union UND1016	Does She Have A Friend For Me/CARLTON HUNTER: You Know Why (12")	£40

ROY CAMPBELL (& JAZZBO JASPERS)

68	Giant GN 41	Another Saturday Night/Wonderful World (with Jazzbo Jaspers)	£15
68	Jolly JY 003	Suzette/Engine Engine Number Nine	£18

PATRICK CAMPBELL-LYONS

73	Sovereign SOV 115	Everybody Should Fly A Kite/I Think I Want Him Too	£15
73	Sovereign SOV 119	Out On The Road/Me And My Friend	£15
73	Sovereign SVNA 7258	ME AND MY FRIEND (LP, gatefold sleeve)	£250
81	Public PUBL 1	THE ELECTRIC PLOUGH (LP)	£20

(see also Nirvana [U.K.], Pica, Hat & Tie, Aquila)

CAMPER VAN BEETHOVEN

86	Rough Trade RT 161	TAKE THE SKINHEADS BOWLING (12" EP)	£15
86	Rough Trade ROUGH 95	TELEPHONE FREE LANDSLIDE VICTORY (LP, with insert)	£18
87	Rough Trade ROUGH 109	CAMPER VAN BEETHOVEN (LP)	£15

CAN

73	United Artists UP 35596	Moonshake/Future Days (Edit)	£20
73	United Artists UP 35506	Spoon/I'm So Green	£20
83	Cherry Red CHERRY 57	Moonshake/Turtles Have Short Legs/One More Night (12")	£20
69	United Artists UAS 29094	MONSTER MOVIE (LP, burgundy label)	£175
70	United Artists UAS 29283	SOUNDTRACKS (LP)	£50
71	United Artists UAS 29094	MONSTE MOVIE (LP, repress by 'the can', sleeve has laminated front)	£50
71	United Artists UAD 60009/10	TAGO MAGO (2-LP, flip-top sleeve)	£150
72	United Artists UAS 29414	EGE BAMYASI (LP, with inner sleeve)	£100
73	United Artists UAS 29505	FUTURE DAYS (LP)	£80
74	United Artists UAG 29673	SOON OVER BABALUMA (LP, original silver sleeve)	£50
74	United Artists USP 103	LIMITED EDITION (LP)	£50
75	Virgin V 2041	LANDED (LP)	£40
76	Caroline CAD 3001	UNLIMITED EDITION (2-LP, gatefold sleeve)	£40
76	Sunset SLS 50400	OPENER (LP)	£20
76	Virgin V 2071	FLOW MOTION (LP, some stickered stating "featuring the hit single I Want More")	£18
77	Virgin V 2079	SAW DELIGHT (LP, with insert)	£30
78	Lightning LIP 4	OUT OF REACH (LP)	£15
78	United Artists UDM 105/6	CANNABALISM (2-LP, gatefold sleeve)	£35
81	Virgin OVED 195	INCANDESCENCE (LP)	£15
89	Mercury 838883	RITE TIME (LP)	£20
97	Mute SPOON39/40	SACRILEGE (3-LP, gatefold)	£30
07	Mute SPOON 008	EGE BAMYASI (LP, reissue)	£15
12	Mute SPOON 55	THE LOST TAPES (5-LP box set, booklet)	£100
12	Spoon CDSPOON5	THE LOST TAPES (3-CD boxed set, booklet)	£25
14	Spoon XSPOON 4	MONSTER MOVIE (LP, reissue, inner with download card)	£15
14	Spoon XSPOON 5	SOUNDTRACKS (LP, reissue, inner with download card)	£15
14	Spoon XSPOON 6/7	TAGO MAGO (2-LP, reissue, download card)	£20
14	Spoon XSPOON 8	EGE BAMYASI (LP, reissue, inner, download card)	£15
14	Spoon XSPOON 9	FUTURE DAYS (LP, inner, download card)	£15
14	Spoon XSPOON 10	SOON OVER BABALUMA (LP, reissue, inner with download card)	£15
14	Spoon XSPOON 25	LANDED (LP, reissue, inner with download card)	£15
14	Spoon XSPOON 23/24	UNLIMITED EDITION (2-LP reissue)	£20
17	Spoon SPOON 60	THE SINGLES (3-LP)	£25

CANAAN

73	Dovetail DOVE 3	CANAAN (LP)	£25
76	Myrrh MYR 1042	OUT OF THE WILDERNESS (LP, with inner sleeve)	£20

LOS CANARIOS

67	Major Minor MM 502	Three Two One Ah/What Can I Do For You	£50
67	Major Minor MM 532	Get On Your Knees/Keep On The Right Side	£35

CANCER

90	Vinyl Solution SOL 22	TO THE GORY END (LP)	£25
91	Vinyl Solution SOL 28	DEATH SHALL RISE (LP)	£20
93	Vinyl Solution SOL 35	THE SINS OF MANKIND (LP)	£25

CANDIDO

79	Salsoul Sa 8520	DANCIN AND PRANCIN (LP)	£18

CANDLE FACTORY

77	CAVS 020	NIGHTSHIFT (LP, private pressing)	£80

CANDLELIGHT

67	CBS 2002507	That's What I Want/The Happy Days Of Summer	£25

CANDLEMASS

87	Active ATV 3	NIGHTFALL (LP)	£15
89	Music For Nations MFN 95	TALES OF CREATION (LP)	£15

MINT VALUE £

88	Active Records ACT LP7	ANCIENT DREAMS (LP, insert)	£20
03	Powerline PRLP 010	DIAMONDS OF DOOM (2-LP, white vinyl, gatefold sleeve with iron-on transfer)	£20

ICHO CANDY
88	Selah DEX 007	Cool Down Sufferer/FISH CLARKE: Carry You Woman Go A Dance (12")	£20
93	Jah Shaka SHAKA 948	GLORY TO THE KING (LP)	£18

CANDY (1)
69	Emerald MD 1119	Little Bit Of Soul/Signs Of Love	£20

CANDY (2)
69	Grape GR 3017	Ace Of Hearts/BILLY JACK: Bet Yer Life I Do	£20

CANDY CHOIR
66	Parlophone R 5472	Silence Is Golden/Shake Hands (And Come Out Crying)	£15

(see also Summer Set, Barry Ryan)

CANDY & KISSES
65	Cameo Parkway C 336	The 81/Two Happy People	£150
65	Cameo Parkway C 336	The 81/Two Happy People (DJ copy)	£200
85	Kent TOWN 104	Mr Creator/CHUCK JACKSON: Hand It Over (withdrawn)	£40

CANE
78	Lightning GIL 31	3 BY 3 EP (p/s)	£25

CANIS MAJOR
80	Gem GEMLP 109	BUTTERFLY QUEEN (LP)	£30

(see also Girlschool)

JAMES CANN BAND
82	LJS LJS 001	Love Don't Know Your Name/Hush Hush We Can Boogie	£15

CANNED HEAT
68	Liberty	Rollin' And Tumblin'/Bullfrog Blues (unreleased)	£0
67	Liberty LBL/LBS 83059E	CANNED HEAT (LP)	£100
68	Liberty LBL/LBS 83103	BOOGIE WITH CANNED HEAT (LP)	£50
69	Liberty LDS 84001E	LIVING THE BLUES (2-LP, gatefold sleeve)	£40
69	Liberty LBS 83239	HALLELUJAH (LP, gatefold sleeve)	£25
70	Pye Intl. NSPL 28129	VINTAGE HEAT (LP)	£30
70	Liberty LBS 83303	CANNED HEAT COOKBOOK (LP)	£15
70	Liberty LBS 83364	FUTURE BLUES (LP, gatefold sleeve)	£20
71	Liberty LPS 103/4	HOOKER'N'HEAT (2-LP, gatefold sleeve, with John Lee Hooker)	£50
72	United Artists UAG 29304	HISTORICAL FIGURES AND ANCIENT HEADS (LP, gatefold sleeve)	£15
73	United Artists UAS 29455	THE NEW AGE (LP)	£15

(see also Harvey Mandel, John Lee Hooker)

CANNIBAL & HEADHUNTERS
65	Stateside SS 403	Land Of A Thousand Dances/I'll Show You How To Love Me	£30
67	CBS 62942	LAND OF A 1000 DANCES (LP)	£40

CANNIBAL CORPSE
90	Metal Blade ZORRO 12	EATEN BACK TO LIFE (LP, inner)	£25
91	Metal Blade ZORRO 26	BUTCHERED AT BIRTH (LP)	£40
92	Metal Blade ZORRO 49	TOMB OF THE MUTILATED (LP, inner)	£45
94	Metal Blade ZORRO 67	THE BLEEDING (LP)	£45

PHIL CANNING
79	Woodbine St. WSR 002	Sell Out/Underground (p/s)	£40

FREDDY CANNON
59	Top Rank JAR 135	Tallahassee Lassie/You Know	£15
59	Top Rank JAR 135	Tallahassee Lassie/You Know (78)	£25
61	Top Rank JAR 568	Buzz Buzz A Diddle It/Opportunity	£20
63	Stateside SS 201	Patty Baby/Betty Jean	£20
60	Top Rank JKP 2058	THE EXPLOSIVE FREDDY (BOOM! BOOM!) CANNON (EP)	£15
60	Top Rank JKP 2066	FOUR DIRECT HITS (EP)	£15
61	Top Rank JKP 3010	ON TARGET (EP)	£15
62	Stateside SE 1002	BLAST OFF WITH FREDDY CANNON (EP)	£20
60	Top Rank 25/018	THE EXPLOSIVE FREDDY CANNON (LP)	£20
61	Top Rank 35/106	FREDDY CANNON SINGS HAPPY SHADES OF BLUE (LP)	£30
61	Top Rank 35/113	FREDDY CANNON FAVOURITES (LP)	£25
63	Stateside SL 10013	BANG ON (LP)	£35
64	Stateside SL 10062	STEPS OUT (LP)	£40
64	Warner Bros WM/WS 8153	FREDDY CANNON (LP)	£25

(see also Danny & Juniors)

JUDY CANNON
65	Pye 7N 15900	The Very First Day I Met You/Hello Heartache	£50

SEAN CANNON
77	Cottage COT 411	ROVING JOURNEYMAN (LP)	£30

CANNON BALL & JOHNNY MELODY
69	Big Shot BI 518	Parapinto/Cool Hand Luke	£100

(see also Carl Bryan, King Cannon, Johnny Moore, Jackie Mittoo, Royals)

CANNON BROTHERS
65	Brit WI 1003	Turn Your Eyes To Me/Don't Stop Now	£18

CANNONS
60	Decca F 11269	I Didn't Know The Gun Was Loaded/My Guy's Come Back	£15

			MINT VALUE £

61 Columbia DB 4724 — **Bush Fire/Juicy** £20

CANNY FETTLE
75 Tradition TSR 023 — **VARRY CANNY** (LP) £30
77 Tradition TSR 027 — **TRIP TO HARROGATE** (LP) £18

CANYON
75 RCA RCA 2112 — **Top Of The World/Boogie Down Broadway** £15

CAPABILITY BROWN
72 Charisma CAS 1056 — **FROM SCRATCH** (LP, lyric inner sleeve, pink 'scroll' label) £50
73 Charisma CAS 1068 — **VOICE** (LP, gatefold sleeve, large 'Mad Hatter' label) £40
74 Charisma Perspective CS 5 — **LIAR** (LP) £15
(see also Unit 4+2, Tony Rivers & Castaways, Fuzzy Duck)

JIM CAPALDI
72 Island ILPS 9187 — **OH HOW WE DANCED** (LP, gatefold sleeve, pink rim label) £20
74 Island ILPS 9254 — **WHALE MEAT AGAIN** (LP, pink rim label) £15
77 Island ILPS 9497 — **PLAY IT BY EAR** (LP) £15
(see also Hellions, Traffic)

CAPDOWN
00 Peter Bower PBR 006 — **CIVIL DISOBEDIENTS** (LP, blue vinyl) £35
03 Rugger Bugger SEEP35LP — **POUND FOR THE SOUND** (LP) £25

DEE CAPE
84 GroovATron GAI 1 — **TIC TOC** (12" EP p/s) £40

CAPE KENNEDY CONSTRUCTION CO.
69 President PT 265 — **First Step On The Moon/Armageddon** £70

CAPES & MASKS
65 Fontana TL 5339 — **COMIC BOOK HEROES** (LP) £50
65 Nevis NEV R005 — **COMIC BOOK HEROES** (LP) £18

CAPES OF GOOD HOPE
66 Stateside SS 577 — **Winter's Children/If My Monique Could Only Dance** £15

CAPITAL LETTERS
77 Greensleeves GRED 2 — **Smoking My Ganja/Natty Walk** (12") £30
79 Greensleeves GRED 16 — **UK Skanking/Run Run Run** (12") £30
79 Greensleeves GREL 7 — **HEADLINE NEWS** (LP) £28

CAPITOLS (U.K.)
66 Pye 7N 17025 — **Honey And Wine/Boulavogue** £15

CAPITOLS (U.S.)
66 Atlantic 584 004 — **Cool Jerk/Hello Stranger** £25
(see also Three Caps)

CAPLO BANAAL
83 Rambert RAM THREE — **She Loves The Money/Is This Love** (p/s) £45

CAPOEIRA TWINS
99 Blowpop BLOWP 001 — **4 x 3** (12", with hand-sprayed Banksy artwork, beware of bootlegs) £3000
99 Blowpop BLOWP 001 — **4 x 3** (12") £15

CAPONE
98 Hardleaders HL 028 — **Friday/Alaska** (12") £30

EDDIE CAPONE'S TREATMENT
85 Treatment SOB 004 — **I Won't Give You Up/We Would Like To Spend Some Time With You** (12", p/s featuring Diane Jones) £80
85 Treatment SOB 0045P — **I Won't Give You Up/We Would Like To Spend Some Time With You** (p/s featuring Diane Jones) £20

ANDY CAPP
69 Treasure Isle TI 7052 — **Pop-A-Top/RICO: The Lion Speaks** £25
70 Duke DU 69 — **The Law Parts 1 & 2** £25

CAPPO
99 Son Records SON011 — **CAP 3000** (12" EP, die-cut sleeve) £15
00 Son Records SON016 — **CODEX** (12" EP) £15
00 Blunted Astronaut BAR 12 TWE 0007 — **THOUSAND WORD EXODUS** (12"EP) £15
14 Boot BEP 011 — **THE BOOT** (12" EP, 100 copies only) £60
14 Boot BEP 012 — **UN:PROGRAMMABLE RAW** (12" EP, p/s) £20
10 Son Records 047 — **GENGHIS** (2LP, 200 only, each with message from Cappo) £30
16 YNR Productions YNR 068 — **DRAMATIC CHANGE OF FORTUNE** (2LP, hand-numbered 100 copies, screen-printed sleeve) £50

CAPPO & NAPPA
15 King Underground KU0-13 — **REBEL BASS** (2-LP) £20

CAPPO & STYLY CEE
11 SON 050 — **FALL OUT** (LP, 200 only hand-sprayed sleeve) £25

CAPRIS
61 Columbia DB 4605 — **There's A Moon Out Tonight/Indian Girl** £80

CAPTAIN BEEFHEART & HIS MAGIC BAND
22 RCV 2115 — **CLEAR SPOT** (clear vinyl, LP of out-takes, g/f, RSD Black Friday 2022) £45
SINGLES
68 Pye International 7N 25443 — **Yellow Brick Road/Abba Zabba** £40
68 A&M AMS 726 — **Moonchild/Who Do You Think You're Fooling** £30

EPs
71	A&M AME 600	DIDDY WAH DIDDY (EP promo only in p/s)	£250
79	Virgin SIXPACK 1	SIX-PACK/SIX TRACK (picture disc, die-cut p/s with stand, 5,000 only)	£15
84	A&M AMY 226	THE LEGENDARY A&M SESSIONS (12" EP/mini-LP, Diddy Wah Diddy EP plus "Here I Am, I Always Am")	£15
86	Edsel BLIMP 902	THE LEGENDARY A&M SESSIONS (12" EP, reissue)	£15

ALBUMS
68	Pye Intl. NPL 28110	SAFE AS MILK (mono, flipback sleeve)	£150
68	Liberty LBL 83172	STRICTLY PERSONAL (gatefold sleeve, mono)	£120
68	Liberty LBS 83172	STRICTLY PERSONAL (gatefold sleeve, stereo)	£80
69	Straight STS 1053	TROUT MASK REPLICA (2-LP, gatefold sleeve)	£200
69	Buddah 623171	SAFE AS MILK (LP, reissue, stereo)	£40
69	Pye/Marble Arch MAL 1117	SAFE AS MILK (LP, reissue, mono, 10 tracks not 12)	£40
70	Straight STS 1063	LICK MY DECALS OFF, BABY	£100
70	Buddah 2349 002	DROPOUT BOOGIE (stereo reissue of "Safe As Milk")	£30
71	Buddah 2365 002	MIRROR MAN (gatefold die-cut sleeve)	£50
71	Sunset SLS50208	STRICTLY PERSONAL (LP, reissue)	£20
72	Reprise K 44162	THE SPOTLIGHT KID (tan 'riverboat' label, with lyric card insert)	£40
72	Reprise K 44162	THE SPOTLIGHT KID (tan 'riverboat' label, without lyric card insert)	£15
72	Reprise K 54007	CLEAR SPOT (PVC sleeve with card insert)	£40
73	Reprise K 44244	LICK MY DECALS OFF, BABY (reissue)	£18
74	Virgin V 2015	UNCONDITIONALLY GUARANTEED ('two virgins' label)	£35
74	Buddah BDLP 4004	MIRROR MAN	£20
74	Virgin V 2023	BLUEJEANS & MOONBEAMS ('two virgins' label)	£30
75	Reprise K 64026	TROUT MASK REPLICA (2-LP, gatefold sleeve, tan 'riverboat' label, matt sleeve, 'Captain Beefhart' on labels)	£50
76	Reprise K 84006	TWO ORIGINALS OF CAPTAIN BEEFHEART (2-LP, reissue of Lick My Decals Off, Baby & "The Spotlight Kid")	£20
77	Pye FILD 008	THE FILE SERIES (2-LP, reissue of "Safe As Milk" & "Mirror Man", die-cut sleeve with inners)	£25
78	Reprise K 64026	TROUT MASK REPLICA (2-LP, gatefold sleeve, 2nd re-pressing, tan 'riverboat' label, soft laminated sleeve)	£30
79	Virgin V 2149	SHINY BEAST (BAT CHAIN PULLER) (LP, inner)	£20
80	Virgin V 2172	DOC AT THE RADAR STATION	£25
81	PRT NCP 1004	SAFE AS MILK (LP, reissue, 10 track version omits 'I'm Glad' and 'Grown So Ugly')	£15
82	Virgin OVED 19	BLUEJEANS AND MOONBEAMS (LP, reissue, Green/Red labels)	£15
82	Virgin V 2237	ICE CREAM FOR CROW (with inner sleeve)	£18
84	PRT NCP 1004	SAFE AS MILK (LP, reissue)	£20
85	Virgin OVED 66	UNCONDITIONALLY GUARANTEED (LP, reissue, green/red labels)	£15
85	Virgin OVED 67	SHINY BEAST (BAT CHAIN PULLER) (LP, reissue, green/red labels)	£15
85	Virgin OVED 68	DOC AT THE RADAR STATION (LP, reissue)	£15
85	Virgin OVED 121	ICE CREAM FOR CROW (LP, reissue, green/red labels)	£15
99	Simply Vinyl/BMG SVLP 122	SAFE AS MILK (2LP, reissue, PVC outer)	£30
08	Oz It Morpheus OZITLP 8006	DUST SUCKER (2LP, gatefold, black or green vinyl, first 1000 numbered))	£30

(see also Mu, Frank Zappa, Jack Nitzsche)

CAPTAIN BEYOND
72	Capricorn K 47503	CAPTAIN BEYOND (LP)	£30

(see also Deep Purple, Iron Butterfly)

CAPTAIN JESUS AND THE SUNRAY TEAM
92	Criminal Jesus 2	ALL THANKS TO THE LORD JESUS CHRIST AMEN (LP)	£40
94	Criminal (No Cat. No.)	THE DAY THAT NEBULON EXPLODED (LP)	£40

(see also Hawkwind)

CAPTAIN LOCKHEED & THE STARFIGHTERS
73	United Artists UP 35543	Ejection/Catch A Falling Starfighter (p/s)	£25

(see also Robert Calvert)

CAPTAIN MARRYAT
74	Thor THOR 1007 S	CAPTAIN MARRYAT (LP, 200 only)	£2000
10	Shadoks S114	CAPTAIN MARRYAT (LP, reissue)	£35

CAPTAIN SINBAD
83	Rusty Intl. RI 006	Sister Maracle/ASHANTI WAUGH: Funny Love (Version) (12")	£18
83	Oak Sound OSLP 002	AGAIN (LP)	£25
84	Greensleeves GREL 34	THE SEVEN VOYAGES OF SINBAD (LP)	£25

C.A. QUINTET
83	Psycho PSYCHO 12	TRIP THROUGH HELL (LP, reissue of U.S. 60s LP)	£15

CARAVAN
69	Verve VS 1518	A Place Of My Own/Ride	£60
70	Decca F 13063	If I Could Do It All Over Again, I'd Do It All Over You/Hello, Hello	£20
71	Decca F 23125	Love To Love You (And Tonight Pigs Will Fly)/Golf Girl	£20
68	Verve VLP 6011	CARAVAN (LP, 'pillar' sleeve, mono, brown/white label, with "sold in the U.K." text)	£500
68	Verve SVLP 6011	CARAVAN (LP, 'pillar' sleeve, stereo)	£400
70	Decca SKL 5052	IF I COULD DO IT ALL OVER AGAIN, I'D DO IT ALL OVER YOU (LP, boxed logo)	£80
71	Deram SDL-R 1	IN THE LAND OF GREY AND PINK (LP, gatefold sleeve, 1st pressing with brown/white label)	£120
71	Deram SDL-R 1	IN THE LAND OF GREY AND PINK (LP, gatefold sleeve, later pressing with red/white label)	£40
72	Deram SDL 8	WATERLOO LILY (LP, gatefold sleeve, 1st pressing brown/white large Deram labels. SDL8 on sleeve and label)	£150
72	Deram SDL 8	WATERLOO LILY (LP, gatefold sleeve later pressing with red/white labels and SDL-R 8 on	£20

		labels and sleeves)	
72	MGM 2353 058	CARAVAN (LP, reissue, blue/gold label)	£25
73	Deram SDL-R 12	FOR GIRLS WHO GROW PLUMP IN THE NIGHT (LP, gatefold sleeve, red/white label)	£30
74	Deram SML-R 1110	CARAVAN AND THE NEW SYMPHONIA (LIVE AT DRURY LANE) (LP, red/white label)	£20
75	Decca SKL-R 5210	CUNNING STUNTS (LP)	£20
76	Decca DKL-R 8/1 & 8/2	CANTERBURY TALES (2-LP)	£18
76	BTM BTM 1007	BLIND DOG AT ST. DUNSTAN'S (LP)	£15
80	Kingdom KVL 9003	THE ALBUM (LP, laminated sleeve)	£20
11	Music On Vinyl MOVLP 385	CARAVAN (LP, reissue)	£18
11	Decca 375 069-3	IF I COULD DO IT ALL OVER AGAIN, I'D DO IT ALL OVER YOU (LP, reissue).................	£18
11	Deram 533 420	IN THE LAND OF GREY AND PINK (2-LP reissue, 'splatter pink' vinyl)	£20

(see also Gringo, Matching Mole, Hatfield & The North, Spiro Gyra)

CARAVELLES
68	Pye 7N 17654	The Other Side Of Love/I Hear A New Kind Of Music	£25
63	Decca LK 4565	THE CARAVELLES (LP)	£25

(see also Lois Lane)

GUY CARAWAN
58	Topic 10T 24	MOUNTAIN SONGS AND BANJO TUNES (10" LP)..	£20
57	77 Records LP8	GUY CARAWAN, HIS BANJO AND GUITAR (10" LP).....................................	£30
67	Columbia SX 6065	A GUY CALLED CARAWAN (LP)	£20

(see also Peggy Seeger & Guy Carawan)

CARBARETTA
78	Ignition IR 1	You Must Be Kidding Me/Scat (die-cut sleeve)	£20

CARCASS
89	Strange Fruit SFPS073	PEEL SESSION (12")	£20
94	Earache MOSH 108T	THE HEARTWORK EP (12")	£15
88	Earache MOSH 06	REEK OF PUTREFACTION (LP)	£40
89	Earache MOSH 18	SYMPHONIES OF SICKNESS (LP, picture disc)	£30
91	Earache MOSH 42	NECROTICISM - DESCANTING THE INSALUBRIOUS (LP)	£30

CORNELIUS CARDEW
71	Deutsche Grammaphon 2538 216	THE GREAT LEARNING (LP, with the Scratch Orchestra)	£40
85	Impetus IMP 28204	MEMORIAL CONCERT (2-LP)..	£45
86	Matchless MR 10	THALMANN VARIATIONS (LP)	£25

CARDIAC ARREST (1)
79	Tortch TOR 002	A BUS FOR A BUS ON A BUS (EP)	£200

(see also Cardiacs)

CARDIAC ARREST (2)
79	Another AN 1	Running In The Street/TV Friends (p/s)	£50

CARDIACS
86	Alphabet ALPH 002	SEASIDE TREATS (12" EP, with poster & lyric insert)	£50
87	Alphabet ALPH 006	THERE'S TOO MANY IRONS IN THE FIRE (12" EP, with poster)......................	£40
88	Alphabet ALPHT 008	Is This The Life/Loosefish Googesash/I'm Eating In Bed (12", p/s)	£20
88	Alphabet ALPH 009T	Susannah's Still Alive/Blind In Safety And Leafy In Love/All His Geese Are Swans (12", p/s)	£15
88	Strange Fruit SFNT 013	RADIO 1 SESSIONS/THE EVENING SHOW (12", p/s)	£25
89	Alphabet ALPH 011T	Baby Heart Dirt/I Hold My Love In My Arms/Horse Head/The Safety Bowl (12", p/s)....	£15
91	Alphabet ALPH 015	Day Is Gone/No Bright Side/Ideal/Joining The Plankton (12" EP, with lyric sheet)	£25
81	private label	THE OBVIOUS IDENTITY (cassette, as Cardiac Arrest)	£100
81	private label	TOY WORLD (cassette)	£100
84	Alphabet ALPH 001	THE SEASIDE (cassette)	£80
87	Alphabet ALPH 004	BIG SHIP (mini LP, with lyric insert)...	£50
88	Night Tracks SFNT 013	RADIO ONE EVENING SESSION: R.E.S./ Buds And Spawn/In A City Lining/Is This The Life/Cameras (12" EP)........	£20
87	Alphabet ALPH 005	RUDE BOOTLEG - LIVE AT READING '86 (LP, stamped sleeve with insert)	£80
87	Alphabet ALPH MC005	RUDE BOOTLEG - LIVE AT READING '86 (cassette)	£35
88	Alphabet ALPHLP 010	CARDIACS LIVE (LP)..	£30
88	Alphabet ALPH 007	A LITTLE MAN AND A HOUSE AND THE WHOLE WORLD WINDOW (LP)............	£60
88	Alphabet ALPH 012	ON LAND AND IN THE SEA (LP)	£40
89	Alphabet ALPH 000	ARCHIVE CARDIACS (cassette, fan club issue, compilation of "Toy World" & "The Obvious Identity")........	£40
90	Alphabet ALPH 013	THE SEASIDE (LP)	£50
91	Alphabet ALPHLP 014	SONGS FOR SHIPS AND IRONS (LP)	£60
92	Alphabet ALPHLP 017	HEAVEN BORN AND EVER BRIGHT (LP)...	£40
14	Alphabet Business Concern ALPH DLP 022	SING TO GOD (2-LP, 1st pressing, 200 copies only)	£40
15	Alphabet Business Concern ALPH DLP 027	GUNS (2-LP, 200 only)	£30

(see also Cardiac Arrest 1, Mr and Mrs Smith and Mr Drake)

CARDIGANS
95	Trampoliene 523 556-1	LIFE (LP)...	£25
96	Stockholm 533117-1	FIRST BAND ON THE MOON (LP)	£40
03	Stockholm 067 101-1	LONG GONE BEFORE DAYLIGHT (LP)	£80
00	Stockholm/Simply Vinyl SVLP 175	GRAN TURISMO (LP, with inner sleeve)..	£80

CARDINAL
94	Dedicated DEDLP 018	CARDINAL (LP)	£25

CARDINALS

71	Nelmwood Audio NWA 1	**SWEET & REFRESHING** (LP)	£30
72	Nelmwood Audio NWA 012	**ON TOP OF THE WORLD** (LP)	£22

JACK CARDWELL

54	Parlophone CMSP 24	**Whiskey, Women And Loaded Dice/Slap-Ka-Dab** (export issue)	£20
54	Parlophone CMSP 27	**Blue Love/Diddle Diddle Dumpling** (export issue)	£20

CAREFREES

63	Oriole CB 1916	**We Love You Beatles/Hot Blooded Lover**	£25
64	Oriole CB 1931	**Aren't You Glad You're You/Paddy Whack**	£15

THE CARETAKER

01	V/VM Test Record OFFAL 07	**A STAIRWAY TO THE STARS** (2-LP, blue vinyl)	£50
11	History Always Favors The Winners HAFTW008-LP	**AN EMPTY BLISS BEYOND THIS WORLD** (LP, blue vinyl)	£45
11	History Always Favors The Winners HAFTW008-LP	**AN EMPTY BLISS BEYOND THIS WORLD** (LP, repressing, clear vinyl)	£35
12	History Always Favors The Winners HAFTW 013	**PATIENCE** (AFTER SEBALD) (LP, blue vinyl, 300 only)	£30
12	History Always Favors The Winners HAFTW 013	**PATIENCE** (AFTER SEBALD) (LP, black vinyl)	£20

DAVE CAREY (JAZZ BAND)

55	Tempo LAP 4	**JAZZ IN THE TRADITIONAL SPIRIT** (10" LP)	£20
58	Tempo TAP 16	**JAZZ AT THE RAILWAY ARMS NO. 2** (LP)	£20

CAREY & LLOYD

72	Attack ATT 8032	**Do It Again** (as Carey/Lloyd)**/GARY RANGLIN: Watch It**	£15
72	Grape GR 3025	**Come Down Part 1/DYNAMITES: Come Down Part 2**	£15

(see also Carey Johnson, Lloyd Young, Lloyd & Carey)

MARIAH CAREY

94	Columbia 661070 7	**All I Want For Christmas Is You/Miss You Most** (At Christmas Time) (jukebox issue)	£50
98	Columbia MARIAH 1	**12s** (10x12" in box)	£70
93	Columbia 474270 1	**MUSIC BOX** (LP)	£50
94	Columbia 477342 1	**MERRY CHRISTMAS** (LP)	£100
95	Columbia 481367 1	**DAYDREAM** (LP)	£100
97	Columbia 488537-1	**BUTTERFLY** (LP)	£100
98	Columbia 4926041	**#1's** (2-LP)	£80
99	Columbia 495065-1	**RAINBOW** (2-LP)	£50
01	Virgin VUSLP 201	**GLITTER** (2-LP)	£30

CARGO (1)

70	No Label, LS 1674	**Killing Time/Love Will Turn You Round** (Unissued, white labels only)	£300

CARIBBEANS (1)

69	Doctor Bird DB 1181	**Let Me Walk By/AMBLINGS: Tell Me Why**	£70
69	Crab CR 14	**Please Please/MATADORS: The Destroyer**	£60

CARIBBEANS (2)

68	Group One G1 501	**A Trembling Feeling/Hoping**	£40

CARIBBEATS

66	Ska Beat JB 246	**The Bells Of St. Mary's/WINSTON RICHARDS: Loki**	£60
67	Double D DD 101	**Highway 300/I Think Of You** (actually by Marlene McKenzie and Caribbeats)	£75
67	Double D DD 103	**I'll Try/If You Did Look**	£60
68	Double D DD 111	**One Step/HAZEL WRIGHT: Please Help Me**	£60

(see also Bobby Aitken, Itals)

CARIBOES

71	Bullet BU 479	**Let It Be Me/All I Have To Do Is Dream**	£15

CARIBOU

14	Jialong JIALONG 012	**Can't Do Without You** (Extended Mlx) (12" 1-sided)	£15
05	Leaf BAY 42V	**THE MILK OF HUMAN KINDNESS** (LP)	£20
07	City Slang SLANG 1047981	**ANDORRA** (LP)	£15
10	City Slang SLANG 9550055	**SWIM** (2-LP)	£20
14	City Slang SLANG 500070LP	**OUR LOVE** (LP, CD)	£20

(see also Manitoba)

CARIBS

60	Starlite ST45 012	**Taboo/Mathilda Cha Cha Cha!**	£25

CARL & COMMANDERS

61	Columbia DB 4719	**Farmer John/Cleanin' Up**	£20

DONOVAN CARLESS

71	Tropical ALO31	**How Can I Tell Her About It/Be Thankful For What You Got**	£15

BILL CARLISLE & CARLISLES

59	Mercury AMT 1063	**Down Boy/Union Suit**	£30

JIM CARLISLE

78	Billy Goat 001	**Don't Start Crying Now/She Knows How To Rock Me**	£15
79	Billy Goat 003	**Train Whistle Boogie/Hillbilly Boogie**	£15

CARLISLE BROTHERS

59	Parlophone GEP 8799	**FRESH FROM THE COUNTRY** (EP)	£20

DON CARLOS

78	Dove 511	**Plantation/Version**	£20
80	Pirate PIR 001	**Nice Time/Get Up** (12")	£20

MINT VALUE £

80	Negus Roots NERT 003	I Love Jah/I Don't Care (12", as Don McCarlos)..£40
80	Ethnic ETH 2236	Grief My Heart/Spread Out (12")..£15
81	Negus Roots NERT 004	Gimme Gimme Your Love/PAPA TULLO: Gimme More Love (12")..........£30
82	Negus Roots NERT 015	Magic Man/Magic Dub (12")..£15
82	Cha Cha CHAD 52	Can't Waste Time/PAPA BRUCE : No Time To Waste (10")..............£20
83	Shuttle SH 008	Money & Women (with John Wayne)/CORNELL CAMPBELL/PURPLEMAN: Keep On Working (12")..£20
83	Blacker Dread SCOM 003	From Creation/Versions (12")..£30
83	Youth In Progress YP001	Jordan River/LITTLE JOHN: Reasons/LADY ANNE AND SANTANA; Love Life (12") £20
85	Blacker Dread SCOM 020	Strictly Culture (Love We Culture Version)/MIKEY DREAD: Dubuling Mix (12") £30
80s	Rusty International RI 001	Isabel/BILLY BOYO: One Morning/CAPTAIN SINBAD & ROOTS RADICALS: Radication Dehbout (12")..£20
81	Blue Moon BM 001	PROPHET (LP)..£40
82	Negus Roots NERLP 001	SUFFERING (LP)..£40
82	Greensleeves GREL 45	DAY TO DAY LIVING (LP)..£15
82	Negus Roots NERLP 005	HARVEST (LP)..£60
83	Burning Sounds BRD 1053	SPREAD OUT INA DANCEHALL STYLE (LP)..............£20
84	Real Authentic Sound RAS 3008	JUST A PASSING GLANCE (LP)..£15
84	Saxon International 5550	SAMMY DREAD MEETS DON CARLOS (LP, not released in sleeve)...............£25

(see also Black Uhuru)

DAVE CARLSEN
73	Spark SRLP 110	A PALE HORSE (LP, yellow/blue label)..£40

MAGNUS CARLSON
11	Acid Jazz AJX268S	From Now On/Barbajagel (with the Ray Moon Quintet)..............£30

CARL CARLTON (LITTLE)
68	Action ACT 4501	Competition Ain't Nothin'/Three Way Love £50
68	Action ACT 4514	46 Drums 1 Guitar/Why Don't They Leave Us Alone £35
69	Action ACT 4537	Look At Mary Wonder/Bad For Each Other (as Carl Carlton) £20

CARLTON & HIS SHOES
68	Coxsone CS 7065	Love Me Forever/Happy Land..£175
68	Studio One SO 2062	This Feeling/You And Me (Love Is A Treasure)..£100
80s	Live & Love LLDIS 116	What A Day/Version (12")..£40
79	Studio One PSOL 003	LOVE ME FOREVER (LP, laminated sleeve, 1st UK press through Peckings)............£80
85	Studio One PSOL 002	LOVE ME FOREVER (LP, reissue, Peckings)..£30

(see also Lee 'Scratch' Perry, Roy & Enid, Abyssinians)

CARMEN
73	R. Zonophone SRZA 8518	FANDANGOS IN SPACE (LP, gatefold sleeve, red/silver label) £35
75	R. Zonophone SLRZ 1040	DANCING ON A COLD WIND (LP, with inner sleeve, red/silver label)............£45

(see also Jethro Tull)

ROGER CARMEN, ROCK KEELING, MO THOMAS & ANN & STEVE MITCHELL
71	Mosart Music MM 1	FROST LAND (LP)..£25

JEAN CARN
79	Philadelphia Int. S PIR 13 8840	Was That All It Was/Whats On Your Mind (12")..£15

CARNABY
65	Piccadilly 7N 35272	Jump And Dance/My Love Will Stay..£120

CARNABY STREET POP ORCHESTRA & CHOIR
69	Carnaby CNLS 6003	THE LONDON THEME (LP) £40

CARNAGE
84	Creative Reality REAL 07	FACE THE FACTS (LP)..£20

CARNATIONS
65	Blue Beat BB 285	Mighty Man/What Are You Selling..£22

CARNIVAL
70	Liberty LBS 83305	THE CARNIVAL (LP)..£20

SASHA CARO
68	Decca F12744	Molotov Molotov/Never Play A B Side..£15

CAROL & MEMORIES
66	CBS 202086	Tears On My Pillow/Crying My Eyes Out £22

CAROLINA SLIM
72	Flyright LP 4702	CAROLINA BLUES AND BOOGIE (LP)..£20

CAROLINES
65	Polydor BM 56027	Love Made A Fool Of Me/Believe In Me..£20

CAROLLS
65	Polydor BM 56046	Give Me Time/Darling I Want You So Much £20

(see also Carrols)

CAROUSELS
67	Pye 7N 17353	Holiday Romance/The Run Run £15

CAR PARK
81	Carrrere CAR 202T	Let's Do What You Do So Well/Fun City (12")..£15

BOB CARPENTER
76	Celtic Music CM 027	SILENT PASSAGE (LP)..£20

CARPENTER JOE
87	Solo SOLO 2	MAVERICK GENIUS (EP)..£20

(See also Doubt)

CARPENTER'S APPRENTICE
72   SRS 12107   CHANGES (LP, with insert)..£200

CARPET BAGGERS
67   Spin SP 2006   Flea Teacher/On Sunday £30

CARPETTES
77   Small Wonder SMALL 3   THE CARPETTES (EP) £15
78   Small Wonder SMALL 9   Small Wonder?/2 Ne 1 (p/s, 2,000 only)......................£35
79   Beggars Banquet BEGA 14   FRUSTRATION PARADISE (LP) £18
80   Beggars Banquet BEGA 21   FIGHT AMONGST YOURSELVES (LP) £20

CATHY CARR
56   London HLH 8274   Ivory Tower/Please, Please Believe Me......................£15

DEREK CARR
01   Trident 001   COPPER BEECH EP (12")..£40
02   Digital Soul DS 04   INITIAL TRANSMISSIONS EP (12") £45
03   Geek GEEK 006   DESTINY EP (12") £40
03   Nice & Nasty DB3 008T   FUTURISTIC OVERTONES EP (12") £40
04   Headspace HS 015   PLANET JUMP EP (12") £35
17   Revoke REVOKE 001   WARM MACHINES EP (12" white labels,150 only) £40

JAMES CARR
66   Stateside SS 507   You've Got My Mind Messed Up/That's What I Want To Know £80
66   Stateside SS 507   You've Got My Mind Messed Up/That's What I Want To Know (DJ Copy) £150
66   Stateside SS 535   Love Attack/Coming Back To Me Baby £40
66   Stateside SS 535   Love Attack/Coming Back To Me Baby (DJ copy)......£70
66   Stateside SS 545   You're Pouring Water On A Drowning Man/Forgetting You......£20
67   Stateside SS 2001   The Dark End Of the Street/Loveable Girl £30
67   Stateside SS 2038   Let It Happen/A Losing Game £15
67   Stateside SS 2052   I'm A Fool For You/Gonna Send You Back To Georgia £25
68   Bell BLL 1004   A Man Needs A Woman/Stronger Than Love............£20
69   B&C CB 101   Freedom Train/That's The Way Love Turned Out For Me (DJ Copy) £50
67   Stateside SL 10205   YOU GOT MY MIND MESSED UP (LP) £100
69   Bell MBLL/SBLL 113   A MAN NEEDS A WOMAN (LP)....................................£60

JOHNNY CARR (& CADILLACS)
64   Decca F 11854   Remember That Night/Respectable £20
65   Fontana TF 600   Do You Love That Girl?/Give Him A Little Time £15
67   Fontana TF 823   Things Get Better/You Got Me Baby (solo)................£35

LEROY CARR
63   CBS BPG 62206   BLUES BEFORE SUNRISE (LP) £50

LINDA CARR
67   Stateside SS 2058   Everytime/Trying To Be Good For You £40

LODY CARR
60   Top Rank 35-111   LADYBIRD (LP)..£15

MIKE CARR
68   Columbia SCX 6248   UNDER PRESSURE (LP) £20
73   Ad-Rhythm ARPS 1020   MIKE CARR (LP) £18

PETER CARR
69   DJM DJS213   Angel And The Woman/Imagine Yourself....................£20

ROMEY CARR
70   Columbia DB 8710   These Things Will Keep Me Loving You/Stand Up And Fight £30
70   Columbia DB 8710   These Things Will Keep Me Loving You/Stand Up And Fight (DJ Copy) £50

WYNONA CARR
85   Ace CH 130   HIT THAT JIVE, JACK! (LP)..£15

CARRAIG AONAIR
77   Gwerin   CARRAIG AONAIR (LP, insert) £25

CARRIAGE COMPANY
70   CBS 5209   In Your Room/Feel Right £30

ANDREA CARROLL
63   London HLX 9772   It Hurts To Be Sixteen/Why Am I So Shy (some copies have Why Am I So Sorry as the B-side) £25

BERNADETTE CARROLL
64   Stateside SS 311   Party Girl/I Don't Wanna Know £20

BOB CARROLL
56   London HLU 8299   Red Confetti, Pink Balloons And Tambourines/Handwriting On The Wall £25
58   London HLT 8724   Hi Yo Silver/Tonto The Brave......................................£15

CATH CARROLL
91   Factory FACT 210   ENGLAND MADE ME (LP) £18

GINA CARROLL
65   Decca F 12297   Bye Bye Big Boy/Down The Street £20

JOHNNY CARROLL & HOT ROCKS
56   Brunswick 05580   Corrine Corrina/Wild Wild Women £600
56   Brunswick 05580   Corrine Corrina/Wild Wild Women (78) £70
56   Brunswick 05603   Crazy, Crazy Lovin'/Hot Rock £600

MINT VALUE £

56	Brunswick 05603	Crazy, Crazy Lovin'/Hot Rock (78) £70

TONI CARROLL

58	MGM EP 689	THIS ONE IS TONI (EP) £15

CARROLLS

66	Polydor BM 56081	Surrender Your Love/The Folk I Love £25
66	Polydor BM 56081	Surrender Your Love/The Folk I Love (DJ Copy) £50
68	CBS 3875	A Lemon Balloon And A Blue Sky/Make Me Belong To You.....................£20
69	CBS 4401	We're In This Thing Together/We Know Better £15
67	CBS 3414	So Gently Falls The Rain/Nice To See You Darling £15
67	CBS 3414	So Gently Falls The Rain/Nice To See You Darling (DJ Copy) £25

(see also Carolls, Brotherly Love)

BEN CARRUTHERS & DEEP

65	Parlophone R 5295	Jack O' Diamonds/Right Behind You...£50

CHAD CARSON

63	HMV POP 1156	They Were Wrong/Stop Picking On Me £50

JOE CARSON

63	Liberty LIB 55578	I Gotta Get Drunk (And I Shore Do Dread It)/Who Will Buy My Memories £25

KEN CARSON

55	London HLF 8213	Hawkeye/I've Been Working On The Railroad £70
56	London HLF 8237	Let Her Go, Let Her Go/The Song Of Daniel Boone (The Daddy Of Them All)...........£60

MINDY CARSON & GUY MITCHELL

53	Columbia SCM 5022	That's A Why/Train Of Love £15

(see also Guy Mitchell)

CARTE BLANCHE

79	Pye 7NL46193	Get Up On Your Feet/Do It Like You Like It (p/s).......................................£15

BENNY CARTER

62	HMV CLP 1624/CSD1480	FURTHER DEFINITIONS (LP, mono/stereo) £20

(see also Helen Humes)

CAROLINE CARTER

65	Decca F 12239	The Ballad Of The Possibilities/We Want Love.............................£20

CAROLYN CARTER

65	London HL 9959	It Hurts/I'm Thru £40

CHRIS CARTER

81	Industrial IRC 32	THE SPACE BETWEEN (cassette) £30
85	Conspiracy International CTILP3	MONDO BEAT (LP)..£25
10	Optimo OM CC01	THE SPACES BETWEEN (LP, reissue)...£15

(see also Throbbing Gristle, Chris & Cosey)

CLARENCE CARTER

68	Atlantic 584 154	Thread The Needle/Don't Make My Baby Cry.....................................£18
68	Atlantic 584 176	Looking For A Fox/I Can't See Myself (Crying About You) £20
68	Atlantic 584 187	Funky Fever/Slip Away..£15
68	Atlantic 584 223	Too Weak To Fight/Let Me Comfort You...£15
69	Atlantic 584 248	Snatchin' It Back/Making Love (At The Dark End Of The Street) £15
83	Certain ACERT 1	Messin' With My Mind/Messin' (Instrumental Version)......................£15
68	Atlantic 588 152	THIS IS CLARENCE CARTER (LP) £30
69	Atlantic 588 172	THE DYNAMIC CLARENCE CARTER (LP) £25
69	Atlantic 588 191	TESTIFYIN' (LP)...£20
70	Atlantic 2400 027	PATCHES (LP)..£20

ERROL CARTER

73	Cactus CT 71	Hold Up Your Head/SUCCESS ALL STARS: Tank Skank £30
76	Cactus CT 96	Ram Goat Malish Water/Ranking Dub £60

HERBIE CARTER

68	Duke DU 4	Happy Time (actually by Keble Drummond)/BOYS: Smashville £50

JEAN CARTER & CENTREPIECES

68	Stateside SS 2114	No Good Jim/And None £15
68	Stateside SS 2114	No Good Jim/And None (DJ Copy) £30

JOHN CARTER & RUSS ALQUIST

68	Spark SRL 1017	The Laughing Man/Midsummer Dreaming £30

(see also Carter-Lewis & Southerners, Ivy League)

LYNDA CARTER

78	CBS EPC 83052	LYNDA CARTER (LP, as aka WONDER WOMAN) £18

MARTIN CARTER

71	Tradition TSR 008	SOMEONE NEW (LP) £30
72	Tradition TSR 012	UPS & DOWNS (LP)..£25

MEL CARTER

63	Pye International 7N 25212	When A Boy Falls In Love/So Wonderful £50
66	Liberty LIB 66113	Hold Me, Thrill Me, Kiss Me/Sweet Little Girl £20

NELL CARTER

74	RCA 2503	Dreams/Send Him Back To Me £15
74	RCA 2503	Dreams/Send Him Back To Me (DJ Copy)......................................£25

NICK CARTER

79	NC 001	ABSTRACTS & EXTRACTS (LP, insert 250 only)................................£150

SHEILA CARTER & EPISODE SIX
66   Pye 7N 17194   I Will Warm Your Heart/Incense £30
(see also Episode, Episode Six)

SONNY CARTER WITH EARL BOSTIC & HIS ORCHESTRA
55   Parlophone MSP 6167   There Is No Greater Love/Oh Baby £20
(see also Earl Bostic)

CARTER STEPHENS CHORALE
68   Fontana TF 936   Peace! (Dream Of The Common Man)/The Promised Land £15

CARTERHALL
76   Thor 1010S   I WISH YOU COULD SEE (LP, 200 only) £700

CARTER-LEWIS & SOUTHERNERS
61   Piccadilly 7N 35004   So Much In Love/Back On The Scene £30
61   Ember EMB S 145   Two Timing Baby/Will It Happen To Me? £50
62   Piccadilly 7N 35085   Here's Hopin'/Poor Joe £30
62   Ember EMB S 165   Tell Me/My Broken Heart £50
63   Oriole CB 1835   Sweet And Tender Romance/Who Told You? £20
63   Oriole CB 1868   Your Momma's Out Of Town/Somebody Told My Girl £20
64   Oriole CB 1919   Skinny Minnie/Easy To Cry £40
(see also Ivy League, White Plains, John Carter & Russ Alquist, Jimmy Page, Dawn Chorus)

CARTER TUTTI VOID
12   Mute STUMM 340   TRANSVERSE (LP, CD) £18
15   Industrial IRCTVLP 01   f(x) (LP, white vinyl) £20
(see also Chris & Cosey, Factory Floor, Nik Colk Void)

MARTIN CARTHY
65   Fontana (S)TL 5269   MARTIN CARTHY (LP, black/silver label) £30
71   Philips 6308 049   LANDFALL (LP, black/silver label) £30
72   Peg PEG 12   SHEARWATER (LP, with insert, purple label) £25
74   Deram SML 1111   SWEET WIVELSFIELD (LP, red/white label) £15

MARTIN CARTHY & DAVE SWARBRICK
67   Fontana TE 17490   NO SONGS (EP) £30
66   Fontana STL 5362   SECOND ALBUM (LP, black/silver label) £30
67   Fontana STL 5434   BYKER HILL (LP) £30
68   Fontana STL 5477   BUT TWO CAME BY (LP) £30
70   Fontana STL 5529   PRINCE HEATHEN (LP, black/silver label) £35
71   Pegasus PEG 6   SELECTIONS (LP, gatefold sleeve) £30
(see also Dave Swarbrick, Three City Four, Steeleye Span, Leon Rosselson, Alex Campbell, Nigel Denver)

CARTOONE
69   Atlantic 588 174   CARTOONE (LP) £25
(see also Jimmy Page)

CARTOONS (1)
80   Hot HOT 001   Lunchtime Love Affair/Dark Alleys (p/s) £15

DAVE CARTWRIGHT
70   Harmony DB 0001   MIDDLE OF THE ROAD (LP, private pressing, 99 only, with insert) ... £200
72   Transatlantic TRA 255   A LITTLE BIT OF GLORY (LP, with inner sleeve) £20
73   Transatlantic TRA 267   BACK TO THE GARDEN (LP, with lyric inner sleeve) £20
74   Transatlantic TRA 284   DON'T LET YOUR FAMILY DOWN (LP, with lyric insert) £20
(see also Bev Pegg, Away From The Sand)

TRISTRAM CARY
70   Galliard GAL 4006   3 4 5 (LP, with booklet) £100
70   Galliard GAL 4007   NARCISSIS (LP, gatefold, with insert) £100
71   EMS (No Cat No)   TRIOS (2-LP, with booklet/instructions, warped copies worth half this price) ... £400
10   Trunk JBH 035 LP   IT'S TIME FOR TRISTRAM CARY (LP, 500 only, black vinyl) £18
10   Trunk JBH 035 LP   IT'S TIME FOR TRISTRAM CARY (LP, reissue, 300 only, clear vinyl) ... £20

CASABLANCA
74   Rocket PIGL 7   CASABLANCA (LP, die-cut sleeve with inner lyric sleeve) £20
(see also Trees, Ginger Bakers Airforce)

JULIAN CASABLANCAS
09   Rough Trade RTRADS 563   I Wish It Was Christmas Today/Old Hollywood (p/s, 500 only, white vinyl) ... £50

CASCADES
63   Warner Bros WEP 6106   RHYTHM OF THE RAIN (EP, mono) £20
63   Warner Bros WSE 6106   RHYTHM OF THE RAIN (EP, stereo) £25
63   Warner Bros WM 8127   RHYTHM OF THE RAIN (LP, mono) £30
63   Warner Bros WM 8127   RHYTHM OF THE RAIN (LP, stereo) £35

HOWIE CASEY & SENIORS
62   Fontana H 364   Double Twist/True Fine Mama £25
62   Fontana H 381   I Ain't Mad At You/Twist At The Top £20
63   Fontana TF 403   The Boll Weevil Song/Bony Moronie £20
62   Fontana TFL 5180   TWIST AT THE TOP (LP, mono) £80
62   Fontana STFL 592   TWIST AT THE TOP (LP, stereo) £100
(see also Freddie Starr)

ALVIN CASH (& REGISTERS)
65   Stateside SS 386   Twine Time/The Bump (as Alvin Cash & Crawlers) £30
65   Stateside SS 386   Twine Time/The Bump (as Alvin Cash & Crawlers) (DJ Copy) £60
66   Stateside SS 543   Philly Freeze/No Deposits, No Returns (as Alvin Cash & Registers) ... £25

MINT VALUE £

| 66 | Stateside SS 543 | Philly Freeze/No Deposits, No Returns (as Alvin Cash & Registers) (DJ Copy) | £50 |
| 67 | President PTL 1000 | THE PHILLY FREEZE (LP) | £35 |

JOHNNY CASH (SOLO & WITH TENNESSEE TWO)

78s

57	London HL 8358	I Walk The Line/Get Rhythm	£20
57	London HLS 8427	Train Of Love/There You Go	£20
57	London HLS 8461	Next In Line/Don't Make Me Go	£20
57	London HLS 8514	Home For The Blues/Give My Love To Rose	£20
58	London HLS 8586	Ballad Of A Teenage Queen/Big River (with Tennessee Two)	£20
58	London HLS 8656	Guess Things Happen That Way/Come In, Stranger	£20
58	London HLS 8709	The Ways Of A Woman In Love/You're The Nearest Thing To Heaven	£15
59	Philips PB 874	All Over Again/What Do I Care	£20
59	Philips PB 897	Don't Take Your Guns To Town/I Still Miss Someone	£20
59	London HLS 8789	It's Just About Time/I Just Thought You'd Like To Know	£20
59	London HLS 8847	Luther Played The Boogie/Thanks A Lot	£40
59	Philips PB 928	Frankie's Man, Johnny/You Dreamer You	£20
59	London HLS 8928	Katy Too/I Forgot To Remember To Forget	£40
59	Philips PB 953	I Got Stripes/Five Feet High And Rising	£40
59	London HLS 8979	You Tell Me/Goodbye, Little Darlin', Goodbye	£40
59	Philips PB 979	The Little Drummer Boy/I'll Remember You	£40

SINGLES

57	London HL 8358	I Walk The Line/Get Rhythm (gold label lettering)	£80
57	London HL 8358	I Walk The Line/Get Rhythm (silver label lettering)	£20
57	London HLS 8427	Train Of Love/There You Go	£30
57	London HLS 8461	Next In Line/Don't Make Me Go	£50
57	London HLS 8514	Home For The Blues/Give My Love To Rose	£40
58	London HLS 8586	Ballad Of A Teenage Queen/Big River (with Tennessee Two)	£20
58	London HLS 8656	Guess Things Happen That Way/Come In, Stranger (with Tennessee Two)	£20
58	London HLS 8709	The Ways Of A Woman In Love/You're The Nearest Thing To Heaven (with Tennessee Two)	£15
59	London HLS 8789	It's Just About Time/I Just Thought You'd Like To Know (with Tennessee Two)	£20
59	London HLS 8847	Luther Played The Boogie/Thanks A Lot	£20
59	London HLS 8928	Katy Too/I Forgot To Remember To Forget	£20
60	London HLS 9182	Down The Street To 301/Story Of A Broken Heart	£15
60	Philips PB 1075	Going To Memphis/Loading Coal	£15

EXPORT SINGLES

57	London HL 7020	Next In Line/Don't Make Me Go	£30
57	London HL 7023	Home For The Blues/Give My Love To Rose	£30
58	London HL 7032	Ballad Of A Teenage Queen/Big River	£25
58	London HL 7053	The Ways Of A Woman In Love/You're The Nearest Thing To Heaven	£20
57	London HL 7131	Folsom Prison Blues/I Walk The Line	£40

EPs

58	London RES 1120	JOHNNY CASH (triangular centre)	£25
58	London RES 1120	JOHNNY CASH (round centre)	£15
59	London RES 1193	JOHNNY CASH SINGS HANK WILLIAMS (triangular centre)	£25
59	London RES 1193	JOHNNY CASH SINGS HANK WILLIAMS (round centre)	£15
59	London RES 1212	COUNTRY BOY (triangular centre)	£25
59	London RES 1212	COUNTRY BOY (round centre)	£15
59	London RES 1230	JOHNNY CASH NO. 2 (triangular centre)	£25
59	London RES 1230	JOHNNY CASH NO. 2 (round centre)	£15
60	Philips BBE 12377	THE TROUBADOR	£20
60	Philips BBE 12318	GRANDFATHER'S CLOCK	£15
60	Philips BBE 12395	SONGS OF OUR SOIL	£15

ALBUMS

59	London HA-S 2157	SINGS THE SONGS THAT MADE HIM FAMOUS	£40
59	London HA-S 2179	WITH HIS HOT AND BLUE GUITAR	£40
59	Philips BBL 7298	THE FABULOUS JOHNNY CASH (mono)	£20
59	Philips SBBL 554	THE FABULOUS JOHNNY CASH (stereo)	£20
59	Philips BBL 7353	SONGS OF OUR SOIL	£15
60	Philips BBL 7358	NOW THERE WAS A SONG! (mono)	£15
60	Philips SBBL 580	NOW THERE WAS A SONG! (stereo)	£20
60	Philips BBL 7417	RIDE THIS TRAIN	£15
61	CBS (S)BPG 62042	THE FABULOUS JOHNNY CASH (mono/stereo)	£15
62	CBS (S)BPG 62073	THE SOUND OF JOHNNY CASH (mono/stereo)	£15
63	CBS BPG 62119	BLOOD SWEAT AND TEARS	£15
63	CBS (S)BPG 62171	RING OF FIRE (mono/stereo)	£15
68	CBS LP 63308	LIVE AT FOLSOM PRISON (LP)	£20
69	CBS LP 63629	LIVE AT SAN QUENTIN (LP)	£20
84	Charly SUN BOX-105	THE SUN YEARS (5-LP box set)	£25
94	American 0731458679028	AMERICAN RECORDINGS (LP, inner)	£30
96	American 51011 2793-1	UNCHAINED (LP, inner)	£30
00	American 51011 279-14	AMERICAN III: SOLITARY MAN (LP)	£25
06	American 0602517005099	AMERICAN V: A HUNDRED HIGHWAYS (LP)	£25

CASINOS

| 67 | Ember EMB S 241 | That's The Way/Too Good To Be True | £30 |
| 68 | President PTL 1007 | THEN YOU CAN TELL ME GOODBYE (LP) | £25 |

CASPAR
79	Rock Steady MICK 007	Messin' Around/Make You Feel Like You're Mine (p/s)	£20

(see also 10cc)

PAUL CASS
75	Rainbow Records RBW 2000	Mini Marianne/Riverboat Rock	£30

CASSANDRA
76	Lucky LY 6034	Love Me Sweeter Tonight/Albatross	£30
79	D Roy DRDD 19	Sitting In The Park/D ROY BAND: Hyde Park Dub	£30
80	D Roy DRDD 29	My Angel Baby/Thank You For The Many Things You've Done (12")	£30
80	D Roy DRDD 31	I Must Be Dreaming/Trading Dub (12")	£30

(see also Johnny Clarke)

CASSETTE
79	1 track CAS 001	THE FAST FORWARD EP: What's The Point/Product/All The Rage	£35

CASSETTES (1)
81	Zip ZIP 101	Reverberate/Don't Label Me (die-cut sleeve)	£50

CASSETTES (2)
82	X-Ray X 001	Call On Me/Fast Forward	£20

CASSIBER
84	Recommended RE 0110	BEAUTY AND THE BEAST (LP)	£18
86	Recommended RE 0000	PERFECT WORLDS (LP)	£18

DITCH CASSIDY
71	Decca F13240	Pisces Apple Lady/Hamburger Midnight	£20

TED CASSIDY
65	Capitol CL 15423	The Lurch/Wesley	£30
65	Capitol CL 15423	The Lurch/Wesley (DJ Copy)	£40

CAST
93	No label or cat no	Sandstorm/Follow Me Down/Tell It Like It Is (10", white label sold at gigs)	£20
95	Polydor INV137 LP COL	ALL CHANGE (2-LP, gatefold, inners, postcard)	£60
97	Polydor 537567 1	MOTHER NATURE CALLS (LP)	£40
99	Polydor 547 176-1	MAGIC HOUR (2-LP)	£50
01	Polydor 589096 1	BEETROOT (LP)	£25

(see also La's)

CASTANARC
74	Peninsula PENCIL 10	JOURNEY TO THE EAST (LP, private pressing)	£18

CASTAWAYS
65	London HL 10003	Liar Liar/Sam	£50
65	London HL 10003	Liar Liar/Sam (DJ Copy)	£80

JOEY CASTELL
57	Decca F 10966	I'm Left, You're Right, She's Gone/Tryin' To Get To You	£200
57	Decca F 10966	I'm Left, You're Right, She's Gone/Tryin' To Get To You (78)	£25

LACKSLEY CASTELL
79	Sufferers Heights SUFF 01	What A Great Day/PRINCE JAMMY: Slaughter House 5 (12")	£50
79	Sound Off SOFD 003	My Collie Tree/RISING SUN: Stop Cheating (12")	£50
80	Negus Roots NERT 001	African Queen/Queen In Dub (12")	£25
80	Negus Roots NERT 003	I Love Jah/Version	£40
80	Black Joy DH 805	Jah Love Is Sweeter/ROCKERS BAND: Sweeter Rockers (12")	£60
81	Negus Roots NERT 005	Jah Is Watching You/PAPA TULLO: Sweet Reggae Music (12")	£30
81	Negus Roots NERT 008	Government Man/P. TULLO: Straight To The Government (12" blue/black vinyl)	£40
82	Negus Roots NERT 013	Speak Softly/Money A The Remedy (with PAPA TULLO/Take This Message To My Woman (12")	£30
83	Negus Roots NERT 019	Johnny Brown/Mrs Brown (12")	£20
83	Csa SPCSA 12006	Tug A War Game/EARL SIXTEEN: Rise In The Morning (12")	£50
82	Negus Roots NERT LP 002	MORNING GLORY (LP)	£100
83	Negus Roots NERT LP 008	AFRICAN LADY (LP)	£50

CASTELLS
61	London HLN 9392	Sacred/I Get Dreamy	£20
62	London HLN 9551	So This Is Love/On The Street Of Tears	£25

BEBETO CASTILHO
02	What Music WMLP 0016	BEBETO (LP)	£15

CASTLE FARM
72	Farm FARM 1	Hot Rod Queen/Mascot (p/s, lyric insert)	£60

ROY CASTLE
65	CBS 201736	Doctor Terror's House Of Horrors/Voodoo Girl (with Tubby Hayes)	£50

CASTLE SISTERS (JAMAICA)
66	Ska Beat JB 257	Stop Your Lying/Don't Be A Fool	£60

CAST OF THOUSANDS
66	Stateside SS 546	My Jenny Wears A Mini/Girl Do What You Gonna Do	£40

CASTON & MAJORS
75	Tamla Motown TMG 938	Child Of Love/No One Will Know	£15

(see also Radiants)

JIMMY CASTOR (BUNCH)
66	Philips BF 1543	Hey Leroy, Your Mama's Callin'/Ham Rock's Espanol	£20

MINT VALUE £

67	Philips BF 1590	**Magic Saxophone/Just You Girl** £25
73	RCA Victor APD1 0103	**DIMENSION III** (LP, quadrophonic) £20

MARIO CASTRO NEVES & HIS ORCHESTRA
73 Decca PFS 4294 **BRAZILIAN MOOD** (LP) £15

CASUAL FOUR
70s Specially Made For Us 102 **I Can Tell/Love Potion No. 9** £20

CASUALS
74 Dawn DNS 1069 **Witch/Good Times** £20
69 Decca LK-R/SKL-R 5001 **HOUR WORLD** (LP, large unboxed logo on label) £50
(see also American Jam, Kansas Hook)

JOHNNY CASWELL
85 Kent TOWN 106 **You Don't Love Me No More/STEINWAYS: You've Been Leading Me On** £20

CAT POWER
98 Matador OLE 286-1 **MOON PIX** (LP, printed inner) £25

CATACOMB
13 Macabre Unit MUV 005 **Music Mi Luv/Badman Culture Pt 2/Cursed** (12") £20

CATAPILLA
71 Vertigo 6360 029 **CATAPILLA** (LP, gatefold sleeve, small swirl label) £600
72 Vertigo 6360 074 **CHANGES** (LP, die-cut gatefold sleeve, small swirl label) £1500
(see also Jon Stevens, Liar)

CATAPULT
75 Box BOX 7 **Put On The Lights/Linda** £15

CATATONIA
96 Blanco Y Negro 16305-1 **WAY BEYOND BLUE** (LP, deleted after one week, with free 7") £40
98 Blanco Y Negro 20834-1 **INTERNATIONAL VELVET** (LP, 1,000 only, with free 12") £80
99 Blanco Y Negro 3984270941 **EQUALLY CURSED AND BLESSED** (LP, with free 1-sided 7") £50
01 Blanco Y Negro 8573888481 **PAPER SCISSORS STONE** (LP) £35

CATCH
77 Logo GO 103 **Borderline/Black Blood** (company sleeve) £40
(see also Tourists, Eurythmics)

CAT CLUB
87 Jive 155 **One Last Kiss/Wild** (p/s) £60
87 Jive JIVE T 155 **One Last Kiss/(Extended Version)/Wild** (12", p/s) £200

CATE BROTHERS
76 Asylum 13062 **Where Can We Go/Instrumental** £15

CATFISH
70 CBS 64006 **GET DOWN** (LP, orange label) £15
71 Epic 64408 **LIVE CATFISH** (LP) £15

CATHEDRAL
11 Rise Above ROSE 12 141 **A NEW ICE AGE EP: Open Mind Surgery/Sabbadaius Sabbatum** (12", poster 100 clear/100 white or 100 transluscent blue vinyl, sold at farewell gig) £60
91 Earache MOSH 43 **FOREST OF EQUILIBRIUM** (LP, gatefold) £40
93 Earache MOSH 77C **THE ETHEREAL MIRROR** (LP, blue vinyl, 1000 copies) £80
94 Rise Above RISE 8 **IN MEMORIAM** (LP, purple vinyl) £25
95 Earache MOSH 130 **THE CARNIVAL BIZARRE** (2 x 10" LP, gatefold sleeve) £20
96 Earache MOSH 156 **SUPERNATURAL BIRTH MACHINE** (2 x 10" test pressings, 10 copies only, release cancelled) £350

CATHERINE WHEEL
92 Fontana 510903-1 **FERMENT** (LP, initially with free 12") £50
92 Fontana 510903-1 **FERMENT** (LP, without free 12") £40
93 Fontana 518 039-1 **CHROME** (LP with inner sleeve) £150
97 Chrysalis 7243 4 93099 1 3 **ADAM & EVE** (2-LP) £80
00 Chrysalis 7243526776 1 0 **WISHVILLE** (LP) £40
17 Music On Vinyl MOVLP1880 **FERMENT** (LP, reissue, numbered, orange vinyl) £35
17 Music On Vinyl MOVLP1880 **FERMENT** (LP, reissue, 180gm) £30
17 Music On Vinyl MOVLP1881 **CHROME** (LP, reissue, numbered, silver vinyl) £40
17 Music On Vinyl MOVLP1881 **CHROME** (LP, reissue, 180gm) £30
19 Music On Vinyl MOVLP2288 **ADAM AND EVE** (2-LP, reissue) £20

RAY CATHODE (BBC RADIOPHONICS)
62 Parlophone R 4901 **Time Beat/Waltz In Orbit** £20
(see also BBC Radiophonic Workshop, George Martin)

CAT IRON
69 Xtra XTRA 1087 **CAT IRON** (LP) £25

CAT MOTHER & ALL NIGHT NEWSBOYS
69 Polydor 184 300 **THE STREET GIVETH AND THE STREET TAKETH AWAY** (LP) £30
70 Polydor 2425 021 **ALBION DOO-WAH** (LP, gatefold sleeve) £15
72 United Artists UAG 29313 **CAT MOTHER & ALL NIGHT NEWS BOYS** (LP, gatefold sleeve) £20
73 United Artists UAG 29381 **LAST CHANCE DANCE** (LP) £15
(see also Jimi Hendrix)

CATS 'N' JAMMER KIDS
77 Ebony EYEC 3 **Disco Drum/Disco Drum** (Part 5) (12") £30

CATS EYES (1)
69 Deram DM 251 **Where Is She Now?/Tom Drum** £25

| 70 | MCA MK 5056 | The Wizard/Hey (Open Your Eyes) | £20 |

CAT'S PYJAMAS
| 68 | Direction 58-3235 | Virginia Water/Baby I Love You | £40 |
| 68 | Direction 58-3482 | Camera Man/House For Sale | £40 |

(see also Kenny Bernard)

CATS (2)
69	Baf BAF 1	Swan Lake/Swing Low	£15
69	Baf BAF 2	My Girl/The Hog	£15
69	Baf BAF 3	The Hig/Blues For Justice	£15
69	Baf BAF 4	William Tell/Love Walk Right In	£15
70	Crystal CR 7009	Sherman/What Can I Do	£40
75	Groove GVE 1001	Swan Lake/Swan Lake (Disco Version) (reissue)	£15

CATS EYES (2)
| 11 | Polydor 2763913 | BROKEN GLASS EP (2 x 7") | £20 |
| 11 | Polydor 2766263 | CAT'S EYES (LP) | £20 |

(see also Horrors)

CLEM CATTINI ORK
| 65 | Decca F 12135 | No Time To Think/Impact | £50 |

(see also Tornados, Aquarian Age, Rumplestiltskin, Spaghetti Head, Sounds Nice)

NADIA CATTOUSE
| 66 | Reality RY 1001 | NADIA CATTOUSE (LP) | £40 |
| 70 | RCA Victor SF 8070 | EARTH MOTHER (LP, orange/white label) | £30 |

THE CAUSE
| 82 | Rising Sun RS 001 | METRO POLICE EP (original copies with insert sleeve) | £30 |
| 82 | Rising Sun RS 001 | METRO POLICE EP (without insert sleeve) | £15 |

CAUSE N EFFECT
| 90 | Foxadelic JTF1 | Hype/That's What It Is | £60 |
| 91 | Foxadelic JTF2 | Some Bite The Bullet (EP) | £50 |

CAUSTIC WINDOW
92	Rephlex CAT 004	JOYREX J4 EP (12", 6-track)	£40
92	Rephlex CAT 005	JOYREX J5 EP (12, 4-track, black vinyl)	£40
92	Rephlex CAT 005	JOYREX J5 EP (12, 4-track, white vinyl)	£30
93	Rephlex CAT 009 i	JOYREX J9 EP (10", picture disc, with bonus track "HMNA", 300 only)	£100
93	Rephlex CAT 009 ii	JOYREX J9 EP (12" 4-track, initial 100 in card mailer with bag of "space dust")	£70
93	Rephlex CAT 009 ii	JOYREX J9 EP (12" 4-track)	£50
94	Rephlex CAT 023	CAUSTIC WINDOW (2-LP, test pressing only, 10 pressed, 5 known copies)	£5000

(see also Aphex Twin)

EDDIE CAVE & FYX
| 66 | Pye 7N 17161 | Fresh Out Of Tears/It's Almost Good | £35 |

NICK CAVE (& BAD SEEDS)
86	Lyntone LYN 18038	Scum (green vinyl flexidisc, with poster, concert freebie)	£18
88	Muite 12MUTE 52	The Mercy Seat (Full Length Version)/New Day/The Mercy Seat (Video Mix) (12", p/s)	£15
94	Mute PMUTE 172	Red Right Hand (1-sided promo, with postcard and press release)	£20
94	Mute MUTE 172	Red Right Hand/That's What Jazz Is To Me (red vinyl, p/s, with 2 different stickers & labels, 2,000 only)	£15
01	Mute 10MUTE 262	Fifteen Feet Of Pure Snow/God Is In The House/And No More Shall We Part (10", p/s numbered)	£20
84	Mute STUMM 17	FROM HER TO ETERNITY (LP, with inner sleeve)	£40
85	Mute STUMM 21	THE FIRSTBORN IS DEAD (LP, with inner sleeve)	£40
86	Mute STUMM 28	KICKING AGAINST THE PRICKS (LP)	£40
86	Mute STUMM 34	YOUR FUNERAL...MY TRIAL (2-LP, gatefold sleeve, with inner sleeves)	£30
88	Mute LSTUMM 52	TENDER PREY (LP, with bonus spoken word 12" And The Ass Saw The Angel [P STUMM 52]: "Autumn"/Animal Static/Mah Sanctum/Lamentation, 5,000 only)	£60
88	Mute STUMM 52	TENDER PREY (LP, without bonus spoken word 12")	£40
90	Mute LSTUMM 76	THE GOOD SON (LP, with bonus 7" "Acoustic Versions From Tender Prey" [P STUMM 76]: "The Mercy Seat"/"City Of Refuge"/"Deanna")	£60
90	Mute STUMM 76	THE GOOD SON (LP, inner sleeve, without free 7")	£40
92	Mute STUMM 92	HENRY'S DREAM (LP, with inner sleeve and art print)	£70
94	Mute LSTUMM 123	LET LOVE IN (LP, inner, with set of postcards or poster)	£100
96	Mute STUMM 138	MURDER BALLADS (LP, with insert)	£100
97	Mute STUMM 142	THE BOATMANS CALL (LP)	£100
98	Mute MUTEL4	THE BEST OF NICK CAVE AND THE BAD SEEDS (2-LP, inners)	£75
01	Mute STUMM 164	NO MORE SHALL WE PART (2-LP, with inner sleeves)	£75
03	Mute STUMM 207	NOCTURAMA (2-LP, inners)	£60
04	Mute STUMM 233	ABBATOIR BLUES/THE LYRE OF ORPHEUS (2-LP, inner sleeves and insert)	£80
08	Mute STUMM 277	DIG LAZARUS DIG (LP, printed inner, booklet, and free 7")	£80
13	Bad Seed Ltd. BS001 DLX	PUSH THE SKY AWAY (2-LP, 2x7", DVD, book numbered and signed box set)	£150
13	Bad Seed Ltd. BS001 DLX	PUSH THE SKY AWAY (2-LP, 2x7", DVD, book numbered and unsigned box set)	£100
13	Bad Seed Ltd. DSC001CE	PUSH THE SKY AWAY (LP, with free 7")	£25
16	Bad Seed Ltd. BS009V	SKELETON TREE (LP, mispressing, A-side plays on both sides, labels correct)	£30

(see also Birthday Party, Annie Hogan, Burmoe Brothers)

STUART & SANDY CAVE
| 77 | Profile GMOR 143 | DAWN ON SUNDAY (LP) | £60 |

ANDY CAVELL
| 62 | HMV POP 1024 | Hey There Cruel Heart/Lonely Soldier Boy | £40 |
| 62 | HMV POP 1080 | Always On Saturday/Hey There, Senorita | £40 |

MINT VALUE £

63	Pye 7N 15539	Andy/There Was A Boy	£30
64	Pye 7N 15610	Shut Up/Tell The Truth	£30

JIMMY CAVELLO & HIS HOUSE ROCKERS
| 57 | Vogue Coral Q 72226 | Rock, Rock, Rock/The Big Beat | £250 |
| 57 | Vogue Coral Q 72240 | Foot Stompin'/Ooh-Wee | £250 |

(see also Alan Freed)

CAVE OF THE LIVING STREAMS
| 74 | Indigo Sound Studios UHC 1 | SIXTEEN SONGS (LP, private pressing with booklet) | £20 |

CAVERN OF ANTI MATTER
13	Associated Electronic AER-2	YOU'RE AN ART SOUL EP (12")	£40
14	Deep Distance DD19	Interlude Music 1/Interlude Music 2 (12")	£25
14	Peripheral Conserve PH24	Total Availability And The Private Future/Cluster Of Rainbows (12")	£20
15	Ghost Box GBX 716	Pulsing River Velvet Phase/Photones	£15
16	Duophonic DUHFLP33RT	VOID BEATS/INVOCATION TREX (3-LP, hand-made sleeve, 80 only)	£80
17	Duophonic DUHFLP 35	BLOOD DRUMS (3-LP reissue, clear vinyl)	£25

(see also Stereolab)

MONTE CAZAZZA
| 79 | Industrial IR 0005 | To Mom On Mother's Day/Candy Man (p/s, with outer polystyrene sleeve & insert, 2,500 only) | £20 |
| 80 | Industrial IR 0010 | SOMETHING FOR NOBODY (EP) | £20 |

(see also Psychic TV)

C.C.S. (COLLECTIVE CONSCIOUSNESS SOCIETY)
70	Rak SRAK 6751	C.C.S. (LP, gatefold sleeve)	£25
72	Rak SRAK 503	C.C.S. (LP)	£25
73	Rak SRAK 504	THE BEST BAND IN THE LAND (LP)	£15

(see also Alexis Korner)

CEDARS
| 68 | Decca F 22720 | For Your Information/Hide If You Want To Hide | £50 |
| 68 | Decca F 22772 | I Like The Way/I Don't Know Why | £50 |

(see also Seaders)

TONY CEE
| 81 | Cheeseman CT 1 | Holiday/One Way Street | £30 |

CELIBATES
| 81 | ALPLP 1001 | A SHAMELESS FASHION (LP) | £40 |

CELITIA
| 96 | Diesel DES LP 03 | CELITIA (LP) | £15 |

CELTIC FROST
84	Noise N 0017	MORBID TALES (mini LP, with poster)	£40
84	Noise N 0017	MORBID TALES (mini LP, without poster)	£25
86	Combat MX 8091	TO MEGA THERION (LP, gatefold, with inner sleeve)	£25
87	NOISE NOISE 065	INTO THE PANDEMONIUM (LP, gatefold sleeve, with insert)	£25
06	Century Media 9979951	MONOTHEIST (2-LP, gatefold, brown marbled vinyl, 100 only)	£50

CENOTAPH CORNER
| 76 | Cottage COT 501 | UPS AND DOWNS (LP) | £20 |
| 79 | Cottage COT 031 | EVERY DAY BUT WEDNESDAY (LP) | £25 |

CENTIPEDE
71	RCA Neon NE 9	SEPTOBER ENERGY (2-LP, gatefold sleeve, black inner sleeve)	£80
74	RCA DPS 2054	SEPTOBER ENERGY (2-LP, reissue, different cover)	£25
13	Klint MJJ358LP	SEPTOMBER ENERGY (2-LP)	£18

(see also Mark Charig, Elton Dean, Zoot Money, Alan Skidmore, Keith Tippett, Julie Tippetts, Mike Patto, Robert Wyatt)

CENTRY
| 93 | Conscious Sounds DNC 002 | THUNDER MOUNTAIN : CENTRY IN DUB (LP) | £25 |
| 95 | Conscious Sounds DNC 005 | RELEASE THE CHAINS (LP) | £15 |

CENTURION
| 82 | Centurion 0001 | Two Wheels/Bitch (private pressing) | £50 |
| 82 | Centurion 0001 | Two Wheels/Bitch (private pressing, mislabelled 'Nikki') | £30 |

CENTURY 21 (GERRY ANDERSON TV SPIN-OFFS)
65	Century 21 MA 100	JOURNEY TO THE MOON (EP)	£15
65	Century 21 MA 102	A TRIP TO MARINEVILLE (EP)	£15
65	Century 21 MA 103	INTRODUCING THUNDERBIRDS (EP)	£15
65	Century 21 MA 104	MARINA SPEAKS (EP)	£15
65	Century 21 MA 105	TV CENTURY 21 THEMES (EP)	£15
66	Century 21 MA 106	THE DALEKS (EP)	£50
66	Century 21 MA 107	F.A.B. (EP)	£18
66	Century 21 MA 108	THUNDERBIRD 1 (EP)	£18
66	Century 21 MA 109	THUNDERBIRD 2 (EP)	£18
66	Century 21 MA 110	THE STATELY HOME ROBBERIES (EP)	£25
66	Century 21 MA 111	LADY PENELOPE & OTHER TV THEMES (EP)	£25
66	Century 21 MA 112	THUNDERBIRD 3 (EP)	£25
66	Century 21 MA 113	THUNDERBIRD 4 (EP)	£25
66	Century 21 MA 114	THE PERILS OF PENELOPE (EP)	£25
66	Century 21 MA 115	TOPO GIGIO IN LONDON (EP)	£40
67	Century 21 MA 116	GREAT THEMES FROM GERRY ANDERSON'S THUNDERBIRDS (EP)	£30
67	Century 21 MA 117	SPACE AGE NURSERY RHYMES (EP)	£30
67	Century 21 MA 118	LADY PENELOPE AND PARKER (EP)	£30

67	Century 21 MA 119	BRAINS AND TIN TIN (EP)	£30
67	Century 21 MA 120	INTERNATIONAL RESCUE (EP)	£30
67	Century 21 MA 121	THUNDERBIRDS (EP)	£30
67	Century 21 MA 122	LADY PENELOPE (EP)	£30
67	Century 21 MA 123	BRAINS (EP)	£30
67	Century 21 MA 124	BRINK OF DISASTER (EP)	£30
67	Century 21 MA 125	ATLANTIC INFERNO (EP)	£30
67	Century 21 MA 126	RICOCHET (EP)	£30
67	Century 21 MA 127	TINGHA & TUCKER & THE WOMBAVILLE BAND (EP)	£30
67	Century 21 MA 128	ONE MOVE & YOU'RE DEAD (EP)	£30
67	Century 21 MA 129	30 MINUTES AFTER NOON (EP)	£30
67	Century 21 MA 130	TINGHA & TUCKER IN NURSERY RHYME TIME (EP)	£30
67	Century 21 MA 131	INTRODUCING CAPTAIN SCARLET (EP)	£25
67	Century 21 MA 132	CAPTAIN SCARLET AND THE MYSTERONS (EP)	£25
67	Century 21 MA 133	CAPTAIN SCARLET IS INDESTRUCTIBLE (EP)	£20
67	Century 21 MA 134	CAPTAIN SCARLET OF SPECTRUM (EP)	£20
67	Century 21 MA 135	CAPTAIN SCARLET VS. CAPTAIN BLACK (EP)	£20
67	Century 21 MA 136	THEMES FROM GERRY ANDERSON'S CAPTAIN SCARLET (EP)	£20
65	Century 21 LA 100	JOURNEY TO THE MOON (LP)	£50
66	Century 21 LA 1	THE WORLD OF TOMORROW (LP)	£40
66	Century 21 LA 2	LADY PENELOPE PRESENTS (LP)	£40
66	Century 21 LA 3	JEFF TRACY INTRODUCES INTERNATIONAL RESCUE (LP)	£40
66	Century 21 LA 4	LADY PENELOPE INVESTIGATES (LP)	£40
66	Century 21 LA 5	THE TINGHA & TUCKER CLUB SONG BOOK (LP)	£40
67	Century 21 LA 6	FAVOURITE TELEVISION THEMES (LP)	£40
68	Marble Arch MAL 770	TV FAVOURITES VOL. 1 (LP)	£20
68	Marble Arch MAL 771	TV FAVOURITES VOL. 2 (LP)	£20

(see also Barry Gray, Dr. Who)

CEOLBEG
| 90 | Ceolbeg Music CB 001 | NOT THE BUNNY HOP (LP) | £20 |

CEREBRAL FIX
| 88 | Vinyl Solution SOL 15 | LIFE SUCKS AND THEN YOU DIE! (LP) | £15 |

CERTAIN LIONS & TIGERS
| 70 | Polydor 2344 002 | SOUL CONDOR (LP) | £40 |

CEYLEIB PEOPLE
| 68 | Vocalion SAVL 8072 | TANYET (LP) | £200 |

CHAD (STUART) & JEREMY (CLYDE)
| 65 | United Artists UEP 1008 | CHAD STUART AND JEREMY CLYDE (EP) | £20 |

(see also John Barry)

ERNIE CHAFFIN
| 57 | London HLS 8409 | Feelin' Low/Lonesome For My Baby | £80 |
| 57 | London HLS 8409 | Feelin' Low/Lonesome For My Baby (78) | £15 |

CHAIN OF STRENGTH
| 91 | First Strike FS010 | WHAT HOLDS US APART (EP, blue vinyl) | £30 |
| 91 | First Strike FS010 | WHAT HOLDS US APART (EP, white vinyl) | £40 |

CHAIN REACTION
77	Gull GULS 77	Never Lose Never Win/Chase A Miracle	£15
77	Gull GULS 53	Why Can't We Be Lovers/Hogtied	£40
77	Gull GULS 43	This Eternal Flame/Never Lose, Never Win	£15
77	Gull GULP 1021	INDEBTED TO YOU (LP)	£100
80	Congress CPLPS1	CHANGE OF ACTION (LP)	£15
81	Congress CPLPS2	CHASE A MIRACLE (LP)	£15
12	Vocalion VOCLP 3302	INDEBTED TO YOU (LP, reissue)	£15

CHAINSAW
80	Square SQSP 2	Police And Politicians/Hole In The Road (p/s)	£45
80	Pot Belly EJSP 9462	Lonely Without You/On The Highway	£35
84	GMC CS 001	Long Legged Woman/Midnight Blue	£30

CHAIRMEN OF THE BOARD
70	Invictus INV 501	Give Me Just A Little More Time/Since The Days Of Pigtails (DJ Copy)	£20
70	Invictus INV 504	You've Got Me Dangling On A String/Patches (DJ Copy)	£20
71	Invictus INV 507	Everything's Tuesday/Bless You (DJ Copy)	£15
71	Invictus INV 511	Pay To The Piper/When Will She Tell Me She Needs Me? (DJ Copy)	£15
70	Invictus SVT 1002	CHAIRMEN OF THE BOARD (LP)	£20
71	Invictus SVT 1003	IN SESSION (LP)	£20
72	Invictus SVT 1006	BITTERSWEET (LP)	£15
74	Invictus SVT 65868	SKIN I'M IN (LP)	£15

(see also Showmen, Norman Johnson)

CHAKACHAS
| 72 | Polydor 2489 050 | JUNGLE FEVER (LP) | £20 |
| 73 | Young Blood SYB 3003 | CHAKACHAS (LP) | £20 |

GEORGE CHAKIRIS
| 60 | Triumph RGM 1010 | Heart Of A Teenage Girl/I'm Always Chasing Rainbows | £30 |

CHALAWA
| 78 | Skynote SKYLP 14 | EXODUS DUB (LP) | £50 |

BRYAN CHALKER('S NEW FRONTIER)
71   Avenue AVE 071   THE HANGING OF SAMUEL HALL (LP, textured sleeve, as Bryan Chalker's New Frontier) .£15

CHALLENGER
81   CMC CM 0001   So Sure Of Yourself/Out To Kill £40

CHALLENGERS (U.S.)
65   Vocalion V 9253   The Man From U.N.C.L.E./The Streets Of London £20
63   Stateside SL 10030   SURFBEAT (LP) £50
67   Vocalion VA-N 8069   WIPE OUT (LP, mono) £50
67   Vocalion SAV-N 8069   WIPE OUT (LP, stereo)...£55

CHAMBERPOT
76   Bead Records BEAD 2   CHAMBERPOT (LP)..£50

JAMES CHAMBERS
71   Summit SUM 8523   Bongo Man/KEN BOOTHE: Now I Know £15
(see also Jimmy Cliff)

CHAMBERS BROTHERS
66   Vocalion VL 9267   Love Me Like The Rain/Pretty Girls Everywhere £20
66   Vocalion VL 9276   Call Me/Seventeen £20
71   CBS 5389   Funky/Love, Peace And Happiness £15
66   Vocalion VA-L/SAV-L 8058 PEOPLE GET READY (LP)..£60
68   Liberty LBS 83272   SHOUT! (LP, blue label)..£30
68   Direction 8-63407   THE TIME HAS COME (LP)..£30
69   Direction 8-63451   A NEW TIME - A NEW DAY (LP) £30
70   Direction 8-66228   LOVE PEACE AND HAPPINESS (Live At Bill Graham's Fillmore West) (2-LP) £30
70   Liberty LBS 83276   FEELIN' THE BLUES (LP) £15
71   CBS 64156   A NEW GENERATION (LP) £15

CHAMELEON
71   CBS 5428   Who Am I/Coogans Keep £20

CHAMELEONS
82   Epic EPCA 2210   In Shreds/Less Than Human (p/s) £15
83   Statik TAK 6/12   A Person Isn't Safe Anywhere These Days/Thursday's Child/Prisoners Of The Sun (12",
                               p/s)...£15
83   Statik TAK 11/12   Up The Down Escalator/Monkeyland/Prisoner Of The Sun (12", p/s)................£15
85   Statik TAK 29   In Shreds/Nostalgia (p/s) £15
86   Geffen GEF 4F/SAM 287   Tears/Paradiso//Swamp Thing/Inside Out (double pack, gatefold p/s)............£15
90   Glass Pyramid EMC 1   TONY FLETCHER WALKED ON WATER (12" EP) £40
90   Strange Fruit SFRLP 114   PEEL SESSIONS (LP) £15
83   Statik STATLP 17   SCRIPT OF THE BRIDGE (LP, 1st pressing, textured sleeve, insert)...................£80
85   Statik STATLP 17   SCRIPT OF THE BRIDGE (LP, picture disc) £20
85   Statik STATLP 22   WHAT DOES ANYTHING MEAN? BASICALLY (LP, gatefold sleeve, with insert)...................£20
86   Geffen 924119   STRANGE TIMES (LP, pink or blue sleeves) £20
90   Glass Pyramid EMC 2   TRIPPING DOGS (LP)..£25
93   Imaginary ILLUSION 042   AUFFUHRUNG IN BERLIN (LP) £45
(see also Reegs, Mark Burgess and the Sons Of God)

TEDDY CHAMES
68   Blue Cat BS 141   I Want It Girl/She Is Gone (actually by Teddy Charmes) £100

CHAMPAGNE BUBBLER PART 1
97   Strictly Limited SHQ 4   RUMP FUNK EP (12")...£25

CHAMPIONS OF NATURE
00   White FOFF 1   The Fuck Off Song/An Undercurrent/360/Carpe Diem (EP) £30
00   White FOFF 2   Finalisation/Cold Dessert/Breakfast Of Champions (EP) £30

CHAMPS (JAMAICA)
64   Blue Beat BB 267   Walk Between Your Enemies/Do What I Say..£40

CHAMPS (U.S.)
59   London RE 1176   FOUR BY THE CHAMPS (EP)..£20
59   London RE-H 1209   ANOTHER FOUR BY THE CHAMPS (EP)...£20
59   London RE-H 1223   STILL MORE BY THE CHAMPS (EP)..£20
61   London RE-H 1250   KNOCKOUTS! (EP)..£20
58   London HA-A 2152   GO CHAMPS GO! (LP) £40
59   London HA-A 2184   EVERYBODY'S ROCKIN' WITH THE CHAMPS (LP) £40
62   London HA-H 2451   GREAT DANCE HITS (LP, early issue with flipback cover) £30

BOB CHANCE
12   Trunk JBH 044   IT'S BROKEN (LP, 1000 only) £35

ROB CHANCE & CHANCES-R
67   CBS 3130   At The End Of The Day/I've Got The Power..£15
(see also Chances-R)

CHANCES ARE
67   Columbia DB 8144   Fragile Child/What Went Wrong..£40

CHANCES-R
67   CBS 202614   Talking Out The Back Of My Head/I Aimed Too High £20
(see also Rob Chance & Chances-R)

CHANCIS
64   Decca F 11860   Everybody's Laughing/Tell Me £15

TIM CHANDELL
78   Orbitone 05   Keep Me/Let's Make Love £20

DANY CHANDELLE
65   Columbia DB 7540   Lying Awake/I Love You £30

KERRI CHANDLER
96   Freetown FTILP2   HEMISPHERE (LP as 2 x 12") £30

BARBARA CHANDLER
63   London HLR 9823   Do You Really Love Me Too?/I Live To Love You £30
64   London HLR 9861   I'm Going Out With The Girls/Lonely New Year £30

GENE CHANDLER
62   Columbia DB 4793   Duke Of Earl/Kissing In The Kitchen £25
63   Stateside SS 185   Rainbow/You Threw A Lucky Punch £40
64   Stateside SS 331   Just Be True/A Song Called Soul £25
64   Stateside SS 364   Bless Our Love/London Town £25
65   Stateside SS 388   What Now/If You Can't Be True (Find A Part Time Love) £35
65   Stateside SS 401   You Can't Hurt Me No More/Everybody Let's Dance £25
65   Stateside SS 425   Nothing Can Stop Me/The Big Lie £60
65   Stateside SS 425   Nothing Can Stop Me/The Big Lie (DJ copy) £150
65   Stateside SS 458   Good Times/No One Can Love You (Like I Do) £35
66   Stateside SS 500   (I'm Just A) Fool For You/Buddy Ain't It A Shame £35
66   Chess CRS 8047   I Fooled You This Time/Such A Pretty Thing £40
66   Chess CRS 8047   I Fooled You This Time/Such A Pretty Thing (DJ copy) £100
67   Coral Q 72490   The Girl Don't Care/My Love £20
68   Soul City SC 102   Nothing Can Stop Me/The Big Lie (reissue) £15
69   Action ACT 4551   I Can't Save It/I Can Take Care Of Myself £60
71   Mercury 6052 098   You're A Lady/Stone Cold Feeling £15
76   Brunswick BR 39   There Was A Time/ARTISTICS: I'm Gonna Miss You £15
65   Fontana TL 5247   DUKE OF EARL (LP) £80
67   Coral LVA 9236   THE GIRL DON'T CARE (LP) £60
69   MCA MUPS 367   THERE WAS A TIME (LP) £30
69   Action ACLP 6010   LIVE ON STAGE (LP) £50
71   Mercury 6338 037   SITUATION (LP) £20
74   Joy JOYS 136   A GENE CHANDLER ALBUM (LP) £15
86   Kent 049   60s SOUL BROTHER (LP) £15

GEORGE CHANDLER
82   Polydor 436   This Could Be The Night/Can't Go Back No More £15

JEFF CHANDLER
58   London HA-U 2100   JEFF CHANDLER SINGS TO YOU (LP) £20

KENNY CHANDLER
63   Stateside SS 166   Heart/Wait For Me £15
68   Stateside SS 2110   Beyond Love/Charity £40
68   Stateside SS 2110   Beyond Love/Charity (DJ Copy) £60

LEN CHANDLER
67   CBS 62931   TO BE A MAN (LP) £20

LORRAINE CHANDLER
97   Kent 6T 13   You Only Live Twice/METROS: My Imagination £30

CHANGE (1)
73   Orange OAS 221   Lazy London Lady/Arkmaker £40
73   Orange OAS 222   Sunshine/Get Your Gun £25

CHANGE (2)
80   WEA K 79141   A Lovers Holiday/The Glow Of Love (12") £15
80   Warner Bros. K99107   THE GLOW OF LOVE (LP) £15

CHANGIN' TIMES
65   Phillips BF 1442   Pied Piper/Thank You Babe £25

BRUCE CHANNEL
62   Pye International 7N 25137 Run Romance Run/Don't Leave Me £15
63   London HLU 9776   I Don't Wanna/Blue And Lonesome £15
64   London HLU 9841   Going Back To Louisiana/Forget Me Not £15
62   Mercury MMC 14104   HEY! BABY! (LP) £50
68   Bell MBLL/SBLL 110   KEEP ON (LP) £20

CHANNEL 3
82   No Future PUNK 2   I'VE GOT A GUN (LP) £18

CHANTAYS
64   King KG 1018   Beyond/I'll Be Back Someday £15
63   London RED 1397   PIPELINE (EP) £35
63   London HA-D 8087   PIPELINE (LP, mono) £40
63   London SH-D 8087   PIPELINE (LP, stereo) £50

CHANTELLES
65   Parlophone R 5271   I Want That Boy/London My Home Town £25
65   Parlophone R 5303   The Secret Of My Success/Sticks And Stones £15
65   Parlophone R 5350   Gonna Get Burned/Gonna Give Him Some Love £15
66   Parlophone R 5431   I Think Of You/Please Don't Kiss Me £15
66   Polydor 56119   There's Something About You/Just Another Fool £20

MINT VALUE £

67	CBS 2777	Blue Mood/The Man I Love	£25

(see also Lana Sisters)

CHANTELLS
78	Sagittarius SUS 6A	Man In Love/Natty Supper (12")	£15
82	Phase 1 SUS 4	Children Of Jah/Desperate Time (12")	£20

CHANTELS
58	London HLU 8561	Maybe/Come My Little Baby	£250
58	London HLU 8561	Maybe/Come My Little Baby (78)	£35
62	London HLL 9428	Look In My Eyes/Glad To Be Back	£50
62	London HLL 9480	Well I Told You/Still	£50
62	London HLL 9532	Here It Comes Again/Summertime	£30
63	Capitol CL 15297	Swamp Water/Eternally	£30

(see also Richard Barrett)

CHANTERS (1)
66	CBS 202454	Every Night (I Sit And Cry)/Where	£30
67	CBS 202616	You Can't Fool Me/All Day Long	£20

(see also Birds Of A Feather)

CHANTERS (2)
79	Burning Rockers BRD 011	Mash Down Babylon/I Told You So (12")	£25

CHANTS (U.K.)
63	Pye 7N 15557	I Don't Care/Come Go With Me	£15
64	Pye 7N 15591	I Could Write A Book/A Thousand Stars	£15
64	Pye 7N 15643	She's Mine/Then I'll Be Home	£15
64	Pye 7N 15691	Sweet Was The Wine/One Star	£15
66	Fontana TF 716	Come Back And Get This Loving Baby/Love Light	£20
67	Decca F 12650	A Lover's Story/Wearing A Smile	£20
67	Page One POF 016	Ain't Nobody Home/For You	£15
68	RCA Victor RCA 1754	A Man Without A Face/Baby I Don't Need Your Love	£100
68	RCA Victor RCA 1754	A Man Without A Face/Baby I Don't Need Your Love (DJ Copy)	£130
69	RCA Victor RCA 1823	I Get The Sweetest Feeling/Candy	£25
76	Chipping Norton CHIP 2	I've Been Trying/Lucky Old Me	£30

(see also Real Thing)

CHANTS (U.S.)
58	Capitol CL 14876	Close Friends/Lost And Found	£25

CHAOS U.K.
79	Chaotic Records VD 1	Summer Of Hate/I Wanna To Be Left Alone (p/s, 500 only)	£200

CHAOS U.K. (BRISTOL)
83	Riot City CITY 002	CHAOS U.K. (LP)	£30
85	C.O.R. GURT 1	SHORT SHARP SHOCK (LP)	£20
86	Manic Ears ACHE 1	RADIOACTIVE (LP, with inner, split with EXTREME NOISE TERROR)	£20

CHAOTIC DISCHORD
81	Riot City 12 ROT 30	Don't Throw It Away (12")	£15
83	Riot City CITY 004	FUCK RELIGION, FUCK POLITICS, AND FUCK THE LOT OF YOU (LP)	£18
84	Syndicate SYNLP 12	FUCK OFF YOU CUNT WHAT A LOAD OF BOLLOCKS (LP)	£15

CHAOTIC YOUTH
83	Beat The System YOUTH 1	SAD SOCIETY (EP)	£50

PAUL CHAPLAIN & HIS EMERALDS
60	London HLU 9205	Shortnin' Bread/Nicotine	£15

CHARLIE CHAPLIN
82	Kingdon KVL 9012	PRESENTING CHARLIE CHAPLIN (LP)	£18
82	Tamoki Wambesi TWLP 1014	RED POND (LP)	£15
82	Tamoki Wambesi TWLP 1020	CHAPLIN CHANT (LP)	£15
83	Trojan TRLS 216	ONE OF A KIND (LP)	£30
84	Vista VSLP 4063	ROOTS & CULTURE (LP)	£25

CHAPMAN AND WHITNEY
74	Reprise K54017	STREETWALKERS (LP, with inner)	£20

(see also Streetwalkers)

GENE CHAPMAN
63	Starlite ST45 102	Oklahoma Blues/Don't Come Crying	£25

GRADY CHAPMAN
60	Mercury AMT 1107	Sweet Thing/I Know What I Want	£30

MICHAEL CHAPMAN
69	Harvest HAR 5002	It Didn't Work Out/Mozart Lives Upstairs	£18
69	Harvest SHVL 755	RAINMAKER (LP, gatefold sleeve, with "Sold in U.K..." label text on 4 lines, No EMI on label)	£100
69	Harvest SHVL 755	RAINMAKER (LP, gatefold sleeve, later pressing with EMI on label)	£40
69	Standard ESL 146	SOLO GUITAR (LP, library issue)	£60
70	Harvest SHVL 764	FULLY QUALIFIED SURVIVOR (LP, gatefold sleeve, 1st pressing with no EMI on label)	£90
70	Harvest SHVL 764	FULLY QUALIFIED SURVIVOR (LP, gatefold sleeve, later pressing with EMI on label)	£30
70	Harvest SHVL 786	WINDOW (LP, gatefold sleeve, with no EMI on label)	£80
70	Harvest SHVL 786	WINDOW (LP, gatefold sleeve, with EMI on label)	£25
71	Harvest SHVL 798	WRECKED AGAIN (LP, gatefold sleeve, EMI on label)	£60
73	Deram SML 1105	MILLSTONE GRIT (LP, red/white label)	£20

74	Deram SML 1114	**DEAL GONE DOWN** (LP)..£20
76	Decca SKL-R 5242	**SAVAGE AMUSEMENT** (LP, with lyric sheet, blue/silver label)...........£20
77	Decca SKL-R 5290	**THE MAN WHO HATED MORNINGS** (LP)..............................£15
78	Criminal STEAL 2	**PLAYING GUITAR THE EASY WAY** (LP)..............................£15
79	Criminal TAKE 3	**FULLY QUALIFIED SURVIVOR** (LP, reissue) £15

CHAPTER FIVE

66	CBS 202395	Anything You Do Is Alright/You Can't Mean It £800
67	CBS 2696	One In A Million/Hey Hey (unissued, demos only) £250
00s	Goldmine Soul Supply GS 009	You Can't Mean It/One In A Million (reissue)...........................£15

CHAPTER FOUR (U.K.)

60s	GSP 11009/10	CHAPTER FOUR (EP, no p/s)...£90

CHAPTER FOUR (U.K.)

80	Bridge BR 001	HANGING AROUND STERLING (LP) £35

CHAPTER FOUR (U.S.)

66	United Artists UP 1143	In My Life/In Each Other's Arms £250

(see also Jay & Americans)

CHAPTER THREE (U.K.)

67	CBS BPG 63007	RAMBLE AWAY (LP) £25

CHAPTERHOUSE

91	Dedicated DEDLP 001	WHIRLPOOL (LP with bonus 12")..£30
91	Dedicated DEDLP 001	WHIRLPOOL (LP, without free 12")......................................£20
93	Dedicated DEDLP 011D	BLOOD MUSIC (2-LP) £35

(see also Slowdive)

CHAPTERS

65	Pye 7N 15815	Can't Stop Thinking About Her/Dance Little Lady.......................£60

CHARACTERS

86	BEM BEM 101	Love Talk/Where Has All The Love Gone (500 only) £30

CHARGE (1)

73	SRT private pressing	CHARGE (LP, 1 known copy)..£1500
92	Kissing Spell KSLP 9205	CHARGE (LP, reissue, revised sleeve, 500 only).........................£20

CHARGE (2)

70	Private pressing	Zeugma/Boring Song (art sleeve) £20

CHARGE (3)

80	YCAFO Records	You Get What You Deserve/Rather B Crazy/Angel Deceast (foldout p/s).........£65
81	Test Pressing	You Deserve More Than A Maybe (p/s, 500 only, existence unconfirmed) £30

CHARGERS

84	Charge BCSK 01	Desperaroes/Are You Out There (p/s) £60

MARK CHARIG

77	Ogun OG 710	PIPEDREAM (LP) £15

(see also Bluesology, B.B. Blunder, Reg King, Centipede, Keith Tippett, Julie Tippett, Brotherhood Of Breath, Elton Dean, Ninesense)

CHARIOT

84	Shades SHADE 1	THE WARRIOR (LP)...£15
86	Shades SHADE 4	BURNING AMBITION (LP) £15

CHARLATANS (U.K.)

90	Situation Two SITU 30L	SOME FRIENDLY (LP, 'some friendly edition' in white PVC sleeve with inner)..........£25
90	Situation Two SITU 30	SOME FRIENDLY (LP)..£20
92	Situation Two SITU 37	BETWEEN 10TH AND 11TH (LP)..£25
91	Live Live Good CB 2	ISOLATION 21.2.91 (LP, official live bootleg, sold via fan club, 1,000 only)......£25
94	Beggars Banquet BBQLP 147	UP TO OUR HIPS (LP, textured sleeve) £25
95	Beggars Banquet BBQLP 174	THE CHARLATANS (2-LP, inners)......................................£80
97	Beggars Banquet BBQLP 190	TELLIN' STORIES (LP) £40
98	Beggars Banquet BBQLP 198	MELTING POT (2-LP) £40
99	Universal 1538650-1	US & US ONLY (LP) £50
01	Universal 014911-1	WONDERLAND (2-LP) £30
04	MCA MCA 60093	UP AT THE LAKE (LP) £20
08	Cooking Vinyl COOK 462	YOU CROSS MY PATH (LP)..£25
10	Music On Vinyl MOVLP 185	WHO WE TOUCH (LP) £20
15	BMG 538014171	MODERN NATURE (2-LP, gold vinyl)...................................£20
15	BMG 538014171	MODERN NATURE (2-LP, signed, gold vinyl with CD).....................£35
17	Beggars Banquet BBQLP 147E	UP TO OUR HIPS (LP, reissue, green vinyl, 250 only) £80

(see also Electric Crayons, Makin' Time, Tim Burgess)

CHARLATANS (U.S.)

69	Philips SBL 7903	THE CHARLATANS (LP) £90

(see also Mike Wilhelm, Tongue & Groove, Dan Hicks & His Hot Licks)

BOBBY CHARLES

56	London HLU 8247	See You Later, Alligator/On Bended Knee £1000
56	London HLU 8247	See You Later, Alligator/On Bended Knee (78) £150

CHILLI CHARLES

74	Virgin V2009	BUSY CORNER (LP) £15
75	Virgin V2028	QUICKSTEP (LP)...£15

DON CHARLES

68	Parlophone R 5688	The Drifter/Great To Be Livin' £150

MINT VALUE £

68	Parlophone R 5688	**The Drifter/Great To Be Livin'** (DJ Copy)	£200
68	Parlophone R 5712	**Your Name Is On My Heart/How Can I**	£15
63	Decca DFE 8530	**DON CHARLES** (EP)	£50
67	Parlophone PMC/PCS 7021	**HAVE I TOLD YOU LATELY** (LP, mono/stereo)	£25

EVAN CHARLES
83	Naive NAV 6	**Intimacy/Ask Yourself** (Revisited) (p/s)	£80

JIMMY CHARLES
60	London HLU 9206	**A Million To One/Hop Scotch Hop**	£25

LEON CHARLES
80	Rokel ROK 15	**Disco Carnival/Instrumental** (12")	£20

RAY CHARLES
78s
58	London HLE 8768	**Rockhouse** (Parts 1 & 2)	£25
59	London HLE 8917	**What'd I Say** (Parts 1 & 2)	£30
59	London HLE 9009	**I'm Movin' On/I Believe To My Soul**	£40
60	HMV POP 792	**Georgia On My Mind/Carry Me Back To Old Virginny**	£50

SINGLES
58	London HLE 8768	**Rockhouse** (Parts 1 & 2)	£30
59	London HLE 8917	**What'd I Say** (Parts 1 & 2)	£25
59	London HLE 9009	**I'm Movin' On/I Believe To My Soul**	£20
60	London HLE 9058	**Let The Good Times Roll/Don't Let The Sun Catch You Cryin'**	£20
60	HMV POP 774	**Sticks And Stones/Worried Life Blues**	£15
60	London HLK 9181	**Tell The Truth/You Be My Baby**	£15
61	HMV POP 838	**Them That Got/I Wonder**	£25
61	London HLK 9364	**Early In The Mornin'/A Bit Of Soul**	£15
61	HMV POP 862	**One Mint Julep/Let's Go**	£15
66	HMV POP 1519	**Together Again/You're Just About To Lose Your Clown**	£20
66	HMV POP 1537	**Let's Go Get Stoned/The Train**	£20
66	HMV POP 1551	**I Chose To Sing The Blues/Hopelessly**	£25
66	HMV POP 1566	**Please Say You're Fooling/I Don't Need No Doctor**	£50
66	HMV POP 1566	**Please Say You're Fooling/I Don't Need No Doctor** (DJ Copy)	£80

EPs
59	London Jazz EZK 19043	**THE GREAT RAY CHARLES**	£15
59	London Jazz EZK 19048	**SOUL BROTHERS** (with Milt Jackson)	£15
61	London REK 1306	**WHAT'D I SAY**	£20
61	London REK 1317	**RAY CHARLES AT NEWPORT**	£15
62	HMV 7EG 8729	**HIT THE ROAD JACK**	£15
62	HMV 7EG 8781	**I CAN'T STOP LOVING YOU**	£15

ALBUMS
58	London Jazz LTZ-K 15134	**THE GREAT RAY CHARLES**	£50
59	London Jazz LTZ-K 15146	**SOUL BROTHERS** (with Milt Jackson, mono)	£25
59	London Jazz SAH-K 6030	**SOUL BROTHERS** (with Milt Jackson, stereo)	£25
59	London Jazz LTZ-K 15149	**RAY CHARLES AT NEWPORT** (mono)	£25
59	London Jazz SAH-K 6008	**RAY CHARLES AT NEWPORT** (stereo)	£25
59	London HA-E 2168	**YES INDEED**	£50
59	London HA-E 2226	**WHAT'D I SAY**	£40
60	London Jazz LTZ-K 15190	**THE GENIUS OF RAY CHARLES**	£40
60	HMV CLP 1387/CSD 1320	**THE GENIUS HITS THE ROAD** (mono)	£15
60	HMV CLP 1387/CSD 1320	**THE GENIUS HITS THE ROAD** (stereo)	£18
60	London HA-K 2284	**RAY CHARLES IN PERSON**	£30
61	HMV CLP 1449/CSD 1362	**DEDICATED TO YOU** (mono)	£15
61	HMV CLP 1449/CSD 1362	**DEDICATED TO YOU** (stereo)	£20
61	HMV CLP 1475/CSD 1384	**GENIUS + SOUL = JAZZ** (mono)	£15
61	HMV CLP 1475/CSD 1384	**GENIUS + SOUL = JAZZ** (stereo)	£20
62	HMV CLP 1520/CSD 1414	**RAY CHARLES AND BETTY CARTER** (mono)	£15
62	HMV CLP 1520/CSD 1414	**RAY CHARLES AND BETTY CARTER** (stereo)	£18
62	London Jazz LJZ-K 15238	**THE GENIUS SINGS THE BLUES**	£25
62	HMV CLP 1580/CSD 1451	**MODERN SOUNDS IN COUNTRY & WESTERN** (mono)	£15
62	HMV CLP 1580/CSD 1451	**MODERN SOUNDS IN COUNTRY & WESTERN** (stereo)	£18
63	HMV CLP 1613/CSD 1477	**MODERN SOUNDS IN COUNTRY & WESTERN VOL. TWO** (mono)	£15
63	HMV CLP 1613/CSD 1477	**MODERN SOUNDS IN COUNTRY & WESTERN VOL. TWO** (stereo)	£15
63	London HA-K 8022	**THE ORIGINAL RAY CHARLES**	£15
63	London HA-K 8035	**THE GENIUS AFTER HOURS**	£15
63	London HA-K/SH-K 8045	**SOUL MEETING** (with Milt Jackson)	£15
63	HMV CLP 1678	**INGREDIENTS IN A RECIPE FOR SOUL**	£20

(see also Raelets, Milt Jackson)

SONNY CHARLES (& CHECKMATES LTD)
67	Ember EMB S 240	**Mastered The Art Of Love/Please Don't Take My World Away**	£40

TINA CHARLES
69	CBS 4015	**Nothing In The World/Millions Of Hearts**	£15
69	CBS 4307	**In The Middle Of The Day/Rich Girl**	£40
69	CBS 4658	**Good To Be Alive/Same Old Story**	£50

CHILI CHARLES
75	Virgin V 2028	**QUICKSTEP** (LP)	£15

DICK CHARLESWORTH (& HIS CITY GENTS)
| 61 | Top Rank 35-104 | MEET THE GENTS (LP) | £15 |
| 62 | HMV CLP 1495 | YES INDEED IT'S THE GENTS (LP) | £15 |

CHARLIE
| 72 | Bumble GE 111 | Dream Hero/Lament | £15 |
| 73 | Decca F 13451 | I Need Your Love/I'm So Happy | £20 |

CHARLIE BOY
| 71 | Trojan TR 7823 | Funky Strip/UPSETTERS: Mellow Mood | £25 |

(see also Lee Perry/Upsetters)

CHARLIE PARKAS
| 80 | Paranoid Plastics PPS 1 | The Ballad Of Robin Hood/Space Invaders (mock 2-Tone die cut p/s) | £30 |

(see also Alberto Y Lost Trios Paranoias)

CHARLIES BROTHER
| 84 | Lost Moment LMO 100 | Wishing Tree/Further Adventures Of | £25 |

CHARLY & THE BOURBON FAMILY
| 71 | Decca F 23164 | Acapulco Gold/Boogachi | £15 |

CHARMAINES
| 98 | Kent 6T 18 | I Idolize You/M&M & THE PEANUTS: Can't Say No | £25 |

CHARMERS (JAMAICA)
61	Blue Beat BB 42	Lonely Boy/I Am Going Back Home	£25
62	Blue Beat BB 114	Crying Over You/Now You Want To Cry	£30
63	Blue Beat BB 157	Time After Time/Done Me Wrong (with Prince Buster's Band)	£25
63	R&B JB 118	Angel Love/My Heart	£50
63	R&B JB 121	Oh Why Baby/ROLAND ALPHONSO: Perhaps	£50
64	Blue Beat	How Could I Forget/Why Won't You Come Home? (with Prince Buster's Band) (white label only)	£75
64	R&B JB 151	What's The Use/I Am Through	£50
64	R&B JB 156	In My Soul/Beware	£50
64	Blue Beat BB 204	I'm Back/It's A Dream	£50
64	Blue Beat BB 238	Waiting For You/You Are My Sunshine	£30
64	Blue Beat BB 251	Dig Then Prince (actually Dip Them Prince)/Girl Of My Dreams (as The Charmer)	£60
65	Blue Beat BB 279	Nobody Takes My Baby Away From Me/ BUSTER ALLSTARS: Mules Mules Mules	£75
66	Blue Beat BB 345	Oh My Baby/STRANGER COLE: When The Party Is Over	£50
66	Ska Beat JB 237	Best Friend/MAYTALS: My Darling	£60
66	Rio R 78	You Don't Know/CORNELL CAMPBELL & ROY PANTON: Sweetest Girl	£40
68	Coxsone CS 7043	Things Going Wrong/KEN BOOTHE: You Keep Me Hanging On	£300
68	Treasure Isle TI 7036	Keep On Going (actually by Lloyd Charmers)/SILVERTONES: Don't Say No	£50
70	Duke DU 87	Colour Him Father/Version	£30
70	Trojan TR 7773	Sweeter She Is (actually by Lloyd Charmers, Dave Barker & Slim Smith)/ Fire Fire (actually by Lloyd Charmers)	£20
70	Explosion EX 2035	Sweet Back/Music Talk (actually by Lloyd Charmers)	£15
71	Explosion EX 2045	Skinhead Train/TONY & CHARMERS: Everstrong (B-side with Tony Binns)	£125
71	Explosion EX 2055	Reggae In Wonderland/Wonder (Version)	£15
71	Supreme SUP 220	Just My Imagination/Gotta Get A Message To You (actually by Dave Barker)	£25
71	Green Door GD 4000	Rasta Never Fails (actually by Lloyd Charmers & Ken Boothe)/CHARMERS ALL STARS: Rasta Version	£20
71	Green Door GD 4001	One Big Unhappy Family/CONSCIOUS MINDS: Africa Is Paradise	£15

(see also Spanishtown Skabeats, Lloydie & Lowbites, Lloyd Terrell)

LLOYD CHARMERS
67	Coxsone CS 7023	Time Is Getting Hard/TONY GREGORY: I Sit By The Shore	£100
69	Duke DU 15	Cooyah/UNIQUES: Forever	£50
69	Duke DU 16	Follow This Sound/Why Pretend	£50
69	Duke DU 25	5 To 5/SOUL STIRRERS: Come See About Me	£40
69	Duke DU 36	Safari (The Far East)/Last Laugh	£40
69	Songbird SB 1001	Ling Ting Tong/LLOYD ROBINSON: Sweet Sweet	£40
69	Songbird SB 1007	Duckey Luckey/In The Spirit	£50
69	Camel CA 30	Confidential/TOMMY COWAN: House In Session	£35
69	Explosion EX 2001	Death A Come/Zylon	£50
70	Explosion EX 2034	Ready Talk/There Is Something About You	£20
70	Trojan TR 7788	Oh Me Oh My/I Did It	£20
70	Bullet BU 435	Dollars And Bonds/Sounds Familiar	£35
70	Bullet BU 442	Reggae A Bye Bye/DAVE BARKER:Doctor Jekyll	£40
70	Escort ES 820	Soul Of England/Shang I	£30
70	Escort ES 836	Hi Shan/Soul At Large	£30
70	Smash SMA 2302	Big Red Bum Ball/BUNNIE LEE ALLSTARS: Big Bum Ball Version	£20
71	Black Swan BW 1405	Love You The Most/LOW BITES:Version	£15
71	Expolsion EX 2054	Going In Circles/Doggone Right (actually by Winston Francis)	£20
74	Harry J. HJ 6662	I'm Gonna Love You Just A Little Bit More/Have I Sinned	£150
11	Explosion THB 7009	The Premises/JOKERS: Brixton	£50
70	Trojan TTL 25	REGGAE IS TIGHT (LP, orange/white label)	£40
70	Trojan TTL 30	REGGAE CHARM (LP)	£30
70	Pama SECO 25	HOUSE IN SESSION (LP, with Hippy Boys)	£175
72	Trojan TRLS 86	BEST OF (LP)	£20
73	Trojan TBL 201	IN SESSION (LP)	£20

(see also Charmers, Lloyd Tyrell/Terrell, Ken Boothe, Hippy Boys, Martia Riley, Eric Donaldson)

CHARMERS (U.S.)
58	Vogue V 9095	He's Gone/Oh! Yes	£200
58	Vogue V 9095	He's Gone/Oh! Yes (78)	£20

CHARMETTES
63	London HLR 9820	Please Don't Kiss Me Again/What Is A Tear	£40

CHARMS (JAMAICA)
64	Island WI 154	Carry, Go, Bring Home (actually by Justin Hinds & Dominoes)/Hill And Gully (actually by L. Reid's Group)	£30
66	Rio R 98	Everybody Say Yeah/This World Is Yours	£30

CHARMS (U.S.)
55	Parlophone MSP 6155	Hearts Of Stone/Ko Ko Mo (I Love You So)	£250
55	Parlophone R3988	Hearts Of Stone/Ko Ko Mo (I Love You So) (78)	£20
55	Parlophone DP 412	Hearts Of Stone/Bazoom, I Need Your Lovin' (78) (export issue)	£20
55	Parlophone DP 423	Two Hearts/The First Time We Met (78) (export issue)	£20

(see also Otis Williams & Charms, Harmonizing Four)

CHARTBUSTERS
64	London HLU 9906	She's The One/Slippin' Thru Your Fingers	£15

CHARTERED HURRICANE
83	SRTS 83 CUS 1695	Cathy Come Home/All Smashed Up (stamped plain white sleeve)	£25

CHARTZ
83	Digital ZELSPS 404	Girls World/Girls World (Dance Mix)	£20

LINCOLN CHASE
57	London HLU 8495	Johnny Klingeringding/You're Driving Me Crazy (What Did I Do)	£20
61	Philips PB 1103	Miss Orangutang/Walking Slowly	£20

CHASERS
65	Decca F 12302	Hey Little Girl/That's What They Call Love	£50
66	Parlophone R 5451	Inspiration/She's Gone Away	£150
67	Philips BF 1546	The Ways Of A Man/Summer Girl	£15

CHASERS
84	SRT SRT4KS 304	Raiders/Final Stand (300 only)	£60

CHATEAUX
82	Ebony EBON 9	Young Blood/Fight To The Last	£20
83	Ebony EBON 13	CHAINED AND DESPERATE (LP)	£20
84	Ebony EBON 18	FIRE POWER (LP)	£15
85	Ebony EBON 31	HIGHLY STRUNG (LP)	£15

CHEAP TRICK
78	Epic S EPC 6199	So Good To See You/You're All Talk (withdrawn)	£20

OLIVER CHEATHAM
83	MCA MCAT 828	Get Down Saturday Night/Something About You (12")	£18
83	MCA MCF 3179	SATURDAY NIGHT (LP)	£30

CHUBBY CHECKER
59	Top Rank JAR 154	The Class/Schooldays, Oh, Schooldays	£30
60	Columbia DB 4541	The Hucklebuck/Whole Lotta Shakin' Goin' On	£15
61	Columbia DB 4652	Good Good Loving/Mess Around	£15
64	Cameo Parkway P 922	She Wants T'Swim/You Better Believe It Baby	£15
65	Cameo Parkway P 936	Lovely, Lovely/The Weekend's Here	£20
65	Cameo Parkway P 949	(At The) Discotheque/Do The Freddie (DJ copy)	£150
65	Cameo Parkway P 949	(At The) Discotheque/Do The Freddie	£50
65	Cameo Parkway P 959	Everything's Wrong/Cu Ma La Be Stay (DJ copy)	£120
65	Cameo Parkway P 959	Everything's Wrong/Cu Ma La Be Stay	£50
65	Cameo Parkway P 965	Two Hearts Make One Love/You Just Don't Know (What You Do To Me) (DJ Copy)	£400
65	Cameo Parkway P 965	Two Hearts Make One Love/You Just Don't Know (What You Do To Me)	£300
65	Cameo Parkway P 989	Hey You Little Boogaloo/Pussy Cat	£30
65	Cameo Parkway P 989	Hey You Little Boogaloo/Pussy Cat (DJ Copy)	£60
73	Pye Int 25620	Reggae My Way/Gypsy	£25
78	London HLU 10557	You Just Don't Know (What You Do To Me)/ Two Hearts Make One Love (reissue) (DJ Copy)	£35
78	London HLU 10557	You Just Don't Know (What You Do To Me)/ Two Hearts Make One Love (reissue)	£20
71	London SHZ 8419	CHEQUERED (LP)	£20

CHUBBY CHECKER & DEE DEE SHARP
62	Cameo Parkway C 1029	DOWN TO EARTH (LP)	£20

(see also Dream Lovers, Bobby Rydell, Dee Dee Sharp)

CHECKMATES
64	Decca F 11844	Sticks And Stones/Please Listen To Me	£15
66	Parlophone R 5495	Every Day Is Just The Same/I'll Be Keeping The Score	£15
61	Pye NPL 18061	THE CHECKMATES (LP)	£30

(see also Original Checkmates, Emile Ford)

CHEEKY
80	Woodbine St. WSR 005	Don't Mess Around/Get Outa My 'Ouse (no p/s)	£40

CHEERS
54	Capitol CL 14189	Bazoom (I Need Your Lovin')/Arrivederci	£15
55	Capitol CL 14377	Black Denim Trousers And Motorcycle Boots/Some Night In Alaska	£30
56	Capitol CL 14561	Chicken/Don't Do Anything	£20
56	Capitol EAP1 584	THE CHEERS (EP)	£15

(see also Bert Convy [& Thunderbirds])

CHEETAHS (1)
64	Philips BF 1362	Mecca/Goodnight Kiss	£15
65	Philips BF 1383	Soldier Boy/Johnny	£15

(see also Carl Wayne & Cheetahs)

CHEFS (1)
80	Attatrix RB 10	SWEETIE EP	£15
81	Graduate GRAD 11	24 Hours/Thrush	£15

CHELMSFORD COUNTY HIGH SCHOOL FOLK GROUP
70	Private Pressing	CHELMSFORD COUNTY HIGH SCHOOL FOLK GROUP (LP)	£20

CHELSEA
77	Step Forward SF 2	Right To Work/The Loner (p/s, original pressing in card p/s)	£15
79	Step Forward SFLP 2	CHELSEA (LP, with inner sleeve)	£30
81	Step Forward SFLP 5	ALTERNATIVE HITS (LP)	£20
82	Step Forward SFLP 7	EVACUATE (LP)	£15
16	Let Them Eat Vinyl LETV 403LP	EVACUATE (2-LP. reissue, red vinyl)	£15

CHEMICAL AGENT
96	Alphaphone ALPHA 003	Waterfall/Shock (12")	£15

(see also Cabaret Voltaire, Richard H. Kirk)

CHEMICAL ALICE
81	Acidic GNOME 1	The Judge/Goodnight Vienna/Lands Of Home/Henry The King (12", p/s)	£40

(see also Marillion)

CHEMICAL BROTHERS
91	Eastern Bloc	Sea Of Beats/Sea Of Beats (Justin Robertson Mix) (12", p/s, as Ariel)	£80
91	Deconstruction PT 44888	Rollercoaster/Mustn't Grumble/Mustn't Grumble (God's Grumble Mix) (12", as Ariel)	£30
93	Dust Brothers DB's 333	Song To The Siren (12", as Dust Brothers, no p/s, 500 only)	£60
93	Junior Boys Own JBO 10	Song To The Siren/Song To The Siren (Sabres Of Paradise Mixes) (12", p/s)	£30
94	Boys Own COLLECT 004	14TH CENTURY SKY EP (12", no p/s, as Dust Brothers)	£20
94	Junior Boys Own JBO 20	MY MERCURY MOUTH EP (12", JBO sleeve, as Dust Brothers)	£30
95	Junior Boys Own CHEMS TI	Leave Home/Leave Home (Sabres Of Paradise)/Let Me In Mate (12", p/s)	£15
95	Junior Boys Own	Leave Home (Underworld Mix One)/Leave Home (Underworld Mix Two) (12", p/s)	£15
15	Secret 7" S722	Let Forever Be (100 only, each with unique art sleeve)	£45
95	Junior Boys Own XDUSTLP1	EXIT PLANET DUST (2-LP, inners)	£35
97	Freestyle Dust XDUST LP2	DIG YOUR OWN HOLE (2-LP)	£50
99	Freestyle Dust XDUST LP4	SURRENDER (2-LP, gatefold)	£50
02	Virgin XDUST LP5	COME WITH US (2-LP)	£30
03	Freestyle Dust XDUSTLP 6	SINGLES 93-03 (4-LP box set)	£50
04	Virgin XDUST LP7	PUSH THE BUTTON (2-LP)	£30

CHEMICAL (2)
96	Acme AC 8014LP	CHEMICAL (LP, 500 only)	£15

CHEMISTRY SET
11	Fruits De Mer Winkle1	Impossible Love/We Luv You (folded p/s, inserts)	£15

CLIFTON CHENIER
69	Action ACT 4550	Black Gal/Frogs Legs	£15
70	Specialty SNTF 5012	BAYOU BLUES (LP)	£20
70	Harvest MHSP 4002	CLIFTON CHENIER'S VERY BEST (LP)	£50
79	Flyright FLY 539	ZYDECO BLUES (LP, with other artists)	£20

CHEQUERED PAST
85	Heavy Metal America	CHEQUERED PAST (LP, picture disc, 1,000 only)	£30

(see also Steve Jones)

CHEQUERS (1)
76	Creole CRLP 504	CHECK US OUT (LP)	£40

CHEQUERS (2)
80	Matthias MT 101	Midnight Hour/Move Up	£15
83	Matthias MT 102	Hard Times/If You Want My Love (no p/s)	£200

CHER
69	Atlantic 584 278	Walk On Gilded Splinters/Tonight I'll Be Staying Here With You	£15
66	Liberty LBY 3081	CHER (LP, mono)	£15
66	Liberty (S)LBY 3081	CHER (LP, stereo)	£15

(see also Sonny & Cher, Caesar & Cleo, Nilsson)

CHEROKEES (U.K.)
65	Columbia DB 7473	Wondrous Place/Send Me All Your Love	£40
66	Columbia DB 7822	Land Of A 1000 Dances/Everybody's Needs	£20

(see also Lee Diamond)

CHEROKEES (U.S.)
61	Pye International 7N 25066	Cherokee/Harlem Nocturne	£15

DON CHERRY (2)
73	JCOA/Virgin J2001	RELATIVITY SUITE (LP)	£25
74	Sonet SNTF 653	ETERNAL NOW (LP)	£50
75	DJM DJSLM 2008	KAWAIDA (LP, with Herbie Hancock)	£30
77	Blue Note BNS 40027	WHERE IS BROOKLYN? (LP, reissue)	£35
78	Sonet SNFF 669	LIVE IN ANKARA (LP)	£50
78	Affinity AFF 8	MU: FIRST PART (LP, reissue)	£15

78	Affinity AFF 17	MU: SECOND PART (LP, reissue)	£15
82	Affinity AFFD 82	ORIENT (2-LP, reissue)	£25
89	A&M 395 258-1	ART DECO (LP)	£25
15	Bue Note ST 84225	COMPLETE COMMUNION (LP, reissue)	£18

CHERRY ORCHARD
88	Red Honey (No Cat. No)	So Blind (p/s, 1-sided flexi)	£15
89	Red Honey ORCHARD 1	SING SISTER GLORY (12" EP)	£18
90	Red Honey ORCHARD 3	For What It's Worth/For What It's Worth (Version) (12", no p/s, promo only)	£18
90	Red Honey ORCHARD 2	HEALING FAITH LIKE FIRE (LP)	£15

CHERRY PEOPLE
68	MGM MGM 1438	And Suddenly/Imagination	£40
68	MGM MGM 1438	And Suddenly/Imagination (DJ copy)	£60
69	MGM MGM 1472	Gotta Get Back/I'm The One Who Loves You	£15

CHERRY PIES
64	Black Swan WI 448	Do You Keep Dreaming/Sweeter Than Cherry Pie	£25

CHERRY POPPERS
80	Hiroshima HRH 1	Money In My Pocket/Hiroshima	£20

CHERRY SMASH
67	Track 604 017	Sing Songs Of Love/Movie Star	£20
68	Decca F 12838	Goodtime Sunshine/Little Old Country Home Town	£25
69	Decca F 12884	Fade Away Maureen/Green Plant	£60

VIC CHESNUTT
96	PLR 005-1	ABOUT TO CHOKE (LP)	£15

PETE CHESTER
61	Pye International 7N 25074	Three Old Maids/Forest Fire (as Pete Chester & Group)	£15

(see also Five Chesternuts)

CHESTERFIELD KINGS
85	Ligget & Mayers	THE CHESTERFIELD KINGS (LP)	£18

CHESTERFIELDS (2)
03	Grapevine 45-134	Think It Over/Why Did You Leave Me Baby? (reissue)	£15

MORRIS CHESTNUT
79	Grapevine GRP 128	Too Darn Soulful/You Don't Love Me Anymore	£20
79	Grapevine GRP 128	Too Darn Soulful/You Don't Love Me Anymore (DJ Copy)	£35

CHEVRONS (2)
79	Shy Talk	Sindy's Got An Action Man/No More Tears (p/s)	£25

CHEVY
80	Avatar AAA 104	Too Much Loving/See The Light (company sleeve)	£15
80	Avatar AAA 107	The Taker/Life On The Run (p/s)	£15
80	Avatar AALP 5001	THE TAKER (LP, with inner sleeve)	£18

CHEYNES (1)
63	Columbia DB 7153	Respectable/It's Gonna Happen To You	£125
64	Columbia DB 7368	Going To The River/Cheyne-Re-La	£125
65	Columbia DB 7464	Down And Out/Stop Running Around	£125

(see also Peter Bardens, Peter B's, Fleetwood Mac, Mark Leeman Five, Bo Street Runners)

CHIC
78	Atlantic K 50441	CHIC (LP)	£20
78	Atlantic K 50565	C'EST CHIC (LP, inner)	£20
79	Atlantic K 50634	RISQUE (LP)	£15
79	Atlantic K 50686	GREATEST HITS (LP)	£15
13	Rhino/Atlantic 8122796497	THE 12" SINGLES COLLECTION (Box set, 5 x 12")	£35

CHICAGO
69	CBS 4503	I'm A Man (Parts 1 & 2) (withdrawn)	£20
69	CBS 4715	I'm A Man/Does Anyone Really Know What Time It Is? (promo p/s)	£20
69	CBS 66221	CHICAGO TRANSIT AUTHORITY (2-LP, orange label)	£20
70	CBS 66233	CHICAGO (2-LP)	£20
71	CBS 66405	IV (AT CARNEGIE HALL) (4-LP, orange label)	£20

CHICAGO LINE
66	Philips BF 1488	Shimmy Shimmy Ko Ko Bop/Jump Back	£200

(see also Mike Patto, Bo Street Runners, Viv Prince)

CHICAGO LOOP
66	Stateside SS 564	(When She Needs Good Lovin') She Comes To Me/This Must Be The Place (DJ Copy)	£40
66	Stateside SS 564	(When She Needs Good Lovin') She Comes To Me/This Must Be The Place	£15

CHICAGO UNDERGROUND COUNCIL
96	Peacefrog PF 060	2 DAYS (12" EP)	£15

CHICANES
81	Dinosaur Discs DD 003	Cry A Little/Further Thoughts (p/s)	£20
88	Bam Caruso NRIC 039	Cry A Little/Further Thoughts (p/s)	£20

CHICK WITH TED CAMERON & D.J.'S
60	Pye 7N 15292	Early In The Morning/Cool Water	£40

CHICKEN SHACK
67	Blue Horizon 57-3135	It's OK With Me Baby/When My Left Eye Jumps	£20
68	Blue Horizon 57-3143	Worried About My Woman/Six Nights In Seven	£20

68	Blue Horizon 57-3146	When The Train Comes Back/Hey Baby	£15
70	Blue Horizon 57-3176	Sad Clown/Tired Eyes	£15
68	Blue Horizon 7-63203	FORTY BLUE FINGERS FRESHLY PACKED AND READY TO SERVE (LP, 1st pressing with 'stereo' sticker on sleeve)	£100
68	Blue Horizon 7-63203	FORTY BLUE FINGERS FRESHLY PACKED AND READY TO SERVE (LP, 1st pressing, mono)	£40
69	Blue Horizon 7-63209	O.K. KEN? (LP, gatefold sleeve, 1st pressing with 'stereo' sticker on sleeve)	£100
69	Blue Horizon 7-63209	O.K. KEN? (LP, gatefold sleeve, 1st pressing, mono)	£60
69	Blue Horizon 7-63218	100 TON CHICKEN (LP, gatefold, 1st pressing with 'stereo' sticker on sleeve)	£100
70	Blue Horizon 7-63861	ACCEPT CHICKEN SHACK (LP, gatefold sleeve)	£75
71	Deram SDL 5	IMAGINATION LADY (LP, gatefold sleeve, brown/white label with large Deram label)	£75
71	Deram SDL 5	IMAGINATION LADY (LP, gatefold sleeve, later pressing with red/white label)	£30
73	Deram SML 1100	UNLUCKY BOY (LP)	£40

(see also Errol Dixon, Fleetwood Mac, Christine Perfect, Carmen Macrae, Broken Glass)

CHICKEN SHED
77	Colby AJ 370	ALICE (LP, hand-made sleeves)	£120

CHICKS
63	Oriole CB 1828	What Are Boys Made Of?/Over The Mountain	£20

CHICORY TIP
71	CBS 7118	My Girl Sunday/Doctor Man	£15

CHIEF
81	Swamp WAM 114	Don't Touch The Receiver/Icebreaker (not released in p/s)	£25

CHIEF CHECKER
79	Original WBA 102	Impossibilities/Possibility (dub) (12", die cut sleeve)	£40
79	Original WBL 101	THE SOUND OF CHIEF CHECKER (LP)	£100

CHIEFS
58	London HLU 8624	Apache/Dee's Dream	£20
58	London HLU 8720	Enchiladas!/Moments To Remember	£20

CHIFFONS
63	Stateside SS 230	A Love So Fine/Only My Friend	£15
64	Stateside SS 254	I Have A Boyfriend/I'm Gonna Dry Your Eyes	£15
64	Stateside SS 332	Sailor Boy/When Summer's Through	£20
65	Statside SS 437	Nobody Knows What's Going On (In My Mind But Me)/The Real Thing (DJ copy)	£60
65	Stateside SS 437	Nobody Knows What's Going On (In My Mind But Me)/The Real Thing	£40
66	Stateside SS 533	Out Of This World/Just A Boy	£15
66	Stateside SS 559	Stop, Look And Listen/March	£30
67	Stateside SS 578	My Boyfriend's Back/I Got Plenty Of Nuttin'	£22
64	Stateside SE 1012	THEY'RE SO FINE (EP)	£60
63	Stateside SL 10040	THE CHIFFONS - HE'S SO FINE (LP)	£80
66	Stateside S(S)L 10190	SWEET TALKIN' GUY (LP)	£80
85	Impact ACT 007	FLIPS FLOPS & RARITIES (LP)	£15

(see also Four Pennies)

SONNY CHILDE (& T.N.T.)
65	Decca F 12218	Giving Up On Love/Mighty Nice (Of You To Call)	£150
65	Decca F12218	Giving Up On Love/Mighty Nice (Of You To Call) (DJ Copy)	£300
66	Polydor 56108	Two Lovers/Ain't That Good News	£15
66	Polydor 56141	Heartbreak/I Still Love You (as Sonny Childe & T.N.T.)	£30
66	Polydor 582 003	TO BE CONTINUED (LP)	£40

CHILD HAROLDS
68	Trident TRA 201	Diary Of My Mind/Loophole	£30

BILLY CHILDISH
93	Damaged Books DAMBOOK 1	TREMBLING OF LIFE (3 x 7" box set with book & 2 postcards)	£20
87	Hangman HANG 9-UP	THE 1982 CASSETTES (LP, blue & white sleeve, with poster)	£30
87	Hangman HANG 9-UP	THE 1982 CASSETTES (LP, blue & white sleeve, without poster)	£30
88	Hangman HANG 16-UP	POEMS OF LAUGHTER & VIOLENCE (LP)	£30
91	Hangman HANG 37 UP	50 ALBUMS GREAT (LP)	£30
08	Aquarium AQU 000l-13	LIVE AT THE AQUARIUM (2-LP, 150 only, numbered and signed)	£100

WILD BILLY CHILDISH & HIS FAMOUS HEADCOATS
00	Buff Medway COCK 1-UP	I AM THE OBJECT OF YOUR DESIRE (LP)	£15

BILLY CHILDISH & THE BLACKHANDS
93	Hangman 53 UP	LIVE IN THE NETHERLANDS (LP)	£20

BILLY CHILDISH & THE NATURAL BORN LOVERS
89	Hangman 30 UP	LONG LEGGED BABY (LP)	£20

BILLY CHILDISH & SEXTON MING
87	Hangman HANG 05 UP	WHICH DEAD DONKEY DADDY (LP, poster)	£15
87	Hangman HANG 10 UP	PLUMP PRIZES & LITTLE GEMS (LP)	£15
87	Hangman HANG 12 UP	YPRES 1917 OVERTURE(LP)	£20
98	Damaged Goods DAMGOOD 159LP	THE CHEEKY CHEESE (LP)	£15

BILLY CHILDISH & THE SINGING LOINS
93	Hangmans Daughter SCRAG 1	AT THE BRIDGE (LP)	£20

WILD BILLY CHILDISH & THE BLACKHANDS
88	Hangman HANG-21 UP	PLAY CAPT'N CALYPSO'S HOODOO PARTY	£20

(see also Milkshakes, Thee Mighty Caesars and Billy Childish & entries)

WILD BILLY CHILDISH & BIG RUSS WILKINS
87 Empire CPO 195   **LAUGHING GRAVY** (10" LP)..£20

WILD BILLY CHILDISH & BUFF MEDWAYS
03 Aquarium (No Cat. No)   **You Are All Phonys** (p/s, 1-sided, white label other side etched, 100 numbered and signed by Childish) £50
03 Aquarium (No Cat. No)   **You Are All Phonys** (p/s, 1-sided, white label other side etched, 400 unsigned) £20
04 Aquarium (No Cat. No)   (I'm Not Going To Your Boring) **Private View** (p/s, 1-sided other side etched, 100 numbered and signed by Childish)..£50
04 Aquarium (No Cat. No)   (I'm Not Going To Your Boring) **Private View** (p/s, 1-sided other side etched, 400 unsigned) £20
05 Damaged Goods DAMGOOD 239LP   **MEDWAY WHEELERS** (LP, 50 copies with numbered 'The Poundlands Poets' booklet.....£30
05 Damaged Goods DAMGOOD 239LP   **MEDWAY WHEELERS** (LP, without booklet) £15
(see also Buff Medways)

WILD BILLY CHILDISH
87 Hangman HANG 2 UP   **I'VE GOT EVERYTHING INDEED** (LP) £35
87 Hangman HANG 13 UP   **I REMEMBER** (LP)...£20

CHILDREN
82 C391/1   **Demon Blues/Nightland** (promo version - different catalogue number)........................£15

CHI-LITES
69 Beacon BEA 119   **Pretty Girl/Love Bandit** £70
71 MCA 1143DJ   **What Do I Wish For** (1-sided DJ copy) £15
70 MCA MUPS 397   **GIVE IT AWAY** (LP) £20
71 MCA MUPS 437   (FOR GOD'S SAKE) **GIVE MORE POWER TO THE PEOPLE** (LP)...........................£30
(see also Jackie Wilson)

CHILLIWACK
71 London SHU 8418   **CHILLIWACK** (LP, U.K. issue of US 1970 issue)..£25
71 A&M AMLH 63509   **CHILLIWACK** (LP) £15
(see also Collectors, Electric Prunes)

CHILLI WILLI & RED HOT PEPPERS
72 Revelation REV 002   **KINGS OF THE ROBOT RHYTHM** (LP, with lyric insert, inner sleeve and sticker) £60
72 Revelation REV 002   **KINGS OF THE ROBOT RHYTHM** (LP, with lyric insert, but without inner sleeve and sticker) £30
74 Mooncrest CREST 21   **BONGOS OVER BALHAM** (LP, with inner sleeve) £25
(see also Brinsley Schwarz, Jo-Ann Kelly, Mighty Baby, Hapshash And The Coloured Coat, Attractions, Action)

CHILLS
85 Normal 43   **LOST EP** (12") £15
84 Flying Nun Europe FNE 13   **KALEIDOSCOPE WORLD** (LP, with free 7") £30
84 Flying Nun Europe FNE 13   **KALEIDOSCOPE WORLD** (LP, without free 7") £20
90 Slash 828191   **SUBMARINE BELLS** (LP, with inner sleeve)..£15

CHILLUM
71 Mushroom 100 MR 11   **CHILLUM** (LP, with photo insert) £250
(see also Secondhand)

CHIMES (U.S.)
61 London HLU 9283   **Once In A While/Summer Night** £15

CHIMNEYS
80 Tagmemics 45-003   **Do The Big Baby/Take Your Brain Out For A Walk** (p/s, 500 only)...............£15

CHINA DOLL
80 Wessex WEX 273   **Oysters And Wine/Past Tense** (p/s)..£150

CHINA DOLLS
82 Speed FIRED 1   **One Hit Wonder/Ain't Love Ain't Bad** (p/s) £35
(see also Slade)

CHINA DRUM
96 Mantra MNTLP1002   **GOOSE FAIR** (LP) £15
97 Mantra MNTLP1009   **SELF MADE MANIAC** (LP)..£15

CHINA SOUL
09 Foofar FF 001   **Cold/Be My Husband** (signed sleeve) £15

CHINATOWN
81 Airship AP 138   **Short And Sweet/How Many Times** (p/s) £60
81 Airship AP 343   **PLAY IT TO DEATH** (LP) £85

CHINAWITE
83 Future Earth FER 014   **Blood On The Streets/Ready To Satisfy** (p/s)...£30

CHINNER
77 Third World TWS 924   **STICKY FINGERS** (LP) £40

CHISEL
70 Ariel AR 003   **Turn To The Sun/Nightingale**..£35

CHITINIOUS ENSEMBLE
71 Deram SML 1093   **CHITINOUS ENSEMBLE** (LP) £300

!!! (CHK CHK CHK)
04 Touch And Go TG 234   **LOUDEN UP NOW** (2-LP, with poster) £15
07 Warp WARLP154   **MYTH TAKES** (2-LP) £30
10 Warp WARLP197   **STRANGE WEATHER. ISN'T IT?** (LP) £18

13	Warp WARPLP236	THR!!!LER (LP) £15
15	Warp WARLP260	AS IS (2-LP) £18
17	Warp WARLP283	SHAKE THE SHUDDER (2-LP) £18

CHOC

70	Decca F23106	Way Of Life/I Want You To Be My Girl £30

CHOC ICE

71	Polydor 2056189	Groovy Situation/Look At It My Way £20

CHOCOLATE BOYS

74	Decca F 13556	El Bimbo/Voltaire Pier £25
74	Decca F 13556	El Bimbo/Voltaire Pier (DJ Copy) £35

CHOCOLATE FROG

68	Atlantic 584 207	Butchers And Bakers/I Forgive You £45

(see also Fleur De Lys)

CHOCOLATE MILK

79	RCA RCAT 2592	I'm Your Radio/Actions Speak Louder Than Words (12") £15
77	RCA PL 11830	COMIN' (LP) £15

CHOCOLATE WATCH BAND

67	Decca F 12649	The Sound Of The Summer/The Only One In Sight £50
67	Decca F 12704	Requiem/What's It To You £40
84	Big Beat WIK 25	44 (LP) £15

CHOCOLATS

76	Aquarius AQ 1	Voltaire Pier/Brasilia Carnival £40

(see also chocolate Boys)

CHOIR

68	Major Minor MM 537	It's Cold Outside/I'm Going Home £40
68	Major Minor MM 557	When You Were With Me/Changin' My Mind £30

HENRI CHOPIN

71	Tangent TGS 106	AUDIOPOEMS (LP) £80

CHOPPER

71	Decca F 13161	Singer Wihout A Song/Think I'm A Man £50

CHOPYN

75	Jet LPO 8	GRAND SLAM (LP) £20

(see also Ann Odell, Ray Russell, Simon Phillips, C.M.U)

CHORDETTES

54	Columbia SCM 5158	Mr. Sandman/I Don't Wanna See You Cryin' £100
55	London HLA 8169	Humming Bird/Lonely Lips £15
56	London HLA 8217	Dudelsack Polka/I Told A Lie £25
56	London HLA 8264	Eddie My Love/Our Melody (triangular centre) £25
60	London RE-A 1228	THE CHORDETTES (EP) £30
58	London HA-A 2088	THE CHORDETTES (LP) £60
62	London HA-A 2441	THE CHORDETTES SING NEVER ON SUNDAY (LP) £25
83	Ace CH 82	THE CHORDETTES (LP, compilation) £20

CHORDS (U.K.)

80	Polydor Super POLS 1019	SO FAR AWAY (LP, stickered sleeve & 7" Now It's Gone/Things We Said [KRODS 1]) £30
80	Polydor Super POLS 1019	SO FAR AWAY (LP, without free 7') £20
86	Unicorn PHZA-1	NO ONE IS LISTENING ANYMORE (LP) £20

(see also Rage)

CHORDS (U.S.)

54	Columbia SCM 5133	Sh-Boom (Life Could Be A Dream)/Little Maiden £1500
54	Columbia DB 3512	Sh-Boom (Life Could Be A Dream)/Little Maiden (78) £60

CHORDS FIVE

67	Island WI 3044	I'm Only Dreaming/Universal Vagrant £100
68	Polydor 56261	Same Old Fat Man/Hold On To Everythin' You've Got £40
69	Jay Boy BOY 6	Some People/Battersea Fair £80

(see also Smoke)

CHOSEN FEW (JAMAICA)

70	Songbird SB 1031	Time Is Hard/CRYSTALITES: Time Is Hard Part Two £20
70	Songbird SB 1032	Going Back Home/CRYSTALITES: Going Back Home Part Two £20
70	Songbird SB 1046	Why Can't I Touch You/INNER CIRCLE BAND: Touch You Version £20
71	Fab FAB 14	Babylon/VIN GORDON: Red Blood (promo only, black label) £50
71	Songbird SB 1061	Shaft/Shaft (Version) £25
71	Songbird SB 1067	Everybody Just A Stall/Everybody (Version) £15
72	Songbird SB 1070	Do Your Thing/Your Thing (Version) £25
72	Trojan TR 7864	Ebony Eyes/Ebony Eyes (Version) £15
72	Trojan TR 7882	Everybody Plays The Fool/You're A Big Girl Now £15
72	Grape G£ 3033	You're A Big Girl Now/Version £15
73	Trojan TR 7894	Am I Black Enough For You/Message From A Blackman £15
73	Duke DU 162	Children Of The Night/LLOYD CHARMERS: For The Good Times £20
73	Duke DU 163	Stoned In Love/MIKE CHUNG & NOW GENERATION: Stoned In Love (Version) £15
73	Duke DU 164	It's Too Late/MIKE CHUNG & NOW GENERATION: It's Too Late (Version) £15
73	Trojan TRLS 56	HIT AFTER HIT (LP) £40
75	Trojan TRLS 106	EVERYBODY PLAYS THE FOOL (LP) £60
76	Trojan Records TRLS 131	IN MIAMI (LP, blue labels) £60

CHOSEN FEW (U.K.) (1)
65	Pye 7N 15905	It Won't Be Around You Anymore/Big City	£20
65	Pye 7N 15942	So Much To Look Forward To/Today, Tonight & Tomorrow	£20

(see also Alan Hull, Lindisfarne, Skip Bifferty)

CHOSEN FEW (U.K.) (2)
74	Action ACT 4623	Funky Butter/Wondering	£70
76	Polydor 2058 721	I Can Make Your Dreams Come True/Pretty Face	£20
76	Miami MIA401	Night And Day/Funky Buttercup	£40
78	Polydor 2058 975	You Mean Everything To Me/It Won't Be Long	£30
77	Polydor 2058 752	Miracle Worker/Young And Foolish	£25

CHOSEN PEOPLE
69	Royalty RT 01	When A Dream Ends/Firefly	£35

CHRIS AND MAXINE
67	Philips BF 1587	Only A Thousand Times A Day/I've Made You My Mind	£15

CHRIS & COSEY/CREATIVE TECHNOLOGY INSTITUTE/CARTER TUTTI
81	Rough Trade RT 078	October (Love Song)/Little Houses (p/s)	£30
81	Rough Trade RTT 078	October (Love Song)/Little Houses (12", p/s)	£20
84	Conspiracy International CTI 1	CONSPIRACY INTERNATIONAL ONE (12", p/s, as CTI)	£25
85	Conspiracy International CTI 2	CONSPIRACY INTERNATIONAL TWO (12", p/s, as CTI)	£25
85	Rough Trade RTT 148	Sweet Surprise 1 (1984)/2 (1985) (12", p/s, with Annie Lennox & Dave Stewart)	£15
87	Play It Again Sam BIAS 75	Exotika (Remix)/Workout/Beatbeatbeat (live) (12", p/s)	£15
91	Play It Again Sam BIAS 186	Synaesthesia (Daniel Miller Mix)/Chris & Cosey Mix/D.M. Instrumental Mix (12", p/s)	£20
13	Conspiracy International CTIV045	Coolican A/Coolican Fusion (10", green vinyl, p/s, as Carter Tutti)	£20
81	Rough Trade ROUGH 34	HEARTBEAT (LP, with insert)	£35
82	Rough Trade ROUGH 44	TRANCE (LP)	£40
84	Rough Trade ROUGH 64	SONGS OF LOVE AND LUST (LP)	£40
84	Doublevision DVR3	ELEMENTAL 7 (LP, as CTI)	£75
84	Doublevision DVR8	EUROPEAN RENDEZVOUS CTI LIVE 1983 (LP, as CTI)	£20
85	Rough Trade ROUGH 84	TECHNO PRIMATIV (LP)	£20
87	Play It Again Sam BIAS 69	EXOTIKA (LP)	£20
91	Play It Again Sam BIAS 179	PAGAN TANGO (LP)	£20
95	T&B TBLP 003	TWIST (2-LP)	£20
10	Conspiracy International CTILP016	EXOTICA (LP, reissue)	£15
15	Conspiracy International CTILP012014	PLAYS CHRIS & COSEY (2-LP as Carter Tutti)	£25

(see also Throbbing Gristle, Chris Carter, Eurythmics, Cosey Fanni Tutti)

PETER CHRIS & OUTCASTS
66	Columbia DB 7923	Over The Hill/The Right Girl For Me	£40

CHRISTEL & THE GOLDMASTER
98	Goldmaster GM 002	Government Man/Version	£25

CHRISTIAN
71	Decca F 23137	Other Side Of Life/She	£15

CHARLIE CHRISTIAN
57	Philips BBL 7172	CHARLIE CHRISTIAN (LP)	£20

FUD CHRISTIAN ALL STARS
71	Big Shot BI 571	Never Fall In Love (actually by Winston Heywood)/Never Fall In Love Version	£15

HANS CHRISTIAN
68	Parlophone R 5676	All Of The Time/Never My Love	£80
68	Parlophone R 5698	(The Autobiography Of) Mississippi Hobo/Sonata Of Love	£100

(see also Jon Anderson, Yes)

JOHN CHRISTIAN DEE
68	Pye 7N 17566	Take Me Along/The World Can Pack Its Bags And Go Away	£15
69	Decca F12901	The World Can Pick Up Its Bags And Go Away/Stick To Your Guns	£15

LIZ CHRISTIAN
67	CBS 202520	Suddenly You Find Love/Make It Work Out	£90
67	CBS 202520	Suddenly You Find Love/Make It Work Out (DJ copy)	£120

(see also James Royal)

MARIA CHRISTIAN
85	MCA MCA 974	Wait Until The Weekend Comes/(Instrumental) (p/s)	£15

NEIL CHRISTIAN (& CRUSADERS)
61	Private Pressing	Restless/Red Sails In The Sunset/Your Cheating Heart/Danny (1-sided 4 track 12" demo acetate, 6 made, Jimmy Page's first studio recording)	£3000
62	Columbia DB 4938	The Road To Love/The Big Beat Drum	£40
63	Columbia DB 7075	A Little Bit Of Someone Else/Get A Load Of This (with Crusaders)	£20
66	Strike JH 301	That's Nice/She's Got The Action	£15
67	Pye 7N 17372	You're All Things Bright And Beautiful/I'm Gonna Love You Baby	£15
76	Satril SAT 106	She's Got The Power/Someone Following Me Around	£20
66	Columbia SEG 8492	A LITTLE BIT OF SOMETHING ELSE (EP)	£80

(see also Christian's Crusaders, Guy Hamilton, Jimmy Page, Nicky Hopkins, Miki Dallon, Screaming Lord Sutch)

CHRISTIAN DEATH
83	Future FL 2	ONLY THEATRE OF PAIN (LP, with insert)	£25

CHRISTIAN'S CRUSADERS
64	Columbia DB 7289	Honey Hush/One For The Money	£75

(see also Neil Christian & Crusaders)

CHRISTIE
70	CBS 64108	CHRISTIE (LP)	£15
71	CBS 64397	FOR ALL MANKIND (LP, gatefold sleeve, orange label)	£20

(see also Acid Gallery, Epics)

DAVE CHRISTIE
68	Mercury MF1028	Love And The Brass Band/Penelope Breedlove	£15

JOHN CHRISTIE
74	Polydor 2058 496	4th Of July (written by Paul McCartney)/Old Enough To Know Better (in p/s)	£30
74	Polydor 2058 496	4th Of July (written by Paul McCartney)/Old Enough To Know Better	£15

KEITH CHRISTIE
54	Esquire 20-047	HOMAGE TO THE DUKE (LP)	£20

LOU CHRISTIE
66	MGM MGM 1297	Lightnin' Strikes/Cryin' In The Streets	£15
66	MGM MGM 1297	Lightnin' Strikes/Cryin' In The Streets (DJ Copy)	£50
66	MGM MGM 1325	If My Car Could Only Talk/Song Of Lita	£20
67	CBS 2718	Shake Hands And Walk Away Cryin'/Escape	£15
66	MGM MGM-C(S) 8008	LIGHTNIN' STRIKES (LP)	£25
66	Colpix PXL 551	STRIKES AGAIN (LP)	£25

SUSAN CHRISTIE
66	CBS 202261	I Love Onions/Take Me As You Find Me	£15
06	Finders Keepers FKR007LP	PAINT A LADY (LP)	£60

DEREK CHRISTIEN
70	Major Minor MM 676	When A Woman Has A Baby/Please Don't Go Away	£30
70	Major Minor MM 713	Suddenly There's A Valley/I'll Be Coming Home	£100

CHRISTINES'S CAT
89	Sarah SARAH 13	Your Love Is.... (5" flexi with two fanzines 'Lemonade: A Fanzine' and 'Cold: A Lie')	£50

KEITH CHRISTMAS
69	RCA Victor SF 8059	STIMULUS (LP, with Mighty Baby, orange/white label)	£200
70	B&C CAS 1015	FABLE OF THE WINGS (LP)	£80
71	B&C CAS 1041	PIGMY (LP, gatefold sleeve)	£70
74	Manticore K 53503	BRIGHTER DAY (LP. with inner sleeve)	£20
76	Manticore K 53509	STORIES FROM THE HUMAN ZOO (LP, with insert)	£20

(see also Mighty Baby, Magic Muscle)

CHRISTOPHER
70	Chapter One CH121	Sharkey/The Race	£20

JORDAN CHRISTOPHER
66	United Artists UP 1140	Hello Lover/What That I Was	£20

LYN CHRISTOPHER
73	Paramount SPFL 288	LYN CHRISTOPHER (LP)	£100

CHARA CHRISTOU
71	Somerville SVL 1	CELEBRATE HIS LOVE (LP)	£25

CHROME
80	Red RS 12007	READ ONLY MEMORY (12" EP, with poster)	£40
80	Red RS 12007	READ ONLY MEMORY (12" EP, without poster)	£25
80	Beggars Banquet BEG 36	New Age/Information (p/s)	£15
81	D. F. O. T. Mountain Y3	INWORLDS (12")	£15
82	D. F. O. T. Mountain Z17	Firebomb/Shadows Of A Thousand Years (p/s)	£15
80	Beggars Banquet BEGA 15	RED EXPOSURE (LP, with inner sleeve)	£25
80	Beggars Banquet BEGA 18	HALF MACHINE LIP MOVES (LP, reissue, with poster insert)	£30
80	Beggars Banquet BEGA 18	HALF MACHINE LIP MOVES (LP, reissue, without poster insert)	£20
81	D. F. O. T. Mountain X6	BLOOD ON THE MOON (LP, blue, green or purple labels, with inner sleeve)	£20
82	D. F. O. T. Mountain X18	3RD FROM THE SUN (LP, with insert)	£20

CHEETAH CHROME
85	Children Of The Revolution GURT 3	I REFUSE IT! (Split LP with MOTHERFUCKERS)	£35

CHROME & ILLINSPIRED
15	B-Line Recordings BLN 012	THE ALL C N I (LP)	£30

CHROMEO
07	Back Yard BACK22LPC1	FANCY FOOT WORK (LP)	£60

CHRON GEN
81	Gargoyle GRGL 780	PUPPETS OF WAR (EP, with sticker)	£15
84	Picasso PIK 002	NOWHERE TO RUN (12' EP)	£40
83	Secret SEC 3	CHRONIC GENERATION (LP, with free 7")	£15

CHRYSTAL BELLE SCRODD
86	United Dairies	BELLE DE JOUR (LP with insert)	£40

(see also Nurse With Wound)

CHUBBY & HONEYSUCKERS
65	Venus VE 3	Come On Home/What Shall I Do?	£20
66	Rio R 75	Emergency Ward/LEN & HONEYSUCKERS: One More River	£20

CHUCK & BETTY
59	Brunswick 05815	Sissy Britches/Come Back Little Girl	£20

CHUCK (JOSEPHS) & DOBBY (DOBSON)
60	Blue Beat BB 19	Til The End Of Time (as Chuck & Darby)/DUKE REID & HIS GROUP: What Makes Honey	£20
60	Blue Beat BB 23	Cool School/DUKE REID & HIS GROUP: Joker	£20
61	Starlite ST45 043	Sad Over You/Sweeter Than Honey	£20
61	Starlite ST45 044	Lovey Dovey/Sitting Square	£20
61	Blue Beat BB 39	Du Du Wap/I Love My Teacher (with Aubrey Adams & Du Droppers)	£20
61	Blue Beat BB 59	Oh Fanny/Running Around	£20
64	Blue Beat BB 246	Tell Me/I'm Going Home	£20

CHUCK & GARY
58	HMV POP 466	Teenie Weenie Jeanie/Can't Make Up My Mind	£40

CHUCKA
74	Lemmy LMY2	Switch On The Heat/My Oh My	£30

CHUCKLES (1)
69	Bullet BU 416	Run Nigel Run/Come On Home	£30

CHUCKLES (2)
72	Duke DU 144	Reggae Limbo/ZAP POW: Broken Contract	£30

CHUCKS
64	Decca DFE 8562	THE CHUCKS (EP)	£25

CHUMBAWAMBA
86	Agit Prop PROP 1	PICTURES OF STARVING CHILDREN SELL RECORDS (LP, with inner)	£30
87	Agit Prop PROP 2	NEVER MIND THE BALLOTS... (LP, gatefold)	£15
88	Agit Prop PROP 3	ENGLISH REBEL SONGS 1381-1914 (10" LP, with die-cut sleeve)	£15
90	Agit Prop PROP 7	SLAP! (LP, with poster)	£15
94	One Little Indian TPLP 46	ANARCHY (LP)	£40
95	One Little Indian TPLP 56	SHOWBUSINESS (LP)	£25

MIKIE CHUNG & NOW GENERATION
72	Green Door GD 4032	Breezing/NOW GENERATION: Breezing - Version	£15
73	Duke DU 163	Stoned In Love/CHOSEN FEW: Stoned In Love	£15
73	Duke DU 164	It's Too Late/CHOSEN FEW: It's Too Late	£15

CHUNKY
73	Orange OAS 214	Albatross Baby/Road Runner Girl	£30

CHURCH
86	EMI EMC 3508	HEYDAY (LP)	£15
88	Arista 208895	STARFISH (LP, with bonus 5-track numbered 12")	£15

EUGENE CHURCH
59	London HL 8940	Miami/I Ain't Goin' For That (round centre)	£50
59	London HL 8940	Miami/I Ain't Goin' For That (round centre) (78)	£15

MARK CHURCHER
95	Emote MOTE 001	Nowhere Man/Blue Depression/3D Thought Of Life (12")	£40

(see also SEND/RETURN)

CHICK CHURCHILL
73	Chrysalis CHR 1051	YOU AND ME (LP)	£20

(see also Ten Years After, Cozy Powell, Jethro Tull)

CHVRCHES
12	National Anthem ANTHEM 003	The Mother We Share/(AJD Optimo Remix)/(Miaoux Miaoux Remix) (10" 500 only)	£60
13	Goodbye GR001V	Recover/ZVVL/Recover (Cim Rim Remix)/Recover Curxes 1996 Remix) (12" orange vinyl)	£20
15	Virgin VS 2116	Get Away/Dead Air	£15
15	Secret 7 S729	Clearest View (1-sided, 100 only)	£50
13	Virgin V3116	THE BONES OF WHAT YOU BELIEVE (LP)	£15

SUZANNE CIANI
91	Private Music 21 1973	HOTEL LUNA (LP)	£15
12	Dead Cert VCR 001	VOICES OF PACKAGED SOULS (LP, reissue, play at 45rpm)	£25
12	Bird 015EGGSLP	SEVEN WAVES (LP, reissue)	£25
14	Disposable Music DIM 009	LOGO PRESENTATION REEL 1985 (LP)	£15
16	Finders Keepers FKR082LP-A	BUCHLA CONCERTS (LP, turquoise leatherette sleeve, inserts, 200 only)	£40
16	Finders Keepers FKR082LP	BUCHLA CONCERTS 1975 (LP)	£15
19	Finders Keepers FKR099LP	FLOWERS OF EVIL (LP)	£15

CICPEN
86	SRT 6KS/826/FFACH F	CYMER FI (EP, p/s)	£25

CIGARETTES
78	Dead Good KEVIN 1	THE CIGARETTES (EP, unreleased)	£0
79	Company CIGCO 008	They're Back Again, Here They Come/I've Forgot My Number/All We Want Is Your Money (gatefold p/s, initial pressing with red labels)	£100
79	Company CIGCO 008	They're Back Again, Here They Come/I've Forgot My Number/All We Want Is Your Money (gatefold p/s, later pressing with black labels)	£60
80	Dead Good DEAD 10	Can't Sleep At Night/It's The Only Way To Live (Die) (p/s)	£40
02	Detour DRLP 029	WILL DAMAGE YOUR HEALTH (2-LP)	£30

CIM(M)AR(R)ONS
70	Hot Rod HR 105	Grandfather Clock/Kick Me Or I Kick You (as Cimarrons)	£100

70	Reggae REG 3003	Bad Day At Black Rock (with Cimmaron Kid)/**Fragile**	£70
71	Big Shot BI 562	**Funky Fight/You Turned Me Down**	£30
71	Spinning Wheel SW 107	**Soul For Sale/Bogus-ism**	£30
71	Downtown DT 486	**Oh Mammy Blue/Oh Mammy Blue - Version**	£15
71	Downtown DT 487	**Holy Christmas/Silent Night/White Christmas**	£15
74	Trojan TR7919	**Over The Rainbow/We Are Not The Same**	£15
75	Vulcan VUL 1005	**Tradition/Wicky Wacky**	£15
78	Cimarak CR002	**Paul Bogle/Greedy Man** (12")	£30
83	MPL/Cimarons 12CIM 001	**Love And Affection** (12", less than 1000 pressed)	£30
74	Trojan TRLS 77	**IN TIME** (LP)	£20
76	Vulcan VULA 501	**ON THE ROCKS** (LP)	£40
78	Polydor 2383512	**MAKA** (LP, green vinyl)	£20

(see also Reaction, Winston Groovy)

CINCH
| 80 | SRTS/80/CUS 622 | **SELL OUT EP** | £20 |

CINDERELLAS (1)
| 60 | Philips PB 1012 | **The Trouble With Boys/Puppy Dog** | £25 |

CINDERELLAS (2)
| 64 | Colpix PX 11026 | **Baby, Baby** (I Still Love You)/**Please Don't Wake Me** | £60 |
| 64 | Colpix PX 11026 | **Baby, Baby** (I Still Love You)/**Please Don't Wake Me** (DJ Copy) | £100 |

(see also Cookies)

CINDI AND THE BARBI DOLLS
| 79 | A Not Major Production NOTEM 1 | **ISN'T SHOWBIZ WONDERFUL EP** (hand-made p/s) | £15 |

CINEMATIC ORCHESTRA
99	Ninja Tune ZEN12 084	**Channel 1 Suite/Ode To The Big Sea** (12")	£15
99	Ninja Tune ZEN 45	**MOTION** (2xLP)	£30
00	Ninja Tune ZEN 50	**REMIXES 98 - 2000** (2xLP)	£20
02	Ninja Tune ZEN 59	**EVERY DAY** (2xLP)	£35
03	Ninja Tune ZEN 78	**MAN WITH A MOVIE CAMERA** (2xLP)	£40
07	Ninja Tune ZEN 122	**MA FLEUR** (2xLP)	£25

CINEMATICS
| 82 | Pulsebeat CINE 001 | **FAREWELL TO THE PLAYGROUND** (EP, foldover p/s) | £30 |

(see also Razorcuts)

CINNAMON QUILL
| 69 | Morgan MRS 17 | **Girl On A Swing/Take It Or Leave It** | £20 |
| 69 | Morgan MRS 21 | **Candy/Hello, It's Me** | £50 |

CIRCLE (1)
| 60s | Circle GR 1 | **IN AID OF THE MILLFIELD BUILDING FUND** (EP, private pressing) | £150 |

CIRCLE (2)
| 02 | Static Caravan/Resonance Staticresonance 6 | **PROSPEKT** (2-LP, gatefold sleeve, black vinyl and green vinyl, 1000 only) | £30 |

CIRCLES (1)
| 66 | Island WI 279 | **Take Your Time/Don't You Love Me No More** | £100 |

(see also Plastic Penny, Savages, Tony Dangerfield & Thrills, Screaming Lord Sutch)

CIRCLES (2)
| 72 | Sioux SIOUX 017 | **Mammy Blue/POOCH JACKSON & HARRY J. ALLSTARS: King Of The Road** | £15 |

(see also Bob Andy)

CIRCLES (3)
79	Graduate GRAD 4	**Opening Up/Billy** (p/s)	£20
80	Vertigo ANGRY 1	**Angry Voices/Summer Nights** (p/s)	£20
85	Graduate GRAD 17	**Circles/Summer Nights** (p/s)	£40

CIRCUIT 7
| 84 | Micro Rapp MIC 1 RAPP 023459 | **Video Boys/The Force** (p/s red vinyl) | £40 |
| 84 | Rapp 023462 | **Modern Story/Eastern Dream** (p/s, blue vinyl) | £25 |

CIRCULUS
05	Rise Above RISE 7/064	**Mirl It Is** (Moog Up Mix)/**WITCHCRAFT: Chylde Of Fire**	£18
05	Rise Above RISELP 063	**THE LICK ON THE TIP OF MY ENVELOPE YET TO BE SENT** (LP, clear vinyl gatefold sleeve, poster, 100 only)	£30
06	Rise Above RISELP 093	**CLOCKS ARE LIKE PEOPLE** (LP, white vinyl, free 1-sided 7", "Tapestry", 500 only)	£25
06	Rise Above RISELP 093	**CLOCKS ARE LIKE PEOPLE** (LP, 700 on blue vinyl, 500 on black vinyl)	£18

CIRCUS
67	Parlophone R 5633	**Gone Are The Songs Of Yesterday/Sink Or Swim**	£25
68	Parlophone R 5672	**Do You Dream/House Of Wood**	£45
69	Transatlantic TRA 207	**CIRCUS** (LP, gatefold sleeve, white/lilac label with 'T' logo)	£125

(see also Philip Goodhand-Tait, King Crimson)

CIRCUS MAXIMUS
| 67 | Vanguard VSD 79260 | **CIRCUS MAXIMUS** (LP) | £20 |
| 68 | Vanguard VSD 79274 | **NEVERLAND REVISITED** (LP) | £20 |

CIRKUS
80	Guardian GRCA 4	**Melissa/Amsterdam/Pick Up A Phone** (EP)	£20
73	RCB 1	**CIRKUS ONE** (LP, private pressing with gatefold sleeve, black/white label)	£300
77	Shock SHOCK 1	**FUTURE SHOCK** (LP)	£90

MINT VALUE £

CITATIONS
63   Columbia DB 7068   Moon Race/Slippin' And Slidin' £30

CITIZEN FISH
90   Bluurg FISH 24   FREE SOULS IN A TRAPPED ENVIRONMENT (LP, with cartoon insert) £15
91   Bluurg FISH 26   WIDER THAN A POSTCARD (LP) £15

CITIZENS OF ROME
82   Someone Elses Music SOM   Someone Elses World/St Malo (p/s) £15
     1

CITRUS
92   Pork PORK 010   Adrenachrome/Decoder/Narcosynthesis (12") £20

CITY GENTS
73   Triumph TR02   Shake/Turn It Down £15

CITY GIANTS
87   Give It A Blast BLA 001   Little Next To Nothing/Where Love's Concerned/Have You Got Any Idea? (p/s) £15

CITY LIMITS
79   Luggage RRP 1003   Morse Code Signals/If I Had Time/I Just Can't Say (EP) £125

CITY RAMBLERS SKIFFLE GROUP
57   Tempo A 158   Ella Speed/2.19 Blues £15
57   Tempo A 161   Mama Don't Allow/Tom Dooley £15
57   Tempo A 165   Delia's Gone/Boodle-Am Shake £15
57   Storyville SEP 327   I WANT A GIRL (EP) £25
57   Storyville SEP 345   I SHALL NOT BE MOVED (EP) £25
57   Tempo EXA 59   I WANT A GIRL (EP) £25
57   Tempo EXA 71   GOOD MORNING BLUES (EP) £25
57   Tempo EXA 77   DELIA'S GONE (EP) £25
(see also Henrik Johansen)

CITY WAITES
74   EMI EMC 3027   A GORGEOUS GALLERY OF GALLANT INVENTIONS (LP) £20
76   Decca SKL 5264   THE CITY WAITES (LP) £20
81   Hyperion A 66008   HOW THE WORLD WAGS (LP, gatefold sleeve, some with Hyperion insert).........£40

CIVILIANS
79   Arista ARIST 318   MADE FOR TELEVISION EP £60

CIVILISED SOCIETY?
86   Manic Ears ACHE 2   SCRAP METAL (LP, with inner) £15
87   Manic Ears ACHE 6   VIOLENCE SUCKS (LP, with lyric inner) £15

C-JAM BLUES
66   Columbia DB 8064   Candy/Stay At Home Girl £40

CLAGGERS
71   DJM DJS 260   Some One/Umber Rag £15

CLAIM
89   Esureint Comms PACE 7   Picking Up The Bitter Little Pieces/Losers Corner (p/s, with postcard) £15
90   Caff CAFF 008   Birth Of A Teenager/Mike The Bike £20
87   Trick Bag CU 0388   THIS PENCIL WAS OBVIOUSLY SHARPENED BY A LEFT-HANDED INDIAN KNIFE
                               THROWER (EP) £18
85   Trick Bag TBR 001   ARMSTRONG'S REVENGE AND ELEVEN OTHER SHORT STORIES (LP) £30
88   Esurient Comms PACE 003   BOOMY TELLA (LP) £30

CLAIR OBSCUR
86   All The Madmen MAD 10   THE PILGRIM'S PROGRESS (LP) £15

CLAMS CASINO
11   Tri Angle TRIANGLE 06   RAINFOREST (12" EP. p/s) £18

CLAN (1)
70   Bullet BU 419   Copycats/BUNNY LEE ALLSTARS: Hot Lead £30
70   Bullet BU 430   Na Na Hay Hay Goodbye/KING STITT: Musical Bop £40

CLANCY'S ALLSTARS
68   Pama PM 722   C.N. Express Parts 1 & 2 (B-side actually "You Were Meant For Me" by Lee Perry).........£50
(see also Clancy Eccles)

CLAN OF XYMOX
85   4AD CAD 503   CLAN OF XYMOX (LP) £15

JIMMY CLANTON
58   London HLS 8699   Just A Dream/You Aim To Please (as Jimmy Clanton & His Rockets) £20
58   London HL 7066   A Letter To An Angel/A Part Of Me (as Jimmy Clanton & Aces) (export issue) £20
59   London HLS 8779   A Letter To An Angel/A Part Of Me (as Jimmy Clanton & Aces) £20
59   Top Rank JAR 189   My Own True Love/Little Boy In Love £15
60   Top Rank JAR 269   Go, Jimmy, Go/I Trusted You £15
65   Stateside SS 410   Hurting Each Other/Don't Keep Your Friends Away £20
65   Stateside SS 140   Hurting Each Other/Don't Keep Your Friends Away (DJ Copy) £40
59   London RES 1224   JUST A DREAM (EP) £50

CLAP
79   SRTS SRTS/79/CUS   Hey Little Girl/20 Watts Of Power (p/s) £20

CLAPHAM SOUTH ESCALATORS
81   Upright UP YOUR 1   Get Me To The World On Time/Leave Me Alone/Cardboard Cut Outs (p/s) £15
(see also Meteors, Escalators)

ERIC CLAPTON
66	Purdah 45-3502	**Lonely Years/Bernard Jenkins** (with John Mayall, 500 copies only)	£400
70	Polydor 2001 096	**I Am Yours** (unissued)	£0
70	Polydor 2383 021	**ERIC CLAPTON** (LP, laminated sleeve, red label)	£25
73	RSO 2479 702	**CLAPTON** (LP, withdrawn)	£60
74	RSO QD 4801	**461 OCEAN BOULEVARD** (LP, quadrophonic)	£20
82	RSO RSDX 3	**TIME PIECES** (2-LP, unissued)	£0
84	Aston PD 20118	**TOO MUCH MONKEY BUSINESS** (LP, picture disc, with Yardbirds)	£15
99	Reprise 9362-47564-1	**CHRONICLES** (2-LP)	£60

(see also Yardbirds, John Mayall, Cream, Blind Faith, Delaney & Bonnie, Derek & The Dominos, Viv Stanshall, King Curtis, Randy Crawford)

ERIC CLAPTON & STEVE WINWOOD
09	Resprise 9362 497985	**LIVE FROM MADISON SQUARE GARDEN** (3-LP)	£40

ALAN CLARE GROUP
56	Decca DFE 6368	**THE IMPROVISATIONS OF...** (EP)	£20
56	Decca DFE 6391	**ALAN CLARE TRIO WITH BOB BURNS** (EP)	£20
58	Decca LK 4260	**JAZZ AROUND THE CLOCK** (LP)	£50

KENNY CLARE & RONNIE STEPHENSON
67	Columbia SCX 6168	**DRUM SPECTACULAR** (LP, with Tubby Hayes, stereo)	£40
67	Columbia SX 6168	**DRUM SPECTACULAR** (LP, with Tubby Hayes, mono)	£30
72	Sounds Superb SPR90057	**DRUM SPECTACULAR** (LP, reissue with Tubby Hayes and Stan Tracey)	£18

CLARENDONIANS
65	Ska Beat JB 219	**Muy Bien** (My Friend)/**You Are A Fool**	£50
66	Ska Beat JB 261	**Doing The Jerk/You Won't See Me**	£50
66	Island WI 284	**Try Me One More Time/Can't Keep A Good Man Down**	£50
66	Island WI 3005	**I'll Never Change/Rules Of Life**	£50
67	Island WI 3032	**Shoo-Be-Doo-Be** (I Love You)/**Sweet Heart Of Beauty**	£50
67	Island WI 3041	**You Can't Be Happy/Goodbye Forever**	£50
67	Studio One SO 2004	**The Table's Going To Turn/I Can't Go On**	£70
67	Studio One SO 2007	**He Who Laughs Last/GAYLADS: Just A Kiss From You**	£70
67	Studio One SO 2017	**Love Me With All Your Heart/Love Don't Mean Much To Me**	£70
67	Rio R 112	**Rudie Bam Bam/Be Bop Boy**	£50
67	Rio R 115	**Musical Train/Lowdown Girl**	£50
68	Caltone TONE 114	**Baby Baby/Bye Bye Bye**	£80
69	Duke DU 97	**Come Along/Try To Be Happy**	£45
69	Gas GAS 131	**When I Am Gone/She Brings Me Joy**	£20
70	Trojan TR 7714	**Lick It Back/BEVERLEY'S ALLSTARS: Busy Bee**	£50
70	Trojan TR 7719	**Baby Don't Do It/BEVERLEY'S ALLSTARS: Touch Down**	£50
71	Green Door GD 4009	**Seven In One** (Medley) (both sides)	£15
72	Attack ATT 8039	**Bound In Chains/STUD ALLSTARS: Version**	£15
72	Pama PM 847	**This Is My Story/VAL BENNETT: Caledonia**	£25
73	Pama PM 856	**Good Hearted Woman/CORNELL CAMPBELL: What Happens**	£25
73	Dragon DRA 1006	**Walking Up A One Way Street/DYNAMITES: Instrumental**	£30

(see also Lee & Clarendonians, Desmond Baker & Clarendonians, Four Aces, Prince Buster, Dennis Walks)

CLARITY
85	Bpop BPOB T02	**The Way U Make Me Feel/Turning Over** (12")	£75

ALICE CLARK
69	Action ACT 4520	**You Got A Deal/Say You'll Never**	£60
04	Acid Jazz 01716	**Don't You Care/Never Did I Stop Loving You**	£20
16	BGP HIQLP045	**THE COMPLETE STUDIO RECORINGS 1968-72** (LP, white vinyl)	£20

CHRIS CLARK (1)
67	Tamla Motown TMG 591	**Love's Gone Bad/Put Yourself In My Place**	£200
67	Tamla Motown TMG 591	**Love's Gone Bad/Put Yourself In My Place** (DJ Copy)	£250
67	Tamla Motown TMG 624	**From Head To Toe/The Beginning Of The End**	£45
67	Tamla Motown TMG 624	**From Head To Toe/The Beginning Of The End** (DJ Copy)	£80
68	Tamla Motown TMG 638	**I Want To Go Back There Again/I Love You**	£30
68	Tamla Motown TMG 638	**I Want To Go Back There Again/I Love You** (DJ Copy)	£60
68	T. Motown STML 11069	**SOUL SOUNDS** (LP, stereo)	£90
68	T. Motown TML 11069	**SOUL SOUNDS** (LP, mono)	£100

CHRIS CLARK (2)
01	Warp WARPLP86	**CLARENCE PARK** (LP)	£18
03	Warp WARPLP107	**EMPTY THE BONES OF YOU** (2-LP)	£20
06	Warp WARLP149	**BODY RIDDLE** (LP as 2 x 12")	£18
08	Warp WARLP162	**TURNING DRAGON** (2-LP)	£18
09	Warp WARPLP185	**TOTEMS FLARE** (LP as 2 x 12")	£25
12	Warp WARPLP222	**IRELDELPHIC** (LP)	£15

CLAUDINE CLARK
62	Pye International 7N 25157	**Party Lights/Disappointed**	£20
63	Pye International 7N 25186	**Walk Me Home From The Party/Who Will You Hurt?**	£20
67	Sue WI 4039	**The Strength To Be Strong/Moon Madness**	£75

DAVE CLARK FIVE
62	Ember EMB S 156	**Chaquita/In Your Heart** (grey/pink labels)	£40
62	Ember EMB S 156	**Chaquita/In Your Heart** (red/yellow labels)	£30
62	Piccadilly 7N 35088	**First Love/I Walk The Line**	£30
62	Piccadilly 7N 35500	**That's What I Said/I Knew It All The Time**	£30
63	Columbia DB 7011	**The Mulberry Bush/Chaquita**	£20

MINT VALUE £

65	Columbia DB 7580	Come Home/Mighty Good Loving (in p/s)	£18
67	Columbia DB 8194	Tabatha Twitchit/Man In A Pin-Striped Suit (in export p/s)	£20
69	Columbia DB 8591	Get It On Now/Maze Of Life (unreleased, acetates exist)	£0
72	Columbia DB 8963	All Time Greats Medley (Glad All Over/Do You Love Me/Bits & Pieces/ Glad All Over)/Wild Weekend (p/s)	£15
65	Columbia SEG 8381	THE HITS OF THE DAVE CLARK FIVE (EP)	£15
65	Columbia SEG 8447	WILD WEEKEND (EP)	£20
64	Columbia 33SX 1598	SESSION WITH THE DAVE CLARK FIVE (LP, blue/black label, with "sold in the U.K..." label text)	£20
64	Ember FA 2003	DAVE CLARK FIVE AND THE WASHINGTON D.C.'s (LP)	£20
65	EMI Regal REG 2017	IN SESSION (LP, export issue)	£20
65	Columbia SX 1756	CATCH US IF YOU CAN (LP, soundtrack, blue/black label)	£30
67	Columbia SX 6105	THE DAVE CLARK FIVE'S GREATEST HITS (LP, blue/black label)	£20
68	Columbia SX 6207	EVERYBODY KNOWS (LP, blue/black label)	£30
69	Columbia SX 6309	5 BY 5 1964-69: 14 TITLES BY THE DAVE CLARK FIVE (LP, blue/black label)	£30
70	Columbia SCX 6437	IF SOMEBODY LOVES YOU (LP)	£30
72	Columbia SCX 6494	DAVE CLARK AND FRIENDS (LP, boxed logo on label)	£30

(see also Dave Clark & Friends, Smith D'Abo, Washington D.C.s)

DEE CLARK

59	London HL 8802	Nobody But You/When I Call On You	£30
59	London HL 8915	Just Keep It Up (And See What Happens)/ Whispering Grass(Don't Tell The Trees)	£20
59	Top Rank JAR 196	Hey, Little Girl/If It Wasn't For Love	£15
60	Top Rank JAR 373	At My Front Door/Cling-A-Ling	£25
61	Top Rank JAR 570	Raindrops/I Want To Love You	£15
62	Columbia DB 4768	Don't Walk Away From Me/You're Telling Our Secrets	£40
63	Stateside SS 180	I'm A Soldier Boy/Shook Up Over You	£25
64	Stateside SS 355	Heartbreak/Warm Summer Breeze	£15
65	Stateside SS 400	T.C.B./It's Impossible	£20
60	Top Rank BUY 044	HOW ABOUT THAT! (LP)	£30
70	Joy JOYS 130	YOU'RE LOOKING GOOD (LP)	£20

DUANE CLARK

| 77 | Spark SRL 1152 | Stop Come Down Come Around/Gettin It | £15 |

GAVIN CLARK

| 14 | Club AC30 AC 301 1061 | BEAUTIFUL SKELETONS (2-LP, CD and DVD) | £100 |

GENE CLARK

67	CBS 202523	Echoes/I Found You	£50
67	CBS 62934	GENE CLARK WITH THE GOSDIN BROTHERS (LP)	£60
72	A&M AMLS 64297	WHITE LIGHT (LP)	£30
74	Asylum SYL 9020	NO OTHER (LP)	£35

(see also Byrds, Dillard & Clark)

J. CLARK

| 80 | Cha Cha CHAD 17 | Babylon/One Man Live (12") | £40 |

JIMMY 'SOUL' CLARK

| 76 | Black Magic BM 115 | Sweet Darlin'/Sweet Darlin' (Instrumental) | £20 |

LARENA CLARK

| 66 | Topic 12T 140 | A CANADIAN GARLAND (LP) | £15 |

MICHAEL CLARK

| 66 | Liberty LIB 5893 | None Of These Girls/Work Out | £15 |

PAUL CLARK & FRIENDS

| 77 | Myrrh MYR 1054 | GOOD TO BE HOME (LP, with inner sleeve) | £20 |
| 78 | Myrrh MYR 1059 | HAND TO THE PLOUGH (LP) | £20 |

PETULA CLARK

ALBUMS

56	Pye Nixa NPT 19002	PETULA CLARK SINGS (10")	£60
56	Pye Nixa NPT 19014	A DATE WITH PET (10")	£60
57	Pye Nixa NPL 18007	YOU ARE MY LUCKY STAR	£60
59	Pye Nixa NPL 18039	PETULA CLARK IN HOLLYWOOD	£50
62	Pye NPL 18070	IN OTHER WORDS - PETULA CLARK	£15
63	Pye NPL 18098	PETULA	£15
64	Pye-Vogue VRL 3001	LES JAMES DEAN	£25

ROY CLARK

59	HMV POP 581	Please Mr. Mayor/Puddin'	£100
59	HMV POP 581	Please Mr. Mayor/Puddin' (78)	£15
63	Capitol CL 15288	In The Mood/Texas Twist	£15
63	Capitol CL 15317	Tips Of My Fingers/Spooky Movies	£15
62	Capitol (S)T 1780	THE LIGHTNING FINGERS OF ROY CLARK (LP)	£30

SANFORD CLARK

56	London HLD 8320	The Fool/Lonesome For A Letter (with Al Casey) (gold label print)	£100
56	London HLD 8320	The Fool/Lonesome For A Letter (with Al Casey) (later silver print label)	£30
56	London HL 7014	The Fool/Lonesome For A Letter (with Al Casey) (export issue)	£20
59	London HLW 8959	Run, Boy Run/New Kind Of Fool (triangular centre)	£15
59	London HLW 8959	Run, Boy Run/New Kind Of Fool (78)	£20
60	London HLW 9026	Son-Of-A-Gun/I Can't Help It (If I'm Still In Love With You) (tri centre)	£20
60	London HLW 9026	Son-Of-A-Gun/I Can't Help It (If I'm Still In Love With You) (round centre)	£15
60	London HLW 9095	Go On Home/Pledging My Love	£15

57 London RED 1105	PRESENTING SANFORD CLARK (EP)	£25
60 London REW 1256	LOWDOWN BLUES (EP)	£25

(see also Al Casey)

TERRY CLARK

70 Myrrh MYR 1071	WELCOME (LP)	£15

ALLAN CLARKE

72 RCA SF 8283	MY REAL NAME IS 'AROLD (LP, lyric insert, orange/white label)	£20
73 EMI EMA 752	HEADROOM (LP, gatefold sleeve, lyric inner sleeve)	£15

(see also Hollies)

ANNETTE CLARKE

73 Techniques TE 925	Just One Look/Sinner Man	£25
73 Black Ark BAR 102	Just One Look/Dub Power (white labels more common)	£25

AUGUSTUS 'GUSSIE' CLARKE

77 Burning Sounds BS 1023	BLACK FOUNDATION DUB (LP)	£60
78 Hawkeye HALP 001	DREAD AT THE CONTROLS DUB (LP)	£25

BOB CLARKE

70 CBS 7435	Haunted/Run Colorado	£30

BUNNY CLARKE

75 Dip DL 5064	Be Thankful/UPSETTERS: Dubbing In The Back (Mr. Chang)	£50

DAVE CLARKE

94 Bush 1012	Red 1 (of 3) (Protective Custody)/Zeno Xero (12", p/s, red vinyl)	£15

ERIC CLARKE

75 Torpedo TOR 40	Fight Against Babylon/Babylon Dub (as Eric Clark)	£25
78 Baal BAL 89004	LOVE THAT GROWS AND GROWS (LP)	£60

FREDDIE CLARKE

81 Main Line MLD6	Home We Wanna Go/THE CIRCLE: Legend (12")	£50

FREDDY CLARKE

78 Jungle Beat JBDC 805	Troubles/I Man (12" with I ROY)	£80
81 Jungle Beat JBDC801	Fight I Down/VIN GORDON: Fire Horns (12", red vinyl)	£40
82 Live & Love LLDIS 205	Are We Gonna Make It Up/Mash It Up (Dub Version) (12")	£15

(see also Freddie Clarke)

JAMES CLARK(E) + SOUNDS

68 Fontana SFJL 966	A MAN OF OUR TIMES (LP)	£40

JOHN COOPER CLARKE

78 CBS 83132	DISGUISE IN LOVE (LP)	£20
80 Epic EPC 84083	SNAP, CRACKLE [&] BOP (LP, with 48-page book in sleeve pocket)	£20
81 Epic EPC 84979	ME AND MY BIG MOUTH (LP)	£15

JOHNNY CLARKE

73 Pep PEP 001	Don't Go/SUCCESS ALL STARS: Version	£25
74 Explosion EX 2089	None Shall Escape The Judgement/Every Rasta Is A Star	£15
74 Pyramid PYR 7013	My Desire/Lemon Tree	£15
74 Lord Koos KOOS42	Enter Into This Gate With Praise/KING TUBBY & THE AGGROVATORS : This Is The Hardest Version	£15
74 Cactus CTEP32	Jump Back Baby	£15
74 Harry J HJ6706	Move Out A Babylon/Move Out A Babylon (Instrumental)	£15
75 Horse HOSS86	Move Out Of Babylon/AGGROVATORS:Version	£15
75 Attack ATT 8118	Cold I Up/Cold I Up (Version)	£15
76 Virgin VS159	Crazy Bald Head/Crazy Bald Head(Version)	£15
77 Virgin VS173	Roots, Natty Roots, Natty Congo/Version	£20
77 Third World TW 70	Age is growing/Version	£20
77 Paradise PDIS 002	Empty Chair/Can't Go On Without You (12", p/s with Dillinger)	£15
78 Star PTP1009	Every Knee Shall Bow/Version (With U Roy) (12")	£25
78 Justice JUDIS 109	Pity Fool Fe Get Wise/Satisfaction (12")	£40
78 Third World TW 76	Peace And Love In The Ghetto/Version	£15
79 Justice JUDIS 109	Play Fool Fe Get Wise/Satisfaction/Version (12")	£25
79 Greensleeves GRED20	Jah Love Is With I/Bad Days Are Going (12")	£35
80 Jah Shaka 842	Got To Be Strong/Babylon (12")	£30
80 Cha Cha CHAD17	Babylon/One Man Live (as J. Clark) (12")	£100
81 Chrysalis 122849	Babylon/Than You For The Many Things You've Done - Cassandra (12")	£50
81 Art & Craft ACD 007	Can't Get Enough/Version (12')	£20
81 Art & Craft ACD 014	Guide Us Jah/Version (12")	£40
81 Art & Craft ACD 015	Rude Boy/Version (12")	£20
82 Art & Craft ACD 018	You Better Try/Version (12")	£20
82 Black Joy DH822	Stop Them Jah/Too Much War	£15
82 Cha Cha CHAD 49	Give Me Love/Version (10")	£20
82 Red Nail RN 039	Guidance/DUB BAND: Protection (12")	£30
83 Top Notch TOP005	Young Rebel/Version (10")	£25
84 Ariwa ARISL002	Nuclear Weapon/Reggae Music (12")	£20
04 Trojan TJHTE 011	Blood Dunza/Version/Blood Sweat & Dunza Dub/Don't Trouble Trouble/A Ruffer Version (10" die-cut Trojan sleeve)	£20
13 Attack Gold ATT10 010	Dem A Say/Dub Version/Two Face Rasta/Extended Dub (10")	£18
75 Attack ATLP 1015	ENTER INTO HIS GATES WITH PRAISE (LP)	£60
75 Vulcan VULP 001	PUT IT ON (LP)	£40
76 Virgin V2076	AUTHORISED VERSION (LP, mono)	£20
76 Virgin V2058	ROCKERS TIME NOW (LP, mono credits on label)	£35

MINT VALUE £

77	Justice JUSLP 001	**GIRL I LOVE YOU** (LP)	£40
77	Paradise PDLP 001	**DON'T STAY OUT LATE** (LP)	£25
77	Third World TWS 914	**SWEET CONVERSATION** (LP)	£30
78	Third World TWS 932	**KING IN A ARENA** (LP, as Johnie Clark)	£40
79	Paradise PDLP 008	**SHOWCASE** (LP)	£35
79	Third World TDWD 4	**SATISFACTION** (LP)	£20
82	Art & Craft ACDLP001	**CAN'T GET ENOUGH** (LP)	£50
83	Ariwa ARI 007 LP	**YARD STYLE** (LP)	£30
83	Vista VSLP 4016	**MEETS CORNEL CAMPBELL** (LP)	£30
85	Ariwa ARI LP 022	**GIVE THANKS** (LP)	£15
89	Attack ATLP 105	**ENTER INTO HIS GATES WITH PRAISE** (LP, reissue)	£15
89	Attack ATLP 107	**DON'T TROUBLE TROUBLE** (LP)	£15

KENNY CLARKE
56	London LTZC 15004	**KENNY CLARKE SEXTET** (LP)	£25
56	London LTZC 15008	**KENNY CLARKE AND ERNIE WILKINS** (LP)	£20
57	London LTZC 15038	**KENNY CLARKE** (LP)	£25
57	London LTZC 15047	**KENNY CLARKE** (LP)	£20
57	Vogue LAE 12029	**JAZZ INTERNATIONAL** (LP)	£25

KENNY CLARKE (WITH FRANCY BOLAND BIG BAND)
56	London LTZ C 15047	**BOHEMIA AFTER DARK** (LP)	£15
63	London HA-K 8085	**JAZZ IS UNIVERSAL** (LP, with Francy Boland Big Band)	£15
66	CBS SBPG 62567	**NOW HEAR OUR MEANIN'** (LP)	£18
68	Polydor 583726	**LATIN KALEIDOSCOPE** (LP)	£20
69	Polydor 583727	**ALL SMILES** (LP)	£20
69	Polydor 583738	**FELLINI 712** (LP)	£20
69	Polydor 583054	**LIVE AT RONNIE SCOTT'S - THE FIRST SET** (LP)	£20
69	Polydor 583055	**LIVE AT RONNIE SCOTT'S - THE SECOND SET** (LP)	£20
70	Polydor 583739	**FACES** (LP)	£15
70	Polydor 2310 147	**OFF LIMITS** (LP, reflective sleeve)	£30

(see also Francey Boland, Kenny Clarke)

LINDA CLARKE
| 67 | Decca F 12709 | **Your Hurtin' Kinda Love/Send Me The Pillow You Dream On** | £15 |
| 68 | Decca F 12787 | **Society's Child/Rain In My Heart** | £20 |

LLOYD CLARKE
62	Blue Beat BB 104	**Fool's Day/You're A Cheat** (with Reco's All Stars)	£30
62	Island WI 007	**Love You The Most/LLOYD ROBINSON: You Said You Loved Me**	£50
62	Island WI 045	**Japanese Girl/He's Coming**	£50
63	Rio R 16	**Love Me/Half As Much**	£40
64	Rio R 23	**Stop Your Talking/A Penny**	£40
64	Rio R 24	**Fellow Jamaican/PATRICK & GEORGE: My Love**	£40
68	Island WI 3116	**Summertime/VAL BENNETT: Soul Survivor**	£130
68	Blue Cat BS 136	**Young Love/UNTOUCHABLES: Wall Flower**	£70
70	Escort ERT 849	**Chicken Thief/STRANGER COLE: Tomorrow**	£18

(see also Derrick & Lloyd, Theo Beckford, Soulettes, Delroy Wilson, Laurel Aitken, Sonny Burke, Uniques)

MICKEY CLARKE
| 66 | HMV 1483 | **Help Me/For Me** | £20 |

PAULA CLARKE
| 83 | Oak Sound OSD 013 | **University/Didn't I Blow Your Mind** (12") | £40 |

RICK CLARKE
81	KR 1001	**Potion** (Vocal)/(Instrumental) (12" white label only)	£30
85	Local LR 11	**Love With A Stranger/Dub With A Stranger** (12" p/s)	£20
88	Raven RAVLP 1	**TIME KEEPS MOVING ON** (LP)	£30

RONA CLARKE
| 67 | Westwood WRS 067 | **UTOPIAN DREAM** (LP) | £30 |

TONY CLARKE
64	Pye International 7N 25251	**Ain't Love Good, Ain't Love Proud/Coming Back Strong**	£22
65	Chess CRS 8011	**The Entertainer/This Heart Of Mine**	£30
65	Chess CRS 8011	**The Entertainer/This Heart Of Mine** (DJ Copy)	£50

CLARK-HUTCHINSON
68	Decca LK-R 5006	**CLARK-HUTCHINSON** (LP, red Decca labels, no sleeve Matrix: ARL-8968.P-1A/1B	£500
70	Decca Nova DN-R 2	**A = MH2** (LP, dark green label, mono)	£150
70	Decca Nova DN-R 2	**A = MH2** (LP, turquoise label, stereo)	£100
70	Deram SML 1076	**RETRIBUTION** (LP)	£100
71	Deram SML 1090	**GESTALT** (LP, laminated sleeve)	£100
71	Deram SML 1090	**GESTALT** (LP, non-laminated sleeve)	£80

(see also Vamp, Upp)

CLARO INTELECTO
| 02 | Ai Ai 003 | **PEACE OF MIND** (12", first pressings in blue p/s) | £15 |

CLASH
SINGLES
77	CBS S CBS 5058	**White Riot/1977** (p/s, 'The Clash' or 'The CLASH' on label, 'copyright control' publishing credit)	£30
77	CBS S 5058	**White Riot/1977** (p/s, 'The Clash' or 'The CLASH' on label, 'Nineden/Riva' publishing credits)	£20
77	CBS CL 1	**CAPITAL RADIO** (EP, NME freebie, p/s)	£150

77	CBS S CBS 5293	Remote Control/London's Burning (p/s with 'live version...in mono...for the first time' on rear, 'copyright control' and 'Dunstable' publishing credit)	£20
77	CBS CBS 5293	Remote Control/London's Burning (p/s, with 'Nineden/Riva' publishing credits)	£15
77	CBS S CBS 5664	Complete Control/The City Of The Dead (p/s, 'copyright control' publishing credits)	£20
78	CBS CBS 5834	Clash City Rockers/Jail Guitar Doors (p/s)	£15
78	CBS S CBS 6383	(White Man) In Hammersmith Palais/The Prisoner (initially green, then pink, blue or yellow die-cut sleeve)	£15
78	CBS S CBS 7082	English Civil War/Pressure Drop (p/s)	£15
79	CBS S CBS 7324	THE COST OF LIVING (EP, gatefold p/s & inner sleeve)	£15
79	CBS S CBS 8087	London Calling/Armagideon Time (p/s, green or red shaded sleeve, white or yellow/ orange label)	£15
79	CBS 12 8087	London Calling/Armagidion Time/Armagidion Time (Version) (12")	£40
81	CBS A12 1133	The Magnificent Seven/The Magnificent Dance (12", p/s, with stickers)	£20
81	CBS S 2309	Know Your Rights/First Night Back In London (p/s, with free sticker)	£15
82	CBS A 2479	Rock The Casbah/Long Time Jerk (p/s, with free stickers)	£15
82	CBS A 11 2479	Rock The Casbah/Long Time Jerk (picture disc)	£15
82	CBS A 13 2479	Rock The Casbah/Mustapha Dance (12", p/s)	£18
82	CBS A 2646	Should I Stay Or Should I Go/Straight To Hell (p/s, with dragon sticker)	£15
82	CBS A 11 2646	Should I Stay Or Should I Go/Straight To Hell (picture disc)	£15
82	CBS A 12 2646	Should I Stay Or Should I Go/Straight To Hell (12", p/s with stencil)	£30
85	CBS A 6122	This Is England/Do It Now (poster p/s)	£15
85	CBS TA 6122	This Is England/Do It Now/Sex Mad Roar (12", p/s, with 6 sticker postcard)	£30
85	CBS S CBS 7082	English Civil War/Pressure Drop (reissue, red label with LC0149 on labels, some in p/ s)	£40
88	CBS CLASH 1	I Fought The Law/City Of The Dead/1977 (p/s)	£15
88	CBS CLASH T1	I Fought The Law/City Of The Dead/Police On My Back/48 Hours (12", p/s)	£15
88	CBS CLASH B 2	London Calling/Brand New Cadillac/Rudie Don't Fail (box set)	£40
88	CBS CLASH T2	London Calling/Brand New Cadillac/Rudie Can't Fail/Street Parade (p/s)	£20
90	CBS 656072-1	Return To Brixton/Guns Of Brixton (p/s)	£20
91	Columbia 6569466	London Calling/Brand New Cadillac/Return To Brixton (12", poster p/s)	£20
91	Columbia 6574306	Train In Vain/The Right Profile/Groovy Times/Gates Of The West (12", p/s)	£20
06	Sony 82876 876287	THE SINGLES (Box set 19 x 7" singles)	£200
11	Columbia 88697890297	The Magnificent Seven/The Cool Out (red vinyl, numbered, die-cut sleeve)	£30
12	Columbia 88691959247	London Calling (2012 Mix)/London Calling (2012 Instrumental) (p/s)	£15
18	Secret S 736	I'm Not Down (1-sided, 100 only, each with unique p/s)	£75

ALBUMS

77	CBS 82000	THE CLASH (LP, 10,000 only with sticker on inner sleeve for free NME Capital Radio EP freebie, orange/yellow labels with 'made in England' at bottom)	£100
77	CBS 82000	THE CLASH (LP, 1st issue with orange/yellow labels with 'made in England' at bottom, 'Copyright Control' publishing credits)	£50
77	CBS CBS 82000	THE CLASH (LP, 1st issue with orange/yellow labels with 'made in England' at bottom, 'Nineden/Riva' publishing credits)	£40
78	CBS 82431	GIVE 'EM ENOUGH ROPE (LP, promo-only package with poster in folder)	£1500
78	CBS 82431	GIVE 'EM ENOUGH ROPE (LP)	£40
79	CBS CLASH 3	LONDON CALLING (2-LP, stickered, with inner sleeves, 1st issue with black & white labels, no Train In Vain)	£250
79	CBS CBS CLASH 3	LONDON CALLING (2-LP, stickered, with inner sleeves, 2nd issue with black & white labels, Train In Vain on side 4 but not listed on sleeve or labels, 'Track 5 is Train In Vain' etched in run-out groove on side 4). 'Stagger Lee' reference on rear sleeve after Wrong Em Boyo)	£80
79	CBS CBS CLASH 3	LONDON CALLING (2-LP, stickered, with inner sleeves, 2nd issue with black & white labels, Train In Vain on side 4 but not listed on sleeve or labels, 'Track 5 is Train In Vain' etched in run-out groove on side 4)	£80
79	CBS CBS 32232	THE CLASH (LP, reissue, LC0149 on labels, some with 'Nice Price £2.99' sticker on sleeve)	£15
80	CBS FSLN 1	SANDINISTA (3-LP, stickered sleeve with 'Armagideon Times' insert)	£75
82	CBS FMLN2	COMBAT ROCK (LP, 1st pressing, inner sleeve and poster of band sitting in bar)	£60
82	CBS FMLN2	COMBAT ROCK (LP, 2nd pressing, inner sleeve and poster of front cover artwork)	£50
84	CBS 32444	GIVE 'EM ENOUGH ROPE (LP, reissue, red labels)	£15
85	CBS 26601	CUT THE CRAP (LP, with inner)	£15
85	CBS 4601141	LONDON CALLING (2-LP, reissue, red labels)	£25
85	CBS 4601141	COMBAT ROCK (LP, reissue, red labels)	£15
88	CBS 460244 1	THE STORY OF THE CLASH (2-LP)	£20
91	Columbia 4689461	THE SINGLES (LP, with poster)	£40
92	CBS 32787	COMBAT ROCK (LP, reissue, has barcode on sleeve)	£15
93	Columbia 4745461	SUPER BLACK MARKET CLASH (LP as 3 x 10" with inners, 'police' labels)	£60
99	CBS 49 5344-1	THE CLASH (LP, reissue)	£20
99	Simply Vinyl SVLP 134	GIVE 'EM ENOUGH ROPE (LP, reissue)	£20
99	CBS 495347-1	LONDON CALLING (2-LP, reissue)	£30
99	CBS 495348-1	SANDINISTA (3-LP, reissue)	£25
99	CBS 495349-1	COMBAT ROCK (LP, 2nd reissue)	£20
99	Columbia 4953511	THE STORY OF THE CLASH (2-LP, reissue)	£40
99	Sony 496183-1	FROM HERE TO ETERNITY (2LP, gatefold, printed inners)	£110
99	Columbia 4953521	SUPER BLACK MARKET CLASH (LP as 3 x 10" with inners, reissue, labels replicate front cover artwork)	£50
08	Epic 88697348801	LIVE AT SHEA STADIUM (LP, printed inner)	£30
13	Columbia 88883725981	THE CLASH (8LP box set, stencil, badge)	£180
13	Columbia 88725460002	SOUND SYSTEM (Box set, 11CD, DVD, book, 5 badges, 3 stickers, notebook, booklet & poster)	£100
16	Columbia 88985316611	LONDON CALLING (2-LP, reissue, green and pink vinyl, 'Tesco' exclusive)	£80
16	Columbia 88985316581	THE CLASH LP, reissue, green vinyl, HMV exclusive)	£40
17	Columbia 88985431091	GIVE EM ENOUGH ROPE (LP, reissue, blue vinyl, HMV exclusive)	£35

MINT VALUE £

19	Columbia 19075978671	LONDON CALLING (2-LP, reissue, 40th anniversary edition with plastic outer sleeve) £30
19	Sony 88985391771	COMBAT ROCK (LP, reissue, green vinyl, HMV exclusive) £35
22	Columbia 19439968951	COMBAT ROCK (LP, green vinyl, 2022 edition, printed inner, poster)...............................£20
22	Columbia 19439955131	COMBAT ROCK + THE PEOPLE'S HALL (3LP, 5-sided, printed inners, obi, poster) £35

PROMOS

77	CBS S CBS 5058	White Riot/1977 (A label promo, The Clash on label, p/s)...£70
77	CBS S CBS 5293	Remote Control/London's Burning (Studio Version) ('A' Label Promo) £50
77	CBS S 5664	Complete Control/The City Of The Dead (A label promo, p/s).....................................£50
78	CBS S CBS 5834	Clash City Rockers/Jail Guitar Doors (A label promo, p/s)..£50
78	CBS S CBS 6383	(White Man) In Hammersmith Palais/The Prisoner (A label demo - small black A - in die-cut sleeve)...£60
78	CBS S CBS 6788	Tommy Gun/1 - 2 Crush On You (A label promo, p/s) £60
78	CBS S CBS 7082	English Civil War/Pressure Drop (A label promo, p/s) £50
79	CBS S CBS 7324	I Fought The Law/Gates Of The West (2-track promo for COST OF LIVING EP) £40
80	CBS S CBS 9339	The Call Up/Stop The World (A label promo, p/s) £50
80	CBS S CBS 9480	Hitsville U.K./Radio One (A label promo, die cut sleeve)..£60
81	WEA SAM 144	4 Track White label EP featuring London Calling and tracks by the Beat, Bad Manners and the Jam)..£200
82	CBS A2309	Know Your Rights/First Night Back In London ("promo copy not for sale" , no A, p/s).....£30
82	CBS A2479	Rock The Casbah/Long Time Jerk (promo with small "A", p/s).......................................£30
82	CBS A 2646	Should I Stay Or Should I Go/Straight To Hell (edit) (A label promo, p/s) £40

(see also 101'ers, Janie Jones & Lash, Ellen Foley, Futura 2000, Joe Strummer, Havana 3AM, The Good The Bad And The Queen)

CLASSICS IV

| 66 | Capitol CL 15470 | Pollyanna/Cry Baby (issued as if by the "Classics") ....£40 |
| 69 | Liberty LBF 15177 | Stormy/Twenty Four Hours Of Loneliness...£15 |

(see also Dennis Yost & Classics IV)

CLASSICS (JAMAICA)

69	Doctor Bird DB 1190	Worried Over Me/LAUREL AITKEN: Rice And Peas £40
71	Punch PH 79	Cheerio Baby/Civilization £80
71	Banana BA331	Mr Fire Coal Man/SOUND DIMENSION: Version (actually by Wailing Souls) £40

CLASSICS (U.S.)

| 61 | Mercury AMT 1152 | Life Is But A Dream/That's The Way ....£75 |
| 63 | Stateside SS 215 | Till Then/Enie Minie Mo ....£30 |

CLAUDETTE (& CORPORATION)

69	Jackpot JP 712	Let's Fall In Love/PROPHETS: Purple Moon £30
70	Grape GR 3020	Skinheads A Bash Them (with Corporation)/ CORPORATION: Walkin' Thru Jerusalem .£200
12	Grape THB 701	Hot Bread And Butter/Ashes To Ashes £25

(see also Corporation)

CLAUDIA

| 84 | Rhythmic RMIC5 | Don't Give Up (Your Love) (Club Mix)/Don't Give Up (Your Love)/Do You Wanna Dance With Me (12", p/s)..£15 |

CASSIUS CLAY

| 64 | CBS AAG 190 | Stand By Me/I Am The Greatest ....£20 |
| 63 | CBS BPG 62274 | I AM THE GREATEST! (LP) ....£40 |

OTIS CLAY

69	Atlantic 584 282	Baby Jane/You Hurt Me For The Last Time..£80
72	London HLU 10397	Trying To Live My Life Without You/Let Me Be The One £15
73	London SH-U 8446	TRYING TO LIVE MY LIFE WITHOUT YOU (LP) £30

CLAY FAV

| 79 | Own label | CONSIGNMENT STOCK (EP, 200 stamped "consignment Stock' sleeve) ....£150 |
| 79 | Own label | CONSIGNMENT STOCK (EP, 800 without stamped "consignment Stock' sleeve) ....£50 |

ALASDAIR CLAYRE

| 67 | Elektra EUK 255 | ALASDAIR CLAYRE (LP, some with mail order insert)..£60 |
| 76 | Acorn CF 252 | ADAM AND THE BEASTS (LP) ....£30 |

DOCTOR CLAYTON

| 70 | RCA Intl. INTS 1176 | PEARL HARBOUR BLUES (LP) ....£15 |

MERRY CLAYTON

70	A&M AMS 802	Gimme Shelter/Good Girls...£20
70	A&M AMS 802	Gimme Shelter/Good Girls (DJ Copy)..£30
70	A&M AMLS 995	GIMME SHELTER (LP) £30
72	A&M AMLS 67012	MERRY CLAYTON (LP) £35

(see also Raelets)

PAUL CLAYTON

| 61 | London REU 1276 | PAUL CLAYTON (EP) ....£30 |

VIKKI CLAYTON

| 88 | Dambuster DAM 021 | LOST LADY FOUND (LP)..£20 |

(see also Fairport Convention)

CLAYTON SQUARES

| 65 | Decca F 12250 | Come And Get It/And Tears Fell ....£40 |
| 66 | Decca F 12456 | There She Is/Imagination ....£175 |

(see also Liverpool Scene, Andy Roberts, Mike Hart)

CLAYTOWN TROUPE

| 92 | EMI 12 88007) | SKYBOUND (LP, withdrawn)..£20 |

CLEAN

| 86 | Flying Nun FNE 29 | COMPILATION (LP)..£25 |

89	Flying Nun Europe FNE 29	IN-A-LIVE (Mini-LP)	£20
90	Rough Trade ROUGH 143	VEHICLE (LP)	£25

CLEANERS FROM VENUS

87	Ammunition JANGLE 1	Illya Kurayakin Looked At Me/Black And White And Blue All Over (p/s)	£25
87	Ammunition JANGLE 1T	Illya Kurayakin Looked At Me/Albion's Daughter/Black And White And Blue All Over/Illya Kuryakin Looked At Me (Full Version) (12", p/s)	£15
87	Ammunition JANGLE 2	Living With Victoria Grey/Sunday Afternoon (p/s)	£20
87	Ammunition JANGLE 2T	Living With Victoria Grey/Sunday Afternoon/She's Checking You Out (12", p/s)	£15
88	Ammunition JANGLE 3	Mercury Girl/Gamma Ray Blues	£20
88	Ammunition JANGLE 3T	Mercury Girl/Gamma Ray Blues/The Iceberg Unicorn (12", p/s)	£15
87	Ammunition CLEAN LP 1	GOING TO ENGLAND (LP)	£30
88	Ammunition CLEAN LP 2	TOWN AND COUNTRY (LP)	£30

(see also Gypp, Martin Newall, Brotherhood of Lizards)

CLEAR BLUE SKY

70	Vertigo 6360 013	CLEAR BLUE SKY (LP, gatefold sleeve, large swirl label)	£500
90	Saturn SRLP 101	DESTINY (LP)	£15

CLEAR LIGHT

68	Elektra EKSN 45027	Night Sounds Loud/How Many Days Have Passed	£30
67	Elektra EKL 4011	CLEAR LIGHT (LP, orange label, mono)	£150
67	Elektra EKS 74011	CLEAR LIGHT (LP, orange label, stereo)	£100
87	Edsel ED 245	BLACK ROSES (LP, reissue of original Clear Light LP with 1 bonus track)	£15

CLEARLIGHT

75	Virgin V 2029	SYMPHONY (LP, stickered sleeve)	£20
75	Virgin V 2039	FOREVER BLOWING BUBBLES (LP)	£20

(see also Gong, Steve Hillage)

CLEAR LIGHT SYMPHONY

75	Virgin V 2039	CLEAR LIGHT SYMPHONY (LP)	£15

CLEFS

62	Salvo SLO 1810	Don't Cry/The Dream Train Special (99 copies only)	£20

CLEFS OF LAVENDER HILL

66	CBS 202230	Stop, Get A Ticket/First Tell Me Why	£20

CLEFTONES

56	Columbia SCM 3801	You Baby, You/Little Girl Of Mine	£250
56	Columbia DB 3801	You Baby, You/Little Girl Of Mine (78)	£15
61	Columbia DB 4678	Heart And Soul/How Do You Feel	£100
61	Columbia DB 4720	(I Love You) For Sentimental Reasons/Deed I Do	£100
63	Columbia DB 4988	Lover Come Back To Me/There She Goes	£50

JACK CLEMENT

58	London HLS 8691	Ten Years/Your Lover Boy	£150
58	London HLS 8691	Ten Years/Your Lover Boy (78)	£40

SOUL JOE CLEMENTS

69	Plexium PXM 10	Smoke And Ashes/Ever, Ever	£400

CLEO

64	Decca F 11817	To Know Him Is To Love Him/ANDREW OLDHAM ORCHESTRA: There Are But Five Rolling Stones	£25

(see also Andrew Oldham Orchestra, This 'N' That)

CLERKS

79	Rok ROK VIII/VII	No Good For Me/HAZARD: Gotta Change My Life (company sleeve)	£15

CLICHE

80	Carrere CAR 133	I Know Your Name/Drawing The Line	£100

CLIENTELE

98	Pointy POINT 001	What Goes Up/Five Day Morning (p/s)	£15
99	Johnny Kane KANE 002	Reflections After Jane/An Hour Before The Light (p/s)	£15
99	Pointy POINT 002	I Had To Say This/Monday's Rain (p/s)	£15
00	Pointy POINT 004LP	SUBURBAN LIGHT (LP, insert)	£40
03	Pointy POINT 011LP	THE VIOLET HOUR (LP)	£40
05	Pointy POINT 017LP	STRANGE GEOMETRY (LP)	£20
17	Tapete TR 385	MUSIC FOR THE AGE OF MIRACLES (LP, CD and 7")	£20

CLIENTELLE

79	Quest BRS 003	Can't Forget/Skyline (p/s)	£125
81	Banana BANANA 505	DESTINATION UNKNOWN (LP, with insert)	£100

JIMMY CLIFF

62	Blue Beat BB 78	I'm Sorry (with Cavaliers Combo)/BLUE BEATS: Roarin' (with Red Price)	£30
62	Island WI 012	Hurricane Hatty/Dearest Beverley	£25
62	Island WI 016	Miss Jamaica/Gold Digger	£25
62	Island WI 025	Since Lately/I'm Free	£30
63	Island WI 062	My Lucky Day/One-Eyed Jacks	£30
63	Island WI 070	King Of Kings/SIR PERCY: Oh Yeah	£30
63	Island WI 112	Miss Universe/The Prodigal	£30
63	Black Swan WI 403	The Man (vocal version)/You Are Never Too Old	£30
63	Black Swan WI 403	The Man (Instrumental version)/You Are Never Too Old	£30
64	Stateside SS 342	One Eyed Jacks/King Of Kings	£30
66	Fontana TF 641	Call On Me/Pride And Passion	£15
67	Island WIP 6004	Aim And Ambition/Give And Take	£15

MINT VALUE £

67	Island WIP 6011	I Got A Feeling/Hard Road To Travel	£15
68	Island WIP 6039	Waterfall/Reward	£35
68	Island ILP 962	HARD ROAD TO TRAVEL (LP)	£60
69	Trojan TRLS 16	JIMMY CLIFF (LP)	£30
71	Island ILPS 9159	ANOTHER CYCLE (LP)	£18
72	Island ILPS 9202	THE HARDER THEY COME (LP, pink rim palm tree label)	£20

(see also Jackie Edwards & Jimmy Cliff, James Chambers)

CLIFF DWELLERS
66	Polydor BM 56707	Hang On Stupid/I'm A Superman For You	£15

BUZZ CLIFFORD
61	Fontana TFL 5147	BABY SITTIN' WITH BUZZ CLIFFORD (LP, mono)	£30
61	Fontana STFL 567	BABY SITTIN' WITH BUZZ CLIFFORD (LP, stereo)	£40

JOHN & JULIA CLIFFORD
77	Topic 12TS 311	THE HUMOURS OF LISHEEN (LP)	£20

LINDA CLIFFORD
74	Paramount PARA 3051	After Loving You/Check Out Your Heart	£30

CLIMAX (CHICAGO) BLUES BAND
69	Parlophone R 5809	Like Uncle Charlie/Loving Machine	£30
69	Parlophone PMC 7069	CLIMAX CHICAGO BLUES BAND (LP, yellow/black label, with "sold in the UK.." text, mono)	£150
69	Parlophone PCS 7069	CLIMAX CHICAGO BLUES BAND (LP, yellow/black label, with "sold in the UK.." text, stereo)	£90
70	Parlophone PCS 7084	PLAYS ON (LP, yellow/black labels)	£250
70	Parlophone PCS 7084	PLAYS ON (LP, later issue with boxed Parlophone logo)	£70
70	Harvest SHSP 4009	A LOT OF BOTTLE (LP, no EMI logo on label, fully laminated sleeve)	£60
71	Harvest SHSP 4015	TIGHTLY KNIT (LP, with EMI logo on label, flipback sleeve)	£40
71	Harvest SHSP 4009	A LOT OF BOTTLE (LP, repressing, with EMI logo on label, fully laminated sleeve)	£30
72	Harvest SHSP 4024	RICH MAN (LP)	£25
74	Polydor 2383259	LIVE (LP)	£18
75	BTM 1004	STAMP ALBUM (LP)	£20
76	BTM 1009	GOLD PLATED (LP, gatefold)	£18

(see also Hipster Image)

CLIMAX INVASION
77	Top Secret TS1	The Advertiser (one-sided)	£30

CLIMAX (1)
71	Voice VC1	I'm A Man/I'm A Man Part 2	£45

CLIMB
81	Pinnacle 12 PIN 510	I Can't Forget (A Mother's Crime)/Your Hell (12", p/s)	£15
84	Second Vision SV 004	Poacher Is (As Poacher Does)/The Woodcutter (p/s)	£20

PATSY CLINE
57	Brunswick 05660	A Poor Man's Roses (Or A Rich Man's Gold)/Walkin' After Midnight	£20
61	Brunswick 05861	Crazy/Who Can I Count On	£15
63	Decca 31262	Blue Moon Of Kentucky/Faded Love (export)	£20
62	Brunswick OE 9490	SWEET DREAMS (EP)	£15
62	Brunswick LAT 8394	SHOWCASE (LP)	£15

CLINIC
99	Domino WIGLP 64	CLINIC (LP)	£25
00	Domino WIGLP 78	INTERNATIONAL WRANGLER (LP)	£30
01	Domino WIGLP 100	WALKING WITH THEE (LP)	£20
04	Domino WIGLP 144	WINCHESTER CATHEDRAL (LP)	£18
06	Domino WIGLP 181	VISITATIONS (LP)	£15
10	Domino WIGLP 261X	BUBBLEGUM (2-LP, pink vinyl, transfer, sticker, poster & badge)	£20

BUDDY CLINTON
60	Top Rank JAR 287	Across The Street From Your House/How My Prayers Have Changed	£15

DAVY CLINTON
68	NEMS 56-3855	Can I Bring Back Yesterday/The Girl With The Sun In Her Hair	£35

GEORGE CLINTON
79	ABC ABC 4053	Please Don't Run From Me/Life And Breath (DJ Copy)	£15

(do not see also Parliament, Funkadelic)

LARRY CLINTON
79	Grapevine GRP 120	She's Wanted In Three States/If I Knew	£40
79	Grapevine GRP 120	She's Wanted In Three States/If I Knew (DJ Copy)	£50

CLIQUE (U.K.) (1)
65	Pye 7N 15786	She Ain't No Good/Time Time Time	£100
65	Pye 7N 15853	We Didn't Kiss, Didn't Love, But Now We Do/You've Been Unfair	£175
60s	private pressing	THE CLIQUE (EP, no p/s)	£550
95	Dig The Fuzz DIG 003	THE COMPLETE RECORDINGS 1964/1965 (LP)	£20

(see also Hammersmith Gorillas)

CLIQUE (U.K.) (2)
91	Guild GUIEP 001	INTRODUCING...THE CLIQUE (EP)	£20
94	Detour DR 014	Reggie/She Doesn't Need You Anymore (pic disc, 200 only)	£15
93	Detour DR 006	THE EARLY DAYS (EP)	£15

CLIQUE (U.S.)
69	London HLU 10286	Sugar On Sunday/Superman	£20

CLIVE & DOREEN
68	Treasure Isle TI 7033	What Can I Do/TOMMY MCCOOK: Black Power £60

CLIVE & GLORIA
63	R&B JB 113	Change Of Plan/Little Gloria £40
64	R&B JB 173	Money Money Money/Have I Told You Lately £40
64	King KG 1004	Do The Ska/You Made Me Cry £40

CLIVE & NAOMI
65	Ska Beat JB 181	You Are Mine/Open The Door £50

(see also Desmond Dekker)

CLOCK DVA
81	Fetish FR 2002	THIRST (LP, with insert)..£25
81	Industrial IRC 31	WHITE SOULS IN BLACK SUITS (cassette, with booklet)...............................£30
83	Polydor POLS 1082	ADVANTAGE (LP)..£20

CLOCKWORK CRIMINALS
82	Ace ACE 38	YOUNG AND BOLD (EP) £150

CLOCKWORK ORANGES
66	Ember EMB S 227	Ready Steady/After Tonight £40

CLOCKWORK SOLDIERS
84	Rot ASS 5	Wet Dreams/Suicide/In The Name Of Science (p/s) £15

CLONE 81
81	FMR 058	Product Of Society/Into The Recess (hand-made p/s).................................£25

CLOR
05	Regal REG 122	CLOR (LP as 2 x 12")...£25

CLOSE LOBSTERS
89	Caff CAFF 4	Just Too Bloody Stupid/All The Little Boys And Girls (fold-out, p/s, insert) £20
15	Fire FIRELP 397	FIRESTATION TOWERS (3-LP compilation) £20

CLAUDE CLOUD
57	MGM MGM 946	The Beat/Around The Horn (as Claude Cloud & His Orchestra)........................£15
55	MGM MGM-EP 517	LET'S GO CATSTATIC NO. 1 (EP, as Claude Cloud & Thunderclaps) £15
56	MGM MGM-D 142	ROCK 'N' ROLL (10" LP)..£80

(see also Sonny Thompson, Sam 'The Man' Taylor)

CLOUD CONTROL
11	Infectious INFECT127LP	BLISS RELEASE (LP)...£30
12	Infectious INFECT163LP	DREAM CAVE (LP) £18

CLOUD NINE
93	Acid Jazz JAZID 87P	I Feel It (12", p/s, promo-only, withdrawn)..£18
93	Acid Jazz JAZID 78	MILLENNIUM (LP, withdrawn) £30

CLOUD (1)
75	Kingsway DOVE 16	FREE TO FLY (LP)..£20
77	Kingsway DOVE 44	WATERED GARDEN (LP, gatefold sleeve) £30
78	Kingsway DOVE 62	THE RESTING PLACE (LP)...£20
82	Kingsway KMR 369	HALLOWED GROUND (LP, with insert)..£15
85	Songs Of Fellow SFR103	THE PROMISE (LP) £15

CLOUD (2)
80	Flashback FLASH 001	All Night Long (Vocal)/All Night Long (Instrumental) (12", white labels most with sticker on one side)..£100
81	Flashback FLASH 002	Take It To The Top/All Night Long (Remix) (12")..£50
81	Flashback FLASH 003	Party Life/The Rio (12") £80
83	Rygel RYG 7	Steppin' Out With You/Rico Rico/Steppin' Out Jam (12")..............................£20

(see also Style X)

CLOUDS (1)
69	Island WIP 6055	Heritage/Make No Bones About It £20
69	Island WIP 6067	Scrapbook/Carpenter...£20
69	Island ILPS 9100	THE CLOUDS SCRAPBOOK (LP, gatefold sleeve, first pressing with black/orange circle logo)..£250
69	Island ILPS 9100	THE CLOUDS SCRAPBOOK (LP, second pressing, circle logo)..........................£100
69	Island ILPS 9100	THE CLOUDS SCRAPBOOK (LP, later pressing 'pink rim palm tree')..................£25
71	Chrysalis ILPS 9151	WATERCOLOUR DAYS (LP, gatefold sleeve, green label with Island logo and Island address in white)...£50

CLOVEN HOOF
82	Elemental EM 001	OPENING RITUAL (12" EP) £80
84	Neat NEAT 1013	CLOVEN HOOF (LP)...£20
86	Trojan CH 002	FIGHTING BACK (LP, with poster)...£25
86	Trojan CH 002	FIGHTING BACK (LP, without poster)..£20

CLOVER
69	Liberty LBS 83340	CLOVER (LP) £30
71	Liberty LBS 83487	FORTY-NINER (LP) £30

(see also Huey Lewis & News)

CLOVERS
56	London HLE 8229	Nip Sip/If I Could Be Loved By You (gold label lettering) £400
56	London HLE 8229	Nip Sip/If I Could Be Loved By You (silver label lettering).............................£150
56	London HLE 8229	Nip Sip/If I Could Be Loved By You (78) £20
56	London HLE 8314	Love, Love, Love/Hey, Doll Baby £250
56	London HLE 8314	Love, Love, Love/Hey, Doll Baby (78)..£20

MINT VALUE £

56	London HLE 8334	From The Bottom Of My Heart/Your Tender Lips	£150
56	London HLE 8334	From The Bottom Of My Heart/Your Tender Lips	£20
58	London HL 7048	Wishing For Your Love/All About You (export issue)	£150
58	HMV POP 542	In The Good Old Summertime/Idaho	£30
59	London HLT 8949	Love Potion No. 9/Stay Awhile (triangular centre)	£50
59	London HLT 8949	Love Potion No. 9/Stay Awhile (round centre)	£35
59	London HLT 8949	Love Potion No. 9/Stay Awhile (78 rpm)	£15
60	London HLT 9122	Lovey/One Mint Julep	£30
60	London HLT 9154	Easy Lovin'/I'm Confessin' (That I Love You)	£40
61	HMV POP 883	Honey Dripper/Have Gun	£25
68	Atlantic 584 160	Your Cash Ain't Nothin' But Trash/I've Got My Eyes On You	£15
69	Atlantic 587 162	LOVE BUG (LP)	£50

CLOWN
72	CBS 7906	Lord Of The Ringside/Rumania	£40

CLOX ITALIA
82	B Flat FLAT 2	LookingThe Part/Leave It In (p/s, as Clox)	£15

CLUTHA (FOLK GROUP)
71	Argo ZFB 18	SCOTIA! (LP, as Clutha Folk Group)	£15

CMETRIC
94	B12 B1210	Cmetric (12", pink vinyl, 300 only)	£35
94	B12 B1210	Cmetric (12")	£30

C.M.J.
68	Impression IMP 102	I Can't Do It All By Myself/Nothing At All	£45
71	Mother MOT 3	La La La/Step Around It	£50
65	Impression EPIM 501	THE C.M.J. TRIO (EP)	£50
69	Impression IMPL 1001	C.M.J. LIVE AT THE BANKHOUSE (LP, private pressing)	£80

C.M.U. (CONTEMPORARY MUSIC UNIT)
72	Transatlantic BIG 508	Heart Of The Sun/Doctor Am I Normal?	£15
71	Transatlantic TRA 237	OPEN SPACES (LP, gatefold sleeve, clear plastic with foam inner, this price for mint record that has not reacted and been marked by plastic/foam inner)	£150
71	Transatlantic TRA 237	OPEN SPACES (LP, gatefold sleeve, clear plastic with foam inner, this price for mint sleeve with record that has been marked by chemical reaction to the plastic/foam inner)	£50
72	Transatlantic TRA 259	SPACE CABARET (LP, with lyric insert)	£100

(see also Chopyn)

COACHOUSE RHYTHM SECTION
77	Ice ICE 3 12	Nobody's Got Time/Nobody's Got Time	£20
77	Ice ICE 3 12	Nobody Got Time/Time Warp (12")	£80

(see also Eddy Grant)

COASTERS
57	London HLE 8450	Searchin'/Young Blood	£75
57	London HL 7021	Searchin'/Young Blood (export issue)	£30
58	London HLE 8665	Yakety Yak/Zing! Went The Strings Of My Heart	£15
58	London HLE 8729	The Shadow Knows/Sorry But I'm Gonna Have To Pass	£50
59	London HLE 8882	Along Came Jones/That Is Rock And Roll (silver top label)	£15
59	London HLE 8938	Poison Ivy/I'm A Hog For You	£15

(The above 45s were originally issued with triangular centres, later round centre copies are worth half to two-thirds these values.)

60	London HLE 9020	What About Us/Run Red Run	£20
60	London HLK 9111	Besame Mucho (Parts 1 & 2)	£50
60	London HLK 9111	Besame Mucho (Parts 1 & 2) (78)	£50
60	London HLK 9151	Wake Me, Shake Me/Stewball	£20
60	London HLK 9208	Shoppin' For Clothes/The Snake And The Bookworm	£25
61	London HLK 9293	Wait A Minute/Thumbin' A Ride	£15
61	London HLK 9349	Little Egypt/Keep On Rolling	£15
61	London HLK 9413	Girls! Girls! Girls! (Parts 1 & 2)	£15
62	London HLK 9493	(Ain't That) Just Like Me/Bad Blood	£15
64	London HLK 9863	T'Ain't Nothin' To Me/Speedo's Back In Town	£15
67	CBS 2749	Soul Pad/Down Home Girl	£15
72	Stateside SS 2201	Cool Jerk/Talkin' 'Bout A Woman	£30
59	London REE 1203	THE COASTERS (EP)	£25
60	London HA-E 2237	GREATEST HITS (LP)	£50
63	London HA-K 8033	COAST ALONG WITH THE COASTERS (LP)	£50
66	Atlantic 588 134	COAST ALONG WITH THE COASTERS (LP, reissue)	£15
67	Atlantic 590 015	ALL TIME GREATEST HITS (LP)	£15
71	Joy JOYS 189	HUNGRY (LP)	£15

COASTERS (JAMAICA)
69	Doctor Bird DB 1182	Stoney Hill/RICK RODRIGUES & JOHNNY MOORE : Continental Shuffle	£100

COAST ROAD DRIVE
74	Deram SML 1113	DELICIOUS AND REFRESHING (LP)	£60

C.O.B. (CLIVE'S ORIGINAL BAND)
72	Polydor 2058 260	Blue Morning/Bones	£15
71	CBS 69010	SPIRIT OF LOVE (LP, gatefold sleeve, orange label)	£200
72	Polydor Folk Mill 2383 161	MOYSHE McSTIFF & THE TARTAN LANCERS OF THE SACRED HEART (LP, gatefold sleeve, red label)	£400
06	Sunbeam SBRL2LP 5029	MOYSHE McSTIFF & THE TARTAN LANCERS OF THE SACRED HEART (2-LP, reissue)	£20

(see also Famous Jug Band, Incredible String Band)

COBBLERS
70	Emblem JDR 314	**WARM ARE THE SOUNDS** (LP)	£30

COBBLERS LAST
79	Banshee BAN 1012	**BOOT IN THE DOOR** (LP, with insert)	£80

COBBS
69	Amalgamated AMG 845	**Hot Buttered Corn/COUNT MACHUKI: It Is I**	£40
69	Amalgamated AMG 849	**Space Doctor/LLOYD & DEVON: Baby Reggae**	£100

BILLY COBHAM
74	Atlantic K50037	**CROSSWINDS** (LP)	£15
73	Atlantic K40506	**SPECTRUM** (LP, gatefold)	£20

COBRA (1)
78	Rip Off RIP 3	**Looking For A Lady/Graveyard Boogie** (p/s)	£35

(see also Speed)

COBRA (2)
85	Criminal Response COBRA 2	**WARRIORS OF THE DEAD** (LP)	£18
87	Ebony EBON 39	**BACK FROM THE DEAD** (LP)	£18

COCHISE
70	United Artists UAS 29117	**COCHISE** (LP, gatefold sleeve, orange/pink label)	£30
70	Liberty LBS 83428	**SWALLOW TALES** (LP, black label)	£20
72	United Artists UAS 29286	**SO FAR** (LP)	£25

(see also B.J. Cole, Mick Grabham)

DIB COCHRAN & EARWIGS
70	Bell BLL 1121	**Oh Baby/Universal Love**	£500

(see also Marc Bolan, Tyrannosaurus Rex, Tony Visconti, Rick Wakeman)

EDDIE COCHRAN
78s
57	London HLU 8386	**20 Flight Rock/Dark Lonely Street**	£50
57	London HLU 8433	**Sittin' In The Balcony/Completely Sweet**	£60
58	London HLU 8702	**Summertime Blues/Love Again**	£70
59	London HLU 8792	**C'mon Everybody/Don't Ever Let Me Go**	£90
59	London HLU 8880	**Teenage Heaven/I Remember**	£100
59	London HLU 8944	**Somethin' Else/Boll Weevil Song**	£250
60	London HLW 9022	**Hallelujah, I Love Her So/Little Angel**	£200
95	Cruisin' The 50s CASS 001	**Three Steps To Heaven/Cut Across Shorty** (reissue, 300 only)	£40
96	Cruisin' The 50s CASB 004	**Week-End/Cherished Memories** (reissue, 400 only)	£30

SINGLES
57	London HLU 8386	**20 Flight Rock/Dark Lonely Street** (silver writing, triangular centre)	£100
57	London HLU 8386	**20 Flight Rock/Dark Lonely Street** (silver-top label with triangular centre)	£125
57	London HLU 8386	**20 Flight Rock/Dark Lonely Street** (round centre)	£50
57	London HLU 8433	**Sittin' In The Balcony/Completely Sweet**	£350
58	London HLU 8702	**Summertime Blues/Love Again**	£25
59	London HLU 8792	**C'mon Everybody/Don't Ever Let Me Go**	£25
59	London HLU 8880	**Teenage Heaven/I Remember**	£25
59	London HL 7082	**Teenage Heaven/Boll Weevil Song** (export issue)	£30
59	London HLU 8944	**Somethin' Else/Boll Weevil Song**	£30
60	London HLW 9022	**Hallelujah, I Love Her So/Little Angel** (triangular centre)	£30

(The above 45s were originally issued with triangular centres, later round centre copies are worth half these values unless otherwise stated.)

60	London HLW 9022	**Hallelujah, I Love Her So/Little Angel** (round centre)	£15
60	London HLG 9196	**Sweetie Pie/Lonely**	£40
61	London HLG 9362	**Weekend/Cherished Memories**	£20
61	London HLG 9460	**Jeannie, Jeannie, Jeannie/Pocketful Of Hearts**	£20
61	London HLG 9464	**Pretty Girl/Teresa**	£35
61	London HLG 9467	**Undying Love/Stockin's 'n' Shoes**	£50
62	Liberty LIB 10049	**Never/Think Of Me**	£20
63	Liberty LIB 10088	**My Way/Rock And Roll Blues**	£15
63	Liberty LIB 10108	**Drive-In Show/I Almost Lost My Mind**	£15
64	Liberty LIB 10151	**Skinny Jim/Nervous Breakdown** (black label)	£60
66	Liberty LIB 10249	**Three Stars/Somethin' Else**	£20
67	Liberty LIB 10276	**Three Steps To Heaven/Eddie's Blues**	£20

EPs
59	London REU 1214	**C'MON EVERYBODY** (orange sleeve, triangular centre)	£30
59	London REU 1214	**C'MON EVERYBODY** (orange sleeve, round centre)	£20
59	London REU 1214	**C'MON EVERYBODY** (yellow sleeve, silver-top label)	£30
59	London REU 1214	**C'MON EVERYBODY** (yellow sleeve, round centre)	£20
60	London REU 1239	**SOMETHIN' ELSE** (triangular centre)	£30
60	London REU 1239	**SOMETHIN' ELSE** (round centre)	£20
60	London REG 1262	**EDDIE'S HITS**	£30
61	London REG 1301	**CHERISHED MEMORIES OF EDDIE COCHRAN**	£30
62	Liberty LEP 2052	**NEVER TO BE FORGOTTEN**	£30
63	Liberty LEP 2090	**CHERISHED MEMORIES** (VOL.1)	£20
63	Liberty LEP 2111	**C'MON EVERYBODY** (reissue)	£15
63	Liberty LEP 2122	**SOMETHIN' ELSE** (reissue)	£15
63	Liberty LEP 2123	**CHERISHED MEMORIES OF EDDIE COCHRAN** (reissue)	£15
63	Liberty LEP 2124	**EDDIE'S HITS** (reissue)	£15
64	Liberty LEP 2165	**C'MON AGAIN**	£60

MINT VALUE £

64	Liberty LEP 2180	STOCKIN'S 'N' SHOES	£25

ALBUMS
58	London HA-U 2093	SINGIN' TO MY BABY (initial pressing with laminated rear sleeve)	£250
58	London HA-U 2093	SINGIN' TO MY BABY (without laminated rear sleeve)	£100
60	London HA-G 2267	THE EDDIE COCHRAN MEMORIAL ALBUM	£80
62	Liberty LBY 1109	CHERISHED MEMORIES	£50
63	Liberty LBY 1127	THE EDDIE COCHRAN MEMORIAL ALBUM (reissue)	£15
63	Liberty LBY 1158	SINGIN' TO MY BABY (reissue)	£20
64	Liberty LBY 1205	MY WAY	£40
88	Liberty ECB 1	THE EDDIE COCHRAN BOX SET (6-LP box set with booklet)	£40

HANK COCHRAN
68	Monument LMO 5020	HEART OF HANK (LP)	£15

JACKIE LEE COCHRAN
57	Brunswick 05669	Ruby Pearl (with Jimmy Pruett)/Mama Don't You Think I Know	£2000
57	Brunswick 05669	Ruby Pearl (with Jimmy Pruett)/Mama Don't You Think I Know (78)	£250

COCK & WOODPECKERS
71	Newbeat 93	Every Day And Every Night/I Fall In Love Everyday	£15

BRUCE COCKBURN
71	True North WTN 003	HIGH WINDS WHITE SKY (LP)	£15
71	True North TNX 7	SUNWHEEL DANCE (LP)	£15

JARVIS COCKER
06	Rough Trade RTRADLP 340	THE JARVIS COCKER RECORD (LP, with bonus one-sided 7")	£35
09	Rough Trade RTRADLP 540	FURTHER COMPLICATIONS (LP with free 12")	£25

(see also Pulp, Relaxed Muscle)

JOE COCKER
64	Decca F 11974	I'll Cry Instead/Precious Words	£250
60s	Oak	JOE COCKER (EP, existence unconfirmed)	£500
67	Action ACT 002 EP	RAG GOES MAD AT THE MOJO (33rpm EP, 2 tracks by Joe Cocker's Blues Band, in conjunction with Sheffield University rag magazine Twikker)	£50
69	Regal Zono. LRZ 1006	WITH A LITTLE HELP FROM MY FRIENDS (LP, mono, red/silver label with "sold in the U.K..." text)	£120
69	Regal Zono. SLRZ 1006	WITH A LITTLE HELP FROM MY FRIENDS (LP, stereo, red/silver label with "sold in the U.K..." text)	£70
69	Regal Zono. SLRZ 1011	JOE COCKER! (LP, red/silver label)	£30
70	A&M AMLS 6002	MAD DOGS & ENGLISHMEN (2-LP, multifold gatefold sleeve, brown label)	£20
71	Fly HIFLY 3	COCKER HAPPY (LP, gatefold sleeve)	£20

(see also Grease Band, Made In Sheffield)

COCKERSDALE
85	EFDSS ESLP 001	PROSPECT PROVIDENCE (LP)	£20

COCKNEY REJECTS
79	Small Wonder SW 19	Flares'N'Slippers/Police Star/I Wanna Be A Star (p/s)	£15
80	Zonophone ZONO 101	GREATEST HITS VOLUME 1 (LP)	£20
80	Zonophone ZONO 102	GREATEST HITS VOLUME 2 (LP, with inner sleeve & poster)	£20
81	Zonophone ZEM 101	GREATEST HITS VOLUME 3 (LIVE AND LOUD) (LP, gatefold)	£15
85	Wonderful World WOW LP 2	UNHEARD REJECTS (LP)	£15

COCK SPARRER
77	Decca FR 13710	Runnin' Riot/Sister Suzie (demos in p/s)	£200
77	Decca FR 13710	Runnin' Riot/Sister Suzie (no p/s)	£40
77	Decca FR 13732	We Love You/Chip On My Shoulder (no p/s)	£20
77	Decca LFR 13732	We Love You/Chip On My Shoulder (12" p/s, with photo insert, 7,500 only)	£25
82	Carrere CAR 255	England Belongs To Me/Argy Bargy (p/s, beware of bootlegs With "fuzzy" looking label logo on sleeve)	£40
83	Razor RAZ 9	SHOCK TROOPS (LP)	£30
84	Syndicate SYNLP 7	RUNNIN' RIOT IN 84 (LP)	£35
86	Razor RAZ 26	TRUE GRIT (LP)	£35
87	Link LP 005	LIVE AND LOUD (LP)	£15

COCKTAIL CABINET
67	Page One POF 046	Puppet On A String/Breathalyser	£40

COCOA TEA
88	Live And Love LLD 87	Lonesome Side/ADMIRAL TIBET: Reality Time (12")	£30

COCONUT DOGS
80	Mongrel Music MM 001	Lipstick On The Glass/The Neighbours/Mannequin (no p/s, 1000 only)	£50

COCO STEEL AND LOVEBOMB
89	Instant INST 10	Frenzy/Version	£20
91	Instant VU 004	Feel It/Discotechno/Discodub (12")	£15
91	Instant VU 005	Touch It (African Plain Mix)/(Butch Mix)/(Sandeed Shore Mix) (12")	£20

COCTEAU TWINS
93	Fontana CTX 1	Evangeline/Mud & Dark/Summer Blink (12", p/s, numbered, insert)	£20
94	Fontana CTX 2	Bluebeard/Three Swept/Ice-Pulse (12", gatefold p/s)	£15
95	Fontana CT 3	Rilkean Heart/Golden Vein//Pink Orange Red/Half Gifts (2 x 7", p/s)	£20
96	Fontana CTX 4	OTHERNESS EP (12", p/s, inner)	£20
96	Fontana CTX 6	Violaine/Alice/Tranquil Eye (12", p/s)	£20
91	4AD CT BOX 1	COCTEAU TWINS - SINGLES COLLECTION (9-CD box set)	£40
82	4AD CAD 411	GARLANDS (LP)	£30
83	4AD CAD 313	HEAD OVER HEELS (LP)	£30

84	4AD CAD 412	TREASURE (LP, inner)	£30
86	4AD CAD 602	VICTORIALAND (LP, inner)	£30
88	4AD CAD 807	BLUE BELL KNOLL (LP, tri-foldout sleeve, inner)	£30
90	4AD CAD 0012	HEAVEN OR LAS VEGAS (LP, with inner)	£35
91	4AD CT BOX 1	SINGLES COLLECTION (10-CD box set)	£50
93	Fontana 518259-1	FOUR CALENDAR CAFE (LP)	£125
96	Fontana 514-501-1	MILK AND KISSES (LP, inner)	£125
05	4AD CTBOX 2	LULLABIES TO VIOLAINE (4-CD box set, tactile cover)	£40
10	Vinyl 180 VIN180LP024	BOX SET ONE (5-LP, 1 x 12", box set)	£125
14	4AD CAD 3420	HEAVEN OR LAS VEGAS (LP, 180 gm reissue, inner, download card)	£18
15	4AD CAD 3509	THE PINK OPAQUE (LP, compilation, reissue)	£15
17	Mercury 5735405	FOUR CALENDAR CAFE (2-LP reissue, purple/blue vinyl)	£25
17	Mercury 5735401	MILK AND KISSES (2-LP reissue, white vinyl)	£25

(see also This Mortal Coil, Felt, Massive Attack, Harold Budd, Lonely Is An Eyesore, The Future Sound Of London, Elizabeth Fraser, Drowning Craze)

CODEK
80	MCA MCAT 550	Me Me Me (Full Length Version)/Demo (12", p/s)	£25
82	Island 12WIP 6764	Tim Toum/Closer (12", p/s)	£40

CODE 071
92	Reinforced RIVET 1213	A London Sumtin' (12")	£20

C.O.D.S
66	Stateside SS 489	Michael (The Lover)/Cry No More	£25
66	Stateside SS 489	Michael (The Lover)/Cry No More (DJ copy)	£60

TONY CODY
72	Pye 7N 45153	Walk On By/(Ain't It) Funny How Time Slips By	£30
72	Pye 7N 45153	Walk On By/(Ain't It) Funny How Time Slips By (DJ Copy)	£50

JAMIE COE
59	Parlophone R 4600	Summertime Symphony/There's Gonna Be A Day	£150
60	Parlophone R 4621	School Day Blues/I'll Go On Loving You	£100
61	HMV POP 991	How Low Is Low/Little Dear Little Darling	£25
63	London HLX 9713	The Fool/I've Got That Feeling Again	£20

PETER & CHRIS COE
72	Trailer LER 2077	OPEN THE DOOR AND LET US IN (LP)	£25
76	Trailer LER 2098	OUT OF SEASON, OUT OF RHYME (LP, yellow label)	£20
79	Highway SHY 7007	GAME OF ALL FOURS (LP)	£15

(see also Bandoggs)

TONY COE (QUINTET)
61	Philips B 10784L	SWINGIN' TILL THE GIRLS COME HOME (LP)	£50
67	Columbia SCX 6170	TONY'S BASEMENT (LP)	£100
78	Lee Lambert LAM100	COE-EXISTENCE (LP)	£20

TONY COE & BRIAN LEMON TRIO
68	'77' SEU 12/41	TONY COE AND BRIAN LEMON TRIO (LP)	£30

(see also Robert Farnon & Tony Coe)

JACK & CHARLIE COEN
77	Topic 12TS 337	THE BRANCH LINE (LP)	£22

CARLTON COFFE
78	Justice JUS 110	Chant Away/Version (12")	£45

CARLTON COFFEE
78	Shebazz FME 003	Music Revoluion/Music Revolution Part 2	£25

COFFEE SET
69	Fontana LPS 16503	SAY IT WITH MUSIC (LP)	£15

DENNIS COFFEY
71	A&M AMS 875	Scorpio/Sad Song (with Detroit Guitar Band)	£20
70	A&M AMLS 68035	EVOLUTION (LP)	£25
71	A&M AMLS 68072	GOIN' FOR MYSELF (LP)	£20
74	Sussex LPSX 9	INSTANT COFFEY (LP)	£20

ALMA COGAN
53	HMV 7M 106	I Went To Your Wedding/You Belong To Me	£15
53	HMV 7M 107	To Be Loved By You/The Homing Waltz (B-side with Larry Day)	£15
53	HMV 7M 166	Over And Over Again/Isn't Life Wonderful (with Les Howerd)	£15
54	HMV 7M 173	Ricochet (Rick-O-Shay)/The Moon Is Blue	£15
54	HMV 7M 188	Bell Bottom Blues/Love Me Again	£25
54	HMV 7M 196	Make Love To Me/Said The Little Moment	£15
54	HMV 7M 219	The Little Shoemaker/Chiqui-Chaqui (Chick-ee Chock-ee)	£20
54	HMV 7M 228	Little Things Mean A Lot/Canoodlin' Rag	£15
54	HMV 7M 239	Skinnie Minnie (Fishtail)/What Am I Going To Do, Ma (The Doo-Ma Song)	£20
54	HMV 7M 269	This Ole House/Skokiaan	£20
54	HMV 7M 271	I Can't Tell A Waltz From A Tango/Christmas Cards	£20
55	HMV 7M 301	Tweedlee-Dee/More Than Ever Now	£15
55	HMV 7M 316	Got'n Idea/Give A Fool A Chance	£15
55	HMV 7M 337	Never Do A Tango With An Eskimo/Twenty Tiny Fingers	£15
56	HMV 7M 367	Love And Marriage/Sycamore Tree	£15
56	HMV 7M 415	Why Do Fools Fall In Love?/ (The Same Thing Happen With) The Birds And The Bees?	£20
56	HMV POP 239	Mama Teach Me To Dance/I'm In Love Again	£20
56	HMV POP 261	In The Middle Of The House/Two Innocent Hearts	£20

MINT VALUE £

57	HMV POP 284	You, Me And Us/Three Brothers	£15
57	HMV POP 317	Whatever Lola Wants (Lola Gets)/Lucky Lips	£30
64	Columbia DB 7390	It's You/I Knew Right Away	£20
65	Columbia DB 7652	Snakes And Snails (And Puppy Dog Tails)/How Many Days, How Many Nights	£20
58	HMV CLP 1152	I LOVE TO SING (LP)	£30
61	Columbia 33SX 1345	ALMA SINGS WITH YOU IN MIND (LP, mono)	£20
62	Columbia 33SX 1469	HOW ABOUT LOVE! (LP, mono)	£20
61	Columbia SCX 3391	ALMA SINGS WITH YOU IN MIND (LP)	£30
62	Columbia SCX 3459	HOW ABOUT LOVE! (LP, stereo)	£30
67	Columbia SX 6130	ALMA (LP)	£30

(see also Ronnie Hilton, Angela & Fans)

DON COGAN
58	MGM MGM 984	The Fountain Of Youth/I'm Takin' Over	£25

SHAYE COGAN
60	MGM MGM 1063	Mean To Me/They Said It Couldn't Be Done	£30

(see also Buddy Morrow)

ALAN COHEN BAND
72	Argo ZDA 159	BLACK, BROWN AND BEIGE (LP)	£80

LEONARD COHEN
68	CBS BPG 63241	SONGS OF LEONARD COHEN (LP, orange label, with stickered sleeve; mono)	£35
68	CBS (S)BPG 63241	SONGS OF LEONARD COHEN (LP, orange label, with stickered sleeve; stereo)	£30
68	CBS 63241	SONGS OF LEONARD COHEN (LP, orange label, re-pressing w/out prefix)	£15
69	CBS M 63587	SONGS FROM A ROOM (LP, laminated sleeve, mono)	£45
69	CBS 63587	SONGS FROM A ROOM (LP, laminated sleeve, stereo)	£25
71	CBS S 69004	SONGS OF LOVE & HATE (LP, orange label, with booklet)	£25
73	CBS 65224	LIVE SONGS (LP)	£15
74	CBS 69087	NEW SKIN FOR THE OLD CEREMONY (LP)	£20
75	CBS 69161	GREATEST HITS (LP, inner and insert, orange/yellow vinyl)	£20
77	CBS 86042	DEATH OF A LADIES MAN (LP, gatefold)	£20
79	CBS 86097	RECENT SONGS (LP)	£18
84	CBS 465569	VARIOUS POSITIONS (LP)	£20
88	CBS 460642	I'M YOUR MAN (LP)	£15
92	Columbia COL 472498 1	THE FUTURE (LP)	£40
97	Simply Vinyl SVLP 008	SONGS FROM A ROOM (LP, reissue, 180gm vinyl)	£20
10	Music On Vinyl MOVLP 193	SONGS FROM THE ROAD (2-LP)	£20
12	Columbia C 79871	OLD IDEAS (LP)	£20

PHILIP COHRAN AND THE ARTISTIC HERITAGE ENSEMBLE
10	Jazzman JMAN 077	THE ZULU 45S COLLECTION (3 x 7" box set)	£35

COIL (1)
79	North'ton Wood H. HAV 1	Motor Industry/Alcoholic Stork (p/s)	£25

COIL (2)
85	F & F/K.422 FFK 512	Panic/Tainted Love/Aqua Regis (12", red vinyl, 'hair'-textured p/s)	£25
85	F & F/K.422 FFK 512	Panic/Tainted Love/Aqua Regis (12", black vinyl, 'hair'-textured p/s)	£15
86	Force & Form/K.422	The Anal Staircase/Blood From The Air/Ravenous (12", p/s, on clear vinyl)	£25
86	Force & Form/K.422 ROTA 121	The Anal Staircase/Blood From The Air/Ravenous (12", p/s)	£15
87	Solar Lodge 001	HELLRAISER (10" EP, coloured vinyl [clear or pink, 500 each])	£25
90	Shock SX 002	Wrong Eye/Scope (pink p/s, signed & lettered A-Z, 26 only)	£45
90	Shock SX 002	Wrong Eye/Scope (974 with numbered white p/s)	£15
90	Shock SX 002	Wrong Eye/Scope (green p/s, 300 only, some with gold/black sticker)	£25
92	Clawfist 22	Airborne Bells/Is Suicide A Solution (p/s, 1,250 only)	£25
94	Loci S1	Themes From Blue (p/s, 23 on yellow vinyl)	£60
94	Loci S1	Themes From Blue (p/s, 1,000 on blue vinyl)	£20
94	Eskaton 001	Nasa Arab/First Dark Ride (12", stickered plain black sleeve, 2,500 only)	£15
95	Eskaton 003	PHILM (10" EP, with poster, 50 on clear vinyl in handmade p/s)	£60
84	FFK1	SCATOLOGY (LP, with pasted anal staircase postcard, some with poster)	£200
86	Threshold ROTA 1	HORSE ROTORVATOR (LP, with A5 card insert & stickers)	£20
87	Threshold House LOCI 1	GOLD IS THE METAL (LP, red vinyl; with bonus 7": "The Wheel"/The Wheal, unfinished proof sleeve without writing, 25 only)	£200
87	Threshold House LOCI 1	GOLD IS THE METAL (LP, box set with 7", "The Wheel"/"The Wheal", poster & booklet in black linen folder, embossed sleeve, autographed, 55 only)	£300
87	Threshold House LOCI 1	GOLD IS THE METAL (LP, red vinyl [150 only] with inner sleeve; with bonus 7": "The Wheel"/"The Wheal")	£70
87	Threshold House LOCI 1	GOLD IS THE METAL (LP, clear vinyl [500 only], with inner sleeve; with bonus 7": "The Wheel"/"The Wheal")	£50
90	Normal NORMAL 77	GOLD IS THE METAL (LP, black vinyl re-pressing with 7": The Wheel/"Keel Hauler")	£18
95	Eskaton 007	WORSHIP THE GLITCH (2 x 10" LP, as Coil Vs. Elph, with insert, 50 with white optical plastic cover)	£100
95	Eskaton 007	WORSHIP THE GLITCH (2 x 10" LP, as Coil Vs. Elph, with insert, 2,000 only)	£50
99	Acme/Prescription DRUG8	ASTRAL DISASTER (LP, 99 copies signed and numbered by Balance And Christopherson, with insert, artwork in plastic bag)	£100
99	Chalice GRAAL LP002	MUSICK TO PLAY IN THE DARK VOL 1 (LP, 500 only, white vinyl)	£200
00	Threshold House LOC114	ASTRAL DISASTER (LP re-issue, 100 copies, grey vinyl signed lyric sheet and art	£60
00	Chalice GRAAL LP004	MUSICK TO PLAY IN THE DARK VOL 2 (2 x LP, white vinyl, one side etched)	£200
00	Chalice GRAAL LP004	MUSICK TO PLAY IN THE DARK VOL 2 (2 x LP, 100 copies with blue/green vinyl)	£250
00	Chalice GRAAL LP004	MUSICK TO PLAY IN THE DARK VOL 2 (2 x LP, translucent purple, 4th side etched with picture of moon and has 'gold leaf' attached, art print on cover, 2 part print inserts – signed – 60 copies only)	£300
00	Chalice GRAAL LP004	MUSICK VOL 2 (26 copy "trauma edition" lettered A-Z white sleeves smeared with	£70

		Balance's blood.)..	
02	Eskaton 28	TIME MACHINES (Coil as Time Machines) (2 x LP, 1,000 55 clear, signed)	£50
02	Eskaton 28	TIME MACHINES (Coil as Time Machines) (2 x LP, 1,000 only)	£40

(see also Psychic TV, Throbbing Gristle, Current 93)

ALVADEAN COKER
55	London HLU 8191	Do Dee Oodle De Do I'm In Love/We're Gonna Bop	£750
55	London HLU 8191	Do Dee Oodle De Do I'm In Love/We're Gonna Bop (78)..	£60

SANDY COKER & HIS BAND
54	London HL 8109	Meadowlark Melody/Toss Over	£40

COKI
05	DMZ DMZ 004	Officer/Mood Dub (12")...	£20
06	Tempa TEMPA 024	Tortured/Shattered (12")...	£15
07	Big Apple BAM 009	Red Eye/Beep/The Sign/Hidden Treasure (12")...	£18
07	SMZ DMZ 013	Spongebob/The End (12")..	£20

RIC COLBECK QUARTET
70	Fontana 6383 001	THE SUN IS COMING UP (LP)..	£75

COLD BLOOD
70	Atlantic 588 218	COLD BLOOD (LP, plum/red label)	£50
71	Atlantic 2400 102	SISYPHUS (LP, gatefold sleeve, plum/red label)	£18
74	Warner Bros K 56047	LYDIA (LP)...	£15

COLD CAVE
11	Matador OLE 921 1	CHERISH THE LIGHT YEARS (LP)...	£20

COLDCUT
91	Ninja Tune ZEN12 004	Jade (12")...	£15
94	Ninja Tune ZEN 12	PHILOSOPHY (2xLP, promo, different mixes to commercial release).............................	£20
94	Ninja Tune ZEN 12	PHILOSOPHY (2xLP)...	£15
97	Ninja Tune ZEN 30	LET US PLAY (2-LP)...	£30

COLD FLY
73	Bus Stop BUS 1007	Caterpillar/Yesterday Started For Judy	£15

COLDPLAY
SINGLES
98	private pressing HGCD 633	SAFETY EP: Bigger, Stronger/No More Keeping My Feet On The Ground/Such A Rush (CD, 500 only, slimline jewel case)	£500
99	Fierce Panda NING 68	Brothers And Sisters/Easy To Please (wraparound p/s, 1000 only)	£30
99	EMI EMI CDR 6528	THE BLUE ROOM EP (Bigger, Stronger/Don't Panic/See You Soon/High Speed/Such A Rush) (CD, digipak)	£30
99	EMI EMI 12R 6528	THE BLUE ROOM EP (Bigger, Stronger/Don't Panic/See You Soon/High Speed/Such A Rush) (12", numbered sleeve)	£200
00	Parlophone R 6538	Yellow/Help Is Around The Corner (7" ltd edn. Numbered single p/s).........................	£25
01	COLDXMAS01	Mince Spies/Have Yourself A Merry Little Christmas/Yellow (Alpha Mix) (CD EP, 1000 only, given away with Coldplayground fanzine)	£150
01	Parlophone 07243 879080-6-2	Don't Panic/You Only Live Twice (live)/Bigger Stronger (live) (12" p/s, withdrawn)........	£60
07	Parlophone 388 3247	THE SINGLES 1999 - 2006 (15x7" box set)	£120

ALBUMS
00	Parlophone 5277831	PARACHUTES (LP, printed inner)...	£100
02	Parlophone 540 5041	A RUSH OF BLOOD TO THE HEAD (LP, gatefold, printed inner)	£80
05	Parlophone 474 7861	X&Y (2LP, gatefold, slip case, printed inners, poster).....................................	£70
08	Parlophone 212 1141	VIVA LA VIDA OR DEATH AND ALL HIS FRIENDS (LP, gatefold, printed inners, booklet)	£40
11	Parlophone P729 7262	MYLO XYLOTO (LP picture disc, CD, pop up sleeve, stencil, stickers, book).................	£50
11	EMI 087 5531	MYLO XYLOTO (LP, die-cut sleeve, poster)...	£25
14	Parlophone 825646298815	GHOST STORIES (LP, gatefold, printed inner, 180g)...	£20
15	Parlophone 0825646982158	A HEAD FULL OF DREAMS (2LP, die-cut sleeve, printed inners, lyric insert)	£50
15	Parlophone 0825646982158	A HEAD FULL OF DREAMS (2LP, pink & blue vinyl, die-cut sleeve, limited)....................	£50
18	Parlophone 0190295570422	LIVE IN BUENOS AIRES/LIVE IN SAO PAOLO/A HEAD FULL OF DREAMS (FILM) (3LP, 2DVD box set, gold vinyl, insert)..	£125
19	Parlophone 0190295355487	EVERYDAY LIFE (2LP, printed inners)..	£20
19	Parlophone 0190295355487	EVERYDAY LIFE (2LP, printed inners, limited, silver vinyl, print, some with badge, lyric book)...	£40
21	Parlophone 0190296666964	MUSIC OF THE SPHERES (LP, die-cut sleeve, map, booklet, recycled coloured vinyl).........	£20
21	Parlophone 0190296608384	MUSIC OF THE SPHERES (LP, die-cut sleeve, map, booklet, recycled coloured vinyl, Infinity Station edition, website exclusive)	£30

PROMOS
98	None	Ode To Deodorant/Brothers And Sisters (2-track cassette sent to concert promoters and radio DJs. White label, attributed to 'The Coldplay' with "contact Phil" and 0777 mobile no.)...	£600
99	Parlophone CDRDJ 6528	THE BLUE ROOM EP (Bigger, Stronger/Don't Panic/See You Soon/High Speed/ Such A Rush) (CD digipak)	£40
99	Parlophone 12RDJ 6528	THE BLUE ROOM EP (Bigger, Stronger/Don't Panic/See You Soon/High Speed/Such A Rush) (12", blue cover)	£60
00	Parlophone 12RDJ 6538	Yellow/Help Is Round The Corner/No More Keeping My Feet On The Ground (12")	£40
06	Parlophone (No cat no)	Talk (FK Dub Mix) 12" one-sided acetate 10 only DJ copies)..................................	£40
08	Parlophone VIVA 001	VIVA LA VIDA OR DEATH AND ALL HIS FRIENDS (LP, promo, 300 only)	£150

COLD TURKEY
72	Pye 7N 45142	Nobody's Fool/Sesame Street..	£15

COLD WAR
83	Namedrop NR 4	The Machinist/Illusion (p/s)..	£15

COLD WARRIOR
96 Alphaphone ALPHA 006   **Yellow Square/Walk East/Witch Hunt/Modern Art** (12") **£40**
(see also Cabaret Voltaire, Richard H. Kirk)

ANN COLE
84 Krazy Kat KK 782   **GOT MY MOJO WORKING** (LP) **£15**

BILLY COLE
75 Power Exchange 104   **Extra Careful/Bump All Night** **£20**

B.J. COLE
73 United Artists UAS 29418   **NEW HOVERING DOG** (LP, laminated front sleeve) **£30**
(see also Cochise)

CINDY COLE
65 Columbia DB 7519   **A Love Like Yours/He's Sure The Boy I Love** **£25**
66 Columbia DB 7973   **Just Being Your Baby** (Turns Me On)**/Lonely City Blue Boy** **£30**
(see also Jeannie & Big Guys)

LLOYD COLE & COMMOTIONS
84 Welcome To L. Vegas LC 1   **Are You Ready To Be Heartbroken?/Down At The Mission** (p/s, withdrawn) **£30**
84 Polydor LCLP 1   **RATTLESNAKES** (LP) **£15**
85 Poldyor LCLP 2   **EASY PIECES** (LP) **£15**
93 Phonogram 518318-1   **BAD VIBES** (LP, as Lloyd Cole) **£20**

MJ COLE
00 Talkin Loud 542 591-1   **SINCERE** (4-LP) **£25**

NAT COLE
70 Jackpot JP 717   **Pack Of Cards/RITA & NAT COLE: Spread Joy** **£20**
70 Jackpot JP 718   **Love Making/SONNY BINNS & RITA: My Love** **£30**
70 Jackpot JP 722   **Sugar Sugar/SONNY BINNS & RITA: Sign Off** **£25**
70 Explosion EX 2022   **In The Summertime/Apollo Moon Walk** **£18**
70 Creole CR 1002   **Me And My Life/Instrumental** **£15**
(see also Rita Alston)

NIKKI COLE
70s Dance Centre 023   **ELEMENTARY MODERN DANCE** (LP) **£40**
70s Dance Centre DC020   **CONTEMPORARY DANCE - BEGINNERS VOL 1.** (LP) **£40**

PATSY COLE
66 Island WI 271   **Disappointed Bride/EARL BOSTIC: Honeymoon Night** **£45**

STRANGER COLE
63 R&B JB 133   **Out Of Many/Nothing Tried** **£40**
63 Island WI 110   **Stranger At The Door/Conqueror** **£40**
63 Island WI 114   **Last Love/STRANGER & KEN: Hush Baby** **£40**
63 Island WI 126   **We Are Rolling/Millie Maw** **£40**
64 Island WI 137   **Goodbye Peggy** (actually plays "Goodbye Peggy Darling" by Roy Panton)**/ BABA BROOKS: Portrait Of My Love** **£40**
64 R&B JB 129   **Morning Star/Beat Up Your Gum** **£40**
64 Island WI 133   **Til My Dying Days/STRANGER & PATSY: I Need You** **£45**
64 Black Swan WI 413   **Uno Dos Tres** (act. with Ken Boothe)**/Look** (B-side actually by unknown artist) **£45**
64 Black Swan WI 415   **Summer Day/Loving You Always** (both actually by Dottie & Bonnie) **£45**
64 Black Swan WI 435   **Little Boy Blue/ERIC MORRIS: Words Of Wisdom** **£45**
65 Ska Beat JB 192   **Pussy Cat/MAYTALS: Sweet Sweet Jenny** **£45**
65 Island WI 169   **Koo Koo Doo** (with Owen & Leon)**/GLORIA & DREAMLETTS: Stay Where You Are** **£45**
65 Island WI 177   **Run Joe** (with Baba Brooks)**/Make Believe** **£50**
65 Blue Beat BB 322   **When The Party Is Over/BUSTER'S ALLSTARS: Happy Independence '65** **£50**
65 Blue Beat BB 333   **Matilda** (actually with Prince Buster)**/BUSTER'S ALL STARS: When The Party Is Over** **£45**
66 Doctor Bird DB 1025   **We Shall Overcome/Do You Really Love Me** (as Stranger Cole & Seraphines) **£60**
66 Doctor Bird DB 1040   **Drop The Ratchet/Oh Yee Mahee** (as Stranger Cole & Conquerors) **£60**
67 Doctor Bird DB 1066   **You Took My Love** (actually by Patsy Todd)**/FUGITIVES: Living Soul** **£300**
68 Island WI 3154   **Jeboza Macoo/Now I Know** (B-side actually with Gladdy Anderson) **£80**
68 Amalgamated AMG 801   **Just Like A River** (as Stranger Cole & Gladdy)**/LEADERS: Hope Someday** **£45**
69 Amalgamated AMG 838   **What Mama Na Want She Get/We Two** **£45**
69 Duke DU 27   **Glad You're Living/Help Wanted** **£45**
69 Unity UN 501   **Last Flight To Reggae City** (w/ Tommy McCook)**/JUNIOR SMITH: Watch Dem Go** **£30**
69 Unity UN 514   **When I Get My Freedom/Life Can Be Beautiful** **£40**
69 Escort ES 810   **Pretty Cottage/To Me** **£40**
69 Escort ES 811   **Why Did You/Do You Remember** **£30**
69 Escort ES 819   **Leana Leana/Na Na Na** **£25**
69 Escort ES 826   **Loneliness/Remember** **£25**
70 Escort ES 830   **Little Things/Till The Well Runs Dry** **£15**
70 Camel CA 54   **Everyday Tomorrow/Let Your Head Up High** **£40**
71 Bullet BU 488   **Soul Sop/Stranger Cole Medley** **£15**
71 Camel CA 72   **Crying Every Night/DENNIS ALCAPONE & DELROY WILSON: It Must Come** **£15**
72 Tropical AL 0011   **Mail Man** (with Charlie Ace)**/Mail Man** (Version) **£15**
72 Jackpot JP 791   **My Confession/LASCELS & HORTENSE: The Might Organ** **£15**
72 Pama PM 848   **The House Where Bombo Lives/Our High School Dance** **£19**
(see also Stranger, Stranger & Gladys, Stranger & Patsy, Stranger & Ken, Rob Walker, Charmers, Lloyd Clarke, Don Drummond, Tommy McCook, Delroy Wilson, Lester Sterling, Baba Brooks, Roland Alphonso, Roy Richards)

BOBBY COLEMAN
66 Pye International 7N 25365   (Baby) **You Don't Have To Tell Me/Pleasure Girl** **£70**
66 Pye International 7N 25365   (Baby) **You Don't Have To Tell Me/Pleasure Girl** (DJ Copy) **£100**

LONNIE COLEMAN & JESSE ROBERTSON
56	London HLU 8335	Dolores Diane/Oh Honey, Why Don'tcha	£40

ORNETTE COLEMAN
60	Contemporary LAC 12228	TOMORROW IS THE QUESTION (LP)	£50
61	London Jazz LTZ-K 15199	CHANGE OF THE CENTURY (LP, mono)	£50
61	London Jazz SAH-K 5099	CHANGE OF THE CENTURY (LP, stereo)	£60
61	London Jazz LTZ-K 15228	THIS IS OUR MUSIC (LP, mono)	£50
62	London Jazz LTZ-K 15241	THE ORNETTE COLEMAN QUARTET (LP, mono)	£40
62	London Jazz SAH-K 6235	THE ORNETTE COLEMAN QUARTET (LP, stereo)	£45
62	Atlantic 588121	ORNETTE ON TENOR (LP)	£40
65	Fontana SFJ 923	TOWN HALL DECEMBER 1962 (LP)	£30
66	Atlantic 588022	THE SHAPE OF JAZZ TO COME (LP, mono/stereo)	£40
67	CBS 66023	CHAPPAQUA SUITE (2-LP)	£50
68	Polydor 623 246/7	AN EVENING WITH ORNETTE COLEMAN (2-LP)	£40
69	Impulse SIPL 518	ORNETTE AT 12 (LP)	£35
71	Atlantic 2400 109	THE AT OF THE IMPROVISERS (LP)	£20
72	Atlantic K 40278	TWINS (LP)	£25
77	Blue Note BNS 40021	AT THE GOLDEN CIRCLE STOCKHOLM (LP, reissue)	£20
82	CBS 85934	BROKEN SHADOWS (LP)	£20
82	Antilles AN2001	OF HUMAN FEELINGS (LP)	£20

COLETTE & BANDITS
65	Stateside SS 416	A Ladies Man/Lost Love	£20

COLEY
70s	Coley (Private Pressing)	GOODBYE BRAIN (LP)	£35

NORMAN 'STAR' COLIN & MYSTIC MURPHY
81	Awawak ARK DD 037	You Never Know/Studio 80 Shank (12")	£20

NIK COLK VOID
12	O Genesis OGEN 007	Gold E (7", with playable sleeve)	£15

(see also Factory Floor)

COLLAGE
73	Studio Two TWO 410	MISTY (LP)	£30

(see also Brian Bennett)

COLLECTIVE HORIZONTAL
79	Dolmen DO 1	COLLECTIVE HORIZONTAL EP (gatefold p/s, stickered white labels)	£20

COLLECTORS (CANADA)
69	Warner Bros WS 1774	GRASS AND WILD STRAWBERRIES (LP)	£22

(see also Chilliwack, Electric Prunes)

COLLECTORS (U.K.)
80	Central Collection COL 1	Different World/Talking Hands (p/s)	£15

COLLEGE
11	Valerie (No Cat. No.)	A Real Hero/Instrumental Version (p/s, 300 only)	£60
13	Invada INV113LP	SECRET DIARY (LP)	£15
13	Invada INV 126	HERITAGE (LP)	£15
13	Invada INV 126	HERITAGE (box set, LP, CD and cassette)	£35
14	Invada INV131LP	NORTHERN COUNCIL (LP, clear vinyl, 300 only)	£15

COLLEGE BOYS (JAMAICA)
64	Blue Beat BB 202	Love Is A Treasure/Someone Will Be There	£25

COLLEGE BOYS (U.K.)
64	Columbia DB 7306	I Just Don't Understand/I'm Gonna Cry	£20

GRAHAM COLLIER SEXTET/SEPTET
67	Deram DML/SML 1005	DEEP DARK BLUE CENTRE (LP)	£150
69	Fontana SFJL 922	DOWN ANOTHER ROAD (LP)	£100
70	Fontana 6309 006	SONGS FOR MY FATHER (LP, as Graham Collier Music featuring Harry Beckett)	£80
71	Philips 6308 051	MOSAICS (LP, live, as Graham Collier Music featuring Harry Beckett)	£80
72	Saydisc SDL 244	PORTRAITS (LP)	£25
74	Mosaic GMC 741	DARIUS (LP)	£20
75	Mosaic GCM 751	MIDNIGHT BLUE (LP)	£20
75	Cambridge Univ 521205638	JAZZ LECTURE CONCERT (LP)	£40
12	Whatmusic WMLP 017	DEEP DARK BLUE CENTRE (LP, reissue)	£20

(see also Harry Beckett)

MITTY COLLIER
64	Pye International 7N 25275	I Had A Talk With My Man/Free Girl	£20
64	Pye International 7N 25275	I Had A Talk With My Man/Free Girl (DJ Copy)	£40
69	Peachtree P122	I'd like To Change Places/Share What You Got	£20

ALBERT COLLINS
69	Liberty LBS 585275	TRASH TALKIN (LP)	£30
69	Liberty LBS 83238	LOVE CAN BE FOUND ANYWHERE (LP)	£40
73	Tumbleweed TW 3501	THERE'S GOTTA BE A CHANGE (LP)	£30

ANSEL(L) COLLINS
69	Trojan TR 699	Night Of Love/DERRICK MORGAN: Copy Cat	£35
69	Trojan TR 7712	Cotton Dandy/CARL DAWKINS: Don't Get Weary	£30
70	Trojan TR 7729	Moon Dust/Fat Cat	£35
70	Trojan TR 7730	Monkey (Version I)/(Version II) (plays "High Voltage"/"High Voltage Version"; B-side actually by Beverley All Stars)	£30

CLANCY COLLINS ALL STARS (Actually, Lloyd Chalmers)

70	J-Dan JDN 4401	Cock Robin/KING DENNIS: Seven Zero £20
70	Techniques TE 907	Top Secret/Crazy Rhythm (both actually by Winston Wright).............................. £25
71	Techniques TE 913	Nuclear Weapon/TECHNIQUES ALL STARS: La, La, La.. £20
11	Techniques THB 7011	Double Or Nothing/DANDY: Double Barrel Man £20

(see also Conquerors, Lloyd Young, Prince Buster, Les Foster, Ethiopians, Eternals, Pam Brooks, Dennis Alcapone, Rad Bryan, Immortals)

CLANCY COLLINS ALL STARS (ACTUALLY, LLOYD CHALMERS)
71	Smash SMA 2321	Sir Collins Special/Conqueror (Actually, LENNOX BROWN : Heart of Knights)................ £40

DAVE COLLINS
72	Rhino RNO 103	Shackatac/Smooths And Sorts £15

DAVE & ANSELL COLLINS
72	Techniques TE 915	Karate/Doing Your Own Thing £25
73	Rhino RNO 111	Hot Line/Sunshine Rock (label credits 'Dave Collins') £20
75	Jama JAMA 002	Heavy Boomerang/Version £15
03	Lave LV1	Heavy Boomerang/DYNAMIC ALLSTARS: It's Not Possible £15
71	Trojan TBL 162	DOUBLE BARREL (LP) £25
75	Trojan TRLS12	IN THE GHETTO (LP) £25

(see also Dave Barker, Ansel(l) Collins)

DOROTHY COLLINS
55	Vogue Coral Q 72111	My Boy - Flat Top/In Love £30
56	Vogue Coral Q 72193	Love Me As Though There Were No Tomorrow/Rock And Roll Train £15
56	Vogue Coral Q 72198	The Italian Theme/Cool It, Baby £15
57	Vogue Coral Q 72232	Baby Can Rock/Would You Ever £15

EDWYN COLLINS
87	Creation CRE 047T	Don't Shilly Shally/If Ever You're Ready (7" white label test pressing only) £40
87	Creation CRE 047T	Don't Shilly Shally/If Ever You're Ready (12", white label test pressing only) £35
08	Heavenly HVN 180	Home Again/Searching For The Truth (7" one of 25 copies with hand decorated insert by 25 different people Including John Squire, Nicky Wire, Billy Childish and Jarvis Cocker).. £50
94	Setanta SETLP14	GORGEOUS GEORGE (LP, inner) £25
97	Setanta SETLP039	I'M NOT FOLLOWING YOU (LP, inner).. £35

(see also Orange Juice)

GLENDA COLLINS
60	Decca F 11280	Take A Chance/Crazy Guy £15
61	Decca F 11321	Oh How I Miss You Tonight/Age For Love £15
61	Decca F 11417	Head Over Heels In Love/Find Another Fool £15
63	HMV POP 1163	I Lost My Heart In The Fairground/I Feel So Good £60
63	HMV POP 1233	If You Gotta Pick A Baby/In The First Place... £80
64	HMV POP 1283	Baby It Hurts/Nice Wasn't It £65
64	HMV POP 1323	Lollipop/Everybody's Got To Fall In Love £50
65	HMV POP 1439	Johnny Loves Me/Paradise for Two £50
65	HMV POP 1475	Thou Shall Not Steal/Been Invited To A Party £50
66	Pye 7N 17044	Something I've Got To Tell You/My Heart Didn't Lie £75
66	Pye 7N 17150	It's Hard To Believe It/Don't Let It Rain On Sunday £75
90	Document CSAP LP 108	BEEN INVITED TO A PARTY (LP) £20

HONEY BOY COLLINS
73	Sir Collins SCMW 004	Better Must Come/Lola £30

JOHNNY COLLINS
75	Tradition TSR 020	JOHNNY'S PRIVATE ARMY (LP) £18

JOHNNY COLLINS & FRIENDS
73	Tradition TSR 014	THE TRAVELLER'S REST (LP, dark blue label, laminated sleeve)........................... £18

JUDY COLLINS
65	Elektra EKL 209	MAID OF CONSTANT SORROW (LP) £15

LYN COLLINS
64	Sabre SA 0002	What Am I Gonna Do Without You?/When A Girl Meets A Bad, Bad Boy £20
74	Polydor 2066 490	Rock Me Again And Again And Again And Again And Again And Again/Wide Awake In A Dream £15
72	Polydor 2918 006	THINK (ABOUT IT) (LP) £40
88	Urban URBLP 7	CHECK ME OUT IF YOU DON'T KNOW ME BY NOW (LP, reissue)............................ £15

(see also James Brown)

PETER COLLINS
70	Decca Nova SDN 21	PETER COLLINS (LP, blue/silver label) £60

RODGER COLLINS
67	Vocalion VF 9285	She's Looking Good/I'm Serving Time £40
67	Vocalion VF 9285	She's Looking Good/I'm Serving Time (DJ copy)... £70

SHIRLEY COLLINS
60	Collector JEI 1508	SINGS IRISH (EP) £70
60	Collector JEB 3	THE FOGGY DEW (EP) £70
60	Collector JEB 5	ENGLISH SONGS (EP) £70
64	Collector JEB 9	ENGLISH SONGS VOL. 2 (EP, with Robin Hall) £70
63	Topic TOP 95	HEROES IN LOVE (EP) £70
59	Folkways FG 3564	FALSE TRUE LOVERS (LP) £200
60	Argo RG 150	SWEET ENGLAND (LP, blue/silver label)... £300
64	Decca LK 4652	FOLK ROOTS, NEW ROUTES (LP, insert, with Davy Graham) £320
67	Topic 12T 170	THE SWEET PRIMROSES (LP, original pressing with blue label)............................ £50
67	Topic 12T 170	THE SWEET PRIMROSES (LP) £25

MINT VALUE £

Year	Label	Title	Value
68	Polydor 583 025	**THE POWER OF THE TRUE LOVE KNOT** (LP, with Incredible String Band)	**£250**
71	Pegasus PEG 7	**NO ROSES** (LP, gatefold sleeve, with Albion Country Band)	**£55**
74	Topic 12T 238	**ADIEU TO OLD ENGLAND** (LP, original pressing with blue label)	**£40**
74	Topic 12T 238	**ADIEU TO OLD ENGLAND** (LP)	**£25**
75	Deram SML 1117	**A FAVOURITE GARLAND** (LP)	**£50**
76	Harvest SHSM 2008	**AMARANTH** (LP, textured sleeve)	**£35**
76	Mooncrest CREST 011	**NO ROSES** (LP, reissue, gatefold sleeve)	**£25**
78	Topic 12T 380	**FOR AS MANY AS WILL** (LP)	**£20**
81	Righteous GDC 001	**FOLK ROOTS, NEW ROUTES** (LP, reissue, with Davy Graham)	**£20**
83	Hannibal HNBL 1327	**THE POWER OF THE TRUE LOVE KNOT** (LP, reissue)	**£20**
87	See For Miles SEE 212	**SWEET ENGLAND** (LP, reissue)	**£25**
91	Mooncrest CREST 011	**NO ROSES** (LP, reissue)	**£15**
05	Boweavil WEAVIL 05	**FALSE TRUE LOVERS** (LP, reissue)	**£20**
05	Boweavil WEAVIL 06	**THE POWER OF THE TRUE LOVE KNOT** (LP, reissue)	**£20**
06	Boweavil WEAVIL 09	**THE SWEET PRIMROSES** (LP, reissue)	**£15**
09	6 Spices 6S 229005	**ADIEU TO OLD ENGLAND** (LP, reissue)	**£15**
14	Decca 379 616 3	**FOLK ROOTS, NEW ROUTES** (LP, reissue, with Davy Graham)	**£18**
16	Domino WIGLP 389	**LODESTAR** (LP and CD)	**£15**

SHIRLEY & DOLLY COLLINS

Year	Label	Title	Value
69	Harvest SHVL 754	**ANTHEMS IN EDEN** (LP, gatefold sleeve, with "Sold in U.K..." text on 4 lines)	**£175**
69	Harvest SHVL 754	**ANTHEMS IN EDEN** (LP, gatefold sleeve, later issue with EMI logo on label)	**£100**
70	Harvest SHVL 771	**LOVE, DEATH AND THE LADY** (LP, gatefold sleeve, no EMI logo on label)	**£140**
78	Topic 12T 5380	**FOR AS MANY AS WILL** (LP)	**£30**
87	See for Miles SEE57	**ANTHEMS IN EDEN** (LP, reissue)	**£20**
87	Beat Goes On BGOLP1	**LOVE, DEATH AND THE LADY** (LP, reissue, gatefold)	**£25**

(see also Davy Graham, Albion Country Band, Conundrum)

STEVE COLLINS

Year	Label	Title	Value
73	Big Shot BI 620	Ding A Ling Ting A Ling/Run Rhythm Run	£15

COLLINS BAND & BOB STACKIE

Year	Label	Title	Value
68	Collins Downbeat	Bob Stackie In Soho/LORD CHARLES & HIS BAND: Jamaican Bits And Pieces	£45

COLLOCUTOR

Year	Label	Title	Value
14	On The Corner OTCLP001	**INSTEAD** (LP)	£60

COLLUSION

Year	Label	Title	Value
71	SRT 71114	**COLLUSION** (LP, private pressing, plain sleeve, 99 copies only)	£1500
15	Audio Archives AALP 101	**COLLUSION** (LP, reissue)	£18

JOE COLMAN

Year	Label	Title	Value
90	Blast First FU10	**INFERNAL MACHINE** (LP, picture disc, 1,000 only)	£18

COLONEL ELLIOTT & THE LUNATICS

Year	Label	Title	Value
73	Rhino SRNP 9001	**INTERSTELLAR REGGAE DRIVE** (LP)	£30

COLONEL BAGSHOT

Year	Label	Title	Value
71	Parlophone R 5893	Georgia Fireball/Look In Her Eyes	£15

JERRY COLONNA

Year	Label	Title	Value
55	Brunswick LA 8711	**MUSIC FOR SCREAMING** (10" LP)	£15

COLORADOS

Year	Label	Title	Value
64	Oriole CB 1972	Lips Are Redder Than You/Who You Gonna Hurt?	£30

COLOSSEUM

Year	Label	Title	Value
69	Fontana TF 1029	Walking In The Park/Those About To Die	£15
69	Fontana STL 5510	**THOSE WHO ARE ABOUT TO DIE SALUTE YOU** (LP, laminated gatefold sleeve, black/silver labels)	£150
69	Vertigo VO 1	**VALENTYNE SUITE** (LP, gatefold sleeve, large swirl label with 'A Philips Record Product' credit & inner bag)	£175
69	Vertigo VO 1	**VALENTYNE SUITE** (LP, 2nd pressing, gatefold sleeve, large swirl label without 'A Philips Record Product' credit & inner bag)	£80
70	Vertigo 6360 017	**DAUGHTER OF TIME** (LP, gatefold sleeve, with large swirl label & bag)	£200
70	Vertigo 6360 017	**DAUGHTER OF TIME** (LP, gatefold sleeve, small swirl label)	£60
71	Bronze ICD 1	**COLOSSEUM LIVE** (2-LP, gatefold, plastic inner)	£40
71	Bronze ILPS 9173	**THE COLLECTORS COLOSSEUM** (LP)	£20
72	Bronze HELP 4	**VALENTYNE SUITE** (LP, reissue with rarer HELP 4 cat no, 'Tinsley-Robor Group Ltd' sleeve printing credit)	£20
72	Bronze BRNA 214	**VALENTYNE SUITE** (LP, reissue)	£15
16	Music On Vinyl MOVLP 1684	**THOSE WHO ARE ABOUT TO DIE SALUTE YOU** (LP, reissue, gatefold)	£15

(see also Bakerloo, Colosseum II, Dick Heckstall-Smith, Chris Farlowe, Greenslade, Humble Pie, John Mayall, Howard Riley Trio, Tempest, Mogul Thrash)

COLOSSEUM II

Year	Label	Title	Value
77	MCA MCF 2800	**ELECTRIC SAVAGE** (LP)	£15

COLOURBOX

Year	Label	Title	Value
85	4AD CAD 508	**COLOURBOX** (LP, stickered sleeve, 10,000 only, with bonus LP MAD 509)	£18

COLOURED RAISINS

Year	Label	Title	Value
70	Trojan TR 7700	One Way Love/No More Heartaches	£15

(see also Raisins)

CHRISTOPHER COLT

Year	Label	Title	Value
68	Decca F 12726	Virgin Sunrise/Girl In The Mirror	£40

TONY COLTON('S BIG BOSS BAND)

Year	Label	Title	Value
64	Decca F 11879	Lose My Mind/So Used To Loving You (solo)	£30
65	Pye 7N 15886	I Stand Accused/Further On Down The Track (with Big Boss Band)	£200
66	Pye 7N 17046	You're Wrong There Baby/Have You Lost Your Mind	£100

MINT VALUE £

| 66 | Pye 7N 17117 | I've Laid Some Down In My Time/Run Pony Rider | £150 |
| 68 | Columbia DB 8385 | In The World Of Marnie Dreaming/Who Is She? (solo) | £25 |

(see also Poet & One Man Band, Head Hands & Feet, Real McCoy, Peter B's)

ALICE COLTRANE

17	Moochin' About MOOCHIN 15	Improvised Harp Solo (10" single-sided, etched, p/s, 1000 only, RSD)	£20
72	Impulse! AS-9224	LORD OF LORDS (LP)	£20
76	Impulse! AS 9156	A MONASTIC TRIO (LP, reissue)	£20
21	Impulse! 00602435939766	KIRTAN: TURIYA SINGS (2LP, gatefold, booklet)	£20
23	Impulse! B0036675-01	JOURNEY TO SATCHIDANANDA (with Pharoah Sanders) (LP, tip-on gatefold, 180 g, reissue)	£35
23	Luaka Bop 6 80899 0087-1-6	THE ECSTATIC MUSIC OF ALICE COLTRANE TURIYASANGITANANDA (2LP, gatefold, inserts, reissue)	£30

JOHN COLTRANE

58	Esquire 32-079	THE FIRST TRANE (LP)	£60
58	Esquire 32-089	SOUL TRANE (LP)	£100
59	Esquire 32-091	TRANEING IN (LP)	£40
60	Esquire 32-101	CATTIN' (LP)	£40
60	London Jazz LTZ-K 15197	GIANT STEPS (LP)	£200
61	Esquire 32-129	LUSH LIFE (LP)	£100
61	London Jazz LTZ-K 15219	COLTRANE JAZZ (LP, also stereo SAH-K 6162)	£35
62	London Jazz LTZ-K 15232	BAGS AND TRANE (LP, also stereo SAH-K 6192)	£30
62	Columbia 33SX 1399	THE BIRDLAND STORY VOL. 1: ECHOES OF AN ERA (LP)	£20
62	London Jazz LTZ-K 15239	OLE COLTRANE (LP, mono)	£35
62	London Jazz SAH-K 6223	OLE COLTRANE (LP, stereo)	£40
62	HMV CLP 1548	AFRICA/BRASS (LP, mono)	£40
62	HMV SCD 1431	AFRICA/BRASS (LP, stereo)	£45
62	HMV CLP 1590	LIVE AT THE VILLAGE VANGUARD (LP, mono)	£25
62	HMV CSD 1456	LIVE AT THE VILLAGE VANGUARD (LP, stereo)	£30
63	United Artists (S)ULP 1018	COLTRANE TIME (LP)	£26
63	London HA-K/SH-K 8017	COLTRANE PLAYS THE BLUES (LP, as John Coltrane Group)	£30
63	Esquire 32-179	STANDARD COLTRANE (LP)	£35
63	HMV CLP 1629	COLTRANE (LP, also stereo CSD 1483)	£40
63	HMV CLP 1647	BALLADS (LP, also stereo CSD 1496)	£25
63	HMV CLP 1657	DUKE ELLINGTON & JOHN COLTRANE (LP, mono)	£40
63	HMV CSD 1502	DUKE ELLINGTON & JOHN COLTRANE (LP, stereo)	£70
64	HMV CLP 1695	IMPRESSIONS (LP, mono)	£30
64	HMV CSD 1509	IMPRRESSIONS (LP, stereo)	£40
64	HMV CLP 1700	JOHN COLTRANE WITH JOHNNY HARTMAN (LP)	£30
64	Realm RM 157	ON WEST 42ND STREET (LP)	£25
64	Realm RM 181	TRANE RIDE (LP)	£25
64	HMV CLP 1741	LIVE AT BIRDLAND (LP, also stereo CSD 1544)	£30
65	HMV CLP 1799	CRESCENT (LP, mono)	£40
65	HMV SCD 1567	CRESCENT (LP, stereo)	£45
65	Stateside SL 10124	BLACK PEARLS (LP)	£40
65	HMV CLP 1869	A LOVE SUPREME (LP, mono)	£80
65	HMV CSD 1605	A LOVE SUPREME (LP, stereo)	£200
65	Atlantic ATL/SAL 5022	MY FAVOURITE THINGS (LP)	£25
65	Realm RM 52226	TANGANYIKA STRUT (LP)	£25
65	HMV CLP 1897	COLTRANE PLAYS (LP, also stereo CSD 1619)	£30
66	Stateside SL 10162	BAHIA (LP)	£30
66	HMV CLP/CSD 3543	ASCENSION (LP, as John Coltrane Orchestra)	£50
66	HMV CLP/CSD 3551	NEW THING AT NEWPORT (LP, with Archie Shepp)	£40
66	Atlantic 587/588 004	THE AVANT-GARDE (LP, with Don Cherry)	£40
66	HMV CLP 3575	MEDITATIONS (LP, mono)	£35
66	HMV CSD 3575	MEDITATIONS (LP, flipback sleeve stereo)	£40
67	Atlantic 587/588 039	COLTRANE'S SOUND (LP)	£40
67	HMV CLP/CSD 3599	COLTRANE LIVE AT THE VILLAGE VANGUARD AGAIN! (LP)	£30
67	HMV CLP/CSD 3617	OM (LP, withdrawn)	£60
67	HMV CLP/CSD 3617	KULU SE MAMA (LP)	£30
68	Transatlantic PR 7280	DAKAR (LP)	£30
68	Transatlantic PR 7378	LAST TRANE (LP)	£30
68	Impulse MIPL 502	EXPRESSION (LP, mono)	£30
68	Impulse SIPL 502	EXPRESSION (LP, stereo)	£20
69	Atlantic 588 139	THREE LITTLE WORDS (LP)	£25
69	Impulse MIPL/SIPL 515	COSMIC MUSIC (LP, by Alice & John Coltrane)	£50
70	Impulse SIPL 522	SELFLESSNESS (LP)	£30
71	Probe SPB 1025	AFRO BLUE (LP)	£30
72	Prestige PR 24003	JOHN COLTRANE (2-LP)	£25
74	CBS PR 24037	BLACK PEARLS (2-LP)	£25
76	Atlantic ATL 50239	GIANT STEPS (LP, reissue, gatefold)	£15
77	Blue Note BNS 40009	BLUE TRAIN (LP, reissue)	£18
91	MCA MCL 1648	A LOVE SUPREME (LP, reissue)	£18

(see also Miles Davis, Thelonious Monk, Cannonball Adderley, Archie Shepp)

RAY COLUMBUS INVADERS

| 60s | Zodiac AZ/1009 | She's A Mod/INVADERS : Cruel Sea | £20 |

KEN COLYER'S SKIFFLE GROUP

| 55 | Decca F 10631 | Down By The Riverside/Take This Hammer | £20 |

56	Decca FJ 10711	Streamline Train/Go Down Old Hannah £20
56	Decca FJ 10751	Down Bound Train/Mule Skinner £20
55	Decca DFE 6286	KEN COLYER'S SKIFFLE GROUP (EP, various coloured sleeves) £20

(see also Crane Skiffle Group)

VEE COMA
62	Pun PUN 001	Piccadilly/Independence Day...£15

COMBAT 84
82	Victory VIC 1	ORDERS OF THE DAY (EP, wraparound p/s) £20
83	Victory VIC 2	Rapist/The Right To Choose/Barry Prudom (p/s) £20

COMBE RALEIGH COUNTRY FOLK
76	MJB Recording BEV LP 1334	COMBE RALEIGH COUNTRY FOLK (LP) £250

COMBINATIONS
72	Punch PH 99	1 2 3 A B C/Zee £15

COME
81	Come Org. WDC 883012	Come Sunday (cassette) £60
79	Come Org. WDC 88001	Come Sunday/Shaved Slits (p/s) £40
79	Come Org. WDC 883001	COME PRESENT RAMPTON (cassette) £60
79	Come Org. WDC 88203	PRESENT RAMPTON (LP) £100
81	Come Org. WDC 881012	I'M JACK (LP, orange vinyl with insert) £80

(see also Whitehouse, New Order)

COMET GAIN
95	Wiiija WIJ 042V	CASINO CLASSICS (LP)..£25
99	Fortuna Pop! FPOP 17	TIGERTOWN PICTURES (LP, insert, with free 7") £18
02	Milou Studios 2MILLP	REALISTES (LP) £20

COMETS SHOWGROUP
70	LRC SCG 1	COMETS ON LOCATION (LP, private pressing, handmade sleeve) £50

COMING UP ROSES
89	Utility UTIL 5	I SAID BALLROOM (LP)...£30

(see also Dolly Mixture)

COMMITTED
79	Ace ACE 006	Crash Victim/British Crimes/Fast Lane/Advertising (500 only)...................£100

COMMITTEE (1)
68	Liberty LBF 15154	The Hard Way/Hey You £15

COMMIX
07	Metalheadz METH LP 09	CALL TO MIND (LP as 3 x 12", gatefold sleeve) £30

COMMODORES (1)
55	London HLD 8209	Riding On A Train/Uranium £200
55	London HLD 8209	Riding On A Train/Uranium (78) £15
56	London HLD 8251	Speedo/Whole Lotta Shakin' Goin' On £200
56	London HLD 8251	Speedo/Whole Lotta Shakin' Goin' On (78) £15

COMMODORES (2)
69	Atlantic 584 273	Keep On Dancing/Rise Up £30

COMMOTION UPSTAIRS
89	Saucy SAUCY TT 17	Lift Me Up/Not Like That/Too Bad/Fake (p/s) £100

PERRY COMO
53	HMV 7M 118	Don't Let The Stars Get In Your Eyes/To Know You (Is To Love You) (B-side with Fontane Sisters)..£25
54	HMV 7M 263	There Never Was A Night So Beautiful/Papa Loves Mambo..........................£20
55	HMV 7M 296	Ko Ko Mo (I Love You So)/You'll Always Be My Lifetime Love £15

(see also Fontane Sisters, Betty Hutton)

COMPANY OF COWARDS
87	Company Of Cowards COC 1	18 AGAIN EP (12") £70

COMPANY (1)
79	United Artists BP 326	We Wish You Well/Right Time For Love £30

(see also Whitesnake)

COMPANY (2)
80	Incus INCUS 36	FABLES (LP) £50
80	Incus INCUS 38	FICTIONS (LP) £50
82	Incus INCUS 46	EPIPHANY (LP) £50
82	Incus INCUS 47	EPIPHANIES (LP) £50
83	Incus INCUS 51	TRIOS (LP) £50

COMPAQ
98	X System X SYS 3	JUICY EP (12") £15

COMPLETE CONTROL
85	OI! OIR 1	BRICKS BLOOD N GUTS (mini-LP) £20

COMPLEX
71	CLPM 001	COMPLEX (LP, private pressing, 99 copies only) £4000
71	Deroy	THE WAY WE FEEL (LP, private pressing, 99 copies only) £1000
98	Tenth Planet TP 038	COMPLEX (LP, reissue, 1000, no'd) £40

(see also Monsoon, Misfits)

COMSAT ANGELS
81	Polydor POLS 1038	SLEEP NO MORE (LP) £15

BOBBY COMSTOCK (& COUNTS)
63	Stateside SS 163	Let's Stomp/I Want To Do It	£15
63	Stateside SS 221	Susie Baby/Take A Walk	£15

COMUS
71	Dawn DNX 2506	Diana/In The Lost Queen's Eyes/Winter Is A Coloured Bird (p/s)	£100
71	Dawn DNLS 3019	FIRST UTTERANCE (LP, gatefold sleeve with lyric sheet, orange label)	£1000
74	Virgin V 2018	TO KEEP FROM CRYING (LP, twin Virgin label)	£60
10	Rise Above Relics RARLP 006	FIRST UTTERANCE (LP, reissue, limited edition with 10" and A2 poster, 300 only, black vinyl)	£50
12	Rise Above RISELP 144	OUT OF THE COMA (LP, clear vinyl, 100 only)	£30
12	Rise Above RISELP 144	OUT OF THE COMA (LP, white splatter vinyl)	£20
12	Rise Above RISELP 144	OUT OF THE COMA (LP)	£15

(see also Gong, Henry Cow, Esperanto Rock Orchestra)

CON-CHORDS
65	Polydor BM 56059	You Can't Take It Away/Let Me Walk With You	£25

CONCORDS (1)
66	Emblem JDR 303	SOUL PURPOSE (LP)	£30

CONCORDS (2)
69	Blue Cat BS 170	Buttoo/I Need Your Loving	£50

CONCRETE
81	Concrete CON 001	GHOULISH PRACTICES EP	£15

CONCRETE GOD
87	Phlox CGOD1	FLOOR EP (12" p/s)	£15
87	Phlox CGOD2	TOYTOWN EP (12" p/s)	£25

CONCRETE JUNGLIST
94	Lloyd Crucial LC12 002	Ribbon In The Sky/Just Kick It/Pick A Sound/Screw Face (12")	£20
94	Lloyd Crucial LC12 005	Southern California (Concrete Mix)/(Suburban Mix)/Crucial Archive (Dub Mix) (12")	£35
94	Lloyd Crucial LC12 007	Lick Him Ina Him Head/India Posie Pan De Map (12")	£40

CONCRETE SOX
89	Big Kiss KISS 1	SEWERSIDE (LP, with inner)	£15
87	Manic Ears ACHE 11	WHOOPS, SORRY VICAR! (LP)	£15
88	C.O.R GURT 10	YOUR TURN NEXT (LP, with insert)	£15

CONCRETES
04	EMI LFLP 012	CONCRETES (LP, stickered sleeve)	£20

CONDEMNED
79	Rock Against Racism TRAR 1	Soldier Boys/Endless Revolution/PROLES: Stereo Love/Thought Crime (p/s)	£45

CONDEMNED 84
86	RFB SIN 2	Oi Ain't Dead!/Under Her Thumb/Follow The Leader/The Nutter (12", p/s, blue vinyl)	£25
86	RFB SIN 2	Oi Ain't Dead!/Under Her Thumb/Follow The Leader/The Nutter (7", p/s, blue vinyl)	£20
87	RFB SIN 3	IN SEARCH OF THE NEW BREED (12" EP)	£30
88	Oi! OIR 003	BATTLE SCARRED (LP)	£22
88	Grade 1	FACE THE AGGRESSION (LP)	£22

CONEY ISLAND KIDS
55	London HLJ 8207	Baby, Baby You/Moonlight Beach	£30

CONFESSOR
91	Earache MOSH 44	CONDEMNED (LP)	£40

CONFIDENTIAL/PRIMEA FACEY
90	Catt CATT 013	Jam The Frequency/Jet Black At Birth (12")	£25

CONFLICT
82	Crass 221984/1	THE HOUSE THAT MAN BUILT (EP, foldout poster p/s)	£15
83	Mortarhate MORT EX001	The Serenade Is Dead (12" with insert)	£15
85	Mortarhate MORT 20	Custom Rock/Statement (Ungovernable Force Promo, white label)	£30
83	Corpus Christi CHRIST IT'S 3	IT'S TIME TO SEE WHO'S WHO (LP, gatefold, inner)	£15
86	Mortarhate MORT 20	THE UNGOVERNABLE FORCE (LP, inner)	£20
87	Mortarhate MORT 30	TURNING REBELLION INTO MONEY (LP)	£20
88	Mortarhate LPMORT 50	THE FINAL CONFLICT (LP, gatefold)	£20
15	Jungle FREUS LP 068	THERE MUST BE ANOTHER WAY - THE SINGLES (LP)	£18

CON FUNK SHUN
80	Mercury MERX 14	Got To Be Enough (Think About It - Don't You Doubt It)/Early Morning Sunshine (12")	£15

CONGO ASHANTI ROY
82	On-U Sound DP 08	Hands & Feet/African Blood (10")	£15
80	Pre PREX 8	SIGN OF THE STAR (LP)	£30

DAHWEH CONGO
94	Soljie SOLJ 703	Most Naturally/In These Times (with Anthony John)	£18

CONGOS
77	Black Swan BS 1	Congo Man/Congo Man Chant (12")	£40
78	Go Feet FEET 5	Fisherman/Can't Come In	£15
80	Go-Feet BEAT 2	HEART OF THE CONGOS (LP, some with hype sticker)	£50
96	Blood & Fire BAFLP 009	HEART OF THE CONGOS (2LP, reissue, gatefold)	£90
00	Simply Vinyl SVLP 247	HEART OF THE CONGOS (2LP, reissue, 180g, gatefold)	£60
03	Congos LP 21521	CONGO ASHANTI (2LP, gatefold, UK vinyl issue of 79 album)	£30

ARTHUR CONLEY
67	Atlantic 587 069	SWEET SOUL MUSIC (LP)	£35
68	Atlantic 587 084	SHAKE, RATTLE AND ROLL (LP)	£20
68	Atlantic 587/588 128	SOUL DIRECTIONS (LP)	£20
69	Atco 228 019	MORE SWEET SOUL (LP)	£15

(see also Soul Clan)

CONNARD
68	Spot JW 11	Amadhan/Desdemona	£70

CONNECTION
92	Spare Beat SBRR 006	THE CONNECTION EP (12")	£30
93	Spare Beat SBRR 008	THE CONNECTION EP VOL II (12")	£30

BRIAN CONNELL & ROUND SOUND
68	Philips BF 1718	I Know/Mister Travel Company	£45

TERRY CONNOLLY & THE TRIXONS
67	King KG 1069	You're Gonna Wonder About Me/Mama, I'm Not The Boy I Used To Be	£20

BRIAN CONNOLLY
82	Carrere CAR 231	Hypnotised/Fade Away (p/s)	£18

(see also Sweet)

CHRIS CONNOR
60	London LZ-N 14036	THIS IS CHRIS (10" LP)	£15

EDRIC CONNOR
53	Argo RG 33	SONGS FROM JAMAICA (LP, with the Caribbeans)	£15
55	Argo RG 57	SONGS FROM TRINIDAD (LP, with the Southlanders)	£15
55	Argo RG 58	CALYPSO (LP)	£15

PAUL CONNOR
71	Polydor 2121045	Little Sparrow/I Don't Love You Any More	£35
71	Polydor 2480072	EASY TO REMEMBER (LP)	£40

CAROL CONNORS
62	London HLN 9619	Big Big Love/Two Rivers	£20

(see also Teddy Bears)

NORMAN CONNORS
74	Buddah BDS 5611	SLEWFOOT (LP)	£20
77	Buddah BDLP 4043	YOU ARE MY STARSHIP (LP)	£20
77	Buddha BDLP 4053	THIS IS YOUR LIFE (LP)	£18
79	Pye DISC 06	INVITATION (LP, as 2 x 12")	£20

(see also Aquarian Dream)

CONQUERING LION
93	X Project DUBPLATE 2	Inah Sound/Outasound/King David Dub (12")	£25
93	X Project DUBPLATE 3	Lion Of Judah/Inah Sound/Dub Plate Special (12")	£20

CONQUERORS
67	Doctor Bird DB 1119	Won't You Come Home Now?/Oh That Day	£50
67	Treasure Isle TI 7035	Lonely Street/I Fell In Love	£40
69	Amalgamated AMG 832	Secret Weapon (actually by Ansell Collins)/Jumpy Jumpy Girl	£75
69	High Note HS 016	If You Can't Beat Them/Anywhere You Want To Go	£50
69	High Note HS 025	National Dish/Mr D.J.	£50
72	Fab FAB 22	You Hold The Handles/SOUL REBELS : Bongo Skank	£150

(see also Stranger Cole & Conquerors, Baba Brooks)

JESS CONRAD
63	Decca DFE 8524	THE HUMAN JUNGLE (EP, with Rhet Stoller)	£20
61	Decca LK 4390	JESS FOR YOU (LP)	£30

(see also Guvners)

TONI CONRAD & FAUST
73	Caroline C 1501	OUTSIDE THE DREAM SYNDICATE (LP, as Tony Conrad)	£80

(see also Faust)

CONSCIOUS MINDS
71	Big BG 318	Jamaican Boy/Brainwash	£25
71	Ackee ACK 141	Paul, Marcus And Norman/Version	£15
71	Escort ERT 857	Peace Treaty/Brainwash	£25

(see also Ken Boothe, Jamaicans, B.B.Seaton, Charmers)

CONSORTIUM
69	Pye 7N 17725	When The Day Breaks/Day The Train Never Came	£30
69	Pye 7N 17797	Beggar Man/Cynthia Serenity	£20

CONSTRUCTION
90	White SDT17	Sudden Impact - In A State Of Experimentation	£35
90	White SDT30	Transmission/Revenge Of The Dragon (12")	£250
91	White SDT37	Change Your Attitude/Time To Get Raw (12")	£50

CONSUMATES
68	Coxsone CS 7054	What Is It/SOUL VENDORS: Musical Happiness	£70

CONTACT
79	Object OM 11	FUTURE/PAST EP	£18

CONTINENTALS (1)
62	Oriole 1569	Bye Bye Blackbird/Everybody Loves My Baby	£15
62	Island WI 010	Going Crazy/Give Me All Your Love	£25

MINT VALUE £

CONTINENTAL UPTIGHT BAND
71 Columbia SCX 6454   BEAUTIFUL FRIENDSHIP (LP, black/silver/white boxed Columbia label).......................£30

CONTINUUM (1)
70 RCA Victor SF 8157   CONTINUUM (LP, gatefold, orange labels)...£30
71 RCA Victor SF 8196   AUTUMN GRASS (LP, gatefold sleeve, orange label)..£50

CONTINUUM (2)
14 Tonefloat TF 134   CONTINUUM I & 2 (3-LP)...£60

(see also Steven Wilson, Porcupine Tree, No Man, Blackfield)

CONTOURS
62 Oriole CB 1763   Do You Love Me/Move Mister Man (DJ Copy)...£100
62 Oriole CB 1763   Do You Love Me/Move Mister Man..£40
63 Oriole CB 1799   Shake Sherry/You Better Get In Line...£60
63 Oriole CB 1831   Don't Let Him Be Your Baby/It Must Be Love £75
64 Stateside SS 299   Can You Do It/I'll Stand By You £60
64 Stateside SS 299   Can You Do It/I'll Stand By You (DJ Copy)..£100
65 Stateside SS 381   Can You Jerk Like Me/That Day She Needed Me £60
65 Stateside SS 381   Can You Jerk Like Me/That Day She Needed Me (DJ Copy).......................................£100
65 Tamla Motown TMG 531   First I Look At The Purse/Searching For A Girl £60
65 Tamla Motown TMG 531   First I Look At The Purse/Searching For A Girl (DJ Copy)..£120
66 Tamla Motown TMG 564   Determination/Just A Little Misunderstanding £60
66 Tamla Motown TMG 564   Determination/Just A Little Misunderstanding (DJ Copy).......................................£150
67 Tamla Motown TMG 605   It's So Hard Being A Loser/Your Love Grows More Precious Every Day...................£35
67 Tamla Motown TMG 605   It's So Hard Being A Loser/Your Love Grows More Precious Every Day (DJ Copy)..........£70
70 Tamla Motown TMG 723   Just A Little Misunderstanding/First I Look At The Purse £15
70 Tamla Motown TMG 723   Just A Little Misunderstanding/First I Look At The Purse (DJ Copy)............................£40
74 Tamla Motown TMG 886   Baby Hit And Run/Can You Jerk Like Me £25
65 Tamla Motown TME 2002   THE CONTOURS (EP)..£120
63 Oriole PS 40043   DO YOU LOVE ME (LP)..£250

CONTRABAND
74 Transatlantic TRA 278   CONTRABAND (LP, with lyric insert) £20

CONTRAST (2)
70 Rs LP 6002   A GOOD YEAR (LP)...£25

CONTROLLED BLEEDING
86 Sterile SR 11   HEADCRACK (LP)...£20

CONUNDRUM & RICHARD HARVEY
78 Streetsong No. 1   Black Birds Of Brittany/SHIRLEY COLLINS & ANNIE POWER: The Mariners Farewell
                               (poster p/s) £18

(see also Bert Jansch, Shirley Collins)

BERT CONVY & THUNDERBIRDS
55 London HLB 8190   C'mon Back/Hoo Bop De Bow..£50

(see also Cheers,Thunderbirds)

CONWAY
16 Daupe! DM SP 016   GRISELDA GHOST (12", p/s, 250 copies, with Westside Gunn) £300
16 Daupe! DM SP 016   GRISELDA GHOST (12", p/s, aqua marine vinyl, 150 copies, with Westside Gunn).........£400
16 Daupe! DM SP 016   GRISELDA GHOST (12", p/s, with obi strip, 20 copies, with Westside Gunn) £500
16 Daupe! DM SP 017   HALL & NASH (12", p/s, 230 only, with Westside Gunn)...£250
16 Daupe! DM SP 017   HALL & NASH (12", p/s, liquor coloured vinyl, 150 only, with Westside Gunn)..............£300
16 Daupe! DM SP 017   HALL & NASH (12", p/s, 20 only, with Westside Gunn) £300
17 Daupe! DM SP 027   REJECT ON STEROIDS (12", p/s, white vinyl, 187 copies)..£100
17 Daupe! DM SP 027   REJECT ON STEROIDS (12", p/s, red vinyl, 187 copies)..£150
17 Daupe! DM SP 027   REJECT ON STEROIDS (12", p/s, grey vinyl, 187 copies)..£150
17 Daupe! DM SP 027   REJECT ON STEROIDS (12", p/s, with obi strip, 20 copies) £120
18 Daupe! DM SP 034   DEATH BY MISADVENTURE (12", p/s, with Sonny Jim, 250 copies) £40
18 Daupe! DM SP 034   DEATH BY MISADVENTURE (12", p/s, with Sonny Jim, white vinyl, 250 copies)...........£40
18 Daupe! DM SP 034   DEATH BY MISADVENTURE (12", p/s, with Sonny Jim, picture disc, 250 copies) £50
18 Daupe! DM SP 034   DEATH BY MISADVENTURE (12", p/s, with Sonny Jim, red vinyl, 250 copies)................£40
18 Daupe! DM SP 034   DEATH BY MISADVENTURE (12", p/s, with Sonny Jim, with obi strip, 20 copies)..........£150
16 Daupe! DM SP 015   REJECT 2 (LP, white vinyl, 100 only)...£400
16 Daupe! DM SP 015   REJECT 2 (LP, numbered, 250 only)...£400
16 Daupe! DM SP 015   REJECT 2 (LP, with obi strip, 20 only) £500
18 Daupe! DM SP 033   G.O.A.T. (LP, orange vinyl, 333 copies)..£100
18 Tonefloat DM SP 033   G.O.A.T. (LP, green vinyl, 333 copies)...£100
18 Daupe! DM SP 033   G.O.A.T. (LP, grey vinyl, 333 copies)..£100

MIKE CONWAY
66 Plexium PXM 1   I'm Gonna Get Me A Woman/Reign Of King Sadness £15

JIMMY CONWELL
72 Jay Boy BOY 64   Cigarette Ashes/Second Hand Happiness..£15
72 Jay Boy BOY 64   Cigarette Ashes/Second Hand Happiness (DJ Copy)..£35

RY COODER
71 Reprise RSLP 6402   RY COODER (LP)..£15

(see also Captain Beefheart)

LITTLE JOE COOK (U.K.)
65 Sue WI 385   Stormy Monday Blues (Parts 1 & 2) £50

(see also Chris Farlowe, Beazers)

LITTLE JOE COOK (U.S.)
68 Sonet SON 2002   Don't You Have Feelings?/Hold On To Your Money £20

PETER COOK (1)
65 Pye 7N 15847   Georgia/There And Bach Again.....................£20
(see also Peter London)

PETER COOK (2)
66 Lyntone LYN 776   Watney's Pale Ale (Flexi, p/s) £15

PETER COOK & DUDLEY MOORE
67 Decca F 12551   The L.S. Bumble Bee/The Bee Side £25
67 Decca F 12710   Bedazzled/Love Me £70
68 Decca SKL 4923   BEDAZZLED (LP, stereo, soundtrack) £100
(see also Dudley Moore Trio)

COOK COUNTY
77 Barak BAR 5   Space Dancin'/Star Wars.....................£15

ROGER (JAMES) COOKE
70 Columbia SCX 6388   STUDY (LP, boxed logo on label).....................£25
72 Regal Zono. SRZA 8508   MEANWHILE ... BACK AT THE WORLD (As Roger Cook, LP, gatefold sleeve, red/silver label) £30
73 Regal Zono. SLRZ 1035   MINSTREL IN FLIGHT (LP) £20
(see also David & Jonathan)

SAM COOKE
57 London HLU 8506   You Send Me/Summertime £40
57 London HLU 8506   You Send Me/Summertime (78) £20
58 London HLU 8615   That's All I Need To Know/I Don't Want To Cry £40
58 London HLU 8615   That's All I Need To Know/I Don't Want To Cry (78) £20
58 HMV POP 568   Love You Most Of All/Win Your Love For Me £40
58 HMV POP 568   Love You Most Of All/Win Your Love For Me (78) £20
59 HMV POP 610   Everybody Likes To Cha Cha Cha/The Little Things You Do £40
59 HMV POP 610   Everybody Likes To Cha Cha Cha/The Little Things You Do (78) £25
59 HMV POP 642   Only Sixteen/Let's Go Steady Again (78) £30
59 HMV POP 675   There, I've Said It Again/One Hour Ahead Of The Posse.....................£30
60 London HLU 9046   Happy In Love/I Need You Now £25
60 RCA RCA 1184   Teenage Sonata/If You Were The Only Girl £20
61 RCA RCA 1230   That's It, I Quit, I'm Movin' On/What Do You Say £15
63 RCA RCA 1327   Send Me Some Loving/Baby Baby Baby £20
65 RCA RCA 1436   Shake/A Change Is Gonna Come £30
65 RCA RCA 1452   It's Got The Whole World Shakin'/Ease My Troublin' Mind £20
65 RCA RCA 1476   Sugar Dumpling/Bridge Of Tears £40
65 RCA RCA 1476   Sugar Dumpling/Bridge Of Tears (DJ Copy).....................£70
63 RCA RCX 7117   HEART AND SOUL (EP).....................£20
64 RCA RCX 7128   SWING SWEETLY (EP).....................£25
58 HMV CLP 1261   SAM COOKE (LP, with Bumps Blackwell Orchestra) £100
59 HMV CLP 1273   ENCORE (LP).....................£70
61 RCA RD 27190   COOKE'S TOUR (LP, mono).....................£35
61 RCA SF 5076   COOKE'S TOUR (LP, stereo).....................£45
61 RCA RD 27215   HITS OF THE FIFTIES (LP, mono).....................£25
61 RCA RD SF 5098   HITS OF THE FIFTIES (LP, stereo).....................£40
61 RCA RD 27222   SWING LOW (LP).....................£35
62 RCA RD 27245   MY KIND OF BLUES (LP, mono).....................£30
62 RCA SF 5120   MY KIND OF BLUES (LP, stereo).....................£30
62 RCA RD 27263   TWISTIN' THE NIGHT AWAY (LP, mono).....................£30
62 RCA RD SF 5133   TWISTIN' THE NIGHT AWAY (LP, stereo).....................£40
63 RCA RDF 7539   MR. SOUL (LP, mono).....................£40
63 RCA SF 7539   MR. SOUL (LP, stereo).....................£45
63 RCA RD/SF 7583   NIGHT BEAT (LP).....................£40
63 RCA RD/SF 7583   NIGHT BEAT (LP).....................£45
64 RCA RD 7635   AIN'T THAT GOOD NEWS (LP, mono).....................£25
64 RCA SF 7635   AIN'T THAT GOOD NEWS (LP, stereo).....................£30
65 RCA RD 7674   AT THE COPA (LP, mono).....................£25
65 RCA SF 7674   AT THE COPA (LP, stereo).....................£30
65 RCA RD 7730   SHAKE (LP, mono).....................£40
65 RCA SF 7730   SHAKE (LP, stereo).....................£55
65 London HA-U 8232   THE SOUL STIRRERS FEATURING SAM COOKE (LP).....................£70
66 RCA RD/SF 7764   TRY A LITTLE LOVE (LP).....................£30
66 Immediate IMLP 002   THE WONDERFUL WORLD OF SAM COOKE (LP).....................£80
74 BBC   SAM COOKE AND OTHERS (LP, for radio use).....................£70

COOKIE MONSTER
03 Ninja Tune ZEN 12143   C Is For Cookie (Funky)/DJ Food Edit/Sweet Version (12" reissue, p/s) £20

COOKIES
62 London HLU 9634   Chains/Stranger In My Arms.....................£30
63 London HLU 9704   Don't Say Nothin' Bad About My Baby/Softly In The Night.....................£25
63 Colpix PX 11012   Will Power/I Want A Boy For My Birthday £30
64 Colpix PX 11020   Girls Grow Up Faster Than Boys/Only To Other People £30
(see also Earl-Jean, Cinderellas, Dorothy Jones)

COOKIN SOUL
19 No label or cat no   DOOM XMAS (LP, picture disc) £100

(see also MF Doom, Madvillian)

COOL BREEZE
| | | | |
71 Patheway PAT 103 — People Ask What Love Is/There'll Be No More Sad Tomorrows £20

COOL CATS
68 Jolly JY 007 — What Kind Of Man/HEMSLEY MORRIS: Little Things £125
69 Jolly JY 009 — Hold Your Love/ALVA LEWIS: Hang My Head And Cry......£100

EDDIE COOLEY & DIMPLES
57 Columbia DB 3873 — Priscilla/Got A Little Woman......£150
57 Columbia DB 3873 — Priscilla/Got A Little Woman (78) £30

COOL HAND FLEX
92 In Touch INT 001 — On The Strength/Your Risk/Go Insane (12")......£25

COOLIES
77 Electric WOT 14 — Geisha Girl/Calling Out Your Name £25

COOL MEN
58 Parlophone GEP 8739 — COOL FOR CATS NO. 1 (EP) £25
58 Parlophone GEP 8752 — COOL FOR CATS NO. 2 (EP) £25

COOL NOTES
77 Circle Int. CIR 003 — After Tonight/Jah Lovely Wonderful Marvellous £15
80 Jama JADC 0024 — My Tune (Re-Mix)/Version (12") £30
82 Mass Media Music MMM 12 1008 — I Forgot How To Love/Why Can't We Be Friends (12") £60
82 Mass Media Music MMM 12 1008 — I Forgot How To Love/Why Can't We Be Friends £15
82 Mass Media Music MMM 12 1011 — Morning Child (Radio Mix)/Morning Child (Radio Mix) £25
82 Cool Notes 12CN 1001 — It's Not Unusual/People Make The World Go Round (12") £15
84 Sour Grapes SG 116 — I Wanna Dance/Blowin It £25
84 Sour Grapes SGR 116 — I Wanna Dance (Extended)/Blowin It (12") £80
85 Abstract Dance 12AD 001 — You're Never Too Young/Sound Of Summer (12") £15
84 Mass Media MMLP 2 — DOWN TO EARTH (LP) £60
85 Abstract Dance AD LP1 — HAVE A GOOD FOREVER (LP) £15

COOL RUNNERS
82 MCA MCAT 760 — Play The Game (So You Think It Funny)/Hawaiian Dream (12", p/s) £20
82 MCA MCAT 893 — Checking Out/High On A Feeling (12", p/s)......£40
84 Tai Wan TWD 1949 — Checking Out/High On A Feeling (12", p/s, reissue as Nat King Cool & Cool Runners)......£25

COOL SPOON (JEFF DIXON & ALTON ELLIS)
67 Coxsone CS 7031 — Yakety Yak/SOUL VENDORS: Drum Song £70

COOL STICKY
68 Amalgamated AMG 825 — Train To Soulsville/ERIC MONTY MORRIS: Cinderella (actually by Errol Dunkley) £50

CHRIS COOMBES
65 Holyground HG 110 — WHERE IT'S AT (EP, 99 only)......£35

CHRIS COOMBS
75 Guildhall GHS 11 — CHRIS COOMBS WITH THE GALLERY (LP)......£100

NIGEL COOMBES & STEVE BERESFORD
80 Bead Records BEAD 16 — IMPROVISED VIOLIN AND PIANO DUETS (LP)......£25

ALICE COOPER
71 Straight W 7209 — Eighteen/Body......£100
73 Warner Brothers K16262 — No More Mr. Nice Guy/Raped And Freezin' (possibly export only)......£20
74 Chrysalis CHS 2069 — I'm Flash/ELKIE BROOKS: Sacrifice (p/s, promo only)......£35
69 Straight STS 1051 — PRETTIES FOR YOU (LP, purple label, gatefold sleeve)......£100
69 Straight STS 1061 — EASY ACTION (LP, purple label, gatefold sleeve)......£100
71 Straight STS 1065 — LOVE IT TO DEATH (LP, purple label, gatefold sleeve)......£80
71 Warner Bros K 56005 — KILLER (LP, olive green label, A1/B1 Matrix numbers, gatefold sleeve with perforated foldout calendar that must have '1972' in bottom left hand corner. Any with '1973' are repressings)......£70
72 Warner Bros K 56007 — SCHOOL'S OUT (LP, green label, desktop gatefold, with paper pants inner) £80
73 Warner Bros K 56013 — BILLION DOLLAR BABIES (LP, 1st pressing, A1/B1 matrixes, 'Pil' etched into dead wax side 2, olive green label, gatefold embossed sleeve with round corners and K56013 in top right corner, 'WEA records printed in England' in bottom right on rear, attached perforated cards, with $ billion note & inner sleeve with large thumb notch)......£40
73 Warner Bros K 46177 — LOVE IT TO DEATH (LP, reissue, green label, gatefold sleeve)......£15
73 Warner Bros K 66021 — SCHOOL DAYS (2-LP, gatefold sleeve, reissue of STS 1051 & 1061) £18
74 Warner Bros K 56018 — MUSCLE OF LOVE (LP, 'cardboard box' sleeve, with insert & inner sleeve) £15

BO COOPER
74 Bell 1373 — Don't Call It Love/Christian £15
74 Bell 1373 — Don't Call It Love/Christian (DJ Copy) £30

GARNELL COOPER & KINFOLKS
63 London HL 9757 — Green Monkey/Long Distance £20

LES COOPER & SOUL ROCKERS
62 Stateside SS 142 — Wiggle Wobble/Dig Yourself £20

LINDSAY COOPER
80 Arc ARC 1 — RAGS (LP)......£30
82 Sync Pulse 1789 — LIVE AT THE BASTILLE (LP, with Maggie Nichols and Joelle Leandre) £20
83 Sync Pulse 0617 — MUSIC FROM THE GOLD DIGGERS (LP) £15
86 Sync Pulse SP3 — MUSIC FOR OTHER OCCASIONS (LP)......£15

MARTY COOPER CLAN
63 RCA Victor RD 7596 NEW SOUNDS - OLD GOODIES (LP) £15

MIKE COOPER
60s Saydisc SD 137 UP THE COUNTRY BLUES (EP) £80
68 Matchbox SDM 159 THE INVERTED WORLD (LP, with Ian A. Anderson) £70
69 Pye NSPL 18281 OH REALLY!? (LP, blue/black label with logo banner on top) £40
70 Dawn DNLS 3005 DO I KNOW YOU? (LP, gatefold sleeve, orange label) £30
70 Dawn DNLS 3011 TROUT STEEL (LP, with poster insert, gatefold sleeve, orange label) £50
71 Dawn DNLS 3026 PLACES I KNOW (LP, with insert, lilac label) £40
72 Dawn DNLS 3031 THE MACHINE GUN COMPANY (LP, lilac label) £25
74 Fresh Air 6370 500 LIFE AND DEATH IN PARADISE (LP) £20
81 Matchless MR 4 'AVE THEY STARTED YET? (LP, with Joanna Pyne) £15
(see also Ian A. Anderson, Heron)

TOMMY COOPER
61 Palette PG 9019 Don't Jump Off The Roof Dad/How Come There's No Dog Day? £15

COOPERETTES
75 Brunswick BR22 Shing A Ling/Don't Trust Him (DJ Copy) £20

COOPER TEMPLE CLAUSE
00s private pressing The Crayon Demos/Who Needs Enemies?/Let's Kill Music/Devil Walks In The Sand Demos (CD-R, in hand-crayoned sleeve, 120 only) £40

JULIAN COPE
87 Antar 4503 Interview/Christmas Mourning/Transmitting (fan club box set, with card, biography, membership card, letter, photos & stickers) £30
84 Mercury MERL 48 FRIED (LP, with poster & promo 12" [MADOX 5]) £20
87 Island ILPS 9861 SAINT JULIAN (LP, with free 12" interview LP [JCCLP 1]) £15
89 CopeCo JULP 89 SKELLINGTON (LP, mail order only) £25
90 Mofoco MOFOCO 90 DROOLIAN (LP, mail order only) £20
91 Island ILPSD 9977 PEGGY SUICIDE (2-LP) £20
92 Island ILPSD 9997 JEHOVAHKILL (2-LP, 4th side etched) £25
93 Ma-Gog MA-GOG 2 THE SKELLINGTON CHRONICLES (LP, mail order only) £25
94 Echo ECHLP 1 AUTOGEDDON (LP, gatefold sleeve) £35
95 Echo ECHLP 5 20 MOTHERS (2-LP, black or purple vinyl) £45
96 Echo ECHLP 12 INTERPRETER (LP, with poster) £40
01 Head Heritage HH12 DISCOVER ODIN (CD, mail order only, 10" x 5" package with booklet, signed & numbered, 1000 only) £40
(see also Teardrop Explodes, Brain Donor, Elizabeth, L.A.M.F)

SUZY COPE
61 HMV POP 941 Teenage Fool/Juvenile Delinquent £25
62 HMV POP 1047 Not Never Not Now/Kisses And Tears £25
63 HMV POP 1167 Biggity Big/Doing What You Know Is Wrong £25
65 CBS 201792 You Can't Say I Never Told You/And Now I Don't Want You £25

AL(L)AN COPELAND
59 Pye International 7N 25007 Flip Flop/Lots More Love (as Allan Copeland) £25

KEN COPELAND
57 London HLP 8423 Pledge Of Love/MINTS: Night Air £100

BOB & RON COPPER
63 EFDSS 1002 BOB & RON COPPER (LP) £35

COPPER FAMILY
71 Leader LED 2067 A SONG FOR EVERY SEASON (LP, sampler, tracks from 4-LP set) £40
71 Leader LEAB 404 A SONG FOR ALL SEASONS (4xLP) £50

COPPERFIELD
69 Instant IN 004 Any Old Time/I'm No Good For Her £15
(see also Quartz)

JOHNNY COPPIN
87 Rola RO 15 FOREST & VALE (LP) £20

COPS 'N ROBBERS
64 Decca F 12019 St. James Infirmary/There's Gotta Be A Reason £50
65 Pye 7N 15870 I Could Have Danced All Night/Just Keep Right On £25
65 Pye 7N 15928 It's All Over Now Baby Blue/I've Found Out £25
(see also Fairies)

COPY CATS
69 Bullet BU 419 Copy Cat (with Derrick Morgan)/BUNNY LEE ALL STARRS: Hot Lead £20

C (COPYRIGHT SIGN)
93 Transglobal GLOBAL 1 WITCH (LP) £60

CORAL
02 Deltasonic DLTLP 006 THE CORAL (LP) £40
04 Deltasonic DLTLP 014 MAGIC AND MEDICINE (2-LP, orange vinyl) £45
04 Deltasonic DLTLP 018 NIGHTFREAK AND THE SONS OF BECKER (mini-LP, gatefold) £20
05 Deltasonic DLTLP 036 THE INVISIBLE INVASION (2-LP, gatefold) £35
07 Deltasonic DLTLP 069 ROOTS & ECHOES (2-LP) £50
08 Deltasonic DLTLP 083 SINGLES COLLECTION (3-LP) £30
10 Deltasonic DLTBX 08 BUTTERFLY HOUSE (LP, 2-CD, DVD, box set) £25
10 Deltasonic DLTLP 086 BUTTERFLY HOUSE (LP) £30
14 Skeleton SKL 006 THE CURSE OF LOVE (LP, CD) £25

MINT VALUE £

CORBAN
78   Acorn AC 002   A BREAK IN THE CLOUDS (LP, with insert) £18

HARRY H. CORBETT
67   Decca F 12714   Flower Power Fred/(I'm) **Saving All My Love** (with Unidentified Flower Objects) £15
(see also & Harry H. Corbett, Faraway Folk)

MIKE CORBETT & JAY HIRSH
71   Atlantic 2400 141   MIKE CORBETT & JAY HIRSH (LP, gatefold sleeve) £20
(see also Mr. Flood's Party)

JERRY CORBITT
69   Polydor 583 576   CORBITT (LP) £25

PHIL CORDELL
69   Warner Bros WB 8001   Pumping The Water/Red Lady £35
(see also Thursday's Children)

CORDES
65   Cavern Sound IMSTL 1   Give Her Time/She's Leaving £70

LOUISE CORDET
62   Decca F 11476   I'm Just A Baby/In A Matter Of Moments (export copy in p/s) £15
62   Decca F 11524   Sweet Enough/Someone Else's Fool (export copy in p/s)......................................£15
63   Decca F 11673   Around And Around/Which Way The Wind Blows £15
64   Decca F 11824   Don't Let The Sun Catch You Crying/Loving Baby £15
64   Decca F 11875   Don't Make Me Over/Two Lovers...£20
62   Decca DFE 8515   THE SWEET BEAT OF LOUISE CORDET (EP) £50

CORDUROYS
66   Planet PLF 122   Tick Tock/Too Much Of A Woman...£60

CHICK COREA (& RETURN TO FOREVER)
72   ECM ECM 1018/9   PARIS CONCERT FEBRUARY 1971 (2-LP, as Corea & Braxton & Holland)................£15
74   Atlantic K 60081   INNER SPACE (2-LP) £15
74   People PLEO 9   SUNDANCE (LP)..£15

CORKSCREW
79   Highway SHY 7005   FOR OPENERS (LP) £25

DON CORNEL & ETERNALS
70   Moodisc MU 3506   Christmas Joy/WINSTON & RUPERT: Musically Beat £20

CORNELIUS
98   Matador OLE 3000   FANTASMA (LP)..£20
02   Matador OLE 3321   POINT (LP) £40

EDDIE CORNELIUS
80   GB Records GB 001   That's Love Making In Your Eyes/Hurry Up £15

DON CORNELL
54   Vogue Coral Q 2013   Hold My Hand/I'm Blessed £15
56   Vogue Coral Q 72144   Teenage Meeting (Gonna Rock It Right)/I Still Have A Prayer £30

JERRY CORNELL
55   London HL 8157   Please Don't Talk About Me When I'm Gone/St. Louis Blues £25

LYN CORNELL
60   Decca F 11227   Like Love/Demon Lover...£20
62   Decca F 11469   I Sold My Heart To The Junkman/Step Up And Rescue Me £15

ARNOLD CORNS
71   B&C CB 149   Moonage Daydream/Hang Onto Yourself (Demo copy as 'The Arnold Corns') £150
71   B&C CB 149   Moonage Daydream/Hang Onto Yourself (as 'The Arnold Corns') £125
72   B&C CB 189   Hang Onto Yourself/Man In The Middle (Demo copy).......................................£80
72   B&C CB 189   Hang Onto Yourself/Man In The Middle (reissue)..£75
74   Mooncrest MOON 25   Hang Onto Yourself/Man In The Middle (Demo copy) £40
74   Mooncrest MOON 25   Hang Onto Yourself/Man In The Middle (reissue) £35
(see also David Bowie)

CORONETS (1)
54   Columbia SCM 5117   Do, Do, Do, Do, Do, Do, Do It Again/I Ain't Gonna Do It No More...................£15
(see also Chris Sandford & Coronets, Ronnie Harris, Benny Hill, Eric Jupp, Lee Lawrence)

CORONETS (2)
68   Stresa BEV SP 1104/1105   I Wonder Why/You're Leaving Tomorrow £45

CORPORATION (JAMAICA)
70   Grape GR 3022   Sweet Musille/Walking Thru' Jerusalem £35
(see also Claudette & Corporation, Billy Jack)

CORPORATION (U.S.)
69   Capitol E-T/E-ST 175   THE CORPORATION (LP) £25

CORROSION OF CONFORMITY
85   Toxic Shock TXLP 4   EYE FOR AN EYE (LP) £18
91   Roadrunner RO9236 1   BLIND (LP) £40
96   Columbia 484328 1   WISEBLOOD (2-LP)...£35

CORSAIRS (JAMAICA)
70   Unity UN 558   Goodnight My Love/Lover Girl £15

CORSAIRS (U.K.)
67   CBS 202624   Pay You Back With Interest/I'm Going To Shut You Down £20

CORSAIRS (U.S.)
62   Pye International 7N 25142 **I'll Take You Home/Sitting On Your Doorstep** (with Jay 'Bird' Uzzel) £15

BOB CORT (SKIFFLE GROUP)
58   Decca F 10989   **The Ark** (Noah Found Grace In The Eyes Of God)**/Yes! Suh!** £15
59   William Timpson Ltd   **The Shop In The Cellar** (1-sided 78, 200 only) £15
57   Decca LK 4222   **AIN'T IT A SHAME** (LP) £20
(see also Liz Winters & Bob Cort)

DAVE 'BABY' CORTEZ
60   London HLU 9126   **Deep In The Heart Of Texas/You're Just Right** £15
62   Pye International 7N 25159 **Rinky Dink/Getting Right** £15
60   London RE-U 1233   **DAVE 'BABY' CORTEZ** (EP) £20
64   London HA-U 8142   **THE GOLDEN HITS OF DAVE 'BABY' CORTEZ** (LP) £30

CORTINAS (1)
68   Polydor 56255   **Phoebe's Flower Shop/Too Much In Love** £15

CORTINAS (2)
77   Step Forward SF 1   **Fascist Dictator/Television Families** (p/s, first 1,000 in card sleeve) £25
77   Step Forward SF 1   **Fascist Dictator/Television Families** (p/s) £15
78   CBS CBS 82831   **TRUE ROMANCES** (LP, with photo insert) £20

CORVETTES
82   Bitchin BIT 100   **Surf, Don't Walk/She'll Be Blonde** (p/s) £15
84   Bitchin BIT 101   **Girls Cars Girls Sun Girls Surf Girls Fun Girls/The Beach Is Not Enough** (p/s) £18

LARRY CORYELL
69   Vanguard SVRL 19051 **LADY CORYELL** (LP) £18
69   Vanguard SVRL 19059 **CORYELL** (LP) £18
70   Vanguard 6359 005   **SPACES** (LP) £25
85   Nimbus/Novus AN 3024 **STANDING OVATION** (LP, NImbus Supercut, mail order only sold via Practical Hi Fi
                                 magazine) £40
(see also Jazz Composers Orchestra)

COSMIC BABY/VANGELIS
94   East West SAM 1484   **A TRIBUTE TO BLADERUNNER** (12", double pack, promo only) £20
(see also Vangelis)

COSMIC DEAD
13   Cardinal Fuzz CFUL 010 **THE COSMIC DEAD** (2-LP gatefold, 1st press, black vinyl, 300 only) £30
13   Cardinal Fuzz CFUL 010 **THE COSMIC DEAD** (2-LP gatefold, 1st press, orange vinyl, 200 only) £35

COSMIC EYE
72   Regal Zono. SLRZ 1030 **DREAM SEQUENCE** (LP) £250

COSMIC PSYCHOS
88   What Goes On GOES ON 23 **COSMIC PSYCHOS** (LP) £15

COSMO
63   Blue Beat BB 175   **Gypsy Woman/Do Unto Others** £18
64   Blue Beat BB 244   **One God/BUSTER'S ALL STARS: Prince Royal** (actually "Reincarnation") £50
64   Blue Beat BB 269   **Rice And Badgee/BUSTER'S ALL STARS: The Tickler** £50
(see also Cosmo & Dennis, Denzil Dennis)

COSMO & DENNIS (ALIAS DENZIL)
62   Blue Beat BB 145   **Bed Of Roses/Tonight And Evermore** (as Cosmo & Denzil) £15
65   Blue Beat BB 296   **Sweet Rosemarie/Lollipop I'm In Love** £20
(see also Cosmo)

FRANK COSMO
63   Island WI 058   **Revenge/Laughin' At You** (B-side actually with Bobby Aitken) £30
63   Island WI 073   **Dear Dreams/Go Go Go** £30
63   Island WI 100   **Merry Christmas/Greetings From Beverley's** £30
63   R&B JB 119   **I Love You/DON DRUMMOND: Close Of Play** £45
64   Island WI 135   **Better Get Right/Ameletia** £35
64   Black Swan WI 446   **Alone/Beautiful Book** £35
(see also Two Kings)

COSMOTHEKA
74   Highway SHY 6002   **A LITTLE BIT OFF THE TOP** (LP) £20
77   Shy SHY 7001   **WINES & SPIRITS** (LP) £35
81   Highway SHY 7015   **A GOOD TURN OUT** (LP) £15
85   Dambuster DAM 1   **COSMOTHEKA** (LP) £18

JACK COSTANZO & TUBBY HAYES
62   Fontana TFL 5190   **COSTANZO PLUS TUBBS - EQUATION IN RHYTHM** (LP, mono) £50
62   Fontana STFL 598   **COSTANZO PLUS TUBBS - EQUATION IN RHYTHM** (LP, stereo) £40
(see also Tubby Hayes)

CELIA COSTELLO
75   Leader LEE 4054   **CELIA COSTELLO** (LP, with insert) £20

ELVIS COSTELLO (& ATTRACTIONS)
77   Stiff BUY 14   **Alison/Welcome To The Working Week** (p/s, A-side mispress on white vinyl) £300
77   Stiff BUY 20 DJ   **Watching The Detectives** (short version)**/Blame It On Cain** (live)**/Mystery Dance** (live)
                        (promo copy) £40
78   Radar ADA 24   **Radio Radio/Tiny Steps** (12", promo-only, 500 pressed) £15
80   2-Tone CHS TT 7   **I Can't Stand Up For Falling Down/Girls Talk** (unreleased, later a gig freebie, more
                        common issue (see other price) **has XX1 in run-off groove, 13,000 pressed**) £50
80   2-Tone CHS TT 7   **I Can't Stand Up For Falling Down/Girls Talk** (unreleased, gig freebie, more common
                        issue with XX1 in run-off groove, 13,000 pressed) £20

80	Stiff GRAB 3	**STIFF SINGLES FOUR PACK** (BUY 11, 14, 15 & 20 in clear plastic wallet)	**£20**
77	Stiff SEEZ 3	**MY AIM IS TRUE** (LP, 1st pressing, b/w front photo, red lettering with 'Help us hype Elvis' promo insert)	**£150**
77	Stiff Seez 3	**MY AIM IS TRUE** (LP, 1st pressing, b/w front photo, red lettering)	**£30**
78	Radar RAD 3	**THIS YEAR'S MODEL** (LP, with free 7" "Stranger In The House"/"Neat Neat Neat" (live) [die-cut company sleeve, SAM 83], 50,000 pressed; 1st 5,000 shrinkwrapped and stickered)	**£25**
79	Radar RAD 15	**ARMED FORCES** (LP, foldout stickered sleeve with free EP Live At Hollywood High [p/s, SAM 90] & postcards)	**£20**
79	Radar RAD 15	**ARMED FORCES** (LP, mispress, plays "[What's So Funny 'Bout] Peace, Love & Understanding" instead of "Two Little Hitlers"; sticker on insert)	**£25**
81	F-BEAT E.C. CHAT 1	**ELVIS COSTELLO INTRODUCES TRACKS ON HIS NEW ALBUM ALMOST BLUE** (LP, promo, signed, numbered,insert)	**£60**
82	F-Beat EC CHAT 2	**A CONVERSATION WITH ELVIS COSTELLO** (2LP, promo, numbered, signed, insert)	**£50**
06	Verve Forecast 0602498564547	**THE RIVER IN REVERSE** (2LP, with Allen Toussaint, printed inners)	**£50**

(see also Nick Lowe, George Jones, Coward Brothers)

COTERIE
69	Emerald GEM 1026	**A SWING TO FOLK** (LP)	**£40**

COTTI & CLUEKID
06	$N Format EPV 001	**4N EXCHANGE EP** (12", stickered white label)	**£35**

JAMES COTTON (BLUES BAND)
68	Vanguard SVRL 19035	**CUT YOU LOOSE!** (LP, as James Cotton Blues Band)	**£25**

JIMMY COTTON
62	Columbia SEG 8141	**CHRIS BARBER PRESENTS JIMMY COTTON** (EP)	**£20**
62	Columbia SEG 8189	**CHRIS BARBER PRESENTS JIMMY COTTON NO. 2** (EP)	**£20**

(see also James Cotton Blues Band, Alexis Korner)

JOSEPH COTTON
77	Observer OB 001	**Fit And Ready/OBSERVER: Iron Fist** (12")	**£40**

MIKE COTTON (SOUND)
64	Columbia DB 7267	**I Don't Wanna Know/This Little Pig**	**£60**
64	Columbia DB 7382	**Round And Round/Beau Dudley**	**£50**
65	Columbia DB 7623	**Make Up Your Mind/I've Got My Eye On You**	**£50**
66	Polydor BM 56096	**Harlem Shuffle/Like That**	**£40**
62	Columbia SEG 8144	**COTTON PICKING** (EP)	**£40**
63	Columbia SEG 8190	**THE WILD AND THE WILLING** (EP)	**£40**
64	Columbia 33SX 1647	**MIKE COTTON SOUND** (LP)	**£500**

(see also Lucas & Mike Cotton Sound, Satisfaction)

COUGARMAN AND GENERAL Z
12	Golden Hole GH001	**When Sally Met Mandingo/Afro Symphony**	**£15**
13	Golden Hole GH002	**Seaman Level/Susan Loves To Jack** (12" p/s)	**£15**

COUGARS
63	Parlophone GEP 8886	**SATURDAY NIGHT WITH THE COUGARS** (EP)	**£30**

ROGER COULAM QUARTET
67	CBS 52399	**ORGAN IN ORBIT** (LP)	**£20**
70	Fontana 16009	**BLOW HOT, BLOW COLD** (LP)	**£20**

DENIS COULDRY (& SMILE)
68	Decca F 12734	**James In The Basement** (solo)**/DENIS COULDRY & NEXT COLLECTION: I Am Nearly There**	**£40**
68	Decca F 12786	**Penny For The Wind/Tea And Toast, Mr. Watson?** (as Denis Couldry & Smile)	**£20**

(see also Felius Andromeda)

COULSON, DEAN, MCGUINNESS, FLINT
72	DJM DJLPS 424	**LO AND BEHOLD** (LP, gatefold sleeve)	**£18**

(see also Manfred Mann, McGuinness Flint, Dennis Coulson, Lyle McGuinness Band)

DENNIS COULSON
73	Elektra K 42148	**DENNIS COULSON** (LP, gatefold sleeve)	**£15**

PHIL COULTER ORCHESTRA
68	Pye 7N 17511	**Congratulations/Gold Rush**	**£20**

COUNT BISHOPS
78	Chiswick NS 35	**Mr Jones/Human Bean/Route 66/Too Much Too Soon** (unissued, test pressings only, as Bishops)	**£40**
77	Chiswick WIK 1	**THE COUNT BISHOPS** (LP)	**£18**

COUNT BUSTY & RUDIES
68	Melody MRC 003	**You Like It/The Reggay**	**£200**

COUNT DOWNE & ZEROS
64	Ember EMB S 189	**Hello My Angel/Don't Shed A Tear**	**£40**

(see also Peter & Headlines)

COUNT FIVE
66	Pye International 7N 25393	**Psychotic Reaction/They're Gonna Get You**	**£75**
87	Edsel ED 225	**PSYCHOTIC REACTION** (LP)	**£20**

COUNT HALA
69	Rude Boy RBH 005	**Cut Price Pussy/THE ATTACKERS : Police In Z Cars Blues**	**£50**
70	Rude Boy RBH 006	**Gems Of Christies/Cut Price Meow**	**£25**

COUNT HOUSE FOLK MUSIC CLUB
65	Own label MSCH 2	**MORE SINGING AT THE COUNT HOUSE** (LP, private pressing)	**£150**

COUNT LASHER
59 Caribou 106 — Caribou Calabash/Dalvey Girl £25

COUNT MACHUKI
10 Randys THB 7002 — Pepper Pot/WINSTON SAMUELS: Lick It Back £50

COUNT OSSIE & HIS MYSTIC REVELATION
71 Ashanti ASH 404 — Rasta Reggae/Samia...£25
71 Moodisc MU 3515 — Whispering Drums/SLIM SMITH & UNIQUES: Give Me Some More Loving £20
73 Ashanti NTI 1301 — GROUNATION (3LP, booklet, with Mystic Revelation Of Rastafari)..............£150
76 Dynamic DVLS 1001 — TALES OF MOZAMBIQUE (LP, gatefold)..£40
22 Soul Jazz SJR 495 — GROUNATION (3LP, 7", with Mystic Revelation Of Rastafari, box set, reissue, booklet, print)..£60
(see also Jackie Estick, Gaylads, Soul Defenders)

COUNT OSSIE & THE REVOLUTIONARIES
78 Charmers CH 0012 — Hog Head/TRINITY: Dog Meat (12")...£50
05 Hot Pot HPLP1014 — LEGGO DUB (LP, reissue)...£20

COUNT SUCKLE
70 Q 2200 — Lavender Blues/Humpty Dumpty £15
70 Q 2201 — Please Don't Go/FREDDIE & THE NOTES: Bread On The Table................£15

COUNTING CROWS
93 Geffen GEF 24528 — AUGUST AND EVERYTHING AFTER (LP, inner)..........................£80

COUNTRY BOY
64 Blue Beat BB 236 — I'm A Lonely Boy (actually by Shenley Duffas)/EDWARD'S ALL STARS: He's Gone Ska......£35

COUNTRY FOLK
70s Thule SLP 101 — THE COUNTRY FOLK (LP, private pressing)....................................£180

COUNTRY FUNK
70 Polydor 248 2018 — COUNTRY FUNK (LP)..£18

COUNTRY GAZETTE
72 United Artists UAG 29404 — TRAITOR IN OUR MIDST (LP)..£15
(see also Flying Burrito Brothers)

COUNTRY HAMS
74 EMI EMI 2220 — Walking In The Park With Eloise/Bridge On The River Suite (p/s, red & brown label) £50
82 EMI EMI 2220 — Walking In The Park With Eloise/Bridge On The River Suite (p/s, reissue, beige label)....£15
(see also Paul McCartney/Wings, Floyd Cramer)

COUNTRY JOE & THE FISH
67 Fontana TF 882 — Not So Sweet Martha Lorraine/Love £15
67 Fontana TFL 6081 — ELECTRIC MUSIC FOR THE MIND AND BODY (LP, flipback sleeve, also Stereo STFL 6087)...£40
68 Fontana TFL 6086 — I-FEEL-LIKE-I'M-FIXIN'-TO-DIE (LP, flipback sleeve).................£40
68 Vanguard SVRL 19006 — TOGETHER (LP) £20
69 Vanguard SVRL 19026 — ELECTRIC MUSIC FOR THE MIND AND BODY (LP, reissue) £30
69 Vanguard SVRL 19029 — I-FEEL-LIKE-I'M-FIXIN'-TO-DIE (LP, reissue)...........................£15
69 Vanguard SVRL 19048 — HERE WE ARE AGAIN (LP)..£20
70 Vanguard 6359 002 — C.J. FISH (LP)...£25
72 Vanguard VSD 79244 — ELECTRIC MUSIC FOR THE MIND AND BODY (LP, reissue, 'West Brothers' printing credit)..£20
73 Vanguard VSD 27/28 — THE LIFE AND TIMES OF (2-LP, gatefold sleeve, quadrophonic) £20
75 Vanguard VSD 79244 — ELECTRIC MUSIC FOR THE MIND AND BODY (LP, reissue)..........£15
73 Vanguard VSD 27/28 — THE LIFE AND TIMES OF (2-LP, gatefold sleeve, stereo)..............£15
80 Piccadilly PIC 3009 — THE EARLY YEARS (LP, private pressing, withdrawn) £40
(see also Country Joe McDonald)

WAYNE/JAYNE COUNTY (& ELECTRIC CHAIRS)
78 Safari SAFE 1 — Eddie And Sheena/Rock And Roll Cleopatra (p/s, with cartoon insert) £15
78 Safari SAFE 6 — I Had Too Much To Dream Last Night/Fuck Off (unissued) £0
79 Safari SAFE 18 — So Many Ways/J'Attends Les Marines (p/s, as Electric Chairs)............£20
78 Safari LONG 1 — ELECTRIC CHAIRS (LP)...£20
78 Safari GOOD 1 — STORM THE GATES OF HEAVEN (LP, multicoloured or grey marbled vinyl)......£20
79 Safari GOOD 2 — THINGS YOUR MOTHER NEVER TOLD YOU (LP)............................£18

COURIERS
66 Ember EMB S 218 — Take Away/Done Me Wrong (with p/s)......................................£80
66 Ember EMB S 218 — Take Away/Done Me Wrong £25

COURIERS
69 Ash ALP 201 — PACK UP YOUR SORROWS (LP)..£30

COURTEENERS
07 Loog LOOG 022 — Cavorting/No You Didn't, No You Don't (p/s, 750 only) £50
07 COURT 2 — Bide Your Time (1-sided, in white die-cut sleeve) £75
08 Loog 1764282 — Not Nineteen Forever/If It Wasn't For Me (Demo) (p/s)..................£15
10 Polydor 2758403 — ELECTRIC LICK (EP, 10", numbered)..£30
13 V2 VVR726589 — Lose Control/Chipping Away...£20
08 Polydor 1767024 — ST. JUDE (LP)..£200
10 Polydor 2729354 — FALCON (LP)...£200
13 V2 VVR724852 — ANNA (LP, CD)...£150
16 Ignition IGNLP82 — MAPPING THE RENDEZVOUS (LP, white/cream vinyl, some signed) £35
16 Ignition IGNLP82 — MAPPING THE RENDEZVOUS (LP)...£25
18 A&M 6729515 — ST. JUDE (LP, reissue, red vinyl)...£150
18 Ignition IGNLP127 — ST. JUDE REWIRED (LP)...£60

COURT MARTIAL

			MINT VALUE £
18	Ignition IGNLP127	ST. JUDE REWIRED (LP, picture disc)	£75
19	Polydor 7730574	FALCON (LP, reissue, hate vinyl)	£20
20	Ignition IGNLP186	MORE. AGAIN. FOREVER (LP, clear vinyl)	£20
20	Ignition IGNLP186	MORE. AGAIN. FOREVER (LP, pop-up sleeve)	£30

COURT MARTIAL
| 82 | Riot City RIOT 11 | NO SOLUTION (EP) | £20 |

LOU COURTNEY
| 99 | Soul Brother SBCS2 | I'M IN NEED OF LOVE (LP, reissue) | £20 |

DEAN COURTNEY
| 96 | Kent 6T 12 | Today Is My Day/SHARON SCOTT: (Putting My Heart) Under Lock And Key | £35 |

COURTYARD MUSIC GROUP
| 74 | Deroy | JUST OUR WAY OF SAYING HELLO (LP, private pressing) | £1500 |
| 15 | No Label or Cat no | JUST OUR WAY OF SAYING GOODBYE (LP, reissue, with 48 page booklet, 300 only) | £100 |

DAVE COUSINS
| 72 | A&M AMLS 68118 | TWO WEEKS LAST SUMMER (LP, brown label) | £35 |
| 79 | Old School SLURP 1 | OLD SCHOOL SONGS (LP, private pressing with Brian Willoughby) | £35 |

(see also The Strawbs)

COUSTEAU
| 00 | Palm PALMLP-58-1 | COUSTEAU (LP, numbered) | £18 |

DON COVAY (& GOODTIMERS)
61	Pye International 7N 25075	Pony Time/Love Boat	£30
61	Philips PB 1140	Shake Wid The Shake/Every Which Way	£30
62	Cameo Parkway C 239	The Popeye Waddle/One Little Boy Had Money	£30
64	Atlantic AT 4006	Mercy, Mercy/Can't Stay Away	£20
65	Atlantic AT 4016	Take This Hurt Off Me/Please Don't Let Me Know	£20
65	Atlantic AT 4056	See Saw/I Never Get Enough Of Your Love	£20
66	Atlantic AT 4078	Sookie Sookie/Watching The Late Late Show	£15
66	Atlantic 584 025	You Put Something In Me/Iron Out The Rough Spots	£15
66	Atlantic 584 059	See Saw/Somebody's Got To Love You	£15
65	Atlantic ATL 5025	MERCY! (LP, plum label)	£80
67	Atlantic 587 062	SEE-SAW (LP)	£40
69	Atlantic K 50225	HOUSE OF BLUE LIGHT (LP)	£25

(see also Soul Clan)

DAVID COVERDALE
77	Purple TPS 3509	DAVID COVERDALE'S WHITESNAKE (LP, with inner)	£25
77	Purple TPS 3509TC	DAVID COVERDALE'S WHITESNAKE (LP, white label promo, plain sleeve, with insert)	£40
78	Purple TPS 3513	NORTHWINDS (LP, with inner sleeve)	£20

(see also Whitesnake, Deep Purple, Wizard's Convention, Roger Glover, Jimmy Page)

COVERDALE PAGE
| 93 | EMI EMD 1041 | COVERDALE PAGE (LP, inner) | £50 |

(see also David Coverdale, Jimmy Page, Led Zeppelin, Deep Purple, Whitesnake)

COVERS
| 79 | Decca FR 13880 | Modern Girls/Head Out On The Road | £30 |
| 80 | Small Operations SO 001 | Young Girls/Boyfriend (p/s) | £20 |

JULIEN COVEY & MACHINE
| 67 | Island WIP 6009 | A Little Bit Hurt/Sweet Bacon | £50 |
| 78 | Island WIP 6442 | A Little Bit Hurt/Sweet Bacon (reissue) | £15 |

JULIE COVINGTON
70	Columbia DB 8649	The Magic Wasn't There/The Way Things Ought To Be	£15
70	Columbia DB 8705	Tonight Your Love Is Over/If I Had My Time Again	£15
67	MJB BEVLP 1009	WHILE THE MUSIC LASTS (LP, 99 copies, with Pete Atkin)	£400
71	Columbia SCX 6466	THE BEAUTIFUL CHANGES (LP)	£150

(see also Rock Follies)

COWBOY
| 71 | Atlantic 2466 022 | REACH FOR THE SKY (LP) | £15 |
| 72 | Atlantic K 40312 | 5'LL GETCHA TEN (LP, with insert) | £20 |

COWBOY JUNKIES
| 88 | Cooking Vinyl COOK 011 | THE TRINITY SESSIONS (LP) | £20 |

COWBOYS INTERNATIONAL
| 79 | Virgin V2136 | THE ORIGINAL SIN (LP, stickered PVC outer sleeve) | £15 |

(see also Public Image Ltd.)

STANLEY COWELL
| 72 | Freedom FLP40104 | BRILLIANT CIRCLES (LP) | £25 |

ELLERY COWLES
| 18 | Revoke REVOKE 005 | RELEASED TOXINS (12", stamped white labels, 300 only) | £20 |

COWSILLS
67	MGM MGM 1353	The Rain, The Park And Other Things/River Blue	£30
68	MGM MGM 1383	We Can Fly/A Time For Remembrance	£15
67	MGM C/CS 8059	THE COWSILLS (LP)	£25
68	MGM CS 8077	WE CAN FLY (LP)	£20
68	MGM CS 8095	CAPTAIN SAD AND HIS SHIP OF FOOLS (LP)	£15

BILLY COX
| 71 | Pye Intl. NSPL 25158 | NITRO FUNCTION (LP, blue/black label with logo-banner on left) | £100 |

(see also Jimi Hendrix)
HARRY COX
65	EFDSS LP 1004	ENGLISH FOLK SINGER (LP)	£25
65	DTS Records LFX 4	ENGLISH FOLK SINGER (LP)	£15

IDA COX
54	London AL 3517	SINGS THE BLUES (10" LP)	£30
75	Gannet GEN 5371-5376	PARAMOUNT RECORDINGS (6-LP box set)	£15

(see also Ma Rainey)
IDA COX/ETHEL WATERS
50s	Poydras 104	IDA COX AND ETHEL WATERS (EP)	£25

MICHAEL COX
59	Decca F 11166	Boy Meets Girl/Teenage Love	£20
59	Decca F 11182	Too Hot To Handle/Serious	£20
60	Ember EMB S 103	Angela Jones/Don't Want To Know (export issue)	£50
60	HMV POP 789	Along Came Caroline/Lonely Road	£15
61	HMV POP 830	Teenage Love/Linda	£15
61	HMV POP 905	Sweet Little Sixteen/Cover Girl	£25
64	HMV POP 1293	Rave On/Just Say Hello	£15

WALLY COX
61	Vogue V 9175	I Can't Help It/The Heebie Jeebees	£15
74	Pye Disco Demand DDS 105	This Man/I've Had Enough (DJ Copy)	£15
89	Kent 6T 5	This Man Wants You/SIX TEASERS: Doing The Hundred	£15

LOL COXHILL
78	Chiltern Sound CS 100	MURDER IN THE AIR (12" EP)	£35
71	Dandelion DSD 8008	EAR OF BEHOLDER (2-LP, gatefold sleeve)	£90
72	Mushroom 150 MR 23	TOVERBAL SWEET (LP)	£80
73	Caroline C 1503	COXHILL MILLER (LP, with Stephen Miller)	£20
74	Caroline C 1507	THE STORY SO FAR ... OH REALLY? (LP, with Stephen Miller)	£25
75	Caroline C 1514	LOL COXHILL & WELFARE STATE (LP)	£20
75	Caroline C 1515	FLEAS IN THE CUSTARD (LP)	£20
76	Ogun OG 510	DIVERSE (LP)	£15
78	Ogun OG 525	THE JOY OF PARANOIA (LP)	£25
78	Incus 0008	MOOT (LP)	£25
80	Pipe PIPE 1	SLOW MUSIC (LP)	£30

(see also Stephen Miller & Lol Coxhill, Kevin Ayers, Steve York's Camelo Pardalis)
COXHILL BEDFORD DUO
71	Polydor 2001 253	Pretty Little Girl (Parts 1 & 2)	£25
72	Dandelion 2058 214	Mood/WILL DANDY & DANDYLETTES: Sonny Boy/Oh Mein Papa	£20

(see also David Bedford, Lol Coxhill)
GRAHAM COXON
98	Transcopic TRANLP 005	THE SKY IS TOO HIGH (LP, inner sleeve, 4 postcards)	£45
01	Transcopic TRANLP 010	CROW SIT ON BLOOD TREE (2-LP, with inners & print, signed, 1,000 only)	£50
01	Transcopic TRANLP 010	CROW SIT ON BLOOD TREE (2-LP, with inners & print, 1,000 only)	£40
02	Transcopic TRANLP 018	THE KISS OF MORNING (2-LP, 10" x 10" picture book)	£30
04	EMI 5775191	HAPPINESS IN MAGAZINES (LP)	£50
06	Parlophone 350 5191	LOVE TRAVELS AT ILLEGAL SPEEDS (2-LP)	£45
09	Transcopic TRANS 102X	THE SPINNING TOP (2-LP)	£50
12	Parlophone 5099960278418	A+E (LP)	£18
18	Graham Coxon Records GC1	THE END OF THE F****ING WORLD (LP, gatefold)	£60

(see also Blur)
KEVIN COYNE
72	Dandelion 2310 228	CASE HISTORY (LP)	£150
73	Virgin VD 251/2	MARJORY RAZORBLADE (2-LP, gatefold sleeve with "130 Notting Hill Gate" credit, black/white label)	£25
73	Virgin VD 2501	MARJORY RAZORBLADE (2-LP, gatefold sleeve, later pressing without "130 Notting Hill Gate" credit)	£15
74	Virgin V 2012	BLAME IT ON THE NIGHT (LP, lyric insert, coloured 'twin Virgin' label)	£25
75	Virgin V 2033	MATCHING HEAD AND FEET (LP, laminated sleeve, lyric poster, coloured "twin-Virgin" label)	£15
79	Virgin V 2128	BABBLE (LP, with Dagmar Krause)	£20
80	Dandelion BUTBOX 1	DANDELION YEARS (3-LP, re-issue of Siren LP's Siren, Strange Locomotion and Coynes Case History)	£25

(see also Coyne-, Siren, Gordon Smith)
CRABBY APPLETON
70	Elektra EKS 74067	CRABBY APPLETON (LP)	£20
71	Elektra EKS 74106	ROTTEN TO THE CORE (LP)	£20

CHRIS CRACK
18	Daupe! DM SP 043	THANKS UNCLE TRILL (LP, 125 copies)	£30
18	Daupe! DM SP 043	THANKS UNCLE TRILL (LP, blue, marbled or white vinyl, 125 copies of each)	£35
18	Daupe! DM SP 043	THANKS UNCLE TRILL (LP, with obi strip, 20 copies)	£80

CRACK (3)
82	RCA RCA 214	Don't You Ever Let Me Down/I Can't Take It (die-cut 'Battle of the Bands' sleeve)	£25
82	RCA RCA 255	Going Out/The Troops Have Landed (p/s)	£15
83	RCA CRACK 1	All Or Nothing/I Caught You Out (p/s)	£30
83	Link LP073	IN SEARCH OF THE CRACK (LP)	£20

CRACKED MIRROR
83 CMLP 001   **CRACKED MIRROR** (LP, private pressing, 200 only) £80
CRACKERS
69 Fontana TF 995   **Honey Do/It Happens All The Time** £15
(see also Merseys)
CRACKLES
74 Filo FL2   **Keep Shaking/Hey Hey Little Girl** £20
SARAH CRACKNELL
87 3 Bears TED 001   **Love Is All You Need/Coastal Town** (p/s) £200
15 Cherry Red BRED 662   **RED KITE** (LP, Ltd. Ed., printed inner, signed) £40
16 Cherry Red BREDLP 685   **KITES** (10" EP, limited, flipback sleeve, some with art print) £25
(see also St. Etienne, 50 Year Void)
CRACK THE SKY
76 Lifesong LSLP 6005   **ANIMAL NOTES** (LP, with inner sleeve) £15
(BILLY) 'CRASH' CRADDOCK
59 Philips PB 966   **Boom Boom Baby/Don't Destroy Me** (as 'Crash' Craddock) £30
59 Philips PB 966   **Boom Boom Baby/Don't Destroy Me** (as 'Crash' Craddock) (78) £15
60 Philips PB 1006   **Since She Turned Seventeen/I Want That** (as 'Crash' Craddock) £30
60 Philips PB 1092   **Good Time Billy** (Is A Happiness Fool)/**Heavenly Love**........................£15
CRADLE OF FILTH
94 Cacophonous NIHIL1   **THE PRINCIPLE OF EVIL MADE FLESH** (LP)........................£25
96 Cacophonous NIHIL 6LP   **VEMPIRE** (mini-LP)...£30
96 Music For Nations MFN 108   **DUSK AND HER EMBRACE** (LP, with poster) £30
98 Music For Nations MFN 242   **CRUELTY AND THE BEAST** (LP, stickered sleeve) £25
00 Music For Nations MFN 666   **MIDIAN** (2-LP)..£20
01 AbraCadaver COF 001LP   **BITTER SUITES TO SUCCUBI** (LP)................................£15
CARL CRAIG
94 Open OPENT-001   **Throw/Remake Uno** (as CARL CRAIG PRESENTS PAPERCLIP PEOPLE) (12") £15
04 Carl Craig (White) CCR002   **Volume Two** (2x12") £25
95 Blanco Y Negro 509-99865-1 **LANDCRUISING** (2xLP) £25
01 Obsessive EVSLP20   **ABSTRACT FUNK THEORY** (as CARL CRAIG PRESENTS...) (2xLP) £20
CRAIG (1)
65 King KG 1022   **Ain't That A Shame/International Blues**...£18
66 Fontana TF 715   **I Must Be Mad/Suspense** £250
CRAIG (2)
66 Fontana TF 665   **A Little Bit Of Soap/Ready Steady Let's Go** £80
(see also Galliard)
DON CRAINE'S NEW DOWNLINERS SECT
67 Pye 7N 17261   **I Can't Get Away From You/Roses** £250
(see also Downliners Sect)
FLOYD CRAMER
54 London HL 8012   **Fancy Pants/Five Foot Two Eyes Of Blue** £20
54 London HL 8062   **Jolly Cholly/Oh! Suzanna** £20
55 London HLU 8195   **Rag-A-Tag/Aunt Dinah's Quiltin' Party** £30
58 RCA RCA 1050   **Flip Flop And Bop/Sophisticated Swing** £40
55 London REP 1023   **PIANO HAYRIDE** (EP, with Louisiana Hayride Band)..................£30
(see also Country Hams)
CRAMPS
79 Illegal ILS 12013   **GRAVEST HITS** (12" EP, blue vinyl) £30
79 Illegal ILS 12013   **GRAVEST HITS** (12" EP, black vinyl) £15
80 Illegal ILS 0017   **Fever/Garbage Man** (withdrawn 1st 'full band' p/s).........................£20
80 Illegal ILS 0017   **Fever/Garbage Man** (p/s; re-pressing in different p/s with 4 separate shots)........£15
80 Illegal ILS 0017   **Garbage Man/Mystery Plane** (Unreleased test pressing)..............£150
80 Illegal ILS 021   **Drug Train/Love Me/I Can't Hardly Stand It** (p/s).......................£15
81 IRS PFS 1003   **Goo Goo Muck/She Said** (p/s, yellow vinyl) £15
81 IRS PFSX 1008   **The Crusher/Save It/New Kind Of Kick** (12", p/s) £15
90 Enigma 12ENV22   **Creature From The Black Leather Lagoon/Jailhouse Rock/Beat Out My Love** (12") £15
80 Illegal ILP 005   **SONGS THE LORD TAUGHT US** (LP, white label with "Drug Train" in place of "T.V. Set") ..£175
80 Illegal ILP 005   **SONGS THE LORD TAUGHT US** (LP, with "T.V. Set")...................£30
81 IRS SP 70016   **PSYCHEDELIC JUNGLE** (LP)...£25
83 Illegal ILP 012   **OFF THE BONE** (LP, white label, with different mix of "Drug Train", around 50 copies pressed, unreleased)......£100
83 Illegal ILP 012   **OFF THE BONE** (LP, with 3-D sleeve & glasses) £35
83 Illegal ILP 012   **OFF THE BONE** (LP, picture disc with extra track) £15
84 Big Beat NED 6   **SMELL OF FEMALE** (LP, red see-through vinyl) £20
84 Big Beat BEDP 6   **SMELL OF FEMALE** (LP, picture disc) £20
84 Big Beat NED 6   **SMELL OF FEMALE** (LP, 2nd issue, black vinyl) £15
86 Big Beat WIKA 46   **A DATE WITH ELVIS** (LP, with poster) £20
86 Big Beat WIKA 46   **A DATE WITH ELVIS** (LP, blue vinyl) £25
90 Enigma ENVLP 1001   **STAY SICK** (LP, inner)..£18
91 Big Beat WIKDP 101   **LOOK MOM NO HEAD** (LP)..£15
91 Big Beat WIKPD 101   **LOOK MOM NO HEAD** (LP, picture disc) £18
90 Illigal ILP 5   **SONGS THE LORD TAUGHT US** (LP, reissue)...................................£15
91 Windsong WINDSONG 4   **LUX** (3 x 12" box set, with poster, T-shirt & book, numbered, withdrawn)........£50

CRANBERRIES

91	Xeric XER 014	Uncertain/Nothing Left At All (p/s)	£15
91	Xeric XER 014T	Uncertain/Nothing Left At All/Pathetic Senses/Them (12", p/s)	£20
91	Xeric XER 014CD	Uncertain/Nothing Left At All/Pathetic Senses/Them (CD)	£40
92	Island IS 548	Dreams/What You Were (p/s)	£15
92	Island 12IS 548	Dreams/What You Were/Liar (12")	£20
94	Island IS 600	Zombie/Away (p/s)	£15
94	Island ILPS 8003	EVERYBODY ELSE IS DOING IT... (LP, audiophile edition, black cover, numbered)	£125
92	Island ILPS 8003	EVERYBODY ELSE IS DOING IT... (LP)	£100
94	Island ILPS 8029	NO NEED TO ARGUE (LP)	£100
96	Island ILPS 8048	TO THE FAITHFUL DEPARTED (LP, yellow vinyl, poster)	£100
99	Mercury/Island 524 644 1	BURY THE HATCHET (2-LP)	£100
12	Cooking Vinyl COOK 552	ROSES (LP, CD)	£40
17	BMG 538274061	SOMETHING ELSE (LP)	£60

TONY CRANE

65	Polydor BM 56008	Ideal Love/Little You	£15
66	CBS 202022	Even The Bravest/I Still Remember	£20
67	Pye 7N 17337	Anonymous Mr Brown/In This World	£15
68	Pye 7N 17517	Scratchin' Ma Head/Patterns In The Sky	£20

(see also Bob Miller, Merseys/Merseybeats)

CRANES

89	Bite Back! BB! 017	SELF NON SELF (LP)	£15
91	Dedicated DEDLP 003S	WINGS OF JOY (LP with free 12")	£15
93	Dedicated DEDLP 009S	FOREVER (LP, with free 12")	£15
94	Dedicated DEDLP 016	LOVED (LP)	£20

CRANIUM PIE

09	Fruits De Mer Crustacean 08	Baby You're A Rich Man/Madman Running Through The Fields (poster p/s, 300 only	£60
11	Regal Crabmophone WINKLE 002	MECHANISMS (PART 1) LP, red vinyl card inserts)	£30
11	Regal Crabmophone WINKLE 002	MECHANISMS (PART 1) (LP, black vinyl, 100 only)	£80
12	Lunartica LUNAR LP 001	THE GEOMETRY OF THISTLES (LP, 'down under' edition, 25 copies, hand-numbered, hand-painted/decorated insert and slightly different cover to standard issue)	£60
12	Lunartica LUNAR LP 001	THE GEOMETRY OF THISTLES (LP)	£30

CRANNOG

| 76 | Crannog CR 1 | CRANNOG (LP) | £25 |

CRASH

| 82 | Crash EJSP 9819 | FIGHT FOR YOUR LIFE (EP, no p/s) | £30 |

CRASH COURSE IN SCIENCE

| 79 | Go Go ROO1 | Kitchen Motors/Mechanical Breakdown/Cakes In The Home (p/s) | £15 |

CRASHERS

| 69 | Amalgamated AMG 834 | Hurry Come Up/Off Track | £100 |

CRASS

78	Small Wonder WEENY 2	THE FEEDING OF THE 5000 (12" EP, with 4-page insert with 621984 on front & poster)	£80
78	Small Wonder WEENY 2	THE FEEDING OF THE 5000 (12" EP, reissue, please note that booklet has 621984 on front with the 6 crossed out)	£40
79	Crass 521984/1	Reality Asylum/Shaved Women (brown cardboard gatefold p/s)	£20
80	Crass/Xntrix 421984/1	Bloody Revolutions/POISON GIRLS: Persons Unknown (foldout p/s)	£20
80	Crass 421984/5	Nagasaki Nightmare/Big A Little A (foldout p/s, with patch)	£25
80	Crass 421984/5	Nagasaki Nightmare/Big A Little A (foldout p/s, without patch)	£15
81	Crass 421984/6	Rival Tribal Rebel Revel/Bully Boys Out Fighting (flexidisc with Toxic Graffiti fanzine)	£20
81	Crass 421984/6	Rival Tribal Rebel Revel/Bully Boys Out Fighting (hard vinyl promo, p/s)	£60
81	Crass COLD TURKEY 1	Merry Crassmass/Merry Crassmass - Have Fun (p/s)	£15
81	Crass 321984/IF flexi	Our Wedding (free flexi sent to readers of Loving -'for the price of a Stamp'. By Creative Recording And Sound Services – CRASS' with mailer envelope)	£300
81	Crass 621984	THE FEEDING OF THE 5000 (12" EP, reissue)	£25
82	Crass 221984/6	How Does It Feel (To Be The Mother Of 1000 Dead?)/The Immortal Death/Don't Tell Me You Care (foldout p/s)	£20
83	Crass 121984/3	Sheep Farming In The Falklands/Gotcha! (p/s with lyric insert)	£15
79	Crass 521984	STATIONS OF THE CRASS (2-LP, fold-out sleeve, black and white inners, original issue with "Pay no more than £3.00" on sleeve)	£40
81	Crass 321984/1	PENIS ENVY (LP, original pressing with "pay no more than £2.25 on sleeve)	£40
82	Crass BOLLOX 2U2	CHRIST THE ALBUM (2-LP, box set with poster and booklet, with "pay no more than 5.00" on spine of box)	£50
83	Crass 121984	YES SIR, I WILL (LP, fold-out sleeve, original issue with "Pay no more than £2.75 on sleeve)	£25
83	Crass 521984	STATIONS OF THE CRASS (2-LP reissue)	£25
84	Crass CAT 5	BEST BEFORE 1984 (2-LP, gatefold, 2 inners)	£20
11	Crass 321984	PENIS ENVY (LP, reissue)	£25
12	Crass 121994/2	YES SIR, I WILL (LP, reissue)	£20
17	Crass 621984	FEEDING OF THE 5000 (SECOND SITTING) (LP, reissue, white vinyl)	£15

(see also Anne Anxiety, Joy De Vivre, Eve Libertine, Poison Girls)

CRATOR

| 79 | Recordiau Lloer SEL 0001 | Blas Da/Fy Mreuddwyd I/Gelyn Yr Awyr (EP, 1000 only, no p/s) | £20 |

CRAVATS

| 78 | The Cravats CH 004 | Gordon/Situations (p/s) | £25 |
| 80 | Small Wonder CRAVAT 1 | THE CRAVATS IN TOYTOWN (LP, with inner sleeve) | £25 |

(see also Very Things)

MINT VALUE £

CAROLINE CRAWFORD
79	Mercury 9198 055	Coming On Strong/A Nice Feeling (12")	£18
19	Kent 6T 35	Ready Or Not Here Comes Love/MIKEY STEVENSON: I Stand Blue	£40
90	Motorcity MOTCLP 42	HEARTACHES (LP)	£15

CAROLYN CRAWFORD
19	Kent 6T 35	Ready Or Not Here Comes Love / MICKEY STEVENSON: I Stand Blue (7", mono, promo, given away at 40th Anniversary of 6Ts club all-nighter)	£300
65	Stateside SS 384	When Someone's Good To You/My Heart	£250
65	Stateside SS 384	When Someone's Good To You/My Heart (DJ copy)	£300

HANK CRAWFORD
76	Kudu KU 26	I HEAR A SYMPHONY (LP)	£15

JIMMY CRAWFORD
60	Columbia DB 4525	Long Stringy Baby/Unkind	£70

JOHNNY CRAWFORD
63	London HA 8060	RUMORS (LP)	£35
64	London HA 8197	JOHNNY CRAWFORD - HIS GREATEST HITS (LP)	£30

CRAWFORD BROTHERS
57	Vogue V 9077	Midnight Mover Groover/Midnight Happenings	£200
57	Vogue V 9077	Midnight Mover Groover/Midnight Happenings (78)	£50
59	Vogue V 9140	It Feels Good/I Ain't Guilty (triangular or round centre)	£150
59	Vogue V 9140	It Feels Good/I Ain't Guilty (triangular or round centre) (78)	£50

CRAWLING CHAOS
80	Factory FAC 17	Sex Machine/Berlin (1st pressing, 3000 copies in embossed p/s)	£25
80	Factory FAC 17	Sex Machine/Berlin (repressing, p/s)	£15
84	Foetus FOETUS 3	THE BIG C (LP)	£20
85	Foetus FOETUS 4	WAQQAZ (LP)	£15

PEE WEE CRAYTON
71	Vanguard VSD 6566	THINGS I USED TO DO (LP)	£15

CRAZE
80	Harvest SHSP 4114	SPARTANS (LP, unissued, test pressings only)	£50

(see also Hard Corps)

CRAZY CAVAN AND THE RHYTHM ROCKERS
73	Crazy Rhythm CR 01	Teddy Boy Boogie/Bop Little Baby	£30
74	Crazy Rhythm CR 02	Teddy Boy Rock'N'Roll/Rockabilly Star/Wildest Cat In Town/Little Teddy Girl	£30

CRAZY ELEPHANT
69	Major Minor SMLP 62	CRAZY ELEPHANT (LP, red/white/black label)	£60

CRAZY ENGLISH
82	Crazy English CH 001	Crazy English/Lose Or Win	£40

CRAZY HORSE
72	Reprise RSLP 6438	CRAZY HORSE (LP)	£25
72	Reprise K 44171	LOOSE (LP, gatefold sleeve)	£15

(see also Neil Young, Jack Nitzsche)

CRAZY HOUSE
82	T.W. PROP 2	THEY DANCE LIKE THIS FROM AS FAR OFF AS THE CRAZY HOUSE (LP, insert)	£15

CREAM
66	Reaction 591 007	Wrapping Paper/Cat's Squirrel	£20
67	Reaction 591 015	Strange Brew/Tales Of Brave Ulysses	£15
69	Polydor 56315	Strange Brew/Wrapping Paper (unissued)	£0
66	Reaction 593 001	FRESH CREAM (LP, mono)	£150
66	Reaction 594 001	FRESH CREAM (LP, stereo)	£120
67	Reaction 593 003	DISRAELI GEARS (LP, 1st pressing, with label miscredits to 'Windfall Music' and 'Apple Publishing' , '1967' on side 2 label, A1/B1 matrix, sleeve laminated on front & back, mono)	£250
67	Reaction 694 003	DISRAELI GEARS (LP, 1st pressing, with 'Windfall Music' and 'Apple publishing' label miscredits.Sleeve laminated on front only, stereo)	£120
67	Reaction 594 003	DISRAELI GEARS (LP, 1st pressing, with 'Windfall Music' and 'Apple publishing' label miscredits.Sleeve laminated on front & back, stereo)	£120
67	Reaction 593 003	DISRAELI GEARS (LP, 2nd pressing, with label credits of 'Immediate Music' and 'Apple publishing', sleeve laminated on front & back, mono)	£150
68	Reaction 593 003	DISRAELI GEARS (LP, 3rd pressing, with 'Immediate' and 'Copyright Control' label credits, sleeve laminated on front only, white box with text in top right corner of back sleeve, mono)	£75
68	Reaction 594 003	DISRAELI GEARS (LP, DISRAELI GEARS (LP, 3rd pressing, with 'Immediate' and 'Copyright Control' label credits, sleeve laminated on front only, white box with text in top right corner of back sleeve, stereo)	£60
68	Polydor 582 031/2	WHEELS OF FIRE (2-LP, gatefold sleeve, mono)	£100
68	Polydor 583 031/2	WHEELS OF FIRE (2-LP, gatefold sleeve, stereo)	£80
68	Polydor 582 033	WHEELS OF FIRE - IN THE STUDIO (LP, mono)	£50
68	Polydor 583 033	WHEELS OF FIRE - IN THE STUDIO (LP, stereo)	£40
68	Polydor 582 040	WHEELS OF FIRE - LIVE AT THE FILLMORE (LP, mono)	£50
68	Polydor 583 040	WHEELS OF FIRE - LIVE AT THE FILLMORE (LP, stereo)	£40
69	Polydor 583 033	WHEELS OF FIRE - IN THE STUDIO (LP, 2nd pressing, matt sleeve, stereo)	£30
69	Polydor 583 053	GOODBYE (LP, gatefold sleeve, with poster)	£25
69	Polydor 583 053	GOODBYE (LP, gatefold sleeve, without poster)	£20
69	Polydor 583 060	THE BEST OF CREAM (LP, 1st pressing, red labels)	£18
70	Polydor 2612 001	WHEELS OF FIRE (2-LP, 2nd pressing, matt sleeve, stereo. New catalogue number features on sleeve, spine and labels)	£40

70	Polydor 2383 016	**LIVE CREAM** (LP)	£18
71	Polydor 2855 002	**CREAM ON TOP** (LP, mail-order compilation)	£20
72	Polydor 2383 119	**LIVE CREAM VOL. 2** (LP)	£18
73	Reaction 594 003	**DISRAELI GEARS** (LP, 4th pressing, unlaminated sleeve, printed inner, stereo)	£35
77	RSO 2394 178	**GOODBYE** (LP, 2nd pressing)	£15
77	RSO 2479 160/1	**WHEELS OF FIRE** (2-LP reissue, 'set no. 2671 109' on back sleeve and labels)	£20
80	RSO 2658 142	**CREAM** (7LP, includes Fresh Cream, Disraeli Gears, Wheels Of Fire, Goodbye, Live Cream & Live Cream Vol. 2, German release, widely available in UK)	£80
83	RSO SPDLP 2	**WHEELS OF FIRE** (2-LP reissue, black labels)	£20
88	RSO 18MW 0068	**DISRAELI GEARS** (LP, 5th pressing, unlaminated sleeve, stereo)	£15
97	Polydor/S. Vinyl SVLP 087	**DISRAELI GEARS** (LP, reissue, 180g)	£30
97	Polydor/S. Vinyl SVLP 106	**FRESH CREAM** (LP, reissue with I Feel Free, 180g)	£20
97	Polydor/S. Vinyl SVLP 202	**WHEELS OF FIRE** (2LP, reissue, gatefold, 180g)	£25
97	Polydor/S. Vinyl SVLP 211	**GOODBYE** (LP, reissue, gatefold, 180g)	£20
13	Reprise 9362-49446-0	**ROYAL ALBERT HALL LONDON MAY 2-3-5-6 05** (3LP box set, white vinyl, RSD)	£60
14	Polydor/Back To Black 0600753548417	**CREAM 1966 - 1972** (7LP box set)	£100
15	473 527 1	**THE SINGLES 1967-1970** (10x7" box set, booklet)	£80
17	Polydor 572 266-9	**FRESH CREAM** (6LP box set, booklet)	£80
19	Polydor/UMC 7734197	**BBC SESSIONS** (2LP, gatefold, LP issue of 2003 CD, white/cream vinyl)	£30
20	Polydor/UMC 779 529-9	**GOODBYE TOUR** (LIVE 1968) (4CD box set, booklet)	£40
21	Polydor/UMC 350 753-5	**THE GOODBYE TOUR** (LIVE AT THE FORUM) (2LP, blue vinyl)	£30

(see also Eric Clapton, Jack Bruce, Ginger Baker, Blind Faith)

CREATION (U.K.)

66	Planet PLF 116	**Making Time/Try And Stop Me** (with Planet sleeve)	£80
66	Planet PLF 116	**Making Time/Try And Stop Me** (without Planet sleeve)	£50
66	Planet PLF 119	**Painter Man/Biff Bang Pow** (with Planet sleeve)	£80
66	Planet PLF 119	**Painter Man/Biff Bang Pow** (without Planet sleeve)	£50
67	Polydor 56177	**If I Stay Too Long/Nightmares**	£50
67	Polydor 56207	**Life Is Just Beginning/Through My Eyes**	£100
68	Polydor 56230	**How Does It Feel To Feel/Tom Tom**	£75
68	Polydor 56246	**Midway Down/The Girls Are Naked**	£50
73	Charisma Perspective CS 8	**THE CREATION '66-67** (LP)	£50
82	Edsel ED 106	**HOW DOES IT FEEL TO FEEL** (LP, with foldout insert)	£15

(see also Mark Four, Birds, Ashton Gardner & Dyke, Kennedy Express, Eddy Phillips, Smiley, Spectrum)

CREATION REBEL

79	Hit Run HIT DD8	**Beware/Natty Conscience Free** (12")	£50
81	On-U Sound DP3	**Independent Man Dub/CREATION REBEL : Dub** (10")	£30
82	Cherry Red CHERRY 41	**Love I Can Feel/Read And Learn** (p/s)	£18
78	Hit Run APLP 9001	**DUB FROM CREATION** (LP)	£80
79	Hit Run APLP 9004	**REBEL VIBRATIONS** (LP)	£70
79	Hit Run APLP 9008	**CLOSE ENCOUNTERS OF THE THIRD WORLD** (LP)	£45
81	4D Rhythms 4DLP1	**STARSHIP AFRICA** (LP)	£40
81	Static STATLP 04	**PSYCHOTIC JONKANOO** (LP)	£30
82	On-U Sound ON-U LP08	**STARSHIP AFRICA** (LP)	£30
82	Cherry Red BRED 21	**THREAT TO CREATION** (LP, with the New Age Steppers)	£25
82	Cherry Red/On-U BRED 33	**LOWS & HIGHS** (LP)	£25

CREATIONS

67	Rio R 133	**Meet Me At Eight/Searching**	£50
68	Amalgamated AMG 818	**Holding Out/Get On Up**	£60
69	Punch PH 2	**Mix Up Girl/Qua Kue Shut**	£400

(see also Little Roys)

CREATION STEPPER

79	Tribesman TM 006	**Stormy Night** (with Ranking Jahman)**/Stepper Now** (12", p/s as Creation Stoppers)	£70
79	Tribesman TM 22	**What You Are Not Supposed To Do/Children Obey Your Parents** (12")	£18
80	Nationwide NWD 015	**Homeward Bound/Version** (12")	£80
81	Moa Anbassa MA005	**Treat Me Unkind/Unkind Dub** (12")	£15
04	Jah Tubbys JT 10019	**King Nebuchadnezzar** (with the Disciples Riddim Section)**/The Nebuchadnezzar Skarock** (with the Dread-UK Crew) (12")	£30

(see also Fred Locks)

CREATIVE SOURCE

75	Polydor 2066680	**Don't Be Afraid** (Take My Love)**/Pass The Feelin' On**	£30
73	Sussex LPSX6	**CREATIVE SOURCE** (LP, gatefold)	£20
74	Sussex LPS X7	**MIGRATION** (LP)	£15
75	Polydor 2391196	**PASS THE FEELIN ON** (LP)	£15
76	Polydor 2391221	**CONSIDER THE SOURCE** (LP)	£15

CREATOR

80	Seven Leaves SLPP 001	**Such Is Life/PRODIGAL CREATOR: Such Is Life** (12")	£75

(see also Lord Creator)

CREATOR & NORMA

63	Island WI 105	**We Will Be Lovers/Come On Pretty Baby**	£25

(see also Lord Creator)

MARTIN CREED AND BOX CODAX

11	Telephone/Vinyl Factory VF 031	**Where You Go/Dawning** (12", 100 only labels hand-painted by Martin Creed)	£100

CREEDENCE CLEARWATER REVIVAL

69	Liberty LBF 15223	**Proud Mary/I Put A Spell On You** (withdrawn)	£20

MINT VALUE £

69	Liberty LBS 83259	**CREEDENCE CLEARWATER REVIVAL** (LP, blue label)	£80
69	Liberty LBS 83261	**BAYOU COUNTRY** (LP, blue label)	£40
69	Liberty LBS 83273	**GREEN RIVER** (LP, blue label)	£40
70	Liberty LBS 83338	**WILLY AND THE POORBOYS** (LP, 1st pressing, blue labels, textured sleeve)	£40
70	Liberty LBS 83338	**WILLY AND THE POORBOYS** (LP, 2nd pressing, blue labels, front laminated sleeve)	£35
70	Liberty LBS 83388	**COSMO'S FACTORY** (LP, 1st pressing, black labels, front laminated sleeve)	£40
71	Liberty LBG 83400	**PENDULUM** (LP, gatefold sleeve)	£20
73	Fantasy FT 506	**CREEDENCE CLEARWATER REVIVAL** (LP, reissue)	£15
73	Fantasy FT 507	**BAYOU COUNTRY** (LP, reissue)	£15
73	Fantasy FT 503	**WILLY AND THE POORBOYS** (LP, reissue)	£15

(see also Golliwogs, John Fogerty, Blue Ridge Rangers)

CREEPERS
| 66 | Blue Beat BB 366 | **Beat Of My Soul/LLOYD ADAMS: I Wish Your Picture Was You** | £40 |

CREERY SISTERS
| 70 | High Note BSLP 5004 | **OH WHAT A GLORY** (LP) | £20 |

CREPSOLES
| 71 | Ackee ACK 136 | **The World Gonna Be A Better Place/Invasion** | £75 |

CRESCENDOS
| 58 | London HLU 8563 | **Oh Julie/My Little Girl** | £60 |

CRESCENTS (1)
| 58 | Columbia DB 4093 | **Wrong/Baby, Baby, Baby** | £100 |

CRESCENTS (2)
| 64 | London HLN 9851 | **Pink Dominos/Breakout** | £15 |

CRESSIDA
70	Vertigo VO 7	**CRESSIDA** (LP, gatefold sleeve, large swirl label)	£1000
71	Vertigo 6360 025	**ASYLUM** (LP, gatefold sleeve, large swirl label)	£1000
11	Record Collector RCLP 002	**TRAPPED IN TIME - THE LOST TAPES** (LP)	£70
14	Reportoire REP 2224	**ASYLUM** (LP, reissue)	£20
14	Reportoire REP 2225	**CRESSIDA** (LP, reissue)	£20

(see also Uriah Heep, Black Widow)

CRESTAS
| 65 | Fontana TF 551 | **To Be Loved/When I Fall In Love** | £25 |

CRESTERS
| 64 | HMV POP 1249 | **I Just Don't Understand/I Want You** | £25 |

(see also Mike Sagar & Cresters, Richard Harding)

CRESTS
59	London HL 8794	**Sixteen Candles/Beside You**	£25
59	Top Rank JAR 150	**Flower Of Love/Molly Mae**	£20
59	Top Rank JAR 168	**Six Nights A Week/I Do**	£25
59	London HL 8954	**The Angels Listened In/I Thank The Moon**	£30
60	Top Rank JAR 302	**A Year Ago Tonight/Paper Crown**	£20
60	Top Rank JAR 372	**Step By Step/Gee** (But I'd Give The World)	£20
60	HMV POP 808	**Isn't It Amazing/Molly Mae**	£20
60	HMV POP 768	**Always You/Trouble In Paradise**	£20
61	HMV POP 848	**Model Girl/We've Got To Tell Them**	£15
62	HMV POP 976	**Little Miracles/Baby I Gotta Know**	£20
63	London HLU 9671	**Guilty/Number One With Me**	£20

(see also Johnny Maestro)

CREW-CUTS
| 56 | Mercury MEP 9002 | **PRESENTING THE CREW-CUTS** (EP) | £40 |
| 56 | Mercury MPT 7501 | **THE CREW-CUTS ON PARADE** (10" LP) | £50 |

BOB CREWE (GENERATION)
67	Philips BL 7788	**PLAY THE FOUR SEASONS HITS** (LP, as Bob Crewe Generation)	£25
67	Stateside SL 10210	**MUSIC TO WATCH GIRLS BY** (LP)	£35
68	Stateside S(S)L 10260	**BARBARELLA** (LP, soundtrack)	£75

BERNARD CRIBBINS
| 67 | Parlophone R 5603 | **When I'm Sixty-Four/Oh My Word** | £20 |
| 62 | Parlophone PMC 1186 | **A COMBINATION OF CRIBBINS** (LP, also stereo [PCS 3035]) | £15 |

THE CRIBS
03	Squirrel No 5	**Baby Don't Sweat/You and I** (other 2 tracks by JEN SCHANDE)	£80
04	Wichita WEBB 059S	**You Were Always The One/Song From Practice 1** (p/s)	£20
04	B-Unique KAISER	**Plays Kaiser Chiefs** (gig only 7" given away free, stickered sleeve)	£15
05	Wichita WEBB 097S	**COLLECTORS BOX SET** (8 x 7" box set, coloured vinyl)	£45
12	Wichita WEBB 338S	**Glitters Like Gold/On A Hotel Wall** (clear vinyl)	£15
13	Roots ROOTS 3	**Jaded Youth** (Live)/**THE BLACK BELLES: Leave You With A Letter** (Live) (10" only sold in Jumbo Records, Leeds)	£15
17	Sonic Blew 247 CRIBS 001	**Year Of Hate** (1-sided white label, 247 copies)	£20
06	Wichita WEBB 082LP	**THE NEW FELLAS** (LP)	£100
07	Wichita WEBB 126LP	**MEN'S NEEDS, WOMAN'S NEEDS, WHATEVER** (LP)	£40
09	Wichita WEBB 220LP	**IGNORE THE IGNORANT** (LP)	£30
10	Wichita WEBB 058 LPTEN	**THE CRIBS** (LP, reissue with CD)	£100
12	Wichita WEBB 335LP	**IN THE BELLY OF THE BRAZEN BULL** (2-LP, one side etched with free 7")	£25
13	Wichita WEBB 360LP	**PAYOLA** (2-LP)	£40
15	Sony 88875052921	**FOR ALL MY SISTERS** (2-LP, CD)	£25

(see also The Smiths)

CRICKETS FEATURING BUDDY HOLLY
SINGLES
57	Vogue Coral Q 72279	That'll Be The Day/I'm Lookin' For Someone To Love	£25
57	Coral Q 72298	Oh Boy!/Not Fade Away	£20
58	Coral Q 72307	Maybe Baby/Tell Me How	£20
58	Coral Q 72329	Think It Over/Fool's Paradise	£20
58	Coral Q 72343	It's So Easy/Lonesome Tears	£20

(Originally issued with triangular centres; later round centre copies are worth around half these values.)

| 68 | Decca AD 1012 | Oh, Boy/That'll Be The Day (export issue) | £75 |

EPs
58	Coral FEP 2003	THE SOUND OF THE CRICKETS (triangular or round centre)	£30
59	Coral FEP 2014	IT'S SO EASY (triangular or round centre)	£30
60	Coral FEP 2060	FOUR MORE BY THE CRICKETS	£30
60	Coral FEP 2062	THAT'LL BE THE DAY	£30

ALBUMS
58	Vogue Coral LVA 9081	THE CHIRPING CRICKETS (Vogue-Coral labels & Coral sleeve)	£150
58	Coral LVA 9081	THE CHIRPING CRICKETS (re-pressing with Coral labels & sleeve)	£100

(see also Buddy Holly)

CRICKETS
78s
59	Coral Q 72365	Love's Made A Fool Of You/Someone, Someone	£15
59	Coral Q 72382	When You Ask About Love/Deborah	£18

SINGLES
59	Coral Q 72365	Love's Made A Fool Of You/Someone, Someone	£15
59	Coral Q 72382	When You Ask About Love/Deborah	£15
60	Coral Q 72395	More Than I Can Say/Baby My Heart	£15
61	Coral Q 72417	Peggy Sue Got Married/Don'tcha Know	£15
61	Coral Q 72440	I Fought The Law/A Sweet Love	£15
61	London HLG 9486	He's Old Enough To Know Better/I'm Feeling Better	£15

EPs
60	Coral FEP 2053	THE CRICKETS (initial trangular centre)	£40
61	Coral FEP 2064	THE CRICKETS DON'T EVER CHANGE	£15
63	Liberty (S)LEP 2094	STRAIGHT NO STRINGS (mono/stereo)	£25
64	Liberty LEP 2173	COME ON	£25

ALBUMS
61	Coral LVA 9142	IN STYLE WITH THE CRICKETS	£30
62	Liberty LBY 1120	SOMETHING OLD, SOMETHING NEW, SOMETHING BLUE, SOMETHING ELSE! (mono)	£15
62	Liberty (S)LBY 1120	SOMETHING OLD, SOMETHING NEW, SOMETHING BLUE, SOMETHING ELSE! (stereo)	£20

(see also Buddy Holly, Jerry Allison & Crickets, Ivan, Sonny Curtis, Earl Sinks, Sinx Mitchell, David Box)

CRIME
80	Punk Products PP 1	Johnny Come Home/Generation Gap (p/s, beware of bootlegs)	£100

CRIME (U.S.)
90	Solar Lodge DOOMED 2	SAN FRANCISCO'S DOOMED (LP)	£15

CRIMEAPPLE
18	Daupe! DM SP 035	AGUARDIENTE (12", p/s, 230 copies)	£80
18	Daupe! DM SP 035	AGUARDIENTE (12", p/s, picture disc, 250 copies)	£80
18	Daupe! DM SP 035	AGUARDIENTE (12", p/s, aquamarine vinyl, 250 copies)	£80
18	Daupe! DM SP 035	AGUARDIENTE (12", p/s, with obi strip, 20 copies)	£150
19	Daupe! DM SP 044	WET DIRT (LP, with DJ Skizx, white, pink or yellow vinyl, 125 copies of each)	£50
19	Daupe! DM SP 044	WET DIRT (LP, with DJ Skizx, with obi strip, 20 copies)	£100
20	Daupe! DM SP 059	JAGUAR ON PALISADE (LP, 200 copies)	£40
20	Daupe! DM SP 059	JAGUAR ON PALISADE (LP, picture disc, 250 copies)	£50
20	Daupe! DM SP 059	JAGUAR ON PALISADE (LP, white vinyl, 100 copies)	£40
20	Daupe! DM SP 059	JAGUAR ON PALISADE (LP, red vinyl, 100 copies)	£40
20	Daupe! DM SP 059	JAGUAR ON PALISADE (LP, with obi strip, 20 copies)	£125

THE CRIMEWATCH PROJECT
92	Strategic Dance Initiative SDI 004	Boomzabang/Kis My Neck/Friday Night Style (white label 12", stickered paper sleeve)	£80

CRIMINAL CLASS
82	Inferno HELL 7	Fighting The System/Soldier (p/s)	£15

CRIMINAL JUSTICE
85	Endangered Music EDR 2	HIERARCHY OF HELL (EP)	£35

THE CRIMINAL MINDS
90	TCM SRT90L2748	GUILTY AS CHARGED (EP)	£180
91	TCM EP002	TALES FROM THE WASTELAND (EP)	£80
03	Vinylstore Records VSR001	BREAK SHIT UP (EP)	£30
01	UK Rap Records UKR001	WIDOWMAKER (LP)	£25

CRIMINALS
81	Crush CR 1	No Pleasure/The Criminals Of This World (no p/s)	£100

CRIMINAL SEX
85	Flexi Tits Disc	CRIMINAL SEX EP (white label inside p/s)	£20

CRIMSON BRIDGE
72	Myrrh Ms 6224	FILL YOUR HEAD WITH (LP)	£25

CRINKS

MINT VALUE £

CRINKS
67 Softspot SPO 1 — Pure And Simple/You Can't Cheat — £35

CRISIS (1)
79 Peckham Action NOTH 1 — No Town Hall (Southwark)/Holocaust/P.C. One Nine Eight Four (p/s) — £20
79 Ardkor CRI 002 — UK '79/White Youth (p/s) — £20
80 Ardkor CRI 003 — HYMNS OF FAITH (12" EP) — £20
81 Ardkor CRI 004 — Alienation/Brückwood/Hospital (p/s, with insert) — £20
82 Crisis NOTH 1/CRI 002 — HOLOCAUST UK (12" EP) — £15
(see also Death In June, Current 93, Theatre Of Hate)

CRISIS (2)
70s private pressing — ANOTHER FINE MESS (LP) — £35

MARILYN CRISPELL
83 Leo LR 118 — RHYTHMS HUNG IN UNDRAWN SKY (LP) — £15
85 Leo LR 126 — AND YOUR IVORY VOICE SINGS (LP) — £15

CRISPY AMBULANCE
79 Aural Assault AAR 001 — From The Cradle To The Grave/4 Minutes From The Frontline (glossy p/s) — £15

PETER CRISS
79 Casablanca CAN 139 — You Matter To Me/Hooked On Rock And Roll (p/s, green vinyl with mask) — £20
(see also Kiss)

CRISTINA
78 ZE 12 ZE 001 — Disco Clone (Disco Mix)/(Original Mix)/(Instrumental Mix) (12", p/s) — £15
80 Ze 12WIP 6560 — Is That All There Is/Jungle Love — £15
80 Island/Ze 12WIP 6560 — Is That All There Is?/Jungle Love (12", p/s) — £15
80 Ze ILPS 7004 — CRISTINA (LP) — £15

BOBBY CRISTO & REBELS
64 Decca F 11913 — The Other Side Of The Track/I've Got You Out Of My Mind — £45

CRITICS
81 Moody Music 80C1 — Town Girl/Without You/Plastic Valentine (foldout p/s) — £35

CRITICS & NYAH SHUFFLE
70 Joe JRS 1 — Behold/SEXY FRANKIE: Tea, Patty, Sex And Ganja — £50

CRITICS GROUP
66 Argo ZDA 46 — A MERRY PROGRESS TO LONDON (LP, with insert) — £25
68 Argo ZDA 82 — THE FEMALE FROLIC (LP, with insert) — £20
68 Argo DA 86 — WATERLOO PETERLOO (LP, yellow label with insert) — £20
71 Argo ZDA 138 — YE MARINERS ALL (LP) — £15

CRITTERS
66 London HLR 10047 — Younger Girl/Gone For Awhile — £15
66 London HLR 10071 — Mr. Dieingly Sad/It Just Won't Be That Way — £15
66 London HLR 10101 — Bad Misunderstanding/Forever Or No More — £25
67 London HLR 10119 — Marryin' Kind Of Love/New York Bound — £25
67 London HLR 10149 — Don't Let The Rain Fall Down On Me/Walk Like A Man Again — £15
67 London HA-R 8302 — THE CRITTERS (LP) — £40

JIM CROCE
72 Vertigo 6360 700 — YOU DON'T MESS AROUND WITH JIM (LP, gatefold sleeve, swirl label) — £40
73 Vertigo 6360 701 — LIFE & TIMES (LP, laminated sleeve, with small spiral label) — £200
70s Life Song 135004 — LIFE & TIMES (LP) — £15
70s Life Song 135004 — GREATEST CHARATOR (LP) — £15

CROCHETED DOUGHNUT RING
67 Polydor 56204 — Two Little Ladies (Azalea And Rhododendron)/Nice — £40
67 Deram DM 169 — Havana Anna/Happy Castle — £40
68 Deram DM 180 — Maxine's Parlour/Get Out Your Rock And Roll Shoes — £25
(see also Force Five, Doughnut Ring, Daddy Lindberg)

TONY CROCKET
82 Alternative ALT 010 — Queen Of Hearts/Plane Jane (12", p/s) — £50

CROFT
71 Maple MP 1 — The Dream/Henry And His Friends — £200

CROFTERS
69 Beltona SBE 103 — CROFTERS (LP) — £15

TONY CROMBIE
56 Columbia DB 3822 — Teach You To Rock/Short'nin' Bread Rock (as Tony Crombie & Rockets) — £40
56 Columbia DB 3859 — Sham Rock/Let's You And I Rock (as Tony Crombie & Rockets) — £30
57 Columbia DB 3881 — Lonesome Train (On A Lonesome Track)/We're Gonna Rock Tonight (78, as Tony Crombie & Rockets) — £20
57 Columbia DB 3921 — London Rock/Brighton Rock (as Tony Crombie & Rockets) — £30
57 Columbia SEG 7676 — ROCK ROCK ROCK (EP) — £50
57 Columbia SEG 7686 — LET'S YOU AND I ROCK (EP) — £50
54 Decca LK 4087 — MODERN JAZZ AT THE FESTIVAL HALL (LP, also features Ken Moule Seven and Don Rendell) — £50
56 Columbia 33S 1117 — TONY CROMBIE & HIS SWEETBEAT (10" LP) — £40
57 Columbia 33S 1108 — ROCKIN' WITH TONY CROMBIE & ROCKETS (10" LP) — £150
58 Columbia SCX 3262 — ATMOSPHERE (LP) — £30
59 Top Rank 35/043 — MAN FROM INTERPOL (LP, TV series music, by Tony Crombie & Band) — £20
61 Tempo TAP 30 — JAZZ INC. (LP) — £175
60 Top Rank BUY 027 — DRUMS! DRUMS! DRUMS! (LP, as Tony Crombie & His Band) — £30

61	Decca SKL 4114	**SWEET WIDE AND BLUE** (LP)	**£30**
61	Ember EMB 3336	**WHOLE LOTTA TONY** (LP)	**£40**

(see also Annie Ross, Ray Ellington, London Jazz Quartet)

CROMWELL

75	Cromwell WELL 006	**First Day**	**£20**
75	Cromwell WELL 005	**AT THE GALLOP** (LP, private pressing)	**£120**

(see also Establishment)

LINK CROMWELL (LENNY KAYE)

66	London HLB 10040	**Crazy Like A Fox/Shock Me**	**£25**

(see also Patti Smith Group)

ANDREW CRONSHAW

77	Trailer LER 2104	**EARTHED IN CLOUD VALLEY** (LP)	**£15**

CROOKED OAK

76	Folkland FL 0102	**FROM LITTLE ACORNS GROW** (LP, 500 only)	**£200**
79	Eron ERON 019	**THE FOOT O'WOR STAIRS** (LP)	**£25**

DAVID CROOKS

70	Jackpot JP 759	**I Won't Hold It Against You** (actually by Dave Barker)/ BOBBY JAMES: King Of Hearts	**£20**

(see also Dave Barker)

STEVE CROPPER

69	Stax SXATS 1008	**WITH A LITTLE HELP FROM MY FRIENDS** (LP)	**£30**

STEVE CROPPER & ALBERT KING

69	Stax SXATS 1020	**JAMMED TOGETHER** (LP, with Pops Staples)	**£20**

(see also Booker T. & M.G.'s, Albert King)

BING CROSBY

67	Reprise RS 20645	**What Do We Do With The World/Step To The Rear**	**£15**

(see also Gary Crosby, Louis Armstrong, Bob Hope)

DAVID CROSBY

71	Atlantic 2401 005	**IF I COULD ONLY REMEMBER MY NAME** (LP, gatefold sleeve, red/plum label)	**£50**

(see also Byrds, Crosby [Stills] Nash [& Young])

GARY CROSBY

58	HMV POP 550	**Judy, Judy/Cheatin' On Me**	**£60**
57	Vogue VA 160118	**GARY CROSBY** (LP)	**£15**

(see also Bing Crosby, Louis Armstrong)

CROSBY & NASH

72	Atlantic K 50011	**GRAHAM NASH & DAVID CROSBY** (LP, foldout sleeve)	**£20**

CROSBY, STILLS & NASH

69	Atlantic 588 189	**CROSBY, STILLS & NASH** (LP, gatefold sleeve, with lyric sheet, plum/orange labels)	**£30**
72	Atlantic K40033	**CROSBY, STILLS & NASH** (LP, reissue, green/orange labels)	**£15**
91	Atlantic 7567804871	**CARRY ON** (3-LP, compilation)	**£80**

CROSBY, STILLS, NASH & YOUNG

70	Atlantic 2401 001	**DÉJA VU** (LP, 1st pressing, 'copyright control/Warner Bros.' publishing credits, gatefold sleeve, pasted-on photo on front, plum/red label)	**£80**
70	Atlantic 2401001	**DÉJA VU** (LP, 2nd pressing 'Goldhill/Giving Room/Guerilla/Kinney & Flamingo' publishing credits, gatefold sleeve, pasted-on photo on front, plum/red label)	**£30**
71	Atlantic 2657 004	**FOUR WAY STREET** (2-LP, gatefold sleeve with lyric sheet)	**£25**
72	Atlantic K50001	**DÉJA VU** (LP, reissue, green/orange labels)	**£15**
71	Atlantic 2657004	**4 WAY STREET** (2-LP)	**£18**
99	Atlantic 9362474361	**LOOKING FORWARD** (2-LP)	**£50**

(see also David Crosby, Stephen Stills [Manassas], Graham Nash, Neil Young)

CROSS

90	Parlophone PCS 7342	**MAD, BAD AND DANGEROUS TO KNOW** (LP)	**£15**

(see also Roger Taylor, Queen)

JIMMIE CROSS

66	Red Bird RB 10042	**Super Duper Man/Hey Little Girl**	**£30**

(see also T2)

SANDRA CROSS (1)

85	Ariwa ARILP 026	**COUNTRY LIFE** (LP)	**£18**
87	Ariwa ARILP 031	**STEPPING IN DUBWISE COUNTRY** (LP)	**£18**
88	Ariwa ARILP 034	**COMET IN THE SKY** (LP)	**£15**
91	Ariwa ARILP 066	**THIS IS SANDRA CROSS** (LP)	**£18**

SANDRA CROSS (2)

11	Trunk JBH 040 LP	**THE MMS BAR RECORDINGS** (LP, 300 only)	**£30**

CROSS SECTION

74	Private Pressing AAMA/B	**Loving Song/Rock N Roll Queen**	**£50**

CROSS & ROSS

71	Decca F 13224	**Can You Beleive It/Blind Willie Johnson**	**£30**
72	Decca F 13316	**Peace In The End/Prophets Guiders**	**£15**
72	Decca EPS1	**CROSS & ROSS** (EP) (in demo only p/s)	**£75**
72	Decca EPS 1	**CROSS & ROSS** (EP)	**£60**
72	Decca SKL 5129	**BORED CIVILIANS** (LP, blue/silver labels)	**£300**

CROSS TOWN TRAFFIC

83	Cross Town Traffic CTT 001	**No For An Answer/Hanging On To You**	**£50**

CROW (1)

70	Stateside SSL 10301	**CROW MUSIC** (LP)	**£25**

MINT VALUE £

70	Stateside SSL 10310	CROW BY CROW (LP)	£20

CROW (2)

78	Inferno HEAT 14	Uncle Funk/Your Autumn Of Tomorrow	£20

CROWBAR

84	Skinhead SKIN 1	Hippie Punks/White Riot (p/s)	£45

CROWD (1)

76	Tropical TST 108	Mango Walk/Beefy Dub	£15

CROWDED HOUSE

10	UMGI 00602527415185	INTRIGUER (LP)	£20
88	Capitol EST 2064	TEMPLE OF LOW MEN (LP)	£20
91	Capitol 064-793559-1	WOODFACE (LP)	£35
93	Capitol SVLP 282	TOGETHER ALONE (LP)	£50
96	Capitol EST 2283	RECURRING DREAM - THE VERY BEST OF CROWDED HOUSE (2-LP)	£120
97	EMI LPCENT 6	WOODFACE (LP, reissue EMI 100 Centenary, stickered sleeve)	£25
07	Parlophone 00946-396027-1-1	TIME ON EARTH (2LP, gatefold, printed inners)	£40

(see also Liam Finn)

DON CROWN & HIS BUSKING BUDGIES

70	Orange OA 5507	Budgerigar Man/Piper Call A Tune	£15

CROWNS

68	Pama PM 725	I Know, It's Alright/I Surrender	£25
68	Pama PM 736	Jerking The Dog/Keep Me Going	£35
68	Pama PM 745	She Ain't Gonna Do Right/I Need Your Loving	£25
68	Pama PM 759	Since You Been Gone/Call Me	£25
68	Pama PMLP 6	MADE OF GOLD (LP)	£45

CROWS (1)

54	Columbia SCM 5119	Gee/I Love You So	£1000
54	Columbia DB 3478)	Gee/I Love You So (78)	£150

CROWS (2)

16	Telharmonium HARM 0005	UNWELCOME LIGHT (12", p/s)	£60

STEVE CROWTHER BAND

82	SMK Records SRTS 82 CUS 1584	Red Herring/My Machine	£100

TREVOR CROZIER'S BROKEN CONSORT

72	Argo AFB 60	PARCEL OF OLD CRAMS (LP)	£35

CRUCIAL BUNNY

79	Star PT LP 1008	CRUCIAL BUNNY VERSUS PRINCE JAMMYS (LP)	£40
82	Hawkeye HLP 008	DUB DUAL (LP, as Crucial Bunny Vs Scientist)	£50

(see also Prince Jammy)

CRUCIFIX

83	Corpus Christi CHRIST ITS 11	DEHUMANISATION (LP, poster sleeve)	£25

CRUCIFIXION

80	Miramar MIR 4	The Fox/Death Sentence (no p/s)	£80
84	Neat NEAT 3712	Green Eyes/Jailbait/Moon Rising (12", p/s, purple or green vinyl)	£20

ARTHUR 'BIG BOY' CRUDUP

64	RCA RCA 1401	My Baby Left Me/I Don't Know It	£40
64	RCA RCX 7161	RHYTHM AND BLUES VOL. 4 (EP)	£15
69	Blue Horizon 7-63855	MEAN OLE FRISCO (LP)	£100
70	Delmark DS 614	LOOK ON YONDERS WALL (LP)	£25
71	Delmark DS 621	CRUDUP'S MOOD (LP)	£25
72	RCA RD 8224	THE FATHER OF ROCK 'N' ROLL (LP)	£30
74	United Artists UAS 29092	ROEBUCK MAN (LP)	£35

JULEE CRUISE

89	Warner Bros. 925 859	FLOATING INTO THE NIGHT (LP)	£25

CRUISERS (1)

65	Decca F 12098	It Ain't Me Babe/Baby What You Want Me To Do	£30

(see also Dave Berry, Godley & Creme)

CRUIZE (1)

83	Wait WAIT 1	Strange Little Girl/Standing In The Rain	£35

CRUIZE (2)

89	TSR TSCRT 2	Get Your Lovin/Donyx Soula Muffin Mix (12")	£30

CRUSADERS

71	Rare Earth SRE 3001	OLD SOCKS NEW SHOES (LP)	£15

(see also Jazz Crusaders)

CRUSHED BUTLER

69	EMIDISC	Love Is All Around Me/Factory Grime (acetate)	£150

CRUSTATION

97	Jive HIP 184	BLOOM (LP)	£50

BETTYE CRUTCHER

74	Stax STX 1035	LONG AS YOU LOVE ME (LP)	£18

CRUX/CRASH

82	No Future OI 18	KEEP ON RUNNING (12" EP)	£15

CRY (1)
80 Sayonara S-3221083 Looking To The Future/Alone (p/s) £35
CRY (2)
81 DATO DAT 1A Love Is Necessary/Ends Are Split (no p/s) £80
CRY (3)
87 Crazy Flowerpot CFP 001 Party After Dark (with p/s) £80
87 Crazy Flowerpot CFP 001 Party After Dark £15
87 Crazy Flowerpot CFP 002 Give Her An Ice Cream (no p/s) £20
CRYER
80 Happy Face MM 124 The Single/Hesitate (p/s, with 2 inserts) £65
CRYIN' SHAMES
66 Decca F 12340 Please Stay/What's News Pussycat £20
66 Decca F 12425 Nobody Waved Goodbye/You £30
(see also Paul & Ritchie & Cryin' Shames, Gary Walker & Rain)
CRY OF THE INNOCENT
82 Pagan CUS 1436 The Haunting/Still Forever (p/s) £25
CRYPTIC SLAUGHTER
90 Metal Blade ZORRO 6 SPEAK YOUR PEACE (LP, inner) £15
CRYSBAS
79 Sain 66S Draenog Marw/Y Nhw (p/s) £25
79 Sain 72E Mae'di Bwrw/Blws Ty Golchi//Mor Gryg wr Morgrug/Amser (p/s)............£25
CRY SHARK
81 Radical Wallpaper RD 002 Protect And Survive/One Phone Call (p/s) £20
CRYSTAL CASTLES
07 Merok ME 002 Alice Practice/Air War/Love And Caring (p/s) £60
07 Rough Trade Pre Untrust/S&MSMS (demo)/Fuck Nicole/And Prolapse (7" given away as 'ticket' to Rough Trade In-Store appearance, 500 only)............................£25
10 Polydor/Fiction LC06444/ 2735606 Doe Deer/Mother Knows Best/Insectica/Seed (12" EP, 500 only, p/s) £25
08 Different DIFB 1200PLP CRYSTAL CASTLES (2-LP) £70
10 Fiction 2740406 CRYSTAL CASTLES (2-LP, gatefold) £40
CRYSTAL CLEAR
75 Crystal Clear CC 1 Buena Sera/I Want To Make Clear To You............................£15
CRYSTAL JOY
70 Wren 0346 Little Dreamer/Bite Hard £30
CRYSTAL METHOD
97 S3 VEGLP 1 VEGAS (2-LP) £35
CRYSTAL SET
81 Heart & Soul HSCS 001 Know How/Critical Town..£15
CRYSTALITES
69 Big Shot BI 510 Biafra/Drop Pan...£50
69 Nu Beat NB 036 Splash Down/Finders Keepers £150
69 Songbird SB 1015 Musical Madness Parts 1 & 2 ....£20
69 Songbird SB 1016 The Bad Parts 1 & 2 ....£40
69 Explosion EX 2002 Doctor Who (Parts 1 & 2) £30
69 Explosion EX 2005 Bombshell/Bag-A-Wire (B-side actually by Bobby Ellis & Crystalites) ...£70
69 Explosion EX 2006 A Fistful Of Dollars/The Emperor (B-side actually by Bobby Ellis & Crystalites) £50
70 Explosion EX 2010 The Bad/The Bad Version..£35
70 Bullet BU 424 A Fistful Of Dollars/BOBBY ELLIS: Crystal £50
70 Songbird SB 1017 The Undertaker/Stop That Man (B-side actually "Easy Ride" by Ike Bennett & Crystalites) £50
70 Songbird SB 1020 Lady Madonna/Ghost Rider £50
70 Songbird SB 1024 Isies/Isies (Version 2) £25
70 Songbird SB 1025 Stranger In Town/Stranger In Town (Version 2) £35
70 Songbird SB 1030 Sic Him Rover/Drop Pon..£35
70 Songbird SB 1034 Overtaker (Version I)/Overtaker (Version II) £35
70 Songbird SB 1035 Undertaker's Burial/Ghost Rider £30
70 Songbird SB 1036 Short Story/No Baptism (Version 2)............................£45
71 Songbird SB 1057 Earthly Sounds/Version..£20
72 Songbird SB 1072 Trinity/SCOTTY: Monkey Drop £25
73 Grape GR 3050 Blacula/Version £40
(see also Chosen Few, Ramon & Crystalites, Kingstonians, Bongo Herman, Denzil Laing, Derrick Harriot, Ethiopians, Dennis Brown, Glen Brown, Big Youth)
CRYSTALS
62 Parlophone R 4867 There's No Other Like My Baby/Oh Yeah Maybe Baby................£150
63 London HLU 9661 He's Sure The Boy I Love/Walking Along (La-La-La)................£15
64 London HLU 9837 Little Boy/Uptown (withdrawn) £150
64 London HLU 9852 I Wonder/Little Boy £50
64 London HLU 9909 All Grown Up/PHIL SPECTOR GROUP: Irving (Jaggered Sixteenths) ...£15
65 United Artists UP 1110 My Place/You Can't Tie A Girl Down £50
63 London RE-U 1381 DA DOO RON RON (EP) £50
63 London HA-U 8120 HE'S A REBEL (LP)..£70
(see also Darlene Love, Bob B. Soxx & Blue Jeans, Phil Spector)
CRYTUFF & THE ORIGINALS
79 Hit Run APLP 9006 DUB TO AFRICA (LP) (Pre-release) £45

CSA
78   Goat GOAT 001   STOCKADE (LP)..£40

C-SAIM
83   Summit SUM 3 T   Night Air/Give And Take (p/s) £15

C.S.L.
93   Nucleus NUKE 008   Work It Tough Bitch/Work It (Tough Mix)/Run Free (Original Jump Mix)/(Dark Black
                                          Mix) (12") £40

JOE CUBA SEXTET
66   Pye International 7N 25401 Bang! Bang!/Push, Push, Push £20

CUBAN HEELS
78   Housewives' Choice JY 1/2 Downtown/Do The Smoke Walk (p/s) £30

CUBY & BLIZZARDS
68   Philips BF 1638   Distant Smile/Don't Know Which Way To Go..£15
69   Philips BF 1827   Apple Knocker's Flophouse/Go Down Sunshine £25
69   Philips (S)BL 7874   DESOLATION (LP, black/silver labels)...£80
69   Philips SBL 7918   APPLE KNOCKERS FLOPHOUSE (LP)..£45

'CUDDLY' DUDLEY (HESLOP)
59   HMV POP 586   Lots More Love/Later...£20
60   HMV POP 725   Too Pooped To Pop/Miss In-Between...£25
64   Oriole International ICB 10 Way Of Life/When Will You Say You'll Be Mine £15

CUDDLY TOYS
82   Fresh LP 6   TRIALS AND CROSSES (LP) £15
(see also Raped)

CUES
56   Capitol CL 14501   Burn That Candle/O My Darlin' £250
56   Capitol CL 14651   Crackerjack/The Girl I Love (featuring Jimmy Breedlove) £200
57   Capitol CL 14682   Prince Or Pauper/Why £150
(see also Jimmy Breedlove)

CUFF-LINKS
70   MCA MUP(S) 398   TRACY (LP) £20

CLIVE CULBERTSON
79   Rip Off RIP 9   Time To Kill/Busy Signal (initially came in brown paper bag sleeve) £75
79   Logo GO 364   Time To Kill/Busy Signals (reissue) £25
82   Mint CHEW 66   Kill Me/The Night's No Friend Of Mine £30
84   Mint CHEW 89   Just A Little Bit/The Last Laugh £30
85   Mint CHEW 101   I Can't Fight It/You Don't Have A Dream £20
(see also No Sweat (1))

ELI CULBERTSON
74   EMI 2207   I Need Your Love Tonight/Boogie Queen..£25

CHRIS CULLEN
82   Zim Zam Z1   Coincidence/I'll See You Later (p/s) £15

CULPEPPER'S ORCHARD
72   Polydor 2480 123   SECOND SIGHT (LP)..£175

CULT HERO
79   Fiction FICS 006   I'm A Cult Hero/I Dig You (p/s, 2,000 only) £60
(see also Cure)

CULT MANIAX
82   Elephant Rock ROCK 001 Blitz/Lucy Looe (p/s, with A3 lyric poster)..£30
82   Elephant Rock ROCK 002 American Dream/Elephant Rock £15
82   Next Wave NXT 2/BAK 1   Frenzie/The Russians Are Coming/Black Horse/Death March (p/s, withdrawn most
                                          have band-inflicted scratch through Black Horse) £60

CULT (1)
80   Anti-Hype DL 001   It'll Take Time/Frontier/I Always Lose My Temper (p/s) £100

CULT (2)
94   Beggars Banquet BBQ 45T Star/Breathing Out/The Witch (Full Version) (12", p/s)..................£20
84   Beggars Banquet BEGA 57   DREAMTIME (white label test pressing, with unique version of "Go West") £45
84   Beggars Banquet BEGA 57   DREAMTIME (LP, with free live LP) £30
84   Beggars Banquet BEGA 57P   DREAMTIME (LP)..£20
84   Beggars Banquet BEGA 57P   DREAMTIME (LP, picture disc) £20
85   Beggars Banquet BEGA 65   LOVE (LP, gatefold) £25
87   Beggars Banquet BEGA 80   ELECTRIC (LP, gatefold) £25
87   Beggars Banquet BEGA 80   ELECTRIC (LP, gatefold sleeve gold vinyl, 5,000 only)........................£35
89   Beggars Banquet BEGA 90   SONIC TEMPLE (LP)...£25
91   Beggars Banquet CBOX 1 SINGLES COLLECTION (10-CD box set, picture discs with booklet)................£30
91   Beggars Banquet BEGA 122 CEREMONY (LP) £40
93   Beggars Banquet BEGA   PURE CULT (4-LP box set)...£100
     1230B
94   Beggars Banquet BBQLP 164 THE CULT (2-LP) £100
09   Vinyl 180 VIN180LP013   LOVE (LP, reissue, with 12") £60
09   Vinyl 180 VIN180LP014   LOVE (LP, reissue)..£25
12   Cooking Vinyl COOKLP548 CHOICE OF WEAPON (LP, with 12") £25
16   Cooking Vinyl COOKLP621 HIDDEN CITY (2-LP)...£18
16   Cooking Vinyl COOKLP621 HIDDEN CITY (2-LP, white vinyl)...£35
18   Music On Vinyl MOVLP2322 BORN INTO THIS (LP, reissue, pink vinyl, insert) £25

21   Beggars Banquet BBL 65 LP   **LOVE** (LP, reissue, platinum vinyl) **£40**
(see also Southern , Lonesome No More, Theatre Of Hate, Studio Sweethearts)

CULT MOUNTAIN
15   No label or Cat. No.   **CULT MOUNTAIN** (LP, repressing, white vinyl, p/s)..**£60**
15   No label or Cat. No.   **CULT MOUNTAIN** (LP, stamped and signed white labels) **£100**
16   Daupe! DM SP 013   **CULT MOUNTAIN 2** (LP, with OBI strip 20 only) **£200**
16   No label or Cat. No.   **CULT MOUNTAIN 2** (LP, 100 only) **£50**

CULTS PERCUSSION ENSEMBLE
79   HS 001   **CULTS PERCUSSION ENSEMBLE** (LP) **£100**
12   Trunk JBH 046 LP   **CULTS PERCUSSION ENSEMBLE** (LP, reissue 803 only) **£35**

CULTURAL ROOTS
82   Reggae REG 01   **Ghetto Running/Version** (12") **£25**
83   Music Works MW 007   **Whole Heap A Daughter/**(Version) (12") **£20**
80s   Up Front EX 718   **Mr Liar Man/People Com A Dance** (12", with HUGH CHRIS) **£20**
82   Germain GLP 002   **DRIFT AWAY FROM EVIL** (LP) **£30**
84   Greensleeves GREL 62   **HELL A GO POP** (LP) **£15**

CULTURE
80   Laser LASL 7   **BALDHEAD BRIDGE**..**£20**
77   Sky Note DD 003   **The Cultures Trod On/THE REVOLUTIONARIES, CULTURE AND RANKING TREVOR: Trod
On In Dub** (A-side as "The Cultures") (12" white pasted sleeve) **£25**
78   Sky Note SKY LP 016   **IN DUB** (LP) **£45**
78   Lightning LIP 1   **TWO SEVENS CLASH** (LP) **£25**
78   Virgin FL 1016   **HARDER THAN THE REST** (LP) **£18**
79   Virgin Frontline FL1047   **INTERNATIONAL HERB** (LP) **£15**
81   Virgin VX1001   **VITAL SELECTION** (LP) **£15**
83   Blue Moon BMLP 004   **TWO SEVENS CLASH** (LP, reissue) **£15**

BOBBY CULTURE
82   Leggo LG 003   **Health And Strength/Buenos Dias** (12") **£40**

CULTURE CLUB
84   Virgin VSY 694   **The War Song/La Cancion De Guerra** (picture disc, withdrawn) **£30**
(see also The Edge)

CULTURE PAUL
80s   Music House MH 2   **Mini Van Man** (12") **£40**

PETER CULTURE
84   Ariwa ARI 38   **The Counsel Of The Father/BLACK STEEL: Grooving In Love** (12")..............**£20**
84   Ariwa ARILP 018   **FACING THE FIGHT** (LP) **£15**

CULTURE SHOCK
82   Bluurg FISH 20   **ONWARDS & UPWARDS** (LP) **£15**
87   Bluurg FISH 19   **GO WILD** (LP) **£15**

CULTURED FEW
76   Feelgood FLG 102   **Better No Come/Better Dub** **£25**

ANDREW CULVERWELL
71   Polydor 2343 035   **WHERE IS THE LOVE?** (LP) **£15**

CUMBERLAND THREE
61   Columbia 33 SX 1302   **FOLK SCENE, U.S.A.** (LP, also stereo SCX 3364)......................................**£15**
61   Columbia 33 SX 1325   **CIVIL WAR ALABAMA VOL 2** (LP) **£15**
64   Parlophone PMC 1223   **INTRODUCING** (LP) **£15**

DAVID CUNNINGHAM
80   Piano PIANO 001   **GREY SCALE** (LP) **£40**

EARL CUNNINGHAM
70s   One Top OSM 002   **Got To Know That Place/Gates Are Wide Open** (12") **£100**
79   Freedom Sounds FSD 016   **Vanity Woman/Best Things** (12")..**£15**
80   Freedom Sounds FSD 017   **Never Give Up/Follow Fashion** (12") **£25**
81   Rusty International RI 012   **Cool Profile/School Girl** (12") **£80**
79   Vista Sounds VSLP 4021   **EARL CUNNINGHAM** (LP)..**£25**
84   Time TRLP 002   **JOHN TOM** (LP, insert) **£25**

CUPIDS
58   Vogue V 9102   **Now You Tell Me/Lillie Mae** **£900**
58   Vogue V 9102   **Now You Tell Me/Lillie Mae** (78) **£100**

CUPID'S INSPIRATION
68   NEMS 56-3500   **Yesterday Has Gone/Dream** **£15**
69   CBS 4509   **Boat Trip/Time Only Knows** **£20**
69   NEMS 6-63553   **YESTERDAY HAS GONE** (LP, gatefold, as Cupid's Inspiration Featuring T. Rice-Milton).......**£20**
(see also Gordon Haskell, Paper Blitz Tissue)

CUPOL
80   4AD BAD 9   **Like This For Ages/Kluba Cupol** (12", p/s, 45/33rpm)..............................**£20**
(see also Wire, Dome, Gilbert & Lewis, Bruce Gilbert, P'o)

CUPPA T
67   Deram DM 144   **Miss Pinkerton/Brand New World** **£25**
68   Deram DM 185   **Streatham Hippodrome/One Man Band** **£20**
(see also Overlanders)

CUPS
68   Polydor 56777   **Good As Gold/Life And Times**...**£40**

(see also Gallagher & Lyle)

CURE

SINGLES

78	Small Wonder SMALL 11	**Killing An Arab/10.15 Saturday Night** (p/s, 15,000 only, beware of counterfeits)	£80
79	Fiction FICS 001	**Killing An Arab/10.15 Saturday Night** (p/s, reissue)	£20
79	Fiction FICS 002	**Boys Don't Cry/Plastic Passion** ('soldier' p/s, typed matrix, 'but Bill does' on A side runout and 'land of 1000 motorhomes' on B)	£20
79	Fiction FICS 005	**Jumping Someone Else's Train/I'm Cold** (p/s, typed matrix)	£25
80	Fiction FICS 010	**A Forest/Another Journey By Train** (p/s)	£30
80	Fiction FICS 010	**A Forest/Another Journey By Train** (2nd pressing, "radiophonic' sleeve)	£15
80	Fiction FICSX 010	**A Forest** (Extended Version)/**Another Journey By Train** (12", p/s)	£200
81	Fiction FICS 012	**Primary/Descent** (p/s)	£15
81	Fiction FICSX 012	**Primary** (Extended)/**Descent** (12", p/s)	£25
81	Fiction FICS 014	**Charlotte Sometimes/Splintered In Her Head** (p/s)	£15
81	Fiction FICSX 014	**Charlotte Sometimes/Splintered In Her Head/Faith** (live) (12", p/s)	£18
82	Fiction FICG 015	**The Hanging Garden/100 Years//A Forest/Killing An Arab** (double pack, gatefold p/s, 5,000 only)	£18
82	Lyntone LYN 12011	**Lament** (1-sided flexidisc, red vinyl)	£40
82	Lyntone LYN 12011	**Lament** (1-sided flexidisc, green vinyl)	£15
82	Lyntone LYN 12011	**Lament** (1-sided flexidisc, red vinyl with Flexipop issue 22)	£50
82	Lyntone LYN 12011	**Lament** (1-sided flexidisc, green vinyl, with Flexipop issue 22)	£18
83	Fiction FICS 018	**The Walk/The Dream** (paper labels, poster p/s)	£20
83	Fiction FICSP 018	**The Walk/The Dream** (picture disc)	£35
83	Fiction FICSX 018	**Upstairs Room/The Dream/The Walk/Lament//Let's Go To Bed** (Extended)/ **Just One Kiss** (Extended) (12" double pack, shrinkwrapped with sticker)	£30
83	Fiction FICSP 019	**The Lovecats/Speak My Language** (picture disc, PVC sleeve)	£35
84	Fiction FIXSP 020	**The Caterpillar/Happy The Man** (picture disc, printed PVC sleeve)	£30
85	Fiction 080182-2	**In Between Days/The Exploding Boy/A Few Hours After This/ Six Different Ways** (live)/**Push** (live) (CD Video)	£40
85	Fiction FICSG 23	**Close To Me** (Remix)/**A Man Inside My Mouth** (poster p/s; some copies with blue & white 'Head On The Door' sticker)	£15
85	Fiction FICST 23	**HALF AN OCTOPUS: Close To Me** (Remix)/**A Man Inside My Mouth/New Day/ Stop Dead** (10" EP, p/s)	£18
85	Fiction 080180-2	**Close To Me** (12" Remix)/**A Man Inside My Mouth/Stop Dead/ New Day** (CD Video)	£45
87	Fiction FICSP 26	**Catch/Breathe** (clear vinyl, printed PVC sleeve)	£18
87	Fiction 080186-2	**Catch/Breathe/A Chain Of Flowers/Icing Sugar** (Remix) (CD Video)	£45
87	Fiction FICS 27	**Just Like Heaven/Snow In Summer** (p/s, mispress, A-side plays both sides)	£20
87	Fiction FICSP 27	**Just Like Heaven/Snow In Summer** (picture disc in custom PVC sleeve)	£20
89	Fiction FICSP 29	**Lullaby** (Remix)/**Babble** (clear vinyl, numbered printed 'spider web' PVC sleeve)	£18
89	Fiction FICVX 29	**Lullaby** (Remix)/**Babble/Out Of Mind** (12", pink vinyl, numbered with stickers)	£18
90	Fiction FICPA 34	**Pictures Of You** (Remix)/**Last Dance** (live) (p/s, green vinyl, mispress, plays "Last Dance" both sides)	£30
90	Fiction FICXA 34	**Pictures Of You** (Extended Remix)/**Last Dance** (Live)/**Fascination Street** (Live) (12")	£18
90	Fiction 080184-2	**Why Can't I Be You?** (12" Remix)/**A Japanese Dream** (5.40 Remix)/**Hey You!!!** (CD Video)	£45
92	Fiction FICCD 42	**Friday I'm In Love/Halo/Scared Of You/Friday I'm In Love** (Strangelove Mix) (12", p/s, different coloured or marbled vinyl)	£25
12	Secret 7 S74	**Friday I'm In Love** (1-sided RSD 7" in unique individual art sleeve, 100 only)	£150

ALBUMS

79	Fiction FIX 1	**THREE IMAGINARY BOYS** (with inner sleeve, postcard & badge)	£50
79	Fiction FIX 1	**THREE IMAGINARY BOYS** (LP, with inner sleeve and "Limited edition special price" stamped in gold on cover)	£20
80	Fiction FIXD 004	**SEVENTEEN SECONDS** (LP, textured sleeve, 1st pressing has FIX 004 on rear of sleeve)	£30
80	Fiction FIXD 4	**SEVENTEEN SECONDS** (LP, reissue)	£18
81	Fiction FIX 6	**FAITH** (LP, inner)	£30
82	Fiction FIX D7	**PORNOGRAPHY** (LP, with inner sleeve)	£20
83	Fiction SPELP 26	**BOYS DON'T CRY** (LP)	£20
83	Fiction FIXM 8	**JAPANESE WHISPERS** (LP, insert)	£20
84	Fiction FIXS 9	**THE TOP** (with badge & poster, green inner sleeve)	£20
84	Fiction FIXS 9	**THE TOP** (with promo plastic snake & top)	£35
84	Fiction FIXH 14	**CONCERT** (LP)	£18
85	Fiction FIXH 11	**HEAD ON THE DOOR** (LP, inner)	£20
86	Fiction 815 011-2	**BOYS DON'T CRY** (CD, original non-picture disc, with "Object" & "World War" & without "So What")	£30
86	Fiction FIXH 12	**STANDING ON A BEACH - THE SINGLES** (LP, gatefold with inner sleeve)	£30
87	Fiction FIXH 13/FIXHA 13	**KISS ME, KISS ME, KISS ME** (with bonus orange vinyl 6-track 12" [FIXHA 13], in custom PVC sleeve)	£50
87	Fiction FIXH 13	**KISS ME, KISS ME, KISS ME** (2-LP)	£30
89	Fiction FIXH 14	**DISINTEGRATION** (LP, snakeskin effect sleeve, with inner)	£35
89	Fiction FIXHP 14	**DISINTEGRATION** (picture disc, printed PVC sleeve)	£30
90	Fiction FIXLP 18	**MIXED UP** (2-LP, inners)	£35
92	Fiction FIXH 20	**WISH** (2-LP, inners)	£100
92	Fiction 513 600-0	**LIMITED EDITION CD BOX** (15 x CD hinged box set, 2,500 only)	£200
96	Fiction FIXLP 28	**WILD MOOD SWINGS** (2-LP)	£125
97	Fiction FIXLP 30	**GALORE** (2-LP, inners)	£150
00	Fiction FIX 31	**BLOODFLOWERS** (2LP, lyric insert)	£250
04	Fiction 981463	**JOIN THE DOTS: B-SIDES AND RARITIES 1978-2001** (4CD box set)	£30
04	Geffen 0602498628461	**THE CURE** (2LP, gatefold, printed inners)	£200

PROMOS

79	Fiction FICS 002	**Boys Don't Cry/Plastic Passion**	£45

79	Fiction CUR 1	Grinding Halt/Meat Hook (12", stickered sleeve)	£150
81	Fiction FICS 12	Primary (1-sided, no p/s)	£25
82	Fiction CURE 1	One Hundred Years/The Hanging Garden (12", p/s, promo/gig freebie)	£200
82	Lyntone LYN 12011	Lament (hard vinyl test pressing, no p/s)	£400
84	Fiction KAREN 1	THE TOP (12", 1-sided, 3-track sampler)	£55
88	Fiction FICSDJ 28	Hot Hot Hot!!! (Remix)/Hey You!!! (Remix) (die-cut title p/s)	£15
89	Fiction CIFCD 3	STRANGER THAN FICTION (CD, 6-track sampler, 1000 only)	£100
80s	Fiction FICS DJ 42	Friday I'm In Love (Promo in die-cut Fiction sleeve)	£20
97	Fiction FICSX 54	Wrong Number (Single Mix)/(ISDN Mix)/(Digital Exchange Mix)/ (Dub Analogue Exchange Mix)/(Crossed Line Mix)/(Engaged Mix)/(P2P Mix) (12", double pack, p/s promo only)	£25
97	Fixtion FIXCD.COM 1	FIVE SWING LIVE (CD, 5-track sampler, available via the internet, 5,000 only)	£30

(see also Cult Hero, Siouxsie & Banshees, Glove, Fools Dance, Tim Pope, Lockjaw, Obtainers)

MARTIN CURE & PEEPS

67	Philips BF 1605	It's All Over Now/I Can Make The Rain Fall Up	£40

(see also Peeps, Rainbows)

CURFEW

70	Brent BN 001	Visions/Look Behind You	£200

CURIOSITY SHOPPE

68	Deram DM 220	Baby I Need You/So Sad	£100

JOHNNY CURIOUS & STRANGERS

78	Illegal IL 009	In Tune/Road To Cheltenham/Pissheadsville/Jennifer (p/s)	£20

CURRENT 93

83	L.A.Y.L.A.H. L.A.Y. 1	Lashtal/Salt/Caresse (12", white p/s)	£22
83	L.A.Y.L.A.H. L.A.Y. 1	Lashtal/Salt/Caresse (12", white p/s [reissue from in 1988 with dark p/s and "1988" on label])	£18
85	L.A.Y.L.A.H. L.A.Y. 14	NIGHTMARE CULTURE (12" EP, with Sickness Of Snakes [i.e. Coil feat. Boyd Rice]; matt black & red sleeve)	£22
87	L.A.Y.L.A.H. L.A.Y. 18	HAPPY BIRTHDAY PIGFACE CHRISTUS (12" EP)	£22
87	Maldoror MAL 108	Crowleymass/Christmassacre/Crowleymass (Mix Mix Mix) (12", p/s)	£28
88	Yangki 002	FAITH'S FAVOURITES EP (Ballad Of The Pale Girl/NURSE WITH WOUND: Swamp Rat) (12", laminated p/s)	£28
88	Maldoror MAL 088	The Red Face Of God/The Breath And The Pain Of God (12", p/s, with insert, 666 only)	£40
89	Yangki 003	DEATH OF THE CORN (12" EP, with Sol Invictus; 'art' sleeve)	£18
90	Shock SX 003	She Is Dead And All Fall Down/God Has Three Faces And Wood Has No Name (folded sleeve in bag, 1,000 only, this price for 26 copies that were signed/lettered)	£45
90	Shock SX 003	She Is Dead And All Fall Down/God Has Three Faces And Wood Has No Name (folded sleeve in bag, 1,000 only)	£22
90	Cerne 004	This Ain't The Summer Of Love (live) (with Sol Invictus, gig freebie, printed labels, this price for 93 copies with ticket)	£30
90	Cerne 004	This Ain't The Summer Of Love (live) (with Sol Invictus, gig freebie, printed labels)	£20
92	Durtro DURTRO 004	LOONEY RUNES (12", live EP, 2,000 only, with poster)	£20
94	Durtro DURTRO 022	THE FIRE OF THE MIND (CD EP, free with book 'Simply Being')	£55
95	Durtro DURTRO 025	Tamlin/How The Great Satanic Glory Faded (12", numbered with insert, 2,000 only)	£28
95	Durtro DURTRO 028	Where The Long Shadows Fall (12", 1-sided clear vinyl with insert, 2,000 only)	£18
84	L.A.Y.L.A.H. LAY 008	DOGS BLOOD RISING (LP)	£25
86	Maldoror UDO 22M	IN MENSTRUAL NIGHT (LP, 25 with handmade inserts & cover)	£100
86	Maldoror UDO 22M	IN MENSTRUAL NIGHT (LP)	£20
86	United Dairies UD 022	IN MENSTRUAL NIGHT (LP, picture disc)	£20
87	L.A.Y.L.A.H. LAY 20	SWASTIKAS FOR NODDY (LP, with insert)	£25
88	Maldoror MAL 666	CHRIST AND THE PALE QUEENS MIGHTY IN SORROW (3-sided LP, with inserts, 93 copies only)	£100
88	Maldoror MAL 777	IMPERIUM (LP, black label, with insert)	£28
88	Maldoror MAL 777	IMPERIUM (LP, later pressing with white label)	£18
89	Maldoror MAL 093	DAWN (LP)	£60
89	Durtro DURTRO 001	LIVE AT BAR MALDOROR (LP, white label, 1,000 only)	£55
80s	Maldoror MAL 123	NATURE UNVEILED (LP, with insert & free 7": "No Hiding From The Blackbird/NURSE WITH WOUND: Burial Of The Sardine")	£30
80s	Maldoror MAL 123	NATURE UNVEILED (LP, with insert)	£20
88	United Dairies UD 029	EARTH COVERS EARTH (mini-LP)	£35
90	Dutro 048	I HAVE A SPECIAL PLAN FOR THIS WORLD (LP, limited edition on red vinyl)	£50
90	Dutro 048	I HAVE A SPECIAL PLAN FOR THIS WORLD (LP, limited edition on clear vinyl)	£30
90	Cerne 00123	THE CERNE BOX SET (3-LP set, includes "Horse"; other LPs by Sol Invictus & Nurse With Wound, 2,000 only)	£70
90	NER BADVC 693	1888 (LP, split with Death In June, 500 each on clear & red vinyl)	£35
90	NER BADVC 693	1888 (LP, split with Death In June, black vinyl)	£25
92	Durtro DURTRO 006	ISLAND (LP, with insert, 2,000 only)	£25
92	Durtro DURTRO 011	THUNDER PERFECT MIND (2-LP, with insert)	£25
94	Durtro DURTRO 018	OF RUINE, OR SOME BLAZING STARRE (LP, blue vinyl w/insert, 2,000 only)	£25
94	Durtro DURTO 019	LUCIFER OVER LONDON (LP, red vinyl with insert, 2,000 only)	£30
96	Durtro DURTRO 026	ALL THE PRETTY LITTLE HORSES (LP, clear vinyl with insert, 2,000 only)	£35
98	Durtro DURTRO 042	SOFT BLACK STARS (LP, clear vinyl with free 12" and insert, 2000 only)	£25

(see also Nurse With Wound, 23 Skidoo, Psychic TV, Crisis, Death In June, Sol Invictus, Steven Stapleton & David Tibet, Tibet & Stapleton)

CLIFFORD CURRY

69	Pama PM 797	I Can't Get A Hold Of Myself/Ain't No Danger	£50

TED CURSON QUARTET

64	Fontana 688310 ZL	TEARS FOR DOLPHY (LP)	£35

MINT VALUE £

DAN CURTIN
95	Peacefrog PF 023	PURVEYORS OF FINE FUNK - HEIGHTS TRAX VOL 1 EP (12", plain sleeve)	£15
94	Peacefrog PF 018	THE SILICON DAWN (2-LP)	£50
95	Peacefrog PF 038	WEB OF LIFE (2-LP)	£18

CHRIS CURTIS
66	Pye 7N 17132	Aggravation/Have I Done Something Wrong	£35

(see also Searchers)

CLEM CURTIS & FOUNDATIONS
72	Pye 7N 45150	I've Never Found A Girl (To Love Me Like You)/Point Of No Return	£20
75	Riverdale RS 105	Sweet Happiness/Lady Luck	£20

(See also the Foundations)

JOHNNY CURTIS
66	Parlophone R 5529	Our Love's Disintegrating/(I'd Be) A Legend In My Time	£70
67	Parlophone R 5582	Jack And The Beanstalk/Go On Back	£30

LEE CURTIS (& ALL STARS)
63	Decca F 11690	Let's Stomp/Poor Unlucky Me	£15
64	Decca F 11830	What About Me/I've Got My Eyes On You	£15
64	Philips BF 1385	Ecstasy/A Shot Of Rhythm And Blues	£15

(see also Pete Best Four)

MAC CURTIS
57	Parlophone R 4279	The Low Road/You Ain't Treatin' Me Right	£1500
57	Parlophone R 4279	The Low Road/You Ain't Treatin' Me Right (78)	£200
74	Polydor 2310 293	ROCKABILLY KINGS (LP, with Charlie Feathers)	£30

SONNY CURTIS
60	Coral Q 72400	The Red Headed Stranger/Talk About My Baby	£40
64	Liberty LIB 55710	I Pledged My Love To You/Bo Diddley Bach	£15

(see also Crickets)

T.C. CURTIS
86	Hot Melt CURTIS 1	STEP BY STEP (LP)	£15

WINSTON CURTIS
79	Supreme SUP DC 1001	You're Mine/My Desire/Mine Part II/Desire Part II (with Samantha Rose) (12")	£30
84	World Intl. WIR12D503	Be Thankful (For What You've Got)/This Magic Moment (12")	£50
77	Empire EMP 901	WINSTON'S GREATS (LP)	£60
77	Diamond DMLP 401	INSTRUMENTAL EXPLOSION (LP)	£100
81	Empire EMP 906	PORTRAIT (LP)	£100

CURTISS MALDOON
71	Purple TPS 3501	CURTISS MALDOON (LP)	£30
73	Purple TPS 3502	MALDOON (LP)	£15

ROCKY CURTISS & HARMONY FLAMES
59	Fontana TFE 17172	U.S.A. HIT PARADE (EP)	£40

BOBBY CURTOLA (& MARTELLS)
61	Columbia DB 4672	Don't You Sweetheart Me/My Heart's Tongue-Tied (solo)	£15
62	London HL 9577	Fortune Teller/Johnny Take Your Time (solo)	£15
62	London HL 9639	Aladdin/I Don't Want To Go On Without You (solo)	£15
63	Decca F 11670	Gypsy Heart/I'm Sorry	£15
63	Decca F 11725	Three Rows Over/Indian Giver	£15

CURVE
93	Anxious	FALLING FREE - APHEX TWIN REMIX (12", 1-sided promo only, 500 only)	£15
92	Anxious ANXLP 77	DOPPELGANGER (LP, with poster)	£30
93	Anxious ANXLP 81	CUCKOO (LP)	£30

CURVED AIR
84	Pearl Key PK 07350	Renegade/We're Only Human (p/s)	£15
70	Warner Bros K 56004	AIR CONDITIONING (LP, picture disc, with booklet, 10,000 only)	£70
70	Warner Bros K 56004	AIR CONDITIONING (LP, picture disc)	£30
70	Warner Bros WSX 3012	AIR CONDITIONING (LP, green label, laminated sleeve)	£40
71	Warner Bros K 46092	SECOND ALBUM (LP, die-cut 'leaves' fold-out sleeve, green label)	£40
72	Warner Bros K 46158	PHANTASMAGORIA (LP, green label, with inner lyric card)	£20
73	Warner Bros K 46224	AIR CUT (LP, green label, gatefold sleeve)	£25
75	Deram SML 1119	LIVE (LP, red/white label)	£20

(see also Kirby, Sonja Kristina, [Darryl Way's] Wolf, Trace, Legs, Stretch, Police)

PETER CUSACK
77	Bead Records BEAD 5	AFTER BEING IN HOLLAND FOR TWO YEARS (LP)	£40
84	Bead Records BEAD 22	BIRD JUMPS INTO WOOD (LP, with Clive Bell)	£20

IVOR CUTLER TRIO
59	Fontana TFE 17144	OF Y'HUP (EP)	£20
61	Decca DFE 6677	GET AWAY FROM THE WALL (EP)	£20
89	Strange Fruit SFPS 068	PEE SESSIONS (12")	£15
61	Decca LK 4405	WHO TORE YOUR TROUSERS? (LP)	£100
67	Parlophone PCS 7040	LUDO (LP)	£100
74	Virgin V2021	DANDRUFF (LP, as Ivor Cutler)	£30
75	Virgin V2037	VELVET DONKEY (LP)	£20
76	Virgin V2056	JAMMY SMEARS (LP)	£20
78	Harvest SHSP4084	LIFE IN A SCOTCH SITTING ROOM VOL 2 (LP)	£20
84	Rough Trade ROUGH 59	PRIVILEGE (LP with Linda Hirst)	£25

85	Virgin OVED 12	JAMMY SMEARS (LP, reissue)	£15
86	Virgin OVED 34	VELVET DONKEY (LP, reissue)	£15
86	Rough Trade ROUGH 89	PRINCE IVOR (2-LP)	£25
86	Rough Trade ROUGH 98	GRUTS (LP)	£20

L CUTMORE
90	Fast Forward CUT 1	Subsonic Mix 1/Subsonic Mix 2 (12")	£25

T. TOMMY CUTRER (& GINNY WRIGHT)
54	London HL 8093	Mexico Gal/Wonderful World (B-side with Ginny Wright)	£40

(see also Ginny Wright)

CYAN THREE
66	Decca F 12371	Since I Lost My Baby/Face Of A Loser	£20

CYANIDE
78	Pye 7N 46048	I'm A Boy/Do It (p/s)	£25
78	Pye 7N 46094	Mac The Flash/Hate The State (demo copies in p/s)	£60
78	Pye 7N 46094	Mac The Flash/Hate The State (demo copies no p/s)	£15
79	Pinnacle PIN 23	Fireball/Your Old Man (p/s)	£40
78	Pye NSPL 18554	CYANIDE (LP)	£40

CYBERMEN
78	Rockaway AERE 101	THE CYBERMEN (EP, available in 2 different sleeves with info sheet)	£100
78	Rockaway AERE 101	THE CYBERMEN (EP, available in 2 different sleeves without info sheet)	£40
79	Rockaway LUV 002	You're To Blame/It's You I Want (with inserts)	£45

CYBERNETIC SERENDIPITY GROUP
68	ICA ICA 1/2	CYBERNETIC SERENDIPITY MUSIC (LP, private pressing)	£150

CYBERSONIK
90	Champion CHAMP 264	Technarchy/Algorhythm (p/s)	£18

CYBOTRON FEATURING DILLINJA
00	Valve CYBX 001	NASTY WAYZ (EP)	£15

(see also Dillinja)

CYCLE
70	S.R.T. 71143	CYCLE (LP, 99 copies only)	£1000
20	Rise Above Relics RARLP 21	COSMIC CLOUDS (2-LP, with 7" and booklet)	£40
20	Rise Above Relics RARLP 21	COSMIC CLOUDS (2-LP, silver vinyl)	£20

CYCLONES (1)
64	Oriole CB 1898	Nobody/Little Egypt	£60

CYCLONES (2)
71	Banana BA 338	My Sweet Lord/DENNIS BROWN: Silky (B-side actually by Monty Alexander & Cyclones)	£40

CYGNUS
78	Greensleeves GRED 4	Jah Man/Babylon (12")	£25

CYLOB
96	Rephlex CAT 033 LP	CYLOBIAN SUNSET (LP)	£35

CYMANDE
73	Alaska ALA 4	The Message/Zion I	£20
73	Alaska ALA 10	Bra/Ras Tafarian Folk Song	£18
74	Contempo CS 2019	Brothers On The Slide/Pon De Dungle	£80
99	Sequel NEET 1008	The Message/Brothers On The Slide/Bra/Dove (12")	£25
73	Alaska ALKA 100	CYMANDE (LP)	£100
74	Contempo CLP 508	PROMISED HEIGHTS (LP)	£80
93	Sequel NEXLP 202	CYMANDE (LP, reissue, actually The Best Of)	£40
99	Sequel NEMLP 428	CYMANDE (LP, reissue)	£20
99	Sequel NEMLP 429	SECOND TIME AROUND (LP, reissue)	£20
99	Sequel NEMLP 430	PROMISE HEIGHTS (LP, reissue)	£20
15	Cherry Red BRED 668	A SIMPLE ACT OF FAITH (LP)	£15
18	Mr. Bongo MRBLP 159	SECOND TIME AROUND (LP. reissue, 180gm)	£20
18	Mr. Bongo MRBLP 160	PROMISED HEIGHTS (LP, reissue, 180gm)	£20

JOHNNY CYMBAL
63	London RER 1375	MISTER BASS MAN (EP)	£25
64	London RER 1406	CYMBAL SMASHES (EP)	£15

CYMBALINE
65	Pye 7N 15916	Please Little Girl/Coming Home Baby	£35
65	Mercury MF 918	Top Girl/Can You Hear Me?	£35
67	Philips BF 1624	Matrimonial Fears/You Will Never Love Me	£70
68	Philips BF 1681	Down By The Seaside/Fire	£25

CYMERONS
64	Decca F 11976	I'll Be There/Making Love To Another	£15

CYNIC
83	Cynic CYN 1	Suicide/No Time At All (no p/s)	£75

CYNTHIA & ARCHIE
64	R&B JB 168	Every Beat/DELROY WILSON: Sammy Dead	£60

CYPRESS HILL
91	Columbia 468893 1	CYPRESS HILL (LP)	£20
93	Columbia 474075	BLACK SUNDAY (2-LP, gatefold, inners)	£35
95	Columbia 478127-1	CYPRESS HILL III (TEMPLES OF BOOM) (2-LP, gatefold)	£25

NOHELANI CYPRIOANO
14	Athens Of The North ATH 007	Lihue/Playing With Fire (reissue)	£15
15	Be With BEWITH008LP	NOHELANI (LP, reissue)	£25

CYRKLE
67	CBS 62977	NEON (LP)	£40

CZAR
70	Philips 6006 071	Oh Lord I'm Getting Heavy/Why Don't We Be A Rock'n'Roll Band	£40
70	Fontana 6309 009	CZAR (LP, black/silver label, laminated sleeve)	£1500
11	Sunbeam SBR2LP5040	CZAR (2-LP, reissue)	£40

(see also Hungry Wolf)

HOLGER CZUKAY
79	EMI EMC 3319	MOVIES (LP)	£20
81	EMI EMC 3384	ON THE WAY TO THE PEAK OF NORMAL (LP)	£15
84	Virgin V 2307	DER OSTEN IST ROT (LP)	£15

(see under Jah Wobble, Can)

D

KIM D
65	Pye 7N 15953	The Real Thing/Come On Baby	£30

(see also Kim Davis)

ROB D
95	Mo' Wax MW 037	Clubbed To Death/(Mixes) (12", p/s)	£25

SCHOOLLY D
86	Flame MELT LP 1	SCHOOLLEY D (LP)	£15

TONY D & SHAKEOUTS
64	Piccadilly 7N 35168	Is It True/Never Let Her Go	£25

DA BAND
78	Rip Off RIP 2	I Like It/Pirate's Lullaby (p/s)	£20

DA REBELS
97	Ugly UGM 009	HOUSE NATION UNDER A GROOVE EP (12")	£30
97	Ugly UGM 012	HOUSE NATION UNDER A GROOVE (12", reissue, promo)	£18

DAB HAND
85	Celtic Music CM 025	HIGH ROCK AND LOWATER (LP)	£18

MIKE D'ABO
69	Immediate IM 075	See The Little People — Gulliver's Travels/Anthology Of Gulliver's Travels Part 2 (withdrawn)	£30
70	Uni UNLS 114	D'ABO (LP, gatefold sleeve)	£40
72	A&M AMLH 68097	DOWN AT RACHEL'S PLACE (LP, with lyric insert)	£15
74	A&M AMLH 63634	BROKEN RAINBOWS (LP)	£15

(see also Manfred Mann, Band Of Angels, Gulliver's Travels, Smith & D'Abo)

DADA
71	Atco 2400 030	DADA (LP, mustard/blue label)	£50

(see also Elkie Brooks, Paul Korda, Vinegar Joe)

DADDY COLONEL
85	Bubblers UKMC7	Take A Tip From Me/Lyric Banton (12")	£20

DADDY FREDDY
89	Fashion FAD 7707	Yes We A Blood/Version	£25

DADDY JUNGLE
80s	Daddy Jungle DJ001	Flash It Operator/Jungle Dub	£20

DADDY LONGLEGS
70	Warner Bros WS 3004	DADDY LONGLEGS (LP)	£40
71	Vertigo 6360 038	OAKDOWN FARM (LP, gatefold sleeve, swirl label)	£250
72	Polydor 2371 261	THREE MUSICIANS (LP)	£15
73	Polydor 2371 323	SHIFTING SANDS (LP)	£25

(see also Daylight)

DADDY MAXFIELD
73	Pye 7N 45266	Rave 'N' Rock/Smilin' Again	£50

DADDY TAR
90	Umbra	Zigawya/Full Up The Style (12" with Aytonbridge)	£15

DADDY'S ACT
67	Columbia DB 8242	Eight Days A Week/Gonna Get You	£18

DAEMION
82	SiJenn MSP1001	Dizzy/Human Arcade (p/s)	£50

D.A.F. (DEUTSCHE AMERIKANISCHE FREUNDSCHAFT)
80	Mute STUMM 1	DIE KLEINEN UND DIE BOSEN (LP)	£20
81	Virgin V2202	ALLES IST GUT (LP)	£20
81	Virgin V2218	GOLD UND LIEBE (LP)	£20

CALVIN DAFOS
66	Blue Beat BB 347	Brown Sugar/I'm Gone	£35
69	Doctor Bird DB 1174	Lash Them/CDs: Medicine Master	£45

DAFT PUNK
97	Virgin VSLH 1633	Around The World (Radio Edit)/**Teachers** (Extended Mix) (7", jukebox, large centre hole, moulded injection label)	£40
13	Columbia 88883746911	**Get Lucky** (Daft Punk Remix)/(Album Version)/(Radio Edit) (12", p/s)	£30
96	Virgin V 2821	HOMEWORK (2LP, embossed sleeve, gatefold, printed inners)	£80
01	Virgin V 2940	DISCOVERY (2LP, gatefold, printed inners, insert with Daft Punk credit card)	£75
01	Virgin V 2952	ALIVE 1997 (LP, sticker sheet)	£50
01	Virgin 7243 8 11479 1 7	HOMEWORK/DISCOVERY/ALIVE 1997 (5LP, box set, belly band)	£150
05	Virgin V 2996	HUMAN AFTER ALL (2LP, gatefold, printed inners)	£70
10	Walt Disney Records 5099909792012	TRON:LEGACY (2LP, soundtrack, gatefold, luminous title, insert, limited))	£200
13	Sony 88883 71686 1	RANDOM ACCESS MEMORIES (2LP, gatefold, booklet)	£25
14	Atlantic 0825646225378	ALIVE 2007 (2LP, trifold sleeve, first vinyl issue of 2007 CD)	£70
20	Walt Disney Records 00050087469887	TRON: LEGACY RECONFIGURED (2LP, issue of previous CD only release, RSD, green vinyl)	£50
22	Walt Disney Records 00050087502560	TRON: LEGACY RECONFIGURED (2LP, reissue, gatefold)	£25
23	Sony 1965 880833 1	RANDOM ACCESS MEMORIES (DRUMLESS EDITION) (2LP, gatefold, booklet)	£20
23	Sony 88883 71686 1	RANDOM ACCESS MEMORIES (10TH ANNIVERSARY EDITION) (3LP, gatefold, booklet, poster)	£30

DAGABAND
83	MHM A-M 094	Second Time Around/Reds Under The Beds/I Can See For Miles (p/s)	£25

DAGGERMEN
86	Own Up DAG 001	DAGGERS IN MY MIND (LP)	£15

(see also James Taylor Quartet)

DAGGERS (1)
74	Scotty SC 003	Live Your Life Alone/Circles Of Dust	£50

DAILY FLASH
84	Psycho PSYCHO 32	I FLASH DAILY (LP)	£20

DAISY CLAN
70	Pye Intl. 7N 25532	Love Needs Love/Glory Be	£30
71	Decca F23169	San Francisco China Town/Ridin' A Rainbow	£30

DAISY PLANET
60s	Oak (no cat. no.)	DAISY PLANET (EP, no p/s)	£70

DAKOTA JIM
66	Blue Beat BB 358	Only Soul Can Tell (actually by Slim Smith)/DAKOTA'S ALLSTARS: Call Me Master (actually by Prince Buster All Stars)	£150

(see also Slim Smith)

DAKOTAS
64	Parlophone R 5203	Oyeh/Hello Josephine	£30
67	Page One POF 018	I'm 'N 'Ardworkin' Barrow Boy/Seven Pounds Of Potatoes	£35
68	Philips BF 1645	I Can't Break The News To Myself/The Spider And The Fly	£200
63	Parlophone GEP 8888	MEET THE DAKOTAS (EP)	£40

(see also Billy J. Kramer & Dakotas)

ALAN DALE
57	Vogue Coral Q 72225	Don't Knock The Rock/Your Love Is My Love	£25
57	Vogue Coral Q 72231	The Girl Can't Help It/Lonesome Road	£25

(see also Johnny Desmond)

DICK DALE & HIS DELTONES
63	Capitol CL 15296	Peppermint Man/Surf Beat	£20
63	Capitol CL 15320	The Scavenger/Wild Ideas	£20
63	Capitol T 1886	SURFERS' CHOICE (LP)	£30
63	Capitol T/ST 1930	KING OF THE SURF GUITAR (LP, mono/stereo)	£30

JACKIE DALE
78	Freedom Sounds FSD 020	Stop And Think Me Over/Bucket Bottom (12", with Prince Allah)	£15

JIM DALE
57	Parlophone GEP 8656	JIM DALE (EP)	£20
58	Parlophone PMD 1055	JIM (10" LP)	£40

SYD DALE ORCHESTRA
01	Trunk JBH 01	Theme To Screen Test (Marching There & back) (1-sided 7", 500 only)	£60

DALE & GRACE
63	London HL 9807	I'm Leaving It Up To You/That's What I Like About You	£15
64	London HL 9857	Stop And Think It Over/Bad Luck	£15
64	London RE 1428	DALE AND GRACE NO. 1 (EP)	£30
64	London RE 1429	DALE AND GRACE NO. 2 (EP)	£30
64	London RE 1430	DALE AND GRACE NO. 3 (EP)	£35

DALEKS
80	Exterminated EXPS 1	Rejected/Man Of The World/This Life (fold-out, p/s)	£15

DALES
75	Deroy 953	LUCKY THIRTEEN (LP)	£30

DALE SISTERS
61	Ember EMB S 140	My Sunday Baby/All My Life	£15

DÄLEX
81   Dodgy DODGY 1 | **Juvenile/Action Man/Touched** (p/s) £30

BASIL DALEY
68   Studio One SO 2054 | **Hold Me Baby/HEPTONES: I Got A Feeling**..................................£60

JIMMY DALEY & DING-A-LINGS
57   Brunswick 05648 | **Rock, Pretty Baby/Can I Steal A Little Love**..........................£100

GRAHAM DALLEY
66   Hollick & Taylor HT/LP 1068 | **GRAHAM DALLEY AT THE BARN** (LP)............................£15

SALVADOR DALI
62   Decca SET/MET 230 | **DALI IN VENICE** (LP, mono/stereo, gatefold sleeve with booklet)........£60

DALIDA
57   Felsted ESD 3043 | **DALIDA IS HER NAME** (EP) £20
59   Felsted ESD 3077 | **PARDON MY ENGLISH** (EP) £25
57   Felsted SDL 86053 | **THE GLAMOUROUS DALIDA** (10" LP) £50
66   Fontana TL 5348 | **DALIDA** (LP)..£18

CYNTHIA DALL
96   Domino WIGLP 23 | **UNTITLED** (LP) £20

MIKI DALLON
65   RCA RCA 1438 | **Do You Call That Love?/Apple Pie** £20
65   RCA RCA 1478 | **I Care About You/I'll Give You Love**..................................£40
66   Strike JH 306 | **Cheat And Lie/**(I'm Gonna Find A) **Cave** £40
(see also Neil Christian & Crusaders)

DALMATIANS
81   Dog Rock SD 101 | **What Love Has Taught You/She's Got To Go** (red vinyl) £60
81   Dog Rock SD 101 | **What Love Has Taught You/She's Got To Go** (black vinyl) £30
83   Dog Rock SD 103 | **Colourful World/Women Against The World** £15

DAVID & MARIANNE DALMOUR
65   Columbia 33SX 1715 | **INTRODUCING** (LP) £20
66   Columbia SCX 6005 | **STRANGE ENCHANTMENT** (LP)..£25

KAREN DALTON
71   Paramount SPFL 271 | **IN MY OWN TIME** (LP) £60

DALTONS
67   Fab FAB 30 | **Never Kiss You Again/RIGHTEOUS FLAMES: When A Girl Loves A Boy**.........£150
(see also Prince Buster)

ROGER DALTREY
77   Polydor 2058 948 | **Say It Ain't So Joe/Satin And Lace** (withdrawn, existence unconfirmed) £20
73   Track 2406 107 | **DALTREY** (LP, gatefold sleeve) £15
80   Polydor POLD 5034 | **McVICAR** (LP, soundtrack, clear vinyl)..........................£15
80   Polydor POLD 5034 | **McVICAR** (LP, soundtrack)..£15
(see also Who, High Numbers, McEnroe & Cash)

DAMARIS
83   CBS 4172 | **What About My Love/Hooray For Love** (12") £30

DAMASCUS
80s   Private pressing | **OPEN YOUR EYES** (12" EP, with insert) £100
80s   Private pressing | **OPEN YOUR EYES** (12" EP, later with different back sleeve, with insert)......£75
(see also Thin End Of The Wedge)

DAMBALA
78   Isis ISIS 001 | **Rebel/MILITANT BARRY : Version** £20
78   Music Hive MH001 | **Zimbabwe/GUS ANYIA : Visions Of War**..............................£40
79   Radic RIC 107 | **Babylon/No Go** (As Dambala featuring Gus Anyia) £40
81   Blank IS 1002 | **Rally Round/Version** (12" p/s) £40
83   Dada Music DLP 1 | **AZANIA** (LP) £40

DAMNED (1)
74   Youngblood YB 1067 | **Morning Bird/Theta**..£40

DAMNED (2)
SINGLES
76   Stiff BUY 6 | **New Rose/Help!** (first pressing with push-out centre, 'Street music co' credit on label, 'is this a record' & 'a bilbo boppa' on A side run out, 'Damned Beatles & 'Bilbo master room' credit on B. 'Delga' credit on p/s) £50
77   Stiff BUY 10 | **Neat Neat Neat/Stab Yor Back/Singalongascabies** (glossy p/s, no 'Island' logo on sleeve, first pressing solid centre) £25
77   Stiff BUY 10 | **Neat Neat Neat/Stab Yor Back/Singalongascabies** (glossy p/s, no 'Island' logo on sleeve, second pressing push-out centre) £25
77   Stiff DAMMED 1 | **Stretcher Case Baby/Sick Of Being Sick** (p/s, NME competition & gig freebie) £125
77   Stiff BUY 18 | **Problem Child/You Take My Money** (p/s, originally with press-out centre) £15
77   Stiff BUY 24 | **Don't Cry Wolf/One Way Love** (promo grey label with small "A")........£30
77   Stiff BUY 24 | **Don't Cry Wolf/One Way Love** (push-out centre, black vinyl) £15
78   Dodgy Demo Co. SGS 105 | **Love Song/Burglar** (mail order issue/gig freebie, plain sleeve, stickered labels) £60
79   Chiswick CHIS 120 ADJ-1 | **I Just Can't Be Happy Today/Ballroom Blitz** ('A' Label DJ promo copy) £200
80   Chiswick CHIS 130 | **White Rabbit/Rabid** (Over You)/**Seagulls** (unissued in U.K., Europe-only, 2 x 1-sided white-label test pressings exist, hand-written labels) £400
80   Chiswick CHIS 139 DJ | **There Ain't No Sanity Clause/Hit Or Miss** (double A side demo) £30
81   Stiff GRAB 2 | **Four Pack** (4 x 7" [BUY 6, 10, 18 & 24], in a plastic wallet) £50
82   Big Beat NS 75 | **Love Song/Noise Noise Noise/Suicide** (3 different sleeves, black vinyl with black and white labels) £25

MINT VALUE £

84	Plus One DAMNED 1T	Thanks For The Night/Nasty/Do The Blitz (12", no'd p/s, multicoloured vinyl) £15
84	Plus One DAMNED 1T	Thanks For The Night/Nasty ('woman'-shaped pic disc w/ plinth, 1,000 only)................£25
85	Stiff BUY DJ 238	New Rose/Help!/I'm So Bored (promo reissue) £20
86	Stiff BUY 6/BUY DJ 6A	New Rose/Help!/I'm So Bored (1-sided) (double pack, stickered PVC sleeve with insert, 1st disc on white vinyl, 2nd disc actually plays "I Fall" [live])..................£20
86	Stiff BUYIT 6	New Rose/Neat Neat Neat/Help/Stretcher Case/Sick Of Being Sick (12", p/s)..............£20
88	Sugar & Spite SS 01	History Of The World Part 1 (Psychedelic Mix) (1-sided flexi credited to 'The Dimmed' wraparound p/s free with Sugar & Spite fanzine £35
88	Sugar & Spite SS 01	History Of The World Part 1 (Psychedelic Mix) (1-sided flexi credited to 'The Dimmed' wraparound p/s free without Sugar & Spite fanzine £20
89	Sugar and Spite SS02	No Fun (1-sided flexi)........................£20
90	Deltic DELT 7T	Fun Factory/CAPTAIN SENSIBLE: Freedom/Pasties/A Riot On Eastbourne Pier (p/s).......£15
90	Deltic DELT 7T	Fun Factory/CAPTAIN SENSIBLE: Freedom/Pasties/A Riot On Eastbourne Pier (12" p/s, blue vinyl, mail-order only, 2000 only)..........................£20
02	Stiff FBUPC 004	New Rose/Help! (reissue with free CD single) £15
05	Lively Arts LADAM 1	Little Miss Disaster/Anti-Pope (live) (p/s, red splatter vinyl) £30
08	Devil's Jukebox DJB66619PRO	WHITE EP (p/s, white vinyl) £40
09	Devil's Jukebox DJB66630PRO7	MACHINE GUN ETIQUETTE (p/s, promo single, blue vinyl, 300 only) £30
10	Devil's Jukebox DJB66644	A Nation Fit For Heroes/Time (p/s, blue, white or red vinyl) £20
11	Devil's Jukebox DJBSAMP02	NOT FOR SALE EP (p/s, green vinyl)....................£40
16	Sanctuary BMG CATS V190	New Rose/Amen (Live) (40th Anniversary picture disc)........................£30
17	Union Square SALVOS V17	New Rose/Help (40th Anniversary picture disc) £30

ALBUMS

77	Stiff SEEZ 1	DAMNED DAMNED DAMNED (LP) £75
77	Stiff SEEZ 1	DAMNED DAMNED DAMNED (LP, 2,000 with Eddie & Hot Rods photograph on rear sleeve; shrinkwrapped with title sticker) £400
77	Stiff SEEZ 1	DAMNED DAMNED DAMNED (LP, 2,000 with Eddie & Hot Rods photograph on rear sleeve; not shrinkwrapped with title sticker)..................£200
77	Stiff SEEZ 5	MUSIC FOR PLEASURE (LP, printed inner) £30
79	Chiswick CWK 3011	MACHINE GUN ETIQUETTE (LP, printed inner) £50
80	Chiswick CWK 3015	THE BLACK ALBUM (2LP) £50
81	Ace DAM 1	ANOTHER GREAT RECORD FROM THE DAMNED: THE BEST OF THE DAMNED (LP, red or blue vinyl)........................£30
82	Bronze BRON 542	STRAWBERRIES (LP, scratch and sniff insert) £40
82	Ace DAM 3	THE BLACK ALBUM (LP, single reissue, 12,000 with lyrics & poster) £15
82	Ace DAM 2	MACHINE GUN ETIQUETTE (LP, reissue, blue or clear vinyl with inner) £25
83	Stiff MAIL 2	DAMNED DAMNED DAMNED/MUSIC FOR PLEASURE (2LP, reissue, gatefold, mail-order, 5000 only)...................£30
83	Damned DAMU 2	LIVE IN NEWCASTLE (LP, 5,000 by mail-order only) £15
83	Damned PDAMU 2	LIVE IN NEWCASTLE (LP, picture disc, 5,000 only) £15
85	MCA MCFW 3275	PHANTASMAGORIA (LP, white vinyl, printed inner) £40
86	Stiff MAIL 2	DAMNED, DAMNED, DAMNED/MUSIC FOR PLEASURE (2-LP, reissue, yellow vinyl, 4000 by mail-order only) £25
86	Dojo DOJOPD 46	STRAWBERRIES (LP, reissue picture disc)...................£15
86	Stiff GET 4	THE CAPTAIN'S BIRTHDAY PARTY — LIVE AT THE ROUNDHOUSE (mini-LP, 45rpm, blue vinyl, stickered plain white sleeve) £15
86	MCA MCG 6015	ANYTHING (LP, gatefold with band pop-up, printed inner) £30
87	Demon FIEND 91	DAMNED DAMNED DAMNED (LP, reissue)....................£15
87	Demon PFIEND 91	DAMNED DAMNED DAMNED (LP, reissue picture disc) £15
87	Demon FIEND 108	MUSIC FOR PLEASURE (LP, reissue, orange vinyl)....................£15
89	Essential ESCLP 008	FINAL DAMNATION (LP, green vinyl, poster) £40
89	Essential ESSLP 008	FINAL DAMNATION (LP) £15
92	Receiver RRLP 159	LIVE AT THE LYCEUM (LP, clear vinyl) £15
10	Devil's Jukebox DJB66643LP	SO, WHO'S PARANOID? (2-LP, numbered) £30
16	Live Here Now LHN014LP	40TH ANNIVERSARY TOUR - LIVE IN MARGATE (3LP, trifold sleeve, yellow vinyl) £60
18	Spinefarm SPINE 734043	EVIL SPIRITS (LP, white vinyl, signed, postcard and Damned plectrum) £50
19	BMG BMGCAT 409QLP	BLACK IS THE NIGHT (THE DEFINITIVE ANTHOLOGY) (4LP, gatefold, gold vinyl, printed inners) £50
22	Ear Music 0216982EMU	A NIGHT OF A THOUSAND VAMPIRES (LIVE IN LONDON) (2LP, glow-in-the-dark vinyl, gatefold, printed inners, poster £50
23	Ear Music 0217910EMU	DARKADELIC (LP, gatefold, printed inner, limted edition, clear vinyl, slipmat) £30

(see also Brian James (2), Captain Sensible, Rat & Whale, Edge, Maxim's Thrash, Naz Nomad & Nightmares,, Tank, Eddie & Hot Rods, U.F.O., Motordam)

STUART DAMON
| 70 | Reflection REF L7 | STUART 'CHAMPION' DAMON (LP) ....£20 |

VIC DAMONE
| 57 | Mercury MPT 7514 | ALL-TIME SONG HITS (10" LP) ....£15 |

DAN
| 89 | Meantime COX 013c | KICKING ASS AT TJ'S (LP, with flexi)....................£15 |

RUPIE DAN
| 82 | Flag FLG 101 | My Black Race/Black Race Dub (12")....................£40 |

JONAH DAN
| 96 | Inner Sanctuary ACT10-004 | Meditation Rock/Dub 1/Dub 2 (10") ....£20 |
| 89 | Conscious Sounds JKPD 001 | MEETS THE BUSH CHEMISTS AT CONSCIOUS SOUNDS (LP)...................£25 |

DANCE CONSPIRACY
| 92 | Metamorphosis MORPHO 001 | DUB WAR EP 12" (die cut sleeve) ....£15 |

DANCELAND ROCK GROUP
| 62 | Danceland Y 2032 | Anytime/Because They're Young ....£15 |

MINT VALUE £

63	Danceland Y 2043	William Tell/Last Night Was Made For Love	£15

DANCE PEOPLE
79	Satril SATLP 4013	FLY AWAY (LP)	£15

DANCE SQUAD
93	Mendoza MEN 0026	**Everybody** (Vocal Mix)/**Everybody** (Instrumental)/**Bad Boy** (Hard Mix) (12", as Dance Squad featuring Camilla)	£25
94	Wicked Sounds WS 02	Yu-a Raggamuffin/Ganjaman (12")	£25

DANCETTE
83	Bel BEL 45	Going Green/He's Clever	£30

GRAHAM PHILIP D'ANCEY
81	Blue September BSEP 005	Sacred Heart/Lament Of The Winged Warrior (p/s)	£40
83	Shibui SHS 001	Freedom/False Prophet (p/s)	£30
83	Shibui SHS 001	ALLUMA (LP)	£30

DANCING DID
79	Fruit & Veg F&V 1	Dancing Did/Lorry Pirates (p/s, insert)	£20
82	Stiff BUY 136	The Lost Platoon/The Human Chicken (withdrawn 'cavalry' p/s)	£15
82	Kamera Records KAM 009	AND DID THOSE FEET (LP, with insert)	£25

DANDO SHAFT
70	Youngblood YB 1012	Cold Wind/Cat Song	£15
70	Youngblood SSYB 6	AN EVENING WITH DANDO SHAFT (LP, white/red label)	£120
71	RCA Neon NE 5	DANDO SHAFT (LP, gatefold sleeve, black inner sleeve)	£175
72	RCA Victor SF 8256	LANTALOON (LP, with poster, orange label)	£175
72	RCA Victor SF 8256	LANTALOON (LP, without poster, orange label)	£80
77	Rubber RUB 034	KINGDOM (LP)	£60

(see also Hedgehog Pie)

DANDY (& SUPERBOYS)
64	Dice CC 21	Rudie Don't Go/It's Just Got To Be	£25
65	Dice CC 24	You Got To Pray/I Got To Have You (as Dandy & Barbara)	£25
65	Blue Beat BB 308	To Love You/I'm Looking For Love	£25
65	Blue Beat BB 319	Hey Boy Hey Girl/So Long Baby (as Dandy & Del)	£25
65	Blue Beat BB 327	My Baby/I'm Gonna Stop Loving You	£25
65	Blue Beat BB 336	I Found Love/You've Got Something Nice	£25
66	Dice CC 29	The Operation/A Little More Ska	£25
66	Ska Beat JB 247	The Fight/Do You Know	£25
67	Ska Beat JB 269	One Scotch One Bourbon One Beer/Maximum Pressure	£25
67	Ska Beat JB 273	Rudie A Message To You/Til Death Do Us Part	£25
67	Ska Beat JB 279	You're No Hustler/No No	£25
67	Giant GN 3	My Time Now/East Of Suez (with Superboys)	£45
67	Giant GN 5	Puppet On A String/Have Your Fun (with Superboys)	£25
67	Giant GN 7	We Are Still Rude/Let's Do Rocksteady (with Superboys)	£25
67	Giant GN 10	Somewhere My Love/My Kind Of Love (with Superboys)	£25
67	Giant GN 15	There Is A Mountain/This Music Got Soul (with Superboys)	£25
68	Giant GN 20	Charlie Brown/Groovin' At The Cue	£40
68	Giant GN 23	Propagandist/Giant March	£20
68	Giant GN 27	Sweet Ride/Up The Hill (with Superboys)	£20
68	Giant GN 30	Tears On My Pillow/Mad Them (with Superboys)	£20
68	Giant GN 36	I'm Back With A Bang Bang/Jungle Walk (with Superboys)	£80
68	Trojan TR 618	The Toast/Kicks Out	£25
69	Columbia Blue Beat DB 112	Play It Cool/Rude With Me	£15
68	Downtown DT 401	Move Your Mule/Reggae Me This	£35
69	Downtown DT 402	Come Back Girl/Shake Me Wake Me	£35
69	Downtown DT 404	Tell Me Darling/Cool Hand Luke	£35
68	Downtown DT 405	Copy Your Rhythm/BROTHER DAN ALL STARS: Lovely Lady	£35
69	Downtown DT 406	Doctor Sure Shot/Put On Your Dancing Shoes	£35
69	Downtown DT 410	Reggae In Your Jeggae/DREAMERS: Reggae Shuffle	£35
69	Downtown DT 411	You Don't Care/Tryer (both sides with Audrey)	£20
69	Downtown DT 415	Rocksteady Gone/Walking Down	£20
69	Downtown DT 416	I'm Your Puppet/Water Boy	£30
69	Downtown DT 421	Games People Play/AUDREY: One Fine Day	£20
69	Downtown DT 429	People Get Ready/RUDIES: Near East	£50
69	Downtown DT 434	Be Natural, Be Proud/Who Do You Want To Run To	£20
69	Downtown DT 437	Come On Home/Love Is All You Need	£25
69	Downtown DT 442	Everybody Loves A Winner/Try Me One More Time	£25
69	Downtown DT 445	Let's Come Together (with Israelites)/JAKE WADE: Music Fever	£25
69	Downtown DT 453	Won't You Come Home/Baby Make It Soon	£25
70	Downtown DT 456	Raining In My Heart/First Note	£25
70	Downtown DT 458	Build Your Love (On Solid Foundation)/Let's Talk It Over (p/s)	£20
70	Downtown DT 458	Build Your Love (On Solid Foundation)/Let's Talk It Over	£15
70	Downtown DT 462	Morning Side Of The Mountain (as Dandy & Audrey)/AUDREY: Show Me Baby	£25
70	Downtown DT 468	How Glad I Am/I'm So Glad (as Dandy & Audrey)	£20
71	Downtown DT 483	Could It Be True/Your Eyes Are Dreaming (as Dandy & Jackie)	£15
71	Downtown DT 484	Daddy's Home/Everyman	£15
67	Giant GNL 1000	ROCKSTEADY WITH DANDY (LP)	£100
68	Trojan TRL 2	DANDY RETURNS (LP)	£75
69	Trojan TRL 17	I NEED YOU (LP, with Audrey)	£40
70	Trojan TTL 26	YOUR MUSICAL DOCTOR (LP)	£50

70 Trojan TBL 118   **MORNING SIDE OF THE MOUNTAIN** (LP, with Audrey) £40

(see also Bobby Thompson, Sugar & Dandy, Rub A Dubs, Don Martin,, Little Sal with Dandy & Superboys, Dandy Livingtsone)

DANDY & AUDREY
69	Downtown DT 411	**You Don't Care/Tryer** (both sides with Audrey)	£40
70	Downtown DT 462	**Morning Side Of The Mountain** (as Dandy & Audrey)/**AUDREY: Show Me Baby**	£25
69	Downtown TRLS 17	**I NEED YOU** (LP)	£40
70	Downtown TBL 118	**MORNING SIDE OF THE MOUNTAIN** (LP)	£40

CHRIS DANE
55 London HLA 8165   **Cynthia's In Love/My Ideal** £30

D'ANGELO
95	Cooltempo CTLP46	**BROWN SUGAR** (LP)	£60
00	EMI 523373 1	**VOODOO** (2-LP)	£30
15	Virgin/Back To Black 00602547240811	**BROWN SUGAR** (LP, reissue)	£18

CAL DANGER
62 Fontana 267 225 TF   **Restless/Teenage Girlie Blues** £100

(see also Tony Dangerfield)

DANGERDOOM
05 Lez LEX 036LP   **MOUSE AND THE MASK** (2-LP, printed plastic sleeve, inner & insert) £50

A.P. DANGERFIELD
68 Fontana TF 935   **Conversations** (In A Station Light Refreshment Bar)/**Further Conversations** £30

KEITH DANGERFIELD
68 Plexium P 1237   **No Life Child/She's A Witch** £200

TONY DANGERFIELD & THRILLS
64 Pye 7N 15695   **I've Seen Such Things/She's Too Way Out** £100

(see also Savages, Circles, Cal Danger)

DANGEROUS BROTHERS
80 Sheep Worrying TMS 002   **False Nose/County Councillor** (p/s) £15

PINO D'ANGIO
82 System 12 STEM 2   **Ma Quale Idea/Lezione D'Amore** (12") £20

ERROLL DANIEL
69 Paradox PAR 45902   **No Excuses/Go Back** £20

JULIUS DANIELS
65 RCA RCX 7175   **R.C.A. VICTOR RACE SERIES VOL. 4** (EP) £15

MIKE DANIELS & HIS BAND
57 Columbia 33SX 1256   **MIKE ON MIKE** (LP) £40

ROLY "YO YO" DANIELS
60s Stardisc SD 101   **Yo Yo Boy/The Teacher** (p/s, features Don Rendell) £50

JOHNNY DANKWORTH ORCHESTRA
56	Parlophone MSP 6255	**Experiments With Mice/Applecake**	£15
61	Columbia DB 4695	**The Avengers/Chano**	£15
62	No label 19517	**Music For The New Prestige Film** (1-sided white label)	£15
63	Fontana TF 422	**The Avengers/Off The Cuff**	£15
64	Fontana TF 512	**Beefeaters/Down A Tone**	£35
58	Parlophone GEP 8653	**DANKWORTH WORKSHOP NO. 1** (EP)	£20
58	Parlophone GEP 8697	**DANKWORTH WORKSHOP NO. 2 — EXPERIMENTS WITH DANKWORTH** (EP)	£15
60	Columbia SEG 8037	**THE CRIMINALS** (EP, soundtrack; also stereo ESG 7825)	£15
56	Parlophone PMD 1042	**JOURNEY INTO JAZZ** (10" LP)	£20
58	Parlophone PMC 1076	**THE VINTAGE YEARS** (LP)	£20
59	Parlophone PMC 1043	**FIVE STEPS TO DANKWORTH** (LP)	£20
60	Top Rank 30/019	**LONDON TO NEWPORT** (LP)	£40
61	Columbia 33SX 1280	**JAZZ ROUTES** (LP, also stereo SCX 3347)	£30
64	Encore ENC 165	**FROM 7 ON** (LP)	£20
65	Fontana TL 5229	**THE ZODIAC VARIATIONS** (LP, mono)	£25
65	Fontana STL 5229	**THE ZODIAC VARIATIONS** (LP, stereo)	£30
67	Stateside S(S)L 10213	**FATHOM** (LP, soundtrack)	£40
68	Fontana TL 5445	**THE $1,000,000 COLLECTION** (LP)	£15
69	Fontana LPS 16261	**OFF DUTY** (LP)	£18

(see also Cleo Laine, Philip Green, Kenny Wheeler & Johnny Dankworth)

DANLEERS
58	Mercury AMT 1003	**One Summer Night/Wheelin' And A-Dealin'**	£200
58	Mercury AMT 1003	**One Summer Night/Wheelin' And A-Dealin'** (78)	£40

DAN LE SAC VS SCROOBIUS PIP
07	I ex Records LEX 044 SVN	**Thou Shalt Always Kill/Thou Shalt Always Kill** (Knifehandchop Remix) (p/s)	£15
08	Sunday Best SBESTLP24	**ANGLES** (2-LP, CD)	£40

DANNY BOYS
89 Ugly Man UG 1   **Days Of The Week** (12" EP) £15

DANNY & THE JUNIORS
58	HMV POP 436	**At The Hop/Sometimes** (When I'm All Alone)	£15
58	HMV POP 467	**Rock And Roll Is Here To Stay/School Boy Romance**	£40
58	HMV POP 504	**Dottie/In The Meantime**	£30
60	Top Rank JAR 510	**Twistin' U.S.A./Thousand Miles Away**	£15
61	Top Rank JAR 552	**Pony Express/Daydreamer**	£15

DANNY & JOE/TOMMY MCCOOK'S BAND

61	Top Rank JAR 587	Back To The Hop/The Charleston Fish	£15
62	Top Rank JAR 604	Twistin' All Night Long/Twistin' England (with Freddy Cannon)	£15

(see also Freddy Cannon)

DANNY & JOE/TOMMY MCCOOK'S BAND
12	Jackpot THB 7018	Please Be Mine/More Strings	£25

DANSE MACABRE
88	Wild West/Alchemy 1	THINK ABOUT DEATH EP	£20

DANSE SOCIETY
81	Society SOC 3-81	The Clock/Continent (brown, black & white foldout p/s)	£15
81	Pax PAX 2	There Is No Shame In Death/Dolphins/These Frayed Edges (12", p/s, blue vinyl)	£20
84	Society SOC V 127	2,000 Light Years From Home (12" blue vinyl, 50-150 pressed)	£60

DANSETTE DAMAGE
78	Shoestring LACE 001	New Musical Express/The Only Sound (p/s, Robert Plant on backing vocals)	£150
94	Shoestring BLOO 2LP	SOLD AS SEEN (LP, gatefold sleeve, 500 only)	£30

DANTA
72	Epic EPC 7776	Freeway/Mau Mau	£15
73	Epic SEPC 1466	Crossfire/Daddy's Gone	£15

DANTALIAN'S CHARIOT
67	Columbia DB 8260	The Madman Running Through The Fields/Sun Came Bursting Through My Cloud	£120
95	Tenth Planet TP 015	CHARIOT RISING (LP, numbered, 1,000 only)	£25

(see also Zoot Money's Big Roll Band)

DANTE (2)
71	CBS 7382	Queen Of Sheba/Feelin' The Heat	£15

DANTE & EVERGREENS
60	Top Rank JAR 402	Alley-Oop/The Right Time	£15

DANZIG
88	Def American 838 487-1	DANZIG (LP, gatefold sleeve)	£50
90	Def American 846 374-1	DANZIG II - LUCIFUGE (LP, with inner)	£40
92	Def American 512 270-1	DANZIG III - HOW THE GODS KILL (LP, gatefold, stickered sleeve)	£80

DAPHNI
12	Jialong JIA 05V	JIALONG (2-LP)	£20

DARIEN SPIRIT
73	Charisma CAS 1065	ELEGY TO MARILYN (LP, large "Mad Hatter" label, with lip intact!)	£40

BOBBY DARIN

78s
56	Brunswick 05561	Rock Island Line/Timber (as Bobby Darin & Jaybirds)	£40
58	London HLE 8666	Splish Splash/Judy Don't Be Moody	£15
58	London HLE 8679	Early In The Morning/Now We're One	£15
58	London HLE 8737	Queen Of The Hop/Lost Love	£25
59	London HLE 8793	Mighty Mighty Man/You're Mine (as Bobby Darin with Rinky Dinks)	£30
59	London HLE 8815	Plain Jane/While I'm Gone	£30
59	London HLE 8867	Dream Lover/Bullmoose	£20
59	London HLK 8939	Mack The Knife/Was There A Call For Me	£25
60	London HLK 9034	La Mer (Beyond The Sea)/That's The Way Love Is	£40
60	London HLK 9086	Clementine/Down With Love	£50
60	London HLK 9142	Bill Bailey Won't You Please Come Home/Tall Story	£60

SINGLES
56	Brunswick 05561	Rock Island Line/Timber (as Bobby Darin & Jaybirds)	£30
58	London HLE 8666	Splish Splash/Judy Don't Be Moody	£25
58	London HLE 8679	Early In The Morning/Now We're One (as Rinky-Dinks featuring Bobby Darin)	£25
58	London HLE 8737	Queen Of The Hop/Lost Love	£30
58	London HL 7060	Queen Of The Hop/Lost Love (export issue)	£20
59	London HLE 8793	Mighty Mighty Man/You're Mine (as Bobby Darin with Rinky Dinks)	£25
59	London HLE 8815	Plain Jane/While I'm Gone	£30
59	London HL 7078	Plain Jane/Dream Lover (export issue)	£25

EPs
59	London REE 1173	BOBBY DARIN (tri centre)	£25
59	London REE 1225	BOBBY DARIN NO. 2 (tri centre)	£25
61	London REK 1286	FOR TEENAGERS ONLY	£20

ALBUMS
58	London HA-E 2140	BOBBY DARIN	£30
59	London HA-E 2172	THAT'S ALL	£15
59	London HA-K 2235	THIS IS DARIN (mono)	£15
59	London SAH-K 6067	THIS IS DARIN (stereo)	£18
60	London HA-K 2311	FOR TEENAGERS ONLY	£40
61	London SAH-K 6194	LOVE SWINGS (stereo)	£15
62	London SAH-K 6243	DARIN SINGS RAY CHARLES (stereo)	£15
64	Capitol (S)T 2007	GOLDEN FOLK HITS (stereo)	£15
67	Atlantic 587 073	SOMETHING SPECIAL	£20
69	Bell SBLL 128	COMMITMENT (LP, as Bob Darin)	£30

(see also Rinky Dinks)

DARK (1)
72	SIS 0102	DARK ROUND THE EDGES (LP, private pressing, test pressing with colour gatefold sleeve & booklet)	£6000

72	SIS 0102	**DARK ROUND THE EDGES** (LP, private pressing, test pressing in white sleeve with 'doodles' by Steve Giles)	£6000
72	SIS 0102	**DARK ROUND THE EDGES** (LP, private pressing, 12 copies with colour gatefold sleeve & booklet)	£15000
72	SIS 0102	**DARK ROUND THE EDGES** (LP, private pressing, 12 copies with black & white gatefold sleeve)	£6000
72	SIS 0102	**DARK ROUND THE EDGES** (LP, private pressing, 38 copies with single black & white sleeve)	£4000
90	Swank/Darkside 001	**DARK ROUND THE EDGES** (LP, reissue, U.K. pressing marketed in U.S.)	£200
91	Swank/Darkside 001	**DARK ROUND THE EDGES** (LP, as above, with different insert, 225 only)	£200
95	Acme AC 8009LP	**ARTEFACTS FROM THE BLACK MUSEUM** (LP, 500 only, with insert)	£40

DARK (2)
| 80 | Fresh FRESH 13 | **Hawaii Five O/Don't Look Now** (/s) | £20 |

DARK ANGEL
86	Under One Flag FLAG 6	**DARKNESS DESCENDS** (LP)	£15
91	Under One Flag FLAG 54	**TIME DOES NOT HEAL** (2-LP)	£20
10	Back On Black BOBV 261 LP	**TIME DOES NOT HEAL** (2-LP, reissue, gatefold sleeve)	£15

JOHNNY DARKE
| 79 | Carrere CAR 130 | **I'm Not A Believer/What She Knows** (p/s) | £20 |

DARKNESS
| 03 | Atlantic 745217 | **PERMISSION TO LAND** (LP, gatefold, poster) | £80 |
| (see also Hot Leg) | | | |

DARK SAND
| 72 | Dark DK001 | **Visions Of Tomorrow/Sad Affair** | £30 |

DARK STAR
81	Steel Strike no cat. no.	**Lady Of Mars/Rock 'N' Romancin'** (12", 250 pressed)	£90
81	Avatar AALP 5003	**DARK STAR** (LP, with patch)	£20
81	Avatar AALP 5003	**DARK STAR** (LP)	£15
87	FM WKFMLP 97	**REAL TO REEL** (LP)	£15

DARKTHRONE
91	Peaceville VILE 22	**SOULSIDE JOURNEY** (LP, picture disc)	£50
92	Peaceville VILE 28	**A BLAZE IN THE NORTHERN SKY** (LP)	£50
93	Peaceville VILE 35	**UNDER A FUNERAL MOON** (LP)	£50
94	Peaceville VILE 43	**TRANSILVANIAN HUNGER** (LP)	£80

DARLETTES
| 70 | President PT 317 | **Lost/Sweet Kind Of Loneliness** | £15 |

DARLINGS
| 67 | CBS 2932 | **Saturday Town/Wish You Were Here** | £20 |

BILL DARNEL
55	London HLU 8204	**My Little Mother/Bring Me A Bluebird** (with Frank Weir & His Orchestra)	£15
56	London HLU 8234	**The Last Frontier/Rock-A-Boogie Baby**	£25
(see also Frank Weir & His Orchestra)			

GUY DARRELL (& MIDNIGHTERS)
63	Oriole CB 1932	**Go Home Girl/You Won't Come Home** (as Guy Darrell & Midnighters)	£15
64	Oriole CB 1964	**Sorry/Sweet Dreams** (as Guy Darrell & Midnighters)	£15
66	CBS 202082	**I've Been Hurt/Blessed**	£40
66	CBS 202082	**I've Been Hurt/Blessed** (demo)	£45
67	Piccadilly 7N 35406	**Evil Woman/What You Do About That**	£30
73	Santa Ponsa PNL 502	**I'VE BEEN HURT** (LP)	£15

EARL DARREN SOUND
| 77 | GTKTEP 1003 | **EARL DARREN SOUND EP** (no p/s) | £15 |

CHRIS DARROW
73	United Artists UAG 29453	**CHRIS DARROW** (LP, gatefold)	£20
74	United Artists UAG 29634	**UNDER MY OWN DISGUISE** (LP)	£20
(see also Kaleidoscope, Nitty Gritty Dirt Band)			

DARRYL RAYNER STEVE
| 77 | Clubland SJP 776 | **LET THE GOOD STONES ROLL 4 BY 3 77 EP** (fold out, p/s) | £40 |

DARTELLS
| 63 | London HLD 9719 | **Hot Pastrami/Dartell Stomp** | £20 |

BARRY DARVELL
| 60 | London HL 9191 | **Geronimo Stomp/How Will It End?** | £50 |

DARWIN'S THEORY
| 67 | Major Minor MM 503 | **Daytime/Hosanna** | £50 |

DAS EFX
| 92 | East West 7567 91827-1 | **DEAD SERIOUS** (LP, inner) | £30 |

NITAE DASGUPTA
| 72 | Mushroom 100 MR 22 | **SONGS OF INDIA** (LP) | £35 |

DAS KABINETTE
| 83 | Klosette PL0026 | **The Cabinet/Fudge It** (p/s, 500 only) | £100 |

DAS SCHNITZ
| 79 | Ellie Jay EJSP 9249 | **4 AM** (EP, custom sleeve) | £70 |

DATE WITH SOUL
| 67 | Stateside SS 2062 | **Yes Sir, That's My Baby/PRISCILLA: He Noticed Me** | £50 |

(see also Jack Nitzsche, Brian Wilson, Sonny & Cher, Darlene Love/Blossoms, Jackie De Shannon, the Paris Sisters)

DAT POLITICS
04	Chicks On Speed COSR 15	GO PET GO (LP)	£15

DAUGHTERS OF ALBION
69	Fontana STL 5486	DAUGHTERS OF ALBION (LP)	£30

DAVANI & RYAN
72	Philips 6308 132	FUNKY COUNTRY (LP)	£20

DAVE
89	Linkway DAVE 1	WHATEVER HAPPENED TO... (LP, insert, 50 copies only)	£300

DAVE DAVANI & D MEN
63	Columbia DB 7125	Don't Fool Around/She's The Best For Me	£15
64	Decca F 11896	Midnight Special/Sho' Know A Lot About Love	£20

(see also Davani & Ryan)

DAVE DAVANI (FOUR)
65	Parlophone R 5329	Top Of The Pops/Workin' Out	£40
66	Parlophone R 5490	Tossin' And Turnin'/Jupe	£50
66	Parlophone R 5525	One Track Mind/On The Cooler Side	£35
65	Parlophone PMC 1258	FUSED (LP)	£100

(see also Davani & Ryan)

DAVE & DIAMONDS
65	Columbia DB 7692	I Walk The Lonely Night/You Do Love (p/s)	£35
65	Columbia DB 7692	I Walk The Lonely Night/You Do Love	£15

BOB DAVENPORT (& RAKES)
66	Columbia SX 1786	BOB DAVENPORT AND THE RAKES (LP, with Rakes)	£40
71	Trailer LER 3008	BOB DAVENPORT& THE MARSDEN RATTLERS (LP, red label)	£22
73	Trailer LER 2088	PAL OF MY CRADLE DAYS (LP, red label)	£18
77	Topic 12TS 318	POSTCARDS HOME (LP, with lyric sheet)	£15

D.A.V.E. THE DRUMMER
90s	Yolk YOLK 05	Steamliner/Jaws (12", with Jerome Hill)	£40
00	Smitten SMTLTD 02	Effective Therapy (1-sided 12", green vinyl)	£15

ALAN DAVEY
87	Hawkfan HWFB 3/4	THE ELF EP (double pack, 2 x 7" with insert in wraparound p/s in poly bag)	£20

(see also Hawkwind)

DAMIEN DAVEY
87	Pashion PASH 12 71	I'm A Man/Sounds So Fine (12", p/s)	£30

(SHAUN) DAVEY & (JAMES) MORRIS
73	York FYK 417	DAVEY AND MORRIS (LP, with insert)	£400

(see also Strawbs)

DAVID
69	Philips BF 1776	Light Of Your Mind/Please Mister Policeman	£200
70	Fontana TF 1081	I'm Going Back/Selppin	£60

ALAN DAVID
65	Decca F 12084	Hurt/I Found Out Too Late	£50
67	Polydor BM 56201	Flower Power/Completely Free	£30
65	Decca LK 4674	ALAN DAVID (LP)	£40

DAVID & JONATHAN
67	Columbia S(C)X 6031	DAVID AND JONATHAN (LP)	£20

(see also Roger Cook, White Plains)

JUSTIN DAVID
95	Ugly UGM 003	GEEKS 'N' FREAKS EP (12')	£20

DAVID & ROZAA
70	Philips 6006 040	Time Of Our Life/We Can Reach An Understanding	£20
71	Philips 6006 094	The Spark That Lights The Flame/Two Can Share	£20

(see also David Essex, Rozaa & Wine)

DIANNE DAVIDSON
72	Janus 6310 209	BACKWOODS WOMAN (LP)	£18

TOMMY DAVIDSON
56	London HLU 8219	Half Past Kissing Time/I Don't Know Yet But I'm Learning	£20

ALAN DAVIE
70	ADMW ADMW 001	THE ALAN DAVIE MUSIC WORKSHOP (LP)	£300
71	ADMW ADMW 002	SUITE FOR PREPARED PIANO AND MINI DRUMS (LP)	£200
71	ADMW ADMW 003	BIRD THROUGH THE WALL (LP)	£100
71	ADMW ADMW 004	PHANTOM IN THE ROOM (LP)	£100

(see also Tony Oxley and Alan Davie)

ALUN DAVIES
72	CBS 65108	DAYDO (LP, gatefold sleeve)	£30

(see also Cat Stevens, Sweet Thursday)

BARRY DAVIES
70	Beacon BEA 114	I Wish It Would Rain/Strange Days	£30
71	Beacon BEA 185	Strange Days/My Song My Whisky and Me (different A-side version)	£40

BOB DAVIES
63	London HLU 9767	Rock'N'Roll Show/With You Tonight	£25

CYRIL DAVIES (R&B ALLSTARS)
63	Pye International 7N 25194	Country Line Special/Chicago Calling	£25
63	Pye International 7N 25221	Preachin' The Blues/Sweet Mary	£40
69	Pye 7N 17663	Country Line Special/Sweet Mary	£15
64	Pye Intl. NEP 44025	THE SOUND OF CYRIL DAVIES (EP)	£75
57	'77' LP 2	THE LEGENDARY CYRIL DAVIES (10" LP, 99 only, with Alexis Korner)	£300
70	Folklore F-LEAT 9	THE LEGENDARY CYRIL DAVIES (LP, reissue)	£50

(see also Alexis Korner, Beryl Bryden)

DAVE DAVIES
68	Pye 7N 17514	Lincoln County/There's No Life Without Love	£20
69	Pye 7N 17678	Hold My Hand/Creeping Jean	£25
68	Pye NEP 24289	DAVE DAVIES HITS (EP)	£300

(see also Kinks)

JACKIE DAVIES & HIS QUARTET
| 57 | Pye Nixa N 15115 | Land Of Make Believe/Over The Rainbow (78) | £18 |

(see also Chico Arnez)

RON DAVIES
| 70 | A&M AMLS 993 | SILENT SONG THROUGH THE LAND (LP, green label) | £30 |

BARRINGTON DAVIS
| 72 | Montague MONS 2 | TRACKS OF MIND (LP, with lyric inner sleeve) | £60 |

BETTE DAVIS (& DEBBIE BURTON)
| 76 | EMI EMA 778 | MISS BETTE DAVIS (LP) | £15 |

BETTY DAVIS
75	Island ILPS 9329	NASTY GAL (LP)	£60
93	Vinyl Experience UFOXY1LP	NASTY GAL (LP, reissue)	£30
93	Vinyl Experience UFOXY 2LP	BETTY DAVIS (LP, reissue)	£40
93	Vinyl Experience UFOXY 3LP	THEY SAY I'M DIFFERENT (LP, reissue)	£40

BILLIE DAVIS
63	Decca F 11572	Tell Him/I'm Thankful (export copies with p/s)	£20
63	Decca F 11658	He's The One/V.I.P. (export copies with p/s)	£15
63	Columbia DB 7115	Bedtime Stories/You And I	£15
64	Columbia DB 7195	That Boy John/Say Nothin' Don't Tell	£15
64	Columbia DB 7246	School Is Over/Give Me Love	£15
64	Columbia DB 7346	Whatcha Gonna Do/Everybody Knows (as Billie Davis & Le Roys)	£35
65	Piccadilly 7N 35266	No Other Baby/Hands Off	£18
66	Piccadilly 7N 35350	Just Walk In My Shoes/Ev'ry Day	£100
67	Decca F 12696	Angel Of The Morning/Darling Be Home Soon	£15
69	Decca F 12923	I Can Remember/Nobody's Home To Go Home To	£20
69	Decca F 12977	Nights In White Satin/It's Over	£18
70	Decca F 13085	There Must Be A Reason/Love	£20
70	Decca LK 5029	BILLIE DAVIS (LP, mono)	£50
70	Decca SKL 5029	BILLIE DAVIS (LP, stereo)	£45

(see also Le Roys, Mike Sarne)

BLIND GARY DAVIS/REVEREND GARY DAVIS
63	'77' LA 12-14	PURE RELIGION AND BAD COMPANY (LP)	£30
60s	Fontana 688 303 ZL	HARLEM STREET SINGER (LP)	£45
64	Xtra XTRA 1009	REV. GARY DAVIS/SHORT STUFF MACON (LP, 1 side each)	£22
66	Xtra XTRA 5014	SAY NO TO THE DEVIL (LP)	£25
67	Xtra XTRA 5042	A LITTLE MORE FAITH (LP)	£25
69	Fontana SFJL 914	BRING YOUR MONEY HONEY (LP)	£25
71	Transatlantic TRA 244	RAGTIME GUITAR (LP)	£15
71	Transatlantic TRA 249	CHILDREN OF ZION (LP)	£15
77	Kicking Mule SNKF 103	LET US GET TOGETHER (LP)	£18

BOBBY DAVIS (JAMAICA)
71	Banana BA 342	Got To Get Away/We'll Cry Together (with BARBARA DUNKLEY)	£30
71	Banana BA 344	Return Your Love/RILEY'S ALLSTARS: Version	£30
71	Beacon 114	Strange Days/I Wish It would Rain	£15

BOBBY DAVIS (U.S.)
| 61 | Starlite ST45 056 | I Was Wrong/Hype You Into Selling Your Head | £50 |

BONNIE DAVIS
| 55 | Brunswick 05507 | Pepper-Hot Baby/For Always, Darling | £40 |

CLIFFORD DAVIS
| 69 | Reprise RS 27003 | Before The Beginning/Man Of The World | £20 |
| 70 | Reprise RS 27008 | Come On Down And Follow Me/Homework | £15 |

DANNY DAVIS ORCHESTRA (U.S.)
| 64 | London HAR 8204 | THEY'RE PLAYING OUR SONG (LP, with Ruby & Romantics) | £20 |

(see also Ruby & Romantics, Byron Lee)

DANNY DAVIS & BYRON LEE
| 64 | MGM 1256 | Night Train From Jamaica/Ska Dee Dah | £18 |

DANNY DAVIS (U.K.)
| 60 | Parlophone R 4657 | Love Me/You're My Only Girl | £20 |
| 60 | Parlophone R 4796 | Talking In My Sleep/Lullaby Of Love | £15 |

(see also Marauders)

DEL DAVIS
71	Bread BR-1105	Baby Don't Wake Me/Wishing And Hoping	£150
72	Trojan 7870	Baby Don't Wake Me/Sugarloaf Hill	£200

EDDIE ('LOCKJAW') DAVIS
60	Esquire 32-104	THE EDDIE 'LOCKJAW' DAVIS COOK BOOK (LP)	£35
60	Esquire 32-117	VERY SAXY (LP, with Coleman Hawkins, Arnett Cobb & Bobby Tate)	£35
61	Esquire 32-128	JAWS IN ORBIT (LP)	£30
64	Stateside SL 10102	THE FIRST SET — LIVE AT MINTONS (LP, with Johnny Griffin)	£20

(see also Coleman Hawkins, Johnny Griffin)

JESSE DAVIS
71	Atlantic 2400 106	JESSE DAVIS (LP, features Gram Parsons and Eric Clapton)	£18

JESSE (ED) DAVIS
71	Atco 2400 106	JESSE 'ED' DAVIS (LP)	£18
72	Atlantic K 40329	ULULU (LP)	£15

JIMMY DAVIS
66	Bounty BY 6009	MAXWELL STREET (LP)	£25

KIM DAVIS
66	Decca F 12387	Don't Take Your Lovin' Away/Feelin' Blue	£20
67	CBS 202568	Tell It Like It Is/Losing Kind	£25

(see also Kim D, Kim & Kinetics)

LARRY DAVIS/FENTON ROBINSON
72	Python PLP 24	LARRY DAVIS AND FENTON ROBINSON (LP, 99 copies only)	£90

LESLIE A DAVIS
83	Sea View SV2	If I Told You A Live I Am Sorry/Me Nah Tun No Informer (12")	£40

MAXWELL DAVIS
66	Ember FA 2040	BATMAN THEME AND OTHER BAT SONGS (LP)	£30

MELVIN DAVIS
69	Action ACT 4531	Save It/This Love Was Meant To Be	£35

MILES DAVIS
53	Esquire 20-017	MILES DAVIS PLAYS (10")	£75
53	Esquire 20-021	MILES DAVIS ALL STARS (10")	£75
53	Vogue LDE 028	MILES DAVIS ALL STARS (10")	£75
54	Esquire 20-041	MILES DAVIS BLOWS (10")	£75
54	Esquire 20-052	MILES DAVIS ALL STARS (A HIFI MODERN JAZZ JAM SESSION) (10")	£75
54	Esquire 20-056	MILES DAVIS ALL STARS (A SECOND HIFI MODERN JAZZ JAM SESSION) (10")	£75
54	Vogue LDE 064	MILES DAVIS AND HIS ORCHESTRA (10")	£75
54	Capitol LC 6683	CLASSICS IN JAZZ (10")	£40
55	Esquire 20-062	DIG (10")	£100
55	Esquire 20-072	MILES DAVIS QUINTET (10")	£100
56	Esquire 32-012	THE MUSINGS OF MILES	£70
56	Esquire 32-021	HIS NEW QUINTET (10")	£100
56	Philips BBL 7140	'ROUND ABOUT MIDNIGHT	£50
57	Esquire 32-028	CHANGES	£50
57	Esquire 32-030	BIRTH OF THE COOL	£50
57	Vogue LDE 191	NATURE BOY	£40
57	Fontana TFL 5007	MILES AHEAD	£50
58	Fontana TFL 5035	MILESTONES	£50
58	Esquire 32-048	COOKIN'	£100
58	Esquire 32-068	RELAXIN' WITH THE MILES DAVIS QUARTET	£100
59	Esquire 32-090	BAGS' GROOVE	£40
59	Fontana TFL 5056	PORGY AND BESS (mono)	£30
59	Fontana STFL 507	PORGY AND BESS (stereo)	£40
60	Fontana TFL 5081	JAZZ TRACK — "L'ANSCENSEUR POUR L'ECHAFAUD"	£20
60	Fontana TFL 5089	THE MOST OF MILES	£20
60	Fontana TFL 5072	KIND OF BLUE (mono)	£100
60	Fontana STFL 513	KIND OF BLUE (stereo)	£100
60	CBS SBPG 62066	KIND OF BLUE (stereo)	£60
60	CBS BPG 62066	KIND OF BLUE (mono)	£60
60	Esquire 32-088	BLUE HAZE	£25
60	Esquire 32-098	WALKIN'	£80
60	Esquire 32-100	MILES DAVIS AND THE MODERN JAZZ GIANTS VOL. 2	£40
60	Esquire 32-108	WORKIN' WITH THE MILES DAVIS QUINTET	£80
61	Fontana TFL 5100/STFL 531	SKETCHES OF SPAIN	£40
61	Esquire 32-118	EARLY MILES	£20
61	Esquire 32-138	STEAMIN' WITH THE MILES DAVIS QUINTET	£50
61	Fontana TFL 5163	FRIDAY NIGHT AT THE BLACKHAWK, SAN FRANCISCO (VOL. 1) (with Cannonball Adderley & John Coltrane; also stereo STFL 580)	£35
61	Fontana TFL 5164	SATURDAY NIGHT AT THE BLACKHAWK, SAN FRANCISCO (VOL. 2) (with Cannonball Adderley & John Coltrane; also stereo STFL 581)	£35
62	Fontana TFL 5172	SOMEDAY MY PRINCE WILL COME (also stereo STFL 587)	£40
62	Transatlantic PR 7254	THE ORIGINAL QUINTET	£20
63	CBS CL 2106	QUIET NIGHTS (LP)	£35
63	CBS BPG 62389	MILES AND MONK AT NEWPORT (with Thelonious Monk, also stereo SBPG 62389)	£30
64	Vocalion LAEF 584	BLUE MOODS	£20
65	Stateside SL 10111	MILES DAVIS AND JOHN COLTRANE	£35
65	CBS BPG 62510	MY FUNNY VALENTINE - MILES DAVIS IN CONCERT (LP)	£30

66	CBS 62577	E.S.P.	£50
66	CBS SPBG 85560	FOUR & MORE (LP)	£20
66	Stateside SL 10168	MILES DAVIS PLAYS FOR LOVERS	£20
66	Fontana FJL 135	BACK TO BACK	£25
66	Transatlantic PR 7044	COLLECTORS ITEMS (LP, reissue)	£20
67	CBS 62933	MILES SMILES (LP, stereo/mono)	£50
67	CBS 963097	SORCERER (LP)	£50
67	CBS 63248	NEFERTITI (LP)	£50
68	CBS 63352	MILES IN THE SKY (LP)	£50
69	CBS 63551	FILLES DE KILIMANJARO (stereo)	£50
69	CBS 63630	IN A SILENT WAY	£50
70	CBS 64010	BITCHES BREW (2-LP, gatefold)	£50
70	CBS 70089	A TRIBUTE TO JACK JOHNSON	£40
71	CBS 66257	MILES DAVIS AT FILLMORE (2-LP)	£40
72	CBS 64575	LIVE-EVIL (2-LP, gatefold)	£40
72	CBS 65246	ON THE CORNER	£60
72	Prestige PR 24001	MILES DAVIS (2-LP)	£20
72	Prestige PR 24012	TALLEST TREES (2LP, gatefold)	£30
73	CBS CQ 30997/Q 66236	BITCHES BREW (2LP, gatefold, quadrophonic)	£50
73	CBS GQ 30954/Q 67219	LIVE-EVIL (2-LP, quadrophonic)	£40
73	CBS 68222	IN CONCERT (2-LP)	£30
74	Columbia 88024	BIG FUN (LP, gatefold)	£40
74	CBS S80476	GET UP WITH IT (2LP, gatefold)	£40
79	CBS 88471	CIRCLE IN THE ROUND (2-LP)	£20
85	CBS 62066	KIND OF BLUE (LP, Nimbus Supercut, mail order from Practical Hi Fi magazine)	£250
85	Columbia 451126	BITCHES BREW (2LP, reissue, single sleeve)	£30
87	CBS 4606031	KIND OF BLUE (LP, remastered CBS Jazz masterpieces series)	£18
87	CBS 450982-1	IN A SILENT WAY (LP, reissue, CBS Jazz masterpieces series)	£18
89	CBS 463351-1	AURA (2-LP)	£15
91	Beat Goes On BGO LP 30	ON THE CORNER (LP, reissue, gatefold)	£18
92	Warner Bros. WB 7599 26938-1	DOO-BOP (LP)	£50
96	Columbia 67219	LIVE-EVIL (LP, reissue, gatefold)	£25
97	Columbia 069897-1	PANTHALASSA: THE REMIXES (2-LP)	£30
98	Sony C4K 65570	THE COMPLETE BITCHES BREW SESSIONS (5CD box set, booklet)	£40
01	Columbia S3K 65362	THE COMPLETE IN A SILENT WAY SESSIONS (3CD box set in book sleeve)	£30
05	Columbia COL 516253 2	THE COMPLETE JACK JOHNSON SESSIONS (5CD box set, booklet)	£35
06	Columbia C6K 93674	COMPLETE CELLAR DOOR SESSIONS (6-CD box set, booklet)	£80
07	Legacy 88697062392	COMPLETE ON THE CORNER SESSIONS (6-CD, Metal box sleeve)	£100
09	Columbia 88697524922	THE COMPLETE COLUMBIA ALBUM COLLECTION (Box set, 70CD, DVD, Booklet)	£300
18	Fontana 0060075379639	ASCENSEUR POUR L'ECHAFAUD (3x10", trifold sleeve)	£40

MILES DAVIS/ART BLAKEY

| 66 | Fontana FJL 135 | L'ASCENSEUR POUR L'ECHAFAUD/LA FEMME DISPARAISSANTE (LP, soundtrack, 1 side each) | £30 |

(see also Art Blakey, Thelonius Monk, Dizzy Gillespie, Milt Jackson, Cannonball Adderley, Charlie Parker)

NATHAN DAVIS

| 09 | Universal Sound USLP 29 | IF (LP, reissue) | £20 |

RONNIE DAVIS

75	Live & Love LAL 04	Jah Jah Jehovah/Version	£15
77	Third World TWDIS 005	Anywhere Don't Watch Your Woman (with Dillinger)/BARRY BROWN : Mr Money Man (12")	£25
76	Dip DLP 5028	BEAUTIFUL PEOPLE FROM JAMAICA (LP)	£100
77	Third World TWS 917	HARD TIMES (LP)	£20

ROY DAVIS JR

| 97 | XL XLT 88 | GABRIEL (12" EP p/s, featuring Peven Everett) | £20 |

SAMMY DAVIS (JNR.)

63	Reprise R 20227	The Shelter Of Your Arms/Falling In Love With You	£15
69	MCA MK 1072	Rhythm Of Life/Pompeii Club/Rich Man's Frug	£30
70	Tamla Motown STML 11160	SOMETHING FOR EVERYONE (LP)	£30

(see also Dean Martin)

SANDY DAVIS

| 75 | EMI EMC 3070 | BACK ON MY FEET AGAIN (LP) | £15 |

SANGIE DAVIS & LEE PERRY

| 03 | Black Art TJITW006 | Words/DEVON IRONS & DR ALIMANTADO: Vampire (12" reissue) | £50 |

SILKIE DAVIS

| 70 | Torpedo TOR 2 | Conversations/TWIZZLE & HOT ROD ALL-STARS: Peace & Tranquility | £70 |
| 70 | Torpedo TOR 12 | When I Was A Little Girl/I'm So Lonely | £40 |

SKEETER DAVIS & BOBBY BARE

| 65 | RCA RD 7711 | TUNES FOR TWO (LP) | £15 |

SMILEY DAVIS

| 53 | London L 1189 | Big Mamou/Play Girl (78, actually by Smiley Lewis) | £80 |

SPENCER DAVIS (GROUP)

64	Fontana TF 471	Dimples/Sittin' And Thinkin'	£30
64	Fontana TF 499	I Can't Stand It/Midnight Train	£25
65	Fontana TF 530	Every Little Bit Hurts/It Hurts Me So	£15
65	Fontana TF 571	Strong Love/This Hammer	£20

67	Fontana TF 854	Time Seller/Don't Want You No More	£15
65	Fontana TE 17444	YOU PUT THE HURT ON ME (EP)	£25
65	Fontana TE 17450	EVERY LITTLE BIT HURTS (EP)	£25
66	Fontana TE 17463	SITTIN' AND THINKIN' (EP)	£40
65	Fontana TL 5242	THEIR FIRST LP (LP, laminated front, black/silver label)	£90
66	Fontana TL 5295	THE SECOND ALBUM (LP, laminated front cover, flipbacks, island) **label on rear**)	£80
66	Fontana TL 5359	AUTUMN '66 (LP, laminated front sleeve, flipbacks. black/silver label)	£60
67	United Artists ULP 1186	HERE WE GO ROUND THE MULBERRY BUSH (LP, soundtrack, with Traffic, mono)	£50
67	United Artists (S)ULP 1186	HERE WE GO ROUND THE MULBERRY BUSH (LP, soundtrack, with Traffic, stereo)	£40
68	United Artists ULP 1192	WITH THEIR NEW FACE ON (LP, mono, blue/silver label)	£60
68	United Artists (S)ULP 1192	WITH THEIR NEW FACE ON (LP, stereo)	£50
68	Wing WL 1165	EVERY LITTLE BIT HURTS (LP, reissue of "Their First LP")	£15
68	Island ILP 970 9070	THE BEST OF THE SPENCER DAVIS GROUP FEATURING STEVIE WINWOOD (LP, plain pink label, flipback sleeve; sleeve lists "Please Do Something" but plays "Together Till The End Of Time", mono)	£30
68	Island ILPS 9070	THE BEST OF THE SPENCER DAVIS GROUP FEATURING STEVIE WINWOOD (LP, plain pink label, flipback sleeve; sleeve lists "Please Do Something" but plays "Together Till The End Of Time", stereo)	£15
69	CBS 63842	LETTERS FROM EDITH (LP, unissued, 50 white label test pressings only)	£500
71	United Artists UAS 29177	IT'S BEEN SO LONG (LP, solo with Peter Jameson, 'envelope' cover)	£20
72	United Artists UAS 29361	MOUSETRAP (LP, solo)	£20
73	Vertigo 6360 088	GLUGGO (LP, die cut, gatefold sleeve, 'spaceship' label)	£30
74	Vertigo 6360 105	LIVIN' IN A BACK STREET (LP)	£15

(see also Stevie Winwood, Traffic, Anglos, Blind Faith, Ray Fenwick, Pete York, Hardin & York, Murgatroyd Band, Mirage, Portobello Explosion, Shotgun Express)

STEVE DAVIS
| 68 | Fontana TF 922 | Take Time To Know Her/She Said Yeah | £75 |

TYRONE DAVIS (1)
68	Stateside SS 2092	What If A Man/Bet You Win	£45
69	Atlantic 584 253	Can I Change My Mind/A Woman Needs To Be Loved	£20
69	Atlantic 584 265	Is It Something You've Got?/Undying Love	£15
69	Atlantic 584 288	All The Waiting Is Not In Vain/Need Your Lovin' Everyday	£15
70	Atlantic 2091 003	Turn Back The Hands Of Time/I Keep Coming Back	£15
71	Atlantic 2091 078	Could I Forget You/Just My Way Of Loving You	£15
70	Atlantic 588 209	CAN I CHANGE MY MIND (LP)	£30
71	Atlantic 2465 021	TURN BACK THE HANDS OF TIME (LP)	£40
73	Brunswick BRLS 3002	I HAD IT ALL THE TIME (LP)	£35
73	Brunswick BRLS 3005	GREATEST HITS (LP)	£18

TYRONE DAVIS (2) (ACTUALLY TYRONE EVANS)
| 69 | Trojan TR 677 | If This World Were Mine/You Done Me Wrong (label miscredit: this is Tyrone Evans) | £300 |
| 16 | Trojan TR677 | If This World Were Mine/You Done Me Wrong (reissue) | £20 |

WALTER DAVIS
| 64 | RCA RCX 7169 | R.C.A. VICTOR RACE SERIES VOL. 3 (EP) | £15 |
| 70 | RCA Intl. INTS 1085 | THINK YOU NEED A SHOT (LP) | £15 |

WARREN DAVIS MONDAY BAND
60s	Island WI 353	How Can You Forget/Best News (test pressings only)	£50
60s	Island WIP 354	Strain On My Heart/Question (test pressings only)	£50
67	Columbia DB 8190	Wait For Me/I Don't Wanna Hurt You	£30
67	Columbia DB 8270	Love Is A Hurtin' Thing/Without Fear	£20

(see also Boardwalkers)

ALFIE DAVISON
| 00 | Philly Groove PG2 | Love Is A Serious Business/FLASHLIGHT: Beware She's Pulling My Strings (reissue) | £20 |

BRIAN DAVISON
| 70 | Charisma CAS 1021 | BRIAN DAVISON'S EVERY WHICH WAY (LP, pink 'scroll' label) | £40 |

(see also Habits, Nice, Refuge)

DAVISON BROTHERS
| 60 | Philips PB 1053 | Journey Of Love/Seven Days A Week | £60 |

WILD BILL DAVISON
| 55 | Melodisc MLP 501 | WILD BILL DAVISON (LP) | £15 |

TIM DAWE
| 69 | Straight ST(S) 1058 | PENROD (LP) | £70 |

CARL DAWKINS
67	Rio R 136	All Of A Sudden/Running Shoes	£45
67	Rio R 137	Baby I Love You/Hard Time	£45
68	Blue Cat BS 114	I Love The Way You Are/DERMOTT LYNCH: I Can't Stand It	£100
68	Duke DU 3	I'll Make It Up/J.J. ALL STARS: One Dollar Of Music	£70
69	Nu Beat NB 030	Rodney's History/DYNAMITES: Tribute To Drumbano	£80
70	Duke DU 93	Get Together/FAMILY MAN: Instalment Plan	£25
70	Duke DU 95	This Land/J.J. ALL STARS: Land Version	£15
70	Trojan TR 7765	Satisfaction/Things A Get Bad To Worse	£20
71	Big Shot BI 570	Perseverence/J.J. ALL STARS: Perseverence (Version)	£20
71	Explosion EX 2051	I Feel Good/J.J. ALL STARS: I Feel Good Version Two	£15
71	Explosion EX 2059	Make It Great/STONE: What A Day	£15
71	New Beat NB 086	Walk A Little Prouder/YOUTH PROFESSIONALS: Walk (Version)	£15
72	Duke DU 133	My Whole World/Men A Broken Heart	£15
73	Lord Koos KOO 18	I'd Rather Go Blind/DEROY WASHINGTON: Jah Man A Come	£70

(see also Rass Dawkins, Winston Wright, Ansell Collins, Roland Alphonso, West Indians)

HORRELL DAWKINS
66   Ska Beat JB 240   Cling To Me/Butterfly £40

JIMMY DAWKINS
71   Delmark DS 623   FAST FINGERS (LP) £30
78   Sonet SNTF 758   TRANSATLANTIC 770 (LP) £15
82   JSP 1042   PLAY MY BLUES (LP)..£18
86   JSP 1102   ALL BLUES (LP) £15
88   JSP 1085   FEEL THE BLUES (LP) £15

RASS DAWKINS (& WAILERS)
71   Upsetter US 368   Picture On The Wall/UPSETTERS: Picture Version.....................................£50
(see also Bob Marley/Wailers, Carl Dawkins)

DAWN AND CHRISTINE
78   Burning Rockers BRD 002   We Love Collie Weed (with Clint Eastwood)/LAWES ROCKERS: Version (12") £30

DAWN TRADER
80   AFE 1980   NO ONE GONNA BETTER ME (EP, private pressing) £40

DAWNBREAKERS
65   Decca F 12110   Let's Live/Lovin' For You...£15

DAWN CHORUS (1)
69   MCA MK 5004   A Night To Be Remembered/Crying All Night £15
(see also Carter-Lewis)

DAWN CHORUS (2)
85   Dawn DAWN 1   Teenage Kicks/Dream Lover (p/s) £18

DAWN & DEEJAYS
65   RCA RCA 1470   These Are The Things About You/I Will Think Of You £18

DAWNWATCHER
80   Dawnwatcher DWS 001   Spellbound/Hall Of Mirrors £75
82   Dawnwatcher DWS 002   Salvadors Dream/Backlash £20

DAWNWIND
76   Amron ARN 5003   LOOKING BACK ON THE FUTURE (LP, private pressing)...........................£80

DONNA DAWSON
73   Trojan TR 7892   You Can't Buy Me Love/First Cut Is The Deepest..£15

LESLEY DAWSON
67   Mercury MF 965   Run For Shelter/I'll Climb On A Rainbow..£35

DANIELLE DAX
83   Initial IRC 009   POP-EYES (LP, with 'Meat Harvest' cover & lyric sheet)...........................£40
(see also Lemon Kittens)

BING DAY
59   Mercury AMT 1047   I Can't Help It/Mama's Place £60

BOBBY DAY (& SATELLITES)
57   HMV POP 425   Little Bitty Pretty One/When The Swallows Come Back To Capistrano (as Bobby Day
                                    & Satellites)..£150
57   HMV POP 425   Little Bitty Pretty One/When The Swallows Come Back To Capistrano (as Bobby Day &
                                    Satellites) (78) £25
59   London HL 8800   The Bluebird, The Buzzard And The Oriole/Alone Too Long £40
60   London HLY 9044   My Blue Heaven/I Don't Want To £15
61   Top Rank JAR 538   Over And Over/Gee Whiz £20
65   Sue WI 388   Rockin' Robin/Over And Over (reissue) £15

DORIS DAY & JOHNNIE RAY
53   Columbia SCM 5033   Ma Says, Pa Says/A Full Time Job £20
(see also Johnnie Ray)

JACKIE DAY
67   Sue WI 4040   Before It's Too Late/Without A Love..£250
09   Kent 6T 25   Get To Steppin/LARRY BANKS: My Life Is No Better..................................£20
09   Kent TOWN 145   Naughty Boy/Get To Steppin (reissue)..£15

JOHNNY DAY
69   Stax STAX 111   Stay Baby Stay/I Love Love (listed as Johnny Daye on demos) £20

MURIEL DAY
69   CBS 4115   The Wages Of Love/Thinking Of You £15
69   Page One POF 151   Optimistic Fool/Nine Times Out Of Ten £60
69   Page One POF 151   Optimistic Fool/Nine Times Out Of Ten (DJ copy) £100

TERRY DAY
62   CBS AAG 104   That's All I Want/I Waited Too Long £20
(see also Rip-Chords, Rogues)

DAYBREAKERS
67   John Hassell 814/5   DAYBREAKERS (LP)..£60
67   John Hassell HAS LP 1126   VOL 2 (LP)..£60

DAY BROTHERS
60   Oriole CB 1575   Angel/Just One More Kiss £20

JOEL DAYDE
71   Barclay BAR 7   Mammy Blue/You've Got Freedom £25

MINT VALUE £

DAYLIGHT
71   RCA SF 8194   DAYLIGHT (LP, gatefold sleeve, orange label)..£80
(see also Daddy Longlegs)

DAYLIGHTERS
64   Sue WI 343   Oh Mom! (Teach Me How To Uncle Willie)/**Hard-Headed Girl** £45

DAY OF THE PHOENIX
70   Greenwich GSLP 1002   WIDE OPEN N-WAY (LP)..£100
72   Chapter One CHS-R 812 THE NEIGHBOUR'S SON (LP, red/silver label) £70

DAYSHIFT
80   Wot WOT 1   Living In The UK/Cedric Wazza Superstar/Yeah Eh Oh Yeah (p/s)..........................£20

DAYTON
84   Capitol 12CLX 318   The Sound Of Music (X-Tended Remix)/Eyes On You/Love You Anyway (12", p/s)..........£15

DAYTONAS
97   Kalevala KALA 004   Faster Gimpo Faster Kill! Kill! Kill!/Faster Gimpo Faster Kill! Kill! Kill! (version)...............£20

DAZE (1)
79   Motor City Rhythm MCR10S I Wanna Be A Star/At The Seaside £300

DAZE (2)
83   Mynah SDM 001   Deep South/Made In America £20

DAZZLE (3)
89   Jam Today 12 CHIL 16 Dazzle You/Only You (12", p/s) £20
89   Jet Star 12 CHIL 11   Don't Want Your Love/Don't Want Your Love (12" white label)...............................£20
89   Jam Today CHIL LP 7   SOUL SISTERS (LP)...£20
90   Jam City CHIL LP 10   ON SECOND THOUGHTS (LP, white labels, hand-made sleeve, 500 only) £30

D BASE
99   D Base DR 1   Dreaming/Dreaming/(Dream Dub)/(Nightmare Dub) (12") £50
99   D Base BASE 1   Can't Stop/Believe In Yourself/Still Can't Stop (12") £30
99   D Base BASE 2   The Fight (South Central Remix 1)/(Original Mix)/(South Central Remix 2) (12") £30
00   D Base BASE 3   Drop The Bomb/Good Body Girlz (12") £15
00   D Base BASE 4   Dark Riddumx: What's The Time/Base Theory (12")...£15

DBX
93   Peacefrog PF 015   Alien EP (12", plain sleeve) £40
94   Peacefrog PF 022   Losing Control/Beat Phreak/Live Wire/Spock's Brain (12", plain sleeve) £22
95   Peacefrog PR 025   Losing Control Remixes (12", plain sleeve) £20

DC 10'S
80   A Certain Euphoria ACE 451 Bermuda/I Can See Through Walls £20

D DASTARDLEY & P PERFECT
97   Confetti Dubs CO DB01 Tear It Up/Da Beats/Party Time (12")...£30
97   Confetti Dubs CO DB02 THE BEATS AND BREAKS EP (12")..£20

DDR
90s Smitten SMTLTD 05   The Gift (12", 1-sided yellow vinyl, 500 only) £60

CHRISTOPH DE BABALON
97   Digital Hardcore DHR LP8 IF YOU'RE INTO IT. I'M OUT OF IT (2-LP) £40

GEORGE DEACON & MARION ROSS
73   Xtra XTRA 1130   SWEET WILLIAM'S GHOST (LP, with lyric insert)..£60

DEAD PARROTS SOCIETY
92   Private Press MDNLP 001 MUSIC OF A BYGONE AGE (LP) £20

DEAD SKELETONS
10   A Records AUKDS 001-10 Dead Mantra (1-sided 10" other side etched)...£30
12   Fuzz Club Dead 12 12 12 Buddha Christ/Kundalini Eyes (12", p/s Silk Screened B side, 300 only)................£40
11   A Records AUK103LP   DEAD MAGICK (2-LP, burgundy/blue vinyl) £60

DEAD BOYS
77   Sire SRE 1004   Sonic Reducer/Down In Flames (no p/s) £25
77   Sire 6078 609   Sonic Reducer/Little Girl/Down In Flames (12", p/s) £15
78   Sire SRE 1029   Tell Me/Not Anymore/Ain't Nothin' To Do (p/s) £25
77   Sire 9103 329   YOUNG, LOUD & SNOTTY (LP) £30
78   Sire SRK 6054   WE HAVE COME FOR YOUR CHILDREN (LP) £25
87   Line LILP 400200   NIGHT OF THE LIVING DEAD BOYS (LP) £15
99   Rude LP00010   3RD GENERATION NATION (LP, clear vinyl, mail order only) £15
(see also Stiv Bators, Lords Of The New Church, Wanderers)

DEAD CAN DANCE
84   4AD CAD 404   DEAD CAN DANCE (LP) £25
85   4AD CAD 512   SPLEEN AND IDEAL (LP) £25
87   4AD CAD 705   WITHIN THE REALM OF A DYING SUN (LP) £25
88   4AD CAD 808   THE SERPENT'S EGG (LP)..£25
90   4AD CAD 0007   AION (LP, inner)..£40
93   4AD DAD 3013   INTO THE LABYRINTH (2-LP) £60
94   4AD DAD 4015   TOWARDS THE WITHIN (2-LP) £60
96   4AD DAD 608   SPIRITCHASER (2-LP)...£60
05   The Show (No Cat. No.) CHICAGO: 12th OCTOBER 2005 (3-LP, 500 only, signed and numbered)..............£125
08   Vinyl 180 VIN180LP003 DEAD CAN DANCE (LP, reissue on 180gm vinyl, with free 12" on black or clear vinyl).......£20
08   Vinyl 180 VIN180LP007 SPLEEN AND IDEAL (LP, reissue 180gm vinyl) £20
09   Vinyl 180 VIN180LP011 WITHIN THE REALMS OF A DYING SUN (LP, reissue, 180gm vinyl) £20
09   Vinyl 180 VIN180LP016 THE SERPENTS EGG (LP, reissue 180gm vinyl) £30

10	Vinyl 180 VIN180LP029	**DEAD CAN DANCE** (2-LP, 2 x 12" reissue, insert)	£150
11	Vinyl 180 VIN180LP028	**AION** (LP, reissue 180gm vinyl)	£20
12	PIAS PIAS R3313LP	**IN CONCERT** (3-LP box set)	£70
12	PIAS PIASR311DLP	**ANASTASIS** (2-LP)	£25

DEAD FINGERS TALK
79	Pye 46156	**This Crazy World/The Boyfriend** (p/s)	£20

DEAD FLOWERS
91	Mystic Stones RUNE 2	**SMELL THE FRAGRANCE, FREE YOUR MIND** (LP)	£15
92	Mystic Stones RUNE 12	**MOONTAN** (LP)	£15
94	Delerium DELEC LP 022	**ALTERED STATE CIRCUS** (LP)	£15

DEAD KENNEDYS
81	Cherry Red B RED 10	**FRESH FRUIT FOR ROTTING VEGETABLES** (LP, with insert & 'Heads' pic on rear)	£40
80	Cherry Red B RED 10	**FRESH FRUIT FOR ROTTING VEGETABLES** (LP, with insert & without 'Heads' pic on rear)	£20
85	Statik/Alternative Tentacles VIRUS 45	**FRANKENCHRIST** (LP, with poster)	£20
86	Statik/Alternative Tentacles VIRUS 50	**BEDTIME FOR DEMOCRACY** (LP)	£18
87	Alternative Tent. VIRUS 57	**GIVE ME CONVENIENCE...** (LP, with booklet and "Buzzbomb From Pasadena" flexidisc)	£18

(see also Lard)

DEADLINE
60s	Hollick & Taylor HT 137	**Glass Man/I'm In My Element**	£300

DEADLY HEADLEY
82	On-U Sound ONULP 14	**35 YEARS FROM ALPHA** (LP)	£30

DEADLY TOYS
79	Bonhard/Hunt DT 1	**Nice Weather/Roll On Doomsday/I'm Logical/Deadly Mess Around** (EP, in hand-made sleeve)	£125
79	Bonhard/Hunt DT 1	**Nice Weather/Roll On Doomsday/I'm Logical/Deadly Mess Around** (EP)	£50

DEAD MANS SHADOW
81	Pig Records HOG 1	**Neighbours/Morons With Power/Poxy Politics/War Ploys** (p/s and sticker)	£20
81	Subversive Anarcho 1	**HEATHROW TOUCHDOWN** (Shared EP with ACTION PACT)	£20

DEAD MEADOW
03	Matador OLE 566-1	**SHIVERING KING AND OTHERS** (2-LP)	£35
05	Matador OLE 625-1	**FEATHERS** (2-LP)	£25
08	Matador OLE 750-1	**OLD GROWTH** (2-LP)	£20

DEAD OR ALIVE
80	Inevitable INEV 005	**I'm Falling/Flowers** (foldout p/s)	£30
82	Black Eyes BE 1	**It's Been Hours Now/Whirlpool/Nowhere To Nowhere/ It's Been Hours Now** (Alternative Mix) (12", p/s)	£20
83	Epic A 3399	**Misty Circles/Misty Circles** (Instrumental) (p/s)	£18
83	Epic TA 3399	**Misty Circles** (Dance Mix)**/Misty Circles** (Dub Mix)**/Selfish Side** (12", p/s)	£20
83	Epic A 3676	**What I Want/The Stranger** (Remix) (white 'floppy hat' p/s, withdrawn)	£120
83	Epic A 3676	**What I Want/The Stranger** ('dreadlocks' p/s)	£25
83	Epic TA 3676	**What I Want** (Dance Mix)**/The Stranger** (12", p/s, poster)	£75
84	Epic A 4510	**What I Want** (Remix)**/The Stranger** (poster p/s)	£60
84	Epic A 4510	**What I Want** (Remix)**/The Stranger** (2nd issue, p/s)	£15
84	Epic XPR 1257	**MIGHTY MIX: Wish You Were Here/What I Want/Do It/Misty Circles/ Absolutely Nothing/Sit On It/You Make Me Wanna/That's The Way** (I Like It) (12", white label, promo only)	£40
85	Epic A 6086	**Lover Come Back To Me/Far Too Hard** (blue p/s, withdrawn)	£250
87	Epic XPR 1328	**CLEAN AND DIRTY: Something In My House** (Mortevicar Mix)**/Something In My House** (Naughty XXX Mix) (12", white label, plain white sleeve)	£100
88	Epic BURNSQ 4	**Turn Around And Count 2 Ten** (I Had A Disco Dream Mix)**/Something In My House** (Instru-Mental)**/Then There Was You/Come Inside** (12", p/s)	£50
88	Epic BURNSQ 4	**Turn Around And Count 2 Ten** (I Had A Disco Dream Mix)**/Something In My House** (Instru-Mental)**/Then There Was You/Come Inside** (12", p/s)	£40
88	Epic BURNSC 4	**Turn Around And Count 2 Ten/Something In My House** (Instru-Mental)**/ Turn Around And Count 2 Ten** (I Love BPM Mix)**/(Instru-Mental** (CD, picture disc)	£40
88	Epic BURNSP4	**Turn Around And Count 2 Ten/Something In My House** (instrumental) (fold-out poster p/s)	£25
89	Epic BURNSC5	**Come Home With Me Baby** (7" version)**/(12" Version)/(Deadhouse Dub)** (CD)	£30
16	Demon BOOMBOX 01LP	**SOPHISTICATED BOOM BOX** (10LP clear vinyl, box set)	£150
16	Demon BOOMBOX 01LPX	**SOPHISTICATED BOOM BOX** (10LP/1x10" clear vinyl, box set, Amazon exclusive)	£175
16	Demon BOOMBOX 01	**SOPHISTICATED BOOM BOX** (17CD/2DVD box set)	£300

(see also Nightmares In Wax, Sisters Of Mercy, Pauline Murray & Invisible Girls, International Chrysis, Mission)

DEAD PREZ
00	Epic 496864-1	**LET'S GET FREE** (2-LP)	£35

DEAD RESIDENTS
04	Sin Nombre SIN 003	**POLTERGEIST FREQUENCY** (12" EP)	£15

DEAD SEA FRUIT
67	Camp 602 001	**Kensington High Street/Put Another Record On**	£20
68	Camp 602 004	**Love At The Hippiedrome/My Naughty Bluebell**	£20
67	Camp 603 001	**DEAD SEA FRUIT** (LP)	£150

DEAD WEATHER
09	Third Man TMR 001	**Hang You From The Heavens/Are Friends Electric?** (luminous vinyl, 'Halloween' cover, 100-only)	£200

(see also The Kills, White Stripes, Raconteurs)

DEADWOOD
71 Decca F13109 | The Turning Of Them All/They Don't Help Me None £160

DEAD WRETCHED
82 Tempest HELL 2 | NO HOPE FOR ANYONE EP £20

DEAF AIDS
79 Regana REG 1 | DO IT AGAIN EP (250 copies only) £100
80 Conspiracy CONS1 | Heroes/Bored Christine (p/s) £15

BILL DEAL & RHONDELLS
69 MGM MGM 1479 | I've Been Hurt/I've Got My Needs £15

MICHAEL DE ALBUQUERQUE
74 RCA SF 8383 | WE MAY BE CATTLE BUT WE ALL HAVE NAMES (LP, with lyric sheet)............£35
76 Warner Bros K 56276 | STALKING THE SLEEPER (LP, as Albuqerque)................................£20
(see also E.L.O., Ricotti & Albuquerque)

DEALER (1)
79 MCA NCA 517 | Buffalo Bill/Star Dance £20

DEALER (2)
83 Windrush WR 1030 | Better Things To Do/Suspected Foul Play (p/s)...............................£100

ALAN DEAN & HIS PROBLEMS
64 Decca F 11947 | The Time It Takes/Dizzy Heights £40
65 Pye 7N 15749 | Thunder And Rain/As Time Goes By £60

LITTLE BILLY DEAN
67 Strike JH 325 | That's Always Like You/Tic Toc £20

ELTON DEAN
71 CBS 64539 | ELTON DEAN (LP) £60
77 Ogun OG 610 | THE CHEQUE IS IN THE MAIL (LP, with Joe Gallivan & Kenny Wheeler)......£20
78 Ogun OG 530 | THE BOLOGNA TAPE (LP) £25
(see also Bluesology, Soft Machine, Centipede, Ninesense, Julie Tippetts, Hugh Hopper, Mike Hugg, Reg King, Keith Tippett)

HAZEL DEAN
81 Carlin CMC 1004 | THE SOUND OF BACHARACH & DAVID (LP, promo only)........................£25

JIMMY DEAN
61 Philips BBL 7537 | BIG BAND JOHN AND OTHER FABULOUS SONGS AND TALES (LP) £15

NORA DEAN
69 Upsetter US 322 | The Same Thing You Gave To Daddy/UPSETTER PILGRIMS: A Testimony.......£90
70 Trojan TR 7735 | Barbwire/BRONS: Calypso Mama..£50
71 Randy's RAN 508 | Want Man/RANDY'S ALL STARS: Man...£25
71 High Note HS 050 | I Must Get A Man/The Valet £20
71 Bullet BU 472 | Peace Begins Within/SLICKERS: Go Back Home £400
71 Gas GAS 165 | Greedy Boy/KEITH: Please Stay (B-side actually by Slim Smith) £20
72 Big Shot BI 611 | Night Food Reggae/PROPHETS: Jaco £20
73 Bread BR 1117 | Mama/Man A Walk And Talk £20
76 Attack ATT 8126 | Scorpion/Version £20
11 Harry J THB 7013 | Mama/SOUL SYNDICATE: Natty In Hong Kong £25
79 Nationwide NWLP 007 | PLAY ME A LOVE SONG (LP)..£50
(see also Hugh Roy, Ebony Sisters)

PAUL DEAN (& SOUL SAVAGES)
65 Decca F 12136 | You Don't Own Me/Hole In The Head (as Paul Dean & Thoughts) £18
66 Reaction 591 002 | She Can Build A Mountain/A Day Gone By (as Paul Dean & Soul Savages)......£15
(see also Oscar, Thoughts)

PAULA DEAN & NYAH SHUFFLE
70 Joe's JRS 2 | Since I Met You Baby/Jug Head £20

ROGER DEAN'S LYSIS
77 Mosaic GCM 762 | LYSIS LIVE (LP)..£15
77 Mosaic GCM 774 | CYCLE (LP)..£15

TRACEY DEAN
74 Decca FR 13497 | Moonshiner/Boy On The Ball £20

DEAN & JEAN
64 Stateside SS 249 | Tra La La La Suzy/I Love The Summertime..£20
64 Stateside SS 283 | Hey Jean Hey Dean/Please Don't Tell Me How £20
64 Stateside SS 313 | Thread Your Needle/I Wanna Be Loved £25

JASON DEANE
66 King KG 1049 | Make Believe/Don't Ever Want To See You No More....................................£30
67 King KG 1060 | Down In The Street/Ain't Got No Love £40

DEANO
65 Columbia SEG 8470 | DEANO (EP) £25

BLOSSOM DEARIE
67 Fontana TL 5399 | SWEET BLOSSOM DEARIE (LP)..£45
67 Fontana TL 5352 | BLOSSOM TIME AT RONNIE'S (LP)..£50
67 Fontana STL 5454 | SOON IT'S GONNA RAIN (LP)...£40
70 Fontana 6309 015 | THAT'S THE WAY I WANT IT TO BE (LP) £80

DEAR MR. TIME
70 Square SQ 3 | Prayer For Her/Light Up A Light £50
71 Square SQA 101 | GRANDFATHER (LP, black/white label) £200

DEATH
87	Under One Flag FLAG 12	SCREAM BLOODY GORE (LP, with inner sleeve)	£60
88	Under One Flag FLAG 24	LEPROSY (LP, inner)	£50
90	Under One Flag FLAG 38	SPIRITUAL HEALING (LP)	£35
90	Under One Flag FLAG 38	SPIRITUAL HEALING (LP, picture disc)	£30
92	Under One Flag FLAG 71	FATE (LP)	£35
07	Back On Black BOBV 055	SCREAM BLOODY GORE (2-LP, reissue, orange vinyl, 500 only)	£20
07	Back On Black BOBV 055	SCREAM BLOODY GORE (2-LP, red splatter vinyl, 1000 only)	£15
07	Back On Black BOBV 056	LEPROSY (LP, reissue, red and white splatter vinyl, gatefold p/s)	£15
07	Back On Black BOBV 058	HUMAN (LP, reissue, red splatter vinyl)	£15
07	Back On Black BOBV 059	INDIVIDUAL THOUGHT PATTERNS (LP, reissue, red splatter vinyl)	£15
07	Back On Black BOBV 059	INDIVIDUAL THOUGHT PATTERNS (LP, reissue, clear vinyl)	£15
08	Back On Black BOBV 071	THE SOUND OF PERSEVERANCE (2-LP, reissue, red splatter vinyl, gatefold)	£18
09	Black Sleeves BLACK 113	LIVE IN L.A. (DEATH & RAW) (2-LP reissue)	£18

DEATH ANGEL
87	Under One Flag FLAG 14	THE ULTRA-VIOLENCE (LP)	£30

DEATH CAB FOR CUTIE
98	Sonic Boom SBR 002	SOMETHING ABOUT AIRPLANES (LP)	£35
03	Sonic Boom SBR 012	TRANSATLANTICISM (2-LP)	£35

DEATH FROM ABOVE 1979
05	679 679LP100P	YOU'RE A WOMAN, I'M A MACHINE (2-LP, pink vinyl limited edition)	£50

DEATH IN JUNE
84	New European SA 29634	Heaven Street/We Drive East/In The Night Time (12", 2,000 with brown/gold embossed/textured sleeve)	£60
84	New European SA 29634	Heaven Street/We Drive East/In The Night Time (12", later pressing of 2,000 with blue/white sleeve)	£50
84	New European SA 30634	State Laughter/Holy Water (p/s)	£50
84	New European BADVC 6	She Said Destroy/The Calling (p/s)	£25
84	New European 12BADVC 6	The Calling/She Said Destroy/Doubt To Nothing (12", p/s with insert)	£35
85	New European BADVC 69	Born Again/The Calling (Mk II)/Carousel (Bolt Mix) (12", p/s)	£25
85	New European BADVC 73	...And Murder Love/A.M.L. (Instrumental) (p/s)	£25
85	New European 12BADVC73	Come Before Christ And Murder Love/Torture By Roses (12", p/s)	£25
87	New European BADVC 10	To Drown A Rose/Zimmerit/Europa/The Gates Of Heaven (10", p/s)	£20
88	Cenaz CENAZ 09	Born Again/The Calling (Mk II)/Carousel (Remix) (12" picture disc, 1st pressing with silver print & rim, 970 only)	£25
88	Cenaz CENAZ 09	Born Again/The Calling (Mk II)/Carousel (Remix) (12" picture disc, 2nd pressing bronze print & rim)	£20
92	New European BADVC 8	CATHEDRAL OF TEARS (12" EP, picture disc with sticker)	£25
93	New European BADVC 63	PARADISE RISING (12" EP)	£18
96	Twilight. Command NERO XIII	Kapo!/Occidental Martyr (p/s)	£18
85	New European BADVC 3	THE GUILTY HAVE NO PRIDE (LP)	£75
92	Leprosy UBADVC 4	BURIAL (LP, standard sleeve, green vinyl)	£40
80s	Leprosy UBADVC 4	BURIAL (LP, 'quilted' sleeve, brown, pink, white & other coloured vinyl)	£60
90s	Leprosy UBADVC 4	BURIAL (LP, textured sleeve, various coloured vinyl)	£35
85	New European BADVC 13	NADA (LP, blue sleeve)	£50
85	New European BADVC 13	NADA (LP, brown sleeve)	£35
85	New European BADVC 13	NADA (LP, picture disc)	£15
86	New European BADVC 726	LESSON ONE: MISANTHROPY (LP, embossed sleeve with insert)	£25
87	New European BADVC 11	BROWN BOOK (LP, textured sleeve with inner & insert; export copies with extra inserts & postcards)	£50
87	New European BADVC 11	BROWN BOOK (LP, textured sleeve with inner & insert)	£30
88	New European BADVC 9	THE WORLD THAT SUMMER (2-LP, gatefold textured sleeve)	£30
88	New European BADVC 88	WALL OF SACRIFICE (LP, red sleeve)	£70
88	New European BADVC 88	WALL OF SACRIFICE (LP, green/yellow sleeve)	£40
89	New European BADVC 93	93 DEAD SUN WHEELS (mini-LP, with Current 93)	£20
92	Leprosy LEPER 2	NIGHT AND FOG (LP, red vinyl, 1,000 only)	£30
93	New European BADVC 36	BUT WHAT ENDS WHEN THE SYMBOLS SHATTER (LP, with inner & insert, 500 on purple vinyl)	£150
93	New European BADVC 36	BUT WHAT ENDS WHEN THE SYMBOLS SHATTER (LP, with inner & insert, 3,000 on black vinyl)	£20
95	New European BADVC 39	BLACK WHOLE OF LOVE (box set with 12", 10", 7" & CDs with inserts)	£30
96	New European BADVC 96	SOMETHING IS COMING (2-LP, textured sleeve with insert)	£15
99	New European BAD VC44	OPERATION HUMMINGBIRD (LP, with inner and postcards)	£25

(see also Crisis, Current 93, Boyd Rice & Friends, Sol Invictus)

DEATH IN VEGAS
03	Concrete HARD 550	So You Say You've Lost Your Baby (7", pink vinyl, white labels featuring Paul Weller)	£25
97	Concrete HARD 22 LP 12	DEAD ELVIS (2-LP)	£60
99	Concrete HARD 41 LP	CONTINO SESSIONS (2-LP)	£40
02	Concrete HARD 5312	SCORPIO RISING (2-LP, gatefold sleeve with inners)	£35
04	Drone DRONELP ONE	SATAN'S CIRCUS (3-LP)	£35
05	Concrete 82376672671	MIX IT - THE BEST OF DEATH IN VEGAS (2-LP)	£30
11	Portabello PORT 1 LP	TRANS-LOVE ENERGIES (2-LP)	£18

DEATH SENTENCE
82	Beat The System DEATH 1	DEATH & PURE DESTRUCTION (EP)	£30

DEB MUSIC PLAYERS
78	Deb DEB LP 003	UMOJA - LOVE AND UNITY (LP)	£45

DEBONAIRES (U.S.)
70	Track 604 035	I'm In Love Again/Headache In My Heart	£50

DEBRIS
78	Kelly DEB-1	THE FIRST ONE EP (no p/s)	£50

DEB-TONES
59	RCA RCA 1137	Knock, Knock — Who's There?/I'm In Love Again	£25

DECADES BY NIGHT
81	Slip 001	Life Spiral/SONS OF MONKEYS: Me And Mr. Suzuki	£50

DECAMERON
73	Vertigo 6360 097	SAY HELLO TO THE BAND (LP)	£18
73	Mooncrest CREST 19	MAMMOTH SPECIAL (LP, lyric insert)	£30
75	Transatlantic TRA 304	THIRD LIGHT (LP)	£20
76	Transatlantic TRA 325	TOMORROW'S PANTOMIME (LP)	£25

DECAPITATED
02	Earache MOSH 255	NIHILTY (LP, embossed sleeve, 500 only)	£75
10	Earache WICK 011LP	WINDS OF CREATION (LP, reissue)	£25

DE CASTRO SISTERS
54	London HL 8104	Teach Me Tonight/It's Love	£20
55	London HL 8137	Boom Boom Boomerang/Let Your Love Walk In	£20
55	London HL 8158	I'm Bewildered/To Say You're Mine	£15
55	London HLU 8189	If I Ever Fall In Love/Cuckoo In The Clock	£20
55	London HLU 8212	Christmas Is A-Comin'/Snowbound For Christmas	£15
56	London HLU 8228	Give Me Time/Too Late Now	£15
56	London HLU 8296	No One To Blame But You/Cowboys Don't Cry	£15

DECISIONS
71	A&M 844	It's Love That Really Counts In The Long Run/I Can't Forget About You	£18

DIANA DECKER
54	Columbia SCM 5083	Oh, My Papa/Crystal Ball	£15
54	Columbia SCM 5096	The Happy Wanderer/Till We Two Are One	£15
54	Columbia SCM 5145	Sisters/Abracadabra	£15
56	Columbia SCM 5246	Rock-A-Boogie Baby/Willie Can	£30

(see also Ray Burns, Ruby Murray)

DECLINO
85	Children Of the Revolution GURT 7	MUCCHIO SELVAGGIO (split LP with NEGAZIONE)	£75

GAT DECOR
92	Effective 12 EFFS 1	Passion (Naked Mix)/(D Emerson Mix) (12", p/s)	£25
92	Tag TAGO 1	Passion (1-sided white label 12")	£20

NINA DECOSTA
80	Rokel ROK 12	Don't Want To Lose You/Instrumental Version (12")	£40

DECOYS
64	Studio 36 KEP 108	DECOYS (EP, 500 only)	£30

DE DANAAN
75	Polydor 2904 005	DE DANAAN (LP)	£15
77	Decca SKL-R 5287	DE DANAAN — SELECTED JIGS AND REELS (LP)	£18

DEDRINGER
81	DinDisc DID 7	DIRECT LINE (LP)	£15
83	Neat NEAT 1009	SECOND RISING (LP, with inner sleeve)	£15

DAVE DEE, DOZY, BEAKY, MICK & TICH
65	Fontana TF 531	No Time/Is It Love	£25
65	Fontana TF 586	All I Want/It Seems A Pity	£25
66	Fontana TL 5350	DAVE DEE, DOZY, BEAKY, MICK & TICH (LP)	£20
66	Fontana TL 5388	IF MUSIC BE THE FOOD OF LOVE PREPARE FOR INDIGESTION (LP, mono)	£20
66	Fontana STL 5388	IF MUSIC BE THE FOOD OF LOVE PREPARE FOR INDIGESTION (LP, stereo)	£25
67	Fontana (S)TL 5441	GOLDEN HITS OF DAVE DEE, DOZY, BEAKY, MICK & TICH (LP)	£15
68	Fontana (S)TL 5471	IF NO-ONE SANG (LP)	£15

(see also Dozy Beaky Mick & Tich [D,B,M & T])

JEANNIE DEE
69	Beacon BEA 142	Don't Go Home My Little Darling/Come See About Me	£15

JOEY DEE
74	Alaska ALA 14	Baby Don't You Know (I Need You)/Half Moon	£20

JOEY DEE & STARLI(GH)TERS
61	Columbia 33SX 1406	DOIN' THE TWIST LIVE AT THE PEPPERMINT LOUNGE (LP)	£15
62	Columbia 33SX 1461	BACK AT THE PEPPERMINT LOUNGE (LP)	£15
62	Columbia 33SX 1502	ALL THE WORLD IS TWISTIN' (LP)	£15
63	Columbia 33SX 1532	JOEY DEE (LP)	£15
63	Columbia 33SX 1607	DANCE DANCE DANCE (LP, with Starlighters, also with Ronettes uncredited)	£15

(see also Young Rascals)

JOHNNY DEE
57	Oriole CB 1367	Sittin' In The Balcony/A-Plus Love	£150
57	Oriole CB 1367	Sittin' In The Balcony/A-Plus Love (78)	£20

(see also John D. Loudermilk)

KIKI DEE
63	Fontana TF 394	Early Night/Lucky High Heels	£25
64	Fontana TF 443	Miracles/That's Right, Walk On By	£18
64	Fontana TF 490	(You Don't Know) How Glad I Am/Baby I Don't Care	£15
66	Fontana TF 669	Why Don't I Run Away From You?/Small Town	£30
67	Fontana TF 792	I'm Going Out (The Same Way I Came In)/We've Got Everything Going For Us	£20
68	Fontana TF 983	Now The Flowers Cry/On A Magic Carpet Ride	£400
70	Tamla Motown TMG 739	The Day Will Come Between Sunday And Monday/My Whole World Ended (The Moment You Left Me)	£25
65	Fontana TE 17443	KIKI DEE (EP)	£40
66	Fontana TE 17470	KIKI DEE IN CLOVER (EP)	£30
68	Fontana (S)TL 5455	I'M KIKI DEE (LP)	£50
70	Tamla Motown STML 11158	GREAT EXPECTATIONS (LP)	£45

(see also Elton John)

RICKY DEE & EMBERS
62	Stateside SS 136	Workout/JOHN MOBLEY: Tunnel Of Love	£15

TAMMI DEE
71	Downtown DT 479	Val/MUSIC DOCTORS: Bank Raid	£15

TOMMY DEE
59	Melodisc 1516	Three Stars/TEEN JONES (TONES): I'll Never Change (tri centre)	£20

DEE AND THE CHEETAHS
80	MG MO 001	You To Me/Touch Me (ps)	£40

DEE AND THE QUOTIUM
69	Jay Boy Boy 8	Someday You'll Need Someone/Send Some Flowers To Jule	£45

MAURICE DEEBANK
84	Cherry Red MRED 61	INNER THOUGHT ZONE (LP)	£25

(see also Felt)

DEEJAYS
65	Polydor BM 56034	Dimples/Coming On Strong	£60
65	Polydor BM 56501	Blackeyed Woman/I Just Can't Go To Sleep	£110

ANTHONY DEELEY
68	Pama PM 728	Anytime Man/Don't Change Your Mind About Me	£20

CAROL DEENE
65	Columbia DB 7743	He Just Don't Know/Up In The Penthouse	£30
68	CBS 3206	When He Wants A Woman/I'm Not Crying	£15
70	World Records ST 1031	A LOVE AFFAIR (LP)	£20

DEEPART
04	Deepart DEEPART LP	ELECTRIC BATTLE FIELD (LP, test pressings only)	£60

DEEP END
78	Private pressing	BEGGED AND BORROWED (LP, listed as CPLP 016)	£15

DEEP FEELING
69	Page One POF 160	Oh Darlin'/Feelin'	£40
71	DJM DJLPS 419	DEEP FEELING (LP)	£200

(see also Raw Material)

DEEP FREEZE MICE
86	Cordelia ERICAT 002	Zoology/These Floors Are Smooth (500 copies, no sleeve)	£15
86	Cordelia ERICAT 016	NEURON MUSIC (12" EP, also featuring Mr. Concept, Yung Analysts and Rimarimba)	£20
79	Mole Embalming MOLE 1	MY GERANIUMS ARE BULLETPROOF (LP, 1st 250 copies with paste-on sleeve, 8-page booklet & various A4 inserts)	£120
79	Mole Embalming MOLE 1	MY GERANIUMS ARE BULLETPROOF (LP, printed sleeve, 1500 only)	£70
81	Mole Embalming MOLE 2	TEENAGE HEAD IN MY REFRIGERATOR (LP, 400 copies with red cover)	£45
81	Mole Embalming MOLE 2	TEENAGE HEAD IN MY REFRIGERATOR (LP, 800 printed)	£50
81	Inedible MOLE 3	GATES OF LUNCH (LP, 1,000 pressed, various inserts)	£40
82	Mole Embalming MOLE C1	TEENAGE HEAD IN MY REFRIGERATOR/LED ZEPPELIN 2 (cassette, around 30 copies)	£50
83	Mole Embalming MOLE 4	SAW A RANCH BURNING LAST NIGHT (LP, 120 in wraparound sleeve)	£40
83	Mole Embalming MOLE 4	SAW A RANCH BURNING LAST NIGHT (LP, 1,000 copies)	£40
84	Inedible MOLE 3	GATES OF LUNCH (LP, 1,000 pressed, these 150 copies with wraparound poster sleeve with insert)	£55
84	Cordelia ERICAT 001	I LOVE YOU LITTLE BOBO WITH YOUR DELICATE GOLDEN LIONS (2 x LP)	£60
84	Cordelia ERICAT 004	HANG ON CONSTANCE, LET ME HEAR THE NEWS (LP, 120 wraparound poster sleeve with insert)	£20
84	Cordelia ERICAT 004	HANG ON CONSTANCE, LET ME HEAR THE NEWS (LP, 1,000 copies)	£20
84	Mole Embalming MOLE C2	MY GERANIUMS ARE BULLETPROOF (cassette, 30 copies only)	£50
84	Mole Embalming MOLE C3	TEENAGE HEAD IN MY REFRIGERATOR (cassette, around 30 copies)	£50
86	Cordelia/Unlikely CERICAT 001	I LOVE YOU LITTLE BOBO WITH YOUR DELICATE GOLDEN LIONS (double cassette, around 25 copies)	£25
87	Cordelia ERICAT 013	RAIN IS WHEN THE EARTH IS TELEVISION (LP, 1000 copies only)	£20
87	Cordelia ERICAT 024	WAR, FAMINE, DEATH, PESTILENCE & MISS TIMBERLAKE (LP, 1000 copies)	£20
88	Cordelia ERICAT 027	THE TENDER YELLOW PONIES OF INSOMNIA (LP, 1000 copies)	£20
89	Logical Fish 1	LIVE IN SWITZERLAND (LP, 500 copies)	£15

DEEP POCKETS
74	Stadium S77	Loose Change/Run Back To Me	£30

DEEP PURPLE
SINGLES
68	Parlophone R 5708	Hush/One More Rainy Day (in promo-only p/s)	£400

68	Parlophone R 5708	**Hush/One More Rainy Day**	**£40**
68	Parlophone R 5745	**Kentucky Woman/Wring That Neck** (withdrawn)..	**£65**
69	Parlophone R 5763	**Emmaretta/Wring That Neck**	**£40**
69	Harvest HAR 5006	**Hallelujah** (I Am The Preacher)/**April Part 1** (in promo-only p/s)...............	**£275**
69	Harvest HAR 5006	**Hallelujah** (I Am The Preacher)/**April Part 1**...	**£35**
70	Harvest PSR 325	**Concerto, 1st Movement** (edit)/**Concerto, 2nd Movement** (edit) (promo, possibly some commercial)	**£40**
11	EMI 266987 8 HAR 5304	**Hush** (1969 BBC Session)/**Speed King** (1969 BBC Session) (p/s)	**£20**
12	EMI PURRSD 138	**Smoke On The Water/Smoke On The Water** (p/s, purple vinyl)..................	**£15**
13	Ear Music 0208665 ERE	**Hell To Pay/All The Time In The World** (Edit) (p/s, red vinyl)...................	**£15**
13	Ear Music 0210271 ERE	**Out Of Hand/Apres Vous** (Instrumental)/**Laze** (live)/**Hell To Pay** (Instrumental) (10", white vinyl)	**£25**
17	Ear Music 0211854 EMU	**Time For Bedlam/Uncommon Man** (Instrumental)/**Paradise Bar/Hi Boots** (rehearsal) (10", p/s)	**£18**

ALBUMS : PARLOPHONE

68	Parlophone PMC 7055	**SHADES OF DEEP PURPLE** (LP, yellow/black label, mono, with "sold in U.K..." text)........	**£600**
68	Parlophone PCS 7055	**SHADES OF DEEP PURPLE** (LP, yellow/black label, stereo, with "sold in U.K..." text).......	**£400**
69	Parlophone PCS 7055	**SHADES OF DEEP PURPLE** (LP, stereo repressing, laminated sleeve, white/black label)	**£40**

ALBUMS : HARVEST

69	Harvest SHVL 751	**THE BOOK OF TALIESYN** (LP, laminated gatefold sleeve, first pressing with "sold in U.K." text spread over 4 lines, no EMI on label)..	**£200**
69	Harvest SHVL 751	**THE BOOK OF TALIESYN** (LP, laminated sleeve, second pressing with "sold in U.K." text spread over 5 lines)...	**£75**
69	Harvest SHVL 751	**THE BOOK OF TALIESYN** (LP, laminated sleeve, third pressing without "sold in U.K." text)...	**£40**
69	Harvest SHVL 759	**DEEP PURPLE** (LP, laminated gatefold sleeve, no EMI logo on label)........................	**£150**
69	Harvest SHVL 759	**DEEP PURPLE** (LP, laminated gatefold sleeve, later pressing with EMI logo on label)	**£25**
70	Harvest SHVL 767	**CONCERTO FOR GROUP AND ORCHESTRA** (LP, laminated gatefold sleeve, no EMI logo on label)	**£75**
70	Harvest SHVL 767	**CONCERTO FOR GROUP AND ORCHESTRA** (LP, laminated gatefold sleeve, later pressing with EMI logo on label)..	**£25**
70	Harvest SHVL 777	**IN ROCK** (LP, laminated gatefold sleeve with "file under popular: pop groups", "Printed and Made by Garrod & Lofthouse Ltd." A2, B1 matrix, "The Gramophone Co" text around label rim not "EMI Records" no EMI logo on label, advertising inner sleeve with "Patent no's 1,125,555 & 1,072,844" at bottom)	**£100**
70	Harvest SHVL 777	**IN ROCK** (LP, laminated gatefold sleeve, later pressing with EMI logo on label)................	**£25**
71	Harvest SHVL 759	**DEEP PURPLE** (LP, laminated gatefold sleeve, non EMI pressing with indented circular groove around spindle hole)...	**£20**
71	Harvest SHVL 793	**FIREBALL** (LP, textured gatefold sleeve, with lyric insert)	**£125**
71	Harvest SHVL 793	**FIREBALL** (LP, gatefold sleeve, with light or no texture, lyric insert)	**£20**
71	Harvest SHVL 751	**THE BOOK OF TALIESYN** (LP, laminated gatefold sleeve with 'Ernest J. Day' printing credit, fourth pressing with EMI logo on label)...	**£40**
75	Harvest SHVL 751	**THE BOOK OF TALIESYN** (LP, laminated gatefold sleeve, fifth pressing with EMI logo)	**£15**
76	Harvest SHVL 751	**THE BOOK OF TALIESYN** (LP, laminated gatefold sleeve with 'Garrod & Lofthouse Ltd' printing credit, sixth pressing with EMI logo on slightly more yellow label)................	**£15**
78	Harvest SHSM 2026	**THE SINGLES A's AND B's** (LP, purple vinyl)	**£20**
80	Harvest SHSM 2016	**SHADES OF DEEP PURPLE** (LP, 'dismembered doll-limb' sleeve, withdrawn)	**£200**
80	Harvest SHDW 412	**IN CONCERT** (2-LP)	**£22**
82	Harvest SHSP 4124	**LIVE IN LONDON** (LP)	**£15**
99	Harvest 7243 4 99469 10	**BOOK OF TALIESYN** (LP, 180gm vinyl, gatefold sleeve in stickered PVC outer)	**£20**

ALBUMS : PURPLE

75	Purple TPSM 2002	**24 CARAT PURPLE** (LP, with "woman From Tokyo" mis-spelling on label)	**£15**
72	Purple TPSP 3511/12	**MADE IN JAPAN 2-LP, First pressing, "Gramophone Co" on label rim, MATRIX TPS 3511 A-1U/B-1U/TPS 3512 A-1U/B1-U, "Porky" (side 1), "Delta Pork" (side 2), "Pecko" (side 3), "Peckie" (Side 4) etched into dead wax, double gatefold sleeve, many originals with £3.25 price sticker)**	**£100**
72	Purple TSPS 3511/12	**MADE IN JAPAN 2-LP, Contract pressing, no mother or stamper details at 3 and 9 'o' clock,** (just number "3" at 9 "o" clock. Ridge around inside of label half an inch from the rim, no "Made in Gt. Britain" at foot of label, no brackets on "Made In Japan" on labels,double gatefold sleeve)	**£80**
72	Purple TPSA 7504	**MACHINE HEAD** (LP, laminated gatefold sleeve, with fold-out lyric insert, date code 7204 on sleeve, no EMI credit on label, outer rim of label has 'The Gramophone Co. Ltd' at 11 o clock and 'Made in Great Britain' at 6 o clock on label)	**£100**
73	Purple TPSA 7508	**WHO DO WE THINK WE ARE** (LP, 1st pressing with 'The Gramophone Co' on rim of label, -1U matrix numbers on both sides, laminated gatefold sleeve with 'File under popular: pop groups', with lyric insert)	**£50**
74	Purple Q4TPS 7504	**MACHINE HEAD** (LP, laminated gatefold sleeve, quadrophonic)	**£60**
74	Purple TPS 3505	**BURN** (LP, First Pressing: "The Gramophone Co" on rim, MATRIX TPS 3505 A-1U/B-1U, "Porky & Mel * Trish" etched into dead wax side 1/"Pecko" etched into dead wax on side 2. Spine wording on top edge as well as spine)	**£40**
74	Purple TPS 3505	**BURN** (LP, Second Pressing: "EMI Records" on rim, -1U Matrixes)	**£25**
74	Purple TPS 3505	**BURN** (LP, hybrid pressing with: "The Gramophone Co" on one label and "EMI Records" on the other)	**£30**
74	Purple TPS 3505	**BURN** (LP, later pressings with "EMI Records" on both labels)	**£15**
74	Purple TPS 3508	**STORMBRINGER** (LP, 1st pressing, matrixes TPS3508 A-1U/B-1U, 'Kendun' stamped in dead wax, "EMI Records Ltd" on label rim, spine wording on top edge and spine, "7411 Garrod & Lofthouse Ltd" on bottom right corner of sleeve)	**£40**
75	Purple TPSA 7515	**COME TASTE THE BAND** (LP, laminated gatefold sleeve with inner)	**£30**
78	Purple TPS 3510	**POWERHOUSE** (LP)	**£15**
79	Purple TPS 3514	**THE MARK 2 PURPLE SINGLES** (LP, purple vinyl)	**£18**
04	EMI 7243 4 73592	**BURN** (2-LP, remastered anniversary edition)..	**£30**
09	EMI/Purple TPSD 3508	**STORMBRINGER** (2-LP, reissue, extra tracks, gatefold sleeve, inners)	**£20**
10	EMI/Purple TPSD 7515	**COME TASTE THE BAND** (2-LP, reissue, gatefold sleeve)	**£20**
12	EMI 50999 463275 1 2	**MACHINE HEAD** (LP, gatefold sleeve, 180gm 40th anniversary edition, bonus 7")	**£20**
12	EMI TPSAD 7504	**MACHINE HEAD** (4-CD/DVD, 40th Anniversary edition)......................................	**£40**

14	Purple 3769654	**MADE IN JAPAN** (9-LP boxed set)	£200
18	Purple/Universal TPSA 7504	**MACHINE HEAD** (LP, purple vinyl)	£20
18	Purple/Universal TPS 3505	**BURN** (LP, reissue, purple vinyl)	£20
18	Purple/Universal TPSA 7508	**WHO DO WE THINK WE ARE?** (LP, gatefold sleeve, purple vinyl)	£20
18	Purple/Universal TPSA 7515	**COME TASTE THE BAND** (LP, reissue, purple vinyl, gatefold sleeve)	£20
18	Purple/Universal TPSA 7515	**MADE IN JAPAN** (2-LP, purple vinyl)	£18
18	Purple/Universal TPSA 7517	**MADE IN EUROPE** (LP, purple vinyl)	£18
20	Purple/Universal TPS 3505	**BURN** (LP, reissue, orange vinyl)	£20

ALBUMS : OTHER LPS

84	Polydor POLH 16	**PERFECT STRANGERS** (LP, inner)	£15
84	Polydor POLHP 16	**PERFECT STRANGERS** (LP, picture disc, with extra track & die-cut sleeve)	£15
84	Polydor DEEP 1A	**DEEP PURPLE INTERVIEW** (LP, 1-sided, promo-only, stickered white sleeve)	£20
85	EMI EJ 26 0343 0	**IN ROCK** (LP, picture disc with poster)	£25
85	EMI EJ 34 0344 0	**FIREBALL** (LP, picture disc with poster)	£25
85	EMI EG 26 0345 0	**MACHINE HEAD** (LP, picture disc with poster)	£25
85	EMI PUR 1/E 2606131	**DEEP PURPLE — ANTHOLOGY** (2-LP, blue vinyl)	£25
86	Polydor DEEP 2A	**HOUSE OF BLUE LIGHT** (interview LP, promo-only, plays same both sides, stickered black sleeve)	£20
87	Polydor POLH 32	**HOUSE OF BLUE LIGHT** (LP, inner)	£15
88	Connoisseur VSOP 125	**SCANDINAVIAN NIGHTS** (2-LP, gatefold sleeve, with booklet)	£25
90	RCA PL 90535	**SLAVES AND MASTERS** (LP)	£15
91	Connoisseur DPVSOPLP 163	**IN THE ABSENCE OF PINK – KNEBWORTH 85** (2-LP gatefold)	£50
91	EMI 96129	**ANTHOLOGY** (3-LP, gatefold sleeve)	£30
93	BMG 74321 15420-1	**THE BATTLE RAGES ON** (LP, with inner sleeve)	£50
95	EMI 7243 8 34019 18	**DEEP PURPLE IN ROCK** (2-LP, purple vinyl, gatefold sleeve with inners)	£35
97	EMI DEEPP 3	**MACHINE HEAD** (2-LP, 'EMI 100' remixed anniversary edition, purple vinyl, gatefold sleeve, with insert)	£40
97	EMI LPCENT 25	**SHADES OF DEEP PURPLE** (LP, 'EMI 100', 180gm vinyl edition, yellow/black label)	£40
97	EMI DEEPP 2	**FIREBALL** (2-LP, gatefold sleeve with inners & limited edition print)	£30
98	EMI PP 074	**30: THE VERY BEST OF** (2-LP, purple vinyl)	£30
98	EMI 7243 8 57864 19	**MADE IN JAPAN** (2-LP, numbered, purple vinyl, gatefold sleeve with inners)	£35
03	EMI 7243 5 91048 12	**BANANAS** (LP, gatefold sleeve, inner)	£50
11	Music On Vinyl MOVLP 361	**PURPENDICULAR** (2-LP, black vinyl)	£25
11	Music On Vinyl MOVLP 361	**PURPENDICULAR** (2-LP, purple vinyl)	£35
11	EMI/BBC DPBBC 6870	**THE BBC SESSIONS** (2-LP)	£30
12	Back On Black RCV083LP	**TOTAL ABANDON, AUSTRALIA '99** (2-LP)	£25
13	Music On Vinyl MOVLP 668	**THE BATTLE RAGES ON** (LP, reissue, 180gm)	£20
13	Eagle Vision ERDVLP 080	**PERFECT STRANGERS** (2-LP, 2-CD & DVD)	£40
13	Ear Music 0208578 ERE	**NOW WHAT?** (2-LP, gatefold, inner)	£20
14	Edel 0209815 ERE	**RAPTURE OF THE DEEP** (LP, reissue, gatefold sleeve)	£20
14	Ear Music 0209764 ERE	**LIVE IN PARIS 1975** (3-LP)	£20
14	Ear Music 0209658 ERE	**PHOENIX RISING** (2-LP)	£20
14	Ear Music 0209624 ERE	**LIVE IN GRAZ 1975** (2-LP, gatefold, inners)	£20
15	Ear Music 0210539	**FROM THE SETTING SUN...LIVE AT WACKEN** (3-LP)	£20
15	Ear Music 0210534 EMU	**...TO THE RISING SUN IN TOKYO** (3-LP)	£20
15	Ear Music 0210221 EMU	**LIVE IN LONG BEACH 1971** (2-LP, gatefold sleeve)	£20
16	Ear Music 0210976 EMU	**LONG BEACH 1976** (LP, gatefold)	£20
17	Sony 88985438451	**THE BATTLE RAGES ON** (LP, reissue, 180gm)	£15
17	Ear Music 0214725 EMU	**INFINITE** (2-LP)	£18
17	Ear Music 0212506 EMU	**INFINITE LIVE RECORDS VOLUME 1** (3-LP, black or purple vinyl)	£20
18	Ear Music 0212925	**TOTAL ABANDON, AUSTRALIA '99** (2-LP, CD reissue)	£18
19	Ear Music 0213901 EMU	**LIVE IN NEWCASTLE, AUSTRALIA** (3-LP)	£20
19	Ear Music 0214547 EMU	**LIVE IN ROME, ITALY** (3-LP)	£20
20	Ear Music 0214764 EMU	**WHOOSH!** (2-LP, clear or white transparent vinyl)	£18

(see also Rainbow, Gillan, [David Coverdale's] Whitesnake, Tommy Bolin, [Sheila Carter &] Episode Six, Jon Lord, Roger Glover, Green Bullfrog, Wizard's Convention, Elf, M.I. Five, Warhorse, Captain Beyond, John Lawton, Hell Preachers Inc., Glen Hughes, Trapeze, Leading Figures, Paice Ashton & Lord, Silverhead, Pete York Percussion Band)

DEEP RIVER BOYS

54	HMV 7M 280	Shake, Rattle And Roll/St. Louis Blues	£40
56	HMV 7M 361	Rock-A-Beatin' Boogie/Just A Little Bit More!	£40
56	HMV POP 263	That's Right/Honey Honey	£20
57	HMV POP 395	Whole Lotta Shakin' Goin' On/There's A Goldmine In The Sky	£30
58	HMV POP 449	Not Too Old To Rock And Roll/Slow Train To Nowhere	£15
60	Top Rank 35/108	**THE BLUE DEEPS** (LP)	£15

(see also Fats Waller)

DEEP SET

68	Pye 7N 17594	That's The Way Life Goes/Hello Amy	£60
70	Target 7N 45018	Cinnamon Girl/You'll Never Know	£100

DEEP SWITCH

86	SWITCH 1	**NINE INCHES OF GOD** (LP, private pressing)	£40

DEEP THROATS

78	Limp LMP 1	Rock N Roll Discharge/Miami Connection	£15

DEEP TIMBRE

72	Westwood WR 5006	**DEEP TIMBRE** (LP)	£40

DEERHUNTER

07	4AD CAD 2822	**MICROCASTLE/WEIRD ERA CONT.** (LP, CD)	£25

SAM DEES
69	Major Minor MM 655	If It's All Wrong (It's All Right)/Don't Keep Me Hangin' On	£50
75	Atlantic K 10676	Fragile, Handle With Care/Save The Love At Any Cost	£100

SAM DEES & BETTYE SWANN
76	Atlantic K 10719	Storybook Children/Just As Sure	£15

(see also Bettye Swann)

DEE SET
68	Blue Cat BS 146	I Know A Place/ROY BENNETT: I Dangerous	£80

DEF J
92	Kold Sweat KS122	Just Save It (12")	£15

(see also Encona Coarse)

DEF LEPPARD
79	Bludgeon Riffola SRT/CUS/232	THE DEF LEPPARD EP: Ride Into The Sun/Getcha Rocks Off/The Overture (red label, p/s with lyric insert, 150 only)	£400
79	Bludgeon Riffola SRT/CUS/232	THE DEF LEPPARD EP: Ride Into The Sun/Getcha Rocks Off/The Overture (red label, with p/s, 850 only)	£300
79	Bludgeon Riffola SRT/CUS/232	THE DEF LEPPARD EP: Ride Into The Sun/Getcha Rocks Off/The Overture (red label, without p/s, 850 only)	£100
79	Bludgeon Riffola MSB 001	Ride Into The Sun/Getcha Rocks Off/The Overture (reissue, yellow label, 15,000 pressed, no p/s)	£35
79	Phonogram 6059 240	Getcha Rocks Off/Ride Into The Sun/The Overture (mispressing, both sides play "The Overture")	£40
81	Phonogram LEPP 2	Let It Go/Switch 625 (p/s, 10,000 shrinkwrapped with patch)	£15
82	Phonogram LEPP 3	Bringin' On The Heartbreak/Me And My Wine (p/s)	£35
82	Phonogram LEPP 312	Bringin' On The Heartbreak/Me And My Wine/You Got Me Runnin' (12", p/s)	£18
83	Phonogram VERP 5	Photograph/Bringin' On The Heartbreak (camera-shaped fold-out/pop-up sleeve, 500 only)	£25
83	Phonogram VERX 5	Photograph/Bringin' On The Heartbreak/Mirror, Mirror (12", p/s)	£20
83	Phonogram VERP 6	Rock Of Ages/Action! Not Words (guitar-shaped picture disc)	£35
83	Phonogram VERQ 6	Rock Of Ages/Action! Not Words (foldout 'rock box' cube sleeve, 500 only)	£40
83	Phonogram VERX 6	Rock Of Ages/Action! Not Words (12", p/s)	£18
83	Phonogram VERDJ 8	Too Late/Foolin' (p/s, DJ-only promo with rear band photo in football kit)	£150
83	Phonogram VERX 8	Too Late For Love/Foolin'/High And Dry (12", p/s)	£20
84	Phonogram VERG 9	Photograph/Bringin' On The Heartbreak (g/fold printed 'wallet' p/s, 500 only)	£35
84	Phonogram VERX 9	Photograph/Bringin' On The Heartbreak/Mirror, Mirror (12", p/s)	£15
87	Phonogram LEPC 1	Animal/Animal (Extended Mix)/Tear It Down (12", p/s, red vinyl)	£15
87	Phonogram LEPPX 2	Pour Some Sugar On Me (Extended Version)/Pour Some Sugar On Me (Extended)/I Wanna Be Your Hero (12", picture disc, unissued)	£0
87	Phonogram LEPX 313	Hysteria/Ride Into The Sun (1987 Version)/Love And Affection (live) (12", envelope box sleeve with poster & international discography, 5,000 only)	£15
88	Phonogram LEPXB 4	Armageddon It!/Armageddon It! (The Atomic Mix)/Ring Of Fire (12", numbered box set with poster, enamel badge & 5 postcards, 5,000 only)	£18
88	Phonogram LEPXB 5	Love Bites/Billy's Got A Gun (live)/Excitable (Orgasmic Mix) (12", box set with 4 cardboard inserts, 5,000 only)	£15
89	Phonogram LEPXP 6	Rocket (The Lunar Mix)/(Radio Edit)/Release Me (12", picture disc, numbered)	£15
80	Vertigo 9102 040	ON THROUGH THE NIGHT (LP)	£15
81	Vertigo 6359 045	HIGH 'N' DRY (LP)	£15
83	Vertigo VERS 2	PYROMANIA (LP)	£20
87	Phonogram HYSLP 1	HYSTERIA (LP, Jack Adams cut. A side Matrix HYSLP 1 A 2U 1 1))	£35
87	Bludgeon Riffola HYSLP 1	HYSTERIA (LP, Dennis Blackham cut A side matrix: HYSLP 1 A - 3U - 1)	£15
87	Phonogram HYSPD 1	HYSTERIA (LP, picture disc)	£15
92	Bludgeon Riffola 510 978 1	ADRENALIZE (LP, inner)	£30
92	Phonogram 510 978-1	ADRENALIZE (LP, picture disc, 5,000 only, numbered, die-cut sleeve)	£15
93	Bludgeon Riffola 518 305 1	RETRO ACTIVE (LP)	£50
94	Phonogram (no cat. no.)	ADRENALIZE — MAHOGANY BOX SET (CD, picture disc, with interview picture CD, 3 booklets, signed/no'd certificate, signed photo & plectrum, 1,000 only)	£200
95	Mercury 528 656-1	VAULT 1980 - 1995 (2-LP, inners)	£100
96	Mercury 532 486-1	SLANG (LP, inner)	£60

(see also Lucy, Gogmagog, Johnny Kalendar Band)

DEF TEX
91	Sound Clash SCR 003	MASTER BLASTER (EP)	£70
01	Son SONCD018	SERENE BUG (LP)	£15

DEFECTS
81	Casualty CR 001	Dance 'Til You Drop/Guilty Conscience/Brutality (p/s)	£20
85	WXYZ LMNOP2	DEFECTIVE BREAKDOWN (LP, with insert)	£25

DEFENDERS
68	Doctor Bird DB 1104	Set Them Free/Don't Blame The Children (actually by Lee Perry & Sensations)	£50

(see also Lee Perry)

DEFIANT
77	Angry LIG 1	L.S.D./Social-Climber (unissued and both tracks unrecorded, 20 sets of labels stuck on pre-existing singles by other artists)	£50

DEFIANT POSE
81	Groucho Marxist WH 4	Someone Else's War/After The Bang (p/s)	£15

ZION DE GALLIER
68	Parlophone R 5686	Me/Winter Will Be Cold	£25
68	Parlophone R 5710	Dream Dream Dream/Geraldine	£20

(see also Mark Wirtz)

DE-HEMS
72	President PT 388	Don't Cross That Line/Lover Let Me Go	£20

DEIGHTON TASK FORCE
89	White REACT1	Neighbourhood (12")	£50

(see also Unique 3)

JACK DE JOHNETTE
70	CBS 64076	COMPLEX (LP)	£20

RICK DE JONGH
83	Challenge TALL 3	So Easy/So Easy (Bonus Beats) (12")	£15

DESMOND DEKKER (& ACES)
63	Island WI 054	Honour Your Mother And Father (as Desmond Decker & Beverley's Allstars)/ Madgie ('63) (with Beverley's Allstars)	£30
63	Island WI 111	Parents/Labour For Learning (solo)	£45
64	Island WI 158	Jeserine/King Of Ska (as Desmond Dekkar & His Cherry Pies)	£50
64	Black Swan WI 455	Dracula (as Desmond Dekkar)/DON DRUMMOND: Spitfire	£60
65	Island WI 181	Get Up Adine (as Desmond Dekkar, actually with Four Aces)/Be Mine Forever (as Patsy & Desmond; song is act. "Down Down Down" by Clive & Naomi)	£60
65	Island WI 202	This Woman (as Desmond Dekkar & Four Aces)/UPSETTERS: Si Senora (B-side actually by Ossie & Upsetters)	£60
67	Pyramid PYR 6003	Wise Man/ROLAND ALPHONSO: Middle East	£40
67	Pyramid PYR 6004	007 (Shanty Town)/ROLAND ALPHONSO: El Torro	£15
67	Pyramid PYR 6006	It's A Shame/ROLAND ALPHONSO: On The Move	£40
67	Pyramid PYR 6008	Rudy Got Soul/ROLAND ALPHONSO: The Cat	£50
67	Pyramid PYR 6011	Rude Boy Train/ROLAND ALPHONSO: Nothing For Nothing	£45
67	Pyramid PYR 6012	Mother's Young Girl/SOUL BROTHERS: Confucious	£45
67	Pyramid PYR 6017	Unity/Sweet Music	£40
67	Pyramid PYR 6020	Sabotage/Pretty Africa	£40
67	Pyramid PYR 6020	Sabotage/It Pays	£35
67	Pyramid PYR 6026	It Pays/Young Generation	£35
68	Pyramid PYR 6031	Beautiful And Dangerous/I've Got The Blues	£30
68	Pyramid PYR 6035	Bongo Gal/Shing A Ling	£30
68	Pyramid PYR 6037	To Sir, With Love/Fu Manchu	£175
68	Pyramid PYR 6044	Mother Pepper/Don't Blame Me	£30
68	Pyramid PYR 6045	Try Me/I'm Leaving	£30
68	Pyramid PYR 6047	Hey Grandma/Young Generation	£30
68	Pyramid PYR 6051	Music Like Dirt (Intensified)/Coconut Water	£25
68	Pyramid PYR 6054	It Mek/Writing On The Wall	£25
68	Pyramid PYR 6059	Christmas Day/I've Got The Blues	£20
70	Trojan TR 7777	You Can Get It If You Really Want/Perseverance	£15
10	Trojan THB 7001	Sugar & Spice/Sentimental Reasons	£20
10	Trojan THB 7005	Dancing Time/Beverley's Special (Nothing For Nothing)	£20
13	Island WI 3161	007/Wise Man	£18
67	Doctor Bird DLM 5007	007 SHANTY TOWN (LP)	£150
69	Doctor Bird DLM 5013	THE ISRAELITES (LP, solo)	£130
69	Trojan TTL 4	THIS IS DESMOND DEKKAR (LP, label credits Dekker)	£30
70	Trojan TBL 146	YOU CAN GET IT IF YOU REALLY WANT (LP)	£30
80	Stiff SEEZ 26	BLACK AND DEKKER (LP)	£15
85	Trojan TRLS 226	ORIGINAL REGGAE HITSOUND (LP)	£15
91	Trojan TRLS 292	KING OF SKA (LP)	£18
93	Trojan TRLS 324	KING OF KINGS (LP, with the Specials)	£15

(see also Al Barry, Skatalites, Maytals)

DEL
73	Uk UK 40	Motorbike Annie/Gypsy Girl (some in p/s)	£20

LANA DEL REY
11	Stranger 2783433	Video Games/Blue Jeans (picture disc, 100 copies signed)	£20
12	Polydor 2793 491	Born To Die/Born To Die (Remix) (Picture disc, stickered PVC sleeve)	£60
12	Polydor 279 3424	BORN TO DIE (2LP, gatefold, printed inners)	£25
12	Interscope 00602537181223	BORN TO DIE (THE PARADISE EDITION) (LP, slipcase)	£30
14	Interscope/Polydor 3787448	ULTRAVIOLENCE (2LP, gatefold, printed inners)	£30
14	Interscope/Polydor 00 6025 378 556-8 1	ULTRAVIOLENCE (2LP, picture disc, CD, art prints)	£400
15	Interscope/Polydor 4748829	HONEYMOON (2LP, gatefold, translucent red vinyl)	£70
17	Interscope/Polydor 5765501	LUST FOR LIFE (2LP, gatefold, printed inners, coke bottle clear vinyl)	£150
19	Interscope/Polydor 0806833	NORMAN FUCKING ROCKWELL! (2LP, gatefold, printed inners, blue vinyl, indies exclusive)	£120
19	Polydor 0806831	NORMAN FUCKING ROCKWELL! NFR! (2LP, gatefold, printed inners, lIme green vinyl, uncensored sleeve print)	£100
19	Interscope/Polydor 0806834	NORMAN FUCKING ROCKWELL! (2LP, gatefold, printed inners, pink vinyl, alternate artwork, Urban Outfitters exclusive)	£100
20	Interscope/Polydor 0742981	VIOLET BENT BACKWARDS OVER THE GRASS (LP. gatefold, printed inner, cream vinyl)	£25
20	Interscope/Polydor 0742982	VIOLET BENT BACKWARDS OVER THE GRASS (LP. gatefold, printed inner, green vinyl, limited edition)	£30
20	Interscope/Polydor 0742983	VIOLET BENT BACKWARDS OVER THE GRASS (LP, picture disc, PVC sleeve)	£30
21	Polydor 3865950	BLUE BANISTERS (2LP, gatefold, printed inners, re vinyl, HMV Exclusive)	£90
21	Polydor 3865952	BLUE BANISTERS (2LP, gatefold, printed inners, translucent or paque white vinyl, Amazon Exclusive)	£50
21	Interscope/Polydor 3553404	CHEMTRAILS OVER THE COUNTRY CLUB (LP, gatefold, printed inner, grey vinyl, website exclusive)	£30

MINT VALUE £

21	Interscope/Polydor 3549798	**CHEMTRAILS OVER THE COUNTRY CLUB** (LP, gatefold, printed inner, yellow vinyl, indies exclusive)	£30
21	Interscope/Polydor 3553403	**CHEMTRAILS OVER THE COUNTRY CLUB** (LP, gatefold, printed inner, red vinyl, poster, HMV exclusive)	£50
21	Interscope/Polydor 3549784	**CHEMTRAILS OVER THE COUNTRY CLUB** (LP, picture disc, PVC sleeve, Sound Of Vinyl exclusive)	£60
21	Interscope/Polydor 3559271	**CHEMTRAILS OVER THE COUNTRY CLUB** (LP, picture disc 2, PVC sleeve, 12x12 artcard, website exclusive)	£50
21	Interscope/Polydor B0033910-01	**CHEMTRAILS OVER THE COUNTRY CLUB** (LP, gatefold, printed inner, RSD, cobalt blue vinyl)	£60
23	Interscope/Polydor 4859191	**DID YOU KNOW THAT THERE'S A TUNNEL UNDER OCEAN BLVD** (2LP, gatefold, printed inners)	£25
23	Interscope/Polydor 4859192	**DID YOU KNOW THAT THERE'S A TUNNEL UNDER OCEAN BLVD** (2LP, gatefold, printed inners, white vinyl, alternate artwork)	£30
23	Interscope/Polydor 4859193	**DID YOU KNOW THAT THERE'S A TUNNEL UNDER OCEAN BLVD** (2LP, gatefold, printed inners, dark pink vinyl, alternate artwork)	£30
23	Interscope/Polydor 4859194	**DID YOU KNOW THAT THERE'S A TUNNEL UNDER OCEAN BLVD** (2LP, gatefold, printed inners, pink vinyl, alternate artwork, Amazon exclusive)	£50
23	Interscope/Polydor 4859195	**DID YOU KNOW THAT THERE'S A TUNNEL UNDER OCEAN BLVD** (2LP, gatefold, printed inners, green vinyl, alternate artwork, indies exclusive)	£30
23	Interscope/Polydor 4859197	**DID YOU KNOW THAT THERE'S A TUNNEL UNDER OCEAN BLVD** (2LP, picture disc, PVC sleeve, Spotify 'Fans First' exclusive)	£40
23	Interscope/Polydor 5553396	**DID YOU KNOW THAT THERE'S A TUNNEL UNDER OCEAN BLVD** (2LP, explicit artwork, gatefold, printed inners, website exclusve)	£150

DELACARDOS
| 61 | HMV POP 890 | **Hold Back The Tears/Mister Dillon** | £30 |

SIMON DE LACY
| 68 | Spark 1001 | **Baby Come Back To Me/Goodbye Love** | £25 |

JUNIOR DELAHAYE
| 80 | Solid Groove SG 015 | **Love/I Love You** (12") | £20 |

DEL AMITRI
83	No Strings NOSP 1	**Sense Sickness/The Difference Is** (p/s)	£30
95	A&M 540 311-1	**TWISTED** (LP, with poster)	£60
97	A&M 540 705-1	**SOME OTHER SUCKER'S PARADISE** (LP)	£70

DELANEY & BONNIE (& FRIENDS)
69	Elektra EKSN 45066	**Get Ourselves Together/Soldiers Of The Cross** (withdrawn)	£20
69	Apple SAPCOR 7	**THE ORIGINAL DELANEY & BONNIE** (LP, unreleased, no sleeve)	£1500
69	Elektra EKS 74039	**THE ORIGINAL DELANEY & BONNIE — ACCEPT NO SUBSTITUTE** (LP, commercial release of above LP)	£25
69	Stax SXATS 1029	**HOME** (LP)	£20
70	Atlantic 2400 013	**ON TOUR WITH ERIC CLAPTON** (LP)	£25
71	Atco 2400 029	**TO BONNIE FROM DELANEY** (LP)	£15

(see also Eric Clapton, Delaney Bramlett, King Curtis with Delaney & Friends, Shindogs)

ERIC DELANEY BAND
| 56 | Pye NIAX NP 19018 | **HI-FI DELANEY** (10" LP) | £20 |

SIMON DELANO
| 70 | Jay Boy JSX2001 | **BANGARANG REGGAE** (LP, with the Gassers) | £20 |

DELAYS
| 06 | Rough Trade RTRADLP 214 | **YOU SEE COLOURS** (LP) | £20 |

DELEGATION
77	State STAT 25	**The Promise Of Love/It Only Happens**	£25
78	State STAT 82	**Oh Honey/Love Is Like A Fire** (12")	£40
78	State STAT 82	**Oh Honey/Love Is Like A Fire**	£15

DELFONICS
70	Bell BLL 1467	**With These Hands/Let It Be Me**	£20
68	Bell SBLL 106	**LA-LA MEANS I LOVE YOU** (LP)	£25
69	Bell SBLL 121	**THE SOUND OF SEXY SOUL** (LP)	£20
70	Bell SBLL 137	**THE DELFONICS** (LP)	£20
72	Bell SBLL 217	**TELL ME THIS IS A DREAM** (LP)	£20
74	Bell BELLS 245	**ALIVE AND KICKING** (LP)	£15

DELGADOS
96	Chemikal Underground CHEM 009	**DOMESTIQUES** (LP, inner)	£20
98	Chemikal Underground CHEM 024	**PELOTON** (LP, inner)	£25
00	Chemikal Underground CHEM 040	**THE GREAT EASTERN** (LP)	£25

DELICATES
| 59 | London HLT 8953 | **Ronnie Is My Lover/Black And White Thunderbird** | £50 |
| 60 | London HLT 9176 | **Too Young To Date/The Kiss** | £30 |

DE LITE
| 89 | Circa YRTPRX 35 | **Wild Times** (12") | £30 |

DE-LITES
| 79 | Destiny 1022 | **Lover/Do The Zombie** | £20 |
| 80 | Grapevine GRP 127 | **Lover/Tell Me Why** | £20 |

DELIVERANCE
| 92 | European Rhyme ERR001 | **Serious Public Disorder/Do Not Disturb** (12") | £20 |
| 94 | Nut Cracker NUT001 | **Dead Funny/Up And Down The Country** (12") | £20 |

ANNA DELL
66	Hollick & Taylor HT/LP S 1166	CRUISIN WITH ANNA DELL (LP)	£40

DENNIS D'ELL
67	CBS 202605	It Breaks My Heart In Two/Better Use Your Head (withdrawn)	£400
67	CBS 202605	It Breaks My Heart In Two/Better Use Your Head (withdrawn: DJ copy)	£300
67	Decca F 12647	A Woman Called Sorrow/The Night Has A Thousand Eyes (as Denny D'ell)	£15

(see also Honeycombs)

JIMMY DELL
58	RCA RCA 1066	Teeny Weeny/BARRY DE VORZON: Barbara Jean	£50
58	RCA RCA 1066	Teeny Weeny/BARRY DE VORZON: Barbara Jean (78)	£20

DELL-VIKINGS
57	London HLD 8405	Come Go With Me/How Can I Find A True Love (gold label lettering)	£100
57	London HLD 8405	Come Go With Me/How Can I Find A True Love (silver label lettering)	£20
57	London HLD 8464	Whispering Bells/Little Billy Boy	£30
59	Mercury AMT 1027	Flat Tyre/How Could You	£40

(see also Chuck Jackson)

PETE DELLO & FRIENDS
71	Nepentha 6437 001	INTO YOUR EARS (LP, gatefold sleeve)	£750
89	See For Miles 257	INTO YOUR EARS....PLUS (2-LP, reissue)	£40

(see also Honeybus, Lace, Red Herring, John Killigrew, Grant Tracy & Sunsets, Sunsets)

DELLS
63	Pye International 7N 25178	The (Bossa Nova) Bird/Eternally	£25
67	Chess CRS 8066	O-O I Love You/There Is	£15
68	Chess CRS 8071	Wear It On Our Face/Please Don't Change Me Now	£20
68	President PT 223	It's Not Unusual/Stay In My Corner	£15
73	Chess 6145 022	Give Your Baby A Standing Ovation/Run For Cover	£20
80	20th Century TC 2478	Your Song/Look At Us Now	£40
68	Chess CRLS 4554	GREATEST HITS (LP)	£25
69	Chess CRLS 4555	LOVE IS BLUE/OH, WHAT A NIGHT (LP)	£25
71	Joy JOYS 186	OH WHAT A NIGHT (LP)	£15

ELAINE DELMAR
63	Columbia DB 7101	Hum Drum Blues/Amor Amor	£30
68	CBS 63511	Sneakin' Up On You/Very Slowly	£40
60	Columbia SEG 8060	A SWINGING CHICK (EP)	£20
68	EMI SX6222	LA BELLE ELAINE (LP)	£20
68	CBS 63511	SNEAKIN' UP ON YOU (LP)	£35

DEL MONAS
85	Empire JLM 14	Sally Sue Brown/Dangerous Charms (7" die cut sleeve)	£15
85	Big Beat WIK 35	DANGEROUS CHARMS (LP)	£20
85	Empire SYF 95	5 (LP)	£25
88	Hangman HANG 20 UP	5 (LP, reissue)	£15
89	Hangman HANG 28 UP	DEL MONAS (LP)	£18
99	Vinyl Japan ASKLP 107	DANGEROUS CHARMS (LP, reissue)	£15

DELMONTS
72	Spiral DIT 2	Gimmie Gimmie Your Loving/Now Is The Time For Love	£15

JOEY DELORENZO
02	Fab-U-Lus FBU07007	Wake Up To The Sunshine Girl/Lost My Sense Of Direction (reissue)	£15

AL DE LORY
65	London HLU 9999	Yesterday/Traffic Jam	£20

DELROY & SPORTY
71	Banana BA 322	Lovers Version/DUDLEY SIBLEY: Having A Party	£40

DELROY & TENNORS
71	Camel CA 62	Donkey Shank/MURPHY'S ALL STARS: Donkey Track	£50

DELTA 5
79	Rough Trade RT 031	Mind Your Own Business/Now That You've Gone (p/s)	£30
80	Rough Trade RT 041	Anticipation/You (p/s)	£15
80	Rough Trade RT 061	Try/Colour (p/s)	£15
81	Pre PRE 16	Shadow/Leaving (yellow p/s)	£20
82	Pre PRE 24	Powerlines/The Heart Is A Lonely Hunter (p/s)	£15
81	PRE PREX 6	SEE THE WHIRL (LP)	£25

DELTA CATS
69	Bamboo BAM 3	I Can't Re-Live (song actually "I Can't Believe")/I've Been Hurt	£75

(see also Thrillers)

DELTA RHYTHM BOYS
52	Esquire 15-001	DELTA RHYTHM BOYS WITH THE METRONOME ALLSTARS (10" LP)	£15

DELTAS
64	Blue Beat BB 265	Georgia/The Party	£40
65	Blue Beat BB 275	The Visitor/SKATALITES: Hanging The Beam	£60

DELTA SKIFFLE GROUP
58	Esquire EP 162	DELTA SKIFFLE GROUP (EP)	£40

DELTONES (U.K.)
70	Columbia DB 8719	Gimme Some Lovin'/Have A Little Talk With Myself	£20

DEL-TONES (U.S.)
59	Top Rank JAR 171	Moonlight Party/Rockin' Blues £100
59	Top Rank JAR 171	Moonlight Party/Rockin' Blues (78) £20

(see also Beau-Marks)

DELUXE
90	Heaven Sent HSX 001	Love Forever/1-2-1 (12") £15
89	Unyque UNQ LP1	JUST A LITTLE MORE (LP) £25
96	Leap Of Faith LEAP 004LP	SHOW ME (LP) £80

DEM 2
94	New York Soundclash NYSC001	REACH (12") £25
97	New York Soundclash NYSC004	BOSTON EXPERIMENTS EP (12") £30
97	New York Soundclash NYSC005	24 SEVEN EP (12") £30
03	New York Soundclash NYSC010	Luv's Hard/Luv's Hard In Destiny's Bed (12") £25

DEMENSIONS
60	Top Rank JAR 505	Over The Rainbow/Nursery Rhyme Rock £40

(see also Wheels, Fox)

DEMENTED ARE GO
86	ID NOSE 9	IN SICKNESS AND IN HEALTH (LP) £20
88	ID NOSE 21	KICKED OUT OF HELL (LP) £20
89	Link MLP 084	THE DAY THE EARTH SPAT BLOOD (LP, as the Demon Teds) £15
90	Link LRM 05	GO GO DEMENTED (LP, blue vinyl) £15
91	Fury F 3016	ORGASMIC NIGHTMARE (LP, blue vinyl) £15
93	Fury DAGLP 1	TANGENTAL MADNESS ON A PLEASANT SIDE OF HELL (LP, white vinyl) £15

(ROD) DEMICK & (HERBIE) ARMSTRONG
71	Mam MAM-AS 1001	LITTLE WILLY RAMBLE (LP, black/silver labels) £25
72	A&M AMLH 68908	LOOKIN' THROUGH (LP, inner sleeve, brown label) £50

DEMOB
81	Round Ear ROUND 1	Anti Police/Teenage Adolescence (foldout p/s) £15
81	Round Ear EAR 3	No Room For You/Think Straight/New Breed (p/s) £18

DEMOLISHED MEN
84	Anthem ANTHEM 2	Ghost Train/Yours In Haste £15

DEMOLITION
81	Demolition ZEL SPS 296	Hooker Hater/Axeman (p/s) £250

DEMON BOYZ
89	Music Of Life DEMON1	RECOGNITION (LP) £25
92	Tribal Bass Tribe11	ORIGINAL GUIDANCE – THE SECOND CHAPTER (LP) £40

DEMON D
95	Voyager VOD 94	Let The Jazz Take You/Together (12") £20

DEMON FUZZ
70	Dawn DNX 2504	I Put A Spell On You/Message To Mankind/Fuzz Oriental Blues (p/s) £60
70	Dawn DNLS 3013	AFREAKA! (LP, laminated gatefold, orange label) £500

DEMON PACT
81	Slime PACT 1	Eaten Alive/Raiders (p/s) £50
81	Slime PACT 2	Escape/Demon Pact (unreleased, labels only) £0

DEMON PREACHER
78	Illegal SRTS/CUS/78110	Royal Northern (N7)/Laughing At Me/Steal Your Love/Dead End Kidz (numbered p/s) £125
78	Small Wonder SMALL TEN	Little Miss Perfect/Perfect Dub (p/s) £20

(see also Demons, Alien Sex Fiend, Fenzyx)

DEMON (1)
81	Carrere CA 651	NIGHT OF THE DEMON (LP, pressed in France) £20
83	Clay CLAYLP 6	THE PLAGUE (LP, gatefold sleeve, with insert) £15
83	Clay CLAYLP 6P	THE PLAGUE (LP, picture disc) £20
90	Sonic SONICLP 1	NIGHT OF THE DEMON (LP, reissue) £15
90	Flametrader LP 1	ONE HELLUVA NIGHT (2-LP) £18

DEMON (2)
12	Macabre Unit MUV 003	Frostbite/DCULT: Sliver (12") £20

DEMONS (JAMAICA)
69	Big Shot BI 523	You Belong To My Heart/Bless You £60

TERRY DENE
57	Decca F 10964	Lucky Lucky Bobby/Baby, She's Gone £25
61	Oriole CB 1594	Like A Baby/Next Stop Paradise £15
63	Aral PS 107	The Feminine Look/Fever (all in p/s) £15
57	Decca DFE 6459	THE GOLDEN DISC (EP) £20
57	Decca DFE 6507	TERRY DENE NO. 1 (EP) £30
66	Herald ELR 107	TERRY DENE NOW (EP) £30

DENE BOYS
57	HMV POP 374	Bye Bye Love/Love Is The Thing £20

DENE FOUR
59	HMV POP 666	Hush-a-bye/Something New £25

(see also Dene Boys)

DENIGH
80	Ace ACE 16	No Way/Running (no p/s)	£50

DENIM
97	EMI RADIODJ 1	Summer Smash (promo, withdrawn)	£20
97	Emidisc DISC009	Summer Smash/Sun's Out (p/s, yellow vinyl)	£60
92	Boys Own 828349	BACK IN DENIM (LP)	£50
96	Echo ECH LP8	DENIM ON ICE (LP)	£45
97	EMI ADISC 001	NOVELTY ROCK (LP)	£75
97	EMI ADISCCD 001	NOVELTY ROCK (CD)	£30

(see also Felt, Go-Kart Mozarts)

DENIMS
65	CBS 201807	I'm Your Man/Ya Ya	£70

ROGER DENISON
67	Parlophone R 5566	It Just Doesn't Seem To Be My Day/She Wanders Through My Mind	£50

SUE DENNING
65	Columbia DB 7486	Kiss Me Once Again/Goodtime Johnny	£20

WADE DENNING & PORT WASHINGTONS
67	MGM MGM 1339	Tarzan's March/Batman	£15

D.D. (DENZIL) DENNIS
70	Crab CRAB 53	Rain Is Ginna Fall/This Game Ain't Free	£25
70	Crab CRAB 60	Having A Party/Man With Ambition	£25
70	Pama Supreme PS 301	My Way/Happy Days	£25
71	Punch PH 93	Christmas Message/Cool It Girl	£15
71	Pama Supreme PS 330	I'm A Believer/I'll Make The Way Easy	£15
74	Pama Supreme PS 391	Women And Money/UPSETTERS: Ten Cent Skank	£15

(see also Denzil Dennis)

D D DENNIS - BROTHER LLOYD'S ALL STARS
68	Mercury MF 1064	Save The Last Dance For Me/Will You Still Love Me Tomorrow	£15

DENZIL DENNIS
63	Blue Beat BB 181	Seven Nights In Rome/Love Is For Fools (as DENZIL)	£25
68	Trojan TR 614	Donkey Train/Down By The Riverside	£25
68	Trojan TR 615	Me Nah Worry/Hush Don't You Cry	£25
68	Jolly JY 011	Oh Carol/Where Has My Little Girl Gone	£25
70	Mary Lyn ML 100	I Guess I'd Better Start Believing/When Will You Ever Learn	£25
71	Pama Supreme PS 350	South Of The Border/GRAHAM: Long Island	£15
72	Pama Supreme PS 375	Mama We're All Crazy Now/ROY SHIRLEY: A Lady's A Man's Best Friend	£15

(see also D.D. Dennis, Cosmo & Dennis, Denzil & Pat, Denzil & Jennifer, Les & Silkie)

JACKIE DENNIS
58	Decca DFE 6513	JACKIE DENNIS NO. 1 (EP)	£25

DENNIS & LIZZY
70	Camel CA 56	Everybody Bawlin'/Mr Brown	£20
73	Pyramid PYR 7002	Ba-Ba-Ri-Ba-Shank/TOMMY McCOOK ALL STARS: Buck And The Preacher	£25

(see also Dennis Alcapone, Lizzy & Dennis)

DENNISONS
64	Decca F 11880	Walkin' The Dog/You Don't Know What Love Is	£15
64	Decca F 11990	Nobody Like My Babe/Lucy (You Sure Did It This Time)	£20

SANDY DENNY
72	Island WIP 6141	Here In Silence/Man Of Iron (theme from Pass Of Arms film, in p/s)	£50
72	Island WIP 6141	Here In Silence/Man Of Iron (theme from Pass Of Arms film)	£25
74	Island WIP 6195	Like An Old Fashioned Waltz (unissued)	£0
77	Island WIP 6391	Candle In The Wind/Still Waters Run Deep (unissued, promo only)	£30
67	Saga EROS 8041	SANDY AND JOHNNY (LP, with Johnny Silvo, black/silver label)	£30
70	Saga EROS 8153	SANDY DENNY (LP)	£30
71	Island ILPS 9165	THE NORTH STAR GRASSMAN AND THE RAVENS (LP, gatefold sleeve, 'pink rim palm tree' label)	£60
72	Island ILPS 9207	SANDY (LP, gatefold sleeve, original pressing with 'pink rim palm tree' label)	£50
72	Island ILPS 9207	SANDY (LP, reissue, gatefold sleeve)	£15
73	Island ILPS 9258	LIKE AN OLD FASHIONED WALTZ (LP, gatefold sleeve, 'pink rim palm tree' label)	£40
73	Hallmark SHM 813	ALL OUR OWN WORK (LP, with Strawbs)	£25
77	Island ILPS 9433	RENDEZVOUS (LP, with lyric inner sleeve)	£25
78	Mooncrest CREST 28	THE ORIGINAL SANDY DENNY (LP)	£25
97	Strange Fruit SFRSCD 006	THE BBC SESSIONS 1971-73 (CD, limited edition, withdrawn – beware of bootlegs)	£30
85	Island SDSP 100	WHO KNOWS WHERE THE TIME GOES (4-LP, box set with booklet)	£60

(see also Fairport Convention, Strawbs, Fotheringay, Alex Campbell, Trevor Lucas, Richard Thompson)

SUSAN DENNY
65	Melodisc MEL 1596	Don't Touch Me/Johnny	£35

DENTISTS
85	Spruck SP 003	Strawberries Are Growing In My Garden (And It's Wintertime)/Burning The Thoughts From My Skin/Doreen (p/s, with folded insert)	£30
85	Spruck SPR 001	SOME PEOPLE ARE ON THE PITCH THEY THINK IT'S ALL OVER IT IS NOW (LP)	£30

NIGEL DENVER
64	Decca DFE 8580	FOLK SINGER (EP)	£15
66	Decca LK 4728	MOVIN' ON (LP, featuring Martin Carthy)	£40
67	Decca LK 4844	REBELLION (LP)	£20

DENYM
82	Occult S 82 CUS 1351	Beauty/Selassie Hi	£30
83	Real Wax RW003	Why Boy/Why Dub (12")	£50

DENZIL & JENNIFER
70	Escort ES 824	Young, Gifted And Black/OWEN GRAY: I Am Satisfied	£100

DENZIL (DENNIS) & PAT (RHODEN)
69	Downtown DT 403	Dream/Sincerely	£25

DEPECHE MODE
SINGLES

81	Lyntone LYN 10209	Sometimes I Wish I Was Dead/FAD GADGET: King Of The Flies (test pressing)	£500
81	Lyntone LYN 10209	Sometimes I Wish I Was Dead/FAD GADGET: King Of The Flies (red flexidisc free with Flexipop magazine, issue 11)	£25
81	Lyntone LYN 10209	Sometimes I Wish I Was Dead/FAD GADGET: I Wish I Was Dead (red vinyl flexidisc free without Flexipop magazine, issue 11)	£15
81	Mute MUTE 013	Dreaming Of Me/Ice Machine (p/s)	£15
83	Mute L12BONG 2	Get The Balance Right/My Secret Garden (live)/See You (live)/Satellite (live) (12", numbered p/s)	£20
83	Mute L12 BONG 3	Everything Counts/Boys Say Go (live)/New Life (live)/Nothing To Fear (live)/The Meaning Of Love (live) (12", numbered p/s)	£20
84	Mute L12BONG 5	People Are People (On-U-Sound Remix)/In Your Memory/ People Are People (12", numbered in die-cut p/s)	£15
84	Mute L12BONG 6	Master And Servant (On-U-Sound Science Fiction Dancehall Classic)/Are People People?/(Set Me Free) Remotivate Me (12", numbered p/s)	£20
85	Mute L 12 BONG 8	Shake The Disease (Edit The Shake)/Master And Servant (Live)/Flexible (Pre-Deportation Mix)/Something To Do (Metalmix) (12", p/s)	£15
85	Mute D12BONG 9	It's Called A Heart (Mixes)/Fly On The Windscreen (Mixes) (12", p/s, dbl-pack)	£15
86	Mute CBONG 11	A Question Of Lust/Christmas Island/If You Want (Live)/Shame (Live)/Blasphemous Rumours (live) (Cassette)	£35
87	Mute P12 BONG 14	Never Let Me Down Again (7" Mix)/Pleasure Little Treasure (7" Mix)/Never Let Me Down Again (12" Split Mix) (12")	£50
88	Mute 12 LITTLE 15	Little 15/Stjarna/Sonata 14 IN CM - MOONLIGHT SONATA (12", p/s)	£15
89	Mute 10BONG 16	Everything Counts (Absolute Mix)/(1983 12" Mix)/Nothing (US 7" Mix) (10", envelope p/s, with 2 postcards & window sticker)	£40
89	Mute LCDBONG 16	Everything Counts (Tim Simenon & M. Saunders Remix)/Nothing (Justin Strauss Remix)/Strangelove (Tim Simenon & M. Saunders Remix) (3" CD 'filofax' page- p/s)	£15
89	Mute L12BONG 17	Personal Jesus (Mixes)/Dangerous (Hazchemix) (12", p/s)	£15
90	Mute 12 BONG 18	Enjoy The Silence/Enjoy The Silence (Hands And Feet Mix)/(Ecstatic Dub)/Sibeling (12", p/s)	£30
90	Mute XL12BONG 18	Enjoy The Silence (The Quad: Final Mix) (12", 1-side etched, p/s)	£30
90	Mute L12BONG 20	World In My Eyes (Dub In My Eyes)/(Mode To Joy)/Happiest Girl (The Pulsating Orbital Mix) (12", p/s with inner, in sealed blue PVC pack)	£25
93	Mute 12 BONG 21	I Feel You (Throb Mix)/(Seven Inch Mix)/(Babylon Mix)/One Caress (12", p/s)	£20
93	Mute L12 BONG 21	I Feel You (Life's Too Short Mix)/(Swamp Mix)/(Renegade Soundwave Afghan Surgery Mix)/(Helmet At The Helm Mix) (12", gatefold p/s)	£40
93	Mute 12 BONG 22	Walking In My Shoes (Grungy Gonads Mix)/(Seven Inch Mix)/My Joy (Seven Inch Mix)/(Slow Slide Mix) (12", p/s)	£80
93	Mute L12 BONG 22	Walking In My Shoes (Extended)/(Random Carpet Mix)/(Anadamidic Mix)/(Ambient Whale Mix) (12", p/s, gatefold) Mix	£40
93	Mute 12 BONG 22	Walking In My Shoes (Grungy Gonads Mix)/(Seven Inch Mix)/My Joy (Seven Inch Mix)/(Slow Slide Mix) (12", p/s, repressing with 'Olympus Studios' misprint))	£60
93	Mute 12 BONG 63	Condemnation (Paris Mix)/Death's Door (Jazz Mix)/Rush (Spiritual Guidance Mix)/Rush (Amylnitrate Mix)/Rush (Wild Panet Mix) (12", p/s)	£60
94	Mute 12 BONG 25	In Your Room (Zephyr Mix)/(Apex Mix)/(Jeep Rock Mix)/Higher Love (Adrenaline Mix)/In Your Room (Extended Zephyr Mix) (12", p/s, black inner sleeve)	£100
94	Mute L12 BONG 24	In Your Room/Policy Of Truth/World In My Eyes/Fly On The Windscreen/Never Let Me Down Again/Death's Door (12", p/s, black inner)	£100
97	Mute L12 BONG 25	Painkiller (Plastikman Mix)/Painkiller/Barrel Of A Gun (One inch Punch Mix)/(United Mix) (12", p/s)	£20
97	Mute 12 BONG 25	Barrel Of A Gun/(Underworld Hard Mix)/(3 Phase Mix)/(One Inch Punch Mix 2)/(Underworld Soft Mix) (12", p/s, gatefold)	£15
97	Mute 12 BONG 26	It's No Good (Hardfloor Mix)/(Speedy J Mix)/(Motor Bass Mix)/(Andrea Parker Mix)/(Dom T Mix) (12", p/s)	£20
97	Mute 12 BONG 27	Home (Jedi Knights Remix)/(Air Remix)/(LFO Mix)/(Grantby Mix) (12", p/s)	£30
97	Mute 12 BONG 28	Useless (Kruder Dorfmeister Session)/(CJ Bolland Funky Sub Mix)/(Air 20 Mix) (12", p/s)	£35
98	Mute 12 BONG 29	Only When I Lose Myself (Subsonic Legacy Remix)/(Dan The Automator Remix)/(LUke Slater Remix) (12", p/s)	£20
98	Mute L BONG 29	Only When I Lose Myself (Gus Gus Long Play Mix)/Painkiller (DJ Shadow Mix)/Surrender (Catalan FC Out Of Reah Mix (12", p/s)	£40
01	Mute 12 BONG 30	Dream On (Bushwacka Tough Guy Mix)/(Dave Clarke Remix)/(Bushwacka Blunt Mix) (12", p/s)	£15
01	Mute 12 BONG 32	Freelove (Console Remix)/Schlammpeitziger Remix)/Zenstation (Atom's Stereonerd Remix)/Freelove (Bertrand Burgalat Version)/(DJ Muggs Remix) (12", p/s)	£30
01	Mute L12 BOONG 31	I Feel Love (Umek Mix)/(Thomas Brinkmann Remix)/(Chamber's Remix) (12", p/s)	£25
01	Mute 12 BONG 31	I Feel Loved (Danny Tenaglia Labor Of Love Edit)/(Danny Tenaglia Labour Of Dub Edit) (12", p/s)	£15
02	Mute MUTE 12BONG 33	Goodnight Lovers (ISAN Falling Leaf Mix)/When The Body Speaks (Acoustic Version)/The Dead Of Night (Electronicat Remix) (12", red vinyl, p/s)	£40
04	Mute 12 BONG 34	Enjoy The Silence (Timo Maas Extended Remix)/(Ewan Pearson Extended Remix) (12", p/s)	£20
05	Mute 12 BONG 35	Precious (Sasha's Spooky Mix)/(Sasha's Gargantuan Vocal Mix) (12", p/s)	£20
05	Mute BONG 35	Precious/(Michael Mayer Ambient Mix) (picture disc)	£20
05	Mute 12 BONG 36	A Pain That I'm Used To (Jacques Lu Cont Remix)/(Jacques Lu Cont Dub) (12", p/s)	£20
05	Mute L12 BONG 36	A Pain That I'm Used To (Bitstream Threshold Mix)/(Bistream Spansule Mix (12", p/s)	£25
06	Mute BONG 38	John The Revelator (UNKLE Dub)/Lilian (Robag Wruhme Slomoschen Killer) (Picture	£15

disc in sealed PVC band, stickered) ....

06	Mute 12 BONG 38	**John The Revelator** (Dave Is In The Disco Tiefschwartz Remix)/(Tiefschwartz Dub)/**Lilian** (Chab Dub) (12", p/s)	£20
06	Mute L12 BONG 38	**John The Revelator** (Murk Mode Dub)/(Boosta Club Remix)/**Lilian** (Chab Vocal Remix) (12", p/s)	£25
06	Mute BONG 37	**Suffer Well** (Metope Vocal Remix)/**The Darkest Star** (Monolake Remix) (picture disc)	£20
06	Mute 12 BONG 37	**Suffer Well** (Tiga Remix)/(Tiga Dub)/(Narcotic Thrust Vocal Dub (12", p/s)	£25
06	Mute L12 BONG 36	**Suffer Well** (Metope Remix)/(Metope Vocal Remix)/(M83 Remix)/**Better Days** (12", p/s)	£35
06	Mute 12 BONG 37	**The Darkest Star** (Holden Remix)/(Holden Dub) (12", p/s)	£30
06	Mute 12 BONG 39	**Martyr** (Booka Shade Dub Mix)/(Dreher and Smart BN Reload Mix)/(Alex Smoke Gravel Mix (12", embossed or non-embossed p/s)	£15
09	Mute 12 BONG 40	**Wrong**/(Thin White Duke Remix)/(Trentmoller Club Remix)/(Caspa Remix) (12", p/s)	£30
09	Mute 12 BONG 42	**Fragile Tension/Hole To Feed/Perfect/Peace** (Mixes) (2x12", p/s)	£60
11	Mute 12 BONG 43	**Personal Jesus** (Alex Metric Remix)/**MAN Remix**)/(Stargate Mix)/(Eric Prydz Remix)/(Sie-Medway Smith Remix) (12", purple vinyl, p/s)	£40
13	Mute 88883 75834 1	**Should Be Higher** (Truss Remix)/(MP3IA Definition)/(Koen Groenveveld Massive Remix)/(Pangea Dub Remix)/(Uberzone Remix)/(DJMREX Remix) (12", p/s)	£25
23	Columbia19658792641	**MEMENTO MORI** (2LP, fourth side etched, red vinyl, trifold sleeve, printed inners, poster, 180g)	£40

ALBUMS

82	Mute STUMM 5	**SPEAK AND SPELL** (LP)	£30
82	Mute STUMM 9	**A BROKEN FRAME** (LP)	£30
83	Mute STUMM 13	**CONSTRUCTION TIME AGAIN** (LP)..	£30
84	Mute STUMM 19	**SOME GREAT REWARD LP, lyric inner)**	£30
85	Mute MUTEL1	**SINGLES 81-85** (LP, gatefold, inner)	£35
86	Mute STUMM 26	**BLACK CELEBRATION** (LP, embossed cover, lyric inner)	£40
87	Mute STUMM 47	**MUSIC FOR THE MASSES** (LP, clear vinyl)	£200
87	Mute STUMM 47	**MUSIC FOR THE MASSES** (LP, with bonus 12" "Strangelove (Maximix)"/"Never Let Me Down Again (Split Mix)" [HMV1])	£60
89	Mute STUMM 101	**101** (2-LP, stickered gatefold sleeve, inner sleeves and 16-page booklet)	£60
89	Mute STUMM 101	**101** (2-LP, envelope sleeve, inner sleeves and 16-page booklet)	£70
90	Mute STUMM 64	**VIOLATOR** (LP, inner)	£80
90	Mute STUMM 47	**MUSIC FOR THE MASSES** (LP, reissue, withdrawn, 'budget' sleeve)	£3000
93	Mute STUMM 106	**SONGS OF FAITH AND DEVOTION** (LP, inner)	£80
93	Mute STUMM 106	**SONGS OF FAITH AND DEVOTION LIVE** (LP)	£150
97	Mute STUMM 148	**ULTRA** (LP, inner sleeve with transfer)	£200
98	Mute P12MUTEL5	**REMIXES 86-98** (3-LP)	£40
98	Mute MUTEL 5	**THE SINGLES 86-98** (3 x LP, box set with booklet, numbered)	£250
01	Mute STUMM 190	**EXCITER** (2-LP)	£100
05	Mute STUMM 260	**PLAYING THE ANGEL** (2-LP)	£100
04	Mute MUTEL 8	**MUTE REMIXES 81-04** (6LP box set, numbered)	£350
07	Mute MUTEL 15	**THE BEST OF** (3LP, printed inners, booklet)	£150
09	Mute STUMM 300	**SOUNDS OF THE UNIVERSE** (2LP/CD, gatefold, printed inners, 180g))	£60
09	Mute BXSTUMM 300	**SOUNDS OF THE UNIVERSE** (4CD/DVD box set, book, badges, poster, ephemera)...........	£50
11	Mute MUTEL 18	**REMIXES 2: 81-11** (6LP box set, liner note insert)	£200
13	Mute 88765460631	**DELTA MACHINE** (2LP, gatefold, printed inners, download card)	£35
17	Mute 88985 41165 1	**SPIRIT** (2LP, fourth side etched, gatefold, printed inners 180g)	£30
21	Mute19439902039	**101** (2CD/2DVD/BD box set, book, ephemera)	£60
23	Columbia19658784211	**MEMENTO MORI** (2LP, fourth side etched, trifold sleeve, printed inners, 180g)	£30
23	Columbia 19658789791	**MEMENTO MORI** (2LP, fourth side etched, transparent red vinyl, printed inners, trifold sleeve, poster, 180g, exclusive to DM store)	£50
23	Columbia 19658789801	**MEMENTO MORI** (2LP, fourth side etched, clear vinyl, printed inners, trifold sleeve, poster, 180g, Amazon exclusive)	£50

PROMOS

82	Mute 12MUTE 018	**See You/This Is Fun** (12", white label promo)	£40
82	Mute 12 BONG 1	**Leave In Silence** (Stripped Mix)/**Instrumental** (12" white label promo)	£50
84	Mute 12 BONG 8	**Blasphemous Rumours/Somebody** (Live)/**Two Minute Warning** (Live)/**Ice Machine** (Live)/**Everything Counts** (Live) (12" white label promo)	£60
85	Mute BONG 9	**It's Called A Heart/Fly On The Windscreen** (12" white label promo with stamped labels)..	£100
86	Mute BONG 10	**Stripped/But Not Tonight** (white label test pressing)	£250
86	Mute RR BONG 10	**Breathing In Fumes/Stripped** (Highland Mix) (12", white labels, some stamped)	£80
86	Mute 7BONG 12	**A Question Of Time** (Edited)/**Black Celebration** (Live) (white label)...................	£100
86	Mute L12 BONG 12	**A Question Of Time** (New Town Mix)/**A Question Of Time** (Live)/**Black Celebration** (Black Tulip Mix)/**More Than A Party** (Live) (12", printed labels with stamped number, plain black die-cut sleeve)	£150
87	Mute CLUB BONG 13	**Strangelove** (12 Inch Maxi Mix)/(7 Inch Mix) (12" promo)...............................	£100
87	Mute DANCE BONG 13	**Strangelove** (Blind Mix)/(Fresh Ground Mix) (12" promo)	£100
87	Mute R BONG 13	**Strangelove** (Radio Edit)/**Strangelove** (p/s)	£200
87	Mute DANCE BONG 13	**Strangelove** (Blind Mix)/(Fresh Ground Mix) (12", promo-only remix some on blue vinyl)	£80
87	Mute CLUB BONG 13	**Strangelove** (12 Inch Maxi Mix)/**Strangelove** (Pain Mix) (12", promo)	£80
87	Mute BONG 14	**Never Let Me Down Again/Pleasure Little Treasure**	£125
87	Mute P 12 BONG 14	**Never Let Me Down Again** (7" Mix)/**Pleasure, Little Treasure** (7" Mix)/**Never Let Me Down Again** (12" Split Mix) (12" promo)...	£150
87	Mute 12BONG 14	**Never Let Me Down Again** (Split Mix)/**Pleasure Little Treasure** (Glitter Mix)/**Never Let Me Down Again** (Aggro Mix) (12")..	£100
87	Mute DJBONG 15	**Behind The Wheel** (DJ Remix)/**Behind The Wheel** (LP Mix) ('DJ Bong' ethed in A-side run out groove)..	£1000
87	Mute D BONG 15	**Behind The Wheel** (Shep Mix)/**Behind The Wheel** (LP Mix)/**Route 66** (7" Mix) (12").......	£80
87	Mute (no cat. no.)	**THE B-SIDES** (4-LP test pressings in title box)	£800

MINT VALUE £

87	Mute (no cat. no.)	THE B-SIDES (4-cassette set)	£200
87	Mute L 12 BONG 15	Behind The Wheel (Beatmasters Mix)/Route 66 (Casualty Mix) (12" promo stamped white labels)	£60
89	Mute S BONG 13	Strangelove (12 Inch Maxi Mix)/(7 Inch Mix)/Pimpf (12" promo)	£100
89	Mute BONG 16R	Everything Counts (Live – Radio Edit)/Nothing (Live Mix) (stickered p/s)	£100
89	Mute P12 BONG 16	Everything Counts (Tim Simenon/Mark Saunders Remix)/(Alan Moulder Remix) (12", black die-cut sleeve)	£80
89	Mute P12 BONG 17	Personal Jesus (Pump Mix)/Dangerous (Hazchemix) (12", black die-cut sleeve)	£60
89	Mute BONG 17	Personal Jesus/Dangerous (censored black rear p/s)	£200
89	Mute PP 12 BONG 16	Strangelove (Hijack Mix)/Nothing (12", promo)	£80
89	Mute CD BONG !7	Personal Jesus (Holier Than Thou Approach)/Dangerous (Sensual Mix)/Personal Jesus (Acoustic) (Promo Cd with censored artwork)	£300
90	Mute BONG 18	Enjoy The Silence/Memphisto ('A' label)	£200
90	Mute P12 BONG 18	Enjoy The Silence (Bass Line)/(Ricki Tik Tik Mix)/(7" Mix) (12", die-cut Mute sleeve)	£70
90	Mute R7 BONG 19	Policy Of Truth (Radio Edit)/Kaleid (p/s)	£50
90	Mute BONG 19R	Policy Of Truth (7" Version)/Kaleid (Remix) (CD)	£30
90	Mute P12 BONG 19	Policy Of Truth (Capitol Mix)/(Pavlov's Dub)/(Trancentral)/Kaleid (Remix) (12", die-cut Mute sleeve)	£80
90	Mute 12BONG 20	World In My Eyes (Oil Tank Mix)/Happiest Girl (Kiss-A-Mix)/Sea Of Sin (Sensoria) (12", white label, numbered, stickered sleeve)	£100
90	Mute BONG 20R	World In My Eyes (7" Version)/Happiest Girl (Jack Mix)/Sea Of Sin (Tonal Mix) (p/s, 33rpm)	£60
90	Mute PSTUMM 64	VIOLATOR (12" EP, 4-track sampler)	£30
90	Mute (no cat. no.)	VIOLATOR (LP, CD & cassette in 12" x 12" picture box with insert)	£1000
90	Mute P12 BONG 20	World In My Eyes (Mayhem Mode Mix)/Happiest Girl (The Pulsating Orbital Mix) (12", die-cut Mute sleeve)	£80
93	Mute P12 BONG 21	I Feel You (Throb Mix)/(Seven Inch Mix)/(Babylon Mix)/One Caress (12", die-cut Mute sleeve)	£30
93	Mute BONG 22	Walking In My Shoes/My Joy (large centre hole)	£60
93	Mute BONG 23	Condemnation (Paris Mix)/Death's Door (Jazz Mix) (large centre hole)	£60
93	Mute PL12BONG 23	Rush (Spiritual Guidance Mix)/Rush (Amylnitrate Mix)/Rush (Wild Planet Vocal Mix) (12")	£80
93	Mute P12 BONG 22	Walking In My Shoes (Grungy Gonads Mix)/(Seven Inch Mix)/My Joy (Seven Inch Mix)/(Slow Slide Mix) (12", die-cut Mute sleeve)	£60
93	Mute P 12 BONG 23	Condemnation (Paris Mix)/Death's Door (Jazz Mix)/Rush (Spiritual Guidance Mix) (12". die-cut Mute sleeve)	£50
93	Mute VERBONG 1	SONGS OF FAITH & DEVOTION (interview CD)	£50
93	Mute (no cat. no.)	SONGS OF FAITH & DEVOTION (4-CD box set)	£300
94	Mute P12 BONG 24	In Your Room (The Jeep Rock Mix)/Higher Love (Adrenaline Mix)/In Your Room (Extended Zephyr Mix) (12", die-cut Mute sleeve)	£50
94	Mute DEPRO 1	DEPRO 1 (13-track compilation CD)	£50
97	Mute P 12 BONG 25	Barrel Of A Gun/(Underworld Hard Mix)/Painkiller (Plastikman Mix)/(Orignal Edit)/Barrel Of A Gun (Underworld Hard instrumental) (12" promo)	£30
97	Mute PL 12 BONG 25	Barrel Of A Gun (One Inch Punch Mix [Version 2])/Painkiller (Original Mix)/Barrel Of A Gun (3 Phase Mix)/Barrel Of A Gun (Original Mix) (12", p/s)	£30
97	Mute P 12 BONG 26	It's No Good (Club 69 Future Mix)/It's No Good (Club 69 Future Dub)/It's No Good (Club 69 Funk Dub) (12")	£35
97	Mute PL12BONG 26	It's No Good (Club 69 mixes) (12")	£40
97	Mute XLCDBONG 26	It's No Good (Live) (CD)	£70
97	Mute P12 BONG 27	Home (Jedi Knights Remix [Drowning In Time])/(Air "Around The Golf" Remix)/(Meant To Be)/(Grantby Mix) (12", 33rpm, die-cut p/s)	£25
97	Mute P12BONG 28	Useless (CJ Bolland Funky Sub Mix)/Useless (the Kruder & Dorfmeister Session™) (12", die-cut p/s)	£20
97	Mute BXSTUMM 148	ULTRA (box set, with CD, T-shirt, stickers & EPK video, soap box pack)	£250
98	Mute PL 12 BONG 29	Headstar (Luke Slater Remix)/Surrender (Catalan FC Out Of Reach Mix)/Only When I Lose Myself (Gus Gus Mix) (12", promo)	£40
98	Mute P 12 BONG 29	Only When I Lose Myself (Dan The Automator Mix)/Only When I Lose Myself (Subsonic Legacy Mix)/Painkiller (Kill The Pain — DJ Shadow Vs Depeche Mode)/Headstar (12", die-cut p/s)	£50
98	Mute (no cat. no.)	THE SINGLES 86>98 (15" x 6" box set, with 3 CDs, video tape & cards)	£120
01	Mute P12BONG 30	Dream On (Bushwacka Tough Guy mixes) (12", p/s)	£16
01	Mute P12 BONG 30	Dream On (Dave Clarke Club Mix)/Dream On (Bushwacka Blunt Mix) (12", p/s)	£25
01	Mute PXL12 BONG 30	Dream On (Octagon Man Mix)/(Octagon Man Dub)/(Dave Clarke Acoustic Mix)/(Kid 606 Mix) 12" p/s)	£30
01	Mute P 12BONG 31	I Feel Loved (Danny Tenaglia Mixes) (12", p/s)	£25
01	Mute P 12 BONG 34	Freelove (Console Remix)/(Schlammpeitziger Remix)/Zenstation (Atom's Stereonerd Remix)/Freelove (Bertrand Burgalat Version)/(DJ Muggs Remix) (12", p/s)	£30
01	Mute PL12 BONG 32	Freelove (Deep Dish Freedom Mix)/Freelove (Josh Wink Vocal Interpretation)/Freelove (Deep Dish Freedom Dub)/Freelove (Power Productions Remix) (12", doublepack, p/s)	£40
01	Mute PXL12 BONG 31	I Feel Loved (Umek Mix)/(Thomas Brinkman Remix)/(Chamber's Remix) (12", p/s)	£30
01	Mute IPKSTUMM 190	EXCITER (interview CD with bonus multimedia disc)	£30
01	Mute BCDSTUMM 190	EXCITER (interview CD with bonus multimedia disc, in long box)	£60
04	Mute P12BONG 34	REMIXES 81 – 04 SAMPLER : Enjoy The Silence (Richard X Extended Mix)/(Ewan Pearson Extended Instrumental)/Timo Maas Extended Remix)/Ewan Pearson Extended Remix) (2 x 12")	£80
04	Mute ACD MUTEL8	REMIXES 81 – 04 (3 x CD, insert & press release)	£30
05	Mute PL 12 BONG 35	Precious (Full Vocal Mix)/(Michael Mayer Balearic Mix)/(Motor Mix)/(Crunch Mix) (12", promo)	£30
05	Mute P 12 BONG 35	Precious (Sasha's Spooky Mix)/(Sasha's Gargantuan Vocal Mix) (12", promo)	£30
05	Mute P12 BONG 36	A Pain That I'm Used To (Jacques Lu Cont Remix)/(Jacques Lu Cont Dub) (12", promo)	£50
05	Mute PL 12 BONG 36	A Pain That I'm Used To (Bitstream Threshold Mix)/(Bistream Spansule Mix (12", promo)	£50
06	Mute PL BONG 37	Suffer Well (Metope Remix)/(Metope Vocal Remix)/(M83 Remix)/Better Days (12", promo)	£30
06	Mute P 12 BONG 37	Suffer Well (Tiga Remix)/(Tiga Dub)/(Narcotic Thrust Vocal Dub) (12", promo)	£30

06	Mute P 12 BONG 39	**Martyr** (Booka Shade Dub Mix)/(Dreher and Smart BN Reload Mix)/(Alex Smoke Gravel Mix (12", embossed or non-embossed p/s)	**£20**
06	Mute PXL 12 BONG 37	**The Darkest Star** (Holden Remix)/(Holden Dub) (12", promo)	**£40**
06	Mute DMINT06CD	**THE BEST OF VOLUME 1 - Interview Disc CD** (p/s)	**£40**
06	Mute PLCDBONG 39	**THE BEST OF VOLUME 1 REMIXES** (promo, p/s, beware of counterfeits)	**£50**

(see also Martin L. Gore, David Gahan, Erasure, Yazoo)

DEPRAVED
86	Children Of the Revolution GURT 14	**STUPIDITY MAKETH THE MAN** (LP, insert)	**£15**

DEPRESSIONS
78	Barn 2314 105	**THE DEPRESSIONS** (LP)	**£30**

DEPTFORD GOTH
13	Merok V2	**LIFE AFTER DEFO** (LP, with CD)	**£25**

DELIA DERBYSHIRE
19	Electronic Sound ES 759	**Doctor Who Theme/Strange Lines And Distances** (p/s, yellow vinyl)	**£15**

(see also BBC Radiophonic Workshop)

DEREK & THE DOMINOES
70	Polydor 2058 057	**Tell The Truth/Roll It Over** (withdrawn)	**£80**
71	Polydor 2625 005	**LAYLA AND OTHER ASSORTED LOVE SONGS** (2-LP, gatefold sleeve)	**£40**
73	RSO 2659 020	**IN CONCERT** (2-LP, gatefold sleeve)	**£15**
11	Universal 0600753314326	**LAYLA AND OTHER ASSORTED LOVE SONGS** (box set, 4-CD, DVD, Book, art print and badge)	**£45**

(see also Eric Clapton, Bobby Whitlock)

DEREK & FRESHMEN
65	Oriole CB 305	**Gone Away/I Stand Alone**	**£15**

DERRICK (MORGAN) & JENNIFER
70	Crab CRAB 47	**Need To Belong/Let's Have Some Fun**	**£20**
70	Crab CRAB 54	**Rocking Good Way/Wipe These Tears**	**£20**

(see also Derrick Morgan)

DERRICK (MORGAN) & LLOYDS (CLARKE)
62	Blue Beat BB 135	**Love And Leave Me** (actually by Lloyd Clarke)/**Merry Twist** (actually "Whistle Stop Tour" by Roy Richards)	**£25**

(see also Derrick Morgan, Lloyd Clarke)

DERRICK (MORGAN) & NAOMI (CAMPBELL)
65	Island WI 193	**Two Of A Kind/I Want A Lover** (credited to Derrick Morgan)	**£45**
65	Ska Beat JB 185	**Heart Of Stone/DERRICK MORGAN: Let Me Go**	**£45**
65	Ska Beat JB 188	**I Wish I Were An Apple/DERRICK MORGAN: Around The Corner**	**£45**

(see also Derrick Morgan, Naomi, Don Drummond)

DERRICK (MORGAN) & PATSY (TODD)
61	Blue Beat BB 57	**Feel So Fine/ROLAND ALPHONSO & GROUP: Mean To Me**	**£25**
61	Blue Beat BB 65	**Baby Please Don't Leave Me/Let The Good Times Roll**	**£25**
62	Blue Beat BB 97	**Love Not To Brag/DRUMBAGO'S ALL STARS: Duck Soup**	**£25**
62	Blue Beat BB 100	**In My Heart** (actually by Derrick Morgan)/**BELL'S GROUP: Kingston 13**	**£30**
62	Blue Beat BB 106	**Oh Shirley/BASIL GABIDON'S GROUP: Sam The Fisherman** (B-side actually by Roland Alphonso)	**£30**
62	Blue Beat BB 121	**Crying In The Chapel/Come Back My Love**	**£30**
62	Blue Beat BB 123	**Oh My Love/Let's Go To The Party**	**£30**
62	Island WI 018	**Housewife's Choice/Gypsy Woman**	**£30**
63	Blue Beat BB 152	**Little Brown Jug/Mow Sen Wa** (with Lloyd Clarke)	**£25**
63	Blue Beat BB 160	**Trying To Make You Mine** (actually "Baby Please Don't Leave Me" by Derrick Morgan)/**Hold Me**	**£30**
63	Island WI 055	**Sea Wave/Look Before You Leap**	**£35**
64	Blue Beat BB 207	**Lover Boy/The Moon**	**£35**
64	Blue Beat BB 224	**Steal Away/Money**	**£35**
64	Blue Beat BB 247	**Troubles/Right** (B-side actually "Baby Face")	**£35**
65	Blue Beat BB 291	**You I Love/Let Me Hold Your hand** (song actually "Steal Away")	**£40**
65	Blue Beat BB 318	**Eternity/Want My Baby**	**£40**
65	Island WI 224	**The National Dance/DESMOND DEKKER & FOUR ACES: Mount Zion**	**£50**
66	Island WI 288	**I Found A Queen/It's True My Darling**	**£25**
68	Nu Beat NB 008	**Hey Boy, Hey Girl/Music Is The Food Of Life**	**£30**

(see also Derrick Morgan, Patsy Todd)

DERRICK (MORGAN) & PAULETT
69	Nu Beat NB 027	**I'll Do It/Give You My Love**	**£40**

(see also Derrick Morgan, Paulette)

DERRICK (MORGAN) & PAULINE (MORGAN)
68	Pyramid PYR 6027	**You Never Miss Your Water/DERRICK MORGAN: Got You On My Mind**	**£40**
68	JJ PYR 6063	**Don't Say/DERRICK MORGAN: Johnny Pram Pram**	**£85**

(see also Derrick Morgan, Patsy Todd, Basil Gabbidon)

DES (BRYAN) ALLSTARS
70	Grape GR 3014	**Night Food Reggae/Walk With Des**	**£80**
70	Grape GR 3015	**If I Had A Hammer/Hammer Reggae**	**£20**
70	Grape GR 3016	**Henry The Great/Black Scorcher**	**£125**

(see also Rudies (Fanatics))

HENRI DES
70	United Artists UP 35109	**Return/Retour**	**£18**

SUGAR PIE DE SANTO
64	Pye International 7N 25249	Soulful Dress/Use What You Got	£25
64	Pye International 7N 25267	I Don't Wanna Fuss/I Love You So Much	£30
66	Chess CRS 8034	There's Gonna Be Trouble/In The Basement (B-side with Etta James)	£30
69	Chess CRS 8093	Soulful Dress/There's Gonna Be Trouble	£20

(see also Etta James & Sugar Pie De Santo)

DESCENDANTS
| 67 | CBS 202545 | Garden Of Eden/Lela | £50 |

LIZZY MERCIER DESCLOUX
| 79 | Ze ILPS 7001 | PRESS COLOUR (LP) | £35 |
| 83 | CBS 25936 | LIZZY MERCIER DESCLOUX (LP) | £15 |

DESERT SESSIONS (JOSH HOLME)
| 03 | Island IS 835 | Crawl Home/The Whores Hustle And The Hustlers Whore (p/s) | £20 |

(see also P J Harvey)

DESERT WOLVES
87	Ugly Man UGLY 6	Love Scattered Lives/Stopped In My Tracks (p/s)	£20
87	Ugly Man UGLY 6T	Love Shattered Lives/Stopped In My Tracks/Desolation/Sunday Morning (12", p/s)	£25
88	Ugly Man UGLY 9	Speak To Me Rochelle/Besotted (p/s)	£15
88	Ugly Man UGLY 9T	Speak To Me Rochelle/Mexico/Besotted/La Petite Rochelle (12", p/s)	£20

JACKIE DE SHANNON
62	Liberty LIB 55497	You Won't Forget Me/I Don't Think So Much	£20
63	Liberty LIB 55563	Needles And Pins/Did He Call Today Mama?	£20
64	Liberty LIB 55645	When You Walk In The Room/Till You Say You'll Be Mine	£20
64	Liberty LIB 10165	Dancing Silhouettes/Hold Your Head High	£15
64	Liberty LIB 10175	Don't Turn Your Back On Me/Be Good Baby	£18
66	Liberty LIB 66224	Come On Down/Find Me Love	£20
65	Liberty LEP 2233	JACKIE (EP)	£40
64	Liberty LBY 1182 (S)	JACKIE DE SHANNON (LP)	£25
65	Liberty LBY 1245	DON'T TURN YOUR BACK ON ME (LP)	£25
65	Liberty LBY 3063	THIS IS JACKIE DE SHANNON (LP)	£20
66	Liberty SLBY 3085	ARE YOU READY FOR THIS? (LP)	£25
68	Liberty LBS 83117E	GREAT PERFORMANCES (LP)	£20
69	Liberty LBS 83148E	ME ABOUT YOU (LP)	£20
70	Liberty LBS 83304	PUT A LITTLE LOVE IN YOUR HEART (LP)	£20
72	Atlantic K 40396	JACKIE (LP)	£15

(see also Date With Soul)

DESIGN FOR LIVING
| 84 | Anthem 3 | Hold Me Closer/The Girl Who Knew Too Much | £18 |

DESIGN (1)
71	Epic EPC 7119	Jet Song/Minstrel's Theme	£15
71	Epic EPC 64322	DESIGN (LP)	£15
71	Epic EPC64653	TOMORROW IS SO FAR AWAY (LP, with lyric insert, stickered sleeve)	£20
73	Regal Zono. SLRZ 1037	DAY OF THE FOX (LP, textured sleeve, red/silver label)	£15

DESIGN (2)
| 86 | Dental 12DENT001 | I Want You I Need You/Never Gonna Give You Up (12") | £40 |

DESI ROOTS
79	Hawkeye HD 018	Hung-Up/Up-Town Rebel (12")	£50
80	Hawkeye HD 025	Weed Fields/Hawkeye All Stars – Burning (12")	£40
80	Hawkeye HD 029	One In A Million/CAROL COOL: Upside Down (12")	£25
80	Hawkeye HD 033	Go Deh Right/Revolutionaries Go Right Deh (12", blue vinyl)	£30
80	Hakweye HD 037	Youth Attack/TALENT INC: Mobilization/Victory (12")	£25
80	Hawkeye HLP 007	DO IT RIGHT (LP)	£75
82	Hawkeye HLP 009	CHILDREN IN EXILE (LP)	£75

(see also Desi Young)

ANDY DESMOND
| 75 | Konk KONK 103 | LIVING ON A SHOESTRING (LP) | £40 |

(see also Gothic Horizon)

JOHNNY DESMOND
| 60 | Philips PB 1044 | Hawk/Playing The Field | £25 |

LORRAE DESMOND (& REBELS)
| 57 | Parlophone R 4361 | Ding-Dong Rock-a-billy Weddin'/Cabin Boy (as Lorrae Desmond & Rebels) | £15 |
| 58 | Parlophone R 4463 | Soda Pop Hop/Blue, Blue Day | £20 |

PAUL DESMOND
| 65 | RCA RS 7701 | BOSSA ANTIGUA (LP, label with red spot) | £20 |
| 65 | RCA Victor SF 7761 | GLAD TO BE HAPPY (LP, with Jim Hall) | £20 |

(see also Gerry Mulligan, Dave Brubeck)

DESOLATION ANGELS
| 84 | AM AM 266 | Valhalla/Boadicea (p/s) | £40 |
| 85 | Thameside TRR 111 | DESOLATION ANGELS (LP) | £50 |

DESPERATE BICYCLES
77	Refill RR 1	Smokescreen/Handlebars (p/s, same tracks both sides)	£40
77	Refill RR 2	The Medium Was Tedium/Don't Back The Front (p/s, same tracks both sides)	£40
78	Refill RR 3	NEW CROSS NEW CROSS (EP)	£40
78	Refill RR 4	Occupied Territory/Skill (p/s)	£20

78	Refill RR 7	Grief Is Very Private/Obstructive/Conundrum	£20
80	Refill RR 6	REMORSE CODE (LP)	£60

DESSIE & JOHN
| 69 | Downtown DT 440 | Boss Sound/Everything Is Alright | £30 |

DESSUS
| 81 | Ellie Jay EJSP 9710 | Ghetto Children/Dessus Jammin' (with p/s) | £25 |

DESTINY
| 80 | VLM LP VLM 001 | I CAN FEEL HIM (LP) | £200 |

DESTROYER (1)
| 81 | Clean Kill SJP 829 | Evil Place/Stand And Deliver (no p/s) | £50 |

DESTROYER (2)
| 14 | Dead Oceans DOC 046 | KAPUTT (2-LP, white vinyl reissue) | £20 |

DESTROYERS
| 70 | Amalgamated AMG 856 | Niney Special/Danger Zone | £40 |
| 70 | Pressure Beat PR 5505 | Pressure Tonic/Machuki's Cooking (B-side actually with Count Machuki) | £35 |

(see also Soul Brothers, Nicky Thomas)

DESTRUCTORS
82	KILL 3	Electronic Church/Khymer Rouge Boogie (rubber-stamped white label, 500 only given away with copies of Trees And Flowers punkzine)	£50
82	Death DEATH 1	MERRY XMAS & FUCK OFF (LP)	£20
83	Radical Change RCLP 2	ARMAGEDDON IN ACTION (LP)	£20

(see also Blanks)

DETONATORS (2)
| 79 | Burning Rockers BR 1008 | GANGSTER (LP) | £20 |

DETOURS (1)
| 68 | CBS 3213 | Run To Me Baby/Hangin' On | £50 |
| 68 | CBS 3401 | Whole Lotta Lovin'/Pieces Of You | £200 |

(see also Gene Latter)

DETRIUS
| 90 | Under One Flag FLAG 55 | PERPETUAL DEFIANCE (LP, with inner sleeve) | £15 |

DETROIT WITH MITCH RYDER
| 72 | Paramount SPFL 277 | DETROIT (LP) | £20 |

(see also Mitch Ryder)

DETROIT ESCALATOR CO.
| 96 | Ferox FERLP 2 | SOUNDTRACK (313) (LP) | £20 |

DETROIT SPINNERS
65	Tamla Motown TMG 514	Sweet Thing/How Can I? (demo credited to 'Spinners')	£425
65	Tamla Motown TMG 514	Sweet Thing/How Can I? (demo credited to 'Detroit Spinners')	£250
65	Tamla Motown TMG 514	Sweet Thing/How Can I? (stock copies credited to 'Spinners')	£425
65	Tamla Motown TMG 523	I'll Always Love You/Tomorrow May Never Come (as 'Spinners')	£110
65	Tamla Motown TMG 523	I'll Always Love You/Tomorrow May Never Come (as 'Detroit Spinners')	£75
65	Tamla Motown TMG 523	I'll Always Love You/Tomorrow May Never Come (as 'Spinners' or 'Detroit Spinners' DJ Copy)	£250
67	Tamla Motown TMG 627	For All We Know/I'll Always Love You (1st pressing with tall, narrow print)	£25
67	Tamla Motown TMG 627	For All We Know/I'll Always Love You (2nd pressing)	£18
70	Tamla Motown TMG 755	It's A Shame/Together We Can Make Such Sweet Music (unissued)	£0
75	Atlantic K10571	Living A Little, Laughing A Lot/I've Got To Make It On My Own	£20
68	T. Motown TML 11060	THE DETROIT SPINNERS (LP, mono)	£50
68	T. Motown STML 11060	THE DETROIT SPINNERS (LP, stereo)	£60
71	T. Motown STML 11182	SECOND TIME AROUND (LP, as Motown Spinners)	£20

(see also G.C. Cameron)

JIMMY DEUCHAR
54	Esquire EP 53	JIMMY DEUCHAR (EP)	£50
55	Tempo EXA 18	JIMMY DEUCHAR ENSEMBLE (EP)	£50
56	Esquire EP 93	JIMMY DEUCHAR QUARTET (EP)	£50
56	Esquire EP 103	JIMMY DEUCHAR QUARTET (EP)	£50
58	Tempo EXA 79	OPUS DE FUNK (EP, as Jimmy Deuchar Sextet)	£50
58	Tempo EXA 81	SWINGIN' IN STUDIO TWO (EP)	£50
59	Tempo EXA 88	WAIL (EP, with Victor Feldman Quintet)	£50
54	Esquire 20-059	DIG DEUCHAR, DON'T DANCE (10", LP)	£125
55	Tempo LAP 2	JIMMY DEUCHAR ENSEMBLE (10" LP)	£275
56	Tempo TAP 4	TOP TRUMPETS (LP)	£250
56	Vogue LDE 023	SHOWCASE (LP)	£80
58	Tempo TAP 20	PAL JIMMY (LP)	£750

(see also Victor Feldman)

DEUS
94	Island 155981854 018-7	Suds & Soda/Secret Hell (limited edition, numbered)	£25
94	Island 1215598854-019-1	Suds And Soda (Extended Version)/Texan Coffee/Secret Hell/Furniture In The Far West (12")	£20
94	Island ILPS 8028/524-0451	WORST CASE SCENARIO (LP, limited edition with postcard and CD booklet)	£70
96	Island ILPS 8052/52429-1	IN A BAR UNDER THE SEA (LP, with inner sleeve)	£60
99	Island ILPS 8082/524 643-1	THE IDEAL CRASH (LP)	£60
05	V2 VVR 1034711	POCKET REVOLUTION (2-LP)	£40
08	V2 VVR 1050471	VANTAGE POINT (LP)	£30

DEUX
19	Electronic Sound ES 751	Europe/Paris/Orly (p/s, reissue)	£15

DEUX FILLES
82	Papier Mache PULP 81	SILENCE & WISDOM (LP)	£80
83	Papier PULP 32	DOUBLE HAPPINESS (LP)	£25

DEVASTATING AFFAIR
73	Mowest 3010	That's How It Was (RIght From The Start)/It's So Sad (DJ copy)	£20

WILLIAM DEVAUGHN
74	Chelsea 2306 002	BE THANKFUL FOR WHAT YOU'VE GOT (LP)	£40
89	Start CHELV 1001	BE THANKFUL FOR WHAT YOU'VE GOT (LP, reissue)	£20

DEVASTATION
84	Creative Reality REAL 8	DRAG YOU DOWN EP	£20

DEVIANTS
68	Stable STA 5601	You Got To Hold On/Let's Loot The Supermarket	£20
67	Underground Imp. IMP 1	PTOOFF! (LP, foldout sleeve, private pressing via IT magazine)	£400
68	Stable SLP 007	DISPOSABLE (LP, gatefold sleeve, red/black label)	£300
69	Transatlantic TRA 204	THE DEVIANTS (LP, with booklet, white/lilac label with 't' logo)	£300
69	Transatlantic TRA 204	THE DEVIANTS (LP, without booklet, white/lilac label with 't' logo)	£150
69	Decca LK-R/SKL-R 4993	PTOOFF! (LP, reissue, large unboxed logo on label)	£90
78	Logo MOGO 4001	THE DEVIANTS (LP, reissue)	£15
84	Psycho PSYCHO 25	HUMAN GARBAGE (LIVE AT DINGWALLS '84) (LP)	£15
	(see also Mick Farren, Pink Fairies)		

DEVIATED INSTINCT
86	Peaceville WARP 2	WELCOME TO THE ORGY EP	£15
88	Peaceville VILE 3	ROCK 'N' ROLL CONFORMITY (LP, inner)	£25
90	Prophecy PRO 004	NAILED EP (12", p/s)	£20
90	Peaceville VILE 16	GUTTURAL BREATH (LP)	£20

DEVO
78	Stiff DEV 1	Jocko Homo/Mongoloid (foldout p/s)	£15
18	Electronic Sound ES 744	Uncontrollable Urge/Sloppy (I Saw My Baby Gettin') (p/s)	£20
78	Virgin V 2106	Q: ARE WE NOT MEN? (LP, various coloured vinyl)	£30
78	Virgin VP 2106	Q: ARE WE NOT MEN? (LP, picture disc, with 'Flimsy Wrap' 33rpm 1-sided flexidisc [VDJ 27/Lyntone LYN 6260])	£15
79	Stiff ODD 1	B-STIFF (Mini-LP, 6 tracks released as Stiff singles)	£15
79	Virgin V2125	DUTY NOW FOR THE FUTURE (LP, promo version with stock LP but different sleeve from official release)	£20
79	Virgin V2125	DUTY NOW FOR THE FUTURE (LP, with red or blue band on front sleeve, card insert)	£20
80	Virgin V2162	FREEDOM OF CHOICE (LP, stickered sleeve with poster)	£20
81	Virgin V2191	NEW TRADITIONALISTS (LP)	£15
82	Virgin V2241	OH NO. IT'S DEVO! (LP)	£15
90	Enigma ENVLP 1006	SMOOTH NOODLE MAPS (LP)	£18

DEVON (RUSSELL) & SEDRIC (MYTON)
69	Blue Cat BS 158	What A Sin Thing/Short Up Dress	£60
	(see also Congos)		

DEVON (RUSSELL) & TARTANS
68	Nu Beat NB 021	Let's Have Some Fun/Making Love	£25
	(see also Tartans)		

DEVONNES
06	Kent 6T 21	Doin The Gittin' Up/MAYBERRY MOVEMENT: I See Him Making Love To You	£20

BARRY DE VORZON
58	RCA RCA 1066	Barbara Jean/JIMMY DELL: Teeny Weeny	£50
60	Philips PB 993	Betty Betty (Go Steady With Me)/Across The Street	£25
	(see also Barry & Tamerlanes, Jimmy Dell)		

DEVOTED
68	Page One POF 076	I Love George Best/United (p/s)	£35
68	Page One POF 076	I Love George Best/United	£15

DEVOTION
79	Sapphire	Devotion/Acid/Energy For The Universe (no p/s)	£50

DEVOTIONS
64	Columbia DB 7256	Rip Van Winkle/(I Love You) For Sentimental Reasons	£100

DEWDROPS
67	Blue Beat BB 381	Somebody's Knocking/By And By	£25

BRIAN DEWHURST
75	Folk Heritage FHR 075	THE HUNTER & THE HUNTED (LP, black label and laminated sleeve)	£20

HARRY DE WIT
79	Bead Records BEAD 11	APRIL '79 (LP)	£25
79	Bead Records BEAD 12	FOR HARM (LP, with Philipp Wachsmann)	£25

RAY DEXTER & LAYABOUTS
62	Decca F 11538	The Coalman's Lament/Lonely Weekend	£30

DEXYS (MIDNIGHT RUNNERS)
14	Absolute 7DEXY 1	Nowhere Is Home/I Love You (Listen To This) (die-cut cover)	£20
80	Parlophone/Late Night Feelings PCS 7213	SEARCHING FOR THE YOUNG SOUL REBELS (LP, 1st issue with inner)	£20
85	Mercury MERH 56	DON'T STAND ME DOWN (LP, lyric insert)	£20

91	Mercury/PolyGram TV 846 460-1	THE VERY BEST OF DEXYS MIDNIGHT RUNNERS (LP)	£30
12	Buback BTT 120-1	ONE DAY I'M GOING TO SOAR (2LP/CD, gatefold, insert)	£60
14	Absolute DEXLP1	NOWHERE IS HOME (4LP, gatefold)	£60
16	100% Records 100LP51	LET THE RECORD SHOW: DEXYS DO IRISH COUNTRY AND SOUL (2LP, gatefold, printed inners)	£25
19	Mercury/UMC 602577309755	AT THE BBC 1982 (2LP, RSD)	£30
22	Mercury/UMC 243885674	TOO-RYE-AYE (AS IT SHOULD HAVE SOUNDED) (4LP, box, booklet, replica programme, prints)	£90
23	100% Records 100LPX133	THE FEMININE DIVINE (LP, Ltd ed., 'fire goddess flame' vinyl, printed inner, signed by Kevin Rowland)	£40
24	100 % 100LP 152B	THE FEMININE DIVINE + DEXYS CLASSICS LIVE! (3LP, trifold sleeve, red, white and blue vinyl)	£35

(see also Killjoys, The Bureau)

TRACEY DEY
64	Stateside SS 287	Go Away/Gonna Get Along Without You Now	£18

DEZZI D
05	Vibes House VH008	Judas/Dub Version	£15

DHAIMA
78	Lightning LIG 528	Ina Jah Children/MIGHTY TWO: Save The Children	£60

DHARMA BLUES BAND
69	Major Minor SMCP 5017	DHARMA BLUES (LP, yellow/white/black label)	£125

(see also Hawkwind)

ALI BEN DHOWN
67	Piccadilly 7N 35395	Musapha/Turkish Delight	£30

DIABOLIKS
00	Vinyl Japan ASKLP P116	THREE FUR BURGERS...AND A HOT CHILLI DOG TO GO! (LP)	£15

DIAGRAM BROTHERS
80	Construct CON 1	We Are All Animals/There Is No Shower/Would I Like To Live In Prison	£15

BRIAN DIAMOND & THE CUTTERS
63	Decca F 11724	Jealousy Will Get You Nowhere/Brady Brady	£15
64	Fontana TF 452	Shake, Shout And Go/Wotcha Gonna Do Now Pretty Baby	£150
65	Pye 7N 15779	Big Bad Wolf/See If I Care	£15
65	Pye 7N 15952	Bone Idol/Sands Of Time	£15

GREGG DIAMOND'S BIONIC BOOGIE
79	Polydor POSPX 50	Chains/Hot Butterfly (12")	£15
79	Polydor 2391322	BIONIC BOOGIE (LP)	£15
78	Polydor 2391373	HOT BUTTERFLY (LP)	£15

JERRY DIAMOND
57	London HLE 8496	Sunburned Lips/Don't Trust Love	£20

NEIL DIAMOND
66	London HA-Z 8307	THE FEEL OF NEIL DIAMOND (LP)	£20

DIAMOND BOYS
62	Parlophone GIB 102	Fool In Love/New Orleans (export issue)	£25
63	RCA RCA 1351	Hey Little Girl/What'd I Say	£15

(see also Albert Ammons)

DIAMOND HEAD
80	Happy Face MMDH 120	Shoot Out The Lights/Helpless (p/s)	£15
80	Media SCREEN 1	Sweet And Innocent/Streets Of Gold (p/s)	£15
81	DHM DHM 005	DIAMOND LIGHTS EP (Diamond Lights/We Won't Be Back/I Don't Got/It's Electric) (12", p/s)	£20
83	MCA DHMT 103	Makin' Music/(Andy Peebles Interview) (12", p/s)	£15
83	MCA DHMT 104	Out Of Phase/The Kingmaker/Sucking My Love (live) (12", p/s)	£25
80	DHM MMDHLP 105	LIGHTNING TO THE NATIONS (LP, plain or printed white labels, plain white sleeve, sold at gigs, signed in blue ink & available via Sounds)	£100
80	DHM MMDHLP 105	LIGHTNING TO THE NATIONS (LP, plain or printed white labels, plain white sleeve, sold at gigs)	£50
81	MCA DH 1001	LIVING ON BORROWED TIME (LP, gatefold sleeve with inner sleeve, with poster & fan club insert)	£25
81	MCA DH 1001	LIVING ON BORROWED TIME (LP, gatefold sleeve with inner sleeve)	£15
82	MCA DH1001	BORROWED TIME (LP, with poster)	£25
83	MCA DH 1002	CANTERBURY (LP, with lyric and tour dates sheet, first pressing faulty and jumps)	£15
86	Metal Masters METALP 110	BEHOLD THE BEGINNING (LP, remixed reissue of 1st LP)	£20
87	FM WKFMLP 92	AM I EVIL (LP, with inner sleeve)	£20

DIAMONDS (JAMAICA)
72	Songbird SB 1079	Mash Up/DYNAMITES: Mash Up (Version)	£15
75	Attack ATT 8108	Jah Jah Bless Your Dreadlocks/Version	£18
75	Attack ATT 8113	Just Can't Figure Out/Just Can't Figure Out (Version)	£15
75	Black Wax WAX 5	Country Living/A Living Version	£15
78	Virgin V2102	PLANET EARTH (LP)	£20

(see also Dymonds, Mighty Diamonds)

DIAMONDS (U.S.)
55	Vogue Coral Q 72109	Black Denim Trousers And Motorcycle Boots/Nip Sip	£30
58	Mercury 7MT 187	Silhouettes/Honey Bird	£25
58	Mercury 7MT 208	Straight Skirts/Patsy	£50
60	Mercury AMT 1086	Tell The Truth/Real True Love	£30

DIANA

61	Mercury AMT 1156	One Summer Night/It's A Doggone Shame	£15
57	Mercury MEP 9515	PRESENTING THE DIAMONDS (EP)	£20
57	Mercury MEP 9523	THE DIAMONDS VOL. 1 (EP)	£20
58	Mercury MEP 9527	THE DIAMONDS VOL. 2 (EP)	£20
58	Mercury MEP 9530	THE DIAMONDS VOL. 3 (EP)	£20
59	Mercury ZEP 10003	DIG THE DIAMONDS (EP)	£20
59	Mercury ZEP 10020	THE DIAMONDS MEET PETE RUGOLO (EP)	£15
60	Mercury ZEP 10053	STAR STUDDED DIAMONDS (EP)	£15
59	Mercury ZEP 10026	DIAMONDS ARE TRUMPS (EP)	£15
57	Mercury MPT 7526	THE DIAMONDS (10" LP)	£40

(see also Pete Rugolo)

DIANA

82	Oak Sounds OSD 003	When Music Hits You/Feel No Pain Combination (12")	£60
83	A1 A1002	Flowers/A1 Dub (12")	£15
83	A1 A1003	The Feeling/Dubbing Feeling (12")	£15

DIANE & JAVELINS

66	Columbia DB 7819	Heart And Soul/Who's The Girl	£55

(PAUL) DI'ANNO

84	FM WKFM LP1	DI'ANNO (LP, blue vinyl, stickered sleeve)	£15
84	FM WKFM PD1	DI'ANNO (LP, picture disc)	£18

(see also Gogmagog, Iron Maiden)

DIATONES

61	Starlite ST45 057	Ruby Has Gone/Oh Baby Come Dance With Me	£100

DIATRIBE

84	Criminal Damage CRI 12 123	DIATRIBE EP	£15

DANNY DIAZ & THE CHECKMATES

69	Pye 7N 17690	Solomon Grundy/Goodbye Baby	£15

MANU DIBANGO

73	London SH 8451	O BOSO (LP)	£25
75	Creole CRLP 503	MAKOSSA MUSIC (LP)	£15
78	Decca SKL-R 5296	AFROVISION (LP)	£15
78	Decca SKL-R 5303	SUN EXPLOSION (LP)	£15
86	Gallo GSL 289	SUPER KUMBA (LP, reissue)	£15

BILLY DICE & SHENLEY DUFFUS

73	Pama 874	Women Smarter/Standing On The Hill (B-side with uncredited Silvertones)	£15

(see also Billy Dyce)

DICE THE BOSS

69	Joe DU 50	Brixton Cat Big And Fat/JOES ALL STARS : Solitude	£55
69	Duke/Joe DU 51	Gun The Man Down/JOE MANSANO: The Thief	£50
69	Duke/Joe DU 52	But Officer/JOE'S ALL STARS: Reggae On The Shore	£50
70	Duke/Joe DU 57	Your Boss D.J./TITO SIMON: Read The News	£80
70	Joe's JRS 17	The Informer/Cool It	£40
70	Explosion EX 2017	Funky Monkey/JOE'S ALL STARS: Funky Monkey Version	£30
70	Explosion EX 2020	Funky Duck/Dunkier Than Duck	£15

(see also Joe The Boss, Ray Martel)

LLOYD DICE

70	Joe JRS 5	Trial Of Pama Dice/JOE: Jughead Returns	£40

(see also Trevor Lloyd)

PAMA DICE

70	Reggae 3002	Brixton Pum Pum Wrecker/JOE ALLSTARS: Version (White label, possibly unreleased)	£100
69	Jackpot JP 715	Honky Tonk Popcorn/Bongo Man	£40
69	Jackpot JP 715	Bongo Man/Bear De Pussy	£30
69	Jackpot JP 716	Sin, Sun And Sex/Reggae Popcorn	£30
70	Reggae REG 3001	Brixton Fight/OPENING: Tea House	£150

(see also Dice The Boss, Joe The Boss)

DICEMEN

83	Random MCPS RR1	Number 19/A Year Without You/Sunrise/Today	£15

DICK & DEE DEE

63	Warner Bros WM 8132	YOUNG AND IN LOVE (LP, mono)	£25
63	Warner Bros WS 8132	YOUNG AND IN LOVE (LP, stereo)	£25

CHARLES DICKENS

65	Pye 7N 15887	That's The Way Love Goes/In The City	£25
66	Immediate IM 025	So Much In Love/Our Soul Brothers	£40

(see also Habits)

DICKIES

79	A&M AMLE 64742	THE INCREDIBLE SHRINKING DICKIES (LP, black or yellow vinyl)	£20
79	A&M AMLE 64742	THE INCREDIBLE SHRINKING DICKIES (LP, blue vinyl, with black or red-and-black on sleeve)	£20
79	A&M AMLE 64742	THE INCREDIBLE SHRINKING DICKIES (LP, orange vinyl, with black or red-and-black on sleeve)	£20
79	A&M AMLH 68510	DAWN OF THE DICKIES (LP, blue vinyl)	£25
79	A&M AMLH 68510	DAWN OF THE DICKIES (LP, black vinyl)	£15

(see also Chuck Wagon)

BRUCE DICKINSON
90	EMI EMPD 138	Tattooed Millionaire/Ballad Of Mutt (uncut shaped picture disc)	£40
90	EMI EMPD 142	All The Young Dudes/Darkness Be My Friend (uncut shaped picture disc)	£25
94	EMI EMD 1057	BALLS TO PICASSO (LP, gatefold sleeve)	£50
95	Raw DV 102	ALIVE IN STUDIO (2-LP, gatefold with inners)	£60
97	RCA 21527987 JB	Torn/Sometimes (7", jukebox, paper label, large centre hole)	£100
97	Raw Power RAWLP 124	ACCIDENT OF BIRTH (LP)	£75

(see also Iron Maiden, Samson, Xero, Speed)

BARBARA DICKSON
70	Decca SKL 5041	THRO' RECENT YEARS (LP, with Archie Fisher)	£50
71	Decca SKL 5058	DO RIGHT WOMAN (LP)	£40
72	Decca SKL 5116	FROM THE BEGGAR'S MANTLE FRINGED WITH GOLD (LP)	£35
74	RSO 2394 141	JOHN, PAUL, GEORGE, RINGO AND BERT (LP, with London cast)	£30

DICK TURPIN
| 70 | Evolution E 2446 | If You've Got The Time/Madeline | £180 |

DICTATORS WITH TONY & HOWARD
| 63 | Oriole CB 1934 | So Long Little Girl/Say Little Girl | £20 |

(see also Tony & Howard)

DICTATORS
75	Epic S EPC 80767	GO GIRL CRAZY (LP)	£20
77	Asylum K 53061	MANIFEST DESTINY (LP, lyric inner)	£15
78	Asylum K 53083	BLOOD BROTHERS LP, inner)	£15

BO DIDDLEY
59	London HLM 8913	The Great Grandfather/Crackin' Up	£50
59	London HLM 8913	The Great Grandfather/Crackin' Up (78)	£20
59	London HLM 8975	Say Man/The Clock Strikes Twelve	£70
59	London HLM 8975	Say Man/The Clock Strikes Twelve (78)	£20
59	London HLM 9035	Say Man, Back Again/She's Alright	£80
60	London HLM 9112	Road Runner/My Story	£50
62	Pye Intl. 7N 25165	You Can't Judge A Book By The Cover/I Can Tell	£15
63	Pye Intl. 7N 25193	Who Do You Love?/The Twister	£20
63	Pye Intl. 7N 25210	Bo Diddley/Detour	£20
64	Pye Intl. 7N 25243	Mona/Gimme Gimme	£15
67	Chess CRS 8057	Wrecking My Love Life/Boo-Ga-Loo Before You Go	£20
56	London RE-U 1054	RHYTHM AND BLUES WITH BO DIDDLEY (EP, gold label lettering)	£200
63	Pye Intl. NEP 44014	HEY! BO DIDDLEY (EP)	£20
64	Pye Intl. NEP 44019	THE STORY OF BO DIDDLEY (EP)	£20
64	Pye Intl. NEP 44031	BO DIDDLEY IS A LUMBERJACK (EP)	£20
64	Pye Intl. NEP 44036	DIDDLING (EP)	£20
65	Chess CRE 6008	I'M A MAN (EP)	£20
66	Chess CRE 6023	ROOSTER STEW (EP)	£20
59	London HA-M 2230	GO BO DIDDLEY (LP)	£350
62	Pye Jazz NJL 33	BO DIDDLEY IS A GUNSLINGER (LP)	£50
63	Pye Intl. NPL 28025	HEY! BO DIDDLEY (LP)	£25
63	Pye Intl. NPL 28026	BO DIDDLEY (LP)	£25
63	Pye Intl. NPL 28029	BO DIDDLEY RIDES AGAIN (LP)	£25
63	Pye Intl. NPL 28032	BO DIDDLEY'S BEACH PARTY (LP)	£25
64	Pye Intl. NPL 28034	BO DIDDLEY IN THE SPOTLIGHT (LP)	£25
64	Pye Intl. NPL 28049	16 ALL-TIME HITS (LP)	£15
64	Chess CRL 4002	HEY GOOD LOOKIN' (LP)	£20
65	Chess CRL 4507	LET ME PASS (LP)	£25
67	Chess CRL 4525	THE ORIGINATOR (LP)	£25
68	Chess CRL 4529	SUPER BLUES (LP, with Muddy Waters & Little Walter)	£20
68	Chess CRL 4537	THE SUPER SUPER BLUES BAND (LP, with Muddy Waters & Howlin' Wolf)	£20
71	Chess 6310107	ANOTHER DIMENSION (LP)	£20

(see also Chuck Berry & Bo Diddley)

DIDO
| 00 | Cheeky 74321 86823 1 | NO ANGEL (LP, gatefold) | £75 |

DIE ELECTRIC EELS
| 78 | Rough Trade RT 008 | Agitated/Cyclotron (p/s) | £15 |

DIE LAUGHING
| 80 | Ocean OC 003 | Hard Living Man/You Got The Power (p/s) | £50 |

DIESEL M
| 94 | Choci's Chewns CCB 001 | M for Multiple (12", blue vinyl, 666 only) | £25 |
| 95 | Choci's Chewns DDL 001 | M For Mangoes (12", red vinyl, 666 only) | £25 |

DIF JUZ
| 81 | 4AD BAD 116 | VIBRATING AIR: Heset/Diselt/Gunet/Soarn (12" EP) | £15 |

DIFFERENT EYES
| 79 | Tuzmadoner TUZMADONER 001 | Open The Box/Uncomfortable//ROYSTON: Snake's Song/Gerald's Eyes (stapled photocopied cover, rubber -stamped labels) | £100 |

DIGA RHYTHM BAND
| 76 | United Artists UAG 29975 | DIGA RHYTHM BAND (LP) | £25 |

(see also Grateful Dead, Mickey Hart, Jerry Garcia)

DIGABLE PLANETS
| 93 | Pendulum 7243 8-3-654 1 7 | REACHIN' (A NEW REFUTATION OF TIME AND SPACE) (LP) | £50 |

MINT VALUE £

94   Pendulum 7243 8 30654 1 7 **BLOWOUT COMB** (2-LP, inners) £35

DIGGA
97   Groove Yard GYARD 14   **DIG A GROOVE EP** (12") £20

STEVE DIGGLE
80   Faulty Products FEP 7000   **Fifty Years Of Comparative Wealth/Shut Out The Light/Here Comes The Fire Brigade** (unreleased) £0

(see also Buzzcocks)

DIGITAL MYSTIKZ
04	Big Apple BAM 004	**Pathways/Ugly/Mawo Dub/Da Wrath** (12")	£20
05	DMZ DMZ 005	**Neverland/Struck** (12")	£25
06	DMZ DMZ 005	**Haunted/Anti War Dub** (12")	£100
06	DMZ DMZ 008	**Ancient Memories/Ancient Memories** (Skream Remix) (12")	£25
10	DMZ DMZLP 001	**RETURN II SPACE** (3-LP)	£18
10	DMZ DMZLP 001	**RETURN II SPACE** (3-LP, picture discs, 200 only but no indication on sleeve if you get picture discs or black vinyl!)	£40

DIGITAL MYSTIKZ & LEOFAH
04	DMZ DMZ 001	**Twisup/B/Chainba** (with Loefah) (12" white labels)	£45
04	DMZ DMZ 002	**Lost City/Jah Fire/Horror Show/Dread Commands** (EP)	£25

DILATED PEOPLES
00	Capitol 7243 5 23310 1 7	**THE PLATFORM** (2-LP)	£25
01	Capitol 531477	**EXPANSION TEAM** (3-LP)	£30

DILLARD & CLARK
69	A&M AMS 764	**Radio Song/Why Not Your Baby**	£40
69	A&M AMLS 939	**THE FANTASTIC EXPEDITION OF DILLARD & CLARK** (LP)	£40
69	A&M AMLS 966	**THROUGH THE MORNING, THROUGH THE NIGHT** (LP)	£35

(see also Gene Clark, Byrds, Dillards)

MOSES & JOSHUA (DILLARD)
67	Stateside SS 2059	**My Elusive Dreams/What's Better Than Love** (as Moses & Joshua Dillard)	£25
67	Stateside SS 2059	**My Elusive Dreams/What's Better Than Love** (as Moses & Joshua Dillard) (DJ Copy)	£40
68	Bell BELL 1018	**Get Out Of My Heart/They Don't Want Us Together** (as Moses & Joshua)	£25
72	Mojo 2092 054	**My Elusive Dreams/Get Out Of My Heart**	£15

DILLARDS
66	Bounty BY 6019	**BACK PORCH BLUEGRASS** (LP)	£20
68	Elektra EKS 7265	**LIVE!!! ALMOST!!!** (LP)	£15
72	United Artists UAG 29366	**ROOTS AND BRANCHES** (LP, textured gatefold sleeve)	£15

(see also Dillard & Clark)

DILLINGER
73	Duke DU 149	**Headquarters** (as Dellenger)/**CHENLEY DUFFAS: Black Girl In My Bed**	£30
73	Downtown DT 512	**Tighten Up Skank/Middle East Rock** (actually by Dillinger)	£45
77	Black Swan WIP 6416	**Cokane In My Brain/Buckingham Palace/Ragnampiza**	£15
77	Black Swan BS 7	**Cocaine In My Brain/Buckingham Palace/Ragnampiza** (12")	£20
77	Third World TW 65	**Flat Foot Hustling/Under Tight Wraps**	£15
76	Black Swan ILPS 9385	**CB200** (LP)	£20
76	Black Swan ILPS 9455	**BIONIC DREAD** (LP)	£25
76	Island ILPS 9385	**CB200** (LP, reissue)	£15
77	Magnum DEAD 1001	**TALKIN' BLUES** (LP)	£30
77	Magnum BB27	**TALKIN' BLUES** (LP, reissue)	£20
77	Third World TWS 919	**TOP RANKING** (LP)	£30
78	Third World TWS 928	**ANSWER ME QUESTION** (LP)	£30
79	Jamaica Sound JSLP 002	**MARIJUANA IN MY BRAIN** (LP)	£15
79	Jamaica Sound JSLP 009	**FUNKY PUNK/ROCK TO THE MUSIC** (LP)	£18

(see also David Isaacs)

DILLINGER, TRINITY, WAYNE WADE. AL CAMPBELL & JUNIOR TAMLIN
82   Oak OSD 002   **Five Man Army/Send Another Moses/Five Man Dub** (12") £30

DILLINGER V TRINITY
78   Burning Sounds BSLP 1003   **CLASH** (LP) £30

TODD DILLINGHAM
95   Woronzow WOO 25   **SGT. KIPPER** (2-LP, 400 only, with bonus track - Speaking In Tongues - not on CD) £15

DILLINJA
93	Cybotron DILL 01	**Steal The Way/Forever Fierce** (1-sided 12")	£20
93	Cybotron DILL 03	**From Beyond/Ride It Hard** (1-sided 12")	£20
93	Cybotron DILL 04	**Sinewave/Dark Science** (1-sided 12")	£100
93	Tough Toonz TT 02	**DILLINJA EP** (12", promo only, four untitled tracks)	£40
93	Wave Form DIL 08	**TEST [2] EP** (12", as Dillinger)	£15
94	Deadly Vinyl D2	**Deadly Ceremonies/Soverign Melody** (12")	£100
94	Deadly Vinyl D3	**Deadly Deep Subs/Calculus Beats** (12")	£30
94	Logic Productions DM 003	**You Don't Know** (Remix)/**Heavenly Bass** (12")	£15
94	JA 1	**South Side** (Riffin Mix)/**Stompers Delight** (12")	£15
95	Deadly Vinyl D4	**Deadly Deep Subs** (Remix)/**Perfect Match** (12")	£15
95	Philly Blunt PB 005	**Muthaf*cka/Sky** (12")	£15
95	Metalheadz MET 006	**The Angel Fell/Ja Know Ya Big/Brutal Bass** (12")	£18

(See also Cybotron featuring Dillinja)

LEONARD DILLON
66   Island WI 285   **Beggars Have No Choice** (by Leonard Dillon & Wailers)/ **MARCIA GRIFFITHS: Funny** £120

(see also Ethiopians)

PHYLLIS DILLON

66	Doctor Bird DB 1061	Don't Stay Away (as Phillis Dillon)/TOMMY McCOOK & SUPERSONICS: What Now	£70
67	Trojan TR 006	This Is A Lovely Way/Thing Of The Past (as Phyllis Dellon)	£70
67	Treasure Isle TI 7003	This Is A Lovely Way/Thing Of The Past	£60
67	Treasure Isle TI 7015	Perfidia/It's Rocking Time	£60
68	Treasure Isle TI 7041	I Wear This Ring/Don't Touch Me Tomato	£50
69	Trojan TR 651	Love Is All I Had/Boys And Girls Reggae (as Phillis Dylon)	£50
69	Trojan TR 671	Get On The Right Track/TOMMY McCOOK & SUPERSONICS: Moonshot	£60
69	Trojan TR 686	Lipstick On Your Collar (as Phillis Dillon)/TOMMY McCOOK & SUPERSONICS: Tribute To Rameses	£45
70	Duke Reid DR 2508	This Is Me/Skabuvie (act. "If Your Name Is Andy"/"Ska Vovi" by Dorothy Reid)	£30
70	Duke DU 76	Walk Through This World/The Rooster	£40
71	Treasure Isle TI 7058	One Life To Live, One Love To Give/TOMMY McCOOK: My Best Dress	£30
71	Treasure Isle TI 7070	Midnight Confession/TOMMY McCOOK & SOUL SYNDICATE: Version	£40
72	Sioux SI 009	In The Ghetto (actually by Judy Mowatt)/NYAH EARTH: Knight Of The Long Knives	£60
72	Trojan TRL 41	ONE LIFE TO LIVE (LP)	£60
91	Treasure Isle LG2 1014	ONE LIFE TO LIVE (LP, reissue)	£20

DIMENSIONS

65	Parlophone R 5294	Tears On My Pillow/You Don't Have To Whisper	£25

DIMPLES & EDDIE WITH RICO'S COMBO

62	Planetone RC 3	Fleet Street/Good Bye World	£40

DIMPLES (1)

66	Decca F 12537	The Love Of A Lifetime/My Heart Is Tied To You	£40

(see also Gospel Garden, Amazing Blondel)

DIMPLES (2)

76	Hybrid HB09	Doctor Dark Eyes/Devil You	£20

D'INFLUENCE

97	Echo ECHLP 16	LONDON (2-LP, gatefold, inners)	£30

DINGER

85	Face Value FVRA 221	Air Of Mystery/I Love To Love (no p/s)	£35

(see also Erasure)

MARK DINNING

61	MGM MGM 1125	Top Forty, News, Weather And Sport/Suddenly	£15

DINNING SISTERS

55	London HLF 8179	Drifting And Dreaming/Truly	£20
56	London HLF 8218	Hold Me Tight/Uncle Joe	£20

(see also Tennessee Ernie Ford)

KENNY DINO

61	HMV POP 960	Your Ma Said You Cried In Your Sleep Last Night/Dream A Girl	£15

DINOSAUR JR

89	Blast First BFFP 31	BUG (LP)	£20
91	Blanco Y Negro BYN 24	GREEN MIND (LP)	£30
93	Blanco Y Negro BYN 28	WHERE YOU BEEN (LP)	£35
94	Blanco Y Negro 4509 96933-1	WITHOUT A SOUND (LP)	£40
97	Blanco Y Negro 0630183121	HAND IT OVER (LP)	£45
01	Strange Fruit SFRSLP078	IN SESSION (LP)	£30
07	Play It Again Sam PIL070LP	BEYOND (LP, with 7")	£20
09	PIAS 110LP	FARM (2-LP, white vinyl 7")	£20
12	PIAS PIASR575LP	I BET ON SKY (LP, purple vinyl)	£15

DINOSAUR L

78	Sire SRE 1034 (T)	Kiss Me Again/(Version) (12", as Dinosaur)	£30
86	City Beat CBE 1205	Go Bang! 5/Clean On Your Bean 1 (12", p/s)	£15

(see also Arthur Russell)

DIO

75	Purple PUR 128	Sitting In A Dream (as Ronnie Dio featuring Roger Glover & Guests)/JOHN LAWTON: Little Chalk Blue	£15
83	Vertiho VERS 5	HOLY DIVER (LP, inner)	£30
93	Vertigo 518486-1	STRANGE HIGHWAYS (LP, on 'swirl' label, with inner sleeve)	£80

(see also Elf, Rainbow, Roger Glover, Black Sabbath, John Lawton)

DION (& BELMONTS)

78s

58	London HL 8646	I Wonder Why/Teen Angel (as Dion & Belmonts)	£20
58	London HL 8718	I Can't Go On (Rosalie)/No One Knows (as Dion & Belmonts)	£20
59	London HL 8799	Don't Pity Me/Just You (as Dion & Belmonts)	£20
59	London HLU 8874	A Teenager In Love/I've Cried Before (as Dion & Belmonts)	£20
59	Pye International 7N 25038	A Lover's Prayer/Every Little Thing I Do (as Dion & Belmonts)	£40
60	London HLU 9030	Where Or When/That's My Desire (as Dion & Belmonts)	£50

SINGLES

58	London HL 8646	I Wonder Why/Teen Angel (as Dion & Belmonts)	£40
58	London HL 8718	I Can't Go On (Rosalie)/No One Knows (as Dion & Belmonts)	£40
59	London HL 8799	Don't Pity Me/Just You (as Dion & Belmonts)	£40
59	London HL 8874	A Teenager In Love/I've Cried Before (mispressing as Dion & Delmonts)	£30
59	London HLU 8874	A Teenager In Love/I've Cried Before (as Dion & Belmonts)	£30

(The above 45s were originally issued with triangular centres, round-centre re-pressings are worth half to two-thirds of these values.)

MINT VALUE £

59	Pye International 7N 25038	A Lover's Prayer/Every Little Thing I Do (as Dion & Belmonts)	£50
60	London HLU 9030	Where Or When/That's My Desire (as Dion & Belmonts)	£25
60	Top Rank JAR 368	When You Wish Upon A Star/My Private Joy (as Dion & Belmonts)	£20
60	Top Rank JAR 503	In The Still Of The Night/Swinging On A Star (as Dion & Belmonts)	£20
60	Top Rank JAR 521	Lonely Teenager/Little Miss Blue	£20
61	Top Rank JAR 545	Havin' Fun/North-East End Of The Corner	£15
63	Stateside SS 161	Sandy/Faith	£20
63	Stateside SS 209	Come Go With Me/King Without A Queen	£15

EPs

| 62 | HMV 7EG 8745 | SWINGALONG WITH DION | £40 |
| 63 | Stateside SE 1006 | DION'S HITS | £20 |

ALBUMS

59	London HA-U 2194	PRESENTING DION AND THE BELMONTS (as Dion & Belmonts)	£150
60	Top Rank 25-027	THE TOPPERMOST — VOL. 1 (as Dion & Belmonts, with others)	£40
61	HMV CLP 1539	RUNAROUND SUE	£50
63	Stateside SL 10034	LOVERS WHO WANDER	£40
63	CBS (S) BPG 62137	RUBY BABY (mono/stereo)	£25
64	CBS (S) BPG 62203	DONNA THE PRIMA DONNA (mono/stereo)	£25
67	HMV CLP 3618	TOGETHER AGAIN (as Dion & Belmonts, also stereo CSD 3618)	£20
75	Phil Spector Intl. 2307 002	BORN TO BE WITH YOU (LP, printed inner)	£30

(see also Belmonts)

DION (CAMERON) & THREE TOPS

| 67 | Doctor Bird DB 1101 | Miserable Friday/This World Has A Feeling | £60 |
| 72 | Big BG 331 | Three Tops Time/UNDERGROUND PEOPLE: Tops (Version) | £15 |

(see also Three Tops)

CELINE DION

| 93 | Columbia 474743 | COLOUR OF MY LOVE (LP) | £25 |

DIPLOMATS (1)

67	Caltone TONE 108	Meet Me At The Corner/Do It To Me Baby (by Lloyd & Groovers)	£60
68	Caltone TONE 109	Going Alone/My Heart My Soul (by Lloyd & Groovers)	£60
68	Caltone TONE 112	Strong Man/Listen To The Music (by Lloyd & Groovers)	£60
68	Direction 58-3899	I Can Give You Love/I'm So Glad I Found You	£20

DIPLOMATS (3)

| 98 | Kent 6T 19 | I Really Love You/DEBRA JOHNSON: To Get Love | £30 |

DIRECT ACTION

| 85 | Second Coming SCP 78501 | THE ALBUM (LP, with booklet) | £18 |

DIRECT CURRENT MCS

| 90 | Underground TUBE1 | Keep In Step/Gangland Rap (12") | £30 |

DIRECT HITS

82	Whaam! WHAAM 007	Modesty Blaise/Sunny Honey Girl (p/s)	£60
80	Bootleg BOOT 004	COLLISIONS AT TEEN JUNCTION (LP, white card sleeve with home made printed front and back, lyric insert)	£30
84	Whaam! BIG 7	BLOW UP (LP)	£30

(see also Exits)

DIRECTIONS

| 79 | Tortch TOR 004 | Three Bands Tonite/On The Train (p/s, with badge) | £80 |
| 79 | Tortch TOR 004 | Three Bands Tonite/On The Train (p/s) | £75 |

(see also Big Sound Authority)

DIRECTIONS IN JAZZ UNIT

| 64 | Philips BL 7625 | DIRECTIONS IN JAZZ (LP) | £50 |

DIRE STRAITS

78	Vertigo 9102 021	DIRE STRAITS (LP)	£20
82	Vertigo HS 6359 034	MAKING MOVIES (LP, half-speed master recording)	£30
82	Vertigo HS 9102 021	DIRE STRAITS (LP, half-speed master recording)	£30
85	Vertigo VERH 25	BROTHERS IN ARMS (LP, insert)	£25
91	Vertigo 510 160-1	ON EVERY STREET (LP)	£30
93	Vertigo 514 766-1	ON THE NIGHT (2-LP)	£60
95	Vertigo 528 323 2	LIVE AT THE BBC (LP)	£100

(see also Mark Knopfler, Notting Hillbillies)

DIRK & STIG

| 78 | Ring O' 2017 109/DIB 1 | Ging Gang Goolie/Mr. Sheene (unissued) | £0 |
| 79 | EMI EMI 2852 | Ging Gang Goolie/Mr. Sheene (p/s, khaki vinyl) | £18 |

(see also Rutles, Neil Innes)

DIRT

82	Crass 221984/7	NEVER MIND THE DIRT HERE'S THE BOLLOCKS (LP, inner)	£25
85	Dirt DIRT 1	JUST AN ERROR (LP)	£25
95	Dirt DIRT 3	DRUNKS IN RUSTY TRANSITS (LP)	£15

DIRTY BLUES BAND

| 68 | Stateside S(S)L 10234 | DIRTY BLUES BAND (LP) | £100 |
| 69 | Stateside S(S)L 10268 | STONE DIRT (LP) | £100 |

(see also Bacon Fat and Juicy Lucy)

DIRTY DOG

| 78 | Lightning GIL 511 | Let Go Of My Hand/Shouldn't Do It/Gonna Quit/Guitar In My Hand (p/s) | £25 |

DIRTY PRETTY THINGS
| 06 | Mercury 9856418 | WATERLOO TO ANYWHERE (LP, with free 7") | £25 |
| 08 | Vertigo 177 236-7 | ROMANCE AT SHORT NOTICE (LP) | £18 |

(see also Libertines)

DIRTY THREE
| 96 | big Cat ABB 107 | SAD AND DANGEROUS (LP) | £30 |

DIRTY TRICKS
| 75 | Polydor 2383351 | DIRTY TRICKS (LP, red label) | £30 |

DIRTY BEACHES
10	Italian Beach Babes IBB 006	Golden Desert Sun/Night Drive (p/s, 300 only)	£20
10	Italian Beach Babes IBB 010	No Fun/No Where Fast (100 hand-numbered copies, risograph cover)	£20
13	A Records AUK 104LP	WATER PARK OST EP (10" white vinyl)	£15
11	Zoo ZM 010	BADLANDS (LP)	£20

DIRTY FUNKER
06	Spirit DF006	Let's Get Dirty (Vocal)/Let's Get Dirty (Dirty Dub) (12", p/s, Unofficial Banksy artwork, without headband)	£800
06	Spirit DF006	Let's Get Dirty (Vocal)/Let's Get Dirty (Dirty Dub) (12", p/s, Unofficial Banksy artwork, with headband)	£400
08	Spirit DF008	Future (Remixes) (12", white/grey or brown sleeve with Banksy artwork)	£200

DIRTY PROJECTORS
| 11 | Domino RUG 418T | MOUNT WITTENBERG (LP, with Bjork, 3D sleeve, insert, first 500 hand-numbered with signed print) | £20 |

DISASTER
| 91 | Tone Deaf TONE DEAF 1 | WAR CRY (LP) | £50 |

DISCHARGE (1)
81	Clay PLATE 2	WHY (12" EP)	£15
83	Clay PLATE 5	WARNING: HER MAJESTY'S GOVERNMENT CAN SERIOUSLY DAMAGE YOUR HEALTH (12")	£15
82	Clay CLAYLP 3	HEAR NOTHING, SEE NOTHING, SAY NOTHING (LP, original issue has "Pay no more than £3.99" on top right of sleeve)	£40
84	Clay CLAYLP 12	NEVER AGAIN (LP, red vinyl)	£20
86	Clay CLAY LP 19	GRAVE NEW WORLD (LP)	£15
87	Clay CLAY LP 24	1980-1986 (LP)	£20
89	Clay CLAY LP 103	LIVE AT THE CITY GARDEN NEW JERSEY (LP, red vinyl)	£18
90	Clay CLAY 107	THE NIGHTMARE CONTINUES...LIVE (LP)	£20
91	Clay CLAY LP 110	MASSACRE DIVINE (LP)	£15
03	Earmark 40024	DISCHARGE (LP)	£15

(see also Broken Bones)

DISCHARGE (2)
| 80 | Go Round ROUND 001 | DISCHARGE/THE FILTH (split 7, wraparound p/s) | £175 |

(not the Discharge that punks know and love!)

DISCIPLE (1)
| 69 | Parlophone R 5760 | Cherie Alamayonaika/Caucasoid Junkie | £45 |

DISCIPLES
93	Boom Shacka Lacka BSL 001	Prowling Lion/Downbeat Rock (12")	£35
94	Boom Shacka Lacka BSL 002	Return To Addis Ababa/Africa Macka (12")	£30
94	Boom Shacka Lacka BSL 003	Dub Revolution/(Innovation Mix)/(Chamber Of Echoes Mix) (10")	£20
95	Boom Shacka Lacka BSL 004	Chant Of Freedom/Unshackled Version (10")	£20
95	Boom Shacka Lacka BSL 005	Sunrise/Message (12")	£45
02	Boom Shacka Lacka BSL 006	Ilodica Theme Pt.1/Ilodica Theme Pt.2/Fearless Dub Pt.1/Fearless Dub Pt.2 (12")	£15
04	Boom Shacka Lacka BSL 009	Almighty Dub/Zion Rock Dub (12")	£20
95	Cloak & Dagger NLX5 004	RESONATIONS (LP)	£20
96	Boom Shacka Lacka BSL 101	FOR THOSE WHO UNDERSTAND (LP)	£30

DISCIPLES OF BELIAL
| 95 | Praxis PRAXIS 17 | GOAT OF MENDES EP (12") | £40 |
| 97 | Praxis PRAXIS 7 | Lucifer We Praise Thee/Sell Your Soul To The Devil/One God (p/s) | £50 |

DISCIPLES RIDDIM SECTION
| 03 | Jah Tubbys JT 10018 | Roots Workout/Mission Of Dub (10") | £25 |

DISCO DREAM AND ANDROIDS
| 79 | Wake Up WUR 3 | Love Dance/Android Love (12" p/s) | £15 |
| 79 | Wake UP WUR 2 | DISCO DREAM AND THE ANDROIDS (LP) | £50 |

DISCO DUB BAND
| 76 | Movers MO 1 | For the Love Of Money/For The Love Of Money Part 2 | £40 |

DISCO INFERNO
| 91 | Che CHE 2 | OPEN DOORS (LP) | £18 |
| 94 | Rough Trade R 3071 | D.I. GO POP (LP) | £40 |

DISCORDS
| 91 | Hangman 41 UP | SECOND TO NO-ONE (LP) | £15 |

DISCO STUDENTS
| 79 | Yeah Yeah Yeah UHHUH 1 | South Africa House/Kafkaesque (no p/s) | £15 |
| 80 | Yeah Yeah Yeah UHHUH 2 | A Boy With A Penchant For Open-Necked Shirts/Pink Triangles/Credit (no p/s) | £15 |

DISCO/VERY
| 79 | Pinnacle PIN 15 12 | Get It On/Part 2 (12") | £20 |

DISCO VOLANTE
84	Catalyst Box CBR 001	No Motion/Click Punishment Tank Live! (p/s)	£50

DISCO ZOMBIES
79	South Circular SGS 106	Drums Over London/Heartbeats Love (black, white & pink or black, white & green handmade wraparound p/s)	£40
79	Uptown/Wizzo WIZZO 1	THE INVISIBLE (EP)	£25
81	Dining Out TUX 2	Here Come The Buts/Mary Millington (p/s)	£15

(see also Fifty Fantastics)

BABA DISE
69	Gas GAS 118	Wanted/SENSATIONS: I'll Always Love You	£45

DISGUISE
78	Chiswick CHIS 107	Hey Baby/Juvenile Delinquent	£30

DISORDER (1)
80	Ace ACE 12	Air Raid/Law And Disorder (1st 100 in custom 'War Book' p/s)	£200
80	Ace ACE 12	Air Raid/Law And Disorder	£70
80	Durham Book Centre BOOK 1	Reality Crisis/1984 (over sized p/s)	£30

DISORDER (2)
84	Disorder AARGH 1	UNDER THE SCALPEL BLADE (LP, with poster)	£15
85	Disorder AARGH 2	GI FAEN I NASJONALITENTEN DIN (LP)	£15
86	Disorder AARGH 3	ONE DAY SON ALL THIS WILL BE YOURZ (split LP with KAFKA PROCESS)	£15

DISRUPTERS
85	Radical Change 12 RC 8	ALIVE IN THE ELECTRIC CHAIR (12" EP, with insert)	£20
83	Radical Change RCLP1	UNREHEARSED WRONGS (LP)	£30
84	Radical Change RCLP3	PLAYING WITH FIRE (LP)	£20

TOM DISSEVELT
62	Philips 430 736 PE	ELECTRONIC MOVEMENTS (EP)	£20
65	Philips BL 7681	FANTASY IN ORBIT (LP)	£60

DISTAINERS
79	Beck 885	Say Goodbye/Spies In Your Eyes (no p/s, 300 copies)	£60

DISTANT COUSINS
66	CBS 202352	She Ain't Loving You/Here Today, Gone Tomorrow	£18

DISTANT DRUMS
82	Rhythmic RMNS 3	Perfect Eyes/Halloween (p/s)	£25

DISTANT MEMORIES
72	N&G 01	Someone Who Knows/Escape From Reality	£60

DISTINCTION
80	En Ay AM 262	Destiny/Destiny (Dub) (12", p/s)	£70

DISTINCTIVE DRONE
79	No label, no cat no	DISTINCTIVE DRONE (cassette LP, 20 only)	£60

(see also Guardians Of The Ancient Wisdom)

DISTORHAUS
94	Mystic MRD 99401	PLASTIC ANGEL EP (12")	£20

DISTORTED WAVES OF OHM
94	Eurk 12EK 001	ZYRCON (12" EP)	£50
95	Eurk 12EK 002	STRANGE ROTATION (12" EP)	£30
95	Eurk 12EK 003	WITH INTENT TO DISTORT (12" EP)	£20

DISTRACTIONS
79	Factory FAC 12	Time Goes By So Slow/Pillow Fight (p/s)	£18
80	Island ILPS 9604	NOBODY'S PERFECT (LP, sleeve designed by Peter Saville)	£15

DISTRAINERS
79	DJ Records BECK 885	Say Goodbye/Spies In Your Eyes (no p/s, 300 only)	£125

DIVINE COMEDY
92	Setanta SET 011	Europop: New Wave/Intifada/Monitor/Timewatch/Jerusalem/The Rise And Fall (12", p/s)	£15
93	Setanta DC 001	Indulgence No. 1: Hate My Way/Untitled Melody/Europe By Train (picture disc)	£20
94	Setanta DC 002	Indulgence No. 2: A Drinking Song/When The Lights Go Out All Over Europe/Tonight We Fly (handfinished wraparound p/s, stamped labels)	£15
90	Setanta SETLPM 002	FANFARE FOR THE COMIC MUSE (LP, with inner sleeve)	£40
93	Setanta SET LP 11	LIBERATION (LP)	£40
94	Setanta SETLP 13	PROMENADE (LP)	£45
96	Setanta SETLP 25	CASSANOVA (LP)	£35
97	Setanta SETLP 36	A SHORT ALBUM ABOUT LOVE (LP)	£50
98	Setanta SETLP 57	FIN DE SIECLE (LP)	£80
10	Divine Comedy DCRP 101LP	BANG GOES THE KNIGHTHOOD (LP)	£30

DIVISION
72	Wren WR1	Under Your Influence/Dark Dreams	£35

DIVORCE BROTHERS
87	Separation	To Understand/That First Kiss/Walk Out Of The Door/The Divorce/The Liquidator (12")	£20

DIXIEBELLES
64	London REU 1434	THE DIXIE BELLES (EP)	£25
64	London HA-U/SH-U 8152	DOWN AT PAPA JOE'S (LP, with Cornbread & Jerry)	£30

DIXIE CUPS

64	Pye International 7N 25245	Chapel Of Love/Ain't That Nice	£15
64	Red Bird RB 10012	You Should Have Seen The Way He Looked At Me/No True Love	£15
64	Red Bird RB 10017	Little Bell/Another Boy Like Mine	£15
65	Red Bird RB 10024	Iko Iko/Gee Baby Gee	£15
65	Red Bird RB 10032	Gee The Moon Is Shining Bright/I'm Gonna Get You Yet	£20
65	HMV POP 1453	Two Way Poc A Way/That's Where It's At	£15
66	HMV POP 1524	What Kind Of Fool/Danny Boy	£25
66	HMV POP 1557	Love Ain't So Bad (After All)/Daddy Said No	£25
65	Red Bird RB 20100	CHAPEL OF LOVE (LP)	£60
66	HMV CLP 1916	RIDING HIGH (LP)	£50
79	Charly CRM 2004	TEEN ANGUISH (LP)	£15

DIXIE FOUR

| 60s | Rarities RA 3 | THE DIXIE FOUR (EP) | £25 |

DIXIE HUMMINGBIRDS

| 64 | Vogue LAE-P 588 | PRAYER FOR PEACE (LP) | £20 |

DIXIELANDERS

| 63 | Vocalion V 9209 | Cyclone/Mardyke | £35 |

DIXIE PEACH

85	Jah Tubbys JT 005	Just Worries/Pure Worries (12")	£60
85	Jah Tubbys JT 014	Spin Spin/Spin Style (12", with the Offbeat Posse)	£40
86	Jah Tubbys JT 018	Slaughter/Slaughter Mix (12")	£45
86	Y&D YDD 0102	Raggamuffin And Rambo/Ragamuffin Style (12")	£40
87	Y&D YDD 0106	Get Up And Skank/LONG MAN AND THE OFFBEAT POSSE: Skank With Me/OFFBEAT POSSE: The Skank (12")	£40
87	Y&D YDD 0112	Hold Onto Your Man/Tonight Is The Night (12")	£30
88	Y&D YDD 0119	Running Around/Run Come Follow Me Now (12")	£30
00	Jah Tubbys JT 7003	Every Step/DISCIPLES RIDDIM SECTION: Step Dub	£20
01	Jah Tubbys JT 7008	I Heard Them Bawling/OFFBEAT POSSE: Bawling For Riddim	£18
03	Jah Tubbys JT 10013	Sufferers Time/What Am I to Do? (10", with the Offbeat Posse)	£30
03	Jah Tubbys JT 10017	Jah Jah Army/Who's Gonna Stop Us? (10", with the Offbeat Posse)	£30
06	Jah Tubbys JT 10027	Roots Vibration (with the Roots Squad)/Got To Be Humble (with WD Production)	£20

DONALD DIXON

| 71 | Fab FAB 19 | Trouble A Fe You/CORNELL CAMPBELL: Just Can't Find Love (unissued, white label only. Beware: this is not the only Fab 45 with this cat. no)) | £350 |

ERROL DIXON

60	Blue Beat BB 27	Midnight Track/Anytime Anywhere	£20
61	Blue Beat BB 46	Mama Shut Your Door/Too Much Whisky	£20
62	Blue Beat BB 86	Bad Bad Woman/Early This Morning	£20
62	Island WI 017	Morning Train/Lonely Heart	£20
63	Island WI 069	I Love You/Tell Me More	£25
63	Carnival CV 7001	Oo Wee Baby/Twisting And Shaking	£15
63	Carnival CV 7004	Mean And Evil Woman/Tutti Frutti	£15
64	Oriole CB 1945	Rocks In My Pillow/Give Me More Time (as Errol Dixon & Bluebeaters)	£70
66	Blue Beat BB 337	Gloria/Heavy Shuffle	£25
66	Blue Beat BB 344	You're No Good/Midnight Bus	£25
66	Rainbow RAI 104	I Need Someone To Love/I Want (as Errol Dixon & Goodtime Band)	£30
66	Fab EP 1	I Need Someone To Love/I Want (reissue)	£25
67	Ska Beat JB 271	Midnight Party/It Makes No Difference	£25
67	Direct DS 5002	I Don't Want/The Hoop	£60
67	Decca F 12613	Six Questions/Not Again	£15
68	Decca F 12826	Back To The Chicken Shack (as Big City Blues Of Errol Dixon)/ I Done Found Out	£20
69	Doctor Bird DB 1197	Why Hurt Yourself/She Started To Scream	£25
65	Decca DFE 8626	SINGS FATS (EP, with Honeydrippers)	£60
68	Decca LK/SKL 4962	BLUES IN THE POT (LP, with Chicken Shack)	£100
70	Transatlantic TRA 225	THAT'S HOW YOU GOT KILLED BEFORE (LP)	£30

(see also Chicken Shack)

JEFF DIXON

| 67 | Coxsone CS 7015 | The Rock/HAMBOYS: Harder On The Rock | £70 |
| 68 | Studio One SO 2051 | Tickle Me/ENFORCERS: Forgive Me | £80 |

WILLIE DIXON & ALLSTARS

56	London HLU 8297	Walking The Blues/Crazy For My Baby	£1500
56	London HLU 8297	Walking The Blues/Crazy For My Baby (78)	£150
64	Pye International 7N 25270	Crazy For My Baby/Walkin' The Blues (reissue)	£25

DJ ASSASSIN

| 96 | Ugly UGM 007 | THE STALKER EP (12") | £20 |

DJ ASSAULT

| 00 | Mo Wax MWR 115LP | BELLE ISLE TECH (LP as 3 x 12") | £30 |

DJ B AND EZM.

| 92 | Industrial Noize DE 001 | Can't Beat Ruff Beats/Shockin' To The Break Of Dawn (12", stamped white label) | £35 |

DJ CRYSTL

92	Lucky Spin LSR 001	Suicidal/Drop XTC (12")	£20
93	Dee Jay Recordings DJX 008	Crystalize/Deep Space (12")	£30
93	Dee Jay Recordings DJX 010	Meditation/Warpdrive (12")	£50
93	Force Ten FTR 001	The Dark Cryst/Inna Year 3000 (12")	£15

MINT VALUE £

93	Lucky Spin STU-1	**LIVE EP** (12" 1-sided white label)	**£45**
94	Lucky Spin STU-2	**Give It Up** (12" 1-sided white label)	**£50**
94	Dee Jay Recordings DJX 016	**Your Destiny/Sweet Dreamz** (12")	**£25**
94	Dee Jay Recordings DJX 020	**Let It Roll/Paradise** (12")	**£25**
94	Dee Jsy DJX 019	**Meditation/Warpdrive** (Remixes) (12")	**£15**
94	Lucky Spin STU 5	**Let It Roll** (Remix) (12" 1-sided white label)	**£20**

DJ CRYSTL & SLIPMASTER J
92	Lucky Spin LSR 004	**Frantic Situation/Drop XTC** (12")	**£25**

DJ CYCLONE
96	Acid Fever MDMA 9612	**909 TRAX EP: Trak 101/Trak 3/4/Trak 303/Trak 23** (12")	**£20**
96	Acid Fever MDMA 9613	**Innersense** (Halfcore Remix)/**Innersense** (Original Hardcore Mix)/**Mushroom Of Fire/Non-sense** (12")	**£20**
96	Acid Fever MDMA 9614 303	**Joy Ride/Cycloid Spiral Motion/Circular Motion/Cycloid Spiral Slow Motion** (12")	**£20**
97	Acid Fever MDMA 9703	**STATE OF THE PLANET EP** (12" two tracks, other two tracks by OCTODRED)	**£15**

DJ DADO
96	Steppin' Out IAN 045T	**Face It** (Club Mix)/(Radio Edit)/(Alternative Mix)/(Status Mix) (12")	**£15**

DJ DEVICE & DEVIBES
95	Stronghouse STR12 006	**POSITIVE INFLUENCES 2** (12" EP)	**£35**

DJ DEXTROUS & H PEE
95	Subversive SUBVR 001	**Hot Flame/Junglist** (12")	**£40**

DJ DM
08	Not on label PC 2	**LAUGH NOW EP** (12", gold, silver, bronze or green p/s, artwork by Banksy)	**£1600**

DJ EXCEL
91	(No company) EDUC 2	**Just When You Thought It Was Safe/Breakbeat 1/Breakbeat 2/Breakbeat 3/Breakbeat 4** (12")	**£30**

DJ FOKUS
95	Lucky Spin LSR 022	**I Want/Pulse** (12")	**£50**

DJ FOOD
90s	Ninja Tune 106267	**REFRIED FOOD LUNCHBOX** (3-LP)	**£15**
90	Ninja Tune ZEN 02	**JAZZ BRAKES VOL. 1** (LP)	**£15**
91	Ninja Tune ZEN 03	**JAZZ BRAKES VOL. 2** (LP)	**£20**
92	Ninja Tune ZEN 04	**JAZZ BRAKES VOL. 2** (2xLP)	**£15**
92	Ninja Tune ZEN 5	**JAZZ BRAKES VOL. 3** (2-LP)	**£15**
93	Ninja Tune ZEN 06	**JAZZ BRAKES VOL. 4** (2xLP)	**£15**
94	Ninja Tune ZEN 10	**JAZZ BRAKES VOL. 5** (2-LP)	**£15**

DJ FORCE & EVOLUTION
93	Knifeforce KF 003	**Fall Down On Me/The Force Will Be With You/Escape The Feeling/Mine All Mine** (12")	**£30**
93	Knifeforce KF 003	**Fall Down On Me/The Force Will Be With You/Escape The Feeling/Mine All Mine** (12", red vinyl, 200 only)	**£35**
93	Knifeforce KF 011	**Twelve Midnight/Lost It** (12")	**£20**
93	Knifeforce KF 16	**Poltergeist/Perfect Dreams** (10", some on clear vinyl)	**£20**
93	Knifeforce KF 024	**High On Life/Raining Smiles** (12")	**£15**

DJ FORMAT
03	Genuine GEN 005 DLP	**MUSIC FOR THE MATURE B-BOY** (2-LP)	**£30**

DJ GOLLUM
96	UK44 UK44 07	**Pleasant Experience/Mystic Fusion** (12")	**£30**

(see also M-Zone & DJ Gollum)

DJ GUNSHOT
93	GOD 1	**Untitled/Untitled** (White label with Dread Or Dead stamp) (12")	**£15**
94	No U Turn NUT 009	**Wheel N Deal/Marble Mix** (10")	**£15**
95	DAT II DISC D2D 001	**Bad Boy/**(Smooth Mix) (12")	**£15**

DJ GWANGE
94	Legend LEG 007	**Motionless/Adrenaline** (12")	**£60**

DJ HARVEY
96	Noid Recordings NOID 0066	**I Am A Man/MONSIEUR D: Hot Love** (12", black or green vinyl)	**£30**
98	Black Cock Records BK 016	**LOVE HOTEL EP** (12", with Gerry Rooney)	**£15**
98	Black Cock Records BK 017	**LOVE HOTEL EP 2** (12")	**£20**
00	Weekend Inc WKD 069	**Done Turn Me/Protect And Survive** (Fuck Loop) (12")	**£20**

(see also Black Cock, Ersatz)

DJ ILEAGLE
93	Dee Jsy DJX 005	**Crazy/Testify** (12")	**£50**

DJ JINX
92	Music Madness MM 003	**Devotion/Paradise Project/Paradise Project** (Bounty Remix) (12")	**£40**

DJ KRUSH
94	Mo' Wax MWLP 025	**STRICTLY TURNTABLIZED** (2-LP)	**£25**
95	Mo' Wax MWLP 039	**MEISO** (2-LP, inner sleeves)	**£18**
97	Mo' Wax MW 077 LP	**MILIGHT** (2-LP)	**£15**
98	Mo' Wax MW 088 LP	**HOLONIC** (LP)	**£15**
99	Columbia 492893 1	**KAKUSEI** (2-LP)	**£15**

(see also DJ Shadow)

DJ LEWI
95	Jet Star ELT1	**You Better Run/After Hours/Ganja** (12", white label)	**£200**

DJ LJT
93 KIN 2   Untitled/Untitled (stamped white labels "DJ LJT FEATURING KINETIC") (12")................£20

DJ MAYHEM
92 Basement BRSS 008   Damage/Metrix: The Remix/Signal Generator (12")....................£15
92 Basement BRSS 016   Storm Trooper/Cold Acid (12") £15

DJ NUT NUT
94 Production House PNT 058 R   The Rumble (Remixes) (12")........................£25
94 Babylon BR 001   Press Up (VIP Mix)/Press Up (Dub Mix) (12", stamped white labels)........£15
94 Hard Step HRD 001   Special Dedication (Ladies Mix)/Bloodclart Hour (12") £20

DJ POOCH
93 LUcky Spin LSR 014   LUCKY SPIN EP (12") £30

DJ RON
92 Pure BR001   Crackman (Mix 1)/Crackman (Mix 2)/Bad Boy/Untitled (12", stamped white label)........£15
93 Rough Tone RT007   Crackman The Return (Remix D.J. Ron)/Crackman The Return (Booyaka Mix) (E.Q.P. Mix) (12")...........£40

DJ SHADOW
93 Mo' Wax MW 014   In/ Flux/Hindsight (12" picture disc, plastic sleeve, with the Groove Robbers)...............£25
94 Mo' Wax MW 027 P1/2/3   What Does Your Soul Look Like (3 x 10" forming DJ Shadow tag)................£70
02 none   Monosylabik/First Letter From Home (acetate, with letter, 10 copies only) £100
06 Gabacradabra CT 010   Gabracadabra/Acappella Version (7", 500 only hand-stamped white label given away at door of London Indig02 gig 2007)...............£50
10 TNF-1   Def Surrounds Us/I've Been Trying (100 only, hand-made cover) £70
10 New Futility TNF2   Def Surrounds Us/Def Surrounds US (Neil Landstrumm Remix) (12" promo, 100 only electric blue sleeve, green vinyl)...............£40
12 A&M/Talenthouse S75   Come On Riding (Through The Cosmos) (1-sided, 100 only, each with unique art sleeve)...............£70
96 Mo' Wax MW059LP   ENDTRODUCING (2-LP, gatefold, centre opening sleeve)................£40
98 Mo' Wax MW059LP   ENDTRODUCING (2-LP, gatefold, spine opening sleeve)................£40
12 Island 3708138   RECONSTRUCTED (6-CD, DVD, 12" in perspex box with signed certificate, 500 only)........£80
02 Island ILPSD8118586981-1   THE PRIVATE PRESS (2-LP, gatefold)................£45
02 none   PRESS CUTTINGS ('The Private Press' Compacted, 5 copies only) £200
06 Island 1704960   THE OUTSIDER (2-LP)...............£25
(see also Q-Bert, U.N.K.L.E.)

DJ SIDE PHONE/DJ CYDER CLONE
97 Acid Fever MDMA 9705   ACID FLUFF EP (12", three tracks each) £20

DJ TOKEN PACE & TOXIC KEV
92 Face The Bass FBR 001   Losing You/Dreamers Revenge (12") £40

DJ TRACE
91 Orbital 12 ORBIT 11   Inception/Ain't Gonna Wait No More/Love Dove Sound (12") £20
92 Orbital 12OUT 997   Teach Me To Fly/Inception (After Dark Remix) (12")................£18
93 Lucky Spin LSR 003   Lost Entity (London side)/Lost Entity (New York side) (12") £20
93 Dee Jay Recordings DJX 007   Never Felt This Way (One Step Ahead)/Never Felt This Way (Intel Mix)........£18
94 Lucky Spin LSR 017   Coffee (Full Of Flavour Mix)/Coffee (Bonus Beat Mix) (12")..............£40
95 Dee Jay DJX 023   Final Chapta (Rollers)/Final Chapta (Chronic) (12", black, red, yellow or purple vinyl) £40
95 Dee Jay DJX 027   By Any Means Necessary (Speed)/By Any Means Necessary (Original) (12")................£30

DJ TRACE & ED RUSH
93 Lucky Spin LSR 008   Don Bad Man/Clean Gun (12") £25

DJ TRACE/DEFENDER
94 Lucky Spin LSR/BM01   Inside Information/DEFENDER: Feel It (12")...............£20

DJ TREMA & THE AVENGER
93 DBS 22   Untitled/Untitled (12", white label, "DBS 22" etched in run-out groove)................£45

DJ VADIM
98 Ninja Tune ZEN 31/2   U.S.S.R. RECONSTRUCTION (2 x 12")...............£15

DJAGO
72 Duke DU 134   Rebel Train/Babylon Version.......................£15

DJANGO DJANGO
09 Shadazz SHAD 09   Storm/Love's Dart £15
13 Because ILMVF004   Love's Dart (Sal P Liquid Liquid Remix) (12" 1-sided, 50 copies only)................£25
15 Because BEC 5156060   BORN UNDER SATURN (2-LP, orange vinyl with bonus CD) £25

RICHIE D-JAY
79 Arawak ARK DD 004   Grooving In Love/Grooving Version (12")...............£25

DJD
99 Noid NOID 007   Ginger Tree/Feelin The Party Groove (12") £15

D-LIVIN
92 D-Livin DL01   Why/Up Their Head/Make A Joyful Noize/Yard An Gorage (12")................£25

DMS
91 Production House PNT 032   Exterminate (12") £15
92 Production House PNT 039   Vengeance/Love Overdose (Remix) (12") £15

DMX KREW
07 Revoke REVOKE 004   SYNTHE SOUND EP (12", test pressing) £50
96 Rephlex CAT 029LP   SOUND OF THE STREET (2-LP) £30
97 Rephlex CAT 053LP   FFRESSSHH! (2-LP) £30
98 Rephlex CAT 061LP   NU ROMANTIX (LP) £25

			MINT VALUE £

D.N.A.

| 99 | Rephlex CAT 086LP | WE ARE DMX (LP) | £35 |

D.N.A.

| 80 | CPEP 002 | SHOCK ROCK EP | £30 |

DNA (1)

| 81 | Rough Trade RTO 86 | A TASTE OF DNA (12" EP, p/s) | £15 |

DNA (3)

| 83 | Confidential FILE 001 | EXTENDED PLAY | £15 |

DNV

| 79 | New Pleasures Z2 | Mafia/Death In Venice/Goodbye 70s (foldout p/s) | £20 |

(see also Another Pretty Face, Waterboys, TV21)

D.O.A.

| 83 | Alt. Tentacles VIRUS 31 | BLOODIED BUT UNBOWED — THE DAMAGE TO DATE 1978-84 (LP) | £15 |

CARL DOBKINS JNR.

| 59 | Brunswick 05811 | If You Don't Want My Lovin'/Love Is Everything | £15 |
| 60 | Brunswick LAT 8329 | CARL DOBKINS JNR. (LP) | £21 |

BONNIE DOBSON

70	RCA SF 8079	BONNIE DOBSON (LP)	£35
72	Argo ZFB 79	BONNIE DOBSON (LP)	£30
76	Polydor 2383 400	MORNING DEW (LP)	£15

DOBBY DOBSON (& DELTAS)

65	King KG 1008	Cry A Little Cry/Diamonds And Pearls (as Dobby Dobson & Deltas)	£25
67	Trojan TR 011	Loving Pauper/TOMMY McCOOK & SUPERSONICS: Sir Don	£65
68	Studio One SO 2068	Walking In The Footsteps/SOUL VENDORS: Studio Rock	£80
68	Coxsone CS 7058	Seems To Me I'm Losing You/GAYLADS: Red Rose	£80
69	Blue Cat BS 171	Strange/Your New Love	£40
69	Punch PH 12	The Masquerade Is Over/Love For Ambition	£15
70	Success RE 906	Crazy/RUPIE EDWARDS ALL STARS: Your New Love	£15
70	Big BG 303	That Wonderful Sound/I Wasn't Born Yesterday	£15
69	Pama SECO 33	STRANGE (LP)	£80
70	Trojan TBL 145	THAT WONDERFUL SOUND (LP)	£60

(see also Chuck & Dobby, Ernest Wilson & Freddy)

LYN DOBSON

| 74 | Fresh Air 6370 501 | JAM SANDWICH (LP) | £40 |

(see also Manfred Mann, Soft Machine, Miller Anderson)

DOC SCOTT

92	Absolute 2 ABS 006DJR	The N.H.S. EP Vol 2 - The Second Chapter (Remix) EP (12")	£60
94	Metalheadz MET 004	Far Away (Fourteen Flavors Of Funk)/It's Yours (12")	£18
95	Metalheadz METH 015	Drumz '95 (Nasty Habits Remix)/Blue Skies (12")	£15
94	Reinforced RIVET 1256	Last Action Hero EP (12")	£15
94	Metalheadz MH 001	Doc Scott/GOLDIE : Unreleased Metal (12")	£20

ROY DOCKER

| 68 | Domain D3 | Mellow Moonlight/MUSIC THROUGH SIX: Riff Raff | £30 |
| 69 | Pama PM 750 | When/Go | £15 |

DR. ALIMANTADO

73	Atra ATRA 007	Return Of Muhummad Ali/Black Love	£20
75	Sun & Star ST 003	Best Dress Chicken/She Wreng-Ep	£25
77	Greensleeves GRE 002	Born For A Purpose/Reason For Living (with the Rebels)	£15
78	Greensleeves GRE 13	Best Dressed Chicken In Town/Can't Conquer Natty Dreadlocks (yellow vinyl)	£15
79	Greensleeves GRED 10	Born For A Purpose/Reason For Living/Still Alive/Life All Over (12", with the Rebels)	£25
78	Greensleeves GREL 1	BEST DRESSED CHICKEN IN TOWN (LP, some copies wit promo pic)	£40
79	Ital ISDA 5000	KINGS BREAD (LP)	£30
81	Greensleeves GREL 22	SONS OF THUNDER (LP)	£30

DR. ATOMIC

| 93 | Guerilla GRRR42 | Schudelfloss (12") | £20 |

DOCTOR BIRDS

| 77 | JS JSM 001 | Smoking (Smoking My Ganja)/Rock With Me (12") | £30 |

DOCTOR BROWN

| 95 | Magic Gnome | ANOTHER REALM (LP, 500 only) | £15 |

DR. FEELGOOD & THE INTERNS (U.S.)

62	Columbia DB 4838	Dr. Feelgood/Mister Moonlight	£25
64	Columbia DB 7228	Blang Dong/The Doctor's Doogie	£25
66	CBS 202099	Don't Tell Me No Dirty/Where Did You Go	£20
68	Capitol CL 15569	Sugar Bee/You're So Used To It	£20
64	Columbia SEG 8310	DR. FEELGOOD AND THE INTERNS (EP)	£70

(see also Piano Red)

DR. FEELGOOD (U.K.)

75	United Artists UAS 29727	DOWN BY THE JETTY (LP, mono only)	£40
75	United Artists UAS 29880	MALPRACTICE (LP)	£25
76	United Artists UAS 29990	STUPIDITY (LP, with stickered covers & bonus 7": "Riot In Cell Block No. 9"/"Johnny B. Goode" [FEEL 1])	£50
77	United Artists UAS 30075	SNEAKIN' SUSPICION (LP)	£15
79	United Artists UAK 30239	AS IT HAPPENS (LP, with inner sleeve & bonus 7" "Encore EP": "Riot In Cell Block No. 9"/"The Blues Had A Baby And They Named It Rock'N'Roll"/"Lights Out"/"Great Balls Of Fire" [p/s, FEEL 2], with inner sleeve)	£20

85	Edsel ED 160	DOWN BY THE JETTY (LP, reissue)	£15

(see also Wilko Johnson, Lew Lewis)

DR. JOHN (THE NIGHT TRIPPER)

68	Atlantic 587/588 147	GRIS GRIS (LP, plum label, mono/stereo)	£80
69	Atco 228 018	BABYLON (LP, plum label)	£40
70	Atco 2400 015	REMEDIES (LP, plum label)	£40
71	Atlantic 2400 161	THE SUN, MOON AND HERBS (LP, plum label, gatefold sleeve with insert)	£40
72	Atlantic K 40384	GUMBO (LP, green & orange label, gatefold sleeve)	£30
72	Atlantic K 40168	GRIS GRIS (LP, reissue, green & orange label)	£25
72	Atlantic K 40250	THE SUN, MOON AND HERBS (LP, reissue, green & orange label, gatefold sleeve with insert)	£30
73	Atco K 50017	IN THE RIGHT PLACE (LP, U.K. disc in U.S. stickered 3-way gatefold sleeve)	£40
73	CBS 65659	TRIUMVIRATE (LP, with John Hammond & Mike Bloomfield)	£20
74	Atlantic K 50035	DESITIVELY BONNAROO (LP)	£20
75	DJM DJSLM 2019	CUT ME WHILE I'M HOT (LP)	£22
75	United Artists UAG 29902	HOLLYWOOD BE THY NAME (LP, with inner sleeve)	£20

DR. K'S BLUES BAND

68	Spark SRLP 101	DR. K'S BLUES BAND (LP, red/silver label)	£120

DR. MIX & THE REMIX

79	Rough Trade ROUGH 6	Wall Of Noise (12")	£20

DR. OCTAGON

96	Mo' Wax MW 046LP	DR OCTAGON (3-LP)	£30
96	Mo' Wax MW064LP	INSTRUMENTALYST (OCTAGON BEATS) (LP)	£25

DOCTOR PABLO

84	On U-Sound ON U 30	NORTH OF THE RIVER THAMES (LP, with Dub Syndicate)	£25

DR. STRANGELY STRANGE

69	Island CIR 15006	KIP OF THE SERENES (cassettte promo)	£50
69	Island ILPS 9106	KIP OF THE SERENES (LP, pink label, with black/orange circle logo)	£400
69	Island ILPS 9106	KIP OF THE SERENES (LP, pink label, with white 'i' logo)	£200
69	Island ILPS 9106	KIP OF THE SERENES (LP, later 'palm-tree' label with remix)	£100
70	Vertigo 6360 009	HEAVY PETTING (LP, gatefold sleeve, large swirl label; original pressing has machine etched matrix in the run out grooves, beware of counterfeits)	£600
86	Timeless TIME 702	KIP OF THE SERENES (LP, reissue)	£20

(see also Sweeney's Men, Gary Moore)

DR. TECHNICAL & MACHINES

83	Hawkfan HWFB 1	Zones/Processed (1-sided with insert, mail-order issue, no p/s)	£25

(see also Hawkwind)

DR. WEST'S MEDICINE SHOW & JUNK BAND

68	Page One POF 061	Bullets La Verne/Jigsaw	£50
69	Page One POLS 017	THE EGGPLANT THAT ATE CHICAGO (LP)	£25

(see also Norman Greenbaum)

DR. WHO

76	Argo ZSW 564	DR. WHO AND THE PESCATONS (LP, spoken word, read by Tom Baker & Elizabeth Sladen)	£18
79	BBC REC 364	GENESIS OF THE DALEKS (LP, spoken word)	£15
81	RNIB	TALKING BOOK (reel-to-reel tape, read by Gabriel Wolf)	£20
82	BBC 2LP-22001	DOCTOR WHO COLLECTOR'S EDITION (2-LP, includes "Genesis Of The Daleks" [BBC 22364], "Sound Effects" [BBC 22316], & bonus 7" "Doctor Who"/"The Astronauts" [RESL 451], with poster)	£30

(see also BBC Radiophonic Workshop, Century 21, Jon Pertwee)

DR. Z

70	Fontana 6007 023	Lady Ladybird/People In The Street	£100
71	Vertigo 6360 048	THREE PARTS TO MY SOUL (LP, gatefold, small swirl label)	£2000

(see also Gorilla Grip)

DODD'S ALLSTARS

69	Coxsone CS 7096	Mother Aitken (actually by Lord Power)/What A Love (actually by Denzil Laing)	£80

NELLA DODDS

65	Pye 7N 25281	Come See About Me/You Don't Love Me Anymore	£50
65	Pye 7N 25281	Come See About Me/You Don't Love Me Anymore (DJ Copy)	£75
65	Pye 7N 25291	Finders Keepers, Losers Weepers/A Girl's Life	£35
65	Pye 7N 25291	Finders Keepers, Losers Weepers/A Girl's Life (DJ Copy)	£60

DODGERS (1)

60	Downbeat CHA 2	Let's Make A Whole Lot Of Love/You Make Me Happy	£25

DODGY

93	A&M 540 0821	THE DODGY ALBUM (LP, printed inner)	£30
94	A&M 540 02821	HOMEGROWN (LP, printed inner)	£60
96	A&M 540 577-1	FREE PEACE SWEET (2LP, printed inners)	£40

DODO'S

67	Polydor BM 56153	I Made Up My Mind/Can't Make It Out	£30

DOES IT OFFEND YOU, YEAH?

08	Does It . . . DIOYYT5002	LIVE @ THE FEZ (12", p/s)	£20
08	Virgin V3045	YOU HAVE NO IDEA WHAT YOU'RE GETTING YOURSELF INTO (LP, printed inner, download card)	£100

DOGFEET

71	Reflection HRS 7	Sad Story/On The Road	£15

MINT VALUE £

71	Reflection HRS 12	Since I Went Away/Evil Woman	£35
70	Reflection REFL 8	DOGFEET (LP, white/brown label)	£1000
94	Kissing Spell CA 36001	DOGFEET (LP, reissue)	£25

DOGGEREL BANK
73	Charisma CAS 1079	SILVER FACES (LP, gatefold sleeve, large "Mad Hatter" label)	£25
75	Charisma CAS 1102	MISTER SKILLCORN DANCES (LP, small "Mad Hatter" label)	£30

BILL DOGGETT
56	Parlophone CMSP 39	Honky Tonk (Parts 1 & 2) (gold label lettering, export issue)	£25
56	Parlophone R 4231	Honky Tonk (Parts 1 & 2) (gold label lettering, later silver)	£15
61	Warner Bros WB 46	You Can't Sit Down (Parts 1 & 2)	£15
58	Parlophone PMD 1067	DAME DREAMING (10" LP)	£15
59	Parlophone PMD 1073	DANCE AWHILE WITH DOGGETT (10" LP)	£20

(see also Ella Fitzgerald, Earl Bostic)

DOGHEAD
73	Sacred SC 01	Come Out Shooting/Passing The Buck	£20

DOGMA CATS
80	Leisure Sounds SRS 33	Experts/Choke (p/s)	£20

DOGMATIC ELEMENT
82	Cattle Company CC001/ 562CUS 1412	Strange Passion/Just Friends (p/s, 1000 only)	£15

DOG ON A ROPE
98	Chase Out DAN 1	SPIKE (LP)	£15

DOGROSE
72	Satril SAT 2	Paradise Row/Sunday Morning	£15
73	Satril SAT 6	All For The Love Of City Lights/All Of The Love Of Each Other	£20
72	Satril SATL 4002	ALL FOR THE LOVE OF DOGROSE (LP)	£30

DOGS D'AMOUR
88	China WOL 7	THE (UN)AUTHORISED BOOTLEG (LP)	£30

DOG SOLDIER
75	United Artists UA 29769	DOG SOLDIER (LP)	£25

(see also Miller Anderson, Keef Hartley)

THE DOG THAT BIT PEOPLE
71	Parlophone R 5880	Lovely Lady/Merry-Go-Round	£45
71	Parlophone PCS 7125	THE DOG THAT BIT PEOPLE (LP, black/silver label with boxed logo)	£800

(see also Norman Haines, Locomotive)

DOGWATCH
79	Bridgehouse BHLP 002	PENFRIEND (LP, with insert)	£20

JIM DOHERTY TRIO
65	Decca LK 4684	EXECUTIVE SUITE (LP)	£60

DOLE
78	Ultimate ULT 402	New Wave Love/Hungry Men No Longer Steal Sheep But Are There Hanging Judges? (die-cut p/s)	£30

ANDY DOLL
63	Starlite STLP II	ON STAGE (LP, by Andy Doll Band & Guests)	£15

LINDA DOLL & SUNDOWNERS
64	Piccadilly 7N 35166	Bonie Maronie/He Don't Want Your Love Anymore	£15

DOLLY MIXTURE
80	Chrysalis CHS 2459	Baby It's You/New Look Baby (p/s)	£30
81	Respond RESP 1	Been Teen/Honky Honda/Ernie Ball (p/s)	£25
82	Respond RESP 4	Everything And More/You And Me On The Sea Shore (p/s)	£20
83	Dead Good Dolly Platters DMS 1	Remember This/Listening Pleasure/Borinda's Lament (p/s)	£40
84	Cordelia ERICAT 017	FIRESIDE EP (12" p/s)	£30
84	DM 1	DEMONSTRATION TAPES (2-LP, rubber stamped, hand-numbered signed sleeves with insert)	£150
10	DMBOX 1	EVERYTHING AND MORE (3-CD box set)	£90
10	Germs Of Youth GERMOS 08	DEMONSTRATION TAPES (2-LP, rubber stamped, hand-numbered signed sleeves with poster, 300 only)	£100
11	For Us FU 043	REMEMBER THIS: THE SINGLES 1980-1984 (LP, black vinyl)	£80
11	For Us FU 043	REMEMBER THIS: THE SINGLES 1980-1984 (LP, white vinyl)	£100
19	Sealed SEAL 005	OTHER MUSIC (LP)	£20
19	Sealed SEAL 005	OTHER MUSIC (LP, yellow vinyl)	£30
19	Spa Green SPA 001	DEMONSTRATION TAPES (2-LP, red vinyl)	£50
19	Spa Green SPA 001	DEMONSTRATION TAPES (2-LP)	£35

(see also Coming Up Roses)

DOLPHINS
65	Stateside SS 375	Hey Da Da Dow/I Don't Want To Go On Without You	£15

ERIC DOLPHY
60	Esquire 21-123	OUTWARD BOUND (LP)	£150
61	Esquire 32-153	OUT THERE (LP)	£100
61	Esquire 32-173	AT THE 5 SPOT VOL. 1.(LP)	£150
64	Fontana TL5284	LAST DATE (LP)	£60
65	Fontana 688521XL	MEMORIAL ALBUM (LP)	£35
69	Transatlantic PR 7311	OUTWARD BOUND (LP)	£20
67	Xtra 5039	SCREAMING THE BLUES (LP, with Oliver Nelson Sextet)	£25

ERIC DOLPHY & BOOKER LITTLE
66   Stateside SL 10160   ERIC DOLPHY AND BOOKER LITTLE MEMORIAL ALBUM (LP).........................£15

DOME
80   Dome DOME 1   DOME (LP)...£25
80   Dome DOME 2   DOME 2 (LP)...£25
81   Dome DOME 3   DOME 3 (LP)...£25
(see also Wire, Gilbert & Lewis, Cupol, Bruce Gilbert, P'o, Duet Emmo)

DOMESTIC BLISS
80   Woodbine ST WSR 004   Child Battery/Life (p/s)...£15

DOMINIC WAXING LYRICAL
86   Neptune LPPIE 020   DOMINIC WAXING LYRICAL (LP)...£15

FATS DOMINO
78s
54   London HL 8007   Rose Mary/You Said You Love Me £40
54   London HL 8063   Little School Girl/You Done Me Wrong.................................£40
54   London HL 8096   Don't Leave Me This Way/Something's Wrong £30
55   London HL 8124   Love Me/Don't You Hear Me Calling You..............................£30
55   London HL 8133   Thinking Of You/I Know £25
58   London HLP 8727   Young School Girl/It Must Be Love £15
58   London HLP 8759   Whole Lotta Loving/Coquette..£15
59   London HLP 8822   When The Saints Go Marching In/Telling Lies £20
59   London HLP 8865   Margie/I'm Ready...£20
59   London HLP 8942   I Want To Walk You Home/I'm Gonna Be A Wheel Some Day ...£20
59   London HLP 9005   Be My Guest/I've Been Around £40
60   London HLP 9073   Country Boy/If You Need Me £40
60   London HLP 9163   Walking To New Orleans/Don't Come Knockin' £60

SINGLES
55   London 45-HL 8124   Love Me/Don't You Hear Me Calling You.............................£175
55   London HL 8133   Thinking Of You/I Know £125
55   London HLU 8173   Ain't That A Shame/La La £80
56   London HLU 8256   Bo Weevil/Don't Blame It On Me £100
56   London HLU 8280   I'm In Love Again/My Blue Heaven £100
56   London HLU 8309   When My Dream Boat Comes Home/So Long £50
56   London HLU 8330   Blueberry Hill/I Can't Go On (Rosalie)..................................£50
57   London HLU 8356   Honey Chile/Don't You Know..£100
57   London HLP 8377   Blue Monday/What's The Reason I'm Not Pleasing You.......£50
(Originally issued with triangular centres & gold lettering labels; later silver-label re-pressings are worth around half these values.)
57   London HLP 8407   I'm Walkin'/I'm In The Mood For Love £15
57   London HLP 8449   The Valley Of Tears/It's You I Love £15
57   London HLP 8519   Wait And See/I Still Love You £15
58   London HLP 8575   The Big Beat (From The Film)/I Want You To Know £20
58   London HLP 8628   Sick And Tired/No, No..£20
58   London HLP 8663   Little Mary/The Prisoner's Song £20
58   London HLP 8727   Young School Girl/It Must Be Love £30
58   London HLP 8759   Whole Lotta Loving/Coquette...£20
(HLP 8407 through to 8822 45s were issued with triangular centres & silver lettering on all-black labels; later copies are worth around half these values.)
59   London HLP 9005   Be My Guest/I've Been Around (triangular centre)...........£20
61   London HLP 9374   It Keeps Rainin'/I Just Cry £20
64   HMV POP 1303   If You Don't Know What Love Is/Something You Got Baby...£40
67   Liberty LBF 12055   It Keeps Rainin'/Blue Monday £15
67   Liberty LBF 12055   It Keeps Rainin'/Blue Monday (DJ Copy).............................£30
68   Reprise RS 20696   Honest Mamas Love Their Papas Better/One For The Highway ...£20
68   Reprise RS 20763   Lady Madonna/One For The Highway £15
69   Reprise RS 20810   Everybody's Got Something To Hide Except Me And My Monkey/ So Swell When You're Well..£30

EXPORT SINGLES
57   London HL 7028   Wait And See/I Still Love You £30
58   London HL 7040   Sick And Tired/No, No..£30
58   London HL 7054   The Big Beat (From The Film)/Little Mary £30

EPs
55   London RE-P 1022   BLUES FOR LOVE (1st pressing with gold lettering label)...........£30
55   London RE-P 1022   BLUES FOR LOVE (2nd pressing with silver lettering label).......£20
56   London RE-U 1062   BLUES FOR LOVE VOL. 2 (1st pressing with gold label)..........£30
56   London RE-U 1062   BLUES FOR LOVE VOL. 2 (2nd pressing with silver label).......£20
57   London RE-U 1073   FATS (export issue, plain sleeve) £40
57   London RE-P 1079   HERE COMES FATS VOL. 1...£30
58   London RE-P 1080   HERE COMES FATS VOL. 2...£30
58   London RE-P 1115   CARRY ON ROCKIN' PART 1 ....£60
58   London RE-P 1116   CARRY ON ROCKIN' PART 2 ....£60
58   London RE-P 1117   BLUES FOR LOVE VOL. 3 ....£30
58   London RE-P 1121   BLUES FOR LOVE VOL. 4 ....£30
58   London RE-P 1138   HERE COMES FATS VOL. 3...£30
59   London RE-P 1206   THE ROCKIN' MR. D VOL. 1...£30
59   London RE-P 1207   THE ROCKIN' MR. D VOL. 2...£30
(The above EPs were originally issued with triangular centres; round-centre re-pressings are worth two-thirds these values.)
60   London RE-P 1261   BE MY GUEST £30

MINT VALUE £

60	London RE-P 1265	THE ROCKIN' MR. D VOL. 3	£30
62	London RE-P 1340	WHAT A PARTY	£30
64	HMV 7EG 8862	RED SAILS IN THE SUNSET	£15
65	Liberty LEP 4026	MY BLUE HEAVEN	£20
66	Liberty LEP 4045	ROLLIN'	£20

ALBUMS

56	London HA-U 2028	FATS' ROCK AND ROLLIN'	£90
56	London HA-P 2041	CARRY ON ROCKIN'	£100
57	London HA-P 2052	HERE STANDS FATS DOMINO	£90
56	London HA-P 2073	THIS IS FATS DOMINO	£60
58	London HA-P 2087	THIS IS FATS	£60
58	London HA-P 2135	THE FABULOUS "MR. D"	£50
59	London HA-P 2223	LET'S PLAY FATS DOMINO	£50
60	London HA-P 2312	A LOT OF DOMINOES!	£40
61	London HA-P 2364	I MISS YOU SO	£40
61	London HA-P 2420	LET THE FOUR WINDS BLOW	£40
61	London HA-P 2426	WHAT A PARTY	£40
62	London HA-P 2447	TWISTIN' THE STOMP	£40
63	London HA-P 8039	JUST DOMINO	£40
63	London HA-P 8084	WALKING TO NEW ORLEANS	£40
63	HMV CLP 1690	HERE COMES FATS DOMINO (also stereo CSD 1520)	£25
63	HMV CLP 1740	FATS ON FIRE (also stereo CSD 1543)	£25
65	HMV CLP 1821	GETAWAY WITH FATS DOMINO (also stereo CSD 1580)	£18
65	Mercury (S)MCL 20070	DOMINO '65 (mono/stereo)	£15
68	Stateside (S)SL 10240	FANTASTIC FATS	£15

DOMINOES (JAMAICA)

68	Melody MRC 001	Tears In Your Eyes/Johnny Darling	£30
68	Melody MRC 002	A Tribute (actually by Ann Reid)/**Hooray** (actually by Uniques)	£110

DOMINOES (U.K.)

60	Reading Rag LYN 545	Bye Bye Johnny/Yakety Yak	£15

DOMINOES (U.S.)

51	Vogue V 9012	Sixty Minute Man/I Can't Escape From You (78)	£50
52	Vogue V 2135	Have Mercy, Baby/That's What You're Doing To Me (78)	£40
67	Vogue V 212	Sixty Minute Man/I Can't Escape From You	£30

(see also Billy Ward & Dominoes, Clyde McPhatter, Jackie Wilson)

DON, DICK & JIMMY

55	London HL 8117	You Can't Have Your Cake And Eat It Too/That's What I Like	£20
56	London RE-U 1043	DON, DICK AND JIMMY (EP)	£20

MIKE DONALD & BOB SIDDALL

74	Tradition Century TSC 2	A BUG'S EYE VIEW (LP, 100 copies only)	£30

(see also Mike Donald)

MIKE DONALD

71	Folk Heritage FHR 021	YORKSHIRE SONGS OF THE BROAD ACRES (LP, first pressing, textured sleeve with black and white photo)	£25
71	Folk Heritage FHR 021	YORKSHIRE SONGS OF THE BROAD ACRES (LP, second pressing, laminated sleeve with colour photo)	£15
72	Galliard GAL 4020	NORTH BY NORTH EAST (LP)	£15

ERIC DONALDSON

70s	Serengeti SGTI 01	Penny Farthing/Evil Eyes (12")	£80
05	Black Art/Trojan TJLBX 244/6	Stand Up (with the Keystones)/**UPSETTERS: Dub Fo Yo Right** (reissue)	£30
72	Trojan TRL 42	ERIC DONALDSON (LP)	£30

(see also Prunes, Satchmo)

DON & DENNY

60s	Loop LOO 504	(Ain't That)**Just Like Me**/Feeling Groovy	£40

DON & DEWEY

64	London HL 9897	Get Your Hat/Annie Lee	£20
66	Cameo Parkway CP 750	Soul Motion/Stretchin' Out	£50
67	Sue WI 4032	Soul Motion/Stretchin' Out (reissue)	£30
71	Specialty SNTF 5006	DON AND DEWEY (LP)	£15

(see also Dewey Terry)

DON & JUAN

62	London HLX 9529	What's Your Name?/Chicken Necks	£15

DONAVAN/FULLWOOD

76	Stop Point	Deeper And Deeper/Hit After Hit	£35

DONAYS

62	Oriole CBA 1770	Devil In His Heart/Bad Boy	£150

DON CABALLERO

93	City Slang 04929-08	FOR RESPECT (LP)	£15

LONNIE DONEGAN

SINGLES

55	Decca F 10647	Rock Island Line/John Henry (as Lonnie Donegan Skiffle Group) (tri-centre)	£15
56	Decca FJ 10695	Diggin' My Potatoes/Bury My Body (as Lonnie Donegan Skiffle Group) (tri-centre)	£15
56	Columbia DB 3850	On A Christmas Day/Take My Hand, Precious Lord (as Lonnie Donegan with Chris Barber's Jazz Band)	£20

58	Pye Jazz 7NJ 2006	Midnight Special/When The Sun Goes Down	£25

ALBUMS

56	Pye Nixa NPT 19012	LONNIE DONEGAN SHOWCASE (10")	£15
57	Pye Nixa NPTs19027	LONNIE (10" LP, stereo)	£20
58	Pye Nixa NPT 19027	LONNIE (10" LP)	£15
62	Pye NPL 18073	SING HALLELUJAH (LP)	£15
65	Pye NPL 18126	THE LONNIE DONEGAN FOLK ALBUM	£18

(see also Chris Barber)

JIMMY DONLEY

57	Brunswick 05715	South Of The Border/The Trail Of The Lonesome Pine	£20
59	Brunswick 05807	The Shape You Left Me In/What Must I Do	£100
59	Brunswick 05807	The Shape You Left Me In/What Must I Do (78)	£20

DONNA & FREEDOM SINGERS

70	Bamboo BAM 53	Oh Me Oh My (actually by Jerry Jones)/JACKIE MITTOO: Gold Mine	£25

RAL DONNER

61	Parlophone R 4859	Please Don't Go/I Didn't Figure On Him (To Come Back)	£15
62	Parlophone R 4889	I Don't Need You/She's Everything (I Wanted You To Be)	£15
62	Stateside SS 109	Bells Of Love/Loveless Life	£20
63	Reprise R 20141	I Got Burned/A Tear In My Eye	£30

DONNIE & DREAMERS

61	Top Rank JAR 571	Count Every Star/Dorothy	£50

DON & OLLIE

79	Cartridge CR D 106	Superman/Have A Party (12")	£100

DO NOTHING

19	No label or Cat no	Gangs/Handshakes (p/s)	£20
20	Exact Truth DNLJ00212	ZERO DOLLAR BILL EP (12", p/s)	£20

DONOVAN

66	Pye 7N 17088	Remember The Alamo/The Ballad Of A Crystal Man	£15
68	Pye 7N 17660	To Susan On The West Coast Waiting/Atlantis (unreleased)	£0
72	private pressing	The Music Makers (one-sided, paper sleeve, 50 only)	£50
75	Epic EPC 2661	Rock'n'Roll With Me/Divine Daze Of Deathless Delight (in p/s)	£20
65	Pye NEP 24229	COLOURS (EP)	£15
66	Pye NEP 24239	DONOVAN VOL. 1 (EP)	£15
68	Pye NEP 24287	CATCH THE WIND (EP)	£15
68	Pye NEP 24299	HURDY GURDY DONOVAN (EP)	£20
65	Pye NPL 18117	WHAT'S BIN DID AND WHAT'S BIN HID (LP, some with misprinted Side 2 label)	£35
65	Pye NPL 18128	FAIRYTALE (LP, some copies with blank rear sleeve)	£50
66	World Records ST 951	DONOVAN (LP)	£18
67	Pye NPL 18181	SUNSHINE SUPERMAN (LP)	£50
68	Pye NPL 20000	A GIFT FROM A FLOWER TO A GARDEN (2-LP, black or navy blue box set, separate halves or with taped hinge; with 12 inserts in folder, mono)	£125
68	Pye N(S)PL 20000	A GIFT FROM A FLOWER TO A GARDEN (2-LP, black or navy blue box set, separate halves or with taped hinge; with 12 inserts in folder, stereo)	£100
68	Pye NPL 18237	DONOVAN IN CONCERT (LP, mono)	£20
68	Pye N(S)PL 18237	DONOVAN IN CONCERT (LP, stereo)	£18
70	Dawn DNLS 3009	OPEN ROAD (LP, gatefold sleeve)	£30
71	Dawn DNLD 4001	H.M.S. DONOVAN (2-LP, First pressing, orange label, MATRIX: DNLP 4001 A-1 *T/B-1 *T/C-1*T/D-1*T :gatefold sleeve, with foldout poster)	£150
72	Dawn DNLD 4001	H.M.S. DONOVAN (2-LP, Second pressing, lilac label, gatefold sleeve, with foldout poster)	£60
72	Dawn DNLD 4001	H.M.S. DONOVAN (2-LP, Second pressing, lilac label, gatefold sleeve, without foldout poster)	£20
73	Dawn DNLD 4001	H.M.S. DONOVAN (2-LP, Third pressing, white label with pink and blue sunrise, gatefold sleeve)	£40
71	Dawn DNLD 4001	H.M.S. DONOVAN (2-LP, gatefold sleeve, without foldout poster)	£25
73	Pye 11PP 102	FOUR SHADES ("H.M.S. Donovan"/"Greatest Hits"/"Open Road") (4-LP box set)	£50
73	Epic EPC 69050	ESSENCE TO ESSENCE (LP, gatefold sleeve, lyric insert, with sticker)	£15

(see also Jeff Beck, Open Road)

DONTELLS

65	Fontana TF 566	In Your Heart/Nothing But Nothing	£50

DICKY DOO & DON'TS

58	London HLU 8589	Click Click/Did You Cry	£20
58	London HLU 8754	Leave Me Alone/Wild, Wild Party (with Orchestra)	£25

DOOF

80	Namedrop NR1	EXIST (10" mini-LP, with booklet)	£25

(see also Exhibit A)

DOOKIE SQUAD

94	Dookie DS 001	6FT Under/Mad Shit (12")	£15

DOOLEY SISTERS

55	London HL 8128	Ko Ko Mo (I Love You So)/Heart Throb	£30

DOOM (1)

89	Discard DISC 001	POLICE BASTARD EP	£15
88	Peaceville VILE 4	WAR CRIMES INHUMAN BEINGS (LP, white vinyl)	£35
89	Strange Fruit SFPMA 203	DOUBLE PEEL SESSIONS (LP, with insert)	£15
89	Peaceville VILE 11	BURY THE DEBT NOT THE DEAD (split LP with NO SECURITY)	£18

DOOM (2)
93	Discipline DISCLP10	THE GREATEST INVENTION (mini-LP)	£20

JOHN DOONAN
72	Leader LEA 2043	FLUTE FOR THE FEIS (LP)	£15

DOOR & THE WINDOW
79	NR NR 1	Subculture/Fashion Slaves/Nostradamus/Don't Kill Colin/Wurst Ban	£25
80	NB Records NB 5	DETAILED TWANG (LP, blank labels)	£18
80	NB Records NB 9	MUSIC AND MOVEMENT (live cassette)	£15

(see also Alternative TV)

DOORS

SINGLES
67	Elektra EKSN 45009	Break On Through (To The Other Side)/End Of The Night	£50
67	Elektra EKSN 45012	Alabama Song (Whisky Bar)/Take It As It Comes	£25
67	Elektra EKSN 45014	Light My Fire/The Crystal Ship	£20
67	Elektra EKSN 45017	People Are Strange/Unhappy Girl	£20
67	Elektra EKSN 45022	Love Me Two Times/Moonlight Drive	£15
68	Elektra EKSN 45030	We Could Be So Good Together/The Unknown Soldier	£15

ALBUMS
67	Elektra EKL 4007	THE DOORS (1st mono pressing, orange labels with black lettering, 'manufactured by Elektra records' on label, in U.S. printed sleeve, mono)	£200
67	Elektra EKL 4007	THE DOORS (2nd mono pressing, orange labels with black lettering, 'manufactured by Polydor' on label records' on label in fully laminated UK printed sleeve, mono)	£150
67	Elektra EKS 4007	THE DOORS (1st stereo pressing, orange labels with black lettering, 'manufactured by Elektra records' on label, in U.S. sleeve, stereo)	£140
67	Elektra EKS 74007	THE DOORS (2nd stereo pressing, orange labels with black lettering, 'manufactured by Polydor' on label, in fully laminated UK printed sleeve)	£80
68	Elektra EKL 4014	STRANGE DAYS (1st mono pressing, orange labels with black lettering, 'THE DOORS' in regular typeface and 'manufactured by Polydor' on label, with printed inner sleeve, fully laminated UK printed sleeve)	£200
68	Elektra EKL 4014	STRANGE DAYS (2nd mono pressing, lighter orange labels with black lettering, 'THE DOORS' as logo and 'manufactured by Polydor' on label, with printed inner sleeve, fully laminated UK printed sleeve)	£150
68	Elektra EKS 4014	STRANGE DAYS (1st stereo pressing, orange labels with black lettering, 'THE DOORS' in regular typeface and 'manufactured by Polydor' on label, with printed inner sleeve, fully laminated UK printed sleeve)	£180
68	Elektra EKS 74014	STRANGE DAYS (2nd stereo pressing, lighter orange labels with black lettering, 'THE DOORS' as logo and 'manufactured by Polydor' on label, with printed inner sleeve, full laminated UK printed sleeve)	£120
68	Elektra EKL 4024	WAITING FOR THE SUN (1st - and only - mono pressing, orange labels with black lettering, 'Polydor Records Ltd' on label, in non laminated gatefold sleeve, with or without 'Ernest J. Day' credit)	£200
68	Elektra EKS 4024	WAITING FOR THE SUN (1st stereo pressing, orange labels with black lettering. 'Polydor Records Ltd' on label, in non laminated gatefold sleeve)	£120
69	Elektra EKS 75005	THE SOFT PARADE (1st pressing, orange labels with silver lettering, with lyric insert, non laminated gatefold sleeve)	£150
69	Elektra EKS 74007	THE DOORS (3rd stereo pressing, orange labels with silver lettering, 'manufactured by Polydor' on label, in fully laminated UK printed sleeve)	£80
70	Elektra EKS 74014	STRANGE DAYS (3rd stereo pressing, red labels, white 'E' logo, in fully laminated UK printed sleeve)	£60
70	Elektra EKS 75007	MORRISON HOTEL (1st stereo pressing, red labels, white 'E' logo, in laminated gatefold sleeve)	£100
70	Elektra 2665 002	ABSOLUTELY LIVE (2-LP, 1st pressing, red labels, white 'E' logo, in non laminated gatefold sleeve. Early copies have 2409-004 & 2409-004 on the respective discs, both with SET NO 2665 002 beneath in brackets. Some also have a white sticker with EKS 9002 on the back sleeve)	£80
70	Elektra EKS 74007	THE DOORS (4th stereo pressing, red labels, white 'E' logo in fully laminated sleeve)	£50
71	Elektra EKS 74079	13 (1st pressing, 'butterfly' labels, p.1970* on labels, non laminated sleeve)	£35
71	Elektra K 42090	L.A. WOMAN (1st pressing, Butterfly labels, embossed round-cornered, die-cut PVC 'window' sleeve & yellow and black inner sleeve)	£80
71	Elektra K 42012	THE DOORS (5th stereo pressing, Butterfly labels, non laminated sleeve)	£35
71	Elektra K 42104	OTHER VOICES (Butterfly labels, gatefold sleeve)	£15
71	Elektra K 42016	STRANGE DAYS (4th stereo pressing. Butterfly labels, non laminated sleeve)	£35
71	Elektra K 42012	WAITING FOR THE SUN (2nd stereo pressing, Butterfly labels, non laminated gatefold sleeve)	£40
72	Elektra K 62009	WEIRD SCENES INSIDE THE GOLDMINE (1st pressing, 2-LP, Butterfly labels, gatefold sleeve)	£40
72	Elektra K 62005	ABSOLUTELY LIVE (2-LP, 2nd pressing, Butterfly labels, 'EMI records Ltd' on back sleeve)	£40
72	Elektra K 62116	FULL CIRCLE (Butterfly labels, gatefold sleeve)	£15
73	Ekektra K 42090	L.A. WOMAN (2nd pressing, Butterfly labels, embossed round-cornered die cut acetate window sleeve with yellow and black inner sleeve. 'EMI' Records Ltd' in label copyright text)	£60
74	Elektra K 42090	LA WOMAN (3rd pressing, Butterfly labels, non embossed, 'round cornered' burgundy, black and white sleeve, no window. Yellow and black inner sleeve. 'EMI Records Ltd' on label copyright text)	£35
74	Elektra K 62009	WEIRD SCENES INSIDE THE GOLDMINE (2nd pressing, 2-LP set, 'EMI Records Ltd' in copyright text on label and on back cover)	£35
74	Elektra K 75007	MORRISON HOTEL (2nd pressing, Butterfly labels, non laminated gatefold sleeve)	£40
74	Elektra K 42062	13 (2nd pressing, Butterfly labels, p.1970 on labels, 'EMI records Ltd' on label copyright text, some with 'EMI Records Ltd' sticker on back sleeve)	£20
76	Elektra K 42062	13 (3rd pressing, Butterfly labels, WEA pressing, p.1971 and 'W' Warner logo added to copyright text on label, non laminated sleeve)	£20
76	Elektra K42012	THE DOORS (6th stereo pressing, Butterfly labels, p.1971 and 'W' Warners logo added to copyright text on label, non laminated sleeve)	£20
76	Elektra K42016	STRANGE DAYS (5th stereo pressing, Butterfly labels, 'W' Warner logo added to copyright text on label, non laminated sleeve)	£20

76	Elektra K42080	**MORRISON HOTEL** (3rd pressing, Butterfly labels, 'W' Warner logo added to copyright text on label, non laminated gatefold sleeve)	£15
76	Elektra K42079	**THE SOFT PARADE** (2nd pressing, Butterfly labels, 'W' Warner logo added to copyright text on label, non laminated gatefold sleeve)	£25
76	Elektra K42041	**WAITING FOR THE SUN** (3rd stereo pressing, 'Butterfly' labels, p.1971 and 'W' Warner logo added to copyright text on label, non laminated gatefold sleeve)	£25
76	Elektra K 62009	**WEIRD SCENES INSIDE THE GOLDMINE** (3rd pressing, 2-LP set WEA pressing, 'W' added to label copyright text)	£25
76	Elektra K42090	**L.A. WOMAN** (4th pressing, Butterfly labels, standard 'square' burgundy, black and yellow sleeve. No inner sleeve. WEA pressing with 'W' Warner logo in copyright text on label)	£25
76	Elektra K 42143	**THE BEST OF THE DOORS** (Butterfly labels)	£20
78	Elektra K52111	**AN AMERICAN PRAYER** ('Butterfly' label, gatefold sleeve, with 8-page booklet)	£20
76	Elektra K 62005	**ABSOLUTELY LIVE** (2-LP, 3rd pressing, Butterfly labels, 'W' Warner logo added to copyright text on label)	£25
83	Elektra 96-0269-1	**ALIVE SHE CRIED** (cream labels, with inner sleeve)	£20

(see also Ray Manzarek)

DOORS OF PERCEPTION
91	Lizard Nation LN 001	**SO JOIN MR. DREAMS** (LP, with inner sleeve and booklet)	£15

DOPE ON PLASTIC
94	Wave DJC 001	**Wave Dub/Out Of Time/East A Bit/It's A Dream** (12")	£70

M.J. DORANE
76	Rockers RRLP 2	**AVONMORE DUB** (LP, pre-release, white labels only)	£400
76	Rockers RRLP 3	**REGGAE TIME** (LP)	£150

MIKE DORANE & CIMARONS
71	Ackee ACK 144	**Penguin Funk/Ad-Lib**	£18

DOREEN (CAMPBELL) & ALL STARS
67	Rainbow RAI 114	**Rude Girls/Please Stay**	£20

DOREEN (SHAFFER) & JACKIE (OPEL)
65	Ska Beat JB 208	**Welcome Home/You And I**	£55

(see also Jackie & Doreen)

DORIS
82	ABCD ABCD 3	**GYPSY LADY** (LP, actually credited to A Band Called Doris)	£250
98	EMI/Mr. Bongo MRBLP 010	**DID YOU GIVE THE WORLD SOME LOVE TODAY, BABY?** (LP, reissue of Swedish 60s LP)	£15

HAROLD DORMAN
60	Top Rank JAR 357	**Mountain Of Love/To Be With You**	£25
61	London HLS 9386	**There They Go/I'll Stick By You**	£15

DOROTHY
80	Industrial IR 0014	**I Confess/Softness** (p/s)	£15

RALPH DORPER
83	Operation Twilight OPT 18	**THE ERASERHEAD EP** (12")	£20

(see also Propaganda)

DIANA DORS
64	Fontana TF 506	**So Little Time/It's Too Late**	£50
60	Pye NPL 18044	**SWINGIN' DORS** (LP, foldout sleeve, red vinyl)	£100

RAY DORSET (WITH MUNGO JERRY)
72	Dawn DNLS 3033	**COLD BLUE EXCURSION** (LP, solo; gatefold sleeve with lyric inner, lilac label)	£50

(see also Mungo Jerry, Good Earth, County Jug,,, Made In England)

DORSETS
65	Sue WI 391	**Pork Chops/Cool It**	£50

GERRY DORSEY
59	Decca F 11108	**Mister Music Man/Crazy Bells**	£25
65	Hickory 45-1337	**Baby Turn Around/Things I Wanna Do**	£35

JACK DORSEY ORCHESTRA
66	Polydor 56090	**Alfie's Theme/Alfie's Theme Too**	£15

LEE DORSEY
62	Top Rank JAR 606	**Do-Re-Mi/People Gonna Talk**	£25
65	Sue WI 367	**Do-Re-Mi/Ya Ya**	£40
66	Sue WI 399	**Messed Around/When I Meet My Baby**	£40
66	Stateside SS 528	**Working In A Coalmine/Mexico** (yellow vinyl)	£50
69	Bell BLL 1074	**Everything I Do Gonna Be Funky/There Should Be A Book**	£15
66	Stateside SE 1038	**RIDE YOUR PONY** (EP)	£30
66	Stateside SE 1043	**YOU'RE BREAKING ME UP** (EP)	£30
65	Sue ILP 924	**THE BEST OF LEE DORSEY** (LP)	£60
66	Stateside S(S)L 10177	**LEE DORSEY — RIDE YOUR PONY** (LP)	£30
66	Stateside S(S)L 10192	**THE NEW LEE DORSEY** (LP)	£25
71	Polydor 2489 006	**YES WE CAN** (LP, black/red/white Polydor logo on bottom left of front sleeve)	£50
84	Polydor 2482 280	**YES WE CAN** (LP, reissue, 'Special Polydor' in top right hand corner)	£20

LEE DORSEY & BETTY HARRIS
69	Buffalo BFS 1002	**Love Lots Of Lovin'/Take Care Of Your Love**	£20

(see also Betty Harris)

D.O.S.E.
95	Colosseum TOGA 001TJX	**Plug Myself In** (with Mark E. Smith) (p/s, numbered, 1-sided, 500 only)	£20

(see also The Fall)

DOSSERS
83	Secret SHH 168-12	Red Night/Punk Rocker/Running Running/Armada (12" in Secret records house bag)	£25

JOHNNY DOT & DASHERS
62	Salvo SLO 1805	I Love An Angel/Just For You (99 copies only)	£50

DOTTY & BONNIE
64	Rio R 43	I'm So Glad/DOUGLAS BROTHERS: Got You On My Mind	£30
64	Island WI 143	Your Kisses/Why Worry	£35
64	Island WI 148	Dearest/Tears Are Falling	£35
65	Ska Beat JB 183	Foul Play/ROLAND ALPHONSO & GROUP: Yard Broom	£50
67	Ska Beat JB 274	I'll Know/Love Is Great	£50
70	Ackee ACK 110	I'm So Glad/Lonely Road	£20

(see also Bonnie Frankson, Eric Morris, Don Drummond, Skatalites, Baba Brooks)

DOUBLE EXPOSURE
76	Salsoul SZS 5503	TEN PERCENT (LP)	£18

DOUBLE FEATURE
67	Deram DM 115	Baby Get Your Head Screwed On/Come On Baby	£70

DOUBLE VISION
97	Big Drum BDRUM 01	HOW SHOULD I START EP (12")	£25

DOUBLES WITH GAY BLADES
59	HMV POP 613	Hey Girl!/Little Joe	£100

DOUBT
80	Solo SOLO 1	Fringes/Lookaway/Contrast Disorder/Time Out (EP, with no p/s but insert)	£20

(See also Carpenter Joe)

DOUGHNUT RING
68	Deram DM 215	Dance Around Julie/The Bandit	£35

(see also Crocheted Doughnut Ring)

JOHNNY DOUGHTY
77	Topic 12TS 324	ROUND RYE BAY FOR MORE (LP, with insert)	£15

CARL DOUGLAS (& BIG STAMPEDE)
66	Go AJ 11401	Crazy Feeling/PETER PERRY SOUL BAND: Keep It To Myself	£35
67	Go AJ 11408	Let The Birds Sing/Something For Nothing	£50
67	United Artists UP 1206	Nobody Cries/Serving A Sentence Of Life	£250
67	United Artists UP 1206	Nobody Cries/Serving A Sentence Of Life (DJ Copy)	£300
68	United Artists UP 2227	Sell My Soul To The Devil/Good Hard Worker	£30
68	Pye 7N 45551	Witchfinder General/Crazy Feeling	£20
71	CBS 7101	Do You Need My Love (To Get Better)/Lean On Me	£70

CRAIG DOUGLAS
59	Top Rank JKR 8033	CRAIG SINGS FOR 'ROXY' (EP)	£15
60	Decca DFE 6633	CRAIG (EP)	£15
62	Decca DFE 8509	CUDDLE UP WITH CRAIG (EP)	£15
63	Columbia SEG 8219	CRAIG MOVIE SONGS (EP)	£20
60	Top Rank BUY 049	CRAIG DOUGLAS (LP)	£25
61	Top Rank 35-103	BANDWAGON BALL (LP)	£25
62	Columbia 33SX 1468	OUR FAVOURITE MELODIES (LP)	£40

(see also Bert Weedon)

KEITH DOUGLAS
84	Zip ZIP001	Frontline/Dub Version (12")	£40

MARK DOUGLAS
62	Ember EMB S 166	It Matters Not/Upside Down	£75

NORMA DOUGLAS
57	London HLZ 8475	Be It Resolved/Joe He Gone	£15

ROBB & DEAN DOUGLAS
67	Deram DM 132	I Can Make It With You/Phone Me	£50

DOUGLAS BROTHERS
66	Rio R 57	Valley Of Tears/CHARMERS: Where Do I Turn	£40
66	Rio R 63	Down And Out/RONALD WILSON: Lonely Man	£125

(see also Dotty & Bonnie)

RONNIE DOVE
65	Stateside SL 10149	RONNIE DOVE (LP)	£40

DOVELLS
61	Columbia DB 4718	The Bristol Stomp/Out In The Cold Again	£20
62	Columbia DB 4810	Do The New Continental/Mopitty Mope Stomp	£20
62	Columbia DB 4877	Bristol Twistin' Annie/The Actor	£20
63	Cameo Parkway P 867	You Can't Sit Down/Stompin' Everywhere	£25
63	Cameo Parkway P 901	Be My Girl/Dragster On The Prowl	£25
79	London HAU 8515	CAMEO PARKWAY SESSIONS (LP)	£15

(see also Len Barry)

DOVES
98	Casino CHIP 001	CEDAR EP: Cedar Room/Rise/Zither (10", wraparound p/s)	£35
99	Casino CHIP 002	SEA EP (10", p/s)	£20
00	Heavenly HVNLP 26	LOST SOULS (2-LP, gatefold)	£100
02	Heavenly HVNLP 35	THE LAST BROADCAST (2-LP)	£50
05	Heavenly HVNLP 50	SOME CITIES (2-LP)	£50

09 Heavenly HVNLP 67 KINGDOM OF RUST (2-LP) £30

(see also Badly Drawn Boy, Sub Sub)

NICK DOW
79 Dingles DIN 306 BURD MARGARET (LP) £15

BRENT DOWE
71 Summit SUM 8521 Knock Three Times/GAYLADS: This Time I Won't Hurt You £15
73 Green Door GD 4061 Reggae Makossa/No Nola (B-side actually by Melodians) £15
74 Trojan TRLS 76 BUILD ME UP (LP) £15

(see also Melodians)

JOHN DOWIE
81 Factory FAC 19 It's Hard To Be An Egg/Mind Sketch (white vinyl, clear sleeve, with white feather) £15

DOWLANDS
62 Oriole CB 1748 Little Sue/Julie (as Dowlands & Soundtracks) £50
62 Oriole CB 1781 Big Big Fella/Don't Ever Change £100
63 Oriole CB 1815 Break Ups/A Love Like Ours £50
63 Oriole CB 1892 Lonely Johnny (song actually titled "Lucky Johnny")/Do You Have To Have Me Blue? ...£500
64 Oriole CB 1897 All My Loving/Hey Sally (as Dowlands & Soundtracks)......................£15
64 Oriole CB 1926 I Walk The Line/Happy Endings £40
64 Oriole CB 1947 Wishing And Hoping/You Will Regret It £80
65 Columbia DB 7547 Don't Make Me Over/Someone Must Be Feeling Sad £40

DOWNBEATS
61 Starlite ST45 051 Thinkin' Of You/Midnight Love £200

ROLAND DOWNER & COUNT OSSIE
68 Doctor Bird DB 1130 Ethiopian Kingdom/A Ju Ju Wah £90

BOB DOWNES
70 Vertigo 6059 011 No Time Like The Present/Keep Off The Grass £35
70 Philips SBL 7922 BOB DOWNES' OPEN MUSIC (LP) £200
70 Vertigo 6360 005 ELECTRIC CITY (LP, gatefold sleeve, large swirl label)....................£300
70 Music For Pleasure MFP DEEP DOWN HEAVY (LP, red/silver label) £25
      1412
73 Ophenian BDOM 001 DIVERSIONS (LP) £25
74 Ophenian BDOM 002 EPISODES AT 4AM (LP, with insert)......................................£22
75 Ophenian BDOM 003 HELLS ANGELS (LP)..£30

(see also Rock Workshop)

DOWNHILL
79 Bead Records BEAD 8 DOWNHILL (LP) £30

BIG AL DOWNING
64 Sue WI 341 Yes I'm Loving You/Please Come Home £45

DOWNLINERS SECT
64 Columbia DB 7300 Baby What's Wrong/Be A Sect Maniac £30
64 Columbia DB 7347 Little Egypt/Sect Appeal £15
64 Columbia DB 7415 Find Out What's Happening/Insecticide £35
65 Columbia DB 7509 Wreck Of The Old '97/Leader Of The Sect £30
65 Columbia DB 7597 I Got Mine/Waiting In Heaven Somewhere £35
65 Columbia DB 7712 Bad Storm Coming/Lonely And Blue £35
66 Columbia DB 7817 All Night Worker/He Was A Square £30
66 Columbia DB 7939 Glendora/I'll Find Out £70
66 Columbia DB 8008 The Cost Of Living/Everything I've Got To Give £25
64 Contrast Sound RBCSP 1 NITE IN GREAT NEWPORT STREET (EP) £300
65 Columbia SEG 8438 THE SECT SING SICK SONGS (EP) £100
64 Columbia 33SX 1658 THE SECT (LP) £200
65 Columbia 33SX 1745 THE COUNTRY SECT (LP) £150
66 Columbia SX 6028 THE ROCK SECT'S IN (LP, mono, black/blue label with "sold in the U.K..." text)............£200
66 Columbia S(C)X 6028 THE ROCK SECT'S IN (LP, stereo, blue/black label with "sold in the U.K..." text) £250
93 Hangman HANG 42 UP BIRTH OF SUAVE (LP) £15

(see also Don Crane's Downliners Sect)

DOWNTOWN ALL STARS
69 Downtown DT 426 Everybody Feel Good/RUDIES: Downtown Jump £30

LAMONT DOZIER
73 Probe SPB 1086 OUT HERE ON MY OWN (Probe oeiginal).................................£20
74 ABC ABCL 5042 OUT HERE ON MY OWN (LP, ABC reissue with sticker over Probe logo)).....£20
75 ABC ABCL 5096 BLACK BACH (LP) £15
76 Warner Bros. K56225 RIGHT THERE (LP) £15
99 Sequel NEMLP 989 LOVE AND BEAUTY (LP) £18

(see also Holland & Dozier)

DOZY, BEAKY, MICK & TICH (D.B.M.&T.)
70 Philips 6308 029 FRESH EAR (LP, gatefold sleeve, credited to D.B.M.&T) £25

(see also Dave Dee Dozy Beaky Mick & Tich)

DP'S
78 Barn 2314107 IF YOU KNOW WHAT I MEAN (LP) £15

(see also The Depressions)

DR. DOG
05 Rough Trade RTRADLP 258 EASY BEAT (LP, textured sleeve, inner) £15

DRACULAS DAUGHTER
97	Kalevala KALA 001	Candy/Candy (version)	£20

DRAGON
76	Acorn CF 268	DRAGON (LP, gatefold sleeve)	£60

DRAGONFLY
74	Retreat RTS 257	Gondola/Almost Abandoned (demo)	£15
74	Retreat RTL 6002	ALMOST ABANDONED (LP)	£25
80s	Dragonfly DF 001	SILENT NIGHTS EP (p/s, private pressing)	£150

DRAGONS
69	Page One	Heart Transplantation/Hello I Love Maria	£40

DRAGONSFIRE
82	Belltree BTR 001	RISING PHOENIX (LP, with insert)	£20

(see also Spinning Wheel)

DRAGONSLAYER
83	Cavalier CAV 017	Broken Hearts/Satan Is Free/I Want Your Life (Early copies with band name as 'Slayer'. NO STICKER)	£120
83	Cavalier CAV 017	Broken Hearts/Satan Is Free/I Want Your Life (Early copies had band name as 'Slayer', these later copies have sticker with new name – Dragonslayer – covering it)	£80

DRAG SET
66	Go AJ 11405	Get Out Of My Way/Day And Night	£250

(see also Open Mind)

DRAGSTER
81	Heavy Metal HEAVY 4	Ambition/Won't Bring You Back (p/s)	£30

CHARLES DRAIN
75	RCA 2750	Is This Really Love/Only You	£15

CHARLIE DRAKE
75	Charisma CB 270	You Never Know/I'm Big Enough For Me (produced by Peter Gabriel)	£30

NICK DRAKE
79	Island RSS 7	Introduction/Hazy Jane II/Time Has Told Me/Fruit Tree/Rider On The Wheel (12", p/s, single-sided "Fruit Tree" sampler, promo only)	£200
04	Island IS 854	Magic/Northern Sky (die-cut picture bag)	£15
04	Island IS 871	River Man/River Man (1968 Recording) (die-cut picture bag)	£20
12	Antar 11	Plaisir D'Amour (1-sided, die cut sleeve, promo)	£80
13	Secret 7 S713	Rider On The Wheel (1-sided, 100 only, each sleeve decorated by different artist)	£100
14	Antar ANTARSP 012	Cello Song (Peel session version, 1-sided, p/s, booklet)	£50
14	Antar ANTARMP 003	The John Peel Session: Time Of No Reply/River Man/Three Hours/Bryter Later/'Cello Song (5-track 10" vinyl EP – sometimes offered separately from the 'Signature Box Edition' set)	£250
22	Feral Child 19	Nick Drake Monologue/Joe Boyd Discusses Five Leaves Left (7", Lathe Cut, clear vinyl, p/s, numbered, 99 copies only)	£80
69	Island ILPS 9105	FIVE LEAVES LEFT (LP, 1st pressing, pink label, black 'circle' logo, matrix numbers ILPS 9105 A//2/ILPS 9105 B//2, gatefold printed by Ernest J. Day, track order of Day Is Done and Way To Blue reversed)	£1500
69	Island ILPS 9105	FIVE LEAVES LEFT (LP, gatefold, 2nd pressing, 'pink rim label', 'palm tree' logo)	£200
70	Island ILPS 9134	BRYTER LAYTER (LP, 1st pressing, 'pink rim label, 'palm tree' logo, 'stereo' on label and Joe Boyd credit on one line, Matrixes: ILPS 9134 A-1U/ILPS 9134 B-1U)	£450
71	Longman (no cat. No.)	INTERPLAY ONE (2LP, educational recording for schools, Drake plays guitar on three tracks, booklets, 'teachers' notes)	£450
72	Island ILPS 9134	BRYTER LAYTER (LP, 2nd pressing 'pink rim label, 'palm tree' logo, no 'stereo' on right hand side of label and Joe Boyd credit on two lines)	£200
72	Island ILPS 9184	PINK MOON (LP, 1st pressing, pink rim label, palm tree logo, gatefold)	£500
76	Island 9105	FIVE LEAVES LEFT (LP, reissue, gatefold,3rd pressing blue rim palm tree label)	£80
76	Island ILPS 9134	BRYTER LATER (LP, reissue, 3rd pressing, blue rim palm tree label, textured sleeve)	£50
76	Island ILPS 9184	PINK MOON (LP, gatefold, reissue, blue rim, palm tree logo)	£50
78	Island ILPS 9105	FIVE LEAVES LEFT (LP, reissue, gatefold, 4th pressing blue rim palm tree label)	£60
78	Island ILPS 9134	BRYTER LATER (LP, reissue, blue label)	£30
78	Island ILPS 9184	PINK MOON (LP, gatefold, reissue)	£50
79	Island NDSP 100	FRUIT TREE: THE COMPLETE RECORDED WORKS (3LP, box set, booklet)	£120
85	Island ILPS 9826	HEAVEN IN A WILD FLOWER (AN EXPLORATION OF NICK DRAKE) (LP)	£25
86	Hannibal HNBX 5302	FRUIT TREE (4LP box set, expanded reissue, booklet)	£100
86	Hannibal HNCD 5402	FRUIT TREE (4CD box set, booklet, 12" x 12" box)	£70
86	Hannibal HNBL 1318	TIME OF NO REPLY (LP, lyric insert, poster)	£50
86	Island ILPM 9826	HEAVEN IN A WILD FLOWER (AN EXPLORATION OF NICK DRAKE) (LP, Island Life Edition, Island printed inner))	£20
89	Island ILPS 9105	FIVE LEAVES LEFT (LP, gatefold, reissue, 'blue with white palm tree' label)	£35
89	Island ILPS 9134	BRYTER LAYTER (LP, reissue, 'blue with white palm tree' label)	£35
89	Island ILPS 9184	PINK MOON (LP, reissue, 'blue with white palm tree' label)	£35
99	Island/Simply Vinyl SVLP 094	BRYTER LAYTER (LP, 180g repress, Simply Vinyl PVC)	£35
00	Island/Simply Vinyl SVLP 163	FIVE LEAVES LEFT (LP, gatefold,180g repress, Simply Vinyl PVC)	£40
00	Island/Simply Vinyl SVLP 172	PINK MOON (LP, gatefold,180g repress, Simply Vinyl PVC)	£50
04	Island ILPS 8141	MADE TO LOVE MAGIC (LP, gatefold, printed inner)	£35
07	Sunbeam SBR2LP5041	FAMILY TREE (2LP, gatefold, insert, numbered, 1000-only 'Founders' edition))	£50
07	Sunbeam SBR2LP 5041	FAMILY TREE (2LP, gatefold, insert)	£30
07	Island 1745703 0	FRUIT TREE (LP/DVD box set, remaster, book)	£150
12	Island ReDISCovered 537134335	PINK MOON (LP, box set,180g, poster, lyric inserts, facsimile master tape insert)	£60

13	Island 537326044	NICK DRAKE (LP, 180g, gatefold, poster, facsimile bio with download code,4000 only, RSD)	£25
13	Island ReDISCovered 537134359	BRYTER LAYTER (LP, box set,180g, poster, lyric inserts, facsimile master tape insert)	£80
13	Island ReDISCovered 537134366	FIVES LEAVES LEFT (LP, box set,180g, poster, lyric inserts, facsimile master tape insert)	£50
13	Island 537538546	TUCK BOX (5CD box set, card sleeves, posters)	£60
14	Island ILPS 8149	NICK DRAKE – A TREASURY (LP, printed inner)	£25
23	Chrysalis BRVC 75	THE ENDLESS COLOURED WAYS (THE SONGS OF NICK DRAKE) (2LP, various artists + 1-sided Nick Drake 7" 'Tomorrow Is A Long Time', grey vinyl)	£35

(see also Molly Drake)

MOLLY DRAKE

11	Bryter Music no.cat.no	MOLLY DRAKE (CD, envelope sleeve, sealed with sticker, booklet, edition of 500)	£40
18	Fledg'ling FLED 3105	THE TIDE'S MAGNIFICENCE: THE SONGS AND POEMS OF MOLLY DRAKE (2CD, booklet)	£50

(see also Nick Drake)

DRAMATICS

72	Stax 2362 025	WHATCHA SEE IS WHATCHA GET (LP)	£25
74	Stax STX 1021	A DRAMATIC EXPERIENCE (LP)	£15
75	ABC ABCL 5121	DRAMATIC JACKPOT (LP, gatefold sleeve)	£15
75	ABC ABCL 5150	DRAMA V (LP, gatefold sleeve)	£15

BARRY DRANSFIELD

72	Polydor Folk Mill 2383 160	BARRY DRANSFIELD (LP, red label)	£350
78	Topic 12TS 386	BOWIN' AND SCRAPIN' (LP)	£25
02	Spinney SPINNEY 003	BARRY DRANSFIELD (LP, reissue)	£20
20	Glass Modern GLAMLP 020	BARRY DRANSFIELD (LP, reissue, green vinyl)	£15

(see also Robin & Barry Dransfield)

ROBIN DRANSFIELD

80	Topic 12TS 414	TIDEWAVE (LP)	£15

(see also Robin & Barry Dransfield)

ROBIN & BARRY DRANSFIELD

70	Trailer LER 2011	THE ROUT OF THE BLUES (LP, first pressing, white Trailer 'test' label)	£50
70	Trailer LER 2011	THE ROUT OF THE BLUES (LP, second pressing, dark red label/silver logo and text)	£40
71	Trailer LER 2026	LORD OF ALL I BEHOLD (LP)	£40
73	Trailer LER 2026	LORD OF ALL I BEHOLD (LP, red/black labels)	£20
73	Trailer LER 2011	THE ROUT OF THE BLUES (LP, red and black labels)	£30
75	Trailer LER 2011	THE ROUT OF THE BLUES (LP, yellow labels)	£20
75	Trailer LER 2026	LORD OF ALL I BEHOLD (LP, yellow labels)	£15
82	Highway	THE ROUT OF THE BLUES (LP, 80s repressing, black and white 'Highwayman' labels)	£15
82	Highway/Trailer LER 2011	THE ROUT OF THE BLUES (LP, Trailer labels and sleeves with 'Highway Records' stickers over 'Trailer' logo on sleeve)	£15

(see also Robin Dransfield, Barry Dransfield)

RUSTY DRAPER

58	Mercury 7MT 229	Chicken-Pickin' Hawk/June, July And August	£15
59	Mercury AMT 1019	Shoppin' Around/With This Ring	£30
56	Mercury MEP 9506	PRESENTING RUSTY DRAPER (EP)	£40
59	Mercury ZEP 10016	RUSTY DRAPER (EP)	£20
60	Mercury ZEP 10059	RUSTY IN GAMBLING MOOD (EP)	£20
60	Mercury ZEP 10095	MULE SKINNER BLUES (EP)	£25
64	London RE-U 1431	RUSTY DRAPER NO. 1 (EP)	£20
64	London RE-U 1432	RUSTY DRAPER NO. 2 (EP)	£20

MIKEY DREAD (AKA MICHAEL CAMPBELL)

79	Do It DUNE 24	Heavyweight Style/Rub A Dub (12")	£20
79	Warrior WAR 125	Barber Saloon/CARLTON PATTERSON: Wash Wash (12")	£20
80	Dread At The Controls DREAD 1	Break Down The Walls/Jumping Master (12")	£15
81	Dread At The Controls DATC 003	Warrior Stylee/Israel Stylee (12")	£25
82	Dread At The Controls DATCD 008	Roots & Culture/Jungle Dread (12")	£40
83	Earthquake EQ 001	RAINBOW STEPPER: And Behold/MIKEY DREAD: Paradise (12")	£50
77	Hawkeye HALP 001	DUB (LP)	£15
79	Dread At The Controls DTCLP 002	AFRICAN ANTHEM – THE MIKEY DREAD SHOW DUBWISE (LP)	£40
79	Trojan TRLS178	DREAD AT THE CONTROLS (LP)	£30
80	Dread At The Controls DTCLP 006	WORLD WAR III (LP)	£30
80	Dread At The Controls DTLP 001	MASTER SHOWCASE (LP)	£30
82	Dread At The Controls DATCD 005	DUB CATALOGUE VOLUME 1 (LP)	£20
82	Dread At The Controls DATCLP 008	JUNGLE SIGNAL (LP)	£30
82	Dread At The Controls RIDE 19	SWALK (LP)	£15
83	Dread At The Controls DTLP 009	DUB MERCHANT (LP)	£30

DREAD AND THE BALDHEAD

94	Slam SLM5	I The Conqueror/Ganja Plant (Drum & Bass Mix)/Ganja Plant (Hard Step Mix) (12")	£50
95	Slam SLM7	Wicked Piece A Tune/Twenty Four Seven (12")	£120

DREAD & FRED
92	Ironworks D&F 001	Down Too Long/CREATIVE STEPPERS: Creative Version (12")	£30
89	Jah Shaka SHAKA 875	IRON WORKS (LP)	£20
89	Jah Shaka SHAKA 937	AFRICAN CHANT (LP)	£30
93	Jah Shaka SHAKA 937	IRON WORKS PART 3 (LP)	£15

DREADZONE
93	Creation CRELP 162	360 DEGREES (LP)	£40
94	Totem TTPLP 002	PERFORMANCE (LP)	£30
95	Virgin V 2778	SECOND LIGHT (2-LP)	£70

DREAMBOYS
80	St Vitus SV1	Bela Lugosi's Birthday/Outer Limits/Shall We Dance	£25

DREAMERS (2)
69	Downtown DT 407	Sweet Chariot/Let's Go Downtown	£40
69	Downtown DT 408	I Second That Emotion/Dear Love (as Audrey and the Dreamers)	£30

DREAMLETS
65	Ska Beat JB 182	Really Now/SKATALITES: Street Corner	£85

DREAMLOVERS
61	Columbia DB 4711	When We Get Married/Just Because	£200

(see also Chubby Checker)

DREAMS
68	United Artists UP 2249	I Will See You There/A Boy Needs A Girl	£35
69	CBS 4247	Baby I'm Your Man/Softly, Softly	£25
70	CBS 64203	DREAMS (LP)	£20
72	CBS 64597	IMAGINE MY SURPRISE (LP)	£20

DREAM SYNDICATE
82	Rough Trade ROUGH 53	THE DAYS OF WINE AND ROSES (LP)	£15

DREAM THEATER
89	MCA MCF 3445	WHEN DREAM AND DAY UNITE (LP)	£30
92	Atco 7567 92148 1	IMAGES AND WORDS (LP)	£15

DREAMTIMERS
61	London HLU 9368	The Dancin' Lady/An Invitation	£20

DREAM WEAVERS
56	Brunswick 05515	It's Almost Tomorrow/You've Got Me Wondering (gold label lettering)	£30
56	Brunswick 05515	It's Almost Tomorrow/You've Got Me Wondering (silver label lettering)	£15

DREGS
79	Disturbing DRO 1	THE DREGS EP (p/s, numbered, stamped sleeve, 500 only)	£50

D-REN
97	Ugly UGM 011	BROTHERS AND SISTERS EP (12")	£25

JOHN DREVAR('S EXPRESSION)
67	MGM MGM 1367	The Closer She Gets/When I Come Home	£200
67	MGM MGM 1367	The Closer She Gets/When I Come Home (DJ Copy)	£300

KENNY DREW
14	Blue Note MMBST 84059	UNDERCURRENT (LP, reissue, gatefold)	£20

PATTI DREW
68	Capitol CL 15557	Workin' On A Groovy Thing/Without A Doubt	£15

DREXCIYA
96	Warp WP 57	JOURNEY DOWN EP (12", p/s)	£18
93	Rephlex Cat 017	3 - MOLECULAR ENHANCEMENT EP (12", 4-track)	£25

DRIFTERS (U.K.)
59	Columbia DB 4263	Feelin' Fine/Don't Be A Fool (With Love)	£50
59	Columbia DB 4263	Feelin' Fine/Don't Be A Fool (With Love) (78)	£50
59	Columbia DB 4325	Driftin'/Jet Black	£45

(see also Shadows, Cliff Richard, Jet Harris)

DRIFTERS (U.S.)
78s
56	London HLE 8344	Soldier Of Fortune/I Gotta Get Myself A Woman	£50
58	London HLE 8686	Moonlight Bay/Drip-Drop	£50
59	London HLE 8892	There Goes My Baby/Oh, My Love	£70
59	London HLE 8988	Dance With Me/True Love, True Love	£80
60	London HLE 9081	This Magic Moment/Baltimore	£100

SINGLES
56	London HLE 8344	Soldier Of Fortune/I Gotta Get Myself A Woman	£1000
58	London HLE 8686	Moonlight Bay/Drip-Drop	£150
59	London HLE 8892	There Goes My Baby/Oh, My Love	£30
60	London HLE 9081	This Magic Moment/Baltimore	£18
60	London HLK 9145	Lonely Winds/Hey Senorita	£18
61	London HLK 7115	I Count The Tears/Dance With Me (export issue)	£20
61	London HLK 9287	I Count The Tears/Sadie My Lady	£25
61	London HLK 9326	Some Kind Of Wonderful/Honey Bee	£15
61	London HLK 9382	Please Stay/No Sweet Lovin'	£15
63	London HLK 9699	On Broadway/Let The Music Play	£15
63	London HLK 9750	Rat Race/If You Don't Come Back	£15

64	Atlantic AT 4008	I've Got Sand In My Shoes/He's Just A Playboy	£15
65	Atlantic AT 4019	At The Club/Answer The Phone	£15
65	Atlantic AT 4034	Follow Me/The Outside World	£15
66	Atlantic AT 4062	We Gotta Sing/Nylon Stockings	£15
66	Atlantic AT 4084	Memories Are Made Of This/My Island In The Sun	£15
66	Atlantic 584 020	Up In The Streets Of Harlem/You Can't Love 'Em All	£15
67	Atlantic 584 065	Baby What I Mean/Aretha	£20
77	Arista 94	I'll Know When True Love Really Passes By/A Good Song Never Dies	£18
79	Epic EPC 7806	Pour Your Little Heart Out Parts 1 & 2	£50

EPs

61	London RE-K 1282	THE DRIFTERS' GREATEST HITS	£20
63	London RE-K 1355	THE DRIFTERS	£20
63	London RE-K 1385	DRIFTIN'	£20
64	Atlantic AET 6003	DRIFTIN' VOL. 2	£25
65	Atlantic AET 6012	TONIGHT	£25

ALBUMS

60	London HA-K 2318	THE DRIFTERS' GREATEST HITS	£50
62	London HA-K 2450	SAVE THE LAST DANCE FOR ME	£30
65	Atlantic ATL 5015	OUR BIGGEST HITS	£20
65	Atlantic ATL/STL 5023	THE GOOD LIFE WITH THE DRIFTERS (mono/stereo)	£20
66	Atlantic ATL/STL 5039	I'LL TAKE YOU WHERE THE MUSIC'S PLAYING (mono/stereo)	£20
67	Atlantic 587 038	BIGGEST HITS	£15
67	Atlantic 590 010	SOUVENIRS	£18
68	Atlantic 587 123	ROCKIN' AND DRIFTIN'	£35
68	Atlantic 587 144	GOOD GRAVY (as Clyde McPhatter & Drifters)	£45
69	Atlantic 587/588 160	UP ON THE ROOF	£15

(see also Clyde McPhatter, Ben E. King, Bobby Hendricks)

DRIFTING SLIM

| 66 | Blue Horizon 45-1005 | Good Morning Baby/My Sweet Woman (99 copies only) | £175 |

DRIFTWOOD

| 70 | Decca SKL 5069 | DRIFTWOOD (LP, blue/silver label with boxed logo) | £100 |

DRINKING ELECTRICITY

| 82 | Survival SUR LP 001 | OVERLOAD (LP) | £20 |

JULIE DRISCOLL

63	Columbia DB 7118	Take Me By The Hand/Stay Away From Me	£30
65	Parlophone R 5296	Don't Do It No More/I Know You	£30
66	Parlophone R 5444	I Didn't Want To Have To Do It/Don't Do It No More	£25
67	Parlophone R 5588	I Know You Love Me Not/If You Should Ever Leave Me	£20
67	Marmalade 598 005	Save Me Pts 1 & 2	£30
71	Polydor 2383077	JULIE DRISCOLL — 1969 (LP)	£60

JULIE DRISCOLL, BRIAN AUGER & TRINITY

69	Marmalade 598 018	Take Me To The Water/Indian Rope Man	£60
67	Marmalade 607002	OPEN (mono, first pressing, with 1-sided insert and non laminated cover produced by "Upton Printing")	£175
67	Marmalade 607 002	OPEN (LP, mono)	£125
67	Marmalade 608 002	OPEN (LP, stereo)	£100
68	M. For Pleasure MFP 1265	JOOLS/BRIAN (LP, tracks shared by Julie Driscoll & Brian Auger)	£20
69	Marmalade 608 005/6	STREET NOISE (2-LP, gatefold sleeve)	£300
69	Marmalade 608 014	STREET NOISE PART 1 (LP)	£35
69	Marmalade 608 015	STREET NOISE PART 2 (LP)	£35
70	Polydor 2334004	BEST OF (LP, 99p series)	£20

(see also Brian Auger & Trinity, Working Week, Julie Tippetts, B.B. Blunder)

DRIVE

| 77 | NRG NE 467 | Jerkin'/Push'N'Shove (no p/s) | £50 |

DRIVER

79	Rods ROD 1	Like A Mirror/Here I Am (p/s)	£20
79	Rods ROD 2	I'm Not Dreaming/So They Say	£15
80	Rods HOT 1	YOU BETTER TAKE IT (LP, 300 only)	£60

DRIVESHAFT

| 80 | Undercover DC 02 | Cold As Ice/I Know What You Are After (features Noel Redding) | £50 |
| 82 | Undercover DC 03 | Heartbreaker/Now That It's Over (p/s) | £25 |

DRIZABONE

| 94 | 4th & Broadway 12 BRW 264 | Pressure (Roger's Soul Sensation Mix)/Pressure (Album Version)/Pressure (Bonus Beats Mix)/Pressure (Bone Idol Remix)/Pressure (Nu Solution Mix)/Pressure (Underground Network Mix) (12", p/s) | £30 |

DROME

| 94 | Ninja Tune ZEN 11 | THE FINAL CORPORATE COLONIZATION OF THE UNCONSCIOUS (2 x LP) | £15 |

FRANK D'RONE

| 60 | Mercury MMC 14053 | AFTER THE BALL (LP) | £15 |

DRONES (1)

77	Fifth Avenue CAS 107	Bone Idol/I Just Wanna Be Myself (cassette, flip-open 'cigarette box' sleeve)	£30
77	Valer VRSP 1	Be My Baby/Lift Off The Bans (12", white label, unreleased)	£50
77	Valer	Be My Baby (Take Two)/The Clique (white label, unreleased, many autographed)	£20
77	Ohms GOOD MIX 1	TEMPTATIONS OF A WHITE COLLAR WORKER (EP, different coloured sleeves, some with writing on inner sleeve)	£20

MINT VALUE £

| 77 | Valer VRLP 1 | FURTHER TEMPTATIONS (LP) | £35 |

DRONES (2)
| 06 | ATP ATPRLP 22 | GALA MILL (2-LP) | £30 |

DRONGOS FOR EUROPE
| 81 | Kite DFE 001 | ADVERSE CHORUS EP | £40 |

DROP
| 81 | Dropped SRTS/81/CUS 929 | He Doesn't Know He's Trendy/Death In The Afternoon/I'm Wearing An Appliance | £20 |

DROP NINETEENS
92	Hut HUTLP 4	DELAWARE (LP)	£40
93	Hut HUTLP 14	NATIONAL COMA (LP, clear vinyl)	£25
93	Hut HUTLP 14	NATIONAL COMA (LP)	£20

DROWNING CRAZE
81	Situation 2 SIT 3	Storage Case/Damp Bones (p/s)	£15
81	Situation 2 SIT 13	Trance/I Love The Fjords (foldout p/s)	£15
82	Situation 2 SIT 16	Heat/Replays (p/s)	£15

DRUDGE
| 90 | Deaf DEAF 01 | SUPPOSE IT WAS YOU (split LP with Agathocles) | £20 |

DRUID
| 75 | EMI EMC 3081 | TOWARDS THE SUN (LP, textured, with inner sleeve) | £20 |
| 76 | EMI EMC 3128 | FLUID DRUID (LP, with inner sleeve) | £20 |

DRUID CHASE
| 67 | CBS 3053 | Take Me In Your Garden/I Wanna Get My Hands On You | £30 |

DRUIDS (1)
| 63 | Parlophone R 5097 | Long Tall Texan/Love So Blue | £20 |
| 64 | Parlophone R 5134 | It's Just A Little Bit Too Late/See What You've Done | £20 |

DRUIDS (2)
| 71 | Argo ZFB 22 | BURNT OFFERING (LP) | £80 |
| 73 | Argo ZFB 39 | PASTIME WITH GOOD COMPANY (LP) | £60 |

(see also Giles Farnaby's Dream Band)

DRUM CLUB
| 93 | Big Life DC PROMO 2 | Big Life (2 x 12" promo) | £15 |

DRUMBAGO
63	Island WI 085	I Am Drunk (actually by Raymond Harper & Drumbago's Group)/Sea Breeze (actually by Sammy & Drumbago's Group)	£20
68	Blue Cat BS 145	Reggae Jeggae (with Blenders)/TYRONE TAYLOR: Delilah	£100
69	Trojan TR 638	Dulcemania (with Dynamites)/CLANCY ECCLES: China Man	£40

(see also Derrick Patsy, Dennis Walks)

BILL DRUMMOND
| 87 | Creation CRE 039T | King Of Joy/The Manager (12", p/s) | £20 |
| 86 | Creation CRELP 014 | THE MAN (LP) | £30 |

(see also Big In Japan,, KLF, Timelords)

DON DRUMMOND
62	Island WI 021	Schooling The Duke/Bitter Rose (as Don Drummond Orchestra; B-side is actually by Shenley Duffus)	£45
63	Black Swan WI 406	Scrap Iron/DRAGONAIRE: Prevention	£45
63	Blue Beat BB 179	Reload/Far East	£50
63	Island WI 094	Scandal/My Ideal (B-side actually by W. Sparks)	£45
63	R&B JB 103	Royal Flush/MAYTALS: Matthew Mark	£55
63	R&B JB 105	The Shock/TONETTES: Tell Me You're Mine	£55
64	Ska Beat JB 178	Silver Dollar/TOMMY McCOOK: My Business	£45
64	Island WI 149	Eastern Standard Time/DOTTY & BONNIE: Sun Rises	£50
64	Island WI 153	Musical Storeroom/STRANGER COLE: He Who Feels	£50
64	Island WI 162	Garden Of Love/STRANGER COLE: Cherry May	£50
65	Island WI 192	Stampede (with Drumbago)/JUSTIN HINDS & DOMINOES: Come Bail Me	£50
65	Island WI 204	Coolie Baby/LORD ANTICS: You May Stray	£50
65	Island WI 208	Man In The Street/RITA & BENNY: You Are My Only Love	£50
65	Island WI 242	University Goes Ska/DERRICK & NAOMI: Pain In My Heart	£50
69	Studio One SO 2078	Heavenless/GLEN BROWN & DAVE BARKER: Lady Lovelight	£70
69	Trojan TR 678	Memory Of Don/JOHN HOLT: Darling I Love You	£45
69	Coxsone CSL 8021	IN MEMORY OF DON DRUMMOND (LP)	£150
69	Studio One SO 9008	THE BEST OF DON DRUMMOND (LP)	£200
69	Trojan TTL 23	MEMORIAL ALBUM (LP)	£200

(see also Joe White, Rhythm Aces, Roy & Millie, Movers, Desmond Dekker, Shenley Duffas, Hi-Tones, Duke Reid, Soul Brothers, Baba Brooks, Bonnie & Skitto, Eric Morris, Pioneers, Stranger & Patsy, Techniques, Winston Wright)

DON DRUMMOND JUNIOR
67	Caltone TONE 104	Sir Pratt Special/HEMSLEY MORRIS: Love Is Strange	£90
68	Caltone TONE 124	Dirty Dozen/PHIL PRATT: Reach Out	£90
70	Jackpot JP 710	Memory Of Don Drummond/TOBIES: Resting	£20
82	Rush NIBZ 001	The Clash And The Specials Go To Jail/Jailbird Dub/Rudies Ska (12", p/s)	£25

(see also Vincent Gordon)

KEITH DRUMMOND
| 82 | Bengad | Love Grows/(Version) (12") | £20 |

PETE DRUMMOND & THE VHF BAND
| 72 | Warner Bros K 16232 | Rocking At The BBC/Goodbye (vinyl 78) | £20 |

DRY CLEANING

18	It's OK	SWEET PRINCESS (cassette)	£60
21	4AD 4AD0415MCE	Bug Eggs/Tony Speaks! (cassette)	£50
21	4AD – 4AD0334SE	Scratchcard Lanyard/Bug Eggs (p/s, yellow vinyl)	£15
19	It's OK OK 002	BOUNDARY ROAD SNACKS AND DRINKS & SWEET PRINCESS (LP, compilation of two EPs, black splatter vinyl, limited) (LP)	£150
21	4AD 4AD0254LP	NEW LONG LEG (LP, yellow vinyl, some with free 7")	£25
21	4AD 0254LPE2	NEW LONG LEG (LP, clear vinyl, with CD)	£25
22	4AD no cat no.	STUMPWORK (LP, Blood Records exclusive, 500 numbered, alternate sleeve, clear vinyl, piece of mastertape included)	£30
22	4AD 4AD 0504LP	STUMPWORK (LP, white vinyl, with bonus 7" Don't Press Me/Swampy)	£35
24	It's OK 4AD 0571LP	BOUNDARY ROAD SNACKS AND DRINKS & SWEET PRINCESS (LP, repress, printed inners)	£20

DRY FRUIT

70	Staple ST 004	Magic Thimble/The Die Is Cast	£40

DRY ICE

69	B&C CB 115	Running To The Convent/Nowhere To Go	£25

(see also Pluto)

DRY RIB

79	Clockwork COR 001	THE DRY SEASON (EP, 33rpm, photocopied foldover p/s, screen-printed labels)	£30

(see also Television Personalities, Times, L'Orange Mechanik)

DRY THE RIVER

12	RCA 88691934251	SHALLOW BED (2-LP)	£60

DRY WATERS

72	Denby DEN 003	Crystal Ball/The Magic Valley	£150

AMANCIO D'SILVA

69	Columbia SX 6322	INTEGRATION (LP, mono)	£1500
69	Columbia SCX 6322	INTEGRATION (LP, stereo)	£1200
71	Columbia SCX 6465	REFLECTIONS - THE ROMANTIC GUITAR OF AMANCIO D'SILVA (LP)	£50

(see also Cosmic Eye, Joe Harriott)

D.S.K.F.

92	WG 001	NEW SCIENCE EP (12", stickered white label)	£100

D.S.P.

92	FX FXUKT 10	Obsession/Revenge Attack/Intravenus/Kebab (12")	£20

D TO THE K

88	BPM BP12004	Hard But Live/Ease Up Your Mind (12")	£25

D12

01	Shady 493080-1	DEVILS NIGHT (2-LP)	£30

DUALS

61	London HL 9450	Stick Shift/Cruising	£25

DUBBING IN THE U.K.

81	Star Light SDLP 902	DUBBING IN THE U.K.(LP)	£30

DUB FACTORY

95	Dub Factory GEMCD 001	VOYAGE INTO DUB - THE 1st JOURNEY (LP)	£18

DUB JUDAH

90	Dub Jockey DJ012	No Tresspassers/FOUNDATION PLAYERS: Version (12")	£15
92	Dub Jockey DJ021	Babylon Is A Trap/Version	£15
92	Dub Jockey DJLP 002	BABYLON IS A TRAP (LP)	£40
93	Dub Jockey DJLP 003	DUBTECH DUB (LP)	£30
94	Dub Jockey DJLP 004	BETTER TO BE GOOD (LP)	£30

DUBKASM

04	Sufferah's Choice DUBK02	Displaced African/Higher Judgement (12")	£20
05	Sufferah's Choice DUBK03	Deh Inna De Lion's Den/Iration Steppas MIx (12" featuring Iration Steppas)	£20

DUBS

57	London HLU 8526	Could This Be Magic/Such Lovin'	£250
57	London HLU 8526	Could This Be Magic/Such Lovin' (78)	£40
58	London HL 8684	Gonna Make A Change/Beside My Love	£200
58	London HL 8684	Gonna Make A Change/Beside My Love (78)	£30

DUB SYNDICATE

84	On-U Sound ON-U LP 18	POUNDING SYSTEM (LP)	£30
86	On-U Sound ON-U LP 38	TUNES FROM THE MISSING CHANNEL (LP)	£30
89	On-U Sound ON-U LP 47	STRIKE THE BALANCE (LP)	£30
91	On-U Sound ON-U LP 56	STONED IMMACULATE (LP)	£30
93	On-U Sound ON ULP G4	ECHOMANIA (LP, with free 7")	£30

DUBTRONIX

94	QDance DUBTLP 1	INTERFAZE - JUNGLISM VOL 1 (LP)	£20

DIANE DUCANE

79	Contact WN 2	Better Late Than Never/One Day	£30

JOHNNY DU CANN

77	Arista ARIST 128	Throw Him In Jail/Street Stutter	£25
77	Arista ARIST 145	Where's The Show/Hang Around	£30

(see also Attack, Andromeda, Five Day Week Straw People, Atomic Rooster, Hard Stuff, Status Quo)

MINT VALUE £

DUCKS DELUXE
74	RCA LPL1 5008	DUCKS DELUXE (LP)	£15
74	RCA SF 8402	TAXI TO THE TERMINAL ZONE (LP)	£15
79	Blue Moon BMLP 001	LAST NIGHT OF A PUB ROCK BAND (2-LP)	£15

(see also Brinsley Schwarz)

DUET EMMO
81	Mute MUTE 25	OR SO IT SEEMS (12" EP)	£18

(see also Dome, Wire)

D DUFFUS
79	Jay Dee JD 009	Is It Just A Dream/Cheaters (12")	£50

SHENLEY DUFFAS
62	Island WI 036	Give To Get/What You Gonna Do (as S. Duffas; B-side actually with Millie Small)	£30
63	Island WI 063	Fret Man Fret/Doreen	£35
63	Island WI 093	What A Disaster/I Am Rich	£35
63	Island WI 115	Know The Lord/TOMMY McCOOK: Ska Ba	£55
63	Island WI 125	Easy Squeal/Things Ain't Going Right	£45
63	R&B JB 134	No More Wedding Bells/Let Them Fret	£50
64	R&B JB 146	Big Mouth/FRANKIE ANDERSON: Peanut Vendor	£50
64	R&B JB 152	Christopher Columbus/CARL BRYAN ORCHESTRA: Barber Chair	£50
64	R&B JB 154	Mother-In-Law/DON DRUMMOND & GROUP: Festival	£50
64	Black Swan WI 440	Digging A Ditch/He's Coming Down	£40
64	Black Swan WI 443	Gather Them In/Crucifixion	£40
64	Rio R 41	I Will Be Glad/Heariso (as Shandly Duffas)	£40
65	Island WI 182	La La La/UPCOMING WILLOWS: Jonestown Special	£50
65	Island WI 184	You Are Mine/UPCOMING WILLOWS: Red China	£60
65	Island WI 186	Rukumbine/One Morning	£45
72	Upsetter US 380	Bet You Don't Know/UPSETTERS: Ring Of Fire	£40
72	Dynamic DYN 451	Peace (with Soul Avengers)/UPSETTERS: Peace — Version	£15
72	Pama PM859	At The End/Good Night My Love	£20
72	Grape GR 3031	Sincerely/Sincerely — Version (with Upsetters)	£20

(see also Chenley Duffus, Billy Dyce)

CHRIS DUFFIN
76	Deroy ADM LP 864	HEY SANDY (LP)	£250

CHENLEY DUFFUS
72	Upsetter US-386	To Be A Lover/Baby Lose Burning	£20

(see also Shenley Duffas)

DUFFY (1)
73	Chapter One SCHR 184	The Joker/Running Away	£18
70	Chapter One CHS-R 814	SCRUFFY DUFFY (LP, red/silver label)	£300

DUFFY (2)
08	A&M 176 696-9	ROCKFERRY (LP, printed inner)	£30

STEPHEN 'TIN TIN' DUFFY
85	10	She Loves Me/She Loves It (p/s, withdrawn)	£40
85	10	Baby Impossible (p/s, withdrawn)	£40

(see also Hawks, Lilac Time)

DUFFY'S NUCLEUS
67	Decca F 22547	Hound Dog/Mary Open The Door	£50

(see also Duffy Power, Pentangle, John McLaughlin)

DUGZ
14	Time and Matter T&M 015	The Berlin Lights : Caught In A War/Hit The Floor	£20

DENVER DUKE & JEFFREY NULL BLUEGRASS BOYS
63	Starlite STEP 33	DENVER DUKE & JEFFREY NULL BLUEGRASS BOYS (EP)	£15

DORIS DUKE
71	Mojo 2092 017	If She's Your Wife Who Am I?/It Sure Was Fun	£15
71	Mojo 2916 001	I'M A LOSER (LP)	£30
71	Mojo 2916 006	A LEGEND IN HER OWN TIME (LP)	£30
75	Contempo CRM 111	A LEGEND IN HER OWN TIME (LP, reissue)	£20
75	Contempo CLP 519	WOMAN (LP)	£30

GEORGE DUKE
75	MPS MC 25671	I LOVE THE BLUES SHE HEARD MY CRY (LP)	£15
75	MPS BAP 5064	THE AURA WILL PREVAIL (LP)	£25

JAMES DUKE
86	Creole CR 93	Hold On/Zyzafon (p/s)	£150
86	Creole CRT 93	Hold On/Zyzafon (12", p/s)	£250

PATTY DUKE
65	United Artists (S)ULP 1123	DON'T JUST STAND THERE (LP, mono/stereo)	£50

DUKE ALL STARS
68	Blue Cat BS 111	Letter To Mummy And Daddy (Parts 1 & 2)	£80

DUKE & DUCHESS
55	London HLU 8206	Borrowed Sunshine/Get Ready For Love (with Sir Hubert Pimm)	£40

(see also Sir Hubert Pimm)

DUKE OF BURLINGTON
71	Decca F23120	Flash/Slot Machine	£15

AGGIE DUKES
57	Vogue V 9090	John John/Well Of Loneliness...£250
57	Vogue V 9090	John John/Well Of Loneliness (78)..£40

DUKES NOBLEMEN
69	Philips BF 1691	City Of Windows/Thank You For Your Loving...£25

DUKES OF ILLYRIA
70	IAMBIG 0001	Food Of Love/Come Away Death...£20

DUKES OF STRATOSPHEAR
85	Virgin VS 763	The Mole From The Ministry/My Love Explodes (die-cut bag, 70s Virgin label)..............£15
87	Virgin VSY 982	You're A Good Man Albert Brown/Vanishing Girl (p/s, 5,000 on marbled lilac vinyl)......£20
85	Virgin WOW 1	25 O'CLOCK (LP, no barcode on first editions, 70s Virgin logo)...........................£30
87	Virgin VP 2440	PSONIC PSUNSPOT (LP, gatefold, 5,000 on marbled vinyl)................................£30
87	Virgin VP 2440	PSONIC PSUNSPOT (LP, gatefold)..£20
10	Ape House APELPP023	25 O'CLOCK (LP, reissue)...£20
10	Ape House APELPP024	PSONIC PSUNSPOT (LP, reissue)...£25
10	Ape House APEBOX 002	THE COMPLETE AND UTTER DUKES (LP/2CD/12"/7" box set, ephemera, jigsaw))........£300

(see also XTC)

DUKE SPIRIT
05	Loog 987099	CUTS ACROSS THE LAND (LP, textured gatefold sleeve)...................................£20
12	Fiction 3700883	DRESDEN LIVE (LP, 300 only)..£30

DULCIMER
71	Nepentha 6437 003	AND I TURNED AS I HAD TURNED AS A BOY (LP, gatefold sleeve)........................£300
80	Happy Face MMLP 1021	A LAND FIT FOR HEROES (LP, private pressing)..£15

DUM DUM
72	Phillips 6414-318	Peter Gunn/Cosa Nostra..£15

MARTIN DUMAS JR
15	BBE 304SLP	Attitude Belief And Determination/Non-Stop To The Top (12", p/s reissue)...................£20

DUMB ANGELS
88	Fierce FRIGHT 033	Love And Mercy/Love And Mercy (p/s, numbered)..£55

(see also Pooh Sticks)

JOHN DUMMER (BLUES BAND)
68	Mercury MF 1040	Travelling Man/40 Days (as John Dummer Blues Band)..................................£20
69	Mercury MF 1119	Try Me One More Time/Riding At Midnight (as John Dummer Blues Band)............£15
70	Fontana 6007 027	Happy/Nightingale (unissued in U.K.; France-only)......................................£0
69	Mercury SMCL 20136	CABAL (LP, black/silver label)...£200
69	Mercury SMCL 20167	JOHN DUMMER BAND (LP, black/silver label)...£200
70	Philips 6309 008	FAMOUS MUSIC BAND (LP, gatefold sleeve, black/silver labels)..........................£150
72	Philips 6382 039	THIS IS THE JOHN DUMMER BLUES BAND (LP)...£20
73	Philips 6382 040	VOLUME II — TRY ME ONE MORE TIME (LP)...£20
72	Vertigo 6360 055	BLUE (LP, gatefold sleeve, small swirl label)..£600
73	Vertigo 6360 083	OOBLEEDOOBLEE JUBILEE (LP, as John Dummer Oobleedooblee Band, small swirl label)..£250

(see also Nick Pickett, Dave Kelly, Tony McPhee)

DUMMY RUN
97	Hot Air BSE LP 002	ICE CREAM HEADACHE (LP)...£15

(see also Stock, Hausen & Walkman)

DUNAMIS
79	Daybreak DB 2602	I CAN FLY (LP, signed)..£60
79	Daybreak DB 2602	I CAN FLY (LP, un-signed)..£15

AYNSLEY DUNBAR (RETALIATION)
67	Blue Horizon 3109	Warning/Cobwebs (in p/s)...£60
67	Blue Horizon 3109	Warning/Cobwebs...£30
68	Liberty LBF 15132	Watch 'N' Chain/Roamin' And Ramblin'..£15
68	Liberty LBL/LBS 83154	AYNSLEY DUNBAR RETALIATION (LP, mono/stereo).....................................£130
68	Liberty LBL/LBS 83177	DR. DUNBAR'S PRESCRIPTION (LP, mono/stereo).......................................£150
69	Liberty LBS 83223	TO MUM FROM AYNSLEY AND THE BOYS (LP)..£150
70	Liberty LBS 83316	REMAINS TO BE HEARD (LP)..£150
71	Warner Bros WS 3010	BLUE WHALE (LP, green label)..£70

(see also John Mayall & Bluesbreakers, Heavy Jelly, Annette & Victor Brox, Exchequers)

SCOTT DUNBAR
71	Ahura Mazda AMS SDS 1	FROM LAKE MARY (LP)..£30

JOHNNY DUNCAN (& BLUE GRASS BOYS)
57	Columbia DB 3925	Kaw-Liga/Ella Speed (gold label lettering)..£20
57	Columbia DB 3959	Last Train To San Fernando/Rock-A-Billy Baby (gold label lettering)...................£20
57	Columbia 33S 1122	TENNESSEE SONG BAG (10" LP)..£30
58	Columbia 33S 1129	JOHNNY DUNCAN SALUTES HANK WILLIAMS (10" LP)..................................£30
61	Columbia 33SX 1328	BEYOND THE SUNSET (LP)..£15

LESLEY DUNCAN (& JOKERS)
63	Parlophone R 5034	I Want A Steady Guy/Movin' Away (as Lesley Duncan & Jokers).......................£15
64	Parlophone R 5106	Tell Me/You Kissed Me Boy...£15
65	Mercury MF 847	Just For The Boy/See That Guy...£20
65	Mercury MF 876	Run To Love/Only The Lonely And Me...£20
65	Mercury MF 939	Hey Boy/I Go To Sleep...£60
71	CBS 64202	SING CHILDREN SING (LP, gatefold sleeve, orange labels)...........................£20

MINT VALUE £

| 72 | CBS 64807 | EARTH MOTHER (LP, gatefold sleeve, orange labels) | £15 |
| 74 | GM GML 1007GM | EVERYTHING CHANGES (LP) | £15 |

(see also Mitchell/Coe Mysteries, Pete Townshend, Phil Lynott, Madeline Bell, Joe Brown & Vicki Brown)

TOMMY DUNCAN
| 66 | Sue WI 4002 | Dance, Dance, Dance/Let's Try It Over Again | £40 |

DIANE DUNCANE
| 79 | Contact 2 | Better Late Than Never/One Day (We're Gonna Do It Again) | £15 |

DELROY DUNKLEY
| 70 | Hot Rod HR 109 | I Wish You Well/TONY & DELROY: Impossible Love | £20 |

ERROL(L) DUNKLEY
67	Rio R 109	Love Me Forever/VIETNAM ALLSTARS: The Toughest	£100
67	Rio R 131	You're Gonna Need Me/Seek And You'll Find	£55
68	Island WI 3150	Once More/I'm Not Your Man	£60
68	Amalgamated AMG 800	Please Stop Your Lying/Feel So Fine (B-side actually by Tommy McCook & Band)	£50
68	Amalgamated AMG 805	I'm Going Home/I'm Not Your Man	£50
68	Amalgamated AMG 807	The Scorcher/Do It Right Tonight	£80
68	Amalgamated AMG 820	Love Brother/I Spy	£45
69	Fab FAB 117	I'll Take You In My Arms/KING CANNON: Daphney Reggae	£40
70	Unity UN 554	My Special Prayer/Never Hurt The One You Love	£15
70	Banana BA 302	Satisfaction/CECIL LOCKE: Sing Out Loud	£35
71	Big BG 324	Deep Meditation/RUPIE EDWARDS ALL STARS: Meditation Version	£25
72	Camel CA 87	Black Cinderella/PHIL PRATT ALLSTARS: Our Anniversary (B-side actually Tropic Shadows)	£25
73	Grape GR 3039	Why Did You Do It/One Love	£15
73	Count Shelley CS 3039	Girl You Cried/Where Must I Go	£15
73	Ackee 507	Keep The Pressure Down/Version	£55
75	Kiss KISS 11	Praise Jah All The Time/KISS ALLSTARS : Jah Rockers (12")	£25
77	Aries ARI 001	Hard Luck Story/To Hell And Forward (p/s both with Jah Steach, actually Jah Stitch)	£100
78	Arawak ARK DD 002	Little Way Different/Differentiah (with Dreadful Julio) (12")	£25
79	Success SRLD 004	Down Below/The End/Untitled (12")	£20
80	Third World TW DIS 01	Little Angel/GENE RONDO: Rebel Woman (12")	£25
82	Success SRLD 014	If You Say So/AFRICAN BROTHERS: Mystery Or Nature	£15
80s	PC Music PCDD 006	You Have Been Bad/Militant Man (12")	£20
73	Attack ATLP 1003	DARLING OOH! (LP)	£60
79	Black Joy DH 802	DISCO SHOWCASE (LP)	£30
76	Third World TWLP 101	SIT AND CRY OVER YOU (LP)	£40
79	Trojan TR 179	DARLING OOH! (LP, reissue)	£25
91	Attack ATLP 116	DARLING OOH! (LP, reissue)	£15

(see also Errol & His Group, Gaynor & Erroll], Mister Versatile, Don Lee, Ken Parker, Bongo Herman)

GEORGE DUNN
| 73 | Leader LEE 4042 | GEORGE DUNN (LP, with insert) | £18 |

MIKE DUNN
| 90 | Desire LUVLP 8 | FREE YOUR MIND (LP, die-cut front) | £20 |

DUNNO
| 71 | M&M FFMS 100013 | Sunday Girl/Magic Beat | £20 |

BLIND WILLIE DUNN'S GIN BOTTLE FOUR WITH KING OLIVER
| 54 | Columbia SCM 5100 | Jet Black Blues/Blue Blood Blues | £25 |
| 54 | Columbia DB3440 | Jet Black Blues/Blue Blood Blues (78) | £15 |

(see also Eddie Lang & Lonnie Johnson)

DUPARS
| 76 | Contempo 2104 | Love Cookin'/Instrumental | £30 |

CHAMPION JACK DUPREE
51	Jazz Parade B 16	Fisherman's Blues/County Jail Special (78)	£30
62	Storyville A 45051	Whiskey Head Woman/Shirley May	£20
67	Decca F 12611	Barrelhouse Woman/Under Your Hood	£25
67	Blue Horizon 45-1007	Get Your Head Happy/Easy Is The Way (with T.S. McPhee)	£120
68	Blue Horizon 57-3140	I Haven't Done No-One No Harm/How Am I Doing It (with Stan Webb)	£20
69	Blue Horizon 57-3152	Ba'la Fouche/Kansas City	£30
69	Blue Horizon 57-3158	I Want To Be A Hippy/Goin' Back To Louisiana	£25
61	Storyville SEP 381	BLUES ANTHOLOGY VOL. 1 (EP)	£15
64	RCA RCX 7137	RHYTHM AND BLUES VOL. 1 (EP)	£15
64	Decca DFE 8586	LONDON SPECIAL (EP, with Keith Smith Climax Band)	£60
65	Ember EMB 4564	JACK DUPREE (EP)	£25
59	London Jazz LTZ-K 15171	BLUES FROM THE GUTTER (LP)	£50
61	London Jazz LTZ-K 15217	CHAMPION JACK'S NATURAL AND SOULFUL BLUES LP, mono)	£65
61	London Jazz SAH-K 6150	CHAMPION JACK'S NATURAL AND SOULFUL BLUES LP, stereo)	£75
65	Storyville SLP 145	TROUBLE TROUBLE (LP)	£25
65	Xtra XTRA 1028	CABBAGE GREENS (LP)	£25
65	Storyville SLP 161	PORTRAITS IN BLUES (LP)	£40
66	Decca LK/SKL 4747	FROM NEW ORLEANS TO CHICAGO (LP)	£100
67	Storyville 670 194	CHAMPION JACK DUPREE (LP)	£25
67	Decca SKL 4871	CHAMPION JACK DUPREE AND HIS BIG BLUES BAND (LP)	£125
68	Blue Horizon 7-63206	WHEN YOU FEEL THE FEELING YOU WAS FEELING (LP)	£90
69	Blue Horizon 7-63214	SCOOBYDOOBYDOO (LP)	£120

(see also T.S. McPhee)

CHAMPION JACK DUPREE/JIMMY RUSHING
64	Ember CJS 800	TWO SHADES OF BLUE (LP)	£18

(see also Jimmy Rushing)

SIMON DUPREE & BIG SOUND
67	Parlophone R 5574	Reservations/You Need A Man	£15
67	Parlophone PMC/PCS 7029	WITHOUT RESERVATIONS (LP, yellow & black label, with "sold in the U.K..." text, laminated sleeve)	£125

(see also Moles, Gentle Giant, Shape Of The Rain)

DUPREES
62	HMV POP 1073	You Belong To Me/Take Me As I Am	£25
62	Stateside SS 143	My Own True Love/Ginny	£15
63	London HLU 9678	I'd Rather Be Here In Your Arms/I Wish I Could Believe You	£15
63	London HLU 9709	Gone With The Wind/Let's Make Love Again	£15
63	London HLU 9774	Why Don't You Believe Me?/My Dearest One	£15
63	London HLU 9813	Have You Heard?/Love Eyes	£15
64	London HLU 9843	It's No Sin/The Sand And The Sea	£15
65	CBS 201803	Around The Corner/They Said It Couldn't Be Done	£15
66	CBS 202028	She Waits For Him/Norma Jean	£15
70	Polydor 2058 077	Check Yourself/The Sky's The Limit	£35

DURAN DURAN
87	EMI TRADEX 1	Skin Trade/We Need You (poster p/s)	£15
93	Parlophone DD 16	Ordinary World/My Antarctica (p/s)	£15
93	Parlophone DD 17	Come Undone/Ordinary World (Acoustic Version) (p/s)	£20
90	Parlophone PCSD 112	LIBERTY (LP, inner)	£30
93	Parlophone 7988761	THE WEDDING ALBUM (LP, inner)	£150
95	Parlophone 72438518981	THANK YOU (LP, with poster)	£100
11	Tape Modern DURANLP01	ALL YOU NEED IS NOW (2-LP)	£150
14	EMI DDLIVEX82	LIVE 2011 (2-LP, screen printed sleeve)	£80
15	Warner Bros. 9362 49251 5	PAPER GODS (2-LP)	£30
15	Vinyl Factory VF 212	PAPER GODS (box set, 2 x 12", prints, booklet, magnets, signed, 350 only)	£250
18	Warner Bros. 9362 49078 8	BUDOKAN (LP)	£25
19	Parlophone DDRSD2019	AS THE LIGHTS GO DOWN (2-LP, one side etched)	£40
21	BMG 4050538693669/3652	FUTURE PAST (LP, red or white vinyl)	£20
22	Tape Modern/BMG 538805881	MEDAZZALAND (2-LP, 45rpm, g/f, pink vinyl)	£30

ALLISON DURBIN
69	Decca LK-R/SKL-R 4996	I HAVE LOVED ME A MAN (LP)	£40

JUDITH DURHAM
74	Pye NSLP 18431	THE HOTTEST BAND IN TOWN (LP)	£15

TERRY DURHAM
69	Deram DML/SML 1042	CRYSTAL TELEPHONE (LP, with insert, red/white label with large logo)	£40

(see also Storyteller)

LAWRENCE DURRELL
70	Turret TRT 102	ULYSSES COME BACK (LP)	£40

DURUTTI COLUMN
80	Factory FACT 14	THE RETURN OF THE DURUTTI COLUMN (LP, with sandpaper sleeve, with Martin Hannett's "Testcard" flexidisc [FACT 14C])	£500
80	Factory FACT 14	THE RETURN OF THE DURUTTI COLUMN (LP, with sandpaper sleeve, without Martin Hannett's "Testcard" flexidisc [FACT 14C])	£400
80	Factory FACT 14	THE RETURN OF THE DURUTTI COLUMN (reissue, different sleeve)	£20
82	Factory FACT 44	LC (LP, 1st pressing with misspelt 'Durrutti Column' on spine, with inner)	£30
83	Factory FACT 74	ANOTHER SETTING (LP, with perfumed cut-out insert)	£30
83	VU VINI 1	LIVE AT THE VENUE LONDON (LP)	£25
84	Factory FACT 84	WITHOUT MERCY (LP, pasted on picture)	£20
86	Factory FACT 164c	VALUABLE PASSAGES (cassette in box with insert)	£35
86	Factory FACT 14C	THE RETURN OF THE DURUTTI COLUMN (reissue, cassette in box with insert)	£35
86	Factory FACT 44c	LC (reissue, cassette in box with insert)	£35
86	Factory FACT 74c	ANOTHER SETTING (reissue, cassette in box with insert)	£35
86	Factory FACT 84c	WITHOUT MERCY (reissue, cassette in box with insert)	£35
87	Factory FACT 204	THE GUITAR AND OTHER MACHINES (LP, inner)	£30
88	Factory FACT 244	VINI REILLY (LP, with free p/s 7" "I Know Very Well How I Got My Note Wrong" [FAC 244++] by Vincent Gerard & Steven Patrick)	£50
88	Factory FACD 244	VINI REILLY (CD, with 3" CD "I Know Very Well How I Got My Note Wrong" [FAC CD 244++] by Vincent Gerard & Steven Patrick)	£45
88	Factory FACT 244	VINI REILLY (LP, without 7")	£20
90	Factory FACT 274	OBEY THE TIME (LP)	£35
19	Factory FBN 274	OBEY THE TIME (2-LP, reissue. yellow/purple vinyl)	£20
20	Demon DEMREC743	REBELLION (LP, reissue, blue vinyl)	£15
20	Factory Benelux FBN 244	VINI REIILLY (2-LP, clear vinyl, 7", reissue)	£35

(see also Nosebleeds, Morrissey)

IAN DURY (& THE BLOCKHEADS)
77	Stiff BUY 23	Sweet Gene Vincent/You're More Than Fair (solid centre)	£30
78	Stiff BUY 2712	What A Waste/Wake Up (12", plain white sleeve, 100 only)	£100
78	Stiff FREEBIE 1	Sex And Drugs And Rock And Roll/England's Glory/Two Steep Hills (p/s, free at NME party/competition, 1500 only)	£20
77	FREEBIE 1	Sex And Drugs And Rock And Roll/England's Glory/Two Steep Hills (white label 7" vinyl test pressing, one copy known)	£300
78	Stiff BUY 38	Hit Me With Your Rhythm Stick/There Ain't Half Been Some Clever Bastards (red	£800

MINT VALUE £

		vinyl, p/s, one, poss two copies known)	
85	MT1	**Fuck Off Noddy/SUN RA: Nuclear War** (white label, 500 only)	£50
77	Stiff SEEZ 4	**NEW BOOTS AND PANTIES!!** (LP, with bonus track 'Sex And Drugs And Rock And Roll') ...£20	
77	Stiff SEEZ 4	**NEW BOOTS AND PANTIES!!** (LP, limited edition gold vinyl)	£25

(see also Kilburn & The High Roads, Greatest Show On Earth, Loving Awareness)

BAXTER DURY, ETIENNE DE CRECY & DELILAH HOLLIDAY
18	PIAS LL116LP	**BED**	£20

ANDREW DURYER
75	Real RR 2003	**BALLADS OF A WANDERER** (LP)...	£25

JEAN DUSHON
65	Chess CRL 4000	**MAKE WAY FOR JEAN DUSHON** (LP)	£40

LA DÜSSELDORF
78	Radar ADA 5	**La Düsseldorf/Silver Cloud** (unissued, white label promo only)	£25
78	Radar RAD 7	**DUSSELDORF** (LP)	£25
78	Radar RAD 10	**VIVA** (LP, with lyric inner)	£25
80	Albion ALB 107	**INDIVIDUELLOS** (LP)...	£25

(see also Neu!)

DUST (1)
68	Full Stop FS 039	**Before Time/There You Are**	£45

DUST (2)
72	Kama Sutra 2319	**DUST** (LP)	£20

DUST BROTHERS
93	Diamond DBS 333	**Song To The Siren** (12" single sided).................................	£40
93	Diamond DBS 333	**Song To The Siren** (12", no p/s, 500 only)..........................	£40
93	Junior Boys Own JBO 10	**Song To The Siren/Song To The Siren** (Sabres Of Paradise Mixes) (12", p/s) ...	£15
94	Dust Up Beats NS 1	**Loops Of Fury** (12")..	£25
94	Boys Own COLLECT 004	**14TH CENTURY SKY EP** (12", no p/s)	£15
94	Junior Boys Own JBO 20	**MY MERCURY MOUTH EP** (12", JBO sleeve)	£15

(see also Chemical Brothers)

DUSTY LEDGE
71	Axes AX 114	**Sign Here/Look To The Sun**	£50

DUSTY SHELF
74	Sprint SP 2	**Jacobs Ladder/You Don't Realise**	£25

SLIM DUSTY
60	Columbia SEG 8009	**SLIM DUSTY AND HIS COUNTRY ROCKERS** (EP)	£15

DUTCH SWING COLLEGE BAND
51	Saturn EGX 106	**Alexander's Ragtime Band/Birthday Blues** (78 picture disc, probably the first issued in the UK)	£15

DUTCHESS
81	B'kreig Waxworks EJSP 9580	**Your Love/Dead And Gone**	£150

JACQUES DUTRONC
66	Vogue VRS 7015	**Et Moi, Et Moi, Et Moi/Mini-Mini-Mini**	£15
67	Vogue VRL 3029	**JACQUES DUTRONC** (LP)	£60

JOSE DUVAL
57	London HLR 8458	**Message Of Love/That's What You Mean To Me**.....................	£25

D&V
83	Crass 121984/1	**Jekyll And Hyde/Wake Up/High Above/Today's Conclusion/Step Inside/DignityS21RN** (fold-out sleeve)..	£15
85	Crass CATNO 1	**INSPIRATION GAVE THEM THE MOTIVATION TO MOVE OUT OF THEIR ISOLATION** (LP, inner)	£15

JOHNNY MBIZO DYANI
87	Cadillac SGC 1016	**WITCHDOCTORS SON TOGETHER** (LP)................................	£18
88	Cadillac SCG 1017	**REJOICE** (LP)..	£20

JUDY DYBLE
06	Fungus AGFLP001	**SONGS FROM THE SPINDLE AND THE WHORL** (LP, handmade sleeve, 250 only, numbered)...	£60
13	Plane Groovy PLG 025	**FLOW AND CHANGE** (LP, printed inner, 198g)	£25
15	Starcrazy SC001-003	**GATHERING THE THREADS** (FIFTY YEARS OF STUFF) (3CD, foldout digipak, booklet) £50	
17	Acid Jazz AJXLP 416	**SUMMER DANCING** (with Andy Lewis) (LP)...........................	£18
18	Acid Jazz AJXLP447	**EARTH IS SLEEPING** (LP, printed inner)	£15
20	Plane Groovy PLG 084	**BETWEEN A BREATH AND A BREATH** (with David Longdon) (LP, blue vinyl, 200 copies) ...£40	

(see also Fairport Convention, Giles, Giles & Fripp)

BILLY DYCE
72	G.G. GG 4532	**Be My Guest/HUGH ROY: Way Down South**	£15
72	Pama PM 835	**Be My Guest/HUGH ROY: Way Down South**...........................	£15

DYKE & BLAZERS
67	Pye International 7N 25413	**Funky Broadway** (Parts 1 & 2)	£20

MICHAEL DYKE
70s	Attack ATT 8112	**Saturday Night Special/CHINNA : Saturday Night Version**	£40

BOB DYLAN
SINGLES
66	CBS 201900	**Can You Please Crawl Out Your Window/Highway 61 Revisited**..............	£15
66	CBS 202053	**One Of Us Must Know** (Sooner Or Later)**/Queen Jane Approximately**	£20

MINT VALUE £

66	CBS 202258	I Want You/Just Like Tom Thumb's Blues (live)	£15
66	CBS 2700	Leopard-Skin Pill-Box Hat/Most Likely You Go Your Way And I'll Go Mine (p/s)	£45
67	CBS 2476	Mixed Up Confusion/Corrine Corrina (unissued in U.K.)	£0
84	CBS A 4055	Jokerman (Special Faded Radio Version)/Licence To Kill (p/s, promo only)	£15
89	CBS 6553588	Everything Is Broken/Dead Man, Dead Man/I Want You (Live) (12" with limited edition album sleeve print)	£20
20	Secret 7 S744	Blind Willie McTell (single-sided 'secret 7"' with unique covers, edition of 100))	£200

EPs

64	CBS 6051	DYLAN (Bob Dylan below song titles, solid/push-out centre, designer credits in bottom right corner, p/s)	£60
64	CBS 6051	DYLAN (Bob Dylan vertically on left; 'EXTENDED PLAY' on 1 line above 'EP 6051', push out centre – no designer credits, p/s)	£45
65	CBS 6051	DYLAN (Bob Dylan vertically on left; 'EXTENDED PLAY' on 2 lines above 'EP 6051', solid centre, no designer credits, p/s)	£45
66	CBS 6070	ONE TOO MANY MORNINGS (Only EP in Europe with five songs, p/s)	£50
66	CBS 6070	MR. TAMBOURINE MAN (length of EP on both sides: 27mm 'EXTENDED PLAY' on 1 line, 'Blossom Music LTD' on both sides. Solid/push-out centre, p/s)	£50
66	CBS 6078	MR. TAMBOURINE MAN (length of EP on side 1, 'EXTENDED PLAY' divided over 2 lines, 'Blossom Music' (side 1) 'Bossom Music Ltd' (Side 2),	£50
65	Fontana TFE 18009	WITH GOD ON OUR SIDE (Joan Baez and Bob Dylan title track)/PETE SEEGER: The Bells of Rhymney/JOAN BAEZ: Waggoner's Lad, p/s)	£75
65	Fontana TFE 18010	BLOWIN' IN THE WIND (BOB DYLAN: Blowin' In The Wind/JOAN BAEZ: Oh Freedom/ PETE SEEGER: Careless Love, p/s)	£75
65	Fontana TFE 18011	YE PLAYBOYS AND PLAYGIRLS (Bob Dylan and Pete Seeger title track/JOAN BAEZ: Te Ador, Te Manha/PETE SEEGER: This Land Is Mine, p/s)	£75

ALBUMS

62	CBS BPG 62022	BOB DYLAN (mono)	£75
62	CBS SBPG 62022	BOB DYLAN (stereo)	£75
63	CBS BPG 62193	THE FREEWHEELIN' BOB DYLAN (mono)	£60
63	CBS SBPG 62193	THE FREEWHEELIN' BOB DYLAN (stereo)	£50
63	CBS BPG 62251	THE TIMES THEY ARE A-CHANGIN' (mono)	£60
63	CBS SBPG 62251	THE TIMES THEY ARE A-CHANGIN' (stereo)	£50
64	CBS BPG 62429	ANOTHER SIDE OF BOB DYLAN (mono)	£60
64	CBS SBPG 62429	ANOTHER SIDE OF BOB DYLAN (stereo)	£50
65	CBS BPG 62515	BRINGING IT ALL BACK HOME (mono, flipback sleeve)	£60
65	CBS SBPG 62515	BRINGING IT ALL BACK HOME (stereo, flipback sleeve)	£50
65	CBS BPG 62572	HIGHWAY 61 REVISITED (mono)	£80
65	CBS SBGP 62572	HIGHWAY 61 REVISITED (stereo)	£70
66	CBS DDP 66012	BLONDE ON BLONDE (2LP, gatefold, 8 or 9 photos on inside, laminated outer sleeve, mono)	£150
66	CBS (S)DDP 66012	BLONDE ON BLONDE (2LP, gatefold, 8 or 9 photos to inside, laminated outer, stereo)	£100
67	CBS BPG 62847	BOB DYLAN'S GREATEST HITS (mono)	£18
68	CBS BGP 63252	JOHN WESLEY HARDING (mono)	£40

(The above LPs were originally issued with rough textured orange labels & flipback sleeves, without 'CBS Records' credit on rear sleeve & with inner sleeves advertising other CBS LPs. First pressings of Bob Dylan, The Freewheelin Bob Dylan, The Times They Are A-Changin', Another Side Of Bob Dylan, Bringing It All Back Home and Blond On Blond have '33' on the labels rather than 33 and a third which denote later 60s repressings. These copies are worth around half the value of the above LPs.)

68	CBS (S)BGP 63252	JOHN WESLEY HARDING (stereo)	£20
69	CBS (M) 63601	NASHVILLE SKYLINE (mono)	£30
69	CBS (S) 63601	NASHVILLE SKYLINE (stereo)	£15
70	CBS S 64085/6	SELF PORTRAIT	£15
71	CBS S 67239	MORE BOB DYLAN GREATEST HITS	£15
73	CBS S 69049	DYLAN	£15
73	CBS 69042	PAT GARRETT & BILLY THE KID	£20
74	Island ILPS 9261	PLANET WAVES ('pink rim palm tree' label, with inner sleeve)	£15
74	Island IDBD-1	BEFORE THE FLOOD (2-LP, gatefold)	£20
75	CBS 69097	BLOOD ON THE TRACKS (orange label, red inner with painting on rear sleeve)	£20
75	CBS 69097	BLOOD ON THE TRACKS (orange label, red inner with liner notes on rear sleeve)	£25
75	CBS S 88147	THE BASEMENT TAPES	£35
76	CBS S 86003	DESIRE (LP, inner)	£25
76	CBS CBS 86016	HARD RAIN (LP, with inner)	£15
78	CBS CBS 86067	STREET-LEGAL (printed inner)	£15
79	CBS CBS 96004	AT BUDOKAN (with poster and 16 page booklet)	£25
83	CBS 25539	INFIDELS (LP, inner)	£15
91	Columbia 468086	THE BOOTLEG SERIES VOLUMES 1-3 (5-LP box set, booklet)	£125
92	Columbia 472710	GOOD AS I BEEN TO YOU (LP, inner)	£30
93	Columbia 4748571	WORLD GONE WRONG (LP)	£100
95	Columbia 478374 1	MTV UNPLUGGED (2-LP)	£80
98	CBS CK265759-1	LIVE 1966 (2-LP)	£40
01	Columbia COL 504364 1	LOVE AND THEFT (2-LP, inners)	£40
06	Columbia 82876 87606 1	MODERN TIMES (2LP, gatefold, printed inners, 180g)	£30
09	Columbia 88697 43893 1	TOGETHER THROUGH LIFE (2LP, CD, printed inners, 180g)	£80
09	Columbia 88697 57323 1	CHRISTMAS IN THE HEART (LP/CD, printed inner)	£100
12	Sony No Cat No	THE 50th ANNIVERSARY COLLECTION (4xCD-R, barcode 88765460722, 100 copies only, beware of bootlegs)	£600
12	Columbia 88725457601	TEMPEST (2LP, CD, printed inners, insert)	£30
13	Columbia 88883799701	50th ANNIVERSARY COLLECTION (6LP box set, printed inners)	£400
15	Columbia 88750057961	SHADOWS IN THE NIGHT (LP/CD, printed inner, 180g)	£20
16	Columbia 88985316001	FALLEN ANGELS (LP, printed inner)	£20
17	Columbia 88985 41351 1	TRIPLICATE (3LP, hardback packaging, numbered edition)	£40
20	Columbia 19439780991	ROUGH AND ROWDY WAYS (2LP, gatefold, printed inners, olive vinyl)	£25

MINT VALUE £

| 23 | Columbia19658767481 | SHADOW KINGDOM (2LP, fourth side etched, gatefold, printed inners) | £25 |

ALBUMS : REISSUES

64	CBS BPG 62066	BOB DYLAN (LP, mono repressing)	£25
67	CBS SBGP 62572	HIGHWAY 61 REVISITED (LP, reissue, flipback sleeve, stereo with 33 and a third on the label)	£25
68	CBS S BPG 62022	BOB DYLAN (LP, stereo, repressing)	£20
68	CBS BPG 62193	THE FREEWHEELIN' BOB DYLAN (LP, reissue, not flipback sleeve witth 33 and a third on the label)	£18
68	CBS 62515	BRINGING IT ALL BACK HOME (LP, reissue, non-flipback sleeve, orange label)	£18
69	CBS 66012	BLONDE ON BLONDE (2-LP, stereo, smooth label, gatefold with no flipback, 9 photos)	£25
70	70s	BOB DYLAN (LP, reissue, orange/yellow labels)	£15
70	CBS SBPG 62251	THE TIMES THEY ARE A-CHANGIN' (LP, reissue, orange/yellow labels)	£15
70	CBS 62515	BRINGING IT ALL BACK HOME (LP, 70s reissue, non-flipback sleeve, orange/yellow label)	£15
70	CBS SBGP 62572	HIGHWAY 61 REVISITED (LP, 2nd reissue, orange/yellow labels, stereo)	£20
75	CBS S62429	ANOTHER SIDE OF BOB DYLAN (LP, reissue, orange/yellow labels)	£15
75	CBS 66012	BLONDE ON BLONDE (2-LP, gatefold, stereo reissue, orange/yellow labels, 7 photos)	£20
85	CBS 66509	BIOGRAPH (5-LP, box set, 2 booklets)	£35
98	Simply Vinyl SVLP 063	BLONDE ON BLONDE (2LP, gatefold, 9 photos, reissue)	£50

(see also Dick Farina, Band, George Harrison, Traveling Wilburys, Doug Sahm)

DYMONDS

| 71 | Big BG 326 | Girl You Are Too Young/RUPIE EDWARDS ALL STARS: Version | £15 |

(see also Diamonds)

DYNAMIC GANG

| 71 | Moodisc MU 3511 | I'll Never Believe In You/LLOYD WILLIS: Black Attack | £15 |

DYNAMIC MCS

| 87 | Tuff Groove TUFF002 | I Feel Dynamic (12") | £60 |

DYNAMIC SUPERIORS

| 77 | Motown PSLP 233 | Nowhere To Run/MANDRE: Solar Flight (Opus 1) (12") | £80 |
| 76 | Tamla Motown STNL 12007 | PURE PLEASURE (LP) | £15 |

DYNAMICS (JAMAICA)

| 68 | Blue Cat BS 104 | My Friends/NEVILLE IRONS: Soul Glide | £70 |
| 69 | Punch PH 1 | The Burner/Juckie Juckie (B-side actually by Tommy McCook & Carl Bryan) | £150 |

DYNAMICS (U.S.)

63	London HLX 9809	Misery/I'm The Man	£50
64	King KG 1007	So In Love With Me/Say You Will	£25
69	Atlantic 584 270	Ice Cream Song/The Love That I Need	£20

DYNAMITES

69	Duke DU 30	John Public/CLANCY ECCLES: Fire Corner (B-side actually by King Stitt)	£30
69	Duke DU 31	I Don't Care (actually by Dingle Brothers)/CLANCY ECCLES: Shoo-Be-Do	£40
69	Clandisc CLA 200	Mr. Midnight (Skokiaan)/KING STITT: Who Yeah	£20
70	Clandisc CLA 212	Black Beret/BARRY & AFFECTIONS: Love Me Tender	£15
70	Clandisc CLA 219	Sha La La La/Pop It Up	£15
69	Trojan/Clandisc TTL 21	FIRE CORNER (LP, with King Stitt)	£60

(see also Clancy Eccles & Dynamites, Baba Brooks, Dennis Alcapone, Diamonds, Joe Higgs, Silvertones, Carl Dawkins, Hopeton Lewis, Melodians, Cynthia Richards, Soul Twins, Stranger & Gladys, Carey & Lloyd)

DYNASTY

| 72 | Top Nix 134 | Tutankhamen/Let's Boogie | £15 |

DYNATONES

| 59 | Top Rank JAR 149 | Steel Guitar Rag/The Girl I'm Searching For (78) | £20 |
| 66 | Pye International 7N 25389 | The Fife Piper/And I Always Will | £50 |

ALAN DYSON

| 68 | Pye NPL 18218 | THE STILL SMALL VOICE OF...(LP) | £20 |

RONNIE DYSON

| 71 | CBS S 64779 | WHEN YOU GET RIGHT DOWN TO IT (LP) | £30 |

E

VINCE EAGER (& THE VAGABONDS)

58	Decca F 11023	Tread Softly Stranger & Yea Yea (as Vince Eager & The Vagabonds; unissued, 2 x 1-sided demos only)	£30
58	Parlophone R 4482	Five Days, Five Days/No More	£30
11	Stateside SS 2242	MORRISSEY: Glamorous Glue (2011 remaster)/VINCE EAGER: The World's Loneliest Man (Retro A label 'Stateside' promo in die-cut 'Stateside' sleeve, 150 only)	£250
58	Decca DFE 6504	VINCE EAGER AND THE VAGABONDS NO. 1 (EP)	£100

EAGLE

| 70 | Pye International 7N 25530 | Kickin' It Back To You/Come In, It's All For Free | £15 |
| 69 | Pye Intl. NSPL 28138 | COME UNDER NANCY'S TENT (LP) | £40 |

EAGLES (JAMAICA)

| 69 | Songbird SB 1006 | Rudam Bam/Prodigal Boy (B-side actually "Any Little Bit" by Crystals) | £50 |
| 72 | Duke Reid DR 2522 | Your Enemies Can't Hurt You/Version | £15 |

(see also Roy Richards)

EAGLES (U.K.)
63	Pye 7N 15571	Eagles Nest/Poinciana (unreleased) £0
63	Pye NPL 18084	SMASH HITS (LP) £30

EAGLES (U.S.)
75	Asylum K 53008	DESPERADO (LP, audiophile pressing, mail-order via Hi-Fi Today mag) £400
98	Simply Vinyl SVLP 050	HELL FREEZES OVER (2-LP, reissue) £100

EAGLES OF DEATH METAL
04	AntAcidAudio AAA 999	PEACE LOVE AND DEATH METAL (LP) £35

SNOOKS EAGLIN
60s	Storyville A 45056	Country Boy/Alberta (some with p/s) £15
60s	Storyville SEP 386	BLUES ANTHOLOGY VOL. 6 (EP) £20
61	Heritage HLP 1002	SNOOKS EAGLIN (LP, 99 only) £100
63	Storyville SLP 119	NEW ORLEANS STREET SINGER (LP) £25
64	Storyville SLP 140	VOL. 2 — BLUES FROM NEW ORLEANS (LP) £15
70s	Storyville 670 146	PORTRAITS IN BLUES VOLUME 1 (LP) £18

EARCANDY
93	Poor Person Prod. PPPR 1	SPACE IS JUST A PLACE (LP, handmade sleeve, 500 only) £20
94	Poor Person Prod. PPPR 2	TIME IS JUST A STATE OF MIND (LP, handmade sleeve) £20
95	Poor Person Prod. PPPR 5	SOUND IS JUST THE WAY YOU EAR IT (LP, handmade sleeve with insert, numbered, 600 only) £20
95	Poor Person Prod. PPPR 8	TASTING 1,2,3, TASTING (LP, handmade sleeve & insert, numbered, 500 only) £20

JON EARDLEY SEVEN
56	Esquire 32040	DOWN EAST (LP) £150

EARGASM
81	Venture EAR 26	This Is Lovers Rock/Name That Tune (as Eargasm, P Pop & Beagle) £20
80	Venture CUT 007	LOVERS DUB (LP) £40

CHARLES EARLAND
78	Mercury 9199831	Let The Music Play/Broken Heart (12") £15
80	CBS 84815	COMING TO YOU LIVE (LP) £15

EARL-JEAN
64	Colpix PX 729	I'm Into Somethin' Good/We Love And Learn £30
64	Colpix PX 748	Randy/They're Jealous Of Me £30

(see also Cookies)

JOSEPH EARLOCKS
80s	Freedom Sounds FSD014	Free Up The Blackman/JAMAICANS & I DAUGHTER : Country Life (12") £20

EARLS
63	Stateside SS 153	Remember Then/Let's Waddle £40
63	London HL 9702	Never/I Keep-A Tellin' You £50

EARLY B
82	Black Solidarity BSI 001	Imitator/Mi Huh Know (with Papa San) £40

EARTH (1)
69	CBS 4671	Resurrection City/Comical Man £40
69	Decca F 22908	Everybody Sing The Song/Stranger Of Fortune £15

EARTH (2)
15	Record Collector RCLP 019	ELEMENTAL (LP, silver sleeve) £30

EARTH & FIRE
70	Polydor 56790	Seasons/Paradise £15
71	Nepentha 6129 001	Invitation/Wild And Exciting £15
71	Nepentha 6437 004	EARTH AND FIRE (LP, gatefold sleeve, artwork by Roger Dean) £1000
73	Polydor 2310 262	ATLANTIS (LP, laminated sleeve) £30

EARTH & STONE
78	Different HAED 5	Back To Africa/Still In Slavery (12") £20
79	Cha Cha CHAD 09	Sweet Africa/Dance With Me (12") £35
79	Cha Cha CHAD 013	False Ruler/Don't Let Them Fool You (12") £50
79	Cha Cha CHAD 015	Slave Driver/Magic Woman (12") £30
77	Different DIFF 105	BACK TO AFRICA (LP) £50
79	Cha Cha CHADLP 007	KOOL ROOTS (LP, gatefold) £80

EARTHBOUND
79	Archway AR 17945	The Robot/Liberated Lady/Song For South Kensington (12" p/s with inserts) £25

EARTH BOYS
59	Capitol CL 14979	Barbara Ann/Space Girl £25

EARTH LEAKAGE TRIP
91	Moving Shadow SHADOW 1	PSYCHOTRONIC EP (12", p/s) £15

EARTHLING SOCIETY
11	Fruits De Mer Crustacean 19	The Green Manalishi (With The Two-Prong Crown)/And I Heard The Fire Sing (orange vinyl, folded p/s, inserts) £15

EARTHLINGS
65	Parlophone R 5242	Landing Of The Daleks/March Of The Robots £50

EARTH MAN
80	Feast	Life Is For Living/Love Is For Giving £100

EARTH OPERA
68	Elektra EKS 74016	EARTH OPERA (LP, stereo, gatefold sleeve)	£35
68	Elektra EKL 4016	EARTH OPERA (LP, mono, gatefold sleeve)	£40
69	Elektra EKS 74038	GREAT AMERICAN EAGLE TRAGEDY (LP)	£30

(see also Rowan Brothers)

EARTHQUAKES
69	Duke DU 54	Pair Of Wings/I Can't Stop Loving You	£50
69	Duke DU 56	Earthquake/Simmering	£25

(see also Sir Collins & Earthquakes)

EARTH, WIND & FIRE
71	Warner Bros. WS 1905	EARTH, WIND & FIRE (LP)	£30
72	CBS S 65208	LAST DAYS AND TIME (LP, gatefold)	£15
73	Columbia KC32194	HEAD TO THE SKY (LP, gatefold)	£15
74	CBS 65844	OPEN OUR EYES (LP)	£15
75	CBS 80575	THAT'S THE WAY OF THE WORLD (LP)	£15

EAST COAST ANGELS
77	Ruby RUB 207	Punk Rockin'/To Nite's The Nite (Irish pressing, no p/s)	£60

EASTER AND THE TOTEM
82	Ark Music (No Cat. No.)	HIP REPLACEMENT (LP)	£25
86	Ideologically Sound ET 1	THE SUM IS GREATER THAN ITS PARTS (LP)	£15

EASTER MONDAY
89	SRT TTWW001	EASTER MONDAY EP (numbered foldover p/s, 500 only)	£15

EASTERN VARIATION
86	Cartridge CRD 15	Baby I Love You/Version (12")	£30
86	XL 180	Creation/V.A.R.I.O.U.S. (12", p/s)	£40

EAST OF EDEN
68	Atlantic 584 198	King Of Siam/Ballad Of Harvey Kaye	£150
69	Deram DML 1038	MERCATOR PROJECTED (LP, mono, red/white label with large logo)	£200
69	Deram SML 1038	MERCATOR PROJECTED (LP, stereo, red/white label with large logo)	£100
70	Deram SML 1050	SNAFU (LP, mono, red/white label with small logo)	£200
70	Deram SML 1050	SNAFU (LP, stereo, red/white label with small logo)	£100
71	Decca SPA 157	WORLD OF EAST OF EDEN (LP, credited on sleeve and blue/silver label as a Deram release)	£15
71	Harvest SHVL 792	EAST OF EDEN (LP, gatefold sleeve, early copies with EMI box on side 1 label but no EMI box on side 2)	£80
71	Harvest SHVL 792	EAST OF EDEN (LP, gatefold sleeve)	£50
72	Harvest SHVL 792	EAST OF EDEN (LP, gatefold sleeve, non EMI 2nd pressing with indented centre perimeter)	£50
71	Harvest SHVL 796	NEW LEAF (LP, gatefold sleeve, with EMI on label)	£70

EAST RIVER PIPE
93	Sarah SARAH 75	Helmet On/Happytown/Axl Or Iggy (foldover p/s, insert)	£20
93	Sarah SARAH 78	She's A Real Good Time/My Life Is Wrong/Times Square Go-Go Boy (foldover p/s in poly bag, insert)	£20
93	Sarah SARAH 405	GOODBYE CALIFORNIA (10" LP)	£50
94	Sarah SARAH 621	POOR FRICKY (LP)	£60
95	Sarah SARAH 407	EVEN THE SUN WAS AFRAID (10" LP)	£45

EASTWOOD
70	SRT SRTS7332	Little Miss Lucy/Living To Learn	£200
71	CBS 7076	I Am Free/Gypsy	£45
72	CBS 7325	Orphan/Another Day In My Life	£25

ALAN JAMES EASTWOOD
72	President PT 379	Closer To The Truth/Strange News	£20
71	President PTLS 1037	SEEDS (LP)	£40

CLINT EASTWOOD (1)
62	Cameo SC 1056	COWBOY FAVOURITES... (LP)	£30

CLINT EASTWOOD (2)
79	Greensleeves GRED 25	True True Love/Me Go Deh Already (12")	£15
77	Jamaica Sounds JSLP 0010	JAH LIGHTS SHINING (LP)	£15
78	Live & Love LAP 011	STEP IT IN A ZION! (LP)	£15
78	Cha Cha CHALP003	DEATH IN THE ARENA (LP)	£45
78	Third World TWS933	AFRICAN YOUTH (LP)	£35
79	Burning Vibrations BV 1001	LOVE AND HAPPINESS (LP)	£20
80	Greensleeves GREL 17	SEX EDUCATION (LP)	£15

EASYBEATS
66	United Artists UP 1144	Come And See Her/Make You Feel Alright (Women)	£20
67	United Artists (S)ULP 1167	GOOD FRIDAY (LP)	£175
68	United Artists (S)ULP 1193	VIGIL (LP)	£100
70	Polydor Special 2482 010	FRIENDS (LP)	£80

(see also , Grapefruit)

EASY LIFE
18	Chess Club CC089	RINGTONES (10". p/s, teal coloured vinyl)	£100
18	Universal 6787818	CREATURE HABITS (12", p/s)	£80
19	Island 6789085	SPACESHIPS (12", p/s, flow in the dark vinyl)	£80
19	Island 6789085	Frank/Ojpl (10", p/s, white vinyl)	£40
20	Island 0848479	JUNK FOOD (LP, red or mustard vinyl)	£40

EASY STREET
70s	Muscle Music AP 591	Person To Person/Easy Come Easy Go	£30

EATER
78	The Label TLRLP 001	THE ALBUM (LP, with inner sleeve)	£40
85	De Lorean EAT 1	THE HISTORY OF EATER (LP, 1,000 each on red, white & blue vinyl, with bonus 7" [EAT FREEBIE 1])	£15
85	De Lorean EAT 1	THE HISTORY OF EATER (LP, green vinyl)	£15

(see also Andy Blade)

EATHOPIANS
69	Nu Beat NB 038	Buss Your Mouth (actually "Contention" by Ethiopians)/REGGAE BOYS: Rough Way Ahead (B-side actually by Keith Blake & Hi-Tals)	£45
68	Crab 4	Reggie Hit The Town/Ding Dong Bell	£40

(see also Ethiopians)

KOOKIE EATON
68	Condor PS 1002	Cream Machine/Joke B Side	£15

EAT STATIC
91	Alien HAB 1	Monkey Man/Habi Beep (12")	£30
91	Alien AR 1	Inanna/Medicine Wheel (12")	£20
92	Alien AR 2	ALMOST HUMAN EP (12")	£20
93	Planet Dog BARK 002T	LOST IN TIME EP (12", p/s)	£20
95	Planet Dog BARK 581 023-1	EYSYLON EP (2x12", p/s)	£15
93	Planet Dog BARK LP 001	ABDUCTION (2-LP)	£25
95	Planet Dog BARK LP 005	IMPLANT (2-LP)	£25
97	Planet Dog BARK LP 029	SCIENCE OF THE GODS (3-LP)	£25

EAZIE RYDER
78	Graduate GRAD 1	Motorbikin'/City Lights (p/s)	£15

EAZYSTREET
84	Private Pressing	Quest For Glory/Let 'Em Rock (no p/s)	£100

EBONY
84	Touched TOUCH 1	Dream Girl/We'll Fight Back (p/s)	£15

EBONY DUBSTERS
03	Ebony EBR 028	EBONY DUBS VOL. 2 (12", p/s one side etched)	£20

EBONY SISTERS
69	Bullet BU 401	Let Me Tell You Boy/RHYTHM RULERS: Mannix	£30
70	Bullet BU 420	Each Time/BUNNY LEE ALLSTARS: Boss Walk	£35

(see also Sister)

EBONY DIAMONDS
16	Super Disco Edits EDI 101	I'm So Lucky/I'm So Lucky (p/s)	£15

EBONY STEEL BAND
82	TJ ESBLP 001	A TOUCH OF CLASS (LP)	£40
19	OM Swagger OMSLP 001	PAN MACHINE (LP, gatefold)	£15
19	OM Swagger OMSLP 001	PAN MACHINE (LP, gatefold, red vinyl, 100 only)	£35

KATJA EBSTEIN
70	Liberty LBF 15317	No More Love For Me/Without Love	£25

ECCENTRICS
65	Pye 7N 15850	What You Got/Fe Fi Fo Fum	£45

CLANCY ECCLES (& DYNAMITES)
61	Blue Beat BB 34	River Jordan/I Live And I Love (with Hersan & His City Slickers)	£30
61	Blue Beat BB 67	Freedom/More Proof	£40
63	Island WI 044	Judgement/Baby Please (B-side actually with Paulette)	£40
63	Island WI 098	Glory Hallelujah/Hot Rod (B-side actually by Roland Alphonso)	£40
65	Ska Beat JB 194	Sammy No Dead/Roam Jerusalem	£40
65	Ska Beat JB 198	Miss Ida/KING ROCKY: What Is Katty	£40
67	Doctor Bird DB 1156	Feel The Rhythm/Easy Snapping (B-side actually by Theo Beckford)	£55
67	Pama PM 701	What Will Your Mama Say/Darling Don't Do That	£35
67	Pama PMB 703	Western Organ/Mother's Advice (actually by The Clancy Set)	£35
68	Pama PM 712	The Fight/Great	£35
68	Nu Beat NB 006	Festival '68/I Really Love You	£35
69	Trojan TR 639	Sweet Africa/Let Us Be Lovers	£40
69	Trojan TR 647	Bangarang Crash/DYNAMITES: Rahthid	£100
69	Trojan TR 648	Constantinople/Deacon Sun	£50
69	Trojan TR 649	Demonstration/VAL BENNETT: My Girl	£50
69	Trojan TR 658	Fattie Fattie/SILVERSTARS: Last Call	£50
69	Duke DU 9	Auntie Lulu/SLICKERS: Bag A Boo	£100
69	Duke DU 31	Shoo-Be-Do/DYNAMITES: I Don't Care (B-side actually by Dingle Brothers)	£40
69	Clandisc CLA 201	The World Needs Loving/DYNAMITES: Dollar Train (B-side actually by Clancy Eccles)	£20
69	Clandisc CLA 206	Dance Beat/KING STITT: The Ugly One	£45
70	Clandisc CLA 209	Open Up/HIGGS & WILSON: Agane (B-side actually "Again")	£20
70	Clandisc CLA 212	Black Beret (with Dynamites)/BARRY & AFFECTIONS: Love Me Tender	£15
70	Clandisc CLA 213	Phantom/Skank Me (both sides with Dynamites) (B-side actually by Barry & Affections)	£25
70	Clandisc CLA 227	Credit Squeeze/DYNAMITES: Credit Squeeze	£15
71	Clandisc CLA 235	John Crow Skank/KING STITT: Merry Rhythm	£25
71	Pama Supreme PS 332	What Will Your Mama Say/TIGER: United We Stand	£25
72	Attack ATT 8037	Ganja Free/DYNAMITES: Ganja (Version)	£15

MINT VALUE £

69	Clandisc TTL 22	FREEDOM (LP)	£60
69	Trojan TTL 22	FREEDOM (LP)	£60
70	Clandisc TBL 124	HERBSMAN REGGAE (LP)	£60
73	Big Shot BILP 101	TOP OF THE LADDER (LP)	£30
88	Trojan TRLS 262	FATTY FATTY (LP)	£15

(see also Dynamites, Drumbago, Marlene Webber, Westmorelites)

ECHO & BUNNYMEN

88	WES YZ175TW	People Are Strange/Paint It Black (live)/Run Run Run (live)/Friction (live) (12", p/s with free poster, in shrinkwrap)	£60
80	Korova KODE 1	CROCODILES (LP, with bonus 7", "Do It Clean"/"Read It In Books" [SAM 128] & inner sleeve)	£30
80	Korova KODE 1	CROCODILES (LP, with inner)	£20
81	Korova KODE 2	HEAVEN UP HERE (LP)	£20
83	Korova KODE 6	PORCUPINE (LP, with bonus Peel Session [KOW 26C])	£20
83	Korova KODE 6	PORCUPINE (LP, with inner)	£15
84	Korova KODE 8	OCEAN RAIN (LP, inner)	£20
85	Korova KODE 13	SONGS TO LEARN AND SING (LP, with lyric booklet & 7": "The Pictures On My Wall"/"Read It In Books" [p/s, yellow/blue labels, CAGE 004], no "Voodoo Billy" run-off groove message; signed)	£30
85	Korova KODE 13	SONGS TO LEARN AND SING (LP)	£20
01	Cooking Vinyl COOK 208	FLOWERS (LP)	£60
06	Let Them Eat Vinyl LEN 007LP	SIBERIA (2-LP)	£80
13	Vinyl 180 VIN180LP063	CROCODILES (2-LP, reissue, hardback cover)	£40
13	Vinyl 180 VIN180LP068	HEAVEN UP HERE (2-LP, reissue, hardback cover)	£40
13	Vinyl 180 VIN180LP068	HEAVEN UP HERE (LP, reissue, blue vinyl)	£30
13	Vinyl 180 VIN180LP068	HEAVEN UP HERE (LP, reissue,180gm)	£20
14	Vinyl 180 VIN180LP070	PORCUPINE (LP. reissue, white vinyl)	£25
14	Vinyl 180 VIN180LP071	PORCUPINE (2-LP, reissue, harback cover)	£40
14	Vinyl 180 VIN180LP075	OCEAN RAIN (LP, reissue)	£20
14	Vinyl 180 VIN180LP075	OCEAN RAIN (LP, reissue, silver vinyl)	£25
14	Vinyl 180 VIN180LP075R	OCEAN RAIN (LP, reissue, blue vinyl)	£30
14	429 FTN 17992	METEORITES (2-LP, CD)	£18
15	Vinyl 180 VIN180LP076	OCEAN RAIN (2-LP, reissue, hardback cover)	£40
15	Vinyl 180 VIN180LP082	ECHO & THE BUNNYMEN (LP, reissue, clear vinyl)	£25
15	Vinyl 180 VIN180LP082	ECHO & THE BUNNYMEN (LP, reissue)	£18

(see also Will Sergeant)

ECHO BASE

85	DEP International LPDEP 9	BUY ME (LP)	£15

(see also Ocean Colour Scene)

ECHOBELLY

94	Fauve FAUV 3LPS	EVERYONE'S GOT ONE (LP, printed inner, poster)	£80
94	Fauve FAUV 3LP	EVERYONE'S GOT ONE (LP, printed inner, without poster)	£40
95	Rhythm King FAUV 6LX	ON (LP/7", printed inner)	£70

ECHOES (U.S.)

60	Top Rank JAR 399	Born To Be With You/My Guiding Light	£15
61	Top Rank JAR 553	Baby Blue/Boomerang	£15

ECHOES & CELESTIALS (JAMAICA)

61	Hornet H 1004	Are You Mine/I'll Love You Forever	£25
62	Blue Beat BB 89	Are You Mine/I'll Love You Forever (reissue)	£20

CHUCK E

94	White House WYHS 038	THE CHUCK EP (12")	£20

BILLY ECKSTINE

65	Tamla Motown TMG 533	Had You Been Around/Down To Earth	£100
65	Tamla Motown TMG 533	Had You Been Around/Down To Earth (DJ copy)	£150
66	T. Motown TML 11025	THE PRIME OF MY LIFE (LP, mono)	£55
66	T. Motown STML 11025	THE PRIME OF MY LIFE (LP, stereo)	£65
67	T. Motown TML 11046	MY WAY (LP, mono)	£50
67	T. Motown STML 11046	MY WAY (LP, stereo)	£60
69	T. Motown (S)TML 11101	GENTLE ON MY MIND (LP, mono/stereo)	£45

ECLECTION

68	Elektra EKL 4023	ECLECTION (LP, gatefold sleeve, also stereo EKS 74023)	£100

(see also Fotheringay, Dorris Henderson, Trevor Lucas, Mogul Thrash)

ECLIPSE

78	Baal BAL 89005	ECLIPSED (LP)	£50

ECOLOGY

92	Vicious Pumpin'	THE COMMUNAL MIND EP (12", stamped white label)	£20
92	Vicious Pumpin' OBS 004	ECOLOGY EP (12", stamped white label)	£30
92	Vicious Pumpin' VIC 002	THE SMOKIN' JAM EP (12", stamped white label)	£20
93	Vicious Pumpin' VIC 010	Vicious House/Take Me Higher (12", stamped white label)	£15

ECSTACY OF SAINT THERESA

94	FREE LP FRE4	FREE D (LP)	£80

ECSTASY CLUB

88	Swordfish DROP 1	JESUS LOVES THE ACID (EP, 12")	£15
88	Flim Flam FFR1207	JESUS LOVES THE ACID (EP, 12")	£20
88	Flim Flam FFR1207	JESUS LOVES THE ACID (EP, 12" picture disc)	£20

89	LD Records	JESUS LOVES THE ACID (EP, 12")	£20

ECTOMORPH
90s	Woronzow WOO 15	THE FURIOUS SLEEPER (LP, with poster & inserts, 500 only)	£20

ED SHEERAN
17	Asylum 01902958 59015	÷ (DIVIDE) (2LP, 45rpm, gatefold, printed inners)	£25

EDAN
02	Lewis LEWISLP001	PRIMITIVE PLUS (2-LP)	£35
05	Lewis LEWISLP 007	BEAUTY & THE BEAT (LP)	£25

EDDIE
82	PC PCDD 001	I Don't Want To Lose You/I Don't Lost In Dub You (12")	£30

EDDIE & THE HOT RODS
76	Island WIP 6270DJ	Writing On The Wall/Cruisin' (In The Lincoln) (promos in generic title p/s)	£25
76	Island WIP 6270	Writing On The Wall/Cruisin' (In The Lincoln) (in black & white p/s)	£15
76	Island WIP 6333	Get Out Of Denver/96 Tears (with 'Collectors item' and 'jukebox special' on label)	£80
76	Island ILPS 9457	TEENAGE DEPRESSION (LP, with poster)	£25
76	Island ILPS 9457	TEENAGE DEPRESSION (LP, without poster)	£15
77	Island ILPS 9509	LIFE ON THE LINE (LP, gatefold)	£20

(see also Lew Lewis)

JASON EDDIE & THE CENTREMEN
65	Parlophone R 5388	Whatcha Gonna Do Baby/Come On Baby (as Jason Eddie & the Centremen)	£175
66	Parlophone R 5473	Singing The Blues/True To You (as Jason Eddy & the Centremen)	£175
69	Tangerine DP 0010	Heart And Soul/Playing The Clown (solo)	£50

EDDIE'S CROWD
66	CBS 202078	Baby Don't Look Down/Take It Easy Baby	£90

DUANE EDDY (& THE REBELS)

78s
58	London HL 8669	Rebel-Rouser/Stalkin'	£15
59	London HLW 8821	The Lonely One/Detour	£20
59	London HLW 8879	Peter Gunn/Yep!	£40
59	London HLW 8929	Forty Miles Of Bad Road/The Quiet Three	£30
59	London HLW 9007	Some Kind-A Earthquake/First Love, First Tears	£30
60	London HLW 9050	Bonnie Came Back/Movin 'N' Groovin'	£40
60	London HLW 9104	Shazam!/The Secret Seven	£60
60	London HLW 9162	Because They're Young/Rebel Walk	£80

SINGLES
58	London HL 8669	Rebel-Rouser/Stalkin' (initially with triangular centre)	£15
60	London HLW 9050	Bonnie Came Back/Movin 'N' Groovin' (tri centre)	£15
59	London HLW 9007	Some Kind-A Earthquake/First Love, First Tears (tri centre)	£15
64	RCA RCA 1425	Guitar Star/The Iguana	£15
65	Colpix PX 779	Trash/South Phoenix	£15
65	Colpix PX 788	The House Of The Rising Sun/Don't Think Twice, It's All Right	£15

EXPORT SINGLES
58	London HL 7057	Ramrod/The Walker (as Duane Eddy & Rebels)	£20
59	London HL 7072	The Lonely One/Detour	£20
59	London HL 7076	Yep!/Three-30-Blues	£30
59	London SLW 4001	Peter Gunn/Yep! (stereo)	£90
59	London HL 7080	Forty Miles Of Bad Road/The Quiet Three	£15
60	London HL 7090	Bonnie Come Back/Lost Island	£15
60	London HL 7096	Because They're Young/Rebel Walk	£15

EPs
58	London RE 1175	REBEL ROUSER (as Douane Eddy)	£20
59	London RE-W 1216	THE LONELY ONE	£20
59	London RE-W 1217	YEP!	£15
60	London RE-W 1257	TWANGY	£15
61	London RE-W 1287	PEPE	£15
61	London RE-W 1303	DUANE EDDY PLAYS MOVIE THEMES	£15
61	London RE-W 1341	TWANGY NO. 2	£15
63	RCA RCX 7115	A COUNTRY TWANG	£15
63	RCA RCX 7129	MR. TWANG	£15
64	RCA RCX 7146	TWANGIN' UP A SMALL STORM	£15
65	Colpix PXE 304	COTTONMOUTH	£30

ALBUMS
58	London HA-W 2160	HAVE 'TWANGY' GUITAR, WILL TRAVEL	£40
59	London HA-W 2191	ESPECIALLY FOR YOU (mono)	£20
59	London SAH-W 6045	ESPECIALLY FOR YOU (stereo with different version of "Tuxedo Junction")	£25
60	London HA-W 2236	THE "TWANG'S" THE "THANG!" (mono)	£20
60	London SAH-W 6068	THE "TWANG'S" THE "THANG" (stereo)	£30
60	London HA-W 2285	SONGS OF OUR HERITAGE (gatefold sleeve, mono)	£20
60	London SAH-W 6119	SONGS OF OUR HERITAGE (gatefold sleeve, stereo)	£20
61	London HA-W 2325	A MILLION DOLLARS' WORTH OF TWANG	£25
61	London HA-W 2373	GIRLS, GIRLS, GIRLS (mono)	£25
61	London SAH-W 6173	GIRLS, GIRLS, GIRLS (stereo)	£30
62	London HA-W 2435	A MILLION DOLLARS' WORTH OF TWANG VOL. 2	£25
62	RCA RD 27264/SF 5134	TWISTIN' AND TWANGIN' (mono/stereo)	£25

MINT VALUE £

62	RCA RD/SF 7510	TWANGY GUITAR — SILKY STRINGS (mono)	£15
62	RCA SF 7510	TWANGY GUITAR — SILKY STRINGS (stereo)	£20
63	RCA RD/SF 7545	DANCE WITH THE GUITAR MAN (mono)	£20
63	RCA SF 7545	DANCE WITH THE GUITAR MAN (stereo)	£25
63	RCA RD/SF 7560	TWANG A COUNTRY SONG (mono)	£20
63	RCA SF 7560	TWANG A COUNTRY SONG (stereo)	£25
63	RCA RD/SF 7568	TWANGIN' UP A STORM (mono)	£20
63	RCA SF 7568	TWANGIN' UP A STORM (stereo)	£25
64	RCA RD/SF 7621	LONELY GUITAR (mono)	£20
64	RCA SF 7621	LONELY GUITAR (stereo)	£20
64	RCA RD/SF 7656	WATER SKIING (mono)	£25
64	RCA SF 7656	WATER SKIING (stereo)	£30
65	RCA RD/SF 7689	TWANGIN' THE GOLDEN HITS (mono)	£15
65	RCA SF 7689	TWANGIN' THE GOLDEN HITS (stereo)	£15
65	RCA RD/SF 7754	TWANGSVILLE (mono)	£20
65	RCA SF 7754	TWANGSVILLE (stereo)	£20
65	Colpix PXL 490	DUANE A-GO-GO-GO	£20
66	Colpix PXL 494	DUANE EDDY DOES BOB DYLAN	£20
67	Reprise R(S)LP 6218	THE BIGGEST TWANG OF THEM ALL (mono)	£15
67	Reprise R(S)LP 6218	THE BIGGEST TWANG OF THEM ALL (stereo)	£18
67	Reprise RLP 6240	THE ROARIN' TWANGIES (mono only)	£25

(see also Lee Hazlewood)

EDDY & TEDDY
61	London HLU 9367	Bye Bye Butterfly/Star Crossed Lovers	£15

DAVID EDE BAND
60	Pye 7N 15280	Easy Go/The Blue Bird (as David Ede & Robin Rock)	£15
61	Pye 7N 15370	Last Night/Ding Dong John (as David Ede & Go Man Go Men)	£20
62	Pye 7N 15417	Twistin' Those Meeces To Pieces/Twistin' The Trad (as David Ede & Rabin Band)	£15

(see also Oscar Rabin)

EDEN
87	Den 3DEN	FORM FOLLOWS FUNCTION EP	£35

EDEN STREET SKIFFLE GROUP
57	Headquarter & General Stores	SKIFFLE ALBUM NO. 1 (10 x 7" 78rpm clear flexidiscs in p/s)	£35

TONI EDEN
60	Columbia DB 4409	Teen Street/No One Understands (My Johnny)	£25
60	Columbia DB 4458	Grown Up Dreams/Whad'ya Gonna Do	£20

EDEN'S CHILDREN
68	Stateside (S)SL 10235	EDEN'S CHILDREN (LP)	£80

EDGE (1)
80	Hurricane FLAK 102	SQUARE 1 (LP, some on white vinyl)	£15

(see also Damned, Culture Club)

EDGE (2)
78	Chiltern Sound CSLP 1	UNEASY PEACE (LP)	£20

EDIKANFO
81	Editions EG EGED 12	THE PACE SETTERS (LP)	£20

EDITORS
05	Kitchenware SKX 77	Bullet/You Are Fading	£20
05	Kitchenware SKCD77	Bullets/You Are Fading/Dust In The Sunlight (CD, 500 only)	£35
05	Kitchenware SKX77	You Are Fading/Dust In The Sunlight (500 only)	£35
13	Independent Label Market ILMVF008	A Ton Of Love (Acoustic) (12" 1-sided, 50 only)	£60
15	PIAS (No Cat. No.)	Life Is A Fear/Marching Orders (Michael Price Rework) (picture disc free with Sonic Seducer magazine)	£15
16	PIAS (No Cat. No.)	Dream Dark As Your Heaven (numbered, 2 copies only)	£100
05	Kitchenware KWX 34	THE BACK ROOM (LP, gatefold sleeve)	£30
07	Kitchenware KWX 37	AN END HAS A START (LP, CD)	£30
09	Kitchenware KWX 43	IN THIS LIGHT AND ON THIS EVENING (LP)	£20
11	PIAS PIASR 250 BOX	UNEDITED (7-LP, 7-CD, book, box set 200 with hand-written insert)	£200
11	PIAS PIASR 250 BOX	UNEDITED (7-LP, 7-CD, book, box set without hand-written insert)	£125
13	Play It Again Sam PIASR660DLP	THE WEIGHT OF YOUR LOVE (2-LP, CD)	£18
15	Play It Again Sam PIASR830LP	IN DREAM (LP, gold vinyl)	£20

LADA EDMUND JR
75	MCA MU 172	The Larue/Soul Au Go-Go (DJ Copy)	£20

DAVE EDMUNDS (& ROCKPILE)
90	Capitol 10CL 568	King Of Love/Stay With Me Tonight (45rpm)/King Of Love (78 rpm) (10", p/s)	£30
71	Regal Zono. SRZA 8503	ROCKPILE COLLECTION (LP, unreleased)	£0
72	Regal Zono. SLRZ 1026	ROCKPILE (LP)	£60
75	Rockfield RRL 101	SUBTLE AS A FLYING MALLET (LP)	£20
82	Arista SPART 1184	DE 7TH (LP, with bonus EP "Live At The Venue" [JUKE 1])	£15

(see also Image, Human Beans, Love Sculpture, Rockpile)

EDQ
77	Ogun OG 410	THEY ALL BE ON THIS OLD ROAD (LP)	£30

EDSELS
61	Pye International 7N 25086	Rama Lama Ding Dong/Bells	£60

EDWARD H. DAFIS
78	Sain SAIN 67S	Uffern Ar Y Ddaear/VC 10 (p/s, as 'Edward H.')	£20
79	Macym/Sain MACYM 3	Breuddwyd Roc A Rol/Smo Fi Ishe Mynd	£25
74	Sain SAIN 1016M	HEN FFORDD GYMREIG O FYW (LP)	£30
75	Sain SAIN 1034	FFORD NEWYDD EINGL-AMERICANAIDD GRÊT O FYW (LP)	£15
76	Sain SAIN 1053M	SNEB YN BECSO DAM (LP, gatefold, as 'Edward H.')	£30
79	Sain SAIN 1144M	YN ERBYN Y FFACTORE (LP, as ' Edward H.', insert)	£25
80	Sain SAIN 1196M	PLANT Y FFLAM (LP, printed inner, as 'Edward H.')	£25
05	Sain SCD 2428	MEWN BOCS (6CD box set)	£30

J VINCENT EDWARD
69	CBS 4388	Run To The Sun/I Never Thought I'd Fall In Love	£15

ADINA EDWARDS
60s	Tabernacle TLP 1005	JESUS IS MINE (LP)	£15

(see also Coxsone Dodd)

C EDWARDS & SYMBOLIC
80	Symbolic BS 02	Loving Jah/Loving One & All (12")	£80

CHUCK EDWARDS
68	Soul City SC 104	Downtown Soulville/I Need You	£30
68	Soul City SC 104	Downtown Soulville/I Need You (DJ Copy)	£100

DEVON EDWARDS
82	CF 12	Bad Boy Lay Down Flat/JAH RUBAL : Burst Shot	£35

IDIATER EDWARDS
85	Pressure HAVE 2	Loving Sweet Devotion/Version (12")	£200

(WILFRED) JACKIE EDWARDS
60	Starlite ST45 016	We're Gonna Love/Your Eyes Are Dreaming (as Wilfred Edwards & Caribs)	£30
60	Starlite ST45 026	I Know/Tell Me Darling (as Wilfred Edwards)	£30
61	Starlite ST45 046	Whenever There's Moonlight/Heaven Just Knows (as Wilfred Edwards)	£30
61	Starlite ST45 062	More Than Words Can Say/I Love You No More (as Wilfred Edwards)	£30
62	Starlite ST45 076	Little Bitty Girl/Never Go Away (as Wilfred Edwards)	£30
62	Island WI 008	All My Days/Hear Me Cry (as Wilfred Jackie Edwards)	£25
62	Island WI 019	One More Week/Tears Like Rain (as Wilfred Edwards)	£25
62	Decca F 11547	Lonely Game/Suddenly	£25
63	Black Swan WI 404	Why Make Believe/Do You Want Me (as Wilfred Jackie Edwards & Velvetts)	£25
64	Black Swan WI 416	The Things You Do/Little Smile (as Wilfred Jackie Edwards)	£25
64	Black Swan WI 426	Why Make Believe/Do You Want Me Again	£25
64	Fontana TF 465	Sea Cruise/Little Princess	£25
64	Sue WI 329	Stagger Lee/Pretty Girl	£40
65	Aladdin WI 601	He'll Have To Go/Gotta Learn To Love Again	£25
65	Aladdin WI 605	Hush/I Am In Love With You No More (p/s)	£15
65	Aladdin WI 611	The Same One/I Don't Know	£15
65	Island WI 255	White Christmas/My Love And I	£20
66	Island WI 270	Sometimes/Come On Home	£40
66	Island WI 274	L-O-V-E/What's Your Name	£40
66	Island WI 287	Think Twice/Oh Mary	£20
66	Island WI 3006	I Feel So Bad/I Don't Want To Be Made A Fool Of	£300
66	Island WI 3018	Royal Telephone/It's No Secret	£15
67	Island WI 3030	Only A Fool Breaks His Own Heart/The End	£15
67	Island WIP 6008	Come Back Girl/Tell Him You Lied	£25
68	Island WIP 6026	Julie On My Mind/If This Is Heaven	£15
68	Island WI 3157	You're My Girl/Heaven Only Knows	£15
69	Direction 58-4402	Too Experienced/Someone To Love	£15
71	Horse HOSS 1	I Must Go Back/Baby I Want To Be Near You (in p/s)	£20
71	Horse HOSS 1	I Must Go Back/Baby I Want To Be Near You	£15
71	Bread BR 1107	Johnny Gunman/JACKIE'S BOYS: Johnny Gunman Version	£15
76	Island WIP 6285	I Feel So Bad/Come On Home (reissue)	£20
76	Grounation GRO 2056	Invasion/JACKIE EDWARDS & THE AGGROVATORS: Version	£25
66	St. Mary's IEP 701	SACRED HYMNS VOL. 1 (EP, in p/s)	£40
66	St. Mary's IEP 701	SACRED HYMNS VOL. 1 (EP)	£15
66	St. Mary's IEP 702	SACRED HYMNS VOL. 2 (EP, with St. Mary's label, in p/s)	£40
66	St. Mary's IEP 702	SACRED HYMNS VOL. 2 (EP, with St. Mary's label)	£15
66	St. Mary's IEP 702	SACRED HYMNS VOL. 2 (EP, with red-and-white Island label; in p/s)	£40
66	St. Mary's IEP 702	SACRED HYMNS VOL. 2 (EP, with red-and-white Island label)	£15
66	Island IEP 708	HUSH! (EP)	£45
64	Island ILP 906	THE MOST OF WILFRED JACKIE EDWARDS (LP)	£50
64	Island ILP 912	STAND UP FOR JESUS (LP)	£50
66	Island ILP 931	COME ON HOME (LP)	£50
66	Island ILP 936	THE BEST OF JACKIE EDWARDS (LP)	£50
66	Island ILP 940	BY DEMAND (LP)	£50
67	Island ILP(S) 960	PREMATURE GOLDEN SANDS (LP)	£40
69	Island IWPS 4	PUT YOUR TEARS AWAY (LP)	£40
69	Direction 8-63977	LET IT BE ME (LP)	£20
70	Trojan TTL 40	THE MOST OF WILFRED JACKIE EDWARDS (LP, as Wilfred Jackie Edwards)	£25
70	Trojan TTL 45	COME ON HOME (LP)	£25
70	Trojan TTL 46	BY DEMAND (LP)	£25

MINT VALUE £

70	Trojan TTL 57	**PREMATURE GOLDEN SANDS** (LP, reissue)	£25
72	Trojan TRLS 47	**I DO LOVE YOU** (LP)	£30
78	Trojan TRLS 47	**SINCERELY** (LP)	£15
82	Black Music BMLP 801	**KING OF THE GHETTO** (LP)	£60

(see also Wilfred & Millie, Jackie & Millie, Jackie's Boys)

JACKIE EDWARDS & JIMMY CLIFF
| 68 | Island WIP 6036 | **Set Me Free/Here I Come** | £20 |

(see also Jackie & Millie, Millie, Jimmy Cliff, Wilfred & Millie, Jackie's Boys)

JIMMY EDWARDS (& PROFILE)
| 79 | Warner Bros K 17415 | **Nora's Diary/Call Me A Fraud** (features Sham 69) (p/s) | £20 |

(see also Time U.K., Pretenders, Sham 69)

JIMMY EDWARDS (U.S.)
58	Mercury 7MT 193	**Love Bug Crawl/Honey Lovin'** (demo - hand-written label)	£700
58	Mercury 7MT 193	**Love Bug Crawl/Honey Lovin'**	£500
58	Mercury MT 193	**Love Bug Crawl/Honey Lovin'** (78)	£50

JOHN EDWARDS
| 95 | Kent 6T 11 | **Ain't That Good Enough/LOLEATTA HOLLOWAY: This Man's Arms** | £25 |
| 08 | Kent TOWN 115 | **Tin Man/BILL BRANDON: The Streets Got My Lady** | £45 |

MILL EDWARDS
| 73 | Action ACT 4617 | **I Found Myself/Don't Forget About Me** | £25 |

NOKIE EDWARDS
| 77 | Cream CR 9006 | **NOKIE** (LP) | £15 |

(see also Ventures)

O.G. EDWARDS
| 88 | Dance Yard YARDT 4 | **Only You** (Know What I Like)/**Only You** (Know What I Like) (Extended Version) (12") | £40 |

PAUL EDWARDS
| 76 | Cottage COT 301 | **LONGSTONE FARM** (LP) | £40 |
| 77 | Cottage COT 021 | **BUTTERFLY DAYS** (LP) | £30 |

RUPIE EDWARDS (ALL STARS)
62	Blue Beat BB 90	**Guilty Convict/Just Because** (as Rupert Edwards & Smithie's Sextet)	£25
68	Doctor Bird DB 1163	**I Can't Forget/I'm Writing Again**	£25
69	Crab CRAB 35	**Long Lost Love/Uncertain Love**	£60
70	Crab CRAB 41	**Sharp Pan Ya Machete/Redemption**	£20
70	Explosion EX 2030	**Full Moon/Baby**	£20
70	Success RE 902	**Grandfather Clock/Promoter's Grouse**	£25
70	Success RE 905	**Handicap/If You Can't Beat Them**	£25
70	Success RE 909	**Pop Hi** (as Rupie Edwards All Stars)/**VAL BENNETT AND BUNNY LEE ALL STARS: High Tide**	£15
71	Big BG 320	**Soulful Stew/Soulful Stew — Version Two** (as Rupie Edwards Allstars)	£15
71	Big BG 324	**Deep Meditation** (version)/**ERROLL DUNKLEY: Deep Meditation**	£25
72	Big BG 335	**Jimmy As Job Card** (actually titled "Jimmy Has A Job Card")/ **Riot** (as Rupie Edwards Allstars)	£50
78	Success SLD 016	**Oh Black People/NOEL TEMPO : It's Time To Be Free** (12")	£65
75	Cactus CTLP 106	**IRE FEELING** (LP)	£20
75	Cactus CTLP 107	**DUB BASKET** (LP)	£80
76	Cactus CTLP 117	**DUB BASKET CHAPTER 2** (LP)	£40
76	Cactus CTLP 120	**JAMAICA SERENADE** (LP)	£40
77	Success SUCLP	**101 DUB CLASSICS** (LP)	£60

(see also Gaylads, Heptones, Ethiopians, Dymonds, Dobby Dobson, Country Boy, Laurel Aitken, Dennis Alcapone, Gregory Isaacs, Itals, Hugh Roy, Kingstonians, Little George, Winston Blake, Mediators, Max Romeo, I Roy)

SAMUEL EDWARDS
| 69 | Blue Cat BS 159 | **Want It Want It/SPARKERS: Israel** | £60 |

SANDRA EDWARDS
| 85 | Soultown SAND 001 | **Give Me Some Emotion/I Love You** (p/s) | £20 |
| 85 | Sir George SG034 | **Give Me Some Emotion/Reggae Give Me Some Emotion/Georgie Rock** (12") | £20 |

SIMON EDWARDS
| 70 | Jayboy JSX 2001 | **NO RETURN** (LP) | £30 |

VINCE EDWARDS (U.K.)
| 67 | United Artists UP 1179 | **I Can't Turn Back Time/The Lively One** | £20 |

VINCE EDWARDS (U.S.)
| 62 | Brunswick LT 8515 | **VINCE EDWARDS SINGS** (LP) | £15 |

WINSTON EDWARDS
| 75 | Studio 16 WE 0010 | **DUB CONFERENCE** (with BLACKBEARD) | £50 |

EDWARDS HAND
| 71 | RCA SF 8154 | **STRANDED** (LP, orange label) | £20 |
| 73 | Regal Zono. SRZA 8513 | **RAINSHINE** (LP, unissued, demos only) | £150 |

(see also Picadilly Line)

WINSTON EDWARS
| 75 | Fay FLP 2004 | **NATTY LOCKS DUB** (LP) | £200 |

EDWICK RUMBOLD
| 66 | CBS 202393 | **Specially When/Come Back** | £120 |
| 67 | Parlophone R 5622 | **Shades Of Grey/Boggle Woggle** | £300 |

EEK A MOUSE
| 80 | Greensleeves GRED 42 | **Noah's Ark/FLICK WILSON: My Lady** (12", green vinyl) | £20 |

81	Love Linch LL019	No Wicked/Trying To Be Free (12")..£50
81	Greensleeves GRED 74	Christmas A Come/LEE VAN CLEEF: Water Gone (12")........................£15
82	Greensleeves GRED 88	Do You Remember/TOYAN : Strictly The Dread (12").........................£15
82	Echo 12 008	Georgie Porgie (with LUI LEPKI)/Version (12")......................................£15
83	Greensleeves GRED 98	Anarexol/Teacher (12")..£15
91	Mango 12MNG790	Rude Boys A Foreign/Version/Gangster Chronicles/Version (12") £50
81	Greensleeves GREL 31	WA-DO-DEM (LP)...£25
82	Greensleeves GREL 41	SKIDIP! (LP)...£20
83	Greensleeves GREL 86	ASSASSINATOR (LP)..£15
84	Greensleeves GREL 65	MOUSEKETEER (LP) £20

EELS
96	Dreamworks DRMS 22174	Novocaine For The Soul/Fucker (p/s) £20
96	Dreamworks DRLP 50001	BEAUTIFUL FREAK (LP)..£100
01	Dreamworks 450 335-1	SOULJACKER (LP)..£40
10	Eworks CSDLP 1145	TOMORROW MORNING (LP and free 7")...£18
14	Dreamworks 533 771	BEAUTIFUL FREAK (LP, reissue)..£20

E.F. BAND
80	Rok ROK XI/XII	Another Day Gone/SYNCHROMESH: October Friday (die-cut co. sleeve)......£40
80	Aerco/EF Band EF 1	Night Angel/Another Day Gone (p/s) £30
80	Aerco/EF Band EF 1	Night Angel/Another Day Gone £15
80	Redball RR 026	Self Made Suicide/Sister Syne (with wraparound p/s)............................£30
80	Redball RR 036	The Devil's Eye/Comprende (with wraparound p/s)................................£25
82	Bullet CULP 2	DEEP CUT (LP)...£15

WILLIE EGANS
| 70s | Flyright LP 6000 | ROCKS, BOOGIES AND ROLLS (LP) ....£15 |

JOSEPH EGER
| 70 | Charisma CAS 1008 | CLASSICAL HEADS (LP, gatefold sleeve, "pink scroll" label) ....£25 |

EGG
69	Deram DM 269	Seven Is A Jolly Good Time/You Are All Princes £40
70	Deram Nova SDN 14	EGG (LP, stereo, 1st pressing, red/silver labels, with sticker on rear sleeve correcting credits)...£175
70	Deram Nova DN 14	EGG (LP, mono, 1st pressing, blue/silver labels, with sticker on rear sleeve correcting credits)...£300
70	Deram Nova SDN 14	EGG (LP, stereo, 2nd pressing, orange label with black print)...............£80
70	Deram Nova DN 14	EGG (LP, mono, 2nd pressing, blue/silver labels).................................£150
71	Deram SML 1074	THE POLITE FORCE (LP, 1st pressing, red/white label)..........................£150
71	Deram SML 1074	THE POLITE FORCE (LP, 2nd pressing, red/white label with small 'r' in circle to right of 'M' in 'Deram' at top of label)..£70
74	Caroline C 1510	THE CIVIL SURFACE (LP, 1st pressing, red/white/red "twin" label with 'E.J.D' printers text on rear)...£80
76	Caroline C 1510	THE CIVIL SURFACE (LP, 2nd pressing) £40
85	See For Miles SEE 47	SEVEN IS A JOLLY GOD TIME (LP) £18

(see also Hatfield & The North, Arzachel, Bunch Of Fives, Khan)

EGGS OVER EASY
| 86 | Edsel ED 199 | GOOD 'N' CHEAP (LP, reissue)...£15 |

EGGY
| 69 | Spark SRL 1024 | Hookey/You're Still Mine ....£40 |

EG OBLIQUE GRAPH
| 82 | Recloose LOOSE 2 | TRIPTYCH EP ....£30 |

(see also Muslim Gauze)

EGYPT
| 88 | HTD HTD LP 1 | EGYPT (LP, with inner)..£15 |

(see also Paul Samson)

EGYPTIAN EMPIRE
| 91 | Fokus FKFR 1 | The Horn Track (Original Mix)/The Horn Track (Mickey Finn Fog Horn Mix) (12")....£20 |
| 92 | FFRR TABX 115 | The Horn Track (Original Mix)/The Horn Track (Foghorn Mix)/The Horn Track (Toxic 2 Mix) (12")..£15 |

8-EYED SPY
| 81 | Fetish FR 2003 | 8-EYED SPY (LP, with inner sleeve)..£20 |

(see also Lydia Lunch)

808 STATE
88	Creed STATE 002	NEWBUILD (LP) £25
89	Creed STATE 004	QUADRASTATE (LP)..£20
89	ZTT ZTT 2	90 (LP) £15
91	ZTT ZTT6D	EX:EL (2-LP) £20
96	ZTT 0630 14356-1	DON SOLARIS (LP)..£18
99	Rephlex CAT 080 LP	NEWBUILD (LP, reissue as 3 x 12")..£30

(see also Hit Squad)

EIGHTH WONDER
| 88 | CBS SCARE Y1 | I'm Not Scared/I'm Not Scared (Disco Mix)/J'ai Pas Peur (10", p/s, with Pet Shop Boys) ....£15 |

(see also Pet Shop Boys)

EIGHTIES LADIES
| 86 | Music Of Life MOLIF 6 | Turned On To You/Sing Me/And I Knew That Love (12", p/s) ....£20 |
| 10 | Universal Sound USLP 33 | LADIES OF THE EIGHTIES (LP, reissue)...£20 |

(see also Roy Ayers)

EINSTEIN & CHEWY
96	Groove Yard GYARD 007	KUTZ FROM THE LAB VOL. I (12")...	£15
96	Groove Yard GYARD 12	KUTZ FROM THE LAB VOL. 2 (12", white label)	£20

EINSTÜRZENDE NEUBAUTEN
83	Mute STUMM 14	STRATEGIES AGAINST ARCHITECTURE (LP)	£15
85	Some Bizarre BART 331	HALBER MENSCH (LP)	£25
87	Some Bizarre BART 332	FUENF AUF NACH OBEN OFFEN RICHTERSKALA (LP)	£15
89	Some Bizarre BART 333	HAUS DER LUEGE (LP)	£15
92	Mute BETON 106	TABULA RASA (LP)	£120
96	Mute BETON 504	ENDE NEU (LP)	£40
97	90s	ENDE NEU REMIXES (2-LP)	£40
04	Mute STUMM 221	PERPETUUM MOBILE (2-LP, printed inners)	£100
18	80s	GRUNDSTÜCK (LP/DVD, reissue, g/f, printed inner, 180g)........................	£35

EIRE APPARENT
67	Track 604 019	Follow Me/Here I Go Again...	£25
69	Buddah 201 039	Rock'N'Roll Band/Yes I Need Someone	£20
69	Buddah 203 021	SUN RISE (LP, featuring Jimi Hendrix, black/silver labels)	£200

(see also Ernie Graham, Henry McCulloch)

EJECTED
82	Riot City CITY 003	A TOUCH OF CLASS (LP)	£20
83	Riot City CITY 007	THE SPIRIT OF REBELLION (LP)	£25

LIVY EKEMEZIE
17	Odion Livingstone ODILIV001LP	FRIDAY NIGHT (LP, reissue, blue vinyl)	£30

EKSEN TRICK BRICK BAND
78	Aerco AERL 17	SKY STORY (LP, with insert)	£30

EKSEPTION
69	Philips 6314 001	BEGGAR JULIAN'S TIME TRIP (LP)	£15
70	Philips 6314 005	EKSEPTION (LP)	£18
71	Philips 6423 005	EKSEPTION III (LP, laminated sleeve)	£15
72	Philips 6423 019	00.04 (LP)	£15
72	Philips 6423 042	V (LP, gatefold sleeve)	£15

EL PAS(S)O
71	Big Shot BI 572	Out De Light, Baby/Mosquito I (both actually by Dennis Alcapone) £25	
71	Punch PH 61	Mosquito One/Out De Light (reissue)..	£18

(see also Dennis Alcapone)

ELAINE & DEREK
61	Parlophone PMC 1160	ELAINE & DEREK (LP)	£20

ELANO B
81	Ellie Jay EJSP 9639	Diane/Too Late (p/s, insert)	£20

ELASTICA
95	Deceptive BLUFF 014LP	ELASTICA (LP, with flexidisc & booklet, no'd & stickered sleeve, 5,000 only, mispressed labels)...	£75
95	Deceptive BLUFF 014LP	ELASTICA (LP)...	£40
00	Deceptive BLUFF 075LP	THE MENACE (LP, printed inner, poster, stickered sleeve)	£80

(see also Suede)

ELASTIC BAND
68	Decca F 12763	Think Of You Baby/It's Been A Long Time Baby	£45
68	Decca F 12815	Do Unto Others (From "Mr. Rose" T.V. Series)/81/2 Hours Of Paradise......	£60
69	Decca Nova (S)DN 6	EXPANSIONS ON LIFE (LP, mono)..	£300
69	Decca Nova (S)DN 6	EXPANSIONS ON LIFE (LP, stereo)	£200

(see also Mayfield's Mule, Sweet, Love Affair, Northwind)

ELASTICK BAND
67	Stateside SS 2056	Spazz/Papier Mache (unissued, demos only)...	£300

EL-B
00	Scorpion SCORPION 001	Ghetto Girl/Show A Little Love (12")	£20
00	Shelflife 001	South West/Reality (12")	£15
00	Scorpion SCORPION 003	Bubble/Bubble (Dub) (12")	£20
00	777 001	When I Fall In Love (Vocal)/(Dub Mix) (12", white label with J DA FLEX)	£35
00	BD009	El-Brand (Vocal)/El-Brand (Dub) (12" white labels only)	£30
00	El Breaks ELB 001	EL BREAKS VOL. 1 (12" white label, some with sticker)..........................	£35
00	Bison B001	Breakbeat Science/Cuba (12" as Roxy Vs El-B).......................................	£15
09	Tempa TEMPALP 012	THE ROOTS OF EL-B (2-LP)	£40

DONNIE ELBERT
58	Parlophone R 4403	Let's Do The Stroll/Wild Child	£100
58	Parlophone R 4403	Let's Do The Stroll/Wild Child (78)...	£40
65	Sue WI 377	A Little Piece Of Leather/Do Wat'cha Wanna	£35
65	Sue WI 396	You Can Push It (Or Pull It)/Lily Lou	£30
67	CBS 2807	Get Ready/Along Came Pride	£30
68	Polydor BM 56234	In Between The Heartaches/Too Far Gone	£30
69	Deram DM 235	Without You/Baby Please Come Home (reissue)	£45
97	Joe Boy JBV 1	So Soon/Can't Get Over Losing You (p/s with numbered certificate, 300 only)	£20
69	Polydor 236 560	TRIBUTE TO A KING (LP)	£50
73	Ember EMB 3421	THE ROOTS OF DONNIE ELBERT (LP)	£20

ELBOW

98	Soft Records Softrec001	**NOISEBOX EP: Powder Blue/Red/George Lassoes The Moon** (Original version)/**Theme From Munroe Kelly/Can't Stop** (CD, 200 copies – 150 numbered)	£100
98	Soft Records Softrec001	**NOISEBOX EP: Powder Blue/Red/George Lassoes The Moon** (Original version)/**Theme From Munroe Kelly/Can't Stop** (CD, 200 copies – 50 un-numbered)	£50
08	Fiction 1767731	**One Day Like This/Every Bit The Little Girl**	£15
08	Fiction 1773700	**One Day Like This/L'il Pissed Charmin' Tune**	£15
14	Secret 7" S716	**Grounds For Divorce** (100 only, each with unique art sleeve)	£50
01	V2 VVR 101588-1	**ASLEEP IN THE BACK** (2LP)	£55
03	V2 VVR 102181-1	**CAST OF THOUSANDS** (LP)	£60
05	V2 VVR 103255-1	**LEADERS OF THE FREE WORLD** (LP)	£55
08	Fiction 176 472-8	**THE SELDOM SEEN KID** (LP, 2 x 12" 45rpm, gatefold)	£50
11	Fiction 2763747	**BUILD A ROCKET BOYS!** (2-LP, mispressing side B and D have same labels)	£30
11	Fiction 2763747	**BUILD A ROCKET BOYS!** (2-LP)	£25
12	Fiction 3711518	**THE DEFINITIVE VINYL ALBUM BOX SET** (7 x 2-LP, USB stick box set)	£200

EL CAMINO

20	Daupe! DM SP 058	**MARTYR'S PRAYER** (LP, with 38 Spesh, 100 copies)	£40
20	Daupe! DM SP 058	**MARTYR'S PRAYER** (LP, with 38 Spesh, orange vinyl, 100 copies)	£40
20	Daupe! DM SP 058	**MARTYR'S PRAYER** (LP, with 38 Spesh, blue vinyl, 100 copies)	£40
20	Daupe! DM SP 058	**MARTYR'S PRAYER** (LP, with 38 Spesh, yellow vinyl, 100 copies)	£40
20	Daupe! DM SP 058	**MARTYR'S PRAYER** (LP, with 38 Spesh, splatter vinyl, 100 copies)	£70
20	Daupe! DM SP 058	**MARTYR'S PRAYER** (LP, with 38 Spesh, with obi strip, 20 copies)	£100

EL CHICANO

72	MCA MUPS 445	**REVOLUCION** (LP)	£15

ELCORT

66	Parlophone R 5447	**Tammy/Searchin'**	£20

ELDORADOS (JAMAICA)

70	Bullet BU 428	**Savage Colt/The Clea Hog**	£25

ELDORADOS (RHODESIA)

63	Decca DFE 8543	**THE ELDORADOS** (EP)	£100

ROY ELDRIDGE QUINTET

55	Columbia/Clef 33C 9005	**ROY ELDRIDGE QUINTET** (LP)	£15

ELECAMPANE

75	Dame Jane ODJ 1	**WHEN GOD'S ON THE WATER** (LP, private pressing with insert)	£50
78	Dame Jane ODJ 2	**FURTHER ADVENTURES OF MR PUNCH** (LP, private pressing with booklet)	£20

ELECKTROIDS

95	Warp WARPLP 35	**ELEKTROWORLD** (2-LP)	£100

ELECTRIC BANANA

67	De Wolfe DW/LP 3040	**ELECTRIC BANANA** (LP, 10", original issue, tricolour label)	£100
67	De Wolfe DWLP 3040	**ELECTRIC BANANA** (LP, second issue, with other artists)	£50
68	De Wolfe DWLP 3069	**MORE ELECTRIC BANANA** (LP)	£200
69	De Wolfe DWLP 3123	**EVEN MORE ELECTRIC BANANA** (LP)	£60
73	De Wolfe DWLP 3284	**HOT LICKS** (LP)	£60
76	De Wolfe DWLP 3381	**THE RETURN OF THE ELECTRIC BANANA** (LP)	£50
79	Butt NOTT 001	**THE SEVENTIES** (LP)	£20
80	Butt NOTT 003	**THE SIXTIES** (LP)	£20
97	Tenth Planet TP 031	**THE ELECTRIC BANANA BLOWS YOUR MIND** (LP, numbered, 1,000 only)	£35

(see also Pretty Things)

ELECTRIC CRAYONS

89	Emergency MIV 3	**Hip Shake Junkie/Happy To Be Hated** (p/s)	£20

(see also Charlatans)

ELECTRIC FLAG

68	CBS 62394	**A LONG TIME COMIN'** (LP, mono)	£30
68	CBS S 63294	**A LONG TIME COMIN'** (LP, stereo)	£35
69	CBS 63462	**THE ELECTRIC FLAG — AN AMERICAN MUSIC BAND** (LP)	£15

(see also Mike Bloomfield, Buddy Miles, Barry Goldberg)

ELECTRIC JOHNNY

61	London HLU 9384	**Black-Eyes Rock/Johnny On His Strings**	£25

ELECTRIC LIGHT ORCHESTRA (E.L.O.)

77	Jet UP 36342	**Mr Blue Sky/One Summer Dream** (p/s, blue vinyl)	£15
79	Jet S JET 12144	**Shine A Little Love/Jungle** (12", die-cut Jet bag, white vinyl)	£15
79	Jet S JET 12144	**Shine A Little Love/Jungle** (12", die-cut Jet bag, black vinyl)	£100
80	Jet JET 10-185	**Xanadu/Fool Country** (10" pink vinyl, die-cut p/s, with Olivia Newton-John)	£30
71	Harvest SHVL 797	**ELECTRIC LIGHT ORCHESTRA** (LP, gatefold sleeve, with inner sleeve & lyric insert)	£50
71	Harvest SHVL 797	**ELECTRIC LIGHT ORCHESTRA** (LP, gatefold sleeve, without inner sleeve & lyric insert)	£50
72	Harvest SHVL 806	**ELO 2** (LP, 1st pressing, gatefold sleeve with EMI box but no 'stereo' on label)	£50
73	Harvest SHVL 806	**ELO 2** (LP, 2nd pressing, gatefold sleeve with EMI box and 'stereo' on label)	£30
73	Harvest Q4SHVL 797	**ELECTRIC LIGHT ORCHESTRA** (LP, quadrophonic, promo only)	£100
74	Harvest SHSP 4037	**SHOWDOWN** (LP)	£20
76	Jet JETLP 19	**OLE ELO** (LP, withdrawn)	£15
77	Jet UAG 30091	**ON THE THIRD DAY** (LP, new mix, new sleeve & inner sleeve)	£15
78	Jet JETBX 1	**THREE LIGHT YEARS** (3LP box set of "On The Third Day", "Eldorado" & "Face The Music", in printed nostatic inners, booklet, insert)	£30
78	Jet JETLP 200	**A NEW WORLD RECORD** (LP, red vinyl, printed inner)	£30
78	Jet JETLP 201	**FACE THE MUSIC** (LP, green vinyl, printed inner)	£40

MINT VALUE £

78	Jet JETLP 202	**ON THE THIRD DAY** (LP, clear vinyl, printed inner)	£30
78	Jet JETLP 203	**ELDORADO** (LP, yellow vinyl, printed inner)	£30
78	Jet JETDP 400	**OUT OF THE BLUE** (2LP, clear or dark blue vinyl, printed inners, push-out cardboard spaceship, poster, insert)	£80
79	JETLX 500	**DISCOVERY** (LP, gatefold, printed inner, insert)	£15
99	Eagle EDGCD 097	**LIVE AT THE BBC** (2CD)	£40
13	L.T.E LETV 097LP	**ZOOM** (2LP, gatefold, white vinyl, reissue of 2001 CD only release)	£200
15	L.T. E. Vinyl LETV 097LP	**ZOOM** (2LP, reissue, gatefold, clear vinyl)	£80
15	Big Trilby/Sony 88875145121	**ALONE IN THE UNIVERSE** (as Jeff Lynne's ELO) (LP, gatefold, printed inner, download card)	£20
17	Columbia 88985 48742 1	**WEMBLEY OR BUST** (as Jeff Lynne's ELO) (3LP, download card)	£40
19	Big Trilby 19075987131	**FROM OUT OF NOWHERE** (as Jeff Lynne's ELO) (LP, gatefold, printed inner, gold vinyl, 180g)	£30

(see also Idle Race, Move, Roy Wood, Michael D'Albuquerque, Wilson Gale & Co., Tandy-Morgan)

ELECTRIC PRUNES

66	Reprise RS 20532	**I Had Too Much To Dream** (Last Night)/**Luvin'**	£35
67	Reprise RS 20564	**Get Me To The World On Time/Are You Lovin' Me More** (But Enjoying It Less)	£30
67	Reprise RS 20607	**The Great Banana Hoax/Wind-Up Toys**	£20
67	Reprise RS 23212	**A Long Day's Flight/The King Is In His Counting House**	£18
68	Reprise RS 20652	**Everybody Knows You're Not In Love/You Never Had It Better**	£30
67	Reprise R(S)LP 6248	**THE ELECTRIC PRUNES** (LP, mono/stereo)	£200
68	Reprise R(S)LP 6275	**MASS IN F MINOR** (LP, mono/stereo)	£120
68	Reprise RSLP 6316	**RELEASE OF AN OATH** (LP)	£120
86	Edsel ED 179	**LONG DAY'S FLIGHT** (LP)	£15
97	Heartbeat HB 67	**STOCKHOLM '67** (LP, gatefold sleeve with booklet)	£20

ELECTRIC SIX

02	XL XLS 151	**Danger! High Voltage/I Lost Control** (Of My Rock And Roll) (p/s)	£20
03	XL XLS 158	**Gay Bar/The Living End** (p/s)	£25
03	XL XLLP 169	**FIRE** (LP, printed inner)	£150

ELECTRIC TOILET

83	Psycho PSYCHO 8	**IN THE HANDS OF KARMA** (LP, reissue of U.S. LP)	£15

ELECTRIC WIZARD

95	Rise Above RISE 11	**Demon Lung/OUR HAUNTED KINGDOM: Aquatic Fanatic** (blue vinyl, p/s)	£60
98	Bad Acid TRIP 1	**Supercoven/Burnout** (12", p/s)	£80
08	Rise Above RISE 12/116	**The Processean** (Procession) (1-sided 12", 500 only sold at Rise Above 20th Anniversary Gig, ULU London 13th December 2008)	£60
08	Rise Above RISE 12/116	**The House On The Border/REVEREND BIZARRE: The Gates Of Nanna** (12", 500 clear, 500 purple, 500 silver and 500 black vinyl, censored p/s)	£20
08	Rise Above RISE 12/116	**The House On The Border/REVEREND BIZARRE: The Gates Of Nanna** (12", 350 red vinyl, uncensored p/s, poster)	£50
95	Rise Above RISE 009	**ELECTRIC WIZARD** (LP, green vinyl)	£50
04	Rise Above RISELP 48	**WE LIVE** (2-LP, purple vinyl)	£70
04	Rise Above RISELP 52	**DOPETHRONE** (2-LP, white vinyl, reissue, first issued on CD in 2000)	£70
04	Rise Above RISELP 52	**DOPETHRONE** (2-LP, black vinyl, reissue, first issued on CD in 2000)	£40
06	Rise Above RISELP 48	**WE LIVE** (2-LP, gatefold sleeve, reissue on green vinyl with 1-sided 7" "The Living Dead At Manchester Morgue")	£60
06	Rise Above RISELP 072	**COME MY FANATICS...** (2-LP, reissue, with balck vinyl 7", black/dark red/violet space dust vinyl)	£50
06	Rise Above RISELP 072	**COME MY FANATICS...** (2-LP, reissue, with coloured 7", violet space dust vinyl, 100 only)	£100
07	Rise Above RISELP 74	**LET US PREY** (2-LP, 100 clear vinyl, reissue first issued on CD in 2002)	£60
07	Rise Above RISELP 74	**LET US PREY** (2-LP, 500 dark red, 500 black vinyl, reissue first issued on CD in 2002)	£40
07	Rise Above RISELP 100	**WITCHCULT TODAY** (2-LP, 200 green vinyl, foil gatefold sleeve, poster, patch)	£50
07	Rise Above RISELP 100	**WITCHCULT TODAY** (2-LP, 500 silver vinyl, foil gatefold sleeve, poster, patch)	£40
07	Rise Above RISELP 52	**DOPETHRONE** (2-LP, reissue, purple sink vinyl, 50 only)	£80
07	Rise Above RISELP 52	**DOPETHRONE** (2-LP, reissue, transparent amber or clear, 100 only of each)	£40
07	Rise Above RISELP 52	**DOPETHRONE** (2-LP, black vinyl, reissue)	£25
10	Rise Above RISELP 130 BOX	**BLACK MASSES** (2-LP, gatefold p/s, poster, comic, embroidered patch in box, clear vinyl, 100 only)	£350
10	Rise Above RISELP 130	**BLACK MASSES** (2-LP, gatefold p/s, poster, comic, embroidered patch in box, 400 only)	£120
11	Rise Above RISELP 072	**COME MY FANATICS...** (2-LP, reissue, green or black 195 gram vinyl)	£35
14	Spinefarm SPINE 788083	**TIME TO DIE** (2-LP, with poster)	£20
15	Rise Above RISELP 073	**DOPETHRONE** (2-LP, reissue, clear vinyl)	£50
17	Witchfinder W004	**WIXARD BLOODY WIZARD** (LP)	£20

ELECTRIX

79	ELX 001	**HOLLAND** (EP)	£30

ELECTRO HIPPIES

87	Strange Fruit SFPS 042	**PEEL SESSIONS** (12", metallic finish with insert)	£15
88	Peaceville VILE 02	**THE ONLY GOOD PUNK... IS A DEAD ONE** (LP)	£15
89	Peaceville VILE 13	**LIVE** (LP, clear vinyl)	£15
89	Necrosis NECR 0001	**PLAY FAST OR DIE** (LP)	£15

ELECTRONIC

91	Factory FAC 287r/7	**Get The Message** (Edit) (DNA Groove Mix)/(DNA Sin Mix) (promo only)	£50
99	Parlophone 12R651	**Late At Night/Make It Happen** (Original Version)/**Make It Happen** (Darren Price Mix) (12" withdrawn)	£20
91	Factory FACT 290	**ELECTRONIC** (LP, inner)	£25
96	Parlophone PCS 7382	**RAISE THE PRESSURE** (LP)	£100

(see also New Order, Smiths, Pet Shop Boys, Joy Division)

ELECTRONIC CIRCUS
81   Scratch SCR 002 — **Direct Lines/Le Chorale** (p/s)...................£50

ELECTRONIC EXPERIENCED
93   Basement BRSS 025 — **V-10 Overload/No. 303** (12")...................£25
94   Basement BRSS 032 — **I.Q./I.Q. More** (12")...................£25

ELECTRONIC DUB
94   Rising High RSN LP 21 — **ELECTRONIC DUB** (2-LP)...................£70

ELECTRONIC EYE
94   Beyond RBADLP8 — **CLOSED CIRCUIT** (4-LP)...................£50
95   Beyond RBADLP14 — **THE IDEA OF JUSTICE** (2-LP)...................£30
(see also Cabaret Voltaire, Sandoz, Richard H. Kirk, Sweet Exorcist)

ELEGANTS
58   HMV POP 520 — **Little Star/Getting Dizzy**...................£15
58   HMV POP 551 — **Please Believe Me/Goodnight**...................£40

ELEKTRAS
63   United Artists UP 1027 — **All I Want To Do Is Run/It Ain't Easy**...................£30

ELEKTRIC MUSIC
93   East West SAM 1252 — **Lifestyle** (Edit-Style Mix)/(Club-Style Mix)/(Phoneme-Style Mix) (10", promo)...................£20
(see also Kraftwerk)

ELEMENTS
81   Look LK/LP 6649 — **ELEMENTARY** (LP)...................£30

ELENA
65   Columbia DB 7598 — **Evening Time/Road Of Love**...................£20

ELEPHANT BAND
72   Mojo 2092 036 — **Stone Penguin/Groovin' At The Apollo**...................£45

ELEPHANT NOISE
91   Own Label — **This Song Is Our Friend/Halloween Day/Remember The Big Time/Cactus Talk** (12" EP)...................£100

ELEPHANT'S MEMORY
69   Buddah 201067 — **Old Man Willow/Jungle Gym At The Zoo**...................£25
70   CBS 5207 — **Mongoose/I Couldn't Dream**...................£25
72   Apple APPLE 45 — **Power Boogie/Liberation Special**...................£20
69   Buddah 203 022 — **ELEPHANT'S MEMORY** (LP)...................£30
72   Apple SAPCOR 22 — **ELEPHANT'S MEMORY** (LP, gatefold sleeve with inner sleeve)...................£40
(see also John Lennon, Yoko Ono)

ELERGY
94   Applied Rhythmic Technology ART 6 — **ENSEMBLE EP** (12")...................£15

ELERI, JANET & DIANE
70s   Fanfare FR 2196 — **THE ANSWER** (LP)...................£100

ELEVATORS
80   Koala KOA 401 — **Your I's Are Too Close Together/That's My Baby**...................£60

11.59
74   Dovetail DOVE 4 — **THIS IS OUR SACRIFICE OF PRAISE** (LP, with insert)...................£40

11 PARANOIAS
14   Ritual RITE 028 — **SPECTRALBEASTIARIES** (LP)...................£20
14   Ritual RITE 31 — **STEALING FIRE FROM HEAVEN** (2-LP)...................£20

ELF
74   Purple TPS 3506 — **CAROLINA COUNTRY BALL** (LP)...................£30
(see also Roger Glover, Dio, Rainbow, Deep Purple, Black Sabbath)

ELGINS
66   Tamla Motown TMG 551 — **Put Yourself In My Place/Darling Baby** (4-prong pushout centre)...................£150
66   Tamla Motown TMG 551 — **Put Yourself In My Place/Darling Baby** (DJ Copy, red 'A' out of white)...................£300
66   Tamla Motown TMG 583 — **Heaven Must Have Sent You/Stay In My Lonely Arms** (4-prong pushout centre, says 'Producer' instead of 'Producers' Side A)...................£80
66   Tamla Motown TMG 583 — **Heaven Must Have Sent You/Stay In My Lonely Arms** (DJ Copy)...................£150
67   Tamla Motown TMG 615 — **It's Been A Long Long Time/I Understand My Man** (4-prong pushout centre)...................£35
67   Tamla Motown TMG 615 — **It's Been A Long Long Time/I Understand My Man** (DJ Copy)...................£50
68   Tamla Motown TMG 642 — **Put Yourself In My Place/Darling Baby** (reissue, 4-prong pushout)...................£35
68   T. Motown (S)TML 11081 — **DARLING BABY** (LP, mono/stereo, flipback sleeve)...................£100

ELIAS HULK
70   Youngblood SSYB 8 — **UNCHAINED** (LP, laminated front cover, red/white label)...................£1000
(see also Babe Ruth)

ELIFFANT
79   Sain 1130M — **M.O.M.** (LP, printed inner)...................£20

ELIJAH
71   Ackee ACK 121 — **Selassie High/Mount Zion**...................£20

ELIMINATORS (1)
66   Pye NPL 18160 — **GUITARS AND PERCUSSION** (LP, pink black label)...................£25

ELIMINATORS (2)
99   Soul Brother SBC 54 — **LOVING EXPLOSION** (LP, reissue)...................£20

ELITE
79	L&S	ANY PORT IN A STORM (LP, 500 only)	£20

ELIXIA
83	Record Shack SOHO 4	Soho Phase/Soho Nights (p/s)	£15
83	Record Shack SOHOT 4	Soho Phase/Soho Nights (12")	£30

ELIXIR
85	Elixir ELIXIR 1	Treachery (Ride Like The Wind)/Winds Of Time (folded p/s with insert)	£80
86	Elixir ELIXIR 2	THE SON OF ODIN (LP, private pressing with insert)	£60
90	Sonic SONICLP 9	LETHAL POTION (LP, features Clive Burr)	£15

(see also Iron Maiden)

ELIZABETH (1)
68	Vanguard SVRL 19010	ELIZABETH (LP)	£150

ELIZABETH (2)
77	Creole CR 139	God Save The Sex Pistols/Silver Story	£15

ELIZABETH (3)
94	Echo Special Prods ESPLP2	QUEEN ELIZABETH (LP, mail order only, with inner sleeve)	£18
97	Head Heritage HH2	QUEEN ELIZABETH 2 - ELIZABETH VAGINA (2-CD mail order, 1000 only)	£30

(see also Julian Cope)

JIMMY ELLEDGE
62	RCA RCA 1274	Swanee River Rocket/Funny How Time Slips Away	£15
64	RCA RCX 7132	FUNNY HOW TIME SLIPS AWAY (EP)	£20

ELLI
67	Parlophone R 5575	Never Mind/I'll Be Looking Out For You	£20
99	Dig The Fuzz DIG 038	ELLI (LP, 500 only)	£18

YVONNE ELLIMAN
73	Purple PUR 114	I Can't Explain/Hawaii	£25
73	Purple TPS 3504	FOOD OF LOVE (LP)	£15

DUKE ELLINGTON & HIS (FAMOUS) ORCHESTRA
60	Philips SBBL 514	ANATOMY OF A MURDER (soundtrack)	£25

MARC ELLINGTON
69	Philips (S)BL 7883	MARC ELLINGTON (LP, black/silver labels)	£100
71	B&C CAS 1033	RAINS, REINS OF CHANGES (LP, envelope cover with lyric insert)	£100
72	Philips 6308 120	A QUESTION OF ROADS (LP, gatefold sleeve, black/silver label)	£100
72	Xtra XTRA 1154	MARC TIME (LP, with Fairport Convention)	£40
73	Philips 6308 143	RESTORATION (LP, blue/silver label)	£80

(see also Fairport Convention, Matthews Southern Comfort)

RAY ELLINGTON QUARTET
53	Columbia SCM 5050	The Little Red Monkey/Kaw-Liga	£20
54	Columbia SCM 5088	All's Going Well (My Lady Montmorency) (with Marion Ryan)/Ol' Man River	£20
54	Columbia SCM 5104	Rub-A-Dub-Dub/The Owl Song	£15
54	Columbia SCM 5147	A.B.C. Boogie/Christmas Cards	£20
55	Columbia SCM 5177	Ko Ko Mo (I Love You So)/Woodpecker	£20
55	Columbia SCM 5187	Play It Boy, Play/The Irish Were Egyptians Long Ago	£20
55	Columbia SCM 5199	Cloudburst/Pet	£15
56	Columbia DB 3821	Stranded In The Jungle/Left Hand Boogie	£20
56	Columbia DB 3838	Giddy-Up-A Ding Dong/The Green Door	£20
57	Columbia DB 3905	Marianne/That Rock 'N' Rollin' Man	£20
58	Columbia DB 4057	Living Doll/Long Black Nylons (solo)	£20
59	Pye Nixa NPL 83011	THAT'S NICE (LP, with Judd Proctor, mono)	£20
59	Pye Nixa NPL 18032	THAT'S NICE (LP, with Judd Proctor, stereo)	£20

(see also Tony Crombie, Marion Ryan)

ELLINGTONS
79	Grapevine GRP 114	(I'm Not) Destined To Become A Loser/MILLIONAIRES: You've Got To Love Your Baby (DJ Copy)	£20

BILL ELLIOT & ELASTIC OZ BAND
71	Apple APPLE 36	God Save Us/Do The Oz (initially with p/s)	£60
71	Apple APPLE 36	God Save Us/Do The Oz	£20

(see also Splinter, John Lennon/Yoko Ono)

DEREK & DOROTHY ELLIOT
72	Trailer LER 2023	DEREK & DOROTHY ELLIOT (LP)	£15
76	Tradition TSR 025	YORKSHIRE RELISH (LP)	£15

MAMA CASS (ELLIOT)
68	Stateside S(S)L 5004	DREAM A LITTLE DREAM (LP)	£20
69	Stateside S(S)L 5014	BUBBLEGUM, LEMONADE AND SOMETHING FOR MAMA (LP)	£18
72	RCA SF 8306	THE ROAD IS NO PLACE FOR A LADY (LP)	£15

(see also Mamas & Papas, Big Three, Dave Mason & Cass Elliot, Mugwumps)

N. ELLIOT & N. BAILEY
71	Moodisc HME 111	People Let Love Shine/MUDIES ALL STARS: Too Much	£80

BERN ELLIOTT (& FENMEN)
65	Decca F 12171	Lipstick Traces/Voodoo Woman (solo)	£20
64	Decca DFE 8561	BERN ELLIOTT AND THE FENMEN (EP)	£30

(see also Fenmen)

DAVID ELLIOTT
72	Atlantic K40374	DAVID ELLIOTT (LP, with lyric insert)	£20

JACK ELLIOTT
69	Leader LEA 4001	JACK ELLIOTT OF BIRTLEY (LP, with booklet)	£20

(see also Elliotts Of Birtley)

(RAMBLIN') JACK ELLIOTT
56	Topic TRC 98	Talking Miner Blues/Pretty Boy Floyd (78)	£20
57	Topic TRC 103	Old Blue/Rambling Blues (78)	£20
57	Topic TRC 104	Streets Of Laredo/Boll Weevil (78)	£20
58	77 Records EP/1	JACK ELLIOTT SINGS Vol 1. (EP)	£100
58	77 Records EP/2	JACK ELLIOTT SINGS Vol. 2. (EP)	£100
61	Collector JEA 5	RAMBLING JACK ELLIOTT (EP)	£20
64	Collector JEA 6	BLUES AND COUNTRY (EP)	£20
55	Topic T 5	WOODY GUTHRIE'S BLUES (8" mini-LP)	£40
57	Topic 10T 15	JACK TAKES THE FLOOR (10" LP)	£40
59	Columbia 33SX 1166	RAMBLIN' JACK ELLIOT IN LONDON (LP)	£20
62	Encore ENC 194	IN LONDON (LP, reissue of Columbia 33SX 1166)	£20
60	Columbia 33SX 1291	RAMBLIN' JACK ELLIOTT SINGS WOODY GUTHRIE & JIMMIE RODGERS (LP)	£40
61	77 LP 1	JACK ELLIOT SINGS (10" LP, spelt 'Elliot' on sleeve)	£175
65	Fontana TFL 6044	JACK ELLIOTT (LP)	£20
65	Stateside SL 10143	JACK ELLIOTT COUNTRY STYLE (LP)	£20
66	Stateside SL 10167	SINGS THE SONGS OF WOODY GUTHRIE (LP)	£20
57	Topic 10T 14	THE RAMBLING BOYS (10" LP, stickered Topic sleeve, insert)	£60
63	Topic 12T 105	THE RAMBLING BOYS (LP, reissue of above with 2 extra tracks)	£50
64	Topic 12T 106	MULESKINNERS (LP)	£30
67	Bounty BY 6036	ROLL ON BUDDY - THE JACK ELLIOTT AND DERROLL ADAMS STORY VOL. 1 (LP)	£50

KEN ELLIOTT
79	RCA PL 25262	BODY MUSIC (LP)	£30

MARI ELLIOTT
76	GTO GT 58	Silly Billy/Half Past One	£30

(see also Poly Styrene, X Ray Spex)

MIKE ELLIOTT
72	Ackee ACK 151	Milk And Honey/Burst A Shirt	£15

VERNON ELLIOTT ENSEMBLE
07	Trunk JBH029 LP	IVOR THE ENGINE & POGLES WOOD (LP)	£15

ELLIOTTS OF BIRTLEY
69	Xtra XTRA 1091	A MUSICAL PORTRAIT OF A DURHAM MINING FAMILY (LP)	£15

(see also Jack Elliott)

ELLIS
72	Epic S EPC 64878	RIDING ON THE CREST OF A SLUMP (LP)	£20

(see also Steve Ellis)

ALTON ELLIS (& FLAMES)
65	Island WI 239	Dance Crasher (with Flames)/BABA BROOKS: Vitamin A	£60
65	Island WI 241	You Are Not To Blame/BABA BROOKS: Teenage Ska	£70
66	Doctor Bird DB 1044	Blessings Of Love/Nothing Sweeter (as Alton & Flames)	£60
66	Doctor Bird DB 1049	The Preacher (as Alton & Flames)/LYNN TAITT & COMETS: Tender Loving Care	£60
66	Doctor Bird DB 1055	Shake It (with Flames)/SILVERTONES: Whoo Baby	£60
66	Doctor Bird DB 1059	Girl I've Got A Date (with Flames)/LYNN TAITT & TOMMY McCOOK: The Yellow Basket	£40
67	Island WI 3046	Cry Tough (with Flames)/TOMMY McCOOK & SUPERSONICS: Mr Solo	£150
67	Treasure Isle TI 7004	Rocksteady (with Flames)/TOMMY McCOOK & SUPERSONICS: Wall Street Shuffle	£60
67	Treasure Isle TI 7010	Duke Of Earl/All My Tears (with Flames)	£60
67	Treasure Isle TI 7016	Ain't That Loving You/TOMMY McCOOK/SUPERSONICS: Tommy's Rocksteady	£60
67	Treasure Isle TI 7030	Oowee Baby/How Can I (with Flames)	£60
67	Treasure Isle TI 7044	Willow Tree/I Can't Stop Now	£60
67	Trojan TR 004	Ain't That Loving You (with Flames)/TOMMY McCOOK & SUPERSONICS: Comet Rocksteady	£60
67	Trojan TR 009	Wise Birds Follow Spring/TOMMY McCOOK & SUPERSONICS: Soul Rock	£60
67	Studio One SO 2028	I Am Just A Guy/SOUL VENDORS: Just A Bit Of Soul	£120
67	Studio One SO 2033	Only Sixteen/Baby (both actually by Heptones)	£40
68	Studio One SO 2037	Live And Learn/HEPTONES: Cry Baby Cry	£65
68	Trojan TR 630	I Can't Stand It/Trying To Reach My Goal	£40
68	Trojan TR 642	Breaking Up/Party Time	£40
68	Nu Beat NB 010	I Can't Stand It/Tonight	£45
68	Nu Beat NB 013	Bye Bye Love/MONTY MORRIS: My Lonely Days	£50
68	Nu Beat NB 014	La La Means I Love You/Give Me Your Love	£40
68	Pama PM 707	The Message/Some Talk	£50
68	Pama PM 717	My Time Is The Right Time/JOHNNY MOORE: Tribute To Sir Alex	£45
68	Coxsone CS 7071	A Fool/SOUL VENDORS: West Of The Sun	£150
69	Studio One SO 2084	Change Of Plans/CABLES: He'll Break Your Heart (B-side act. by Mad Lads)	£160
69	Gas GAS 105	Diana/English Talk	£60
69	Bamboo BAM 2	Better Example/DUKE MORGAN: Lick It Back	£70
69	Duke DU 14	Diana/Personality	£55
70	Duke DU 72	Remember That Sunday/TOMMY McCOOK & SUPERSONICS: Last Lick	£40
70	Gas GAS 151	Suzie/Life Is Down In Denver (some copies credit Alton Ellis & Flames)	£15
70	Gas GAS 161	Deliver Us/NEVILLE HINDS: Originator	£15
70	Duke Reid DR 2501	What Does It Take To Win Your Love/TOMMY McCOOK: Reggae Meringue	£25
70	Duke Reid DR 2512	You Made Me So Very Happy/TOMMY McCOOK & SUPERSONICS: Continental	£35

MINT VALUE £

70	Bamboo BAM 29	Tumbling Tears/SOUND DIMENSION: Today Version	£50
70	Techniques TE 903	It's Your Thing/TECHNIQUES ALL STARS: Get Left	£25
70	Techniques TE 905	I'll Be Waiting/TECHNIQUES ALL STARS: I'll Be Waiting Version	£25
71	Banana BA 318	Sunday Coming/CARL BRYAN: Sunday Version	£35
71	Banana BA 330	Bam Bye/Keep On Yearning	£30
71	Banana BA 347	Hey World/Harder And Harder	£30
71	Gas GAS 164	Back To Africa/NEVILLE HINDS: Originator	£15
71	Fab FAB 165	Good Good Loving/Since I Fell For You	£40
71	Bullet BU 466	Black Man's Pride/LEROY PALMER: Groove With It	£25
71	Bullet BU 485	Don't Care/True Born African	£35
71	Smash SMA 2319	A Little Loving/DELROY WILSON & ALTON ELLIS: Loving Version	£20
71	Smash SMA 2320	I'll Be There/ITALS: Rude Boy Train	£20
71	Big Shot BI 589	Be True/Be True — Version	£20
72	Big Shot BI 602	I'm Trying/Luna's Mood	£15
72	Count Shelly CS 004	Follow My Heart/KOOS ALL STARS: Sincerely	£15
72	Spur SP 3	All That We Need Is Love/KEITH HUDSON: Better Love	£30
72	Grape GR 3029	Big Bad Boy/HUDSON'S ALLSTARS: Big Bad Version	£15
72	Ackee ACK 145	Oppression/Oppression Version (both with Zoot Simms)	£45
72	Ackee ACK 148	Let's Stay Together/Version	£35
72	Ackee ACK 502	Too Late To Turn Back Now/IMPACT ALLSTARS: Version	£15
72	Jackpot JP 796	Play It Cool/AGGROVATORS: King Of The Zozas	£15
72	Camel CA 94	Wonderful World/FAB DIMENSION: Wonderful Version	£15
72	Pama Supreme PS 361	Working On A Groovy Thing/HARLESDEN SKANKERS: Version	£20
73	Ackee ACK 511	Alton's Official Daughter/Aquarius Dub (both with Herman)	£15
73	Pyramid PYR 7003	Truly/LLOYD COXSONE SIX: Cruising	£25
73	A&M AMS 7093	Shoo BeDoo Be Doo/I Love You True	£25
75	Bam Bam BAM 02	I'm Still In Love With You/Version	£25
75	Atra ATRA 26	Rasta Spirit/WILD BUNCH: Jal Dub	£40
79	Cha Cha	Children Are Crying/Mr. Ska Beana	£20
67	Coxsone CSL 8008	SINGS ROCK AND SOUL (LP)	£200
69	Coxsone CSL 8019	THE BEST OF ALTON ELLIS (LP)	£100
71	Bamboo BDLPS 214	SUNDAY COMING (LP)	£100
80	Cha Cha	MR. SKABEANA (LP)	£30
77	Trojan HRLP 708	STILL IN LOVE (LP)	£30
73	Count Shelly SSLO 02	ALTON ELLIS'S GREATEST HITS (LP)	£50
84	Jet Star SKYLP46	25TH SILVER JUBILEE (LP)	£15
95	Horse HRLP 708	STILL IN LOVE (LP, reissue)	£50

(see also Alton & Eddy, Hortense Ellis, Hortense & Alton, Flames [Jamaica], Righteous Flames,Tony Gordon, Soul Flames)

ALTON ELLIS & THE HEPTONES
80	Cha Cha CHAD 21	Mr. Ska Beana/ALTON ELLIS: Ain't No Music (12")	£25

ALTON ELLIS & DENNIS ALCAPONE
72	Lord Koos KOO 21	Big Bad Boy Version/TAPPER ZUKIE: Ira Lion	£35

(see also Tapper Zukie)

BOBBY ELLIS
68	Island WI 3136	Dollar A Head (with Crystalites)/RUDY MILLS: I'm Trapped	£70
74	Dragon DRA 1033	Up Park Camp/Verse 4	£15
77	Third World TWS 9	MEET THE REVOLUTIONARIES (LP)	£40

(see also Jerry Lewis, Derrick Harriot, Rudy Mills, Crystalites, Keith & Tex, Eric Morris, Roy Richards, Soul Vendors)

DAVE ELLIS
72	Sonet SNTF 646	ALBUM (LP)	£25

ELLIS DEE PROJECT
92	Ellis Dee Project LSD 001	Do You Want Me/Rock To The Max (12")	£20
92	Ellis Dee Project LSD 003	Dance Factor (1-sided 12")	£20

DON ELLIS (ORCHESTRA)
68	Liberty LBL 8306OE	LIVE IN THREE QUARTER TIME (LP)	£20
68	CBS 63230	ELECTRIC BATH (LP)	£25
68	CBS 63356	SHOCK TREATMENT (LP)	£15
69	CBS 63680	THE NEW DON ELLIS BAND GOES UNDERGROUND (LP)	£15
71	CBS 66261	DON ELLIS AT FILLMORE (2-LP)	£15

HERB ELLIS-JIMMY GIUFFRE ALL STARS
59	HMV CLP 1337	HERB ELLIS MEETS JIMMY GIUFFRE (LP)	£18

HORTENSE ELLIS
63	R&B JB 101	I'll Come Softly/I'm In Love (with Alton Ellis)	£50
65	Blue Beat BB 295	I've Been A Fool/Hold Me Tenderly	£35
67	Fab FAB 20	Somebody Help Me (with Buster's All Stars)/ PRINCE BUSTER & ALL STARS: Rock & Shake	£80
68	Coxsone SC 7033	A Man Of Chances(as Tree Tops)/HORTENSE ELLIS: A Groovy Kind Of Love	£300
70	Bullet BU 427	Last Date/PAT SATCHMO: Cherry Pink	£50
71	Gas 166	I Shall Sing/Stand By Your Man	£40
73	Tropical AL020	Woman in The Ghetto/Instrumental Version	£25
76	Third World TWS 918	JAMAICA'S FIRST LADY OF SONG (LP)	£20

(see also Hortense & Alton, Hortense & Delroy, Hortense & Jackie, Alton Ellis, Duke Reid, Three Tops, Jackie Opal)

JOANNE ELLIS
82	RCA 247	Self Service Love/Bye Baby	£15

JO-JO ELLIS
72	Fury FY 302	The Fly/Perdona Mia	£30

LARRY ELLIS
58 Felsted AF 110 Buzz Goes The Bee/Nothing You Can Do £15

LARRY ELLIS AND THE BLACK HAMMER
03 Jazzman JMANLP 014 Funky Thing 1/Funky Thing 2 (reissue) £18

MATTHEW ELLIS
71 Regal Zonophone RZ 3033 Avalon/You Are £15
71 Regal Zono. SRZA 8501 MATTHEW ELLIS (LP, gatefold sleeve, red/silver labels) £40
72 Regal Zono. SRZA 8505 AM I...? (LP, gatefold sleeve, red/silver labels) £50
(see also Procol Harum, Chris Spedding)

SHIRLEY ELLIS
65 London HLR 9946 The Name Game/Whisper To Me Wind £15
67 CBS 202606 Soul Time/Waitin' (DJ copy, 4 prong push-out centre, large red A to front label)) £180
67 CBS 202606 Soul Time/Waitin' (4-prong push-out centre) £100
67 CBS 2817 Sugar, Let's Shing-A-Ling/How Lonely Is Lonely (4-prong push-out centre) £20
71 CBS 7463 Soul Time/Waitin' (reissue, 4-prong push-out centre) £30
77 CBS 4901 Soul Time/Waitin' (2nd reissue, blue vinyl, sold centre) £20
67 CBS (S)BPG 63044 SOUL TIME WITH SHIRLEY ELLIS (LP. stereo/mono, CBS 'world of entertainment' inner) .. £70
(see also Love Affair, Widowmaker, Zoot Money, Peter Bardens)

(STEVE) ELLIS
70 CBS 4992 Loot/More More More £70
72 Epic EPC 64878 RIDING ON THE CREST OF A SLUMP (LP, as Ellis) £20
73 Epic EPC 65650 WHY NOT? (LP, as Ellis) £20
18 Sony 19075827551 BOOM! BANG! TWANG! (LP, printed inner) £15
22 Edsel Records EDSL 0108 FINCHLEY BOY (10CD box set, 36 page booklet, signed print) £25
(see also Ellis, Love Affair)

ANDY ELLISON
68 Track 604 018 It's Been A Long Time/JOHN'S CHILDREN: Arthur Green £70
68 CBS 3357 Fool From Upper Eden/Another Lucky Lie £45
68 S.N.B. 55-3308 You Can't Do That/Casbah £75
68 S.N.B. 55-3308 You Can't Do That/Cornflake Zoo (second issue, different B-side) £85
(see also John's Children, Jet, Radio Stars, Beau Brummel)

LORRAINE ELLISON
66 Warner Bros WB 5850 Stay With Me/I Got My Baby Back £15
71 Mercury 6052 073 Call Me Anytime You Need Some Lovin'/Please Don't Teach Me To Love You £30
70 Warner Bros WS 1821 STAY WITH ME (LP) £40

ELMER HOCKETT'S HURDY GURDY
68 Parlophone R 5716 Fantastic Fair/MOOD MOSAIC: The Yellow Spotted Capricorn £15
(see also Mood Mosaic, Mark Wirtz)

IAN ELMS
82 Squid Marks SMT 013 GOOD NIGHT (LP, with insert) £180

ELOY
82 Heavy Metal HMILP 1 PLANETS (LP, clear vinyl with inner sleeve) £15
82 Heavy Metal HMIPD 1 PLANETS (LP, picture disc) £18
82 Heavy Metal HMIPD 3 TIME TO TURN (LP, picture disc) £18
83 Heavy Metal HMIPD 12 PERFORMANCE (LP, picture disc) £15
84 Heavy Metal HMIPD 21 METROMANIA (LP, picture disc) £18
89 FM Revolver REV PD120 RA (LP, picture disc) £15

RAS ELROY
81 Arawak DD 030 Stepping/Walking On (12") £30
(see also Elroy Baily)

JEFF ELROY & BOYS BLUE
66 Philips BF 1533 Honey Machine/Three Woman £30
(see also Boys Blue)

LEE & JAY ELVIN
59 Fontana H 191 So The Story Goes/When You See Her £20
59 Fontana H 191 So The Story Goes/When You See Her (78) £15
(see also Jerry Lordan)

ELVIS HITLER
90 GWR GWLP 37 DISGRACELAND (LP) £20

EMANON
77 Clubland SJP 777 Raging Pain/Rip A Bough (stamped sleeve) £30

ROBERT EMANUEL
80 Black Roots BRD 1 Illiteracy/RANKING SIMEON: Cultural Dread/Unknown Artist: Progress Road Dub/Don't Get Weary/RANKING SIMEON: Don't Get Jumpy/Unknown Artist: Strictly Rub-A-Dub (12") £20
81 Black Roots BR 25 Never Get Away/Jah Is My Light (12" as Robert Emanuel & Ranking Simeon) £45
85 CF CMF 02 Fashion Dread/No Beggy Beggy (12") £50
84 Black Roots BR 181262 Leave Natty Business/BARRINGTON LEVY & DARBAZ: Jah Black (12") £20

EMBERS
63 Decca F 11625 Chelsea Boots/Samantha £20
(see also Three's A Crowd)

EMBRACE
98 BBC BOX SET EMBRACE EP'S (6 x 12"s in black box, numbered, 100 only) £60
98 Hut HUTLP 46 THE GOOD WILL OUT (2-LP) £50

MINT VALUE £

00	Hut HUTLP 60	DRAWN FROM MEMORY (LP)	£50
01	Hut HUTLP 68	IF YOU'VE NEVER BEEN (LP)	£50
04	Independiente ISOM 45LP	OUT OF NOTHING (LP)	£60
06	Independiente ISOM 60LP	THIS NEW DAY (LP)	£30

EMBRYO

80	Rampant RAM 001	I'm Different/You Know He Did (p/s)	£15

(see also Jump Squad)

EMCEE 5

62	Columbia SEG 8153	LET'S TAKE FIVE (EP)	£175
62	Alpha International DB 92	VOLUME ONE (EP)	£150

(see also Rendell-Carr, Ian Carr's Nucleus)

EMERALD

78	Look LK/SP 6365	The Tempter/Rolling Stone (no p/s)	£20

EMERALDS (U.K.)

65	Decca F 12304	King Lonely The Blue/Someone Else's Fool	£40

AVALON EMERSON

16	Whities WHYT006	WHITIES 006 (12", p/s)	£40

KEITH EMERSON

15	Record Collector RCLP015	THE KEITH EMERSON TRIO (10", brown die-cut sleeve, with certificate, 750 only)	£15

(see also Emerson Lake & Palmer, Nice, V.I.P.'s)

EMERSON, LAKE & PALMER

70	Island ILPS 9132	EMERSON, LAKE AND PALMER (LP, pink label)	£150
70	Island ILPS 9123	EMERSON, LAKE AND PALMER (LP, later 'pink rim palm tree')	£40
71	Island ILPS 9155	TARKUS (LP, 1st pressing, gatefold sleeve, 'pink rim palm tree' label with 'side 1' and 'side 2' on labels)	£100
71	Island ILPS 9155	TARKUS (LP, 2nd pressing, gatefold sleeve, 'pink rim palm tree' label with 'A' and 'B' on label)	£50
71	Island HELP 1	PICTURES AT AN EXHIBITION (LP, gatefold sleeve, black label and pink "i")	£75
72	Island ILPS 9186	TRILOGY (LP, gatefold sleeve. pink rim label)	£50
73	Manticore K 53501	BRAIN SALAD SURGERY (LP, fold-out die cut sleeve with poster)	£40
73	Epic S EPC 65450	WELCOME BACK MY FRIENDS TO THE SHOW THAT NEVER ENDS (3-LP, trifold sleeve)	£30
73	Manticore K 43503	EMERSON, LAKE AND PALMER (LP, reissue)	£20
73	Manticore K 443504	TARKUS (LP, reissue)	£20
73	Manticore K 33501	PICTURES AT AN EXHIBITION (LP, repressing)	£20
73	Manticore K 43505	TRILOGY (LP, repressing)	£20
92	Victory 828 318-1	BLACK MOON (LP)	£30

(see also Emerson Lake & Powell, Nice, Keith Emerson, Shame, Asia, King Crimson, Stray Dog, Atomic Rooster)

DICK EMERY

69	Pye NPL (NSPL) 18277	DICK EMERY SINGS (LP)	£15

KATHLEEN EMERY

97	Jazzman JM001	Sometimes I Feel Like A Motherless Child/Evil Ways (hand numbered sticker on paper sleeve, 500 only)	£20

EMILY (1)

74	Emily (No cat no)	If All The World/Long Tall Glasses/Smoke On The Water (p/s)	£70

EMJAYS

59	Top Rank JAR 145	All My Love All My Life/Cross My Heart	£50

ENDAF EMLYN

71	Wren WRL 537	HIRAETH (LP)	£300
74	Sain 1012M	SALEM (LP)	£50

DAVID EMMANUEL

83	White Lodge WLT 1	Giving It Up For Love/Stir It Around (12")	£50

EMMET SPICELAND

68	Page One POLS 011	THE FIRST (LP, with stickered sleeve, blue/silver labels)	£60
68	Page One POLS 011	THE FIRST (LP, without sticker on sleeve, blue/silver labels)	£50
77	Hawk HALP 166	THE EMMET SPICELAND ALBUM (LP, reissue of above LP)	£35

FRED EMNEY

58	Decca TRI DFE 6554	FRED EMNEY (EP)	£20

E-MOTIONS

90s	Slammin 1	E-MOTIONS (EP)	£20

EMOTIONS

69	Downtown DT 446	Give Me Love/HORACE FAITH: Daddy's Home	£40

EMOTIONS (JAMAICA)

66	Ska Beat JB 263	Rude Boy Confession/Heartbreaking Gypsy	£55
67	Caltone TONE 100	A Rainbow/TONY & DOREEN: Just You And I	£60
68	Caltone TONE 118	Soulful Music/No Use To Cry	£60
68	Caltone TONE 120	Careless Hands/TOMMY McCOOK & SUPERSONICS: Caltone Special	£60
69	High Note HS 018	The Storm/Easy Squeeze	£40
69	High Note HS 026	Rum Bay/PATSY: Find Someone	£40
70	Supreme SUP 209	Halleluiah/MATADOR ALLSTARS: Boat Of Joy	£20
71	Prince Buster PB 22	Walking Along/Sometimes	£20
11	Big Shot THB 7010	You Are The One/PHIL PRATT ALL STARS: Girls Like Dirt Stars	£25

(see also Romeo & Emotions, Horace Faith, Max Romeo)

EMOTIONS (U.K.)

62	London HLR 9640	Echo/Come Dance Baby	£40

| 63 | London HLR 9701 | L-O-V-E/A Million Reasons | £30 |
| 63 | Stateside SS 237 | A Story Untold/One Life One Love One You | £20 |

EMOTIONS (U.S.)
| 69 | Deep Soul DS 9104 | Somebody New/Brushfire | £30 |
| 70 | Stax SXATS 1030 | SO I CAN LOVE YOU (LP) | £20 |

EMPEROR (NORWAY)
93	Candlelight 002	EMPEROR (LP)	£20
95	Candlelight 008	IN THE NIGHTSIDE ECLIPSE (LP)	£20
98	Candlelight 023	ANTHEMS TO THE WELKIN AT DUSK (LP, gatefold sleeve)	£20
99	Candlelight 035	IX : EQUILIBRIUM (LP, gatefold sleeve)	£20
01	Candlelight 052	EMPERIAL VINYL PRESENTATION (Numbered box set with 5 picture disc LPs and booklet)	£60

EMPERORS
| 66 | Stateside SS 565 | Karate/I've Got To Have Her | £30 |
| 68 | Pama 786 | I've Got To Have Her/Karate | £25 |

EMPHASIS
| 76 | Jaycee JC 002 | EMPHASIS (LP) | £40 |

EMPIRE OF THE SUN
| 09 | Capitol 50999 | WALKING ON A DREAM (LP) | £60 |
| 13 | EMI 3748461 | ICE ON THE DUNE (LP) | £60 |

EMS STUDIOS
| 72 | (No label or cat no) | SOUNDS FROM EMS (7" flexi in printed sleeve) | £120 |
| 72 | EMS | EMS SYNTHI AND THE COMPOSER (LP) | £500 |

EN ROUTE
| 79 | Barn BARN 006 | Break Down Your Defences/Rusty Capri | £30 |

ENCHANTED FOREST
| 68 | Stateside SS 2080 | You're Never Gonna Get My Lovin'/Suzanne | £15 |

ENCHANTERS
| 67 | Warner Bros WB 2054 | We Got Love/I've Lost All Communications | £25 |

ENCONA COURSE (FEATURING DEF J)
| 91 | Edutainment EDUT001 | Rhyme Grenade/Taste Of The Future/Hit Men (EP) | £40 |
| 92 | White (No Cat. No.) | VIA COARSEVILLE (EP) | £41 |

END RESULT
| 73 | Priory PRY 1 | Towards The Sun/Please Go | £175 |

THE END
65	Philips BF 1444	I Can't Get Any Joy/Hey Little Girl	£30
68	Decca F 22750	Shades Of Orange/Loving, Sacred Loving	£50
69	Decca LK 5015	INTROSPECTION (LP, large unboxed logo on label, mono)	£700
69	Decca SKL-R 5015	INTROSPECTION (LP, large unboxed logo on label, stereo)	£500
96	Tenth Planet TP 025	IN THE BEGINNING ... THE END (LP, gatefold sleeve, numbered, 1,000 only)	£20
97	Tenth Planet TP 033	RETROSPECTION (LP, numbered, 1,000 only)	£15

(see also Tucky Buzzard, Bill Wyman, Innocents, Bobby Angelo, Tuxedo)

END (THE)
| 81 | No label or cat no | I Can't Take Any More/Take A Look (no p/s) | £30 |

ENDEVERS
| 68 | Decca F 12817 | Remember When We Were Young/Taking Care Of Myself | £30 |
| 68 | Decca F 12859 | She's My Girl/She's That Kind Of Girl | £30 |

ENDGAMES
| 83 | Virgin VS 640 | Miracle In My Heart/Ecstacy (Centurion MIx) (12") | £20 |

END PHENOMENA
| 70 | Hollick And Taylor | END PHENOMENA (LP) | £50 |

MELVIN ENDSLEY
| 57 | RCA RCA 1004 | I Like Your Kind Of Love/Is It True? | £25 |
| 58 | RCA RCA 1051 | I Got A Feelin'/There's Bound To Be | £20 |

END TO END
87	T.S. TS3	Are You Gonna Be/Version/We Can Work It Out/Verion (12")	£60
88	Sure Delight SDT 7	Confusion/(7" Mix)/(Instrumental Version) (12" white label)	£40
88	TS 7TS 1	Confuzzion/Confuzzed	£40

ENEMY (1)
| 83 | Fallout FALL LP 015 | THE GATEWAY TO HELL (LP) | £20 |

ENERGETIC KRUSHER
| 89 | Vinyl Solution SOL 17 | PATH TO OBLIVION (LP, with insert, features Danny McCormack) | £20 |

(see also Wildhearts)

ENERGY
81	GRN 1	CONQUER THE WORLD: Conquer The World/Make It/Law Breaker (EP, no p/s)	£75
80	BIPS BECK 927	ENERGISED (EP)	£50
83	Aros AROS 11233	Nowhere To Hide/Fight For Your Freedom (no p/s)	£50

SCOTT ENGEL
58	Vogue V 9125	Blue Bell/Paper Doll	£150
58	Vogue V 9125	Blue Bell/Paper Doll (78)	£80
59	Vogue V 9145	The Livin' End/Good For Nothin' (with Count Dracula & Boys)	£400
59	Vogue V 9145	The Livin' End/Good For Nothin' (with Count Dracula & Boys) (78)	£60

MINT VALUE £

59	Vogue V 9150	Charlie Bop/All I Do Is Dream Of You	£200
59	Vogue V 9150	Charlie Bop/All I Do Is Dream Of You (78)	£40
66	Liberty LEP 2261	SCOTT ENGEL (EP)	£35

(see also Scott Walker, Walker Brothers)

SCOTT ENGEL & JOHN STEWART
| 66 | Capitol CL 15440 | I Only Came To Dance With You/Greens | £40 |

(see also Scott Walker, Walker Brothers)

ENGINEERS (2)
04	Echo ECHLP 55	FOLLY (6-Track mini-album)	£20
05	Echo ECHLP61	ENGINEERS (2-LP, g/f)	£40
14	KScope KSCOPE 868	ALWAYS RETURNING (LP)	£15

ENGINEERS WITHOUT FEARS
| 94 | Dee Jay DJX 015 | Spiritual Aura/Rhythm (12") | £25 |

ENGLAND (1)
| 76 | Deroy DER 1356 | ENGLAND (LP, private pressing) | £1000 |

ENGLAND (2)
| 77 | Arista ARTY 153 | GARDEN SHED (LP, allegedly with booklet) | £60 |
| 77 | Arista ARTY 153 | GARDEN SHED (LP, without alleged booklet) | £40 |

ENGLAND FOOTBALL SQUAD
| 70 | Pye 7N 17920 | Back Home/Cinnamon Stick (with 'football centre and p/s) | £15 |
| 70 | Pye 7N 17920 | Back Home/Cinnamon Stick (in promo 'BOAC' sleeve) | £50 |

ENGLAND'S GLORY
| 73 | Venus VEN 105 | ENGLAND'S GLORY (LP, private pressing, pink label, 25 copies only, Venus VEN 105 in run-out groove; beware of white label counterfeits) | £1000 |

(see also Only Ones)

ENGLAND SISTERS
| 60 | HMV POP 710 | Heartbeat/Little Child | £30 |

BARBARA JEAN ENGLISH
| 73 | Contempo CLP 507 | BARBARA JEAN ENGLISH (LP) | £25 |

ENGLISH COUNTRY BLUES BAND
| 83 | Rogue FMSL 2004 | HOME AND DERANGED (LP) | £15 |

ENGLISH DOGS
83	Clay PLATE 6	MAD PUNX AND ENGLISH DOGS (12")	£25
84	Ros ASS 17	TO THE ENDS OF THE EARTH (12" EP, p/s)	£20
83	Clay LP 10	INVASION OF THE PORKY MEN (LP, inner)	£20
85	Rot ASS 20	FORWARD INTO BATTLE (LP)	£15
86	Under One Flag FLAG 4	WHERE LEGEND BEGAN (LP)	£15

ERROL(L) ENGLISH
70	Torpedo TOR 8	Open The Door To Your Heart/That Will Do	£30
70	Torpedo TOR 9	Where You Lead Me/Hitchin' A Ride	£30
70	Torpedo TOR 16	Sad Girl/Welcome Me Back Home	£30
70	Torpedo TOR 22	Sha La La La Lee/BOVVER BOYS: A.G.G.R.O.	£100

(see also Junior English, Errol & Champions)

MR JOE ENGLISH
| 69 | Fontana TF 3034 | Lay Lady Lay/Two Minute Silence | £15 |

JUNIOR ENGLISH
69	Camel CA 35	Nobody Knows (with Tony Sexton)/Somewhere	£25
78	Ethnic Fight ETH 1228	Keep On Trying/HORSE MOUTH WALLACE: Herb Vendor (12")	£35
79	Burning Rockers BRD 004	Love And Key/Key Down (12", red vinyl)	£20
74	Cactus CTLP 102	THE DYNAMIC (LP)	£25
75	Horse HRLP 707	THE GREAT (LP)	£15
80	Burning Rockers BR 1010	LOVERS KEY (LP)	£25
83	Sunsplash SNSLP01	TWO OF A KIND (LP)	£40

(see also Errol English, Tony Sexton)

ENGLISH MCCOY
| 88 | Nowyertalkin' 7TALK 2 | Give Me Something To Believe In/Breaking Down (p/s) | £100 |
| 88 | Nowyertalkin' 12TALK 2 | GIVE ME SOMETHING TO BELIEVE IN (12" EP) | £200 |

ENID
76	Buk BULP 2014	IN THE REGION OF THE SUMMER STARS (LP, 1st issue, white label, with insert, without mention of "Enid" on front cover; distributed by Decca)	£35
77	Buk BULP 2014	IN THE REGION OF THE SUMMER STARS (2nd issue, black label, with "Enid" on front cover)	£20
77	honeybee INS 3005	IN THE REGION OF THE SUMMER STARS (3rd pressing, brown label with poster)	£18
84	The Stand LE 1	"THE LIVERPOOL ALBUM" (untitled mini-album, sold at gigs, 800 only)	£20
84	The Stand THE STAND 1	THE STAND (fan club issue, 5,000 only, autographed)	£25
84	The Stand THE STAND 1	THE STAND (fan club issue, 5,000 only, some autographed)	£15
85	The Stand THE STAND 2	THE STAND 1985-1986 (fan club issue, 2,000 only, autographed)	£25
85	The Stand THE STAND 2	THE STAND 1985-1986 (fan club issue, 2,000 only)	£15

(see also Robert John Godfrey, Godfrey & Stewart, William Arkle, Glen Baker)

ETHEL ENNIS
| 64 | RCA SF 7654 | ONCE AGAIN (LP) | £15 |

RAY ENNIS & BLUE JEANS
| 68 | Columbia DB 8431 | What Have They Done To Hazel?/Now That You've Got Me (You Don't Seem To Want Me) | £25 |

(see also Swinging Blue Jeans, Blue Jeans)

BRIAN ENO

74	Island WIP 6178	Seven Deadly Finns/Later On	£15
75	Island WIP 6233	The Lion Sleeps Tonight (Wimoweh)/I'll Come Running	£15
78	Polydor 2001 762	King's Lead Hat/R.A.F. (B-side with Snatch)	£15
73	Island ILPS 9268	HERE COME THE WARM JETS (LP, pink rim, palm tree label, MATRIX A-1E/B-1E)	£50
74	Island ILPS 9309	TAKING TIGER MOUNTAIN (BY STRATEGY) (LP, gatefold sleeve, pink rim, Island label)	£50
75	Island ILPS 9351	ANOTHER GREEN WORLD (LP, 1st pressing, blue rim, palm tree label)	£75
75	Island HELP 22	EVENING STAR (LP, as Fripp & Eno)	£30
75	Obscure OBS 3	DISCREET MUSIC (LP, 1st pressing with grey labels)	£75
75	Obscure OBS 3	DISCREET MUSIC (LP, 2nd pressing, red labels)	£40
76	Editions EG EGM 1	MUSIC FOR FILMS (LP, private pressing)	£250
77	Polydor 2302 071	BEFORE AND AFTER SCIENCE (LP, with 4 Peter Schmidt prints in envelope)	£100
77	Polydor 2302 071	BEFORE AND AFTER SCIENCE (LP, without prints)	£35
77	Polydor 2683082	HERE COME THE WARM JETS/BEFORE & AFTER SCIENCE (2-LP reissue)	£30
77	Polydor 2302 063	HERE COME THE WARM JETS (LP, reissue)	£25
77	Polydor 2302 668	TAKING TIGER MOUNTAIN (BY STRATEGY) (LP, reissue, red label)	£25
77	Polydor 2302 069	ANOTHER GREEN WORLD (LP, reissue, red label)	£25
78	Polydor 2310623	MUSIC FOR FILMS (LP, textured sleeve)	£35
78	EG AMB 001	AMBIENT 1 - MUSIC FOR AIRPORTS (LP, inner)	£50
82	EG EGED 20	AMBIENT 4 (LP)	£30
82	Editions EG EGED 17	AMBIENT 1 - MUSIC FOR AIRPORTS (LP, reissue)	£25
82	EG EGED 5	MUSIC FOR FILMS (LP, reissue)	£20
83	EG EGLP 53	APOLLO (LP)	£40
83	EG EGBS 002	WORKING BACKWARDS 1983-1973 (9-LP box set with "Music For Films, Vol. 2" LP & "Rarities" 12")	£200
84	EG EGLP 17	TAKING TIGER MOUNTAIN (BY STRATEGY) (LP, reissue)	£15
86	EG EGLP 65	MORE BLANK THAN FRANK (LP)	£20
87	Editions EG EGED 23	DISCREET MUSIC (LP, reissue)	£20
87	EG EGLP 32	BEFORE AND AFTER SCIENCE (LP, reissue)	£20
87	Editions EG EGED 20	AMBIENT 4 (LP. reissue, barcode on rear of sleeve)	£20
89	Standard Music Library ESL 168	TEXTURES (LP)	£400
89	Standard Music Library SML ESL 003CD	TEXTURES (CD)	£50
93	Virgin ENOBX 1	I: INSTRUMENTAL (3CD, box set, booklet)	£30
93	Virgin ENOBX 2	II: VOCAL (3CD box set, booklet)	£40
92	Opal 9362 45010-1	THE SHUTOV ASSEMBLY (LP)	£50
95	All Saints AS 23	SPINNER (LP, with Jah Wobble as Eno/Wobble)	£35
11	Warp WARPLP207R	SMALL CRAFT ON A MILK SEA (2-LP)	£20
11	Warp WARPLP214	DRUMS BETWEEN THE BELLS (2-LP with Rick Holland)	£18
14	All Saints	NERVE NET (2LP, gatefold, printed inners, first UK issue of 1992 CD)	£20
15	Opal ENORSD2015	MY SQUELCHY LIFE (2LP, RSD, gatefold, printed inners, download card, hype sticker))	£30
15	Opal/Warp WARPLP 272	THE SHIP (2LP, gatefold, printed inners, clear vinyl, 4 art prints)	£40
17	Opal/Warp WARPLP 280	REFLECTION (2LP, printed inners, download card, album title in square sticker to shrink)	£20
20	Opal/UMC 085 524-9	RAMS - ORIGINAL SOUNDTRACK ALBUM (LP, white vinyl, printed inner, DL card, RSD)	£30
22	Opal/UMC 4801370	FOREVERANDEVERNOMORE (LP, ltd, ed. clear vinyl, compostable plastic wrap, gatefold, printed inner)	£30
23	Opal/Netflix/At The Movies MOVATM 376	TOP BOY (2LP, gatefold, silver vinyl, printed inners)	£40
23	Opal/Netflix/At The Movies MOVATM 376	TOP BOY (2LP, gatefold, crystal clear vinyl, printed inners)	£35

(see also Ayers Cale Nico & Eno, Roxy Music, Passengers, Robert Fripp, Lady June, David Toop, Gavin Bryars, Toto, Eno & Cale, Brian Eno & David Byrne, David Byrne & Brian Eno, Harold Budd & Brian Eno, Eno.Hyde)

BRIAN ENO & DAVID BYRNE

81	EG ECOX 1	The Jezebel Spirit/Regiment/Very Very Hungry (12", p/s)	£18
81	EG EGLP 48	MY LIFE IN THE BUSH OF GHOSTS (LP, 1st pressing, later pressings have barcode on sleeve)	£30

(see also David Byrne, Talking Heads, David Byrne & Brian Eno)

BRIAN ENO & JOHN CALE

90	Land LAND 12	WRONG WAY UP (LP)	£20

(see also Brian Eno. John Cale)

ENO.HYDE

14	Warp WARPLP 249X	SOMEDAY WORLD (2LP, gatefold, ltd ed. of 750 w/print)	£30
14	Warp WARPLP 255X	HIGH LIFE (2LP, gatefold, indie store exclusive w/print)	£20

(see also Brian Eno, Karl Hyde, Underworld)

ENOS & SHEILA

68	Blue Cat BS 138	Tonight You're Mine/UNTOUCHABLES: Your Love	£80

(see also Enos McLeod)

ENOUGH'S ENOUGH

68	Tattoo TT 101	Please Remember/Look Around You Baby	£700

ENSEMBLE

82	Stiff WIN 1	Viva Scotland, England, Ireland/Viva Scotland, England, Ireland ("A" label promo)	£15

ENSLAVED

90s	Candlelight 001MLP	HORDANES LAND (EP)	£60

ENTER SHIKARI

09	Ambush Reality LPAMBR006V	COMMON DREADS (LP)	£150
12	Ambush Reality LPAMBR015	A FLASH FLOOD OF COLOUR (LP, blue, transparent pink or white vinyl)	£30

MINT VALUE £

13	Ambush Reality LPAMBR001	**TAKE TO THE SKIES** (2-LP reissue, with CD, green/beige vinyl)	£60
13	Ambush Reality LPAMBR001	**TAKE TO THE SKIES** (2-LP reissue, with CD, orange/blue vinyl)	£50
13	Ambush Reality ESBS002LP	**LIVE AT ROCK CITY 2009** (LP, grey vinyl)	£20
13	Ambush Reality EBS004LP	**LIVE IN LONDON** (LP/DVD)	£20
15	Ambush Reality AMBR031	**THE MINDSWEEP** (LP)	£15
15	Ambush Reality PIASR835DLP	**THE MINDSWEEP: HOSPITALIZED** (2-LP, orange vinyl)	£20
15	Ambush Reality LPAMBR001	**TAKE TO THE SKIES** (2-LP reissue, with CD, clear vinyl)	£40
17	Ambush Reality LPAMBR001	**TAKE TO THE SKIES** (2-LP reissue, with CD, violet vinyl)	£35
17	Ambush Reality PIASR990LP	**THE SPARK** (LP, silver vinyl)	£20
19	Ambush Reality LPAMBR006V	**COMMON DREADS** (LP, repressing, splatter vinyl, with 7")	£60

ENTICERS
72	Atlantic 2091 136	**Calling For Your Love/Storyteller**	£40

JIMI ENTLEY SOUND
02	Espionage Disk ESP 001	**Apache/Charlie's Theme**	£25

(see also Portishead)

ENTOMBED
93	Earache MOSH 94 T	**HOLLOWMAN EP** (6 track 12", p/s)	£15
89	Earache MOSH 21P	**LEFT HAND PATH** (LP, picture disc)	£20
90	Earache MOSH 21	**LEFT HAND PATH** (LP, insert)	£25
91	Earache MOSH 21	**LEFT HAND PATH** (LP, white vinyl, stickered sleeve, 2000 only)	£30
91	Earache MOSH 37	**CLANDESTINE LP, embossed sleeve, insert)**	£20
93	Earache MOSH 82	**WOLVERINE BLUES** (LP, lyric insert)	£50
97	Music For Nations MFN 216	**TO RIDE, SHOOT STRAIGHT AND SPEAK THE TRUTH** (LP, with "Family Favourites" 12")	£50
98	Music For Nations MFN 244	**SAME DIFFERENCE** (LP)	£40
07	Back On Black BOBV 067 LP	**SERPENT SAINTS/THE TEN AMENDMENTS** (LP, red vinyl)	£15

JOHN ENTWISTLE('S OX)
71	Track 2406 005	**SMASH YOUR HEAD AGAINST THE WALL** (LP, gatefold, black/silver label)	£30
72	Track 2406 104	**WHISTLE RYMES** (LP, gatefold sleeve, black/silver labels)	£25
73	Track 2406106	**RIGOR MORTIS SETS IN** (LP, gatefold, inner)	£15
75	Decca TXS 114	**MAD DOG** (LP, as John Entwistle's Ox, with poster, lyric insert)	£25
75	Decca TXS 114	**MAD DOG** (LP, as John Entwistle's Ox, without poster, lyric insert)	£15

(see also Who, Rigor Mortis)

ENYA
87	BBC REB 605	**ENYA** (LP)	£20

EPEE MD
87	Cooltempo COOL 156	**It's My Thing** (Club)**/You're A Customer** (Club) (p/s)	£50

EPICS (JAMAICA)
70	Bamboo BAM 37	**Your Love/Driving Me Crazy**	£45

EPICS (U.K.)
68	CBS 3564	**Travelling Circus/Henry Long**	£20

(see also Acid Gallery, Christie)

EPIDEMIC
89	Metalcore CORE 4	**THE TRUTH OF WHAT WILL BE** (LP)	£20

EPILEPTICS
80	Stortbeat/Mirror BEAT 8	**1970'S EP** (black & white p/s, stencilled white labels)	£20
81	Spiderleg SDL 1	**1970'S EP** (re-recorded, printed labels, folded different printed b&w p/s)	£15

(see also Licks, Flux Of Pink Indians)

EPISODE
68	MGM MGM 1409	**Little One/Wide Smiles**	£30

(see also Episode Six)

EPISODE FOUR
86	Lenin & McCarthy LENM 001T	**STRIKE UP MATCHES EP** (p/s with insert, 500 only, many destroyed)	£150

(see also East Village)

EPISODE SIX
66	Pye 7N 17018	**Put Yourself In My Place/That's All I Want**	£25
66	Pye 7N 17110	**I Hear Trumpets Blow/True Love Is Funny That Way**	£20
66	Pye 7N 17147	**Here, There And Everywhere/Mighty Morris Ten**	£20
67	Pye 7N 17244	**Love, Hate, Revenge/Baby Baby Baby**	£40
67	Pye 7N 17330	**Morning Dew/Sunshine Girl**	£25
67	Pye 7N 17376	**I Can See Through You/When I Fall In Love**	£40
68	Chapter One CH 103	**Lucky Sunday/Mr. Universe**	£20
69	Chapter One CH 104	**Mozart Versus The Rest/Jak D'Or**	£20
87	PRT PYL 6026	**PUT YOURSELF IN MY PLACE** (LP)	£15

(see also Episode, Sheila Carter & Episode Six, Neo Maya, Roger Glover, Jon Lord, Gillan, Deep Purple, Quatermass)

EPMD
89	Sleeping Bag SBUK 17	**The Big Payback/You Had Too Much To Drink**	£100
88	Sleeping Bag SBUK LP 1	**STRICTLY BUSINESS** (LP)	£20
89	Sleeping Bag SBUK LP 8	**UNFINISHED BUSINESS** (LP)	£20
90	Def Jam 467697 1	**BUSINESS AS USUAL** (LP)	£20
92	Def Jam 471963 1	**BUSINESS NEVER PERSONAL** (LP)	£25

MINNIE EPPERSON
68	Action ACT 4503	**Grab Your Clothes** (And Get On Out)**/No Love At All**	£75

KAT EPPLE AND BOB STOHL
13   Dead Cert VCR 004   SANCTUS SPIRITUS (LP) £18

PRESTON EPPS
60   Top Rank JKP 2060   RUSHING FOR PERCUSSION (EP, with Sandy Nelson)...£20
(see also Sandy Nelson)

EQUA
83   Mr Fox FOX 1   In The Red/City Dub £20
83   Mr Fox FOX 1   In The Red/City Dub/City Lights (12")...£60

EQUALS
67   President ZAM 2   I'm A Poor Man/Can't Find A Girl To Love Me (Export only) £30
70   President PT 303   I Can See But You Don't Know/Gigolo Sam £40
70   Presiden ZAM 1   Let's Go To The Moon/Watching The Girls (export) £25
73   President PT 414   Diversion/Here Today Gone Tomorrow £15
76   Mercury 6007 106   Funky Like A Train/If You Didn't Miss Me £15
76   Phonogram EQUAL 001   EQUALS PARTY (12", promo only) £100
88   Club JAB 58   Funky Like A Train/Born Ya! (p/s, reissue, green moulded injection labels)).....£15
88   Club JABX 58   Funky Like A Train/Funky Like A Train (extended)/Born Ya! (12", p/s, reissue) £20
68   President PTE 1   BABY COME BACK (EP) £20
68   President PTE 2   THE EQUALS (EP)...£25
67   President PTL 1006   UNEQUALLED EQUALS (LP)...£30
68   President PTL 1015   EQUALS EXPLOSION (LP)..£30
68   President PTL(S) 1020   SENSATIONAL EQUALS (LP)...£30
68   President PTL(S) 1025   SUPREME (LP) £30
69   President PTLS 1030   THE EQUALS STRIKE AGAIN (LP) £30
69   President PTLS 1050   BEST OF THE EQUALS (LP)...£20
70   President PTLS 1038   EQUALS AT THE TOP (LP, gatefold, poster)...£40
76   Mercury 9109 601   BORN YA! (LP, printed inner)..£50
78   Ice ICEL 1002   MYSTIC SISTER (LP)..£120
(see also Little Grants & Eddie, Pyramids, Hickory, Little Brother Grant, Zappata Schmitt, Seven Letters/Syramip, Thirty-Second Turn-Off)

EQUATORS
76   Klik KL 620   Father Oh Father/Version £25

EQUINOX
73   Boulevard BLVD 4118   HARD ROCK (LP, black/silver labels) £25

EQUIPE 84
67   Major Minor MM 517   Auschwitz/Twenty Ninth Of September..£20

ERAMUS HALL
96   Westbound SEWD 112   YOUR LOVE IS MY DESIRE (LP, reissue)...£35
16   Expansion ERAMUS LP !   YOUR LOVE IS MY DESIRE (LP, reissue)..£20
16   Expansion ERAMUS LP !   YOUR LOVE IS MY DESIRE (LP, reissue, with free 7").....................................£35

ERASMUS CHORUM
72   Chapter 1 SCM 173   Oh Lord, The Holy House On Sunday/Mary Jane £20
73   Alaska ALA 13   Jungle/That Is Why...£40

ERASURE
SINGLES
85   Mute L12MUTE 40   Who Needs Love (Like That) (Mexican Mix)/Push Me Shove Me (Tacos Mix) (12", p/s) ...£20
85   Mute L12MUTE 42   Heavenly Action (Yellow Brick Mix)/Don't Say No (Ruby Red Mix) (12", p/s, L12 cat. no. must be listed on sleeve & label) £75
85   Mute D12 MUTE 42   Heavenly Action/Don't Say No (Ruby Red Mix)//Who Needs Love (Like That) (Mexican Mix)/Push Me Shove Me (Tacos Mix) (12" shrinkwrapped double pack).........£100
94   Mute MUTE 166   I Love Saturday/Dodo/Because You're So Sweet (unreleased, p/s only) £60
ALBUMS
91   Mute STUMM 95   CHORUS (LP) £20
92   Mute L2   POP! - THE FIRST 20 HITS (2LP, gatefold, printed inners)...............................£100
94   Mute STUMM 115   I SAY I SAY I SAY (LP, booklet) £40
95   Mute STUMM 145   ERASURE (2LP, gatefold, printed inners) £40
97   Mute STUMM 155   COWBOY (LP)..£50
PROMOS
86   Mute P12MUTE 45   Oh L'Amour/March On Down The Line/Gimme! Gimme! Gimme! (12", plain white sleeve, dark blue vinyl) £30
89   Mute (no cat. no.)   WILD (CD/LP/12" box set, promo, stickers, postcard, photo, info sheet) £350
90s Mute P12MUTE 195   Don't Say Your Love Is Killing Me (Tall Paul Mix)/(John Pleased Wimmin Flashback Vox) Oh L'Amour (Tin Tin Out Remix)/(Matt Darey Mix) (12", white label test pressing with press release & release sheet, 10 copies only) £70
91   Mute CDSTUMM 95   CHORUS (promo CD, with and booklet) £60
92   Mute (no cat. no.)   POP! THE FIRST 20 HITS (2LP/CD, promo-only box set, T-shirt, info sheets, video tape,)..£350
20   Mute FSTUMM455   Welcome To The Neon - 1-track promo with Hey Now (Think I Got A Feeling) (500 only) £35
(see also Depeche Mode, Dinger)

ERIC (SYKES) & HATTIE (JACQUES)
63   Decca LK 4507   ERIC, HATTIE AND THINGS!!! (LP, laminated flipback sleeve)............................£15

ERIC & THE VIKINGS
86   Kool Kat 5   Hurting/My Baby Ain't No Play Thing (red vinyl)..£25

ROKY ERICKSON (& THE ALIENS)
80   CBS SCBS 84463   ROKY ERICKSON & THE ALIENS (LP) £20
86   Demon FIEND 66   GREMLINS HAVE PICTURES (LP) £15

MINT VALUE £

87	5 Hours Back TOCK 007	CASTING THE RUNES (LP)	£15
87	5 Hours Back TOCK 7P	CASTING THE RUNES (LP, picture disc)	£25
92	Swordfish SFMD LP 1	MAD DOG (LP)	£25
92	Swordfish SFMD LP 2	LOVE TO SEE YOU BLEED (LP)	£25

(see also 13th Floor Elevators)

ROLF ERICSON

| 59 | Pye NIxa NJL 14 | SESSION IN STOCKHOLM (LP, with Freddie Redd) | £100 |

ERIN PERYGLUS

87	OFN OFN 3	Bronson/Y Dyn Newydd (p/s)	£30
88	OFN OFN 6	Dafydd Yn Gwneud Teisen/Merthyr (p/s)	£20
89	OFN OFN 07B	Y LLOSG (12" picture disc)	£20

ERNIE & ED

| 72 | Jay Boy BOY 58 | Beautiful World/Indication | £50 |

ERROL (ENGLISH) & CHAMPIONS

| 70 | Jackpot JP 732 | Lonely Boy/Da Boo | £15 |

(see also Errol English)

ERROL (DUNKLEY) & HIS GROUP

| 65 | Blue Beat BB 284 | Gypsy/Miss May (actually by Errol Dunkley & Roy Shirley) | £40 |

(see also Errol Dunkley)

ERROL (DUNKLEY) & U ROY

| 72 | Punch PH 105 | Darling Ooh Wee/GOD SONS: Merry Up Version | £15 |

E.R. & THE ROUGH RIDERS

| 69 | Polydor 56361 | Heya/I'm Alive | £15 |

ERSATZ

| 81 | Raw RAW 35 | Motorbody Love/One Good Reason/Gimme A Chance (poster p/s) | £35 |

(see also DJ Harvey)

BOOKER ERVIN

| 61 | Parlophone PMC 1170 | THE BOOK (LP) | £80 |

DEE ERVIN

| 72 | Signpost SG 4356 | DEE ERVIN SINGS (LP) | £20 |

ESCALATORS

| 83 | Big Beat WIKM15 | MOVING STAIRCASES (LP) | £25 |

(see also Clapham South Escalators, The Meteors)

ESCAPE FROM NEW YORK

| 84 | Rollerball BALL 1 | Fire In My Heart/Won't Be Your Fool/Fire In My Heart (Instrumental) (12") | £50 |

ESCORTS (JAMAICA)

| 70 | Big Shot BI 535 | I'm So Afraid/Mother Nature | £40 |
| 74 | Fab FAB 245 | Sixpense/Loving Feeling | £15 |

(see also Sensations)

ESCORTS (U.K.)

64	Fontana TF 453	Dizzy Miss Lizzy/All I Want Is You	£25
64	Fontana TF 474	The One To Cry/Tell Me Baby	£25
64	Fontana TF 516	I Don't Want To Go On Without You/Don't Forget To Write	£25
65	Fontana TF 570	C'Mon Home Baby/You'll Get No Lovin' That Way	£25
66	Fontana TF 651	Let It Be Me/Mad Mad World	£25
66	Columbia DB 8061	From Head To Toe/Night Time	£45

(see also Big Three, Paddy Klaus & Gibson, Swinging Blue Jeans)

ESCORTS (U.S.)

| 63 | Coral Q 72458 | Submarine Race Watching/Somewhere | £25 |

ESCORTS & KAY JUSTICE

| 54 | Columbia SCM 5132 | If You Took Your Love From Me/Yes, Indeed | £15 |

ESG

81	Factory FAC 34	You're No Good/UFO (p/s)	£25
93	C.T. CTT42	Moody (Original Mix)/(Spaced Out Mix)/(CT Remix 1)/CT Remix 2) (12")	£20
15	Fire BLAZE 221	MOODY EP (12" splatter green vinyl)	£20
00	Universal Sounds USLP 10	ESG: A SOUTH BRONX STORY (2-LP, insert)	£50
02	Soul Jazz SJR LP 65	STEP OFF (2-LP)	£20
06	Soul Jazz SJR LP 138	KEEP ON MOVING (2-LP)	£18
06	Soul Jazz SJR LP 150	COME AWAY WITH ESG (2-LP reissue)	£30
07	Soul Jazz SJR LP 167	ESG: A SOUTH BRONX STORY VOLUME 2 (2-LP, insert)	£30
10	Fire FIRELP 156	DANCE TO THE BEST OF ESG (3-LP)	£45
11	Fire F222	ESG (LP, reissue)	£25

ESKIMOS & EGYPT

| 81 | Village VILS 102 | The Cold/A Year/Screams And Whispers (EP, p/s) | £60 |

ESOTERIC/ESOTERIK

96	Club Craft OR 100	Dancing With The Devil/Esoteric Vs. Hybrid (12")	£50
96	Club Craft OR 200	Ultimate Straightness/Playing With Voices (12")	£40
96	Club Craft OR 300	Elegant Panning/3 After That One (12")	£30
96	Club Craft OR 400	Odd Sins/Odd Sins (12")	£80
96	Crowd Control CROWD 005T	Desert Planet/Mayhem (12", as Esoterik)	£40
96	Utmostfear UTMOST 1301	Falling, Floating, Flying/Ultimate Straightness (12")	£40
96	Utmostfear UTMOST 1302	Curley And Ramon/Mad Strings (12")	£40
97	Crowd Control CROWD 006	Mayhem/Purdey's Effect/In The Hills (12", as Esoterik)	£80

98　Utmostfear UTMOST 1303　**Untitled/Untitled** (12", label bears legend "Curley Truly Unique 1973-1998")............**£40**
(See also Spiral Tribe)

ESOTERIC (2)
11　Aesthetic Death ADLP 003　**EPISTEMOLOGICAL DESPONDENCY** (2-LP, reissue of 1994 CD release, numbered gatefold sleeve, insert, 350 only) **£25**

ESP
89　Radical DJ INT 14　**It's You** (12", p/s) **£40**

ESPERANTO ROCK ORCHESTRA
73　A&M AMLH 68175　**ESPERANTO ROCK ORCHESTRA** (LP, gatefold sleeve, brown label) **£20**
74　A&M AMLH 63624　**DANSE MACABRE** (LP, as Esperanto, silver/gold labels) **£15**
75　A&M AMLS 68294　**LAST TANGO** (LP, as Esperanto, silver/brown labels) **£20**
(see also Keith Christmas, Comus)

ESPERS
05　Wichita WEBB084LP　**ESPERS** (LP) **£60**

ESPRIT DE CORPS (1)
73　Jam JAM 24　**If** (Would It Turn Out Wrong)/**Picture On The Wall** **£15**
(see also David Ballantyne, Just Plain Smith, Just Plain Jones)

ESPRIT DE CORPS (2)
81　Come COME 1　**Anxiety/The Tea Cup Song** (hand-made silk-screened sleeve) **£30**

ESQUERITA
58　Capitol CL 14938　**Rockin' The Joint/Esquerita And The Voola** **£100**
72　Specialty SPE 6603　**WILDCAT SHAKEOUT** (LP) **£30**

ESQUIRES
67　Stateside SS 2048　**Get On Up/Listen To Me** **£20**
68　Stateside SS 2077　**And Get Away/Everybody's Laughing** **£20**
73　Action ACT 4618　**My Sweet Baby/Henry Ralph** **£50**
68　London HA-Q/SH-Q 8356　**GET ON UP AND GET AWAY** (LP) **£40**

ESQUIVEL
63　Reprise R 6046　**MORE OF OTHER WORLDS, OTHER SOUNDS** (LP) **£15**

ESSENTIAL LOGIC
79　Rough Trade ROUGH 5　**BEAT RHYTHM NEWS** (LP) **£20**
(see also X-Ray Spex, Lora Logic)

ESSER
09　Transgressive TRANS094X　**BRAVEFACE** (LP, 300 only, numbered) **£30**

ESSEX
63　Columbia DB 7077　**Easier Said Than Done/Are You Going My Way** **£15**
63　Columbia DB 7122　**A Walkin' Miracle/What I Don't Know Won't Hurt Me** (with Anita Humes) **£20**
63　Columbia DB 7178　**She's Got Everything/Out Of Sight, Out Of Mind** **£20**
63　Columbia 33SX 1593　**EASIER SAID THAN DONE** (LP) **£50**
64　Columbia 33SX 1613　**A WALKIN' MIRACLE** (LP) **£50**

DAVID ESSEX
65　Fontana TF 559　**And The Tears Came Tumbling Down/You Can't Stop Me Loving You** **£50**
65　Fontana TF 620　**Can't Nobody Love You/Baby I Don't Mind** **£45**
66　Fontana TF 680　**This Little Girl Of Mine/Brokenhearted** **£45**
66　Fontana TF 733　**Thigh High/De Boom Lay Boom** **£40**
68　Uni UN 502　**Love Story/Higher Than High** **£20**
68　Pye 7N 17621　**Just For Tonight/Goodbye** **£20**
69　Decca F 12935　**That Takes Me Back/Lost Without Linda** **£40**
69　Decca F 12967　**The Day The Earth Stood Still/Is It So Strange?** **£30**
79　Vertigo 6059 233　**M.O.D./M.O.D.** (2) (as M.O.D., songwriting credited to D. Cook, p/s, allegedly mispressed on 2-Tone label) **£75**
(see also David & Rozaa, Us)

ESSJAY
71　DJM DJS 254　**Twins Of Evil/Fastback** **£35**

ASTON ESSON
80　Studio 16 STD 01　**Woman Of My Dreams/Version** (12") **£30**

NEVILLE ESSON
61　Blue Beat BB 37　**Lover's Jive/Wicked And Dreadful** (with Clue J. & His Blues Busters) **£18**

ESTABLISHMENT
81　Foetain　**BAD CATHOLICS** (LP) **£30**
(see also Cromwell)

'SLEEPY' JOHN ESTES
66　Delmark DJB 3　**SLEEPY JOHN'S GOT THE BLUES** (EP) **£40**
63　Esquire 32-195　**THE LEGEND OF SLEEPY JOHN ESTES** (LP) **£60**
63　'77' LA 12-27　**TENNESSEE JUG BUSTERS — BROKE AND HUNGRY** (LP) **£40**
65　Storyville SLP 172　**PORTRAITS IN BLUES VOLUME 10** (LP) **£22**
72　Delmark DS 619　**ELECTRIC SLEEP** (LP) **£20**
71　Delmark DS 613　**BROWNSVILLE BLUES** (LP) **£25**

JOHN ESTES/FURRY LEWIS/WILL SHADE
71　Revival RVS 1008　**OLD ORIGINAL TENNESSEE BLUES** (LP) **£20**

JACKIE ESTREK
61　Blue Beat BB 64　**Boss Girl/COUNT OSSIE & GROUP: Cassavubu** **£35**
63　Island WI 042　**Since You've Been Gone/Daisy I Love You** **£45**

66	Ska Beat JB 256	The Ska/Daisy I Love You...£50

ETCETERAS

64	Oriole CB 1950	Where Is My Love/Bengawan Solo £15
64	Oriole CB 1973	Little Lady/Now I Know £20

ETERNAL

90	Sarah SARAH 031	Sleep/Breathe/Take Me Down (p/s) £30

(see also Slowdive)

ETERNAL BASS

93	Volatile VILE 003	Way Of The Future/Deep Sensation (12") £40

ETERNALS (JAMAICA)

69	Coxsone CS 7091	Queen Of The Minstrels/Stars £90
71	Moodisc MU 3507	Push Me In The Corner/MUDIE'S ALL STARS: Mudie's Madness (B-side actually by Ansell Collins) £45
71	Moodisc MU 3508	Keep On Dancing/HAZEL WRIGHT: My Jealous Eyes.............................£35

(see also Don Cornel & Eternals, Cornel Campbell)

ETERNALS (U.S.)

59	London HL 8995	Rockin' In The Jungle/Rock 'N' Roll Cha-Cha (triangular centre) £150
59	London HL 8995	Rockin' In The Jungle/Rock 'N' Roll Cha-Cha (round centre) £50
59	London HL 8995	Rockin' In The Jungle/Rock 'N' Roll Cha-Cha (78) £35

ETERNAL SCREAM

81	Eternal 01	Hypocrite/Action In My Life (p/s) £15
81	Eternal 02	How I Wish/Child (p/s) £20

ETERNITY'S CHILDREN

68	Capitol CL 15558	Mrs Bluebird/Little Boy £25

ETHEL THE FROG

80	Best SRTSFMR 014	Eleanor Rigby/Whatever Happened To Love...£60
80	EMI EMC 3329	ETHEL THE FROG (LP, with Terry Hopkinson & Doug Sheppard)............£22

ETHIOPIAN IRATION BLOOD RELATIVE & IDREN

79	Greensleeves GRED 21	This Foundation/Elders and Deacons/How Can A Man/Jah Children Come (12") £40

ETHIOPIANS

66	Coxsone DIR 2003	Let The Light Shine/Let's Get Together (white labels only)....................£200
66	Ska Beat JB 260	Live Good (credited to the Etheopians)/SOUL BROTHERS: Soho £70
66	Island WI 3015	I Am Free/SOUL BROTHERS: Shanty Town..£70
67	Rio R 110	Owe Me No Pay Me/SHARKS: I Wouldn't Baby......................................£30
67	Rio R 114	I'm Gonna Take Over Now/JACKIE MITTOO: Home Made £70
67	Rio R 123	What To Do/JACKIE MITTOO: Got My Bugaloo £225
67	Rio R 126	Dun Dead A'Ready/BOB ANDY: Stay In My Lonely Arms £60
67	Rio R 130	Train To Skaville/You Are The Girl (B-side actually by Gladiators) £30
67	Doctor Bird DB 1092	I Need You/Do It Sweet..£100
67	Doctor Bird DB 1096	The Whip/Cool It, Amigo £25
67	Doctor Bird DB 1103	Stay Loose, Mama/The World Goes Ska £50
68	Doctor Bird DB 1141	Come On Now/Sh'Boom £45
68	Doctor Bird DB 1147	Engine 54/Give Me Your Love £150
68	Doctor Bird DB 1148	Train To Glory/You Got The Dough £75
68	Doctor Bird DB 1169	Everything Crash/I'm Not Losing You..£22
68	Crab CRAB 2	Fire A Muss Tail/Blacker Black (B-side actually by Count Ossie) £45
68	Crab CRAB 5	Reggie Hit The Town/Ding Dong Bell £40
69	Crab CRAB 7	I Am A King/What A Big Surprise £50
69	Doctor Bird DB 1172	Not Me/Cut Down £200
69	J J Records DB 1185	Hong Kong Flu/Clap Your Hands £18
69	J J Records DB 1186	What A Fire/You £20
69	Doctor Bird DB 1199	Everyday Talking/Sharing You £25
69	Trojan TR 666	Woman Capture Man/One £20
69	Trojan TR 697	Well Red/J.J. ALLSTARS: R.F.K. £30
69	Nu Beat NB 031	My Testimony (credited to the Maytals)/J.J. ALL STARS: One Dollar Of Soul £30
69	Nu Beat NB 038	Buss Your Mouth/GLEN ADAMS (Actually REGGAE BOYS) Rough Way Ahead...............£60
69	Duke DU 35	My Girl/ANSELL COLLINS: Bigger Boss £60
70	Duke DU 61	Mek You Go On So/WINSTON WRIGHT & J.J. ALL STARS: Neck Tie £50
70	Duke Reid DR 2507	Mother's Tender Care/TOMMY McCOOK: Soldier Man £15
70	Bamboo BAM 26	Walkie Talkie/SOUND DIMENSION: Moan And Groan............................£25
70	Bamboo BAM 38	You'll Want To Come Back/JACKIE MITTOO: Baby Why (Instrumental) (B-side actually by Sound Dimension).............................£35
70	J.J. JJ 3302	Wreck It Up/Don't Go £90
70	J.J. JJ 3303	Hong Kong Flu/Everything Crash £20
70	Songbird SB 1040	No Baptism/CRYSTALITES: No Baptism (Version Two)..........................£15
71	Fab FAB 180	Monkey Money/Version £20
71	Big Shot BI 569	He's Not A Rebel/J.J. ALL STARS: He's Not A Rebel — Version...............£15
71	Big Shot BI 574	The Selah/Don't Let Me Go £18
71	Duke DU 102	Drop Him/J.J. ALL STARS: Drop Him Version..£15
71	Supreme SUP 226	Starvation/MAXIE & GLEN: Jordan River..£15
71	Big BG 330	Solid As A Rock/RUPIE EDWARDS ALL STARS: Solid As A Rock Version £15
71	Punch PH 96	Solid As A Rock/RUPIE EDWARDS ALL STARS: Solid As A Rock Version £15
72	G.G. GG 4533	Israel Want To be Free/TYPHOON ALL STARS: Israel (Version)...............£15
72	Prince Buster PB 38	You Are For Me/Playboy £20
72	Techniques TE 919	Promises/TIVOLIS: Promises — Version £15
76	Attack ATT 8131	Another Moses/SYLFORD WALKER: I Can't Understand £15

MINT VALUE £

78	Sensation SSD015	Hail Rasta/Version (12")	£15
78	Treasure Isle TRE 010	The Whip/Cool It, Omigo/BOBBY ELLIS: Shank I Sheck (12")	£15
11	Smash THB 7012	I'm Shocking/Sign The Cheque	£20
68	Doctor Bird DLM 5011	THE ETHIOPIANS GO ROCK STEADY/ENGINE 54 (LP, this is a UK pressing in a Jamaican sleeve)	£450
69	Trojan TTL 10	REGGAE POWER (LP)	£75
70	Trojan TBL 112	WOMAN CAPTURE MAN (LP)	£80
77	Third World TWS 15	SLAVE CALL (LP)	£35
86	Trojan TRLS 228	ORIGINAL REGGAE HITSOUND (LP)	£20
92	Trojan TRLS 312	THE WORLD GOES SKA (LP)	£15

(see Eathopians, Soul Brothers, Soul Vendors, Hamlins)

ETHNIC FIGHT BAND
75	Ethnic Fight EF 4416	OUT OF ONE MAN COMES MANY DUBS (LP)	£80
77	Ethnic Fight EF 4444	MUSIC EXPLOSION DUB (LP)	£100

ETIVES
81	Ayrespin AYRC 106	A BREATH OF FRESH AIR (LP)	£20
84	Ayrespin AYRC 015	AN GAOL A THUG MI OG (MY LOVE OF EARLY DAYS) (LP)	£20

ETTA (JAMES) & HARVEY (FUQUA)
60	London HLM 9180	If I Can't Have You/My Heart Cries	£50

(see also Etta James, Moonglows, Harvey & Moonglows)

EUGENE & BURST
71	Supreme SUP 225	Let It Fall/DENZIL & BURST: Can't Change	£15

EUGENIUS
92	Paperhouse PAPLP 011	OOMALAMA (LP)	£15
94	August Rust 008	MARY QUEEN OF SCOTS (LP)	£15

(see also Teenage Fanclub)

EUROPEAN TOYS
84	Backs 12NCH 009	KOREA EP (12")	£15

EURYTHMICS
81	RCA RCAT 68	Never Gonna Cry Again (Extended)/Le Sinistre (Extended) (12", p/s)	£15
82	RCA RCAT 199	This Is The House/Your Time Will Come (live)/Never Gonna Cry Again/4/4 In Leather (live)/Take Me To Your Heart (live) (12", p/s)	£25
82	RCA RCAT 230	The Walk/Invisible Hands/Dr Trash/The Walk (Part 2) (12", printed die-cut sleeve)	£25
83	RCA DA 4/EUC 001	Right By Your Side/Right By Your Side (Party Mix) (stickered p/s with free shrinkwrapped (RCA EUC 001)	£25
84	RCA PLP 70109	TOUCH (LP, picture disc)	£20

(see also ACatch, Tourists, Chris & Cosey, Stewart & Harrison, Vegas)

JOHN EVAN BAND
90	A New Day NRS/CD 1	THE JOHN EVAN BAND LIVE '66 (CD, 500 only)	£30

(see also Jethro Tull)

ADRIANA EVANS
97	RCA 07863 66958-1	ADRIANA EVANS (2-LP)	£25

BARBARA EVANS
59	RCA RCA 1122	Souvenirs/Pray For Me, Mother (triangular centre)	£25

BILL EVANS
59	Fontana FJL 104	DIG IT (LP)	£20
59	Riverside 12-315	PORTRAIT IN JAZZ (LP)	£150
60	Riverside 291	EVERYBODY DIGS BILL EVANS (LP)	£150
61	Riverside RLP 9399	WALTZ FOR DEBBY (LP)	£200
61	Riverside RLP 351	EXPLORATIONS (LP)	£100
61	Riverside RLP 376	SUNDAY AT THE VILLAGE VANGUARD (LP)	£80
62	Riverside RLP 428	MOONBEAMS (LP)	£80
63	Verve VLP 9054	CONVERSATIONS WITH MYSELF (LP)	£40
64	Riverside RLP 473	HOW MY HEART SINGS (LP)	£50
67	Verve VLP 9161	A SIMPLE MATTER OF CONVICTION (LP)	£30
64	Verve VLP 9077	TRIO 64 (LP)	£50

BRIAN EVANS
71	CBS 5392	We're Going Wrong/Paradise Lost	£50

DAVE EVANS
71	Village Thing VTS 6	THE WORDS IN BETWEEN (LP)	£40
72	Village Thing VTS 14	ELEPHANTASIA (LP)	£45
74	Kicking Mule SNKF 107	SAD PIG DANCE (LP, with booklet)	£20
76	Kicking Mule SNKF 122	TAKE A BITE OUT OF LIFE (LP)	£18

GIL EVANS ORCHESTRA
60	Vogue LAE 12234	GREAT JAZZ STANDARDS (LP)	£20
61	HMV CLP 1456	OUT OF THE COOL (LP)	£20

LARRY EVANS
56	London HLU 8269	Crazy 'Bout My Baby/Henpecked	£750
56	London HLU 8269	Crazy 'Bout My Baby/Henpecked (78)	£75

MAUREEN EVANS
67	CBS 3222	I Almost Called Your Name/Searching For Home (Demo copy)	£50
68	CBS 3222	I Almost Called Your Name/Searching For Home	£40
63	Oriole EP 7076	MELANCHOLY ME (EP)	£30
63	Oriole PS 40046	LIKE I DO (LP)	£30

MILL EVANS
01	Kent 6T 17	Ain't You Glad/MILLIONAIRES: I'm The One Who Loves You	£20

PAUL EVANS (& CURLS)
59	London HLL 8968	Seven Little Girls Sitting In The Back Seat/Worshipping An Idol (78)	£15
60	London HLL 9045	Midnite Special/Since I Met You, Baby	£30
60	London HLL 9239	Hushabye Little Guitar/Blind Boy	£20
63	London RE-R 1349	PAUL EVANS (EP)	£40
60	London HA-L 2248	PAUL EVANS SINGS THE FABULOUS TEENS (LP)	£100

RICHARD EVANS
78	AMS 7438	Burning Spear/Do Re Me For Soul (12")	£20

RUSSELL EVANS & NITEHAWKS
66	Atlantic 584 010	Send Me Some Cornbread/The Bold	£30

TONY EVANS BAND
71	Polydor 2058 101	Hot Pants/Beach Bird	£15

VIC EVANS & THE HASTINGS
64	Airborne NBP 006	Caribbean Child/Hurry Along Belinda	£20

EVEN AS WE SPEAK
90	Sarah SARAH 37	Nothing Ever Happens/Blue Suburban Skies/Bizarre Love Triangle/ Goes So Slow/A Stranger Calls (p/s, insert)	£15
91	Sarah SARAH 49	One Step Forward/Must Be Something Else/Best Kept Secret (p/s, insert)	£15
91	Sarah SARAH 59	Beautiful Day/Nothing Much At All (p/s, insert)	£15
93	Sarah SARAH 79	(All You Find Is) Air/Getting Faster/Blue Eyes Deceiving Me (p/s, insert)	£15
93	Sarah SARAH 614	FERAL POP FRENZY (LP)	£40

EVEN DOZEN JUG BAND
66	Bounty BY 6023	THE EVEN DOZEN JUG BAND (LP)	£25

(see also Lovin' Spoonful, John Sebastian)

EVENING OUTS
80	Refill RR5	Channel/Stammer (no p/s, hand stamped labels)	£100

EVENSONG
73	Philips 6006 276	I Was Her Cowboy/Gypsy	£15

EVER RED
88	Supertone STR 007	Dem No Ruff Like We/Hot Number (12")	£40

BETTY EVERETT
64	Stateside SS 259	You're No Good/Chained To Your Love	£20
64	Stateside SS 280	It's In His Kiss (The Shoop Shoop Song)/Hands Off	£20
64	Stateside SS 321	I Can't Hear You/Can I Get To Know You	£25
64	Fontana TF 520	Getting Mighty Crowded/Chained To A Memory	£20
64	King KG 1002	Happy I Long To Be/Your Loving Arms	£20
65	Sue WI 352	I've Got A Claim On You/Your Love Is Important To Me	£60
71	Liberty LBF 15428	I Got To Tell Somebody/Why Are You Leaving Me	£15
65	Fontana TL 5236	IT'S IN HIS KISS (LP)	£60
68	Joy JOYS 106	IT'S IN HIS KISS (LP, reissue)	£15
69	Uni UNLS 109	THERE'LL COME A TIME (LP)	£25

BETTY EVERETT & JERRY BUTLER
65	Fontana TL 5237	DELICIOUS TOGETHER (LP)	£50

(see also Jerry Butler)

EVERGREEN BLUES
68	Mercury 20122 SMCL	7 DO ELEVEN (LP)	£20

EVERGREEN BLUESHOES
69	London HA-U/SH-U 8399	THE BALLAD OF THE EVERGREEN BLUESHOES (LP)	£20

(see also Skip Battin, Byrds)

EVERLY BROTHERS
78s
58	London HLA 8554	Should We Tell Him/This Little Girl Of Mine	£15
59	London HLA 8863	Poor Jenny/Take A Message To Mary	£20
59	London HLA 8934	('Til) I Kissed You/Oh, What A Feeling	£30
60	London HLA 9039	Let It Be Me/Since You Broke My Heart	£60
60	Warner Bros WB 1	Cathy's Clown/Always It's You	£100
60	London HLA 9157	When Will I Be Loved/Be-Bop-A-Lula	£60
60	Warner Bros WB 19	Lucille/So Sad (To Watch Good Love Go Bad)	£200

SINGLES
58	London HLA 8554	Should We Tell Him/This Little Girl Of Mine (triangular centre)	£20
64	Warner Bros WB 143	You're The One I Love/Ring Around My Rosie (withdrawn)	£20
66	Warner Bros WB 5682	It's All Over/I Used To Love You (unissued)	£0
70	Warner Bros WB 7425	Yves/Human Race	£15
80	Old Gold SET 1	THE EVERLY BROTHERS SINGLES SET (15 x p/s 7", box set with book)	£15

EPs
58	London RE-A 1113	THE EVERLY BROTHERS	£15
58	London RE-A 1148	THE EVERLY BROTHERS — NO. 2	£15
58	London RE-A 1149	THE EVERLY BROTHERS — NO. 3	£15
59	London RE-A 1174	THE EVERLY BROTHERS — NO. 4	£15
59	London RE-A 1195	SONGS OUR DADDY TAUGHT US PART 1	£15
59	London RE-A 1196	SONGS OUR DADDY TAUGHT US PART 2	£15

| 59 | London RE-A 1197 | SONGS OUR DADDY TAUGHT US PART 3 | £15 |
| 60 | London RE-A 1229 | THE EVERLY BROTHERS — NO. 5 | £15 |

(The above EPs were originally issued with triangular centres, later round-centre editions are worth half to two-thirds of these values.)

61	Warners WEP 6034	ESPECIALLY FOR YOU (mono)	£20
61	Warners W(S)EP 6034	ESPECIALLY FOR YOU (stereo)	£20
61	London RE-A 1311	THE EVERLY BROTHERS — NO. 6	£15
62	Warners WEP 6049	FOREVERLY YOURS (mono)	£15
62	Warners W(S)EP 6049	FOREVERLY YOURS (stereo)	£15
62	Warners WEP 6056	IT'S EVERLY TIME (mono)	£15
62	Warners W(S)EP 6056	IT'S EVERLY TIME (stereo)	£15
63	Warners WEP 6107	A DATE WITH THE EVERLY BROTHERS VOL. 1 (mono)	£15
63	Warners W(S)EP 6107	A DATE WITH THE EVERLY BROTHERS VOL. 1 (stereo)	£15
63	Warners WEP 6109	A DATE WITH THE EVERLY BROTHERS VOL. 2 (mono)	£15
63	Warners W(S)EP 6109	A DATE WITH THE EVERLY BROTHERS VOL. 2 (stereo)	£18
63	Warners WEP 6111	INSTANT PARTY VOL. 1 (mono)	£15
63	Warners W(S)EP 6111	INSTANT PARTY VOL. 1 (stereo)	£20
63	Warners WEP 6113	INSTANT PARTY VOL. 2 (mono)	£15
63	Warners W(S)EP 6113	INSTANT PARTY VOL. 2 (stereo)	£20
63	Warners WEP 6115	BOTH SIDES OF AN EVENING — FOR DANCING VOL. 1 (mono)	£15
63	Warners W(S)EP 6115	BOTH SIDES OF AN EVENING — FOR DANCING VOL. 1 (stereo)	£18
64	Warners WEP 6117	BOTH SIDES OF AN EVENING — FOR DREAMING VOL. 2 (mono)	£15
64	Warners W(S)EP 6117	BOTH SIDES OF AN EVENING — FOR DREAMING VOL. 2 (stereo)	£18
64	Warners WEP 6128	THE EVERLY BROTHERS SING GREAT COUNTRY HITS VOL. 1	£15
64	Warners WEP 6131	THE EVERLY BROTHERS SING GREAT COUNTRY HITS VOL. 2	£15
64	Warners WEP 6132	THE EVERLY BROTHERS SING GREAT COUNTRY HITS VOL. 3	£15
65	Warner Bros WEP 608	ROCK'N'SOUL VOL. 1	£15
65	Warner Bros WEP 609	ROCK'N'SOUL VOL. 2	£15
66	Warner Bros WEP 610	LOVE IS STRANGE	£15
66	Warner Bros WEP 612	PEOPLE GET READY	£15
66	Warner Bros WEP 618	WHAT AM I LIVING FOR?	£20
67	Warner Bros WEP 622	LEAVE MY GIRL ALONE	£20
67	Warner Bros WEP 623	SOMEBODY HELP ME	£20

ALBUMS

58	London HA-A 2081	THE EVERLY BROTHERS	£40
58	London HA-A 2150	SONGS OUR DADDY TAUGHT US	£30
60	Warner Bros WM 4012	IT'S EVERLY TIME (Mono)	£30
60	Warner Bros WS 8012	IT'S EVERLY TIME (Stereo)	£30
60	London HA-A 2266	THE FABULOUS STYLE OF THE EVERLY BROTHERS	£30
60	Warner Bros WM 4028	A DATE WITH THE EVERLY BROTHERS (mono)	£30
60	Warner Bros WS 8028	A DATE WITH THE EVERLY BROTHERS (stereo)	£35
61	Warner Bros WM 4052	BOTH SIDES OF AN EVENING (Mono)	£20
61	Warner Bros WS 8052	BOTH SIDES OF AN EVENING (stereo)	£25
62	Warner Bros WM 4061	INSTANT PARTY (also stereo WS 8061)	£20
62	Warner Bros WM 4061	INSTANT PARTY (also stereo WS 8061)	£25
62	Warner Bros WM 8116	CHRISTMAS WITH THE EVERLY BROTHERS AND THE BOYS TOWN CHOIR (mono)	£20
62	Warner Bros WS 8116	CHRISTMAS WITH THE EVERLY BROTHERS AND THE BOYS TOWN CHOIR (stereo)	£25
63	Warner Bros WM 8138	SING GREAT COUNTRY HITS (mono)	£20
63	Warner Bros WS 8138	SING GREAT COUNTRY HITS (stereo)	£25
65	Warner Bros WM 8169	GONE GONE GONE (mono)	£20
65	Warner Bros WS 8169	GONE GONE GONE (stereo)	£25
65	Warner Bros WM 8171	ROCK 'N' SOUL (mono)	£20
65	Warner Bros WS 8171	ROCK 'N' SOUL (stereo)	£25
65	Warner Bros W(S) 1605	BEAT 'N' SOUL	£15
65	Warner Bros W 1620	IN OUR IMAGE (mono)	£15
65	Warner Bros W(S) 1620	IN OUR IMAGE (stereo)	£18

EVERREADY'S
| 80 | Taaga TAG 3 | Don't Do It Again/Martian Girl (gatefold p/s) | £15 |

EVERVESSENCE
| 69 | Priory 02 | Strange One/My Illusive Life | £50 |

EVERYBODY
| 70 | Page One POF 163 | The Shape Of Things To Come/Do Like The Little Children Do | £15 |

EVERY MOTHER'S SON
67	MGM MGM 1341	Come And Take A Ride In My Boat/I Believe In You	£25
67	MGM MGM 1350	Put Your Mind At Ease/Proper Four Leaf Clover	£25
67	MGM C(S) 8044	EVERY MOTHER'S SON (LP)	£40
68	MGM C(S) 8061	EVERY MOTHER'S SON'S BACK (LP)	£35

EVERYONE
| 71 | B&C CAS 1028 | EVERYONE (LP, gatefold sleeve, attached envelope with booklet) | £50 |

(see also Andy Roberts)

EVERYONE ELSE
| 79 | Woodbine St WSR 001 | Schooldays/Brainwashed/Out Of My Mind/Don't Call Us (p/s) | £100 |

EVERYONE INVOLVED
| 72 | Arcturus ARC 3 | The Circus Keeps On Turning/Motor Car Madness | £30 |
| 72 | Arcturus ARC 4 | EITHER OR (LP, private pressing, embossed plain white sleeve with inserts) | £250 |

EVERYTHING BUT THE GIRL
| 96 | Virgin V 2803 | WALKING WOUNDED (LP) | £80 |

MINT VALUE £

99	Virgin V 2892	TEMPERAMENTAL (LP)	£80
01	DMC BACKLP06	BACK TO MINE (3-LP, compilation - non EBG tracks)	£60

(see also Ben Watt, Marine Girls, Tracey Thorn)

EVERYTHING EVERYTHING

08	Saliva TIC 008	Suffragette Suffragette/Luddites & Lambs (p/s, poster)	£40
09	Young & Lost Club YALC 0044	My Keys, Your Boyfriend/Nasa Is On Your Side (p/s)	£25
09	Another AMAK 014	Photoshop Handsome/DNA Dump! (p/s)	£25
10	Geffen 2743110	Schoolin/Lee Zero Dub (p/s)	£25
10	Geffen 2748166	My Kz, Yr Bf/My Kz, Yr Bf (Clock Opera Remix) (p/s)	£30
11	Geffen 2758306	MAN ALIVE (LP, gatefold, printed inner, poster, booklet, first 500 signed)	£200
13	RCA Victor 88725473731	ARC (LP, gatefold, booklet)	£40
15	RCA 88875061171	GET TO HEAVEN (LP, gatefold, booklet, download card, limited edition)	£200
23	Geffen/UMR UMCLP067	MAN ALIVE (2LP, expanded reissue, gatefold, printed inner, booklet, poster)	£50

EVERYTHING IS EVERYTHING

69	Vanguard VA 1	Witchi Tai To/Oooh Baby	£15
68	Vanguard SVRL 19036	EVERYTHING IS EVERYTHING (LP)	£25

EVIL ED

01	YNR YNR4	THE TOURNAMENT ROUND 1 (12", EP stickered black die-cut sleeve)	£16
02	Hidden Identity HID1	THE TOURNAMENT ROUND 2 (12" EP)	£15

EVOLUTION

90	Positive Vinyl PV 001	Came Outa Nowhere (12")	£20
91	Positive Vinyl PV 002	Metropolis (12")	£20

EWAN (MCDERMOTT) & DENVER

67	Giant GN 17	I Want You So Bad/ERIC McDERMOTT: I'm Gonna Love You	£40

EWAN (MCDERMOTT) & JERRY (MCCARTHY)

67	Blue Beat BB 385	Oh Babe/Dance With Me (with Carib Beats)	£40
67	Giant GN 5	The Right Track/We Got To Be One	£40
67	Giant GN 10	Rock Steady Train/My Baby Is Gone	£45
67	Giant GN 14	Tennessee Waltz/You've Got Something	£40

EX

86	Ron Johnson ZRON 11	'1936' THE SPANISH REVOLUTION (double pack with book)	£20

EX/ALERTA

84	CNT CNT 017	THE RED DANCE PACKAGE (12", split EP)	£15

EXCALIBUR

88	Clay PLATE 1	HOT FOR LOVE (Hot For Love/Early In The Morning/Come On And Rock/Death's Door (12" EP)	£15
85	Conquest QUEST 5	THE BITTER END (mini-LP)	£20

EXCEL

79	ARSS XL1	If It Rains/Rolling Home/She's One Of The Boys/Rock Show (EP, p/s)	£100

EXCELS

67	Atlantic 584 133	California On My Mind/The Arrival Of Mary	£25

EXCELSIOR SPRING

69	Instant IN 002	Happy Miranda/It	£35

EXCEPTIONS

65	Decca F 12100	What More Do You Want?/Soldier Boy	£25

(see also Orchids)

EXCEPTION(S)

67	CBS 202632	The Eagle Flies On Friday/Girl Trouble	£70
67	CBS 2830	Gaberdine Saturday Night Street Walker/Sunday Night At The Prince Rupert	£30
69	President PTLS 1026	THE EXCEPTIONAL EXCEPTION (LP, yellow/black labels)	£40

(see also Fotheringay, Fairport Convention)

EXCHANGE AND MART

72	President PT 385	Yeah My Friend/I Know That I'm Dreaming	£15

EXCHECKERS

64	Decca F 11871	All The World Is Mine/It's All Over	£25

(see also Aynsley Dunbar Retaliation)

EXCITER

85	Music For Nations MFN 47	LONG LIVE THE LOUD (LP, inner)	£15
86	Music For Nations MFN 61	UNVEILING THE WICKED (LP, with inner)	£15

EXCITERS

63	United Artists UP 1011	Tell Him/Hard Way To Go	£15
63	United Artists UP 1017	He's Got The Power/Drama Of Love	£15
63	United Artists UP 1026	Get Him/It's So Exciting	£20
64	United Artists UP 1041	Do-Wah-Diddy/If Love Came Your Way	£25
65	Columbia DB 7479	I Want You To Be My Boy/Tonight, Tonight	£25
65	Columbia DB 7544	Just Not Ready/Are You Satisfied	£20
65	Columbia DB 7606	Run Mascara/My Father	£20
66	London HLZ 10018	A Little Bit Of Soap/I'm Gonna Get Him Someday	£20
66	London HLZ 10038	You Better Come Home/Weddings Make Me Cry	£40
71	Jay Boy BOY 38	Soul Motion/You Know It Ain't Right	£20
74	Contempo CS 2033	Blowing Up My Mind (Vocal)/Blowing Up My Mind (Instrumental)	£20
65	United Artists UEP 1005	DO WAH DIDDY DIDDY (EP)	£60
64	United Artists ULP 1032	THE EXCITERS (LP)	£100

(see also Jerry Allen)

EXCURSION
68	Morgan MX 7001	NIGHT TRAIN (LP)	£30
69	Gemini GMX 5029	NIGHT TRAIN (LP, reissue)	£18

(see also Jerry Allen)

EXECUTE/INFERNO
86	Pusmort 0012-06	SPLIT LP	£20

EXECUTIVE(S) (2)
67	CBS 202652	Smokey Atmosphere/Sensation	£30
67	CBS 3067	Ginza Strip/I'll Always Love You	£25
68	CBS 3431	Tracy Took A Trip/Gardena Dreamer (as Executive, with promo only p/s)	£40
68	CBS 3431	Tracy Took A Trip/Gardena Dreamer (as Executive)	£30
69	CBS 4013	I Ain't Got Nobody/To Kingdom Come (as Executive)	£30

EXECUTIVES (3)
80	Attrix RB 05	Shy Little Girl/Never Go Home/JONNIE & LUBES: I Got Rabies/Terror In The Parking Lot (p/s)	£15

EXECUTIVE SUITE
74	Polydor 2310400	EXECUTIVE SUITE 1 (LP)	£50

EXHIBIT A
80	Irrelevant Wombat DAMP 1	NO ELEPHANTS THIS SIDE OF THE WATFORD GAP (EP, with insert)	£25
80	Irrelevant Wombat DAMP 2	DISTANCE (EP)	£15

(see also Doof)

EXILE
77	Boring BO 1	DON'T TAX ME (EP, 1,000 only p/s)	£30
78	Charly CYS 1033	The Real People/Tomorrow Today/Disaster Movie (p/s)	£18

EXILES
66	Topic 12T 143	FREEDOM, COME ALL YE (LP)	£15
67	Topic 12T 164	THE HALE AND THE HANGED (LP)	£15

EXILES INTACT
86	Chri$ Dixon EX 1 (T)A	Who Is There/On Broadway/Who''s Dub (12" p/s)	£30
86	Chri$ Dixon EX 1A	Who Is There/On Broadway	£15

(see also Royal Blood (1))

EXIT (1)
80	Kik KIK 010	Look Inside/Three In A Bed	£20

EXIT (2)
83	Red Beret REB 1	Planetoid Passion/Social Graces	£50

EXITS (1)
78	Way Out WOO 1	YODELLING (EP, numbered, gatefold p/s, hand-stamped labels)	£60

EXITS (2)
78	Red Lightning GIL 519	The Fashion Plague/Cheam (p/s, labels on wrong sides)	£100

(see also Direct Hits)

EXIT STANCE (1)
84	Mortarhate MORT 11	WHILE BACKS ARE TURNED (LP, with insert)	£20
84	Fight Back FIGHT 4	CRIME AGAINST HUMANITY (EP)	£15

EXIT STANCE (2)
84	Exit Stance ES 002	Esthetics/Conspiracy Of Silence	£30

EXIT 13
82	Artlos Music LOS 001	CELIA'S LAST WEDNESDAY (LP)	£25

EXOCET
86	Exocet EXO 1PS12	STALEMATE (EP)	£50

EXODUS
85	Music For Nations MFN 44	BONDED BY BLOOD (LP)	£20

EXODUS (JAMAICA)
71	Duke DU 103	Pharaoh's Walk/Little Caesar	£15
72	Sioux SI 001	Pharaoh's Walk No. 9/SAMMY JONES: Worried Over You	£15
72	Sioux SI 010	Julia Sees Me/LLOYD THE MATADOR: The Train (Engine 54)	£50

EXORDIUM
72	Face To Face FTF 1001	TROUBLE WITH ADAM (LP, private pressing)	£30

EXOTICS (1)
68	Columbia DB 8418	Don't Lead Me On/You Can Try	£25

EXPERIMENTS WITH ICE
81	United Dairies EX 001	EXPERIMENTS WITH ICE (LP)	£25

EXPLOITED
83	Secret SHH145-12	Troops Of Tomorrow (DJ Edit)/Troops Of Tomorrow (12", promo, no p/s)	£25
81	Exploited EXP 1001	PUNK'S NOT DEAD (LP)	£20
81	Exploited EXP 1002	ON STAGE (LP, some on yellow vinyl)	£20
82	Secret SEC 8	TROOPS OF TOMORROW (LP)	£20
83	Pax PAX 18	LET'S START A WAR (LP)	£20
86	Dojo DOJOLP 37	HORROR EPICS (LP)	£15
87	Rough Justice JUST 6	DEATH BEFORE DISHONOUR (LP, inner)	£15
90	Rough Justice JUST 15	THE MASSACRE (LP)	£15
96	Rough Justice JUST 22	BEAT THE BASTARDS (LP, inner)	£25

EXPLORER
| 84 | Rock Shop RSR 006 | EXPLODING (LP) | £50 |

EXPLOSIVE
69	President PT 244	Cities Make The Country Colder/Step Out Of Line	£20
69	President PT 262	Who Planted Thorns In Miss Alice's Garden?/I Get My Kicks From Living	£15
71	Plexium PXM 20	Hey Presto, Magic Man/Get It Together	£300

(see also Watson T. Browne & Explosive)

EXPORT
79	Atlantic K 11344	Julie Bitch/Nice To Know You	£15
80	His Master's Vice VICE 2	You've Got To Rock/Wheeler Dealer (title sleeve)	£18
80	His Master's Vice VICE 1	EXPORT (LP)	£18

EXTERNAL MENACE
| 82 | Beat The System!! MENACE 1 | YOUTH OF TODAY (EP) | £15 |
| 83 | Beat The System!! MENACE 2 | NO VIEWS (EP) | £15 |

EXTREEM
| 66 | Strike JH 326 | On The Beach/Don't You Ignore Me | £20 |

EXTREME NOISE TERROR
88	Strange Fruit SFPS 048	PEEL SESSION (12" EP p/s)	£18
15	Quagga Curious QCS 039	Chained And Crazed/Nih Nightmare (lathe cut 7", 31 copies only)	£30
88	Head Eruption HURT 1	A HOLOCAUST IN YOUR HEAD (LP, with inner)	£20
91	Vinyl Japan/Discipline DISC1T	PHONOPHOBIA (LP, insert)	£15

EXTREME NOISE TERROR/CHAOS U.K.
| 86 | Manic Ears ACHE 01 | EAR SLAUGHTER — RADIOACTIVE (LP) | £15 |

EXUMA
| 70 | Mercury 6338 018 | EXUMA (LP, gatefold) | £35 |
| 71 | Kama Sutra 2319 010 | DU WAH NANNY (LP, gatefold) | £20 |

EYEHATEGOD
| 00 | People Like You 772521 | SOUTHERN DISCOMFORT (LP, white vinyl with inner) | £20 |

EYELESS IN GAZA
| 80 | Ambivalent Scale ASR 2 | Kodak Ghosts Run Amok/China Blue Vision/The Feeling's Mutual (wraparound p/s) | £20 |
| 81 | Cherry Red BRED 18 | CAUGHT IN THE FLUX (LP, with bonus 12" EP [12 BRED 18], with inner) | £15 |

EYES OF BLUE
66	Deram DM 106	Heart Trouble/Up And Down	£60
67	Deram DM 114	Supermarket Full Of Cans/Don't Ask Me To Mend Your Broken Heart	£70
68	Mercury MF 1049	Largo/Yesterday	£15
69	Mercury SMCL 20134	THE CROSSROADS OF TIME (LP, black/silver labels with 'Mercury' logo)	£200
69	Mercury SMCL 20164	IN FIELDS OF ARDATH (LP, black/silver label with Mercury logo)	£250

(see also Ancient Grease, Big Sleep, Man, Ritchie Francis, Gary Pickford-Hopkins, Gentle Giant)

EYES (1)
65	Mercury MF 881	When The Night Falls/I'm Rowed Out	£200
66	Mercury MF 897	The Immediate Pleasure/My Degeneration	£150
66	Mercury MF 910	Man With Money/You're Too Much	£175
65	Mercury MF 934	Good Day Sunshine/Please Don't Cry	£100
66	Mercury 10035 MCE	THE ARRIVAL OF THE EYES (EP)	£350
84	Bam Caruso KIRI 028	BLINK (LP, 2 different sleeves)	£18
87	Bam Caruso MARI 038	SCENE BUT NOT HEARD (mini-LP)	£15

(see also Pupils)

EYNESBURY GIANT
| 78 | Ultimate URL 602 | FROM THE CASK (LP, with insert) | £20 |

EZRA COLLECTIVE
| 16 | EZCOLCHP7 | CHAPTER 7 (12", p/s) | £100 |

EZY MEAT
| 84 | Electric Storm ES 0001 | NOT FOR WIMPS (LP, with insert, Irish only) | £50 |
| 86 | Electric Storm ES 0002 | ROCK YOUR BRAINS OUT (LP, with insert, Irish only) | £40 |

EZY RIDER
| 82 | English Steel | POWER (LP) | £150 |

F

F.F.S.
| 15 | Domino WIGLP 349 | FFS (2LP, gatefold) | £20 |
| 15 | Domino WIGLP 349X | FFS (2LP, gatefold, red vinyl, indie and website exclusive) | £30 |

(see also Franz Ferdinand, Sparks)

FABIAN
59	HMV POP 587	I'm A Man/Hypnotized	£20
59	HMV POP 587	I'm A Man/Hypnotized (78)	£20
59	HMV POP 612	Turn Me Loose/Stop Thief!	£20

59	HMV CLP 1301	**HOLD THAT TIGER** (LP)..**£40**
60	HMV CLP 1345	**THE FABULOUS FABIAN** (LP)..**£40**
61	HMV CLP 1433	**YOUNG AND WONDERFUL** (LP, mono)......................................**£30**
61	HMV CSD 1352	**YOUNG AND WONDERFUL** (LP, stereo).....................................**£30**

FABIAN (JAMAICA)

77	Tribesman TM 004	**Prophecy/Prophecy Dub**..**£30**
77	Black Swan BS 8	**Prophecy/JIMMY LINDSAY : Easy** (12")...............................**£15**
78	Tribesman TM 08	**Prophecy/JIMMY LINDSAY : Easy** (12")...............................**£35**
78	Island 12 WIP 6431	**Prophecy/JIMMY LINDSAY : Easy** (12")...............................**£25**
96	Tribesman TM 01	**Prophecy/Prophecy Dub** (12" reissue)...............................**£40**

FABIONS

| 69 | Bullet BU 410 | **V. Rocket/Smile** (B-side actually "My Baby" by Tennors) .....**£200** |

FABLE

| 73 | Magnet MAG 5002 | **FABLE** (LP, gatefold sleeve, white/red labels)....................**£20** |

(see also Trapeze, Uriah Heep)

GREGORY FABULOUS

03	Jah Tubbys JT 10015	**Get Up/Moving To Zion** (10", with the Offbeat Posse)........**£20**
04	Jah Tubbys JT 10022	**Love Jah/Tra-La-La** (10", with Prof. Natty)........................**£20**
06	Jah Tubbys JT 10026	**Jah Lead I Forward/Bless We Oh Jah** (12")........................**£15**
11	Jet Star TK50	**Give Your Face A Rest/**(Jungle Mix) (12" white label) **£18**

FABULOUS DIALS

| 63 | Pye International 7N 25200 | **Bossa Nova Stomp/Forget Me Not** ....**£25** |

FABULOUS FIVE INC.

| 73 | Ahanti SHAN 104 | **FABULOUS FIVE INC.** (LP)..**£30** |

FABULOUS FLAMES

| 70 | Clandisc CLA 224 | **Holly Holy/LORD CREATOR: Kingston Town** ....**£15** |
| 71 | Trojan TR 7822 | **Growing Up/Lovitis**...**£15** |

(see also Dynamites)

FABULOUS IMPACT

| 90 | Kent 6T 6 | **Baby Baby, I Want You/HAMPTONS: No No No No No No Not My Girl** (100 Club 6T's All-nighter anniversary disc) ....**£30** |

FABULOUS ORIGINALS

| 02 | Funk 45 FUNK45 006 | **It Ain't Fair But It's Fun Parts I and II** (reissue)................**£15** |

FABULOUS SWINGTONES

| 58 | HMV POP 471 | **Geraldine/You Know Baby** ....**£250** |
| 58 | HMV POP 471 | **Geraldine/You Know Baby** (78)...**£50** |

FABULOUS TALBOT BROTHERS

| 50s | Melodisc M 1507 | **Bloodshot Eyes/She's Got Freckles** ....**£20** |

FACES

70	Warner Bros WB 8014	**Wicked Messenger/Nobody Knows** (unissued) **£0**
73	Warner Bros K 16281	**Borstal Boys** (withdrawn, any pressed?) **£0**
70	Warner Bros WS 3000	**FIRST STEP** (LP, orange label, gatefold sleeve) **£100**
71	Warner Bros WS 3011	**LONG PLAYER** (LP, blue & silver label, stitched die-cut '78rpm' style sleeve) **£50**
71	Warner Bros K 46053	**FIRST STEP** (LP, reissue, green label, gatefold sleeve) **£20**
71	Warner Bros K 56006	**A NOD IS AS GOOD AS A WINK ... TO A BLIND HORSE** (LP, green label, with poster)........**£40**
72	Warner Bros K 46064	**LONG PLAYER** (LP, reissue, blue & silver label, stitched die-cut '78rpm'-style sleeve).........**£20**
73	Warner Bros K 56011	**OOH-LA-LA** (LP, green label, die-cut fold out 'Faces' sleeve with lyric poster, 'can can' picture label)..**£90**
74	Warner Bros K 56011	**OOH-LA-LA** (LP, 'Burbank' label, 'Faces' sleeve with lyric poster) **£20**
74	Warner Bros K 56006	**A NOD IS AS GOOD AS A WINK ... TO A BLIND HORSE** (LP, reissue, 'Burbank' label)......**£15**
75	Warner Bros K 66027	**TWO ORIGINALS OF . . .** (2-LP, reissue of "First Steps" & "Long Player", gatefold sleeve)..**£20**

(see also Small Faces, Rod Stewart, Ronnie Lane & Slim Chance, Ron Wood, Jeff Beck Group)

FACE TO FACE

| 71 | Face To Face FTF 1000 | **FACE TO FACE** (LP, 1000 only)..**£150** |

FACTOR FICTION

| 81 | TKS 001 | **FACTOR FICTION EP** (Pressed in Ireland but imported into U.K) ....**£15** |

FACTORY FLOOR

08	Outside OUT 0015	**Bipolar/You Were Always Wrong** (p/s, orange vinyl, 500 only) **£30**
08	One Of One ON 01	**PLANNING APPLICATION EP** (12" p/s, 500 only) **£25**
10	Blast First Petite PTVT 048	**Lying** (Stephen Morris Mix)/**Lying** (Original)/**Lying** (Chris Carter Mix)/**A Wooden Box** (Original) (2x12" in plastic sleeve, 200 only)..................**£15**
11	DFA DAF 2318	**Two Different Ways/Second Way** (12", limited edition screen printed sleeve, numbered and signed by one member of the band)..................**£20**
14	Vinyl Factory VF 079	**o/o/o/o//o/o/o/o/** (NVC Remix") (12" signed, numbered, 100 only) **£20**
13	DFA DFA 2392	**FACTORY FLOOR** (2-LP, yellow vinyl, with CD and CD-R, 300 only) **£30**
13	DFA DFA 2392	**FACTORY FLOOR** (2-LP, white vinyl, with CD and CD-R) **£25**
16	DFA DFA2525X	**25 25** (2-LP, blue plastic sleeve , white vinyl) **£18**
18	H/O/D HOD003COL	**A SOUNDTRACK FOR A FILM** (4-LP, grey vinyl) **£30**

(see also Nik Colk Void)

FACTORY (1)

| 68 | MGM MGM 1444 | **Path Through The Forest/Gone**..**£1000** |
| 69 | CBS 4540 | **Try A Little Sunshine/Red Chalk Hill**................................**£1400** |

(see also Peter & Wolves, Norman Conquest, John Pantry, Velvet Hush)

FACTORY (2)

| 70 | OAK RGJ718 | **Time Machine/Castle On The Hill** (99 copies only)..............**£450** |

FACTORY (3)
82	Future Earth FER 011	You Are The Music/History Of The World (silver die-cut sleeve)	£20

FACTORY (4)
86	Strike Back SBR10	Hold Out/Burn Me Up (p/s)	£20
86	Strike Back SBR 10T	Hold Out (Extended)/Burn Me Up/Outcast (12", p/s)	£25

FACTOTUMS
65	Immediate IM 009	In My Lonely Room/Run In The Green And Tangerine Flaked Forest	£40
65	Immediate IM 022	You're So Good To Me/Can't Go Home Anymore My Love	£30
66	Piccadilly 7N 35333	Here Today/In My Room	£30
66	Piccadilly 7N 35355	I Can't Give You Anything But Love/Absolutely Sweet Marie	£20
67	Pye 7N 17402	Cloudy/Easy Said, Easy Done	£25
69	CBS 4140	Mr And Mrs Regards/Driftwood	£20

FADED TAPES
13	Box Bedroom BBR 2	5 TRACK EP (p/s, numbered, 100 only)	£20

FADERS
79	Rip Off RIP 8	Cheatin'/Library Book (in bag p/s)	£75

FAD GADGET
81	Lyntone LYN 10209	King Of The Flies/DEPECHE MODE: Sometimes I Wish I Was Dead (red vinyl flexidisc free with Flexipop magazine, issue 11)	£25
81	Lyntone LYN 10209	King Of The Flies/DEPECHE MODE: Sometimes I Wish I Was Dead (red vinyl flexidisc free without Flexipop magazine, issue 11)	£15
80	Mute STUMM 3	FIRESIDE FAVOURITES (LP)	£25
81	Mute STUMM 6	INCONTINENT (LP)	£20
82	Mute STUMM 8	UNDER THE FLAG (LP)	£20
84	Mute STUMM 15	GAG (LP)	£15

FADING COLOURS
66	Ember EMB S 229	(Just Like) Romeo And Juliet/Billy Christian	£20

(see also Orange Seaweed)

DONALD FAGEN
93	Resprise 9362 45230-1	KAMAKIRIAD (LP)	£40
05	Reprise 9362-49975-1	MORPH THE CAT (2-LP)	£60
17	Reprise 081227932824	CHEAP XMAS: DONALD FAGEN COMPLETE (7-LP box set)	£150

(see laos Steely Dan)

BRIAN FAHEY (& HIS ORCHESTRA)
60	Parlophone R 4686	At The Sign Of The Swingin' Cymbal/The Clanger	£20
67	Parlophone R 5615	The Plank/Stay On the Island	£15
69	Major Minor MM 656	Open House/Countdown	£25
67	Studio Two TWO 175	TIME FOR TV (LP)	£20

JOHN FAHEY
67	Transatlantic TRA 173	THE TRANSFIGURATION OF BLIND JOE DEATH (LP, with booklet)	£40
67	Transatlantic TRA 173	THE TRANSFIGURATION OF BLIND JOE DEATH (LP, without booklet)	£20
68	Vanguard SVRL 19033	YELLOW PRINCESS (LP)	£25
68	Vanguard SVRL 19055	REQUIA (LP)	£30
69	Takoma SNTF 607	BLIND JOE DEATH (LP)	£20
69	Sonet SNTF 608	VOLUME 2 DEATH CHANTS,BREAKDOWNS AND MILITARY WALTZES(LP)	£20
72	Sonet SNTF 628	AMERICA (LP)	£25
72	Reprise K 44213	OF RIVERS AND RELIGION (LP)	£20
73	Reprise K 44246	AFTER THE BALL (LP)	£20
74	Takoma SNTF 675	JOHN FAHEY, PETER LANG AND LEO KOTTKE (LP)	£15
74	Sonet SNTF 656	FARE FORWARD VOYAGERS (LP)	£20
76	Sonet SNTF 702	THE NEW POSSIBILITY (LP)	£20
77	Transatlantic TRA 173	THE TRANSFIGURATION OF BLIND JOE DEATH (LP, reissue, picture label)	£25

MIATTA FAHNBULLEH
79	EMI EMC 3294	MIATTA (LP)	£80
80	Pan African PAF 001	THE MESSAGE OF THE REVOLUTION (LP)	£75

JAD FAIR & PASTELS
91	Paperhouse PAPER 013T	THIS COULD BE THE NIGHT EP (12", p/s)	£15

(see also Pastels)

YVONNE FAIR
75	Tamla Motown STML 12008	THE BITCH IS BLACK (LP)	£25

WERLY FAIRBURN & DELTA BOYS
56	London HLC 8349	I'm A Fool About Your Love/All The Time	£1000
56	London HLC 8349	I'm A Fool About Your Love/All The Time (78)	£150

JOHNNY FAIRE
58	London HLU 8569	Bertha Lou/Till The Law Says Stop	£500
58	London HLU 8569	Bertha Lou/Till The Law Says Stop (78)	£150

FAIRFIELD PARLOUR
70	Vertigo 6059 003	Bordeaux Rosé/Chalk On The Wall	£20
70	Vertigo 6059 008	Just Another Day/Caraminda/I Am All The Animals/Song For You	£40
70	Vertigo 6360 001	FROM HOME TO HOME (LP, textured gatefold sleeve, large swirl label)	£400
91	UFO BFTP 003	FROM HOME TO HOME (LP, reissue)	£30
03	Circle CPWL 104	PLEASE LISTEN TO THE PICTURES (2-LP, BBC sessions, split release with Kaleidoscope)	£20

(see also Kaleidoscope [U.K.], I Luv Wight)

FAIRIES
64	Decca F 11943	Don't Think Twice, It's Alright/Anytime At All	£125
65	HMV POP 1404	Get Yourself Home/I'll Dance	£200
65	HMV POP 1445	Don't Mind/Baby Don't	£175

(see also Twink, Cops 'N Robbers)

FAIRPORT CONVENTION

SINGLES
67	Track 604 020	If I Had A Ribbon Bow/If (Stomp)	£75
68	Island WIP 6047	Meet On The Ledge/Throwaway Street Puzzle (pink label)	£20
78	Hawk HASP 423	Jam's O'Donnell's Jig/The Last Waltz (Irish-only)	£15

ALBUMS : POLYDOR ALBUMS
68	Polydor 582 035	FAIRPORT CONVENTION (mono, laminated sleeve)	£300
68	Polydor 582/583 035	FAIRPORT CONVENTION (stereo, laminated sleeve)	£250
76	Polydor Special 2384 047	FAIRPORT CONVENTION (LP, reissue)	£15

ALBUMS : ISLAND ALBUMS
69	Island ILPS 9092	WHAT WE DID ON OUR HOLIDAYS (1st pressing, laminated front cover, pink label with orange/black 'circle')	£250
69	Island ILPS 9092	WHAT WE DID ON OUR HOLIDAYS (2nd pressing, pink label with black 'block' logo)	£100
69	Island ILPS 9092	WHAT WE DID ON OUR HOLIDAYS (3rd pressing, pink label with 'i' logo)	£60
70	Island ILPS 9092	WHAT WE DID ON OUR HOLIDAYS (4th pressing, pink rim label with 'palm tree' logo)	£20
69	Island ILPS 9102	UNHALFBRICKING (1st pressing, pink label with black 'block' logo)	£250
69	Island ILPS 9102	UNHALFBRICKING (2nd pressing, pink label with 'i' logo)	£100
70	Island ILPS 9102	UNHALFBRICKING (3rd pressing, pink rim label with 'palm tree' logo)	£40
69	Island ILPS 9115	LIEGE AND LIEF (gatefold sleeve, 1st pressing, pink label with 'i' logo)	£150
70	Island ILPS 9115	LIEGE AND LIEF (gatefold sleeve, 2nd pressing, pink rim label with 'palm tree' logo)	£20
70	Island ILPS 9130	FULL HOUSE (white label test pressing, with "Poor Will & The Jolly Hangman")	£300
70	Island ILPS 9130	FULL HOUSE (1st pressing, pink 'i' label, gatefold sleeve lists "Poor Will & The Jolly Hangman")	£60
70	Island ILPS 9130	FULL HOUSE (2nd pressing, with pink 'i' label, gatefold sleeve without reference to "Poor Will & The Jolly Hangman")	£30
70	Island ILPS 9130	FULL HOUSE (gatefold sleeve, 3rd pressing, pink rim label with 'palm tree' logo)	£15
71	Island ILPS 9162	ANGEL DELIGHT (gatefold sleeve with 'stuck-on' photos, pink rim label)	£20
71	Island ILPS 9176	BABBACOMBE LEE (gatefold sleeve, with innersleeve and booklet, with sticker, pink rim label)	£35
71	Island ILPS 9176	BABBACOMBE LEE (gatefold sleeve, with innersleeve and booklet, without sticker)	£20
72	Island ICD 4	THE HISTORY OF FAIRPORT CONVENTION (2-LP, with 12-page booklet & blue ribbons)	£20
72	Island ICD 4	THE HISTORY OF FAIRPORT CONVENTION (2-LP, later pressing with book & green, red or light blue ribbons)	£18
73	Island ILPS 9208	ROSIE	£15
73	Island ILPS 9246	FAIRPORT NINE (gatefold sleeve)	£18
74	Island ILPS 9285	LIVE CONVENTION (with insert)	£15
75	Island ILPS 9313	RISING FOR THE MOON (with insert, 'palm tree' label)	£15
75	Island ISS 2	FAIRPORT TOUR SAMPLER (free in NME competition, 500 only)	£150
76	Island HELP 28	LIVE AT THE L.A. TROUBADOR 1974	£30
00	Simply Vinyl SVLP 164	UNHALFBRICKING (LP, reissue)	£15

ALBUMS : OTHER ALBUMS
77	Vertigo 9102 015	BONNY BUNCH OF ROSES (gatefold sleeve)	£18
78	Vertigo 9102 022	TIPPLER'S TALES (with lyric insert)	£15
79	Woodworm BEAR 22	FAREWELL FAREWELL (gatefold sleeve)	£20
79	Simons GAMA 1	FAREWELL FAREWELL (reissue, gatefold sleeve)	£18
83	Woodworm WRC 1	AT 2 (AIRING CUPBOARD TAPES 2)	£15
84	Woodworm (no cat. no.)	THE BOOT (2- cassette in video box, 1,000 only)	£20

(see also Richard Thompson, Ian Matthews, Dave Swarbrick, Sandy Denny, Ashley Hutchings, Trevor Lucas, Albion Band. Bunch, Fotheringay. Vashti Bunyan, Trader Horne, Allan Taylor, Krysia, Marc Ellington, Brian Maxine, Steeleye Span, Vikki clayton)

FAIRUZ
61	Parlophone 45 VDL 309	Am Betdawui Eshams/Shatty Ya Deney (export only)	£15
61	Parlophone 45 VDL 322	Lwayn Rayheem/Medwiyyeh (export only)	£15
57	Parlophone LPVD 1	FAIRUZ SINGS (10" LP, Export)	£50
58	Parlophone LPVD 4	FAIRUZ SINGS AGAIN (10" LP, Export)	£60
66	Parlophone LPVDX 106	DAMASCUS FESTIVAL (LP)	£30

FAIR WARNING
87	Areba ERA 2	Rocking At The Speed Of Light EP (12", p/s)	£30

FAIR WEATHER
71	RCA Neon NE 1000	Lay It On Me/Looking For The Red Label Pt 2	£15
70	RCA Victor SF 8155	BEGINNING FROM AN END (LP, withdrawn, different cover and one less track than Neon issue)	£175
71	RCA Neon NE 1	BEGINNING FROM AN END (LP, gatefold sleeve, black inner sleeve)	£125

(see also Amen Corner, Wynder K. Frog)

FAIRY'S MOKE
75	Deroy 1175	FAIRY'S MOKE (LP, private pressing, actually various artists LP)	£80

(see also Baby Sunshine)

FAIRYTALE
67	Decca F 12644	Guess I Was Dreaming/Run And Hide	£125
67	Decca F 12665	Lovely People/Listen To Mary Cry	£70

ADAM FAITH (& ROULETTES)
SINGLES
58	HMV POP 438	(Got A) **Heartsick Feeling/Brother Heartache And Sister Tears**	£80
58	HMV POP 438	(Got A) **Heartsick Feeling/Brother Heartache And Sister Tears** (78)	£30
58	HMV POP 557	**High School Confidential/Country Music Holiday**	£100
58	HMV POP 557	**High School Confidential/Country Music Holiday** (78)	£30
59	Top Rank JAR 126	**Ah, Poor Little Baby!/Runk Bunk** (blue label)	£25
59	Top Rank JAR 126	**Ah, Poor Little Baby!/Runk Bunk** (blue label) (78)	£40
59	Parlophone R 4591	**What Do You Want?/From Now Until Forever** (78)	£30
60	Parlophone R 4623	**Poor Me/The Reason** (78)	£30
60	Parlophone R 4665	**Made You/When Johnny Comes Marching Home** (78, existence unconfirmed)	£0
67	Parlophone R 5635	**Cowman Milk Your Cow/Daddy, What'll Happen To Me**	£30

EPs
62	Columbia SEG 8138	**BEAT GIRL** (2 Faith tracks, with John Barry Orchestra)	£20
64	Parlophone GEP 8904	**FOR YOU — ADAM**	£15
65	Parlophone GEP 8929	**A MESSAGE TO MARTHA — FROM ADAM**	£15
65	Parlophone GEP 8939	**SONGS AND THINGS**	£15

ALBUMS
60	Parlophone PMC 1128	**ADAM** (mono)	£15
60	Columbia 33SX 1225	**BEAT GIRL** (soundtrack, with John Barry Orchestra)	£40
64	Parlophone PMC 1228	**ON THE MOVE** (with Roulettes)	£30
65	Parlophone PMC 1249	**FAITH ALIVE!** (with Roulettes)	£30

(see also Roulettes, John Barry)

GEORGE FAITH
77	Island IPR 2034	**Diana/To Be A Lover** (12")	£15
77	Black Swan BS 2	**To Be A Lover/UPSETTERS: Rastaman Shuffle** (12")	£25
77	Black Swan BS 3	**I've Got The Groove/Diana** (12")	£20
77	Black Swan BS 4	**Midnight Hour/Turn Back The Hands Of Time** (12")	£20
77	Black Swan BS 5	**All The Love I've Got/So Fine** (12")	£20
79	Warrior WAR 134	**Don't Be Afraid/BUNNY SCOTT : What's The Use/Never Had It So Good** (act. Jimmy Riley) (12")	£25
77	Black Swan ILPS 9504	**TO BE A LOVER** (LP)	£30

(see also Earl George, George Ferris. Winston Reedy)

HORACE FAITH
69	B&C CB 104	**Spinning Wheel/Like I Used To Do**	£15
69	Downtown DT 446	**Daddy's Home/EMOTIONS: Give Me A Love**	£30
76	DJM DJS 10687	**I Can't Understand It/Gimme Good Lovin'**	£30
78	Ultra PFU 7501	**Rich Man Poor Man/No More**	£15

PALOMA FAITH
12	RCA 88725412231	**FALL TO GRACE** (2-LP)	£40
14	RCA 88843043981	**A PERFECT CONTRADICTION** (2-LP)	£100

FAITH BROTHERS
67	Tabernacle TS 1002	**I Am Saved Now/Too Near My Heavenly Home**	£20

AUSTIN FAITHFUL
68	Blue Cat BS 140	**Uncle Joe/Can't Understand**	£250
68	Pyramid PYR 6016	**I'm In A Rocking Mood/ROLAND ALPHONSO: Stream Of Life**	£80
69	Pyramid PYR 6028	**Eternal Love/ROLAND ALPHONSO: Goodnight My Love**	£80
69	Pyramid PYR 6042	**Ain't That Peculiar/Miss Anti-Social** (as Austin Faithful & the Hippies)	£100

FAITHFUL DAWN
94	Dawn 001	**The Sequel** (Original mix)**/Dark Beat Mix** (12", white label – 300 only	£20

MARIANNE FAITHFULL
66	Decca F 12443	**Counting/I'd Like To Dial Your Number**	£20
69	Decca F 12889	**Something Better/Sister Morphine** (withdrawn)	£50
65	Decca DFE 8624	**GO AWAY FROM MY WORLD** (EP)	£35
65	Decca LK 4688	**COME MY WAY** (LP)	£100
65	Decca LK 4689	**MARIANNE FAITHFULL** (LP)	£80
66	Decca LK 4778	**NORTH COUNTRY MAID** (LP)	£75
67	Decca LK/SKL 4854	**LOVEINAMIST** (LP)	£120
69	Decca PA 17	**THE WORLD OF MARIANNE FAITHFULL** (LP, mono)	£20
69	Decca SPA 17	**THE WORLD OF MARIANNE FAITHFULL** (LP, stereo)	£15
76	NEMS NEL 6007	**DREAMIN' MY DREAMS** (LP)	£15
78	NEMS NEL 6012	**FAITHLESS** (LP)	£15
92	Island ILPM 9570	**BROKEN ENGLISH** (LP)	£15

FAITH NO MORE
90	London/Slash 850 228	**KING FOR A DAY, FOOL FOR A LIFETIME** (7 x 7" box set)	£40
89	Slash 828154	**THE REAL THING** (LP)	£35
89	Slash 828 217-1	**THE REAL THING** (LP, picture disc)	£25
92	Slash LASHP18	**ANGEL DUST** (LP, insert with free 12")	£30
95	Slash 828 560-1	**KING FOR A DAY FOOL FOR A LIFETIME** (2-LP, red vinyl)	£50
97	Slash 828 901	**ALBUM OF THE YEAR** (LP)	£40

FAKES
79	Deep Cuts DEEP TWO	**Production/Look-Out/Tony Blackburn/Sylvia Clark** (p/s)	£15

FALCONS (U.K.)
64	Philips BF 1297	**Stampede/Kazutzka**	£20

FALCONS (U.S.)
59	London HLT 8876	You're So Fine/Goddess Of Angels	£100
59	London HLT 8876	You're So Fine/Goddess Of Angels (78)	£70
62	London HLK 9565	I Found A Love/Swim (some labels credit B-side as "Swin")	£50

(see also Wilson Pickett, Eddie Floyd)

THE FALL
85	Beggars Banquet BEG 134	Rollin' Dany/Couldn't Get Ahead (p/s)	£20

SINGLES
78	Step-Forward SF 9	It's The New Thing/Various Times (p/s)	£25
79	Step-Forward SF 11	Rowche Rumble/In My Area (p/s)	£25
80	Step-Forward SF 13	Fiery Jack/Second Dark Age/Psykick Dancehall 2 (colour outline p/s)	£40
80	Step-Forward SF 13	Fiery Jack/Second Dark Age/Psykick Dancehall 2 (b/w p/s, repress)	£20
80	Rough Trade RT 048	How I Wrote 'Elastic Man'/City Hobgoblins (p/s)	£25
80	Rough Trade RT 056	Totally Wired/Putta Block (die-cut p/s)	£30
81	Kamera ERA 001	Lie Dream Of A Casino Soul/Fantastic Life (p/s)	£20
82	Kamera ERA 004	Look, Know/I'm Into C.B. (p/s)	£20
82	Kamera ERA 014	Marquis Cha Cha/Papal Visit (p/s, B-side plays 'Room To Live', withdrawn in 82, limited release 83)	£150
83	Rough Trade RT 133	The Man Whose Head Expanded/Ludd Gang (p/s)	£25
83	Rough Trade RT 143	Kicker Conspiracy/Wings//Container Drivers/New Puritan (2x7", gatefold)	£40
84	Beggars Banquet BEG 110	Oh! Brother/God Box (p/s)	£15
84	Beggars Banquet BEG 110T	Oh! Brother/ O! Brother (12" mix)/God-Box (12", p/s)	£15
84	Beggars Banquet BEG 116	C.R.E.E.P./Pat-Trip Dispenser (p/s)	£20
84	Beggars Banquet BEG 116T	C.R.E.E.P./ Pat-Trip Dispenser/ C.R.E.E.P. (long version)(12", p/s, green vinyl)	£25
84	Beggars Banquet BEG 116TP	C.R.E.E.P./Pat-Trip Dispenser/C.R.E.E.P. (long version)(12", p/s, with art print)	£25
85	Beggars Banquet BEG 134T	Couldn't Get Ahead/Rollin' Dany/Petty Thief Lout (12", p/s)	£20
85	Beggars Banquet BEG 150	Cruiser's Creek/LA (p/s)	£15
85	Beggars Banquet BEG 150T	Cruiser's Creek/Vixen/LA (12", p/s)	£15
86	Beggars Banquet BEG 165T	Living Too Late/Hot Aftershave Bop/Living Too Long (12", p/s)	£15
86	Beggars Banquet BEG 168T	Mr. Pharmacist/Lucifer Over Lancashire/Auto-Tech Pilot (12", p/s)	£15
86	Beggars Banquet BEG 176T	Hey! Luciani/Entitled/Shoulder Pads #1B (12", p/s)	£15
87	Beggars Banquet BEG 187H	There's A Ghost In My House/Haf Found Bormann (hologram p/s)	£15
87	Beggars Banquet BEG 187T	There's A Ghost In My House/Sleep Debt Snatches/Mark'll Sink Us/Haf Found Boorman (12", gatefold p/s)	£15
87	Beggars Banquet BEG 200	Hit The North Part 1/Hit The North Part 2 (p/s)	£15
87	Beggars Banquet BEG 200P	Hit The North (Parts 1 & 2) (picture disc, printed PVC sleeve)	£15
87	Beggars Banquet BEG 200T	Hit The North Part 1/Australians In Europe/Hit The North Part 3/ Northerns In Europ (12", gatefold, p/s)	£18
87	Beggars Banquet BEG 206TR	Hit The North Part 4/Hit The North Part 5/Hit The North Part 1 (12", p/s)	£15
87	Beggars Banquet BEG 206B	Victoria/Tuff Life Boogie (7" box set, inserts, badge)	£20
88	Beggars Banquet BEG 206T	Victoria/Guest Informant/Tuff Life Boogie/Twister (12", p/s)	£15
88	Beggars Banquet FALL 2B	Jerusalem/Acid Priest 2088/Big New Prinz/Wrong Place, Right Time No 2 (2 x 7" box set, postcard, numbered)	£15
89	Beggars Banquet BEG 226	Cab It Up/Dead Beat Descendant (p/s)	£15
89	Beggars Banquet BEG 226T	Cab It Up/Dead Beat Descendant/ Kurious Oranj (Live)/Hit The North (Live) (12", p/s)	£15
90	Cog Sinister SIN 4	Telephone Thing/British People In Hot Weather (p/s)	£15
90	Cog Sinister SIN 412	Telephone Thing (Extended Mix)/British People In Hot Weather/Telephone Dub	£15
90	Cog Sinister SINR 5	Popcorn Double Feature/Zandra (alternate p/s, ltd. edition)	£15
90	Cog Sinister SINR 512	Popcorn Double Feature/Zandra/Black Monk Theme Pt. II (12", different p/s, ltd edition)	£20
90	Cog Sinister SINX 612	White Lightning/Zagreb/Blood Outta Stone/Funeral Mix (12", p/s)	£25
90	Cog Sinister SIN 7	High Tension Line/Xmas WIth Simon (p/s)	£15
90	Cog Sinister SIN 712	High Tension Line/Xmas With Simon/Don't Take The Pizza (12", p/s)	£18
91	Cog Sinister FALL 1	So What About It/Edinburgh Man (promo only)	£30
91	Cog Sinister NICE 1	So What About It (Remix 1/2/3) (12" white label promo, typed sticker to label)	£100
92	Cog Sinister SIN 8	Free Range/Everything Hurtz (7", hand painted p/s)	£15
92	Cog Sinister SIN 812	Free Range/Return/Everything Hurtz/Dangerous (12", p/s, ltd numbered)	£15
92	Cog Sinister SIN 912	Ed's Babe/Pumpkin Head Xscapes/The Knight The Devil And Death/Free Ranger (12", p/s, ltd edition)	£20
93	Strange Fruit SFPS 787	Kimble/C'n'C-Hassle Schmuk (7", p/s)	£15
93	Strange Fruit SFPS 087	Kimble/C'n'C-Hassle Schmuk/Spoilt Victorian Child/Words Of Expectation (12", p/s)	£20
93	Permanent 12SPERM 9	Why Are People Grudgeful?/Glam Racket/The Re-Mixer/Lost In Music (12", p/s)	£25
94	Permanent 10SPERM 14	15 Ways/Hey! Student/The $500 Bottle Of Wine (10", p/s, clear vinyl)	£15
96	Jet JET 500	The Chiselers/Chilinist (p/s)	£15
98	Artful 10ARTFUL 1	Masquerade (Mr. Natural mix)/Masquerade (PWL mix)/Masquerade (10", p/s)	£15
99	Artful 12ARTFUL 2	Touch Sensitive Dance Mix/Antidote/Touch Sensitive (12", p/s)	£15
01	Flitwick MK45 1FG	Rude (All The Time)/I Wake Up In The City (7", p/s, limited to 500)	£125
02	Action TAKE 20	Susan vs Youthclub/Janet vs Johnny (7", p/s)	£40
03	Action Action TAKE 22	(We Wish You) A Protein Christmas/(We Are) Mod Mock Goth/(Birtwistle's) Girl In Shop/Recovery Kit 2# (2x7", gatefold p/s, limited to 1000 copies)	£30
04	Action TAKE 23	Theme From Sparta F.C. #2 /My Ex Classmate's Kids (live) (7", p/s)	£60
05	Slogan SLOS 005	I Can Hear The Grass Grow/Clasp Hands (p/s)	£15
07	Slogan SLOTW 009	Reformation! (Uncut)/Over Over (Rough Mix)/My Door Is Never (Rough Mix)/Reformation! (Edit) (12", p/s)	£40
09	Action ACTOUR 01V	Slippy Floor (Mark Mix)/Hot Cake - Part 2 (7", p/s, ltd edition)	£20
10	Domino RUG 363	Bury! #2+4 /Cowboy Gregori (7", p/s, RSD)	£15
11	Cherry Red CHERRY 500	Laptop Dog/Cosmos 7/Monocard (Lunatic Mix) (7", p/s, 33rpm)	£30
12	Cherry Red CHERRY 501	Night Of The Humerons: Victrola Time/Taking Off (Live) (7", p/s, RSD)	£20
13	Cherry Red CHERRY 501	Sir William Wray (Single Mix)/Jetplane/Hittite Man (Single Mix) (7", p/s, RSD)	£20

EPS : EXTENDED PLAYS

78	Step-Forward SF 7	**Bingo-Masters' Breakout!** (EP, p/s)	£60
84	Beggars Banquet BEG 120E	**CALL FOR ESCAPE ROUTE** (7"/12" EP, p/s)	£25
87	Strange Fruit SFPS 028	**THE PEEL SESSIONS** (12" EP, p/s)	£25
90	Cog Sinister SIN 612	**THE DREDGER EP** (12" EP, poster, flyer, numbered)	£25
93	Permanent 12SPERM 13	**BEHIND THE COUNTER EP Vol 1** (12", p/s)	£25
93	Permanent 12SPERMX 13	**BEHIND THE COUNTER EP Vol 2** (12", p/s)	£20
81	Rough Trade RTO 71	**SLATES** (10" EP, 33rpm)	£30
13	Cherry Red BREDEP 600	**THE REMAINDERER** (10" EP, gatefold p/s)	£30
16	Cherry Red BREDEP 666	**WISE OL' MAN** (12" EP, p/s)	£20
23	Cherry Red 10CHERRY 533	**O-MIT** (10" EP, p/s, red vinyl)	£35
24	Popstock POP 01VRT	**'SLATES' LIVE** (10"EP/CD, blue vinyl, PVS outer, Rough Trade exclusive)	£35

ALBUMS : COMPILATIONS

81	Step Forward SFLP 6	**THE EARLY YEARS 1977-79** (LP)	£35
85	Situation 2 SITU 13	**HIP PRIEST AND KAMERADS** (LP)	£20
87	Cog Sinister COG 1	**THE FALL IN: PALACE OF SWORDS REVERSED** (LP)	£30
90	Beggars Banquet BEGA 111	**458489 - A SIDES** (LP, printed inner)	£30
90	Beggars Banquet BEGA 116	**458489 - B SIDES** (2LP, printed inners)	£50
96	Receiver RRLP 209	**SINISTER WALTZ** (LP)	£20
96	Receiver RRLP 211	**FIEND WITH A VIOLIN** (LP)	£20
96	Receiver RRLP 213	**OSWALD DEFENCE LAWYER** (LP)	£25
05	Castle CMXBX982	**THE COMPLETE PEEL SESSIONS 1978 - 2004** (6CD box set, booklet)	£100
07	Castle CMXBX1558	**THE FALL BOX SET 1976-2007** (5CD box set, booklet)	£70

ALBUMS : LIVE/PART-LIVE ALBUMS

80	Rough Trade ROUGH 10	**TOTALE'S TURNS** (IT'S NOW OR NEVER) (LP, 1st pressing, matt sleeve))	£35
82	Chaos LIVE 006	**LIVE IN LONDON 1980** (cassette, numbered edition of 4000)	£30
89	Beggars Banquet BBL 102	**SEMINAL LIVE** (LP)	£15
95	Permanent PERMLP 36	**THE TWENTY-SEVEN POINTS** (2LP, gatefold)	£80
13	Dandelion OZITDANLP 8014	**LIVE IN SAN FRANCISCO** (2LP/CD, gatefold, purple)	£25
14	Secret SECLP 104	**YARBLES** (LP)	£20
14	Cherry Red BRED 599	**LIVE UUROP VIII-XII PLACES IN SUN & WINTER, SON** (2LP, as The Fall Group)	£25
16	Dandelion OZITDANLP 8027	**BINGO MASTERS AT THE WITCH TRIALS** (LP, gatefold, orange vinyl)	£20
21	Castle Face CF 133	**LIVE AT ST. HELENS TECHNICAL COLLEGE, 1981** (LP/7", gatefold, clear vinyl)	£30
23	Cherry Red BRED 836	**LIVE 1977** (LP, printed inner, red vinyl, RSD)	£25

ALBUMS

79	Step-Forward SFLP 1	**LIVE AT THE WITCH TRIALS** (LP, 1st pressing)	£80
79	Step-Forward SFLP 4	**DRAGNET** (LP, 1st pressing, with insert, Lyntone version with LYN 7552/3 and SFLP 4 in run-out groove)	£70
79	Step Forward SFLP4	**DRAGNET** (LP, 1st pressing, with insert. Non-Lyntone version with SFLP 4 in run-out groove)	£40
80	Rough Trade ROUGH 18	**GROTESQUE** (AFTER THE GRAMME) (LP)	£60
82	Kamera KAM 005	**HEX ENDUCATION HOUR** (LP)	£100
82	Kamera KAM 011	**ROOM TO LIVE** (LP)	£40
83	Rough Trade ROUGH 62	**PERVERTED BY LANGUAGE** (LP, printed inner)	£50
84	Beggars Banquet BEGA 58	**THE WONDERFUL AND FRIGHTENING WORLD OF . . . THE FALL** (LP)	£35
85	Beggars Banquet BEGA 67	**THIS NATION'S SAVING GRACE** (LP, gatefold, printed inner)	£40
86	Beggars Banquet BEGA 75	**BEND SINISTER** (LP, printed inner)	£35
88	Beggars Banquet BEGA 91	**THE FRENZ EXPERIMENT** (LP, with free 7", sticker to seal sleeve)	£40
88	Beggars Banquet BEGA 91	**THE FRENZ EXPERIMENT** (LP)	£20
88	Beggars Banquet BEGA 96	**I AM KURIOUS ORANJ** (LP, gatefold)	£35
90	Cog Sinister 842 204-1	**EXTRICATE** (LP, printed inner)	£30
91	Cog Sinister/Fontana 848 594-1	**SHIFT-WORK** (LP)	£30
92	Fontana 512 162-1	**CODE: SELFISH** (LP, printed inner)	£80
93	Permanent PERMLP 12	**THE INFOTAINMENT SCAN** (LP)	£100
94	Permanent PERMLP 16	**MIDDLE CLASS REVOLT** (LP)	£90
95	Permanent PERMLP 30	**CEREBRAL CAUSTIC** (LP)	£80
96	Jet JETLP 1012	**THE LIGHT USER SYNDROME** (LP)	£90
97	Artful ARTFUL LP 9	**LEVITATE** (LP)	£100
99	Artful ARTFUL LP 17	**THE MARSHALL SUITE** (2LP, one side etched)	£150
02	Cog Sinister COGVP 131	**ARE YOU ARE MISSING WINNER** (LP, picture disc, die-cut sleeve, numbered)	£120
03	Action TAKE 21	**THE REAL NEW FALL LP FORMERLY 'COUNTRY ON THE CLICK'** (LP, printed inner)	£100
05	Slogan SLOLP 003	**FALL HEADS ROLL** (LP)	£150
07	Slogan SLODV 007	**REFORMATION POST-TLC** (2LP)	£70
08	Castle 1766796	**IMPERIAL WAX SOLVENT** (LP)	£100
10	Domino WIGLP 245	**YOUR FUTURE OUR CLUTTER** (2LP)	£30
11	Cherry Red BRED 500	**ERSATZ GB** (LP)	£100
13	Cherry Red BRED 580	**RE-MIT** (LP)	£70
15	Cherry Red BRED 660	**SUB-LINGUAL TABLET** (2LP, insert)	£60
17	Cherry Red BRED 706	**NEW FACTS EMERGE** (2x10" LP)	£30

ALBUMS : REISSUES

85	Step Forward SFLP 1	**LIVE AT THE WITCH TRIALS** (LP, repressing, with 'Made in France' on bottom of labels)	£30
85	Step Forward SFLP 4	**DRAGNET** (LP, reissue, printed inner, 'Made in France' on bottom of labels)	£30
02	Turning Point TPM 02208	**LIVE AT THE WITCH TRIALS** (LP, reissue, 180g)	£25
02	Turning Point TPM 02209	**DRAGNET** (LP, reissue, gatefold)	£25
02	Turning Point TPM 02210	**GROTESQUE** (AFTER THE GRAMME) (LP, reissue)	£20
05	Earmark 40040	**HEX ENDUCATION HOUR** (2LP, reissue, 180g)	£40

10	Beggars Banquet BBQCD 2066	THE WONDERFUL AND FRIGHTENING WORLD OF . . . THE FALL (Omnibus Edition) (4CD, box set, booklet))	£50
10	Beggars Banquet BBQCD 2067	THIS NATION'S SAVING GRACE (OMNIBUS EDITION) (3CD box set, booklet reissue)	£50
14	L.T.E.Vinyl LETV 109LP	THE UNUTTERABLE (2LP, vinyl issue of 2000 CD, gatefold)	£150
15	B. Banquet BBQLP 2136	THE WONDERFUL AND FRIGHTENING WORLD OF . . . THE FALL (2LP, reissue)	£30
18	Cherry Red BREDT 725	LEVITATE (3LP, printed inners, reissue)	£30
19	Cherry Red BRED749	IMPERIAL WAX SOLVENT (LP, yellow vinyl, RSD, reissue)	£45
19	L.T.E. Vinyl LETV 569LP	THE UNUTTERABLE: TESTA ROSSA MONITOR MIXES (LP, gatefold, RSD)	£20
19	Cherry Red BRED 752	LIVE AT THE WITCH TRIALS (LP, reissue, red vinyl, some with badge)	£25
19	Cherry Red BRED 744	DRAGNET (LP, reissue, printed inner, b/w splatter vinyl, with 7", some with badge)	£30
19	Cherry Red BREDT 780	HEX ENDUCTION HOUR (3LP/7", trifold sleeve, green splatter vinyl, reissue)	£70
19	Cherry Red BREDD 781	ROOM TO LIVE (2LP, reissue, brown marbled vinyl)	£25
19	Beggars Banquet BBQ 2153LP	BEND SINISTER/THE 'DOMESDAY' PAY-OFF TRIAD PLUS! (2LP, gatefold, printed inners sleeves, reissue)	£25
20	Beggars Banquet BBQ 2171LP	THE FRENZ EXPERIMENT (2LP, gatefold, printed inners, reissue)	£25
20	L.T.E.Vinyl LETV 574LP	INTERIM (LP, vinyl issue of 2004 CD)	£15
20	Demon DEMREC 657	CEREBRAL CAUSTIC (LP, reissue, printed inner, splatter vinyl, 180g, RSD)	£70
20	Cherry Red BREDD811	IMPERIAL WAX SOLVENT (2LP, printed inners, green splatter vinyl, reissue)	£50
20	Cherry Red BREDD800	REFORMATION POST-TLC (2LP, red/blue vinyl, printed inners, reissue)	£40
21	Demon DEMREC 747	THE INFOTAINMENT SCAN (LP, reissue, printed inner, clear vinyl, hype sticker)	£20
21	Demon DEMREC 748	MIDDLE CLASS REVOLT (LP, reissue, printed inner, clear vinyl)	£20
21	Demon DEMREC 749	THE TWENTY-SEVEN POINTS (2LP, reissue, gatefold, printed inners, clear vinyl))	£25
21	Cherry Red BREDD 834	ARE YOU ARE MISSING WINNER (2LP, purple/grey vinyl, printed inners, reissue)	£50
24	Cherry Red BRED 892	THE REAL NEW FALL LP FORMERLY 'COUNTRY ON THE CLICK' (LP, yellow vinyl, printed inner, reissue)	£50

(see also D.O.S.E., Fates, Von Sudenfed, House of All)

FALLEN ANGELS (U.S.)
| 68 | London HA-Z/SH-Z 8359 | THE FALLEN ANGELS (LP) | £50 |

JOHNNY FALLIN
| 59 | Capitol CL 15043 | Party Kiss/The Creation Of Love | £60 |
| 59 | Capitol CL 15091 | Wild Streak/If I Could Write A Love Song | £60 |

FALLING LEAVES (1)
| 65 | Parlophone R 5233 | She Loves To Be Loved/Not Guilty | £75 |

FALLING LEAVES (2)
| 66 | Decca F 12420 | Beggar's Parade/Tomorrow Night | £50 |

FALLOUT (1)
| 81 | No label or Cat. No.) | Conscription/Democracy?/Nuclear Power/Them & Us/Laughable Attack/Sign Away (fold-out sleeve) | £15 |
| 83 | Own Label F3 LP 1 | HOME COOKED MEAT (LP, with 2 inserts) | £30 |

FALLOUT (2)
| 90 | Azuli AZ001 | The Morning After (12") | £20 |

FALLOUT CLUB
| 80 | Secret SHH104 | The Falling Years/The Beat Boys (p/s) | £15 |
| 81 | Happy Birthday UR 3 | Dream Soldiers/Pedestrian Walk Way (p/s) | £15 |

AGNETHA FALTSKOG
13	0602537367900	A	£60
13	0602537376940	When You Really Loved Someone (single sided picture disc)	£20
83	Epic EPC WA 3436	The Heat Is On/Man (picture disc)	£30
83	Epic EPC A 3812	Can't Shake Loose/To Love (poster p/s)	£15
83	Epic EPC WA 3812	Can't Shake Loose/To Love (picture disc)	£25
98	Polydor POLPROCD 2	The Queen Of Hearts (Nar Du Tar Mej I Din Fam) (CD, promo only)	£30
74	Embassy EMB 31094	AGNETHA (LP)	£40

(see also Abba)

GEORGIE FAME (& THE BLUE FLAMES)
SINGLES
64	Columbia DB 7193	Do The Dog/Shop Around	£25
64	Columbia DB 7255	Green Onions/Do-Re-Mi	£18
64	Columbia DB 7328	Bend A Little/I'm In Love With You (solo)	£20
67	CBS 5946/7	Knock On Wood/Didn't Want To Have To Do It (promo only)	£20
70	CBS 5035	Entertaining Mr. Sloane/Somebody Stole My Thunder (DJ Copy)	£175
70	CBS 5035	Entertaining Mr. Sloane/Somebody Stole My Thunder	£150
77	Island WIP 6384	Daylight/Three Legged Mule	£40
77	Island WIP 6384	Daylight/Three Legged Mule (12")	£30

EPs
64	Columbia SEG 8334	RHYTHM AND BLUE BEAT	£60
64	Columbia SEG 8382	RHYTHM AND BLUES AT THE FLAMINGO	£50
64	Columbia SEG 8393	FAME AT LAST	£25
65	Columbia SEG 8406	FATS FOR FAME	£25
65	Columbia SEG 8454	MOVE IT ON OVER	£25
66	Columbia SEG 8518	GETAWAY	£25
67	CBS EP 6363	KNOCK ON WOOD	£25

ALBUMS
| 64 | Columbia 33SX 1599 | RHYTHM AND BLUES AT THE FLAMINGO | £90 |
| 64 | Columbia 33SX 1638 | FAME AT LAST | £35 |

Georgie FAME & ANNIE ROSS

66	Columbia SX 6043	SWEET THINGS	£25
66	Columbia SX 6076	SOUND VENTURE	£40
67	Columbia SX 6120	HALL OF FAME	£20
67	CBS (S)BPG 63018	TWO FACES OF FAME	£20
68	CBS (S) 63293	THE THIRD FACE OF FAME (mono/stereo)	£15
69	CBS S 63786	SEVENTH SON	£15
69	Regal Starline SRS5002	GEORGIE FAME AND THE BLUE FLAMES	£15
71	CBS S 64350	GOING HOME	£15
72	Reprise K 44183	ALL ME OWN WORK (LP, gatefold sleeve)	£20
74	Island ILPS 9293	GEORGIE FAME	£20

(see also Blue Flames, Jimmy Nicol, Perry Ford & Sapphires, Annie Ross)

GEORGIE FAME & ANNIE ROSS
81	Bald Eagle	Drip Drop/One Morning In May (12" p/s 50 copies only)	£40

FAMILY
06	Mystic MYS CD191	OLD SONGS NEW SONGS. THE DEFINITIVE BOX SET (5-CD)	£35
13	Snapper FAMILY 1	ONCE UPON A TIME (14-CD box set and book, signed by Roger Chapman, 2000 only)	£300
67	Liberty LBF 15031	Scene Through The Eye Of A Lens/Gypsy Woman (mispress, B-side plays "Let Me Be Good To You" by Otis Redding)	£150
67	Liberty LBF 15031	Scene Through The Eye Of A Lens/Gypsy Woman	£200
68	Reprise RS 23270	Me My Friend/Hey Mr. Policeman	£20
68	Reprise RS 23315	Second Generation Woman/Home Town	£15
69	Reprise RS 27001	No Mule's Fool/Good Friend Of Mine (p/s)	£15
70	Reprise RS 27005	Today/Song For Lots (p/s)	£15
71	Reprise SAM 1	Larf And Sing/Children (promo only)	£15
68	Reprise RLP 6312	MUSIC IN A DOLL'S HOUSE (LP, 1st pressing with 'Steamboat' label, insert, mono)	£250
68	Reprise R(S)LP 6312	MUSIC IN A DOLL'S HOUSE (LP, 1st pressing, with 'Steamboat' label, insert, stereo)	£150
69	Reprise RLP 6340	FAMILY ENTERTAINMENT (LP, 1st pressing, with 'Steamboat' label mono, with poster)	£150
69	Reprise RSLP 6340	FAMILY ENTERTAINMENT (LP, 1st pressing with 'Steamboat' label, stereo, with poster)	£90
70	Reprise RSLP 9001	A SONG FOR ME (LP, 1st pressing with 'Steamboat' label, with lyric sheet)	£90
70	Reprise RSX 9005	ANYWAY (LP, custom polythene sleeve)	£35
71	Reprise RMP 9007	OLD SONGS NEW SONGS (LP)	£30
71	Reprise K 54003	FEARLESS (LP, multi gatefold sleeve, lyric insert)	£50
72	Reprise K 54006	BANDSTAND (LP, 'window' die-cut sleeve, lyric inner)	£30
73	Raft RA58501	IT'S ONLY A MOVIE (LP, lyric inner and 'banger' insert)	£40
73	Raft RA 58501	IT'S ONLY A MOVIE (LP, lyric inner and no 'banger' insert)	£15

(see also Farinas, Stud, Mogul Thrash, Hellions, Ashton Gardner & Dyke, Revolution, Streetwalkers)

FAMILY AFFAIR
68	Saga STFID 2124	THE FAMILY AFFAIR (LP)	£15

FAMILY CHOICE
78	Union UND 1003	I'm Still Waiting/Don't Give Up Your Right (12")	£35
77	S-Fa SOLP 001	DO IT AGAIN (LP)	£40
78	BB BBL1R	LET'S DO IT TOGETHER (LP)	£30

FAMILY CIRCLE
69	Attack AT 8001	Phoenix Reggae/BIG L: Music Box	£45
69	Attack AT 8002	Reggae Krishna/Official	£45
69	JJ DB 1300	Give Peace A Chance/GEORGE LEE: Reggae Groove	£45

FAMILY DOGG
67	MGM MGM 1360	The Storm/Family Dogg	£20
68	Fontana TF 921	I Wear A Silly Grin/Couldn't Help It	£15
69	Bell SBLL 122	A WAY OF LIFE (LP, with members of Led Zeppelin, gatefold)	£30
72	Buddah 2318 061	THE VIEW FROM ROWLAND'S HEAD (LP, gatefold, lyric insert)	£20

(see also Steve Rowland)

FAMILY FODDER
79	Fresh Records FRESH 9	SUNDAY GIRLS (12")	£15
80	Fresh LP 3	MONKEY BANANA KITCHEN (LP)	£25
83	Jungle FREUD 2	ALL STYLES (2-LP)	£20

FAMILY MAN (ASTON BARRETT)
70	Escort ERT 834	Midnight Sunshine/GREGORY ISAACS & STICKY: You Are My Sunshine	£15
72	Downtown DT 491	Herb Tree/STUDIO SOUND: Holy Poly (reissue)	£15

(see also Hippy Boys, Upsetters, Bob Marley & Wailers, Carl Dawkins)

FAMILY ON HOLIDAY
81	Fabidoo S81CUS 1140	Who's A Pretty Boy Then/You're As Cute As A Dead Gerbil (p/s)	£15

FAMOUS JUG BAND
69	Liberty LBS 83263	SUNSHINE POSSIBILITIES (LP, blue labels)	£100
70	Liberty LBS 83355	CHAMELEON (LP, textured sleeve, blue labels)	£100

(see also Incredible String Band, C.O.B.)

FAMOUS PLAYERS
80	Page 45 AH 1001	Who's Kissing You/Angel In Black (p/s)	£70

FANATICS
89	Chapter 22 12 CHAP 38	SUBURBAN LOVE SONGS (12" EP)	£18

(see also Ocean Colour Scene)

FAN-CLUB
78	M&S SJP 791B	Avenue/Night Caller (p/s, photocopied insert)	£15

FANCY
73	Sticky STY 3	Starlord/Brother John	£30
73	Atlantic K 51502	WILD THING (LP)	£20
75	Arista ARTY 102	SOMETHING TO REMEMBER (LP)	£20

(see also Ray Fenwick, Judas Priest)

COSEY FANNI TUTTI
83	Flowmotion	TIME TO TELL (cassette with booklet)	£50

(see also Throbbing Gristle, Chris & Cosey)

FANS
79	Fried Egg EGG 3	Giving Me That Look In Your Eyes/Stay The Night/He'll Have To Go (p/s)	£50
79	Albion ION 0004	True (dayglo inner, inc bonus 7" & lyric sheet)	£20
80	Albion FAN 01	Cars And Explosions/Dangerous Goodbyes (p/s)	£20
81	Fried Egg EGG 10	You Don't Live Here Anymore/Following You (p/s)	£60

FANTASIA (1)
67	Stateside SS 2031	Gotta Get Away/She Needs My Love	£15

FANTASIA (2)
88	Greenwood SRT8KL 1456	THIS OLD TOWN (LP)	£50
89	Greenwood SRT9KL2225	PICTURES IN MY MIND (LP)	£100

FANTASTIC FOUR
68	Tamla Motown TMG 678	I Love You Madly/I Love You Madly (Instrumental)	£22
68	T. Motown TML 11105	THE FANTASTIC FOUR (LP, mono)	£60
69	T. Motown STML 11105	THE FANTASTIC FOUR (LP, stereo)	£50

FANTASTIC PUZZLES
76	Right On 106	Come Back/Come Back Part 2	£35

FANTASTICS
68	MGM MGM 1434	Baby Make Your Own Sweet Music/Who Could Be Lovin' You	£20
68	MGM MGM 1434DJ	Baby Make Your Own Sweet Music/ Who Could Be Lovin' You (DJ promo)	£30
70	Deram DM 283	Waiting Round For Heartaches/Ask The Lonely	£20

FANTASY
73	Polydor 2058 405	Politely Insane/I Was Once Aware	£40
73	Polydor 2383 246	PAINT A PICTURE (LP, gatefold sleeve, red label)	£1000
21	Record Collector RCLP 033	PAINT A PICTURE (LP, gatefold, reissue, red vinyl)	£20

BARRY FANTONI
66	Fontana TF 707	Little Man In A Little Box/Fat Man	£35

FAPARDOKLY
83	Psycho PSYCHO 5	FAPARDOKLY (LP, 300 only)	£20

(see also Mu)

FARAWAY FOLK
70	RA EP 7001	INTRODUCING THE FARAWAY FOLK (EP)	£26
70	RA LP 6006ST	LIVE AT THE BOLTON (LP)	£30
70	RA LP 6012ST	TIME AND TIDE (LP)	£30
74	RA LP 6019	ON THE RADIO (LP)	£30
75	RA LP 6022	ONLY AUTHORISED EMPLOYEES TO BREAK BOTTLES (LP, with Harry H. Corbett)	£22
75	RA LP 6029	SEASONAL MAN (LP, gatefold sleeve with insert)	£200
80s	RA	BATTLE OF THE DRAGONS (LP)	£15

(see also Harry H. Corbett)

FAR CRY
69	Vanguard SVRL 19041	THE FAR CRY (LP)	£30

DON FARDON
69	Pye International 7N 25483	We Can Make It Together/Coming On Strong	£25
69	Youngblood YB 1003	I'm Alive/Keep On Loving Me	£40
69	Young Blood YB 1007	It's Been Nice Loving You/Let The Love Live	£25
70	Young Blood YB 1010	Belfast Boy/Echoes Of The Cheers	£20
70	Young Blood SSYB 4	I'VE PAID MY DUES! (LP)	£20
70	Young Blood SSYB 13	RELEASED (LP)	£15

(see also Sorrows)

FAR EAST FAMILY BAND
75	Vertigo 6370 850	NIPPONJIN (LP)	£40

DICK FARINA & ERIC VON SCHMIDT
63	Folklore F-LEUT/7	DICK FARINA & ERIC VON SCHMIDT (LP, featuring 'Blind Boy Grunt')	£100

(see also Bob Dylan, Richard & Mimi Farina, Four For Fun)

RICHARD & MIMI FARINA
65	Fontana STFL 6060	CELEBRATIONS FOR A GREY DAY (LP)	£30
65	Fontana STFL 6075	REFLECTIONS IN A CRYSTAL WIND (LP)	£30
73	Vanguard VSD 21/22	THE BEST OF RICHARD & MIMI FARINA (2-LP)	£15

(see also Dick Farina & Eric Von Schmidt)

FARINAS
64	Victor Buckland Sound Studio	Bye Bye Johnny/All You Gotta Do/Twist And Shout (as James King & Farinas)	£400
64	Fontana TF 493	You'd Better Stop/I Like It Like That	£80

TAL FARLOW
57	Columbia 33CX 10029	THE INTERPRETATIONS OF (LP)	£15

CHRIS FARLOWE (& THUNDERBIRDS)

62	Decca F 11536	Air Travel/Why Did You Break My Heart?	£60
63	Columbia DB 7120	I Remember/Push Push (as Chris Farlowe & Thunderbirds)	£40
64	Columbia DB 7237	Girl Trouble/Itty Bitty Pieces (as Chris Farlowe & Thunderbirds)	£40
64	Columbia DB 7311	Just A Dream/What You Gonna Do? (as Chris Farlow & Thunderbirds)	£40
64	Columbia DB 7379	Hey, Hey, Hey, Hey/Hound Dog (as Chris Farlow & Thunderbirds)	£30
65	Columbia DB 7614	Buzz With The Fuzz/You're The One (withdrawn, as Chris Farlow & Thunderbirds, demos more common £100)	£200
65	Immediate IM 016	The Fool/Treat Her Good	£15
66	Immediate IM 023	Think/Don't Just Look At Me	£30
66	Columbia DB 7983	Just A Dream/Hey, Hey, Hey, Hey	£15
67	Immediate IM 041	My Way Of Giving/You're So Good To Me	£15
68	Immediate IM 066	The Last Goodbye/Paperman Fly In The Sky (B-side with Thunderbirds)	£15
69	Immediate IM 074	Dawn/April Was The Month	£15
65	Decca DFE 8665	CHRIS FARLOWE (EP)	£100
65	Immediate IMEP 001	FARLOWE IN THE MIDNIGHT HOUR (EP)	£50
66	Immediate IMEP 004	CHRIS FARLOWE HITS (EP)	£40
66	Island IEP 709	STORMY MONDAY (EP)	£120
66	Columbia SX 6034	CHRIS FARLOWE AND THE THUNDERBIRDS (LP, black/blue labels with "sold in the U.K..." text)	£150
66	Music For Pleasure MFP 1186	STORMY MONDAY (LP, reissue of Chris Farlowe & Thunderbirds LP)	£20
66	Immediate IMLP 005	14 THINGS TO THINK ABOUT (LP, lilac label)	£75
66	Immediate IMLP 006	THE ART OF CHRIS FARLOWE (LP, mono, lilac label)	£70
66	Immediate IMSP 006	THE ART OF CHRIS FARLOWE (LP, stereo, lilac label)	£100
67	EMI Regal REG 2025	CHRIS FARLOWE (LP, export issue)	£40
68	Immediate IMCP 010	THE BEST OF CHRIS FARLOWE VOLUME ONE (LP, lilac label)	£30
69	Immediate IMLP 021	THE LAST GOODBYE (LP, pink label with "sold in U.K..." text)	£100
70	Polydor 2425 029	FROM HERE TO MAMA ROSA (LP, as Chris Farlowe & Hill, gatefold sleeve, insert)	£60

(see also Thunderbirds, Beazers, Little Joe Cook, Atomic Rooster, Colosseum, Dave Greenslade, Spectrum)

FARM

74	Spark SRL1105	Fat Judy/Gysy Mountain Woman	£30

ART FARMER

54	Esquire 20-033	ART FARMER SEXTET — WORK OF ART (10" LP)	£50
55	Esquire 32 042	CHARTS (LP)	£30
55	Esquire 32-037	WILD PARTY (LP)	£50
56	Esquire 32-072	TWO TRUMPETS (LP, with Donald Byrd)	£50
56	Esquire 32-137	FARMERS MARKET (LP)	£75
58	Contemporary LAC 12197	PORTRAIT OF ART FARMER (LP)	£30
59	London SAH-T 6028	MODERN ART (LP)	£35
60	London Jazz LTZ-T 15184	BRASS SHOUT (LP)	£35
60	London Jazz LTZ-T 15198	THE AZTEC SUITE (LP)	£35
60	Pye Jazz NJL 45	MEET THE JAZZTET (with Benny Golson)	£35
61	Esquire 32 197	EARLY ART (LP)	£40
61	Esquire 32-120	EARTHY (LP)	£35
64	London HA-K/SH-K 8135	INTERACTION (LP, as Art Farmer Quartet featuring Jim Hall)	£25
73	Mainstream MSL 1013	GENTLE EYES (LP, gatefold)	£20
77	CTI CTI 7073	CRAWL SPACE (LP, gatefold)	£15

(see also Clifford Brown, Benny Golson, Donald Byrd)

MYLENE FARMER

91	Polydor 873 738 7	Desenchantee (Edited Version)/Desenchantee (Chaos Mix) (Promo only)	£20

FARMLIFE

83	Whaam! WHAAM 13	Big Country 1 & 2 (unreleased; Echantillan test pressings only)	£40

GILES FARNABY'S DREAM BAND

73	Argo ZDA 158	GILES FARNABY'S DREAM BAND (LP)	£60

(see also Druids)

FARNBOROUGH FIREWORK FACTORY

72	Decca F13290	Too Many People/She's Against The Law	£15

(see also Mike Batt)

ROBERT FARNON ORCHESTRA

55	Decca LK 4119	CANADIAN IMPRESSIONS (LP)	£20
56	Vogue Coral LVA 9003	GENTLEMEN MARRY BRUNETTES (LP, soundtrack)	£30
60	Delyse ECB 3157/DS 6057	CAPTAIN HORATIO HORNBLOWER (LP, soundtrack, mono)	£30
60	Delyse DS 6057	CAPTAIN HORATIO HORNBLOWER (LP, soundtrack, stereo)	£30
68	Philips SBL 7867	SHALAKO (LP, soundtrack)	£15

(see also Jack Saunders)

ROBERT FARNON & TONY COE

70	Chapter One CHS 804	POP MAKES PROGRESS (LP)	£30

(see also Tony Coe)

FARON'S FLAMINGOS

63	Oriole CB 1834	Do You Love Me?/See If She Cares	£25
63	Oriole CB 1867	Shake Sherry/Give Me Time	£30

(see also Big Three, Mojos)

WAYNE FARO'S SCHMALTZ BAND

69	Deram DM 222	There's Still Time/Give It Time	£40

GARY FARR (& THE T-BONES)
65	Columbia DB 7608	**Give All She's Got/Don't Stop And Stare** (as Gary Farr & T-Bones) (demo in p/s)	£100
65	Columbia DB 7608	**Give All She's Got/Don't Stop And Stare** (as Gary Farr & T-Bones)	£50
68	Marmalade 598 007	**Everyday/Green** (with Kevin Westlake)	£25
69	Marmalade 598 017	**Hey Daddy/The Vicar And The Pope**	£25
65	Columbia SEG 8414	**DEM BONES, DEM BONES, DEM T-BONES** (EP)	£120
69	Marmalade 608 013	**TAKE SOMETHING WITH YOU** (LP)	£300
71	CBS 64138	**STRANGE FRUIT** (LP, with Richard Thompson & Mighty Baby)	£200
08	Sunbeam SBR2LP5051	**TAKE SOMETHING WITH YOU** (2-LP, reissue)	£20

(see also T-Bones, Richard Thompson, Mighty Baby, Meic Stevens, Kevin Westlake & Gary Farr)

FARRAGO
79	ESP 9269	**I Wouldn't Wanna Be Like You/If I Can't Have You** (no p/s)	£15

MARY ANN FARRAR & SATIN SOUL
76	Brunswick BR 38	**Stoned Out Of My Mind/Living In The Footsteps Of Another Girl** (DJ Copy)	£30
76	Brunswick BR 38	**Stoned Out Of My Mind/Living In The Footsteps Of Another Girl**	£20
76	Brunswick BRLS 3022	**NEVER GONNA LEAVE YOU** (LP)	£30

BILLY FARRELL
58	Philips PB 828	**Yeah Yeah/Someday** (You'll Want Me To Want You)	£22

DO & DENA FARRELL
57	HMV POP 427	**Young Magic/New Love Tonight**	£15

MICK FARREN
70	Transatlantic TRA 212	**MONA** (THE CARNIVOROUS CIRCUS) (LP, lilac label with "t" logo)	£150
78	Logo LOGO 2010	**VAMPIRES STOLE MY LUNCH MONEY** (LP, with lyric insert)	£25
84	Psycho PSYCHO 20	**MONA** (THE CARNIVOROUS CIRCUS) (LP, reissue)	£20

(see also Deviants, Twink)

FARRIERS
69	Broadside BRO 112	**FARRIERS** (LP)	£20
76	Broadside BRO 119	**KEMPION BRUMMAGEM BALLADS** (LP, featuring Dick Brice)	£50

FARTZ
82	Alt. Tentacles VIRUS 17	**WORLD FULL OF HATE** (12" EP with poster)	£25

FASCINATIONS
67	Stateside SS 594	**Girls Are Out To Get You/You'll Be Sorry**	£75
67	Stateside SS 594	**Girls Are Out To Get You/You'll Be Sorry** (DJ copy)	£150
68	Sue WI 4049	**Girls Are Out To Get You/You'll Be Sorry** (reissue)	£40

FASCINATORS (1)
58	Capitol CL 14942	**Chapel Bells/I Wonder Who**	£300
59	Capitol CL 15062	**Oh, Rose Marie/Fried Chicken And Macaroni**	£150

FASCINATORS (2)
81	Penthouse PENT 9	**Blue Movies/Monochrome Moon** (p/s)	£70

FASHAWN
10	High Water HWM013	**BOY MEETS WORLD** (2-LP)	£50

FASHION
79	Fashion FML001	**PRODUCT PERFECT** (LP)	£15

FAST BREEDERS
82	Breeder BMS 82001 S82 CUS 1570	**How Could You/Strange Party**	£20

FAST BREEDERS & RADIO ACTORS
78	Nuke NUKE 235	**Nuclear Waste/Digital Love** (in p/s, with insert)	£18

(see also Radio Actors)

FAST CARS
79	Streets Ahead SA 3	**The Kids Just Wanna Dance/You're So Funny** (1,000 only, p/s)	£200

FAST EDDIE (2)
88	Westside DJINT 04	**Acid Thunder** (Smooth Thunder)**/AA Aacid/Fast Thunder/Tyree's Supercooper Mix** (12")	£25
88	Westside PROMO 18	**My Melody/Halloween House** (12") (with Slick Master Rick)	£20
88	DJ International DJART 902	**JACK TO THE SOUND** (LP with free 12")	£15

FAST LINE
70	Highwire HW 001	**Look Into My Mind/A Nice Time To Die** (p/s)	£40

FAST SET
80	Axis AXIS 1	**Junction One/Children Of The Revolution** (p/s)	£25

FAT
71	RCA LSA 3009	**FAT** (LP)	£50

FATAL CHARM
89	Fatal 1	**THIS STRANGE ATTRACTION** (LP)	£25

FATAL MICROBES
79	Small Wonder SMALL 20	**Violence Grows/Beautiful Pictures/Cry Baby** (p/s)	£20

(see also Pete Fender)

FATAL MICROBES/POISON GIRLS
79	Small Wonder WEENY 3	**FATAL MICROBES MEET THE POISON GIRLS** (12" EP, with insert)	£15

(see also Poison Girls)

FATBACK BAND
74	Polydor 2391 143	**KEEP ON STEPPIN'** (LP)	£15

75   Polydor 2391 184   YUM YUM (LP) £15

FATES
85   Taboo HAG 1   FURIA (LP) £25

FATHEAD
83   Greensleeves GRED 118   Champion/Stop All The Fight (12") £20

FATHER THOMAS
70   Candidate 1   Look For The Sun/There's A Dream £70

FATHER JOHN MISTY
15   Bella Union BELLA 487V   I Loved You Honeybee/I've Never Been A Woman (heart-shaped red vinyl) £40
15   Bella Union BELLA 476VX   I LOVE YOU HONEYBEAR (2-LP, CD coloured vinyl and musical pop up sleeve) £50
15   Bella Union BELLA 476V   I LOVE YOU HONEYBEAR (LP, with CD, poster) £25
15   Bella Union BELLA 527V   LIVE AT ROUGH TRADE (LP) £18
17   Bella Union BELLA 628VX   PURE COMEDY (2-LP, aluminium/copper vinyl, poster, tarot card and 4 sleeve
variations) £30
(see also Fleet Foxes)

FATHER'S ANGELS
68   MGM MGM 1459   Don't Knock It/Bok To Bach £250
68   MGM MGM 1459   Don't Knock It/Bok To Bach (DJ Copy) £300

FATHER'S BROWN
70   Decca F23059   Maybe/The Yellow Moon Is High £20

FAT LARRY'S BAND
82   WMOT VS 491   Act Like You Know/Get Down And Get Funky £20

FATMAN VERSUS JAH SHAKA
80   Live & Love LAP12   IN A DUB CONFERENCE (LP) £35

FAT MATTRESS
69   Polydor 56367   Magic Forest/Bright New Way £15
70   Polydor 2058 053   Highway/Black Sheep Of The Family £15
69   Polydor 582/583 056   FAT MATTRESS (LP, open-out sleeve, red label) £50
70   Polydor 2383 025   FAT MATTRESS II (LP, red label) £50
(see also Jimi Hendrix Experience, Juicy Lucy)

ERIC FATTER
69   Camel CA 20   Since You've Been Gone (actually Eric Fratter)/WINSTON HINES: Cool Down (B-side
actually by Winston Hinds) £25
(see also Eric Fratter, Afrotones)

FAT TULIPS
88   Sweet William BILLY 001   You Opened My Eyes/ROSEHIPS: Ask Johnny Dee (33rpm flexi, p/s w/insert) £15

FAUST
72   Faust/Polydor 2001-299   It's A Bit Of A Pain/So Far...£25
96   Die Stadt 011   Right Between Yr Eyes (p/s, Uberschall Festival single,with Stereolab and Foetus) £20
90   Chemical Imbalance CI 08   Live In Hamburg (issued free with Chemical Imbalance magazine) £25
71   Polydor 2310 142   FAUST (LP, initial pressing on clear vinyl, with clear sleeve & clear insert) £150
71   Polydor 2310 142   FAUST (LP, insert) £70
72   Polydor 2310 196   SO FAR (LP, with 9 prints in wallet) £150
73   Virgin VC 501   THE FAUST TAPES (LP) £25
73   Virgin V 2004   FAUST IV (LP) £40
79   Recommended R.R. 1   FAUST (LP, reissue, clear vinyl, clear sleeve, insert) £30
79   Recommended R.R. 2   SO FAR (LP, reissue, with 10 insert prints, numbered, 600 only) £50
80   Recommended R.R. 6   THE FAUST TAPES (LP, plastic bag cover)...£20
86   Recommended R.R. 125   MUNICH AND ELSEWHERE (LP) £20
88   ReR Megacorp Rer 36   THE LAST LP (LP, numbered) £20
10   ReR Megacorp VF2   THE FAUST TAPES (LP, reissue, 180 gm vinyl) £18
(see also Toni Conrad & Faust)

FAVOURITES
80   4 Play FOUR 002   S.O.S./Favourite Shoes (p/s) £80
80   4 Play FOUR 003   Angelica/Cold (p/s)...£30

FAVOURITE SONS
66   Mercury MF 911   That Driving Beat/Walkin' Walkin' Walkin' £250

DAVE FAWCETT
81   DMF MK 1   My Car/Danger In The Night (no p/s) £30

WALLY FAWKES (& HIS TROGLODYTES)
58   Decca LF 312   FAWKES ON HOLIDAY (LP) £15
(see also Sandy Brown)

BILL FAY
67   Deram DM 143   Some Good Advice/Screams In The Ears £60
70   Deram Nova SDN 12   BILL FAY (LP, stereo) £400
70   Deram Nova DN 12   BILL FAY (LP, mono) £500
71   Deram SML 1079   TIME OF THE LAST PERSECUTION (LP, red/white label) £1500
09   Deram Nova SDN 12   BILL FAY (LP, reissue, stereo) £25

ALMA FAYE
79   Flamingo FM 5   Don't Fall In Love/I Believed (DJ copy)...£60
78   Flamingo FM 5   Don't Fall In Love/I Believed £50
79   Flamingo 12 FM 5   Don't Fall In Love/I Believed (12") £15

FRANCIS FAYE
65   Stateside SL 10129   YOU GOTTA GO! GO! GO! (LP)..£20

FAZE ACTION
99	Nuphonic NUX 139	MOVING CITIES (2xLP) £15

FAZED IDJUTS
99	U Star USR 002	Dust Of Life (12", single sided) £20

FBD PROJECT
92	Bang In Tunes BT 001	F.B.D./Blasted (12" white label) £20
93	Bang In Tunes BT 002	Terminate/F-B-D Remix/Blasted (Remix) (12" white label) £40
93	Bang In Tunes BT 003	Breakin Up/The Core (12", black labels) £50
93	FBD Project FBD 03	Deep Dance EP (12", pink labels)..£40
93	Bang In Tunes BT 004	Ruff To Da Smooth (The Remixes) (12") £35
94	Bang In Tunes BT 005	Journeys/Just Wanna Live (12")..£35
94	Bang In Tunes BIT 009	She's So (Revisited)/Ruffguide (12")..£25
98	Bang In Tunes BITRP 001	The Core/Terminate (12") £40
16	Bang In Tunes BITRLP002	The Core - 2016 Remixes (2 x 12")...£30

F.B.I. (FOLK BLUES INC.)
66	Eyemark EMS 1006	Don't Hide/When The Ship Comes In £25
76	Good Earth GD 6	F.B.I./The Time Is Right To Leave The City £25
77	Good Earth GDS 802	F.B.I. (LP) £60

FEAR FACTORY
95	Roadrunner RR 8856-1	DEMANUFACTURE (LP) £35

FEARN'S BRASS FOUNDRY
68	Decca F 12721	Don't Change It/John White £50
68	Decca F 12835	Now I Taste The Tears/Love, Sink And Drown £25

FEAR OF FALLING
83	Excellent XL 7	Like A Lion/You My Prodigal Son (p/s)..£20

CHARLIE FEATHERS/MAC CURTIS
74	Polydor 2310 293	ROCKABILLY KINGS (LP) £20

(see also Mac Curtis)

FEATURES (1)
77	Progress PR 01	Drab City/Job Satisfaction £50

FEATURES (2)
80	ASM HIT 06	She Makes Me Blue/Don't Let Them Know...£20
81	AFM PET 01	Monday-Friday/Cue The Next Army £20

FEDERALS (JAMAICA)
67	Island WI 3126	Penny For Your Song/I've Passed This Way Before £55
68	Island WI 3152	Shocking Love/By The River..£50
69	High Note HS 024	Wailing Festival/Me And My Baby (B-side actually "By The River")...........£30
70	Camel CA 40	In This World/You Better Call On Me (B-side actually "Shocking Love") £100

FEDERALS (U.K.)
63	Parlophone R 4988	Brazil/In A Persian Market £15
63	Parlophone R 5013	Boot Hill/Keep On Dancing With Me £15
64	Parlophone R 5100	The Climb/Dance With A Dolly £15
64	Parlophone R 5139	Marlena/Please Believe Me..£15
64	Parlophone R 5193	Twilight Time/Lost And Alone £15
65	Parlophone R 5320	Bucket Full Of Love/Leah £25

(see also Winston's Fumbs, Yes)

FEEDER
96	Echo ECS 13	TWO COLOURS: Pictures Of Rain/Chicken On A Bone (p/s, clear vinyl) £40
96	Echo ECSCD 13	TWO COLOURS: Pictures Of Rain/Chicken On A Bone (CD, 1,000 only) £40
04	Echo ECS157A/B -1	Tumble and Fall/Victoria (12" white label promos auctioned for Warchild charity) £15
96	Echo ECHLP 9	SWIM (LP, inner) £40
97	Echo ECHLP 15	POLYTHENE (LP, vinyl re-issue of original CD album, with free High 7", 500 only) £120
97	Echo ECHLP 15	POLYTHENE (LP, vinyl re-issue of original CD album, without free 7")................£80
99	Echo ECHLP 28	YESTERDAY WENT TOO SOON (LP, top opening sleeve, inner)....................£80
01	Echo ECHLP 34	ECHO PARK (LP, gatefold, inner)...£75
02	Echo ECHLP 43	COMFORT IN SOUND (LP, white vinyl)...£60
04	Echo ECHLP 52	PICTURE OF PERFECT YOUTH (3xLP) £40
05	Echo ECHLP 60	PUSHING THE SENSES (LP) £40
08	Echo ECHLP 79	SILENT CRY (LP) £30

FEELIES
79	Rough Trade RT 024	Raised Eyebrows/Fa Cé La (p/s) £15
80	Stiff BUY 65	Everybody's Got Something To Hide (Except For Me & My Monkey)/Original Love (die-cut p/s)...£15
80	Stiff SEEZ 20	CRAZY RHYTHMS (LP, printed inner, 'pay no more than £3.99' sticker) £60
86	Rough Trade ROUGH 104	THE GOOD EARTH (LP)...£20
89	A&M 395214-1	ONLY LIFE (LP) £20
91	A&M 395 344-1	TIME FOR A WITNESS (LP)...£25
09	Domino REWIGLP 65	CRAZY RHYTHMS (LP, reissue, stickered sleeve, printed inner, download card)............£20
09	Domino REWIGLP 66	THE GOOD EARTH (LP, reissue, download card with bonus covers) £15

FELDER'S ORIOLES
65	Piccadilly 7N 35247	Down Home Girl/Misty £40
65	Piccadilly 7N 35269	Sweet Tasting Wine/Turn On Your Lovelight £20
66	Piccadilly 7N 35311	I Know You Don't Love Me No More/Only Three Can Play £20
66	Piccadilly 7N 35332	Back Street/Something You Got £25

MINT VALUE £

(see also V.I.P.s, Mike Patto)

VICTOR FELDMAN BIG BAND/QUARTET

56	Tempo A 142	Big Top/Cabaletto	£15
57	Tempo A 154	Jackpot/You Are My Heart's Desire	£15
55	Tempo EXA 29	BIG BAND (EP)	£50
57	Tempo EXA 57	VICTOR FELDMAN IN LONDON -- THE QUARTET VOLUME 1 (EP)	£60
57	Tempo EXA 67	VICTOR FELDMAN IN LONDON VOLUME 2 (EP)	£60
58	Tempo EXA 85	MUTUAL ADMIRATION (EP, with Dizzy Reece)	£75
53	Esquire EP 43	MODERN JAZZ QUARTET (EP)	£40
53	Esquire EP 54	MODERN JAZZ QUARTET (EP)	£20
53	Esquire EP 64	MODERN JAZZ QUINTET/SEXTET (EP)	£25
53	Esquire EP 84	MODERN JAZZ QUARTET/SEXTET (EP)	£20
54	Esquire EP 104	MODERN JAZZ QUARTET (EP)	£40
54	Esquire EP 114	VIC FELDMAN ENCORE (EP)	£20
54	Esquire 20 - 046	MULTIPLE TALENTS (LP)	£60
55	Esquire 20 - 064	EXPERIMENT IN TIME (LP)	£60
55	Tempo LAP 5	VICTOR FELDMAN'S SEXTET (10" LP)	£300
56	Tempo LAP 6	VICTOR FELDMAN MODERN JAZZ QUARTET (10" LP)	£200
57	Tempo TAP 8	VICTOR FELDMAN IN LONDON VOL. 1 (LP)	£150
57	Tempo TAP 12	VICTOR FELDMAN IN LONDON VOL. 2 (LP)	£150
58	Tempo TAP 19	TRANSATLANTIC ALLIANCE (LP)	£350
59	Contemporary LAC 12172	THE ARRIVAL OF VICTOR FELDMAN (LP)	£20
61	Riversode RLP 366	MERRY OLDE SOUL (LP)	£20
63	MGM C 8954	SOVIET JAZZ THEMES (LP)	£15
64	Contemporary LAC 580	LATINSVILLEI (LP)	£50
67	United Artists UAS 529006	PLAYS EVERYTHING IN SIGHT (LP)	£15
82	Jasmine JASM 2023	IN LONDON VOL. 1 (LP, reissue)	£15
82	Jasmine JASM 2023	IN LONDON VOL. 2 (LP, reissue)	£15

(see also Dizzy Reece, Tubby Hayes)

VICTOR FELDMAN, TERRY GIBBS & LARRY BUNKER
60	Top Rank 30/007	VIBES TO THE POWER OF THREE (LP)	£20

FELICE BROTHERS
07	Loose VJLP 171	LIVE AT THE ARIZONA (LP)	£100

JOSE FELICIANO
74	RCA RCA PB10094	Golden Lady/Virgo	£60

FELIUS ANDROMEDA
67	Decca F 12694	Meditations/Cheadle Heath Delusions	£60
72	Cactus CT 2	After The Storm/Rainbow Chasing (as Andromeda)	£15

(see also Denis Couldry)

LENNIE FELIX, BRIAN LEMON, KEITH INGHAM, RALPH SUTTON
75	77 77S 58	PIANO SUMMIT (LP)	£20

JULIE FELIX
71	RAK 108	Snakeskin/Watching Waiting	£40
72	RAK 14	Clothos Web/Windy Morning	£25
64	Decca LK 4626	JULIE FELIX (LP)	£20
65	Decca LK 4683	SINGS DYLAN AND GUTHRIE (LP)	£20
65	Decca LK 4724	SECOND ALBUM (LP)	£20
66	Decca LK 4820	THIRD ALBUM (LP)	£20
66	Fontana TL 5386	CHANGES (LP, mono/stereo)	£20
67	Fontana (S) TL 5437	FLOWERS (LP)	£20
72	Rak SRKA 6752	CLOTHOS WEB (LP)	£20

MIKE FELIX
66	Pye 7N 17058	You Belong To Me/Booga Dee	£25

(see also Migel 5)

RORY FELLOWES
68	S n B 55-3877	Nina/Endlessly Friendlessly Blue	£20

GRAHAM FELLOWS
79	EMI INT 598	Men Of Oats And Creosote/Rebecca (promo, in envelope p/s)	£40
85	Wicked Frog FROG 01	LOVE AT THE HACIENDA (LP)	£50

(see also Jilted John)

FELT
79	Shanghai S79/CUS 321	Index/Break It (hand-made p/s, early copies with poem on rear sleeve 100 only, yellow labels)	£300
79	Shanghai S79/CUS 321	Index/Break It (hand-made p/s, no poem on rear sleeve)	£150
81	Cherry Red CHERRY 26	Something Sends Me To Sleep/Red Indians/Something Sends Me To Sleep (Version)/Red Indians (p/s)	£40
82	Cherry Red CHERRY 45	My Face Is On Fire/Trails Of Colour Dissolve (p/s)	£40
83	Cherry Red CHERRY 59	Penelope Tree/A Preacher In New England (p/s)	£25
83	Cherry Red 12CHERRY 59	Penelope Tree/A Preacher In New England/Now Summer's Spread Its Wings Again (12")	£25
84	Cherry Red CHERRY 78	Mexican Bandits/The World Is As Soft As Lace (p/s)	£30
84	Cherry Red CHERRY 81	Sunlight Bathed The Golden Glow/Fortune (p/s)	£25
84	Cherry Red 12CHERRY 81	Sunlight Bathed The Golden Glow/Fortune/Sunlight Strings (12", p/s)	£20
85	Cherry Red 12CHERRY 89	Primitive Painters/Cathedral (12", p/s, with Liz Frazer)	£15
86	Creation CRE 027	Ballad Of The Band/I Didn't Mean To Hurt You (p/s)	£15
86	Creation CRE 027T	Ballad Of The Band/I Didn't Mean To Hurt You/Candles In A Church/Ferdinand (12")	£15

86	Creation CRE 032	Rain Of Crystal Spires/I Will Die With My Head In Flames (p/s)	£15
86	Creation CRE 032T	Rain Of Crystal Spires/Gather Up Your Wings And Fly/I Will Die With My Head In Flames/Sandman's On The Rise Again (12", p/s)	£18
88	Creation CRE 060T	Space Blues/Be Still/Female Star/Tuesday's Secret (12")	£25
82	Cherry Red MRED 25	CRUMBLING THE ANTISEPTIC BEAUTY (LP, 1st pressing, full photo, white label)	£50
82	Cherry Red MRED 25	CRUMBLING THE ANTISEPTIC BEAUTY (LP, 2nd pressing, black rectangle on right side of photo, white label)	£30
84	Cherry Red MRED 57	THE SPLENDOUR OF FEAR (LP)	£40
84	Cherry Red BRED 63	THE STRANGE IDOLS PATTERN AND OTHER SHORT STORIES (LP)	£50
84	Cherry Red MRED 25	CRUMBLING THE ANTISEPTIC BEAUTY (LP, reissue, black labels)	£18
85	Cherry Red B-RED 65	IGNITE THE SEVEN CANNONS AND SET SAIL FOR THE SUN (LP, textured sleeve with lyric insert)	£40
86	Creation CRELP 009	LET THE SNAKES CRINKLE THEIR HEADS TO DEATH (LP)	£40
86	Creation CRELP 011	FOREVER BREATHES THE LONELY WORD (LP, with inner sleeve)	£40
87	Creation CRELP 017	POEM OF THE RIVER (LP)	£40
87	Cherry Red BRED 79	GOLD MINE TRASH (LP, with inner)	£40
88	Creation CRELP 030	PICTORIAL JACKSON REVIEW (LP)	£40
88	Creation CRELP 033	TRAIN ABOVE THE CITY (LP)	£35
89	el ACME 24	ME AND A MONKEY ON THE MOON (LP)	£40
90	Creation CRELP 069	BUBBLEGUM PERFUME (LP)	£40
18	Cherry Red FLT180	CRUMBLING THE ANTISEPTIC BEAUTY (LP, reissue)	£20
18	Cherry Red FLT181	THE SPLENDOUR OF FEAR (LP, reissue)	£20
18	Cherry Red FLT182	THE STRANGE IDOLS PATTERN AND OTHER SHORT STORIES (LP, reissue)	£20
18	Cherry Red FLT183	IGNITE THE SEVEN CANNONS AND SET SAIL FOR THE SUN (LP, reissue)	£20
18	Cherry Red FLT184	THE SEVENTEETNTH CENTURY (LP, reissue)	£20
18	Cherry Red FLT185	FOREVER BREATHES THE LONELY WORLD (LP, reissue)	£20
18	Cherry Red FLT186	POEM OF THE RIVER (LP, reissue)	£20
18	Cherry Red FLT187	PICTORIAL JACKSON REVIEW (LP, reissue)	£20
18	Cherry Red FLT188	TRAIN ABOVE THE CITY (LP, reissue)	£20
18	Cherry Red FLT189	ME AND A MONKEY ON THE MOON (LP, reissue)	£20

(see also Denim, Versatile Newts, Maurice Deebank, Cocteau Twins, Go-Kart Mozart)

FENCE
| 80 | BFD BFD 2 | Thinking That I Shouldn't/Thru With You/Hey Girl (p/s) | £15 |

JAN FENDER
71	Prince Buster PB 5	Sea Of Love/PRINCE BUSTER: Heaven Help Us All	£25
71	Fab FAB 164	Sweet P/CLIFF & ORGANIZERS: Mr Brown	£40
71	Fab FAB 166	Holly Holy Version/Old Kentrone Version (as Jal Fender)	£20

PETE FENDER
| 81 | Xntrix 2002 | FOUR FORMULAS (EP, in 8" silk-screened book p/s) | £30 |

(see also Fatal Microbes, Omega Tribe)

FENDERMEN
| 60 | Top Rank JAR 513 | Don't You Just Know It/Beach Party | £20 |

FENMEN
64	Decca F 11955	Rag Doll/Be My Girl	£20
65	Decca F 12269	I've Got Everthing You Need Babe/Every Little Day Now	£15
66	CBS 202236	Rejected/Girl Don't Bring Me Down	£25

(see also Bern Elliott & Fenmen, Pretty Things)

DAVID FENTON
| 83 | Razor RZS 106 | Fresh Air/Buried In The Snow (p/s) | £20 |

PETER FENTON
| 66 | Fontana TF 748 | Marble Breaks, Iron Bends/Small Town | £20 |
| 67 | Fontana TF 789 | I Was Lord Kitcheners Valet/Walking In Circles | £15 |

SHANE FENTON (& FENTONES)
| 74 | Contour 2870 409 | GOOD ROCKIN' TONIGHT (LP) | £15 |

FENWAYS
| 65 | Liberty LIB 66082 | Walk/Whip And Jerk | £25 |

RAY FENWICK
| 71 | Decca SKL 5090 | KEEP AMERICA BEAUTIFUL, GET A HAIRCUT (LP, blue/silver label with small logo) | £60 |

(see also Spencer Davis Group, After Tea, Fancy, Ian Gillan Band, Wizard's Convention, Murgatroyd Band,, Syndicats, South Coast Ska Kings, Rupert's People)

FENWYCK
| 68 | ERA ERA 100 | State Of Mind/Away | £80 |

FENZYX
| 81 | Ellie Jay EJSP 9655 | Soldiers/Angels Of Mercy (p/s) | £25 |

FERDIA
| 78 | Polydor 2904 012 | A SIGH FOR OLD TIMES (LP) | £15 |

WINSTON FERGUS
78	Arawak ARK DD 001	Fly Natty Dread/Loving Pauper (12")	£40
79	Burning Rockers BRD 016	Corner Girl/Corner Dub (12")	£20
82	Burning Rockers BRD 037	Pay To Live/Earth In Dub (12")	£40
82	Fergie Music FM 002	In Ting Sound/My Own Way Heart (12")	£150
83	Burning Sounds BSD 060	Keep On Dancing/One Day Up (12")	£20
85	John Dread JPD 002	I WILL SING (LP)	£15

HELENA FERGUSON
| 67 | London HLZ 10164 | Where Is The Party?/My Terms | £50 |

MAYNARD FERGUSON ORCHESTRA
58	Emarcy EJL 1270	JAM SESSION (LP)	£15
58	Emarcy EJL 1275	AROUND THE HORN (LP)	£20
58	Emarcy EJL 1287	DIMENSIONS (LP)	£20
59	Columbia 33SX 1146	MESSAGE FROM NEWPORT (LP)	£20
60	Mercury MMC 14050	THE BOY WITH LOTS OF BRASS (LP, also stereo CMS 18034)	£20
60	Columbia 33SX 1210	MESSAGE FROM BIRDLAND (LP, also stereo SCX 3245)	£15
60	Columbia 33SX 1270	JAZZ FOR DANCING (LP, also stereo SCX 3338)	£20
61	Columbia 33SX 1301	NEWPORT SUITE (LP, also stereo SCX 3368)	£20
62	Columbia 33SX 1439	MAYNARD 62 (LP)	£20
66	Fontana TL 5274	BLUES ROAR (LP)	£20
66	Fontana TL 5293	COLOR HIM WILD (LP)	£20
67	Fontana TL 5310	SEXTET (LP)	£20
68	Atlantic 2464008	FREAKY (LP)	£20
69	CBS 63514	BALLAD STLYE OF MAYNARD FERGUSON (LP)	£40
71	CBS 64432	ALIVE AND WELL IN LONDON (LP)	£20
72	CBS 65027	M.F. HORN 2 (LP, gatefold)	£15
73	CBS 65589	M.F. HORN 3 (LP)	£20
73	CBS 65952	M.F. HORN 4 (LIVE AT JIMMYS) (LP)	£20

ALEX FERGUSSON
92	Private Pressing AF 001	ALEX FERGUSSON (LP, white label, 500 copies, no sleeve)	£30

(see also Alternative TV, Psychic TV)

FERKO STRING BAND
55	London HL 8140	Alabama Jubilee/Sing A Little Melody	£25
55	London HLF 8183	Ma (She's Making Eyes At Me)/You Are My Sunshine	£25
55	London HLF 8215	Happy Days Are Here Again/Deep In The Heart Of Texas	£25
58	London HL 7052	Happy Days Are Here Again/Alabama Jubilee (export issue)	£18
57	London HB-C 1064	THE FERKO STRING BAND VOL. 1 (10" LP)	£15

ANDY FERNBACH
69	Liberty LBL/LBS 83233	IF YOU MISS YOUR CONNEXION (LP, blue label)	£200

(see also Groundhogs)

MAJA FERNICK
72	Philips 6006 196	Give Me Your Love Again/Flowers In The City	£20

PIERRE FEROLDI
94	Disco Magic DISK 001	Moving Now (Extended)/Moving Now (Italian Version) (12" featuring Linda Ray)	£20

CHRISTIAN FERRAS
61	HMV ASD 427	MOZART VIOLIN CONCERTOS NO 4 & 6 (LP, stereo)	£400
63	HMV ASD 531	FERRAS & BARBIZET : ENESCO & DEBUSSY SONATAS ETC (LP, Stereo with Pierre Barbizel)	£800
64	HMV ASD 572	BERG: CONCERTO FOR VIOLIN AND ORCHESTRA (LP, stereo)	£150

JOE FERRER & HIS DEVILS BOYS
61	Oriole CB 1629	Rockin' Crickets/Blue Guitar	£20

EUGENE FERRIS
66	Planet PLF 112	There Was A Smile In Your Eyes/Soft Moonlight (without p/s)	£15
66	Planet PLF 112	There Was A Smile In Your Eyes/Soft Moonlight (with p/s)	£30

GEORGE FERRIS
71	Ackee ACK 117	With Every Dream/Diana	£20

(see also George Faith)

FERRIS WHEEL
67	Pye 7N 17387	I Can't Break The Habit/Number One Guy	£30
67	Pye NPL 18203	CAN'T BREAK THE HABIT (LP)	£100
70	Polydor 583 066	FERRIS WHEEL (LP, lyric insert, red label)	£60

(see also Linda Lewis, West Five)

BRYAN FERRY
73	Island IDJ 1	These Foolish Things/Sympathy For The Devil/Baby I Don't Care/ Loving You Is Sweeter Than Ever (promo)	£30
75	Island WIP 6234	You Go To My Head/Re-Make, Re-Model (DJ copies in generic promo p/s)	£20
78	Polydor PPSP 10	Hold On I'm Coming/Take Me To The River (12", unissued, promo only, numbered stamped p/s)	£20
76	Island ILPS 9367	LET'S STICK TOGETHER (LP, original issue)	£15
93	Virgin V2700	TAXI (LP, inner)	£40
94	Virgin V2751	MAMOUNA (LP)	£150
95	Virgin V 2791	MORE THAN THIS - THE BEST OF BRYAN FERRY AND ROXY MUSIC (2-LP)	£100
99	Virgin 8482711	AS TIME GOES BY (LP)	£200
02	Virgin LPVIR 167	FRANTIC (LP)	£100
07	Virgin V3026	DYLANESQUE (LP, inner)	£150
10	Virgin/Vinyl Factory VF 021	OLYMPIA (LP, gatefold)	£150
14	BMG 538013701	AVONMORE (LP, with CD)	£35

(see also Roxy Music)

MANFREDO FEST
79	Bluebird BRT 1	Jungle Kitten (5.30)/Jungle Kitten (3.36)/Send In The Clowns (12")	£60
79	Bluebird BRT 1	Send In The Clowns/Jungle Kitten	£40

FESTIVAL (1)
72	RCA 2275	Today/Warm Me (demo only)	£90

(see also 10cc)

FESTIVAL (2)
78   Nevis NEV 107 — **Something In Your Smile/Let's Make Love** **£60**

FEVER TREE
68   Uni UNLS 102 — **FEVER TREE** (LP) **£100**
68   MCA MUPS 347 — **ANOTHER TIME, ANOTHER PLACE** (LP) **£70**

FEWS
15   Speedy Wunderground SW012 — **III** (Part 1)/(Part 2) **£18**

FFWD
94   Inter Modo INTA001 — **FFWD** (2-LP, inners) **£35**
(see also King Crimson, Orb)

FICKLE PICKLE
70   Fontana TF 1069 — **Millionaire/Sam And Sadie** **£15**

FIDD
69   Polydor 56320 — **Guai Guai** (From the film 'Baby Love')/**Happy Walk** **£25**

FI-DELS
72   Jay Boy BOY 69 — **Try A Little Harder/You Never Do Right** **£15**
72   Jay Boy BOY 69 — **Try A Little Harder/You Never Do Right** (DJ Copy) **£30**
76   DJM DJS 689 — **Try A Little Harder/KEYMAN STRINGS: Instrumental Version** (DJ copy p/s £20) **£30**

KEITH FIELD
68   Polydor 56278 — **The Day That War Broke Out/Stop Thief** **£30**

JERRY FIELDING & HIS ORCHESTRA
54   London HL 8017 — **When I Grow Too Old To Dream/Button Up Your Overcoat** **£30**
55   London HL 7003 — **Tea For Two/Here In My Arms** (export issue) **£15**
55   London HL 7004 — **I'm In Love/Blue Prelude** (export issue) **£15**

FIELD MICE
88   Sarah SARAH 012 — **Emma's House/When You Sleep/Fabulous Friend/The Last Letter** (p/s, with poster) **£50**
88   Sarah SARAH 18 — **Sensitive/When Morning Comes To Town/Penguins** (foldout p/s, with poster) **£60**
89   Caff CAFF 2 — **I Can See Myself Alone Forever/Everything About You** (foldaround p/s in poly bag with insert) **£30**
90   Sarah SARAH 024 — **Autumn Store Pt. 1/If You Need Someone/World In Me** (p/s) **£25**
90   Sarah SARAH 025 — **Autumn Store Pt. 2/Anyone Else Isn't You/Bleak** (p/s) **£25**
91   Sarah SARAH 44 — **September's Not So Far Away/Hello And Goodbye** (p/s, with insert) **£25**
91   Sarah SARAH 57 — **Missing The Moon/A Wrong Turn And Raindrops/An Earlier Autumn** (12", p/s) **£20**
90   Sarah SARAH 38 — **SO SAID KAY EP 10", p/s)** **£30**
90   Sarah SARAH 402 — **SNOWBALL** (10" LP) **£30**
90   Sarah SARAH 601 — **SKYWRITING** (LP) **£40**
90   Sarah SARAH 606 — **COASTAL** (LP) **£50**
91   Sarah SARAH 607 — **FOR KEEPS** (LP) **£45**
(see also Northern Picture Library)

FIELD MUSIC
05   Memphis Industries NI 043LP — **FIELD MUSIC** (LP) **£18**
07   Memphis industries NI 074LP — **TONES OF MUSIC** (LP) **£25**
10   Memphis Industries MI0149LP — **FIELD MUSIC** (MEASURE) (2-LP) **£25**
12   Memphis Industries MI0208LP — **PLUMB** (LP, purple vinyl) **£15**
16   Memphis Industries MIO 387LPX — **COMMONTIME** (2-LP orange vinyl) **£20**
16   Memphis Industries MIO 387LPX — **COMMONTIME** (2-LP green vinyl with signed poster) **£30**
16   Memphis Industries MIO 387LPX — **COMMONTIME** (2-LP green vinyl without signed poster) **£20**
18   Memphis Industries MIO 476LPX — **OPEN HERE** (LP, blue vinyl) **£25**

ERNIE FIELDS & HIS ORCHESTRA
60   London RE 1260 — **SAXY** (EP) **£30**
60   London HA 2263 — **IN THE MOOD** (LP) **£30**

FIELDS OF THE NEPHILIM
87   SITUP18 — **DAWNRAZOR** **£0**
85   Tower N1 — **BURNING THE FIELDS** (12" EP, red/black p/s) **£200**
85   Tower N1/Jung. JUNG 28T — **BURNING THE FIELDS** (12" EP, green p/s with insert & band photo label) **£40**
85   Tower N1/Jung. JUNG 28T — **BURNING THE FIELDS** (12" EP, green & other coloured vinyl export issue) **£40**
86   Situation 2 SIT 42 — **Power/Secrets** (7", white label promos only, stickered plain sleeve) **£15**
87   Situation 2 SIT 46 — **Preacher Man/Laura II** (p/s, swith Beggars Banquet sticker) **£35**
87   Situation 2 SIT 46 — **Preacher Man/Laura II** (p/s) **£25**
87   Situation 2 SIT 48T — **Blue Water** (1 track 12" promo) **£20**
87   Situation 2 SIT 48T — **Blue Water** (Electrostatic)/**In Every Dream Home A Heartache** (live)/**Blue Water** (Hot Wire) (12", p/s, with poster) **£15**
87   Situation 2 SITUP 18 — **DAWNRAZOR** (LP) **£20**
88   Situation 2 SITU 22 — **THE NEPHILIM** (LP, gatefold, printed inner) **£30**
88   Situation 2 SITU 22L — **THE NEPHILIM** (2LP, 45rpm, gatefold, numbered, stickered shrinkwrap) **£60**
90   Beggars Banquet BEGA 115 — **ELIZIUM** (LP, printed inner, early copies with print) **£30**
91   Beggars Banquet BEGA 120 — **EARTH INFERNO** (2LP, printed inners) **£40**
02   Jungle FREUD 063 — **FALLEN** (LP) **£30**
12   Sacred Symphony SS LP — **CEROMONIES** (2LP, gatefold) **£40**

12	Sacred Symphony SS CD 0666	0666	
		CEROMONIES (2LP/2CD/2DVD box set, red vinyl, wooden case, ephemera)	£400

FIELDS (1)

69	Uni UNLS 104	FIELDS (LP)	£100

FIELDS (2)

71	CBS 7555	A Friends Of Mine/Three Minstrels	£15
71	CBS 69009	FIELDS (LP, with poster)	£125
71	CBS 69009	FIELDS (LP, without poster)	£50
16	Black Gold BG 008	FIELDS (LP, reissue)	£18

(see also Rare Bird, Greenslade)

FIEND

84	Endangered EDR 1	STAND ALONE EP	£18

FIESTAS

59	London HL 8870	So Fine/Last Night I Dreamed	£40
59	London HL 8870	So Fine/Last Night I Dreamed (78)	£20

FIFE REIVERS

69	Columbia SCX 6371	FIFE REIVERS (LP)	£15

15 16 17

76	Morpheus MOR 1022	If You Love Me Smile/Version	£25
77	Morpheus DEB 06	Black Skin Boy/Version	£25
78	DEB DEB 003	Emotion/Castro Black Speaks To Dennis Bovell	£20
78	DEB DEB 012	Good Times/Black Skin Boys (12")	£20
79	DEB DBR 101	Someone Special/Suddenly Happiness	£20
79	DEB RIC 103	Baby Love/I'm Hurt	£25
80	Cha Cha CHAD 24	I Need A Man/OVERNIGHT PLAYERS: Next Cut (12")	£25
06	DEB DEB LP 101	MAGIC TOUCH (LP, issue of unreleased LP from 1978)	£20

FIFTH AVENUE

65	Immediate IM 002	The Bells Of Rhymney/Just Like Anyone Would Do (in blue/white Immediate sleeve)	£40
65	Immediate IM 002	The Bells Of Rhymney/Just Like Anyone Would Do (in black/white Immediate sleeve)	£30

(see also Denny Gerrard, Warm Sounds)

FIFTH AVENUE BAND

69	Reprise RSPL 6369	FIFTH AVENUE BAND (LP)	£35

FIFTH COLUMN

66	Columbia DB 8068	Benjamin Day/There's Nobody Here	£50

(see also Gerry Rafferty)

5TH DIMENSION

67	Liberty LIB 12051	Go Where You Wanna Go/Too Poor To Die	£35
67	Liberty LIB 12051	Go Where You Wanna Go/Too Poor To Die (DJ Copy)	£45
67	Liberty LIB 15037	Paper Cup/Poor Side Of Town	£20
68	Liberty LBF 15052	Carpet Man/Magic Garden	£15
70	Liberty LBF 15356	I'll Be Lovin' You Forever/Train Keep On Movin'	£25
68	Liberty LBL/LBS 83098E	MAGIC GARDEN (LP)	£15
67	Liberty LBL/LBS 83038	UP UP AND AWAY (LP)	£15
68	Liberty LBL/LBS 83155E	STONED SOUL PICNIC (LP)	£15

5TH OF HEAVEN

88	Mix Out 12 FOH 1	Just A Little More/(Surrender Mix) (12', p/s)	£40

FIFTY FANTASTICS

79	South Circular SGS 108	God's Got Religion/STEPPES: The Beat Drill (white label)	£15
80	Dining Out TUX 5	God's Got Religion/The Beat Drill (reissue, foldout p/s, hand made labels)	£15

(see also Disco Zombies)

FIFTY FIVE DEGREES

79	No label or cat number	There's Gonna Be A Showdown/There's Gonna Be A Showdown (p/s)	£20

FIFTY FOOT HOSE

69	Mercury SLML 4030	CAULDRON (LP)	£200

53 BUS

83	Custom Cars 100MPH	Horizontal Dancing/Horizontal D.I.Y.	£50

50 YEAR VOID

92	BLADE 1	Blade's Love Machine (1-sided 12", white label promo, 100 only)	£30

(see also St. Etienne, Sarah Cracknell)

57TH PARALLEL

81	Rising sun RS 005	In This Light/Psalm Fifty Seven	£20

FIGGY DUFF

80	Dingles DIN 326	FIGGY DUFF (LP)	£25
85	Celtic CM 023	AFTER THE TEMPEST (LP, with insert)	£30

FIGHT

93	Epic EPC 474547	WAR OF WORDS (LP, white vinyl)	£60

(see also Judas Priest, Halford)

NESTOR FIGUERAS, DAVID TOOP & PAUL BURWELL

77	Bead Records BEAD 6	NESTOR FIGUERAS, DAVID TOOP & PAUL BURWELL (LP)	£40

PAULINE FILBY

68	Herald ELR 1081	MY WORLD BY PAULINE FILBY (EP)	£20
69	Herald LLR 567	SHOW ME A RAINBOW (LP)	£100

PHILIP JOHN FILBY

(see also Narnia, Accolade, Gordon Giltrap)

PHILIP JOHN FILBY
71   Dart ART2007   David McKenzie/Close My Eyes And Stick With Me.................................£20

FILM CAST
84   True Friends TF 004   The Distant Heart/World Of Light...£25

FILTHY RICH
87   JM TR 102   She's 17/Love Ain't A Fool (p/s)...£20

(see also Trident)

FILTHY SIX
10   Acid Jazz AJXLP229   THE FILTHY SIX (LP)..£15
12   Acid Jazz AJXLP288   THE FOX (LP)...£15

FIN
82   4AD BAD 205   In Camera: The Fatal Day/Coordinates/Apocalypse................................£20

FINAL ACADEMY
83   Spectrum SPEC 005   Night Cafe/The Collector...£40

FINAL CONFLICT
89   Futuresound VFS 001   My England/Across The Room (stickered white sleeve) £20

FINAL PROGRAM
81   Program FINAL 001   PROTECT AND SURVIVE (EP) £40

FINAL TOUCH
70s Myrrh MYR 1188   LOVE SONG (LP)...£25

FINCH
78   Rockburgh ROC 103   GALLEONS OF PASSION (LP) £18

FINDERS KEEPERS (U.K.)
66   CBS 202249   Light/Power Of Love (withdrawn, promos may exist)............................£65
66   CBS 202249   Light/Come On Now..£20
67   Fontana TF 892   Friday Kind Of Monday/On The Beach £40
68   Fontana TF 938   Sadie (The Cleaning Lady)/Without Her..£20

(see also Trapeze, Glenn Hughes, News)

JEM FINER
03   Artangel no cat. no.   LONGPLAYER (LP, book, 1000 only)..£20

(see also Pogues)

FINESSE
82   CBS A13 2169   Feel It/Inside Your Head (12")..£15

FINGERS (1)
66   Columbia DB 8026   I'll Take You Where The Music's Playing/My Way Of Thinking £20
67   Columbia DB 8112   All Kinds Of People/Circus With A Female Clown £45

(see also Crocheted Doughnut Ring, Legend)

FINGERS (2)
79   Ratched RAT 101   Marching Band/The Bandleader (Baz's Tune) (no p/s)............................£40
79   Ratchet RAT 102   Saints Alive/We're Alright £40

FINGERS INC.
87   Jack Trax 12 J TRAX 8   Distant Planet Club Mix/Distant Planet Dub MIx (12", stickered die-cut company
                                sleeve)..£45
88   Desire WANTX 6   Can You Feel It/My House (Acapella) (12", die-cut p/s)........................£30
88   Jack Trax JTX 8   Distant Planet (Remix, 4 Mixes) (12")..£60
88   Jack Trax JTX 20   Can You Feel It (4 Mixes) (12", p/s)...£25
89   Jack Trax JTX 2   Never No More Lonely/Music Takes Me Up/Distant Planet (Club Mix) (12").................£30
88   Jack Trax FING 1   ANOTHER SIDE (2-LP, gatefold sleeve)...£40

(see also Mr. Fingers, Larry Heard)

LEE FINN & RHYTHM MEN
63   Starlite ST45 103   High Class Feelin'/Pour Me A Glass Of Wine £50

LIAM FINN
08   Transgressive TRANS 080X I'LL BE LIGHTNING (LP with CD-R) £25

FINN MACCUILL
76   Radio Edinburgh REL 451   FINN MACCUILL (LP) £150
77   Radio Edinburgh REL 460   SINK YE - SWIM YE (LP)..£200

SIMON FINN
70   Mushroom 100 MR 2   PASS THE DISTANCE (LP, with lyric insert, white/brown labels)...........£500

LARRY FINNEGAN
62   HMV POP 1022   Dear One/Candy Lips £15
62   London HLU 9613   Pretty Suzy Sunshine/It's Walkin' Talkin' Time......................................£20
65   Ember EMB S 207   The Other Ringo (A Tribute To Ringo Starr)/When My Love Passes By (p/s) £20

FINS
81   SRTS 81 CUS 1075   Voice Of America/Omega Man £25

FIRE
68   Decca F 12753   Father's Name Is Dad/Treacle Toffee World £500
68   Decca F 12856   Round The Gum Tree/Toothie Ruthie £70
70   Pye NSPL 18343   THE MAGIC SHOEMAKER (LP, blue/black labels with logo banner at top) £600
90   See For Miles SEE 794   THE MAGIC SHOEMAKER (LP, reissue) £20
97   Tenth Planet TP 029   UNDERGROUND AND OVERHEAD: THE ALTERNATE FIRE (LP, gatefold sleeve,
                                numbered, 1,000 only) £18

(see also Strawbs, Paul Brett's Sage)

FIREBALLS
59	Top Rank JAR 218	Torquay/Cry Baby	£15
68	Stateside SS 2106	Goin' Away/Groovy Motions	£15
61	Top Rank 35/105	VAQUERO (LP)	£25

(see also Jimmy Gilmer, Buddy Holly)

FIREBIRD (2)
79	Rat SRTS79/CUS576	Change/Nightride (in p/s)	£150
79	Rat SRTS79/CUS576	Change/Nightride	£40

FIREBRAND
85	What WR 71	Never Felt This Way Before/I'm Leaving (p/s)	£50

FIRE ENGINES
80	Codex Comms. CDX 01	Get Up And Use Me/Everything's Roses (p/s)	£20
81	Pop:Aural POP 010	Candy Skin/Meat Whiplash (foldout p/s in poly bag)	£15
81	Accessory ACC 001	LUBRICATE YOUR LIVING ROOM (LP, in plastic bag)	£30
92	Rev-Ola CREV 001LP	FOND (LP)	£30

FIRE EXIT
79	Time Bomb Explosion 1	Timewall/Talkin' About Myself (p/s, stamped labels)	£100

FIREFLIES
59	Top Rank JAR 198	You Were Mine/Stella Got A Fella	£20
59	Top Rank JAR 198	You Were Mine/Stella Got A Fella (78)	£20
60	London HLU 9057	I Can't Say Goodbye/What Did I Do Wrong	£35

FIREFOX
96	Philly Blunt PB 006	Bonanza Kid/Buck Rogers (12")	£20

FIRE HYDRANT MEN
85	MCHMLP 3	BACKS (LP)	£20

FIREMAN
98	Hydra HYPRO 12 007	Rushes: Bison/Fluid/Appletree Cinnabar Amber (12" with massive fold-out poster)	£100
98	Hydra HYPRO 12 007	Rushes: Bison/Fluid/Appletree Cinnabar Amber (12" without massive fold-out poster)	£20
99	Hydra HYPRO 12 008	Fluid (12", p/s, promo only)	£35
93	Parlophone FIRE 1	STRAWBERRIES OCEANS SHIPS FOREST (2-LP, clear vinyl, numbered white sleeve, with inners, promo only)	£150
93	Parlophone PCSD 145	STRAWBERRIES OCEANS SHIPS FOREST (2-LP, clear vinyl, red sleeve, with inners)	£150
98	Hydra 4970551	RUSHES (2-LP, inners)	£200
08	One L. Indian TPLP 1003	ELECTRIC ARGUEMENTS (2-LP, CD, numbered)	£50
08	One L. Indian TPLP1016	ELECTRIC ARGUEMENTS (2-LP, CD, un-numbered)	£30
09	One L. Indian TPLPDE1016	ELECTRIC ARGUEMENTS (Box set, 2-LP, 2-CD, DVD in paper satchel)	£200

(see also Paul McCartney, Youth, Killing Joke, Brilliant, Twin Freaks)

FIRE SESSION
70	Revolution REVR 009	Honey Don't/Maximum Serenade	£25
70	Revolution REV 10	Souvenir/Bad Girl	£25
70	Revolution REV 13	Sleeping Reggae/CAROLS: Everyday I Have To Cry Some	£25
70	Revolution REV 14	Death Of The Ugly One/Big Feet	£35

FIRESIGN THEATRE
72	CBS CQ 30737	FIRESIGN THEATRE (LP, quadrophonic)	£15

FIRING SQUAD (1)
64	Parlophone R 5152	A Little Bit More/Bull Moose	£50

FIRING SQUAD (3)
83	Instant IMR 002	A Piece Of The Night/Muscle Talk (no p/s)	£30

FIRKIN THE FOX
84	Woodworm WR 005	BEHIND BARS (LP)	£25

FIRM (1)
80	SRTS 80 CUS 806	Angry Young Man/Not Gonna Turn Back Anymore/Mainstream (stamped paper sleeve)	£20

FIRST AID
77	Decca TXS 117	NOSTRADAMUS (LP)	£50

FIRST AID KIT
14	Columbia 88843066611	STAY GOLD (LP, CD gold vinyl)	£20

FIRST CHOICE
73	Pye International 7N 25613	This Is The House Where Love Died/One Step Away (unissued, demos may exist, this price for acetate)	£400
73	Bell BELLS 229	ARMED AND EXTREMELY DANGEROUS (LP)	£18
76	Warner Bros. K 56226	SO LET US ENTERTAIN YOU (LP)	£15
78	Salsoul SSLP 1503	DELUSIONS (LP)	£15
79	Salsoul SSLP 1514	HOLD YOUR HORSES (LP)	£15
93	Charly CPLP 8060	DELUSIONS (LP, reissue)	£15

FIRST CLASS
74	UK UKAL 1008	THE FIRST CLASS (LP)	£18
76	UK UKAL 1022	S.S.T. (LP)	£18

(see also White Plains, Brotherhood Of Man, Carter-Lewis & Southerners, Ivy League)

FIRST DOWN
90	Cobden Capers FD1	Jaw Warfare/From Now On/Dedication	£70
93	Ill Gotten Gains FD002	LET THE BATTLE BEGIN (EP)	£25
94	Blitz Vinyl EFA61009	WORLD SERVICE (LP)	£18

FIRST EDITION
68	Reprise RS 20655	**Just Dropped In** (To See What Condition My Condition Was In)/**Shadow In The Corner Of Your Mind**	**£40**
68	Reprise RSLP 6276	**THE FIRST EDITION** (LP)	**£15**

(see also Kenny Rogers)

FIRST GEAR
64	Pye 7N 15703	**A Certain Girl/Leave My Kitten Alone**	**£200**
65	Pye 7N 15763	**The 'In' Crowd/Gotta Make Their Future Bright**	**£70**

FIRST IMPRESSION/GOOD EARTH
68	Saga FID 2117	**SWINGING LONDON** (LP)	**£25**

(see also Good Earth, Mungo Jerry)

FIRST IMPRESSIONS
65	Pye 7N 15797	**I'm Coming Home/Looking For Her**	**£25**

(see also Legends)

FIRST OFFENCE
88	Metal Other OTH 11	**FIRST OFFENCE** (LP, with insert)	**£30**
88	Metal Other OTH 11	**FIRST OFFENCE** (LP, without insert)	**£25**

1ST OFFENCE
82	Chaos	**NIGHT THE PUNKS TURNED UGLY EP** (fold out sleeve)	**£15**

1ST QUOTE
96	Groove Yard GYARD 10	**BUMP AND GRIND EP** (12")	**£20**

FIRST REFUSAL
78	Rainbow RSL 015	**FIRST REFUSAL EP** (500 only)	**£40**

FIRST STEPS
80	English Rose ER I	**The Beat Is Back/She Ain't In Love/Let's Go Cuboids** (p/s, with insert)	**£30**
81	English Rose ER III	**Anywhere Else But Here/Airplay/I Got The News** (p/s)	**£20**

FIRST COLLABORATION
72	Cavendish CAV 8	**FIRST COLLABORATION** (LP)	**£50**

CLARE FISCHER
62	Fontana 688124 ZL	**FIRST TIME OUT** (LP)	**£15**

WILD MAN FISCHER
69	Reprise RSLP 6332	**AN EVENING WITH WILD MAN FISCHER** (LP, gatefold sleeve)	**£60**

(see also Frank Zappa)

FISCHERSPOONER
01	International Deejay Gigolo Records GIGOLO 70	**#1** (2-LP)	**£40**
02	FS Studios FSMOSLP1	**#1** (LP, remastered and re-sequenced)	**£35**
05	FS Studios FSLPDJ 2	**ODYSSEY** (2-LP, picture disc)	**£45**

F F & Z (FISHBAUGH FISHBAUGH & ZORN)
72	CBS 8163	**Everybody Got Out Of Bed/Spaced On Happy**	**£20**
72	CBS 64783	**FISHBAUGH, FISHBAUGH & ZORN** (LP)	**£25**

ARCHIE FISHER
68	Xtra XTRA 1070	**ARCHIE FISHER** (LP)	**£25**
70	Decca SKL 5057	**ORFEO** (LP)	**£50**
76	Topic 12TS 277	**WILL YE GANG LOVE** (LP)	**£20**
82	Celtic Music CM 007	**ARCHIE FISHER** (LP, reissue)	**£20**

(see also Barbara Dickson)

ARCHIE FISHER, BARBARA DICKSON & JOHN MACKINNON
69	Trailer LER 3002	**THE FATE O' CHARLIE: SONGS OF THE JACOBITE REBELLIONS** (LP, first pressing, white label)	**£60**
69	Trailer LER 3002	**THE FATE O' CHARLIE: SONGS OF THE JACOBITE REBELLIONS** (LP, second pressing, red label)	**£30**

CHIP FISHER
59	Parlophone R 4604	**Poor Me/No One**	**£15**
59	RCA RCX 143	**AT THE SUGAR BOWL** (EP)	**£60**

CILLA FISHER & ARTIE TREZISE
76	Trailer LER 2100	**BALCANQUHAL** (LP, yellow label)	**£15**
79	Kettle KAC 1	**FOR FOUL DAY AND FAIR** (LP)	**£15**

EDDIE FISHER
53	HMV 7M 101	**I'm Yours/That's The Chance You Take**	**£15**
53	HMV 7M 117	**Outside Of Heaven/Lady Of Spain**	**£15**
56	HMV POP 273	**Cindy, Oh Cindy/Fanny**	**£15**

MARY ANN FISHER
11	Jukebox Jab JBJ 1018	**Put On My Shoes/Wild As You Can Be** (reissue)	**£20**

MATTHEW FISHER
73	RCA SF8380	**JOURNEY'S END** (LP)	**£18**
74	RCA APL 1	**I'LL BE THERE** (LP)	**£15**

(see also Procol Harum, Green Bullfrog)

RAY FISHER
72	Trailer LER 2038	**THE BONNY BIRD** (LP, red label)	**£25**

SONNY FISHER
77	Ace NST 59	**Rockin' Daddy/I Can't Lose** (78)	**£18**

MINT VALUE £

WILLIE FISHER
77	Jama JA 35	Put Your Lovin' On Me/Take Time To Know Her	£30

FISH GOAT & SUFFURAH
93	Sound N Presuure SNP 001	Warm The Nation/Version (12")	£20

FISH TURNED HUMAN
79	Sequel PART 1	TURKEYS IN CHINA (EP)	£15

FIST
80	Neat NEAT 04	Name Rank And Serial Number/You'll Never Get Me In One Of Those (p/s, with poster insert)	£15
80	MCA MCA 615	Name Rank And Serial Number/You'll Never Get Me (In One Of Those) (p/s, reissue, with poster insert)	£30
80	MCA MCA 615	Name Rank And Serial Number/You'll Never Get Me (In One Of Those) (p/s, reissue, without poster insert)	£20
81	MCA MCA 663	Collision Course/Law Of The Jungle (p/s)	£100
81	MCA MCA 663	Collision Course/Law Of The Jungle	£30
80	MCA MCF 3082	TURN THE HELL ON (LP)	£15
82	Neat NEAT 1003	BACK WITH A VENGEANCE (LP, yellow vinyl)	£30
82	Neat NEAT 1003	BACK WITH A VENGEANCE (LP)	£15

JOHN FITCH & ASSOCIATES
71	Beacon BEA 117	Romantic Altitude/Stoned Out Of It	£90

FITS
82	Rondelet ABOUT 6	YOU'RE NOTHING, YOU'RE NOWHERE (LP)	£15

FITZ & COOLERS
68	Nu Beat NB 003	Cover Me/Darling	£20

ELLA FITZGERALD
SINGLES
66	Stateside SS 569	These Boots Were Made For Walkin'/Stardust (DJ Copy)	£50
69	Reprise RS 20850	Get Ready/Open Your Window	£30

ALBUMS
53	Brunswick LA 8581	SOUVENIR ALBUM (10")	£15
54	Brunswick LA 8648	ELLA SINGS GERSHWIN (10")	£15
55	Brunswick LAT 8056	ELLA — SONGS IN A MELLOW MOOD	£15
56	Brunswick LAT 8091	SWEET AND HOT	£15
56	Brunswick LAT 8115	LULLABIES OF BIRDLAND	£15
68	Polydor 583737	SUNSHINE OF YOUR LOVE (LP)	£20

(see also Count Basie)

ELLA FITZGERALD & LOUIS ARMSTRONG
56	HMV CLP 1098	ELLA AND LOUIS (LP)	£20

ELLA FITZGERALD/BILLIE HOLIDAY
58	Columbia Clef 33CX 10100	AT NEWPORT (LP)	£15

G.F. FITZGERALD
70	Uni UNLS 115	MOUSEPROOF (LP, gatefold sleeve, with insert, yellow swirl label)	£200

PATRIK FITZGERALD
79	Polydor 2383 533	GRUBBY STORIES (LP)	£15
82	Red Flame EF8	GIFTS & TELEGRAMS (LP)	£20

FITZROY (STERLING) & HARRY
70	Bullet BU 439	Reggae Sounds Are Boss/Goodbye My Love	£30
70	Escort ERT 827	Pop A Top Train/Doing The Moonwalk	£25

FIVE AMERICANS
66	Pye International 7N 25354	I See The Light/The Outcasts	£25
66	Pye International 7N 25373	Evol — Not Love/Don't Blame Me	£20

5 A.M. EVENT
66	Pye 7N 17154	Hungry/I Wash My Hands (In Muddy Water)	£325

FIVE & A PENNY
68	Polydor 56282	You Don't Know Where Your Interest Lies/Mary Go Round	£75
77	Polydor 56282	You Don't Know Where Your Interest Lies/Mary Go Round (2nd pressing injection moulded)	£25

FIVE BLIND BOYS
64	Vocalion EPVP 1276	NEGRO SPIRITUALS (EP, 2 tracks by Spirits Of Memphis)	£20

FIVE BLOBS
58	Philips PB 881	The Blob/Saturday Night In Tijuana	£20

FIVE BY FIVE
68	Pye International 7N 25477	Fire/Hang Up	£70

FIVE CARD STUD
67	Philips BF 1567	Beg Me/Once	£15

FIVE CHESTERNUTS
58	Columbia DB 4165	Jean Dorothy/Teenage Love	£200
58	Columbia DB 4165	Jean Dorothy/Teenage Love (78)	£100

(see also Shadows, Pete Chester)

FIVE COUNTS
62	Oriole CBA 1769	Watermelon Walk/Spanish Nights	£30

FIVE CRESTAS
66   Excel ES SP 288/289   How Sweet It Is (To Be Loved By You)/**You Used To Love Me** (private pressing)..............£100

FIVE DAY RAIN
70   Private pressing   **FIVE DAY RAIN** (LP, no sleeve, 20-30 copies only)..£2000
93   Private pressing   **FIVE DAY RAIN** (LP, re-pressing in signed, numbered sleeve, signed note in run-out groove & letter of authenticity, 25 only)..........£80

(see also Scots Of St. James, Hopscotch, One Way Ticket, Glencoe)

FIVE DAY WEEK STRAW PEOPLE
68   Saga FID 2123   **FIVE DAY WEEK STRAW PEOPLE** (LP, black/silver labels) £200

(see also Attack, Andromeda, John Du Cann)

FIVE DU-TONES
63   Stateside SS 206   **Shake A Tail Feather/Divorce Court** £20

FIVE EMPREES
65   Stateside SS 470   **Little Miss Sad/Hey Lover**...£20

FIVE FINGER DEATH PUNCH
09   Park/Spinefarm   **WAR IS THE ANSWER** (2-LP, red vinyl) £20
     SPI360LP.272045

FIVE FLEETS
58   Felsted AF 103   **Oh What A Feeling/I Been Cryin'** £100
58   Felsted AF 103   **Oh What A Feeling/I Been Cryin'** (78) £40

FIVE GO DOWN TO THE SEA
83   Kabuki KAFIVE 5   **KNOT A FISH** (EP) £15

FIVE KEYS
54   Capitol CL 14184   **Ling, Ting, Tong/I'm Alone** £300
54   Capitol CL 14184   **Ling, Ting, Tong/I'm Alone** (78) £50
55   Capitol CL 14313   **The Verdict/Make Me Um Pow Pow** (triangular centre) £300
55   Capitol CL 14313   **The Verdict/Make Me Um Pow Pow** (78) £50
55   Capitol CL 14325   **(Close Your Eyes) Take A Deep Breath/Doggone It, You Did It** (tri centre) £300
55   Capitol CL 14325   **(Close Your Eyes) Take A Deep Breath/Doggone It, You Did It** (78) £40
56   Capitol CL 14545   **Gee Whittakers!/'Cause You're My Lover**...£300
56   Capitol CL 14545   **Gee Whittakers!/'Cause You're My Lover** (78) £25
56   Capitol CL 14582   **She's The Most/I Dreamt I Dwelt In Heaven** £250
56   Capitol CL 14582   **She's The Most/I Dreamt I Dwelt In Heaven** (78) £25
56   Capitol CL 14639   **That's Right/Out Of Sight, Out Of Mind** £150
56   Capitol CL 14639   **That's Right/Out Of Sight, Out Of Mind** (78) £20
57   Capitol CL 14686   **The Wisdom Of A Fool/Now Don't That Prove I Love You?** £150
57   Capitol CL 14686   **The Wisdom Of A Fool/Now Don't That Prove I Love You?** (78) £25
57   Capitol CL 14736   **Four Walls/Let There Be You** £100
57   Capitol CL 14736   **Four Walls/Let There Be You** (78) £30
57   Capitol CL 14756   **The Blues Don't Care/This I Promise You**...£150
57   Capitol CL 14756   **The Blues Don't Care/This I Promise You** (78) £40
58   Capitol CL 14829   **From Me To You/Whippety Whirl** £150
58   Capitol CL 14829   **From Me To You/Whippety Whirl** (78)...£45
58   Capitol CL 14967   **One Great Love/Really-O Truly-O** £150
57   Capitol T 828   **THE FIVE KEYS ON STAGE!** (LP) £200

FIVE MILES OUT
73   Action ACT 4614   **Super Sweet Girl Of Mine/Set Your Mind Free**...£25

FIVE NITES
64   Decca F 11963   **With A Loving Kiss/Let's Try Again**...£15

FIVE OF DIAMONDS
65   Oak RGJ 150 FD   **FIVE OF DIAMONDS** (EP) £400

FIVE ROYALES
60   Ember EMB S 124   **Dedicated To The One I Love/Miracle Of Love** £150

FIVE SATINS
57   London HL 8501   **To The Aisle/Wish I Had My Baby**..£450
57   London HL 8501   **To The Aisle/Wish I Had My Baby** (78)...£40
59   Top Rank JAR 199   **Wonderful Girl/Weeping Willow** £30
59   Top Rank JAR 239   **Shadows/Toni My Love** £50
60   MGM MGM 1087   **Your Memory/I Didn't Know** £60

FIVE SMITH BROTHERS
54   Decca F 10403   **A.B.C. Boogie/Veni-Vidi-Vici** (with Dennis Wilson Quartet) £20

FIVE STAIRSTEPS (& CUBIE)
70   Buddah 201 083   **Dear Prudence/O-o-h Child**...£15

(see also Stairsteps)

FIVE STEPS BEYOND
67   CBS 202490   **Not So Young Today/Meanwhile Back In My Heart** £25
95   Tenth Planet TP 019   **FAINT HEARTS AND FAIR MAIDS** (LP, 600 only)..£20
96   Tenth Planet TP 021   **SMILE** (LP, with A4 booklet, 600 only)...£20

FIVE THIRTY/5.30
87   Other 12 OTH 2   **THE CATCHER IN THE RYE EP** (12", p/s) £20

FIVE YEAR PLAN
87   Breaking Down Break 3   **Hit The Bottle/Swallow Your Pride** £20

FIVE'S COMPANY
66	Pye 7N 17118	Sunday For Seven Days/The Big Kill	£15
66	Pye 7N 17199	Session Man/Dejection	£20
69	Saga FID 2151	THE BALLAD OF FRED THE PIXIE (LP)	£20

(see also Brunning Hall Sunflower Blues Band)

5 SECONDS OF SUMMER
14	Capito l3797518	Amnesia/American Idiot (p/s)	£50
15	Capitol 4746076	She's Kinda Hot/The Girl Who Cried Wolf (p/s, red vinyl)	£30

THE 5, 6, 7, 8'S
04	Sweet Nothing 7SN028	Woo Hoo/Guitar Date (p/s)	£15
02	Sweet Nothing SNLP 035	TEENAGE MOJO WORKOUT (LP)	£15

FIVE STAR GAS
79	Warp Records SRTS/79/CUS - 540WARP 001	Smokey Bubble Shoo Fly Pie/Sledge Hammer (500 only, no p/s)	£20

5UU'S
88	RER Megacorp RER 33	ELEMENTS (LP)	£25

FIXED PENALTY
92	FPT 001	Man Of Action/All Of Us (12")	£18
92	FPT 002	To You/Bubble Up (12")	£20

FIXER
78	Rainbow RSL 116	Bright And Rosy/Peaceful Atom Bomb (no p/s)	£40

FIXIT
79	Ellie Jay SJSP9246	Eighteen Plus/April Fool	£50

FKA TWIGS
14	Young Turks YTLP 118X	LP 1 (LP, with free 7" and prints, gatefold)	£40

ROBERTA FLACK
69	Atlantic 588 204	FIRST TAKE (LP, 1st pressing, orange/plum label)	£40
71	Atlantic K 40097	CHAPTER TWO (LP)	£20
72	Atlantic K 40297	QUIET FIRE (LP)	£20
72	Atlantic K 40040	FIRST TAKE (LP, 2nd pressing, turquoise/orange label)	£15
73	Atlantic K 50021	KILLING ME SOFTLY (LP, folding piano sleeve)	£20
75	Atlantic K 50049	FEEL LIKE MAKIN' LOVE (LP)	£15

(see also Donny Hathaway)

FLACK OFF
80	Sofa SEAT 003	FLACK OFF EP: COCKTAILS AT SIX	£25

FLAIRS
57	Oriole CB 1392	Swing Pretty Mama/I'd Climb The Hills And Mountains	£500
57	Oriole CB 1392	Swing Pretty Mama/I'd Climb The Hills And Mountains (78)	£100

LES FLAMBEAUX
71	Mushroom 100 MR 13	LES FLAMBEAUX (LP, 2 different sleeve designs)	£30

FLAME
70	Stateside SS 2183	See The Light/Get Your Mind Made Up	£18
71	Stateside SSL 10312	THE FLAME (LP)	£40

(see also Flames [South Africa], Beach Boys)

FLAME 'N' KING & BOLD ONES
79	Grapevine GRP 123	Ho Happy Day/Ain't Nobody Jivin'	£30

FLAMES (SOUTH AFRICA)
68	Flame FAN 101/1	Streamliner/Follow The Sun (p/s)	£20
68	Page One FOR(S) 009	BURNING SOUL (LP)	£50

(see also Beach Boys)

FLAMES (1)
64	Island WI 130	He's The Greatest/Someone Going To Bawl (both actually by the Maytals)	£90
64	Island WI 136	Little Flea/Good Idea (both actually by the Maytals)	£40
64	Island WI 138	When I Get Home/Neither Silver Nor Gold (both actually by the Maytals)	£40
64	Island WI 139	Broadway Jungle/Beat Lied (both actually by the Maytals)	£200
64	Blue Beat BB 205	Helena Darling/My Darling (both actually by Plamers)	£40

(see also Maytals, Vikings)

FLAMES (2)
69	Nu Beat NB 028	You've Lost Your Date/Little Girl (B-side actually Stars by Cornel Campbell and Eternals)	£70
73	Ackee ACK 528	Feeling Good/Zig Zag	£30

(see also Alton Ellis & Flames, Righteous Flames, Larry Marshall, Winston Jarrett)

FLAMING GNOMES
09	Fruits De Mer Crustacean 05	Care Of Cell 44/Love Song With Flute (300 only, purple vinyl)	£30

FLAMING STARS
96	Vinyl Japan ASKLP 62	SONGS FROM THE BAR ROOM FLOOR (LP)	£25
99	Vinyl Japan ASKLP 83	PATHWAY (LP)	£20
00	Vinyl Japan ASKLP 121	A WALK ON THE WIRED SIDE (LP)	£20
02	Vinyl Japan ASKLP 139	SUNSET & VOID (LP)	£20
04	Vinyl Japan ASKLP 146	NAMED AND SHAMED (LP)	£20

FLAMING LIPS
89	Glitterhouse EFA 40153	Drug Machine In Heaven/Strychnine/What's So Funny (About Peace, Love And Understanding) (p/s)	£20

92	Warner Bros. PRO S 5452	**Ballrooms Of Mars/MR BUNGLE: Sudden Death** (promo, grey vinyl, no p/s)	£15
94	Warner Bros. SAM 1431	**She Don't Use Jelly/Translucent Egg/Turn It On** (Bluegrass Version)/**The Process** (12" promo)	£15
86	Enigma 2173-1	**HEAR IT IS** (LP with poster)	£15
89	Enigma ENVLP523	**TELEPATHIC SURGERY** (LP)	£20
90	City Slang SLANG 005	**IN A PRIEST DRIVEN AMBULANCE** (2-LP)	£18
03	Warner Bros. 9362481411	**YOSHIMI BATTLES THE PINK ROBOTS** (LP, inner sleeve, pink vinyl)	£30
06	Warner Bros. WEA 9362 49966-1	**AT WAR WITH THE MYSTICS** (2-LP, one orange & one turquoise LP)	£25
10	Warner Bros. 520857-1	**EMBRYONIC** (2-LP, blue/yellow vinyl)	£20
10	Warner Bros. 523541-1	**THE DARK SIDE OF THE MOON** (LP/CD, green vinyl, insert, 5000 only, RSD, worldwide release)	£40
13	Bella Union BELLAV 388	**THE TERROR** (2-LP, 7" and CD)	£25

JOHNNY FLAMINGO

57	Vogue V 9089	**My Teen-Age Girl/When I Lost You**	£100
57	Vogue V 9089	**My Teen-Age Girl/When I Lost You** (78)	£30
58	Vogue V 9100	**So Long/Make Me A Present Of You**	£75
58	Vogue V 9100	**So Long/Make Me A Present Of You** (78)	£40

FLAMINGOS

57	London HLN 8373	**Would I Be Crying?/Just For A Kick**	£600
57	London HLN 8373	**Would I Be Crying?/Just For A Kick** (78)	£100
57	Brunswick 05696	**The Ladder Of Love/Let's Make Up**	£500
57	Brunswick 05696	**The Ladder Of Love/Let's Make Up** (78)	£80
59	Top Rank JAR 213	**Love Walked In/Yours**	£50
60	Top Rank JAR 263	**I Only Have Eyes For You/I Was Such A Fool**	£60
60	Top Rank JAR 367	**Nobody Loves Me Like You/You, Me And The Sea**	£40
60	Top Rank JAR 519	**Mio Amore/At Night**	£35
66	Philips BF 1483	**Boogaloo Party/Nearness Of You**	£25
69	Philips SBL 7906	**HITS NOW AND THEN** (LP)	£30

FLAMIN' GROOVIES

72	United Artists UP 35392	**Slow Death/Talahassie Lassie** (in promo only p/s)	£60
71	Kama Sutra 2683 003	**FLAMIN' GROOVIES** (2-LP)	£20
76	Sire 9103 251	**SHAKE SOME ACTION** (LP)	£30
78	Sire 9103 333	**THE FLAMIN' GROOVIES NOW!** (LP)	£20
86	Edsel ED 173	**SUPERSNAZZ** (LP, reissue)	£18
88	Dojo DOJOLP 58	**TEENAGE HEAD** (LP, reissue)	£15

(see also Mike Wilhelm)

FLAMING YOUTH

69	Fontana TF 1057	**Guide Me Orion/From Now On** (Immortal Invisible)	£20
70	Fontana 6001 002	**Every Man, Woman And Child/Drifting**	£18
70	Fontana 6001 003	**From Now On/Space Child**	£18
69	Fontana STL 5533	**ARK II** (LP, with laminated multifold plastic window sleeve)	£150
69	Fontana STL 5533	**ARK II** (LP, later sleeve pressing with unlaminated multifold plastic window sleeve)	£60
69	Fontana STL 5533	**ARK II** (LP, gatefold sleeve, white front, black/silver labels)	£50

(see also Genesis, Jackson Heights)

FLAMMA-SHERMAN

68	SNB 55-3488	**No Need To Explain/Bassa Love**	£20
68	SNB 55-3769	**Love Is In The Air/Super Day**	£18
69	SNB 55-4142	**Move Me/Where Is He**	£18
69	SNB 55-4142	**Move Me/Where Is He** (DJ copy)	£50

TOMMY FLANAGAN

59	Esquire 32-156	**THE CATS** (LP, with John Coltrane)	£75

FLANAGAN BROTHERS

58	Vogue Coral Q 72342	**Salton City/Early One Evening**	£20

TOMMY FLANDERS

69	Verve SVLP 6020	**MOONSTONE** (LP)	£25

(see also Blues Project)

FLARES

61	London HLU 9441	**Foot Stompin'/Hotcha Cha-Cha Brown**	£25
63	London HA-U 8034	**FOOT STOMPIN' HITS** (LP)	£75

FLASH

72	Sovereign SVNA 7251	**FLASH** (LP, laminated outer gatefold sleeve)	£35
72	Sovereign SVNA 7255	**FLASH IN THE CAN** (LP, in unissued 'band in studio' proof sleeve)	£25
72	Sovereign SVNA 7255	**FLASH IN THE CAN** (LP, gatefold sleeve)	£20
73	Sovereign SVNA 7260	**OUT OF OUR HANDS** (LP, gatefold sleeve)	£30

(see also Peter Banks, Yes)

FLASH CADILLAC & THE CONTINENTAL KIDS

75	Private Stock PVLP 1002	**SONS OF THE BEACHES** (LP)	£15

FLASHBACK

82	Aaron FB 001	**Angel/You Won't Change Me/Don't Mess With The Best** (no p/s)	£30

FLASHPOINT

87	Private pressing FP 01	**NO POINT OF REFERENCE** (LP)	£40

FLAT EARTH SOCIETY

83	Psycho PSYCHO 17	**WALEECO** (LP)	£20

FLATMATES
13	Optic Nerve OPT4 007	POTPOURRI (2-LP, pink vinyl)	£20

JACKIE FLAVELLE
72	York FYK 408	ADMISSION FREE (LP)	£25

FLAVOR (1)
68	Direction 58-3597	Sally Had A Party/Shop Around	£15

FLAVOR (2)
77	Tamla Motown STML 12066	IN GOOD TASTE (LP)	£15

FLEE REKKERS
60	Triumph RGM 1008	Green Jeans/You Are My Sunshine (as Fabulous Flee-Rakkers)	£25
60	Top Rank JAR 431	Green Jeans/You Are My Sunshine (reissue, as Fabulous Flea-Rakkers)	£30
60	Pye 7N 15288	Sunday Date/Shiftless Sam	£20
61	Piccadilly 7N 35006	Lone Rider/Miller Like Wow	£15
62	Piccadilly 7N 35048	Stage To Cimarron/Twistin' The Chestnuts	£15
62	Piccadilly 7N 35081	Sunburst/Black Buffalo	£15
63	Piccadilly 7N 35109	Fireball/Fandango	£15
61	Pye NEP 24141	THE FABULOUS FLEE-REKKERS (EP)	£40
91	C5 C5 564	JOE MEEK'S FABULOUS FLEE REKKERS (LP)	£15

FLEETWOOD MAC
SINGLES
67	Blue Horizon 57-3051	I Believe My Time Ain't Long/Rambling Pony (as Peter Green's Fleetwood Mac, p/s)	£100
67	Blue Horizon 57-3051	I Believe My Time Ain't Long/Rambling Pony (as Peter Green's Fleetwood Mac)	£20
69	Blue Horizon 57-3157	Need Your Love So Bad/Black Magic Woman (unissued)	£0
69	Blue Horizon 57-3157	Black Magic Woman/No Place To Go (unissued)	£0
70	Reprise RS 27007	The Green Manalishi (With The Two-Prong Crown)/ World In Harmony (with p/s)	£30

ALBUMS
68	Blue Horizon 7-63200	PETER GREEN'S FLEETWOOD MAC (mono, laminated front cover)	£250
68	Blue Horizon 7-63200	PETER GREEN'S FLEETWOOD MAC (stereo, with stereo sticker, laminated front)	£175
68	Blue Horizon 7-63205	MR. WONDERFUL (LP, mono, gatefold sleeve)	£100
68	Blue Horizon (S)7-63205	MR. WONDERFUL (LP, stereo, gatefold sleeve)	£75
69	Blue Horizon S 7-63215	THE PIOUS BIRD OF GOOD OMEN	£40
69	Reprise RSLP 9000	THEN PLAY ON (gatefold sleeve, 'steamboat' label)	£100
70	Reprise RSLP 9004	KILN HOUSE (gatefold sleeve, with insert)	£80
70	Reprise RSLP 9004	KILN HOUSE (gatefold sleeve, without insert)	£60
71	CBS Blue Horizon 63875	THE ORIGINAL FLEETWOOD MAC	£30
72	Reprise K 44181	BARE TREES	£20
77	Reprise K 54043	FLEETWOOD MAC (white vinyl with lyric sheet)	£20
77	Warner K 56344	RUMOURS (LP, textured sleeve, 4-page lyric insert)	£35
77	Warner Bros K 56344	RUMOURS (white vinyl with lyric sheet)	£40
79	Warner Bros. K 66088	TUSK (2LP, embossed sleeve, printed inners within inners)	£25

(see also Peter Green, Buckingham-Nicks, Jeremy Spencer, Christine Perfect, Danny Kirwan, John Mayall, Otis Spann, Eddie Boyd, Duster Bennett, Chicken Shack, Shotgun Express, Bo Street Runners, Cheynes, Tramp, Brunning Hall Sunflower Blues Band)

FLEETWOODS
59	London HLU 4003	Come Softly To Me/I Care So Much (stereo export issue)	£15
60	Top Rank JAR 294	Outside My Window/Magic Star (in p/s)	£20
60	Top Rank BUY 028	MR BLUE (LP, with 3 tracks by Little Bill & Bluenotes, Frantics and Bonnie Guitar)	£20
61	London HA-G 2388	SOFTLY (LP, mono)	£30
61	London SAH-G 6188	SOFTLY (LP, stereo)	£40
61	London HA-G 2419	DEEP IN A DREAM (LP)	£30

GARFIELD FLEMING
19	Becket BKD 505	Don't Send Me Away/You Got Dat Right (12", reissue)	£15
18	Cordial CORD 12001	GARFIELD FLEMING (LP)	£15

HELEN FLEMING
66	Blue Beat BB 341	Eve's Ten Commandments/Don't Take Your Love Away	£35

WADE FLEMONS
60	Top Rank JAR 371	Easy Lovin'/Woops Now	£15

FLESHEATERS
81	Initial IRC 007	A MINUTE TO PRAY, A SECOND TO DIE (LP)	£18

AMELIA FLETCHER
91	Fierce FRIGHT 052	Can You Keep A Secret/Wrap My Arms Around Him (p/s)	£20

(see also Heavenly, Talulah Gosh)

DARROW FLETCHER
66	London HLU 10024	The Pain Gets A Little Deeper/My Judgement Day	£75
66	London HLU 10024	The Pain Gets A Little Deeper/My Judgement Day (DJ copy)	£150

DON FLETCHER
66	Vocalion VP 9271	Two Wrongs Don't Make A Right/I'm So Glad	£25

GUY FLETCHER
71	Philips 6303013	GUY FLETCHER (LP, gatefold sleeve, black/silver labels)	£25

FLEUR-DE-LYS
65	Immediate IM 020	Moondreams/Wait For Me	£300
66	Immediate IM 032	Circles/So Come On	£800
66	Polydor 56124	Mud In Your Eye/I've Been Trying	£800
67	Polydor 56200	I Can See A Light/Prodigal Son	£100

MINT VALUE £

68	Polydor 56251	Gong With The Luminous Nose/Hammer Head	£300
68	Atlantic 584 193	Stop Crossing The Bridge/Brick By Brick (Stone By Stone)	£60
69	Atlantic 584 243	Liar/One Girl City	£300

(see also John Bromley, Terry Durham, Tony & Tandy, Sharon Tandy, Rupert's People, Shyster, Quotations, Chocolate Frog, Gordon Haskell, Waygood Ellis)

FLEURITY
| 94 | Aesthetic Death ADEP 001 | A DARKER SHADE OF EVIL EP (p/s) | £20 |
| 08 | Aesthetic Death ADLP 001 | MIN TID SKAL KOMME (2-LP, numbered sleeve, insert, 600 only) | £18 |

VIC FLICK SOUND
67	Rediffusion International RIM 1	Sexton Blake/West Of Winward	£15
70	Chapter One CH 136	Hang On/Wonderful World	£15
68	Rediffusion ZS5	WEST OF WINWARD (LP)	£20

FLICK OF THE WRIST
| 81 | Do Nutt 0101 | Movietone/Ruth (no p/s) | £100 |

FLIES
66	Decca F 12533	I'm Not Your Stepping Stone/Talk To Me	£175
67	Decca F 12594	House Of Love/It Had To Be You	£80
68	RCA RCA 1757	The Magic Train/Gently As You Feel	£75

(see also Bulldog Breed, T2)

FLIGHT 77
| 82 | Flight 77 | Looking For The Aliens/Stranger (p/s) | £25 |

MICK FLINN BAND
| 78 | EMI EMI 2805 | Doin' It Right/Do What You Wanna Do | £20 |

(see also Mixtures)

SHELBY FLINT
| 66 | London HLT 10068 | Cast Your Fate To The Wind/The Lilly | £20 |

FLINT (2)
| 03 | Coolkills 980009-9 | ASTEROIDS (1-sided pink neon 10", p/s with inner) | £30 |

(see also The Prodigy)

FLINTSTONES
| 64 | HMV POP 1266 | Safari/Work Out | £20 |

BUNNY FLIP
| 72 | Pressure Beat PB 5510 | Shanky Dog (actually "Skanky Dog" by Winston Scotland)/JOE GIBBS & NOW GENERATION: Boney Dog | £15 |

(see also Winston Scotland, Peter Tosh)

FLIP & DATELINERS
| 64 | HMV POP 1359 | My Johnny Doesn't Come Around Anymore/Please Listen To Me | £60 |

FLIPPER
| 81 | Alt. Tentacles VIRUS 8 | Ha Ha Ha/Love Canal (p/s, with insert) | £15 |
| 82 | Subterranean SUB UK1 | ALBUM GENERIC FLIPPER (LP) | £25 |

FLIRTATIONS
68	Deram DM 216	Nothing But A Heartache/Christmas Time Is Here Again	£35
71	Polydor 2058 167	Little Darlin'/Take Me In Your Arms And Love Me	£20
69	Deram DML/SML 1046	SOUNDS LIKE THE FLIRTATIONS (LP)	£40
72	Deram SPA 218	THE WORLD OF THE FLIRTATIONS (LP)	£15
75	RCA SF8448	LOVE MAKES THE WORLD GO ROUND (LP)	£15

(see also Gypsies)

FLO & EDDIE
| 72 | Reprise K 44201 | THE PHLORESCENT LEECH AND EDDIE (LP) | £15 |
| 73 | Reprise K 44234 | FLO AND EDDIE (LP) | £15 |

(see also Turtles, Frank Zappa/Mothers Of Invention)

FLOATING BRIDGE
| 69 | Liberty LBS 83271 | FLOATING BRIDGE (LP) | £100 |

FLOATING OPERA
| 74 | DJM DJS 321 | Keep On Streaking/Home Run | £20 |

FLOATING POINTS
11	Eglo EGLO 22	SHADOWS EP (2 x 12", 1st pressing, 180gram, gatefold)	£30
15	Pluto FPLP 01	ELAENIA (LP)	£18
17	Pluto RE001LP	REFLECTIONS - MOJAVE DESERT (LP, with DVD)	£18
19	Ninja Tune ZEN 259	CRUSH (LP)	£18
20	Luaka Bop 6 80899 0097-1-3	PROMISES (LP, with London Symphony Orchestra and Pharoah Saunders)	£20
21	Luaka Bop 6 80899 0097-1-3/0097	PROMISES (LP, reissue, blue marbled or yellow marbled vinyl with London Symphony Orchestra and Pharoah Saunders)	£80

(see also Maalem Mahmoud Guinia)

FLOCK
70	CBS 4932	Tired Of Waiting For You/Store Bought — Store Thought	£15
69	CBS 63733	THE FLOCK (LP, orange label)	£15
70	CBS 64055	DINOSAUR SWAMPS (LP, orange label, gatefold sleeve)	£20

(see also Mahavishnu Orchestra)

FLORENCE AND THE MACHINE
08	Moshi Moshi MOMO15	Kiss With A Fist/Hospital Beds (p/s)	£15
08	Moshi Moshi 171	Dog Days Are Over/You've Got The Love (p/s)	£15
09	Moshi Moshi 2710003	Rabbit Heart (Raise It Up)/Are You Hurting The One You Love? (p/s)	£15
09	Moshi Moshi 2718895	Drumming Song (Acoustic)/My Boy Builds A Coffin (Acoustic)	£15

MINT VALUE £

09	Moshi Moshi 2726062	You've Got The Love/You've Got The Love (Jamie XX Re-Write) (p/s)	£20
10	Moshi Moshi 2736273	Dog Days Are Over/Dog Days Are Over (Optimo Mix)	£15
10	Moshi Moshi 2744152	Cosmic Love/Cosmic Love (Isa Machine Mix)	£15
11	Vinyl Factory VF-04X	Never Let Me Go/Never Let Me Go (Clams Casino Mix) (12" white vinyl, hand numbered, 500 only)	£60
11	Vinyl Factory VF-04Y	Spectrum/Spectrum (Calvin Harris Mix)/Spectrum (Aluna George Mix)/Spectrum (Mary Jane Coles Mix (12" white vinyl hand numbered, 500 only)	£50
11	Vinyl Factory VF 035	Shake It Out/Shake It Out (Weekend Remix) (12" white vinyl, hand numbered, 500 copies)	£60
12	Universal/Talenthouse S76	Only If For A Night (1-sided, 100 only)	£60
12	Vinyl Factory VF 038	No Light, No Light/No Light, No Light (DAS Mix) (12" white vinyl, hand numbered, 500 only)	£70
12	Vinyl Factory VF 044	Never Let Me Go/Clams Casino Remix (12" p/s, white vinyl, numbered)	£35
09	Island 2709106	LUNGS (LP)	£20
11	Island 2784790	CEREMONIALS (2-LP)	£20
15	Island GB-UM7-15-00288	HOW BIG, HOW BLUE, HOW BEAUTIFUL (LP as 6 x 7")	£60
15	Island 602547244956	HOW BIG, HOW BLUE, HOW BEAUTIFUL (2-LP)	£20

FLORIBUNDA ROSE

| 67 | Piccadilly 7N 35408 | One Way Street/Linda Loves Linda | £60 |

(see also Scrugg, John T. Kongos)

FLOWERS FOR AGATHA

| 85 | Off Beat OB 10 | Presentation/The Thickest Head (p/s) | £20 |
| 86 | Leeds Independent 12 LIL 8 | YOUNG FOOLISH OLD AND STUPID EP (12" p/s) | £15 |

FLOWERS & FROLICS

| 77 | Free Reed FRR 016 | BEES ON HORSEBACK (LP, featuring June Tabor & Bob Davenport) | £35 |

FLOWERS IN THE DUSTBIN

| 84 | All The Madmen MAD 7 | FREAKS RUN WILD IN THE DISCO (12" EP) | £20 |

LLOYD FLOWERS & RECO'S RHYTHM GROUP

| 62 | Blue Beat BB 88 | I'm Going Home/Lover's Town | £15 |

PHIL FLOWER(S)

| 69 | A&M AMS 766 | Like A Rolling Stone/Keep On Sockin' It Children | £20 |

FLOWERS OF EVIL

| 82 | Marching Men MAME 001 | First Blood/Joy (p/s) | £20 |

FLOWER TRAVELLING BAND

| 71 | Atlantic 2091 128 | Satori (Enlightment) (Parts 1 & 2) | £20 |

BOBBY FLOYD

| 72 | Pama PM 860 | Sound Doctor/YOUNG DILLINGER: Doctor Skank | £50 |

EDDIE FLOYD

67	Speciality SPE 1001	Never Get Enough Of Your Love/Bye Bye Baby	£20
67	Stax 601 016	Things Get Better/Good Love, Bad Love	£15
67	Stax 601 024	On A Saturday Night/Under My Nose	£15
68	Stax 601 035	Big Bird/Holding On With Both Hands	£30
68	Stax STAX 104	I've Never Found A Girl (To Love Me Like You Do)/I'm Just The Kind Of Fool	£15
67	Stax 589 006	KNOCK ON WOOD (LP)	£50
68	Stax (S)XATS 1003	I'VE NEVER FOUND A GIRL (LP)	£30
69	Stax SXATS 1023	YOU'VE GOT TO HAVE EDDIE (LP)	£30
70	Stax SXATS 1036	CALIFORNIA GIRL (LP)	£20
74	Stax STX 1002	SOUL STREET (LP)	£15
88	Stax SX 010	THE BEST OF EDDIE FLOYD (LP)	£15

(see also Falcons, Primettes/Eddie Floyd)

WOLFGANG FLUR

| 15 | Cherry Red SFELP 046D | ELOQUENCE - COMPLETE WORKS (2-LP, clear vinyl) | £18 |

(see also Kraftwerk)

FLUX OF PINK INDIANS

| 83 | Spiderleg SDL 8 | STRIVE TO SURVIVE CAUSING THE LEAST SUFFERING POSSIBLE (LP, with booklet) | £35 |
| 84 | Spiderleg SDL 13 | THE FUCKING CUNTS TREAT US LIKE PRICKS (2-LP) | £20 |

(see also Epileptics, Licks)

FLY ON THE WALL

| 79 | Next Wave NEXT 1 | DEVON DUMB (EP, numbered, 1000 only) | £35 |

FLYING BRIX

| 80 | Modello MHMS 194 | BLACK COLOURS EP (p/s, with booket, 500 only) | £20 |

FLYING BURRITO BROTHERS

69	A&M AML(S) 931	THE GILDED PALACE OF SIN (LP)	£30
70	A&M AMLS 983	BURRITO DELUXE (LP)	£18
71	A&M AMLS 64295	THE FLYING BURRITO BROTHERS (LP)	£15

(see also Byrds, Gram Parsons, Gene Parsons, Stephen Stills & Manassas, Country Gazette, Skip Battin)

FLYING CIRCUS

| 71 | Harvest SHSP 4010 | PREPARED IN PEACE (LP, no EMI box on label) | £75 |

FLYING COLOURS

| 81 | No Records NO 1 | Abstract Art/Ape Notes (p/s) | £25 |

FLYING IS EASY

| 70 | High Key HK1 | Stone Cross/Magic Pastures | £50 |

FLYING LIZARDS

| 80 | Virgin V2150 | FLYING LIZARDS (LP) | £20 |

| 81 | Virgin V2190 | FOURTH WALL (LP) | £18 |

FLYING LOTUS
07	Warp WAP 228	Reset (12")	£15
08	Warp WARPLP 165	LOS ANGELS (2-LP)	£25
10	Warp WARPLP 195	COSMOGRAMMA (2-LP, plastic sleeves and grease proof sleeve, MP3 download)	£20
12	Warp WARPLP230	UNTIL THE QUIET COMES (2-LP)	£20
14	Warp WARPLP 256	YOU'RE DEAD (2-LP)	£20
19	Warp WARPLP 291	FLAMAGRA (2-LP)	£20

FLYING MACHINE
| 70 | Pye 7N 45001 | The Devil Has Possession Of Your Mind/Hey Little Girl | £30 |
| 70 | Pye NSPL 18328 | DOWN TO EARTH WITH THE FLYING MACHINE (LP, blue/black label with logo-banner on top) | £40 |

(see also Pinkertons, Pinkerton's Assorted Colours, Tony Newman)

FLYING SAUCER ATTACK
92	Heartbeat FSA 6	Soaring High/Standing Stone (p/s, 500 only, 1st few with autographed postcards)	£25
92	Heartbeat FSA 6	Soaring High/Standing Stone (p/s, 500 only, with various different designs)	£20
93	Heartbeat FSA 61	Wish/Oceans (p/s, 700 only)	£20
93	Heartbeat FSA 62	FLYING SAUCER ATTACK (LP, 1st pressing, 1,000 only, black and white sleeve, hand numbered, booklet insert)	£50
93	FSA FAS 62	FLYING SAUCER ATTACK (LP, 2nd pressing, 923 copies, coloured sleeve, insert)	£25
93	FSA FAS 62	FLYING SAUCER ATTACK (LP, 3rd pressing, 1,000 only, blue vinyl, stamped white sleeve, photocopied insert)	£25
94	Domino WIGLP 12	DISTANCE (LP)	£15
94	Domino WIGLP 20	FURTHER (LP, gatefold sleeve, insert)	£20
95	Domino WIGLP 22	CHORUS (LP, inert)	£15
97	Domino WIGLP 38	NEW LANDS (LP)	£20
00	FSA 64	MIRROR (LP, clear vinyl)	£18

FLYING SAUCERS
| 76 | Nevis NEV LP 114 | PLANET OF THE DRAPES (LP) | £15 |
| 91 | Rawking Music | THE ROCKING SANDY FORD (LP) | £25 |

JOHNNY FLYNN
| 08 | Vertigo 1766662 | A LARUM (LP, pop up sleeve) | £80 |

STEVE FLYNN
| 67 | Parlophone R 5625 | Mr Rainbow/Let's Live For Tomorrow | £50 |

(see also Mark Wirtz)

FLYS
78	EMI EMI 2747	Love And A Molotov Cocktail/Can I Crash Here?/Civilisation (p/s)	£20
79	EMI EMI 2936	Name Dropping/Fly V Fly (p/s, some on green vinyl)	£15
77	Zama ZA 10 EP	BUNCH OF FIVE (33rpm EP, die-cut p/s)	£50
80	Parlophone R 6063	FOUR FROM THE SQUARE (demo copies)	£20
78	EMI EMC 3249	WAIKIKI BEACH REFUGEES (LP)	£15

FLYTE REACTION
| 91 | Woronzow W0014 | SONGS IN A CIRCLE (LP) | £20 |

FOALS
06	Try Harder	Try This On Your Piano/Look At My Furrows Of Worry (700 only, hand-numbered)	£35
07	Transgressive TRANS 049	FOALS LIVE (12" promo, 1000 only p/s)	£25
07	Transgressive TRANS 050	Hummer/Astronaut And All (p/s, 1000 only)	£20
07	Transgressive TRANS 053	Mathletics/Big Big Love (1,500 only)	£18
08	Transgressive TRANS 071LP	ANTIDOTES (LP, insert, poster, stickered sleeve)	£50
10	Warner Bros. 5051865913900	TOTAL LIFE FOREVER (LP)	£35
13	Warner Bros. 825646522248	HOLY FIRE (LP)	£20
13	Warner Bros. 825646521388	HOLY FIRE (Box set, marbled vinyl LP, CD, DVD, 7", numbered)	£60

FOAMPLATE
| 16 | System SYSTM 012 | Lionize/696 (12") | £40 |

GREG FOAT GROUP
11	Jazzman JMANLP041	DARK IS THE SUN (LP, 1st pressing)	£40
12	Jazzman JMANLP054	GIRL AND ROBOT WITH FLOWERS (LP)	£20
15	Jazzman JMANLP041	DARK IS THE SUN (LP, repressing, purple and silver screen printed cover)	£15

FOCAL POINT
| 68 | Deram DM 186 | Love You Forever/Sycamore Sid | £60 |

FO'C'SLE
| 72 | Tradition TSC 1 | FROM THE FOREST (LP, 100 copies only) | £25 |

FOCUS
71	Blue Horizon 2094 006	Hocus Pocus/Janis	£15
72	Blue Horizon 2096 008	Tommy/Focus II	£15
71	Polydor 2344 003	IN AND OUT OF FOCUS (LP, gatefold sleeve)	£15
71	Blue Horizon 2096 2931	MOVING WAVES (LP, 1st pressing, white/blue labels, Matrixes: Side 1, 2931002 A etched (with 2431011 crossed out) A/1 V 420 1 1 2, Side 2 2931002 B etched (243101 stamped not crossed out) B/1 V 420 11 4, Blue Horizon logo on rear of E.J. Group sleeve)	£25
72	Polydor 2659 016	FOCUS III (2-LP, gatefold sleeve)	£15
76	Harvest SHSP 4068	SHIP OF MEMORIES (LP)	£15
73	Polydor 2442 118	AT THE RAINBOW (multifold sleeve)	£15

(see also Jan Akkerman, Brainbox, Robin Lent)

THE FOCUS GROUP
| 11 | Ghost Box GBX 002 | SKETCHES AND SPELLS (LP) | £30 |
| 13 | Ghost Box GBX 018 | ELEKTRIK KAROUSEL (LP) | £18 |

FOCUS THREE
| 67 | Columbia DB 8279 | 10,000 Years Behind My Mind/The Sunkeeper | £80 |

FOETUS UNDER GLASS
| 85 | Self Immolation. WOMB S201 | Spite Your Face/OKFM (p/s) | £15 |

(see also You've Got Foetus On Your Breath, Philip & His Foetus Vibrations, Scraping Foetus Off The Wheel)

FOGCITY
| 93 | Houseplant/Mighty Force HP1061/MF005 | FOGCITY EP (12", white label, 250 only) | £20 |

FOGCUTTERS
| 64 | Liberty LIB 55793 | Cry Cry Cry/You Say | £15 |

JOHN FOGERTY
| 75 | Fantasy FT 526 | JOHN FOGERTY (LP) | £15 |

(see also Creedence Clearwater Revival, Blue Ridge Rangers)

FOGGY
73	York SYK 542	Kitty Starr/She's Far Away (p/s)	£15
72	York FYK 411	SIMPLE GIFTS (LP, with insert, featuring Strawbs)	£30
75	Canon CNN 5759	PATCHWORK (LP)	£20

(see also Strawbs, Foggy Dew-O)

FOGGY DEW-O
| 68 | Decca LK/SKL 4940 | THE FOGGY DEW-O (LP, blue/silver labels with large unboxed logo) | £25 |
| 70 | Decca LK/SKL 5035 | BORN TO TAKE THE HIGHWAY (LP, blue/silver label with small boxed logo) | £15 |

(see also Strawbs, Foggy)

FOGHAT
| 72 | Bearsville K45503 | FOGHAT (LP) | £40 |

(see also Black Cat Bones, Warren Philips & The Rockets)

FOKUS
95	Lucky Spin LRS 025	Trigger Happy (Original)/Trigger Happy (Voyager Remix) (12")	£35
95	Lucky SPin LSR 025	Wired/Brave New World (12")	£45
95	Dee Jay DJX 028	On Line (Original)/On Line Drum N Bass)/On Line (Trip Hop) (12")	£40

ELLEN FOLEY (& CLASH)
| 81 | Epic SEPC 84809 | SPIRIT OF ST. LOUIS (LP, with inner sleeve) | £20 |

(see also Clash)

RED FOLEY
| 55 | Brunswick 05363 | Hearts Of Stone/RED FOLEY & BETTY FOLEY: Never | £18 |

(see also Roberta Lee)

RED FOLEY & ERNEST TUBB
| 55 | Brunswick OE 9148 | COUNTRY DOUBLE DATE (EP, with Minnie Pearl) | £15 |

(see also Ernest Tubb)

SIMON FOLEY
| 77 | Look LKLP 6324 | TO STRIVE WITH PRINCES (LP, with booklet) | £20 |

FOLKAL POINT
| 72 | Midas MR 003 | FOLKAL POINT (LP) | £1500 |

FOLK DEVILS
| 84 | Ganges RAY 1 | Hank Turns Blue/Chewin' The Fat (with p/s) | £15 |

CALVIN FOLKES
63	Rio R 5	Someone/Kentucky Home	£25
63	Rio R 8	You'll Never Know/Is It Time?	£25
64	Port-O-Jam PJ 4117	My Bonnie/What A Day	£30
64	Port-O-Jam PJ 4118	Hello Everybody/IRVING SIX: King's Boogie	£30

FOLKLORE
| 77 | Tank BSS 210 | ROOM FOR COMPANY (LP) | £20 |

FOLK(S) BROTHERS
| 61 | Blue Beat BB 30 | Carolina/I Met A Man (original, blue label, as Folks Brothers) | £25 |
| 60s | Fab BB 30 | Carolina (as Folks Brothers)/ERIC 'HUMPTY DUMPTY' MORRIS: Humpty Dumpty | £15 |

FOLK SONG CLUB
| 65 | white label (no cat. no.) | IMPERIAL COLLEGE (LP, private pressing) | £100 |

FOLKUS
| 70 | Thule SLP 102 | ALIVE (LP) | £100 |

ROY FONTAINE
| 86 | Abstract ADT 9 | One Is A Lonely Number (Vocal)/(Instrumental Version) (12" white label only) | £40 |

CLAUDIA FONTAINE
| 89 | SC 001 | I You Wanna Lover/(Instrumental)/(Dub Mix) (12" stamped white labels as Serious Chocolate featuring Claudia Fontaine) | £20 |

EDDIE FONTAINE
55	HMV 7M 304	Rock Love/All My Love Belongs To You (with Neal Hefti & Excels)	£150
55	HMV B 10852	Rock Love/All My Love Belongs To You (with Neal Hefti & Excels) (78)	£20
56	Brunswick 05624	Cool It, Baby/Into Each Life Some Rain Must Fall	£100
56	Brunswick 05624	Cool It, Baby/Into Each Life Some Rain Must Fall (78)	£20
58	London HLM 8711	Nothin' Shakin' (But The Leaves On The Trees)/Don't Ya Know	£50

FONTAINES
87	51st Parallel FONT 1	I Want Everything/Bernadette (p/s)	£30

WAYNE FONTANA & THE MINDBENDERS
63	Fontana TF 404	Hello! Josephine/Road Runner	£25
63	Fontana TF 418	For You, For You/Love Potion No.9	£15
64	Fontana TF 436	Little Darlin'/Come Dance With Me	£20
64	Fontana TE 17421	ROAD RUNNER (EP)	£50
64	Fontana TE 17435	UM, UM, UM, UM, UM, UM (EP)	£20
65	Fontana TE 17449	THE GAME OF LOVE (EP)	£15
65	Fontana TE 17453	WALKING ON AIR (EP)	£40
64	Fontana TL 5230	WAYNE FONTANA AND THE MINDBENDERS (LP)	£60
65	Fontana TL 5257	ERIC, RICK, WAYNE, BOB — IT'S WAYNE FONTANA AND THE MINDBENDERS (LP)	£65
67	Wing WL 1166	WAYNE FONTANA AND THE MINDBENDERS (LP, reissue)	£15

(see also Wayne Fontana, Mindbenders)

WAYNE FONTANA
68	Fontana TF 976	Never An Everyday Thing/Waiting For A Break In The Clouds	£40
69	Fontana TF 1054	Charlie Cass/Linda (withdrawn issue)	£25
70	Philips 6006 035	Give Me Just A Little More Time/I'm In Love (withdrawn)	£150
70	Philips 6006 035	Give Me Just A Little More Time/I'm In Love (withdrawn) (DJ Copy)	£100
66	Fontana (S)TL 5351	WAYNE ONE (LP, black/silver labels)	£25

(see also Mindbenders)

FONTANE SISTERS
54	London HL 8099	Happy Days And Lonely Nights/If I Didn't Have You	£30
55	London HL 8113	Hearts Of Stone/Bless Your Heart	£30
55	London HL 8126	Rock Love/You're Mine	£30
55	London HLD 8177	Seventeen/If I Could Be With You	£35
55	London HLD 8211	Rolling Stone/Daddy-O	£30
56	London HLD 8225	Adorable/Playmates	£20
56	London HLD 8265	Eddie My Love/Yum Yum	£20
56	London HL 7009	Eddie My Love/Yum Yum (export issue)	£20
56	London HLD 8289	I'm In Love Again/You Always Hurt The One You Love (gold lettering label)	£25
56	London HLD 8318	Voices (with narration by Pat Boone)/Willow Weep For Me (gold lettering label)	£20
55	London RE-D 1029	FONTANE SISTERS NO. 1 (EP)	£25
55	London RE-D 1037	FONTANE SISTERS NO. 2 (EP)	£25
57	London HA-D 2053	THE FONTANES SING (LP)	£50

(see also Pat Boone, Perry Como)

BILLY FONTEYNE
63	Oriole CB 1917	Little Child/Look Before You Leap	£15

FOO FIGHTERS
SINGLES
95	Roswell 12CL 753	This Is A Call/Winnebago/Podunk (12", luminous vinyl)	£20
95	Roswell 12CL 757	I'll Stick Around/How I Miss You (12" p/s)	£15
97	Roswell CL 788	Monkey Wrench/Up In Arms (red vinyl, p/s)	£15
97	Roswell CL 792	Everlong/Drive Me Wild (blue vinyl, p/s)	£80
97	Roswell CL 796	My Hero/Dear Lover (red vinyl, stickered poly sleeve, with insert)	£30

ALBUMS
95	Roswell EST 2266	FOO FIGHTERS (LP)	£70
97	Roswell EST 2295	THE COLOUR AND THE SHAPE (LP)	£100
99	RCA 07863678921	THERE IS NOTHING LEFT TO LOSE (LP, stickered gatefold sleeve, with tattoo transfer)	£60
02	RCA 74321973481	ONE BY ONE (LP, gatefold sleeve with inner)	£40
05	BMG 82876680381	IN YOUR HONOUR (4-LP)	£40
07	RCA 88697 22526 1	ECHOES, SILENCE, PATIENCE & GRACE (2-LP)	£20
11	RCA 8869784493 1	WASTING LIGHT (LP, 2 x 12")	£20
11	RCA 869798322 1	THE COLOUR AND THE SHAPE (2-LP, reissue, download card)	£20
11	Roswell 88697983211RE1	FOO FIGHTERS (LP, reissue, download card)	£15
14	RCA 88843 09008 18	SONIC HIGHWAYS (LP, various different sleeve designs)	£18
15	RCA 88697983241RE1	THERE IS NOTHING LEFT TO LOOSE (LP, reissue)	£18
15	RCA 88697983261RE1	ONE BY ONE (2-LP, reissue)	£18
15	RCA 8869798327RE1	IN YOUR HONOUR (2-LP, reissue)	£18
15	RCA 8869711516 -1	ECHOES, SILENCE, PATIENCE & GRACE (2-LP, 180 gram, reissue)	£18
15	RCA 8869798328	SKIN & BONE (2-LP, reissue)	£18

(see also Nirvana, Probot)

FOOL
69	Mercury SMCL 20138	THE FOOL (LP, gatefold sleeve. black/silver labels)	£100

FOOLS DANCE
87	L. T. T. Slaughter LTS 22T	They'll Never Know/The Collector/Empty Hours/The Ring (12", p/s)	£15
85	Top Hole Turn TURN 19	FOOLS DANCE (mini-LP)	£20

(see also Cure, Stranglers)

FOOT IN COLD WATER
74	Elektra K 52011	OR ALL AROUND US (LP)	£20

FOOT SOLDIER
93	Blipton Factor Wreckords BLIP 002	SO WHAT HAPPENS NOW EP (stamped white labels)	£18
93	Blipton Factor Wreckords BLIP 004	WE HAVE SUCH SIGHTS TO SHOW YOU EP (12" stamped white labels)	£35

MINT VALUE £

FOR CARNATION
00	Domino WIGLP 77	FOR CARNATION (LP, stickered sleeve)	£15

FORBIDDEN
88	Under One Flag FLAG 27	FORBIDDEN EVIL (LP)	£15

FORCE/CASH CREW
88	Vinyl Lab VL04T	Mission Impossible/Microphone Maniac (12")	£15

FORCE FIVE
64	United Artists UP 1051	Don't Make My Baby Blue/Shaking Postman	£30
65	United Artists UP 1089	Yeah, I'm Waiting/I Don't Want To See You Again	£35
65	United Artists UP 1102	Baby Don't Care/Come Down To Earth	£35
65	United Artists UP 1118	I Want You Babe/Gee Too Tiger	£50
66	United Artists UP 1141	Don't Know Which Way To Turn/Baby Let Your Hair Down	£45

(see also Crocheted Doughnut Ring)

FORCE MAJOR
82	Harbour City 14	Put It In Your Pipe/Say What You Feel	£15

FORCE OF MUSIC
78	Ballistic UAS 530190	FREEDOM FIGHTERS DUB (LP)	£20

FORCE WEST
66	Columbia DB 7908	Gotta Find Another Baby/Talkin' About Our Love	£15
67	Columbia DB 8174	All The Children Sleep/Desolation	£15

DEAN FORD (& GAYLORDS)
64	Columbia DB 7264	Twenty Miles/What's The Matter With Me?	£25
64	Columbia DB 7402	Mr Heartbreak's Here Instead/I Won't	£25
65	Columbia DB 7610	The Name Game/That Lonely Feeling	£25
75	EMI EMC 3079	DEAN FORD (LP)	£15

(see also Gaylords, Marmalade, Junior Campbell)

DEE DEE FORD
60	London HLU 9245	Good-Morning Blues/I Just Can't Believe	£40

(see also Don Gardner & Dee Dee Ford)

DONETTE FORD
91	Jah Works JW 007	Rhythm Of Resistance/Dub Wilderness (10")	£15

EMILE FORD (& THE CHECKMATES)
60	Pye NPL 18049	NEW TRACKS WITH EMILE (LP)	£20
61	Piccadilly NPL 38001	EMILE (LP)	£30

(see also Original Checkmates, Checkmates)

'TENNESSEE' ERNIE FORD
54	Capitol CL 14005	Give Me Your Word/River Of No Return	£15
54	Capitol CL 14006	Catfish Boogie/Kiss Me Big	£25
56	Capitol CL 14500	Sixteen Tons/You Don't Have To Be A Baby To Cry	£20
56	Capitol CL 14506	The Ballad Of Davy Crockett/Farewell	£20
61	Capitol CL 15210	Little Red Rockin' Hood/I Gotta Have My Baby Back	£20

(see also Dinning Sisters)

'TENNESSEE' ERNIE FORD & BETTY HUTTON
54	Capitol CL 14133	This Must Be The Place/The Honeymoon's Over (green label)	£18

FRANKIE FORD
59	London HL 8850	Sea Cruise/Roberta (with Huey 'Piano' Smith & Clowns) (black triangular centre)	£60
59	London HL 8850	Sea Cruise/Roberta (with Huey 'Piano' Smith & Clowns) (later silver-top triangular centre)	£30
60	Top Rank JAR 282	Cheatin' Woman/HUEY 'PIANO' SMITH & CLOWNS: Don't You Just Know Kokomo	£20
60	London HLP 9222	If You've Got Troubles/You Talk Too Much	£20
65	Sue WI 366	Sea Cruise/Roberta (with Huey 'Piano' Smith & Clowns) (reissue)	£25
65	Sue WI 369	What's Going On?/Watchdog	£40

(see also Huey Piano Smith)

JON FORD
70	Philips 6006 030	You've Got Me Where You Want Me/You're All Alone Tonight	£100
70	Philips 6006 030	You've Got Me Where You Want Me/You're All Alone Tonight (DJ Copy)	£150

LITA FORD & OZZY OSBOURNE
89	Dreamland PA 49396	Close My Eyes Forever (Remix)/Under The Gun/Blueberry (12", picture disc)	£20

(see also Ozzy Osbourne, Runaways)

MIKE FORD & THE CONSULS
63	Piccadilly 7N 35127	Jump Jeremiah/The Greenman	£20

PERRY FORD (& SAPPHIRES)
59	Parlophone R 4573	Bye, Bye Baby, Goodbye/She Came As A Stranger	£15
60	Parlophone R 4633	Crazy Over You/Garden Of Happiness	£15
60	Parlophone R 4683	Don't Weep (Little Lady)/Little Grown-Up	£15
62	Decca F 11497	Baby, Baby (Don't You Worry)/Prince Of Fools (with Sapphires & Blue Flames)	£15

(see also Ivy League, Georgie Fame)

SIR TED FORD
79	Ardent ADS 9001	Disco Music/I've Got A Goal	£80

JOHN FORDE
77	EMI EMI 2656	Stardance/Flight Of The Jumping Bean (12", p/s, some on blue vinyl)	£25
78	EMI EMI 2763	Atlantis/Atlantis (Instrumental)	£30
79	Sidewalk 12 YSID 107	Woman/Stardance/Don't You Know Who Did It (12", p/s)	£30

79	Sidewalk SID 107	Woman/Don't You Know Who Did It £20

EDDIE 'BUSTER' FOREHAND
69	Action ACT 4519	Young Boy Blues/You Were Meant For Me £35

FOREIGN BODIES
84	Alien 1	Take A Look/Love By Love (p/s) £25

FOREIGN LEGION
90	Venture VR/FL 100	WELCOME TO FORT ZINDERNEUF (LP) £15

FOREIGN PRESS
80	Streets Ahead SA 1	Downpour/Crossfire/Behind The Glass (1st pressing, gatefold sleeve)..............................£15

FORELAND
77	Flams	FORELAND (LP) £35

JOHN FOREMAN
66	Reality RY 1004	THE 'OUSES IN BETWEEN (LP) £15

FORERUNNERS
64	Solar SRP 100	Bony Maronie/Pride..£60

FORERUNNERS
60s	Key KL 008	THE FORERUNNERS (LP) £18
60s	Key KL 004	RUNNING BACK (LP) £18

FOREST (1)
69	Harvest HAR 5007	Searching For Shadows/Mirror Of Life £20
69	Harvest SHVL 760	FOREST (LP, gatefold sleeve, no EMI logo on label) £400
70	Harvest SHVL 784	FULL CIRCLE (LP, gatefold sleeve, no EMI logo on label) £700
88	Zap! ZAP 3	FULL CIRCLE (LP, reissue)..£25

SHARON FORESTER
73	Ashanti ASH 403	Silly Wasn't I?/NOW-GEN: Silly Wasn't I? — Version £25
74	Ashanti ASH 411	Put A Little Love Away/Words With No Meaning £20
74	Ashanti ASH 416	Don't Let Me Be Lonely Tonight/Which Craft Is Witchcraft?...£20
75	Ashanti ASH 420	Silly Wasn't It/Funny £30
76	Vulcan VUL 1011	Here Comes The Sun/Next Time £20
74	Ashanti SHAN 105	SHARON (LP)..£30

FOREVER AMBER
69	Advance (no cat. no.)	THE LOVE CYCLE (LP, private pressing, 99 copies only) £2500
07	10th Planet TP060	THE LOVE CYCLE (LP, reissue) £20

FOREVER MORE
70	RCA SF 8016	YOURS FOREVER MORE (LP, gatefold sleeve, orange label) £75
71	RCA LSA 3015	WORDS ON BLACK PLASTIC (LP, laminated front sleeve) £60
(see also Scots Of St. James, Hopscotch)		

FOREVER PEOPLE
92	Sarah SARAH 54	Invisible/Sometimes (p/s, insert) £25

FORK IN THE ROAD
70	Ember EMB 311	I Can't Turn Around/Skeleton In My Closet (test pressing) £150
70	Ember EMB S 311	I Can't Turn Around/Skeleton In My Closet £100

FORMATIONS
68	MGM MGM 1399	At The Top Of The Stairs/Magic Melody £120
68	MGM MGM 1399	At The Top Of The Stairs/Magic Melody (DJ Copy) £220

FORMERLY FAT HARRY
71	Harvest SHSP 4016	FORMERLY FAT HARRY (LP, with EMI logo on label) £100
(see also Country Joe and the Fish)		

FORMINX
65	Vocalion V 9235	Jenka Beat/Geronimo Jenka £30
(see also Aphrodite's Child, Vangelis)		

FORMIX
72	Tulip TP 001	What Would You Want Of Me/Shake £40

FORMULA 1
65	Warner Bros WB 155	I Just Can't Go To Sleep/Sure Know A Lot About Love £30

ANDY FORRAY
68	Parlophone R 5729	The Proud One/Messin' Round With Me £15
68	Decca F 12733	Epitaph To You/Dream With Me £80

HELEN FORREST
56	Capitol LC 6834	VOICE OF THE NAME BANDS (10" LP) £15

BRUCE FORSYTH
60	Parlophone PMC 1132	MR ENTERTAINMENT (LP, also stereo PCS 3031) £15

FORTES MENTUM
68	Parlophone R 5684	Saga Of A Wrinkled Man/Mr. Partridge Passed Away Today £50
68	Parlophone R 5726	I Can't Go On Loving You/Humdiggle We Love You £15
69	Parlophone R 5768	Gotta Go/Marrakesh £15
(see also Angel Pavement, Pussy)		

FORTUNATE PEOPLE
69	Dukesbury DB 002	Simple Skies/Stop...£90

JOHNNY FORTUNE
60s	Sonet SON 2139	Soul Surfer/Dragster £15

MINT VALUE £

LANCE FORTUNE
61	Pye 7N 15347	Who's Gonna Tell Me?/Love Is The Sweetest Thing	£15

FORTUNES
63	Decca F 11718	Summertime Summertime/I Love Her Still (as Fortunes & Cliftones) (in p/s)	£30
63	Decca F 11718	Summertime Summertime/I Love Her Still (as Fortunes & Cliftones)	£15
64	Decca F 11809	Caroline/If You Don't Want Me Now	£30
64	Decca F 11912	Come On Girl/I Like The Look Of You (curved logo)	£15
64	Decca F 11985	Look Homeward Angel/I'll Have My Tears To Remind Me	£15
69	United Artists UP 35054	Lifetime Of Love/Sad Sad Sad (withdrawn, existence unconfirmed)	£0
65	Decca LK 4736	THE FORTUNES (LP, mono)	£35
65	Decca SKL 4736	THE FORTUNES (LP, stereo)	£60
72	Capitol ST 21891	THE FORTUNES (LP)	£15

FORUM
67	London HLM 10120	The River Is Wide/I Fall In Love (All Over Again)	£15

FORWARD INTENSE
92	Harm HARM1	Stated/Imply The Calm (12")	£50

SHIRLEY FORWOOD
57	London HLD 8402	Two Hearts (With An Arrow Between)/Juke Box Lovers	£20

FOSSIL
74	Pennine PSS14	Black Night/For Your Love/Smile On Me/Wishing Well	£75

FRANK FOSTER
60s	Esquire 32 033	WAIL FRANK WAIL (LP)	£18

JACKIE FOSTER
63	Sway SWAY 001	Dry Up Your Tears/Try To Understand	£40
63	Planetone RC 13	Oh Leona/I Fell In Love	£35

JOHN FOSTER
66	Island ILP 939	JOHN FOSTER SINGS (LP)	£40

LES FOSTER
70	Torpedo TOR 7	Run Like A Thief/Nobody's Fool	£80

LES FOSTER & ANSELL COLLINS
73	Camel CA 102	The Man In Your Life/Version	£15

(see also Sugar Simone, Lance Hannibal)

RONNIE FOSTER
95	Blue Note 7243 8 30282 1	TWO HEADED FREAP (LP, reissue)	£50

VINCENT FOSTER
69	Escort ES 803	Shine Eye Gal/Who Nest (B-side actually "Who Next" by Carl Bryan)	£100

FOTHERINGAY
70	Island WIP 6085	Peace In The End/Winter Winds	£15
70	Island ILPS 9125	FOTHERINGAY (LP, pink label/'i' logo, gatefold sleeve)	£150
70	Island ILPS 9125	FOTHERINGAY (LP, later issue, pink rim label/'palm tree' logo, gatefold sleeve)	£30
86	Hannibal HNBL 4426	FOTHERINGAY (LP, reissue)	£18

(see also Sandy Denny, Trevor Lucas, Eclection, Exception[s], Fairport Convention, Mick Greenwood)

FOTOSTAT
79	Sour Grape SG 112	Fotostat/Fotostat II (p/s)	£20

FOUL PLAY
92	Oblivion OR 001	VOLUME 1 EP: The Alchemist/Ragatere/Ricochet/Feel The Vibe (12")	£25
92	Oblivion OR 002	VOLUME 2 EP: Survival/Dubbing You/Ricochet (No Stopping The Remix)/Feel The Vibe (Again) (12")	£25
93	Section 5 SECTION 04	Finest Illusion/Screwface (12" white label)	£60
93	Section 5 SECTION 04	Finest Illusion/Screwface (12" printed labels)	£50
93	Section 5 SECTION 4	Finest Illusion/Screwface (12", 2nd pressing, black labels, actually no labels at all!)	£50
94	Moving Shadow SHAD 49R1	VOLUME 4 - Remixes Part 1 (10")	£20
95	Moving Shadow ASHADOW 2 LP	SUSPECTED (LP as 2 x 12")	£18

FOUNDATIONS
71	MCA MCA 5075	Stoney Ground/I'll Give You Love	£20
78	Psycho P 2603	Closer To Loving You/Change My Life	£250
68	Pye NEP 24297	IT'S ALL RIGHT (EP)	£25
67	Pye NPL 18206	FROM THE FOUNDATIONS (LP)	£25
68	Pye NPL 18227	ROCKING THE FOUNDATIONS (LP, mono)	£20
68	Pye NSPL 18227	ROCKING THE FOUNDATIONS (LP, stereo)	£25
69	Pye N(S)PL 18290	DIGGING THE FOUNDATIONS (LP, gatefold sleeve)	£20

(see also Pluto, Clem Curtis)

FOUNDED
82	Heroes ER 02	Looking For Love/Run To Hell	£60

THE 4
64	Decca F 11999	It's Alright/There's Nothing Like It	£20

4 BY FOUR
60s	Victor Buckland	Roll Over Beethoven/Till There Was You/You Better Move On/Chains	£75

FOUR ACES (JAMAICA)
65	Island WI 178	Hoochy-Koochy-Kai-Po/River Bank Coberly Again	£60
65	Island WI 178	Hoochy-Koochy-Kai-Po/SKATALITES: Sucu Sucu (different B-side)	£60
65	Island WI 179	Sweet Chariot/Peace And Love	£60

MINT VALUE £

65	Island WI 180	Little Girl/CLARENDONIANS: Day Will Come £60
(see also Desmond Dekker)		

FOUR ACES (U.K.)
60s	Anton/E.R.S. EAG 178/179	Why Do You/Fortune Teller (private pressing) £250

FOUR ACES (U.S.)
54	Brunswick 05308	Three Coins In The Fountain/Wedding Bells (Are Breaking Up This Gang Of Mine) £15
54	Brunswick 05355	Mister Sandman/(I'll Be With You) In Apple Blossom Time £15
55	Brunswick 05480	Love Is A Many Splendored Thing/Shine On Harvest Moon £15
53	Brunswick LA 8614	JUST SQUEEZE ME (10" LP)..£15

FOURBEATS (1)
63	Oxford University UTF 164	Do You Love Me/Mr Postman/Baby Its Me/They Say (p/s) £30

FOURBEATS (2)
82	SRTS 82 CUS 1460	Back Door/If Pigs Could Fly £20

FOUR BELOW ZERO
01	Expansion EXPAND 82	My Baby's Got E.S.P./CHARLES JOHNSON: Never Had A Love So Good (12") £20
16	Soul Jazz SJR391-7	E.S.P. Part 1/E.S.P. Part 2 (reissue) £20

4 DEGREES
65	Oak RGJ 187	4 DEGREES (LP, 1-sided, no sleeve) £425

FOUR ESQUIRES
55	London HL 8152	The Sphinx Won't Tell/Three Things (A Man Must Do).....................................£20
57	London HL 8376	Look Homeward Angel/Santo Domingo (78) (unreleased on both 78 and 45) £0

FOUR EVERS
66	CBS 202549	A Lovely Way To Say Goodnight/The Girl I Wanna Bring Home.............................£45

FOUR FOR FUN
63	Waverley ELP 113	FOUR FOR FUN (EP) £60
(see also Dick Farina, Carolyn Hester)		

FOUR GEES
67	President PT 160	Ethiopia/Rough Rider £20
(see also eddy Grant)		

FOUR GIBSON GIRLS
58	Oriole CB 1447	No School Tomorrow/June, July And August £20
58	Oriole CB 1453	Safety Sue/VARIOUS ARTISTS: Safety Sue £15

FOUR GUNS
85	Gun 001	Sign Of The Crimes/Spirit Of The Thing (no'd p/s, 500 only)...............................£20

4 HERO
91	Reinforced RIVET 1203	IN ROUGH TERRITORY (LP, with free 12")...£25
95	Reinforced LP 004	PARALLEL UNIVERSE (2-LP)...£60
98	Reinforced/Talking Loud	TWO PAGES (LP as 4x12")..£30
99	Talkin Loud 5860571	CREATING PATTERNS (3-LP) £40

4 HORSEMEN OF THE APOCALYPSE
93	Tone Def 013DJ	Drowning In Her/We Are The Future (12")..£100

FOUR INSTANTS
66	Society SOC 1016	DISCOTHEQUE (LP) £60
69	Allied OPP 3013	DISCOTHEQUE (LP, reissue)..£15

FOUR JACKS
58	Decca F 10984	Hey! Baby/The Prayer Of Love £15
58	Decca DFE 6460	HEY! BABY (EP) £50

FOUR JONES BOYS
56	Decca F 10717	Tutti Frutti/Are You Satisfied?...£15
(see also Jones Boys, Annette Klooger)		

FOUR JUST MEN
64	Parlophone R 5186	That's My Baby/Things Will Never Be The Same £80
(see also Just Four Men, Wimple Winch)		

FOUR KENTS
68	RCA RCA 1705	The Moving Finger Writes/Searchin' £20

FOUR KINSMEN
67	Decca F 22671	It Looks Like The Daybreak/Forget About Him £15
67	Herald ELR 1080	WHEREVER HE GOES EP £15
(see also Kinsmen)		

FOUR KNIGHTS
54	Capitol CL 14076	I Get So Lonely/Till Then £20
54	Capitol CL 14154	Easy Street/In The Chapel In The Moonlight...£15
54	Capitol CL 14204	I Don't Wanna See You Cryin'/Saw Your Eyes £15
55	Capitol CL 14244	Honey Bunch/Write Me, Baby £15
55	Capitol CL 14290	Inside Out/Foolishly Yours £15
56	Capitol CL 14516	Guilty/You..£15
59	Coral Q 72355	Foolish Tears/O' Falling Star £15
55	Capitol EAP1 506	THE FOUR KNIGHTS (EP)..£15
53	Capitol LC 6604	SPOTLIGHT SONGS (10" LP)...£20

FOUR LEAVED CLOVER
65	Oak RGJ 207	Alright Girl/Why £500

MINT VALUE £

FOUR MATADORS
66	Columbia DB 7806	A Man's Gotta Stand Tall/Fast Cars And Money	£70

FOURMOST
68	CBS 3814	Apples, Peaches, Pumpkin Pie/He Could Never	£15
69	CBS 4041	Rosetta/Just Like Before	£50
69	CBS 4461	Easy Squeezy/Do I Love You?	£20
64	Parlophone GEP 8917	THE FOURMOST (EP)	£35
64	Parlophone GEP 8892	THE FOURMOST SOUND (EP)	£35
65	Parlophone PMC 1259	FIRST AND FOURMOST (LP)	£100
75	Fourmost SOF 001	THE FOURMOST (LP)	£15

(see also Format)

FOURMYULA
69	Columbia DB 8549	Honey Chile/Come With Me	£20

FOUR OWLS
11	High Focus HFREP 001	NATURES GREATEST MYSTERY EP (12", 300 only)	£50
14	High focus HFRLP 026	NATURES GREATEST MYSTERY (2-LP)	£35

FOUR PALMS
58	Vogue V 9116	Jeanie, Joanie, Shirley, Toni/Consideration	£600
58	Vogue V 9116	Jeanie, Joanie, Shirley, Toni/Consideration (78)	£150

FOUR PENNIES (U.K.)
64	Philips BF 1322	Juliet/Tell Me Girl (What Are You Gonna Do) (p/s, A- & B-sides supposedly flipped after original release)	£20
66	Philips BL 7734	MIXED BAG (LP)	£60

(see also Fritz Mike & Mo)

FOUR PENNIES (U.S.)
63	Stateside SS 198	My Block/Dry Your Eyes	£40
63	Stateside SS 244	When The Boy's Happy (The Girl's Happy Too)/Hockaday Part 1	£30

(see also Chiffons)

FOUR PLUGS
80	Disposable THROWAY ONE	Wrong Treatment/Biking Girl (p/s)	£20

FOUR + ONE
65	Parlophone R 5221	Time Is On My Side/Don't Lie To Me	£100

(see also In Crowd, Tomorrow, Keith West)

FOUR SEASONS

SINGLES
63	Stateside SS 241	Santa Claus Is Coming To Town/Christmas Tears	£15
64	Stateside SS 262	Peanuts/Silhouettes	£15
64	Stateside SS 343	Since I Don't Have You/Sincerely	£15
67	Philips BF 1556	Beggin'/Dody (as the 4 Seasons)	£15
67	Philips BF 1600	Around And Around/WONDER WHO: Lonesome Road	£15
67	Philips BF 1621	Watch The Flowers Grow/Raven	£15
68	Philips BF 1651	Will You Love Me Tomorrow?/Silhouettes	£15
68	Philips BF 1685	Saturday's Father/Goodbye Girl	£15
69	Philips BF 1743	Electric Stories/Pity	£15
71	Warner Bros K 16107	Whatever You Say/Sleeping Man (withdrawn, 300 only) As Frankie Valli and the...)	£45
64	Stateside SE 1011	THE FOUR SEASONS SING (EP)	£40

ALBUMS
63	Stateside SL 10033	SHERRY AND 11 OTHERS	£30
63	Stateside SL 10042	AIN'T THAT A SHAME	£40
63	Stateside SL 10051	THE FOUR SEASONS' GREETINGS	£30
64	Philips BL 7611	BORN TO WANDER	£20
64	Philips BL 7621	DAWN (GO AWAY) AND 11 OTHER GREAT SONGS	£20
64	Philips BL 7643	RAG DOLL	£18
65	Philips BL 7663	ENTERTAIN YOU	£20
65	Philips (S)BL 7687	SING BIG HITS BY BURT BACHARACH ... HAL DAVID ... BOB DYLAN	£20
65	Philips BL 7699	WORKING MY WAY BACK TO YOU	£18
67	Philips (S)BL 7753	CHRISTMAS ALBUM	£25
69	Philips (S)BL 7880	THE GENUINE IMITATION LIFE GAZETTE	£25

(see also Beverly Hills Blues Band, Frankie Valli, Wonder Who)

FOUR SIGHTS
64	Columbia DB 7227	But I Can Tell/And I Cry	£15

4-SKINS
81	Clockwork Fun CF 101	One Law For Them/Brave New World (p/s)	£20
82	Secret SEC 4	THE GOOD, THE BAD AND THE 4-SKINS (LP, with photo inner)	£25
83	Syndicate SYN 1	A FISTFUL OF ... 4-SKINS (LP)	£18
89	Link LINK LP 090	LIVE AND LOUD!! (THE BRIDGEHOUSE TAPES) (LP)	£18
84	Syndicate SYN LP 5	FROM CHAOS TO 1984 (LP)	£20
01	Captain Oi! AHOY PD3	THE GOOD THE BAD AND THE 4-SKINS (LP, reissue, clear vinyl picture disc)	£15

(see also Plastic Gangsters)

FOURSOME
76	Fanfare FR 6490	UPSIDE DOWN (LP)	£40

FOUR SPICES
57	MGM MGM 944	Armen's Theme (Yesterday And You)/Fire Engine Boogie	£100

FOUR SQUARES
64	Hollick & Taylor HT 1009	FOUR SQUARES (EP)	£100

(see also Pink People)

FOURTEEN (14)
68	Olga OLE 002	Through My Door/Meet Mr. Edgar	£20
68	Olga OLE 006	Umbrella/Drizzle (Rain)	£20
68	Olga OLE 006	Umbrella/Drizzle (Rain) (Demo)	£45
68	Olga S 051	Easy To Fool/Frosty Stars On A Window Pane	£15

14 ICED BEARS
86	Frank COPPOLA 101	Inside/Blue Suit/Cut (hand-printed paper bag sleeve)	£25
88	Sarah SARAH 005	Come Get Me/Unhappy Days/Sure To See (poster p/s)	£80
89	Thunderball 7TBL 2	Mother Sleep (7", unreleased, Mayking test pressings only)	£25
88	Thunderball TBLP 1	14 ICED BEARS (LP)	£20
91	Borderline BORD 002	WONDER (LP)	£15

FOUR TET
98	Output OPR 14	THIRTYSIXTWENTYFIVE EP (2 one-sided 12", p/s)	£15
09	Text TEXT 006	Moth/Wolf Cub (12", black label, plain black sleeve with Burial)	£15
11	Text TEXT 010	Ego/Mirror (12", with Thom Yorke and Burial, black labels on both sides)	£18
11	Text TEXT 009	Pinnacles/DAPHNI: Ya Ya (12")	£15
12	Text TEXT 013	Nova (1-sided 12", with Burial)	£20
99	Output OPR21	DIALOGUE (LP, inner)	£30
01	Domino WIGLP94	PAUSE (LP, inner)	£20
02	Domino WIGLP126	ROUNDS (2-LP, gatefold)	£25
05	Domino WIGLP154	EVERYTHING ECSTATIC (2xLP, one sided etched, with bonus CD)	£20
10	Domino WIGLP254	THERE IS LOVE IN YOU (2-LP)	£25
13	Text TEXT 025	BEAUTIFUL REWIND (LP)	£20
13	Four Tet FTC 001	COMPILATION ONE (LP, pink vinyl)	£20
13	Domino REWIGLP88	ROUNDS (2-LP, reissue with live CD)	£20
15	Text TEXT018	PINK (2-LP, reissue)	£18
15	Text TEXT 036	MORNING/EVENING (LP)	£20
17	Text TEXT 046	NEW ENERGY (2-LP)	£25
20	Text TEXT 051	SIXTEEN OCEANS (2-LP)	£20

(see also Fridge, Percussions, Thom Yorke)

4TH STREET ORCHESTRA
77	Rama RM 001	AH WHO SEH? GO-DEH! (LP)	£70
77	Rama RM 002	AH FE WE DIS (LP)	£75
77	Rama RM 004	(SCIENTIFIC) HIGHER RANKING DUB (LP)	£200
77	Rama RMLP 005	YUH LEARN! (LP)	£100

(see also Dennis Bovell, Matumbi)

FOURTH WORLD
| 95 | B&W BWR 030 | FOURTH WORLD (LP) | £15 |

(see also Arto Moreira)

FOUR TONES
| 58 | Decca F 11074 | Voom Ba Voom/Rickshaw Boy | £15 |

FOUR TOPHATTERS
55	London HLA 8163	Leave-a My Gal Alone/Go Baby Go	£200
55	London HLA 8163	Leave-a My Gal Alone/Go Baby Go (78)	£15
55	London HLA 8198	Forty Five Men In A Telephone Booth/Wild Rosie	£200
55	London HLA 8198	Forty Five Men In A Telephone Booth/Wild Rosie (78)	£15

FOUR TOPS
SINGLES
64	Stateside SS 336	Baby I Need Your Lovin'/Call On Me (DJ Copy)	£70
64	Stateside SS 336	Baby I Need Your Lovin'/Call On Me	£50
65	Stateside SS 371	Without The One You Love (Life's Not Worthwhile)/Love Has Gone (DJ Copy)	£130
65	Stateside SS 371	Without The One You Love (Life's Not Worthwhile)/Love Has Gone	£60
65	Tamla Motown TMG 507	Ask The Lonely/Where Did You Go? (DJ copy)	£150
65	Tamla Motown TMG 507	Ask The Lonely/Where Did You Go?	£90
65	Tamla Motown TMG 515	I Can't Help Myself/Sad Souvenirs (DJ copy)	£150
65	Tamla Motown TMG 515	I Can't Help Myself/Sad Souvenirs	£25
65	Tamla Motown TMG 528	It's The Same Old Song/Your Love Is Amazing (DJ copy)	£100
65	Tamla Motown TMG 528	It's The Same Old Song/Your Love Is Amazing	£25
65	Tamla Motown TMG 542	Something About You/Darling I Hum Our Song (DJ copy)	£100
65	Tamla Motown TMG 542	Something About You/Darling I Hum Our Song	£30
66	Tamla Motown TMG 553	Shake Me, Wake Me (When It's Over)/Just As Long As You Need Me (DJ copy)	£100
66	Tamla Motown TMG 553	Shake Me, Wake Me (When It's Over)/Just As Long As You Need Me)	£35
66	Tamla Motown TMG 568	Loving You Is Sweeter Than Ever/I Like Everything About You (DJ copy £100)	£100
66	Tamla Motown TMG 568	Loving You Is Sweeter Than Ever/I Like Everything About You	£30
66	Tamla Motown TMG 579	Reach Out, I'll Be There/Until You Love Someone (DJ copy)	£100
66	Tamla Motown TMG 579	Reach Out, I'll Be There/Until You Love Someone (small print, later large print = £15)	£18
67	Tamla Motown TMG 589	Standing In The Shadows Of Love/Since You've Been Gone (DJ copy)	£100
67	Tamla Motown TMG 589	Standing In The Shadows Of Love/Since You've Been Gone (small print)	£15
67	Tamla Motown TMG 601	Bernadette/I Got A Feeling (DJ copy)	£100
67	Tamla Motown TMG 601	Bernadette/I Got A Feeling	£15
67	Tamla Motown TMG 612	Seven Rooms Of Gloom/I'll Turn To Stone (DJ copy)	£65
67	Tamla Motown TMG 612	Seven Rooms Of Gloom/I'll Turn To Stone	£15
67	Tamla Motown TMG 623	You Keep Running Away/If You Don't Want My Love (DJ copy)	£65

FOUR TUNES

67	Tamla Motown TMG 634	Walk Away Renee/Mame (DJ copy)	£60
68	Tamla Motown TMG 647	If I Were A Carpenter/Your Love Is Wonderful (DJ copy)	£60
68	Tamla Motown TMG 665	Yesterday's Dreams/For Once In My Life (DJ copy)	£60
68	Tamla Motown TMG 665	Yesterday's Dreams/For Once In My Life	£15
68	Tamla Motown TMG 675	I'm In A Different World/Remember When (DJ copy)	£60
68	Tamla Motown TMG 675	I'm In A Different World/Remember When	£15
69	Tamla Motown TMG 698	What Is A Man?/Don't Bring Back Memories (DJ copy)	£70
69	Tamla Motown TMG 710	Do What You Gotta Do/Can't Seem To Get You Out Of My Mind (DJ copy)	£70
69	Tamla Motown TMG 710	Do What You Gotta Do/Can't Seem To Get You Out Of My Mind	£18
70	Tamla Motown TMG 736	It's All In The Game/Love (Is The Answer) (DJ copy)	£40
70	Tamla Motown TMG 752	Still Water (Love)/Still Water (Peace) (DJ copy)	£40
71	Tamla Motown TMG 770	Just Seven Numbers (Can Straighten Out My Life)/I Wish I Were Your Mirror (DJ copy)	£30
71	Tamla Motown TMG 785	Simple Game/You Stole My Love (DJ copy)	£30
72	Tamla Motown TMG 803	Bernadette/I Got A Feeling/It's The Same Old Song (DJ copy)	£30
72	Tamla Motown TMG 829	I'll Turn To Stone/Love Feels Like Fire (DJ copy)	£30
74	Probe PRO 612	I Just Can't Get You Out Of My Mind/Am I My Brother's Keeper	£15
83	Tamla Motown TMG 1320	Medley/TEMPTATIONS: Papa Was A Rolling Stone	£35
84	Calibre 124	Your Song/I'm Here Again (p/s, withdrawn)	£100
84	Calibre 124	Your Song/I'm Here Again (withdrawn)	£50

EPs

66	Tamla Motown TME 2012	THE FOUR TOPS (EP, flipback sleeve)	£30
67	Tamla Motown TME 2018	FOUR TOP HITS	£35

ALBUMS

65	Tamla Motown TML 11010	THE FOUR TOPS	£80
66	Tamla Motown TML 11021	SECOND ALBUM (mono)	£40
66	Tamla Motown STML 11021	SECOND ALBUM (stereo)	£50
66	Tamla Motown TML 11037	FOUR TOPS ON TOP (mono)	£35
66	Tamla Motown STML 11037	FOUR TOPS ON TOP (stereo)	£45
67	Tamla Motown TML 11041	FOUR TOPS LIVE! (mono)	£25
67	Tamla Motown (S)TML 11041	FOUR TOPS LIVE! (stereo)	£30
67	Tamla Motown TML 11056	REACH OUT (mono)	£25
67	Tamla Motown TML 11056	REACH OUT (stereo)	£30
68	Tamla Motown STML 11061	FOUR TOPS GREATEST HITS (stereo)	£25
68	Tamla Motown TML 11061	FOUR TOPS GREATEST HITS (mono)	£20
69	Tamla Motown (S)TML 11087	YESTERDAY'S DREAMS (mono/stereo)	£25
69	Tamla Motown TML 11113	FOUR TOPS NOW (mono)	£25
69	Tamla Motown TML 11113	FOUR TOPS NOW (stereo)	£20
70	Tamla Motown TML 11138	SOUL SPIN (mono)	£25
70	Tamla Motown STML 11138	SOUL SPIN (stereo)	£20
70	Tamla Motown STML 11149	STILL WATERS RUN DEEP	£20
71	Tamla Motown STML 11173	CHANGING TIMES	£20
72	Tamla Motown STML 11206	NATURE PLANNED IT	£15
73	Probe SPB 1064	KEEPER OF THE CASTLE	£15
73	Probe SPB 1077	SHAFT IN AFRICA (soundtrack, with Johnny Pate)	£40
74	Probe SPBA 6283	MEETING OF THE MINDS	£15
74	ABC ABCL 5035	SHAFT IN AFRICA (soundtrack, reissue)	£15

(see also Supremes & Four Tops)

FOUR TUNES

54	London L 1231	I Gambled With Love/Marie (78)	£15
54	London HL 8050	Do, Do, Do, Do, Do Do It Again/My Wild Irish Rose (78)	£15
55	London HL 8151	I Sold My Heart To A Junkman/The Greatest Feeling In The World	£100
55	London HL 8151	I Sold My Heart To A Junkman/The Greatest Feeling In The World (78)	£20
55	London HLJ 8164	Tired Of Waitin'/L'Amour, Toujours L'Amour (Love Everlasting)	£50
55	London HLJ 8164	Tired Of Waitin'/L'Amour, Toujours L'Amour (Love Everlasting) (78)	£20

FOURUM

78	Sirius SP 519	FOURUM (LP)	£20
81	Guardian GRC 95	SINGING THE DALES (LP)	£20

FOUR WINDS

58	London HLU 8556	Short Shorts/Five Minutes More	£25

KIM FOWLEY

66	Parlophone R 5521	Lights/Something New And Different	£30
66	CBS 202243	They're Coming To Take Me Away Ha-Haaa!!/You Get More For Your Money On The Flip Side Of This Record Talking Blues	£15
66	CBS 202338	Lights (The Blind Can See)/Something New And Different (reissue)	£15
66	Island WI 278	The Trip/Beautiful People	£20
77	Island WIP 278	The Trip/Beautiful People (p/s, reissue)	£15
73	Capitol E-ST 11159	INTERNATIONAL HEROES (LP)	£25

(see also Freaks Of Nature, Hollywood Argyles, Napoleon XIV)

(THE) FOX

68	CBS 3381	Mister Carpenter/Seek And You Find	£300

FOX (1)

70	Fontana 6007 016	Second Hand Love/Butterfly	£25
70	Fontana 6309 007	FOR FOX SAKE (LP, laminated sleeve, black/silver labels)	£300
03	RPM RPM 254LP	FOR FOX SAKE (LP, gatefold, reissue)	£15

FOX (2)
75	GTO GTLP 006	TAILS OF ILLUSION (LP, textured sleeve, lyric inner)	£25
77	GTO GTLP 020	BLUE HOTEL (LP)	£20

(see also Wooden Horse, Demick & Armstrong)

BOB FOX & STU LUCKLEY
78	Rubber RUB 028	NOWT SO GOOD'LL PASS (LP)	£15

DON FOX
60	Triumph RGM 1022	T'ain't What You Do/Out There	£40

PAUL FOX
90	Sound Business SB 1	Writing On The Wall/Version/LIBERATION TRIBE: African Mask (12")	£40

(see also Tafari & Paul Fox)

UFFA FOX
60	Parlophone PMC 1112	UFFA SINGS (LP)	£15

FOX IN SOCKS
81	Jest 001	Sound Patterns/Lonely House (p/s)	£25

FOXX
71	MCA MUPS 419	REVOLT OF EMILY YOUNG (LP)	£15

INEZ FOXX
63	Sue WI 301	Mockingbird/He's The One You Love (actually by Inez & Charlie Foxx)	£25
64	Sue WI 304	Jaybirds/Broken-Hearted Fool (actually by Inez & Charlie Foxx)	£25
64	Sue WI 314	Ask Me/Hi Diddle Diddle (actually by Inez & Charlie Foxx)	£25
64	Sue WI 323	Hurt By Love/Confusion (actually by Inez & Charlie Foxx)	£25

INEZ & CHARLIE FOXX
64	Sue WI 307	Competition/Here We Go Round The Mulberry Bush (as Charlie & Inez Foxx)	£30
64	Sue WI 356	La De Da I Love You/Yankee Doodle Dandy	£30
66	Stateside SS 556	Come By Here/No Stranger To Love	£30
67	Stateside SS 586	Tightrope/My Special Prayer	£30
67	Stateside SS 586	Tightrope/My Special Prayer (DJ copy)	£75
69	Direction 58-4042	Baby Give It To Me/You Fixed My Heartache	£40
69	London HLC 10250	Mockingbird/Hummingbird (unissued)	£0
83	Sue ENS 2	Mockingbird (EP)	£15
64	Sue ILP 911	MOCKINGBIRD (LP)	£100
65	London HA-C 8241	INEZ AND CHARLIE FOXX (LP, plum label)	£70
65	London HA-C 8241	INEZ AND CHARLIE FOXX (LP, later black label)	£40
68	Direction 8-63085	COME BY HERE (LP)	£30
68	Direction 8-63281	GREATEST HITS (LP)	£20
69	United Artists UA(S) 29025	MOCKINGBIRD (LP)	£15

JOHN FOXX
80	Virgin VS 338	No-One Driving (2.53 DJ Version)/Glimmer//This City/Mr. No (double pack, stickered gatefold p/s, matrix no. VS 338 A5DJ)	£15
18	Electronic Sound ES 748	Underpass/Film One (p/s, red vinyl, reissue)	£15
80	Virgin V 2146	METAMATIC (LP)	£20
81	Virgin V 2194	THE GARDEN (LP)	£20
83	Virgin V 2233	THE GOLDEN SECTION (LP)	£20
85	Virgin V 2355	IN MYSTERIOUS WAYS (LP)	£15

(see also Ultravox)

FRABJOY & RUNCIBLE SPOON
69	Marmalade 598 019	I'm Beside Myself/Animal Song	£50

(see also Godley & Creme, Hotlegs, Mockingbirds, 10cc)

FRAGILE FRIENDS
83	KC KCT1	NOVELTY WEARS OFF (12" EP)	£25
84	KC KC 001	Paper Doll/What I Call Beautiful	£35

FRAME
66	RCA RCA 1556	My Feet Don't Fit In His Shoes/She	£18
67	RCA RCA 1571	Doctor Doctor/I Can't Go On	£65
74	Seven Sun SSUN 12	Billy The Dreamer/Rocking Machine	£20

FRAMED
82	Thunderbay TBR 020A	Into My Life (1-sided)	£60
82	Thunderbay TBR 021	Wonderland (1-sided)	£60
82	Thunderbay TBR 021	Into My Life/Wonderland (test pressings)	£50

(see also Girlschool, Sham 69)

FRANCIS
67	Blue Beat BB 379	Warn The People (actually by Willie Francis)/SWINGERS: Simpleton (actually by Peter Tosh & Crackers)	£120
72	Fab FAB 182	Rocking Machine/SOUL CLANS: Flying Rhythm	£25
73	Fab FAB 251	Locks/Version	£30

B. FRANCIS
65	Ska Beat JB 193	Judy Crowned/Who Crunch	£40

BOBBY FRANCIS
67	JJ DB 1153	Chain Gang/Venus	£175

(see also Winston Francis)

CONNIE FRANCIS
SINGLES
56	MGM SP 1169	My First Real Love (with Jaybirds)/Believe In Me (Crede Mi)	£60

MINT VALUE £

56	MGM MGM 932	My Sailor Boy/Everyone Needs Someone	£30
57	MGM MGM 945	Little Blue Wren/I Never Had A Sweetheart	£30
57	MGM MGM 962	Eighteen/Faded Orchid	£30

CONNIE FRANCIS & MARVIN RAINWATER
58	MGM MGM 969	The Majesty Of Love/You My Darling You	£35

(see also Marvin Rainwater)

(KING) JOE FRANCIS
65	Blue Beat BB 323	Wicked Woman/King Joe's Ska (as King Joe Francis)	£25
65	Ska Beat JB 184	Waggling Tails/I Don't Want You No More	£35
66	Ska Beat JB 262	Scarborough Ska/I Got A Scar (as Joe Francis & Ricky Logan & Snowballs)	£35
66	Rio R 90	Have My Body (song actually "Have Mercy Baby")/Everybody's Got To Know (as King Joe Francis & Hijackers)	£50
66	Rio R 94	Days Are Lonely/My Baby	£30
67	Rainbow RAI 114	My Granny/Pull It Out (as J. Francis & Rico's Boys)	£25

LEE FRANCIS (2)
78	Lonely I & I L 1	Be My Wife Little Girl/Loneliness	£40
79	Lonely I & I L 2	A Lonely I & I/Paradise (12")	£50
79	Lee & Roy L 3	Shadows Of My Youth/Deception Of Consciousness (12")	£45
79	Lonely I & I L 4	Throwing Stones/No, You Don't Know (12")	£80

NAT FRANCIS
66	Blue Beat BB 346	Mama Kiss Him Goodnight/Tra La La (with Prince Buster Junior & Sunsets)	£30
66	Blue Beat BB 361	Just To Keep You (credited to B. Junior)/You Only Want My Money	£30
67	Blue Beat BB 376	Seven Nights Of Love/Feeling Blue	£30

RITCHIE FRANCIS
72	Pegasus PEG 11	SONGBIRD (LP, gatefold textured sleeve)	£40

(see also Eyes Of Blue, Big Sleep)

RUDOLPH FRANCIS
79	Kim A 024	Time To Realise/Motherless Children (12")	£125

WILBERT FRANCIS & VIBRATORS
66	Ska Beat JB 267	Memories Of You/CHUCK JACQUES: Now That You're Gone	£50

(see also Little Willie, Vibrators [Jamaica])

WILLIE FRANCIS
69	Bullet BU 415	Motherless Children/I Am Not Afraid	£90
71	Escort ERT 848	Burn Them/Poor Boy	£15
71	Bullet BU 489	Willie's Rouster/Rouster Version	£15

(see also Martin Riley)

WINSTON FRANCIS
69	Coxsone CS 7089	Reggae And Cry/FREEDOM SINGERS: Easy Come Easy Go (B-side actually by Righteous Flames)	£150
69	Studio One SO 2086	Games People Play/GLADIATORS: The Kicks	£125
69	Punch PH 5	Too Experienced/JACKIE MINTO: Mule Jerk (B-side actually by Jackie Mittoo)	£50
69	Bamboo BAM 10	The Same Old Song/SOUND DIMENSION: Rattle On	£60
70	Bamboo BAM 46	Turn Back The Hands Of Time/Soul Bowl	£50
70	Bamboo BAM 48	California Dreaming/JACKIE MITTOO & SOUND DIMENSION: Soul Stew	£50
72	Camel CA 99	Ten Times Sweeter Than You/Fat Boy	£25
73	Fab FAB 271	Mr Fix It/Version	£30
74	Ashanti ASH 415	California Dreaming/SOUND DIMENSION: Soul Food (reissue)	£30
70	Bamboo BDLP 207	MR FIX IT (LP)	£80
71	Bamboo BDLPS 216	CALIFORNIA DREAMING (LP)	£90

(see also Bobby Francis, Jerry & Freedom Singers, Band Of Mercy & Salvation)

CLAUDE FRANCOIS
66	Fontana TF 725	In My Memory/Gone From My Mind	£30
67	Fontana TF 799	Bench Number 3 Waterloo Station/Run To Daddy	£80
78	EMI 2773	Bordeaux Rose/Magnolias (demo in p/s)	£20
77	EMI EMC 3189	HIS HITS IN ENGLISH (LP)	£30

FRANCOIS K
02	Azuli AZLP 13	AZULI PRESENTS FRANCOIS K " CHOICE " A COLLECTION OF CLASSICS (4xLP)	£15

JACKSON C. FRANK
78	B&C BCS 0012	Blues Run The Game/Milk & Honey	£20
65	Columbia DB 7795	Blues Run The Game/Can't Get Away From My Love	£100
65	Columbia 33SX 1788	JACKSON C. FRANK (LP)	£400
78	B&C BCLP 4	AGAIN (LP, reissue of above LP)	£40

FRANK & BARBARIANS
62	Oriole CB 1758	The Bouncer/Concerto In The Stars	£15

FRANKIE & CLASSICALS
67	Philips BF 1586	I Only Have Eyes For You/What Shall I Do?	£200

FRANKIE GOES TO HOLLYWOOD
SINGLES
84	ZTT XZIP 1	Two Tribes (Hibakusha)/War (Hide Yourself)/Two Tribes/ One February Friday (12", ZTT sleeve)	£15

(see also Spitfire Boys)

FRANKIE & JOHNNY
66	Decca F 22376	Never Gonna Leave You/I'll Hold You	£400
66	Decca F 22376	Never Gonna Leave You/I'll Hold You (DJ Copy)	£500
66	Parlophone R 5518	Climb Ev'ry Mountain/I Wanna Make You Understand	£25

(see also Maggie Bell)

ARETHA FRANKLIN

SINGLES

61	Fontana H 271	Love Is The Only Thing/Today I Sing The Blues (with Ray Bryant Combo)......................£15
65	CBS 201732	Can't You Just See Me/You Little Miss Raggedy Anne...£20
69	Atlantic 584 239	Don't Let Me Lose This Dream/The House That Jack Built £25
70	Atlantic 2091 042	Border Song (Holy Moses)/You And Me (unissued)...£0
70	Atlantic 2091 044	Oh No, Not My Baby/You And Me £40

EPs

62	Fontana TE 467217	TODAY I SING THE BLUES £50

ALBUMS

61	Fontana TFL 5173	ARETHA..£70
65	CBS (S)BPG 62566	YEAH!!! — IN PERSON £40
67	CBS (S)BPG 62744	SOUL SISTER £40
67	Atlantic 587/588 066	I NEVER LOVED A MAN £20
67	CBS (S)BPG 62969	TAKE IT LIKE YOU GIVE IT..£20
67	CBS 63160	LEE CROSS £20
67	Atlantic 587/588 085	ARETHA ARRIVES £20
67	CBS 64536	GREATEST HITS £20
68	Atlantic 587/588 099	LADY SOUL..£40
68	CBS 63269	TAKE A LOOK AT ARETHA FRANKLIN £20
68	Atlantic 587/588 114	ARETHA NOW £30
68	CBS 63064	GREATEST HITS VOL. 2 ....£15
68	Atlantic 587/588 149	ARETHA IN PARIS — LIVE AT THE OLYMPIA £20
69	Atlantic 588 169	SOUL '69 ....£20
72	Atlantic K40323	YOUNG GIFTED AND BLACK (LP) £25
73	Atlantic K40504	HEY NOW HEY (THE OTHER SIDE OF THE SKY) (LP, gatefold) £18
75	Atlantic K50191	YOU (LP) £20
76	Atlantic K56248	SPARKLE (LP) £20
77	Atlantic K50368	SWEET PASSION (LP) £15

CAROLYN FRANKLIN

69	RCA RD/SF 8035	BABY DYNAMITE! (LP) £30

ERMA FRANKLIN

67	London HLZ 10170	Piece Of My Heart/Big Boss Man...£15
69	Soul City SC 118	Don't Wait Too Long/Time After Time £25
69	MCA MU 1073	Gotta Find Me A Lover (24 Hours A Day)/Change My Thoughts From You £15
70	MCA MUP MUPS 394	SOUL SISTER (LP) £25

JOHNNY FRANKS

55	Melodisc P 230	Tweedle Dee/Shake, Rattle And Roll (78) £25
58	Melodisc 1459	Good Old Country Music/Cheatin' On Me (78) £20

BONNIE (BLUE) FRANKSON

68	Jolly JY 014	Loving You/Shoo Be Do (both with Joe Nolan and his Band) £20
69	Jolly JY 021	London City/Dearest (both with Joe Nolan & Dynamic Heatwave) £20
69	Columbia Blue Beat DB 114	Dearest/London City £20
70	Ackee ACK 110	I'm So Glad/Lonely Road (both with Dotty) £15
73	Ackee ACK 512	Getting Things Together/Version £15

(see also Dotty & Bonnie)

FRANTIC ELEVATORS

79	TJM TJM 5	Voice In The Dark/Passion/Every Day I Die (p/s)..................................£40
80	TJM TJM 6	Hunchback Of Notre Dame/See Nothing And Everything/Don't Judge Me (unreleased; demos only) £150
80	Eric's ERIC'S 6	You Know What You Told Me/Production Prevention (p/s) £50
81	Crackin' Up CRAK 1	Searching For The Only One/Hunchback Of Notre Dame (p/s)..................£20
82	No Waiting WAIT 1	Holding Back The Years/Pistols In My Brain (p/s)..................................£20
87	TJM TJM 101	THE EARLY YEARS (mini-LP) £20
88	Receiver KNOB 2	THE EARLY YEARS (mini-LP, reissue with new sleeve & interview disc, as Mick Hucknall & Frantic Elevators) £15

FRANZ FERDINAND

22	Domino WIGLP 473XM	HITS TO THE HEAD (2LP, booklet, gold vinyl exclusive to website) £40
04	Domino RUG 172	Take Me Out/Truck Stop (3,000 only, p/s) £25
04	Domino RUG 172TDAFT	Take Me Out (Daft Punk Remix)/(Album Version)/(Naum Gabo Remix) (12", p/s) £20
06	Domino FC 001	Swallow Smile/Take Me Out (Acoustic) (p/s, fan club release)..................£20
03	Chateau CHAT001	LIVE 2003 (LP, 10-track official bootleg/promo 500 copies) £15
04	Domino WIGLP 136	FRANZ FERDINAND (LP, embossed sleeve, printed inner) £50
05	Domino WIGLP 161	YOU COULD HAVE IT SO MUCH BETTER (LP, printed inner) £30
09	Domino WIGIP 205	TONIGHT: FRANZ FERDINAND (2LP, gatefold, fold-out insert) £25
09	Domino WIG 205X	TONIGHT: FRANZ FERDINAND (6x7"/2CD/DVD box set, book, dink) £20
09	Domino WIGLP 239	BLOOD: FRANZ FERDINAND (LP, mirrorboard sleeve, 1000 copies, RSD).....£30
13	Domino WIGLP 255X	RIGHT THOUGHTS, RIGHT WORDS, RIGHT ACTIONS (2LP/CD/12"/2x7" 'passport' box set, postcards)...£100
13	Domino WIGLP 255X	RIGHT THOUGHTS, RIGHT WORDS, RIGHT ACTIONS (2LP, 180g, hand numbered edition of 500)..£60
18	Domino WIGLP 408	ALWAYS ASCENDING (LP, 180g, booklet, poster).................................£15
18	Domino WIGLP 408XXM	ALWAYS ASCENDING (LP, blue/white vinyl, deluxe edition, booklet, poster, tote bag) £30

(see also The Ampheta Meanies, F.F.S.)

ANDY FRASER BAND
75   CBS 80731   THE ANDY FRASER BAND (LP) £20
(see also Free, Sharks)

ELIZABETH FRASER
00   Blancy Y Negro SAM 00346 **Underwater** (Charlie May Mix)/**Underwater** (Charlie May Instrumental) (12", stamped
                                 white label, 200 only) £150
(see also Cocteau Twins)

TERRY FRASER
69   Rude Boy RBH 001   Beng Beng Chitty/Soul Food £25

FRATELLIS
06   No Label   Cigarillo/Got Ma Nuts From A Hippy (Demo) (gig freebie, 500 only) £15

ERIC FRATTER
69   Trojan TR 655   Since You've Been Gone/AFROTONES: Things I Love £50
(see also Eric Fatter)

FRAYS
65   Decca F 12153   Keep Me Covered/Walk On £150
65   Decca F 12229   My Girl Sloopy/For Your Precious Love £50
(see also Mike Patto)

DEAN FRAZER
79   Cha Cha CHALP 006   PURE HORN (LP) £40

NORMA FRAZER
65   Ska Beat JB 223   Heartaches/Everybody Loves A Lover £200
67   Coxsone CS 7017   The First Cut Is The Deepest/BUMPS OAKLEY: Rag Doll £70
67   Studio One SO 2024   Come By Here/WAILERS: I Stand Predominate £250
68   Coxsone CS 7060   Respect/Time £250
(see also Sound Dimension, Righteous Homes, Viceroys, Tommy McCook, Soul Vendors)

CALVIN FRAZIER AND SAMSON PITTMAN
80   Flyright FLY LP 542   I'M IN THE HIGHWAY MAN (LP) £40

FREAK POWER
94   4th & Broadway BRLP 606   DRIVE THRU BOOTY (2-LP) £35

FREAKS OF NATURE
66   Island WI 3017   People! Let's Freak Out/The Shadow Chasers £100
(see also Kim Fowley, Belfast Gypsies, Jackie McAuley)

FREAK SISTERS
92   Nucleus NUKE 003   Freak Boutique/We've Got To Live Together (12") £20

JOHN FRED & HIS PLAYBOY BAND
68   Pye International 7N 25453 Hey Hey Bunny/No Letter Today £20
67   Pye Intl. NPL 28111   AGNES ENGLISH (LP) £20

FRED LOCKS
78   Tribesman TM 20   Love & Only Love/Stricker Ishion (12") £25
78   Revelations FRW 375   Love & Harmony/Joy & Harmony (featuring Brigadier Jerry) (p/s) £25
78   Lloyd Coxsone LC 001   Voice Of The Poor/LEVI ROOTS: Poor Man's Story £25
81   Omega OM3   Redemption/Nice Up The Dance (12") £25
78   Form FORM 1091   LOVE & HARMONY (LP) £30
80   Rev 001 LP   NEBUCHADNEZZER KING OF BABYLON (FRED LOCKS MEETS CREATORS) (LP)...........£60
82   Regal RLP 002   LOVE AND ONLY LOVE (LP, with CREATION STEPPERS) £45
83   Vulcan VULA 502   BLACK STAR LINER (LP, inner with poster) £20

FREDDIE & THE DREAMERS
65   Columbia SEG 8457   FREDDIE AND THE DREAMERS (EP) £15
67   EMI Regal   SEE YOU LATER ALLIGATOR (Export issue)..£20
63   Columbia 33SX 1577   FREDDIE AND THE DREAMERS (LP) £15
64   Columbia 33SX 1663   YOU WERE MAD FOR ME (LP) £15
66   Columbia SX 6069   IN DISNEYLAND (LP, mono) £15
66   Columbia S(C)X 6069   IN DISNEYLAND (LP, stereo) £20
67   Columbia SX 6177   KING FREDDIE AND THE DREAMING KNIGHTS (LP) £20
(see also Freddie Garrity, Dreamers)

FREDDIE & THE DREAMERS/PETER & GORDON
64   Columbia SEG 8337   JUST FOR YOU (EP, 2 tracks each) £15
(see also Peter & Gordon)

FREDDIE & FITZY
66   Dr Bird 1033   Do Good/SOUL BROTHERS: On The Town £60
(see also Clarendonians, Young Freddie, Freddie McGregor)

DOTTY FREDERICK
59   Top Rank JAR 106   Ricky/Just Wait £40

TOMMY FREDERICK & HI-NOTES
58   London HLU 8555   Prince Of Players/I'm Not Pretending £50
58   London HLU 8555   Prince Of Players/I'm Not Pretending (78) £20

BILL FREDERICKS
76   Polydor 2058 946   Love With You/Someone Like You £15
77   Polydor 2058 895   Lovers/It's Just A Matter Of Time £30
78   Polydor 2059 035   Almost/Wind Of Change £75

DOLORES FREDERICKS
56   Brunswick 05540   Cha Cha Joe/Whole Lotta Shakin' Goin' On £30

MARC FREDERICKS
56	London HLD 8281	Mystic Midnight/Symphony To Anne	£20

FREE (HOLLAND)
69	Philips BF 1738	Soul Party/Down To The Bone	£15
69	Philips BF 1754	Keep In Touch/Taking It Away	£40

FREE (U.K.)
69	Island WIP 6054	Broad Daylight/The Worm	£60
69	Island WIP 6062	I'll Be Creepin'/Sugar For Mr Morrison	£60
78	Island IEPJB 6	All Right Now/Wishing Well (jukebox copy, short version)	£25
69	Island ILPS 9089	TONS OF SOBS (LP, gatefold sleeve, 1st pressing, pink label/ black & orange 'circle' logo)	£300
69	Island ILPS 9089	TONS OF SOBS (LP, gatefold sleeve, 2nd pressing, pink label/black 'block' logo)	£90
70	Island ILPS 9089	TONS OF SOBS (LP, gatefold sleeve, 3rd pressing, pink label/'i' logo)	£35
71	Island ILPS 9089	TONS OF SOBS (LP, gatefold sleeve, 4th pressing, pink rim label/ 'palm tree' logo)	£15
69	Island ILPS 9104	FREE (LP, gatefold sleeve, 1st pressing, pink label/'i' logo)	£200
70	Island ILPS 9104	FREE (LP, gatefold sleeve, 2nd pressing, pink rim label/'palm tree' logo)	£15
70	Island ILPS 9120	FIRE AND WATER (LP, 1st pressing, pink label/'i' logo)	£120
70	Island ILPS 9120	FIRE AND WATER (LP, 2nd pressing, pink rim label/'palm tree' logo)	£15
70	Island ILPS 9138	HIGHWAY (LP, pink rim, palm tree label)	£20
71	Island ILPS 9160	LIVE (LP, in envelope sleeve with inner, pink rim, palm tree label)	£40
72	Island ILPS 9192	FREE AT LAST (LP)	£25
72	Island ILPS 9217	HEARTBREAKER (LP, lyric inner sleeve, pink rim, palm tree label)	£20
74	Island ISLD 4	THE FREE STORY (2-LP, gatefold, with 4-page booklet, numbered)	£25
09	Island 0600753181850	FIRE AND WATER (LP, 180 gram reissue with Island pink 'i' logo on label)	£15
11	Music On Vinyl MOVLP 415	FREE (LP, reissue, single sleeve)	£15

(see also Paul Kossoff, Rabbit, Kossoff Kirke Tetsu & Rabbit, Sharks, Andy Fraser Band, Black Cat Bones)

FREE WINDS
66	Jon Hassell HAS 818/818	Blood Red River/Romping Roving Days/Till It's Time For You To Go/Abiline	£100
66	MJB REV LP 397	FROM A NEW DIRECTION (10" LP)	£200

FREE AGENTS
80	Groovy STP 1	FREE AGENTS (LP, 1000 only, hand-made sleeve)	£20

(see also Pete Shelley)

ALAN FREED & HIS ROCK'N'ROLL BAND
57	Vogue Coral Q 72219	Teen Rock/Right Now, Right Now (with Alan Freed's Rock'n'Rollers)	£100
57	Vogue Coral Q 72230	Rock'n'Roll Boogie/Teener's Canteen (with Alan Freed's Rock'n'Rollers)	£100
56	Vogue Coral LVA 9033	ROCK'N'ROLL DANCE PARTY VOL. 1 (LP, featuring Modernaires)	£60
57	Vogue Coral LVA 9066	ROCK'N'ROLL DANCE PARTY VOL. 2 (LP, with Jimmy Cavello)	£60

(see also Jimmy Cavello)

FREE DESIGN
69	Project 3	HEAVEN/EARTH (LP)	£30

BOB FREEDMAN ORCHESTRA
63	Island ILP 101	MUSIC TO STRIP BY (LP, with free G string)	£40

J.A. FREEDMAN
69	Decca F12963	When You Walked Out Of My Life/Love's Got A Minf Of It's Own	£25
69	Decca LK 5021	MY NAME IS J.A. FREEDMAN, I ALSO SING (LP)	£40

FREEDOM
68	Mercury MF 1033	Where Will You Be Tonight/Trying To Get A Glimpse Of You (in p/s)	£45
68	Mercury MF 1033	Where Will You Be Tonight/Trying To Get A Glimpse Of You	£30
70	Probe PRO 504	Frustrated Woman/Man Made Laws	£20
71	Vertigo 6059 051	Thanks/Miss Little Louise	£30
70	Probe SPBA 6252	FREEDOM (LP, gatefold sleeve, pink label)	£200
71	Vertigo 6360 049	THROUGH THE YEARS (LP, gatefold sleeve, small swirl label)	£300
72	Vertigo 6360 072	FREEDOM IS MORE THAN A WORD (LP, die cut gatefold sleeve, small swirl label)	£400
94	Tenth Planet TP 011	NEROSUBIANCO (LP, reissue, 500 only, booklet)	£20

(see also Mick Abrahams, Procol Harum, Snafu)

FREEDOM SINGERS (JAMAICA)
67	Studio One SO 2010	Have Faith/Work Crazy (B-side actually Dinah by Joe Higgs)	£80
70	Bamboo BAM 21	Give Peace A Chance/SOUND DIMENSION: In Cold Blood	£50

(see also Winston Francis, Leroy Sibbles)

FREED UNIT
99	Out-There OTT 06	MASONIC YOUTH (9" EP, triangular clear vinyl, 100 only)	£50
01	Out-There OTT 09	SIX SIDED (9" EP, clear vinyl, 100 only)	£25
98	Out-There OTTLP 04	FIELD REPORTS FROM OUT-THERE (LP, clear vinyl)	£18
98	Enraptured RAPTLP 19	THINGS ARE LOOKING UP... (LP, orange vinyl)	£15

FREEEZ
80	Pink Rhythm 12 PINKY 2	Stay/Hot Footing It (12")	£100
80	Pink Rhythm EL PEE 1	SOUTHERN FREEEZ (LP)	£50
80	Beggars Banquet BEGA 22	SOUTHERN FREEEZ (LP, reissue gatefold)	£15
83	Beggars Banquet BEGA 48	GONNA GET YOU (LP)	£15
84	Beggars Banquet BEGA 53	ANTI FREEEZ (LP)	£15
85	Beggars Banquet BEGA 62	IDLE VICE (LP)	£15

(see also Pink Rhythm, Gamer 3, Midi Rain)

FREE FERRY
70	CBS 4647	Haverjack Drive/Flying	£20

FREEFORM
95	Skam SKA 3	Fane/Recut/Rail/Siamese Telebox/The Brink/Many/Freeform Dub (12")......	£25
95	Skam SKA 4	FREE EP (12")......	£25

FREELANCE
83	Chav KMG S 83 CUS 1765	Writing On The Wall/Elinor/One More Time (die-cut cover)......	£40

ART FREEMAN
66	Atlantic 584 053	Slippin' Around/Can't Get You Out Of My Mind......	£200

BOBBY FREEMAN
58	London HLJ 8644	Do You Want To Dance?/Big Fat Woman......	£30
58	London HLJ 8644	Do You Want To Dance?/Big Fat Woman (78)......	£15
58	London HLJ 8721	Betty Lou Got A New Pair Of Shoes/Starlight......	£40
58	London HLJ 8721	Betty Lou Got A New Pair Of Shoes/Starlight (78)......	£15
59	London HLJ 8782	Shame On You Miss Johnson/Need Your Love......	£50
59	London HLJ 8782	Shame On You Miss Johnson/Need Your Love (78)......	£15
59	London HLJ 8898	Mary Ann Thomas/Love Me......	£40
59	London HLJ 8898	Mary Ann Thomas/Love Me (78)......	£15
60	London HLJ 9031	Sinbad/Ebb Tide (The Sea)......	£15
60	Parlophone R 4684	(I Do The) Shimmy Shimmy/You Don't Understand Me......	£20
64	Pye International 7N 25260	C'mon And Swim (Parts 1 & 2)......	£25
64	Pye International 7N 25280	S-W-I-M/That Little Old Heartbreaker Me......	£25
66	Pye International 7N 25347	The Duck/Cross My Heart......	£30

BUD FREEMAN
66	Fontana TL 5370	BUD FREEMAN ESQ. (LP)......	£20
68	Fontana TL 5414	FREEMAN & CO (LP)......	£20

CAROL FREEMAN
67	CBS 202579	The Rolling Sea/Leaving You Now......	£15

ERNIE FREEMAN
57	London HLP 8523	Raunchy/Puddin'......	£20
57	London HL 7029	Dumplin's/Beautiful Weekend (export issue)......	£15
58	London HLP 8558	Dumplin's/Beautiful Weekend......	£15
56	London RE-U 1059	ERNIE FREEMAN AND HIS RHYTHM GUITAR (EP)......	£30
59	London RE-P 1210	ERNIE FREEMAN VOL. 2 (EP)......	£30

GEORGE FREEMAN
71	Jay Boy BOY 54	I'm Like A Fish/Why Are You Doing This To Me......	£15

MARGARET FREEMAN
61	Starlite ST45 040	Forbidden Fruit/Mister Ting A Ling......	£40

PAUL FREEMAN
71	Punch PH 82	Don't Give Up/UPSETTERS: Give Up (Version)......	£20

FREE MOVEMENT
72	CBS 7768	The Harder I Try/Comin' Home......	£30

FREE 'N EASY (1)
68	Oak RGJ 628	FREE 'N EASY (LP, private pressing [Warren Coley W.C.P. 001])......	£100

FREE 'N' EASY (2)
81	SRT/Clovis S81 CUS 1222 BMC 003	FOUR EASY MOVES EP......	£30

FREE SOULS
64	Blue Beat BB 264	I Want To Be Free/Angel......	£50

FREESTYLE FELLOWSHIP
93	4th & Broadway BRLP 595	INNERCITY GRIOTS (LP, printed inner)......	£85
93	4th & Broadway BRW 274	Hot Potato/Way Cool (p/s)......	£40

FREESTYLE ORCHESTRA
89	SBK 12SBKDJ 7011	Keep On Pumping It Up (12", promo only)......	£15

FREEWAY
79	Decca TXS 131	FREEWAY (LP)......	£18

(see also Terry Melcher)

FREEZE
79	A1.A.1.1.A.1	IN COLOUR (EP, p/s)......	£15

ACE FREHLEY
78	Casablanca CAN 135	New York Groove/Snow Blind (p/s, blue vinyl with mask)......	£30

(see also Kiss)

DON FRENCH
59	London HLW 8884	Lonely Saturday Night/Goldilocks......	£40
59	London HLW 8989	Little Blonde Girl/I Look Into My Heart......	£100
59	London HLW 8989	Little Blonde Girl/I Look Into My Heart (78)......	£20

ROBERT FRENCH
85	Uptemp UTO 10	Something On My Mind/Help Yourself (12")......	£40

FRENCH IMPRESSIONISTS
82	Operation Twilight OPT 020	Santa Baby/THICK PIGEON: Jingle Bell Rock/MONKS IN THE SNOW: A Theme For This Special Evening (P/s, last track uncredited)......	£20

(see also Aztec Camera)

FRENCH REVOLUTION
69	Decca F 22898	Nine Till Five/Why?......	£70

FRENZY (1)
76	DJM DJS 633	Poser/Things You Do (To Me)	£15

FRENZY (2)
81	Frenzy FRENZY 1	This Is The Last Time/Gypsy Dancer (no p/s)	£50
81	Frenzy FRENZY 2	Blackburn Rovers/Up The Rovers	£35
81	Frenzy FRENZY 3	Without You/Thanks For Nothing (no p/s)	£50
86	I.D. NOSE 8	CLOCKWORK TOY (LP)	£15
87	I.D. NOSE 19	SALLY'S PINK BEDROOM (LP)	£15

FRESH
70	RCA RCA 2003	Stoned In Saigon/Just A Note	£20
70	RCA SF 8122	FRESH OUT OF BORSTAL (LP)	£20
71	RCA LSA 3027	FRESH TODAY (LP)	£18

(see also Paul Korda, Brother Bung, Fruit Machine)

FRESH AIR
69	Pye 7N 17736	Running Wild/Stop, Look, Listen	£200

FRESH GROUND
70	Dortell DT1	Inside Out/Ways Of Man	£80

FRESH MAGGOTS
71	RCA RCA 2150	Car Song/What Would You Do	£40
71	RCA SF 8205	FRESH MAGGOTS (LP, orange label)	£750
07	Sunbeam SBR2LP5002	FRESH MAGGOTS - HATCHED (2-LP, reissue)	£18

FRESH SKI & MO ROCK
88	Tuff GrooveTUFF003	Talking Pays/Pick Up On This (12")	£100
91	Conscious CON003	THE LONG AWAITED PAROXYSM (EP)	£20
11	Diggers With Gratitude DWG 010	THE COARSE SELECTORS (EP)	£15

FRESH WINDOWS
67	Fontana TF 839	Fashion Conscious/Summer Sun Shines	£200

FRESHIES
78	Razz RAZZXEP 1	BAISER (EP, with Chris Sievey solo tracks, 33rpm, no'd, handwritten labels)	£40
79	Razz RAZZXEP 2	STRAIGHT IN AT NO. 2 (EP, handwritten labels with inserts, 1,000 only, numbered, green or orange p/s)	£30
79	Razz RAZZ 3	THE MEN FROM BANANA ISLAND WHOSE STUPID IDEAS NEVER CAUGHT ON IN THE WESTERN WORLD AS WE KNOW IT (EP, black & white photocopied p/s or numbered blue p/s)	£15
79	Razz RAZZ 5	We're Like You/CHRIS SIEVEY: Hey (p/s)	£15
80	Razz RAZZ 8	RED INDIAN MUSIC (EP, with Chris Sievey)	£18
80	Razz RAZZ 11	I'm In Love With The Girl On The Virgin Manchester Megastore Checkout Desk/Singalong Version (p/s, with free lyric book)	£15
80	Razz RAZZ 12	I'm In Love With The Girl On The Virgin Megastore Manchester Checkout Desk (Radio Version)/Singalong Version ('bleeped') (white label radio issue, 200 only)	£15
80	Razz RAZZ 13	One To One/House Beautiful (unreleased)	£0
84	HANNA 1	Virgin Megastore/Wrap Up The Rockets/Buy Me A Shirt/Tell Her I'm Ill/Frank Talks To Chris (Conversation) (12", white label, stickered sleeve)	£30
85	ETS 1	JOHNNY RADAR STORY (20-track, with bonus Frank Sidebottom 8-track: "Firm Favourites")	£20

(see also Chris Sievey)

FRESHMEN
68	Pye N(S)PL 18263	MOVIN' ON (LP)	£100
70	CBS 64099	PEACE ON EARTH (LP)	£40

STEPHEN FRETWELL
03	Tape Recordings TAPE 001	Something's Got To Give/Whenforever/Honey	£20

FRIDA
84	Epic EPC A 4886	Heart Of The Country/Slowly (p/s)	£15
84	Epic EPC TA 4886	Heart Of The Country/Slowly/I Know There's Something Going On (Extended) (12")	£20

(see also Abba)

CAROL FRIDAY
65	Parlophone R 5369	Everybody I Know/Wasted Days	£30

FRIDAY CLUB
85	2 Tone CHSTT28	Window Shopping/Window Shopping (instrumental) (p/s)	£100
85	2 Tone CHSTT1228	Window Shopping (extended version)/Window Shopping (instrumental) 12" (p/s)	£100

FRIDGE
97	Output OPR 06	CEEFAX (LP)	£25
98	Output OPR 12	SEMAPHORE (2-LP)	£25
99	Go Beat 547 1141	EPH (2-LP)	£25
00	Text TEXT002LP	HAPPINESS (2-LP)	£20

(see also Four Tet)

BRIAN JOSEPH FRIEL
74	Dawn DNLS 3054	BRIAN JOSEPH FRIEL (LP, gatefold sleeve with insert, pink 'sun' label)	£20

FRIEND & LOVER
68	Verve VS 1515	Reach Out Of The Darkness/Time Is On Your Side	£15

TERRY FRIEND & FRIENDS
77	Tramp (no cat. no.)	COME THE DAY (LP, private pressing, 100 only)	£40

(see also Stonefield Tramp)

FRIENDLY FIRES
08	XL XLT 395	Paris (Aeroplane Remix)/Paris (Justus Kohncke Remix) (12", p/s)......................£15
08	XL XLLP 383	FRIENDLY FIRES (LP)..£25

FRIENDS (1)
68	Deram DM 198	Piccolo Man/Mythological Sunday...£30

(see also Ivy League)

FRIENDS (3)
74	Merlin HF 4	FRIENDS (LP, white label test pressing, 1 copy only!)..........................£2000

(see also Ithaca, Alice Through The Looking Glass, Agincourt, Tomorrow Come Someday, BBC Radiophonic Workshop)

FRIENDS (4)
75	Caroline C1511	FRIENDS (LP, stickered with £1.49 price tag and quote from Jazz Forum)........£20

FRIENDS (5)
83	Rock Shop RSR 002	Night Walker/Wasted Time (no p/s)...£25

FRIENDS O' MINE
72	Westwood WRS 021	FRIENDS O' MINE (LP, 250 copies only)..£100

FRIENDS OF DISTINCTION
69	RCA SF 8032	GRAZIN' (LP)..£20

FRIENDSHIP LEAGUE
75	Luggage (no cat no)	FRIENDSHIP LEAGUE 5 TRACKS (plays at 33rpm)...............................£35

FRIGHTY
01	Jah Tubbys JT 7009	Call On Jah Name/OFFBEAT POSSE: Call On Dub..............................£25
03	Jah Tubbys JT 10012	Jah Jah Is Coming/Fright Jah Jah Is Coming Version/Dub Is Coming (10", with the Offbeat Posse)..£20

FRIJID PINK
70	Deram SML 1062	FRIJID PINK (LP)..£100
70	Deram SML 1077	DEFROSTED (LP)...£100

THOMAS FRIMPONG
84	Damfo Domino DDP 006	SASAKRROMA (LP)..£40
85	Asona ASR 2010	AYE YI (LP)..£100
86	Asona ASR 5010	ANASI SHUFFLE (LP)..£50

(ROBERT) FRIPP & (BRIAN) ENO
73	Island HELP 16	NO PUSSYFOOTING (LP, gatefold sleeve, black label with pink 'i' logo)........£40
75	Island HELP 22	EVENING STAR (LP, black label with pink 'i' logo)..............................£30
77	Polydor 2343095	NO PUSSYFOOTING (LP, reissue)..£15
86	Editions EG EGED 3	EVENING STAR (LP, reissue)...£15
14	Discipline Global Mobile/ Opal DGM LP 1	NO PUSSYFOOTING (LP, reissue, 200gm vinyl)................................£15
14	Discipline Global Mobile/ Opal DGM LP 3	THE EQUATORIAL STARS (LP)...£15

(see also Giles Giles & Fripp, King Crimson, Brian Eno, Roxy Music, Robert Fripp)

ROBERT FRIPP
79	EG PRO 090	FOUR FROM EXPOSURE (12", p/s, promo)......................................£15
85	EG EGODJ 23	North Star/Heptaparaparshinokh (7" promo, blue injection labels)........£15
79	EG EGLP 101	EXPOSURE (LP, postcard, printed inner)..£20
80	EG EGLP 105	GOD SAVE THE QUEEN/UNDER HEAVY MANNERS (LP, printed inner, postcard)........£20
81	Editions EG EGED 10	LET THE POWER FALL (LP, postcard)...£15
85	EG EGMLP 4	NETWORK (LP, mini album)...£15
85	EG EGLP 41	EXPOSURE (1983 remixed edition) (LP, printed inner)......................£15
86	Editions EG EGED 43	LIVE! (Robert Fripp And The League Of Crafty Guitarists) (LP)..........£18
91	Editions EG EEG 2102-1	SHOW OF HANDS (Robert Fripp & The League Of Crafty Guitarists) (LP)........£30
20	Panegyric DGMLPX101	EXPOSURE (2LP, augmented reissue, gatefold, printed inners)........£30
21	Panegyric RFXP5010	MUSIC FOR QUIET MOMENTS (8CD box set, booklet)......................£60
22	Panegyric RFBX101	EXPOSURES: STUDIO, LIVE 1977-1983 (25CD/3DVD/3BD box set, book, ephemera)......£150

(see also Giles, Giles & Fripp, King Crimson, Fripp & Eno, League Of Gentleman (2), David Sylvian & Robert Fripp)

JACKIE FRISCO
63	Decca F 11566	You Can't Catch Me/Sugar Baby...£15

VONNIE FRITCHIE
55	London HLU 8178	Sugar Booger Avenue/There I Stood (To Throw Old Shoes And Rice)........£40

FRED FRITH
74	Caroline C 1508	GUITAR SOLOS (LP)..£30
76	Caroline C 1518	GUITAR SOLOS 2 (LP)...£25

(see also Henry Cow)

FROCK
78	Frock Music FM 7848	SILKIE (LP, 250 only)..£300

EDGAR FROESE
74	Virgin V 2016	AQUA (LP, gatefold)...£15
75	Virgin V 2040	EPSILON IN MALAYSIAN PALE (LP beige "mirror" girl label)..............£15

(see also Tangerine Dream)

FROG
73	Jam JAM 39	Witch Hunt (Theme From Psychomania)/Living Dead (die-cut company sleeve)........£150

(see also John Cameron)

FROG ISLAND SKIFFLE GROUP
57	77 Records EP 4	FROG ISLAND SKIFFLE GROUP (EP)...£200

RAYMOND FROGGATT
68	Polydor 583 044	THE VOICE AND WRITING OF RAYMOND FROGGATT (LP, gatefold)	£15
72	Bell BELLS 207	BLEACH (LP)	£15
74	Reprise K 44257	ROGUES AND THIEVES (LP)	£15

(see also Monopoly)

FROGMEN
61	Oriole CB 1617	Underwater/Mad Rush (withdrawn)	£100

FROGMORTON
76	Philips 6308 261	AT LAST (LP, blue/silver labels)	£25

FROM WEST TO EAST
72	Zella JHPS 128	FROM WEST TO EAST (LP)	£20

DOM FRONTIERE & HIS ORCHESTRA
57	London HLU 8385	Jet Rink Ballad/Uno Mas	£15

FRONT LINE
65	Atlantic AT 4057	I Don't Care/Got Love	£40

FRONTLINE ORCHESTRA
81	Ice ICET 50	Don't Turn You Back On Me/No Entry (12")	£40

FROST
69	Vanguard SVRL 19052	FROST MUSIC (LP)	£18
69	Vanguard SVRL 19056	ROCK AND ROLL MUSIC (LP)	£18

(see also Alice Cooper)

BERNIE FROST
74	Vertigo 6059 108	The House/What Do You Want To Hear Today	£50

(see also Status Quo, Rossi & Frost, Boz Frost)

BOZ FROST
73	Vertigo 6059 089	Foreign Lady/Big White Seagull	£25

(see also Status Quo, Rossi & Frost, Bernie Frost)

FROST LANE
71	Cutty Wren MM 1	FROST LANE (LP, actually various artists LP)	£45

MAX FROST & TROOPERS
68	Capitol CL 15565	Shape Of Things To Come/Free Lovin'	£30

(see also Millicent Martin)

FROZEN TEAR
69	Ra RA 5001	The Hunter/You Know What Has To Be (99 copies only)	£450

FRUGAL SOUND
66	Pye 7N 17062	Norwegian Wood/Cruel To Be Kind	£15

FRUIT EATING BEARS
78	DJM DJS 857	Door In My Face/Going Through The Motions (company sleeve)	£45
78	Lightning GIL 509	Chevy Heavy/Fifties Cowboy (p/s)	£40

FRUIT MACHINE
69	Spark SRL 1003	Follow Me/Cuddly Toy	£80
69	Spark SRL 1027	I'm Alone Today/Sunshine Of Your Love (in title p/s)	£200
69	Spark SRL 1027	I'm Alone Today/Sunshine Of Your Love	£80

(see also Rare Bird)

FRUMPY
71	Philips 6003 133	Life Without Pain/Morning	£20
71	Philips 6305 067	ALL WILL BE CHANGED (LP, black/silver labels)	£120
72	Philips 6305 098	FRUMP 2 (LP, black & blue vinyl)	£100

(see also Atlantis)

FRUUPP
73	Dawn DNLS 3053	FUTURE LEGENDS (LP, gatefold sleeve)	£150
74	Dawn DNLS 3058	SEVEN SECRETS (LP, with lyric insert)	£150
74	Dawn DNLH 2	THE PRINCE OF HEAVEN'S EYES (LP, gatefold sleeve, with book)	£150
74	Dawn DNLH 2	THE PRINCE OF HEAVEN'S EYES (LP, gatefold sleeve, without book)	£100
75	Dawn DNLS 3070	MODERN MASQUERADES (LP, gatefold sleeve, with lyric insert)	£100

MARK FRY
06	Sunbeam SBRLPS 028	DREAMING WITH ALICE (LP, 180 gram vinyl reissue of original 1972 Italian pressing)	£20

FUCHSIA
71	Pegasus PEG 8	FUCHSIA (LP)	£400
17	Fruits De Mer CRUSTACEAN 82	FUCHSIA II (200 only, 100 on magenta and 100 on green vinyl)	£40
18	Fruits De Mer CRUSTACEAN 86	FUCHSIA (reissue, 2-LP gatefold, with DVD, poster)	£50

FUCK BUTTONS
10	Rock Action ROCKACT 43	Colours Move (Shibuya Drunk Mix)/Mogwai Fear Satan (10", white vinyl p/s)	£18
08	ATP ATPRLP 28	STREET HORRSING (2-LP)	£25
09	ATP ATPRLP 35	TAROT SPORT (2-LP)	£35
13	Epic Electronic ATPRLP 49	SLOW FOCUS (2-LP)	£25

FUCKED UP
11	Fucked Up FU 010	The Other Shoe/The Truest Road (p/s, lyric sheet, original U.K. tour 7")	£20

THE FUCKERS
97	Kalevala KALA 002	Sexy Roy Orbison/Sexy Roy Orbison (Version)	£20

MINT VALUE £

FUDGE TUNNEL
91	Earache MOSH 36	HATE SONGS IN E MINOR (LP, with free hand-painted 7").....................................£40
92	Earache MOSH 64	CREEP DIETS (LP, insert)...£25
94	Earache MOSH 119LP	THE COMPLICATED FUTILITY OF IGNORANCE (LP)...£30

FUGAZI
89	Dischord DIS 44	REPEATER (LP)...£20
91	Dischord DIS 60V	STEADY DIET OF NOTHING (LP, inner) £25
93	Dischord DIS 60V	IN ON THE KILL TAKER (LP) £30
95	Dischord DIS 90V	RED MEDICINE (LP) £35
98	Dischord DIS 110V	END HITS (LP, gatefold) £25

FUGEES
| 96 | Columbia 483549-1 | THE SCORE (2-LP)..£60 |

(see also Lauryn Hill)

FUGI
| 71 | Blue Horizon 2096 005 | Red Moon (Parts 1 & 2)...£30 |

FUGITIVE
| 81 | Private pressing FMR 050 | Need My Freedom..£20 |

FUGITIVES (JAMAICA)
| 67 | Doctor Bird DB 1082 | Musical Pressure/LESLIE BUTLER & FUGITIVES: Winchester Rocksteady ....£70 |
| 67 | Doctor Bird 1097 | Lecture/Canteloupe Rock..£80 |

(see also Jo Jo Bennett & Fugitives, Two Kings, Jo Jo Bennett, Stranger Cole)

FUGITIVES (U.S.)
| 61 | Vogue V 9176 | Freeway/Fugitive..£30 |

FUGS
68	Big T BIG 115	Crystal Liaison/When The Mode Of The Music Changes £15
68	Transatlantic TRA 180	TENDERNESS JUNCTION (LP, with poster)..............................£55
68	Transatlantic TRA 180	TENDERNESS JUNCTION (LP, without poster)...........................£25
68	Transatlantic TRA 181	IT CRAWLED INTO MY HAND, HONEST (LP)...............................£40
69	Fontana (S)TL 5501	VIRGIN FUGS (LP)..£30
69	Fontana (S)TL 5513	THE FUGS ... FIRST ALBUM (LP).....................................£40
69	Fontana (S)TL 5524	FUGS II (LP) £35
69	Reprise RSLP 6359	THE BELLE OF AVENUE A (LP) £35
70	Reprise 6396	GOLDEN FILTH - LIVE AT THE FILLIMORE EAST (LP) £35

FULHAM FURIES
| 78 | GM GMS 9050 | These Boots Are Made For Walking/Under Pressure (no p/s) ....£35 |

(see also Lurkers)

BLIND BOY FULLER
57	Philips BBL 7512	BLIND BOY FULLER 1935-40 (LP) £25
68	Matchbox SDR 143	BLIND BOY FULLER ON DOWN VOLUME 1 (LP) £15
69	Matchbox SDR 168	BLIND BOY FULLER ON DOWN VOLUME 2 (LP) £15
60s	Flyright LP 105	CAROLINA BLUES (LP)..£15

BOBBY FULLER FOUR
66	London HLU 10030	I Fought The Law/Little Annie Lou £30
66	London HLU 10041	Love's Made A Fool Of You/Don't You Ever Let Me Know.................£15
67	President PTL 1003	MEMORIAL ALBUM (LP) £40

CURTIS FULLER/TOMMY FLANAGAN
| 58 | Pye NPL28009 | IT'S MAGIC (LP) ....£30 |

JERRY FULLER
| 62 | Salvo SLO 1802 | Lipstick And Rouge/Mother Goose At The Bandstand (99 copies only).........£150 |

JESSE FULLER
58	Good Time Jazz LAG 12159	JESSE FULLER (LP) £25
60	Good Time Jazz LAG 12279	LONE CAT (LP) £25
60	Topic 10T 59	WORKING ON THE RAILROAD (10" LP) £35
63	Good Time Jazz LAG 574	SAN FRANCISCO BAY BLUES (LP) £25
65	Stateside SL 10154	JESSE FULLER'S FAVOURITES (LP) £20
66	Fontana TL 5313	SESSION WITH JESSE FULLER (LP).......................................£25
66	Topic 12T 134	MOVE ON DOWN THE LINE (LP) £35
60s	Vocalion VRLP 574	SAN FRANCISCO BAY BLUES (LP) £20
60s	Evolution Z 1004	LIVE IN LONDON (LP) £20

FULL EXPERIENCE
| 12 | Attack THB 7016 | Young Gifted And Broke/Can't See You ....£20 |

FULL MOON (1)
| 79 | SRTS/79/CUS 279 | Stand Up/Fly Away (p/s) ....£35 |

FULL MOON (2)
87	Luna SRT 7K51283	The Eternal Now/Nemesis £25
89	Voices Of Wonder VOW11	FULL MOON (LP, insert) £25
92	Demi Monde DMLP 1031	EUPHORIA (LP)...£20

LOWELL FULSON/FULSOM
65	Sue WI 375	Too Many Drivers/Key To Your Heart £40
66	Sue WI 4023	Talking Woman/Blues Around Midnight £40
66	Outasite 45-502	Stop And Think/Baby (with Leon Blue) £70
66	Polydor 56515	Black Nights/Little Angel £20
67	Fontana TF 795	Tramp/Pico £20

69	Fontana SFJL 920	**SAN FRANCISCO BLUES** (LP)	**£30**
69	Polydor 2384 038	**IN A HEAVY BAG** (LP, as Lowell Fulsom)	**£20**

MAURICE FULTON
00	Spectrum RAJLP 001	**LIFE IS WATER FOR GERBADAISIES WHEN THEY ARE DANCING** (2-LP)	**£40**
01	Transfusion TFLP 001	**WHY PUT ME THROUGH IT** (2-LP)	**£20**

FUMME
83	Sanity 12STY 008	**Only You** (Make It Right)**/Only You** (Make It Right - Instrumental)**/Only You** (Make It Right - Instrumental) (12")	**£70**

FUNBOY FIVE
80	Cool Cat Daddy-O PHUN 1	**Life After Death/Compulsive Eater** (foldover green, yellow, pink, blue and white p/s)	**£70**

FUNERAL FOR A FRIEND
03	Infectious EW 269	**Juneau/Getaway Plan** (white vinyl, p/s)	**£15**
03	Warner EW 274	**She Drove Me To Daytime TV/Bullet Theory** (blue vinyl, p/s)	**£15**
03	Infectious INFEC 126S	**Four Ways — This Year's Most Open Heartbreak/She Drove Me To Daytime Television//Kiss And Make Up** (All Bets Are Off)**/Escape Artists Never Die** (2 x 7" red vinyl, gatefold p/s)	**£20**
03	Infectious 2564609471	**CASUALLY DRESSED AND DEEP IN CONVERSATON** (2-LP)	**£20**
05	Atlantic 5050467844	**HOURS** (2-LP)	**£50**
08	Roadrunner RRCAR 7911-1	**MEMORY AND HUMANITY** (LP)	**£20**

FUN FOUR
80	NMC NMC 010	**Singing In The Showers/By Products/Elevator Crush** (p/s)	**£100**

(see also Orange Juice)

FUNGUS
73	Fungus FUN 1	**PREMONITIONS** (LP, private pressing)	**£200**

(see also Secondhand)

FUNKADELIC
70	Pye Intl. NSPL 28137	**FUNKADELIC** (LP)	**£200**
71	Pye Intl. NSPL 28144	**FREE YOUR MIND AND YOUR ASS WILL FOLLOW** (LP)	**£200**
71	Janus 6310 201	**MAGGOT BRAIN** (LP)	**£200**
75	20th Century W 215	**LET'S TAKE IT TO THE STAGE** (LP)	**£20**
78	Warner Bros K 56299	**HARDCORE JOLLIES** (LP)	**£20**
78	Warner Bros K 56539	**ONE NATION UNDER A GROOVE** (LP, with free 12" "One Nation Under A Groove")	**£30**
06	Westbound SEW 002	**MAGGOT BRAIN** (LP, reissue)	**£15**
17	Westbound SEW3 158	**REWORKED BY DETROITERS** (3-LP)	**£20**

(see also Parliament, Parlet, Bootsy's Rubber Band, Dolby's Cube, P-Funk Allstars)

FUNKALOO
79	Rouge RMS 122	**ROBOT DANCER** (LP)	**£40**

FUNKEES
75	Contempo CS 2058	**Tu Lay/Cool It Down**	**£25**
74	Amba AM 001	**POINT OF NO RETURN** (LP)	**£200**

FUNKGUS
76	Baal BAL 89002	**II** (LP)	**£25**

FUNKY BOTTOM CONGREGATION
69	Beacon BEA 122	**Hare-Krishna/Things About Yourself**	**£20**

FINBAR & EDDIE FUREY
68	Transatlantic TRA 168	**FINBAR AND EDDIE FUREY** (LP, laminated front sleeve, white/lilac labels)	**£15**
72	Dawn DNLS 3037	**THE DAWNING OF THE DAY** (LP, with lyric insert, lilac label)	**£20**

FURNITURE
80	Para 1	**Shaking Story/Take A Walk Down Town** (p/s)	**£30**
83	Premonition PREM 4CA	**WHEN THE BOOM WAS ON** (Mini-LP)	**£20**
86	Premonition PREM 6	**THE LOVEMONGERS** (LP)	**£20**

TOMMY FURTADO
57	London HLA 8418	**Sun Tan Sam/Isabella**	**£40**

BILLY FURY
78s
59	Decca F 11102	**Maybe Tomorrow/Gonna Type A Letter**	**£200**
59	Decca F 11128	**Margo/Don't Knock Upon My Door**	**£150**
59	Decca F 11158	**Angel Face/Time Has Come**	**£250**
59	Decca F 11189	**My Christmas Prayer/Last Kiss**	**£300**

SINGLES
59	Decca F 11102	**Maybe Tomorrow/Gonna Type A Letter** (triangular centre)	**£25**
59	Decca F 11102	**Maybe Tomorrow/Gonna Type A Letter** (later pressing with round centre)	**£15**
59	Decca F 11128	**Margo/Don't Knock Upon My Door** (triangular centre)	**£30**
59	Decca F 11128	**Margo/Don't Knock Upon My Door** (later pressing with round centre)	**£20**
59	Decca F 11158	**Angel Face/Time Has Come** (triangular centre)	**£30**
59	Decca F 11158	**Angel Face/Time Has Come** (later pressing with round centre)	**£20**
59	Decca F 11189	**My Christmas Prayer/Last Kiss** (triangular centre)	**£50**
59	Decca F 11189	**My Christmas Prayer/Last Kiss** (later pressing with round centre)	**£25**
60	Decca F 11200	**Colette/Baby How I Cried** (triangular centre)	**£40**
60	Decca F 11200	**Colette/Baby How I Cried** (later pressing with round centre)	**£15**
60	Decca F 11237	**That's Love/You Don't Know** (as Billy Fury & Four Jays)	**£20**
60	Decca F 11267	**Wondrous Place/Alright, Goodbye**	**£20**
61	Decca F 11334	**Don't Worry/Talkin' In My Sleep** (with Four Kestrels)	**£15**
62	Decca F 11437	**Letter Full Of Tears/Magic Eyes**	**£15**

64	Decca F.11888	I Will/Nothin' Shakin' (But The Leaves On The Trees) (some B-sides list "Nothin' Shakin' ")	£15
64	Decca F 40719	Hippy Hippy Shake/Glad All Over (export-only, with p/s)	£80
64	Decca F 40719	Hippy Hippy Shake/Glad All Over (export-only)	£50
66	Decca F 12459	Give Me Your Word/She's So Far Out She's In	£15
67	Parlophone R 5560	Hurtin' Is Loving/Things Are Changing	£30
67	Parlophone R 5605	Loving You/I'll Go Along With It Now	£20
67	Parlophone R 5634	Suzanne In The Mirror/It Just Don't Matter Now	£40
67	Parlophone R 5658	Beyond The Shadow Of A Doubt/Baby Do You Love Me?	£40
68	Parlophone R 5681	Silly Boy Blue/One Minute Woman	£40
68	Parlophone R 5723	Phone Box/Any Morning Now	£40
68	Parlophone R 5747	Lady/Certain Things	£40
69	Parlophone R 5788	I Call For My Rose/Bye Bye	£50
69	Parlophone R 5819	All The Way To The U.S.A./Do My Best For You	£50
70	Parlophone R 5845	Why Are You Leaving?/Old Sweet Roll (Hi-De-Ho)	£50
70	Parlophone R 5874	Paradise Alley/Well ... All Right	£50
72	Fury FY 301	Will The Real Man Please Stand Up/At This Stage	£40
74	Warner Bros WB 16402	I'll Be Your Sweetheart/Fascinating Candle Flame	£30
83	Polydor POSP 558	Let Me Go Lover/Your Words (same p/s as above but diff. A-side, 500 only)	£20
83	Lyntone LYN 13078/BF 1	Devil Or Angel/Lost Without You (flexi free within memorial concert booklet)	£20
83	Private pressing	BILLY FURY IN INTERVIEW WITH STUART COLEMAN (10", 500 white label copies only, 1st 200 numbered)	£30
83	Private pressing	BILLY FURY IN INTERVIEW WITH STUART COLEMAN (10", 500 white label copies only, un-numbered)	£20

EPs

59	Decca DFE 6597	MAYBE TOMORROW (triangular centre, orange/red p/s)	£80
59	Decca DFE 6597	MAYBE TOMORROW (round centre, orange/red p/s)	£60
59	Decca DFE 6597	MAYBE TOMORROW (round centre, yellow p/s)	£100
61	Decca DFE 6694	BILLY FURY	£45
62	Decca DFE 6699	BILLY FURY NO. 2	£45
62	Decca DFE 6708	PLAY IT COOL	£25
62	Decca DFE 6708	PLAY IT COOL (export issue, blue/green 'crouching' cover)	£70
62	Decca DFE 8505	BILLY FURY HITS	£20
63	Decca DFE 8525	BILLY FURY AND THE TORNADOS	£20
63	Decca DFE 8558	AM I BLUE	£50
65	Decca DFE 8641	BILLY FURY AND THE GAMBLERS	£100

ALBUMS

60	Decca LF 1329	THE SOUND OF FURY (10")	£250
60	Ace Of Clubs ACL 1047	BILLY FURY	£30
61	Ace Of Clubs ACL 1083	HALFWAY TO PARADISE	£30
63	Decca LK 4533	BILLY	£40
63	Decca LK 4548	WE WANT BILLY! (with Tornados, mono)	£40
63	Decca SKL 4548	WE WANT BILLY! (with Tornados, stereo)	£45
65	Decca LK 4677	I'VE GOTTA HORSE (soundtrack)	£40
76	Decca DPA 3033/4	THE BILLY FURY STORY (2-LP)	£15
81	Decca LFT 1329	THE SOUND OF FURY (10", reissue)	£20

(see also Tornados, Gamblers)

FURYS

72	Jay Boy BOY 68	I'm Satisfied With You/Just A Little Mixed Up	£15
72	Jay Boy BOY 68	I'm Satisfied With You/Just A Little Mixed Up (DJ Copy)	£30

F.U.S.E.

93	Warp LP12LTD	Dimension Intrusion (2-LP, white vinyl)	£15

FUSION ORCHESTRA

73	EMI EMA 758	A SKELETON IN ARMOUR (LP, gatefold sleeve)	£100

FUSION (1)

80	Telephone TEL 101	TILL I HEAR FROM YOU (LP, blue vinyl)	£20

FUSION FARM

71	SRT 71169	RUSH JOB (LP)	£400

FUT

70	Beacon BEA 160	Have You Heard The Word/Futting Around	£30

(see also Graham Bonnet, Bee Gees, Maurice Gibb, Steve & Stevie; this record has NO Beatles involvement)

FUTURA 2000

83	Celluloid CYZ 104	The Escapades of Futura 2000/Instrumental Version (12", p/s, featuring The Clash)	£15
83	Celluloid CYZ-7-104	The Escapades of Futura 2000/Instrumental Version (p/s, featuring The Clash)	£15

(see also The Clash)

FUTURE BEAT ALLIANCE

96	Void VOID 002	Mode 2/Volatile Memory/Electric Blues/Deep Enuf (12")	£20
97	Void VOID 006	Inside Out/Advance/Intruder (12")	£15
97	Void VOID 009	HIDDEN EMOTION (LP as 2 x 12", white label only)	£60

FUTURE BODIES

80	SGS 111	Terrorist/Science Of Romance (p/s, lyric insert, rubber stamped labels)	£45

FUTURE OF THE LEFT

06	Too Pure PURE 206LP	CURSES! (LP)	£30
09	4AD CAD2913	TRAVELS WITH MYSELF AND ANOTHER (LP)	£25
12	Xtra Mile Recordings – XMR058LP	THE PLOT AGAINST COMMON SENSE (LP)	£15

FUTURE PAST
91	B12 03	Our Paths Meet/Harmony Park/Your Hand In My Mind/Dance Intellect/TV People (12", black vinyl)......£50

FUTURE SOUND OF HARDCORE
93	Dee Jay DJX 013	VOLUME 1 (12").....£30
94	Dee Jay DJX 014	VOLUME 2 (12").....£20
94	Dee Jay DJX 016A	Promised Land (Remix) (12" 1-sided).....£50

FUTURE SOUND OF LONDON
92	Jumpin' & Pumpin' 12TOT 17R	Papua New Guinea (Andrew Weatherall Mix)/(Dub Mix)/(Journey To Pyramid)/(Monsoon Mix)/(Graham Massey Mix)/(Dumb Child Of Q Mix) (p/s).....£15
94	Virgin promo 500	Slider/Snake Hips/You're Creeping Me Out/Herd Killing/Live In New York (2 x 12" p/s, promo only, 500 copies, FSOL under different names).....£15
94	Virgin VST 1540P	Far Out Son Of Lung And The Ramblings Of A Madman/Snake Hips/Smokin' Japanese Babe/Amoeba (white vinyl, promo only).....£20
95	Virgin SEMTEX DJ 1	Semtex (Part 1)/Semtex (Part 2)/We Have Explosive/Semtex (stamped sleeve, promo only, 500 copies).....£15
92	Jumpin'/Pumpin' LPTOT 2	ACCELERATOR (LP).....£20
94	Virgin V 2722	LIFEFORMS (2-LP, stickered gatefold sleeve with inner sleeves).....£80
94	Virgin V 2755	ISDN (LP, embossed, fold-out black sleeve with insert).....£50
94	Virgin VX 2755	ISDN (2-LP version).....£50
96	Virgin V 2814	DEAD CITIES (2-LP, gatefold sleeve with inners).....£40
15	LP TOT 59	ENVIROMENTS (LP, reissue).....£20
19	Virgin 0602557787078	LIFEFORMS (2-LP, reissue).....£20

(see also Amorphous Androgynous, Art Science Technology, Humanoid,

FUTUREHEADS
04	679 579 L07T	FUTUREHEADS (2-LP).....£30

FUZZ (1)
71	Mojo 2916 010	FUZZ (LP).....£25

FUZZTONES
85	ABC LP 4	LYSERGIC EMANATIONS (LP).....£15
91	Music Maniac MMLP 044	BRAINDROPS (LP).....£20

FUZZY DUCK
71	MAM MAM 37	Double Time Woman/Just Look Around You.....£15
71	MAM MAM 51	Big Brass Band/One More Hour.....£15
71	MAM AS 1005	FUZZY DUCK (LP, laminated front sleeve, black/silver labels).....£700
90	Reflection MM 05	FUZZY DUCK (LP, reissue with booklet & single "Double Time Woman"/ "One More Hour" [MMS 01]).....£25

(see also Andromeda, Greatest Show On Earth, Alvin Lee, Capability Brown, Cockney Rebel))

FX
79	Southern Rock SR 4501	THE SOUTH'S GONNA RISE AGAIN (EP, oversized 8" folding p/s).....£200

HILTON FYLE BAND
87	Nadiya NADLP 1002	FRESH (LP).....£60
88	Finesse FIN 401	SALUT AFRICA (LP).....£30

FYNN MCCOOL
70	RCA SF 8112	FYNN McCOOL (LP, gatefold sleeve).....£200

(see also Shakespears, Grapefruit, Sleepy)

G

TOMMY G & CHARMS
67	London HLB 10107	I Know What I Want/I Want You So Bad.....£40

WINSTON G (& WICKED)
65	Parlophone R 5266	Please Don't Say/Like A Baby.....£35
66	Parlophone R 5330	Until You Were Gone/That Way Too (as Winston G. & Wicked).....£18
66	Decca F 12444	Cloud Nine/I'll Make You Cry Tomorrow.....£18
67	Decca F 12559	Mother Ferguson's Love Dust/Judge And Jury.....£75
67	Decca F 12623	Riding With The Milkman/Bye Bye Baby.....£20

B(ASIL) GABBIDON
61	Blue Beat BB 069-A	Warpaint Baby (miscredited to B. Cabbidon & Buster's Group)/ I Was Wrong (miscredited to Chuck & Dobbie with Buster's Group).....£25
62	Blue Beat BB 111-A	Ivoree/Lover Man.....£25
62	Blue Beat BB 124	Independence Blues/For My Love (as B. Gabbidon).....£30
62	Blue Beat BB 129-A	Our Melody/Going Back To Ja (with Randy's All Stars).....£40
62	Island WI 033	I Found My Baby (actually by Roy Braham)/No Fault Of Mine.....£45
63	Island WI 076	I Bet You Don't Know/3 x 7.....£45
63	Island WI 089	St. Louis Woman/Get On The Ball.....£45
63	Blue Beat BB 155-A	Eana Mena/Since You Are Gone (with Prince Buster All Stars).....£50
63	Blue Beat BB 161	I'll Find Love (with Prince Buster All Stars)/ MELLOW LARKS: What You Gonna Do?.....£50
65	Blue Beat BB 288	Tick Tock (actually by Theo Beckford)/The Streets Of Glory (actually by Theo Beckford & Yvonne Harrison).....£50

(see also Derrick Patsy & Basil, Mellow Larks, Derrick Morgan)

MINT VALUE £

PETER GABRIEL
77	Charisma CB 302	Modern Love/Slowburn (no p/s, 'nude' picture label, withdrawn)	£30
78	Charisma CB 319	D.I.Y. (Remix)/Mother Of Violence/Teddy Bear (no p/s, withdrawn)	£20
15	Secret 7" S725	Sledgehammer (100 only, each with unique art sleeve)	£50
92	Virgin PG 7	US (2-LP, inners)	£30
16	Real World PGLPR5X	SO (2-LP, half-speed remaster, numbered)	£40

(see also Genesis, Youssou 'Ndour & Peter Gabriel, Colin Scot, Charlie Drake)

RUSS GABRIEL
| 93 | Ferox FER 002 | PEACE EP (12", plain sleeve) | £18 |
| 95 | Input Neuron INMLP 004 | VOLTAGE CONTROL (2-LP) | £40 |

(see also Fusion, Too Funk)

RUSS GABRIEL & AFFIE YUSUF
| 94 | Ferox FER 005 | Sian's Tune/Deep Space (12") | £18 |

GABRIEL & ANGELS
| 63 | Stateside SS 150 | That's Life (That's Tough)/Don't Wanna Twist No More | £20 |

GABRIELLI BRASS
| 68 | Polydor 56252 | 'Canterbury Tales' Theme/Working My Way Back To You | £15 |

GABY & CABLES
| 72 | Duke DU 129 | Only Love Can Make You Smile/Only Love Version | £15 |

PABLO GAD
78	Burning Sounds BDS 009	Bloodsuckers/Jail House Pressure (12", red vinyl)	£20
79	Burning Rockers BRD 007	Visions Of Pablo/Tru I De A Jail (12")	£20
79	Burning Rockers BRD 008	Natty Loving/Trodding On Home (12")	£20
79	Burning Rockers BRD 020	Riddle I Dis/Iration (12")	£20
79	Burning Sounds BSD 015	Throw Your Dreams/What Makes A Natty Dread Cry (12", red vinyl)	£20
79	Burning Rockers BRD 014	Trafalgar Square/Chereene (12", red vinyl)	£20
80	Burning Rockers BRD 043	Hard Time/Lighter Shade Of Black (12")	£20
80	His Majesty HMD 010	Crisis Time/Saddest Mistake (12")	£25
80	Burning Rockers BRD 044	Black Before Creation/Reggae Music (12")	£15
80	Greensleeves GRED 33	Fly Away Home/Well Insane (12")	£40
80	His Majesty HMD 012	Oh Jah/Little Young Girl (12")	£35
80	FORM D001	Gun Fever/Fever Dub (12", red vinyl)	£20
81	FORM D005	P.G. In Love/RANKING SIMEON: Ranking Love (12")	£20
86	Jah Shaka SHAKA 853	King Of Kings/Lord Of Lords (12")	£15
80	Burning Sounds BS 1038	TRAFALGAR SQUARE (LP)	£25
80	Federation Of Reggae FORM LP 1099	HARD TIMES (LP, red vinyl)	£30

GADGETS
79	Final Solution FSLP 001	GADGETREE (LP, with insert, blue or beige picture on sleeve)	£20
80	Final Solution FSLP 002	LOVE, CURIOSITY, FRECKLES & DOUBT (LP)	£25
83	Glass GLALP 006	THE BLUE ALBUM (LP, with inner sleeve)	£15

(see also The The, Matt Johnson, Colin Lloyd Tucker)

MEL GADSON
| 60 | London HLX 9105 | Comin' Down With Love/I'm Gettin' Sentimental Over You | £20 |

GAFFA
77	Cleverly Bros CBM 002	NORMAL SERVICE WILL NEVER BE RESUMED EP (various hand-made p/s)	£20
79	Gaffa ZZZZ S001	Hearts Of Stone/You Know I Love You (But I Don't Know How I Know) (various p/s)	£15
79	Gaffa ZZZZ S002	ATTITUDE DANCING (LAND OF 1000 DUNCES)/LONG WEEKEND (four different p/s of 250 copies to go with pressing of 1000 records)	£15
80	Gaffa ZZZZ 5003	Man With A Motive/Your Side/My Side	£20
78	ZZZZ 001	NEITHER USE NOR ORNAMENT (LP)	£15

GAGALACTYCA
| 90 | Holyground HG 1135/Magic Mixture MM 3 | GAGALACTYCA (LP, with booklet, actually by Lightyears Away & Thundermother, 425 only) | £40 |

(see also David John & Mood)

MAJOR YURI GAGARIN
| 61 | Britone MK 100 | CONQUEST OF SPACE (EP) | £20 |

GAGS
| 79 | Look LKLP 6312 | DEATH IN BUZZARD'S GULCH (LP) | £30 |

DAVID GAHAN
03	Mute STUMM 216	PAPER MONSTERS (LP)	£40
08	Mute STUMM 288	HOURGLASS (2-LP, gatefold with CD)	£30
08	Mute LSTUMM 288	HOURGLASS REMIXES (2-LP & CD of remixes)	£18

(see also Depeche Mode)

GAH-GA
| 85 | Everbimes EVB 003 | Give Your Love To Me/Transition (p/s) | £40 |

SLIM GAILLARD (QUARTET/TRIO)
56	Parlophone GEP 8595	SLIM GAILLARD NO. 1 (EP)	£15
56	Columbia Clef SEB 10046	MUSICAL AGGREGATIONS (EP)	£15
60	London RED 1251	SLIM GAILLARD RIDES AGAIN (EP)	£25

(see also Meade 'Lux' Lewis & Slim Gaillard)

DONNA GAINES
| 71 | MCA MK 5060 | Sally Go Round The Roses/So Said The Man | £200 |

(see also Donna Summer)

PEGGY GAINES
98	Kent 6T 14	When The Boy That You Love/SAN FRANCISCO TKOS: Make Up Your Mind	£25

GAINORS
58	London HLU 8734	The Secret/Gonna Rock Tonite	£100
58	London HLU 8734	The Secret/Gonna Rock Tonite (78)	£25

SERGE GAINSBOURG
79	Island ILPS 9581	AUX ARMES ET CAETERA (LP)	£20

(see also Jane Birkin and Serge Gainsbourg)

CHARLOTTE GAINSBOURGH
09	Because BEC5772607	IRM (2-LP)	£15

GAK
94	Warp WAP 48	GAK EP (12")	£60
94	Warp WAP 48CD	GAK (CD)	£40

(see also Aphex Twin)

GALACTIC FEDERATION
66	Polydor BM 56093	The March Of The Sky People/Moon Shot	£25

GALACTIC MUTHERLAND
20	UEG VALP008	A MUTHER'S PEARL (2-LP, purple vinyl, poster, 200 only)	£40

GALACTIC SYMPOSIUM
80	Vague VOG 2	Money/In The Navy (gatefold p/s)	£15

GALAHAD (1)
73	Bell BLL 1273	Rocket Summer/Elephant Stomp	£30

DIAMANDA GALAS
82	Y Y 18	LITANIES DU SATAN (LP)	£40
86	Mute STUMM 27	THE DIVINE PUNISHMENT (LP)	£20
86	Mute STUMM 33	SAINT OF THE PIT (LP)	£18
88	Mute STUMM 46	YOU MUST BE CERTAIN OF THE DEVIL (LP)	£20
91	Mute STUMM 83	PLAGUE MASS (2-LP)	£60
92	Mute STUMM 103	THE SINGER (LP)	£40
93	Mute STUMM 119	VENA CAVA (LP, inner)	£40
94	Mute STUMM 127	THE SPORTING LIFE (LP, with John Paul Jones)	£60

GALAXIE 500
90	Caff CAFF 9	Rain/Don't Let Your Youth Go To Waste (p/s, with insert in bag)	£40
89	Shimmy Disc Europe SDE 8908 LP	TODAY (LP)	£25
89	Rough Trade ROUGH 146	ON FIRE (LP)	£30
90	Rough Trade ROUGH 156	THIS IS OUR MUSIC (LP, with sticker and 3 postcards)	£25
91	Rough Trade ROUGH 146L	ON FIRE (LP, reissue with shrinkwrapped CD single)	£20
10	Domino REWIGLP69	TODAY (LP, reissue)	£15

(see also Luna)

GALAXIES
60	Capitol CL 15158	The Big Triangle/Until The Next Time	£15

EDDIE GALE
69	Blue Note BST 84294	GHETTO MUSIC (LP)	£15

ERICA GALE
81	Santic SAN 0020	Stranger In The Night/SANTIC ALLSTARS: Midnight Serenade (12")	£40
82	Ital ITD 015	It's Allright/Moving Up (12")	£30
82	Sanity STY 003	Tonight Tonight/Instrumental (12", as Erica)	£20
83	Cassia CAS 001	Ain't Gonna Loose My Head/Instrumental Version (12")	£30

GALENS
63	London HLH 9804	Baby I Do Love You/Love Bells	£30

LIAM GALLAGHER
17	Warner Bros. 0190295793708	Wall Of Glass (1-sided 7", other side etched, die-cut sleeve, 500 only)	£40
17	Warner Bros. 0190295768140	AS YOU WERE (LP, white vinyl, with 7" CD and book)	£35

(see also Oasis, Beady Eye)

LIAM GALLAGHER, JOHN SQUIRE
24	Warner 5054197893964	LIAM GALLAGHER JOHN SQUIRE (LP, gatefold, bioplastic, orange, poster, Amazon exclusive)	£30
24	Warner 5054197893971	LIAM GALLAGHER JOHN SQUIRE (LP, gatefold, red/blue vinyl, poster/sticker sheet, artist store exclusive)	£40
24	Warner 5054197893988	LIAM GALLAGHER JOHN SQUIRE (LP, alternative artwork, Zoetrope disc)	£50

(See also Oasis, Beady Eye, Stone Roses, Seahorses, Liam Gallagher)

NOEL GALLAGHER'S HIGH FLYING BIRDS
12	Sour Mash JDNC 14T	SONGS FROM THE GREAT WHITE NORTH EP (12", p/s numbered)	£15
12	Sour Mash JDNC 11	Dream On/Shoot A Hole Into The Sun (12" p/s, numbered)	£20
14	Sour Mash JDNC 19	In The Heat Of The Moment/Do The Damage (p/s, blue vinyl, mail-order only)	£30
15	Sour Mash JDNC21TE	The Dying Of The Light (Demo) (10" 1-sided)	£20
11	Sour Mash JDNCLP10	NOEL GALLAGHER'S HIGH FLYING BIRDS (LP)	£15
14	Sour Mash JDNCLP18	CHASING YESTERDAY (LP, CD)	£15
15	Sour Mash JDNC25T	WHERE THE CITY MEETS THE SKY - CHASING YESTERDAY - THE REMIXES (LP, 2 x 12")	£15

(see also Oasis)

RORY GALLAGHER
71	Polydor 2814 004	It's You/Just The Smile/Sinner Boy (promo only)	£50

MINT VALUE £

75	Chrysalis CDJ 102	Souped Up Ford/I Take What I Want (p/s, promo only)	£40
79	Chrysalis CXP 2281	Shadow Play/Brute Force And Ignorance/Moonchild/Souped-Up Ford (10", p/s)	£20
80	Chrysalis CHS 2453	Wayward Child/Keychain (p/s, as Rory Gallagher Live, clear vinyl)	£20
82	Chrysalis CHS 2612	Big Guns/The Devil Made Me Do it (p/s, with free 'Jinx' LP patch)	£20
71	Polydor 2383 044	RORY GALLAGHER (LP)	£50
71	Polydor 2383 076	DEUCE (LP)	£50
72	Polydor 2383 112	LIVE! IN EUROPE (LP, gatefold sleeve)	£40
73	Polydor 2383 189	BLUEPRINT (LP)	£50
73	Polydor 2383 230	TATTOO (LP)	£50
74	Polydor 2659 031	IRISH TOUR '74 (2-LP)	£35
75	Chrysalis CHR 1098	AGAINST THE GRAIN (LP)	£18
76	Chrysalis CHR 1124	CALLING CARD (LP)	£15
78	Chrysalis CHR 1170	PHOTO-FINISH (LP)	£18
79	Chrysalis CHR 1235	TOP PRIORITY (LP)	£20
80	Chrysalis CHR 1280	STAGE STRUCK (LP)	£20
82	Chrysalis CHR 1359	JINX (LP)	£20
87	Capo/Demon XFIEND 98	DEFENDER (LP, with bonus 7", "Seems To Me"/"No Peace For The Wicked")	£20
90	Capo CAPO LP 14	FRESH EVIDENCE (LP)	£18
92	Demon FIEND 719	EDGED IN BLUE (LP)	£25
18	Universal RGBUND 001	RORY GALLAGHER (Box set, 15 LPs, remastered, 300 only, numbered)	£200

(see also Taste, Killing Floor, Joe O'Donnell)

GALLAGHER-LYLE

67	Polydor BM 56170	Trees/In The Crowd	£18
72	Capitol ST 21906	GALLAGHER AND LYLE (LP)	£20
73	A&M AMLH 68148	WILLIE AND THE LAPDOG (LP, with booklet)	£18

(see also James Galt, McGuinness Flint, Cups)

GALLAHADS

55	Capitol CL 14282	Ooh-Ah/Careless	£15

RONNIE GALLANT

62	Warner Bros WB 61	In The Night/The Hole In The Wall	£20

GALLANTS

65	Capitol CL 15408	Man From U.N.C.L.E. Theme/Vagabond	£15

GALLERY (1)

72	Midas MFHR 046	THE WIND THAT SHAKES THE BARLEY (LP)	£800
78	Look LK LP 6029	EACH DAY THROUGH (LP)	£100

GALLERY (2)

82	Cobweb AP163/CWB814	EGYPTIAN THEORY (LP, with insert)	£40

GALLEY

75	Guildhall GHS 10	HAIL SMILING MORN (LP, 50 only)	£300

GALLIANO

91	Talkin Loud 848 493-1	IN PURSUIT OF THE 13TH NOTE (LP)	£15
92	Talkin Loud 848 080-1	A JOYFUL NOISE UNTO THE CREATOR (LP)	£25
94	Talkin Loud 522 452-1	THE PLOT THICKENS (2-LP)	£30

GALLIARD

70	Deram DM 306	I Wrapped Her In Ribbons/The Hermit And The Knight	£20
70	Deram Nova (S)DN 4	STRANGE PLEASURE (LP, red/silver labels)	£300
70	Deram SML 1075	NEW DAWN (LP, white/red labels with small logo)	£450

(see also Craig)

VINCENT GALLO

01	Warp 7261-WARP01-7	Honey Bunny (Mono)/Honey Bunny (Stereo) (p/s)	£15
01	Warp WAP 149	So Sad/So Sad (12", p/s)	£18
01	Warp WAPLP 87	WHEN (LP, 'book' cover)	£200
02	Warp WAPLP 99	RECORDINGS OF MUSIC FOR FILMS (2-LP)	£45

GALLON DRUNK

93	Clawfist XPIG 21	Known, Not Wanted/TINDERSTICKS: We Have All The Time In The World ('singles club' release, p/s, 1,400 only)	£15
91	Clawfist HUNKA LP2	TONITE...THE SINGLES BAR (LP)	£15
96	City Slang EFA04982-1	IN THE LONG STILL NIGHT (LP)	£15
02	Sweet Nothing SNLP 012	FIRE MUSIC (2-LP)	£18

GALLOWS

07	Holy Roar HRR 006V	DEMO 2005 (white vinyl, 500 only)	£40
07	Thirty Days Of Night TDON 015	Sick Of Feeling Sick/If Credits What Matters I'll Take Credit/NOVEMBER COMING FIRE: Return Of The Black Dog/Bear Away (split 7", p/s, various coloured vinyl)	£15
10	Thirty Days Of Night TDON015	Sick Of Feeling Sick/If Credits What Matters I'll Take Credit/NOVEMBER COMING FIRE: Return Of The Black Dog/Bear Away (repressing, white/blue vinyl, 20 only)	£15
07	Warner Bros. 25646 9846 3	ORCHESTRA OF WOLVES (LP & CD, green vinyl)	£30
09	Reprise 519232-1	GREY BRITAIN (LP, red/grey vinyl)	£35

JAMES GALT

65	Pye 7N 17021	With My Baby/A Most Unusual Feeling	£75
65	Pye 7N 17021	With My Baby/A Most Unusual Feeling (DJ Copy)	£100

(see also Gallagher-Lyle)

CHILDISH GAMBINO

12	Glassnote GLS012102IV	CAMP (2LP, double gatefold)	£25
17	Glassnote GLS-0221-01	AWAKEN, MY LOVE ! (LP, insert)	£20
20	Glassnote GLS-0152-01R	BECAUSE THE INTERNET (2LP, insert, UK reissue of 2013 album)	£20

GAMBIT OF SHAME
82   Dead Hedgehog DHE 7009   **No Bounds/18 Out Of 20** (p/s) £15

GAMBLER
72   Spaceward SRS24   **TOMMY** (LP)...£100

GAMBLERS
63   Decca F 11780   **You've Really Got A Hold On Me/Can I See You Tonight?** £15
64   Decca F 11872   **Nobody But Me** (Kissin' Time)**It's So Nice** £15
65   Decca F 12060   **Now I'm All Alone/Find Out What's Happening**...........£30
66   Decca F 12399   **Doctor Goldfoot** (And His Bikini Machine)**/It Seems So Long** £30
67   Parlophone R 5557   **Cry Me A River/Who Will Buy**...........£30
(see also Billy Fury)

GAME
65   Pye 7N 15889   **But I Do/Gotta Keep On Moving Baby** £80
66   Decca F 12469   **Gonna Get Me Someone/Gotta Wait** £300
67   Parlophone R 5553   **The Addicted Man/Help Me Mummy's Gone** (withdrawn)...........£1000
67   Parlophone R 5553   **The Addicted Man/Help Me Mummy's Gone** (withdrawn) (demo copy)...........£700
67   Parlophone R 5569   **It's Shocking What They Call Me/Help Me Mummy's Gone** £500
97   Dig The Fuzz DIG 026   **IT'S SHOCKING WHAT THEY CALL US** (LP, gatefold, poster and free 7")...........£20

GAMER 3
91   Chemical CHEM 001   **ACID FOR BLOOD EP** (12")...........£30
(see also Freeez, Pink Rhythm)

GAMES
80   Games 001   **Childsplay/First Law Of Games** (p/s)...........£80
82   Open Eye OE 7   **Dance This Way/Love Canal** (p/s)...........£40

GAMMITT
73   Solar SL1   **Queen Of Rock/We Dance** £15

GANDALF THE GREY
80s   Heyoka   **THE GREY WIZARD AM I** (LP, reissue of U.S. LP)...........£25

LITTLE JIMMY GANDY
69   Roulette RO 510   **Cool Thirteen/I'm Not Like The Others** (Existence unconfirmed)...........£20

GANELIN TRIO
80   Leo LR 102   **CATALOGUE, LIVE IN EAST GERMANY** (LP) £15
83   Leo LR 112   **NEW WINE...**(LP)...........£30

GANG STARR
89   Bellaphon BENNLP 1   **NO MORE MISTER NICE GUY** (LP, with free 12")...........£25
90   Cooltempo CTLP 21   **STEP IN THE ARENA** (LP)...........£35
92   Cooltempo CTLP 27   **DAILY OPERATION** (LP)...........£25
94   Chrysalis CTLP 38   **HARD TO EARN** (2-LP)...........£30
98   Noo Trybe 7243 8 59032 1 2   **MOMENT OF TRUTH** (3-LP) £40
99   EMI 7243 5 21189 15   **FULL CLIP: A DECADE OF GANG STARR** (4-LP) £50

GANG OF FOUR
78   Fast Product FAST 5   **DAMAGED GOODS** (EP, 1st pressing, with b&w labels and 'dp delga press' credit some with sticker insert)...........£50
78   Fast Product FAST 5   **DAMAGED GOODS** (EP, 2nd pressing, with b&w labels, no 'dp delga press limited' credit,no sticker)...........£30
79   EMI EMC 3313   **ENTERTAINMENT!** (LP, 1st pressing with 'crowd' image on b-side label, with inner sleeve)...........£60
79   EMI EMC 3313   **ENTERTAINMENT!** (LP, 2nd pressing without 'crowd' image on b-side label, with inner sleeve)...........£35
82   EMI EMC 3412   **SONGS OF THE FREE** (LP, with inner sleeve)...........£20
81   EMI EMC 3364   **SOLID GOLD** (LP, with insert) £20
83   EMI EMC 1652191   **HARD** (LP) £15
84   Mercury MERL 51   **AT THE PALACE** (LP)...........£15
19   Parlophone EMC 3313   **ENTERTAINMENT!** (LP, reissue, red vinyl) £25

GANGSTERS (1)
79   Stortbeat A45/B45   **Harlow Town/Record Company** £20
79   Stortbeat BEAT 2   **GANGSTERS** (LP) £20

ALAN GANLEY QUARTET
58   Pye Nixa NJE 1046   **GONE GANLEY** (EP)...........£100

ELMER GANTRY'S VELVET OPERA
67   Direction 58-3083   **Flames/Salisbury Plain** £20
68   Direction 58-3481   **Mary Jane/Dreamy**...........£20
69   Direction 58-3924   **Volcano/A Quick 'B'** £20
68   Direction 8-63300   **ELMER GANTRY'S VELVET OPERA** (LP, laminated front sleeve, yellow/black labels)...........£175
(see also Velvet Opera, Stretch, Strawbs, Hudson-Ford, Paul Brett's Sage)

GANTS
65   Liberty LIB 55829   **Road Runner/My Baby Don't Care** £35
67   Liberty LIB 55940   **I Wonder/Greener Days** £15

GARBAGE
95   Discordant CORD 001   **Vow/Torn Apart** (embossed metal 'G' logo sleeve, with insert, 3,000 pressed [934 issued], stickered, sealed)...........£20
95   Discordant CORD 001   **Vow/Torn Apart** (embossed metal 'G' logo sleeve, with insert, 3,000 pressed [934 issued], stickered, unsealed)...........£20
95   Mushroom SX 1138   **Subhuman/1 Crush** (embossed rubber 'G' logo sleeve, with SX 1138 insert, some in white 'G' logo carrier bag, 3,000 only; with incorrect insert [S1138])...........£15

MINT VALUE £

GARBO
95	Mushroom L 31450	GARBAGE (LP) (as 2 x 45rpm 12", with inner sleeves)	£20
95	Mushroom LX 31450	GARBAGE (LP) (as 6 x 7" singles in box set with 3 inserts [now import only], sealed)	£20
95	Mushroom LX 31450	GARBAGE (LP) (as 6 x 7" singles in box set with 3 inserts [now import only], unsealed)	£15
98	Mushroom MUSH29LP	VERSION 2.0 (LP)	£40
99	Simply Vinyl SVLP 140	VERSION 2.0 (LP, 180 gram reissue)	£40
01	Mushroom MUSH95LP	BEAUTIFUL GARBAGE (2-LP)	£40

(see also Goodbye Mr. MacKenzie)

GARBO
| 82 | Rarn RARN 201 | Dancing Strange/Why Don't You Call Me?/Everyday Hallucinations (with p/s) | £200 |
| 82 | Rarn RARN 201 | Dancing Strange/Why Don't You Call Me?/Everyday Hallucinations (without p/s) | £50 |

JERRY GARCIA
| 71 | Douglas DGL 69013 | HOOTEROLL? (LP, with Howard Wales) | £20 |
| 72 | Warner Bros K 46139 | GARCIA (LP) | £15 |

(see also Grateful Dead, Diga Rhythm Band, Old & In The Way)

NUBYA GARCIA
| 18 | Nyasha NYASHA0001 | When We Are/Source/When We Are (K15 Remix)/Source (Maxwell Owin Remix) (12", p/s) | £20 |
| 17 | Jazz Refreshed JRF00012 | NUBYAS 5IVE (LP | £60 |

RUSS GARCIA ORCHESTRA
| 58 | London HAU 2141 | FANTASTICA! (LP) | £15 |

GARDEN ODYSSEY (ENTERPRISE)
| 69 | Deram DM 267 | Sad And Lonely/Sky Pilot (8/M/1) (as Garden Odyssey Enterprise) | £80 |
| 72 | RCA RCA 2159 | Joker/Have You Ever Been To Georgia (as Garden Odyssey) | £70 |

(see also Graham Gouldman)

BORIS GARD(I)NER (& LOVE PEOPLE)
10	Jazzman JMANLP 036	EVERY NIGGER IS A STAR (LP, reissue)	£40
69	High Note HS 010	Lucky Is The Boy/Bobby Sox To Stockings	£100
69	Doctor Bird DB 1205	Elizabethan Reggae/Hooked On A Feeling	£25
69	Duke DU 21	Never My Love/The Bold One	£35
69	Duke 39	Elizabethan Reggae/BYRON LEE : Soul Serenade	£15
70	Big Shot BI 537	Sweet Soul Special/Memories Of Love (with Love People)	£30
70	Big Shot BI 538	Darkness/Watch This Music (B-side actually "Keep Out") (with Love People)	£30
70	Big Shot BI 539	Hot Shot/Watch This Music (with Love People)	£40
70	Dynamic DYN 404	Commanding Wife/Band Of Gold (as Boris Gardner & Happening)	£20
70	Trojan TBL 121	REGGAE HAPPENING (LP)	£20

PAUL GARDINER
| 81 | Beggars Banquet BEG 61T | Stormtrooper In Drag/Night Talk (12", unreleased, white label promos only) | £700 |

(see also Tubeway Army, Gary Numan)

DAVE GARDNER
| 58 | Brunswick 05740 | Hop Along Rock/All By Myself (B-side with Anita Kerr Singers) | £30 |

DON GARDNER
| 02 | Grapevine G2K-45-120 | Cheatin Kind/Is This Really Love (reissue) | £25 |

DON GARDNER & DEE DEE FORD
| 62 | Stateside SS 114 | I Need Your Loving/Tell Me | £20 |
| 62 | Stateside SS 130 | Don't You Worry/I'm Coming Home To Stay | £20 |

(see also Baby Washington & Don Gardner, Dee Dee Ford)

JOHNNY GARFIELD
| 65 | Pye 7N 15758 | Stranger In Paradise/Anyone Can Lose A Heart | £45 |

(see also Simon & Garfunkel, Tom & Jerry)

ART GARFUNKEL
| 74 | CBS CQ 31474/Q 69021 | ANGEL CLARE (LP, quadrophonic) | £20 |

JUDY GARLAND
| 59 | Capitol (S)T 1188 | THE LETTER (LP, with paste-on letter intact) | £25 |

RED GARLAND
56	Esquire 32 056	GROOVY! (LP)	£50
57	Esquire 32 046	A GARLAND OF RED (LP)	£50
60	Esquire 32-096	MANTECA (LP)	£40
60	Esquire 32-099	ALL MORNING LONG (LP)	£150
61	Esquire 32-116	RED IN BLUES VILLE (LP)	£60
61	Esquire 32-126	AT THE PRELUDE (LP)	£40
61	Esquire 32-136	SOUL JUNCTION (LP)	£40
62	Esquire 32-146	ROJO (LP)	£30
62	Esquire 32-166	HIGH PRESSURE (LP)	£30

BILLY GARNER
| 00 | BGPS 006 | Brand New Girl/JACQUELINE JONES : Can't Stop The Show | £15 |

REGGIE GARNER
| 76 | Capitol CL 15874 | Hot Line/Blessed Be The Name Of My Baby (DJ Copy) | £15 |

GALE GARNETT
65	RCA RCA 1451	I'll Cry Alone/Where Do You Go To Go Away?	£60
65	RCA RCA 1451	I'll Cry Alone/Where Do You Go To Go Away? (DJ Copy)	£100
65	RCA RD 7726	MY KIND OF FOLK SONGS (LP)	£30
66	RCA RD 7750	LOVIN' PLACE (LP)	£20

RACHELLE GARNIEZ
| 09 | Third Man TMR 004 | My House Of Peace (1-sided, 100 only, luminous vinyl) | £70 |

CHRIS GARRETT AND SWEET POISON
75	Mandala MDS 59	Family Man/Cold N Rainy (p/s)	£100

VERNON GARRETT
67	Stateside SS 2006	If I Could Turn Back The Hands Of Time/You And Me Together	£40
67	Stateside SS 2006	If I Could Turn Back The Hands Of Time/You And Me Together (DJ copy)	£80
67	Stateside SS 2026	Shine It On/Things Are Lookin' Better	£50
67	Stateside SS 2026	Shine It On/Things Are Lookin' Better (DJ copy)	£75
68	Action ACT 4508	Shine It On/Things Are Lookin' Better (reissue)	£30

DAVID GARRICK
67	Piccadilly NEP 34056	DAVID (EP)	£30
66	Piccadilly NPL 38024	A BOY CALLED DAVID (LP, mono)	£20
66	Piccadilly N(S)PL 38024	A BOY CALLED DAVID (LP, stereo)	£25
67	Piccadilly N(S)PL 38035	DON'T GO OUT INTO THE RAIN, SUGAR (LP)	£25
68	Pye NSPL 18223	LIVE! (LP, blue/black label)	£30

MICHAEL GARRICK
63	Airborne NBP 002	A CASE OF JAZZ (EP, with Shake Keane)	£350
65	Argo EAF/ZFA 92	ANTHEM - MICHAEL GARRICK QUINTET (EP, mono/stereo with Shake Keane)	£100
66	Argo EAF 115	BEFORE NIGHT/DAY (EP)	£100
64	Airborne NMP 004	MOONSCAPE (LP)	£3000
64	Argo ZDA 26	POETRY AND JAZZ IN CONCERT - RECORD ONE (LP)	£60
64	Argo ZDA 27	POETRY AND JAZZ IN CONCERT - RECORD TWO (LP)	£100
65	Argo DA 33	OCTOBER WOMAN (LP, mono, as Michael Garrick Quintet, with Joe Harriott)	£300
65	Argo ZDA 33	OCTOBER WOMAN (LP, stereo, as Michael Garrick Quintet, with Joe Harriott)	£350
65	Argo DA 36	PROMISES (LP, mono, as Michael Garrick Sextet, with Ian Carr)	£300
65	Argo ZDA 36	PROMISES (LP, stereo, as Michael Garrick Sextet, with Ian Carr)	£300
66	Argo DA 88	BLACK MARIGOLDS (LP, mono, as Michael Garrick Septet)	£500
66	Argo ZDA 88	BLACK MARIGOLDS (LP, stereo, as Michael Garrick Septet)	£400
68	Airborne NBP 0021	JAZZ PRAISES AT ST. PAULS (LP)	£150
69	Erase EO 254 S	JAZZ CANTATA (LP, 'Farnham Festival' release, music by Garrick words by John Smith)	£300
70	Argo ZPR 264/5	POETRY AND JAZZ IN CONCERT 250 (2LP, as Michael Garrick Quintet)	£100
70	Argo ZDA 135	THE HEART IS A LOTUS (LP, as Michael Garrick Sextet with Norma Winstone)	£400
72	Argo ZDA 153	COLD MOUNTAIN (LP, as Michael Garrick Trio)	£300
72	Argo ZDA 154	HOME STRETCH BLUES (LP, as Michael Garrick Band with Norma Winstone)	£450
74	Argo ZDA 163	TROPPO (LP)	£300
81	Hep Records HEP2011	YOU'VE CHANGED (LP)	£30
07	Trunk JBH 022LP	MOONSCAPE (LP, reissue 500 only)	£60
11	Trunk JBH 041LP	RISING STARS (LP, with Shake Keane, 750 only)	£20
13	Gearbox GB 1517	PRELUDE TO HEART IS A LOTUS (LP, 180g, limited edition)	£30

(see also Norma Winstone, Joe Harriott, Garrick's Fairground, Shake Keane)

GARRICK'S FAIRGROUND
71	Argo AFW 105	Epiphany/Blessed Are The Peacemakers	£100
72	Argo ZAGF 1	MR. SMITH'S APOCALYPSE (LP)	£100

(see also Michael Garrick)

FREDDIE GARRITY
74	Bus Stop BUSLP 5002	LITTLE BIG TIME (LP)	£15

(see also Freddie & Dreamers)

ROBIN GARSIDE & PAUL GOUGH
77	Northern Sound NSR 01	SEA SONGS (LP)	£15

MORT GARSON
69	A & M AMLS 960	ELECTRIC HAIRPIECES (LP)	£20

GARUDA
77	EMI EMC 3174	GARUDA (LP)	£50

GUY GARVEY
15	Fiction 4758702	COURTING THE SQUALL (LP, lenticular sleeve)	£25
15	Fiction 4758702	COURTING THE SQUALL (LP, signed)	£30

REX GARVIN & MIGHTY CRAVERS
66	Atlantic 584 028	Sock It To 'Em J.B. (Parts 1 & 2)	£25
67	Atlantic 584 097	I Gotta Go Now (Up On The Floor)/Believe It Or Not	£25

SAM GARY
56	Esquire 32 017	SAM GARY SINGS (LP)	£20

GARY & ARIELS
64	Fontana TF 476	Say You Love Me/Town Girl	£15

(see also Garry Mills)

GARY & STU
72	Carnaby 6302 012	HARLAN FARE (LP, white label with 'crab' logo)	£100

(see also Koobas, March Hare)

GAS
80	Polydor POSP 192	It Shows In Your Face/Tomorrow (p/s)	£15
81	Polydor POSP 264	Ignore Me/Do It, Don't Tell Me (p/s)	£15
81	Polydor POSP 344	The Finger/Knock It Down (p/s)	£18
81	Polydor POLE 1052	EMOTIONAL WARFARE (LP)	£15
83	Good Vibrations GAS LP 1	FROM THE CRADLE TO THE GRAVE (LP)	£15

GASKIN
81	Rondelet ROUND 7	I'm No Fool/Sweet Dream Maker (p/s)	£25

82	Rondelet ROUND 21	Mony Mony/Queen Of Hams (p/s)	£18
81	Rondelet ABOUT 4	END OF THE WORLD (LP, gatefold sleeve)	£25
82	Rondelet ABOUT 8	NO WAY OUT (LP, with inner)	£20

GASLIGHT
69	Jay Boy BOY 17	Move/And So To Sleep	£18
70	SDE 32732	GASLIGHT (2-LP, private pressing, gatefold sleeve with inserts, 2nd disc by Gaslight Choir)	£50

GASLIGHT ANTHEM
12	Mercury B0016941-01	HANDWRITTEN (LP, blue vinyl and free blue vinyl 7")	£20

GAS MASK
71	Polydor 2383 068	THEIR FIRST ALBUM (LP)	£20

GASOLIN
71	CBS 64685	GASOLIN (LP, gatefold sleeve, orange/black label)	£50
72	CBS 65229	2 (LP, gatefold sleeve, orange/black label)	£40
73	CBS 65798	3 (LP, orange label)	£30
75	Epic SEPC 81436	WHAT A LEMON (LP, yellow/black label)	£40

GASOLINE BAND
72	Cube HIFLY 9	GASOLINE BAND (LP, cube label)	£200

GASP
79	Storm SR 028	Gaz's Boots/Jimmy The Fish (no p/s)	£20

GASS COMPANY
68	President PT 170	Everybody Needs Love/Nightmare	£60

(see also Wake)

GASS (1)
65	Parlophone R 5344	One Of These Days/I Don't Know Why	£30
66	Parlophone R 5456	The New Breed/In The City	£60
67	CBS 202647	Dream Baby (How Long Must I Dream?)/Jitterbug Sid	£30
70	Polydor 2383 022	JUJU (LP, featuring Peter Green)	£150
70	Polydor 2383 022	JUJU (LP, featuring Peter Green, alternative sleeve, black/gold with Gass logo on front and drawing on rear, record has same matrix as other issue and red Polydor labels)	£250
71	Polydor 2383 035	CATCH MY SOUL - THE ROCK-OTHELLO (LP, cast recording featuring Gass)	£30

(see also Hummingbird, Humble Pie, Streetwalkers, Peter Green)

GASS (2)
97	Public Demand PPDT 28	Dark (2as1 & MJ Cole)/(Nocturnal Mix)/(Mascara Mix) (12")	£30

GAS WORKS
73	Regal Zono. SRLZ 1036	GAS WORKS (LP)	£25

DAVID GATES
60	Top Rank JAR 504	The Happiest Man Alive/The Road That Leads To Love	£30

(see also Bread)

RAY GATES
66	Decca F 12502	It's Such A Shame/Have You Ever Had The Blues	£40

GATES OF EDEN
66	Pye 7N 17195	Too Much On My Mind/I'm Warning You	£25
67	Pye 7N 17278	1 To 7/Hey Now	£30

GATEWAY
18	Super Disco Edits SDE 32	Show Is Over Part 1/Part 2 (demo only, release cancelled)	£25

GATHERERS
73	Duke DU 153	Words Of My Mouth/UPSETTERS: Version	£110

GATOR CREEK
71	Mercury 6052 058	Danny's Song/Take A Look	£15
71	Mercury 6338 035	GATOR CREEK (LP)	£15

DICK GAUGHAN
72	Trailer LER 2072	NO MORE FOREVER (LP, red label)	£25
76	Rubber RUB 019	FIVE HAND REEL (LP)	£20
78	Topic 12TS384	GAUGHAN (LP, tan label)	£15
81	Topic 12TS419	HANDFUL OF EARTH (LP)	£15

GEORGES GAVARENTZ
69	Philips SBL 7898	THEY CAME TO ROB LAS VEGAS (LP, soundtrack)	£40

JIMMY GAVIN
57	London HLU 8478	I Sit In My Window/Lonely Chair	£80

MAC GAYDEN
73	EMI EMA 760	McGAVOCK GAYDEN (LP)	£50

MARVIN GAYE
63	Oriole CBA 1803	Stubborn Kind Of Fellow/It Hurt Me Too	£100
63	Oriole CBA 1803	Stubborn Kind Of Fellow/It Hurt Me Too (DJ Copy)	£200
63	Oriole CBA 1846	Pride And Joy/One Of These Days	£100
63	Oriole CBA 1846	Pride And Joy/One Of These Days (DJ Copy)	£200
63	Stateside SS 243	Can I Get A Witness?/I'm Crazy 'Bout My Baby	£90
63	Stateside SS 243	Can I Get A Witness?/I'm Crazy 'Bout My Baby (DJ Copy)	£100
64	Stateside SS 284	You're A Wonderful One/When I'm Alone I Cry	£50
64	Stateside SS 284	You're A Wonderful One/When I'm Alone I Cry (DJ Copy)	£100
64	Stateside SS 326	Try It Baby/If My Heart Could Sing	£40
64	Stateside SS 326	Try It Baby/If My Heart Could Sing (DJ Copy)	£70

MINT VALUE £

64	Stateside SS 360	How Sweet It Is (To Be Loved By You)/**Forever**...£30
64	Stateside SS 360	How Sweet It Is (To Be Loved By You)/**Forever** (DJ Copy)...........................£90
65	Tamla Motown TMG 510	**I'll Be Doggone/You've Been A Long Time Coming**.........................£40
65	Tamla Motown TMG 510	**I'll Be Doggone/You've Been A Long Time Coming** (DJ Copy)..............£120
65	Tamla Motown TMG 524	**Pretty Little Baby/Now That You've Won Me**..............................£40
65	Tamla Motown TMG 524	**Pretty Little Baby/Now That You've Won Me** (DJ Copy)....................£90
65	Tamla Motown TMG 539	**Ain't That Peculiar?/She's Got To Be Real**................................£30
65	Tamla Motown TMG 539	**Ain't That Peculiar?/She's Got To Be Real** (DJ Copy)......................£90
66	Tamla Motown TMG 552	**One More Heartache/When I Had Your Love**...............................£30
66	Tamla Motown TMG 552	**One More Heartache/When I Had Your Love** (DJ Copy)....................£80
66	Tamla Motown TMG 563	**Take This Heart Of Mine/Need Your Lovin'** (Want You Back).............£35
66	Tamla Motown TMG 563	**Take This Heart Of Mine/Need Your Lovin'** (Want You Back) (DJ Copy)....£80
66	Tamla Motown TMG 574	**Little Darling** (I Need You)/**Hey Diddle Diddle**.........................£35
66	Tamla Motown TMG 574	**Little Darlin'** (I Need You)/**Hey Diddle Diddle** (DJ Copy)...............£120
67	Tamla Motown TMG 618	**Your Unchanging Love/I'll Take Care Of You**...............................£20
67	Tamla Motown TMG 618	**Your Unchanging Love/I'll Take Care Of You** (DJ Copy)....................£50
68	Tamla Motown TMG 640	**You/Change What You Can**...£20
68	Tamla Motown TMG 640	**You/Change What You Can** (DJ Copy)......................................£40
68	Tamla Motown TMG 676	**Chained/At Last** (I Found A Love)..£18
69	Tamla Motown TMG 686	**I Heard It Through The Grapevine/Need Somebody** (DJ Copy)............£30
70	Tamla Motown TMG 734	**Abraham, Martin And John/How Can I Forget?** (DJ Copy)..................£30
71	Tamla Motown TMG 775	**What's Going On/God Is Love** (DJ Copy)...................................£40
73	Tamla Motown TMG 868	**Let's Get It On/I Wish It Would Rain** (DJ Copy)............................£40
74	Tamla Motown TMG 882	**Come Get To This/Distant Lover**...£15
86	Tamla Motown ZB 40757	**Lonely Lover/The World Is Rated X** (p/s)..................................£25
94	Tamla Motoen TMG 1426	**Lucky Lucky Me** (Radio Edit)/(Pure Soul Mix) (p/s)........................£15
96	Chriskings 81156 DJ	**This Love Starved Heart Of Mine/This Love Starved Heart Of Mine** (promo, 500 only ...£20
66	Tamla Motown TME 2016	**MARVIN GAYE** (EP)..£60
67	Tamla Motown TME 2019	**ORIGINALS FROM MARVIN GAYE** (EP).....................................£50
64	Stateside SL 10100	**MARVIN GAYE** (LP)...£200
65	Tamla Motown TML 11004	**HOW SWEET IT IS TO BE LOVED BY YOU** (LP).............................£60
65	Tamla Motown TML 11015	**HELLO BROADWAY** (LP)...£80
66	Tamla Motown TML 11022	**A TRIBUTE TO THE GREAT NAT KING COLE** (LP, mono)...................£65
66	Tamla Motown STML 11022	**A TRIBUTE TO THE GREAT NAT KING COLE** (LP, stereo).................£80
66	Tamla Motown TML 11033	**MOODS OF MARVIN GAYE** (LP, mono)....................................£50
66	Tamla Motown STML 11033	**MOODS OF MARVIN GAYE** (LP, stereo)..................................£60
68	Tamla Motown TML 11065	**MARVIN GAYE'S GREATEST HITS** (LP, mono)..............................£20
68	Tamla Motown STML 11065	**MARVIN GAYE'S GREATEST HITS** (LP, stereo)............................£20
69	Tamla Motown (S)TML 11091	**IN THE GROOVE** (LP, mono/stereo)......................................£30
69	Tamla Motown (S)TML 1111	**M.P.G.** (LP, mono/stereo)..£25
69	Tamla Motown TML 11123	**MARVIN GAYE AND HIS GIRLS** (LP, mono, with T. Terrell, M. Wells & K. Weston).....£25
70	Tamla Motown STML 11123	**MARVIN GAYE AND HIS GIRLS** (LP, stereo, with T. Terrell, M. Wells & K. Weston)...........£22
70	Tamla Motown TML 11136	**THAT'S THE WAY LOVE IS** (LP, mono)....................................£30
70	Tamla Motown STML 11136	**THAT'S THE WAY LOVE IS** (LP, stereo)..................................£20
71	Tamla Motown STML 11190	**WHAT'S GOING ON?** (LP, textured sleeve A1/B1 matrixes, with lyric sheet)...........£40
73	Tamla Motown STMA 8013	**LET'S GET IT ON** (LP, gatefold)...£30
73	Tamla Motoen STML 11225	**TROUBLE MAN** (LP, soundtrack)..£20
74	Tamla Motown STMA 8018	**MARVIN GAYE LIVE!** (LP, gatefold)..£15
76	Tamla Motown STML 12025	**I WANT YOU** (LP)..£20
78	Tamla Motown TMSP 6008	**HERE, MY DEAR** (2-LP)...£25
81	Tamla Motown STML 12149	**IN OUR LIFETIME** (LP)...£15
82	CBS 85977	**MIDNIGHT LOVE** (LP, insert)...£15

MARVIN GAYE & TAMMI TERRELL

67	Tamla Motown TMG 611	**Ain't No Mountain High Enough/Give A Little Love**.......................£30
67	Tamla Motown TMG 611	**Ain't No Mountain High Enough/Give A Little Love** (DJ Copy)............£80
67	Tamla Motown TMG 625	**Your Precious Love/Hold Me Oh My Darling**..............................£25
67	Tamla Motown TMG 625	**Your Precious Love/Hold Me Oh My Darling** (DJ Copy)....................£50
67	Tamla Motown TMG 635	**If I Could Build My Whole World Around You/If This World Were Mine**.....£15
67	Tamla Motown TMG 635	**If I Could Build My Whole World Around You/If This World Were Mine** (DJ Copy).........£30
68	Tamla Motown TMG 655	**Ain't Nothin' Like The Real Thing/Little Ole Boy, Little Ole Girl** (DJ Copy).........£30
69	Tamla Motown TMG 715	**The Onion Song/I Can't Believe You Love Me** (demo in p/s)...............£50
68	T. Motown TML 11062	**UNITED** (LP, mono)..£40
68	T. Motown STML 11062	**UNITED** (LP, stereo)...£45
68	T. Motown (S)TML 11084	**YOU'RE ALL I NEED** (LP, mono/stereo)...................................£40
70	T. Motown TML 11132	**EASY** (LP, mono)..£20
70	T. Motown STML 11132	**EASY** (LP, stereo)...£18
70	T. Motown (S)TML 11153	**GREATEST HITS** (LP)...£15

MARVIN GAYE & MARY WELLS

64	Stateside SS 316	**Once Upon A Time/What's The Matter With You, Baby?**..................£35
64	Stateside SS 316	**Once Upon A Time/What's The Matter With You, Baby?** (DJ Copy).......£80
64	Stateside SL 10097	**TOGETHER** (LP)..£75

MARVIN GAYE & KIM WESTON

64	Stateside SS 363	**What Good Am I Without You?/I Want You Around**.......................£40
64	Stateside SS 363	**What Good Am I Without You?/I Want You Around** (DJ Copy).............£80
67	Tamla Motown TMG 590	**It Takes Two/It's Got To Be A Miracle** (This Thing Called Love) (DJ Copy)...........£70
67	T. Motown TML 11049	**TAKE TWO** (LP, mono)...£40
67	T. Motown STML 11049	**TAKE TWO** (LP, stereo)...£45

(see also Diana Ross, Tammi Terrell, Mary Wells, Kim Weston)

GAYLADS

64	R&B JB 159	There'll Come A Day/BILLY COOKE: Iron Bar	£50
64	R&B JB 165	What Is Wrong With Me?/Whap Whap	£60
66	Island WI 281	Goodbye Daddy/Your Eyes	£30
66	Island WI 291	You Never Leave Him/Message To My Girl	£35
66	Island WI 3002	Stop Making Love/They Call Her Dawn	£40
66	Doctor Bird DB 1014	Lady With The Red Dress/Dinner For Two	£25
66	Doctor Bird DB 1031	You Should Never Do That/WINSTON STEWART: I Don't Know Why I Love You	£25
66	Rymska RA 104	You Should Never Do That/TECHNIQUES: So Many Times	£35
67	Island WI 3022	Don't Say No/SONNY BURKE: You Rule My Heart	£40
67	Island WI 3025	You No Good Girl/Yes Girl	£35
67	Studio One SO 2002	Tears From My Eyes/Never Let Your Country Down	£125
67	Studio One SO 2009	Won't You Come Home(actually DELROY WILSON)/PETER & HORTENSE : I've Been Lonely	£70
67	Studio One SO 2013	I Am Going To Cool It (actually by Little Roy)/ MELODIANS: Let's Join Together	£60
67	Studio One SO 2017	Love Me With All Your Heart/I Don't Care	£45
67	Studio One SO 2021	IF You Knew/Festival Day	£80
67	Rio R 125	Put On Your Style/SOUL BROTHERS: Soul Serenade	£65
68	Blue Cat BS 110	Go Away/SOUL VENDORS: Julie On My Mind	£50
68	Doctor Bird DB 1124	It's Hard To Confess/I Need Your Loving	£40
68	Doctor Bird DB 1145	She Want It/Joy In The Morning	£45
68	Fab FAB 62	Looking For A Girl/Aren't You The Guy	£100
68	Hi Note HS 001	A B C Rocksteady/LESLIE BUTLER & COUNT OSSIE: Soul Drums	£35
69	Upsetter US 323	The Same Things/I Wear My Slanders	£40
70	Trojan TR 7743	Young, Gifted And Black/BEVERLEY'S ALLSTARS: Moon Glow	£25
70	Trojan TR 7771	Soul Sister/BEVERLEY'S ALLSTARS: Soul Version	£15
67	Coxsone CSL 8005	ROCKSTEADY (LP)	£400
67	Coxsone CSL 8006	SUNSHINE IS GOLDEN (LP)	£300
79	Ballistic UAG 30236	UNDERSTANDING (LP)	£15

(see also Gaylords, Rockstones, Delano Stewart, Ken Boothe, B.B. Seaton, Brent Dowe, Dobby Dobson, Jackie Mittoo, Heptones, Clarendonians, Soul Vendors)

BONNIE GAYLE

75	Treble C CCC 008	Mellow Up Yourself/Version	£20
76	Love LOV 0024	How Many Strong/CONSCIOUS MINDS: Version	£50

VINLEY GAYLE

64	Black Swan WI 453	Go-Go/BABA BROOKS: Take Five	£30

GAYLET(T)S

68	Island WI 3129	Silent River Runs Deep/You're Kind Of Man	£45
68	Island WI 3141	I Like Your World/Lonely Feeling	£25
69	Big Shot BI 516	Son-Of-A-Preacher-Man/That's How Strong My Love Is	£18

(see also Judy Mowatt)

GAYLORDS (DOMINICA)

75	Cosmos C.S.P. 1001	I Man Suffering/Dread Lucks Version	£200

GAYLORDS (JAMAICA)

66	Island WI 269	Chipmunk Ska/What Is Wrong? (both actually by Gaylads)	£25

(see also Gaylads)

GAYLORDS (U.K.)

66	Columbia DB 7805	He's A Good Face But He's Down And Out/You Know It Too	£15

(see also Dean Ford & Gaylords, Marmalade)

WILTON 'BOGEY' GAYNAIR QUARTET

61	Tempo EXA 103	BLUE BOGEY VOLUME ONE (EP)	£60
59	Tempo TAP 25	BLUE BOGEY (LP)	£500
83	Jasmine JASM 2016	BLUE BOGEY (LP, reissue)	£20

GAYNOR (JUNIOR ENGLISH) & ERROL (DUNKLEY)

65	Blue Beat BB 286	My Queen/ROLAND ALPHONSO: Roland Plays Prince (B-side actually "Hanging The Beam" by Skatalites)	£60

(see also Errol Dunkley)

GLORIA GAYNOR

78	Polydor 2066922	For The First Time In My Life/This Love Affair	£20
75	MGM 2315 321	NEVER CAN SAY GOODBYE (LP)	£15

ROSEMARY GAYNOR

55	Columbia SCM 5196	Ain't That A Shame/A Happy Song	£15

PAUL GAYTEN

57	London HL 8503	Yo, Yo, Walk/TUNE WEAVERS: Happy Happy Birthday Baby	£80
59	London HLM 8998	The Hunch/Hot Cross Buns	£50

GAYTONES (JAMAICA)

70	High Note HS 037	Target (actually "Musical Fight" by Crashers)/PATSY: Find Someone (song actually "True Love")	£30
71	High Note HS 055	Heart Of The Knights/One Toke Over The Line (B-side actually by Stranger & Gladdy)	£15

(see also Righteous Flames, Max Romeo, Ethiopians, Jean & Gaytones, Huxborn & Scotty, Charlie Ace, Delano Stewart, Teddy & Conquerors)

GAYTONES (U.S.)

73	Action ACT 4610	Soul Makossa/Soul Makossa (Version)	£15

GBH

81	Clay PLATE 3	LEATHER, BRISTLES, STUDS AND ACNE (LP)	£18
82	Clay CLAYLP 4	CITY BABY ATTACKED BY RATS (LP)	£20

G-CLEFS
56	Columbia DB 3851	Ka-Ding Dong/Darla, My Darlin'	£750
56	Columbia DB 3851	Ka-Ding Dong/Darla, My Darlin' (78 rpm)	£35
62	London HLU 9563	Make Up Your Mind/Call Me Away	£15

GEDDES AXE
80	ACS ACS 1	Return Of The Gods/Wildfire/Aftermath (p/s, with insert)	£20
81	Steel City AXE 1	Sharpen Your Wits/Rock 'N' Roll (p/s)	£50

RON GEESIN
65	RRG 319/320	RON GEESIN (EP, handmade p/s, 100 only)	£100
67	Transatlantic (S)TRA 161	A RAISE OF EYEBROWS (LP)	£50
72	KPM KPM 1102	ELECTROSOUND (LP, library issue, 1,000 only)	£60
73	Ron Geesin RON 28	AS HE STANDS (LP)	£30
75	KPM KPM 1154	ELECTROSOUND VOL. 2 (LP, library issue, 1,000 only)	£60
75	Ron Geesin RON 31	PATRUNS (LP)	£15
77	Ron Geesin RON 323	RIGHT THROUGH (LP)	£18
77	KPM KPM 1201	ATMOSPHERES (LP, library issue, 1,000 only)	£30
08	Glo Spot 1102	ELECTROSOUND (LP, reissue, different sleeve art, blue vinyl)	£20

(see also Bridget St. John, Pink Floyd, Original Downtown Syncopators, Amory Kane)

RON GEESIN & ROGER WATERS
70	Harvest SHSP 4008	MUSIC FROM THE BODY (LP, soundtrack; green labels with Waters/Geesin photos)	£50
87	Harvest SHSP 4008	MUSIC FROM THE BODY (LP, reissue, black label, barcode on rear of sleeve)	£15

(see also Roger Waters, Pink Floyd)

AVIV GEFFEN
09	2006 Records 012 LP	AVIV GEFFEN (LP)	£30

HERB GELLER QUARTET
56	London RE-U 1067	SENSATIONAL SAX OF HERB GELLER (EP)	£15

HERB GELLER
75	Atlantic SD 1681	RHYME & REASON (LP)	£25

GEMAGE
80	Private pressing BGA 1	Story So Far/Bring Me Death (no p/s)	£50

GEMINI (U.K.) (1)
65	Columbia DB 7638	Space Walk/Goodbye Joe (demos may credit the 'Original Tornados')	£50

(see also Tornados)

GEMINI (U.K.) (3)
81	Airship AP 345	COUNTER BALANCE (LP)	£60

GEMINI (4)
97	Peacefrog PF 061	HIBERNATION EP (12")	£70
97	NRK 003	REVOLUTION EP (12", p/s)	£25
97	Peacefrog PF 065	ON THE NORTH STAR WITH GEMINI EP (12")	£25
98	Cyclo CYC 005.6	TAKE YOUR TIME EP (12")	£15
98	Classic CMG 81	IN MY HEAD EP (12")	£35
97	Substance SUB 4844.1	IN NEUTRAL (2-LP)	£30
97	Peacefrog PF 070	IN AND OUT OF FOG AND LIGHTS (2-LP)	£50
99	Cyclo CYC 005.1	THE MUSIC HALL (LP as 2 x 12")	£15
16	Anothertheday 004AD	IMAGINE-A-NATION (LP, reissue as 2 x 12")	£20
17	Peacefrog PF 070	IN AND OUT OF FOG AND LIGHTS (2-LP, reissue)	£20

GENE
96	Costermonger GENE 1LP	OLYMPIAN (LP)	£50
96	Polydor GENE 2LP	TO SEE THE LIGHTS (2-LP)	£50
97	Polydor GENELP 3	DRAWN TO THE DEEP END (2-LP)	£60
99	Polydor GENELP 4	REVELATIONS (LP, with booklet)	£60

GENE & GARY
09	Kent 6T 26	Baby Without You/PARAMOUNT FOUR: Sorry Ain't The Word	£20

GENE & EUNICE
56	Vogue V 9062	I Gotta Go Home/Have You Changed Your Mind?	£200
56	Vogue V 9062	I Gotta Go Home/Have You Changed Your Mind? (78)	£40
57	Vogue V 9066	Move It Over, Baby/This Is My Story	£150
57	Vogue V 9066	Move It Over, Baby/This Is My Story (78)	£40
57	Vogue V 9071	Let's Get Together/I'm So In Love With You	£150
57	Vogue V 9071	Let's Get Together/I'm So In Love With You (78)	£30
57	Vogue V 9083	Doodle Doodle Doo/Don't Treat Me This Way	£150
57	Vogue V 9083	Doodle Doodle Doo/Don't Treat Me This Way (78)	£30
58	Vogue V 9106	I Mean Love/The Angels Gave You To Me	£150
58	Vogue V 9106	I Mean Love/The Angels Gave You To Me (78)	£30
58	Vogue V 9126	Strange World/The Vow	£50

(The above 45s were originally issued with triangular centres; later issues with round centres are worth about half the values listed.)

58	Vogue V 9126	Strange World/The Vow (78)	£30
59	Vogue V 9136	Bom Bom Lulu/Hi Diddle Diddle	£100
59	Vogue V 9136	Bom Bom Lulu/Hi Diddle Diddle (78)	£40
59	London HL 8956	Poco-Loco/Go-On Kokomo	£50
59	London HL 8956	Poco-Loco/Go-On Kokomo (78)	£40

GENE LOVES JEZEBEL
82	Situation 2 SIT 18T	Shavin' My Neck/Sun & Insanity/Machismo/Glad To Be Alive (12", p/s)	£15

GENERAL HAVOC
91	Chapati Heat BIRD 1	Moonshine/Vacuum Cleaner/Another Cup Of Tea Arch Deacon?.................................£40

GENERAL LEVY
90	Musik Street MS 005	**You Can't Hurry Love** (with Junior Dunn)/**JAZWAD: You Can't Hurry Dub** (12", red or blue labels)...£70
93	Ffrr/Fashion F214	**Monkey Man** (Fashion Radio Edit)/**Mad Them** (p/s)...£20
93	Ffrr/Fashion FX 214	**WICKEDER GENERAL EP** (12", p/s)...£25
92	Fashion FADLP 024	**THE WICKEDER GENERAL** (LP)...£40

(see also M-Beat)

MIKEY GENERAL
85	Jagan Intl. J.I. 001	**Bag A Respect/Yard A Yard** (12")...£35

GENERAL T
88	Realistic RR09	**Nah Tek De Coke/Version** (12")..£30

GENERATION X
77	GX 2	**Perfect Hits 2: Rock On/No No No/Gimmie Some Truth/From The Heart** (no p/s).........£15
77	GX 1	**Perfect Hits: Your Generation/Save My Life/Ready Steady Go** (no p/s) £15
77	GX 101	**Your Generation/Listen!** (white label test pressing, official bootleg sold at gigs, no p/s)...£100
77	Chrysalis CHS 2165	**Your Generation/Day By Day** (sleeve only, unissued, featuring 'pre-peroxide' Billy Idol; 4 copies known to exist)...£1000
77	Chrysalis CHS 2189	**Wild Youth/Wild Dub** (Version) (p/s, mispressing, plays "No No No", B-side matrix: CHS 2189 B/1)..£40
79	Chrysalis CHS 2310	**Valley Of The Dolls/Shakin' All Over** (multi-coloured vinyl, p/s).............................£50
79	Chrysalis CHS 2330	**Friday's Angels/Trying For Kicks/This Heat** (p/s, black vinyl)................................£15
78	Chrysalis CHR 1169	**GENERATION X** (LP, with rare obi at bottom of sleeve) £40
78	Chrysalis CHR 1169	**GENERATION X** (LP)..£25
79	Chrysalis CHR 1193	**VALLEY OF THE DOLLS** (LP, inner) £15

(see also Billy Idol, Sigue Sigue Sputnik, Westworld)

GENESIS (1)
23	BBC/EMI/UMC 00602435686417	**BBC BROADCASTS** (5CD box set, booklet) £40

SINGLES
68	Decca F 12735	**The Silent Sun/That's Me** £450
68	Decca F 12735	**The Silent Sun/That's Me** (promo copy) £500
68	Decca F 12775	**A Winter's Tale/One Eyed Hound** £600
68	Decca F 12775	**A Winter's Tale/One Eyed Hound** (promo copy. push out centre)..................£750
68	Decca F 12775	**A Winter's Tale/One Eyed Hound** (promo copy, solid centre) £950
68	London F12775	**A Winter's Tale/One Eyed Hound** (export promo single)............................£2000
69	Decca F 12949	**Where The Sour Turns To Sweet/In Hiding** £750
69	Decca F 12949	**Where The Sour Turns To Sweet/In Hiding** (promo copy) £600
70	Charisma GS 1/2	**Looking For Someone/Visions Of Angels** (promo only, push out centre)........£900
70	Charisma GS 1/2	**Looking For Someone/Visions Of Angels** (promo only, solid centre)...........£1200
71	Charisma CB 152	**The Knife** (Parts 1 & 2) (in p/s, push out or solid).....................................£600
71	Charisma CB 152	**The Knife** (Parts 1 & 2, push out or solid)..£100
72	Charisma CB 181	**Happy The Man/Seven Stones** (promo copy, push out centre 'DJ Not For Sale' on both labels or A dise only)..£150
72	Charisma CB 181	**Happy The Man/Seven Stones** (push out or solid centre, JOHN ANTHONY in capitals) ..£125
72	Charisma CB 181	**Happy The Man/Seven Stones** (p/s, solid or push out centre, with JOHN ANTHONY in capitals)...£500
73	Charisma (no cat. no.)	**Twilight Alehouse** (1-sided flexidisc free with Zig Zag magazine)..................£35
73	Charisma (no cat. no.)	**Twilight Alehouse** (1-sided flexidisc free with Zig Zag & later via fan club, without magazine)...£20
73	Charisma (no cat. no.)	**Twilight Alehouse** (black vinyl, white label test pressings)............................£70
73	Charisma (no cat. no.)	**Twilight Alehouse** (1-sided flexidisc free via fan club, with letter, sticker, poster and Genesis "revolver")..£80
74	Charisma CB 224	**I Know What I Like** (In Your Wardrobe)/**Twilight Alehouse** (promos with press release)...£100
74	Charisma CB 238	**Counting Out Time/Riding The Scree** (solid centre) £20
74	Charisma CB 238	**Counting Out Time/Counting Out Time** (promo, push out centre) £75
75	Charisma CB 251	**The Carpet Crawlers/The Waiting Room** (Evil Jam) £28
75	Charisma CB 251	**The Carpet Crawlers/The Waiting Room** (Evil Jam) (7" A-label promo) £70
82	Charisma CB 393	**Man On The Corner/Submarine** (blue injection labels, large centre hole)......£90
82	Charisma CB 93	**Man On The Corner/Submarine** (p/s, green injection labels, solid centre) £25
83	Lyntone LYN 13143	**Firth Of Fifth** (live edit) (flexidisc, with numbered gatefold p/s) £18
83	Virgin TATAY 1	**That's All/Taking It All Too Hard** (uncut picture disc)................................£75
83	Charisma/Virgin TATA Y-1	**That's All/Taking It All Too Hard** (shaped picture disc) £15
84	Charisma/Virgin CB 300	**Your Own Special Way/It's Yourself** (blue label reissue, push out or solid centre no p/s)...£25
84	Charisma CB 356	**Turn It On Again/ Behind The Lines Part 2** (blue paper label reissue) £15
84	Charisma/Virgin CB 369	**Misunderstanding/Evidence Of Autumn** (blue label reissue, no p/s) £20
87	Virgin CDEP 1	**Tonight, Tonight, Tonight** (Edit)/**In The Glow Of The Night/ Invisible Touch** (12" Remix)/**Tonight, Tonight, Tonight** (CD, gatefold p/s) £40
98	Virgin SOLO2	**Live Rehearsal: Mama** (live)/**Calling All Stations** (live)/**Invisible Touch** (live)/ **Follow You, Follow Me** (live)/**Turn It On Again** (live) (CD 5-track promo) £50

ALBUMS : COMPILATIONS/BOX SETS
74	Decca SKL 4990	**IN THE BEGINNING** (reissue of 1st LP, 'snake' sleeve, lyric insert)................£20
75	Charisma CGS 102	**GENESIS COLLECTION VOLUME ONE** (2LP, boxed set of Trespass & Nursery Cryme in original sleeves, poster)...£100
75	Charisma CGS 103	**GENESIS COLLECTION VOLUME TWO** (2LP, boxed set of Foxtrot & Selling England By The Pound, poster)...£120

98	Virgin CDBOX6	GENESIS ARCHIVE 1967-1975 (4CD box set, booklet)	£60
98	Virgin IVCDJBOX 6	GENESIS ARCHIVE 1967-1975 The Interviews (2CD promo, p/s)	£40
00	Virgin CDBOX 7	GENESIS ARCHIVE #2: 1976-1992 (3CD box set, booklet)	£40
07	Virgin CDBOX 12	GENESIS 1976-1982 (6 SACD/6DVD box set, booklet)	£300
07	Virgin CDBOX13	GENESIS 1983-1998 (5 SACD/5DVD box set, booklet)	£200
08	Virgin LPBOX 14	1970-1975 (6LP box set, original gatefolds, printed inners & inserts)	£200
08	Virgin CDBOX 14	1970-1975 (7SACD/6DVD box set, booklet)	£300
09	Virgin VDVDBOX 1	1981-2007 THE MOVIE BOX (5DVD box set, booklet, space for When In Rome)	£140
09	Virgin CDBOX 17	LIVE 1973-2007 (8 SACD/3DVD box set, booklet, with space for 'Live Over Europe')	£150
12	Virgin LPBOX 12	1976-1982 (5LP box set, original gatefolds & printed inners)	£220
15	Not Bad BADBOX 001	FROM GENESIS TO REVELATION (3LP, 3x7" box set, booklet)	£70
15	Virgin LPBOX 13	1983-1998 (6LP, original gatefolds & printed inners, pressed originally on 150gm vinyl, later repressed on 180gm vinyl)	£100

ALBUMS

69	Decca LK 4990	FROM GENESIS TO REVELATION (mono, with 'mono' peephole, with red/pink lyric sheet, red/silver unboxed logo)	£1500
69	Decca SKL 4990	FROM GENESIS TO REVELATION (stereo, with stereo 'peephole', with lyric sheet, unboxed logo)	£500
70	Decca SKL 4990	FROM GENESIS TO REVELATION (stereo, with lyric sheet, blue/silver boxed logo)	£100
70	Decca KSKC 4990	FROM GENESIS TO REVELATION (cassette, boxed logo)	£25
70	Charisma CAS 1020	TRESPASS (1st pressing, original pink scroll label & gatefold sleeve with lyric sheet, with bolder (p) 1970)	£200
70	Charisma CAS 1020	TRESPASS (2nd pressing, original pink scroll label & gatefold sleeve with lyric sheet, with less bold (p) 1970 with more spaced text)	£165
71	Charisma CAS 1052	NURSERY CRYME (LP, 1st pressing, textured sleeve, original pink scroll label, gatefold sleeve)	£200
72	Charisma CAS 1058	FOXTROT (LP, textured gatefold, large 'Mad Hatter' logo and B&C credit on label)	£70
72	Charisma CAS 1058	FOXTROT (LP, gatefold sleeve, 'Mad Hatter' logo and B&C credit on label, Michael Rutherford credited as Micheal Rutherford. Horizons listed as Horizon's)	£30
72	Charisma CAS 1020	TRESPASS (LP, repressing, large 'Mad Hatter' label with 'Printed and made by the Bruin B.V - Zaandam/Holland' on label)	£18
72	Charisma CAS 1052	NURSERY CRYME (LP, 1st reissue, large 'Mad Hatter' label, gatefold sleeve)	£20
72	Charisma CAS 1052	NURSERY CRYME (LP, 1st reissue, large 'Mad Hatter' label, gatefold sleeve, mispressing plays 'Cabaret' OST)	£60
73	CAS 1074	SELLING ENGLAND BY THE POUND (LP, first pressing, green card printed inner (not insert), B&C credit to label)	£50
73	Charisma CAS 1074	SELLING ENGLAND BY THE POUND (LP, dark green card insert, large 'Mad Hatter' logo)	£25
73	Charisma CLASS 1	LIVE (LP, non laminated sleeve, large 'Mad Hatter' logo, with 'Charisma Live Giants - £1.99' sticker on front cover)	£30
73	Charisma CLASS 1	LIVE (LP, non laminated sleeve, large 'Mad Hatter' logo)	£25
74	Charisma CGS 101	THE LAMB LIES DOWN ON BROADWAY (2LP, gatefold, printed inners 'Mad Hatter' label, original pressing with 'Marketed by B&C Records' label text on both LPs and 'Printed and Made by Bruin B.V. Zaandam/Holland" credit on sleeve, some with Gold Chase contest insert)	£110
74	Charima CAS 1052	NURSERY CRYME (LP, reissue, small 'Mad Hatter' label, gatefold sleeve)	£15
75	Charisma CAs 1074	SELLING ENGLAND BY THE POUND (LP, insert, small 'Mad Hatter' logo)	£18
75	Charisma CGS 101	THE LAMB LIES DOWN ON BROADWAY (2LP, gatefold, printed inners, 'Mad Hatter' label, Phonogram credits,'Printed and Made by Bruin B.V Zaandam/Holland' credit on sleeve)	£25
76	Charisma CDS 4001	A TRICK OF THE TAIL (LP, textured gatefold sleeve, inner,sleeve printed by "Bruin BV or Robor Ltd")	£15
76	Charisma CAS 1020	TRESPASS (LP, repressing, small 'Mad Hatter' label, pressed by PRS or Phonodisc)	£15
80	Charisma CAS 1058	FOXTROT (LP, reissue, gatefold sleeve, blue label)	£15
83	Charisma CHC 12	TRESPASS (LP, repressing, blue label, insert)	£15
91	Virgin GENLP 3	WE CAN'T DANCE (2LP, printed inners)	£30
91	Virgin EDITS 1	WE CAN'T DANCE - SPECIAL EDITION VOLKSWAGEN (6-track promo tour edition CD)	£50
91	Virgin GEN CD	WE CAN'T DANCE (CD & tape, housed in custom promo box With three hand numbered watercolours)	£90
92	Virgin GEN LP 4	LIVE/THE WAY WE WALK VOLUME ONE: THE SHORTS (LP, printed inner, 'Longs' insert)	£100
93	Virgin GENLP 5	LIVE/THE WAY WE WALK VOLUME 2: THE LONGS (LP, printed inner)	£100
93	Virgin GENBOX 1	LIVE/THE WAY WE WALK (2CD, wooden box, certificate, badge, 1000 only)	£80
97	Virgin GENLP6	CALLING ALL STATIONS (2LP, fourth sided etched, gatefold, printed inners)	£150
97	EMI LPCENT 17	SELLING ENGLAND BY THE POUND (LP, reissue, EMI Centenary pressing, stickered sleeve)	£40
99	Virgin VGP 000270	TURN IT ON AGAIN - THE HITS (CD, instore promo, p/s - each song played for 1 min)	£60
07	Charisma GENLPY 2	NURSERY CRYME (LP, remastered reissue, gatefold sleeve, 180gm vinyl)	£35
07	Charisma 4790193	A TRICK OF THE TAIL (LP, reissue, gatefold, inner, 180gm)	£18
08	Charisma GENPLY 3	FOXTROT (LP, reissue, gatefold sleeve)	£18
08	Charisma GENLP 4	SELLING ENGLAND BY THE POUND (LP, reissue, 18ogm vinyl, insert)	£20
13	Charisma GENLPY 1	TRESPASS (LP, repressing, half-speed master, gatefold sleeve, insert)	£22
13	Back To Black 00600753454503	SELLING ENGLAND BY THE POUND (LP, picture disc)	£35
13	Charisma GENLPY 5	THE LAMB LIES DOWN ON BROADWAY (2LP, reissue, gatefold, printed inners,180g)	£25
18	Charisma 00602567489849	NURSERY CRYME (LP, reissue, half speed master)	£20
21	Virgin/UMC 354 286 7	THE LAST DOMINO? (4LP, 180g vinyl, double gatefold, printed inners)	£75
23	BBC/EMI/UMC 00602435686370	BBC BROADCASTS (3LP, trifold sleeve, printed inners)	£50
24	Craft Recordings RCV1 83244	TURN IT ON AGAIN (THE HITS) (2LP, printed inners, clear vinyl, first vinyl release of 1999 CD)	£35

(see also Flaming Youth, Tony Banks,, Peter Gabriel, Anthony Phillips, Quiet World)

GENESIS (2)

77	Pilgrim 438	ENJOY CHRISTMAS WITH GENESIS (LP)	£15

GENEVEVE
66	CBS 202061	Once/Just A Whisper (in p/s)	£25
66	CBS 202061	Once/Just A Whisper	£15

GENGHIS KHAN (U.K.)
83	Genghis Khan GK 1	DOUBLE DEALIN' (If Heaven Is Hell/Highway Passion//Midnight Rendezvous Mean Streak) (EP, double pack)	£80
83	Wabbit WAB 61/63	Love You/Lady Lady/Mongol Nation/Gone For A Drive (double pack)	£40

GENITAL DEFORMITIES
89	Fair Dinkum FD 001	SHAG NAST OI! (LP)	£15

GENIUS/GZA
95	Gaffe GEF 24813	LIQUID SWORDS (2-LP)	£40
99	MCA MCA 2111969	BENEATH THE SURFACE (2-LP)	£25

GENOCIDE EXIT
80	Slam SEM 016	Future Vibes/I'm Not Really Here/Dream Song/All I Want	£50

GENTLE DESPITE
90	Sarah SARAH 26	THE DARKEST BLUE EP (p/s, insert)	£25
91	Sarah SARAH 45	Torment To Me/Bittersweet Kiss/Shadow Of A Girl (p/s, insert)	£25

JOHNNY GENTLE
59	Philips BBE 12345	THE GENTLE TOUCH (EP)	£25

(see also Darren Young)

GENTLE ONES
70	Solar SL 3	Roundabout/Time To Spare	£25

GENTLE WAVES
99	Jeepster JPRLP 006	THE GREEN FIELDS OF FOREVERLAND...(LP)	£20
00	Jeepster JPRLP 011	SWANSONG FOR YOU (LP)	£50

(see also Belle & Sebastian, Isobel Campbell)

GENTLE GIANT
73	WWA WWP 1001	In A Glass House/An Inmate's Lullaby	£30
70	Vertigo 6360 020	GENTLE GIANT (LP, 1st pressing, gatefold sleeve, large swirl label)	£400
71	Vertigo 6360 020	GENTLE GIANT (LP, 2nd pressing, gatefold sleeve, small swirl label)	£70
71	Vertigo 6360 041	ACQUIRING THE TASTE (LP, gatefold sleeve, small swirl label)	£300
72	Vertigo 6360 070	THREE FRIENDS (LP, 1st pressing, no "made in England" under 1972 on top right hand side of label, gatefold sleeve, small swirl label)	£200
72	Vertigo 6360 070	THREE FRIENDS (LP, 2nd pressing, "made in England" under 1972 on top right hand side of label, gatefold sleeve, small swirl label)	£50
72	Vertigo 6360 080	OCTOPUS (LP, gatefold sleeve, small swirl label)	£200
73	WWA WWA 002	IN A GLASS HOUSE (LP, silk-screen cover, with photo insert & lyric inner)	£50
74	WWA WWA 010	THE POWER AND THE GLORY (LP, with insert, sleeve has 2 rounded corners)	£40
74	Vertigo 6360041	ACQUIRING THE TASTE (LP, reissue, 'spaceship' label)	£25
75	Vertigo 6360 020	GENTLE GIANT (LP, reissue, gatefold sleeve, spaceship label)	£30
75	Vertigo 6360080	OCTOPUS (LP, reissue, 'spaceship' label)	£30
75	Vertigo 6641 334	GIANT STEPS - (THE FIRST FIVE YEARS) 1970-1975 (2-LP, gatefold sleeve, spaceship label)	£25
75	Chrysalis CHR 1093	FREE HAND (LP, lyric insert, green label)	£15
77	Vertigo 9286 946	PRETENTIOUS (2-LP, gatefold sleeve)	£15
77	Chrysalis CTY 1133	LIVE (PLAYING THE FOOL) (2-LP, with 12-page booklet)	£20
77	Chrysalis CHR 1152	THE MISSING PIECE (LP, with inner sleeve)	£15
78	Chrysalis CHR 1186	GIANT FOR A DAY (LP, with mask insert & lyric inner sleeve)	£15
80	Chrysalis CHR 1285	CIVILIAN (LP, with lyric inner sleeve)	£15
10	Tapestry TPT 255	ACQUIRING THE TASTE (LP, reissue)	£15
12	Tapestry TPT 271	THREE FRIENDS (LP, reissue)	£15

(see also Simon Dupree & Big Sound, Moles)

GENTLE INFLUENCE
69	Pye 7N 17666	Never Trust In Tomorrow/Easy To Love	£15
69	Pye 7N 17743	Always Be A Part Of My Living/Captain Reale	£22

GENTLE PEOPLE (2)
97	Rephlex CAT 045 LP	SOUNDTRACKS FOR LIVING (2-LP)	£15
99	Rephlex CAT 088 LP	SIMPLY FABOO (2-LP)	£15

GENTLE POWER OF SONG
67	Polydor 2310 285	CIRCUS (LP)	£25

GENTLE RAIN
73	Polydor 2310 285	MOODY (LP)	£200

BILL GENTLES
69	Gas GAS 104	Long Life/SCHOOLBOYS: O Tell Me	£18
70	Pama PM 801	What A Woman/Sleepy Cat	£40

(see also Bill Jentles)

ERROL GENTLES
79	Attack TACK 11	Tell Me Why/Far Far Away (12")	£20

GENTRY
70	Dolphin DO571	Long Road/Sing Me A Sad Song/Attempt Contact (EP, Irish pressing)	£250
70	Dolphin DOS 35	Sing Me A Sad Song/Attempted Contact	£150

ART GENTRY
72	Mojo 2092 048	Breakthrough/Wonderful Dream	£15

BOBBIE GENTRY
67	Capitol (S)T 2830	ODE TO BILLIE JOE (LP)	£15
68	Capitol ST2964	LOCAL GENTRY (LP)	£15
68	Capitol (S)T 2842	THE DELTA SWEETE (LP)	£15

GENTRY ICE
| 88 | Jack Trax JTX 15 | Do You Wanna Jack/Lost In The Sound (with Adonis) (12") | £20 |

GENTRYS
65	MGM MGM 1284	Keep On Dancing/Make Up Your Mind	£20
66	MGM MGM 1296	Brown Paper Sack/Spread It On Thick	£25
66	MGM MGM 1312	Everyday I Have To Cry/Don't Let It Be	£15

GENTS
| 81 | Posh POSH 001 | The Faker/The Pink Panther | £20 |

GEOFFREY
| 78 | Music Bank BECK 694 | ABH (Who Wants To Listen To Punk Rock?)/Colt 45 Rock (p/s) | £15 |

GEORDIE
73	EMI EMC 3001	HOPE YOU LIKE IT (LP)	£30
74	EMI EMA 764	DON'T BE FOOLED BY THE NAME (LP)	£80
76	EMI EMC 3134	SAVE THE WORLD (LP)	£40
83	Neat NEAT 1008	NO SWEAT (LP)	£40

(see also Influence, AC/DC)

BARBARA GEORGE
| 62 | London HL 9513 | I Know (You Don't Love Me No More)/Love (Is Just A Chance You Take) | £25 |
| 64 | Sue WI 316 | Send For Me/Bless You | £50 |

EARL GEORGE
| 73 | Count Shelly CS 025 | Gonna Give Her All The Love/PRINCE JAZZBO: Wise Shepherd | £15 |
| 78 | Burning Sounds BS 1015 | ONE AND ONLY (LP) | £20 |

(see also George Faith, George Ferris, Winston Reedy)

GEORGE GOLDEN
| 64 | R&B JB145 | Fire In My Feet/ One More Chance | £15 |
| 64 | R&B JB157 | Don't You Know/ Nancy Tell Me | £15 |

LLOYD GEORGE
| 62 | London HLP 9562 | Lucy Lee/Sing Real Loud | £60 |

GEORGE T
| 99 | Refried WOK1200499 | UNDER ELEVATOR EP (12") | £20 |
| 00 | Under The Counter UTC 024 | SOME LUNAR PURSUITS EP (12") | £35 |

GEORGETTES
| 58 | London HL 8548 | Love Like A Fool/Oh Tonight | £50 |
| 58 | London HL 8548 | Love Like A Fool/Oh Tonight (78) | £30 |

GEORGIA TOM
| 60s | Riverside RLP 8803 | GEORGIA TOM AND FRIENDS (LP) | £20 |

(see also Paramount Allstars)

GERALDINE
| 71 | Beltona Sword SBE 128 | GERALDINE (LP) | £150 |

WESLEY GERMS
| 72 | Upsetter US 390 | Whiplash/UPSETTERS: Whiplash Version | £25 |

GERONIMO BLACK
| 72 | Uni UNLS 127 | GERONIMO BLACK (LP) | £75 |

(see also Frank Zappa/Mothers Of Invention)

DENNY GERRARD
| 70 | Deram Nova DN 10 | SINISTER MORNING (LP, mono, with High Tide, Deram Nova on top right hand corner of sleeve with either Deram Nova or Decca Nova on label) | £300 |
| 70 | Deram Nova SDN 10 | SINISTER MORNING (LP, stereo, with High Tide, Deram Nova on top right hand corner of sleeve with either Deram Nova or Decca Nova on label) | £150 |

(see also Warm Sounds, High Tide, Open Road, Fifth Avenue)

GERRY & THE HOLOGRAMS
| 79 | Absurd ABSURD 4 | Gerry And The Holograms/Increased Resistance (p/s) | £30 |
| 79 | Absurd ABSURD 5 | The Emperor's New Music (unplayable record, glued into p/s) | £30 |

GERRY & THE PACEMAKERS
64	Columbia SEG 8295	YOU'LL NEVER WALK ALONE (EP, in misprinted sleeve listing "It's All Right" instead of "Jambalaya" on front)	£25
64	Columbia SEG 8295	YOU'LL NEVER WALK ALONE (EP)	£15
64	Columbia SEG 8311	I'M THE ONE (EP)	£15
64	Columbia SEG 8346	DON'T LET THE SUN CATCH YOU CRYING (EP)	£15
64	Columbia SEG 8367	IT'S GONNA BE ALRIGHT (EP)	£20
65	Columbia SEG 8388	GERRY IN CALIFORNIA (EP)	£30
65	Columbia SEG 8397	HITS FROM 'FERRY CROSS THE MERSEY' (EP)	£30
65	Columbia SEG 8426	RIP IT UP (EP)	£35
63	Columbia 33SX 1546	HOW DO YOU LIKE IT? (LP, mono)	£20
63	Columbia 33SCX 1546	HOW DO YOU LIKE IT? (LP, stereo)	£30
65	Columbia 33SX 1693	FERRY CROSS THE MERSEY (LP, soundtrack, with Cilla Black & Fourmost, mono)	£25
65	Columbia 33SCX 1693	FERRY CROSS THE MERSEY (LP, soundtrack, with Cilla Black & Fourmost, stereo)	£35
65	EMI Regal REG 2018	YOU'LL NEVER WALK ALONE (LP, export issue)	£25

(see also Gerry Marsden)

GERVASE
68 Decca F12822   **Pepper Grinder/Visions** **£20**

GESCOM
94	Skam SKA 2	**Dan One/Five/Cicada/Sciew Spo** (12", card folder p/s).. **£35**
95	Skam SKA 3	**Snackwitch/Mag** (12", bubblewrap sleeve with insert) **£40**
95	Skam SKA 3	**Snackwitch/Mag** (12", second issue, black sleeve) **£20**
95	Clear CLR 408	**THE SOUNDS OF MACHINES OUR PARENTS USED** (12", p/s)....................................... **£40**
96	Skam SKA 7	**KEY NELL 1/2/3/4** (12", bubblewrap sleeve) **£15**
98	Skam SKA010 THAT	**THAT** (EP) (12", p/s 2 inserts)... **£15**
98	Skam SKA010 THIS	**THIS** (EP) (12", p/s) **£15**

(see also Autechre)

GESTURES
65 Stateside SS 379   **Run Run Run/It Seems To Me** **£25**

STAN GETZ (QUARTET/QUINTET)
53	Esquire 20-007	**STAN GETZ PLAYS** (LP, 10").. **£25**
54	Vogue LDE 089	**AT STORYVILLE** (LP, 10").. **£25**
55	Vogue LDE 147	**STAN GETZ QUARTET** (LP, 10").. **£25**
55	Columbia Clef 33CX 10000	**AT THE SHRINE NO. 1** (LP, as Stan Getz Quintet) **£25**
55	Columbia Clef 33CX 10001	**AT THE SHRINE NO. 2** (LP, as Stan Getz Quintet) **£25**
58	HMV CLP 1292	**STAN GETZ/CHET BAKER** (LP) **£20**
62	HMV CLP 1577	**FOCUS** (LP, also stereo CSD 1448) **£20**
63	Verve VLP 9013	**JAZZ SAMBA** (LP, with Charlie Byrd, mono) **£20**
63	Verve (S)VLP 9013	**JAZZ SAMBA** (LP, with Charlie Byrd, stereo)... **£20**
63	Verve VLP 9024	**BIG BAND BOSSA NOVA** (LP) **£20**
63	Verve VLP 9038	**JAZZ SAMBA ENCORE!** (LP, with Luiz Bonfa, mono).. **£20**
63	Verve (S)VLP 9038	**JAZZ SAMBA ENCORE!** (LP, with Luiz Bonfa, stereo) **£20**
64	Verve VLP 9065	**GETZ-GILBERTO** (LP) **£25**
65	MGM MGM-C 8001	**MICKEY ONE** (LP, soundtrack, mono, with booklet) **£20**
65	MGM MGM-C(S) 8001	**MICKEY ONE** (LP, soundtrack, stereo, with booklet)... **£25**

(see also Dizzy Gillespie, Astrud Gilberto, Joao Gilberto, Johnny Smith)

GEZLIM
72 Helm 001   **Dark Side Of Your Face** (1-sided) **£200**

G-FORCE
80	Jet JET 183	**Hot Gossip/Because Of Your Love** (p/s) **£20**
80	Jet JET 7005	**White Knuckles/Rockin' And Rollin'/I Look At You** (p/s).................................... **£15**
80	Jet JETLP 229	**G-FORCE** (LP, with inner sleeve and patch).. **£20**
80	Jet JETPD 229	**G-FORCE** (LP, picture disc)... **£18**

(see also Gary Moore)

G.G. ALLSTARS
70	Explosion EX 2012	**Champion/MAYTONES: Funny Man**.. **£25**
70	G.G. GG 4505	**I Don't Like To Interfere/Version II**... **£20**
70	G.G. GG 4501	**Music Keep On Playing** (actually by Cornell Campbell)**/ Music Keep On Playing Version** **£70**
71	G.G. GG 4510	**Rocking On The G.G. Beat** (actually by Maytones)**/WINSTON WRIGHT: Rocking On The G.G. Beat Version II** **£15**
71	G.G. GG 4526	**Rod Of Righteousness** (actually "Stretch Forth His Hand" by Jah Huntly)**/ DENNIS ALCAPONE: King Of Kings** (B-side actually "King Of Glory")............................... **£25**
70	Trojan TBL 129	**MAN FROM CAROLINA** (LP).. **£70**

(see also Billy Dyce, Maytones, Charlie Ace, Monty Morris, Starlights, Lloyd & Carey, Gladdy & Stranger, Heptones, Shorty Perry, Barbara Jones)

G.G.F.H.
94 Peaceville CC8   **Welcome To The Process/Too Much Punch/Dread** (green vinyl, p/s) **£15**

G.G. RHYTHM SECTION
69 Blue Cat BS 165   **T.N.T./MAYTONES: Botheration** **£35**

GHETTO FUNK
00 G-Funk GFUNK 001   **Doing My Thing** (Light Side)/(Heavy Side) (12") **£45**

GHETTO PRIEST
03 On U Sound ON-ULP 1003   **VULTURE CULTURE** (LP) **£15**

GHETTO TEARS
84 Ghetto Tears GT 001   **Ghetto Children/Ghetto Prayers** (12" p/s) **£80**

GHOST DANCE
88 Karbon KAR XL 303   **GATHERING DUST** (LP) **£15**

(see also Skeletal Family, All About Eve, Sisters Of Mercy)

GHOST (1)
69	Gemini GMS 007	**When You're Dead/Indian Maid** **£50**
70	Gemini GMS 014	**I've Got To Get To Know You/For One Second**... **£40**
70	Gemini GME 1004	**WHEN YOU'RE DEAD - ONE SECOND** (LP, laminated front cover, with extra track, "I've Got To Get To Know Her").. **£750**
70	Gemini GME 1004	**WHEN YOU'RE DEAD - ONE SECOND** (LP, laminated front cover, without extra track, "I've Got To Get To Know Her") **£500**
87	Bam Caruso KIRI 077	**FOR ONE SECOND** (LP, reissue of "When You're Dead" with extra track)........... **£20**

(see also Velvett Fogg, Shirley Kent, Virginia Tree, Wizzard)

GHOST (2)
10 Rise Above RISELP 124   **OPVS EPONYMOVS** (LP, 'Die Hard Edition', 300 only)................................... **£200**

GHOSTFACE KILLAH
96 Razor Sharp EPC 485389 1   **IRONMAN** (2-LP) **£50**

00	Epic EPC 491955	**SUPREME CLIENTELE** (2-LP)	**£150**
01	Epic EPC 501941 1	**BULLETPROOF WALLETS** (2-LP)	**£20**
18	Daupe! DM SP 039	**THE LOST TAPES** (LP)	**£20**
18	Daupe! DM SP 039	**THE LOST TAPES** (LP, gold vinyl)	**£20**
18	Daupe! DM SP 039	**THE LOST TAPES** (LP, silver vinyl)	**£20**
18	Daupe! DM SP 039	**THE LOST TAPES** (LP, white vinyl)	**£20**
18	Daupe! DM SP 039	**THE LOST TAPES** (LP, yellow vinyl)	**£20**
18	Daupe! DM SP 039	**THE LOST TAPES** (LP, glow in the dark vinyl)	**£30**
18	Daupe! DM SP 039	**THE LOST TAPES** (LP, with obi strip, 40 copies)	**£250**

GHOSTPOET
11	Brownswood BWOOD057LP	**PEANUT BUTTER BLUES AND MELONCOLY JAM** (LP, 1st pressing, 2014 reissue has different barcode)	**£30**

GHOSTS
80	Arista ARIST 347	**My Town/I'm Your Man** (no p/s)	**£20**

GHOSTS OF DANCE
82	Plastic Canvas PC001	**Ghosts Of Dance/Walking Through Gardens** (p/s)	**£20**

BILLY GIANT
65	Pye 25337	**Leave My Girl Alone/Nice Girls**	**£20**

GIANT CRAB
68	Uni UN 509	**Hot Line Conversation/E.S.P.**	**£35**

GIANTS
60s	Polydor LPHM 46426	**IN GERMANY** (LP, mono)	**£25**
60s	Polydor SLPHM 237626	**IN GERMANY** (LP, stereo)	**£30**

GIANT SIZE C
91	Afrocentric AFRO 1	**Perspective/(Bedroom Mix)/(Rough Mix)** (12")	**£150**
93	Afrocentric AFRO 3	**Hate** (12")	**£15**

GIANT SUNFLOWER
67	CBS 2805	**February Sunshine/Big Apple**	**£20**

BARRY GIBB
70	Lyntone LYN 2375	**King Cathy/Summer Ends/I Can Bring Love**	**£100**

(see also Bee Gees)

MAURICE GIBB
84	Audiotrax ATX 05	**Hold Her In Your Hand/Instrumental** (gatefold sleeve)	**£15**

(see also Bee Gees, Fut)

ROBIN GIBB
69	Polydor 56337	**Saved By The Bell/Alexandria Good Time** (withdrawn)	**£20**
69	Polydor 583 085	**ROBIN'S REIGN** (LP)	**£25**

(see also Bee Gees)

BETH GIBBONS
19	Domino WIGLP 395X	**GORECKI SYMPHONY NO. 3** (SYMPHONY OF SORROWFUL SONGS) (LP/DVD, tip on sleeve, booklet, 180gm)	**£40**
24	Domino WIGLP287XM	**LIVES OUTGROWN** (LP, gatefold, printed inner, signed postcard, Ltd. Ed)	**£70**

(see also Portishead, Beth Gibbons & Rustin Man)

STEVE GIBBONS (BAND)
71	Wizard SWZA 5501	**SHORT STORIES** (LP, gatefold sleeve, lyric insert, yellow vinyl)	**£100**
71	Wizard SWZA 5501	**SHORT STORIES** (LP, gatefold sleeve, lyric insert, black vinyl)	**£30**

(see also Uglys, Magic Christians, B,L&G)

CALY GIBBS
71	Amalgamated AMG 870	**Seeing Is Believing/JOE GIBBS ALLSTARS: Ghost Capturer**	**£35**

(see also Carlton Gibbs)

CARLTON GIBBS
70	Amalgamated AMG 872	**Ghost Walk/Joy Stick**	**£45**

GEORGIA GIBBS
58	RCA RCA 1029	**Great Balls Of Fire/I Miss You**	**£45**
56	Mercury MPT 7500	**SINGS THE OLDIES** (10" LP)	**£15**
57	Mercury MPT 7511	**HER NIBS MISS GIBBS** (10" LP)	**£15**
57	Mercury MPL 6508	**SWINGING WITH HER NIBS** (LP)	**£15**

JOE GIBBS (& DESTROYERS)
68	Amslgamated AMG 822	**People Grudgeful** (as Sir Joe)/**Pan-Ya Machete** (actually the Pioneers)	**£65**
70	Amalgamated AMG 855	**Nevada Joe** (act. by Johnny Lover)/**Straight To The Head** (act. by Destroyers)	**£60**
70	Amalgamated AMG 858	**Franco Nero** (actually by Count Machuki & Destroyers)/ **Version Two** (actually by Destroyers)	**£30**
70	Amalgamated AMG 859	**Rock The Clock/Version Two**	**£50**
70	Amalgamated AMG 860	**Let It Be/Turn Back The Hands Of Time** (both actually by Nicky Thomas)	**£25**
70	Amalgamated AMG 861	**La La/Reggae Fever** (as Joe Gibbs All Stars)	**£40**
70	Amalgamated AMG 865	**Hijacked/Life Is Down In Denver**	**£50**
70	Amalgamated AMG 867	**Movements/Caesar**	**£160**
70	Amalgamated AMG 869	**Perfect Born Yah/Red Red Wine** (as Jo Gibs All Stars)	**£65**
70	Amalgamated AMG 868	**Gift Of God** (actually by Lizzy)/**The Raper**	**£15**
70	Pressure Beat PR 5504	**News Flash/Version Two**	**£15**
72	Pressure Beat DB5513	**Money In My Pocket** (actually by Dennis Brown)/**Money Love**	**£25**
72	Pressure Beat PB 5514	**Tipatone/Do It To Me** (as Joe Gibbs All Stars)	**£15**
04	Amalgamated TJSE 022	**Movements/Caesar** (reissue)	**£25**
78	Lightning LIP 10	**AFRICAN DUB ALMIGHTY** (LP, with The Professionals)	**£20**
78	Lightning LIP 11	**AFRICAN DUB ALMIGHTY - CHAPTER TWO** (LP)	**£15**

Michael GIBBS

78	Lightning LIP 12	AFRICAN DUB ALMIGHTY - CHAPTER THREE (LP)	£15
88	Trojan TRLS 261	REGGAE TRAIN 1968 - 71 (LP)	£15

(see also Lizzy, Reggae Boys, Bunny Flip, Destroyers, Dennis Brown, Caly Gibbs, Nicky Thomas)

MICHAEL GIBBS
70	Deram DML/SML 1063	MICHAEL GIBBS (LP)	£50
71	Deram SML 1087	TANGLEWOOD '63 (LP)	£50
72	Polydor 2683 011	JUST AHEAD (2-LP)	£35
74	Polydor 2383 252	IN THE PUBLIC INTEREST (LP, with Gary Burton)	£35
75	Bronze ILPS 9353	ONLY CHROME ... WATERFALL (LP)	£15

(see also Neil Ardley, Gary Burton)

TERRY GIBBS SEXTET
56	Vogue Coral LVA 9013	TERRY (LP)	£20
56	Vogue Coral LVA 9009	JAZZTIME USA (LP, as Terry Gibbs Quartet & Sextet)	£20

(see also Terry Gibbs Big Band)

TERRY GIBBS BIG BAND
59	Mercury CMS 18016	LAUNCHING A NEW BAND (LP)	£15

DON GIBSON
56	MGM SP 1177	Sweet Dreams/The Road Of Life Alone	£125
58	RCA RCA 1056	Oh Lonesome Me/I Can't Stop Lovin' You	£15
58	RCA RCA 1098	Give Myself A Party/Look Who's Blue	£20
59	RCA RCA 1150	Don't Tell Me Your Troubles/Heartbreak Avenue	£18
59	RCA RCA 1158	Big Hearted Me/I'm Movin' On	£15

(Originally issued with triangular centres; later round-centre copies are worth half these values.)

59	RCA RCA 1158	Big Hearted Me/I'm Movin' On (78)	£15
60	RCA RD 27158	THE GIBSON BOY (LP)	£40

GINNY GIBSON
55	MGM SP 1121	Like Ma-a-d/Once There Was A Little Girl	£15
58	MGM MGM 953	Whatever Lola Wants (Lola Gets)/If Anything Should Happen	£15

JODY GIBSON & MULESKINNERS
59	Parlophone R 4579	Kissin' Time/Man On My Trail	£15
60	Parlophone R 4645	If You Don't Know/So You Think You've Got Troubles	£15

LORNE GIBSON TRIO
66	Decca F12450	Roses From A Stranger/Jingle Jangle	£20

STEVE GIBSON & RED CAPS
57	HMV POP 417	Silhouettes/Flamingo	£150
57	HMV POP 417	Silhouettes/Flamingo (78)	£30

WAYNE GIBSON (& DYNAMIC SOUNDS)
63	Decca F 11713	Linda Lu/Beachcomber	£20
64	Decca F 11800	Come On Let's Go/DYNAMIC SOUNDS : Pop The Whip	£20
64	Pye 7N 15680	Kelly/See You Later Alligator	£20
65	Columbia DB 7683	One Little Smile/Baby, Baby, Baby Pity Me	£30
66	Columbia DB 7911	Under My Thumb/It Always Happens (Icey) (solo)	£60
66	Columbia DB 7911	Under My Thumb/It Always Happens (Icey) (solo) (DJ copy)	£120

GIBSONS
67	Major Minor MM 524	Night And Day/City Life	£25
67	Major Minor MM 538	Lazy Summer Day/She's Not Like Any Girl	£25

GIDIAN (& UNIVERSALS)
66	Columbia DB 7826	Try Me Out/There Isn't Anything	£20

(see also Universals, Chris Lamb & Universals)

COLIN GIFFIN
69	CBS 4030	Changes In Our Time/When I Was So Young	£40

GIFT (1)
81	Venus ORBIT 1	Crashing Down/It'll End In Tears (p/s)	£20

GIFT (2)
88	Red Communications RED 001	You Don't Feel For Me/Torn Apart (p/s)	£20

GIFTED CHILDREN
81	Whaam! WHAAM 001	Painting By Numbers/Lichtenstein Girl (p/s)	£60

(see also Television Personalities)

GIGGETTY
75	GE 100	DAWN TO DUSK IN THE BLACK COUNTRY (LP, with insert, credited to Giggetty and Jim Wm. Jones)	£40
77	Bridge GE 101	TAMBOURINE (LP)	£30
80	Bridge GE 103	BLACK COUNTRY TIME (LP, also listed as Revolver REV LP1)	£30

GIGGLES
74	EMI 2246	Giggle Wiggle/For Just One Day	£100

GILBERTO GIL
82	WEA K 79285 (T)	Palco/Samba De Los Angeles/Maracatu Atomico (12")	£40
82	WEA K 79285	Palco/Samba De Los Angeles	£20
71	Famous SFM 1001	GILBERTO GIL (LP)	£40

GILBERT
67	CBS 3089	Disappear/You	£15
68	CBS 3399	What Can I Do?/You	£15
69	Major Minor MM 613	Mister Moody's Garden/I Wish I Could Cry	£15

BRUCE GILBERT
84	Mute STUMM 18	THS WAY (LP)	£20
86	Mute STUMM 39	THE SHIVERING MAN (LP)	£35
91	Mute STUMM 71	INSIDING (LP)	£20
91	Mute STUMM 77	MUSIC FOR FRUIT (LP)	£30

(see also Wire, Cupol, Dome, Gilbert & Lewis, Duet Emmo)

GEORGE GILBERT
74	Mime LPMS 7041	MEDWAY FLOWS SOFTLY (LP, with insert)	£15

GILBERT & LEWIS
80	4AD CAD 16	3R4 (LP as B. C. Gilbert and G. Lewis)	£30
82	Cherry Red BRED 27	MZUI (LP, PVC cover, insert sleeve)	£25

(see also Wire, Dome, Cupol, Duet Emmo)

ASTRUD GILBERTO
65	Verve VLP 9087	THE ASTRUD GILBERTO ALBUM (LP, mono, 'tip-on' sleeve)	£25
65	Verve VLP 9107	THE SHADOW OF YOUR SMILE (LP)	£20
66	Verve (S)VLP 9163	A CERTAIN SMILE AND A CERTAIN SADNESS (LP)	£20
67	Verve SVLP 9137	BEACH SAMBA (LP)	£20
68	Verve 2317 021	WINDY (LP)	£20
69	Verve (S)VLP 9242	I HAVEN'T GOT ANYTHING BETTER TO DO (LP)	£20
70	Verve SVLP 9252	HOLIDAY (LP)	£20
72	CT. CTL 1	GILBERTO WITH TURRENTINE (LP, with Stanley Turrentine)	£20

(see also Stan Getz, Stanley Turrentine)

JOAO GILBERTO
61	Parlophone PMC 1248	BOSSA-FINADO (LP)	£15
62	Parlophone PMC 1247	THE LEADER OF THE REVOLUTION (LP)	£20

(see also Stan Getz)

GILDED CAGE
69	Tepee TPR 1003	Long Long Road (For The Broken Heart)/Baby Grumpling	£40

(see also She Trinity)

GILES, GILES & FRIPP
68	Deram DM 188	One In A Million/Newly-Weds	£100
68	Deram DM 210	Thursday Morning/Elephant Song	£80
68	Deram DML 1022	THE CHEERFUL INSANITY OF GILES, GILES AND FRIPP (LP, mono)	£150
68	Deram SML 1022	THE CHEERFUL INSANITY OF GILES, GILES AND FRIPP (LP, stereo)	£150
70	Deram SPA 423	THE CHEERFUL INSANITY OF GILES, GILES AND FRIPP (LP, stereo reissue)	£40
13	Cherry Red CRP 203	THE CHEERFUL INSANITY OF GILES, GILES AND FRIPP (LP, reissue)	£15

(see also Brain, Trendsetters Ltd, League Of Gentlemen, King Crimson, Fripp & Eno, McDonald & Giles)

GILGAMESH
75	Caroline CA 2007	GILGAMESH (LP)	£30

(see also Hugh Hopper, Colosseum, Whitesnake)

TERRY GILKYSON & EASY RIDERS
58	Philips JK 1007	Marianne/Goodbye Chaquita (jukebox issue)	£18
53	Brunswick LA 8618	GOLDEN MINUTES OF FOLK MUSIC (10" LP)	£25
61	London HA-R 2301	ROLLIN' (LP, also stereo SAH-R 6111)	£15
61	London HA-R 2323	REMEMBER THE ALAMO (LP, as Easyriders Including Terry Gilkyson)	£15

JONATHAN GILL
73	Pye 7N 45206	I've Got To Please You/Isandulu Road	£15

(IAN) GILLAN (BAND)
78	Island R 553-B	Twin Exhausted (live)/Smoke On The Water (live)/ILLUSION: Madonna Blue/Revolutionary (12", promo only, as Ian Gillan Band)	£20
79	Acrobat BAT 1212	She Tears Me Down/Puget Sound/Vengeance/Mr. Universe (12", stickered card sleeve, promo only)	£20
81	Lyntone LYN 10599	Higher And Higher/Spanish Guitar (same tracks both sides, hard vinyl test pressing, handwritten white labels)	£35
76	Polydor/Oyster 2490 136	CHILD IN TIME (LP, gatefold sleeve, as Ian Gillan Band)	£15
77	Island ILPS 9511DJ	IAN GILLAN BAND SAMPLER (LP, 1-sided promo for "Scarabus", company sleeve)	£20
77	Island ILPS 59511	SCARABUS (LP, as Ian Gillan Band)	£15
78	Island ILPS 9545	LIVE AT THE BUDO-KAN (LP, unissued)	£0
79	Acrobat ACRO 3	MR UNIVERSE (LP, inner)	£15
80	Virgin V 2171	GLORY ROAD (LP, with bonus LP "For Gillan Fans Only" [VDJ 32], stickered, embossed sleeve & inner sleeves)	£15
82	Virgin VP 2236	MAGIC (LP, picture disc)	£15
81	Virgin V2196	FUTURE SHOCK (LP, gatefold sleeve, booklet)	£15
12	Virgin VIN 180 LP P048	FUTURE SHOCK (2-LP, reissue, hardback book edition)	£18
12	Virgin VIN 180 LP P 055	DOUBLE TROUBLE (2-LP, reissue, hardback book edition)	£18

(see also Episode Six, Deep Purple, Ray Fenwick, John McCoy, Johnny Gustafson, Bernie Tormé, Jerusalem, Quatermass, Colin Towns, White Spirit, Zzebra)

DANA GILLESPIE
65	Pye 7N 15872	Donna Donna/It's No Use Saying If	£15
65	Pye 7N 15962	Thank You Boy/You're A Heartbreak Man	£15
68	Decca F 12847	You Just Gotta Know My Mind/He Loves Me, He Loves Me Not	£60
69	Decca LK 5012	BOX OF SURPRISES (LP, mono)	£100
69	Decca SLK 5012	BOX OF SURPRISES (LP, stereo)	£150
73	RCA APL1 0354	WEREN'T BORN A MAN (LP, insert)	£20
74	RCA APL1 0682	AIN'T GONNA PLAY NO SECOND FIDDLE (LP, gatefold sleeve)	£15

(see also David Bowie)

DIZZY GILLESPIE & CHARLIE PARKER
61	Vogue LAE 12252	DIZ 'N BIRD IN CONCERT (LP)	£15

(see also Charlie Parker)

JIMMY GILMER & FIREBALLS
62	London HLD 9632	I'm Gonna Go Walkin'/Born To Be With You (as Chimmy Gilmer)	£15
64	London HA-D/SH-D 8150	SUGAR SHACK (LP)	£30
65	Dot DLP 3577	BUDDY'S BUDDY - BUDDY HOLLY SONGS BY JIMMY GILMER (LP)	£30

(see also Fireballs, Jim & Monica)

DAVID GILMOUR
84	Harvest DG 1	Blue Light (Special 12" Mix)/Blue Light (Instrumental) (12", stamped sleeve)	£40
06	EMI EMDJ 733	Take a Breath (single-sided clear vinyl promo)	£200
06	EMI EM 717 0946 384878 7 6	Arnold Layne (vocal by David Bowie)/Arnold Layne (vocal by Richard Wright)//Dark Globe (p/s)	£20
20	David Gilmour Records/Sony DGRS1	Yes, I Have Ghosts/Yes, I Have Ghosts (Andy Jackson mix) (with Romany Gilmour) (7", RSD)	£15
78	Harvest SHVL 817	DAVID GILMOUR (LP, gatefold)	£20
06	EMI 094635569513	ON AN ISLAND (LP, gatefold, printed inner, poster)	£80
08	EMI 50999 2 35484 1 1	LIVE IN GDANSK (5LP box set, booklet, poster. laminated web-pass)	£600
17	Columbia/Sony 88985464971	LIVE AT POMPEII (4LP, box set, booklet, 180g)	£50

(see also Pink Floyd, Joker's Wild, Unicorn, The Orb)

GORDON GILTRAP (BAND)
95	Munchkin MRC 1	THE BROTHERHOOD SUITE (cassette, 300 only)	£30
73	Philips 6006 344	No Way Of Knowing/I See A Road	£15
68	Transatlantic TRA 175	GORDON GILTRAP (LP, lilac label with 't' logo)	£50
69	Transatlantic TRA 202	PORTRAIT (LP)	£45
71	MCA MKPS 2020	A TESTAMENT OF TIME (LP, red/pink 'dogbone' label)	£40
73	Philips 6308 175	GILTRAP (LP, with lyric insert, blue/silver label)	£20

(see also Accolade, Pauline Filby, Catherine Andrews)

GIMIK
79	Mik MIK 003	Schools Out Forever/Jaqui	£20

GIMMICKS
70	Decca Eclipse ECS-R 2054	BRAZILIAN SAMBA (LP)	£30

W. GIMMICS
65	Polydor EPH 27 125	HOT RODS (EP, manufactured in Europe)	£60

GIMMIX
79	Elektra K 12377	Too Much/Testing Testing 1 2 3	£15

GIMPO
97	Kaleval KALA 003	Gimpo/Gimpo (version)	£25

GINGER HOBBY HORSE
70	Ra RALP 6004	GINGER HOBBY HORSE AND FRIENDS (LP)	£40

GINGER JUG BAND
70s	GJB 001	GINGER JUG BAND (LP, private pressing)	£25

GINGER SNAPS
65	RCA RCA 1483	The Sh Down Down Song/I've Got Faith In Him	£20

GINHOUSE
71	Charisma CAS 1031	GINHOUSE (LP, gatefold sleeve)	£200

(see also Kestrel. Mouse, Sammy)

GINNUNGAGAP
06	Aurora Borealis ABX 007	REMEINDRE (LP, clear folder cover, white vinyl)	£15

GINO & GINA
58	Mercury 7MT 230	Pretty Baby/Love's A Carousel	£20

ALLEN GINSBERG
60s	Cape Goliard	Wales: A Visitation (single issued with book of same title)	£15
65	Better Books (no cat. no.)	ALLEN GINSBERG READING AT BETTER BOOKS (LP)	£20
65	Love Books Ltd. LB 0001	ALLEN GINSBERG, LAURENCE FERLINGHETTI, GREGORY CORSO & ANDREI VOZNESENSKY READING AT THE ARCHITECTURAL ASSOCIATION (LP)	£20
68	Transatlantic TRA 192	GINSBERG'S THING (LP)	£15

(see also Ginsbergs)

GINSBERGS
67	Saga Psyche PSY 3002	THE GINSBERGS AT THE ICA (LP)	£15

(see also Allen Ginsberg)

GINSENG SPARTA
83	Guardian GRC 210	Forbidden Fruit/Lazy Hazy Day	£25

GIORGIO
69	MCA 5025	Moody Trudy/Stop	£20

(see also Giorgio Moroder, Giorgio & Marco's Men)

GIORGIO & MARCO'S MEN
68	Electratone EP 1003	Baby I Need You/Maureen	£70

GIPSY LOVE
72	BASF BAP 5026	GIPSY LOVE (LP)	£20

CHUCK GIRARD
75	Myrrh MYR 1025	CHUCK GIRARD (LP)	£15
70s	Myrrh MYR 1065	WRITTEN ON THE WIND (LP)	£15

MINT VALUE £

| 70s | myrrh MYR 1089 | THE STAND (LP) | £15 |

GIRL BAND
15	Rough Trade RTRADST 736	THE EARLY YEARS (12", 500 only)	£18
15	Rough Trade RTRADLP770	HOLDING HANDS WITH JAMIE (LP, yellow vinyl with booklet, signed)	£35
15	Rough Trade RTRADLP770	HOLDING HANDS WITH JAMIE (LP, yellow vinyl with booklet, unsigned)	£30

GIRL GUIDED MISSILES
| 79 | Seandee CND 01 | Desperate Men/Fully Qualified Robot (p/s, 1000 only) | £80 |

GIRLFRIENDS
| 63 | Colpix PX 712 | Jimmy Boy/For My Sake (DJ Copy) | £125 |
| 63 | Colpix PX 712 | Jimmy Boy/For My Sake | £60 |

GIRLIE
69	Treasure Isle TI 7053	Boss Cocky/LOVE SHOCKS: Musical True	£100
69	Bullet BU 400	Madame Stragga/LAUREL AITKEN: Stupid Married Man	£20
69	Duke DU 42	African Meeting (as Girlie & Junior)/JOSH: Higher And Higher	£15
70	Joe JRS 7	Small Change/Mind Your Business (as Girlie & Joe [Mansano])	£15
70	Ackee ACK 124	Decimilization/Decimilization Version (as Girlie & Paul)	£15

(see also Laurel Aitken & Girlie, Madame Dracula)

GIRLS ALOUD
03	Polydor JUMP 2	Jump (Almighty Vocal Mix)/Jump/Girls Allowed (Almighty Vocal Mix)/Jump (Almighty Dub Mix) (12" pink glitter promo)	£20
05	Polydor 9874045	Long Hot Summer/Long Hot Summer - Tony Lamezma Rides Again/Jump - Almighty Vocal Mix) (12", p/s)	£15
04	Polydor WHATGA 3	WHAT WILL THE NEIGHBOURS SAY? (LP, promo, pink vinyl)	£20

GIRLS AT OUR BEST
| 80 | Record Records RR 001 | Getting Nowhere Fast/Warm Girls (p/s) | £15 |
| 81 | Happy Birthday RULP 1 | PLEASURE (LP, with lyric insert, 1st 10,000 with free 'pleasure bag' with 2 postcards, sticker & stencil) | £20 |

GIRLSCHOOL
| 81 | Bronze BRON 534 | HIT AND RUN (LP, red vinyl) | £20 |

(see also Motorhead, Killjoys, Framed)

GIRLS IN SYNTHESIS
17	Blank/Own It BETBC008	SUBURBAN HELL EP (p/s)	£40
18	Blank/Own It BETBC014	WE MIGHT NOT MAKE TOMORROW EP (p/s)	£40
18	Blank/Own It BETBC015	FAN THE FLAMES EP (p/s, numbered)	£40

GIST
| 83 | Rough Trade ROUGH 25 | EMBRACE THE HERD (LP) | £15 |

GITS
| 89 | Stig STIG 0019 | Too Many People/Happy Song (p/s) | £40 |

JIMMY GIUFFRE
55	Capitol LC 6699	JIMMY GIUFFRE (10" LP)	£20
57	London Jazz LTZK 15059	THE JIMMY GIUFFRE CLARINET (LP)	£15
58	London Jazz LTZK 15130	JIMMY GIUFFRE (LP)	£25
58	London Jazz LTZK 15137	TRAV'LIN' LIGHT (LP)	£20

(see also Shelly Manne)

GLADDY (ANDERSON) & FOLLOWERS
| 69 | Blue Cat BS 172 | Judas/The World Come To An End | £40 |

(see also Stranger & Glady)

GLADE
| 72 | Glade 1 | Touching The Sky/Evil | £80 |

GLADIATORS (1)
| 63 | HMV POP 1134 | Bleak House/Tovaritch | £25 |

(see also Nero & Gladiators)

GLADIATORS (2)
| 68 | Direction 58-3854 | Girl Don't Make Me Wait/Can't Get Away From Heartbreak | £18 |
| 69 | Direction 58-4308 | Waiting On The Shores Of Nowhere/I'll Always Love You | £18 |

GLADIATORS (JAMAICA)
69	Studio One SO 2072	Hello Carol/RICHARD ACE: More Reggae	£50
69	Studio One SO 2086	Kicks/Gladions People Play	£45
69	Doctor Bird DB 1114	The Train Is Coming/Feeling So Fine	£30
69	Bamboo BAM 7	Any Where/SOUND DIMENSION: Baby Face	£30
70	Rock Steady Rev. REVR 12	Unusual Reggae/Andue	£20
70	Duke DU 58	My Girl (actually by Glen Adams)/You Were To Be	£25
72	Ackee ACK 149	Sonia/SOUND DIMENSION: Solas	£30
77	Virgin VS 19312	Pocket Money/Money Version Disco Mix/Evil Doers/Disco Mix (12")	£30
76	Virgin V2062	TRENCHTOWN MIX UP (LP, 1st pressing with white rim around labels)	£60
76	Virgin V2062	TRENCHTOWN MIX UP (LP, 2nd pressing without white rim around labels)	£40
78	Virgin Frontline FL 1002	PROVERBIAL REGGAE (LP)	£30
78	Virgin Frontline FL 1035	NATURALITY (LP)	£30
79	Virgin Frontline FL 1048	SWEET SO TILL (LP)	£25
81	Virgin VX 1003	VITAL SELECTION (LP)	£25
82	Nighthawk NIGHTHAWK	SYMBOL OF REALITY (LP)	£20

GLADIOLAS
| 57 | London HLO 8435 | Little Darlin'/Sweetheart, Please Don't Go | £100 |
| 57 | London HLO 8435 | Little Darlin'/Sweetheart, Please Don't Go (78 rpm) | £25 |

(see also Maurice Williams & Zodiacs)

MINT VALUE £

GLAM SLAM
91   Good Vibrations GOT 25   The Leader/Tell Him/Coz I Love You (fold out p/s) £30

GLASGOW
84   Neat NEAT 40   Stranded/Heat Of The Night (p/s).. £15

LUD GLASKIN
62   UPC 3428   To My Good Friend Jack Cotton, the 'Allo Twist (1-sided private pressing)...................... £25

GLASS
82   Glass GLASS1   New Colours/Sweet Entropy (p/s) £22

PHILIP GLASS
76	Caroline CA 2010	MUSIC IN 12 (PARTS 1 & 2) (LP, 1st pressing in matt textured sleeve)............................ £35
76	Caroline CA 2010	MUSIC IN 12 (PARTS 1 & 2) (LP, 2nd pressing in glossy sleeve)................................... £20
77	Virgin V 2085	NORTH STAR (LP, 1st issue, with green "mirror" girl label)... £15
78	Shandar SHAN 83515	SOLO MUSIC (LP) £15
79	CBS M4 38875	EINSTEIN ON THE BEACH (4-LP box set, with booklet).. £40
82	CBS 73640	GLASSWORKS (LP) £15
83	Island ISTA 4	KOYAANISQATSI (LP, soundtrack).. £25
85	CBS 13M39672	SATYAGRAHA (3-LP box set, booklet) £40
85	Nonsuch 979113-1	MISHIMA (LP) £15
86	CBS M342457	AKHNATEN (3-LP box set, booklet) £40
15	Music On Vinyl MOVCL015	HEROES SYMPHONY (LP, reissue, white vinyl).. £35

GLASS ANIMALS
12	Kaya Kaya KKT001	LEAFLINGS EP (12", p/s)... £60
13	Wolf Tone WOLFPROM01	Psylla/Black Mambo/Exxus/Woozy (10", p/s).. £60
13	Wolf Tone WOLFTONE 1	Black Mambo/Exxus/Black Mambo (Zodiac Remix)/Exxus (Pattern Remix) (12", p/s, many signed)... £70
14	Wolf Tone WOLFTONE 2	GOOEY (12", p/s) £60
15	Wolf Tone WOLFSTONERSD1	REMIXES EP (12", p/s).. £40
19	Wolf Tone 7736623	ZABA STRIPPED (12", p/s)... £20
14	Wolf Tone WOLFTONE001LP	ZABA (2-LP, 1st pressimg) £30
16	Wolf Tone WOLFTONE012LP	HOW TO BE A HUMAN BEING (2-LP)... £30

GLASS HARP
72   MCA MUPS 431   GLASS HARP (LP)... £25
72   MCA MUPS 449   SYNERGY (LP) £22

GLASS MENAGERIE
68   Pye 7N 17615   Frederick Jordan/I Said Goodbye To Me... £240
69   Polydor 56341   Do My Thing Myself/Watching The World Pass By £25
(see also Paladin, Toe-Fat)

GLASS OPENING
68   Plexium P 1236   Silver Bells And Cockle Shells/Does It Really Matter £250

GLASVEGAS
04	Rebelstance J 21091979	I'm Gonna Get Stabbed/Ina Lvs Rab (CD-R, self release with lyric inner)........................ £80
06	Waks WAKS 0035	Go Square Go/Legs 'N' Show (400 only, with lyric insert).. £50
07	Sane Man SAN 001	Daddy's Gone/Flowers And Football Tops (p/s, 1,000 only, numbered) £20
08	Columbia GOWOW012	GLASVEGAS (LP)... £30

GLAXO BABIES
79   Heartbeat PULSE 3   THIS IS YOUR LIFE (12" EP) £15
80   Heartbeat HBM 3   PUT ME ON THE GUEST LIST (LP)... £25
80   Heartbeat HB 2   NINE MONTHS TO THE DISCO (LP) £25

GLEN (BROWN) & LLOYD (ROBINSON)
66   Ska Beat JB 250   Live And Let Others Live/Too Late £45
67   Doctor Bird DB 1099   Feel Good Now/What You've Got (credited as Lloyd Glen) £45

GLENCOE
72   Epic EPC 65207   GLENCOE (LP)... £25
73   Epic EPC 65717   SPIRIT OF GLENCOE (LP) £15
(see also Hopscotch, Five Day Rain, Greatest Show On Earth, Loving Awareness)

GLIDE
95   Ochre OCH 001L   SPACE AGE FREAK OUT (LP)... £20
(see also Echo & Bunnymen)

GLITTERHOUSE
68   Stateside SS 2129   Barbarella/BOB CREWE: An Angel Is Love £20
68   Stateside SS 2129   Barbarella/Love Drags Me Down (different B-side) £18

GLOBAL COMMUNICATION
92	Evolution EV 004	KEONGAKU EP (12", 4-track, plain sleeve) £25
94	Dedicated DEDLP 014L	76: 14 (2LP, embossed gatefold with bonus 12" [DEDLP 0145]) £100
94	Dedicated DEDLP 014	76: 14 (2LP, gatefold)... £50
96	Dedicated DED 21LP	REMOTION - THE GLOBAL COMMUNICATION REMIX ALBUM (2LP)........................... £30
20	Evolution EVOR 11	TRANSMISSIONS (7LP box set, 1000 copies only) £150
20	Music On Vinyl MOVLP 2546	76: 14 (2LP, reissue, 180gm, embossed gatefold, MOV sticker and sleeve)................. £25
(see also Mystic Institute, Link, Reload, Reload & E621, Jedi Knights, Tom Middleton)

GLOBAL METHOD
92   Not On Label GM1   VIBE TRIBE (EP) £110

GLOBAL VILLAGE TRUCKING COMPANY
76   Caroline C 1516   GLOBAL VILLAGE TRUCKING COMPANY (LP, with lyric insert, b/s & red label, twins logo)... £30

(see also Byzantium, Man)
GLOBE SHOW
69   Page One POF 128   Yes Or No/Gettin' On Back £30
(see also Chris Shakespeare Globe Show)
GLOBE TROTTERS
54   Parlophone GEP 8528   SATURDAY NIGHT HOP (EP)..£15
GLOBETROTTERS
71   RCA SF 8158   THE GLOBETROTTERS (LP) £15
GLOK
19   Bytes BYTES02LP   DISSIDENT (LP, green vinyl)..£20
20   Bytes BYTES02LP   DISSIDENT REMIXED (2-LP, splatter vinyl) £30
(see also Ride)
GLOOMYS
68   Columbia DB 8391   Daybreak/Queen And King £15
GLORIA
69   Columbia DB 8568   The Last Seven Days/Merry Dance £15
GLORIA MUNDI
78   RCA PL2 5157   I INDIVIDUAL (LP, with inner sleeve)...£15
79   RCA PL2 5244   THE WORD IS OUT (LP, with lyric inner) £15
GLORIANA
72   No label or cat no   MUSIC FOR A WHILE (LP, black labels) £200
GLORIAS ALLSTARS
70   Camel CA 48   Jumping Dick/News Room £25
GLORIES
67   CBS 2786   I Stand Accused (Of Loving You)/Wish They Could Write A Song............£15
67   CBS 2786   I Stand Accused (Of Loving You)/Wish They Could Write A Song (DJ Copy)....£20
67   Direction 58-3084   (I Love You Babe But) Give Me My Freedom/Security £20
68   Direction 58-3300   Sing Me A Love Song/Oh Baby That's Love £15
GLORY HUNTER
79   Rock Hard CPS 027   Thoughts Of Destiny/At The Crossroads (no p/s) £800
GLORY LANDERS
69   IBA SECC 1203   VOLUME 1 (LP)...£15
GLOVE
83   Wonderland SHELP 2   BLUE SUNSHINE (LP, mispressing with double-printed sleeve) £20
(see also Cure, Siouxsie & Banshees)
ROGER GLOVER (& GUESTS)
74   Purple TPSA 7514   THE BUTTERFLY BALL (AND THE GRASSHOPPER'S FEAST) (LP, g/fold sleeve)....£15
84   Polydor POLD 5139   THE MASK (LP, solo, with insert) £15
(see also [Sheila Carter &] Episode [Six], Deep Purple, Elf, Eddie Hardin, Whitesnake, Rainbow, Glenn Hughes, John Lawton, Wizard's Convention, Green Bullfrog, David Coverdale, Dio)
JEREMY GLUCK
86   Flicknife SHARP 037   I KNEW BUFFALO BILL (LP)..£15
(see also Barracudas)
G MEN
82   Cro Magnon   G-MEN (EP, 1000 only) £20
GNIDROLOG
72   RCA SF 8261   IN SPITE OF HARRY'S TOE-NAIL (LP, gatefoldsleeve, orange label)....£200
72   RCA SF 8322   LADY LAKE (LP, with lyric insert) £350
72   RCA SF 8322   LADY LAKE (LP, without lyric insert) £250
(see also Pork Dukes, Steeleye Span)
GNOMES OF ZURICH
66   Planet PLF 121   Please Mr Sun/I'm Coming Down With The Blues (with custom 'Planet' sleeve) £60
66   Planet PLF 121   Please Mr Sun/I'm Coming Down With The Blues (without custom 'Planet' sleeve)....£30
67   CBS 202556   Hang On Baby/Blues For My Baby £30
67   CBS 2694   High Hopes/Pretender £30
67   RCA Victor RCA 1606   Second Fiddle/Publicity Girl..£60
G-NOTES
58   Oriole CB 1456   Ronnie (How I Wish He'd Notice Me)/I Would............................£20
GOAT
12   Rocket LAUNCH 048   WORLD MUSIC (LP 1st pressing on orange vinyl, 300 only) £40
GOBBLEDEGOOKS
64   Decca F 12023   Now And Again/Where Have You Been.....................................£15
GOBBLINZ
79   Pinnacle P 8454   London/Women In Love (p/s) £80
79   Bacon SLICE 01   Love Me Too/All Of This And More (p/s) £80
GO-BETWEENS
80   Postcard 80-4   I Need Two Heads/Stop Before You Say It (brown label & brown co. sleeve) ...£25
80   Postcard 80-4   I Need Two Heads/Stop Before You Say It (b/w A side label, yellow/red B side label, cream co. sleeve)....£35
82   Rough Trade RT 108   Hammer The Hammer/By Chance (p/s)....................................£18
83   Rough Trade RT 144   Man O'Sand To Girl O'Sea/This Girl Black Girl (p/s) £18
83   Rough Trade RT 124   Cattle And Cane/Heaven Says (p/s) £18
84   Sire W9156T   Bachelor Kisses/Rare Breed/Unkind And Unwise (Instrumental) (12", p/s) £15

MINT VALUE £

84	Sire W9211T	Part Company/Just A King In Mirrors/Newton Told Me (12", p/s)	£15
86	Situation 2 SIT 44T	ABLE LABEL SINGLES (12" EP, gatefold sleeve)	£30
05	Lo-Max 022V	WORLDS APART (12", p/s)	£25
89	Strange Fruit SFPS 074	PEEL SESSIONS (12" EP)	£20
82	Rough Trade ROUGH 45	SEND ME A LULLABY (LP, inner)	£40
83	Rough Trade ROUGH 54	BEFORE HOLLYWOOD (LP)	£40
84	Sire 925 197-1	SPRING HILL FAIR (LP)	£35
86	Beggars Banquet BEGA 72	LIBERTY BELLE AND THE BLACK DIAMOND EXPRESS (LP, textured sleeve)	£30
87	Beggars Banquet BEGA 81	TALLULAH (LP, inner)	£30
88	Beggars Banquet BEGA 95	16 LOVERS LANE (LP, inner)	£35
88	Beggars Banquet BBL 72	LIBERTY BELLE AND THE BLACK DIAMOND EXPRESS (LP, reissue, matt sleeve)	£20
90	Beggars Banquet BEGA 104	1978 - 1990 (2-LP)	£25
15	Domino REWIG89X	G STANDS FOR GO-BETWEENS VOLUME 1 (box set, 3-LP, 4, CD, booklet, print, insert, download card and book from Grant McLennan's library)	£600
15	Domino REWIG90X	G STANDS FOR GO-BETWEENS VOLUME 1 (box set, 3-LP, 4, CD, booklet, songbook download card but no book from Grant McLennan's library)	£500
19	Domino REWIG90X	G STANDS FOR GO-BETWEENS VOLUME 2 (box set, 5-LP, 4CD, booklet, songbook download card but no book from Grant McLennan's library)	£200
19	Domino REWIG90X	G STANDS FOR GO-BETWEENS VOLUME 2 (box set, 5-LP, 4CD, booklet, songbook download card and book from Grant McLennan's library)	£250

GOBLIN
79	EMI EMC 3222	SUSPIRIA (LP, soundtrack)	£35

VIC GODARD (& SUBWAY SECT)
80	Oddball/MCA MCF 3070	WHAT'S THE MATTER BOY? (LP, with Subway Sect)	£20
82	London SH 8549	SONGS FOR SALE (LP, with Subway Sect)	£18
85	Rough Trade ROUGH 56	A RETROSPECTIVE (LP, inner sleeve, with Subway Sect)	£20
85	MCA/El 01	HOLIDAY HYMN (LP, 10 test pressings only; abandoned issue of "T.R.O.U.B.L.E.")	£40
86	Rough Trade ROUGH 86	T.R.O.U.B.L.E. (LP)	£15
93	Postcard DUBH 936	END OF THE SURREY PEOPLE (LP)	£15

(see also Subway Sect)

KEITH & DONNA GODCHAUX
75	Round RX 104	KEITH & DONNA GODCHAUX (LP)	£18

(see also Grateful Dead)

GEOFF GODDARD
61	HMV POP 938	Girl Bride/For Eternity	£50
62	HMV POP 1068	My Little Girl's Come Home/Try Once More	£50
63	HMV POP 1160	Saturday Dance/Come Back To Me	£40
63	HMV POP 1213	Sky Men/Walk With Me My Angel	£80

GODFATHER DON
07	Diggers With Gratitude DWG 002	SLAVE OF NEW YORK (EP, 150 only)	£180
09	Diggers With Gratitude DWG 005	BILLY BATHGATE (12", 20 only, green vinyl)	£120
09	Diggers With Gratitude DWG 005	BILLY BATHGATE (12", 280 only, black vinyl)	£30

GODFLESH
91	Earache MOSH 56T	Cold World/Nihil/Nihil (Total Belief Mix)/Nihil (No Belief Mix) (12", p/s)	£15
94	Earache MOSH 116	Merciless/Blind/Unworthy/Flowers (2 x 7", white vinyl, gatefold p/s)	£15
88	Swordfish FLESH LP 1	GODFLESH (LP, textured sleeve, inner)	£20
89	Earache MOSH 15	STREETCLEANER (LP)	£15
92	Earache MOSH 32	PURE (LP, poster, insert)	£20
94	Earache MOSH 85	SELFLESS (LP, insert)	£20

HUGH GODFREY
67	Coxsone CS 7001	A Dey Pon Dem/SOUL BROTHERS: Take Ten	£100
67	Studio One SO 2008	My Time/MARCIA GRIFFITHS: Hound Dog	£80
67	Studio One SO 2015	Go Tell Him/MARCIA GRIFFITHS: After Laughter (b-side actually by Freddie McGregor)	£80

(see also Soul Brothers)

ROBERT JOHN GODFREY
74	Charisma CAS 1084	FALL OF HYPERION (LP)	£40

(see also Enid, Godfrey & Stewart, Don Bradshaw)

GODFREY & STEWART
88	The Enid ENID 11	THE SEED AND THE SOWER (LP)	£15
80s	The Stand HEARTLP	JOINED BY THE HEART (LP, fan club issue, 2,000 only)	£20

(see also Robert John Godfrey, Enid)

GODLEY & CREME
68	Blinkers 1215	Goodnight Blinkers/Hello Blinkers (die-cut sleeve)	£300

(see also Mockingbirds, Hotlegs, 10cc, Dave Berry, Frabjoy & Runcible Spoon, Cruisers, Whirlwinds)

GOD MACHINE
91	Eve EVER 8T	PURITY: Home/The Blind Man/Purity (12", p/s)	£20
92	Fiction FICSX 44	Desert Song/Prostitute/Commitment/Pictures Of A Bleeding Boy (12", p/s)	£20
93	Fiction FICSX 47	Home/All My Colours/Train/Fever (12", p/s)	£20
93	Fiction FIXH 23	SCENES FROM THE SECOND STOREY (2-LP)	£150
94	Fiction FIXH 27	ONE LAST LAUGH IN A PLACE OF DYING (LP)	£175

GODS
67	Polydor 56168	Come On Down To My Boat Baby/Garage Man	£180
68	Columbia DB 8486	Baby's Rich/Somewhere In The Street	£60
69	Columbia DB 8544	Hey! Bulldog/Real Love Guaranteed	£40

MINT VALUE £

69	Columbia DB 8572	Maria/Long Time, Sad Time, Bad Time	£40
68	Columbia SX 6286	GENESIS (LP, mono, blue/black label with "sold in U.K..." text)	£600
70	SCX 6286	GENESIS (LP, stereo, silver/black label)	£350
70	Columbia SCX 6372	TO SAMUEL A SON (LP, black/silver labels with boxed logo)	£600
76	Harvest SHSM 2011	GODS (LP)	£30
15	Parlophone 0825646172375	GENESIS (LP, reissue, multicoloured vinyl)	£15

(see also Uriah Heep, Shame, Toe-Fat, Birds Birds, Carmen, Jethro Tull)

GODS GIFT
| 79 | Newmarket NEW 101 | THESE DAYS EP | £15 |

GODSONS
| 71 | Philips 6006155 | All Dressed In White/We've Not Made It | £15 |

(see also Orange Bicycle)

GODZ
| 67 | Fontana STL 5500 | CONTACT WITH THE GODZ (LP) | £40 |
| 69 | Fontana STL 5512 | GODZ II (LP) | £40 |

GOGMAGOG
| 85 | F. For Thought YUMT 109 | I Will Be There/Living In A Timewarp/It's Illegal, It's Immoral, It's Unhealthy But It's Fun (12", p/s & insert) | £35 |

(see also Iron Maiden, Di'Anno, Def Leppard, Whitesnake, Gillan, White Spirit)

GO GO THUNDER
| 75 | RCA RCA 2494 | The Race/Mrs. Mann | £20 |

GO-GO'S (U.K.)
| 64 | Oriole CB 1982 | I'm Gonna Spend My Christmas With A Dalek/Big Boss Man (in p/s) | £60 |
| 64 | Oriole CB 1982 | I'm Gonna Spend My Christmas With A Dalek/Big Boss Man | £40 |

HERBIE GOINS & NIGHT-TIMERS
66	Parlophone R 5478	No. 1 In Your Heart/Cruisin'	£150
66	Parlophone R 5478	No. 1 In Your Heart/Cruisin' (DJ Copy)	£200
66	Parlophone R 5533	The Incredible Miss Brown/Comin' Home To You	£120
67	Parlophone PMC 7026	NUMBER ONE IN YOUR HEART (LP)	£200

(see also Night-Timers, Alexis Korner's Blues Incorporated)

GO-KART MOZART
| 99 | West Midlands Records BRUM 1 | INSTANT WIGWAM AND IGLOO MIXTURE (LP, 1,000 only, with poster and small sealing sticker over opening) | £40 |
| 04 | West Midlands BRUM 4 | ON THE HOT DOG STREETS (2-LP) | £30 |

(see also Felt, Denim)

DAVID GOLD
| 97 | Fat Cat 10FAT 001 | Respect City Police (10") | £40 |

BARRY GOLDBERG (REUNION)
| 68 | Pye Intl. NSPL 28116 | BARRY GOLDBERG REUNION (LP) | £20 |
| 69 | Buddah 203 020 | TWO JEWS BLUES (LP, with Mike Bloomfield) | £15 |

(see also Electric Flag, Mike Bloomfield)

GOLDEN APPLES OF THE SUN
| 65 | Decca F 12194 | Monkey Time/Chocolate Rolls, Tea And Monopoly (unissued, test pressings only) | £100 |
| 65 | Immediate IM 010 | Monkey Time/Chocolate Rolls, Tea And Monopoly | £70 |

GOLDEN DAWN
| 88 | Sarah SARAH 009 | My Secret World/Spring-Heeled Jack/The Railway Track (p/s, with poster) | £45 |
| 89 | Sarah SARAH 017 | George Hamilton's Dead/The Sweetest Touch/Let's Build A Dyonsphere (p/s, with poster) | £25 |

GOLDEN EARRING(S)
68	Capitol CL 15552	I've Just Lost Somebody/The Truth About Arthur (as Golden Earrings)	£25
68	Capitol CL 15567	Dong Dong Di Ki Di Gi Dong/Wake Up - Breakfast (as Golden Earrings)	£20
69	Major Minor MM 601	Just A Little Peace In My Heart/Remember My Friend (as Golden Earrings)	£20
70	Major Minor MM 679	Another Forty-Five Miles/I Can't Get Hold Of Her	£25
70	Polydor BM 56514	That Day/Words I Need	£20
69	Major Minor SMLP 65	EIGHT MILES HIGH (LP)	£150
70	Polydor 2310049	GOLDEN EARRING (LP, gatefold sleeve)	£70
71	Polydor 2310 135	SEVEN TEARS (LP)	£30
72	Polydor 2310 210	TOGETHER (LP)	£18
73	Track 2406 109	HEARING EARRING (LP, braille sleeve)	£18
73	Track 2406 112	MOONTAN (LP, gatefold sleeve with insert)	£18

GOLDEN GATE STRINGS
| 65 | Columbia DB 7634 | Mr. Tambourine Man/With God On Our Side | £30 |

GOLDFRAPP
00	Mute STUMM 188	FELT MOUNTAIN (LP, with inner)	£100
03	Mute STUMM 196	BLACK CHERRY (LP)	£100
05	Mute STUMM 250	SUPERNATURE (LP, gatefold)	£100
08	Mute STUMM 280	SEVENTH TREE (LP, with poster)	£50
10	Mute STUMM 320	HEAD FIRST (LP, with CD insert)	£30
13	Mute STUMM 356	TALES OF US (LP with CD)	£15

GOLDIE
| 95 | FFRR 828 614-1 | TIMELESS (2-LP, gatefold) | £40 |

GOLDIE (AND THE GINGERBREADS)
65	Decca F 12070	Can't You Hear My Heartbeat/Little Boy	£15
65	Decca F 12126	That's Why I Love You/The Skip	£25
65	Decca F 12199	Sailor Boy/Please Please	£15

MINT VALUE £

66	Immediate IM 026	Going Back/Headlines (solo)	£40
66	Fontana TF 693	I Do/Think About The Good Times (solo)	£30

(see also Ten Wheel Drive)

JOHN GOLDING

74	Cottage 101S	DISCARDED VERSE (LP, 2,000 only)	£20

GOLD IN THE SHADE

90	TSR TSCRT 4	Shining Through/Dance Mix (12")	£50
91	TSR TSCRT 5/4	Over You/Shining Through (12")	£60
91	TSR TSCRT 5/3	Over You/Mix 2/SPECIAL TOUCH: You're So Good (12")	£50
92	DEEP 001	I Really Love You So/Mix 2/Mix 3/Mix 4 (12")	£40

(see also Special Touch, Out Of The Shade)

GOLD LEAF

73	Pembrook PEM 1	After The Rain/The Sun (p/s)	£200
73	Pembrook PEM 1	After The Rain/The Sun (no p/s)	£50

VIVIEN GOLDMAN

81	Window WIN 1	Launderette/Private Armies (gatefold p/s, with PiL)	£40
81	Window 12WIN 1	Launderette/Private Armies (12", different p/s, with PiL)	£30

(see also Public Image Ltd)

ANNA GOLDRICK

70s	Polydor 2384030	IT'S HERSELF (LP)	£30

BOBBY GOLDSBORO

63	Stateside SS 193	The Runaround/The Letter	£20
65	United Artists UP 1079	Little Things/I Just Can't Go On Pretending	£15
66	United Artists UP 1128	It's Too Late/I'm Goin' Home	£15
66	United Artists UP 1128	It's Too Late/I'm Goin' Home (DJ copy)	£30
66	United Artists UP 1146	Take Your Love/Longer Than Forever	£25
67	United Artists UP 1166	No Fun At The Fair/Hold On	£35
67	United Artists UP 1177	Too Many People/Goodbye To All You Women	£200
67	United Artists UP 1177	Too Many People/Goodbye To All You Women (DJ copy)	£250
69	United Artists UP 2264	Love Arrester/Dissatisfied Man	£15
65	United Artists UEP 1006	LITTLE THINGS (EP)	£45
66	United Artists UEP 1016	THE TALENTED BOBBY GOLDSBORO (EP)	£45
65	United Artists ULP 1118	I CAN'T STOP LOVING YOU (LP)	£35
66	United Artists (S)ULP 1135	IT'S TOO LATE (LP)	£35
67	United Artists (S)ULP 1163	SOLID GOLDSBORO - GREATEST HITS (LP)	£22
68	United Artists (S)ULP 1195	HONEY (LP, black label)	£15
68	United Artists (S)ULP 1206	WORD PICTURES (LP)	£20
69	United Artists UAS 29008	TODAY (LP)	£18

GOLDSMITH

83	Bedlam BLM 001	Life Is Killing Me/Music Man (p/s)	£50

GOLGOTHA

84	Golgotha GOTH 002	DANGEROUS GAMES (Dangerous Games/Old England's Green/Air/The Great Divide (EP, no p/s)	£90
90	Communique CMGLP 003	UNMAKER OF WORLDS (EP, p/s)	£15

GOLIARD

76	Broadside BRO 127	FORTUNE MY FOE (LP, with booklet)	£18

GOLIATH

70	CBS 64229	GOLIATH (LP)	£200

GOLINSKI BROTHERS

80	Badge BAD 6	Bloody/Toy	£20

GOLLIWOGS

66	Vocalion VF 9266	Brown-Eyed Girl/You Better Be Careful	£50
67	Vocalion VF 9283	Fragile Child/Fight Fire	£50
72	Fantasy FAN 5996	GOLLIWOGS (LP, pressed in U.S. for U.K. distribution)	£15

(see also Creedence Clearwater Revival)

BENNY GOLSON

59	Esquire 32-125	GONE WITH GOLSON (LP)	£35
60	Esquire 32-105	GROOVIN' WITH GOLSON (LP)	£35

GOMEZ

98	Hut HUTDLP 49	BRING IT ON (2-LP)	£40
99	Hut HUTDLP 54	LIQUID SKIN (2-LP, gatefold, inner)	£60
02	Hut HUTDLP 72	IN OUR GUN (2-LP, gatefold)	£40
04	Hut HUTDLP 84	SPLIT THE DIFFERENCE (LP)	£40

GONG

71	Philips 6332 033	CONTINENTAL CIRCUS (LP, soundtrack)	£20
71	Caroline C1520	CAMEMBERT ELECTRIQUE (LP, 'twin' label)	£30
73	Virgin V 2002	RADIO GNOME INVISIBLE PART 1 - THE FLYING TEAPOT (LP, gatefold sleeve, 1st pressing original with black & white label design)	£100
73	Virgin V 2002	RADIO GNOME INVISIBLE PART 1 - THE FLYING TEAPOT (LP, gatefold sleeve, 2nd pressing with colour girl and dragon label design)	£40
73	Virgin V 2007	RADIO GNOME INVISIBLE PART 2 - ANGEL'S EGG (LP, 1st pressing, stickered gatefold sleeve, initially with b&w label; with booklet)	£80
73	Virgin V 2007	RADIO GNOME INVISIBLE PART 2 - ANGEL'S EGG (LP, 1st pressing, gatefold sleeve, initially with b&w label; without booklet)	£50
74	Virgin V 2007	RADIO GNOME INVISIBLE PART 2 - ANGEL'S EGG (LP, 2nd pressing, coloured "girl/dragon label")	£20

74	Caroline C 1505	CAMEMBERT ELECTRIQUE (LP, unissued, released as Virgin VC 502 with 1505 matrix struck through and 502 added as well as a V in front of the C)	£0
74	Virgin VC 502	CAMEMBERT ELECTRIQUE (LP)	£35
74	Virgin V 2019	YOU (LP, 1st pressing, with lyric insert, coloured 'twin' label)	£30
76	Virgin V 2046	SHAMAL (LP, gatefold)	£25
76	Virgin V 2074	GAZEUSE (LP, green "mirror" girl label, with poster)	£30
76	Virgin V 2074	GAZEUSE (LP, "two Virgins" round label, with poster)	£20
77	Charly CRM 2000	LIVE FLOATING ANARCHY (LP, as Planet Gong)	£18
77	Virgin VGD 3501	LIVE ETC. (2-LP, with cut-out cover & inner sleeves)	£30
77	Affinity AFF 4	MAGICK BROTHER (LP, reissue)	£25
78	Virgin V 2099	EXPRESSO II (LP)	£20
78	Virgin V 2019	YOU (LP, repressing, with blue label)	£20
82	Ottersongs	GONG LIVE A LYONS (cassette LP)	£30
82	Charly C£ 30220	YOU (LP, reissue, different cover art)	£20
84	Virgin OVED 14	RADIO GNOME INVISIBLE PART 1 - THE FLYING TEAPOT (LP, reissue)	£20
84	Virgin OVED 15	ANGEL'S EGG (LP, reissue)	£20
84	Virgin OVED 16	YOU (LP, reissue, green/red labels)	£20
84	Virgin OVED 17	SHAMAL (LP, reissue)	£15
84	Virgin OVED 18	GAZEUSE (LP, reissue)	£15
89	Demi Monde DMLP 1018	THE MYSTERY AND THE HISTORY OF THE PLANET GONG (2-LP)	£25
90	Ottersongs	HAUNTED CHATEAU (cassette LP)	£25
92	Gas GL 1	LIVE AT ANGERS (cassette LP)	£20
92	Gas GL 2	YOU DO HAVE TO GIVE UP DOPE!? (cassette LP)	£20
09	Snapper 900501	ZERO TO INFINITY (2-LP)	£40
09	G-Wave AAGWLPX001	2032 (2-LP, booklet, CD, poster, numbered)	£70
09	G-Wave AAGWLPX001	2032 (2-LP, booklet, CD, poster, with A5 postcards, 200 only, numbered)	£100
13	Celluloid CEL 7000	GONG EST MORT (2-LP, reissue)	£20
14	Maddish SMALP1024	I SEE YOU (2-LP)	£20

(see also Gilli Smyth & , Daevid Allen, Steve Hillage, Clearlight, Radio Actors, Sphynx, Tim Blake, Comus)

GONG/CAMEL/HENRY COW/GLOBAL TRUCKING COMPANY
73	Greasy Truckers GT 4997	GREASY TRUCKERS (2-LP, 1 side each; with insert)	£18

(see also Camel, Henry Cow, Global Trucking Company)

GONJASUFI
10	Warp WARPLP172	A SUFI AND A KILLER (2-LP)	£30

GONKS
64	Decca F 11984	The Gonk Song/That's All Right, Mamma	£30

(see also Twinkle)

PAUL GONSALVES
63	His Master's Voice CLP 1758	TELL IT THE WAY IT IS! (LP, laminated flipback sleeve)	£40
63	His Master's Voice CLP 1688	CLEOPATRA FEELIN' JAZZY (LP, laminated flipback sleeve)	£25
64	Vocalion LAE 587	BOOM-JACKIE-BOOM-CHICK (LP, laminated flipback sleeve, mono))	£2000
70	Deram SML 1064	HUMMING BIRD (LP, laminated flipback sleeve)	£100
17	Spellbound SPELL 4004LP	BOOM-JACKIE-BOOM-CHICK (LP, reissue)	£30

(see also Tubby Hayes & Paul Gonsalves)

GONZALEZ
74	EMI EMC 3046	GONZALEZ (LP)	£40
75	EMI EMC 3100	OUR ONLY WEAPON IS OUR MUSIC (LP)	£18

BELLE GONZALEZ
65	Jupiter JEPOC 37	POETS SET IN JAZZ (EP, as Belle Gonzalez & Sextet)	£18
66	Jupiter JEPOC 39	CONTEMPORARY POETS SET IN JAZZ (EP)	£18
72	Columbia SCX 6484	BELLE (LP)	£100

(see also Mark Wirtz)

GOODBYE MR. MACKENZIE
84	Scruples YTS 1	Death Of A Salesman/LINDY BERGMAN: Locked Inside Your Prison (no p/s, 500 only)	£15
90	Parlophone PCS 7345	HAMMER AND TONGS (LP, unreleased, white label test pressings only)	£30

(see also Garbage)o

GOOD EARTH
68	Saga FID 2112	IT'S HARD ROCK AND ALL THAT (LP)	£40

(see also First Impression/Good Earth, Mungo Jerry, Ray Dorset)

GOOD GUYS
70	Duke DU 82	Death Rides/Destruction	£20
70	Duke DU 83	Wreck It Up/Dynamic Groove	£20
70	Duke DU 84	Happiness/Latissimo	£20

(see also Byron Lee & Dragonaires)

PHILLIP GOODHAND-TAIT (& STORMSVILLE SHAKERS)
66	Parlophone R 5448	I'm Gonna Put Some Hurt On You/It's A Lie (with Stormsville Shakers)	£20
66	Parlophone R 5498	No Problem/What More Do You Want (with Stormsville Shakers)	£25
66	Parlophone R 5547	You Can't Take Love/J.C. Greaseburger (solo)	£20
70	DJM DJLPS 411	REHEARSAL (LP)	£15
71	DJM DJLPS 416	I THINK I'LL WRITE A SONG (LP, gatefold)	£15
72	DJM DJLPS 425	SONGFALL (LP, gatefold)	£20

(see also Circus, Larry Williams, Love Affair)

JOHNNY GOODISON
70	Deram DM 319	A Little Understanding/One Mistake	£20

(see also Quotations, Johnny B. Great)

JOHN GOODLUCK
74	Tradition TSR 015	SUFFOLK MIRACLE (LP, with insert)	£20
75	Sweet Folk & Country SFA 047	SPEED THE PLOUGH: TRADITIONAL SONGS OF SUFFOLK (LP)	£20

GOOD MISSIONARIES
80	Unormality NORM 002	DERANGED IN HASTINGS: Keep Going Backwards/Attitudes (hand made p/s)	£15
80	Unnormality NORM 001	VIBING UP THE SENILE WORLD (The Good Missionary Part 1 [live]/The Good Missionary Part/Kif Kif's Free Freak Out [live]) (EP, 1,000 only)	£15
79	Deptford Fun City DLP 04	FIRE FROM HEAVEN (LP)	£20

(see also Mark Perry, Alternative TV)

GOOD RATS
69	London HLR 10237	The Hobo/The Truth Is Gone	£15

THE GOOD, 2 BAD & HUGLY
93	Ruff Kut! RUF T6	THE RETURN OF THE DRUNKEN MASTER (12", p/s)	£15

ROD GOODWAY
90	Woronzow WOO 12	ETHEREAL COUNTERBALANCE (LP)	£18

RON GOODWIN CONCERT ORCHESTRA
53	Parlophone MSP 6035	Limelight/The Song From Moulin Rouge	£18
61	Parlophone R 4821	Murder She Says/Double Scotch	£25
54	Parlophone PMD 1014	FILM FAVOURITES (10" LP)	£15
56	Parlophone PMD 1038	MUSIC TO SET YOU DREAMING (10" LP)	£15
58	Parlophone PCS 3002	MUSIC FOR AN ARABIAN NIGHT (LP)	£15
58	Parlophone PCS 3006	OUT OF THIS WORLD! (LP)	£20
64	United Artists ULP 1071	633 SQUADRON (LP, soundtrack)	£20
65	Stateside SL 10136	THOSE MAGNIFICENT MEN IN THEIR FLYING MACHINES (LP, soundtrack)	£20
66	Polydor 582 004	THE TRAP (LP, soundtrack)	£40
68	Stateside (S)SL 10259	DECLINE AND FALL ... OF A BIRDWATCHER (LP, soundtrack)	£125
69	Paramount SPFL 255	MONTE CARLO OR BUST! (LP, soundtrack)	£25

(see also 20th Century Fox Orchestra, Parlophone Pops Orchestra)

GOOFERS
55	Vogue Coral Q 72051	Hearts Of Stone/You're The One	£50
55	Vogue Coral Q 72074	Flip, Flop And Fly/My Babe	£50
55	Vogue Coral Q 72094	Goofy Drybones/Nare	£30
56	Vogue Coral Q 72124	Sick! Sick! Sick!/Twenty One	£15
56	Vogue Coral Q 72171	Tear Drop Motel/Tennessee Rock And Roll	£25
57	Vogue Coral Q 72267	Wow!/Push, Push, Push Cart	£15
57	Vogue Coral Q 72289	The Dipsy Doodle/Take This Heart	£15

GOOM
72	Pye 7N 25587	Massai Part 1/Massai Part 2	£15

SAM GOPAL
69	Stable STA 5602	Horse/Back Door Man (unissued, existence unconfirmed)	£0
69	Stable SLE 8001	Escalator/Angry Faces/Cold Embrace/The Sky is Burning (LP sampler)	£70
69	Stable SLE 8001	ESCALATOR (LP, gatefold sleeve, black/silver label)	£400
68	Stable SLE 8001	ESCALATOR (LP, gatefold sleeve, label stating "DJ Copy not for resale")	£400

(see also Hawkwind, Motorhead, Vamp, Isaac Guillory, Clark-Hutchinson, G. F. Fitzgerald)

CHANCE GORDON
63	Pye 7N 15475	Instant Love/You Don't Want My Love	£20

CHRIS GORDON
68	Derpy ADMLP 390	IN THE EARLY MORNING RAIN (LP)	£200

DEXTER GORDON
66	Fontana Jazz FJL 907	MASTER SWINGERS (LP, with Wardell Gray)	£20
79	Blue Note BNS 40032	GO! (LP, reissue)	£20

(see also Wardell Gray)

PHIL GORDON
56	Brunswick 05545	Down The Road Apiece/I'm Gonna Move To The Outskirts Of Town	£50

ROBERT GORDON WITH LINK WRAY
77	Private Stock PVLP 1027	ROBERT GORDON WITH LINK WRAY (LP)	£15

(see also Link Wray)

RONNIE GORDON
63	R&B JB 127	Shake Some Time/Comin' Home	£100

ROSCO(E) GORDON
60	Top Rank JAR 332	Just A Little Bit/Goin' Home (as Rosco Gordon)	£25
63	Stateside SS 204	Just A Little Bit/What I Wouldn't Do	£25
65	Vocalion V-P 9245	Keep On Doggin'/Bad Dream	£30
65	Island WI 256	Surely I Love You/What You Do To Me	£25
66	Island WI 272	No More Doggin'/Goin' Home	£30

TONY GORDON
73	Grape GR 3056	Be True (actually by Alton Ellis)/Navajo Trail	£35

(see also Alton Ellis)

VINCENT GORDON
69	Coxsone CS 7085	Soul Trombone/LARRY & ALVIN: Your Cheating Heart	£300
69	Duke DU 37	Everybody Bawlin'/SILVERTONES: Come Look Here	£40
69	Crab CRAB 16	Walking By/VICEROYS: Promises Promises	£40
71	Fab FAB 14	Red Blood/CHOSEN FEW: Babylon (promo only, black label)	£50

MINT VALUE £

79	Attack TACK 10	**Liquid Horns** (as Vin Gordon & Corner Shots)/**JUNIOR & CORNER SHOTS: Liquidator** (12").............£18
79	Third World TWDIS 17	**Grass In The Sun/Split Second** (12")...........£60
79	Third World TWDIS 18	**Vin Cosmic/Enforcement** (12")...........£20
75	DIP DLP 5001	**MUSICAL BONES** (LP, plain sleeve, white label with word 'upsetters' in red type)...........**£300**

(see also Don Drummond Junior)

TREV GORDON
66	Pye 7N 17168	**Floating/Everyone Knows** (possibly demo only) £15

CHARLIE GORE
54	Parlophone CMSP 19	**I'll Find Somebody/Heaven Sent You To Me** (export issue)...........£25
54	Parlophone CMSP 26	**Two Of A Kind/It's A Long Walk Back To Town** (export issue)...........£20
54	Parlophone CMSP 30	**I Didn't Know/Oh! Mis'rable Love** (export issue)...........£20

(see also Hawkshaw Hawkins, Ruby Wright)

LESLEY GORE
64	Mercury MF 803	**You Don't Own Me/Run Bobby Run** £15
65	Mercury MF 846	**The Look Of Love/Little Girl Go Home** £20
65	Mercury MF 862	**Sunshine Lollipops And Rainbows/You've Come Back**...........£15
65	Mercury MF 872	**My Town, My Guy And Me/Girl In Love** £15
65	Mercury MF 889	**I Won't Love You Anymore** (Sorry)/**No Matter What You Do** £15
66	Mercury MF 984	**I'm Fallin' Down/Summer And Sandy** £20
64	Mercury 10017 MCE	**LESLEY GORE** (EP) £35
63	Mercury MMC 14127	**I'LL CRY IF I WANT TO** (LP) £40
63	Mercury 20001 MCL	**SINGS OF MIXED-UP HEARTS** (LP) £30
64	Mercury 20020 MCL	**BOYS BOYS BOYS** (LP) £30
64	Mercury 20033 MCL	**GIRL TALK** (LP) £30
65	Mercury 20071 MCL	**MY TOWN, MY GUY & ME** (LP) £30
65	Mercury 20076 MCL	**ALL ABOUT LOVE** (LP) £30

GORGONI, MARTIN & TAYLOR
72	Buddah 2318 067	**GORGONI, MARTIN AND TAYLOR** (LP)...........£15

GORILLA GRIP
78	Birnback KOM 019	**King Of The Pipes/Birnback Island** (500 only no p/s) £20

(see also DR Z)

GORILLAS
75	Chiswick NS 4	**She's My Gal/Why Wait 'Til Tomorrow**...........£15
78	Chiswick NS 8	**Gatecrasher/Gorilla Got Me** £15
78	Raw RAW 14	**It's My Life/My Son's Alive** £15
78	Raw RWLP 103	**MESSAGE TO THE WORLD** (LP, with insert) £20

(see also Hammersmith Gorillas, Jesse Hector)

GORILLAZ
00	Parlophone 10RDJ 6545	**Tomorrow Comes Today/Rock The House/Latin Simone/12D3** (10", promo. p/s) £25
00	Parlophone 12R 6545	**Tomorrow Comes Today/Rock The House/Latin Simone/12D3** (12", p/s)...........£20
05	Parlophone R 6663	**Feel Good Inc./68 State** (picture disc in die-cut card sleeve) £30
06	Parlophone R 6685	**Kids With Guns/El Manana** (p/s, red vinyl, poster) £15
11	Parlophone P7300787	**THE SINGLES COLLECTION 2001-2011** (8 x 7" box set) £30
01	Parlophone 724353113810	**GORILLAZ** (2-LP) £30
02	Parlophone 539 9821	**LAIKA COME HOME** (2-LP with comic) £40
05	Parlophone 07243 87383814	**DEMON DAYS** (2-LP) £150
05	Parlophone 07243 873838	**DEMON DAYS INSTRUMENTALS** (2-LP, promo die-cut stickered sleeve) £50
10	Parlophone 5099962616614	**PLASTIC BEACH** (2-LP) £30
11	Parlophone 5099909758810	**THE FALL** (LP, numbered) £30
11	Parlophone P730 0781	**THE SINGLES COLLECTION 2001-2011** (2-LP) £40
17	Parlophone 9029585118	**HUMANZ** (2-LP, artbook version) £25
17	Parlophone 0190295818845	**HUMANZ** (LP as 14 x 12", coloured vinyl, hardback book, vinyl case) £200

(see also Blur, Damon Albarn)

GORKY'S ZYGOTIC MYNCI
93	Ankst ANKST/GZM 040	**PATIO** (10" EP)...........£15
95	Ankst ANKST 056	**LLANFFWROG** (10" EP) £15
95	Ankst ANKST 059	**BWYD TIME** (LP, gatefold sleeve) £40
97	Fontana 534 769	**BARAFUNDLE** (LP) £60
98	Fontana 558 822-1	**GORKY 5** (LP) £40
99	Mantra MNTPL 1015	**SPANISH DANCE TROUPE** (LP) £60
00	Mantra MNTLPM 1023	**THE BLUE TREES** (LP) £25
01	Mantra MNTLP 1025	**HOW I LONG TO FEEL THAT SUMMER IN MY HEART** (LP)...........£40

JOHN GORMAN
77	DJM DJF 20491	**GO MAN GORMAN** (LP) £15

(see also Scaffold, Grimms)

EYDIE GORMÉ
56	London HL 8227	**Sincerely Yours/Come Home** £15

GORP
83	Beet Bop 1	**THE WILD MEN OF GORP** (LP) £15

FRANK GORSHIN
66	Pye International 7N 25402	**The Riddler/Never Let Her Go** (in p/s) £50
66	Pye International 7N 25402	**The Riddler/Never Let Her Go** £25

MINT VALUE £

GOSPEL CLASSICS
68   Chess CRS 8080   More Love, That's What We Need/You Need Faith...£150
68   Chess CRS 8080   More Love, That's What We Need/You Need Faith (DJ copy) £200

GOSPELFOLK
69   Emblem 7DR 324   PRODIGAL (LP) £150

GOSPEL GARDEN
68   Camp 602 006   Finders Keepers/Just A Tear £40
(see also Dimples, Amazing Blondel)

GOSPEL OAK
70   Uni UNLS 113   GOSPEL OAK (LP) £125

GOSPEL PEARLS
63   Liberty LBY 1191   THE GOSPEL PEARLS (LP) £25

RACHEL GOSWELL
04   4AD CAD 2414   WAVES ARE UNIVERSAL (LP) £25
(see also Slowdive)

GOTAN PROJECT
01   XL XLLP 148   LA REVANCHA DEL TANGO (2-LP, gatefold) £25

GOTHIC GIRLS
84   Backs 12NCH 011   GLASS BABY EP (12", p/s) £15

GOTHIC HORIZON
71   Argo ZFB 26   THE JASON LODGE POETRY BOOK (LP) £100
72   Argo ZDA 150   TOMORROW IS ANOTHER DAY (LP) £150

GOTH TRAD
07   Deep Medi Musik MEDI 05 Cut End/Flags (12")..£20

DALE GOULDER & LIZ DYER
70   Argo ZFB 10   JANUARY MAN (LP) £40
71   Argo ZFB 30   RAVEN & CROW (LP)...£40

GRAHAM GOULDMAN
66   Decca F 12334   Stop! Stop! Stop! (Or Honey I'll Be Gone...)/Better To Have Loved And Lost £150
68   RCA Victor RCA 1667   Upstairs, Downstairs/Chestnut...£40
69   Spark SRL 1026   Windmills Of Your Mind/Harvey's Theme (as Graham Gouldman Orchestra) £15
(see also 10cc, Whirlwinds, Mockingbirds, High Society, Frabjoy & Runcible Spoon, Manchester Mob, Garden Odyssey Enterprise, Friday Browne)

DUSKO GOYKOVICH
67   Columbia SX 6260   SWINGING MACEDONIA (LP) £500
01   Cosmic CS14   BELGRADE BLUES (LP, reissue) £15

MICK GRABHAM
72   United Artists UAS 29341 MICK THE LAD (LP, laminated front cove sleeve) £20
(see also Plastic Penny, Cochise, Procol Harum)

GRACE
77   Zipp ZB 003   Old Stories/Rule Britannia (in p/s) £60
77   Zipp ZB 003   Old Stories/Rule Britannia (no p/s) £20
81   MCA MCA 667   Billy Boy/Ad Mad (p/s)..£15

GRAME GRACE
75   RCA SF 8418   HAIL ME (LP, with insert) £15

CHARLIE GRACIE
57   Parlophone R 4290   Butterfly/Ninety-Nine Ways (initially gold lettering on label)...........................£40
57   Parlophone R 4290   Butterfly/Ninety-Nine Ways (later pressing with silver lettering on label)........£20
57   Parlophone R 4313   Fabulous/Just Lookin' (initially gold lettering on label) £40
57   Parlophone R 4313   Fabulous/Just Lookin' (later pressing with silver lettering on label) £15
57   London HLU 8521   Cool Baby/You Got A Heart Like A Rock (tri-centre) £20
58   London HLU 8596   Crazy Girl/Dressin' Up (tri-centre)...£30
59   Coral Q 72362   Doodlebug/Hurry Up, Buttercup (tri-centre) £30
59   Coral Q 72362   Doodlebug/Hurry Up, Buttercup (78)..£30
59   Coral Q 72373   Angel Of Love/I'm A Fool, That's Why (tri-centre)..£15
59   Coral Q 72373   Angel Of Love/I'm A Fool, That's Why (78) £20
59   Coral Q 72381   Oh-Well-A/Because I Love You So...£15
59   Coral Q 72381   Oh-Well-A/Because I Love You So (78) £25
62   London HLU 9603   Pretty Baby/Night And Day, U.S.A...£20
65   Stateside SS 402   He'll Never Love You Like I Do/Keep My Love Next To Your Heart £75
65   Stateside SS 402   He'll Never Love You Like I Do/Keep My Love Next To Your Heart (DJ copy) £150
57   Parlophone GEP 8630   THE FABULOUS CHARLIE GRACIE (EP) £40
83   Rollercoaster ROLL 2005 LIVE AT THE STOCKHOLM GLOBE AUGUST 26 1957 (LP)......................................£15

GRACIOUS!
68   Polydor 56333   Beautiful/What A Lovely Rain...£35
70   Vertigo 6059 009   Once On A Windy Day/Fugue In D Minor..£30
70   Vertigo 6360 002   GRACIOUS! (LP, gatefold sleeve, large swirl label) £500
72   Philips Intl. 6382 004   THIS IS ... GRACIOUS!! (LP, black/silver labels) £350
88   Beat Goes On BGO LP 34 GRACIOUS! (LP, reissue)..£15

GRADUATE
79   Blue Hat 5 BHR   Mad One/Somebody Put Out The Fire £150
(see also Tears For Fears)

GRAFITTI
76   Beeb 19   Dear Prudence/Come Together £20

BILLY GRAHAM & ESCALATORS
| 67 | Atlantic 584 073 | Ooh Poo Pah Doo/East 24th Avenue | £15 |

BOBBY/BOBBIE GRAHAM
| 65 | Fontana TF 521 | Skin Deep/Zoom Widge And Wag (as Bobbie Graham) | £25 |
| 66 | Fontana TF 667 | Teensville/Grotty Drums (as Bobby Graham) | £15 |

(see also Outlaws, Jimmy Page)

DAV(E)Y GRAHAM
62	Golden Guinea GGL 0224	THE GUITAR PLAYER (LP)	£50
64	Decca LK 4649	FOLK, BLUES AND BEYOND (LP)	£175
66	Decca LK 4780	MIDNIGHT MAN (LP)	£100
68	Decca LK/SKL 4969	LARGE AS LIFE AND TWICE AS NATURAL (LP)	£150
69	Decca LK/SKL 5011	HAT (LP)	£100
70	Decca SKL 5056	HOLLY KALEIDOSCOPE (LP, as Davy Graham & Holly)	£120
70	Decca LK 4649	FOLK, BLUES AND BEYOND (LP, 2nd issue, boxed Decca logo, laminated front cover)	£100
70	President PTLS 1039	GODINGTON BOUNDARY (LP, with Holly)	£150
76	Eron ERON 007	ALL THAT MOODY (LP, private pressing)	£200

(see also Shirley Collins)

DAVY GRAHAM/THAMESIDERS
| 63 | Decca DFE 8538 | FROM A LONDON HOOTENANNY (EP, 2 tracks each) | £18 |

DAVY GRAHAM & ALEXIS KORNER
62	Topic TOP 70	3/4 A.D. (EP, first pressing in mauve sleeve with cream label)	£90
62	Topic TOP 70	3/4 A.D. (EP, later pressings with lilac sleeve and blue label)	£60
62	Topic TOP 70	3/4 A.D. (EP, later pressings with bronze sleeve and blue label)	£30

(see also Alexis Korner)

ERNIE GRAHAM
| 71 | Liberty LBS 83485 | ERNIE GRAHAM (LP, textured sleeve, black label) | £250 |

(see also Clancy, Eire Apparent, Brinsley Schwarz, Help Yourself, Nick Lowe)

KENNY GRAHAM'S AFRO-CUBISTS
57	Pye Jazz NJE 1053	PRESENTING KENNY GRAHAM PART 1 (EP)	£20
57	Esquire EP 34	CARIBBEAN SUITE (EP)	£20
57	Esquire EP 68	KENNY GRAHAM'S AFRO CUBISTS (EP)	£20
57	Esquire EP 83	KENNY GRAHAM'S AFRO CUBISTS (EP)	£25
56	MGM MGM-C 764	MOONDOG AND SUNCAT SUITES (LP, as Kenny Graham & His Satellites)	£150
57	Nixa NJL 12	PRESENTING KENNY GRAHAM (LP)	£120
57	Esquire 20-012	KENNY GRAHAM AFRO CUBISTS (LP)	£90
57	Esquire 20-023	CARIBBEAN SUITE (LP)	£120
10	Trunk JBH 036 LP	MOONDOG AND SUNCAT SUITES (LP, 800 only, as Kenny Graham And His Satellites)	£20
10	Trunk JBH 036 LP	MOONDOG AND SUNCAT SUITES (LP, reissue, 500 only yellow vinyl, as Kenny Graham And His Satellites)	£25

(see also Yolanda)

LEO GRAHAM
73	Upsetter US 399	News Flash/UPSETTERS: Flashing Echo	£28
73	Summit SUM 8539	Three Blind Mice/UPSETTERS: Mice Skank	£15
75	Ethnic Fight EF 026	Big Tongue Buster/KING SCRATCH BAND: Bus-A-Dub	£25
78	PM Records PMS DD 496	My Little Sandra/Dubbing Sandra (12")	£35

(see also Bleechers)

LOU GRAHAM
| 58 | Coral Q 72322 | Wee Willie Brown/You Were Mean Baby | £400 |
| 58 | Coral Q 72322 | Wee Willie Brown/You Were Mean Baby (78) | £50 |

GRAHAM CENTRAL STATION
| 74 | Warner Bros K 46206 | GRAHAM CENTRAL STATION (LP) | £15 |

(see also Sly & Family Stone)

RON GRAINER ORCHESTRA
67	RCA Victor RCA 1635	The Prisoner/Happening Sunday	£75
79	Six Of One 6 OF 1	THE PRISONER ARRIVAL (EP, fan club issue)	£30
69	RCA Intl. INTS 1020	THEMES LIKE... (LP)	£15
78	RK LB 003	TALES OF THE UNEXPECTED (LP)	£15

BILLY GRAMMER
| 59 | Felsted GEP 1005 | BILLY GRAMMER HITS (EP) | £15 |
| 67 | Monument LMO 5010 | TRAVELIN' ON (LP) | £15 |

GERRY GRANAHAN
| 58 | London HL 8668 | No Chemise, Please/Girl Of My Dreams | £20 |
| 60 | Top Rank JAR 262 | It Hurts/RICHIE ROBIN: Strange Dream | £15 |

GRANDADDY
98	Big Cat ABB 152	UNDER THE WESTEN FREEWAY (LP, printed inner, sticker with single offer)	£50
00	V2 VVR 1012231	SOPHTWARE SLUMP (LP, printed inner)	£80
03	V2 VVR 1012251	SUMDAY (2LP, printed inners)	£50
11	Mercury 00602527797038	SOPHTWARE SLUMP (2LP, reissue)	£50

GRAND FUNK RAILROAD
69	Capitol E-ST 307	ON TIME (LP)	£50
70	Capitol E-ST 406	GRAND FUNK (LP)	£40
70	Capitol E-ST 471	CLOSER THAN HOME (LP)	£40
71	Capitol E-SW 764	SURVIVAL (LP)	£25
72	Capitol E-AS 853	E PLURIBUS FUNK (LP, circular 'silver coin' sleeve)	£50
73	Capitol E-AST 11099	PHOENIX (LP, gatefold sleeve)	£18

GRANDMASTER FLASH
99   Sequel NXTLP 305   BACK TO THE OLD SCHOOL (4-LP) £50

GRAND PRIX
80   RCA RCA 7   Thinking Of You/Feels Good (p/s) £15
(see also McAuley Schenker Group, Praying Mantis, Stratus, Uriah Heep)

GRAND UNION
68   CBS 3956   Slowly But Surely/She Said £40
(see also Enough's Enough)

GERRI GRANGER
63   London HLX 9759   Just Tell Him Jane Said Hello/What's Wrong With Me £15

GRANNIE
71   SRT 71138   GRANNIE (LP, private pressing of 99 copies only, homemade sleeve) £2500
12   SRT 71138   GRANNIE (LP, reissue, hand-made sleeve, 750 only, insert, and signed numbered
                                certificate) £100

GRANNY
73   DJM DJS. 291   Lady/Weirdie Deirdre's Dilemma £15

GRANNY'S INTENTIONS
67   Deram DM 158   The Story Of David/Sandy's On The Phone Again £25
68   Deram DM 184   Julie Don't Love Me Anymore/One Time Lovers £18
68   Deram DM 214   Never An Everyday Thing/Hilda The Bilda £25
70   Deram DM 293   Take Me Back/Maybe £20
70   Deram SML 1060   HONEST INJUN (LP, white/red label with small logo) £125
(see also Gary Moore)

AMY GRANT
82   Myrrh MYR 1124   AGE TO AGE (LP, with lyric insert) £15

DOMINIC GRANT
68   Mercury MF 1032   I've Been There/Don't Stop Girl £50

EDDY GRANT
75   Torpedo TOR 53   Nobody's Got Time (Part 1)/Nobody's Got Time (Part 2) £80
77   Ice GUY 2   Curfew/Jamaican Child (with GUY 2 sticker over ICE 2 catalogue number on both
                                sides) £20
17   Torpedo TOR 53   Nobody's Got Time (Part 1)/Nobody's Got Time (Part 2) (reissue, 300 only) £20
75   Torpedo TOL 500   EDDY GRANT (LP) £200
92   Ice 920201   PAINTINGS OF THE SOUL (LP, printed inner) £25
(see also Equals, Coach House Rhythm Section)

ERKEY GRANT & EARWIGS
63   Pye 7N 15521   I'm A Hog For You/I Can't Get Enough Of You £25

GOGI GRANT
56   London HLB 8282   Wayward Wind/No More Than Forever £20
(see also Tony Martin)

JANIE GRANT
61   Pye International 7N 25093 Triangle/She's Going Steady With You £18
62   Pye International 7N 25148 That Greasy Kid Stuff/Trying To Forget You £18

JOHN GRANT
13   Bella Union BELLAV 395   STRONGROOM EP (12") £20
15   Bella Union BELLA 514V   JOHN GRANT WITH ROYAL NORTHERN SINFONIA (12") £20
10   Bella Union BELLAV 235   QUEEN OF DENMARK (2-LP, gatefold, inners) £20
13   Bella Union BELLAV 377   PALE GREEN GHOSTS (2-LP, CD, green vinyl) £20
15   Bella Union BELLA 478V   WITH THE BBC PHILHARMONIC LIVE IN CONCERT (2-LP, silver vinyl) £50
15   Bella Union BELLA 505V   GREY TICKLES, BLACK PRESSURE (2-LP, lavender vinyl) £20
(see also Midlake)

JULIE GRANT
65   Pye 7N 15937   Stop/When The Lovin' Ends £15
62   Pye NEP 24171   THIS IS JULIE GRANT (EP) £25

LEE GRANT (& CAPITOLS)
66   Parlophone R 5531   Breaking Point/Don't Cry Baby (with Capitols) £20

LITTLE BROTHER (GRANT)
70   Torpedo TOR 27   Baby Don't Let Me Down/Brother Strong Man (as Little Brother) £15
70   Torpedo TOR 28   Let's Do It Together/Hey Man, Why (as Little Brother Grant & Zapatta Schmidt) £35
(see also Equals)

NEVILLE GRANT
73   Attack ATT 8058   Baby Don't Get Hooked On Me/Happy Hippie £20
73   Downtown DT 509   Sick And Tired/PRINCE DJANGO: Hot Tip £80

TOP GRANT
62   Island WI 034   Searching/David & Goliath £15
62   Island WI 052   Suzie/Jenny £15
63   Island WI 072   Riverbank Coberley (as Top-Grant)/Nancy £15
63   Island WI 074   Money Money Money/Have Mercy On Me £18
63   Island WI 077   War In Africa/The Birds £15
(see also Rhythm Aces)

GEORGE GRANT
77   Deroy DER 1366   90768 (LP, private pressing, 50 copies) £2500

GRAPE
92   Pencil Toast PENT 001   **Baby In A Plastic Bag/Listen To Your Heart** (p/s) £25

GRAPEFRUIT
68   RCA Victor RCA 1677   **Elevator/Yes**...£25
69   Stateside-Dunhill S(S)L 5008   **AROUND GRAPEFRUIT** (LP, black/white/red label with "sold in the U.K..." text)....£100
69   RCA Victor SF 8030   **DEEP WATER** (LP) £80
(see also Tony Rivers & Castaways, Easybeats, Fynn McCool, Sleepy)

GRAPHIC DESIGN
83   SRTS/83/CUS/1952   **Lonely Life/Shock** (p/s)..£100

GRAPHITE
72   Beacon BEA 109   **Gimme Your Number/Chestnut Loke** (possibly promo only)..........................£40

GRASS CUTTERS
72   Malbury MB 1   **Inside A Dream/The Silence Is Over** (p/s) £25

GRASSROOTS
68   RCA Victor RCA 1737   **Midnight Confessions/Who Will You Be Tomorrow** £15
69   Stateside S(S)L 5005   **GOLDEN GRASS** (LP) £25
70   Stateside SSL 5012   **LEAVING IT ALL BEHIND** (LP)...£25
(see also P.F. Sloan)

GRATEFUL DEAD
67   Warner Bros WB 7186   **Born Cross-Eyed/Dark Star**...£50
71   Warner Bros.   **Truckin'/Johnny B. Goode** (unissued) £0
77   Warner Bros SAM 79   **Dark Star/Born Cross-Eyed** (p/s, mail-order issue with Dark Star magazine) £40
67   Warner Bros. W 1689   **THE GRATEFUL DEAD** (LP, 1st pressing, mono, gold labels, front laminated flipback sleeves, mono)....................................£100
68   Warner Bros. W 1689   **THE GRATEFUL DEAD** (2nd pressing, mono, orange labels, front laminated flipback sleeve)..£80
68   Warner Bros. WS 1749   **ANTHEM OF THE SUN** (LP, 1st pressing, orange labels, front laminated flipback sleeve, stereo)..£100
69   Warner Bros. WS 1790   **AOXOMOXOA** (LP, 1st pressing orange labels, front laminated flipback sleeve, original mix)..£70
70   Warner Bros. WS 1830   **LIVE/DEAD** (2-LP, 1st pressing, orange labels) £60
70   Warner Bros. WS 1869   **WORKINGMAN'S DEAD** (LP, 1st pressing, orange labels) £50
70   Warner Bros. WS 1749   **ANTHEM OF THE SUN** (LP, 2nd pressing, green labels, front laminated flipback sleeve) ...£50
71   Warner Bros. WS 1893   **AMERICAN BEAUTY** (LP, 1st pressing, green labels, front laminated sleeve) £45
71   Warner Bros. K 66009   **GRATEFUL DEAD** (SKULL AND ROSES) (2-LP, green labels)..........................£45
71   Warner Bros. K66002   **LIVE/DEAD** (LP, 2nd pressing, green labels reissue) £35
72   Warner Bros. K 46049   **WORKINGMAN'S DEAD** (LP, 2nd pressing, green labels)...........................£30
72   Warner Bros. K 46021   **ANTHEM OF THE SUN** (LP, 3rd pressing, green labels, matt sleeve)...............£30
72   Warner Bros. K 46027   **AOXOMOXOA** (LP, 2nd pressing, green labels, matt sleeve, original mix, reissue)......£35
72   Warner Bros. K 46074   **AMERICAN BEAUTY** (LP, 2nd pressing, green labels, front laminated sleeve)..........£30
72   Polydor 2310 171   **HISTORIC DEAD** (LP)...£25
72   Polydor 2310 172   **VINTAGE DEAD** (LP)..£30
72   Warner Bros. K 66019   **EUROPE '72** (3-LP, 1st pressing, green labels, triple fold-out sleeve, with 8 page booklet)......................................£35
73   Warner Bros. K 46021   **ANTHEM OF THE SUN** (LP, 4th pressing, 'Palm tree' labels, matt sleeve)...........£20
73   Warner Bros. K 46246   **HISTORY OF GRATEFUL DEAD VOL. 1** (BEAR'S CHOICE) (LP)..........................£20
73   Warner Bros. K 49301   **WAKE OF THE FLOOD** (LP, 1st pressing, matt sleeve 'picture' labels) £25
73   Warner Bros. K 46049   **WORKINGMAN'S DEAD** (LP, 3rd pressing, 'Palm tree' labels) £20
73   Warner Bros. K 66009   **GRATEFUL DEAD** (SKULL AND ROSES) (2-LP, 2nd pressing, 'Palm tree' labels)......£25
73   Warner Bros. K 66002   **LIVE/DEAD** (2-LP, 3rd pressing, 'Palm tree' labels).............................£25
73   Warner Bros. K 46074   **AMERICAN BEAUTY** (LP, 3rd pressing, 'Palm tree' labels).........................£25
74   Warner Bros. K 66019   **EUROPE '72** (3-LP, 2nd pressing, fold-out sleeve, 'Palm tree' labels)...........£25
74   Warner Bros. K 56024   **SKELETONS FROM THE CLOSET: THE BEST OF GRATEFUL DEAD** (LP, 1st pressing 'Palm tree' labels) £15
74   Warner Bros. K 59302   **FROM THE MARS HOTEL** (LP, 1st pressing, 'Picture' labels).......................£20
75   United Artists UA 29895   **BLUES FOR ALLAH** (LP, 1st pressing, laminated front sleeve, 'Picture' label).....£20
76   United Artists UAD 60131/2   **STEAL YOUR FACE** (2-LP, 1st pressing, 'Picture labels' gatefold sleeve with bonus sampler LP For Dead Heads Only [FREE 2] in printed sleeve) £20
77   Arista 1016   **TERRAPIN STATION** (LP)...£18
81   Arista DARTY 9   **RECKONING** (2-LP) £15
81   Arista DARTY 11   **DEAD SET** (2-LP gatefold sleeve) £18
81   Warner Bros. K 46027   **AOXOMOXOA** (LP, 3rd pressing, cream labels, glossy sleeve)......................£15
81   Warner Bros. K 46049   **WORKINGMAN'S DEAD** (LP, 4th pressing, cream labels, glossy sleeve) £15
81   Warner Bros. K 46021X   **ANTHEM OF THE SUN** (LP, 5th pressing, cream labels, glossy sleeve)..............£15
87   Edsel ED 221   **THE GRATEFUL DEAD** (LP, reissue of debut LP, glossy sleeve).....................£18
(see also Jerry Garcia, Mickey Hart, Kingfish, Robert Hunter, Keith & Donna Godchaux, Silver [U.S.], Diga Rhythm Band)

GRATIS
79   B.P.M. BPM 1   **Downtown/Please Call My Number** (1000 only, p/s) £40

GRATTITUDE
70   Moth NT 1   **Dark Approaches/Sit Still** (p/s) £100

GRAUZONE
81   EMI 3408   **GRAUZONE** (LP) £40

GRAVE
03   Century Media   **MORBID WAYS TO DIE** (Numbered box set with 6 picture disc LPs and booklet) £60

GRAVEDIGGAZ
94   Gee Street GEEA 14   **NIGGAMORTIS** (LP, with inner sleeve) £20

NICK GRAVENITES
69	CBS 63818	MY LABORS (LP)	£22

(see also Big Brother & Holding Company)

BILLY GRAVES
59	Felsted AF 119	The Shag (Is Totally Cool)/Uncertain (export issue)	£25

GRAVY TRAIN
71	Vertigo 6059049	Alone In Georgia/Can Anybody Hear Me	£30
70	Vertigo 6360 023	GRAVY TRAIN (LP, gatefold sleeve, large swirl label)	£400
71	Vertigo 6360 051	BALLAD OF A PEACEFUL MAN (LP, gatefold sleeve, small swirl label)	£900
73	Dawn DNLS 3046	SECOND BIRTH (LP)	£125
74	Dawn DNLH 1	STAIRCASE TO THE DAY (LP, gatefold sleeve, pink 'sun' label)	£125

(see also Mandalaband)

BARRY GRAY (ORCHESTRA)
62	Lyntone LYN 249/250	Sabotage/Supercar Song/Supercar Twist (flexi, with p/s may exist)	£30
62	Lyntone LYN 249/250	Sabotage/Supercar Song/Supercar Twist (flexi)	£15
64	Melodisc MEL 1591	Fireball/Zero G (by Barry Gray & His Spacemakers; in p/s)	£55
64	Melodisc MEL 1591	Fireball/Zero G (by Barry Gray & His Spacemakers)	£20
65	Pye 7N 17016	Thunderbirds/Parker - Well Done (in p/s)	£35
65	Pye 7N 17016	Thunderbirds/Parker - Well Done	£15
67	Pye 7N 17391	Captain Scarlet/The Mysterons Theme (in p/s)	£35
67	Pye 7N 17391	Captain Scarlet/The Mysterons Theme	£15
68	Pye 7N 17625	Joe 90 - Title Theme/Joe 90 - Hijacked (in p/s)	£50
68	Pye 7N 17625	Joe 90 - Title Theme/Joe 90 – Hijacked	£25
62	Golden Guinea GGL 0106	SUPERCAR - FLIGHT OF FANCY (LP, with Edwin Astley)	£50
67	United Artists ULP 1159	THUNDERBIRDS ARE GO! (LP, soundtrack, mono)	£100
67	United Artists (S)ULP 1159	THUNDERBIRDS ARE GO! (LP, soundtrack, stereo)	£120
98	Fanderson FANSF6	SUPERCAR & FIREBALL XL5 (CD, mail order only)	£30

(see also Century 21, Mary Jane with Barry Gray, Richard Harvey)

BARRY GRAY
04	Trunk JBH 010	UFO: THE ORIGINAL TELEVISION SERIES SOUNDTRACK (LP, 500 on clear vinyl)	£60
04	Trunk JBH 010	UFO: THE ORIGINAL TELEVISION SERIES SOUNDTRACK (LP, 500 on black vinyl)	£60
11	Trunk JBH 039	STAND BY FOR ADVERTS (LP, 500 only)	£15

CHRIS GRAY
97	Music Is... MULP 01	A DEEPER LEVEL OF UNDERSTANDING (2-LP)	£35

DAVID GRAY
93	Hut HUTLP 9	A CENTURY ENDS (LP, inner)	£60

DOBIE GRAY
65	London HL 9953	The "In" Crowd/Be A Man (DJ Copy)	£40
65	Pye International 7N 25307	See You At The Go Go/Walk With Love	£25
65	Pye International 7N 25307	See You At The Go Go/Walk With Love (DJ Copy)	£50

DOLORES GRAY
55	Brunswick 05382	Heat Wave/After You Get What You Want, You Don't Want It	£15
55	Brunswick 05407	Rock Love/One	£30
57	Capitol T 897	WARM BRANDY (LP)	£15

HERBIE GRAY
68	Giant GN 38	We're Staying Here/Life Ska	£30

(see also Gene Rondo, Owen & Dandy, Tony Tribe)

JIMMIE GRAY
82	JKO 12JKO 100	The Kool People (Vocal)/The Kool People (Instrumental) (12")	£40

OWEN GRAY
60	Starlite ST45 015	Far Love/Please Let Me Go	£35
60	Starlite ST45 019	Jenny Lee/The Plea	£40
60	Blue Beat BB 8	Cutest Little Woman/Running Around (with Ken Richards Band)	£20
61	Blue Beat BB 43	Sinners Weep/Get Drunk (with Hersan & His City Slickers)	£20
61	Starlite ST45 032	Mash It (Parts 1 & 2)	£40
62	Starlite ST45 078	I Feel Good/Someone To Help Me	£40
62	Starlite ST45 088	Let Me Go Free/In My Dreams	£40
62	Blue Beat BB 75	Rockin' In My Feet/Nobody Else (with Jets)	£20
62	Blue Beat BB 91	Millie Girl (with Buster's Group)/DERRICK MORGAN: Headache	£25
62	Blue Beat BB 103	Lonely Days/No Good Woman (with Sonny Bradshaw Quartet)	£18
62	Blue Beat BB 108	Keep It In Mind/Do You Want To Jump (with Les Dawson Combo)	£18
62	Blue Beat BB 113	Best Twist/Grandma-Grandpa (B-side with Hersan & His City Slickers)	£18
62	Blue Beat BB 127	Pretty Girl/Twist So Fine	£18
62	Blue Beat BB 136	They Got To Move/I Love Her	£18
62	Blue Beat BB 139	Tree In The Meadow/Lizebella (with Buster's Group)	£18
62	Island WI 002	Patricia/Twist Baby	£20
62	Island WI 020	Audrey/Dolly Baby (with Ernest Rauglin [sic] Orchestra)	£20
62	Island WI 030	Midnight Trail/Time Will Tell	£20
62	Chek TD 101	Come On Baby/My One Desire	£15
62	Dice CC 3	On The Beach/Young Lover	£30
63	Blue Beat BB 147	Big Mabel/Don't Come Knocking (with Edwards' Groupe)	£15
63	Blue Beat BB 188	Call Me My Pet/Give Me Your Love	£15
63	Blue Beat BB 201	Snow Falling/Oowee Baby (as Owen Gray & His Big Brother)	£15
64	Blue Beat BB 217	Draw Me Nearer/Daddy's Girl	£15
65	Blue Beat BB 290	Daddy's Gone/BUSTER'S ALLSTARS: Johnny Dark	£85

MINT VALUE £

65	Aladdin WI 603	Gonna Work Out Fine/Dolly Baby	£20
65	Aladdin WI 607	Can I Get A Witness/Linda Lu	£100
65	Island WI 252	Shook Shimmy And Shake/I'm Going Back	£35
65	Island WI 258	You Don't Know Like I Do/Take Me Serious (with Sound System)	£15
66	Island WI 252	Shook, Shimmy And Shake/Gonna Work Out Fine	£35
67	Island WIP 6000	Help Me/Incense	£45
67	Collins Downbeat CR 003	Collins Greetings/Rock It Down (with Sir Collins & Band)	£50
67	Collins Downbeat CR 004	I'm So Lonely (with Sir Collins & Band)/EL RECO, SIR COLLINS & J. SATCH: Shock Steady	£90
68	Collins Downbeat CR 007	Am Satisfy (with Sir Collins & Band)/BOB STACKIE & SIR COLLINS & BAND: Sweet Music	£150
68	Collins Downbeat CR 009	Grab It, Hold It, Feel It (with Bob Stackie)/DAN SIMMONS: Way Out Sound	£65
68	Collins Downbeat CR 010	I'm Gonna Take You Back (with Bob Stackie)/GLEN ADAMS: King Sized	£125
68	Coxsone CS 7047	Give Me A Little Sign/Ain't Nobody Home	£300
68	Coxsone CS 7053	Give It To Me/Isn't It So	£160
68	Blue Cat BS 123	These Foolish Things/This I Promise	£100
69	Blue Cat BS 156	I Can't Stop Loving You/Tell Me Darling	£30
68	Trojan TR 632	Lovey Dovey/Grooving	£20
68	Revolution REV 001	Sitting In The Park/You've Got It	£20
69	Fab FAB 90	Three Coins In The Fountain/Tennessee Waltz	£15
69	Fab FAB 120	Understand My Love/Apollo 12	£30
69	Fab FAB 96	Ay Ay Ay/Let It Be Me (with Rudies)	£25
69	Fab FAB 126	Swing Low/Release Me	£20
69	Duke DU 12	Reggae Dance/I Know	£40
69	Downtown DT 423	Groovin'/HERBIE GRAY & RUDIES: These Memories	£15
69	Camel CA 25	Girl What You Doing To Me/Woman A Grumble	£25
69	Camel CA 34	Don't Take Your Love Away/Two Lovers	£25
69	Camel CA 37	Every Beat Of My Heart/Don't Cry	£20
70	Camel CA 50	Don't Sign The Paper/Packing Up Loneliness	£20
70	Camel CA 51	Bring Back Your Love/Got To Come Back	£20
70	Upfront UPF 3	Dream Lover/Mudda-Granma-Reggae (with Maximum Breed)	£20
70	Ackee ACK 102	No More/Don't Leave Me (both as Owen Gray & Omen)	£15
71	Camel CA 60	Groove Me/No Other One	£20
71	Camel CA 73	Nothing Can Separate Us/Girl I Want You To Understand	£35
78	Bushranger BAR 101	The Greatest Love Of All (with RANKING JAH SON)/TONY SEXTON & SUPERSTAR: Segregation (12")	£30
61	Starlite STLP 5	OWEN GRAY SINGS (LP)	£120
63	Melodisc MLP 12-153	CUPID (LP)	£45
69	Trojan TTL 24	REGGAE WITH SOUL (LP)	£30
77	Trojan TRLS 139	FIRE AND BULLETS (LP)	£20
78	Trojan TRLS 150	DREAMS OF OWEN GRAY (LP)	£25

(see also Laurel & Owen, Gray Brothers, Elki & Owen, Owen & Milie, Owen & Dandy, Dennis Lowe, Survivors, Denzil & Jennifer, Brother Dan, Glen Adam)

VERA GRAY
| 66 | HMV CLP3531 | LISTEN, MOVE & DANCE 4 (LP) | £25 |

WARDELL GRAY
| 54 | Brunswick LA 8646 | THE CHASE (LP, with Dexter Gordon) | £25 |

LARRY GRAYSON
| 72 | York MYK 602 | WHAT A GAY DAY (LP) | £15 |

RUDY GRAYZELL
| 54 | London HL 8094 | Looking At The Moon And Wishing On A Star/The Heart That Once Was Mine | £200 |
| 54 | London HL 8094 | Looking At The Moon And Wishing On A Star/The Heart That Once Was Mine (78) | £30 |

GRAZINA
| 63 | HMV POP 1212 | Be My Baby/I Ain't Gonna Knock On Your Door | £20 |

(see also Lady Murray, Le Roys, Cliff Richard)

GREASE BAND
71	Harvest SHVL 790	THE GREASE BAND (LP, textured sleeve first pressing)	£60
72	Harvest SHVL 790	THE GREASE BAND (LP, second pressing with EMI boxed logo)	£20
75	Goodear EAR 2902	AMAZING GREASE (LP)	£15

(see also Joe Cocker, Wynder K. Frog, Made In Sheffield)

GREAT ACES
72	Fab FAB 200	Liberty Rock/Rock My Soul	£25
72	Fab FAB 201	I Didn't Mean It/Boots And Shoes	£20
73	Fab FAB 203	Banana/My Sweet Lord	£20

GREAT BRITISH HEROES (AKA GBH)
| 78 | Lightning Records GIL 534 | Eric Miller/Don't Give A Damn (unreleased, 1 known only) | £1500 |

GREATEST SHOW ON EARTH
70	Harvest HAR 5012	Real Cool World/Again And Again	£20
70	Harvest SHVL 769	HORIZONS (LP, gatefold sleeve, no EMI on label)	£150
70	Harvest SHVL 783	THE GOING'S EASY (LP, gatefold sleeve, no EMI logo on label)	£150
75	Harvest SHSM 2004	THE GREATEST SHOW ON EARTH (LP)	£15

(see also Ian Dury & Blockheads, Fuzzy Duck, Glencoe, Naturals)

GREAT EXPECTATIONS
| 81 | Phillips (no cat no) | Midnight Man/Pt. 2 | £15 |

GREAT METROPOLITAN STEAM BAND
| 69 | MCA MNP/S 403 | THE GREAT METROPLITAN STEAM BAND (LP) | £25 |

GREAT SOCIETY
68	CBS 63476	CONSPICUOUS ONLY IN ITS ABSENCE (LP)	£35

(see also Jefferson Airplane)

GREAT UNCLE FRED
67	Strike JH 324	I'm In Love With An Ex-Beauty Queen/Singalong Version	£20

ADAM GREEN
03	Rough Trade RTRADLP 107	FRIENDS OF MINE (LP, inner)	£40
05	Rough Trade RTRADLP 194	GEMSTONES (LP)	£25

AL GREEN(E)
68	Stateside SS 2079	Back Up Train/Don't Leave Me (as Al Greene & Soul Mates)	£25
68	Stateside SS 2079	Back Up Train/Don't Leave Me (as Al Greene & Soul Mates) (DJ copy)	£40
69	Action ACT 4540	Don't Hurt Me No More/Get Yourself Together (by Al Greene)	£20
71	London SHU 8424	AL GREEN GETS NEXT TO YOU (LP)	£30
69	Action ACLP 6008	BACK UP TRAIN (LP)	£60
72	London SHU 8430	LET'S STAY TOGETHER (LP)	£30
72	London SHU 8443	I'M STILL IN LOVE WITH YOU (LP)	£30
73	London SHU 8457	CALL ME (LP)	£20
74	London SHU 8464	LIVIN' FOR YOU (LP)	£20
74	London SHU 8479	EXPLORES YOUR MIND (LP)	£20
75	London SHU 8481	GREATEST HITS (LP)	£20
76	London SHU 8493	FULL OF FIRE (LP)	£15
76	London SHU 8505	HAVE A GOOD TIME (LP)	£20
86	Hi HI UK LP 401	GREEN IS BLUES (LP, reissue)	£15
86	Hi HI UK LP 405	LET'S STAY TOGETHER (LP, reissue)	£15
86	Hi HI UK LP 409	CALL ME (LP, reissue)	£15

BARRY GREEN
71	Ember TBS 713	Together/Sexopolis	£100
71	Decca F13171	I Wanna Join The Cavalry/When The Morning Returns (demo only)	£15

BENNIE GREEN
61	Parlophone PMC 1180	HORNFUL OF SOUL (LP)	£30

BRIAN GREEN
68	Fontana SFJL 912	BRIAN GREEN DISPLAY (LP)	£40

CARL GREEN AND THE SCENE
79	Sirius SP 516	RECORD NOT FOUND EP	£20
80	Benton Fun/Ginnis Bucka GRCGCS1	All The Tea In China/Business Aquaintance/Fish In The Sea (p/s, double sided insert)	£100

GARLAND GREEN
98	Kent 6T 16	Come Through Me/JUNIOR MCCANTS: Try Me For Your New Love	£40
90	Kent KEND 097	THE SPRING SIDES (LP)	£20

GRANT GREEN
65	Verve VLP 9111	HIS MAJESTY KING FUNK (LP)	£25
93	Blue Note 89622	STREET FUNK AND JAZZ GROOVES (2-LP)	£20

IAN GREEN (REVELATION)
67	Polydor 56194	Last Pink Rose/Green Blues (solo)	£30
70	CBS 63840	REVELATION (LP)	£30

(see also Madeline Bell, Rosetta Hightower)

JIMMY GREEN
73	Green Door GD 4062	I'll Be Standing By/LLOYD'S ALL STARS: I'll Be Standing By "Version"	£15

(see also Jimmy London)

KATHE GREEN
69	Deram SML 1039	RUN THE LENGTH OF YOUR WILDNESS (LP, white/red label)	£35

KEITH GREEN
60s	Bird 118	NO COMPROMISE (LP)	£30

LLOYD GREEN
75	Monument S MNT 81245	STEEL RIDES (LP)	£20

PETER GREEN
71	Reprise RS 27012	Heavy Heart/No Way Out	£25
72	Reprise K 14092	Heavy Heart/No Way Out (repressing)	£20
72	Reprise K 14141	Beast Of Burden/Uganda Woman (with Nigel Watson)	£25
70	Reprise RSLP 9006	THE END OF THE GAME (LP, with Nigel Watson)	£150
79	PVK PVLS 101	IN THE SKIES (LP, gatefold, green vinyl)	£30
80	PVK PVLS 102	LITTLE DREAMER (LP, with inner sleeve)	£15
81	PVK PET 1	WHATCHA GONNA DO? (LP)	£20
82	Headline HED 1	WHITE SKY (LP)	£20
83	Headline HED 2	KOLORS (LP)	£20
85	Nightflight NTFL 2001	A CASE FOR THE BLUES/KATMANDU (LP)	£20

(see also Fleetwood Mac, Peter B's, Shotgun Express, John Mayall & Bluesbreakers, Gass, Peter Bardens, Gass)

SALLY GREEN
62	Philips PB 1243	It Hurts Too Much To Laugh/When's He Gonna Kiss Me	£15

TOM GREEN
74	Action ACT 4621	Rock Springs Railroad Station/Endless Confusion	£100

GREEN ANGELS
65	Parlophone R 5390	Rockin' Red Wing/Let It Happen	£15

NORMAN GREENBAUM
70	Reprise RSLP 6365	SPIRIT IN THE SKY (LP)	£20
70	Page One POLS 017	WITH DR. WEST'S MEDICINE SHOW & JUNK BAND (LP)	£22

(see also Dr. West's Medicine Show & Junk Band)

GREENBEATS
67	Spin SP 2007	Pretty Woman/Thing	£15

GREEN BULLFROG
72	MCA MKPS 2021	GREEN BULLFROG (LP, black/blue 'hexagon' label)	£175

(see also Deep Purple, Roger Glover, Matthew Fisher)

GREEN DAY
94	Reprise W 0247 T	Longview/Going To Pasalacqua (Infatuation)/FOD (Live)/ Christy Road (Live) (10", green vinyl, stickered PVC sleeve)	£20
94	Reprise W 0257	Basket Case/Tired Of Waiting For You (Green vinyl, numbered p/s)	£15
94	Reprise W 0269 T	Welcome To Paradise/Chump (Live)/Emenius Sleepus (green vinyl 12", stickered PVC sleeve)	£15
94	Reprise 9362 45529 1	DOOKIE (LP, with crowd photo on back cover, green vinyl, numbered sticker)	£50
95	Reprise 9362 46046 1	INSOMNIAC (LP, with inner)	£50
97	Reprise 9362 46794 1	NIMROD (LP, with inner)	£50
01	Reprise 48145	INTERNATIONAL SUPERHITS! (LP, insert, purple vinyl)	£40
04	Reprise 9362-41777-1	AMERICAN IDIOT (2-LP)	£35

CLAUDE 'FATS' GREENE & ORCHESTRA
66	Island WI 290	Fats Shake 'Em Up Parts 1 & 2 (actually with Al Thomas)	£15

LORNE GREENE
63	RCA RD 7566	YOUNG... AT HEART (LP)	£15
65	RCA RD 7709	THE MAN (LP)	£15

GREEN EYE
73	Whirl WH01	Sinister Jack/Run Run Run	£25

GREENFIELD
71	Philips 6113002	Sweet America/Dorothys Daughter	£15

GREEN GINGER THREE
65	Decca DFE 8623	FROM THE LAND OF GREEN GINGER (EP)	£15

GREEN LINES
80	CMS MR 016X	A PIECE OF THE NIGHT (EP, folded p/s)	£15

GREEN MAN
75	Private pressing	WHAT AILS THEE? (LP, 100 copies, Matrix Vem 107-A2/B2)	£200
00	Slightly Discoloured FADE 01	WHAT AILS THEE? (LP, reissue)	£18

GREEN PAJAMAS
89	Ubik Records BAKTUN 1	SUMMER OF LUST (LP, reissue)	£15
99	Woronzow WOO 36 LP	SEVEN FATHOMS DOWN AND FALLING (LP)	£20

GREEN RIVER
85	Homestead HMS 031	COME ON DOWN (EP, with insert)	£20
88	Glitterhouse GR 0031	REHAB DOLL (LP)	£20

(see also Mudhoney)

GREENSLADE
73	Warner Bros K 46207	GREENSLADE (LP, gatefold sleeve, green label)	£25
73	Warner Bros K 46259	BEDSIDE MANNERS ARE EXTRA (LP, gatefold sleeve 'Burbank' label)	£20
74	Warner Bros K 56055	SPYGLASS GUEST (LP, gatefold sleeve)	£15
76	Warner Bros K 56306	CACTUS CHOIR (LP, lyric insert)	£15
80	EMI EMSP 332	THE PENTATEUCH OF THE COSMOGONY (2-LP, with 47-page book, as Dave Greenslade)	£40

(see also Wes Minster Five, Alan Price Set, Geno Washington & Ram Jam Band, Chris Farlowe, Colosseum, Samurai, Web, King Crimson, Stackridge)

ARTHUR GREENSLADE (& GEE MEN)
66	Columbia DB 7865	Watermelon Man/Serenade To A Broken Jaw	£30

GREENTEA PENG
19	Different DIF433EP	RISING (12", 1st pressing, green vinyl)	£80

GREEN VELVET
95	Open OPENP 017	Flash (The Relief Remixes) (12")	£15

ELLIE GREENWICH
67	United Artists UP 1180	I Want You To Be My Baby/Goodnight, Goodnight	£25
73	MGM 2315 243	LET IT BE WRITTEN, LET IT BE SUNG (LP)	£30

(see also Popsicles, Raindrops [U.S.])

GREEN WILLOW
80	Cotswold Music SFA 115	COTSWOLD MUSIC (LP)	£30

JONNY GREENWOOD
03	Parlophone 5951471	BODYSONG (LP)	£60

(see also Radiohead)

MICK GREENWOOD
71	MCA MDKS 8003	THE LIVING GAME (LP, gatefold sleeve, pink/orange 'dogbone' label)	£30
72	MCA MKPS 2026	TO FRIENDS (LP, black/blue 'hexagon' label)	£20

(see also Fotheringay)

NICHOLAS GREENWOOD
72	Kingdom KVLP 9002	COLD CUTS (LP, laminated sleeve)	£3000
18	Swordfish SWFLP 36	COLD CUTS (LP, reissue, printed inner, limited edition)	£30

(see also Crazy World Of Arthur Brown, Khan, Bryn Howarth)

STOCKER GREENWOOD & FRIENDS
79   Changes   BILLY + NINE (LP)..£20

GREGER
66   Polydor 249 1103   IN THE NIGHT (LP)..£25

BOBBY GREGG & FRIENDS
62   Columbia DB 4825   The Jam (Parts 1 & 2)...£15

IA(I)N GREGORY
60   Pye 7N 15295   Time Will Tell/The Night You Told A Lie (as Ian Gregory)......................£30
61   Pye 7N 15397   Can't You Hear The Beat Of A Broken Heart/Because..........................£25
62   Pye 7N 15435   Mr. Lovebug/Pocketful Of Dreams £35

JANE GREGORY
84   D Sharp DSS 1004   Do Not Go/After A Dream (p/s) £150

JOHNNY GREGORY & HIS ORCHESTRA
72   Philips 6308 111   SPIES AND DOLLS (LP)...£15
74   United Artists UAG 29546   A MAN FOR ALL SEASONS (LP)...£25
74   United Artists QUAG 29546   A MAN FOR ALL SEASONS (LP, quadrophonic)....................................£75

TONY GREGORY
66   Doctor Bird DB 1007   Baby Come On Home/Marie Elena £30
66   Doctor Bird DB 1016   Give Me One More Chance/I've Lost My Love £30
67   Island WI 3029   Get Out Of My Life/SOUL BROTHERS: Sugar Cane £40
67   Coxsone CS 7013   Only A Fool (Breaks His Own Heart)/Pure Soul £50
67   Coxsone CSL 8011   TONY GREGORY SINGS (LP) £100
(see also Lloyd Charmers)

STAN GREIG'S JAZZ BAND
59   Tempo EXA 90   STAN GREIG'S JAZZ BAND (EP) £25
80s   Calligraph CLGLP 004   BLUES EVERY TIME (LP) £20

GREMLINS
66   Mercury MF 981   The Coming Generation/That's What I Want £20
67   Mercury MF 1004   You Gotta Believe It/I Can't Say £20

JOEL GREY
54   MGM SPC 1   Last Night In The Back Porch/Two-Faced (export issue)......................£18
58   Capitol CL 14832   Be My Next/Shoppin' Around (demos is picture sleeves = £40)..........£20

RONNIE GREY & JETS
55   Capitol CL 14329   Run, Manny, Run/Sweet Baby £20

SARAH GREY & ELLIE ELLIS
86   Greenwich Village GVR 231   YOU GAVE ME A SONG (LP, with insert) £15

GREY BROTHERS
68   Blue Cat BS 124   Always/Big Man £80
(see also Owen Gray)

GREYHOUND
72   Trojan TRLS 27   BLACK AND WHITE (LP) £30
(see also Tillermen)

GREY PARADE
85   Plan B GREY 1   THE REASON (LP) £25

GRIDS
80   Kings Head   NEW ANTHEMS (EP) £20

MERVA GRIER
83   Hawkeyes HD 053   Feeling Like A Million/HOPETON LINDO: We Are One (12") £25

ROOSEVELT GRIER
68   Action ACT 4515   People Make The World/Hard To Forget £15
69   Pama PM 774   Who's Got The Ball £15
69   Pama PM 784   C'mon Cupid/High Society Woman...£20

GRIFFIN
69   Bell BLL 1075   I Am The Noise In Your Head/Don't You Know....................................£35
(see also Heavy Jelly, Skip Bifferty, Bell & Arc, Happy Magazine, Ginger Baker's Airforce)

JOHNNY GRIFFIN
62   Riverside RLP 420   THE KERRY DANCERS (LP)...£80
69   Polydor 583734   THE MAN I LOVE (LP) £60
70   Youngblood SSYB 11   FOOT PATTING (LP) £50

JOHNNY GRIFFIN BIG SOUL BAND
61   Riverside RLP 12-3331   THE BIG SOUL BAND (LP, also stereo [RLP 9331] £20
(see also Eddie 'Lockjaw' Davis)

JOE GRIFFITHS
69   Philips SBL 7902   OUT OF THE HEAD OF...(LP, black/silver labels).................................£20

MARCIA GRIFFITHS
66   Island WI 285   Funny/KING SPARROW: Beggars Have No Choice (B-side actually by Leonard Dillon & Wailers; some copies credit Marcia Griffiths on both sides)...........£120
67   Studio One SO 2008   Hound Dog (actually by Norma Fraser)/HUGH GODFREY: My Time...............£100
67   Studio One SO 2015   After Laughter/HUGH GODFREY: Go Tell Him......................................£80
68   Coxsone CS 7035   Mojo Girl (actually Nora Dean)/HAMLINS: Tell Me That You Love Me.........£200
68   Coxsone CS 7055   Feel Like Jumping/HORACE TAYLOR: Thundering Vibrations £75

MINT VALUE £

68	Coxsone CS 7062	Hold Me Tight/BASIES: Home Sweet Home (B-side actually by Basses) £400
68	Studio One SO 2047	Words (as Marcia Griffiths & Jeff Dixon)/SHARKS: How Could I Live £150
68	Studio One SO 2059	Truly/SIMMS & ROBINSON: Drought..£70
69	Gas GAS 111	Tell Me Now/STAN HOPE: The Weight...£100
69	High Note HS 029	Talk (Parts 1 & 2) (correct title is actually "Toil")..............................£15
69	Escort ES 808	Don't Let Me Down/REGGAEITES: Romper Room (B-side actually by Peter Tosh).........£100
69	Trojan TR 693	Put A Little Love In Your Heart/J BOYS: Jay Fever...................................£15
70	Harry J. HJ 6613	Put A Little Love In Your Heart/JAY BOYS: Bah Oop Ah...............................£15
70	Harry J. HJ 6623	Band Of Gold/JAY BOYS: Cowboy (Version II)......................................£25
70	Bamboo BAM 59	Shimmering Star/SOUND DIMENSION: Mun-Dun-Gu (B-side actually Im & David).......£100
75	Torpedo TOR 47	Survival/Version...£40
70	Trojan TRLS 94	SWEET BITTER LOVE (LP)...£50
74	Trojan TRLS 94	SWEET BITTER LOVE (LP, orange/white label).......................................£30
78	Sky Note KYLP 17	STEPPIN' (LP)...£20
79	Sky Note SKYLP 09	NATURALLY (LP)...£25

(see also Bob & Marcia, Peter Touch/Tosh, Roy Richards, Soul Vendor, Bob Andy, Della Humphrey, Mr. Foundation, Bob Marley)

VICTOR GRIFFITHS
70	Punch PH 29	I Am Proud Of You/KING VICTOR ALL STARS: Version £20

GRIMES
10	No Pain In Pop – NPIP024	GEIDI PRIMES (LP)..£75
11	Lo LCD 87	HALFAXA (LP)..£20
12	4AD CAD3208	VISIONS (LP)...£18
15	4AD CAD3535	ART ANGELS (LP)...£20

CAROL GRIMES (& DELIVERY)
70	Charisma CAS 1023	FOOLS MEETING (LP, with Delivery, gatefold sleeve)..............................£250
74	Caroline CA 2001	WARM BLOOD (LP, black/white/red 'twins' labels) £25
75	Decca SKL-R 5268	CAROL GRIMES (LP, blue/silver labels) £20

(see also Uncle Dog, Babylon)

GRIMMS
73	Island ILPS 9248	ROCKIN' DUCK (LP, die cut 'duck' sleeve outside single sleeve, pink rim, palm tree logo)..£20
76	DJM DJLPS 470	SLEEPERS (LP)...£15

(see also Neil Innes, Liverpool Scene, Scaffold, Mike McGear, McGough & McGear, John Gorman, Zoot Money, Patto, Viv Stanshall, Andy Roberts, Bashers)

GRIM REAPER (1)
83	Ebony EBON 16	SEE YOU IN HELL (LP)..£20
85	Ebony EBON 32	FEAR NO EVIL (LP)...£20

GRIM REAPER (2)
94	No label or cat no	Free/Mighter Than Mighty/Go Chew/My Soul (12")..............................£35

GRINDERMAN
07	Mute MUTE 370	Get It On (1-sided 7" other side etched, p/s)...................................£15
07	Mute STUMM 272	GRINDERMAN (LP)..£35
11	Mute STUMM 299	GRINDERMAN 2 (LP & CD with poster and print)................................£25
11	Mute XCDSTUMM299	GRINDERMAN 2 RMX (2-LP & CD)...£25

(see also Nick Cave)

JANNY GRINE
70s	Sparrow BIRD 104	FREE INDEED (LP)..£25

GRINGO
71	MCA MKPS 2107	GRINGO (LP, red/pink 'dogbone' label)..£80

(see also Caravan)

JOE GRINNE
69	Coxsone CS 7098	Mr Editor/How I Feel (both sides actually by Melodians).........................£250

GRIP
80	Mrs. Dixon MDR 3001	File It Under Maybe, Baby/Pavement Princess/Hole in The Wall (p/s) £25

GRIPPIN
72	Priory PR1	I See What You See/Times Over £80

GRISBY DYKE
69	Deram DM 232	The Adventures Of Miss Rosemary La Page/Mary Anne She.......................£30

GRISSLE
74	Roach RC 3	Crazy Lady/She Goes £40

GROBBERT & DUFF
72	Sunlamp GRA 101	I Am I Think/The Man From Naz £100

DEWEY GROOM
62	Starlite ST45 085	Butane Blues/That's All I Want Out Of Life £20

GROOP (1)
68	CBS 3204	Woman You're Breaking Me/Mad Over You......................................£30
78	CBS 3351	Lovin' Tree/Night Life £20

GROOP (2)
69	Bell BLL 1070	A Famous Myth/Tears And Joys £15
69	Bell BLL 1080	The Jet Song (When The Weekend's Over)/Nobody At All £18

GROOVE CHRONICLES
96	Old Dog NOOD 1	The Beginings Part 1/Part 2/Tidy Vibes (12")..................................£15
97	DPR DPR 001	Angel Body/Natural (12" white label)..£15
97	Groove Chronicles GC 001	Stone Cold/Hold On (12", white label)...£35

MINT VALUE £

98   Groove Chronicles GC 001e   **Stone Cold/Hold On** (12")..£30

GROOVE (1)
69   Parlophone R 5783   **The Wind/Play The Song**..£50

GROOVE (2)
80   Trendy WHIP 1   **Heart Complaint/I Wanna Be Your Pygmy**..£15

GROOVE ARMADA
98   Tummy Touch TUCH 103   **NORTHERN STAR** (2-LP)..£30
99   Pepper 0530331   **VERTIGO** (2-LP, inners)..£40
00   Pepper 9230100   **THE REMIXES** (2-LP)..£20
01   Pepper 9230491   **GOODBYE COUNTRY** (HELLO NIGHTCLUB) (3-LP)..£50
02   Zomba 9230661   **LOVEBOX** (3-LP)..£50
10   Music On Vinyl MOVLP223   **WHITE LIGHT** (LP)..£80
10   Work It GABLP1   **BLACK LIGHT** (2-LP)..£80

GROOVERIDER
97   Higher Ground 487219 1   **THE PROTOTYPE YEARS** (3-LP)..£40
98   Higher Ground HIGH LP 6   **MYSTERIES OF FUNK** (4-LP)..£30

GROOVERS
68   Amalgamated AMG 816   **Having A Party/Day By Day**..£85
71   Camel CA 83   **Put Me Down Easy/I Want To Go Back Home**..£15
71   Escort ERT 863   **Bend Down Low/The Burning Feeling**..£20
(see also Lloyd & Groovers, Alva Lewis, Junior Byles, Dennis Walks)

WINSTON GROOV(E)Y
69   Grape GR 3005   **Leaving Me Standing/Little Girl**..£20
69   Grape GR 3008   **Merry X-mas/I Am Lonely**..£15
69   Nu Beat NB 041   **Island In The Sun/Work It Up**..£15
70   Attack ATT 8019   **You Can't Turn Your Back On Me/PAMA DICE: The Worm**..£20
70   Jackpot JP 708   **Funky Chicken/CIMARRONS: Part 2** (B-side actually unknown instrumental)..£25
70   Torpedo TOR 11   **Please Don't Make Me Cry/Motion On The Ocean**..£20
69   Pama PMP 2011   **FREE THE PEOPLE** (LP)..£40
78   Trojan TRLS 155   **THE GROOVEY COLLECTION** (LP)..£20
(see also King Horror, Upsetters)

PAUL GROOVY AND THE POP ART EXPERIENCE
87   Bite Back! – BB!012   **Andy Watch Out!/Take Away The Pain** (wrap-around p/s, sticker, lyric sheet)..£30

GROSS CLUB
81   Caveman CMR 01   **Second Chance/Look Away** (sleeve is a paper insert glued on white inner sleeve)..£100

G.G. GROSSETT
69   Crab CRAB 10   **Run Girl Run/DENNIS WALKS: The Drifter**..£100
69   Crab CRAB 33   **Greater Sounds/Live The Life I love**..£50

STEFAN GROSSMAN
68   Fontana (S)TL 5463   **AUNT MOLLY'S MURRAY FARM** (LP)..£25
69   Fontana STL 5485   **THE GRAMERCY PARK SHEIK** (LP)..£20
70   Transatlantic TRA 217   **YAZOO BASIN BOOGIE** (LP)..£15
71   Transatlantic TRA 246   **THOSE PLEASANT DAYS** (LP, with lyric insert)..£15
(see also John Renbourn)

LUTHER GROSVENOR
71   Island ILPS 9168   **UNDER OPEN SKIES** (LP, gatefold sleeve pink rim palm tree logo)..£50
(see also Hellions, Revolution, Art, Spooky Tooth, Mott The Hoople, Widowmaker)

CARL GROSZMANN
75   Ring O' 2017 103   **I've Had It/C'mon And Roll**..£15
77   Ring O' 2017 107   **Face Of A Permanent Stranger/Your Own Affair** (promo p/s)..£15
75   Ring O' 2320 102   **CARL GROSZMANN** (LP, unreleased)..£0

GROUND ATTACK
81   Ground Attack GAR 001   **THE RED LION EP** (Red Lion/Every Mother's Son) (gatefold p/s)..£100
81   Ground Attack GAR 001   **THE RED LION EP** (Red Lion/Every Mother's Son) (later pressing with no p/s)..£20

GROUND CONTROL
81   Sycamore SRS 001   **Cover Girl/Lonely Guy**..£40

GROUNDHOGS
68   Liberty LBF 15174   **You Don't Love Me/Still A Fool**..£30
69   Liberty LBF 15263   **B.D.D./TONY McPHEE: Gasoline**..£35
70   Liberty LBF 15346   **Eccentric Man/Status People**..£20
68   Liberty LBL 83199E   **SCRATCHING THE SURFACE** (LP, mono, blue label)..£125
68   Liberty LBS 83199E   **SCRATCHING THE SURFACE** (LP, stereo, blue label)..£75
69   Liberty LBS 83253   **BLUES OBITUARY** (LP, blue label)..£100
70   Liberty LBS 83295   **THANK CHRIST FOR THE BOMB** (LP, gatefold sleeve, 1st pressing blue label)..£150
71   Liberty LBG 83401   **SPLIT** (LP, gatefold sleeve, black label)..£50
70   Liberty LBS 83295   **THANK CHRIST FOR THE BOMB** (LP, gatefold sleeve, 2nd pressing black label)..£50
72   United Artists UAG 29347   **WHO WILL SAVE THE WORLD...** (LP, gatefold sleeve)..£40
72   United Artists UAG 29419   **HOGWASH** (LP, tri-fold sleeve)..£30
73   United Artists UDF 31   **GROUNDHOGS' BEST 1969-1972** (2-LP, red HK/DA/73 inside sleeve))..£15
74   W. Wide Artists WWA 004   **SOLID** (LP, with lyric insert)..£15
76   United Artists UAS 29917   **CROSSCUT SAW** (LP)..£15
84   Psycho PSYCHO 24   **HOGGIN' THE STAGE** (2-LP, with EP, stickered gatefold sleeve)..£18
89   BGO BGOLP 67   **THANK CHRIST FOR THE BOMB** (LP, reissue, gatefold)..£20
(see also Tony McPhee, Herbal Mixture, Home, Andy Fernbach, John Lee Hooker)

GROUP (FEATURING CECIL WASHINGTON)
98　Goldmine Soul Supply GS
　　209　　　I Don't Like To Lose/Can't Loose My Head (reissue) £15

GROUP B
67　Vocalion VF 9284　　I Know Your Name Girl/I Never Really Knew £25
(see also Blue Cheer)

GROUP 1850
69　Philips SBL 7884　　AGEMO'S TRIP TO MOTHER EARTH (LP, gatefold sleeve) £600

GROUP IMAGE
69　Stable SLE 8005　　A MOUTH IN THE CLOUDS (LP) £90

GROUP ONE
58　HMV POP 463　　She's Neat/Made For Each Other £30

GROUP SIX
59　Oriole CB 1488　　Rock-A-Boogie/Rockin' The Blues £20

GROUP THERAPY
69　Philips SBL 7888　　YOU'RE IN NEED OF GROUP THERAPY (LP) £20

GROUP X
63　Fontana 267 274 TF　　There Are 8 Million Cossack Melodies - And This Is One Of Them/Teneriffe (in p/s) £15

GROUPER
07　Type TYPE 020V　　WAY THEIR CREPT (LP, clear vinyl, 100 only) £50
07　Type TYPE 020V　　WAY THEIR CREPT (LP) £20
08　Type TYPE 038V　　DRAGGING A DEAD DEER UP A HILL (LP) £30

GROUP SOUNDS FOUR AND FIVE
21　Jazz In Britain JB 14 M LP　　BLACK AND WHITE RAGA (LP) £20

GROUT
79　Urinating Vicar　　DO IT YOURSELF (EP) (100 only, sound quality very poor) £400

GROW UP
79　Object Music OBJ 5　　THE BEST THING (LP) £20
81　UP Records GROWL 1　　WITHOUT WINDS (LP) £15

GRUDGE
73　Black Label BL 002　　When Christine Comes Around/I'm Gonna Smash Your Face In £50

GRUMBLEWEEDS
71　Phillips 78434　　Never Before/Fiona McLaughlin £15
74　Decca F13513　　(Hey Babe) Follow Me/Won't Say No Again £20
72　Philips 6308091　　IN A TEKNIKOLOR DREAM (LP) £40

GRUNT FUTTOCK
72　Regal Zonophone RZ 3042　　Rock 'N' Roll Christian/Free Sole £40
(see also Move, Roy Wood)

GRUNTRUCK
92　Roadrunner RR 9130 1　　PUSH (LP) £60

DAVE GRUSIN
85　Arista GRP 5610　　MOUNTAIN DANCE (LP, Nimbus Supercut, mail order only through Practical Hi Fi
　　　　magazine) £40

GRUVY BEATS
70　Nu Beat NB 048　　Share Your Popcorn/LAUREL AITKEN: Mr. Popcorn £15
70　Nu Beat NB 049　　Blue Mink/LAUREL AITKEN: I've Got Your Love £20

GIGI GRYCE
60　Esquire 32-151　　SAYIN' SOMETHIN' (LP) £100
60　Esquire 32-181　　RAT RACE BLUES (LP) £100

GRYPHON
73　Transatlantic TRA 262　　GRYPHON (LP, gatefold sleeve) £25
74　Transatlantic TRA 282　　MIDNIGHT MUSHRUMPS (LP) £15
74　Transatlantic TRA 287　　RED QUEEN TO GRYPHON THREE (LP) £15
75　Transatlantic TRA 302　　RAINDANCE (LP) £15
77　Harvest SHSP 4063　　TREASON (LP, with lyric inner sleeve) £20
(see also Richard Harvey, The Banned)

G.T.O.'S
67　Polydor 56721　　She Rides With Me/Rudy Vadoo £75
(see also Joey & Continentals)

G.T.O.'S (GIRLS TOGETHER OUTRAGEOUSLY)
70　Straight STS 1059　　PERMANENT DAMAGE (LP) £150
(see also Jeff Beck, Frank Zappa)

GUARDIANS OF THE ANCIENT WISDOM
15　154 001　　DESCEND THE STAIRWAY TO DARKNESS WITH... (2-LP, handmade sleeve, booklet and
　　　　CD) £20

GUERNICA
87　Idol 12 ID 2　　ORANGE AND RED EP (12") £150
88　Miss Pedestal MP 001　　HUMMING OF THE ENGINE (12", p/s) £50

GUESS WHO
65　Pye International 7N 25305　　Shakin' All Over/Till We Kissed £25
66　King KG 1044　　His Girl/It's My Pride £25
67　Fontana TF 831　　This Time Long Ago/There's No Getting Away From You £15

MINT VALUE £

69	RCA SF 8037	WHEATFIELD SOUL (LP)	£15
70	RCA SF 8107	AMERICAN WOMAN (LP)	£15

EARL GUEST
64	Columbia DB 7212	Begin The Beguine/Foxy	£20

GUEST & EDWARDS
72	Phillips 6006231	All Alone/Sing You A Picture	£20

REG GUEST SYNDICATE
65	Mercury MF 927	Underworld/Guys, Guns, Dolls And Danger	£125
66	Mercury 20089MCL	UNDERWORLD (LP)	£40

GUGGENHEIM
72	Indigo GOLP 7001	GUGGENHEIM (LP, private pressing)	£75

GUIDED BY VOICES
94	Domino RUG 11	CLOWN PRINCE OF THE MENTHOL TRAILER EP (p/s)	£30
96	Fear & Loathing RCRPA 17	BRIGHTON ROCKS: Hot Freaks/Game Of Pricks (50 copies on blue vinyl with fanzine)	£60
96	Fear & Loathing RCRPA 17	BRIGHTON ROCKS: Hot Freaks/Game Of Pricks (450 copies on black vinyl with fanzine)	£40
99	Creation CRE 325	Teenage FBI/Flying Into Ashes/Tropical Robots (p/s)	£20
99	Creation CRE 328	Hold On Hope/Perfect This Time (p/s, release cancelled)	£200
94	Matador OLE 084 1	BEE THOUSAND (LP, blue vinyl)	£60
96	Matador OLE 161 1	UNDER THE BUSHES UNDER THE STARS (LP, with free 12")	£40
97	Matafor OLE 241-1	MAG EARWHIG! (LP)	£40
99	Creation CRELP 251	DO THE COLLAPSE (LP)	£50
02	Matador OLE 547-1	UNIVERSAL TRUTHS AND CYCLES (LP, gatefold)	£80

GUILLEMOTS
05	Fantastic Plastic FPS050	I SAW SUCH THINGS IN MY SLEEP EP (10", 300 only p/s)	£15
06	Polydor IC00309	THROUGH THE WINDOWPANE (2-LP, gatefold sleeve, inner sleeves & booklet)	£25
11	Polydor 2769730	WALK THE RIVER (2-LP)	£15

ISAAC GUILLORY
74	Atlantic K 40521	ISAAC GUILLORY (LP)	£18

(see also Shames)

GUILLOTEENS
65	Pye International 7N 25324	I Don't Believe/Hey You	£60

GUILT EDGE
79	Fragile FRAG 001	Bye Bye/Wires (p/s)	£15

MAALEM MAHMOUD GUINIA
15	Eglo EGBC001	MARHABA (12", p/s, with 20 page booklet, with Floating Points and James Holden)	£30

BONNIE GUITAR
58	London HLD 8591	A Very Precious Love/Johnny Vagabond	£15
58	London HA-D 2122	MOONLIGHT AND SHADOWS (LP)	£15

GUITAR CRUSHER WITH JIMMY SPURRILL
69	Blue Horizon 57-3149	Since My Baby Hit The Numbers/Hambone Blues	£45

(see also Wild Jimmy Spurrill)

GUITAR RED
63	Pye International 7N 25219	Just You And I/Old Fashioned Love	£35

GUITAR SHORTY
72	Flyright LP 500	CAROLINA SLIDE GUITAR (LP)	£15

GUITAR GANGSTERS
89	Link LP 105	PROHIBITION (LP)	£20

GULLIVER
70	Elektra 2410 006	GULLIVER (LP)	£18

GULLIVER'S PEOPLE
66	Parlophone R 5435	Splendor In The Grass/Took This Land	£20

GULLIVER'S TRAVELS
69	Instant INLP 003	GULLIVER'S TRAVELS (LP, withdrawn, front laminated sleeve, flipbacks)	£200

(see also Mike D'Abo, Andrew Oldham)

GUMBAE CULTURE
85	Leyson LR 0105	Take It Easy/Ghetto Youth (12")	£15

GUN
69	CBS M63552	GUN (LP, mono, laminated front sleeve, orange label)	£200
69	CBS 63552	GUN (LP, stereo, laminated front sleeve, orange label)	£100
69	CBS 63683	GUNSIGHT (LP)	£75

(see also Baker-Gurvitz Army, Parrish & Gurvitz, Rupert's People, Three Man Army, Knack)o

GUN CLUB
82	Beggars Banquet BEG 80	Ghost On The Highway/Sex Beat (p/s)	£20
81	Beggars Banquet BEGA 37	THE FIRE OF LOVE (LP)	£35
82	Animal CHR 1398	MIAMI (LP)	£35
83	ABC ABC LP 1	THE BIRTH THE DEATH THE GHOST (LP)	£25
84	Animal CHR 1398	LAS VEGAS STORY (LP)	£20
87	Red Rhino REDLP 84	MOTHER JUNO (LP)	£25
85	Castle DOJOLP 8	TWO SIDES OF THE BEAST (LP)	£15
90	Fire FIRELP 28	PASTORAL HIDE AND SEEK (LP)	£15
08	Retro Delux RDBX 004	THE LIFE AND TIMES OF JEFFREY LEE PIERCE AND THE GUN CLUB (4-CD box set)	£30

(see also Jeffrey Lee Pierce)

JIM GUNNER
60	Decca F 11276	Hoolee Jump/Footloose (as Jim Gunner & Echoes)	£15
61	Fontana H 313	Desperado/Baghdad (as Jim Gunner & His Sidekicks)	£20

TONY GUNNER
62	London HLU 9492	Rough Road/You Gotta Get Home	£20

SARAH OGAN GUNNING
67	Topic 12T 171	A GIRL OF CONSTANT SORROW (LP, mono, blue label)	£20

GUNSHIP
16	Horsie in The Hedge LLP HITH002LP	GUNSHIP (LP, picture disc)	£70
17	Horsie in The Hedge LLP HITH003LP	GUNSHIP (2-LP)	£25
18	Horsie in The Hedge LLP HITH008LPS	DARK ALL DAY (2-LP)	£30

GUNSHOT
94	Vinyl Solution STEAM 92	SINGLES CONNECTION (LP, red vinyl)	£15
17	Naked Ape NAR 017	INTERNATIONAL RESCUE (2-LP, reissue)	£30

GUNSHY
87	Silverstar CMS 001	Where Are The Glory Boys/If You Leave Me (no p/s)	£30

GUNSLINGER
84	Clyde CLY 001	Never A Dull Moment/Shake Some Action (no p/s)	£20

GUNS N' ROSES
87	Geffen GEF 22TP	It's So Easy/Mr Brownstone/Shadow Of Your Love/ Move To The City (12", picture disc with stickered PVC sleeve)	£40
87	Geffen GEF 30T	Welcome To The Jungle/Whole Lotta Rosie (live)/It's So Easy (live)/Knockin' On Heaven's Door (live) (12", red p/s)	£20
87	Geffen GEF 30P	Welcome To The Jungle/Whole Lotta Rosie (live)/It's So Easy (live)/Knockin' On Heaven's Door (live) (12", picture disc)	£40
88	Geffen GEF 43TE	Sweet Child O' Mine/Out Ta Get Me/Rocket Queen (10", revolving p/s)	£15
89	Geffen GEF 50P	Paradise City/I Used To Love Her (gun-shaped white picture disc in 'holster' sleeve)	£15
89	Geffen GEF 55P	Sweet Child O' Mine/Out Ta Get Me/Rocket Queen (12" uncut shaped pic disc)	£100
87	Geffen 9240 148	APPETITE FOR DESTRUCTION (LP, withdrawn 'robot' sleeve, with stickers)	£50
91	Geffen GEF 24415	USE YOUR ILLUSION I (2-LP)	£50
91	Geffen GEF 24420	USE YOUR ILLUSION II (2-LP)	£50
93	Geffen GEF24617	THE SPAGHETTI INCIDENT? (LP)	£40
08	Geffen 0602517906136	CHINESE DEMOCRACY (2-LP)	£50

ARTHUR GUNTER
72	Blue Horizon 2431 012	BLUES AFTER HOURS (LP)	£75
70s	Contempo COLP 119	BLACK AND BLUES (LP)	£25

HARDROCK GUNTER
55	Brunswick OE 9167	MOUNTAIN MUSIC (EP)	£25

(see also Red Foley, Roberta Lee)

G.I. GURDJIEFF AND THOMAS DE HARTMANN
87	Editions EG EGED 45	JOURNEY TO INACCESSIBLE PLACES AND OTHER MUSIC (LP)	£15

(see also Robert Fripp)

GURU
93	Cooltempo COOL 282	No Time To Play/Jazz Thing (p/s)	£50
93	Cooltempo CTLP 34	JAZZMATAZZ VOL. 1 (LP)	£80
95	Capitol 7243 8 34806 1 6	JAZZMATAZZ VOL. 2 (2-LP)	£100
00	Virgin VUSLP 178	JAZZMATAZZ (STREETSOUL) (2-LP)	£50
07	7 Grand VVR1046851	JAZZMATAZZ VOL 4: THE HIP HOP MESSENGER (2-LP)	£80
18	Music On Vinyl MOVLP1111	JAZZMATAZZ VOL 1 (LP, reissue, blue vinyl)	£30
18	Virgin 00600753820254	JAZZMATAZZ VOL 1 (3-LP, reissue, booklet)	£50

GURU GURU
73	Atlantic K 50022	DON'T CALL US WE'LL CALL YOU (LP)	£20
74	Atlantic K 50044	DANCE OF THE FLAMES (LP)	£20

GURU GURU/ULI TREPTE
80s	United Dairies UDT 07	LIVE 72 & 73 (LP, 1 side each)	£18

GURU JOSH
90	Deconstruction PT 44140	Freaky Dreamer (12")	£15

GURUS
66	United Artists UP 1160	Blue Snow Night/Come Girl	£30

GUS GUS
97	4AD DAD 7005	POLYDISTORTION (2-LP, inners)	£50
99	4AD CAD 9006	THIS IS NORMAL (2-LP)	£40
00	4AD CAD 2K02	GUS GUS VS T WORLD (2-LP)	£30
02	Underwater H20 020 LP	ATTENTION (2-LP)	£30

JOHNNY GUSTAFSON
65	Polydor 56022	Just To Be With You/Sweet Day	£20
65	Polydor 56043	Take Me For A Little While/Make Me Your Number One	£35

(see also Big Three, Merseybeats, Quotations, Hard Stuff, Johnny & John, Ian Gillan Band, G-Force)

ARLO GUTHRIE
67	Reprise RSLP 6267	ALICE'S RESTAURANT (LP, mono)	£20
67	Reprise RLP 6267	ALICE'S RESTAURANT (LP, stereo)	£20
68	Reprise RSLP 6269	ARLO (LP)	£20

MINT VALUE £

69	Reprise RSLP 6346	RUNNING DOWN THE ROAD (LP)	£15
70	Reprise RSLP 6411	WASHINGTON COUNTY (LP)	£15

GWEN GUTHRIE
86	4th & Broadway BRW 52	Seventh Heaven/Getting Hot (p/s or die-cut sleeve)	£15
86	4th & Broadway BRW 1252	Seventh Heaven/It Should Have Been You/Getting Hot (12", p/s)	£40

WOODY GUTHRIE
51	Melodisc 1141	Ramblin' Blues/Talkin' Columbia Blues (78)	£15
55	Melodisc EPM7 84	HARD AIN'T IT HARD (EP)	£20
55	Melodisc EPM7 85	WORRIED MAN BLUES (EP)	£20
55	Melodisc EPM7 91	HEY LOLLY LOLLY (EP)	£20
55	Melodisc MLP 12-106	MORE SONGS BY GUTHRIE (LP)	£40
58	Topic 12T 31	BOUND FOR GLORY (LP)	£35
64	RCA RD 7642	DUST BOWL BALLADS (LP)	£25

GUTTERSNIPE ARMY
89	Link LUNK LP 076	NEVER DIE (LP)	£50

GUTTERSNYPES
94	Liberty Grooves LIB004	The Trials Of Life (Green vinyl radio edit) (12")	£15
94	Liberty Grooves LIB005	The Trials Of Life (White vinyl, promo version, limited edition, personalised by band) (12")	£25
94	Liberty Grooves LIB006	The Trials Of Life (Clear vinyl, instrumentals) (12")	£15

GUV'NERS
63	Piccadilly 7N 35117	Let's Make A Habit Of This/The Kissing Had To Stop	£15

(see also Jess Conrad, Dickie Pride, Nelson Keene)

BARRY GUY
76	Incus INCUS 22	STATEMENTS V-XI FOR DOUBLE BASS AND VIOLONE (LP)	£50

(see also Derek Bailey Barry Guy & Paul Rutherford)

BUDDY GUY
65	Chess CRS 8004	Let Me Love You Baby/Ten Years Ago	£20
68	Fontana TF 951	Mary Had A Little Lamb/Sweet Little Angel	£18
65	Chess CRE 6004	CRAZY MUSIC (EP)	£40
68	Vanguard SVRL 19001	COMING AT YOU (LP)	£40
68	Vanguard SVRL. 19002	A MAN AND THE BLUES (LP)	£40
68	Vanguard SVRL 19004	BLUES TODAY (LP)	£40
69	Vanguard SVRL 19008	THIS IS BUDDY GUY! (LP)	£40
69	Vanguard SVRL 79290	HOT AND COOL (LP)	£40
69	Chess CRL(S) 4546	I LEFT MY BLUES IN SAN FRANCISCO (LP)	£30
69	Python KM 2	FIRST TIME I MET THE BLUES (LP)	£70
70	Harvest SHSP 4006	BUDDY AND THE JUNIORS (LP, with Junior Mance & Junior Wells)	£65
70	Red Lightnin' RL 001	IN THE BEGINNING (LP)	£15
72	Atlantic K 40240	PLAY THE BLUES (LP, with Junior Wells)	£20
73	Vanguard VSD 79323	HOLD THAT PLANE (LP)	£20

(see also Junior Wells, Eddie Boyd/Buddy Guy)

GUYS
69	Tepee TPR SP 1001	You Go Your Way/Little Girl	£20

GEORGE GUZMAN
68	London HA 8384	INTRODUCING GEORGE GUZMAN (LP, mono)	£100
68	London SH 8384	INTRODUCING GEORGE GUZMAN (LP)	£100

GWAR
91	Metal Blade ZORRO 37	AMERICA MUST BE DESTROYED (LP)	£60

GWENNO
14	Peski PESK1030	Y DYFF OLAF (LP)	£20
15	Heavenly HVNLP 118B	Y DYDD OLAF (LP, CD)	£18

(see also Pipettes)

GWIGWIS BAND
67	77 AFRO/101	KWELA (LP)	£100

GXFR
18	Daupe DM SP 018	DON'T GET SCARED NOW (LP, numbered on grey vinyl, 150 only)	£200
16	Daupe DM SP 018	DON'T GET SCARED NOW (LP, numbered on black vinyl, 230 copies)	£200
16	Daupe DM SP 018	DON'T GET SCARED NOW (LP, numbered with obi strip, 20 only)	£250

KIKI GYAN
77	PVP ILPS 7777	AFRO REGGAE (LP)	£40
12	Soundway SNDWLP047	24 HOURS IN A DISCO 1978-82 (LP)	£20

(see also Osibisa, Kofi & Kiki)

GYGAFO
75	Look LK SP 6061	Broken Smiles/Wing	£40
89	Holyground HG 1155	LEGEND OF THE KINGFISHER (LP, 160 copies only, posthumously designed semi-gatefold sleeve with insert)	£60

GYMSLIPS
83	Abstract ABT 006	ROCKING WITH THE RENEES (LP, with insert)	£20

GYPP
79	Shy Talk AC 1065	YAAH EP: Marigoldz/Titania/Sister Darling (p/s)	£20

(see also Martin Newell, Cleaners From Venus, Brotherhood Of Lizards)

GYPPO
79	United Artists UP36510	High Rise Love/Free Enterprise	£100

GYPSIES
67   CBS 201785   Jerk It/Diamonds, Rubies, Gold And Fame £40
(see also Flirtations)

GYPSY (1)
71   United Artists UAG 29155   GYPSY (LP)..£15
72   United Artists UAS 29420   BRENDA AND THE RATTLESNAKE (LP) £15
(see also Legay)

GYPSY (2)
84   Private Pressing   We Came To Be Free/Get It Right £50

H

HABIBIYYA
72   Island HELP 7   IF MAN BUT KNEW (LP, with inner sleeve, black/silver label, pink 'i' logo) £40
07   Sunbeam SBR2LP5043   IF MAN BUT KNEW (2-LP, reissue)...£18
(see also Mighty Baby)

HABITS
66   Decca F 12348   Elbow Baby/Need You...£40
(see also Charles Dickens, Nice, Brian Davison)

HACKENSACK
71   Polydor 2383 263   UP THE HARD WAY (LP, with inner sleeve) £100
74   Zel UZ 003   HERE COMES THE JUDGE (LP, private pressing, as Hack & Sack) £125
(see also Megaton, Tiger [U.K.], Samson)

MARIKA HACKMAN
13   Dirty Hits DH0031   THAT IRON TASTE (LP, gatefold, blue vinyl, numbered) £30

VERNON HADDOCK'S JUBILEE LOVELIES
65   Columbia SX 6011   VERNON HADDOCK'S JUBILEE LOVELIES (LP)..............................£125

IDA HAENDEL
58   HMV CLP 1021   IDA HAENDEL WITH GERALD MOORE AT THE PIANO (LP)...............£800
59   HMV CLP 1032   BRAHMS VIOLIN CONCERTO (LP) £250
60   HMV DLP 1190   TCHAIKOVSKY VIOLIN CONCERTO (LP) £450
77   HMV ASD 3352   A CLASSICAL RECITAL (LP) £150
80   EMI ASD 3785   BRAVISSIMA! (LP) £200

HAFLER TRIO
84   Doublevision DVR 4   BANG! - AN OPEN LETTER (LP, with insert)....................................£25
86   Charrm 3   THREE WAYS OF SAYING TWO - THE NETHERLANDS LECTURES (LP, stickered sleeve with booklet)..£25
86   Touch T 05   THE SEA ORG (10", 'audio/visual' package with booklet) £20
(see also Cabaret Voltaire)

HAGAR THE WOMB
84   Abstract Sounds 12ABS 029 FUNNERY IN THE NUNNERY (12" EP) £15
84   Mortarhate MORT 2   WORD OF THE WOMB (12" EP) £15

HA HA MONO
82   SRTS 82 CUS 1481   Run For Miles/Snakes (p/s)..£60

PAUL HAIG
98   Syntactic NICE 49   Listen To Me (Looking/Irresponsible) (handmade p/s, with Billy McKenzie) £20
81   Rational no cat. no.   DRAMA (cassette mini-LP)...£15
(see also Josef K, Rhythm Of Life, Billy McKenzie)

ROBERT HAIGH
85   Laylah LAY 09   JULIET OF THE SPIRITS EP (12")..£25
86   Laylah LAY 21   MUSIC FROM THE ANTE CHAMBER EP (12") £25
87   United Dairies UDT 034   THE BEST OF ROBERT HAIGH (cassette) £20
88   United Dairies UD 026   VALENTINE OUT OF SEASON (LP) £40
89   Le Rey LR 103   A WALTZ IN PLAIN C (CD)..£50
(see also SEMA)

HAIM
13   Secret 7" S79   Better Off (100 only, each with unique art sleeve)........................£30

NORMAN HAINES (BAND)
70   Parlophone R 5871   Daffodil/Autumn Mobile (as Norman Haynes Band) £25
71   Parlophone SPSR 338   Den Of Iniquity/Everything You See (Mr. Armageddon) (promo only) £60
72   Parlophone R 5960   Give It To You Girl/Elaine (as Norman Haines) £20
71   Parlophone PCS 7130   DEN OF INIQUITY (LP, black/silver label with boxed logo).........£1250
94   Shoestring BL001   DEN OF INIQUITY (LP, reissue)...£30
14   Acid Nightmare ANM 011   DEN OF INIQUITY (LP, reissue, 400 only) £20
(see also Avalanche, Brumbeats, The Dog That Bit People, Locomotive)

HAIR (1)
69   Pye NSPL 18314   RAVE UP (LIVE FROM THE SHAFTESBURY THEATRE) (LP)................£70
(see also Alex Harvey, Hairband)

HAIR (2)
70   Columbia SCX 6452   HAIRPIECE (LP, black/silver labels with boxed logo) £350

HAIRBAND

| 69 | Bell BLL 1076 | Big Louis/Travelling Song | £18 |
| 69 | Bell SBLL 69 | BAND ON THE WAGON (LP, blue/silver/black label with "sold in on the U.K..." text) | £60 |

(see also Alex Harvey, Hair)

HAIR & SKIN TRADING COMPANY

| 94 | Beggars Banquet BBQLP 141 | OVER VALENCE (LP with free 12") | £15 |

I. HALCIDEONS AND I. JARZIF

| 78 | Greensleeves GRED 7 | Rise Ethiopians/Signs Of The Messiah (12") | £40 |

WILLIE 'BEAVER' HALE

| 01 | Soul Brother 12-SBT-3 | Groove On/Let The Good Times Roll (12" reissue) | £18 |
| 80 | T.K. S TKR 83392 | BEAVER FEVER (LP) | £15 |

BILL HALEY (& HIS COMETS)

78s

53	London L 1190	Crazy Man, Crazy/Whatcha Gonna Do (as Bill Haley with Haley's Comets) (gold label lettering)	£30
53	London L 1216	Pat-A-Cake/Fractured (as Bill Haley with Haley's Comets, gold label)	£30
54	London HL 1190	Crazy Man, Crazy/Whatcha Gonna Do (as Bill Haley with Haley's Comets) (reissue, silver label lettering)	£20
54	London HL 1216	Pat-A-Cake/Fractured (reissue, silver label lettering, as Bill Haley with Haley's Comets)	£20
55	London HL 8142	Green Tree Boogie/Sundown Boogie	£15
55	London HLF 8161	Farewell, So Long, Goodbye/I'll Be True	£18
55	London HLF 8194	Ten Little Indians/Rocking Chair On The Moon	£15
56	Melodisc 1376	I'm Gonna Dry Ev'ry Tear With A Kiss/Why Do I Cry Over You	£40
57	London HLF 8371	Rock The Joint/Yes Indeed!	£15
58	Brunswick 05735	Mary, Mary Lou/It's A Sin	£15
58	Brunswick 05742	Skinny Minnie/How Many	£15
58	Brunswick 05752	Lean Jean/Don't Nobody Move	£15
58	Brunswick 05766	Whoa Mabel!/Chiquita Linda	£15
59	Brunswick 05788	I Got A Woman/Charmaine	£20
59	Brunswick 05805	Shaky/Caldonia	£20
59	Brunswick 05810	Joey's Song/Ooh! Look-A There, Ain't She Pretty	£20

SINGLES

54	Brunswick 05317	(We're Gonna) Rock Around The Clock/Thirteen Women (gold lettering on label)	£60
54	Brunswick 05317	(We're Gonna) Rock Around The Clock/Thirteen Women (silver lettering on label)	£25
54	Brunswick 05338	Shake, Rattle And Roll/A.B.C. Boogie (gold lettering on label)	£40
54	Brunswick 05338	Shake, Rattle And Roll/A.B.C. Boogie (silver lettering on label)	£20
55	Brunswick 05373	Happy Baby/Dim, Dim The Lights (I Want Some Atmosphere) (gold lettering on label)	£40
55	Brunswick 05373	Happy Baby/Dim, Dim The Lights (I Want Some Atmosphere) (silver lettering on label)	£20
55	Brunswick 05405	Birth Of The Boogie/Mambo Rock (gold lettering on label)	£40
55	Brunswick 05405	Birth Of The Boogie/Mambo Rock (silver lettering on label)	£20
55	London HL 8142	Green Tree Boogie/Sundown Boogie (gold lettering on label)	£150
55	London HL 8142	Green Tree Boogie/Sundown Boogie (silver lettering on label)	£50
55	Brunswick 05453	Two Hound Dogs/Razzle Dazzle (gold lettering on label)	£40
55	Brunswick 05453	Two Hound Dogs/Razzle Dazzle (silver lettering on label)	£20
55	London HLF 8161	Farewell, So Long, Goodbye/I'll Be True (gold lettering on label)	£100
55	London HLF 8161	Farewell, So Long, Goodbye/I'll Be True (silver lettering on label)	£50
55	London HLF 8194	Ten Little Indians/Rocking Chair On The Moon (gold lettering on label)	£100
55	London HLF 8194	Ten Little Indians/Rocking Chair On The Moon (silver lettering on label)	£50
55	Brunswick 05509	Rock-A-Beatin' Boogie/Burn That Candle (gold lettering on label)	£40
55	Brunswick 05509	Rock-A-Beatin' Boogie/Burn That Candle (silver lettering on label)	£20
56	Brunswick 05530	See You Later, Alligator/The Paper Boy (On Main Street, USA) (gold lettering on label)	£40
56	Brunswick 05530	See You Later, Alligator/The Paper Boy (On Main Street, USA) (silver lettering on label)	£20
56	Brunswick 05565	The Saints Rock 'N' Roll/R-O-C-K	£15
56	Brunswick 05582	Rockin' Through The Rye/Hot Dog Buddy Buddy	£15
56	Brunswick 05615	Rip It Up/Teenager's Mother	£15
56	Brunswick 05616	Rudy's Rock/Blue Comet Blues	£15
57	Brunswick 05640	Don't Knock The Rock/Calling All Comets	£15
57	Brunswick 05641	Hook, Line And Sinker/Goofin' Around	£15
57	London HLF 8371	Rock The Joint/Yes Indeed! (gold label)	£150
57	London HLF 8371	Rock The Joint/Yes Indeed! (silver label)	£50
57	Brunswick 05658	Forty Cups Of Coffee/Choo Choo Ch'Boogie	£15
57	Brunswick 05688	(You Hit The Wrong Note) Billy Goat/Rockin' Rollin' Rover	£15
57	Brunswick 05719	Miss You/The Dipsy Doodle	£15
58	Brunswick 05735	Mary, Mary Lou/It's A Sin	£15
58	Brunswick 05742	Skinny Minnie/How Many	£20
58	Brunswick 05752	Lean Jean/Don't Nobody Move	£15
58	Brunswick 05766	Whoa Mabel!/Chiquita Linda	£15
59	Brunswick 05788	I Got A Woman/Charmaine	£15
59	Brunswick 05805	Shaky/Caldonia	£15
59	Brunswick 05810	Joey's Song/Ooh! Look-A There, Ain't She Pretty	£15

(The above 45s were originally issued with triangular centres; later round centres are worth two-thirds of these values.)

64	Brunswick 05910	Happy Baby/Birth Of The Boogie	£15
64	Brunswick 05917	The Green Door/Yeah! She's Evil	£15
68	Pye International 7N 25455	Crazy Man, Crazy/Dance With A Dolly (With A Hole In Her Stocking)	£15

EXPORT SINGLES

| 54 | Decca BM 05317 | (We're Gonna) Rock Around The Clock/Thirteen Women | £60 |

55	Decca BM 05405	Birth Of The Boogie/Mambo Rock..£40
55	Decca BM 05509	Rock-A-Beatin' Boogie/Burn That Candle..£40
56	Decca BM 05530	See You Later Alligator/The Paper Boy (On Main Street, USA).........................£40
56	Decca BM 31163	The Saints Rock 'N' Roll/R-O-C-K...£30
56	Decca BM 31164	Rockin' Through The Rye/Hot Dog Buddy Buddy...£30
56	Decca BM 31171	Rip It Up/Teenager's Mother..£30
57	Decca BM 31174	Don't Knock The Rock/Choo Choo Ch'Boogie...£30

EPs

55	Brunswick OE 9129	DIM, DIM THE LIGHTS (gold lettering label, 'stage' p/s, various colours).........................£40
55	Brunswick OE 9129	DIM, DIM THE LIGHTS (silver lettering label, 'stage' or 'cameo' p/s)...........................£25
55	London REF 1031	ROCK AND ROLL...£50
56	London REF 1049	LIVE IT UP PART 1...£30
56	London REF 1050	LIVE IT UP PART 2...£30
56	Brunswick OE 9214	ROCK AND ROLL WITH BILL HALEY £25
56	Brunswick OE 9250	ROCK AROUND THE CLOCK £20
56	Brunswick OE 9250	ROCK AROUND THE CLOCK (round centre, different sleeve, same design as "Bill Haley" [OE 9459])..£35
56	London REF 1058	LIVE IT UP PART 3...£35
56	Brunswick OE 9278	ROCK'N'ROLL STAGE SHOW PART 1...£20
56	Brunswick OE 9279	ROCK'N'ROLL STAGE SHOW PART 2...£20
56	Brunswick OE 9280	ROCK'N'ROLL STAGE SHOW PART 3...£20
58	Brunswick OE 9349	ROCKIN' THE OLDIES PART 1..£25
58	Brunswick OE 9350	ROCKIN' THE OLDIES PART 2..£25
58	Brunswick OE 9351	ROCKIN' THE OLDIES PART 3..£25

(Originally issued with triangular centres, later round-centre copies are worth two-thirds this value.)

59	Brunswick OE 9446	ROCKIN' AROUND THE WORLD...£60
59	Brunswick OE 9459	BILL HALEY..£50

(The above EPs were originally issued with triangular centres, later round-centre copies are worth half to two-thirds these values.)

60	Warners WEP 6001	BILL HALEY AND HIS COMETS £30
61	Warners WEP 6025	BILL HALEY'S JUKE BOX (mono)..£30
61	Warners WSEP 6025	BILL HALEY'S JUKE BOX (stereo)...£40
64	Warners WEP 6133	BILL HALEY VOLUME 1..£30
64	Warners WEP 6136	BILL HALEY VOLUME 2..£30

ALBUMS

55	London H-APB 1042	LIVE IT UP (10", gold lettering on label)..£80
55	London H-APB 1042	LIVE IT UP (10", silver lettering on label) £25
56	Brunswick LAT 8117	ROCK AROUND THE CLOCK £30
56	Brunswick LAT 8139	ROCK AND ROLL STAGE SHOW..£30
57	London HA-F 2037	ROCK THE JOINT...£80
57	Brunswick LAT 8219	ROCKIN' THE OLDIES..£60
57	Brunswick LAT 8268	ROCKIN' THE JOINT..£60
59	Brunswick LAT 8295	BILL HALEY'S CHICKS (mono)..£60
59	Brunswick STA 3011	BILL HALEY'S CHICKS (stereo)...£70
60	Brunswick LAT 8326	STRICTLY INSTRUMENTAL...£40
62	Columbia 33SX 1460	TWISTIN' KNIGHTS AT THE ROUNDTABLE (LIVE!)...£30
65	Warner Bros W 1391	BILL HALEY'S JUKE BOX £20

(see also Kingsmen, Jodimars, Nick Nantos & His Fireballs)

HALF JAPANESE

81	Armageddon ABOX 1	1/2 GENTLEMEN NOT BEASTS (3-LP box set with poster, booklet & lyric insert)..............£50
81	Armageddon ARM 7	LOUD (LP)...£15

HALFBREED

75	United Artists UAG 29877	HALFBREED (LP, fold out sleeve)..£20

HALFORD

00	Metal Is MISLP 001	RESURRECTION (LP)..£100

(see also Judas Priest)

HALF PINT

85	Greensleeves GRED 178	Freedom Fighter/Hold On (12")..£25

HAL HOPPERS

54	London HL 8107	More Love/Do Nothin' Blues £40
55	London HL 8129	Mother Of Pearl/Baby I've Had It £40

AUDREY HALL AND DON EVANS

86	Trojan TRLS229	THE DYNAMIC DUO (LP) £20

DEREK HALL & MIKE COOPER

60s	Kennet KRS 766	OUT OF THE SHADES (EP) £35

ERASMUS HALL

96	Westbound SEWD 112	YOUR LOVE IS MY DESIRE (LP, reissue)..£40

GERRI HALL

66	Sue WI 4026	Who Can I Run To/I Lost A Key (unissued) £0
04	Grapevine 2000 143	Who Can I Run To/JADES: Lucky Fellow (reissue)..£18

JIM HALL

59	Vogue LAE 12072	JAZZ GUITAR (LP)..£50
64	Fontana FJL 121	THE WINNER! (LP, reissue of Jazz Guitar) £18

(see also Modest Jazz Trio)

JIMMY GRAY HALL

74	Epic EPC 2312	Be That Way/Possessed By The Moon..£20

MINT VALUE £

LARRY HALL
60	Parlophone R 4625	Sandy/Lovin' Tree	£15
62	Salvo SLO 1811	Ladder Of Love/The One You Left Behind (99 copies only)	£20

TERRY HALL AND MUSHTAQ
03	Honest Jons HJRLP5	THE HOUR OF TWO LIGHTS (2-LP, inners)	£18

(see also Specials)

RENE HALL'S ORCHESTRA
58	London HLU 8581	Twitchy/Flippin'	£30

ROBIN HALL (& JIMMY MACGREGOR)
66	Island PBM	A Little Bit Of Paper/Going Into Paper (promotional p/s, given away by British Paper and Board Maker's)	£30

ROY HALL
56	Brunswick 05531	See You Later, Alligator/Don't Stop Now (gold label lettering)	£500
56	Brunswick 05531	See You Later, Alligator/Don't Stop Now (78)	£50
56	Brunswick 05555	Blue Suede Shoes/Luscious	£300
56	Brunswick 05627	Diggin' The Boogie/Three Alley Cats	£500
56	Brunswick 05627	Diggin' The Boogie/Three Alley Cats (78)	£50

TONY HALL
77	Free Reed FRR 012	FIELDVOLE MUSIC (LP, with insert)	£20

CHANCE HALLADAY
62	Vogue V 9203	John Henry/Thirteen Women	£25

HALLELUJAH SKIFFLE GROUP
58	Oriole CB 1429	I Saw The Light/A Closer Walk With Thee (with Clinton Ford)	£20

HALLIARD
67	Saga SOC 1058	IT'S THE IRISH IN ME (LP)	£30
68	Broadside BRO 106	THE HALLIARD AND JON RAVEN (LP)	£60
06	Olde Musick OMMCD 05	THE LAST GOODNIGHT! (CD)	£30

(see also Jon Raven, Nic Jones)

GERRY HALLOM
84	Fellside FE 036	A RUN A MINUTE (LP)	£15

HALLUCINOGEN
94	Dragonfly BFLT 14	Alpha Centauri/LSD (12")	£20
95	Dragonfly BFLT 29	LSD (Live Mix)/(LS Doof Remix)/(Original Version) (12")	£15
96	Twisted TWST 1	Deranger/Gamma Goblins (12")	£15
95	Dragonfly BFLLP 15	TWISTED (2-LP, yellow vinyl or one green and one pink or black vinyl)	£50
97	Twisted TWSLP1	THE LONE DERANGER (2-LP)	£100

JOHNNY HALLYDAY
62	Philips 432 813BE	ROCKING (EP)	£100
66	Vogue VRE 5013	JOHNNY HALLYDAY (EP)	£100
61	Philips BBL 7556	SINGS AMERICA'S ROCKIN' HITS (LP)	£100

HALOES
83	Thor 1003 S	THE HALOES (LP, 200 only)	£50

HALOS
61	London HLU 9424	Nag/Copycat	£30

STUART HAMBLEN
54	HMV 7MC 20	This Ole House/When My Lord Picks Up The 'Phone (export issue)	£25
56	HMV 7M 394	Hell Train/A Few Things To Remember	£15

CLAIRE HAMILL
72	Island ILPS 9182	ONE HOUSE LEFT STANDING (LP, lyric inner sleeve)	£40
73	Island ILPS 9225	OCTOBER (LP, gatefold sleeve, pink rim palm tree label)	£20
74	Konk KONK 101	STAGE DOOR JOHNNIES (LP, gatefold sleeve, blue label)	£15
75	Konk KONK 104	ABRACADABRA (LP, featuring Cafe Society, with lyric insert, blue label)	£15

(see also Cafe Society, Gary Numan, Wishbone Ash)

HAMILTON
79	Muscle SJP 806/MUS 001	Jet Set Girl/Methodone And Coconuts (500 only, no p/s)	£100

CHICO HAMILTON QUINTET
57	Decca DL 8614	SWEET SMELL OF SUCCESS (LP)	£20
58	Vogue LAE 12045	CHICO HAMILTON QUINTET IN HIFI (LP)	£20
64	HMV CLP 1807	MAN FROM TWO WORLDS (LP)	£20

EDWARD HAMILTON & ARABIANS
80	Grapevine GRP 134	Baby Don't You Weep/I'm Gonna Love You	£20

GAVIN HAMILTON
67	King KG 1067	It Won't Be The Same/Turn The Key Softly	£150

GEORGE HAMILTON IV
57	London HL 8361	A Rose And A Candy Bar/If You Don't Know (gold label print)	£125
57	London HL 8361	A Rose And A Candy Bar/If You Don't Know (later silver label print)	£30
59	HMV CLP 1263	SING ME A SAD SONG - A TRIBUTE TO HANK WILLIAMS (LP)	£20

GUY HAMILTON
65	HMV POP 1418	A Lifetime Of Loneliness/Give The Game Away	£15

(see also Neil Christian)

(KINGSIZE) HAMILTON & PLATTERMEN
66	Emerald MD 1048	Shake/I Got To Know	£25

M. HAMILTON

67	Ska Beat JB 265	Something Gotta Ring/DENNIS LYNWARD & HIS GROUP: Jazz Session	£35

ROY HAMILTON (1)

58	Fontana H 113	Don't Let Go/The Right To Love	£25
58	Fontana H 143	Crazy Feelin'/In A Dream	£15
59	Fontana H 180	Pledging My Love/My One And Only Love	£15
59	Fontana H 193	I Need Your Loving/Somewhere Along The Way	£15
61	Fontana H 298	You Can Have Her/Abide With Me	£15
61	Fontana H 320	You're Gonna Need Magic/To The One I Love	£15
63	MGM MGM 1210	Theme From "The VIPs"/The Sinner	£15
64	MGM MGM 1251	There She Is/The Panic Is On	£175
64	MGM MGM 1251	There She Is/The Panic Is On (DJ copy)	£600
65	MGM MGM 1268	A Thousand Tears Ago/Sweet Violet	£15
66	RCA RCA 1500	And I Love Her/Tore Up Over You	£15
69	Deep Soul DS 9106	Dark End Of The Street/100 Years Ago	£40
59	Fontana TFE 17160	WHY FIGHT THE FEELING (EP)	£20
60	Fontana TFE 17163	THE MOOD MOVES (EP)	£20
61	Fontana TFE 17170	COME OUT SWINGING (EP)	£20
63	Columbia 33SX 1473	GREATEST HITS (LP)	£40
64	MGM MGM-C 960	WARM SOUL (LP)	£60

ROY HAMILTON (2)

83	HBS K CAP 1	Turn Up The Music/Instrumental Version (12", with Capiche)	£20

RUSS HAMILTON

58	Oriole MG 20031	WE WILL MAKE LOVE (LP)	£20

HAMILTON & MOVEMENT

65	Polydor BM 56026	Really Saying Something/I Won't See You Tonight	£80
67	CBS 202573	I'm Not The Marrying Kind/My Love Belongs To You	£40

HAMLET

67	Decca F12571	She Won't See The Light/Go Play In Your Own Yard	£20

HAMLETT

72	Pye 7N45171	Where'd The Day Go/Vampire Man	£20

HAMLINS

67	Coxsone CS 7021	Trying To Keep A Good Man Down/SUMMERTAIRS: Oh My Darling (actually by Bob & Rita Marley)	£90
67	Coxsone CS 7022	Soul And Inspiration/ETHIOPIANS: Let's Get Together	£35
68	Coxsone CS 7048	Sentimental Reasons/SOUL VENDORS: Last Waltz	£200
68	Blue Cat BS 115	Sugar And Spice/SOUL VENDORS: Mercy Mercy Mercy	£200

(see also Minstrels)

JACK HAMMER

61	Oriole CB 1634	Young Only Once/Juliette	£15
62	Oriole CB 1753	Don't Let Baby Know/Number 2539	£15
66	Polydor 56091	Thanks/Love Ladder	£20
67	Polydor 56158	Joe Poor Loves Daphne Rich/Ode To A Discotheque	£50
69	United Artists UP 35029	What Greater Love/The Mason Dixon Line	£30
71	Youngblood B 1023	Swim/Colour Combination (solid centre)	£60
63	Oriole PS 40020	HAMMER + BEAT = TWIST (LP)	£80
66	Polydor 582001	BRAVE NEW WORLD (LP)	£120

HAMMER (2)

85	Ebony EBON 29	CONTRACT WITH HELL (LP)	£15

HAMMERHEAD

81	Linden Sounds LS 009	Time Will Tell/Lonely Man (p/s)	£60

HAMMERS (JAMAICA)

70	Gas GAS 162	Hotter Than Scorcher/Someday Could See You	£40

(see also Joan Ross)

HAMMERSMITH GORILLAS

74	Penny Farthing PEN 849	You Really Got Me/Leavin' 'Ome (p/s)	£25
77	Raw RAW 2	You Really Got Me/Leavin' 'Ome (reissue, company sleeve)	£15

(see also Gorillas, Helter Skelter, Jesse Hector)

PETER HAMMILL

75	Charisma CB 245	Birthday Special/Shingle Song (as Rikki Nadir)	£20
77	Charisma PH 001	Crying Wolf/This Side Of The Looking Glass (promo only)	£40
79	Charisma PH 339	The Polaroid (as Rikki Nadir)/The Old School Tie	£15
86	Foundry FOUND 312	Painting By Numbers (Extended)/You Hit Me Where I Live/Shell (12", p/s)	£15
71	Charisma CAS 1037	FOOL'S MATE (LP, textured gatefold, pink 'scroll' label)	£100
73	Charisma CAS 1067	CHAMELEON IN THE SHADOW OF THE NIGHT (LP, gatefold, large 'Mad Hatter' label)	£60
73	Charisma CAS 1037	FOOL'S MATE (LP, reissue, 'Mad Hatter' label, gatefold)	£40
74	Charisma CAS 1083	THE SILENT CORNER AND THE EMPTY STAGE (LP, gatefold, printed inner, large 'Mad Hatter' label)	£40
74	Charisma CAS 1089	IN CAMERA (LP, with inner sleeve, small 'Mad Hatter' label)	£20
75	Charisma CAS 1099	NADIR'S BIG CHANCE (LP, laminated sleeve, printed inner, small 'Mad Hatter' label)	£30
77	Charisma CAS 1125	OVER (LP, printed inner, small 'Mad Hatter' label)	£30
78	Charisma CAS 1137	THE FUTURE NOW (LP, fold-out lyric insert)	£20
79	Charisma CAS 1146	pH7 (LP, printed inner)	£20
80	S-Type PHS 1	A BLACK BOX (LP, fold-out lyric insert ordered separately)	£20
81	Virgin V 2205	SITTING TARGETS (LP, lyric insert, £3.99 sticker to top right)	£20

MINT VALUE £

82	Naive Records NAVL 1	ENTER K (LP, printed inner)	£15
82	Sofa Sound SS4	LOOPS AND REELS (Cassette, mail-order only)	£15
83	Naive NAVL 3	PATIENCE (LP, lyric insert)	£15
84	Charisma CAS 1166	THE LOVE SONGS (LP, insert)	£20
85	Foundry FONDL 1	THE MARGIN (LIVE) (2LP, as Peter Hammill & K Group, gatefold)	£25
86	Foundry FONDL 3	SKIN (LP, printed inner)	£15
86	Virgin V 2409	AND CLOSE AS THIS (LP, lyric insert available by mail order)	£15
88	Red Hot ZCRH 102	SPUR OF THE MOMENT (with Guy Evans) (Cassette)	£20
88	Enigma ENVLP 512	IN A FOREIGN TOWN (LP, printed inner)	£15
90	Enigma ENVLP 1003	OUT OF WATER (LP, lyric insert)	£20
91	Some Bizzare SBZ-LP 007	THE FALL OF THE HOUSE OF USHER (2LP, printed inners, edition of 500)	£50
95	Strange Fruit SFRCD 136	THE PEEL SESSIONS (CD)	£30
11	Fie! FIE 9135	PNO GTR VOX BOX (EIGHTY-FOUR LIVE PERFORMANCES) (7CD box set, booklet)	£200
14	E. Antenna EANTLP 1026	OTHER WORLD (with Gary Lucas) (LP, gatefold, ltd. ed.)	£20
14	Fie! FIE 9137V	. . . ALL THAT MIGHT HAVE BEEN . . . (LP, printed inner)	£25
14	Fie! FIE 9137X	. . . ALL THAT MIGHT HAVE BEEN . . . (3CD box set, booklet)	£30
17	Fie! FIE 9138V	FROM THE TREES (LP, 4-panel lyric insert)	£25
19	Fie! FIE 9140	NOT YET NOT NOW (8CD box set, booklet)	£80
19	Ataraxia ATX 3LP	IN AMAZONIA (with Isildurs Band) (LP, gatefold, green vinyl)	£40
20	fsoldigital.com LP TOT 79	WE PERSUADE OURSELVES WE ARE IMMORTAL (with Amorphous Androgynous) (LP, printed inner)	£25
21	Fie! FIE 9141V	IN TRANSLATION (LP, printed inner, white vinyl)	£25
21	Ataraxia ATX 4LP	IN DISEQUILIBRIUM (with Isildurs Bane) (LP, gatefold, red vinyl)	£35

(see also Van Der Graaf Generator, Rikki Nadir, Colin Scot, Amorphous Androgynous, Robert Fripp)

JOHN HAMMOND

65	Fontana TF 560	Baby Won't You Tell Me/I Love The Life I Live	£15
68	Atlantic 584 190	Brown Eyed Handsome Man/Crosscut Saw	£18
64	Fontana TFL 6046	BIG CITY BLUES (LP)	£60
65	Fontana TFL 6059	SO MANY ROADS (LP)	£50
71	CBS 64365	SOURCE POINT (LP)	£25
72	CBS 65051	I'M SATISFIED (LP)	£25
72	Vanguard VSD 11/12	THE BEST OF JOHN HAMMOND - SOUTHERN FRIED (2-LP)	£20

JOHNNY HAMMOND

93	Milestone MX 9062	GEARS (LP, reissue)	£35
01	Soul Brother LP SBCS 9	GAMBLERS LIFE (LP, reissue)	£18

BILLY HAMON

78	Bronze BRO 58	Butch Things/Amusement Arcade (p/s)	£20

SLIDE HAMPTON & HIS BAND

62	London HA-K/SH-K 8008	JAZZ WITH A TWIST (LP)	£18
62	London LZT-K 15225	LONDON JAZZ (LP, as Slide Hampton Octet)	£18

HERBIE HANCOCK

70	Warner Bros WB 7358	Fat Mama/Wiggle-Waggle	£15
66	MGM C(S) 78039	BLOW-UP (LP, soundtrack)	£80
71	Warner Bros WS 1834	FAT ALBERT ROTUNDA (LP)	£25
71	Warner Bros K 46077	MWANDISHI (LP)	£25
72	Warner Bros K 46164	CROSSINGS (LP)	£20
74	Warner Bros K 46039	FAT ALBERT ROTUNDA (LP, reissue)	£15
74	CBS 60193	THRUST (LP)	£20
74	CBS 80546	DEATH WISH (LP, soundtrack)	£15
74	CBS 65582	SEXTANT (LP)	£20
74	CBS 65928	HEADHUNTERS (LP)	£20
75	DJM 22008	KAWAIDA (LP, with Don Cherry)	£30
75	CBS 69185	MAN-CHILD (LP)	£20
76	CBS 81591	SECRETS (LP)	£20
77	Blue Note BNS 40020	MAIDEN VOYAGE (LP, reissue)	£15
77	Blue Note BNS 40025	SPEAK LIKE A CHILD (LP, reissue)	£15
78	CBS 82240	SUNLIGHT (LP)	£20
79	CBS 83491	FEETS DON'T FAIL ME NOW (LP)	£15
80	CBS 84237	MONSTER (LP)	£15
80	CBS 84638	MR. HANDS (LP)	£20
81	CBS 85144	MAGIC WINDOWS (LP)	£20
82	CBS 32474	LITE ME UP (LP)	£15
83	CBS 25540	FUTURE SHOCK (LP)	£15
96	Premier 72438 5228018	BLOW-UP (LP, reissue, soundtrack)	£15
97	Blue Note ST 46339	MAIDEN VOYAGE (LP, reissue)	£15
01	Transparent HERBIE LP 1	FUTURE 2 FUTURE (2-LP)	£20
07	Verve 0602517468344	RIVER: THE JONI LETTERS (2-LP)	£20

(see also Headhunters, Kimiko Kasai)

OWEN HAND

61	Transatlantic TRA 127	SOMETHING NEW (LP)	£100
66	Transatlantic TRA	I LOVED A LASS (LP)	£80

JOHNNY HANDLE

75	Topic 12TS 270	THE COLLIER LAD (LP)	£15

(see also Louise Killen & Johnny Handle, High Level Ranters)

HANDSOME BOY MODELLING SCHOOL

99	Tommy Boy TBV 1258	SO...HOWS YOUR GIRL? (2-LP)	£60

04	Eketra 7559629411	**WHITE PEOPLE** (2-LP)..	£18

HANDSOME BEASTS
81	Heavy Metal HEAVY 1	**All Riot Now/Mark Of The Beast** (p/s).......................................	£25
82	Heavy Metal HMRLP 2	**BEASTIALITY** (LP)..	£20

WAYNE HANDY
58	London HL 8547	**Say Yeah/Could It Be** (B-side with King Sisters)........................	£200
58	London HL 8547	**Say Yeah/Could It Be** (B-side with King Sisters) (78)................	£15

HANG DAVID
90	Vacant HANG 01	**HANG DAVID** (12" EP, p/s)..	£18

JOSH HANNA
66	Decca F 12532	**Shut Your Mouth/Sweet To My Soul**....................................	£20

ROSS HANNAMAN
67	Columbia DB 8288	**1969/Probably On A Thursday** (with p/s)................................	£50
67	Columbia DB 8288	**1969/Probably On A Thursday**..	£40
74	Bellwood BW1	**A NIGHT AT FACTOTUM** (LP, 100 only, as John and Rosalind).........	£20

MARTIN HANNETT
80	Factory FACT 14C	**First Aspect Of The Same Thing/Second Aspect Of The Same Thing** (flexi, most included first/second pressing of THE RETURN OF THE DURUTTI COLUMN LP).........	£25

(see also Durutti Column)

HANNIBAL
74	B&C HB 1	**Winds Of Change/Winter**..	£15
70	B&C CAS 1022	**HANNIBAL** (LP, gatefold sleeve)...	£200

(see also Wizzard)

LANCE HANNIBAL
69	Blue Cat BS 148	**Read The News/RECO & RHYTHM ACES: Return Of The Bullet**	£45

(see also Sugar Simone, Les Foster)

JERRY HANSEN & RAMBLERS DANCE BAND
67	Decca WAP 24	**DANCE WITH THE RAMBLERS** (LP)..	£25

HANSON
73	Manticore K43507	**NOW HEAR THIS** (LP, gatefold sleeve)..................................	£20

HANSON & KARLSSON
67	Polydor 184 196	**SWEDISH UNDERGROUND** (LP)..	£15
69	Polydor 462 60	**MONUMENT** (LP)..	£60
69	Polydor 583 564	**MAN AT THE MOON** (LP)...	£60

(see also Bo Hansson)

BO HANSSON
72	Charisma CAS 1059	**LORD OF THE RINGS** (LP, insert, large 'Mad Hatter' label)............	£20
73	Charisma CAS 1073	**MAGICIANS'S HAT** (LP, large 'Mad Hatter' label).......................	£15
76	Charisma CAS 1113	**ATTIC THOUGHTS** (LP, gatefold. 'Mad Hatter' label)...................	£15

HAPPENINGS
67	Fontana TL 5383	**BYE BYE, SO LONG, FAREWELL ... SEE YOU IN SEPTEMBER** (LP)	£35
67	BT Puppy BTLP 1003	**PSYCLE** (LP)..	£40
68	BT Puppy BTLPS 1004	**GOLDEN HITS** (LP)..	£20

HAPPY CATS
78	Grapevine 110	**These Boots Are Made For Walkin'/Destroy That Boy**.................	£20

HAPPY CONFUSION
69	Penny Farthing PEN 706	**Yes Sir/Hereditary Impediment**	£15

HAPPY FAMILY
82	4AD AD 204	**Puritans/Innermost Thoughts/The Mistake** (p/s).....................	£15

(see also Josef K, Momus)

HAPPY MAGAZINE
68	Polydor 56233	**Satisfied Street/Do Right Woman Do Right Man**	£20

(see also Griffin)

HAPPY MONDAYS
87	Factory FACT 170	**SQUIRREL & G-MAN TWENTY FOUR HOUR PARTY PEOPLE PLASTIC FACE CARNT SMILE** (WHITE OUT) (LP, with "Desmond", 5,000 in plastic sleeve)................	£50
87	Factory FACT 170	**SQUIRREL & G-MAN TWENTY FOUR HOUR PARTY PEOPLE PLASTIC FACE CARNT SMILE** (WHITE OUT) (LP, with "Desmond")...	£30
87	Factory FACT 170c	**SQUIRREL & G-MAN TWENTY FOUR HOUR PARTY PEOPLE PLASTIC FACE CARNT SMILE** (WHITE OUT) (cassette)..	£20
87	Factory FACT 170c	**SQUIRREL & G-MAN TWENTY FOUR HOUR PARTY PEOPLE PLASTIC FACE CARNT SMILE** (WHITE OUT) (cassette, in box with insert).................................	£20
88	Factory FACT 220	**BUMMED** (LP, embossed cover)..	£25
90	Factory FACT 320	**PILLS 'N' THRILLS & BELLYACHES** (LP, withdrawn 'sweet wrapper' sleeve).........	£50
90	Factory FACT 320	**PILLS 'N' THRILLS & BELLYACHES** (LP)....................................	£20
91	Factory FACT 322	**LIVE** (2-LP)..	£25
92	Factory FACT 420	**...YES PLEASE** (LP, with inner and lyric insert)	£35
07	Sequel SEQLP 012	**UNCLE DYSFUNKTIONAL** (LP)	£35

(see also Black Grape)

HAPPY REFUGEES
84	Gymnasium HREF 002	**LAST CHANGE SALOON** (LP)...	£15

HAPSHASH & THE COLOURED COAT
69	Liberty LBF 15188	**Colinda/The Wall**...	£25
67	Minit MLS 40001E	**FEATURING THE HUMAN HOST AND THE HEAVY METAL KIDS** (LP, with Art, red vinyl (MLL 40001) **with insert**)...	£200

MINT VALUE £

| 67 | Minit MLS 40001E | **FEATURING THE HUMAN HOST AND THE HEAVY METAL KIDS** (LP, with Art, later pressing on black vinyl) | £60 |
| 69 | Liberty LBL/LBS 83212R | **THE WESTERN FLYER** (LP, with Mike Batt, blue label) | £100 |

(see also Tony McPhee, Warm Sounds, Marc Bolan/T. Rex, Art, Mike Batt)

HARBOUR FOLK
| 70 | Polydor 583 080 | **WAXIE'S DARGLE** (LP) | £30 |

HARD CORPS
84	Hard Corps HC 01	**Dirty/To Breathe** (12", hand-written white labels, numbered)	£20
85	Polydor HARDA 1	**Je Suis Passée** (Hard Mix)/(French Mix)/(Dub Mix) (12", gatefold PVC sleeve, various colours, with poster)	£20
85	Polydor HARD 2	**To Breathe/Metal And Flesh** (unreleased)	£20
85	Polydor HARDX 2	**To Breathe/Metal And Flesh/To Breathe** (Instrumental) (12", unreleased)	£25
90	Concrete P. CPPRODLP 011	**METAL AND FLESH** (LP, clear vinyl)	£35

(see also Craze)

HARD FEELINGS
| 21 | Domino WIGLP491XM | **HARD FEELINGS** (2LP, poster) | £20 |

(see also Joe Goddard, Hot Chip, 2Bears, Black Peaches)

HARD-FI
05	Necessary HARD 05	**Cash Machine** (Album Version)/**Cash Machine** (Roots Manuva Remix) (p/s, yellow vinyl)	£15
05	Necessary 5050467863675	**LIMITED 7" COLLECTOR'S PACK** (4x7" box set)	£30
05	Necessary 5046786911	**STARS OF CCTV** (2LP, gatefold, printed inners)	£100
05	Neccessary 5050467-8691-1-	**STARS OF CCTV** (2LP, gatefold, printed inners HMV exclusive with 7")	£110

HARD HORSE
| 71 | Dart ART 2001 | **Let It Ride/Hang Old Freddy** | £20 |
| 72 | Dart ART 2012 | (Get It) **Up Down/So Long I'm Moving On** | £30 |

(EDDIE) HARDIN & (PETE) YORK
69	Bell BLL 1064	**Tomorrow Today/Candlelight** (as Hardin-York)	£30
69	Bell SBLL 125	**TOMORROW TODAY** (LP, gatefold sleeve, blue/silver/black label, with "Sold in the U.K..." text)	£50
70	Bell SBLL 136	**HARDIN & YORK** (THE WORLD'S SMALLEST BIG BAND) (LP, gatefold)	£50
71	Bell SBLL 141	**FOR THE WORLD** (LP, existence unconfirmed)	£100
71	Decca SKL 5095	**FOR THE WORLD** (LP, reissue, blue/silver label with boxed logo)	£15

(see also Eddie Hardin, Pete York, Spencer Davis Group)

EDDIE HARDIN
| 72 | Decca TXS 106 | **HOME IS WHERE YOU FIND IT** (LP, gatefold sleeve, green/silver label) | £25 |

(see also Hardin-York, Spencer Davis Group, Roger Glover, Wizards Convention)

RICHARD HARDIN
| 61 | HMV POP 887 | **Jezebel/Temptation** | £25 |

(see also Cresters, Mike Sagar & Cresters)

TIM HARDIN
66	Verve (S)VLP 5018	**TIM HARDIN 1** (LP)	£40
67	Verve (S)VLP 6002	**TIM HARDIN 2** (LP)	£35
67	Atlantic 587/588 082	**THIS IS TIM HARDIN** (LP, plum label)	£25
68	Verve (S)VLP 6010	**LIVE IN CONCERT** (LP)	£30
69	Verve (S)VLP 6016	**TIM HARDIN 4** (LP)	£25
69	Verve (S)VLP 6019	**THE BEST OF** (LP)	£20
69	CBS (S/M) 63571	**SUITE FOR SUSAN MOORE AND DAMIAN** (LP, gatefold sleeve, mono/stereo)	£20
70	CBS 64335	**BIRD ON A WIRE** (LP)	£15
72	CBS 65209	**PAINTED HEAD** (LP)	£18
74	Verve 2683 048	**TIM HARDIN 1/2** (2-LP, gatefold reissue)	£20

(see also Eddie Hardin, Pete York, Spencer Davis Group)

MIKE HARDING
| 86 | Moonraker M 003 | **BOMBERS MOON** (LP) | £20 |

ROSEMARY HARDMAN (& BOB AXFORD)
69	Folk Heritage no cat. no.	**QUEEN OF HEARTS** (LP)	£125
71	Trailer LER 2075	**FIREBIRD** (LP)	£40
71	Trailer LER 3018	**SECOND SEASON CAME** (LP, by Rosemary Hardman & Bob Axford)	£20
75	Alida Star Cottage	**JERSEY BURGER** (LP)	£120

HARD MEAT
69	Island WIP 6066	**Rain/Burning Up Years**	£15
70	Warner Bros WS 1852	**HARD MEAT** (LP, gatefold sleeve with photo insert)	£150
70	Warner Bros WS 1879	**THROUGH A WINDOW** (LP, green label)	£150

HARDNOISE
89	White HNX001	**Untitled** (different recording to Music Of Life version - 300 pressed) (12")	£100
90	Music Of Life NOTE40	**Untitled** (12")	£15
91	Music Of Life NOTE48	**Serve Tea, Then Murder/Mice In The Presence Of The Lion** (12")	£15
12	Gibo GIB 001	**Pure Destructive Power** (12")	£20
13	Gibo GIB 002	**Pure Destructive Power** (12", green vinyl, 50 pressed)	£40
13	Gibo GIB 003	**Untitled Sessions** (12" EP, reissue)	£25

HARD RAIN
| 88 | London LONX 185 | **Diamonds/Monkey House/Diamonds** (7" Version) (12", p/s) | £15 |

HARD ROAD
| 79 | Goodstuff LP 1002 | **NO PROBLEM** (LP, private pressing) | £15 |

HARD ROCK
83	Inner Light DLT 103	Feel No Way/Version (12")	£80

HARD SKIN
07	No Future OI 28	New Age/FUCKED UP: Toronto FC (250 copies with fold-out sleeve, 50 with hard cover)	£15
96	Helen Of Oi H0031LP	HARD NUTS AND HARD CUNTS (LP, green vinyl)	£15
13	JT Classics CLASS 003	ON THE BALLS (LP)	£15
13	JT Classics CLASS 004	WHY DO BIRDS SUDDENLY APPEAR (LP)	£15

HARD STUFF
72	Purple PUR 103	Jay Time/The Orchestrator	£30
72	Purple TPSA 7505	BULLETPROOF (LP, gatefold sleeve)	£70
73	Purple TPSA 7507	BOLEX DEMENTIA (LP, textured gatefold sleeve)	£75

(see also Andromeda, Atomic Rooster, John Du Cann, Five Day Week Straw People, Johnny Gustafson, Bullet, Quatermass)

HARD TRAVELLIN'
71	Flams Ltd PR 1065	HARD TRAVELLIN' (LP, private pressing)	£150

HARDWARE (2)
85	Reset 12REST 7	Dance/Hey (12", p/s)	£15

FRANCOISE HARDY
70	United Artists UP 35105	Soon Is Slipping Away/The Bells Of Avignon (misspelling on label)	£50
66	Vogue VRE 5012	CHANTE EN ALLEMAND (EP)	£15
66	Vogue VRE 5015	L'AMITIE (EP)	£15
66	Vogue VRE 5017	MON AMIE LA ROSE (EP)	£15
67	Vogue VRE 5018	AUTUMN RENDEZVOUS (EP)	£15
64	Pye NPL 18094	FRANCOISE HARDY (LP)	£25
64	Pye NPL 18099	IN VOGUE (LP)	£25
65	Vogue VRL 3000	FRANCOISE HARDY (LP)	£25
66	Vogue VRL 3021	FRANCOISE HARDY (LP)	£25
66	Vogue VRL 3023	LE MEILLEUR DE FRANCOISE HARDY (LP)	£25
66	Vogue VRL 3025	SINGS IN ENGLISH (LP)	£30
67	Vogue VRL 3028	FRANCOISE (LP)	£25
67	Vogue VRL 3031	VOILA! FRANCOISE HARDY (LP)	£25
68	United Artists SULP 1191	IL N'Y A PAS D'AMOUR HEUREUX (LP)	£25
68	United Artists SULP 1207	EN ANGLAIS (LP)	£25
70	United Artists UAS 29046	ONE-NINE-SEVEN-ZERO (LP)	£40

LAVELL HARDY
68	Direction 58-3261	Don't Lose Your Groove/Women Of The World	£20

COLIN HARE
70	Penny Farthing PEN 736	Grannie, Grannie/For Where Have You Been	£20
71	Penny Farthing PEN 750	Underground Girl/Fighting For Peace	£20
72	Warner Bros K 16203	Didn't I Tell You/Seek Not In The Wide World	£20
71	Penny Farthing PELS 516	MARCH HARE (LP)	£350

(see also Honeybus)

WINSTON HAREWOOD
71	Camel CA 64	I Will Never Fall In Love Again (actually by Winston Heywood)/LA-FUD-DIL ALL-STARS: La-Fud-Dil (actually "La-Fud-Del")	£15

(see also Winston Heywood)

RON HARGRAVE
58	MGM MGM 956	Latch On/Only A Daydream	£1000
58	MGM MGM 956	Latch On/Only A Daydream (78)	£100

HARLAN COUNTY
70	Nashville 6336 002	HARLAN COUNTY (LP, red/black label)	£25

HARLEM SPEAKEASY
68	Polydor 56270	Aretha/Sight Of Pegasus	£15

HARLESDEN MONKS
72	Pama Supreme PS 352	Rock Me Mister Ping Wing/Breakdown Rock	£40

(see also Lloyd Charmers)

STEVE HARLEY (& COCKNEY REBEL)
74	EMI EMI 2191	Psychomodo/Such A Dream (unreleased)	£0

(see also Anderson Harley & Batt)

IAN G HARLING
80	P.TO. PT 209/EJSP 9410	Heavy Breathing/Black & White (no p/s)	£15

HARLOW
79	Pepper UP 36452	Harry De Mazzio/Nothing To You	£100

JEREMY HARMER
69	JH 001	IDIOSYNCRATICS & SWALLOW WINGS (LP, insert, 99 only)	£300

LEE HARMER'S POPCORN
68	Page One POF 053	Love Is Coming/Hello Sunshine	£20

HARMONIANS
70	Junior JR 112	Music Street/Version	£15
70	Ackee ACK 107	Music Street/Group Of Girls	£150

(see also Tony & Hippy Boys, Winston Shan)

HARMONIC 33
02	Alphabet Zoo AZEP 2002	EXTRAORDINARY PEOPLE (LP)	£15

MINT VALUE £

05	Warp WARPLP 127	MUSIC FOR FILM, TELEVISION AND RADIO VOLUME 1 (LP)	£15

HARMONICA FATS

63	Stateside SS 184	Tore Up/I Get So Tired	£50
68	Action ACT 4507	Tore Up/I Get So Tired (reissue)	£25

HARMONISERS

69	Duke DU 32	Mother Hen/WINSTON SINCLAIR: Chastise Them	£20

HARMONIZING FOUR

66	Rymska RA 102	Who Knows/Heart Of Stone (actually by Charms)	£20

(see also Charms)

HARMONY BEACH

83	Surf King SK 1	HARMONY BEACH (EP, private pressing)	£18

HARMONY GRASS

70	RCA SF 8034	THIS IS US (LP)	£40

(see also Capability Brown, Tony Rivers & Castaways)

HARMONY ROCKETS

95	Big Cat ABB90	PARALYZED MIND OF THE ARCHANGEL VOID (LP)	£30

(see also Mercury Rev)

HARMONY & XTREME

92	Lucky Spin LSR 008	Treats/NRG Rush (12" white labels only)	£60
93	Lucky Spin LSR 010	Love In My Heart/Journey Through Time (12")	£40

JOE HARNELL

78	MCA MCA 397	The Incredible Hulk Theme/Love Theme	£15

BILLY HARNER

71	Kama Sutra 2013 029	What About The Music/Please Spare Me This Time	£20
71	Kama Sutra 2013 029	What About The Music (instrumental)/Please Spare Me This Time (withdrawn)	£1500

BUD HARPER

65	Vocalion VP 9252	Mr. Soul/Let Me Love You	£60
65	Vocalion VP 9252	Mr. Soul/Let Me Love You (DJ copy)	£100

CHARLIE HARPER AND CAPTAIN SENSIBLE

13	Time & Matter T&M 009	TOO MUCH REALITY EP (cream and purple splatter vinyl)	£40

(see also U.K. Subs, Damned)

DON HARPER ORCHESTRA

68	Columbia DB 8519	World Of Sport March/England 88	£15
73	Columbia DB 9023	World Of Sport/"Dr. Who" Theme (as Don Harper's Homo Electronicus)	£25
74	Columbia SCX 6559	HOMO ELECTRONICUS (LP)	£50
74	Impress IA 406	LIVE-NEUTRAL-EARTH (LP)	£20

JANICE HARPER

59	Capitol T 1195	WITH FEELING (LP)	£15

JESSIE HARPER

92	Kissing Spell KSLP 9203	GUITAR ABSOLUTION IN THE SHADE OF A MIDNIGHT SUN (LP, reissue of acetate-only album)	£20

(see also Human Instinct)

ROY HARPER

SINGLES

66	Strike JH 304	Take Me Into Your Eyes/Pretty Baby (in wraparound p/s)	£100
66	Strike JH 304	Take Me Into Your Eyes/Pretty Baby	£35
67	CBS 203001	Midspring Dithering/Zengem	£20
68	CBS 3371	Life Goes By/Nobody's Got Any Money In The Summer	£25

ALBUMS : ORIGINAL LPS

66	Strike JHL 105	SOPHISTICATED BEGGAR	£500
67	CBS BPG 63184	COME OUT FIGHTING GHENGIS SMITH (mono, orange label)	£100
67	CBS SBPG 63184	COME OUT FIGHTING GHENGIS SMITH (stereo, orange label)	£120
69	Liberty LBL 83231	FOLKJOKEOPUS (mono, blue label)	£125
69	Liberty LBS 83231	FOLKJOKEOPUS (stereo, blue label)	£100
69	Harvest SHVL 766	FLAT, BAROQUE AND BERSERK (gatefold sleeve; first pressing with "H. Ash" label credit)	£100
71	Harvest SHVL 789	STORMCOCK (gatefold sleeve with lyric insert, no EMI logo on label)	£50
73	Harvest SHVL 808	LIFEMASK (foldout 'door' sleeve, with insert)	£30
74	Harvest SHSP 4027	VALENTINE (1st pressing, with 'Made in GT. Britain' on bottom of label, initially with lyric booklet)	£40
74	Harvest SHSP 4027	VALENTINE (1st pressing with 'Made in GT. Britain' at bottom of label, without lyric booklet)	£15
74	Harvest SHDW 405	FLASHES FROM THE ARCHIVES OF OBLIVION (2-LP, gatefold sleeve)	£35
75	Harvest SHSP 4046	HQ (with lyric inner sleeve, EMI logo on label)	£20
77	Harvest SHSP 4060	BULLINAMINGVASE (with inner sleeve & "Watford Gap"; some with 7" single, Referendum/"Another Day" (live)/"Tom Tiddler's Ground" [PSR 407])	£20
77	Harvest SHSP 4060	BULLINAMINGVASE (2nd pressing with "Breakfast With You")	£15
77	Harvest SHSP 4077	COMMERCIAL BREAK (unreleased; test pressing with proof sleeve)	£300
78	Harvest	HARPER 1970-1975 (6-LP box set)	£100
84	Hard Up PUB 5002	BORN IN CAPTIVITY (880 only)	£30
92	Hard Up HU 2	BORN IN CAPTIVITY II (LIVE) (cassette)	£15

ALBUMS : REISSUE ALBUMS

71	Harvest SHVL 766	FLAT, BAROQUE AND BERSERK (gatefold sleeve; second pressing with "H. Ash" label credit and boxed EMI logo)	£25
70	Young Blood SSYB 7	RETURN OF THE SOPHISTICATED BEGGAR (LP, with "Hup Hup Spiral" closed run-out	£20

groove, different sleeve) ....

71	Harvest SHVL 789	**STORMCOCK** (gatefold sleeve with lyric inner, with EMI logo on label) **£20**
73	Birth RAB 3	**RETURN OF THE SOPHISTICATED BEGGAR** (LP, 2nd reissue, with "Hup Hup Spiral" closed run-out groove, different sleeve)..**£15**
74	Harvest SHSP 4027	**VALENTINE** (2nd pressing without 'Made in GT. Britain' at bottom of label, without lyric booklet)...**£15**
75	Sunset SLS 50373	**FOLKJOKEOPUS** (LP) **£15**
77	Big Ben BBX 502	**THE SOPHISTICATED BEGGAR** (LP, different rear sleeve)..**£20**
80	CBS (S) BPG 63184	**COME OUT FIGHTING GHENGIS SMITH** (LP, reissue) **£15**
86	Awareness AWL 1002	**WORK OF HEART** (LP, different sleeve with inner; 1st 1,000 with 2 x 7" "No One Gets Out Of Here Alive"/"Casualty (live) **[PUBS 1001])** & **"Still Care"/"Goodbye Ladybird"** **[PUBS2])**...**£15**
86	Awareness AWL 1002	**WORK OF HEART** (LP, different sleeve, 250 only on 'real time' quality tape) **£15**
(see also Pink Floyd)		

TIM HARPER
95	Peacefrog PF 047	**I Feel A Groove** (12", plain sleeve)..**£18**

ROY HARPER & JIMMY PAGE
85	Beggars Banquet BEGA 60	**WHATEVER HAPPENED TO JUGULA?** (LP) **£15**

HARPER'S BIZARRE
67	Warner Bros W 1693	**FEELIN' GROOVY** (LP) **£15**
67	Warner Bros W 1716	**ANYTHING GOES** (LP) **£20**
68	Warner Bros W(S) 1739	**THE SECRET LIFE OF HARPER'S BIZARRE** (LP) **£15**

SLIM HARPO
61	Pye International 7N 25098	**Rainin' In My Heart/Don't Start Cryin' Now** **£25**
63	Pye International 7N 25220	**Don't Start Cryin' Now/Rainin' In My Heart** **£25**
66	Stateside SS 491	**Baby Scratch My Back/I'm Gonna Miss You** (Like The Devil) **£30**
66	Stateside SS 527	**Shake Your Hips/Midnight Blues** **£40**
66	Stateside SS 557	**I'm A King Bee/I Got Love If You Want It** **£50**
67	Stateside SS 581	**I'm Your Breadmaker Baby/Loving You** (The Way I Do) **£30**
68	Liberty LBF 15176	**Something Inside Me/PAPPA LIGHTFOOT: Wine Whisky And Women**................**£30**
68	President PT 187	**Tip On In** (Parts 1 & 2) **£15**
70	Blue Horizon 57-3175	**Folsom Prison Blues/Mutual Friend** **£30**
65	Stateside SL 10135	**A LONG DRINK OF THE BLUES** (LP, with Lightnin' Slim) **£80**
68	President PTL 1017	**TIP ON IN** (LP) **£50**
70	Blue Horizon 7-63854	**HE KNEW THE BLUES** (LP) **£150**
72	Blue Horizon 2431 013	**TRIGGER FINGER** (LP) **£150**
76	Flyright LP 520	**BLUES HANGOVER** (LP) **£18**
78	Sonet SNTF 769	**HE KNEW THE BLUES** (LP) **£20**
80	Flyright FLY 558	**GOT LOVE IF YOU WANT IT** (LP)...**£18**
(see also Lightnin' Slim)		

GEORGE HARRASSMENT & HOMOSEXUALS
80	Black Noise 12 NO 6	**MASAI SLEEP WALKING** (LP)...**£35**
(see also Homosexuals)		

HARRIER
84	Black Horse HARR 1T	**OUT ON THE STREET EP** (Out On The Street/Nickels And Dimes/Shine On) (12", p/s) **£15**

DERRICK HARRIOT(T) (& CRYSTALITES)
62	Blue Beat BB 131	**I Care/Have Faith In Me** (as Derrick Harriott & Vagabonds)................................**£15**
63	Blue Beat BB 178	**Be True/I Won't Cry** **£15**
64	Island WI 157	**What Can I Do** (The Wedding)/**Leona** **£15**
65	Island WI 170	**I Am Only Human** (as Derak Harriott)/**ROY PANTON: Good Man** **£30**
65	Island WI 237	**My Three Loves/The Jerk** **£40**
65	Island WI 245	**Together/Mama Didn't Lie** **£65**
65	Ska Beat JB 199	**Monkey Ska/Derrick!** **£50**
66	Doctor Bird DB 1002	**Jon Tom/AUDREY WILLIAMS: Solas Market** **£20**
67	Island WI 3063	**The Loser/Bless You** **£170**
67	Island WI 3064	**Happy Times/You My Everything**..**£50**
67	Island WI 3077	**Walk The Streets/BOBBY ELLIS: Step Softly** (B-side with Desmond Miles Seven) **£80**
67	Island WI 3089	**Solomon/BOBBY ELLIS: The Emperor** (B-side with Desmond Miles Seven).....................**£75**
68	Island WI 3135	**Do I Worry?/BOBBY ELLIS & CRYSTALITES: Shuntin'** **£150**
68	Island WI 3147	**Born To Love You/IKE & CRYSTALITES: Alfred Hitchcock** (existence unconfirmed) **£40**
68	Island WI 3153	**Tang Tang Festival Song/CRYSTALITES: James Ray** **£125**
69	Big Shot BI 505	**Standing In/Bumble Bee** **£200**
69	Big Shot BI 511	**Another Lonely Night/Been So Long** **£100**
70	Songbird SB 1013	**Riding For A Fall/I'm Not Begging** **£130**
70	Songbird SB 1014	**Sitting On Top/You Were Meant For Me** **£160**
70	Songbird SB 1022	**Go Bye Bye/Laugh It Off** **£15**
70	Songbird SB 1028	**Message From A Black Man/**(Version II) **£15**
70	Songbird SB 1029	**Psychedelic Train** (w/ Chosen Few)/**Psychedelic Train** (Pt. 2) (with Crystalites) **£20**
70	Songbird SB 1043	**Psychedelic Train Chapter Three/CRYSTALITES: Groovy Situation Version II**...........**£15**
71	Songbird SB 1055	**Lollipop Girl/CRYSTALITES: Lollipop Version** **£15**
72	Songbird SB 1071	**Since I Lost My Baby/Baby** (Version) **£15**
73	Attack ATT 8056	**Brown Baby/CRYSTALITES: Brown Baby Version** **£20**
73	Explosion EX 2071	**Let Me Down Easy/Let Me Down Easy - Version** **£20**
65	Island ILP 928	**THE BEST OF DERRICK HARRIOTT** (LP)..**£175**
67	Island ILP 955	**DERRICK HARRIOTT'S ROCKSTEADY PARTY** (LP, actually v/a LP)..........................**£500**
68	Island ILP 983	**THE BEST OF VOLUME TWO** (LP, as Derrick Harriott & Crystalites) **£250**
69	Pama SECO 13	**SINGS JAMAICA REGGAE** (LP)...**£200**

MINT VALUE £

70	Trojan TTL 43	THE BEST OF DERRICK HARRIOTT (LP)	£80
70	Trojan TTL 54	ROCKSTEADY PARTY (LP)	£80
70	Trojan TBL 114	THE UNDERTAKER (LP, as Derrick Harriott & Crystalites)	£75
70	Trojan TBL 141	PSYCHEDELIC TRAIN (LP, as Derrick Harriott & Crystalites)	£90
75	Charmers LP 5	REGGAE DISCO ROCKERS (LP)	£20
75	Trojan TRLS 116	GREATEST REGGAE HITS (LP)	£20
81	Trojan TRTS 198	SONGS FOR MIDNIGHT LOVERS (LP)	£15
95	Dr. Buster Dynamite DBD 108	FOR A FISTFUL OF JAMAICAN DOLLARS (LP, reissue of the Undertaker)	£25

JOE HARRIOTT

56	Jazz Today JTE 106	WITH STRINGS (EP)	£40
56	Pye Jazz NJE 1003	NO STRINGS (EP)	£80
57	Columbia SEG 7665	JOE HARRIOTT QUARTET (EP)	£100
59	Columbia SEG 7939	BLUE HARRIOTT (EP)	£60
60	Melodisc EPM7 117	COOL JAZZ WITH JOE (EP)	£75
61	Columbia SEG 8070	A GUY CALLED JOE (EP)	£45
60	Jazzland JLP 49	FREE FORM (LP)	£200
62	Columbia 33SX 1477	ABSTRACT (LP)	£400
63	Columbia 33SX 1627	MOVEMENT (LP)	£750
64	Columbia 33SX 1692	HIGH SPIRITS (LP)	£750
67	Melodisc SLP 12150	SWINGS HIGH (LP)	£200
66	Columbia SX/SCX 6025	INDO-JAZZ SUITE (LP, with John Mayer)	£75
67	Columbia S(C) 6122	INDO-JAZZ FUSIONS (LP, with John Mayer)	£50
68	Columbia S(C)X 6215	INDO-JAZZ FUSIONS II (LP, with John Mayer)	£50
68	Columbia S(C)X 6249	PERSONAL PORTRAIT (LP)	£100
69	Columbia SCX 6354	HUM-DONO (LP, with Amancio D'Silva)	£1000
73	One Up OU 2011	MEMORIAL 1973 (LP)	£50
89	Cadillac SGC/MLP 12-150	SWINGS HIGH (LP, reissue)	£20
11	Gearbox GB 1506	PARTYING WITH JOE (LP)	£20
11	Moonlighting MT 001	JOURNEY (LP)	£15
14	Doxy DOK 230	FREE FORM (LP, reissue)	£15
14	Doxy ACV 2040	ABSTRACT (LP, reissue, clear vinyl)	£15
15	Vocalion VOCLP 3303	HUM-DONO (LP, reissue, with Amancio D'Silva)	£15

(see also Tony Kinsey Trio & Joe Harriott, John Mayer, Michael Garrick)

JOE HARRIOTT/DON RENDELL QUARTET

57	MGM MGM-EP 615	JAZZ BRITANNIA (EP, 2 tracks each)	£60

(see also Don Rendell)

ANITA HARRIS

66	CBS BGP/SBPG 62894	SOMEBODY'S IN MY ORCHARD (LP)	£15

BETTY HARRIS

63	London HL 9796	Cry To Me/I'll Be A Liar	£20
65	Stateside SS 475	What A Sad Feeling/I'm Evil Tonight	£30
67	Stateside SS 2045	Nearer To You/12 Red Roses	£20
69	Action ACT 4535	Ride Your Pony/Trouble With My Lover	£60
69	Action ACLP 6007	SOUL PERFECTION (LP)	£100

(see also Betty Harris & Lee Dorsey)

CALVIN HARRIS

08	Ministry Of Sound MINISTRY 065	I CREATED DISCO (2-LP)	£50

EDDIE HARRIS

69	Atlantic 584 232	It's Crazy/Live Right Now (unissued)	£0
69	Atlantic 588 177	SILVER CYCLES (LP)	£20

EMMYLOU HARRIS

95	Gravevine GRALP 102	WRECKING BALL (LP)	£50

GENE HARRIS & THE THREE SOUNDS

96	Blue Note BN 724383533817	LIVE AT THE IT CLUB (LP)	£18

JET HARRIS

67	Fontana TF 849	My Lady/You Don't Live Twice	£25
62	Decca DFE 8502	JET HARRIS (EP)	£25
78	Ellie Jay EJSP 8622	INSIDE JET HARRIS - THE LAST CONCERT (LP, 2,500 only)	£20
70s	Q LPMM 1038	ANNIVERSARY ALBUM (LP)	£20

(see also Shadows, Keith Meehan)

JOHNNY HARRIS

65	Mercury MF 942	Mynah Hop/Here Comes The Boot (as the Johnny Harris Orchestra)	£40
69	Warner Bros WB 8000	Footprints On The Moon/Lulu's Theme	£15
70	Warner Bros WB 8016	Fragment Of Fear/Stepping Stones (4-prong push-out centre)	£50
70	Warner Bros WS 3002	MOVEMENTS (LP, 1st pressing, orange labels)	£50
72	Warner Bros K 46054	MOVEMENTS (LP, reissue)	£25
73	Warner Bros K 46187	ALL TO BRING YOU MORNING (LP)	£15
02	Warner/WSM 8122 73602-1	MOVEMENTS (2LP, printed inners, expanded reissue)	£30

PAT HARRIS & BLACKJACKS

63	Pye 7N 15567	The Hippy Hippy Shake/You Gotta See Your Mama Ev'ry Night	£25

ROY HARRIS

72	Topic 12TS 217	THE BITTER AND THE SWEET (LP, blue label)	£15

SCOTT HARRIS
68 Morgan MR7S   Barry Johnson's Sad Eyes Inn/Morning Sun £30

SHAKEY JAKE HARRIS
69 Liberty LBS 83217   FURTHER ON UP THE ROAD (LP) £50
73 Polydor 2391 015   THE DEVIL'S HARMONICA (LP) £20

SUZANNE HARRIS
69 Polydor 56354   Sure That's What God Said/It's A Long Way From The Movies/Go Out And Multiply/
                          Are You £15
70 R.F.S. Records RFS 8270 Here Come The Beautiful People/We're Using Up The World (p/s) £20

THURSTON HARRIS (& SHARPS)
57 Vogue V 9092   Little Bitty Pretty One/I Hope You Won't Hold It Against Me (with Sharps) £200
58 Vogue V 9098   Do What You Did/I'm Asking Forgiveness (as Thurston Harris & Sharps) £250
57 Vogue V 9092   Little Bitty Pretty One/I Hope You Won't Hold It Against Me (with Sharps) (78) £30
58 Vogue V 9098   Do What You Did/I'm Asking Forgiveness (as Thurston Harris & Sharps) (78) £20
58 Vogue V 9108   Be Baba Leba/I'm Out To Getcha £250
58 Vogue V 9108   Be Baba Leba/I'm Out To Getcha (78) £20
58 Vogue V 9122   Smokey Joe's/Only One Love Is Blessed £150
58 Vogue V 9122   Smokey Joe's/Only One Love Is Blessed (78) £20
58 Vogue V 9127   Tears From My Heart/Over Somebody Else's Shoulder £100
58 Vogue V 9127   Tears From My Heart/Over Somebody Else's Shoulder (78) £20
59 Vogue V 9139   Purple Stew (as Thurston Harris & Masters)/I Hear A Rhapsody £150
59 Vogue V 9139   Purple Stew (as Thurston Harris & Masters)/I Hear A Rhapsody (78) £20
59 Vogue V 9144   You Don't Know How Much I Love You/In The Bottom Of My Heart £100
59 Vogue V 9144   You Don't Know How Much I Love You/In The Bottom Of My Heart (78) £20
59 Vogue V 9146   Hey Little Girl/My Love Will Last £150
59 Vogue V 9146   Hey Little Girl/My Love Will Last (78) £30
59 Vogue V 9149   Runk Bunk/Bless Your Heart £150
59 Vogue V 9149   Runk Bunk/Bless Your Heart (78) £30
59 Vogue V 9151   Slip-Slop/Paradise Hill £200
59 Vogue V 9151   Slip-Slop/Paradise Hill (78) £40
66 Sue WI 4016   Little Bitty Pretty One/I Hope You Won't Hold It Against Me (reissue)..................... £50
(see also Sharps)

WEE WILLIE HARRIS
57 Decca F 10970   Rockin' At The Two 'I's/Back To School Again £40
58 Decca F 10980   Love Bug Crawl/Rosie Lee £40
58 Decca F 11044   Got A Match/No Chemise, Please! £20
60 Decca F 11217   Wild One/Little Bitty Girl £20
63 HMV POP 1198   You Must Be Joking/Better To Have Loved £15
66 Polydor 56140   Listen To The River Roll Along/Try Moving Baby (writing in black or white).......... £30
58 Decca DFE 6465   ROCKING WITH WEE WILLIE (EP) £150

WYNONIE 'MR BLUES' HARRIS
56 Vogue V 2127   Bloodshot Eyes/Lollipop Mama (triangular centre).. £100
56 Vogue V 2127   Bloodshot Eyes/Lollipop Mama (round centre).. £40
56 Vogue EPV 1103   WYNONIE 'MISTER BLUES' HARRIS (EP) £60
61 Blue Beat BBEP 301   BATTLE OF THE BLUES (EP) £80

WYNONIE HARRIS/EDDIE 'CLEANHEAD' VINSON
72 Polydor 2343 048   JUMP BLUES (LP) £15
(see also Tiny Bradshaw/Wynonie Harris, Eddie 'Cleanhead' Vinson)

HARRISON
84 Skipping Rope SKIP 1 There Is No Refrain/Simply This (p/s) £40

DANNY HARRISON
65 Coral Q 72479   Speak Of The Devil/I'm A Rollin' Stone £15
62 Starlite STEP 23   INTRODUCING DANNY HARRISON (EP) £20

EARL HARRISON
67 London HL 10121   Humphrey Stomp/Can You Forgive Me £50
67 London HL 10121   Humphrey Stomp/Can You Forgive Me (DJ Copy) £100

GEORGE HARRISON

SINGLES
71 Apple R5912   Bangla-Desh/Deep Blue (Demo copy)... £70
71 Apple R 5912   Bangla-Desh/Deep Blue (with rare p/s [beware of new-looking counterfeits!])........... £80
73 Apple R 5988   Give Me Love (Give Me Peace On Earth)/Miss O'Dell (Demo copy) £70
74 Apple R 6001   Dark Horse/I Don't Care Anymore (unissued) £0
76 Apple R 6012   This Guitar (Can't Keep From Crying)/Maya Love (no p/s).................................. £35
77 Dark Horse K 16967   It's What You Value/Woman Don't You Cry For Me (no p/s).............................. £15
79 Dark Horse K 17284   Love Comes To Everyone/Soft Hearted Hana £15
79 Dark Horse K 17423   Faster/Your Love Is Forever (with charity stickered plain white die-cut sleeve) £15
79 Dark Horse K 17423   Faster/Your Love Is Forever (picture disc, stickered PVC sleeve with insert) £30
81 Dark Horse K 17837DJ Teardrops (Edited Version)/Save The World (DJ promo only, no p/s) £25
86 Ganga Publishing B.V. Shanghai Surprise (with Vicki Brown) (unreleased, 1-sided promo only; no catalogue
                          number, matrix: SHANGHAI 1) £500
87 Dark Horse W 8178B   Got My Mind Set On You/Lay His Head (box set with 2 postcards) £20
87 Dark Horse W 8178T   Got My Mind Set On You (Extended Version)/Got My Mind Set On You (Single
                          Version)/Lay His Head (12", p/s with poster) £15
87 Dark Horse W 8178TP Got My Mind Set On You (Extended Version)/Got My Mind Set On You (Single
                          Version)/Lay His Head (12", picture disc) £20
88 Dark Horse W 8131TP When We Was Fab (Unextended Version)/Zig Zag/That's The Way It Goes £20

		(Remix)/**When We Was Fab** (Reverse End) (12", picture disc)	
88	Dark Horse W 7913T	**This Is Love/Breath Away From Heaven/All Those Years Ago** (12", p/s)	£15
89	Dark Horse W 2696T	**Cheer Down/That's What It Takes/Crackerbox Palace** (12", p/s)	£15
88	Genesis SGH 777	**SONGS BY GEORGE HARRISON** (Limited Edition) (EP, 33rpm, issued with limited edition book Songs By George Harrison)	£900
88	Genesis SGHCD 777	**SONGS BY GEORGE HARRISON** (CD EP, issued with limited edition book)	£800
92	Genesis SGH 778	**SONGS BY GEORGE HARRISON VOL. 2** (EP, with limited edition book Songs By George Harrison Vol. 2)	£400
92	Genesis SGHCD 778	**SONGS BY GEORGE HARRISON VOL. 2** (CD EP, with limited edition book)	£600
03	Parlophone R 6601	**Any Road/Marwa Blues** (p/s)	£30

ALBUMS

68	Apple APCOR 1	**WONDERWALL MUSIC** (LP, insert, black inner, mono)	£250
68	Apple SAPCOR 1	**WONDERWALL MUSIC** (LP, insert, black inner, stereo)	£100
69	Zapple ZAPPLE 02	**ELECTRONIC SOUND** (LP, printed inner)	£150
70	Apple STCH 639	**ALL THINGS MUST PASS** (3LP box set, poster, printed inners; initial batch in U.K. Box)	£200
70	Apple STCH 639	**ALL THINGS MUST PASS** (3LP box set, poster, printed inners; later batch in U.S. box)	£100
72	Apple STCX 3385	**THE CONCERT FOR BANGLA DESH** (3LP box set, orange inside with BMI/ASCAP label credits, booklet)	£75
73	Apple PAS 10006	**LIVING IN THE MATERIAL WORLD** (LP, gatefold, printed inner)	£20
74	Apple PAS 10008	**DARK HORSE** (LP, gatefold, inner sleeve, lyric insert)	£30
75	Apple PAS 10009	**EXTRA TEXTURE** (READ ALL ABOUT IT) (LP, textured sleeve, printed inner)	£40
76	Dark Horse K56319	**THIRTY THREE AND A 1/3** (LP, gatefold, printed inner)	£25
79	Dark Horse K 56562	**GEORGE HARRISON** (LP, printed inner)	£20
81	Dark Horse K 56870	**SOMEWHERE IN ENGLAND** (LP, printed inner)	£20
82	Dark Horse 923734-1	**GONE TROPPO** (LP, printed inner)	£20
87	Dark Horse WX 123	**CLOUD NINE** (LP, printed inner)	£20
89	Dark Horse WX 312	**THE BEST OF DARK HORSE 1976-1989** (LP, printed inner)	£15
91	EPIC EPC 468835 1	**THE CONCERT FOR BANGLA DESH** (3LP, booklet)	£25
92	Dark Horse 759926964-1	**LIVE IN JAPAN** (2LP, printed inners)	£80
92	Apple SAPCOR 1	**WONDERWALL MUSIC** (reissue, gatefold sleeve with inner sleeve)	£20
96	Zapple ZAPPLE 02	**ELECTRONIC SOUND** (reissue, with inner sleeve)	£40
01	GnOM 5304741	**ALL THINGS MUST PASS** (3LP box set, reissue, booklet, printed inners)	£100
02	Dark Horse 7243 5 41969 1 1	**BRAINWASHED** (LP, gatefold, printed inner, booklet, oval sticker to sleeve)	£50
04	Apple/UMC 060253791387	**THE APPLE YEARS 1968-75** (7CD/DVD box set, booklet)	£150
04	Dark Horse GHBOX 1	**THE DARK HORSE YEARS 1976-1992** (5CD/2SACD/1DVD box set, booklet)	£60
10	Dark Horse R2 525469	**COLLABORATIONS** (with Ravi Shankar) (3CD/1DVD box set, certificate of authenticity, booklet)	£80
13	Universal 060253704439	**EARLY TAKES VOL. 1** (LP, clear vinyl)	£40
17	Apple STCH 639	**ALL THINGS MUST PASS** (3LP box set, reissue, printed inners, poster)	£60
17	Apple 0602557090277	**THE VINYL COLLECTION** (16LP/2x12" picture disc box set, remastered, lenticular front cover)	£350
21	Dark Horse/Apple/UMe 356 523 5	**ALL THINGS MUST PASS 50TH ANNIVERSARY** (8LP/5CD/1BD wooden crate 'uber deluxe' box set, books, beads, ephemera, 1/6 scale replica of GH and gnomes from cover)	£800
21	Dark Horse/Apple/UMe 602435652375	**ALL THINGS MUST PASS 50th ANNIVERSARY** (8LP 'super deluxe' box set, 180g, book)	£120
21	Dark Horse/Apple/UMe 3565242	**ALL THINGS MUST PASS 50th ANNIVERSARY** (3LP box set, green splatter vinyl, limited, 180g, printed inners, poly bags, poster, notes insert)	£80
21	Dark Horse/Apple/UMe 3565238	**ALL THINGS MUST PASS 50th ANNIVERSARY** (5CD/1BD 'super deluxe' box, book)	£60
24	Dark Horse DH0033Z	**WONDERWALL MUSIC** (LP, Zoetrope picture disc, die cut sleeve, insert, RSD)	£25
24	Dark Horse DH 0034Z	**ELECTRONIC SOUND** (LP, Zoetrope picture disc, die cut sleeve, insert, RSD)	£25

(see also Beatles, Traveling Wilburys, Billy Connolly & Chris Tummings)

MIKE HARRISON

71	Island ILPS 9170	**MIKE HARRISON** (LP, gatefold sleeve, pink rim, palm tree label)	£40
72	Island ILPS 9209	**SMOKESTACK LIGHTNING** (LP, laminated sleeve, pink rim, palm tree label)	£30
75	Good Ear EAR 7002	**RAINBOW RIDER** (LP)	£20

(see also Art, Spirit, Spooky Tooth)

NOEL HARRISON

57	HMV 7EG 8383	**NOEL HARRISON** (EP)	£15
60	Philips BBL 7399	**AT THE BLUE ANGEL** (LP)	£20
69	Reprise RSLP 6321	**THE GREAT ELECTRIC EXPERIMENT IS OVER** (LP)	£15

REGGIE HARRISON

63	Cameo Parkway P 863	**A Lonely Piano/HIPPIES: Memory Lane**	£20

VALERIE HARRISON

81	B&B BBD 135	**Golden Touch/You're No Good** (12")	£15
81	B&B BBLP 1001	**GOLDEN TOUCH** (LP)	£35

WILBERT HARRISON

59	Top Rank JAR 132	**Kansas City/Listen My Darling**	£20
59	Top Rank JAR 132	**Kansas City/Listen My Darling** (78)	£30
62	Island WI 031	**I'm Broke/Off To School**	£20
65	Sue WI 363	**Let's Stick Together/Kansas City Twist**	£40
70	London HL 10307	**Let's Work Together/Stagger Lee**	£15
70	London HA/SH 8415	**LET'S WORK TOGETHER** (LP)	£40
85	Charly CRB 1102	**LOVIN...PERATOR** (LP)	£15

YVONNE HARRISON

67	Caltone TONE 102	**The Chase/Take My Hand**	£100

HARRIS SISTERS
55	Capitol CL 14232	Kissin' Bug/We've Been Walkin' All Night	£20

KEVIN HARRISION
81	Cherry Red BRED 16	INSCRUTABLY OBVIOUS (LP)	£40

HARRY J. ALL STARS
69	Harry J TR 694	Spyrone/JOHN HOLT: Have Sympathy	£40
70	Harry J. HJ 6601	The Big Three/Lavender (B-side actually "Lavender Blue" by Lloyd Robinson)	£25
70	Harry J. HJ 6621	Return Of The Liquidator (actually "Tons Of Gold" by Val Bennett)/All Day	£30
70	Trojan TBL 104	THE LIQUIDATOR (LP)	£35

(see also Jay Boys, Bob Andy, John Holt, Lizzy)

HARRY & RADCLIFFE
69	Camel CA 26	History/Just Be Alone	£60

WARREN HARRY
76	Sonet SON-2088	I don't Care/Backwards Forwards	£15
78	HAH 1/EJSP-8632	1965/Radio Show (500 only, no p/s)	£30

HARSH REALITY
68	Philips PB 1710	Tobacco Ash Sunday/How Do You Feel	£30
69	Philips PB 1769	Heaven And Hell/Praying For Reprieve	£30
69	Philips (S)BL 7891	HEAVEN AND HELL (LP, gatefold sleeve, blue/silver labels)	£500

(see also Matthews Southern Comfort)

CAJUN HART
69	Warner Bros WB 7258	Got To Find A Way/Lover's Prayer	£700
69	Warner Bros WB 7258	Got To Find A Way/Lover's Prayer (DJ Copy)	£800
06	Warner Bros WB 7258	Got To Find A Way/LINDA JONES: A Last Minute Miracle (A-label reissue)	£20

DERRY HART & HARTBEATS
59	Decca F 11138	Come On Baby/Nowhere In This World	£25

MICKEY HART
73	Warner Bros. K 46182	ROLLING THUNDER (LP)	£15

(see also Grateful Dead, Diga Rhythm Band)

MIKE HART
70	Dandelion 63756	MIKE HART BLEEDS (LP, black/red/silver labels)	£50
72	Dandelion 2310 211	BASHER, CHALKY, PONGO AND ME (LP, as Mike Hart & Comrades)	£50

(see also Clayton Squares, Liverpool Scene)

TIM HART & MADDY PRIOR
68	Tepee TPRM 104	FOLK SONGS OF OLDE ENGLAND VOL. 1 (LP, gatefold sleeve)	£100
69	Tepee TPRM 105	FOLK SONGS OF OLDE ENGLAND VOL. 2 (LP, gatefold sleeve)	£100
69	Ad-Rhythm ARPS 3	FOLK SONGS OF OLDE ENGLAND VOL. 1 (LP, reissue)	£25
69	Ad-Rhythm ARPS 4	FOLK SONGS OF OLDE ENGLAND VOL. 2 (LP, reissue)	£25
71	B&C CAS 1035	SUMMER SOLSTICE (LP, gatefold sleeve)	£30

(see also Steeleye Span)

CIARAN HARTE
80	Glass 003	Love Is Strange/Shimahero (p/s)	£20

KEEF HARTLEY (BAND)
69	Deram DML 1037	HALFBREED (LP, mono, gatefold sleeve, 1st pressing has 'mono/stereo' holes on rear sleeve, white/red label)	£100
69	Deram SML 1037	HALFBREED (LP, stereo, gatefold sleeve, 1st pressing has 'mono/stereo' holes on rear sleeve, white/red label)	£80
69	Deram DML 1054	THE BATTLE OF N.W.6 (LP, mono, gatefold sleeve, 1st pressing with 'mono/stereo' holes on rear sleeve, white/red labels)	£100
69	Deram SML 1054	THE BATTLE OF N.W.6 (LP, stereo, gatefold sleeve, 1st pressing with 'mono/stereo' holes on rear sleeve, white/red labels)	£80
70	Deram SML 1071	THE TIME IS NEAR (LP, with booklet, white/red labels with small logo)	£100
70	Deram SML 1071	THE TIME IS NEAR (LP, without booklet, white/red labels with small logo)	£80
71	Deram SDL 2	OVERDOG (LP, gatefold sleeve, white/brown labels with small logo)	£60
71	Deram SDL 4	LITTLE BIG BAND (LP, white/brown label, gatefold sleeve)	£60
72	Deram SDL 9	SEVENTY SECOND BRAVE (LP, gatefold sleeve)	£50
73	Deram SDL 13	LANCASHIRE HUSTLER (LP, gatefold sleeve, as Keeg Hartley)	£40
74	Deram DPA 3011/2	THE BEST OF (2-LP, gatefold sleeve)	£20

(see also Rory Storm & Hurricanes, Artwoods, John Mayall's Bluesbreakers, Miller Anderson, Dog Soldier, Henry Lowther, Wynder K. Frog)

TREVOR HARTLEY
79	Jah Child JC 002	Africa/Repatriation Version (12")	£35
80	Matumbi MA 006	Selassi I/Skip Away (12". p/s)	£30
80	Jungle Beat JB DC 808	Mama Say Son/Oppression (12")	£80
79	Burning Rockers BR1011	INNOCENT LOVER (LP)	£25

HARVEST
80	Secular Records SEC 001	Fashion Parade/Will You Be The One	£70

HARVEST MINISTERS
92	Sarah SARAH 64	You Do My World The World Of Good/Petticoats (p/s, insert)	£30
92	Sarah SARAH 68	Six O'Clock Is Rosary/The First Star (p/s, insert)	£30
93	Sarah SARAH 84	If It Kills Me And It Will/Can Go It Alone (p/s, insert)	£30
93	Sarah SARAH 616	LITTLE DARK MANSIONS (LP)	£50

HARVESTERS
72	Westwood WRS 015	THE HARVESTERS (LP)	£25

ALEX HARVEY (1) AKA THE SENSATIONAL ALEX HARVEY BAND
64	Polydor NH 52264	I Just Wanna Make Love To You/Let The Good Times Roll	£60

MINT VALUE £

64	Polydor NH 52907	Got My Mojo Working/I Ain't Worried Baby (as Alex Harvey & His Soul Band) £60
65	Polydor BM 56017	Ain't That Just Too Bad/My Kind Of Love (as Alex Harvey & His Soul Band) £60
65	Fontana TF 610	Agent 00 Soul/Go Away Baby £40
66	Fontana TF 764	Work Song/I Can Do Without Your Love £25
67	Decca F 12640	The Sunday Song/Horizon's £50
67	Decca F 12660	Maybe Some Day/Curtains For My Baby...£60
69	Fontana TF 1063	Midnight Moses/Roman Wall Blues £70
72	Vertigo 6059 070	There's No Lights On The Christmas Tree Mother, (They're Burning Big Louie Tonight)/Harp £40
64	Polydor LPHM 46424	ALEX HARVEY AND HIS SOUL BAND (LP)...£250
64	Polydor LPHM 46441	THE BLUES (LP)...£200
69	Fontana (S)TL 5534	ROMAN WALL BLUES (LP)..£400
73	Vertigo 6360 081	FRAMED (LP, as The Sensational Alex Harvey Band, gatefold sleeve, small swirl label) ...£200
72	Vertigo 6360 081	FRAMED (LP, as The Sensational Alex Harvey Band, gatefold sleeve, later spaceship label) £30
73	Vertigo 6360 103	NEXT (LP, as The Sensational Alex Harvey Band, spaceship label, 1st pressing, side 1 Matrix 1Y//1 1 6 3) £20
74	Vertigo 6360 112	THE IMPOSSIBLE DREAM (LP, gatefold sleeve, spaceship label).......................................£15
75	Vertigo 9102 003	TOMORROW BELONGS TO ME (LP, gatefold sleeve, spaceship label) £15
77	K-Tel NE 984	ALEX HARVEY PRESENTS THE LOCH NESS MONSTER (LP, withdrawn, gatefold stickered sleeve, with 16-page 'descriptive diary') £50
78	Mountain TOPS 114	ROCK DRILL (with 'No Complaints Department') £35
78	Mountain TOPS 114	ROCK DRILL (Later copies with revised Track listing stickered on sleeve)..........................£15
83	Power Station AMP 2	THE SOLDIER ON THE WALL (LP, solo) £20

(see also Tear Gas, Hairband, Rock Workshop, Nazareth, Michael Schenker Group, Tandoori)

ALEX HARVEY (2)

71	Capitol E-ST 789	ALEX HARVEY (LP)...£15

CARL HARVEY MEETS THE DUB MASTER

78	Cancer CANLP 003	ECSTACY OF MANKIND (LP) £40

JANCIS HARVEY

73	Pilgrim King KLPS 47	DISTANCE OF DOORS (LP) £45
73	Westwood WRS 029	WORDS YOU LEFT BEHIND (LP) £60
74	Westwood WRS 038	JANCIS HARVEY (LP)..£60
75	Westwood WRS 054	TIME WAS NOW (LP) £60
76	Westwood WRS 107	A PORTRAIT OF JANCIS HARVEY (LP) £45
79	Westwood WRS 144	FROM THE DARKNESS CAME LIGHT (LP) £40

LANCE HARVEY & KINGPINS

64	Lyntone LYN 509	SINCE YOU WALKED OUT ON ME (Keele Rag flexidisc EP, with The Escorts)....................£15

MICK HARVEY

97	Mute STUMM 157	PINK ELEPHANTS (LP, inner) £25

(see also Nick Cave)

HARVEY (FUQUA) & MOONGLOWS

58	London HLM 8730	Ten Commandments Of Love/Mean Old Blues £300
58	London HLM 8730	Ten Commandments Of Love/Mean Old Blues (78)..£50

(see also Moonglows, Etta & Harvey)

P.J. HARVEY

90	Private Pressing	P. J. Harvey (3-track demo , 'wooden' p/s includes pictures of P. J. and lyrics to Dress).....£80
91	Too Pure PURE 5	Dress/Water (demo)/Dry (demo) (12")..£20
92	Too Pure PURES 8	Sheela-Na-Gig/Joe (p/s, 400 only) £45
92	Too Pure PURE 8	Sheela-Na-Gig/Hair (demo)/Joe (demo) (12", p/s)..£25
93	Island 12IS 538	50 Ft Queenie/Mansize (demo)/Hook (demo)/Reeling (12", p/s)...................................£18
93	Island 12IS 569	Mansize/Wang Dang Doodle/Daddy (12", p/s)..£15
95	Island 12IS 614	C'Mon Billy/Darling Be There/Maniac (12", p/s)...£15
95	Island IS 610	Send His Love To Me/Long Time Coming (Evening Session) (picture disc in 12" poster p/s) £15
95	Island CIDD J610	Send His Love To Me (Promo-only CD, exclusive 'rose dress' sleeve) £30
99	Island IS 730	The Wind/Rebecca/Nina In Ecstacy 2 ....£15
00	Island IS 769	Good Fortune/66 Promises £30
01	Island IS 771	A Place Called Home/Kick It To The Ground (demo) (numbered) £25
11	Island 2762434	The Words That Maketh Murder/The Guns Called Me Back Again £15
17	Island 538287631	A Dog Called Money/I'll Be Waiting (tour 7")...£30
92	Too Pure PURE(D) 10	DRY (LP, 1st 5,000 with bonus LP, "Demonstrations", inner sleeve and no'd sticker).......£150
92	Too Pure PURE 10	DRY (LP with inner but without "Demonstrations") £100
92	Too Pure PUREDCD 10	DRY (CD, 1st 5,000 with additional "Demonstrations" LP tracks) £30
93	Island 5146961	RID OF ME (LP)...£150
93	Island ILPM 2079	4 TRACK DEMOS (LP, with inner) £80
95	Island CIDZ 8035	TO BRING YOU MY LOVE & THE B-SIDES CD (2-CD) £40
95	Island ILPS 8035	TO BRING YOU MY LOVE (LP, 1st pressing, with inner and large photo on rear) £150
98	Island ILPS 8076	IS THIS DESIRE? (LP, with inner)..£200
00	Island ILPS 8099	STORIES FROM THE CITY, STORIES FROM THE SEA (LP, with inner) £150
04	Island ILPS 8143	UH HUH HER (LP, with inner) £60
07	Island 1740335	WHITE CHALK (LP, inner) £40
10	Island 2758997	LET ENGLAND SHAKE (LP)...£30
16	Island 4774545	THE HOPE SIX DEMOLITION PROJECT (LP) £20
19	Lakeshore LSINV223LP	ALL ABOUT EVE (LP) £15

(see also Automatic Dlamini, Grape, John Parish & Polly Jean Harvey)

RICHARD HARVEY
75 Transatlantic TRA 292   DIVISIONS ON A GROUND (LP)..£15
(see also Gryphon, Barry Gray, The Banned)

TINA HARVEY
73 UK UK 24   Nowhere To Run/Tina's Second Song £25
76 UK UK 141   I'm Waiting For The Man/Baby, Let Me Follow You Down £15
73 UK UKAL 1002   TINA HARVEY (LP, bule/silver labels) £25

HARVEY BOYS
57 London HLA 8397   Nothing Is Too Good For You/Marina Girl £30

HARVEY & THE PHENOMENALS
04 Funk 45 FUNK45 018   Soul & Sunshine/What Can I Do (reissue)....................................£20

HARVEY'S PEOPLE
69 Galliard GAL 4001   LOVING AND LIVING (LP)..£15

CHRISTINE HARWOOD
70 Birth RAB 1   NICE TO MEET MISS CHRISTINE (LP, white 'rabbit' child' label)............£200
06 Finders Keepers FKR005LP   NICE TO MEET MISS CHRISTINE (LP, reissue)....................£15

ELTON HARWOOD
85 Harwood HARD 01   Just Like Money/Instrumental (12", p/s) £60

GORDON HASKELL
69 CBS 63741   SAILIN' MY BOAT (LP) £125
72 Atlantic K 40311   IT IS AND IT ISN'T (LP, with lyric insert) £40
73 RCA   SERVE AT ROOM TEMPERATURE (LP, unissued) £250
(see also Fleur-De-Lys, Cupid's Inspiration, King Crimson)

JACK HASKELL (& HONEY-DREAMERS)
57 London HL 8426   Around The World/Away Out West...£15

NAZIA HASSAN
80 HMV PEASD 12751   DISCO DEEWANE (LP) £40
82 HMV PEASD 2065   STAR (LP, with Zoheb Hassan) £15

JON HASSELL
81 Editions EG EGED 13   DREAM THEORY IN MALAYA (LP) £25
83 Editions EG EGED 31   AKA/DARBARI/JAVA- MAGIC REALISM (LP)................................£40
90 Land LAND 11   CITY: WORKS OF FICTION (LP) £15

JON HASSELL & BRIAN ENO
80 EG EGED 7   POSSIBLE MUSICS (LP) £35
(see also Roxy Music, Brian Eno, Fripp & Eno)

JOE HASSELVANDER
85 Pentagram DEVIL 3   LADY KILLER (LP) £15

HASSLES
67 United Artists UP 1199   You Got Me Hummin'/I'm Thinkin' £20
(see also Billy Joel)

HAT & TIE
66 President PT 105   Chance For Romance/California Jazz Club U.S.A. £15
67 President PT 122   Bread To Spend/Finding It Rough (demos credit A-side as "Bread") £150
(see also Patrick Campbell-Lyons, Nirvana [U.K.])

TONY HATCH ORCHESTRA
69 Pye 7N 17814   Theme From Who-Dun-It/The Champions £30
(see also Jackie Trent)

HATE
70 Famous SFMA 5752   HATE KILLS (LP, gatefold sleeve, orange labels)............................£125

HATFIELD & THE NORTH
74 Virgin VS 116   Let's Eat (Real Soon)/Fitter Stoke Has A Bath £15
74 Virgin V 2008   HATFIELD AND THE NORTH (LP, laminated gatefold, red 'twin' label)............£80
76 Virgin V 2008   HATFIELD AND THE NORTH (LP, gatefold, repressing on "red mirror girl" label)............£25
75 Virgin V 2030   THE ROTTER'S CLUB (LP, red Virgin inner, coloured 'twin' label) £50
80 Virgin VR 5   AFTERS (LP, A4 lyric insert) £40
05 Hatfield & The North HATCOCD 737501   HATWISE CHOICE: ARCHIVE RECORDINGS 1973-1975, VOLUME 1 (CD, digipak, booklet).....................£30
06 Hatfield & The North HATCOCD 737502   HATTITUDE: ARCHIVE RECORDINGS 1973-1975, VOLUME 2 (CD, digipak, booklet).........£30
(see also Matching Mole, Egg, Khan, Camel, National Health, Caravan)

DONNY HATHAWAY
71 Atco 2465 019   EVERYTHING IS EVERYTHING (LP) £40
71 Atlantic 2400 143   DONNY HATHAWAY (LP)..£20
72 Atlantic K 40369   LIVE (LP) £15
73 Atlantic K 40487   EXTENSION OF A MAN (LP) £20
(see also Roberta Flack)

HAUSFRAUEN EXPERIMENT
10 Fruits De Mer Crustacean 12   Oscillations/Spirit Of The Age//Baby's On Fire/Sebastian (2x7", yellow/blue vinyl, foldover p/s) £30

ANNA VON HAUSSWOLF
14 Touch TONE45.6   KALLAN (LP, white label in white stickered sleeve)............................£50

HAVANA LETS GO
81 Polydor POSP 364   Spanish Cabaret/Continental Shelf (in p/s) £18

HAVANA 3AM
91	IRS EIRSA 1047	HAVANA 3AM (LP)	£25

(see also Clash, The Good The Bad And The Queen)

ALAN HAVEN
65	Fontana TF 590	The Knack/Satin Doll (with John Barry)	£15

RICHIE HAVENS
69	Verve VS 1519	Lady Madonna/Indian Rope Man	£15
68	Verve (S)VLP 6005	SOMETHIN' ELSE AGAIN (LP)	£20
68	Verve (S)VLP 6008	MIXED BAG (LP)	£20
69	Verve (S)VLP 6014	1983 (LP)	£20
69	Verve (S)VLP 6021	STONEHENGE (LP)	£15
69	Transatlantic TRA 187	ELECTRIC HAVENS (LP)	£15
69	Transatlantic TRA 199	THE RICHIE HAVENS RECORD (LP)	£15

HAVENSTREET
76	Rissole KAB 1034	THE END OF THE LINE (LP, private pressing with booklet)	£150

CYRIL HAVERMANS
73	MGM 2315 261	CYRIL (LP, gatefold sleeve, blue/gold 'lion' label)	£25
74	MGM 2315 311	MIND WAVE (LP, blue/gold 'lion' label)	£18

NICK HAWARD
83	Cradle Music CMINH1	Grey Day/Watching Through My Window (p/s)	£30

HAMPTON HAWES
53	Esquire 20 079	HAMPTON HAWES (LP)	£30
57	Contemporary LAC 12056	HAMPTON HAWES TRIO VOL. 1 (LP)	£20
58	Contemporary LAC 12081	THIS IS HAMPTON HAWES VOL. 2 THE TRIO (LP)	£30
56	Contemporary LAC 12091	EVERYBODY LIKES HAMPTON HAWES VOL. 3 - THE TRIO (LP)	£40
62	Contemporary SCA 5028	FOR REAL! (LP)	£40

PAT HAWES WITH DAVE CAREY'S RHYTHM
56	Tempo LAP 9	PAT HAWES (10" LP)	£20

HAWKEYES
57	Capitol CL 14764	Someone Someday/Who Is He?	£20

BUDDY BOY HAWKINS/WILLIAM MOORE
50s	Heritage RE 102	BUDDY BOY HAWKINS/WILLIAM MOORE (EP)	£60

(see also Blind Lemon Jefferson)

COLEMAN HAWKINS
53	Capitol LC 6580	CLASSICS IN JAZZ (10" LP)	£30
53	Capitol LC 6650	CAPITOL PRESENTS COLEMAN HAWKINS AND SONNY GREER (10" LP)	£30
54	HMV DLP 1055	TEN COLEMAN HAWKINS' SPECIALS (10" LP)	£30
58	London LTZ U 15117	THE HAWK FLIES HIGH (LP)	£25
59	HMC CLP 1293	GENIUS OF COLEMAN HAWKINS (LP)	£30
59	Felsted FJA 7005	THE HIGH AND MIGHTY HAWK (LP, also stereo SJA 2005)	£35
61	Esquire 32-095	SOUL (LP)	£35
61	Esquire 32-102	HAWK EYES (LP)	£40
61	Moodsville MV 7	COLEMAN HAWKINS (LP)	£25
62	Swingsville SVLP 2001	COLEMAN HAWKINS WITH THE RED GARLAND TRIO (LP)	£20
62	Swingsville SVLP 2005	THE COLEMAN HAWKINS ALL STARS (LP)	£20
62	Swingsville SVLP 2013	STASCH (LP)	£20
63	HMV CLP 1630	DESAFINADO (LP, also stereo CSD 1484)	£20
64	Verve VLP 9044	ALIVE! AT THE VILLAGE GATE (LP)	£20
64	HMV CLP 1689	TODAY AND NOW (LP)	£20
64	CBS BPG 62157	BACK IN BEAN'S BAG (LP, with Clark Terry)	£15
64	Fontana FJL 102	SWING' (LP)	£15
65	Fontana TL 5273	MEDITATION (LP)	£15
66	Fontana SJL 131	CATTIN' (LP)	£15

(see also Milt Jackson & Coleman Hawkins, Eddie 'Lockjaw' Davis, Sir Charles Thompson)

COLEMAN HAWKINS GROUP
58	London LTZC 15048	COLEMAN HAWKINS GROUP (LP)	£18

(see also Coleman Hawkins)

COLEMAN HAWKINS & LESTER YOUNG
65	Stateside SL 10117	CLASSIC TENORS (LP)	£20

DALE HAWKINS
57	London HL 8482	Susie-Q/Don't Treat Me That Way	£500
57	London HL 8482	Susie-Q/Don't Treat Me That Way (78)	£80
58	London HLM 8728	La-Do-Dada/Cross Ties	£40
58	London HLM 8728	La-Do-Dada/Cross Ties (78)	£15
59	London HLM 8842	Yea-Yea (Class Cutter)/Lonely Nights	£40
59	London HLM 8842	Yea-Yea (Glass Cutter)/Lonely Nights (78)	£15
59	London HLM 9016	Liza Jane/Back To School Blues	£40
59	London HLM 9016	Liza Jane/Back To School Blues (78)	£15
60	London HLM 9060	Hot Dog/Our Turn	£40
69	Bell SBLL 127	L.A., MEMPHIS AND TYLER, TEXAS (LP)	£25
73	Checker 6467 301	OH! SUSIE Q (LP)	£15

ERSKINE HAWKINS QUINTET
60	Brunswick LAT 8374	THE HAWK BLOWS AT MIDNIGHT (LP, also stereo STA 3042)	£15

HAWKSHAW HAWKINS

51	Vogue V 9003	Doghouse Boogie/Yesterday's Kisses (78)	£15
54	Parlophone CMSP 1	Betty Lorraine/CHARLIE GORE & LOUIS INNIS: Mexican Joe (export issue)	£30
58	Parlophone GEP 8742	COUNTRY AND WESTERN (EP)	£30
58	Vogue VE 170117	HAWKSHAW HAWKINS - COUNTRY AND WESTERN (EP)	£30
64	London HA 8181	THE ALL NEW HAWKSHAW HAWKINS (LP)	£20

(see also Charlie Gore, Louis Innis)

RONNIE HAWKINS (& HAWKS)

59	Columbia DB 4319	Forty Days (To Come Back Home)/One Of These Days	£50
59	Columbia DB 4345	Mary Lou/Need Your Lovin' (Oh So Bad)	£50
60	Columbia DB 4412	Southern Love (Whatcha-Gonna' Do)/Love Me Like You Can	£20
60	Columbia DB 4442	Clara/Lonely Hours	£30
63	Columbia DB 7036	Bo Diddley/Who Do You Love?	£30
60	Columbia SEG 7983	ROCKIN' WITH RONNIE (EP, mono)	£70
60	Columbia ESG 7792	ROCKIN' WITH RONNIE (EP, stereo)	£100
60	Columbia SEG 7988	ROCKIN' WITH RONNIE (EP, mono)	£70
60	Columbia ESG 7795	ROCKIN' WITH RONNIE (EP, stereo)	£100
60	Columbia 33SX 1238	MR. DYNAMO (LP, mono)	£70
60	Columbia SCX 3315	MR. DYNAMO (LP, stereo)	£100
60	Columbia 33SX 1295	THE FOLK BALLADS OF RONNIE HAWKINS (LP, mono)	£40
60	Columbia SCX 3358	THE FOLK BALLADS OF RONNIE HAWKINS (LP, stereo)	£50
70	Roulette RCP 1003	ARKANSAS ROCK PILE (LP, with The Band)	£20

(see also Band, Levon & Hawks)

SCREAMIN' JAY HAWKINS

58	Fontana H 107	I Put A Spell On You/Little Demon (78)	£60
64	Columbia DB 7460	The Whammy/Strange	£40
65	Sue WI 379	I Hear Voices/Just Don't Care	£40
66	Sue WI 4008	I Put A Spell On You/Little Demon (unissued)	£0
69	Direction 58-4097	I Put A Spell On You/Little Demon	£20
66	Planet PLL 1001	THE NIGHT AND DAY OF SCREAMIN' JAY HAWKINS (LP)	£125
69	Direction (S) 8-63481	I PUT A SPELL ON YOU (LP, mono or stereo)	£70
69	Mercury SMCL 20178	WHAT THAT IS (LP)	£50

(see also Keith Richards)

H. HAWKLINE

12	Trash Aesthetics TA 1202	BLACK DOMINO BOX EP (12" with poster)	£15
10	Shape SHAPE 013	A CUP OF SALT (LP, numbered)	£35
11	Shape SHAPE 017	THE STRANGE USES OF OX GALL (LP, numbered)	£30
14	Heavenly HVNLPCC 108	SALT GALL BOX GHOULS (LP)	£20

HAWKLORDS

| 78 | Charisma CDS 4014 | 25 YEARS ON (LP, with inner sleeve, sold with separate tour book) | £20 |
| 78 | Charisma CDS 4014 | 25 YEARS ON (LP, with inner sleeve) | £15 |

(see also Hawkwind)

ALAN HAWKSHAW

79	BBC RESL 64	Grange Hill/Stoned (credited to Deluxe)	£20
72	Studio Two TWO 391	27 TOP TV THEMES AND COMMERCIALS (LP)	£30
72	KPM 1080	FLUTE FOR MODERNS (with Alan Parker and Joe Hailer) (LP)	£35

(see also Shadows, Bizarre)

JOHNNY HAWKSWORTH (ORCHESTRA)

| 65 | Pye 7N 15969 | Lunar Walk/It's Murder (as Johnny Hawksworth Orchestra) | £15 |
| 64 | Columbia 33SX 1654 | I'VE GROWN ACCUSTOMED TO MY BASS (LP) | £50 |

HAWKWIND

SINGLES

70	Liberty LBF 15382	Hurry On Sundown/Mirror Of Illusion	£400
72	United Artists UP 35381	Silver Machine/Seven By Seven ('machine' art p/s)	£15
73	United Artists (WD 3637)	Sonic Attack (1-sided promo in cloth sleeve)	£400
73	United Artists UP 35566	Urban Guerilla/Brainbox Pollution	£15
73	United Artists USEP 1	HURRY ON HAWKWIND (EP)	£50
75	United Artists UP 35808	Kings Of Speed/Motorhead (in p/s)	£40
80	Bronze BRO 98	Shot Down In The Night/Urban Guerilla (1-sided gold vinyl flexidisc)	£30
83	Liberty UPP 35381	Silver Machine/Seven By Seven (mispressed picture disc, plays Beatles' "Ask Me Why")	£15
86	Samurai HW 001	Silver Machine/Magnu (motorcycle-shaped picture disc)	£15
90	Receiver REPLAY 3014	THE EARLY YEARS LIVE (12", p/s, blue vinyl)	£15
94	Emerg. Broadcast EBS 110	QUARK, STRANGENESS & CHARM (12" EP, clear vinyl, 200 only)	£15

EPS : ORIGINAL ALBUMS

70	Liberty LBS 83348	HAWKWIND (LP, gatefold sleeve; blue label)	£350
70	Liberty LBS 83348	HAWKWIND (LP, gatefold sleeve; black label)	£60
71	United Artists UAG 29202	IN SEARCH OF SPACE (LP in foldout 'door' sleeve, with 'log book')	£150
71	United Artists UAG 29202	IN SEARCH OF SPACE (LP in foldout 'door' sleeve, without 'log book')	£75
72	United Artists UAG 29364	DOREMI-FASOL-LATIDO (LP, with inner sleeve, with poster)	£200
72	United Artists UAG 29364	DOREMI-FASOL-LATIDO (LP, with inner sleeve, without poster)	£150
73	Utd. Artists UAD 60037/8	SPACE RITUAL ALIVE (2-LP, foldout sleeve with inners)	£100
74	United Artists UAG 29672	HALL OF THE MOUNTAIN GRILL (LP, with inner sleeve)	£40
75	United Artists UAG 29766	WARRIOR ON THE EDGE OF TIME (LP, foldout pop-up sleeve with inner)	£100
76	Charisma CDS 4004	ASTOUNDING SOUNDS. AMAZING MUSIC (LP)	£20
76	United Artists UAK 29919	ROADHAWKS (LP, gatefold sleeve with poster & sticker)	£20

MINT VALUE £

76	Mushroom	THE XENON CODEX (LP, with inner, gatefold sleeve)	£15
77	Charisma CDS 4008	QUARK STRANGENESS AND CHARM (LP, 'Mad Hatter' label)	£40
79	Charisma CDS 4016	P.X.R.5 (LP, with family tree poster, with picture of incorrectly wired plug on rear)	£30
79	Charisma CDS 4016	P.X.R.5 (LP, without family tree poster, but with uncensored wired plug on rear)	£15
80	Bronze BRON 530	LEVITATION (LP, blue vinyl)	£20
82	RCA Active RCALP 9004	CHURCH OF HAWKWIND (LP, with lyric booklet)	£15
82	RCA Active RCALP 6055	CHOOSE YOUR MASQUES (LP)	£18
84	Flicknife PSHARP 014	ZONES (LP, picture disc reissue)	£18
84	Flicknife SHARP 022	STONHENGE: THIS IS HAWKWIND DO NOT PANIC (LP, with 12", gatefold sleeve or single sleeve with poster)	£15
85	Demi Monde DM 002	BRING ME THE HEAD OF YURI GAGARIN (LP)	£15
85	Flicknife SHARP 033	CHRONICLE OF THE BLACK SWORD (LP, with inner sleeve)	£15
86	Hawkfan HWFB 2	HAWKFAN 12 (LP, with poster, sticker insert & carrier bag, 600 only)	£70
86	Samurai SMR 046	APPROVED HISTORY OF HAWKWIND 1967-1982 (3-LP, pic discs & booklet)	£45
87	Flicknife HWBOX 01	OFFICIAL PICTURE LOG BOOK (4-LP box set, [3 picture discs & interview disc] with badge & insert)	£35
92	Essential ESSLP 181	ELECTRIC TEPEE (2-LP, 5,000 only, numbered)	£35
94	Emergency Broadcast System EBS 111	THE BUSINESS TRIP (2-LP, clear vinyl, 1,500 only)	£25
95	Emergency Broadcast System EBSLP 118	ALIEN 4 (2-LP, gatefold sleeve)	£40
96	Emergency Broadcast System EBSLP 120	LOVE IN SPACE (2-LP, gatefold)	£40
16	Cherry Red BRED 688	THE MACHINE STOPS (LP, with free 12")	£25
17	Cherry Red BREDT700	INTO THE WOODS (2-LP)	£20
17	Cherry Red BREDT721	AT THE ROUNDHOUSE (3-LP, poster)	£35

ALBUMS : REISSUES

75	Sunset SLS 50374	HAWKWIND (LP, reissue)	£15
77	United Artists UAG 29364	DOREMI-FASOL-LATIDO (LP, reissue, with poster and inner sleeve)	£15
77	United Artists UAD 6003718	SPACE RITUAL (2-LP)	£15
79	United Artists UAG 29766	WARRIOR ON THE EDGE OF TIME (LP, reissue)	£20
80	Liberty LBR 1012	HAWKWIND (LP, reissue, 'Rock File' different p/s)	£15
80	United Artists UAD 60037	SPACE RITUAL (2-LP, reissue)	£18
81	Liberty UAG 29766	WARRIOR ON THE EDGE OF TIME (LP, reissue)	£15
81	Liberty LBG 29292	IN SEARCH OF SPACE (LP, reissue)	£15
82	Charisma CDS 4008	QUARK STRANGENESS AND CHARM (LP, reissue, blue label)	£15
84	Liberty SLP 1972921	HAWKWIND (LP, reissue, picture disc, die-cut)	£15
84	Liberty SLS 1972921	HAWKWIND (LP, reissue)	£15
00	Simply Vinyl SVLP 266	IN SEARCH OF SPACE (2-LP, 180gm reissue)	£20
09	Let Them Eat Vinyl LETV 024LP	LIVE 1982 (2-LP, green and red vinyl)	£18
11	Back On Black RCV010LP	HAWKWIND (2-LP, reissue, 180gm vinyl)	£20
11	Back On Black RCV012LP	HALL OF THE MOUNTAIN GRILL (2-LP, reissue, black or yellow vinyl)	£20
11	Back On Black RCV013LP	DOREMI-FASOL-LATIDO (2-LP, reissue)	£20
11	Back On Black RCV017LP	SPACE RITUAL VOL 1. (2-LP, reissue, clear, green or black vinyl)	£25
11	Back On Black RCV017LP	SPACE RITUAL VOL 2. (2-LP, reissue, green or yellow vinyl)	£25
15	Let Them Eat Vinyl LETV307LP	WARRIOR ON THE EDGE OF TIME (LP, reissue, black or yellow vinyl)	£15
15	Let Them Eat VInyl LETV 264LP	QUARK STRANGENESS AND CHARM (2-LP, reissue, clear vinyl)	£20

(see also Hawklords, Robert Calvert, Michael Moorcock, Inner City Unit, Sphynx,, Tim Blake, Huw Lloyd Langton Group, Alan Davey, Motorhead, Dr. Technical & Machines, Magic Muscle, Opal Butterfly, Widowmaker, Adrian Shaw, Captain Jesus And The Sunray Team)

RICHARD HAWLEY

12	Parlophone RHSCBOX	THE SINGLE CLUB 1-IV (4 x 10" box set)	£50
03	Setanta SETLP 110	LOWLEDGES (LP)	£70
05	Mute STUMM 251	COLES CORNER (LP)	£150
09	Mute STUMM 312	TRUELOVE'S GUTTER (2-LP, CD & signed print, 1000 only)	£150
12	Parlophone 5099946369819	STANDING AT THE SKY'S EDGE (2-LP)	£25
14	Setanta SETLP 088	LATE NIGHT FINAL (LP, reissue)	£20
14	Setanta SETLP 153	RICHARD HAWLEY (LP, reissue)	£20
18	Live Here Now 030	LIVE AT THE DEVIL'S ARSE (2-LP clear vinyl)	£40
19	Setanta SETLP088	LATE NIGHT FINAL (LP, reissue, red or clear vinyl)	£20
19	Setanta SETLP170	COLES CORNER (LP, reissue, red vinyl)	£40
19	Setanta SETLP110	LOWLEDGES (LP, reissue)	£20

(see also Longpigs)

HAXAN CLOAK

| 13 | Aurora Borealis ABX 050 | HAXAN CLOAK (2-LP, 1st pressing, 300 on black and 300 on clear vinyl) | £15 |

HAYDEN WOOD

| 69 | NEMS 56 4499 | House Beside The Mine/Lady Wants More | £25 |
| 70 | NEMS 4803 | Sixty Years On/The Last One To Know | £25 |

HAYDOCK'S ROCKHOUSE

| 66 | Columbia DB 8050 | Cupid/She Thinks | £70 |
| 67 | Columbia DB 8135 | Lovin' You/Mix A Fix | £60 |

(see also Hollies)

BILL HAYES

53	MGM SP 1036	The Donkey Song/My Ever-Lovin'	£15
55	London HL 8149	The Berry Tree/Blue Black Hair	£25
56	London HLA 8220	Ballad Of Davy Crockett/Farewell	£25
56	London HLA 8239	Kwela Kwela/The White Buffalo	£20

56	London HLA 8300	Das Ist Musik/I Know An Old Lady	£20
56	London HLA 8325	The Legend Of Wyatt Earp/That Do Make It Nice	£15
57	London HL 8430	Wringle Wrangle/Westward Ho The Wagons	£15
56	London RE-A 1051	GREAT PIONEERS OF THE WEST (EP)	£15

ISAAC HAYES

69	Stax SXATS 1028	HOT BUTTERED SOUL (LP)	£40
70	Stax SXATS 1032	THE ISAAC HAYES MOVEMENT (LP)	£30
70	Stax 2465 016	BLUE HAYES (LP, with Presenting Isaac Hayes on labels)	£25
71	Stax 2325 026	TO BE CONTINUED (LP)	£30
71	Stax 2325 014	THE ISAAC HAYES MOVEMENT (LP, reissue)	£15
71	Stax 2659 007	SHAFT - ORIGINAL SOUNDTRACK (2-LP, soundtrack, gatefold sleeve)	£15
72	Atlantic K 40327	IN THE BEGINNING (LP)	£15
72	Stax 2628 004	BLACK MOSES (2-LP, cruciform sleeve)	£50
73	Stax 2362 032	LIVE AT THE SAHARA TAHOE (2-LP)	£25
74	Stax 2325 111	JOY (LP)	£15
74	Stax STXD 4001/2	TRUCK TURNER (2-LP, soundtrack)	£15
95	Virgin VPBLP24	BRANDED (LP)	£30

LINDA HAYES

| 55 | Parlophone MSP 6174 | Please Have Mercy (with Platters)/Oochi Pachi (with Tony Williams) | £300 |
| 55 | Parlophone R 4038 | Please Have Mercy (with Platters)/Oochi Pachi (with Tony Williams) (78) | £50 |

(see also Platters)

TUBBY HAYES

62	Fontana H 397	Sally/I Believe In You (as Tubby Hayes Quintet)	£25
55	Tempo EXA 14	THE LITTLE GIANT (EP)	£75
55	Tempo EXA 17	TUBBY HAYES AND HIS ORCHESTRA (EP)	£30
55	Tempo EXA 27	THE SWINGING GIANT NO. 1 (EP, as Tubby Hayes Quartet)	£50
56	Tempo EXA 28	THE SWINGING GIANT NO. 2 (EP, as Tubby Hayes Quartet)	£50
56	Tempo EXA 36	MODERN JAZZ SCENE (EP, as Tubby Hayes & His Orchestra)	£60
57	Tempo EXA 55	AFTER LIGHTS OUT (EP, as Tubby Hayes Quintet)	£60
57	Tempo EXA 75	TUBBY HAYES AND THE JAZZ COURIERS (EP)	£60
58	Tempo EXA 82	THE EIGHTH WONDER (EP, solo)	£60
09	Trunk TTT005	VOODOO SESSION (EP, 1st pressing 666 copies only)	£30
57	Tempo TAP 6	AFTER LIGHTS OUT (LP, as Tubby Hayes Quintet)	£600
57	Tempo TAP 15	JAZZ COURIERS (LP)	£450
60	Tempo TAP 29	TUBBY'S GROOVE (LP, as Tubby Hayes Quartet)	£450
61	Fontana TFL 5142	TUBBS (LP, also stereo STFL 562)	£200
61	Ember EMB 3337	AN EVENING WITH MR. PERCUSSION (LP, with Tony Kinsey)	£70
61	Fontana TFL 5183	TUBBS IN NEW YORK (LP, also stereo STFL 595)	£120
63	Fontana 680 998 TL	DOWN IN THE VILLAGE (LP, mono)	£350
63	Fontana 886 163TY	DOWN IN THE VILLAGE (LP, stereo)	£250
64	Fontana (S)TL 5195	RETURN VISIT! (LP)	£150
64	Fontana TL 5200	LATE SPOT AT SCOTT'S (LP)	£250
66	Fontana (S)TL 5221	TUBBS' TOURS (LP, with Orchestra)	£70
66	Fontana (S)TL 5410	100% PROOF (LP)	£70
67	Wing WL 1162	TUBBS IN NEW YORK (LP, reissue)	£20
69	Fontana SFJL 911	MEXICAN GREEN (LP)	£100
71	Fontana 6309 002	THE TUBBY HAYES ORCHESTRA (LP)	£30
72	Philips 6382 041	THIS IS JAZZ - 100% PROOF (LP)	£20
81	Mole MOLE 2	MEXICAN GREEN (LP, reissue)	£20
81	Mole MOLE 4	TUBBS' TOURS (LP, reissue)	£20
82	Jasmine JASM 2015	AFTER LIGHTS OUT (LP, reissue)	£20
90	CBS Masterpieces CBS 466363-1	TUBBY HAYES WITH CLARK TERRY THE NEW YORK SESSIONS (LP, reissue)	£25
90	MMO 79	67 LIVE - FOR MEMBERS ONLY (LP)	£20
09	Gearbox GB 1502	BBC JAZZ FOR MODERNS (LP)	£30

(see also Jack Constanzo & Tubby Hayes, Jazz Couriers, London Jazz Quartet, Dave Lee, Ronnie Scott, Roy Castle)

TUBBY HAYES & CLEO LAINE

| 61 | Fontana TFL 5151 | PALLADIUM JAZZ DATE (LP, also stereo STFL 570) | £20 |

(see also Cleo Laine)

TUBBY HAYES & PAUL GONSALVES ALLSTARS

65	Columbia SCX 6003	JUST FRIENDS (LP, stereo, laminated flipback sleeve, as Paul Gonsalves & Tubby Hayes)	£400
65	Columbia SX 6003	JUST FRIENDS (LP, mono, laminated flipback sleeve, as Paul Gonsalves & Tubby Hayes)	£250
67	World Record Club T 631	CHANGE OF SETTING (LP, stereo, laminated flipback sleeve)	£120

(see also Paul Gonsalves, Tubby Hayes)

LOU HAYLES

| 77 | Myrrh MYR 1055 | DON'T HIDE AWAY (LP) | £22 |

ROY HAYNES QUARTET

| 62 | HMV CLP 1628 | OUT OF THE AFTERNOON (LP) | £30 |

ROY HAYNES, PHINEAS NEWBORN, PAUL CHAMBERS TRIO

| 61 | Esquire 32-103 | WE THREE (LP) | £30 |

STEVE HAYNES BAND

| 78 | Black Bear BLA 2005 | Back In My Arms Again/Walk On By (p/s) | £20 |
| 78 | Black Bear BLA 2008 | Save Me Save Me/Strong Good Lovin' (p/s) | £15 |

MINT VALUE £

HAYSTACKS BALBOA
70	Polydor	Spoiler/Bruce's Twist	£25
70	Polydor 2489 002	HAYSTACKS BALBOA (LP)	£100

CHARLES HAYWARD
87	Ink INK 31	SURVIVE THE GESTURE (LP)	£20
17	Care In The Community CARE112LP	IMPROVISATIONS (LP, with Thurston Moore)	£25

(see also This Heat, Camberwell Now)

JUSTIN HAYWARD
65	Pye 7N 17041	London Is Behind Me/Day Must Come	£150
66	Parlophone R 5496	I Can't Face The World Without You/I'll Be Here Tomorrow	£200
80	CBS 11-7731	The Eve Of The War/Horsell (12" picture disc)	£15

(see also Wilde Three)

RICK HAYWARD
71	Blue Horizon 2431 006	RICK HAYWARD (LP)	£200

(see also Accent, Christine Perfect)

JOE HAYWOOD
65	Island WI 218	Warm And Tender Love/I Would If I Could	£35

LEON HAYWOOD
66	Vocalion VL 9280	Ain't No Use/Hey, Hey, Hey	£30
66	Vocalion VL 9280	Ain't No Use/Hey, Hey, Hey (DJ copy)	£50
67	Vocalion VL 9288	Ever Since You Were Sweet Sixteen/Skate Awhile	£30
70	Capitol CL 15634	I Wanna Thank You/I Was Sent To Love You	£15
78	Fantasy FTC 151	Baby Reconsider/Would I	£15
67	Vocalion VAL 8064	SOUL CARGO (LP)	£75
69	MCA MUPS 369	IT'S GOT TO BE MELLOW (LP)	£20
73	Pye Intl. NSPL 28177	BACK TO STAY (LP)	£25
75	20th Century BT 476	COME AND GET YOURSELF SOME (LP)	£15

HAZARD
79	Rok ROK VII/VIII	Gotta Change My Life/CLERKS: No Good For Me	£15

HAZE (1)
74	Haze HAZE 00174	HAZE (LP, 100 only)	£100

HAZE (2)
81	Mushroom MUSH 1	The Night/Dig Them Mushrooms	£20
84	Gabadon GABL 001	C'EST LA VIE (LP)	£25

EDDIE HAZEL
16	Be With BEWTH011LP	GAMES, DAMES AND GUITAR THANGS (LP, reissue)	£40

HAZEL & JOLLY BOYS
67	Doctor Bird DB 1063	Stop Them/Deep Down	£35

LEE HAZLEWOOD
60	London HLW 9223	Words Mean Nothing/The Girl On Death Row (with Duane Eddy)	£35
66	MGM MGM-CS 8014	THE VERY SPECIAL WORLD OF LEE HAZLEWOOD (LP)	£40
68	Reprise RSLP 6297	LOVE AND OTHER CRIMES (LP)	£25
69	London HA-N/SH-N 8398	TROUBLE IS A LONESOME TOWN (LP)	£40
69	Music For Pleasure MFP 1309	THE VERY SPECIAL WORLD OF LEE HAZLEWOOD (LP, reissue)	£15
72	Reprise K 44161	REQUIEM FOR AN ALMOST LADY (LP)	£50
74	Stateside SSL 10315	POET, FOOL OR BUM (LP)	£40
02	City Slang 20194-1	FOR EVERY SOLUTION THERE IS A PROBLEM (LP)	£30

(see also Nancy Sinatra & Lee Hazlewood, Duane Eddy)

OSTERWALK HAZY
72	Jam JAM 22	Oumbalo Oumbalo/Tai Weh	£15

HAZZARD
81	Rammy EJSP9600	Snake In The Grass/Kicked To The Ground (p/s)	£100

TONY HAZZARD
66	Columbia DB 7927	You'll Never Put Shackles On Me/Calling You Home	£20
69	CBS 63608	TONY HARRARD SINGS (LP, orange label)	£60
71	Bronze ILPS 9174	LOUDWATER HOUSE (LP, gatefold sleeve, lyric inner sleeve)	£20
73	Bronze ILPS 9222	WAS THAT ALRIGHT THEN? (LP, gatefold sleeve, lyric inner sleeve)	£20

MICHAEL HEAD & STRANDS
95	Megaphone Music MEGA 01	THE MAGICAL WORLD OF THE STRANDS (LP, gatefold sleeve)	£60

(see also Pale Saints, Shack)

MURRAY HEAD
67	Immediate IM 053	She Was Perfection/Secondhand Monday	£70
73	CBS 65503	NIGEL LIVED (LP, gatefold sleeve and booklet)	£30
75	Island ILPS 9347	SAY IT AIN'T SO (LP, gatefold sleeve, blue rim palm tree label)	£15

ROY HEAD (& TRAITS)
65	Pye International 7N 25340	Just A Little Bit/Treat Me Right	£20
65	Vocalion VP 9248	Treat Her Right/So Long, My Love	£20
66	Vocalion VP 9254	Apple Of My Eye/I Pass The Day	£15
66	Vocalion VP 9269	My Babe/Pain	£20
66	Vocalion VP 9274	Wigglin' And Gigglin'/Driving Wheel	£20
66	London HLZ 10097	To Make A Big Man Cry/Don't Cry No More	£15
66	Pye Intl. NEP 44053	JUST A LITTLE BIT OF ROY HEAD (EP)	£50

70	Stateside SSL 5033	**SAME PEOPLE** (LP)	£25

(see also Traits)

HEAD (1)
73	SRT 72254	**GTF** (LP)	£150
75	Canon CNN 5970	**RED DWARF** (LP)	£60

HEAD (2)
77	HEAD HSLP333333333C	**BLACKPOOL COOL** (LP)	£60

HEAD (3)
79	Ellie Jay MB1	**Nothing To Do In A Town Like Leatherhead/University '79**	£60
96	Headhunter HH 7 01	**Gnu/Demonizer 48/48** (p/s, 1000 only)	£15

HEADACHE
77	Lout 001	**Can't Stand Still/No Reason For Your Call** (p/s)	£20

HEAD ARSE FUSION BAND
00	U-Star US 009	**UNTITLED EP** (12")	£40

HEADCLEANERS
83	Xcentric Noise THIRD 1	**THE INFECTION GROWS EP**	£70

HEADCOATS (THEE)
89	Hangman HANG 29 UP	**HEADCOATS DOWN** (LP)	£18
90	Hangman HANG 32 UP	**THE KIDS ARE ALL SQUARE** (LP)	£18
91	Hangman HANG 40 UP	**W.O.A.H.** (LP)	£18
01	Hangman HANG 54 UP	**LIVE AT THE DIRTY WATER CLUB** (LP)	£18

(see also Milkshakes, Thee Headcoats)

HEADHUNTERS
76	Arista ARTY 116	**SURVIVAL OF THE FITTEST** (LP)	£25
77	Arista SPART 1046	**STRAIGHT FROM THE GATE** (LP)	£15

(see also Herbie Hancock)

HEADLESS CHICKENS
89	Hometown Atrocities 1	**THE HOMETOWN ATROCITIES EP** (wraparound p/s with 3 inserts, 'kylie')	£100
89	Hometown Atrocities 1	**THE HOMETOWN ATROCITIES EP** (wraparound p/s, 'glossy')	£40
89	Maelstrom Storm 1	**THE HOMETOWN ATROCITIES EP** (repress of above)	£15

(see also Radiohead)

HEAD MACHINE
70	Major Minor SMLP 79	**ORGASM** (LP, laminated front sleeve, 'Major Minor' on front sleeve beneath word 'Orgasm' red/white/black labels)	£500

(see also Uriah Heep)

HEAD OF DAVID
89	Blast First WANT 001	**WHITE ELEPHANT** (LP, mail-order only)	£15

HEADS
94	Rooster ROOSTER 1	**Quad/Woke Up/Looking At You** (p/s, 500 only, with "Rizla" papers)	£45
94	Rooster ROOSTER 1	**Quad/Woke Up/Looking At You** (p/s, 500 only, without "Rizla" papers)	£30
95	Headhunter HED 718	**Television/Steamroller '95/Jellystoned Park** (8.47 Edit) (p/s)	£20
95	Rooster ROOSTER 2	**Coogan's Bluff/J Walking/Theme** (p/s 1000 only)	£20
00	Rocket LAUNCH 008	**Spliff Riff** (Conga'd Out)**/75** (All Of It) (p/s, 4 inserts, First press 100 yellow vinyl)	£20
00	Rocket LAUNCH 008	**Spliff Riff** (Conga'd Out)**/75** (All Of It) (p/s, 4 inserts, First press 400 black vinyl)	£15
95	Headhunter HUK 001	**RELAXING WITH...** (LP)	£80
00	Sweet Nothing SNLP 007	**EVERYBODY KNOWS WE GOT NOWHERE** (2-LP)	£35
02	Rocket LAUNCH 015	**SESSIONS 02** (LP, limited edition of 100, blue vinyl with free 7", 10 inserts)	£100
02	Rocket LAUNCH 015	**SESSIONS 02** (LP, 900 copies, black vinyl)	£35
02	Sweet Nothing SNLP 011	**UNDER SIDED** (2-LP)	£30
03	Rocket LAUNCH 018	**AT LAST** (LP)	£35
05	Invada INV 015	**33** (LP, blue or black vinyl)	£20
05	Invada INV 017	**DEAD IN THE WATER** (2-LP, pink marbled vinyl)	£30
06	Rocket LAUNCH 26/INVLP 24	**UNDER THE STRESS OF A HEADLONG DIVE** (2-LP)	£20
09	Rocket LAUNCH 033LP	**COLLISIONS V.1** (LP, one side Heads one side WHITE HILLS, 150 orange vinyl with poster)	£30
09	Rocket LAUNCH 033LP	**COLLISIONS V.1** (LP, one side Heads one side WHITE HILLS, 150 orange vinyl without poster)	£20

HEADS TOGETHER
74	SRT SRTM 73345	**FUNKY STUFF** (LP)	£35

HEADS, HANDS & FEET
71	Island ILPS 9149	**HEADS, HANDS AND FEET** (LP, gatefold, pink rim palm tree label)	£25
72	Island ILPS 9185	**TRACKS** (LP, gatefold, pink rim palm tree label)	£22
73	Atlantic K40465	**OLD SOLIDERS NEVER DIE** (LP, gatefold sleeve, lyric insert)	£15

(see also Tony Colton, Poet & One Man Band)

HEADSTONE
74	EMI EMA 766	**BAD HABITS** (LP, gatefold sleeve)	£20
75	EMI EMC 3673	**HEADSTONE** (LP)	£20

LARRY HEARD
94	Black Market BM1020LP	**SCENERIES NOT SONGS, VOLUME ONE** (LP)	£75
98	Mecca MEC LP 002	**ICE CASTLES** (LP)	£35

(see also Mr Fingers, Fingers Inc.)

HEART (1)
77	Arista SPART 1024	**MAGAZINE** (LP, withdrawn)	£15
77	Arista SPART 1024	**MAGAZINE** (LP, picture disc)	£15

			MINT VALUE £

HEART BEATS
90 Capitol HGIFT 1 HEART BOX SET (3-LP: "Heart", "Bad Animals" & "Brigade" + 24pp booklet) £18

HEART BEATS
81 Nothing Shaking SHAD 1 Go/One Of The People (p/s, blue vinyl) £15

HEARTBREAKERS
77 Track 2094 135T Chinese Rocks/Born To Lose (12", p/s) £15
77 Track 2094 142 It's Not Enough/Let Go (p/s, withdrawn) £250
77 Track 2409 218 L.A.M.F. (LP) £35
79 Beggars Banquet BEGA 9 LIVE AT MAX'S KANSAS CITY (LP, with inner bag) £15
81 Jungle FREUD 1 D.T.K. - LIVE AT THE SPEAKEASY (LP, white or pink vinyl) £20
84 Jungle FREUD 4 L.A.M.F. REVISITED (LP, picture disc) £20
84 Jungle FREUD 4 L.A.M.F. REVISITED (white label with withdrawn test proof sleeve) £150
88 Jungle FREUDP 1 D.T.K. - LIVE AT THE SPEAKEASY (LP, reissue, picture disc) £18
(see also New York Dolls, Johnny Thunders)

HEARTS (U.K.)
64 Parlophone R 5147 Young Woman/Black Eyes £20

HEARTS (U.S.)
64 Stateside SS 268 Dear Abby/Dear Abby (Instrumental) £22

JOHN HEARTSMAN AND CIRCLES
09 Jazzman JMANLP 030 MUSIC OF MY HEART (2-LP) £25

HEARTS OF SOUL
70 Columbia DB 8670 Waterman/Fat Jack £20

HEAT EXCHANGE
79 EMI EMC 3306 ONE STEP AHEAD (LP) £15
(see also Brian Bennett)

HEATERS
70 Upsetter US 329 Melting Pot/UPSETTERS: Kinky Mood £30

JIMMY HEATH
60 Riverside RLP 333 REALLY BIG (LP) £20

HEATWAVE (1)
70 Penny Farthing PEN 738 Sister Simon (Funny Man)/Rastus Ravel £30

HEATWAVE (2)
75 Harp HSP 1055 One-Eyed Man/999 ....£50
76 GTO GT 59 Ain't No Half Stepping/Special Offer £20

HEAVEN
72 CBS 7782 Hangin On/Funny Lines £25
71 CBS 66293 BRASS ROCK 1 (2-LP, ornate fold-out sleeve) £100

HEAVEN & EARTH
73 London SHO 8448 REFUGE (LP) £50

HEAVENLY
89 Sarah SARAH 30 I Fell In Love Last Night/Over And Over (p/s) £20
91 Sarah SARAH 41 Our Love Is Heavenly/Wrap My Arms Around Him (p/s, insert) £20
91 Sarah SARAH 51 So Little Deserve/I'm Not Scared Of You (p/s, insert) £20
93 Sarah SARAH 81 P.U.N.K. Girl/Hearts And Crosses (p/s, insert) £45
93 Sarah SARAH 82 Atta Girl/Dig Your Own Grave/So? (p/s, insert) £18
91 Sarah SARAH 603 HEAVENLY VS SATAN (LP) £20
92 Sarah SARAH 610 LE JARDIN DE HEAVENLY (LP) £30
94 Sarah SARAH 623 THE DECLINE AND FALL OF HEAVENLY (LP) £35
96 Wiiija WIJLP 1053 OPERATION HEAVENLY (LP) £35
(see also Talulah Gosh, Amelia Fletcher)

HEAVEN 17
82 Virgin VS 483 Height Of The Fighting (He-La-Hu)/Honeymoon In New York (unissued, no p/s) £15
(see also B.E.F., Human League, Glenn Gregory & Claudia Brucken)

HEAVY JELLY
69 Head HDS 4001 Time Out Chewn In/The Long Wait £20
69 Island WIP 6049 I Keep Singing The Same Old Song/Blue £30
70 Island HELP HEAVY JELLY (LP, promo only) £250
(see also Jackie Lomax, Aynsley Dunbar Retaliation, Skip Bifferty, Griffin, Graham Bell, Arc)

HEAVY METAL KIDS
74 Atlantic K 50047 HEAVY METAL KIDS (LP, with poster) £15
77 Rak SRAK 523 KITSCH (LP) £15
(see also Kids)

HEAVY PUKE
80 (No label or cat no) Spunk Bunny/Ozymandias (p/s, handwritten white labels) £30

HEAVYWEIGHT
91 One After D ODE3 The Way Of The Future (12") £45

HEAVYWEIGHTS
69 Spark SRL 1033 Utterly Funky/Shambala £30

BOBBY HEBB
66 Philips BF 1522 A Satisfied Mind/Love Love Love £40
68 Philips BF 1702 You Want To Change Me/Dreamy £100
66 Philips BL 7740 SUNNY (LP) £30

DICK HECKSTALL-SMITH (QUINTET)
| 57 | Pye Jazz NJE 1037 | VERY SPECIAL OLD JAZZ (EP, as Dick Heckstall-Smith Quintet) | £40 |
| 72 | Bronze ILPS 9196 | A STORY ENDED (LP, gatefold, printed inner) | £50 |

(see also Graham Bond Organisation, John Mayall & Bluesbreakers, Alexis Korner, Colosseum, Rocket 88)

HECTOR
| 73 | DJM DJS 289 | Wired Up/Ain't Got Time | £30 |
| 74 | DJM DJS 303 | Bye Bye Bad Days/Lady | £30 |

JESSE HECTOR
| 98 | Dig The Fuzz DIG 029 | CRUSHED BUTLER : UNCRUSHED (10" LP gatefold) | £20 |

(see also Crushed Butler, Hammersmith Gorillas, Gorillas, Helter Skelter)

HEDGEHOG AFFAIR
| 94 | Sound Entity SENT 1206 | RUSH TILL DAWN PRESENTS THE HEDGEHOG AFFAIR PT. 5 EP (12") | £20 |

HEDGEHOG PIE
71	Rubber RUB 004	HIS ROUND (LP, with Tony Capstick, gatefold, first pressing with black label on side 1 and white label on side 2)	£20
75	Rubber RUB 009	HEDGEHOG PIE (LP)	£30
75	Rubber RUB 014	GREEN LADY (LP)	£50
78	Rubber RUB 024	JUST ACT NORMAL (LP, with lyric insert)	£20

(see also Dando Shaft)

HEDONE
| 84 | Omgowa Power HEAD 001 | Sensible/Everything's Going To Be Nice (no p/s) | £50 |

HEERA
| 86 | Arishma ARI 004 | DIAMONDS FROM HEERA (LP) | £20 |

HEFNER
97	Boogie Wonderland BWL020	A BETTER FRIEND EP (7" p/s with two inserts)	£15
97	Boogie Wonderland BWL 023	Lee Remick/Schoolgirls Knees (p/s)	£15
98	Sticky STICKY 23	A Hymn For The Alcohol/My Art College Days Are Over (p/s, 500 only)	£15
98	Too Pure PURE 83LP	BREAKING GOD'S HEART (LP)	£35
99	Too Pure PURE 92LP	THE FIDELITY WARS (LP)	£50
00	Too Pure PURE 99LP	BOXING HEFNER (LP)	£35
00	Too Pure PURE 106LP	WE LOVE THE CITY (LP)	£40
01	Too Pure PURE 105LP	DEAD MEDIA (LP)	£35
22	Where It's At Is Where You Are wia101 lp	MAIDA VALE (LP, translucent "Reign In Blood' red vinyl, RSD, ltd to 500 copies, reissue of 2006 CD)	£25

NEAL HEFTI & ORCHESTRA
66	RCA Victor RCA 1521	The Batman Theme/Batman Chase	£30
54	Vogue/Coral LVC 10005	SWINGIN' ON A CORAL REEF (10" LP)	£15
65	Warner Bros W 1599	HARLOW (LP, soundtrack)	£15
65	United Artists (S)ULP 1098	HOW TO MURDER YOUR WIFE (LP, soundtrack)	£15
67	London HA-D 8337	BAREFOOT IN THE PARK (LP, soundtrack)	£15
68	Dot (S)LPD 514	THE ODD COUPLE (LP, soundtrack)	£15

LUCILLE HEGAMIN
| 73 | VJM VLP 50 | BLUE FLAME (LP) | £15 |

DONALD HEIGHT
66	London HLZ 10062	Talk Of The Grapevine/There'll Be No Tomorrow	£130
66	London HLZ 10062	Talk Of The Grapevine/There'll Be No Tomorrow (DJ copy)	£175
67	London HLZ 10116	Three Hundred & Sixty Five Days/I'm Willing To Wait	£100
67	London HLZ 10116	Three Hundred & Sixty Five Days/I'm Willing To Wait (DJ copy)	£140
71	Avco Embassy 6105 005	Dancin' To The Music Of Love/Rags To Riches To Rags	£75
71	Jay Boy BOY 32	Talk Of The Grapevine/There'll Be No Tomorrow (reissue)	£15

HEINZ (& WILD BOYS)
63	Decca F 11652	Dreams Do Come True/Been Invited To A Party	£20
64	Decca F 11920	Please Little Girl/For Loving Me This Way	£20
64	Columbia DB 7374	Questions I Can't Answer/The Beating Of My Heart	£20
65	Columbia DB 7482	Diggin' My Potatoes/She Ain't Comin' Back (with Wild Boys)	£40
65	Columbia DB 7559	Don't Think Twice, It's All Right/Big Fat Spider	£30
65	Columbia DB 7656	End Of The World/You Make Me Feel So Good	£40
65	Columbia DB 7779	Heart Full Of Sorrow/Don't Worry Baby	£40
66	Columbia DB 7942	Movin' In/I'm Not A Bad Guy	£40
63	Decca DFE 8545	HEINZ (EP)	£40
63	Decca DFE 8559	LIVE IT UP (EP)	£30
64	Decca LK 4599	TRIBUTE TO EDDIE (LP)	£50

(see also Tornados, Saints)

HEISENBERG
| 89 | Uncertain HEI 5001 | No More Dreams/Rain (p/s) | £20 |

HELDEN
| 83 | Zica 12 ZICA 01 | Holding On/Once Upon A Time In The ... (12", p/s) | £15 |

(see also Ultravox)

HELICOPTER
| 72 | Maple Annie MA 102 | I Belong To Yesterday/Lonely Tonight | £25 |

(see also Galliard)

HELL
| 83 | Deadly Weapons DWS 666 | Save Us From Those Who Would Save Us/Death Squad | £75 |

RICHARD HELL (& VOIDOIDS)
76	Stiff BUY 7	(I Could Live With You In) **Another World**/(I Belong To The) **Blank Generation/You Gotta Lose** (with p/s, numbered, 5,000 only with 4 point press-out centre)	£30
79	Radar ADA 30	**The Kid With The Replaceable Head/I'm Your Man** (p/s)	£15
77	Sire 9103 327	**BLANK GENERATION** (LP, with inner sleeve)	£40
77	Sire 9103 327	**BLANK GENERATION** (LP, without inner sleeve)	£20
83	I.D. NOSE 2	**DESTINY STREET** (LP)	£15

(see also Neon Boys)

HELLACOPTERS
01	Sweet Nothing 12SN007	**HIGH ENERGY ROCK 'N' ROLL** (mini-LP)	£30
04	Sweet Nothing SNLP 040	**STRIKES LIKE LIGHTNING** (3 x 7" box set, cards, badge & pendant)	£30

(see also Super$hit666)

HELLANBACH
80	Guardian GR/HC56	**Out To Get You/Light Of The World/Let's Get This Show On The Road/Nobody's Fool**	£40
84	Neat NEAT 1006	**NOW HEAR THIS** (LP, with inner sleeve)	£15
84	Neat NEAT 1019	**THE BIG ... H** (LP, with insert)	£15

PETE HELLER'S BIG LOVE
98	Junior London CUT 001	**Big Love/Atlanta** (12")	£40

HELLHAMMER
84	Noise N 008	**APOCALYPTIC RAIDS** (12" EP, 45/33rpm)	£50
08	Century Media 9977392	**DEMON ENTRAILS** (3-LP, 180gm vinyl with booklet and poster)	£80

DAVE HELLING
66	Planet PLF 101	**Christine/The Bells**	£50

HELLIONS
65	Piccadilly 7N 35213	**Daydreaming Of You/Shades Of Blue**	£25
65	Piccadilly 7N 35232	**Tomorrow Never Comes/Dream Child**	£25
65	Piccadilly 7N 35265	**A Little Lovin'/Think It Over**	£25

(see also Revolution, Traffic, Roaring Sixties, Jim Capaldi, Dave Mason, Luther Grosvenor, Spooky Tooth)

HELLO
72	Bell BELL 1238	**You Move Me/Ask Your Mama**	£15
76	Bell BELL 1479	**Teenage Revolution/Keeps Us Off The Streets** (demo copies only)	£100
76	Bell BELLS 263	**KEEP US OFF THE STREETS** (LP)	£15

HELL PREACHERS INC.
69	Marble Arch MALS 1169	**SUPREME PSYCHEDELIC UNDERGROUND** (LP)	£40

HELMET
92	Interscope 7567 92162-1	**MEANTIME** (LP, inner)	£70

BOBBY HELMS
58	Brunswick 05730	**No Other Baby/The Magic Song**	£15
58	Brunswick 05741	**Love My Lady/Just A Little Lonesome**	£15
58	Brunswick 05754	**Schoolboy Crush/Borrowed Dreams**	£15
59	Brunswick 05813	**My Lucky Day/Hurry Baby** (78)	£20
60	Brunswick OE 9461	**BOBBY HELMS** (EP)	£30
57	Brunswick LAT 8250	**SINGS TO MY SPECIAL ANGEL** (LP)	£50

JIMMY HELMS
74	Pye 7N 45440	**Ragtime Girl/Romeo & Juliet**	£60

HELP
71	MCA MWPS 4039	**SECOND COMING** (LP)	£80

HELP YOURSELF
71	Liberty LBF 15459	**Running Down Deep/Paper Leaves**	£20
72	United Artists UP 35355	**Heaven Row/Brown Lady**	£15
72	United Artists UP35466	**Mommy Won't Be Home For Christmas/Johnny B. Goode** (demo in picture sleeve)	£60
72	United Artists UP 35466	**Mommy Won't Be Home For Christmas/Johnny B. Goode**	£40
71	Liberty LBS 83484	**HELP YOURSELF** (LP)	£100
72	United Artists UAS 29287	**STRANGE AFFAIR** (LP, with inner sleeve)	£100
72	United Artists UAS 29413	**BEWARE OF THE SHADOW** (LP)	£75
73	United Artists UDG 4001 [UAS 29487/FREE 1]	**THE RETURN OF KEN WHALEY/HAPPY DAYS** (2-LP set in envelope sleeve with LPs in individual sleeves)	£60
73	United Artists UAS 29487	**THE RETURN OF KEN WHALEY** (LP)	£20

(see also Man, Deke Leonard, Wreckless Eric)

HELPLESS HUW
80	US US 002	**Sid Vicious Was Innocent/Going Through The Motions/Baby We're Not In Love/When You're Weary** (p/s in bag)	£15

HELTER SKELTER (1)
69	Peach PO1	**Between Dreams/Run**	£100

HELTER SKELTER (2)
77	Sticky STY 102	**I Need You/Goodbye Baby**	£40

(see also Gorillas, Hammersmith Gorillas, Jesse Hector)

HEMLOCK
73	Deram SML 1102	**HEMLOCK** (LP, white/red label with small logo)	£150

(see also Miller Anderson, Keef Hartley Band, Dog Soldier)

DORRIS HENDERSON
65	Columbia DB 7567	**The Hangman/Leaves That Are Green**	£25
67	Fontana TF 811	**Message To Pretty/Watch The Stars**	£25
65	Columbia SX 6001	**THERE YOU GO** (LP, with John Renbourn)	£175

| 67 | Fontana (S)TL 5385 | WATCH THE STARS (LP, with John Renbourn) ....£175 |

(see also Eclection, John Renbourn)

JOE HENDERSON
| 63 | London REU 1376 | JOE HENDERSON (EP) ....£30 |

LORNA HENDERSON
| 60 | Oriole CB 1549 | Lollipops To Lipstick/Steady Eddie...£25 |
| 60 | Oriole CB 1549 | Lollipops To Lipstick/Steady Eddie (78)...£18 |

BOBBY HENDRICKS
58	London HL 8714	Itchy Twitchy Feeling/A Thousand Dreams £60
58	London HL 8714	Itchy Twitchy Feeling/A Thousand Dreams (78) £30
59	Top Rank JAR 193	Little John Green/Sincerely, Your Lover £20
64	Sue WI 315	Itchy Twitchy Feeling/Thousand Dreams (reissue, as Bobby Henricks)..............£35

(see also Drifters)

HUGH HENDRICKS & UPSETTERS
| 70 | Spinning Wheel SW 103 | Land Of Kinks/O'NEIL HALL: This Man ....£60 |

JIMI HENDRIX (EXPERIENCE)
SINGLES
66	Polydor 56139	Hey Joe/Stone Free (1st pressing credited to Jimi Hendrix, Polydor printed in black type)..£100
66	Polydor 56139	Hey Joe/Stone Free (1st pressing, variant credited to Jimi Hendrix, Polydor printed in white type)...£40
66	Polydor 56139	Hey Joe/Stone Free (2nd pressing credited to Jimi Hendrix Experience)............£20
67	Track 604 001	Purple Haze (1-sided promo, white label with black text)................................£450
67	Track 604 001	Purple Haze/51st Anniversary (white label) £20
67	Track 604 001	Purple Haze/51st Anniversary (black label) £15
67	Track 604 001	Purple Haze/51st Anniversary (black label, alternative mix, but no way of telling from either label or matrix number))..£25
67	Decca F22652	How Would You Feel?/You Won't Want Me (white label copies with stamped Decca logo and hand-written labels)..£100
67	Track 604 007	The Burning Of The Midnight Lamp/The Stars That Play With Laughing Sam's Dice.......£15
67	Decca F 22652	How Would You Feel/You Don't Want Me (with Curtis Knight, test pressing, unreleased)...£500
67	London HL 10160	Hush Now/Flashing (with Curtis Knight; demo)...£50
70	London HL 7126	Ballad Of Jimi/Gloomy Monday (with Curtis Knight, export issue)....................£30
70	Track 2095 001	Voodoo Chile/Hey Joe/All Along The Watchtower (p/s; later copies have white border on sleeve))...£15
71	RCA RCA 2033	No Such Animal (Parts 1 & 2) (initially in p/s, with Curtis Knight uncredited)...........£25
71	Track 2094 010	Gypsy Eyes/Remember/Purple Haze/Stone Free (in p/s))...............................£25
73	Polydor/Sound For Industry SFI 1572	Red House/Spanish Castle Magic (1-sided flexidisc with Rolling Stone)............£15
80	Polydor 260 8001	6 SINGLES PACK (6 plain sleeve singles [2141 275-280], open-out card p/s) £35
82	CBS A 132749	Fire/Are You Experienced (12", p/s)..£20
82	Polydor POSPX 401	All Along The Watchtower/Foxy Lady/Purple Haze/Manic Depression (12", p/s) £15
82	Polydor POSPX 608	Voodoo Chile (Slight Return)/Gypsy Eyes/Hey Joe/3rd Stone From The Sun (12", p/s) ...£15
90	Polydor PZ 71	Crosstown Traffic/Voodoo Chile/All Along The Watchtower (12", p/s)..............£15
10	Sony MOVLP 225	Little Drummer Boy-Silent Night-Auld Lang Syne/Three Little Bears/Little Drummer Boy-Silent Night-Auld Lang Syne (10", p/s, green vinyl) £15

ALBUMS : TRACK LPS
67	Track 612 001	ARE YOU EXPERIENCED (mono, laminated (front and back) sleeve £700
67	Track 612 001	ARE YOU EXPERIENCED (mono, laminated front but matt rear sleeve) £350
67	Track 612 003	AXIS: BOLD AS LOVE (laminated gatefold sleeve, with gatefold insert mono) £750
67	Track 612 003	AXIS: BOLD AS LOVE (laminated gatefold sleeve, without gatefold insert, mono)..........£150
67	Track 613 003	AXIS: BOLD AS LOVE (laminated gatefold sleeve, with gatefold insert, stereo) £300
67	Track 613 003	AXIS: BOLD AS LOVE (laminated gatefold sleeve, without gatefold insert, stereo).........£120
68	Track 612 004	SMASH HITS (mono) £100
68	Track 613 004	SMASH HITS (stereo) £40
68	Track 612004	SMASH HITS (LP, "Vanenti" credit for Hey Joe)...£100
68	Track 612 008/009	ELECTRIC LADYLAND (2-LP, plain white non-gatefold sleeve, labels marked "Test Pressing", mono)..£2000
68	Track 613 008/009	ELECTRIC LADYLAND (2-LP, laminated gatefold sleeve, stereo, blue text inside sleeve) ..£800
68	Track 613 008/009	ELECTRIC LADYLAND (2-LP, laminated gatefold sleeve, stereo, white text inside sleeve)...£350
68	Track 613 010	ELECTRIC LADYLAND PART 1 (stereo only) £35
68	Track 613 017	ELECTRIC LADYLAND PART 2 (stereo only) £35
70	Track Super 2406 002	BAND OF GYPSYS (original 'puppet' sleeve, beware of 'fake' copies on eBay) £200
70	Track Super 2406 002	BAND OF GYPSYS (repressing, gatefold 'Isle Of Wight' sleeve)..........................£50
70	Track Super 2406 002	BAND OF GYPSYS (2nd repressing, single sleeve)...£20
70	Track 2407 010	BACKTRACK 10: ARE YOU EXPERIENCED? (budget reissue, mono, some state mono but play stereo) £20
70	Track 2407 010	BACKTRACK 10: ARE YOU EXPERIENCED? (budget reissue, stereo, but in Mono sleeve)..£50
70	Track 2407 011	BACKTRACK 11: AXIS: BOLD AS LOVE (budget reissue, stereo)..........................£20
71	Track 2856 002	ELECTRIC JIMI HENDRIX (mail-order only Record Club release) £800
71	Track 2408 101	THE CRY OF LOVE (gatefold sleeve) £30
71	Track 2408 101	THE CRY OF LOVE (red vinyl, factory custom pressing, 5 known copies. The LP was pressed to test dealer reaction to coloured vinyl with a view to marketing the Pink Fairies LP Never Never Land. Although the Cry Of Love is on both sides only side A has the correct (black) Track label with the other side having a red Polydor label stating 'The Very Best Of Bert Kaempfert'. It appears that initially these Hendrix LPs were sleeved in Never Never Land sleeves but over time they have been re-sleeved by owners in Hendrix Cry Of Love sleeves.)..£3000
74	Track 603003	ARE YOU EXPERIENCED (LP, stereo with POLYDOR INT. GmbH on label, this is NOT the £40

		1967 Stereo issue of ARE YOU EXPERIENCED)	
88	Track/HMV C 881-16	ARE YOU EXPERIENCED (LP, box set, ltd. ed. of 2,500, no'd, with certificate)	£30

ALBUMS : POLYDOR LPS

71	Polydor 2302 016	ISLE OF WIGHT...	£25
71	Polydor 2302 018	HENDRIX IN THE WEST (gatefold sleeve)	£15
72	Polydor 2302 020	WAR HEROES	£15
73	Polydor ACB 00219 Super	SMASH HITS (LP, Audio Club Of Great Britain issue)...	£20
73	Polydor 2657 012	ELECTRIC LADYLAND (2-LP, laminated gatefold sleeve, reissue)..............................	£60
73	Polydor 2310 271	ELECTRIC LADYLAND PART 1 (reissue)	£20
73	Polydor 2310 272	ELECTRIC LADYLAND PART 2 (reissue)	£20
74	Polydor 2310 301	LOOSE ENDS	£15
75	Polydor 2310 398	CRASH LANDING	£15
75	Polydor 2310 415	MIDNIGHT LIGHTNING	£15
78	Polydor 2612 034	THE ESSENTIAL JIMI HENDRIX (2-LP, with bonus 1-sided 33rpm 7" Gloria [JIMI 1] in special bag)	£40
78	St. Michael/Poly. 2891 139	JIMI HENDRIX (cassette)	£20
79	St. Michael 2102/0102	JIMI HENDRIX (cat. no. also listed as Polydor 2891 139)	£75
80	Polydor 2625 040	JIMI HENDRIX (13-LP box set [11 x LP + 1 x 2-LP])	£75
80	Polydor POLS 1023	NINE TO THE UNIVERSE	£15
84	Polydor SPDLP 3	ELECTRIC LADYLAND (2-LP, non-laminated gatefold sleeve, 2nd reissue)	£40
87	Polydor 833 004-1	LIVE AT WINTERLAND (LP, with poster)	£18
90	Polydor 847 2311	CORNERSTONES: JIMI HENDRIX 1967-1970	£15
83	Polydor PODV6	SINGLES ALBUM (2-LP, gatefold)	£20
91	Polydor 847 234 1	ARE YOU EXPERIENCED? (LP, reissue with barcode on rear)	£15
93	Polydor 847243	AXIS: BOLD AS LOVE (LP, reissue)	£25

ALBUMS : OTHER LPS

68	London HA 8349	GET THAT FEELING (Mono, with Curtis Knight)..	£50
68	London SH 8369	GET THAT FEELING (Stereo, with Curtis Knight)..	£40
68	London HA 8369	STRANGE THINGS (Mono, with Curtis Knight)	£50
68	London SH 8369	STRANGE THINGS (Stereo, with Curtis Knight)	£40
71	Reprise K 40430	LIVE AT THE MONTEREY INTERNATIONAL POP FESTIVAL (shared with Otis Redding)	£35
71	Reprise K 44159	RAINBOW BRIDGE (matt gatefold sleeve, 'steamboat' label, soundtrack)	£20
73	Reprise K 64017	SOUNDTRACK RECORDINGS FROM THE FILM JIMI HENDRIX (2-LP)	£18
73	Ember NR 5068	IN THE BEGINNING (textured gatefold sleeve)	£15
74	Ember EMB 3428	LOOKING BACK WITH JIMI HENDRIX	£15
75	DJM DJLMD 8011	FOR REAL (2-LP, gatefold sleeve)	£25
89	Castle Comms. HBLP 100	LIVE AND UNRELEASED - THE RADIO SHOW (5-LP)	£30
89	Castle CCSLP 212	RADIO ONE (2-LP, gatefold)	£20

ALBUMS : CDS

84	Track 821 993 2	BAND OF GYPSYS	£35
88	Polydor/HMV C88 LP 1-11	ARE YOU EXPERIENCED? (box set via HMV stores, 1,500 only)	£25
89	Castle Comms. HBCD 100	LIVE AND UNRELEASED - THE RADIO SHOW (3-CD, box set)	£30

(see also Eire Apparent, Jayne Mansfield, McGough & McGear, Fat Mattress, Curtis Knight, Billy Cox, Buddy Miles, Riot Squad)

MARGIE HENDRIX

66	Mercury MF 976	I Call You Lover But You Ain't Nothin' But A Tramp/The Question	£25
67	Mercury MF 1001	Restless/On The Right Track	£20

CHRISTIE HENNESSY

73	Westwood	CHRISTIE HENNESSY (LP)	£35

HENNESSYS

69	Cambrian CLP 593	THE ROADS AND THE MILES (LP)	£80
60s	Music Factory MF 106	KARDIFF AFTER DARK (LP)	£90

ADRIAN HENRI

74	Charivari VAR4982	ADRIAN HENRI (LP)...	£45
74	Argo PLP 1194	ADRIAN HENRI AND HUGO WILLIAMS (LP)	£40

(see also Liverpool Scene, McGough & McGear)

BOB HENRY

65	Philips BF 1450	I Need Me Someone/Built Like A Man	£18

(see also Robert Henry)

CLARENCE ('FROGMAN') HENRY

57	London HLN 8389	Ain't Got No Home/Troubles Troubles (as Clarence Henry) (gold lettering on label)	£150
57	London HLN 8389	Ain't Got No Home/Troubles Troubles (as Clarence Henry) (silver lettering on label)	£100
57	London HLN 8389	Ain't Got No Home/Troubles Troubles (as Clarence Henry) (78)	£40
62	Pye International 7N 25169	The Jealous Kind/Come On And Dance	£15
64	London HLU 9936	Little Green Frog/Have You Ever Been Lonely?	£30
66	London HLU 10025	Ain't Got No Home/Baby, Ain't That Love?	£30
61	Pye Intl. NEP 44007	CLARENCE 'FROGMAN' HENRY HIT PARADE (EP)	£30
61	Pye Intl. NPL 28017	YOU ALWAYS HURT THE ONE YOU LOVE (LP)	£40

DANNY HENRY

81	Three Kings TK50	Sharon My Love/Version/African Gold (12")	£40

MILTON HENRY

76	Cactus CT85	Gypsy Woman/Dub	£25
85	Wackies LP 2450	WHO DO YOU THINK I AM? (LP)	£40
87	Tachyon WR 2741	BABYLON LOOT (LP)..	£55

PIERRE HENRY

66	Philips 4FE 8000	LE VOYAGE FROM THE TIBETAN BOOK OF THE DEAD (LP)...................................	£20

66	Philips 4FE 8504	VARIATIONS FOR A DOOR AND A SIGH (LP, UK record in French sleeve)......................£20
68	Philips 4FE 8004	MASS FOR THE PRESENT TIME (LP)...£40

ROBERT HENRY
66	Philips BF 1476	Walk Away Like A Winner/That's All I Want....................................£70

(see also Bob Henry)

HENRY & LOUIS
80s	2 Kings 2K7001	Jah Jah Never Fail/Dub Never Fail I...............................£15

HENRY COW
73	Virgin V 2005	THE LEGEND (LP)...£50
74	Virgin V 2011	UNREST (LP, gatefold sleeve, black/white 'twin' label) £30
75	Virgin V 2027	IN PRAISE OF LEARNING (LP).....................................£30
76	Caroline CAD 3002	CONCERTS (LP)...£30
79	Broadcast BC 1	WESTERN CULTURE (LP) £20
86	Broadcast BC3	IN PRAISE OF LEARNING (LP, reissue) £15
12	ReR MegacorpRER VHC5 DLP	CONCERTS (2-LP, reissue)...............................£40
17	ReR MegacorpRER VHC2	UNREST (LP, reissue) £18
17	ReR MegacorpRER VHC3	IN PRAISE OF LEARNING (LP, reissue)..................£15

(see also Slapp Happy, Art Bears, Fred Frith, Gong/Henry Cow/Global Trucking Company)

HENRY ESSENCE
79	Ellie Jay Records EJSP9392	Margarita/14 Year Old Lover (500 only, p/s)..................£150

HENRY III
67	Island WI 3078	Thank You Girl/Take Me Back £50
67	Island WI 3081	I'll Reach The End/Won't Go Away (B-side actually Lee's Special by Don Tony Lee) £60
67	RCA RCA 1568	So Much Love/Sitting In The Park............................£20
70	Dynamic DYN 402	Out Of Time/VICEROYS: Love For Everyone (both with Hubcap & Wheels)..........£15

(see also Uniques)

JUDY HENSKE
66	Reprise RS 20485	Road To Nowhere/Sing A Rainbow...............................£15
65	Reprise RS 6203	DEATH DEFYING (LP)...£30

JUDY HENSKE & JERRY YESTER
69	Straight STS 1052	FAREWELL ALDEBARAN (LP)......................................£50

KEN HENSLEY
73	Bronze ILPS 9223	PROUD WORDS ON A DUSTY SHELF (LP, gatefold sleeve, lyric inner, Island credit on label)........£60
75	Bronze ILPS 9307	EAGER TO PLEASE (LP, lyric inner, Island credit on label)..........£50
81	Bronze BRON 533	FREE SPIRIT (LP) £35

(see also Uriah Heep. Wasp)

NICKY HENSON
63	Parlophone R 4976	Till I See You Cry/What Does It Mean?.........................£20

HEPBURNS
89	Let's Zine! (No Cat. No.)	Where You Belong/WALTONES: She Looks Right Through Me (Demo Version) (1-sided flexi, with Zine fanzine issue 10) £15
90	Magic MAGIC 01T	Electrified (From Countryside To City)/London Welshman/Dive (12", p/s)..........£25
88	Cherry Red BRED 83	THE MAGIC OF THE HEPBURNS (LP)...............................£15

HEP STARS
66	Decca F 22446	Sunny Girl/No Response £45
67	Olga OLE 001	Wedding/Consolation £25
68	Olga OLE 013	Let It Be Me/Groovy Summertime (withdrawn, supposedly reissued 1969) £45
68	Olga OLE 014	Malaika/It's Nice To Be Back (in export p/s)..........£55
68	Olga OLE 014	Malaika/It's Nice To Be Back.................................£25

(see also Abba)

HEPTONES
66	Rio R 104	Gunmen Coming To Town/TOMMY McCOOK & SUPERSONICS: Riverton City.............£100
67	Ska Beat JB 266	We've Got Love/I Am Lonely £180
67	Caltone TONE 105	Schoolgirls/Ain't That Bad?..................................£60
67	Studio One SO 2005	A Change Is Gonna Come/Nobody Knows..........................£150
67	Studio One SO 2014	Fat Girl/DELROY WILSON: Mother Word..........................£30
67	Studio One SO 2021	If I Knew/Festival Day.......................................£50
67	Studio One SO 2026	Why Did You Leave?/GAYLADS: Don't Try To Reach Me £30
67	Studio One SO 2027	Why Must I?/SLIM SMITH: Try Again............................£65
67	Studio One SO 2031	Take Me (actually by The Soul Vendors)/DELROY WILSON: I'm Not A King..........£50
67	Studio One SO 2033	Only Sixteen/Baby...£30
68	Studio One SO 2040	Tripe Girl/DELROY WILSON: Mr. D.J...........................£110
68	Studio One SO 2049	Cry, Baby, Cry/Mama...£50
68	Studio One SO 2052	Dock Of The Bay/KING ROCKY (ELLIS): The Ruler £170
68	Studio One SO 2055	Party Time/Oil In Your Lamp £50
68	Coxsone CS 7052	Love Won't Come Easy/Gee Wee................................£100
68	Coxsone CS 7068	Equal Rights/Ting-A-Ling £60
68	Coxsone CS 7082	Soul Power/Love Me Always £125
69	Coxsone CS 7092	Sweet Talking/Ob-La-Di.......................................£70
69	Studio One SO 2083	I Shall Be Released/Love Me Always £50
69	Bamboo BAM 11	I Shall Be Released/Love Me Always (Power) (reissue) £30
70	Bamboo BAM 28	Young, Gifted and Black/SOUND DIMENSION: Joyland £30
70	Bamboo BAM 39	Young Generation/You Turned Away............................£45
70	Bamboo BAM 43	Message From A Blackman/SOUND DIMENSION: Jamaica Underground..........£30

MINT VALUE £

70	Upsetter US 339	Hurry Up/Thanks We Get	£30
70	Banana BA 311	Be A Man/U ROY: Shock Attack	£20
71	Banana BA 325	Suspicious Minds/Haven't You Any Fight Left?	£30
71	Banana BA 349	Freedom Line/SOUND DIMENSION: Version	£20
72	Prince Buster PB 37	Our Day Will Come/PRINCE BUSTER: Protection	£18
73	Downtown DT 515	Meaning Of Life/Version Of Life	£20
73	Jaguar JAG 103	Drifting Away/BONGO LES: Zion Drum	£18
73	Smash SMA 2328	Soul Sister/IMPACT ALLSTARS: Soul Sister (Version)	£15
73	Count Shelley CS 017	Now I Know/AUGUSTUS PABLO: Version	£15
74	Pama Supreme PS 390	Thanks We Get/Oppression (B-side by Delroy Butler)	£25
70s	Third World TWDIS 13	Losing You/Mount Zion (12")	£15
67	Studio One SOL 9002	THE HEPTONES (LP)	£300
68	Studio One SOL 9010	ON TOP (LP)	£400
72	Trojan TBL 183	THE HEPTONES AND THEIR FRIENDS MEET THE NOW GENERATION (LP)	£35
75	Island ILPS 9297	BOOK OF RULES (LP)	£30
76	Island ILPS 9456	PARTY TIME (LP)	£25
76	Island ILPS 9381	NIGHT FOOD (LP)	£20
76	Trojan TRLS 128	COOL RASTA (LP)	£15
78	Third World TDWD1	BETTER DAYS (LP)	£20

(see also Soul Vendors, Ronald & Lloyd, Ed Nangle, Love Generation, Alton Ellis, Basil Daley, Ken Boothe, Jackie Mittoo)

HERB & KAY
54	Parlophone MSP 6127	This Ole House/Angels In The Sky	£20
54	Parlophone CMSP 23	This Ole House/Angels In The Sky (export issue)	£20
55	Parlophone CMSP 31	Coffee Blues/Juke Box Jig (export issue)	£20

HERBAL MIXTURE
| 66 | Columbia DB 8021 | A Love That's Died/Tailor Made | £250 |
| 66 | Columbia DB 8083 | Machines/Please Leave My Mind | £350 |

(see also Tony McPhee, Groundhogs)

HERBALISER
95	Ninja Tune ZEN 18	REMEDIES (2-LP)	£20
97	Ninja Tune ZEN 28	BLOW YOUR HEADPHONES (LP)	£20
99	Ninja Tune ZEN 41	VERY MERCENARY (2-LP)	£20

HERBIE & ROYALISTS
| 68 | Saga FID 2121 | SOUL OF THE MATTER (LP) | £30 |

HERBIE'S PEOPLE
| 65 | CBS 202005 | Sweet And Tender Romance/You Thrill Me To Pieces | £25 |
| 66 | CBS 202058 | One Little Smile/You Never Know | £20 |

HERD
65	Parlophone R 5284	Goodbye Baby, Goodbye/Here Comes The Fool	£50
65	Parlophone R 5353	She Was Really Saying Something/It's Been A Long Time Baby	£50
66	Parlophone R 5413	So Much In Love/This Boy's Always Been True	£60
67	Fontana TF 819	I Can Fly/Diary Of A Narcissist	£15
67	Fontana TF 887	Paradise Lost/Come On - Believe Me (in p/s)	£20
68	Fontana (S)TL 5458	PARADISE LOST (LP, flipback sleeve, black/silver labels)	£80
72	Bumble GEMP 5001	NOSTALGIA (LP)	£25

(see also Humble Pie, Judas Jump, Andy Bown, Preachers)

HERE & NOW
| 78 | Deptford Fun City DLP 02 | WHAT YOU SEE ... IS WHAT YOU ARE (LP, 1 side by Alternative TV) | £15 |
| 83 | Chick CHRL 003 | FANTASY SHIFT (LP) | £20 |

(see also Daevid Allen)

HERESY
85	Earache EAR 01	NEVER HEALED EP (Flexi)	£20
88	In Your Face FACE 01	FACE UP TO IT! (LP)	£15
89	In Your Face FACE 07	13 ROCKING ANTHEMS (LP)	£15

HERESY/CONCRETE SOX
| 87 | Manic Ears MOSH 2 | HERESY/CONCRETE SOX (LP, inner, 1 side each) | £15 |

HERETIC
| 84 | Thunderbolt THBE 1004 | BURNT AT THE STAKE EP (Water Of Vice/Keep On Telling Those Lies/Fever Of Love/ Watch Me Grow (12", p/s) | £25 |

HERITAGE
81	Rondelet ROUND 8	Strange Place To Be/Misunderstood (p/s)	£20
82	Rondelet ABOUT 12	REMORSE CODE (LP, with lyric insert)	£35
82	Plant Life PLR 040	LIVING BY THE AIR (LP)	£15

HERMAN (CHIN-LOY)
71	Big Shot BI 573	El Fishy/HERMAN'S ALLSTARS: Nightmare (B-side actually "In The Spirit" by Lloyd Charmers)	£15
71	Big Shot BI 578	New Love/AUGUSTUS PABLO: The Mood	£25
71	Big Shot BI 579	East Of The River Nile Version/AUGUSTO PABLO: East Of The River Nile	£50
71	Duke DU 107	To The Fields/HERMAN'S VERSION MEN: Fields Version	£40
71	Punch PH 55	Hold The Ghost/AQUARIUS SOUL BAND: Duppy Dance	£15

(see also Jimbilin)

PRIEST HERMAN
| 64 | Blue Beat BB 266 | We Are Praying/BUSTER'S ALLSTARS: Dallas, Texas | £60 |

WOODY HERMAN
| 54 | London HL 8013 | Wooftie/Moten Stomp (as Woody Herman & New Third Herd) | £20 |

54	London HL 8031	Fancy Woman/Eight Babies To Mind (as Woody Herman's Woodchoppers)	£20
55	London HL 8122	Sorry 'Bout The Whole Darned Thing/Love's A Dog (with New Third Herd)	£15
66	CBS 202522	Sidewinder/Greasy Sack Blues	£30

HERMAN'S HERMITS
74	Buddah BDS 700	Train/Ride On The Water (withdrawn)	£30
65	Columbia 33SX 1727	HERMAN'S HERMITS (LP)	£20
66	Columbia SX 6084	BOTH SIDES OF HERMAN'S HERMITS (LP)	£15
67	Columbia S(C)X 6174	THERE'S A KIND OF HUSH ALL OVER THE WORLD (LP)	£15

(see also Peter Noone)

HERMITS
71	RCA 2135	She's A Lady (Say What You Want To Say)/Gold Mandela	£15
72	RCA 2265	The Man/Effen Curly	£50

TED HEROLD
60	Polydor NH 66817	I Don't Know Why/Moonlight	£15

HERON
70	Dawn DNS 1015	Take Me Back Home/Minstrel And A King	£15
71	Dawn DNX 2509	Bye And Bye/Through Time/Only A Hobo/I'm Ready To Leave (p/s)	£25
71	Dawn DNLS 3010	HERON (LP, with insert, some with "this album was recorded live in a field" sticker)	£250
72	Dawn DNLS 3025	TWICE AS NICE & HALF THE PRICE (2-LP, with postcard)	£300
72	Dawn DNLS 3025	TWICE AS NICE & HALF THE PRICE (2-LP, without postcard)	£150

(see also Mike Cooper)

DIANA HERON
79	Ethnic Fight DD4432	Be Thankful/Dub (12")	£15

MIKE HERON('S REPUTATION)
71	Island ILPS 9146	SMILING MEN WITH BAD REPUTATIONS (LP, gatefold sleeve, pink rim, palm tree label)	£40
75	Neighborhood 80637	MIKE HERON'S REPUTATION (LP)	£20

(see also Incredible String Band)

BERNARD HERRMANN
69	Phase 4 Stereo PFS 4173	THE GREAT MOVIE THRILLERS (LP)	£18
75	Phase 4 Stereo PFS 4309	THE FANTASY FILM WORLD OF BERNARD HERRMANN (LP)	£30
76	Phase 4 Stereo PFS 4337	THE MYSTERIOUS FILM WORLD OF BERNARD HERRMANN (LP)	£18

KRISTIN HERSH
94	4AD CAD 4002	HIPS & MAKERS (LP)	£50
12	Music On Vinyl MOVLP489	HIPS & MAKERS (LP, reissue)	£20

(see also Throwing Muses)

KIM HERTE
85	RMO 12-ZAM 1	Do You Wanna Danvce With Me/(Electro Mix) (12")	£30

HESITATIONS
69	London HLR 10180	Born Free/Push A Little Bit Harder	£20
68	London HA-R/SH-R 8360	THE NEW BORN FREE (LP)	£30

CAROLYN HESTER
66	CBS (S)BPG 62033	CAROLYN HESTER (LP)	£30
69	Pye Intl. NSPL 28121	THE CAROLYN HESTER COALITION (LP)	£20

(see also Four For Fun)

HEWETT SISTERS
59	HMV POP 567	Baby-O/Jerri-Lee (I Love Him So)	£25

KEVIN HEWICK
82	Factory FAC 48	Ophelia's Drinking Song/Cathy Clown/He Holds You Tighter (p/s)	£15

BEN HEWITT
59	Mercury AMT 1041	You Break Me Up/I Ain't Givin' Up Nothin'	£50
59	Mercury AMT 1055	For Quite A While/Patricia June	£35
59	Mercury AMT 1084	I Want A New Girl Now/My Search	£50
60	Mercury ZEP 10035	BREAK IT UP WITH BEN HEWITT (EP)	£200
84	Bear Family BFX 15150	THEY WOULD CALL ME ELVIS (LP, gatefold)	£15
85	Bear Family BFX 15187	GOOD TIMES AND SOME MIGHTY FINE ROCK 'N' ROLL (LP, gatefold)	£15

GARTH HEWITT
70s	Myrrh MYR 1051	LOVE SONGS FOR THE EARTH (LP)	£30
78	Myrrh MYR 1078	I'M GRATEFUL (LP, insert)	£30

RICHARD HEWSON ORCHESTRA
76	Splash CPLP 1002	LOVE IS (LP)	£30

PETER HEWSON
83	Reset RES 2	Take My Hand/Her (p/s)	£40
83	Reset REST 2	Take My Hand/Her (12", p/s)	£60

HEX
93	Ninja Tune ZEN 05	SOUNDTRACK TO GLOBAL CHAOS (LP)	£20
93	Ninja Tune ZEN 07	DIGITAL LOVE (LP)	£20

NICK HEYWARD
17	Gladsome Hawk GHAWKV 001	WOODLAND ECHOES (LP, printed inner, numbered edition of 500)	£20

LENNIE HIBBERT & COUNT OSSIE BAND
69	Doctor Bird DB 1113	Pure Sole/PATSY: A Man Is Two Faced	£200

(see also Sound Dimension)

AL HIBBLER
55	Brunswick 05420	Unchained Melody/Daybreak (gold label)	£20
55	London HL 8184	Now I Lay Me Down To Dream/Danny Boy	£35

ERSEL HICKEY
59	Fontana H 198	You Threw A Dart/Don't Be Afraid Of Love	£70
59	Fontana H 198	You Threw A Dart/Don't Be Afraid Of Love (78)	£20

HICKORY
68	Lyntone 1928	Scottish Magic (Promo flexi for Tartan Ale, p/s)	£20
69	CBS 3963	Green Light/Key	£30

(see also Equals)

HICKORY SIX
64	Oak RGJ 149	Feelin Blue/Hello My Darling	£80

COLIN HICKS (& CABIN BOYS)
57	Pye 7N 15114	Wild Eyes And Tender Lips/Empty Arms Blues (with Cabin Boys)	£15

DAN HICKS & HIS HOT LICKS
72	Blue Thumb ILPS 9204	STRIKING IT RICH (LP)	£18

(see also Charlatans (U.S.)

JIMMY HICKS
72	London HLU 10396	I'm Mr. Big Stuff/Tell Her That I Love You	£15

MARVA HICKS
78	Infinity 102	Looking Over My Shoulder/Here I Go Again	£15

HIDDEN CAMERAS
03	Rough Trade RTRADLP 077	THE SMELL OF OUR OWN (LP, hand stencilled sleeve)	£30

HIDDEN IDENTITY
94	Pure Rudeness HIDBBB1	BLUNTED BUMPKIN BUSTERS (EP)	£20

(see also Evil Ed)

HIDEAWAYS
69	Action ACT 4544	Hide Out/Jolly Joe	£25

HI-FI FOUR
56	Parlophone MSP 6210	Band Of Gold/Davy, You Upset My Life	£70

HI FI (1)
78	Aura AUS 106	Run Run/Sole Kitchen (p/s)	£20

HI FI'S
64	Pye 7N 15710	I Keep Forgettin'/Why Can't I Stop Loving You?	£35
65	Pye 7N 15788	Baby's In Black/Kiss And Run	£15
66	Alp 595 010	It's Gonna Be Morning/I Wanna Hear You Say Yeah	£70

JOE HIGGS
67	Coxsone CS 7004	Neighbour Neighbour/MELODIANS: I Should Have Made It Up	£200
67	Island WI 3026	I Am The Song/Worry No More	£80
68	Island WI 3131	You Hurt My Soul/LYNN TAITT: Why Am I Treated So Bad?	£100
70	Clandisc CLA 208	Mademoiselle/DYNAMITES: Lion	£30
71	Big BG 312	Burning Fire/RUPIE EDWARDS ALL STARS: Version	£15
72	Sioux SI 005	The World Is Spinning Around/THE REACTION: Hallelujah	£20
72	Sioux SI 014	The Wave Of War/JUMBO STERLING: Shaft	£25
72	Sioux SI 021	Lay A Foundation/JACKIE ROWLAND: Lay A Foundation (Version)	£15
75	TorpedoTOR 41	My Baby Still Love Me/Hard Time	£30
76	Ethnic Fight EF 038	Creation/AUGUSTUS PABLO & SUPER 8 CORPORATION: Creative Version	£20
75	Grounation GROL 508	LIFE OF CONTRADICTION (LP)	£50
78	1 STOP STOP 1002	UNITY IS POWER (LP)	£25

(see also Higgs & Wilson, Bob Marley/Wailers, Soul Vendors)

(JOE) HIGGS & (ROY) WILSON
60	Blue Beat (B)B 3	Manny Oh/When You Tell Me Baby (yellow label/blue writing [B3] or blue label/silver writing [BB 3]) (with Ken Richards & His Comets)	£20
61	Starlite ST45 035	Pretty Baby/I Long For The Day	£20
61	Starlite ST45 036	Lover's Song/It Is A Day	£20
61	Starlite ST45 042	Come On Home/The Robe	£20
61	Starlite ST45 053	Sha Ba Ba/Change Of Mind	£20
62	Blue Beat BB 95	How Can I Be Sure/Mighty Man	£25
63	R&B JB 109	Let Me Know/Bye And Bye	£25
63	Blue Beat BB 190	If You Want Pardon/BABA BROOKS BAND: Musical Communion	£20
63	Island WI 081	Last Saturday Morning/Praise The Lord	£20
64	Rio R 29	Love Is Not For Me/Gone Is Yesterday	£15
65	Blue Beat BB 277	Pain In My Heart/BUSTER ALL STARS: Going West	£30

(see also Clancy Eccles)

HIGH
69	CBS 4164	Long Live The High/Beggar Man Dan	£30

HIGH & MIGHTY
66	HMV POP 1548	Tryin' To Stop Cryin'/Escape From Cuba	£35

HIGH BROOM
70	Island WI 6088	Dancing In The Moonlight/Percy's On The Run	£15

(see also Leviathan, Jason Crest, Holy Mackerel)

HIGHER INTELLEGENCE AGENCY
93	Beyond HIA 1	SPEEDLEARN EP (12", p/s)	£35

94	Beyond HIA 2	COLOUR REFORM (12" EP) £15
93	Beyond RBADLP 5	COLOURFORM (2-LP) £40
95	Beyond RBADLP 13	FREEFLOATER (2-LP) £40

HIGH FASHION

83	Capitol 1A 064-7122871	MAKE UP YOUR MIND (LP) £20
82	Capitol ST 12214	FEELIN LUCKY (LP) £20

HIGH KEYS

63	London HLK 9768	Que Sera Sera/Daddy, Ooh Long Legs £30

HIGH LEVEL RANTERS

68	Topic 12TS 186	NORTHUMBERLAND FOR EVER (LP, blue label, 2 different sleeves) £15
69	Leader/Trailer LER 2007	THE LADS OF NORTHUMBERLAND (LP) £18
75	Topic 2-12TS 271/2	THE BONNY PIT LADDIE (2-LP, blue label) £18
77	Broadside BRO 128	ENGLISH SPORTING BALLADS (LP, 1-side Martin Wyndham-Read, 2,000 only) £25

HIGH NUMBERS

64	Fontana TF 480	Zoot Suit/I'm The Face (textured labels with "Mono" on labels) £1500
80	Back Door DOOR 4	I'm The Face/Zoot Suit (reissue, picture sleeve, silver plastic labels) £20
92	Fontana TF 480	I'm The Face/Zoot Suit (reissue, smooth labels with "stereo" on labels, die-cut sleeve from Fontana Box) £20

(see also Who)

HIGH SHELF

70	Sprint SP 2	Suddenly You/Wendy £40

HIGH SOCIETY (1)

66	Fontana TF 771	People Passing By/Star Of Eastern Street £22

(see also Friday Browne, Graham Gouldman, Manchester Mob)

HIGH SOCIETY (2)

70	CBS 4746	Only You Only You/Tell Me Now £15

HIGH STREET EAST

69	Rubber RUBBER ONE	Newcastle Brown/Everybody Knows (p/s) £70
69	Rubber RUBBER ONE	Newcastle Brown/Everybody Knows (no p/s) £45

HIGH TIDE (1)

69	Liberty LBS 83264	SEA SHANTIES (LP, gatefold sleeve, blue label) £250
70	Liberty LBS 83294	HIGH TIDE (LP, blue label) £175

(see also Hawkwind, Misunderstood, Denny Gerrard, Magic Muscle, Third Ear Band)

DEAN HIGHTOWER

60	HMV CLP 1360	TWANGY - WITH A BEAT (LP) £50

DONNA HIGHTOWER

60	Capitol ST 1273	GEE BABY (LP) £15

ROSETTA HIGHTOWER

68	Toast TT 506	Pretty Red Balloons/How Can You Mistreat (The One You Love)? £30
68	Toast TT 509	I Can't Give Back The Love I Feel For You/Big Bird £100
71	CBS 64201	HIGHTOWER (LP) £100
71	Rediffusion ZS 88	ROSETTA HIGHTOWER (LP) £30

(see also Orlons, Ian Green [Revelation])

HIGH TREASON

80	Burlington BURLS 001	Saturday Night Special/Waste My Love (p/s) £140
80	Burlington BURLS 001	Saturday Night Special/Waste My Love (no p/s) £80

HIGHWAY (1)

74	EMI EMC 3019	HIGHWAY (LP) £20
75	EMI EMA 770	SMOKING AT THE EDGE (LP, gatefold sleeve) £35

HIGHWAY (2)

88	Highway (no cat no)	Midnight Girl/Can't Let Go (p/s) £35

HIGSONS

83	Two Tone CHSTT 1224	Run Me Down (extended)/Instrumental/Put The Punk Back Into Funk (1 & 2) (12", p/s) £15
82	Two Tone CHS TT 1	Tear The Whole Thing Down/Ylang Ylang (12" promo shared with Apollinaires) £35

(see also New York New York, Serious Drinking)

HIJACK

88	Music Of Life NOTE016	Style Wars (12") £15
88	Music Of Life NOTE021	Hold No Hostage/Doomsday Of Rap (12") £15
91	Rhyme Syndicate 6555176	HORNS OF JERICHO (LP) £35
96	Reservoir RES 18	THE ORIGINAL HORNS OF JERICHO (LP) £80

HILARY HILARY

80	Modern STP 2	How Come You're So Dumb/Rich Kid Blues (p/s) £60

(see also Roger Taylor, Queen)

RAY HILDEBRAND

70s	Myrrh MST 6508	SPECIAL KIND OF MAN (LP) £20

DIANE HILDEBRANDE

69	Elektra EKL 4031	EARLY MORNING BLUES AND GREENS (LP) £20

HI-LITERS

58	Mercury AMT 1011	Dance Me To Death/Cha Cha Rock £150
58	Mercury AMT 1011	Dance Me To Death/Cha Cha Rock (78) £35

HI LITES

65	London HL 9967	Hey Baby/Groovey £20

ALEX HILL
53   Vocalion V 1027   Stompin' 'Em Down/Track Head Blues (78) £18
(see also Paramount Allstars)

BENNY HILL
65   Decca LK 4723   BENNY AT THE BBC (LP) £15
(see also Coronets)

BUNKER HILL & RAYMEN
62   Stateside SS 135   Hide & Go Seek Parts 1 & 2..£25

DAVID HILL
57   Vogue V 9076   All Shook Up/Melody For Lovers (with Ray Ellis Orchestra, probably unreleased) £200
57   Vogue V 9076   All Shook Up/Melody For Lovers (78, with Ray Ellis Orchestra) £35
58   RCA RCA 1041   That's Love/Keep Me In Mind (with Joe Relsman's Orchestra & Chorus)....................£100
58   RCA RCA 1041   That's Love/Keep Me In Mind (78, with Joe Relsman's Orchestra & Chorus)..................£30

JEFF HILL BAND
79   Baloon BLOW 1/SRTS/79/
     CUS-557   Something's Wrong With My Baby/Whatever She Wanted (p/s, 500 only) £60

JESSIE HILL
60   London HLU 9117   Ooh Poo Pah Doo Parts 1 & 2..£25

LAURYN HILL
98   Columbia COL 489843 1 THE MISEDUCATION OF LAURYN HILL (2-LP) £50
(see also Fugees)

Z.Z. HILL
65   R&B MRB 5005   Someone To Love Me/Have Mercy Someone..£30
69   Action ACT 4532   Make Me Yours/What Am I Living For?..£100
66   Sue IEP 711   GIMME GIMME (EP, 2 tracks each by Z.Z. Hill & Intentions; in p/s) £300
66   Sue IEP 711   GIMME GIMME (EP, 2 tracks each by Z.Z. Hill & Intentions) £100
69   Action ACLP 6004   WHOLE LOT OF SOUL (LP)...£60
72   Mojo 2916 013   THE BRAND NEW Z.Z. HILL (LP) £20
75   Contempo CLP 515   THE BRAND NEW Z.Z. HILL (LP, reissue)..£15
84   Kent KENT 018   DUES PAID IN FULL (LP, compilation)..£20
(see also Intentions)

STEVE HILLAGE
75   Virgin V 2031   FISH RISING (LP, lyric insert, coloured 'twin' label)...£30
77   Virgin VGD 3501   LIVE HERALD (2-LP, with limited edition mail order lyric sheet in English, French or
                            German)...£30
78   Virgin V 2098   GREEN (LP, green vinyl, with insert)..£15
79   Virgin VR1   RAINBOW DOME MUSIC (LP, clear vinyl, stickered sleeve) £15
(see also Gong, Khan, Arzachel, Clearlight, Radio Actors, System 7)

JANE HILLERY
66   Columbia DB 7918   You've Got That Hold On Me/Take Me Away £40
(see also Magistrates)

MABLE HILLERY
69   Xtra XTRA 1063   IT'S SO HARD TO BE A NIGGER (LP)..£50

CHRIS HILLS
72   Atlantic 2400208   EVERYTHING IS EVERYTHING (LP) £25

HILLTOPPERS
54   London HL 8026   From The Vine Came The Grape/Time Will Tell..£15
54   London HL 8070   Poor Butterfly/Wrapped Up In A Dream £20
54   London HL 8081   Will You Remember?/The Old Cabaret...£20
54   London HL 8092   If I Didn't Care/Bettina £20
55   London HL 8116   Time Waits For No One/You Try Somebody Else...£20
55   London HLD 8168   The Kentuckian Song/I Must Be Dreaming £20
55   London HLD 8208   Searching/All I Need Is You £35
56   London HLD 8221   Only You (And You Alone)/(It Will Have To Do) Until The Real Thing Comes Along (gold
                            label lettering)..£30
56   London HLD 8221   Only You (And You Alone)/(It Will Have To Do) Until The Real Thing Comes Along (silver
                            label lettering)..£15
56   London HLD 8255   My Treasure/Last Word In Love £50
56   London HLD 8278   Do The Bop/When You're Alone £100
56   London HLD 8298   Tryin'/D-A-R-L-I-N'..£30
56   London HLD 8333   So Tired/Faded Rose £30
57   London HLD 8381   Marianne/You're Wasting Your Time £15
57   London HLD 8441   I'm Serious/I Love My Girl £15
57   London HLD 8455   A Fallen Star/Footsteps £15
57   London HLD 8528   The Joker/Chicken, Chicken £40
58   London HLD 8603   You Sure Look Good To Me/Starry Eyes £20
55   London RE-P 1012   PRESENTING THE HILLTOPPERS £20
55   London RE-D 1030   THE HILLTOPPERS VOL. 2..£20
57   London RE-D 1099   THE HILLTOPPERS VOL. 3..£20
57   London HA-D 2029   THE TOWERING HILLTOPPERS £20
57   London HA-D 2071   TOPS IN POPS £20
(see also Sacca, Billy Vaughn)

RONNIE HILTON
55   HMV 7M 285   Prize Of Gold/A Blossom Fell £15
67   HMV POP 1600   If I Were A Rich Man/Laughing Gnome (Bowie penned B-side) £40
(see also Alma Cogan)

HILTONAIRES
67	Coxsone CSL 8004	THE BEST OF THE HILTONAIRES (LP)	£80

HIM & THE OTHERS
66	Parlophone R 5510	I Mean It/She's Got Eyes That Tell Lies	£850

JUSTIN HINDS/HINES (& DOMINOES)
64	Ska Beat JB 176	King Samuel/River Jordan	£25
65	Ska Beat JB 187	Mother Banner/DON DRUMMOND & HIS GROUP: Apanga	£55
65	Island WI 171	Botheration/Satan (as Justin Hines & Dominoes)	£30
65	Island WI 174	Jump Out Of The Frying Pan/Holy Dove (as Justin Hines & Dominoes)	£30
65	Island WI 194	Rub Up, Push Up/The Ark	£30
65	Island WI 232	Turn Them Back/TOMMY McCOOK: Rocket Ship	£60
65	Island WI 236	Peace And Love/Skalarama (B-side actually by Lyn Taitt & Comets)	£40
66	Doctor Bird DB 1048	The Higher The Monkey Climbs/Fight For Your Right	£30
67	Island WI 3048	On A Saturday Night/Save A Bread	£22
67	Treasure Isle TI 7002	Here I Stand/No Good Rudie	£25
67	Treasure Isle TI 7005	Carry Go Bring Come/Fight Too Much	£40
67	Treasure Isle TI 7014	On A Saturday Night/Save A Bread	£20
67	Treasure Isle TI 7017	Once A Man/TOMMY McCOOK & SUPERSONICS: Persian Cat	£25
68	Treasure Isle TI 7063	Botheration/VINCENT HINDS: Mouth Trombone	£15
68	Treasure Isle TI 7068	Mighty Redeemer (Parts 1 & 2)	£15
69	Trojan TR 652	You Should've Known Better/TOMMY McCOOK & SUPERSONICS: Third Figure	£18
70	Duke Reid DR 2511	Say Me Say/I Want It	£15
70	Duke DU 67	Drink Milk/Everywhere I Go (as Justin Hines & Dominoes)	£18
12	Duke THB 7023	Sufferation 1969/Warm Up	£30
76	Island ILPS 9416	JEZEBEL (LP)	£30

(see also Lyn Taitt, Skatalites, Don Drummond)

NEVILLE HINDS
70	Duke Reid DR 2503	Sunday Gravy (as Neville Hines)/JOHN HOLT: Write Her A Letter	£30
70	Camel CA 44	London Bridge/SCORCHERS: Things And Time (B-side act. by Wailing Souls)	£20
72	Upsetter US 384	Blackman's Time/UPSETTERS: Version	£25

(see also Neville Irons & Byron Lee & The Dragonaires, Lloyd Robinson, Marvels, Alton Ellis)

RUPERT HINE
71	Purple TPSA 7502	PICK UP A BONE (LP, with David MacIver, textured gatefold sleeve)	£50
73	Purple TPSA 7509	UNFINISHED PICTURE (LP, gatefold sleeve)	£50

(see also Jon Pertwee, Quantum Jump)

FRAZER HINES
68	Major Minor MM 579	Who's Dr. Who?/Punch And Judy Man	£70

SONNY HINES
65	King KG 1009	Anytime, Any Day, Anywhere/Nothing Like Your Love	£25

MICAH P HINSON
06	Sketch 013LP	MICAH P HINSON AND THE OPERA CIRCUIT (LP)	£40
06	Full Time Hobby FTH 056LP	MICAH P HINSON AND RED EMPIRE ORCHESTRA (LP)	£35
10	Full Time Hobby FTH 093LP	MICAH P HINSON AND THE PIONEER SABOTEURS (2-LP)	£25

JOE HINTON
64	Vocalion VP 9224	Funny How Time Slips Away/You Gotta Have Love	£30
66	Vocalion VA-P 8043	FUNNY HOW TIME SLIPS AWAY (LP)	£120

HI-NUMBERS
65	Decca F 12233	Heart Of Stone/Dancing In The Street	£60

HIPPIES
63	Cameo Parkway P 863	Memory Lane/REGGIE HARRISON: A Lonely Piano	£20

HIPPY BOYS
69	Trojan TR 668	Love/The Whole Family	£25
69	Trojan TR 669	Michael Row The Boat Ashore/Who Is Coming To Dinner	£40
69	Bullet BU 412	Hog In A Me Minte/Lorna Run	£50
69	Bullet BU 413	What's Your Excuse?/Tell Me Tell	£60
69	Camel CA 29	Cat Nip/Cooyah (both as Hippie Boys)	£40
69	High Note HS 021	Doctor No Go/Sailing (B-side actually "Faberge" by Baba Brooks & Band)	£50
69	High Note HS 030	Chicken Lickin'/BABA BROOKS: Old Man Flint	£30
69	High Note HS 035	Reggae Pressure/SOUL RHYTHMS: It Hurts	£30
69	Unity UN 528	Dreams To Remember/Peace Maker	£70
70	High Note HS 038	Piccadilly Hop/Nigeria	£100
70	Duke DU 92	Cloud Burst/LLOYD CHARMERS: Message From A Black Man	£80
70	Explosion EX 2032	Vengeance/Look-Ea-Py-Py	£50
71	Big Shot 580	Voodoo/LITTLE ROY: Hard Fighter	£40
69	Big Shot BSLP 5005	REGGAE WITH THE HIPPY BOYS (LP, actually on High Note label)	£200
11	Sunspot LP 003	REGGAE WITH THE HIPPY BOYS, (LP reissue, 350 only, signed insert)	£30

(see also Upsetters, Family Man, Danny Williams, Tony, Hippy Boys, Cynthia Richards, Pioneers)

HIPSTER IMAGE
65	Decca F 12137	Can't Let Her Go/Make Her Mine	£500
65	Lyntone LYN 951	KEELE RAG RECORD (4 tracks but 2 by Hipster Image - All For You/A Little Piece Of Leather)	£30

(see also Climax Chicago Blues Band)

HI RHYTHM
76	London SHU 8506	ON THE LOOSE (LP)	£20

HIRSCHE NICHT AUFS SOFA
86 United Dairies UD 018 MELCHIOR (LP, with Insert) £30

HI-RYZE
93 General Production GPR(X) 15 PROGRESS EP (12") £60

HI-SPOTS
58 Melodisc 1457 Lend Me Your Comb/I Don't Hurt Anymore £22
58 Melodisc 1473 Secretly/I Got £22

HIS WORD
87 Lyn 14747 Loving In Degrees/Life + 1 = 3 ....£60

ALFRED HITCHCOCK
58 London HA-P 2130 MUSIC TO BE MURDERED BY (LP, music by Jeff Alexander Orchestra, mono) £20
58 London SH-P 6012 MUSIC TO BE MURDERED BY (LP, music by Jeff Alexander Orchestra, stereo)...........£20
60 Wonderland LP 89 ALFRED HITCHCOCK PRESENTS GHOST STORIES FOR YOUNG PEOPLE (LP, read by Peter Allen)..£30

(see Jeff Alexander)

ROBYN HITCHCOCK (& THE EGYPTIANS)
84 Bucketfull/Brains BOB 8 Happy The Golden Prince (hard vinyl white label test pressing, 20 only) £30
81 Armageddon ARM 4 BLACK SNAKE DIAMOND RÔLE (LP)..£15

(see also Soft Boys)

HI-TONES
62 Island WI 029 Going Steady/Darlin' Elaine £25
62 Wasp W 004 I'm In Love With You/Singing A Song..£30
63 Island WI 086 Ten Virgins (actually by Angelic Brothers)/Too Young To Love (actually by Larry Marshall) £25
63 R&B JB 123 You Hold The Key/DON DRUMMOND: Rock Away £50

HIT PACK
65 Tamla Motown TMG 513 Never Say No To Your Baby/Let's Dance £150
65 Tamla Motown TMG 513 Never Say No To Your Baby/Let's Dance (DJ copy) £200

HIT PARADE (1)
90 Sarah SARAH 90 Autobiography/The Dispossessed/Now The Holiday's Over (p/s, insert)....£40
91 Sarah SARAH 58 In Gunnersbury Park/Harvey (ps, insert) £20
91 Vinyl Japan ASKLP 5 MORE POP SONGS (LP)..£18
94 Sarah SARAH 622 THE SOUND OF THE HIT PARADE (LP) £75

HIT PARADE (2)
82 Crass 221984/12 BAD NEWS (EP)...£25
84 Crass 1984/2 PLASTIC CULTURE : Product of The Troubles/Media Son (12") £18
86 Crass No 9 NICK NACK PADDY WHACK (LP, with lyric inner) £25

HIT SQUAD
88 Eastern Bloc EASTERN 01 Wax On The Melt/SPM MC Tunes/Shure.4 (12", white label promo only, plain stickered sleeve)...£30

(see also 808 State)

HITTERS
73 United Artists UP 35530 Hypocrite/The Version £22

(see also Brinsley Schwarz)

HIVES
01 Poptones MC5055LP YOUR NEW FAVOURITE BAND (LP)...£15
04 Polydor 9866988 TYRANNOSAURUS HIVES (LP, inner with free 7")................................£20

HMC
93 New Electronica ELEC 03P Science Funktion (12", promo) £30

HOAX
80 Hologram HOAX 1 ONLY THE BLIND CAN SEE IN THE DARK (EP, 2000 only) £30
81 Hologram HOAX 3 SO WHAT (12" EP, p/s, blue vinyl, 2000 only) £15
81 Hologram HOAX 6 BLIND PANIC EP (p/s, 2000 only) £15
82 Hologram HOAX 4 QUIET IN THE SIXPENNY'S (p/s, 2000 only) £15

HOBBIES OF TODAY
79 Waxworks H.O.T. WAX 01 Metal Boys/Tightrope Walker (p/s) £30
85 Rune CAST 02/LYN 16721/2 In My Minds Eye/You (Company sleeve).................................£15
14 Waxworks H.O.T. WAX 00 HOBBIES OF TODAY (EP, deluxe edition in handmade sleeve with insert, photos and badge)..£30

HOBBIT
71 Deroy 709 FIRST AND LAST (LP, private pressing, 99 only) £250

HOBBITS
68 Decca AD 1004 Daffodil Days (The Affection Song)/Sunny Day Girl (export issue)..........£20
67 MCA MUP 301 DOWN TO MIDDLE EARTH (LP) £35

CHRISTOPHER HOBBS/JOHN ADAMS/GAVIN BRYERS
75 Obscure OBS 2 ENSEMBLE PIECES (LP) £30

PAUL HOBBS
72 Deroy 759 HAVING SAID THAT (LP)...£600

LES HOBEAUX
58 HMV POP 444 Dynamo/Two Ships £15
57 HMV 7EG 8297 SOHO SKIFFLE (EP) £35

HOBO
| 76 | United Artists UAS 29809 | HOBO (LP) | £15 |

HOBOKEN
| 73 | Oak | HOBOKEN (LP, 6 copies only) | £450 |

TREVOR HOCKEY
| 70s | Beau Brummie TET 120ST | Happy 'Cos I'm Blue/BLUES PLAYERS: Keep Right On To The End Of The Road (p/s) | £40 |

CHRIS HODGE
| 72 | Apple APPLE 43 | We're On Our Way/Supersoul (in p/s) | £30 |
| 72 | Apple APPLE 43 | We're On Our Way/Supersoul | £20 |

CHARLES HODGES
| 69 | Major Minor MM 654 | Try A Little Love/Someone To Love | £20 |

(see also Outlaws, Cliff Bennett's Rebellion)

EDDIE HODGES
| 62 | London REA 1353 | EDDIE HODGES (EP) | £30 |

JOHNNY HODGES & HIS ORCHESTRA
| 52 | Vogue LD 011 | JOHNNY HODGES (10" LP) | £15 |

INGFRIED HOFFMAN
| 67 | Polydor 583 015 | SOUL BOND (LP) | £15 |

ANNIE HOGAN
| 85 | Doublevision DVR 9 | PLAYS KICKABYE (12" EP) | £15 |

(see also Marc Almond, Nick Cave, Soft Cell)

SILAS HOGAN
| 71 | Blue Horizon 2431 008 | TROUBLE AT HOME (LP) | £125 |
| 70s | Flyright FLY 595 | I'M A FREE-HEARTED MAN (LP) | £15 |

JAMES HOGG
| 72 | Regal Zonophone RZ 3054 | Lovely Lady Rock/Happy Sad | £15 |

SMOKEY HOGG
64	Realm RM 197	I'M SO LONELY (LP)	£25
72	Ember EMB 3405	SINGS THE BLUES (LP)	£20
70s	Specialty SNTF 5018	U BETTER WATCH THAT JIVE (LP)	£15

(see also John Lee Hooker/Lightnin' Hopkins/Smokey Hogg)

HOGGS
| 80 | Now PRR 2001 | See It Now/Time On The Line (p/s) | £20 |

HOGS
| 69 | Jay Boy BOY 5 | It's All Coming To Me Now/Motor Cycle Rider | £15 |

SUZI JANE HOKUM
| 66 | MGM MGM 1323 | Need All The Help I Can Get/Home | £50 |

HOKUS POKE
| 72 | Vertigo 6360 064 | EARTH HARMONY (LP, die-cut gatefold sleeve, small swirl label) | £450 |

RON HOLDEN
| 60 | London HLU 9116 | My Babe/Love You So | £60 |

MARK HOLDER & THE POSITIVES
| 73 | Atlantic K10280 | Whatever's Fair/Why Dear Lord | £20 |

RAM HOLDER BROTHERS
| 66 | Parlophone R 5471 | Just Across The River/Ram Blues | £30 |

(see also Ram Jam Band, Ram John Holder)

RAM JOHN HOLDER
67	Columbia DB 8262	My Friend Jones/It Won't Be Long Before I Love You	£40
63	Melodisc MLP 12-133	RAM BLUES GOSPEL AND SOUL (LP)	£60
69	Beacon BEAS 2	BLACK LONDON BLUES (LP, white/black label with "Sold in U.K..." text)	£70
70	Beacon BEAS 17	BOOTLEG BLUES (LP, gatefold sleeve with lyric poster, white/black labels)	£80
70	Beacon BEAS 17	BOOTLEG BLUES (LP, gatefold sleeve without lyric poster, white/black labels)	£30

(see also Ram Jam Band, Ram Holder Brothers, Geno Washington)

HOLE
91	City Slang EFA 04070-45	Teenage Whore/Drown Soda (p/s, lilac, clear or green vinyl, 500 of each)	£15
91	City Slang SLANG 012	PRETTY ON THE INSIDE (LP, blue vinyl)	£35
94	City Slang EFA 04935-1	LIVE THROUGH THIS (LP, 3000 on white vinyl)	£100
94	City Slang EFA 04935-1	LIVE THROUGH THIS (LP, black vinyl)	£40
98	Geffen GEF 25164	CELEBRITY SKIN (LP)	£50
14	Music On Vinyl MOVLP 999	CELEBRITY SKIN (LP, orange vinyl repressing)	£20

BILLIE HOLIDAY
56	Vogue V 2408	Detour Ahead/Blue, Turning Grey Over You	£15
54	Columbia 33S 1034	BILLIE HOLIDAY (10" LP)	£30
54	Brunswick LA 8676	LOVER MAN (10" LP)	£30
55	Philips BBR 8032	FAVOURITES (10" LP)	£35
56	Columbia Clef 33C 9023	AT JAZZ AT THE PHILHARMONIC (10" LP)	£20
56	Columbia Clef 33CX 10019	MUSIC FOR TORCHING (LP)	£25
57	Columbia Clef 33CX 10064	VELVET MOOD (LP)	£25
57	Columbia Clef 33CX 10076	SOLITUDE (LP)	£20
57	Columbia Clef 33CX 10092	LADY SINGS THE BLUES (LP)	£20
59	Columbia Clef 33CX 10145	SONGS FOR DISTINGUÉ LOVERS (LP)	£20
66	Island ILP 929	LAST LIVE RECORDING (LP)	£30

MINT VALUE £

CHICO HOLIDAY
59	RCA RCA 1117	Young Ideas/Cuckoo Girl	£30
61	Coral Q 72443	God, Country And My Baby/Fools (withdrawn)	£30
59	RCA RCX 171	CHICO HOLIDAY (EP)	£80

JIMMY HOLIDAY
63	Vocalion POP V 9206	How Can I Forget/Janet	£30
64	London HLY 9868	I Lied/Alison	£20
66	Liberty LIB 12040	Baby I Love You/You Won't Get Away	£20
67	Liberty LIB 12048	Give Me Your Love/The Turning Point	£20
67	Liberty LIB 12053	Everybody Needs Help/I'm Gonna Move To The City	£20
68	Minit MLF 11008	Give Me Your Love/The Beauty Of A Girl In Love	£15
69	Minit MLL/MLS 40010	SPREAD YOUR LOVE (LP)	£60

JIMMY HOLIDAY & CLYDIE KING
67	Liberty LIB 12058	Ready, Willing And Able/We Got A Good Thing Goin'	£30
67	Liberty LIB 12058	Ready, Willing And Able/We Got A Good Thing Goin' (DJ copy)	£50

HOLIDAYS
66	Polydor 56720	I'll Love You Forever/Makin' Up Time	£100

(see also Edwin Starr)

EDDIE HOLLAND
62	Fontana H 387	Jamie/Take A Chance On Me	£400
63	Oriole CBA 1808	If It's Love (It's All Right)/It's Not Too Late	£500

LYNN HOLLAND
67	Polydor 56166	One Man In My Life/Wand'rin Boy	£20
67	Polydor 56187	Come And Love/May God Help You And Protect You	£25
67	Polydor 236217	OH DARLING HOW I MISS YOU (LP)	£25

(see also Holly)

TONY HOLLAND
63	HMV POP 1135	Sidewalk/Time Goes By	£40

SU(SAN) HOLLIDAY
64	Columbia DB 7363	Dark Despair/The Other Side (demos list A-side as "[Street Of] Dark Despair")	£15
64	Columbia DB 7403	Any Day Now/Don't Come Knocking At My Door	£15
66	Columbia SX 6067	I WANNA SAY HELLO (LP, as Su Holliday)	£40

(see also Susan Singer)

TIM HOLLIER
68	United Artists (S)ULP 1211	MESSAGE TO A HARLEQUIN (LP, laminated front sleeve, blue/silver labels)	£70
70	Fontana 6309 003	TIM HOLLIER (LP, laminated sleve, black/silver labels)	£225
71	Philips 6308 044	SKY SAIL (LP, laminated sleeve, black/silver labels)	£45

(see also Amory Kane)

HOLLIES

SINGLES
63	Parlophone R 5030	(Ain't That) Just Like Me/Hey, What's Wrong With Me	£15
66	United Artists UP 1152	After The Fox (with Peter Sellers)/BURT BACHARACH: The Fox-Trot	£35

EPs
64	Parlophone GEP 8909	THE HOLLIES	£40
64	Parlophone GEP 8911	JUST ONE LOOK	£35
64	Parlophone GEP 8915	HERE I GO AGAIN	£35
64	Parlophone GEP 8927	WE'RE THROUGH	£35
65	Parlophone GEP 8934	IN THE HOLLIES STYLE	£50
65	Parlophone GEP 8942	I'M ALIVE	£35
66	Parlophone GEP 8951	I CAN'T LET GO	£50

ALBUMS
64	Parlophone PMC 1220	STAY WITH THE HOLLIES (mono)	£100
64	Parlophone PCS 3054	STAY WITH THE HOLLIES (stereo, large 'stereo' on sleeve)	£175
65	Parlophone PMC 1235	IN THE HOLLIES STYLE (mid-sized mono on front sleeve, "Sold in U.K..." text)	£125
65	Parlophone PMC 1261	THE HOLLIES (small mono on front sleeve, "Sold in U.K..." text)	£125
66	Parlophone PMC 7008	WOULD YOU BELIEVE? (mono, with "Sold in U.K..." text)	£80
66	Parlophone PCS 7008	WOULD YOU BELIEVE? (stereo, "Sold in U.K..." text)	£150
66	Parlophone PMC 7011	FOR CERTAIN BECAUSE (gatefold sleeve, mono, with "Sold in U.K..." text)	£50
66	Parlophone PCS 7011	FOR CERTAIN BECAUSE (gatefold sleeve, stereo, with "Sold in U.K..." text)	£80
67	Parlophone PMC 7022	EVOLUTION (mono, with "Sold in U.K..." text)	£50
67	Parlophone PCS 7022	EVOLUTION (stereo, with "Sold in U.K..." text)	£100
67	Parlophone PMC 7039	BUTTERFLY (mono, with "Sold in U.K..." text)	£50
67	Parlophone PCS 7039	BUTTERFLY (stereo, with "sold in U.K..." text)	£100
67	EMI Regal SREG 2024	THE HOLLIES (export compilation)	£25
67	World Records ST 979	THE VINTAGE HOLLIES (stereo reissue of "In The Hollies Style")	£35
68	World Records ST 1035	STAY WITH THE HOLLIES (record club reissue)	£30
68	Parlophone PCS 7057	THE HOLLIES' GREATEST (stereo, with outtake version of Yes I Will)	£15
69	Parlophone PMC 7078	THE HOLLIES SING DYLAN (mono, with "Solid in U.K..." text)	£35
69	Parlophone PCS 7078	THE HOLLIES SING DYLAN (stereo, with "Sold in U.K..." text)	£30
69	Parlophone PCS 7092	HOLLIES SING HOLLIES (gatefold sleeve)	£20

(All Parlophone LPs listed above were originally issued with yellow/black labels; 1970s pressings with silver & black labels are worth £8)

70	Parlophone PCS 7116	CONFESSIONS OF THE MIND (with colour insert)	£20
71	Parlophone PAS 10005	DISTANT LIGHT (gatefold sleeve)	£18
72	Parlophone PCS 7148	THE HOLLIES' GREATEST HITS VOL. 2	£15
72	Polydor 2383 144	ROMANY (gatefold sleeve)	£15

74	Polydor 2383 262	**HOLLIES** (with lyric insert)	£15
75	Polydor 2442 128	**ANOTHER NIGHT** (gatefold sleeve)	£15
76	Polydor 2442 141	**WRITE ON** (with lyric inner)	£15
76	Polydor 2383 421	**RUSSIAN ROULETTE** (with lyric inner)	£15
78	Polydor 2383 474	**A CRAZY STEAL** (with lyric inner)	£15
87	BGO BGOLP4	**STAY WITH THE HOLLIES** (LP, reissue)	£15
87	BGO BGOLP8	**IN THE HOLLIES STYLE** (LP, reissue)	£15
88	BGO BGOLP25	**HOLLIES** (LP, reissue)	£15
88	BGO BGOLP9	**FOR CERTAIN BECAUSE...** (LP, reissue, gatefold)	£15
88	BGO BGOLP24	**WOULD YOU BELIEVE?** (LP, reissue)	£15
90	BGO BGOLP79	**BUTTERFLY** (LP, reissue)	£15
90	BGO BGOLP80	**EVOLUTION** (LP, reissue)	£15

(see also Allan Clarke, Graham Nash, Terry Sylvester, Haydock's Rockhouse, Peter Sellers & Sophia Loren)o

HOLLINGWORTH

71	Columbia DB 8808	**Jump On My Wagon/This Town**	£18

MARK HOLLIS

03	Polydor 537 688-1	**MARK HOLLIS** (LP, reissue of 1998 CD, 180gm, printed inner)	£200
19	Polydor/UMC 080 288-0	**MARK HOLLIS** (LP, second reissue, 180gm, printed inner, download card)	£25

(see also Talk Talk)

BRENDA HOLLOWAY

64	Stateside SS 307	**Every Little Bit Hurts/Land Of A Thousand Boys**	£80
64	Stateside SS 307	**Every Little Bit Hurts/Land Of A Thousand Boys** (DJ Copy)	£150
65	Tamla Motown TMG 508	**When I'm Gone/I've Been Good To You**	£100
65	Tamla Motown TMG 508	**When I'm Gone/I've Been Good To You** (DJ copy)	£200
65	Tamla Motown TMG 519	**Operator/I'll Be Available**	£100
65	Tamla Motown TMG 519	**Operator/I'll Be Available** (DJ copy)	£200
66	Tamla Motown TMG 556	**Together Till The End Of Time/Sad Song**	£150
66	Tamla Motown TMG 556	**Together Till The End Of Time/Sad Song** (DJ copy)	£200
66	Tamla Motown TMG 581	**Hurt A Little Everyday/Where Were You** (demos credit Brenda Holiday)	£100
66	Tamla Motown TMG 581	**Hurt A Little Everyday/Where Were You** (demos credit Brenda Holiday) (DJ copy)	£125
67	Tamla Motown TMG 608	**Just Look What You've Done/Starting The Hurt All Over Again**	£80
67	Tamla Motown TMG 608	**Just Look What You've Done/Starting The Hurt All Over Again** (DJ copy)	£125
67	Tamla Motown TMG 622	**You've Made Me So Very Happy/I've Got To Find It**	£45
69	Tamla Motown TMG 700	**Just Look What You've Done/You've Made Me So Very Happy**	£18
68	T. Motown (S)TML 11083	**THE ARTISTRY OF BRENDA HOLLOWAY** (LP, mono/stereo)	£150

LAURIE HOLLOWAY

79	Hobo HO 503	**CUMULUS** (LP)	£100

LOLEATTA HOLLOWAY

96	Kent 6T 11	**This Man's Arms/JOHN EDWARDS: Ain't That Good Enough**	£25
76	Salsoul SZS 5513	**LOLEATTA** (LP)	£20

PATRICE HOLLOWAY

66	Capitol CL 15484	**Love And Desire/Ecstasy**	£150
66	Capitol CL 15484	**Love And Desire/Ecstasy** (DJ Copy)	£250

HOLLOW GROUND

80	Guardian GR/HG C57	**FLYING HIGH EP** (Flying High/Warlord/Rock On/Don't Chase The Dragon) (in p/s)	£150
80	Guardian GR/HG C57	**FLYING HIGH EP** (Flying High/Warlord/Rock On/Don't Chase The Dragon)	£45

BUDDY HOLLY

78s

56	Brunswick 05581	**Blue Days - Black Nights/Love Me**	£300
57	Vogue Coral Q 72293	**Peggy Sue/Everyday**	£150
58	Coral Q 72293	**Peggy Sue/Everyday**	£15
58	Coral Q 72288	**Listen To Me/I'm Gonna Love You Too**	£25
58	Coral Q 72325	**Rave On/Take Your Time**	£30
58	Coral Q 72333	**Early In The Morning/Now We're One**	£35
58	Coral Q 72346	**Heartbeat/Well ... All Right**	£50
59	Coral Q 72360	**It Doesn't Matter Anymore/Raining In My Heart**	£30
59	Brunswick 05800	**Rock Around With Ollie Vee/Midnight Shift**	£200
59	Coral Q 72376	**Peggy Sue Got Married/Crying, Waiting, Hoping**	£200
60	Coral Q 72392	**Heartbeat/Everyday**	£350

SINGLES

56	Brunswick 05581	**Blue Days - Black Nights/Love Me**	£800
57	Vogue Coral Q 72293	**Peggy Sue/Everyday**	£50
58	Coral Q 72293	**Peggy Sue/Everyday**	£20
58	Coral Q 72288	**Listen To Me/I'm Gonna Love You Too**	£25
58	Coral Q 72325	**Rave On/Take Your Time**	£25
58	Coral Q 72333	**Early In The Morning/Now We're One**	£25
58	Coral Q 72346	**Heartbeat/Well ... All Right**	£25
59	Brunswick 05800	**Rock Around With Ollie Vee/Midnight Shift**	£40
59	Coral Q 72376	**Peggy Sue Got Married/Crying, Waiting, Hoping**	£25

(The above 45s were originally issued with triangular centres; reissues with round centres are worth two-thirds these values.)

60	Coral Q 72392	**Heartbeat/Everyday**	£20
61	Coral Q 72445	**Look At Me/Mailman, Bring Me No More Blues**	£15
62	Coral Q 72449	**Listen To Me/Words Of Love**	£15
64	Coral Q 72472	**You've Got Love/An Empty Cup** (as Buddy Holly & The Crickets)	£25
64	Coral Q 72475	**Love's Made A Fool Of You/You're The One**	£20

MINT VALUE £

66	Coral Q 72483	Maybe Baby/That's My Desire	£40
68	Decca AD 1009	Rave On/Peggy Sue (p/s, export reissue)	£40
84	MCA BHB 1	THAT'LL BE THE DAY (10 x 7" box set, comprising BH1-10 in p/s)	£40

EPs

58	Coral FEP 2002	LISTEN TO ME (brown cover, sleeve shows Holly without glasses; disc credits title as "Buddy Holly")	£400
58	Coral FEP 2002	LISTEN TO ME (re-pressing, various shades of green/brown p/s, shows Holly with glasses; disc credits title as "Buddy Holly")	£40
58	Coral FEP 2005	RAVE ON (various shades of green/brown p/s)	£40
58	Coral FEP 2014	IT'S SO EASY	£40
59	Coral FEP 2015	HEARTBEAT	£40
59	Coral FEP 2032	BUDDY HOLLY	£40
59	Brunswick OE 9456	BUDDY HOLLY NO. 1	£60
59	Brunswick OE 9457	BUDDY HOLLY NO. 2	£60

(The above EPs were originally issued with triangular centres; later pressings with round-centres are worth between half and two thirds of these values.)

60	Coral FEP 2044	THE LATE GREAT BUDDY HOLLY (tri centre)	£50
60	Coral FEP 2044	THE LATE GREAT BUDDY HOLLY (round centre)	£15
64	Coral FEP 2065	BUDDY - BY REQUEST	£40
64	Coral FEP 2066	THAT TEX-MEX SOUND	£50
64	Coral FEP 2067	WISHING	£50
64	Coral FEP 2068	SHOWCASE VOLUME 1	£40
64	Coral FEP 2069	SHOWCASE VOLUME 2	£40
65	Coral FEP 2070	BUDDY HOLLY SINGS	£40

ALBUMS

58	Vogue Coral LVA 9085	BUDDY HOLLY (Vogue-Coral labels & Coral sleeve)	£100
58	Coral LVA 9085	BUDDY HOLLY	£45
59	Coral LVA 9105	THE BUDDY HOLLY STORY ('High Fidelity Coral' logo on sleeve)	£25
60s	Coral LVA 9105	THE BUDDY HOLLY STORY (reissue, different 'roll-neck sweater' sleeve with small 'Coral' logo)	£40
60	Coral LVA 9127	THE BUDDY HOLLY STORY VOL. II	£20
61	Ace Of Hearts AH 3	THAT'LL BE THE DAY	£25
63	Coral LVA 9212	REMINISCING	£25
64	Coral LVA 9222	SHOWCASE	£25
65	Coral LVA 9227	HOLLY IN THE HILLS (with Bob Montgomery, withdrawn mispressing, sleeve & label list "Wishing", plays "Reminiscing"; matrix no's end with 1B both sides)	£40
65	Coral LVA 9227	HOLLY IN THE HILLS (corrected edition, with Bob Montgomery, plays "Wishing", matrix numbers end with 1B on one side & 2B on other)	£60
68	MCA MUP 320	WISHING (mono only, reissue of "Holly In The Hills")	£18
69	MCA MUPS 371	GIANT	£18

(Originally issued with yellow labels; later variations exist with various twin-toned designs.)

75	World Records SM 301/5	THE BUDDY HOLLY STORY (5-LP box set)	£20
79	MCA Coral CDMSP 807	THE COMPLETE BUDDY HOLLY (6-LP box set with sepia-tinted book)	£30

(see also Crickets, Fireballs)

STEVIE HOLLY

66	Planet PLF 107	A Strange World/Little Man	£80

HOLLY (2)

79	Eric's ERIC'S 003	Yankee Rose/Treasure Island/Desperate Dan (p/s)	£25
79	Eric's ERIC'S 007	Hobo Joe/Stars Of The Bars (p/s)	£20

(see also Frankie Goes To Hollywood, Big In Japan)

HOLLY & THE ITALIANS

81	Virgin VS 411	I Wanna Go Home/Fanzine (p/s)	£15
81	Virgin V 2186	THE RIGHT TO BE ITALIAN (LP, with lyric insert)	£15

HOLLYWOOD ARGYLES

60	Top Rank JAR 530	Gun Totin' Critter Called Jack/GARY PAXTON: Bug-Eye	£20

(see also Kim Fowley, Skip & Flip, Gary Paxton)

HOLLYWOOD BRATS

80	Cherry Red 12 CHERRY 6	Then He Kissed Me/Another School Day/Sick On You (12", p/s)	£35
80	Cherry Red A RED 6	HOLLYWOOD BRATS (LP)	£40

HOLLYWOOD FLAMES

57	London HL 7030	Buzz Buzz Buzz/Crazy (export issue)	£50
58	London HL 8545	Buzz Buzz Buzz/Crazy	£75
58	London HL 8545	Buzz Buzz Buzz/Crazy (78)	£15
59	London HLW 8955	Much Too Much/In The Dark	£75
59	London HLW 8955	Much Too Much/In The Dark (78)	£25
60	London HLE 9071	If I Thought You Needed Me/Every Day Every Way	£50

KENNY HOLLYWOOD

62	Decca F 11546	Magic Star/The Wonderful Story Of Love	£25

HOLLYWOOD KILLERS

78	Rollerball ROLL 2	Goodbye Suicide/Tramp	£50

(see also Jim Penfold & The Hollywood Killers)

PETER HOLM

67	Major Minor MM504	This Is Not The Way/You Will Be Mine	£15

EDDIE HOLMAN

65	Cameo Parkway P 960	This Can't Be True/A Free Country	£50
69	Action ACT 4547	I Love You/I Surrender	£125
00	Grapevine G2K 45-138	Hold Me In Your Arms/MRS BAND: Diggin It	£35

CARL HOLMES
04   Soul On 45 S 102   Soul Dance Number 2/PARISIANS: Twinkle Litte Star £15

DAVID HOLMES
02   13 Amp APM 001LP   COME GET IT I GOT IT (2xLP) £40
(see also Mogwai)

ELDRIDGE HOLMES
68   Pama PM 746   Beverley/Wait For Me Baby...................£18

JAKE HOLMES
70   Ember EMB S 269   Saturday Night/Diner Song (p/s)...................£20
70   Polydor 583 579   JAKE HOLMES (LP)...................£30
70   Polydor 2425 036   SO CLOSE SO VERY FAR TO GO (LP)...................£22
72   CBS 64905   HOW MUCH TIME (LP)...................£20

RICHARD 'GROOVES' HOLMES
67   Transatlantic PR 7435   SOUL MESSAGE (LP)...................£25
68   Transatlantic PR 7493   RICHARD 'GROOVES' HOLMES (LP)...................£20

HOLOCAUST (1)
80   Phoenix PSP 1   Heavy Metal Mania/Only As Young As You Feel (p/s)...................£20
80   Phoenix 12 PSP 1   Heavy Metal Mania/Love's Power/Only As Young As You Feel (12", p/s) £30
80   Phoenix 12 PSP 2   Smokin' Valves/Friend Or Foe/Out My Book (12", p/s) £30
81   Phoenix PSP 3P   HOLOCAUST LIVE (EP)...................£25
82   Phoenix 12 PSP 4   Comin' Through/Don't Wanna Be A Loser/Good Thing Going (12", p/s)...................£30
81   Phoenix PSLP 1   THE NIGHTCOMERS (LP)...................£40
83   Phoenix PSPLP 4   LIVE (HOT CURRY AND WINE) (LP)...................£25
84   Phoenix PSPLP 5   NO MAN'S LAND (LP)...................£20

HOLOCAUST (2)
79   Pile Driver HOL 201   Slay That Dragon/Take Me To Your Lawyer/So Called Civilised Way (12", no p/s) £1000

ERROL HOLT
76   Olympic MOR 1015   Those Who Have Eyes To See/Dub To See £35
77   Lior ROAR 111   Come Rock Me/Congo Dread (12")...................£50
78   Star Time EHLF 427   I Am Not A King (with PRINCE FAR I)/Version (12")...................£40
79   Hit Run HIT DD16   Yes Yes Yes/ROD TAYLOR: No One Can Tell I About Jah (12")...................£80
79   Hit Run HIT DD25   Sweet Reggae Music/PRINCE FAR I: Hairdressing Salon £90
70s   Dread DDLP 102   VISION OF AFRICA (LP) £50

JOHN HOLT
63   Island WI 041   I Cried A Tear/I'll Stay £30
68   Trojan TR 643   Tonight/Oh How It Hurts (B-side actually by Paragons) £25
69   Trojan TR 661   Ali Baba/I'm Your Man £75
69   Harry J TR 694   Have Sympathy/HARRY J ALLSTARS: Spyrone £40
70   Duke Reid DR 2506   Come Out Of My Bed/WINSTON WRIGHT: Hide And Seek £18
70   Duke DU 73   Stealing, Stealing/WINSTON WRIGHT: Stealing, Stealing (Volume 2)...................£25
70   Duke DU 77   The Working Kind/Open Jaw £25
70   Jackpot JP 735   A Little Tear/JEFF BARNS: Get In The Groove £15
70   Bamboo BAM 44   A Love I Can Feel/JOHNNY LAST: Long Liver Man (B-side act. by Hugh Black) £25
70   Bamboo BAM 55   A Stranger In Love/WAILERS: Jailhouse (Good Rudy) £50
70   Bamboo BAM 62   Holly Holy/Do You Love Me? £20
70   Banana BA 314   Why Can't I Touch You/SOUND DIMENSION: Touching Version £15
70   Supreme SUP 212   Share My Rest/AL BROWN: Allways £40
70   Unity UN 548   Sometimes/BUNNY LEE ALL STARS: Lash-La-Rue £30
70   Unity UN 552   Walking Along/LEE'S ALL STARS: Warefare...................£50
70   Unity UN 556   Give Her All The Love/BUSTY BROWN: Nobody But You £15
70   Success RE 903   Fat Girl, Sexy Girl/Man And Woman £30
71   Banana BA 340   O.K. Fred/Fancy Make-Up £15
71   Banana BA 345   Build Our Dreams/LEROY SIBBLES: Love In Our Nation £25
71   Treasure Isle TI 7061   Let's Build Our Dreams/TOMMY McCOOK & SUPERSONICS: Testify Version...................£25
71   Treasure Isle TI 7065   Sister Big Stuff/TOMMY McCOOK & SUPERSONICS: Black River £25
71   Treasure Isle TI 7066   Paragons Medley/TOMMY McCOOK & SUPERSONICS: Medley Version...................£15
71   Punch PH 60   Strange Things/WINSTON WRIGHT: Want Money (B-side act. G.G. All Stars)...................£25
72   Blue Beat BB 424   O.K. Fred/BIG YOUTH: Chi Chi Run £20
72   Fab FAB 188   A Little Happiness/DELROY WILSON: Diamond Rings £15
83   Greensleeves GRED 120   Police In Helicopter/Youth Pon The Corner (12")...................£20
70   Bamboo BDLP 210   A LOVE I CAN FEEL (LP)...................£60
72   Melodisc MLP 12170   GREATEST HITS (LP)...................£40
72   Melodisc MLP 12180   OK FRED (LP)...................£45
70s   Melodisc MLP 12191   JOHN HOLT & FRIENDS (LP)...................£45
71   Trojan TRL(S) 37   STILL IN CHAINS (LP)...................£15
72   Trojan TBL 184   PLEDGING MY LOVE (LP)...................£15
73   Trojan TRLS 75   1000 VOLTS OF HOLT (LP)...................£20
74   Attack ATLP 1010   A LOVE I CAN FEEL (LP)...................£15
80   Lord Koos KLP 4   DON'T BREAK YOUR PROMISE (LP, colour or black and white cover) £40
83   Greensleeves GRED 120   POLICE IN HELICOPTER (LP)...................£25
(see also Jay & Joya, Neville Hinds, Jeff Barnes, Danny Simpson, Hugh Roy, U Roy Junior, Don Drummond, Interns)

ROOSEVELT HOLTS
68   Blue Horizon 7-63201   PRESENTING THE COUNTRY BLUES (LP) £85

HOLY MACKEREL
72   CBS 65297   HOLY MACKEREL (LP)...................£40

MINT VALUE £

93	Tenth Planet TP 005	CLOSER TO HEAVEN (LP, numbered, 500 only)	£20

(see also Jason Crest, High Broom)

HOLY MODAL ROUNDERS
68	Elektra EKL 4026	THE MORAY EELS EAT THE HOLY MODALS (LP, mono)	£40
68	Elektra EKS 74026	THE MORAY EELS EAT THE HOLY MODALS (LP, stereo)	£40
70	Transatlantic TRA 7451	HOLY MODAL ROUNDERS (LP)	£40
70	Transatlantic TRA	HOLY MODAL ROUNDERS 2 (LP)	£35

HOMBRES
67	Verve VS 1510	Let It Out (Let It All Hang Out)/Go Girl Go	£15

HOME
72	(No Cat No)	You'll Get A Helping Hand At Barclays/Dreamer (p/s)	£15
71	CBS 64356	PAUSE FOR A HOARSE HORSE (LP, gatefold sleeve)	£40
72	CBS 64752	HOME (LP)	£25
73	CBS 65550	THE ALCHEMIST (LP)	£30

(see also Groundhogs, AC/DC, WIshbone Ash, Blue Rondos)

HOMERS KNODS
69	Pye 7N 17731	All She Said Was Goodbye/Mr Rainbow	£20

HOME SERVICE
84	Coda NAT 001	THE MYSTERIES (LP)	£15

HOMESICK JAMES
64	Sue WI 319	Crossroads/My Baby's Sweet	£75
65	Sue WI 330	Set A Date/Can't Afford To It	£50

HOMESICK JAMES/SNOOKY PRYOR
74	Caroline C 1502	HOMESICK JAMES AND SNOOKY PRYOR (LP)	£20

HOMESTEAD
68	Road R3946	She/Will You Leave	£15

HOMOSEXUALS
78	L'Orelei PF 151	Hearts In Exile/South South Africans (p/s, with insert)	£15
81	Black Noise BN 1	BIGGER THAN THE NUMBER YET MISSING THE DOT (EP, clear vinyl, fold-around hand-painted sleeve)	£20
82	Black Noise BLACKNOISE 2	THE HOMOSEXUALS EP (12")	£30
84	Recommended RR 18	THE HOMOSEXUALS RECORD (LP, with inserts)	£20

(see also George Harrassment & Homosexuals, Ice La Bas, Amos & Sara, L-Voag, Sir Alick & Phraser)

MINAKO HONDA
87	Columbia DB 9153	Golden Days (English Version)/Crazy Nights (English Version) (p/s, features Brian May)	£35

HONDELLS
64	Mercury MF 834	Little Honda/Hot Rod High	£25
65	Mercury MF 925	Younger Girl/All American Girl	£20
66	Mercury MF 967	Cheryl's Goin' Home/Show Me Girl	£20

HONEST MEN
69	Tamla Motown TMG 706	Cherie/Baby	£50
69	Tamla Motown TMG 706	Cherie/Baby (DJ Copy)	£60

HONEY BEES
02	Fab-U-Lus FBU07014	Never In A Million Years/MELBA MOORE: The Magic Touch (reissue)	£15

HONEYBOY
71	Trojan TR 7835	Jamaica/ITALS: Sea Wave	£18
72	Banana BA 375	Homeward Bound/Peace In The Land	£100
73	Sir Collins Music SCMW 004	Better Must Come/Lola (as Honeyboy Collins)	£40
73	Count Shelly CS 030	Feeling High Version/Bush Ranger At His Workshop (with Tapper Zukie)	£50
75	B & C BC 002	Darlin' Coming Home/SIR COLLINS: We A Come Dread	£25
73	Count Shelly SSLP 101	THIS IS HONEY BOY (LP)	£60
74	Cactus CTLP 101	IMPOSSIBLE LOVE (LP)	£25

HONEYBUS
69	Deram DM 254	She Sold Blackpool Rock/Would You Believe	£25
70	Deram DML/SML 1056	STORY (LP)	£150
73	Warner Bros K 46248	RECITAL (LP, withdrawn, test pressings only)	£300
79	See For Miles SEE 264	AT THEIR BEST (LP)	£15

(see also Pete Dello, Colin Hare, Lace, Red Herring)

HONEYCOMBAK
69	Carousel CAR 1	Sex Change Sadie/It's My Life	£50

HONEYCOMBS
65	Pye 7N 15781	Don't Love You No More/I'll See You Tomorrow (withdrawn, promo only)	£120
66	Pye 7N 17089	Who Is Sylvia?/How Will I Know	£15
66	Pye 7N 17138	It's So Hard/I Fell In Love	£15
66	Pye 7N 17173	That Loving Feeling/Should A Man Cry	£18
65	Pye NEP 24230	THAT'S THE WAY (EP)	£35
64	Pye NPL 18097	THE HONEYCOMBS (LP)	£40
65	Pye NPL 18132	ALL SYSTEMS GO! (LP)	£70

(see also Lemmings, Dennis D'Ell)

HONEYCONE
71	Hot Wax SHW 5002	HONEYCONE (LP)	£20
71	Hot Wax SHW 5004	SWEET REPLIES (LP)	£20
72	Hot Wax SHW 5005	SOULFUL TAPESTRY (LP)	£20
73	Hot Wax SHW 5010	LOVE, PEACE AND SOUL (LP)	£20

HONEYCRACK
| 96 | Epic 484230 0 | PROZAC (LP, with inner sleeve, white vinyl, 2000 only) | £25 |
| 96 | Epic 484230 1 | PROZAC (LP, with inner sleeve, black vinyl) | £25 |

(see also Jellys, Wildhearts)

HONEYDEW
| 70 | Argo AFW 101 | Part Of This Game/To Make You Mine | £20 |
| 70 | Argo ZFB 15 | HONEYDEW (LP) | £150 |

HONEYEND
| 72 | Spark SRL 1072 | Heartbreaker/Beautiful Downtown | £20 |

HONEYS
| 63 | Capitol CL 15299 | Surfin' Down The Swanee River/Shoot The Curl | £50 |

(see also American Spring, Beach Boys)

HONEYTONES
| 58 | London HLX 8671 | Don't Look Now, But.../I Know, I Know | £60 |
| 58 | London HLX 8671 | Don't Look Now, But.../I Know, I Know (78) | £35 |

HONEYTREE
| 70s | Myrrh MYR 1039 | EVERGREEN (LP) | £20 |

HOOD
00	Jonathan Whiskey 04	I Can't Find My Brittle Youth/Song Of The Sea/STEWARD: Silver Soda Pop/I'm A Woman Not Just A Toy/Flatter Me With Concern For Prejudice (envelope sleeve, 250 only)	£20
94	Fluff ARC 01	CABLED LINEAR TRACTION (LP, 200 only)	£50
98	Domino WIGLP 42	RUSTIC HOUSES FORLORN VALLEYS (LP)	£30
99	Domino WIGLP 61	THE CYCLE OF DAYS AND REASONS (LP)	£25
01	Domino WIGLP 102	COLD HOUSE (LP)	£20
05	Domino WIGLP 148	OUTSIDE CLOSER (LP)	£18
12	Domino REWIGLP85	COLD HOUSE (reissue, 2x12")	£20

ROBBIN HOOD
| 56 | MGM SP 1178 | The Rock-A-Bye Blues/Beautiful, Beautiful Love | £15 |

HOODOO RHYTHM DEVILS
| 78 | Fantasy FTC 147 | Gotta Lot Of Love In My Soul/MDR Of Love | £15 |

MARCUS HOOK ROLL BAND
| 72 | Regal Zonophone RZ 3061 | Natural Man/Boogalooing Is For Wooing | £30 |
| 74 | EMI 2119 | Can't Stand The Heat/Moonshine Blues | £20 |

EARL HOOKER
69	Blue Horizon 57-3166	Boogie Don't Blot/Funky Blues	£30
70	Blue Horizon 7-63850	SWEET BLACK ANGEL (LP)	£120
70	Stateside SSL 10298	DON'T HAVE TO WORRY (LP)	£60

(see also John Lee Hooker)

JOHN LEE HOOKER
| 89 | Silvertone Records ZL 74307 | THE HEALER (LP) | £15 |

78s
| 52 | Vogue V 2102 | Hoogie Boogie/Whistlin' And Moanin' Blues | £40 |
| 54 | London HL 8037 | Need Somebody/Too Much Boogie | £40 |

SINGLES
63	Stateside SS 203	Boom Boom/Frisco Blues	£25
64	Stateside SS 297	Dimples/I'm Leaving	£20
64	Stateside SS 341	I Love You Honey/Send Me Your Pillow	£20
64	Pye International 7N 25255	High Priced Woman/Sugar Mama	£20
64	Polydor NH 52930	Shake It Baby/Let's Make It Baby	£20
65	Sue WI 361	I'm In The Mood/Boogie Chillun	£40
66	Chess CRS 8039	Let's Go Out Tonight/In The Mood	£20
66	Planet PLF 114	Mai Lee/Don't Be Messing With My Bread (with Groundhogs)	£100

EPs
60	Riverside REP 3202	WEDNESDAY EVENING	£30
60	Riverside REP 3207	DEMOCRAT MAN	£30
64	Stateside SE 1019	THE BLUES OF JOHN HOOKER	£30
64	Stateside SE 1023	I'M JOHN LEE HOOKER	£30
64	Ember EP 4561	THINKING BLUES	£40
65	Pye Intl. NEP 44034	LOVE BLUES	£35
65	Chess CRE 6000	DOWN AT THE LANDING	£35
65	Atlantic AET 6010	JOHN LEE HOOKER	£35
66	Chess CRE 6007	WALKING THE BOOGIE	£30
66	Chess CRE 6014	THE JOURNEY	£30
66	Chess CRE 6021	REAL FOLK BLUES VOL. 3	£30
73	Impulse 9103	SERVES YOU RIGHT TO SUFFER	£15

ALBUMS
60	Advent LP 2801	JOHN LEE HOOKER AND HIS GUITAR	£80
62	Riverside RLP 12-838	THE FOLK BLUES OF JOHN LEE HOOKER	£45
62	Stateside SL 10014	THE FOLK LORE OF JOHN LEE HOOKER	£70
63	London HA-K 8097	DON'T TURN ME FROM YOUR DOOR	£80
64	Stateside SL 10053	THE BIG SOUL OF JOHN LEE HOOKER	£80
64	Stateside SL 10074	I WANT TO SHOUT THE BLUES	£60
64	Pye Intl. NPL 28042	HOUSE OF THE BLUES	£60

MINT VALUE £

64	Fontana 688 700 ZL	THE FOLK-BLUES OF HOOKER	£45
65	Fontana FJL 119	BLUE!	£70
65	Ember EMB 3356	SINGS THE BLUES	£35
65	Riverside RLP 008	BURNING HELL	£35
65	Chess CRL 4500	JOHN LEE HOOKER PLAYS AND SINGS THE BLUES	£60
66	HMV CLP 5032	IT SERVES YOU RIGHT TO SUFFER (mono)	£150
66	HMV CSD 3542	IT SERVES YOU RIGHT TO SUFFER (stereo)	£135
66	Ember (ST)EMB 3371	DRIFTIN' THROUGH THE BLUES	£25
67	Chess CRL 4527	THE REAL FOLK BLUES	£40
67	HMV CLP/CSD 3612	LIVE AT THE CAFE A GO GO	£40
67	Atlantic Special 590 003	DRIFTIN' BLUES	£18
68	Joy JOY(S) 101	I'M JOHN LEE HOOKER	£15
68	Joy JOY(S) 124	BURNIN'	£15
68	Stateside (S)SL 10246	URBAN BLUES	£40
69	Stateside (S)SL 10280	SIMPLY THE TRUTH	£50
69	Joy JOYS 133	THE FOLKLORE OF JOHN LEE HOOKER	£15
69	Joy JOYS 142	CONCERT AT NEWPORT	£15
69	Joy JOYS 147	THE BIG SOUL OF JOHN LEE HOOKER	£15
69	Storyville 673 005	YOU'RE LEAVIN' ME BABY	£15
69	Joy JOYS 152	IN PERSON	£15
70	Storyville 673 020	TUPELO BLUES	£30
70	Stax SXATS 1025	THAT'S WHERE IT'S AT	£20
71	Probe SPB 1016	IF YOU MISS 'IM . . . I GOT 'IM (with Earl Hooker)	£30
71	Probe SPB 1034	ENDLESS BOOGIE	£15
71	Stax 2362 017	THAT'S WHERE IT'S AT!	£20
71	Xtra XTRA 1114	JOHN LEE HOOKER	£40
71	United Artists UAS 29235	COAST TO COAST BLUES BAND	£22
72	Probe SPB 1057	NEVER GET OUT OF THESE BLUES ALIVE	£18
73	Green Bottle GN 4002	JOHNNY LEE	£18
75	ABC ABCL 5059	FREE BEER AND CHICKEN	£20
77	DJM DJD 28026	DIMPLES (2LP, gatefold)	£15
91	Silvertone ZL 75087	MR. LUCKY (LP)	£30
95	Virgin VPBLP 22	CHILL OUT (LP, printed inner)	£120

(see also Canned Heat, Carlos Santana & Buddy Miles)

JOHN LEE HOOKER/LIGHTNIN' HOPKINS/SMOKEY HOGG
| 73 | Specialty SNTF 5013 | HOOKER HOPKINS HOGG (LP) | £20 |

(see also Lightnin' Hopkins, Smokey Hogg)

HOOKFOOT
71	DJM DJLPS 413	HOOKFOOT (LP, gatefold sleeve)	£30
72	DJM DJLPS 422	GOOD TIMES A' COMIN' (LP, gatefold sleeve)	£25
73	DJM DJLPS 428	COMMUNICATION (LP, gatefold sleeve)	£20
75	DJM DJLMD 8013	HEADLINES (2XLP)	£18

(see also Elton John, Loot, Caleb, Soul Agents)

MARSHALL HOOKS & CO.
| 71 | Blue Horizon 2096 002 | I Want The Same Thing Tomorrow/Hookin' It | £20 |
| 71 | Blue Horizon 2431 003 | MARSHALL HOOKS & CO. (LP) | £100 |

HOOKY
| 72 | RCA Victor SF 8247 | THE COLLECTED TALES OF HOOKY NO.1 (LP, gatefold sleeve) | £20 |

HOOTEN(ANNY) SINGERS
| 64 | United Artists UP 1082 | Gabrielle/Darling (most copies list artist as Hooten Singers) | £35 |

(see also Abba, Hep Stars, Northern Lights)

BOB HOPE
| 63 | Brunswick LAT 8539 | IN RUSSIA AND ONE OTHER PLACE (LP) | £15 |

(see also Bing Crosby)

LYN(N) HOPE
57	Vogue V 9081	Blue Moon/Blues For Anna Bacca	£20
57	Vogue V 9082	Eleven Till Two/Blues For Mary	£20
60	Blue Beat BB 21	Shockin'/Blue And Sentimental	£20
57	Vogue VE 170103	LYNN HOPE AND HIS TENOR SAX (EP)	£40
60	Vogue VE 170146	LYNN HOPE AND HIS TENOR SAX (EP)	£40

HOPE BLISTERS
| 98 | 4AD CAD 8008 | ...SMILES OK (LP) | £30 |

HOPETOWN (LEWIS) & GLENMORE (BROWN)
| 68 | Fab FAB 43 | Skinny Leg Girl/Live Like A King | £90 |

MARY HOPKIN
69	Apple APPLE 7	Lontana Dagli Occhi/Game (Europe-only, unreleased in U.K.)	£0
69	Apple APPLE 9	Prince En Avignon/The Game (France-only, unreleased in U.K.)	£0
69	Apple APPLE 16	Que Sera Sera/Fields Of St. Etienne (unreleased)	£0
69	Cambrian CSP 703	Aderyn Llwyd/Y Blodyn Gwyn (p/s)	£18
70	Cambrian CSP 712	Pleserau Serch/Tyrd Yn Ôl (p/s)	£18
70	Apple APPLE 27	Que Sera Sera/Fields Of St. Etienne (unreleased in U.K., acetates only)	£0
71	Apple APPLE 34	Let My Name Be Sorrow/Kew Gardens (p/s)	£15
71	Apple APPLE 39	Water, Paper And Clay/Jefferson (p/s)	£25
68	Cambrian CEP 414	LLAIS SWYNOL MARY HOPKIN (EP)	£15
69	Cambrian CEP 420	MARY AC EDWARD (EP, with Edward Morris Jones)	£15
69	Apple APCOR 5	POST CARD (LP, laminated sleeve, with black or white inner sleeve, mono)	£25

MINT VALUE £

69	Apple SAPCOR 5	POST CARD (LP, laminated sleeve, with black or white inner sleeve, stereo)	£20
71	Apple SAPCOR 21	EARTH SONG - OCEAN SONG (LP, gatefold sleeve, 'Apple' inner sleeve)	£50
72	Apple SAPCOR 23	THOSE WERE THE DAYS (LP, with 'Apple' inner sleeve)	£90
77	Decca SPA 546	THE WELSH WORLD OF MARY HOPKIN (LP)	£30
89	Trax Modem 1045	SPIRIT (LP)	£20
91	Apple SAPCOR 5	POST CARD (LP, reissue, gatefold sleeve with bonus 12" [SAPCOR 52])	£30
92	Apple SAPCOR 21	EARTH SONG/OCEAN SONG (LP, reissue, gatefold sleeve with inner)	£30

(see also Sundance, Oasis, Bob Johnson & Pete Knight, Roy Budd, Elmer Bernstein)

JOEL & LIGHTNIN' HOPKINS

60	Heritage H 1000	BLUES FROM EAST TEXAS (LP, 99 copies only)	£120

(see also Lightnin' Hopkins)

LIGHTNIN' HOPKINS

61	Bluesville BVLP 1019	LIGHTNIN' HOPKINS (LP)	£80
62	'77' LA 12/1	SAM LIGHTNIN' HOPKINS - THE ROOSTER CROWED IN ENGLAND (LP 99 copies only)	£150
63	Stateside SL 10031	LIGHTNIN' STRIKES (LP)	£90
63	Realm RM 128	LIGHTNIN' HOPKINS SINGS THE BLUES (LP)	£35
63	Realm RM 171	DIRTY HOUSE BLUES (LP)	£30
64	Stateside SL 10076	BLUES HOOT (LP, some tracks by Sonny Terry & Brownie McGhee)	£60
65	Stateside SL 10110	HOOTIN' THE BLUES (LP)	£60
65	Stateside SL 10155	DOWN HOME BLUES (LP)	£60
65	Fontana AH 183	THE BLUES (LP)	£40
65	FONTANA 688 007 ZL	PENITENTIARY BLUES (LP)	£35
65	Fontana 688 301 ZL	LAST NIGHT BLUES (LP)	£40
65	Fontana 688 801 ZL	BURNIN' IN L.A. (LP)	£40
66	Fontana 688 803 ZL	BLUE BIRD BLUES (LP)	£40
66	Fontana 688 807 ZL	BLUES PARTY (LP)	£40
66	Ember EMB 3389	A TIME FOR BLUES (LP)	£25
66	Ember EMB 3416	LIVE AT THE BIRD LOUNGE (LP)	£25
67	Ember EMB 3423	I'VE BEEN BUKED AND SCORNED (LP)	£25
66	Verve (S)VLP 5003	ROOTS OF HOPKINS (LP)	£25
66	Verve (S)VLP 5014	LIGHTNIN' STRIKES (LP, reissue)	£18
66	Saga ERO 8001	LIGHTNIN' HOPKINS (LP)	£15
67	Xtra XTRA 5036	BLUES IN MY BOTTLE (LP)	£18
68	Xtra XTRA 5044	GOT TO MOVE YOUR BABY (LP, reissue of Fontana 688 301 ZL)	£20
68	Minit MLL/MLS 40006	EARTH BLUES (LP)	£40
69	Liberty LBL 83254	KING OF DOWLING STREET (LP)	£30
69	Joy JOY(S) 115	LIGHTNIN' STRIKES (LP, 2nd reissue)	£15
69	Polydor 545 019	THAT'S MY STORY (LP)	£25
70	Ace Of Hearts AH 183	THE BLUES (LP)	£15
70	Poppy PYS 11000	LIGHTNIN'! VOLUME 1 (LP)	£20
70	Poppy PYS 11002	LIGHTNIN'! VOLUME 2 (LP)	£20
71	Liberty LBS 83293	THE CALIFORNIA MUDSLIDE (AND EARTHQUAKE) (LP)	£30
71	Mayfair AMLB 4000 1/2	LIGHTNIN' STRIKES (2-LP)	£18
71	Blue Horizon 2431 005	LET'S WORK AWHILE (LP)	£120
71	Xtra XTRA 1127	THE ROOTS OF LIGHTNIN' HOPKINS (LP)	£18
72	Carnival 2941 005	LONESOME LIGHTNIN' (LP)	£18

(see also Sonny Terry & Brownie McGhee, Joel & Lightnin' Hopkins, Lightnin' Hopkins & John Lee Hooker, Big Joe Williams)

LIGHTNIN' HOPKINS & JOHN LEE HOOKER

69	Storyville 616 001	THERE'S GOOD ROCKIN' TONIGHT! (LP)	£35
72	Storyville SLP 174	LIGHTNIN' HOPKINS AND JOHN LEE HOOKER (LP)	£35

(see also John Lee Hooker/Lightnin' Hopkins/Smokey Hogg)

LINDA HOPKINS

61	Coral Q 72423	I Diddle Dum Dum/All In My Mind	£20
62	Coral Q 72448	Mama's Doin' The Twist/My Mother's Eyes	£20

LINDA HOPKINS & JACKIE WILSON

63	Coral Q 72464	Shake A Hand/Say I Do	£15
65	Coral Q 72480	Yes Indeed/When The Saints Go Marching In	£15

(see also Jackie Wilson)

NICKY HOPKINS

66	CBS 202055	Mr Big/Jenni	£18
67	Polydor 56175	Mister Pleasant/Nothing As Yet	£18
66	CBS (S)BPG 62679	THE REVOLUTIONARY PIANO OF NICKY HOPKINS (LP)	£70
73	CBS 65416	THE TIN MAN WAS A DREAMER (LP, gatefold sleeve)	£30

(see also Aquarian Age, Neil Christian & Crusaders, Cyril Davies R&B All-Stars, Poet & One Man Band, Quicksilver Messenger Service, Sweet Thursday)

WASH HOPKINS SINGERS

69	Action ACT 4546	He's Got Blessing/Rock In A Weary Land	£20

HOPKIRK AND LEE

98	Rough Trade/For Us 001	Beneath The Apple Tree (7" 1,000 copies)	£18

HUGH HOPPER

73	CBS 65466	1984 (LP)	£40
76	Compendium FIDARDO 4	CRUEL BUT FAIR (LP)	£20
77	Compendium FIDARDO 7	HOPPERTUNITY BOX (LP)	£20
78	Ogun OG 527	ROGUE ELEMENT (LP, as Hopper, Dean, Gowen, Sheen - 'Soft Heap')	£20
80	Red ROUGE 1	TWO RAINBOWS DAILY (LP, with Alan Gowen)	£30

(see also Caravan, Elton Dean, Gilgamesh, Isotope, Matching Mole, Ninesense, Soft Machine)

HOPSCOTCH
69	United Artists UP 2231	Look At The Lights Go Up/Same Old Fat Man	£140

(see also Scots Of St. James, Five Day Rain, Forever More, Glencoe)o

HORACE & IMPERIALS
68	Nu Beat NB 012	Young Love/Days Like These	£15

HORDEN RAIKES
73	Folk Heritage FHR 042	KING COTTON (LP)	£15
72	Folk Heritage FHR 026	HORDEN RAIKES (LP)	£20

PAUL HORN
68	Liberty LBL 83084E	COSMIC CONSCIOUSNESS (LP)	£30

LENA HORNE
65	United Artists UP 1101	The Sand And The Sea/It Had Better Be Tonight	£25

HORNSEY AT WAR
79	War WAR 001	DEAD BEAT REVIVAL (EP, numbered p/s)	£40

HORRORCOMIC
77	Lightning/B&C BVZ 0007	I'm All Hung Up On Pierrepoint/The Exorcist/Sex In The Afternoon (p/s)	£40
78	Lightning GIL 512	I Don't Mind/England 77 (p/s)	£90
79	B&C BCS 18	Jesus Crisis/Cut Your Throat (p/s)	£400

HORRORS
06	Loog LOOG 015	Sheena Is A Parasite/Jack The Ripper (p/s, insert, 500 only)	£80
06	Loog LOOG 18-7X	Count In Fives/A Knife In Their Eye (p/s, inner p/s, stickered PVC sleeve)	£15
06	Loog LOOG 18-7	Count In Fives/Who Says (black sleeve, barcode sticker, with sticker inside)	£18
13	XL XLBX 587	HIGHER (4 x 12", 2-CD, DVD box set)	£50
07	Polydor 172 417-9	STRANGE HOUSE (LP, stickered gatefold sleeve, inner)	£80
09	XL XLLP 418	PRIMARY COLOURS (2-LP, poster)	£25
11	XL XLLP 539	SKYING (2-LP with 5 prints)	£20
14	XL XLLP 640	LUMINOUS (2-LP)	£18

(see also Spider & The Flies)

FRANK HORROX
60	Embassy WEP 1038	JAZZ SESSION (EP, featuring Don Rendell)	£20

HORSE
70	RCA Victor SF 8109	HORSE (LP, laminated sleeve)	£400

(see also Saturnalia, Atomic Rooster)

HORSEBEACH
13	Box Bedroom BBR 5	HORSEBEACH EP (p/s, numbered, 125 copies)	£20

HORSE MOUTH
75	Fight FT 010	Herb Vendor/DELROY BUTLER: Give Thanks	£50

(see also Mad Roy, Silvertones)

HORSLIPS
73	Oats MOO 3	HAPPY TO MEET ... SORRY TO PART (LP, booklet octagonal sleeve)	£45
73	Oats MOO 5	THE TAIN (LP, gatefold sleeve, lyric inner sleeve)	£20
75	RCA Victor SF 8432	THE UNFORTUNATE CUP OF TEA (LP, orange label)	£15

HORTENSE (ELLIS) & ALTON (ELLIS)
65	Island WI 230	Don't Gamble With Love/Something You Got (B-side actually by Alton Ellis & Flames)	£40

(see also Hortense Ellis, Alton Ellis, Mr. Foundation)

HORTENSE (ELLIS) & DELROY (WILSON)
66	Rio R 119	We're Gonna Make It/SOUL BROTHERS: Ska Shuffle	£35

(see also Hortense Ellis, Delroy Wilson)

HORTENSE (ELLIS) & JACKIE (OPEL)
64	R&B JB 138	Stand By Me/JACKIE OPEL: Solid Rock	£50

(see also Hortense Ellis, Jackie Opel)

JOHNNY HORTON
60	Mercury ZEP 10074	THE FANTASTIC JOHNNY HORTON (EP)	£40
64	Mercury 10008 MCE	COUNTRY AND WESTERN ACES (EP)	£20
60	Philips BBL 7464	THE SPECTACULAR JOHNNY HORTON (LP)	£40
61	Philips BBL 7536	HONKY TONK MAN (LP)	£40
63	London HA-U 8096	DONE ROVIN' (LP)	£25

WALTER 'SHAKEY' HORTON
70	London HAK/SHK 8405	SOUTHERN COMFORT (LP, as Shakey Horton)	£100
74	Xtra XTRA 1135	WALTER 'SHAKEY' HORTON WITH HOT COTTAGE (LP)	£30
74	Sonet SNTF 677	BIG WALTER HORTON (LP, with Carey Bell)	£25

JOHN HOSIER
70	Universal Editions LYN 2177	NEW SOUNDS IN CLASS (with St. Anne's Girls School)	£30

HOT CHIP
12	Domino RUG 473T	Flutes/Flutes (instrumental) (12", 200 only)	£15
12	Last Night On Earth LNOE009V	Flutes (Sasha Remix) (1-sided white vinyl 12", p/s)	£100
04	Moshi Moshi MOSHILP 06	COMING ON STRONG (LP, silkscreened cover, 500 only)	£100
06	EMI 094634741811	THE WARNING (2-LP with free 7", Won't Wash/Bally)	£80
06	EMI 094634741811	THE WARNING (2-LP)	£70
08	EMI 5099952057717	MADE IN THE DARK (LP)	£35
10	Vinyl Factory VF 012	ONE LIFE STAND (2-LP with free 7" Bubble/Do Not Wait, no'd gatefold sleeve)	£50
10	Vinyl Factory VF012	ONE LIFE STAND (2-LP, 200gm, 250 only)	£50

10	Moshi Moshi MOSHILP06	COMING ON STRONG (LP, reissue, different cover)	£25
15	Domino WIGLP 313X	WHY MAKE SENSE? (LP, with free 12")	£20
12	Domino WIGLP 293X	IN OUR HEADS (2-LP with 7")	£25
15	Domino WIGLP 313	WHY MAKE SENSE? (LP)	£15
17	Moshi Moshi MOSHILP06X	COMING ON STRONG (LP, reissue, different cover, yellow vinyl)	£35

(see also 2 Bears)

HOT CHOCOLATE (BAND)

69	Apple APPLE 18	Give Peace A Chance/Living Without Tomorrow (as Hot Chocolate Band)	£80
73	Rak RAK 139	You'll Always Be A friend/Go Go Girl	£15

(see also Tony Wilson)

HOT CITY

71	London HLU 10344	Leaving/I Believe In Life	£15

HOT LEG

09	Barbeque Rock BRR0003V	RED LIGHT FEVER (LP, red)	£25

(see also Darkness)

HOTLEGS

71	Philips 6308 047	THINKS: SCHOOL STINKS (LP, gatefold sleeve, black/silver label)	£50
71	Philips 6308 080	SONG (LP, gatefold sleeve, black/silver label)	£60

(see also 10cc, Mindbenders, Godley & Creme, Ramases)

HOT NATURED

13	Hot Creations HNLP 001	DIFFERENT SIDES OF THE SUN (3-LP)	£30

HOT POTATO

73	PMTB 1	HOT POTATO (LP, private pressing)	£200

HOT RAIN

90	Pine Tree TWIG 002	STAY TRUE (12", EP)	£25

HOT ROCKS & JAH LOXLEY

80s	Gemini GSM 025	Jah Jah No Parcial/Badda Badda	£20

HOT ROD

69	Joe's DU 41	The Judge/RON: Soul Of Soul Of Joel	£20

HOT ROD ALLSTARS

69	Duke DU 59	Lick A Pop/Treasure	£50
70	Duke DU 65	Paint Your Wagon/Organ Man (Setters as artist on label)	£150
70	Duke DU 66	Return Of The Bad Man/Caysoe Reggae	£125
70	Trojan TR 7732	Strong Man/Sentimental	£35
70	Trojan TR 7733	Virgin Soldier/Brixton Reggae Festival	£50
70	Torpedo TOR 1	Pussy Got Nine Life/BOSS SOUNDS: Lick It Back	£200
70	Torpedo TOR 5	Skinheads Don't Fear/Ten Commandments From The Devil	£200
70	Torpedo TOR 10	Moonhop In London/Skinhead Moondust	£300
70	Torpedo TOR 14	Control Your Doggy/Follow The Stars	£75
70	Hot Rod HR 104	Skinhead Speaks His Mind/CARL LEVEY: Carnaby Street	£200
70	Hot Rod HR 107	Strictly Invitation/PATSY & PEGGY: Dog Your Woman	£100
70	Hot Rod HR 108	Beautiful World/Shocks Of A Drugs Man	£100

(see also Setters, Betty Sinclair)

HOTRODS

65	Columbia DB 7693	I Don't Love You No More/Ain't Coming Back No More	£50

HOT SPRINGS

66	Columbia DB 7821	It's All Right/All I Know About Love	£20

HOT THUMBS O'RILEY

73	Charisma CAS 1071	HOT THUMBS O'RILEY (LP, gatefold sleeve, large 'Mad Hatter' label)	£30

HOT-TODDYS

59	Pye International 7N 25020	Rockin' Crickets/Shakin' And Stompin'	£30

(see also Rockin' Rebels)

HOT TUNA

70	RCA SF 8125	HOT TUNA (LP)	£20

(see also Jefferson Airplane)

HOT VULTURES

77	Red Rag RRR 015	THE EAST STREET SHAKES (LP)	£20
79	Plant Life PLR 018	UP THE LINE (LP)	£20

(see also Ian (A) Anderson)

HOUNDHEAD HENRY/FRANKIE JAXON

60	Jazz Collector JEL 10	THE MALE BLUES VOLUME 6 (EP)	£18

HOUR GLASS

68	Liberty LBL83129/LBS 83129E	THE HOUR GLASS (LP)	£40
74	United Artists USD 303/4	THE HOUR GLASS (2-LP)	£25

(see also Allman Brothers)

HOUSE CREW

91	Production House PNT 029R	Keep The Fires Burning (Remixes) (12")	£20
92	Production House PNT 035	We Are Hardcore/Maniac (Hypermix) (12")	£15
92	Production House PNT 035R	We Are Hardcore/Maniac (Remixes) (12")	£15
93	Production House PNT 047	The Theme/Euphoria (12")	£25
93	Production House PNT 047R	The Theme/Euphoria (Remixes) (12")	£25
94	Production House PNT 060	Superhero (My Knight) (12")	£15
94	Production House PNT 060R	Superhero (Remixes) (12")	£15

94	Production House PNT 060RX	**Superhero** (Remixes II) (12")...	**£15**

HOUSEMARTINS
86	Go Discs! AGOLP 7	**LONDON 0 HULL 4** (LP)	**£18**
86	Go! Discs GODB 16	**THE HOUSEMARTINS' CHRISTMAS BOX SET** (4 singles in foldout sleeve, signed)	**£25**
07	Mercury 175 252-3	**SOUP** ('deluxe Fan Edition', in sealed/stickered tin: CD, DVD, T-shirt and mug)	**£60**

(see also Beautiful South)

HOUSEMASTER BALDWIN
88	Koolkat KOOLT 21	**DELTA HOUSE** (12", p/s)...	**£15**
88	Koolkat KOOLT 22	**DON'T LEAD ME** (12", p/s)...	**£15**

HOUSE OF ALL
23	Tiny Global Productions PICI 0050 LP1	**HOUSE OF ALL** (LP, orange/clear vinyl, download card)	**£35**
23	Tiny Global Productions LSE 0005 CD	**BAY CITY PISTOLS** (CD, 16-page A5 booklet, limited)................................	**£35**
24	Tiny Global Productions PICI 0061 LP	**CONTINUUM** (LP, violet vinyl. download card)	**£30**

(see also The Fall, Blue Orchids)

HOUSE OF LORDS
69	B&C CB 112	**In The Land Of Dreams/Ain't Gonna Wait Forever**..............................	**£25**

HOUSE OF LOVE
87	Creation CRE 043T	**Shine On/Love/Flow** (12", p/s, 4,000 only)....................................	**£20**
87	Creation CRE 044T	**Real Animal/Plastic/Nothing To Me** (12", p/s, 4,000 only)..................	**£20**
92	Love 1	**ROYAL ALBERT HALL EP** (10" gig freebie, stickered)	**£25**
88	Creation CRELP 034	**HOUSE OF LOVE** (LP, with free 7", "Shine On/Christine", matt sleeve).........	**£20**
88	Creation CRELP 034	**HOUSE OF LOVE** (LP, without 7")...	**£15**
89	Fontana 842 293-1	**THE HOUSE OF LOVE** (LP, stickered sleeve)...................................	**£18**
92	Fontana 512 549-1	**BABE RAINBOW** (LP)..	**£30**
93	Fontana 514 880-1	**AUDIENCE WITH THE MIND** (LP)..	**£40**

CISCO HOUSTON
60	Top Rank 30/028	**THE CISCO SPECIAL** (LP)	**£50**
62	Fontana TFL 6007	**CISCO SPECIAL!** (LP)	**£25**
62	Fontana TFL 6014	**SINGS SONGS OF WOODY GUTHRIE** (LP)	**£20**
68	Fontana FJL 412	**I AIN'T GOT NO HOME** (LP)..	**£15**
69	Ember CW 135	**CISCO HOUSTON AND WOODY GUTHRIE** (LP)	**£15**

CISSY HOUSTON
70	Pye International 7N 25537	**I Just Don't Know What To Do With Myself/This Empty Place**	**£45**
70	Major Minor SMLP 80	**PRESENTING CISSY HOUSTON** (LP)	**£30**

(see also Sweet Inspirations)

DAVID HOUSTON
55	London HL 8147	**Blue Prelude/I'm Sorry I Made You Cry**	**£30**

THELMA HOUSTON
73	Mowest MW 3004	**Black California/I'm Letting Go** (withdrawn)................................	**£60**
69	Stateside (S)SL 5010	**SUNSHOWER** (LP)	**£25**
73	Mowest MWS 7003	**THELMA HOUSTON** (LP)...	**£30**

HOVERCRAFT
97	Blast First BFFP 135	**AKATHISIA** (2-LP)	**£18**
98	Blast First BFFP 160	**EXPERIMENT BELOW** (LP)...	**£15**

BEN HOWARD
11	Communication COMM009	**Old Pine/Further Away/Follation Wood/Three Tree Down** (2 x 7", p/s)	**£60**
12	Island 3721238	**THE BURGH ISLAND EP** (12", 1-sided, download card, 1000 only)................	**£70**
12	Secret 7" S71	**Black Flies** (100 only, each with unique art sleeve)	**£80**
11	Island 2782648	**EVERY KINGDOM** (LP, download card, pink rim palm tree logo)	**£15**
14	Island 4701043	**I FORGOT WHERE WE WERE** (2-LP, download code with bonus track Am I In Your Light?)	**£18**

BRIAN HOWARD & SILHOUETTES
62	Columbia DB 4914	**Somebody Help Me/Young And Evil**	**£25**
63	Columbia DB 7067	**The Worryin' Kind/Come To Me**	**£25**
64	Fontana TF 464	**Back In The U.S.A./Hooked**	**£20**

JAN HOWARD
60	London HL 7088	**The One You Slip Around With/I Wish I Could Fall In Love Again** (export issue)	**£25**

JOHN HOWARD
75	CBS 80473	**KID IN A BIG WORLD** (LP, with insert)...	**£25**

JOHNNY HOWARD BAND
65	Decca LK 4735	**THE EASY BEAT SOUND** (LP)	**£15**
67	Deram DML/SML 1001	**THE VELVET TOUCH OF JOHNNY HOWARD** (LP)............................	**£15**

KEITH HOWARD
80	Rods HOT 2	**LOOKING FOR YOU** (LP, some sleeves contain Driver artwork inside sleeve)	**£35**

(see also Victory)

NOAH HOWARD
69	Polydor Super 2383093	**THE BLACK ARK** (LP)...	**£40**

HOWDY BOYS
80	Spectacle SP 1	**Spectacle/Dancing In The Depression** (p/s).................................	**£15**

CATHERINE HOWE
71	Reflection HRS 11	Nothing More Than Strangers/It Comes With The Breezes	£20
71	Reflection REFL 11	WHAT A BEAUTIFUL PLACE (LP, laminated front sleeve 'correction' sticker on rear sleeve)	£1000
75	RCA Victor SF 8407	HARRY (LP)	£18

STEVE HOWE
75	Atlantic K50151	BEGINNINGS (LP, gatefold sleeve)	£15

(see also Yes)

HOWEEFEEL
75	Contempo CS2065	The Devil's On The Run/Just Can't Do Without Love	£15

EDDY HOWELL
69	Parlophone R5756	Easy Street/Judy's Good	£45

FRANKIE HOWERD
63	HMV CLP 1685	A FUNNY THING HAPPENED ON THE WAY TO THE FORUM (LP)	£15

HOWLIN' WOLF
61	Pye International 7N 25101	Little Baby/Down In The Bottom	£25
63	Pye International 7N 25192	Just Like I Treat You/I Ain't Superstitious	£25
64	Pye International 7N 25244	Smokestack Lightnin'/Going Down Slow ('Slow' on B-side label)	£25
64	Pye International 7N 25244	Smokestack Lightnin'/Going Down Slow ("South" on B-side label)	£20
64	Pye International 7N 25269	Little Girl/Tail Dragger	£22
64	Pye International 7N 25283	Love Me Darling/My Country Sugar Mama	£22
65	Chess CRS 8010	Killing Floor/Louise	£15
65	Chess CRS 8016	Ooh Baby/Tell Me What I've Done	£15
69	Chess CRS 8097	Evil/Tail Dragger	£15
56	London REU 1072	RHYTHM AND BLUES WITH HOWLIN' WOLF (EP)	£200
63	Pye Intl. NEP 44015	SMOKESTACK LIGHTNIN' (EP)	£40
64	Pye Intl. NEP 44032	TELL ME (EP)	£30
66	Chess CRE 6017	REAL FOLK BLUES (EP)	£30
64	Chess CRL 4006	MOANIN' IN THE MOONLIGHT (LP)	£100
65	Chess CRL 4508	POOR BOY (LP)	£45
66	Ember EMB 3370	BIG CITY BLUES (LP)	£25
69	Chess CRLS 4543	THE HOWLIN' WOLF ALBUM (LP)	£25
71	Syndicate Chapter SC 003	GOING BACK HOME (LP)	£20
71	Chess 6310 108	MESSAGE TO THE YOUNG (LP)	£22
71	Rolling Stones COC 49101	THE LONDON SESSIONS (LP)	£20
71	Python PLP 13	HOWLIN' WOLF (LP)	£60

(see also Hubert Sumlin)

HOWLIN' WOLF/JUNIOR PARKER/BOBBY BLAND
74	Polydor 2383 257	BLUES FOR MR. CRUMP (LP)	£30

HOWLIN' WOLF, MUDDY WATERS & BO DIDDLEY
68	Chess CRL 4537	THE SUPER SUPER BLUES BAND (LP)	£45

(see also Muddy Waters, Bo Diddley)

LINDA HOYLE
70	Vertigo 6059 018	Eli's Coming/United States Of Mind (as Linda Hoyle & Affinity)	£40
71	Vertigo 6360 060	PIECES OF ME (LP, gatefold sleeve, small swirl label)	£1000

(see also Affinity, Nucleus)

H.P. LOVECRAFT
68	Philips BF 1639	The White Ship (Parts 1 & 2) (unissued)	£0
68	Philips BF 1639	The White Ship/I've Been Wrong Before	£15
67	Philips (S)BL 7830	H.P. LOVECRAFT (LP)	£80
68	Philips SBL 7872	H.P. LOVECRAFT II (LP, without watermark at start of each side)	£50
68	Philips SBL 7872	H.P. LOVECRAFT II (LP, with watermark at start of each side)	£20
72	Philips 6336 210	THIS IS H.P. LOVECRAFT (LP)	£40
72	Philips 6336 213	H.P. LOVECRAFT VOL. 2 (LP)	£25
88	Edsel DED 256	AT THE MOUNTAINS OF MADNESS (2-LP)	£20

HQ SQUAD
89	Music Of Life NOTE33	Burial Proceedings In The Course Of Three Knights/Onslaught (12")	£15

HTRK
07	Fire FIRELP 104	NOSTALGIA (LP, reissue)	£15

H.T. SPLIFF
79	Septic SP 002	OUT OF THE EARTH'S WOMB (LP)	£60

FREDDIE HUBBARD
70	CTI 6001	RED CLAY (LP)	£25
74	MSP/BASF BAP 5036	THE HUB OF HUBBARD (LP)	£20

HUBCAP & WHEELS
70	Dynamic DYN 403	One Pound Weight/VICEROYS: Come Dance	£20

(see also Byron Lee & Dragonaires)

HUDDERSFIELD TRANSIT AUTHORITY
72	Polydor 2001284	Runaway/Bayou Farm	£15

AL HUDSON
78	ABC 5251	Spread Love (slow start 3.25 version)/Spread Love (2.38 version)	£30

JACK HUDSON
72	Folk Heritage FHR 041	SUMMER DAYS AND YOU (LP)	£20

MINT VALUE £

KEITH HUDSON (& CHUCKLES)

69	Big Shot BI 528	Tambourine Man/Old Fashioned Way (both actually by Ken Boothe)	£35
70	Smash SMA 2311	Don't Get Me Confused/D. SMITH: Ball of Confusion (B-side actually by Dennis Alcapone)	£20
71	Smash SMA 2526	Light Of Day/I Thought You Knew	£35
72	Spur SP 1	Darkest Night On A Wet Looking Road/Version	£50
72	Duke DU 145	Satan Side (with Chuckles)/DON T. JUNIOR: Evil Spirit	£40
72	Downtown DT 492	True True To My Heart/BIG YOUTH: Ace 90 Skank	£22
73	Summit SUM 8541	Melody Maker/Uncover Me	£30
75	Faith FA 025	Blackbelt Jones/Version	£20
77	Tunde TR 1000	I Wanna Be Where You Are/Still Water (12")	£25
78	Greensleeves GRED 8	Bloody Eyes/Dub	£25
78	Greensleeves GRED 8	Bloody Eyes/Dub (12")	£25
79	Greensleeves GRED 26	Nuh Skin Up/Felt We Felt The Strain (12")	£25
75	Magnet MGT 007	ENTER THE DRAGON (LP)	£200
75	Mamba KH1	FLESH OF MY SKIN, BLOOD OF MY BLOOD (LP)	£150
75	Mamba MAM 002	TORCH OF FREEDOM (LP)	£50
75	Atra LP1001	TORCH OF FREEDOM (LP)	£50
75	Atra ATLP 1002	PICK A DUB (LP)	£100
76	Third World TWL 106	REBEL DUB (LP, produced by Keith Hudson)	£100
76	Virgin V2056	TOO EXPENSIVE (LP)	£25
77	BRAND BRD 001	BRAND (LP)	£75
79	Greensleeves GREL 5	RASTA COMMUNICATION (LP)	£25
88	Atra LP 1004	FLESH OF MY SKIN BLOOD OF MY BLOOD (LP, reissue)	£30
94	Blood & Fire LP 003	PICK A DUB (LP, reissue)	£30
01	Simply Vinyl SVLP 283	PICK A DUB (LP, reissue)	£15

(see also Big Youth, Alton Ellis, Delroy Washington, Hugh Roy, Delroy Wilson)

KEITH HUDSON & I ROY

73	Randy's RAN 534	Silver Platter/Jean You Change Everything	£30

(see also I Roy)

MIKE HUDSON

65	Columbia DB 7622	One Sided Love/I'll Wait Until Tomorrow	£15

HUDSON-FORD

73	A&M AMLH 68208	NICKELODEON (LP, lyric insert, brown label)	£15
77	Arnakata ARN 5001	REPERTOIRE (LP, for publishers' use)	£20

(see also Strawbs, Monks, Elmer Gantry's Velvet Opera)

HUDSON PEOPLE

79	Ensign ENY 27	Trip To Your Mind/Part 2	£25
78	Hithouse HIT 1	Trip To Your Mind/Power To The Hour (12")	£60
79	Ensign ENY 2712	Trip To Your Mind/Power To The Hour (12", different mix)	£40

HUDSONS

83	Epic A3373	Don't Try To Fight It/You Keep Me Up (promo only)	£20
83	Epic TA 3373	Don't Try To Fight It (Vocal)/Instrumental/You Keep Me Up (12")	£25

HUG

75	Polydor 2383 330	NEON DREAM (LP)	£20

(see also Mike Hugg)

MIKE HUGG

72	Polydor 2383 140	SOMEWHERE (LP, gatefold sleeve)	£30
73	Polydor 2383 213	STRESS AND STRAIN (LP)	£30

(see also Manfred Mann, Hug, Elton Dean)

BOB HUGHES

76	Puddlebrook 3SLP8	MY OLD MAN (LP, plain cover with pasted-on A4 information sheet)	£200
78	Puddlebrook IRPH 16	THE KIDS ARE OK! (LP)	£100

BOBBY HUGHES EXPERIENCE

99	Ultimate Diler UDRLP 008	FUSA RIOT (2xLP)	£20

CAROL HUGHES

58	Columbia DB 4094	Lend Me Your Comb/First Date	£15

DANNY HUGHES

69	Pye 7N 17750	Hi Ho Silver Lining/I Washed My Hands In Muddy Water	£15

(see also Orange Machine)

FRED HUGHES

65	Fontana TF 583	Oo Wee Baby I Love You/Love Me Baby	£30

GLENN HUGHES

77	Safari LONG 2	PLAY ME OUT (LP, with inner sleeve)	£15

(see also Deep Purple, News, Finders Keepers, Trapeze, Roger Glover, Hughes-Thrall)

GUY HUGHES

79	Admiral AMC 01	The Last Admiral/Just Call Me (no p/s)	£25

JIMMY HUGHES

63	London HL 9680	I'm Qualified/My Loving Time	£30
64	Pye International 7N 25254	Steal Away/Lollipops, Lace And Lipstick	£25
66	Sue WI 4006	Goodbye My Love/It Was Nice	£50
66	Atlantic 584 017	Neighbour, Neighbour/It's A Good Thing	£22
67	Atlantic 584 135	Hi-Heel Sneakers/Time Will Bring You Back	£15
67	Atlantic 587 068	WHY NOT TONIGHT? (LP)	£80

| 69 | Stax SXATS 1010 | SOMETHING SPECIAL (LP) | £30 |

RHETTA HUGHES
| 69 | Polydor 184 223 | RELIGHT MY FIRE (LP) | £80 |

HUGHES-THRALL
| 82 | Epic EPC 25052 | HUGHES-THRALL (LP, with inner sleeve) | £15 |
(see also Glenn Hughes)

HUGO & LUIGI
| 57 | Columbia DB 3978 | Rockabilly Party/Shenandoah Rose | £15 |

ALAN HULL
| 73 | Charisma CAS 1069 | PIPEDREAM (LP, gatefold sleeve, booklet, large 'Mad Hatter' label) | £20 |
| 75 | Warner Bros K56121 | SQUIRE (LP, 'Burbank' label) | £15 |
(see also Lindisfarne, Chosen Few)

HUMAN BEANS
| 67 | Columbia DB 8230 | Morning Dew (Take Me For A Walk)/It's A Wonder | £50 |
(see also Love Sculpture)

HUMAN BEAST
| 70 | Decca LK/SKL 5053 | VOLUME ONE (LP) | £1000 |
| 07 | Sunbeam SBRLP 5044 | VOLUME ONE (LP, reissue) | £20 |
(see also Bread Love & Dreams)

HUMAN BEINZ
67	Capitol CL 15529	Nobody But Me/Sueno	£60
67	Capitol CL 15529	Nobody But Me/Sueno (DJ Copy)	£100
68	Capitol CL 15542	Turn On Your Lovelight/It's Fun To Be Clean	£25
86	Decal LIK 5	EVOLUTIONS (LP, reissue)	£15

HUMAN CONDITION
| 81 | THC 1 | THE HUMAN CONDITION (Live at Collegiate Theatre 13th September 1981) (cassette, black inlay, white writing) | £25 |
| 81 | THC 1 | THE HUMAN CONDITION (Live in Europe November 1981) (cassette, white inlay, black writing) | £25 |
(see also Jah Wobble)

HUMAN INSTINCT
65	Mercury MF 951	Can't Stop Around/I Want To Be Loved By You My Friend	£50
66	Mercury MF 972	The Rich Man/Illusions	£70
67	Mercury MF 990	Go-Go/I Can't Live Without You	£50
68	Deram DM 167	A Day In My Mind's Mind/Death Of The Seaside	£140
68	Deram DM 177	Renaissance Fair/Pink Dawn	£80
(see also Jessie Harper)

HUMAN LEAGUE
78	Fast Product FAST 4	Being Boiled/Circus Of Death (p/s, original issue with b&w picture labels)	£20
79	Fast Product FAST 10	THE DIGNITY OF LABOUR (12" EP, with spoken-word flexidisc [F10x/VF 1])	£30
80	Virgin SV 105	HOLIDAY '80 (EP, double pack, purple & blue labels, 10,000 only)	£15
80	Virgin VS 351	Empire State Human/Introducing//Only After Dark/Toyota City (Long Version) (double pack, p/s, shrinkwrapped, sealed copies are incredibly scarce)	£75
81	Virgin SV 105-12	HOLIDAY '80 (12", 5-track EP, withdrawn)	£100
79	Virgin VS 2133	REPRODUCTION (LP)	£15
80	Virgin VS 2160	TRAVELOGUE (LP)	£15
81	Virgin V 2192	DARE (LP, gatefold, printed inner)	£20
90	Virgin V2624	ROMANTIC? (LP)	£20
95	EastWest 4509987501	OCTOPUS (LP)	£100
11	Wall Of Sound WOS085DLP	CREDO (2LP, trifold cover, download coupon)	£600
16	Virgin 571 111-5	A VERY BRITISH SYNTHESISER GROUP (3LP box set)	£70
18	Demon DEMREC 305	SECRETS (2LP, gatefold, printed inners, reissue)	£25
20	East West 0190295402341	OCTOPUS (LP, reissue)	£15
(see also Heaven 17, Men, Respect)

HUMAN CABBAGES
| 81 | Boys and Girls BAG TWO | The Witch/Air Raid Shelter/One More Fool (p/s) | £40 |

HUMANOID
| 88 | Westside Human 1989 | GLOBAL (LP) | £15 |
| 03 | Rephlex CAT 130 LP | SESSIONS 84-88 (2-LP) | £25 |
(see also Future Sound Of London)

HUMANTE & RABBIT IN THE MOON
| 95 | Rising High RSN 106 | East (The Remixes) (12") | £15 |

HUMBLEBUMS
69	Transatlantic TRA 201	THE NEW HUMBLEBUMS (LP, lilac/white label with 't' logo)	£20
70	Transatlantic TRA 218	OPEN UP THE DOOR (LP, laminated sleeve)	£15
74	Transatlantic TRA 288	THE COMPLETE HUMBLEBUMS (3-LP, box set of above albums)	£20
(see also Gerry Rafferty)

HUMBLE PIE
69	Immediate IMSP 025	AS SAFE AS YESTERDAY IS (LP, lyric inner sleeve, pink label)	£80
69	Immediate IMSP 027	TOWN AND COUNTRY (LP, lyric inner sleeve, pink label)	£75
70	A&M AMLS 986	HUMBLE PIE (LP, textured gatefold sleeve, brown label)	£75
71	A&M AMLS 2013	ROCK ON (LP)	£25
71	A&M AMLH 63506	PERFORMANCE - ROCKIN' THE FILLMORE (2-LP)	£25
72	A&M AMLS 64342	SMOKIN' (LP)	£25
73	A&M AMLD 6004	EAT IT (2-LP, gatefold sleeve, booklet, brown label)	£25

MINT VALUE £

74	A&M AMLH 63611	THUNDERBOX (LP)	£15
75	A&M AMLS 68282	STREET RATS (LP)	£15
79	Jet LP231	ON TO VICTORY (LP)	£20
80	Atco SD 38 131	GO FOR THE THROAT (LP)	£20

(see also Steve Marriott, Small Faces, Herd, Natural Gas)

HUMBUG
70	CBS 4811	Groovin' With Mr Bloe/Marianna	£20
70	CBS 5208	I Got A Feeling (Vocal)/I Got A Feeling (Instrumental)	£20

HELEN HUMES
61	Contemporary LAC 12245	HELEN HUMES AND THE BENNY CARTER ALL STARS (LP)	£15

(see also Benny Carter, Jimmy Witherspoon/Helen Humes)

BOBBI HUMPHREY
75	Blue Note UAG 20003	FANCY DANCER (LP)	£25
98	Blue Note 7243 4 94706 1 3	BLUE BREAKBEATS (LP)	£15
92	Blue Note B1 80503	THE BEST OF (LP)	£18

DELLA HUMPHREY
69	Action ACT 4525	Don't Make The Good Girls Go Bad/Your Love Is All I Need	£50
72	Fab FAB 183	Dreamland/Version	£55

HUMPY BONG
70	Parlophone R 5859	Don't You Be Too Long/We're Alright 'Till Then	£15

(see also Bee Gees, Jonathan Kelly, Morgan)

HUNGER
84	Psycho PSYCHO 14	STRICTLY FROM HUNGER (LP, reissue of U.S. LP)	£15

HUNGRY TOUCH
88	Firehorse HT 188	Shake The System/She's Got The Hungry Touch/Riding High (12" p/s)	£50

HUNGRY WOLF
70	Philips 6308 009	HUNGRY WOLF (LP, laminated sleeve, black/silver labels)	£250

(see also Czar, Alan Parker, Ugly Custard)

PETER HUNNINGALE
86	Cosmic COSMIC 001	Untamed Love/Untamed Dub (12")	£75

FRED HUNT TRIO
68	77 88LEU12/27	PEARLS ON VELVET (LP)	£35

MARSHA HUNT
69	Track 604 030	Walk On Gilded Splinters/Hot Rod Poppa	£15
69	Track 604 034	Desdemona/Hippy Gumbo	£20
73	Vertigo 6059 080	(Oh, No! Not) The Beast Day/Somebody To Love (as Marsha Hunt's 22)	£20
73	Vertigo 6059 093	Medusa/Bop City (as Marsha Hunt's 22)	£25
71	Track 2410 101	WOMAN CHILD (LP)	£100

TOMMY HUNT
62	Top Rank JAR 605	The Door Is Open/I'm Wondering	£20
68	Direction 58-3216	I Need A Woman Of My Own/Searchin' For My Baby Looking Everywhere	£30
75	Spark SRLP 117	LIVE AT THE WIGAN CASINO (LP)	£25
86	Kent KENT 059	YOUR MAN (LP)	£30

(see also Ivorys)

WILLIE AMOS HUNT
67	Camp 602 003	Would You Believe/My Baby Wants To Dance	£75

HUNT & TURNER
72	Village Thing VTS 11	MAGIC LANDSCAPE (LP)	£60

CAROL HUNTER
73	Purple TPS 3503	THE NEXT VOICE YOU HEAR (LP)	£15

DANE HUNTER
65	Oriole CB 1985	The Evergreen Tree/Too Late	£20
65	CBS 201777	Silly Little Girl/Cryin Sobbin Wailin	£15
65	CBS 202004	Because You're Mine/Look The Other Way	£15

DANNY HUNTER (& GIANTS)
60	HMV POP 722	Make It Up/Little Girl (as Danny Hunter & Giants)	£20
60	HMV POP 775	Who's Gonna Walk Ya Home?/Lonely And Blue	£20
61	Fontana H 300	Lost Weekend/Age For Love	£15

DAVE HUNTER
68	RCA RCA 1766	Love Me A Lifetime/She's A Heartbreaker	£35

IAN HUNTER
76	CBS 4479	You Nearly Did Me In/Letter To Britannia From The Union Jack	£15

(see also Mott The Hoople, At Last The 1958 Rock & Roll Show, Apex Rhythm & Blues All Stars, Mick Ronson, Roger Taylor)

IVORY JOE HUNTER
50	MGM MGM 271	I Almost Lost My Mind/S.P. Blues (78, with Orchestra)	£20
56	London HLE 8261	A Tear Fell/I Need You By My Side	£300
56	London HLE 8261	A Tear Fell/I Need You By My Side (78)	£20
57	Columbia DB 3872	Since I Met You, Baby/You Can't Stop This Rockin' And Rollin'	£250
57	Columbia DB 3872	Since I Met You, Baby/You Can't Stop This Rockin' And Rollin' (78)	£20
57	London HLE 8486	Love's A Hurting Game/Empty Arms	£150
57	London HLE 8486	Love's A Hurting Game/Empty Arms (78)	£20
61	Capitol CL 15220	I'm Hooked/Because I Love You	£30
61	Capitol CL 15226	You Better Believe It, Baby/May The Man Win	£30

ROBERT HUNTER
74	Round RX 101	TALES OF THE GREAT RUM RUNNERS (LP)	£15
80	Dark Star DSLP 8001	JACK O'ROSES (LP)	£15

(see also Grateful Dead)

TAB HUNTER
57	London HLD 8380	Young Love/Red Sails In The Sunset (gold label)	£15
61	Warner Bros WSEP 2023	TAB HUNTER (EP, stereo)	£15
60	Warner Bros WS 8008	TAB HUNTER (LP, stereo)	£15
61	London HA-D 2401	YOUNG LOVE (LP, mono)	£15
61	London SAH-G 6201	YOUNG LOVE (LP, stereo)	£15

HUNTER MUSKETT
70	Decca Nova SDN 20	EVERY TIME YOU MOVE (LP, blue/silver labels)	£300
73	Bradleys BRADL 1003	HUNTER MUSKETT (LP, lyric inner sleeve)	£35

HUNTERS (HOLLAND)
66	RCA RCA 1541	Russian Spy And I/Spring	£20

(see also Jan Akkerman, Brainbox)

HUNTERS (U.K.)
60	Fontana H 276	Teen Scene/Santa Monica Flyer	£15
61	Fontana H 303	Golden Ear-rings/Tally Ho	£15
61	Fontana H 323	The Storm/How's M'Chicks?	£20
64	Fontana TF 514	Teen Scene/Someone Else's Baby	£15
61	Fontana TFL 5140	TEEN SCENE: THE HUNTERS PLAY THE BIG HITS (LP, mono)	£30
61	Fontana STFL 561	TEEN SCENE: THE HUNTERS PLAY THE BIG HITS (LP, stereo)	£50
62	Fontana TFL 5175	HITS FROM THE HUNTERS (LP, mono)	£50
62	Fontana STFL 572	HITS FROM THE HUNTERS (LP, stereo)	£50

(see also Dave Sampson & Hunters)

HUNTING LODGE
85	Sterile SER 04	NOMAD SOULS (LP)	£20

HURDY GURDY
72	CBS 64781	HURDY GURDY (LP, gatefold sleeve)	£200

HURRICANE STRINGS
63	Columbia DB 7027	Venus/In The Carrick	£15

HURRICANES
71	Upsetter US 363	Got To Be Mine/UPSETTERS: Version	£30

(see also Dave Barker)

MISSISSIPPI JOHN HURT
65	Vanguard SVRL 19005	THE IMMORTAL MISSISSIPPI JOHN HURT (LP)	£35
66	Vanguard SVRL 19032	MISSISSIPPI JOHN HURT (LP)	£35
67	Fontana TFL 6079	MISSISSIPPI JOHN HURT (LP)	£35
71	Spokane SPL 1001	THE ORIGINAL 1928 RECORDINGS (LP)	£50
71	Vanguard VSD 19/20	THE BEST OF MISSISSIPPI JOHN HURT (2-LP)	£18
73	Vanguard VSD 79327	LAST SESSIONS (LP)	£20
72	Vanguard VSD 79220	TODAY (LP)	£20

HURTS
10	Major MAJRE 017	Wonderful Life/(Mantronix Remix) (p/s, no'd)	£15
10	Major MAJREC031	HAPPINESS (LP & CD)	£40

(see also Daggers (2))

HUSH
68	Fontana TF 944	Elephant Rider/Grey	£500

HÜSKER DÜ
81	Alt. Tentacles VIRUS 25	LAND SPEED RECORD (LP)	£18
82	Bespoke BES 03 LP	EVERYTHING FALLS APART (LP)	£20
83	SST SST 020	METAL CIRCUS (LP)	£30
84	SST SST 027	ZEN ARCADE (2-LP, gatefold)	£40
86	Warner Bros WX40	CANDY APPLE GREY (LP)	£20
87	Warner Bros WB 925544	WAREHOUSE SONGS & STORIES (2-LP)	£18

(see also Bob Mould, Sugar)

HUS KINGPIN
17	Daupe! DM SP 026	COCAINE BEACH (LP, 125 copies)	£100
17	Daupe! DM SP 026	COCAINE BEACH (LP, with obi strip 20 copies)	£200
17	Daupe! DM SP 026	COCAINE BEACH (LP, yellow, white or blue vinyl 125 copies)	£100

FERLIN HUSKY (& HIS HUSH PUPPIES)
58	Capitol CL 14824	Wang Dang Doo/What'cha Doin' After School	£20
58	Capitol T 880	BOULEVARD OF BROKEN DREAMS (LP)	£15

HUSSARS
82	Sunny EON 103	The Charge Of The Light Brigade/Your Country Needs You	£30

NIPSEY HUSSLE
17	Omerta Inc. OMINC 013	CRENSHAW (2-LP, reissue 500 only, red and white vinyl, numbered)	£100

JACQUES HUSTIN
74	EMI EMI 2143	Fleur De Liberté/Freedom For The Man	£15

HUSTLERS
64	Mercury MF 817	Sick Of Giving/Easy To Find	£20

MINT VALUE £

WILLIE HUTCH
73	Tamla Motown TMG 862	Brother's Gonna Work It Out/I Choose You	£20
78	ABC 4206	Love Runs Out/BOBBY HUTTON: Lend A Hand (DJ copy)	£15
78	Whitfield K17318	Come On And Dance With Me/Easy Does It	£30
73	Tamla Motown STMA 8003	THE MACK (LP, soundtrack)	£35
73	Tamla Motown STML 11247	FULLY EXPOSED (LP)	£25
74	Tamla Motown STML 11269	FOXY BROWN (LP, soundtrack)	£40
74	Tamla Motown STML 11280	THE MARK OF THE BEAST (LP)	£20
75	Tamla Motown STML 12015	ODE TO MY LADY (LP)	£20
76	Tamla Motown STML 12023	CONCERT IN BLUES (LP)	£15

ASHLEY HUTCHINGS
72	Island HELP 5	MORRIS ON (LP, actually by various folk artists)	£20
76	Island HELP 24	RATTLEBONE (LP)	£25
76	Harvest SHSM 2012	SON OF MORRIS ON (LP, actually by various folk artists)	£18

(see also Albion Band, Fairport Convention, Steeleye Span)

HUTCH HUTCHINGS
77	Goodwood GM 12324	FEELS LIKE RAIN (LP)	£35

DON HUTCHINSON
84	Pep 7001	What You Gonna Do/What You Gonna Do (Version) (dinked 7")	£55

LEROY HUTSON
75	Warner Bros. K16536	All Because Of You/All Because Of You (Theme Instrumental)	£30
74	Buddah BDLP 4013	THE MAN (LP)	£20
75	Warner Bros K 56139	HUTSON (LP)	£50
97	Deep Beats DEEP X 007	THE VERY BEST OF LEROY HUTSON (2-LP)	£20
98	Deep Beats DEEP X 033	MORE WHERE THIS CAME FROM - THE BEST OF VOL. 2 (2-LP)	£25
99	Sequel NEMLP 442	HUTSON II (LP, reissue)	£20

J.B. HUTTO & HIS HAWKS
73	Delmark DS 617	HAWK SQUAT (LP)	£30

BETTY HUTTON
54	Capitol LC 6639	CAPITOL PRESENTS BETTY HUTTON (10" LP)	£15

(see also Hutton Sisters, Perry Como, 'Tennessee' Ernie Ford)

BOBBY HUTTON
78	ABC 4206	Lend A Hand/WILLIE HUTCH: Love Runs Out (DJ copy)	£15

DANNY HUTTON
66	MGM MGM 1314	Funny How Love Can Be/Dreamin' Isn't Good For You	£15

(see also Three Dog Night)

HUTTON SISTERS (BETTY & MARION)
55	Capitol CL 14250	Ko Ko Mo (I Love You So)/Heart Throb	£25

(see also Betty Hutton)

ALDOUS HUXLEY
73	Lansdowne LSR003/4	SPEAKING PERSONALLY (2-LP)	£40

HYACINTH GIRLS
88	Red RED 002	HAPPY NOW?	£40

CHARLIE HYATT
65	Island IEP 707	RASS! (EP, as Bam & Charlie Hyatt)	£30
66	Island ILP 932	KISS ME NECK (LP)	£35

LEON HYATT
76	Nationwide NW 1014	40 Days And Nights/Third World Affairs	£15

HYBRID KIDS
80	Cherry Red BRED 11	CLAWS (LP)	£15

KARL HYDE
13	Universal 3729832	EDGELAND (2LP, 45rpm, die-cut gatefold, 180g)	£20

(see also Underworld, Lemon Interrupt, Eno . Hyde, Underworld & Iggy Pop)

TANYA HYDE
79	Waldo's DS 008	Herr Wunderbar/Auf Der Anderen Seite (p/s)	£15

HYGRADES
65	Columbia DB 7734	She Cared/We're Through	£15

BRIAN HYLAND
60	London HLR 9161	Itsy Bitsy Teeny Weeny Yellow Polka Dot Bikini/Don't Dilly Dally, Sally (78)	£100
60	London HLR 9113	Rosemary/Library Love Affair	£20
66	Philips BF 1508	The Joker Went Wild/I Can Hear The Rain	£20
62	HMV 7EG 8780	SEALED WITH A KISS (EP)	£20
61	London HA-R 2289	THE BASHFUL BLONDE (LP)	£80
62	HMV CLP 1553	LET ME BELONG TO YOU (LP)	£30
63	HMV CLP 1759	COUNTRY MEETS FOLK (LP)	£30
66	Philips BL 7762	THE JOKER WENT WILD (LP)	£20
68	Fontana SFL 13008	HERE'S TO OUR LOVE (LP)	£20

C. HYMAN
65	Ska Beat JB 200	The Ska Rhythm/The Ska Is Moving On	£40

DICK HYMAN TRIO
67	Command SCMD 105	BRAZILIAN IMPRESSIONS (LP)	£15
69	Command SCMD 508	MOOG - THE ELECTRIC ECLECTICS OF DICK HYMAN (LP)	£20
70	Command SCMD 946	THE AGE OF ELECTRONICUS (LP)	£30

PHYLLIS HYMAN

79	Arista ARIST 323	You Know How To Love Me/Give A Little More	£15
77	Buddah BDLP 4046	PHYLLIS HYMAN (LP)	£15
78	Buddah BDLP 4058	SING A SONG (LP)	£40
79	Arista SPART 1114	YOU KNOW HOW TO LOVE ME (LP)	£15
81	Artista SPART 1154	CAN'T WE FALL IN LOVE AGAIN (LP)	£15

HYPA KONCEPT

91	No Label L8 001	Party People (Come Together) (3 Mixes) (12", hand written labels)	£20
92	Club State CSR 12001	Love Addict (4 Mixes) (12", stamped white label)	£40

HYPER ON EXPERIENCE

93	Moving Shadow SHADOW 30	DEAF IN THE FAMILY EP (12", white label stamped with cat. no. only as Hyper On exp.)	£60
93	Moving Shadow SHADOW 30	DEAF IN THE FAMILY EP (12", p/s as Hyper-On Experience)	£40
93	Moving Shadow SHADOW 40	THE FAMILY WE NEVER HAD EP (12", p/s, as Hyper-On Experience)	£15
94	Moving Shadow SHADOW 40	THE FAMILY WE NEVER HAD (12" picture disc)	£50

HYPER VYPER

88	SRTS SRT/DIY/NWOBHM	EASY LIVIN EP	£15

HYSTERIA

84	Sculpture SCT4-1	BEHIND THE VEIL (12" EP, p/s)	£20

I

I AM KLOOT

01	We Love You AMOUR 5	NATURAL HISTORY (LP)	£40
03	Echo ECHLP 46A	I AM KLOOT (LP, gatefold, black sleeve and black vinyl)	£60
03	Echo ECHLP 46A	I AM KLOOT (LP, gatefold, white sleeve and white vinyl)	£40
05	Echo ECHLP 62	GODS AND MONSTERS (LP)	£25
08	Pias 556 4763.010	PLAY MOOLAH ROUGE (LP)	£35
10	Pias 556 A003 012	B (2-LP)	£20
10	Pias PIASR 210 LP	SKY AT NIGHT (LP)	£25
13	Pias PIASR330LP	LET IT ALL IN (LP)	£15
14	Kudos Film & Television 4705387	FROM THERE TO HERE (LP)	£15

(see also Johnny Dangerously)

JANIS IAN

67	Verve Folkways VS 1503	Society's Child (Baby I've Been Thinking)/Letter To Jon	£20
67	Verve Forecast (S)VLP 6001	JANIS IAN (LP)	£30
67	Verve Forecast (S)VLP 6003	FOR ALL THE SEASONS OF YOUR MIND (LP)	£30
68	Verve Forecast (S)VLP 6009	THE SECRET LIFE OF J. EDDY FINK (LP)	£20
70	Verve Folkways SVLP 6023	WHO REALLY CARES (LP)	£15
71	Capitol E-ST 683	PRESENT COMPANY (LP)	£15
85	CBS 60636	BETWEEN THE LINES (LP, Nimbus Supercut, mail order only through Practical Hi Fi magazine)	£40

IAN (EDWARD) & ZODIACS

63	Oriole CB 1849	Beechwood 4-5789/You Can Think Again	£35
65	Fontana TF 548	Just The Little Things/This Won't Happen To Me (as Ian Edward with Zodiacs)	£30
66	Fontana TF 708	No Money, No Honey/Where Were You?	£50
66	Fontana TF 753	Wade In The Water/Come On Along, Girl	£60
65	Wing WL 1074	GEAR AGAIN - 12 HITS (LP)	£25

(see also Koppykats, Wellington Wade)

IAN (MEESON) & BELINDA (GILLET)

89	Odeon ODO 112	Who Wants To Live Forever?/Who Wants To Live Forever? (Instrumental) (p/s, feat. Brian May, handful signed by Brian May for Blood Transfusion staff)	£40

(see also Brian May)

IAN & SYLVIA

65	Fontana TFL 6053	EARLY MORNING RAIN (LP)	£30

I BENJAHMAN

82	Lion Kingdom LK 002	Give Love A Try/Mind Blowing Dub/Version (12")	£40
83	Lion Kingdom LKLP 01	INTRODUCING A FRACTION OF JAH ACTION (LP)	£35

IBIBIO SOUND MACHINE

14	Soundway SNDWYLP057	IBIBIO SOUND MACHINE (LP)	£15

IBM 7090 COMPUTER & DIGITAL TO SOUND TRANSCUDER

62	Brunswick STA 8523	MUSIC FOR MATHEMATICS (LP)	£40

RAS IBUNA

77	Grove Music GM003	Diverse Doctrine/Version	£35
78	Grove Music GMDM7	Pay Dem Dues/Diverse Doctrine (12", with Jah Woosh)	£40

ICARUS

69	Spark SRL 1012	The Devil Rides Out/You're In Life	£175
72	Pye Int. NSPL 28161	THE MARVEL WORLD OF ICARUS (LP, laminated sleeve, blue/black labels)	£200

12	Acme ADLP 1082	THE MARVEL WORLD OF ICARUS (LP, reissue)	£15

(see also Soft Machine)

ICE (1)

67	Decca F 12680	Anniversary (Of Love)/So Many Times	£80
68	Decca F 12749	Ice Man/Whisper Her Name (Maria Laine)	£120

(see also Affinity)

ICE (2)

79	Storm SR 3307	SAGA OF THE ICE KING (LP, private pressing with booklet)	£250
04	Kissing Spell KSLP9602	SAGA OF THE ICE KING (LP, repressing)	£20

ICE BABIES

81	Groove Digger GOD 1	Genius Of Lies/Reason Not Rhyme	£20

ICEBREAKERS

78	Virgin Frontline FL1010	PLANET MARS DUB (LP, as Icebreakers with the Diamonds)	£20

ICE CREAM

74	Fontana 6007 039	Shout It Out/Hold Yourself Tight	£25

ICE CUBE

90	4th & Broadway BRW 192	AmeriKKKa's Most Wanted/Once Upon A Time In The Projects (p/s)	£20
91	4th & Broadway BRW 239	Steady Mobbin'/Us (p/s)	£30
90	Island/Priority BRLP 551	AMERIKKKA'S MOST WANTED (LP)	£20
91	Island/Priority 510 656-1	DEATH CERTIFICATE (LP)	£20
92	Island/Priority BRLP 592	THE PREDATOR (LP)	£30
93	Priority 74321 16191-1	LETHAL INJECTION (LP)	£30

ICE FACTORY

83	No Label	JERUSALEM EP	£35

ICEPICK

97	Backbone BR971AA	Phenomenal Criminal/Brixtonites Pt 1(12")	£20
98	Backbone ICEEP1 BB002	ICEPICK (EP)	£18

(see also Bodysnatchers)

ICE THE FALLING RAIN

83	Future FS 7	Lifes Illusion/Illusions (p/s)	£20

ICI LA BAS

79	Black Noise NO 4	ICI LA BAS (12" EP, with booklet)	£45

(see also Homosexuals)

ICONS OF FILTH

97	BBP/Yellow Fever BBPV3/YF1	SHOW US YOU CARE EP (12 test pressings with red fold-out p/s and inserts)	£25
84	Mortarhate MORT 5	ONWARD CHRISTIAN SOLDIERS (LP)	£25

ICQ

82	Unsquare ICQ 1201	Final Approach/Loveland/One Finger Snap (12" white label)	£25

IDEAL HUSBANDS

80	Discovery DIK 001	Town Planning/Out Of The Factory And Into The Wood (p/s)	£50

IDEALS

61	Pye International 7N 25103	Knee Socks/Mary's Lamb	£40

IDES OF MARCH (1)

66	London HLU 10058	You Wouldn't Listen/I'll Keep Searching (as I'des Of March)	£15
70	Warner Bros WS 1863	VEHICLE (LP)	£25

(see also Survivors)

IDIOT DANCERS

81	Retrospect HP 1001	Glances/Up And Down/Imagination (hand-stamped die cut sleeve)	£15

IDJUT BOYS

94	U Star US 001	IDJUT BOY EP (12")	£50
94	U Star US 003	PHANTOM SLASHER EP (12")	£40
96	Noid NOID ONE	Girth Soup/Crouton Bonus/DJ HARVEY: Keep On Trying/Drums in 6 Twelve (12")	£20
98	Noid NOIDLP 001	NOID LONG PLAYER (LP, as 2x12")	£30

IDJUT BOYS & LAJ

95	U Star US 004	NOT REGGAE (12")	£30
95	U Star US 006	FOOLIN' (12")	£30
95	U star US 007	BEARD LAW (EP)	£15
96	U Star US 008	JAZ FOOK (12")	£15
96	U Star US 010	WHOK TISH EP (12")	£20
00	U Star USRLP 001	MORE OR LESS (LP, as 3 x 12")	£50

IDLE RACE

67	Liberty LBF 15026	The Imposters Of Life's Magazine/Sitting In My Tree	£80
68	Liberty LBF 15054	The Skeleton And The Roundabout/Knocking Nails Into My House	£30
68	Liberty LBF 15101	The End Of The Road/The Morning Sunshine	£20
68	Liberty LBF 15129	I Like My Toys/The Birthday (unissued)	£0
69	Liberty LBF 15218	Days Of Broken Arrows/Warm Red Carpet (B-side act. "Worn Red Carpet")	£20
69	Liberty LBF 15242	Come With Me/Reminds Me Of You	£25
68	Liberty LBL 83132	THE BIRTHDAY PARTY (LP, mono)	£125
68	Liberty LBS 83132	THE BIRTHDAY PARTY (LP, stereo)	£100
69	Liberty LBS 83221	THE IDLE RACE (LP)	£150
71	Regal Zono. SLRZ 1017	TIME IS (LP)	£200
73	Sunset SLS 50354	ON WITH THE SHOW (LP)	£15

76	Sunset SLS 50381	THE BIRTHDAY PARTY (LP, reissue)	£15
85	See For Miles SEE 60	LIGHT AT THE END OF THE ROAD (LP)	£15

(see also Mike Sheridan &, Mike Sheridan's Lot, Lemon Tree, Move, E.L.O., Trevor Burton, Steve Gibbons Band, Wizzard)

IDLES
17	Bailey BALLEY 002	Divide & Conquer/Untitled (gold vinyl, 500 copies)	£75
17	Bailey BALLEY 003	Well Done/Untitled (end vinyl)	£25
17	Bailey BALLEY 004	Moter/Untitled (white vinyl)	£25
17	Bailey BALLEY 001	BRUTALISM (LP)	£20
18	Partisan PTKF2158-6	JOY AS AN ACT OF RESISTANCE (LP, pink vinyl)	£20

IDLEWILD
97	Human Condition HC 0017	Queen Of The Troubled Teens/Faster/Self Healer (p/s, 1,000 only)	£30
98	Food FOODLP 28	HOPE IS IMPORTANT (LP)	£35
00	Food FOODLP 32	100 BROKEN WINDOWS (LP)	£30
02	Parlophone 5402431	THE REMOTE PART (LP, with inner sleeve)	£30
09	Diverse DIV 020LP	POST ELECTRIC BLUES (LP)	£25
16	Empty Words EWR 007	IDLEWILD LIVE (2-LP)	£30

BILLY IDOL
93	Chrysalis CHR 6000	CYBERPUNK (LP, inner)	£25

(see also Generation X)

IDOL DEATH
80	ID Records ID DISY 1234	Ignorance Is Bliss/Sticky Death	£30

IDOLS (1)
65	Mercury MF 840	Don't Walk Away/You Don't Care	£20

I. E.M. (INCREDIBLE EXPANDING MINDFUCK)
96	Chromatic CHR 001	I.E.M. (LP)	£30
03	Gates Of Dawn GOD 007	HAVE COME FOR YOUR CHILDREN (2-LP, no sleeve, 2 postcards, 90 only)	£35

(see also Steven Wilson, Porcupine Tree, No-Man, Blackfield, Continuum (2))

IF
70	Island ILPS 9129	IF (LP, 1st pressing, pink label/'i' logo)	£100
71	Island ILPS 9129	IF (LP, 2nd pressing, pink rim label/'palm tree' logo)	£40
71	Island ILPS 9137	IF 2 (LP, pink label, pink rim label/'palm tree' logo)	£50
71	United Artists UAG 29158	IF 3 (LP, gatefold sleeve)	£50
72	United Artists UAG 29315	IF 4 (LP, gatefold sleeve with inner)	£40
75	Gull GULP 1007	TEA-BREAK OVER - BACK ON YOUR 'EADS (LP)	£15
74	Gull GULP 1004	NOT JUST ANOTHER BUNCH OF PRETTY FACES (LP, with inner sleeve)	£15

(see also Ferris Wheel, Terry Smith)

TECWYN IFAN
76	Sain Sain 1071	DREF WEN (LP, with insert)	£80

KRIS IFE
67	MGM MGM 1369	Hush/The Spectator	£50
68	Music Factory CUB 3	Give And Take/Sands Of Time	£20
68	Parlophone R 5741	Imagination/I'm Coming 'Round	£20
73	Bumlade GE122	Wherever You Are/The Sun, The Sea, The Sand And The Wine	£25

(see also Quiet Five, Judd)

I GAD
92	Nuff Tuff TUF 006	Brutality/ENHANCERS: Brutal Dub/Wicked Man/MANDINKA: Rootsman Corner/ ENHANCERS: Wicked Dub (12")	£50

IGANDA
79	021 Records OTO1	Slow Down/Mark Of Slavery (p/s)	£50

'IGGINBOTTOM
69	Deram SML 1051	'IGGINBOTTOM'S WRENCH (LP, stereo)	£350
69	Deram DML 1051	'IGGINBOTTOM'S WRENCH (LP, mono)	£400

(see also Soft Machine)

IGNERANTS
79	Rundown ACE 008	Radio Interference/Wrong Place, Wrong Time (p/s)	£30

IGUANA
72	Polydor 2383 108	IGUANA (LP, gatefold sleeve)	£50

IGUANAS
65	RCA RCA 1484	This Is What I Was Made For/Don't Come Runnin' To Me	£40

I HAICIDEONS & I JARZIF
78	Greensleeves GRED 7	Rise Ethiopians/Signs Of The Messiah (12")	£40

I JAH MAN (LEVI)
76	Lucky LY 6016	Jah Heavy Load/Heavy Dub	£80
76	Concrete Jungle CJ 750	Jah Heavy Load/Straight To Blackwax Locks	£40
76	Concrete Jungle CJ 756	I Am Levi/Part 2	£100
77	Ghetto Rocker PRE 1	Africa/Afrodub (handwritten labels)	£40
78	Island WIP 6458	Heavy Load/I'm A Levi	£20
80	Jahmani JMI 304	Moulding (as Ijahman)/HIS MAJESTERIANS: Jah Is Coming Again (12")	£60
85	Jahmani JMI 501	Moulding/Jah Is Coming Again (12")	£40
78	Island ILPS 9521	HAILE I HYMN (LP)	£18

I-JOG & TRACKSUITS
80	Tyger TYG 1	Red Box/Worrying Man (p/s)	£20

LEIAH IKAFA
| 79 | Hobo HOS 002 | Disco 2000/Together In Love | £15 |
| 79 | Hobo HOSD 002 | Disco 2000/Together In Love (12" clear vinyl) | £35 |

IKE (B) & CRYSTALITES
| 68 | Island WI 3134 | Illya Kuryakin/Anne Marie (B-side miscredited to Bobby Ellis & Crystalites) | £60 |
| 68 | Island WI 3151 | Try A Little Merriness/Patricia (as Ike B & Crystalites) | £20 |

IKETTES
62	London HLU 9508	I'm Blue/Find My Baby	£25
65	Stateside SS 407	Peaches'N'Cream/The Biggest Players	£40
65	Stateside SS 434	(He's Gonna Be) Fine Fine Fine/How Come	£30
65	Sue WI 389	Prisoner In Love/Those Words	£40
66	Polydor 56506	I'm So Thankful/Don't Feel Sorry For Me	£20
66	Polydor 56516	(Never More) Lonely For You/Sally Go Round The Roses	£20
66	London HLU 10081	What'cha Gonna Do?/Down, Down	£80
85	Kent 6T1	MARY LOVE: Hey Stoney Face/IKETTES: It's Been So Long/ETTA JAMES: Wallflower	£20
65	Stateside SE 1033	FINE FINE FINE (EP)	£175

(see also Ike & Tina Turner, P.P. Arnold)

I LIFE
| 64 | R&B JB 140 | Kiss You Gave Me/No More | £18 |

ILLUSION
70	Dot DOT 137	Let's Make Each Other Happy/Beside You (unissued)	£0
69	Dot (S)LPD 531	ILLUSION (LP)	£25
70	Dot SLPD 537	TOGETHER (AS A WAY OF LIFE) (LP)	£22
70	Paramount SPFL 264	IF IT'S SO (LP, originally planned for Dot SLPD 539)	£15

ILLUSIONS
| 83 | Zella ZEL LPS 405 | ILLUSIONS (LP, 100 only, with insert) | £50 |

ILLUSIVE DREAM
| 69 | RCA Victor RCA 1791 | Electric Garden/Back Again | £30 |

(see also Christine Perfect)

ILLUSTRATION
| 69 | Pye Int. NSPL 28140 | ILLUSTRATION (LP) | £25 |

ERIK ILOTT, SHANTYMAN
| 73 | Folk'sle Records FOR 7 | SHIPSHAPE & BRISTOL FASHION (LP, card sleeve, pasted photo & booklet) | £40 |

I LUV WIGHT
| 70 | Philips 6006 043 | Let The World Wash In/Mediaeval Masquerade (in p/s) | £75 |
| 70 | Philips 6006 043 | Let The World Wash In/Mediaeval Masquerade | £35 |

(see also Kaleidoscope, Fairfield Parlour)

IMAGE
65	Parlophone R 5281	Come To The Party/Never Let Me Go	£50
65	Parlophone R 5352	Home Is Anywhere/I Hear Your Voice Again	£50
66	Parlophone R 5442	I Can't Stop Myself/Let's Make The Scene	£60

IMAGES
| 65 | Polydor 56011 | I Only Have Myself To Blame/Head Over Heels | £30 |

IMAGINATION (1)
| 68 | Status ST 001 | Flying/The Magic Wand | £50 |

IM & COUNT OSSIE
| 71 | Banana CA 357 | So Long Rastafari Calling/Give Me Back My Language & Culture | £50 |

IM (CEDRIC BROOKS) & DAVID
| 70 | Bamboo BAM 57 | Candid Eye/SOUND DIMENSION: Federated Backdrop | £40 |

NATALIE IMBRUGLIA
| 97 | RCA 21527987 JB | Torn/Sometimes (7", jukebox, paper label, large centre hole) | £100 |

IMMORTALS (1)
| 69 | Amalgamated AMG 851 | Bongo Jah/ANSELL COLLINS: My Last Waltz | £40 |
| 77 | Hawkeye HE 10 | Why Keep A Good Man Down/Good Man | £20 |

IMMORTALS (2)
| 86 | MCA MCA 1057 | No Turning Back/No Turning Back (The Chocks-Away Mix) (p/s) | £25 |
| 86 | MCA MCAT 1057 | No Turning Back (Joy Stick Mix)/No Turning Back/No Turning Back (The Chocks-Away Mix) (12", p/s) | £30 |

(see also Queen)

IMPAC
| 66 | CBS 202402 | Too Far Out/Rat Tat Ta Tat | £80 |

IMPACT
| 83 | Cyanide | PUNK CHRISTMAS EP | £20 |

IMPACT ALL STARS
| 71 | Randy's RAN 519 | Go Back Version 4/Version 3 | £15 |
| 71 | Supreme SUP 223 | Go Back/Version | £15 |

(see also Randy's All Stars, Alton Ellis, Gregory Issacs, Errol Dunkley, C. Danovan, Heptones, Dennis Brown, Horace Andy)

IMPALAS
59	MGM MGM 1015	Sorry (I Ran All The Way Home)/Fool, Fool, Fool	£15
59	MGM MGM 1015	Sorry (I Ran All The Way Home)/Fool, Fool, Fool (78)	£25
59	MGM MGM 1031	Oh, What A Fool/Sandy Went Away	£30
60	MGM MGM 1068	Peggy Darling/'Bye Everybody	£30
59	MGM MGM-EP 696	SORRY (I RAN ALL THE WAY HOME) (EP)	£400

IMPERIAL POMPADOURS
80	Pompadour POMP 001	ERSATZ (LP, actually Inner City Unit with Robert Calvert & Barney Bubbles).....................£40

(see also Inner City Unit, Robert Calvert)

IMPERIALS (JAMAICA)
69	Bullet BU 417	Black Is Soul/Always With You...£50

IMPERIALS (1)
72	Key KL 012	TIME TO GET IT TOGETHER (LP) £18
74	Key KL 025	FOLLOW THE MAN WITH THE MUSIC (LP) £15

IMPERIALS (2)
68	Nu Beat NB 012	Young Love/Days Like These £25

IMPOSTERS
69	Mercury MF 1080	Apache '69/Q Three £20

IMPRESSIONS
58	London HL 8697	For Your Precious Love/Sweet Was The Wine (as Jerry Butler & Impressions) £200
58	London HL 8697	For Your Precious Love/Sweet Was The Wine (78, as Jerry Butler & Impressions) £100
61	HMV POP 961	Gypsy Woman/As Long As You Love Me £50
63	HMV POP 1129	I'm The One Who Loves You/I Need Your Love £40
63	HMV POP 1226	It's Alright/You'll Want Me Back £25
64	HMV POP 1262	Talkin' About My Baby/Never Too Much Love £20
64	HMV POP 1295	I'm So Proud/I Made A Mistake...£20
64	HMV POP 1317	Keep On Pushing/I Love You (Yeah) £20
64	HMV POP 1343	You Must Believe Me/See The Real Me £18
65	HMV POP 1408	People Get Ready/I've Been Trying £18
65	HMV POP 1429	Woman's Got Soul/Get Up And Move..£18
65	HMV POP 1446	A Meeting Over Yonder/I Found That I've Lost £20
65	HMV POP 1472	I Need You/Never Could You Be...£20
66	HMV POP 1498	You've Been Cheatin'/Just One Kiss From You £40
66	HMV POP 1498	You've Been Cheatin'/Just One Kiss From You (DJ Copy)..£100
66	HMV POP 1516	Since I Lost The One I Love/Falling In Love With You £15
66	HMV POP 1526	Too Slow/No One Else £15
66	HMV POP 1545	Can't Satisfy/This Must End £40
66	HMV POP 1545	Can't Satisfy/This Must End (DJ Copy)...£100
67	HMV POP 1581	You Always Hurt Me/Little Girl £40
67	HMV POP 1581	You Always Hurt Me/Little Girl (DJ Copy)..£100
68	Stateside SS 2083	We're A Winner/You've Got Me Runnin'..£18
69	Stateside SS 2139	Can't Satisfy/You've Been Cheatin'...£20
69	Buddah 201 062	Choice Of Colors/Mighty Mighty Spade And Whitey £15
65	HMV 7EG 8896	IT'S ALL RIGHT (EP) £100
66	HMV 7EG 8954	SOULFULLY (EP)...£100
64	HMV CLP 1743	THE NEVER ENDING IMPRESSIONS (LP) £80
65	HMV CLP 1935	BIG SIXTEEN (LP, mono) £40
65	HMV CSD 1642	BIG SIXTEEN (LP, stereo) £50
66	HMV CLP/CSD 3548	RIDIN' HIGH (LP) £60
67	HMV CLP/CSD 3631	THE FABULOUS IMPRESSIONS (LP)..£60
68	Stateside (S)SL 10239	WE'RE A WINNER (LP) £35
68	Joy JOYS 104	FOR YOUR PRECIOUS LOVE (LP, with Jerry Butler) £15
69	Buddah 203 012	THIS IS MY COUNTRY (LP) £30
69	Stateside (S)SL 10279	BIG SIXTEEN (VOL. 2) (LP) £30
70	Buddah 2359 003	THE YOUNG MOD'S FORGOTTEN STORY (LP) £30
70	Buddah 2359 009	AMEN (LP) £18
71	Buddah 2318 017	CHECK OUT YOUR MIND (LP) £20
72	Buddah 2318 059	TIMES HAVE CHANGED (LP)..£18
73	Buddah BDLP 4003	FINALLY GOT MYSELF TOGETHER (LP) £15
75	ABC ABCL 5104	BIG SIXTEEN (LP, reissue) £15

(see also Curtis Mayfield, Jerry Butler)

IMPROVING SILENCE
77	Perky Pat CS LP 145/6	IMPROVING SILENCE EP (1,000, p/s with 8 page book insert) £40

IMPS
58	Parlophone R 4398	Dim Dumb Blonde/Let Me Lie £20

INADEQUATES
59	Capitol CL 15051	Pretty Face/Audie...£25

INCANDESCENT LUMINAIRE
82	Clock House CHR 0501	Famous Names/The Warning..£18

INCAS (1)
65	Lyntone LYN 765/6	KEELE RAG RECORD (EP, flexidisc, with 3 other bands) £30
66	Parlophone R 5551	One Night Stand/I'll Keep Holding On £60

INCAS (2)
75	Tank BSS 112	X CERTIFICATE (LP, private pressing) £50

ERROL INCE
65	Ember EMB 3360	DANCE TRINIDAD (LP, as Errol Ince and his Music Makers) £18

INCEE WINCEE SPIDER
88	Overspill SPILL1	Don't Know Anythin'/See My Love Shine (p/s) £30

INCH BY INCH
81	Blue Of London BOL 1	If It's Magic (We Don't Want It)/War's Not Inevitable (12". p/s)..................................£30

INCOGNITO (2)

81	Ensign ENVY 504	JAZZ FUNK (LP)	£20
91	Talkin Loud 848 546-1	INSIDE LIFE (LP)	£15

INCREDIBLE BONGO BAND

72	MGM 2315 255	BONGO ROCK (LP)	£25
76	DJM DJS 20452	BONGO ROCK (LP, reissue)	£15

INCREDIBLE CHERRY TREE BAND

76	Look LKLP 6037	INCREDIBLE CHERRY TREE BAND (LP)	£30

INCREDIBLE HOG

73	Dart ART 2026	Lame/Tadpole	£15
73	Dart 65372	VOLUME 1 (LP, laminated sleeve, pink/white/black label)	£300
11	Rise Above Relics RARLP 009	VOLUME 1- 4 (LP, with 10")	£25
11	Rise Above Relics RARLP 009	VOLUME 1- 4 (LP, with blue vinyl 10")	£35
11	Rise Above Relics RARLP 009	VOLUME 1- 4 (LP, with 10" and 7" all on pink vinyl, 300 only)	£35

INCREDIBLE KIDDA BAND

78	Psycho P 2608	Everybody Knows/No Nerve (in p/s)	£100
78	Psycho P 2608	Everybody Knows/No Nerve (no p/s)	£30
79	Carrere CAR 119	Fighting My Way Back/Saturday Night Fever (as KIDDA BAND)	£130

INCREDIBLES

67	Stateside SS 2053	There's Nothing Else To Say/Heart And Soul	£200
67	Stateside SS 2053	There's Nothing Else To Say/Heart And Soul (DJ copy)	£300
74	Contempo CS 9008	There's Nothing Else To Say/Another Dirty Deal	£20
74	Contempo CLP 512	HEART AND SOUL (LP)	£25

INCREDIBLE STRING BAND

SINGLES

67	Elektra EKSN 45013	Way Back In The 1960s/Chinese White (white-label promo)	£60
68	Elektra EKSN 45028	Painting Box/No Sleep Blues	£15

ALBUMS : ORIGINAL ALBUMS

66	Elektra EUK 254	THE INCREDIBLE STRING BAND (1st pressing, white label, green logo, black lettering)	£225
67	Elektra EUK 257	THE 5000 SPIRITS OR THE LAYERS OF THE ONION (mono, orange label)	£150
67	Elektra EUKS 7257	THE 5000 SPIRITS OR THE LAYERS OF THE ONION (LP, stereo, orange label, laminated sleeve)	£150
68	Elektra EUKS 258	THE HANGMAN'S BEAUTIFUL DAUGHTER (mono, orange label, with lyric insert)	£70
68	Elektra EUKS 7258	THE HANGMAN'S BEAUTIFUL DAUGHTER (stereo, orange label, laminated sleeve with lyric insert)	£80
68	Elektra EKL 4036/7	WEE TAM/THE BIG HUGE (2-LP, orange label, laminated gatefold sleeve, with insert; also stereo EKS 74036/7)	£45
69	Elektra EKS 74057	CHANGING HORSES (red/white label, gatefold sleeve)	£45
70	Elektra 2469 002	I LOOKED UP (red/white label)	£50
70	Elektra 2665 001	U (2-LP, red/white label, gatefold sleeve, with foldover lyric insert)	£35
70	Elektra 2665 001	U (2-LP, red label, gatefold sleeve, without foldover lyric insert)	£25
70	Island ILPS 9140	BE GLAD FOR THE SONG HAS NO ENDING (pink rim label/'palm tree' logo)	£18
71	Island ILPS 9172	LIQUID ACROBAT AS REGARDS THE AIR (gatefold sleeve, with inner, pink rim label/'palm tree' logo)	£30
72	Island ILPS 9211	EARTHSPAN (with lyric inner sleeve, pink rim label/'palm tree' logo)	£18
73	Island ILPS 9229	NO RUINOUS FEUD (with inner sleeve, pink rim label/'palm tree' logo)	£15
74	Island ILPS 9270	HARD ROPE AND SILKEN TWINE (with inner sleeve, pink rim label/'palm tree' logo)	£15
76	Island ISLD 9	SEASONS THEY CHANGE (2-LP, gatefold sleeve)	£25

ALBUMS : REISSUE ALBUMS

66	Elektra EUK 254	THE INCREDIBLE STRING BAND (2nd pressing, orange label)	£60

(All other 'butterfly' label re-issues £8-£10 each)

68	Elektra EKL 254	THE INCREDIBLE STRING BAND (3rd pressing, red label)	£20
68	Elektra EKS 7257	THE 5000 SPIRITS OR THE LAYERS OF THE ONION (LP, stereo, red label)	£150
68	Elektra EKL 257	THE 5000 SPIRITS OR THE LAYERS OF THE ONION (LP, mono, red label)	£50
68	Elektra EKL 4036	WEE TAM (red label, also stereo EKS 74036)	£15

(All other 'butterfly' label re-issues £8-£10 each)

68	Elektra EKL 4037	THE BIG HUGE (red label, also stereo EKS 74037)	£15

(All other 'butterfly' label re-issues £8-£10 each)

72	Elektra K 62002	U (2-LP, 'butterfly' label, gatefold sleeve, with foldover lyric insert)	£15

(see also Robin Williamson, Mike Heron, Famous Jug Band, C.O.B., Shirley Collins)

IN CROWD (JAMAICA)

71	Spinning Wheel SW 105	Bush Jacket/Soul Face	£25
78	Cactus CT 111	Back A Yard/Yard (12")	£18
78	Cactus CTLP 125	HIS MAJESTY IS COMING (LP)	£25

IN CROWD (U.K.)

65	Parlophone R 5276	That's How Strong My Love Is/Things She Says	£80
65	Parlophone R 5328	Stop! Wait A Minute/You're On Your Own	£70
65	Parlophone R 5364	Why Must They Criticize?/I Don't Mind	£60

(see also Tomorrow, Keith West, Steve Howe, Four + One)

INCROWD (U.K.)

69	Deram DM 272	Where In The World/I Can Make Love To You	£15

INCUBUS

84	Guardian GRC 2165	TO THE DEVIL A DAUGHTER (LP)	£18

PETER IND

61	Esquire 32 159	LOOKING OUT (LP)	£120

68	Wave LP 3	**IMPROVISATION** (LP)	£30
69	Wave LP 4	**TIME FOR IMPROVISATION** (LP)	£30
69	Wave LP 5	**JAZZ AT THE RICHMOND FESTIVAL** (LP, with Charlie Burchell, Bernie Cash & Derek Phillips)	£30
70	Wave LP 20	**COTRA-BACH** (LP, with Bernard Cash)	£30
74	Wave LP 29	**NO KIDDING** (LP, with Chas Burchell, Tox Drohar & Dave Cliff)	£30

IN DEPTH PERCEPTION

| 93 | Lucky Spin GP 001 | **Entropy/Rhizone** (12") | £20 |

INDEX (1)

| 78 | Index INDY 001 | **Jetlag/Total Bland** (1st pressing, 500 only, push out centre, die cut stickered sleeve) | £30 |
| 78 | Index INDY 001 | **Jetlag/Total Bland** (2nd pressing, 500 only, solid centre, die cut sleeve) | £15 |

INDEX (2)

| 81 | Record Shack SHACK 128 | **Starlight/Starlight** (The Break) (12") | £40 |
| 81 | Record Shack SHACK 8 | **Starlight/Starbright Instrumental Mix** | £30 |

INDIAN SUMMER

| 71 | RCA Neon NE 3 | **INDIAN SUMMER** (LP, gatefold sleeve) | £250 |

(see also Badfinger)

INDIFFERENT DANCE CENTRE

| 81 | Recluse RECLUSE 1 | **Flight & Pursuit/Release** (p/s) | £25 |

INDO-BRITISH ENSEMBLE

| 69 | MFP 1307 | **CURRIED JAZZ** (LP) | £20 |

INDO JAZZMEN

| 68 | Saga FID 2145 | **RAGAS AND REFLECTIONS** (LP) | £15 |

INDUSTRIAL

| 92 | Kinetix KNT 007 | **TIME TO ROCK EP** (12") | £20 |

IN EMBRACE

82	Glass GLASS 019	**THE INITIAL CARESS** (12" EP)	£15
82	Glass GLALP 001	**PASSIONFRUIT PASTELS** (LP)	£18
83	Glass GLALP 004	**TOO** (LP)	£15

INERTIA (1)

| 80 | ERT 2 | **DANCEBEAT ATTITUDE EP** | £50 |

INEVITABLES

| 82 | Honk 1 | **The Fourth Contender/The Puppeteer/Neutral News** (p/s) | £25 |

INFANTES JUBILATE

| 68 | Music Factory CUB 5 | **Exploding Galaxy/Take It Now** | £60 |

INFA RIOT

| 82 | Secret SEC 7 | **STILL OUT OF ORDER** (LP) | £15 |
| 88 | Link LINKLP 052 | **LIVE AND LOUD!!** (LP) | £15 |

(see also Infas)

INFAS

| 84 | Panache PANLP 501 | **SOUND AND FURY** (LP) | £15 |

(see also Infa Riot)

INFERNAL BLUES MACHINE

| 76 | London SHU 8496 | **ADIOS AMIGOS** (LP) | £15 |

INFINITY PROJECT

| 95 | Blue Room BRO005LP | **MYSTICAL EXPERIENCES** (2-LP) | £35 |
| 95 | TIP TIPLP 3 | **FEELING WEIRD** (2-LP) | £25 |

IN FLAMES

| 72 | Pama PM 842 | **Rocket Man/I'm All Broke Up** | £30 |

INFLUENCE

| 69 | Orange OAS 201 | **I Want To Live/Driving Me Wild** | £25 |

(see also John Miles, Geordie)

INFORMATION

| 69 | Beacon BEA 121 | **Orphan/Oh Strange Man** | £30 |
| 70 | Evolution E 2461S | **Lovely To See You/Face To The Sun** | £20 |

INFRA RED HELICOPTERS

| 79 | 1979 | **BRACKNELL** (EP) | £25 |

NICK INGMAN

| 75 | Studio Two TWOX 1045 | **TERMINATOR** (LP) | £40 |

JORGEN INGMANN

| 59 | Pye Int. NPT 29000 | **GUITAR IN HI-FI** (10" LP) | £25 |

INGRAM

| 83 | Streetwave WAVLP 001 | **WOULD YOU LIKE TO FLY** (LP, with bonus 12") | £40 |
| 83 | Streetwave WAVLP 001 | **WOULD YOU LIKE TO FLY** (LP, without bonus 12") | £25 |

LUTHER INGRAM

| 08 | Kent Select CITY 007 | **Baby Don't You Weep/CHET POISON' IVY: Mata Hari** | £20 |
| 72 | Koko KOS 2202 | **IF LOVING YOU IS WRONG I DON'T WANT TO BE RIGHT** (LP, photo insert) | £20 |

I 'N' I ONENESS MEETS UK PLAYERS

| 97 | Jah Works JW 018S | **Further/Further Into Dub** (12") | £20 |

INITIALS

| 64 | London HLR 9860 | **School Day/Song Is Number One** | £18 |

AUTREY INMAN
63   Decca DFE 8571   AMERICAN COUNTRY JUBILEE NO. 1 (EP) £15

JOHN INMAN
75   DJM DJLPS 465   ARE YOU BEING SERVED SIR? (LP) £15

INMATE AND THE GENERAL
97   Groove Yard GYARD 15   OHMS EP (12") £30

INMATES
79   Radar RAD 25   FIRST OFFENCE (LP) £15

INNER CIRCLE & FATMAN
00   Blood & Fire SVLP 293   HEAVY WEIGHT DUB KILLER DUB (2-LP) £20

INNER CITY BAND
78   Key KS 101   Happiness/Night At The Disco £25

INNER CITY EXPRESS
78   Ebony EYE 5   Fat On Funk/Sho' Dig Dancin' (12") £20

INNER CITY UNIT
79   Riddle RID 002   PASS OUT (THE 360° PSYCHO DELERIA SOUND) (LP) £15
(see also Hawkwind, Sphynx, Radio Actors, Imperial Pompadours, Catherine Andrews, Big Amongst Sheep)

INNER LIFE
18   Salsoul SALSBMG12LP   INNER LIFE - THE STARS OF SALSOUL (2-LP) £20

INNER MIND
70   New Beat NB 069   Pum Pum Girl/Freedom £15
72   Shades SHA 12   Jesse James Hits Back/Let Me In £15

INNERSOULS
06   Funk 45 FUNK45 028   Just Take Your Time/Thoughts (reissue) £25

NEIL INNES
72   United Artists UP 35358   Slush/Rawlinson's End (different version from that on the Vivian Stanshall LP) £30
73   United Artists UAG 29492 HOW SWEET TO BE AN IDIOT (LP) £30
82   MMC MMC 001   OFF THE RECORD (2-LP) £30
(see also Grimms, Bonzo Dog [Doo Dah] Band, Rutles, World, Dirk & Stig)

INN KEEPERS
71   Banana BA 328   Duppy Serenade/Sunshine Version (actually by Dennis Alcapone) £20
(see also WInston Matthews)

INNOCENCE IN AFRICA
81   S/81/KUS 1205   Larger Than Life/Strangers Now (p/s) £25

INNOCENT VICARS
80   No Brain INV 001   She's Here/Antimatter (p/s, hand-stamped labels) £60

INNOCENTS (U.K.)
63   Columbia DB 7098   Stepping Stones/Grazina £15
63   Columbia DB 7173   A Fine, Fine Bird/Spanish Holiday £15
(see also Mike Berry)

INNOCENTS (U.S.)
60   Top Rank JAR 508   Honest I Do/My Baby Hully Gullys £30
61   Top Rank JAR 541   Gee Whiz/Please Mr Sun £40
(see also Kathy Young)

INSANE
82   Insane INSANE 1   Why Die?/War And Violence (p/s) £15
82   No Future OI 10   El Salvador/Nuclear War/Chinese Rock (p/s, with Rising Free Fanzine)..........£25

INSANE CLOWN POSSE
98   Island ISP 705   Hokus Pokus/Prom Queen (picture disc) £15

INSANE MACBETH
00   Insane LP1   THE RETARDATION PROJECT (LP, 100 only) £100
(see also Kinetic Effect)

INSECT TRUST
69   Capitol E-(S)T 109   THE INSECT TRUST (LP) £80

INSERTS
80   Supermusic SUP 26   N.M.E/The Plague/Teenage Girls (with p/s) £35
80   Supermusic SUP 26   N.M.E/The Plague/Teenage Girls (without p/s) £25

INSIDE OV A COFFIN
98   Out-There OTT 1   Banking On Death (7", existence unconfirmed) £0
(see also Freed Unit)

INSPIRAL CARPETS
80s   Own label   SONGS OF SHALLOW INTENSITY (p/s, demo) £20
80s   Own label   WAITING FOR OURS (p/s, demo) £20
80s   Own label   COW (p/s, demo) £20
88   Playtime AMUSE 2T   PLANE CRASH EP £20
89   Dung 4   DUNG 4 (cassette LP) £15
92   Mute/Cow DUNG 19   REVENGE OF THE GOLDFISH (LP) £35
94   Mute/Cow LDUNG 25   DEVIL HOPPING (LP) £40
94   Mute/Cow LDUNG 25   DEVIL HOPPING (LP, with free red vinyl 10" EP) £60
95   Mute MOOTEL 3   THE SINGLES (2-LP, with free 7") £50
14   Cherry Red CRDUNG4   DUNG 4 (LP, 7", reissue) £30

INSPIRATION
73 Tavern STA 1004   Love Don't Grow On Trees/Dambusters March/Guitar Man/America £15

INSPIRATIONS (JAMAICA)
69 Camel CA 11   Down In The Park/Love Oh Love...£80
69 Camel CA 21   Wonder Of Love/Cinderella...£80
70 Amalgamated AMG 857   Take Back Your Duck/Nothing For Nothing £35
70 Amalgamated AMG 861   La La/Reggae Fever..£35
70 Amalgamated AMG 862   The Train Is Coming/Man Oh Man...£50
71 Upsetter US 355   Confusion/THE UPSETTERS: Confusion Version £40
70 Trojan TTL 27   REGGAE FEVER (LP) £50
(see also Niney)

INSPIRATIONS (U.S.)
67 Polydor 56730   Touch Me, Kiss Me, Hold Me/What Am I Gonna Do With You? £200

INSTANT AUTOMATONS
80 Deleted DEP 001   PETER PAINTS HIS FENCE EP (2x7", numbered, fold-out sleeve with inserts and
                             stickers) £25

INSTANT FUNK
79 Salsoul SSLP 1511   I GOT MY MIND MADE UP (LP) £15

INSTITUTION
79 Industrial Accident SGS 112 Jane and John/Stephanie (500 only, hand stamped labels).....................£30
(see also Jazz Butcher)

INSYNC
92 Irdial Discs 27IRD INS 1 Storm/Warm (12") £50
93 Irdial Discs INS 2   UNTITLED EP (12", test pressings only) £150

INSYNC VS MYSTERON
97 Fat Cat 12FAT 004   TALES FROM THE CRYPT (12", custom sleeve) £15

INTELLIGENT COMMUNICATION
91 Jumpin & Pumpin 12 TOT 15 PRINCIPLES OF MOTION (12" EP)..£30
(see also Future Sound Of London)

INTENSE DEGREE
88 Earache MOSH 9   WAR IN MY HEAD (LP, with inner) £15

INTENSITY
73 Eden EDEN LP 68   TURN ABOUT INSIDE OUT PLASTIC COATED HUMANS (LP) £150

INTENTIONS (U.S.)/Z.Z. HILL
66 Sue IEP 711   GIMME GIMME (EP, 2 tracks each by Intentions & Z.Z. Hill; 2 tracks mistakenly
                             credited to Jackie Day on sleeve; in p/s)..£300
66 Sue IEP 711   GIMME GIMME (EP, 2 tracks each by Intentions & Z.Z. Hill; 2 tracks mistakenly
                             credited to Jackie Day on sleeve; no p/s)..£100

INTERFACE
81 Blue Beat HIT 2358   Automaton/Electric Dreamland (p/s) £40

INTERNATIONAL CHRYSIS
94 PWL PWLT 303   Rebel Rebel (The Hole Mix)/Rebel Rebel (Extended Mix) (12", promo only) £15
(see also Dead Or Alive)

INTERNATIONAL SPARES
81 Spare KF 001   No Time At All/The Windmill..£50

INTERNS (JAMAICA)
75 Attack ATT 8097   Nothing Is Impossible/HARDY BOYS: Black Out £20
79 Burning Rockers BR 1003 DETOUR (LP) £30
(see also Viceroys, Bob Marley & Wailers)

INTERNS (U.K.)
64 Philips BF 1320   Don't You Dare/Here There Everywhere £15
64 Philips BF 1345   Cry To Me/There's Love For You £15
66 Parlophone R 5479   Is It Really What You Want?/Just Like Me £50
(see also Shadows)

INTERPOL
00 CHEM047CD   fukd i.d #3 PDA/Precipitate/Roland/5 (CD, stickered card sleeve, 1,000 only) £80
02 Matador OLE 546-7   INTERPOL EP: PDA/Specialist (p/s) £25
02 Matador OLE 541   TURN ON THE BRIGHT LIGHTS (LP) £50
03 Black Sessions 1803   LIVE - BLACK SESSIONS (LP, red splatter vinyl)...£30
04 Matador OLE 616-1   ANTICS (LP) £50
04 Matador (no. Cat. No)   ANTICS (5 x 7" box set, only from Interpol Space Art Gallery, London) £40
05 Matador OLE 675   ANTICS - REMIXES (LP) £30
07 Capitol/Parlophone 0946 3 OUR LOVE TO ADMIRE (2-LP) £50
    96248 1

INTESTINES
81 Alternative Capitalists AC51 Life In A Cardboard Box/New Recruit (p/s) £25

IN THE GYM
81 Taaga Records TAG 2   Playing The Fool/Don't Go Slow (no sleeve) £50

IN THE NURSERY
84 Paragon VIRTUE 5   Witness To A Scream/1984 (p/s)..£15
83 Paragon VIRTUE 2   WHEN CHERISHED DREAMS COME TRUE (mini-LP, silk-screened g/fold p/s).................£25

IN THE WOODS...
95 Misanthropy AMAZON 4   HEART OF THE AGES (LP, with booklet) £70

MINT VALUE £

97   Misanthropy AMAZON 11   **OMNIO** (2-LP, gatefold sleeve, 1-sided etched disc) £50

INTIMATE OBSESSIONS
85   Third Mind TMLP 11   **EREBUS TO HADES** (LP)..£15

INTIMATE STRANGERS
75   Alaska ALA 1005   **Love Sounds/The Track** £50

INTRA VEIN
79   Bum FP 001   **Speed Of The City/Sick** (printed PVC sleeve)...£45
79   Bum FP 001   **Speed Of The City/Sick** (stamped plain sleeve)..£35
(see also Veins)

INTRIGUE
82   Pressure PRESS D 1003   **I Like It** (Vocal)/**I Like It** (Instrumental) (12").................................£60
84   Music Power MPR(T) 1   **No Turning Back/Call Of The Heart** (12")......................................£25
86   Intrigue INT 12-001   **One Touch/Touch Down** (12")..£15

INTRODUCING DRAGONS
81   Zebra ZEBRA 3001   **Via Media/Time Hangs** (p/s) £20

INTROZE
82   Monarch MON 037   **Doin' The Lambeth Walk/Kids In Uniform** £50

INTRUDERS (2)
66   London HL 10069   **Up And Down The Ladder/United** £40
69   Action ACT 4523   **Slow Drag/So Glad I'm Yours** £15
69   Ember EMB S 254   **Cowboys To Girls/Turn Back The Hands Of Time** £15

INVADERS (JAMAICA)
68   Studio One SO 2044   **Soulful Music/SOUL VENDORS: Happy Organ** £200

INVISIBLE MAN
92   Timeless DJ 005   **On A Mission/Twisted/Intro** (Think About It)/ **The End** (Drug Induced Psychosis Mix)/**Bonus Turbo Cut** (12")...£30
93   Timeless DJ 006   **The Beginning/The End** (12")..£20
93   Timeless DJ 007   **Skyliner/Power** (12")...£20
93   Timeless DJ 008   **Skyliner** (Remix)/**MYSTERON: U Don't Know** (12").............................£20

INVITATIONS (JAMAICA)
71   Crab CRAB 66   **Birmingham Cat/Now You're On Your Own** £20

INVITATIONS (U.S.)
65   Stateside SS 453   **Hallelujah/Written On The Wall** £50
65   Stateside SS 478   **What's Wrong With My Baby?/Why Did My Baby Turn Bad?** £150
65   Stateside SS 478   **What's Wrong With My Baby?/Why Did My Baby Turn Bad?** (DJ copy)........£300
70   Jay Boy BOY 24   **How'd We Ever Get This Way?/Picking Up** £35

INVOGUE
82   Street Life S 82 CUS 1474   **EXPRESSIONS OF YOUTH EP** £50

INXS
87   Mercury MERH 114   **KICK** (LP, gatefold) £15
94   Mercury 526 230-1   **THE GREATEST HITS** (2-LP)..£40

IONA
78   Silver Scales   **CUCKOO** (LP) £35
70s   Celtic Music CM 001   **IONA** (LP) £35

I.O.W. CHEROKEES
66   69 69EP 001   **I.O.W. CHEROKEES** (EP, private pressing)..£40

IPSISSIMUS
69   Parlophone R 5774   **Hold On/Lazy Woman** £70

IPSO FACTO
84   IF IF 7 84   **Noir Dior/Craving** £15

IQ
84   Jim White/IQ PROMO 101   **Awake And Nervous/Through The Corridors** (12", no p/s, 500 only)....£30
84   IQFREEB 1   **Hollow Afternoon** (1-sided, Marquee gig freebie) £30
86   STAL Other Boxer 1   **Nomzamo** (Demo) (1-sided fan club single) £18
86   Sahara IQSD 1   **It All Stops Here/Intelligence Quotient** (shaped picture disc) £18
87   RLOG Another Boxer 1   **Fascination/The Bold Grenadier Pt. 1** (fan club single)....................£18
85   STAL BOXER 1   **NINE IN A POND IS HERE** (2-LP, 1,000 copies only) £20
(see also Niadem's Ghost)

IQ ZERO
79   Object Music OM 9   **(Everybody Kills) Insects/Electromotion/Quirky Pop Music** (p/s) £20
80   Phony Gram SRTS/80/CUS 623   **She's So Rare/Crazy Dolls** £25
79   Logo GO 374   **She's So Rare/Crazy Dolls** (p/s) £15

IRATION STEPPAS
94   Iration Steppa BS 159   **Scud Missile/High Rise Vibrations** (12") £35
95   Iration Steppa IS 003   **Kilimanjaro/High Altitude Mix/Summit Mix** (10")......................£80
03   Tandori Space TS 012   **Too Much War/Stop The War Dub/What's Wrong/What's Wrong Dub** (10").......£25
(see also Dubkasm)

IRATION STEPPAS & TENA STELIN
01   Tandori Space TSR 001   **War Inna Babylon/Dub Version** £20
01   Tandori Space TSR 002   **Jungle Jungle/Dub Version**..£20
(see also Tena Stelin)

DAVID IRELAND
73	Sovereign SOV 120	Shoot The Family Man/Coming Up Strong	£15

IRINI
95	Here It Is HIILP 023	DON'T MAKE ME WISH (LP)	£15

IRON BUTTERFLY
68	Atco 2091 024	In-A-Gadda-Da-Vida/Termination (first pressing with Atco label and Polydor Records Limited type)	£20
68	Atlantic 584 188	Possession/Unconscious Power	£15
68	Atco 2465 015	HEAVY (LP)	£25
68	Atlantic 587/588 116	IN-A-GADDA-DA-VIDA (LP)	£80
69	Atco 228 011	BALL (LP, gatefold sleeve)	£25
70	Atlantic 2400 014	LIVE (LP)	£18
71	Atlantic 2401 003	METAMORPHOSIS (LP)	£50

(see also Ramatam, Captain Beyond)

IRON CROSS
74	Spark 1112	Everybody Rock On/All The Time	£20

IRON HORSE
71	Bell BLL1148	The Obeah Man/Magic Love	£20

IRON MAIDEN (1)
70	Gemini GMS 006	Falling/Ned Kelly	£45

IRON MAIDEN (2)
SINGLES
80	EMI EMI 5032	Running Free/Burning Ambition (p/s)	£25
80	EMI EMI 5065	Sanctuary/Drifter (live)/I've Got The Fire (live) (uncensored p/s)	£45
80	EMI EMI 5065	Sanctuary/Drifter (live)/I've Got The Fire (live) (censored p/s)	£15
80	EMI EMI 5105	Women In Uniform/Invasion (p/s)	£18
80	EMI 12EMI 5105	Women In Uniform/Phantom Of The Opera (live)/Invasion (12", p/s)	£15
81	EMI EMI 5145	Twilight Zone/Wrathchild (p/s)	£15
81	EMI EMI 5145	Twilight Zone/Wrathchild (p/s, clear vinyl)	£25
81	EMI EMI 5145	Twilight Zone/Wrathchild (p/s, red vinyl)	£30
81	EMI EMI 5145	Twilight Zone/Wrathchild (p/s, brown vinyl mispressing)	£800
81	EMI EMI 5184	Purgatory/Genghis Khan (p/s)	£35
82	EMI EMIP 5263	Run To The Hills/Total Eclipse (picture disc, mispressed, b-side picture both sides)	£30
82	EMI EMIP 5263	Run To The Hills/Total Eclipse (picture disc)	£20
83	EMI 12EMIP 5378	Flight Of Icarus/I've Got The Fire (12", picture disc)	£20
83	EMI EMIP 5397	The Trooper/Cross-Eyed Mary (soldier-shaped picture disc)	£25
83	EMI EMIP 5397	The Trooper/Cross-Eyed Mary (uncut shaped picture disc)	£800
84	EMI 12EMI 5489	2 Minutes To Midnight/Rainbow's Gold/Mission From 'Arry (12", picture disc)	£15
84	EMI 12EMIP 5502	Aces High/King Of Twilight/The Number Of The Beast (live) (12", picture disc)	£20
85	EMI 12EMIP 5532	Running Free (live)/Sanctuary (live)/Murders In The Rue Morgue (live) (12", picture disc)	£20
85	EMI 12EMIP 5542	Run To The Hills (live)/Phantom Of The Opera (live)/Losfer Words (The Big 'Orra) (live) (12", picture disc)	£20
86	EMI EMIP 5583	Wasted Years/Reach Out (computer-shaped picture disc)	£20
86	EMI EMIP 5583	Wasted Years/Reach Out (uncut computer-shaped picture disc)	£1000
86	EMI 12EMIP 5589	Stranger In A Strange Land/That Girl/Juanita (12", picture disc)	£18
88	EMI EMP 49	Can I Play With Madness/Black Bart Blues (shaped picture disc)	£18
88	EMI EMP 49	Can I Play With Madness/Black Bart Blues (uncut shaped picture disc)	£400
88	EMI EMP 64	The Evil That Men Do/Prowler '88 (uncut shaped picture disc)	£200
88	EMI EMP 79	The Clairvoyant (live)/The Prisoner (live) (shaped picture disc)	£15
88	EMI EMP 79	The Clairvoyant (live)/The Prisoner (live) (uncut shaped picture disc)	£200
89	EMI EMPD 117	Infinite Dreams (live)/Killers (live) (uncut shaped picture disc)	£200
90	EMI CDEM 171	Bring Your Daughter...To The Slaughter/I'm A Mover (UK pressed CD single)	£100
92	EMI EMPD 240	From Here To Eternity/I Can't See My Feeling (uncut shaped picture disc)	£150
92	EMI EMPD 263	Fear Of The Dark (live)/Hooks In You (live) (uncut shaped picture disc)	£150
92	EMI EMPD 263	Fear Of The Dark (live)/Hooks In You (live) (shaped picture disc, with mispressed B-side "Tailgunner" [live])	£18
95	EMI 12EM 398	Man On The Edge/I Live My Way (12", picture disc, with poster, die-cut sleeve)	£15
95	EMI CDMAN 2	Man On The Edge/The Edge Of Darkness/Sign Of The Cross (CD)	£50
98	EMI EM 507	The Angel And The Gambler/Blood On The World's Hands (Live) (picture disc)	£15
98	EMI 8860690	Futureal/ The Evil That Men Do(live)/ Man On The Edge(live)/ The Angel And The Gambler (video) (CD digi-pack Fan Club only issue with poster)	£50

SINGLES : PROMOS
80	EMI EMI 5032 DJ	Running Free (One-sided 7" DJ copy)	£50
80	EMI EMI 5065	Sanctuary/Drifter (live)/I've Got The Fire (live) (DJ copy, censored p/s)	£50
90	EMI EMDJ 153	Holy Smoke (1-sided 7" DJ copy, radio edit, censored)	£50
90	EMI 12EMP 153	Holy Smoke/All In Your Mind/Kill Me Ce Soir (12", gold vinyl test pressing, promo only)	£150
90	EMI EM 171	Bring Your Daughter ... To The Slaughter/I'm A Mover (Clear or white vinyl Test pressing for 12" picture disc)	£100
90	EMI (no cat. no.)	NO PRAYER FOR THE DYING (CD, with interview , photos & bio, promo only)	£100
92	EMI (no cat. No.)	FEAR OF THE DARK (CD, interview , EPK video, colour booklet, A4 poster in luminous flip top box)	£150
96	EMI BEST 001	BEST OF THE BEAST (CD, Steve Harris interview disc, commercial CD, video, in 40cm x 30cm, flip-up 3D presentation box with 60-page book, 2 photographs, biography, promo only)	£200
97	EMI CDINPROF 001	In Profile (CD, 31 track edit band history picture disc custom sleeve)	£35
98	EMI CDONPROF 001	IN PROFILE (CD)	£30

MINT VALUE £

98	EMI HELLROM001	Maiden Hell promotional CD-Rom in full colour custom card sleeve	£25
99	EMI EDHUNTER 666	ED HUNTER DEMO (CD-Rom, card p/s with booklet, press info and photo)	£40
00	EMI no cat. no.	Tommy Vance Previews: The Wicker Man/Ghost Of The Navigator/ Brave New World/ Dream Of Mirrors/The Nomad (CD-R with Thomas The Vance intros)	£50
02	EMI RIOINTCD 001	ROCK IN RIO (Promo interview CD, with colour booklet)	£50
02	EMI CDSP255	EDDIE'S ARCHIVE (CD, 8 track sampler in card sleeve)	£50
04	BMG PUB049	Int Iron Maiden 10 track promo CD in custom sleeve	£50

EPs

79	Rock Hard ROK.1	THE SOUNDHOUSE TAPES (EP mispressing with labels on wrong sides, Matrix numbers ROK-1A SA LYN 7627-1T/ROK-1B EG SA LYN 7628-1T, p/s)	£1200
79	Rock Hard ROK.1	THE SOUNDHOUSE TAPES (EP, p/s; Matrix ROK-1A EG SA LYN 7627-1T/ ROK-1B EG SA LYN 7628-1T. Counterfeits have slightly glossier sleeves. Any with different p/s and coloured vinyl are also counterfeit; with T-shirt offer insert)	£1000
79	Rock Hard ROK 1	THE SOUNDHOUSE TAPES (EP, p/s; Matrix ROK-1A EG SA LYN 7627-1T/ ROK-1B EG SA LYN 7628-1T. counterfeits have slightly glossier sleeves. Any with different p/s and coloured vinyl are also counterfeit)	£750
81	EMI 12EMI 5219	MAIDEN JAPAN EP (12" EP, p/s)	£15

ALBUMS

80	EMI EMC 3330	IRON MAIDEN (LP, with 24" x 24" poster, hype sticker)	£300
80	EMI EMC 3330	IRON MAIDEN (LP, without poster)	£35
81	EMI EMC 3357	KILLERS (LP)	£40
82	EMI EMC 3400	NUMBER OF THE BEAST (LP, inner and Iron Maiden fan club flyer)	£50
82	EMI EMCP 3400	THE NUMBER OF THE BEAST (LP, picture disc, with inner)	£50
83	EMI EMA 800	PIECE OF MIND (LP, gatefold, black card inner)	£35
84	EMI EJ 2402001	POWERSLAVE (LP, textured sleeve, printed inner)	£40
84	EMI POWERP 1	POWERSLAVE (LP, picture disc)	£50
85	EMI ES 24 0426 3	LIVE AFTER DEATH (2LP, gatefold, printed inners, booklet)	£40
86	EMI EMC 3512	SOMEWHERE IN TIME (LP, printed inner)	£45
88	EMI EMD 1006	SEVENTH SON OF A SEVENTH SON (LP, printed inner)	£40
88	EMI EMDP 1006	SEVENTH SON OF A SEVENTH SON (LP, picture disc, with banner)	£45
90	EMI EMD 1017	NO PRAYER FOR THE DYING (LP, printed inner)	£35
90	EMI EMPD 1017	NO PRAYER FOR THE DYING (LP, picture disc, die-cut sleeve)	£45
90	EMI (no cat. no.)	THE FIRST TEN YEARS - UP THE IRONS (10 x 12" double packs, box set available by mail order with tokens from records)	£175
90	EMI (no cat. no.)	THE FIRST TEN YEARS - UP THE IRONS (10 x CD, box set available by mail order with tokens from CDs)	£100
92	EMI EMD 1032	FEAR OF THE DARK (2-LP with merchandise leaflet)	£100
93	EMI DON 1	LIVE AT DONINGTON (3-LP, numbered)	£200
93	EMI EMD 1042	A REAL LIVE ONE (LP, gatefold sleeve with inner sleeve)	£200
93	EMI EMD 1048	A REAL DEAD ONE (LP, gatefold sleeve and inner sleeve)	£200
95	EMI 724383581917	THE X FACTOR (2-LP, clear vinyl, gatefold with poster)	£200
96	EMI (no cat. No.)	THE STORY SO FAR PART 1 (5CD box set, 1000 copies only, exclusive to HMV)	£300
96	EMI (no cat. No.)	THE STORY SO FAR PART 2 (5CD box set, 1000 copies only, exclusive to HMV)	£300
96	EMI EMDX 1097	BEST OF THE BEAST (4LP box set, printed inners, book, bonus tracks)	£400
97	EMI LPCENT 35	IRON MAIDEN (LP, reissue, EMI centenary, stickered sleeve)	£30
97	EMI LPCENT 7	THE NUMBER OF THE BEAST (LP, reissue, 180gm vinyl)	£35
98	EMI LPCENT 35	IRON MAIDEN (LP, reissue, 180gm vinyl)	£30
98	EMI 4979990	EDDIE'S HEAD (13 CD boxset, plastic skull with flashing eyes)	£175
98	EMI 4939151	VIRTUAL XI (2-LP gatefold, with inner sleeves)	£250
00	EMI 526 6051	BRAVE NEW WORLD (2LP, picture disc, gatefold, printed inners)	£200
02	EMI 538 64316	ROCK IN RIO (3LP, picture discs, trifold sleeve)	£130
02	EMI 7243 5412772 4	EDDIE'S ARCHIVE (6CD tin box, insert, shot glass, pewter ring, parchment. 1st issue blue lining, numbered)	£200
02	EMI 544 2772	EDDIE'S ARCHIVE (6-CD, tin box with insert, shot glass, pewter ring and Parchment. 2nd issue red lining)	£80
03	EMI 592 3401	DANCE OF DEATH (2-LP, picture disc, gatefold sleeve and inner sleeves)	£125
05	EMI 336 4371	DEATH ON THE ROAD (2LP, picture disc, gatefold)	£40
06	EMI 372 3211	A MATTER OF LIFE AND DEATH (2-LP, picture disc, gatefold, inner sleeves)	£60
10	EMI 50999 6477701 6	THE FINAL FRONTIER (2-LP, picture disc)	£80
12	EMI 50999 301587 1 9	EN VIVO! (2LP, picture disc, gatefold, printed inners)	£40
12	EMI 5099941648001	PICTURE DISC COLLECTION 1980 - 1988 (10LP box set)	£500
14	Parlophone 2564622290	THE COMPLETE ALBUMS COLLECTION 1980 - 1988 (box set, only contains Iron Maiden, Killers and The Number Of The Beast with space for 5 additional reissues. This price for original box that was manufactured too small to hold all the LPs)	£70
14	Parlophone 2564622290	THE COMPLETE ALBUMS COLLECTION 1980 - 1988 (box set, only contains Iron Maiden, Killers and The Number Of The Beast with space for 5 additional reissues. This price for 'replacement' box that was manufactured the right size to hold all the LPs)	£50
15	Parlophone 0825646089208	THE BOOK OF SOULS (3LP, trifold sleeve, printed inners)	£50
17	Parlophone 0190295760878	THE BOOK OF SOULS: LIVE CHAPTER (3LP, trifold sleeve, printed inners)	£35
17	Parlophone 0190295849498	THE COMPLETE ALBUMS COLLECTION 1990 - 2015 (Box set, only contains No Prayer For The Dying and Fear Of The Dark with additional space left for subsequent reissues)	£30
20	Parlophone 0190295163037	NIGHTS OF THE DEAD, LEGACY OF THE BEAST: LIVE IN MEXICO CITY (3LP, red/white/ green vinyl, trifold sleeve, printed inners	£30
21	Parlophone 0190295015916	SENJUTSU (2LP, triple gatefold, printed inners)	£30
21	Parlophone 0190296718632	SENJUTSU (2LP, triple gatefold, printed inners,black & red marble vinyl, exclusive to HMVC sticker)	£45
21	Parlophone 0190296718649	SENJUTSU (2LP, triple gatefold, printed inners, silver &black marble vinyl, exclusive to Amazon sticker)	£60
21	Parlophone 0190295015947	SENJUTSU (2CD/blu-ray, Fanclub Edition in hand crafted wooden box with pendant, prints, engraved Eddie teak stamp, banner, certificate, ltd to 2021 copies worldwide	£500

(see also Bruce Dickinson, Di'Anno, Gogmagog, Samson, Urchin, Xero, Lionheart, Stratus, Nicko McBrain, Money, White Spirit, McEnroe & Cash, Speed)

IRON VIRGIN
74	Deram DM 408	Jet/Midnight Hitcher	£15
74	Deram DM 416	Rebels Rule/Ain't No Clown	£25

NEVILLE IRONS
68	Blue Cat BS 104	Soul Glide/DYNAMICS: My Friends	£45

(see also Neville Hinds)

IRRESTIBLE FORCE
92	Rising High RSNLP 5	FLYING HIGH (2-LP)	£60
94	Rising High RSN LP 24	GLOBAL CHILLAGE (2-LP)	£40
98	Ninja Tune ZEN 28	IT'S TOMORROW ALREADY (2-LP)	£25

ANDY IRVINE
80	Tara 3002	RAINY SUNDAYS, WINDY DREAMS (LP, lyric insert)	£15

ANDY IRVINE & PAUL BRADY
76	Mulligan LUN 008	ANDY IRVINE & PAUL BRADY (LP)	£30

(see also Dr. Strangely Strange)

WELDON IRVINE
96	Hubbub HUB 12 LP	LIBERATED BROTHER (LP, reissue)	£20
96	Hubbub HUB 13 LP	TIME CAPSULE (LP, reissue)	£35

LONNIE IRVING
60	Melodisc MEL 1546	Pinball Machine/I Got Blues On My Mind	£40

IRVING 6
70s	Port O Jam PJ4116	Ossie's Special/Trouble	£20

(BIG) DEE IRWIN
65	Stateside SS 450	You Satisfy My Needs/I Wanna Stay Right Here With You	£125
65	Stateside SS 450	You Satisfy My Needs/I Wanna Stay Right Here With You (DJ copy)	£200
68	Minit MLF 11013	I Can't Stand The Pain/My Hope To Die Girl (as Dee Irwin)	£15

BIG DEE IRWIN & LITTLE EVA
63	Colpix PXE 301	SWINGING ON A STAR (EP)	£20
70	Golden Guinea GSGL 10497	SWINGING ON A STAR (LP)	£15

(see also Little Eva, Suzi & Big Dee Irwin)

DAVID ISAACS
66	Island WI 261	I'd Rather Be Lonely/See That Man	£80
68	Trojan TR 616	Place In The Sun/UPSETTER ALL STARS: Handy-Cap	£50
69	Upsetter US 302	Good Father/SLIM SMITH: What A Situation	£40
69	Upsetter US 305	I've Got Memories/I'm Leaving	£30
69	Upsetter US 311	He'll Have To Go/Since You're Gone	£40
69	Upsetter US 319	Who To Tell/BUSTY BROWN: I Can't See Myself Cry	£35
69	Punch PH 6	I Can't Take It Anymore/LLOYD DOUGLAS: Anyway	£15
71	Bullet BU 459	Just Enough/ROY PATIN: Standing (B-side actually by Roy Panton)	£35
73	Upsetter US 400	Stranger On The Shore/DILLINGER: John Devour	£70
73	Bread BR 1118	Just Enough/We Are Neighbours	£30
79	Attack TACK 13	Just Like A Sea (with Jah Thomas)/WITTY'S ALL STARS: Just Like A Sea (Version) (12")	£18

(see also Upsetters)

GREGORY ISAACS
70	Escort ERT 833	While There Is Life/HARRY YOUNG: Come On Over	£15
70	Success RE 914	Too Late/KINGSTONIANS: You Can't Wine	£25
70	Bullet BU 448	Set Back/SYDNEY'S ALLSTARS: Version II	£30
75	Torpedo TOR 34	Tomorrow's Sun (May Never Shine)/Way Of Life	£20
75	Torpedo TOR 50	Help Up Get Over/All I Have Is Love	£20
76	Third World TW 032	Look Before You Leap/K. SMILEY: Sata	£20
76	Morpheus MOR 1016	Rasta Business/Version	£15
76	Morpheus MOR 1017	Black Kill A Black/Version	£25
77	Golden Age GAM 05	Mr. Cop/Mr. Cop Dub	£15
77	Observer OBMM-1000	Soul On Fire/CHRISTINE: Saturday Night/TYRONE TAYLOR: Sufferation/ In Style (12")	£40
77	GGs GG 040	The Border/Out Of Rome (12", with U BROWN)	£15
78	Observer	Rock On/Murder Observer Style/DENNIS BROWN & DILLINGER: Jah Is Watching/ Hustling (12")	£50
78	DEB DEB 004	Mr Know It All/OSSIE HIBBERT & REVOLUTIONARIES: War Of The Stars (12")	£25
78	Star PTP 1002	Lonely Days/U ROY: Nanny Skank (12")	£15
79	Front Line FLS 12112	Soon Forward/Uncle Joe/Come Off Mi Toe (Feat. Prince Far I) (12")	£15
79	Niagra NIADD 104	Going Down Town/Motherless Children (12")	£20
80	African Museum (no number)	If You See My Mary/Mary's Special (12", blue vinyl)	£20
80	Solomonic SM 002	Sunday Morning/DENNIS BROWN: Running Around (12")	£25
84	Fu Manchu PC 15484	No One But Me/Version (12", p/s)	£15
85	African Museum AF 0050	G.P./Version (12")	£25
86	Greensleeves GRED 230	Mind Ju Dis/Version (12")	£18
88	Greensleeves GRED 221	Rumours/More Rumours (12")	£30
88	Greensleeves GRED 225	Rough Neck/Version (12" with the Mighty Diamonds)	£30
89	Jah Shaka SHAKA 874	Just Infatuation/Just Dub (12")	£15
89	Greensleeves GRED 256	Report To Me/Report To Me (continued) (12")	£30
75	Trojan TRLS 102	IN PERSON (LP)	£15
76	Trojan TRLS 121	ALL I HAVE IS LOVE (LP)	£20
78	Conflict COLP 2002	EXTRA CLASSIC (LP)	£20
78	Burning Sounds BS1010	SLUM - GREGORY ISAACS IN DUB (LP)	£30
78	DEB DEB LP 04	MR ISAACS (LP)	£30

IKE ISAACS
78	Virgin Front Line FL 1020	COOL RULER (LP)	£18
79	Virgin Front Line FL 1044	SOON FORWARD (LP)	£30
80	Shack BITE 200	EXTRA CLASSIC (LP, reissue)	£20
82	Island 9721	NIGHT NURSE (LP, blue vinyl with poster)	£20
83	Burning Sounds BS 1051	SLUM DUB (LP)	£25
83	Pre PREX 1	THE LONELY LOVER (LP)	£20

(see also Tony Brevett)

IKE ISAACS
68	Morgan MR 116P	I LIKE IKE (LP)	£15

ISCA FAYRE
76	Candle CAN 761	THEN AROUND ME YOUNG AND OLD (LP)	£15

JON ISHERWOOD
70	Decca LK/SKL 5051	A LAUGHING CRY (LP)	£15

ISHMAEL UNITED
79	Kingsway 5NIL	Song Of The Last Generation/Crowd Trouble	£20

ISHMAEL & ANDY
73	Myrrh MYR 1005	READY SALTED (LP)	£20

JIMMY ISLE
59	London HLS 8832	Diamond Ring/I've Been Waiting (78)	£70
59	London HLS 8832	Diamond Ring/I've Been Waiting (tri centre)	£20
60	Top Rank JAR 274	Billy Boy/Oh Judy	£15

ISLEY BROTHERS
59	RCA RCA 1149	Shout (Parts 1 & 2) (tri centre)	£30
59	RCA RCA 1149	Shout (Parts 1 & 2) (round centre)	£25
59	RCA RCA 1149	Shout (Parts 1 & 2) (78)	£200
60	RCA RCA 1172	Respectable/I'm Gonna Knock On Your Door	£20
60	RCA RCA 1190	How Deep Is The Ocean/He's Got The Whole World In His Hands	£20
60	RCA RCA 1213	Tell Me Who/Say You Love Me Too	£20
62	Stateside SS 112	Twist And Shout/Spanish Twist	£15
62	Stateside SS 132	Twistin' With Linda/You Better Come Home	£15
63	Stateside SS 218	Nobody But Me/I'm Laughing To Keep From Crying	£20
63	United Artists UP 1034	Tango/She's Gone	£18
64	United Artists UP 1050	Shake It With Me Baby/Stagger Lee	£20
64	Atlantic AT 4010	The Last Girl/Looking For A Love	£45
66	Tamla Motown TMG 555	This Old Heart Of Mine (Is Weak For You)/There's No Love Left (1st press with narrow print on label)	£20
66	Tamla Motown TMG 566	Take Some Time Out For Love/Who Could Ever Doubt My Love	£35
66	Tamla Motown TMG 572	I Guess I'll Always Love You/I Hear A Symphony (1st pressing with "sold subject to" on centre piece)	£25
67	Tamla Motown TMG 606	Got To Have You Back/Just Ain't Enough Love	£20
68	Tamla Motown TMG 652	Take Me In Your Arms (Rock Me A Little While)/Why When Love Is Gone	£30
64	RCA RCX 7149	THE ISLEY BROTHERS (EP)	£80
60	RCA RD 27165	SHOUT (LP, mono)	£60
60	RCA SF 7055	SHOUT (LP, stereo)	£100
64	United Artists ULP 1064	THE FAMOUS ISLEY BROTHERS - TWISTING AND SHOUTING (LP)	£80
66	Tamla Motown TML 11034	THIS OLD HEART OF MINE (IS WEAK FOR YOU) (LP, mono)	£30
66	STML 11034	THIS OLD HEART OF MINE (IS WEAK FOR YOU) (LP, stereo)	£35
68	T. Motown TML 11066	SOUL ON THE ROCKS (LP, mono)	£30
68	T. Motown STML 11066	SOUL ON THE ROCKS (LP, stereo)	£35
69	Major Minor SMLP 59	IT'S OUR THING (LP)	£25
69	T. Motown TML 11112	BEHIND A PAINTED SMILE (LP, mono)	£25
69	T. Motown (S)TML 11112	BEHIND A PAINTED SMILE (LP, stereo)	£22
70	Stateside SSL 10300	THE BROTHERS: ISLEY (LP)	£22
15	Sony 88875043972	THE RCA VICTOR AND T-NECK ALBUM MASTERS 1959-83 (box set, 23-CD, booklet)	£40

ISOLATION
73	Riverside HASLP 2083	ISOLATION (LP, private pressing with insert)	£800

ISOTOPE
74	Gull GULP 1002	ISOTOPE (LP)	£20
74	Gull GULP 1006	ILLUSION (LP)	£20
75	Gull GULP 1017	DEEP END (LP, 1976 on both labels)	£20

(see also Brian Auger, Hugh Hopper)

ISRAELITES
69	Downtown DT 413	Moma Moma/Melody For Two	£25
69	Downtown DT 421	Games People Play/AUDREY: One Fine Day	£25
69	Downtown DT 433	Seven Books/Chucka Beat	£20

(see also Music Doctors)

ISRAEL VIBRATION
78	Harvest HAR 184	The Same Song/Weep And Moan	£15
79	Harvest 12 HAR 5189	Crisis/Crisis Dub (12", feat. Augustus Pablo)	£30
79	Harvest SHSP 4099	THE SAME SONG (LP, black and red Harvest label)	£25
88	RAS RAS 3037	STRENGTH OF MY LIFE (LP)	£40
90	RAS RAS 3054	PRAISES (LP)	£30
90	Greensleeves GREL 148	UNCONQUERED PEOPLE (LP, reissue)	£15

HUGHIE ISSACHAAR
82	House Of Asher HA2	Don't Pretent You Love/Dub (12")	£15

HUGHY ISSACHAR
86 Melody Muzik MM 001   Mountain Rock/ORIGINAL ROCKERS: So Shall It Be (12")................................£50
ITAL MICK
16 System SYSTM 013   Babylon Ways/Dub Ways/Kingly Character/Dub Character (12") £18
ITALS (JAMAICA)
67 Giant GN 8   New Loving (with Soul Brothers)/I Told You Little Girl.................................£40
67 Giant GN 12   Don't Throw It Away/Make Up Your Mind (both with Carib-Beats)..............£60
70 Big Shot BI-561   Put It On/Rasta Isies (as Hitals)..£25
70 Big BG304   Everytime/Version...£15
(see also Alton Ellis, Honeyboy)
ITHACA
73 Merlin HF 6   A GAME FOR ALL WHO KNOW (LP, with insert)....................................£1000
93 Background HBG 01LP   A GAME FOR ALL WHO KNOW (LP, reissue)...£25
(see also Friends, Alice Through The Looking Glass, Agincourt, Tomorrow Come Someday, BBC Radiophonic Workshop)
IT'S A BEAUTIFUL DAY
70 CBS 4933   Soapstone Mountain/Do You Remember The Sun...............................£15
69 CBS 63722   IT'S A BEAUTIFUL DAY (LP, gatefold sleeve) £35
70 CBS 64065   MARRYING MAIDEN (LP)..£30
72 CBS 64314   CHOICE QUALITY STUFF - ANYTIME (LP, insert) £25
IVAN
58 Coral Q 72341   Real Wild Child/Oh, You Beautiful Doll £200
58 Coral Q 72341   Real Wild Child/Oh, You Beautiful Doll (78) £50
(see also Jerry Allison, Crickets)
IVAN D. JUNIORS
63 Oriole CB 1874   Catch You If I Can/On My Mind...£20
IVANS MEADS
65 Parlophone R 5342   A Little Sympathy/The Sins Of A Family £50
66 Parlophone R 5503   We'll Talk About It Tomorrow/The Bottle...£40
IVEYS
68 Apple APPLE 5   Maybe Tomorrow/And Her Daddy's A Millionaire...............................£60
69 Apple APPLE 14   Dear Angie/No Escaping Your Love (unreleased; Europe & Japan only)....£0
68 Apple SAPCOR 8   MAYBE TOMORROW (LP, unissued; Europe & Japan only) £0
92 Apple SAPCOR 8   MAYBE TOMORROW (LP, reissue, gatefold sleeve & bonus 12" [SAPCOR 82]) £25
(see also Badfinger, Pleasure Garden)
IVOR & SHEILA
81 Eron 027   CHANGING TIMES (LP, with insert) £30
JACKIE IVORY
66 Atlantic AT 4075   Hi-Heel Sneakers/Do It To Death £20
65 Atlantic ATL 5046   SOUL DISCOVERY (LP)...£60
65 Atlantic ATL 5046   SOUL DISCOVERY (LP, 1966 reissue) £25
IVORY SUN
70 Jupiter   Another Yesterday/ Rainy Tomorrow/Black Gold £60
IVY
94 Sarah SARAH 91   Wish You Would/Nowhere To Mourn (p/s)...£40
94 Sarah SARAH 92   Avenge/Sound The Deep Waters..£15
IVY LEAGUE
65 Piccadilly NEP 34038   FUNNY HOW LOVE CAN BE (EP) £15
65 Piccadilly NEP 34042   TOSSING AND TURNING (EP) £15
66 Piccadilly NEP 34048   OUR LOVE IS SLIPPING AWAY (EP)...£20
65 Piccadilly NPL 38015   THIS IS THE IVY LEAGUE (LP) £30
(see also Carter-Lewis, White Plains,, Kestrels, One & One, Johnny Shadow, Perry Ford, First Class, Friends, Warm Sensations)
IVY THREE
60 London HLW 9178   Yogi/Was Judy There £15
IZZY POUND
69 Plexium PXM 9   Pumpkin Miny/Na Na Na Na...£40

CLUE J. & HIS BLUES BLASTERS
60 Blue Beat BB 15   Easy Snappin'/Goin' Home (with vocal by Theophilus Beckford)......£15
DAVID J. (& J. WALKERS)
84 GLASS 12032   V For Vendetta: This Viscious Cabaret/V's Theme/Incidental/V's Theme (12" p/s)........£15
83 Situation 2 SIT U 8   ETIQUETTE OF VIOLENCE (LP) £15
85 Glass GLALP 010   CROCODILE TEARS AND THE VELVET COSH (LP)................................£15
90 Beggars Banquet BEGA 112 SONGS FROM ANOTHER SEASON (LP) £15
(see also Bauhaus)
JABBERWOCK
77 MCA MCA 264   Sneakin' Snaky/Fortune Teller £15

JABULA
75	Caroline CA 2004	JABULA (LP)	£20
76	Caroline CA 2009	THUNDER INTO OUR HEARTS (LP)	£15
78	Jabula JBL 2003	AFRIKA AWAKE (LP)	£18

JOY JACINTH
83	Zebratone ZTD 93	Baby Boy/Red Lights (12")	£15

JACK (BERNARD) & BEANSTALKS
69	Supreme SUP 203	Work It Up/Chatty Chatty	£18

(see also Kingstonians)

BILLY JACK (& CIMARONS)
70	Grape GR 3018	Let's Work Together/CORPORATION: Jam Monkey	£15

(see also Candy)

JACKAL (2)
86	Crim. Damage CRI 12-134	Underneath The Arches/Thunder Machine (12", p/s)	£15

(see also Renegade Soundwave)

JACKIE (1)
78	Fashion FAD 002	It's Too Late Baby/Fashion On Fine Style (12")	£20

JACKIE (2)
80	Cha Cha CHAD 28	Who Can I Run To/OVERNIGHT PLAYERS: Dub Cuts (12", yellow vinyl)	£25

JACKIE & BRIDIE
64	Fontana TL 5212	HOLD BACK THE DAWN (LP)	£25
70	Concord CONS 1002	FOLK WORLD OF JACKIE AND BRIDIE (LP)	£15
71	Galliard GAL 4009	THE PERFECT ROUND (LP)	£15

JACKIE & DOREEN
64	Ska Beat JB 168	Every Beat Of My Heart	£20
65	Ska Beat JB 209	The New Vow/Adorable You	£50

(see also Doreen Shaffer, Jackie Opel)

JACKIE (EDWARDS) & MILLIE (SMALL)
65	Island WI 253	This Is My Story/SOUND SYSTEM: Never Again	£45
66	Island WI 265	My Desire/MILLIE: That's How Strong My Love Is	£15
67	Island WIP 6012	In A Dream/Ooh Ooh	£20
67	Island ILP 941	PLEDGING MY LOVE (LP, as Jackie Edwards & Millie Small)	£60
68	Island ILP 963	THE BEST OF JACKIE AND MILLIE VOLUME TWO (LP)	£60
70	Trojan TTL 52	THE BEST OF JACKIE AND MILLIE VOLUME TWO (LP, reissue)	£20
70	Trojan TBL 155	JACKIE & MILLIE (LP)	£40

(see also Jackie Edwards, Millie)

JACKIE AND NICKY
74	Bradleys BRAD 313	Break Out In The Morning/Children Of Love	£15

(see also Jackie Lee (& Raindrops))

JACKIE & ROY
58	Vogue V 9101	You Smell So Good/Let's Take A Walk Around The Block	£20
59	Vogue VE 1-70131	JACKIE AND ROY (EP)	£30
58	Vogue VA 1-60111	JACKIE AND ROY (LP)	£40

DAVID JACKMAN
96	Speed Pig SP 001	TEN CUT (10" clear vinyl, serrated edge, signed, no'd 80 only)	£50

JACKPOTS
69	Sonet SON 2006	Jack In The Box/Henbanes Sacrifice	£25

ALEXANDER JACKSON & TURNKEYS
65	Sue WI 386	The Whip/Tell It Like It Is (actually "Flea Pot"/"Sweetie Lester" by Lala Wilson)	£100

BOBBY JACKSON
10	Jazzman JMANLP 035	BOBBY JACKSON'S THE CAFE EXTRA-ORDINAIRE STORY (LP, reissue)	£20

CHRIS JACKSON
69	Soul City SC 112	I'll Never Forget You/Forever I'll Stay With You	£50
70	444 Label	Since There's No Doubt/We Will Be Together (unissued, acetate only - 2 known copies)	£800
70	Soul City 120	Since There's No Doubt/We Will Be Together (unissued)	£0

CHUCK JACKSON
61	Top Rank JAR 564	I Don't Want To Cry/Just Once	£40
62	Top Rank JAR 607	The Breaking Point/My Willow Tree	£40
62	Stateside SS 102	Any Day Now/The Prophet	£30
62	Stateside SS 127	I Keep Forgettin'/Who's Gonna Pick Up The Pieces	£30
63	Stateside SS 171	Tell Him I'm Not Home/Getting Ready For The Heartbreak	£25
64	Pye International 7N 25247	Beg Me/For All Time	£25
64	Pye International 7N 25276	Any Day Now/The Prophet (reissue)	£20
65	Pye International 7N 25287	Since I Don't Have You/Hand It Over	£100
65	Pye International 7N 25287	Since I Don't Have You/Hand It Over (DJ Copy)	£150
65	Pye International 7N 25301	I Need You/Chuck's Soul Brothers Twist	£20
65	Pye International 7N 25321	If I Didn't Love You/Just A Little Bit Of Your Soul	£25
66	Pye International 7N 25384	Chains Of Love/I Keep Forgettin'	£100
66	Pye International 7N 25384	Chains Of Love/I Keep Forgettin' (DJ copy)	£150
67	Pye International 7N 25439	Shame On Me/Candy	£25
68	Tamla Motown TMG 651	Girls, Girls, Girls/(You Can't Let The Boy Overpower) The Man In You	£30
70	Tamla Motown TMG 729	Honey Come Back/What Am I Gonna Do Without You	£20
75	All Platinum 6146 310	I've Got The Need/Beautiful Woman	£15

85	Kent TOWN 104	Hand It Over/CANDY & KISSES: Mr Creator (withdrawn)	£30
86	Kent 6T2	MELBA MOORE: Magic Touch/CHUCK JACKSON: Little By Little	£20
80s	Inferno SIN 1	Chains Of Love/Good Things Come To Those Who Wait/Hand It Over/Any Day Now	£20
92	Kent 8	What's With This Loneliness/Surf And Soul	£20
66	Pye Intl. NPL 28082	TRIBUTE TO RHYTHM AND BLUES (LP)	£60
68	T. Motown (S)TML 11071	CHUCK JACKSON ARRIVES! (LP, mono/stereo)	£45
69	T. Motown TML 11117	GOIN' BACK TO CHUCK JACKSON (LP, mono)	£50
69	T. Motown STML 11117	GOIN' BACK TO CHUCK JACKSON (LP, stereo)	£50
72	Probe SPB 1084	THROUGH ALL TIMES (LP)	£25
84	Kent 003	MR. EMOTION (LP)	£15
87	Kent KENT 073	A POWERFUL SOUL (LP)	£20

(see also Del[l]-Vikings)

CHUCK JACKSON & MAXINE BROWN
| 65 | Pye International 7N 25308 | Something You Got/Baby Take Me | £20 |
| 65 | Pye Intl. NPL 28091 | SAYING SOMETHING (LP) | £50 |

(see also Maxine Brown, Tammi Terrell)

DAVID JACKSON
| 82 | Butt NOTT 5 | THE LONG HELLO VOLUME 3 (LP) | £20 |

(see also Van Der Graaf Generator)

DEON JACKSON
66	Atlantic AT 4070	Love Makes The World Go Round/You Said You Loved Me	£45
66	Atlantic 584 012	Love Takes A Long Time Growing/Hush Little Baby	£25
68	Atlantic 584 159	Ooh Baby/All On A Sunny Day	£30
76	Contempo CS 9031	Love Makes The World Go Round/I Can't Go On	£25

EARL JACKSON
| 76 | ABC 410 | Soul Self Satisfaction/Looking Thru' The Eyes Of Love (DJ Copy) | £30 |
| 76 | ABC ABC 4110 | Soul Self Satisfaction/Looking Thru' The Eyes Of Love | £20 |

GEORGE JACKSON
| 69 | Capitol CL 15605 | Find 'Em, Fool 'Em And Forget 'Em/My Desires Are Getting The Best Of Me | £25 |

GIDEON JACKSON
| 99 | Conceive CON 001 | Touch Me/Connextion (12", white labels) | £40 |

GORDON JACKSON
69	Marmalade 598 010	Me And My Zoo/A Day At The Cottage	£20
69	Marmalade 598 021	Song For Freedom/Sing To Me Woman	£25
69	Marmalade 608 012	THINKING BACK (LP)	£250
06	Sunbeam SBRLP5001	THINKING BACK (LP, reissue)	£15

(see also Hellions, Jane Relf, Traffic)

HAROLD JACKSON & TORNADOES
| 58 | Vogue V 9105 | Move It On Down The Line Parts 1 & 2 | £100 |
| 58 | Vogue V 9105 | Move It On Down The Line Parts 1 & 2 (78) | £40 |

JACKIE JACKSON
| 74 | T. Motown STML 11249 | JACKIE JACKSON (LP) | £15 |

(see also Jacksons, Jackson 5)

JANET JACKSON
| 93 | Virgin V 2720 | JANET (2-LP, gatefold, inners) | £80 |
| 97 | Virgin V 2860 | VELVET ROPE (2-LP, gatefold, inners) | £100 |

JERRY JACKSON
63	London HLR 9689	Gypsy Eyes/Turn Back	£40
66	Cameo Parkway P 100	It's Rough Out There/I'm Gonna Paint A Picture	£175
66	Cameo Parkway P 100	It's Rough Out There/I'm Gonna Paint A Picture (DJ copy)	£300

JIMMY JACKSON('S ROCK 'N' ROLL SKIFFLE)
57	Columbia DB 3898	California Zephyr/I Shall Not Be Moved	£20
57	Columbia DB 3937	Sittin' In The Balcony/Good Morning Blues	£25
57	Columbia DB 3957	River Line/Lonely Road	£15
58	Columbia SEG 7750	ROCK 'N' SKIFFLE (EP)	£60
58	Columbia SEG 7768	COUNTRY AND BLUES (EP)	£60

J.J. JACKSON (& GREATEST LITTLE SOUL BAND IN THE LAND)
67	Polydor 56718	But It's Alright/Do The Boogaloo	£20
67	Strike JH 329	Come See Me/Try Me	£30
67	Warner Bros WB 2082	Sho Nuff (Got A Good Thing Going)/Here We Go Again	£15
68	Warner Bros WB 2090	Down, But Not Out/Why Does It Take So Long?	£15
68	Warner Bros WB 6029	Courage Ain't Strength/You Do It 'Cause You Wanna	£15
70	RCA RCA 1924	Bow Down To The Dollar/Indian Thing (as J.J's DILEMMA)	£20
67	Strike JLH 104	J.J. JACKSON WITH THE GREATEST LITTLE SOUL BAND (LP)	£40
69	MCA SKA 100	GREATEST LITTLE SOUL BAND (LP)	£25
70	RCA Victor SF 8093	J.J. JACKSON'S DILEMMA (LP)	£30

(see also Greatest Little Soul Band)

LEVI JACKSON
| 71 | Columbia DB 8807 | This Beautiful Day/Don't You Be A Sinner | £100 |
| 71 | Columbia DB 8807 | This Beautiful Day/Don't You Be A Sinner (DJ copy) | £150 |

(see also Solomon King)

MAHALIA JACKSON
| 52 | Vogue LDE 005 | QUEEN OF THE GOSPEL SINGERS (10" LP) | £30 |

MICHAEL JACKSON

SINGLES

79	Epic 12EPC 7763	Don't Stop 'Til You Get Enough/I Can't Help It (12")	£15
82	Epic EPCA 11-2729	The Girl Is Mine (with Paul McCartney)/Can't Get Outta The Rain (picture disc)	£30
83	Epic EPC 2906	GREATEST ORIGINAL HITS: Don't Stop 'Til You Get Enough/ She's Out Of My Life/Off The Wall/Rock With You (EP)	£15
83	Epic TA 3643	Thriller (Album Version)/Thriller (Remix Short Version)/JACKSONS: Things I Do For You (live) (12", 'calendar' p/s)	£50
83	Epic MJ 1 (1-9)	MICHAEL JACKSON'S 9 SINGLES PACK (9 x 7", p/s, each on red vinyl, in PVC foldout wallet)	£40
87	Epic 650 202-6	I Just Can't Stop Loving You (with Siedah Garratt)/Baby Be Mine (12", p/s with poster)	£15
88	Epic 651 389-9	Man In The Mirror (Single Mix)/Man In The Mirror (Instrumental) (Uncut 12", square-shaped picture disc)	£250
88	Epic 651 388-9	Man In The Mirror (Single Mix)/Man In The Mirror (Instrumental) (square-shaped picture disc)	£35
88	Epic 651 546-7	Dirty Diana/Dirty Diana (p/s, with 13" cardboard figure)	£20
88	Epic 652 864-6	Dirty Diana/Dirty Diana (Instrumental)/Bad (Extended Dance Mix With False Fade) (12", with tour poster p/s)	£15
88	Epic MJ 5	THE MICHAEL JACKSON BAD SOUVENIR SINGLES PACK (5 x 7" square picture discs in foldout PVC wallet, with lyric book)	£45
88	Epic 652 844-9	Another Part Of Me/(Instrumental) (p/s, with Bad tour backstage pass)	£25
88	Epic 653 026-0	Smooth Criminal/Smooth Criminal (Instrumental) (pack with 4 postcards)	£20
88	Epic 653 170-6	Smooth Criminal (Extended Dance Mix)/ Smooth Criminal Extended (Dance Mix Dub Mix)/Smooth Criminal (A Capella) (12" with "Moonwalker" advert calendar)	£20
89	Epic 654 672-0	Leave Me Alone/Human Nature (pop-up pack)	£50
89	Epic 654 947-9	Liberian Girl (Edit)/Girlfriend (star mobile foldout card pack)	£20
92	Epic MJ 4 (658 281-1/4)	TOUR SOUVENIR PACK (CD, 4-picture disc, box set with booklet)	£40
97	Epic 665 130 6	Smile/It It Scary (Deep Dish Dark And Scary Remix)/Is It Scary (Eddie's Rub-a-Dub Mix)/Is It Scary (Eddie's Love Mix)/Off The Wall (Junior Vasquez Remix) (12" p/s withdrawn. Beware of counterfeits with poor print quality on label, sleeve and especially the barcode)	£200
03	Epic 674480-8	One More Chance (Album Version)/Billie Jean (album Version) (12" picture disc, numbered)	£15
03	Epic XPR 3744	TWELVES (7 x 12" p/s in box with insert)	£200

ALBUMS

78	Epic S EPC 83468	OFF THE WALL (LP, gatefold)	£20
79	Epic EPC 83458/83468	OFF THE WALL (LP, gatefold sleeve, with 7" picture disc "You Can't Win (Parts 1)/(Part 2)" [S EPC 7135], some with information sheet)	£25
82	Epic EPC 85930	THRILLER (LP, gatefold, insert)	£20
82	Epic EPC 11-85930	THRILLER (LP, picture disc in PVC sleeve)	£30
83	MCA MCA 70000	E.T. - THE EXTRA TERRESTRIAL (LP, box set with booklet & poster, narration & "Someone In The Dark", with music by John Williams)	£30
87	Epic 450 290-8	BAD GIFT PACK (pack, with note pad, highlighter pen & calendar)	£15
87	Epic EPC 450290 1	BAD (LP, gatefold, insert)	£20
87	Epic 450 290-0	BAD (LP, picture disc)	£30
87	Epic 450 290-9	BAD (CD, picture disc, sealed in long PVC blister pack)	£45
87	Epic 450 290-9	BAD (CD, picture disc, unsealed in long PVC blister pack)	£25
91	Epic 465802 1	DANGEROUS (2-LP, inners)	£25
95	Epic EPC 474709 1	HISTORY (3-LP, inners, 52-page booklet)	£70
08	Sony 88697233441	THRILLER (2-LP 25th Anniversary special edition)	£20
09	Sony 88697616541	THIS IS IT (4-LP box set with 36 page book, numbered)	£45

PROMOS

82	Epic XPR 1242	Billie Jean/Rock With You/Burn This Disco Out/Off The Wall/Don't Stop Till You Get Enough/Shake Your Body (Down To The Ground)/Blame It On The Boogie/Thriller/Billie Jean (Disco Mix Club DJ 12", same tracks on both side, 1000 pressed most destroyed at request of Michael Jackson, 6 known copies)	£400
92	Epic XPR 1814	Jam: (More Than Enuff Mix)/(Roger's Club Mix)/(E-Smoov Jazzy Jam) (Atlanta Techno Mix)/(Roger's Underground Mix)/(Silky 12")/(More Than Enuff Dub)/(Maurice's Jammin' Dub Mix)/(Roger's Club Dub)/(Atlanta Techno Dub)/(Roger's Slam Jam Mix)/(Silky Dub)/(A Capella Mix) (12", double pack, black & orange stickered white sleeve)	£15
95	Epic XPR 2184	Scream: (Classic Club Mix)/(DM R&B Extended Mix)/(Def Radio Mix)/ (Naughty Main Mix)/(Naughty Main Mix No Rap)/Dave 'Jam' Hall's Extended Urban Remix)/(Pressurised Dub Part 1)/(Pressurised Dub Part 2)/(Album Version)/(Single Edit No. 2)/(Naughty Pretty-Pella)/(Naughty A Capella) (12" double pack, red title sleeve)	£20
96	Epic XPR 2207	Mj Club Megamix (MJ Mega Remix)/(MJ Urban Megamix) (12", blue & purple title sleeve)	£15
97	Epic XPR 3159	HIStory (Tony Moran's HIStory Lesson)/(Tony Moran's HIStorical Dub) Is It Scary (Eddie's Love Mix)/(Eddie's Rub-A-Dub Mix)/(Eddie's Love Mix) (Radio Edit) (12", white embossed title p/s)	£20
97	Epic XPR 3196	Is It Scary (Deep Dish Dark & Scary Remix)/(Deep Dish Dark & Scary Remix)/ (Deep Dish Double-O-Jazz Dub)/(Radio Edit) (12", black embossed title p/s)	£35
04	Epic YPR 3829	Cheater (Demo)/One More Chance (R Kelly Remix) (12" p/s)	£50

(see also Jackson 5, Paul McCartney, Jacksons)

MILLIE JACKSON

76	Spring 2066 713	A House For Sale/There You Are	£40
72	Mojo 2918 005	MILLIE JACKSON (LP)	£20
74	Polydor 2391 147	CAUGHT UP (LP)	£20
75	Polydor 2391 183	STILL CAUGHT UP (LP)	£20
89	Jive HIP 77	BACK TO THE S..T (LP)	£20

(see also Elton John)

MILT JACKSON

53	Vogue LDE 044	MILT JACKSON AND HIS NEW GROUP (10" LP)	£20
55	Esquire 20-042	MILT JACKSON QUINTET (10" LP)	£20

55	London Jazz LZ-C 14006	**MILT JACKSON QUARTET** (10" LP)	**£20**

(see also Ray Charles, Modern Jazz Quartet, Stanley Turrentine, Miles Davis/Art Blakey, Coleman Hawkins)

PAPA CHARLIE JACKSON

50	Tempo R 30	**Long Gone Lost John/I'm Looking For A Woman Who Knows How To Treat Me Right** (78)	**£15**
60	Heritage R 100	**PAPA CHARLIE JACKSON** (EP) 99 only	**£80**
60	Heritage HLP 1011	**PAPA CHARLIE JACKSON** (LP) 99 only	**£100**

(see also Paramount Allstars, Blind Blake)

POOCH JACKSON

72	Sioux SI 013	**You Just Gotta Get Ready/BROTHER DAN: Django's Valley**	**£15**
72	Sioux SI 017	**King Of The Road/Circles/Mammy Blue**	**£15**
72	Sioux SI 016	**Once Bitten** (with Harry J. Allstars)**/KING REGGAE: Slave Driver**	**£15**

(see also Circles)

PYTHON LEE JACKSON

72	Young Blood YB 3001	**IN A BROKEN DREAM** (LP, featuring Rod Stewart who is not credited on front or rear sleeve)	**£20**

RALPH 'SOUL' JACKSON

69	Atlantic 584258	**'Cause I Love You/Sunshine Of Your Love**	**£30**

SIMONE JACKSON

62	Piccadilly 7N 35087	**Pop Pop Pop Pie/He Ain't Got No Time For Love**	**£15**
63	Piccadilly 7N 35124	**Ain't Gonna Kiss Ya/Slow Motion**	**£15**

TONY JACKSON (& VIBRATIONS)

64	Pye 7N 15685	**Bye Bye Baby/Watch Your Step**	**£25**
64	Pye 7N 15745	**This Little Girl Of Mine/You Beat Me To The Punch**	**£40**
65	Pye 7N 15766	**Love Potion No. 9/Fortune Teller**	**£50**
65	Pye 7N 15876	**Stage Door/That's What I Want** (as Tony Jackson Group)	**£40**
66	CBS 202039	**You're My Number One/Let Me Know** (as Tony Jackson Group)	**£40**
66	CBS 202069	**Never Leave Your Baby's Side/I'm The One She Really Thinks A Lot Of** (solo)	**£40**
66	CBS 202297	**Follow Me/Walk Walk Walk Walk** (solo)	**£60**
66	CBS 202408	**Anything Else You Want/Come On And Stop** (solo)	**£40**
91	Strange Things STZ 5005	**JUST LIKE ME** (LP)	**£15**

(see also Searchers)

TOTLYN JACKSON

66	Airborne NBP 00010	**Cha Cha In Bataseya/Little Boy**	**£40**

VIVIAN JACKSON & THE PROPHETS

78	Roots TS 100	**72 Nation Bow/Ya Be Yoo**	**£50**
78	Nationwide PRO 001	**CHANT DOWN BABYLON KINGDOM** (LP)	**£120**
78	Grove Music GMLP 4	**BEWARE** (LP)	**£40**

(See also Yabby U.)

WALTER JACKSON

65	Columbia DB 7620	**Welcome Home/Blowin' In The Wind**	**£40**
66	Columbia DB 7949	**Tear For Tear/It's An Uphill Climb To The Bottom**	**£75**
66	Columbia DB 7949	**Tear For Tear/It's An Uphill Climb To The Bottom** (DJ copy)	**£125**
66	Columbia DB 8054	**A Corner In The Sun/Not You**	**£30**
67	Columbia DB 8154	**Speak Her Name/They Don't Give Medals** (To Yesterday's Heroes)	**£30**

WANDA JACKSON

59	Capitol CL 15033	**You're The One For Me/A Date With Jerry**	**£20**
59	Capitol CL 15090	**Reaching/I'd Rather Have You**	**£20**
60	Capitol CL 15147	**Let's Have A Party/Cool Love**	**£20**
61	Capitol CL 15176	**Mean Mean Man/Honey Bop**	**£30**
61	Capitol CL 15223	**Right Or Wrong/Funnel Of Love**	**£15**
58	Capitol EAP1 1041	**WANDA JACKSON** (EP)	**£75**
62	Capitol EAP1 20353	**A LITTLE BITTY TEAR** (EP)	**£60**
58	Capitol T 1041	**WANDA JACKSON** (LP)	**£150**
60	Capitol T 1384	**ROCKIN' WITH WANDA** (LP)	**£120**
61	Capitol T 1511	**THERE'S A PARTY GOIN' ON** (LP, mono)	**£80**
61	Capitol (S)T 1511	**THERE'S A PARTY GOIN' ON** (LP, stereo)	**£100**
61	Capitol T 1596	**RIGHT OR WRONG** (LP, mono)	**£50**
61	Capitol (S)T 1596	**RIGHT OR WRONG** (LP, stereo)	**£60**
62	Capitol T 1776	**WONDERFUL WANDA** (LP)	**£30**
64	Capitol T 2030	**TWO SIDES OF WANDA** (LP, mono)	**£50**
64	Capitol (S)T 2030	**TWO SIDES OF WANDA** (LP, stereo)	**£55**
64	Capitol (S)T 2306	**BLUES IN MY HEART** (LP)	**£15**
66	Capitol (S)T 2438	**SINGS COUNTRY SONGS** (LP, black label)	**£15**
67	Capitol (S)T 2606	**SALUTES THE COUNTRY MUSIC HALL OF FAME** (LP, black label)	**£15**
67	Capitol (S)T 2812	**YOU'LL ALWAYS HAVE MY LOVE** (LP)	**£15**
69	Capitol (S)T 2976	**CREAM OF THE CROP** (LP, with Party Timers)	**£15**

JACKSON BROTHERS

59	London HLX 8845	**Tell Him No/Love Me**	**£25**

JACKSON 5

SINGLES

70	Tamla Motown TMG 738	**ABC/The Young Folks** (promo only p/s)	**£60**
71	Tamla Motown TMG 769	**Mama's Pearl/Darling Dear** (promo only p/s)	**£60**
72	Tamla Motown TMG 833	**Lookin' Through The Windows/Love Song** (promo only p/s)	**£15**
73	Tamla Motown TMG 865	**Skywriter/Ain't Nothin' Like The Real Thing** (promo only p/s)	**£20**

MINT VALUE £

74	Lyntone LYN 2639	Talk And Sing Personally To Valentine Readers (33rpm flexidisc free with 'Valentine' magazine)	£15
75	Rice Krispies (no cat. Nos.)	Sugar Daddy/Goin' Back To Indiana/Who's Loving You/Mama's Pearl/ ABC/The Love You Save (6 different Rice Krispies cut-out card discs, price is for each)	£30
80	Motown SPTMG 2	THE MOTOWN 20TH ANNIVERSARY SINGLES BOX (15 x 7")	£30

ALBUMS

70	Tamla Motown TML 11142	DIANA ROSS PRESENTS THE JACKSON 5 (flipback sleeve, mono)	£30
70	Tamla Motown (S)TML 11142	DIANA ROSS PRESENTS THE JACKSON 5 (flipback sleeve, /stereo)	£20
70	Tamla Motown TML 11156	ABC (flipback sleeve, mono, existence unconfirmed)	£40
70	Tamla Motown STML 11156	ABC (flipback sleeve, stereo)	£15
70	Tamla Motown STML 11168	THE JACKSON 5 CHRISTMAS ALBUM (flipback sleeve)	£20
71	Tamla Motown STML 11174	THIRD ALBUM (original with flipback sleeve)	£20
71	Tamla Motown STML 11188	MAYBE TOMORROW	£20
72	Tamla Motown STML 11214	LOOKIN' THROUGH THE WINDOWS	£20
73	Tamla Motown STML 11243	GET IT TOGETHER (with photo insert)	£20
74	Tamla Motown STML 11275	DANCING MACHINE	£15
75	Tamla Motown STML 11290	MOVING VIOLATIONS	£15
77	Tamla Motown TMSP 6004	THE JACKSON 5 ANTHOLOGY (2-LP, original issue)	£15
77	Motown STMX 6006	MOTOWN SPECIAL - THE JACKSON 5	£15
79	MFP MFP 50418	ZIP-A-DEE-DOO-DAH	£15
81	Motown PR 84	JACKSON 5: HISTORY OF MOTOWN (4-LP box set, with 1 Michael Jackson LP)	£30

(see also Michael Jackson, Jacksons)

JACKSON HEIGHTS

72	Vertigo 6059 068	Maureen/Long Time Dying	£25
70	Charisma CAS 1018	KINGS PROGRESS (LP, pink 'scroll' label)	£70
72	Vertigo 6360 067	5TH AVENUE BUS (LP, gatefold sleeve, swirl label)	£250
72	Vertigo 6360 077	RAGAMUFFIN'S FOOL (LP, swirl label, with poster)	£250
72	Vertigo 6360 077	RAGAMUFFIN'S FOOL (LP, swirl label, without poster)	£80
73	Vertigo 6360 092	BUMP'N'GRIND (LP, g/f, laminated cover, 'spaceship label')	£60

(see also Nice)

JACKSONS

81	Epic EPC A 1294	Walk Right Now/Your Ways (picture disc)	£15
84	Epic WA 4431	State Of Shock/Your Ways (7" picture disc)	£15
79	Epic S XPR 1207	EPIC HITS FROM THE JACKSONS & MICHAEL JACKSON (LP, promo only)	£20
84	Epic EPC 86303	VICTORY (LP, picture disc)	£35
85	Epic SAI 7561	A TASTE OF VICTORY (LP, picture disc, promo only via Kelloggs offer)	£60

(see also Jackson 5, Michael Jackson)

JACKSON SISTERS (1)

73	Mums SMUM 1829	I Believe In Miracles/Day In The Blue	£50
87	Urban URBX 4	I Believe In Miracles/Boy You're Dynamite (12", p/s)	£20
87	Urban URBX 4	I Believe in Miracles/MACEO & THE MACS: Across The tracks/URBAN ALL STARS: It All Began In Africa (12" promo)	£25

JACK THE LAD

| 74 | Charisma CAS 1085 | IT'S JACK THE LAD (LP, small 'Mad Hatter' label) | £15 |
| 74 | Charisma CAS 1094 | OLD STRAIGHT TRACK (LP, with lyric sheet, Charsima inner) | £15 |

(see also Lindisfarne)

JACKY

| 68 | Philips SBL 7851 | WHITE HORSES (LP) | £35 |

(see also Raindrops, Jackie Lee, Emma Rede)

DEBBIE JACOBS

| 79 | MCA MCF 3019 | UNDERCOVER LOVER (LP) | £15 |

DICK JACOBS (& HIS ORCHESTRA)

57	Vogue Coral Q 72245	The Big Beat/The Tower Trot	£15
57	Vogue Coral Q 72260	Rock-a-billy Gal/The Golden Strings	£15
57	Vogue Coral LVA 9076	THE SKIFFLE SOUND (LP, as Dick Jacobs & His Skiffle Group)	£30
59	Coral LVA 9102	THEMES FROM HORROR MOVIES (LP)	£25

HANK JACOBS

| 64 | Sue WI 313 | So Far Away/Monkey, Hips And Rice | £40 |

JACQUELINE & BRIDIE

| 64 | Fontana TL 5212 | HOLD BACK THE DAWN (LP) | £20 |

(see also Jackie & Bridie)

CHUCK JACQUES & LYNN TAITT & COMETS

| 67 | Ska Beat JB 264 | Dial 609/VIBRATORS & TOMMY McCOOK & COMETS: Wait For Me | £20 |

(see also Wilbert Francis & Vibrators)

JADE

| 70 | DJM DJS 227 | Alan's Song/Amongst Anemones | £15 |
| 70 | DJM DJLPS 407 | FLY ON STRANGE WINGS (LP, gatefold sleeve) | £200 |

JADE WARRIOR

72	Vertigo 6059 069	The Demon Trucker/Snake	£15
71	Vertigo 6360 033	JADE WARRIOR (LP, gatefold sleeve, swirl label)	£200
71	Vertigo 6360 062	RELEASED (LP, multi-poster sleeve, small swirl label)	£500
72	Vertigo 6360 079	LAST AUTUMN'S DREAM (LP, gatefold sleeve, swirl label)	£175
74	Island ILPS 9290	FLOATING WORLD (LP, textured sleeve, pink rim palm tree label)	£30
75	Island ILPS 9318	WAVES (LP, pink rim palm tree label)	£20
76	Island ILPS 9393	KITES (LP)	£18

79	Butt BUTT 001	REFLECTIONS (LP, lyric inner)	£18

(see also July, Joe O'Donnell)

JADIS

| 90 | Back Beat 004-12 | THE JADIS ALBUM (LP, numbered) | £15 |

JAFFREY

| 76 | Tank | ALICE AT JAFFREY (LP) | £100 |

CHRIS JAGGER

| 73 | GM GML 1003 | CHRIS JAGGER (LP) | £15 |

MICK JAGGER

70	Decca F 13067	Memo From Turner/Natural Magic (in export p/s)	£40
70	Decca F 13067	Memo From Turner/Natural Magic	£15
70	United Artists UAS 29108	NED KELLY (LP, various artists soundtrack, only 1 Jagger track)	£30
70	Warner Bros WS 2554	PERFORMANCE (LP, first pressing, orange label, soundtrack)	£40
70	Warner Bros WS 2554	PERFORMANCE (LP, second pressing, green label, soundtrack)	£30
93	Atlantic 7567 82436-1	WANDERING SPIRIT (LP)	£50
01	Virgin 7243 8 11288 2 4	GODDESSINTHDOORWAY (2-LP)	£50

(see also Rolling Stones)

JAGS (2)

| 80 | Island WIP 6666 | I Never Was A Beach Boy/Tune Into Heaven (p/s) | £18 |

JAGUAR

81	Heavy Metal HEAVY 10	Back Street Woman/Chasing The Dragon (p/s)	£40
82	Neat NEAT 16	Axe Crazy/War Machine (p/s)	£20
83	Neat NEAT 1007	POWER GAMES (LP, some on purple vinyl)	£30
83	Neat NEAT 1007	POWER GAMES (LP, black vinyl)	£18
84	Roadrunner RR 9851	THIS TIME (LP)	£15

JAGUARS

| 63 | Impression IMP 101 | Opus To Spring/The Beat (1,000 only) | £35 |
| 65 | Contest RGJ 152 | We'll Live On Happily/Now You Wonder Why | £300 |

(see also Dave Mason)

JAH BUNNY

| 80 | White Label | DUBBS INTERNATIONAL (LP) | £40 |

JAH DAVE

| 85 | Solid Groove SG 019 | Informer/RANKING REUBEN: Taken Away (12") | £40 |

JAH ELEMENT

| 86 | Jah Element JE 001 | Jah Alone/Summertime (12") | £35 |

JAH FATTA & THE BLACK BROTHERS

| 79 | Rite Sound RS DD 002 | Free Rasta Free/BLACK BROTHER ALL STARS: Free Dub (12") | £60 |

JAH FISH

| 72 | Grape GR 3034 | Vampire Rock/MOD STARS: El-Sisco Rock | £20 |

JAH FRANKIE JONES

| 77 | Third World TWS 916 | SATTA & PRAISE JAH (LP) | £45 |

JAH FREE

| 93 | Jah Free | Lightning Clap/Lightning Dub/Jubilation/Jubilation Dub (12") | £25 |

JAH GLEN

| 76 | Love 0021 | Jah Jah Bring Everything/RICHARD MCDONALD: Natty Lead The Way | £25 |

(see also Glenmore Brown)

JAH GLOBE

| 84 | Pyramid PAD 002 | More People Are Walking/Keep It In Reality (12", with the Pyramid Posse) | £25 |

JAH LARRY

| 79 | Charmers LP 10 | STAR LORD (LP) | £20 |

JAH LION

83	Congo COS 2	Melody For Negus/Negus Dub	£30
76	Island ILPS 9386	COLUMBIA COLLY (LP)	£40
83	Kongo KLP 001	PRAISE JAH (LP)	£100

(see also Jah Lloyd)

JAH LLOYD

74	DIP PL DL 1001	HERBS OF DUB...MORE HERBS (LP)	£80
78	Virgin Frontline FL 1005	THE HUMBLE ONE (LP)	£25
79	Virgin Frontline FL 1031	BLACK MOSES (LP)	£15
79	His Majesty MH 1003	DREAD LION DUB (LP)	£40
79	His Majesty MH 1004	REGGAE STICK (LP)	£30

(see also Jah Lion)

JAH PALM

| 79 | Soul & Fire SF 7 | Cumbaya/Version (12") | £30 |
| 85 | Soul & Fire SF4 | ALL CREATURE (LP) | £60 |

JAH RUBY

| 77 | Dynamic DYLP 3011 | DREAD AFFAIR (LP) | £25 |

JAH SHAKA

82	Jah Shaka 821	Revelation 18/Revelation Dub (12", red vinyl)	£20
82	Jah Shaka 823	Jah Children (with Sister Pat)/SHAKA RIDIM SECTION : Jah Works (12")	£35
82	Jah Shaka 828	Lion Youth/MAD PROFESSOR : Beyond The Realms (12")	£20
82	Jah Shaka LP 824	THE COMMANDMENTS OF DUB (LP)	£25

MINT VALUE £

82	Rough Trade ROUGH 50	COMMANDMENTS OF DUB (LP)	£18
83	Jah Shaka 833	REVELATION SONGS (LP)	£15
84	Jah Shaka 841	COMMANDMENTS OF DUB PART 2 (LP)	£15
84	Jah Shaka 845	KINGS MUSIC (VOCALS AND DUBS) (LP)	£18
84	Jah Shaka 848	MESSAGE FROM AFRICA (LP)	£15
84	Ariwa SALP 84	JAH SHAKA MEETS MAD PROFESSOR (LP)	£20
85	Jah Shaka 847	COMMANDMENTS OF DUB PART 3 (LP)	£15
85	Jah Shaka 849	JAH SHAKA MEETS PEPPER IN ADDIS ABABA STUDIOS (LP)	£20
85	Jah Shaka 850	JAH SHAKA MEETS ASWAD (LP)	£15
85	Jah Shaka 851	DUB ALMIGHTY - COMMANDMENTS OF DUB VOLUME 4 (LP)	£15
85	Jah Shaka 856	JAH DUB CREATOR (LP)	£15
86	Jah Shaka 860	DELIVERANCE - COMMANDMENTS OF DUB 6 (LP)	£15
86	Jah Shaka 867	WARRIOR - COMMANDMENTS OF DUB 7 (LP)	£15
88	Jah Shaka 777	MUSIC MESSAGE (LP)	£15
89	Jah Shaka 887	DISCIPLES (LP)	£20
89	Mango MPLM 1001	PRESENTS DUB MASTERS VOL. 1 (LP)	£15
90	Jah Shaka SHAK 872	CORONATION DUB (LP)	£20
91	Original OMLP 021	SENSI DUB VOLUME 5 (LP, with The Revolutionaries)	£20
92	Jah Shaka SHAKA 924	DISCIPLES PART 2 - ADDIS ABABA (LP)	£15
92	Jah Shaka SHAKA 923	NEW TESTAMENTS OF DUB PART 1 (LP)	£15
93	Jah Shaka SHAKA 936	NEW TESTAMENTS OF DUB CHAPTER 2 (LP)	£15

JAH SHAKA VS FATMAN
80	Live & Love LP 10	LIVE (LP)	£30

JAH STITCH
75	Third World TWS 401	NO DREAD CAN'T DEAD (LP)	£30
78	Cancer CANSLP 002	MY PRECIOUS LOCKS (LP)	£25
78	Third World TWLP 701	WATCH YOUR STEP YOUTHMAN (LP)	£20

JAH THOMAS
78	Greensleeves GREL 3	STOP YU LOAFIN' (LP)	£25
80	Daddy Kool DKLP 16	DANCE HALL STYLEE (LP)	£25
83	Silver Camel SCLP 03	DANCE HALL CONNECTION (LP)	£15

JAH WALTON
81	Music Force MFLP 02	TOUCH HERE WHERE SHE WANT IT MOST (LP)	£80

JAH WARRIOR
96	Jah Warrior JW701	Babylon Shall Fall/Tumble Down Dub	£20
96	Jah Warrior JWD 003	Judgement Day/Conquering Lion (12")	£20
96	Jah Warrior JWD 004	Zulu/Equal Rights (12")	£15
96	Jah Warrior JWLP 005	AFRICAN TRIBES DUB (LP)	£15

JAH WOBBLE
83	Lago LAGO4	INVADERS OF THE HEART EP (12", p/s)	£15
80	Virgin V 2158	THE LEGEND LIVES ON (LP)	£18
91	Oval OVLP601	RISING ABOVE BEDLAM (LP)	£20
94	Island ILSD 8044	HEAVEN & EARTH (2-LP)	£30

JAH WOBBLE, THE EDGE & HOLGER CZUKAY
83	Island IMA 1	SNAKE CHARMER (LP)	£20

(see also Joolz, Public Image Ltd, The Edge, Orb, Can)

JAH WOOSH
76	Sunshot SS002	Religious Dread/Religious Dub	£15
76	Attack ATT 8124	I'm Alright/Version	£18
78	Grove Music GMDM 7	Pay Them Dues/Diverse Doctrine (with Ras Ibuna) (12")	£20
78	Freedom Sounds FSD 001	Ales Skank/Different Style (12")	£15
79	Yard International YI 02	Jah Is The Ruler/Ruling Power/Jammys At The Control (12")	£30
74	Cactus CTLP 103	JAH WOOSH (LP)	£30
76	Student STULP 1003	CHALIS BLAZE (LP)	£30
76	Trojan TRLS 133	DREADLOCKS AFFAIR (LP)	£15
76	Black Wax WAX LP2	PSALMS OF WISDOM (LP)	£100
76	Cactus CTLP 116	JAH JAH DEY DEY (LP)	£25
77	K&B KBLP 002	LICK HIM WITH THE DUSTBIN (LP)	£25
78	Trojan TRLS 157	RELIGIOUS DREAD (LP)	£30
79	Creation Rebel CRBLP900	MARIJUANA WORLD TOUR (LP)	£25
79	Dread & Dread 002	GATHERING ISRAEL (LP, multi-coloured vinyl)	£35
90	Reggae Collectors RCLP 338	JAH WOOSH (LP, reissue)	£15

JAHFA CULTURE & THE OFFBEAT POSSE
86	Jah Tubbys JT 017	Listen To We/Listen Mix (12")	£175

JAHMA
97	Groove Yard GYARD 13	KEEP ON WALKING EP (12")	£30

JAIDEV
99	Saregama CDF 131167	THE GOLDEN COLLECTION (2CD)	£30

JAILHOUSE RECIPES
89	First Strike FS 01	ENERGY IN AN EMPTY TANK WORLD (LP)	£15

JAKE & FAMILY JEWELS
70	Polydor 2425 027	JAKE AND THE FAMILY JEWELS (LP)	£15

JAKLIN
69	Stable SLE 8003	JAKLIN (LP, laminated sleeve, black/silver labels)	£400

JAKOB
78	SRTS 78 CUS 152	I Am A Child/Day By Day	£25

JAKSZYK FRIPP AND COLLINS
11	Panegyric KCLP 21	A SCARCITY OF MIRACLES (A KING CRIMSON PROJEKT) (LP, gatefold, insert, 200g)	£60

(see also King Crimson)

(THE) JAM
SINGLES : ORIGINAL SINGLES
73	Fanfare	Taking My Love (From Me)/Blueberry Rock (acetate)	£5000
73	Fanfare	Some Kinda Lovin'/Making My Way Back Home (acetate 6 copies only)	£5000
75	Fanfare	When I Needed You/Please Don't Treat Me Bad/Taking My Love/Again (acetate)	£5000
78	Polydor 2059 054	David Watts/"A" Bomb In Wardour Street (1st pressing, double-A-sided 7"; A-side songwriter miscredited as "Ray Davis" without an "e")	£15
78	Polydor POSP 8 (2059 068)	Down In The Tube Station At Midnight/So Sad About Us/The Night (7"; misprinted with erroneous B-side ref. to All Mod Cons)	£15

SINGLES : REISSUES & RETROSPECTIVE SINGLES
97	Polydor 5715987	The Bitterest Pill (I Ever Had To Swallow)/The Butterfly Collector	£20
06	Polydor 9831170	THE SINGLES 1977-79 (9 x 7" box set)	£80
06	Polydor 9831404	THE SINGLES1980-82 (9 x 7" box set)	£80
08	Genesis Publications (No Cat. No.)	FANFAREEP: In The City/Time For Truth/So Sad About Us/Sounds From The Street (12", 2000 only, this price with A Thousand Things book)	£300
16	Secret S 732	Art School (1-sided, 100 only, numbered each with unique sleeve)	£75

ALBUMS
77	Polydor 2383 447	IN THE CITY (LP)	£25
77	Polydor 2383 475	THIS IS THE MODERN WORLD (LP)	£25
78	Polydor POLD 5008	ALL MOD CONS (LP, inner)	£25
79	Polydor POLD 5028	SETTING SONS (LP, embossed sleeve, sticker on rear, inner, insert)	£20
80	Polydor POLD 5035	SOUND AFFECTS (LP)	£20
80	Polydor 2683074	IN THE CITY/THIS IS THE MODERN WORLD (2-LP, gatefold)	£20
82	Polydor POLD 5075	DIG THE NEW BREED (LP, die-cut cover)	£15
82	Polydor POLD 5055	THE GIFT (LP, initial copies in pink/white striped paper bag)	£40
82	Polydor POLD 5055	THE GIFT (LP)	£20
83	Polydor SNAP 1/ SNAPL 45	SNAP! (2-LP, gatefold, with bonus 7" EP: Live! Wembley Arena 2 & 3.12.82 [SNAPL 45])	£40
83	Polydor SNAP 1	SNAP! (2-LP)	£15
91	Polydor 8495541	GREATEST HITS (LP)	£25
91	Receiver RRLP 141	LIVE AT THE ROXY (LP, unreleased, white label test pressings exist with printed proof sleeve shelved before release as the recording was actually only half a show from the 100 club 11/9/77)	£500
92	Polydor 513 177-1	EXTRAS (2-LP, single sleeve with picture inners)	£100
93	Polydor 519 667-1	LIVE JAM (2-LP, single sleeve with picture inners)	£100
96	Polydor 531 493-1	THE JAM COLLECTION (2-LP, single sleeve, picture inners)	£75
02	Simply Vinyl SVLP 108	ALL MOD CONS (LP, 180g vinyl, PVC sleeve, 2002)	£18
02	Simply Vinyl SVLP 209	SETTING SONS (LP, 180g vinyl, PVC sleeve, 2002)	£18
02	Polydor 5897811	THE SOUND OF THE JAM (2-LP)	£80
12	Polydor/UMC 0602537185955	COPENHAGEN APRIL 1982 (LP)	£100
14	Polydor/UMC 0602537946983	LIVE AT THE BRIGHTON CENTRE DECEMBER 1979 (2-LP)	£150
15	Polydor/UMC 4747449	LIVE AT THE NEWCASTLE CITY HALL 28TH OCTOBER 1980 (2-LP)	£125
16	Polydor/UMC 0602547930569	LIVE AT THE MUSIC MACHINE 2ND MARCH 1978 (2-LP)	£35
16	Polydor/UMC 0602549726685	LIVE AT THE 100 CLUB 11TH SEPTEMBER 1977 (2-LP)	£80
16	Polydor/UMC 5705857	ABOUT THE YOUNG IDEA - THE VERY BEST OF THE JAM (3-LP)	£30
16	Polydor/UMC 0602547930620	LIVE AT READING UNIVERSITY 16TH FEBRUARY 1979 (2-LP)	£70
17	Polydor/UMC 602557141092	LIVE AT THE HAMMERSMITH PALAIS 14TH DECEMBER 1981 (2-LP)	£50
17	Polydor/UMC 0602557141122	LIVE AT THE WEMBLEY ARENA 2ND DECEMBER 1982 (2-LP)	£60
19	Polydor/UMC SNAP 1/ 7752702	SNAP! (2-LP, with 7")	£30

PROMOS
78	Polydor 2059 054DJ	David Watts/'A' Bomb In Wardour Street (p/s, with Ray Davies spelt as Davis in credits)	£125
81	WEA SAM 144	4-Track white label EP featuring Little Boy Soldiers as well as tracks by the Beat, Bad Manners and the Clash)	£200
82	Polydor POSP 400	Precious (1-sided 7", company sleeve)	£50
82	Polydor DEN 1	Town Called Malice (Live at Hammersmith Palais 14.12.81)/ Precious (Extended Version) (12", white label promo)	£30
82	Polydor PODJ 54	Beat Surrender (Censored)/Shopping (7", radio promo)	£20
82	Polydor POSPX 540	Beat Surrender/Shopping/Move On Up/Stoned Out Of My Mind/War (12", white label promo)	£15
83	Polydor LEE 1	Medley of Jam Songs to promote SNAP LP. 1-sided, plain white label)	£60
83	Polydor SNAPL 45	LIVE! WEMBLEY ARENA (bonus Snap! EP, white label promo)	£30
97	Polydor 2058 266/	In The City (1-sided 7", "20th anniversary party invite", co. sleeve; some copies with 'tax disc'-style card invite (ADMITS 1)	£40
97	Polydor 2058 266/ ADMITS 1	In The City (1-sided 7", "20th anniversary party invite", co. sleeve; some copies with 'tax disc'-style card invite (ADMITS 1)	£30

MISPRESSINGS
78	Polydor 2058 995	News Of The World/Aunties And Uncles (Impulsive Youths)/ Innocent Man (plays B-side on both sides)	£40

MINT VALUE £

78	Polydor POSP 8	**Down In The Tube Station At Midnight/So Sad About Us/The Night** (A-side plays John Travolta's "Sandy")	£30
78	Polydor POSP 6	**Sandy/Can't Let You Go** (by John Travolta, B-side mispressed with "So Sad About Us")	£30
79	Polydor POSP 69	**When You're Young/Smithers-Jones** (p/s, plays B-side both sides)	£40
82	Polydor POSP 400	**Town Called Malice/Precious** (7", both sides play "Precious")	£30

FLEXIDISCS

80	Lyntone (no cat. no.)	**When You're Young** (live) (1-sided fan club flexi)	£25
80	Lyntone LYN 9048	**Boy About Town/Pop Art Poem** (hard vinyl white label test pressing, same tracks both sides, without mailer, 1980)	£60
80	Lyntone LYN 9048	**Boy About Town/Pop Art Poem** (hard vinyl white label test pressing, same tracks both sides, with mailer, 1980)	£80
82	Lyntone (no cat. no.)	**Tales From The Riverbank** (re-recorded) (1-sided fan club flexi	£15

(see also Style Council, Paul Weller, Time U.K., Sharp)

JAMAICA BAND

73	Action ACT 4611	**Sticky Fingers Part 1/Part 2**	£20

JAMAICA FATS

66	Blue Beat BB 368	**Jacqueline/Please Come Home** (actually by Al T. Joe & Celestials)	£22

(see also Al T. Joe)

JAMAICA JUBILEE STOMPERS

67	Amusicon AMU 1002	**Give Your Love To Me/I Cry To My Heart**	£15

JAMAICAN ACTIONS

68	Coxsone CS 7070	**Catch The Quinella/JACKIE MITTOO: Songbird**	£100

JAMAICAN FOUNDATIONS

68	Coxsone CS 7036	**Take It Cool/VICEROYS: Try Hard To Leave**	£200

JAMAICANS

66	Doctor Bird DB 1109	**Cool Night/Ma And Pa**	£75
67	Trojan TR 007	**Dedicated To You/The Things I Said To You**	£35
67	Treasure Isle TI 7007	**Things You Say You Love/I've Got A Pain**	£35
67	Treasure Isle TI 7012	**Baba Boom** (Festival Song 1967) (actually by Baba Boom)/ **TOMMY McCOOK & SUPERSONICS: Real Cool**	£25
67	Treasure Isle TI 7037	**Peace And Love/Woman Gone Home**	£35
69	Escort ES 806	**Early In The Morning/Mr. Lonely**	£15

(see also Norris Weir & Jamaicans, Tommy Cowan)

JAMAICAN SHADOWS

67	Coxsone CS 7005	**HUGH GODFREY : Have Mercy/Blending Love**	£65
69	Upsetter US 320	**Dirty Dozen** (actually by Upsetters)**/Crying Too Long**	£40

JAMAICA'S OWN VAGABONDS

64	Decca DFE 8588	**BEHOLD** (EP)	£30
64	Decca LK 4617	**SKA TIME** (LP)	£50
70	Decca Eclipse ECM 7028	**SKA TIME** (LP, reissue)	£20

(see also Vagabonds, Jimmy James & Vagabonds)

AHMED JAMAL

59	London Jazz LTZ-M 15162	**BUT NOT FOR ME : AHMED JAMAL AT THE PERSHING** (LP)	£18
59	London Jazz LTZ-M 15170	**AHMED JAMAL** (LP)	£18
62	Pye Jazz NJL 38	**ALHAMBRA** (LP)	£15
62	Pye Jazz NJL 47	**ALL OF YOU** (LP)	£15
63	Pye Jazz NJL 52	**POINCIANA** (LP)	£15

JAMES

16	Fontana 4760131	**THE GREENPEACE PALACE CONCERT** (23 NOVEMBER 1992) (2-LP, clear vinyl)	£60
85	Factory FAC 119	**Hymn From A Village/If Things Were Perfect** (p/s)	£15
86	Sire JIM 3T	**Chain Mail/Uprising/Hup Springs** (12", p/s)	£15
86	Sire JIM 4	**So Many Ways/Withdrawn** (p/s)	£25
86	Sire JIM 4T	**So Many Ways/Just Hipper/Withdrawn** (12", p/s)	£15
89	Rough Trade ONEMAN 1LP	**ONE MAN CLAPPING** (LP, with inner sleeve)	£15
93	Fontana 5149431	**LAID** (LP, with mailing card insert)	£45
93	Fontana 5149431	**LAID** (LP, without mailing card insert)	£40
94	Fontana 5228271	**WAH WAH** (2-LP)	£40
97	Fontana 534 3541	**WHIPLASH** (LP)	£80
03	Simply Vinyl SVLP 158	**LAID** (2-LP, reissue)	£25
12	Universal 2753129	**THE GATHERING SOUND** (12", 3-CD, DVD, memory stick, book, badges, stickers, signed art print, 500 only box set)	£200

B.B. JAMES

70	Upsetter US 328	**Consider Me/Consider Me Version**	£20

BOB JAMES

76	CTI 6063	**THREE** (LP, gatefold)	£20

BRIAN JAMES (2)

82	Illegal ILS 0026	**Why? Why? Why?/When Did I Find A Girl Like You** (p/s)	£30

(see also The Damned)

CALVIN JAMES

65	Columbia DB 7516	**Some Things You Never Get Used To/Remember**	£25

DAVID JAMES

69	Crystal CR 7008	**Nothing Left To Lose/Go With The Times**	£25

DES JAMES

67	Fontana TF 847	**My Au Pair/City Street**	£40

DICK JAMES
56	Parlophone MSP 6199	Robin Hood/The Ballad Of Davy Crockett...........£15

ELMORE JAMES
64	Sue WI 335	Dust My Blues/Happy Home (as Elmore James & Broom Dusters) £50
65	Sue WI 383	It Hurts Me Too/Bleeding Heart...........£40
65	Sue WI 392	Knocking At Your Door/Calling The Blues (B-side actually by Junior Wells & Earl Hooker)...........£120
66	Sue WI 4007	I Need You/Mean Mistreating Mama £40
65	Sue ILP 918	THE BEST OF ELMORE JAMES (LP) £80
65	Sue ILP 927	THE ELMORE JAMES MEMORIAL ALBUM (LP) £80
68	Blue Horizon 7-63204	TOUGH (LP, with 4 tracks by John Brim) £70
68	Bell MBLL/SBLL 104	SOMETHING INSIDE OF ME (LP) £45
68	Ember EMB 3397	THE LATE FANTASTICALLY GREAT ELMORE JAMES (LP) £25
70	United Artists UAS 29109	THE LEGEND OF ELMORE JAMES (LP)...........£50
70	Blue Horizon 7-66230	TO KNOW A MAN (2-LP)...........£75
73	Polydor 2383 200	COTTON PATCH HOTFOOTS (LP, shared with Walter Horton)...........£20
75	DJM DJLMD 8008	ALL THEM BLUES (2-LP) £18

ETTA JAMES
60	London HLM 9139	All I Could Do Was Cry/Tough Mary...........£50
60	London HLM 9234	My Dearest Darling/Girl Of My Dreams £30
61	Pye International 7N 25079	At Last/I Just Want To Make Love To You £50
61	Pye International 7N 25080	Trust In Me/Anything To Say You're Mine £20
61	Pye International 7N 25113	Dream/Fool That I Am £20
62	Pye International 7N 25131	Something's Got A Hold On Me/Waiting For Charlie To Come Home £40
62	Pye International 7N 25162	Stop The Wedding/Street Of Tears £20
63	Pye International 7N 25205	Pushover/I Can't Hold It In Any More...........£25
65	Sue WI 359	Roll With Me Henry/Good Rockin' Daddy £60
67	Chess CRS 8052	I Prefer You/I'm So Glad (I Found Love In You)...........£20
67	Chess CRS 8063	Tell Mama/I'd Rather Go Blind £25
67	Chess CRS 8069	Security/I'm Gonna Take What He's Got £15
68	Chess CRS 8076	I Got You Babe/I Worship The Ground You Walk On...........£15
68	Chess CRS 8082	You Got It/Fire £15
72	Chess 6145 016	Tell Mama/I'd Rather Go Blind/I Found A Love...........£15
85	Kent 6T1	MARY LOVE: Hey Stoney Face/IKETTES: It's Been So Long/ETTA JAMES: Wallflower £20
65	Chess CRL 4502	ETTA JAMES ROCKS THE HOUSE (LP)...........£75
67	Chess CRL 4524	AT LAST (LP) £70
68	Ember EMB 3390	THE SOUL OF ETTA JAMES (LP) £50
68	Chess CRL 4536	TELL MAMA (LP) £40
73	Chess 6671 003	PEACHES (2-LP) £25

(see also Etta & Harvey)

ETTA JAMES & SUGAR PIE DESANTO
65	Chess CRS 8025	Do I Make Myself Clear/Somewhere Down The Line...........£30

(see also Sugar Pie DeSanto)

GARY JAMES
68	Polydor 56134	Nicole/You're Gone £20
67	Polydor S6208	Teddy Bear/In The Rain £15

JASON JAMES
67	CBS 2705	Miss Pilkington's Maid/Count Me Out £30

JERRY JAMES & BANDITS
64	Solar SRP 101	Sweet Little Sixteen/Three Steps To Heaven £15

JESSE JAMES
54	Vocalion V 1037	Southern Casey Jones/Lonesome Day Blues (78)...........£20

JIMMY JAMES (& THE VAGABONDS)
62	Dice CC 4	Bewildered And Blue/I Don't Want To Cry (solo)...........£20
63	R&B JB 112	Jump Children/Tell Me (solo)...........£25
64	Black Swan WI 437	Thinking Of You/Shirley (solo) £30
65	Columbia DB 7653	Shoo Be Doo You're Mine/We'll Never Stop Loving You £20
66	Ska Beat JB 242	Your Love/Someday (solo) £18
66	Piccadilly 7N 35298	I Feel Alright/I Wanna Be Your Everything (p/s) £75
66	Piccadilly 7N 35298	I Feel Alright/I Wanna Be Your Everything £30
66	Piccadilly 7N 35320	Hi Diddley Dee Dum Dum (It's A Good Good Feelin')/Come To Me Softly £20
66	Piccadilly 7N 35331	This Heart Of Mine/I Don't Wanna Cry (p/s) £100
66	Piccadilly 7N 35331	This Heart Of Mine/I Don't Wanna Cry...........£75
66	Piccadilly 7N 35349	Ain't Love Good, Ain't Love Proud/Don't Know What I'm Gonna Do £20
71	Trojan TR 7806	Help Yourself/Why £25
72	Stateside SS 2209	A Man Like Me/Survival £15
72	Stateside SS 2209	A Man Like Me/Survival (DJ copy) £35
75	Pye 7N 45472	Hey Girl/I Am Somebody £50
66	Piccadilly NEP 34053	JIMMY JAMES AND THE VAGABONDS (EP) £40
66	Piccadilly NPL 38027	THE NEW RELIGION (LP) £40
68	Pye N(S)PL 18231	OPEN UP YOUR SOUL (LP) £25

JIMMY JAMES & THE VAGABONDS/ALAN BOWN SET
67	Pye N(S)PL 18156	LONDON SWINGS - LIVE AT THE MARQUEE CLUB (LP, 1 side each) £30

(see also Vagabonds, Jamaica's Own Vagabonds, Alan Bown Set)

MINT VALUE £

JOHN JAMES
70	Transatlantic TRA 219	MORNING BRINGS THE LIGHT (LP)	£30
71	Transatlantic TRA 242	JOHN JAMES (LP)	£20
76	Kicking Mule SNKF 128	DESCRIPTIVE GUITAR INSTRUMENTALS (LP)	£15
78	Kicking Mule SNKF 136	LIVE IN CONCERT (LP)	£18
84	Stoptime STOP 101	ACOUSTICA ECLECTICA (LP, signed)	£35
84	Stoptime STOP 101	ACOUSTICA ECLECTICA (LP)	£20

JONI JAMES
54	MGM MGM-D 127	LET THERE BE LOVE (10" LP)	£15

JOSE JAMES
08	Brownsville BWOOD026LP	THE DREAMER (LP)	£35

NICKY JAMES (MOVEMENT)
63	Pye 7N 15560	My Colour Is Blue/Take Me Back	£80
65	Columbia DB 7747	Stagger Lee/I'm Hurtin' Inside (as Nicky James Movement)	£30
68	Philips BF 1635	Would You Believe/Silver Butterfly	£18
71	Philips 6308 069	NICKY JAMES (LP, black/silver labels)	£100
73	Threshold THS 10	EVERY HOME SHOULD HAVE ONE (LP, gatefold sleeve)	£30
76	Threshold THS 19	THUNDERTHROAT (LP)	£15

(see also Move)

PHILIP JAMES & BLUES BUSTERS
65	Island WI 219	Wide Awake In A Dream/MAYTALS: Tell Me The Reason	£75

(see also Blues Busters)

RICKY JAMES
57	HMV POP 306	Knee Deep in The Blues/Bluer Than Blue	£20
57	HMV POP 334	Party Doll/Ninety-Nine Ways	£20

ROGER JAMES FOUR
66	Columbia DB 7813	Better Than Here/You're Gonna Come Home Cryin' (withdrawn)	£70
66	Columbia DB 7829	Better Than Here/You're Gonna Come Home Cryin'	£100

(see also Danny Storm)

ROGER JAMES
71	NEMS 563719	If I Didn't Have You/I Know It's Love	£20
71	Chapter One CHS 807	RIDING FREE (LP, red/silver labels)	£25

(see also Danny Storm, Prestons)

RUBY JAMES
69	Fontana TF 1051	Gettin' Mighty Crowded/Don't Play That Song	£20

SKIP JAMES
65	Vanguard VSD 79219	SKIP JAMES TODAY (LP)	£40
67	Private PR3	1964-67 (LP, 99 copies only)	£100
67	Vanguard SVRP 19001	SKIP JAMES TODAY (LP, reissue)	£30
68	Vanguard VSD 79273	DEVIL GOT MY WOMAN (LP)	£45
70	Spokane SPL 1003	THE ORIGINAL 1930/31 RECORDINGS (LP)	£50
78	Vanguard VDP 20001	I'M SO GLAD (LP)	£20
69	Storyville 670 185	THE GREATEST OF THE DELTA BLUES SINGERS (LP)	£18

SONNY JAMES
56	Capitol CL 14635	The Cat Came Back/Hello Old Broken Heart	£20
56	Capitol CL 14664	Twenty Feet Of Muddy Water/For Rent (One Empty Heart)	£15
57	Capitol CL 14708	First Date, First Kiss, First Love/Speak To Me	£15
57	Capitol CL 14814	Uh-Huh-Mm/Why Can't They Remember?	£30
58	Capitol CL 14848	Kathaleen/Walk To The Dance	£15
57	Capitol EAP1 827	YOUNG LOVE (EP)	£20
57	Capitol T 779	SOUTHERN GENTLEMAN (LP)	£20
57	Capitol T 867	SONNY (LP)	£20
63	London HA-D 8049	YOUNG LOVE (LP)	£20

TOMMY JAMES & SHONDELLS
66	Roulette RK 7000	Hanky Panky/SHONDELLS: Thunderbolt	£15
68	Major Minor MMLP/SMLP 27	SOMETHING SPECIAL (LP)	£35
68	Roulette RRLP/SRLP 1	MONY MONY (LP)	£30
68	Roulette RRLP/SRLP 2	CRIMSON AND CLOVER (LP)	£40
69	Roulette RRLP/SRLP 3	CELLOPHANE SYMPHONY (LP)	£20
72	Roulette 2432 002	THE BEST OF TOMMY JAMES & THE SHONDELLS (LP)	£15

TONY JAMES
68	Jolly JY 002	Treat Me Right/Me Donkey's Dead	£20

WINSTON JAMES
70	Hot Rod HR 106	Prison Sentence/JANET FERRON: Darling I Need You	£45
70	Torpedo TOR 6	I May Never/Longest Day	£80
70	Torpedo TOR 4	Gal You Think You Nice/White Silver Sands	£100

BOBBY JAMES & DAVE (BARKER)
71	Smash SMA 2314	You Said It/AGGRO BAND: Hot Sauce	£40

JAMES BOYS (1)
63	Direction 58-3721	The Mule (Instrumental)/The Horse (Vocal)	£15

JAMES GANG
70	Stateside SS 2158	Funk No. 48/Collage	£15
70	Stateside SS 2173	Stop/Take A Look Around (withdrawn)	£15

70	Stateside SSL 10295	YER' ALBUM (LP)	£20
70	Probe SPB 6253	RIDES AGAIN (LP)	£18
71	Probe SPB 1038	THIRDS (LP)	£15
71	Probe SPB 1045	LIVE IN CONCERT (LP, textured sleeve, flipback sleeve)	£15
72	Probe SPB 1056	STRAIGHT SHOOTER (LP)	£15

(see also Tommy Bolin)

BOBBY JAMESON

64	Decca F 12032	All I Want Is My Baby/Each And Every Day	£40
64	London HL 9921	I Wanna Love You/I'm So Lonely	£30
65	Brit WI 1001	Rum-Pum/Please Mr. Mailman	£20
69	Joy JOYS 193	TOO MANY MORNINGS (LP)	£100

STEPHEN JAMESON

| 73 | Dawn DNLS 3044 | STEPHEN JAMESON (LP) | £15 |

JAMESON RAID

80	Blackbird BRAID 001	The Hypnotist/The Raid/Gettin' Hotter/Straight From The Butchers (p/s)	£40
81	GBH GBH 1	Seven Days Of Splendour/It's A Crime/Catcher In The Rye (p/s, with lyric sheet, white sleeve)	£50
81	GBH GBH 1	Seven Days Of Splendour/It's A Crime/Catcher In The Rye (p/s, with lyric sheet, later pressing with black sleeve)	£30

JAMIES

| 58 | Fontana H 153 | Summertime Summertime/Searching For You | £40 |
| 62 | Columbia DB 4885 | Summertime Summertime/Searching For You (reissue) | £20 |

JAMIROQUAI

93	Sony 474069 1	EMERGENCY ON PLANET EARTH (2-LP)	£50
94	Sony 477813 - 1	THE RETURN OF THE SPACE COWBOY (2-LP)	£50
96	Sony 4839991	TRAVELLING WITHOUT MOVING (2-LP with bonus track Do You Know Where You're Coming From)	£80
99	Sony S2 494517 1	SYNKRONIZED (2-LP)	£80
00	Simply Vinyl SVLP 267	EMERGENCY ON PLANET EARTH (2-LP, reissue)	£50
01	Sony 504069 1	A FUNK ODYSSEY (LP, numbered/un-numbered)	£150
02	Simply Vinyl SVLP 365	THE RETURN OF THE SPACE COWBOY (2-LP, reissue)	£50
05	Epic BL 96532	DYNAMITE (LP)	£80
12	Art Vinyl AVLP14	A FUNK ODYSSEY (LP, reissue, with CD)	£60
10	Mercury 2754292	ROCK DUST LIGHT STAR (2-LP)	£30
17	Virgin/EMI V3178	AUTOMATON (2-LP)	£30

JAMME

| 70 | Stateside-Dunhill SSL 5024 | JAMME (LP) | £25 |

JOE JAMMER

| 73 | Regal Zono. SRZA 8514 | BAD NEWS (LP, gatefold sleeve, red/silver labels) | £50 |

(see also Mitchell/Coe Mysteries)

JAM TODAY

| 81 | Stroppy Cow SCJT 1 | Stereotyping/Song About Myself (p/s, with insert) | £50 |

JAN & ARNIE

| 58 | London HL 8653 | Jennie Lee/Gotta Getta Date | £40 |
| 58 | London HL 8653 | Jennie Lee/Gotta Getta Date (78) | £35 |

(see also Jan & Dean)

JAN & DEAN

59	London HLN 8936	Baby Talk/Jeanette, Get Your Hair Done	£20
59	London HLN 8936	Baby Talk/Jeanette, Get Your Hair Done (78)	£20
59	London HLU 8990	There's A Girl/My Heart Sings	£25
59	London HLU 8990	There's A Girl/My Heart Sings (78)	£40
60	London HLU 9063	Clementine/You're On My Mind	£20
61	London HLH 9395	Heart And Soul/Midsummer Night's Dream	£15
62	Liberty LIB 55397	A Sunday Kind Of Love/Poor Little Puppet	£20
63	Liberty LIB 55531	Linda/When I Learn How To Cry	£15
64	Liberty LIB 55641	Drag City/Schlock Rod Pt 1	£15
66	Liberty LIB 10225	Norwegian Wood/A Beginning From An End	£20
66	Liberty LIB 55860	Batman/Bucket 'T'	£25
66	Liberty LIB 10244	Popsicle/The Joker Is Wild	£25
67	CBS 202630	Yellow Balloon/A Taste Of Rain	£25
65	Liberty LEP 2213	SURF 'N' DRAG HITS (EP)	£30
66	Liberty LEP 2258	THE TITANIC TWOSOME (EP)	£30
63	Liberty LBY 1163	SURF CITY AND OTHER SWINGING CITIES (LP)	£30
64	Liberty LBY 1220	DEAD MAN'S CURVE/NEW GIRL IN SCHOOL (LP)	£35
64	Liberty LBY 1229	RIDE THE WILD SURF (LP)	£30
65	Liberty LBY 1279	GOLDEN HITS (LP)	£30
65	Liberty LBY 1304	FOLK 'N' ROLL (LP)	£30
66	Liberty LBY 1309	JAN AND DEAN MEET BATMAN (LP)	£40
66	Liberty LBY 1339	FILET OF SOUL (A LIVE ONE) (LP)	£25

(see also Legendary Masked Surfers, Jan & Arnie)

BRUCE JANAWAY

| 78 | Deep Range SRTX/CUS/216 | PURITANICAL ODES (LP, with insert) | £350 |

JAN DUKES DE GREY

| 70 | Decca Nova (S)DN 8 | SORCERERS (LP) | £350 |
| 71 | Transatlantic TRA 234 | MICE AND RATS IN THE LOFT (LP, gatefold sleeve, plastic inner/foam opening) | £350 |

JANE
82	AM 106	It's A Fine Day (Jane)/It's A Fine Day (Lou) no p/s	£15

MARY JANE WITH BARRY GRAY & SPACEMAKERS
63	Philips 326 587 BF	Robot Man/Just The Same As I Do (in p/s)	£25
63	Philips 326 587 BF	Robot Man/Just The Same As I Do (no p/s)	£15

(see also Barry Gray)

PETER JANES
68	CBS 3299	Do You Believe/For The Sake Of Time	£20

BUSTER JANGLES' FLYING MATTRESS
72	RCA RCA 2112	Love Has Taken Over My Brain/The Little World I Knew	£25

JANGLETTIES
81	Eskimo Vinyl	Happy All The Time/Backseat (p/s)	£30

JANIE
70	President PT 309	Back On My Feet Again/Psycho	£20

JANINE
81	Stiletto JAN 001	Crazy On You/Candy (p/s)	£170

JOHNNY JANIS
58	HMV 7EG 8365	JOHNNY JANIS (EP)	£30
66	London HA-U 8270	ONCE IN A BLUE MOON (LP)	£20

BERT JANSCH
66	Transatlantic EP 145	NEEDLE OF DEATH (EP)	£40
65	Transatlantic TRA 125	BERT JANSCH (LP)	£80
65	Transatlantic TRA 132	IT DON'T BOTHER ME (LP)	£50
66	Transatlantic TRA 143	JACK ORION (LP, 1st pressing with purple globe on top of labels)	£70
66	Transatlantic TRA 143	JACK ORION (LP, 2nd pressing with purple and white globe around centre of labels)	£40
67	Transatlantic TRA 157	NICOLA (LP)	£40
69	Transatlantic TRA 179	BIRTHDAY BLUES (LP)	£50
69	Vanguard VSD 79292	STEPPING STONES (LP)	£40
69	Transatlantic TRASAM 10	THE BERT JANSCH SAMPLER (LP)	£15
71	Transatlantic TRA 235	ROSEMARY LANE (LP)	£40
72	Transatlantic TRASAM 27	BOX OF LOVE - THE BERT JANSCH SAMPLER VOL. 2 (LP)	£20
73	Reprise K 44225	MOONSHINE (LP, with lyric insert)	£25
74	Charisma CAS 1090	L.A. TURNAROUND (LP, with lyric insert)	£35
75	Charisma CAS 1107	SANTA BARBARA HONEYMOON (LP)	£15
77	Charisma CAS 1127	A RARE CONUNDRUM (LP, lyric inner)	£15
79	Charisma CLASS 6	AVOCET (LP)	£15
80	Kicking Mule SNKF 162	THIRTEEN DOWN (LP, as Bert Jansch Conundrum)	£30
81	Logo LOGO 1035	HEARTBREAK (LP)	£15
85	Konexion KOMA 788006	FROM THE OUTSIDE (LP, 500 only)	£15
88	Demon TRANDEM1	BERT JANSCH (LP, reissue)	£15

BERT JANSCH & JOHN RENBOURN
66	Transatlantic TRA 144	BERT AND JOHN (LP, 1st pressing, purple/white label with 'Transatlantic' logo on top)	£75
66	Transatlantic TRA 144	BERT AND JOHN (LP, 2nd pressing, purple/white label with 'Transatlantic' logo on centre)	£50
72	Transatlantic TRA 144	BERT & JOHN (LP, reissue with 'World globe' label)	£15

(see also Conundrum, Pentangle, John Renbourn)

BERT JANSCH AND ROD CLEMENTS
88	Black Crow CRO 218	LEATHER LAUNDERETTE (LP)	£40

JAPAN
78	Ariola Hansa AHA 510	Don't Rain On My Parade/Stateline (solid or press-out centre, no p/s)	£15
78	Ariola Hansa AHA 525	The Unconventional/Adolescent Sex (with p/s)	£20
80	Virgin VS 379	Gentlemen Take Polaroids/The Experience of Swimming (autographed by band, p/s)	£75
19	Electronic Sound ES 757	European Son/Suburban Berlin (p/s, red vinyl)	£15
78	Ariola Hansa AHAL 8004	ADOLESCENT SEX (LP, 1st pressing, 'Damont' etched in run out groove, inner sleeve or lyric insert)	£20
78	Ariola Hansa AHAL 8007	OBSCURE ALTERNATIVES (LP)	£15
80	Virgin V 2180	GENTLEMEN TAKE POLAROIDS (LP)	£20
80	Virgin V 2180	GENTLEMEN TAKE POLAROIDS (LP, with misprinted sleeve with sticker, Some Kind Of Fool listed instead of "Burning Bridges")	£25
80	Ariola Hansa AHAL 8011	QUIET LIFE (LP, gatefold)	£20
81	Virgin V 2209	TIN DRUM (LP)	£15
83	Virgin VD 2513	OIL ON CANVAS (2-LP, gatefold)	£18
84	Virgin VGD 3510	EXORCISING GHOSTS (LP)	£15

(see also David Sylvian, Rain Tree Crow)

JARMAZ
84	Rash ITCH 1	Night City Life/Night City Life (Disco Remix) (p/s)	£80

JARMELS
61	Top Rank JAR 560	She Loves To Dance/Little Lonely One	£30
61	Top Rank JAR 580	A Little Bit Of Soap/The Way You Look Tonight	£30

JEAN-MICHEL JARRE
88	Polydor C88 1-3	OXYGENE (LP, HMV-only box set with booklet, 3,300 only)	£15
97	Epic EPC 486984 1	OXYGENE 7-13 (LP)	£18

MAURICE JARRE
65	Fontana (S)TL 5259	THE COLLECTOR (LP, soundtrack)	£25
66	CBS (S)BPG 62843	IS PARIS BURNING? (LP, soundtrack)	£18

67	RCA RD 7848	NIGHT OF THE GENERALS (LP, soundtrack) £30
67	RCA Victor RD/SF 7876	THE PROFESSIONALS (LP, soundtrack) £50
68	Dot (S)LPD 515	VILLA RIDES (LP, soundtrack) £15

ECCLETON JARRETT
86	CF CFD 010	Greedy Girl/Fling It Up (12") £40

KILLERMAN JARRETT
86	Trojan TROT 9086	War Ina South Africa/Dub/Bub 2 (12") £40

WAYNE JARRETT
79	Kingley Sounds REX 3	Anyone Who Had A Heart (with Tommy McCook)/WAYNE JARRETT/GLEN BROWN: Flute From South Side/Youth Man (12") £30
80	Greensleeves GRED 41	Saturday Night Jamboree (12") £20
82	Echo ECHO 011	Satta Dread/Sadat (12") £35
82	Wackies W 191	BUBBLE UP (LP, blue label) £25
98	Wackies WR 191	BUBBLE UP (LP, reissue, black label) £15

(see also Winston Jarrett)

WINSTON JARRETT
74	Atra AR 21	No Time To Waste/Time Dub £30
77	Carib Gems CG 012	Sleepers/Sleepers Version (with the Righteous Flames) £20
78	Write Sounds WTS 1002	Spanish Town Road/Version £15
78	Ballistic UP 36416	War/Version (12") £15
80	Warrior WAR 144	Wise Man/I Shen Galore (12") £20
80	Kingley Sounds REX 3	Youth Man/Melodica (12") £18
80	Wambesi TWLP 1001	WISE MAN (LP) £25
84	VSLP 5008	ROCKING VIBRATION (LP) £15

(see also Righteous Flames)

MARIAN JARVIS
75	Chelsea 2005 038	A Penny For Your Thoughts/A Good Man To Wake Up To £30

STEVE JARVIS
74	Torpedo TOR 32	Every Step I Made/BABA BROOKS BAND: One Eyed Giant £20

JASARO PEOPLE
77	Timba T001	Suffering/Timba Version £200

JASMIN T
69	Tangerine DP 13	Some Other Guy/Evening (with p/s) £50
69	Tangerine DP 13	Some Other Guy/Evening £20

JASMINE MINKS
84	Creation CRE 008	Where Traffic Goes/Mr. Magic (foldout p/s) £15

JASON & THE SCORCHERS
10	Blue Rose BLULP 0508	HALCYON TIMES (2-LP, CD, features Ginger Wildheart) £30

JASON CREST
68	Philips BF 1633	Turquoise Tandem Cycle/Good Life (in export p/s) £175
68	Philips BF 1633	Turquoise Tandem Cycle/Good Life £60
68	Philips BF 1650	Juliano The Bull/Two By The Sea £40
68	Philips BF 1687	(Here We Go Round) The Lemon Tree/Patricia's Dream £60
69	Philips BF 1752	Waterloo Road/Education £40
69	Philips BF 1809	A Place In The Sun/Black Mass £200

(see also Holy Mackerel, High Broom)

JASON'S GENERATIONS
66	Polydor BM 56042	It's Up To You/Insurance Co.'s Are Very Unfair £80

JASPER
69	Spark SRLP 103	LIBERATION (LP, laminated front sleeve, blue/silver labels) £750

JEROME JASPER
82	NYC 1	I'll Do Anything/I'll Do Anything (Instrumental) (12" promo white label) £25
82	Rak 12RAK 354	I'll Do Anything For You/Treasure The Moment (12") £15

JAVAROO
80	Capitol 12CL 16142	Breakin' In/Change It Up/Bring Out The Woman (12") £50
80	Capitol CL 16168	Javaroo/The Buzz £20
80	Capitol E-ST 12052	OUT! (LP) £25

JAWBONE
70	Carnaby CNLS 6004	JAWBONE (LP) £200

(see also Mirage, Portobello Explosion)

BOB JAXON (& HI-TONES)
55	London HL 8156	Ali Baba/Why Does A Woman Cry (as Bob Jaxon & Hi-Tones) £40
55	London HL 8156	Ali Baba/Why Does A Woman Cry (as Bob Jaxon & Hi-Tones) (78) £15
57	RCA RCA 1019	Beach Party/(Gotta Have Something In The) Bank Frank £80
57	RCA RCA 1019	Beach Party/(Gotta Have Something In The) Bank Frank (78) £15

JAY (BLACK)
64	Coral Q 72471	I Rise, I Fall/How Sweet It Is £35

(see also Jay & The Americans)

ABNER JAY
63	London HLN 9791	Cleo/Thresher £40

LAURIE JAY COMBO
63	HMV POP 1234	Teenage Idol/Think Of Me (Demo copy) £60
63	HMV POP 1234	Teenage Idol/Think Of Me £75

MINT VALUE £

65   Decca F 12083   A Song Called Soul/Just A Little Bit £25
(see also Nero & Gladiators)

PATSY DEE JAY
77   Rama RMS 005   Peace Talking/EVE ORCHESTRA: Jumpers In Session £25

PETER JAY (& BLUE MEN)
60   Triumph RGM 1000   Just Too Late/Friendship (as Peter Jay & Blue Men) £40
60   Pye 7N 15290   Paradise Garden/Who's The Girl? £45
(see also Blue Men)

PETER JAY & JAYWALKERS
65   Piccadilly 7N 35220   Parchman Farm/What's Easy For Two Is So Hard For One £20
(see also Terry Reid, Miller, Big Boy Pete)

JAY (JOHN HOLT) & JOYA (LANDIS)
68   Trojan TR 633   I'll Be Lonely/SUPERSONICS: Second Fiddle £45
(see also John Holt, Joya Landis)

JAY & TECHNIQUES
67   Philips PB 1597   Apples, Peaches, Pumpkin Pie/Stronger Than Dirt £25
67   Philips PB 1618   Keep The Ball Rollin'/Here We Go Again £15
67   Philips (S)BL 7834   APPLES, PEACHES, PUMPKIN PIE (LP) £30

JAY & THE AMERICANS
62   HMV POP 1009   She Cried/Dawning £40
64   United Artists UP 1039   Come Dance With Me/Look Into My Eyes Maria £18
66   United Artists UP 1129   Why Can't You Bring Me Home/Baby Stop Your Crying £20
66   United Artists UP 1142   Livin' Above Your Head/She's The Girl (That's Messing Up My Mind) £30
67   United Artists UP 1191   (We'll Meet In The) Yellow Forest/Got Hung Up Along The Way £60
65   United Artists UEP 1003   COME A LITTLE BIT CLOSER (EP) £40
66   United Artists UEP 1017   LIVING WITH JAY AND THE AMERICANS (EP) £40
66   United Artists (S)ULP 1117   JAY AND THE AMERICANS (LP) £50
66   United Artists (S)ULP 1128   SUNDAY AND ME (LP) £30
67   United Artists (S)ULP 1150   LIVIN' ABOVE YOUR HEAD (LP) £40
67   United Artists (S)ULP 1164   TRY SOME OF THIS (LP) £30
(see also Jay, Chapter Four)

JAYBIRDS
66   Sue WI 4013   Somebody Help Me/The Right Kind (without writer credits) £125
66   Sue WI 4013   Somebody Help Me/The Right Kind (with writer credits) £150

JAY BOYS
69   Trojan TR 665   Splendour Splash/TREVOR SHIELD: Please £40
70   Harry J. HJ 6607   Jack The Ripper/Don't Let Me Down £80
70   Harry J. HJ 6609   Jay Moon Walk/Elcong £20
70   Harry J. HJ 6610   Je T'Aime/It Ain't Me Babe £15
70   Harry J. HJ 6617   Del Gago/Killer Version £50
72   Harry J. HJ 6644   African People/HARRY J. ALL STARS: African (Version) £15
72   Ashanti AHS 407   Rough Road/TREVOR SHIELD: Rough Road £18
(see also Roy Panton, Bob & Marcia, Cables)

JERRY JAYE
67   London HLU 10128   My Girl Josephine/Five Miles From Home £40

JAYE SISTERS
59   London HLT 9011   Sure Fire Love/G-3 .... £60
59   London HLT 9011   Sure Fire Love/G-3 (78) £30

JAYHAWKS (1)
56   Parlophone R 4228   Stranded In The Jungle/My Only Darling £800
56   Parlophone R 4228   Stranded In The Jungle/My Only Darling (78) £100

JAYHAWKS (2)
92   Def American 512.986-1   HOLLYWOOD TOWN HALL (LP, with inner) £100
03   American B00000801   RAINY DAY MUSIC (2-LP) £30

JAYLADS
71   Punch PH 95   Royal Chord (actually by Melodians)/Version (actually "In The Spirit" by Lloyd
                                            Charmers) £18
(see also Melodians)

JAYNETTS
63   Stateside SS 227   Sally Go Round The Roses/Sally Go Round The Roses (Instrumental) £15

ROY JAY
82   self released ROY-JAY 1   Vehicle/You Might Need Somebody (p/s, white label, sold at gigs) £20
82   Clubland SJP 837   ROY JAY (LP, some copies signed) £20

JAZZ BUTCHER
83   Glass GLASS 027   Southern Mark Smith/Jazz Butcher Meets Count Dracula (p/s) £20
85   Glass GLASS 12041   Real Men/The Jazz Butcher V The Prime Minister/Southern Mark Smith (Original)
                                            (12") £20
(see also Institution)

JAZZ COMPOSERS ORCHESTRA
74   JCOA/Virgin JDA 3001   JAZZ COMPOSERS ORCHESTRA (2-LP, gatefold sleeve) £20
(see also Carla Bley, Mike Mantler, Larry Coryell)

JAZZ COURIERS
50s (no cat. no.)   Top Spot Blues/Monk Was Here/Last Minute Blues (square flexi) £100
57   Tempo EXA 75   JAZZ COURIERS (EP) £60

59	Tempo EXA 87	JAZZ COURIERS (EP)	£60
58	Tempo TAP 22	IN CONCERT (LP)	£400
59	Tempo TAP 26	THE LAST WORD (LP)	£350
60	London Jazz LTZ-L 15188	THE COURIERS OF JAZZ! (LP)	£200
67	M. For Pleasure MFP 1072	IN CONCERT (LP)	£15
80s	Jasmine JASM 2004	THE JAZZ COURIERS (LP, reissue)	£20
80s	Jasmine JASM 2024	THE LAST WORD (LP, reissue)	£15

(see also Tubby Hayes, Ronnie Scott)

JAZZ CRUSADERS

| 66 | Fontana 688 149 ZL | THE THING (LP) | £20 |
| 66 | Fontana 688 117 ZL | LOOKIN' AHEAD (LP) | £18 |

(see also Crusaders)

JAZZ DEFEKTORS

| 87 | Factory FACT 205 | THE JAZZ DEFEKTORS (LP) | £15 |

JAZZ FIVE

| 61 | Tempo TAP 32 | THE FIVE OF US (LP) | £400 |

(see also Vic Ash Quartet, Harry Klein Quartet)

JAZZ HIP TRIO

| 67 | Major Minor MMLP 8 | JAZZ IN RELIEF (LP) | £125 |

JAZZ MAKERS

| 66 | Ember FA 2023 | SWINGIN' SOUNDS (LP) | £20 |

JAZZ MODES

| 60 | London Jazz LTZ-K 15191 | THE MOST HAPPY FELLA (LP) | £20 |

JAZZ ROCK EXPERIENCE

| 70 | Deram Nova SDN 19 | JAZZ ROCK EXPERIENCE (LP) | £100 |

J & B

| 66 | Polydor 56095 | Wow Wow Wow/There She Goes | £50 |

(see also State Of Micky & Tommy)

THE JB

| 95 | Back 2 Basics B2B12022 | Back 2 Life (The Dedication) (Linarz Cru Remix)/(Original 12" Mix) (12", p/s) | £30 |

J.B.'S

72	Mojo 2918 004	PASS THE PEAS (LP)	£20
72	Polydor 2391 034	FOOD FOR THOUGHT (LP)	£20
74	Polydor 2391 087	DOING IT TO DEATH (LP)	£20
75	Polydor 2391 194	HUSTLE WITH SPEED (LP)	£20
76	Polydor 2391 204	GIVIN' UP FOOD FOR FUNK - THE BEST OF THE JB's (LP)	£20

(see also Fred Wesley & JB's, James Brown, Bobby Byrd)

J.B'S ALLSTARS

| 85 | 2 Tone CHSTT29 | The Alphabet Army/Al Arm (p/s) | £40 |
| 85 | 2 Tone CHSTT1229 | The Alphabet Army (extended mix)/The Alphabet Army (string mix)/The Alphabet Army/Al Arm (12" p/s) | £40 |

J.D. (THE ROC)

| 72 | Sioux SI 008 | Superbad/MONTEGO MELON: Lucky Dip | £30 |

(see also Jeff Dixon)

CATHY JEAN & ROOMATES

| 61 | Parlophone R 4764 | Please Love Me Forever/Canadian Sunset | £60 |

JEAN & GAYTONES

| 71 | Trojan TR 7817 | I Shall Sing (actually by Judy Mowatt & Gaytones)/GAYTONES: Target | £15 |

LANA JEAN

| 63 | Pye International 7N 25214 | It Hurts To Be Sixteen/Bad Boy | £25 |

JEAN & STATESIDES

64	Columbia DB 7287	Putty In Your Hands/One Fine Day	£40
64	Columbia DB 7439	You Won't Forget Me/Cold, Cold Winter	£30
65	Columbia DB 7651	Mama Didn't Lie/Just Let Me Cry	£30

JEANNIE (& BIG GUYS)

| 63 | Piccadilly 7N 35147 | Don't Lie To Me/Boys (as Jeannie & Big Guys) | £15 |
| 64 | Piccadilly 7N 35164 | I Want You/Sticks And Stones (as Jeannie & Big Guys) | £15 |

(see also Cindy Cole)

JEANNIE & REDHEADS

| 64 | Decca F 11829 | Animal Duds/ANDREW OLDHAM GROUP: Funky And Fleopatra | £30 |

(see also Andrew Oldham Orchestra)

JEDDAH

| 83 | Death RIP 2001 | Eleanor Rigby/Ghosts (Never Leave You Behind) (with poster, no p/s) | £25 |

JEDI KNIGHTS

| 95 | Clear CLR 406X | MAY THE FUNK BE WITH YOU (12" EP, clear vinyl, embossed sleeve) | £20 |

(see also Global Communications)

JEEPS

| 66 | Strike JH 308 | He Saw Eesaw/The Music Goes Round | £15 |
| 66 | Strike JH 315 | Ain't It A Great Big Laugh/I Put On My Shoes | £15 |

JEFFERSON

68	Pye 7N 17634	Montage/Did You Hear A Heartbreak Last Night	£15
71	Pye 7N 45022	Spider/Can't Get You Out Of My Mind	£30
69	Pye NSPL 18316	THE COLOUR OF MY LOVE (LP)	£15

MINT VALUE £

73	Philips 6308 166	**I LOVE YOU THIS MUCH** (LP, blue/silver labels)	**£20**

(see also Rockin' Berries, Sight & Sound)

JEFFERSON AIRPLANE

67	RCA Victor RCA 1594	**Somebody To Love/She Has Funny Cars**	**£15**
67	RCA Victor RCA 1631	**White Rabbit/Plastic Fantastic Lover**	**£15**
67	RCA Victor RD 7889	**SURREALISTIC PILLOW** (LP, black label, mono)	**£80**
67	RCA Victor SF 7889	**SURREALISTIC PILLOW** (LP, black label, stereo)	**£50**
68	RCA Victor RD 7926	**AFTER BATHING AT BAXTERS** (LP, black label, mono)	**£70**
68	RCA Victor SF 7926	**AFTER BATHING AT BAXTERS** (LP, black label, stereo)	**£40**
68	RCA Victor RD 7976	**CROWN OF CREATION** (LP, black label, mono)	**£70**
68	RCA Victor SF 7976	**CROWN OF CREATION** (LP, black label, stereo)	**£30**
69	RCA RD/SF 8019	**BLESS ITS POINTED LITTLE HEAD** (LP)	**£20**
69	RCA Victor SF 7889	**SURREALISTIC PILLOW** (LP, repressing, orange label)	**£35**
69	RCA Victor SF 7926	**AFTER BATHING AT BAXTERS** (LP, repressing, orange label)	**£25**
69	RCA Victor SF 7976	**CROWN OF CREATION** (LP, repressing, orange label, 'SR Ltd' printing credit on sleeve)	**£40**
70	RCA SF 8076	**VOLUNTEERS** (LP, gatefold sleeve)	**£20**
71	Grunt FTR 1001	**BARK** (LP, bag cover with lyric sheet & brown inner sleeve)	**£15**
71	RCA SF 8195	**JEFFERSON AIRPLANE TAKES OFF** (LP)	**£18**
72	Grunt FTR 1007	**LONG JOHN SILVER** (LP, open-out box cover with inner lyric sleeve)	**£15**

(see also Great Society, Paul Kantner, Hot Tuna)

ALAN JEFFERSON

15	Trunk JBH 056 LP	**GALACTIC NIGHTMARE** (2-LP)	**£20**

BLIND LEMON JEFFERSON

50	Tempo R 38	**Weary Dog Blues/Change My Luck Blues** (78)	**£25**
50	Tempo R 39	**Lock Step Blues/Hangman's Blues** (78)	**£25**
51	Tempo R 46	**Shuckin' Sugar Blues/Rabbit Foot Blues** (78)	**£25**
52	Tempo R 54	**Gone Dead On You Blues/One Dime Blues** (78)	**£25**
53	Jazz Collector L 91	**Shuckin' Sugar Blues/Rabbit Foot Blues** (78)	**£20**
53	Jazz Collector L 103	**Jack O'Diamonds Blues/Clock House Blues** (78)	**£20**
54	Jazz Collector L 126	**Gone Dead On You Blues/One Dime Blues** (78)	**£20**
50s	Poydras 99	**BLIND LEMON JEFFERSON** (10" LP)	**£50**
53	London Jazz AL 3508	**FOLK BLUES OF BLIND LEMON JEFFERSON** (10" LP)	**£50**
55	London Jazz AL 3546	**PENITENTIARY BLUES** (10" LP)	**£50**
57	London Jazz AL 3564	**SINGS THE BLUES** (10" LP)	**£50**
69	CBS 63738	**THE IMMORTAL** (LP)	**£20**
70s	Roots Matchbox RL 301	**BLIND LEMON JEFFERSON VOLUME 1** (LP)	**£20**
70s	Roots Matchbox RL 306	**BLIND LEMON JEFFERSON VOLUME 2** (LP)	**£18**
70s	Roots Matchbox RL 331	**BLIND LEMON JEFFERSON VOLUME 3** (LP)	**£18**

(see also Paramount Allstars)

BLIND LEMON JEFFERSON & RAMBLING THOMAS

50s	Heritage HLP 1007	**BLIND LEMON JEFFERSON AND RAMBLING THOMAS** (LP, 99 only)	**£100**

GEORGE PAUL JEFFERSON

68	Fontana TF 923	**Looking For My Mind/Out Of Place**	**£45**

MARSHALL JEFFERSON

88	FFRR FFRX 18	**Open Our Eyes** (Celestial Mix)/(Spiritual Mix)/(Marshall's Elevated Dub) (12", p/s)	**£15**

JE FRENCHIE

80	Guardian GFR 18	**JE FRENCHIE EP**	**£15**

JEGA

96	Skam SKA 6	**Phlax/Nortom Midgate/Bluette/Ionic/Evil Lee Kirtcele/Steel Drum/In With The In** (12", custom sleeve)	**£45**
98	Planet Mu ZIQ 001	**TYPE XERO EP** (12")	**£20**
00	Planet Mu ZIQ 012	**GEOMETRY** (2-LP)	**£20**

JEHST

99	Y n R Productions YNR 001	**PREMONITIONS EP:** (12", stickered (white die-cut sleeve, 1st pressing blue text)	**£50**
99	Y n R YNR 1	**PREMONITIONS** (EP, 2nd pressing black text on label)	**£15**
01	Lowlife LOW 12	**THE HIGH PLAINS DRIFTER** (EP, p/s)	**£40**
01	Lowlife LOW 12 PRO	**The Trilogy Remix** (1-sided 12", 2 mixes 500 pressed)	**£30**
02	Y n R YNR008	**Alcoholic Author/Night Breed** (12", p/s)	**£18**
14	Y n R YNR 062	**Dolph Lundgren/Instrumental** (gig-only 7" with STRANGE U)	**£20**
17	Y n R BH71854-01	**44th Floor/44th Floor** (Instrumental) (100 only)	**£35**
03	Lowlife LOW30	**FALLING DOWN** (LP)	**£50**
05	High Plains REPHP 001	**NUKE PROOF SUIT** (LP)	**£30**
11	YNR YNR 047LP	**THE DRAGON OF AN ORDINARY FAMILY** (LP, red & blue vinyl)	**£75**
12	YNR YNR 052	**THE DRAGON OF AN ORDINARY FAMILY** (LP, remixes 300 only)	**£15**

JELLIES

81	Jelli 1	**Jive Baby On A Saturday Night/Conversation** (die-cut sleeve)	**£80**
10	Trunk TTT 006	**JIVE BABY ON A SATURDAY NIGHT** (12" EP)	**£15**

JELLY

72	Mother MOT9	**I'll Meet You Half Way/Chicago Calling**	**£40**

JELLY BABIES

81	De Nada	**DE NADA EP** (hand-made p/s, white labels)	**£60**

JELLY BEANS

64	Pye International 7N 25252	**I Wanna Love Him So Bad/So Long**	**£30**
64	Red Bird RB 10011	**The Kind Of Boy You Can't Forget/Baby Be Mine**	**£30**

JELLYBREAD

69	Blue Horizon 57-3162	Chairman Mao's Boogaloo/No One Else	£15
70	Blue Horizon 57-3169	Comment/Funky Wasp	£15
70	Blue Horizon 57-3174	Rockin' Pneumonia And The Boogie-Woogie Flu/Readin' The Meters	£15
70	Blue Horizon 57-3180	Old Man Hank/Faded Grace	£15
71	Blue Horizon 2096 001	Creepin' And Crawlin'/The Loser/The Clergyman's Daughter	£15
72	Blue Horizon 2096 006	Down Along The Cove/Sister Lucy	£15
72	Liphook 1	JELLYBREAD (mini-LP)	£325
69	Blue Horizon 7-63853	FIRST SLICE (LP)	£100
71	Blue Horizon 2431 002	SIXTY-FIVE PARKWAY (LP, with lyric insert)	£110
71	Blue Horizon 2431 002	SIXTY-FIVE PARKWAY (LP, without lyric insert)	£70
72	Blue Horizon 2931 004	BACK TO THE BEGINNING AGAIN (LP, gatefold sleeve)	£150

JELLYS

98	Mission Impossible MIRVL1	WELCOME TO OUR WORLD (LP, with inner sleeve, mail-order only)	£18

(see also Honeycrack, Wildhearts)

JENA

88	Abacush AB 008	Reggae Vibes/Abacush (12")	£150

JOHNNY JENKINS

71	Atco 2400 033	TON-TON MACOUTE (LP)	£25

LEROY JENKINS

76	JCOA/Virgin J 2005	FOR PLAYERS ONLY (LP)	£15

BARBARA JENKYNS

67	Newbreed NB1	Shoult About It/Groovy Boy	£50

JENNIFERS

92	Nude NUD 2T	Just Got Back Today/Rocks And Boulders/Danny's Song/Tomorrow's Rain (12")	£20
92	Nude NUD 2CD	Just Got Back Today/Rocks And Boulders/Danny's Song/Tomorrow's Rain (CD)	£30

(see also Supergrass)

JENNORS

67	Coxsone CS 7024	Pressure And Slide (actually by Tennors)/SOUL BROTHERS: One Stop	£40

(see also Tennors)

KRIS JENSEN

62	Fontana 267 241 TF	Torture/Let's Sit Down	£15
63	Fontana 267 267 TF	Don't Take Her From Me/Claudette	£15
64	Hickory 45-1224	Donna Donna/Big As I Can Dream	£15
64	Hickory 45-1243	Lookin' For Love/In Time	£15

BILL JENTLES

70	Pama PM 809	True True Train/JEFF BARNES: Give And Take	£25
70	Pama PM 801	What A Woman/Sleepy Cat	£40

JEREMIAH R

13	Organic Analogue OA 001	THE NEW WAY EP (12", white label, 400 only)	£20

JEREMIAHS

85	No Label or catalogue number	Over The Stove/Wipe Away Your Tears/Never Come Back (printed insert and photo stuck on cover 25-50 copies only)	£150
87	Abstract ABCT 112	DRIVING INTO THE SUN (12" EP)	£45
87	Abstract ABS 053	DRIVING INTO THE SUN EP	£25

JERICHO (JONES)

71	A&M AMLH 68050	JUNKIES, MONKEYS & DONKEYS (LP, as Jericho Jones, gatefold, brown label)	£200
72	A&M AMLS 68079	JERICHO (LP, beware of counterfeits with slightly thicker sleeves)	£200

JERKS

78	Underground URA 1	Get Your Woofing Dog Off Me/Hold My Hand (p/s)	£35
78	Lightning GIL 549	Cool/Jerkin' (p/s)	£30
80	Laser LAS 25	Come Back Bogart (I Wish You Would)/Are You Strong Enough?/The Strangest Man Of All (p/s)	£15
97	Overground OVER 65	JERK OFF (LP, 600 only pressed in U.K. for export to Japan)	£20

JERMZ

78	One Way EFP 1	Power Cut/Me And My Baby (with p/s)	£200
78	One Way EFP 1	Power Cut/Me And My Baby (without p/s)	£80

JERRY THE FERRET

78	Jerry The Ferret EGH 919	One Step Forward/I Think You're Lyin' (1000 only, no p/s)	£50
80	Dead Horse	THE MUSIC GOES ON AND ON (EP)	£20

JERRY & THE BLUEBELLS

75	Torpedo TOR 44	Girls/Girls Version	£40

JERRY & FREEDOM SINGERS

70	Banana BA 308	It's All In The Game (duet Winston Francis)/ IM: The Way To My Heart (pseudonym for Cedric Brooks)	£60

(see also Jerry Jones, Winston Francis)

JERUSALEM (2)

72	Deram DM 358	Kamakazi Moth/Frustration	£50
72	Deram SDL 6	JERUSALEM (LP, gatefold sleeve, white/brown label with large 'Deram' logo)	£400
72	Deram SDL 6	JERUSALEM (LP, gatefold sleeve, later red/white label)	£200

(see also Pussy, Ian Gillan)

JESS & JAMES

68	MGM MGM 1389	Move/What Was I Born For	£25
68	MGM MGM 1420	Something For Nothing/I Let The Day Go By (with J.J. Band)	£20

JESSUP
72	Beacon BEA 108	Little Friend/On The Run	£15

JESTERS
62	R&L RL 15/16	Little Girl/Casa Pedro (blue and white labels)	£30
73	Jam JAM 35	Fool For A Day/Can't Live Without You	£15

JESUS & MARY CHAIN
84	Creation CRE 012	Upside Down/Vegetable Man (black & white wraparound p/s in poly bag with address on rear & name in red)	£40
84	Creation CRE 012	Upside Down/Vegetable Man (red & white wraparound p/s in poly bag with address on rear & name in black)	£40
84	Creation CRE 012	Upside Down/Vegetable Man (pink, blue or yellow wraparound p/s in poly bag; with small T-shirt offer insert)	£25
85	Fierce FRIGHT 004	RIOT (EP, with 'LSD bar' & badge; 2 different sleeves)	£100
85	Blanco Y Negro NEG 17F	Just Like Honey/Head//Inside Me/Just Like Honey (Demo Oct 84) (double pack, gatefold p/s)	£15
86	Creation CRE 012T	Upside Down/Vegetable Man/Upside Down (demo) (12" white label, no sleeve)	£100
91	Strange Fruit SFPMA210	PEEL SESSIONS (12")	£15
85	Creation CRE(T) 1	LIVE (UNTITLED) (100 only, numbered, with press sheet)	£100
85	Blanco Y Negro BYN 7	PSYCHOCANDY (LP, with inner)	£25
87	Blanco Y Negro BYN 11	DARKLANDS (LP, with inner)	£25
88	Blanco Y Negro BYN 15	BARBED WIRE KISSES (B-SIDES AND MORE) (LP)	£15
89	Blanco Y Negro BYN 20W	AUTOMATIC (LP, gatefold sleeve, with insert)	£20
92	Blanco Y Negro BYN 26	HONEY'S DEAD (LP)	£30
94	Warner Bros. 4509-96717-4	STONED & DETHRONED (LP)	£80
98	Creation CRELP 232	MUNKI (2-LP)	£100
00	Strange Fruit SFRSLP092	THE COMPLETE PEEL SESSIONS (LP)	£18
13	Demon CANDY 1	PSYCHOCANDY (LP, reissue, red splatter vinyl, poster)	£25
13	Demon JAMCLPBOX01	THE VINYL COLLECTION (11LP box set)	£180
15	Demon DEMREC76	BARROWLANDS LIVE (LP, RSD, 340 copies red vinyl out of 1500)	£60
15	Edsel JAMCLIVEBOOK1	BARROWLANDS LIVE (10", CD, 40 page hardback book)	£35

(see also Primal Scream, Meat Whiplash)

JESUS LIZARD
91	Touch & Go T&GLP #43	PURE (EP purple vinyl, numbered sticker on sleeve, 1500 only)	£18
93	Touch & Go TG 83	Puss/NIRVANA: Oh, The Guilt (p/s, blue vinyl, with poster)	£25
90	Touch & Go T&GLP 54	HEAD (LP, red & white vinyl, numbered sticker on sleeve, 1500 only)	£18
91	Touch & Go T&GLP 68	GOAT (LP, orange vinyl, numbered sticker on sleeve, 1000 only)	£40
91	Touch & Go TG68P	GOAT (LP, picture disc)	£18
92	Touch & Go TGLP 100	LIAR (LP, maroon vinyl, stickered no'd sleeve)	£20
94	Touch & Go TG 131	DOWN (LP, with 4 postcards)	£25

(see also Nirvana)

JET
75	CBS 80699	JET (LP, with lyric insert)	£20

(see also Andy Ellison,John's Children, Nice, Radio Stars, Sparks)

JET (AUSTRALIA)
03	Elektra 7559-62956-1	GET BORN (2-LP, white vinyl, stickered, gatefold with inners)	£30

JETHRO TULL
SINGLES
68	MGM MGM 1384	Sunshine Day/Aeroplane (miscredited to 'Jethro Toe'; counterfeits credit 'Jethro Tull')	£600
68	Island WIP 6043	A Song For Jeffrey/One For John Gee	£40
68	Island WIP 6048	Love Story/A Christmas Song (mispressing, B-side or both sides credited to Ian Henderson)	£18
69	Island WIP 6056	Living In The Past/Driving Song (2 different pink labels)	£15
70	Chrysalis WIP 6077	The Witch's Promise/Teacher (in p/s)	£20
70	Chrysalis WIP 6077	The Witch's Promise/Teacher	£15
71	Chrysalis WIP 6098	Lick Your Fingers Clean/Up To Me (unissued)	£0
77	Chrysalis CHS 2135	The Whistler/Strip Cartoon (in p/s)	£25
86	Chrysalis TULLX 2	Coronach (with David Palmer)/Jack Frost And The Hooded Crow/ Living In The Past/ Elegy (12", p/s)	£40
87	Chrysalis TULLP 3	Steel Monkey/Down At The End Of Your Road (die-cut picture disc)	£20
87	Chrysalis ZTULL 3	Steel Monkey/Down At The End Of Your Road/Too Many Too/I'm Your Gun (numbered edition of 3,000 with competition pack & badge)	£15
88	Chrysalis TULLCD 4	Said She Was A Dancer/Dogs In The Midwinter/Down At The End Of The Road/Too Many Too (CD, picture disc, limited issue)	£25
89	Chrysalis TULLX5	Another Christmas Song/Intro-A Christmas Song/Cheap Day Return-Mother Goose/ Outro-Locomotive Breath (12" p/s)	£20

ALBUMS
68	Island ILP 985	THIS WAS (1st pressing, pink label/black & orange 'circle' logo, mono)	£400
68	Island ILPS 9085	THIS WAS (1st pressing, pink label/black & orange 'circle' logo, stereo, laminated gatefold flipback sleeve, some sleeves as mono issues with stereo stickers)	£250
69	Island ILPS 9103	STAND UP (1st pressing, gatefold sleeve pop-up inside, pink label/black & orange 'circle' logo)	£225
70	Chrysalis ILPS 9123	BENEFIT (green Chrysalis or Island pink rim label)	£100
70	Chrysalis ILPS 9123	BENEFIT (Island pink rim label 'palm tree' logo)	£45
71	Island ILPS 9145	AQUALUNG (1st pressing, Matrixes ILPS 9145 A//1U and ILPS B//3U, Chrysalis labels with white 'i' at top of label, with textured E.J. Day Group gatefold sleeve with ILPS 9145 on top right hand corner, inner bag)	£100
71	Island ILPS 9145	AQUALUNG (pink rim palm tree label, gatefold sleeve)	£150
72	Chrysalis CHR 1003	THICK AS A BRICK (LP, 1st pressing with white 'i' at top of label, Matrixes: CHR1003 A-3U/CHR1003 B-2U, 'Porky' etched into dead wax side 1, 'Pecko' etched into dead wax	£80

		side 2, textured sleeve with fold-out newspaper sleeve)	£30
72	Chrysalis CJT 1	**LIVING IN THE PAST** (2-LP, with hard sleeve & booklet)	£30
73	Chrysalis CHR 1040	**A PASSION PLAY** (gatefold sleeve with matt finish, with Linwell theatre booklet, Matrix CHR1040 A4U/B4, green label without small white "i", later presses have red wording on rim and A2U matrix)	£45
77	Chrysalis CJT 4	**LIVE - BURSTING OUT** (2-LP, gatefold sleeve with inners)	£15

(First pressings of all above Chrysalis LPs have a white 'I' logo on the label. Second pressings without this are worth slightly less.)

78	Chrysalis CHR 1175	**HEAVY HORSES** (LP, with insert)	£15
84	Chrysalis CDLP 1461	**UNDER WRAPS** (picture disc)	£15
88	Chrysalis Tbox1	**20 YEARS OF JETHRO TULL** (5-LP box set with 24-page booklet)	£75
88	Chrysalis Tbox CD1	**20 YEARS OF JETHRO TULL** (3-CD box set with 24-page booklet)	£50
89	Chrysalis CHRP 1708	**ROCK ISLAND** (Picture disc)	£18
91	Chrysalis DCHR 1886	**CATFISH RISING** (Ltd edn. With 3-track 12" and lyric sheet inner sleeve)	£20
93	Chrysalis CDCHR 6004	**JETHRO TULL 25th ANNIVERSARY** (4-CD cigar box set with 48-page booklet)	£55
95	Chrysalis CHR 6109	**ROOTS TO BRANCHES** (2-LP)	£80

ALBUMS : LP REPRESSINGS

68	Island ILP 985	**THIS WAS** (pink label/'i' logo, mono)	£70
69	Island ILPS 9085	**THIS WAS** (pink label/black 'block' logo, 1st mix)	£40
70	Island ILPS 9085	**THIS WAS** (pink label/'i' logo)	£20
70	Chrysalis ILPS 9103	**STAND UP** (pop-up sleeve, pink label/black 'block' logo or pink label/'i' logo)	£18
96	Chrysalis LP25AQUA1	**AQUALUNG** (2-LP, 25th anniversary edition)	£50
97	EMI LPCENT 8	**STAND UP** (LP, reissue, EMI centenary, stickered sleeve)	£30
97	EMI LPCENT 31	**AS THICK AS A BRICK** (LP, reissue, EMI centenary, stickered sleeve)	£30
16	Chrysalis AQUA 1	**AQUALUNG** (LP, repressing, Steve Wilson mix, green vinyl, Sainsburys sticker)	£20

PROMOS

76	Chrysalis CHS 3 PDJ	**Ring Out/Solstice Bells/March, The Mad Scientist/Christmas Song/ Pan Dance** (12")	£25
79	Chrysalis CHS018-PDJ	**Dark Ages** (Special edited version) **12" promo**	£15
87	Chrysalis VAS 2866	**Farm On The Freeway** (Special Rock Radio Edit) (12" promo)	£15
88	Chrysalis VAS 1170	**Part Of The Machine/Part Of The Machine** (Edit) (12" promo with tour dates sticker)	£18

(see also Mick Abrahams, Blodwyn Pig, Wild Turkey, The John Even Band)

JETLINERS

66	Blue Beat BB 367	**Meditation** (actually by Sugar & Dandy)**/GIRL SATCHMO: Nature Of Love** (actually with Jetliners)	£35

JETS (1)

73	Cube BUG 35	**Yeah!/Rusty Corinthian Pillar**	£15

JETS (2)

79	Decca FR 13867	**Tearaway/Impossible**	£100

JET SET

62	Delta DW 5001	**VC 10/Cruising 600** (some in p/s)	£15
64	Parlophone R 5199	**You Got Me Hooked/True To You**	£25

JETSET

85	Dance Network WORK 1	**THERE GOES THE NEIGHBOURHOOD** (LP, pink sleeve, poster)	£20
86	Dance Network WORK 4	**4 GO BANANAS** (LP, with lyric insert)	£20

JETSTREAMS

59	Decca F 11149	**Bongo Rock/Tiger**	£15

JETZ

78	Pollen PBM 019	**Down By The River/Brother John/You Ain't Seen Nothing Yet/Easy Feeling**	£25

JEVUTSHTA

78	Zel-La JHSPS 226	**Fight Your Way Out/Stomp**	£30

JEWELLS (JAMAICA)

77	Observer OB 005	**Black is The Highest Culture** (Culture Version)**/One Little Lick Version** (12")	£45
77	Observer OB 1101	**Jah I/LEROY SMART: Jah Is My Light/I-ROY: Wicked Eat Dirt** (12")	£25

JEWELS

64	Colpix PX 11034	**Opportunity/Gotta Find A Way**	£30
65	Colpix PX 11048	**But I Do/Smokey Joe**	£18

JIGSAW

68	Polydor 56241	**I Need Your Love/I've Gotta Get Me Some Money** (as Jig-Saw Band)	£15
68	Music Factory CUB 4	**Mister Job/Great Idea**	£15
68	Music Factory CUB 6	**Let Me Go Home/Tumblin'**	£80
68	MGM MGM 1410	**One Way Street/Then I Found You**	£100
70	Philips 6006 033	**One Way Street/Coffucious Confusion**	£70
70	Fontana 6007 017	**Lollipop And Goody Man/Seven Fishes**	£40
71	Philips 6308 033	**LETHERSLADE FARM** (LP)	£80
72	Philips 6308 072	**AURORA BOREALIS** (LP)	£50
73	BASF 29106-5	**BROKEN HEARTED** (LP, gatefold sleeve)	£15

JILL & BOULEVARDS

62	Columbia DB 4823	**And Now I Cry/Eugene**	£25

JILL & Y'VERNS

60s	Oak RGJ 503	**My Soulful Dress/Anything He Wants Me To Do**	£100

JILTED JOHN

78	Rabid TOSH 105	**Jilted John/Going Steady** (p/s)	£15
78	EMI Intl. INS 3024	**TRUE LOVE STORIES** (LP, with board game insert)	£25
78	EMI Intl. INS 3024	**TRUE LOVE STORIES** (LP)	£15

JIM & JEAN
68   Verve Folkways VLP 5017   CHANGES (LP) £40

JIM & JOE
64   London HL 9831   Fireball Mail/Daisy Mae £20
(see also James Burton)

JIM & MONICA
64   Stateside SS 266   Slippin' And Slidin'/Sing Along Without Jim & Monica £20
(see also Jimmy Gilmer & Fireballs)

JIMBILIN
71   Bamboo BAM 68   Human Race/Let Love In (both actually by Herman Chin-Loy & Aquarians) £15
75   Ashanti ASH 421   Balaclava/Tacku £15

JIMMIE & NIGHT HOPPERS
59   London HLP 8830   Cruisin'/Night Hop £30
59   London HLP 8830   Cruisin'/Night Hop (78) £30

JIMMY J & CRU-L-T
94   Kniceforce KF 027   Take Me Away (Slipmatt Remix)/FUTURE PRIMITIVE: Life Me Up (Slammin' Vinyl Remix) (12", p/s) £15

JIV-A-TONES
58   Felsted AF 101   Flirty Gertie/Fire Engine Baby £150
58   Felsted AF 101   Flirty Gertie/Fire Engine Baby (78) £50

JIVE FIVE
61   Parlophone R 4822   My True Story/When I Was Single £150
62   Stateside SS 133   What Time Is It?/Begging You Please £90
65   United Artists UP 1106   I'm A Happy Man/Kiss Kiss Kiss £45

JIVERS (JAMAICA)
68   Trojan TR 604   Wear My Crown/Down On The Beach £30
(see also Brother Dan Allstars)

JIVERS (U.S.)
56   Vogue V 9060   Little Mama/Cherie £650
56   Vogue V 9060   Little Mama/Cherie (78) £150
57   Vogue V 9068   Ray Pearl/Dear Little One £600
57   Vogue V 9068   Ray Pearl/Dear Little One (78) £150

JIVING JUNIORS
60   Blue Beat BB 4   Lollipop Girl/Dearest Darling £30
60   Blue Beat BB 5   My Heart's Desire/I Love You £40
60   Starlite ST45 028   Lovers Line/Tu-Woo-Up-Tu-Woo £40
61   Starlite ST45 049   Slop & Mash/My Sweet Angel £40
61   Blue Beat BB 36   Over The River/Hip Rub (with Hersan & His City Slickers) £30
62   Island WI 003   Sugar Dandy/Valerie £25
62   Island WI 027   Andrea/Don't Leave Me £25
63   Island WI 129   Sugar Dandy/Valerie (reissue) £20
(see also Duke Reid)

J.J. ALLSTARS
68   Duke DU 3   One Dollar Of Music/CARL DAWKINS: I'll Make It Up £70
69   Trojan TR 691   Memphis Underground (Parts 1 & 2) £25
69   Doctor Bird DB 1308   Five miles High/CARL DAWKINS: Only Girl £50
70   Duke DU 94   Collecting Coins/Cabbage Leaf £15
70   Escort ES 821   Mango Tree/The Removers (both actually by Winston Wright & J.J. All Stars)..........£50
71   Duke DU 135   Soup/Soup (Version) (with Lloyd Young) £20
(see also Lloyd Young, Bleechers, Ethiopians)

J.J. BAND
71   CBS S 64396   THE J.J. BAND (LP) £25

JJ72
00   Lakota LAKLP 0017   JJ72 (LP) £20

JJ'S POWERHOUSE
83   Sillysybin COX 1657   Running For The Line/Blackrods (no p/s).. £250

JME
15   Boy Better Know JME 051   INTEGRITY (LP, clear vinyl) £50
15   Boy Better Know JME 052   INTEGRITY - INSTRUMENTALS (LP, clear vinyl) £15

JOBRIATH
74   Elektra K 12156   Ooh La La/Gone Tomorrow (demo) £20
73   Elektra EKS 75070   JOBRIATH (LP) £20
74   Elektra K 42163   CREATURES OF THE STREET (LP) £20

JO'BURG HAWK
73   Charisma CAS 1064   JO'BURG HAWK (LP, gatefold sleeve, large 'Mad Hatter' label) £20

JOCELYNE JOCYA
69   CBS 4177   I Have Loved Me A Man/Time £60
69   CBS 4177   I Have Loved Me A Man/Time (DJ copy)... £150

JODECI
92   MCA MCA 10534   FOREVER MY LADY (LP) £20
93   MCA MCA 11019   DIARY OF A MAD BAND (LP) £20
95   MCA MCA 11258   THE SHOW THE AFTER PARTY THE HOTEL (2-LP) £20

JODEY
79	Elliejay EJSP 9242	The Rocker/Front Man	£150

JODIMARS
56	Capitol CL 14518	Well Now, Dig This/Let's All Rock Together	£75
56	Capitol CL 14518	Well Now, Dig This/Let's All Rock Together (78)	£15
56	Capitol CL 14627	Rattle My Bones/Lotsa Love	£75
56	Capitol CL 14627	Rattle My Bones/Lotsa Love (78)	£15
56	Capitol CL 14641	Rattle Shakin' Daddy/Eat Your Heart Out Annie	£75
56	Capitol CL 14641	Rattle Shakin' Daddy/Eat Your Heart Out Annie (78)	£15
56	Capitol CL 14642	Dance The Bop/Boom, Boom My Bayou Baby	£75
56	Capitol CL 14642	Dance The Bop/Boom, Boom My Bayou Baby (78)	£15
56	Capitol CL 14663	Midnight/Clarabella	£75
56	Capitol CL 14663	Midnight/Clarabella (78)	£15
57	Capitol CL 14700	Cloud 99/Later	£70
57	Capitol CL 14700	Cloud 99/Later (78)	£15
72	Specialty SPE 6608	WELL NOW DIG THIS (LP)	£20

(see also Bill Haley & Comets)

JODY GRIND
69	Transatlantic TRA 210	ONE STEP ON (LP, gatefold sleeve, lilac label with 't' logo)	£175
70	Transatlantic TRA 221	FAR CANAL (LP, white/lilac label with 't' logo)	£175

(see also Vinegar Joe, Hummingbird, Heads, Hands & Feet)

JODY ST
81	Lips LIPS1	Fight Back/Granny Did It (private pressing)	£150
81	Private Pressing	STREET (LP, private pressing)	£125

AL T. JOE (& CELESTIALS)
62	Dice CC 9	Rise Jamaica/I'm On My Own	£15
62	Blue Beat BB 126	You Cheated On Me/This Heart Of Mine (as Al T. Joe & Celestials)	£15
63	Blue Beat BB 166	Goodbye Dreamboat/Please Forgive Me	£15
72	Duke DU 148	Vision/Young And Unlearned	£15
72	Dynamic DYN 429	Oh What A Price/The Prisoners Song	£15

(see also Jamaica Fats)

JOE & ANN
65	Black Swan WI 468	Gee Baby/Wherever You May Be	£20

JOE COOL (& THE KILLERS)
77	Ariola ARO 105	I Just Don't Care/My Way (p/s)	£25

JOE CROW
82	Cherry Red CHERRY 48	Compulsion/Absent Friends	£25

JOE & DELLA
65	Doctor Bird DB 1043	So Close/BABA BROOKS : Eight Games	£20

JOE & EDDIE
65	Vocalion VAN 8046	WALKIN' DOWN THE LINE (LP)	£30

JOE 9T & THUNDERBIRDS
79	Gemme JOE 9T/LYN 6526	Joe 9T Theme/THEY MUST BE RUSSIANS: Psycho Analysis (p/s, stamped white label)	£15

(see also They Must Be Russians)

JOE 90
92	Full Effect FERT 112	Good Times/New Found Strength (12")	£20

JOE PUBLIC (2)
85	Capital Class	Anti CND/Champagne Charlie	£30

JOE (MANSANO) THE BOSS
70	Joe JRS 6	Son Of Al Capone/All My Enemies	£30
70	Joe JRS 10	If Life Was A Thing/LLOYD KINGPIN: Daisy Bothering	£120

(see also Joe's Allstars, Joe Mansano, Dice The Boss)

BILLY JOEL
74	Philips 6078 018	The Ballad Of Billy The Kid/If I Only Had The Words (To Tell You) (in p/s)	£35
74	Philips 6078 018	The Ballad Of Billy The Kid/If I Only Had The Words (To Tell You)	£25
79	CBS 7150	Honesty/Root Beer Rag (withdrawn)	£20
72	Philips 6369 150	COLD SPRING HARBOR (LP)	£15
73	Philips 6369 160	PIANO MAN (LP, withdrawn)	£20
78	CBS H 82311	THE STRANGER (LP, half-speed master version)	£20

(see also Hassles)

JOE'S ALLSTARS
69	Joe/Duke DU 24	Hey Jude/Musical Feet	£75
69	Joe/Duke DU 28	Battle Cry Of Biafra/Funky Reggae Part 1	£40
69	Joe/Duke DU 50	Brixton Cat/Solitude	£50
70	Joe JRS 9	Tony B's Theme/JOE THE BOSS: Skinhead Revolt	£180
70	Trojan TBL 106	BRIXTON CAT (LP)	£50

(see also Joe The Boss, Dice The Boss, King Horror)

JOE SOAP
73	Polydor 2383 233	KEEP IT CLEAN (LP, laminated sleeve, correction sticker on rear)	£150

JOE SOPE
79	Redball RR 022	Gotta Be Something Else/Don't Understand	£40

JOEY & CONTINENTALS
70	Polydor 56520	She Rides With Me/Rudy Vadoo	£85

MINT VALUE £

(see also G.T.O.'s)

ANDREW JOHN
| 72 | CBS 64835 | THE MACHINE STOPS (LP) | £20 |

CLIVE JOHN
| 75 | United Artists UAS 29733 | YOU ALWAYS KNOW WHERE YOU STAND WITH A BUZZARD (LP) | £25 |

(see also Man)

COURTNEY JOHN
| 09 | Peckings PTI 059 | Lucky Man/LADY LEX: Don't Know Why | £40 |

DAVID JOHN & MOOD
64	Vocalion V 9220	To Catch That Man/Pretty Thing	£220
65	Parlophone R 5255	Bring It To Jerome/I Love To See You Strut	£275
65	Parlophone R 5301	Diggin' For Gold/She's Fine	£275

(see also Gagalactyca, Astral Navigations, Little Free Rock)

ELTON JOHN

SINGLES
68	Philips BF 1643	I've Been Loving You/Here's To The Next Time	£250
69	Philips BF 1739	Lady Samantha/All Across The Havens	£70
69	DJM DJS 205	It's Me That You Need/Just Like Strange Rain (in p/s)	£120
69	DJM DJS 205	It's Me That You Need/Just Like Strange Rain	£50
70	DJM DJS 217	Border Song/Bad Side Of The Moon	£25
70	DJM DJS 222	Rock And Roll Madonna/Grey Seal	£30
73	DJM DJ X502	Saturday Night's Alright For Fighting/Jack Rabbit/Whenever You're Ready (We'll Go Steady Again) (non-laminated p/s)	£20
77	Rocket GOALD 1	The Goaldigger Song/Jimmy, Brian, Elton, Eric (mail-order, signed, 500 only, solid centre copies are counterfeits)	£250
77	Rocket GOALD 1	The Goaldigger Song/Jimmy, Brian, Elton, Eric (mail-order, unsigned, 500 only, solid centre copies are counterfeits)	£150
78	DJM EJ 12	THE ELTON JOHN SINGLES COLLECTION (12 x 7" box set [DJS 10901-12])	£50
79	Rocket XPRES 20	Mama Can't Buy You Love/Strangers (p/s; withdrawn, misspelt "Mamma")	£350
80	Rocket XPRES 45	Dear God/Tactics (company sleeve)	£40
83	Rocket XPRES 91	That's Why They Call It The Blues/Lord Choc Ice Goes Mental ('raised musical note' sleeve with shorter A-side title)	£15
83	Rocket EJPIC 1	I'm Still Standing/Earn While You Learn (piano-shaped picture disc)	£15
85	Rocket EJSP 10	Wrap Her Up/Restless (live) (with George Michael, oblong-shaped picture disc, with pictures on wrong sides)	£25
86	Rocket EJSP 13	Slow Rivers (with Cliff Richard)/Billy & The Kids (picture disc)	£30
88	Rocket EJS 1612	I Don't Wanna Go On With You Like That (Remix)/(7" Version)/ Rope Around A Fool (12", blue vinyl factory custom pressing, no p/s)	£150
90	Rocket EJS 21	Club At The End Of The Street/Give Peace A Chance (p/s, withdrawn)	£200
90	Rocket EJS 2112	Club At The End Of The Street/Give Peace A Chance (12", p/s, withdrawn)	£500
97	Rocket EJSCD 41	Something About The Way You Look Tonight (Edited Version)/ I Know Why I'm In Love/No Valentines/Something About The Way You Look Tonight (Album Version) (CD, card sleeve, unreleased)	£40
97	Rocket EJSCX 41	Something About The Way You Look Tonight (Edited Version)/ I Know Why I'm In Love/You Can Make History (Young Again)/Something About The Way You Look Tonight (Album Version) (CD, digipak, unreleased)	£75
13	Secret 7" S78	Bennie And The Jets (100 only, each with unique art sleeve)	£70

ALBUMS
69	DJM DJLP 403	EMPTY SKY (gatefold sleeve, mono)	£150
69	DJM DJLPS 403	EMPTY SKY (gatefold sleeve, stereo, with 'stereo' sticker on sleeve)	£30
70	Warlock Music WMM 101/2	WARLOCK MUSIC SAMPLER (untitled publishing sampler, 7 tracks by Elton, 4 by Linda Peters)	£1000
70	DJM DJLPS 406	ELTON JOHN (textured gatefold sleeve)	£35
70	DJM DJLPS 406	ELTON JOHN (later smooth gatefold sleeve)	£20
70	DJM DJLPS 410	TUMBLEWEED CONNECTION (LP, with booklet)	£35
71	DJM DJLPH 420	MADMAN ACROSS THE WATER (LP, gatefold, booklet)	£35
72	DJM DJLPH 423	HONKY CHATEAU (LP, gatefold)	£35
73	DJM DJLPD 1001	GOODBYE YELLOW BRICK ROAD (2-LP, tri-fold)	£25
73	DJM DJLPH 427	DON'T SHOOT ME I'M ONLY THE PIANO PLAYER (LP, with booklet)	£35
75	DJM DJLPX 1	CAPTAIN FANTASTIC AND THE BROWN DIRT COWBOY (LP, gatefold)	£35
76	DJM DJE 29001	GOODBYE YELLOW BRICK ROAD (2-LP, yellow vinyl, triplefold sleeve)	£60
78	DJM DJV 2300	CAPTAIN FANTASTIC AND THE BROWN DIRT COWBOY (picture disc)	£40
78	DJM LSP 14512	ELTON JOHN (5-LP, box set)	£40
90	Rocket 846 947 1	THE VERY BEST OF ELTON JOHN (2-LP)	£20
91	Rocket 848 236-2	TO BE CONTINUED ... THE VERY BEST OF ELTON JOHN (4-CD, 12" x 8" box set with large colour booklet)	£100
93	Happenstance HAPP 001	PLAYS THE SIRAN (private pressing, 50 only)	£1000
93	Happenstance HAPP 002	THE FISHING TRIP (4-CD set, private pressing, 100 only, existence unconfirmed)	£700
93	Rocket 518 478-1	DUETS (2-LP)	£35
95	Mercury 526 185 1	MADE IN ENGLAND (LP)	£100
95	Rocket 528 788 2	LOVE SONGS (2-LP)	£80
97	Rocket ELTON 50	CELEBRATING ELTON JOHN'S 50TH BIRTHDAY (promo only)	£50
99	Mercury ADV 1999/1	AIDA (with Sir Tim Rice) (box set with wallet, plinth stand, interview CD, booklet and calender cards, promo only)	£50
99	Mercury ADV 1999/1	AIDA PRESS KIT (card box set with wallet, plinth stand, interview CD, booklet, calender cards, scented candle and broadcast CD-R, promo only)	£50
05	Rocket 9872301	PEACHTREE ROAD (LP)	£200
06	Mercury 1705730	THE CAPTAIN & THE KID (LP)	£70
10	Mercury 2750475	THE UNION (2-LP, with Leon Russell)	£25
21	Rocket RSDRSZ 2021	REGIMENTAL SGT. ZIPPO (LP, mono, RSD, Laminated 'tip-on' sleeve)	£28

(see also [Stu Brown &] Bluesology, Bread & Beer Band, Neil Sedaka, Kiki Dee, Aretha Franklin, Dionne Warwick Radio Heart, Argosy)

JOHN LEE'S GROUNDHOGS
66   Planet PLF 104   Over You Baby/I'll Never Fall In Love Again...£100
(see also Groundhogs, Tony McPhee)

LITTLE WILLIE JOHN
56   Parlophone R 4209   Fever/Letter From My Darling £150
56   Parlophone R 4209   Fever/Letter From My Darling (78)..£20
58   Parlophone R 4396   Uh, Uh, Baby/Dinner Date (With His Girl Friend)...............................£50
58   Parlophone R 4396   Uh, Uh, Baby/Dinner Date (With His Girl Friend) (78) £15
58   Parlophone R 4432   Talk To Me, Talk To Me/Spasms £40
58   Parlophone R 4432   Talk To Me, Talk To Me/Spasms (78)..£15
58   Parlophone R 4472   Let's Rock While The Rockin's Good/You're A Sweetheart...............£60
58   Parlophone R 4472   Let's Rock While The Rockin's Good/You're A Sweetheart (78)........£15
59   Parlophone R 4571   Leave My Kitten Alone/Let Nobody Love You £50
60   Parlophone R 4674   Heartbreak (It's Hurtin' Me)/Do You Love Me £30
60   Parlophone R 4699   Sleep/There's A Difference £30
61   Parlophone R 4728   Walk Slow/HANK BALLARD: The Hoochie Coochie Coo £40
59   Parlophone PMC 1163   SURE THINGS (LP)..£175
64   London HA 8126   COME ON AND JOIN LITTLE WILLIE JOHN (LP)...................................£70

MABLE JOHN
66   Atlantic 584 022   It's Catching/Your Good Thing (Is About To End) £15
67   Stax 601 010   Same Time Same Place/Bigger And Better (dark blue label)...........£15
68   Stax 601 034   Able Mable/Don't Get Caught £15

MAVIS JOHN & JOANNE WILSON
81   Red Stripe SON 2222   How Can I Love Again?/JOANNE WILSON: Gotta Have You Back....£15

ROBERT JOHN (1)
68   CBS 3436   If You Don't Want My Love/Don't..£15
68   A&M AMS 835   Raindrops Love And Sunshine/When The Party Is Over (DJ Copy)...£100
68   A&M AMS 835   Raindrops Love And Sunshine/When The Party Is Over £50

ROBERT JOHN (2)
80   John 1   The Aliens Stalk The Wrecked Planet/The Aliens Stalk The Wrecked Planet (same track both sides, no p/s) £25

SAMMIE JOHN
67   Stateside SS 585   Little John/Boss Bag £20

JOHN & PAUL
65   London HLU 9997   People Say/I'm Walkin' £15

JOHNNIE & JOE
58   London HLM 8682   Over The Mountain, Across The Sea/My Baby's Gone, On, On £150
58   London HLM 8682   Over The Mountain, Across The Sea/My Baby's Gone, On, On (78)...£20

JOHNNY DANGEROUSLY
90   Village (no cat no)   Introducing Jane/Tear It Down/Subway Life (12" p/s) £20
89   Village (no cat no)   YOU, ME AND THE ALARM CLOCK (mini LP p/s with photo insert, 1,000 only) £35
(see also I Am Kloot)

JOHNNY & THE ROCCOS
78   SRT SRTX/78/CUS 212   JOHNNY & THE ROCCOS (LP)...£40

JOHNNY (OSBORNE) & ATTRACTIONS
67   Doctor Bird DB 1118   Young Wings Can Fly/DUDLEY WILLIAMSON: I'm Moving On £200
68   Doctor Bird DB 1117   Coming On The Scene/Anything You Want £400

JOHNNY (STEVENS) & THE BLUE BEATS
64   Blue Beat BB 229   Shame/Ball And Chain £15

JOHNNY & CHAZ & GUNNERS
61   Decca F 11365   Bobby/Out Of Luck..£22

JOHNNY & THE COPYCATS
64   Norco AB 102   I'm A Hog For You Baby/I Can Never See You £60
(see also My Dear Watson)

JOHNNY & THE HURRICANES
59   London HL 8899   Crossfire/Lazy (triangular-centre)..£20
59   London HL 9017   Reveille Rock/Time Bomb (78)..£20
60   London HLI 9072   Beatnick Fly/Sand Storm (78) £40
60   London HLX 9134   Down Yonder/Sheba (78)...£80
60   London HLX 9190   Rocking Goose/Revival (78) £100
60   London HL 7099   The Hep Canary/Catnip (export issue) £25
62   London HLX 7116   You Are My Sunshine/Farewell, Farewell (export issue) £20
61   London REX 1284   ROCKING GOOSE (EP)..£20
62   London REX 1347   JOHNNY AND THE HURRICANES (EP)..£20
64   London REX 1414   JOHNNY AND THE HURRICANES VOL. 2 (EP)..£25
60   London HA 2227   RED RIVER ROCK (LP, plum label) £25
60   London HA-I 2269   STORMSVILLE (LP) £25
61   London HA-X 2322   THE BIG SOUND OF JOHNNY AND THE HURRICANES (LP)...............£20

JOHNNY & JACK
54   HMV 7MC 21   Honey, I Need You/Goodnight, Well It's Time To Go (export issue) ...£20

JOHNNY & JOHN
66   Polydor 56087   Bumper To Bumper/Scrape My Boot...£25
(see also Johnny Gustafson, Big Three)

MINT VALUE £

JOHNNY & JUDY
59	Vogue Pop V 9128	Bother Me Baby/Who's To Say	£500
59	Vogue Pop V 9128	Bother Me Baby/Who's To Say (78)	£150

(see also John Walker)

JOHNNY & THE SELF ABUSERS
77	Chiswick NS 22	Saints And Sinners/Dead Vandals (p/s)	£40

(see also Simple Minds)

JOHNNY F & KLM
92	Liberty Grooves LIB003	TAKIN' LIBERTIES VOL 1 (LP)	£15

JOHNNY MOPED
76	Chiswick PROMO 3	BASICALLY, THE ORIGINAL JOHNNY MOPED TAPE (33rpm, no p/s)	£20
77	Chiswick S 15	No-One/Incendiary Device (first pressing has laminate p/s)	£20
78	Chiswick WIK 8	CYCLEDELIC (LP, with free single [PROMO 3])	£30
90	Deltic DELTLP 6	THE SEARCH FOR XERXES (LP)	£20

(see also Maxim's Trash)

JOHNNY P
88	Unity EE 07	Rude Boy/Talk About We (with Richie Davis)	£35

JOHN'S CHILDREN
66	Columbia DB 8030	The Love I Thought I'd Found/Strange Affair (very few in p/s)	£500
66	Columbia DB 8030	The Love I Thought I'd Found/Strange Affair	£300
67	Columbia DB 8124	Just What You Want - Just What You'll Get/But She's Mine	£160
67	Track 604 003	Desdemona/Remember Thomas A'Beckett (in p/s)	£150
67	Track 604 003	Desdemona/Remember Thomas A'Beckett	£60
67	Track 604 005	Midsummer Night's Scene/Sara Crazy Child (withdrawn)	£4000
67	Track 604 005	Come And Play With Me In The Garden/Sara Crazy Child (in p/s)	£200
67	Track 604 005	Come And Play With Me In The Garden/Sara Crazy Child	£90
67	Track 604 010	Go Go Girl/Jagged Time Lapse	£80
82	Cherry Red BRED 31	ORGASM (LP, with inner)	£20
87	Bam Caruso KIRI 095	MIDSUMMER NIGHT'S SCENE (LP)	£30

(see also Marc Bolan, Andy Ellison, Radio Stars, Jook, Tyrannosaurus Rex)

GLYN JOHNS
65	Immediate IM 013	Mary Anne/Like Grains Of Yellow Sand	£25

LYNDON JOHNS (& ISRAELITES)
69	Downtown DT 444	Don't Gamble With Love/Song Bird	£40
69	Downtown DT 451	Oh Mama Oh Papa/Bring Back The Night (with The Israelites)	£30

JOHN'S RADIO
82	Epidemic EPC 001	Song In My Head/Strange	£20

ANTHONY JOHNSON
82	Rusty R 005	Dread Locks Fight/ANTHONY JOHNSON & RANKING TOYAN: Babyloving (12"	£35
81	Greensleeves GRED 76	Let Go This One/BILLY BOYO: One Spliff A Day (12")	£20
89	Unity UNI 7	Dance Hall Vibe/Version//TONTO IRIE: Wrap It UP Mix (12")	£20
83	Rusty RILP 003	I'M READY (LP)	£25
82	Midnight Rock MRLP 002	GUN SHOT (LP)	£30

BETTY JOHNSON
56	London HLU 8307	I'll Wait/Please Tell Me Why	£40
56	London HLU 8326	Honky Tonk Rock/Say It Isn't So, Joe	£100
56	London HLU 8326	Honky Tonk Rock/Say It Isn't So, Joe (78)	£30
57	London HLU 8365	I Dreamed/If It's Wrong To Love You	£20
58	London HLE 8678	Dream/How Much	£15
58	London HLE 8701	There's Never Been A Night/Mr. Brown Is Out Of Town	£25
58	London HLE 8725	Hoopa Hoola/One More Time	£20
59	London HLE 8839	Does Your Heart Beat For Me?/You And Only You	£20
59	London HLE 8839	Does Your Heart Beat For Me?/You And Only You (78)	£20
59	London RE-E 1221	DREAM (EP)	£75
59	London HA-E 2163	THE SONG YOU HEARD WHEN YOU FELL IN LOVE (LP)	£40

BLIND WILLIE JOHNSON
70	Xtra XTRA 1098	BLIND WILLIE JOHNSON (LP)	£20

BOB JOHNSON & PETE KNIGHT
77	Chrysalis CHR 1137	THE KING OF ELFLAND'S DAUGHTER (LP, lyric insert, green label)	£15

(see also Steeleye Span, Mary Hopkin)

BOBBY JOHNSON & ATOMS
67	Ember EMB S 245	Do It Again A Little Bit Slower/Tramp (in p/s)	£20

BROWNIE JOHNSON
62	Longhorn BLH 0004	Best Dressed Beggar/Just Pretending (estimated that around 1000 pressed)	£40

BUBBER JOHNSON
57	Parlophone R 4259	Confidential/Have A Little Faith In Me	£35

BUDDY JOHNSON
59	Mercury ZEP 10009	BUDDY JOHNSON WAILS (EP, with Ella Johnson)	£50
57	Mercury MPT 7515	ROCK AND ROLL (10" LP, with Ella Johnson)	£150

CAREY JOHNSON
72	Banana BA 369	Correction Train/SOUL DEFENDERS: Version	£25

DANIEL JOHNSON
65	Island WI 250	Come On My People/Brother Nathan	£15

DEBRA JOHNSON
98	Kent 6T 19	To Get Love/DIPLOMATS: I Really Love You	£30

DOMINO JOHNSON
72	Green Door GD 4045	Summertime/SWANS: Grazing	£25
73	Count Shelly	I've Seen The Light/BARRY CRUBER: This Yah Daughter	£50

GENERAL JOHNSON
73	Invictus SVT 1008	GENERALLY SPEAKING (LP)	£20

(see also Norman Johnson, Showmen, Chairmen Of The Board)

GINGER JOHNSON AND HIS AFRICAN MESSENGERS
67	Masquerade SM 02001	AFRICAN PARTY (LP)	£125

HOWARD JOHNSON
71	Jay Boy BOY 47	The Slide/That Magic Touch Can Send You Flying	£15

JIMMY JOHNSON
65	Sue WI 387	Don't Answer The Door Parts 1 & 2	£35

J.J. JOHNSON
55	Vogue LDE 124	J.J. JOHNSON SEXTET (10" LP)	£15
55	Vogue LDE 162	J.J. JOHNSON QUINTET (10" LP)	£15
72	United Artists UAS 29451	ACROSS 110TH STREET (LP, soundtrack, with Bobby Womack)	£20

(see also Sonny Stitt)

(JOHNNY JOHNSON &) THE BANDWAGON
72	Stateside SS 2207	Honey Bee/I Don't Know Why	£20
74	EMI EMI 2114	Strong Love, Proud Love/Fast Running Out Of World	£25
69	Direction 8-63500	JOHNNY JOHNSON AND THE BANDWAGON (LP)	£30
70	Bell SBLL 138	SOUL SURVIVOR (LP)	£25

JUDI JOHNSON (& PERFECTIONS)
64	HMV POP 1371	My Baby's Face/Make The Most Of It (solo)	£30
65	HMV POP 1399	How Many Times/A Way Out (as Judi Johnson & Perfections)	£20

LARRY JOHNSON
70	Blue Horizon 7-63851	PRESENTING THE COUNTRY BLUES (LP)	£150

LAURIE JOHNSON ORCHESTRA
65	Pye 7N 17015	The Avengers/Minor Bossa Nova (in p/s)	£50
65	Pye 7N 17015	The Avengers/Minor Bossa Nova	£30
69	MGM MGM 1457	There Is Another Song/Caesar Smith	£25
71	Columbia DB 8826	The Jason King Theme/There Comes A Time	£50
63	Pye NPL 18088	THE NEW BIG SOUND OF THE LAURIE JOHNSON ORCHESTRA (LP)	£15
65	Pye NPL 18103	THE BIG NEW SOUND STRIKES AGAIN (LP)	£15
67	Marble Arch MAL 695	THE AVENGERS AND OTHER FAVOURITES (LP)	£25
69	MGM C(S) 8104	THEMES AND ... (LP)	£25
70	Columbia SCX 6412	LAURIE JOHNSON/LONDON JAZZ ORCHESTRA - SYNTHESIS (LP, with Joe Harriott, Tubby Hayes, Stan Tracey & Tony Coe)	£60
80	Unicorn Kachana KPM 7009	MUSIC FROM THE AVENGERS, THE NEW AVENGERS AND THE PROFESSIONALS (LP, gatefold sleeve, with London Studio Orchestra)	£20

LINTON KWESI JOHNSON
78	Virgin VX 1002	DREAD BEAT AN' BLOOD (LP, as Poet & The Roots)	£25
79	Island ILPS 9566	FORCES OF VICTORY (LP, with inner sleeve)	£15
80	Island ILPS 9605	BASS CULTURE (LP)	£20
80	Island ILPS 9650	LKJ IN DUB (LP)	£15

LONNIE JOHNSON
57	Parlophone GEP 8635	LONESOME ROAD (EP)	£20
57	Parlophone GEP 8663	LONNIE'S BLUES (EP)	£20
58	Parlophone GEP 8693	LONNIE'S BLUES NO. 2 (EP)	£20
64	Storyville SLP 162	PORTRAITS IN BLUES VOL. 6 (LP)	£20
64	Storyville 616 010	SEE SEE RIDER (LP, with Otis Spann)	£40
60s	Xtra XTRA 1037	LONNIE JOHNSON (LP)	£25

(see also Eddie Lang & Lonnie Johnson)

LORRAINE JOHNSON
78	EPIC S EPC 7089	FEED THE FLAME (LP)	£25

LOU JOHNSON
63	London HLX 9805	Reach Out For Me/Magic Potion	£50
63	London HLX 9805	Reach Out For Me/Magic Potion (DJ copy)	£100
64	London HLX 9917	(There's) Always Something There To Remind Me/Wouldn't That Be Something	£25
64	London HLX 9929	A Message To Martha (Kentucky Bluebird)/The Last One To Be Loved	£15
65	London HLX 9965	Please Stop The Wedding/Park Avenue	£20
65	London HLX 9994	A Time To Love, A Time To Cry/Unsatisfied	£80
65	London HLX 9994	A Time To Love, A Time To Cry/Unsatisfied (DJ copy)	£150
64	London REX 1438	THE MAGIC POTION OF LOU JOHNSON (EP)	£150

LUTHER 'GEORGIA BOY SNAKE' JOHNSON
69	Transatlantic TRA 188	THE MUDDY WATERS BLUES BAND (LP, credits Muddy Waters on label)	£30

MARV JOHNSON
59	London HLT 8856	Come To Me/Whisper (tri-centre)	£100
59	London HLT 8856	Come To Me/Whisper	£30
59	London HLT 9013	You Got What It Takes/Don't Leave Me (tri centre)	£20
59	London HLT 9013	You Got What It Takes/Don't Leave Me (78)	£20
60	London HLT 9109	I Love The Way You Love/Let Me Love You	£20

60	London HL 7095	I Love The Way You Love/Let Me Love You (export issue)	£20
60	London HLT 9165	Ain't Gonna Be That Way/All The Love I've Got	£20
60	London HLT 9187	(You've Got To) Move Two Mountains/I Need You	£20
61	London HLT 9265	Happy Days/Baby, Baby	£20
61	London HLT 9311	Merry-Go-Round/Tell Me That You Love Me	£30
65	Tamla Motown TMG 525	Why Do You Want To Let Me Go/I'm Not A Plaything	£100
60	London HA-T 2271	MARVELLOUS MARV JOHNSON (LP)	£150
69	T. Motown TML 11111	I'LL PICK A ROSE FOR MY ROSE (LP, mono)	£30
69	T. Motown STML 11111	I'LL PICK A ROSE FOR MY ROSE (LP, stereo)	£25

MATT JOHNSON

81	4AD CAD 113	BURNING BLUE SOUL (LP, original 'psychedelic eye' cover)	£80

(see also Gadgets, The The)

MIRRIAM JOHNSON

61	London HLW 9337	Lonesome Road/Young And Innocent	£15

NORMAN JOHNSON (& SHOWMEN)

69	Action ACT 4529	You're Everything/Our Love Will Grow	£100
69	Action ACT 4545	Take It Baby/In Paradise	£50
71	Action ACT 4601	You're Everything/Our Love Will Grow (reissue)	£40

(see also Chairmen Of The Board, Showmen)

PETE JOHNSON

56	Vogue V 2007	J.J. Boogie/Yancey Special	£35
56	Vogue V 2008	Swanee River Boogie/St. Louis Boogie	£30
55	Vogue EPV 1039	PETE JOHNSON (EP)	£30
59	Top Rank JKR 8009	ROLL 'EM BOY (EP)	£25
55	London AL 3549	JUMPIN' WITH PETE JOHNSON (10" LP)	£50
55	Vogue Coral LRA 10016	BOOGIE WOOGIE MOOD (LP)	£30

(see also Joe Turner & Pete Johnson, Albert Ammons & Meade Lux Lewis)

PHILIP JOHNSON

82	Namedrop NR3	YOUTH IN MOURNING (LP, with 4 double sided A4 sheets)	£20

PLAS JOHNSON (ORCHESTRA)

57	Capitol CL 14772	The Big Twist/Come Rain Or Come Shine	£20
57	Capitol CL 14816	Swanee River Rock/You Send Me	£20
58	Capitol CL 14836	Popcorn/Hoppin' Mad	£20
58	Capitol CL 14903	Little Rockin' Deacon/Dinah	£20
57	London HB-U 1078	BOP ME DADDY (10" LP)	£60

PROFESSOR JOHNSON & HIS GOSPEL SINGERS

51	Vocalion V 1013	Give Me That Old Time Religion/Where Shall I Be (78)	£20
58	Brunswick OE 9352	PROFESSOR JOHNSON AND HIS GOSPEL SINGERS (EP)	£20

RAY JOHNSON

57	Vogue V 9073	If You Don't Want Me Baby/Calypso Joe	£40
58	Vogue V 9093	Calypso Blues/Are You There	£40

ROBERT JOHNSON

62	Philips BBL 7539	ROBERT JOHNSON 1936-1937 (LP)	£100
65	CBS BPG 62456	KING OF THE DELTA BLUES SINGERS (LP)	£60
67	Kokomo K 1000	ROBERT JOHNSON (LP)	£50
60s	Smokestack SS/LP 1	BLUES LEGEND 1936-1937 (LP)	£40
70	CBS 64102	KING OF THE DELTA BLUES SINGERS VOL. 2 (LP)	£30
85	Blue Diamond/CBS 22190	KING OF THE DELTA BLUES SINGERS VOLUMES 1 & 2 (2-LP)	£20

ROY LEE JOHNSON

69	Action ACT 4518	So Anna Just Love Me/Boogaloo No. 3 (Red label)	£40
69	Action ACT 4518	So Anna Just Love Me/Boogaloo No. 3 (Yellow label)	£30

RUBY JOHNSON

67	Stax 601 020	If I Ever Needed Love (I Sure Do Need It Now)/Keep On Keeping On	£30

SYL JOHNSON

73	London HL 10403	We Did It/Anyway The Wind Blows	£15
74	London SHU 8469	BACK FOR A TASTE OF YOUR LOVE (LP)	£20
74	London SHU 8477	DIAMOND IN THE ROUGH (LP)	£30
75	London SHU 8494	TOTAL EXPLOSION (LP)	£15
80	Flyright FLY LP 569	BRINGS OUT THE BLUES IN ME (LP)	£15
86	Charly CRD 1125	IS IT BECAUSE I'M BLACK (LP)	£15

(see also Lula Reed)

T J JOHNSON

83	Switch DSW 003	I Can Make It/Good For You (12")	£50

THEO JOHNSON

65	Aladdin WI 604	Masters Of War/The Water Is Wide	£15

TOMMY JOHNSON

60s	Saydisc SDM 224	THE LEGACY OF TOMMY JOHNSON (LP)	£20

WILCO JOHNSONS SOLID SENDERS

78	Virgin V 2105	SOLID SENDERS (LP, with free 'Live LP' stickered sleeve)	£15
80	Fresh FRESH LP 4	ICE ON THE MOTORWAY (LP, with free 7", as Wilco Johnson)	£15

(see also Dr. Feelgood)

BRUCE JOHNSTON COMBO

63	London HL 9780	Original Surfer Stomp/Pajama Party	£60

(see also Beach Boys,, Sagittarius)

DANIEL JOHNSTON
93	Ay Carramba! EL BARTO 001	**RESPECT** (10" LP)	£15
02	Pickled Egg EGG 22	**REJECTED UNKNOWN** (2-LP)	£20
06	Coppertree CTR 007	**FEAR YOURSELF** (LP, 1000 only)	£25

JOHNSTON BROTHERS
54	Decca F 10364	**Sh-Boom** (Life Could Be A Dream)/**Crazy 'Bout Ya Baby**	£15
55	Decca F 10608	**Hernando's Hideaway/Hey There**	£15

(see also Vera Lynn, Joan Regan, Lita Roza, Suzi Miller, Ted Heath)

JOHNSTONS
68	Transatlantic TRA 169	**THE JOHNSTONS** (LP)	£22
68	Transatlantic TRA 184	**GIVE A DAMN** (LP)	£18
68	Transatlantic TRA 185	**THE BARLEYCORN** (LP)	£18
70	Transatlantic TRA 211	**BITTER GREEN** (LP)	£20
71	Transatlantic TRA 231	**COLOURS OF THE DAWN** (LP)	£15

(see also Adrienne Johnston)

JOINT PROJECT
92	Soapbar SBR 001	**Total Feeling/Good Feeling** (12")	£35
93	Soapbar SBR 005	**Dark In Da Jungle/Fantasize** (12")	£25

JOKE SHOP
72	Access ACC 01	**Lame Dog/Tell Her To Leave** (p/s)	£15

JOKER (2)
93	Skanna 06	**The Joker/Roots** (12")	£40

(see also Skanna)

JOKERS
62	Salvo SLO 1806	**Blue Moonbeam/Dog Fight** (99 only)	£35

JOKER'S WILD
66	Regent Sound RSR 0031	**Don't Ask Me/Why Do Fools Fall In Love** (handwritten labels, 50 only)	£500
66	Regent Sound RSLP 007	**JOKER'S WILD: Why Do Fools Fall In Love/Walk Like A Man/Don't Ask Me/Big Girls Don't Cry/Beautiful Delilah** (12", 1-sided, 50 copies only)	£1000

(see also Dave Gilmour, Pink Floyd)

JOLLIVER ARKANSAS
69	Bell SBLL 119	**HOME** (LP)	£30

(see also Leslie West, Mountain)

JOLLY BOYS
70	Moodisc MU 3504	**On The Water/MUDIES ALL STARS: Cash Register**	£15

JOLLY BROTHERS
78	Ballistic FORCE 2002	**Conscious Man/PRODIGAL CREATOR: Life** (actually dub to Lee Perry's Ne Jah Go Run) (12")	£18
81	Seven Leaves SL 008	**Have A Litte Faith/Right Before My Eyes** (12")	£18
93	Roots RRLP 001	**LEE PERRY PRESENTS THE JOLLY BROTHERS** (LP)	£20

JOLT
77	Polydor 2058 936	**You're Cold/All I Can Do** (p/s)	£15
78	Polydor 2383 504	**THE JOLT** (LP, flip-back sleeve)	£30

JON
67	Parlophone R 5604	**So Much For Mary/Polly Sunday** (in p/s)	£50
67	Parlophone R 5604	**So Much For Mary/Polly Sunday**	£25
67	Columbia DB 8249	**Is It Love/Sing Out**	£150

(see also Titus Groan, Still Life)

JON & ALUN
63	Decca LK 4547	**RELAX YOUR MIND** (LP, mono)	£22
63	Decca SKL 4547	**RELAX YOUR MIND** (LP, stereo)	£30

JON & ROBIN & IN-CROWD
67	Stateside SS 2027	**Do It Again A Little Bit Slower/If I Need Someone It's You**	£15

JONAH
85	MW MW 7853	**Tough/This Is Love** (no p/s)	£280

JONATHAN & CHARLES
69	Herald LLR 566	**ANOTHER WEEK TO GO** (LP)	£30

A JONES
04	Jah Tubbys JT 10020	**Jah Bless I/MA-KAYA CREW: Iron Dub**	£25

AL JONES (1)
58	HMV POP 451	**Mad, Mad, World/Lonely Traveller**	£200
58	HMV POP 451	**Mad, Mad, World/Lonely Traveller**(78)	£20

AL JONES (2)
69	Parlophone PMC/PCS 7081	**ALUN ASHWORTH JONES** (LP, black/yellow label with "Sold in U.K..." text)	£175
72	Village Thing VTS 19	**JONESVILLE** (LP)	£175

BARBARA JONES
72	Bullet BU 516	**Sad Movies/SIR HARRY: Deejay Version**	£20
76	Trojan TRLS 136	**THE BEST OF BARBARA JONES** (LP)	£20

BETTY HALL JONES
50	Capitol CL 13266	**This Joint's Too Hip For Me/You've Got To Have What It Takes** (78)	£15

BEVERLEY JONES (& PRESTONS)
63	HMV POP 1140	**Why Do Lovers Break Each Other's Heart/I'm Just An In-Between**	£20
63	HMV POP 1201	**Wait 'Til My Bobby Gets Home/A Boy Like You**	£15

MINT VALUE £

64	Parlophone R 5189	Heatwave/Hear You Talking (with Prestons)	£20

(see also Roger James)

CAROL JONES
60	Triumph RGM 1012	The Boy With The Eyes Of Blue/I Gave Him Back His Ring	£125

CASEY JONES & THE ENGINEERS
63	Columbia DB 7083	One Way Ticket/I'm Gonna Love	£35

CASEY JONES & THE GOVERNERS
64	Golden 12LP 106	DON'T HA HA (LP)	£60

(see also Casey Jones & The Engineers)

CURTIS JONES
66	RCA RCX 7184	R.C.A. VICTOR RACE SERIES VOL. 9 (EP)	£15
64	Decca LK 4587	CURTIS JONES IN LONDON (LP)	£125
68	Blue Horizon 7-63207	NOW RESIDENT IN EUROPE (LP, mono)	£80
68	Blue Horizon (S)-63207	NOW RESIDENT IN EUROPE (LP, stereo)	£50

DAVIE JONES & THE KING BEES
64	Vocalion V 9221	Liza Jane/Louie, Louie Go Home (Demo copy)	£2000
64	Vocalion Pop V 9221	Liza Jane/Louie, Louie Go Home (beware of counterfeits without centres)	£1500
78	Decca F 13807	Liza Jane/Louie, Louie Go Home (reissue)	£25

(see also David Bowie, Manish Boys, Calvin James)

DAVY JONES (U.K.) (1)
65	Parlophone R 5250	You've Got A Habit Of Leaving/Baby Loves That Way (Demo)	£900
65	Parlophone R 5315	You've Got A Habit Of Leaving/Baby Loves That Way	£1000

(see also David Bowie)

DAVY JONES (U.K.) (2)
67	Pye International 7N 25432	Theme For A New Love/Dream Girl (reissue, withdrawn)	£20
67	Pye NPL 18178	DAVY JONES (LP)	£20

(see also Davy Jones & Micky Dolenz, Monkees)

DAVY JONES (U.K.) & THE LOWER THIRD/MANISH BOYS
79	EMI 2925	You've Got A Habit Of Leaving/Baby Loves That Way/MANISH BOYS: I Pity The Fool/Take My Tip (Demo copy, p/s)	£20
82	Charly CYM 1	You've Got A Habit Of Leaving/Baby Loves That Way/MANISH BOYS: I Pity The Fool/Take My Tip (10", p/s)	£20

(see also David Bowie, Davie Jones & King Bees, Manish Boys, Calvin James)

DAVY JONES (U.S.)
62	Piccadilly 7N 35038	Jezebel/Don't Come Crying To Me	£40

(see also Thelonious Monk)

DILL JONES TRIO
56	Jazz Today JTE 104	PIANO MOODS VOL. 2 (EP)	£25
56	Pye Jazz NJE 1024	PIANO MOODS VOL. 5 (EP)	£25
60	Columbia 33SX 1336	JONES THE JAZZ (LP)	£60
78	77 77SEU 12/45	UP JUMPED YOU WITH LOVE (LP)	£20

DOROTHY JONES
61	Philips PB 1169	Takin' That Long Walk Home/It's Unbearable	£30

(see also Cookies)

GEORGE JONES
59	Mercury AMT 1036	White Lightning/Long Time To Forget	£25
59	Mercury AMT 1058	Who Shot Sam/Into My Arms Again	£15
65	United Artists UP 1080	The Race Is On/She's So Lonesome Again	£15
59	Mercury ZEP 10036	GEORGE JONES (EP)	£80
59	Melodisc EPM7 109	COUNTRY SONG HITS (EP)	£40
64	Mercury 10009 MCE	C & W ACES (EP)	£20
62	United Artists ULP 1007	THE NEW FAVOURITES OF GEORGE JONES (LP)	£20
63	United Artists ULP 1014	MY FAVOURITES OF HANK WILLIAMS (LP)	£20
63	Ember CW 101	THE CROWN PRINCE OF COUNTRY MUSIC (LP, original pressings have grey & orange label)	£20

(see also Gene Pitney, Elvis Costello)

JONES GIRLS
82	Philadelphia Intl. PIR 12-2031	Nights Over Egypt/Love Don't Ever Say Goodbye (12")	£20
79	Phil. Intl. PIR 83831	THE JONES GIRLS (LP)	£15

GLORIA JONES
66	Capitol CL 15429	Heartbeat (Parts 1 & 2)	£50
66	Stateside SS 555	Finders Keepers/Run One Flight Of Stairs	£80
77	EMI 2570	Go Now (album version)/Drive Me Crazy (12" demos only)	£65
79	Inferno HEAT 6	Tainted Love/SANDY WYNNS: A Touch Of Venus (reissue)	£15
14	Champion 5350752	Tainted Love/Come Go With Me (reissue)	£15
74	Tamla Motown STML 11254	SHARE MY LOVE (LP)	£25
76	EMI EMC 3159	VIXEN (LP, produced by Marc Bolan)	£20

(see also Marc Bolan & Gloria Jones)

GRACE JONES
77	RCA 2058856	Sorry/That's The Trouble	£15
04	DPRO WL 12004	Clandestine Affair (Vocal)/(Instrumental)/We Know (12", clear with Tricky)	£25
77	Island ILPS 9470	PORTFOLIO (LP)	£15
78	Island ILPS 9525	FAME (LP)	£15
80	Island ILPS 9592	WARM LEATHERETTE (LP, 1st pressing, blue labels)	£18
81	Island ILPS 9624	NIGHTCLUBBING (LP, 1st pressing, gold 'picture' labels)	£18

82	Island PILPS 9722	**LIVING MY LIFE** (LP, picture disc)	£18
82	Island ILPS 9722	**LIVING MY LIFE** (LP, 1st pressing, blue labels, inner and 'video ad' insert)	£15
85	Island GRACE 1	**SLAVE TO THE RHYTHM** (LP)	£15
85	Island 207 572	**ISLAND LIFE** (LP)	£20
10	Vinyl Factory VF 016	**HURRICANE** (2-LP, numbered)	£150
11	Wall Of Sound WOS050DLPX	**HURRICANE DUB** (2-LP)	£100
14	Island/Back To Black 0600753480540	**NIGHTCLUBBING** (2-LP reissue)	£35
14	Island/Back To Black 535 142-8	**ISLAND LIFE** (LP, reissue)	£25
16	Island 0600753660713	**WARM LEATHERETTE** (4-LP box set in 'leather finished' box)	£50

GRANDPA JONES
57	Brunswick 05676	**Eight More Miles To Louisville/Dark As A Dungeon**	£15
62	London HA-U/SH-U 8010	**MAKES THE RAFTERS RING** (LP)	£20
64	London HA-U/SH-U 8119	**YODELLING HITS** (LP)	£20

(see also Brown's Ferry Four)

HEATHER JONES
68	Welsh Teldisc TEP 872	**CANEUON EP** (p/s)	£15
71	Newyddion Da ND 2	**HEATHER EP** (p/s, with Meic Stevens)	£45
71	Sain SAIN 20	**COLLI LAITH EP** (p/s)	£15
72	Sain SAIN 30	**PAN DDAWR DYDD EP** (p/s)	£15
74	Sain SAIN 1008M	**MAE'R OLYWYN YN TROI** (LP)	£50
76	Sain SAIN 1047M	**JIAWL!** (LP)	£40

JAKE JONES
| 71 | MCA MVPS 432 | **JAKE JONES** (LP) | £25 |

JANET JONES
| 74 | Midas MR 005 | **SING TO ME LADY** (LP, red or yellow labels) | £250 |
| 74 | Midas MFHR 059 | **JANET JONES** (LP, yellow label, released on Folk Heritage label) | £250 |

JANIE JONES (& LASH)
65	HMV POP 1495	**Witches Brew/Take-A My Tip**	£15
66	HMV POP 1514	**Gunning For You/Go Go Away From Me**	£15
67	Columbia DB 8173	**Tickle Me Tootsie Wootsies/High And Dry**	£15
83	Big Beat NS 91	**House Of The Ju-Ju Queen/Sex Machine** (as Janie Jones & Lash, p/s)	£20

(see also The Clash)

JERRY JONES
70	Banana BA 316	**Still Waters** (Love)**/SOUND DIMENSION: Wig Wam**	£30
71	Bamboo BAM 65	**Still Waters** (Love)**/BRENTFORD ALLSTARS: Wig Wam** (reissue)	£40
71	Bamboo BALPS 213	**AT THE KINGSTON HOTEL, JAMAICA** (LP)	£65

JIMMY JONES
60	MGM MGM 1051	**Handy Man/The Search Is Over** (78)	£40
60	MGM MGM 1103	**Ready For Love/For You**	£15
61	MGM MGM 1123	**I Told You So/You Got It**	£15
61	MGM MGM 1146	**Mr Music Man/Holler Hey**	£15
65	Columbia DB 7592	**Walkin'/Pardon Me**	£30
65	Cameo Parkway P 988	**Don't You Just Know It**	£15
67	Stateside SS 2041	**39-21-46/Personal Property**	£18
60	MGM MGM-EP 745	**JIMMY HANDYMAN JONES** (EP)	£30
61	MGM MGM-EP 787	**ORIGINAL HITS** (EP)	£30
60	MGM MGM-C 832	**GOOD TIMIN'** (LP)	£50

JO JONES TRIO
| 59 | Top Rank 25/039 | **JO JONES** (LP) | £18 |

JOE JONES
| 60 | Columbia DB 4533 | **You Talk Too Much/I Love You Still** | £15 |

JOHN PAUL JONES
| 64 | Pye 7N 15637 | **Baja/A Foggy Day In Vietnam** (B-side by Andrew Oldham Orchestra, white label promo) | £200 |
| 64 | Pye 7N 15637 | **Baja/A Foggy Day In Vietnam** (B-side actually by Andrew Oldham Orchestra) | £150 |

(see also Led Zeppelin, Andrew Oldham Orchestra)

JUSTIN JONES
| 61 | London HLU 9463 | **Dance By Yourself/Love** | £150 |

LEATH JONES
| 81 | All That DAT 1 EJSP 9772 | **Bad Boys/First Time** (p/s) | £20 |

LESLIE JONES
| 59 | Pye NSPL 83008/9 | **THE MUSIC OF ROBERT FARNON** (2-LP) | £20 |

LINDA JONES
67	Warner Bros WB 2070	**Hypnotised/I Can't Stop Lovin' My Baby**	£60
72	London HLU 10368	**For Your Precious Love/Don't Go**	£15
75	Warner Bros WB 16621	**I Just Can't Live My Life/My Heart Will Understand**	£20
15	Soul Brother SB 701	**I Just Can't Live My Life/My Heart Needs A Break**	£15

LLOYD JONES
| 70 | Bullet BU 429 | **Rome/RHYTHM RULERS: Version** | £30 |

LOUIS JONES ROCK & ROLL BAND
| 50s | Vogue VE1 70111 | **ROCK AND ROLL** (EP) | £100 |

MAGGIE JONES
| 70 | VJM VLP 23 | COLUMBIA RECORDINGS IN CHRONOLOGICAL ORDER VOL. 1 (LP) | £15 |
| 70 | VJM VLP 25 | COLUMBIA RECORDINGS IN CHRONOLOGICAL ORDER VOL. 2 (LP) | £15 |

NIC JONES
70	Trailer LER 2014	BALLADS AND SONGS (LP, white label)	£60
70	Trailer LER 2014	BALLADS AND SONGS (LP, red label)	£50
70	Trailer LER 2014	BALLADS AND SONGS (LP, later pressing with 'highway' label)	£15
71	Trailer LER 2027	NIC JONES (LP, yellow label)	£40
71	Trailer LER 2027	NIC JONES (LP, red label)	£50
73	Trailer LER 2083	SONGS OF A CHANGING WORLD (LP, with Jon Raven & Tony Rose, red label with insert)	£30
77	Trailer LER 2091	NOAH'S ARK TRAP (LP)	£50
77	Trailer LER 2091	NOAH'S ARK TRAP (LP, reissue with Highway label)	£15
78	Transatlantic LTRA 507	FROM THE DEVIL TO A STRANGER (LP)	£60
80	Topic 12TS411	PENGUIN EGGS (LP)	£50
09	Three Black Feathers TBFLP001	PENGUIN EGGS (LP, reissue, 200gm vinyl)	£20
17	Topic 12TS 411	PENGUIN EGGS (LP, reissue white vinyl)	£15

(see also Jon Raven, Halliard)

NIGEL MAZLYN JONES
76	Isle Of Light IOL 666/1	SHIP TO SHORE (LP)	£50
78	Avada AVA 105	SENTINEL (LP, with inner sleeve, b/w picture label)	£20
82	Isle Of Light IOL 0230	BREAKING COVER (LP)	£20
91	Isle Of Light 1OL 0232LP	MAZLYN JONES (LP)	£20

NORAH JONES
| 04 | Blue Note 7243 5 3208813 | COME AWAY WITH ME (LP) | £25 |

PALMER JONES
| 68 | Direction 58-3603 | The Great Magic Of Love/Dancing Master | £30 |

PAUL JONES
67	HMV PSR 5307	Privilege (1-sided demo)	£20
68	Columbia DB 8379	And The Sun Will Shine/The Dog Presides	£25
67	HMV 7EG 8975	PRIVILEGE (EP)	£20
66	HMV CLP 3586	MY WAY (LP, mono)	£25
66	HMV CSD 3586	MY WAY (LP, stereo)	£30
67	HMV CLP 3602	LOVE ME, LOVE MY FRIENDS (LP, mono)	£35
67	HMV CSD 3602	LOVE ME, LOVE MY FRIENDS (LP, stereo)	£40
67	HMV CLP/CSD 3623	PRIVILEGE (LP, soundtrack, with George Bean Group & Mike Leander)	£40
69	Columbia SX/SCX 6347	COME INTO MY MUSIC BOX (LP, mono/stereo)	£20
71	Vertigo 6360 059	CRUCIFIX IN A HORSESHOE (LP, gatefold sleeve, swirl label)	£150
70	President PTLS 1068	DRAKE'S DREAM (LP, soundtrack)	£30

(see also Manfred Mann, Blues Band)

QUINCY JONES
72	A&M AMS 888	Ironside/Cast Your Fate To The Wind	£15
60	Mercury MMC 14038	THE BIRTH OF A BAND (LP, mono)	£20
60	Mercury CMS 18026	THE BIRTH OF A BAND (LP, stereo)	£25
65	Mercury 20047 MCL	GOLDEN BOY (LP)	£15
65	Mercury 20063 SMCL	THE PAWNBROKER (LP, soundtrack)	£30
66	Mercury 20072 (S)MCL	MIRAGE (LP, soundtrack)	£25
66	Mercury 20078 (S)MCL	QUINCY'S GOT A BRAND NEW BAG (LP)	£15
66	Fontana FJL 127	FAB! (LP)	£15
67	Mercury SMWL 30003	TRAVELLIN' ON THE QUINCY JONES BANDWAGON (LP)	£15
68	RCA Victor RD/SF 7931	IN COLD BLOOD (LP, soundtrack)	£20
68	United Artists (S)ULP 1181	IN THE HEAT OF THE NIGHT (LP, soundtrack, with Ray Charles)	£25
69	Uni UNLS 103	LOST MAN (LP, soundtrack)	£25
69	Paramount SPFL 256	THE ITALIAN JOB (LP, soundtrack, with Matt Monro)	£75
70	United Artists UAS 29128	THEY CALL ME MISTER TIBBS (LP, soundtrack)	£60
72	WEA K 44168	THE HEIST (LP, soundtrack, with Little Richard)	£15
72	Atlantic K 40371	HOW TO STEAL A DIAMOND IN FOUR UNEASY LESSONS (LP, soundtrack)	£15
85	Nimbus/A&M AMLH 64485	SOUNDS AND STUFF LIKE THAT (LP, Nimbus Supercut, mail order only from Practical Hi Fi magazine)	£40

(see also Annie Ross, Eddie Barclay & Quincy Jones, Diana Ross & Quincy Jones, John & Joan Shakespeare)

RICK JONES
| 73 | Argo ZDA 156 | HIYA MAYA (LP) | £15 |

RICKIE LEE JONES
| 84 | Warner Bros. K56628 | RICKIE LEE JONES (LP, Nimbus Supercut, mail order only through Practical Hi-Fi magazine) | £90 |

ROBIN JONES & HIS QUINTET
71	Apollo Sound APPS5012	DENGA (LP)	£40
71	Apollo Sound APP S 5016	EL MAJA (LP, as Robin Jones Seven)	£125
20	Jazz Room JAZZR 004	EL MAJA (reissue)	£15

RONNIE JONES
64	Decca F 12012	Let's Pin A Rose On You/I Need Your Loving (B-side with Night Timers)	£20
65	Decca F 12066	My Love/It's All Over	£40
65	Decca F 12146	Anyone Who Knows What Love Is/Nobody But You	£20
65	Parlophone R 5326	You're Lookin' Good/I'm So Clean (with Blue Jays)	£40
67	CBS 2699	Little Bitty Pretty One/Put Your Tears Away	£18

MINT VALUE £

67	Polydor 56222	In My Love Mind/Mama Come On Home	£15

(see also Night-Timers)

SALENA JONES
67	Decca F 12708	The Glory Of Love/I've Got The Blues	£70
71	CBS 7542	Baby Don't Ya Get Crazy/Fire And Rain	£15
73	Indigo GOPOP	Live And Let Die/Some Other World (in p/s)	£15
69	CBS 63613	THE MOMENT OF TRUTH (LP)	£35
70	CBS 63901	EVERYBODY'S TALKIN' ABOUT SALENA JONES (LP)	£30
71	CBS 64435	PLATINUM (LP)	£20
73	RCA Victor SF 8335	ALONE & TOGETHER (LP)	£20
74	RCA LPL 1 5025	THIS'N'THAT (LP)	£20

SAM JONES
60	Riverside 12-324	SOUL SOCIETY (LP)	£20

SAMANTHA JONES
65	United Artists UP 1072	It's All Because Of You/I Woke Up Crying	£15
65	United Artists UP 1087	Don't Come Any Closer/Just Call And I'll Be There	£15
67	United Artists UP 1185	Surrounded By A Ray Of Sunshine/How Do You Say Goodbye	£80
67	United Artists UP 1185	Surrounded By A Ray Of Sunshine/How Do You Say Goodbye (DJ Copy)	£150
68	United Artists UP 2258	And Suddenly/Go Ahead And Love Me	£50
80	Ford SLE 19	Ford Leads The Way/Go Ahead And Love Me (p/s, Ford cars promo disc)	£15
68	United Artists	CALL IT SAMANTHA (LP)	£25
72	Contour 2870 303	MY WAY (LP)	£15

(see also Vernons Girls, Krimson Kake)

SOLOMON JONES
70	Pama PM 812	Here Comes The Night/RECO RODRIQUEZ: Jaded Ramble	£18

STAN JONES
58	Pye Disneyland DPL 39000	CREAKIN' LEATHER (LP)	£15

STEVE JONES (1)
84	P Flight PFD01	I Need You (By My Side)/FAT BOYS: The Challenge	£90
84	P flight PFD 01	I Need You (By My Side)/FAT BOYS: The Challenge (12")	£150

STEVE JONES (2)
87	MCA MCF 3384	MERCY (LP)	£15

(see also Sex Pistols, Professionals)

TAMIKO JONES
76	Contempo CX 15	Let It Flow/DORIS DUKE: Woman Of The Ghetto	£15

THAD JONES
57	Esquire 32-065	OLIO (LP)	£60
58	Esquire 32-080	AFTER HOURS (LP)	£60
59	Pye Nixa NJL 13	MAD THAD (LP)	£70

THELMA JONES
68	Sue WI 4047	Stronger/Never Leave Me	£60
69	Soul City SC 110	The House That Jack Built/Give It To Me Straight	£40
76	CBS 4711	Salty Tears/You're The Song	£15

TOM JONES
64	Decca F 11966	Chills And Fever/Breathless	£60
65	Columbia DB 7566	Little Lonely One/That's What We'll All Do	£20
65	Columbia DB 7733	Lonely Joe/I Was A Fool	£20
66	Decca F 12461	This And That/City Girl	£15
65	Decca DFE 8668	WHAT A PARTY (EP)	£15
79	EMI1A 062 63224	DO YOU TAKE THIS MAN? (LP)	£40

JONES TOWN MALE QUARTET/FRANKLIN LADIES TOWN TRIO
62	Son TD 104	We'll Never Say Goodbye/Living For J (split 45 rpm single)	£25

U.K. JONES
69	Deram DM 231	Let Me Tell Ya/And The Rains Came Down	£15

(see also Mike Berry)

VIVIAN JONES
79	White Rum/Red Stripe 101 PROOF	Jah Music/Vibes (as V. Jones)	£20
80s	Virgo Stomach VG 1003	Who's Gonna Get Caught/Horn Fingers (12", blue vinyl)	£15
81	Cha Cha CHAD 37	One Of These Days/Dub (12")	£40
85	Leo LEO 008	Physical/Energy (Instrumental)/Energy (Dub) (12")	£200
86	Jah Shaka 859	Red Eye/Got A Light (12")	£35
92	Imperial House IH 006	Ethiopian Eyes African Smile/African Love/African Dub (12")	£15
87	Jah Shaka SHAKA 861	JAH WORKS (LP)	£60
89	Ruff Cutt RCLP 001	BANK ROBBERY (LP)	£120

WIZZ JONES
69	United Artists (S)ULP 1209	WIZZ JONES (LP)	£175
70	Village Thing VTS 4	LEGENDARY ME (LP)	£100
72	CBS 64809	RIGHT NOW (LP)	£100
74	Village Thing VTS 24	WHEN I LEAVE BERLIN (LP)	£90
77	Plant Life PLR 009	MAGICAL FLIGHT (LP, with insert)	£25

(see also Pete Stanley & Wizz Jones, Accolade)

JONES BOYS
57	Columbia DB 4046	Cool Baby/Rock-A-Hula Baby (Ukulele Lady)	£15

(see also Four Jones Boys)
JONES BROTHERS
69	Pye Intl. 7N 25696	Lucky Lady/Good Old Days **£75**

JONESES
81	Champagne FIZY 507	Summer Groove/Summer Grove (12") **£40**
81	Champagne FIZY 507	Summer Groove (Moving On)/Summer Groove Music/Summer Groove **£25**

JONESY
73	Dawn DNS 1030	Ricochet/Every Day's The Same **£20**
72	Dawn DNLS 3042	NO ALTERNATIVE (LP, gatefold sleeve) **£80**
73	Dawn DNLS 3048	KEEPING UP (LP, with lyric insert, lilac label) **£100**
73	Dawn DNLS 3048	KEEPING UP (LP, without lyric insert, lilac label) **£60**
73	Dawn DNLS 3055	GROWING (LP, gatefold sleeve, with lyric insert, pink 'sun' label) **£80**
73	Dawn DNLS 3055	GROWING (LP, gatefold sleeve, without lyric insert, pink 'sun' label) **£50**

(see also Alan Bown, Ray Thomas)
JONIE D
89	Positive Beat PBEP 001	WHICH BASE (EP) **£15**

JONJO
72	Bumble GE 119	Nine Years Old/Flash In The Pan **£80**

KEN JONNART
69	Mercury MF 1118	From The Very First Time/There's A Place **£30**

JONNIE & THE LUBES
79	Attrix RB 05	I Got Rabies/Terror In T/EXECUTIVES: Shy Little Girl/Never Go Home **£15**

HARLEM JONNS RESHUFFLE
68	Fontana TF 970	You Are The One I Love/Good Lovin' **£30**
69	Fontana TF 1004	Everything Under The Sun/Let Love Come Between Us **£20**
69	Fontana (S)TL 5509	HARLEM JONNS RESHUFFLE (LP) **£50**

JONSI
10	Parlophone 5099962617819	GO (LP) **£20**

(see also Sigur Ros)
JONSTON MCPHILBRY
66	Fontana TF 663	She's Gone/Woke Up At Eight **£75**

JON THE POSTMAN
78	Bent BIG BENT 2	PUERILE (12" EP, stamped brown paper bag p/s, with inserts) **£20**
78	Bent BIG BENT 4	PSYCHEDELIC ROCK'N'ROLL FIVE SKINNERS (12" EP, white label, foldover p/s in bag) **£20**

JOOK
72	RCA RCA 2279	Alright With Me/Do What You Can **£15**
73	RCA RCA 2344	Shame/City And Suburban Blues **£20**
73	RCA RCA 2368	Oo-Oo-Rudi/Jook's On You **£15**
74	RCA RCA 5024	Bish Bash Bosh/Crazy Kids **£18**

(see also John's Children, Sparks)
JANIS JOPLIN
69	CBS 3683	Turtle Blues/Piece Of My Heart (withdrawn) **£30**
69	CBS 63546	I GOT DEM OL' KOZMIC BLUES AGAIN, MAMA! (LP) **£45**
72	CBS 64792	JOPLIN IN CONCERT (2-LP) **£20**
71	CBS S 64188	PEARL (LP) **£20**
73	CBS CQ 30322/Q 64188	PEARL (LP, quadrophonic) **£25**
75	CBS 88115	JANIS (2-LP) **£20**
81	CBS S 64188	PEARL (LP, reissue) **£15**
82	CBS 85354	FAREWELL SONGS (LP) **£15**
99	Simply Vinyl SVLP 062	PEARL (LP, reissue, 180gm) **£15**
07	Columbia CS 9913	I GOT DEM OL' KOZMIC BLUES AGAIN, MAMA! (LP, reissue, 180gm) **£20**
07	Music On Vinyl MOVLP010	PEARL (LP, reissue, 180gm) **£15**
15	music On Vinyl MOVLP466	PEARL (LP, reissue, red vinyl, 300 numbered copies) **£40**

(see also Big Brother & Holding Company)
JORDAN BROTHERS
59	London HLW 8908	Never, Never/Please Tell Me Now **£30**
59	London HLW 8908	Never, Never/Please Tell Me Now (78) **£25**

CLIFFORD JORDAN
72	Polydor 2383206	CLIFFORD JORDAN IN THE WORLD (LP) **£60**

DICK JORDAN
60	Oriole CB 1534	Hallelujah, I Love Her So/Sandy **£15**
60	Oriole CB 1548	Little Christine/I'll Love You Forever **£15**
61	Piccadilly 7N 35035	Some Of These Days/I Want Her Back **£75**
66	Parlophone R5475	Progress/Something's Going On In There **£25**

EARL JORDAN
72	Sovereign SVN 6501	JORDAN (LP, textured sleeve with flipbacks) **£30**

LOUIS JORDAN (& HIS TYMPANY FIVE)
54	Melodisc 1031	Dad Gum Ya Hide Boy/Whiskey Do Your Stuff (78) **£15**
56	Melodisc 1349	Messy Bessy/I Seen What'cha Done (78) **£20**
60	Downbeat CHA 3	Ooo-Wee/I'll Die Happy **£20**
50s	Melodisc EPM7 66	LOUIS JORDAN (EP, as Louis Jordan Tympany Five, 3 different covers) **£90**
57	Mercury MPT 7521	SOMEBODY UP THERE DIGS ME (10" LP, with Tympany Five) **£100**
58	Mercury MPL 6541	MAN, WE'RE WAILIN' (LP, with Tympany Five) **£60**

| 64 | HMV CLP 1809 | HALLELUJAH, LOUIS JORDAN IS BACK (LP) | £40 |

(see also Louis Armstrong)

LOUIS JORDAN & CHRIS BARBER'S BAND

| 63 | Melodisc 45-1616 | Is She Is Or Is She Ain't Your Baby/Fifty Cents | £18 |

(see also Chris Barber)

RONNY JORDAN

92	Island ILPS 9988	THE ANTIDOTE (LP)	£15
93	Island ILPSD 8009	THE QUIET REVOLUTION (2-LP)	£20
94	Island IMA 8024	BAD BROTHERS (Mini-LP with D.J. Krush)	£15
96	Island 524 212-1	LIGHT TO DARK (LP)	£15
00	Blue Note 7243 5 20208 1 2	A BRIGHTER DAY (LP)	£20

JORDANAIRES

57	Capitol CL 14687	Sugaree/Baby, Won't You Please Come Home?	£40
57	Capitol CL 14773	Summer Vacation/Each Day	£20
58	Capitol CL 14921	Little Miss Ruby/All I Need Is You	£20
63	Capitol CL 15281	Don't Be Cruel/Don't Worry	£20
62	Capitol T 1742	SPOTLIGHT ON THE JORDANAIRES (LP)	£40

(see also Elvis Presley, Patsy Cline, Don Gibson, Marty Robbins)

JOSEF K

79	Absolute ABS 1	Chance Meeting/Romance (p/s, 1,000 only)	£45
80	Postcard 80-3	Radio Drill Time/Crazy To Exist (hand-coloured foldaround p/s, blue labels)	£50
80	Postcard 80-3	Radio Drill Time/Crazy To Exist (cream/yellow sleeve & labels)	£20
80	Postcard 80-5	It's Kinda Funny/Final Request (in poly bag, with picture insert)	£35
81	Postcard 81-4/TWI 023	Sorry For Laughing/Revelation (p/s)	£20
81	Postcard 81-5	Chance Meeting/Pictures (die-cut sleeve, with postcard)	£30
81	Postcard 81-1	SORRY FOR LAUGHING (LP, unreleased, a few with proof sleeve)	£400
81	Postcard 81-7	THE ONLY FUN IN TOWN (LP, with inner sleeve)	£50
87	Supreme Intl. Edit. 87-6	YOUNG AND STUPID (LP, 'Endless Soul' on rear sleeve and labels)	£15
12	Les Disques Du Crépuscule LTV 2549	SORRY FOR LAUGHING (LP, reissue, inner, with CD)	£25
14	Les Disques Du Crépuscule TWI 052	THE ONLY FUN IN TOWN (2-LP, reissue with art print)	£40

(see also Orange Juice, Paul Haig, Happy Family, Rhythm Of Life)

KATHRYN JOSEPH

| 15 | Hits The Fan (no cat no) | BONES YOU HAVE THROWN ME AND BLOOD I'VE SPILLED (LP, white vinyl, with 42-page booklet) | £60 |

MARGIE JOSEPH

75	Atlantic K10646	I Can't Move No Mountains/Just As Soon As The Feelings Over	£20
72	Stax 2362 008	MAKES A NEW IMPRESSION (LP)	£25
73	Atlantic K 40462	MARGIE JOSEPH (LP)	£20
88	Stax SX 015	IN THE NAME OF LOVE (LP)	£15

NERIOUS JOSEPH

| 85 | Fashion FAD 042 | You're My Special Lady/Danger Man (12") | £20 |

JOSH

| 69 | Duke DU 41 | Judge/RON: Soul Of Joemel | £15 |
| 70 | Hot Rod HR 111 | Leaving Everything/HOT ROD ALL STARS : Psychedelic Bird | £45 |

(see also Girlie)

JOSHUA

| 73 | Key KL 014 | JOSHUA (LP) | £100 |

MARVA JOSIE

| 66 | Polydor 56711 | Crazy Stockings/I'll Get By | £15 |

JOY & DAVID/DAVE

58	Parlophone R 4477	Whoopee!/My Oh My! (as Joy & David)	£25
59	Decca F 11123	Rocking Away The Blues/If You Pass Me By (as Joy & David)	£25
60	Triumph RGM 1002	Let's Go See Gran'ma/Believe Me (as Joy & Dave)	£25
60	Decca F 11291	My Very Good Friend The Milkman/Doopey Darling (as Joy & Dave)	£15
61	Parlophone R 4855	Joe's Been A-Gittin' There/They Tell Us Not To Love (as Joy & Dave)	£20
61	Parlophone R 4855	Joe's Been A-Gittin' There/They Tell Us Not To Love (demo copies with alternate take of B-side)	£30

MABEL JOY

| 75 | Real RR 2004 | MABEL JOY (LP) | £25 |

JOY OF LIFE

| 85 | New European BAD VC 62 | ENJOY EP (12", p/s) | £18 |
| 88 | Cadre CR JOL67 | HEAR THE CHILDREN (LP) | £20 |

RODDIE JOY

| 65 | Red Bird RB 10021 | Come Back Baby/Love Hit Me With A Wallop | £60 |

JOHNNY JOYCE

| 76 | Freedom FLP 99003 | JOYCE'S CHOICE MIXTURE (LP) | £22 |

(see also Velvet Opera, Levee Breakers)

ROSALINE JOYCE

84	Hartone HAR 01	Are You Really Going/Version (12")	£20
88	Jam Today 12 ROS 2	Falling In Love Again (12" Remix)/I Need All Your Loving/Falling In Love Again (Soulful Lovers Mix) (12")	£30
88	Intrigue IGE 3T	This Time I Feel Love/Try (12")	£20
89	Jam Today 12 ROS 1	No Questions No Answers (Yankee Style)/(Yankee Mix)/(London Mix)/(B-Boy Mix) (12")	£25

MINT VALUE £

| 91 | Unyque UNQ 14T | **Waiting So Long** (Nemesis Mix)/(Original Mix) (12")..£20 |
| 87 | Jam Today ROSLP 1 | **LOVERS SOUL** (LP)..£40 |

JOYCE'S ANGELS
| 67 | Major Minor MM 526 | **Flowers For My Friends/Rodney Reginald Smithfield Harvey Jones**.................£15 |

(see also Chris White)

JOY DE VIVRE
| 81 | Crass CR & SS ENVY 1 | **Our Wedding** (flexidisc, white vinyl, no p/s, with mailer)....................................£300 |
| 81 | Crass CR & SS ENVY 1 | **Our Wedding** (flexidisc, white vinyl, no p/s, without mailer) ....£200 |

(see also Crass)

JOY DIVISION

SINGLES
78	Enigma PSS 139	**AN IDEAL FOR LIVING** (Warsaw/No Love Lost/Leaders Of Men/Failures) (EP, 1,000 only, foldout p/s; beware of counterfeits)...£2000
78	Anonymous ANON 1	**AN IDEAL FOR LIVING** (Warsaw/No Love Lost/Leaders Of Men/Failures) (12" EP reissue, 1,200 only)...£700
79	Factory FAC 13	**Transmission/Novelty** (1st pressing, 10,000 in textured p/s) £20
80	Factory FACUS T2	**She's Lost Control/Atmosphere** £15
80	Factory FAC23.12	**Love Will Tear Us Apart/These Days/Love Will Tear Us Apart** (12", laminated sleeve) £25
80	Factory FACUS 2/UK	**Atmosphere/She's Lost Control** (UK variant, 12", black vinyl) £30
80	Factory FACUS 2/UK	**Atmosphere/She's Lost Control** (UK variant, 12", red vinyl) £20
82	Factory FAC 13 12	**Transmission/Novelty** (12")..£20
88	Factory FAC213	**Atmosphere/The Only Mistake/Sound Of Music** (12", p/s)...................................£15
87	Strange Fruit SFPS 033	**PEEL SESSIONS** (12" EP)..£15
11	Rhino FAC .33	**Ceremony** (Original Version)**/In A Lonely Place** (12" Version)**//Ceremony** (Heart & Soul Rehearsal Version)**/In A Lonely Place** (Unreleased Rehearsal Version) (12", 800 only) £25
10	Rhino 5186595937	**SINGLES 1978-80** (10 x 7", art piece, 2 x CD-R, box set, 500 only)..........................£200

ALBUMS
79	Factory FACT 10	**UNKNOWN PLEASURES** (LP with inner sleeve, textured sleeve, 1st press turns a deep translucent red when held over a light)...£150
79	Factory FACT 10	**UNKNOWN PLEASURES** (LP with inner sleeve, textured sleeve, 2nd non transluscent issue)...£80
80	Factory FACT 25	**CLOSER** (LP, hard textured sleeve & inner, some 1st pressing turns a deep translucent red when held over a light)...£100
80	Factory FACT 25	**CLOSER** (LP, hard textured sleeve & inner, 1st pressing, solid black vinyl) £50
81	Factory FACT 40	**STILL** (2-LP, hessian sleeve, card inners & white/blue ribbon)...........................£150
81	Factory FAC 40	**STILL** (2-LP, gatefold)...£40
85	Factory FACT 10c	**UNKNOWN PLEASURES** (reissue, cassette in box with insert)..............................£30
85	Factory FACT 25c	**CLOSER** (reissue, cassette in box with insert)..£30
85	Factory FACT 40c	**STILL** (reissue, cassette in box with insert)..£30
88	Factory FACT 250	**SUBSTANCE** (LP)...£40
90	Strange Fruit SFRLP 111	**PEEL SESSIONS** (LP, reissue of both EPs)...£20
95	London 828624 1	**PERMANENT** (2-LP, insert)..£50
01	Strange Fruit SFRSLP 094	**THE COMPLETE BBC RECORDINGS** (LP)..£30
07	London 2564699291	**JOY DIVISION: IN MEMORY** (4xLP boxed set, 3000 only).....................................£150
07	London 25646 40151	**UNKNOWN PLEASURES** (LP, remastered reissue on 180gm vinyl) £20
07	London 25645 4014 1	**CLOSER** (LP, remastered reissue on 180gm vinyl) £20
07	Ozit Morpheus OZIT 8797	**MARTIN HANNETT'S PERSONAL MIXES** (2-LP)..£20

(see also New Order, Electronic, Other Two, Revenge, Bad Lieutenant, Monaco)

COL JOYE & JOYBOYS
| 59 | Brunswick 05806 | (Rockin' Rollin') **Clementine/Bye Bye Baby Goodbye** ....£20 |

JOYFUL SOUND
| 73 | SRT SRT 73278 | **IT WILL BE WORTH IT ALL** (LP)..£300 |

JOYRIDE
| 69 | RCA SF 8027 | **FRIEND SOUND** (LP)..£20 |

JOYRIDE GOODBYE
| 80 | Joyride SRTS80/CUS 659 | **Goodbye/Something Special** (no p/s)..£30 |

JOY UNLIMITED
69	Page One POF 147	**Daytime Night Time/Mister Pseudonym** £30
69	Page One POF 160	**Oh Darlin'/Feelin'** £40
70	Page One POLS 028	**TURBULENCE** (LP)..£80

J P SUNSHINE
| 95 | Uncle Glitch Records UG 1 | **UNCLE GLITCH PRESENTS** (LP, 500 only) ....£30 |

J.S.D. BAND
71	Regal Zono. SRLZ 1018	**COUNTRY OF THE BLIND** (LP, textured sleeve, first press with flipbacks).............£90
71	Regal Zono. SRLZ 1018	**COUNTRY OF THE BLIND** (LP, textured sleeve, later press without flipbacks).......£50
72	Cube HIFLY 11	**J.S.D. BAND** (LP)...£15
73	Cube HIFLY 14	**TRAVELLING DAYS** (LP, fully laminated sleeve) £15

JUAN & JUNIOR
| 68 | CBS 3223 | **To Girls/Andurina** ....£15 |

JUDAS JUMP
| 70 | Parlophone R 5828 | **Run For Your Life/Beer Drinking Woman**..£15 |
| 70 | Parlophone PAS 10001 | **SCORCH** (LP, gatefold sleeve, black/silver label with boxed logo)........................£80 |

(see also Herd, Amen Corner, Andy Bown)

JUDAS PRIEST
| 74 | Gull GULS 6 | **Rocka-Rolla/Never Satisfied**..£30 |
| 76 | Gull GULS 31 | **The Ripper/Island Of Domination**..£30 |

MINT VALUE £

83	Gull GULS 7612	**Tyrant/Rocka-Rolla/Genocide** (12", p/s, white vinyl)	£15
74	Gull GULP 1005	**ROCKA ROLLA** (LP, 1st pressing, 'bottle top' sleeve, with 'Thanks for the words Al!" credit on rear sleeve)	£60
76	Gull GULP 1015	**SAD WINGS OF DESTINY** (LP)	£25
76	Gull PGULP 1015	**SAD WINGS OF DESTINY** (LP, picture disc)	£22
77	CBS 82008	**SIN AFTER SIN** (LP)	£20
78	CBS 82430	**STAINED CLASS** (LP)	£15
78	CBS 83135	**KILLING MACHINE** (LP, red vinyl)	£20
79	CBS 83852	**UNLEASHED IN THE EAST** (LP, with free single "Rock Forever"/ Hell Bent For Leather/"Beyond The Realms Of Death" [SJP 1], and tour advertising flyer)	£30
79	CBS 66357	**BOX SET** (3-LP, reissue of "Sin After Sin"/"Stained Class"/"Killing Machine")	£25
80	CBS 84160	**BRITISH STEEL** (LP)	£20
86	Shanghai PGLP 1026	**JUDAS PRIEST** (LP, picture disc)	£20
88	CBS 461108	**RAM IT DOWN** (LP, with inner)	£20
90	CBS 467290 1	**PAINKILLER** (LP)	£35
93	CBS 473050	**METAL WORKS** (2xLP, gatefold sleeve)	£40
98	SPV 0891 8542	**98 LIVE MELTDOWN** (2xLP)	£40
04	Sony 5128933	**METALOGY** (4xCD, DVD, booklet, leather studded box set)	£45
08	Sony 88697315572	**NOSTRADAMUS** (3-LP, 2-CD boxed set)	£30
11	Sony 88697967872	**COMPLETE ALBUMS COLLECTION** (19 x CD box set. booklet)	£50

(see also Trapeze, Fancy, Fight, Halford)

JUDD
70	Penny Farthing PELS 504	**JUDD** (LP, die-cut sleeve, insert, red/black/yellow labels)	£175

(see also Kris Ife)

F.C. JUDD
60	Castle EFX 1	**ELECTRONIC SOUNDS AND MUSIC** (EP)	£50
60	Castle EFX 2	**ELECTRONIC THEMES AND MUSIQUE CONCRETE** (EP)	£50
60	Castle EFX 3	**RHYTHMIC ELECTRONIC MUSIC** (EP)	£50
60	Castle HMX 1	**HAUNTED HOUSE, MYSTERY SOUNDS AND MUSIC** (EP)	£25
67	(No label or cat no)	**ELECTRONIC SOUNDS AND EFFECTS** (flexi, free with Practical Electronics)	£15

PAA JUDE
92	Asona ARC 019	**SEAMAN JOLLY** (LP)	£60

JUDGE HAPPINESS
85	Mynah SCS 8501	**Hey Judge/Pig In Pink** (very few with p/s)	£25

(see also Mock Turtles)

JUICE CREW
08	Diggers With Gratitude DWG 004	**THE JUICE CREW** (EP, 75 only, red vinyl)	£90
08	Diggers With Gratitude DWG 004	**THE JUICE CREW** (EP, 75 only, blue vinyl)	£90
08	Diggers With Gratitude DWG 003	**THE JUICE CREW** (EP, 75 only, white vinyl)	£90
08	Diggers With Gratitude DWG 002	**THE JUICE CREW** (EP, 125 only, black vinyl)	£60

JUICY LUCY
70	Fontana TF 1068	**Who Do You Love/Walking Down The Highway** (unissued)	£0
70	Vertigo 6059 015	**Pretty Woman/I'm A Thief**	£18
69	Vertigo VO 2	**JUICY LUCY** (LP, first press with 'Philips' credit on large swirl label, gatefold sleeve)	£200
69	Vertigo VO 2	**JUICY LUCY** (LP, later press without 'Philips' credit on large swirl label, gatefold sleeve)	£70
70	Vertigo 6360 014	**LIE BACK AND ENJOY IT** (LP, large swirl label, gatefold poster sleeve)	£200
71	Bronze ILPS 9157	**GET A WHIFF OF THIS** (LP, textured sleeve, Island credit on label)	£30
72	Polydor 2310 160	**PIECES** (LP)	£25

(see also Misunderstood, Van Der Graaf Generator, Ray Owen, Paul Williams' Big Roll Band)

TM JUKE
03	Try Thoughts TRULP 050	**MAPS FROM THE WILDERNESS** (2-LP)	£70

JIMMY JUKEBOX
75	Sonet SON 2057	**Motorboat/25 Hours A Day**	£40
77	Sonet SON 2057	**Motorboat/25 Hours A Day** (1977 re-issue with new Savage Pencil p/s sleeve but original 1975 records inside)	£20

(see also Kim Fowley)

JULIAN (SCOTT)
59	Pye Nixa 7N 15236	**Sue Saturday/Can't Wait**	£30
59	Pye Nixa N 15236	**Sue Saturday/Can't Wait** (78)	£20

(see also Brian Bennett)

JULIAN (JUDY MOWATT) & GAYTONES
72	High Note HS 059	**She Kept On Talking/Version**	£20

JULIAN'S TREATMENT
70	Young Blood YB 1009	**Phantom City/Alda, Dark Lady Of The Outer Worlds**	£25
70	Young Blood SYB 2/3	**A TIME BEFORE THIS** (2-LP, laminated gatefold sleeve, white/red labels)	£400

(see also Julian Jay Savarin)

JULIET & GRACE
80	Atra 32 DA	**What Can I Do/MILITANT BARRY: Lovers Styly** (12". p/s)	£20

(see also Militant Barry)

JULY
68	Major Minor MM 568	**My Clown/Dandelion Seeds**	£200
68	Major Minor MM 580	**Hello, Who's There?/The Way**	£80
68	Major Minor MMLP 29	**JULY** (LP, laminated front sleeve, red/white/black labels)	£1000

MINT VALUE £

87	Bam Caruso KIRI 097	**DANDELION SEEDS** (LP, reissue of above LP with extra tracks & different sleeve) **£25**
95	Essex 1011LP	**JULY** (LP, reissue with bonus 7": "Hello Who's There?"/"The Way" [p/s, 10117]) **£20**

(see also Jade Warrior, Tom Newman)

ISSA JUMA
90	Discafrique AFRILP 008	**SIGALAME 2** (LP) **£60**

JUMBLE LANE
71	Holyground HG 115	**JUMBLE LANE** (LP, 99 copies only) **£600**

JUMP
80	Caveman CLUB 1	**Shake Up/All In Vain** (p/s) **£25**

JUMPBACKS
73	Maxi M3	**Shake/Hello Stranger** **£30**

JUMPIN' JACKS
58	HMV POP 440	**My Girl, My Girl/Tried And Tested** **£25**

JUMPLEADS
82	Ock OC 001	**THE STAG MUST DIE** (LP, with insert) **£15**

JUMP SQUAD
81	101 UR 2	**Lord Of The Dance/Debt** (p/s) **£20**

(see also Embryo)

JUNCO PARTNERS
65	Columbia DB 7665	**As Long As I Have You/Take This Hammer** **£70**
71	Philips 6308 032	**JUNCO PARTNERS** (LP, laminated sleeve, black/silver labels) **£150**

JUNCTION
87	New Youth NYJ 175	**PANDORAS BOX EP** **£20**

JUNCTION 32
75	Holyground HGS 119	**JUNCTION 32** (LP, 100 copies only) **£550**

JUNCUNO
71	Banana BA 361	**The End** (as Joncuno)/**HORACE ANDY: See A Man's Face** **£50**

ROSANNE JUNE
56	London HLU 8352	**The Charge Of The Light Brigade/Broken Windows** **£20**

JUNE BRIDES
85	Pink PINKY 5	**THERE ARE EIGHT MILLION STORIES...** (LP, insert) **£15**

JUNG COLLECTIVE
02	Nanny Tango NT 1	**Injustice/Street Preacher** (Plaid Mix) (clear vinyl, poly sleeve w/sticker insert) **£20**

CARL GUSTAV JUNG
63	Piccadilly FTF 38505	**FACE TO FACE** (LP) **£20**

JUNGLE BROTHERS
88	Gee St. GEEA 001	**STRAIGHT OUT THE JUNGLE** (LP, with free 12") **£15**

JOHNNY JUNGLE
93	Dee Jay DJX 005	**REMIXES 1** (12") **£20**
93	Dee Jay DJX 006	**REMIXES 2** (12") **£15**

JUNGLE WARRIOR
94	Strictly Underground STUR 38	**No Surrender/New Style** (12") **£25**
95	Strictly Underground STUR 47	**Jungle Jesus** (Pope John Paul Mix)/(Absolution Mix) (12") **£35**

JUNIOR (SIMPSON)
68	Giant GN 18	**I'm Gonna Leave You Girl/I Love You I Love You** **£20**
68	Giant GN 25	**Come Cure Me/I Want Your Loving** **£25**

JUNIOR B
92	Eastern Sher ES 001	**Meditation/Black And White** (12") **£40**

JUNIOR BROWN
78	Tempus TEMD 01	**Jah Find Babylon Guilty** (feat. Ranking Ruben)/**Dub** (12") **£18**
80	Jah Shaka SHAKA 829	**Fly Me Away/Travelling Dub** (12") **£30**
82	Jah Shaka SHAKA 822	**Warrior/Right Fight** (12") **£15**

JUNIOR AND THE COOL NOTES
75	Torpedo TOR 36	**Curley Locks/Version Locks** **£15**

JUNIOR DELGADO
77	Deb TIC 1001	**Tiction/Tiction Volume 2** **£18**
78	Deb DEB 001	**Tonight & Tune In/Armed Robbery** (12") **£20**
78	Deb DEB 019	**Trickster/CARLTON & HIS SHOES: Better Days** (12") **£35**
79	Greensleeves GRED 15	**Love Tickles Like Magic/PRINCE JAMMY & AGGROVATORS : Prince Jammy's Magic** (12") **£20**
79	Burning Sounds BRD 005	**Raiders/Warrior** (12") **£20**
79	DEB 026	**Warrior** (with Ras Bug)/**DEB PLAYERS: Version** (12") **£30**
80	Greensleeves GRED 39	**Midnight Raver/365 days** (12", blue vinyl) **£15**
80	Niagra NIADD 108	**Fort Augustus/Escape Prisioners** (12") **£35**
82	Incredible Jux 04	**Trouble Part 1/Trouble Part 2** (12") **£20**
86	Incredible IM001	**Poverty/Version** (12") **£30**
87	Fashion FAD 040	**Hot Stuff/It Takes Two To Tango** (12") **£15**
88	Mango IS 368	**Hanging Tree/Hey Good Looking** (12") **£20**
89	Fashion FAD 066	**Dub School/We A Blood** (12") **£25**
79	Deb DEBLP 05	**TASTE OF THE YOUNG HEART** (LP) **£40**
79	Deb DEBLP 010	**EFFORT** (LP) **£40**

82	Incredible Jux HBLP 001	BUSHMAN REVOLUTION (LP)	£40
86	Mango ILPS 9856	RAGAMUFFIN YEAR (LP)	£15
86	Fashion FADLP 003	IT TAKES TWO TO TANGO (LP)	£18

JUNIOR DISPROL
| 01 | SFDB AO27658 | Fight Club/Junq Waffle | £25 |

JUNIOR ENGLISH
| 79 | Ethnic Fight ETH 1328 | Keep On Trying/HORSEMOUTH: Herb Vendor (12") | £20 |

JUNIOR GEE
| 86 | Scorcher 1032 | The Truth (12") | £50 |

JUNIOR GEE & THE CAPITAL BOYS
| 84 | Tai Wan 1948 | Check Us Out/The Break (12") | £15 |

HUGH ROY JUNIOR
72	Duke DU 137	Live It Up/DENNIS BROWN: Baby Don't Do It	£15
72	Ashanti ASH 405	King Of The Road/ROOSEVELT ALL STARS: Version	£15
72	Jackpot JP 806	Two Ton Guletto/Version	£20
(see also U Roy Junior)

JUNIOR KEITHING
| 80 | Grand Masters GM 001 | Jah Wrote Me A Letter/Letter Dub (12") | £20 |

JUNIOR MCCANTS
| 98 | Kent 6T 16 | Try Me For Your New Love/GARLAND GREEN: Come Through Me | £40 |

JUNIOR MURVIN
68	Doctor Bird DB 1112	Miss Cushie (as Junior Soul)/LYNN TAITT & JETS: Dr. Paul	£250
68	Big Shot BI 503	Chattie Chattie/The Magic Touch	£300
69	Big Shot BI 527	The Hustler/The Magic Touch	£200
77	Island IPR 2001	Tedious/Memories	£30
77	Island 12WIP 2010	Upsetter Revue Feat. Junior Murvin: Dread Locks In Moonlight/Closer Together (12")	£20
80	Black Ark ARK 007	Cross Over/I Am In Love (12")	£25
82	Dread At The Controls DATCD 009	Bad Man Posse/Riddim Request To All Posse Smoker Posse (12")	£18
86	Greensleeves GRED 199	Apartheid/Jack Slick (12")	£15
77	Island ILPS 9499	POLICE AND THIEVES (LP)	£35
82	Dread At The Controls DATC 007	BADMAN POSSE (LP)	£30
84	Greensleeves GREL 70	MUGGERS IN THE STREET (LP)	£20

JUNIOR REID
80	Negus Roots NERT 02	Sister Dawn/Dub Version (12")	£20
81	Negus Roots NERT 09	IF I/Versions (12")	£40
82	King Imperial KG 008	Jail House/We Got To Leave (12")	£50
84	Greensleeves GRED 163	Boom Shack A Lack/Old Time Something (12")	£15
85	Greensleeves GREL 78	BOOM SHACK A LACK (LP)	£20

JUNIOR ROOTS
| 81 | Black Roots BR 24 | Natty Dread Time/BLACK TRAP: Into The Light (12") | £15 |

JUNIOR ROSS AND THE SPEARS
| 76 | K&B KB 5529 | Judgement Time/Version | £25 |

JUNIOR SENIOR
| 03 | Mercury 0679201 | D-D-DON'T STOP THE BEAT (LP) | £30 |

TREVOR JUNIOR
| 84 | Tonos TON 002 | Ghetto Living/Have Faith In Jah (12") | £50 |

JUNIORS
| 64 | Columbia DB 7339 | There's A Pretty Girl/Pocket Size | £55 |

JUNIOR'S EYES
69	Regal Zonophone RZ 3009	Mr. Golden Trumpet Player/Black Snake	£30
69	Regal Zonophone RZ 3018	Woman Love/White Light Part 2 (withdrawn B-side)	£30
69	Regal Zonophone RZ 3018	Woman Love/Circus Days	£20
69	Regal Zonophone RZ 3023	Star Child/Sink Or Swim	£20
69	Regal Zono. SLRZ 1008	BATTERSEA POWER STATION (LP, laminated front, flipbacks, "Sold in U.K..." label text)	£200
(see also David Bowie, Tickle, Bunch Of Fives, Outsiders)

JUNIPER GREEN
| 71 | Columbia DB 8809 | Dreams In The Sky/Cascade Of Ice | £20 |

JUNK SHOP RADIOS
| 91 | Junk JUNK 001 | Summer Rain/Missed Again (die-cut hand-stamped sleeve) | £15 |

LENA JUNOFF
| 68 | Olga OLE 8 | Yesterday Has Gone/Good Kind Of Hurt | £40 |

JUNO REACTOR
95	Blue Room BR009LP	BEYOND THE INFINITE (4-LP)	£30
97	Blue Room Released BR042LP	BIBLE OF DREAMS (3-LP)	£20
00	Electric M.E.L.T. ELM 8033LP	SHANGO (2-LP)	£20

JUNO'S CLAW
| 79 | MPA EMP 081 | Barbara/The Master/Big City (EP, no p/s) | £100 |

JUPITER
| 72 | Parlophone R 5967 | The Meteor Song/Life Is Getting Better Every Day | £25 |

JURASSIC 5
98	Pan/PIAS PAN 015LP	JURASSIC FIVE (LP, postcard)	£50
00	Interscope 490 710 1	QUALITY CONTROL (2LP, gatefold, insert)	£35
02	Interscope 493 437-1	POWER IN NUMBERS (2LP, insert)	£50

JUS BADD
87	Tuff GrooveTUFF001	Freestyle/Proud (12")	£50

JUST MEASURES
83	It's War Boy £5	FLAGELLATION (LP)	£20

JUST THE JOB
80	KIK 2	Fears Of The Years/Street Feelings/London Lights (with p/s)	£50
80	KIK 2	Fears Of The Years/Street Feelings/London Lights (without p/s)	£30

SAMANTHA JUSTE
66	Go AJ 11402	No One Needs My Love Today/If Trees Could Talk	£25

JUST FOUR MEN
64	Parlophone R 5186	That's My Baby/Things Will Never Be The Same (withdrawn, as Four Just Men)	£80
64	Parlophone R 5208	That's My Baby/Things Will Never Be The Same	£60
65	Parlophone R 5241	There's Not One Thing/Don't Come Any Closer	£60

(see also Wimple Winch, Four Just Men, Pacific Drift)

JUST FRANK
79	Rok ROK III/IV	You/SPLIT SCREENS: Just Don't Try (die-cut company sleeve)	£35

JIMMY JUSTICE
60	Pye 7N 15301	I Understand Just How You Feel/Bloodshot Eyes (as Jimmy Justice & Jury)	£20
61	Pye 7N 15351	When Love Has Left You/The Teacher	£15
61	Pye 7N 15376	A Little Bit Of Soap/Little Lonely One	£15
68	RCA Victor RCA 1681	I'm Past Forgetting You/Walking Away With My Heart	£25
62	Pye NPL 18080	TWO SIDES OF JIMMY JUSTICE (LP)	£30
62	Pye NPL 18085	SMASH HITS (LP)	£20

JUSTIFIED ANCIENTS OF MU MU (J.A.M.S)
87	KLF Comm. JAMS 23	All You Need Is Love (Original) (12", white label, 1-sided, 500 only)	£50
87	KLF Comm. JAMS 23T	All You Need Is Love/Ivum Naya/Rap, Rhyme And Scratch Yourself (12", 'James Anderton' p/s, 5,000 only)	£15
87	KLF Comm. JAMS 24T	Whitney Joins The JAMs (120 bpm) (12", 1-sided, 'Scottish' issue, 500 only)	£15
87	KLF Comm. JAMS 25T	1987 - The 45 Edits (12", p/s)	£15
87	KLF Comm. JAMS 27T	Down Town (118 bpm)/Down Town (12",mispressed 'album' label, generic sleeve)	£15
90	KLF Comm.	It's Grim Up North (Original Vocal Mix) (1st pressing, 12", grey vinyl, 1-sided, 350 pressed but most sent back and destroyed due to error matrix in run-out groove. This one has "IT'S GRIM UP NORTH JA" and no cat no)	£500
90	KLF Comm. JAMS 28T	It's Grim Up North (Original Vocal Mix) (2nd pressing, 12", grey vinyl, 1-sided, 350 only, "IT'S GRIM UP NORTH JAMS-28T JA" in run out groove)	£100
87	KLF Comm. JAMS DS 1	Deep Shit (flexidisc, unreleased)	£150
87	KLF Comm. JAMS LP 1	1987 (WHAT THE FUCK IS GOING ON?) (LP, withdrawn)	£100
88	JAMS CLP 1	1987 (WHAT THE FUCK IS GOING ON?) (cassette LP)	£30
88	KLF Comm. JAMS LP 2	WHO KILLED THE JAMS? (LP, stickered sleeve with insert)	£20
89	KLF Comm. JAMS DLP 3	SHAG TIMES (2-LP)	£50
89	KLF Comm. JAMS CD 3	SHAG TIMES (CD)	£40

(see also KLF, Timelords, Space, Orb, Bill Drummond)

JUSTIN CASE
80	Rok ROK XIX	TV/STRAIGHT UP: One Out All Out (die-cut company sleeve)	£40

JUSTIN & KARLSSON
66	Piccadilly 7N 35295	Somewhere They Can't Find Me/What More Do You Want	£40

JUSTINE
69	Buffalo BFS 1001	Right Now/Place Where Sorrow Hides	£30
70	Uni UNLS 111	JUSTINE (LP)	£90

JUSTIN'S TIMEPEICE
68	Reverberation CKS 20001	Lonely Man/Bull Durham's Workout	£40

JUSTINS
71	Punch PH 65	Cholera/LLOYD ALL STARS: Black Bird	£20

BILL JUSTIS & HIS ORCHESTRA
57	London HLS 8517	Raunchy/The Midnight Man	£20
58	London HLS 8614	College Man/The Stranger (B-side with Spinners)	£25

JUST LIKE THAT
76	Tank BS 122	JUST LIKE THAT (LP)	£20

JUST OTHERS
74	Goodwill Records WS 1	AMALGAM (LP, 250 only)	£1000

JUST PLAIN JONES
71	CBS CBS 7480	Crazy, Crazy/Should Have Stayed With Mary	£20

(see also Just Plain Smith, Esprit De Corps)

JUST PLAIN SMITH
69	Sunshine SUN 7702	February's Child/Don't Open Your Mind (with p/s)	£135
69	Sunshine SUN 7702	February's Child/Don't Open Your Mind	£60

(see also Just Plain Jones, Esprit De Corps)

JUST WILLIAM
68	Spark SRL 1018	I Don't Care/Cherrywood Green	£30

JUVENILES
66   Pye International 7N 25349   **Bo Diddley/Yes I Believe** £100

JYL
84   Thunderbolt THBL 036   **JYL** (LP)...£50

JYNX
64   Columbia DB 7304   **How/Do What They Don't Say** £75

CAROLINE K
87   Earthly Delights EARTH 1   **NOW WAIT FOR LAST YEAR** (LP, 1,500 only)........................£15

MOSES K & PROPHETS
65   Decca F 12244   **I Went Out With My Baby Tonight/So Long** £25
(see also Them)

SIMON K
69   B&C CB 111   **You Know I Do/Bring Your Love Back**...£40

K VARIOUS ARTISTS SINGLES & EPS 70S/80S/90S/00S
18   UMC 675 523-4   **A KALEIDOSCOPE OF SOUND: PSYCHEDELIC & FREAKBEAT MASTERPIECES** (7x7" box set, booklet)..............................£50

KABBALA
82   Red Flame RF 1211   **Ashewo Ara/Voltan Dance** (12", black or red p/s).............£60
83   Red Flame RFB 37 12   **Yen-Nbo-Ose/Yo You Dance** (12", p/s)......................£20
88   INK 1228   **Ashewo Ara** (Mix 88)/**Voltan Dance** (12", p/s)..............................£20
97   MAMA MAMT 015   **ASHEWO ARA: Side Afro Funk/Side House** (12", p/s)............£15

KABUKI
82   Kabaret Noir KAB 1   **I Am A Horse/My Hair** (p/s)..£30

KADDO STRINGS
80   Grapevine GRP 146   **Nothing But Love/Crying Over You** £15
(see also Duke Browner, Tartans)

KADENZA
82   PRT 12P 247   **Let's Stay Together** (Night Club Mix)/**Let's Stay Together** (Vocal 2)/(Instrumental Version) (12")..................................£30
82   PRT 12P 261   **Let's Do It**/(Instrumental) (12")..£40
82   PRT 12P 261   **Let's Do It**/(Instrumental) £20

KAISER CHIEFS
04   B-Unique BUN088-7   **I Predict A Riot/Take My Temperature** (150 signed 7" with p/s)........£15
05   B-Unique BUN 093LP   **EMPLOYMENT** (LP, gatefold, printed inner)......................£40
07   B-Unique BUN 122LP   **YOURS TRULY, ANGRY MOB** (2LP, gatefold, printed inners) £30
08   B-Unique BUN 144LP   **OFF WITH THEIR HEADS** (2LP, gatefold, printed inners) £25
11   B-Unique GUM 003   **THE FUTURE IS MEDIEVAL** (2LP, numbered, 500 only)............£80
14   Caroline EDUCATE 03   **EDUCATION, EDUCATION, EDUCATION & WAR** (LP/7", printed inner)........£25
19   Polydor 7705205   **DUCK** (LP, limited tricolour Leeds edition, printed inner, poster) £35
24   V2 VVNL 46971   **KAISER CHIEFS' EASY EIGHTH ALBUM** (LP, clear splatter vinyl, indies exclusive, stickers)..£25

KAISERS
94   No Hit Records NO HIT 14   **IN STEP WITH THE KAISERS** (LP) £15
93   No Hit NO HIT 012   **SQUAREHEAD STOMP!** (LP) £18

KAJANUS/PICKETT
72   Signport SGA 5001   **HI HO SILVER** (LP, sleeve with cut flap) £20

KAKKO
90   CBS 655 710 8   **We Should Be Dancing** (mixes) (12", p/s)..............................£18

KALA
73   Bradleys BRADL 1002   **KALA** (LP) £15
(see also Quintessence)

KALANI BOB AND REMEGEL
95   Groove Yard GYARD 005   **THE CHEESE AND PICKLE EP** (12")...........................£50

ALAN KALANI
59   Vogue V 9147   **A Touch Of Pink/SURFERS: Mambo Jambo**................................£20
59   Vogue V 9147   **A Touch Of Pink/SURFERS: Mambo Jambo** (78) £20

KALEIDOSCOPE (U.K.)
67   Fontana TF 863   **Flight From Ashiya/Holidaymaker** (in p/s)........................£100
67   Fontana TF 863   **Flight From Ashiya/Holidaymaker** £60
68   Fontana TF 895   **A Dream For Julie/Please Excuse My Face** £40
68   Fontana TF 964   **Jenny Artichoke/Just How Much Are You**............................£50
69   Fontana TF 1002   **Do It Again For Jeffrey/Poem** £50
69   Fontana TF 1048   **Balloon/If You So Wish** £110
69   Decca (No Cat. No.)   **Black Fjord** (1-sided)..£130
67   Fontana (S)TL 5448   **TANGERINE DREAM** (LP, unlaminated sleeve, flipbacks, black/silver label) £1000
69   Fontana STL 5491   **FAINTLY BLOWING** (LP, laminated gatefold sleeve; without watermark on beginning of each side)........£1000

KALEIDOSCOPE (U.S.)

MINT VALUE £

69	Fontana STL 5491	FAINTLY BLOWING (LP, laminated gatefold sleeve; with watermark on beginning of each side)	£400
87	5 Hours Back TOCK 005	TANGERINE DREAM (LP, stereo reissue)	£20
87	5 Hours Back TOCK 006	FAINTLY BLOWING (LP, reissue, single sleeve)	£20
03	Circle CPWL 104	PLEASE LISTEN TO THE PICTURES (2-LP, BBC sessions, split LP with Fairfield Parlour)	£20

(see also Fairfield Parlour, I Luv Wight)

KALEIDOSCOPE (U.S.)

| 70 | CBS 64005 | BERNICE (LP, as American Kaleidoscope) | £30 |

JOHNNY KALENDAR BAND

| 79 | CJMO PX 109` | FOOLING YOURSELF EP (p/s) | £50 |

(see also Def Leppard)

KALIN TWINS

59	Brunswick 05814	The Meaning Of The Blues/Why Don't You Believe Me? (78)	£15
61	Brunswick 05862	One More Time/I'm Forever Blowing Bubbles	£15
58	Brunswick OE 9383	WHEN (EP)	£20
59	Brunswick OE 9449	THE KALIN TWINS (EP)	£25

KITTY KALLEN

54	Brunswick 05261	Are You Looking For A Sweetheart/In The Chapel In The Moonlight	£15
54	Brunswick 05287	Little Things Mean A Lot/I Don't Think You Love Me Anymore	£20
54	Brunswick 05357	Heartless Heart/The Spirit Of Christmas	£15

DICK KALLMAN

| 63 | HMV CLP 1642 | SPEAK SOFTLY (LP) | £20 |

BOBBY KALPHAT

68	Nu Beat NB 007	Rhythm And Soul/BUNNY & RUDDY: True Romance	£80
73	Tropical AL 049	Natty Rock/Natty Dub	£15
74	Faith FA 008	Zion Hill/Dub Hill	£20

BOBBY KALPHAT & PHIL PRATT

| 76 | Terminal TERM 001 | ZION HILL DUB (LP) | £350 |
| 79 | Phil Pratt SSLP 1007 | THE WAR IS ON DUB STYLE (LP) | £75 |

CAROL KALPHAT

| 78 | Hit Run HIT DD 1 | African Land (featuring Clint Eastwood)/DOCTOR PABLO AND THE CRYTUFF ALLSTARS -African Melody (12", title sleeve) | £70 |

YUSSEF KAMAAL

| 16 | Brownswood BWOOD0157LP | BLACK FOCUS (LP, white vinyl) | £70 |
| 16 | Brownswood BWOOD0157LP | BLACK FOCUS (LP) | £15 |

KAMARAS

| 69 | CBS 4199 | Let This Moment Pass Away/I Just Can't Break Away From This Lovin' | £25 |

KAMIKAZE

| 05 | No Cat or label number | Ghetto Kyote (Instrumental)/(Remix)/(Vocal Mix) (12" white labels) | £30 |

INI KAMOZE

| 84 | Island IMA 7 | INI KAMOZE (LP) | £20 |

KANDAHAR

| 74 | Sounds Superb 4M048-97401 | LONG LIVE THE SLICED HAM (LP) | £30 |

AMORY KANE

68	MCA MU 1036	Reflections Of Your Face/Four Ravens	£15
68	MCA MUP(S) 348	MEMORIES OF TIME UNWOUND (LP, with insert)	£50
70	CBS 63849	JUST TO BE THERE (LP)	£40

(see also Ron Geesin)

DOUG KANE

| 80 | Video VIDEO 2 | ONE BETWEEN THE EYES (LP) | £35 |

EDEN KANE

60	Pye 7N 15284	Hot Chocolate Crazy/You Make Love So Well	£35
64	Decca DFE 8567	SIX GREAT NEW SWINGERS (EP)	£15
64	Fontana TFE 17424	IT'S EDEN (EP)	£15
62	Ace Of Clubs ACL 1133	EDEN KANE (LP)	£25
64	Fontana TL 5211	IT'S EDEN (LP)	£20

(see also Brothers Kane, Sarstedt Brothers)

HELEN KANE

| 55 | MGM EP 549 | THE BOOP BOOP A DOOP GIRL (EP) | £15 |

JEFF KANE

| 69 | Tangerine DP 0006 | Pretty Young Lady/On My Darkest Day | £35 |

MILES KANE

| 11 | Columbia 886978276414 | COLOUR OF THE TRAP (LP, gatefold) | £50 |

(see also Arctic Monkeys, Rascals (3))

STEPHANIE KANE

| 64 | Oriole CB1908 | It's Love/Think Of Me | £25 |

KAN KAN

| 80 | Kabaret Music TRAIN 1 | Film Noir/The Watchmaker | £20 |

KANSAS HOOK

| 71 | Decca F13117 | Nervous Shaking/Mr. Universe | £40 |

KANTATA
84	Oval OVLP 508	ASIKO (LP)	£15
86	Asona ASR 3010	IT'S HIGH TIME NOW (LP)	£20

PAUL KANTNER
71	RCA Victor SF 8163	BLOWS AGAINST THE EMPIRE (LP, gatefold sleeve with booklet, as Paul Kantner & Jefferson Starship)	£20
71	Grunt FTR 1002	SUNFIGHTER (LP, gatefold sleeve with booklet & inner sleeve; as Paul Kantner, Grace Slick & Jefferson Starship)	£15

(see also Jefferson Airplane/Starship)

PANDIT KANWAR SAIN TRIKHA
71	Mushroom 100 MR 7	THREE SITAR PIECES (LP)	£45

KAPLAN
68	Philips BF 1636	Do You Believe In Magic/I Like	£18
68	Philips BF 1699	I Love It/Trousers Down	£20

KAPT. KOPTER & FABULOUS TWIRLY BIRDS
73	Epic EPC 65381	KAPT. KOPTER & THE FABULOUS TWIRLY BIRDS (LP)	£20

(see also Spirit)

JASMINE KARA
12	Acid Jazz AJX281S	Ain't No More Room/Ordinary Joe	£20

LAKIS KARALIS
71	KAR 1	SUPERMARKET 14 (LP, name, title track listing and liner notes written in Greek)	£40

KAREEM
97	Exploding Plastic EXP8	Never Give Up On Love/Restless Soul (Peaktime Radio Mix)/Hipster Mix	£30

KENNY KAREN
61	Philips PB 1213	Oh Susie Forgive Me/The Light In Your Window	£15

KARINA
71	United Artists UP 35205	Tomorrow I'm Coming Your Way/Something	£15

BORIS KARLOFF
60	Caedmon CAL 102/1	HANS CHRISTIAN ANDERSEN (LP)	£15
67	Brunswick LAT 8678	AN EVENING WITH BORIS KARLOFF AND FRIENDS (LP)	£30

KARMA SUTRA
87	Paradoxical PARODY 1	DAYDREAMS OF A PRODUCTION LINE WORKER (LP, with booklet)	£40

KAROO
65	Oak RGJ 193	Mamma's Out Of Town/Lonely Weekend	£200

KARPET KETCHUP
85	Newspaper KK1	Penny Drops/Deep Inside	£15

KARRIER
84	Unit TRANS 101	I'm Back/Dreaming (no p/s)	£30
86	Status JEMS 101	Poor Little Rich Girl/Endless Shadow	£30
85	Unit TRALP 2001	WAY BEYOND THE NIGHT (LP)	£15

KASABIAN
03	BMG Paradise 02	Processed Beats (10" 45 rpm screen print sleeve with elastic bands)	£25
04	BMG Paradise 04	Reason Is Treason (10" p/s 1,000 only)	£18
04	BMG Paradise 06	Club Foot (Jagz Kooner Mix) (12" with man-shaped hole sleeve)	£20
07	No label	Fast Fuse/Thick As Thieves (10" 200 only die-cut sleeve, stamped labels given away at Somerset House gig 2007)	£35
04	BMG Paradise 18	KASABIAN (LP, 2 x 10", embossed gatefold sleeve)	£35
06	Paradise PARADISE 38	EMPIRE (LP, 2x10")	£18
09	Paradise PARADISE 59	WEST RYDER PAUPER LUNATIC ASYLUM (LP, 2x10")	£25
11	Paradise PARADISE 72	VELOCIRAPTOR! (2-LP)	£25

KIMIKO KASAI
18	Be With BEWITH028LP	BUTTERFLY (LP, reissue, with Herbie Hancock)	£20

(see also Herbie Hancock)

KASHIF
83	Arista 205 347	KASHIF (LP)	£20

KASHMERE
06	Receptor RR 005	20 MINUTES OF CHAOS (12", p/s)	£20
04	Low Life LOW 35 LP	BACKHAND SLAP TALK/TECHNICAL ILLNESS (LP, with VERB T)	£30
10	Boot BLP 003	GALAKTUS: POWER COSMIC (LP, numbered)	£30

EDWARD KA-SPEL
84	In Phaze HAZ 6	DANCE CHINA DOLL (EP 12")	£20
84	In Phaze PHA 6	EYES CHINA DOLL (LP)	£25

KATATONIA
96	Misanthropy AMAZON 010	Scarlet Heavens/PRIMORDIAL: To Enter Pagan MCMXCVI (10", p/s)	£20
06	Peaceville VILELP 128	THE GREAT COLD DISTANCE (LP, gatefold, red vinyl)	£40

KATCH-22 (1)
66	Fontana TF 768	Major Catastrophe/Hold Me	£90
67	Fontana TF 874	Makin' Up My Mind/While We're Friends	£25
68	Fontana TF 930	The World's Gettin' Smaller/Don't Bother	£20
68	Fontana TF 984	Pumpkin Mini/100,000 Years	£25
69	Fontana TF 1005	Out Of My Life/Baby Love	£15
69	CBS 4644	It's The Sunshine/Mrs. Jones	£20
68	Saga EROS 8047	IT'S SOFT ROCK & ALLSORTS (LP, with insert, Saga inner sleeve)	£20

KATCHIES
79 Chart PSS 162   Shambles/To Be A Musician..£20

KATE
68 CBS 3631   Strange Girl/I Don't Make A Sound £100
68 CBS 3815   Hold Me Now/Empty World £20
69 CBS 4123   Shout It/Sweet Little Thing £70
(see also Viv Prince, Pretty Things)

KATZ (1)
60s Tetlow TET 118   LIVE AT THE RUM RUNNER (EP) £75

KATZ (2)
79 SRTS/79/CUS/533   Talkin' About You/I'm So Nasty (no p/s, 200 only) £250

BARBARA KAY
65 Pye 7N 15914   Yes I'm Ready/Someone Has To Cry..£20

JANET KAY
82 Solid Groove SGL 103   CAPRICORN WOMAN (LP) £20

JANET K(AY)
78 Bushays BFM 108   Silhouette (with Rico)/PRINCE JAZEBO & RICO: Silhouette Gone Clear (12") £20

JOHN KAY
72 Probe SPB 1054   FORGOTTEN SONGS AND UNSUNG HEROES (LP) £15
(see also Steppenwolf)

SHIRLEY KAY
68 Trojan TR 015   Make Me Yours/We Have Happiness...£75
(see also Phyllis Dillon)

KAYAK
74 Harvest SHSP 4033   SEE SEE THE SUN (LP) £20
74 Harvest SHSP 4036   KAYAK (LP)..£20

DAVE KAYE (& DYKONS)
64 Decca F 11866   A Fool Such As I/It's Nice Isn't It (as Davy Kaye) £35
65 Decca F 12073   In My Way/All The Stars In Heaven (as Dave Kaye) £25

LINDA KAYE
66 Columbia DB 7915   I Can't Stop Thinking About You/When We Meet Again..............................£25

KAYE SISTERS
58 Philips PB 806   Are You Ready, Freddy?/The Pansy £15
(see also Three/Three Kaye Sisters, Frankie Vaughan)

LAINIE KAZAN
69 MGM MGM 1476   Window Of My Mind/It's You £30

ERNIE K-DOE
61 London HLU 9330   Mother-In-Law/Wanted, $10,000.00 Reward £15
61 London HLU 9390   Te-Ta-Te-Ta-Ta/Real Man £20
65 Vocalion VP 9233   My Mother In Law (Is In My Hair Again)/Looking Into The Future £20
68 Action ACT 4502   Dancing Man/Later For Tomorrow £25
68 Action ACT 4512   Gotta Pack My Bags/How Sweet You Are £25

KEANE
00 Zoomorphic (No cat. no)   Call Me What You Like/Rubbernecking/Closer Now (CD, 500 only) £80
01 Zoomorphic ZOO12101   Wolf At The Door/Call Me What You Like/She Has No Time (CD, 500 only p/s) £80
05 Island KEANE2   The Sun Ain't Gonna Shine Anymore/Your Eyes Open (Fan club issue 1000 only p/s) £40
06 Island (no cat no)   Nothing In My Way (512MB memory stick, 1500 only, numbered in title sleeve) £20
06 Universal KEANEBX1   Is it Any Wonder? Fan club box set 2 x 7" with Is It Any Wonder/Let It Slide (IS 934) with art print and 1-sided Atlantic (ATLANTIC001), 2,500 copies)..........................£15
06 Island 1723054   A Bad Dream (512MN memory stick, numbered in title sleeve)....................£20
06 Island KEANEBX1   Atlantic (single sided 7" in box) £15
08 Universal PSBOX1   Spiralling (1-sided 7" in box, 2,000 only, numbered)...............................£20
04 Island ILPS 8145   HOPES AND FEARS (LP, 1000 only) £150
04 Island (no cat no)   HOPES AND FEARS (CD promo, 200 only) £30
04 Island (no cat no)   HOPES AND FEARS (DVD sampler, jewel case, promo).............................£30
05 Island   SINGLES BOX SET (1000 only, 5x7" from HOPES AND FEARS LP) £120
06 Island (no cat no)   THE VIDEOS (Fan club issue only) £50
06 Island ILPS 8167   UNDER THE IRON SEA (2-LP) £70
08 Island 1785966   PERFECT SYMMETRY (LP)...£30

SHAKE KEANE
55 HMV 7MC 38   Akinla/Fire, Fire (export issue) £15
62 Columbia SEG 8239   BOSSA NEGRA (EP) £40
62 Columbia SEG 8140   IN MY CONDITION (EP)...£40
64 Airborne NBP 002   A CASE OF JAZZ (EP, as Shake Keane and MIchael Garrick Quartette, 99 copies only) £350
65 Decca SKL 4720   SHAKE KEANE WITH THE KEATING SOUND (LP)....................................£20
66 Ace Of Clubs ACL 1219   THAT'S THE NOISE (LP)..£25
69 Phase 4 Stereo PFS 4154   DIG IT (LP, with Ivor Raymonde Orchestra)...£40
70 Pama SECO 30   RISING STARS AT EVENING TIME (LP with Gordon Langford and Hastings Girl Choir) £30
91 KLJ LP 008   REAL KEEN REGGAE INTO JAZZ (LP)..£15
11 Trunk JBH 041 LP   RISING STARS (LP, with Michael Garrick, 750 only) £20
(see also Marie Bryant, Michael Garrick)

JOHNNY KEATING ORCHESTRA
57 Oriole MG 20011   BRITISH JAZZ (LP)..£60
58 London LTZ-15122   SWINGIN' SCOTS (LP)...£25

64	Ace Of Clubs ACL 1160	SIXTEEN HITS FOR YOUR DANCE PARTY (LP)	£20
64	Decca PFS 4038	SWING REVISITED (LP)	£25
64	Decca PFS 4078	STRAIGHT AHEAD (LP)	£30
72	Studio Two TWO 393	SPACE EXPERIENCE (LP)	£15
72	Studio Two Q4 TWO 393	SPACE EXPERIENCE (LP, quadrophonic)	£25
75	Studio Two TWOX 1044	SPACE EXPERIENCE 2 (LP)	£15

PAUL KEELEY

08	Anjunadeep ANJDEE-023	A Sort Of Homecoming (Michael Cassette Mix)/(Radio Edit)/(Jaytech Saturday Mix) (12", p/s)	£50

KEEN

90	Scaredy Cat PUR 003	FELINE GROOVY EP (12")	£30

JEFF KEEN

12	Trunk JBH 047 LP	NOISE ART (LP, 500 only silkscreened sleeves. 100 black sleeve/clear vinyl, 100 red sleeve/red and clear vinyl, 100 yellow sleeve/clear/red/yellow vinyl, 100 blue sleeve/ clear/red/yellow and 100 blue vinyl and silver sleeve with clear/red/yellow/blue and silver vinyl)	£40

SPEEDY KEEN

71	Track 2406 105	PREVIOUS CONVICTIONS (LP)	£15

(see also Thunderclap Newman)

NELSON KEENE

60	HMV POP 771	Image Of A Girl/Ocean Of Love	£15
60	HMV POP 814	Keep Loving Me/Teenage Troubles	£15
61	HMV POP 916	Miracles Are Happening To Me/Poor Little Rich Boy	£15

(see also Guv'ners)

KEETY ROOTS

94	Black Legacy BL 003	African Blood/TENASTELIN: Spirit of	£80

ACE KEFFORD STAND

69	Atlantic 584 260	For Your Love/Gravy Booby Jam (small centre hole)	£50
69	Atlantic 584 260	For Your Love/Gravy Booby Jam (large centre hole)	£40

(see also Move, Cozy Powell, Young Blood, Big Bertha, Bedlam, Carl Wayne)

KEITH

67	Mercury MF 989	Daylight Savin' Time/Happy Walking Around	£15
67	Mercury MCL 20103	98.6/AIN'T GONNA LIE (LP)	£30

BRYAN KEITH

63	London HLU 9707	Sad Sad Song/Mean Woman	£20

RON KEITH

76	A&M AMS 7217	Party Music/Gotta Go By What You Tell Me	£90

KEITH (STEWART) & ENID (CUMBERLAND)

63	Island ILP 901	KEITH & ENID SING (LP)	£50
70	Trojan TTL 37	KEITH & ENID SING (LP, reissue)	£20

KEITH (LYN) & KEN (LAZARUS)

65	London HA-R/SH-R 8229	YOU'LL LOVE JAMAICA (LP)	£40

KEITH (ROWE) & TEX (DIXON)

67	Island WI 3085	Tonight/LYN TAIT & JETS: You Have Caught Me	£175
68	Island WI 3091	Stop That Train/BOBBY ELLIS: Feeling Peckish (with Desmond Miles Seven)	£175
68	Island WI 3137	Hypnotizing Eyes/Lonely Man	£150
70	Explosion EX 2008	Tighten Up Your Gird/Look To The Sky	£50
03	Trojan TJGSE 009	Stop That Train/Leaving On That Train (reissue, die-cut Trojan sleeve)	£20

KEITHY

77	Xamayca XAD 002	Struggling In A Babylon (with Imperial Hudson)/XAMAYCA BAND: Togetherness	£25

KELEKETIA!

20	Ahead Of Our Time AHED 024RT	KELEKETIA! (2-LP, multi-coloured vinyl, ltd.to 300)	£30

(see also Coldcut, Shabaka Hutchings)

ROGER KELLAWAY

67	Liberty LBS 583061E	SPIRIT FEEL (LP)	£25

JERRY KELLER

60	London HA-R 2261	HERE COMES JERRY KELLER (LP, mono)	£35
60	London SAH-R 6083	HERE COMES JERRY KELLER (LP, stereo)	£40

PAT KELL(E)Y

68	Giant GN 37	Little Boy Blue/You Are Not Mine (as Pat Kelley & Uniques)	£80
68	Island WI 3121	Somebodies Baby (as Pat Kelly)/BEVERLY SIMMONS: Please Don't Leave Me	£45
68	Island WI 3124	Twelfth Of Never/VAL BENNETT: Caledonia	£50
69	Gas GAS 110	The Workman Song/Never Give Up (as Pat Kelly)	£15
69	Gas GAS 115	How Long/Try To Remember (as Pat Kelly)	£20
69	Gas GAS 124	Festival Time (Parts 1 & 2) (as Pat Kelly)	£20
69	Gas GAS 125	If It Don't Work Out/I Am Coming Home (as Pat Kelley)	£15
70	Gas GAS 144	Tammy/I Am Not Your Guy (as Pat Kelly)	£15
70	Gas GAS 145	Striving For The Right/When A Boy Fall In Love (as Pat Kelley)	£15
71	Camel CA 65	Talk About Love (as Pat Kelley)/PHIL PRATT ALL STARS: Version	£15
71	Punch PH 88	Soulful Love (as Pat Kelly)/HUGH ROY & PARAGONS: One For All	£20
69	Pama PMLP 12	PAT KELLEY SINGS (LP)	£100
71	Pama PMP 2013	COOL BREEZING (LP)	£60
77	Burning Rockers BR 007LP	SO PROUD (LP)	£25
78	Burning Sounds BS1001	LONELY MAN (LP)	£30

MINT VALUE £

| 78 | KG Imperial KGLP 001 | TALK ABOUT LOVE (LP) | £30 |

PETER KELLEY

| 69 | London HAK 8402 | PATH OF THE WAVE (LP) | £40 |
| 71 | Polydor 2310 119 | DEALIN' BLUES (LP) | £25 |

MURRAY KELLUM

| 64 | London HLU 9830 | Long Tall Texan/GLEN SUTTON: I Gotta Leave This Town | £15 |

KELLY

| 69 | Deram DM 277 | Mary Mary/Reverend Richard Baily | £30 |

CHARLIE KELLY

| 68 | Island WI 3155 | So Nice Like Rice/STRANGER & GLADDY: Over Again | £25 |

DAVE KELLY

| 69 | Mercury 20151 SMCL | KEEPS IT IN THE FAMILY (LP, laminated sleeve, black/silver labels) | £200 |
| 71 | Mercury 6310 001 | DAVE KELLY (LP, with Jo-Ann Kelly & Brunning-Hall Sunflower Band) | £250 |

(see also John Dummer Blues Band, Brunning-Hall Sunflower Blues Band)

DAVID WILLIAM KELLY

| 83 | Ethereal ETH 1 | Heart Of Hearts/Chemistry Of MInd (no p/s) | £50 |

FRANK KELLY & HUNTERS

| 63 | Fontana 267 261 TF | I Saw Linda Yesterday/Good And True | £15 |

JO-ANN KELLY

64	GW EP 1	BLUES AND GOSPEL (EP, live at the Bridge House Club)	£150
66	Harlequin HAL 1/HW 349	NEW SOUNDS IN FOLK (LP, with other artists)	£80
69	CBS 63841	JO-ANN KELLY (LP, laminated front sleeve)	£200
76	Red Rag RRR 006	DO IT (LP, with Peter Emery)	£35

(see also Chilli Willi & Red Hot Peppers, Dave Kelly, Tramp)

JO-ANN KELLY & TONY MCPHEE

| 72 | Sunset SLS 50209 | THE SAME THING ON THEIR MINDS (LP) | £30 |

(see also Tony McPhee, Dave Kelly)

JONATHAN KELLY

70	Parlophone R 5851	Don't You Believe It?/Billy (Eric Clapton on guitar)	£40
70	Parlophone PCS 7114	JONATHAN KELLY (LP, black/silver labels with boxed logo)	£100
72	RCA SF 8262	TWICE AROUND THE HOUSES (LP, laminated cover)	£20
73	RCA SF 8353	WAIT TILL THEY CHANGE THE BACKDROP (LP, gatefold sleeve)	£20

(see also Humpy Bong, Boomerang)

KEITH KELLY

60	Parlophone R 4640	(Must You Always) Tease Me/Ooh-La-La	£25
60	Parlophone R 4676	Listen Little Girl/Uh-Huh	£30
60	Parlophone R 4713	With You/You'll Break My Heart	£20
61	Parlophone R 4797	Cold White And Beautiful/When You First Fall In Love	£20

PAUL KELLY

| 65 | Atlantic AT 4053 | Chills And Fever/Only Your Love | £45 |
| 67 | Philips BF 1591 | Sweet Sweet Lovin'/Cryin' For My Baby | £25 |

PETE KELLY'S SOULUTION

| 68 | Decca F 12755 | Midnight Confessions/If Your Love Don't Swing | £30 |
| 68 | Decca F 22829 | Midnight Confessions/BERNIE & BUZZ BAND: The House That Jack Built (export issue) | £20 |

(see also Bernie & Buzz Band, Rhythm & Blues Inc.)

R. KELLY

93	Jive HIP 144	12 PLAY (2-LP)	£20
95	Jive HIP 166	R KELLY (2-LP)	£25
95	Jive 0517931	R. (3-LP)	£30

SEYMOUR KELLY

| 68 | Columbia DB8445 | Indian Scene/Worlds Apart | £15 |

TABBY CAT KELLY

| 78 | Arawak ARK DD005 | Don't Call Us Immigrants/Version | £25 |

WYNTON KELLY TRIO

| 60 | Top Rank 35-107 | KELLY GREAT (LP) | £40 |
| 65 | Verve VLP 9103 | UNDILUTED (LP) | £20 |

KELLY BROTHERS

67	Sue WI 4034	Falling In Love Again/Crying Days Are Over	£150
68	President PT 143	You Put Your Touch On Me/Hanging In There	£25
70	Blue Horizon 57-3177	That's What You Mean To Me/Comin' On In	£30
68	President PTL 1019	SWEET SOUL (LP)	£100

KELV

| 81 | Axis Industries AXLP1 | ATTACKING VESSELS (LP, 250 only, insert) | £18 |

KEMPION

| 77 | Broadside BRO 123 | KEMPION (LP) | £18 |
| 77 | Sweet Folk & C. SFA 044 | CAM YE O'ER FRAE FRANCE (LP) | £15 |

KEN & NEW ESTABLISHMENT

| 73 | Fab FAB 264 | Soul Mood/Golden Locks | £35 |

KEN & STEPPING TONY

| 78 | Rama RMD 005 | Sticks Man Affair/ROCKA & DAVE & GIRL WONDER: Skip-A Dip (12") | £30 |

KENDALL SISTERS
58	London HLM 8622	Won't You Be My Baby/Yea, Yea	£30
58	London HLM 8622	Won't You Be My Baby/Yea, Yea (78)	£20

ANDY KENDRICK
94	Fence Beater FBKA 001	Another Night In The Ghetto/Re-Incarnation	£15
94	Fence Beater FBKLP 001	ANOTHER NIGHT IN THE GHETTO (LP)	£20

LINDA KENDRICK
66	Polydor 56076	It's The Little Things/When Your Love Is Warm	£30
66	Polydor 56076	It's The Little Things/When Your Love Is Warm (DJ copy)	£50
71	Philips 6006-078	Generation (Light Up The Sky)/Come With The Beautiful People	£25
70	Philips SBL 7921	LINDA KENDRICK (LP)	£15

NAT KENDRICK & SWANS
60	Top Rank JAR 351	(Do The) Mashed Potatoes Parts 1 & 2	£30
60	Top Rank JAR 387	Dish Rag Parts 1 & 2	£20

(see also James Brown)

EDDIE KENDRICKS
72	Tamla Motown TMG 845	If You Let Me/Just Memories (DJ Copy)	£45
72	Tamla Motown TMG 845	If You Let Me/Just Memories	£20
71	T. Motown STML 11186	ALL BY MYSELF (LP)	£15
72	T. Motown STML 11213	PEOPLE...HOLD ON (LP, UK-only artwork, sides reversed)	£75
73	T. Motown STML 11245	EDDIE KENDRICKS (LP)	£15

KENICKIE
97	EMI ADISC 002	AT THE CLUB (LP)	£30

CALUM KENNEDY
62	Ember EMB 5167	The Celtic Chorus/Danny Boy	£25

JOHN F. KENNEDY
64	Stateside SL 10064	THE PRESIDENTIAL YEARS 1960-1963 (LP)	£15

JON KENNEDY
01	Tru Thoughts TRU LP 017	WE'RE JUST WAITING FOR YOU NOW (2xLP)	£15

MIKE KENNEDY
72	Youngblood YB 1035	Louisiana/Look Up In The Sky	£20

CHRIS KENNER
61	London HLU 9410	I Like It Like That Parts 1 & 2	£35
65	Sue WI 351	Land Of 1,000 Dances/That's My Girl	£35
66	Atlantic 587 008	LAND OF 1000 DANCES (LP)	£40

KENNY & DENY
65	Decca F 12138	Try To Forget Me/Little Surfer Girl	£70

(see also Jimmy Page, Tony Rivers & The Castaways, Harmony Grass, Capability Brown)

KENNY & WRANGLERS
64	Parlophone R 5224	Somebody Help Me/Who Do You Think I Am?	£25
65	Parlophone R 5275	Doobie Doo/Moonshine	£25

(see also Kenny Bernard & Wranglers)

JERRI BO KENO
75	Phil Spector Intl. 2010 001	Here It Comes (And Here I Go)/I Don't Know Why	£20

KENT
99	RCA 7432164593-7	747/Unprofessional (p/s)	£30

AL KENT
67	Track 604 016	You Got To Pay The Price/Where Do I Go From Here	£50
71	Mojo 2092 015	You Got To Pay The Price/Where Do I Go From Here (unissued)	£0

CINDY KENT
73	York FYK 418	I AM YOUR SERVANT (LP)	£125

KLARK KENT
78	A&M AMS 7376	Don't Care/Office Girls/Thrills (p/s or die-cut sleeve, black vinyl)	£20

(see also Police)

PAUL KENT
70	RCA SF 8083	P.C. KENT (LP)	£60
71	B&C CAS 1044	PAUL KENT (LP)	£50

RICHARD KENT STYLE
66	Columbia DB 7964	No Matter What You Do/Go, Go Children	£200
66	Columbia DB 8051	You Can't Put Me Down/All Good Things	£150
67	Columbia DB 8182	Marching Off To War/I'm Out	£120
68	MCA MU 1032	Love Will Shake The World Awake/Crocodile Tears	£40
69	Mercury MF 1090	A Little Bit O' Soul/Don't Tell Lies	£40

SHIRLEY KENT
66	Keele University 103	THE MASTER SINGERS AND SHIRLEY KENT SING FOR CHAREC 67 (EP)	£35

(see also Ghost, Virginia Tree)

KENT (BROWN) & DIMPLE (HINDS)
63	Island WI 046	Day Is Done/Linger A While	£20

KENT (BROWN) & JEANNIE WITH CITY SLICKERS
62	Blue Beat BB 98	Daddy/Hello Love	£20

(see also Kent Brown & Rainbows)

KENTUCKY COLONELS

74	United Artists UAS 29514	THE KENTUCKY COLONELS (LP)	£18

(see also Byrds)

PATRICK KERR

65	Decca F 12069	Magic Potion/It's No Trouble To Love You	£30

RICHARD KERR

66	Decca F12538	Hard Lovin'/Auntie's Insurance Policy	£15
67	Deram DM 138	Happy Birthday Blues/Mother's Blue-Eyed Angel	£20
73	Warner Bros K 46206	FROM NOW UNTIL THEN (LP, laminated cover, foldout lyric insert)	£15

JOHN KERRUISH

70	A&M AMS 604	Time To Wander/Today, Tonight And Tomorrow Morning	£70

CHRIS KERRY

65	Mercury MF 957	Seven Deadly Sins/The Place	£15
66	Mercury MF 985	Watermelon Man/I've Got My Pride	£25

KEN KESEY

83	Psycho PSYCHO 4	THE ACID TEST (LP, 300 only)	£30

BARNEY KESSEL

54	Vogue LDE 085	BARNEY KESSEL (10" LP)	£20
55	Contemporary LDC 153	BARNEY KESSEL VOLUME 2 (10" LP)	£20
77	Phil Spector Intl. 2307 011	SLOW BURN (LP)	£15

(see also Rick Nelson)

KESTREL

75	Cube HIFLY 19	KESTREL (LP)	£800

KESTRELS

60s	Donegal MAU 500	THE KESTRELS (EP)	£20
63	Piccadilly NPL 38009	SMASH HITS (LP)	£30

(see also Ivy League, White Plains)

JACK KETCH & CROWMEN

87	Hangmen HANG 19 UP	BRIMFULL OF HATE (LP)	£35

KEYBOARD

75	Eyelett EYE 4	Will You Shut Up/Move On	£20

EBONY KEYES

66	Piccadilly 7N 35358	Sitting In The Ring/If You Knew	£100

KAROL KEYES

64	Fontana TF 517	You Beat Me To The Punch/No-One Can Take Your Place (in p/s)	£30
64	Fontana TF 517	You Beat Me To The Punch/No-One Can Take Your Place	£20
66	Columbia DB 7899	A Fool In Love/The Good Love, The Bad Love	£20
66	Columbia DB 8001	One In A Million/Don't Jump	£75

(see also Volunteers)

TROY KEYES

68	Stateside SS 2087	Love Explosions/I'm Crying (Inside)	£22

KEY LARGO

71	Blue Horizon 57-3178	Voodoo Rhythm/As The Years Go Passing By	£20
70	Blue Horizon 7-63859	KEY LARGO (LP)	£60

KEY MASSIVE

89	Hat Music HT 001	Oh Girl/Sweet Sensi (12")	£25
97	Wild Bunch WBRTDJ8	Risingson/Instrumental/Single Mix/Neanderthal Mix/Darren Emerson Mix/Underdog Mix/Underdog Instrumental (2 x 12", clear vinyl promo)	£18

KEYMEN

57	Vogue Coral LVA 9048	THE VOCAL SOUNDS OF THE KEYMEN (LP)	£15

KEYNOTES

63	Planetone 14	I'm In Love/In The Valley	£15

BOBBY KEYS

72	Warner Bros K 46141	BOBBY KEYS (LP)	£25

KEYS (1)

64	Oriole CB 1968	Sleep Sleep My Baby/Colour Slide	£20

KEYS (2)

80	A&M AMS 7511	Just A Camera/It Ain't So (p/s)	£15
81	A&M AMS 8142	I Don't Wanna Cry/Listening In (p/s)	£15
81	A&M AMLH 68526	THE KEYS ALBUM (LP)	£15

KEYTONES

85	Keytone KEY 3	Good To Be Alive/Now's The Time	£15

KEYWI

83	Virgin VS 623	Lets Get It Right/Dub Version/Short Version (12")	£15

K GROOVE

91	The White Label KG 1	The Future/On FB/10 To 10/BYS (12")	£60

KHAN

72	Deram SDL-R 11	SPACE SHANTY (LP, gatefold, white/red label, small logo)	£70
72	Deram SDL 11	SPACE SHANTY (LP, gatefold, white/red label, small logo, later stickered sleeve)	£35

(see also Steve Hillage, Egg, Nick Greenwood, Arzachel, Hatfield & The North)

ASHISH KHAN
68	Liberty LBL 83083E	ASHISH KHAN (LP)	£15

CHAKA KHAN
80	Warner Bros. 17617T	Clouds/What You Did (12")	£15
81	Warner Bros. LV 48	Wha'cha Gonna Do For Me/We Got The Love/I'm Every Woman (12", p/s)	£15
18	Diary no cat no	Like Sugar (Extended)/(Switch Remix) (12", 100 only, hand-numbered)	£150
80	Warner Bros. K 56713	NAUGHTY (LP, printed inner)	£15
89	Warner Bros. WX 268	LIFE IS A DANCE - THE REMIX PROJECT (2LP, printed inners)	£18
81	Warner Bros. K 56888	WHAT CHA' GONNA DO FOR ME (LP)	£15
92	Warner Bros.WX 472	THE WOMAN I AM (LP, printed inners)	£15
19	Island/Diary 6757801	HELLO HAPPINESS (LP, ltd.ed.,coral vinyl, poster)	£40

(see also Rufus, Rufus & Chaka Khan)

USTAD ALI AKBAR KHAN
69	HMV ASD 2367	MUSIC FROM INDIA NO. 5 (LP)	£15
69	Transatlantic TRA 183	DHUN PALAS KAFI (LP)	£20
71	Mushroom 100 MR 14	THE PEACEFUL MUSIC OF USTAD ALI AKBAR KHAN (LP)	£35

(see also Ravi Shankar)

USTAD VILAYET KHAN
70	Transatlantic TRA 239	RAGA TILAKKAMOD (LP)	£15

STEVE KHAN
85	Nimbus AN 3023	EVIDENCE (LP, Nimbus Supercut, mail order only from Practical Hi Fi Magazine)	£25

KHANDARS
65	Blue Beat BB 332	Don't Dig A Hole For Me/BUSTER'S ALL STARS: Skara	£60

KHANS
62	London HLU 9555	New Orleans, 2 AM/Blue Mist	£18

KIASMOS
12	Erased Tapes ERATP044LP	THROWN (12", p/s)	£30

KICK (1)
79	EMI 2962	ROUGH N SMOOTH EP	£15

KICKER BOYS
89	Link LINKLP 071	KICKER BOYS (LP)	£25

KICKS
80	Carrere CAR 138	Get Off The Telephone/Big Boys Don't Cry (p/s)	£30
81	Blue Chip BC 102	If Looks Could Kill/Don't She Look Fab	£70

JOHNNY KIDD (& PIRATES)
59	HMV POP 615	Please Don't Touch/Growl	£30
59	HMV POP 674	Feelin'/If You Were The Only Girl In The World (solo)	£25
60	HMV POP 698	You Got What It Takes/Longin' Lips	£18
60	HMV POP 753	Shakin' All Over/Yes Sir, That's My Baby	£15
60	HMV POP 790	Restless/Magic Of Love	£18
61	HMV POP 853	Linda Lu/Let's Talk About Us	£20
61	HMV POP 919	Please Don't Bring Me Down/So What	£20
62	HMV POP 978	Hurry On Back To Love/I Want That (with The Mike Sammes Singers)	£25
62	HMV POP 1088	A Shot Of Rhythm And Blues/I Can Tell (blue or black label)	£15
64	HMV POP 1309	Jealous Girl/Shop Around	£15
64	HMV POP 1353	Whole Lotta Woman/Your Cheatin' Heart	£20
65	HMV POP 1397	The Birds And The Bees/Don't Make The Same Mistake As I Did	£20
65	HMV POP 1424	Shakin' All Over '65/Gotta Travel On	£40
65	HMV POP 1520	It's Got To Be You/I Hate To Get Up In The Morning (solo)	£30
66	HMV POP 1559	Send For That Girl/The Fool	£40
60s	HMV JO 674	Feelin'/If You Were The Only Girl In The World (export issue, black label)	£30
97	Cruisin' 50 CASB 005	Shakin' All Over/Please Don't Touch (78rpm, 300 only)	£30
60	HMV 7EG 8628	SHAKIN' ALL OVER (EP)	£30
64	HMV 7EG 8834	JOHNNY KIDD AND THE PIRATES (EP)	£40

(see also Pirates)

KIDDA BAND
79	Carrere CAR 119	Fighting My Way Back/Saturday Night Fever	£130

KID DYNAMITE
73	Pye 7N 45274	Call Me Sunshine Superman/Breaking The Ice	£15

KID GUNGO
69	Escort ES 801	Hold The Pussy/KING CANNON: Wha Pen (B-side actually by Carl Bryan)	£18

KID 'N' PLAY
88	Cooltempo COOLXR 175	2 Hype (12" promo)	£20

KIDROCK
73	Youngblood YB 1058	Ice Cream Man/Dream Dream	£35

KIDS
75	Atlantic K 50143	ANVIL CHORUS (LP, with inner, stickered sleeve)	£25

(see also Heavy Metal Kids)

KIDZ
79	P 1099	I'll Get Caught/Prototype Pete (no p/s)	£35

KIDZ NEXT DOOR
79	Warner Bros K 17492	What's It All About?/The Kidz Next Door (p/s)	£50

KIKROKOS
78 Polydor 2393 208   JUNGLE DJ AND DIRTY KATE (LP)..£15

KILBURN & HIGH ROADS
75 Dawn DNLS 3065   HANDSOME (LP, pink 'sun' label)..£40
78 Warner Bros. K56513   WOTABUNCH (LP)..£15
(see also Ian Dury & Blockheads, 999, Nine Days Wonder)

ROY KILDARE
64 Blue Beat BB 226   I Won't Leave/What About It...£15

JUDY KILEEN
56 London HLU 8328   Just Walking In The Rain/A Heart Without A Sweetheart.............£35

MERLE KILGORE
54 London HL 8103   Seeing Double, Feeling Single/It Can't Rain All The Time £300
54 London HL 8103   Seeing Double, Feeling Single/It Can't Rain All The Time (78)......£20
57 London HLP 8392   Ernie/Trying To Find (Someone Like You).....................................£100
57 London HLP 8392   Ernie/Trying To Find (Someone Like You) (78)...............................£29
62 Mercury AMT 1193   42 In Chicago/A Girl Named Liz..£15
65 London HA-B 8244   THERE'S GOLD IN THEM THAR HILLS (LP) £15

THEOLA KILGORE
67 Sue WI 4035   I'll Keep Trying/He's Coming Back To Me £40

KILLA INSTINCT
92 Music Of Life NOTE061 The Bambi Murders (12")...£15
92 Music Of Life NOTE063 Den Of Thieves/Ununited Kingdom (12")......................................£15
93 European Rhyme ERR02 WHISPERS OF HATRED (EP) £18
(see also Total Fiasco)

KILLER
77 Ariola ARL 5003   KILLER (LP) £35
(see also Joe Cool & The Killers)

KILLERHERTZ
92 FX FXUKT 9   Distant Dream (X-Static Mix)/Love Byte (Apocalypse Mix)/Love Byte (Stronthium Mix)/Distant Dream (Flying Fader Mix) (12")......................£40

KILLERMETERS
79 Psycho P 2620   Why Should It Happen To Me/Cardiac Arrest (in p/s) £100
79 Psycho P 2620   Why Should It Happen To Me/Cardiac Arrest £30
80 Gem GEMS 22   Twisted Wheel/SX 225 (p/s, demo copies £50) £90
97 Detour DRLP 013   METRIC NOISE (2xLP, gatefold, 'sparkly' clear vinyl) £20

KILLERS (2)
03 Lizard King LIZARD007X Mr Brightside/Smile Like You Mean It (white vinyl, 500 only p/s).........£80
04 Lizard King LIZARD009X Somebody Told Me/The Ballad Of Michael Valentine (pink vinyl, 2,000 only, p/s and poster).....................£20
04 Lizard King LIZARD010X Mr Brightside/Who Let You Go (red vinyl, p/s and poster).........£25
04 Lizard King IND1ERR   Glamorous Indie Rock & Roll (1-sided promo, 400 only) £15
09 Vertigo 2714744   A Dustyard Fairytale/Forget About What I Said (picture disc) £15
04 Lizard King LIZARD011X HOT FUSS (LP, blue vinyl)..£125
05 Island B0005491-21   HOT FUSS (LP as 11 x 7" box set) £80
08 Island 602517902534 DAY & AGE (LP) £30
12 Island 602537118762 BATTLE BORN (2-LP, red and black vinyl, 200 only autographed for Wembley concert) £40
17 Island 00602557937572 WONDERFUL WONDERFUL (LP, pink vinyl) £30

KILLER WATT
87 Raglan RGS 312   DEATH (EP) £25

JOHN KILLIGREW
71 Penny Farthing PELS 513 JOHN KILLIGREW (LP, with Pete Dello, red/black/yellow labels) ...£175
(see also Pete Dello)

KILLING FLOOR
70 Penny Farthing PEN 745 Call For The Politicians/Acid Bean £20
69 Spark (S)RLP 102   KILLING FLOOR (LP, blue/silver labels) £500
70 Penny Farthing PELS 511 OUT OF URANUS (LP, gatefold sleeve, red/black/yellow label) £450
73 Spark Replay SRLM 2004 ORIGINAL KILLING FLOOR (LP, reissue).......................................£30
(see also Rory Gallagher)

KILLING JOKE
79 Malicious Damage MD 410 Nervous System/Turn To Red/Are You Receiving (10" EP in bag, with picture & 4 cards) £35
80 Island WIP 6550   Turn To Red/Nervous System ('A' label)......................................£15
80 Malicious Damage MD 540 Wardance/Psyche (p/s, with 'call up paper' insert)......................£15
80 Malicious Damage MD 540 Wardance/Psyche (Mispressed B-side plays 'unknown artist', p/s) £25
83 E.G. EGOXD 14   Me Or You/Feast Of Blaze/Wilful Days//Let's All Go (To The Fire Dances)/The Fall Of Because (live)/Dominator (Version) (12", sealed double pack) ...£15
80 E.G. EGM5.45   KILLING JOKE (LP, gatefold)...£30
81 E.G. EGMD 5.50   WHAT'S THIS FOR...! (LP) £30
82 E.G. EGMD 3   REVELATIONS (LP)...£15
83 E.G. EGMD 5   FIRE DANCES (LP) £15
90 AG -54-1   EXTREMITIES DIRT AND VARIOUS REPRESSED EMOTIONS (2-LP) ...£15
85 E.G. EGLP 61   NIGHT TIME (LP, inner) £20
86 EG EGLP 57   KILLING JOKE (LP, reissue, black and red EG labels, gatefold).......£15
86 EG EGLP 58   WHAT'S THIS FOR...! (LP, reissue, black and red EG labels) £15
94 Butterfly BFLLP9   PANDEMONIUM (2-LP)..£30

06	Let Them Eat Vinyl LETV005LP	HOSANNAS FROM THE BASEMENTS OF HELL (2-LP, gatefold blue vinyl)	£30
08	Let Them Eat Vinyl LETV003LP	DEMOCRACY (2-LP gatefold, white vinyl, reissue)	£25
08	Let Them Eat Vinyl LETV014LP	KILLING JOKE (2-LP, reissue, black and white vinyl, gatefold sleeve)	£30
08	Let Them Eat Vinyl LETV015LP	WHAT'S THIS FOR...! (2-LP reissue, red and green vinyl, gatefold)	£25
08	Let Them Eat VInyl LETV016LP	REVELATIONS (2-LP, reissue, blue and yellow vinyl)	£18

(see also Youth, Peyr, Brilliant, Firemen)

KILLJOYS (1)

77	Raw RAW 3	Johnny Won't Get To Heaven/Naive (p/s, 4 different label designs)	£35
91	Dam. Goods FNARR LP10	NAIVE (LP, green vinyl)	£20

(see also Girlschool)

KILLS

16	Domino RUG 759	Doing It To Death (1-sided, B-side etched)	£15
03	Domino WIGLP 124	KEEP ON YOUR MEAN SIDE (LP, with fold-out insert)	£25
05	Domino WIGLP 140	NO WOW (LP, with DVD)	£30
08	Domino WIGLP 184	MIDNIGHT BOOM (LP)	£15
11	Domino WIGLP 249	BLOOD PRESSURES (LP, gatefold, download card)	£15
16	Domino WIGLP 289X	ASH & ICE (2-LP, pink and blue vinyl)	£20

(see also Dead Weather)

KILOWATTS

68	JJ DB 1140	Bring It On Home/What A Wonderful World (with Doctor Bird label cat no)	£30

(see also West Indians)

PAT KILROY

67	Elektra EKL 311	LIGHT OF DAY (LP)	£80

KILTIES

56	Beltona BL 2666	Teach You To Rock/Giddy-Up-A Ding Dong	£15

KIM & KINETICS

60s	Mortonsound 3032/3033	Without A Song/Stormy Monday	£60
60s	Mortonsound 3036/3033	Wee Wee Hours/Stormy Monday	£60

(see also Kim Davis)

STEVIE KIMBLE

66	Decca F 12378	Some Things Take A Little Time/All The Time In The World (DJ Copy)	£50
66	Decca F 12378	Some Things Take A Little Time/All The Time In The World	£25

KINESPHERE

76	Kinesphere KIN 5001	ALL AROUND YOU (LP)	£100

KINETIC EFFECT

93	Insane 1201	Borderin' Insanity/Beyond The Parameters (12" green vinyl, 500 pressed)	£30
93	Insane 1201	Borderin' Insanity/Beyond The Parameters (12")	£18
97	Insane 1202	Man Bites Dog/The Effect Of Fear (12")	£18
12	Insane 1001	A Physical Exorcise/The Catalyst (clear vinyl 10")	£15

(see also 2 The Top and Insane Macbeth)

AL KING

68	Sue WI 4045	Think Twice Before You Speak/The Winner	£40

ALBERT KING

67	Atlantic 584 099	Crosscut Saw/Down Don't Bother Me	£20
67	Polydor 2343 026	TRAVELLIN' TO CALIFORNIA (LP)	£40
68	Stax (S)XATS 1002	LIVE WIRE - BLUES POWER (LP)	£40
69	Atlantic 588 173	KING OF THE BLUES GUITAR (LP)	£40
69	Stax SXATS 1017	KING DOES THE KING'S THINGS (LP)	£35
69	Stax SXATS 1022	YEARS GONE BY (LP)	£35
71	Stax 2363 003	LIVE WIRE - BLUES POWER (LP, reissue)	£15
71	Stax 2325 042	LOVEJOY (LP)	£35
73	Stax 2325 089	I'LL PLAY THE BLUES FOR YOU (LP)	£20
74	Stax STX 1003	I WANNA GET FUNKY (LP)	£20

(see also Steve Cropper & Albert King)

ANNA KING

65	Philips BF 1402	If Somebody Told You/Baby, Baby, Baby (as Anna King & Bobby Byrd)	£15
65	Philips BBE 12584	BACK TO SOUL (EP)	£40
65	Philips (S)BL 7655	BACK TO SOUL (LP)	£60

(see also Bobby Byrd)

ANTHONY KING

70s	Peer Intl.	ELECTRICAL BAZAAR - SYNTHESIZERS UNLIMITED (LP, library issue)	£20

B.B. KING

62	HMV POP 1101	Tomorrow Night/Mother's Love	£25
64	Ember EMB S 196	Rock Me Baby/I Can't Lose	£25
65	Sue WI 358	The Letter/You Never Know	£30
66	HMV POP 1568	Don't Answer The Door Parts 1 & 2	£20
67	HMV POP 1580	Night Life/Waitin' On You	£15
67	HMV POP 1594	I Don't Want You Cuttin' Your Hair/Think It Over	£15
67	Polydor 56735	Jungle/Long Gone Baby	£15
68	Blue Horizon 57-3144	The Woman I Love/Blues For Me	£20
69	Blue Horizon 57-3161	Everyday I Have The Blues/Five Long Years	£20

MINT VALUE £

65	HMV CLP 1870	LIVE AT THE REGAL (LP)	£50
66	HMV CLP 3514	CONFESSIN' THE BLUES (LP)	£30
67	HMV CLP 3608	BLUES IS KING (LP)	£30
68	Stateside (S)SL 10238	BLUES ON TOP OF BLUES (LP)	£30
67	Ember EMB 3379	THE R&B AND SOUL OF B.B. KING (LP)	£30
68	Blue Horizon 7-63216	THE B.B. KING STORY CHAPTER 1 (LP)	£50
69	Stateside (S)SL 10272	LUCILLE (LP)	£40
69	Stateside SSL 10284	HIS BEST - THE ELECTRIC B.B. KING (LP)	£20
69	Blue Horizon 7-63226	THE B.B. KING STORY CHAPTER 2 - BEALE STREET BLUES (LP)	£75
70	Stateside SSL 10297	LIVE AND WELL (LP)	£30
70	Stateside SSL 10299	COMPLETELY WELL (LP)	£30
70	Probe SPBA 6255	INDIANOLA MISSISSIPPI SEEDS (LP)	£30
71	Blue Horizon 2431 004	TAKE A SWING WITH ME (LP, mono)	£100
71	Probe SPB 1032	LIVE IN COOK COUNTY JAIL (LP)	£30

(see also U2)

B.B. KING & BOBBY BLAND

| 74 | ABC ABCD 605 | TOGETHER FOR THE FIRST TIME (2-LP) | £18 |

(see also Bobby Bland)

BEN E. KING

61	London HLK 9358	Stand By Me/On The Horizon	£15
61	London HLK 9457	Here Comes The Night/Young Boy Blues	£15
62	London HLK 9586	Too Bad/My Heart Cries For You	£15
63	London HLK 9631	I'm Standing By/Walking In The Footsteps Of A Fool	£15
63	London HLK 9691	How Can I Forget/Gloria, Gloria	£15
64	London HLK 9840	Around The Corner/Groovin'	£20
64	Atlantic AT 4007	It's All Over/Let The Water Run Down	£22
65	Atlantic AT 4018	Seven Letters/River Of Tears	£22
65	Atlantic AT 4025	The Record (Baby I Love You)/The Way You Shake It	£20
65	Atlantic AT 4043	Cry No More/(There's) No Place To Hide	£40
66	Atlantic AT 4065	Goodnight My Love, Pleasant Dreams/I Can't Break The News To Myself (demos with blank label on different B-side)	£400
66	Atlantic 584 008	So Much Love/Don't Drive Me Away	£15
67	Atlantic 584 106	Tears, Tears, Tears/A Man Without A Dream	£15
68	Atlantic 584 184	Don't Take Your Love From Me/Forgive This Fool	£25
75	Atlantic K 10618	Happiness Is Where You Find It/Drop My Heart Off	£15
03	Atco 67855	I Can't Break The News Myself/BOBBY SHEEN: Something New To Do	£15
63	London REK 1361	BEN E. KING (EP)	£40
63	London REK 1386	I'M STANDING BY (EP)	£40
64	Atlantic AET 6004	WHAT NOW MY LOVE (EP)	£40
61	London HA-K 2395	SPANISH HARLEM (LP, mono)	£50
61	London SAH-K 6195	SPANISH HARLEM (LP, stereo)	£70
62	London HA-K 8012	DON'T PLAY THAT SONG! (LP)	£50
63	London HA-K 8026	SONGS FOR SOULFUL LOVERS (LP, cover credits Sings For Soulful Lovers; mono)	£50
63	London SH-K 8026	SONGS FOR SOULFUL LOVERS (LP, cover credits Sings For Soulful Lovers; stereo)	£70
65	Atlantic ATL 5016	GREATEST HITS (LP, plum label)	£40
65	Atlantic ATL 5024	SEVEN LETTERS (LP)	£50
66	Atlantic 587/588 055	SONGS FOR SOULFUL LOVERS (LP, cover credits Sings For Soulful Lovers; reissue)	£18
67	Atlantic 587 072	WHAT IS SOUL? (LP)	£25
70	Crewe CRWS 203	ROUGH EDGES (LP)	£15

(see also Drifters, Soul Clan)

BOB KING & THE COUNTRY KINGS

| 59 | Oriole CB 1497 | My Petite Marie/Hey Honey | £80 |
| 59 | Oriole CB 1497 | My Petite Marie/Hey Honey (78) | £20 |

BUZZY KING

| 60 | Top Rank JAR 278 | Schoolboy Blues/Your Picture | £20 |

CANNON BALL KING

69	Camel CA 14	Danny Boy/Reggae Happiness	£40
69	Gas GAS 133	Stagger Back/The Creeper	£50
70s	Junior JR 103	Reggay Got Soul/Land Of Love (actually by Soul Cats)	£15

(see also Carl Bryan, King Cannon, Cannon Ball & Johnny Melody)

CARL KING

| 66 | CBS 202407 | Out Of My Depth/Keep It Coming | £25 |

CAROLE KING

| 66 | London HLU 10036 | Road To Nowhere/Some Of Your Lovin' | £40 |

CLAUDE KING

| 65 | CBS EP 6067 | TIGER WOMAN (EP) | £15 |
| 62 | CBS BPG 62114 | MEET CLAUDE KING (LP) | £20 |

DANNY KING('S MAYFAIR SET)

64	Columbia DB 7276	Tossin' And Turnin'/Young Blood	£35
65	Columbia DB 7456	Pretty Things/Outside Of My Room	£40
65	Columbia DB 7792	Amen (My Teenage Prayer)/It's Such A Shame (as Danny King's Mayfair Set)	£25

(see also Trevor Burton, Lemon Tree, Roy Wood)

DENNIS KING

| 77 | EMI EMI 2578 | Regan's Theme From The Film 'Sweeney'/F.J.'s Tune | £20 |

(see also King Brothers)

DR. MARTIN LUTHER KING
68 Tamla Motown TML 11076 **THE GREAT MARCH TO FREEDOM** (LP)..**£60**

FREDDY/FREDDIE KING
61	Parlophone R 4777	**Hideaway/I Love The Woman**	**£50**
65	Sue WI 349	**Driving Sideways/Hideaway**	**£40**
69	Atlantic 584 235	**Play It Cool/Funky**	**£15**
69	Atlantic 588 186	**FREDDIE IS A BLUES MASTER** (LP)	**£45**
69	Polydor 2343 009	**KING OF R&B VOL. 2** (LP)	**£15**
69	Python PLP-KM 5	**FREDDY KING VOLUME 1** (LP, 99 copies only)	**£100**
69	Python PLP-KM 7	**FREDDY KING VOLUME 2** (LP, 99 copies only)	**£100**
69	Python PLP-KM 11	**FREDDY KING VOLUME 3** (LP, 99 copies only)	**£100**

(Pre-1970 releases are usually credited to Freddy King, post-1970 releases to Freddie King.)

72	A&M AMLS 68113	**TEXAS CANNONBALL** (LP)	**£15**
72	Black Bear 904	**LIVE PERFORMANCES VOLUME 1** (LP)	**£15**
72	Black Bear 905	**LIVE PERFORMANCES VOLUME 2** (LP)	**£15**

(see also Lula Reed & Freddy King)

HANK KING
63 Starlite STEP 41 **COUNTRY AND WESTERN** (EP)...**£25**

JAY W. KING
66 Stateside SS 505 **I'm So Afraid/I Don't Have To Worry** (Not Anymore)..................**£15**

MORGAN KING
93 OM Records 12OM0006 T **I Am Free** (8 Mixes) (2 x12")...**£40**

P. RUFUS KING
73 Dawn DNS 1031 **Look At Me Now/Nobody Knows** **£25**

(see also Paul King, Mungo Jerry)

PAUL KING
72 Dawn DNLS 3035 **BEEN IN THE PEN TOO LONG** (LP, textured sleeve with lyric insert).....**£40**

(see also Mungo Jerry, P. Rufus King, King Earl Boogie Band, D'Jurann Jurran, Jigilo Jug Band)

PETER KING (1)
68 Crab CRAB 3 **Reggae Limbo/DERRICK MORGAN: River To The Bank** **£20**

PETER KING (2)
78 Miles Music MM 076 **BROTHER BERNARD** (LP, with Alan Skidmore)..........................**£20**

PETER KING (3)
75	Orbitone OTLP 007	**MILIKI SOUND** (LP)	**£100**
76	Orbitone OTLP 010	**OMU LEWA** (LP)	**£150**
77	Orbitone OTLP 012	**A SOULFUL PETER KING** (LP)	**£20**
93	Spindle LP 07	**MILIKI SOUND** (LP, reissue)	**£30**
93	Spindle LP 08	**OMO LEWA** (LP, reissue)	**£35**

PETER KING (4)
85	Fashion FAD 029	**Step On The Gas/Ten Commandments Of An MC** (12")	**£30**
85	Fashion FAD 045	**Bad Memory/Rewind/Jack It Up** (12")	**£30**

RAMONA KING
64 Warner Bros WB 125 **It's In His Kiss/It Couldn't Happen To A Nicer Guy** **£25**

RAY KING SOUL BAND
67	Piccadilly 7N 35394	**Behold/Soon You'll Be Gone**	**£20**
68	Direction 8-63394	**LIVE AT THE PLAYBOY CLUB** (LP)	**£20**

REG KING
71	United Artists UP 35204	**Little Boy/10,000 Miles** (as Reg King & B.B. Blunder)	**£25**
71	United Artists UAG 29157	**REG KING** (LP)	**£120**

(see also Action, Andy Leigh, B.B. Blunder, Mark Charig, Elton Dean, Mighty Baby)

SID KING & FIVE STRINGS
56 Philips PB 589 **Booger Red/Oobie-Doobie** (78) **£50**

SOLOMON KING
70	Columbia DB 8676	**Say A Prayer/This Beautiful Day**	**£100**
70	Columbia DB 8676	**Say A Prayer/This Beautiful Day** (demo copy)	**£150**
72	Polydor 2058258	**When You Gotta Go/Life Child**	**£30**

(see also Levi Jackson)

TEDDY KING & BUSTER'S ALLSTARS
67 Fab FAB 27 **Mexican Divorce/SOUL TOPS: Baby I Got News**................**£35**

TONY KING (& HIPPY BOYS)
69 Trojan TR 667 **Proud Mary/My Devotion** (as Tony King & Hippy Boys).......**£20**

(see also Maytals)

TRACY KING
86 DMD 002 **Don't Stop/Love Again** (12") **£20**

KING AND QUEEN
79 Decca F 13863 **Reunited/Reunited** (Dub)...**£40**

KINGBEES
66	Tempo TPO 103	**I'm A Kingbee/My Little Red Book** (Irish-only, in p/s)	**£350**
66	Tempo TPO 103	**I'm A Kingbee/My Little Red Book** (Irish-only)	**£250**

KING BISCUIT BOY
70	Paramount SPFL 270	**OFFICIAL MUSIC** (LP)	**£18**
71	Paramount SPFA 7001	**GOODUNS** (LP)	**£18**

(see also Bobby Bland)

KING BROTHERS
58	Parlophone PMC 1060	THREE KINGS AND AN ACE (LP)	£15

(see also Jim Dale, Dennis King)

KING CANNON
69	Trojan TR 663	Soul Scorcher/GLEN & DAVE: Lucky Boy	£60
69	Harry J TR 664	Soul Special/TREVOR SHIELD: Moon Is Playing Tricks On Me	£60
69	Crab CRAB 6	Mellow Trumpet/VAL BENNETT: Reggae City	£80
71	Hillcrest HCT 2	Reggay Got Soul/SOUL CATS: Land Of Love	£18
71	Moodisc HME 109	Raw Deal (as King Cannon Allout; actually by Carl Bryan)/ MUDIE'S ALL STARS: Shirley's Hide Out	£18

(see also Cannon Ball & Johnny Melody, Carl Bryan, Max Romeo, Lester Sterling, Kid Gungo, Erroll Dunkley)

KING CANNON (BALL)
68	Trojan TR 636	Thunderstorm/BURT WALTERS: Honey Love	£65

KING CC
76	Concrete Jungle CJ 751	Rasta Poker/LUCKY ALL STARS: Babylon Fall Down	£100

(see Prince Far I, King Cry Cry)

KING CHUBBY
70	Pama Supreme PS 297	What's The World Coming To/Live As One	£15

(see also Junior Byles)

KING CRIMSON
19	DGM KCCBX 14	HEAVEN AND EARTH (18CD/2DVDA/4BD, box, ephemera)	£180

SINGLES : SINGLES/EPS
69	Island WIP 6071	The Court Of The Crimson King (Parts 1 & 2)	£40
70	Island WIP 6080	Cat Food/Groon (in p/s)	£40
76	Island WIP 6274	21st Century Schizoid Man/Epitaph (in p/s)	£30
76	Island WIP 6274	Epitaph/21st Century Schizoid Man (7", promo, 'DJ Copy' on label, die cut company sleeve)	£75
15	DGM DGMP 121	CYCLOPS (12" EP, picture disc)	£20
18	DGM KC 10X2	UNCERTAIN TIMES (2x10" EP, gatefold p/s)	£20

ALBUMS : ORIGINAL ALBUMS
69	Island ILPS 9111	IN THE COURT OF THE CRIMSON KING (LP, 1st pressing, Matrixes ILPS 9111 A 2 1 2 4/ ILPS 9111B//4 1 1 1or ILPS 9111 A//3 1 1 3/ILPS 9111 B//3 123 gatefold sleeve, 'Printed and made by E.J. Day, London.' sleeve credit , pink label/'i' logo)	£600
70	Island ILPS 9111	IN THE COURT OF THE CRIMSON KING (LP, 2nd pressing, gatefold sleeve no printer credits, pink rim label/'palm tree' logo)	£70
70	Island ILPS 9127	IN THE WAKE OF POSEIDON (LP, 1st pressing, textured gatefold sleeve made by E.J. Day, A1/B1 matrixes deep pink lightly texturred label with 'i' logo)	£250
70	Island ILPS 9127	IN THE WAKE OF POSEIDON (LP, 2nd pressing, pink rim label/'palm tree' logo)	£40
70	Island ILPS 9141	LIZARD (LP, 1st pressing with E. J. Day Co sleeves, Matrix ILPS9141 A-2U/B-2U, laminated gatefold sleeve, pink rim label/'palm tree' logo. Sleeve variation with title 'Lizard' inverted on spine)	£200
70	Island ILPS 9141	LIZARD (LP, 1st pressing with E. J. Day Co sleeves, Matrix ILPS9141 A-2U/B-2U, laminated gatefold sleeve, pink rim label/'palm tree' logo)	£100
70	Island ILPS 9141	LIZARD (LP, 2nd pressing with Robor sleeves, laminated gatefold sleeve, pink rim label/'palm tree' logo)	£30
71	Island ILPS 9175	ISLANDS (LP, pink rim label/'palm tree' logo, with fold-out gatefold inner)	£60
71	Island ILPS 9111	IN THE COURT OF THE CRIMSON KING (LP, 3rd pressing, pink rim palm tree label with rough finish, no printers credits, Matrixes: ILPS+9111+A2/ILPS+9111+B2, Basing Street London W11 address)	£40
72	Island ILPS 9111	IN THE COURT OF THE CRIMSON KING (LP, 4th pressing, smooth labels, PRINTED IN ENGLAND by ROBOR LIMITED sleeve credit, Matrixes ILPS 9111 A-4U PD 2/ILPS 9111 B-4U HM 2)	£30
72	Island HELP 6	EARTHBOUND (LP, 1st pressing, black/pink label, Matrixes: HELP 6A - 2U GM 1/HELP 6 B - 1U PR 1)	£60
73	Island ILPS 9230	LARKS' TONGUES IN ASPIC (LP, 1st pressing in shrinkwrap with 'King Crimson' sticker, pink rim label/'palm tree' logo, with inner)	£150
73	Island ILPS 9230	LARKS' TONGUES IN ASPIC (LP, 1st pressing, no shrinkwrap without 'King Crimson' sticker, pink rim label/'palm tree' logo, with inner)	£60
74	Island ILPS 9275	STARLESS AND BIBLE BLACK (LP, textured gatefold sleeve printed by Robor, palm tree logo, matrixes: A/3U, B/3U, 'Garc' etched into dead wax side A, 'Sean & Ray' etched into dead wax side B, with inner)	£60
74	Island ILPS 9308	RED (LP, pink rim label/'palm tree' logo, with inner sleeve)	£45
75	Island ILPS 9316	U.S.A. (LP, pink rim label/'palm tree' logo, with inner)	£35
81	EG EGLP 49	DISCIPLINE (LP, yellow labels, Polydor logo at 6 O'clock on labels)	£50
82	EG EGLP 51	BEAT (LP, blue labels, Polydor logo on labels, blue printed inner)	£25
84	EG EGLP 55	THREE OF A PERFECT PAIR (LP, Polydor logo on label, printed inner, later pressings have black labels and Virgin logo)	£20
19	DGM KCLPX 13	THRAK (2LP, 200g, gatefold, printed inners, first vinyl issue of 95 CD)	£30
19	DGM KCLPX 15	THE POWER TO BELIEVE (2LP, 200g, gatefold, printed poly lined inners, vinyl issue of 03 CD)	£35

ALBUMS : REISSUES, BOX SETS AND COMPILATIONS
76	Island ISLP 7	A YOUNG PERSON'S GUIDE TO KING CRIMSON (2LP, gatefold, booklet, black polylined inner sleeves with pink Island logo)	£30
80	Polydor 2683 080	IN THE COURT OF THE CRIMSON KING/LARKS TONGUES IN ASPIC (2LP, gatefold)	£20
77	Polydor 2302 059	LIZARD (LP, reissue, gatefold sleeve)	£15
77	Polydor 2302 060	ISLANDS (LP, reissue)	£15
77	Polydor 2343 092	EARTHBOUND (LP, reissue)	£15
77	Polydor 2302 061	LARKS TONGUES IN ASPIC (LP, reissue)	£15
77	Polydor 2302 065	STARLESS AND BIBLE BLACK (LP, reissue)	£15
77	Polydor 2302 066	RED (LP, reissue)	£15
87	EG EGLP 5	ISLANDS (LP, reissue)	£15

87	EG EGLP 15	**RED** (LP, reissue)	£15
89	EG EGLP 4	**LIZARD** (LP, reissue, gatefold sleeve)	£15
91	EG EGLP 7	**LARKS TONGUES IN ASPIC** (LP, reissue)	£15
91	Virgin KCBOX 1	**FRAME BY FRAME** (THE ESSENTIAL KING CRIMSON) (4CD box set, booklet, reissued 1994)	£40
92	Discipline KDIS 1	**THE GREAT DECEIVER** (4CD box set, booklet, repressed 1994)	£50
09	DGM KCCBX1	**IN THE COURT OF THE CRIMSON KING** (5CD/DVD box set, booklet, reissue)	£70
11	DGM KCLP 2	**IN THE WAKE OF POSEIDON** (LP, reissue, gatefold, 200g)	£20
12	Discipline Global Mobile KCLP3	**LIZARD** (LP, reissue, gatefold, 200g)	£15
13	DGM KCLP 5	**LARKS TONGUES IN ASPIC** (LP, reissue, 200g)	£15
13	Discipline Global Mobile/ Opal DGM KCLP7	**RED** (LP, reissue, 200gm vinyl)	£15
13	Discipline Global Mobile KCCBX7	**THE ROAD TO RED** (21CD/DVD/2BD box set, reissue, booklet, prints)	£150
14	Discipline Global Mobile DGM KCLP4	**ISLANDS** (LP, reissue, 200gm vinyl)	£18
14	Discipline Global Mobile KCCBX6	**STARLESS** (23CD/2DVD/2BD box set, booklet)	£125
15	Discipline Global Mobile/ Opal DGM KCLP6	**STARLESS AND BIBLE BLACK** (LP, reissue 200gm vinyl)	£20
15	Discipline Global Mobile KCCBX13	**THRAK BOX** (LIVE AND STUDIO 1994-1997) (12CD/2DVD/2BD box set, booklet)	£160
16	DGM KCCBX 8	**ON** (AND OFF) **THE ROAD** (11CD/3DVDA/2DVD/3BD, box set, ephemera)	£100
17	DGM KCCBX 4	**SAILORS' TALES** (21CD/2DVDA/4BD, box, ephemera)	£225
18	DGM KCLPBX 502	**1969-1972** (6LP box set, 200g, booklet)	£150
19	DGM KCLPBX 503	**1972-1974** (6LP box set, booklet, poster, 200g)	£170
20	DGM KCCBX 9111	**THE COMPLETE 1969 RECORDINGS** (20CD/4BD/2DVD box set, booklet, ephemera)	£150
22	DGM KCLP 11	**EARTHBOUND** (LP, 200g, reissue)	£20

(see also Giles Giles & Fripp, Fripp & Eno, Gordon Haskell, Shame, McDonald & Giles, Emerson Lake & Palmer, Uriah Heep, Boz, Trendsetters Ltd., Pete Sinfield, Jakszyk, Fripp and Collins)

KING CRY CRY (PRINCE FAR I)
| 71 | Banana BA 356 | I Had A Talk/BURNING SPEAR: Zion Higher | £35 |

(see also King C C)

KING CURTIS
62	London HLU 9547	**Soul Twist/Twistin' Time** (as King Curtis & Noble Knights)	£20
64	Capitol CL 15346	**Soul Serenade/More Soul**	£20
67	Atlantic 584 134	**Memphis Soul Stew/Blue Nocturne**	£15
70	Atco 2091 012	**Teasin'/Soulin'** (as King Curtis & Delaney Bramlett, Eric Clapton & Friends)	£15
60	London RE-K 1307	**HAVE TENOR SAX, WILL BLOW** (EP)	£40
60	London HA-K 2247	**HAVE TENOR SAX, WILL BLOW** (LP)	£70
62	RCA RD 27252	**ARTHUR MURRAY'S MUSIC FOR DANCING - THE TWIST** (LP)	£30
62	Esquire 32-161	**THE NEW SCENE OF KING CURTIS** (LP)	£40
67	Atlantic 587 067	**PLAYS THE GREAT MEMPHIS HITS** (LP)	£20
68	Ember SPE/LP 6600	**SOUL SERENADE** (LP)	£20
68	Atlantic 587 093	**KINGSIZE SOUL** (LP, as King Curtis & Kingpins)	£20
69	Atco 228 002	**BEST OF KING CURTIS** (LP)	£15
68	Atlantic 587/588 115	**SWEET SOUL** (LP)	£20
69	Atco 228 027	**INSTANT GROOVE** (LP)	£20
71	Atlantic 2400159	**LIVE AT FILLMORE WEST** (LP, gatefold)	£20

(see also Champion Jack Dupree, Eric Clapton)

KING CURTIS, OLIVER NELSON & JIMMY FORREST
| 63 | Esquire 32-189 | **SOUL BATTLE** (LP) | £30 |

KING DIAMOND
| 89 | Roadrunner RR 9461-1 | **CONSPIRACY** (LP, inner) | £15 |
| 89 | Roadrunner RR 94616 | **CONSPIRACY** (LP, picture disc) | £20 |

KINGDOM
| 70 | United Artists UP 35145 | All I Need/Nothing Could Be Better | £25 |

BOBBY KINGDOM/BLUE BEATS
| 61 | Blue Beat BB 44 | Honey Please/BLUE BEATS: That's My Girl | £25 |

KINGDOM COME (U.K.)
72	Polydor 2310 130	**GALACTIC ZOO DOSSIER** (LP, gatefold sleeve, with poster)	£100
72	Polydor 2310 130	**GALACTIC ZOO DOSSIER** (LP, gatefold sleeve, without poster)	£30
72	Polydor 2310 178	**KINGDOM COME** (LP)	£30
73	Polydor 2310 254	**JOURNEY** (LP)	£25

(see also Arcadium. Arthur Brown, Kiki Dee, Spirit Of John Morgan, Arcadium)

KING-EARL BOOGIE BAND
| 72 | Dawn DNLS 3040 | **TROUBLE AT MILL** (LP, with poster) | £30 |
| 72 | Dawn DNLS 3040 | **TROUBLE AT MILL** (LP, without poster) | £20 |

(see also Mungo Jerry, Paul King)

KING EDWARDS ALL STARS
| 66 | Rio R 077 | North Coast/Kingston 11 | £150 |

(KING) EDWARDS GROUP
63	Island WI 040	**Dear Hearts/Oh Mary** (B-side actually by Ransford Barnett)	£25
63	Island WI 047	**Russian Roulette** (actually by King Edwards All Stars)/**You're Mine** (actually by Douglas Brothers)	£30
63	Island WI 082	**He Gave You To Me/Kings Priests And Prophets** (both actually by The Schoolboys)	£20
63	Island WI 087	**Hey Girl/Skies Are Grey** (both actually by Ransford Barnett)	£18

KINGFISH
76	United Artists UAG 29922	KINGFISH (LP)	£15
77	Jet UAG 30080	LIVE AND KICKIN' (LP, early copies with picture inner sleeve)	£15

(see also Grateful Dead)

KING FLOYD
71	Atlantic 2466014	GROOVE ME (LP)	£20

KING GENERAL
96	Conscious Sounds DNC EP 01	Gunman/Dub/Conscious Ites Cut 5/CULTURE FREEMAN: The Fittest/High Speed Dubbing/C23000 Dubbing (12")	£30

KING GENERAL & BUSH CHEMISTS
96	Conscious Sounds DNC 006	MONEY RUN TINGS (LP, 1st pressing)	£35

KING GEORGE
67	RCA RCA 1573	Drive On James/I'm Gonna Be Somebody Someday	£30

KING GIZZARD AND THE LIZARD WIZARD
14	Heavenly HVN 281	Head On/Pill (1-sided 12" picture disc)	£100
14	Heavenly HVN 296	Cellophane/The Wholly Ghost (3D p/s, comes with 3D glasses)	£60
14	Heavenly 5414939920240	I'M IN YOUR MIND FUZZ (LP)	£25
15	Heavenly HVNLP 114	QUARTERS! (LP)	£20
15	Heavenly HVNLP 124	PAPER MACHE DREAM BALOON (LP)	£25
16	Heavenly HVNLP 127	NONAGON INFINITY (LP)	£20
17	Wizard 01	POLYGONWANALAND (LP, blue, pink, clear, red and green vinyl - 100 each)	£25
17	Shake Appeal SA 1	POLYGONWANALAND (LP, smoke effect marbled vinyl)	£25
17	Static Caravan VAN 327	POLYGONWANALAND (LP, limited edition of 20 numbered lathe cut copies)	£60
17	Hyperloop HL 1	POLYGONWANALAND (LP, limited edition of 50 numbered lathe cut copies)	£40
17	Phwoar And Peace BWR 039	POLYGONWANALAND (LP, limited edition of 300 copies on red/black vinyl)	£20

KING HARVEST
73	Pye NSPL 28174	DANCING IN THE MOONLIGHT (LP)	£15

KING HORROR
69	Joe/Duke DU 34	Dracula Prince Of Darkness/JOE'S ALL STARS: Honky	£50
69	Grape GR 3003	Cutting Blade/Vampire	£50
69	Grape GR 3006	The Hole/WINSTON GROOVY: Lover Come Back	£30
69	Grape GR 3007	Lochness Monster/VISIONS: Zion I	£60
69	Jackpot JP 713	Wood In The Fire/The Naked City	£25
69	Jackpot JP 714	Police/PAMA DICE: Honky Tonk Popcorn	£40
70	Nu Beat NB 051	Frankenstein/WINSTON GROOVY: I Can't Stand It	£60
70	Reggae REG 3005	Slave Driver	£20

(see also Laurel Aitken)

KING IWAH
72	Upsetter US 382	Give Me Power # 2/UPSETTERS: Public Enemy Number One	£30

KING KONG
86	Greensleeves GRED 206	Paro Them Paro/BUBBLERS COMPUTER STARS : Paranoia (12")	£30
87	Digikal DIG 006	Digital We Digital/FRANKIE PAUL: Rambo (12")	£20

KING KURT
82	Thin Sliced TSR 2	Zulu Beat/Rockin' Kurt (first pressing, orange vinyl with hand-painted sleeves by band members)	£125
82	Thin Sliced TSR 2	Zulu Beat/Rockin' Kurt (second, green vinyl, 159 copies, with hand-painted sleeves by band members)	£100
82	Thin Sliced TSR 2	Zulu Beat/Rockin' Kurt (second pressing, green vinyl, 1529 copies, sleeves not hand painted by band members)	£40
82	Thin Sliced TSR 2	Zulu Beat/Rockin' Kurt (later pressings, yellow/gold/purple vinyl, different sleeves)	£30

KINGLY BAND
69	Decca LK 5002	ROCKSTEADY (LP)	£25

KINGPINS (U.K.)
65	Oriole CB 1986	Two Right Feet/That's The Way It Should Be	£35

KINGPINS (U.S.)
58	London HLU 8658	Ungaua Parts 1 & 2	£15

KING ROCK & WILLOWS
67	Caltone TONE 111	You Are The One/ALVA LEWIS: Return Home	£130

KING ROCKY
68	Studio One SO 2045	The King Is Back/THREE TOPS: Vex Till Yuh Buss	£85

(see also Leroy & Rocky, Clancy Eccles, Heptones)

KINGS OF TOMORROW
01	Defected DFECT 37X	FINALLY EP (2x12")	£20

KINGS COUNTY CARNIVAL
69	United Artists UP 2267	Don't Vote For Luke McCabe/The Proof Of The Pudding	£18

KING SCRATCH
70s	Ethnic ETH 16	Spiritual Whip/Version	£18
70s	Ethnic ETH 30	Mash Finger/Version	£20

(see also Lee Perry/Upsetters, Skatalites)

KING'S HENCHMEN
59	Coral FEP 2025	ALAN FREED PRESENTS VOL. 1 (EP)	£150

KINGSIGHTER
78	Trojan TRLS 166	THE ONE EYED GIANT (LP)	£15

KING SISTERS
57	Capitol T 808	ALOHA (LP)	£15
60	Capitol ST 1333	BABY THEY'RE SINGING OUR SONG (LP)	£15

PADDY KINGSLAND
74	Studio 2 TWOX 1024	SUPERCHARGED (LP)	£20

CHARLES KINGSLEY CREATION
65	Columbia DB 7758	Summer Without Sun/Still In Love With You	£70

EVELYN KINGSLEY & TOWERS
58	Capitol CL 14944	To Know Him Is To Love Him/FRANK PERRY & TOWERS: Let Me Be The One	£20

(see also Towers)

KINGSMEN (1)
58	London HLE 8735	Better Believe It/Week-End	£30
59	London HLE 8812	Conga Rock/The Cat Walk	£30
59	London REE 1211	THE KINGSMEN (EP)	£100

(see also Bill Haley & Comets)

KINGSMEN (2)
63	Pye International 7N 25231	Louie Louie/Haunted Castle	£30
64	Pye International 7N 25262	Little Latin Lupe Lu/David's Mood	£15
66	Pye International 7N 25366	Little Latin Lupe Lu/Louie Louie	£15
64	Pye Intl. NEP 44023	THE KINGSMEN (EP)	£30
65	Pye Intl. NEP 44040	MOJO WORKOUT (EP)	£35
66	Pye Intl. NEP 44063	FEVER (EP)	£40
63	Pye Intl. NPL 28050	THE KINGSMEN IN PERSON (LP, live)	£25
64	Pye Intl. NPL 28054	THE KINGSMEN VOLUME II (LP)	£25
65	Pye Intl. NPL 28068	THE KINGSMEN ON CAMPUS (LP)	£25
66	Pye Intl. NPL 28085	15 GREAT HITS (LP)	£20

(see also Touch)

KINGS OF CONVENIENCE
01	Source SOURLP 019	QUIET IS THE NEW LOUD (LP)	£40
01	Source SOURLP 040	VERSUS (LP, gatefold sleeve)	£30
04	Source SOURLP 099	RIOT ON AN EMPTY STREET (LP)	£50

KINGS OF LEON
08	RCA 88697 36890 7	Sex On Fire/Beneath The Surface (p/s)	£15
03	Handmedown HMD 26	YOUTH & YOUNG MANHOOD (LP, 2 x 10", p/s with picture inners)	£35
04	Handmedown HMD 40	AHA SHAKE HEARTBREAK (2-LP, 10" clear vinyl, gatefold sleeve)	£35
08	RCA 88697 32712 1	ONLY BY THE NIGHT (2-LP)	£20
10	RCA 88697 78241 1	COME AROUND SUNDOWN (2-LP, gatefold, inners)	£25
12	Music On Vinyl MOVLP 473	BECAUSE OF THE TIMES (2-LP, reissue)	£18

KING SOUNDS
78	Grove Music GMDM 5	Spend One Night In Babylon (feat. Trinity)/Keep Us Down In Poverty (feat. Jah Woosh) (12")	£25
79	Grove Music GMDM 11	They That Hate Us (wrongfully)/Ungrateful Bretheren (12")	£15
79	Grove Music GMDM 20	Kill Them Dead/Look Into Youself (12")	£20
79	Grove GMLP 22	COME ZION SIDE HAPPINESS (LP)	£15

KING SPORTY
70	Banana BA 321	Inspiration/Choice Of Music	£20
70	Banana BA 322	Lover's Version (as Sporty & Wilson)/DUDLEY SIBLEY: Having A Party	£22
70	Punch PH 44	For Our Desire/WINSTON WRIGHT: Version	£15
71	Banana BA 323	D.J. Special/RICHARD & MAD: Creation Version	£20
86	Dancefloor DFLP 3002	MEET ME AT THE DISCO (LP)	£15

(see also Delroy Wilson)

KING STITT
69	Clandisc CLA 200	Who Yea/DYNAMITES: Mr Midnight	£20
69	Clandisc CLA 202	Vigerton Two/On The Street	£20
69	Clandisc CLA 203	On The Street/CYNTHIA RICHARDS: Foolish Fool	£25
69	Clandisc CLA 206	The Ugly One/CLANCY ECCLES: Dance Beat	£45
70	Clandisc CLA 207	Herbsman Shuffle (with Andy [Capp])/HIGGS & WILSON: Don't Mind Me	£20
70	Clandisc CLA 223	King Of Kings/DYNAMITES: Reggaedelic	£20
71	Clandisc CLA 235	Merry Rhythm/CLANCY ECCLES: John Crow Skank	£15
71	Banana BA 332	Back Out Version/VEGETABLES: Holly Rhythm	£25
71	Banana BA 334	Rhyming Time/Reality	£30

(see also Kurass)

KINGSTON JOE
64	Blue Beat BB 253	Time Is On My Friend (actually by Lloyd Barnes)/Wear And Tear (B-side actually by Lascelles Perkins)	£30

KINGSTON PETE & BUSTER'S ALL STARS
67	Blue Beat BB 403	Little Boy Blue/I'm A Lover Try Me (actually by Larry Marshall)	£200

(see also Larry Marshall)

KINGSTON ALLSTARS
66	Dice CC 25	Happy Hunter/LITTLE NORMA: Ten Commandments Of Woman	£125

KINGSTONIANS
67	Rio R 140	Winey Winey/I Don't Care	£30
68	Coxsone CS 7066	Mother Miserable/I Make A Woman	£300
68	Doctor Bird DB 1120	Put Down Your Fire/Girls Like Dirt	£150
68	Doctor Bird DB 1123	Mummy And Daddy/False Witness	£100

MINT VALUE £

68	Doctor Bird DB 1126	Fun Galore/Crime Don't Pay	£100
68	Trojan TR 627	Mix It Up/I'll Be Around	£40
69	Big Shot BI 508	Sufferer/Kiss A Little Finger	£75
69	Big Shot BI 526	Nice Nice/I'll Be Around	£80
69	Crab CRAB 19	Hold Down/BARRY YORK: Who Will She Be	£150
69	Bullet BU 409	I Am Just A Minstrel/Yesterday	£25
69	Crab CRAB 43	The Clip/KEITH & TEX: Tighten Up Your Gird (white labels only)	£300
69	Songbird SB 1011	The Clip/BRUCE ANTHONY: Little Miss Muffett	£50
70	Songbird SB 1019	Singer Man/CRYSTALITES: Version	£15
70	Songbird SB 1041	Rumble Rumble/CRYSTALITES: Version	£35
70	Songbird SB 1045	Out There/CRYSTALITES: Out There Version II	£35
70	Duke DU 88	You Can't Wine/RUPIE EDWARDS ALLSTARS: Bee Sting	£20
72	Duke DU 126	Lion's Den/Version	£15
70	Trojan TBL 113	SUFFERER (LP)	£70

(see also Jack (Bernard) & Beanstalks, Gregory Isaacs, Jackie Bernard)

KING TRUMAN
89	Acid Jazz JAZID 9T	Like A Gun (Safe Sax Mix)/(Dub Version)/(Radio Edit) (12", p/s)	£80

(see also Style Council, Paul Weller)

KING TUBBY
75	Grounation GROL 502	THE ROOTS OF DUB (LP)	£35
75	Live & Love LALP 02	MEETS THE AGGROVATORS AT THE DUB STATION (LP)	£100
76	Fay FMLP 307	SURROUNDED BY DREAD AT THE NATIONAL ARENA (LP)	£80
76	Klik KLIP 9002	SHALOM DUB (LP)	£45
77	Fay Music FMLP 304	KING TUBBY MEETS THE UPSETTER AT THE GRASS ROOTS OF DUB (LP, with Lee Perry)	£60
78	Studio 16 WE 100	KING TUBBY MEETS THE UPSETTER AT THE GRASS ROOTS OF DUB (LP, reissue, with Lee Perry)	£35
78	Studio 16 WE 102	SURROUNDED BY DREAD AT THE NATIONAL ARENA (LP, re-issue)	£35
79	Star PTLP 1029	MAJESTIC DUB (LP)	£25
81	Live & Love LAP 015	UPSETS THE UPSETTER (LP)	£35
81	Vista Sounds VSLP 2006	KING AT THE CONTROL (LP)	£50
94	Blood & Fire BAFLP 002	DUB GONE CRAZY (LP)	£20
99	Blood & Fire SVLP 260	DUB LIKE DIRT (2-LP)	£25

KING TUBBY & THE AGGROVATORS
82	Black Music BMLP 804	DUBBING IN THE BACKYARD (LP)	£50

KING TUBBY, PRINCE JAMMY & SCIENTIST
81	K&G Imperial KGLP 002	FIRST, SECOND AND THIRD GENERATION OF DUB (LP)	£60

KING TUBBY MEETS ROOTS RADICS
81	Copasetic COPLP 5002	DANGEROUS DUB (LP)	£50

KING TUBBY & YABBY U
76	Prophets (No Cat No)	PROPHECY OF DUB (LP, green label in plain sleeve)	£140

KINKS

SINGLES : PYE SINGLES
64	Pye 7N 15611	Long Tall Sally/I Took My Baby Home	£120
64	Pye 7N 15611	Long Tall Sally/I Took My Baby Home (Demo copy)	£150
64	Pye 7N 15636	You Still Want Me/You Do Something To Me	£200
64	Pye 7N 15636	You Still Want Me/You Do Something To Me (Demo copy)	£150
64	Pye 7N 15673	You Really Got Me/It's All Right	£15
64	Pye 7N 15673	You Really Got Me/It's All Right (Demo copy)	£150
64	Pya 7N 15673	All Day And All Of The Night/I Gotta Move (Demo copy)	£150
65	Pye 7N 15759	Tired Of Waiting For You/Come On Now (Demo copy)	£100
68	Pye 7N 17468	Wonderboy/Polly	£15
68	Pye 7N 17573	Days/She's Got Everything	£15
69	Pye 7N 17724	Plastic Man/King Kong	£15
69	Pye 7N 17776	Drivin'/Mindless Child Of Motherhood	£35
69	Pye 7N 17812	Shangri-La/Last Of The Steam-Powered Trains (unissued, acetates only)	£0
69	Pye 7N 17812	Shangri-La/This Man He Weeps Tonight	£25
69	Pye 7N 17865	Victoria/Mr Churchill Says	£15
71	Pye 7NX 8001	PERCY (33rpm 4-track maxi-single, p/s)	£20
74	Pye 7N 45313	Where Have All The Good Times Gone/Lola (p/s)	£20

SINGLES : EXPORT SINGLES
65	Pye 7N 15981	Till The End Of The Day/Where Have All The Good Times Gone (export p/s)	£150
66	Pye 7N 17100	Well Respected Man/Milk Cow Blues	£120
67	Pye 7N 17314	Mr. Pleasant/This Is Where I Belong	£100
67	Pye 7N 17405	Autumn Almanac/David Watts	£100
71	Pye 7N 8001	God's Children/Moments (in p/s)	£60
71	Pye 7N 8001	God's Children/Moments	£30

EPs
64	Pye NEP 24200	KINKSIZE SESSION	£30
64	Pye NEP 24203	KINKSIZE HITS	£40
65	Pye NEP 24221	KWYET KINKS	£45
66	Pye NEP 24258	DEDICATED KINKS	£120
68	Pye NEP 24296	THE KINKS	£275
75	Pye AMEP 1001	THE KINKS ('Yesteryear' export issue, red or blue vinyl)	£22

ALBUMS : PYE ALBUMS
64	Pye NPL 18096	THE KINKS (mono)	£175

64	Pye NSPL 83021	THE KINKS (stereo, export only)	£250
65	Pye NSPL 18096	THE KINKS (stereo, export only, reissue)	£275
65	Pye NPL 18112	KINDA KINKS...	£150
65	Pye NPL 18131	THE KINK KONTROVERSY...	£100
65	Pye NSPL 18131	THE KINK KONTROVERSY (reprocessed stereo with stickered catalogue number, export only)	£300
66	Pye NPL 18149	FACE TO FACE (mono)	£120
66	Pye NSPL 18149	FACE TO FACE (stereo, stickered sleeve "export only")	£225
66	Pye NSLP 18149	FACE TO FACE (LP original issue)	£100
67	Golden Guinea GGL 0357	THE KINKS (reissue, mono)	£25
67	Golden Guinea GGGL 10357	THE KINKS (reissue, stereo)	£30
67	Pye NPL 18191	LIVE AT KELVIN HALL (mono)	£100
67	Pye N(S)PL 18191	LIVE AT KELVIN HALL (stereo)	£150

(The Pye LPs listed above were originally issued with laminated flipback sleeves, pink labels & light blue labels.)

67	Pye NPL 18193	SOMETHING ELSE BY THE KINKS (mono)	£200
67	Pye N(S)PL 18193	SOMETHING ELSE BY THE KINKS (stereo)...	£150
68	Pye N(S)PL 18233	THE KINKS ARE THE VILLAGE GREEN PRESERVATION SOCIETY (unissued, 12-track version, test pressings only)	£1000
68	Pye NPL 18233	THE KINKS ARE THE VILLAGE GREEN PRESERVATION SOCIETY (15-track version, mono)	£500
68	Pye N(S)PL 18233	THE KINKS ARE THE VILLAGE GREEN PRESERVATION SOCIETY (15-track version, stereo)..	£300
69	Pye NPL 18317	ARTHUR (mono, gatefold sleeve "Quiien Victoria" insert)...........................	£300
69	Pye N(S)PL 18317	ARTHUR (stereo, gatefold sleeve "Quiien Victoria" insert)........................	£250
70	Pye NPL 18326	THE KINKS (2-LP, gatefold sleeve)	£20
70	Pye NSPL 18359	THE KINKS PT 1 - LOLA VS POWERMAN & THE MONEY-GO-ROUND (gatefold sleeve)...	£150
71	Pye NSPL 18365	SOUNDTRACK FROM THE FILM 'PERCY' (soundtrack)...................................	£50
73	Pye 11PP 100	ALL THE GOOD TIMES (4-LP, box set)	£80
83	PRT KINK 1	GREATEST HITS (with bonus 10" EP of unreleased material).......................	£40

ALBUMS : OTHER ALBUMS

71	RCA SF 8243	MUSWELL HILLBILLIES (gatefold sleeve)..	£100
72	RCA DPS 2035	EVERYBODY'S IN SHOWBIZ, EVERYBODY'S A STAR (2-LP, gatefold sleeve).......	£25
73	RCA SF 8392	PRESERVATION ACT 1 (gatefold sleeve)	£40
74	RCA LPL2 5040	PRESERVATION ACT 2 (2-LP, gatefold sleeve)	£35
75	RCA SF 8411	SOAP OPERA (gatefold sleeve)	£35
75	RCA RS 1028	SCHOOLBOYS IN DISGRACE	£40
76	RCA RS 1059	CELLULOID HEROES	£20
77	Arista SPART 1002	SLEEPWALKER (LP, with photo inner sleeve)	£25
78	Arista SPARTY 1055	MISFITS (LP, photo inner sleeve)	£20
79	Arista SPART 1099	LOW BUDGET (LP, with photo inner sleeve)	£20
80	Arista DARTY 6	ONE FOR THE ROAD (2-LP, gatefold)...	£30
81	Arista SPART 1171	GIVE THE PEOPLE WHAT THEY WANT (LP)	£20
83	Arista 205 275	STATE OF CONFUSION (LP)	£15
84	Arista 206 685	WORD OF MOUTH (LP)...	£15
86	London LONLP 27	THINK VISUAL (LP, inner)...	£15
89	London LONLP 49	LIVE: ON THE ROAD (LP)...	£15
89	London 828 165 1	UK JIVE (LP)..	£20
93	Sony 472489-1	PHOBIA (omits 2 tracks from CD)	£35
94	Konk KNKLP 1	TO THE BONE (LP)...	£70
98	Earmark 42004	FACE TO FACE (LP, reissue)...	£18
01	Sanctuary SANTV 010	BBC SESSIONS 1964-1977 (3-LP)...	£80

ALBUMS : REISSUES

79	Pye NPL 18096	THE KINKS (LP, reissue, mono, grey labels)	£15
79	Pye NPL 18131	KINDA KINKS (LP, reissue, grey labels)	£15
79	Pye NPL1831	THE KINK KONTROVERSY (LP, reissue, grey labels)......................................	£15
79	Pye NPL 18131	FACE TO FACE (LP, reissue, grey labels)...	£15
79	Pye NSPL 18191	LIVE AT KELVIN HALL (LP, reissue, grey labels)...	£15
79	Pye NSPL 18193	SOMETHING ELSE BY THE KINKS (LP, reissue, stereo, grey labels)	£15
79	Pye NSPL 18233	THE KINKS ARE THE VILLAGE GREEN PRESERVATION SOCIETY (LP, reissue, stereo, grey labels)...	£15
81	Precision NSPL 18191	LIVE AT KELVIN HALL (LP, reissue, blue/white labels).................................	£15
82	Fame FA 3048	SLEEPWALKER (LP, reissue)	£15
82	PRT 18096	THE KINKS (LP, reissue, green/red labels)	£15
82	PRT NPL 18149	FACE TO FACE (LP, reissue, red/green labels)	£15
82	Pye NSPL 18191	LIVE AT KELVIN HALL (LP, reissue, green/red labels)..................................	£15
82	PRT NSPL 18233	THE KINKS ARE THE VILLAGE GREEN PRESERVATION SOCIETY (LP, reissue, green/red labels)...	£15
85	PRT FBLP 8091	THE KINKS ARE THE VILLAGE GREEN PRESERVATION SOCIETY (LP, reissue, different cover)	£20
87	PRT 6002	THE KINKS (LP, reissue, grey labels)	£15
87	PRT PYL 6003	KINDA KINKS (LP, reissue, green/red labels)..	£15
87	PRT PYL 6004	THE KINK KONTROVERSY (LP, reissue, green/red labels)...........................	£15
87	Pye PYL 6005	FACE TO FACE (LP, reissue)..	£15
87	Pye PYL 6008	LIVE AT KELVIN HALL (LP, reissue, grey labels)...	£15
87	PRT PYL 6008	THE KINKS ARE THE VILLAGE GREEN PRESERVATION SOCIETY (LP, reissue).......	£15
87	PRT NSPL 18193	SOMETHING ELSE BY THE KINKS (LP, reissue, green/red labels)	£15
97	Castle ORLP 005	THE KINKS ARE THE VILLAGE GREEN PRESERVATION SOCIETY (LP, reissue, free 7").........	£25
00	Castle ESMLP 482	THE KINKS (LP, reissue)	£15
00	Castle ESLP 483	KINDA KINKS (LP, reissue)...	£15

			MINT VALUE £
00	Castle ESMLP 484	THE KINK KONTROVERSY (LP, reissue)	£15
00	Castle ESMLP 485	FACE TO FACE (LP, reissue)	£15
00	Castle ESMLP 875	SOMETHING ELSE BY THE KINKS (LP, reissue)	£15
00	Castle CMHLP 001	ARTHUR (LP, reissue)	£15
00	Castle CMHLP 012	LIVE AT KELVIN HALL (LP, reissue)	£15
00	Castle ESMLP 890	THE KINKS PT 1 - LOLA VS POWERMAN & THE MONEY-GO-ROUND (LP, reissue)	£15
00	Castle ESMLP 891	PERCY (LP, reissue)	£15
11	UMC/Sanctuary 273220	THE KINKS ARE THE VILLAGE GREEN PRESERVATION SOCIETY (2-LP, reissue, marbled green vinyl, 1000 only)	£60
12	UMC/Sanctuary 2732148	SOMETHING ELSE BY THE KINKS (2-LP, reissue, red vinyl, 500 only)	£50
12	UMC/Sanctuary 2732277	ARTHUR (2-LP, reissue, white vinyl, 500 only)	£40
16	Sanctuary/BMG KINKSBOX003	THE MONO COLLECTION (10-LP, box set)	£350
12	UMC/Sanctuary 2783111	FACE TO FACE (2-LP, reissue, blue vinyl, 500 only)	£40
18	BMG BMGAA 09 BOX	THE KINKS ARE THE VILLAGE GREEN PRESERVATION SOCIETY (3-LP, 5-CD, 3 x 7" reissue box set)	£100
19	BMG BMGCAT 407 BOX	ARTHUR (3-CD, 3 x 7", box set reissue)	£40

(see also Dave Davies, Maple Oak, Leapy Lee)

TONY KINSEY (QUARTET)

55	Decca F 10548	She's Funny That Way/Fascinatin' Rhythm	£15
55	Decca F 10606	Close Your Eyes/Pierrot	£15
55	Decca F 10648	Hey! There/Ballet	£25
62	Ember JBS 707	Girl In Blue/Weber The Great	£20
56	Decca DFE 6282	PRESENTING THE TONY KINSEY QUARTET NO. 1 (EP)	£40
56	Decca DFE 6285	PRESENTING THE TONY KINSEY QUARTET NO. 2 (EP)	£40
58	Decca DFE 6461	MY FAIR LADY (EP)	£15
59	Parlophone SGE 2004	RED BIRD - JAZZ AND POETRY (EP, mono [GEP 8765]/stereo, with Christopher Logue)	£40
59	Parlophone SGE 2008	FOURSOME (EP, stereo, also mono GEP 8895)	£15
57	Decca LK 4186	INTRODUCING THE QUINTET (LP)	£100
57	Decca LK 4207	JAZZ AT THE FLAMINGO (LP)	£150
58	Decca LK 4274	TIME GENTLEMEN PLEASE (LP)	£100
61	Ember EMB 3337	AN EVENING WITH ... (LP)	£70
63	Decca LK 4534	HOW TO SUCCEED IN BUSINESS WITHOUT REALLY TRYING (LP, with Gordon Beck)	£50

TONY KINSEY TRIO & JOE HARRIOTT

54	Esquire EP 36	TONY KINSEY TRIO & JOE HARRIOTT (EP)	£50
54	Esquire EP 52	TONY KINSEY TRIO & JOE HARRIOTT (EP)	£50
54	Esquire EP 82	TONY KINSEY TRIO & JOE HARRIOTT (EP)	£50

(see also Joe Harriott)

KINSMEN

68	Decca F 22724	Glasshouse Green, Splinter Red/It's Started To Rain Again	£45

(see also Four Kinsmen)

KIPPINGTON LODGE

67	Parlophone R 5645	Shy Boy/Lady On A Bicycle	£40
68	Parlophone R 5677	Rumours/And She Cried	£40
68	Parlophone R 5717	Tell Me A Story/Understand A Woman	£40
68	Parlophone R 5750	Tomorrow Today/Turn Out The Light	£40
69	Parlophone R 5776	In My Life/I Can See Her Face	£90

(see also Brinsley Schwarz, Nick Lowe)

KIRBY

78	Hot Wax HW 2	COMPOSITION (LP)	£75
94	Backtrack Archive HW 2	COMPOSITION (LP, reissue)	£30

(see also Curved Air, Stretch)

KATHY KIRBY

60	Pye 7N 15313	Love Can Be/Crush Me	£20
61	Pye 7N 15342	Danny/Now You're Crying	£20
66	Decca F 12432	The Adam Adamant Theme/Will I Never Learn?	£25
73	Orange OAS 216	Singer With The Band/Hello Morning	£60
67	Decca LK 4746	MAKE SOMEONE HAPPY (LP)	£25
68	Columbia S(C)X 6259	MY THANKS TO YOU (LP)	£40

LARRY KIRBY & ENCORES

59	Top Rank JAR 143	My Baby Don't Love Me/My Rose Of Kentucky	£15

BASIL KIRCHIN (BAND)

71	Columbia SCX 6463	WORLD WITHIN WORLDS (LP)	£800
74	Island HELP18	WORLD WITHIN WORLDS (not a reissue but second LP)	£80
03	Trunk JBH 003 LP	QUANTUM LP, hand numbered, 500 only)	£80
04	Trunk JBH 005 LP	CHARCOAL SKETCHES/STATES OF MIND (LP, 500 only)	£60
05	Trunk JBH 012 LP	ABSTRACTIONS OF THE INDUSTRIAL NORTH (LP)	£75
06	Trunk JBH 021 LP	PARTICLES (LP)	£20
10	Trunk JBH 038 LP	PRIMITIVE LONDON (LP, 500 only)	£18
19	Trunk JBH 080 LP	WORLDS WITHIN WORLDS PARTS 1 & 2 (LP, gold vinyl)	£50
19	Trunk JBH 080 LP	WORLDS WITHIN WORLDS PARTS 1 & 2 (LP, black vinyl)	£20

(see also Basil Kirchin, London Studio Group)

(IVOR & BASIL) KIRCHIN BAND

55	Decca F 10434	Minor Mambo/Mother Goose Jumps (as Kirchin Band)	£15
56	Parlophone R 4237	Rockin' & Rollin' Thru The Darktown Strutters' Ball/Ambush	£20
57	Parlophone R 4266	Rock Around The World Medley (with Shani Wallis)	£18
55	Psrlophone GEP 8556	THE BIGGEST LITTLE BAND IN THE WORLD (EP)	£15

55	Decca DFE 6237	**MEET THE KIRCHINS** (EP)	£15
55	Parlophone GEP 8531	**KIRCHIN BANDBOX** (EP)	£15
56	Parlophone GEP 8569	**THE IVOR AND BASIL KIRCHIN BAND** (EP)	£30

DEE KIRK

62	Salvo SLO 1809	**I'll Cry/My Used To Be** (99 copies only)	£15

RICHARD H. KIRK

86	Rough Trade RTT 199	**Hypnotic/Martyrs Of Palestine** (12", p/s)	£15
81	Industrial IRC 34	**DISPOSABLE HALF TRUTHS** (cassette)	£20
83	Doublevision DVR 2	**TIME HIGH FICTION** (2-LP)	£30
86	Rough Trade RTM 189	**UGLY SPIRIT** (LP)	£15
86	Rough Trade ROUGH 99	**BLACK JESUS VOICE** (LP)	£15
94	Warp WARPLP 19	**VIRTUAL STATE** (2-LP)	£25
95	Warp WARPLP 32	**THE NUMBER OF MAGIC** (2-LP)	£30
17	Intone LP1	**DASEIN** (2-LP)	£18

(see also Cabaret Voltaire,, Cold Warrior, Chemical Agent,, Multiple Transmission, Papdoctrine, Robots and Humanoids, Sandoz, Electronic Eye, Sweet Exorcist)

(RAHSAAN) ROLAND KIRK

62	Esquire 32-164	**KIRK'S WORK** (LP, with Jack McDuff)	£30
63	Mercury MMC 14126	**WE FREE KINGS** (LP)	£30
64	Mercury MCL 20002	**THE KIRK QUARTET MEETS THE BENNY GOLSON ORCHESTRA** (LP)	£30
64	Mercury MCL 20021	**KIRK IN COPENHAGEN** (LP)	£20
64	Mercury SMWL 21020	**GIFTS & MESSAGES** (LP)	£15
65	Mercury MCL 20045	**DOMINO** (LP)	£20
65	Fontana FJL 114	**HIP!** (LP)	£20
66	Mercury (S)LML 4005	**I TALK WITH THE SPIRITS** (LP)	£15
66	Mercury (S)LML 4015	**RIP, RIG AND PANIC** (LP)	£15
67	Mercury (S)LML 4019	**SLIGHTLY LATIN** (LP)	£20
67	Verve 9193	**NOW PLEASE DON'T YOU CRY BEAUTIFUL EDITH** (LP)	£18
68	Atlantic 588112	**THE INFLATED TEAR** (LP)	£20
69	Atlantic 588 207	**VOLUNTEERED SLAVERY** (LP)	£20
70	Atlantic 588178	**LEFT & RIGHT** (LP)	£25

KIRKBYS

66	RCA RCA 1542	**It's A Crime/I've Never Been So Much In Love**	£150

(see also 23rd Turnoff, Jimmy Campbell, Rockin' Horse, Merseybeats)

JOHN KIRKPATRICK (& SUE HARRIS)

72	Trailer LER 2033	**JUMP AT THE SUN** (LP, with Sue Harris, first pressing with red/black label)	£25
75	Trailer LER 2033	**JUMP AT THE SUN** (LP, with Sue Harris, repressing with yellow label)	£15
76	Topic 12TS 295	**AMONG THE MANY ATTRACTIONS AT THE SHOW WILL BE A REALLY HIGH-CLASS BAND** (LP, with Sue Harris)	£20

(see also Jon Raven)

JULIAN KIRSCH

69	Columbia DB 8541	**Clever Little Man/The Adventures Of A Young Cuckoo**	£40

DANNY KIRWAN

75	DJM DJLPS 454	**SECOND CHAPTER** (LP, gatefold sleeve)	£15

(see also Fleetwood Mac, Tramp)

KISS

85	Vertigo VERH 32	**ASYLUM** (LP, printed inner)	£15

SINGLES

75	Casablanca CBX 503	**Nothin' To Lose/Love Theme From Kiss**	£25
75	Casablanca CBX 510	**Rock And Roll All Nite/Anything For My Baby**	£25
76	Casablanca CBX 516	**Shout It Out Loud/Sweet Pain**	£15
76	Casablanca CBX 519	**Beth/God Of Thunder**	£18
77	Casablanca CAN 102	**Hard Luck Woman/Calling Dr Love/Beth** (in p/s)	£35
77	Casablanca CAN 110	**Then She Kissed Me/Hooligan/Flaming Youth**	£15
78	Casablanca CAN 126	**Rock And Roll All Nite/C'Mon And Love Me** (in p/s)	£25
79	Casablanca CANL 152	**I Was Made For Lovin' You** (extended)/**Charisma** (12", die-cut Casablanca house bag)	£15
80	Casablanca NB 1001	**2000 Man/I Was Made For Lovin' You/Sure Know Something** (p/s)	£15
82	Casablanca KISS 312	**Killer/I Love It Loud/I Was Made For Lovin' You** (12", p/s)	£15
82	Casablanca KISS 412	**Creatures Of The Night/War Machine/Rock And Roll All Nite** (live) (12", p/s)	£15
82	Casablanca KISSD 4	**Creatures Of The Night/Rock And Roll All Nite** (live) (12", double groove, autographs engraved on 1 side)	£20
83	Vertigo KPIC 5	**Lick It Up/Not For The Innocent** (tank-shaped picture disc)	£20

ALBUMS

75	Casablanca CBC 4003	**KISS** (LP, blue 'Bogart' label, EMI address on rear sleeve)	£45
75	Casablanca CBC 4004	**DRESSED TO KILL** (LP, blue 'Bogart' label, embossed sleeve, EMI address on rear sleeve)	£40
76	Casablanca CBC 4008	**DESTROYER** (LP, blue 'Bogart' label with inner sleeve)	£30
76	Casablanca CBC 4011/2	**ALIVE!** (2LP, blue 'Bogart' label, gatefold, insert, sleeve also lists CBSP 401)	£30
77	Casablanca CALH 2001	**ROCK AND ROLL OVER** (LP, 'lovegun' label, red vinyl)	£50
77	Casablanca CAL 2006	**KISS** (LP, reissue, 'lovegun' label, red vinyl)	£50
77	Casablanca CAL 2007	**HOTTER THAN HELL** (LP, 'lovegun' label, red vinyl)	£50
77	Casablanca CAL 2008	**DRESSED TO KILL** (LP, reissue, 'lovegun' label, red vinyl)	£40
77	Casablanca CAL 2009	**DESTROYER** (LP, reissue, different sleeve, 'lovegun' label, red vinyl)	£20
77	Casablanca CALD 5001	**ALIVE!** (2LP, reissue, 'lovegun' label, red vinyl)	£50
77	Casablanca CALH 2017	**LOVE GUN** (LP, 'lovegun' label, printed inners)	£22
77	Casablanca CALH 2017	**LOVE GUN** (LP, 'lovegun' label, red vinyl, printed inner)	£50

MINT VALUE £

77	Casablanca CALD 5004	KISS ALIVE II (2LP, 'lovegun' label, booklet, transfers)	£35
77	Casablanca CALD 5004	KISS ALIVE II (2LP, 'lovegun' label, red vinyl, booklet)	£40
78	Casablanca CALD 5005	DOUBLE PLATINUM (2LP, 'lovegun' label, silver foil embossed sleeve, insert; sleeve & insert pressed in U.S. with U.K. cat. no. sticker)	£40
79	Casablanca CALH 2051	DYNASTY (LP, 'lovegun' label, printed inner, poster)	£30
80	Mercury 6302 032	UNMASKED (LP, poster)	£25
81	Casablanca 6302 163	(MUSIC FROM) THE ELDER (LP, single sleeve or gatefold)	£25
82	Casablanca CANL 4	CREATURES OF THE NIGHT (LP, 'make-up' sleeve, printed inner)	£30
87	Vertigo 832 903-1	CRAZY NIGHTS (LP, picture disc, stickered PVC wallet)	£25
92	Mercury 848 037 1	REVENGE (LP, printed inner)	£60
98	Mercury PLP 31453 8137-2	PSYCHO CIRCUS (LP, promo only picture disc)	£70

(see also Gene Simmons, Ace Frehley, Peter Criss, Paul Stanley)

KISS THE BLADE

85	Incision CUT 1-7	The Party's Begun/The Night Comes Down (p/s)	£15
85	Incision CUT 1	The Party's Begun/The Night Comes Down/The Bridge (12", p/s)	£25
86	Incision CUT 3	Young Soldier/The Love I Give (12" p/s)	£40

KIT KATS

66	London HLW 10075	Won't Find Better Than Me/That's The Way	£18

(see also New Hope)

KITCHENS

79	Red Square RS 001	DEATH OF ROCK AND ROLL EP	£30

KITE

78	Solent SS 050	KITE (LP)	£25

EARTHA KITT

54	HMV 7M 234	Santa Baby/Let's Do It (Let's Fall In Love)	£15
56	HMV 7M 422	Honolulu Rock-A-Roll-A/Je Cherche Un Homme (I Want A Man)	£20
70	Spark SRL 1039	Hurdy Gurdy Man/Catch The Wind	£20

KITTENS

64	Decca F 12036	Round About Way/Don't Stop Now	£15

KLAATU

77	Capitol E ST 11542	KLAATU (LP, insert)	£15

KLAN (2)

74	Flux 301	Hey Diddle Diddle/Lord	£20

KLAXONS

07	RINSELP1T	MYTHS OF THE NEAR FUTURE (2-LP, 1 side etched)	£25
10	RINSELP2T	SURFING THE VOID (2-LP, 500 only, white vinyl)	£20

SUSIE KLEE

66	Polydor BM 56082	Mr Zero/Punch And Judy Girl	£15

KLEEER

81	Atlantic K 60614	I LOVE TO DANCE (LP)	£15
84	Atlantic 7801451	INTIMATE CONNECTION (LP)	£20

KLEENEX

79	Rough Trade/Sunrise RT 9	Ain't You/Hedi's Head (poster p/s)	£15

(see also Liliput)

ALAN KLEIN

62	Oriole CB 1719	Striped Purple Shirt/You Gave Me The Blues	£15
62	Oriole CB 1737	Three Coins In The Sewer/Danger Ahead	£15
64	Decca LK 4621	WELL, AT LEAST IT'S BRITISH (LP)	£15

HARRY KLEIN QUARTET

56	Jazz Today JTE 105	BRASH BARITONE (EP)	£30
56	Nixa NJE 1009	NEW SOUND (EP)	£25
56	Nixa NJE 1022	HARRY KLEIN QUARTET (EP)	£25
57	Columbia SEG 7647	BARITONE SAX (EP)	£20

(see also Jazz Five)

KLEPTOMANIA

92	Hypno-Genesis HG 001	Amadeus (Martini Mix)/Amadeus (Stringi Wingi Mix)/Morf (Plastascene Mix)/Morf (Scratchi Waxi Mix) (12")	£70

KLF

89	KLF Comms 004M	What Time is Love (Monster Attack Mix) (1-sided 12", 3 only)	£300
89	KLF Comms. KLF 006T	Love Trance/What Time Is Love (12", p/s, 3 copies known)	£500
89	KLF Comms. KLF 008R	Last Train To Trancentral (Remixes 1 & 2) (12", p/s, 'Pure Trance 5', 2,000 pressed, some warped, price is for unwarped copy)	£40
89	KLF Comms. KLF 010IR	Deep Shit Deep Shit Part 3 (the Illegal Remix)/Deep Shit Part 2/The Lovers' Side (unreleased 12", 6 copies only)	£700
89	KLF PROMO 2	Kylie Said To Jason (Full Length)/Kylie Said Trance (12", promo & press sheet)	£15
89	KLF Comms. KLF 010T	Kylie Said To Jason (Full Length)/Kylie Said Trance (12", stickered p/s & pstr)	£15
89	KLF Comms. KLF 010R	Kylie Said To Jason (Trance Kylie Express)/Kylie In A Trance/ Kylie Said Harder (12" remix, p/s, export issue)	£15
89	KLF Comms. KLF 010RR	Kylie In A Trance/Kylie Said Mu (12", p/s, export edition, 500 only)	£40
89	KLF Comms. KLF 010RR	Kylie In A Trance/Kylie Said Mu (12", p/s, export edition, 500 only, shrinkwrapped with KLF 010R)	£70
89	KLF Comms. KLF 010CD	Kylie Said To Jason (Full Length)/Madrugada Eterna/Kylie Said Trance (CD)	£40
90	KLF Comms. KLF 011T	Madrugada Eterna (Club Mix)/Madrugada Eterna (Edit)/Madrugada Eterna (Ambient House Mix) (12", 20 only, beware of counterfeits!)	£150
90	KLF Comms. ETERNA 1	Madrugada Eterna (Club Mix) (12", 1-sided, white label, 6 pressed, beware of counterfeits!)	£200

90	KLF Comms. KLF 004X	**What Time Is Love?** (Live At Trancentral)/**Techno Gate Mix** (12", p/s, mispressing, B-side actually plays "Wandafull Mix", matrix no.: KLF 004X-B)	**£25**
91	KLF Comms. CHOC ICE 3	**Justified And Ancient** (Anti-Acapella Version) (12", 1-sided, w/l, 200 only)	**£50**
91	KLF Comms. LP PROMO 1	**Make It Rain/No More Tears** (12", promo only, 1,729 pressed)	**£20**
91	KLF Comms. 92PROMO 2	**America: What Time Is January?** (12", 1-sided, white label promo, 50 - 250 only)	**£100**
91	KLF Comms. 3AM 1	**3AM Eternal** (feat. Extreme Noise Terror) (p/s, mail order only)	**£20**
92	KLF Comms. KLF 5 TOTP	**3AM Eternal** (Xmas Top Of The Pops Version) (1-sided, with Extreme Noise Terror, mail-order only, with insert & mailing envelope; beware of bootlegs!)	**£30**
92	KLF Comms. 92PROMO 3	**What Time Is Love** (Acid Mix) (12", 1-sided, w/l promo, perhaps 20 only)	**£300**
92	KLF Comms. USA 4X/ CHOC ICE 2	**Justified And Ancient/America: What Time Is Love?** (12", 'longboat' picture disc, export edition, 4,000 only)	**£30**
97	KLF Comms.	**Fuck The Millennium** (4-track CD, in white carrier bag Fuck The Millennium kit, with T-shirt, window sticker, certificate)	**£50**
89	KLF Comms. JAMS LP 4	**THE WHAT TIME IS LOVE STORY** (LP)	**£30**
89	KLF Comms. JAMS CD 4	**THE WHAT TIME IS LOVE STORY** (CD)	**£30**
89	KLF Comms. JAMS LP 5	**CHILL OUT** (LP)	**£80**
89	KLF Comms. JAMS CD 5	**CHILL OUT** (CD)	**£40**
89	KLF Comms. JAMS LP 6	(TUNES FROM) **THE WHITE ROOM** (LP, 9-track white label, unreleased, promo only, beware of counterfeits!)	**£50**
91	KLF Comm. JAMS LP 006	**THE WHITE ROOM** (LP)	**£40**

(see also Timelords, Bill Drummond, Space, Orb)

TONY KLINGER & MICHAEL LYONS
72	Deram SML 1095	**EXTREMES** (LP, soundtrack)	**£100**

KLINGONS
80	Kang KLING001	**Dr. Jekyl And Mr Hyde/The First Question** (p/s)	**£15**

PETER KLINT (QUINTET)
66	Mercury MF 997	**Walkin' Proud/Shake**	**£20**
68	Atlantic 584 208	**Hey Diddle Diddle/Just Holding On** (solo)	**£18**

ANNETTE KLOOGER
56	Decca F 10701	**The Rock And Roll Waltz/Rock Around The Island** (with Ted Heath Music)	**£15**
56	Decca F 10733	**The Magic Touch/We'll Love Again** (with Four Jones Boys)	**£15**
56	Decca F 10738	**Why Do Fools Fall In Love?/Lovely One** (with Four Jones Boys)	**£15**

(see also Four Jones Boys)

KLUBS
68	Cam CAM 681	**I Found The Sun/Ever Needed Someone**	**£200**

EARL KLUGH
85	Blue Note UAG 20009	**LIVING INSIDE YOUR LOVE** (LP, Nimbus Supercut, mail order only with Hi Fi Today magazine)	**£50**

KMA PRODUCTIONS
96	Urban Beat URB 004	**Cape Fear/Phantasy Trip** (12", stamped white labels)	**£35**
96	Urban Beat URB 004	**Phantasy Trip/Cape Fear** (12")	**£30**
97	KMA Productions KMA001	**BREAKING OUT EP** (12")	**£25**

KNACK (U.K.)
65	Decca F 12234	**She Ain't No Good/Who'll Be The Next In Line**	**£60**
65	Decca F 12278	**It's Love Baby** (24 Hours A Day)/**Time Time Time**	**£50**
66	Piccadilly 7N 35315	**Did You Ever Have To Make Up Your Mind?/Red Hearts**	**£15**
66	Piccadilly 7N 35322	**Stop!** (Before You Get Me Going)/**Younger Girl**	**£15**
66	Piccadilly 7N 35347	**Save All My Love For Joey/Take Your Love**	**£15**
67	Piccadilly 7N 35367	(Man From The) **Marriage Guidance And Advice Bureau/ Dolly Catch Her Man**	**£15**

(see also Gun, Sky)

KNICKERBOCKERS
66	London HLH 10013	**Lies/The Coming Generation**	**£20**
66	London HLH 10035	**One Track Mind/I Must Be Doing Something Right**	**£20**
66	London HLH 10061	**High On Love/Stick With Me**	**£30**
66	London HLH 10093	**Rumours, Gossip, Words Untrue/Love Is A Bird**	**£18**
67	London HLH 10102	**Can You Help Me/Please Don't Love Him**	**£18**
66	London HA-H 8294	**THE FABULOUS KNICKERBOCKERS** (LP)	**£60**

KNIFE
06	Brille BRILLP 103	**SILENT SHOUT** (2-LP)	**£35**
06	Brille BRILLP 105	**DEEP CUTS** (2-LP, inners)	**£70**
13	Brille BRILLP 117	**SHAKING THE HABITUAL** (3-LP, 2 booklets, 2 x CD)	**£20**

KNIFE EDGE
80	No Hessle F001	**Favourite Girl/Say You Will** (p/s)	**£40**

KNIFEWORLD
09	Believers Roast BRR002LP	**BURIED ALONE: TALES OF CRUSHING DEFEAT** (LP)	**£15**
14	Inside Out IOMLP 402	**THE UNRAVELLING** (LP, with CD)	**£15**

CURTIS KNIGHT (& ZEUS)
70	RCA RCA 1950	**Down In The Village/No Point Of View**	**£15**
74	Dawn DNLS 3060	**THE SECOND COMING** (LP, laminated sleeve, lyric insert, pink 'sun' label)	**£100**
74	Dawn DNLS 3060	**THE SECOND COMING** (LP, laminated sleeve, no lyric insert, pink 'sun' label)	**£45**

(see also Jimi Hendrix, Blue Goose)

GLADYS KNIGHT (& PIPS)

SINGLES
64	Stateside SS 318	**Giving Up/Maybe Maybe Baby**	**£35**
64	Stateside SS 352	**Lovers Always Forgive/Another Love**	**£35**
65	Sue WI 394	**Letter Full Of Tears/You Broke Your Promise**	**£40**

MINT VALUE £

66	Tamla Motown TMG 576	Just Walk In My Shoes/Stepping Closer To Your Heart	£60
66	Tamla Motown TMG 576	Just Walk In My Shoes/Stepping Closer To Your Heart (DJ copy)	£150
67	Tamla Motown TMG 604	Take Me In Your Arms And Love Me/Do You Love Me Just A Little Honey	£15
67	Tamla Motown TMG 619	Everybody Needs Love/Stepping Closer To Your Heart (demo-only B-side)	£100
67	Tamla Motown TMG 619	Everybody Needs Love/Since I've Lost You	£20
67	Tamla Motown TMG 629	I Heard It Through The Grapevine/It's Time To Go Now	£25
68	Tamla Motown TMG 645	The End Of Our Road/Don't Let Her Take Your Love From Me	£20
68	Tamla Motown TMG 660	It Should Have Been Me/You Don't Love Me No More	£18
68	Tamla Motown TMG 674	I Wish It Would Rain/It's Summer	£18
72	Tamla Motown TMG 805	Make Me The Woman That You Go Home To/I Don't Want To Do Wrong	£15
73	Tamla Motown TMG 864	Take Me In Your Arms And Love Me/No One Could Love You More	£200
75	Tamla Motown TMG 945	You've Lost That Loving Feeling/This Child Needs A Father	£15

ALBUMS

67	T. Motown TML 11058	EVERYBODY NEEDS LOVE (mono)	£35
67	T. Motown STML 11058	EVERYBODY NEEDS LOVE (stereo)	£40
68	Bell MBLL 103	TASTIEST HITS	£40
68	T. Motown TML 11080	FEELIN' BLUESY (mono)	£30
68	T. Motown STML 11080	FEELIN' BLUESY (stereo)	£35
69	T. Motown TML 11100	SILK 'N' SOUL (mono)	£40
69	T. Motown STML 11100	SILK'N'SOUL (stereo)	£35
69	T. Motown TML 11135	THE NITTY GRITTY (mono)	£30
69	T. Motown (S)TML 11135	THE NITTY GRITTY (stereo)	£22
70	T. Motown STML 11148	GREATEST HITS (original with flipback sleeve)	£20
71	T. Motown STML 11187	IF I WERE YOUR WOMAN	£20
74	T. Motown STML 1120	STANDING OVATION (LP)	£20

(see also Pips, Dionne Warwick)

JASON KNIGHT

67	Pye 7N 17399	Love Is Getting Stronger/Standing In My Shoes	£150
67	Pye 7N 17399	Love Is Getting Stronger/Standing In My Shoes (DJ copy)	£250

JEAN KNIGHT

72	Stax 2362 022	MR. BIG STUFF (LP)	£20

MARIE KNIGHT

61	Fontana H 354	Nothing/Come Tomorrow	£20
65	Stateside SS 419	Cry Me A River/Comes The Knight	£20
85	Kent TOWN 102	That's No Way To Treat A Girl/JACK MONTGOMERY: Dearly Beloved	£15

PETER KNIGHT ORCHESTRA/SINGERS

67	Mercury SML 30023	SGT. PEPPER'S LONELY HEARTS CLUB BAND (LP)	£15

ROBERT KNIGHT

62	London HLD 9496	Free Me/The Other Half Of Man	£30
68	Monument MON 1008	Everlasting Love/Somebody's Baby	£15
68	Monument MON 1017	The Power Of Love/Love On A Mountain Top	£35

SONNY KNIGHT

57	London HLD 8362	Confidential/Jail Bird (gold label print)	£200
57	London HLD 8362	Confidential/Jail Bird (silver label print)	£60
57	London HLD 8362	Confidential/Jail Bird (78 rpm)	£20
57	London HL 7016	Confidential/Jail Bird (export issue)	£60
59	Vogue Pop V 9134	But Officer/Dear Wonderful God	£150
59	Vogue Pop V 9134	But Officer/Dear Wonderful God (78)	£40

TERRY KNIGHT & PACK

66	Cameo Parkway C 102	I (Who Have Nothing)/Numbers	£60

(see also Grand Funk Railroad)

TONY KNIGHT

64	Decca F 11989	Did You Ever Hear The Sound?/I Feel So Blue (as Tony Knight & Live Wires)	£40
65	Decca F 12109	How Sweet/Surfer Street (as Tony Knight's Chessmen)	£35

KNIGHT BROTHERS

65	Chess CRS 8015	Sinking Low/Temptation 'Bout To Get Me	£30
66	Chess CRS 8046	That'll Get It/She's A1	£30

KNIGHTRIDER

87	Omega KS 1299	Shout Out Loud	£30

K9'S

79	Dog Breath WOOF 1	The K9 Hassle/Idi Amin/Sweeney Todd (1st issue in numbered blue p/s, with insert, 1000 only)	£45
79	Dog Breath WOOF 1	The K9 Hassle/Idi Amin/Sweeney Todd (reissue, 500 only in stamped die cut sleeve)	£15

KNOCKER JUNGLE

71	Ember NR 5052	KNOCKER JUNGLE (LP, gatefold sleeve)	£75

KNOCKOUTS

60	Top Rank JAR 279	Riot In Room 3C/Darling Lorraine	£25

KNOCK UP

82	Movie Music MM 002	Telling Lies/Need Your Love (no p/s)	£30

MARK KNOPFLER

84	Vertigo MARK ONE	Comfort And Joy (12", 1-sided promo)	£25
02	Mercury 063292-1	THE RAGPICKERS DREAM (2-LP, numbered)	£80
04	Mercury 9867262	SHANGRI-LA (2-LP)	£45

(see also Dire Straits, Randy Newman)

KENNY KNOTS
86	Unity UNO 18	Watch How The People Dancing/ERROL BELLUT: A Weh Do She (12")	£30
88	Unity UNO 22	Ring Up My Number/MIKEY MURKA: We Try (12")	£15
06	Jah Tubby's JT 10023	Babylon Fall Down/Gully Bank Rock (10" with Bush Chemists)	£25

KNOTT SISTERS
58	London HLX 8713	Undivided Attention/SHADES with KNOTT SISTERS: Sun Glasses	£40

KNOWLEDGE
78	A&M AMLH 68500	HAIL DREAD (LP)	£30
96	Tamoki Wambesi TWLP 1034	STUMBLING BLOCK (LP)	£50

BUDDY KNOX
57	Columbia DB 3914	Party Doll/My Baby's Gone (gold label print)	£50
57	Columbia DB 3952	Rock Your Little Baby To Sleep/Don't Make Me Cry (as Lieutenant Buddy Knox, gold label print)	£50
57	Columbia DB 4014	Hula Love/Devil Woman	£25
58	Columbia DB 4077	Swingin' Daddy/Whenever I'm Lonely	£25
58	Columbia DB 4180	Somebody Touched Me/C'mon Baby	£20
59	Columbia DB 4302	To Be With You/I Think I'm Gonna Kill Myself	£15
62	Liberty LIB 55473	She's Gone/Now There's Only Me	£20
57	Columbia SEG 7732	ROCK-A-BUDDY KNOX (EP)	£50
62	Liberty LBY 1114	GOLDEN HITS (LP)	£20

KNUCKLEHEAD
93	Saucerman ART 01	Red Eye, Dead Eye/Spirit Matter (p/s, hand-painted label, 150 copies only)	£15

FRANKIE KNUCKLES
89	Radical Records TRAXT 3	Your Love/Baby Wants To Ride (12", p/s)	£25
89	Trax TRAX 3	Your Love/Baby Wants To Ride (p/s)	£30
11	Nocturnal Groove NCTGD 064V	Your Love (Director's Cut Signature Mix)/(Belocca And Soneec Vocal Club Nocturnal Groove) (12" p/s reissue)	£30
91	Virgin America VUSLP 36	BEYOND THE MIX (LP)	£18

KNXWLEDGE
16	All City ACKWTLPX1	WRAPTAYPES (2-LP, gatefold)	£25

KOBALT 60
91	Music Of Life NOTE57	Chaos From Order/Concrete Show (12")	£15

KODA
94	Lucky Spin STU 8 1	Untitled (12" 1-sided white label)	£20
94	Dee Jay DJX 019	The Deep/Spacetek (12")	£40

KODIAKS
69	Decca F 12942	All Because You Wanna See Me Cry/Tell Me Rhonda	£20

(SPIDER) JOHN KOERNER
67	Elektra EKSN 45005	Won't You Give Me Some Love/Don't Stop	£25
66	Elektra EKL 267	(LOTS MORE) BLUES RAGS AND HOLLERS (LP, with Dave Ray and Tony Glover, US sleeve but UK pressed record with golden Elektra "guitar player' logo)	£45
65	Elektra EKL 290	SPIDER BLUES (LP)	£50
68	Elek. EKL 4041/EKS 74041	RUNNING JUMPING STANDING STILL (LP, with Willie Murphy)	£30

KOFI
87	Ariwa ARI 73	Didn't I/PROFESSOR DOPPLER: I'm A Dropout (12")	£35
89	Ariwa ARI LP 042	BLACK...WITH SUGAR (LP)	£30
93	Ariwa ARILP 092	WISHING WELL (LP)	£30
94	Ariwa ARILP064	FRIDAY'S CHILD (LP)	£25

KOFI & KIKI
79	Bronze 12 BRO 70	24 Hours In A Disco/(Instrumental Version) (12")	£15

(see also Koki Gyan)

LEONID KOGAN
58	Columbia 33CX 1562	PAGANINI VIOLIN CONCERTO NO. 1 IN D MAJOR (LP, mono)	£150
60	Columbia SAX 2307	BRAHMS VIOLIN CONCERTO (LP, stereo)	£1000
60	Columbia SAX 2329	LALO: SYMPHONIE ESPAGNOLE/TCHAIKOVSKY: SERENADE MELANCOLIQUE, LP, stereo, turquoise/silver label)	£1500
60	Columbia SAX 2323	TCHAIKOVSKY: VIOLIN CONCERTO OP 35 & MEDITATION D MINOR OP 42 with Paris Conservatoire Orchestra, turquoise/silver label) LP, stereo)	£1500
60	Columbia 33CX 1711	TCHAIKOVSKY: VIOLIN CONCERTO OP 35 & MEDITATION D MINOR OP 42 with Paris Conservatoire Orchestra, LP, blue label, mono)	£50
60	Columbia SAX 2386	BEETHOVEN VIOLIN CONCERTO (LP, stereo, turquoise/silver label)	£2000
64	Columbia SAX 2531	SONATAS FOR TWO VIOLINS (with ELISABTH GILELS) (LP, stereo, turquoise/silver label)	£1500
64	Odeon SAX 2388	SONATAS FOR TWO VIOLINS (with ELISABTH GILELS) (LP, stereo export edition, black label)	£500

KOKO TAYLOR
87	Chess CH-9263	KOKO TAYLOR (LP, reissue, first UK pressing)	£30

KO KO TAYLOR
66	Chess CRS 8035	Wang Dang Doodle/Blues Heaven	£35
66	Chess CRS 8035	Wang Dang Doodle/Blues Heaven (DJ copy)	£60

KOLETTES
64	Pye International 7N 25278	Who's That Guy?/Just How Much	£50

BONNIE KOLOC
72	London SHO 8432	AFTER ALL THIS TIME (LP)	£25

72	London SHO 8440	**HOLD ON TO ME** (LP)	£20

MO KOLOURS

17	22a 018	**AXUM** (p/s, 300 only, with insert)	£15

MO KOLOURS/R.O. MAMODE IV

14	22a 003	**MO KOLOURS/R.O. MAMODE IV** (12" split EP, stamped white labels)	£15

CHRISTOPHER KOMEDA

66	Polydor 580001	**CUL DE SAC** (soundtrack EP)	£150
68	Dot (S)LPD 519	**ROSEMARY'S BABY** (LP, as Kryzstophe Komeda)	£50

KOMYTEA

08	Anjunaseep ANJDEE 027	**Professional Killers/My Personal Summer** (12")	£80

MANJEET KONDAL

86	Multitone MUT 1018	**HOLLE HOLLE** (LP)	£30
88	Arishma ARI 1006	**WICKED AND WILD** (LP)	£30
91	Nachural LNR 0206	**SPECIAL BREW** (LP)	£40

KONGAS

74	Barclay 80524	**AFRO ROCK** (LP)	£15

JOHN (T.) KONGOS

69	Dawn DNLS 3002	**CONFUSIONS ABOUT A GOLDFISH** (LP, with sticker)	£50
69	Dawn DNLS 3002	**CONFUSIONS ABOUT A GOLDFISH** (LP, without sticker)	£40
71	Fly HIFLY 7	**KONGOS** (LP, gatefold sleeve, insert, Fly label)	£20

(see also Scrugg, Floribunda Rose)

V. KONGS

63	Halagala HG 18	**Tomorrow Will Soon Be Here/Pretty Little Girl**	£20

LEE KONITZ

56	London LTZK 15025	**LEE KONITZ WITH WAYNE MARSH** (LP)	£20

KONK

84	4th & Broadway BRW 7	**Your Life/Dub**	£15
04	Soul Jazz SJR LP 90	**THE SOUND OF KONK** (2-LP)	£20

KONKRETE CANTICLE

71	Arts Council Of Great Britain AC 1971	**EXPERIMENTS IN DISINTEGRATING LANGUAGE** (LP)	£70

KONRADS

65	CBS 201812	**Baby It's Too Late Now/I'm Over You**	£50

KONSTRUKTIVITS

83	Flowmotion FM 001	**VOLUME 1** (cassette)	£60
83	Flowmotion FM 002	**A DISSEMBLY** (LP)	£35
83	Third Mind TMLP 02	**PSYKO GENETIKA** (LP)	£35
84	Third Mind TMLP 05	**BLACK DECEMBER** (LP)	£30
85	Sterile SR 10	**GLENNASCAUL** (LP)	£15

(see also Whitehouse)

KOOBAS

65	Pye 7N 17012	**Take Me For A Little While/Somewhere In The Night**	£50
66	Pye 7N 17087	**You'd Better Make Up Your Mind/A Place I Know**	£60
66	Columbia DB 7988	**Sweet Music/Face**	£60
67	Columbia DB 8103	**Sally/Champagne And Caviar**	£35
67	Columbia DB 8187	**Gypsy Fred/City Girl**	£30
68	Columbia DB 8419	**The First Cut Is The Deepest/Walking Out**	£55
69	Columbia S(C)X 6271	**THE KOOBAS** (LP, black/silver label, boxed logo, "Sold in U.K..." text)	£1500
88	Bam Caruso KIRI 047	**BARRICADES** (LP)	£18

(see also Kubas, Van Der Graaf Generator, Gary & Stu, Juicy Lucy, March Hare)

KOOKS

06	Virgin VX 3016	**INSIDE IN/INSIDE OUT** (LP, with 'bonus' live LP)	£70
08	Virgin V3043	**KONK** (LP)	£30

KOOL

67	CBS 203003	**Look At Me, Look At Me/Room At The Top**	£20
69	CBS 2865	**Step Out Of Your Mind/Funny** (What A Fool A Man Can Be)	£80

BO KOOL

81	Tania TAN 001S	**(Money) No Love/Love Money** (12", purple vinyl)	£20

KOOL KEITH/PHAROE MONCH/AKINYELLE

95	Liberty Grooves	**Freestyle Frenzy/Gotta Go Down** (7")	£45

KOOL & THE GANG

71	Mojo 2347 001	**LIVE AT P.J.'S** (LP)	£20
71	Mojo 2347 002	**THE BEST OF KOOL AND THE GANG** (LP)	£15
72	Mojo 2347 003	**LIVE AT THE SEX MACHINE** (LP)	£15
73	Mojo 2347 004	**MUSIC IS THE MESSAGE** (LP)	£15
74	Polydor 2310299	**WILD AND PEACEFUL** (LP)	£20
74	Poydor 2310 357	**LIGHT OF WORLDS** (LP)	£18
75	Polydor 2310 416	**SPIRIT OF THE BOOGIE** (LP)	£20
76	Polydor 2310 441	**LOVE & UNDERSTANDING** (LP)	£18

AL KOOPER

65	Mercury MF 885	**Parchman Farm/You're The Lovin' End** (as Alan Kooper)	£20
69	CBS 63538	**I STAND ALONE** (LP, orange label)	£30
69	CBS 63651	**YOU NEVER KNOW WHO YOUR FRIENDS ARE** (LP, orange label)	£20

70	CBS 63797	KOOPER SESSION - WITH SHUGGIE OTIS (LP, orange label)	£20
70	CBS 66252	EASY DOES IT (2-LP, orange label)	£20
71	United Artists UAS 29120	THE LANDLORD (LP, soundtrack, with Staple Singers & Lorraine Ellison)	£20
71	CBS 64340	NEW YORK CITY (YOU'RE A WOMAN) (LP, gatefold sleeve, orange label)	£15
72	CBS 64208	A POSSIBLE PROJECTION OF THE FUTURE/CHILDHOOD'S END (LP, orange label)	£15
73	CBS 65193	NAKED SONGS (LP)	£15

(see also Blues Project, Blood Sweat & Tears, Shuggie Otis)

AL KOOPER, MIKE BLOOMFIELD & STEPHEN STILLS

| 68 | CBS 63396 | SUPER SESSION (LP) | £20 |
| 73 | CBS CQ 30991 | SUPER SESSION (LP, quadrophonic) | £25 |

(see also Mike Bloomfield & Al Kooper, Stephen Stills)

KOPPYKATS

| 68 | Fontana SFT 13052/3 | BEATLES' BEST (2-LP) | £35 |

(see also Ian [Edward] & Zodiacs)

TAMARA KORAN WITH PERCEPTION

| 68 | Domain D7 | Veils Of Mourning Lace/Don't Throw Our Love Away (DJ copy) | £400 |
| 68 | Domain D7 | Veils Of Mourning Lace/Don't Throw Our Love Away | £350 |

PAUL KORDA

66	Columbia DB 7994	Go On Home/Just Come Closer To Me	£30
69	Parlophone R5778	Seagull (West Coast Oil Tragedy Of '68)/Night Of The Next Day (with p/s)	£30
69	Parlophone R 5778	Seagull (West Coast Oil Tragedy Of '68)/Night Of The Next Day	£15
71	MAM AS 1003	PASSING STRANGER (LP, gatefold sleeve)	£75

(see also Dada)

KOREA

| 84 | Romac (No cat no) | I Don't Know/Deep In Your Heart (no p/s) | £50 |

KORELESS

| 11 | Pictures Music PICT 005 | 4D (12", stamped white labels) | £20 |
| 13 | Young Turks YT088 | YUGEN (12") | £20 |

KORN

| 95 | Epic KORN 1 | Blind/Fake/Sean Olson (10", p/s numbered) | £18 |
| 96 | Epic 6638450 | No Place To Hide/Proud (white vinyl, 7,500 only) | £15 |

ALEXIS KORNER (BLUES INCORPORATED)

58	Tempo A 166	I Ain't Gonna Worry No More/County Jail (as Alexis Korner Skiffle Group)	£100
58	Tempo A 166	I Ain't Gonna Worry No More/County Jail (78)	£50
63	Lyntone LYN 299	Blaydon Races/Up-Town (as Blues Incorporated With Alexis Korner, free with women's magazine Trio)	£100
63	Parlophone R 5206	I Need Your Loving/Please Please Please (as Alexis Korner's Blues Inc.)	£40
65	Parlophone R 5247	Little Baby/Roberta (as Alexis Korner's Blues Inc.)	£40
65	King KG 1017	See See Rider/Blues A La King (as Alexis Korner's All Stars)	£45
66	Fontana TF 706	River's Invitation/Everyday (I Have The Blues)	£25
67	Fontana TF 817	Rosie/Rock Me	£25
58	Tempo EXA 76	BLUES FROM THE ROUNDHOUSE VOL. 1 (EP, as Alexis Korner Skiffle Group)	£175
59	Tempo EXA 102	BLUES FROM THE ROUNDHOUSE VOL. 2 (EP, as Alexis Korner's Blues Inc.)	£300
62	Topic TOP 70	3/4 A.D. (EP, with Davy Graham, first pressing in mauve sleeve with cream label)	£90
62	Topic TOP 70	3/4 A.D. (EP, with Davy Graham, later pressing with lilac sleeve and blue label)	£60
62	Topic TOP 70	3/4 A.D. (EP, with Davy Graham, later pressings with bronze sleeve and blue label)	£30
57	'77' LP/2	BLUES FROM THE ROUNDHOUSE (10" LP, 99 only, as Alexis Korner Breakdown Group)	£1000
62	Ace of Clubs ACL 1130	R&B FROM THE MARQUEE (LP, claret labels, with Long John Baldry)	£120
64	Transatlantic TRA 117	RED HOT FROM ALEX (LP, with Herbie Goins)	£150
64	Oriole PS 40058	AT THE CAVERN (LP, live, with Herbie Goins, laminated sleeve with flipbacks)	£375
65	Ace of Clubs ACL 1187	ALEXIS KORNER'S BLUES INCORPORATED (LP)	£100
65	Spot JW 551	SKY HIGH (LP, featuring Duffy Power)	£400
67	Fontana TL 5381	I WONDER WHO (LP, mono)	£150
67	Fontana (S)TL 5381	I WONDER WHO (LP, stereo)	£200
67	Polydor Special 236 206	BLUES INCORPORATED (LP, 1st issue, listing 4 tracks on Side A on sleeve/label)	£80
67	Polydor Special 236 206	BLUES INCORPORATED (LP, 2nd issue, listing 5 tracks on Side A on sleeve/label)	£50
68	Liberty LBL/LBS 83147	A NEW GENERATION OF BLUES (LP)	£75
69	Transatlantic TRASAM 7	ALEXIS KORNER'S ALL STAR BLUES INCORPORATED (LP, reissue of "Red Hot From Alex", different cover)	£30
71	Rak SRAK 501	ALEXIS KORNER (LP, textured sleeve)	£45
72	Rak SRAKSP 51	BOOTLEG HIM! (2-LP, with booklet)	£55
73	Transatlantic TRA 269	ACCIDENTALLY BORN IN NEW ORLEANS (LP, as Snape)	£35
75	CBS 69155	GET OFF MY CLOUD (LP)	£25

(see also Cyril Davies, C.C.S., Herbie Goins, Duffy Power, Long John Baldry, Rocket 88, Davy Graham, Beryl Bryden, Jimmy Cotton, Ken Colyer, Jack Bruce, Snape & Little Brother Montgomery)

ARTIE KORNFELD'S TREE

| 70 | Probe SPB 1022 | A TIME TO REMEMBER (LP) | £20 |

KORPERAYSHUN

| 89 | BPM BP12007 | K Factor/Non Stop (12") | £30 |

KOSMICHER LAUFER

13	Unknown Capability UCKL001V	THE SECRET MUSIC OF THE EAST GERMAN OLYMPIC PROGRAMME 1972-83 VOLUME ONE (LP, CD with postcards)	£60
13	Unknown Capability UCKL001V	THE SECRET MUSIC OF THE EAST GERMAN OLYMPIC PROGRAMME 1972-83 VOLUME ONE (LP)	£35
14	Unknown Capability UCKL002V	THE SECRET MUSIC OF THE EAST GERMAN OLYMPIC PROGRAMME 1972-83 VOLUME TWO (LP, red vinyl)	£35

15	Unknown Capability UCKL003V	THE SECRET MUSIC OF THE EAST GERMAN OLYMPIC PROGRAMME 1972-83 VOLUME THREE (LP, yellow vinyl with CD) £40
18	Unknown Capability UCKL004V	THE SECRET MUSIC OF THE EAST GERMAN OLYMPIC PROGRAMME 1972-83 VOLUME FOUR (LP, blue vinyl, some with CD) £35

KOSMIK KOMMANDO
93	Rephlex MX 202	UNIVERSAL INDICATOR YELLOW EP (12") £18
01	Machine Codes CODE 1010	ANALOGUE ANDROID (LP, 100 only, signed insert) £50

(see also Aphex Twin)

LEE KOSMIN
78	Polydor 2059034	Ain't No Way/How Fine I Feel £20

DAVID KOSSOFF
60	Oriole MG 20043	LARKIN SINGIN' (LP) £15

PAUL KOSSOFF
73	Island ILPS 9264	BACK STREET CRAWLER (LP, pink rim palm tree label) £15
77	DJM DJE 29002	KOSS (2-LP) £15

(see also Free, Kossoff Kirke Tetsu & Rabbit, Creepy John Thomas)

KOSSOFF, KIRKE, TETSU & RABBIT
71	Island ILPS 9188	KOSSOFF, KIRKE, TETSU AND RABBIT (LP, gatefold sleeve, pink rim palm tree label) £50

(see also Paul Kossoff, Rabbit, Free)

CHIM KOTHARI
66	Deram DML 1002	SOUND OF THE SITAR (LP) £40

KRACKER
74	Rolling Stones COC 49102	KRACKER BRAND (LP, gatefold sleeve)...£20

KRAFTWERK
SINGLES
74	Vertigo 6147 012	Autobahn/Kometenmelodie 1 ....£15
75	Vertigo 6147 015	Comet Melody 2/Kristallo £30
76	Capitol CL 15853	Radio Activity/Antenna (in p/s) £15
77	Capitol CL 15917	Trans-Europe Express/Europe Endless..£20
77	Capitol CLX 104	Showroom Dummies/Europe Endless (12", 'train station' p/s) £18
78	Capitol CL 15981	The Robots (edited version)/Spacelab (demo copy, special die cut sleeve).......£35
78	Capitol CL 15981	The Robots/Spacelab (foldout p/s) £15
78	Capitol CL 15981	The Robots (alternative mix)/Spacelab (foldout p/s) £30
78	Capitol 12CL 15998	Neon Lights/Trans-Europe Express/The Model (12", luminous vinyl, dayglo sleeve) £30
78	Capitol 12CL 16098	Showroom Dummies/Spacelab/Europe Endless (12", reissue, 'red shirts' p/s).............£15
81	EMI TCEMI 5175	Pocket Calculator/Numbers/Dentaku (cassette in cigarette'-pack style box)...................£35
81	Vertigo VER 3	Kometenmelodie 2/Vom Himmel Hoch (p/s) £15
83	EMI TCEMI 5413	Tour De France/Tour De France (Short Version)/ Tour De France (2" Etape) £15
83	EMI 12EMI 5413	Tour De France (Long Version)/(7" Version)/(2" Etape) (12", p/s, red or yellow labels) £18
84	EMI 12EMI 5413	Tour De France (Kevorkian Remix)/Tour De France (Different Extended Version)/Tour De France (Original 7" Version) (12", reissue, 'Breakdance' p/s) £18
86	EMI 12EMI 5588	Musique Non-Stop (6.15)/Musique Non-Stop (7" Version) (12", p/s)..................£15
87	EMI EMI 5602	The Telephone Call/Der Telefon Anruf (p/s) £15
87	EMI 12EMI 5602	The Telephone Call (Remix)/House Phone/Der Telefon Anruf (12", p/s).............£20
97	EMI KLANG BOX 101	KRAFTWERK (4 x 12" box set, including "Trans Europe Express", Numbers, "Musique Non Stop" & "Homecomputer"; with separate white or black T-shirt, promo only) £100
97	EMI KLANG BOX 101	KRAFTWERK (4 x 12" box set, including "Trans Europe Express", "Numbers", Musique Non Stop & "Homecomputer"; without T-shirt, promo only) £60

ALBUMS
72	Vertigo 6641 077	KRAFTWERK (2-LP, gatefold sleeve, small 'swirl') £400
72	Vertigo 6641 077	KRAFTWERK (2-LP gatefold sleeve, 'spacecraft' labels) £100
74	Vertigo 6360 616	RALF AND FLORIAN ('spacecraft' label, embossed sleeve) £150
74	Vertigo 6360 620	AUTOBAHN (embossed blue sleeve) £50
75	Vertigo 6360 629	EXCELLER 8 (some with stickered sleeve) £35
76	Capitol E-ST 11457	RADIO-ACTIVITY (with insert)...£30
77	Capitol E-ST 11603	TRANS-EUROPE EXPRESS (LP, inner)..£30
78	Capitol E-ST 11728	MAN MACHINE (LP, inner with round edges) £30
81	EMI EMC 3370	COMPUTER WORLD (LP, inner)..£25
81	Vertigo 6449 066	ELEKTROKINETIK (LP)...£25
81	Vertigo 6641077	KRAFTWERK (2-LP, reissue in single sleeve, spaceship labels)........................£50
83	EMI EMC 3407	TECHNOPOP (unissued, sleeves only)...£0
83	Fame FA 4131031	RADIO-ACTIVITY (LP, reissue) £15
83	Fame 41 31511	TRANS-EUROPE EXPRESS (LP, reissue) £15
85	Fame FA4131181	MAN MACHINE (LP, reissue) £15
86	EMI EMD 100130	ELECTRIC CAFE (LP, gatefold)...£25
91	EMI EM 1408	THE MIX (2-LP, with inner sleeves) £30
03	EMI EMI 591 708 1	TOUR DE FRANCE SOUNDTRACKS (2-LP, single stickered sleeve with inners)...................£50
04	EMI KLANG BOX 001	THE CATALOGUE (8-CD, in card box, 1,000 only) £80
05	EMI 560 6111	MINIMUM - MAXIMUM (4-LP box set)..£100
05	EMI 45855	MINIMUM - MAXIMUM (2-CD, DVD box set) £35

(see also Organisation, Electric Music, Karl Bartos, Wolfgang Flur)

KRAFTY KUTS
99	Lacerba CERBAL 14	SLAM THE BREAKS ON (3-LP) £20

KRAKEN
80	Knave EJSP 9370	FANTASY REALITY (EP, no p/s)...£50

BILLY J. KRAMER & THE DAKOTAS

67	Reaction 591 014	Town Of Tuxley Toymakers/Chinese Girl	£50
64	Parlophone GEP 8907	LITTLE CHILDREN (EP)	£15
64	Parlophone GEP 8921	FROM A WINDOW (EP)	£15
65	Parlophone GEP 8928	BILLY J. PLAYS THE STATES (EP)	£50
63	Parlophone PMC 1209	LISTEN (LP, mono)	£25
65	Regal REG 1057	BILLY J (LP, export only)	£30

(see also Dakotas)

KRAVIN AS

91	Hangman HANG 39 UP	KRAVE ON! (LP)	£15

KRAY CHERUBS

88	Fierce FRIGHT 014	No (p/s, 1-sided)	£20
89	Forced Exposure FE 18	Teen Camel/I Hate My Job (p/s)	£15

(see also Art Attacks, Savage Pencil)

BILL KRENZ & HIS RAGTIMERS

56	London HLU 8258	There'll Be No New Tunes On This Old Piano/Goofus	£35

KREW KATS

61	HMV POP 840	Trambone/Peak Hour	£15
61	HMV POP 894	Samovar/Jack's Good	£25

(see also Shadows, Brian Bennett)

VEIRA KREW

85	VK 1000	Sexy Lady (Vocal)/(Instrumental)/Welcome To A Dream (12")	£100

KRIMSON KAKE

69	Penny Farthing PEN 707	Feelin' Better/Waiter	£30

(see also Samantha Jones, Vernons Girls)

KRIS

79	V-KRIS VKR 1	Okay/Trouble With The Law	£30

DAVE KRISS

72	Deroy	EMIGRATING (2-LP)	£40

SONJA KRISTINA

68	Polydor 56299	Let The Sunshine In/Frank Mills	£15
80	Chopper CHOPE 5	SONJA KRISTINA (LP)	£35

(see also Curved Air)

DANNY KRIVIT

03	Strut STRUTLP 016	EDITS BY MR K (3 x 12")	£40

KROKODIL

69	Liberty LBS 83306	KROKODIL (LP)	£50
70	Liberty LBS 83417	SWAMP (LP)	£50

KROME & TIME

92	Suburban B. SUBBASE 011	This Sound Is For The Underground/Manic Stampede (12", p/s)	£25
92	Suburban B. SUBBASE 11R	This Sound Is For The Underground (E.5 Remix)/Manic Stampede (DJ Hype's Sandringham Road Mix) (12")	£20
93	Suburban B. SUBBASE 26	The Slammer/Into The Night (12", p/s as DJ Krome & Mr Time)	£20

KROMESTAR

06	Deep Medi Musik medi 01	Kalawanji/Surgery (12")	£30
15	System SYSTM 006	Mere Sher/Flute Song (12")	£30

KRONSTADT UPRISING

83	Spiderleg SDL 12	THE UNKNOWN REVOLUTION EP (fold-out p/s)	£30
85	Dog Rock SD 108	Part Of The Game/The Horsemen (fold out p/s)	£20

KRS-ONE

93	Jive HIP 142	RETURN OF THE BOOM BAP (2-LP)	£20
95	Jive HIP 165	KRS ONE (2-LP)	£20

KRUDER & DORFMEISTER

93	G-Stone- Recordings G-Stone 001	G-STONED EP: Definition/Deep Shit Pt .1 & Pt. 2/High Noon/Original Bedroom Rockers (12", p/s)	£40
15	!K7/G-Stone Recordings !K7073LP,	THE K&D SESSIONS (5LP, compilation, trifold sleeve, reissue, 180g)	£60
22	!K7/G-Stone Recordings !K7073LP,	THE K&D SESSIONS (5LP, compilation, trifold sleeve, reissue, 20th Anniversary edition, 180g, hype sticker)	£60

(see also Tosca, The Peace Orchestra)

KRU POPS

82	Electric Bubble Gum EB 101	Yummy Yummy Yummy/Gimme One More Dance	£40

KRUZA

79	Black Hole Records BHE 101	Movies in The Night/Sun In My Eyes/Someone's There/All Stood Up (p/s)	£20

KRYPTIC MINDS

09	Swamp 81 SWAMP 001	One Of Us/Six Degrees (12", p/s)	£20
10	Swamp 81 SWAMP LP 001	ONE OF US (LP as 3 x 12")	£40
11	Black Box BLACKBOX012	CAN'T SLEEP (LP as 3 x 12")	£30

KRYSIA (KOCJAN)

74	RCA LPL1 5052	KRYSIA (LP)	£18

(see also Natural Acoustic Band, Fairport Convention)

BOB KUBAN & INMEN

66	Stateside SS 488	The Cheater/Try Me Baby	£60
66	Stateside SS 488	The Cheater/Try Me Baby (DJ copy)	£110

MINT VALUE £

66	Stateside SS 514	The Teaser/All I Want £20

KUBAS
| 65 | Columbia DB 7451 | I Love Her/Magic Potion .... £60 |

(see also Koobas)

DAVE KUBINEC
| 69 | Parlophone R5762 | Schopi/The Lady Loves .... £20 |

KUF-LINX
| 58 | London HLU 8583 | So Tough/What'cha Gonna Do .... £80 |
| 58 | London HLU 8583 | So Tough/What'cha Gonna Do (78) .... £25 |

KUKL
| 84 | Crass 1984/1 | THE EYE (LP, foldout sleeve) .... £20 |
| 85 | Crass No. 4 | HOLIDAYS IN EUROPE (LP, with inner sleeve) .... £20 |

(see also Sugarcubes)

KULA SHAKER
96	Columbia SHAKER 1LP	K (LP, inner) £30
99	Columbia SHAKER 2LP	PEASANTS, PIGS & ASTRONAUTS (LP, gatefold) £30
10	Strangefolk SFKS003LP	PILGRIM'S PROGRESS (LP, 300 only with signed screenprinted cover) ... £80
10	Strangefolk SFK S003LP	PILGRIM'S PROGRESS (LP) £40

KULT
| 69 | CBS 4276 | No Home Today/Mister Number One .... £300 |

KURASS
| 70 | Escort ES 825 | Stampede/KING STITT: You Were Meant For Me (B-side actually by Lee Perry) .... £40 |

KUSTOM
| 82 | Red Bus RBUS 71 | Let The Girl Dance/Arrested .... £20 |

KUT
| 81 | Half Kut HKR 001 | Can't Sleep at Night/Faithful (no p/s) .... £35 |

FELA RANSOME KUTI (& AFRICA '70)
72	Regal Zonophone RZ 3052	Egbe Mi O/Chop And Quench (with Africa '70 & Ginger Baker) £20
72	Regal Zonophone RZ 3052)	Egbe Mi O/Chop And Quench (with Africa '70 & Ginger Baker) (promo, large red 'A' to A-side) £50
72	Regal Zono. SLRZ 1023	FELA RANSOME-KUTI & THE AFRICA '70 WITH GINGER BAKER LIVE! (LP) £50
73	Regal Zono. SLR2 1034	AFRODISIAC (LP, red/silver labels with EMI boxed logo) £200
75	Decca/Aphrodisia DWAPS 2005	UPSIDE DOWN (LP) £25
75	Creole CRLP 501	SHAKARA (LP, with Africa '70) £40
77	Creole CRLP 509	EVERYTHING SCATTER (LP) £30
77	Creole CRLP 511	ZOMBIE (LP, with Africa '70) £40
78	Phase 4 Stereo PFS 4412	YELLOW FEVER (LP) £50
79	Creole CRLP 502	GENTLEMEN (LP) £20
81	Arista SPART 1167	BLACK PRESIDENT (LP) £30
82	Arista SPART 1177	ORIGINAL SUFFERHEAD (LP) £30
83	EMI EDP 1547203	FELA ANIKULAPO KUTI (2-LP) £25
93	Sterns STERNS 3005	THE 69 LOS ANGELES SESSIONS (with Nigeria 70, reissue) £30
97	Talkin Loud 547 035-1	BOX SET 1 (Box set, 6-LP, booklet, postcards) £80

(see also Ginger Baker)

BEN KWELLER
| 02 | 679 777201 | SHA SHA (LP) .... £25 |

JIM KWESKIN JUG BAND
65	Fontana TFL 6036	JIM KWESKIN JUG BAND (LP) £20
67	Fontana (S)TFL 6080	SEE REVERSE SIDE FOR TITLE (LP) £18
68	Vanguard SVRL 19046	WHATEVER HAPPENED TO THOSE GOOD OLD DAYS AT CLUB 47 (LP) ... £18

KWICK
| 80 | EMI America 12 EA 117 | We Ought To Be Dancing/Can't Help Myself/Let This Moment Be Forever (12") ... £15 |
| 81 | EMI America | Night Life/Here I Go Again (Another Weekend)/Split Decision (12") ... £15 |

(THE) KYDDS
| 69 | NEMS 56-4095 | The Sun Is A Laughing Child/Touch Of The Sun .... £15 |

CHARLES KYNARD
72	Mainstream MSL 1009	WOGA (LP) £30
73	Mainstream MSL 1017	YOUR MAMA DON'T DANCE (LP) £25
96	BGP BGPD 1056	REELIN' WITH THE FEELIN' (LP, reissue) £15
96	BGP BGPD 1057	WA-TU-WA-ZUI (BEAUTIFUL PEOPLE) (LP, reissue) £15

KYTES
66	Pye 7N 17136	Blessed/Call Me Darling £15
66	Pye 7N 17179	Frosted Panes/I'll Give You Better Love £35
68	Island WI 6027	Running In The Water/The End Of The Day £80

KYTTOCK KYND
| 70 | Dorian 4782 | KYTTOCK KYND (LP) .... £40 |

KYUSS
94	Elektra EKR 192	Demon Cleaner/Freedom Run (live) (p/s, sky blue vinyl) £40
94	Elektra SAM 1371	SKY VALLEY PART 2 (1-sided 12" sampler, stated white labels, stickered die-cut sleeve) .. £40
95	Elektra 7559-61571-1	WELCOME TO SKY VALLEY (2-LP) £80

PATTI LA BELLE (& BLUE BELLES)
64	Sue WI 324	Down The Aisle/C'est La Vie	£30
65	Cameo Parkway P 935	Danny Boy/I Believe	£20
65	Atlantic AT 4055	All Or Nothing/You Forgot How To Love (as Patty La Belle & Her Belles)	£30
66	Atlantic AT 4064	Over The Rainbow/Groovy Kind Of Love (as Patty La Belle & Her Belles)	£15
66	Atlantic 587 001	OVER THE RAINBOW (LP)	£50

(see also Blue-Belles)

LABRADFORD
95	Flying Nun FN 329	A STABLE REFERENCE (LP, reissue, numbered sleeve)	£30
96	Blast First BFFP 136	LABRADFORD (LP, die-cut sleeve, 2 inserts)	£30
97	Blast First BFFP 144	MI MEDIA NARANJA (LP)	£40
99	Blast First BFFP 157	E LUXO SO (LP)	£40
00	Blast First BFFP 167	FIXED :: CONTENT (LP)	£20

LACE
68	Columbia DB 8499	People People/The Nun	£25

(see also Universals, Pete Dello, Honeybus, Red Herring, Gary Walker & Rain)

LACKEY & SWEENEY
73	Village Thing VTS 23	JUNK STORE SONGS FOR SALE (LP, inner)	£50

LACK OF KNOWLEDGE
81	LOK LOK 1	The Uninvited/Ritual (with A4 photocopied inserts)	£30
83	Crass Records 121984/6	GREY (EP)	£20
84	Corpus Christi CHRIST 15	SIRENS ARE BACK (LP)	£20

JUNIOR LACY
77	Aries ARI 003	You Will See Jah Light/Jah Love Version (12")	£35

STEVE LACY
57	Esquire 32 143	SOPRANO TODAY (LP)	£50
72	Emanem 301	SOLO (LP)	£25
73	Emanem 304	THE CRUST (LP)	£35

STEVE LACY & DEREK BAILEY
76	Incus 26	COMPANY 4 (LP)	£25

(see also Derek Bailey)

LADD'S BLACK ACES
56	London AL 3556	LADD'S BLACK ACES (10" LP)	£15

LA-DE-DA BAND
69	Parlophone R 5810	Come Together/Here Is Love	£18

LADIES
80s	Music Of Life MOLIS 6	Turned On To You/I Knew That Love (12")	£15

TOMMY LADNIER
54	London AL 3524	BLUES AND STOMPS VOLUME ONE - TOMMY LADNIER (10" LP)	£20
55	London AL 3548	PLAYS THE BLUES WITH MA RAINEY & EDMONIA HENDERSON (10" LP)	£20

(see also Ma Rainey)

LADY BLACKBIRD
21	Foundation Music FM0008	BLACK ACID SOUL (LP, orange vinyl, limited edition, "collectors issue". printed inner)	£80
21	Foundation Music FM0008	BLACK ACID SOUL (LP, 'A Kind Of Blue' vinyl, limited edition 500 copies, printed inner)	£60
21	Foundation Music FM 0008	BLACK ACID SOUL (LP, 'Crystal Blue Persuasion' vinyl, limited edition 500 copies)	£50
21	Foundation Music FM 0008	BLACK ACID SOUL (LP, 'smokey black' vinyl, limited edition 500 copies)	£50
22	Foundation/BMG 538830160,	BLACK ACID SOUL (2LP, gatefold, Deluxe Edition)	£25

LADY GAGA
08	Interscope LGDANCEUP1	JUST DANCE - THE REMIXES (LP, promo, pink vinyl)	£45

LADY JANE
84	Schizoid SCHIZ 01	For You Tonight/Out For The Count/Whisky And Leather (private pressing)	£60

LADY JUNE
74	Caroline C 1509	LADY JUNE'S LINGUISTIC LEPROSY (LP, with perforated lyric sheet)	£35

(see also Kevin Ayers, Eno)

LADY PENELOPE
97	Emitta EMT 100	Devotion To Love/Up & Down/Deeper Part 2 (12:")	£18

(see also Abstrac & Lady Penelope)

LADYHAWKE
08	Modular MODVL 104	LADYHAWKE (LP, gatefold, booklet)	£40

LADY LEX
04	Peckings PT 1013	Love Doctor/NATIJAH: Open My Gate	£15
09	Peckings PTI 059	COURTNEY JOHN: Lucky Man/LADY LEX: Don't Know Why	£40

LADYTRON
01	Invicta Hi Fi LIQ 014	604 (2-LP, white vinyl)	£40
02	Telstar TELP 3296	LIGHT & MAGIC (LP)	£70

MINT VALUE £

11	Nettwork 0 6700 30924 2 5	**GRAVITY THE SEDUCER** (LP, black vinyl)	£60
11	Nettwork 0 6700 30924 2 5	**GRAVITY THE SEDUCER** (LP, clear vinyl)	£70
12	Nettwork 0 6700 30946 1 0	**WITCHING HOUR** (LP, reissue, red vinyl)	£30

LAFAYETTE AFRO ROCK BAND
99	Strut STRUTLP 003	**DARKEST LIGHT - THE BEST OF** (2-LP)	£40

JACK LA FORGE
65	Stateside SS 444	Our Crazy Affair/Bossa Bossa Nova (withdrawn)	£25

L.A. GUNS
88	Vertigo VERH 55	**L.A. GUNS** (LP)	£20

FRANCIS LAI
67	Brunswick LAT/STA 8689	**I'LL NEVER FORGET WHAT'S 'ISNAME** (LP, soundtrack)	£50
69	United Artists SULP 1231	**HANNIBAL BROOKS** (LP)	£30
69	Philips SBL 7876	**MAYERLING** (LP)	£20
70	United Artists UAS 29137	**RIDER IN THE RAIN** (LP)	£25

LAIBACH
86	Cherry Red BRED 67	**NOVA AKROPOLA** (LP)	£15
86	Side Effects SER 08	**OCCUPIED EUROPE TOUR '85** (LP)	£15
87	Mute STUMM 44	**OPUS DEI** (LP)	£20
88	Mute STUMM 58	**LET IT BE** (LP)	£15
92	Mute STUMM 82	**KAPITAL** (2-LP, printed inners)	£50
94	Mute STUMM 121	**NATO** (LP)	£50
96	Mute STUMM 136	**JESUS CHRIST SUPERSTARS** (LP)	£80
03	Mute STUMM 223	**WAT** (2-LP)	£100
14	Mute STUMM358	**SPECTRE** (LP & CD)	£20
18	Mute STUMM430	**THE SOUND OF MUSIC** (LP, gold vinyl)	£20

LAIKA
94	Too Pure PURE 42	**SILVER APPLES ON THE MOON** (LP)	£30
97	Too Pure PURE 62	**SOUNDS OF THE SATELLITES** (2-LP)	£30
00	Too Pure PURE 89	**GOOD LOOKING BLUES** (2-LP)	£30

CLEO LAINE
71	Philips 6006 077	**Model City's Programme/Night Owl**	£50
57	Pye Nixa Jazz NJE 1026	**THE APRIL AGE** (EP, as Cleo Laine & Dave Lee Quintet)	£20
57	Esquire EP 102	**CLEO LAINE** (EP, as Cleo Laine & Keith Christie Quintet)	£20
57	Esquire EP 122	**CLEO LAINE** (EP, as Cleo Laine & Keith Christie Quintet)	£20
55	Esquire 15-007	**CLEO LAINE** (10" LP)	£40
58	Pye Nixa NPT 19024	**CLEO'S CHOICE** (10" LP)	£40
58	MGM MGM-C 765	**SHE'S THE TOPS** (LP)	£25
62	Fontana 680 992 TL	**ALL ABOUT ME** (LP, also stereo 886 159 TY)	£15
64	Fontana (S)TL 5209	**SHAKESPEARE AND ALL THAT JAZZ** (LP)	£15
66	Fontana (S)TL 5316	**WOMAN TALK** (LP)	£15
68	Fontana STL 5483	**SOLILOQUY** (LP)	£15

(see also Johnny Dankworth, Tubby Hayes & Cleo Laine, Dudley Moore)

DENNY LAINE
67	Deram DM 122	**Say You Don't Mind/Ask The People**	£15
68	Deram DM 171	**Too Much In Love/Catherine's Wheel**	£30
73	Wizard WIZ 104	**Find A Way Somehow/Move Me To Another Place**	£15
73	Wizard SW2 2001	**AHH...LAINE** (LP, yellow labels)	£20

(see also Paul McCartney/Wings, Balls, Trevor Burton, Magic Christians, Ginger Baker's Airforce, BL&G)

LINDA LAINE (& SINNERS)
64	Columbia DB 7204	**Doncha Know, Doncha Know, Doncha Know/Ain't That Fun**	£20
64	Columbia DB 7370	**Low Grades And High Fever/After Today**	£20
65	Columbia DB 7549	**Don't Do It Baby/All I Want To Do Is Run**	£20

SCOTT LAINE
63	Windsor WB 114	**Tearaway Johnnie/John Silver**	£40

DENZIL LAING
71	Songbird SB 1054	**Medicine Stick/CRYSTALITES: Short Cut**	£15

(see also Soul Vendors, Dennis Alcapone)

ALAN LAKE
70	Ember EMB S 278	**Good Times/Got To Have Tenderness** (p/s)	£15

BONNIE LAKE & HER BEAUX
56	Brunswick 05622	**Thirteen Black Cats/The Miracle Of Love**	£20

(see also Jack Pleis)

LAKELANDERS
60s		**THE LAKELANDERS IN CONCERT** (LP, hand-typed labels)	£80

JOYCE LALOR
66	Airbourne NBP 006	**Carribean Child/Evening Time** (with the Fabulous Frats Quintet)	£30

LEE LAMAR & HIS ORCHESTRA
57	London HLB 8508	**Teenage Pedal Pushers/Sophia**	£75

GENE LAMARR
72	Injun 112	**You Don't Love Me Anymore/Crazy Little House On The Hill**	£15

LAMB
96	Fontana PY 281	**LAMB** (2-LP, inner)	£30
99	Mercury 558 821-1	**FEAR OF FOURS** (2-LP)	£30

MINT VALUE £

01	Mercury 586 4351	**WHAT SOUND** (2-LP)...	£60
03	Mercury 986 591-7	**BETWEEN DARKNESS AND WONDER** (LP)........................	£25

CHRIS LAMB & UNIVERSALS
65	Decca F 12176	**Mysterious Land/If You Ask Me**	£15

(see also Universals, Gidian)

KEVIN LAMB
72	Birth RAB 4	**WHO IS THE HERO?** (LP, white label with 'rabbit' child logo)	£40

LAMBCHOP
10	City Slang SLANG 0680056	**TOUR BOX** (8-CD, 2-DVD in canvas box, 1000 only sold on 2010 tour).............	£90

JEANNIE LAMBE
67	CBS 202636	**Miss Disc/Montano Blues** (with Gordon Beck Orchestra)......	£25
67	CBS 2731	**Day After Day After Day/City At Night**	£20

DAVE LAMBERT, JON HENDRICKS & ANNIE ROSS
60	Philips BBL 7368	**DAVE LAMBERT, JON HENDRICKS & ANNIE ROSS** (LP, stereo SBBL 562)............	£15

(see also Annie Ross)

LAMBERT & NUTTYCOMBE
70	A&M AMLS 997	**AT HOME** (LP)...	£60

LAMBRETTAS
79	Rocket XPRES 23	**Go Steady/Listen Listen/Cortinas** (p/s).....................	£15
80	Rocket XPRES 25	**Poison Ivy/Runaround** (with '2-Stroke' die-cut sleeve & label)	£20
80	Rocket XPRES 36	**Page 3/Steppin' Out** (Of Line) (withdrawn; one copy known to exist with p/s)............£1000	
80	Rocket TRAIN 10	**BEAT BOYS IN THE JET AGE** (LP, with inner)	£15

LAME DUCK
73	Perth PR 001	**Sitting Still/Hold Out Your Hand**	£25

LAMELLA
80	Direct DO B1	**When Julie Dances/Wasting Your Time** (no p/s, 500 only).............	£50

TONI LAMOND
68	Philips BF 1722	**Silent Voices/They Don't Give Medals** (To Yesterday's Heroes)...........	£15

DUNCAN LAMONT
68	Morgan MRSAM 2	**THIS GUY** (LP)...	£15

LA MORTGAGE
79	Metro 0501/EJSP 9289	**Fallin/The Shady Lane** (p/s).......................................	£30

LAMPLIGHTERS
55	Parlophone DP 416	**Salty Dog/Ride Jockey Ride** (78, export issue)	£40

(see also Thurston Harris)

LAMP SISTERS
68	Sue WI 4048	**A Woman With The Blues/I Thought It Was All Over**...........	£40

LANA SISTERS
58	Fontana H 148	**Ring-A My Phone/Chimes Of Arcady**	£25
59	Fontana H 176	**Buzzin'/Cry, Cry, Baby**...	£25
59	Fontana H 176	**Buzzin'/Cry, Cry, Baby** (78)	£15
59	Fontana H 190	**Mister Dee-Jay/Tell Him No**	£25
59	Fontana H 221	(Seven Little Girls) **Sitting In The Back Seat** (with Al Saxon)/ **Sitting On The Sidewalk**.....	£20
59	Fontana H 221	(Seven Little Girls) **Sitting In The Back Seat** (with Al Saxon)/ **Sitting On The Sidewalk** (78).............	£15

(see also Al Saxon, Dusty Springfield, Chantelles)

LANCASHIRE FAYRE
80	Folk Heritage FHR 113	**LANCASHIRE FAYRE** (LP)...	£20

STEVE LANCASTER
67	Polydor 56215	**San Francisco Street/Miguel Fernando San Sebastian Brown**	£15

LANCASTRIANS
64	Pye 7N 15732	**We'll Sing In The Sunshine/Was She Tall**	£20
66	Pye 7N 17043	**The World Keeps Going Round/Not The Same Anymore**...........	£40

MAJOR LANCE
63	Columbia DB 7099	**The Monkey Time/Mama Didn't Know**	£35
63	Columbia DB 7099	**The Monkey Time/Mama Didn't Know** (DJ copy)............	£60
63	Columbia DB 7168	**Hey Little Girl/Crying In The Rain**...........................	£25
64	Columbia DB 7205	**Um, Um, Um, Um, Um, Um/Sweet Music**	£30
64	Columbia DB 7271	**The Matador/Gonna Get Married**	£40
64	Columbia DB 7365	**Rhythm/Please Don't Say No More**	£40
65	Columbia DB 7463	**I'm So Lost/Sometimes I Wonder**	£35
65	Columbia DB 7527	**Come See/You Belong To Me, My Love**	£40
65	Columbia DB 7609	**Pride And Joy/I'm The One**	£60
65	Columbia DB 7688	**Too Hot To Hold/Dark And Lonely**	£80
65	Columbia DB 7787	**Everybody Loves A Good Time/I Just Can't Help It**	£30
65	Columbia DB 7787	**Everybody Loves A Good Time/I Just Can't Help It** (DJ Copy)............	£75
66	Columbia DB 7967	**Investigate/Little Young Lover**	£100
66	Columbia DB 7967	**Investigate/Little Young Lover** (DJ copy)	£200
67	Columbia DB 8122	**Ain't No Soul** (Left In These Ole Shoes)/**You'll Want Me Back**............	£100
67	Columbia DB 8122	**Ain't No Soul** (Left In These Ole Shoes)/**You'll Want Me Back** (DJ copy)	£175
69	Atlantic 584 277	**Follow The Leader/Since You've Been Gone**	£15
69	Atlantic 584 302	**Sweeter As The Days Go By/Shadows Of A Memory**	£20
69	Soul City SC 114	**The Beat/You'll Want Me Back**	£25

MINT VALUE £

70	Buddah 2011 046	Gypsy Woman/Stay Away From Me	£15
72	Stax 2025 124	I Wanna Make Up/That's The Story Of My Life	£15
73	Contempo C 26	Dark And Lonely/My Girl	£20
74	Warner Bros K 16385	Without A Doubt/Open The Door To Your Heart	£15
74	Contempo CS 2017	Gimme Little Sign/How Can You Say Goodbye	£25
75	Contempo CS 2045	Don't You Know I Love You (Parts 1 & 2)	£20
75	Pye 7N 45487	You're Everything I Need (Parts 1 & 2)	£15
64	Columbia SEG 8318	UM UM UM UM UM UM (EP)	£100
65	Columbia 33SX 1728	THE RHYTHM OF MAJOR LANCE (LP)	£150
73	Contempo COLP 1001	GREATEST HITS LIVE AT THE TORCH (LP, sitting under a tree is first pressing)	£50

RICK LANCELOT & SEVEN KNIGHTS
66	RCA RCA 1502	Say Girl/Live Like A Lion	£15

LANCERS
54	London HL 8027	Stop Chasin' Me Baby/Peggy O'Neil	£15
54	London HL 8079	So High, So Low, So Wide/It's You, It's You I Love	£15
54	Vogue Coral Q 2038	Mister Sandman/The Little White Light	£15
55	Vogue Coral Q 72062	Timberjack/C-r-a-z-y Music	£20
55	Vogue Coral Q 72081	Get Out Of The Car (as Lancers & Georgie Auld)/Close Your Eyes	£20
56	Vogue Coral Q 72128	Alphabet Rock/Rock Around The Island	£40
55	London REP 1027	PRESENTING THE LANCERS (EP)	£20
54	London H-APB 1029	OH SWEET MAMA (10" LP)	£25
61	London HA-P 2307	CONCERT IN CONTRASTS (LP)	£15

HAROLD LAND
58	Contemporary LAC 12178	HAROLD IN THE LAND OF JAZZ (LP)	£15

BOB LANDER & SPOTNICKS
62	Oriole CB 1784	Midnight Special/My Old Kentucky Home	£15

(see also Spotnicks)

BILL & BRETT LANDIS
59	Parlophone R 4516	Since You've Gone/Bright Eyes	£15
59	Parlophone R 4570	Baby Talk/Love Me True	£15

JERRY LANDIS
62	Oriole CB 1930	Carlos Dominguez/He Was My Brother	£40

(see also Paul Simon)

JOYA LANDIS
68	Trojan TR 620	Kansas City/Out The Light	£20
68	Trojan TR 622	Angel Of The Morning/ALTON PHILLIPS: Love Letters	£40
69	Trojan TR 641	Moonlight Lover/I Love You True	£45

(see also Jay & Joya, Hugh Roy)

HOAGY LANDS
67	Stateside SS 2030	The Next In Line/Please Don't Talk About Me When I'm Gone	£250
67	Stateside SS 2030	The Next In Line/Please Don't Talk About Me When I'm Gone (DJ copy)	£400
68	Stateside SS 2085	I'm Yours/Only You	£20
72	Action ACT 4605	Why Didn't You Let Me Know/Do You Know What Life Is All About	£35
75	UK USA 13	Friends And Lovers Don't Go Together/True Love At Last	£30

NEIL LANDSTRUMM
95	Mosquito MSQ 02	PASCAL EP (12", custom sleeve)	£20

(see also Blue Arsed Fly)

ANITA LANE
93	Mute STUMM 81	DIRTY PEARL (LP)	£35

GARY LANE & GARRISONS
61	Fontana H 338	Start Walking Boy/How Wrong Can You Be	£15

LOIS LANE
68	Mercury SMCL 20125	LOIS LANE (LP)	£20

(see also Caravelles)

MICKEY LEE LANE
64	Stateside SS 354	Shaggy Dog/Oo Oo	£20
65	Stateside SS 456	Hey Sah-Lo-Ney/Of Yesterday	£75
65	Stateside SS 456	Hey Sah-Lo-Ney/Of Yesterday (DJ copy)	£150

RONNIE LANE & SLIM CHANCE
74	GML 1013	ANYMORE FOR ANYMORE (LP)	£30
75	Island ILPS 9321	RONNIE LANE AND SLIM CHANCE (LP, gatefold)	£30
75	Island ILPS 9366	ONE FOR THE ROAD (LP)	£20
76	Atlantic K 50308	MAHONEY'S LAST STAND (LP, with Ron Wood, soundtrack)	£15
80	Gem GEMLP 107	SEE ME (LP, with insert)	£15

(see also Small Faces, Faces, Pete Townshend & Ronnie Lane)

TONY LANE & DELTONES
64	Sabre SA-45-5	It's Great/Now She's Mine	£30

PATTIE LANE
68	Polydor 56260	Paper Dreams/My Four Walls	£40

MARK LANEGAN
99	Beggars Banquet BBQLP215	I'LL TAKE CARE OF YOU (LP)	£70
03	Beggars Banquet BBQ 373T	THERE COMES THAT WEIRD CHILL (10" LP, as Mark Lanegan Band)	£60
04	Beggars Banquet BBQLP 237	BUBBLEGUM (LP, as Mark Lanegan Band)	£70

(see also Screaming Trees, Soulsavers, Isobel Campbell & Mark Lanegan)

DON LANG (& HIS "FRANTIC" FIVE)
56	HMV 7M 354	Four Brothers/I Want You To Be My Baby (solo)	£30
56	HMV 7M 381	Rock Around The Island/Jumpin' To Conclusions (solo)	£30
56	HMV 7M 416	Rock And Roll Blues/Stop The World I Wanna Get Off (solo)	£30
56	HMV POP 260	Sweet Sue - Just You/Lazy Latin (solo)	£20
57	HMV POP 289	Rock Around The Cookhouse/Rock Mister Piper	£30
57	HMV POP 335	Rock-A-Billy/Come Go With Me (B-side with Skifflers)	£30
57	HMV POP 350	School Day (Ring! Ring! Goes The Bell)/Six-Five Special	£30
57	HMV POP 382	White Silver Sands/Again 'N' Again 'N' Again	£15
57	HMV POP 414	Red Planet Rock/Texas Tambourine	£25
58	HMV POP 434	Ramshackle Daddy/6-5 Hand Jive	£25
58	HMV POP 465	Tequila/Junior Hand Jive	£25
58	HMV POP 465	Tequila/Junior Hand Jive (78)	£15
58	HMV POP 547	Queen Of The Hop/La-Do-Da-Da (solo)	£15
59	HMV POP 585	Wiggle Wiggle/(You Were Only) Teasin' (solo)	£15
59	HMV POP 623	Percy Green/Phineas McCoy (solo)	£15
59	HMV POP 682	Reveille Rock/Frankie And Johnny	£15
60	HMV POP 714	Sink The Bismarck!/They Call Him Cliff (solo)	£30
60	HMV POP 805	Time Machine/Don't Open That Door	£15
57	HMV 7EG 8208	ROCK 'N' ROLL (EP)	£100
57	HMV DLP 1151	SKIFFLE SPECIAL (LP, 10", by Don Lang & His Skiffle Group)	£120
58	HMV DLP 1179	INTRODUCING THE HAND JIVE (LP, 10")	£150
62	Ace Of Clubs ACL 1111	TWENTY TOP-TWENTY TWISTS (LP)	£20

(see also Gordon Langhorn)

EDDIE LANG & LONNIE JOHNSON
67	Parlophone PMC 7019	BLUE GUITARS (LP)	£20
70	Parlophone PMC 7106	BLUE GUITARS VOLUME 2 (LP)	£20

(see also Blind Willie Dunn's Gin Bottle Four)

GORDON LANGHORN
55	Decca F 10591	Give A Fool A Chance/Don't Stay Away Too Long	£15

(see also Don Lang, Cyril Stapleton)

PERPETUAL LANGLEY
66	Planet PLF 110	We Wanna Stay Home/So Sad	£40
66	Planet PLF 115	Surrender/Two By Two	£150

(HUW) LLOYD LANGTON (GROUP)
83	Flicknife SHARP 015	OUTSIDE THE LAW (LP, 1,000 with bonus 7": "Working Time"/ I See You [FREE 001], as Huw Lloyd Langton)	£15

(see also Hawkwind, Widowmaker)

PHIL LANGTON TRIO
60s	Holyground	PHIL LANGTON TRIO (LP)	£18

SNOOKY LANSON
56	London HLD 8223	It's Almost Tomorrow/Why Don't You Write	£100
56	London HLD 8236	Stop (Let Me Off The Bus)/Last Minute Love	£200
56	London HLD 8249	Seven Days/Tippity Top	£200
56	London HL 7005	Seven Days/Tippity Top (export issue)	£80

(see also Teresa Brewer)

JENNIFER LARA
79	Hit Run HIT DD 14	Jah Will Lead Us Home/RANKING PURPLE: Ah Fi We Jah (12")	£60

LARAAJI
80	Editions EG EGAMB 003	AMBIENT 3 - DAY OF RADIANCE (LP)	£15
10	Universal Sound USLP 30	CELESTRAL VIBRATION (LP, reissue)	£15
13	All Saints WAST 037LP	ESSENCE/UNIVERSAL (LP, reissue, clear vinyl)	£18

LARD
89	Alternative Tentacles VIRUS 72T	POWER OF LARD (12" EP)	£15
90	Alternative Tentacles VIRUS 84	LAST TEMPTATION OF REID (LP, with free 12")	£20

PHILIP LARKIN
58	Mervell Press	LESS DECEIVED (LP, 100 only, numbered)	£125
68	Listen	LESS DECEIVED (LP)	£40
75	Argo PLP 1202	HIGH WINDOWS (LP)	£25

LARKS (1)
64	Pye International 7N 25284	The Jerk/Forget Me	£50
64	Pye International 7N 25284	The Jerk/Forget Me (DJ copy)	£80

LARKS (2)
87	Exaltation 12LARX 3	PAIN IN THE NECK EP (12", p/s)	£20
87	Exaltation LARX 3	Pain In The Neck/I Am A Clean Boy	£20

JULIUS LA ROSA
55	London HL 8154	Mobile/Pass It On	£15
55	London HLA 8170	Domani/Mama Rosa	£15
55	London HLA 8193	Suddenly There's A Valley/Everytime I Kiss Carrie	£15
56	London HLA 8272	No Other Love/Rosanne	£15
57	London HA-A 2031	JULIUS LA ROSA (LP)	£20

LARRY'S ALL STARS
71	Ackee ACK 125	In The Fields/Teardrops Got The Feeling	£15

MINT VALUE £

71	Ackee ACK 130	Pre-Fight/The Prayer	£20

(see also Larry Lawrence, Delroy Wilson, Hugh Roy, Sensations)

LARRY (MARSHALL) & ALVIN

68	Studio One SO 2065	Nanny Goat/Smell You Crep	£30
68	Studio One SO 2067	Can't You Understand/Hush Up	£70
69	Studio One SO 2080	Lonely Room (No One To Give Me Love)/You Mean To Me	£45
69	Coxsone CS 7081	Love Got Me/BOB ANDY: Lady With The Bright Light (both sides actually by Glen [Brown] & Dave [Barker])	£150
70	Bamboo BAM 22	Girl Of My Dream/SOUND DIMENTION: Give It Away	£60

(see also Larry Marshall, Sound Dimension, Vincent Gordon)

LARRY & JOHNNY

65	Outasite 45 501	Beatle Time Parts 1 & 2 (99 copies only)	£150

(see also Larry Williams & Johnny 'Guitar' Watson)

LARRY & TOMMY

68	Polydor 56741	You've Gotta Bend A Little/Yo-Yo (A side written and produced by John Cale)	£35

KIM LARSEN & JUNGLE DREAMS

82	CBS A 2232	Rock 'N' Roll City/Time Bomb	£20

LAS

14	System SYSTM 004	FIREPUSHER EP (12" with GANTZ)	£20
14	System SYSTM 007	Backyard/Tic (12")	£30
17	System SYSTM 016	Crowded/Recsystem (12")	£20

LA'S

88	Go! Discs GOLAS 2	There She Goes/Come In Come Out (red p/s)	£15
89	Go! Discs GOLAS 3	Timeless Melody/Clean Prophet (p/s, unissued; 10 test pressings only)	£60
89	Go! Discs LASEP 3	Timeless Melody (10", unissued)	£0
89	Go! Discs LASDJ 312	Timeless Melody/Clean Prophet/Knock Me Down/Over (12", promo, 500 only)	£15
91	Go! Discs 828 202-1	THE LA'S (LP)	£50
99	Viper VLP 002	LOST LA's 1984-1986 BREAKLOOSE (LP)	£20
01	Viper VLP 008	LOST LA's 1986-1987: CALLIN' ALL (LP)	£20
17	Viper VIPERLP 124	1987 (LP)	£20

(see also Cast)

BONGO LES (CHEN) & BUNNY (HERMAN)

72	Attack ATT 8041	Feel Nice (Version)/WINSTON SCOTLAND: Quick And Slick	£20

(see also Bongo Herman)

DENISE LASALLE

71	Janus 6310206	TRAPPED BY A THING CALLED LOVE (LP)	£25
72	Westbound 6309 102	DOIN' IT RIGHT (LP)	£20

LAST DINNER PARTY

23	Island 5556335	Nothing Matters/Prelude To Ecstasy (p/s, ltd ed.)	£30
24	Island 6508055	PRELUDE TO ESCTASY (LP/CD,'Roundhouse edition',alternate artwork, ltd to 500 copies))	£150
24	Island BLOOD 269	PRELUDE TO ESCTASY (LP, red wine stain vinyl, numbered ltd ed of 2000)	£60

LAST EXIT

75	Wudwink WUD 01	Whispering Voices/Evensong (no p/s, push-out centre)	£60
79	Wudwink WUD 01	Whispering Voices/Evensong (reissue, solid centre)	£30
75	Wudwink WUD.C.101	FIRST FROM LAST EXIT (cassette only, pink card insert, sold at gigs, only 3 copies known to exist)	£500

(see also Newcastle Big Band, Police, Sting)

LAST MAN IN EUROPE

85	Cocteau CO 22	A Certain Bridge/TV Addict (p/s)	£18

LAST POETS

72	Douglas DGL 69012	THIS IS MADNESS (LP)	£30

LAST RESORT (1)

78	Red Meat RMRS 01	Having Fun?/F.U.2 (die-cut printed paper sleeve)	£30

LAST RESORT (2)

82	Last Resort LR 1	SKINHEAD ANTHEMS (LP, red vinyl)	£30
82	Last Resort LR 1	SKINHEAD ANTHEMS (LP, white vinyl)	£30
82	Last Resort LR 1	SKINHEAD ANTHEMS (LP, blue vinyl)	£30
82	Last Resort LR 1	SKINHEAD ANTHEMS (LP, black vinyl)	£40

LAST RITES

83	Flicknife FLS 219	We Don't Care/Step Down (p/s)	£20
84	Essential 004	FASCISM MEANS WAR (No Right To Take/Convicted Without Trial/Protest And Survive/The Dreams Of Many) (EP, gatefold p/s)	£25
84	Essential 001	THIS IS THE REACTION (LP)	£30

LAST ROUGH CAUSE

85	LRC 001	THE VIOLENT FEW (EP, with lyric sheet)	£40

LAST STAND

81	Silly Symbol SJP 825	Just A Number/Caviare (p/s)	£40

LAST STRAW

78	Solent SS 049	Oh Lady/Fly By Night (p/s)	£50

LAST WORDS

81	Armageddon ARM 2	THE LAST WORDS (LP)	£15

LAST LAUGH

85	Hmmm! HA 1	GLEE SWITCH EP	£25

LAST SHADOW PUPPETS
08	Domino WIGLP 208	AGE OF THE UNDERSTATEMENT (LP, insert)	£20
16	Domino WIGLP371X	EVERYTHING YOU'VE COME TO EXPECT (LP/yellow vinyl 7", tip on gatefold sleeve, 32 page booklet, ltd. ed))	£80

(see also Arctic Monkeys)

BILL LASWELL
84	Rough Trade ROUGH 51	BASELINES (LP)	£15
88	Venture VE12	HEAR NO EVIL (LP)	£25

(see also Material)

LATE ARRIVALS
67	Highlight HL1	No One Cares/Voices Above	£25

LATE OF THE PIER
08	EMI 228 0331	FANTASY BLACK CHANNEL (LP, inner, stickered sleeve)	£60

LATE SHOW
78	Decca F 13777	Drop Dead/Ain't Gonna Stamp On His Face (p/s)	£15

YUSEF LATEEF
58	Esquire 32-069	THE SOUNDS OF YUSEF (LP)	£150
58	Columbia Clef 33CX 10124	BEFORE DAWN (LP)	£50
59	Esquire 32-139	CRY! TENDER (LP)	£60
64	Realm RM 228	FABRIC OF JAZZ (LP)	£25
64	Transatlantic PR 7319	EASTERN SOUNDS (LP)	£30
67	HMV CSD 3615	THE GOLDEN FLUTE (LP)	£20
72	Atlantic K 40359	GENTLE GIANT (LP)	£20
73	Prestige PR 24007	YUSEF LATEEF (LP)	£15
74	Atlantic K 50041	PART OF THE SEARCH (LP)	£15
76	Impulse IMPL 8013	CLUB DATE (LP)	£15

THE LATHUMS
21	Island 3830562	HOW BEAUTIFUL CAN LIFE BE (2-LP, gold vinyl)	£35

LATIMORE
73	President PTLS 1058	S.T. (LP)	£15
74	President PTLS 1062	MORE MORE MORE (LP)	£15

GENE LATTER
66	Decca F 12364	Just A Minute Or Two/Dream Lover	£30
66	Decca F 12397	Mother's Little Helper/Please Come Back To Me Again	£25
67	CBS 2843	A Little Piece Of Leather/Funny Face Girl	£40
67	CBS 2843	A Little Piece Of Leather/Funny Face Girl (DJ copy)	£60
69	Spark SRL 1031	Holding A Dream/The Old Iron Bell	£350

(see also Detours)

THE LAUGHING APPLE
81	Autonomy AUT 001	HA HA HEE HEE (EP)	£15
81	Autonomy AUT 002	Participate!/Wouldn't You? (foldover p/s)	£15
82	Essential ESS 001	Precious Feeling/Celebration (p/s)	£15

(see also Biff Bang Pow!, Revolving Paint Dream)

LAUGHING MOTHERS
85	Motherkare MUM 1	Tunnel/Cats Cradle (p/s)	£20

LAUREL (AITKEN) & OWEN (GRAY)
62	Blue Beat BB 149	She's Going To Napoli/Have Mercy Mr Percy	£15

(see also Laurel Aitken, Owen Gray)

LAURELS
68	RCA Victor RCA 1741	Sunshine Thursday/Threepence A Tune	£15
69	RCA Victor RCA 1836	Making It Groovy/Rainmaker	£40
71	Pye 45034	The Devil's Well/Underground	£60

JOHN LAURENZ
55	London HL 8138	Goodbye, Stranger, Goodbye/Red Roses	£20

MISS LAVELL
65	Vocalion VP 9236	Everybody's Got Somebody/The Best Part Of Me	£25

ROGER LA VERN & MICRONS
63	Decca F 11791	Christmas Stocking/Reindeer Ride	£25

(see also Tornados)

BETTY LAVETTE
67	Stateside SS 2015	I Feel Good All Over/Only Your Love Can Save Me	£60
67	Stateside SS 2015	I Feel Good All Over/Only Your Love Can Save Me (DJ copy)	£75
68	Pama PM 748	Only Your Love Can Save Me/I Feel Good All Over (reissue)	£60
72	Mojo 2092 030	Let Me Down Easy/I Feel Good All Over/What I Don't Know Won't Hurt Me	£20

LAW AND AUDER
95	Sub + Bleep BLEEP 12 002	Gimme (The Weed) (Mix 1)/(Mix 2)/Cant Tekkie (12")	£25
95	Sub + Bleep BLEEP 12 003	Sunshine/Lively Body (12")	£20
95	G-Fource 951	Feel It/Acid Jungle (12", white label)	£80
95	G-Fource 952	Who Gose/Untitled (12", white label)	£35
95	G-Fource 953	Too Right/Untitled (12", white label)	£40
95	Slamming Wreck SLAM 003	It's Alright/Bust The New Jam (12", stamped white labels)	£15

LAW (THE)
79	Smile SR011	Be My Girl/Dead City Kicks/I Just Want Your Body (500 pressed)	£50

MINT VALUE £

GASPAR LAWAL
80   Cap   AJOMASE (LP) £20

AZIE LAWRENCE
60   Starlite ST45 022   West Indians In England/Jump Up (with Carib Serenaders) £15
64   Blue Beat BB 222   Pempelem/Lovers Understand £400

DIANE LAWRENCE
67   Doctor Bird DB 1075   I Won't Hang Around Like A Hound Dog/Read It Over £35

EARL LAWRENCE
85   Ariwa ARI 44   Dancing On A Bassline/Dancing On A Bassline (Version) (12") £80

LARRY LAWRENCE (JAMAICA)
63   Island WI 091   Garden Of Eden/DERRICK MORGAN: Sendin' This Message....................£15
(see also Larry's Allstars, McBean Scott & Champions)

LARRY LAWRENCE (U.S.)
60   Ember EMB S 106   Squad Car Theme/Jug-A-Roo (with Beatniks, in art p/s).......................£15

LEE LAWRENCE (& CORONETS)
57   Columbia DB 3855   Rock 'n' Roll Opera/Don't Nobody Move £40

ZACK LAWRENCE
73   Pemini Organisation   ASSASSIN EP (with p/s) £70
73   Pemini Organisation   ASSASSIN EP (without p/s) £30

LAWRENCE AND COMFORTABLE SOCIETY
86   LC LC 1   Sleeper/Heartache (handmade p/s) £225

BILLY (M.) LAWRIE
69   Polydor 56363   Roll Over Beethoven/Come Back Joanna (as Billy M. Lawrie) £25
73   RCA SF 8395   SHIP IMAGINATION (LP, die-cut gatefold sleeve)...........................£25

JOHN LAWSON
79   SRTX 79 CUS 617 FMR 024   1 X 6 (LP) £25

JULIET LAWSON
72   Sovereign SVNA 7257   BOO (LP, textured gatefold sleeve) £200
(see also Trees)

SHIRLEY LAWSON
68   Soul City SC 108   The Star/One More Chance £200

LAWSON-HAGGART ROCKIN' BAND
59   Brunswick OE 9451   BOPPING AT THE HOP (EP) £15
59   Brunswick STA 3010   BOPPING AT THE HOP (LP) £30

LOU LAWTON
67   Ember EMB S 232   Doin' The Philly Dog/I Am Searching £30
68   Speciality SPE 1005   I'm Just A Fool/Wrapped In A Dream £30

LAXTON & OLIVER
69   Blue Cat BS 168   Wickeder/Stay In My Arms £20

OSSIE LAYNE
65   R&B MRB 5006   Come Back/Never Answer That 'Phone £35

PAUL LAYTON
68   Paradox PAR 45901   Mister Mister/Sing Sadman Sing (p/s) £25

KEN LAZ(A)RUS (& CREW)
65   Island WI 220   Funny (as Ken Lazrus & Byron Lee Orchestra)/ BYRON LEE ORCHESTRA: Walk Like A
                                               Dragon £15
70   London HA-J 8412   REGGAE SCORCHER (LP, unissued) £0
70   London ZGJ 107   REGGAE - GREATEST HITS VOL. 1 (LP) £20

PETER LAZONBY
96   Brainiak BRAINK 40R   Wavespeech (12") £30

LAZY FOUR
79   SGS SGS 110   Callow Capital/I Won't Shed A Tear £15

LAZY LATINS
67   Morgan MR 110 P   LAZY LATIN (LP) £15

LAZY SMOKE
80s Heyoka   CORRIDOR OF FACES (LP, reissue of U.S. LP)..............................£15

LCD SOUNDSYSTEM
05   DFA DFAEMIDJ 2138LP   LCD SOUNDSYSTEM (2-LP promo, die-cut sleeve)............................£35
05   DFA DFAEMI2138LP   LCD SOUNDSYSTEM (2-LP)...£30
07   EMI DFAEMI 2163lp   45:33 (2 x 12")..£15
07   EMI 0946 3 85114 1 0   SOUND OF SILVER (2-LP, inners, poster) £30
10   DFA DFA 22502   THIS IS HAPPENING (2-LP) £25
14   DFA DFA2362LP   THE LONG GOODBYE - LCD LIVE AT MADISON SQUARE GARDEN (5-LP box set) £150

LE TIGRE
99   Wiiija WIJ LP 1108   LE TIGRE (LP) £35

BARBARA LEA
56   London HB-U 1058   A WOMAN IN LOVE (10" LP)...£20
56   Esquire 32/043   NOBODY ELSE BUT ME (LP) £20
57   Esquire 32/063   IN LOVE (LP) £20

JIMMY LEA
85   Trojan KANE 001   Citizen Kane/Poland (p/s) £15

(see also Slade)

LEADBELLY (HUDDIE LEDBETTER)

EPs

| 62 | Storyville SEP 387 | STORYVILLE BLUES ANTHOLOGY VOL. 7 | £15 |

ALBUMS

53	Capitol LC 6597	LEADBELLY SINGS CLASSICS IN JAZZ (10")	£40
57	Melodisc MLP 511	LEADBELLY VOL. 1 (10", green & silver labels)	£30
57	Melodisc MLP 512	LEADBELLY VOL. 2 (10", green & silver labels)	£30
58	Melodisc MLP 515	LEADBELLY VOL. 3 (10", green & silver labels)	£30
58	Melodisc MLP 517	PLAYS PARTY SONGS (10", green & silver labels)	£30
58	Melodisc MLP 12-107	THE SAGA OF LEADBELLY (green & silver or blue & black labels)	£20
59	Melodisc MLP 12-113	LEADBELLY'S LAST SESSIONS VOLUME 2 PART 1	£20
59	Melodisc MLP 12-114	LEADBELLY'S LAST SESSIONS VOLUME 2 PART 2	£20
62	Storyville SLP 124	A DEMON OF A MAN - BLUES ANTHOLOGY	£20
63	Storyville SLP 139	LEADBELLY 2 - T.B. BLUES	£20
63	Capitol T 1821	HIS GUITAR, HIS VOICE, HIS PIANO: HUDDIE LEDBETTER'S BEST	£15
63	RCA Victor RD 7567	GOOD MORNING BLUES	£20
65	Verve (S)VLP 5002	TAKE THIS HAMMER	£20
66	Elektra EKL 301/2	THE LIBRARY OF CONGRESS RECORDINGS (3-LP)	£30
67	Verve (S)VLP 5011	KEEP YOUR HANDS OFF HER	£15
69	Xtra XTRA 1046	LEADBELLY SINGS FOLK SONGS	£18
69	Xtra XTRA 1126	SHOUT ON	£15

LEADERS (JAMAICA)

| 68 | Amalgamated AMG 804 | Tit For Tat (actually by Lynn Taitt & Jets)/MARVETTS: You Take Too Long | £35 |

(see also Pioneers, Stranger Cole)

LEADING FIGURES

| 67 | Deram DML/SML 1006 | OSCILLATION 67! (LP) | £65 |
| 67 | Ace Of Clubs ACL 1225/SCL 1225 | SOUND AND MOVEMENT (LP, mono/stereo) | £65 |

(see also Jon Lord, Deep Purple)

LEAF HOUND

| 05 | Rise Above 7/68 | Freelance Fiend/Too Many Rock N Roll Times | £40 |
| 71 | Decca SKL-R 5094 | GROWERS OF MUSHROOM (LP) | £2500 |

(see also Brunning Sunflower Blues Band, Black Cat Bones, Atomic Rooster, Cactus)

LEAF DOG

| 14 | High Focus HFRFP003 | FROM A SCARECROW'S PERSPECTIVE (2-LP) | £35 |

LEAGUE

| 67 | President PT 167 | Nothing On/Hey Conductor | £25 |

LEAGUE OF GENTLEMEN (1)

| 65 | Columbia DB 7666 | Each Little Falling Tear/And I Do Now | £70 |
| 66 | Planet PLF 109 | How Can You Tell/How Do They Know (with Planet company sleeve) | £100 |

LEAGUE OF GENTLEMEN (2)

| 80 | Editions EG EGEDS 1 | Heptaparaparshinokh/ROBERT FRIPP: Marriagemuzic | £15 |
| 81 | Editions EG EGED 9 | THE LEAGUE OF GENTLEMEN (LP,postcard) | £25 |

(see also Giles Giles & Fripp, King Crimson, Robert Fripp, Brain, XTC, Gang of 4)

LEAGUE OF NATIONS

| 84 | Glaze GZLP 102 | MUSIC FOR THE NEW DEPRESSION (LP) | £50 |

BOB LEAPER

| 65 | Pye 7N 15700 | High Wire (Theme From 'Danger Man')/The Lost World | £40 |
| 64 | Decca LK 4639 | BIG BAND, BEATLE SONGS (LP) | £20 |

LEAPERS CREEPERS SLEEPERS

| 66 | Island WI 275 | Precious Words/Ba Boo | £30 |

KEVIN 'KING' LEAR

67	Polydor 56203	Count Me Out/Pretty Woman	£15
68	Page One POF 087	Power Of Love/Mr. Pearly	£20
68	Page One POF 109	Cry Me A River/Shoe Shine Sam	£20
69	Page One POF 132	The Snake/Man In The Funnies	£15

LEARGO

| 79 | Motor City DNS 87903 | The Artist/Played Out Angel (p/s) | £40 |

LEATHERCOATED MINDS

| 67 | Fontana (S)TL 5412 | A TRIP DOWN THE SUNSET STRIP (LP) | £80 |

(see also J.J. Cale)

LEATHERFACE

90	Roughneck HYPE 1	Razor Blades And Asprin/Colorado Joe, Leningrad Vlad/Post War Product Of A Fat Man's Wallet	£15
90	Meantime COXEP 3	BEERPIG (EP, with insert)	£30
91	Roughneck HYPE 9T	NOT SUPERSTITIOUS (12" EP)	£15
93	Roughneck HYPE 22T	DO THE RIGHT THING (12", pls)	£15
89	Meantime COX 017	CHERRY KNOWLE (LP)	£20
90	Roughneck NECKLP 1	FILL YOUR BOOTS (LP, with insert)	£30
91	Roughneck NECKLP 5	MUSH (LP, inner)	£50
93	Roughneck NECK 11LPS	MINX (LP, with bonus 7" Can't Help Falling In Love/Dreaming (HYPE 24)	£40
93	Roughneck NECKLP 11	MINX (LP)	£30

(see also Frankie Stubbs)

LEATHERHEAD
74	Philips 6006 371	Gimme Your Money Please/Epitaph (die-cut 'Leatherhead' sleeve)	£20

LEATHER NUN
79	Industrial IR 0006	SLOW DEATH (EP)	£20
84	Criminal Damage CRI MLP 113	SLOW DEATH (Reissue, mini LP)	£25

LEA VALLEY SKIFFLE GROUP
58	Esquire EP 163	LEA VALLEY SKIFFLE GROUP (EP)	£40

LEAVES
66	Fontana TF 713	Hey Joe/Funny Little World	£40

CATE LE BON
07	Recordiau Reandomonium 70300h	No One Can Drag Me Down/Disappear (p/s, 500 only)	£20
08	Pesky Peski 009	Edrych Yn Llygaid Ceffyl Benthyg EP (10" white vinyl)	£25
12	Ovni/Turnstile OVNI 012/ 796.A032.133	CYRK II (12" EP with download)	£30
14	Turnstile TS005S1	He's Leaving/Solitude (die-cut p/s. tour 7")	£20
12	Ovni / Turnstile OVNI010LP/ 796.A028.010	CYRK (LP, with inner)	£20
13	Turnstile TS005S1	MUG MUSEUM (LP, pink vinyl with insert and CD)	£25
16	Turnstile//Caroline TS022LP	CRAB DAY (LP, with inner and download)	£20
19	Mexican Summer MEX 250	REWARD (LP, splatter vinyl, limited linked sleeve with inner and insert)	£20
22	Mexican Summer MEX 315	POMPEII (LP, pink/white marbled vinyl with inner. Mail order only)	£45
22	Mexican Summer MEX 315	POMPEII (LP, clear vinyl, Rough Trade exclusive)	£30

LECUONDA CUBAN BOYS
55	Columbia 33S 1075	BENEATH THE CUBAN MOON (10" LP)	£15

CHRIS LEDOUX
79	Westwood WRS 143	RODEO'S SINGING BRONC RIDER (LP)	£60

LED ZEPPELIN
SINGLES
69	Atlantic 584 268	Good Times, Bad Times (unissued, 1-sided EMIdisc and LDC acetates only)	£2000
69	Atlantic 584 269	Communication Breakdown/Good Times, Bad Times (unissued, promo only)	£700
69	Atlantic/Emidisc	Whole Lotta Love (Edit)/Whole Lotta Love (Edit) (Acetate)	£2000
69	Atlantic 584 309	Whole Lotta Love (Edit)/Livin' Lovin' Maid (She's A Woman) (withdrawn, large centre hole, clean label or "5th Dec 1969" stamp on label)	£600
69	Atlantic 584 309	Whole Lotta Love (Edit)/Livin' Lovin' Maid (She's A Woman) (withdrawn, solid centre with small centre hole, 1 copy known)	£1500
69	Atlantic 584 309	Whole Lotta Love (Edit)/Living Loving Maid (She's A Woman) (withdrawn, large centre hole, mispressing with Living Loving Maid labels on both sides)	£600
70	Emidisc	Immigrant Song (unissued one sided acetate, scheduled to be released as Atlantic 2091 043 on 27th November 1970)	£3000
73	Trident	D'Yer Mak'er (Unissued one sided acetate)	£1200
73	Atlantic K 10296	D'Yer Mak'er/Over The Hills And Far Away (unreleased, promo only)	£350
75	Swan Song DC 1	Trampled Underfoot/Black Country Woman (white label test pressing)	£350
75	Swan Song DC 1	Trampled Underfoot/Black Country Woman (Red label test pressing)	£500
75	Swan Song SSK 19403	Trampled underfoot/Black Country Woman (withdrawn first pressing)	£150
75	Swan Song DC 1	Trampled Underfoot/Black Country Woman (Limited edition dealer incentive promo, die-cut title sleeve)	£25
75	Swan Song SSK 19403	Trampled Underfoot/Black Country Woman (push mispressed cat. no.)	£150
79	Swan Song SSK 19421	Wearing And Tearing/Darlene (cancelled Knebworth 45, existence unconfirmed)	£0
90	Atlantic LZ 3	Stairway To Heaven/Whole Lotta Love (white label test pressing)	£350
90	Atlantic LZ 2	Stairway To Heaven/Immigrant Song/Whole Lotta Love/Good Times Bad Times (10", p/s, promo only)	£40
90	Atlantic LZ 2	Stairway To Heaven/Immigrant Song/Whole Lotta Love/Good Times Bad Times (10", test pressing, white labels)	£350
90	Atlantic CD LZ 1	Stairway To Heaven/Immigrant Song/Whole Lotta Love/Good Times Bad Times (CD, promo only, in Zeppelin-design long box)	£30
90	Atlantic LZ 3	Stairway To Heaven/Whole Lotta Love (with East West Records internal memo, 150 copies only, promo)	£175
90	Atlantic LZ 3 LC	Stairway To Heaven/Whole Lotta Love (jukebox single, push-out centre)	£30
97	Atlantic AT 0013 LC	Whole Lotta Love/Whole Lotta Love (jukebox promo)	£25
97	Atlantic AT 0031LC	Whole Lotta Love (Edit)/Whole Lotta Love (Edit) (jukebox issue, with pushout centre)	£15
03	Warner Vision PR 03945	What Is And What Should Never Be/In My Time Of Dying/Rock And Roll (DVD, promo sampler)	£25
18	Atlantic R 7566332	Rock And Roll (Sunset Sound Mix)/Friends (Olympic Studio Mix) RSD, yellow vinyl	£20

ALBUMS
69	Atlantic 588 171	LED ZEPPELIN (LP, 1st pressing, red/maroon label, turquoise sleeve lettering, "Superhype" publishing credit)	£3000
69	Atlantic 588 171	LED ZEPPELIN (LP, 2nd pressing, red/maroon label, orange sleeve lettering, "Superhype" publishing credit)	£300
69	Atlantic 588 171	LED ZEPPELIN (LP, 2nd pressing, red/maroon label, orange sleeve lettering, "Warner Bros" publishing credit)	£300
69	Atlantic 588 198	LED ZEPPELIN II (LP, 1st pressing, red/maroon label, with "Living Loving Wreck" miscredit, light brown gatefold sleeve with blue-green edge)	£500
69	Atlantic 588 198	LED ZEPPELIN II (LP, 1st pressing, red/maroon label, with "The Lemon Song" credit, light brown gatefold sleeve with blue-green edge)	£200
70	Atlantic 588 198	LED ZEPPELIN II (LP, light brown sleeve, 2nd pressing, credits "Killing Floor" instead of "The Lemon Song" on label)	£40
70	Atlantic Deluxe 2401 002	LED ZEPPELIN III (LP, 1st pressing, red/maroon label, gatefold rotating-wheel sleeve, 'Do What Thou Wilt' in run-off side 1, "Produced by Jimmy Page" and "Executive Producer Peter Grant" on top of label. Catalogue number "2401002" on label)	£400

70	Atlantic Deluxe 2401 002	LED ZEPPELIN III (LP, 2nd pressing, red/maroon label, gatefold rotating-wheel sleeve, no Peter Grant Credit. Catalogue number 2401 002 on label) £200
70	Atlantic K50002	LED ZEPPELIN III (LP, reissue, gatefold, green/orange labels) £25
71	Atlantic Deluxe 2401 012	LED ZEPPELIN IV (FOUR SYMBOLS) **(1st pressing, 1st labels, LP, gatefold sleeve, red/ maroon label with 2 'stickers' covering Peter Grant credit and also revised publishing details to "Kinney Music Ltd/Superhype Music Inc."** £500
71	Atlantic Deluxe 2401 012	LED ZEPPELIN IV (FOUR SYMBOLS) (1st Pressing, 1st labels, LP, gatefold sleeve, red/ maroon label with Peter Grant credit, 'Led Zeppelin' at bottom, "Pecko Duck" etched onto run out groove on side 1 and "Porky" on side 2. Matrix numbers A//3 and B//3) ...£400
71	Atlantic Deluxe 2401 012	LED ZEPPELIN IV (FOUR SYMBOLS) (1st pressing, 2nd labels, LP, gatefold sleeve, red/ maroon label without Peter Grant credit, 'Led Zeppelin' at top, 'Atlantic Recording' credit in central white band, full 'Kinney Music Ltd/Superhype Music Inc' credit. 'Misty Mountain Hop' spelt as 'Misty Mountain Top') £100
71	Atlantic Deluxe 2401 012	LED ZEPPELIN IV (FOUR SYMBOLS) (1st pressing, 3rd labels, with 'Misty Mountain Top' corrected to 'Misty Mountain Hop') £65
71	Atlantic Deluxe 2401 012	LED ZEPPELIN IV (FOUR SYMBOLS) (1st pressing, 4th labels, stickered sleeve, some corrected pressings with a sticker on the sleeve that has the Atlantic logo, K50008, audio information and record label credits) £75
72	Atlantic K50008	LED ZEPPELIN IV (FOUR SYMBOLS) (2nd pressing, first green/orange labels, no four symbols, 'Misty Mountain Top' spelling error, matrix 2401012/K 50008 in run-out grooves) £75
72	Atlantic K50008	LED ZEPPELIN IV (FOUR SYMBOLS) (2nd pressing mispressing on 'Asylum' label) £150
72	Atlantic K40037	LED ZEPPELIN II (LP, first reissue on green/orange label) £25
72	Atlantic K40031	LED ZEPPELIN (LP, repressing) £25
73	Atlantic K 50014	HOUSES OF THE HOLY (LP, original pressing, unlaminated sleeve with 'obi' around the sleeve, textured inner sleeve with thumb notch, matrix A2/B2) £150
73	Atlantic K50014	HOUSES OF THE HOLY (LP, original pressing, unlaminated sleeve with 'obi') £40
75	Swan Song SSK 89400	PHYSICAL GRAFFITI (2LP, First pressing MATRIXES:SSK89400 A1/B5/C1/D1 (There are some with A1/B4/C1/D1). (Sleeve must have "Swan Song/484 Kings Road, London SW10", inner wraparound on thick card with a matt finish and a spine at the bottom, inner sleeves on thick card, labels have "Made in UK" at 9 "o" clock and NO Warners logo at 3 "o" clock. die-cut sleeve, inner sleeve, folded insert) £100
76	Swan Song SSK 59402	PRESENCE (LP, shrinkwrapped gatefold sleeve with 'Led Zeppelin Presence' sticker) £50
76	Swan Song SSK59402	PRESENCE (LP, shrinkwrapped gatefold sleeve without 'led Zeppelin Presence' sticker) ...£30
76	Swan Song SSK 89402	THE SONG REMAINS THE SAME (2LP, textured gatefold, booklet, black inners) £35
78	Atlantic K 50008	LED ZEPPELIN IV (FOUR SYMBOLS) (LP, purple vinyl testpressing or mispressing of lilac vinyl reissue) £250
78	Atlantic K 50008	LED ZEPPELIN IV (FOUR SYMBOLS) (LP, lilac vinyl reissue) £50
79	Swan Song SSK 59410 A-F	IN THROUGH THE OUT DOOR (LP, 6 different covers with inner sleeves; set labelled 'A' to 'F', each in individual paper outer; available separately with paper outer £25 each) ..£350
82	Swansong A0051	CODA (LP, embossed gatefold sleeve, inner) £40
88	Atlantic K 50008/C 88 1-4	FOUR SYMBOLS (LP, HMV 'Classic Collection' box set, with booklet, numbered) £25
88	Atlantic 250008/C 88 1-4	FOUR SYMBOLS (CD, HMV 'Classic Collection' box set, with booklet, numbered) £30
90	Atlantic ZEP 1	REMASTERS (3LP, trifold sleeve) £60
90	Atlantic 7567 82144-1	LED ZEPPELIN (6LP box set, book, printed inners) £150
97	Atlantic 7567 83061-1	BBC SESSIONS (4-LP, box set, book and print) £150
99	Atlantic 7567 83268-1	EARLY DAYS - THE BEST OF LED ZEPPELIN VOLUME 1 (LP) £40
00	Atlantic 7567 83278-1	LATTER DAYS - THE BEST OF LED ZEPPELIN VOLUME 2 (LP) £35
08	Rhino/Atlantic/Swan Song 8122799489	SOUNDTRACK FROM 'THE SONG REMAINS THE SAME' (4-LP. 180gm expanded edition) £75
08	Swan Song R1 357564	SOUNDTRACK FROM 'THE SONG REMAINS THE SAME' (4LP 180g expanded edition, white vinyl, 200 only, US only, but 100 sent randomly worldwide through website) £600
08	Rhino/Atlantic/Swan Song 8122799513	MOTHERSHIP (4LP, 180g) £70
14	Atlantic 8122796435	LED ZEPPELIN III (box set reissue, 2-CD, 2-LP, download, 30,000 with art print) £80

(see also Jimmy Page, Robert Plant, John Paul Jones, Dansette Damage, Listen, Family Dogg, Ian Whitcomb, P.J. Proby, Lord Sutch,Yardbirds, Coverdale Page, Page & Plant)

ALVIN LEE

73	Chrysalis CHR 1054	ON THE ROAD TO FREEDOM (LP, with Myron Le Fevre) £20

(see also Ten Years After)

LEE & CLARENDONIANS

72	Green Door GD 4038	Night Owl/Night Owl Version £15

LEE (PERRY) & JIMMY (RILEY)

75	Dip DL 5075	Rasta Train/Yagga Yagga £25

LEE (PERRY) & JUNIOR (BYLES)

75	Dip DL 5060	Dreader Locks/Militant Rock £20

ARTHUR LEE

72	A&M AMLS 64356	VINDICATOR (LP) £35

(see also Love)

BRENDA LEE

78s

56	Brunswick 05628	I'm Gonna Lasso Santa Claus/Christy Christmas (as Little Brenda Lee) £15
57	Brunswick 05685	Dynamite/Love You Til I Die £15
57	Brunswick 05720	Ain't That Love/One Teenager To Another £15
58	Brunswick 05755	Ring-A-My-Phone/Little Jonah (Rock On Your Little Steel Guitar) £50
59	Brunswick 05780	Bill Bailey, Won't You Please Come Home/Hummin' The Blues Over You £40
60	Brunswick 05819	Sweet Nuthin's/Weep No More My Baby £80

SINGLES

56	Brunswick 05628	I'm Gonna Lasso Santa Claus/Christy Christmas (triangular centre) £75
57	Brunswick 05685	Dynamite/Love You Til I Die (with Anita Kerr Singers, triangular centre) £60
57	Brunswick 05720	Ain't That Love/One Teenager To Another (w/ Anita Kerr Singers, tri-centre) £60
58	Brunswick 05755	Ring-A-My-Phone/Little Jonah (Rock On Your Little Steel Guitar) (tri-centre) £60

MINT VALUE £

58	Decca BM 31186	**Fairyland/One Step At A Time** (export issue, triangular centre)	£40
66	Brunswick 05957	**Too Little Time/Time And Time Again**	£20
67	Brunswick 05976	**Where's The Melody?/Born To Be By Your Side**	£15

EPs

59	Brunswick OE 9462	**ROCK THE BOP** (green p/s & tri-centre)	£35
59	Brunswick OE 9462	**ROCK THE BOP** (blue p/s & round centre)	£15

BUNNY LEE ALLSTARS

69	Unity UN 541	**Daydream/Joy Ride**	£40
69	Unity UN 543	**Ivan Itler The Conqueror/The Spice**	£70
70	Camel CA39	**Three Stooge/Isle Of Love**	£25
70	Pama PM 803	**Annie Pama/Mr Magoo**	£25
70	Unity UN 543	**Ivan Itler The Conqueror/The Spice**	£75
71	Smash SMA 2304	**Stanley** (Parts 1 & 2) (as Bunnie Lee Allstars)	£15
78	Jamaica Sound JS 013	**SUPER DUB DISCO STYLE** (LP, with the Aggrovators)	£50

(see also Lloyd Charmers, Sonny Binns & Rudies, Copy Cats, John Holt, Delroy Wilson)

BYRON LEE & DRAGONAIR(E)S

60	Blue Beat B 2	**Dumplin's/Kissin' Gal** (vocal: Buddy Davidson) (white label, blue print)	£20
60	Blue Beat BB 2	**Dumplin's/Kissin' Gal** (vocal: Buddy Davidson) (2nd pressing, blue label, silver print)	£15
61	Blue Beat BB 28	**Mash! Mr. Lee/Help Me Forget** (vocal: Keith Lyn)	£20
61	Starlite ST45 045	**Joy Ride/Over The Rainbow**	£15
64	Parlophone R 5124	**River Bank/Musical Communion**	£20
64	Parlophone R 5125	**Sour Apples/Hanging Up My Heart**	£20
64	Parlophone R 5140	**Sammy Dead/Say Bye Bye** (both actually by Eric Morris with Byron Lee)	£20
64	Parlophone R 5177	**Beautiful Garden/Too Late**	£20
64	Parlophone R 5182	**Come Back/Jamaica Ska**	£20
64	MGM MGM 1256	**Night Train From Jamaica/Ska Dee Wah** (with Danny Davis)	£20
66	Doctor Bird DB 1003	**Sloopy/Gold Finger**	£20
70	Trojan TR 7731	**Squeeze Up** (Parts 1 & 2)	£20
70	Trojan TR 7747	**Bond In Bliss/Musical Scorcher**	£15
72	Dynamic DYN 435	**Make It Reggae/DENNIS ALCAPONE: Go Johnny Go**	£15
65	Atlantic AET 6014	**SKA TIME** (EP, as Byron Lee Ska Kings)	£35
64	Island ILP 905	**CARIBBEAN JOY RIDE** (LP)	£35
66	Atlantic 587018	**JUMP UP** (LP)	£35
69	Trojan TTL 5	**ROCKSTEADY EXPLOSION** (LP)	£40
69	Major Minor SMLP 53	**BYRON LEE & THE DRAGONAIRES** (LP)	£20
70	Trojan TRLS 18	**REGGAE WITH BYRON LEE** (LP)	£20
71	Trojan TRL 28	**REGGAE SPLASH DOWN** (LP)	£25

(see also Mighty Avengers, Ken Lazarus, Hopeton Lewis, Danny Davis Orchestra, Good Guys, Neville Hinds, Hubcaps & Wheels, Mighty Sparrow, Blues Busters)

LITTLE MR. LEE & CHEROKEES

66	Vocalion VP 9268	**Young Lover/I Don't Want To Go**	£40

CHRISTOPHER LEE

74	Studio Two TWOA Q4 5001	**HAMMER PRESENTS DRACULA** (LP, gatefold sleeve, quadrophonic)	£15

CURTIS LEE

60	Top Rank JAR 317	**With All My Heart** (I Love You)**/Pure Love**	£60
61	London HLX 9313	**Pledge Of Love/Then I'll Know**	£25
61	London HLX 9397	**Pretty Little Angel Eyes/Gee How I Wish You Were Here**	£20
61	London HLX 9445	**Under The Moon Of Love/Beverly Jean**	£20
62	London HLX 9533	**A Night At Daddy Gee's/Just Another Fool**	£20
67	CBS 2717	**Get My Bag/Everybody's Going Wild** (as Curtis Lee & K.C.P.s)	£40
67	CBS 2717	**Get My Bag/Everybody's Going Wild** (as Curtis Lee & K.C.P.s) (DJ copy)	£80

DAVE LEE SOUND

74	Sea Cruise SCDL 100	**DAVE LEE SOUND EP**	£20
73	Southern Sound 401	**PLAY ROCK N ROLL REQUESTS** (LP, white labels)	£30
73	Southern Sound SSLP 204	**LIVE AT THE STARDUST** (LP)	£20
75	Throstle Nest TN 001	**CARRY ON** (LP)	£20

DAVE LEE (& STAGGERLEES)

66	Fontana TF 723	**Adam Adamant/Georgie's Theme** (as Dave Lee & His Orchestra)	£15

DAVE LEE

66	Colpix PXL 550	**OUR MAN CRICHTON** (LP, with Tubby Hayes)	£80

(see also Tubby Hayes)

DINAH LEE

65	Aladdin WI 606	**I'll Forgive You Then Forget You/Nitty Gritty**	£35
65	Brit 1005	**I Can't Believe What You Say/Pushin' A Good Thing Too Far** (unissued)	£0
65	Aladdin WI 608	**I Can't Believe What You Say/Pushin' A Good Thing Too Far**	£40

DON (TONY) LEE

68	Big Shot BI 504	**It's Reggae Time** (as Don Tony Lee)**/ERROL DUNKLEY: The Clamp Is On**	£50
68	Doctor Bird DB 1106	**Lee's Special** (as Don Tony Lee)**/LLOYD & GROOVERS: My Heart And Soul**	£40
68	Island WI 3160	**It's Reggae Time** (as D. Tony Lee)**/ERROL DUNKLEY: The Clamp Is On**	£45
69	Unity UN 519	**Peyton Place/Red Gal In The Ring** (as Don Tony Lee)	£20
70	Gas 163	**Work Out/Too Long** (as Donald Lee)	£35

(FREDDIE) 'FINGERS' LEE (& UPPER HAND)

65	Fontana TF 619	**The Friendly Undertaker/Little Bit More** (as 'Fingers' Lee)	£25
66	Fontana TF 655	**I'm Gonna Buy Me A Dog/I Can't Drive** (as 'Fingers' Lee)	£40
66	Columbia DB 8002	**Bossy Boss/Don't Run Away** (as Fingers Lee & Upper Hand)	£40

(see also At Last The 1958 Rock & Roll Show)

GEORGE LEE (& MUSIC DOCTORS)
69	Downtown DT 443	**Talking Boss/Jungle Fever** (solo)	£45
70	J-Dan JDN 4407	**Johnny Dollar/Tough Of Poison** (with Music Doctors)	£25

(see also Desmond Riley)

JACKIE LEE & RAINDROPS (U.K.) (FEMALE)
62	Oriole CB 1757	**Party Lights/Midnight**	£15
72	ICI Pharmacuticals Division ICI 1	**Space Age Lullaby/Sleep** (p/s)	£15

(see also Jacky, Jackie Lee [U.K.], Raindrops [U.K], Emma Rede, Boeing Duveen and the Beautiful Soup)

JACKIE LEE (U.S.) (MALE)
65	Fontana TF 646	**The Duck/Let Your Conscience Be Your Guide**	£40
68	London HLM 10233	**The Duck/Dancing In The Street**	£15
72	Jay Boy BOY 66	**Oh! My Darlin'/Don't Be Ashamed**	£15
72	Jay Boy BOY 66	**Oh! My Darlin'/Don't Be Ashamed** (DJ copy)	£30
85	Kent TOWN 107	**Darkest Days/EDDIE BISHOP: Call Me**	£25
67	London HA-M 8336	**THE DUCK** (LP)	£50

(see also Bob & Earl, Earl Nelson)

JAMIE LEE & ATLANTICS
63	Decca F 11571	**In The Night/Little Girl In Blue**	£45

JIMMY LEE
61	Starlite ST45 059	**All My Life/Chicago Jump**	£30

JULIA LEE (& HER BOYFRIENDS)
51	Capitol LC 6535	**PARTY TIME** (10" LP, 2 different sleeves)	£50

LAURA LEE (U.K.)
60	Triumph RGM 1030	**Tell Tommy I Miss Him/I'm Sending Back Your Roses**	£50
62	Decca F 11513	**Too Young To Be In Love/Brand New Heartbeat**	£15

LAURA LEE (U.S.)
72	Tamla Motown TMG 831	**To Win Your Heart/So Will I**	£60
72	Tamla Motown TMG 831	**To Win Your Heart/So Will I** (DJ copy)	£150
71	Hot Wax SHW 5006	**WOMEN'S LOVE RIGHTS** (LP)	£15
73	Hot Wax SHW 5009	**TWO SIDES OF LAURA LEE** (LP)	£15

LEAPY LEE
66	Decca F 12369	**King Of The Whole Wide World/Shake Hands** (featuring the Kinks)	£50
68	MCA MUIPS 354	**LITTLE ARROWS** (LP)	£15

NICKIE LEE
69	Deep Soul DS 9103	**And Black Is Beautiful/Faith Within**	£25

ROBERT LEE
87	Josiah KJ 008	**Easy Norman/MICHAEL MARTIN ALLSTARS: Version** (12")	£40

ROBERTA LEE
53	Brunswick 05076	**Sixty Minute Man** (with Hardrock Gunter)/**RED FOLEY: Hot Toddy** (78)	£15

(see also Red Foley, Hardrock Gunter)

RUDY LEE & STEPPER
89	Wau! Mr. Modo MOWLP 003	**TEAM WORKS PRESENTS** (LP)	£25

VINNY LEE & RIDERS
61	HMV POP 856	**Mule Train/Gambler's Guitar**	£15

WARREN LEE
69	Pama PM 762	**Underdog Backstreet/Come Put My Life In Order**	£20

MARK LEEMAN FIVE
65	Columbia DB 7452	**Portland Town/Gotta Get Myself Together**	£50
65	Columbia DB 7648	**Blow My Blues Away/On The Horizon**	£60
66	Columbia DB 7812	**Forbidden Fruit/Goin' To Bluesville**	£40
66	Columbia DB 7955	**Follow Me/Gather Up The Pieces**	£40
64	No label or cat no	**RHYTHM AND BLUES PLUS** (LP, private pressing)	£500

(see also Cheynes)

LEEPERS
23	Detour DR143PD	**Paint A Day/Going Through The Motions/Ronnie's House /On My Own** (EP, picture disc)	£15

(see also Le Mat)

THOMAS LEER
78	Oblique ER 101	**Private Plane/International** (folded photocopied p/s, hand-stamped labels)	£60
78	Company/Oblique OBCO 1	**Private Plane/International** (reissue, printed p/s)	£20
82	Cherry Red ERED 26	**CONTRADICTIONS EP** (12", double pack)	£15
79	Industrial IR 0007	**THE BRIDGE** (LP, with Robert Rental)	£40

(see also Act, Robert Rental)

JOHN LEES
74	Polydor 2058 513	**Best Of My Love/You Can't Get It**	£15
73	Harvest SHVL 811	**A MAJOR FANCY** (LP, released as SHSM 2018)	£20

(see also Barclay James Harvest)

LEFT BANKE
67	Philips (S)BL 7773	**WALK AWAY RENEE/PRETTY BALLERINA** (LP)	£50

LEFTFIELD
90	Outer Rhythm FOOT 3	**Not Forgotten** (12")	£15
95	Hard Hands HANDLP 2	**LEFTISM** (2-LP, gatefold sleeve)	£30

MINT VALUE £

95	Hard Hands HANDLP 2T	LEFTISM (3-LP, gatefold sleeve)..	£40
99	Hard Hands HANDLP 4	RHYTHM AND STEALTH (2-LP)...	£20
99	Hard Hands HANDLP 4T	RHYTHM AND STEALTH (5 x 10" box set, limited edition)...................	£25
00	Simply Vinyl SVLP 194	LEFTISM (2-LP reissue)...	£20
15	Infectious INFECT223DLP	ALTERNATIVE LIGHT SOURCE (2-LP)..	£15

(see also Curve)

LEFT HAND DRIVE
| 77 | Bankrupt Records BECK 611 | Jailbait/Motorway Crow (1,000 only, no p/s) .... | £50 |

LEFT-HANDED MARRIAGE
| 67 | Private pressing | ON THE RIGHT SIDE OF THE LEFT-HANDED MARRIAGE (LP)................. | £500 |
| 96 | Tenth Planet TP 022 | ON THE RIGHT SIDE OF THE LEFT-HANDED MARRIAGE (LP, reissue, gatefold sleeve) .... | £25 |

(see also Queen)

LEGAL AID
| 81 | Earshot ERA 1 | That's Life/Limbo... | £15 |

LEGATO
| 85 | Adelphi ADE T002 | Buttercup/Butterdub (12").. | £45 |

LEGAY
| 69 | Fontana TF 904 | No-One/The Fantastic Story Of The Steam Driven Banana................ | £175 |

(see also Gypsy)

LEGEND!
| 83 | Creation CRE 001/Lyntone LYN 12903 | '73 In '83/You (Chunka Chunka) Were Glamorous (foldaround p/s in poly bag, with 33rpm flexidisc "I Wonder Why! (live)" by The Pastels/"Wouldn't You? By Laughing Apple).. | £15 |

LEGEND (1)
69	Bell BLL 1048	National Gas/Wouldn't You	£20
69	Bell BLL 1082	Georgia George Part 1/July	£15
70	Vertigo 6059 021	Life/Late Last Night	£20
71	Vertigo 6059 036	Don't You Know/Someday	£15
69	Bell MBLL/SBLL 115	LEGEND (LP, blue/silver labels with "Sold in U.K..." text)................	£175
71	Vertigo 6360 019	LEGEND ('RED BOOT') (LP, gatefold sleeve, large swirl label)..........	£300
72	Vertigo 6360 063	MOONSHINE (LP, gatefold sleeve, small swirl label).......................	£400

(see also Procol Harum)

LEGEND (2)
| 81 | Legend LEG 1 | Hideaway/Heaven Sent (p/s) .... | £70 |

LEGEND (3)
82	Workshop WR 3478	FRONTLINE EP (Frontline/Sabre & Chatila/ Stormers Of Heaven/Open The Skies (12")	£25
81	Workshop WR 2007	LEGEND (LP)...	£90
82	Workshop WR 3477	DEATH IN THE NURSERY (LP, with insert)	£20

LEGENDARY FLOBS
| 79 | Flobs FLO 1 | Dead Popes/You're In Danger (p/s)... | £25 |

LEGENDARY HEARTS
| 88 | Surfin' Pict | IN A WORLD LIKE THIS (12" EP) .... | £30 |

LEGENDARY MASKED SURFERS
| 73 | United Artists UP 35542 | Gonna Hustle You/Summertime, Summertime............................. | £18 |

(see also Beach Boys, Jan & Dean)

LEGENDARY PINK DOTS
81	Mirrordot MD 01	ONLY DREAMING (cassette, all different hand-made covers)............	£100
81	Mirrordot MD02/03	CHEMICAL PLAYSCHOOL 1/2 (double cassette, 24 copies all different handmade covers)...	£120
81	Cassetteking CK04	DOTS ON THE EYE (cassette)...	£45
82	Flowmotion FMC 09	PREMONITION (cassette, around 60 copies).................................	£45
82	Mirrordot MD/03/II	CHEMICAL PLAYSCHOOL 2 EDITION 2 (cassette, 9 copies, different handmade copies)..	£120
82	Mirrordot MD 02-03	CHEMICAL PLAYSCHOOL 3/4 (double cassette, 120 copies, different covers)....	£75
82	Mirrordot MD 04	KLEINE KRIEG (cassette, 120 copies, individual hand-made covers)	£80
82	In Phaze 4	BRIGHTER NOW (cassette, 300 copies, different mixes on some tracks)	£45
82	In Phaze IPNER 1	BRIGHTER NOW (LP)...	£25
83	Third Mind TMT 08	BASILISK (cassette, 1000 copies)...	£30
83	In Phaze PHA 2	CURSE (LP, 2500 copies)..	£20
84	In Phaze PHA	THE TOWER (LP, 2500 copies)..	£20

LEGENDS
65	Pye 7N 15904	I've Found Her/Something's Gonna Happen	£20
67	Parlophone R 5581	Tomorrow's Gonna Be Another Day/Nobody Laughs Anymore	£40
67	Parlophone R 5613	Under The Sky/Twenty-Four Hours A Day	£20

(see also First Impressions)

B. LEGGS
| 71 | Green Door GD 4004 | Drums Of Passion/Love And Emotion (Version) .... | £18 |

(see also Morgan's All Stars. Righteous Flames)

LEGION
| 84 | Off Beat S LEG 003 | Yesterday/Anticks (p/s) .... | £15 |

LEGION OF PARASITES
84	Fight Back FIGHT 2	UNDESIRABLE GUESTS (12" EP)	£15
85	Thrash THRASH 1	THE PRISON OF LIFE! (LP)..	£15
87	Stud STUDLP 3	DAWN TO DUST (LP)..	£15

LEGO FEET
91	Skam SKA 001	LEGO FEET (LP, in black die-cut sleeve like a 12")	£175
12	Skam SKA 001	LEGO FEET (2-LP, reissue)	£25

MICHEL LEGRAND
64	Mercury SML 30020	VIOLENT VIOLINS (LP)	£18
66	Philips (S)BL 7792	THE YOUNG GIRLS OF ROCHEFORT (LP, soundtrack)	£25
68	United Artists SULP 1218	THE THOMAS CROWN AFFAIR (LP, soundtrack)	£35
70	Sunset SLS 50519	THE THOMAS CROWN AFFAIR (LP, reissue)	£20
70	United Artists UAS 29084	THE HAPPY ENDING (LP, soundtrack)	£20

LE GRIFFE
83	Bullet BOLT 1	Fast Bikes/Where Are You?/The Actor (12", p/s)	£15
84	Bullet BOLT 7	You're Killing Me/E.T.A. (12", p/s)	£15
84	Bullet BULP 2	BREAKING STRAIN (mini-LP)	£20

LEGS
74	Warner Bros K 16317	So Many Faces/You Bet You Have	£15

(see also Curved Air, Stretch)

LEIBER-STOLLER ORCHESTRA
62	HMV 1050	Cafe Expresso/Blue Baion	£25

LEIBSTANDARTE SS MB
81	Come Organisation WDC 881015	TRIUMPH OF THE WILL (LP, 500 only)	£100
81	Come Organisation WDC 881018	WELTANSCHAUUNG (LP)	£100
82	Come Organisation WDC 883023	MENSES (cassette)	£70

ANDREW LEIGH
70	Polydor 2343 034	MAGICIAN (LP)	£75

(see also Reg King, Spooky Tooth)

ROBERTA LEIGH
58	HMV EH 8339	THE ADVENTURES OF TWIZZLE (EP)	£15

LEISURE ADDICTS
80	Addictive ADIC 1	Subway Suicide/Prefab 13 (no p/s)	£20

LEISURE RESEARCH
84	Innocent INNOC 1	Discontent/Reasons (p/s)	£20

LEITMOTIV
83	Paragon VIRTUE 3	CARESS AND CURSE EP (12")	£15

LELU/LU'S
86	Possum POST 001	Africa/Fragile Thigs/Blipverts (12", p/s)	£15

LE MAT
82	Whaam! WHAAM 008	Waltz Of The Fool/Ev'ry Dream (p/s)	£15
83	Whaam! BIG 6	THE WALTZ OF THE FOOL (LP, printed inner)	£20

(see also The Leepers)

GARY LEMEL
67	London HLM 7124	Beautiful People/Take Me With You (export issue)	£20

JOHN LE MESURIER
76	Reprise K54080	WHAT IS GOING TO BECOME OF US ALL (LP)	£20

LEMMINGS
65	Pye 7N 15837	Out Of My Mind/My Little Girl	£20
65	Pye 7N 15899	You Can't Blame Me For Trying/Bring Your Heart With You	£20

(see also Honeycombs)

LEMON D
92	Planet Earth PEDJ 01	DJ ON WAX (12" EP)	£60
93	Planet Earth PDJ 02	PURSUIT OF A VISION (12" EP)	£60
95	Conqueror OC 9	VOL II (12" EP)	£15
95	Metalheadz METH 014	Urban Style Music/This Is LA (12")	£15

LEMON DIPS
69	De Wolfe DW/LP 3114	WHO'S GONNA BUY? (10" LP, library issue)	£75

LEMONHEADS
90	Atlantic 82137	LOVEY (LP)	£15
93	Atlantic 82537	COME ON FEEL (LP)	£30

LEMON INTERRUPT
93	Junior Boys Own JBO 12002	Eclipse/Bigmouth (12")	£15
93	Junior Boys Own JBO 712	Dirty/Minneapolis/Minneapolis (Airwaves) (12")	£15

(see also Underworld)

LEMON JELLY
01	Soft Rock SOFTROCK 001	Soft/Rock (blue vinyl, denim sleeve with condom, 1000 only)	£40
03	Rolled Oats RO 01	Rolled/Oats (gold vinyl, hessian sleeve, 1200 only)	£15
98	Impotent Fury IF 001	THE BATH EP: In The Bath/Nervous Tension/A Tune For Jack (10", 1000 only, stickered cardboard sleeve, 1st 250 hand-printed p/s)	£80
98	Impotent Fury IF 001	THE BATH EP: In The Bath/Nervous Tension/A Tune For Jack (10", 1000 only, stickered)	£30
99	Impotent Fury IF 002	THE YELLOW EP: His Majesty King Raam/The Staunton Lick/Homage To Patagonia (10", 1000 only, stickered cardboard sleeve, 1st 240 in hand-printed p/s)	£70
99	Impotent Fury IF 002	THE YELLOW EP: His Majesty King Raam/The Staunton Lick/Homage To Patagonia	£20

MINT VALUE £

		(10", 1000 only, stickered cardboard sleeve)	
00	Impotent Fury IF 003	THE MIDNIGHT EP: Kneel Before Your God/Page One/Come (10", 1000 only, stickered cardboard sleeve, 1st 350 in hand-printed p/s)	£80
00	Impotent Fury IF 003	THE MIDNIGHT EP: Kneel Before Your God/Page One/Come (10", 1000 only, stickered cardboard sleeve)	£20
00	XL IXXLLP 139	KY (2-LP gatefold sleeve with insert)	£100
02	XL IFXLLP 160	LOST HORIZONS (2-LP, gatefold sleeve, with booklet, 'Lemon Jelly' sticker on front)	£100
05	XL IFXLLP182	'64 - '95 (4 x 10" box set)	£100

LEMON KITTENS

79	Step Forward SF 10	SPOONFED AND WRITHING (EP)	£25
81	United Dairies UD 07	CAKE BEAST (12" EP, with inner sleeve & insert)	£25
80	United Dairies UD 02	WE BUY A HAMMER FOR DADDY (LP, with inner sheet)	£35
83	Illuminated JAMS 131	THE BIG DENTIST (LP)	£35

(see also Danielle Dax, Underneath, Gland Shrouds, Karl Blake)

LEMON LINE

67	Decca F 12688	For Your Precious Love/You Made Me See The Light	£15

LEMON MEN

69	Polydor 56365	I've Seen You Cut Lemons/Lemon Strip/Lemon Walk	£15

LEMON PIPERS

68	Pye Intl. NPL 28112	GREEN TAMBOURINE (LP)	£30
68	Pye Intl. NSPL 28118	JUNGLE MARMALADE (LP)	£20

(see also Ram Jam)

LEMON PIPERS/1910 FRUITGUM CO.

68	Pye Intl. NEP 44091	PRESENTING ... (EP, 1 side each)	£15

(see also 1910 Fruitgum Co.)

LEMONS

81	Race RB 004	My Favourite Band/English Summer (p/s)	£20

LEMON TREE

68	Parlophone R 5671	I Can Touch A Rainbow/William Chalker's Time Machine	£50
68	Parlophone R 5739	It's So Nice To Come Home/Come On Girl	£40

(see also Idle Race, Uglys, Danny King's Mayfair Set, Balls)

LEN & HIS SEXTET

63	Melotone ME 100	Blowin' The Top/Don't Stop	£25

FREDDIE LENNON

66	Piccadilly 7N 35290	That's My Life (My Love And My Home)/The Next Time You Feel Important	£40

(see also Loving Kind)

JIMMY LENNON & ATLANTICS

64	Decca F 11825	Louisiana Mama/I Learned To Yodel	£35

JOHN LENNON/PLASTIC ONO BAND

SINGLES

69	Apple APPLE 13	Give Peace A Chance/Remember Love (p/s, as Plastic Ono Band; with Parlophone catalogue number, dark green label, only second pressings have R5795 added to catalogue number)	£18
69	Apple APPLE 13	Give Peace A Chance/Remember Love (p/s, as Plastic Ono Band, first press with "sold in UK..." label text)	£40
69	Apple APPLES 1001	Cold Turkey/Don't Worry Kyoko (Mummy's Only Looking For A Hand In The Snow) (p/s, as Plastic Ono Band)	£15
69	Apple APPLES 1002	You Know My Name (Look Up The Number)/What's The New Mary Jane? (as Plastic Ono Band, unreleased; vinyl test pressings only with typed Apple 'Custom Recording' labels & hand written catalogue number)	£3000
71	Apple R 5892	Power To The People/YOKO ONO & PLASTIC ONO BAND: Open Your Box (p/s, full apple label both sides or full/half apple label)	£15
72	Apple R 5970	Happy Xmas (War Is Over) (as John & Yoko/Plastic Ono Band with Harlem Community Choir)/YOKO ONO & PLASTIC ONO BAND: Listen, The Snow Is Falling (p/s green vinyl)	£15
72	Apple R 5953	Woman Is The Nigger Of The World/Sisters O Sisters (unreleased, test pressings only)	£2500
73	Apple R 5994	Mind Games/Meat City (demo copy)	£30
74	EMI PSR 369	Interview With John Lennon By Bob Mercer And Message To The Salesmen/Whatever Gets You Thru' The Night (promo only)	£500
74	Apple R5998	Whatever Gets You Thru The Night/Beef Jerky (demo copy)	£40
75	Apple R 6005	Stand By Me/Move Over Ms. L (demo copy)	£45
75	Apple R 6003	9 Dream (Edited Version)/What You Got (demo only)	£80
75	Apple R 6009	Imagine/Working Class Hero (demo copy)	£30
80	WEA Geffen K 79186	(Just Like) Starting Over/YOKO ONO : Kiss Kiss Kiss (Green vinyl, promo)	£500
81	WEA K 79207	Watching The Wheels/YOKO ONO: I'm Your Angel (Pink vinyl "in house" promo)	£500
84	Polydor PODJ 700	Nobody Told Me (1-sided white label promo)	£60
84	Polydor PODJ 701	Borrowed Time (Edited Version)/YOKO ONO: Your Hands (promo only)	£25
88	Parlophone RP 6199	Imagine/Jealous Guy (picture disc)	£15
88	Parlophone 12R 6199	Imagine/Jealous Guy/Happy Xmas (War Is Over) (12" p/s)	£18
24	UMR/Calderstone 00602465151831	MIND GAMES EP (12", RSD, glow-in-the-dark vinyl)	£40

ALBUMS

68	Apple APCOR 2	UNFINISHED MUSIC NO. 1: TWO VIRGINS (with Yoko Ono, mono; black inner, no track listing, with "Merrie In England..." blurb on front sleeve)	£3000
68	Apple SAPCOR 2/Track 613 012	UNFINISHED MUSIC NO. 1: TWO VIRGINS (with Yoko Ono, stereo; black inner, with track listing & "Merrie In England..." blurb on back sleeve & Track Records logo on label, dark green label, "Sold in U.K..." "Mfd in UK" label text)	£700
69	Zapple ZAPPLE 01	UNFINISHED MUSIC NO. 2: LIFE WITH THE LIONS (with Yoko Ono, with inner sleeve, dark green label, "Sold in U.K..." "Mfd in UK" label text)	£250

69	Apple SAPCOR 11	**WEDDING ALBUM** (with Yoko Ono; gatefold sleeve in box set, includes wedding certificate glued to inside box lid, press booklet, poster, white 'Bagism' bag, passport photographs, postcard & picture of wedding cake)	£800
69	Apple CORE 2001	**LIVE PEACE IN TORONTO 1969** (as Plastic Ono Band, with stapled calendar, sealed, 1st pressing with rough surface label and Apple publishing credit on side 2, dark green label with "Sold in U.K..." text)	£200
69	Apple CORE 2001	**LIVE PEACE IN TORONTO 1969** (as Plastic Ono Band, with stapled calendar, unsealed)	£20
70	Apple PCS 7124	**JOHN LENNON : PLASTIC ONO BAND** (LP, with inner)	£60
72	Apple PAS 10004	**IMAGINE** (LP, with inner sleeve, poster & postcard, 1st pressing with laminated sleeve/'sniped' spine edges)	£80
72	Apple PAS 10004	**IMAGINE** (LP, with inner sleeve, without poster & postcard)	£30
72	Apple Q4PAS 10004	**IMAGINE** (LP, quadrophonic, with inner sleeve, poster & postcard)	£150
72	Apple PCSP 716	**SOMETIME IN NEW YORK CITY** (2-LP, gatefold, inner sleeve & postcard)	£45
72	Apple PCSP 716	**SOMETIME IN NEW YORK CITY** (2-LP, gatefold, inner sleeve & without postcard)	£20
73	Apple PCS 7165	**MIND GAMES** (LP, inner, 1U/1U matrix)	£20
75	Apple PCS 7169	**ROCK 'N' ROLL** (LP)	£25
74	Apple PCTC 253	**WALLS AND BRIDGES** (LP, gatefold, with booklet and inner sleeve)	£25
75	Apple PCS 7173	**SHAVED FISH** (LP, lyric inner)	£30
81	Parlophone JLB 8	**THE JOHN LENNON BOX** (9-LP set, with insert)	£100
84	Polydor POLH P5	**MILK AND HONEY** (picture disc, original pressing, thin vinyl, 2,000 only)	£40
84	Polydor POLH P5	**MILK AND HONEY** (picture disc, 2nd pressing, thicker vinyl, 1,000 only)	£50
86	Parlophone PCS 7301	**LIVE IN NEW YORK CITY** (LP, with inner)	£15
86	Parlophone PCS 7308	**MENLOVE AVENUE** (LP, with inner)	£20
88	Parlophone PCSP 722	**IMAGINE : JOHN LENNON** (2xLP with inner)	£20
90	Parlophone CDS 79 5220	**LENNON** (4 x CD set)	£70
97	Parlophone 8 21954 2	**LENNON LEGEND** (2-LP with inner)	£150
97	EMI LPCENT 9	**ROCK 'N' ROLL** (LP, reissue, EMI Centenary, stickered sleeve)	£40
97	EMI LPCENT 27	**IMAGINE** (LP, reissue, EMI centenary, stickered sleeve)	£40
98	Parlophone 8306142	**ANTHOLOGY** (4-CDR, jewel cases with Abbey Road studio inlays, incorrect track listing and missing "Grow Old With Me" from CD4, promo only)	£80
99	Capitol 497 6391	**WONSAPONETIME** (2-LP with inner)	£50
99	Apple PCTC 253	**WALLS AND BRIDGES** (LP, reissue, inner & booklet)	£30

(see also Beatles,Yoko Ono, Bill Elliott/Elastic Oz Band, Elephant's Memory, Musketeer Gripweed, Elton John)

JOHN LENNON & BLEECHERS (JAMAICA)
| 70 | Punch PH 23 | **Ram You Hard/UPSETTERS: Soul Stew** | £100 |

(see also Bleechers, Lee Graham)

LENNON SISTERS
| 61 | London HLD 9417 | **Sad Movies/I Don't Know Why** | £15 |

ANNIE LENNOX
| 04 | Simply Vinyl SVLP 081 | **DIVA** (LP, reissue) | £25 |
| 09 | Sony 88697368051 | **THE ANNIE LENNOX COLLECTION** (2-LP, inners) | £80 |

LENNY AND THE LAWBREAKERS
| 79 | Rip Off RIP 11 | **Me And Bobby McGee/Suzy D** (die cut p/s) | £50 |

J.B. LENOIR (& AFRICAN HUNCH RHYTHM)
65	Sue WI 339	**I Sing Um The Way I Feel/I Feel So Good** (with His African Hunch Rhythm)	£50
65	Bootleg 503	**Man Watch Your Woman/Mama Talk To Your Daughter** (99 copies only)	£60
66	Blue Horizon 45-1004	**Mojo Boogie/I Don't Care What Nobody Say** (99 copies only)	£150
68	Python PLP 25	**J.B. LENOIR** (LP, 99 copies only)	£75
70	Polydor 2482 014	**CRUSADE** (LP)	£40
75	Rarity LP 2	**J.B. LENOIR** (LP)	£25
70s	CBS 62593	**ALABAMA BLUES** (LP)	£40

ROBIN LENT
| 71 | Nepentha 6347 002 | **SCARECROW'S JOURNEY** (LP, gatefold sleeve, with Focus) | £175 |

(see also Focus, Jan Akkerman)

VAN LENTON
| 65 | Immediate IM 008 | **Gotta Get Away/You Don't Care** | £80 |

LEON (SILVERA) & OWEN (GRAY)
| 62 | Blue Beat BB 117 | **Murder** (with Drumbago All Stars)/**ROY PANTON: Forty Four** | £15 |

(see also Owen & Leon, Owen & Millie)

DEKE LEONARD
| 73 | United Artists UAG 29464 | **ICEBERG** (LP, gatefold sleeve) | £15 |
| 74 | United Artists UAG 29544 | **KAMIKAZE** (LP, gatefold sleeve) | £15 |

(see also Man, Marty Wilde, Help Yourself, Pete Brown's Piblokto)

ANN LEONARDO
| 57 | Capitol CL 14723 | **Straws In The Wind/Travelling Stranger** | £15 |

LE ORME
| 73 | Charisma CAS 1072 | **FELONA AND SORONA** (LP, gatefold, large 'Mad Hatter' label) | £60 |

(see under 'O')

LEO'S SUNSHIPP
80	Grapevine RED 3	**Give Me The Sunshine/I'm Back For More**	£35
80	Grapevine REDC 3	**Give Me The Sunshine/I'm Back For More** (12")	£20
86	Expansion EXAPND 03	**Give Me The Sunshine/I'm Back For More** (Mini-Trio)/**I'm Back For More** (Vocal)/**Give Me The Sunshine** (Mini-Trio) (12", reissue)	£15
96	Expansion EXLPM 2	**WE NEED EACH OTHER** (LP, reissue)	£30

LEPRECHAUN
| 81 | Excalibur EXC 508 | **Loc It Up/Party Freaks** (12") | £15 |

LE RITZ
77 Breaker BS 2001   Punker/What A Sucker (p/s) £15

LEROY & ROCKY (ELLIS)
68 Studio One SO 2042   Love Me Girl/WRIGGLERS: Reel Up £80
(see also King Rocky, Leroy Sibbles, Alva Lewis)

LE ROYS
64 HMV POP 1312   Chills/Lost Out On Love £15
(see also Mike Sarne, Simon Scott, John Leyton, Mike Berry, Grazina, Billie Davis, Billy Boyle, Don Spencer)

LES & SILKIE
70 Torpedo TOR 13   I Don't Want To Tell You/DENZIL DENNIS: Come On In £30

LES KITTIES
81 Camille CAM 1   What's That?/Little Claw (500 only, no p/s) £15

BILL LE SAGE
64 World Records T/ST 346   PRESENTING THE BILL LESAGE/RONNIE ROSS QUARTET (LP, stereo sticker on front) £40
(see also Ronnie Ross)

LORNE LESLEY
59 Parlophone R 4581   So High, So Low/I Don't Know £30

DESMOND LESLIE
05 Trunk JBH 014 LP   MUSIC OF THE FUTURE (LP) £25

JOHN & CHRIS LESLIE
76 Cottage COT 901   THE SHIP OF TIME (LP) £15

MICHAEL LESLIE
65 Pye 7N 15959   Make Up Or Break Up/She Can't See Me £25

LES ROCKETS
77 Decca FR 13752   Space Rock/Let's Be Sad (Please note demos, state Let's Be Sade) £40
77 Decca FR 13752   Space Rock (extended)/Don't Be Sad (12") £20

KETTY LESTER
64 RCA Victor RCA 1394   Some Things Are Better Left Unsaid/The House Is Haunted £60
64 RCA Victor RCA 1394   Some Things Are Better Left Unsaid/The House Is Haunted (DJ copy) £100
64 RCA Victor RCA 1403   Roses Grow With Thorns/Please Don't Cry Anymore £40
64 RCA Victor RCA 1421   I Trust You Baby/Theme From "The Luck Of Ginger Coffey" £15
65 Capitol CL 15427   West Coast/I'll Be Looking Back £30
62 London RE-N 1348   KETTY LESTER (EP) £40
63 London HA-N 2455   LOVE LETTERS (LP) £60
64 RCA Victor RD 7669   THE SOUL OF ME (LP) £40
65 RCA Victor RD 7712   WHERE IS LOVE (LP) £40
67 Stateside S(S)L 10196   WHEN A MAN LOVES A WOMAN (LP) £80

LAZY LESTER
64 Stateside SS 277   I'm A Lover Not A Fighter/Sugar Coated Love £40
71 Blue Horizon 2431 007   MADE UP MY MIND (LP) £150
77 Flyright FLYLP 526   THEY CALL ME LAZY (LP) £15
79 Flyright FLYLP 544   POOR BOY BLUES (LP) £15

LESTER AND THE BREW
81 PL EP 001   A BAD DAY AT THE CITY (EP) £25

LETHAL
94 White BAD 1   Portrait Of A Young Man As An Artist (12") £15

JOE LETHAL
78 Lethal CI 200526   Don't Come Back/You Ain't Free (no p/s) £35

LETIMOV
85 Reconciliation RECONCILE 2 To The Suffering/The Gift Of Life (p/s) £15

LET'S WRESTLE
09 Stolen SR666   IN THE COURT OF THE WRESTLING LETS (LP, silkscreen sleeve, 300 only) £25

LETTERMEN (2)
74 Stag SG 10075   FIRST CLASS (LP, private pressing) £90

LETTERS
79 Heartbeat PULSE 9   Nobody Loves Me/Don't Want You Back (p/s) £90

JANE LEUNG
70 Jane (No cat on)   Heaven Help Up All/Now You're Gone (no p/s) £30

LARRY LEVAN
85 Garage IMA 2   PADLOCK (LP, with Sly Dunbar, Robbie Shakespeare, Gwen Guthrie, Wally Badarou,
                             Darryl Thompson) £15
00 Strut STRUTLP 006   LARRY LEVAN LIVE AT THE PARADISE GARAGE (3LP, compilation, printed inners) £60

LEVEE BREAKERS
65 Parlophone R 5291   Babe I'm Leaving You/Wild About My Loving £25
(see also Beverley, Johnny Joyce)

LEVEE CAMP MOAN
69 County Recording Service LEVEE CAMP MOAN (LP, private pressing) £750
    COUN LP 133
69 County Recording Srvice PEACOCK FARM (LP, private pressing) £750
    COUN LP 158

LEVEL 42
79 Elite DAZZ 4   Sandstorm/Journey To The Powerline (Remix) (12", white label test pressing, no p/s) £75

80	Elite DAZZ 5	Love Meeting Love/Instrumental Love (7", unreleased)	£0
80	Elite DAZZ 5	Love Meeting Love/Instrumental Love (12", company die-cut stickered sleeve)	£25
91	Polydor 511 635-2	THE COMPLETE LEVEL 42 (9-CD box set)	£40

LEVELLERS

91	On The Fiddle OTF EP 1	Police On My Back/Where The Hell Are We Going To Love?/Travelogue (4am Mix) (12", fan club issue, p/s)	£15
92	On The Fiddle OTF LP 2	LIVE 1992 (LP, fan club issue, 2,000 only)	£18

GERRY LEVENE (& AVENGERS)

64	Decca F 11815	It's Driving Me Wild (solo)/Dr. Feelgood	£40

LEVERS

79	Bead Records BEAD 10	LEVERS (LP)	£25

CARL LEV(E)Y & CIMARRONS

70	Hot Rod HR 100	Walk The Hot Street/PEGGY & CIMARRONS: You Say You Don't Love Me	£35
70	Hot Rod HR 101	Remember Easter Monday/PEGGY & JIMMY: Pum Pum Lover	£20

(see also Hot Rod Allstars, Rita Alston, Peggy)

FRANKIE LEVI

86	Firm (no cat no)	Steady Rock/KEVIN GAD: Bloodlines Connections (12")	£150

LEVIATHAN

68	Elektra EKSN 45052	Remember The Times/Second Production	£45
69	Elektra EKSN 45057	The War Machine/Time	£30
69	Elektra EKSN 45052/45057	(WAY IN) THE FOUR FACES OF LEVIATHAN (Remember The Times/Second Production/ The War Machine/Time) (2 x 7" press pack, A4 folder sleeve, some overprinted with 'Harrods' logo, with bio & photo, promo, some commercial)	£250
69	Elektra EKSN 45075	Flames/Just Forget Tomorrow	£30
69	Elektra EKS 74046	LEVIATHAN (2-LP, unissued, acetates only, 1 copy known)	£2000
12	Record Collector RCLP004	UNLEASHED (2-LP, 1 side etched, gatefold)	£50

(see also High Broom)

LEVITICUS

94	Philly Blunt PB 001	Burial (Lovers Rock Mix)/(Mademoiselle Mix) (12")	£30

LEVITTS

69	ESP Disk/Fontana STL 5518	WE ARE THE LEVITTS (LP)	£25

LEVON & HAWKS

65	Atlantic AT 4054	The Stones I Throw/He Don't Love You	£70

(see also Band)

BARRINGTON LEVY

79	Bushays BFM 128	Sister Debby/Blacksin Dub (12", with Jah Thomas)	£20
70s	Burning Vibrations BVD 003	A Ya We Deh/Give Thanks And Praise (12", with Trinity)	£25
79	Burning Sounds BRD 029	Hunting Man (feat. Jah Thomas)/Hunting Dub (12")	£25
79	Greensleeves GRED 27	Lose Respect (feat. Trinity)/ROMAN STEWART & TRINITY: Since You're Gone (12")	£15
80	Greensleeves GRED 28	Englishman/SCORCHER & ROOTS RADICS BAND: The Daughter Them Ire (12")	£20
80	Greensleeves GRED 35	Mary Long Tongue/Look Youthman (12")	£20
80	Greensleeves GRED 40	Crucifixion/Eventide Fire A Disaster (red vinyl 12")	£18
80	Cha Cha CHAD 22	Warm and Sunny Day/GENERAL SAINT - DJ cut (12")	£50
80	His Majesty HMD 004	Shaolin Temple/Version (12")	£25
80	Strong Like Sampson SLSD8	Wicked Intention/ROD TAYLOR (12")	£40
80	Lovelinch LL 03	Skylarking/HORTENSE ELLIS - You Done Me Wrong (12")	£25
82	Greensleeves GRED 80	Tomorrow Is Another Day/PAPA TULLO: Delaware (12")	£20
80	Strong Like Sampson SLSD 017	She Rob And Gorn/PAPPA TULLO: Cat Called Francella (12")	£15
82	Oak Sounds OSD 008	Open Book/Open version (12")	£20
84	Greensleeves GRED 136	Prison Oval Rock (master mix)/Prison Oval Rock (dub plate mix) (12")	£15
84	Greensleeves GRED 145	Pon Your Toe/Girl I Love You (12")	£18
85	Time TR009	Here I Come/Trouble A Come/Run Come Dub/Rub A Dub (12")	£18
87	Live & Learn LLD014	Juggling Soldier/Version (12")	£20
79	Greensleeves GREL 9	ENGLISHMAN (LP)	£30
79	Burning Sounds BS 1039	SHINE EYE GAL (LP)	£30
80	JB JBLP 01	DOH RAY ME (LP)	£60
80	Jah Guidance JA CC 14	ROBIN HOOD (LP)	£40
82	Trojan TRLS 209	POOR MAN STYLE (LP)	£15
83	GG's GG 0032	BARRINGTON LEVY'S LIFE STYLE (LP)	£40
83	Burning Sounds BS 1050	HUNTER MAN (LP)	£20
85	Time Records TRLP 003	HERE I COME (LP)	£30

BEN LEVY

66	Ska Beat JB 245	Doreen/Never Knew Love	£20
66	Ska Beat JB 255	I'll Make You Glad/Keep Smiling	£20

JONA LEWIE

78	Stiff BUY 37	Halleluja Europe/Police Trap (Unreleased, test pressings only)	£50
79	Stiff SEEZ 8	ON THE OTHER HAND THERE'S A FIST (LP, yellow vinyl)	£15
78	Stiff SEEZ 8	ON THE OTHER HAND THERE'S A FIST (LP, picture disc)	£15

(see also Brett Marvin & Thunderbolts)

ALVA (REGGIE) LEWIS

67	Caltone TONE 111	Return Home/KING ROCK & WILLOWS: You Are The One	£100
67	Island WI 3080	I'm Indebted/GROOVERS: You've Got To Cry	£50
68	Blue Cat BS 125	She Is leaving/UNIQUES: Girls Like Dirt	£80
68	Jolly HY 009	Hang My Head And Cry/COOL CATS: Hold Your Love	£100
72	Upsetter US 391	Natty Natty (as Reggie Lewis)/UPSETTERS: Version	£20

(see also Reggae Boys, Webber Sisters, Lester Sterling, Cool Cats)

LEWIS & CLARKE EXPEDITION
67	RCA 1633	Blue Revelations/I Feel Good (I Feel Bad)	£20

ANDY LEWIS & PAUL WELLER
97	Acid Jazz AJX 193P	Are You Trying To Be Lonely?/Tell Me Once Again You Love Me (7" promo, A-label in Acid Jazz sleeve, 50 copies only)	£40

(see also Paul Weller)

BARBARA LEWIS
63	London HLK 9724	Hello Stranger/Think A Little Sugar	£25
63	London HLK 9724	Hello Stranger/Think A Little Sugar (DJ Copy)	£60
63	London HLK 9779	Straighten Up Your Heart/If You Love Her	£25
64	London HLK 9832	Snap Your Fingers/Puppy Love	£25
64	Atlantic AT 4013	Pushin' A Good Thing Too Far/Come Home	£40
65	Atlantic AT 4031	Baby I'm Yours/Hello I Say Love	£20
65	Atlantic AT 4041	Make Me Your Baby/Love To Be Loved	£20
66	Atlantic AT 4068	Don't Forget About Me/It's Magic	£20
66	Atlantic 584 037	Make Me Belong To You/Girls Need Loving Care	£20
67	Atlantic 584 061	Baby What Do You Want Me To Do/I Remember The Feeling	£60
68	Atlantic 584 174	Sho Nuff (It's Got To Be Your Love)/Thankful For What I Got	£20
71	Atlantic 2091 143	Someday We're Gonna Love Again/Baby I'm Yours	£15
65	Atlantic AET 6015	SNAP YOUR FINGERS (EP)	£70
66	Atlantic ATL 5042	BABY I'M YOURS (LP)	£40
66	Atlantic 587 002	IT'S MAGIC (LP, mono)	£50
66	Atlantic 588 002	IT'S MAGIC (LP, stereo)	£60
70	Stax SXATS 1035	THE MANY GROOVES OF BARBARA LEWIS (LP)	£50

BOBBY LEWIS
61	Parlophone R 4794	Tossin' And Turnin'/Oh Yes, I Love You	£20
61	Parlophone R 4831	One Track Mind/Are You Ready	£25
62	Stateside SS 126	I'm Tossin' And Turnin' Again/Nothin' But The Blues	£25

CAPPY LEWIS
61	Vogue V 9184	Bullfight/OLYMPICS: Little Pedro	£20

(see also Olympics)

DAVE LEWIS (1)
66	Pye Intl. NEP 44057	GIVIN' GAS (EP)	£40
64	Pye Intl. NPL 28053	LITTLE GREEN THING(LP)	£30

DAVE LEWIS (2)
76	Polydor 2383 420	FROM TIME TO TIME (LP, with lyric sheet)	£18

DAVID LEWIS
70	AX 1	SONGS OF DAVID LEWIS (LP, private pressing, paste-on sleeve)	£400

(see also Andwella['s Dream], David Baxter)

FURRY LEWIS
69	Blue Horizon 7-63228	PRESENTING THE COUNTRY BLUES (LP)	£80
70	Matchbox SDR 190	IN MEMPHIS (LP)	£30
71	Xtra XTRA 1116	FURRY LEWIS (LP)	£20
71	Spokane SPL 1004	THE EARLY YEARS 1927-1929 (LP)	£30

(see also John Estes)

GARY LEWIS & PLAYBOYS
66	Liberty LIB 55846	She's Just My Style/I Won't Make That Mistake Again	£20
66	Liberty LIB 55898	My Heart's Symphony/Tina	£20
65	Liberty LBY 1259	THIS DIAMOND RING (LP)	£30
66	Liberty LBY 1322	JUST OUR STYLE (LP)	£25

GEORGE LEWIS/FREDDIE KOHLMAN
53	Brunswick LA 8627	NEW ORLEANS JAZZ CONCERT (10" LP)	£15

HOPETON LEWIS
67	Island WI 3054	Rock Steady/Cool Collie	£150
67	Island WI 3055	Finder's Keepers/ROLAND ALPHONSO: Shanty Town Curfew	£100
67	Island WI 3056	Let Me Come On Home/Hardships Of Life (with Merritone All Stars)	£75
67	Island WI 3057	Run Down/Pick Yourself Up	£150
67	Island WI 3059	Let The Little Girl Dance/This Music Got Soul	£125
67	Island WI 3068	Rock A Shacka/I Don't Want Trouble	£125
68	Island WI 3076	Everybody Rocking/Stars Shining So Bright	£125
68	Fab FAB 43	Skinny Leg Girl/Live Like A King (as Hopetown Lewis & Glenmore Brown)	£90
70	Duke Reid DR 2505	Boom Shaka Lacka/TOMMY McCOOK QUINTET: Dynamite	£25
70	Duke Reid DR 2516	Testify/TOMMY McCOOK: Super Soul	£25
71	Duke DU 112	Grooving Out Of Life (with Byron Lee & Dragonaires) (actually titled Grooving Out On Life)/BYRON LEE & DRAGONAIRES: Fire Fire	£15
71	Treasure Isle TI 7060	To The Other Man/TOMMY McCOOK: Stampede	£15
72	Treasure Isle TI 7071	Judgement Day (actually by Hopeton Lewis & Dennis Alcapone)/ EARL LINDO: Version Day	£15
12	Duke Reid THB 7015	Live It Up/JOHN HOLT WITH TOMMY MCCOOK AND THE SUPERSONICS: Ali Baba/ Dub	£18
67	Island ILP 957	TAKE IT EASY: ROCKSTEADY WITH HOPETON LEWIS (LP)	£200
71	Trojan TRL 36	GROOVING OUT ON LIFE (LP)	£30

(see also Glenmore Brown & Hopeton Lewis)

JERRY LEWIS
53	Capitol LC 6591	CAPITOL PRESENTS JERRY LEWIS (10" LP)	£20

57	Brunswick LAT 8173	JUST SINGS (LP)	£15
58	Brunswick LAT 8222	MORE JERRY LEWIS (LP)	£15

(see also Dean Martin)

JERRY LEWIS (JAMAICA)

72	Pama PM 862	The Godfather/ALTON ELLIS: Some Day	£20
73	Explosion EX 2077	Rhythm Pleasure/AGGROVATORS: Doctor Seaton	£20

(see also I Roy)

JERRY LEE LEWIS

78s

57	London HLS 8457	Whole Lotta Shakin' Goin' On/It'll Be Me	£18
57	London HLS 8529	Great Balls Of Fire/Mean Woman Blues	£20
58	London HLS 8559	You Win Again/I'm Feelin' Sorry	£30
58	London HLS 8592	Breathless/Down The Line	£20
58	London HLS 8700	Break-Up/I'll Make It All Up To You	£35
59	London HLS 8780	High School Confidential/Fools Like Me	£50
59	London HLS 8840	Lovin' Up A Storm/Big Blon' Baby	£50
59	London HLS 8941	Let's Talk About Us/The Ballad Of Billy Joe	£60
59	London HLS 8993	Little Queenie/I Could Never Be Ashamed Of You	£100
96	Cruisin' The 50s CASB 002	Wild One/Old Black Joe (numbered, 300 only)	£35

SINGLES

57	London HLS 8457	Whole Lotta Shakin' Goin' On/It'll Be Me	£30
57	London HLS 8529	Great Balls Of Fire/Mean Woman Blues	£20
58	London HLS 8559	You Win Again/I'm Feelin' Sorry	£25
58	London HLS 8592	Breathless/Down The Line	£20
58	London HLS 8700	Break-Up/I'll Make It All Up To You	£20
59	London HLS 8780	High School Confidential/Fools Like Me	£20
59	London HLS 8840	Lovin' Up A Storm/Big Blon' Baby	£20
59	London HLS 8941	Let's Talk About Us/The Ballad Of Billy Joe (no triangular centre)	£20
59	London HLS 8993	Little Queenie/I Could Never Be Ashamed Of You (no triangular centre)	£20

(Originally issued with triangular centres; round-centre pressings are worth two-thirds of these values.)

60	London HLS 9083	I'll Sail My Ship Alone/It Hurt Me So	£15
60	London HLS 9131	Baby, Baby, Bye Bye/Old Black Joe	£20
60	London HLS 9202	John Henry/Hang Up My Rock And Roll Shoes	£20
64	London HLS 9867	Lewis Boogie/Bonnie B	£20

SINGLES : EXPORT SINGLES

58	London HL 7050	High School Confidential/Fools Like Me	£20
62	London HL 7117	Save The Last Dance For Me/Hello Josephine	£30
63	London HL 7120	Good Golly Miss Molly/I Can't Trust Me (In Your Arms Anymore)	£20
63	London HL 7123	In The Mood/I'm Feelin' Sorry	£40

EPs

58	London RE-S 1140	JERRY LEE LEWIS - NO. 1 (with triangular centre)	£40
58	London RE-S 1140	JERRY LEE LEWIS - NO. 1	£20
59	London RE-S 1186	JERRY LEE LEWIS - NO. 2 (with triangular centre)	£40
59	London RE-S 1186	JERRY LEE LEWIS - NO. 2	£25
59	London RE-S 1187	JERRY LEE LEWIS - NO. 3 (with triangular centre)	£40
59	London RE-S 1187	JERRY LEE LEWIS - NO. 3	£25
61	London RE-S 1296	JERRY LEE LEWIS - NO. 4	£30
62	London RE-S 1336	JERRY LEE LEWIS - NO. 5	£30
63	London RE-S 1351	JERRY LEE LEWIS - NO. 6	£30
63	London RE-S 1378	FOUR MORE FROM JERRY LEE LEWIS	£30
66	Philips BE 12599	COUNTRY STYLE	£30

ALBUMS

59	London HA-S 2138	JERRY LEE LEWIS	£100
62	London HA-S 2440	JERRY LEE'S GREATEST	£50
64	Philips (S)BL 7622	GOLDEN HITS	£20
65	Philips (S)BL 7646	LIVE AT THE STAR CLUB, HAMBURG (with Nashville Teens)	£25
65	Philips BL 7650	THE GREATEST LIVE SHOW ON EARTH	£15
65	Philips BL 7668	THE RETURN OF ROCK	£15
65	London HA-S 8251	WHOLE LOTTA SHAKIN' GOIN' ON	£50
67	London HA-S 8323	BREATHLESS	£30

(see also Nashville Teens)

JIMMY LEWIS

68	Minit MLF 11002	The Girls From Texas/Let Me Know	£20

JOHN LEWIS

60	London Jazz LTZ-K 15186	IMPROVISED MEDITATIONS AND EXCURSIONS (LP)	£15
61	London Jazz LTZ-K 15218	THE GOLDEN STRIKER (LP, also stereo SAH-K 6152)	£15

(see also Modern Jazz Quartet)

JOHN LEWIS AND SACHA DISTEL

59	UK Oriole MG20036	AFTERNOON IN PARIS (LP)	£25

LEW LEWIS (REFORMER)

78	Lew Lewis LEW 1	Lucky Seven/Night Talk (500 only, plain white sleeve, handwritten-style white label)	£20

(see also Dr. Feelgood, Eddie & the Hot Rods)

LINDA LEWIS

67	Polydor 56173	You Turned My Bitter Into Sweet/Do You Believe In Love	£150
71	Reprise K 44130	SAY NO MORE (LP)	£25

MINT VALUE £

72	Reprise K 44208	LARK (LP, textured gatefold sleeve)	£20
75	Artista ARTY 109	NOT A LITTLE GIRL ANYMORE (LP)	£15
77	Arista SPARTY 1003	WOMAN OVERBOARD (LP)	£15
73	Raft RA 48501	FATHOMS DEEP (LP, die-cut sleeve with inner)	£18
79	Ariola ARL 5033	HACIENDA VIEW (LP)	£15
83	Epic EPC 25478	A TEAR AND A SMILE (LP)	£20
95	Turpin TPN 3	SECOND NATURE (LP)	£15
96	Turpin TPN 5	WHATEVER (2-LP)	£25

(see also Ferris Wheel)

LOUISE LEWIS
79	Inferno HEAT 120	Wee Oo I'll Let It Be You Babe/Instrumental Version (unissued and unconfirmed, this price for test pressings may exist)	£100

MARGARET LEWIS
62	Starlite ST45 081	Sometin's Wrong Baby/John De Lee	£30

MEADE 'LUX' LEWIS
55	Vogue EPV 1065	MEADE 'LUX' LEWIS (EP)	£15
56	Melodisc EPM7 107	BOOGIE WOOGIE AND BLUES (EP)	£15

(see also Albert Ammons, [Big] Joe Turner)

MEADE 'LUX' LEWIS & SLIM GAILLARD
56	Columbia Clef 33C 9021	JAZZ AT THE PHILHARMONIC (10" LP)	£20

(see also Slim Gaillard)

MIA LEWIS
66	Parlophone R 5526	Nothing Lasts Forever/(Baby) I'm Feeling Good	£15

MICHAEL LEWIS
73	United Artists UP 35569	Theatre Of Blood Theme/Edwina's Theme	£15

NIGEL LEWIS
86	Media Burn MB10	WHAT I FEEL NOW (LP)	£25

NORMA LEWIS
81	Challenge LOVER 1	This Feelings Killing Me/The Girl's A Fool/(Instrumental) (12")	£30
82	Jive JIVE T 11	This Feelings Killing Me/The Girl's A Fool/T.B.C. Magic Bullet (features Atmosfear uncredited) (12")	£18

(see also Atmosfear)

RAMSEY LEWIS (TRIO)
65	Chess CRS 8020	The 'In' Crowd/Since I Fell For You (as Ramsey Lewis Trio)	£15
66	Chess CRS 8041	Wade In The Water/Ain't That Peculiar (as Ramsey Lewis Trio)	£60
66	Chess CRS 8041	Wade In The Water/Ain't That Peculiar (as Ramsey Lewis Trio) (DJ copy)	£200
67	Chess CRS 8051	Day Tripper/Hurt So Bad	£20
69	Chess CRS 8096	Cry Baby Cry/Wade In The Water	£20
69	Chess CRS 8096	Cry Baby Cry/Wade In The Water (DJ copy)	£45
72	Chess 6145 004	Wade In The Water/Ain't That Peculiar (paper label)	£15
66	Chess CRE 6019	A HARD DAY'S NIGHT (EP, as Ramsey Lewis Trio)	£30
65	Pye Jazz NJL 55	AT THE BOHEMIAN CAVERNS (LP)	£20
65	Chess CRL 4511	THE 'IN' CROWD (LP)	£25
65	Chess CRL 4518	CHOICE! THE BEST OF RAMSEY LEWIS (LP)	£25
66	Chess CRL 4520	HANG ON RAMSEY! (LP)	£20
66	Chess CRL 4522	WADE IN THE WATER (LP)	£40
67	Chess CRL 4528	GOIN' LATIN (LP)	£25
67	Chess CRL 4531	THE MOVIE ALBUM (LP)	£20
68	Chess CRL(S) 4533	DANCIN' IN THE STREET (LP)	£25
68	Chess CRLS 4535	UP POPS RAMSEY LEWIS (LP)	£25
68	Chess CRLS 4539	MAIDEN VOYAGE (LP)	£25
69	Chess CRLS 4545	MOTHER NATURE'S SON (LP)	£30
68	Fontana SFJL 962	DOWN TO EARTH (LP)	£20
72	Chess 6310 106	BACK TO THE ROOTS (LP)	£15
72	Chess 6310 114	THE BEST OF RAMSEY LEWIS (LP)	£15
72	Chess 6310 124	TOBACCO ROAD (LP)	£15
73	CBS 65307	FUNKY SERENITY (LP)	£20
73	CBS CQ 31096	UPENDO NI PAMOJA (LP, quadrophonic)	£15
74	CBS S80677	SUN GODDESS (LP)	£30
76	CBS 81406	SALONGO (LP)	£18

(see also Young-Holt Unlimited)

RICHARD LEWIS & HIS BAND
60	Downbeat CHA 1	Hey, Little Girl/Hey, Little Boy	£40

SHIRLEY LEWIS
83	High Energy	Loves Warming Up/Dub Mix (12")	£15

SMILEY LEWIS
53	London L 1189	Big Mamou/Play Girl (78, some copies miscredited to Smiley Davis)	£100
56	London HLU 8312	One Night/Ain't Gonna Do It	£800
56	London HLU 8312	One Night/Ain't Gonna Do It (78)	£100
56	London HLU 8337	Down Yonder We Go Ballin'/Don't Be That Way (Please Listen To Me)	£800
56	London HLU 8337	Down Yonder We Go Ballin'/Don't Be That Way (Please Listen To Me) (78)	£100
57	London HLP 8367	Shame, Shame, Shame/No, No (gold lettering)	£500
57	London HLP 8367	Shame, Shame, Shame/No, No (silver lettering)	£400
57	London HLP 8367	Shame, Shame, Shame/No, No (78)	£70
70	Liberty LBS 83308	SHAME, SHAME, SHAME (LP)	£25
78	United Artists UAS 30167	I HEAR YOU KNOCKING (LP)	£15

STEVIE LEWIS
| 65 | Mercury MF 871 | Take Me For A Little While/My Whole World Seems To Be Tumbling Down | £22 |

TAMALA LEWIS
| 79 | Destiny DS 1010 | You Won't Say Nothing/If You Can Stand Me (DJ copy) | £15 |

TINY LEWIS
| 60 | Parlophone R 4617 | Too Much Rockin'/I Get Weak | £150 |

VIC LEWIS
69	NEMS 56-4057	Blackbird/I Will	£20
55	Decca LF 1216	PROGRESSIVE JAZZ (10" LP)	£30
62	HMV CLP 1641	PLAY BOSSA NOVA HOME AND AWAY (LP, features Tubby Hayes)	£50
70	Ember CJS 807	AT THE BEAULIEU FESTIVAL (LP)	£25
60s	Ember SE 8018	BIG BAND EXPLOSION (LP)	£30
70s	DJM SPECB 103	MY LIFE MY WAY (LP)	£15

LEWIS SISTERS
| 65 | Tamla Motown TMG 536 | You Need Me/Moonlight On The Beach (DJ Copy) | £150 |
| 65 | Tamla Motown TMG 536 | You Need Me/Moonlight On The Beach | £120 |

DAVE LEWRY
| 72 | Westwood WRS 019 | ALL I WANT TO DO IS PLAY GUITAR (LP) | £35 |

LEYTON BUZZARDS
| 79 | Chrysalis CHR 1213 | JELLIED EELS TO RECORD DEALS (LP, as Buzzards) | £15 |

JOHN LEYTON
60	Top Rank JAR 426	Tell Laura I Love Her/Goodbye To Teenage Love	£30
60	HMV POP 798	The Girl On The Floor Above/Terry Brown's In Love With Mary Dee	£50
64	HMV POP 1374	All I Want Is You/Every Day Is A Holiday (with Grazina Frame & Mike Sarne)	£15
73	York SYK 551	Dancing In The Graveyard/Riversong	£15
74	York YR 210	Rock 'N' Roll/Highway Song	£15
62	Top Rank JKP 3016	JOHN LEYTON (EP)	£30
62	HMV 7EG 8747	HIT PARADE (EP)	£20
64	HMV 7EG 8843	BEAUTIFUL DREAMER (EP)	£20
64	HMV 7EG 8854	TELL LAURA I LOVE HER (EP)	£25
61	HMV CLP 1497	THE TWO SIDES OF JOHN LEYTON (LP)	£30
62	HMV CLP 1664	ALWAYS YOURS (LP, with Charles Blackwell's Orchestra)	£40

(see also Le Roys)

L.F.O.
90	Warp WAP 5	L.F.O. (The Leeds Warehouse Mix)/L.F.O. (Track 4)/Probe (The Cuba Edit) (12", p/s)	£20
91	Warp WARPLP3	FREQUENCIES (LP)	£35
96	Warp WARPLP39	ADVANCE (2-LP)	£30
03	Warp WARPLP110	SHEATH (LP)	£15

LG & LOPEZ
| 06 | Sit Tight STRLP 03 | SMOKE RINGS (LP) | £15 |

LIAISON
| 82 | Catweazle CR 001 | Play It With A Passion/Caught In A ... (grey p/s) | £35 |
| 84 | Liaison LSN 0020 | Only Heaven Knows/Ease The Pain Away (p/s) | £100 |

LIAR
| 79 | Bearsville K 55524 | SET THE WORLD ON FIRE (LP, picture disc) | £15 |

LIARS
14	Mute 12MUTE 511	Mess On A Mission/Blah Vets/Mess On A Mission (Black Bananas Freezer Jam Remix)/Mess On A Mission (Silent Servant Remix) (12" clear vinly with embedded coloured strings)	£25
04	Mute STUMM 225	THEY WERE WRONG SO WE DROWNED (LP, gatefold, white vinyl, booklet)	£20
05	Mute STUMM 246	DRUM'S NOT DEAD (LP with DVD)	£25
07	Mute STUMM 287	LIARS (LP, white vinyl, inner)	£15
13	Mute STUMM 343	WIXIW (LP & CD, all dipped in wax, 355 copies)	£50
14	Mute (No Cat. No.)	MESS (LP, clear vinyl, vacuum sealed with coloured string)	£35

SVEN LIBAEK
| 06 | Trunk JBH 020 LP | INNER SPACE: THE LOST FILM MUSIC OF SVEN LIBAEK (LP, 500 only) | £30 |

LIBERACE COUGHS UP BLOOD
| 81 | Vital VTL 0002 | Messerschmidt/Too Many Places/NIK TOWNEND: Gunslinger (p/s) | £15 |

LIBERATION SUITE
| 75 | Myrrh MYR 1027 | LIBERATION SUITE (LP) | £20 |

LIBERATORS
| 65 | Stateside SS 424 | It Hurts So Much/You Look So Fine | £15 |

(see also Pinkerton's Assorted Colours)

EVE LIBERTINE & CRASS
| 84 | Crass 1984/4 | ACTS OF LOVE (LP, with book) | £15 |

(see also Crass)

LIBERTINES
02	Rough Trade RTRADES 054	What A Waster/I Get Along (p/s, 2000 only)	£25
02	Rough Trade RTRADES 064	Up The Bracket/Boys In The Band (p/s)	£15
03	Rough Trade RTRADES 074	Time For Heroes/The 7 Deadly Sins (demo version) (p/s)	£20
03	Rough Trade RTRADS 119	Don't Look Back Into The Sun/Death On The Stairs (blue vinyl, fold-out poster sleeve in PVC slipcase, 3000 only)	£30
04	Rough Trade RTRADS 163	Can't Stand Me Now/(I've Got) Sweets (p/s)	£15
16	Virgin/EMI (no cat no)	LIVE FROM NOTTINGHAM 2015: Can't Stand Me Now/Time For Heroes (p/s, 250	£15

		only)	
16	Virgin EMI (no cat no)	**Don't Look Back In To The Sun** (Live)/ **What A Waster** (Live) (p/s, Live at O2 Academy Bristol 8th September 2015, 250 copies only)	£30
02	Rough Trade RTRADELP 065	**UP THE BRACKET** (LP, printed inner)	£60
04	Rough Trade RTRADELP166	**THE LIBERTINES** (LP, printed inner)	£30
04	Rough Trade RTRADELPX166	**THE LIBERTINES** (LP, gatefold, 180g, numbered, 3000 only)	£60
04	Rough Trade RTRADELP166	**THE LIBERTINES** (White label test pressing, 10 only)	£100
07	Rough Trade RTRADLP 421	**TIME FOR HEROES - THE BEST OF THE LIBERTINES** (LP, red vinyl, printed inner)	£50
15	Virgin/EMI 4746281	**ANTHEMS FOR DOOMED YOUTH** (LP, printed inner)	£20
15	Virgin/EMI 4746282	**ANTHEMS FOR DOOMED YOUTH** (LP/2CD box set, 4000 only)	£35
15	Virgin/EMI 4769576	**ANTHEMS FOR DOOMED YOUTH** (6 x 7" box set, 1000 only)	£35
24	EMI BN04768	**ALL QUIET ON THE EASTERN ESPLANADE** (LP, alternate sleeve)	£30
24	EMI/Blood EMIV 2111	**ALL QUIET ON THE EASTERN ESPLANADE** (LP, yellow, black and blue splatter vinyl, numbered, 2000 only, tattoo)	£40

(see also Babyshambles)

LIBERTY
80s	Mortarhate MORT 25	**THE PEOPLE WHO CARE ARE ANGRY** (LP)	£25

LIBIDO 1
73	Mooncrest MOON 2	**Hold On To Your Fire/Weren't Born A Man**	£20

LICKS
79	Stortbeat BEAT 8	**1970S EP**	£15

(see also Epileptics, Flux Of Pink Indians)

GARETH LIDDIARD
10	ATP ATPRLP41	**STRANGE TOURIST** (2-LP)	£80

LIDJ INCORPORATED
89	Youth Sound YSR 001	**Black Liberation/Version 1/Version 2/Version 3** (12", white labels only)	£40
90	Youth Sound YSR 002	**Line Up/Version/Ole Pan Sound/Version** (12")	£30
90	Youth Sound YSR 003T	**General Penitentiary/Version/G.P.** (12")	£30
90	Youth Sound YOLP 002	**DUB LIBERATION - LIDJ INCORPORATED MEETS SOUND IRATION** (LP)	£25
95	Eastern Sher ES 001	**BLACK LIBERATION** (LP)	£25

BUNNY LIE LIE
81	Greensleeves GRED 52	**Babylonian/WAYNE WADE: Poor And Humble** (12")	£20

LIEUTENANT PIGEON
73	Decca SKL 5154	**MOULDY OLD MUSIC** (LP)	£20
73	Decca SKL 5174	**PIGEON PIE** (LP)	£20
74	Decca SKL 5196	**PIGEON PARTY** (LP)	£25

(see also Shel Naylor)

LIFE
69	Polydor 56778	**Hands Of The Clock/Ain't I Told You Before**	£22
72	Philips 6006247	**Hold On** (I'll Find You)/**Love Nest**	£30
73	Philips 6006 280	**Cats Eyes/Death In The Family** (paper label)	£20
74	Polydor 2383 295	**LIFE AFTER DEATH** (LP)	£60

LIFE AFTER LIFE
85	Timetrack SRTSKL 453	**LIFE AFTER LIFE** (LP, private pressing)	£120

LIFE 'N' SOUL
67	Decca F 12659	**Ode To Billy Joe/Peacefully Asleep**	£25
68	Decca F 12851	**Here Comes Yesterday Again/Dear Paul**	£15

LIFE STUDIES
83	Occasion OCC 001	**Girl On Fire/Inside Out/Citizen Of Love**	£20

LIFE SUPPORT
79	Slug SLUG 1	**Leader Deceiver/Confusion** (p/s, white labels)	£25

LIFE WITHOUT BUILDINGS
00	Tugboat TUGLP 023	**ANY OTHER CITY** (LP)	£30

LIFESTYLE
77	MCA MCA 308	**Katrina/Love Can Make You Cry**	£20

LIFETIME
70	Polydor 2066 050	**One Word/Two Worlds**	£20

(see also Tony Williams [Lifetime], Jack Bruce, John McLaughlin)

LIFETONES
83	Tone Of Life LTM 001	**FOR A REASON** (LP)	£100

LIFT TO EXPERIENCE
01	Bella Union BELLAV 23	**THE TEXAS JERUSALEM CROSSROADS** (2-LP)	£50

JOE LIGES
63	Blue Beat BB 172	**Spit In The Sky/Tell Me What** (both actually by Delroy Wilson)	£25

(see also Delroy Wilson)

(THE) LIGHT
96	AAA Recordings TRIP 002	**Dusk** (12")	£15

LIGHT BEARER
11	Eyes Of Sound EOSLP 035	**LAPSUS** (2-LP, 'wings' cover, inserts, 200 only)	£30

ENOCH LIGHT
65	Pye Command PCLS 873	**DISCOTHEQUE** (LP)	£20
69	Studio Two TWO 312	**SPACED OUT** (LP)	£20
70	Project 3	**PERMISSIVE POLYPHONICS** (LP)	£20

LIGHT FANTASTIC
73 RCA RCA 2331   Jeanie/You Don't Care £20

LIGHT OF THE WORLD
80 Ensign ENVY 14   ROUND TRIP (LP) £18
82 EMI EMC 3410   CHECK US OUT (LP) £20

GORDON LIGHTFOOT
62 Decca F 11527   (Remember Me) I'm The One/Daisy-Doo (as Gord Lightfoot)....................£20

PAPA (GEORGE) LIGHTFOOT
69 Liberty LBF 15176   Wine Whiskey And Woman/SLIM HARPO: Something Inside Me £25
60s Jan & Dil JR 451   MORE DOWN HOME BLUES (EP)........................£35
71 Liberty LBS 83353   NATCHEZ TRACE (LP, as Papa George Lightfoot) £30

TERRY LIGHTFOOT'S (NEW ORLEANS) JAZZMEN
61 Columbia 33SX 1290   TRAD PARADE (LP, with New Orleans Jazzmen, also stereo SCX 3354) £15
61 Columbia 33SX 1353   WORLD OF TRAD (LP) £15
62 Columbia 33SX 1449   LIGHTFOOT AT LANSDOWNE (LP)....................£15

LIGHTHOUSE
72 Philips 6073 153   Take It Slow/Sweet Lullaby £20
70 RCA SF 8103   SUITE FEELING (LP) £15
71 Vertigo 6342 010   ONE FINE MORNING (LP, gatefold sleeve, swirl label) £150
71 Vertigo 6342 011   THOUGHTS OF MOVIN' ON (LP, gatefold sleeve, swirl label) £100

LIGHTNIN' SLIM
72 Blue Horizon 2096 013   Just A Little Bit/You're Old Enough To Understand/Mind Your Own Business....£30
65 Stateside SL 10135   A LONG DRINK OF BLUES (LP, with Slim Harpo) £80
69 Python PLP 8   THE DOWNHOME BLUES PART 1 (LP, 99 copies only) £60
70 Blue Horizon 7-63863   ROOSTER BLUES (LP)....................................£85
72 Blue Horizon 2931 005   LONDON GUMBO (LP)....................................£150
78 Flyright FLYLP 533   TRIP TO CHICAGO (LP)....................................£18
79 Flyright FLYLP 583   THE FEATURE SIDES 1954 (LP)....................£15
80 Flyright FLYLP 612   WE GOTTA ROCK TONIGHT (LP)....................£18
(see also Slim Harpo)

LIGHTNING LEON
60s Jan & Dil JR 450   DOWN HOME BLUES - SIXTIES STYLE (EP)....................£35

LIGHTNING RAIDERS
80 Arista ARIST 341   Psychedelik Musik ('adult' version)/Views (p/s)....................£18
80 Arista ARIST 341DJ   Psychedelik Musik ('censored' version)/Views (promo only, no p/s)....£35
81 Revenge RSS 39   Sweet Revenge/Rowdies/Addiction/Soul Rescue (12", promo only)....£45
(see also Pink Fairies, Professionals)

LIGOTAGE
84 Picasso PIKM005   FORGIVE AND FORGET (LP, lyric insert) £15

LIJADU SISTERS
78 Afrodisia DWPS 2046   SUNSHINE (LP) £50
12 Soul Jazz SJR LP 246   AFRO-BEAT SOUL SISTERS (2-LP)....................£40

LIKE
10 Geffen 2740655   He's Not A Boy/Why When Love Is Gone £15

LIKE A SONG
73 De Wolfe DW/LP 3273   LIKE A SONG (LP, library issue)....................£18

LIL LOUIS
89 Rough TOUGH 4   Frequency (Remix) (12", 3,000 copies)....................£15

LILAC TIME
90 Caff CAFF 12   Madresfield/Bird On The Wire (p/s, with insert)....................£25
88 Swordfish SWF LP 6   THE LILAC TIME (LP, original issue)....................£15
(see also Hawks, Stephen Duffy)

LILIPUT
81 Rough Trade RT 062   Eisiger Wind/When The Cat's Away Then The Mice Will Play £15
82 Rough Trade ROUGH 43   LILIPUT (LP) £20
(see also Kleenex)

LILLIAN AXE
92 Music For Nations MFN 131   POETIC JUSTICE (LP)....................£40
93 Music For Nations MFN 151   PSYCHOSCHITZOPHRENIA (LP)....................£80

LILLY AK & YOUTH
84 Intrigue 12 84 1/2   Take Me Now/(Remix) (12")....................£15

LIMELIGHT (2)
80 Future Earth FER 008   LIMELIGHT (LP) £22
81 Avatar AALP 5005   LIMITED LIMELIGHT (LP, with bonus single) £20
81 Avatar AALP 5005   LIMITED LIMELIGHT (LP)....................£15

LIMEYS
66 Decca F 12382   Cara-Lin/Feel So Blue £30

LIMIT (1)
78 Private Stock PVT 156   Please Please Me/My World At Night (company sleeve) £45

LIMIT (2)
81 Survival 002   Shockwaves/Ok Go (p/s)....................................£15
81 Survival SUR 004   Taki It/Do It (p/s)....................................£15

LIMMIE
78 Psycho P 2604 **Saturday Night's The Night/Party** £50
14 Super Disco Edits CATS DE6 **Saturday Night's The Night/Can't Turn You Loose** (reissue, as Limmie Funk Ltd) £40

LIMPS/NO SUPPORT
79 Matchbox Classics MC 1 **OPPOSITE SIDES EP** (Split 7" with 2 tracks by Limps and 2 tracks by No Support, p/s) £20
79 Matchbox Classics MC 2 **ANOTHER MATCHBOX CLASSIC?** (Split EP, 2 tracks by Limps and 2 by No Support, with folded p/s) £40
79 Matchbox Classics MC 2 **ANOTHER MATCHBOX CLASSIC?** (Split EP, 2 tracks by Limps and 2 by No Support, without folded p/s, just die-cut stamped sleeve) £15

PETER LINCOLN
67 Major Minor MM 520 **In The Day Of My Youth/My Monkey Is A Junkie** £30
(see also Peter Sarstedt, Sarstedt Brothers, Brothers Kane)

PHILAMORE LINCOLN
68 NEMS 56-3711 **Running By The River/Rainy Day** £70
70 CBS 5007 **The County Jail Band/You're The One** £40

BOB LIND
66 Fontana (S)TL 5340 **DON'T BE CONCERNED** (LP) £20
66 Verve F'ways (S)VLP 5015 **THE ELUSIVE BOB LIND** (LP) £15

LINDA AND THE DARK
80 Crash Point **Horror Movies/I Don't Want To See You Out With Somebody Else** (p/s) £20

DADDY LINDBERG
67 Columbia DB 8138 **Shirl/Wade In The Shade** £120
(see also Crocheted Doughnut Ring)

LINDISFARNE
70 Charisma CB 137 **Clear White Light Part II/Knackers Yard Blues** £15
70 Charisma CAS 1025 **NICELY OUT OF TUNE** (LP, pink 'scroll' label) £35
71 Charisma CAS 1050 **FOG ON THE TYNE** (LP, gatefold textured sleeve, pink 'scroll' label)................£25
72 Charisma CAS 1057 **DINGLY DELL** (LP, with inner sleeve & poster)...£15
(see also Alan Hull, Jack The Lad, Chosen Few, Radiator)

WILLIE LINDO
76 Klik KLP 9019 **FAR AND DISTANT** (LP)...£15
78 Black Wax WAX 21 **Midnight/After Midnight** £25

JIMMY LINDSAY AND THE BEANS
70 Q 2203 **Peace To You Brother/Tribute To Jimi Hendrix** £15

JIMMY LINDSAY
77 Black Swan BS 8 **Easy/FABIAN: Prophecy** (12")..£30
77 Tribesman TM 008 **Easy/FABIAN: Prophecy** (12")...£30
78 Music Hive MH002 **Ain't No Sunshine/EXODUS : Take Six/DIMBALA : And Ting** (12")................£30
82 Music Hive MH004 **Turn Out The Lights/Dole Queue** (12")...£30
80 Gem GEMLP 110 **CHILDREN OF RASTAFARI** (LP) £15

TERRY LINDSEY
69 President PT 232 **It's Over/One Day Up, Next Day Down**...£15

DAVID LINDUP ORCHESTRA
66 Polydor 56106 **Survival Theme/New Forest**...£20
70 Aristocrat AR 1021 **WHEN THE SAINTS GO** (LP) £20

LINDYS
60 Decca F 11253 **The Train Of Love/You Know How Things Get Around**...................................£15
60 Decca F 11272 **Boy With The Eyes Of Blue/Someone Else's Roses** £15

LINES
83 Red ROUGE 3 **ULTRAMARINE** (LP) £15

BUZZY LINHART
69 Philips SBL 7885 **BUZZY** (LP, laminated gatefold sleeve, black/silver labels) £40
71 Kama Sutra 2319011 **THE TIME TO LIVE IS NOW** (LP, textured gatefold sleeve, yellow/red label) £25
71 Buddah 2318028 **MUSIC** (LP)..£15

LINK
92 Evolution EVO 05 **THE FIRST LINK EP** (12", plain sleeve) £35
95 Warp WAP 59 **ANTACID EP** (12", p/s)...£15
(see also Reload, Global Communications, Mystic Institute)

LINKERS
71 Big Shot BI 567 **Bongo Man/FUD CHRISTIAN ALLSTARS: Creation Version** £20

LINN COUNTY
68 Mercury SMCL 20142 **PROUD FLESH SOOTHSEER** (LP) £25
69 Mercury SMCL 20165 **FEVER SHOT** (LP) £20
70 Philips SBL 7923 **TILL THE BREAK OF DAWN** (LP) £18

ELMO LINN
63 Starlite ST45 101 **Another Man's Arms/Sam Houston**...£18

JOE LINTHECOME
50s Poydras 87 **Pretty Mama Blues/Hummingbird Blues** £15

LIONHEART
84 Epic EPC26214 **HOT TONIGHT** (LP)...£15
(see also Iron Maiden,Wildfire)

LIONS
| 69 | Polydor 56757 | Twisted Nerve/My Friend The Blackbird | £30 |

LIONS (JAMAICA)
| 77 | Truth & Right L 001 | Natty Congo I/Version | £150 |

LIONS OF JUDAH
| 69 | Fontana TF 1016 | Our Love's A Growin' Thing/Katja | £20 |

LION TAMERS
| 68 | Polydor 56283 | Speak Your Mind/Light | £50 |

LION YOUTH
78	Virgo Stomach VG 104	Rat Cut A Bottle/Rub A Dub (12", black or purple vinyl)	£30
79	Virgo Stomach VG 013	Three Million On The Dole/Three Million Posse On Employed In A Dub (12")	£15
83	Music Hawk MH 04	I Don't Like It/Government Dub (12")	£15
81	Virgo Stomach VGLP 001	LOVE COMES AND GOES (LP)	£25

LIP MOVES
| 79 | Tichonderoga HP 1 | Guest/What Is (p/s with insert, stickered white labels, signed) | £40 |
| 79 | Tichonderoga HP 1 | Guest/What Is (p/s with insert, stickered white labels) | £30 |

PEGGY LIPTON
| 70 | CBS 4779 | Lu/Let Me Pass By | £15 |

LIQUID
| 95 | XL XLT 28 | Sweet Harmony/Phog/Sweet Harmony (Remix)/Feel 3 (12") | £15 |
| 95 | XL XLLP 113 | CULTURE (2-LP) | £20 |

LIQUID CRYSTAL
91	Bizarre BIZZ 2	Inner Sense/Dischord (12")	£25
92	Bizarre BIZZ 3	The Power Within/Let It Go/Inner Sense ('92 remix) (12")	£25
92	Bizarre BIZZ 3R T	The Power Within (Remix)/Radiate/Inner Sense (Original) (12", p/s)	£25
92	Ruff On Wax ROWT 1	CHROMATIC EP (12", stickered plain sleeve)	£70
92	Ruff On Wax ROWTR 1	CHROMATIC 2 EP: (12", stickered plain sleeve)	£60

LIQUID LIQUID
97	Mo Wax MWLP 078	Cavern (Remix)/Lock Groove (Live)/New Walk (U.N.K.L.E) (12", promo only)	£15
97	Mo Wax MW 078LP	LIQUID LIQUID (2-LP)	£30
08	Domino REWIGLP 34	SLIP IN AND OUT OF PHENOMENON (LP, 12", CD)	£20
97	Mo Wax MW 078LP	LIQUID LIQUID (2-LP)	£20

LIQUID SMOKE
| 70 | Avco Embassy 646 6003 | LIQUID SMOKE (LP) | £50 |

LIQUID STONE
| 81 | Liquid Stone LIQ 001 | Here Comes The Weekend/Because Of You (no p/s, hand stickered labels) | £350 |

LIQUORICE (2)
| 95 | 4AD CAD 5008 | LISTENING CAP (LP) | £15 |

LISTEN
| 65 | CBS 202456 | You'd Better Run/Everybody's Gonna Say | £300 |
| (see also Robert Plant, Led Zeppelin) |

LIT
| 99 | RCA 74321 678591 | A PLACE IN THE SUN (LP) | £50 |

LITMUS
| 09 | Rise Above RISELP 125 | AURORA (2-LP, 1 side etched) | £20 |

LITTER
| 69 | Probe CLPS 4504 | EMERGE (LP) | £75 |

LITTLE ANNIE
| 92 | On U Sound ON UP LP 60 | SHORT AND SWEET (LP) | £20 |
| (see also Annie Anxiety) |

'BIG' TINY LITTLE
| 57 | Vogue Coral Q 72263 | School Day/That's The Only Way To Live | £40 |
| 57 | Vogue Coral Q 72263 | School Day/That's The Only Way To Live (78) | £20 |

SHARON LITTLE
81	One Love (no number)	Don't Mash Up Creation/Version (12")	£150
81	One Love	Don't Mash Up Creation/Version	£100
10	Jah Shaka SHAKA 108	Mash Up Creation/YOUNG WARRIOR: Creation Dub (12", 1st reissue, blue ink on white label)	£30
13	Jah Shaka SHAKA 108	Don't Mash Up Creation/YOUNG WARRIOR: Creation Dub (12", 2nd reissue, black ink)	£20

LITTLE SIMZ
| 17 | Age 101 Music AGE1011X | STILLNESS IN WONDERLAND (2-LP, signed) | £80 |
| 17 | Age 101 Music AGE1011X | STILLNESS IN WONDERLAND (2-LP, unsigned) | £60 |

LITTLE ANGELS
| 87 | Little Angels LAN 001 | LITTLE ANGELS '87 (12" EP) | £30 |
| 87 | Powerstation AMP 14 | TOO POSH TO MOSH (mini-LP) | £18 |

LITTLE ANN
| 98 | Kent TOWN 111 | What Should I Do/O.C. TALBOT: I'm Shooting High (I Reach For The Sky) | £15 |
| 99 | Kent TOWN 112 | Who Are You Trying To Fool/I Got To Have You | £30 |

LITTLE ANTHONY & IMPERIALS
| 58 | London HLH 8704 | Tears On My Pillow/Two People In The World | £40 |
| 58 | London HLH 8704 | Tears On My Pillow/Two People In The World (78) | £30 |

LITTLE ARCHIE

59	London HL 8848	So Much/Oh Yeah	£50
59	London HL 8848	So Much/Oh Yeah (78)	£40
59	Top Rank JAR 256	Shimmy, Shimmy, Ko-Ko Bop/I'm Still In Love With You	£25
60	Top Rank JAR 366	My Empty Room/Bayou, Bayou, Baby	£15
64	United Artists UP 1065	I'm On The Outside Looking In/Please Go	£15
64	United Artists UP 1073	Goin' Out Of My Head/Make It Easy On Yourself	£15
65	United Artists UP 1083	Hurt So Bad/Reputation	£25
65	United Artists UP 1098	Take Me Back/Our Song	£20
65	United Artists UP 1112	I Miss You/Get Out Of My Life	£15
66	United Artists UP 1126	Hurt/Never Again	£40
66	United Artists UP 1137	Better Use Your Head/The Wonder Of It All	£80
66	United Artists UP 1137	Better Use Your Head/The Wonder Of It All (DJ copy)	£150
66	United Artists UP 1151	Gonna Fix You Good (Every Time You're Bad)/You Better Take It Easy Baby	£75
65	United Artists UEP 1004	LITTLE ANTHONY AND THE IMPERIALS (EP)	£100
64	United Artists ULP 1089	I'M ON THE OUTSIDE LOOKING IN (LP)	£100
66	United Artists ULP 1100	GOIN' OUT OF MY HEAD (LP)	£80

LITTLE ARCHIE
68	Atlantic 584 209	I Need You/I Am A Carpet	£40

LITTLE AXE
94	Wired WIRED 17	THE WOLF THAT HOUSE BUILT (2-LP)	£25
96	Wired WIRED 133	SLOW FUSE (2-LP)	£35

LITTLE BEAVER
72	President PTLS 1060	JOEY (LP)	£25
75	President PTLS 1063	PARTY DOWN (LP)	£100

LITTLE BIG HORN
70	Polydor 2058042	Another Man's Song/Just A Game	£40

LITTLE BILL & BLUE NOTES
59	Top Rank JAR 176	I Love An Angel/Bye, Bye Baby	£25
59	Top Rank JAR 176	I Love An Angel/Bye, Bye Baby (78)	£25

(see also Blue Notes)

LITTLE BOOTS
08	50 Bones 4BONES	Meddle/Meddle (Toddla T & Ross Orton Mix) (green vinyl with tattoo set, 500 only)	£35

LITTLE BOY BLUE
69	Jackpot JP 701	Dark End Of The Street/MR VERSATILE: Apple Blossoms	£25

LITTLE CLARKIE & THE OFFBEAT POSSE
86	Jah Tubbys JT 015	Selector Him Good/COLONEL MITE: Bless The Selector/JAH TUBBY: Select The Rhythm (12")	£80
86	Jah Tubbys JT 20	Live Stock Party/Bounty Hunter (12")	£50
87	Y&D YDD 0107	Bubble-N-Rock/Cowboy Stylee (12")	£50
88	Y&D YDD 0134	Can't Come A Dance And Stand Up/Never Give You Up (12")	£30

LITTLE DARLING
65	Blue Beat BB 325	No One/BUSTER'S ALL STARS: Congo Revolution	£150

LITTLE DARLINGS
65	Fontana TF 539	Little Bit O' Soul/Easy To Cry	£100

LITTLE DIPPERS
61	London HLG 9269	Lonely/I Wonder, I Wonder, I Wonder	£15

LITTLE EVA
64	Colpix PX 11035	Making With The Magilla/Run To Her	£15
65	Stateside SS 477	Stand By Me/That's My Man	£20
63	London HA-U 8036	L-L-L-L-LOCO-MOTION (LP, original with plum label & laminated sleeve)	£30

(see also Big Dee Irwin & Little Eva)

LITTLE FEAT
72	Warner Bros. K 46072	LITTLE FEAT (LP)	£15
72	Warner Bros. K 46156	SAILIN' SHOES (LP, gatefold)	£15
75	Warner Bros. K 66038	THE LAST RECORD ALBUM (LP)	£15
77	Warner Bros. K 56349	TIME LOVES A HERO (LP)	£15
86	Nimbus 80027	FEATS DON'T FAIL ME NOW (LP, reissue, Nimbus Supercut, mail order only through Practical Hi Fi magazine)	£70

LITTLE FISH
72	Plant Life PLR 011	HERTFORDSHIRE FOLK SONGS (EP, with insert)	£50

LITTLE FOLK
71	Studio Republic CR 1001	LEAVE THEM A FLOWER (LP)	£18

LITTLE FRANKIE (& COUNTRY GENTLEMEN)
65	Columbia DB 7490	The Kind Of Boy You Can't Forget/I'm Not Gonna Do It	£20
65	Columbia DB 7578	Make-A-Love/Love Is Just A Game (with Country Gentlemen)	£40
65	Columbia DB 7681	It Doesn't Matter Anymore/Happy, That's Me	£20

(see also Chimes featuring Denise)

LITTLE FREE ROCK
69	Transatlantic TRA 208	LITTLE FREE ROCK (LP, laminated sleeve, white/lilac labels, 't' logo)	£175

(see also David John & Mood)

LITTLE GEORGE
64	Rio R 45	Mary Anne/EDWARDS ALLSTARS: Blue Night	£20

LITTLE GRANT
70	Torpedo TOR 27	Baby Don't Let Me Down/Brother Strong Man	£30

LITTLE GRANTS & EDDIE (GRANT)
(see also Equals, Pyramids, Eddy Grant)

67	President PT 159	Rudy's Dead/Everything's Alright	£20
67	President PT 172	Rock Steady '67/Bingo	£20

(see also Equals, Pyramids, Eddy Grant)

LITTLE HANK
66	London HLU 10090	Mr. Bang Bang Man/Don't You Know (withdrawn)	£150
66	London HLU 10090	Mr. Bang Bang Man/Don't You Know (withdrawn) (DJ copy)	£150
70	Monument MON 1045	Mr. Bang Bang Man/Don't You Know (reissue)	£15

LITTLE HOWIE
85	Look To Afrika LTAF 03	Original Love Me/EARL ANTHONY Sensi Man Rock (12")	£100

LITTLE JOE BLUE
78	Flyright FLY LP 534	DON'T TAX ME IN (LP)	£20

LITTLE JOE (JAMAICA)
70	Torpedo TOR 15	Bad Blood/Maxi-Mini War	£40

(see also Sexy Girls)

LITTLE JOE (& THRILLERS)
57	Philips PB 759	Peanuts/Lilly Lou (78)	£15
60	Fontana H 281	Stay (as Little Joe & Thrillers)/Cherry	£25
63	Reprise R 20142	Peanuts/No No I Can't Stop	£20

LITTLE JOHN
67	Pama PM 702	Let's Get Married/Around The World	£20
70	Unity UN 561	No Love/A Little Tear (both sides actually by John Holt)	£15
84	Greensleeves GRELD 139	Form A Line/YELLOWMAN: Rub & Go Down (12")	£15
84	Music Hawk MH15	Walk Away/Version (12")	£20
84	Vista VSLP 4061	UNITE (LP)	£20

(see also John Holt)

ALAN LITTLEJOHN BAND
62	Oriole CB 1734	Out Of The Blue/There Ain't No Sweet Man Worth The Salt Of My Tears	£15

LITTLE JOHN & BILLY BOYO
82	Greensleeves GRED 86	Bushmaster Connection/BILY BOYO: Little Girl (12")	£18
82	Greensleeves GRED 92	Janet Sinclair/Agony Column Dub (12")	£25
82	Rusty International RI 003	What You Want To Be/PROFESSOR & ROOTS RADICS: Combination (12")	£20

LITTLE JOHN ANTHONY
60	Ember EMB 3302	TEENAGE DANCE PARTY (LP)	£20

LITTLE JOHNNY & THREE TEENAGERS
58	Decca F 10990	Baby Lover/Rickety Rackety Rendezvous	£20

LITTLE KIRK
70s	Ruddys RM 004	Ghetto People Broke/Version (12")	£45
70s	Ruddys RM 001	Weed Them Out/Version (12")	£50

LITTLE LULU
72	FAB FAB 21	Love & Obey/AL CAMPBELL & FREDDIE MCGREGOR: Free Man	£200

LITTLE LUMAN
64	Rio R 44	Hurry Harry/R. ALPHONSE: Hucklebuck (B-side actually by Roland Alphonso)	£15

LITTLE LUTHER
64	Pye International 7N 25266	Eenie Meenie Minie Moe/Twirl	£70

LITTLE MACK & BOSS SOUNDS
66	Atlantic 584 031	In The Midnight Hour/You Can't Love Me (In The Midnight Hour)	£25

MARIE LITTLE
71	Argo ZFB 19	FACTORY GIRL (LP)	£150
73	Trailer LER 2084	MARIE LITTLE (LP, red or yellow label)	£50

LITTLE MILTON
65	Pye International 7N 25289	Blind Man/Blues In The Night	£15
65	Chess CRS 8013	We're Gonna Make It/Can't Hold Back The Tears	£20
65	Chess CRS 8013	We're Gonna Make It/Can't Hold Back The Tears (demo copy)	£35
65	Chess CRS 8018	Who's Cheating Who?/Ain't No Big Deal On You	£20
66	Sue WI 4021	Early In The Morning/Bless Your Heart (actually by Roy Milton)	£40
69	Chess CRS 8087	Grits Ain't Groceries/I Can't Quit You Baby	£25
69	Chess CRS 8100	Let's Get Together/I'll Always Love You	£25
69	Chess CRLS 4552	GRITS AIN'T GROCERIES (LP)	£80
72	Chess 6310 120	GOLDEN DECADE (LP)	£15
74	Stax STX 1013	BLUES 'N' SOUL (LP)	£25

LITTLE RICHARD
78s
56	London HLO 8336	Rip It Up/Ready Teddy	£15
57	London HLO 8366	Long Tall Sally/Tutti Frutti	£15
57	London HLO 8382	The Girl Can't Help It/She's Got It	£15
57	London HLO 8446	Lucille/Send Me Some Lovin' (as Little Richard & His Band)	£20
57	London HLO 8470	Jenny, Jenny/Miss Ann (as Little Richard & His Band)	£20
57	London HLO 8509	Keep A Knockin'/Can't Believe You Wanna Leave	£15
58	London HLO 8560	Good Golly Miss Molly/Hey-Hey-Hey-Hey	£15
58	London HLO 8647	Ooh! My Soul/True, Fine Mama	£30
58	London HLU 8770	Baby Face/I'll Never Let You Go	£15

MINT VALUE £

59	London HLU 8831	By The Light Of The Silvery Moon/Early One Morning	£30
59	London HLU 8868	Kansas City/She Knows How To Rock	£50
60	London HLU 9065	Baby/I Got It	£90

SINGLES

56	London HLO 8336	Rip It Up/Ready Teddy (gold label print)	£150
56	London HLO 8336	Rip It Up/Ready Teddy (later pressing with silver label print)	£30
50s	London HLO 8336	Rip It Up/Ready Teddy (repressing, silver-top label, round centre)	£25
57	London HLO 8366	Long Tall Sally/Tutti Frutti (gold label print)	£125
57	London HLO 8366	Long Tall Sally/Tutti Frutti (later silver label print)	£40
50s	London HLO 8366	Long Tall Sally/Tutti Frutti (repressing, silver-top label, round centre)	£20
57	London HLO 8382	The Girl Can't Help It/She's Got It (gold label print)	£125
57	London HLO 8382	The Girl Can't Help It/She's Got It (later silver label print)	£30
50s	London HLO 8382	The Girl Can't Help It/She's Got It (repressing, silver-top label, round centre)	£20
57	London HLO 8446	Lucille/Send Me Some Lovin' (as Little Richard & His Band)	£30
57	London HLO 8470	Jenny, Jenny/Miss Ann (as Little Richard & His Band)	£30
57	London HLO 8509	Keep A Knockin'/Can't Believe You Wanna Leave	£30
58	London HLU 8560	Good Golly Miss Molly/Hey-Hey-Hey-Hey	£30
58	London HLO 8647	Ooh! My Soul/True, Fine Mama	£15
60	London HLU 9065	Baby/I Got It	£15
66	Fontana TF 652	I Don't Know What You've Got But It's Got Me (Parts 1 & 2)	£30
66	Stateside SS 508	Holy Mackeral/Baby, Don'tcha Want A Man Like Me?	£20
66	Sue WI 4001	Without Love/Dance What You Wanna	£40
66	Sue WI 4015	It Ain't Watcha Do (It's The Way How You Do It)/Crossover	£40
66	Columbia DB 7974	Poor Dog/Well	£25
66	Columbia DB 8058	I Need Love/The Commandments Of Love	£20
67	Columbia DB 8116	Get Down With It/Rose Mary	£25
67	Columbia DB 8240	A Little Bit Of Something/Money	£50
67	Columbia DB 8240	A Little Bit Of Something/Money (DJ copy)	£75
67	Columbia DB 8263	I Don't Want To Discuss It/Hurry Sundown	£50
67	Columbia DB 8263	I Don't Want To Discuss It/Hurry Sundown (DJ copy)	£85

SINGLES : EXPORT SINGLES

57	London HL 7022	Jenny, Jenny/Miss Ann (as Little Richard & His Band)	£30
58	London HL 7049	Ooh! My Soul/True, Fine Mama	£15
58	London HL 7056	Baby Face/I'll Never Let You Go	£15
59	London HL 7074	She Knows How To Rock/Early One Morning	£20
59	London HL 7079	By The Light Of The Silvery Moon/Kansas City	£20
59	London HL 7085	Whole Lotta Shakin' Goin' On/All Around The World	£40
68	Decca AD 1006	She's Together/Try Some Of Mine	£25

EPs

57	London RE-O 1071	LITTLE RICHARD AND HIS BAND VOL. 1 (gold tri-centre)	£40
57	London RE-O 1071	LITTLE RICHARD AND HIS BAND VOL. 1 (later silver label)	£30
57	London RE-O 1074	LITTLE RICHARD AND HIS BAND VOL. 2 (later silver label)	£40
57	London RE-O 1074	LITTLE RICHARD AND HIS BAND VOL. 2 (gold tri-centre, later silver)	£20
57	London RE-O 1103	LITTLE RICHARD AND HIS BAND VOL. 3	£25
57	London RE-O 1106	LITTLE RICHARD AND HIS BAND VOL. 4	£25
59	London RE-U 1208	LITTLE RICHARD AND HIS BAND VOL. 5	£25
60	London RE-U 1234	LITTLE RICHARD AND HIS BAND VOL. 6	£30
60	London RE-U 1235	LITTLE RICHARD AND HIS BAND VOL. 7	£35

(The above EPs were originally issued with triangular centres; later round-centre pressings are worth between half to two thirds of these listed values.)

63	London REK 1400	HE'S BACK	£40
64	Vocalion VEP 170155	MEMPHIS SLIM AND LITTLE RICHARD	£80
66	Stateside SE 1042	DO YOU FEEL IT	£60

ALBUMS

89	Ace ABOXLP 1	THE SPECIALITY SESSIONS (8-LP box set, booklet)	£35
57	London HA-O 2055	HERE'S LITTLE RICHARD (flipback, rear sleeve in gloss red)	£100
57	London HA-O 2055	HERE'S LITTLE RICHARD (flipback)	£50
57	London HA-O 2055	HERE'S LITTLE RICHARD (small flipback sleeve)	£55
57	London HA-O 2055	HERE'S LITTLE RICHARD (non-flipback sleeve)	£35
58	London HA-U 2126	LITTLE RICHARD VOL. 2 (flipback sleeve)	£75
58	London HA-U 2126	LITTLE RICHARD VOL. 2 (non-flipback sleeve)	£40
59	RCA Camden CDN 125	LITTLE RICHARD (8 tracks only; others by Buck Ram Orchestra, picture of Richard in "frame" on sleeve, brown wooden effect is first pressing)	£25
59	London HA-U 2193	THE FABULOUS LITTLE RICHARD (flipback sleeve)	£75
59	London HA-U 2193	THE FABULOUS LITTLE RICHARD (non-flipback sleeve)	£40
60	Top Rank 25/025	PRAY ALONG WITH LITTLE RICHARD VOL. 1: A CLOSER WALK WITH THEE (plain white sleeve, mail-order only)	£40
60	Top Rank 25/026	PRAY ALONG WITH LITTLE RICHARD VOL. 2: I'M QUITTING SHOW BUSINESS (plain white sleeve, mail-order only)	£80
64	Stateside SL 10054	SINGS GOSPEL	£25
64	Coral LVA 9220	COMING HOME	£25
65	Mercury MCL 20036	IT'S REAL	£15
65	Fontana TL 5235	IS BACK!	£25
67	Columbia SX/SCX 6136	THE EXPLOSIVE LITTLE RICHARD	£40
68	Fontana SFL 13010	KING OF THE GOSPEL SINGERS	£15
70	Reprise RSLP 6406	THE RILL THING	£15

(see also Canned Heat, Sister Rosetta Tharpe, Buck Ram's Ramrocks)

LITTLE ROY

69	Crab CRAB 39	Without My Love (actually by Roy & Joy)/WINSTON SAMUELS: Here I Come Again	£35

70	Bullet BU 445	Keep Trying/Version (actually by the Matadors)	£20
70	Bullet BU 445	Keep Trying/THE MATADORS: Version II	£15
70	Camel CA 43	Scrooge/In The Days Of Old	£20
70	Camel CA 52	Fight Them/Dreadlock	£20
70	Camel CA 46	You Run Come/THE LITTLE ROYS: Skank King (actually "Skank Me" by Little Roy)	£20
81	Copasetic COP 5001	COLUMBUS SHIP (LP)	£40

LITTLE ROYS

69	Camel CA 36	Bongonyah/CREATIONS: Dad Name (B-side actually "Bad Name")	£25
70	Camel CA 42	Gold Digger (actually by Wailing Soul)/MATADORS: The Mine	£25
70	Camel CA 57	Selassie Want Us Back/ROY AND JOY: Make It With You	£25

(see also Little Roy, Hippy Boys)

LITTLE SAL WITH DANDY & SUPERBOYS

| 68 | Giant GN 19 | I'm In The Mood/I'm A Lover | £30 |

(see also Dandy & Superboys, Superboys)

LITTLE SONNY

| 71 | Stax 2363 005 | NEW KING OF THE BLUES HARMONICA (LP) | £20 |

LITTLE TONY & HIS BROTHERS

59	Durium DC 16639	Who's That Knockin'/The Beat	£25
59	Durium DC 16657	Four An' Twenty Thousand Kisses/Bella Marie	£20
58	Durium U 20058	PRESENTING LITTLE TONY AND HIS BROTHERS (EP)	£20

LITTLE WALTER

60	London HLM 9175	My Babe/Blue Midnight	£70
64	Pye International 7N 25263	My Babe/You Better Watch Yourself	£20
56	London RE-U 1061	LITTLE WALTER AND HIS JUKES (EP)	£200
64	Pye Intl. NPL 28043	LITTLE WALTER (LP)	£70
67	Chess CRL 4529	SUPER BLUES (LP, with Bo Diddley & Muddy Waters)	£45
68	Marble Arch MAL 815	LITTLE WALTER (LP, reissue)	£15
69	Python PLP-KM 20	LITTLE WALTER AND HIS DUKES (LP, 99 copies only)	£55

LITTLE WILBUR (& PLEASERS)

57	Vogue V 9091	Plaything/I Don't Care	£500
57	Vogue V 9091	Plaything/I Don't Care (78)	£100
58	Vogue V 9097	Heart To Heart/Alone In The Night (solo)	£600
58	Vogue V 9097	Heart To Heart/Alone In The Night (solo) (78)	£150

(see also Wilbur Whitfield)

LITTLE WINSTON

| 79 | Crazy Lane SP 001 | Time And Time Again/Come Back Baby (no p/s) | £20 |

LIVELY ONES

63	London HA 8082	SURF DRUMS (LP)	£70
63	London HA 8107	SURF RIDER (LP, mono)	£70
63	London SH 8107	SURF RIDER (LP, stereo)	£85

LIVERPOOL ECHO

| 73 | Spark | LIVERPOOL ECHO (LP) | £20 |

(see also Mandrake Paddle Steamers)

LIVERPOOL EXPRESS

| 76 | Warner Brothers K 56281 | TRACKS (LP) | £15 |

LIVERPOOL F.C.

| 65 | Seddon SED 100 | EE AYE ADDIO: SEVENTY YEARS WAITING (LP) | £20 |

LIVERPOOL FISHERMEN

| 71 | Mushroom 150 MR 9 | SWALLOW THE ANCHOR (LP) | £50 |

LIVERPOOL SCENE

67	CBS BPG 63045	THE INCREDIBLE NEW LIVERPOOL SCENE (LP)	£40
68	RCA SF 7995	THE AMAZING ADVENTURES OF THE LIVERPOOL SCENE (LP)	£18
68	RCA SF 7995	THE AMAZING ADVENTURES OF THE LIVERPOOL SCENE (LP, unlaminated cover)	£18
69	RCA SF 8057	BREAD ON THE NIGHT (LP)	£18
70	RCA SF 8100	ST. ADRIAN AND CO. BROADWAY & 3RD (LP)	£18
70	RCA SF 8134	HEIRLOON (LP)	£18

(see also Clayton Squares, Adrian Henri, Brian Patten, Mike Hart, Andy Roberts, Grimms)

LIVES OF ANGELS

| 86 | Fire FIRE LP 2 | ELEVATOR TO EDEN (LP) | £45 |

LIVING DAYLIGHTS (1)

67	Philips BF 1561	Let's Live For Today/I'm Real (B-side actually titled "It's Real")	£30
79	E.S.R. S/79/CUS 523	HEARTSTOP EP (Personality Changes/Outdoor Girl/Don't Fit/Let Me Know (33 rpm, die-cut p/s, also listed as ESR 3)	£45
67	Philips BF 1613	Always With Him/Baila Maria	£50

(see also Greatest Show On Earth, Naturals)

LIVING DAYLIGHTS (2)

| 79 | E.S.R. S/79/CUS 523 | HEARTSTOP EP (Personality Changes/Outdoor Girl/Don't Fit/Let Me Know (33 rpm, die-cut p/s, also listed as ESR 3) | £200 |

LIVING FORCE

| 84 | Chapter 1 SCH 161 | Ride Ride Ride/Some People | £20 |

LIVING INTENTS

| 81 | Powerful Pierre PPP 01 | (All The) Nice Boys/Genine/Said It's So (p/s) | £20 |

DANDY LIVINGSTONE

| 79 | More Cuts RIC 109 | Instant Music/Living In Sus | £15 |

70s	Night Owl NOR 5002	Calling Africa/Yee Fre Afrikafo Nde	£25
80	Mint Music MMD2	Fever/Righteous Man (12")	£200
81	Trojan TMX 4008	RUDY, A MESSAGE TO YOU (EP, p/s)	£15
72	Trojan TRLS 45	DANDY LIVINGSTONE (LP)	£25

(see also RD Livingstone, Dandy)

J C LIVINGSTONE
| 73 | Penny Farthing Pen 824 | Momma Was A Steamroller Lady/OO La La Me .... | £15 |

LIVIN STONES
| 65 | Oak | I Can't Hold Out/The Music Played On (acetate only) .... | £50 |

LIZA & JET SET
| 65 | Parlophone R 5248 | How Can I Know?/Dancing Yet .... | £15 |

(see also Liza Strike)

LIZZARD
| 76 | Black Wax WAX 14 | Satta I/I And Eye (p/s as Lizard) .... | £25 |
| 76 | Trojan TRLS 138 | SATTA (LP) .... | £40 |

LIZZIE & DELROY WILSON
| 71 | Jackpot JP 771 | Double Attack/AGGRAVATORS: The Sniper .... | £20 |

(see also Lizzy)

LIZZY
70	Harry J HJ 6625	More Heartaches/HARRY J ALL STARS: Version	£30
70	Pressure Beat PB 5508	Ten Feet Tall (actually "Wear You From The Ball"/JOE GIBBS & DESTROYERS: Chapter (actually "Harmony Hall" by Mr Nigel)	£15
73	Duke DU 161	Love Is A Treasure/FREDDIE McKAY: Love Is A Treasure	£20

LIZZY & DENNIS (ALCAPONE)
| 70 | Ackee ACK 114 | Happy Go Lucky Girl/BOBBY & DAVE: Sammy .... | £20 |

LIZZY & PARAGONS
| 71 | Ackee ACK 118 | On The Beach/DAVE BARKER: Maria .... | £30 |

LJ IV
| 69 | CBS 63512 | AN ELIZABETHAN SONGBOOK (LP) .... | £125 |

(see also London Jazz Four)

LLAN
| 66 | CBS 202405 | Realise/Anytime .... | £40 |

(see also Vogues)

A.L. LLOYD
57	Topic T7	A.L. LLOYD EWAN MACCOLL (10" LP with insert)	£30
57	Topic T8	THE BLACK BALL LINE (8" EP, insert, with Ewan MaCColl)	£25
60	Topic 12T 51	OUTBACK BALLADS (LP, blue label)	£40
64	Topic 12T 103	ENGLISH AND SCOTTISH FOLK BALLADS (LP, with Ewan MacColl, with blue label & booklet)	£30
64	Topic 12T 103	ENGLISH AND SCOTTISH FOLK BALLADS (LP, with Ewan MacColl) ...	£20
65	Topic 12T 135	BIRD IN THE BUSH (LP, with Anne Briggs & Frankie Armstrong, blue label) ...	£60
66	Topic 12T 118	FIRST PERSON (LP, blue label)	£30
67	Topic 12T 174	LEVIATHAN! (LP, blue label with booklet)	£35

(see also Frankie Armstrong, Anne Briggs)

A.L. LLOYD & MARTYN WYNDHAM-READ
| 71 | Topic 12TS 203 | THE GREAT AUSTRALIAN LEGEND (LP, blue label with booklet) .... | £65 |

(see also Ewan MacColl, Peggy Seeger, Martin Wyndham-Read)

LLOYD ALEXANDER REAL ESTATE
| 67 | President PT 157 | Whatcha Gonna Do/Gonna Live Again .... | £100 |

LLOYD & CLAUDETTE
| 70 | Big Shot BI 546 | Queen Of The World/PROPHETS: Top Of The World .... | £80 |

LLOYD (ROBINSON) & DEVON (RUSSELL)
| 69 | Punch PH 14 | Love Is The Key/VIRTUES: High Tide .... | £30 |
| 69 | Blue Cat BS 151 | Out Of The Fire/Can't Understand (B-side actually by Austin Faithful) .... | £100 |

(see also Cobbs, Derrick Morgan)

LLOYD (ROBINSON) & GLEN (BROWN)
67	Coxsone CS 7011	That Girl/You Got Me Wrong	£200
67	Doctor Bird DB 1058	Jezebel/TOMMY McCOOK & SUPERSONICS: Jam Session	£50
67	Doctor Bird DB 1071	Keep On Pushing/BOBBY AITKEN & CARIBBEATS: You Won't Regret (B-side actually by Lloyd & Glen)	£60
67	Doctor Bird DB 1099	Feel Good Now/What You've Got	£40
68	Doctor Bird DB 1105	Successful Man/I'll Give You Love	£60

LLOYD (JACKSON) & GROOVERS
67	Caltone TONE 108	Do It To Me Baby/DIPLOMATS: Meet Me At The Corner	£50
68	Caltone TONE 109	My Heart My Soul/DIPLOMATS with TOMMY McCOOK & SUPERSONICS: Going Along ..	£60
68	Caltone TONE 112	Listen To The Music/DIPLOMATS: Strong Man	£60

(see also Groovers, Don Lett)

LLOYD & JOHNNY
| 68 | Island WI 3158 | My Argument (actually by Lloyd Terrell)/JOHNNY MELODY: Foey Man (actually by George Dekker) .... | £300 |

(see also Lloyd Terrell)

LLOYD & LARRY
| 71 | New Beat NB 080 | Monkey Spanner/LLOYD & LARRY'S ALL STARS: Version .... | £22 |

LLOYD & THE PROPHETS
70	Big Shot BI 553	Bush Beat/PATRICK & PROPHETS: Please Come Come	£50
70	Big Shot BI 556	Jaco/Soul Reggae	£40

(see also Prophets [Jamaica], Patrick & Lloyd)

CAROL LLOYD
83	Philly World PWLP 1004	LOVE CAROL (LP)	£50

CHARLES LLOYD (QUARTET)
66	Atlantic 588025	DREAMWEAVER (LP)	£20
67	Atlantic 587/588 077	LOVE-IN (LP)	£20
68	Atlantic 587/588 101	JOURNEY WITHIN (LP)	£20
68	Atlantic 588 108	IN EUROPE (LP)	£15
70	MCA MUPS 421	MOON MAN (LP)	£15
71	Atlantic 2400 108	IN THE SOVIET UNION (LP)	£20

LLOYD, DICE & THE BARRISTER
70	Joe JRS 14	Appeal Of Pama Dice/BOSS ALL STARS: Young And Strong Version 2	£20

LLOYD, DICE & HIS MUM
70	Joe JRS 5	Trial Of Pama Dice/NYAH SHUFFLE: Jughead Returns Version 1	£25
72	Sioux SI 022	Trial Of Pama Dice/Lonely Man (reissue)	£15

LLOYD & JOY
71	Explosion EX 2047	Back To Africa (actually by Alton Ellis)/Born To Lose	£20

LLOYD (CAMPBELL) THE MATADOR
72	Sioux SI 010	The Train/EXODUS: Julia Sees Me	£50

RUE LLOYD
72	Green Door GD 4033	Loving You/Version	£15

(see also Joe White)

TREVOR LLOYD
70	Explosion EX 2018	Chinee Brush/DICE & CUMMIE: Real Colley	£60
70	Explosion EX 2019	Give Me Back Your Love/Hold Me	£20

LLOYDIE & LOWBITES
71	Lowbite LOW 001	CENSORED! (LP, green/silver label)	£40

(see also Lloyd Tyrell/Charmers)

LLOYD'S ALLSTARS
69	Doctor Bird DB 1178	Love Kiss Blue/UNIQUES: Secretly	£80

(see also Justins, U Roy Junior, Jimmy Green, Victors)

ELERI LLWYD
77	Sain 1073	AM HEDDIW MAE NGHAN (LP)	£25

LLYGOD FFYRNIG
78	Pwdwr PWDWR 1	N.C.B./Sais/Cariad Y Bus Stop (p/s, white rubber stamped labels)	£100
78	Pwdwr PWDWR 1	N.C.B./Sais/Cariad Y Bus Stop (p/s, printed green labels)	£150

DICKIE LOADER
61	Palette PG 9015	Heatwave/Happiness	£30

EDU LOBO
71	A&M AMLS63035	SERGIO MENDES PRESENTS (LP)	£20

LOCAL HEROES
80	Junior Records	Blast The Pop!/Tomorrow (p/s)	£50

LOCKETS
63	Pye International 7N 25232	Don't Cha Know/Little Boy	£40

LOCKJAW
77	Raw RAW 8	Radio Call Sign/The Young Ones (p/s)	£20
78	Raw RAW 19	Journalist Jive/I'm A Virgin/A Doonga Doonga (p/s, beware of counterfeits)	£100

(see also the Cure)

GERRY LOCKRAN
69	Decca F 12919	Standing On Your Own/You're Not There	£20
67	Planet PLL 1002	HOLD ON, I'M COMING (LP)	£150
68	Waverley ZLP 2091	BLUES VENDETTA (LP)	£60
69	Spark SRLP 104	THE ESSENTIAL GERRY LOCKRAN (LP)	£50
72	Polydor 2383 122	WUN (LP)	£60
76	Decca SKL-R 5257	RAGS TO GLADRAGS (LP)	£40
80	BML 2536	ACROSS THE TRACKS (LP)	£15

ANNA LOCKWOOD
70	Tangent TGS 104	THE GLASS WORLD OF ANNA LOCKWOOD (LP)	£40

MALCOLM LOCKYER ORCHESTRA
65	Columbia DB 7552	The Intelligence Men/Brighton Run	£20
65	Columbia DB 7663	The Eccentric Dr. Who/Daleks And Thals	£60

LOCOMOTIVE
67	Direction 58-3814	Rudy A Message To You/Broken Heart	£25
68	Parlophone R 5718	Rudi's In Love/Never Set Me Free	£20
69	Parlophone R 5758	Mr. Armageddon/There's Got To Be A Way (in promos p/s)	£30
69	Parlophone R 5758	Mr. Armageddan/There's Got To Be A Way	£15
69	Parlophone R 5801	I'm Never Gonna Let You Go/You Must Be Joking	£20
71	Parlophone R 5915	Rudi's In Love/You Must Be Joking	£20
69	Parlophone PCS 7093	WE ARE EVERYTHING YOU SEE (LP, laminated front sleeve)	£1000

MINT VALUE £

| 88 | Zap! ZAP 5 | WE ARE EVERYTHING YOU SEE (LP, reissue) | £20 |

(see also Norman Haines Band, Dog That Bit People)

LOCOMOTIVE GT
| 74 | Epic EPC 80229 | LOCOMOTIVE GT (LP) | £15 |

LOEFAH
04	Big Apple BAM 006	Jungle Inflitrator/Jazz Lick/Indian Dub/Life Dub (12")	£60
05	DMZ DMZ 006	Root/The Goat Stare (12")	£40
05	Tectonic TEC 003	28g/Fearless (12")	£15
06	DMZ DMZ 009	Mud/Rufage (12")	£50
06	Six Six SIx 001	Voodoo/Voodoo (Omen Mix)	£25
06	Tectonic TEC 008	System/DIGITAL MYSTIKZ: Molten (10")	£30

LOFT
| 84 | Creation CRE 009 | Why Does The Rain/Like (foldaround p/s in poly bag) | £15 |

(see also Weather Prophets)

CRIPPLE CLARENCE LOFTON
59	Vogue EPV 1209	CRIPPLE CLARENCE LOFTON (EP)	£50
54	London AL 3531	A LOST RECORDING DATE (10" LP)	£50
55	Vogue LDE 122	JAZZ IMMORTALS NO. 1 (10" LP)	£50

LORA LOGIC
| 81 | Rough Trade Rt087 | Wonderful Offer/Stereo/Rather Than Repeat (12", p/s) | £15 |
| 82 | Rough Trade ROUGH 28 | PEDIGREE CHARM (LP) | £20 |

(see also Essential Logic)

LOGIC (1)
| 83 | Okey Doke LOGIC 03 | Pied Piper/Backstabber | £20 |
| 83 | Okey DokeLOGIG 01 OD 3 | Hi Ho Hi Ho/Never Break My Love | £40 |

LOG 10
| 83 | Sonic SR 77 | In The Dark/Dark Step Dub (p/s, with insert) | £25 |
| 84 | Sonic SR 78 | You're Not There/Freefall (die-cut sleeve) | £20 |

LOL
| 73 | Columbia DB 9009 | Naughty Nola/Bumbler | £60 |

(see also 10cc)

LOLLIPOP SHOP
| 85 | Big Beat WIK36 | JUST COLOUR (LP) | £15 |

LAURIE LOMAN
| 54 | London HL 8101 | Whither Thou Goest/I Was The Last One To Know (gold triangular centre) | £50 |

ALAN LOMAX (& RAMBLERS)
| 57 | Nixa Jazz NJL 11 | MURDERER'S HOME (LP) | £15 |
| 58 | HMV CLP 1192 | GREAT AMERICAN BALLADS (LP, with Alexis Korner & Guy Carawan) | £30 |

LOMAX ALLIANCE
| 67 | CBS 2729 | Try As You May/See The People | £50 |

(see also Jackie Lomax)

JACKIE LOMAX
68	CBS 2554	Genuine Imitation Life/One Minute Woman	£20
68	Apple APPLE 3	Sour Milk Sea/The Eagle Laughs At You	£35
69	Apple APPLE 11	New Day/I Fall Inside Your Eyes	£15
70	Apple APPLE 23	How The Web Was Woven/Thumbin' A Ride (in p/s)	£30
70	Apple APPLE 23	How The Web Was Woven/Thumbin' A Ride	£15
69	Apple APCOR 6	IS THIS WHAT YOU WANT (LP, with inner sleeve)	£200
69	Apple (S)APCOR 6	IS THIS WHAT YOU WANT (LP, with inner sleeve, stereo, 'McNeill Press', on sleeve)	£150
91	Apple SAPCOR 6	IS THIS WHAT YOU WANT (LP, reissue, gatefold sleeve with bonus 12" [SAPCOR 62])	£40

(see also Lomax Alliance, Undertakers, Takers, Heavy Jelly, Badger)

AL LOMBARDY & HIS ORCHESTRA
| 54 | London HL 8076 | The Blues/The Boogie | £40 |
| 55 | London HL 8127 | In A Little Spanish Town/Flying Home | £20 |

LONDON
| 78 | MCA MCF 2823 | ANIMAL GAMES (LP) | £15 |

JIMMY LONDON
71	Randy's RAN 517	Bridge Over Troubled Waters/RANDY'S ALLSTARS: War	£20
72	Trojan TRL 39	BRIDGE OVER TROUBLED WATERS (LP)	£30
78	Burning Sounds BS 1016	WELCOME TO MY WORLD (LP)	£18
79	Jama JALP 003	JIMMY IN LONDON (LP)	£35
80	JB JBLP 03	CHILDREN CRYING IN THE GHETTO (LP)	£15

(see also Jimmy Green, The Inspirations)

JOE LONDON
| 59 | London HLW 9008 | Lonesome Whistle/It Might Have Been | £15 |

JULIE LONDON

SINGLES
56	London HLU 8240	Cry Me A River/S'Wonderful (gold label print)	£80
56	London HLU 8240	Cry Me A River/S'Wonderful (later silver label print)	£20
56	London HLU 8279	Baby, Baby All The Time/Shadow Woman (gold label print)	£40
57	London HLU 8394	The Meaning Of The Blues/Now! Baby, Now! (gold label print)	£30
57	London HLU 8394	The Meaning Of The Blues/Now! Baby, Now! (later silver label print)	£15

EPs
57	London RE-U 1076	JULIE SINGS FILM SONGS (gold label print)	£20
57	London RE-N 1092	LONDON'S GIRL FRIENDS VOL. 1	£20

ALBUMS
56	London HA-U 2005	JULIE IS HER NAME	£30
57	London HA-U 2038	CALENDAR GIRL	£30
58	London HA-U 2083	MAKE LOVE TO ME	£30
58	London HA-U 2099	ABOUT THE BLUES	£30
58	London HA-U 2112	JULIE	£30
59	London HA-U 2171	LONDON BY NIGHT	£25
59	London HA-U 2186	JULIE IS HER NAME VOL. 2 (also stereo SAH-U 6042)	£30
60	London HA-W 2225	SWING ME AN OLD SONG	£20
60	London HA-W 2229	YOUR NUMBER PLEASE	£25
60	London HA-G 2280	JULIE AT HOME (mono)	£18
60	London SAH-G 6097	JULIE AT HOME (stereo)	£20
61	London HA-G 2299	AROUND MIDNIGHT	£20
61	London HA-G 2353	SEND FOR ME (mono)	£18
61	London SAH-G 6154	SEND FOR ME (stereo)	£20
62	London HA-G 2405	WHATEVER JULIE WANTS (mono)	£18
62	London SAH-G 6205)	WHATEVER JULIE WANTS (stereo)	£20
63	Liberty (S)LBY 1113	LOVE ON THE ROCKS	£20
63	Liberty (S)LBY 1136	SINGS LATIN IN A SATIN MOOD	£15
66	Liberty (S)LBY 1300	ALL THROUGH THE NIGHT	£15
67	Liberty (S)LBY 1334	FOR THE NIGHT PEOPLE	£15
67	Liberty (S)LBY 1364	NICE GIRLS DON'T STAY FOR BREAKFAST	£15
69	Liberty LBL/LBS 83183E	YUMMY, YUMMY, YUMMY	£15

LAURIE LONDON
58	Parlophone GEP 8689	LITTLE LAURIE LONDON No. 2 (EP)	£20

MARK LONDON
65	Pye 7N 15825	Stranger In The World/Moanin'	£15

PETER LONDON
65	Pye 7N 15957	Bless You/Baby I Like The Look Of You	£50

(see also Peter Cook)

LONDONAIRES
66	Decca F12379	Dearest Emma/Bugles A Go-Go	£15

LONDON & BRIDGES
66	CBS 202056	It Just Ain't Right/Leave Her Alone	£40

LONDON FUNK ALLSTARS
96	Ninja Tune ZEN 24	FLESH EATING DISCO ZOMBIES VERSUS THE BIONIC HOOKERS FROM MARS (3xLP)	£30

LONDON HOSPITAL
60s	Private Pressing WAD 9-1	LONDON HOSPITAL CHRISTMAS FACTOR (EP)	£60

LONDON JAZZ CHAMBER GROUP
72	Ember CJS 823	ADAM'S RIB SUITE (LP)	£20

(see also Ken Moule's London Jazz Chamber Group, Ken Moule Seven)

LONDON JAZZ COMPOSERS ORCHESTRA
70s	Incus 7	ODE (LP, with insert)	£50

LONDON JAZZ FOUR
66	Polydor 56092	Norwegian Wood/I Feel Fine	£25
67	Polydor 56214	It Strikes A Chord/Song For Hilary	£30
67	Polydor 582 005	TAKE A NEW LOOK AT THE BEATLES (LP)	£60

(see also London Jazz Quartet, LJ IV)

LONDON JAZZ QUARTET
60	Tempo TAP 28	LONDON JAZZ QUARTET (LP, with Tubby Hayes & Tony Crombie)	£350
60s	Ember EMB 3306	LONDON JAZZ QUARTET (LP)	£150

(see also London Jazz Four, Tubby Hayes, Tony Crombie)

LONDON POSSE
88	Justice JT003	Money Mad (12")	£50
96	Bullet BULT 5	Style (12")	£20
90	Mango MLPS1066	GANGSTER CHRONICLE (LP)	£15

(see also Rodney P)

LONDON PX
80	New Puritan NP 1	Orders/Eviction (p/s)	£25

LONDON STUDIO GROUP
66	De Wolfe DW/LP 2974	THE WILD ONE (10" LP, tricolour label)	£60

(see also Ivor & Basil Kirchen Band)

LONDON UNDERGROUND
83	On-U Sound LP 22	AT HOME WITH THE LONDON UNDERGROUND (LP)	£20

LONDON WAITS
66	Immediate IM 030	Softly Softly/Serenadio	£30

LONE ARCHER
74	Strand ST11	I'll Come To You/Glass Web	£15

LONE PIGEON
01	Sketchbook SKETCH 001	CONCUBINE RICE (LP)	£25

			MINT VALUE £

LONE RANGER
10 Domino REWIGCD77X   TIME CAPSULE (7-CD box set)..£35
(see also Beta Band)

LONE RANGER
80 GG's GG 021   BARNABAS COLLINS (LP) £20
81 Black Joy DHLP 002   ROSEMARIE (LP) £18

LONE WOLF (1)
80 Wolf Music LW 001   Cash For Candy/Pipedream Mary (p/s) £150
82 Guardian GRC 144   Leave Me Behind/High Class Hooker.....................................£20
84 Neat NEAT 44-12   Nobody's Move/Town To Town/Leave Me Behind (12")............£20

LONE WOLF (2)
81 Kai KR 02   Fighting For Sommerlund/Vonotar The Traitor (p/s) £15

LONERS
67 Stone ST 1   Visions Of You/Falling £100

JOHNNY LONESOME
61 HMV POP 837   Marie Marie/Doctor Heartache £20

LONESOME STONE
73 Reflection RL 306   LONESOME STONE (LP, stage production recording)............£18
(see also Sheep)

LONESOME SUNDOWN
71 Blue Horizon 7-63864   LONESOME LONELY BLUES (LP) £100
77 Flyright LP 529   BOUGHT ME A TICKET (LP) £18
83 Flyright LP 587   LONESOME WHISTLER (LP)..£18

LONESOME TONE
81 Stiff BUY DJ 111   Mum Dad Love Hate And Elvis/Ghost Town (promo only) £20

LONESOME TRAVELLERS
70 Tradition TSR 004   THE LONESOME TRAVELLERS (LP) £25
70s Nebula NEB 100   THE LOST CHILDREN (LP) £15

LONG & SHORT
64 Decca F 11964   The Letter/Love Is A Funny Thing £35
64 Decca F 12043   Choc Ice/Here Comes The Fool £40

LONG BLONDES
04 Thee Sheffield SPC 005   New Idols/Long Blonde (p/s pink vinyl, playing card & newsletter insert) £20
04 Angular Recording ARC 007   Giddy Stratospheres/Polly/Darts (p/s, 500 only, blue vinyl)............£15

FITZROY D. LONG & BUSTER ALL STARS
68 Fab FAB 32   Get A New Girl/BUSTER'S ALL STARS: Come And Do It With Me £50
(see also Larry Marshall)

LONG HELLO
73 Private pressing   THE LONG HELLO (LP, mail-order only, numbered white sleeve)......................£20
(see also Van Der Graaf Generator)

SHORTY LONG
65 Tamla Motown TMG 512   Out To Get You/It's A Crying Shame £125
65 Tamla Motown TMG 512   Out To Get You/It's A Crying Shame (DJ copy) £200
66 Tamla Motown TMG 573   Function At The Junction/Call On Me £45
66 Tamla Motown TMG 573   Function At The Junction/Call On Me (DJ copy) £60
67 Tamla Motown TMG 600   Chantilly Lace/Your Love Is Amazing £20
68 Tamla Motown TMG 644   Night Fo' Last (Vocal)/Night Fo' Last (Instrumental) £25
68 Tamla Motown TMG 663   Here Comes The Judge/Sing What You Wanna £18
68 T. Motown (S)TML 11086   HERE COMES THE JUDGE (LP, mono/stereo) £45
70 T. Motown STML 11144   THE PRIME OF SHORTY LONG (LP) £35
(see also Art Mooney)

LONG TALL SHORTY
79 Warner Bros K 17491   By Your Love/1970's Boy (p/s, withdrawn) £80
81 Ramkup CAC 007   Win Or Lose/Ain't Done Wrong (p/s).....................................£50
85 Diamond DIA 002   On The Streets Again/I Fought The Law/Promises (p/s, with poster) £25
86 Diamond DIA 005   What's Going On/Steppin' Stone/Win Or Lose/England (p/s)............£15
88 001   ROCKIN' AT THE SAVOY (LP, official bootleg, with poster)............£25
88 001   ROCKIN' AT THE SAVOY (LP, official bootleg, without poster) £20
(see also Case, Rage)

LONGBOATMEN
66 Polydor 56115   Take Her Any Time/Only In Her Home Town £500

LONGDANCER
73 Rocket PIG 1   If It Was So Simple/Silent Emotions (p/s) £15
74 Rocket PIG 11   Puppet Man/Cold Love £15
77 Rocket PIGL 6   TRAILER FOR A GOOD LIFE (LP, die cut gatefold sleeve)............£15

DAVID LONGDON
20 Plane Groovy   BETWEEN A BREATH AND A BREATH (with Judy Dyble) (LP, blue vinyl, 200 copies)..........£40
22 Plane Groovy PLG112   DOOR ONE (LP, gatefold, insert, white vinyl, limited edition)................£25
23 Plane Groovy PLG 119   WILD RIVER (2LP, yellow/green vinyl, vinyl release of 2004 CD) £25
(see also Big Big Train)

CLAUDINE LONGET
67 A&M AML 903   CLAUDINE (LP) £20

LONGPIGS
96 Mother MUM 9602   THE SUN IS OFTEN OUT (LP)...£100

(see also Richard Hawley)

LONGPORT BUZZ

78	Buzz 13	**CANTERBURY POP EP** (White labels, most handwritten)	£30
80	Criminal Records SWAG 14	**Fun/Who Is He** (different sleeve to Canterbury Pop version, with sticker)	£25

LOOK BACK IN ANGER

81	L.B.A. LBA 1	**Caprice/Mannequin** (oversized card sleeve)	£25
84	Criminal Damage CRI MLP 118	**CAPRICE** (mini-LP)	£15

LOOKING GLASS (1)

72	Epic 65041	**LOOKING GLASS** (LP)	£20

LOOP

86	Head HEAD 5	**16 Dreams/Head On/Burning World** (12", p/s)	£18
87	Head HEAD 7L	**Spinning Parts 1 & 2** (juke box centre, plain black die-cut sleeve)	£15
87	Head HEAD 7	**Spinning/Deep Hit/I'll Take You There** (12", p/s)	£20
87	Head HEAD LP 1	**HEAVEN'S END** (LP, with inner sleeve)	£25
87	Head HEAD LP 2	**WORLD IN YOUR EYES** (LP)	£20
88	Chapter 22 CHAPLLP 34	**FADE OUT** (LP, 2 x 45rpm 12", gold stickered gatefold sleeve, signed)	£40
88	Chapter 22 CHAPLLP 34	**FADE OUT** (LP, 2 x 45rpm 12", gold stickered gatefold sleeve)	£30
88	Chapter 22 CHAPL 44	**ETERNAL - SINGLES** (LP)	£15
90	Situation 2 SITU 27	**A GILDED ETERNITY** (2-LP with free 7")	£40
90	Situation 2 SITU 27	**A GILDED ETERNITY** (2-LP, without free 7")	£30
91	Reactor REACTORLP 3	**WOLF FLOW - JOHN PEEL SESSIONS 1987-90** (2-LP, contains merchandise sheet)	£20
91	Reactor REACTOR LP1	**HEAVEN'S END** (LP, reissue)	£20
92	Reactor REACTOR LP5	**DUAL** (LP, blue vinyl)	£30
92	Reactor REACTOR LP4	**FADE OUT** (LP, reissue, grey vinyl)	£15
14	Reactor REACTOR 04 LP	**A GILDED ETERNITY** (2 x 12", 7", reissue)	£20

LOOP OF SOUND

95	SECRET 007	**VOL 1.** (12")	£25

LOOSE ENDS (1)

66	Decca F 12437	**Send The People Away/I Ain't Gonna Eat My Heart Out Anymore**	£40
66	Decca F 12476	**Taxman/That's It**	£150

LOOSE ENDS (2)

82	Virgin VS 497-12	**In The Sky/Only A Day Away/In The Sky** (Instrumental) (12", p/s, as Loose End)	£15

LOOSE FITTINGS

69	Amber AM 01	**Sightings Of Emily/It's Down To Us**	£50

LOOSE RAIL

68	Denby DB 002	**Leave Me/A Place To Die** (p/s)	£100
72	Homewatch HW 1	**Silence In The Sky/Magic Well** (p/s)	£75

LOOSE TAPESTRIES

12	Sony 88691969131	**THE LUXURY COMEDY TAPES** (2-LP, gatefold)	£60

LOOT

66	Page One POF 013	**Baby Come Closer/Baby**	£15
67	Page One POF 026	**I've Just Gotta Love You/You Need Someone To Love**	£20
67	CBS 2938	**Whenever You're Ready/I Got What You Want**	£18
68	Page One POF 095	**She's A Winner/Radio City** (withdrawn B-side)	£30
68	Page One POF 095	**She's A Winner/Save Me**	£22
68	CBS 3231	**Don't Turn Around/You Are My Sunshine Girl**	£25
69	Page One POF 115	**Try To Keep It A Secret/Radio City**	£40

(see also Soul Agents, Hookfoot)

TRINI LOPEZ

65	Stateside SE 1013	**SINNER NOT A SAINT** (EP)	£30

KENNY LORAN

59	Capitol CL 15081	**Mama's Little Baby/Magic Star**	£30

L'ORANGE MECHANIK

86	Art Pop POP 44	**Symphony/Intermezzo** (Sprechstimme)/**Scherzo** (p/s)	£15

(see also Times)

JON LORD

71	Purple TPSA 7501	**GEMINI SUITE** (LP, textured gatefold sleeve)	£70
74	Purple TPSA 7513	**WINDOWS** (LP, gatefold sleeve)	£20
76	Purple TPSA 7516	**SARABANDE** (LP, die-cut sleeve)	£15

(see also Artwoods, Deep Purple, [Paice] Ashton & Lord, Wizard's Convention, Episode Six, Leading Figures, Whitesnake, Cozy Powell)

TONY LORD

66	Planet PLF 102	**World's Champion/It Makes Me Sad**	£40

JERRY LORDAN

61	Parlophone R 4748	**You Came A Long Way From St. Louis/Let's Try Again**	£15
62	Parlophone R 4903	**One Good Solid 24 Carat Reason/Second Hand Dress**	£20
70	CBS 5057	**The Old Man And The Sea/Harlequin Melodies**	£30
61	Parlophone PMC 1133	**ALL MY OWN WORK** (LP, mono)	£70
61	Parlophone PCS 3014	**ALL MY OWN WORK** (LP, stereo)	£100

(see also Lee & Jay Elvin)

LORD BEGINNER

51	Esquire 5-034	**Randolph Turpin's Victory/West Indians And The Steel Band** (78, with Kenny Graham's Afro-Cubists)	£15
51	Esquire 5-041	**Fifty Women To One Man/1951 Festival Of Britain** (78, with Kenny Graham's Afro-	£15

Cubists) ....

53	Esquire 5-091	England Regains The Ashes/Nobody Wants To Grow Old (78)	£15
54	Melodisc 1333	Sir Winston Churchill Calypso/Rhythm Dance (78)	£15

(see also Lord Kitchener)

LORD BRISCO(E)

64	Rio R42	Fabulous Eyes/What You See	£20
64	Black Swan WI 447	Spiritual Mambo/BABA BROOKS: Fly Right	£20
64	Black Swan WI 450	My Love Has Come/BABA BROOKS: Sweet Eileen	£25
64	Black Swan WI 454	Trojan/I Am The Least	£20
64	Island WI 131	Praise For I/Tell You The Story	£35
65	Island WI 187	Jonah (The Master)/Mr. Cleveland	£15

LORD BRYNNER & SHEIKS

66	Island WI 266	Congo War/Teach Me To Ska	£40

(see also Roland Alphonso)

LORD BUCKLEY

62	Fontana 688 010ZL	IN CONCERT (LP)	£20
67	Fontana TL 5396	BLOWING HIS MIND (AND YOURS, TOO) (LP)	£20

LORD COMIC

70	Bamboo BAM 66	Rhythm Rebellion/ROY RICHARDS: Reggae Children	£50
70	Pressure Beat PR 5507	Jack Of My Trade/CYNTHIA RICHARDS: United We Stand	£70

(see also Sir Lord Comic)

LORD CREATOR

62	Island WI 001	Independant [sic] Jamaica Calypso/Remember (B-side is actually Remember Your Mother And Father)	£20
63	Kalypso XX 24	Peeping Tom/Second Hand Piano	£25
64	Port-O-Jam PJ 4119	Jamaica's Anniversary/Mother's Love	£22
64	National Calypso NC 2001	Drive With Care/Sweet Jamaica	£20
65	Blue Beat BB 292	Evening News/Good For Creator	£45
65	Black Swan WI 463	Wicked Lady/MAYTALS: My Little Ruby	£25
67	Jump Up JU 503	Jamaica Jump Up/Laziest Man	£25
67	Jump Up JU 524	Big Bamboo/Marjorie And Harry	£25

(see also Creator, Kentrick Patrick, Fabulous Flames)

LORD CRISTO

67	Jump Up JU 515	Dumb Boy And The Parrot/General Hospital	£35
67	Jump Up JU 517	Election War Zone/Bad Luck Man	£35

LORDE

14	Secret 7" S718	Team (100 only, each with unique art sleeve)	£20

LORD GANDA

57	Melodisc MEL 1417	Everybody Is Rockin' & Rollin'/Landlady Don't Steal My Clothes (78)	£15

LORD KITCHENER

63	Melodisc CAL 5	Drink A Rum/Your Wife	£15
60s	Jump Up JU 504	Love In The Cemetery/Jamaica Woman	£15
60s	Jump Up JU 506	Road On Carnival Day/Neighbour, Neighbour	£15
64	Jump Up JU 511	Dr. Kitch/Come Back Home Meh Boy	£15
65	Jump Up JU 530	Kitch You So Sweet/Ain't That Fun	£15
65	Aladdin WI 612	Dr. Kitch/Come Back Home Meh Boy (reissue)	£15
55	Melodisc MLP 500	KITCH - KING OF CALYPSO (10" LP)	£25
57	Melodisc MLP 510	KING OF CALYPSO VOL. 2 (10" LP)	£25
60s	Melodisc 12-129	CALYPSOS TOO HOT TO HANDLE (LP)	£30
60s	Melodisc 12-130	CALYPSOS TOO HOT TO HANDLE VOL. 2 (LP)	£30
60s	Melodisc 12-199	CALYPSOS TOO HOT TO HANDLE (LP, reissue with extra tracks)	£30
60s	Melodisc 12-200	CALYPSOS TOO HOT TO HANDLE VOL. 2 (LP, reissue with extra tracks)	£30

(see also Lord Beginner)

LORD KITCHENER/FITZROY COLEMAN BAND

56	no label	City And United 1956/The Manchester Football Double (78)	£60

LORD LEBBY

58	Kalypso RL 101	Dr Kinsey Report/Ethiopia	£15
60	Starlite ST45 018	Caldonia/One Kiss For My Baby	£150

LORD NELSON

64	Stateside SS 281	It's Delinquency/Proud West Indian	£15
64	Stateside SE 1024	PROUD WEST INDIAN (EP)	£30

LORD POWER

69	Coxsone CS 7079	Temptation/AL & VIBRATORS: Change Everything	£80

LORD RIGBY

64	National Calypso NC 1001	Carnival Jamaica/Music Teacher	£20

LORD ROCKINGHAM'S XI

58	Decca DFE 6555	OH BOY! (EP)	£25
68	Columbia S(C)X 6291	THE RETURN OF LORD ROCKINGHAM'S XI (LP, mono/stereo)	£25

LORD ROSE

60s	Kalypso XX 25	Independent Jamaica/Twistin' Uncle	£40

LORDS

67	Columbia DB 8121	Don't Mince Matters/No One Knows	£140
68	Columbia DB 8367	Gloryland/Gypsy Boy	£18

LORDS OF RAP
92 Mad Dog MADDOG001 **STIX 'N' STONES** (EP) **£15**

LORDS OF THE UNDERGROUND
93 Pendulum7243 8 27757 1 3 **HERE COME THE LORDS** (2-LP) **£18**
94 Pendulum 7243 8 30710 1 2 **KEEPERS OF THE FUNK** (2-LP) **£35**

LORD SASSAFROST
82 Star Light SDLP 911 **HORSE MAN CONNECTION** (LP) **£20**

LORD SITAR
68 Columbia SX/SCX 6256 **LORD SITAR** (LP) **£40**

LORD SPOON
70 Escort ERT 839 **Woman A Love In The Night Time/World On A Wheel** **£15**

LORD TANAMO
60 Kalypso XX 20 **Blues Have Got Me Down/Sweet Dreaming** **£20**
64 Ska Beat JB 177 **Night Food Ska/My Business** **£60**
65 Ska Beat JB 217 **Mattie Rag/BABA BROOKS BAND: Mattie Rag** **£25**
65 Ska Beat JB 224 **I'm In The Mood For Ska/You Never Know** **£150**
66 Ska Beat JB 243 **Mother's Love/Downtown Gal** **£30**
60s Caribou CRC 3 **I Love You Truly/If You Were Only Mine** **£150**
70 Bamboo BAM 45 **Rainy Night In Georgia/KEN PACKER: When You're Gone** **£30**
71 Banana BA 319 **Keep On Moving/JACKIE MITTOO: Totaly [sic] Together** **£125**

LORELEI
74 CBS 2048 **S.T.O.P.** (Stop)**/I'll Never Let You Down** **£15**

MYRNA LORRIE
55 London HLU 8187 **Underway/I'm Your Man, I'm Your Gal** (B-side with Buddy DeVal) **£25**
56 London HLU 8294 **Life's Changing Scene/Listen To My Heartstrings** **£25**

DICK LORY
56 London HLD 8348 **Cool It Baby/Ball Room Baby** **£400**
56 London HLD 8348 **Cool It Baby/Ball Room Baby** (78) **£50**
61 London HLG 9284 **My Last Date/Broken Hearted** **£30**

LOS DOURADOS
70 EMI Regal/Starline SRS 5018 **INTRODUCING LOS DOURADOS** (LP) **£15**

LOS LOBOS
92 London/Slash 828 298-1 **KIKO** **£40**

JOE LOSS (& HIS ORCHESTRA)
66 HMV POP 1500 **Thunderbirds Theme/"The Avengers" Theme** **£15**

LOST
94 Tenth Planet TP 009 **LOST IN ACTION** (LP, with free 7") **£20**

LOST CHERREES
84 Fight Back FIGHT 6 **ALL PART OF GROWING UP** (LP, with lyric inner) **£15**

LOST DOG
71 Phoenix SNIX 143 **Latch Key Child/One More Time** **£60**

LOST FAMOUS
82 Silent SR6703 **Anywhere Else/A Warning** **£30**

LOST HORIZONS
17 Bella Union BELLA700RT **OJALA** (2-LP, die-cut sleeve, sky blue and silver vinyl, Rough Trade version, with CD) **£20**

LOTHAR & THE HAND PEOPLE
69 Capitol CL 15610 **Sdrawkcab** (Backwards)**/Today Is Only Yesterday's Tomorrow** **£20**
69 Capitol E-ST 247 **SPACE HYMN** (LP) **£80**

LOTUS CRUISE
83 Armbury ARM 603 **Billy's Got A Gun/Tonight** **£50**

BONNIE LOU
53 Parlophone MSP 6021 **Seven Lonely Days/Dancin' With Someone** **£50**
53 Parlophone MSP 6036 **Hand-Me-Down Heart/Scrap Of Paper** **£50**
53 Parlophone MSP 6048 **Tennessee Wig Walk/Just Out Of Reach** **£50**
53 Parlophone MSP 6051 **Pa-Paya Mama/Since You Said Goodbye** **£40**
54 Parlophone MSP 6072 **The Texas Polka/No Heart At All** **£30**
54 Parlophone MSP 6095 **Don't Stop Kissing Me Goodnight/The Welcome Mat** **£30**
54 Parlophone MSP 6108 **No One/Huckleberry Pie** **£30**
54 Parlophone MSP 6117 **Blue Tennessee Rain/Wait For Me, Darling** **£30**
54 Parlophone MSP 6132 **Two Step - Side Step/Please Don't Laugh When I Cry** **£30**
55 Parlophone MSP 6151 **Tennessee Mambo/Train Whistle Blues** **£40**
55 Parlophone MSP 6157 **Tweedle Dee/The Finger Of Suspicion Points At You** **£40**
55 Parlophone MSP 6173 **Drop Me A Line/Old Faithful And True Love** **£25**
55 Parlophone MSP 6178 **The Barnyard Hop/Tell The World** **£20**
55 Parlophone MSP 6188 **Dancin' In My Socks/Daddy-O** **£40**
56 Parlophone MSP 6223 **Darlin' Why/Miss The Love** (That I've Been Dreaming Of) **£20**
56 Parlophone MSP 6234 **Bo Weevil** (A Country Song)**/Chaperon** **£20**
56 Parlophone MSP 6253 **Lonesome Lover/Little Miss Bobby Sox** **£25**
56 Parlophone R 4215 **No Rock 'N' Roll Tonight/One Track Love** **£25**
57 Parlophone R 4350 **Teenage Wedding/Runnin' Away** **£25**
58 Parlophone DP 545 **I'm Available/Waiting In Vain** (export issue) **£20**

MINT VALUE £

BONNIE LOU & RUSTY YORK
58	Parlophone R 4409	Let The School Bell Ring Ding-A-Ling/La Dee Dah	£80
58	Parlophone R 4409	Let The School Bell Ring Ding-A-Ling/La Dee Dah (78)	£30

BUBBA LOU & THE HIGHBALLS
81	Stiff BUY 114	Love All Over The Place/Over You (Unissued)	£25

LOUD E
08	Ambassador's Reception ABR 001	Robotlove/Au Paradise/Jungleman Life (12")	£18

JOHN D. LOUDERMILK
62	RCA RD 27248/SF 5123	THE LANGUAGE OF LOVE (LP)	£20

(see also Johnny Dee)

(THE) LOUDWATER TERN
68	Morgan MR 6S	Senorita/I'll Be Where You Are (some demos credit Damon J Hardy and Polly Perkins)	£40

LISA LOUGHEED
87	Ariola 111 713	Run With Us (Remix)/Ain't No Planes	£20

JOE HILL LOUIS
65	Bootleg 502	Heartache Baby/I Feel Like A Million (99 copies only)	£40
67	Advent LP 2803	MEMPHIS BLUES AND BREAKDOWNS (LP)	£70
74	Polydor 2383 214	BLUE IN THE MORNING (LP)	£30

LOUISIANA RED
64	Columbia DB 7270	Keep Your Hands Off My Woman/Don't Cry	£40
64	Sue WI 337	I Done Woke Up/I Had A Feeling	£40
64	Columbia 33SX 1612	LOWDOWN BACK PORCH BLUES (LP)	£45
72	Atlantic K 40436	SINGS THE BLUES (LP)	£20
72	Carnival 2941 002	THE SEVENTH SON (LP)	£20

LOUNGE SOCIETY
20	Speedy Wunderground SW034	Generation Game Part 1/Part 2 (die-cut p/s)	£15

JACQUES LOUSSIER
69	Decca F 12920	Theme From Tu Seras Terriblement Gentille / Ballet Photo Rouge	£50

LOUVIN BROTHERS
59	Capitol CL 14989	Knoxville Girl/I Wish It Had Been A Dream	£20
84	Stetson HAT 3043	TRAGIC SONGS OF LIFE (LP, reissue)	£25

LOVABLES
68	Stateside SS 2108	You're The Cause Of It/Beautiful Idea	£25

ARNIE LOVE AND THE LOVELESS
12	Soul Spectrum SLSP008	We Had Enough/Invisible Wind (reissue)	£35

CHRISTOPHER LOVE
69	London HLU 10263	The Curse Goes On/You May Be The Next	£18

DARLENE LOVE
63	London HLU 9725	(Today I Met) The Boy I'm Gonna Marry/Playing For Keeps	£40
63	London HLU 9765	Wait 'Til My Bobby Gets Home/Take It From Me	£40
63	London HLU 9815	A Fine Fine Boy/Marshmallow World	£50
69	London HLU 10244	Wait 'Til My Bobby Gets Home/(Today I Met) The Boy I'm Gonna Marry	£15
74	Warner Bros K 19011	Christmas (Baby Please Come Home)/Wait Till My Bobby Comes Home (blue vinyl)	£20
77	Phil Spector Intl. 2010 019	Lord If You're A Woman/Johnny Baby Please Come Home	£20
77	Phil Spector Intl. 2010 019	Lord If You're A Woman/Johnny Baby Please Come Home (12", some copies 1-sided)	£15
90	Warner Brothers W 9535	Mr Fix-It/K.D. LANG with TAKE SIX: Ridin' The Rails (with p/s)	£20
90	Warner Brothers W 9535	Mr Fix-It/K.D. LANG with TAKE SIX: Ridin' The Rails	£20
64	London RE-U 1411	WAIT TILL MY BOBBY GETS HOME (EP)	£250

(see also Bob B. Soxx & Blue Jeans, Crystals, Phil Spector, Blossoms, Allisons [U.S.], Date With Soul)

GARFIELD LOVE & JIMMY SPRUILL
69	Blue Horizon 57-3150	Next Time You See Me/Part Time Love	£35

MARY LOVE
65	King KG 1024	You Turned My Bitter Into Sweet/I'm In Your Hands	£250
67	Stateside SS 2009	Lay This Burden Down/Think It Over Baby	£75
67	Stateside SS 2009	Lay This Burden Down/Think It Over Baby (DJ copy)	£125
68	Stateside SS 2135	The Hurt Is Just Beginning/If You Change Your Mind	£15
82	Kent TOWN 501	You Turned My Bitter Into Sweet/SWEETHEARTS: This Couldn't Be Me (green vinyl)	£25
85	Kent 6T1	Hey Stoney Face/IKETTES: It's Been So Long/ETTA JAMES: Wallflower	£20

NANA LOVE
77	Golden Age GAM 01	When The Heart Decides/Give Me The Chance	£80
78	Nestor NES 01	Chains Of Love/Sahara	£50
78	Nestor NES 0201	DISCO DOCUMENTARY - FULL OF FUNK (LP)	£200
14	BBE BBE250ALP	DISCO DOCUMENTARY - FULL OF FUNK (2-LP, CD, reissue)	£20

RONNIE LOVE
61	London HLD 9272	Chills And Fever/Pledging My Love	£50

SYLVIA LOVE
79	RCA PC 5168	Extraterrestial Lover/(Instrumental) (12")	£15

WILLIE LOVE/WILLIE NIX
66	Highway 51 H 700	THE TWO WILLIES FROM MEMPHIS (LP, 99 copies only)	£75

LOVE (1)

SINGLES

66	London HLZ 10053	My Little Red Book/Hey Joe	£60
66	London HLZ 10073	7 And 7 Is/No. Fourteen	£60
67	Elektra EKSN 45010	She Comes In Colours/Orange Skies	£30
67	Elektra EKSN 45016	Softly To Me/The Castle	£30
68	Elektra EKSN 45024	Alone Again Or/Bummer In The Summer	£30
68	Elektra EKSN 45026	The Daily Planet/Andmoreagain	£60
68	Elektra EKSN 45038	Your Mind And We Belong Together/Laughing Stock	£45
70	Elektra EKSN 45086	I'm With You/Robert Montgomery	£15
70	Harvest HAR 5014	Stand Out/Doggone	£15
70	Harvest HAR 5030	The Everlasting First/Keep On Shining	£15

ALBUMS : ORIGINAL ALBUMS

67	Elek. EKL 4001/EKS 74001	LOVE (LP, 1st pressing, gold labels, in U.S. sleeve)	£150
66	Elek. EKL 4001/EKS 74001	LOVE (LP, 2nd pressing, orange labels in U.S. sleeve or fully laminated UK sleeve)	£75
67	Elek. EKL 4005/EKS 74005	DA CAPO (LP, 1st pressing, mono/stereo, orange label with 'Manufactured in England by Elektra Records (U.K.) Ltd' at the bottom of labels in U.S. sleeves)	£120
67	Elek. EKL 4005/EKS 74005	DA CAPO (LP, 2nd pressing with 'Manufactured in Gt Britain' and 'Polydor Records Ltd' at the bottom of labels in either US or fully laminated UK sleeves)	£120
68	Elektra EKL 4013	FOREVER CHANGES (LP, 1st pressing, orange labels, laminated sleeve, mono)	£200
68	Elektra EKS 74013	FOREVER CHANGES (LP, 1st pressing, orange labels, laminated sleeve, stereo)	£150
69	Elektra EKS 74013	FOREVER CHANGES (LP, 2nd pressing, lighter orange label with silver lettering, stereo, laminated sleeve)	£70
70	Elektra EKS 74013	FOREVER CHANGES (LP, 3rd pressing, red labels, laminated sleeve, stereo)	£70
71	Elektra K 42015	FOREVER CHANGES (LP, 4th pressing, 'butterfly' labels, matt sleeve, band picture on rear)	£35
76	Elektra K 42015	FOREVER CHANGES (LP, 5th pressing, butterfly labels, matt sleeve, Arthur Lee picture on rear)	£30
69	Elektra EKL 4049	FOUR SAIL (LP, orange label, mono, existence unconfirmed)	£70
69	Elektra EKS 74049	FOUR SAIL (LP, orange label, stereo)	£70
70	Harvest SHDW 3/4	OUT HERE (2-LP, gatefold sleeve)	£50
71	Harvest SHVL 787	FALSE START (LP, gatefold sleeve)	£70
71	Elektra 2469 009	LOVE REVISITED (LP, gatefold sleeve)	£18
73	Elektra K 32002	LOVE MASTERS (LP)	£18
74	RSO 2394 145	REEL TO REAL (LP)	£20

ALBUMS : REISSUES

71	Elektra EKS 74005	DA CAPO (LP, 'butterfly' label)	£18
72	Elektra K 42011	DA CAPO (LP, 'butterfly' label)	£15
72	Elektra K 42068	LOVE (LP, 'butterfly' label)	£25
72	Elektra K 42030	FOUR SAIL (LP, 'butterfly' label)	£15
81	Elektra K 42011	DA CAPO (LP, reissue)	£15
87	Edsel ED 218	LOVE (LP, reissue)	£15
87	Elektra 7559 60656-1	DA CAPO (LP, reissue)	£15
88	Big Beat WIKA 69	OUT THERE (LP)	£15
13	Music On Vinyl MOVLP677	LOVE (LP, reissue)	£15
15	Elektra 8122797115	FOREVER CHANGES (LP, reissue)	£15
16	Music On Vinyl MOVLP1002	DA CAPO (LP, reissue, gold vinyl, 500 only)	£15

(see also Arthur Lee)

LOVE (2)

90	Fierce FRIGHT 036	Welsh Girl (1-sided, p/s in bag, hand-finished labels, mail-order only)	£20

LOVE AFFAIR

67	Decca F 12558	She Smiled Sweetly/Satisfaction Guaranteed	£70
68	CBS 3366	Rainbow Valley/Someone Like Me (in p/s, says 'Someone Like Us' on p/s)	£20
68	CBS 63416	THE EVERLASTING LOVE AFFAIR (LP, mono/stereo)	£35
70	CBS 64109	NEW DAY (LP)	£40

(see also Ellis, Steve Ellis, Elastic Band, Widowmaker, Morgan, Phillip Goodhand-Tait, Rainbow Ffolly)

LOVE & UNITY

79	Studio 16 WE 0014	Can't Let You Go/Dub Version (12")	£30
80	Studio 16 WE 001	Put It On/(feat Ranking Bogart)/Dub	£35
80	Studio 16 WE N1	Just Don't Care/Cut From The Master Tape (12")	£25
80	Studio 16 WEA 347	I Adore You/CAPTAIN DESMOND : Lover In Dance (12")	£25

LOVE AND WAR

80s	SRT SRT9KS 2323	Touch Of Class (p/s)	£100

LOVE CHILDREN

69	Deram DM 268	Easy Squeezy/Every Little Step	£15
70	Deram DM 303	Paper Chase/My Turkey Snuffed It	£20

LOVE CONNECTION

77	Strong Like Sampson SLS01	It's My House/Fall In Love (12")	£20

LOVE DIMENSION

79	Black Bear BLA 2010	You Stepped Into My Life/The Game	£15

LOVE GENERATION (U.S.)

68	Liberty LBL/LBS 83121E	LOVE GENERATION (LP)	£25

JOY LOVEJOY

72	Chess 6145 010	In Orbit/Uhl Hum (paper label/moulded label)	£30

LOVEJOYS

80s	Solid Groove SG 016	Stranger/Let Me Rock You (12")	£20

LOVELACE GREEN
69 Concord CON 003   Sister George/Pauper Millionaire £20

LOVELY BODIES
81 Shark Hits LB 1   Swelter In The Shelter/Come On Too Strong (p/s) £30

LOVE OF LIFE ORCHESTRA
81 Beggars Banquet TBET 2   Beginning Of The Heartbreak/Don't, Don't/Extended Niceties/Reprise (12", p/s).........£15
(see also David Byrne)

LOVE PARADE
90 Turntable Friend TURN 03   GUILT CHEST (EP) £25

JOHNNY LOVER
70 Amalgamated AMG 871   Pumpkin Eater/Version £20
70 Amalgamated AMG 873   Two Edged Sword/Version £35
(see also Heptones)

LOVERS
58 Vogue Pop V 9111   Let's Elope/I Wanna Be Loved £500
58 Vogue Pop V 9111   Let's Elope/I Wanna Be Loved (78) £150

LOVERS DUB
80 Venture   CUT 7 (LP) (actually by Eargasm)...£40
(see also Tradition)

LOVE SCULPTURE
68 Parlophone R 5664   River To Another Day/Brand New Woman £20
68 Parlophone R 5731   Wang-Dang-Doodle/The Stumble..£20
69 Parlophone R 5807   Seagull/Farandole £15
70 Parlophone R 5831   In The Land Of The Few/People People £20
68 Parlophone PMC 7059   BLUES HELPING (LP, 1st pressing, yellow/black label, mono) £80
68 Parlophone PCS 7059   BLUES HELPING (LP, 1st pressing, yellow/black label, stereo) £50
69 Parlophone PCS 7090   FORMS AND FEELINGS (LP, 1st pressing, yellow/black label) £100
70 Parlophone PCS 7059   BLUES HELPING (LP, 2nd pressing, silver/black label) £25
70 Parlophone PCS 7090   FORMS AND FEELINGS (LP, 2nd pressing, silver/black label)....................£25
(see also Human Beans)

EDDIE LOVETTE
69 Big Shot BI 519   You're My Girl/Let Them Say £15
70 London HA-J 8413   TOO EXPERIENCED (LP, unissued) £0

LENE LOVICH
76 Polydor 2058 812   I Saw Mommy Kissing Santa Claus/The Christmas Song (Merry Christmas To You)/Happy Christmas (p/s) £40
78 Stiff BUYJ 32   I Think We're Alone Now (Japanese)/Lucky Number (mail-order promo only) £25
78 Stiff BUY 35   Home/Lucky Number (unreleased, test pressings only) £100

LOVIN'
67 Page One POF 035   Keep On Believing/I'm In Command £35
67 Page One POF 041   All You've Got/Do It Again £75
(see also Nerve)

LOVIN' SPOONFUL
66 Pye International 7N 25344   You Didn't Have To Be So Nice/My Gal..£15
66 Kama Sutra KEP 300   DID YOU EVER HAVE TO MAKE UP YOUR MIND (EP)......................£20
66 Kama Sutra KEP 301   JUG BAND MUSIC (EP)...£20
66 Kama Sutra KEP 302   SUMMER IN THE CITY (EP) £20
67 Kama Sutra KEP 303   DAY BLUES (EP) £20
67 Kama Sutra KEP 304   NASHVILLE CATS (EP) £25
67 Kama Sutra KEP 305   LOVIN' YOU (EP)...£30
67 Kama Sutra KEP 306   SOMETHING IN THE NIGHT (EP) £35
65 Pye Intl. NPL 28069   DO YOU BELIEVE IN MAGIC? (LP)..£25
66 Pye Intl. NPL 28078   DAYDREAM (LP) £35
67 Kama Sutra KLP 401   HUMS OF THE LOVIN' SPOONFUL (LP) £20
67 Kama Sutra KLP 402   YOU'RE A BIG BOY NOW (LP, soundtrack) £18
68 Kama Sutra KLP 404   EVERYTHING PLAYING (LP)..£15
68 Kama Sutra K(S)LP 405   THE BEST OF THE LOVIN' SPOONFUL VOL. 2 (LP)........................£15
69 Kama Sutra 602 009   REVELATION: REVOLUTION '69 (LP) £15
(see also John Sebastian, Mugwumps, Zalman Yanovsky, Even Dozen Jug Band)

LOVING AWARENESS
76 More Love ML 001   LOVING AWARENESS (LP, gatefold sleeve with 2 posters)......................£15
(see also Glencoe, Skip Bifferty, Ian Dury)

LOVING KIND
66 Piccadilly 7N 35299   Accidental Love/Nothing Can Change This Love £15
66 Piccadilly 7N 35318   I Love The Things You Do/Treat Me Nice £18
66 Piccadilly 7N 35342   Ain't That Peculiar/With Rhyme And Reason..................................£25
(see also Freddie Lennon)

LOW
96 Vernon Yard YARD 22   FINALLY... (EP) £20
98 Rough Trade RTRADELP 061   TRUST (2-LP) £30
99 Tugboat TUGLP 007   SECRET NAME (2-LP)...£35
01 Tugboat TUGLP 027   THINGS WE LOST IN THE FIRE (2-LP, 4th side etched with lyrics)..............£25
05 Rough Trade RTRADELP 206   THE GREAT DESTROYER (2-LP) £18

BRUCE LOW
56 HMV JO 464   Just Walking In The Rain/Cindy Oh Cindy (export issue) £20

LOW NUMBERS
79 Warner Brothers K 17493 | Keep In Touch/Nine All Out (p/s) £25

LOW PROFILE
80 Ellie Jay EJSP 9434 | Hangin' Around/Substitute (p/s) £50

LOWBITES
80 Black Joy DH 800 | Can I Go With You?/BOBBY DODSON & TRINITY: Having My Baby (12") £15

DENNIS LOWE
70 Downtown DT 465 | What's Your Name/MUSIC DOCTORS: Mr Locabe £20
70 Downtown DT 468 | Stand Up For The Sound/OWEN & DENNIS: Old Man Trouble £20

EARL LOWE
75 Tafari WL 708 | Jah Can Count On I/Bongo Nyah (12") £70

JEZ LOWE
80 Fellside FE 034 | JEZ LOWE (LP, textured sleeve, light green label, large 'Rams Horn' logo)...........£15
83 Fellside FE 034 | THE OLD DURHAM ROAD (LP) £15
85 Fellisde FE 049 | GALLOWAYS (LP, with lyric insert)..£15

JIM LOWE
55 London HLD 8171 | Close The Door/Nueva Laredo (gold label print) £40
56 London HLD 8276 | Blue Suede Shoes/Maybellene (silver label print) £100
56 London HLD 8276 | Blue Suede Shoes/Maybellene (silver label print) (78) £20
56 London HLD 8288 | Love Is The $64,000 Dollar Question/Rene La Rue (gold label print) £80
56 London HLD 8317 | The Green Door/The Little Man In Chinatown (as Jim Lowe & High Fives, gold label print) £50
56 London HLD 8317 | The Green Door/The Little Man In Chinatown (as Jim Lowe & High Fives, later silver print label) £25
57 London HLD 8368 | I Feel The Beat/By You, By You, By You (gold label print) £50
57 London HLD 8368 | I Feel The Beat/By You, By You, By You (later silver print label) £30
57 London HLD 8431 | Four Walls/Talkin' To The Blues £25
58 London HLD 8538 | Roc-A-Chicka/The Bright Light (with Billy Vaughan's Orchestra) £125
58 London HLD 8538 | Roc-A-Chicka/The Bright Light (with Billy Vaughan's Orchestra) (78) £15
58 London HA-D 2108 | SONGS THEY SING BEHIND THE GREEN DOOR (LP) £30
59 London HA-D 2146 | WICKED WOMEN (LP)..£20
(see also John Barry Seven)

NICK LOWE
76 Stiff BUY 1 | So It Goes/Heart Of The City (promo, 'plug' copy) £40
76 Stiff BUY 1 | So It Goes/Heart Of The City, (push-out centre) £15
77 Stiff LAST 1-12 | Bowi EP (Born A Woman//Marie Provost/Endless Sleep, 12" promo, 50 only)........£100

MUNDELL LOWE QUARTET
56 London American LTZ U 15020 | MUNDELL LOWE QUARTET (LP) £30

LOWER LEVELS
81 Pushover 1 | Get It/So Bloody Lazy (p/s) £20

LOWLIFE
89 LOLIF DEMO 1 | THE DEMOS (LP, white label test pressings only, hand-written white sleeve) £60

LOWRELL
80 AVI AVLP 504 | LOWRELL (LP)...£20

HENRY LOWTHER BAND
70 Deram SML 1070 | CHILD SONG (LP) £175
(see also Manfred Mann, John Mayall & Bluesbreakers, Keef Hartley Band, Ricotti & Albuquerque)

MARK LOYD
65 Parlophone R 5332 | Everybody Tries/She Said No £60
66 Parlophone R 5423 | When Evening Falls/When I'm Gonna Find Her £400
66 Parlophone R 5423 | When Evening Falls/When I'm Gonna Find Her (DJ copy) £500

L7
92 London/Slash 828 307-1 | BRICKS ARE HEAVY (LP, green marbled vinyl with poster).......................£40

LUCA C & BRIGANTE
12 Southern Fried ECB 346 | Flash Of Light (Original Mix)/(Tales Of Us And Minds Against Mix)/(Solomon Mix) (12", featuring Roisin Murphy) £35

LUCAS (& MIKE COTTON SOUND)
66 Polydor 56114 | I Saw Pity In The Face Of A Friend/Dance Children Dance (solo)........................£20
67 Pye 7N 17313 | Step Out Of Line/Ain't Love Good, Ain't Love Proud £50
68 MGM MGM 1398 | Soul Serenade/We Got A Thing Going Baby £45
68 MGM MGM 1427 | Jack And The Beanstalk/Mother-In-Law...£30
(see also Mike Cotton Sound, Artwoods)

BUDDY LUCAS BAND
60 Pye International 7N 25045 | I Want To Know/Deacon John £20

LUCAS AND THE DYNAMOS
91 SRTS 91 S2904 | Rock And Roll Is Good For The Soul/Blood Shot/My Gal/Baby Baby £15

TREVOR LUCAS
66 Reality RE 505 | Waltzing Matilda/It's On £20
66 Reality RY 1002 | OVERLANDER (LP)...£275
(see also Eclection, Fotheringay, Fairport Convention, Bronco, Sandy Denny)

JON LUCIEN
74 RCA ALP1-0493 | MINDS EYE (LP)..£30

LUCIFER (1)
71	Lucifer L 001	Don't Care/Hypnosis	£15
72	Lucifer L 005/006/L 003/004	Prick/Want It/Fuck You/Bad (double pack, black box set)	£40
73	Lucifer L007	Mr Jack/Mr Jack	£50
72	Lucifer LLP 1	BIG GUN (LP, private pressing, with poster/inserts, sold via Oz mag)	£125
72	Lucifer LLP 1	BIG GUN (LP, private pressing, without poster/inserts, sold via Oz mag)	£80
72	Lucifer LLP 2	EXIT (LP, private pressing, with poster, sold via Oz magazine)	£150
72	Lucifer LLP 2	EXIT (LP, private pressing, without poster, sold via Oz magazine)	£70

LUCIFER'S FRIEND
| 71 | Philips 6003 092 | Ride The Sky/Horla | £15 |
| 71 | Philips 6305 068 | LUCIFER'S FRIEND (LP) | £250 |

(see also John Lawton, Uriah Heep)

THE LUCK OF EDEN HALL
| 11 | Fruits De Mer Winkle 03 | She Comes In Colours/Never My Love/Chrysalide/The Ottoman Girl (folded p/s, green vinyl, insert) | £20 |

LUCY SHOW
| 85 | A&M AMY 261 | Ephemeral/White Space (12", p/s) | £20 |

LUCY (2)
77	Lightning BCS 008	Really Got Me Goin'/Oy (export only p/s)	£15
78	Lightning GIL 516	Never Never/Feel So Good (with export p/s)	£100
78	Lightning GIL 516	Never Never/Feel So Good (without export p/s)	£30

(see also Def Leppard)

LUCY PEARL
| 00 | Pookie 7243 8 49393 1 1 | LUCY PEARL (2-LP) | £30 |

LUDDITES
| 83 | Xcentric Noise SECOND 1 | STRENGTH OF YOUR CRY (EP, black foldout p/s) | £15 |

LUDLOWS
| 61 | Pye NEP 24252 | THE SEA AROUND US (EP) | £20 |
| 66 | Pye NPL 18150 | THE WIND AND THE SEA (LP) | £18 |

(see also Jim McCann)

LUDUS
| 82 | New Hormones ORG 20 | DANGER CAME SMILING (LP, insert) | £18 |

ROBIN LUKE
58	London HLD 8771	Chicka Chicka Honey/My Girl	£30
58	London HLD 8771	Chicka Chicka Honey/My Girl (78)	£20
59	London RED 1222	ROBIN LUKE (EP)	£50

LUKIE D
| 89 | Uptempo TEMP 030 | Rough Neck A Town/Love Will Find A Way (12") | £75 |
| 89 | Original Sounds OS 1003 LP | GOLDEN RULE (LP) | £30 |

LULU (& LUVVERS)
64	Decca F 11965	Can't Hear You No More/I Am In Love	£20
64	Decca F 12017	Here Comes The Night/That's Really Some Good	£15
65	Decca F 12128	Satisfied/Surprise Surprise (as Lulu & Luvers)	£18
65	Decca F 12254	Tell Me Like It Is/Stop Fooling Around	£20
65	Decca DFE 8597	LULU (EP)	£35
65	Decca LK 4719	SOMETHING TO SHOUT ABOUT (LP)	£50
67	Ace Of Clubs ACL 1232	LULU! (LP)	£20
67	Fontana (S)TL 5446	TO SIR, WITH LOVE (LP, soundtrack, with Ron Grainer & Mindbenders)	£35
67	Columbia S(C)X 6201	LOVE LOVES TO LOVE LULU (LP, John Paul Jones arrangements)	£30
69	Columbia S(C)X 6365	LULU'S ALBUM (LP)	£25
69	Atco 228 031	NEW ROUTES (LP)	£15
70	Atco 2400017	MELODY FAIR (LP)	£15

(see also Luvvers)

LULU BELLE & SCOTTY
| 65 | London HA-B 8277 | SWEETHEART STILL (LP) | £15 |

BOB LUMAN
60	Warner Bros WB 12	Dreamy Doll/Buttercup	£15
62	Warner Bros WB 60	Louisiana Man/Rocks Of Reno (unissued)	£0
61	Warner Bros WEP 6046	LET'S THINK ABOUT LIVIN' (EP, mono)	£15
61	Warner Bros WSEP 2046	LET'S THINK ABOUT LIVIN' (EP, stereo)	£25
62	Warner Bros WEP 6055	LET'S THINK ABOUT LIVIN' NO. 2 (EP, mono)	£15
62	Warner Bros WSEP 2055	LET'S THINK ABOUT LIVIN' NO. 2 (EP, stereo)	£20
62	Warner Bros WEP 6102	LET'S THINK ABOUT LIVIN' NO. 3 (EP, mono)	£15
62	Warner Bros WSEP 2102	LET'S THINK ABOUT LIVIN' NO. 3 (EP, stereo)	£20
60	Warner Bros WM 4025	LET'S THINK ABOUT LIVIN' (LP, mono)	£20
60	Warner Bros WS 8025	LET'S THINK ABOUT LIVIN' (LP, stereo)	£25

RUFUS LUMLEY
66	Stateside SS 516	I'm Standing/Let's Hide Away (Me And You)	£200
66	Stateside SS 516	I'm Standing/Let's Hide Away (Me And You) (DJ copy)	£400
78	EMI International INT 556	I'm Standing/Let's Hide Away (Me And You) (reissue)	£15

LUNA
95	Beggars Banquet BBQLP 178	PENTHOUSE (LP)	£20
97	Beggars Banquet BBQLP 194	PUP TENT (LP)	£20
99	Beggars Banquet BBQLP 209	THE DAY OF OUR NIGHTS (LP, white vinyl)	£20

(see also Galaxie 500)
LUNA C
93	Knifeforce KF 001	THE LUNA C PROJECT EP (12")	£40
93	Knifeforce KF 002	LUNA C PROJECT 2 - MISSION OF MADNESS (12")	£40

LUNAR TWO
60s	Spot JWS 551	Get It Take It/Don't Ever Leave Me	£20

LUNATIC FRINGE
84	COR 1	CRINGE WITH THE FRINGE (EP)	£15

LYDIA LUNCH
80	Celluoid CEL 2 6561	QUEEN OF SIAM (LP)	£25
82	Situation 2 SITU 6	13.13 (LP, with inner sleeve)	£20
84	Doublevision DVR 5	IN LIMBO (LP, red vinyl with inner sleeve)	£20
86	Widowspeak SWP 01/07	THE INTIMATE DIARIES OF THE SEXUALLY INSANE (cassette, box set with book, signed)	£25
87	Widowspeak WSP 8	HYSTERIE (2-LP, with inners and poster)	£20

(see also Eight-Eyed Spy, Roland S. Howard, No Trend)
ART LUND
57	Vogue Coral LVA 9056	THIS IS ART (LP)	£20

LUNG LEG
97	Versuvius POMPLP 007	MAID TO MINX (LP)	£15

LARRY LUREX
73	EMI EMI 2030	I Can Hear Music/Goin' Back (demo)	£400
73	EMI EMI 2030	I Can Hear Music/Goin' Back (press-out centre; beware of solid-centered counterfeits)	£350

(see also Queen)
LURKERS
77	Beggars Banquet BEG 1	Free Admission Single: Shadow/Love Story (p/s, black vinyl)	£15
78	Beggars Banquet BEGA 2	FULHAM FALLOUT (LP, gatefold sleeve, some with picture disc flexi 'Chaos Brothers Fulham Fallout Forty Free' [BEG 6 ½] & stickered sleeve)	£20

(see also Fulham Furies, Rowdies)
LUSH
89	4AD JAD 911	SCAR (mini-LP)	£15
90	4AD CAD 0017	GALA (LP)	£30
92	4AD CAD D 2002	SPOOKY (LP as 2x10")	£30
94	4AD CAD 2002	SPOOKY (LP)	£35
94	4AD CAD 4011	SPLIT (LP)	£50
96	4AD CAD 6004	LOVELIFE (LP, clear vinyl)	£40
16	4AD LUSH BOX 2	ORIGAMI (5-LP box set)	£80

DON LUSHER BAND
55	Decca F 10560	Rock 'n' Roll/On With The Don	£20
67	CBS 62883	FROM LUSHER WITH LOVE (LP)	£15

LUSTMØRD
81	Sterile SR 3	LUSTMØRD (LP, 1st pressing, white cover with 2 postcards)	£60
81	Sterile SR 3	LUSTMØRD (LP, 2nd pressing, grey cover)	£35
86	Side Effects SER 07	PARADISE DISOWNED (LP)	£20

NELLIE LUTCHER (& HER RHYTHM)
60	Capitol EAP 20066	REAL GONE (EP)	£15
56	Philips BBE 12045	NELLIE LUTCHER (EP)	£15
51	Capitol LC 6506	REAL GONE! (10" LP)	£30
57	London HA-U 2036	OUR NEW NELLIE (LP)	£25

LUTHER & LITTLE EVA
57	Parlophone R 4292	Love Is Strange/Ain't Got No Home	£400
57	Parlophone R 4292	Love Is Strange/Ain't Got No Home (78)	£100

LUV MACHINE
71	Polydor 2058 080	Witches Wand/In The Early Hours	£30
71	Polydor 2460 102	LUV MACHINE (LP)	£300
06	Rise Above Relics RARLP 001	TURNS YOU ON (2-LP)	£20

LUVVERS
66	Parlophone R 5459	The House On The Hill/Most Unlovely	£70

(see also Lulu)
LUXURY
91	Spare Beat SBRR 001	LUXURY EP 1 (12")	£15
92	Spare Beat SBRR 003	The Silencer/You And Me (12")	£15

L-VOAG
79	Sesame Songs MOVE 1	MOVE (EP, p/s with handmade labels & insert)	£30
81	Axis No. 9	THE WAY OUT (LP, with booklet & poster)	£40

(see also Homosexuals)
LYADRIVE
84	Bridge BR 003	Anytime/White Dress (no p/s)	£30

LYDS
96	Dig The Fuzz DIG 014	Fly Away With Me/Seperations (p/s)	£15

ARTHUR LYMAN GROUP
59	Vogue VA 160142	TABOO VOL. 1 (LP, mono)	£15
59	Vogue SAV 8002	TABOO VOL. 1 (LP, stereo)	£18

Rare Record Price Guide 2026

MINT VALUE £

61	Vogue VA 160174	TABOO VOL. 2 (LP, also stereo SAV 8003)	£15

FRANKIE LYMON (& TEENAGERS)

56	Columbia SCM 5265	Why Do Fools Fall In Love?/Please Be Mine (as Teenagers featuring Frankie Lymon)	£60
56	Columbia SCM 5285	I Want You To Be My Girl/I'm Not A Know It All	£50
56	Columbia DB 3819	Who Can Explain?/I Promise To Remember	£50
56	Columbia DB 3858	Share/The A.B.C.'s Of Love	£50
57	Columbia DB 3878	I'm Not A Juvenile Delinquent/Baby, Baby	£30
57	Columbia DB 3910	Teenage Love/Paper Castles	£40
57	Columbia DB 3942	Miracle In The Rain/Out In The Cold Again	£40
57	Columbia DB 3983	Goody Goody/Creation Of Love	£20
57	Columbia DB 4028	My Girl/So Goes My Love	£25
58	Columbia DB 4073	Thumb Thumb/Footsteps (solo)	£30
58	Columbia DB 4134	Mama Don't Allow It/Portable On My Shoulder (solo)	£20
59	Columbia DB 4245	Melinda/The Only Way To Love (solo)	£20
59	Columbia DB 4295	Up Jumped A Rabbit/No Matter What You've Done (solo)	£25
60	Columbia DB 4499	Little Bitty Pretty One/Creation Of Love (solo)	£25
57	Columbia SEG 7662	TEENAGE ROCK (EP)	£30
57	Columbia SEG 7694	THE TEENAGERS FEATURING FRANKIE LYMON (EP)	£35
57	Columbia SEG 7734	FRANKIE LYMON AND THE TEENAGERS (EP)	£30
58	Columbia 33S 1127	FRANKIE LYMON IN LONDON (10" LP, solo)	£50
58	Columbia 33S 1134	ROCKIN' WITH FRANKIE LYMON (10" LP, solo)	£300

LEWIS LYMON & TEENCHORDS

58	Oriole 45-CB 1419	Too Young/Your Last Chance	£400
58	Oriole CB 1419	Too Young/Your Last Chance (78)	£75

DERMOTT LYNCH

68	Blue Cat BS 101	Hot Shot/I've Got Your Number	£100
68	Blue Cat BS 122	I Got Everything/Echo	£200
68	Doctor Bird DB 1115	Adults Only/Cool It	£50

(see also Trevor, Carl Dawkins, Joe White)

E D LYNCH

66	Fontana TF688	Sad Songs/Shoe Of True Love	£15

KENNY LYNCH

62	HMV POP 1057	Puff/Happy That's Me	£15
64	HMV POP 1367	My Own Two Feet/So Much To Love You For	£40
67	HMV POP 1577	I Just Wanna Love You/It's Too Late	£15
67	HMV POP 1604	Movin' Away/Could I Count On You	£150
68	Columbia DB 8329	Mister Moonlight/The Other Side Of Dreamland	£15
68	Columbia DB 8498	Along Comes Love/Sweet Situation	£15
69	Columbia DB 8599	The Drifter/Did I Stay Too Long?	£30
64	HMV 7EG 8855	KENNY LYNCH (EP)	£15
63	HMV CLP 1635	UP ON THE ROOF (LP, mono)	£45
63	HMV CSD 1489	UP ON THE ROOF (LP, stereo)	£50

LYNCH MOB

90	Elektra EKT 81	WICKED SENSATION (LP)	£30
92	Elektra7559 61322 1	LYNCH MOB (LP)	£40

LINDA LYNDELL

68	Stax 601 041	Bring Your Love Back To Me/Here I Am	£75

ANDREA LYNN

83	Sanity STY 007	Feel Your Love (Mix 1)/(Mix 2)/(Mix 3) (12" stamped white labels)	£50

BARBARA LYNN

64	London HLW 9918	Oh! Baby (We Got A Good Thing Goin')/Unfair	£40
65	Immediate IM 011	You Can't Buy My Love/That's What A Friend Will Do	£45
66	London HLU 10094	You Left The Water Running/Until I'm Free	£35
67	Sue WI 4028	Letter To Mommy And Daddy/Second Fiddle Girl	£50
67	Sue WI 4038	You'll Lose A Good Thing/Lonely Heartaches	£55
71	Atlantic 2091 133	Take Your Love And Run/(Until Then) I'll Suffer	£25
67	Sue ILP 949	THE BARBARA LYNN STORY (LP)	£200
76	Oval OVLM 5002	HERE IS (LP)	£20

BOBBI LYNN

68	Stateside SS 2088	Earthquake/Opportunity Street	£50
68	Stateside SS 2088	Earthquake/Opportunity Street (DJ copy)	£75

CHERYL LYNN

78	CBS S CBS 83145	CHERYL LYNN (LP)	£15

JESSE LYNN DEAN

79	Creole CR 176	Do It/My Boyfriend's Back In Town (p/s)	£20

(see also the Wasps)

KARI LYNN

61	Oriole CB 1632	Yo Yo/Summer Day	£15
61	Oriole CB 1644	You've Got To See Mamma Every Night/Lonesome And Sorry	£15

PATTI LYNN

62	Fontana H 370	I See It All Now/Someone Else's Valentine	£15
62	Fontana H 391	Johnny Angel/Tonight You Belong To Me	£15
62	Fontana 267 247 TF	Tell Me Telstar/Big Big Love	£20
62	Fontana TFE 17392	PATTI (EP)	£40

TAM(M)I LYNN
66	Atlantic AT 4071	I'm Gonna Run Away From You/The Boy Next Door	£70
66	Atlantic AT 4071	I'm Gonna Run Away From You/The Boy Next Door (DJ Copy)	£100
71	Mojo 2916 007	LOVE IS HERE AND NOW YOU'RE GONE (LP)	£30

VERA LYNN
54	Decca F 10372	My Son, My Son/Our Heaven On Earth (with Frank Weir & His Saxophone)	£15

(see also Johnstone Brothers, Frank Weir & His Orchestra)

GLORIA LYNNE
59	Top Rank JKP 2024	MEET GLORIA LYNNE (EP, with Wild Bill Davis)	£20
60	Top Rank BUY 031	LONELY AND SENTIMENTAL (LP)	£25
64	London HA-Y 8112	AT THE LAS VEGAS THUNDERBIRD (LP, with Herman Foster Trio)	£15
65	Fontana TL 5315	INTIMATE MOMENTS (LP)	£15
72	Mojo 2916 016	HAPPY AND IN LOVE (LP)	£25

SUE LYNNE
69	RCA Victor RCA 1822	You/Don't Pity Me	£300
69	RCA Victor RCA 1822	You/Don't Pity Me (DJ copy)	£400

PHIL LYNOTT
80	Vertigo PHIL 1	SOLO IN SOHO (LP, picture disc, die-cut sleeve)	£15

(see also Thin Lizzy, Gary Moore & Phil Lynott, John Sykes, Rockers)

JACKIE LYNTON
67	Columbia DB 8224	Answer Me/I Never Loved A Girl Like You	£25
74	WWA WWA 012	THE JACKIE LYNTON ALBUM (LP)	£15

(see also Savoy Brown Blues Band)

LYNX
78	ST Products SRTS/78/CUS 112	See The Light/C.I.A. (no p/s, 500 only)	£250

LYNYRD SKYNYRD
74	MCA MCG 3502	PRONOUNCED LEH-NERD SKIN-NERD (LP, gatefold sleeve)	£20
74	MCA MCF 2547	SECOND HELPING (LP)	£20
77	MCA MCG 3525	STREET SURVIVORS (LP, gatefold sleeve with tour dates on inner sleeve)	£15

BARBARA LYON
56	Columbia DB 3865	Falling In Love/Letter To A Soldier	£15
60	Triumph RGM 1027	My Charlie/Tell Me	£40
56	Columbia SEG 7640	MY FOUR FRIENDS (EP)	£15

RICHARD LYON
59	Fontana H 206	All My Own/Private Eye	£22

LYONS & MALONE
69	Jay Boy BOY 9	Doctor Gentle/She's Alright	£60

LYRICS
67	Coxsone CS 7003	A Get It/KEN PARKER: How Strong	£75
68	Coxsone CS 7067	Music Like Dirt/TONETTES: I Give It To You	£150
70	Randy's RAN 504	Give Thanks And Praises/TOMMY McCOOK: Get Ready	£15
71	Randy's RAN 511	Give Thanks/RANDY'S ALL STARS: Give - Version	£15

(see also Randy's All Stars, Viceroys, Jackie Mittoo, Fred Locks)

JOHNNY LYTLE
68	Minit MLF 11006	Gonna Get That Boat (Parts 1 & 2)	£15

HUMPHREY LYTTELTON (& HIS BAND)
SINGLES
51	Saturn EGX 105	When The Saints Go Marching In/Careless Love (78, picture disc)	£60
58	Parlophone CMSP 41	Bad Penny Blues/Baby Doll (export issue)	£20

ALBUMS : LPS
53	Parlophone PMD 1006	JAZZ CONCERT (10" LP)	£30
54	Parlophone PMC 1012	HUMPH AT THE CONWAY (LP)	£30
55	Parlophone PMD 1032	JAZZ AT THE ROYAL FESTIVAL HALL (10" LP)	£20
56	Parlophone PMD 1035	JAZZ SESSION WITH HUMPH (10" LP)	£15
56	Parlophone PMD 1044	HUMPH SWINGS OUT (10" LP)	£25
57	Parlophone PMD 1049	HERE'S HUMPH (10" LP)	£15
58	Parlophone PMD 1052	KATH MEETS HUMPH (10" LP, with Kathy Stobart)	£20
58	Parlophone PMC 1070	HUMPH IN PERSPECTIVE (LP)	£20
58	Decca LK 4276	I PLAY AS I PLEASE (LP)	£20
59	Parlophone PMC 1110	TRIPLE EXPOSURE (LP)	£70
54	Esquire 32-007	HUMPHREY LYTTELTON AND HIS BAND (LP)	£20
60	Columbia 33SX 1239	BLUES IN THE NIGHT (LP)	£20
60	Columbia 33SX 1305	HUMPH PLAYS STANDARDS (LP)	£20
60	Columbia 33SX 1364	HUMPH MEETS CAB (LP)	£30
61	Columbia 33SX 3382	HUMPH RETURNS TO THE CONWAY (LP)	£18
62	Columbia 33SX 1484	LATE NIGHT FINAL (LP)	£18

(see also George Brown, Helen Shapiro, Radiohead)

MINT VALUE £

WILLIE MABON
64	Sue WI 320	Got To Have Some/Why Did It Happen To Me	£50
65	Sue WI 331	Just Got Some/That's No Big Thing	£50
65	Sue WI 382	I'm The Fixer/Some More	£50

MABRAK
78	Different GET A101	DRUM TALK (mixed by King Tubby) (LP, cover laminated front and back)	£150

SPENCER MAC
70	Penny Farthing PEN 723	Blues Up In Down Town/Ka Ka Kabya Mow Mow	£100
70	Penny Farthing PEN 742	Commuter/Better By You - Better By Me	£60

MACABRE
87	Vinyl Solution SOL 18	GRIM REALITY (LP, with insert)	£18
89	Vinyl Solution SOL 020	GLOOM (LP)	£15

GLO MACARI
65	Piccadilly 7N 35218	He Knows I Love Him Too Much/I've Lost You	£15
71	Columbia DB 8821	Looking For Love/People Like You	£15

NEIL MACARTHUR
69	Deram DM 225	She's Not There/World Of Glass	£25
69	Deram DM 262	Don't Try To Explain/Without Her	£15
69	Deram DM 275	It's Not Easy/12.29	£15

(see also Colin Blunstone, Zombies)

MACATTACK
86	Baad! Records 12HIP1AZ	ART OF DRUMS (12" EP)	£15

MACC LADS
85	FM Revolver FMLP 56	BEER AND SEX AND CHIPS'N'GRAVY (LP, white vinyl)	£15
88	FM Revolver WKFMLP 115	LIVE AT LEEDS (LP, blue vinyl)	£15

MACCABEES
06	Promise PROM 001	X-Ray/Lego	£15
08	Fiction 174 653-4	Toothpaste/Kisses/Mary (Live At The Roundhouse) (picture disc)	£30
09	Fiction 2710467	CAN YOU GIVE IT (box set 2 x 7" with CD)	£20
15	Secret 7" S724	Go (100 only, each with unique art sleeve)	£40
09	Fiction 2703065	WALL OF ARMS (LP)	£25
15	Fiction COLOUR LP 1	COLOUR IT IN (LP, numbered, black and white cover)	£80
15	Fiction COLOUR LP 2	COLOUR IT IN (LP, colour cover)	£80
12	Fiction 2787390	GIVEN TO THE WILD (2-LP)	£75
15	Fiction MACC4001	MARKS TO PROVE IT (LP)	£25
17	Fiction MACCBOX 1	THE COMPLETE COLLECTION (4-LP box set, with 12" and DVD)	£100

EWAN MACCOLL
58	Topic 10T 26	BARRACK ROOM BALLADS (10" LP)	£20
58	Topic 10T 36	BOLD SPORTSMEN ALL (10" LP, with A.L. Lloyd)	£20
58	Topic 10T 50	STILL I LOVE HIM (10" LP with booklet, with Isla Cameron)	£20
60	Topic 12T 41	STREETS OF SONG (LP, with Dominic Behan, with booklet and original blue label)	£15
62	Topic 12T 79	THE JACOBITE REBELLIONS (LP, with original blue label)	£15
64	Topic 12T 103	ENGLISH AND SCOTTISH FOLK BALLADS (LP, with A.L. Lloyd, initial pressing with blue label & booklet)	£15
64	Topic 12T 103	ENGLISH AND SCOTTISH FOLK BALLADS (LP, with A.L. Lloyd)	£15
67	Topic 12T 130	BUNDOOK BALLADS (LP, originally with blue label)	£15
67	Argo ZFB 12	SOLO FLIGHT (LP; reissued 1972)	£15
67	Xtra 1052	BLOW BOYS BLOW - SONGS OF THE SEA (LP, with A.L. Lloyd)	£15
68	Argo (Z)DA 85	THE WANTON MUSE (LP, with booklet)	£15

(see also A.L. Lloyd)

EWAN MACCOLL & PEGGY SEEGER (& CHARLES PARKER)
57	Topic 10T 13	SHUTTLE AND CAGE (10" LP)	£20
61	Topic 12T 16	CHORUS FROM THE GALLOWS (LP, original pressing with blue label, insert)	£15
64	Topic 12T 104	STEAM WHISTLE BALLADS (LP, blue label)	£15
64	Topic 12T 104	STEAM WHISTLE BALLADS (LP, later reissue with booklet)	£15
65	Argo RG 474	THE BALLAD OF JOHN AXON (LP, by Ewan MacColl & Charles Parker)	£18
67	Topic 12T 147	THE MANCHESTER ANGEL (LP, original pressing with blue label)	£18
67	Argo DA 140	THE BIG HEWER - A RADIO BALLAD BY EWAN MacCOLL, PEGGY SEEGER, CHARLES PARKER (LP, documentary with music)	£20
67	Argo (Z)DA 66	LONG HARVEST 1 (LP)	£15
67	Argo (Z)DA 67	LONG HARVEST 2 (LP)	£15
67	Argo (Z)DA 68	LONG HARVEST 3 (LP)	£15
67	Argo (Z)DA 69	LONG HARVEST 4 (LP)	£15
67	Argo RG 502	SINGING THE FISHING (LP, with Charles Parker)	£25
67	Argo DA 142	SINGING THE FISHING (LP, reissue, with Charles Parker)	£18
60s	XTRA 1054	SCOTS BALLADS (LP)	£20
60s	Folkways FW 8958	SONGS OF ROBERT BURNS (LP)	£30
70	Argo DA 133	THE TRAVELLING PEOPLE (LP, with Charles Parker)	£15

71 Argo DA 136   ON THE EDGE (LP)..£15
(see also Peggy Seeger, A.L. Lloyd)

KIRSTY MACCOLL
79 Stiff BUY 47   They Don't Know/Motor On (yellow label, 'plug copy' promo, p/s) £15
79 Stiff BUY 57   You Caught Me Out/Boys (with Boomtown Rats, unreleased, demos only)......£50
81 Polydor POSP 368   You Still Believe In Me/Queen Of The High Teas (p/s) £15
83 Stiff BUY DJ 190   Terry/Quietly Alone (Pink promo. "A" label)..................................£15
85 Polydor SEPLP 95825 791   KIRSTY MACCOLL (LP)..£15

GALT MACDERMOT
73 Decca SKLR 5164   TWO GENTLEMEN OF VERONA (LP) £30

GAVIN MACDONALD
72 Regal Zono. SLRZ 1027   LINES (LP, red/silver label)..£25
(see also Country Joe & Fish)

RALPH MACDONALD
76 T.K. XL 14030   SOUND OF A DRUM (LP) £15

MACEO & ALL THE KING'S MEN
72 Pye International 7N 25571   Got To Get 'Cha/Thank You For Letting Me Be Myself Again (Part 1) £18
72 Mojo 2916 017   FUNKY MUSIC MACHINE (LP) £30
75 Contempo CRM 114   FUNKY MUSIC MACHINE (LP, reissue) £15
(see also Maceo & The Macks, James Brown, Maceo Parker)

MACEO & THE MACKS
87 Urban URB 1   Cross The Tracks (We Better Go Back)/Soul Power (printed die-cut sleeve)......£15
87 Urban URBX 1   Cross The Tracks (We Better Go Back) (Extended Version)/Party Part 1/ Soul Power
                                (12", printed die-cut sleeve) £15
74 Polydor 2391 122   US (LP)...£30
(see also Maceo & All The King's Men, James Brown)

TEO MACERO
57 Esquire 32-113   TEO (LP)...£30

MACEYS WINDOW
72 Parlophone R 5893   It's Getting Harder/Pray For Sister Sunshine £60

SHANE MACGOWAN & THE POPES
97 ZTT MACG003P   MORE SONGS ABOUT DRINKING AND THINKING (10" EP, p/s).......£15
(see also Pogues, Nick Cave & Shane MacGowan)

MACH HOMMY
17 Daupe! DM SP 022   DOLLAR MENU (12", p/s, 200 copies) £150
17 Daupe! DM SP 022   DOLLAR MENU (12", p/s, green vinyl, 100 copies) £150
17 Daupe! DM SP 022   DOLLAR MENU (12", p/s, grey vinyl, 100 copies) £150
17 Daupe! DM SP 022   DOLLAR MENU (12", p/s, with obi strip, 20 copies) £200

MACHINE MEN
71 AXE 1   Counting Time/Young Blood £15

MACHINE (1)
67 Granta GR 7STD   Stupidity/Please Stay (private pressing) £40

MACHINE (2)
69 Polydor 56760   Spooky's Day Off/Nobody Wants You......................................£18
(see also Swinging Soul Machine)

MACHINE (3)
78 Plastic SRTS/78/CUS/198   Bored With The City/Brown Eyed Girl (100 only, no p/s) £275

MACHINES
78 Wax EAR 1   True Life/Everything's Technical/You Better Hear/Evening Radio (stamped p/s, white
                                labels)..£150

CHRIS MACK
97 Confetti CO EP 010   RYDIM 4 YA EP (12" as Chris Mac) £25
97 Confetti CODB 03   Plenty More/Get It (Come) (Remix) (12") £30
98 Suspect SUS 001   Every Day/Every Day (12", no artist name on labels) £20
98 First Class FC 002   KA-BOOM EP (12") £35
98 Main Ingredient MAIN 011   Feel Good/Alright/Alright Mix (12") £30

FREDDY MACK
67 Rayrik TPMLP 143   LIVE AT TOFT CLUB FOLKSTONE (LP, as Freddy Mack Show, 99 copies only)......£300

LONNIE MACK
63 Stateside SS 207   Memphis/Down In The Dumps...£25
63 Stateside SS 226   Wham!/Susie-Q...£25
64 Stateside SS 312   Lonnie On The Move/Say Something Nice To Me £18
65 Stateside SS 393   Sa-Ba-Hoola/Chickin' Pickin' £20
67 President PTL 1004   THE WHAM OF THAT MEMPHIS MAN (LP) £30
69 Elektra EKL 4040   GLAD I'M IN THE BAND (LP, orange label, also stereo EKS 74040) £30
69 Elektra EKS 74050   WHATEVER'S RIGHT (LP, orange label) £30

MACK SISTERS
56 London HLU 8331   Long Range Love/Stop What You're Doing £60

WARNER MACK
58 Brunswick 05728   Roc-A-Chicka/Since I Lost You (with Anita Kerr Quartet) £200
58 Brunswick 05728   Roc-A-Chicka/Since I Lost You (with Anita Kerr Quartet) (78)...........£50
58 Decca   Roc-A-Chicka/Since I Lost You (export issue, with Anita Kerr Quartet)......£60

DUNCAN MACKAY
80	Edge EDGE 5	Visa/Gin Sing (12")	£150
81	Edge EDGE 14	Sirius II Mark II/In The Pink (no p/s)	£20
80	Edge HOG 3	VISA (LP)	£15

RABBIT MACKAY
68	MCA MUPS 351	BUG CLOTH (LP)	£15

MACKENZIE JET COMBO
70	Torpedo TOR 18	Milkman's Theme/Capadulah Recipe	£30

JUDY MACKENZIE
70	Key KL 005	JUDY (LP)	£22
71	Key KL 009	PEACE AND LOVE AND FREEDOM (LP, with poster)	£22

KEN MACKINTOSH (& HIS ORCHESTRA)
57	HMV POP 327	Almost Paradise/Rock Man Rock	£15
56	HMV 7EG 8170	TEENAGER'S SPECIAL (EP)	£15
55	HMV DLP 1093	KEN MACKINTOSH (10" LP)	£15
58	HMV DLP 1178	ONE NIGHT STAND (10" LP)	£15

DOUGIE MACLEAN
88	Dunkeld DUN 008	REAL ESTATE (LP)	£20

PATRICK MACNEE & HONOR BLACKMAN
64	Decca F 11843	Kinky Boots/Let's Keep It Friendly	£35

(see also Honor Blackman)

MADELINE MACNEIL
69	Skyline DD 103	PATCHWORK (LP)	£30

MADAME DRACULA
73	Sunbeam SB 004	Big Ten/Version	£50

(see also Girlie)

OSIBERT MADDO
84	Sunsplash SNS 003	King In The Ring/PAPA SAN: Ghetto Life (12")	£100

MAD DOG (1)
74	Chappell LPC 1053	POP SOUNDS (LP, library edition)	£40

MAD DOG (2)
85	Brainy CUTN 1	Sheriff/You're A Beautiful Sight (p/s)	£50
86	Stud STUDLP1	MAD DOG (LP)	£40

JOHNNY MADDOX (& HIS ORCHESTRA)
55	London MSD 1503/1504	Nickelodeon Tango/Solitude (unissued, demos only)	£30
55	London HL 8134	The Crazy Otto - Medley/Humoresque	£15
55	London HLD 8203	Do, Do, Do/When You Wore A Tulip (And I Wore A Big Red Rose)	£15
56	London HLD 8277	Hop Scotch Boogie/Hands Off	£25
56	London HLD 8347	Heart And Soul/Dixieland Band	£20
58	London HLD 8540	Yellow Dog Blues/Sugar Train	£15

MADE IN BRITAIN
91	White MIB001	Break The Crunch/Mellow Infection (12")	£50

MADE IN ENGLAND (1)
81	Gargoyle GARG 1	Dance Of The Warriors/The Quest (p/s)	£50

MADE IN SHEFFIELD
67	Fontana TF 871	Amelia Jane/Right Satisfied	£30

(see also Joe Cocker, Grease Band, Chris Stainton)

MADE IN SWEDEN
69	Sonet SLP 71	MADE IN SWEDEN (LP)	£40
69	Sonet SLP 2504	SNAKES IN A HOLE (LP)	£30
70	Sonet SLP 2506	LIVE AT THE GOLDEN CIRCLE (LP)	£30
70	Sonet SLP 2512	MADE IN ENGLAND (LP)	£35
71	Sonet SNTF 621	MAD RIVER (LP)	£45

MAD JOCKS & ENGLISHMEN
80	Wild Dog DOGLP 18	TONGUE IN CHEEK (LP)	£18
80s	Wild Dog DOGLP 50	THUD & BLUNDER (LP)	£18

MAD LADS (JAMAICA)
69	Coxsone CS 7099	Losing You/WINSTON JARRETT: Peck Up A Pagan	£180

MAD LADS (U.S.)
65	Atlantic AT 4051	Don't Have To Shop Around/Tear Maker	£18
66	Atlantic AT 4083	I Want Someone/Nothing Can Break Through	£18
66	Atlantic 584 038	Sugar Sugar/Get Out Of My Life Woman	£25

MADLIB
03	Blue Note 7243 5 36447 1 0	SHADES OF BLUE (2-LP)	£35
14	Blue Note 0602537781997	SHADES OF BLUE (2-LP, reissue, 180gm)	£25
19	Keep Cool 190759349212BT	BANDANA (LP, with Freddie Gibbs, variant cover by Tom J Newall, 250 only, signed)	£60

(see also Madvillain)

MADNESS
SINGLES
79	2-Tone TT 3	The Prince/Madness (paper label, company sleeve)	£20
79	2-Tone TT 3	The Prince/Madness (later blue plastic label, company sleeve)	£100
79	Stiff BUY IT 56	One Step Beyond/Mistakes/Nutty Theme (12", p/s)	£15

79	Stiff MAD 1	Don't Quote Me On That/Swan Lake (12", promo only, 500 copies)................................£50
80	Stiff BUY 84	Baggy Trousers/The Business (p/s, blue labels instead of green, Mike Barson not credited as songwriter)...£75
81	Stiff BUY IT 112	Grey Day/Baggy Trousers/Take It Or Leave It/Un Paso Adelante (12", p/s, white or yellow labels)...£20
81	Stiff BUY 112	Grey Day/Memories (p/s, rare edition with legs instead of feet on label)....................£15
82	Stiff GRAB 1	THE MADNESS PACK (6 x 7" in clear plastic folder) £20
85	Zarjazz JAZZF 7	Uncle Sam/Please Don't Go ('flag bag' edition) £20
85	Zarjazz JAZZY 7	Uncle Sam/Please Don't Go/Insanity Over Christmas (picture disc) £18
86	Zarjazz JAZZS 9	(Waiting For) The Ghost Train/Maybe In Another Life (square picture disc)...................£50
86	Zarjazz JAZZY 8	Sweetest Girl/Jenny (A Portrait Of) (picture disc, stickered PVC sleeve)......................£18
87	Virgin VS 876	Our House/Walking With Mr. Wheeze £15
88	Virgin VSJ 1078	What's That/Flashings ('Jig' disc, 1st of 2 interlocking shaped picture discs) £30
88	Virgin VSS 1078	What's That/Be Good Boy 'Saw' disc, 2nd of 2 interlocking shaped picture discs)........£30
89	2-Tone TTP1	THE SPECIALS: Rudi, A Message To You/Ghost Town//SELECTER: On My Radio/ MADNESS: One Step Beyond (promo, 40 only)..£200

ALBUMS

79	Stiff SEEZ 17	ONE STEP BEYOND (LP, first pressing, sleeve lists 'Bed & Breakfast' not 'Bed & Breakfast Man')..£20
80	Stiff SEEZ 29	ABSOLUTELY (LP, first pressing with slightly different front cover image) £15
82	M.I.S. (no cat. no)	THIRTY MINUTES OF CULTURE (fan club cassette)..£25
84	Stiff PSEEZ 53	KEEP MOVING (LP, picture disc, U.S. running order) £15
85	Zarjazz JZLP1	MAD NOT MAD (LP, withdrawn edition, alternative sleeve omitting gold on front) £75
86	M.I.S. (no cat. no)	SONGS FROM AROUND THE PLONET (fan club cassette, live compilation) £35
90	Virgin VVIP 107	IT'S MADNESS (LP, 1000 copies) £70
90	Virgin TPAK 8	ONE STEP BEYOND/ABSOLUTELY/RISE & FALL (3-CD box set, picture discs) £50
92	Virgin V2692	DIVINE MADNESS (2-LP, gatefold) £25
92	Virgin 463 166	DIVINE (Digital compact cassette) £20
92	Virgin MDV 2692	DIVINE (Mini disc)..£20
92	Go! Discs 828 367-1	MADSTOCK (LP, with picture inner sleeve) £20
94	Simply Vinyl SVLP 309	DIVINE (LP, reissue)..£15
99	Virgin MADBOX 2	THE LOT (6-CD box set of first 6 studio albums) £40
09	Lucky Seven 003SE	THE LIBERTY OF NORTON FOLGATE (LP, 3-CD box set including poster, membership card, rule book, letter & badge)..£50
09	Lucky Seven LUCKY7003LP	THE LIBERTY OF NORTON FOLGATE (LP)...£25
10	Size 12 SIZE 1001	ONE STEP BEYOND (LP, reissue as 2 x 10")..£25

FLEXIDISCS

82	Lyntone LYN 11546	My Girl (Ballad) (hard vinyl test pressing of Flexipop free flexi)...............................£200
85	Lyntone LYN 16676	From Us ... To You (Mad Not Mad tour disc, with tour programme) £18
86	Lyntone LYN 18251	Last Christmas With Madness:Ghost Train (The Demo)/The Final Goodbye (fan club disc)..£20

(see also Argonauts)

MADONNA

SINGLES : SIRE SINGLES

82	Sire W 9899	Everybody/Everybody (Dub Version) (WEA sleeve, no p/s) £175
82	Sire W 9899T	Everybody/Everybody (Dub Version) (12", WEA sleeve, no p/s) £125
83	Sire W 9522	Lucky Star (Edit)/I Know It ('sunglasses' p/s with no Jellybean credit on label)..............£900
83	Sire W 9522T	Lucky Star (Full Length Version)/I Know It (12", 'sunglasses' p/s; £50
83	Sire W 9522TV	Lucky Star (U.S Remix)/I Know It (12", stickered plain white die-cut sleeve)...............£35
84	Sire W 9522T	Lucky Star (Full Length Version)/I Know It (12" reissue, stickered 'TV screen' p/s, with poster)..£30
84	Sire W 9260F	Borderline (Edit)/Physical Attraction//Holiday (Edit)/Think Of Me ('map' p/s, double pack with European p/s, copies of "Holiday", shrinkwrapped & stickered: beware of counterfeits with less than Mint picture sleeves)...£100
84	Sire W 9210T	Like A Virgin (U.S. Dance Remix)/Stay (12", p/s, with poster & sticker) £35
85	Sire W 9083T	Material Girl (Jellybean Dance Mix)/Pretender (12", with poster p/s) £35
85	Sire WA6323	Crazy For You/Sammy Hagar "I'll Fall In Love Again" (7" Madonna shaped picture Disc in stickered PVC sleeve. No p/s.)...£50
85	Sire WA6323	Crazy For You/Sammy Hagar "I'll Fall In Love Again" (Uncut 7" Picture disc on 10" vinyl in PVC sleeve. No p/s.)..£800
85	Sire W 8934P	Into The Groove/Shoo-Be-Doo (heart-shaped picture disc with 2 stickers) £40
85	Sire W 8934P	Into The Groove/Shoo-Be-Doo (12" uncut heart-shaped picture disc, very few copies)..£1000
85	Sire W 8934T	Into The Groove/Everybody/Shoo-Be-Doo (12", p/s, with poster) £25
85	Sire W 9405T	Holiday (Full Length Version 6.08)/Think Of Me (12", 'cross earring' p/s reissue)...........£15
85	Sire W 9405P	Holiday (Full Length Version 6.08)/Think Of Me (12", picture disc) £30
85	Sire W 8881P	Angel (Edit)/Burning Up (shaped pic disc, with cardboard plinth)............................£45
85	Sire W 8881P	Angel (Edit)/Burning Up (shaped pic disc) £35
85	SireW8881P	Angel (Edit)/Burning Up (Uncut 7" pic disc on 12" vinyl in PVC sleeve, no p/s)..........£1000
85	Sire QA6585	Gambler/Black 'n' Blue:Nature Of The Beach (7" foldout poster p/s) £30
85	Sire TA6585	Gambler (Extended Dance Mix)/(Instrumental Remix) Black 'n' Blue: Nature Of The Beach (12" p/s)...£20
85	Sire W 8848TF	Dress You Up (12" Formal Mix)/(Casual Instrumental)/I Know It (12", foldout p/s with Virgin Tour Video Advert on back)..£35
85	Sire W 8848P	Dress You Up/I Know It ('Xmas tree star'-shaped picture disc) £35
85	Sire W 8848P	Dress You Up (Uncut 7" picture disc on 12" vinyl, no p/s)......................................£750
86	Sire W 9560P	Borderline/Physical Attraction (Madonna-shaped picture disc in pvc sleeve no p/s) £50
86	Sire W 9560P	Borderline/Physical Attraction (Uncut 7" picture disc on 12" vinyl,pvc sleeve no p/s) .£1000
86	Sire W 8717T(W)	Live To Tell (LP Version)/(Edit)/(Instrumental) (12", p/s, with poster) £20
86	Sire W8636T	Papa Don't Preach(Extended Version)/(LP Vesion) Ain't No Big Deal (12" with poster in stickered p/s)...£20

MINT VALUE £

86	Sire W 8636T(W)	**Papa Don't Preach** (Extended Version)/**Papa Don't Preach** (LP Version)/ **Ain't No Big Deal** (12", p/s, initially with free poster)	£15
86	Sire W 8636TP	**Papa Don't Preach** (Extended Remix)/**Ain't No Big Deal** (LP Version)/ **Papa Don't Preach** (LP version) **(12", picture disc)**	£20
86	Sire W 8550TP	**True Blue** (Extended Dance Version)/**Holiday** (Full Length Version) (12" picture disc)	£20
87	Sire W 8378TP	**La Isla Bonita** (Extended Remix)/(Extended Instrumental) (12", picture disc)	£20
87	Sire W 8341TX	**Who's That Girl** (Extended Version)/**Who's That Girl** (Dub Mix)/ **White Heat** (12" Remix) (12", p/s)	£20
87	Sire W 8341TP	**Who's That Girl** (Extended Version)/**White Heat** (12", picture disc; beware of original decaying PVC sleeves)	£40
87	Sire W 8224	**Causing A Commotion** (Silver Screen Single Mix)/**Jimmy Jimmy** (withdrawn p/s, with sticker stating 'Free personality poster W 8224W', most destroyed when withdrawn in favour of 'badge' insert, no poster))	£100
87	Sire W 8224	**Causing A Commotion** (Silver Screen Single Mix)/**Jimmy Jimmy** (p/s, with badge shrinkwrapped to p/s)	£60
87	Sire W 8224TP	**Causing A Commotion** (Silver Screen Single Mix)/**Causing A Commotion** (Movie House Mix)/**Jimmy Jimmy** (Fade) (12", picture disc)	£15
87	Sire W 8115TW	**The Look Of Love/Love Don't Live Here Anymore/I Know It** (12", p/s & poster)	£15
87	Sire W 8115TP	**The Look Of Love/Love Don't Live Here Anymore/I Know It** (12", picture disc)	£20
89	Sire 925 681-2	**Papa Don't Preach** (7" Version)/(12" Version)/**Pretender** (Video)(5" CD-Video p/s)	£40
89	Sire W 7539TP	**Like A Prayer** (12" Extended Remix)/(12" Club Version)/ **Act Of Contrition** (12", picture disc)	£15
89	Sire W 2948X	**Express Yourself** (7" Remix)/**The Look Of Love** (LP) (poster p/s)	£25
89	Sire W 2948C	**Express Yourself** (7" Remix)/**The Look Of Love** (LP) ('jeans zipper' p/s)	£40
89	Sire W 2948CX	**Express Yourself** (Non-Stop Express Mix)/(Stop + Go Dubs) (cassette)	£20
89	Sire W 2948TP	**Express Yourself**/(Non-Stop Express Mix)/(Stop + Go Dubs) (12", 'nude' picture disc)	£15
89	Sire W 2268CDX	**Dear Jessie/Till Death Do Us Part/Holiday** (12" Version) (CD, picture disc)	£125
89	Sire 925 681-2	**Papa Don't Preach** (7" Version)/(12" Version)/**Pretender** (LP Version)/ **Papa Don't Preach** (CD Video)	£35
90	Sire W 9851TW	**Vogue** (12" Version)/**Keep It Together** (12" Remix) (12", p/s, with 'Face of the 80s' poster)	£15
90	Sire W 9851TX	**Vogue** (12" Version)/**Vogue** (Strike-A-Pose Dub) (12", p/s, with 'X-rated' 30" x 20" poster)	£20
90	Sire W 9851TP	**Vogue** (12" Version)/**Keep It Together** (12" Remix) (12", picture disc)	£20
90	Sire W 9789TP	**Hanky Panky** (Bare Bottom 12" Mix)/(Bare Bones Single Mix)/**More** (LP Version) (12", picture disc with gatefold insert & foldout poster)	£20
91	Sire W 0008P	**Crazy For You** (Remix)/**Keep It Together** (Single Remix) (shaped picture disc with plinth & insert)	£15
91	Sire W 0037TP	**Holiday/True Blue** (12", clear vinyl picture disc with insert in PVC sleeve)	£15

SINGLES : MAVERICK SINGLES
92	Maverick W 0138TP	**Erotica** (Album Version 5.12)/**Erotica** (Instrumental 5.12)/**Erotica** (Radio Edit 4.31) (12", picture disc with gold insert, withdrawn, 138 only)	£2500
92	Maverick W 0146TP	**Deeper And Deeper** (Shep's Classic 12")/(Shep's Deep Makeover Mix)/ (Shep's Deep Beats)/(David's Klub Mix)/(David's Deep Mix)/(Shep's Deeper Dub) (12", picture disc)	£15
93	Maverick W0154TW	**Bad Girl** (Edit)/**Erotica** (William Orbit 12")/**Erotica** (William Orbit Dub)/ **Erotica** (Madonna's In My Jeep Mix) (12", Free Poster, p/s)	£30
95	Warner Bros W0285TX	**Bedtime Story** (Junior's Sound Factory Mix)/(Junior's Sound Factory Dub)/ (Orbital Mix)/**Junior's Wet Dream Mix)** (12" Glitter Holographic Sleeve)	£15

SINGLES : OTHER SINGLES
92	Reciever RRSPT 1007	**Shine A Light/On The Ground/Little Boy** (12", picture disc)	£15

ALBUMS
85	Sire WX 20P	**LIKE A VIRGIN** (LP, picture disc in die-cut sleeve)	£50
86	Sire WX 54	**TRUE BLUE** (LP, with tour poster)	£15
87	Sire WX 76	**YOU CAN DANCE** (LP, poster, gold 'obi')	£20
90	Sire 7599 264932	**ROYAL BOX** (box set with "Immaculate Collection" CD in satin digipak, video, poster & postcards)	£75
90	Sire 7599-26440 1	**THE IMMACULATE COLLECTION** (2LP, gatefold, printed inners)	£30
92	Sire WX 491	**EROTICA** (Dirty Version) (2LP, gatefold, printed inners, stickered)	£45
92	Sire WX491	**EROTICA** (Clean Version) (2LP, gatefold, printed inners, stickered)	£50
94	Sire 9362 45767 1	**BEDTIME STORIES** (LP)	£35
95	Sire 9362 46100-1	**SOMETHING TO REMEMBER** (LP)	£40
98	Sire 9362 46847-1	**RAY OF LIGHT** (2-LP with inner sleeve, stickered)	£15
00	Maverick 9362-47865-1	**MUSIC** (LP, gold die-cut inners, stickered)	£30
03	Maverick 9362-48439-1	**AMERICAN LIFE** (2LP, gatefold, printed inner)	£30
04	Sire 9362 46847-1	**RAY OF LIGHT** (Reissue, 2-LP with inner sleeve 180 gram deluxe vinyl, stickered)	£30
06	Warner 9362 494601	**CONFESSIONS ON A DANCE FLOOR** (2LP, gatefold, pink vinyl)	£50
08	Warner 440444-2	**HARD CANDY** (CD, 'Candy Box' edition, booklet, bonus mixes, bag of sweets)	£30
09	Warner 9362-49729-3	**CELEBRATION** (4LP, gatefold)	£150
12	Interscope 0602527977515	**MDNA** (2LP, gatefold,180g)	£200
15	Interscope 0602547211699	**REBEL HEART** (2LP, gatefold, 200g)	£80
16	Sire 8122 797358	**TRUE BLUE** (LP, blue vinyl, 'Sainsbury's' sticker, printed inner, poster)	£100
16	Sire 8122 79731-7	**LIKE A PRAYER** (LP, red vinyl, 'Sainsburys' sticker, printed inner)	£100
17	Sire 8122-79735-9	**LIKE A VIRGIN** (LP, clear vinyl, 'Sainsburys' sticke, printed inner)	£60
17	Maverick/Sire/Warner 9362-46847-1	**RAY OF LIGHT** (2LP, blue vinyl, 'Sainsburys' sticker)	£100
18	Maverick/Sire/Warner 8122-79735-6	**EROTICA** (2LP, reissue, white vinyl, 'Sainsburys' sticker, printed inners)	£100
18	Maverick 9362-47865-1	**MUSIC** (LP, reissue, printed inner, blue vinyl, 'Sainsbury's' sticker)	£80
19	Maverick B0030045-01	**MADAME X** (2LP, gatefold, printed inners, clear vinyl, limited edition, website exclusive)	£30
19	Maverick 00602577582837	**MADAME X** (2LP, picture discs, PVC outer, sticker)	£25
22	Warner R1 694981	**FINALLY ENOUGH LOVE: 50 NUMBER ONES** (6LP box set, three red, three black vinyl, booklet, 6000 worldwide)	£250

| 22 | Warner R1 695110 | **FINALLY ENOUGH LOVE** (2LP, gatefold, printed inner, red vinyl) | £30 |

PROMOS

85	Sire SAM 251	**Into The Groove** (Edit) **Holiday** (Edit) **(12" white label, die-cut sleeve, stickered**	£100
87	Sire SAM 412	**Spotlight** (Dub)/**Holiday** (Dub)/**Over And Over** (Dub)/**Into The Groove** (Dub) **12" white label, die-cut WEA sleeve, no p/s)**	£50
89	Sire SAM 641	**Keep It Together** (12" Remix)/(Dub)/(Extended Remix)/(12" Mix)/ (Bonus Beats)/(Instrumental) (12")	£15
90	Sire SAM 659	**Vogue** (12" Version)/**Vogue** (Strike A Pose Dub) (12")	£15
90	Sire SAM 738	**Justify My Love** (Remix) (One-sided 12" die-cut sleeve, p/s)	£15
91	Sire SAM 800	**Holiday** (Edit) (CD)	£50
92	Sire SAM 1103	**Erotica** (Album Version) (12")	£25
92	Sire SAM 1118	**Deeper And Deeper** (Edit)/**Shep's Deep Makeover Mix**/**Shep's Classic 12")** David's Klub Mix)/**David's Love Dub**/**David's Deeper Dub) 12" white label no p/s**	£25
93	Sire SAM 1131	**Fever** (Hot Sweat 12" Mix)/(Shep's Remedy Dub)/(Dub One)/(Dub Two)/ (Bugged Out Bonzai Mix)/(Peggy's Nightclub Mix)/(Radio Edit)/(Murk Boys Miami Mix)/(Murk Boys Deep South Mix)/(Album Version)/(Oscar G's Dope Dub)/(Back To The Dub Two) (2x12")	£50
95	Warner Bros SAM 1653	**Human Nature: The Remixes**/(Mixes) (12", stickered title sleeve)	£15
95	Warner Bros SAM 1526	**Bedtime Story** (Junior's Sound Factory Mix)/(Junior's Sound Factory Dub)/ (Orbital Mix)/**Junior's Wet Dream Mix**/(Junior's Wet Dream Dub) (12")	£15
96	Sire SAM 1880	**Love Don't Live Here Anymore** (Mark!s It's A Girl Dub)/(Mark!s It's A Boy Dub)/(Mark!s Full On Vocal) (12")	£25
98	Warner Bros 3331000037	**Drowned World/Substitute For Love** (BT & Sasha's Bucklodge Ashram Remix)/ **Sky Fits Heaven** (Sasha Remix)/**Substitute For Love** (Victor Calderone Remix Edit) (12")	£20
98	Warner Bros SAM 3247	**Ray Of Light** (Sasha's Ultra Violet Mix)/(William Orbit's Liquid Mix) (12")	£15
98	Warner Bros SAM 3248	**Ray Of Light** (Calderone Club Mix)/(Album Version) (12" no p/s)	£15
98	Warner Bros SAM 3268	**Ray Of Light** (Sasha's Twilo Mix)/(Victor Calderone Drum Mix) (12")	£15
98	Warner Bros SAM 3269	**Ray Of Light** (Sasha's Strip Down Mix)/(Orbit's Ultra Violet Mix) (12")	£15
98	Maverick W0444 LC	**Ray Of Light/Has To Be** (jukebox promo)	£15
00	Warner Bros PRO 6584	**Music** (mixes) (12" doublepack, title-stickered sleeve)	£15
01	Warner Bros MADZ 01	**What It Feels Like For A Girl** (Perfecto Mix)/(Above & Beyond Remix) (12" stickered white label, A4 press release, die-cut sleeve no p/s)	£25
01	Warner Bros SAM 00586	**GHV2** (CD, 10" x 10" gatefold p/s)	£50
02	Warner Bros SAM 00721	**Die Another Day** (Dirty Vegas Main Mix)/(Mixes) (12" double pack, stickered title sleeve)	£15
06	Warner PRO 15953	**Get Together** (Tiefschwarz Remix)/(James Holden Remix) (12" 'mirrorball' p/s)	£200

PROMOS : ALBUM PROMO

| 89 | Sire MER 0272 | **LIKE A PRAYER** (CD/cassette box set, press release, badge, slides, Rolling Stone reprint, 2 photos) | £400 |

MADONNA & MISSY (ELLIOTT)

| 08 | Warner 440444-2 | **HARD CANDY** (CD, 'Candy Box' edition, booklet, bonus mixes, bag of sweets) | £30 |
| 03 | Maverick RRCG 0301 | **Into The Hollywood Groove/Hollywood** (Jack Lu Cont's Thin White Dick Mix) (GAP in-store promo) | £25 |

MAD PROFESSOR

82	Ariwa ARILP 001	**DUB ME CRAZY** (LP)	£20
82	Ariwa ARILP 002	**BEYOND THE REALMS OF DUB** (LP)	£20
83	Ariwa ARILP 005	**THE AFRICAN CONNECTION - DUB ME CRAZY PART 3** (LP)	£25
83	Ariwa ARILP 011	**ESCAPE TO THE ASYLUM OF DUB** (LP)	£20
85	Ariwa ARILP 025	**CARIBBEAN TASTE OF TECHNOLOGY GONE CRAZY** (LP)	£25
86	Ariwa ARILP 030	**SCHIZOPHRENIC DUB ME CRAZY VOL. 6** (LP)	£15
85	Ariwa ARILP 021	**DUB ME CRAZY - VOLUME 5** (LP)	£15
93	Ariwa ARILP 095	**BLACK LIBERATION DUB** (LP)	£15
94	Ariwa ARILP 057	**PSYCHEDELIC DUB DUB - DUB ME CRAZY PART 10** (LP)	£15
09	Ariwa AROLP 001LP	**DUB ME CRAZY** (LP, reissue)	£15

MAD PROFESSOR & JAH SHAKA

| 96 | Ariwa AEILP 116 | **NEW DECADE OF DUB** (LP) | £25 |

MAD RAGGA JON

| 92 | Mad House M/HSE 001 | **Original Bad Boy/So Good** (12") | £15 |
| 93 | Mad House HTP07 | **Fall Down On Me/The Power** (12") | £15 |

MADRIGAL

71	Decca F13110	**Blue Eyes In Paradise/Wendy**	£20
72	Sovereign SOV 1071	**Time Of The Season/Tapestry**	£20
73	Madrigal MAD 100	**BENEATH THE GREENWOOD TREE** (LP, private pressing)	£60

MAD RIVER

| 69 | Capitol (S)T 2985 | **MAD RIVER** (LP) | £125 |
| 85 | Edsel ED 140 | **MAD RIVER** (LP, reissue) | £15 |

MAD SEASON

| 95 | Columbia 478 5071 | **ABOVE** (LP, with free 1-sided etched 12") | £80 |

MADVILLAIN

| 04 | PIAS PIASX 040 | **MADVILLAINY** (2-LP) | £40 |
| (see also Madlib, Cookin Soul) |

JOHNNY MAESTRO

61	HMV POP 875	**What A Surprise/The Warning Voice**	£25
61	HMV POP 909	**Mr. Happiness/Test Of Love**	£25
64	United Artists UP 1004	**Before I Love Her/Fifty Million Heartbeats**	£25
(see also Crests)

MAGAZINE

| 78 | Virgin VS 200 | **Shot By Both Sides/My Mind Ain't So Open** (card p/s) | £15 |

MINT VALUE £

78	Virgin V2100	REAL LIFE (LP, original blue labels)	£30
78	Virgin V2100	REAL LIFE (LP, reissue, green/red labels)	£15
79	Virgin V2121	SECONDHAND DAYLIGHT (LP, gatefold)	£30
80	Virgin V2156	THE CORRECT USE OF SOAP (LP)	£25
80	Virgin V2184	PLAY (LP)	£20
81	Virgin V2200	MAGIC, MURDER AND THE WEATHER (LP)	£20
82	Virgin VM 1	AFTER THE FACT (LP)	£20
11	Wire Sound WIRED 22	NO THYSELF (LP)	£15

(see also Buzzcocks)

MAGENTA
78	Cottage COT 821	CANTERBURY MOON (LP, with insert)	£40
80	Little Stan LSP 811	RECOLLECTIONS (2-LP, gatefold sleeve with insert)	£35
81	Little Stan LSP 831	WOT'S NEXT THEN (LP, with insert)	£25

MAGIC CARPET
72	Mushroom 200 MR 20	MAGIC CARPET (LP, white/brown labels)	£300
95	Magic Carpet MC 1001 LP	MAGIC CARPET (LP, reissue)	£25

(see also Clem Alford)

MAGIC CHRISTIANS
69	Major Minor MM 673	Come And Get It/Nuts (2nd pressing with correct title)	£20
70	Major Minor SMLP 71	THE MAGIC CHRISTIANS (LP)	£40

(see also Trevor Burton, Gary Wright, Denny Laine, Steve Gibbons)

MAGIC DISCO MACHINE
75	Motown TML 11289	DISC-O-TECH (LP)	£18

MAGIC LANTERNS
66	CBS 202250	Rumplestiltskin/I Stumbled	£40
67	CBS (S)BPG 62935	LIT UP WITH THE MAGIC LANTERNS (LP)	£40

MAGIC MIXTURE
68	Saga STFID 2125	THIS IS MAGIC MIXTURE (LP, black/silver labels)	£150
08	Sunbeam SBR2LP 5059	THIS IS THE MAGIC MIXTURE (2-LP, reissue)	£18

MAGIC MUSCLE
88	Five Hours Back TOCK 009	THE PIPE, THE ROAR, THE GRID (LP, with booklet)	£18
89	One Big Guitar OBGLP 9005	100 MILES BELOW (LP)	£15
90	Pilgrim (no cat. no.)	LIVING WEEDS FROM ANCIENT SEEDS (cassette, box set, autographed with booklet, posters & postcard)	£15
91	Woronzow WOO 17	GULP! (LP)	£20

(see also Keith Christmas, Hawkwind, High Tide, Twink)

MAGIC MUSHROOM BAND
86	Pagan PM 003	THE POLITICS OF ECSTASY (LP, 100 with A1 poster)	£50
86	Pagan PM 003	THE POLITICS OF ECSTASY (LP, 500 with A3 insert)	£25
87	Aftermath AFT 3	BOMSHAMKAR (LP)	£15
91	Fungus FUN 005	SPACED OUT (LP, foldout sleeve with A4 booklet)	£15

THE MAGIC NUMBERS
05	Heavenly HVNLP53	MAGIC NUMBERS (2-LP with free 1-sided 7" HVBLP53X)	£18

MAGIC SAM
69	Python PEN 701	Twenty One Days In Jail/Easy Baby (99 copies only)	£45
69	Rooster 707	MEAN MISTREATER (EP)	£20
70	Blue Horizon 7-63223	MAGIC SAM: 1937-1969 (LP)	£100
70	Delmark DS 615	WEST SIDE SOUL (LP, blue label)	£30
71	Delmark DS 620	BLACK MAGIC (LP, blue label)	£35

MAGICIAN
79	Hobo HOS 008	House Of The Purple Mist (Part 1)/(Part 2)	£40
79	Hobo HO 501	MAGICIAN (LP)	£40

MAGICIANS
68	MCA MU 1046	Painting On Wood/Slow Motion	£40

MAGISTRATES
68	MGM MGM 1437	After The Fox/Tear Down The Walls (with Jean Hillary)	£15

(see also Jane Hillery)

MAGITS
79	Outer H. SRTS/79/CUS/401	Fragmented/Disconnected/Disjointed/Detached (p/s, with 3 page magazine insert)	£140
79	Outer H. SRTS/79/CUS/401	Fragmented/Disconnected/Disjointed/Detached (p/s, without magazine)	£100

(see also Rudimentary Peni)

MAGMA
74	A&M AMS 7119	Mekanik Machine/Mekanik Machine (Version)	£20
70	Philips 6359 051/2	MAGMA (2-LP)	£70
71	Philips 6397 031	1001 CENTIGRADE (LP)	£40
74	A&M AMLH 64397	MEKANIK DESTRUCTIW KOMMANDOH (LP, gatefold sleeve, lyric insert)	£40
74	A&M AMLH 68260	KOHN TARKOSZ (LP)	£20

MAGNA CARTA
69	Fontana TF 1060	Romeo Jack/7 O'Clock Man	£20
69	Mercury MF 1096	Mid-Winter/Spinning Wheels Of Time	£20
69	Mercury MCL 20166 S	MAGNA CARTA (LP, laminated sleeve, black/silver labels)	£200
70	Vertigo 6360 003	SEASONS (LP, 1st pressing, gatefold sleeve, large swirl label, "Vertigo" at base of label)	£120
70	Vertigo 6360 003	SEASONS (LP, 2nd pressing, gatefold sleeve, small swirl label, "Vertigo" beneath swirl above centre hole)	£50

71	Vertigo 6360 040	SONGS FROM WASTIES ORCHARD (LP, multifold sleeve, large swirl label)	£150
72	Vertigo 6360 068	IN CONCERT (LP, gatefold sleeve, small swirl label)	£18
73	Vertigo 6360 093	LORD OF THE AGES (LP, 1st pressing, side 1 matrix, 1 (crossed out 2) Y//1 1 1 1 1, gatefold sleeve, lyric insert, spaceship label)	£15
74	Vertigo 6360 003	SEASONS (LP, 3rd pressing, 'spaceship label)	£15

MAGNET
| 69 | CBS 4472 | Let Me Stay/Mr Guy Fawkes | £30 |

MAGNETIC FORCE
| 97 | Time 2 Flex TTFLEX 01 | REFLECTIONS EP (12") | £20 |

MAGNETS
| 79 | Hurricane FIRE 1 | Who's The Fool (Me Or You)/Best (with insert, round white cut-out sheet) | £25 |

MAGNIFICENT
| 88 | Link LINKLP 027 | HIT AND RUN (LP) | £20 |

MAGNIFICENT MEN
| 66 | Capitol CL 15462 | Peace Of Mind/All Your Lovin's Gone To My Head | £30 |

MAGNUM
75	CBS S CBS 2959	Sweets For My Sweet/Movin' On (no p/s)	£45
86	Polydor POSPP 833	Midnight (Remix)/Back Street Kid/Kingdom Of Madness (live)/Midnight (You Won't Be Sleeping)(12", picture disc)	£15
78	Jet JETLP 210	KINGDOM OF MADNESS (LP, original 'king' sleeve)	£25
83	FM WKFMPD 111	THE ELEVENTH HOUR (LP, picture disc)	£25
85	FM WKFM LP 34	ON A STORYTELLER'S NIGHT (LP, with bonus single)	£20
85	FM WKFMG/CLP34	ON A STORYTELLER'S NIGHT (LP, clear vinyl)	£20
85	FM WKFM G/C LP 34	ON A STORYTELLER'S NIGHT (LP, gold or clear vinyl, with poster)	£15
85	FM WKFM PD 34	ON A STORYTELLER'S NIGHT (LP, picture disc)	£18
86	Polydor POLD 5198	VIGILANTE (LP, with inner)	£15
87	FM Revolver WKFMHP 106	MIRADOR (LP, blue vinyl, gatefold sleeve, poster and blue vinyl 12" (12HP106)	£18
88	FM Revolver WKFMPD 119T	MAGNUM II (LP, reissue, picture disc)	£15
90	FM Revolver WKFMBX 145	FOUNDATION (6-LP box set)	£45
92	Music For Nations MFN 143	SLEEPWALKING (LP)	£80

MAGPIES
| 68 | Doctor Bird DB 1129 | Lulu/Must I Be Lonely | £18 |
| 68 | Doctor Bird DB 1132 | Blue Boy/I Guess I'm Crazy | £18 |

MAG SPIES/MAGAZINE SPIES/MAGSPIES
| 79 | Dance Fools Dance GLITCH 1 | LIFEBLOOD (12" EP, 2 tracks by Mag Spies/2 by Obtainers) | £400 |

(see also The Cure)

ALEX MAGUIRE
| 87 | Incus INCUS 52 | LIVE AT OSCARS (LP) | £35 |

MAGUS
| 80 | Northern Sound NSR 200 | BREEZIN' AWAY (LP, private pressing) | £50 |

(see also Blue Epitaph)

TAJ MAHAL
67	Direction 8-63279	TAJ MAHAL (LP)	£30
69	Direction 8-63397	THE NATCH'L BLUES (LP)	£30
69	Direction 8-66226	GIANT STEP/DE OLE FOLKS AT HOME (2-LP)	£25
71	CBS 66288	THE REAL THING (2-LP)	£18

MAHAVISHNU ORCHESTRA
| 72 | CBS 64717 | THE INNER MOUNTING FLAME (LP, with insert) | £15 |
| 74 | CBS CQ 31996 | BIRDS OF FIRE (LP, quadrophonic) | £20 |

(see also John McLaughlin)

SKIP MAHONEY & CASUALS
| 76 | Contempo CLP 539 | LAND OF LOVE (LP) | £20 |

MAIL
| 71 | Parlophone R 5916 | Omnibus/Life Goes On | £25 |

MAIN
| 96 | Beggars Banquet HERTZ 16LP | Hz (2-LP) | £25 |

MAIN ATTRACTIONS
| 77 | Solid Sound SS 001 | Love/Doug's Love (with Augustus Pablo) | £20 |

MAIN INGREDIENT
| 71 | RCA LSA 3020 | TASTEFUL SOUL (LP) | £15 |

MAINFRAME (1)
83	MC Squared MC 004	Radio (Will Bring Me Home)/The Message/The Room (Part 2) (p/s)	£15
83	MC Squared MC 005	TALK TO ME EP	£15
83	MC Squared MC 007	TENANTS OF THE LATTICE WORK (LP)	£20

MAINHORSE
| 71 | Polydor 2383 049 | MAINHORSE (LP) | £45 |

MIKE MAINIERI
| 69 | Solid State USS 7006 | INSIGHT (LP) | £30 |

MAINLAND
| 79 | Christy ACML 0200 | EXPOSURE (LP) | £15 |

MAINLINER
| 03 | Remorse LP 01 | MELLOW OUT (LP, red vinyl) | £15 |

MINT VALUE £

JULIE MAIRS & CHRIS STOWELL
(see also Acid Mothers Temple)
77	Cottage COT 211	SOFT SEA BLUE (LP)	£25

MAJAMOOD
66	Doc. Bird/W.I.R.L. DB 1052	Two Hundred Million Red Ants/Faces Amassed	£30

MAJESTERIANS
81	Daddy Kool DKR 125	So Many Times/Flute On Fire (12")	£30

MAJESTIC CHOIR AND SOUL STIRRERS
69	Chess CRS 8101	Why Am I Treated So Bad/We Can All Walk A Little Prouder	£15

MAJESTICS (1)
73	Cube BUG 34	Living It All Again/She Troubles My Mind	£25

MAJOR
78	North Star NS 104	MAJOR EP	£50

MAJOR ACCIDENT
82	M. Melodies MAME 1001	Warboots/Terrorist Gang (unissued, test pressings only)	£40
83	Flicknife FLS 016	Fight To Win/Free Man (p/s)	£15
83	Step Forward SFLP 9	MASSACRED MELODIES (LP)	£30
84	Syndicate SYNLP 9	TORTURED TUNES LIVE (LP)	£25
85	Flicknife SHARP 027	PNEUMATIC PNEUROSIS (LP)	£25

(see also Accident)

MAJORETTES
63	Lyntone LYN 982	White Levi's (flexidisc)	£15

MAJOR FORCE
94	Mo' Wax MW 082LP	Return Of The Original Artform/(Mixes) (5 x 12" box set)	£25

MAJORINE
69	Pyramid 6069	Loving Shrine/I Live	£20

MAJORITY
65	Decca F 12186	Pretty Little Girl/I Don't Wanna Be Hurt No More	£20
65	Decca F 12271	A Little Bit Of Sunlight/Shut 'Em Down In London Town	£25
66	Decca F 12313	We Kiss In A Shadow/Ring The Bells	£15
66	Decca F 12453	Simplified/One Third	£100
66	Decca F 12504	To Make Me A Man/Tears Won't Help	£15
67	Decca F 12573	I Hear A Rhapsody/Wait By The Fire	£20
67	Decca F 12638	Running Away With My Baby/Let The Joybells Ring	£20
68	Decca F 12727	All Our Christmases/People	£25

MAJORS (1)
62	London HLP 9602	A Wonderful Dream/Time Will Tell	£20
62	London HLP 9627	She's A Troublemaker/A Little Bit Now	£20
63	London HLP 9693	What In The World/Tra La La	£20
64	Liberty LBF 66009	Ooh Wee Baby/I'll Be There	£30
63	London RE-P 1358	MEET THE MAJORS (EP)	£50
63	London HA-P 8068	MEET THE MAJORS (LP)	£80

MAJORS (2)
77	Magnet MAG 79	It Only Happens/One Sided Love Affair	£20

MAJOR SURGERY
77	Next 104	NEXT CUT (LP)	£40

MAJOR TOM
76	Satril SAT 113	Spaceman Boy/Spaceman Boy (Instrumental)	£25

MAKIN' TIME
85	Countdown DOWN 1	RHYTHM 'N' SOUL (LP)	£15
86	Ready To Eat READY 1	NO LUMPS OF FAT OR GRISTLE GUARANTEED (LP)	£18
87	Re-Elect/President ELECT 1	TIME, TROUBLE AND MONEY (LP)	£18

(see also Charlatans)

MAKKA BEES
77	Congo CO 1	Nation Fiddler/Fire	£20

MAL & PRIMITIVES
65	Pye 7N 15915	Every Minute Of Every Day/Pretty Little Face	£80

(see also Primitives, Mal Ryder & Spirits)

MALA
05	DMZ DMZ 003	Da Wrath Souljahz Vip Mix/LOEFAH: Twisup Vip (12")	£25
06	DMZ DMZ 010	Left Leg Out/Vlue Notez (12")	£20
07	DMZ DMZ 011	Bury Da Bwoy/Hunter (12")	£25
07	DMZ DMZ 012	Lean Forward/Learn (12")	£30

MALARIA!
82	Jungle JUNG 3	NEW YORK PASSAGE (12" EP)	£20
19	Electronic Sound ES 753	Your Turn To Run/GUDRUN GUT: Boys Keep Swinging (p/s)	£15

CARL MALCOLM
77	Grove Music GMDM 1	Repatriation (feat. Ranking Trevor)/Take A Tip From Me (feat. Ranking Trevor) (12")	£40

CARLOS MALCOLM & AFRO CARIBS
65	Island WI 173	Bonanza Ska/Papa Luiga	£20

HUGH MALCOLM
68	Amalgamated AMG 827	Good Time Rock/LYNN TAITT & JETS: Sleepy Ludy	£50

		MINT VALUE £
68	Amalgamated AMG 829	Mortgage/CANNONBALL BRYAN TRIO: Man About Town £50

MALIBU
| 78 | Cleverly Bros CBSP 1000 100 | Skateboarding/Billy...£20 |

MALLARD
| 76 | Virgin V 2045 | MALLARD (LP)...£15 |

(see also Captain Beefheart & His Magic Band)

MALLET
| 80 | Rox ROX 014 | C C Rider/Route 66 ....£25 |

STEPHEN MALLINDER
| 82 | Fetish FM 2010 | POW-WOW (LP) ....£30 |

(see also Cabaret Voltaire)

SIW MALMKVIST
| 59 | Oriole CB 1486 | Sermonette/The Preacher...£20 |

WIL MALONE
| 70 | Fontana STL 5541 | WIL MALONE (LP) ....£1500 |
| 10 | Morgan Bluetown BT 5005 | WIL MALONE (LP, reissue, 750 only with signed certificate) ....£35 |

(see also Motherlight, Wilson Malone Voiceband)

WILSON MALONE VOICEBAND
| 68 | Morgan MR 112P | FUNNY SAD MUSIC (LP)..£50 |

(see also Motherlight, Wil Malone)

MALPRACTICE
| 80 | SRTS/80/CUS 762 | It's OK/Wish You Would/Don't Take It Out ....£100 |

MAMA LAPATO
| 82 | Bead Records BEAD 20 | MAMA LAPATO (LP) ....£20 |

MAMA LION
| 72 | Philips 6369 153 | PRESERVE WILDLIFE (LP) ....£20 |

MAMAS & PAPAS
66	RCA Victor RD 7803	IF YOU CAN BELIEVE YOUR EYES AND EARS (LP)............................£20
66	RCA Victor RD/SF 7834	CASS, JOHN, MICHELLE, DENNY (LP) £20
67	RCA Victor RD/SF 7880	DELIVER (LP) £20
68	RCA Victor RD/SF 7960	THE PAPAS AND THE MAMAS (LP) £20
68	Stateside (S)SL 5002	THE MAMAS AND THE PAPAS GOLDEN ERA VOL. 2 (LP).............£15
70	Probe SPB 1013/14	A GATHERING OF FLOWERS (2-LP) £20
71	Probe SPB 1048	PEOPLE LIKE US (LP)...£15
78	St. Michael MO 101225	CALIFORNIA DREAMIN' (LP, exclusive to Marks & Spencer)...........£15

(see also Mama Cass [Elliot], John Phillips, Michelle Phillips, Scott McKenzie, Barry McGuire, Mugwumps, Big Three [U.S], Spanky & Our Gang)

MAMMOTH
| 89 | Jive MOTHX 4 | All The Days/Fatman/Bet You Wish (12", picture disc, PVC sleeve, withdrawn)..............£20 |

(see also John McCoy, Gillan, Samson, Tiger, Hackensack)

BATTI MAMZELLE
| 74 | Fly 17 | I SEE THE LIGHT (LP) ....£20 |

MAN
69	Pye 7N 17684	Sudden Life/Love..£35
71	Liberty LBF 15448	Daughter Of The Fireplace/Country Girl.................................£18
74	United Artists UP 35643	Don't Go Away (possibly unissued) £15
69	Pye N(S)PL 18275	REVELATION (LP, mono, original pressing with sky blue label with black at top) £100
69	Pye N(S)PL 18275	REVELATION (LP, stereo, original pressing with sky blue label with black at top)..............£80
69	Dawn DNLS 3003	2 OZS OF PLASTIC WITH A HOLE IN THE MIDDLE (LP, orange label, gatefold sleeve) £50
69	Dawn DNLS 3003	2 OZ'S OF PLASTIC WITH A HOLE IN THE MIDDLE (LP, later pressings with lilac then pink 'sun' labels, gatefold sleeve) £20
70	Liberty LBG 83464	MAN (LP, gatefold textured sleeve)..£40
72	United Artists UAS 29236	DO YOU LIKE IT HERE NOW (ARE YOU SETTLING IN ALRIGHT?) (LP)...........£40
72	United Artists USP 100	LIVE AT THE PADGET ROOMS, PENARTH (LP) £30
72	United Artists UAG 29417	BE GOOD TO YOURSELF AT LEAST ONCE A DAY (LP, fold out 'map' in gatefold sleeve with 'family tree' inner)...£45
73	United Artists UDX 205/6	CHRISTMAS AT THE PATTI (LP, 2 x 10", with other artists)...............£22
73	Utd Artists UAD 60053/4	BACK INTO THE FUTURE (2-LP, gatefold sleeve, some stickered) £20
74	United Artists UAG 29631	RHINOS WINOS AND LUNATICS (LP, laminated gatefold)...........£15
74	United Artists UAG 29675	SLOW MOTION (LP, lyric inner sleeve).....................................£15
75	United Artists UAG 29872	MAXIMUM DARKNESS (LP, gatefold sleeve, with poster) £15
77	MCA MCF 2815	ALL'S WELL THAT ENDS WELL (LP, initial batch with History Of Man booklet) £20

(see also Bystanders, Eyes Of Blue, Ancient Grease, Big Sleep, Clive John, Alkatraz, Help Yourself, Deke Leonard, Neutrons, Wild Turkey)

T. MAN & T. BONES
| 72 | Sioux SI 007 | True Born African (actually by Winston Jarrett & Righteous Flames)/JAYBOYS:Tropical Chief...£70 |

MAN UPSTAIRS
82	Clock House CH 0502	Summa/The Gospel According To Mark (p/s)...........................£15
85	Sideline SIDE 1	Sad In My Heart/Country Boy (p/s) £15
85	Sideline 1SIDE12	CONSUMERS EP (12", p/s)...£40

(STEPHEN STILLS') MANASSAS
| 72 | Atlantic K 60021 | MANASSAS (2-LP, with 2 inner sleeves & lyric poster) ....£25 |
| 73 | Atlantic K 40440 | DOWN THE ROAD (LP, with inner sleeve) ....£20 |

(see also Stephen Stills, Crosby Stills & Nash, Flying Burrito Brothers)

MINT VALUE £

MANASSEH
77   Genesis 12   MANASSEH (LP, with insert) £20

JUNIOR MANCE
60   HMV CLP 1342   JUNIOR (LP)..£25
71   Atlantic 2400 028   WITH A LOTTA HELP FROM MY FRIENDS (LP) £20

STEVE MANCHA/J.J. BARNES
69   Stax SXATS 1012   RARE STAMPS (LP) £60
(see also J.J. Barnes)

MANCHESTER MEKON
79   Newmarket NEW 102   No Forgetting/Have A Go-Go/Jonathan Livingstone Seafood (hand-painted p/s with
                          insert, 1,000 only) £25

MANCHESTER MOB
67   Parlophone R 5552   Bony Maronie At The Hop/Afro Asian £40
(see also Graham Gouldman, High Society, 10cc, Friday Browne)

MANCHESTERS
66   Ember   TRIBUTE TO THE BEATLES (LP) £20

MANCHESTER'S PLAYBOYS
66   Fontana TF 745   I Feel So Good/I Close My Eyes £150

HENRY MANCINI & HIS ORCHESTRA
57   Brunswick LAT 8162 ROCK, PRETTY BABY (LP, soundtrack, with Rod McKuen)...............................£80

DAVID MANCUSO
99   Nuphonic NUX 136   DAVID MANCUSO PRESENTS THE LOFT (4 x 12")...£100
00   Nuphonic NUX 154   DAVID MANCUSO PRESENTS THE LOFT VOL. 2 (4 x 12") £100

MANDALABAND
75   Chrysalis CHR 1095 MANDALABAND (LP) £20
78   Chrysalis CHR 1181 THE EYE OF WENDOR: PROPHECIES (LP, with booklet).................................£20

MANDARIN KRAZE
70   Carnaby CNS 4008   How Long Does It Take/Magazine Cottage £25

HARVEY MANDEL
68   Philips SBL 7873   CRISTO REDENTOR (LP) £45
69   Philips SBL 7904   RIGHTEOUS (LP)..£20
70   Philips SBL 7915   GAMES GUITARS PLAY (LP) £15
71   Dawn DNLS 3015   BABY BATTER (LP)..£40
71   Philips 6336 009   CRISTO REDENTOR (LP, reissue)...£15
72   London SH-O 8426   GET OFF IN CHICAGO (LP) £15
72   Janus 6310 210   THE SNAKE (LP)..£15
(see also Canned Heat, Dewey Terry)

DAVE MANDELL & STEVE WILSON
72   Wilfa WIL 50   NUCLEAR POWER STATION (LP) £50

MANDINGO
73   EMI EMI 2014   Medicine Man/Black Rite..£15
73   Studio Two TWO 400 PRIMEVAL RHYTHM OF LIFE (LP)...£40
73   Studio Two Q4TWO 400 PRIMEVAL RHYTHM OF LIFE (LP, quadrophonic)......................................£40
73   EMI EMC 3010   SACRIFICE (LP)...£20
75   EMI EMC 3038   MANDINGO 3: STORY OF SURVIVAL (LP) £30
77   EMI EMC 3217   SAVAGE RITE (LP) £25
(see also Geoff Love)

MANDRAGORA
89   SAB 01   OVER THE MOON (LP, 1st pressing with white label/cream sleeve)...................£50
89   Babbleon Bab 1   OVER THE MOON (LP, 2nd pressing with blue label/yellow/blue/white/cream sleeve) £30
91   Resonance 33-9133 HEAD FIRST (LP) £20
93   Mystic Stones RUNE 13 EARTHDANCE (LP)..£15
95   Mystic Stones RUNE 14 TEMPLE BALL (LP) £15

MANDRAKE MEMORIAL
69   RCA SF 8028   MEDIUM (LP) £125
70   RCA/Poppy PYS 11003 PUZZLE (LP)..£140

MANDRAKE PADDLE STEAMERS
69   Parlophone R 5780 Strange Walking Man/Steam £130
(see also Liverpool Echo)

MANDRILL
72   Polydor 2391 030   MANDRILL IS (LP, gatefold) £40
73   Polydor 2391 061   COMPOSITE TRUTH (LP) £20
73   Polydor 2391 092   JUST OUTSIDE OF TOWN (LP) £15
73   United Artists UAS 29923 SOLID (LP) £15
75   United Artists UAS 29920 BEAST FROM THE EAST (LP) £20
75   Polydor 2391 188   THE BEST OF (LP) £15
77   Arista SPART 1035 WE ARE ONE (LP) £15
78   Arista ARTY 162   NEW WORLDS (LP)..£25

MANEATERS
82   Editions EG EGO 8 Nine To Five/SUZI PINNS: Jerusalem (withdrawn 'Adam & Toyah' p/s).........................£100
(see also Adam & The Ants)

MAN FRIDAY & JIVE JUNIOR
83   Malaco MAL 011   Picking Up Sounds/Picking Up Sounds (Radio Mix) (p/s, features John Deacon)..............£20

83	Malaco MAL 1211	**Picking Up Sounds** (Extended)/**Picking Up Sounds** (Radio Mix) (12", p/s, features John Deacon)	**£35**

(see also Queen)

MAN FROM DELMONTE
87	Ugly Man UGLY 3	**Drive Drive Drive** (22 And Still In Love With You)/**Sun Serious** (p/s)	**£25**
87	Ugly Man UGLY 5T	**Water In My Eyes/Bored By You/The Country** (12", p/s)	**£18**
88	Ugly Man UGLY 7T	(Will Nobody Save) **Louise/Good Things In Life/Like A Millionaire** (12", p/s)	**£25**
89	Bop Cassettes BIP 502	**WAITING FOR ANN** (12" EP)	**£15**

RAY MANG
96	Noid NOID 099	**NUMBER ONE EP** (12")	**£20**
08	Mangled REG 008	**Angel/Cerela Lover** (12")	**£15**

MANGO GREEN
70	Ackee ACK 109	**Birds Of A Feather/Run Down**	**£15**

MANHATTANS
65	Sue WI 384	**I Wanna Be** (Your Everything)/**Searchin' For My Baby**	**£50**
66	Carnival CAR 100	**Baby I Need You/Teach Me** (The Philly Dog)	**£20**
66	Carnival CAR 101	**That New Girl/Can I**	**£20**
73	London SHB 8449	**A MILLION TO ONE** (LP)	**£30**

MANHATTEN BROTHERS
65	Columbia 33SX 1704	**EMERGENT VOICES** (LP)	**£40**

MANIACS
77	United Artists UP 36327	**Chelsea 1977/Ain't No Legend** (p/s)	**£20**
77	United Artists UP 36327	**Chelsea 1977/Ain't No Legend** (p/s, green labels, demo versions different mixes)	**£30**

(see also Rings)

MANIAX
66	White Label WLR 101/102	**Out Of Reach/The Devil's Home**	**£20**

MANIC STREET PREACHERS
SINGLES
88	SBS Records SBS 002	**Suicide Alley/Tennessee** (I Get Low) (hand-made p/s with press-cuttings glued to plain card cover)	**£1000**
88	SBS Records SBS 002	**Suicide Alley/Tennessee** (I Get Low) (blue p/s, 200 only)	**£600**
88	SBS SBS 002	**Suicide Alley/Tennessee** (I Get Low) (no p/s, 100 only)	**£300**
90	Hopelessly Devoted 1	**UK Channel Boredom/LAURENS: I Don't Know What The Trouble Is** (p/s flexidisc, free with Hopelessly Devoted fanzine; later repressed)	**£35**
90	Hopelessly Devoted 1	**UK Channel Boredom/LAURENS: I Don't Know What The Trouble Is** (p/s flexidisc, without Hopelessly Devoted fanzine; later repressed)	**£45**
90	Damaged Goods YUBB 4	**NEW ART RIOT EP: New Art Riot/Strip It Down/Last Exit On Yesterday/Teenage 20/20** (12", white label, 100 copies, plain sleeves rubber stamped with "Made In Wales")	**£35**
90	Damaged Goods YUBB 4	**NEW ART RIOT EP: New Art Riot/Strip It Down/Last Exit On Yesterday/Teenage 20/20** (12" EP, p/s, 1st 1,000 black & white label)	**£20**
90	Damaged Goods YUBB 4	**NEW ART RIOT EP: New Art Riot/Strip It Down/Last Exit On Yesterday/Teenage 20/20** (12" EP, p/s, 2nd 1,000 on black-on-yellow labels)	**£15**
91	Damaged Goods YUBB 004P	**NEW ART RIOT EP: New Art Riot/Strip It Down/Last Exit On Yesterday/Teenage 20/20** (12" EP, p/s, reissue on pink vinyl)	**£25**
91	Heavenly HVN 812	**Motown Junk/Sorrow 16/We Her Majesty's Prisoners** (12", withdrawn p/s)	**£35**
91	Heavenly HVN 8CD	**Motown Junk/Sorrow 16/We Her Majesty's Prisoners** (CD, withdrawn sleeve)	**£125**
91	Heavenly HVN 10	**You Love Us/Spectators Of Suicide** (p/s)	**£15**
91	Heavenly HVN 1012	**You Love Us/Spectators Of Suicide/Starlover/Strip It Down** (live) (12", p/s)	**£20**
91	Columbia 657337 6	**Stay Beautiful/R.P. McMurphy/Soul Contamination** (12", p/s)	**£15**
91	Columbia 657337 8	**Stay Beautiful/R.P. McMurphy/Soul Contamination** (12", stickered poster p/s)	**£30**
91	Columbia 657582 8	**Repeat/Democracy Coma/Love's Sweet Exile/Stay Beautiful** (live) (12", gatefold, stickered p/s)	**£15**
91	Caff CAFF 15	**FEMININE IS BEAUTIFUL: Repeat After Me/New Art Riot** (p/s, 500 only)	**£250**
92	Columbia 658083 6	**Motorcycle Emptiness/Bored Out Of My Mind/Under My Wheels** (12")	**£15**
92	Columbia 658083 6	**Motorcycle Emptiness/Bored Out Of My Mind/Under My Wheels** (12", picture disc, stickered PVC sleeve)	**£25**
93	Columbia 6594776	**La Tristesse Durera** (Scream To A Sigh)/**Parick Bateman/Repeat** (Live)/**Tennessee** (12", with 20 x 30 inch poster)	**£20**
94	Columbia 6600706	**Life Becoming A Landslide/Comfort Comes/Are Mothers Saints** (12" with poster)	**£18**
94	Epic 6604470	**P.CP./Faster/Sculpture Of Man** (10")	**£20**
94	Epic 6608950	**She Is Suffering/Love Torn Us Under/The Drowners/Stay With Me** (10")	**£20**
98	Epics MSP 12	**If You Tolerate This Your Children Will Be Next** (Massive Attack Remix)/(Massive Attack Instrumental Remix)/(Class Reunion Of Of The Sunset Marquise Mix) (12")	**£15**
07	Columbia 8697075597	**Underdogs** (1-sided, p/s)	**£20**
11	Heavenly HVN 8	**Motown Junk/Sorrow 16** (reissue, 1000 only, p/s)	**£20**
11	Columbia 88697946142	**NATIONAL TREASURES - THE COMPLETE SINGLES** (box set, 38 x CD, DVD and 3 x 7" singles)	**£300**
11	SEAT UMPC 014	**ON TRACK WITH SEAT** (12")	**£200**
14	Phantasy Sound PH 36	**Europa Geht Durch Mich** (Erol Alkan's Mesmerise Eins Rework)/(Erol Alkan's Mesmerise Eins Rework) (12")	**£25**
18	Secret S 741	**No Surface All Feeling** (1-sided, unique p/s)	**£300**

ALBUMS
92	Epic 471060 1	**GENERATION TERRORISTS** (2-LP)	**£60**
92	Columbia 471060 0	**GENERATION TERRORISTS** (2-LP, picture discs, inner sleeves, 5,000 only)	**£40**
93	Columbia 474064 1	**GOLD AGAINST THE SOUL** (LP, inner sleeve)	**£100**
94	Epic 477421 0	**THE HOLY BIBLE** (LP, picture disc)	**£70**
96	Epic 483930	**EVERYTHING MUST GO** (LP)	**£70**
98	Epic 4917031	**THIS IS MY TRUTH TELL ME YOURS** (LP)	**£80**
01	Epic 501880	**KNOW YOUR ENEMY** (LP, inner)	**£50**

MINT VALUE £

02	Epic 5095511	FOREVER DELAYED - THE GREATEST HITS (2-LP)	£50
03	Sony 5123861	LIPSTICK TRACES (3 x LP, 1,000 only with tactile sleeve)	£350
04	Sony 519995 1	LIFEBLOOD (2-LP, with booklet)	£175
07	Columbia 88697 07563 1	SEND AWAY THE TIGERS (LP)	£50
09	Columbia 88697520581	JOURNAL FOR PLAGUE LOVERS (LP)	£60
10	Columbia 88697778601	POSTCARDS FROM A YOUNG MAN (LP)	£40
10	Music On Vinyl MOVLP 129	KNOW YOUR ENEMY (LP, reissue)	£50
10	Music On Vinyl MOVLP 221	FOREVER DELAYED - THE GREATEST HITS (2-LP, repressing)	£80
11	Columbia QMAGMANIACS	NATIONAL TREASURES - THE SELECTED SINGLES (LP, exclusive to Q magazine)	£80
11	Music On Vinyl MOVLP 261	THIS IS MY TRUTH TELL ME YOURS (LP, reissue)	£60
12	Music On Vinyl MOVLP 194	EVERYTHING MUST GO (LP, reissue)	£60
12	Columbia 88725471251	GENERATION TERRORISTS (2-LP, reissue, adds Theme From MASH)	£40
13	Columbia 888834745291	REWIND THE FILM (LP)	£35
14	Columbia 88843049621	FUTUROLOGY (LP)	£35
14	Columbia 88875036002	THE HOLY BIBLE 20 (LP, reissue, with 2CD, misprint with 4st 7lb listed as last track on side 1)	£100
14	Columbia 88875036002	THE HOLY BIBLE 20 (LP, reissue, with 2 x CD)	£50
15	Columbia 88875140661	THE HOLY BIBLE 20 (LP, reissue, US mix, picture disc)	£30
16	Columbia 88985317831	EVERYTHING MUST GO (2LP, reissue)	£80
16	Columbia 88985317831	EVERYTHING MUST GO (LP, reissue, blue vinyl)	£50
16	Columbia 88875036002	EVERYTHING MUST GO (LP/4CD, reissue, book)	£40
17	Sony 88985435081	THIS IS MY TRUTH TELL ME YOURS (LP, reissue)	£35
18	Sony 19075895241	THIS IS MY TRUTH TELL ME YOURS (2-LP, reissue, misprint without band name and title)	£60
18	Sony 190758909911	THIS IS MY TRUTH TELL ME YOURS (2-LP)	£40
18	Columbia 19075809891	RESISTANCE IS FUTILE (LP)	£25
18	Columbia 19075809891	RESISTANCE IS FUTILE (LP, white or red vinyl)	£20
21	Columbia 19439895431	THE ULTRA VIVID LAMENT (LP)	£20
21	Columbia 19439906001	THE ULTRA VIVID LAMENT (LP, alternative artwork HMV exclusive)	£30
21	Columbia 19439895461	THE ULTRA VIVID LAMENT (LP, picture disc)	£20

PROMOS

90	Damaged Goods YUBB 4	NEW ART RIOT EP (12", white label, 100 copies with press kit)	£300
91	Heavenly HVN 10P	You Love Us (Radio Edit) (promo-only, some with stickered p/s, 1-sided white label, 500 only)	£25
93	Columbia/Damont XPS 272	Symphony Of Tourette (1-sided, white label, no p/s)	£80
93	Columbia XPR 1966	Roses In The Hospital (OG Psychoval Mix(51 Funk Salute Mix)/Filet-O-Gang Mix/(ECG Mix)(Original Version) (12	£40
94	Columbia	DONE AND DUSTED (12", Chemical Brothers Remixes)	£15
96	Columbia XPR 3043	A Design For Life (Stealth Sonic Orchestra Remix)/(Instrumental) (12")	£25
96	Columbia XPR 3081	Kevin Carter (Stealth Sonic Orchestra Remix) (12", white label, 1-sided, stickered card sleeve, 30 only)	£20
96	Columbia XPR 3094	Australia (Lionrock Remix) (12", white label, 1-sided, stickered card sleeve, 20 only)	£30
97	Columbia MANIC 1-6CD	SIX SINGLES FROM GENERATION TERRORISTS (6-CD box set)	£90
98	Epic 6666865	The Everlasting (Deadly Avenger Remixes)/Psalm 315/Psalm 215 Instrumental/69th St Mix/69th St Instrumental (12")	£25
99	Epic XPR 3307	You Stole The Sun From My Heart (David Holmes Mixes) (12")	£20
99	Epic XPR 3320	Tsunami (Cornelius Remix)/(Electron Ray Tube Mix by Stereolab) (12", p/s, sealed with sticker, promo only)	£22
09	Columbia MSP 02	COOKING- CLEANING - FLOWER ARRANGING: JOURNAL FOR PLAGUE LOVERS (2 x 12", white labels)	£100

(see also James Dean Bradfield)

MANISH BOYS

65	Parlophone R 5250	I Pity The Fool/Take My Tip	£1000
65	Parlophone R 5250	I Pity The Fool/Take My Tip (Demo copy)	£500

(see also David Bowie)

MANISH BOYS/DAVY JONES & LOWER THIRD

79	EMI 2925	I Pity The Fool/Take My Tip/DAVY JONES You've Got A Habit Of Leaving/Baby Loves That Way (Demo copy p/s)	£20

(see also David Bowie, Davie Jones & King Bees)

MANITOBA (2)

01	Leaf BAY 16V	STOP BREAKING MY HEART (LP)	£20
03	Leaf BAY 26V	UP IN FLAMES (LP)	£20
03	Leaf BAY 26VX	UP IN FLAMES (LP, clear vinyl)	£20

(see also Caribou)

MANIX

92	Reinforced RIVET 1221	Rainbow People (12")	£15

EARLE MANKEY

78	Bronze BRO 53	Mau Mau/Crazy	£15

SYDNEY MANKIND

82	Musical Ambassador MAPD 001	The Truth/EDI FITZROY: Chant It To The Rhythm (12")	£40

BARRY MANN

61	HMV POP 911	Who Put The Bomp (In The Bomp Bomp)/Love True Love	£25
61	HMV POP 949	Little Miss U.S.A./Find Another Fool	£20
62	HMV POP 1084	Hey Baby I'm Dancin'/Like I Don't Love You	£15
63	HMV POP 1108	Bless You/Teenage Has Been	£15
64	Colpix PX 776	Talk To Me Baby/Amy	£15
66	Capitol CL 15463	Angelica/Looking At Tomorrow	£15
63	HMV CLP 1559	WHO PUT THE BOMP IN THE BOMP BOMP BOMP? (LP)	£125

72	CBS 64805	LAY IT ALL OUT (LP, gatefold)	£15

CARL MANN

59	London HLS 8935	Mona Lisa/Foolish One	£50
59	London HLS 8935	Mona Lisa/Foolish One (78)	£15
59	London HLS 9006	Pretend/Rockin' Love	£35
59	London HLS 9006	Pretend/Rockin' Love (78)	£30
60	London HLS 9170	South Of The Border/I'm Comin' Home	£25
60	London HA-S 2277	LIKE MANN - CARL MANN SINGS (LP)	£250

GLORIA MANN

56	Brunswick 05569	Why Do Fools Fall In Love/Partners For Life	£20

HERBIE MANN

75	Atlantic K 10580	Hijack/Orient Express	£15
75	Atlantic SAM 26	Hijack (Disco Cut)/Bertha Boogie Part 1 (12", "Disco Special Cut" on label)	£60
58	Fontana TFL 5013	SALUTE TO THE FLUTE (LP)	£15
60	Top Rank 25/015	FLUTE FOR ETERNITY (10" LP, with Buddy Collette)	£20
63	London HA-K/SH-K 8043	RIGHT NOW (LP)	£20
64	Atlantic ATL 5008	HERBIE MANN AT NEWPORT (LP)	£15
65	Atlantic ATL/SAL 5035	THE ROAR OF THE GREASE PAINT (LP)	£20
66	CBS (S)BPG 62585	LATIN MANN (LP)	£20
66	Atlantic ATL/SAL 5038	STANDING OVATION AT NEWPORT (LP)	£15
66	Atlantic 587/588 003	MONDAY NIGHT AT THE VILLAGE GATE (LP)	£15
66	Atlantic 587/588 028	NIRVANA (LP, with Bill Evans)	£15

MANFRED MANN

63	HMV POP 1189	Why Should We Not/Brother Jack	£30
63	HMV POP 1225	Cock-A-Hoop/Now You're Needing Me	£20
65	HMV 7TEA 2124	There's No Living Without Your Loving/Tired Of Trying, Bored With Lying, Scared Of Dying (demo-only EP sampler)	£30
68	Fontana TF 908	Up The Junction/Sleepy Hollow (in p/s)	£18
64	HMV 7EG 8848	MANFRED MANN'S COCK-A-HOOP WITH 54321 (EP)	£25
65	HMV 7EG 8876	GROOVIN' WITH MANFRED MANN (EP)	£20
65	HMV 7EG 8922	NO LIVING WITHOUT LOVING (EP)	£18
66	HMV 7EG 8942	MACHINES (EP)	£25
66	HMV 7EG 8949	INSTRUMENTAL ASYLUM (EP, with Jack Bruce)	£25
66	HMV 7EG 8962	AS WAS (EP)	£25
64	HMV CLP 1731	THE FIVE FACES OF MANFRED MANN (LP)	£60
64	Odeon PCLP 1731	THE FIVE FACES OF MANFRED MANN (LP, export issue gold/red odeon sticker on cover)	£90
65	HMV CLP 1911	MANN MADE (LP, mono)	£30
65	HMV CSD 1628	MANN MADE (LP, stereo)	£40
66	HMV CLP 3559	MANN MADE HITS (LP)	£35
66	Fontana TL 5377	AS IS (LP, 'alcove' cover, mono)	£20
66	Fontana (S)TL 5377	AS IS (LP, 'alcove' cover, stereo)	£30
66	Fontana (S)TL 5377	AS IS (LP, 'locomotive' cover, mono/stereo)	£60
67	HMV CLP 3594	SOUL OF MANN (LP, mono)	£50
67	HMV CSD 3594	SOUL OF MANN (LP, stereo)	£70
68	Fontana (S)TL 5460	UP THE JUNCTION - ORIGINAL SOUNDTRACK RECORDING (LP)	£50
68	Fontana SFL 13003	WHAT A MANN (LP)	£20
68	Fontana TL 5470	MIGHTY GARVEY! (LP, mono)	£25
68	Fontana (S)TL 5470	MIGHTY GARVEY! (LP, stereo)	£15
70	Fontana 6852 005	UP THE JUNCTION - ORIGINAL SOUNDTRACK RECORDING (LP, reissue)	£25

(see also Paul Jones, Blues Band, Mike Hugg, Henry Lowther, Mike D'Abo, McGuinness Flint, Jack Bruce, Coulson & Dean, Lyn Dobson, Paddy Klaus & Gibson)

MANFRED MANN & MIKE HUG(G)

71	Ski SKI 1	Ski 'Full-Of-Fitness' Theme/Baby Jane (in p/s)	£15
71	Michelin MIC+01	The Michelin Theme (Go Radial, Go Michelin) (1-sided, gatefold p/s)	£15

MANFRED MANN'S CHAPTER III

69	Vertigo VO 3	MANFRED MANN CHAPTER III (LP, 1st pressing, "Manfred Mann Chapter Three" and VO 3 847 902 VTY" in large type on B side, gatefold sleeve, large swirl label)	£175
70	Vertigo VO 3	MANFRED MANN CHAPTER III (LP, 2nd pressing, "Manfred Mann Chapter Three" and VO 3 847 902 VTY" in smaller type on B side, gatefold sleeve, large swirl label)	£125
70	Vertigo VO 3 847 902 VTY	MANFRED MANN CHAPTER III (LP, 3rd pressing, without 'A Philips Record Product' text, gatefold sleeve, large swirl label)	£80
70	Vertigo 6360 012	MANFRED MANN CHAPTER III VOL. 2 (LP, gatefold sleeve, large swirl label)	£175

MANFRED MANN'S EARTH BAND

71	Philips 6308 062	STEPPING SIDEWAYS (LP, unissued)	£0
72	Philips 6308 086	MANFRED MANN'S EARTH BAND (LP, black/silver labels)	£40
72	Philips 6308 125	GLORIFIED MAGNIFIED (LP, gatefold sleeve, 1st pressing, black/silver labels)	£50
72	Philips 6308 086	GLORIFIED MAGNIFIED (LP, gatefold sleeve, 2nd pressing, blue/silver labels)	£20
73	Vertigo 6360 087	MESSIN' (LP, die cut gatefold sleeve, 'spaceship' label)	£25
73	Bronze ILPS 9265	SOLAR FIRE (LP, gatefold sleeve, lyric inner sleeve, Island label credit)	£20
74	Bronze ILPS 9306	THE GOOD EARTH (LP, lyric inner sleeve with uncut corner, Island label credit)	£20
75	Bronze ILPS 9337	NIGHTINGALES AND BOMBERS (LP, 1st pressing with Island matrix numbers ILPS 9337 A-2U/B-2U, "MELYS I.B.C" etched into dead wax)	£20

(see also Australian Playboys, Trifle, AC/DC, Thin Lizzy, Alan Parsons Project, Jeff Wayne)

ROBERTO MANN ORCHESTRA

68	Decca F13904	Love Theme From Witchfinder General/Both Sides Now	£30

SHELLY MANNE

54	Vogue LDE 072	SHELLY MANNE AND HIS MEN VOL. 1 (10" LP)	£15

MINT VALUE £

55	Contemporary LDC 143	SHELLY MANNE VOL. 2 (10" LP, with Andre Previn & Leroy Vinegar)	£15
56	Contemporary LDC 190	SHELLY MANNE, SHORTY ROGERS AND JIMMY GIUFFRE - THE THREE (10" LP)	£15
56	Contemporary LDC 192	SHELLY MANNE AND RUSS FREEMAN (10" LP)	£15
56	Contemporary LAC 12075	SHELLY MANNE AND HIS FRIENDS (LP, with Andre Previn & Leroy Vinegar)	£15
61	Contemporary LAC 12305/6	AT THE MANNE HOLE (2-LP)	£15
62	Contemporary LAC12315	CHECKMATE (LP)	£15

(see also Gerry Mulligan & Shelly Manne, Shorty Rogers & His Orchestra)

MANNIN FOLK
| 76 | Kelly MAN 2 | KING OF THE SEA (LP) | £35 |
| 70s | Kelly KEP 1 | MANNIN FOLK SING (LP) | £20 |

BERNARD MANNING
| 72 | Decca SKL 5030 | SINGS 16 FAVOUORITE SONGS (LP) | £15 |

EDDIE MANNION
| 60 | HMV POP 804 | Just Driftin'/Quiet Girl | £50 |

CAROL MANNS
| 79 | SRTS 79 CUS 425 | You Me And The Boogie/Seagulls | £20 |

WINGY MANONE ORCHESTRA
| 57 | Brunswick 05655 | Party Doll/Real Gone | £20 |

MAN...OR ASTROMAN
94	One Louder LOUDER 4	YOUR WEIGHT ON THE MOON (10 LP", pink, silver or luminous vinyl)	£15
95	One Louder LOUDER 8	INTRAVENOUS TELEVISION CONTINUUM (LP)	£15
96	One Louder LOUDER 12	EXPERIMENTAL ZERO (LP, yellow vinyl, with poster)	£15

MANOWAR
87	Atlantic BT 9463	Blow Your Speakers/Violence And Bloodshed (12", embossed p/s, with poster)	£25
87	Atlantic BT 9463	Blow Your Speakers/Violence And Bloodshed (12", embossed p/s, without poster)	£15
83	Music For Nations MFN 6	INTO GLORY RIDE (LP, with inner)	£25
84	Music For Nations MFN 19	HAIL TO ENGLAND (LP, inner)	£30
84	10 Records 206 639	SIGN OF THE HAMMER (LP)	£15
87	Atco 790 563	FIGHTING THE WORLD (LP)	£20
07	SPV 85601	GODS OF WAR (3-LP)	£20

MAN PARRISH
| 82 | Polydor POLD 5101 | MAN PARRISH (LP) | £15 |

JOE MANSANO
| 69 | Blue Cat BS 150 | Life On Reggae Planet/RECO & RHYTHM ACES: Z.Z. Beat | £50 |
| 72 | Sioux SI 022 | The Trial Of Pama Dice/JACKIE ROWLAND: Lonely Man | £20 |

(see also Joe The Boss, Joe's Allstars, Dice The Boss)

JAYNE MANSFIELD
| 67 | London HL 10147 | As The Clouds Drift By/Suey (with Jimi Hendrix, demos more common, £35) | £50 |
| 62 | World Record Club TP 262 | JAYNE MANSFIELD IN LAS VEGAS (LP) | £60 |

(see also Jimi Hendrix)

KEITH MANSFIELD ORCHESTRA
68	CBS 3895	Beautiful/Soul Thing	£20
68	CBS 63426	ALL YOU NEED IS KEITH MANSFIELD (LP)	£40
70	CBS 70073	LOOT (LP, soundtrack, with Steve Ellis)	£40
79	Amphonic AMPS 123	NIGHT BIRD (LP)	£125

MANSFIELD ORGANISATION
| 67 | President PT131 | Daddy Russian Stoned/Ol' Nick | £20 |

CHARLES MANSON
80	Come Org. WDC 883008	LIE (cassette)	£50
86	Fierce FRIGHT 006	Rise/Sick City (p/s, 1 side etched, handwritten labels)	£20
88	Fierce FRIGHT 012	It's Comin' Down Fast (Helter Skelter) (p/s, 1 side etched, hand-made labels)	£20
86	Fierce FRIGHT 001	LOVE AND TERROR CULT (LP)	£30

JEANE MANSON
| 79 | CBS S CBS 7222 | I've Already Seen It In Your Eyes/J'ai Deja Vu Ca Dans Tes Yeux | £15 |

MARILYN MANSON
98	Simply Vinyl SVLP 055	ANTICHRIST SUPERSTAR (2-LP, 180 gm vinyl, gatefold sleeve)	£250
98	Simply Vinyl SVLP 195	MECHANICAL ANIMALS (2-LP, 180 gm vinyl)	£150
99	Interscope ADV 490 394-2	MECHANICAL ANIMALS (CD, promo, numbered, card sleeve, with comic, PVC slipcase)	£45
99	Simply Vinyl SVLP 121	PORTRAIT ON AN AMERICAN FAMILY (2-LP)	£200
00	Nothing 490 790 1	HOLY WOOD (2-LP)	£200
01	Simply Vinyl SVLP 208	SMELLS LIKE CHILDREN (LP, 180 gm vinyl)	£200
04	Interscope 9864285	LEST WE FORGET - THE BEST OF (2-LP)	£150
12	Cooking Vinyl COOKLP 554	BORN VILLAIN (2-LP)	£40

MANSUN
95	Polygram no cat. no.	Take It Easy Chicken (Demo)/Naked Twister/Drastic Sturgeon (cassette, promo only, with title inlay)	£20
95	Sci Fi Hi Fi MANSON 1	Take It Easy Chicken/Take It Easy Chicken (as Manson, same track both sides, die-cut sleeve, 500 only; promos with "Manson Promo" on label £30)	£15
99	Fan club MANSUN 001	Taxloss/Everyone Must Win (live) (fanclub-only release)	£18
97	Parlophone CPCS 7387	ATTACK OF THE GREY LANTERN (2-LP, gatefold sleeve, with inners and poster)	£60
98	EMI 749672314	SIX (2-LP, gatefold, inners)	£60
00	Parlophone 724352778218	LITTLE KIX (2-LP)	£40

MIKE MANTLER
| 75 | Watt WATT 3 | 133/4 (LP, with Carla Bley; with insert) | £20 |

(see also Carla Bley, Jazz Composers Orchestra)

MANUELLA
65   Decca F 22275   The Nitty Gritty/Two Shadows...£150

MANYANA
80   Modello AVR 1938   LIVE CARROTS (LP, cat. no MHR 101 on sleeve)...£15

PHIL MANZANERA (& 801)
76   Island ILPS 9444   801 LIVE (LP) £15

(see also Roxy Music, Quiet Sun)

RAY MANZAREK
74   Mercury SRM 1703   THE WHOLE THING STARTED WITH ROCK'N'ROLL (LP)..............................£15

(see also Doors, Philip Glass)

MAP OF AFRICA
05   Whatever We Want WEWW Black Skin Blue Eyed Boys (12") £30
     004

THOMAS MAPFUMO
86   Earthworks EMW 5506   GWINDINGWI RINE SHUMBA (LP, insert)..£50

MAPLEOAK
70   Decca F 13008   Son Of A Gun/Hurt Me So Much..£20
71   Decca SKL 5085   MAPLEOAK (LP, blue/silver label, boxed logo)..£300

LUCILLE MAPP
59   Columbia DB 4261   Chinchilla/Follow Me £15

MARATHONS
61   Pye International 7N 25088 Peanut Butter/Down In New Orleans..£20
61   Vogue V 9185   Peanut Butter/Talkin' Trash £25

MARAUDERS
63   Decca F 11695   That's What I Want/Hey What D'ya Say £15
63   Decca F 11748   Always On My Mind/Heart Full Of Tears £15
64   Decca F 11836   Lucille/Little Egypt £15
65   Fontana TF 609   Baby I Wanna Be Loved/Somebody Told My Girl £20

(see also Danny Davis)

MARC & MAMBAS
82   Some Bizzare BZS 512   Fun City/Sleaze (Take It, Shake It)/Taking It And Shaking It (12", p/s, fan club issue,
                                        mail-order only)..£20
82   Some Bizzare BZS 15   Big Louise/Empty Eyes (unreleased, artwork only)......................................£0
82   Some Bizzare BZS 1512   Big Louise/Empty Eyes/The Dirt Behind The Neon (Sleaze Revisited) (12", unreleased,
                                        artwork only)..£0
82   Some Bizzare B2A 4   UNTITLED (2-LP, gatefold sleeve) £15
83   Some Bizzare BZA 13   TORMENTS & TOREROS (2-LP) £15
84   Gutterhearts GH 1   BITE BLACK AND BLUES - RAOUL & THE RUINED LIVE (LP, fan club issue).......£15

(see also Soft Cell, Marc Almond)

LYDIA MARCELLE
66   Sue WI 4025   Another Kind Of Fellow/I've Never Been Hurt Like This Before £80

MUZZY MARCELLINO
56   London HLU 8355   Mary Lou/MR. FORD & MR. GOON-BONES: Ain't She Sweet £25

MARCELS
61   Pye International 7N 25105 You Are My Sunshine/Find Another Fool £15
61   Pye International 7N 25114 Heartaches/My Love For You £15
62   Pye International 7N 25124 My Melancholy Baby/Really Need Your Love £15
63   Pye International 7N 25201 I Wanna Be The Leader/Give Me Back Your Love £30
61   Pye Intl. NPL 28016   BLUE MOON (LP) £50

(see also Tommy Regan)

GLORIA MARCH
58   London HLB 8568   Baby Of Mine/Nippon Wishing Well £25

HAL MARCH
58   London HLD 8534   Hear Me Good/One Dozen Roses £25

(LITTLE) PEGGY MARCH
68   RCA RCA 1687   If You Loved Me/Thinking Through My Tears £30
68   RCA RCA 1687   If You Loved Me/Thinking Through My Tears (DJ copy) £60

BOBBY MARCHAN
69   Action ACT 4533   Ain't No Reason For Girls To Be Lonely Parts 1 & 2 ....£20

(see also Huey 'Piano' Smith & Clowns)

MARCH HARE
68   Chapter One CH 101   Cry My Heart/With My Eyes Closed £20
69   Deram DM 258   I Could Make It There With You/Have We Got News For You...................£30

(see also Gary & Stu, Koobas)

MARCHING GIRLS
81   Pop:Aural POP 011   True Love/First In Line (p/s) £45

MARCH VIOLETS
82   Merciful Release MR 013   Religious As Hell/Fodder/Children On Stun/Bon Bon Babies (p/s) £30

MARCIA & JEFF
68   Studio One SO 2047   Words/SHARKS: How Could I Live..£150

MARCO
74   Torpedo 31   Do Me Bump/Bump On £15

MINT VALUE £

75	Torpedo TOR 33	I'm Coming Home/I'm Coming Home Again..£50

MARCUS

76	United Artists UAS 30000	MARCUS (LP) £15

JANIE MARDEN

65	Decca F 12101	They Long To Be Close To You/This Empty Place £15
65	You Really Didn't Mean It/ Only The One You Love	You Really Didn't Mean It/Only The One You Love (promo) £50

MARDEN HILL

88	El ACME 13	CADAQUEZ (LP)...£20

ERNIE MARESCA

62	London HLU 9531	Shout Shout Knock Yourself (Out) /Crying Like A Baby Over You £20
62	London HLU 9579	Mary Jane/Down On The Beach £30
63	London HLU 9720	Love Express/Lorelei £22
64	London HLU 9834	Rovin' Kind/Please Be Fair £15
66	Stateside SS 560	Rockin' Boulevard Street/Am I Better Off Than Them £25

MARGAH MAN

93	Margah MMTB1	Funky Bumpkin (12")..£15

MARGARET AND ANGLE

72	Zella JHLPS 128	KNOCK GOD UP (LP) £75

MARGO

69	Deram DM 274	The Spark That Lights The Flame/Left Over Love £20

MARGO & MARVETTES

64	Parlophone R 5154	Say You Will/Cherry Pie £18
64	Parlophone R 5227	Copper Kettle/So Fine £15
67	Piccadilly 7N 35387	Seven Letters/That's How Love Goes..£15
67	Pye 7N 17423	When Love Slips Away/I'll Be Home (When You Call)....................................£50
67	Pye 7N 17423	When Love Slips Away/I'll Be Home (When You Call) (DJ copy) £75

MARGUERITA

64	Black Swan WI 431	Woman Come/ERIC MORRIS: Number One £30

MARIANNE

68	Columbia DB 8420	As For Marionettes/You Know My Name £18
68	Columbia DB 8456	You Had Better Change Your Evil Ways/Like A See Saw £25

CHARLIE MARIANO

56	London LTZN15031	CHARLIE MARIANO QUARTET (LP)...£70

A.C. MARIAS

81	Dome DOM 451	Drop/So (black die cut distressed sleeve)..£15

MARIE CELESTE

71	Private pressing	AND THEN PERHAPS (LP)...£400

TEENA MARIE

79	Motown STML 12109	WILD AND PEACEFUL (LP)..£15

MARILLION

08	EMI 50999 2 43084 2 7	EARLY STAGES (THE OFFICIAL BOOTLEG BOX SET1982-1987) (6-CD set, booklet)...........£110
82	EMI 12 EMIP 5351	Market Square Heroes/Three Boats Down From The Candy/Grendel (12", picture disc, 3,000 only) £25
83	EMI 12 EMIP 5362	He Knows, You Know/Charting The Single/He Knows, You Know (Full Length Version) (12", picture disc, unreleased).. £0
83	EMI EMIP 5393	Garden Party/Margaret (live) ('jester'-shaped picture disc) £35
84	EMI 12 MARIL 2	Assassing (Full Length Version)/Cinderella Search (Full Length Version) (12", p/s)...........£15
88	EMI MARLIP 9	Freaks (live)/Kayleigh (live) (Uncut 'jester'-shaped picture disc) £50
83	EMI EMC 3429	SCRIPT FOR A JESTER'S TEAR (LP, gatefold) £20
84	EMI EMCP 3429	SCRIPT FOR A JESTER'S TEAR (LP, picture disc)..£20
84	EMI EG 2603031	REEL TO REEL (LP) £15
85	EMI JESTP 1	REAL TO REEL (LP, picture disc) £25
84	EMI EMC 2400851	FUGAZI (LP)..£20
84	EMI MRLP 1	FUGAZI (LP, picture disc) £25
85	EMI EJ 2403401	MISPLACED CHILDHOOD (LP)...£15
85	EMI MRLP 2	MISPLACED CHILDHOOD (LP, picture disc) £15
87	EMI EMD 1002	CLUTCHING AT STRAWS (LP)...£20
88	EMI MARL 1	THE THIEVING MAGPIE (2-LP) £20
89	EMI 064 7 92877 1	SEASONS END (LP, gatefold) £20
91	EMI EMD 1022	HOLIDAYS IN EDEN (LP) £40
94	EMI 7243 8 280321 8	BRAVE (2-LP, gatefold) £175
95	EMI EMD 1079	AFRAID OF SUNLIGHT (LP, inner) £100
97	EMI LPCENT 25	MISPLACED CHILDHOOD (LP, reissue, EMI 100 Centenary, stickered sleeve)..................£100
04	Chocolate Frog FRC 015	CURTAIN CALL (A LIVE ARCHIVE 1983 - 1988) (6-CD box set) £150
06	Intact Records IntactLP 01	MARBLES (2-LP, marbled vinyl, numbered) £150
09	Intact Records IntactLP 02	HAPPINESS IS THE ROAD VOLUME 1 (LP as 2 x 12")..£40
09	Intact Records IntactLP 03	HAPPINESS IS THE ROAD VOLUME 2 (LP as 2 x 12") £45
12	Madfish SMALP982	MARILLION.COM (2-LP, reissue) £20
12	Madfish SMALP991	ANORAKNOPHOBIA (2-LP, reissue) £20
13	Madfish SMALP996	RADIATION 2013 (2-LP, reissue, blue vintl, 180gm) £20
17	Parlophone 0190295865511	MISPLACED CHILDHOOD (box set, remaster, 4-LP) £100

(see also Chemical Alice)

MARINA & THE DIAMONDS
09	Neon Gold GOLD 004	**CROWN JEWELS** (EP, 200 only) **£30**
09	679 Recordings 679L168	**Mogwli's Road/Space And The Woods** (200 only, in envelope, numbered and signed)....**£40**
10	679 Recordings 679L173X	**I Am Not A Robot/I Am Not A Robot** (Clock Opera Remix) (p/s, signed edition).............**£15**
10	679 Recordings 679L17OX	**Hollywood/Hollywood** (Gonzales Remix) (signed edition) **£15**

MARINE GIRLS
82	In Phaze COD 2	**On My Mind/The Lure Of The Rockpools** (p/s, with insert)........................**£15**
80	private release	**A DAY BY THE SEA** (cassette, 50 copies only)..**£50**
81	In Phaze Tapes 002	**BEACH PARTY** (cassette, with photocopied drawings, game & handmade sleeve) **£40**
81	Whaam!/In Phaze COD 1	**BEACH PARTY** (LP, black & white sleeve & labels, with 2 inserts)......................**£25**
83	Cherry Red BRED 44	**LAZY WAYS** (LP, textured sleeve)...**£20**

(see also Tracey Thorn, Everything But The Girl, Jane)

MARINO MARINI QUARTET
| 59 | Durium DLU 96034 | **COME PRIMA** (10" LP) ....**£15** |

MARION (FINLAND)
| 73 | Columbia DB 8987 | **Tom Tom Tom/My Son John**...**£15** |

MARIONETTES (1)
| 66 | Parlophone R 5416 | **Like A Man/Tonight It's Going To Storm** ....**£25** |

(see also Rag Dolls [U.K.])

MARIONETTES (2)
| 90 | Maze Music DSMBC | **AVE DEMENTIA** (LP)..**£20** |

LOUISA MARK
75	Safari SF 1105	**Caught You In A Lie/Caught Dubbing** **£20**
77	Trojan TRO 9005	**Keep It Like It Is/TROJANS: Fatty Bum Bum Gone To Jail** **£15**
78	Bushays BFM 100	**Even Though You're Gone/Gone Clear** (12")......................................**£30**
81	Bushays BFM LP 101	**BREAKOUT** (LP)...**£40**
12	Universal Sound USLP 51	**BREAKOUT** (2-LP, reissue)..**£18**

MARK-ALMOND
| 71 | Harvest SHSP 4011 | **MARK-ALMOND** (LP, no EMI logo on label) ....**£25** |
| 73 | Harvest SHVL 809 | **RISING** (LP, EMI logo on label) ....**£20** |

(see also Johnny Almond Music Machine, John Mayall)

MARKETTS
62	Liberty LIB 55401	**Surfer's Stomp/Start** (as Mar-kets) **£15**
62	Liberty LIB 55443	**Balboa Blue/Stompede**..**£15**
64	Warner Bros WB 120	**Out Of Limits/Bella Delana** **£25**
64	Warner Bros WB 130	**Vanishing Point/Borealis**..**£20**
66	Warner Bros WB 5696	**The Batman Theme/Richie's Theme** (with p/s) **£40**
66	Warner Bros WB 5696	**The Batman Theme/Richie's Theme** **£20**
67	Warner Bros WB 5847	**Tarzan's March/Stirrin' Up Some Soul** **£40**
67	Warner Bros WB 5847	**Tarzan's March/Stirrin' Up Some Soul** (DJ copy)................................**£50**
63	Warner Bros WM 8140	**THE MARKETTS TAKE TO WHEELS** (LP)..**£50**
64	Warner Bros WM 8147	**OUT OF LIMITS** (LP)...**£40**
66	Warner Bros W 1642	**BATMAN** (LP)...**£50**

MAR-KEYS
61	London HLK 9399	**Last Night/Night Before** **£20**
61	London HLK 9449	**Morning After/Diana** **£15**
62	London HLK 9510	**Foxy/One Degree North** **£15**
66	Atlantic AT 4079	**Philly Dog/Honey Pot** **£15**
62	London HA-K 8011	**DO THE POP-EYE** (LP)..**£50**
66	Atlantic 587/588 024	**THE GREAT MEMPHIS SOUND** (LP) **£20**
68	Atlantic 587/588 135	**MELLOW JELLY** (LP)...**£20**
69	Stax SXATS 1021	**DAMNIFIKNOW!** (LP)...**£25**
69	Stax 2363 008	**DAMNIFIKNOW!** (LP, reissue)...**£15**

(see also Booker T. & M.G.'s)

MARK FIVE
| 64 | Fontana TF 513 | **Baby What's Wrong/Tango** ....**£65** |

(see also Nazareth)

MARK FOUR
64	Mercury MF 815	**Rock Around The Clock/Slow Down** **£30**
64	Mercury MF 825	**Try It Baby/Crazy Country Hop** **£65**
65	Decca F 12204	**Hurt Me If You Will/I'm Leaving**..**£70**
66	Fontana TF 664	**Work All Day** (Sleep All Night)**/Going Down Fast**............................**£100**

(see also Creation)

PIGMEAT MARKHAM
| 68 | Chess CRS 8085 | **Sock It To 'Em Judge/The Hip Judge** ....**£15** |

MARKSMEN
| 63 | Parlophone R 5075 | **Smersh/Orbit Three** ....**£20** |

(see also Mark Rogers & Marksmen, Houston Wells & Marksmen)

MARLEY MARL
| 87 | MCA 1135 | **He Cuts So Fresh/FINESSE & SYNQUIS: Bass Game** (p/s, moulded silver label) ....**£40** |
| 87 | MCA 1135 | **He Cuts So Fresh/FINESSE & SYNQUIS: Bass Game** (p/s, paper label) ....**£50** |

MIKE MARLAN
| 73 | Bronze ILPS 9221 | **FAIR WARNING** (LP, gatefold sleeve, label with Island credit) ....**£20** |

BOB MARLEY/WAILERS
SINGLES

63	Island WI 088	Judge Not/Do You Still Love Me (as Robert Marley)	£300
63	Island WI 128	ERNEST RANGLIN: Exodus/R. MARLEY: One Cup Of Coffee	£300
65	Island WI 188	It Hurts To Be Alone/Mr. Talkative	£90
65	Island WI 206	Play Boy/Your Love	£100
65	Island WI 211	Hoot Nanny Hoot (actually by Peter Tosh & Wailers)/ BOB MARLEY: Do You Remember (actually with Wailers)	£160
65	Island WI 212	Hooligan/Maga Dog (B-side actually by Peter Tosh & Wailers)	£70
65	Island WI 215	Shame And Scandal (as Peter Touch [Tosh] & Wailers)/The Jerk	£100
65	Island WI 216	Donna/Don't Ever Leave Me	£60
65	Island WI 254	What's New Pussycat/Where Will I Find	£70
65	Ska Beat JB 186	Simmer Down/I Don't Need Your Love	£60
65	Ska Beat JB 211	Lonesome Feelings/There She Goes	£70
65	Ska Beat JB 226	I Made A Mistake/SOUL BROTHERS: Train To Skaville	£200
66	Ska Beat JB 228	Love And Affection/Teenager In Love	£70
66	Ska Beat JB 230	And I Love Her/Do It Right	£70
66	Ska Beat JB 249	Lonesome Tracks/Zimmerman	£80
66	Island WI 260	Jumbie Jamboree/SKATALITES: Independent Anniversary Ska (I Should Have Known Better)	£100
66	Island WI 268	Put It On/Love Won't Be Mine	£50
66	Island WI 3001	He Who Feels It Knows It/Sunday Morning	£90
66	Island WI 3009	Let Him Go (Rude Boy Get Bail)/Sinner Man (B-side matrix: WI-3009B+)	£70
66	Island WI 3009	Let Him Go (Rude Boy Get Bail)/The Masher (actually by Beverley's All Stars or Soul Brothers) (B-side matrix: WI-3009 B+2)	£70
66	Rio R 116	Dancing Shoes/Don't Look Back	£45
66	Doctor Bird DB 1013	Rude Boy/ROLANDO AL & SOUL BROTHERS: Ringo's Theme (This Boy)	£90
66	Doctor Bird DB 1021	Good Good Rudie (Jailhouse)/CITY SLICKERS: Oceans II	£75
66	Doctor Bird DB 1039	Rasta Put It On/ROLAND AL & SOUL BROTHERS: Ska With Ringo	£150
67	Island WI 3035	Baby I Need You (credited to Ken Boothe)/KEN BOOTHE: I Don't Want To See You Cry	£100
67	Island WI 3042	I Am The Toughest (by Peter Touch [Tosh] & Wailers)/ MARCIA GRIFFITHS: No Faith	£70
67	Island WI 3043	Bend Down Low/Freedom Time	£80
67	Coxsone CS 7021	Oh My Darling/HAMLINS: Trying To Keep A Good Man Down	£90
67	Doctor Bird DB 1091	Nice Time/Hypocrite	£65
67	Studio One SO 2010	Have Faith In The Lord (with Heavenly Sisters; actually by Peter Austin)/ JOE HIGGS: Dinah	£70
67	Studio One SO 2024	I Stand Predominate/NORMA FRAZER: Come By Here	£250
68	Fab FAB 34	Pound Get A Blow/Funeral (white label only)	£150
68	Fab FAB 36	Thank You Lord/Mellow Mood (white label only)	£170
68	Fab FAB 37	Nice Time/Hypocrites (white label only)	£80
68	Fab FAB 41	Burial/Bus Them Shut (existence unconfirmed)	£0
68	Trojan TR 617	Stir It Up/This Train	£45
70	Bamboo BAM 55	Jailhouse (Good Rudy)/JOHN HOLT: A Stranger In Love	£50

(Credited to Wailers unless stated.)

70	Trojan TR 7759	Soul Shake Down Party/BEVERLY'S ALLSTARS: Version	£30
70	Escort ERT 842	Run For Cover/To The Rescue	£70
70	Unity UN 562	Duppy Conqueror/UPSETTERS: Duppy Conqueror (Version)	£40
70	Jackpot JP 730	Mr Chatterbox (as Interns)/DOREEN SHAEFFER: Walk Thru' This World	£35
70	Upsetter US 340	My Cup (solo)/LEE PERRY & WAILERS: Son Of Thunder	£35
70	Upsetter US 348	Doppy Conqueror (song actually titled "Duppy Conqueror" but plays Runaway Child by Dave Barker)/UPSETTERS: Justice	£20
70	Upsetter US 349	UPSETTERS: Upsetting Station (actually plays "Dig Your Grave" by Bob Marley & Wailers/UPSETTERS: Justice (Instrumental)	£40
71	Upsetter US 354	Mr. Brown/UPSETTERS: Dracula	£50
71	Upsetter US 356	Kaya/UPSETTERS: Version	£45
71	Upsetter US 357	Small Axe/All In One	£35
71	Upsetter US 368	Picture On The Wall (as Rass Dawkins & Wailers)/UPSETTERS: Version	£45
71	Upsetter US 369	More Axe (as Bob Marley)/UPSETTERS: Axe Man	£30
71	Upsetter US 371	Dreamland (as Wailers)/UPSETTERS: Version	£35
71	Upsetter US 372	More Axe (as Bob Marley, different version)/UPSETTERS: Axe Man	£30
71	Bullet BU 464	Soultown/Let The Sun Shine On Me	£40
71	Bullet BU 493	Lick Samba/Samba	£40
71	Punch PH 69	Small Axe/DAVE BARKER: What A Confusion	£65
71	Punch PH 77	Down Presser (as Wailers)/JUNIOR BYLES: Got The Tip	£40
71	Summit SUM 8526	Stop The Train/Caution (as Wailers)	£35
71	Green Door GD 4005	Trench Town Rock/Grooving Kingston 12	£25
71	Green Door GD 4022	Lively Yourself Up/TOMMY McCOOK: Lively	£25
72	Green Door GD 4025	Guava Jelly/Redder Than Red	£20
72	Upsetter US 392	Keep On Moving/African Herbsman	£35
72	CBS 8114	Reggae On Broadway/Oh Lord, I Got To Get There (as Wailers)	£25
73	Blue Mountain BM 1021	Baby Baby We've Got A Date/Stop That Train	£15
73	Punch PH 101	Screw Face/Face Man	£25
73	Punch PH 102	Lively Up Yourself/TOMMY McCOOK: Version	£20
73	Supreme SUP 216	I Like It Like This (as Bob Marley)/BUNNY GALE: Am Sorry	£60
73	Island IDJ 2	I Shot The Sheriff/Pass It On/Duppy Conqueror (promo only)	£30
76	Island WIP 6478	Stir It Up/Rat Race (withdrawn, demos only)	£15
77	Island WIP 6402 1DJ	Promotional Advert For "Exodus" (handwritten label, same track both sides, with Marley commentary)	£30
84	Daddy Kool DK 12101	Rainbow Country (Vocal)/Rainbow Country (Dub)/PABLO & UPSETTERS: Lama Lava	£20

		(12", p/s)	£20
84	Daddy Kool DK 12102	Natural Mystic/Natural Mystic Rhythm (12", p/s)	£20
03	Trojan/Sanctuary TJITV005	LEE PERRY: Disco Devil/BOB MARLEY & WU CHU: Keep On Moving (12" reissue)	£40

ALBUMS

71	Upsetter/Trojan TBL 126	SOUL REBELS (LP)	£100
71	Trojan TBL 126	SOUL REBELS (reissue)	£65
71	Trojan TTL 66A/B	SOUL REVOLUTION (LP, white label, test pressing only)	£125
72	Island ILPS 9241	CATCH A FIRE (original 'pink rim' label, 'zippo lighter' sleeve)	£250
73	Island ILPS 9256	BURNIN' (original label, gatefold sleeve with photos on innner)	£20
73	Trojan TRLS 62	AFRICAN HERBSMAN (original issue with "12 Neasden Lane" address and rough orange/white paper labels)	£60
73	BBC TS 133425/6	POP SPECTACULAR IN CONCERT (LP, in buff sleeve with printed sheets)	£300
73	Black Power PW2	WAILERS (LP, no title, no sleeve, pink label)	£50
74	Trojan TRLS 89	RASTA REVOLUTION (reissue of TBL 126 with 2 extra tracks)	£25
75	Island ISS 3	BOB MARLEY & THE WAILERS RADIO SAMPLER (with photos & press release, promo only)	£40
75	Island ISS 3	BOB MARLEY & THE WAILERS RADIO SAMPLER (promo only)	£20
77	Island ILPS 9498	EXODUS (LP, embossed sleeve)	£15
77	BBC	ROCK GOES TO COLLEGE IN CONCERT (LP, re-issue of BBC TS 133425/6)	£80
79	Island ILPS 9542	SURVIVAL (LP)	£15
83	Island PILPS 97690	CONFRONTATION (picture disc)	£25
83	Trojan TRLS 62	AFRICAN HERBSMAN (LP, reissue)	£20
84	Island BMSP 100	THE BOX SET (All 9 Island albums in presentation box - 10,000 only)	£125
84	Island PBMW 1	LEGEND - THE BEST OF BOB MARLEY (picture disc)	£15
87	Receiver RRPL 106	SOUL REBELS (LP, reissue)	£20

(see also Peter Tosh, Rita Marley, Ernest Ranglin, Interns, Skatalites, Rass Dawkins & Wailers, Family Man, Norma Frazer)

RITA MARLEY

65	Island WI-226	One More Chance (as Rita and Soulettes)/SKALITES: Dick Tracey	£80
67	Rio R 108	Pied Piper/It's Alright	£90
67	Island WI 3052	Come To Me/SOUL BOYS: Blood Pressure	£150

(see also Soulettes, Soul Brothers)

LAURA MARLING

07	Way Out West WOW 003	LONDON TOWN EP (500 only)	£60
07	Virgin VS 1956	MY MANIC AND I EP (with separate promotional booklet)	£50
07	Virgin VS 1956	MY MANIC AND I EP (signed with booklet)	£35
07	Virgin VS 1956	MY MANIC AND I EP (unsigned with booklet)	£15
08	Virgin VS 1979	Night Terror/Alpha Shallows	£20
10	Third Man TMR 044	Blues Run The Game/The Needle And The Damage Done (US pressing but 100 shipped over and sold in UK, black/white/gold vinyl, signed)	£150
13	Secret 7 S711	The Beast (1-sided, Secret Seven, 100 only, each with unique art sleeve)	£100
08	Virgin/FMinor V 3040	ALAS I CANNOT SWIM (LP/DVD, printed inner)	£100
10	Diverse DIV 028LP	I SPEAK BECAUSE I CAN (LP, gatefold)	£18
11	Virgin CDVX 3091	A CREATURE I DON'T KNOW (Box set, picture disc LP, CD, DVD, postcard, slide viewer and booklet)	£40

MICKI MARLO

55	Capitol CL 14271	Prize Of Gold/Foolish Notion	£15
57	London HL 8481	That's Right/What You've Done To Me (B-side with Paul Anka)	£25

(see also Paul Anka)

ROBERT MARLOW

85	Reset 12REST 6	Calling All Destroyers/In Retrosepct (12", p/s, existence unconfirmed)	£0

(see also Vince Clarke, Erasure)

MARION MARLOWE

56	London HLA 8306	The Hands Of Time/Ring, Phone, Ring (withdrawn)	£100
56	London HLA 8306	The Hands Of Time/Ring, Phone, Ring (78)	£50

MARMALADE

66	CBS 202340	It's All Leading Up To Saturday Night/Wait A Minute Baby	£20
67	CBS 202643	Can't Stop Now/There Ain't No Use In Hangin' On	£25
67	CBS 2948	I See The Rain/Laughing Man	£25
67	CBS 3088	Man In A Shop/Cry (The Shoob Doroorie Song)	£15
68	CBS 63414	THERE'S A LOT OF IT ABOUT (LP)	£25
70	CBS PR 36	THE BEST OF THE MARMALADE (LP)	£15
70	Decca LK 5047	REFLECTIONS OF MARMALADE (LP, mono)	£30
70	Decca SKL 5047	REFLECTIONS OF THE MARMALADE (LP, stereo)	£15
71	Decca SKL 5111	SONGS (LP)	£20
99	Tenth Planet TP 044	KALEIDOSCOPE (LP)	£15

(see also Dean Ford [& Gaylords], Gaylords, Junior Campbell, Chris McClure Section)

MARQUIS DE SADE

81	Xpose XP-02	Somewhere Up In The Mountain/Black Angel (p/s with insert)	£200

MARQUIS OF KENSINGTON

67	Immediate IM 052	Changing Of The Guard/Reverse Thrust	£30

HANK MARR

60	Blue Beat BB 26	Tonk Game/Hob-Nobbin	£15

MARRATXI

79	Clubland SJP 901	Rock With Me/Swedish Lady	£150

RICARDO MARRERO

09	Jazzman JMANLP 027	A TASTE (LP, reissue as Ricardo Marrero And The Group)	£45

MINT VALUE £

STEVE MARRIOTT
63	Decca F 11619	Give Her My Regards/Imaginary Love	£200
76	A&M AMLH 64572	MARRIOTT (LP)	£25

(see also Small Faces, Humble Pie, Spectrum)

MARS
86	Windowspeak WSP 10	78 (LP)	£20

JOHNNY MARS
72	Polydor 2460 168	BLUES FROM MARS (LP)	£15

BERYL MARSDEN
63	Decca F 11707	I Know (You Don't Love Me No More)/I Only Care About You	£15
64	Decca F 11819	When The Lovelight Starts Shining Through His Eyes/ Love Is Going To Happen To Me	£20
65	Columbia DB 7718	Who You Gonna Hurt?/Gonna Make Him My Baby	£35
65	Columbia DB 7797	Music Talk/Break-A-Way	£35
66	Columbia DB 7888	What's She Got/Let's Go Somewhere	£35

(see also Shotgun Express, She Trinity)

GERRY MARSDEN
67	CBS 2946	Gilbert Green/What Makes Me Love You	£15

(see also Gerry & Pacemakers)

PETER MARSH
81	Polydor POSP 210	You Say You Wanna Love Me/I Won't Let You Go	£15

WARNE MARSH
57	London LTZ-P 15080	JAZZ OF TWO CITIES (LP)	£30

WAYNE MARSH
70	Wave LP 6	RELEASE RECORD SEND TAPE (LP)	£35
75	Wave LP 10	JAZZ FROM THE EAST VILLAGE (LP)	£30

CHUCK MARSHALL & TWIST STARS
62	Brunswick STA 3062	TWIST TO SONGS EVERYBODY KNOWS (LP)	£15

JOY MARSHALL
65	Decca F12189	Heartache Hurry On By/He's For Me	£40
66	Decca F 12422	The More I See You/Taste Of Honey	£20
68	Toast 512	And I'll Find You/I'm So Glad You're Back	£15
65	Decca LK 4678	WHO SAYS THEY DON'T WRITE GOOD SONGS ANY MORE? (LP)	£35

LARRY MARSHALL
67	Blue Beat BB 374	Move Your Feet/Find A New Baby	£70
67	Blue Beat BB 380	Suspicion/Broken Heart	£175
67	Doctor Bird DB 1008	Snake In The Grass/ROLAND ALPHONSO: V.C. 10	£125
68	Caltone TONE 126	No One To Give Me Love/PHIL PRATT: Safe Travel	£175
70	Bamboo BAM 22	Girl Of My Dreams/SOUND DIMENSON: Give It Away	£30
70	Bamboo BAM 52	Man From Galilee/Give It Away (as Larry Marshall & Enid Cumberland)	£30
70	Bamboo BAM 61	Let's Make It Up/BURNING SPEAR: Free	£35
70	Banana BA 300	Stay A Little Longer/MAYTALS: He'll Provide	£20
71	Banana BA 364	Maga Dog/OSSIE ROBINSON: Economical Heatwave	£25
73	Pama PM 873	True Believer/FLAMES: Water Your Garden	£15
75	Ocean OC 004	Can't You Understand/KING TUBBY : Locks Of Dub	£18
79	Yard International YI 103	Birdsong/She's Gone (12")	£15
86	Java LM001LP	I ADMIRE YOU (LP, reissue, blue or black labels)	£40
95	Original OMLP 029	THROW MI CORN (LP)	£30

(see also Larry & Alvin, Irving Brown, Fitzroy D. Long, Kingston Pete & Buster's Allstars, Max Romeo, Jackie Mittoo)

OWEN MARSHALL
12	Jazzman JMANLP 048	THE NAKED TRUTH (LP, with free 7", reissue)	£30

WAYNE MARSHALL
85	Jah Tubbys JT 013	Give Me The Mix/Mike In My Hand (12", with the Offbeat Posse)	£75

WILLIE MARSHALL
70	Torpedo TOR 20	Loosen Up Strong Man/Strong Man	£40

MARSHMELLOW HIGHWAY
68	London HLR 10204	I Don't Wanna Live This Way/Loving You Makes Everything Alright	£18

MARSUPILAMI
70	Transatlantic TRA 213	MARSUPILAMI (LP, white/lilac label, 't' logo)	£200
71	Transatlantic TRA 230	ARENA (LP, white/lilac label, 't' logo)	£200

RAY MARTELL
70	Joe JRS 3	She Caught The Train/PAMA DICE: Tea House From Emperor Rosko	£100

MARTELLS
66	Decca F 12463	Time To Say Goodnight/The Cherry Song	£40

MARTHA (REEVES) & VANDELLAS
63	Oriole CBA 1814	I'll Have To Let Him Go/My Baby Won't Come Back	£450
63	Oriole CBA 1819	Come And Get These Memories/Jealous Lover	£275
63	Stateside SS 228	Heatwave/A Love Like Yours (Don't Come Knockin' Every Day)	£50
63	Stateside SS 228	Heatwave/A Love Like Yours (Don't Come Knockin' Every Day) (DJ copy)	£150
64	Stateside SS 250	Quicksand/Darling, I Hum Our Song	£55
64	Stateside SS 250	Quicksand/Darling, I Hum Our Song (DJ copy)	£125
64	Stateside SS 272	Live Wire/Old Love (Let's Try It Again)	£60
64	Stateside SS 272	Live Wire/Old Love (Let's Try It Again) (DJ copy)	£100
64	Stateside SS 305	In My Lonely Room/A Tear For The Girl	£80

64	Stateside SS 305	In My Lonely Room/A Tear For The Girl (DJ copy)	£150
64	Stateside SS 345	Dancing In The Street/There He Is (At My Door)	£20
64	Stateside SS 345	Dancing In The Street/There He Is (At My Door) (DJ copy)	£125
65	Stateside SS 383	Wild One/Dancing Slow	£50
65	Stateside SS 383	Wild One/Dancing Slow (DJ copy)	£200
65	Tamla Motown TMG 502	Nowhere To Run/Motoring	£25
65	Tamla Motown TMG 502	Nowhere To Run/Motoring (DJ copy)	£120
65	Tamla Motown TMG 530	You've Been In Love Too Long/Love (Makes Me Do Foolish Things)	£35
65	Tamla Motown TMG 530	You've Been In Love Too Long/Love (Makes Me Do Foolish Things) (DJ copy)	£100
66	Tamla Motown TMG 549	My Baby Loves Me/Never Leave Your Baby's Side	£40
66	Tamla Motown TMG 549	My Baby Loves Me/Never Leave Your Baby's Side (DJ copy)	£120
66	Tamla Motown TMG 567	What Am I Going To Do Without Your Love/Go Ahead And Laugh	£35
66	Tamla Motown TMG 567	What Am I Going To Do Without Your Love/Go Ahead And Laugh (DJ copy)	£100
66	Tamla Motown TMG 582	I'm Ready For Love/He Doesn't Love Her Anymore	£20
66	Tamla Motown TMG 582	I'm Ready For Love/He Doesn't Love Her Anymore (DJ copy)	£50
67	Tamla Motown TMG 621	Love Bug Leave My Heart Alone/One Way Out	£35
67	Tamla Motown TMG 621	Love Bug Leave My Heart Alone/One Way Out (DJ copy)	£75
68	Tamla Motown TMG 636	Honey Chile/Show Me The Way	£18
68	Tamla Motown TMG 657	I Promise To Wait, My Love/Forget Me Not	£18
68	Tamla Motown TMG 669	I Can't Dance To That Music You're Playing/I Tried	£25
73	Tamla Motown TMG 843	No One There/(I've Given You) The Best Years Of My Life	£125
73	Tamla Motown TMG 843	No One There/(I've Given You) The Best Years Of My Life (DJ Copy)	£200
65	Tamla Motown TME 2009	MARTHA AND THE VANDELLAS (EP)	£120
66	Tamla Motown TME 2017	HITTIN' (EP)	£150
63	Oriole PS 40052	COME AND GET THESE MEMORIES (LP)	£400
65	Tamla Motown TML 11005	HEATWAVE (LP)	£60
65	Tamla Motown TML 11013	DANCE PARTY (LP)	£70
67	Tamla Motown TML 11040	GREATEST HITS (LP, original with flipback sleeve, mono)	£25
67	Tamla Motown (S)TML 11040	GREATEST HITS (LP, original with flipback sleeve, stereo)	£30
67	Tamla Motown (S)TML 11040	GREATEST HITS (LP, re-pressing non-flipback sleeve)	£15
67	Tamla Motown TML 11051	WATCH OUT! (LP, mono)	£50
67	Tamla Motown STML 11051	WATCH OUT! (LP, stereo)	£50
68	Tamla Motown TML 11078	RIDIN' HIGH (LP, mono)	£30
68	Tamla Motown STML 11078	RIDIN' HIGH (LP, stereo)	£35
69	Tamla Motown (S)TML 11099	DANCING IN THE STREET (LP, mono/stereo)	£25
70	Tamla Motown TML 11134	SUGAR N' SPICE (LP, mono)	£35
70	Tamla Motown STML 11134	SUGAR N' SPICE (LP, stereo)	£25
70	Tamla Motown STML 11166	NATURAL RESOURCES (LP)	£25
72	Tamla Motown STML 11204	BLACK MAGIC (LP)	£30

MARTIN
| 68 | Coxsone CS 7056 | I Second That Emotion (actually by Martin Riley)/ROY TOMLINSON: I Stand For I | £150 |

ALAN MARTIN
| 66 | Rio R 94 | Days Are Lonely/My Baby | £15 |
| 66 | Rio R 96 | Rome Wasn't Built In A Day/I'm Hurt | £15 |

MARTIN & DERRICK
| 61 | Blue Beat BB 48 | Times Are Going/I Love You Baby (with Cavaliers Combo) | £15 |
| 62 | Island WI 024 | Come On/MONTY & CYCLONES: Organisation | £20 |

(see also Derrick Morgan)

MARTIN & FINLEY
| 73 | Tamla Motown TMG 867 | It's Another Sunday/Best Friends (withdrawn, demo only) | £350 |

DAVE MARTIN
| 64 | Port-O-Jam PJ 4112 | Let Them Fight/OSSIE IRVING SIX: Why I Love You | £18 |
| 64 | Port-O-Jam PJ 4115 | All My Dreams/Take Your Belongings | £18 |

DEAN MARTIN
SINGLES
| 54 | Capitol CL 14123 | Hey Brother, Pour The Wine/I'd Cry Like A Baby (green label) | £15 |
| 54 | Capitol CL 14138 | Sway/Pretty As A Picture | £40 |

(see also Jerry Lewis, Frank Sinatra)

DEREK MARTIN
64	Sue WI 308	Daddy Rolling Stone/Don't Put Me Down Like This (credited as Derak Martin)	£100
65	Columbia DB 7694	You Better Go/You Know	£40
68	Stax 601 039	Soul Power/Sly Girl	£30

DON MARTIN & DANDY (& SUPERBOYS)
| 67 | Giant GN 6 | Got A Feelin'/CONNECTIONS: At The Junction | £25 |
| 68 | Giant GN 24 | Keep On Fighting/Rock Steady Boogie (with Superboys) | £25 |

(see also Dandy & Superboys)

GEORGE MARTIN & HIS ORCHESTRA
65	Parlophone R 5222	All Quiet On The Mersey Front/Out Of The Picture	£15
65	Parlophone R 5375	Yesterday/Another Girl	£15
66	United Artists UP 1154	By George! - It's The David Frost Theme/Double Scotch	£15
66	United Artists UP 1165	Love In The Open Air/Theme From "The Family Way"	£20
67	United Artists UP 1194	Theme One/Elephants And Castles	£20
65	Parlophone GEP 8930	MUSIC FROM "A HARD DAY'S NIGHT" (EP)	£35

64	Parlophone PMC 1227	OFF THE BEATLE TRACK (LP, mono)	£18
64	Parlophone PCS 3057	OFF THE BEATLE TRACK (LP, stereo)	£20
65	Columbia SX 1775	PLAYS HELP! (LP, mono)	£20
65	Studio Two TWO 102	PLAYS HELP! (LP, stereo)	£20
66	United Artists (S)ULP 1157	INSTRUMENTALLY SALUTES THE BEATLES GIRLS (LP)	£30
66	Studio Two TWO 141	AND I LOVE HER (LP)	£20
67	Decca LK 4847	THE FAMILY WAY (LP, mono, soundtrack)	£70
67	Decca SKL 4847	THE FAMILY WAY (LP, stereo, soundtrack)	£90
68	United Artists (S)ULP 1196	BRITISH MAID (LP)	£25
70	Sunset SLS 50182	BY GEORGE! (LP)	£20
73	United Artists UAS 29475	LIVE AND LET DIE (LP, soundtrack, gatefold sleeve)	£25
74	Polydor Super 2383 304	BEATLES TO BOND AND BACH (LP)	£15
78	St. Michael IMP 105	BEATLES TO BOND AND BACH (LP, exclusive to Marks & Spencer)	£20

(see also Beatles, Ray Cathode)

GRADY MARTIN & THE SLEWFOOT FIVE

56	Brunswick 05535	Nashville/Don't Take Your Love From Me	£15

HONEYBOY MARTIN

67	Caltone TONE 103	Dreader Than Dread (and the Voices)/DANDY: In The Mood	£50

(see also Lynn Tait & Jets)

JANIS MARTIN

60	Palette PG 9000	Here Today And Gone Tomorrow Love/Hard Times Ahead	£25
80	RCA PL 43153	THE COMPLETE RCA JANIS MARTIN (2-LP)	£25

JERRY MARTIN

63	London HLU 9692	Shake-A Take-A/Exchange Student	£15

MILES MARTIN FOLK GROUP

71	Amber	MILES MARTIN FOLK GROUP (LP, private pressing)	£70

MILLICENT MARTIN

63	Parlophone R5033	Get Lost My Love/Gravy Waltz	£15
59	Columbia 33SX 1145	MILLICENT (LP)	£150
64	Philips BL 7591	MR & MRS (LP)	£15

(see also David Frost)

PAUL MARTIN

67	Sue WI 4041	Snake In The Grass/I've Got A New Love	£70

REMY MARTIN

82	Cartridge CRD 14	I Want You/I Want You (Dub) (12")	£60

RICKY MARTIN & TYME MACHINE

68	Olga OLE 4	Something Else/Blue Suede Shoes	£15

RON MARTIN & JUBILEE STOMPERS

68	Doctor Bird DB 1151	Give Your Love To Me/I Cry My Heart	£20

RUPIE MARTIN('S ALLSTARS)

69	Ackee ACK 101	The Arena/Naturally	£60
70	Torpedo TOR 24	Last Flight/Super Lotus	£30
70	Torpedo TOR 26	Musical Container (Parts 1 & 2)	£100
70	Punch PH 43	Death In The Arena (actually by Rupie Martin All Stars)/ MAN COMETH: Julia Caesar (actually by Charlie Ace)	£30

SETH MARTIN

68	Page One POF 073	Another Day Goes By/Look At Me	£15

SHANE MARTIN

68	CBS 2894	You're So Young/I Need You	£275
68	CBS 2894	You're So Young/I Need You (DJ copy)	£350

TONY MARTIN

65	Stateside SS 394	Talkin' To Your Picture/Our Rhapsody	£120
65	Tamla Motown TMG 537	The Bigger Your Heart Is (The Harder You'll Fall)/The Two Of Us	£220
65	Tamla Motown TMG 537	The Bigger Your Heart Is (The Harder You'll Fall)/The Two Of Us (DJ copy)	£300

(see also Gogi Grant)

TRADE MARTIN

63	London HL 9662	Hula Hula Dancin' Doll/Something In The Wind	£15

MARTIN & THE BROWNSHIRTS

78	Lightning GIL 507	Taxi Driver/Boring	£40

WINK MARTINDALE

60	London HA-D 2240	WINK MARTINDALE (LP)	£20

MARTIN ISLAND

83	Contraband CON 1	Don't Give It Up/Part 2 (p/s)	£200

AL MARTINO

54	Capitol CL 14163	The Story Of Tina/Destiny (No One Can Change) (Green label, tri centre)	£15
55	Capitol CL 14343	The Man From Laramie/To Please My Lady	£15

(Originally issued with triangular centres; round-centre reissues are worth around half these values.)

67	Capitol 15516	More Than The Eye Can See/Red Is Red	£20

MARTINS

65	Studio 66 KEP 113/4	MARTINS EP (no p/s)	£50

JOHN MARTYN

71	Island WIP 6116	May You Never/Just Now	£20
81	Island IPR 2046	Johnny Too Bad (Extended Dub Version)/Big Muff (Extended Mix) (12", promo)	£25

86	Island CID 265	Classic John Martyn: Angeline/Tight Connection To My Heart (Has Anybody Seen My Love)/May You Never/Solid Air/Glistening Glyndebourne (CD, foldout sleeve)	£15
67	Island ILP 952	LONDON CONVERSATION (LP, 1st pressing, with black & orange 'circle' logo)	£350
68	Island ILP 991	THE TUMBLER (LP, 1st pressing, with black 'circle' logo, mono)	£250
68	Island ILPS 9091	THE TUMBLER (LP, 1st pressing, with black 'circle' logo, stereo)	£60
69	Island ILP 952	LONDON CONVERSATION (LP, 2nd pressing, pink label, white 'i' logo)	£70
69	Island ILP 952	LONDON CONVERSATION (LP, 3rd pressing, 'pink rim' label, 'palm tree' logo)	£40
70	Island ILPS 9091	THE TUMBLER (LP, 2nd pressing, 'pink rim' label, 'palm tree' logo, fully laminated sleeve)	£40
71	Island ILPS 9167	BLESS THE WEATHER (LP, 'pink rim' label, 'palm tree' logo)	£80
73	Island ILPS 9226	SOLID AIR (LP, gatefold sleeve with lyric sheet 'pink rim' label, 'palm tree' logo)	£100
73	Island ILPS 9253	INSIDE OUT (LP, gatefold sleeve with inner, 'pink rim' label, 'palm tree' logo)	£30
74	Island ILPS 9296	SUNDAY'S CHILD (LP, printed inner, 'palm tree' label)	£30
75	Island ILPS 9343	LIVE AT LEEDS (LP, mail-order, 10,000 only, numbered & some signed)	£30
77	Island ILPS 9492	ONE WORLD (LP, printed inner, first press, dark/light blue Island labels)	£40
86	Body Swerve JMLP 001	PHILENTROPY (LP, red sleeve, matrix number etched on record only)	£15
90	Permanent PERM LP 1	THE APPRENTICE (LP, printed inner)	£25
91	Permanent PERMLP 4	COOLTIDE (LP, printed inner)	£25
21	Craft CR 00371	THE CHURCH WITH ONE BELL (LP, 180g, obi strip, printed inner, half-speed master, RSD)	£35

JOHN & BEVERLEY MARTYN

70	Island ILPS 9113	STORMBRINGER (LP, 1st pressing, pink label with 'i' logo)	£100
70	Island ILPS 9113	STORMBRINGER (LP, 2nd pressing, 'pink rim' label, 'palm tree' logo)	£15
70	Island ILPS 9133	THE ROAD TO RUIN (LP, 'pink rim' label, 'palm tree' logo)	£25

(see also Beverley)

KID MARTYN

62	77 77LA 12/20	IN NEW ORLEANS WITH KID SHEIK'S BAND (LP)	£15

MARVELETTES

61	Fontana H 355	Please Mr Postman/So Long Baby	£55
62	Fontana H 386	Twistin' Postman/I Want A Guy	£70
62	Oriole CBA 1764	Beechwood 4-5789/Someday Someway	£155
63	Oriole CBA 1817	Locking Up My Heart/Forever	£400
64	Stateside SS 251	As Long As I Know He's Mine/Little Girl Blue (DJ copy)	£90
64	Stateside SS 251	As Long As I Know He's Mine/Little Girl Blue	£60
64	Stateside SS 273	He's A Good Guy (Yes He Is)/Goddess Of Love (DJ copy)	£100
64	Stateside SS 273	He's A Good Guy (Yes He Is)/Goddess Of Love	£60
64	Stateside SS 334	You're My Remedy/A Little Bit Of Sympathy, A Little Bit Of Love (DJ copy)	£100
64	Stateside SS 334	You're My Remedy/A Little Bit Of Sympathy, A Little Bit Of Love	£45
65	Stateside SS 369	Too Many Fish In The Sea/Need For Love (DJ copy)	£125
65	Stateside SS 369	Too Many Fish In The Sea/Need For Love	£40
65	Tamla Motown TMG 518	I'll Keep Holding On/No Time For Tears (DJ copy)	£400
65	Tamla Motown TMG 518	I'll Keep Holding On/No Time For Tears	£120
65	Tamla Motown TMG 535	Danger Heartbreak Dead Ahead/Your Cheating Ways (DJ copy)	£200
65	Tamla Motown TMG 535	Danger Heartbreak Dead Ahead/Your Cheating Ways	£100
66	Tamla Motown TMG 546	Don't Mess With Bill/Anything You Wanna Do (DJ copy)	£85
66	Tamla Motown TMG 546	Don't Mess With Bill/Anything You Wanna Do	£50
66	Tamla Motown TMG 562	You're The One/Paper Boy (DJ copy)	£75
66	Tamla Motown TMG 562	You're The One/Paper Boy	£45
67	Tamla Motown TMG 594	The Hunter Gets Captured By The Game/I Think I Can Change You (DJ copy)	£60
67	Tamla Motown TMG 594	The Hunter Gets Captured By The Game/I Think I Can Change You	£30
67	Tamla Motown TMG 609	When You're Young And In Love/The Day You Take One, You Have To Take The Other	£15
68	Tamla Motown TMG 639	My Baby Must Be A Magician/I Need Someone	£22
68	Tamla Motown TMG 659	Here I Am Baby/Keep Off, No Trespassing	£25
69	Tamla Motown TMG 701	Reachin' For Something I Can't Have/Destination Anywhere	£15
73	Tamla Motown TMG 860	Reachin' For Something I Can't Have/Here I Am Baby (DJ copy, plays "My Baby Must Be A Magician")	£100
75	Tamla Motown TMG 1000	Finders Keepers, Losers Weepers/KIM WESTON: Do Like I Do	£100
65	Tamla Motown TME 2003	THE MARVELETTES (EP)	£110
65	Tamla Motown TML 11008	THE MARVELLOUS MARVELETTES (LP)	£250
67	Tamla Motown TML 11052	THE MARVELETTES (LP, mono)	£50
67	Tamla Motown STML 11052	THE MARVELETTES (LP, stereo)	£55
69	Tamla Motown (S)TML 11090	SOPHISTICATED SOUL (LP, mono/stereo)	£40
70	Tamla Motown STML 11145	IN FULL BLOOM (LP)	£30
71	Tamla Motown STML 11177	THE RETURN OF THE MARVELETTES (LP, unissued)	£0
75	Tamla Motown STML 11258	THE BEST OF THE MARVELETTES (LP)	£40

MARVELLOUS CAIN

95	Suburban Base SUBBASELP3	GUN TALK (2-LP)	£20

MARVELOWS

65	HMV POP 1433	I Do/My Heart	£30
65	HMV POP 1433	I Do/My Heart (DJ Copy)	£40

MARVELS (JAMAICA)

64	Blue Beat BB 221	Millie/Saturday	£20
70	Gas GAS 138	Sail Away/Fight A Broke	£15
70	Gas GAS 139	Someday We'll Be Together/MOHAWKS: The Rhythm	£20
71	Pama Supreme PS 338	Rocksteady/ Be My Baby	£30

MARVELS (U.K.)

68	Columbia DB 8341	Keep On Searching/Heartache	£120

MARVELS FIVE
65	HMV POP 1452	Don't Play That Song/(You Lied) I Forgive	£15

MARVETTE
68	Amalgamated AMG 804	Tit For Tat (actually by Lyn Taitt & Jets)/You Take So Long To Know	£50
68	Tabernacle TS 1001	I Want A Revival/Tell It	£15
60s	Coxsone TLP 1002	IT'S REVIVAL TIME (LP)	£60

MARVIN & FARRAR
73	EMI EMA 755	HANK MARVIN AND JOHN FARRAR (LP, with Olivia Newton-John on recorder)	£20

(see also Shadows, Hank Marvin, Marvin Welch & Farrar)

MARVIN & JOHNNY
57	Vogue V 9074	Yak Yak/Pretty Eyes	£300
57	Vogue V 9074	Yak Yak/Pretty Eyes (78)	£75
58	Vogue V 9099	Smack, Smack/You're In My Heart	£300
58	Vogue V 9099	Smack, Smack/You're In My Heart (78)	£75
65	Black Swan WI 467	Cherry Pie/Ain't That Right	£20

BRETT MARVIN & THUNDERBOLTS
70	Sonet SNTF 616	BRETT MARVIN AND THE THUNDERBOLTS (LP)	£15
71	Sonet SNTF 619	12 INCHES OF BRETT MARVIN & THE THUNDERBOLTS (LP)	£20

(see also Jona Lewie)

HANK (B.) MARVIN
68	Columbia DB 8326	London's Not Too Far/SHADOWS: Running Out Of World	£15
70	Columbia DB 8693	Break Another Dawn/Would You Believe It? (demo-only, unissued B-side)	£100
69	Columbia SCX 6352	HANK MARVIN (LP, blue/black label, mono)	£35
69	Columbia SCX 6352	HANK MARVIN (LP, blue/black label, stereo)	£30

(see also Shadows, Marvin & Farrar, Marvin Welch & Farrar, Bruce Welch, Cliff Richard, Spaghetti Junction, Jean-Michel Jarre)

JOEL MARVIN
70	Explosion EX 2028	Too Late/Each Day (both actually by Gregory Isaacs)	£15

(see also Gregory Isaacs)

MARVIN, WELCH & FARRAR
72	Regal Zono. Q4SRZA 8504	SECOND OPINION (LP, quadrophonic)	£25

(see also Shadows, Marvin & Farrar, Bruce Welch [& Hank Marvin])

MARY JANE GIRLS
83	Tamla Motown TMGT 1309	All Night Long/Musical Love (12")	£18

MARZ
80	Frozen Owl SRR 0023	Lady Of The Night/On The Road To Freedom/Daydreamer (p/s, with badge)	£90

MASAI (1)
74	Contempo CS 2007	Across The Track (We Better Go Back) (Parts 1 & 2)	£30

MASAL
23	Sonic Cathedral SCR248	Hallogallo (Part One)/Hallogallo (Part Two) (with Andy Bell, p/s, orange vinyl)	£30
20	Courier PACKET 07	CHARITY SHOP (LP, lathe cut limited pressing)	£15
24	Up In Her Room UIHR024	THE GALLOPING CAT (LP, pink vinyl)	£25

(see also Andy Bell)

MASCARA
79	Ensign ENVY 9	SEE YOU IN LA (LP)	£40

MASCOTS
63	Pye International 7N 25189	Hey Little Angel/Once Upon A Love	£20

HUGH MASEKELA
68	Uni UNL(S) 101	ALIVE AND WELL AT THE WHISKEY (LP)	£20
69	Fontana SFL 13056	HUGH MASEKELA (LP)	£20
71	Rare Earth SRE 3002	HUGH MASEKELA AND THE UNION OF SOUTH AFRICA (LP)	£25
72	Blue Thumb ICD 3	HOME IS WHERE THE MUSIC IS (LP)	£30

MASHMAKAN
70	CBS S 5170	As The Years Go By/Days When We Are Free	£15

JIMMIE LEE MASLON
74	Southern Sound SSR 501	Long Gone Daddy/Down The Line/Don't Mean Maybe Baby	£15

MASON
73	Dawn DNLS 3050	MASON (LP, export issue, do finished copies exist?)	£20

BARBARA MASON
65	London HL 9977	Yes, I'm Ready/Keep Him	£40
65	London HL 9977	Yes, I'm Ready/Keep Him (DJ copy)	£75
68	Direction 58-3382	Oh How It Hurts/Ain't Got Nobody	£50
69	Action ACT 4542	Slipping Away/Half A Love	£25
69	Action ACLP 6002	OH HOW IT HURTS (LP)	£75
75	Buddah BDLP 4027	TRANSITION (LP)	£20
75	Buddah BDLP 4032	LOVE'S THE THING (LP)	£20
84	Other End OEBM1	TIED UP (LP)	£20

BARRY MASON
66	Deram DM 104	Over The Hills And Far Away/A Collection Of Recollections	£45

(see also Sounds Of Les & Barry)

BILL MASON BAND
79	Kingsway KMS 903	Out On The Streets/Mr. G (p/s)	£15

DAVE MASON

70	Harvest SHTC 251	**ALONE TOGETHER** (LP, gatefold sleeve with 'gimmick' die cut, ' Gramophone Co' on label rim, no EMI logo, both matrix numbers end in -1 as well as crossed out matrix numbers SHVL 778 A-1/B-1)	£45
72	Blue Thumb ILPS 9203	**HEAD KEEPER** (LP)	£15
72	Island ICD 5	**SCRAPBOOK** (2-LP)	£15

(see also Hellions, Revolution, Traffic, Fox, Jaguars)

DAVE MASON & CASS ELLIOT

71	Probe SPBA 6259	**DAVE MASON AND CASS ELLIOT** (LP, gatefold sleeve, pink label)	£15

(see also Dave Mason, Mama Cass [Elliot])

JAMES MASON

96	Mighty Fine MFR 002	**I Want Your Love/Nightgruv** (12")	£60
00	Soul Brother 12SBT1	**I Want Your Love/Nightgruv/I Want Your Love** (Blacksmith Edit)	£15
17	Dynamite Cuts DYNAM7001/7002	**Sweet Power Your Embrace/Free/I've Got Me Eyes On You/Slick City** (2 x 7", p/s)	£15
93	Sureshot SURE1LP	**RHYTHM OF LIFE** (LP, reissue)	£30
99	Soul Brother LP SBC53	**RHYTHM OF LIFE** (LP, reissue)	£40

NICK MASON

81	Harvest SHSP 4116	**NICK MASON'S FICTITIOUS SPORTS** (LP, with printed inner)	£20
85	EMI MAF 1	**PROFILES** (with Rick Fenn) (LP, printed inner)	£20
18	Parlophone 0190295660222	**UNATTENDED LUGGAGE** (3LP, box set, 180g)	£30
20	Legacy 19075982711	**LIVE AT THE ROUNDHOUSE** (as Nick Mason's Saucerful Of Secrets) (2LP, gatefold, die-cut slipcase, printed inners)	£25

(see also Pink Floyd)

MASONICS

91	Hangman HANG 43 UP	**MASONICS** (LP)	£20

(see also Milkshakes)

MASS

80	4AD AD 14	**You And I/Cabbage** (with poster insert in die-cut sleeve)	£25
81	4AD CAD 107	**LABOUR OF LOVE** (LP, with inner sleeve)	£15

(see also Models, Rema-Rema, Wolfgang Press)

MASSIVE ATTACK

88	Massive Attack MASS 001	**Any Love/Any Love** (Bonus)**Any Love** (Instrumental)/**Any Love** (Acapella) (12", stickered plain black die-cut sleeve)	£15
91	Wild Bunch WBRT 2	**Unfinished Sympathy/Instrumental** (12", p/s, as MASSIVE)	£15
91	Wild Bunch WBRR 2	**Unfinished Sympathy** (Nellee Hooper 12" Mix)/ (Nellee Hooper Instrumental Mix)/(Original) (12", p/s)	£15
98	Wild Bunch WBRT 9	**Teardrop:** (LP Version)/**Euro Zero Zero/Tear Drop** (Scream Team Remix)/**Teardrop** (Mad Professor Remix) (12")	£15
98	Wild Bunch WBRLH 9	**Teardrop/Euro Zero Zero** (jukebox issue)	£15
98	Circa MASBOX 2	**SINGLES 90/98** (11 x 12" singles in numbered heat sensitive box)	£80
02	Melankolic SADT 15	**I Against I/I Against I** (Inst.) (12", 300 only)	£15
09	Vinyl Factory VF 006	**SPLITTING THE ATOM EP** (12", numbered p/s. 180 gram vinyl, 1000 only)	£35
11	Vinyl Factory	**Four Walls/Paradise Circus** (12" as Massive Attack V Burial, silk-screened glitter sleeve, 1000 only)	£125
11	Vinyl Factory VF 020	**ATLAS AIR EP** (12", numbered)	£40
14	Secret 7" S719	**Karmacoma** (100, only, each with unique art sleeve)	£45
16	Vinyl Factory VF 250	**Dear Friend/Dear Friend** (Version) (12" blue vinyl)	£40
16	Virgin VST 2129	**RITUAL SPIRIT EP** (12" numbered, grey vinyl, 300 copies, 4 different sleeves)	£100
91	Wild Bunch WBRLP1	**BLUE LINES** (LP, as 'Massive')	£80
94	Wild Bunch WBRLP2	**PROTECTION** (LP)	£80
96	Wild Bunch WBRLP3	**NO PROTECTION** (LP)	£50
98	Wild Bunch WBRLP4	**MEZZANINE** (2-LP)	£80
98	Circa/Virgin MASBOX 2	**SINGLES 90/98** (11 12" set, heat sensitive sleeve, hype sticker)	£180
98	Circa/Virgin MASBOX 1	**SINGLES 90/98** (11CD set, heat sensitive sleeve)	£30
03	Virgin V 2967	**100th WINDOW** (3LP, trifold sleeve, 45rpm)	£150
06	Virgin V3017	**COLLECTED** (3-LP, gatefold)	£75
10	Vinyl Factory VF013	**HELIGOLAND** (2-LP, CD and booklet deluxe edition)	£125
12	Wild Bunch Records WBRCDX 1	**BLUE LINES - 2012 MIX/MASTER** (2LP, CD, DVD, poster)	£80

MASSIVE DREAD

79	His Majesty HM 1001	**MASSIVE DREAD** (LP)	£30
83	Upfront UPF 10	**IT'S MASSIVE** (LP)	£30

MASTERFLEET

73	Sussex LPSX 5	**HIGH ON THE SEA** (LP)	£25

MASTERMINDS

65	Immediate IM 005	**She Belongs To Me/Taken My Love**	£40

(see also Badfinger)

CARL MASTERS

72	Big Shot BI 604	**Va Va Voom/GOD SONS: Rebel**	£15

(see also Max Romeo, Dennis Alcapone)

SAMMY MASTERS

60	Warner Bros WB 10	**Rockin' Red Wing/Lonely Weekend**	£25
60	Warner Bros WB 10	**Rockin' Red Wing/Lonely Weekend** (78)	£100
65	London HLR 9949	**I Fought The Law** (And The Law Won)/**Big Man Cried**	£15

VALERIE MASTERS

64	Columbia DB 7426	**Christmas Calling/He Didn't Fool Me**	£50

MINT VALUE £

65	Polydor 56056	It's Up To You/Next Train Out	£30
66	Polydor 56135	Don't Ever Go/Say Hello	£75

MASTERSAFE
92	Formation FORM 12014	ASPERATIONS EP (12")	£20

MASTER'S APPRENTICES
71	Regal Zonophone RZ 3031	I'm Your Satisfier/Because I Love You	£35
71	Regal Zono. SLRZ 1016	MASTER'S APPRENTICES (LP, red/silver labels with no EMI logo)	£300
71	Regal Zono. SLRZ 1022	A TOAST TO PANAMA RED (LP, red/silver label with EMI logo)	£250

MASTERS AT WORK
96	Talkin' Loud 578795-1	NUYORICAN SOUL (6-LP box set)	£30

MASTERS OF REALITY
88	Def American 838 474-1	THE MASTERS OF REALITY (LP)	£20

MASTERS OF THE MONOTONAL GROOVE
94	3 Beat 3BTT32	VOL V (12")	£35

MASTERSTROKE
80s	DTS DTS 043	Prisoner Of Love/Burning Heart (no p/s)	£75

MASTERSWITCH
78	Epic S EPC 6259	Action Replay/Mass Media Meditation (no p/s)	£25

MATADORS
69	Crab CRAB 27	Death A Come (actually by Lloyd Robinson)/The Sword (actually "Zylon" by Lloyd Tyrell [Charmers])	£80
70	Camel CA 45	Dark Of The Sun (actually by Jackie Mittoo)/Dreader Than Dread	£30
71	Green Door GD 4017	I'm Sorry (actually by Tony Brevett)/JOE WHITE: I'm Sorry Version	£20

(see also Emotions, Little Roys, Ethiopians)

MATATA (AIR-FIESTA)
72	President PT 380	Wanna Do My Thing/Wild River	£20
73	President PT 406	I Feel Funky/I Want You	£20
74	President PT 417	Return To You/Something In Mind (as Matata)	£20
75	President PT 438	Good Good Understanding/Gimme Some Lovin' (as Matata)	£20
72	President PTLS 1052	MATATA: AIR FIESTA (LP)	£60
75	President PTLS 1057	INDEPENDENCE (LP)	£80

MATAYO
75	RAK RAK 222	Matayo/I Like Rock 'N' Roll	£20

MATCHBOX (1)
69	Polydor 56327	Run Much Faster/Every Little Thing She Does	£150

MATCHBOX (2)
71	Rak 113	Don't Shut Me Out/Rod	£15

MATCHBOX (3)
78	Raw	Rock Rollin' Boogie/Troublesome Bay (p/s)	£15

MATCHING MOLE
72	CBS 8101	O Caroline/Signed Curtain	£22
72	CBS 64850	MATCHING MOLE (LP, slightly textured sleeve, orange label)	£80
72	CBS 65260	MATCHING MOLE'S LITTLE RED RECORD (LP, orange label with red inner sleeve)	£80
79	CBS 32105	MATCHING MOLE (LP, reissue)	£20

(see also Robert Wyatt, Soft Machine, Caravan, Hatfield & The North, Quiet Sun)

MATCHMAKERS
71	Chapter One	BUBBLEGUM A GO GO (LP)	£25

(see also Mark Wirtz, Philwit & Pegasus)

MATERIAL
81	Red RS 12.006	TEMPORARY MUSIC (12", EP. p/s)	£20
81	Red RS 12.008	TEMPORARY MUSIC 2 (12", EP. p/s)	£20
81	Celluoid ILPS 59693	MEMORY SERVES (LP)	£15
86	Jungle FREUD 11	SECRET LIFE (2-LP)	£20
89	Virgin V 2596	SEVEN SOULS (LP)	£15
94	Axiom 518 351 1	HALLUCINATION ENGINE (LP, with booklet)	£40
12	Music On Vinyl MOVLP541	HALLUCINATION ENGINE (LP, reissue)	£30

(see also Bill Laswell)

MATHEMATIQUES MODERNES
81	Celluloid 12WIP 6743	Disco Rough (Long Version)/Jungle Hurt (12")	£30
81	Celluloid ILPS 9690	LES VISITEURS DU SOIR (LP)	£30

MATHETAI
77	Cavs CAV 017	KNOWING (LP)	£50

JODI MATHIS
75	Capitol CL 15827	Mama/Don't You Care Anymore (DJ Copy)	£20

JOHNNY MATHIS
84	CBS A4889	Love Never Felt So Good/One Love (p/s)	£40

MATIC 16
82	Music Hive (No cat. No)	Jahovah/Ten Man (12")	£50
82	Regent RGTDS 1001	No Money Today/Matic Rock (12")	£40

MATRIX RISE
92	Mutant 12 MUTATE 6	D.O.Y.L.E. Factor/Reality (12")	£25
92	Mutant 12 MUTATE 8	Moments Of Pleasure/The Preacher (12")	£40

AL MATTHEWS
78   Electric Co 23   Run To You/People Are People £15

CARL MATTHEWS
88   ICR ICR 25   OLD & NEW (cassette) £35
80   M 601   AKSU (cassette)...£70
81   Mirage   FREEWHEEL TO FREEDOM (cassette, either black or bespoke Mirage sleeve and details on cassette)..£40
81   Mirage   INTERVENTION '87 (cassette)..£40
82   Mirage M606   EASTWEST (cassette) £40
83   Mirage M609   IRIDESCENCE (cassette) £50
84   Mirage M 412   CALL FOR WORLD SAVIOURS (Cassette)..£40
89   Electronical Dreams 010 LAST WORD FROM MOTHERSHIP (cassette)......................................£40
92   Electronical Dreams 029 COL (cassette) £20

IAN MATTHEWS
71   Vertigo 6360 034   IF YOU SAW THRO' MY EYES (LP, 1st pressing textured gatefold sleeve, large swirl label)..£150
71   Vertigo 6360 034   IF YOU SAW THRO' MY EYES (LP, 2nd LP textured gatefold sleeve, small swirl label) £40
72   Vertigo 6360 056   TIGERS WILL SURVIVE (LP, textured gatefold sleeve, small swirl label) £150
73   Elektra K 42144   VALLEY HI (LP, textured gatefold sleeve, 'butterfly' label).......................£30
74   Elektra K 42160   SOME DAYS YOU EAT THE BEAR, SOME DAYS THE BEAR EATS YOU (LP) £20
74   Mooncrest CREST 18   JOURNEYS FROM GOSPEL OAK (LP)..£20
76   CBS 81316   GO FOR BROKE (LP) £18
(see also Pyramid, Fairport Convention, Matthews Southern Comfort, Plainsong)

JOE MATTHEWS
68   Sue WI 4046   Sorry Ain't Good Enough/You Better Mend Your Ways £90

RANDY MATTHEWS
70s Myrrh MXX 1035   NOW DO YOU UNDERSTAND (LP, gatefold sleeve)..................................£25

WINSTON MATTHEWS
71   Banana BA 329   Sun Is Shining/INN KEEPERS: My Friend (B-side actually "The Pressure Is On" by Purpleites)..£18

MATTHEWS SOUTHERN COMFORT
70   Uni UNLS 108   MATTHEWS SOUTHERN COMFORT (LP, gatefold, lyric insert, yellow swirl label) £40
70   Uni UNLS 112   SECOND SPRING (LP, textured sleeve, lyric insert, yellow swirl label) £30
70   Uni MKPS 2015   LATER THAT SAME YEAR... (LP, red/pink 'dogbone' label)........................£20
(see also Ian Matthews, Marc Ellington, Southern Comfort)

MATUMBI
73   Horse HOSS 39   (I Can't Get Enough Of That) Reggae Stuff/Wipe Them Out £20
73   G.G. GG 4540   Brother Louie Parts 1 & 2 ....£25
77   Matumbi Music MA 004   Music In The Air/Guide Us (12") £40
78   Matumbi Music 12 MR 1 After Tonight (Pts 1-3)/Take It From Me (12") £30
77   Trojan TRLS 145   THE BEST OF MATUMBI (LP)..£15
78   EMI SHSP 4090   SEVEN SEALS (LP, red/black label with inner, some on green vinyl) £20
80   Extinguish MR 007   DUB PLANET ORBIT 1 (LP) £200

DENNIS MATUMBI
77   More Cut MCT 001   Raindrops/Eye Water £25
77   Rama CJ6N   Blood Ah Go Run/Blood Dem £30
78   Serious Business SBD004 Blood Ah Go Run/Blood Dem £30
78   Serious Business SBD004 Rolling Down The River/Choose Me £40

HARVEY MATUSOW'S JEWS HARP BAND
69   Head HDLS 6001   WAR BETWEEN THE FATS & THE THINS (LP) £40

MA2
95   Formation FORM 12057   Rollers Music/Hearing Is Believing (12") £20

MAUDS
67   Philips BL 7791   HEY, LOOK ME OVER (LP)...£25

SUSAN MAUGHAN
61   Philips BF 1216   Mama Do The Twist/Blue Night In Yokohama....................................£15
62   Philips BF 1236   Baby Doll Twist/Some Of These Days £15
62   Philips 326 533BF   I've Got To Learn To Forget/I Didn't Mean What I Said £15
62   Philips BBE 12525   HI, I'M SUSAN MAUGHAN AND I SING (EP) £15
63   Philips BBE 12549   FOUR BEAUX AND A BELLE (EP) £15
62   Philips 433 621 BE   EFFERVESCENT MISS MAUGHAN (EP)..£15
63   Philips 433 641 BE   MORE OF MAUGHAN (EP)...£15
63   Philips 632 300 BL   I WANNA BE BOBBY'S GIRL BUT ... (LP)...£25
64   Philips BL 7577   SWINGIN' SUSAN (LP)..£20
65   Philips BL 7637   SENTIMENTAL SUSAN (LP)..£20

MAU-MAUS
82   Pax PAX 6   SOCIETY'S REJECTS (EP, black or blue sleeve) £15
82   Pax PAX 8   No Concern/Clampdown/Why Do We Suffer (p/s) £15
83   Pax/Paragon PAX 12   FACTS OF WAR (EP)..£15
85   Rebellion REBEL 701   TEAR DOWN THE WALLS (EP) £15
85   Rebellion REBEL 1202   NOWHERE TO RUN (12" EP)..£15
83   Pax PAX 16   LIVE AT THE MARPLES (LP)..£20
84   Pax PAX 20   RUNNING WITH THE PACK (LP)...£25
85   Rebellion REBLP01   FEAR NO EVIL (LP)..£15

MAUREENY WISHFULL
68   Moonshine WO 2388   **THE MAUREENY WISHFULL ALBUM** (LP, 300 copies, beware of counterfeits) **£100**
(see also Jimmy Page, Big Jim Sullivan)

JOHN MAUS
06   Upset The Rhythm UTR 003   **SONGS** (LP, pink vinyl) **£40**
08   Upset The Rhythm UTR   **LOVE IS REAL** (LP, clear or white vinyl) **£50**
     015V
11   Upset The Rhythm UTR 003   **SONGS** (LP, reissue) **£25**
11   Upset The Rhythm UTR   **LOVE IS REAL** (LP, reissue, pink vinyl) **£40**
     015V
11   Upset The Rhythm UTR 049   **WE MUST BECOME THE PITILESS CENSORS OF OURSELVES** (LP, blue vinyl with CD, 100
                                only) **£30**
11   Upset The Rhythm UTR 049   **WE MUST BECOME THE PITILESS CENSORS OF OURSELVES** (LP, clear vinyl with CD) **£20**

MAVE & DAVE
80   Red Stripe SON 2215   **Do Ypu Really Want My Love/You Are Delicious** **£60**

MAWAMBA DUB
78   Warrior DRLP 1001   **MAWANDA DUB** (LP) **£70**
(see also Dennis Bovell, Alton Ellis)

MAX
74   Caroline C1506   **MAX** (LP, black Virgin inner, black/red 'Twin' label, artist is Max Handley) **£20**

MAX HEADROOM & CARPARKS
82   Bandwagon B001   **Soldier** (no p/s) **£20**

SMILEY MAXEDON & HIS OKAW VALLEY BOYS
54   Columbia SCMC 3   **Crazy To Care/In The Window Of My Heart** (export issue) **£15**

JOE S. MAXEY
73   Action ACT 4607   **Sign Of The Crab/May The Best Man Win** (actually plays Packers' "Hole In The
                                Wall"/"Go Ahead On") **£20**

MAXIE, SCIENTIST AND BARNABAS
81   Silver Camel SCLP 001   **THREE THE HARD WAY** (LP) **£80**

MAXIMILIAN
61   London HLX 9356   **The Snake/The Wanderer** **£35**

MAXIMO PARK
03   Billingham Records   **Graffiti/Going Missing** (red vinyl, 500 only, p/s) **£35**
04   Warp 7WAP 183   **The Coast Is Always Changing/The Night I Lost My Head** (500 only, p/s) **£15**
05   Warp WARPLP 130   **A CERTAIN TRIGGER** (LP, inner) **£25**
07   Warp WARPLP 130   **OUR EARTHLY PLEASURES** (LP) **£30**

MAXIM'S TRASH
79   Gimp GIMP 1   **Disco Girls/Blu Shoes** (plastic p/s & inner, hand-stamped white labels, tracks actually
                                recorded in 1975) **£40**
(see also Captain Sensible, Johnny Moped)

MAXIMUM BAND
68   Fab FAB 51   **Cupid/Hold Me Tight** **£20**

MAXIMUM JOY
81   Y 11   **Stretch/Silent Street** (p/s) **£20**
81   Y Y 11   **Stretch/Silent Street** (12", p/s) **£20**
82   Y Y 15   **White And Green Place/Building Bridges** (12", p/s) **£20**
82   Y 12 Y 26   **In The Air** (Extended)/**Simmer Till Done** (p/s) **£15**
82   Y 28   **STATION MXJY** (LP) **£35**

BRIAN MAXINE
72   EMI Starline SRS 5140   **BRIAN MAXINE SINGS** (LP) **£40**
75   Columbia SCX 6575   **RIBBON OF STAINLESS STEEL** (LP) **£30**
(see also Fairport Convention)

MAXINE (2)
97   0181 12 0181 R1   **Crazy** (Sky Joose Remix)/**Crazy** (DHSS Remix) (12, white label) **£20**
97   12 0181 R2   **Fade Away** (Vocal)/**Fade Away** (Instrumental) (12", white label) **£40**

MAXWELL
96   Columbia 483699 1   **MAXWELL'S URBAN HANG SUITE** (2-LP) **£80**
98   Columbia 489420-1   **EMBRYA** (2-LP) **£30**
01   Columbia 497454-1   **NOW** (LP) **£30**
09   Columbia 88697518521   **BLACKSUMMER'S NIGHT** (LP, CD) **£50**

BRIAN MAY
83   EMI EMI 5436   **Starfleet** (Single Version)/**Son Of Starfleet** (p/s) **£15**
91   Parlophone RDJ 6304   **Driven By You** (Edited Version)/(Pollarded Version)/(Special Version)/(Proper Version)
                                (promo only, no stars on p/s) **£70**
92   Parlophone CDRS 6320   **Too Much Love Will Kill You** (Album Version)/**I'm Scared** (Single Version)/**Too Much
                                Love Will Kill You** (Guitar Version)/**Driven By You** (New Version) (CD, red circular
                                gatefold card p/s) **£18**
92   Parlophone RDJ 6329   **Back To The Light** (Radio Version)/**Nothin' But Blue** (Guitar Version) (promo only, p/s) ...**£50**
93   Parlophone 0 7777 80400   **BACK TO THE LIGHT** (LP, textured sleeve) **£30**
     19
98   EMI 4949731   **ANOTHER WORLD** (LP, picture disc, with inner sleeve) **£100**
(see also Queen, MC Spy-D & 'Friends', Holly Johnson,, Ian & Belinda, Cozy Powell, Black Sabbath)

JOHN MAYALL (& BLUESBREAKERS)
SINGLES
64   Decca F 11900   **Crawling Up A Hill/Mr. James** (as John Mayall & Blues Breakers) **£75**

65	Decca F 12120	**Crocodile Walk/Blues City Shakedown**	**£45**
65	Immediate IM 012	**I'm Your Witchdoctor/Telephone Blues**	**£60**
66	Purdah 45-3502	**Lonely Years/Bernard Jenkins** (as John Mayall & Eric Clapton, 500 copies only)	**£450**
66	Decca F 12490	**Parchman Farm** (solo)**/Key To Love** (B-side with Bluesbreakers)	**£30**
66	Decca F 12506	**Looking Back/So Many Roads** (as John Mayall's Bluesbreakers & Peter Green)	**£18**
67	Decca F 12545	**Sitting In The Rain/Out Of Reach** (as John Mayall's Bluesbreakers)	**£15**
67	Decca F 12621	**Double Trouble/It Hurts Me Too** (as John Mayall's Bluesbreakers)	**£20**
67	Immediate IM 051	**I'm Your Witchdoctor/Telephone Blues** (reissue, as John Mayall with Eric Clapton)	**£30**
67	Decca F 12684	**Suspicions** (Parts 1 & 2) (as John Mayall's Bluesbreakers)	**£15**
76	Decca F12120	**Crocodile Walk/Blues City Shakedown** (reissue, with boxed Decca logo, uninverted label matrix numbers, double A side)	**£15**

EPs
| 67 | Decca DFE-R 8673 | **THE BLUESBREAKERS WITH PAUL BUTTERFIELD** (EP) .... | **£60** |

ALBUMS
65	Decca LK 4680	**PLAYS JOHN MAYALL - LIVE AT KLOOKS KLEEK!**	**£120**
66	Decca LK 4804	**BLUES BREAKERS WITH ERIC CLAPTON** (original label, mono, "Beano" cover)	**£150**
67	Decca LK/SKL 4853	**A HARD ROAD** (as John Mayall & Bluesbreakers)	**£50**
67	Decca LK 4890	**CRUSADE** (Mono, as John Mayall & Bluesbreakers)	**£50**
67	Decca SKL 4890	**CRUSADE** (Stereo, as John Mayall & Bluesbreakers)	**£30**
67	Ace of Clubs ACL/SCL 1243	**THE BLUES ALONE** (LP, "A Hard Road" on back cover)	**£30**
68	Decca LK/SKL 4918	**THE DIARY OF A BAND VOL. 1**	**£30**
68	Decca LK/SKL 4919	**THE DIARY OF A BAND VOL. 2**	**£30**
68	Decca LK/SKL 4945	**BARE WIRES** (gatefold sleeve, as John Mayall & Blues Breakers)	**£40**
68	Decca LK/SKL 4972	**BLUES FROM LAUREL CANYON** (LP, unboxed logo, gatefold sleeve)	**£40**
(The Decca LPs listed above were originally issued with unboxed Decca label logos.)			
69	Decca LK/SKL 5010	**LOOKING BACK** (gatefold sleeve)	**£25**
69	Polydor 583 571	**THE TURNING POINT**	**£20**
69	Decca SKL 4804	**BLUES BREAKERS WITH ERIC CLAPTON** (reissue, original label, stereo)	**£40**
70s	Decca LK 4804	**BLUES BREAKERS WITH ERIC CLAPTON** (reissue, boxed logo, mono)	**£20**
71	Decca SKL 4804	**BLUES BREAKERS WITH ERIC CLAPTON** (reissue, boxed logo, stereo)	**£15**
70	Polydor 583 580	**EMPTY ROOMS** (with lyric insert)	**£15**
70	Polydor 2425 020	**U.S.A. UNION**	**£20**
71	Polydor 2657 005	**BACK TO THE ROOTS** (2-LP)	**£30**
71	Polydor 2425 085	**MEMORIES**	**£15**
71	Polydor 2483 016	**BEYOND THE TURNING POINT**	**£15**
71	Decca SKL 5086	**THRU THE YEARS**	**£25**
72	Polydor 2425 103	**JAZZ-BLUES FUSION**	**£15**
73	Polydor 2391 047	**MOVING ON**	**£15**
73	Polydor 2482 111	**TEN YEARS ARE GONE**	**£15**
74	Polydor 2391 141	**THE LATEST EDITION**	**£15**

(see also Paul Butterfield, Eric Clapton, Jack Bruce, Peter Green, McGuinness Flint, Johnny Almond Music Machine, Alan Skidmore, Mick Taylor, Dick Heckstall-Smith, Keef Hartley, Paul Williams, Ray Warleigh, Colosseum, Henry Lowther, Jon Mark, Aynsley Dun

MAYBERRY MOVEMENT
| 06 | Kent 6T 21 | **I See Him Making Love To You/THE DEVONNES: Doin' The Gittin' Up** .... | **£20** |

MAY BLITZ
| 70 | Vertigo 6360 007 | **MAY BLITZ** (LP, gatefold sleeve, large swirl label) .... | **£400** |
| 71 | Vertigo 6360 037 | **THE 2ND OF MAY** (LP, gatefold sleeve, swirl label) .... | **£450** |

(see also Jeff Beck,Boxer, Sounds Inc.)

MAYDAY
| 80 | Reddingtons R.R. DAN 2 | **Day After Day/Love In The Spaceage** (p/s) .... | **£20** |

JOHN MAYER (GROUP)
66	Columbia DB 8037	**Acka Raga** (as John Mayer's I-J-7)**/Gana** (as John Mayer & Joe Harriott Quintet)	**£30**
66	Columbia S(C)X 6025	**INDO-JAZZ SUITE** (LP, with Joe Harriott)	**£75**
67	Columbia SX 6122	**INDO-JAZZ FUSIONS** (LP, with Joe Harriott)	**£50**
67	Columbia S(C)X 6215	**INDO-JAZZ FUSIONS II** (LP, with Joe Harriott)	**£50**
69	Sonet SNTF 603	**ETUDES** (LP, as John Mayer Indo-Jazz Fusions)	**£15**
71	Columbia SCX 6462	**RADHA KRISHNA** (LP)	**£20**

(see also Joe Harriott & John Mayer, Radha Krishna)

NATHANIEL MAYER & FABULOUS TWILIGHTS
| 62 | HMV POP 1041 | **Village Of Love/I Want A Woman** .... | **£50** |

CURTIS MAYFIELD
71	Buddah 2318 015	**CURTIS** (LP, 1st pressing, black and silver labels, gatefold sleeve)	**£50**
71	Buddah 2659 004	**CURTIS/LIVE** (2-LP)	**£20**
72	Buddah 2318 045	**ROOTS** (LP, gatefold sleeve)	**£30**
72	Buddah 2318 065	**SUPERFLY** (LP, soundtrack, gatefold sleeve)	**£20**
73	Buddah 2318 085	**BACK TO THE WORLD** (LP, gatefold sleeve)	**£20**
73	Buddah 2318 091	**CURTIS IN CHICAGO** (LP, TV soundtrack, gatefold sleeve, with Impressions, Jerry Butler, Gene Chandler & Leroy Hutson)	**£15**
74	Buddah BDLH 5001	**SWEET EXORCIST** (LP)	**£30**
74	Buddah BDLP 2001	**CURTIS/LIVE** (2-LP, reissue)	**£18**
74	Buddah BDLH 5005	**CURTIS** (LP, 2nd pressing, pink rim 'Buddah' label, 1974 on labels, gatefold)	**£30**
74	Buddah BDLP 4010	**CLAUDINE** (LP, soundtrack, with Gladys Knight)	**£15**
75	Buddah BDLP 4033	**THERE'S NO PLACE LIKE AMERICA TODAY** (LP)	**£20**
76	Buddah BDLP 4042	**GIVE, GET TAKE AND HAVE** (LP)	**£15**

(see also Impressions)

PERCY MAYFIELD
| 67 | HMV CLP/CSD 3572 | **MY JUG AND I** (LP) .... | **£40** |

MAYFIELD'S MULE

69	Parlophone R 5817	Double Dealing Woman/(Drinking My) Moonshine (in p/s)	£30
69	Parlophone R 5817	Double Dealing Woman/(Drinking My) Moonshine	£15
70	Parlophone R 5843	I See A River/"Queen" Of Rock'n'Roll	£15

(see also Elastic Band, Sweet, Amen Corner)

JUDY MAYHAN

71	Atlantic 2466006	MOMENTS (LP)	£15

MAYHEM

83	Riot City RIOT 24	PULLING PUPPETS STRINGS EP	£15
85	Vigilante VIG 1T	Bloodrush/Addictive Risk/I Defy (12", p/s)	£15
96	Black Metal BMR 002	Freezing Moon/Carnage (12", picture disc)	£20
97	Misanthropy HH 666	Ancient Skin/Necrolust (CD single in printed PVC sleeve, hand numbered insert, gig freebie, 500 only, beware of bootleg 7" singles)	£40
97	Misanthropy AMAZON 012	WOLF'S LAIR ABYSS (LP)	£40
97	Misanthropy AMAZON CPD 012	WOLF'S LAIR ABYSS (LP, picture disc)	£50

(TOOTS &) THE MAYTALS

63	Blue Beat BB 176	Hallelujah/Helping Ages Past	£20
64	Blue Beat BB 215	He Is Real/Domino	£20
64	Blue Beat BB 220	Pain In My Belly/BUSTER'S ALL STARS: City Riot	£100
64	Blue Beat BB 231	Dog War/RECO & CREATORS: I'll Be Home	£70
64	Blue Beat BB 245	Little Slea (song actually "Little Flea")/Don't Talk (song actually Pain In My Belly) (both sides miscredited as V. Maytals)	£25
64	Blue Beat BB 254	Sweet Love/PRINCE BUSTER: Wings Of A Dove	£35
64	Blue Beat BB 255	Judgement Day/Goodbye Jane	£20
64	Blue Beat BB 270	You've Got Me Spinning/Lovely Walking	£40
64	R&B JB 130	Hurry Up/Love Divide	£20
64	R&B JB 141	Another Chance/FRANKIE ANDERSON: Always On A Sunday	£20
64	R&B JB 153	Give Me Your Love/He Will Provide	£20
64	R&B JB 164	Hello Honey/ROLAND ALPHONSO: Crime Wave	£50
64	R&B JB 174	Christmas Feelings/Let's Kiss	£25
65	Blue Beat BB 281	Looking Down The Street/PRINCE BUSTER: Blues Market	£50
65	Blue Beat BB 299	Light Of The World/Lovely Walking	£30
65	Blue Beat BB 306	Ska War (song actually "Treating Me Bad")/SKATALITES: Perhaps	£90
65	Ska Beat JB 202	Let's Jump/Joy And Jean	£25
65	Island WI 200	Never You Change/What's On Your Mind	£25
65	Island WI 213	My New Name/It's No Use	£35
65	Black Swan WI 464	John James/THEO BECKFORD: Sailing On	£25
66	Doctor Bird DB 1019	If You Act This Way/SIR LORD COMIC & HIS COWBOYS: Ska-ing West	£45
66	Doctor Bird DB 1038	Bam Bam/So Mad In Love (with Byron Lee and the Dragoniares)	£40
68	Pyramid PYR 6030	54-46, That's My Number/ROLAND ALPHONSO: Dreamland	£30
68	Pyramid PYR 6043	Struggle/ROLAND ALPHONSO: Stream Of Life	£50
68	Pyramid PYR 6048	Just Tell Me/Reborn	£80
68	Pyramid PYR 6050	Bim Today, Bam Tomorrow/Hold On	£25
68	Pyramid PYR 6052	We Shall Overcome/DESMOND DEKKER & ACES: Fu Manchu	£125
68	Pyramid PYR 6055	Schooldays/Big Man	£35
68	Pyramid PYR 6056	Ben Johnson Day (actually by Derrick Morgan and George Dekkar)/MAYTALS: Ain't Got No Tip	£125
68	Pyramid PYR 6057	Do The Reggay/BEVERLEY'S ALLSTARS: Motoring	£55
68	Pyramid PYR 6064	Scare Him/In My Heart	£20
68	Pyramid PYR 6066	Don't Trouble Trouble/BEVERLEY'S ALLSTARS: Double Action	£110
69	Pyramid PYR 6070	Aldina/Hold On	£45
69	Pyramid PYR 6073	Pressure Drop/BEVERLEY'S ALLSTARS: Express	£30
69	Pyramid PYR 6074	Sweet And Dandy/Oh Yeah	£30
69	Trojan TR 7709	Pressure Drop/BEVERLEY'S ALLSTARS: Smoke Screen	£25
69	Nu Beat NB 031	My Testimony/JOHNSON BOYS: One Dollar Of Soul (actually by Ethiopians)	£35
69	Trojan TR 7711	Monkey Man/Night And Day	£30
70	Trojan TR 7726	Sweet And Dandy/54-46, That's My Number	£16
70	Trojan TR 7741	Bla Bla Bla/Reborn	£15
70	Trojan TR 7757	Water Melon/She's My Scorcher	£18
70	Trojan TR 7786	Doctor Lester/Sun, Moon And Star	£15
70	Summit SUM 8510	Peeping Tom/BEVERLEY'S ALLSTARS: Version	£15
71	Trojan TR 7808	54-46 Was My Number/BEVERLEY'S ALLSTARS: 54-46 Instrumental	£25
71	Summit SUM 8513	Monkey Girl/BEVERLEY'S ALLSTARS: Version	£20
72	Trojan TR 7865	Louie Louie/Pressure Drop '72	£30
73	Dragon DRA 1013	Country Road/Funky Kingston (as Toots & Maytals)	£40
80	Island 1EP 11 DJ	Pressure Drop (1-sided promo)	£20
11	Beverlys THB 7008	Do The Boogaloo/Bim Today Bam Tomorrow	£20
64	Ska Beat JBL 1113	PRESENTING THE MAYTALS (NEVER GROW OLD) (LP)	£1000
66	Doctor Bird DLM 5003	THE SENSATIONAL MAYTALS (LP)	£300
70	Trojan TBL 107	MONKEY MAN (LP, laminated front cover)	£60
73	Trojan TRLS 65	FROM THE ROOTS (LP)	£35
73	Dragon DRLS 5002	FUNKY KINGSTON (LP)	£40
74	Dragon DRLS 5004	IN THE DARK (LP)	£25
74	Prince Buster PB 11	ORIGINAL GOLDEN OLDIES VOLUME 3 (LP)	£20
77	State ETAT16	TOOTS PRESENTS THE MAYTALS (LP)	£15
85	Island IRG 1	REGGAE GREATS (LP)	£15

(see also Vikings, Flames, Philip James & Blues Busters, Don Drummond, Stranger, Lord Creator, Larry Marshall, Derrick Morgan, Brentwood Road Allstars,

Roland Alphonso, Charmers)

MAYTONES

68	Blue Cat BS 149	Billy Goat/Call You Up	£100
69	Blue Cat BS 152	Loving Reggae/Musical Beat	£75
69	Blue Cat BS 166	Copper Girl/Love	£80
69	Blue Cat BS 173	We Nah Tek You Lick/Dig Away De Money	£80
69	Camel CA 27	Sentimental Reason/Lover Girl	£30
70	Explosion EX 2012	Funny Man/G.G. ALLSTARS: Champion	£20
70	Explosion EX 2014	Barrabus/G.G. ALLSTARS: Barrabus Part 2 (B-side actually "This Kind Of Life")	£60
70	Camel CA 47	Black And White/GLORIA'S ALLSTARS: Jumbo Jet	£15
70	Camel CA 49	Since You Left/GLORIA'S ALL STARS: Bird Wing	£20
71	Duke DU 116	Babylon A Fall/TONY KING: Version Buggy	£18
71	Camel CA 61	Judas (actually by Gladstone Anderson & Followers)/Mi Nah Tek	£15
71	Camel CA 63	Cleanliness/Sister Hold On	£20
77	GG's GG 021	Money Trouble (with I Roy)/GG'S ALL STARS: Dub Part Two (12")	£25
82	Burning Sounds BS 1052	BEST OF (LP)	£15

(see also Vern & Alvin, Roland Alphonso, G.G. Rhythm Section, Cynthia Richards, Max Romeo, Charlie Ace, Dennis Alcapone)

MAZE (U.K.)

66	Reaction 591 009	Hello Stranger/Telephone	£100
67	MGM MGM 1368	Catari Catari/Easy Street	£40

(see also M.I. Five, Deep Purple, Paice, Ashton & Lord)

MAZE (FEATURING FRANKIE BEVERLY)

77	Capitol E-ST 11607	MAZE FEATURING FRANKIE BEVERLY (LP)	£20
78	Capitol E ST 11710	GOLDEN TIME OF DAY (LP)	£15
79	Capitol EST 11912	INSPIRATION (LP)	£15
80	Capitol EST 12087	JOY AND PAIN (LP, printed inner)	£15
81	Capitol EST SP22	LIVE IN NEW ORLEANS (2LP, gatefold)	£20
83	Capitol EST 12262	WE ARE ONE (LP, printed inner)	£15
95	Mastercuts CUTLEGLP 1	LIVE IN NEW ORLEANS (2LP, gatefold, Mastercuts 'Legends' reissue)	£15
21	Capitol 3532600	LIVE IN NEW ORLEANS (2LP, gatefold, reissue)	£25

(See also Frank Beverly)

ANA MAZZOTTI

99	Treasure Trove LPR 184	NINGUEM VAI ME SEGURAR (LP, reissue)	£40

MAZZY STAR

93	Rough Trade Singles Club 45 rev 19	Five String Serenade/Under My Car (p/s)	£15
94	Capitol 10CL720	Fade Into You/Five String Serenade/Under My Car/Bells Ring (Acoustic) (10" p/s, numbered)	£100
96	Capitol CL 781	FLOWERS IN DECEMBER (EP, blue vinyl)	£25
90	Rough Trade ROUGH 158	SHE HANGS BRIGHTLY (LP)	£100
93	Capitol EST2206	SO TONIGHT THAT I MIGHT SEE (LP)	£150
96	Capitol 8272241	AMONG MY SWAN (LP)	£150
13	Rhymes RHYMES 004	SEASONS OF YOUR DAY (2-LP, transparent purple vinyl)	£40
17	Capitol 00602557537574	SO TONIGHT THAT I MIGHT SEE (LP, reissue)	£40

M.B.C. BAND AND CHICHIRI QUEENS

73	Ng Omo MBC 002	Angwazi Kawiri-Kawiri	£20
74	Ng Omo MWLP 1	KOKOLIKO KU MALAWI (LP)	£50

M-BEAT

94	Renk 12RENKT 42	Incredible (Original Mix)/(Booyaka Mix)/(Instrumental Version) (12", featuring General Levy)	£18
94	Renk RENK LP1	ALBUM (LP)	£20
94	Renk RENK LP2	WICKED ALBUM (LP)	£18

M.B.P. MIX

69	Major Minor MM66	Light My Fire/There's A Baby	£30

MBT

85	MBT MBT 1	You Know Too Much/(Extended Version) (12")	£100

MC FYRE

88	DTI MAC 3	It's My Rhythm/Kold Rockin' The Crowd (12")	£40

MC SOLAAR

94	Talkin Loud 523 979-1	PROSE COMBAT (2-LP)	£150

MC X

92	Pound Sterling POUND T002	F**K AmMeriKKAA (Version 1)/F**K AmMERIKKAA (Version 2) (12")	£50

MCALMONT AND BUTLER

95	Hut HUTLP 32	THE SOUND OF...MCALMONT AND BUTLER (LP, inner)	£30

(see also Bernard Butler, Suede)

WINSTON MCANUFF

79	Third World	I Love Jah/FREDDIE McGREGOR : Massachusetts (12")	£30

JACKIE MCAULEY

71	Dawn DNLS 3023	JACKIE McAULEY (LP, gatefold sleeve)	£150

(see also Them, Belfast Gypsies, Trader Horne, Freaks Of Nature)

MCAULEY SCHENKER GROUP

90	EMI EMPD 127	Anytime/What We Need/Anytime (Edit) (uncut picture disc)	£30

(see also Group, Grand Prix)

JOHNNY MCBEE

63	Airborne NBP 0001	Nothing But Love/Rose-A-Lee	£80

MINT VALUE £

CECIL MCBEE
79 Inner City IC3023   MUSIC FROM THE SOURCE (LP) £15

NICKO MCBRAIN
91 EMI NICKOPD 1   Rhythm Of The Beast/McBrain Damage Interview (shaped picture disc with insert & plinth)..£15

(see also Iron Maiden, Streetwalkers)
JERRY MCCAIN
69 Python 02   Homogenised Love/728 Texas (99 copies only) £50

CASH MCCALL
67 Chess CRS 8056   It's Wonderful (To Be In Love)/Let's Try It Over £20

TOUSSAINT MCCALL
67 Pye International 7N 25420 Nothing Takes The Place Of You/Shimmy..£30

DAVID MCCALLUM
66 Capitol (S)T 2432   MUSIC ... A PART OF ME (LP)..£25
66 Capitol (S)T 2498   MUSIC ... A BIT MORE OF ME (LP)..£15

MCCALMANS
70 CBS 564145   TURN AGAIN (LP) £35
73 One Up OU 2161   McCALMANS' FOLK (LP) £15

JIM MCCANN
72 Polydor 2489 053   McCANNED! (LP)..£40
(see also Ludlows)

LES MCCANN (LTD)
67 Mercury MF 973   All/Bucket O'Grease £15
69 Atlantic 584 284   With These Hands/Burnin' Coal £15

DON MCCARLOS
80 Negus Roots NERT 003   I Don't Care/I Love Jah (12")..£45

MCCARTHY
86 Wall Of Salmon MAC 001   In Purgatory/The Comrade Era/Something Wrong Somewhere (foldover p/s in poly bag, white labels)..£25

(see also Stereolab)
KEITH MCCARTHY
67 Coxsone CS 7014   Everybody Rude Now/BASES: Beware..£25

MARY MCCARTHY
67 CBS 2832   The Folk I Love/You Know He Did £100
67 CBS 2987   Happy Days And Lonely Night/Easy Kind Of Love £70

CECIL MCCARTNEY
68 Columbia DB 8474   Hey Aleuthia I Want You/Liquid Blue £25
69 Columbia DB 8595   Orange And Green/Cloudy £15
68 Columbia S(C)X 6283   OM (LP, first pressing with blue/black label with "Sold in UK..." text)........................£150
68 Columbia S(C)X 6283   OM (LP, second pressing with black/silver label, boxed logo) £40

LINDA MCCARTNEY
98 Parlophone 4979101   WILD PRAIRIE (LP) £80
(see also Suzy & The Red Stripes)

PAUL MCCARTNEY/WINGS
78 PAS 10012   London Town £0
18 MPL 00602567731184   RED ROSE SPEEDWAY 'DOUBLE ALBUM' (2LP, gatefold, different sleeve, 180g vinyl, bonus tracks, reissue)..£40

SINGLES
72 Apple R 5932   Love Is Strange/I Am Your Singer (unreleased)...£1500
73 Apple R 5985   My Love/The Mess (as McCartney's Wings, demos and early retail copies shipped in a plain red sleeve)..£20
78 Parlophone R 6018   Mull Of Kintyre/Girls School (yellow juke box 'Best selling British single ever' p/s) £60
80 Parlophone 12R 6039   Temporary Secretary/Secret Friend (12", p/s) £35
82 Parlophone R 6054   Ebony And Ivory/Rainclouds (unreleased sepia-toned 'studio photo' p/s; beware of clever counterfeits) £50
82 Epic A 11-2729   The Girl Is Mine (with Michael Jackson)/MICHAEL JACKSON: Can't Get Outta The Rain (picture disc) £30
84 Parlophone 12RP 6080   No More Lonely Nights (Extended Version)/Silly Love Songs/ No More Lonely Nights (Ballad) (12", picture disc)...£20
84 Parlophone RP 6086   We All Stand Together/We All Stand Together (Humming Version) (with Frog Chorus, shaped picture disc, in printed PVC sleeve)...£18
85 Parlophone RP 6118   Spies Like Us/My Carnival (shaped picture disc)...£15
85 Parlophone 12RP 6118   Spies Like Us/Spies Like Us (Alternative Mix)/Spies Like Us (DJ Version)/My Carnival (Party Mix) (12", picture disc) £20
89 Parlophone 12RS 6235   Figure Of Eight/Ou Est Le Soliel? (12" etched vinyl) £25
05 GRA2010   Really Love You/Lalula (1-side etched, McCartney remixes by TWIN FREAKS 2,500 only)..£20
13 MPL/Universal   Maybe I'm Amazed - Short Version (mono)/Album Version (mono)//Maybe I'm Amazed - Short Version (stereo)/Album Version (stereo) (12" die cut sleeve).........................£15
15 No label or cat no   Sweet Thrash/Sweet Thrash (12, hand-written labels, RSD secret release, 100 only, plain die-cut sleeve) £800
22 Capitol/MPL/UMe   THE 7" SINGLES BOX (80 x 7", booklet, wooden crate, 1 random white label 7", global
    0060244529652   edition of 3000) £1500

ALBUMS : ARCHIVE COLLECTION
12 MPL HRM 33451-01   RAM (2LP, reissue, gatefold, 180g, bonus tracks) £30
12 MPL HRM-33452-01   RAM (LP, mono, mock white labels, numbered, white inner, insert) £50
18 Capitol/MPL/UMe   WINGS 1971-73 (Wild Life & Red Rose Speedway 7CD/3DVD/BD) £1100

	B-002822602		
20	Parlophone 00602508617720	FLAMING PIE (3LP, 180g vinyl, bonus tracks, reissue).	£40
20	MPL 0861756	FLAMING PIE (3LP/12"/5CD/2DVD, deluxe edition, 3000 only, box, prints, webstore exclusive)	£350

ALBUMS

70	Apple PCS 7102	McCARTNEY (LP, gatefold sleeve)	£50
70	Apple TA 7102	McCARTNEY (reel-to-reel tape, jewel case, mono)	£120
70	Apple TD-PCS 7102	McCARTNEY (reel-to-reel tape, jewel case, stereo)	£50
70	Parlophone PPCS 7102	McCARTNEY (LP, export edition, black/silver label, 'Parlophone' and 'EMI' boxed logos)	£200
71	Apple PAS 10003	RAM (LP, laminated gatefold sleeve)	£40
71	Apple PCS 7142	WILD LIFE (LP, sleeve with 'sniped' spine edges, yellow inner)	£60
73	Apple PCTC 251	RED ROSE SPEEDWAY (LP, laminated gatefold sleeve, with booklet)	£100
73	Apple PCTC 251	RED ROSE SPEEDWAY (LP, gatefold sleeve, without booklet)	£70
73	Apple PAS 10007	BAND ON THE RUN (LP, with lyric inner sleeve & poster)	£50
73	Apple PAS 10007	BAND ON THE RUN (LP, export edition, Apple logo on textured label above catalogue number, circle indent on label, etched not stamped matrix ZYEX-929-3/ZYEX-930-3, 'BLAIR' etched onto dead wax)	£60
75	Capitol PCTC 254	VENUS AND MARS (LP, gatefold sleeve, inner sleeve, 2 posters & stickers)	£50
76	MPL PCSP 720	WINGS OVER AMERICA (3-LP, with poster)	£35
79	Parlophone PCTC 257	BACK TO THE EGG (LP, with inner)	£30
80	Parlophone PCTC 258	MCCARTNEY II (LP, with inner)	£20
80	Parlophone CHAT 1	MCCARTNEY INTERVIEW (LP)	£30
84	Fame FA 413100-1	McCARTNEY (LP, gatefold sleeve)	£15
84	Nimbus PAS 10007	BAND ON THE RUN (LP, with 'Nimbus' sticker)	£300
87	Fame FA 3191	RED ROSE SPEEDWAY (LP, gatefold sleeve)	£20
89	Parlophone PCSDX 106	FLOWERS IN THE DIRT (LP, World Tour pack with outer folder, 'Part' 7" single, poster, family tree, sticker, postcards & tour itinary)	£50
90	Parlophone PCST 7346	TRIPPING THE LIVE FANTASTIC (3-LP in slip sleeve with inners and 12" x 12" booklet)	£40
91	EMI PAUL 1	LIVERPOOL ORATORIO (2-LP, box set with booklet)	£20

(With Carl Davis and others. McCartney does not play on this record which is his first classical composition in collaboration with Carl Davis)

93	Parlophone PCSD 125	OFF THE GROUND (LP, gatefold)	£100
93	Parlophone PCSD 147	PAUL IS LIVE (2 x LP)	£120
97	Parlophone PCSD 171	FLAMING PIE (LP, gatefold)	£100
99	Parlophone 5223511	RUN DEVIL RUN (LP, gatefold)	£100
99	Parlophone 5232291	RUN DEVIL RUN (8 x 7", box set with booklet)	£70
99	EMI Classics 5568971	WORKING CLASSICAL (2 x LP, gatefold)	£40
99	Parlophone 4991761	BAND ON THE RUN (2 x LP, gatefold, 25th Anniversary)	£30
01	Parlophone 5355101	DRIVING RAIN (2 x LP)	£150
01	Parlophone 5328501	WINGSPAN (4LP, gatefold, 3D image insert, printed inners)	£120
05	Parlophone 3383452	CHAOS AND CREATION IN THE BACKYARD (LP, gatefold with 4 art prints)	£80
12	Universal 088072335981	KISSES ON THE BOTTOM (LP)	£20
24	MPL 602455435620	BAND ON THE RUN 50TH ANNIVERSARY EDITION (2LP, wide-spine sleeve, posters)	£50
24	MPL 602465081633	ONE HAND CLAPPING(2LP/7", printed die-cut inners, booklet, webstore exclusive)	£70

PROMOS : PROMO SINGLES

71	Apple R 5889	Another Day/Oh Woman, Oh Why (demo)	£70
71	Apple R 5914	The Back Seat Of My Car/Heart Of The Country (demo)	£50
73	Apple R5993	Helen Wheels/Country Dreamer (demo)	£40
74	EMI R 5997	Band On The Run (Edited Version)/(Full Version) (demo)	£150
74	Apple R 5999	Junior's Farm (Edited Version)/Junior's Farm (Full Version) (demo)	£100
75	Apple R 5999	Sally G/Junior's Farm (reversed sides, demo)	£150
75	Capitol R 6010	Venus And Mars; Rock Show/Magneto And Titanium Man (demo)	£30
76	Parlophone R 6015	Let 'Em In (Edited Version)/Let 'Em In (Full Version) (demo)	£55
76	Parlophone R 6014	Silly Love Songs (Edited Version)/Silly Love Songs (Full Version) (demo)	£50
77	MPL Publishing MPL 1	We've Moved! (music publishing sampler with excerpts by Wings, Peggy Lee, Gene Vincent, Frank Sinatra, etc.; with press pack and insert)	£350
77	MPL Publishing MPL 1	We've Moved! (music publishing sampler with excerpts by Wings, Peggy Lee, Gene Vincent, Frank Sinatra, etc.; without press pack and insert)	£250
77	Capitol R 6018	Mull Of Kintyre (Edited Version)/Girls' School (Edited Version) (demo)	£50
78	Parlophone R 6019	With A Little Luck (Edited Version)/Backwards Traveller-Cuff Link (demo)	£40
80	Parlophone R 6037DJ	Waterfalls (3.22) (edit)/Check My Machine (demo)	£40
80	Parlophone R 6039A	Temporary Secretary (1-sided demo, no p/s)	£80
84	Parlophone 12RDJ 6080T	No More Lonely Nights (Mole Mix) (12", 1-sided, plain white numbered sleeve with plain white inner sleeve & insert, 250 only; beware of counterfeits with scratched [not stamped] matrix)	£250
84	Parlophone 12R(DJ) 6080	No More Lonely Nights (Extended Version)/Silly Love Songs/No More Lonely Nights (Ballad) (12", promo, blue 'Give My Regards To Broad Street' label, black die-cut sleeve)	£50
85	Parlophone RDJ 6118	Spies Like Us (DJ Version 3.46)/My Carnival (demo, white printed die-cut sleeve)	£35
88	Parlophone PMBOX 11-19	ALL THE BEST! ('Special Edition') (9 x 7" box set, in black die-cut sleeves, with signed 7" print; with genuine signatures)	£200
88	Parlophone PMBOX 11-19	ALL THE BEST! ('Special Edition') (9 x 7" box set, in black die-cut sleeves, with signed 7" print)	£75
89	Parl. 12R LOVE 6223	This One (Lovejoy's Remix) (12", 1-sided, plain label, black die-cut sleeve)	£35
89	Parlophone GOOD 1	Good Sign (6.51)/Good Sign (Groove Mix) (7.22) (12", black die-cut sleeve)	£45
89	Parlophone RDJ 6235	Figure Of Eight (Edited Version 3.59)/Ou Est Le Soleil? (Edited Version 3.57) (demo, standard p/s)	£30
89	Parlophone RDJ 6238	Party (Remix By Bruce Forest)/Party (different remix) (12", some listed as 'Party Party', with insert)	£40
89	Parlophone RDJ 6238	Party (Remix By Bruce Forest)/Party (different remix) (12")	£30
89	Parlophone R 6213	My Brave Face/Flying To My Home (promo in retro Parlophone sleeve)	£50

MINT VALUE £

90	Parlophone 12 SOL 1	**Où Est Le Soleil?** (Tub Dub Mix)/**Où Est Le Soleil?** (Instrumental Mix) (12", black die-cut stickered sleeve, with insert)	£40
90	Parlophone 12 SOL 1	**Où Est Le Soleil?** (Tub Dub Mix)/**Où Est Le Soleil?** (Instrumental Mix) (12", black die-cut stickered sleeve, some without insert)	£20
90	Parlophone R 6271	**Birthday Boy/Good Day Sunshine** (promo in repro Parlophone sleeve)	£30
90	Parlophone R 6278	**All My Trials/C Moon** (promo in repro Parlophone sleeve)	£20
93	Parlophone CDRDJ 6338	**C'mon People** (Radio Edit)/**C'mon People** (CD)	£30
93	Parlophone CDRS 6347	**Biker Like An Icon/Things We Said Today/Mean Woman Blues/ Midnight Special** (CD, unissued)	£0
93	Parlophone CDRDJ 6347	**Biker Like An Icon/Things We Said Today/Mean Woman Blues/ Midnight Special** (CD, no inlay, jewel case with large sticker; beware of counterfeits with thicker blurred label print & smaller sticker on case)	£70
93	Parlophone 12 DELIVDJ 1	**Deliverance/Deliverance** (Dub Mix) (12", green label, plain black die-cut sleeve)	£20
99	Parlophone RDR03	**Run Devil Run/Blue Jean Bop** (mock 50's Parlophone label/sleeve)	£30
00	Hydra FREE 02	**Free Now** (as Liverpool Sound Collage, 1-sided, p/s)	£25
01	WINDJ 002	**Silly Love Songs** (Loop Da Loop Mix)/**Coming Up** (Linus Loves Mix) (12" 50 copies)	£150
03	Parlophone TEMPSEC 01	**Temporary Secretary** (Re-edited by Radio Slave) (12", 1-sided)	£40

PROMOS : PROMO ALBUMS

79	Parlophone PCTCP 257	**BACK TO THE EGG** (LP, as Wings, MPL in-house picture disc; die-cut sleeve, matrix numbers YEX 987-2 & YEX 988-4 or -1; beware counterfeits)	£950
79	Parlophone PCTC 257	**BACK TO THE EGG** (LP, box set with badge, booklet, sticker, postcard & 5 cigarette cards; with or without T-shirt; beware of counterfeits with blurred printing)	£300
79	Capitol (no cat. no.)	**MPL PRESENTS** (6-LP, box set, hand-numbered, 25 only)	£700

(see also Beatles, Country Hams, Percy 'Thrills' Thrillington, Fireman, Mike McGear, Suzy & The Red Stripes, George Martin, Spirit Of Play, Ferry Aid, Michael Jackson, Twin Freaks)

CAROLINE MCCAUSLAND

60s	Happy Face MMLP 1022	**SONGS FOR GALA** (LP)	£40

DAVE MCCLAREN

71	Big BG 323	**Love Is What I Bring** (actually by Dave Barker & Uniques)/ **RUPIE EDWARDS ALL STARS: Love Version** (with U Roy Junior)	£18

CHRIS MCCLURE (SECTION)

68	Polydor 56227	**Hazy People/I'm Just A Country Boy**	£15

(see also Marmalade)

TOMMY MCCOOK (& SUPERSONICS)

63	Island WI 102	**Adam's Apple/MAYTALS: Every Time** (B-side actually by Tonettes)	£30
63	Island WI 118	**Below Zero/LEE PERRY: Never Get Weary**	£40
63	Island WI 124	**Junior Jive/HORACE SEATON: Power**	£25
64	R&B JB 139	**Sampson/ROY & ANNETTE: My Arms Are Waiting**	£50
64	R&B JB 163	**Bridge View/NAOMI & CO: What Can I Do** (B-side actually by Naomi & Clive)	£45
64	Port-O-Jam PJ 4001	**Exodus** (& His Group)/**LEE PERRY: Help The Weak**	£60
64	Port-O-Jam PJ 4003	**Jam Rock/LEE PERRY: Band Minded People**	£40
64	Port-O-Jam PJ 4010	**Road Bloack/LEE PERRY: Chatty Chatty Woman**	£70
64	Black Swan WI 422	**Two For One/LASCELLES PERKINS: I Don't Know**	£25
65	Island WI 232	**Rocket Ship/JUSTIN HINDS & DOMINOES: Turn Them Back**	£60
66	Rio R 100	**Jerk Time** (with Supersonics)/**UNIQUES: The Journey**	£70
66	Rio R 101	**Out Of Space** (with Supersonics)/**UNIQUES: Do Me Good**	£100
66	Rio R 103	**Ska Jam/Smooth Sailing** (with Supersonics)	£100
66	Rio R 104	**Riverton City/HEPTONES: Gunmen Coming To Town**	£100
66	Doctor Bird DB 1028	**More Love/SILVERTONES: True Confession**	£80
66	Doctor Bird DB 1032	**Naked City** (with Supersonics)/**NORMA FRASER: Heartaches**	£45
66	Doctor Bird DB 1047	**Spanish Eyes** (with Lynn Taitt)/**STRANGER & HORTENSE: Loving Wine**	£30
66	Doctor Bird DB 1051	**A Little Bit Of Heaven** (& His Band)/**LLOYD WILLIAMS: Sad World**	£30
66	Doctor Bird DB 1053	**Indian Love Call** (with Supersonics)/**OWEN & LEON: How Would You Feel**	£25
66	Doctor Bird DB 1056	**Danger Man** (with Supersonics)/**ERIC MORRIS: If I Didn't Love You**	£40
66	Doctor Bird DB 1061	**What Now/Don't Stay Away**	£70
67	Doctor Bird DB 1058	**Jam Session** (with Supersonics)/**LLOYD & GLEN: Jezebel**	£50
67	Island WI 3047	**One Two Three Kick/TREASURE ISLE BOYS: What A Fool** (B-side actually by Silvertones)	£50
67	Island WI 3049	**Saboo** (with Supersonics)/**MOVING BROTHERS: Darling I Love You**	£40
67	Treasure Isle TI 7017	**Persian Cat/JUSTIN HINDS: Once A Man**	£20
67	Treasure Isle TI 7018	**Saboo** (with Supersonics)/**MOVING BROTHERS: Darling I Love You** (reissue)	£25
67	Treasure Isle TI 7020	**Shadow Of Your Smile/SILVERTONES: Cool Down**	£60
68	Treasure Isle TI 7027	**Soul For Sale/SILVERTONES: In The Midnight Hour**	£25
68	Treasure Isle TI 7032	**Venus/Music Is My Occupation** (with Supersonics)	£30
68	Treasure Isle TI 7039	**Our Man Flint** (with Supersonics)/**SILVERTONES: Old Man River**	£150
68	Treasure Isle TI 7042	**Moving** (with Supersonics)/**SILVERTONES: Slow And Easy**	£80
68	Doctor Bird DB 1135	**Mad Mad World/Wonderful World** (with Lloyd Williams)	£30
68	Unity UN 501	**Last Flight To Reggie** (Reggae) **City** (with Stranger Cole)/**Watch Dem Go**	£80
69	Trojan TR 642	**Breaking Up/Party Time** (with Supersonics) (both actually by Alton Ellis)	£40
69	Trojan TR 652	**Third Figure/You Should've Known Better**	£25
69	Trojan TR 657	**When The Saints Go Marching In/SOUL OFROUS: Ease Me Up Officer** (B-side actually by Righteous Flames)	£40
69	Trojan TR 671	**Moonshot/PHYLLIS DILLON: Get On The Right Shot**	£60
69	Trojan TR 686	**Tribute To Rameses/PHYLLIS DILLION: Lipstick On Your Collar**	£25
69	Trojan TR 7706	**Black Coffee** (with Supersonics)/**VIC TAYLOR: Heartaches**	£20
69	Unity UN 506	**The Avengers/LAUREL AITKEN: Donkey Man**	£30
69	Unity UN 534	**Dream Boat/Tommy's Dream**	£25
69	Unity UN 535	**Peanut Vendor/100,000 Tons Of Rock**	£40
70	Duke DU 77	**Open Jaw** (with Supersonics)/**JOHN HOLT: The Working Kind**	£25
71	Treasure Isle TI 7058	**My Best Dress/PHYLISS DILLON: One Life To Live**	£20

MINT VALUE £

71	Treasure Isle TI 7061	Testify Version/JOHN HOLT: Let's Build Our Dreams	£25
71	Treasure Isle TI 7065	Black River/JOHN HOLT: Sister Big Stuff	£25
71	Treasure Isle TI 7066	Paragon's Medley Version/JOHN HOLT: Paragon's Medley	£18
71	Treasure Isle TI 7070	Midnight Confession Version/PHYLLIS DILLON: Midnight Confession	£30
71	Big Shot BI 585	Psalm Nine To Keep In Mind (with Observers)/Psalm Nine (Version)	£20
71	Spinning Wheel SW 109	Crying Everynight (with Supersonics) (actually by Stranger Cole)/ HERMAN MARQUIS: Tom's Version	£50
71	Spinning Wheel SW 110	Stupid Doctor (with Supersonics)/ROB WALKER: Grooving In Style (B-side actually by Ken Parker)	£125
79	Grove Music GMDM 26	Sensimena/TONY TUFF: You Wrong (12")	£20
70	Trojan TBL 111	GREATER JAMAICA (MOONWALK REGGAE) (LP, actually by various artists)	£60
74	Attack ATLP 1007	TOMMY McCOOK (LP)	£35
75	Trojan HRLP 706	COOKIN' (LP)	£30
77	Third World TWS 920	HOT LAVA (LP)	£30
77	Justice JUS LP 07	INSTRUMENTAL (LP)	£45

(see also Denis Alcapone, Dave Barker, Dennis Brown, Shenley Duffas, Dennis & Lizzy, Dobby Dobson, Dynamics, Alton Ellis, Ethiopians, Eagles, Emotions, Herman, Heptones, Jamaicans, Hopeton Lewis, Lloyd & Glen, Lloyd & Groovers, Bob Marley, Maytals, Melodians, Mellodites, Millions, Paragons, Hugh Roy, Karl Walker Allstars)

TOMMY MCCOOK & GLEN BROWN
76	Groundation GROL 10	HORNY DUB (LP, white label)	£300

TOMMY MCCOOK & BOBBY ELLIS
77	Grove Music GM 006	Blazing/No Water	£40
75	Grove Music GMLP 002	BLAZING HORNS (LP)	£80

JASON MCCORD
65	Pye 7N 15925	It Was A Very Good Year/Song Of The Pine Tree	£35

MCCORMICK BROTHERS
63	Polydor NH 66986	Red Hen Boogie/Blue Grass Express	£50
66	Hickory LPE 1509	AUTHENTIC BLUEGRASS HITS (EP)	£22

GEORGE MCCORMICK
55	MGM SPC 6	Don't Fix Up The Doghouse/Gold Wedding Band (export issue)	£18

CLYDE MCCOY
57	Mercury MEP 9513	DANCING TO THE BLUES (EP)	£15

JOE MCCOY
59	Collector JDL 81	One In A Hundred/One More Greasing	£30

VIOLA MCCOY
50s	Ristic LP 27	VIOLA McCOY 1923-1927 (10" LP)	£40

N MCCOY & ALBIANS
78	K&K K001	The People/Talk To The People (12")	£70

(see also Albians)

MCCOYS
67	Immediate IM 046	I Got To Go Back/Dynamite	£15
67	London HLZ 10154	Say Those Magic Words/I Wonder If She Remembers Me	£25
66	Immediate IMEP 002	HITS VOL. 1 (EP)	£40
66	Immediate IMEP 003	HITS VOL. 2 (EP)	£40
65	Immediate IMLP 001	HANG ON SLOOPY (LP)	£55
68	Mercury (S)MCL 20128	THE INFINITE McCOYS (LP)	£40
71	Joy JOYS 196	HANG ON SLOOPY (LP, reissue)	£15

(see also Rick Derringer)

JIMMY MCCRACKLIN
58	London HLM 8598	The Walk/I'm To Blame (as Jimmy McCracklin & His Band)	£50
58	London HLM 8598	The Walk/I'm To Blame (as Jimmy McCracklin & His Band) (78)	£15
58	London HL 7035	The Walk/I'm To Blame (export issue, as Jimmy McCracklin & His Band)	£15
62	Top Rank JAR 617	Just Got To Know/The Drag	£25
65	R&B MRB 5001	I Got Eyes For You/I'm Gonna Tell Your Mother	£25
66	Outasite 45 120	Christmas Time (Parts 1 & 2) (99 copies only)	£40
65	Vocalion VEP 170160	JIMMY McCRACKLIN (EP)	£100
68	Minit MLL/MLS 40003	A PIECE OF JIMMY McCRACKLIN (LP)	£40

GWEN MCCRAE
82	Atlantic FLAM 1T	Keep The Fire Burning/Funky Sensation (12")	£20

DANNY MCCULLOCH
69	Capitol E-(S)T 174	WINGS OF A MAN (LP, black/silver label with boxed logo)	£40

(see also Animals)

IAN MCCULLOCH
64	Decca F11855	Come On Home/Down By The River	£50

ED MCCURDY
66	Bounty BY 6017	BLOOD BOOZE N BONES (LP)	£20
60s	Elektra ELK 110	WHEN DALLIANCE WAS IN FLOWER AND MAIDENS LOST THEIR HEADS (LP, with insert)	£40
60s	Elektra ELK 140	WHEN DALLIANCE WAS IN FLOWER VOL 2 (LP)	£40

LUKE MCDANIEL
55	Parlophone CMSP 29	The Automobile Song/I Can't Steal Another's Bride (export issue)	£40

EUGENE MCDANIELS
71	Atlantic 2465 022	OUTLAW (LP, plum labels, Polydor Records on rim)	£60
71	Atlantic 2400 163	HEADLESS HEROES OF THE APOCALYPSE (LP, US sleeve with sticker over US cat no. UK pressed record)	£150

MINT VALUE £

02 Warner Bros. 756793113-1 **HEADLESS HEROES OF THE APOCALYPSE** (LP, reissue) £20

GENE MCDANIELS
61	London HLG 9396	A Tear/She's Come Back	£15
62	Liberty LIB 55480	Point Of No Return/Warmer Than A Whisper	£15
63	Liberty LIB 55597	It's A Lonely Town/False Friends	£30
64	Liberty LIB 55723	In Times Like These/Make Me A Present Of You	£15
65	Liberty LIB 55752	(There Goes The) Forgotten Man	£45
65	Liberty LIB 55805	Walk With A Winner/A Miracle	£100
65	Liberty LIB 55805	Walk With A Winner/A Miracle (DJ copy)	£250
61	London REG 1298	GENE McDANIELS (EP)	£40
62	Liberty LEP 2054	A CHANGE OF MOOD (EP)	£40
61	London HA-G 2384	A HUNDRED POUNDS OF CLAY (LP, mono)	£60
61	London SAH-G 6184	A HUNDRED POUNDS OF CLAY (LP, stereo)	£80
62	Liberty LBY 1003	... SOMETIMES I'M HAPPY (LP)	£40
62	Liberty LBY 1021	TOWER OF STRENGTH (LP)	£40
63	Liberty (S)LBY 1128	SPANISH LACE (LP)	£40
63	Liberty LBY 1179	THE WONDERFUL WORLD OF GENE McDANIELS (LP)	£40
68	Sunset SLS 50017E	FACTS OF LIFE (LP)	£15

CHAS MCDEVITT (SKIFFLE GROUP)
57	Oriole CB 1352	Freight Train (with Nancy Whiskey)/The Cotton Song	£15
58	Oriole CB 1457	Real Love (with Shirley Douglas)/Juke-Box Jumble	£15
57	Oriole EP 7002	CHAS AND NANCY (EP, with Nancy Whiskey)	£20
57	Oriole MG 10018	THE INTOXICATING MISS WHISKEY (10" LP, with Nancy Whiskey)	£30
65	Columbia 33SX 1738	SIXTEEN BIG FOLK HITS (LP, with Shirley Douglas)	£15
(see also Nancy Whiskey)

(COUNTRY) JOE MCDONALD
71	Vanguard 6359 004	TONIGHT I'M SINGING JUST FOR YOU (LP)	£15
71	Sonet SNTF 622	QUIET DAYS IN CLICHY (LP, soundtrack)	£15
71	Vanguard VSD 79314	HOLD ON - IT'S COMING (LP)	£15
71	Vanguard VSD 79315	WAR WAR WAR (LP)	£15
(see also Country Joe & The Fish)

RITCHIE MCDONALD
79	Warrior WAR 137	Hard Road/WIRE LINDO: African Sound (12")	£80
72	Duke DU 141	Boat To Progress/Boat To Progress - Version (with Glen Brown)	£20

RORY MCDONALD
71	Philips 6006 117	Your Love Is Indescribably Delicious/If I Had A Mind To	£30

SHELAGH MCDONALD
70	B&C CAS 1019	THE SHELAGH McDONALD ALBUM (LP, textured sleeve)	£200
71	B&C CAS 1043	STAR GAZER (LP, with inner sleeve)	£200
(see also Keith Christmas)

SKEETS MCDONALD
59	Capitol EAP1 1040	GOING STEADY WITH THE BLUES (EP)	£40

TESFA MCDONALD
72	Dynamic DYN 455	Life Is The Highest/Recarnate (Re-Incarnate) (actually by Bobby Ellis and Tommy McCook)	£30

MCDONALD & GILES
70	Island ILPS 9126	McDONALD AND GILES (LP, 1st pressing, pink label, with 'i' logo)	£200
73	Island ILPS 9126	McDONALD AND GILES (LP, 2nd pressing, 'pink rim' label, 'palm tree' logo)	£40
77	Polydor 2302 070	McDONALD AND GILES (LP, repressing)	£25
(see also King Crimson; Giles, Giles & Fripp)

(MISSISSIPPI) FRED MCDOWELL
66	Bounty BY 6022	MY HOME IS IN THE DELTA (LP)	£45
66	Fontana 688 806 ZL	MISSISSIPPI DELTA BLUES (LP)	£40
69	CBS 63735	LONG WAY FROM HOME (LP)	£30
69	Polydor 236 278	GOING DOWN SOUTH (LP)	£30
70	Capitol E-ST 409	I DO NOT PLAY NO ROCK & ROLL (LP)	£25
70	Transatlantic TRA 194	LONDON 1 (LP)	£18
71	Transatlantic TRA 203	LONDON 2 (LP)	£18
71	Revival RVS 1001	EIGHT YEARS RAMBLIN' (LP, with Johnny Woods)	£18
74	Xtra XTRA 1136	MISSISSIPPI FRED McDOWELL 1904-1972 (LP)	£15

FRED & ANNIE MAE MCDOWELL
64	Polydor 236 570	GOING DOWN SOUTH (LP)	£18

BROTHER JACK MCDUFF
64	Stateside SL 10060	BROTHER JACK McDUFF LIVE! (LP)	£20
64	Stateside SL 10101	THE DYNAMIC JACK McDUFF (LP, as Brother Jack McDuff Quartet)	£20
65	Stateside SL 10121	BROTHER JACK McDUFF QUARTET LIVE! AT THE JAZZ WORKSHOP (LP)	£20
65	Stateside SL 10142	PRELUDE (LP)	£20
66	Stateside SL 10165	THE CONCERT McDUFF (LP)	£20
66	Atlantic 587 030	A CHANGE IS GONNA COME (LP)	£20
67	Transatlantic PR 7404	SILK AND SOUL (LP)	£15
67	Transatlantic PR 7476	WALK ON BY (LP)	£15
68	Transatlantic PR 7286	AT THE JAZZ WORKSHOP (LP)	£15
68	Transatlantic ATRA 5056	DYNAMIC JACK McDUFF (LP)	£15
(see also Roland Kirk, Kenny Burrell, Jimmy Witherspoon)

JOHNNY MCEVOY
| 73 | Hawk HALPX 112 | JOHNNY McEVOY (LP) | £15 |
| 74 | Hawk HALPX 117 | SOUNDS LIKE JOHNNY McEVOY (LP) | £20 |

BOB MCFADDEN & DOR
| 59 | Coral Q 72378 | The Mummy/The Beat Generation (tri centre) | £20 |

(see also Rod McKuen)

MC5
69	Elektra EKSN 45056	Kick Out The Jams/Motor City Is Burning	£50
69	Elektra EKSN 45067	Ramblin' Rose/Borderline	£35
69	Elektra EKL 4042	KICK OUT THE JAMS (LP, orange label, gatefold sleeve, mono)	£200
69	Elektra EKS 74042	KICK OUT THE JAMS (LP, orange label, gatefold sleeve, stereo)	£100
70	Atlantic 2400 016	BACK IN THE U.S.A. (LP)	£100
71	Atlantic 2400 135	HIGH TIME (LP)	£80
77	Atlantic K50346	BACK IN THE USA (LP, reissue)	£25
77	Elektra K42027	KICK OUT THE JAMS (LP, reissue with 'Brothers & Sisters' edit)	£30

MIKE MCGEAR
72	Island WIP 6131	Woman/Kill	£15
75	Warner Bros K 16658	Simply Love You/What Do We Really Know (in p/s)	£15
80	Carrere CAR 144	All The Whales In The Ocean/I Juz Want What You Got - Money! (in p/s)	£30
80	Carrere CAR 144	All The Whales In The Ocean/I Juz Want What You Got - Money!	£15
81	Conn SRTS/81/CUS 1112	No Lardidar/God Save The Gracious Queen (in p/s)	£55
81	Conn SRTS/81/CUS 1112	No Lardidar/God Save The Gracious Queen	£35
72	Island ILPS 9191	WOMAN (LP, gatefold, pink rim palm tree label)	£50
74	Warner Bros K 56051	McGEAR (LP, gatefold sleeve with folded lyric insert)	£25
74	Warner Bros KMG 1	McGEAR'S LIMITED EDITION (7-track white label sampler & press kit)	£45
80s	Centre Labs	McGEAR (LP, 6-track reissue, 500 only, numbered & signed)	£60

(see also Grimms, Scaffold, McGough & McGear, Paul McCartney)

FRANCINE MCGEE
| 77 | RCA PC 0216 | Feelin Good (Disco Mix)/Delerium (Disco Mix) (12") | £20 |
| 78 | RCA PB 9216 | Feelin Good/Delerium | £20 |

LARRY MCGEE REVOLUTION
| 05 | Liquorice Soul LSD 010T | The Burg (Nick Faber Edit)/(Original Version)/(Fat Camp Re-edit)/(Bonus Beats) (12", reissue) | £20 |

BROWNIE MCGHEE
51	Melodisc 1127	Secret Mojo Blues/Me And My Dog (78)	£15
63	Columbia SEG 8226	BLUES ON PARADE NO. 1 (EP)	£20
60s	Xtra 1021	BROWNIE McGHEE (LP)	£20

BROWNIE MCGHEE & DAVE LEE
| 57 | Pye Jazz NJE 1060 | THE BLUEST (EP) | £22 |

(see also Sonny Terry & Brownie McGhee)

DONNA MCGHEE
78	Anchor ANC 1061	Do As I Do/Mr Blindman	£25
78	Anchor ANCT 1061	Do As I Do/Mr Blindman (12")	£35
78	Anchor ANCL 2027	MAKE IT LAST FOREVER (LP)	£100

HOWARD MCGHEE
| 61 | Parlophone PMC 1811 | DUSTY BLUE (LP, black/gold label) | £70 |
| 61 | Fontana FJL906 | THE SHARP EDGE (LP) | £40 |

(see also Scaffold, Adrian Henri, Mike McGear, Jimi Hendrix, Grimms)

(ROGER) MCGOUGH & (MIKE) MCGEAR
| 68 | Parlophone PMC/PCS 7047 | McGOUGH AND McGEAR (LP, with phasing on "So Much"; black/yellow label with "Sold in U.K..." text) | £275 |
| 89 | Parlophone PCS 7332 | McGOUGH AND McGEAR (LP, stereo reissue with inner sleeve, without phasing on "So Much") | £15 |

ROGER MCGOUGH & BRIAN PATTEN
| 75 | Argo ZPL 1190 | READ THEIR OWN VERSE - BRITISH POETS OF OUR TIME (LP) | £25 |

CHRIS MCGREGOR('S BROTHERHOOD OF BREATH)
68	Polydor 184 137	VERY URGENT (LP, as Chris McGregor Group)	£80
68	Polydor 583 072	UP TO EARTH (LP, unreleased, test pressings only)	£150
71	RCA Neon NE 2	CHRIS McGREGOR'S BROTHERHOOD OF BREATH (LP, gatefold sleeve)	£70
72	RCA SF 8260	BROTHERHOOD (LP, gatefold sleeve, as Chris McGregor's Brotherhood of Breath)	£70
74	Ogun OG 100	LIVE, WILLISAU (LP)	£25
77	Ogun OG 521	IN HIS OWN TIME (LP)	£25
78	Ogun OG 524	PROCESSION (LP)	£25

(see also Brotherhood Of Breath, Tunji)

FREDDIE MCGREGOR
73	Fab FAB 261	Wise Words/NEW ESTABLISHMENT: Version	£35
75	Sol Fa SA 02	Get Involved/BAILEY'S ALL STARS: Part 2	£30
79	Observer OBS 903	Run Come Rally (12")	£60
81	Yashemabeth YM01	Wine Of Violence/Once A Man (12")	£15
81	JB JBD 030	Leave Yah/20 Miles Blackstar Liner/U BROWN: Step It Up (12", blue/yellow vinyl)	£40
84	Real Authentic Sound RAS 7008	Across The Border/Version (12")	£30
96	Blacker Dread BDTL 05	Mr. Pressure Man/CLIVE HYLTON: Babylon Keep On Knocking (12")	£35
79	Jackal JALP 7000	FREDDY McGREGOR (LP)	£30

(see also Soul Brothers, Young Freddie)

Rare Record Price Guide 2026

JIMMY MCGRIFF

64	Sue WI 303	All About My Girl/M.G. Blues	£40
64	Sue WI 310	Last Minute (Parts 1 & 2)	£40
64	Sue WI 317	I've Got A Woman (Parts 1 & 2)	£40
64	Sue WI 333	'Round Midnight/Lonely Avenue	£40
66	United Artists UP 1170	See See Rider/Hallelujah	£20
70	United Artists UP 35025	The Worm/What's That	£30
64	Sue ILP 907	I'VE GOT A WOMAN (LP)	£100
64	Sue ILP 908	GOSPEL TIME (LP)	£100
65	London HA-C 8247	BLUES FOR MISTER JIMMY (LP)	£60
66	London HA-C 8242	AT THE APOLLO (LP)	£75
66	United Artists (S)ULP 1158	A BAG FULL OF SOUL (LP)	£30
68	United Artists (S)ULP 1170	THE BIG BAND (LP)	£25
72	Groove Merchant GM 503	GROOVE GREASE (LP)	£15
74	People PLEO 14	FLY DUDE (LP)	£15
74	People PLEO 19	LET'S STAY TOGETHER (LP)	£15
74	People PLEO 23	IF YOU'RE READY COME GO WITH ME (LP)	£15

BILL MCGUFFIE (TRIO)

67	Philips BF 1550	Fugue For Thought (from the film 'Dalek Invasion Earth 2150AD')/ Fair's Fair	£25
55	Philips BBR 8054	JAZZ WITH McGUFFIE (LP)	£15
56	Philips BBR 8087	McGUFFIE MAGIC (LP)	£20
56	Philips BBL 7072	MORE JAZZ WITH McGUFFIE (LP)	£20
58	Philips BBL 7261	CONTINENTAL TOUR (LP)	£20

MCGUINNESS FLINT

70	Capitol EA-ST 22625	McGUINNESS FLINT (LP, gatefold sleeve)	£20
71	Capitol ST 22794	HAPPY BIRTHDAY, RUTHY BABY (LP)	£15

(see also Manfred Mann, Blues Band, John Mayall, Coulson Dean McGuinness Flint, Gallagher & Lyle, Paladin)

BARRY MCGUIRE

66	RCA Victor RCA 1525	Cloudy Summer Afternoon/You've Got To Hide Your Love Away (B-side with Mamas & Papas)	£15
65	RCA Victor RD 7751	SINGS EVE OF DESTRUCTION (LP)	£30
76	Sparrow BIRD 105	C'MON ALONG (LP)	£15

(see also Mamas & Papas)

MCGUIRE SISTERS

54	Vogue Coral Q 2028	Lonesome Polecat/Muskrat Ramble	£15
56	Vogue Coral LVA 9024	DO YOU REMEMBER WHEN? (LP)	£20
57	Vogue Coral LVA 9072	CHILDREN'S HOLIDAY (LP)	£20
58	Coral LVA 9073	TEENAGE PARTY (LP)	£20

MCIB

88	Unyque UNQ 1	Word/Men From The Boys/Money/Like This (12")	£15

KEN MCINTIRE

60	Esquire 32-133	LOOKING AHEAD (LP, with Eric Dolphy)	£60

DAVID MCIVOR

69	Warner Bros WB8002	Closing My Eyes/Love That Burns	£30

MCKAY

03	Go! Beat GOBX 57	Take Me Over/Thinking Of You (D.R.U.N.K. Remix/Thinking Of You (12", p/s)	£25
03	Go! Beat TAKE 7	Take Me Over/(Mafia & Fluxy Remix)	£70
03	Go! Beat 065 631 1	MCKAY (LP)	£25

FREDDIE MCKAY

71	Banana BA 348	Picture On The Wall/SOUND DIMENSION: Version	£25
71	Banana BA 353	Sweet You, Sour You/High School Dance	£20
71	Banana BA 358	High School Dance/SOUND DIMENSION: High School Version	£20
71	Moodisc HM 110	Old Joe/Too Much Fire	£15
72	Banana BA 370	Drunken Sailor/SOUND DIMENSION: Version	£60
73	Bullet BU 525	Go On This Way/SANTIC ALL STARS: Santic Dub	£20
73	Dragon DRA 1012	Our Rendezvous/Black Beauty	£15
73	Atra ATRA 003	I'm A Freeman/SWEET HARMONY: Santic Special	£25
81	Greensleeves GRED 46	Another Weekend/EARL SIXTEEN: Live Together (12")	£30
82	Live & Love LLDIS 2014	In Times Of Trouble/Version (12")	£30
71	Banana BALPS 01	PICTURE ON THE WALL (LP)	£65
73	Attack ATLP 1013	PICTURE ON THE WALL (LP, reissue)	£40
78	GG GG 009	BEST OF (LP)	£40
79	Plant PLAN 10003	CREATION (LP)	£40
85	Move MVLP 6	TRIBAL INNA YARD (LP)	£80

(see also Lizzy)

SCOTT MCKAY

67	Columbia DB 8147	I Can't Make Your Way/Take A Giant Step	£40

LONETTE MCKEE

75	Sussex SXX 4	Save It (Don't Give It Away)/Do It To Me	£15

VAL MCKENNA

65	Piccadilly 7N 35237	Baby Do It/I Believe In Love	£15
65	Piccadilly 7N 35256	Mixed Up Shook Up Girl/Now That You've Made Up Your Mind	£15
66	Piccadilly 7N 35286	I Can't Believe What You Say/Don't Hesitate	£15
70	Spark SRL 1038	Love Feeling/It's All In My Imagination (silver label)	£25

MCKENNA MENDELSON MAINLINE
69   Liberty LBS 83251   STINK (LP) £50

CANDY MCKENZIE
10   Trojan THB 7003   Breakfast In Bed/Ice Cream £25
11   Upsetter TBL 210   LEE PERRY PRESENTS (LP)...£55

MERLENE MCKENZIE
68   Double D DD 106   Left Me For Another/BOBBY AITKEN & CARIBBEATS: Cell Block Eleven..........£20

SCOTT MCKENZIE
67   Capitol CL 15509   Look In Your Eyes/All I Want Is You.................................£20
67   CBS (S)BPG 63157   THE VOICE OF SCOTT McKENZIE (LP) £20
70   A&M AMLS 999   STAINED GLASS MORNING (LP) £18
(see also Mamas & Papas)

TOMMY MCKENZIE
68   Pama PM 720   Fiddlesticks/Please Stay £35

MCKENZIE, DOUG & BOB
82   Mercury HOSER 1   Take Off/Elron McKenzie (p/s) £20
(see also Rush)

MCKENZIE & GARDINER
83   Sound Of London TSOLL 501 From Time/From TIme (Version) (12") £80
83   Sound Of London TSOL 501 From Time/(Special Instrumental Remix) £30

LESLIE MCKEOWN
79   Ego Trip EGO 001   ALL WASHED UP (LP, gatefold, with poster)...................£20

MCKINLEYS
64   Columbia DB 7230   Someone Cares For Me/A Million Miles Away £20
65   Columbia DB 7583   Give Him My Love/Once More £15

ROD MCKUEN
57   London HLU 8390   Happy Is A Boy Named Me/Jaydee................................£15
(see also Bob McFadden & Dor, Mike Sarne, Henri Mancini)

(MAHAVISHNU) JOHN MCLAUGHLIN
69   Marmalade 608 007   EXTRAPOLATION (LP)..£200
70   Polydor 02343 012   EXTRAPOLATION (LP, reissue).......................................£25
71   Douglas DGL 65075   DEVOTION (LP, gatefold sleeve) £20
71   Douglas DGL 69014   MY GOAL'S BEYOND (LP, as Mahavishnu John McLaughlin, gatefold sleeve)......£15
74   CBS Q 69037   LOVE, DEVOTION, SURRENDER (LP, quadrophonic issue) £15

JACKIE MCLEAN QUINTET
55   Esquire 32-041   LIGHTS OUT (LP) £150
56   Esquire 32-111   JACKIE'S PALS (LP) £50
(see also Lifetime, Tony Williams [Lifetime], Mahavishnu Orchestra, John Surman, Santana)

NANA MCLEAN
71   Banana BA 355   A Little Love/SOUND DIMENSION: Heavy Beat £50

CRAIG MCLEARIE
79   Wealden WS 187   WARP FACTOR (LP) £125

GERALD MCLEASH
71   G.G. GG 4516   False Reaper/G.G. ALL STARS: Reaping Version..............£25

LARIS MCLENNON
67   CBM 04   Confusion/Turn Me Loose...£15

ENOS MCLEOD
68   Blue Cat BS 135   You Can Never Get Away/ENOS & SHEILA: La La La Bamba.........£200
83   Stewmac SB 003   BY THE LOOK IN YOUR EYES (LP) £50
96   Pressure Sounds PSLP 008 THE GENIUS OF ENOS (LP) £20
(see also Enos & Sheila)

SEAN MCLEOD
69   Aurora 4594   Living Without You/Love Songs From Another Planet ...£30

OSCAR MCLOLLIE & HIS HONEYJUMPERS
55   London HL 8130   Take Your Shoes Off, Pop/Love Me Tonight £250
55   London HL 8130   Take Your Shoes Off, Pop/Love Me Tonight (78)..........£40

BOBBY MCLURE
66   Chess CRS 8048   Peak Of Love/You Got Me Baby..................................£45
66   Chess CRS 8048   Peak Of Love/You Got Me Baby (DJ copy) £75
75   Island USA 006   You Bring Out The Love In Me/SURVIVAL KIT: Daybreak £20
(see also Fontella Bass)

MCLUSKY
02   Too Pure PURE 117LP   MCLUSKY DO DALLAS (LP) £40
02   Too Pure PURE 117LP   MCLUSKY DO DALLAS (LP, orange or white vinyl).........£50
03   Too Pure PURE 132LP   MY PAIN AND SADNESS IS MORE SAD AND PAINFUL THAN YOURS (LP, vinyl reissue of CD release)...£30
04   Too Pure PURE 154LP   THE DIFFERENCE BETWEEN YOU AND ME IS THAT I'M NOT ON FIRE (LP, with poster).....£35

MCLYNNS
70   CBS 63836   OLD MARKET ST. (LP)..£50

ROSS MCMANUS
72   Rediffusion ZS 122   THE LEAVING OF LIVERPOOL (LP)...............................£15

MC MELLO
92	Funki Dreds PA6640	Gone Crazy/Talk Dem Way/Firm Stance (EP)	£20
94	Natural Response MELLO 1	I Hear Voices/Live At Portland (promo only)	£18
90	Republic 4353ILE	THOUGHTS RELEASED (LP)	£15

BARBARA MCNAIR
66	Tamla Motown TMG 544	You're Gonna Love My Baby/The Touch Of Time (DJ copy)	£400
66	Tamla Motown TMG 544	You're Gonna Love My Baby/The Touch Of Time	£350
59	Coral FEP 2021	FRONT ROW CENTRE VOL. 1 (EP)	£40
64	Warner Bros WEP 6129	I ENJOY BEING A GIRL (EP)	£40

(see also Billy Williams & Barbara McNair)

HAROLD MCNAIR
68	RCA Victor RCA 1742	The Hipster/Indecision	£80
65	Island ILP 926	AFFECTIONATE FINK (LP, with Ornette Coleman's Sidemen)	£500
68	RCA SF 7969	HAROLD McNAIR (LP, 1st pressing, black RCA red dot label)	£300
68	RCA SF 7969	HAROLD McNAIR (LP, 2nd pressing, orange label)	£150
70	RCA Intl. INTS 1096	FLUTE AND NUT (LP)	£50
70	B&C CAS 1016	THE FENCE (LP, gatefold with pink envelope containing balloon)	£80
70	B&C CAS 1016	THE FENCE (LP, gatefold with pink envelope without balloon)	£40
72	B&C CAS 1045	HAROLD McNAIR (LP)	£70

(see also Ginger Baker's Airforce)

BIG JAY MCNEELY
59	Top Rank JAR 169	There Is Something On Your Mind/...Back...Shack...Track ('vocal: Little Sonny')	£40
59	Top Rank JAR 169	There Is Something On Your Mind/...Back...Shack...Track ('vocal: Little Sonny') (78)	£15
65	Sue WI 373	There Is Something On Your Mind/...Back...Shack...Track ('vocal: Little Sonny') (reissue)	£20
64	Warner Bros WM 8143	BIG JAY'S PARTY (LP)	£30

DAVID MCNEIL
68	President PT 212	Don't Let Your Chance Go By/Space Plane	£40

LLOYD MCNEIL QUARTET
10	Universal Sound USLP 31	ASHA (LP, reissue)	£20
11	Universal Sounds USLP39	WASHINGTON SUITE (LP, reissue)	£25

PAUL MCNEILL
66	Decca LK 4803	TRADITIONALLY AT THE TROUBADOUR (LP)	£40

RONNIE MCNEIR
75	Tamla Motown STML 2036	RONNIE MCNEIR (LP)	£30
76	Motown STML 12041	LOVES COMIN DOWN (LP)	£15

MCPEAKE FAMILY/FOLK GROUP
60s	Topic	IRISH TRADITIONAL FOLK SONGS AND MUSIC (LP, blue label)	£30
60s	Topic 12T 87	THE McPEAKE FAMILY (LP)	£20
64	Fontana TL 5214	IRISH FOLK! (LP, as McPeake Family)	£20
65	Fontana TL 5358	AT HOME WITH THE McPEAKES (LP)	£20
67	Fontana TL 5433	PLEASANT AND DELIGHTFUL (LP, as McPeake Family)	£20
69	Evolution Z 1002	WELCOME HOME (LP, as McPeake Folk Group)	£40

CLYDE MCPHATTER
SINGLES
56	London HLE 8250	Seven Days/I'm Not Worthy Of You	£400
56	London HLE 8250	Seven Days/I'm Not Worthy Of You (78)	£30
56	London HL 7006	Seven Days/I'm Not Worthy Of You (export issue)	£125
56	London HLE 8293	Treasure Of Love/When You're Sincere (gold label lettering)	£150
56	London HLE 8293	Treasure Of Love/When You're Sincere (silver label lettering)	£60
57	London HLE 8462	Just To Hold My Hand/No Matter What (triangular centre)	£150
57	London HLE 8462	Just To Hold My Hand/No Matter What (78)	£20
57	London HLE 8476	Long Lonely Nights/Heartaches (triangular centre)	£100
57	London HLE 8476	Long Lonely Nights/Heartaches (triangular centre) (78)	£20
57	London HLE 8525	Rock And Cry/You'll Be There (triangular centre)	£90
57	London HLE 8525	Rock And Cry/You'll Be There (later round centre)	£40
57	London HLE 8525	Rock And Cry/You'll Be There (78)	£20
58	London HLE 8707	Come What May/Let Me Know (triangular centre)	£60
58	London HLE 8707	Come What May/Let Me Know (78)	£25
58	London HLE 8755	A Lover's Question/I Can't Stand Up Alone (triangular centre)	£30
58	London HLE 8755	A Lover's Question/I Can't Stand Up Alone (78)	£20
59	MGM MGM 1014	I Told Myself A Lie/(I'm Afraid) The Masquerade Is Over	£20
59	London HLE 8878	Lovey Dovey/My Island Of Dreams (triangular centre)	£30
59	London HLE 8878	Lovey Dovey/My Island Of Dreams (78)	£25
59	London HLE 8906	Since You've Been Gone/Try Try Baby (triangular centre)	£40
59	London HLE 8906	Since You've Been Gone/Try Try Baby (78)	£30
59	MGM MGM 1040	Twice As Nice/Where Did I Make My Mistake	£18
59	London HLE 9000	You Went Back On Your Word/There You Go	£40
59	London HLE 9000	You Went Back On Your Word/There You Go (78)	£40
59	MGM MGM 1048	Bless You/Let's Try Again	£18
60	London HLE 9059	Just Give Me A Ring/Don't Dog Me	£45
60	MGM MGM 1061	Think Me A Kiss/When The Right Time Comes Along	£18
60	Mercury AMT 1108	I Ain't Givin' Up Nothin' (If I Can't Get Something)/Ta Ta	£15
60	Mercury AMT 1120	You're For Me/I Just Want To Love You	£18
61	Mercury AMT 1136	Tomorrow Is A-Comin'/I'll Love You Till The Cows Come Home	£40

62	Mercury AMT 1174	Lover Please/Let's Forget About The Past	£20
62	Mercury AMT 1181	Little Bitty Pretty One/Next To Me	£20
66	Stateside SS 487	Everybody's Somebody's Fool/I Belong To You	£18
66	Stateside SS 567	A Shot Of Rhythm And Blues/I'm Not Going To Work Today	£30
67	Stateside SS 592	Lavender Lace/Sweet And Innocent	£20
68	Deram DM 202	Only A Fool/Thank You Love	£25
69	Deram DM 223	Baby I Could Be So Good At Loving You/Baby You've Got It	£25

EPs
59	London RE-E 1202	CLYDE McPHATTER	£250
60	London RE-E 1240	CLYDE McPHATTER NO. 2 (unissued)	£0
59	MGM MGM-EP 705	TWICE AS NICE	£60
60	MGM MGM-EP 739	THIS IS NOT GOODBYE	£60

ALBUMS
63	Mercury MMC 14120	LOVER PLEASE	£100
64	Atlantic ATL 5001	THE BEST OF CLYDE McPHATTER	£90
71	MCA MUPS 418	WELCOME HOME	£20
73	Atlantic K 30033	A TRIBUTE TO CLYDE McPHATTER	£20

(see also Drifters, Jackie Wilson, Dominoes, Billy Ward & Dominoes, Jackie Wilson/Clyde McPhatter)

TONY (T.S.) MCPHEE
66	Purdah 45-3501	Someone To Love Me/Ain't Gonna Cry No Mo' (as T.S. McPhee)	£200
68	Liberty LBL/LBS 83190	ME AND THE DEVIL (LP)	£60
71	Sunset SLS 50209	THE SAME THING ON THEIR MINDS (LP, with Jo-Ann Kelly)	£30
73	World Wide Artists WWA 1	THE TWO SIDES OF TONY (T.S.) McPHEE (LP, with insert)	£25

(see also Groundhogs, Champion Jack Dupree, Jo-Ann Kelly, John Dummer Blues Band, Hapshash & Coloured Coat, Herbal Mixture)

CHARLES MCPHERSON
| 65 | Stateside SL 10151 | BEBOP REVISITED (LP) | £15 |

GILLIAN MCPHERSON
| 71 | RCA Victor SF 8220 | POETS AND PAINTERS AND PERFORMERS OF THE BLUES (LP) | £80 |

HERB MCQUAY
| 75 | Bell 1398 | Runnin' Away From You/Storm Clouds | £18 |

RON MCQUINN
| 77 | Decca F13693 | Look At Love Bleed/Banshee | £20 |

CARMEN MCRAE
| 57 | London RE-N 1094 | LONDON'S GIRL FRIENDS (EP) | £15 |
| 56 | Brunswick LAT 8133 | TORCHY (LP) | £15 |

(see also Sammy Davis Jnr.)

MC SPY-D & 'FRIENDS'
| 95 | Parlophone 12RDJ 6404 | The Amazing Spider-Man (Solution Mix)/(Solution Chilled Mix)/(B&J White Trouser Mix) (12", no p/s, promo only) | £25 |

(see also Brian May)

BLIND WILLIE MCTELL
66	Transatlantic PR 1040	LAST SESSION (LP)	£35
67	Storyville 670 816	BLIND WILLIE McTELL 1940 (LP)	£22
60s	Roots RL 324	BLIND WILLIE McTELL 1929-1935 (LP)	£20
73	Atlantic K 40400	ATLANTA TWELVE STRING GUITAR (LP)	£18

RALPH MCTELL
68	Transatlantic TRA 165	8 FRAMES A SECOND (LP, white/lilac label with 't' logo)	£35
69	Transatlantic TRA 177	SPIRAL STAIRCASE (LP, laminated sleeve, with insert)	£25
69	Transatlantic TRA 209	MY SIDE OF YOUR WINDOW (LP, textured sleeve)	£20
70	Transatlantic TRA 227	REVISITED (LP)	£20

RAY MCVAY SOUND
65	Pye 7N 15777	Raunchy/Revenge (Promo copies have "Macvay" spelling)	£45
65	Pye 7N 15816	Kinda Kinky/Kinkdom Come	£50
71	Philips 6006 083	They Call Me Mr. Tibbs (as Ray McVay & Orchestra)	£25

CARL MCVOY
| 58 | London HLU 8617 | Tootsie/You Are My Sunshine | £200 |
| 58 | London HLU 8617 | Tootsie/You Are My Sunshine (78) | £40 |

BRIGETTE MCWILLIAMS
| 97 | Virgin VUSLP 137 | TOO MUCH WOMAN (2-LP) | £18 |

DAVID MCWILLIAMS
67	Major Minor MM 533	Harlem Lady/The Days Of Pearly Spencer (some copies later 'flipped')	£15
67	Major Minor MMLP 2	SINGING SONGS BY DAVID McWILLIAMS (LP, laminated sleeve, also stereo SMLP 2)	£15
67	Major Minor MMLP 10	DAVID McWILLIAMS VOL. 2 (LP, laminated front cover, also stereo SMLP 10)	£15
68	Major Minor MMLP 11	VOLUME III (LP, also stereo SMLP 11)	£15
69	Major Minor MCP 5026	THE DAYS OF DAVID McWILLIAMS (LP)	£15
72	Dawn DNLS 3039	LORD OFFALY (LP, textured gatefold sleeve)	£20
73	Dawn DNLS 3047	THE BEGGAR AND THE PRIEST (LP)	£20
74	Dawn DNLS 3059	LIVING'S JUST A STATE OF MIND (LP)	£18

MEADOW SWEET
| 73 | Sunday SUN 1 | Behind You/Dreams In Colour | £40 |

ME & THEM
64	Pye 7N 15596	Feels So Good/I Think I'm Gonna Kill Myself	£18
64	Pye 7N 15631	Everything I Do Is Wrong/Show You Mean It Too	£15
64	Pye 7N 15683	Get Away/Tell Me Why	£15

MEANIES
79 Vendetta VD 002 | **Waiting For You/It's True** (p/s) **£100**

MEANSTREAK
81 Meanstreak MS1 | (Time I) **Played It Right/You Took The Fire/I Know** (p/s) **£50**

MEAN STREET
77 Vortex/NEMS NES 115 | **Bunch Of Stiffs/WASPS: Can't Wait 'Til '78** (p/s)................................. **£18**

MEAN STREET DEALERS
79 Graduate GRAD 5 | **Japanese Motorbikes/Tight Skirts** (p/s).. **£20**
79 Mean St. Dealers MSD 001 | **BENT NEEDLES** (LP)... **£25**
79 Graduate GRADLP 1 | **BENT NEEDLES** (LP, reissue) **£18**
(see also Tea & Sympathy)

MEASLES
65 Columbia DB 7531 | **Casting My Spell/Bye Birdie Fly** **£40**
65 Columbia DB 7673 | **Night People/Dog Rough Dan** **£25**
66 Columbia DB 7875 | **Kicks/No Baby At All** **£35**
66 Columbia DB 8029 | **Walkin' In/Looking For Love** **£25**

MEAT LOAF
75 Ode ODS 66304 | **Clap Your Hands, Stamp Your Feet/Stand By Me** (withdrawn)............. **£25**
82 Epic EPC 11 82419 | **BAT OUT OF HELL** (LP, picture disc)...................................... **£15**
(see also Stoney & Meat Loaf, Rocky Horror Show)

MEAT WHIPLASH
85 Creation CRE 020 | **Don't Slip Up/Here It Comes** (foldaround p/s in poly bag; 1st pressing has photo of band by fence) **£20**
(see also Jesus & Mary Chain)

MECANO
82 CBS A 3140 | **The Uninvited Guest/London** (p/s) **£20**

MECHANICAL HEARTS
91 Mechanartz 017 | **Precious Time/Pay The Driver**... **£60**

MEDDY EVILS
65 Pye 7N 15941 | **Find Somebody To Love/A Place Called Love** **£125**
66 Pye 7N 17091 | **It's All For You/Ma's Place**.. **£160**
(see also Stu James and the Mojos, the Quik)

MEDIA (1)
79 Takeaway TA 001 | **TV Kids/Don't Sit Back/Just For You/Rose And Crown** (500 only, p/s) **£100**

MEDIATORS
69 Coxsone CS 7101 | **Darling, There I Stand/PRINCE CHARLIE: Hit And Run** **£100**
70 Supreme SUP 210 | **When You Go To A Party** (actually by Meditators)/ **RUPIE EDWARDS ALLSTARS: Stop The Party** **£15**
(see also Meditators)

MEDICINE HEAD
69 Dandelion S 4661 | **His Guiding Hand/This Love Of Old** **£20**
69 Dandelion 63757 | **NEW BOTTLES, OLD MEDICINE** (LP).. **£60**
71 Dandelion DAN 8005 | **HEAVY ON THE DRUM** (LP, gatefold sleeve, 1st pressing with lyric insert with DAN 8005 on sleeve, label and matrix).. **£125**
71 Dandelion DAN 8005 | **HEAVY ON THE DRUM** (LP, gatefold sleeve, later pressing listed as K 49005; without lyric insert).. **£50**
71 Dandelion 2310 166 | **DARK SIDE OF THE MOON** (LP, with insert) **£35**
73 Polydor 2310 248 | **ONE & ONE IS ONE** (LP, fold-out sleeve) **£15**
74 Polydor 2383 272 | **THRU' A FIVE** (LP)... **£15**
(see also Ashton Gardner & Dyke, British Lions)

MEDITATIONS (2)
78 Island IPR 2022 | **Life Is Not Easy/Much Smarter** (12").. **£25**
70s GG's GG 097 | **Justice/Version** (12") **£25**
80 JB JBD21 | **Vanity Lover/Part 2** (12") **£15**
81 Kingdom KV 8020 12 | **Stranger In Love/Unity** (12") **£15**
77 United Artists UAS30178 | **MESSAGE FROM THE MEDITATIONS** (LP) **£20**
78 Third World TWS 929 | **WAKE UP!** (LP) **£25**
79 Tad's TRDLP 101579 | **GUIDANCE** (LP) **£25**
83 Greensleeves GREL52 | **NO MORE FRIEND** (LP)... **£15**

MEDITATORS
69 Bullet BU 403 | **Duba Duba/CECIL NICKY THOMAS: Running Alone**....................... **£20**
69 Success RE 901 | **Look Who Bust A Style/RUPIE EDWARDS ALL STARS: Look Who Bust A Style** **£35**
70 Big BG 302 | **When You Go To A Party/Good Morning Mother Cuba** **£20**
71 Big BG 305 | **Music Alone Shall Live/RUPIE EDWARDS AND ALL STARS: Music Alone - Version** **£20**
(see also Busty Brown, Pat Satchmo)

MEDIUM
68 CBS 3404 | **Edward Never Lies/Colours Of The Rainbow**............................. **£40**

MEDIUM MEDIUM
81 Cherry Red BRED 19 | **THE GLITTERHOUSE** (LP) **£15**

MEDIUM WAVE
69 Ember EMB 5265 | **Walk In The Sunshine/Looking Towards The Sky** (p/s).................... **£15**

BILL MEDLEY
69 MGM MGM-C(S) 8091 | **BILL MEDLEY 100%** (LP) **£20**
(see also Righteous Brothers, Garnet Mimms)

JOE MEDLIN
59   Mercury AMT 1032   I Kneel At Your Throne/Out Of Sight, Out Of Mind £25

KEITH MEEHAN
69   Marmalade 598 016   Darkness Of My Life/TONY MEEHAN: Hooker Street £30

JOE MEEK ORCHESTRA
63   Decca F 11796   The Kennedy March/The Theme Of Freedom £30
(see also Blue Men)

CARL MEEKS
88   Redman Intl. RED LP 12   WEH DEM FAH (LP) £22
89   Greensleeves GREL 132   JACKMANDORA (LP) £20

MEET JESUS MUSIC
72   Echo ECH 002   MEET JESUS MUSIC (LP) £20

MEGA CITY 2
92   Hear Dis HDR 001   London To Essex In 3 Hours/Darker Side Of Evil (12") £20
93   Extra Terrestrial ETR 002 Nightwalker/Atmospheric Disturbance (12") £40
93   Extra Terrestrial   DEMONS BY DAYLIGHT EP (12") £30
     VERYDARK001

MEGADETH
87   Capitol CLP 476   Wake Up Dead/Black Friday (live) (skull-shaped picture disc with insert)...........£18
87   Capitol 12CL 476   Wake Up Dead/Black Friday (live)/Devil's Island (live)/Wake Up Dead/Black Friday (live) (12", p/s, allegedly shrink-wrapped with 7" picture disc) £25
87   Capitol 12CL 476   Wake Up Dead/Black Friday (live)/Devil's Island (live)/Wake Up Dead/Black Friday (live) (12", p/s) £15
87   Capitol 12CL 476   Wake Up Dead/Black Friday (Tommy Vance Show)/Devil's Island (Tommy Vance Show) (12", stickered p/s, with 'Deth' certificate) £15
88   Capitol CLP 480   Anarchy In The U.K./Liar (U.K.-shaped picture disc) £15
90   SBK SBKPD 4   No More Mr. Nice Guy/DEAD ON: "Different Breed" (chair-shaped pic disc) ...£15
91   Capitol CLS 604   Hangar 18 (MJ 12 Edit)/The Conjuring (live) (p/s, shrinkwrapped with patch)........£15
91   Capitol CLPD 604   Hangar 18 (MJ 12 Edit)/The Conjuring (live) (Vic-shaped picture disc)...........£20
92   Capitol 12CLS 662   Symphony Of Destruction/Breakpoint/Go To Hell (12", p/s, clear vinyl with giant autographed poster) £20
92   Capitol CLP 669   Skin O' My Teeth (LP Version)/Holy Wars... The Punishment Due (The General Schwarzkopf Mix)/High Speed Dirt (live)/The Passes (Mustaine Remarks On Game) (10" bronze Megadeth box with passes & game rules) £20
88   M. For Nations MFN 46P   KILLING IS MY BUSINESS ... AND BUSINESS IS GOOD (LP, picture disc with insert)...........£20
88   Capitol ESTP 2022   PEACE SELLS ... BUT WHO'S BUYING? (LP, picture disc with insert) £20
88   Capitol ESTP 2053   SO FAR, SO GOOD ... SO WHAT (LP, picture disc with insert) £30
90   Capitol EST 2132   RUST IN PEACE (LP) £40
90   Capitol ESTPD 2132   RUST IN PEACE (LP, picture disc, die cut sleeve) £30
94   Capitol ESTPD 2244   YOUTHANASIA (LP, picture disc) £50
94   Capitol ESTPD 2244   YOUTHANASIA (LP, gatefold sleeve, blue vinyl, 1000 only) £150
97   Capitol EST 2297   CRYPTIC WRITINGS (LP, gatefold) £200
07   EMI 50995 13187 28   WARCHEST ('ammo' box set with 4 CD's, DVD and booklet) £35

MEGATON (1)
71   Deram DM-R 331   Out Of Your Own Little World/Niagara £30
71   Deram SML-R 1086   MEGATON (LP, white/red label with small logo)............................£2000

MEGATON (2)
81   Hot Metal HMM 69   Aluminium Lady/Diehard (p/s) £80

MEGATONS (JAMAICA)
70   Downtown DT 464   Take It Easy/Funk The Beat £15
70   Downtown DT 469   Militant Man/MUSIC DOCTORS: Reggae Jeggae Version £20
(see also Revelation)

MEGATONS (U.S.)
65   Sue WI 325   Shimmy Shimmy Walk (Parts 1 & 2)...£40

MEKONS
78   Fast Products FAST 1   Never Been In A Riot/32 Weeks/Heart And Soul £50
79   Virgin V2143   THE QUALITY OF MERCY IS NOT STRNEN (LP) £25
82   CNT CNT 009   THE MEKONS STORY (LP) £20
85   Sin 001   FEAR AND WHISKEY (LP) £20
91   Blast First BFFP 80   THE CURSE OF THE MEKONS (LP) £15
(see also Batfish Boys, Ut)

MEL & DAVE
70   Upsetter US 330   Spinning Wheel/Version £40

MEL & TIM
73   Stax 2325 090   STARTING ALL OVER AGAIN (LP) £25

MELANCHOLY MAN
91   Warriors Dance WAFT 22   Precaution/Caution/Extra Precaution (12") £18

TERRY MELCHER
74   Reprise K 54016   TERRY MELCHER (LP) £20
(see also Terry Day, The Rip Chords, Freeway)

GIL MELLE (QUINTET)
55   Vogue LDE 141   GIL MELLE QUINTET (10" LP) £15

SUSAN MELLEN
75   MAM MAMAS 1014   THE MELLEN BIRD (LP, with insert) £30

MELLODITIES
64	R&B JB 179	Vacation/TOMMY McCOOK: Music Is My Occupation £50

MELL(O)TONES
68	Amalgamated AMG 812	Fat Girl In Red/VERSATILES: Trust The Book £35
68	Amalgamated AMG 817	Feel Good (actually maybe by Bleechers)/Soulful Mood (actually by Tommy McCook & Supersonics)...£30
68	Doctor Bird DB 1136	None Such/VAL BENNETT: Popeye On The Shore...£50
68	Trojan TR 612	Uncle Charlie/What A Botheration...£45
68	Pyramid PYR 6060	Let's Join Together/BEVERLEY'S ALLSTARS: I Don't Know £50
69	Camel CA 18	Facts Of Life/TERMITES: I'll Be Waiting...£35
70	Escort ERT 844	Work It/SOUL MAN: Good Lover £15

(see also Sexy Girls)

MELLOW CANDLE
68	SNB 55-3645	Feeling High/Tea With The Sun..£100
72	Deram DM 357	Dan The Wing/Silversong (with promotional p/s) £500
72	Deram DM 357	Dan The Wing/Silversong...£80
72	Deram SDL 7	SWADDLING SONGS (LP) £2000
11	Rise Above Relics RARLP007	SWADDLING SONGS PLUS (Box set, 2-LP, white vinyl, 2 x 7" booklet) £70

(see also Alison O'Donnell)

MELLOW CATS WITH COUNT OSSIE & WARRICKAS
61	Blue Beat BB 68	Rock A Man Soul/MONTO & CYCLONES: Lazy Lou (B-side actually by Monty [Alexander] & Cyclones)...£25

(see also Melo Cats)

MELLOW FRUITFULNESS
67	Columbia S(C)X 6242	MEDITATION (LP, mono/stereo)..£15

MELLOW LARKS
60	Blue Beat BB 16	Time To Pray (Alleluia)/Love You Baby...£20
61	Blue Beat BB 38	No More Wedding/Lite Of My Life £20

(see also Basil Gabbidon)

MELLOW ROSE
80	Studio 16 WE 0018	Too Much Heaven/Strike (12", with Vin Gordon) £25
80	Studio 16 WE 348	Imitation Love/SGT. PEPPER: Dub A Rub Ina Imitation Way (12")......................£25

MELLOW SOUNDS
70	Axe AXE 1	Turn It Down/A Night Of Fear £50

MELO CATS
61	Blue Beat BB 54	Another Moses/ROLAND ALPHONSO & ALLEY CATS: Hully Gully Rock £20

(see also Mellow Cats)

MELODIANS
66	Island WI 3014	Lay It On/Meet Me £40
67	Coxsone CS 7004	I Should Have Made It Up/JOE HIGGS: Neighbour Neighbour £150
67	Treasure Isle TI 7006	You Don't Need Me/I Will Get Along £30
67	Treasure Isle TI 7022	You Have Caught Me/I Know Just How She Feels £50
67	Treasure Isle TI 7023	Last Train To Expo. '67/TOMMY McCOOK & SUPERSONICS: Expo £35
68	Treasure Isle TI 7028	Come On, Little Girl/TOMMY McCOOK & SUPERSONICS: Got Your Soul £30
68	Doctor Bird DB 1125	Little Nut Tree/You Are My Only Love £25
68	Doctor Bird DB 1139	Swing And Dine/I Could Be King £25
68	Masters Time MT 004	Let's Join Hands Together/My Last Word £60
68	Fab FAB 61	Sweet Rose/It Comes And Goes...£30
69	Gas GAS 108	Ring Of Gold/You've Got It..£40
69	Gas GAS 116	Personally Speaking/LLOYD ROBINSON: Trouble Trouble...............................£20
69	Crab CRAB 15	When There Is You/UNIQUES: My Woman's Love £80
69	Trojan TR 660	Everybody Bawlin'/TOMMY McCOOK: Kilowatt £25
71	Summit SUM 8512	It Took A Miracle/BEVERLEY'S ALLSTARS: Miraculous Version...........................£15
72	Punch PH 111	Round And Round/UPSETTERS: Round Version £15
75	Torpedo TOR 46	I'll Take You To Where The Music's Playing/It's All In The Family.......................£20
78	Sky Note SKYLP18	PRE MEDITATION (LP)..£30

(see also Gentiles, Tony Brevett, Brent Dowe, Jaylads, Gaylads, Joe Grinne)

BOBBY MELODY
69	Duke DU 20	The Break (actually by Winston Francis)/BAND OF MERCY AND SALVATION: Suffering Stink £200
79	Hit Run HIT DD5	Anger & Strife (ft. Jah Lion)/JAH LION: Johnnie Walker (12")...........................£30
82	Negus Roots NERT012	True True Loving/I'm Gonna Keep On Trying (12")......................................£20

JOHNNY MELODY
68	Pyramid PYR 6041	You Treating Me Bad/ROLAND ALPHONSO: Peace And Love £40
67	Pyramid PYR 6023	Govern Your Mouth (actually by George Dekker)/ROLAND ALPHONSO: Peace And Love £30

(see also Lloyd & Johnny Melody under 'L', Lloyd Terrell)

RICKY MELODY
88	Wolrd Enterprise WED 61	What An Act/Version (12") £80

MELODY ENCHANTERS
63	Island WI 049	Enchanter's Ball/I'll Be True £20
63	R&B JB 117	Gone Gone/Blueberry Hill £18

KANSAS CITY MELROSE/CASINO SIMPSON
72	Chicago Piano 12-001	KANSAS CITY MELROSE/CASINO SIMPSON (LP)......................................£15

JOE MELSON
61	Polydor NH 66959	Oh Yeah!/What's The Use I Still Love You	£30
61	Polydor NH 66961	Hey Mister Cupid/No One Really Cares	£25

MELTATIONS
87	Meltations MEL 701	32 Sweet Teeth/I'll Take It As A Compliment (p/s)	£80

MELTING BEAR
85	Beggars Banquet BEG 144	It Makes No Difference/Nature's Way/Sea Song (unreleased, test pressings only)	£15

MELTON CONSTABLE
72	SIS Studio 101	MELTON CONSTABLE (LP)	£150

KATIE MELUA
04	Dramatico DRAMLP 001	CALL OFF THE SEARCH (LP)	£100
06	Dramatico DRAMLP 002	PIECE BY PIECE (LP, 180gm, numbered)	£150
08	Dramatico DRAMLP 003	PICTURES (LP)	£100
09	Dramatico DRAMLP 007	LIVE AT THE O2 ARENA (2-LP, 180gm)	£80
10	Dramatico DRAMLP 016	THE HOUSE (LP, with CD)	£60
12	Dramatico DRAMLP 020	SECRET SYMPHONY (LP, with CD)	£50

HAROLD MELVIN & BLUE NOTES
79	Source SRC 102	Prayin/Your Love Is Taking Me On A Journey	£15
73	CBS 65350	HAROLD MELVIN & THE BLUES NOTES (LP)	£15
73	CBS Q 65859	BLACK AND BLUE (LP, quadrophonic)	£15
75	Philadelphia Int. PI SPIR 80399	TO BE TRUE (LP)	£15
75	Philadelphia Int. PIR 69193	WAKE UP EVERYODY (LP, with free 7" EP)	£20
75	Philadelphia Int. PIR 69193	WAKE UP EVERYODY (LP)	£15

(see also Teddy Pendergrass)

MELVINS
90	Tupelo TUPEP 10	Sweet Young Thing Ain't Sweet No More/STEEL POLE BATH TUB: I Dreamed I Dream (12", p/s, green vinyl, 600 only)	£20
89	Tupelo TUPL 7	OZMA (LP)	£25
91	Tupelo TUP LP 26	BULLHEAD (LP)	£25

MEMBERS
78	Stiff/One Off OFF 3	Solitary Confinement/Rat Up A Drainpipe (p/s)	£15

MEMORIES
74	Rex R 11091	Lay It On Me/Did Ya Get It	£20

MEMOS
59	Parlophone R 4616	The Biddy Leg/My Type Of Girl	£60

MEMPHIS HORNS
71	Mojo 2466 010	THE MEMPHIS HORNS (LP)	£25

MEMPHIS JUG BAND
55	HMV 7EG 8073	MEMPHIS JUG BAND (EP, withdrawn)	£30

MEMPHIS MINNIE
64	Heritage H 103	MEMPHIS MINNIE (EP)	£75
69	Limited Edition (no cat. no.)	MEMPHIS MINNIE 1934-1936 (LP)	£40
69	Limited Edition (no cat. no.)	MEMPHIS MINNIE 1934-1941 (LP)	£40
69	Sunflower ET 1400	MEMPHIS MINNIE 1941-1949 (LP, 99 copies only)	£50

MEMPHIS SLIM
53	Esquire 10-319	Harlem Bound/ST. LOUIS JIMMY R&B BAND: Holiday For Boogie (78)	£15
60	Collector JDN 102	Pinetop's Blues/How Long	£15
62	Storyville A 45055	Big City Girl/El Capitan (p/s)	£15
61	Collector JEN 5	GOING TO KANSAS CITY (EP)	£30
62	Storyville SEP 385	STORYVILLE BLUES ANTHOLOGY VOL. 5 - BOOGIE WOOGIE AND THE BLUES (EP)	£22
63	Vocalion VEP 170155	MEMPHIS SLIM AND LITTLE RICHARD (EP)	£80
61	Collector JGN 1004	MEMPHIS SLIM U.S.A. (LP)	£45
61	Collector JGN 1005	MEMPHIS SLIM U.S.A. (VOL. 2) (LP)	£45
62	Bluesville BV 1018	JUST BLUES (LP)	£30
62	Storyville SLP 118	MEMPHIS SLIM (LP)	£22
62	Storyville SLP 138	THIS IS A GOOD TIME TO WRITE A SONG (LP)	£22
62	Fontana 688 302 ZL	NO STRAIN (LP)	£25
63	United Artists ULP 1042	BROKEN SOUL BLUES (LP)	£30
64	Storyville SLP 118	TRAVELLIN' WITH THE BLUES (LP)	£22
64	Xtra XTRA 1008	MEMPHIS SLIM (LP)	£18
64	Fontana 688 701	ALONE WITH MY FRIENDS (LP)	£30
65	Fontana TL 5254	CLAP YOUR HANDS (LP)	£25
65	Melodisc MLPS 12-149	FATTENIN' FROGS FOR SNAKES (LP)	£25
66	Fontana 688 315 ZL	FRISCO BAY BLUES (LP)	£30
67	Polydor 623 211	PINETOP'S BLUES (LP)	£18
68	Polydor 623 263	BLUESINGLY YOURS (LP, with Mickey Baker)	£18
68	Xtra XTRA 5060	ALL KINDS OF BLUES (LP)	£15
69	Xtra XTRA 1085	CHICAGO BLUES (LP)	£15
72	Barclay 920 214	BLUE MEMPHIS (LP, with Peter Green)	£75
72	Barclay 920 332-3	OLD TIMES, NEW TIMES (2-LP)	£18

(see also Washboard Sam, Ivory Joe Hunter, Otis Spann)

MEN
79	Virgin VS 269	I Don't Depend On You/Cruel (p/s)	£25
79	Virgin VS 269-12	I Don't Depend On You/Cruel (12", p/s)	£30

(see also Human League, Heaven 17)

MENACE

77	Illegal IL 004	Screwed Up/Insane Society (p/s)	£15
77	Illegal IL 004	Screwed Up/Insane Society (12", p/s)	£20
77	Small Wonder SMALL 5	G.L.C./I'm Civilized (p/s)	£20
78	Illegal IL 008	I Need Nothing/Electrocutioner (p/s)	£15
82	Fresh FRESH 14	The Young Ones/Tomorrow's World/Live For Today (p/s)	£15
86	Razor RAZ 18	GLC - RIP (LP)	£25

(see also Aces, Vermilion & Aces)

MENACE

01	Plastica DPFT 004	Reap What You Sow (12")	£15

MENACE MAKES 3

92	Danse City DC 1203	Pure Hysteria (Give Me A Mother Mix)/Do You Feel What I'm Feeling? (Matrix Rise Remix)(12")	£50

MENDES PREY

83	MP AM 076	On To The Borderline/Runnin' For You (p/s)	£20
86	Wag WAG 2	Wonderland/Can You Believe It (p/s)	£25
86	Wag 12 WAG 2	Wonderland/Can You Believe It (12", p/s)	£25

E.T. MENSAH & HIS TEMPO'S BAND

58	Decca WAL 1001	A SATURDAY NIGHT (10" LP)	£20
58	Decca WAL 1002	MORE MENSAH (10" LP)	£20
59	Decca WAPS 27	MENSAH's AFRICAN RHYTHMS (LP)	£35

MENTAL

79	Kamikaze Pig RAM 1	God For A Day/18/Kill The Bill/Off The Rails (600 only, p/s)	£80

MENTAL CUBE

90	Debut DEBTX 3104	Chile Of The Bass Generation/Q/Drop Module (12", p/s)	£15

MIKE MERCADO

67	Parlophone 5589	Hey Mister Monk It's Page Nine/Popcorn	£15

MARY MAE MERCER

65	Decca DFE 8599	MARY MAE MERCER (EP)	£50

MICKEY MERCIAN

84	Unity Sound UN 029	Ride The Rhythm/Go Anywhere (12")	£25

FREDDIE MERCURY

84	CBS WA 4735	Love Kills/GEORGIO MORODER: Rotwang's Party (picture disc)	£30
85	CBS DA 6019	I Was Born To Love You/Stop All The Fighting//Love Kills (Extended)/Stop All The Fighting (Extended) (double pack)	£15
85	CBS WA 6413	Made In Heaven (Remix)/She Blows Hot And Cold (shaped picture disc)	£30
85	CBS WA 6413	Made In Heaven (Remix)/She Blows Hot And Cold (uncut shaped picture disc)	£500
85	CBS A 6725	Love Me Like There's No Tomorrow/Let's Turn It On (p/s)	£30
85	CBS TA 6725	Love Me Like There's No Tomorrow (Extended Version)/Let's Turn It On (Extended Version) (12", p/s)	£25
85	CBS DTA 6725	Love Me Like There's No Tomorrow (Extended Version)/Let's Turn It On (Extended Version)//Living On My Own (Extended 6.38)/My Love Is Dangerous (Extended 6.25) (12" double pack, shrinkwrapped with sticker)	£50
85	CBS TA 6725	Love Me Like There's No Tomorrow (Extended Version)/Let's Turn It On (Extended Version) (12", promo, white card sleeve, with sticker)	£50
87	Parlophone RP 6151	The Great Pretender/Exercises In Free Love (Mercury Vocal) (shaped picture disc)	£30
87	Parlophone RP 6151	The Great Pretender/Exercises In Free Love (Mercury Vocal) (shaped picture disc, with unfolded or folded plinth)	£60
87	Parlophone RP 6151	The Great Pretender/Exercises In Free Love (Mercury Vocal) (shaped picture disc, with unfolded or folded plinth)	£40
87	Parlophone RP 6151	The Great Pretender/Exercises In Free Love (Mercury Vocal) (uncut shaped picture disc)	£350
87	Parlophone 10R 6151	The Great Pretender (Extended Version)/(7" Version)/Exercises In Free Love (7" Version) (10", 1-sided, printed white label, plain black die-cut sleeve, promo only)	£25
87	Polydor POSPP 887	Barcelona (7" Version)/Exercises In Free Love (Caballé Vocal) (7" Version)/ Barcelona (Extended Version) (12", picture disc)	£30
87	Polydor POCD 887	Barcelona/Exercises In Free Love (Version 2) (Caballé Vocal)/ Barcelona (Extended) (CD, autographed card p/s, promo only)	£300
87	Polydor PO 23 DJ	The Golden Boy (with Montserrat Caballé) (radio edit) (1-sided DJ sampler, p/s, with sticker)	£100
88	Polydor POSPX 23	The Golden Boy/The Fallen Priest/The Golden Boy (Instrumental) (12", p/s)	£20
88	Polydor PZCD234	The Golden Boy/The Fallen Priest/The Golden Boy (Instrumental) (CD)	£15
88	Polydor PO 29	How Can I Go On/Overture Piccante (with Montserrat Caballe) (p/s)	£15
88	Polydor POSX 29	How Can I Go On/Overture Piccante (with Montserrat Caballe) (picture disc)	£45
89	Polydor PZ 29	How Can I Go On/Guide Me Home/Overture Piccante (12", p/s)	£25
89	Polydor PZCD 29	How Can I Go On/Guide Me Home/Overture Piccante (CD, picture disc)	£35
88	Polydor CD 3 125 211	The Golden Boy/La Japanese/Barcelona (CD promo, unreleased p/s, jewel case)	£100
89	Polydor 0805 548-2	Ensueno/Barcelona (Edit 4.24)/Exercises In Free Love/Barcelona (Extended Version 7.02)/Barcelona (Video) (CD Video)	£40
89	Polydor 0805 580-2	The Fallen Priest/The Golden Boy (Album Version)/The Golden Boy (Instrumental Version)/The Golden Boy (Video) (CD Video)	£40
06	Parlophone KILLS 001	Love Kills (Glimmer Mix)/(Pixel 82 Mix)/I Was Born To Love You (George Demure Mix) (12" promo)	£15
06	Parlophone KILLS 003	Living On My Own (mixes) (12" promo)	£15
92	Parlophone 077778099918	THE FREDDIE MERCURY ALBUM (LP)	£50
94	Parlophone 7234 8 2814 10	FREDDIE MERCURY REMIXES (LP, unreleased)	£150
97	EMI LPCENT 10	THE FREDDIE MERCURY ALBUM (LP, reissue, EMI Centenary, stickered sleeve)	£40
00	Parlophone FMRARE001	THE SOLO COLLECTION (10 CD & 2 DVD box set)	£80

(see also Queen, Larry Lurex, Billy Squier)

MERCURY REV
91	Mint Film MINT 5	Car Wash Hair/Coney Island Cyclone (4 track demo) (200 copies only, p/s)	£15
91	Mint Film MINTLP 4	YERSELF IS STEAM (LP, blue or pink vinyl)	£30
92	Beggars Banquet BBQLP 125	YERSELF IS STEAM (LP, reissue with bonus LP 'Lego My Ego')	£40
92	Beggars Banquet BBQLP 135	LEGO MY EGO (LP)	£20
93	Beggars Banquet BBQLP 140	BOCES (LP, clear red vinyl)	£40
93	Beggars Banquet BBQLP 140	BOCES (LP)	£30
95	Beggars Banquet BBQLP 176	SEE YOU ON THE OTHER SIDE (LP)	£50
95	Beggars Banquet BBQLP176P	SEE YOU ON THE OTHER SIDE (LP, picture disc)	£30
98	V2 VVR 1002771	DESERTERS SONGS (LP)	£50
01	V2 175218	ALL IS DREAM (LP)	£40
05	Virgin VVR1029231	THE SECRET MIGRATION (LP)	£30
08	V2 VVR1051271	SNOWFLAKE MIDNIGHT (2-LP)	£18

(see also Harmony Rockets)

MERCY
69	London HLZ 10273	Love (Can Make You Happy)/Fireball	£20

MERCYFUL FATE
83	Music For Nations MFN 10	MELISSA (LP, inner)	£15
84	Music For Nations MFN 28	DON'T BREAK THE OATH (LP, inner)	£15

MIKEY MERICAN
85	Hands & Hearts HHDD 007	Family Affair/Family Dub (12")	£20
86	Unity UN 024	Control The Dance/Version/Automatic/Version (12")	£20
86	Unity UN 029	Ride The Rhythm/Version/Go Anywhere/Version (12")	£20
86	Regal RG 001	Rub A Dub Party/Money Lover (12", as Mikey Merica)	£15

TRUMAN MERIT
93	Spurt 3	ALIEN BOOGIE (LP and free 7")	£18

MERLIN Q
69	Pye 7N 17828	The Secret/Love's Beautiful	£25

RAY MERRELL
70	Jay Boy BOY 22	Tears Of Joy/Searchin' (withdrawn) (Beware of bootlegs!)	£200
70	Jay Boy BOY 22	Tears Of Joy/Searchin' (withdrawn) (Beware of bootlegs!) (DJ copy)	£350

BOB MERRILL
58	Columbia DB 4086	Nairobi/Jump When I Say Frog	£15

HELEN MERRILL
58	Mercury MMB 12000	THE NEARNESS OF YOU (LP, features Bill Evans)	£40

MERRITTS
70	Hot Rod HR 113	I Don't Want To (Part 1)/HOT ROD ALL STARS: Version	£30

MERRY MAKER
76	Western Kingston WK 505	Untouchable Special/Straight To Music City Head	£20

MERRYMEN
66	Doctor Bird DB 1004	Big Bamboo/Island Woman	£15
68	Island ILP 984	CARIBBEAN TREASURE CHEST (LP)	£30

(see also Soul Brothers)

MERSEYBEATS
64	Fontana TE 17422	ON STAGE (EP)	£25
64	Fontana TE 17423	I THINK OF YOU (EP)	£30
64	Fontana TE 17432	THE MERSEYBEATS (EP)	£30
64	Fontana TL 5210	THE MERSEYBEATS (LP)	£60
69	Wing WL 1163	THE MERSEYBEATS (LP)	£15

(see also Merseys, Rockin' Horse, Tony Crane, Kirkbys, Quotations, Johnny Gustavson)

MERSEYBOYS
64	Ace Of Clubs ACL 1169	15 GREAT SONGS BY JOHN, PAUL AND GEORGE (LP)	£20

MERSEYS
66	Fontana TF 732	So Sad About Us/Love Will Continue	£15
67	Fontana TF 845	The Cat/Change Of Heart	£25
68	Fontana TF 955	Lovely Loretta/Dreaming	£15

(see also Merseybeats, Crackers)

WIM MERTENS
87	Factory FACT 190c	EDUCES ME (cassette, in bespoke box with insert)	£200

MERTON PARKAS
79	Beggars Banquet BEGA 11	FACE IN THE CROWD (LP)	£18

(see also Style Council)

MESCALINE UNITED
92	R&S RS 92019	We Have Arrived (Aphex Twin QQT Reconstruction Mix)/We Have Arrived (Aphex Twin TTQ Reconstruction Mix) (limited issue 12", also known as "PCP Remixed" plain paper sleeve)	£70

MESSAGE (1)
70	Doctor Bird DB 1503	Rum-Bum-A-Loo/Drummer Boy	£125
72	Reggae REG 3004	Wrestling/Tricia	£60

(see also Boris Gardner)

MESSAGE (2)
75	Decca SKL-R 5213	MESSAGE (LP, blue/silver label)	£25

MESSAGE (3)
81	Is It Original...? ISIT1	Empty Promise/War Of The Music	£100

RICKY MESSENGER & SEMI PROFESSIONALS
80s	Kim 019	Now Is The Time For Jah/Mr. Richman (12")	£20

MESSENGERS (JAMAICA)
73	Attack ATT 8057	Crowded City/Thula Thula	£25
73	Mirto MIR 100	Is It Because I'm Black/Just Like A Shelter (actually by Ken Boothe and Lloyd Charmers)	£18

MESSENGERS OF THE CROSS
69	Emblem JDR 21	MESSENGERS OF THE CROSS (LP)	£20

METABOLIST
79	Drömm DRO 1	Drömm/Slaves/Eulam's Beat (p/s, rough screen-printed & folded p/s)	£20
80	Drömm DRO 3	Identity/Tizhoznam (p/s)	£15
79	Drömm NCN	GOATMANAUT (cassette)	£50
80	Drömm DRO 2	HANSTEN KLORK (LP)	£20
81	Cassetteking CK2	STAGMANAUT! (cassette)	£50

METAL HEADS
92	Synthetic SYNTH 003	TERMINATOR (12", p/s)	£20

METALLICA
16	Blackened 00602557156416	HARDWIRED . . . TO SELF DESTRUCT (2LP, gatefold, printed inners, download card)	£25

SINGLES
84	Music For Nations 12 KUT 105	Jump In The Fire/Seek And Destroy (live)/Phantom Lord (live) (12", p/s, initial pressing with beige labels)	£25
84	Music For Nations 12 KUT 105	Jump In The Fire/Seek And Destroy (live)/Phantom Lord (live) (12", p/s, later pressing with red/yellow labels)	£20
84	Music For Nations CV12 KUT 105	Jump In The Fire/Seek And Destroy (live)/Phantom Lord (live) (12", red vinyl, p/s)	£25
84	Music For Nations 12 KUT 112	Creeping Death/Am I Evil?/Blitzkrieg (12", p/s, initial pressing with beige label)	£20
84	Music For Nations 12 KUT 112	Creeping Death/Am I Evil?/Blitzkrieg (12", p/s, later pressing with red/yellow labels)	£18
84	Music For Nations CV12 KUT 112	Creeping Death/Am I Evil?/Blitzkrieg (12", p/s, blue vinyl, red/yellow or 'Special Anniversary Edition' labels)	£35
84	Music For Nations GV12 KUT 112	Creeping Death/Am I Evil?/Blitzkrieg (12", no p/s, 'Anniversary Gold Edition', gold vinyl, 3000 only; mispressing with 1 side gold, 1 side black vinyl)	£80
84	Music For Nations GV12 KUT 112	Creeping Death/Am I Evil?/Blitzkrieg (12", no p/s, 'Anniversary Gold Edition', gold vinyl, 3000 only)	£70
84	Music For Nations P12 KUT 112	Creeping Death/Am I Evil?/Blitzkrieg (12", picture disc, initially without barcode)	£30
84	Music For Nations CD12 KUT 112	Creeping Death/Am I Evil?/Blitzkrieg Jump In The Fire/ Seek And Destroy (live)/Phantom Lord (live) (CD)	£60
86	Music For Nations 12 KUT 105XP	Jump In The Fire/Seek And Destroy (live)/Phantom Lord (live) (12", repressing, stickered sleeve with sew-on patch)	£80
86	Music For Nations PKUT 105	Jump In The Fire/Phantom Lord (live) (shaped picture disc, initial pressing without barcode)	£25
86	Music For Nations PKUT 105	Jump In The Fire/Phantom Lord (live) (shaped picture disc, later pressing with barcode)	£20
86	Music For Nations PKUT 105	Jump In The Fire/Phantom Lord (live) (uncut picture disc)	£150
87	Vertigo METAL 112	$5.98 EP - GARAGE DAYS RE-REVISITED: Helpless/Crash Course In Brain Surgery/The Small Hours/Last Caress - Green Hell (medley) (12" p/s, later copies add "The Wait")	£35
88	Vertigo METAL 212	Harvester Of Sorrow/Breadfan/The Prince (12", p/s, some with 'skull' label)	£18
89	Vertigo 842-219-2	Creeping Death/Am I Evil?/Blitzkrieg/Jump In The Fire/Seek And Destroy (live)/Phantom Lord (live) (CD)	£50
89	Vertigo METAP 5	One/Seek And Destroy (live) (card p/s, some stickered, with rolled poster)	£15
89	Vertigo METPD 510	One/Seek And Destroy (live) (10", picture disc with card)	£30
89	Vertigo METG 512	One (Demo Version)/For Whom The Bell Tolls (live)/Welcome Home (Sanitarium) (live) (12", gatefold p/s, with booklet, mispressed with B-side label on both sides)	£20
90	Vertigo 875 487 1	THE GOOD, THE BAD AND THE LIVE - THE 61/2 YEARS ANNIVERSARY COLLECTION (6 x 12", with live 4-track EP [METAL 612])	£80
91	Vertigo METAL 7	Enter Sandman/Stone Cold Crazy (picture disc in p/s, stickered)	£15
91	Vertigo METBX 712	Enter Sandman/Stone Cold Crazy/Enter Sandman (Demo) (12", box with 4 photo prints)	£30
91	Vertigo METCD 7	Enter Sandman/Stone Cold Crazy/Enter Sandman (Demo) (CD, picture disc in box with room for 3 more CDs)	£30
93	Vertigo METAL 1112	Sad But True/Nothing Else Matters (Elevator Version)/Creeping Death (live)/Sad But True (Demo) (12" picture disc with insert)	£20
97	Vertigo METJB 15	The Memory Remains/For Whom The Bell Tolls (Haven't Heard It Yet Remix) (Jukebox issue no p/s)	£18
03	Columbia GABBA 1	53rd & 3rd/Outsider (by GREEN DAY)/I Wanna Be Sedated (by OFFSPRING) (blue vinyl, stickered p/s withdrawn single)	£400
90s	Vertigo METJB 19	Whiskey In The Jar/Turn The Page (Jukebox issue no p/s)	£20
10	Vertigo 00602527391100	Frantic (UNKLE Remix)/BLACK SABBATH: Paranoid (Alternative Vocal Version (12", 1000 only)	£20

ALBUMS
83	Music For Nations MFN 7	KILL 'EM ALL (LP, 1st issue with beige labels)	£50
83	Music For Nations MFN 7	KILL 'EM ALL (LP, later pressing with red/yellow labels)	£30
84	M. For Nations MFNCD 7	KILL 'EM ALL (CD)	£30
84	Music For Nations MFN 27	RIDE THE LIGHTNING (LP, with inner sleeve, initial pressing with beige labels & without barcode)	£50
86	Music For Nations MFN 60	MASTER OF PUPPETS (LP, with inner sleeve & insert)	£40
86	Music For Nations MFN 60	MASTER OF PUPPETS (LP, mispressing, Side 1 label on both sides)	£30
86	Music For Nations MFN 60P	MASTER OF PUPPETS (LP, picture disc, initially without barcode)	£25

MINT VALUE £

86	Music For Nations MFN 60P	MASTER OF PUPPETS (LP, picture disc, with barcode)	£25
86	M. For Nations MFNCD 60	MASTER OF PUPPETS (CD)	£30
86	Music For Nations MFN 27P	RIDE THE LIGHTNING (LP, picture disc, initial pressing with no barcode)....................	£30
86	Music For Nations MFN 27P	RIDE THE LIGHTNING (LP, picture disc, with barcode)..	£20
86	Music For Nations MFN 7P	KILL 'EM ALL (LP reissue, picture disc, lacking picture on 1 side, initially lacking barcode)..	£25
86	Music For Nations MFN 7P	KILL 'EM ALL (LP reissue, picture disc, with picture on 1 side and barcode)	£22
87	Music For Nations MFN 7DM	KILL 'EM ALL (2-LP, 'direct metal mastered' reissue, gatefold sleeve).......................	£35
87	Music For Nations MFN 60DM	MASTER OF PUPPETS (2-LP, 'direct metal mastered' reissue, gatefold sleeve with poster)...	£30
87	Music For Nations MFN 27DM	RIDE THE LIGHTNING (2-LP, 'direct metal mastered' reissue, gatefold sleeve with insert)..	£30
88	Vertigo VERH 61	...AND JUSTICE FOR ALL (2-LP)	£40
89	Vertigo 838-140-1	RIDE THE LIGHTNING (LP, reissue, mispressing, Side 1 lists Master Of Puppets tracks).....	£20
91	Vertigo 510 022-1	METALLICA (2-LP)...	£70
91	Vertigo MECAN 1/510-022-0	THE METALLICAN (CD, gold disc in metal 'paint can' with video & T-shirt; 35,000 only)..£100
93	Vertigo 518-725-0	LIVE SHIT, BINGE & PURGE (3-CD box set with 3 videos & 72-page book)......................	£80
96	Ekektra 532618	LOAD (2-LP, gatefold)..	£80
97	Elektra 536409	RELOAD (2-LP, gatefold, stickered sleeve with inners)...	£50
98	Vertigo 538 351-1	GARAGE INC. (3-LP, gatefold, inners)	£80
08	Vertigo 00602517737310	DEATH MAGNETIC (Box set, 5x12")	£40
08	Vertigo 00602517800502	DEATH MAGNETIC (LP, coffin-shaped box set, CD, DVD, T-shirt, guitar picks, flag, poster and credit card)...	£75
08	Universal 0600753085201	KILL 'EM ALL (2-LP, reissue, gatefold with obi)..	£20
08	Universal 0600753085240	RIDE THE LIGHTNING (2LP, reissue, gatefold, obi)...	£50
08	Universal 0600753101162	MASTER OF PUPPETS (2LP, reissue, gatefold with obi)..	£50
16	Blackened 00602557156379	HARDWIRED . . . TO SELF DESTRUCT (2LP, gatefold, printed inners, red vinyl, download card, RSD)..	£30
16	Blackened 00602557156454	HARDWIRED . . . TO SELF-DESTRUCT (3LP/CD box set, blue/yellow/red vinyl, lithograph, badges)	£50

PROMOS

88	Vertigo METDJ 2	Harvester Of Sorrow/Harvester Of Sorrow (unique p/s).....................................	£60
88	Vertigo MET CD 100	THE WHIPLASH SAMPLER (CD)..	£70
89	Vertigo METDJ 5	One/One (Edit) (unique blue cover, plus insert)..	£100
89	Vertigo METDJ 512	One (Demo Version)/For Whom The Bell Tolls (live)/Welcome Home (Sanitarium) (live) (12", unissued, promo-only p/s)..	£70
91	Vertigo METDJ 7	Enter Sandman (Radio Edit)/Stone Cold Crazy (p/s B-side actually silent)	£15
91	Vertigo METDJ8	The Unforgiven (edit)/Killing Time (p/s)...	£25
96	Mercury MM CJ-1	MANDATORY METALLICA (CD, 7-track sampler)	£30
96	Vertigo MET INT 1	LOAD - THE INTERVIEW (CD, with cue booklet)	£50
97	Vertigo MMCJ-2	MANDATORY METALLICA 2 (2-CD, 17-track sampler)	£35
03	Vertigo FRANTICDJ 1	Frantic (12" promo)	£15

METAL MIRROR

80	M&M MM 001	Rock 'N Roll Ain't Never Gonna Leave Us/English Booze (in p/s).........................	£80
80	M&M MM 001	Rock 'N Roll Ain't Never Gonna Leave Us/English Booze	£50

METAL URBAIN

77	Rough Trade RT 001	Paris Maquis/Cle De Contact (p/s)	£18

METEORS (3)

81	Ace SWT 65	METEOR MADNESS (10" EP, white label test pressings only, custom p/s)......................	£250
81	Ace SW 65	METEOR MADNESS (EP, on blue vinyl)..	£25
81	Ace SW 65	METEOR MADNESS (EP)...	£15
86	Anagram 12ANA 31	Surf City (Has Beens From Outer Space Mix)/The Edge/Johnny's Here (12", p/s)............	£15
81	Ace MAD 1	THE METEORS MEET SCREAMIN' LORD SUTCH (mini-LP, 1 side each, 1,000 only, stickered cartoon print on plain card sleeve)...	£100
81	Lost Soul LOSTLP 3001	IN HEAVEN (LP)..	£20
86	Big Beat WIKA 47	TEENAGERS FROM OUTER SPACE (LP)	£18
86	Anagram GRAM 27	SEWERTIME BLUES (LP)	£15
88	Anagram GRAM 37	MUTANT MONKEY AND AND THE SURFERS FROM ZORCH (LP)...............................	£20

(see also Clapham South Escalators, [Screamin'] Lord Sutch)

METERS

74	Island IDJ 3	Ride Your Pony/Look-Ka-Py-Py (DJ album sampler)..	£25
72	Reprise K 44242	CABBAGE ALLEY (LP)...	£20
74	Reprise K 54027	REJUVENATION (LP)..	£20
74	Island ILPS 9250	CISSY STRUT (LP)...	£30
75	Reprise K 54044	FIRE ON THE BAYOU (LP)	£15
76	Reprise K 54076	BEST OF THE METERS (LP)	£15
76	Reprise K 54078	TRICK BAG (LP)	£18

METGUMBNERBONE

83	Aeon (No Cat. No.)	COPS OF MATTER (cassette)	£40
83	Amission REV 13:15	LIGELIAHORN (LP, 500 only, with insert)...	£100
84	Private cassette	FOR THE RAVEN (cassette)..	£40

METHOD MAN

94	Def Jam 523 839-1	TICAL (LP)	£25

(see also Wu Tang Clan)

METHODS

70	DJM DJS 225	Chasing The Sun/And That Is Life	£15

METRO
84   CSA SPCSA 12008   The Girl Is Mine (with Yellowman)/AL CAMPBELL: Bad Boy (12") £25
METRO TRINITY
87   Cafeteria CAFF 1   DIE YOUNG EP (12")...£60
METRO AREA
02   Source SOURLP 070   METRO AREA (LP as 2 x 12")...£25
METRO GLIDER
80   Racket RKT 1   Do It Right/Consequences £20
METROPHASE
79   Neo London MS 02   New Age/Frames Of Life (foldout p/s, stamped white labels) £25
(see also Swell Maps)
METROPOLIS
82   Gargoyle GRGL 4   See No Reason/Russian Romance (no p/s)...£20
METROTONE
98   Earworm WORM 21   THE LESS YOU HAVE THE MORE YOU ARE (LP, test pressings only) £25
PAUL METSERS
81   Highway SHY 7014   CAUTION TO THE WIND (LP) £18
MEXICANO
77   Pioneer PIOLP !   MOVE UP STARSKY (LP) £15
MEXICO RED
88   Hummingbird   Eternal Flame/Follow Me To Heaven (p/s, insert) £80
ANTHONY MEYNELL
82   Hi-Lo LO 01   HITS FROM 3000 YEARS AGO (LP, purple sleeve) £15
(see also Squire)
LEE MEZA
67   Stateside SS 589   If It Happens/One Good Thing Leads To Another...£30
M-G-M STUDIO ORCHESTRA
55   MGM SP 1144   Rock Around The Clock/"Blackboard Jungle" Love Theme £25
MIAMI
75   Jay Boy JSL 5   THE PARTY FREAKS (LP) £15
76   Jay Boy JSL 11   NOTORIOUS MIAMI (LP)..£15
GEORGE MICHAEL
87   Epic EPC 460000 1   FAITH (LP, inner & insert) £20
90   Epic 467295 1   LISTEN WITHOUT PREJUDICE (LP) £20
96   Virgin V2802   OLDER (LP) £500
14   Aegean/Virgin 379244-6   SYMPHONICA (2-LP) £500
(see also Wham!, High, Elton John, Queen)
RAS MICHAEL & THE SONS OF NEGUS
75   Grounation GRD 2037   None A Jah Children/Glory Dawn £25
74   Trojan TRLS 118   NYAHBINGHI (LP) £20
75   Trojan TRSL 113   DADAWAH (PEACE & LOVE) (LP, credited to DADAWAH)..£45
75   Vulcan VUL 005   RASTAFARI (LP) £25
75   Grounation GROL 505   RASTAFARI (LP) £25
76   Trojan TRLS 203   TRIBUTE TO THE EMPEROR RASTAFORI (LP, with Jazzbo Abubaka) £20
76   Dynamic DYLP 3004   FREEDOM SOUNDS (LP, as The Sons Of Negus)...£20
91   Greensleeves GREL 158   KIBIR AM LAKE (LP)...£18
MICHAEL SCHENKER GROUP
82   Chysalis PCHR 1393   ASSAULT ATTACK (LP, picture disc)..£18
83   Chysalis CHRP 1441   BUILT TO DESTROY (LP, picture disc, U.S. remixes) £18
(see also McAuley Schenker Group, Scorpions, UFO, Cozy Powell, Graham Bonnet, Alex Harvey Band)
MICHAEL'S TOY
85   Dog Rock SD 105   Excuses/I'll Take All Of Your Time (p/s, with The Nepalese Temple Twists).....................£15
MICHIGAN RAG
72   Blue Horizon 2096 009   Don't Run Away/She's Looking Good £20
MICHIGANS
63   Vogue V 9207   Intermission Riff/Tea For Two £15
MICKEY & LUDELLA
95   Vinyl Japan ASKLP 52   BEDLAM A GO GO (LP) £30
(see also Milkshakes, Billy Childish, Del Monas, Thee Headcoatees)
MICKEY (BAKER) & KITTY (NOBLE)
60   London HLE 9054   Buttercup/My Reverie £35
MICKEY (BAKER) & SYLVIA
57   HMV POP 331   Love Is Strange/I'm Going Home £100
57   HMV POP 331   Love Is Strange/I'm Going Home (78) £30
58   RCA RCA 1064   Rock And Stroll Room/Bewildered £50
58   RCA RCA 1064   Rock And Stroll Room/Bewildered (78) £30
60   RCA RCA 1206   Sweeter As The Day Goes By/Mommy Out De Light...£15
65   RCA Victor RCA 1487   Love Is Strange/Dearest £15
65   RCA Camden CDN 5133   LOVE IS STRANGE (LP) £200
(see also Mickey Baker, Sylvia [Robbins])
MICKEY FINN (1)
64   Blue Beat BB 203   Tom Hark/Please Love Me (as 'Mickey Finn & the Blue Men') £25

64	Oriole CB 1927	Pills/Hush Your Mouth (as 'Mickey Finn & the Blue Men')	£80
64	Oriole CB 1940	Reelin' & A'Rockin'/I Still Want You (as 'Mickey Finn')	£50
65	Columbia DB 7510	The Sporting Life/Night Comes Down (as 'The Mickey Finn')	£100
66	Polydor 56719	I Do Love You/If I Had You Baby (as 'The Mickey Finn')	£100
67	Direction 58-3086	Garden Of My Mind/Time To Start Loving You (as 'The Mickey Finn')	£200

MICKEY FINN (2)

93	Dee Jay DJX 011	D Pressed/Reality (12")	£15

MICRODISNEY

88	Virgin V2505	39 MINUTES (LP)	£18
84	Rough Trade ROUGH 75	EVERYBODY IS FANTASTIC (LP)	£15
84	Rough Trade RTM 155	WE HATE YOU SOUTH AFRICAN BASTARDS (LP)	£20
85	Rough Trade ROUGH 85	THE CLOCK COMES DOWN THE STAIRS (LP)	£15

MICRON

88	White SG045	Eastenders Rap (12")	£15

(see Rebel MC)

STEPHAN MICUS

76	Caroline C 1517	ARCHAIC CONCERTS (LP)	£25

MIDAS MOULD

72	Columbia DB 8868	Information Emily/Love Sweet Love	£15

MIDAS (1)

70	Solar SL003	I've Seen A New Life/Visit The Sun	£40

MIDAS (2)

83	Small Run SRR 0008	Can't Stop Loving You/Power In The Sky (p/s with insert)	£200

MIDDLE OF THE ROAD

72	RCA SF 8305	THE BEST OF (LP)	£15

MAX MIDDLETON & ROBERT AWWAI

79	Harvest SHSP 4103	ANOTHER SLEEPER (LP)	£18

TONY MIDDLETON

65	London HLR 9983	My Little Red Book (as Burt Bacharach Orchestra with Tony Middleton)/BURT BACHARACH ORCHESTRA: What's New Pussycat	£30
66	Polydor BM 56704	To The Ends Of The Earth/Don't Ever Leave Me	£450
66	Polydor BM 56704	To The Ends Of The Earth/Don't Ever Leave Me (DJ copy)	£500

(see also Willows, Burt Bacharach)

MIDI RAIN

94	Vinyl Solution STEAM 56	ONE (2-LP)	£30

(see also John Rocca, Freeez, Pink Rhythm, Gamer 3)

MIDLAKE

10	Is It Balearic? IIBR 002	Roscoe (Beyond The Wizard Sleeve Re:animation) (12", B-side contains 5 silent tracks)	£15
08	Bella Union BELLAV 117	THE TRIALS OF VAN OCCUPANTHER (LP)	£50
10	Bella Union BELLACD224SP	THE COURAGE OF OTHERS (2-LP)	£25
10	Bella Union CD02245P	THE COURAGE OF OTHERS (Box set, 2-LP, DVD, CD & 32 page booklet)	£50

(see also John Grant)

MIDNIGHT

78	Ariola ATTA 514DJ	Don't Bother To Knock/Keep Walking By (DJ Copy, p/s)	£80
78	Ariola ATTA 514	Don't Bother To Knock/Keep Walking By (p/s)	£75
79	Magnet MAG 148	Love's Gonna Hit You Like A Bullet/Minute To Midnight (as Midnite)	£20

THE MIDNIGHT

17	155694	ENDLESS SUMMER LP)	£40

MIDNIGHT SHIFT

66	Decca F 12487	Saturday Jump/Living Fast	£30

MIDNIGHT SUN

71	MCA MKPS 2019	MIDNIGHT SUN (LP, red/pink 'dogbone' label)	£60
72	MCA MKPS 2024	WALKING CIRCLES (LP, black/blue hexagon label)	£60

MIDNIGHTS

66	Ember EMB S 220	(Won'tcha) Show Me Around/Only Two Can Play	£18
63	MEP 101/MN 1/EAG-EP-134	MIDNIGHTS (EP, private pressing)	£130

M.I. FIVE

66	Parlophone R 5486	You'll Never Stop Me Loving You/Only Time Will Tell	£150

(see also Deep Purple)

MI5 (2)

95	Lucky Spin LSR 021	I Can't Understand/Experience (12")	£30

MIGHT OF COINCIDENCE

72	Entropia BM 0001	WHY COULDN'T PEOPLE WAIT (LP)	£100

MIGHTY ABIJANS

80	No 1 Rock	Untamed(vocal & DJ Cut)/Dubwise (12")	£35

MIGHTY AVENGERS (JAMAICA)

66	Rymska RA 101	Scatter Shot (actually by Byron Lee & Dragonaires)/BYRON LEE: Like You Do (B-side actually "No One" by Techniques)	£30

MIGHTY AVENGERS (U.K.)

64	Decca F 11891	Hide Your Pride/Hey Senorita	£18
64	Decca F 11962	So Much In Love/Sometime They Say	£25
65	Decca F 12085	Blue Turns To Grey/I'm Lost Without You	£25

65	Decca F 12198	(Walkin' Thru The) **Sleepy City/Sir Edward And Lady Jane**	£35

(see also Andrew Oldham)

MIGHTY BABY

71	Blue Horizon 2096 003	**Devil's Whisper/Virgin Spring**	£80
69	Head HDLS 6002	**MIGHTY BABY** (LP, gatefold sleeve, yellow label)	£400
71	Blue Horizon 2931 001	**A JUG OF LOVE** (LP, with lyric insert)	£650
71	Blue Horizon 2931 001	**A JUG OF LOVE** (LP)	£400
84	Psycho PSYCHO 31	**EGYPTIAN TOMB** (LP, reissue of "Mighty Baby" in different sleeve)	£30

(see also Action, Robin Scott, Habibiyya, Keith Christmas, Gary Farr, Stone's Masonry, Andy Roberts)

THEE MIGHTY CAESARS

86	Empire LWC 604	**Ten Bears Of The Comanches/Baby What's Wrong** (p/s)	£15
86	Media Burn MB 5	**Little By Little/The Swag/What You've Got/Cyclonic** (12", p/s)	£25
88	Swag SWG 001	**She's Just Fifteen Years Old/The Swag** (flexi in p/s with Pandora's Box fanzine)	£18
16	Empire L WC 604	**Ten Bears Of The Comanches/Baby What's Wrong?** (lathe cut 7", 20 copies only)	£30
85	Milkshakes NER - 0	**S.T.** (LP)	£40
86	Milkshakes APOLL - 0	**THEE CAESARS OF TRASH** (LP)	£20
86	Milkshakes PLAT - 0	**ACROPOLIS NOW** (LP)	£35
86	Big Beat WIK45	**BEWARE OF THE IDES OF MARCH** (LP)	£30
87	Hangman HANG 3 UP	**DON'T GIVE ANY DINNER TO HENRY CHINASKI** (LP)	£50
87	Hangmen HANG 7 UP	**PUNK ROCK SHOWCASE** (LP)	£60
88	Crypt LP 014	**ENGLISH PUNK ROCK EXPLOSION** (LP)	£15
87	Big Beat WIK 60	**LIVE IN ROME** (LP)	£20
87	Ambassador AMBAS 2	**WISE BLOOD** (LP, colour sleeve)	£30
89	Hangman HANG 26 UP	**WISE BLOOD** (LP, reissue, black and silver sleeve)	£20

(see also Milkshakes, Prisoners, Billy Childish, Thee Headcoats)

MIGHTY DIAMONDS

75	Black Wax WAX13	**I Need A Roof/Joe Joe Dub**	£15
77	JAMA JAMA 014	**Hey Girl/JUNIOR BYLES & I ROY: Fade Away** (12")	£20
80	Greensleeves GRED 45	**Gates Of Zion/SLY AND ROBBIE - Zion In Dub** (12", green vinyl)	£40
76	Virgin V 2052	**RIGHT TIME** (LP)	£20
77	Virgin V 2078	**ICE ON FIRE** (LP)	£15
79	Virgin Frontline FLD 6001	**DEEPER ROOTS** (LP, with bonus dub LP)	£25
80	Mobiliser SRE 31	**LEADER OF THE BLACK COUNTRY** (LP)	£20

(see also Diamonds)

MIGHTY 'EM

73	Decca FR 13446	**Jekyll And Hyde/What A Way To Go**	£35

MIGHTY ETHNICZ

88	Good Times EB20	**Freestyle/B Style** (12")	£30

MIGHTY FLEA & MICKEY BAKER

73	Polydor 2460 185	**LET THE GOOD TIMES ROLL** (LP)	£22

MIGHTY FLYERS

74	Myrrh MYR 1016	**LOW FLYING ANGELS** (LP, with insert)	£20

(see also Mick Abrahams)

MIGHTY HARD

70	Pye 7N 17878	**Save The Life Of My Child/House Of The Rising Sun**	£30

MIGHTY MAYTONES

78	GG's GG 029	**Searching In Disco** (with Trinity)**/Madness In Disco** (with U Brown) (12")	£20
76	Burning Sounds BS 1002	**MADNESS** (LP)	£25
78	Burning Sounds BS 1022	**BOAT TO ZION** (LP)	£25

(see also Maytones)

MIGHTY MEN

62	Salvo SLO 1804	**No Way Out/You Too Much** (99 copies only)	£30

MIGHTY MICRO

79	Warner Bros. K18134	**Replaced By A Micro Chip/Everything With Chips** (no p/s)	£20

MIGHTY MIGHTY

87	Sha La La Ba Ba Ba Ba 001	**Throwaway** (Throwaway Version)**/CLOUDS: Jenny Nowhere** (p/s, flexi, with Baby Honey Fanzine 1)	£20

MIGHTY SAM

66	Stateside SS 534	**Sweet Dreams/Good Humor Man**	£15
66	Stateside SS 544	**Fannie Mae/Badmouthin'**	£15
68	Stateside SS 2076	**When She Touches Me/Just Like Old Times**	£15
70	Soul City SC 115	**Papa True Love/I Need A Lot Of Lovin'**	£25
70	Soul City SCM 004	**MIGHTY SOUL** (LP)	£85

MIGHTY 7

84	EMI 12PUSH 1	**Push The Button** (To The Beat)**/Call Me** (12")	£100
84	EMI PUSH 1	**Push The Button** (To The Beat)**/Call Me**	£40

MIGHTY SPARROW

63	Island ILP 902	**THE SLAVE** (LP)	£30
66	RCA RD 7516	**SPARROW COME BACK** (LP)	£15
68	Melodisc MLPWI 12-146	**CALYPSO CARNIVAL** (LP)	£25
68	Melodisc MLPWI 12-148	**MR WALKER** (LP)	£30
72	Trojan TRL49	**HOTTER THAN EVER** (LP)	£15

(see also King)

MIGHTY VIKINGS
67	Island WI 3060	Do Re Mi/The Sound Of Music	£35
67	Island WI 3074	Rockitty Fockitty/Give Me Back My Gal (both actually with Sammy Ismay)	£35

MIGHTY RYEDERS
18	Dynamite Cuts DYNAM7004/7005	Evil Vibrations/The Mighty Ryeders/Lovely/Everybody Groove (reissue, 2 x 7', p/s)	£20

MIGIL FIVE
67	Columbia DB 8196	Together/Superstition	£20
64	Pye NEP 24191	MEET THE MIGIL FIVE (EP)	£15
64	Pye NPL 18093	MOCKING BIRD HILL (LP)	£30

(see also Mike Felix)

MIKE & MODIFIERS
62	Oriole CB 1775	I Found Myself A Brand New Baby/It's Too Bad	£800

MIKE STUART SPAN
66	Columbia DB 8066	Come On Over To Our Place/Still Nights	£100
67	Columbia DB 8206	Dear/Invitation	£80
68	Jewel JL 01	Children Of Tomorrow/Concerto Of Thoughts	£500
68	Fontana TF 959	You Can Understand Me/Baubles And Bangles	£25
93	117 CPAT 1171	EXPANSIONS: Second Production/Rescue Me/Remember The Times/World In My Head (EP)	£15
95	Tenth Planet TP 014	TIMESPAN (LP, gatefold sleeve, numbered, 1,000 copies only)	£25

(see also Leviathan, High Defenders, Tony's Defenders, High Broom)

MIKE & RICH
96	Rephlex CAT 027LP	EXPERT KNOB TWIDDLERS (2-LP)	£40

(see also Aphex Twin, Caustic Window, Polygon Window, Q-Chastic, Kosmic Kommando, Tuss, U-Ziq)

MIKEY B
95	Vision VSN 004	So Wrong/So Much Love (12")	£30

AMOS MILBURN
57	Vogue V 9064	Every Day Of The Week/Girl Of My Dreams (triangular centre)	£150
57	Vogue V 9064	Every Day Of The Week/Girl Of My Dreams (round centre)	£40
57	Vogue V 9064	Every Day Of The Week/Girl Of My Dreams (78)	£15
57	Vogue V 9069	Rum And Coca Cola/Soft Pillow (triangular centre)	£150
57	Vogue V 9069	Rum And Coca Cola/Soft Pillow (triangular centre) (78)	£85
57	Vogue V 9080	Thinking Of You Baby/If I Could Be With You (One Hour Tonight) (triangular centre)	£150
57	Vogue V 9080	Thinking Of You Baby/If I Could Be With You (One Hour Tonight) (78)	£35
60	Vogue V 9163	One Scotch, One Bourbon, One Beer/Bad, Bad Whiskey	£100
57	Vogue VE 1-70102	ROCK AND ROLL (EP)	£250

AMOS MILBURN JNR
63	London HLU 9795	Gloria/Look At Me Fool	£20

MILDRED AND THE MICE
09	Third Man TMR 003	I Like My Mice (Dead)/Spider Bite (100 only, luminous vinyl)	£40

PERCY MILEM
66	Stateside SS 566	Crying Baby, Baby, Baby/Call On Me	£100
66	Stateside SS 566	Crying Baby, Baby, Baby/Call On Me (DJ copy)	£150

BUDDY MILES (EXPRESS)
69	Mercury 20137 SMCL	EXPRESSWAY TO YOUR SKULL (LP)	£20
69	Mercury 20163 SMCL	ELECTRIC CHURCH (LP)	£20
70	Mercury 6338 016	THEM CHANGES (LP)	£15
71	Mercury 6338 028	WE GOT TO LIVE TOGETHER (LP)	£15

(see also Electric Flag, Jimi Hendrix, Carlos Santana & Buddy Miles)

DICK & SUE MILES
79	Sweet Folk & Country SFA 106	THE DUNMOW FLITCH (LP)	£18

GARRY MILES
60	London REG 1264	LOOK FOR A STAR (EP)	£25

JOHN MILES
70	Orange OAS 508	Why Don't You Love Me?/If I Could See Through	£20
73	Orange OAS 213	One Minute Every Hour/Hollywood Queen (DJ Copy)	£60
73	Orange OAS 213	One Minute Every Hour/Hollywood Queen	£20

(see also Influence)

LENNY MILES
61	Top Rank JAR 546	Don't Believe Him Donna/Invisible	£30

LIZZIE MILES
56	HMV 7EG 8178	THE BLUES THEY SANG (EP, 1 side by Billy Young, both with Jelly Roll Morton)	£20

ROBERT MILES
96	Deconstruction 74321429741	DREAMLAND (2-LP, stickered sleeve)	£75
97	S:alt SALTLP 001	ORGANIC (2-LP)	£18

MILITAIRES
66	Airborne 0009	I Need You/Maybe	£15

MILITANT BARRY
77	Conflict COND 2000	Idi Amin Disco/Blood Up/Free Black People (12", die-cut p/s)	£15
78	Conflict COND 2003	Ambition/Can't Stop Me (12")	£15
79	Vista Sounds STLP 1012	GREEN VALLEY (LP)	£30

MINT VALUE £

(see also Juliet & Grace)

MILK FROM CHELTENHAM
83	Its War Boys £3	TRIPTYCH OF POISONERS (LP, silkscreened sleeve red or blue vinyl)	£50

MILKSHAKES
82	Havasong BILK-O	Please Don't Tell My Baby/It's You (p/s)	£25
86	Empire UXF 228	Let Me Love You/She Tells Me She Loves Me (p/s)	£15
83	Big Beat NED 4	14 RHYTHM AND BEAT GREATS (LP, red, lilac and blue sleeves)	£20
83	Upright UPLP 1	AFTER SCHOOL SESSION (LP, laminated sleeve)	£20
84	Milkshake GARB-O	THEE KNIGHTS OF TRASH (LP)	£30
84	Milkshake HARP-O	NOTHING CAN STOP THESE MEN (LP)	£20
84	Big Beat WIK 22	SHOWCASE (LP)	£25
85	Big Beat WIK 30	THEY CAME, THEY SAW, THEY CONQUERED (LP)	£20
86	Media Burn MB 6	THE 107 TAPES (2-LP)	£25
86	Milkshake MILK-O	TALKING 'BOUT MILKSHAKES (LP, with poster)	£40
86	Milkshake MILK-O	TALKING 'BOUT MILKSHAKES (LP, without poster)	£25
87	Hangman HANG 11 UP	LIVE FROM CHATHAM (LP)	£18
87	Hangman HANG 1 UP	REVENGE - TRASH FROM THE VAULT (THE LEGENDARY MISSING 9th ALBUM) (LP)	£25
92	Vinyl Japan ASKLP 10	STILL TALKING 'BOUT (LP)	£25
05	Damaged Goods DAMGOOD 249LP	IN GERMANY (LP)	£15

(see also Prisoners/Milkshakes, Pop Rivits, Len Bright Combo, Billy Childish, Thee Headcoats, Mickey & Ludella, Masonics)

MILK TEETH
74	Bead Records BEAD 1	A TOUCH OF THE SUN (LP)	£150

MILLENIUM
84	Guardian GRC 2163	MILLENIUM (LP)	£20

MILLER
65	Oak RGJ 190	Baby I've Got News For You/The Girl With The Castle	£300
65	Columbia DB 7735	Baby I Got News For You/The Girl With The Castle	£400

(see also Big Boy Pete, Peter Jay & Jaywalkers, Pete Miller, News)

BOBBIE MILLER
65	Decca F 12064	What A Guy/You Went Away	£40
65	Decca F 12252	Every Beat Of My Heart/Tomorrow	£15
66	Decca F 12354	Everywhere I Go/IAN STEWART & RAILROADERS: Stu-Ball	£80

(see also Mongrels, Rolling Stones)

CHUCK MILLER
56	Capitol CL 14543	Rogue River Valley/No Baby Like You	£15
57	Mercury 7MT 153	The Auctioneer/Me Head's In De Barrel	£20
58	Mercury 7MT 215	Down The Road A-Piece/Mad About Her Blues	£100
60	Mercury ZEP 10058	GOING GOING GONE (EP)	£50

FRANKIE MILLER
59	Melodisc MEL 1519	True Blue/Black Land Farmer	£15
59	Melodisc MEL 1519	True Blue/Black Land Farmer (78)	£15
59	Melodisc MEL 1529	Poppin' Johnnie/Family Man	£15
59	Melodisc MEL 1529	Poppin' Johnnie/Family Man (78)	£15
60	Melodisc MEL 1552	Rain, Rain/Baby Rocked Her Dolly	£15
62	Top Rank JKP 3013	COUNTRY MUSIC (EP)	£20
64	Ember CW 107	THE TRUE COUNTRY STYLE OF FRANKIE MILLER (LP)	£20

GARY MILLER
57	Nixa NPL 18008	MEET MISTER MILLER (LP)	£15

GLEN MILLER
67	Doctor Bird DB 1089	Where Is The Love/Funky Broadway	£400
68	Doctor Bird DB 1128	Rocksteady Party(A-side with Booker T & MGs)/Book Of Memories	£50

JACOB MILLER
78	Hawkeye HD 009	Each One Teach One/Matthews Lane Dub/TETRACK: Let's Get It Together/Black Arts Dub (12")	£40
82	Greensleeves GREL 166	WHO SAY JAH NO DREAD (LP)	£15

JIMMY MILLER & (NEW) BARBECUES
57	Columbia DB 4006	Sizzlin' Hot/Free Wheelin' Baby (as Jimmy Miller & Barbecues)	£60
57	Columbia DB 4006	Sizzlin' Hot/Free Wheelin' Baby (as Jimmy Miller & Barbecues) (78)	£15
58	Columbia DB 4081	Jelly Baby/Cry, Baby, Cry (as Jimmy Miller & New Barbecues)	£60
58	Columbia DB 4081	Jelly Baby/Cry, Baby, Cry (as Jimmy Miller & New Barbecues) (78)	£30

(see also Station Skiffle Group)

JODY MILLER
64	Capitol CL 15356	The Fever/In My Room	£15
65	Capitol CL 15415	Home Of The Brave/This Is The Life	£15
65	Capitol T 2416	HOME OF THE BRAVE (LP, mono)	£20
65	Capitol (S) T 2416	HOME OF THE BRAVE (LP, stereo)	£25
66	Capitol T 2446	JODY MILLER SINGS THE GREAT HITS OF BUCK OWENS (LP, mono)	£20
66	Capitol (S) T 2446	JODY MILLER SINGS THE GREAT HITS OF BUCK OWENS (LP, stereo)	£25

KENNY MILLER
65	Stateside SS 405	Restless/Take My Tip	£150

MR MILLER
69	Jackpot JP 707	Feel It/LYN BECKFORD: Kiss Me Quick (actually by Keeling Beckford)	£120

NED MILLER
63	Capitol EAP1 20492	NED MILLER (EP)	£15

MINT VALUE £

63	London RE 1382	NED MILLER (EP)	£15
63	London HA 8072	FROM A JACK TO A KING (LP)	£25

PAULETTE MILLER

79	Burning Rockers PR 157	Woman In Love/In Love Dub (12")	£20

PETE MILLER

97	Tenth Planet TP 030	SUMMERLAND (LP, numbered, 1000 only)	£15

(see also Miller, Big Boy Pete)

RUSS MILLER

57	HMV POP 391	I Sit In My Window/Wait For Me, My Love	£50

STEPHEN MILLER & LOL COXHILL

73	Caroline C 1503	COXHILL MILLER (LP, black/white/red 'Twin' label)	£25
74	Caroline C 1507	THE STORY SO FAR ... OH REALLY? (LP)	£30

(see also Lol Coxhill)

STEVE MILLER BAND

68	Capitol CL 15539	Sittin' In Circles/Roll With It	£15
68	Capitol CL 15564	Living In The U.S.A./Quicksilver Girl	£15
69	Capitol CL 15604	My Dark Hour/Song For Our Ancestors	£15
68	Capitol (S)T 2920	CHILDREN OF THE FUTURE (LP, 'rainbow rim' label)	£50
69	Capitol (S)T 2984	SAILOR (LP, 'rainbow rim' label)	£40
69	Capitol E-ST 184	BRAVE NEW WORLD (LP, mono)	£25
70	Capitol E-ST 184	BRAVE NEW WORLD (LP, stereo)	£20
70	Capitol E-ST 331	YOUR SAVING GRACE (LP)	£20
77	Mercury 9286 455	BOOK OF DREAMS (LP, printed inner)	£15
17	Capitol Records 00602557906356	ULTIMATE HITS (4LP, gatefold, insert)	£40

(see also Boz Scaggs)

SUZI MILLER

54	Decca F 10389	Happy Days And Lonely Nights/Tell Me, Tell Me (with Johnston Brothers)	£20
55	Decca F 10475	Tweedlee-Dee (with Johnston Brothers)/That's All I Want From You	£15
55	Decca F 10512	Dance With Me Henry (Wallflower) (with Johnston Brothers)/ Butterfingers (with Marilyn Sisters)	£15

(see also Johnston Brothers)

STEVE MILLER TRIO

86	Matchless MR 09	MILLERS TALE (LP)	£25

MILLER'S THUMB

76	Tradition TSC 3	SITTING ON THE RIGHT SIDE (LP, 100 copies only)	£20

MILLIE (SMALL)

64	Cadbury's BNVT 01F	The Bournvita Song/Three Nights A Week (p/s)	£25
65	Fontana TF 617	Bloodshot Eyes/Tongue Tied	£18
65	Brit WI 1002	My Street/A Mixed Up, Fickle, Moody, Self-Centred, Spoiled Kind Of Boy	£15
70	Trojan TR 7744	Enoch Power/Mayfair	£25
70	President PT 306	We're All In A Zoo/Piccaninny Man	£15
61	Blue Beat BBEP 302	MILLIE (EP, with Little Roy & Owen Gray; with sleeve)	£140
61	Blue Beat BBEP 302	MILLIE (EP, with Little Roy & Owen Gray; without sleeve)	£20
64	Fontana TE 17425	MY BOY LOLLIPOP (EP)	£50
66	Island IEP 705	MILLIE AND HER BOYFRIENDS (EP)	£40
64	Fontana TL 5220	MORE MILLIE (LP, mono)	£40
64	Fontana (S)TL 5220	MORE MILLIE (LP, stereo)	£50
65	Fontana TL 5276	MILLIE SINGS FATS DOMINO (LP)	£60
67	Island ILP 953	THE BEST OF MILLIE SMALL (LP)	£50
69	Trojan TTL 17	MILLIE AND HER BOYFRIENDS (LP)	£20
69	Trojan TTL 49	THE BEST OF MILLIE SMALL (LP, reissue)	£15
70	Trojan TBL 108	TIME WILL TELL (LP)	£20

(see also Jackie & Millie, Roy & Millie, Owen & Millie)

SPIKE MILLIGAN

61	Parlophone PMC 1148	MILLIGAN PRESERVED (LP, mono)	£15
61	Parlophone PCS 18	MILLIGAN PRESERVED (LP, stereo)	£20

(see also Famous Eccles)

MARY MILLINGTON

99	Trunk/Bonk B 01	COME PLAY ME (EP)	£60

SIR EUGENE MILLINGTON-DRAKE

65	Decca LK 4659	MIXED GRILL (LP)	£60

MILLIONAIRES (IRELAND)

66	Decca F 12468	Wishing Well/Chatterbox	£100

MILLIONAIRES (U.S.)

67	Mercury 6052301	Never For Me/If I Had You Babe (paper labels)	£35
67	Mercury 6052301	Never For Me/If I Had You Babe (plastic labels)	£15

MILLIONS

73	Downtown DT 516	Love Of Jah Jah Children/Jah Jah Version	£30

BARBARA MILLS

65	Hickory 45-1323	Queen Of Fools/Make It Last, Take Your Time	£400
65	Hickory 45-1323	Queen Of Fools/Make It Last, Take Your Time (DJ copy)	£500
65	Hickory 45-1392	Try/Let's Make A Memory	£15

MINT VALUE £

BETTY LOU MILLS
60s	Shal SHAL 1	Where Is My Star/Rock Him	£30
60	Pilgrim JLPS 101	EVERYWHERE I LOOK (LP)	£25

GARRY MILLS
59	Top Rank JAR 119	Hey Baby (You're Pretty)/You Alone	£20
61	Decca F 11383	Bless You/Footprints In The Sand	£15
61	Decca F 11415	Treasure Island/Sad Little Girl	£15
62	Decca F 11471	Never Believed In Love/Save A Dream For Me	£15

(see also Gary & Ariels)

HAYLEY MILLS
62	Decca LK 4426	LET'S GET TOGETHER (LP)	£15

JEFF MILLS
61	Ember EMB S 133	Daddy's Home/TIMMY REYNOLDS: Lullaby Of Love	£70

RUDY MILLS
67	Island WI 3092	A Long Story/BOBBY ELLIS: Now We Know (actually. with Desmond Miles Seven)	£40
68	Island WI 3136	I'm Trapped/BOBBY ELLIS & CRYSTALLITES: Dollar A Head	£55
69	Big Shot BI 509	John Jones/A Place Called Happiness	£70
69	Explosion EX 2007	Lemi Li/Goody Goody	£20
69	Crab CRAB 20	Tears On My Pillow/I'm Trapped	£20
69	Crab CRAB 24	A Heavy Load/Wholesale Love	£60
69	Pama SECO 12	REGGAE HITS (LP)	£150

STEPHANIE MILLS
76	Tamla Motown TMG 1020	This Empty Place/I See You For The First Time (unissued)	£50
76	Tamla Motown STML 12017	FOR THE FIRST TIME (LP)	£20

MILLS BROTHERS
58	London HLD 8553	Get A Job/I Found A Million Dollar Baby	£15

(see also Louis Armstrong)

RONNIE MILSAP
66	Pye International 7N 25392	Ain't No Soul (Left In These Old Shoes)/Another Branch From The Same Old Tree	£60
66	Pye International 7N 25392	Ain't No Soul (Left In These Old Shoes)/Another Branch From The Same Old Tree (DJ copy)	£100

RONNIE MILSAP/ROSCOE ROBINSON
66	Pye Intl. NEP 44078	SOUL SENSATIONS (EP)	£50

NATHAN MILSTEIN
62	Columbia SAX 2518	VIVALDI: FOUR CONCERTI (LP, stereo, turquoise/silver label)	£500
63	Columbia SAX 2563	MUSIC OF OLD RUSSIA (LP, stereo, red label)	£450
65	Columbia SAX 5254	MOZART VIOLIN CONCERTOS (LP, stereo, red label)	£100
66	Columbia SAX 5275	PROKOFIEV: THE TWO CONCERTOS FOR VIOLIN & ORCHESTRA (LP, stereo, red label)	£350
66	Columbia SAX 5285	BACH: TWO VIOLIN CONCERTOS/VIVALDI: TWO VIOLIN CONCERTOS (LP, Stereo)	£400

TED MILTON
79	Echt! ECHT! ONE	Confessions Of An Aeroplane Farter/I Don't Want To Go Poo Poo! (7" in 12" p/s)	£50

MILWAUKEE COASTERS
68	Pama PMLP 2	WEST COAST ROCK'N'ROLL 1968 (LP)	£15

ILHAN MIMAROGLU
69	Turnabout TV34177S	ELECTRONIC MUSIC III (LP)	£20

GARNET MIMMS (& ENCHANTERS)
63	United Artists UP 1033	Cry Baby/Don't Change Your Heart (with Enchanters)	£25
63	United Artists UP 1038	Baby Don't You Weep/For Your Precious Love (with Enchanters)	£20
64	United Artists UP 1048	Tell Me Baby/Anytime You Want Me (with Enchanters)	£25
65	United Artists UP 1090	It Was Easier To Hurt Her/So Close	£30
66	United Artists UP 1130	I'll Take Good Care Of You/Looking For You	£100
66	United Artists UP 1130	I'll Take Good Care Of You/Looking For You (DJ copy)	£200
66	United Artists UP 1147	It's Been Such A Long Way Home/Thinkin'	£20
66	United Artists UP 1153	My Baby/It Won't Hurt Half As Much	£25
66	United Artists UP 1172	All About Love/The Truth Hurts	£20
67	United Artists UP 1181	Roll With The Punches/Only Your Love	£25
67	United Artists UP 1186	As Long As I Have You/Yesterday	£200
68	Verve VS 569	I Can Hear My Baby Crying/Stop And Think It Over	£20
68	Verve VS 574	We Can Find That Love/Can You Top This	£35
63	United Artists ULP 1067	CRY BABY AND 11 OTHER HITS (LP, with Enchanters)	£125
66	United Artists (S)ULP 1145	WARM AND SOULFUL (LP)	£70
67	United Artists (S)ULP 1174	LIVE (LP, as Garnet Mimms & Senate)	£60

MINA
60	Oriole CB 1600	This World We Live In/Please Don't Leave Me	£60
61	Oriole EP 7050	IL CIELO IN UNA STANZA (EP)	£80

MIND OVER MATTER
70	Haflex HF 01	Sunrise/Enter The Dragon	£40

MINDBENDERS
66	Fontana TF 780	I Want Her, She Wants Me/The Morning After	£18
67	Fontana TF 877	Schoolgirl/Coming Back	£40
68	Fontana TF 910	Blessed Are The Lonely/Yellow Brick Road	£20
68	Fontana TF 961	Uncle Joe, The Ice Cream Man/The Man Who Loved Trees	£15
66	Fontana TL 5324	THE MINDBENDERS (LP, mono)	£45
66	Fontana (S)TL 5324	THE MINDBENDERS (LP, stereo)	£55

| 67 | Fontana (S)TL 5403 | **WITH WOMAN IN MIND** (LP) | £60 |

(see also Wayne Fontana & Mindbenders, Hotlegs, Lulu)

MINDSEYE
| 82 | Man 1 | **No One Else/Don't Stop/Risk** (no p/s) | £15 |

SAL MINEO
57	Philips JK 1024	**Start Movin'** (In My Direction)/**Love Affair** (jukebox issue)	£20
58	Fontana H 118	**Little Pigeon/Cuttin' In**	£20
58	Fontana TFL 5004	**SAL** (LP)	£30

SEXTON MING
88	Hangman HANG-1-UP	**OLD HORSE OF THE NATION** (LP)	£15
90	Hangman HANG 36 UP	**BIRDS WITH TEETH** (LP)	£15
98	Hangman's Daughter HANG 018UP	**6 MORE MILES TO THE GRAVEYARD** (LP)	£18

(see also Billy Childish etc.etc. etc.)

CHARLES/CHARLIE MINGUS
56	Vogue LDE 178	**CHARLIE MINGUS PRESENTS JAZZ WORKSHOP VOL. 2** (10" LP)	£40
59	Parlophone PMC 1092	**EAST COASTING** (LP)	£40
59	Philips BBL 7352	**MINGUS AH HUM** (LP)	£80
60	Atlantic 587 166	**REINCARNATION OF A LOVEBIRD** (LP)	£40
60	London Jazz LTZ-K 15194	**BLUES AND ROOTS** (LP, also stereo SAH-K 6087)	£50
62	Atlantic SD 8005	**CHARLES MINGUS PRESENTS CHARLES MINGUS** (LP, U.K. issue of U.S. LP)	£30
62	United Artists ULP 1004	**JAZZ PORTRAITS** (LP)	£25
62	London HA-K/SH-K 8007	**OH YEAH** (LP, by Charlie Mingus & Jazz Group)	£40
63	RCA RD/SF 7514	**TIJUANA MOODS** (LP)	£30
63	Vocalion LAE 543	**CHAZZ** (LP)	£40
64	HMV CLP 1694	**THE BLACK SAINT AND THE SINNER LADY** (LP)	£40
65	United Artists ULP 1068	**TOWN HALL CONCERT** (LP)	£30
65	Vocalion LAEF/SEAF 591	**CHARLIE MINGUS QUINTET WITH MAX ROACH** (LP)	£30
65	HMV CLP 1742	**MINGUS, MINGUS, MINGUS** (LP, also stereo CSD 1545)	£35
65	HMV CLP 1796	**MINGUS PLAYS PIANO** (LP)	£30
65	Atlantic ATL/SAL 5019	**TONIGHT AT NOON** (LP)	£30
66	Realm RM 211	**JAZZ COMPOSERS WORKSHOP** (NO. 1) (LP)	£30
66	CBS (S)BPG 62261	**MINGUS DYNASTY** (LP)	£30
68	Atlantic 587131	**PITHECANTTHROPUS ERECTUS** (LP)	£30

MINI DRESSES
| 14 | Box Bedroom Rebels BBR12 | **MINI DRESSES EP** (p/s, insert, numbered) | £15 |

MINIM
| 67 | Polydor 582 011 | **WRAPPED IN A UNION JACK** (LP) | £30 |

MINIMAL MAN
| 93 | Guerrila GRRR 54 | **MINIMAL MAN EP** (12") | £15 |
| 01 | Vinyl Classics VC 02 | **Treatment Fee** (Remixes) (12") | £20 |

MINISTRY
92	Sire W 0096	**Jesus Built My Hotrod/T.V. Song** (p/s)	£15
83	Arista 205 306	**WORK FOR LOVE** (LP)	£15
89	Sire 926 004 1	**THE MIND IS A TERRIBLE THING TO TASTE** (LP)	£15
92	Sire WX 481	**ΚΕΦΑΛΗΞΘ** (10" LP, limited edition)	£25

MINISTRY OF SOUND
| 66 | Decca F 12449 | **White Collar Worker/Back Seat Driver** | £40 |

MINNY POPS
| 82 | Factory FAC 57 | **Secret Story/Island** | £15 |

KYLIE MINOGUE
SINGLES
89	PWL PWLT 35R	**Hand On Your Heart** (Heartache Mix)/**Hand On Your Heart** (Dub mix) **Just Wanna Love You** (12", with stickered p/s)	£30
89	PWL PWLT 42R	**Wouldn't Change A Thing** (Espagna Mix)/**Wouldn't Change A Thing** (7" Mix)/**It's No Secret** (Extended) (12", stickered p/s)	£20
91	PWL PWLP 72	**What Do I Have To Do** (New Mix)/**What Do I Have To Do** (Instrumental) (stickered p/s, with postcards)	£15
91	PWL PWLT 72R	**What Do I Have To Do** (Between The Sheets Mix) (12", withdrawn, no p/s)	£100
91	PWL PWL P81	**Shocked** (DNA 7" Mix)/**Shocked** (Harding & Curnow 7" Mix) (picture disc)	£15
91	PWL PWLT204R	**Word Is Out** (Summer Breeze Remix) (1-sided 12" Limited Edition with etched Kylie autograph on other side, p/s)	£20
97	DeCon. 7432 1517257	**Some Kind Of Bliss/Love Takes Over Me** (numbered limited edition 7", die-cut p/s)	£30
98	DeConstruction 74321 587151	**KYLIE MIXES** (3x12", printed inners)	£40
23	BMG 538966081	**Padam Padam/Padam Padam** (Extended Mix) (p/s, red vinyl)	£20

ALBUMS
88	PWL HFD 4	**KYLIE** (DAT)	£150
90	PWL HFL 18	**RHYTHM OF LOVE** (LP, gold leaf sleeve, poster, 100 only)	£100
98	30DeCon. 74321 58715 1	**MIXES** (3xLP, inner sleeves, pink silhouette Kylie outer p/s)	£20
94	Deconstruction 74321 22749 1	**KYLIE MINOGUE** (LP, printed inner)	£40
10	Parlophone 642 9051	**APHRODITE** (LP, printed inner)	£150
12	Parlophone P015 8611	**THE ABBEY ROAD SESSIONS** (2LP/CD, gatefold, printed inners, booklet, numbered)	£200
15	Parlophone 0825640048	**KYLIE CHRISTMAS** (LP, white vinyl, printed inner, wrapping paper edition via website)	£150
15	PWL KYLIE 1 X	**KYLIE** (LP/2CD/DVD reissue, picture disc, postcards, book)	£150

MINT VALUE £

15	PWL KYLIE 2 X	**ENJOY YOURSELF** (LP/2CD/DVD reissue, picture disc, postcards, book)	**£100**
15	PWL KYLIE 3 X	**RHYTHM OF LOVE** (LP/2CD/DVD reissue, picture disc, postcards, book)	**£150**
15	PWL KYLIE 4 X	**LET'S GET TO IT** (LP/2CD/DVD reissue, picture disc)	**£400**
17	Parlophone 0190295846428	**FEVER** (LP, white vinyl, 'Sainsburys' sticker)	**£100**
18	Parlophone 0190295680855	**LIGHT YEARS** (2LP, blue vinyl, 'Sainsburys' sticker)	**£150**
18	BMG 538360801	**GOLDEN** (LP, gatefold, clear vinyl)	**£25**
21	BMG 538634041	**DISCO** (LP, die-cut inner sleeves, insert, photo, blue vinyl)	**£25**
21	BMG 538695901	**DISCO** (EXTENDED MIXES) (2LP, gatefold, printed inners, purple vinyl)	**£20**
22	BMG 4050538695854	**INFINITE DISCO** (LP, printed inner, clear vinyl, limited to 6000 copies)	**£25**
21	Parl. 0190295846428	**FEVER** (LP, reissue, 20th Anniversary Edition, printed inner, silver vinyl)	**£100**
21	Parlophone 0190295846428	**FEVER** (LP, National Album Day version, white vinyl, printed inner)	**£40**
22	BMG BMGCAT 586VLP	**IMPOSSIBLE PRINCESS** (LP, gatefold, printed inner, violet transparent vinyl, 25th Anniversary Edition, first vinyl issue of 1997 CD)	**£50**
23	BMG 538948351	**TENSION** (LP, clear vinyl, alternate artwork, 4000 only thru pop-up store)	**£100**
22	BMG 538927921	**TENSION** (LP, printed inner, Coke bottle clear vinyl, Spotify exclusive)	**£60**
23	BMG 538927891	**TENSION** (LP, printed inner, green vinyl, HMV exclusive)	**£30**
23	BMG 538927901	**TENSION** (LP, printed inners, orange vinyl, indies exclusive)	**£25**
24	Parl. 5054197802928	**BODY LANGUAGE** (LP, gatefold sleeve, poster, 20th Anniversary Edition, first vinyl issue of 2003 CD, red vinyl)	**£30**

PROMOS

94	DeConstruction KM 100	**KYLIE MINOGUE** (CD, promo, gatefold sl. in lilac slipcase with silver lettering)	**£50**
88	PWL (no cat. no.)	**Made In Heaven** (3:26) **PWL 1-track in-house promo cassette, custom PWL logo inlay typled/stickered, 1 only)**	**£30**
90	PWL PWLT 56R	**Better The Devil You Know** (KC Cohen 'US' Remix) (1-sided 12" promo, withdrawn, die-cut sleeve, 50 only)	**£30**
91	PWL PWLT 72R	**What Do I Have To Do** (Between The Sheets Mix) (1-sided 12" promo, withdrawn die-cut sleeve)	**£30**
91	PWL ZR-A1	**Keep On Pumpin' It** (12" white label issued under pseudonym of 'Angel K', includes Angelic Remix' & 'Astral Flight Mix', handwritten/stamped labels, Some with 'I Guess I Like It' titles. Die-cut sleeve)	**£30**
91	PWL (no cat. no.)	**I Guess I Like It Like That** (12" 1-sided white label issued under pseudonym of 'Angel K', includes 'Extended/Album Version', 200 only)	**£20**
91	PWL ANGEL-2	**Do You Dare** (12" white label issued under pseudonym of 'Angel K', includes NRG Mix' & 'New Rave Mix', handwritten labels, die-cut sleeve, 100 only)	**£20**
92	PWL PWLT 257	**Celebration** (Have A Party Mix)/**Let's Get To It** (Album Version) ('Black Diamond' limited promo 12", Christmas "leaving PWL" promo p/s, black diamond label)	**£25**
94	DeCon. 21 246577 JB	**Put Yourself In My Place** (Radio Mix)/(All Star Mix) (7" jukebox issue, no p/s)	**£15**
95	DeConstruction FEEL2	**Where Is The Feeling?** (BIR Dolphin Mix)/(Morales Club Mix) (12", die-cut sleeve, limited quantities)	**£30**
95	DeConstruction FEEL3	**Where Is The Feeling?** (Da Klubb Feelin' Mix)/(Aphroheadz Powerlite Mix)/(Three Rad Vid Clash Mix) (12", promo, no p/s, 200 only)	**£25**
95	Deconstruction TIME1	**Time Will Pass You By** (Paul Masterson's 'Wand Silver Screen Remix') (1-sided 12" White Label, handwritten labels, unreleased mix, withdrawn, 20 only)	**£40**
97	DeConstruction DID2	**Did It Again** (Trouser Enthusiasts' Goddess of Contortion Mix)/(Razor N Go Mix) (12" promo, custom Deconstruction die-cut sleeve, limited to 500 only)	**£20**
97	DeCon. 21 535707 JB	**Did It Again** (Radio Edit)/**Tears** (7" jukebox issue, no p/s)	**£20**
98	DeCon. 21 570137 JB	**Breathe** (Radio Edit)/(Tee's Radio Edit) (7" jukebox issue, no p/s)	**£20**
98	DeConstruction TOOFAR 1	**Too Far** (Brothers In Rhythm Mix)/(Junior Vasquez Remix) (12", promo, no p/s)	**£25**
98	Arthrob ART021TJ	**GBI** (Sharp Boys Deee-Liteful Dub)/(Album Version)/(Kylie-Pella) (with Towa Tei) (UK promo 12" part 1, custom Arthrob sleeve)	**£15**
98	Arthrob ART021TJX	**GBI** (Rekut/DJ Krust Mix)/(Ebony Boogie Down Mix)/**Bold Line** (not Kylie) (with Towa Tei) (UK promo 12" part 2, custom Arthrob sleeve)	**£15**
00	Parlophone BUTTERFLO1A	**Butterfly** (Sandstorm Dub) (12" 1-sided DJ white label, butterfly logo stamped die cut paper sleeve)	**£40**
00	Parlophone 12MIND 1	**Spinning Around** (Messy Boyz Remix) (12" 1-sided promo featuring unreleased mix, die cut sleeve, Handwritten label, withdrawn, 10 only)	**£40**
00	Parlophone SHARP DJ 1	**Spinning Around** (Sharp Vocal Mix)/**Spinning Around** (Sharp Double Dub) (12" Pink Promo DJ Vinyl, die-cut sleeve, 100 only)	**£40**
00	Parlophone 12RDJ 6551	**Please Stay** (Metro Mix)/**Please Stay** (7th District Club Flava Mix)/ **Please Stay** (7th District Club Dub) (12" promo, p/s, with inner sleeve)	**£20**
04	Parlophone RDJ6633	**Red Blooded Woman** (Promo 1-sided clear 7" vinyl featuring otherwise unreleased 'Play Paul Radio Edit', 50 only)	**£30**
04	Parlophone (no cat. no)	**Chocolate** (Violanti's Remix) (1-sided 12" white label, unreleased remix, Withdrawn, hand-written label)	**£30**
97	DeConstruction KYLIE 1	**IMPOSSIBLE PRINCESS** (CD, promo, insert, withdrawn, some with Press Release from 'Hall Or Nothing' explaining about the withdrawal of the CD and title due to Princess Diana's death)	**£30**
97	DeConstruction KM 002	**AN INTERVIEW WITH KYLIE MINOGUE** (Promo interview CD for 'Impossible Princess' album, unique p/s)	**£100**
00	Parlophone LIGHTX 001	**LIGHT YEARS** (LP Promo, unique blue outer 'Kylie' logo sleeve, inner picture sleeve, does not include 'Kids' or 'Password', 100 only)	**£30**
00	Parlophone LIGHTX 002	**LIGHT YEARS** (LP Promo, unique blue outer 'Kylie' logo sleeve, inner picture sleeve, includes 'Kids' but not 'Password', 100 only)	**£30**
00	BMG HITS1	**HITS+** (CD promo, original withdrawn artwork, card slip case, withdrawn at Kylie's request when she disliked the picture used, most copies incinerated, less than 5 copies exist)	**£40**
07	Parlophone XINTER 001	**X 'The Interview'** (CD, promo, 42-track interview, custom cover)	**£30**

MINOR CLASSICS

82	Chiswick DICE 4	**Sign Language/This Side Of Paradise**	**£50**

MINORBOPS

58	Vogue V 9110	**Need You Tonight/Want You For My Own**	**£800**
58	Vogue V 9110	**Need You Tonight/Want You For My Own** (78)	**£250**

MINOR THREAT

83	Discord DISCHORD 10	**OUT OF STEP EP** (12", reissue, red print, insert)	**£20**
85	Discord DISCORD 15	**Salad Days/Stumped/Good Guys** (p/s)	**£18**

MINSTRELS
67	Studio One SO 2036	People Get Ready/HAMLINS: Everyone's Got To Be There	£200
68	Studio One SO 2050	Miss Highty Tighty/WESTMORELITES: Let Me Be Yours Until Tomorrow	£90

MINT JULEPS
87	Stiff BUY DJ 264	Docklands/Under Pressure (12" test pressing of last Stiff single for 20 years)	£30

MINT (1)
69	Tangerine 014	Luv/Simone	£20

MINTS
57	London HLP 8423	Night Air/KEN COPELAND: Pledge Of Love	£100

MINUCCI
56	Vogue Coral LVA 9015	GINA LOLLO BRIGIDA PRESENTS MUSIC OF GINO BY MINUCCI (LP, photo of Gina on cover)	£15

MINUTEMEN
83	SST SST 002	PARANOID TIME (8-track EP)	£18

MIRACLE MILE
86	Miracle MIR 001	Bless This Ship/Breaking Down The Barriers (p/s)	£35

(SMOKEY ROBINSON &) MIRACLES
61	London HL9276	Shop Around/Who's Lovin' You (DJ Copy)	£100
61	London HL 9276	Shop Around/Who's Lovin' You	£60
61	London HL 9366	Ain't It Baby/The Only One I Love (DJ Copy)	£200
61	London HL 9366	Ain't It Baby/The Only One I Love	£100
62	Fontana H 384	What's So Good About Goodbye/I've Been So Good To You	£200
63	Oriole CBA 1795	You've Really Got A Hold On Me/Happy Landing	£120

(Credited to The Miracles.)
63	Oriole CBA 1863	Mickey's Monkey/Whatever Makes You Happy	£80
64	Stateside SS 263	I Gotta Dance To Keep From Crying/Such Is Love, Such Is Life (DJ Copy)	£100
64	Stateside SS 263	I Gotta Dance To Keep From Crying/Such Is Love, Such Is Life	£55
64	Stateside SS 282	The Man In You/Heartbreak Road (DJ Copy)	£70
64	Stateside SS 282	The Man In You/Heartbreak Road	£40
64	Stateside SS 324	I Like It Like That/You're So Fine And Sweet (DJ Copy)	£70
64	Stateside SS 324	I Like It Like That/You're So Fine And Sweet	£45
64	Stateside SS 353	That's What Love Is Made Of/Would I Love You (DJ Copy)	£80
64	Stateside SS 353	That's What Love Is Made Of/Would I Love You	£35
65	Stateside SS 377	Come On Do The Jerk/Baby Don't You Go (DJ Copy)	£60
65	Stateside SS 377	Come On Do The Jerk/Baby Don't You Go	£45
65	Tamla Motown TMG 503	Oo Baby Baby/That's All Good (DJ Copy)	£140
65	Tamla Motown TMG 503	Ooo Baby Baby/All That's Good	£40
65	Tamla Motown TMG 522	The Tracks Of My Tears/Fork In The Road (DJ Copy)	£100
65	Tamla Motown TMG 522	The Tracks Of My Tears/A Fork In The Road	£45
65	Tamla Motown TMG 540	My Girl Has Gone/Since You Won My Heart (DJ Copy)	£100
65	Tamla Motown TMG 540	My Girl Has Gone/Since You Won My Heart	£40
66	Tamla Motown TMG 547	Going To A Go-Go/Choosey Beggar (DJ Copy)	£200
66	Tamla Motown TMG 547	Going To A Go-Go/Choosey Beggar	£25
66	Tamla Motown TMG 569	Who Lotta Shakin' In My Heart/Oh Be My Love (DJ Copy)	£80
66	Tamla Motown TMG 569	Whole Lotta Shakin' In My Heart/Oh Be My Love	£45
66	Tamla Motown TMG 584	(Come Round Here) I'm The One You Need/Save Me (DJ Copy)	£80
66	Tamla Motown TMG 584	(Come 'Round Here) I'm The One You Need/Save Me	£25

(All of the singles listed above are credited to The Miracles.)
67	Tamla Motown TMG 598	The Love I Saw In You Was Just A Mirage/Swept For You Baby (DJ Copy)	£80
67	Tamla Motown TMG 598	The Love I Saw In You Was Just A Mirage/Swept For You Baby	£25
67	Tamla Motown TMG 614	More Love/Swept For You Baby (DJ Copy, mislabelled, B-side plays Come Spy With Me)	£80
67	Tamla Motown TMG 614	More Love/Swept For You Baby (mislabelled, B-side plays Come Spy With Me)	£25
67	Tamla Motown TMG 614	More Love/Come Spy With Me	£80
67	Tamla Motown TMG 631	I Second That Emotion/You Must Be Love (DJ Copy)	£70
68	Tamla Motown TMG 648	If You Can Want/When The Words From Your Heart Get Caught Up In Your Throat (DJ Copy)	£40
68	Tamla Motown TMG 648	If You Can Want/When The Words From Your Heart Get Caught Up In Your Throat	£15
68	Tamla Motown TMG 661	Yester-Love/Much Better Of (DJ Copy)	£40
68	Tamla Motown TMG 661	Yester-Love/Much Better Off	£15
68	Tamla Motown TMG 673	Special Occasion/Give Her Up (DJ Copy)	£40
68	Tamla Motown TMG 673	Special Occasion/Give Her Up	£15
69	Tamla Motown TMG 687	Baby, Baby Don't Cry/Your Mother's Only Daughter (DJ Copy)	£40
69	Tamla Motown TMG 687	Baby, Baby Don't Cry/Your Mother's Only Daughter	£15
69	Tamla Motown TMG 696	The Tracks Of My Tears/Come On Do The Jerk (DJ Copy)	£40
70	Tamla Motown TMG 745	The Tears Of A Clown/You Must Be Love (DJ Copy)	£40
70	Tamla Motown TMG 745	The Tears Of A Clown/You Must Be Love (with withdrawn B-side)	£40
71	Tamla Motown TMG 761	(Come Round Here) I'm The One You Need/We Can Make It We Can (DJ Copy)	£35
71	Tamla Motown TMG 774	I Don't Blame You At All/That Girl (DJ Copy)	£35
72	Tamla Motown TMG 811	My Girl Has Gone/Crazy Bout The La La La (DJ Copy)	£30
73	Tamla Motown TMG 853	Going To A Go-Go/Whole Lotta Shakin' In My Heart/Yester-Love (DJ Copy)	£25
61	London RE 1295	SHOP AROUND (EP, as The Miracles)	£200
63	Oriole PS 40044	HI! WE'RE THE MIRACLES (LP)	£250
64	Stateside SL 10099	THE FABULOUS MIRACLES (LP)	£140
65	Tamla Motown TML 11003	I LIKE IT LIKE THAT (LP)	£80
66	Tamla Motown TML 11024	GOIN' TO A GO-GO (LP, as Smokey Robinson & The Miracles, mono)	£45
66	Tamla Motown TML 11024	GOIN' TO A GO-GO (LP, as Smokey Robinson & The Miracles, stereo)	£55

MINT VALUE £

66	Tamla Motown TML 11031	**THE MIRACLES FROM THE BEGINNING** (LP, mono)	**£50**
66	Tamla Motown STML 11031	**THE MIRACLES FROM THE BEGINNING** (LP, stereo)	**£50**
67	Tamla Motown TML 11044	**AWAY WE A-GO-GO** (LP, mono)	**£50**
67	Tamla Motown STML 11044	**AWAY WE A-GO-GO** (LP, stereo)	**£65**
68	Tamla Motown TML 11067	**MAKE IT HAPPEN** (LP, mono)	**£30**
68	Tamla Motown STML 11067	**MAKE IT HAPPEN** (LP, stereo)	**£35**
68	Tamla Motown (S)TML 11072	**GREATEST HITS** (LP, mono/stereo)	**£20**
69	Tamla Motown (S)TML 11089	**SPECIAL OCCASION** (LP, mono/stereo)	**£25**
69	Tamla Motown (S)TML 11107	**SMOKEY ROBINSON & THE MIRACLES LIVE!** (LP, mono/stereo)	**£25**
70	Tamla Motown (S)TML 11129	**TIME OUT FOR SMOKEY ROBINSON & THE MIRACLES** (LP)	**£18**
70	Tamla Motown STML 11151	**FOUR IN BLUE** (LP)	**£25**
70	Tamla Motown STML 11163	**WHAT LOVE HAS JOINED TOGETHER** (LP, unissued)	**£0**
70	Tamla Motown STML 11172	**SMOKEY ROBINSON & THE MIRACLES** (LP)	**£15**
71	Tamla Motown STML 11172	**POCKETFUL OF MIRACLES** (LP)	**£20**
73	Tama Motown STMA 8010	**RENAISSANCE** (LP, gatefold as The Miracles)	**£15**

MIRAGE
65	CBS 201772	**It's In Her Kiss/What Ye Gonna Do 'Bout It**	**£20**
65	CBS 202007	**Go Away/Just A Face**	**£20**
66	Philips BF 1534	**Tomorrow Never Knows/You Can't Be Serious**	**£50**
67	Philips BF 1554	**Hold On/Can You Hear Me**	**£50**
67	Philips BF 1571	**The Wedding Of Ramona Blair/Lazy Man**	**£80**

(see also Caleb, Jawbone, Spencer Davis Group, Portobello Explosion)

MIRETTES
| 69 | MCA MUP(S) 344 | **IN THE MIDNIGHT HOUR** (LP) | **£20** |

(see also Ikettes)

MIRK
| 79 | Mother Earth MUM 1205 | **MODDANS BOWER** (LP) | **£80** |
| 82 | Spring Thyme SPR 1009 | **TAK A DRAM AFOR YE GO** (LP) | **£25** |

MIRKWOOD
| 71 | Flams Ltd PR 1067 | **MIRKWOOD** (LP) | **£1000** |
| 93 | Tenth Planet TP 003 | **MIRKWOOD** (LP, reissue, numbered with insert, 500 only) | **£30** |

MIRO
| 90 | Sacret Heart SH 30008 | **GREETINGS FROM GOLBORNE ROAD EP** (hand-made and signed p/s) | **£20** |

STEVE MIRO & EYES
80	Object Music OBF 008	**RUDE INTRUSIONS** (LP)	**£15**
81	Object Music OBJ 015	**SECOND SENTENCE** (LP)	**£15**
84	Glaze GZLP101	**TRILEMNA** (LP)	**£15**

(see also Eyes, Noyes Bros)

MIRROR
| 68 | Philips BF 1666 | **Gingerbread Man/Faster Than Light** | **£60** |

MIRRORS
| 78 | Lightning GIL 503 | **Cure For Cancer/Nice Vice** (p/s) | **£15** |
| 79 | Lightning GIL 540 | **Dark Glasses/999** (p/s) | **£25** |

MISBELIEVED ONES
| 71 | Croft CR 1 | **Sudddenly It Rains/Doctor Death** | **£70** |

MISA NEGRA
| 98 | People PEOPLE 008 | **Spiritual Vibes** (Aeronaut Dub)/(Original Reprise)/(Afro Boogie House Mix) (12") | **£30** |

MISBELIEVERS
| 71 | Plumett PL01 | **High In The Sky/Devil You** | **£35** |

MI 7
| 91 | Chill TUV 20 | **Rockin Down The House/Rockin Down The House** (Chop Mix) (12") | **£20** |

MISFITS (U.S.)
| 80 | Plan 9/Cherry Red PLP 9 | **BEWARE** (12" EP) | **£250** |

MISHKA
| 99 | Creation CRELP 244 | **MISHKA** (LP) | **£40** |

MISSES MISTY
| 79 | Freedom Sounds FSD 018 | **Mellow Mellow Ride On/FREEDOM FIGHTER BAND: Ladies Night** (12") | **£70** |

MISSING
| 94 | 3rd Party 3RD 11 | **Flex & Relax/Back To Consciousness** (12") | **£15** |

MISSING SCIENTISTS
| 80 | Rough Trade RT 057 | **Big City, Bright Lights/Discotheque X** (p/s) | **£20** |

(see also Television Personalities, Slaughter)

MISSION
| 95 | Equator SMEELP 001 | **NEVERLAND** (2-LP) | **£40** |
| 96 | Equator SMEELP 002 | **BLUE** (LP) | **£40** |

(see also Sisters Of Mercy, Dead Or Alive, Pauline Murray, Artery, Red Lorry Yellow Lorry)

MISSISSIPPI
| 70 | Fox FOX 1 | **Mr. Union Railway Man/Main Street** | **£100** |

MISS JANE
| 68 | Pama PM 704 | **Bad Mind People/My Heart Is Aching** (B-side act. "Witch Doctor" by Coolers) | **£55** |

MISS KATE
79	TJM TJM 10	Ebony Eyes/I Love You £20

MISSPENT YOUTH (1)
79	Sequel PART III	FOREVER EP (p/s) £30

MISSPENT YOUTH (2)
79	Big Bear BB20	Betcha Won't Dance/Birmingham Boys (p/s) £20

MISTAKEN IDENTITY
85	RAM 17CHP 7010	The Answer/The Answer (Club Version) (12") £25

MISTAKES
81	Twist And Shout TN5	Radiation/16 Pins (insert p/s) £15

MISTER VERSATILE
69	Jackpot JP 701	Apple Blossom/LITTLE BOY BLUE: Dark End Of The Street (act. by Pat Kelly) £20

(see also Lester Sterling)

MISTY IN ROOTS
78	People Unite SJP 781	Six One Penny/Six One Penny Version £18
78	People Unite SJP 789	Oh Wicked Man/Version £15
79	People Unite PU 001	See Them A Come/How Long Jah (12", p/s) £25
80	People Unite PU 002	Rich Man/Salvation (12", p/s) £18
81	People Unite PU 006	Wandering Wanderer/Cry Out For Peace (12") £20
81	People Unite PU 003	Peace And Love/Ball Out (12") £15
83	People Unite PU 103	Poor And Needy/Follow Fashion (12") £25
86	People Unite PU 007	Own Them Control Them/Own Them Control Them (Version) £15
79	People Unite PU 003	LIVE AT THE COUNTER EUROVISION '79 (LP) £30
82	People Unite PU 101 ALB	WISE AND FOOLISH (LP, inner) £25
83	People Unite PU 102	EARTH (LP) £25
85	People Unite PU 105	MUSI-O-TUNYA (LP) £25

MISTY MEADOWS
70	Rhone RH 002	Visions/We See The Sun £150

MISTY (1)
70	Parlophone R5852	Hot Cinnamon/Cascades £80

MISTY (2)
77	Cottage COT 511	MISTY (LP) £18

MISUNDERSTOOD
66	Fontana TF 777	I Can Take You To The Sun/Who Do You Love £80
69	Fontana TF 998	Children Of The Sun/I Unseen (small centre hole) £70
69	Fontana TF 998	Children Of The Sun/I Unseen (large centre hole) £50
69	Fontana TF 1028	You're Tuff Enough/Little Red Rooster (as Misunderstood featuring Glenn "Fernando" Campbell, in p/s) £60
69	Fontana TF 1028	You're Tuff Enough/Little Red Rooster (as Misunderstood featuring Glenn "Fernando" Campbell) £35
69	Fontana TF 1041	Never Had A Girl (Like You Before)/Golden Glass (as Misunderstood featuring Glenn "Fernando" Campbell) £45
82	Cherry Red B RED 32	BEFORE THE DREAM FADED (LP, with inner) £25

BLUE MITCHELL
73	Mainstream MSL 1015	THE LAST TANGO = BLUES (LP) £18

DENNY MITCHELL SOUNDSATIONS
64	Decca F 11848	I've Been Crying/For Your Love £25

(see also Preachers, Moon's Train)

GROVER MITCHELL
68	London HLU 10221	Turned On/Blue Over You £18
76	Vanguard VS 5003	What Hurts/Super Hero £50

GUY MITCHELL

SINGLES : SINGLES & EPS
53	Columbia SCM 5018	Feet Up (Pat Him On The Po-Po)/Jenny Kissed Me £15
53	Columbia SCM 5022	Cause I Love Ya, That's A-Why/Train Of Love (both with Mindy Carson) £15
53	Columbia SCM 5032	She Wears Red Feathers/Should I Go Home? £15
53	Columbia SCM 5037	Pretty Little Black-Eyed Susie/MITCH MILLER HORNS: Horn Belt Boogie £20
63	Pye International 7N 25179	Go, Tiger, Go/If You Ever Go Away (unreleased) £0

JONI MITCHELL
68	Reprise RS 20694	Night In The City/I Had A King £15
68	Reprise RSLP 6293	JONI MITCHELL (LP, gatefold sleeve, 'steamboat' label) £50
69	Reprise RSLP 6341	CLOUDS (LP, textured single sleeve, 'steamboat' label) £45
69	Reprise RSLP 6341	CLOUDS (LP, 2nd pressing, stickered U.S. gatefold sleeve, 'steamboat' label) £15
70	Reprise RSLP 6376	LADIES OF THE CANYON (LP, gatefold sleeve, 'steamboat' label) £30
71	Reprise K 44128	BLUE (LP, gatefold sleeve, with blue inner sleeve) £35
71	Reprise K 44128	BLUE (LP, gatefold sleeve) £25
73	Asylum SYLA 8753	FOR THE ROSES (LP, gatefold sleeve) £15
74	Asylum SYLA 8756	COURT AND SPARK (LP, gatefold sleeve) £20
75	Asylum SYLA 8763	THE HISSING OF SUMMER LAWNS (LP) £25
75	Asylum SYSP 902	MILES OF AISLES (2LP, two-page gatefold) £20
76	Asylum K 53053	HEJIRA (LP, gatefold) £30
77	Asylum K 63003	DON JUAN'S RECKLESS DAUGHTER (2LP, gatefold) £20
79	Asylum K 53091	MINGUS (LP, three-page gatefold) £18
80	Asylum K 62030	SHADOWS AND LIGHT (2LP, gatefold, printed inners) £25

MINT VALUE £

82	Asylum/Nimbus K 53018	THE HISSING OF SUMMER LAWNS (LP, audiophile pressing, mail order issue)	£150

McKINLEY 'SOUL' MITCHELL
68	President PTL 1005	McKINLEY 'SOUL' MITCHELL (LP)	£40

PHILIP MITCHELL
71	Jay Boy BOY 37	I'm Gonna Build California From All Over The World/ The World Needs More People Like You	£30
71	Jay Boy BOY 37	I'm Gonna Build California From All Over The World/ The World Needs More People Like You (DJ copy)	£50
74	London HLU 10444	Ain't No Love In My Life/Turning Over The Ground	£40

RED MITCHELL
56	London LTZ N15041	RED MITCHELL (LP)	£80
62	London LZ-N1 4017	HAPPY MINORS (10" LP)	£40
61	Vogue LAE 12286	REJOICE! (LP)	£35
63	London SH-K 8027	HEAR YE!! HEAR YE!! (LP)	£20

ROSCOE MITCHELL (SEXTET)
66	Delmark DL 408	SOUND (LP)	£50

SINX MITCHELL
64	Hickory 45-1248	This Weird Sensation/Love Is All I'm Asking For	£20

(see also Crickets, Earl Sinks)

VALERIE MITCHELL
65	Oak RGJ 160	There Goes My Heart Again/If I Didn't Love You (p/s)	£60

WILLIE MITCHELL
64	London HLU 9926	20-75/Secret Home	£20
64	London HLU 9926	20-75/Secret Home (DJ Copy)	£40
65	London HLU 10004	Everything Is Gonna Be Alright/That Driving Beat (Boxed logo)	£15
65	London HLU 10004	Everything Is Gonna Be Alright/That Driving Beat	£20
65	London HLU 10004	Everything Is Gonna Be Alright/That Driving Beat (DJ copy)	£50
74	London HLU 10545	The Champion (2 parts) (DJ copy)	£30
80	Cream CS 104	That Driving Beat/Mercy/Everything Is Gonna Be Alright	£15
67	London HA-U 8319	THE HIT SOUND OF WILLIE MITCHELL (LP)	£30
68	London HA-U/SH-U 8365	SOUL SERENADE (LP)	£20
68	London HA-U/SH-U 8368	LIVE (LP)	£20
69	London HA-U/SH-U 8372	SOLID SOUL (LP)	£20
70	London HA-U/SH-U 8388	ON TOP (LP)	£20
70	London HA-U/SH-U 8408	SOUL BAG (LP)	£20

MITCHELL/COE MYSTERIES
80	RCA PL 25297	EXILED (LP, with inner sleeve, with gatefold sleeve)	£15

(see also Colin Blunstone, Lesley Duncan, Francis Rossi & Berni Frost, Ray Russell, Joe Jammer, Complex, Monsoon)

ROBERT MITCHUM
67	Monument LMO 5011	THAT MAN (LP)	£20

MITHRANDIR
82	New Leaf SVC 570	Dreamers Of Fortune/After Tomorrow (p/s)	£50
82	New Leaf SVC 01	MAGICK EP (p/s)	£75

JACKIE MITTOO
66	Island WI 293	Killer Diller (as Jackie Mitto & Soul Brothers)/PATRICK HYTTON: Oh Lady	£150
67	Rio R 114	Home Made/ETHIOPIANS: I'm Gonna Take Over Now	£75
67	Rio R 123	Got My Buglaoo/ETHIOPIANS: What To Do	£230
67	Coxsone CS 7002	Somebody Help Me/GAYLADS & SOUL VENDORS: The Sound Of Silence	£125
67	Coxsone CS 7009	Ba Ba Boom/SLIM SMITH & FREEDOM SINGERS: Mercy Mercy	£125
67	Coxsone CS 7019	Ram Jam/SUMMERTAIRES: You're Gonna Leave	£40
67	Coxsone CS 7026	Something Stupid/LYRICS: Money Lover	£50
68	Coxsone CS 7040	Norwegian Wood/GAYLADS: Most Peculiar Man	£60
68	Coxsone CS 7042	Sure Shot/OCTAVES: The Bottle	£200
68	Coxsone CS 7046	Man Pon Spot/BOP & BELTONES: Not For A Moment	£50
68	Coxsone CS 7050	Napoleon Solo/CANNON BALL BRYAN: You're My Everything	£100
68	Coxsone CS 7070	Songbird/JAMAICAN ACTIONS: Catch The Quinella	£100
68	Coxsone CS 7075	Mission Impossible/HEPTONES: Giddy Up (B-side actually by Actions)	£80
68	Studio One SO 2043	Put It One/SOUL VENDORS: Chinese Chicken	£30
68	Studio One SO 2056	Race Track/BASES: I Don't Mind	£40
69	Studio One SO 2082	Hi-Jack/TREVOR CLARKE: Sufferer	£40
69	Doctor Bird DB 1177	Dark Of The Sun/MATADOR ALL STARS: Bridge View	£60
69	Bamboo BAM 6	Our Thing (with Sound Dimension)/C. MARSHALL: Tra La La Sweet '69	£60
69	Bamboo BAM 15	Clean Up/Spring Time (as Jackie Mittoo & Sound Dimension)	£40
70	Bamboo BAM 17	Dark Of The Moon/Moon Walk (as Jackie Mittoo & Sound Dimension)	£40
70	Bamboo BAM 20	Gold Dust/SUPERTONES: Real Gone Loser	£80
70	Bamboo BAM 31	Can I Change My Mind/BRENTFORD ALLSTARS: Early Duckling	£40
70	Bamboo BAM 38	Baby Why/ETHIOPIANS: You'll Want To Come Back	£40
70	Bamboo BAM 51	Dancing Groove/BLACK & GEORGE: Peanut Butter	£50
70	Banana BA 315	Holly Holy/LARRY MARSHALL: I've Got To Make It	£20
71	Banana BA 320	Peenie Wallie/ROY RICHARDS: Can't Go On	£20
79	Justice DIS 001	Disco Jack/Disco Dub (12")	£35
80	Rite Sound RTA 06	Mystic World/Version (12")	£20
81	Black Roots BR20	These Eyes/Wall Street/Killer Thriller (12", p/s)	£30
67	Coxsone CSL 8009	IN LONDON (LP)	£150
68	Coxsone CSL 8014	EVENING TIME (LP, with Soul Vendors)	£150
69	Coxsone CSL 8020	KEEP ON DANCING (LP)	£150

70	Bamboo BDLP 209	NOW (LP)	£80
72	London SHU 8436	WISHBONE (LP)	£25
77	Third World TWS 912	HOT BLOOD (LP)	£30
78	Third World TWS 931	IN COLD BLOOD (LP)	£40
79	Third World TWS 501	KEYBOARD KING (LP)	£35
97	Quartz QRLP 004	IN AFRICA (LP)	£40
00	Universal Sound USLP 8	THE KEYBOARD KING AT STUDIO ONE (2-LP)	£25
21	Soul Jazz Records SJR LP486	THE KEYBOARD KING AT STUDIO ONE (2-LP, reissue, Ltd Ed., transparent blue vinyl)	£30
23	Soul Jazz Records SJR LP 486-BLK	THE KEYBOARD KING AT STUDIO ONE (2-LP, reissue, Ltd Ed.)	£25

(see also Lord Tanamo, Jamaican Actions, Matadors, Jackie Opel, Soul Vendors, Winston Francis, Donna & Freedom Singers, Skatalites)

MIXED FEELINGS
| 73 | Scotty SCO 2 | Make Me Jump/Stop | £20 |

MIXMAN
| 90 | Citizen Kane 12KANE 2 | Bright Child (Manmix)/Bright Child (Dancemix) (12", p/s) | £15 |
| 94 | Blakamix BLKM012 | Carriacou Cargo EP (12") | £15 |

MIXRACE & PRO-TON-ISOSPACE
| 94 | Stronghold STRONG 3 | The Endless Skies (Hyper-On-Experience Remix)/True Jungle (Brown & Dangerman Remix)/The Endless Skies/True Jungle (12") | £20 |

MIXTURES
| 71 | Polydor 205813 | Never Be Untrue/She's Gone Away | £20 |

VIC MIZZY, HIS ORCHESTRA & CHORUS
| 65 | RCA RCA 1440 | Addams Family Main Theme/Kentucky James Main Theme | £20 |

MO2VATION
| 93 | No Noise NNDJ 008 | Lowdown & Funky/That Ruff Track (with L Double, 12") | £15 |

MO2VATION & APEX
| 92 | Hypno Genesis HG 002 | ANIMATION EP (12") | £25 |

MOB (1)
68	Mercury MF 1026	Disappear/I Wish You Would Leave Me Alone	£15
71	Polydor 2001 127	I Dig Everything About You/Love's Got A Hold On Me	£20
71	Polydor 2344 001	MOB (LP)	£15

MOB (3)
80	All The Madmen MAD 1	Youth/Crying Again (p/s)	£40
83	Cause For Concern CFC 2	LIVE AT THE LMC (LP, with the APOSTLES)	£30
83	All The Madmen MAD 4	LET THE TRIBE INCREASE (LP, with lyric poster)	£25
86	All The Madmen MAD 13	CRYING AGAIN (EP)	£30
80s	All/Madmen MADPACK 1	MAD PACK 1 (3 x 7" in 12" pack)	£25

HANK MOBLEY
| 56 | Esquire 32-029 | MOBLEY'S MESSAGE (LP) | £150 |
| 59 | Columbia 33SX 1160 | MONDAY NIGHT AT BIRDLAND (LP, with Billy Root, Chris Fuller & Lee Morgan) | £60 |

JOHN MOBLEY
| 62 | Stateside SS 136 | Tunnel Of Love/Work Out | £15 |

MOBY
93	Equator ATLASLP 001	THE STORY SO FAR (LP)	£25
93	Equator ATLASLP 002	AMBIENT (LP)	£40
95	Mute STUMM 130	EVERYTHING IS WRONG (LP)	£30
96	Mute STUMM 150	ANIMAL RIGHTS (LP)	£40
97	Mute STUMM 168	I LIKE TO SCORE (LP)	£25
99	Mute STUMM 172	PLAY (2-LP, inner, 500 only)	£100
02	Mute STUMM 202	18 (2-LP, gatefold)	£80
05	Mute STUMM 240	HOTEL (LP)	£35
05	Little Idiot MOB2VINIOT03OVXX	HOTEL : AMBIENT (LP)	£20
08	Mute STUMM 275	LAST NIGHT (2-LP)	£30
09	Little Idiot IDIOT 001T	LITTLE IDIOT (2-LP)	£30
11	Little Idiot IDIOT 010LP	DESTROYED (2-LP, CD)	£35
13	Little Idiot IDIOT 110	PLAY (2-LP, gatefold, reissue, 500 only, all signed by Moby)	£80
13	Little Idiot IDIOT 111	18 (2-LP, gatefold, reissue, 500 only, all signed by Moby)	£80
16	Mute STUMM 130	EVERYTHING IS WRONG (LP, reissue)	£15
16	Mute STUMM 150	ANIMAL RIGHTS (LP, reissue)	£18

MOBY DICK
| 82 | Ebony EBON 5 | Nothing To Fear/Can't Have My Body Tonight | £20 |

MOBY GRAPE
67	CBS 2953	Omaha/Hey Grandma	£20
68	CBS 3555	Can't Be So Bad/Murder In My Heart For The Judge	£15
67	CBS (S)BPG 63090	MOBY GRAPE (LP)	£60
68	CBS 63271	WOW (LP, mono & stereo)	£40
69	CBS 63430	69 (LP, mono & stereo)	£40
69	CBS 63698	TRULY FINE CITIZEN (LP, stereo)	£40
69	CBS 63698	TRULY FINE CITIZEN (LP, mono)	£60
71	Reprise K 44152	20 GRANITE CREEK (LP)	£15
74	CBS 64743	GREAT GRAPE (LP)	£15

MOCKINGBIRDS
| 65 | Columbia DB 7480 | That's How It's Gonna Stay/I Never Should Have Kissed You | £50 |
| 65 | Columbia DB 7565 | I Can Feel We're Parting/The Flight Of The Mockingbird | £50 |

MINT VALUE £

65	Immediate IM 015	**You Stole My Love/Skit Skat**	**£150**
66	Decca F 12434	**One By One/Lovingly Yours**	**£60**
66	Decca F 12510	**How To Find A Lover/My Story**	**£50**

(see also 10cc, Graham Gouldman, Whirlwinds, Hotlegs, Godley & Creme)

M.O.D.
79	Vertigo 6059 233	**M.O.D./M.O.D.** (2) (p/s, allegedly mispressed on 2-Tone label)	**£30**

(see also David Essex)

MODE
66	Private pressing	**THE MODE** (EP, white labels, no p/s)	**£400**

MODEL 500
89	Kool Kat KOOL T 507	**The Chase** (Express Mix)/(Neutral Mix)/(Mayday Mix) (12", p/s)	**£15**

MODEL MANIA
79	Boob MM1 A/MM 1AA	**No Pride Slow Suicide/Epic Cowboy** (250 with handmade stamped label)	**£100**
79	Boob MM1 A/MM 1AA	**No Pride Slow Suicide/Epic Cowboy** (750 with black labels)	**£75**

MODEL WORKERS
81	Make It Yourself 007BOND	**Cry/My Winter Of Discontent/** (p/s, yellow, pink and blue variants)	**£50**

MODELS
77	Step Forward SF 3	**Freeze/Man Of The Year** (p/s, 1st pressing with The Models and The Freeze on labels)	**£20**
77	Step Forward SF-3	**Freeze/Man Of The Year** (p/s, 2nd pressing with Models and Freeze on labels)	**£15**

(see also Adam & The Ants, Mass, Rema Rema, Wolfgang Press)

MODE-M
96	Void VOID 001	**Space Based/Cohesion** (12")	**£30**
97	Void VOID 005	**INNER WORLD EP** (2 x 12")	**£20**

MODERATES
80	Open Eye OEEP 1001	**FETISHES** (12" EP)	**£15**

MODERN ART
84	Color Disc COLORS 1	**Dreams To Live/Beautiful Truth** (p/s)	**£25**
87	Color Disc COLOR 3	**STEREOLAND** (LP, hand-stencilled with insert, 300 only)	**£60**
94	Acme 8007 LP	**ALL ABOARD THE MIND TRAIN** (LP, 500 only, numbered)	**£18**

MODERN ENGLISH
79	Limp LMP 2	**Drowning Man/Silent World** (p/s)	**£30**
80	4AD AD 6	**Swans On Glass/Incident** (p/s)	**£15**
80	4AD AD 15	**Gathering Dust/Tranquility Of A Summer Moment** (p/s)	**£15**
81	4AD CAD 105	**MESH AND LACE** (LP)	**£20**

(see also This Mortal Coil)

MODERN EON
80	Modern Eon EON 001	**PIECES** (EP)	**£20**
81	Dinsales 2	**Euthenics/Choreography/Waiting For The Cavalry/The Real Hymn** (12", white label LP sampler)	**£20**

MODERN FOLK QUARTET (M.F.Q.)
64	Warner Bros WB 147	**The Love Of A Clown/If You All Think**	**£25**
66	RCA RCA 1514	**Night Time Girl/Lifetime** (as M.F.Q.)	**£30**
63	Warner Bros WM/WS 8135	**THE MODERN FOLK QUARTET** (LP)	**£20**
85	Off Beat WIK 55	**MOONLIGHT SERENADE** (LP)	**£15**

MODERN JAZZ QUARTET (M.J.Q.)
55	Esquire 20-069	**MODERN JAZZ QUARTET** (10" LP)	**£20**
55	Esquire 20-038	**MODERN JAZZ QUARTET VOL. 2** (10" LP)	**£20**
55	Esquire 20-090	**THE CLASSICAL PERFORMANCES OF...** (10" LP)	**£20**
56	Esquire 320024	**MJQ IN HI FI** (LP)	**£20**
57	London Jazz LTZK 15022	**FONTESSA** (LP, also stereo SAH-K 6031)	**£20**
58	London Jazz LTZK 15085	**AT THE MUSIC INN** (LP)	**£20**
58	London Jazz LTZ 15136	**MODERN JAZZ QUARTET** (LP)	**£20**
59	London Jazz LTZ-K 15140	**PLAYS ONE NEVER KNOWS** (LP, also stereo SAH-K 6029)	**£20**
59	London Jazz LTZK 15181	**ODDS AGAINST TOMORROW** (LP)	**£20**
59	Columbia Clef 33CX 11028	**MODERN JAZZ QUARTET & OSCAR PETERSON AT THE OPERA HOUSE** (LP)	**£20**
60	London Jazz LTZ-K 15193	**PYRAMID** (LP, also stereo SAH-K 6086)	**£20**
61	London Jazz LTZ-K 15207	**THIRD STREAM MUSIC** (LP, with Beaux Arts String Quartet & Jimmy Giuffre Three)	**£20**
63	London HA-K/SH-K 8016	**LONELY WOMAN** (LP)	**£15**
68	Apple APCOR 4	**UNDER THE JASMINE TREE** (LP, mono)	**£50**
68	Apple SAPCOR 4	**UNDER THE JASMINE TREE** (LP, stereo)	**£35**
69	Apple SAPCOR 10	**SPACE** (LP, gatefold sleeve, dark green label, black inner)	**£40**
73	Apple SAPCOR 10	**SPACE** (LP, later pressing, light green label, single sleeve, white 'Apple' inner)	**£50**
93	Apple SAPCOR 4	**UNDER THE JASMINE TREE** (LP, reissue, gatefold sleeve with inner)	**£20**
93	Apple SAPCOR 10	**SPACE** (LP, reissue)	**£20**

(see also John Lewis, Milt Jackson, Sonny Rollins)

MODERN JAZZ SEXTET
56	Columbia Clef 33CX 10048	**MODERN JAZZ SEXTET** (LP)	**£20**

MODERNAIRES (U.K.)
80	Illuminated JAMS 3	**WAY OF LIVING** (LP)	**£15**

MODEST JAZZ TRIO
60	Vogue LAE 12278	**GOOD FRIDAY BLUES** (LP)	**£25**

(see also Jim Hall)

MODEST MOUSE
00	Matador OLE 464-1	**NIGHT ON THE SUN** (12" EP, p/s)	**£15**

| 00 | Matador OLE 4501 | **MOON AND ANTARTICA** (2-LP) | **£30** |

MO-DETTES
| 80 | Deram SML 1120 | **THE STORY SO FAR** (LP, with insert & free colour sticker) | **£20** |

MODS (1)
| 64 | RCA RCA 1399 | **Something On My Mind/You're Making Me Blue** | **£25** |

MODS (2)
| 80 | Bootlegged Records 007 | **LOST TOUCH** (LP; sold only in Portobello Market, London) | **£25** |

MODULATIONS
| 74 | Buddah BDS 406 | **I Can't Fight Your Love/Your Love Has Locked Me Up** (DJ Copy) | **£30** |
| 74 | Buddah BDS 406 | **I Can't Fight Your Love/Your Love Has Locked Me Up** | **£15** |

MOFFAT ALL STARS
| 70 | Jackpot JP 719 | **Riot/IMPERSONATORS: Girls And Boys** | **£200** |

LENROY MOFFATT
| 74 | Atra AR 20 | **What It Takes/I Love You Darling** | **£45** |

MOGUL THRASH
| 70 | RCA RCA 2030 | **Sleeping In The Kitchen/St. Peter** | **£15** |
| 71 | RCA SF 8156 | **MOGUL THRASH** (LP) | **£150** |

(see also Colosseum, Eclection, King Crimson)

MOGWAI
96	Rock Action RAR 01	**Tuner/Lower** (p/s, 500 only)	**£70**
96	Ché CHE 59	**4 TRACK 3 BAND TOUR EP** (with Urusei Yatsura & Backwater, p/s, 50 only)	**£40**
96	Love Train PUBE 014	**Summer/Ithica 27/9** (p/s, 1,500 only, inserts)	**£20**
97	Wurlitzer Jukebox WJ 22	**New Paths To Helicon** (Parts 1 & 2) (foldover p/s in polythene bag, 2 inserts,1,000 only)	**£15**
97	Flotsam/Jetsam SHAG13.04	**Stereo Dee/PH FAMILY: Club Beatroot Part 4** (p/s, 400 only)	**£15**
97	Chemikal CHEM 015	**4 SATIN EP**	**£15**
99	Chemikal CHEM 036	**EP** (12")	**£15**
01	Rock Action ROCKACT 10	**My Father My King** (1-sided 12")	**£15**
13	Rock Action ROCKACT 73	**LES REVENANTS EP** (10")	**£18**
97	Chemikal Underground CHEM 818	**YOUNG TEAM** (2LP, gatefold)	**£200**
98	Eye Q EYEUKLP 019	**KICKING A DEAD PIG** (2LP, with poster)	**£50**
99	Chemikal Underground CHEM 033	**COME ON DIE YOUNG** (2LP, gatefold, printed inners)	**£100**
01	Southpaw PAWLP1	**ROCK ACTION** (LP, printed inner, fold-out poster)	**£40**
03	Pias PIASX 035LP	**HAPPY SONGS FOR HAPPY PEOPLE** (LP, silver mirror sleeve)	**£50**
05	Pias PIAS051LP	**GOVERNMENT COMMISSIONS : BBC SESSIONS 1996-2003** (2LP, gatefold)	**£50**
06	Pias PIAS X062DLP	**MR BEAST** (2LP, one sided etched, gatefold, speech bubble sticker)	**£30**
06	Pias PIAS X067DLP	**ZIDANE - A 21st CENTURY PORTRAIT** (2LP, gatefold)	**£35**
08	Wall Of Sound WOS 040DLP	**THE HAWK IS HOWLING** (2LP, gatefold, printed inners)	**£20**
08	Chemikal Underground CHEM 106	**YOUNG TEAM** (4LP box set, reissue, printed inners)	**£150**
10	Rock Action ROCKACT 48X	**SPECIAL MOVES** (3LP, CD, DVD, box set, signed poster, patch)	**£80**
11	Rock Action ROCKACT 55	**HARDCORE WILL NEVER DIE, BUT YOU WILL** (2LP 2CD 12" box set, art prints, stencil)	**£70**
11	Rock Action ROCKACT 55LP	**HARDCORE WILL NEVER DIE, BUT YOU WILL** (2LP, gatefold, printed inners)	**£20**
12	Rock Action ROCKACT 72LP	**A WRETCHED VILE LORE** (2LP, printed inners)	**£20**
13	Rock Action ROCKACT 74LP	**LES REVENANTS** (LP, printed inner, download card)	**£15**
14	Rock Action ROCKACT80	**RAVE TAPES** (LP, pink vinyl 12", 7", CD, cassette box set, art prints, book, download card)	**£60**
14	Rock Action ROCKACT 80LPX	**RAVE TAPES** (LP, 7", die-cut sleeve, printed inner, download card)	**£20**
15	Rock Action ROCKACT 100LP	**CENTRAL BELTERS** (6LP box set, booklet, printed inners)	**£100**
16	Rock Action ROCKACTION102LPX	**ATOMIC** (2LP, gatefold, orange vinyl)	**£25**
16	Rock Action ROCKACTION 102LP	**ATOMIC** (2LP, gatefold)	**£15**
17	ROCK ACTION ROCKACT 108	**EVERY COUNTRY'S SUN** (white vinyl 2LP, CD, 12" box set, prints)	**£40**
17	ROCK ACTION ROCKACT 108LPX	**EVERY COUNTRY'S SUN** (2LP, gatefold, clear vinyl)	**£20**
18	Rock Action ROCKACT 115LPX	**KIN** (ORIGINAL MOTION PICTURE SOUNDTRACK) (LP, red vinyl)	**£15**
19	Rock Action ROCKACT 5LPX	**TEN RAPID** (COLLECTED RECORDINGS 1996-1997) (LP, first UK vinyl issue of 97 CD, green vinyl, printed inner, NAD)	**£20**
21	Rock Action ROCKACT 134LP	**ZEROZEROZERO** (A MOGWAI SOUNDTRACK) (2LP, white vinyl, RSD)	**£18**
21	Rock Action ROCKACT 140	**AS THE LOVE CONTINUES** (red vinyl 2LP, 12", CD box set, book, ltd.ed.)	**£50**
21	Rock Action ROCKACT 140LPM	**AS THE LOVE CONTINUES** (2LP, gatefold, orange vinyl, ltd. to 500)	**£50**
21	Rock Action ROCKACT 140LPXS	**AS THE LOVE CONTINUES** (2LP, gatefold, gold vinyl, indie store exclusive)	**£25**
21	Rock Action ROCKACT 140LPX	**AS THE LOVE CONTINUES** (2LP, gatefold, yellow vinyl)	**£20**
21	Chemikal Underground CHEM 250	**E.P. x 3** (3x12", curaçao, clear, yellow vinyl, 3EPS in original packaging)	**£25**
23	Rock Action ROCKACT 05LPS	**TEN RAPID** (COLLECTED RECORDINGS 1996-1997) (red vinyl LP, green 7" flexi, numbered print, lanyard, ltd 500 Monorail edition)	**£50**

(see also Fuck Buttons)

ESSRA MOHAWK
| 75 | Mooncrest CREST 24 | **ESSRA MOHAWK** (LP, with insert) | **£15** |
| 77 | Private Stock PVLP 1016 | **ESSRA** (LP) | **£15** |

MOHAWKS
| 68 | Pama PM 309 | **The Clock/Version** | **£35** |

MINT VALUE £

68	Pama PM 719	The Champ/Sound Of The Witchdoctors (blue label)...................................£30
68	Pama PM 719	The Champ/Sound Of The Witchdoctors (purple label)...............................£20
68	Pama PM 739	Baby Hold On (Parts 1 & 2)...£20
68	Pama PM 751	Sweet Soul Music/Hip Jigger..£20
68	Pama PM 757	Mony Mony/Pepsi..£70
69	Pama PM 758	Ride Your Pony/Western Promise...£25
69	Pama PM 798	Skinhead Shuffle/RICO: Red Cow...£40
70	Supreme SUP 205	Wicked Lady/For Our Liberty..£15
70	Pama PM 796	Landscape/Number 1..£25
70	Supreme SUP 204	Let It Be/Looking Back..£15
70	Supreme SUP 207	Give Me Some/(Instrumental)...£120
72	Supreme PS 362	Storm/And I Love Her..£40
73	Supreme PS 376	The Champ/Cherry Pink...£100
70s	Star PTP 1011	Whiter Shade Of Pale/My One Desire...£15
86	Pama PM1	The Champ/Landscape (7", reissue, p/s)...£18
68	Pama PMLP 5	THE CHAMP (LP, flipback sleeve, purple labels)..£200

(see also Sid & Joe & Mohawks)

LOUIS MOHOLO
78	Ogun OG 520	SPIRITS REJOICE (LP)..£80

MOJAVE 3
95	4AD CAD 5013	ASK ME TOMORROW (LP)...£150
98	4AD CAD 8018	OUT OF TUNE (LP)...£150
00	4AD CAD 2K05	EXCUSES FOR TRAVELLERS (LP)..£150
03	4AD CAD 2309 LP	SPOON & RAFTER (LP)..£75
06	4AD CAD 2604	PUZZLES LIKE YOU (LP)..£75
17	Sonic Cathedral SCRO73LP	ASK ME TOMORROW (LP, reissue, green vinyl, 500 only)..............................£25

(see also Slowdive)

MOJO HANNAH
72	Kingdom KV 8004	St. Jeremy/You'll Be Alright..£25
73	Kingdom KVL 9001	SIX DAYS ON THE ROAD (LP, orange label)...£35

MOJO MEN
65	Pye International 7N 25336	Dance With Me/Loneliest Boy In Town...£30
66	Reprise RS 20486	Hanky Panky/She's My Baby..£30
67	Reprise RS 20539	Sit Down I Think I Love You/Don't Leave Me Crying Like Before...................£20
67	Reprise RS 20580	Me About You/When You're In Love...£15

MOJOS
63	Decca F 11732	They Say/Forever...£15
65	Decca F 12127	Comin' On To Cry/That's The Way It Goes..£15
67	Decca F 12557	Goodbye Dolly Gray/I Just Can't Let Her Go..£25
68	Liberty LBF 15097	Until My Baby Comes Home/Seven Park Avenue..£60
64	Decca DFE 8591	THE MOJOS (EP)...£70

(see also Stu James & Mojos, Faron's Flamingos)

MOLDY PEACHES
01	Rough Trade RTRADELP 014	THE MOLDY PEACHES (LP)..£80

MOLES
68	Parlophone R 5743	We Are The Moles (Parts 1 & 2)...£30

MOLOKO
95	Echo ECHLP 7	DO YOU LIKE MY TIGHT SWEATER (2-LP)..£40
98	Echo ECHLP 21	I AM NOT A DOCTOR (2-LP, triple gatefold)...£80
00	Echo ECHLP 31	THINGS TO MAKE AND DO (2-LP)...£80
03	Echo ECHLP 44	STATUES (LP)..£125

MOMENT
86	Rave RAVE UP 1	THE WORK GETS DONE (LP, coloured vinyl)...£15

MOMENT OF TRUTH
77	Salsoul SZS 5509	MOMENT OF TRUTH (LP)...£15

MOMENTS (2)
76	All Platinum SOUL 001	Nine Times (Disco Version)/THE RIMSHOTS: Do What You Feel (Disco Version) (12")......£50
73	London SHU 8471	THE BEST OF THE MOMENTS (LP)..£15

MOMUS
86	Él GPO 9T	Nicky/Don't Leave/See A Friend In Tears (12")..£15
86	el ACME 2	CIRCUS MAXIMUS (LP)...£15
88	Creation CRELP 036	TENDER PERVERT (LP, with free 7")...£15
90	Creation CRELP 052	DON'T STOP THE NIGHT (LP)..£15
91	Creation CRELP 097	HIPPOPOTAMOMUS (LP, with "Michelin Man" track & Michelin Man style inlay, withdrawn)...£15

(see also Happy Family)

MONARCHS
64	London HLU 9862	Look Homeward Angel/What's Made You Change Your Mind.........................£30

GRACHAN MONCUR III
74	JCOA/Virgin J2003	ECHOES OF PRAYER (LP)..£25

MONEY (2)
80	Hobo HOS 011	FAST WORLD (EP, p/s)..£80
79	Gull GULP 1031	FIRST INVESTMENT (LP)..£18

MONEY JANGLE
| 72 | President PT 362 | Home/Away Away | £20 |

ZOOT MONEY('S BIG ROLL BAND)
64	Decca F 11954	The Uncle Willie/Zoot's Suit (solo)	£50
65	Columbia DB 7518	Good/Bring It Home To Me	£40
65	Columbia DB 7600	Please Stay/You Know You'll Cry	£35
65	Columbia DB 7697	Something Is Worrying Me/Stubborn Kind Of Fellow	£30
65	Columbia DB 7768	The Many Faces Of Love/Jump Back (as Paul Williams & Zoot Money Band)	£30
66	Columbia DB 7876	Let's Run For Cover/Self-Discipline	£30
66	Columbia DB 7975	Big Time Operator/Zoot's Sermon	£20
66	Columbia DB 8090	The Star Of The Show (The La La Song)/The Mound Moves	£35
67	Columbia DB 8172	Nick Knack/I Really Learnt How To Cry	£15
80	Magic Moon/MPL MACH 6	The Two Of Us/Ain't Nothin' Shakin' But The Bacon (solo)	£30
66	Columbia SEG 8519	BIG TIME OPERATOR (EP)	£200
66	Columbia S(C)X 6075	ZOOT! - LIVE AT KLOOK'S KLEEK (LP, mono)	£100
66	Columbia S(C)X 6075	ZOOT! - LIVE AT KLOOK'S KLEEK (LP, stereo)	£120
65	Columbia 33SX 1734	IT SHOULD'VE BEEN ME (LP)	£150
68	Direction 8-63231	TRANSITION (LP)	£100
70	Polydor 2482 019	ZOOT MONEY (LP)	£80

(see also Paul Williams & Big Roll Band, Dantalian's Chariot, Eric Burdon & Animals, Grimms, Centipede, Ellis, Johnny Almond Music Machine)

MONGOLFIER BROS
| 84 | Incurable | I Know/Things That Go Bump | £20 |

MONGREL
| 73 | Polydor 2383 182 | GET YOUR TEETH INTO THIS (LP) | £25 |

(see also Wizzard)

MONGRELS
| 64 | Decca F 12003 | I Long To Hear/Everywhere | £30 |
| 65 | Decca F 12086 | My Love For You/Stewball | £30 |

(see also Bobbie Miller)

MONITORS (1)
| 69 | T. Motown TML 11108 | GREETINGS WE'RE THE MONITORS (LP, mono) | £100 |
| 69 | T. Motown STML 11108 | GREETINGS WE'RE THE MONITORS (LP, stereo) | £90 |

MONK BOUGHT LUNCH
| 91 | Own Label | Love And Hate/Paint It White/The Sailor's Tilted Hat (p/s) | £40 |

THELONIOUS MONK
55	Esquire 20-039	THELONIOUS MONK QUINTET (10" LP)	£45
55	Esquire 20-049	THELONIOUS MONK (10" LP)	£45
56	Esquire 20-075	THELONIOUS MONK PLAYS (10" LP)	£45
57	London LTZU 15097	BRILLIANT CORNERS (LP)	£50
60	Esquire 32-109	THELONIOUS MONK QUINTETS (LP)	£50
61	Esquire 32-115	WORK! (LP, with Art Blakey & Sonny Rollins)	£60
61	Esquire 32-119	MONK'S MOODS (LP)	£60
61	Riverside RLP 12-201	MONK PLAYS ELLINGTON (LP)	£50
61	Philips BBL 1510	THELONIOUS MONK VOL. 1 (LP)	£50
61	Riverside RLP 12-226	BRILLIANT CORNERS (LP)	£80
61	Riverside RLP 12-262	MONK IN ACTION (LP)	£40
62	Riverside RLP 12-300	AT THE TOWN HALL (LP, also stereo RLP 1138)	£40
62	Riverside RLP 12-323	AT THE BLACK HAWK (LP, also stereo RLP 1171)	£40
62	Philips BBL 1511	THELONIOUS MONK VOL. 2 (LP)	£40
62	Riverside RLP 12-242	MONK'S MUSIC (LP)	£80
63	CBS (S)BPG 62135	MONK'S DREAM (LP)	£50
63	Riverside RLP 12-235	THELONIOUS HIMSELF (LP)	£50
63	Riverside JLP (9)46	THELONIOUS MONK AND JOHN COLTRANE (LP)	£50
64	Riverside RLP 002	IN EUROPE (VOL. 1)	£35
64	CBS (S)BPG 62173	CRISS-CROSS (LP)	£35
64	Blue Note (B)BLP 1510	THE GENIUS OF MODERN MUSIC (VOL. 1) (LP)	£25
64	Blue Note (B)BLP 1511	THE GENIUS OF MODERN MUSIC (VOL. 2) (LP)	£25
64	Riverside RLP 279	MISTERIOSO (LP)	£25
64	CBS (S)BPG 62248	BIG BAND AND QUARTET IN CONCERT (LP)	£25
65	CBS (S)BPG 62391	IT'S MONK'S TIME (LP)	£25
65	Riverside RLP 305	FIVE BY MONK BY FIVE (LP)	£25
65	Riverside RLP 003	IN EUROPE (VOL. 2) (LP)	£20
65	CBS (S)BPG 62497	MONK (LP)	£20
65	Riverside RLP 312	ALONE IN SAN FRANCISCO (LP)	£20
65	Fontana FJL 113	WAY OUT! (LP)	£20
65	Realm RM 52223	NICA'S TEMPO (LP, with Gigi Gryce)	£20
65	CBS (S)BPG 62549	SOLO (LP)	£20
65	Stateside SL 10152	THE GOLDEN MONK (LP)	£20
67	Transatlantic PR7169	WORK (LP)	£20
69	CBS 63609	MONKS BLUES (LP)	£15

(see also John Coltrane, Sonny Rollins, Art Blakey, Miles Davis)

MONKEES
67	RCA Victor RD 7844	The MONKEES (LP, mono)	£15
67	RCA Victor RD 7868	MORE OF THE MONKEES (LP, mono)	£18
67	RCA Victor SF 7868	MORE OF THE MONKEES (LP, stereo)	£20
67	RCA Victor RD 7886	HEADQUARTERS (LP, mono	£20

MINT VALUE £

67	RCA Victor SF 7886	**HEADQUARTERS** (LP, stereo)	**£22**
67	RCA Victor RD 7886	**HEADQUARTERS** (LP, with different 'beard' photo on back, mono)	**£25**
67	RCA Victor SF 7886	**HEADQUARTERS** (LP, with different 'beard' photo on back, stereo)	**£30**
67	RCA Victor RD/SF 7912	**PISCES, AQUARIUS, CAPRICORN AND JONES LTD.** (LP)	**£22**
68	RCA Victor RD/SF 7948	**THE BIRDS, THE BEES & THE MONKEES** (LP)	**£22**

(The above albums were originally issued with black labels; later orange label copies are worth the same value.)

69	RCA RD 8016	**INSTANT REPLAY** (LP, mono)	**£30**
69	RCA SF 8016	**INSTANT REPLAY** (LP, stereo)	**£25**
69	RCA RD 8051	**HEAD** (LP, soundtrack, mono)	**£90**
69	RCA SF 8051	**HEAD** (LP, soundtrack, stereo)	**£60**
79	Arista MONK-1 1/2	**MONKEEMANIA** (LP)	**£20**
89	Circus BOY 1	**IDOLISED, PLASTICISED, PSYCHOANYLYSED, STERILISED** (LP, spoken-word convention issue, white vinyl)	**£15**
89	Circus BOY 1	**IDOLISED, PLASTICISED, PSYCHOANYLYSED, STERILISED** (LP, spoken-word convention issue, picture disc)	**£18**

(see also Michael Nesmith, Tommy Boyce & Bobby Hart)

MONOCHROME SET

80	Dindisc DID 4	**STRANGE BOUTIQUE** (LP)	**£25**
80	DinDisc DID 8	**LOVE ZOMBIES** (LP, with lithograph)	**£20**
82	Cherry Red BRED 34	**ELIGIBLE BACHELORS** (LP)	**£15**
83	Cherry Red MRED 47	**VOLUME CONTRAST BRILLIANCE** (LP)	**£15**

(see also Art Attacks)

MONOLITH (1)

78	None	(I'm Not Your) **Stepping Stone/Guns Of Time** (no p/s)	**£60**

MONOLITH (2)

10	Rephlex CAT 210EP	**VOLUME 1** (12" EP)	**£30**
15	Central Processing Unit 00010001	**FLEKTRO** (12" EP, as MNLTH)	**£30**
16	Organic Analogue OA04	**LASER 80** (12" EP as MNLTH)	**£30**

MONOPOLY

67	Polydor 56164	**House Of Lords/Magic Carpet**	**£20**
70	Pye 7N 17940	**We Belong Together/Gone Tomorrow**	**£25**

(see also Raymond Froggatt)

MONOTONES (U.S.)

58	London HLM 8625	**Book Of Love/You Never Loved Me**	**£40**
58	London HLM 8625	**Book Of Love/You Never Loved Me** (78)	**£20**

MATT MONRO

61	Ember EMB S 120	**The Ghost Of Your Past/Quite Suddenly**	**£15**
69	capitol CL 15603	**On Days Like These/On A Clear Day** (You Can See Forever)	**£25**
57	Decca LF 1276	**BLUE AND SENTIMENTAL** (10" LP)	**£20**

(see also John Barry)

BILL MONROE (& HIS BLUE GRASS BOYS)

56	Brunswick 05567	**New John Henry Blues/Put My Little Shoes Away**	**£15**

MARILYN MONROE

53	MGM MGM 663	**Diamonds Are A Girl's Best Friend/Bye Bye Baby** (78)	**£15**
54	HMV 7M 232	**The River Of No Return/I'm Gonna File My Claim**	**£60**
54	HMV B 10723	**The River Of No Return/I'm Gonna File My Claim** (78)	**£15**
55	HMV B 10847	**After You Get What You Want/Heat Wave** (78)	**£15**
59	London HLT 8862	**I Wanna Be Loved By You/I'm Thru' With Love**	**£35**
59	London HLT 8862	**I Wanna Be Loved By You/I'm Thru' With Love** (78)	**£15**
55	HMV 7EG 8090	**THERE'S NO BUSINESS LIKE SHOW BUSINESS - SOUNDTRACK EXCERPTS** (EP, company sleeve)	**£25**
59	London RET 1231	**SOME LIKE IT HOT** (EP, soundtrack; first pressing with triangular centre)	**£80**
59	London RET 1231	**SOME LIKE IT HOT** (EP, soundtrack; later round centre)	**£20**
60	Philips BBE 12414	**LET'S MAKE LOVE - FILM SOUNDTRACK** (EP, with Yves Montand & Frankie Vaughan; mono)	**£30**
60	Philips SBBE 9031	**LET'S MAKE LOVE - FILM SOUNDTRACK** (EP, with Yves Montand & Frankie Vaughan; stereo)	**£40**
53	MGM MGM-D 116	**GENTLEMEN PREFER BLONDES** (10" LP, soundtrack with other artists)	**£75**
59	London HA-T 2176	**SOME LIKE IT HOT** (LP, soundtrack with other artists, mono)	**£50**
59	London SAH-T 6040	**SOME LIKE IT HOT** (LP, soundtrack with other artists, stereo)	**£60**
60	Philips BBL 7414	**LET'S MAKE LOVE** (LP, soundtrack, with Yves Montand & Frankie Vaughan; mono)	**£40**
60	Philips SBBL 592	**LET'S MAKE LOVE** (LP, soundtrack, with Yves Montand & Frankie Vaughan; stereo)	**£40**
63	Stateside S(S)L 10048	**MARILYN** (LP, soundtrack, mono)	**£30**
63	Stateside S(S)L 10048	**MARILYN** (LP, soundtrack, stereo)	**£40**

(see also Frankie Vaughan)

VAUGHN MONROE (& HIS ORCHESTRA)

56	HMV 7M 332	**Black Denim Trousers And Motorcycle Boots/All By Myself**	**£20**

MONSOON (1)

72	Blue Mountain BM 1006	**Night Of The Fly/Caroline The Wine Was Good**	**£40**

MONSTER MAGNET

95	A&M 540 315-1	**DOPES TO INFINITY** (2-LP)	**£80**
98	A&M 540 908-1	**POWERTRIP** (2-LP)	**£100**

MONTANAS

66	Pye 7N 17183	**That's When Happiness Began/Goodbye Little Girl**	**£50**
67	Pye 7N 17394	**You've Got To Be Loved/Difference Of Opinion**	**£20**
69	Pye 7N 17697	**Roundabout/Mystery**	**£15**

| 71 | MAM R45 | No Smoke Without Fire/Seaport | £15 |

71 MAM R45   No Smoke Without Fire/Seaport £15
71 MAM MAMR62   Suzanne/Your Love Is Growing £15
(see also Trapeze)

MONTANA SEXTET
83 Virgin VS 600   Who Needs Enemies With A Friend Like You/Friendly Vibes (12") ...£15

MONTCLAIRS
75 Contempo CS 2036   Hung Up On Your Love/I Need You More Than Ever £30
01 Grapevine 114   Hey You Don't Fight It/Never Ending Love £45
74 Contempo CLP 503   DREAMING OF A SEASON (LP)..£15

VINNIE MONTE
63 Stateside SS 156   Joanie Don't Be Angry/Take Good Care Of Her £18

MONTEGO MELON
68 Sioux SI 004   Swan Lake/HONG GANG: Reggae Mento £15

HUGO MONTENEGRO ORCHESTRA
63 Oriole CB 1792   Get Off The Moon/Sherry £20
65 RCA Victor RD 7758   THE MAN FROM U.N.C.L.E. (LP, soundtrack) £40
66 RCA Victor RD 7832   MORE MUSIC FROM THE MAN FROM U.N.C.L.E. (LP, soundtrack)...£45
67 RCA Victor RD/SF 7877 HURRY SUNDOWN (LP, soundtrack) £20
69 RCA SF 8053   MOOG POWER (LP) £20
69 Stateside S(S)L 10267 LADY IN CEMENT (LP, soundtrack)...£40
70 Pye Intl. NSPL 28136   DAWN OF DYLAN (LP) £15

CHRIS MONTEZ
66 Pye International 7N 25348 Call Me/Go 'Head On £15
63 London REU 1392   LET'S DANCE (EP) £40
63 London HA-U 8079   LET'S DANCE AND HAVE SOME KINDA FUN!!! (LP) £30

JACK MONTGOMERY
85 Kent TOWN 102   Dearly Beloved/MARIE KNIGHT: That's No Way To Treat A Girl ...£15
80s Soul City 124   Dearly Beloved/Do You Believe It..£15

LITTLE BROTHER MONTGOMERY
50 Jazz Collector L 44   No Special Rider Blues/Vicksburg Blues (78) £15
61 Columbia DB 4595   Pinetop's Boogie Woogie/Cow Cow Blues £25
61 Columbia 33SX 1289   LITTLE BROTHER MONTGOMERY (LP, with Alexis Korner) £70
62 77' 77LA 12/21   LITTLE BROTHER MONTGOMERY/SUNNYLAND SLIM (LP)...........£30
65 Decca LK 4664   LITTLE BROTHER MONTGOMERY (LP)...£30
66 Xtra XTRA 1018   LITTLE BROTHER MONTGOMERY (LP)..£20
71 Xtra XTRA 1115   FARRO ST. JIVE (LP) £20
71 Saydisc SDR 213   LITTLE BROTHER MONTGOMERY 1930-1969 (LP) £20
72 Saydisc SDM 223   HOME AGAIN (LP)...£20

MARIAN MONTGOMERY
67 Reaction 591 018   Love Makes Two People Sing/Monday Thru Saturday..................£25
72 Polydor 2383 159   MARIAN IN THE MORNING (LP) £20

ROY MONTGOMERY
97 Enraptured RAPT 4510   Trajectory One/Trajectory Two (p/s, 27 in handmade p/s)...........£15

STUART MONTGOMERY
69 Private pressing   CERTAIN SEA WORDS (LP, with insert)..£15

WES MONTGOMERY
60 Riverside RLP 12-320   THE INCREDIBLE JAZZ GUITAR OF WES MONTGOMERY (LP, mono) ...£15
60 Riverside RLP 12-320   THE INCREDIBLE JAZZ GUITAR OF WES MONTGOMERY (LP, stereo) ...£20

MONTY, DERRICK & PATSY
65 Blue Beat BB 280   Stir The Pot/Mercy £50
(see also Monty Morris, Derrick Morgan)

MONTY (MORRIS) & ROY
61 Blue Beat BB 63   Sweetie Pie/ROLAND ALPHONSO'S GROUP: Green Door £18
(see also Monty Morris)

MONTY PYTHON('S FLYING CIRCUS)
79 Warner Bros K 17495   Always Look On The Bright Side Of Life/Brian (p/s) £15
80 Charisma CB 374   I Like Chinese/I Bet You They Won't Play This Song On The Radio/Finland (p/s)...........£15
70 BBC REB 73M   MONTY PYTHON'S FLYING CIRCUS (LP, mono, mustard label) £18
70 Charisma CAS 1049   ANOTHER MONTY PYTHON RECORD (LP, inner sleeve, 3 inserts, 'scroll' label)...............£20
73 Charisma CAS 1063   MONTY PYTHON'S PREVIOUS RECORD (LP, with free flexidisc in p/s, Teach Yourself Heath & inner sleeve) £15
73 Charisma CAS 1080   MATCHING TIE AND HANDKERCHIEF (LP, parallel grooves on side 2, die-cut sleeve, 2 inserts) £15
(see also John Cleese, Rutles)

MONUMENT
71 Beacon BEAS 15   THE FIRST MONUMENT (LP)...£60
(see also Zior)

MONUMENTUM
95 Misanthropy AMAZON 007 IN ABSENTIA CHRISTI (LP) £50

MOOCHE
69 Pye 7N 17735   Hot Smoke And Sasafrass/Seen Through A Light £20

MOOD MOSAIC
66 Columbia DB 7801   A Touch Of Velvet, A Sting Of Brass/Bond Street P.M. £35
66 Columbia DB 7801   A Touch Of Velvet, A Sting Of Brass/Bond Street P.M.(DJ Copy) ...£50

MINT VALUE £

67	Columbia DB 8149	Chinese Chequers/The Real Mr. Smith	£25
68	Parlophone R 5716	The Yellow Spotted Capricorn/ELMER HOCKETT'S HURDY GURDY: Fantastic Fair	£15
69	Columbia DB 8618	A Touch Of Velvet, A Sting Of Brass/Bond Street P.M. (reissue)	£15
67	Columbia SX 6153	MOOD MOSAIC (LP, mono)	£35
67	Studio Two TWO 160	MOOD MOSAIC (LP, stereo)	£25

(see also Mark Wirtz Orchestra & Chorus, Keith West)

MOOD OF HAMILTON
67	Columbia DB 8304	Why Can't There Be More Love?/King's Message	£25

MOOD REACTION
69	Gas 136	Too Much Loving/Roaring Twenties	£20
70	Gas GAS 143	Change Of Heart/Run Away Man	£20
70	Pama PSP 1007	LIVE AT THE CUMBERLAND (LP)	£40

MOOD SIX
82	EMI EMI 5336	She's Too Far/Venus (unreleased; white label copies exist with p/s)	£30

MOODS
63	Starlite ST45 098	Duckwalk/Easy Going	£22

MOODY
73	Polydor 2310 285	THE GENTLE RAIN (LP)	£200

AMEIL MOODY
69	Blue Cat BS 143	Mullo Reggae/Lifeline (as Amiel Moodie)	£250
69	Blue Cat BS 164	Ratchet Knife/Bend The Tree	£750

MOODY BLUES
64	Decca F 11971	Steal Your Heart Away/Loose Your Money (But Don't Loose Your Mind) (as Moodyblues)	£45
67	Decca F 12543	Life's Not Life/He Can't Win (withdrawn)	£60
67	Decca F 12607	Fly Me High/Really Haven't Got The Time	£30
67	Decca F 12670	Love And Beauty/Leave This Man Alone	£20
65	Decca DFE 8622	THE MOODY BLUES (EP, original label)	£30
65	Decca LK 4711	THE MAGNIFICENT MOODIES (LP, unboxed red/silver Decca label logo)	£100
65	Decca LK 4711	THE MAGNIFICENT MOODIES (LP, boxed red/silver Decca label logo)	£20
67	Deram DML 707	DAYS OF FUTURE PASSED (LP, originally with white band on sleeve & 'DSS' labels, mono)	£30
67	Deram SML 707	DAYS OF FUTURE PASSED (LP, originally with white band on sleeve & 'DSS' labels, stereo)	£15
68	Deram DML 711	IN SEARCH OF THE LOST CHORD (LP, gatefold sleeve, mono, 'DSS' label)	£40
69	Deram DML 1035	ON THE THRESHOLD OF A DREAM (LP, gatefold sleeve with stapled booklet, mono. Label is white/brown with large logo)	£30
69	Deram SML 1035	ON THE THRESHOLD OF A DREAM (LP, gatefold sleeve with stapled booklet, stereo)	£20
69	Threshold THM 1	TO OUR CHILDREN'S CHILDREN'S CHILDREN (LP, gatefold, with insert, white/pink label, mono)	£40
69	Threshold THS 1	TO OUR CHILDREN'S CHILDREN'S CHILDREN (LP, gatefold, with insert, white/lilac label, stereo)	£20
70	Threshold THS 3	A QUESTION OF BALANCE (1st pressing, Matrixes 10009P-1W/10010P-1W, 'flap' gatefold sleeve with lyric sheet)	£25
71	Threshold THS 5	EVERY GOOD BOY DESERVES A FAVOUR (LP, gatefold, lyric insert, white/blue label)	£18
72	Threshold THS 7	SEVENTH SOJOURN (LP, gatefold sleeve, lyric insert, white/blue label)	£18

(see also Justin Hayward, Denny Laine, Gerry Levene & Avengers)

JAMES MOODY
55	Esquire 20-071	MOODY HI FI (10" LP)	£20

MOOG MACHINE
69	CBS 63807	SWITCHED ON ROCK (LP)	£20

(THE) MOOG
92	Delirious DELIS 2	Rush Hour/Jungle Muffin/Live Forever/Hopelessly Volatile/Subtone (12")	£30

MOOM
95	Delerium DELEC LP 035	TOOT (LP)	£15

MOON
68	Liberty LBF 15076	Someday Girl/Mothers And Fathers	£25
68	Liberty LBL/LBS 83146	WITHOUT EARTH (LP)	£80

(see also Beach Boys)

KEITH MOON
75	Polydor 2058 584	Don't Worry Baby/Together	£20
75	Polydor 2442 134	TWO SIDES OF THE MOON (LP)	£30

LARRY MOON
63	Ember EMB 171	Tia Juana Ball/Bouquet Of Roses	£20

MOON BOYS
69	Amalgamated AMG 846	Apollo 11/PIONEERS: Love Love Everyday	£150

(see also Hippy Boys)

MOONCHILD
75	Look LKSP 5010	Hourglass/War Orphan (Brother Of The Day)	£20

MOONDOG
54	London REP 1010	ON THE STREETS OF NEW YORK (EP)	£30
59	Esquire 32-055	MOONDOG (LP)	£200
69	CBS 63906	MOONDOG (LP, gatefold sleeve)	£50
04	Honest Jons HJRLP 18	THE VIKING OF SIXTH AVENUE (2-LP)	£20
09	Honest Jons HJRLP 107	THE STORY OF MOONDOG (LP, reissue)	£15

MOONDOGS (1)
78 Lyntone LT 002 — Heads I Win/Two's A Crowd (p/s) £40

MOONDOGS (2)
79 Good Vibrations GOT 10 — She's Nineteen/Ya Don't Do Ya (foldout p/s) £20
81 Real ARE 14 — Talking In The Canteen/Make Her Love Me (p/s, with neckerchief) £35
81 Real ARE 14 — Talking In The Canteen/Make Her Love Me/You Said (p/s)...................£15
81 Real ARE 16 — Imposter/Baby Snatcher (p/s)...£15

ART MOONEY (& HIS ORCHESTRA)
57 MGM MGM 923 — Rebel Without A Cause Theme/"East Of Eden" Theme £15
57 MGM MGM 943 — Giant/There's Never Been Anyone Else But You £15
57 MGM MGM 951 — Rock And Roll Tumbleweed/Is There A Teenager In The House (with Ocie Smith)..........£22
57 MGM MGM 951 — Rock And Roll Tumbleweed/Is There A Teenager In The House (with Ocie Smith) (78) ...£15
(see also Ocie Smith, Shorty Long)

MOONGLOWS
57 London HLN 8374 — I Knew From The Start/Over And Over Again.................................£700
57 London HLN 8374 — I Knew From The Start/Over And Over Again (78) £70
(see also Harvey & Moonglows, Etta & Harvey)

MOONKYTE
71 Mother SMOT 1 — COUNT ME OUT (LP, with insert, cover has a die-cut spire) £600

MOONLIGHTERS (1)
63 Island WI 043 — Going Out/Hold My Hands...£20

MOON ROCKS & PRINCE JAZZBO
78 Bushay's BFM 101 — Unite Jah People/Have No Fear (12") £40

MOONSHADOW
76 Maxi M003 — Chase Me/Fight Hard £15

MICKY MOONSHINE
74 Decca F 13555 — Baby Blue/Name It You Got It...£20
74 Decca F 13555 — Baby Blue/Name It You Got It (DJ copy) £40

MOONSHINE (1)
70 KJ Roberts ZDR56312 — Susannah/Garden Of Men £60

MOONSHINE (2)
76 Moo Records MOO 1 — MOONSHINE EP (EP) £70

MOONSHINERS
67 Page One POLS 004 — HOLD UP (LP) £22

MOONSTOMP
89 Link LINK LP 086 — THEY NEVER SEE (LP) £20

MOON'S TRAIN
67 MGM MGM 1333 — Deed I Do/It's In My Mind £40
98 Tenth Planet TP 037 — MOON'S TRAIN (LP)..£15
(see also Denny Mitchell, Preachers)

MOONTREKKERS
61 Parlophone R 4814 — Night Of The Vampire/Melodie D'Amour.....................................£30
62 Parlophone R 4888 — There's Something At The Bottom Of The Well/Hatashiai £30
63 Decca F 11714 — Moondust/The Bogey Man £20

MICHAEL MOORCOCK('S DEEP FIX)
82 Flicknife EJS P9831 — Brothel In Rosenstrasse/Time Centre (numbered, 500 only, with autographed lyric sheet) £30
92 Cyborg (no cat. no.) — The Brothel In Rosenstrasse (cassette only)...................................£20
75 United Artists UAG 29732 — NEW WORLD'S FAIR (LP, with inner sleeve)......................£40
(see also Hawkwind)

ALICE MOORE
50s Poydras MC 66 — Prison Blues/My Man Blues £22

ANTHONY MOORE
71 Polydor 2310 062 — PIECES FROM THE CLOUDLAND BALLROOM (LP) £60
72 Polydor 2310 079 — SECRETS OF THE BLUE BAG (LP) £40
76 Virgin V 2057 — OUT (LP, unissued) £0

BARBARA MOORE
67 CBS (S) BPG 62839 — A LITTLE MOORE BARBARA (LP)..£40

BOBBY MOORE (& RHYTHM ACES)
66 Chess CRS 8033 — Searching For My Love/Hey Mr D.J. £25
66 Chess CRL 4521 — SEARCHIN' FOR MY LOVE (LP) £75

CHRISTY MOORE
69 Mercury 20170 SMCL — PADDY ON THE ROAD (LP)...£400
72 Trailer LER 3035 — PROSPEROUS (LP) £15
75 Polydor 2383 344 — WHATEVER TICKLES YOUR FANCY (LP) £25
76 Polydor 2383 426 — CHRISTY MOORE (LP) £25
70s WEA WX 286 — VOYAGE (LP)..£15

CURLEY MOORE & THE COOL ONES
71 Pye 25570 — Funky Yeah/Shelly's Rubber Band £35

DOROTHY MOORE
76 Contempo CLP 535 — MISTY BLUE (LP) £15

DUDLEY MOORE (TRIO)
69	Decca F 12882	**Keep It Up/Gently** (as Dudley Moore Trio)	£25
66	Decca LK 4788	**GENUINE DUD** (LP, as Dudley Moore Trio)	£20
68	Decca SKL 4923	**BEDAZZLED** (LP, stereo, soundtrack)	£100
69	Decca LK/SKL 4976	**THE DUDLEY MOORE TRIO** (LP)	£30

(see also Peter Cook & Dudley Moore, Cleo Laine)

GARY MOORE
78	MCA MCA 386	**Back On The Streets/Track Nine** (in p/s)	£30
73	CBS 65527	**GRINDING STONE** (LP, as Gary Moore Band)	£20
78	MCA MCF 2853	**BACK ON THE STREETS** (LP, with inner sleeve)	£18
81	Jet JETLP 245	**LIVE AT THE MARQUEE** (LP, withdrawn test pressing, white sleeve with Jet Info sticker)	£100
82	Virgin V 2245	**CORRIDORS OF POWER** (LP, with free live EP [VDJ 34])	£20
84	EMI OVED 206	**VICTIMS OF THE FUTURE** (LP, with inner & poster)	£20
86	10 DIXP 16	**RUN FOR COVER** (LP, picture disc, die-cut sleeve)	£30
87	10 DIXG 56	**WILD FRONTIER** (2-LP, gatefold sleeve)	£20

(see also Granny's Intentions, Dr. Strangely Strange, Skid Row, Thin Lizzy, Gary Moore & Phil Lynott,, G-Force, Cozy Powell, Jack Bruce. National Head)

GARY MOORE & PHIL LYNOTT
85	10 TENS 49	**Out In The Fields/Military Man** (2 1-sided interlocking shaped picture-disc set, stickered gatefold PVC sleeve)	£15

JACKIE MOORE
74	Atlantic K40544	**SWEET CHARLIE BABE** (LP)	£20
76	RCA RS 1033	**MAKE ME FEEL LIKE A WOMAN** (LP)	£20
79	CBS 83786	**I'M ON MY WAY** (LP)	£15

JERRY MOORE
69	Fontana STL 5502	**LIFE IS A CONSTANT JOURNEY HOME** (LP)	£40

JOHNNY MOORE (1)
67	Caltone TONE 101	**Sound And Soul/ROY SHIRLEY: Get On The Ball**	£60
69	Doctor Bird DB 1180	**Big Big Boss/CARL CANNONBALL BRYON: Reggae This Reggae**	£100

(see also Cannonball & Johnny Melody, Alton Ellis)

MERRILL E. MOORE
54	Capitol CL 14057	**Bell Bottom Boogie/The House Of Blue Lights** (78)	£15
54	Capitol CL 14130	**Nola/Fly Right Boogie** (78)	£15
55	Capitol CL 14369	**Five Foot Two, Eyes Of Blue/Hard Top Race** (as Merrill Moore)	£200
55	Capitol CL 14369	**Five Foot Two, Eyes Of Blue/Hard Top Race** (as Merrill Moore) (78)	£20
56	Capitol F 3397	**King Porter Stomp/Rock Island Line** (export only)	£150
68	Ember EMB S 253	**Down The Road A-Piece/Buttermilk Baby**	£15
67	Ember EMB 3392	**BELLYFUL OF BLUE-THUNDER** (LP)	£40

OSCAR MOORE TRIO
55	London H-APB 1035	**KENYA** (10" LP)	£20

ROGER MOORE
65	CBS 202014	**Where Does Love Go/Tomorrow After Tomorrow** (in p/s)	£20

SCOTTY MOORE
64	Columbia 33SX 1680	**THE GUITAR THAT CHANGED THE WORLD!** (LP)	£60

(see also Elvis Presley)

SYLVIA MOORE
70	Sunshine SUN 3	**JUNGLE MAGIC** (LP)	£40

MELBA MOORE
86	Kent 6T 2	**Magic Touch/CHUCK JACKSON: Little By Little**	£30
87	Horace's 001	**Magic Touch/TOMMY HUNT: The Pretty Part Of You**	£20

BIG MOOSE (WALKER)
68	Python PKM 1	**Puppy Howl Blues/Rambling Woman** (pressed with reversed labels)	£35

MOOSE (1)
70	Escort ERT 840	**Engine No. 9/KUKASS: Do It**	£30

MOOSE (2)
92	Hut HUTLP 5	**XYZ** (LP, without free 7")	£15
92	Hut HUTLP 5	**XYZ** (LP, with free 7")	£20
94	PIAS BIAS 260	**HONEY BEE** (LP, with free 7")	£25

MOQUETTES
64	Columbia DB 7315	**Right String, But The Wrong Yo-Yo/You Came Along**	£50

JOHN MORALES
09	BBE BBE 129CLP	**THE M&M MIXES** (3-LP)	£20

MORAL SUPPORT
79	Round RSR 001	**Just Where It's At Tonight/Sin**	£20

MIKE MORAN
70s	Alba TAR 053	**PENNY WHISTLES OF ROBERT LOUIS STEVENSON** (LP)	£20

MORBID ANGEL
89	Earache MOSH 11	**ALTARS OF MADNESS** (LP, pink splattered vinyl, stickered sleeve)	£30
89	Earache MOSH 11P	**ALTARS OF MADNESS** (LP, picture disc)	£30
91	Earache MOSH 31	**BLESSED ARE THE SICK** (LP)	£20
91	Earache MOSH 31	**BLESSED ARE THE SICK** (LP on 6 x 7" in box with 4 page insert)	£40
91	Earache MOSH 48	**ABOMINATIONS OF DESOLATION** (LP)	£25
94	Earache MOSH 112	**LAIBACH REMIXES EP** (God Of Emptiness/Sworn To The Black/Sworn To The Black [Laibach Remix]/God Of Emptiness [Laibach Remix]) (12", p/s)	£30

| 95 | Earache MOSH 134 LP | DOMINATION (LP) | £20 |

MORE

| 82 | Atlantic K 11744 | Trickster/Hey Joe (p/s) | £15 |

MANDY MORE

72	Philips 6006 199	Come With Me To Jesus/Alone In My Yellow	£25
73	Philips 6006 277	San Francisco 5AM/Coffee Cups	£25
73	Philips 6006 343	Every Mother's Child/Blue Seasons	£25
75	Fresh Air 6121 119	Rose Coloured Window/If I Smiled On Saturday	£25
72	Philips 6308109	BUT THAT IS ME (LP)	£250

AIRTO MOREIRA AND THE GODS OF JAZZ

| 93 | B&W BW 051 | KILLER BEES (LP, in box with prints) | £50 |

(see also Fourth World)

MORGAN

| 73 | RCA SF 8321 | NOVA SOLIS (LP, with insert) | £40 |

(see also Mott The Hoople, Love Affair, Humpy Bong)

MORGAN AND THE MARK 7

| 66 | Polydor BM 56083 | I'm Gonna Turn My Life Around/Undercover Man | £35 |

CARLTON B MORGAN

| 82 | CNT 0666 | DEVILS MUSIC (LP) | £15 |

DAVID/DAVY MORGAN

| 65 | Columbia DB 7624 | Tomorrow I'll Be Gone/Ain't Got Much More To See (as Davy Morgan) | £45 |
| 68 | Parlophone R 5692 | True To Life/Dawning (as David Morgan) | £25 |

(see also Wishful Thinking)

DERRICK MORGAN

60	Blue Beat BB 7	Fat Man/I'm Gonna Leave You	£30
60	Blue Beat BB 12	Don't Cry/I Pray For You (as Derrick Morgan & Ebonies)	£25
60	Blue Beat BB 18	Lover Boy/Oh My!	£25
61	Blue Beat BB 31	Now We Know/Nights Are Lonely (with Trenton Spence Orchestra)	£25
61	Blue Beat BB 35	Leave Earth/Wigger Wee Shuffle (with Clue J. & His Blues Busters)	£25
61	Blue Beat BB 62	Shake A Leg/Golden Rule (as Derrick & Drumbago All Stars)	£25
62	Blue Beat BB 76	Sunday, Monday/Be Still	£25
62	Blue Beat BB 82	Don't You Know Little Girl (actually by Derrick & Basil)/ B. GABBIDON: Hully Gully Miss Molly	£25
62	Blue Beat BB 85	Come On Over/Come Back My Darling (with Buster's Group)	£25
62	Blue Beat BB 91	Headache/OWEN GRAY: Millie Girl	£25
62	Blue Beat BB 94	Meekly Wait/Day In And Day Out (both sides with Yvonne [Sterling])	£20
62	Blue Beat BB 100	In My Heart/BELL'S GROUP: Kingston 13	£30
62	Blue Beat BB 110	Are You Going To Marry Me?/Troubles (as Derrick Morgan & Patsy)	£25
62	Blue Beat BB 130	Should Be Ashamed/Marjorie (with Buster's Group)	£20
62	Blue Beat BB 141	Joybells (with Duke Reid Group)/Going Down To Canaan (with Denzil Dennis)	£20
62	Island WI 004	Travel On/Teach Me Baby	£35
62	Island WI 006	The Hop/Tell It To Me	£35
62	Island WI 011	Forward March/Please Don't Talk About Me (B-side actually with Eric Morris)	£25
62	Island WI 013	Cherry Home/See And Blind	£35
63	Blue Beat BB 148	Jezebell/Burnette	£25
63	Blue Beat BB 177	Patricia My Dear/The Girl I Left Behind	£25
63	Blue Beat BB 187	Tears On My Pillow/You Should Have Known	£25
63	Blue Beat BB 196	Telephone/Life Is Tough (B-side actually "Tough Man Tough")	£35
63	Island WI 037	Dorothy/Leave Her Alone	£25
63	Island WI 051	Blazing Fire/DERRICK & PATSY: I'm In A Jam	£25
63	Island WI 053	No Raise, No Praise/Loving Baby	£25
63	Island WI 080	Angel With Blue Eyes/Corner Stone	£25
63	Rio R 1	Blazing Fire/Edmarine	£20
64	Black Swan WI 402	Street Girl/Edmarine	£25
64	Black Swan WI 425	Cherry Pie (actually by Frederick Hibbert)/BOB WALLS: Beware	£20
64	Blue Beat BB 233	Let Them Talk/Sleeping	£30
64	Blue Beat BB 239	Miss Lulu/DERRICK & PALOY: She's So Young (B-side act. by Derrick & Patsy)	£20
64	Blue Beat BB 261	The Soldier Man/BUSTER'S ALL STARS: Jet 707	£100
64	Blue Beat BB 268	Katy Katy/Call On Me	£18
65	Blue Beat BB 276	Weep No More/I Want A Girl	£18
65	Blue Beat BB 283	Johnny Grave/BUSTER'S ALL STARS: Yeah Yeah	£30
65	Blue Beat BB 311	Throw Them Away/Baby Face	£25
65	Blue Beat BB 329	Sweeter Than Honey/You Never Know (with Prince Buster)	£25
65	Ska Beat JB 185	Heart Of Stone/Let Me Go (with Baba Brooks Group)	£25
65	Ska Beat JB 218	Don't Call Me Daddy/BABA BROOK'S BAND: Girl's Town Ska	£30
65	Island WI 193	Two Of A Kind/I Want A Lover (both actually with Naomi)	£30
65	Island WI 225	Starvation/I Am A Blackhead Again	£30
66	Island WI 277	It's Alright/I Need Someone (both sides actually with Blenders)	£35
66	Island WI 289	Ameletia (actually by Frank Cosmo)/Don't You Worry (B-side with Patsy Todd)	£20
66	Island WI 3010	Gather Together Now (Jamaican Independence Song)/Soft Hand (actually "So Hard") (both sides actually with Blenders)	£30
66	Rio R 122	Cool Off Rudies/Take It Easy	£18
67	Island WI 3079	Someone (actually Derrick & Pauline Morgan)/Do You Love Me (with Pauline)	£18
67	Pyramid PYR 6010	Tougher Than Tough/ROLAND ALPHONSO: Song For My Father	£25
67	Pyramid PYR 6013	Greedy Gal/SOUL BROTHERS: Marcus Junior	£30
67	Pyramid PYR 6014	Court Dismiss/FREDERICK McCLEAN: Fine Fine Fine	£35
67	Pyramid PYR 6019	Judge Dread In Court/Last Chance	£30

MINT VALUE £

67	Pyramid PYR 6021	Kill Me Dead/Don't Be A Fool	£25
67	Pyramid PYR 6024	No Dice/I Mean It	£25
67	Pyramid PYR 6025	Do The Beng Beng/Revenge	£45
68	Island WI 3094	Conquering Ruler/LLOYD & DEVON: Red Rum Ball	£100
68	Island WI 3101	Gimme Back/VICEROYS: Send Requests	£60
68	Island WI 3159	Hold You Jack/One Morning In May	£40
68	Pyramid PYR 6029	I Am The Ruler/I Mean It	£40
68	Pyramid PYR 6039	Woman A Grumble/Don't Be A Fool	£25
68	Pyramid PYR 6040	Want More/ROLAND ALPHONSO: Goodnight My Love	£25
68	Pyramid PYR 6045	Try Me/I'm Leaving (B-side with Pauline)	£25
68	Pyramid PYR 6046	King For Tonight (with Pauline)/Last Chance	£20
68	Pyramid PYR 6053	Me Now Give Up/BEVERLEY'S ALLSTARS: Dreadnaught	£50
68	JJ PYR 6061	What's Your Grouse/BEVERLEY'S ALLSTARS: Sly Mongoose	£30
68	JJ PYR 6063	Johnny Pram Pram/Don't Say (B-side with Pauline Morgan	£85
68	Amalgamated AMG 824	I Want To Go Home/JACKIE ROBINSON: Let The Little Girl Dance	£40
68	Crab CRAB 3	River To The Bank/PETER KING: Reggae Limbo	£20
68	Trojan TR 626	Fat Man/VAL BENNETT: South Parkway Rock	£45
68	Nu Beat NB 016	I Love You/JUNIOR SMITH: Searching	£25
68	Big Shot BI 506	Shower Of Rain/VAL BENNETT: It Might As Well Be Spring	£20
69	Crab CRAB 8	Seven Letters/TARTANS: Lonely Heartaches (B-side act. by Clarendonians)	£20
69	Crab CRAB 11	My First Taste Of Love/TARTANS: Dance All Night	£20
69	Crab CRAB 18	Don't Play That Song/How Can I Forget You?	£20
69	Crab CRAB 23	Send Me Some Loving/Come What May	£20
69	Crab CRAB 22	Mek It Tan Deah/Gimme Back	£20
69	Crab CRAB 28	Hard Time/ROY RICHARDS: Death Rides A Horse	£50
69	Crab CRAB 30	Man Pon Moon/What A Thing	£25
69	Crab CRAB 32	Moon Hop/Harris Wheel	£40
69	Unity UN 507	Belly Woman/PAULETT & LOVERS: Please Stay	£35
69	Unity UN 540	Derrick - Top The Pop/GLEN ADAMS: Capone's Revenge	£22
70	Unity UN 546	Return Of Jack Slade/Fat Man	£20
70	Unity UN 569	The Conqueror/Bedweight (as Derrick)	£50
70	Crab CRAB 44	A Night At The Hop/Telephone	£30
70	Crab CRAB 57	My Dickie (as The Commentator)/THE KURAAS: Brixton Hop	£45
72	Jackpot JP 797	Me Now Run/All Night Long	£15
63	Island ILP 903	FORWARD MARCH (LP)	£250
69	Doctor Bird DLMB 5014	BEST OF DERRICK MORGAN (LP)	£150
69	Island ILP 990	DERRICK MORGAN AND HIS FRIENDS (LP)	£150
69	Pama ECO 10	DERRICK MORGAN IN LONDON (LP)	£100
69	Pama PSP 1006	MOON HOP (LP)	£100
69	Trojan TTL 5	SEVEN LETTERS (LP)	£60
70	Trojan TTL 38	FORWARD MARCH (LP, reissue)	£30
74	Magnet MGT 004	IN THE MOOD (LP)	£90

(see also Roland Alphonso; Frank Cosmo; Copy Cats, Derrick & Lloyd; Derrick, Morris & Patsy; Derrick & Patsy; Derrick & Naomi; Derrick & Paulette; Derrick & Pauline; Morgan's All Stars; Martin & Derrick; Larry Lawrence; Matador, Jackie Robinson)

GEORGE MORGAN
57	Philips BBE 12149	COUNTRY AND WESTERN SPECTACULAR (EP)	£20
68	London HAB 8353	COUNTRY HITS BY CANDLELIGHT (LP)	£22

MORGAN JAMES DUO
68	Philips BF 1707	Let's Ride/After The Storm	£25
66	Fontana SFL 13071	AT THE BAR OF MUSIC (LP)	£30
66	Philips BL 7702	SHHHH...TALENT STRIKES AGAIN (LP)	£20

JANE MORGAN (& TROUBADORS)
55	London HL 8148	Why - Oh Why/The Heart You Break (May Be Your Own)	£15
57	London HLR 8395	From The First Hello To The Last Goodbye/ Come Home, Come Home, Come Home	£20
58	London HLR 8611	I've Got Bells On My Heart/Only One Love	£15
67	Columbia DB 7645	Maybe/Walking The Streets In The Rain	£15
57	London HA-R 2086	FASCINATION (LP)	£15
58	London HA-R 2110	ALL THE WAY (LP, with Troubadors)	£15
58	London HA-R 2133	SOMETHING OLD, SOMETHING NEW, SOMETHING BORROWED, SOMETHING BLUE (LP)	£15
61	London HA-R 2371	JANE MORGAN TIME (LP)	£15

(see also Troubadors)

JAYE P. MORGAN
55	HMV 7M 327	The Longest Walk/Swanee	£15
56	HMV 7M 348	If You Don't Want My Love/Pepper Hot Baby	£25
59	MGM MGM-C 793	SLOW AND EASY (LP)	£15

JOHN MORGAN
72	Carnaby 6302 010	KALEIDOSCOPE (LP, white label with red 'crab' logo)	£100
70s	SWP 1007	LIVE AT DURRANT HOUSE (LP, private pressing)	£100

(see also Spirit Of John Morgan)

LEE MORGAN
61	Columbia 33SX 1399	THE BIRDLAND STORY VOL. 1 (LP)	£20
62	Stateside SL 10016	EXPOOBIDENT (LP)	£30

MACE MORGAN THUNDERBIRDS
63	Starlite STEP 36	SHAKE AND SWING (EP)	£60

TONY MORGAN
69	Beacon BEA 115	Racial Segregation/Racial Segregation (instrumental)	£15
72	Beacon BEA 188	Black Skin Blue Eyed Boys/Why Build A Mountain	£15

MORGAN TWINS
58	RCA RCA 1083	T.V. Hop/Let's Get Going	£60
58	RCA RCA 1083	T.V. Hop/Let's Get Going (78)	£20

MORGAN'S ALL STARS
71	Camel CA 76	I Love You The Most (actually by Lloyd Clarke)/I Love You The Most - Version	£25

(see also B. Leggs, Derrick Morgan, Marvels)

(RON PAUL) MORIN & (LUKE P.) WILSON
72	Sovereign SVNA 7252	PEACEFUL COMPANY (LP)	£20

JOHNNY MORISETTE
62	Stateside SS 107	Meet Me At The Twistin' Place/Any Time Any Day Any Where	£15

ALANIS MORISSETTE
95	Maverick 9362 45901	JAGGED LITTLE PILL (LP, German pressing but imported into U.K.)	£50
12	Maverick 8122797168	JAGGED LITTLE PILL (LP, reissue)	£15

MORNIN
69	CBS 4883	Cheatin' On You/Let Me Love You	£20

MORNING
70	Liberty LBS 83463	MORNING (LP)	£40
72	United Artists UAS 29337	STRUCK LIKE SILVER (LP)	£20

MORNING AFTER
71	Sky SKYLP 71014	BLUE BLOOD (LP)	£300

MORNING GLORY
73	Island ILPS 9237	MORNING GLORY (LP, gatefold, pink rim palm tree label)	£30

(see also John Surman)

MOROCCAN COCO
83	SR 001	Steam Radio/One Day (p/s)	£35

GIORGIO MORODER
66	Page One POF 003	Full Stop/Believe Me	£15
67	Page One POF 028	How Much Longer Must I Wait/Bla Bla Diddley	£15
90s	Cause-N-Effect	I Wanna Rock You (Thee Maddcat Mix)/(Thee DrumDrum Mix) (12", no p/s)	£15

(see also Giorgio)

ENNIO MORRICONE ORCHESTRA
67	RCA Victor RD/SF 7875	A FISTFUL OF DOLLARS (LP, soundtrack)	£30
68	RCA Victor RD 7994	A FISTFUL OF DOLLARS/FOR A FEW DOLLARS MORE/THE GOOD, THE BAD AND THE UGLY (LP, soundtrack)	£15
68	United Artists (S)ULP 1197	THE GOOD, THE BAD AND THE UGLY (LP, soundtrack)	£15
69	United Artists UAS 29005	A PROFESSIONAL GUN (LP, soundtrack)	£25
70	CBS 70067	LOVE CIRCLE (LP, soundtrack)	£50
70	MCA MKPS 2013	TWO MULES FOR SISTER SARA (LP, soundtrack)	£30
72	United Artists UAS 29345	A FISTFUL OF DYNAMITE (LP, soundtrack)	£40

BYRON MORRIS AND UNITY
01	Universal Sound USLP 17	BLOW THRU YOUR MIND (LP, reissue)	£30

ERIC MORRIS
61	Starlite ST45 052	Search The World/Buster's Shack	£40
61	Blue Beat BB 53	Humpty Dumpty/Corn Bread And Butter (as Eric 'Humpty Dumpty' Morris & Drumbago All Stars; [B-side actually by Drumbago All Stars])	£20
62	Blue Beat BB 74	My Forty-Five/I've Tried Everybody (as Eric 'Humpty Dumpty' Morris & Drumbago All Stars)	£30
62	Blue Beat BB 81	Sinners Repent And Pray/Now And Forever More (B-side act. by Alton Ellis)	£20
62	Blue Beat BB 83	Money Can't Buy Life (with Buster's Group)/A. ELLIS: True Love	£25
62	Blue Beat BB 105	Pack Up Your Troubles/Oh What A Smile Can Do (with D. Cosmo & Drumbago's All Stars)	£20
62	Blue Beat BB 115	G.I. Lady/Going To The River	£20
62	Blue Beat BB 128	Over The Hills/Lazy Woman (with Buster's Group)	£20
62	Blue Beat BB 137	Miss Peggy's Grandmother/BUSTER'S GROUP: Megaton	£25
62	Blue Beat BB 140	Seven Long Years/For Your Love	£20
63	Blue Beat BB 153	Lonely Blue Boy/PRINCE BUSTER: Oh We	£22
63	Blue Beat BB 184	Sweet Love/BUSTER, DEREK, ERIC: Country Girl	£15
64	Blue Beat BB 218	Love Can Break A Man/Worried People	£20
64	Blue Beat BB 273	Stitch In Time/For Ever	£20
64	Black Swan WI 412	Sampson/BABA BROOKS: Jelly Beans	£30
64	Black Swan WI 414	Solomon Grundie/BABA BROOKS: Key To The City	£40
64	Black Swan WI 433	Supper In The Gutter/Words Of My Mouth	£20
64	Black Swan WI 439	River Come Down/Seek And You'll Find	£20
64	Black Swan WI 445	Home Sweet Home/LESTER STERLING: '64 Special	£25
64	Island WI 142	Penny-Reel/DUKE REID'S GROUP: Darling When (B-side act. Dotty & Bonnie)	£35
64	Island WI 147	Mama No Fret/FRANKIE ANDERSON: Santa Lucia (B-side w/Roland Alphonso)	£20
64	Island WI 150	Drop Your Sword/Catch A Fire (B-side actually by Roland Alphonso)	£25
64	Island WI 151	What A Man Doeth/DUKE REID'S GROUP: Rude Boy (B-side actually by Baba Brooks)	£25
64	Port-O-Jam PJ 4006	Oh My Dear/Lena Belle	£25
64	Rio R 39	Little District/True And Just	£25
64	Rio R 48	Live As A Man/Man Will Rule	£25
65	Rio R 72	By The Sea/I Wasn't Around	£25

MINT VALUE £

65	Island WI 177	Drop Your Sword/Catch A Fire	£25
65	Island WI 183	Love Can Make A Mansion (actually "Love Can Break A Man")/ Ungodly People	£15
65	Island WI 185	Suddenly/Many Long Years	£25
65	Island WI 199	Fast Mouth/The Harder They Come	£18
65	Island WI 234	Children Of Today/BABA BROOKS: Greenfield Ska	£25
65	Blue Beat BB 298	Those Teardrops/DON DRUMMOND: Ska Town	£50
66	Blue Beat BB 349	I'm The Greatest/BUSTER'S ALL STARS: Picket Line	£60
13	Island WI 3163	Terrible Mistake/Festival Time	£30

(see also Monty Morris, Byron Lee & Dragonaires, Cool Sticky, Tommy McCook, Zoot Simms, Marguerita, Cool Cats)

HELMSLEY MORRIS
67	Caltone TONE 104	Love Is Strange/DON D. JUNIOR: Sir Pratt Special	£90
68	Pama PM 720	Stay Loose Mama/You Think I'm A Fool (as Hainsley Morris)	£35

LIBBY MORRIS
66	RCA RD 7789	AD-LIBBY (LP)	£15

MONTY MORRIS
67	Doctor Bird DB 1067	Play It Cool/BABA BROOKS' BAND: Open The Door	£70
67	Doctor Bird DB 1081	Put On Your Best Dress/BABA BROOKS' BAND: Faberge	£150
68	Doctor Bird DB 1162	Last Laugh/You Really Got A Hold On Me	£150
68	Pama PM 721	Say What You're Saying/Tears In Your Eyes	£40
68	Nu Beat NB 011	Simple Simon/BUNNY & RUDDY: On The Town	£75
69	Doctor Bird DB 1176	Same Face/A Little Bit Of This (miscredited to Tennors)	£60
69	Big Shot BI 513	Deportation/Say I'm Back	£100
69	Camel CA 12	Can't Get No Peace/UPSETTERS: For A Few Dollars More	£70
69	Camel CA 28	No More Teardrops/Love Me Or Leave Me (as Monty Morris & Maples)	£50
70	Explosion EX 2016	Higher Than The Highest Mountain/G.G. ALL STARS: Musical Shot	£25
73	Ackee ACK 527	I'm Ready To Go/TOMMY McCOOK: Flower Pot	£15
10	Duke THB 7004	Deep In My Soul/TOMMY MCCOOK: Reggae To Jeggae	£30

(see also Eric Morris, Monty, Derrick & Patsy, Monty & Roy, Alton Ellis)

NAGGO MORRIS
79	Hit Run DD 111	Jah Will Explain/DOCTOR PABLO: Wicked Feel It (12")	£25
82	S & G SG 12	A True You Na No/Going Places (12")	£50
82	S & G SG 23	False Rasta/Two Time Girl (12")	£70
82	Black Roots BR0036A	A True Them No Know/Version/Africa/Version (12")	£30

ROGER MORRIS
72	Regal Zono. SRZA 8509	FIRST ALBUM (LP, textured gatefold sleeve, red/silver label)	£400

RUSSELL MORRIS
69	Decca F 22964	The Real Thing (Parts I & II)/It's Only A Matter Of Time	£80

VICTOR MORRIS
68	Amalgamated AMG 813	Now I'm Alone/Rise And Fall	£20

MORRIS & MITCH
68	Trend TRE 1010	The Magical Musherishi Tourists/Mister D.J. Man	£15
58	Decca DFE 6486	SIX FIVE NOTHING SPECIAL (EP)	£15

CURLEY JIM MORRISON
61	Starlite ST45 065	Air Force Blues/Didn't I Tell You	£50

DOROTHY MORRISON
71	Elektra K 42094	BRAND NEW DAY (LP)	£18

VAN MORRISON
67	London HLZ 10150	Brown-Eyed Girl/Goodbye Baby (Baby Goodbye)	£50
67	London HLZ 10150	Brown Eyed Girl/Goodbye Baby (Baby Goodbye) (yellow label promo, release date 28-7-67 to right of spindle hole)	£100
70	Warner Brothers WB 7383	Come Running/Crazy Love (orange label)	£20
70	Warner Brothers WB 7434	Domino/Sweet Jannie (orange label)	£20
70	Warner Brothers WB 7434	Domino/Sweet Jannie (DJ Copy)	£35
70	President PT 328	Brown-Eyed Girl/Goodbye Baby (Baby Goodbye) (reissue)	£15
72	Warner Brothers K 16210	Jackie Wilson Said/You've Got The Power (light green label)	£15
74	London HLM 10453	Brown-Eyed Girl/Goodbye Baby (Baby Goodbye) (2nd reissue)	£15
74	Warner Brothers K 16392	Caldonia(What Makes Your Big Head Hard?)/What's Up, Crazy Pup (with the Caledonia Soul Express)	£15
83	Mercury MERX 132	Cry For Home/Summertime In England (Live)/All Saint's Day (12", p/s)	£15
68	London HA-Z 8346	BLOWIN' YOUR MIND (LP)	£180
69	Warner Brothers WS 1768	ASTRAL WEEKS (LP, laminated front sleeve, flipbacks, orange label)	£250
71	Warner Brothers WS 1768	ASTRAL WEEKS (LP, green label)	£50
70	Warner Brothers WS 1835	MOONDANCE (LP, orange label)	£175
70	Warner Brothers WS 1835	MOONDANCE (LP, green label)	£20
71	Warner Brothers WS 1884	HIS BAND AND STREET CHOIR (LP, green label, gatefold)	£35
71	President PTLS 1045	THE BEST OF VAN MORRISON (LP)	£15
71	Warner Brothers K 46114	TUPELO HONEY (LP, gatefold sleeve, green label)	£30
72	Warner Brothers K 46172	SAINT DOMINIC'S PREVIEW (LP, with folded insert, green label)	£35
73	Warner Brothers K 46024	ASTRAL WEEKS (LP, reissue, 'Burbank' label)	£25
73	Warner Brothers K 46040	MOONDANCE (LP, reissue, 'Burbank' label)	£15
73	Warner Brothers K 46066	HIS BAND AND STREET CHOIR (LP, reissue, 'Burbank' label)	£15
73	Warner Brothers K 46242	HARD NOSE THE HIGHWAY (LP, gatefold sleeve, 'Burbank' label)	£15
74	London HSM 5008	T.B. SHEETS (LP, laminated front cover, dark green labels)	£15
74	Warner Brothers K 86007	IT'S TOO LATE TO STOP NOW (2-LP, gatefold sleeve, 'Burbank' label)	£20
74	Warner Brothers K 56068	VEEDON FLEECE (LP, 'Burbank' label)	£20
77	Bang 6467 625	THIS IS WHERE I CAME IN (LP)	£15

| 77 | Warner Brothers K 56322 | **A PERIOD OF TRANSITION** (LP) | **£15** |

77	Warner Brothers K 56322	**A PERIOD OF TRANSITION** (LP)..	**£15**
78	Warner Brothers K 56526	**WAVELENGTH** (LP, printed inner)..	**£15**
79	Mercury 9102 852	**INTO THE MUSIC** (LP, printed inner)	**£20**
80	Mercury 6302 021	**COMMON ONE** (LP, printed inner)...	**£15**
84	Mercury MERL 36	**LIVE AT THE GRAND OPERA HOUSE BELFAST** (LP)	**£15**
84	Mercury MERH 54	**A SENSE OF WONDER** (LP, white label test pressings with "Crazy Jane On God").............	**£40**
84	Mercury MERH 54	**A SENSE OF WONDER** (LP, credits but doesn't play "Crazy Jane On God")......................	**£15**
86	Mercury MERH 94	**NO GURU, NO METHOD, NO TEACHER** (LP, printed inner)	**£15**
87	Mercury MERH 110	**POETIC CHAMPIONS COMPOSE** (LP, printed inner)	**£20**
89	Polydor 839 262 1	**AVALON SUNSET** (LP, printed inner)	**£20**
90	Polydor 841 970-1	**THE BEST OF VAN MORRISON** (LP, printed inner)	**£30**
90	Polydor 847 100 1	**ENLIGHTENMENT** (LP, printed inner)	**£15**
91	Polydor 849 026 1	**HYMNS TO THE SILENCE** (2LP, gatefold, printed inners)...................................	**£80**
93	Polydor 519 219-1	**TOO LONG IN EXILE** (2LP, gatefold)...	**£100**
95	Verve 529 136-1	**HOW LONG HAS THIS BEEN GOING ON** (LP, with Georgie Fame and Friends)...........	**£50**
95	Exile/Polydor 527 307-1	**DAYS LIKE THIS** (LP, printed inner)	**£180**
96	Verve 533 203-1	**TELL ME SOMETHING: THE SONGS OF MOSE ALLISON** (with Georgie Fame, Mose Allison and Ben Sidran) (LP, printed inner)..	**£80**
97	Exile 5371011	**THE HEALING GAME** (LP, printed inner)	**£80**
99	Exile/Simply Vinyl SVLP 253	**BACK ON TOP** (LP, PVC envelope outer, printed inner).....................................	**£300**
02	Exile/Polydor 589177-1	**DOWN THE ROAD** (2LP, gloss printed inners)	**£120**
05	Exile/Polydor 987 1428	**MAGIC TIME** (LP, printed inner)	**£120**
09	Listen To The Lion 50999 6 93423 1 8	**ASTRAL WEEKS LIVE AT THE HOLLYWOOD BOWL** (2LP, gatefold)	**£50**
15	RCA 88875 06844 1	**DUETS: RE-WORKING THE CATALOGUE** (2LP, gatefold)	**£20**
16	Exile/Caroline International 5703575	**KEEP ME SINGING** (LP, lenticular sleeve)	**£20**
17	Exile/Caroline International 5703 575	**ROLL WITH THE PUNCHES** (2LP, gatefold)..	**£20**
17	Exile/Caroine International 670 8156	**VERSATILE** (2LP, gatefold)...	**£20**
18	Exile/Sony 9075820041	**YOU'RE DRIVING ME CRAZY** (with Joey DeFrancesco) (2LP, gatefold).................	**£20**
18	Exile/Caroline International 770 7173	**THE PROPHET SPEAKS** (2LP, gatefold sleeve)...	**£20**
19	Exile/Caroline International 080 1664	**THREE CHORDS & THE TRUTH** (2LP, gatefold, silver vinyl)................................	**£20**
21	Exile/BMG 538666250	**LATEST RECORD PROJECT** (VOLUME ONE) (3LP, trifold sleeve, 12x12 booklet).................	**£25**
22	Exile/BMG 00602445182299	**WHAT'S IT GONNA TAKE?** (2LP, gatefold, dove grey vinyl, indies ltd ed)	**£25**
23	Exile/Caroline International 00602448192363	**MOVING ON SKIFFLE** (2LP, blue vinyl)	**£25**
23	Exile/Caroline International 00602448192349	**MOVING ON SKIFFLE** (2LP, red vinyl)	**£25**
23	Exile/Virgin 3369665	**ACCENTUATE THE POSTIVE** (2LP, gatefold, blue vinyl, Ltd. Ed)	**£25**

(see also Them)

MORRISSEY

SINGLES

88	HMV TCPOP 1618	**Suedehead/I Know Very Well How I Got My Name**..	**£20**
88	HMV TCPOP 1618	**Suedehead/I Know Very Well How I Got My Name/ Hairdresser On Fire/Oh Well, I'll Never Learn** (cassette)...	**£15**
88	HMV TCPOP 1618	**Suedehead/I Know Very Well How I Got My Name/Oh Well, I'll Never Learn** (mispressed cassette, plays "Ordinary Boys" instead of I Know Very Well... withdrawn) ...	**£20**
88	HMV 12 POP 1618	**Suedehead/I Know Very Well How I Got My Name/Hairdresser On Fire** (12", 1st pressings in brown p/s)..	**£20**
91	HMV 12 POP 1627	**Pregnant For The Last Time/Skin Storm/Cosmic Dancer** (live)/ **Disappointed** (live) (12", p/s)..	**£15**
92	EMI CDMOZBX 1	**THE SINGLES COLLECTION 1986-1992** (13 x CD singles set hinged black/purple box with numbered insert)...	**£90**
94	Parlophone 12 R6383	**Hold Onto Your Friends/Moonriver** (12", gatefold sleeve)	**£25**
95	RCA Victor LC 0316	**Dagenham Dave/Nobody Loves Us** (p/s)..	**£15**
97	Island IS 667	**Alma Matters/Heir Apparent** (p/s)	**£25**
97	Parlophone 12 IS 667	**Alma Matters/Heir Apparent/I Can Have Both** (12")......................................	**£25**
97	Island IS 671	**Roy's Keen/Lost** (p/s)	**£25**
97	Island 12 IS 671	**Roy's Keen/Lost/The Edges Are No Longer Paralle** (12")	**£45**
97	Island IS 686	**Satan Rejected My Soul/Now I Am A Was** (p/s)	**£25**
97	Island 12IS 686	**Satan Rejected My Soul/Now I Am A Was/This Is Not Your Country** (12")	**£60**
00	EMI EMI 8872932	**SINGLES 88-91** (10 x CDs, card sleeves)...	**£40**
01	EMI EMI 8797452	**SINGLES 91-95** (9 X CDs, card sleeves, in box)	**£40**
06	Attack ATKTW 020	**First Of The Gang To Die** (12" 4-track EP)	**£20**
06	Attack ATKTW 019	**Irish Blood, English Heart** (12" 4-track EP)	**£20**

ALBUMS

88	HMV CSD 3787	**VIVA HATE** (LP)...	**£40**
90	HMV CLP 3788	**BONA DRAG** (LP)..	**£40**
91	EMI CSD 3789	**KILL UNCLE** (LP, gatefold)	**£40**
92	HMV CSD 3790	**YOUR ARSENAL** (LP)...	**£50**
93	HMV CSD 3791	**BEETHOVEN WAS DEAF** (LP)..	**£60**
94	Parlophone/EMI PCSD 148	**VAUXHALL AND I** (LP, gatefold)	**£100**
95	RCA Victor 74321299531	**SOUTHPAW GRAMMAR** (LP, with limited edition booklet)	**£150**
95	RCA 29953 1	**SOUTHPAW GRAMMAR** (LP)	**£100**
95	Parlophone PCS 7374	**BONA DRAG** (LP, reissue)	**£20**
95	Parlophone PCS 7375	**KILL UNCLE** (LP, reissue)	**£20**

MINT VALUE £

95	Parlophone PCS 7376	VIVA HATE (LP, reissue)	£20
97	Island ILPS 8059	MALADJUSTED (LP)	£40
97	EMI EMC 2771	SUEDEHEAD: THE BEST OF MORRISSEY (2-LP, gatefold)	£50
97	Parlophone PCSD 163	WORLD OF MORRISSEY (LP, classic yellow/black Parlophone label)	£50
04	Attack ATKLP 001	YOU ARE THE QUARRY (LP, 5,000 only)	£150
06	Attack ATKLP 016	RINGLEADER OF THE TORMENTORS (LP, gatefold)	£100
08	Decca SKL 6003	GREATEST HITS (2-LP, inners, download card)	£70
09	Polydor/Decca SKL6014/ 4781581	YEARS OF REFUSAL (LP)	£50
10	Major Minor SMLP70	BONA DRAG (2-LP, 20th aniversary edition, inners, poster)	£20
21	Major Minor SMLP 70	BONA DRAG (2-LP, reissue, teal coloured vinyl, obi)	£30

PROMOS

88	Factory FA 244+	I Know Very Well How I Got My Note Wrong (7" promo, as Vincent Gerrard and Stephen Patrick, 1,000 only)	£50
88	Factory FACD 244+	I Know Very Well How I Got My Note Wrong (CD promo, as Vincent Gerrard and Stephen Patrick, 1,000 only)	£40
88	HMV 12POP DJ 1618	Suedehead/I Know Very Well How I Got My Name/Hairdresser On Fire (12" promo)	£25
88	HMV 12 POP DJ 1619	Everyday Is Like A Sunday (12", promo, 1-sided)	£20
89	Parlophone POP 1620	The Last Of The Famous International Playboys/Lucky Lisp (test pressing with different version of Lucky Lisp to official release - matrixes A-1U-1-1/B-1U-1-1	£200
89	HMV 12POP DJ 1620	The Last Of The Famous International Playboys/Lucky Lisp/Michaels Bones (12" promo)	£20
89	EMI SPM 29	Interesting Drug/Such A Little Thing Makes Such A Big Difference (12" die cut red sleeve, promo)	£15
89	EMI SPM 29	Interesting Drug/etched B side (12", die cut black sleeve, promo)	£60
89	Parlophone 12POPDJ 1622	Ouija Board, Ouija Board/Yes, I Am Blind/East West (12" A label promo)	£30
90	HMV POPDJ1623	November The Second (12" promo, white label 'Dance Mix' destroyed on order of Morrissey, 1 known copy)	£2000
90	Parlophone 12POPDJ 1623	November Spawned A Monster/He Knows I'd Love To See Him/ Girl Least Likely To (12" promo)	£30
90	HMV POPDJ 1624	Piccadilly Palare/Get Off The Stage (promo, in die-cut HMV sleeve)	£35
91	Parlophone POPDJ1625	Our Frank/Journalists Who Lie (red 'A' label promo in die-cut retro sleeve)	£200
91	HMV POP DJ 1626	Sing Your Life/That's Entertainment (promo, die-cut HMV sleeve)	£35
91	HMV POP DJ1627	Pregnant For The Last TIme/Skin Storm (promo)	£50
91	HMV POPDJ1628	My Love Life/I've Changed My Plea To Guilty ('A' label promo in die cut sleeve)	£80
92	HMV POP DJ 1630	You're The One For Me, Fatty/You're The One For Me, Fatty (10", A-side plays at 45rpm, B-side at 78rpm, die-cut sleeve)	£40
92	HMV POP DJ 1629	We Hate It When Our Friends Become Successful/We Hate It When Our Friends Become Sucessful (10", A-side plays at 45rpm, B-side at 78rpm, die-cut sleeve)	£40
92	HMV POPDJ 1631	Certain People I Know/Jack The Ripper (die-cut 'Moz' p/s, 300 only)	£175
93	Parlophone POPDJ1632	Jack The Ripper/Sister I'm A Poet (promo in p/s)	£25
94	Parlophone RDJ 6372	The More You Ignore Me The Closer I Get/Used to Be A Sweet Boy ('photographer' sleeve)	£50
94	Parlophone CDRDJ 6372	The More You Ignore, Me The Closer I Get (CD, with "45rpm" logo on disc, withdrawn)	£45
94	Parlophone R 6383	Hold Onto Your Friends/Moonriver (promo in different p/s, 150 only)	£100
95	Parlophone RDJ 6400	Have-A-Go Merchant/Whatever Happens, I Love You (p/s)	£25
95	Parlophone/EMI RDJ 6400	Have-A-Go Merchant/Whatever Happens, I Love You p/s, promo for unreleased single)	£75
95	RCA SOLO 1	OUTSIDE TOUR SAMPLER (CD promo features Boy Racer)	£60
04	Sanctuary (No Cat. No)	YOU ARE THE QUARRY (CD-R interview promo)	£35
11	Stateside SS 2242	Glamorous Glue (2011 remaster)/VINCE EAGER: The World's Loneliest Man (Retro A label 'Stateside' promo in die-cut 'Stateside' sleeve, 150 only)	£250

(see also Smiths, Durutti Column)

MORRISSEY & SIOUXSIE

94	Parlophone 12R 6365	Interlude/Interlude (Extended)/Interlude (Instrumental) (12")	£15

DICK MORRISSEY

61	77' LEU 12/8	HAVE YOU HEARD? (LP)	£350
61	Fontana TFL 5149	IT'S MORRISSEY MAN! (LP)	£400
67	Mercury 20093	HERE AND NOW AND SOUNDING GOOD (LP)	£300
67	Mercury 20077MCL	STORM WARNING (LP)	£350

(see also If)

ELLA MAE MORSE

55	Capitol CL 14223	Bring Back My Baby To Me/Lovey Dovey	£50
55	Capitol CL 14303	Smack Dab In The Middle/Yes, Yes I Do	£50
55	Capitol CL 14332	Livin', Livin', Livin'/Heart Full Of Hope	£40
55	Capitol CL 14341	Razzle-Dazzle/Ain't That A Shame (with Big Dave & His Music)	£100
55	Capitol CL 14341	Razzle-Dazzle/Ain't That A Shame (with Big Dave & His Music) (78)	£25
55	Capitol CL 14362	Seventeen/Piddily Patter Song (with Big Dave & His Music)	£100
55	Capitol CL 14362	Seventeen/Piddily Patter Song (with Big Dave & His Music) (78)	£25
55	Capitol CL 14376	Birmin'ham/An Occasional Man	£40

(The 45s listed above were originally issued with triangular centres; later round-centres issues are worth around half to two-thirds of these values.)

56	Capitol CL 14508	When Boy Kiss Girl (It's Love)/Sing-Ing-Ing-Ing	£30
56	Capitol CL 14572	Rock And Roll Wedding/Down In Mexico	£40
56	Capitol CL 14572	Rock And Roll Wedding/Down In Mexico (78)	£20
57	Capitol CL 14726	What Good'll It Do Me/Mister Money Maker	£20
57	Capitol CL 14760	I'm Gone/Sway Me	£20
55	Capitol EAP1 513	BARRELHOUSE BOOGIE AND THE BLUES (EP)	£15
54	Capitol LC 6687	BARRELHOUSE BOOGIE AND THE BLUES (10" LP)	£20

(see also 'Tennessee' Ernie Ford)

ELLA MAE MORSE & FREDDIE SLACK
67   Ember SPE 6605 — ROCKIN' BREW (LP) £25

MORTA SKULD
93   Peaceville CC 4 — Sacrificial Rite/VITAL REMAINS: Amulet Of The Conquering (clear vinyl, p/s)...............£15
93   Deaf DEAF 11 — DYING REMAINS (LP) £25
94   Deaf DEAF 15 — HUMANITY FADES (LP) £20

MORTICIANS
87   Tin Soldier TIN 1 — FREAK OUT WITH THE MORTICIANS (LP)...£20

AZIE MORTIMER
60   London HLX 9237 — Lips/Wrapped Up In A Dream £100

MIKE MORTON CONGREGATION
70   Plexium PXM 19 — Burning Bridges/You Gotta Be Mine £15

MANDY MORTON (BAND)
79   Banshee BANS 791 — Song For Me (Music Prince)/Little Inbetween (with Spriguns) £15
78   Banshee BAN 1011 — MAGIC LADY (LP, with lyric insert, 1,000 only) £350
78   Banshee BAN 1011 — MAGIC LADY (LP, with lyric insert, blue vinyl, 20 only) £1000
80   Polydor 2382 101 — SEA OF STORMS (LP, solo, with insert) £70
83   Banshee — VALLEY OF LIGHT (LP, private pressing) £100

MORWELLS
75   Sir Jessus JES 4 — Come On Little Girl/Version '75 ....£15
79   Greensleeves GRED 17 — Thief A Dub (12") £40
77   Burning Sounds BS 1006 — CRAB RACE (LP)...£50
79   Bushays BFMLP 100 — COOL RUNNING (LP) £35
80   Trojan TRLS 193 — A1 DUB (LP) £35

MOSAIC
71   Parlophone R5928 — Blue Bird/Bird Of Fire £15

MOSAICS
66   Columbia DB 7990 — Let's Go Drag Racing/Now That You're Here £35

HARRY MOSCO
80   Samba SA003 — Step On/Sexy Dancer (12") £20

MOSCOVITE FIVE
82   In Phaze — WINTER WEEKENDS (cassette) £20

ADRIAN MOSELY
68   Redcar RC001 — Silent Night/Ellusive Face..£60

JOSHUA MOSES
78   More Cut MCT 6001 — Africa Is Our Land/Home (12", die-cut p/s) £70

LEE MOSES
07   Castle CMFDV1522 — TIME AND PLACE (2-LP, reissue) £100

PABLO MOSES
75   Treble C CCC 01 — I Man A Grasshopper/Grasshopper (Part 2) £20
75   Treble C CCC 09 — Blood Money/Version £20
76   Lizzard 001 — We Should Be In Angola/Dubbing In Angola £25
80   Island 12WIP — Dubbing Is A Must/Revolutionary Step (12") £25
82   Island 10WIP 6781 — Proverbs Extractions/Music Is My Desire (10") £35
77   Klik KLP 9026 — REVOLUTIONARY DREAM (LP)..£60
78   Different GETL 104 — REVOLUTIONARY DREAM (LP)..£20

MOSFETS
82   Sub SUB 1 — The Great War/Power Games (p/s) £60

MOSIAH
79   Big SOLD 6 — Rumours Of War/Channel Dub £35

MOSKOW (2)
82   Rygel RY6 — Heat House/Robot (p/s) £30

MOSS
06   Rise Above RISE7/085 5 — MOSS: Maimed & Slaughtered/THE PLAGUE OF GENTLEMEN: Rainbow Demon (test pressings only) £100
08   Rise Above RISELP 108 — SUB TEMPULUM (2-LP)..£25

BILL MOSS
69   Pama PM 765 — Sock It To 'Em Soul Brother (Parts 1 & 2) £15
70   Pama PM 796 — Number One/MOHAWKS: Lanscape..£20

BUDDY MOSS
60s Kokomo K 1003 — GEORGIA BLUES VOLUME 2 (LP) £50

JENNY MOSS
63   Columbia DB 7061 — Hobbies/Big Boys £40

STIRLING MOSS
61   Redemption RLP 5004 — THE STIRLING MOSS STORY (LP)...£15

GERRY MORRIS
72   York SYK 525 — Come On Home/Nothing To Declare £20
73   York SYK 557 — Sunlove/Only The Beginning...£30
73   York FYK 415 — ONLY THE BEGINNING (LP) £150

MOST
79   SRT SRTS/CUS/570 — Carefree/In And Out (1,000 only stamped lyric insert).............................£60

ABE MOST OCTET
55   London RE-P 1028   PRESENTING THE ABE MOST OCTET (EP) £20

MOST DOMINANT
93   Kold Sweat KSEP210   PUSHED TO DA LIMIT (EP) £15

MICKIE MOST (& GEAR)
63   Decca F 11664   Mr. Porter/Yes Indeed I Do £30
63   Columbia DB 7117   The Feminine Look/Shame On You Boy...£15
63   Columbia DB 7180   Sea Cruise/It's A Little Bit Hot...£15
64   Columbia DB 7245   Money Honey/That's Alright (as Mickey Most & Gear) £20
(see also Most Brothers)

MOST BROTHERS
57   Decca F 10968   Whistle Bait/I'm Comin' Home £20
58   Decca F 10998   Whole Lotta Woman/Teen Angel £20
58   Decca F 11040   Don't Go Home/Dottie...£20
(see also Mickie Most)

MOTHER EARTH
68   Mercury SMCL 20143   LIVING WITH THE ANIMALS (LP) £25

MOTHER FREEDOM BAND
77   All Platinum 6146326   Beautiful Summer Day/Flick Of the Wrist £20

MOTHER LIZA
83   Vista VSLP 2005   MOTHER LIZA MEETS PAPA TOLLO (TULLO) (LP) £15

MOTHER NATURE (2)
84   Ariwa ARILP 017   A BREATH OF FRESH AIR (LP) £15

MOTHER YOD
97   Prescription DRUG 1   MOTHER YOD (LP, 99 copies only) £25

MOTHERLIGHT
69   Morgan Bluetown BT 5003   BOBAK, JONS, MALONE (LP) £600
88   Morgan Blue Town BT5008   BOBAK, JOHNS, MALONE (LP, reissue)..£35
(see also Will Malone [Voice Band], Orange Bicycle)

MOTHERLODE
69   Buddah 2318 043   WHEN I DIE (LP) £15

MOTHER LOVE BONE
90   Polypro 843 191   APPLE (LP)...£80

MOTHER'S RUIN
81   Spectra SPC 1   Streetfighters/Leaving You (in p/s) £55
81   Spectra SPC 1   Streetfighters/Leaving You £40
82   Spectra SPC 6   Street Lights/Turn A Corner (p/s) £20
82   Spectra SPC 7   Say It's Not True/It's Illogical (p/s) £35

MOTHMEN
80s   On-U-Sound LP 2   PAY ATTENTION (LP) £15
(see also Alberto Y Lost Trios Paranoias)

MOTHS
69   Deroy   MOTHS (LP, private pressing in plain white sleeve) £500

MOTIFFE
72   Deroy 777   MOTIFFE (LP, private pressing in hand-illustrated white sleeve, 99 only).......................£1500

MOTIFS
82   MM1   Shadow Of Fear/On The Inside...£50

MOTION
79   DD Records DDLP04   MOTION (LP)...£40
(see also Aswad)

MOTIONS
66   Pye International 7N 25390   Stop Your Crying/Every Step I Take...£25

MOTIVATION
68   Direction 58-3248   Come On Down/Little Man £35

MOTIVES
80   Romantic RR 0001   King Of The Dub/Lies And Stories £15

FRANK MOTLEY & KING HERBERT
98   Jazzman JMANLP 001   CANADA'S MESSAGE TO THE METERS (THE BEST OF...) (LP) £20

MOTLEY CREW (1)
68   MJB BEV 429   MOTLEY CREW (EP, hand made sleeve)...£25

MÖTLEY CRÜE
84   Elektra E 9756T   Looks That Kill/Piece Of The Action/Live Wire (12", p/s with free tattoo)......................£15
84   Elektra E 9756TP   Looks That Kill/Piece Of The Action/Live Wire (12", picture disc) £20
84   Elektra E 9732T   Too Young To Fall In Love/Take Me To The Top (12", p/s, with poster).......£15
86   Elektra EKR 16TP   Smokin' In The Boys' Room/Use It Or Lose It (mask-shaped pic disc & sticker) £15
86   Elektra EKR 33P   Smokin' In The Boys' Room/Home Sweet Home (2 different interlocking mask-shaped picture disc set)........£20
86   Elektra EKR 33T   Smokin' In The Boys' Room/Home Sweet Home/Shout At The Devil (12", p/s with poster).......£20
83   Elektra 9602 89-1   SHOUT AT THE DEVIL (LP, with bonus 12" picture disc & poster) £20

MOTÖRHEAD

SINGLES : SINGLES AND EPS

76	Stiff BUY 9	**Leaving Here/White Line Fever** (Unreleased, but included in Stiff box set of first 10 singles and some also sold via mail order)...£50
77	Stiff BUY 9	**Leaving Here/White Line Fever** (mispressing, A side plays Neat Neat Neat by THE DAMNED)..£100
77	Chiswick S 13	**Motörhead/City Kids** (p/s) £20
77	Chiswick S 13A	**Motörhead/City Kids** (12", p/s)..£20
79	Bronze BRO 78	**No Class/Like A Nightmare** (3 different sleeves)...£50
80	Big Beat NSP 13	**Motörhead/City Kids** (p/s, blue & white picture disc) £15
80	Bronze BRO 92 DJ	**Leaving Here** (live)/**Stone Dead Forever** (live) (2-track promo for Golden Years EP)........£40
83	Bronze BROX 167/BROX 92	**Shine/Hoochie Coochie Man** (live)/**Don't Need Religion** (live)/**THE GOLDEN YEARS** (12", p/s, stickered, shrinkwrapped double pack) £80
84	Bronze BROP 185	**Killed By Death/Under The Knife** (logo skull-shaped picture disc) £20
84	Bronze BROX 185	**Killed By Death** (Full Length Version)/**Under The Knife/Under The Knife** (12", stickered p/s, with poster) £15
84	Bronze BROP 185	**Killed By Death/Under The Knife** (logo skull-shaped picture disc, mispressing, A side plays Banana Banana and B side plays Bo Diddley Goes East by KING KURT)...............£100
88	GWR GWR 15	**Ace Of Spades/Dogs/Traitor** (sold at concerts & through fan club, no p/s)..........£20
90	Epic 656578 0	**The One To Sing The Blues/Dead Man's Hand** (shaped picture disc).............£15
80	Big Beat SWT 61	**BEER DRINKERS EP** (12", p/s, pink or orange vinyl) £15
80	Big Beat SWT 61	**BEER DRINKERS EP** (12", p/s, brown vinyl)..£40
81	Bronze BROX 116	**ST. VALENTINES DAY MASSACRE** (10" EP, with Girlschool)...............................£15

ALBUMS

77	Chiswick WIK 2	**MOTÖRHEAD** (LP, black and silver sleeve with swastika on Snaggletooth, printed inner, 1000 only) £1500
77	Chiswick WIK 2	**MOTÖRHEAD** (LP, black & white laminated sleeve with inner) £75
78	Chiswick CWK 3008	**MOTÖRHEAD** (LP, white vinyl)..£30
78	United Artists LBR 1004	**ON PAROLE** (LP)...£25
79	Bronze BRON 515	**OVERKILL** (LP, green vinyl) £45
79	Bronze BRON 523	**BOMBER** (LP, 3 different shades of blue vinyl)...£40
80	Bronze BRON 531	**ACE OF SPADES** (LP, EMI pressing)...£35
80	Bronze BRONG 531	**ACE OF SPADES** (LP, gold vinyl, stickered sleeve) £80
80	Big Beat WIK 2	**MOTÖRHEAD** (LP, reissue, red or clear vinyl with inner sleeve) £20
81	Bronze BRONG 535	**NO SLEEP 'TIL HAMMERSMITH** (LP, gold vinyl, stickered sleeve) £45
82	Bronze BRNA 539	**IRON FIST** (LP, printed inner, some with biog insert and stickered sleeve))......£25
83	Bronze BRON 546	**ANOTHER PERFECT DAY**(LP, insert, mispressed with Uriah Heep labels) £30
83	Bronze BRON 546	**ANOTHER PERFECT DAY**(LP, insert)...£18
84	Bronze/Pro MOTOR 1	**NO REMORSE** (2LP, leather sleeve with printed inners) £45
83	GWR GWLP1	**ORGASMATRON** (LP, four-page insert) £20
86	GWR GWRLP 1	**ORGASMATRON** (LP, picture disc)..£40
87	GWR GWLP 14	**ROCK'N'ROLL** (LP, printed inner, Eat The Rich hype sticker)..............................£25
90	Castle TFOLP 024	**BOMBER/ACE OF SPADES** (2LP, reissue, gatefold)..£30
91	Epic 467481 1	**1916** (LP, printed inner)...£30
91	Epic 467481-0	**1916** (LP, picture disc, stickered PVC sleeve) £100
91	Epic 467481 9	**1916** (CD, 'tour' picture disc shrinkwrapped with booklet, stickered case) £30
92	Receiver RRLP 005	**LIVE JAILBAIT** (2LP) £100
92	Epic 471723 1	**MARCH OR DIE** (LP, printed inner) £120
93	Castle CTVLP 125	**ALL THE ACES** (LP, gatefold)..£45
93	Castle/Bronze CTVCD 125	**ALL THE ACES** (CD, numbered promo, in box with metal skull, 100 only)........£250
93	ZYX 20263-1	**BASTARDS** (LP, European release, 2 different barcodes)...................................£75
95	Steamhammer SPV 008-76941	**SACRIFICE** (LP, printed inner) £100
96	Steamhammer SPV 085-18301	**OVERNIGHT SENSATION** (LP, printed inner) £120
98	Steamhammer SPV 008-18891	**SNAKE BITE LOVE** (LP, printed inner, side 2 track list over 3 lines on rear) £120
00	Metal-Is MISL 002	**THE BEST OF...**(3LP, numbered with insert & bonus exclusive live EP) £65
00	Steamhammer SPV 078-21821 LP	**WE ARE MOTÖRHEAD** (LP, printed inner)...£120
02	Steamhammer SPV 085-74061 LP	**HAMMERED** (LP, printed inner) £60
04	Steamhammer SPV 22325	**INFERNO** (2LP, printed inners) £40
06	Steamhammer 28777 LP	**KISS OF DEATH** (LP, printed inner) £28
07	Steamhammer SPV 31645 4LP	**BETTER MÖTORHEAD THAN DEAD – LIVE AT HAMMERSMITH** (4LP, gatefold, Cargo logo on labels) £70
08	Steamhammer SPV 91631 LP	**MOTÖRIZER** (LP, gatefold, printed inner)...£55
10	Back To Black 5326582	**ACE OF SPADES** (LP, picture disc, reissue, with download card) £15
10	Motorhead Music UDR – UDR 0005 LP	**THE WÖRLD IS YOURS** (LP, gatefold)..£30
10	Motorhead Music UDR – UDR 0005 LP	**THE WÖRLD IS YOURS** (LP, gatefold, silver vinyl, 1000 only) £75
12	Back On Black BOBV320LP	**MARCH OR DIE** (LP, 180g white vinyl, gatefold sleeve, reissue) £50
13	UDR UDR 0186 LP	**AFTERSHOCK** (LP, gatefold, printed inner, brown marbled vinyl, issued through Nuclear Blast) £60
15	UDR UDR 057P47	**BAD MAGIC** (LP/CD, gatefold, printed inner, white vinyl, CD in paper sleeve) £28
16	UDR UDR062P75	**CLEAN YOUR CLOCK** (2LP/CD/DVD/BD, pop up gatefold, grey vinyl, metal pin, 2 different boxes)..£70
19	BMG BMGCAT 380DBOX	**1979** (7LP/2x7", 180g vinyl, magazine, tour programme, sheet music, badge, Bronze sticker, box, leather jacket outer, deluxe edition) £400
21	BMG BMGCAT522QLP	**EVERYTHING LOUDER FOREVER** (4LP, trifold, printed inners, some mail order copies £45

MINT VALUE £

with poster)..			£100

| 23 | Steamhammer SPV 089-21141 3LP | EVERYTHING LOUDER THAN EVERYTHING ELSE (3LP, printed inners)......................... | £100 |
| 23 | Silver Lining Music SLM777P75 | SERIOUSLY BAD MAGIC (3LP/2CD, bonus tracks, box set, reissue) .... | £85 |

(see also Lemmy & Upsetters, Hawkwind, Girlschool, Wild Horses, Young & Moody, Rocking Vickers, Blue Goose, Persian Risk)

MOTOWN SOUNDS
| 79 | Motown 12TMG 1143 | Space Dance/Bad Mouthin' (12")..£20 |
| 79 | Motown STML 12105 | SPACE DANCE (LP)..£15 |

MOTT THE HOOPLE
69	Island WIP 6072	Rock And Roll Queen/Road To Birmingham £25
71	Island WIP 6105	Midnight Lady/The Debt (in p/s)...£18
69	Island ILPS 9108	MOTT THE HOOPLE (LP, gatefold sleeve, pink label with white 'i' logo; with "Backsliding Fearlessly" in correct order)...........................£100
69	Island ILPS 9108	MOTT THE HOOPLE (LP, pink label; mispress with 5 alternate mixes & Road To Birmingham in place of "Backsliding Fearlessly" or one alternative mix with "Road To Birmingham", and "Rock And Roll Queen" correctly credited. This price for each copy) ...£90
70	Island ILPS 9119	MAD SHADOWS (LP, pink label with pink 'i' logo, gatefold sleeve) £50
71	Island ILPS 9144	WILD LIFE (LP, gatefold, pink rim palm tree label) £50
71	Island ILPS 9178	BRAIN CAPERS (LP, pink rim palm tree label & inner sleeve, with mask)........£100
71	Island ILPS 9178	BRAIN CAPERS (LP, pink rim palm tree label & inner sleeve, without mask).....£40
72	CBS 65184	ALL THE YOUNG DUDES (LP, with inner sleeve)..£40
72	Island ILPS 9215	ROCK AND ROLL QUEEN (LP, 'pink rim palm tree' label) £25
73	CBS 69038	MOTT (LP, die-cut gatefold sleeve with plastic flap, inner sleeve, orange label, stickered) £40
74	CBS 69062	THE HOOPLE (LP, with insert)..£40
80	Island IRSP 8	TWO MILES FROM HEAVEN (LP, early copies listing "Moving On" on rear sleeve) £20
80	Island IRSP 8	TWO MILES FROM HEAVEN (LP)...£15

(see also Ian Hunter, At Last The 1958 Rock & Roll Show, Morgan, Mick Ronson, British Lions, Luther Grosvenor, Charlie Woolfe)

KEN MOULE'S LONDON JAZZ CHAMBER GROUP
| 70 | Ember EMB S 275 | Mae West/Zsa Zsa Gabor (in p/s)...£15 |
| 69 | Ember CJS 823 | ADAM'S RIB SUITE (LP)..£70 |

(see also London Jazz Chamber Group, Ken Moule Seven)

KEN MOULE SEVEN
54	Decca LK 4087	MODERN JAZZ AT THE FESTIVAL HALL (LP, also features Don Rendell and Tony Crombie Orchestra) £50
57	Decca LK 4192	KEN MOULE ARRANGES FOR (LP) £25
58	Decca LK 4261	JAZZ AT TOAD HALL (LP) £30

(see also London Jazz Chamber Group)

MATTIE MOULTRIE
| 67 | CBS 202547 | That's How Strong My Love Is/The Saddest Story Ever Told......................£20 |
| 67 | CBS 202547 | That's How Strong My Love Is/The Saddest Story Ever Told (DJ Copy) ....£40 |

MOUNT KIMBIE
11	Hotflush CNL 003	CARBONATED EP (2 x 12")..£15
13	Beat/Warp WAP 251J	You Took Your Time (Oneman Remix) (12") £30
17	Warp WARPLP 288X	LOVE WHAT SURVIVES (2-LP, white vinyl)...£18

MOUNTAIN
70	Bell BLL 1112	Mississippi Queen/The Laird...£15
70	Bell BLL 1125	Sittin' On A Rainbow/To My Friend £20
70	Bell SBLL 133	MOUNTAIN CLIMBING! (LP) £20
71	Island ILPS 9148	NANTUCKET SLEIGHRIDE (LP, 'pink rim palm tree' label) £20
71	Island ILPS 9179	FLOWERS OF EVIL (LP, 'pink rim palm tree' label).....................................£15

(see also West Bruce & Laing, Leslie West, Jolliver Arkansas)

MOUNTAIN ASH
| 75 | Witches Bane LKLP 6036 | THE HERMIT (LP, private pressing with insert)...£200 |

MOUNTAIN MEN
| 65 | Eos CE 717 | Too Many People/Without You..£250 |

MOURNING PHASE
71	Eden LP 45	MOURNING PHASE (LP, private pressing, white label, cat no. in run-out groove, handful in existence)......................£2000
91	Eden EDEN 001	MOURNING PHASE (LP, reissue, 250 copies, insert).................................£50
21	Seelie Court SCLP 013	MOURNING PHASE (LP, remastered reissue, gatefold) £25

MOUSE
| 73 | Sovereign SOV 122 | We Can Make It/It's Happening To Me And You ....£20 |
| 73 | Sovereign SVNA 7262 | LADY KILLER (LP, gatefold sleeve) ....£800 |

(see also Ginhouse, Ray Russell Quartet, Running Man)

MOUSE & TRAPS
| 68 | President PT 174 | L.O.V.E. Love/Beg Borrow And Steal ....£40 |
| 68 | President PT 210 | Sometimes You Just Can't Win/Crying Inside..£20 |

MOUSE ON MARS
94	Too Pure PURE 36	VULVALAND (LP, with free 12")..£20
97	Too Pure PURE 70	AUTODITACKER (LP)...£20
95	Too Pure PURE 48	LAORA TAHITI (LP)..£20
99	Domino WIGLP 70	NIUN NIGGUNG (LP)...£20

MOUSETRAP
| 71 | Aurora AU 4324 | Susie/Greenfields ....£35 |

MOUTH TO MOUTH
79	Mouth To Mouth MT 1	Gallery Of Dolls/Life In The Subbterrain (hand stamped labels, no p/s) £200

MOVE
67	Regal Zonophone	Cherry Blossom Clinic/Vote For Me (unissued) £0
71	Harvest HAR 5036	Ella James/No Time (unissued) £0
68	Regal Zono. TRZ 2001	SOMETHING ELSE FROM THE MOVE (EP, 33rpm) £75
68	Regal Zono. LRZ 1002	THE MOVE (LP, mono, red/silver labels with "Sold in the U.K..." text) £150
68	Regal Zono. SLRZ 1002	THE MOVE (LP, stereo, red/silver labels with "Sold in the U.K..." text)....................£100
68	Regal Zono. TA-LRZ 1002	THE MOVE (reel-to-reel, mono only) £15
70	Regal Zono. SLRZ 1012	SHAZAM (LP, many with pressing flaw on track "Don't Make My Baby Blue" that makes record skip on this track, red/silver label)..£150
70	Fly HIFLY 1	LOOKING ON (LP, white label, 'Fly' logo) £40
71	Harvest SHSP 4013	MESSAGE FROM THE COUNTRY (LP, with EMI logo on label)..£80
72	Fly TOOFA 5/6	THE MOVE/SHAZAM (2-LP reissue)...£18
74	Harvest SHSP 4035	CALIFORNIA MAN (LP) £20

(see also Roy Wood, ELO, Idle Race, Trevor Burton, Nicky James Movement, Ace Kefford Stand, Grunt Futtock, Rick Price, Uglys, Charlie Wayne)

MOVEMENT (1)
68	Pye 7N 17443	Tell Her/Something You've Got..£120
68	Target 7N 17443	Something You've Got/Tell Her (Irish issue)..£120
68	Big T BIG 112	Head For The Sun/Mister Mann £180

MOVEMENT (2)
80	Ballistic TRIF 2	No Man Is An Island/JAMDOWN PLAYERS: Levi's Choice (dubwise)/Togetherness/ Deviate/Consolidate/Progression (12")..£30

MOVERS (1)
65	Ska Beat JB 191	Jo-Anne/DON DRUMMOND: Don De Lion £45

MOVERS (2)
68	Capitol CL 15562	Birmingham/Leave Me Loose £25

MOVERS (3)
60s	Junior Records Ltd JR 109	Rock Rock/Reggay Rock £200

MOVIE STARS
82	Lansater LG10	No Time To Kill/Heroes (no p/s) £30

MOVIETONE
95	Planet PUNK 010	MOVIETONE (LP)...£30
97	Domino WIGLP 36	DAY AND NIGHT (LP)...£30
00	Domino WIGLP 79	THE BLOSSOM FILLED STREETS (LP) £30
03	Domino WIGLP 131	THE SAND AND THE STARS (LP) £20

MOVING BROTHERS
67	Island WI 3049	Darling I Love You/TOMMY McCOOK & SUPERSONICS: Saboo £40
67	Treasure Isle TI 7018	Darling I Love You/TOMMY McCOOK & SUPERSONICS: Saboo (reissue)..........................£25

MOVING ENGLAND
80	English ER 001	Moving Back/Stretching Back (Part 3) £30

MOVING FINGER
68	Mercury MF 1051	Jeremy The Lamp/Pain Of My Misfortune £50
69	Mercury MF 1077	Higher And Higher/Shake And Fingerpop £70

(see also Anglians)

JUDY MOWATT
71	Trojan GPW 33	The Gardener/Vesion (white label only) £35
80	Grove Music IPR 2041	Black Woman (feat. Joy Tulloch)/My My People (12") £25

(see also Jean & Gaytones, Gaylettes)

MOWREY JNR. & WATSON
76	Riverdale RRL 1000	BUSKER (LP, with insert) £30

MR. BLOE
70	DJM DJLPS 036	GROOVIN' WITH MR. BLOE (LP) £18

(see also Harry Pitch)

MR. BUNGLE
91	London 828 276-1	MR BUNGLE (LP, picture disc) £40

MR. B WACKA
97	Humboldt County BOLDT6	Traffic Jam/Bus Stop (12") £60

MR. CEE
87	Asona ASR 7010	NYE WONKO (LP) £20

MR CHIPPS
77	Spiral SPF 7014	The Way I Am/Lady Elaine (no p/s) £30

MR. CONCEPT
85	Cordelia ERICAT 009	NOVEMBER (LP)..£30

MR. DYNAMITE
67	Sue WI 4027	Sh'mon/DYNAMITE ORCHESTRA: Sh'mon (Part Two)...£300

MR. FINGERS
89	Jack Trax JTX 32	LOVE AND JUSTICE (12")...£20
88	Jack Trax 12 J TRAX 10	SLAM DANCE EP (12") £50
90	FFRR F131	What About This Love/Dub Version (die-cut sleeve) £20
89	Jack Trax FING 2	AMMNESIA (2-LP)..£80
92	MCA MCA 10571	INTRODUCTION (LP with free 12")..£40
94	Black Market BMI 022 LP	BACK TO LOVE (LP)...£35

MR. FLOOD'S PARTY

MINT VALUE £

95	Black Market BMI 024 LP	CLASSIC FINGERS (2-LP)	£30
18	Alleviated ML 9017	CEREBAL HEMISPHERES (3-LP)	£20

(see also Larry Heard, Fingers Inc.)

MR. FLOOD'S PARTY
71	Ember EMB S 312	Compared To What/Unbreakable Toy	£20
71	Ember EMB S 312	Compared To What/Unbreakable Toy (DJ copy)	£40

(see also Mike Corbett & Jay Hirsch)

MR. FORD & MR. GOON-BONES
56	London HLU 8355	Ain't She Sweet/MUZZY MARCELLINO: Mary Lou	£25

(see also Mr. Goon-Bones & Cavaliers)

MR FOUNDATION
67	Studio One SO 2001	See Them A Come/KEN PARKER: Have A Good Time	£70
67	Studio One SO 2003	All Rudies In Jail (actually by Zoot Sims)/HORTENSE & ALTON Easy Squeeze	£90
68	Studio One SO 2061	Timo Oh/DUDLEY SIBLEY & PETER AUSTIN: Hole In Your Soul	£125
68	Studio One SO 2069	Reggae Rumble/MARCIA GRIFFITHS : You Keep Me On The Move	£180
69	Supreme SUP 201	Time To Pray (actually by Lloyd Robinson)/Young Budd (by Leonard Dillon)	£20

(see also Busty & Cool, Simms & Robinson, Sound Dimension)

MR. FOX
70	Transatlantic TRA 226	MR FOX (LP)	£75
71	Transatlantic TRA 236	THE GIPSY (LP, gatefold sleeve, plaatic inner with foam opening)	£125
75	Transatlantic TRA 303	THE COMPLETE MR FOX (2-LP, reissue of "Mr Fox" & "The Gipsy")	£20

(see also Bob Pegg, Bob & Carol Pegg)

MR. MO'S MESSENGERS
67	Columbia DB 8133	Feelin' Good/The Handyman	£15

MISTER MOST
69	Downtown DT 409	Reggae Train/Pushwood	£30

MR. PINK/MR. BLONDE
96	Resevoir BP1	Payin' The Price/Death Before Dishonour (12")	£15

MR. REJECT
71	Private pressing	MR. REJECT (LP)	£40

MR. SCRUFF
99	Ninja Tune ZEN 42	KEEP IT UNREAL (2xLP, gatefold)	£25
99	Ninja Tune ZEN 42	KEEP IT UNREAL (2xLP, gatefold, purple sleeve)	£30
99	Ninja Tune ZEN 65	TROUSER JAZZ (2xLP, gatefold)	£25

MR STONE
79	Strictly Pre PRE 1	Jah Jah Higher Than I/Unbeliever (12")	£60

MR. TWISTER & TORNADOS
63	Starlite ST45 099	Big Twist (Parts 1 & 2)	£15

MR. THING X MICALL PARKNSUN
17	White 157067E2/A	THE RAW EP (12", p/s, 100 only)	£25
18	Village Live TVI 019	FINISH WHAT WE STARTED (LP, with obi strip)	£30

MTUME
78	Epic EPC 84629	IN SEARCH OF THE RAINBOW SEEKERS (LP)	£20
83	Epic EPC 25399	JUICY FRUIT (LP)	£20

MU
74	United Artists UAG 29709	LEMURIAN MUSIC (LP)	£35

MU5
72	Crystal CR 7015	Mrs Watson/Rain Dance	£50

MUCKY DUCK
70	Deram DM314	Jefferson/Psycho's On The Run	£15

MUD
67	CBS 203002	Flower Power/You're My Mother (in p/s)	£50
67	CBS 203002	Flower Power/You're My Mother	£35
68	CBS 3355	Up The Airy Mountain/Latter Days	£30
69	Philips BF 1775	Shangri-La/House On The Hill	£20
70	Philips 6006 022	Jumping Jehosaphat/Won't Let It Go	£20

MUDHONEY
88	Glitterhouse GR 0034	SUPERFUZZ BIGMUFF (12" EP)	£18
95	Reprise 9362 458401	MY BROTHER THE COW (LP, with 6-track EP, [PRO S 7492])	£20

(see also Sonic Youth, Greenriver)

MUD HUTTERS
79	Defensive SRTS/79/CUS 263	INFORMATION EP (paper wrap p/s)	£50
79	Defensive SRTS/79/CUS 496	THE DECLARATION EP (paper wrap p/s)	£30
80	Defensive PACT 1	FACTORY FARMING (LP)	£30

MUDIE'S ALL STARS
70	Moodisc HM 3503	Wha Who Wha - Version/G.G. RUSSELL: Wha Who Wha	£20

(see also I Roy, Eternals, King Cannon, John Holt, Niney, Jolly Boys, Jo Jo Bennett)

MUDLARKS
58	Columbia SEG 7854	THE MUDLARKS! (EP)	£20

MUFF
71	Mother MOT 7	Hurdy Gurdy/Why Did You Leave Me	£15

MUGGINS BLIGHT
79 Look LK/EP 6455   Mr Somebody/They Go Up! They Go Down!/Malcolm Where's the Talcum? (p/s).........£25

MUGWUMPS
67 Warner Bros W 1697   THE MUGWUMPS - AN HISTORICAL RECORDING (LP)....................................£35
70 Valiant VS 134   THE MUGWUMPS - AN HISTORICAL RECORDING (LP, reissue) £18
(see also Mamas & Papas, Mama Cass Elliot, Lovin' Spoonful, Zalman Yanovsky)

IDRIS MUHAMMAD
74 Kudu KU 17   POWER OF SOUL (LP) £50
77 Kudo KU 34   TURN THIS MUTHA OUT (LP) £30
78 Fantasy FT 552   YOU AIN'T NO FRIEND OF MINE (LP) £20
78 Kudu KU 38   BOOGIE TO THE TOP (LP)..£20
79 Fantasy FT 562   FOXHUNTIN' (LP) £15

BOBBY MUIR & BLUEBEATS
61 Blue Beat BB 44   Honey Please/That's My Girl (as Bobby Kingdom & Blue Beats) £25

JAMIE MUIR & DEREK BAILEY
81 Incus INCUS 41   DART DRUG (LP) £50
(see also Derek Bailey)

LINDSAY MUIR'S UNTAMED
66 Planet PLF 113   Daddy Long Legs/Trust Yourself A Little Bit (initial release with plain white white
                             sleeve)...£250
66 Planet PLF 113   Daddy Long Legs/Trust Yourself A Little Bit (with Planet company sleeve)....................£240
(see also Untamed)

MULCAYS
55 London HLF 8188   Harbour Lights/Dipsy Doodle...£20

MULDOONS
65 Decca F 12164   I'm Lost Without You/Come Back Now Baby £30

MULESKINNERS
65 Fontana TF 527   Back Door Man/Need Your Lovin'..£200
65 Keepoint KEE-EP-7104   MULESKINNERS (EP, private pressing, no p/s)..............................£750
(see also Small Faces, Faces)

ARTHUR MULLARD
67 Masquerade MP 2003   ARTHUR MULLARD OF LONDON (LP)..£30

MOON MULLICAN
51 Vogue V 9013   Cherokee Boogie/Love Is The Light That Leads Me Home (78)...............£15
56 Parlophone DP 503   Yearning (Just For You)/Put Your Arms Around Me, Honey (export 78)....£15
56 Parlophone DP 512   San Antonio Rose/Cedarwood Blues (export 78) £15
56 Parlophone MSP 6254   Seven Nights To Rock/Honolulu Rock-A Roll-A (with Boyd Bennett & His Rockets) £300
56 Parlophone R 4195   Seven Nights To Rock/Honolulu Rock-A Roll-A (with Boyd Bennett & His Rockets) (78)...£50
59 Parlophone GEP 8794   COUNTRY ROUND UP (EP)...£60
50s Parlophone CGEP 13   MOON MULLICAN (EP, export issue) £40
50s Parlophone CGEP 15   PIANO BREAKDOWN (EP, export issue, company sleeve) £20
(see also Boyd Bennett & His Rockets)

GERRY MULLIGAN
53 Capitol LC 6621   THE GERRY MULLIGAN TENTETTE - ROCKER (10" LP) £15
53 Vogue LDE 029   THE GERRY MULLIGAN QUARTET VOL. 1 (10" LP) £15
53 Vogue LDE 030   THE GERRY MULLIGAN QUARTET VOL. 2 (10" LP) £15
53 Vogue LDE 031   THE GERRY MULLIGAN QUARTET VOL. 3 (10" LP) £15
54 Vogue LDE 075   THE GERRY MULLIGAN QUARTET (10" LP) £15
54 Vogue LDE 083   THE GERRY MULLIGAN QUARTET VOL. 4 (10" LP) £15
54 Esquire 20-032   GERRY MULLIGAN ALLSTARS - MULLIGAN'S TOO (10" LP) £20
55 Vogue LDE 156   GERRY MULLIGAN QUARTET WITH LEE KONITZ (10" LP)............£20
56 Esquire 32-014   GERRY MULLIGAN ALLSTARS (LP) £20
56 Vogue LAE 12006   THE GERRY MULLIGAN QUARTET (LP) £20
56 Vogue LAE 12015   THE GERRY MULLIGAN QUARTET - PARIS JAZZ FAIR 1954 (LP).....£20
56 Emarcy EJL 101   PRESENTING THE GERRY MULLIGAN SEXTET (LP)......................£25
57 Emarcy EJL 1259   MAINSTREAM OF JAZZ (LP, by Gerry Mulligan Sextet) £25
58 Columbia Clef 33CX 10113 GERRY MULLIGAN AND PAUL DESMOND QUARTET (LP).............£25
58 HMV CLP 1204   PHIL SUNKEL'S "JAZZ CONCERTO GROSSO" (LP, with Bob Brookmeyer) £25
59 Philips SBBL 552   WHAT IS THERE TO SAY? (LP, stereo) £25
59 Vogue SEA 5006   GERRY MULLIGAN SONGBOOK (LP, stereo) £25
59 Vogue SEA 5007   REUNION WITH CHET BAKER (LP, stereo, as Gerry Mulligan Quartet)....£25
59 London Jazz LTZT 15161   I WANT TO LIVE (LP, with Shelly Manne) £20
60 HMV CLP 1373   GERRY MULLIGAN MEETS BEN WEBSTER (LP) £20
61 HMV CLP 1432   THE CONCERT JAZZ BAND (LP, also stereo CSD 1351) £20
61 Vocalion LAE 12268   THE GENIUS OF GERRY MULLIGAN (LP) £20
62 HMV CLP 1465   GERRY MULLIGAN MEETS JOHNNY HODGES (LP, also stereo CSD 1372)........£20
62 HMV CLP 1488   AT THE VILLAGE VANGUARD (LP, also stereo CSD 1396).............£20
62 Riverside RLP 12-247   MULLIGAN MEETS MONK (LP, with Thelonious Monk)..............£20
62 HMV CLP 1549   A CONCERT IN JAZZ (LP, also stereo CSD 1432) £20
62 HMV CLP 1585   ON TOUR (LP, with Zoot Sims) £20
63 Philips BL 7597   NIGHT LIGHTS (LP)..£25
(see also Gerry Mulligan, Chet Baker, Shelly Manne, Annie Ross)

MICK MULLIGAN'S JAZZ BAND
57 Tempo TAP 14   JAZZ AT THE RAILWAY ARMS (LP, with George Melly)...............£50
59 Pye Jazz NJL 21   MEET MICK MULLIGAN (LP) £20

(see also George Melly)

MULTIPLE TRANSMISSION
95	Alphaphone ALPHA 002	Earthloop/Low Load/Antichrist (12")	£25

(see also Cabaret Voltaire, Richard H. Kirk)

MUM
02	Fat Cat FATLP 18	FINALLY WE ARE NO ONE (2 x 10")	£50
07	Fat Cat FATLP46	GO GO SMEAR THE POISON IVY (LP, with bonus 7")	£18

MUMFORD & SONS
08	Chess Club CC 006	LEND ME YOUR EYES EP (10", p/s)	£175
08	Chess Club CC 009	LOVE YOUR GROUND EP (10", p/s)	£150
09	Gentlemen Of The Road/ Island 2728222,	Winter Winds/Hold On To What You Believe (p/s, cream coloured vinyl)	£20
09	Chess Club CC 015	The Cave/My Heart Told My Head (Winter Winds) (1-sided 10", gatefold p/s, 300 only, signed)	£100
09	Chess Club CC 015	The Cave/My Heart Told My Head (Winter Winds) (1-sided 10", gatefold p/s, 300 only, unsigned)	£50
12	Gentlemen Of The Road/ Island 3716215	I Will Wait/I Will Wait (live) (p/s, no'd, 500 only)	£18
12	Gentlemen Of The Road/ Island 3723020	Lover Of The Light/Thistle & Weeds (live) (p/s, 1000 only, no'd)	£15
10	Chess Club WEDDING 1	FIRST DANCE EP (tour 10" as The Wedding Band)	£80
09	V2 VVR 723601	SIGH NO MORE (LP)	£15
12	Gentlemen Of The Road 3710659	BABEL (LP, gatefold)	£15

MUMMIES
89	Hangman HANG 47 UP	FUCKS C.D.S. ITS...(LP)	£20

HUGH MUNDELL
78	Greensleeves GRE9	Let's All Unite/Unity Dub	£15
79	Warrior WAR 131	Stop Them Jah/Push Dawta Push (12")	£30
80	J&F 002	Jah Fire Will Be Burning/King Of Israel (12")	£30
81	Greensleeves GRED 54	Can't Pop No Style/JUNIOR REID: Know Myself (12")	£50
80	Mun Rock MMLP 001	TIME AND PLACE (LP)	£25
80	Live And Love LAP 13	JAH FIRE (LP, with Lacksley Castell and Augustus Pablo)	£60
82	Greensleeves GREL 36	MUNDELL (LP)	£20
86	Greensleeves GREL 94	AFRICA MUST BE FREE BY 1983 (LP, reissue)	£30
88	Atra 1007	ARISE (LP)	£35

(see also Ray Dorset, Good Earth, King Earl Boogie Band, Horizon, Made In England, Jigilo Jug Band, Paul King, P. Rufus King,, Good Earth)

MUNGO JERRY
70	Dwn DNLS 3008	MUNGO JERRY (LP, gatefold sleeve, with 3-D glasses)	£40
71	Dawn DNLS 3028	YOU DON'T HAVE TO BE IN THE ARMY (LP, gatefold sleeve, with lyric insert)	£15
71	Dawn DNLS 3020	ELECTRONICALLY TESTED (LP, gatefold sleeve)	£20
72	Dawn DNLS 3041	BOOT POWER (LP, with 'Dennis The Menace' or 'gun' gatefold sleeve)	£15

(see also Ray Dorset, Good Earth, King Earl Boogie Band, Horizon, Made In England, Jigilo Jug Band, Paul King, P. Rufus King,, Good Earth)

RAY MUNNINGS
79	Tammi TAM 102	It Could Happen To You/Let's Boogie	£20
79	Tammi TAM 103	Funky Nassau/Jump In The Water	£100
79	Tammi Records TAM 103	Funky Nassau/Jump In The Water (promo)	£100
79	Tammi TAM 103	Funky Nassau/Jump In The Water (12")	£50

CAROLINE MUNRO
67	Columbia DB 8189	Tar And Cement/The Sporting Life	£20

(see also Gary Numan)

SHEILA MUNRO
79	Munrover SM 1	Summertime/Vehicle/You Made Me So Very Happy (promo only)	£25

MURCOF
02	Leaf BAY 23	MARTES (2-LP)	£25
05	Leaf BAY 47 V	REMEMBRANZA (2-LP)	£20

BILLY MURE (ORCHESTRA)
61	London HAR 2400	TOUGH STRINGS (LP)	£20

(see also Supersonics)

MURGATROYD BAND
71	Decca F 12809	Magpie (Theme From The TV Series)/Twice A Week (p/s)	£40
71	Decca F 13256	Magpie (Theme From The TV Series)/Twice A Week (without p/s)	£15
71	Decca F 13256	Magpie (Theme From The TV Series)/Twice A Week (with p/s)	£25

(see also Spencer Davis Group, Ray Fenwick)

MURMAIDS
63	Stateside SS 247	Popsicles And Icicles/Comedy And Tragedy	£20

KEITH MURPHY & THE DAZE
68	Polydor 56542	Slightly Reminiscent Of Her/Dirty Old Sam	£40

LYLE MURPHY
58	Contemporary LAC 12135	GONE WITH THE WOODWINDS (LP)	£20

MARK MURPHY
63	Riverside RIF 106908	Fly Me To The Moon/Why Don't You Do Right	£40
64	Fontana TF 489	And Now You've Gone/Midnight Train	£20
65	Fontana TF 572	High On Windy Hill/Broken Heart	£15
67	Fontana TF 803	(Ain't That) Just Like A Woman/Do You Wonder If I Love You	£25
57	Brunswick LAT 8172	MEET MARK MURPHY (LP)	£20

60	Capitol (S)T 5011	HIT PARADE (LP)	£20
64	Fontana (S)TL 5217	MARK TIME! (LP)	£20
66	Immediate IMLP/IMSP 004	WHO CAN I TURN TO (LP)	£40
69	Phoenix PMS 1001	THIS MUST BE EARTH (LP)	£100
71	Riverside RLP 395	RAH (LP)	£30

NOEL MURPHY
67	Fontana TL 5450	NYA-A-A-H! (LP)	£15
73	Village Thing VTS 25	MURF (LP)	£15

PETER MURPHY
86	Beggars Banquet BEGA 69	SHOULD THE WORLD FAIL TO FALL APART (LP, gatefold)	£20
88	Beggars Banquet BEGA 92	LOVE HYSTERIA (LP)	£20
89	Beggars Banquet BEGA 107	DEEP (LP)	£40
92	Beggars Banquet BEGA 123	HOLY SMOKE (LP)	£40
19	Live Here Now LHN065LP	LIVE IN LONDON (3-LP, red vinyl)	£35
21	Beggars Arkive BBQ2209LPX	PETER MURPHY (7-LP box set)	£150

(see also Bauhaus)

ROISIN MURPHY
05	Echo ECHLP 63	RUBY BLUE (2-LP, with booklet)	£50
07	EMI 507 0911	OVERPOWERED (2-LP, promo version on pink/orange vinyl)	£100
14	Vinyl Factory VF 104	MI SENTI (2 x 12", gatefold white vinyl, signed)	£80
14	Vinyl Factory VF 104	MI SENTI (2 x 12", gatefold white vinyl, unsigned)	£50

(see also Moloko)

ROSE MURPHY
52	Oriole/Mercury MG 10004	SONGS BY ROSE MURPHY (10" LP)	£20

MURPHY FEDERATION
81	London Madras LM 1/2	The Fed Up Skank/Slipping Past On The Inside (handmade p/s, cut up wallpaper with artwork on each side stapled together, paper inner sleeve)	£70

DAVID MURRAY
78	Cadillac SGC 1007	CONCEPTUAL SAXOPHONE (LP)	£20
79	Cadillac SGC 1008/9	THE LONDON CONCERT (2-LP)	£20

LADY MURRAY
66	Clan 597 002	Mister Abercrombie Taught Me/In My Imagination	£30

(see also Grazina)

MITCH MURRAY CLAN
66	Clan 597 001	Skyliner/Cherokee	£15

RUBY MURRAY
55	Columbia SCM 5162	Softly, Softly/What Could Be More Beautiful	£30
58	Columbia 33S 1135	ENDEARING YOUNG CHARMS (10" LP)	£15

(see also Norman Wisdom & Ruby Murray, Ray Burns, Ronnie Harris, Diana Decker)

JOHN MURTAUGH
70	Polydor 2482 015	BLUES CURRENT (LP)	£20

MUSCLE SHOALS HORNS
76	Bang SHOT 001	BORN TO GET DOWN (LP)	£20
76	Atlantic K 50283	THE CREAM OF MUSCLE SHOALS (LP)	£20

MUSE
SINGLES
99	Mushroom MUSH 50S	Uno/Agitated (p/s, clear vinyl)	£40
99	Mushroom MUSH 58S	Cave/Cave (Instrumental Remix) (clear vinyl, p/s)	£40
99	Mushroom MUSH 66S	Muscle Museum/Escape (p/s)	£15
99	Mushroom MUSH 66S	Muscle Museum/Minimum (clear vinyl, autographed p/s, 1000 only)	£80
99	Mushroom MUSH 68S	Sunburn/(Live Acoustic Version) (stickered p/s, clear vinyl)	£18
00	Mushroom MUSH 72S	Unintended/Sober (p/s, clear vinyl)	£18
01	Mushroom MUSH 89S	Plug In Baby/Nature 1 (p/s)	£20
01	Mushroom MUSH 92S	New Born/Shrinking Universe (p/s, limited issue)	£18
01	Mushroom MUSH 96S	Bliss/Hyper Chondriac Music (p/s)	£15
01	Mushroom MUSH 96S	Bliss/The Gallery (p/s)	£15
01	Mushroom MUSH 97S	Hyper Music/Feeling Good (numbered p/s)	£18
01	Mushroom MUSH 104S	Dead Star/In Your World (p/s)	£15
03	East West EW 272	Time is Running Out/The Groove (clear vinyl, p/s)	£15
03	East West EW 278	Hysteria/Eternally Missed (clear vinyl, p/s)	£15
04	East West EW 285	Sing For Absolution/Fury (p/s, clear vinyl)	£15
06	Warner Brothers HEL 3003	Starlight/Supermassive Black Hole (Remix) (picture disc, stickered)	£15
06	A & E HEL 3004	Knights of Cydonia/Assassion (picture disc, stickered)	£18
07	Warner Brothers HEL3005	Invincible/Glorious (picture disc, stickered)	£18
07	Warner Brothers HEL3005	Invincible/Glorious (in static shield bag, this price for unopened)	£30
07	Warner Brothers HEL3005	Invincible/Glorious (in static shield bag, this price for opened)	£15

EPs
98	Dangerous DREX CDEP 103	MUSE EP (CD, 999 copies, numbered sticker)	£300
98	Dangerous DREX CDEP 104	MUSCLE MUSEUM EP: Sober/Uno/Unintended/Instant Messenger/Muscle Museum # 2/Muscle Museum (CD, 999 copies, numbered sticker)	£175

ALBUMS : ORIGINAL ALBUMS
00	Mushroom MUSH 59LP	SHOWBIZ (2-LP, clear vinyl, gatefold sleeve, with inners, numbered)	£150
01	Mushroom MUSH 93LP	ORIGIN OF SYMMETRY (2-LP, gatefold sleeve, with lyric inner sleeves, 1500 only)	£100
03	East West 5046 68587-1	ABSOLUTION (2-LP, gatefold sleeve)	£40
09	Warner Bros.	THE RESISTANCE (2-LP)	£30

	825646869664		
09	Warner Bros. 825646869664	THE RESISTANCE (Box set, CD, DVD, USB stick)	£50
12	Warner Bros. 825646568772	THE 2ND LAW (2-LP)	£20
12	Warner Bros. 2564656876	THE 2ND LAW (Box set, 2-LP, DVD, CD, book, print and heat sensitive sleeve)	£50
15	Warner Bros. 0825646121212	DRONES (2-LP, red vinyl, CD, DVD)	£35
15	Warner Bros. 0825646121229	DRONES (2-LP)	£18

ALBUMS : ALBUMS - REISSUES

15	Warner Bros. 0825646912223	SHOWBIZ (2-LP, reissue)	£20
15	Warner Bros. 0825646909452	ORIGIN OF SYMMETRY (2-LP, reissue)	£20
15	Warner Bros. 0825646909445	ABSOLUTION (2-LP, reissue)	£20
15	Warner Bros. 0825646865475	THE RESISTANCE (2-LP, reissue)	£20
15	Warner Bros. 0825646350919	BLACK HOLES AND REVELATIONS (LP)	£18

MUSHROOM

73	Hawk HASP 320	Devil Among The Tailors/Sun Ni Dhuibir/King Of Ireland's Daughter	£25
74	Hawk HASP 340	Kings And Queens/Met A Friend	£25
73	Hawk HALPX 116	EARLY ONE MORNING (LP, with poster inner)	£700
73	Hawk HALPX 116	EARLY ONE MORNING (LP, without poster inner)	£450

(see also Joe O'Donnell)

THE MUSIC

01	Fierce Panda NINGT 107	Take The Long Road And Walk It/The Walls Get Smaller (12", p/s, 250 only)	£18
02	Hut HUTDLP 76	THE MUSIC (2-LP)	£50
04	Virgin 724386437310	WELCOME TO THE NORTH (2-LP)	£25
08	Polydor 1771689	STRENGTH IN NUMBERS (LP)	£30

MUSIC BOX (2)

69	VOY	FUN PALACE (LP)	£1500

MUSIC BOX (1)

72	Westwood MRS 013	SONGS OF SUNSHINE (LP)	£150

MUSIC DOCTORS

69	Downtown DT 447	Music Doctor (Parts 1 & 2)	£20
71	Downtown DT480	The Pliers/Pliers (Version)	£18
70	J-Dan JDN 4402	Electric Shock/KING DENNIS: Black Robin	£20
70	J-Dan JDN 4403	Bush Doctor/Lick Your Stick	£20
70	J-Dan JDN 4411	The Wild Bunch/ISRAELITES: Born To Be Strong	£40
70	J-Dan JDN 4414	In The Summertime/Foundation Track	£15
70	J-Dan JDN 4417	Discretion Version/Doctor Dan, Boy Friday And Friend	£15
70	Trojan TBL 117	REGGAE IN THE SUMMERTIME (LP)	£30

(see also Dennis Lowe, Desmond Riley, Megatons, Prince Of Darkness, Gene Rondo)

MUSIC EMPORIUM

83	Psycho PSYCHO 11	MUSIC EMPORIUM (LP)	£15

MUSIC EXPLOSION

67	Stateside SS 2028	A Little Bit O' Soul/I See The Light	£25
67	Stateside SS 2054	Sunshine Games/Can't Stop Now	£20
67	London HA-P/SH-P 8352	A LITTLE BIT O' SOUL (LP)	£50

MUSIC MACHINE

67	Pye International 7N 25407	Talk Talk/Come On In	£50
67	Pye International 7N 25414	The People In Me/Masculine Intuition	£60

MUSIC MOTOR

70	Deram DM 282	Happy/Where Am I Going?	£15

MUSIC STAND

69	Fresh FR 003	Sunbird/Dreamland	£20

MUSIC THROUGH SIX

68	Domain D3	Riff Raff/ROY DOCKER: Mellow Moonlight	£30

(see also Jason Sims & Music Through Six)

MUSIC UK

82	Fairview FMR 061	Jose/Unemployment/House With A Red Gate	£30

MUSIC WARRIORS

72	Sir Collins SCMW 734	Some Day/Untitled (white labels only)	£80

MUSICA ELETTRONICA VIVA

69	Polydor 583 769	MUSICA ELETTRONICA VIVA (LP)	£100

MUSICAL DOCTORS

69	Downtown DT 447	Musical Doctor Chaper 1/Musical Doctor Chapter 2	£20

JIM MUSICMAN

90	Bosh JIM 101	I Can't Help Myself/I Can't Help Myself (12", purple vinyl)	£80

MUSICOLOGY

91	B12 B1201	Musicology (12")	£40
91	B12 B1201	Musicology (12", clear vinyl)	£60
92	B12 B1204	Outlook (12", green vinyl, 300 only)	£40

| 92 | B12 B1206 | Hall Of Mirrors (12") | £15 |
| 92 | B12 B1206 | Hall Of Mirrors (12" Ltd, yellow vinyl) | £40 |

MUSIQUE CONCRET
81	United Dairies UD 010	BRINGING UP BABY (LP, blue vinyl, 100 only)	£120
81	United Dairies UD 010	BRINGING UP BABY (LP, black vinyl, 400 only)	£100
87	United Dairies UDT 10	BRINGING UP BABY (cassette)	£40

MUSKETEER GRIPWEED & THIRD TROOP
| 66 | United Artists UP 1196 | How I Won The War/Aftermath | £175 |
| 66 | United Artists UP 1196 | How I Won The War/Aftermath (demo copy) | £100 |
(see also John Lennon)

MUSKYTEERS
| 69 | Upsetter US 309 | Endlessly/Kiddy-O | £45 |
(see also Silvertones (Jamaica))

MUSLIMGAUZE
83	Hessian 1	Hammer And Sickle/Fear Of Gadaffi/Nettle Cloth/Baize Tents	£25
84	Limited Editions LIMITED 1	HUNTING OUT WITH AN AERIAL EYE (12" 45rpm EP)	£25
83	Product Kinematograph PKR-1	KABUL (LP, die cut 12" sleeve, some with Facsimile fanzine)	£60
84	Recloose LOOSE 008	BUDDHIST ON FIRE (LP, some with free Triptych EP and inserts)	£60
85	Limited Editions LIMITED 2	BLINDED HORSES (LP)	£40
86	Limited Editions LIMITED 3	FLAJELATA (LP)	£40
86	Limited Editions LIMITED 4	HAJJ (LP)	£40
87	Limited Editions LIMITED 5	JAZIRAT-UL-ARAB (LP)	£40
87	Limited Editions LIMITED 6	ABU NIDAL (LP)	£40
88	Limited Editions LIMITED 7	THE RAPE OF PALESTINE (LP)	£40
(see also Eg Oblique Graph)

CHARLIE MUSSELWHITE BLUES BAND
| 69 | Vanguard SVRL 19012 | STONE BLUES (LP) | £22 |

MUSTANG
| 67 | Parlophone R 5579 | Why/Here, There And Everywhere | £25 |

MUSTARD
| 74 | EMI EMI 2165 | Good Time Comin'/I Saw I Heard | £25 |

MUTANTS
| 77 | Rox ROX 002 | Boss Man/Back Yard Boys (p/s) | £15 |

MUTATION
| 13 | (No label or Cat. No.) | I: THE FRANKENSTEIN EFFECT/II: ERROR 500 (2-LP black.red splatter vinyl) | £40 |
(see also Ginger Wildheart, Wildhearts)

MUTE DRIVERS
| 80s | Mute Drivers MD 001 | MUTE DRIVERS (LP, with insert in handmade painted sleeve, 300 only) | £15 |
(see also Anonymes)

MVP'S
| 71 | Buddah BDS 469 | Turnin' My Heartbeat Up/Every Man For Herself | £35 |

M.W.A.B.
| 83 | M.W.A.B. Records | Angus Young/Is Michael Bum An Apple? | £15 |

MWANAMKE MWFICA
| 82 | African Woman AWLP 101 | AFRICAN WOMAN ABROAD (LP) | £100 |

MX-80 SOUND
| 77 | Island ILPS 9520 | HARD ATTACK (LP, insert) | £30 |

MY BLOODY VALENTINE
86	Fever FEV 5X	No Place To Go/Moonlight (p/s)	£60
86	Fever FEV 5	GEEK! (12" EP)	£40
86	Kaleid. Sound KS 101	THE NEW RECORD BY MY BLOODY VALENTINE (12" EP)	£50
87	Lazy LAZY 04	Sunny Sundae Smile/Paint A Rainbow (p/s)	£30
87	Lazy LAZY 04T	Sunny Sundae Smile/Paint A Rainbow/Kiss The Eclipse/ Sylvie's Head (12", p/s)	£40
87	Lazy LAZY 07	Strawberry Wine/Never Say Goodbye/Can I Touch You (12", p/s)	£50
88	Creation CRE 055	You Made Me Realise/Slow (die-cut company sleeve)	£35
88	Creation CRE 055T	You Made Me Realise/Slow/Thorn/Cigarette/Drive It All Over Me (12", p/s)	£50
88	Creation CRE 061	Feed Me With Your Kiss/Emptiness Inside (plays "I Believe") (die-cut company sleeve)	£30
88	Creation CRE 061T	Feed Me With Your Kiss/I Believe/Emptiness Inside/I Need No Trust (12", p/s)	£35
89	Creation CRE 085	To Here Knows When/Swallow	£15
89	Creation CRE 085T	Tremolo/To Here Knows When (12", p/s)	£30
89	Lyntone CAT 067	Sugar/PACIFIC: December, With The Day (square flexidisc free with The Catalogue magazine, issue 67)	£15
90	Creation CRE 073	Soon/Glider (p/s)	£15
90	Creation CRE 073T	GLIDER EP (12", p/s)	£30
90	Creation CRE 073X	GLIDER EP (12", remixed by Andy Weatherall, stickered die-cut sleeve)	£25
87	Lazy LAZY 08	ECSTACY (mini-LP, 3,000 only)	£50
88	Creation CRELP 040	ISN'T ANYTHING (LP, first pressing with black label, 3,000 copies with bonus 7", "Instrumental"/"Instrumental" [CRE FRE 4, no p/s] & stickered sleeve)	£100
88	Creation CRELP 040	ISN'T ANYTHING (LP, 2nd pressing, brown label, without bonus 7")	£60
89	Lazy LAZY 12	ECSTACY & WINE (LP, compilation of LAZY 07 & LAZY 08)	£30
91	Creation CRELP 060	LOVELESS (LP, inner)	£150
98	Creation CRELP 040	ISN'T ANYTHING (LP, reissue, has new Creation address on rear: 109 Regents Park Road, London NW1 8UR)	£25
11	Lazy LAZY 12	ECSTACY AND WINE (LP, reissue)	£20

MINT VALUE £

13	MBV mbvlp01	M.B.V (LP, gatefold with CD)	£25
18	MBV mbvlp02	ISN'T ANYTHING (LP, alternative mix, white sleeve)	£35

(see also Primal Scream, Collapsed Lung, Snowpony, Dinosaur Jr.)

MY CAPTAINS
81	4AD AD 103	Fall/Converse/History/Nothing (p/s)	£15

MY CHEMICAL ROMANCE
03	20:20 TWENTY 7s 003	Honey, This Mirror Isn't Big Enough For The Two Of Us/This Is The Best Day Ever (p/s)	£50
04	20:20 TWENTY 7S 004	Headfirst For Halos/Our Lady Of Sorrows (Live) (p/s)	£45
04	Reprise W 661	Thank You For The Venom/Jack The Ripper (Live) (red vinyl, p/s)	£40
06	Reprise 116796-1	THE BLACK PARADE (2-LP box set)	£35

MY DEAR WATSON
68	Parlophone R 5687	Elusive Face/The Shame Just Drained	£30
68	Parlophone R 5737	Make This Day Last/Stop, Stop, I'll Be There	£30

(see also Johnny & Copycats)

MY DYING BRIDE
90	Private pressing	Towards The Sinister EP (4 track demo cassette)	£40
92	Peaceville VILE 27	Symphonaire Infernus Et Spera Empyrium Act 1/ Symphonaire Infernus Et Spera Empyrium Act 2 (12", p/s)	£25
93	Peaceville VILE 44T	I Am The Bloody Earth/Transcending (Into The Exquisite) (12", p/s)	£20
93	Peaceville VILE 37T	The Thrash Of Naked Limbs/Le Cerf Malade/Gather Me Up Forever (12", p/s)	£25
93	Unbridled Voyage (No Cat. No)	Unreleased Bitterness: The Bitterness And The Bereavement (1-sided flexidisc, fold-out p/s in poly sleeve, 1150 only)	£20
94	Peaceville CC5	Sexuality Of Bereavement/Crown Of Sympathy (Remix) (p/s)	£25
94	Peaceville VILE 45	THE STORIES EP (box set, 1000 only)	£75
92	Peaceville VILE 30	AS THE FLOWER WITHERS (LP, gatefold sleeve, with poster)	£40
93	Peaceville VILE 39	TURN LOOSE THE SWANS (2-LP)	£50
95	Peaceville VILE 50	THE ANGEL AND THE DARK RIVER (LP)	£40
96	Peaceville VILE 65	LIKE GODS OF THE SUN (LP)	£40
98	Peaceville VILE 74	37.488% (LP)	£40

TIM MYCROFT
71	Parlophone R5919	Shadra/Bournemouth Rock	£15

AMINA CLAUDINE MYERS
80	Leo LR 100	SONG FOR MOTHER E (LP)	£20
80	Leo LR 103	AMINA CLAUDINE MYERS SALUTES BESSIE SMITH (LP)	£45

ROWLAND MYERS
75	MSE MSE 2SSP/P	Give Them A Hand/Pandemonium	£30
74	Deroy DER 1063	JUST FOR THE RECORD (LP, private pressing, also listed as Music Sound Enterprise MSE 1)	£120

STEVE MYERS
86	Pressure P HAVE 7	Cinderella/Shake Me	£60

MY FRIENDS AND I
69	Marroo MR 001	Susan/Wake The Dead	£40

MY KIND OF PEOPLE
70	CBS 555133	Somebodys Coming/Nobody Knows Why The Butterfly Died	£25

BILLY MYLES
57	HMV POP 423	The Joker (That's What They Call Me)/Honey Bee	£50
57	HMV POP 423	The Joker (That's What They Call Me)/Honey Bee (78)	£15

MY LIFE STORY
86	Think Tank CHAPTER 1	HOME SWEET ZOO: Boring Dream/Sliding Bookcase (gatefold p/s, 500 only)	£30

MY LORDE SHERIFFE'S COMPLAINTE
79	Frog FROG 1	MY LORDE SHERIFFE'S COMPLAINTE (LP, private pressing)	£15

MYND MUZIC
94	Poor Person Prod.	IMAGINE THIS (LP, handmade sleeve, 500 only)	£20

MYRON
98	Island 12 MYRON 1	We Can Get Down (Groove Chronicles Remix) (1-sided 12")	£25

MYRTELLES
63	Oriole CB 1805	Don't Wanna Cry Again/Just Let Me Cry	£40

(see also Sue & Sunny, Stockingtops)

MYSTERIES
64	Decca F 11919	Give Me Rhythm And Blues/Teardrops	£30

MYSTERY GIRLS
79	Strange HAM 1	SOUNDS LIKE THE MYSTERY GIRLS EP	£20

MYSTERY JETS (2)
08	No label or cat. no.	TWENTY ONE (LP, 300 copies only, numbered)	£50
08	No label or cat. no.	POWERCUT SERENADES EP (300 only, numbered)	£20
10	Rough Trade RTRADLP 551	SEROTONIN (LP with free 7")	£25
12	Rough Trade RTRADLP 651	RADLANDS (2-LP)	£18
15	Transgressive TRANS 159	LIVE AT THE ROYAL FESTIVAL HALL (2-LP, gold vinyl)	£35

MYSTERY MAKER
77	Caves UHC 3	MYSTERY MAKER (LP, private pressing with booklet)	£120

MYSTERY BLONDE
87	Freshman 7KS1236	Stay With Me/Game Of Life (p/s)	£20

MYSTIC EMP
80	His Majesty HMD 006	Reality/JAH THOMAS: Throw Away Vanity/MYSTIC EMP & JAH THOMAS: Reality Dub (12")	£20

MYSTIC EYES
79	Greensleeves GRED 11	Perilous Times (with Trinity)/REVOLUTIONARIES: Roots Man Version (12")	£30
79	Warrior WAR 135	Elaine/MIKEY DREAD: Schoolgirls (12")	£40
78	Burning Sounds BS 1033	MYSTERIOUS (LP)	£45

MYSTIC HARMONY
83	Clouds CLSD 001	Night Over Egypt/SS BAND: Night Out In London	£200
84	Clouds CLSD 008	Living In The Country/Independent Lady (12")	£20

MYSTIC INSTITUTE
92	Evolution EVO 06	CYBERDON EP (12")	£18

(see also Global Communications, Reload, Link)

MYSTIC MATT & THE ANTHILL MOB
99	Love Peace & Unity LOVE 05	A SHOCK 2 DA SYSTEM EP (12", p/s)	£25

(see also Anthill Mob)

MYSTIC MERLIN
80	Capitol EST 12047	MYSTIC MERLIN (LP)	£15

MYSTIC MOODS
74	Warner Bros K 46250	AWAKENING (LP)	£15

MYSTIC NUMBER NATIONAL BANK
69	Probe SPB 1001	THE MYSTIC NUMBER NATIONAL BANK (LP)	£25

MYSTIC RADICS
81	Water Mount WMT 1	Nation Wide/Dub Version (12")	£250

MYSTIC TOUCH
81	Champagne FIZZ 505	Get Yourself Together/Pary People	£15

MYSTICS
59	HMV POP 646	Hushabye/Adam And Eve	£30
59	Top Rank JAR 243	Don't Take The Stars/So Tenderly	£30

MYSTIC SLOT
93	Black Cock BCOK 007	No Way Back/Disco Adventure (12", beware of US pressed bootlegs)	£45

MYSTREATED
92	Hangman TWISTBIG 4	10 BOSS CUTS (LP)	£20
94	Twist TWISTBIG 4	LOOKING RIGHT THROUGH (LP)	£15
95	Twist TWISTBIG 7	EVERY QUESTIONING WHY (LP)	£15

MYTHRA
80	Streetbeat LAMP 2	Death Or Destiny/Killer/U.F.O. (with p/s)	£90
80	Streetbeat 12 LAMP 2	Death Or Destiny/Killer/Overlord/U.F.O. (12", with p/s)	£125
80	Streetbeat 12 LAMP 2	Death Or Destiny/Killer/Overlord/U.F.O. (12")	£20

MÅNESKIN & IGGY POP
21	Sony Music 19439934277	I Wanna Be Your Slave/I Wanna Be Your Slave (Maneskin only) &7", p/s, ltd.ed.)	£15

(see also Maneskin, Iggy Pop)

N

NABAY
80	Grapevine GRP 143	Believe It Or Not/Believe It Or Not (Instrumental)	£30

ESTEE NACK & SADHU GOLD
18	Daupe! DM SP 053	SURFINONGOLD.WAV (LP, splatter vinyl, 100 copies)	£100
20	Daupe! DM SP 053	SURFINONGOLD.WAV (LP, red vinyl, 100 copies)	£40
20	Daupe! DM SP 053	SURFINONGOLD.WAV (LP, green vinyl, 100 copies)	£50
20	Daupe! DM SP 053	SURFINONGOLD.WAV (LP, with obi strip, 20 copies)	£100

NADRIAN
71	Dolphin DO 514	Something Passing By/You Can't Lose Out	£250

NAFFI
79	Absurd ABSURD 8	Slice 1/Slice 2 (as Naafi Sandwich)	£25
81	Naffi Productions RUM 5	D'ya Hear Me/Freedie's Fever (dub)/The Hutch (dub)	£20
82	Ark DOVE 1	YUM YUM YUM YA (LP)	£25
85	Situation Two DOVE 2	NAFFI-LOCKSMAN (LP, as Naffi Locksman)	£50

NAIL
98	Remote REM 009	BROTHERS AND SISTERS (12", EP, die-cut sleeve)	£18

NAIROBI SISTERS
76	Jamatel JAL 07	Promised Land/Version	£35

NAKED CITY
90	Earache MOSH 28	TORTURE GARDEN EP (12")	£20

NAKED LUNCH
81	Ramkup CAC 003	Rabies/Slipping Again (p/s)	£15

KOICHI NAMIKI, KATSUHIRO HAYASHI & SHIGERU OHWADA
15	Data Discs DAT 004	SUPER HANG ON (LP, die cut sleeve, Obi)	£35

ZBIGNIEW NAMYSLOWSKI MODERN JAZZ QUARTET
64	Decca LK/SKL 4644	LOLA (LP)	£200

NANETTE
70	Columbia DB 8659	Flying Machine/You're Wasting Your Time	£35
70	Columbia SCX 6398	NANETTE (LP)	£30

ED NANGLE
68	Blue Cat BS 120	Good Girl/ENFORCERS: Musical Fever	£225
68	Coxsone CS 7038	Whipping The Prince (actually by Ed Nangle & Alton Ellis & Soul Vendors)/HEPTONES: If You Knew	£100

NICK NANTOS & HIS FIREBALLERS
63	Summit LSE 2042	GUITARS ON FIRE (EP)	£15
64	Summit ATL 4114	GUITARS ON FIRE (LP)	£15

(see also Bill Haley & Comets)

NAOMI
70	Gayfeet GS 207	You're Not My Kind/GAYTONES: You're Not My Kind (Version II)	£20
70	High Note HS 047	Natural Woman/GAYTONES: Natural Woman - Version	£20

(see also Derrick Morgan, Tommy McCook)

NAPALM DEATH
87	Strange Fruit SFPS 049	THE PEEL SESSIONS (12", p/s)	£15
89	Rise Above RISE 001	NAPALM DEATH EP (poster p/s, sold at gigs)	£25
89	Earache MOSH 014	MENTALLY MURDERED EP (Rise Above/The Missing Link/Mentally Murdered Walls Of Confinement/Cause And Effect/No Mental Effort) (12", p/s)	£20
93	Earache 7MOSH 92	Nazi Punks Fuck Off/Aryanisms/Nazi Punks Fuck Off (Live)/Contemptuous (Xtreem Mix) (p/s)	£20
95	Earache MOSH 146	GREED KILLING EP (Greed Killing/My Own Worst Enemy/Self Betrayal/Finer Truths White Lies/Antibody/All Links Severed/Plague Rages [Live]) (10", p/s)	£15
96	Earache 7 MOSH 168	Food Chains/Upward And Uninterested (demo version)/COALESCE: A Safe Place/ Harvest Of Maturity) (p/s, insert, purple vinyl)	£15
87	Earache MOSH 3	SCUM (LP, lyric insert, black/orange, black/green, black red or black/yellow cover)	£20
88	Earache MOSH 8	FROM ENSLAVEMENT TO OBLITERATION (LP, gatefold sleeve, free 7" EP The Curse [7MOSH 8])	£35
90	Earache MOSH 19/19L	HARMONY CORRUPTION (2-LP, with inserts)	£30
90	Earache MOSH 19P	HARMONY CORRUPTION (LP, picture disc)	£20
91	Earache MOSH 3	SCUM (LP, reissue, white and black swirl vinyl, black and gold sleeve, 2000 only)	£18
92	Earache MOSH 53	UTOPIA BANISHED (LP, free 7" EP [MOSH 53L])	£25
02	Feto SLAVE001LP	ORDER OF THE LEECH (LP, purple vinyl)	£20
06	Earache MOSH 003PD	SCUM (LP, 2nd reissue, picture disc, stickered PVC sleeve, 1500 only)	£15

MARTY NAPOLEON
55	London EZ-NI9001	NAPOLEON SINGS AND SWINGS (EP)	£15

NAPOLEON XIV
66	Warner Bros WB 5853	I'm In Love With My Little Red Tricycle/Doin' The Napoleon	£15
66	Warner Bros W 1661	THEY'RE COMING TO TAKE ME AWAY HA-HA-A! (LP)	£40

(see also Jerry Samuels, Kim Fowley)

RAYMOND NAPTALI AND ROY RANKING
81	KG Imperial KG 006	New Cross Fire/Brixton Incident (12", blue vinyl)	£25

NAPTHALI
91	Black Legacy BLLP 001	MENTAL SLAVERY SHOWCASE (LP)	£60

NINO NARDINI
02	Jazzman JM 019	Tropicola/ANTHONY KING: Filigree Funk	£15

PETER NARDINI
80s	Kettle KS 701	I Think You're Great/Ma Maw's A Mod (in p/s)	£15

NARNIA
74	Myrrh MYR 1007	NARNIA - ASLAN IS NOT A TAME LION (LP)	£80

(see also After The Fire, Pauline Filby)

NAS
13	Secret 7" S712	The Don (100 only, each with unique art sleeve)	£40
94	Columbia COL 475959-1	ILLMATIC (LP)	£25
96	Columbia 484196 1	IT WAS WRITTEN (LP)	£30
99	Columbia COL 4953120	NASTRADAMUS (LP)	£30
99	Columbia COL 489419-1	I AM (LP)	£25

GRAHAM NASH
71	Atlantic 2401 011	SONGS FOR BEGINNERS (LP)	£20

(see also Hollies, Crosby Stills Nash & Young)

JOHNNY NASH
62	Warner Bros WB 65	Don't Take Away Your Love/Moment Of Weakness	£20
62	Warner Bros WB 76	Ol' Man River/My Dear Little Sweetheart	£30
63	Warner Bros WB 93	Cigareets, Whuskey And Wild, Wild Women/I'm Moving On	£15
64	Pye International 7N 25250	Love Ain't Nothin'/Talk To Me	£60
65	Chess CRS 8005	Strange Feelin'/Rainin' In My Heart	£25
66	Pye International 7N 25353	Let's Move And Groove (Together)/Understanding	£20
66	Pye International 7N 25363	One More Time/Tryin' To Find Her	£20
69	MGM MGM 1480	(I'm So) Glad You're My Baby/Stormy	£35
64	RCA Victor RCX 7163	PRESENTING JOHNNY NASH (EP)	£100

59	HMV CLP 1251	JOHNNY NASH (LP)	£40
59	HMV CLP 1299	QUIET HOUR WITH JOHNNY NASH (LP)	£25
60	HMV CLP 1325	I GOT RHYTHM (LP, mono)	£30
60	HMV CSD 1288	I GOT RHYTHM (LP, stereo)	£30
62	Encore ENC 2005	LET'S GET LOST (LP)	£15
69	Major Minor MMLP/SMLP 47	YOU GOT SOUL (LP)	£15
69	Major Minor MMLP/SMLP 56	SOUL FOLK (LP)	£15
69	Major Minor MMLP/SMLP 63	PRINCE OF PEACE (LP)	£15

KATE NASH

| 06 | Fiction 1755804 | MADE OF BRICKS (LP, pink vinyl) | £50 |

TONY NASH

| 70 | Hot Rod HR 110 | Keep On Trying/WINSTON JAMES: Just Can't Do Without Your Love | £40 |

NASHVILLE FIVE

| 62 | Decca DFE 6706 | LIKE NASHVILLE (EP) | £40 |

NASHVILLE TEENS

66	Decca F 12316	The Hard Way/Upside Down	£15
66	Decca F 12458	Forbidden Fruit/Revived 45 Time	£25
66	Decca F 12542	That's My Woman/Words	£18
68	Decca F 12754	All Along The Watchtower/Sun-Dog	£15
69	Major Minor MM 599	The Lament Of The Cherokee Reservation Indian/Looking For You	£18
71	Parlophone R 5925	Ella James/Tennessee Woman	£20
72	Parlophone R 5961	You Shouldn't Have Been So Nice/Tell The People (unissued)	£0
65	Decca DFE 8600	THE NASHVILLE TEENS (EP)	£50
75	New World NW 6002	THE NASHVILLE TEENS (LP)	£40

(see also Arizona Swamp Company, Jerry Lee Lewis, Carl Perkins)

NASTY FACTS

| 81 | 5th Column FC 2 | Drive My Car/Gotta Get To You/Crazy 'Bout you (p/s) | £60 |

NASTY HABITS

91	NHS NHS 001	Make Some Noise/Street Knowledge (12")	£25
92	NHS NHS 003	Let's Go/No Dominator (12")	£25
92	Reinforced RIVET 1233	As Nasty As I Wanna Be (12")	£25
92	Reinforced RIVET 1233R	As Nasty As I Wanna Be (Remixes) (12")	£25

NASTY MEDIA

| 78 | Lightning GIL 542 | SPIKED COPY EP (p/s) | £40 |

BARRY NATHAN TRIO

| 80 | EMAL BNT 1 | MORNING SONGRISE (LP) | £50 |

NATIONAL

07	Beggars Banquet BBQ 407	Apartment Story/Mansion On The Hill (live) (yellow vinyl)	£15
07	Beggars Banquet BBQ 408 CDP	EXTRAS EP (tour CD, 1000 only)	£30
17	Beggars Banquet (No Cat. No.)	England (Live)/BELLE & SEBASTIAN: The State I Am In (12" p/s, splatter vinyl, booklet)	£60
03	Brassland HWY 003	SAD SONGS FOR DIRTY LOVERS (LP)	£40
05	Beggars Banquet BBQLP 241	ALLIGATOR (LP)	£20
07	Beggars Banquet BBQLP 252	BOXER (LP, inner)	£20
10	4AD CAD 3X03X	HIGH VIOLET (2-LP, violet vinyl)	£30
13	4AD CAD 3315	TROUBLE WILL FIND ME (2-LP, clear vinyl, card inserts box set)	£40
15	4AD TAD 3504	A LOT OF SORROW (9-LP box set, clear vinyl)	£150
17	4AD 4AD0020LPE	SLEEP WELL BEAST (2-LP, blue vinyl, 7" blue flexi and poster)	£30

NATIONAL ART HATE WEEK

| 09 | No Cat no | God Save Marcel Duchamp/Silent Revolt (p/s, mail order only, 350 copies, numbered) | £15 |

NATIONAL HEAD BAND

| 71 | Warner Bros K 46094 | ALBERT 1 (LP) | £50 |

(see also Caravan, Gary Moore, Toe-Fat, Uriah Heep)

NATIONAL HEALTH

| 78 | Affinity AFF 6 | NATIONAL HEALTH (LP) | £30 |
| 78 | Charly CRL 5010 | OF QUEUES AND CURES (LP) | £25 |

(see also Hatfield & The North)

NATIONAL PINION POLE

| 66 | Planet PLF 111 | Make Your Mark Little Man/I Was The One You Came In With (in Planet sleeve) | £80 |
| 66 | Planet PLF 111 | Make Your Mark Little Man/I Was The One You Came In With | £45 |

NATIONAL FLAG

| 75 | Private Pressing | THANK YOU AND GOODNIGHT (LP, insert, 100 only) | £400 |

NATIVES

| 84 | Fearless FEAR 2 | Here Is The News/Love In A Day | £20 |

NATO

| 81 | DV DVR 1 | Gangland/Tied Down (p/s) | £50 |

NAT RUS & RANKING GLAD

| 77 | Nat Rus | Mash It/Come From Africa/Africa (12") | £40 |

NATURAL ACOUSTIC BAND

| 72 | RCA SF 8272 | LEARNING TO LIVE (LP, textured gatefold sleeve) | £35 |
| 72 | RCA SF 8314 | BRANCHING IN (LP, with lyric insert) | £25 |

(see also Krysia)

CLIVE NATURAL
77	WIRL WIRL 1	Marridge Rekka/No Money (12")	£50

NATURAL FOUR
75	Curtom 16583	Love's So Wonderful/What's Happening Here	£15
75	Curtom K 56142	HEAVEN RIGHT HERE ON EARTH (LP)	£40
76	Custom K56224	NIGHTCHASER (LP)	£15
95	Charlie CPLP 8127	NATURAL FOUR (LP, reissue)	£18

NATURAL GAS
76	Private Stock PVLP 1007	NATURAL GAS (LP, gatefold sleeve with inner sleeve)	£15

(see also Badfinger, Blue Goose, Humble Pie, Uriah Heep, Quiver)

NATURAL HI
81	KBK KBSK 001T	Fame (Got You On My Mind)/Fame (Hi-Re-Mix) (12")	£70

THE NATURAL ITES AND THE REALISTICS
83	CSA 12CSA 501	Picture On My Wall/Jah Works Mama (12")	£18
84	Realistic RR 03	Black Roses/Gwan Do It (12")	£50
85	CSA CSLP 18	PICTURE ON THE WALL (LP)	£25

NATURAL MYSTIC
81	Ethnic Fight ETH 1326	NATURAL LOVE (LP)	£35
85	Starlight SDLP 914	GROOVE ROCKING (LP)	£45

NATURAL MYSTIQUE
82	Dune 2AA	Generals/In This Time (p/s)	£60

NATURAL ROOTS
82	Fasim FS106	Know Yourself/Ain't Got No Money (12")	£20

NATURAL VIBES
83	Suffering & Faith SWEET 1	Sweet Sensation/Version (12")	£30
82	Starlight Records SDLP 907	LIFE HARD IN A YARD (LP)	£40

NATURALITY
69	Ackee ACK 101	The Arena/Natural	£50

NATURALLY
79	Bushays BFM 111	I'll Get By/All I Have Is Written In Your Eyes (12")	£15

NATURALS (U.K.) (1)
64	Parlophone R 5202	It Was You/Look At Me Now	£15
65	Parlophone R 5257	Blue Roses/Shame On You	£15

(see also Greatest Show On Earth)

NATURALS (U.K.) (2)
80	Refined RR2	STRANGE DAYS (EP, 500 only)	£30
81	Just For The Records	Six Girls & Alice (fold-out cover)	£15

NAUGHTY THOUGHTS
82	Maestro MR 004	All Of Nothing/Weekdays (foldover p/s, some with press release inserts)	£30

FATS NAVARRO
56	London LZ-C 14015	MEMORIAL (LP)	£20

NAVY BLUE
82	AP 572	THE PUSSERS (EP)	£15

JERRY NAYLOR
61	Top Rank JAR 591	Stop Your Crying/You're Thirteen	£25

SHEL NAYLOR
63	Decca F 11776	How Deep Is The Ocean/La Bamba	£20
64	Decca F 11856	One Fine Day/It's Gonna Happen Soon	£200

(see also Lieutenant Pigeon)

NAZARETH
72	Pegasus PGS 2	Dear John/Friends	£25
72	Pegasus PGS 2	Dear John/Friends (2nd issue, PEG label, B-side lists 'Occasional Failure')	£30
72	Pegasus BCP 3	Dear John/Witchdoctor Woman/Morning Dew (unreleased, promo only, stamped white labels and insert)	£75
72	Pegasus PGS 4	Morning Dew/Spinning Top (PEG label)	£20
72	Pegasus PGS 5	If You See My Baby/Hard Living (PEG label)	£20
72	Pegasus BCP 8	Fool About You/Woke Up This Morning/Morning Dew (unreleased, promo only, handwritten white labels)	£75
73	Mooncrest MOON 1	Broken Down Angel/Witchdoctor Woman (promo, custom sleeve)	£15
75	Mooncrest MOON 47	My White Bicycle/My White Bicycle (A label promo only)	£15
76	Mountain PSLP191	I Don't Want To Go On Without You/Waiting For The Man (12" promo)	£18
78	Mountain TOP 37	Place In Your Heart/Kentucky Fried Blues (mispressing, B-side plays Bee Gees track, company sleeve)	£20
71	Pegasus PEG 10	NAZARETH (LP, 1st issue, Pegasus picture label, with promo booklet, textured matt sleeve)	£200
71	Pegasus PEG 10	NAZARETH (LP, 1st issue, Pegasus picture label, without promo booklet, textured matt sleeve)	£150
72	Pegasus PEG 10	NAZARETH (LP, 2nd issue, PEG label/glossy sleeve)	£50
72	Pegasus PEG 14	EXERCISES (LP, Peg label, gatefold sleeve)	£100
73	Mooncrest CREST 1	RAZAMANAZ (LP, gatefold sleeve, initial copies with inner and stickered sleeve)	£75
73	Mooncrest CREST 4	LOUD 'N' PROUD (LP, gatefold sleeve)	£70
74	Mooncrest CREST 10	NAZARETH (LP, reissue)	£15
75	Mountain TOPS 103	EXERCISES (LP, reissue)	£15

74	Mooncrest CREST 15	**RAMPANT** (LP, embossed sleeve, inner sleeve, dollar sticker insert)	**£75**
75	Mountain TOPS 104	**RAZAMANAZ** (LP, reissue)	**£15**
75	Mooncrest CREST 27	**HAIR OF THE DOG** (LP, with inner)	**£70**
76	Mountain TOPS 109	**CLOSE ENOUGH FOR ROCK 'N' ROLL** (LP)	**£40**
76	Mountain TOPS 113	**PLAY 'N' THE GAME** (LP, with inner sleeve)	**£30**
77	Mountain TOPS 115	**EXPECT NO MERCY** (LP, with inner sleeve)	**£20**
79	Mountain TOPS 123	**NO MEAN CITY** (LP, with inner sleeve)	**£15**
80	Mountain TOPS 126	**MALICE IN WONDERLAND** (LP, inner sleeve)	**£15**
81	NEMS NELD 102	**SNAZ** (2-LP, gatefold sleeve, inner)	**£20**
85	Sahara SAH 130	**SOUND ELIXIR** (LP, Marimba label, withdrawn)	**£20**
85	Sahara SAH 137	**20 GREATEST HITS** (LP, withdrawn)	**£20**
85	Sahara SAH 131	**LOUD 'N' PROUD** (LP, reissue)	**£15**
92	Mausoleum 3670010.1	**NO JIVE** (LP, insert)	**£15**
01	Receiver RRLT 009Z	**BACK TO THE TRENCHES: LIVE 72-84** (3-LP, gatefold sleeve, booklet)	**£25**

(see also Mark Five, Sensational Alex Harvey Band, Tandoori Cassette)

NAZZ

68	Screen Gems SGC 219001	**Open My Eyes/Hello It's Me**	**£25**
69	Screen Gems SGC 219002	**Hello It's Me/Crowded**	**£15**
69	Screen Gems SGC 221001	**NAZZ** (LP)	**£65**

(see also Todd Rundgren)

'N BETWEENS

66	Columbia DB 8080	**You Better Run/Evil Witchman** (demos credit In-Be-Tweens)	**£400**

(see also Slade, Vendors)

JOHNNY NEAL & STARLINERS

65	Pye 7N 15838	**And I Will Love You/Walk Baby Walk**	**£80**

(see also Storyteller)

TOMMY NEAL

68	Vocalion VL 9290	**Goin' To A Happening/Tee Ta**	**£75**
68	Vocalion VL 9290	**Goin' To A Happening/Tee Ta** (DJ copy)	**£150**

NEARLY NORMAL

80	Insurrection Now! INA 1	**Bedtime/Die Baby Die!**(hand-made p/s)	**£60**

NEAT

80s	Neatbeat LYN 6269	**Hormones In Action/Take Your Chances** (p/s)	**£50**

NEAT CHANGE

68	Decca F 12809	**I Lied To Auntie May/Sandman** (in foldout p/s)	**£120**
68	Decca F 12809	**I Lied To Auntie May/Sandman**	**£60**

(see also Peter Banks)

NEBULA

03	Sweet Nothing SNLP 026	**ATOMIC RITUAL** (LP)	**£30**

NEBULA II

92	Reinforced RIVET 1232R	**X-Plore H-Core/Peace Maker** (Remixes) (12")	**£15**

NECESSARIES

81	Sire SRK 3573	**BIG SKY** (LP)	**£40**
82	Sire SRK 3574	**EVENT HORIZON** (LP)	**£40**

(see also Arthur Russell)

NECROMANDUS

90	Reflection MM 09	**QUICKSAND DREAM** (LP, 500 only)	**£18**

NEDS ATOMIC DUSTBIN

91	Furtive 4681121	**GOD FODDER** (LP)	**£18**
92	Sony Soho Square 4726331	**ARE YOU NORMAL?** (LP)	**£25**
95	Sony Soho Square 478330 1	**BRAINBLOODVOLUME** (LP)	**£35**

NEED

80	SKITZ 1	**Let Them Eat Valium/Seduction** (p/s)	**£30**

NEEDLES (1)

80	Ellie Jay EJSP 9340	**Gotta Know You/Jayneski** (no p/s)	**£100**

LOUIS NEEFS

69	Columbia DB 8561	**Jennifer Jennings/I Love You**	**£25**

SEYOUM NEFTA

81	Mink	**BURNING AN ILLUSION** (LP)	**£30**

NEGATIVE FX

84	Fundamental HOLY 7	**NEGATIVE FX** (LP)	**£25**

NEGATIVES

78	Look LK/SP 6478	**Stakeout** (50 copies with p/s)	**£200**
78	Look LK/SP 6478	**Stakeout** (no p/s)	**£40**

NEGATIVES IN COLOUR

82	NEG 1	**Caught In Possession/Everyman**	**£18**

NEGAZIONE

85	Children Of The Revolution GURT 7	**MUCCHIO SELVAGGIO** (split LP with DECLINO)	**£75**

NEGRIL (1)

75	Torpedo TOR 51	**I Shot The Sheriff/Negril**	**£20**
75	Klik KLP 9005	**NEGRIL** (LP)	**£30**

NEGRIL (2)
80	Tuff Rank TRA 903	Alone Some Time/Dub Ten Thousand (12")	£120

NEGRO
80	Negro NEG 1	Unite/DJ A HUMBLE I: Unite Tonight	£150

NEGUS DAWTAS
78	Natty Congo NATTY 001	I Speak The Truth/Hail Rastafari (Actually by Ranking Reuben)	£20

NEGUS ROOTS MEETS THE MAD PROFESSOR
83	Negus Roots NERLP 009	DUB ROCKERS VOLUME 2 (LP)	£80

(see also Lackley Castell)

CHRISTOPHER NEIL
72	RAK SRKA 6753	WHERE I BELONG (LP)	£25

EARL NEIL
78	Studio 16 We 401	Rough And Tough/PRINE JAZZBO: Suffer Must Live (12")	£30

FRED NEIL
67	Elektra EKS 7293	BLEECKER & MACDOUGAL (LP)	£60
70	Capitol E-ST 657	OTHER SIDE OF THIS LIFE (LP)	£35

NEKTAR
73	United Artists NEK 1	What Ya Gonna Do?/Day In The Life Of A Preacher Pt. One (Edit) (p/s)	£15
73	United Artists UAD 60041/2	SOUNDS LIKE THIS (2-LP)	£40
74	United Artists UAS 29499	A TAB IN THE OCEAN (LP, gatefold sleeve)	£35
74	United Artists UAG 29545	REMEMBER THE FUTURE (LP, gatefold)	£35
74	United Artists UAG 29680	DOWN TO EARTH (LP, gatefold sleeve)	£30
76	Decca SKL-R 5250	RECYCLED (LP)	£15

(see also Robert Calvert)

NELLIE
69	Gas GAS 126	I Who Have Nothing/You Send Me	£60

BILL NELSON('S RED NOISE)
71	Smile LAF 2182/HG 116	NORTHERN DREAM (LP, 250 only, numbered, in foldover gatefold sleeve with booklet)	£70
71	Smile LAF 2182/HG 116	NORTHERN DREAM (LP, 250 second pressing unnumbered, (reissues on the Butt label, £15)	£30
78	Harvest SHSP 4095	SOUND ON SOUND (LP)	£15
85	Cocteau JEAN 2	TRIAL BY INTIMACY (THE BOOK OF SPLENDOURS) (4-LP, box set, with book & postcards, initial copies misspelt as "The Book Splendours")	£20
11	Esoteric COCDBOX 1002	THE PRACTICE OF EVERYDAY LIFE (8-CD box set)	£40

(see also A - Austr, Astral Navigations, Gagalactyca, Be-Bop Deluxe)

EARL NELSON
59	London HLW 8950	No Time To Cry/Come On	£30
59	London HLW 8950	No Time To Cry/Come On (78)	£15

OLIVER NELSON
60	Esquire 32-148	SCREAMIN THE BLUES (LP, as the Oliver Nelson Sextet)	£50
61	His Masters Voice CSD 1422	THE BLUES AND THE ABSTRACT TRUTH (LP)	£40
61	Esquire 32 168	STRAIGHT AHEAD (LP, with Eric Dolphy)	£50
62	Esquire 32 188	MAIN STEM (LP, with Joe Newman)	£25
63	Verve VLP 9053	FULL NELSON (LP)	£15
66	His Masters Voice CSD 3570	OLIVER NELSON PLAYS MICHELLE (LP)	£15
68	HMV CLP 1868	MORE BLUES AND THE ABSTRACT TRUTH (LP)	£18

OZZIE & HARRIET NELSON
59	London HA-P 2145	OZZIE AND HARRIET NELSON (LP)	£30

PETER NELSON
72	Peacock PEA502	Good Scotch Whiskey/I Am A Ship	£20

RICK(Y) NELSON
78s
57	HMV POP 355	I'm Walkin'/A Teenager's Romance	£40
57	HMV POP 390	You're My One And Only Love/BARNEY KESSEL: Honey Rock	£40
57	London HLP 8499	Be-Bop Baby/Have I Told You Lately That I Love You	£20
58	London HLP 8542	Stood Up/Waitin' In School	£20
58	London HLP 8594	Believe What You Say/My Bucket's Got A Hole In It	£20
58	London HLP 8732	Someday/I Got A Feeling	£20
58	London HLP 8738	Lonesome Town/My Babe	£20
59	London HLP 8817	It's Late/Never Be Anyone Else But You	£20
59	London HLP 8927	Just A Little Too Much/Sweeter Than You	£25
60	London HLP 9021	I Wanna Be Loved/Mighty Good	£60
60	London HLP 9121	Young Emotions/Right By My Side	£30
60	London HLP 9188	Yes, Sir, That's My Baby/I'm Not Afraid	£60

SINGLES
57	HMV POP 355	I'm Walkin'/A Teenager's Romance (gold label lettering)	£150
57	HMV POP 355	I'm Walkin'/A Teenager's Romance (silver label lettering)	£40
57	HMV POP 390	You're My One And Only Love/BARNEY KESSEL: Honey Rock	£50
57	London HLP 8499	Be-Bop Baby/Have I Told You Lately That I Love You	£20
58	London HLP 8542	Stood Up/Waitin' In School	£20
58	London HLP 8594	Believe What You Say/My Bucket's Got A Hole In It	£20
59	London HLP 8894	Just A Little Too Much/Sweeter Than You (unreleased)	£0
61	London HLP 9260	You Are The Only One/Milk Cow Blues	£20
61	London HLP 9260	You Are The One And Only/Milk Cow Blues (with different label credit)	£15

EPs

58	London RE-P 1141	RICKY PART 1	£20
58	London RE-P 1142	RICKY PART 2	£20
58	London RE-P 1143	RICKY PART 3	£20
58	London RE-P 1144	RICKY PART 4	£20
59	London RE-P 1168	RICKY NELSON PART 1	£20
59	London RE-P 1169	RICKY NELSON PART 2	£20
59	London RE-P 1170	RICKY NELSON PART 3	£20
59	London RE-P 1200	RICKY SINGS AGAIN PART 1	£20
59	London RE-P 1201	RICKY SINGS AGAIN PART 2	£20
60	London RE-P 1238	I GOT A FEELING	£20
60	London RE-P 1249	RICKY SINGS SPIRITUALS	£20
61	London RE-P 1300	RICKY NELSON PART 4	£20

(The EPs listed above are credited to Ricky Nelson)

62	London RE-P 1339	IT'S A YOUNG WORLD	£20
63	London RE-P 1362	IT'S UP TO YOU	£30
63	Brunswick OE 9502	ONE BOY TOO LATE	£30
64	Liberty LEP 4001	SINGS FOR YOU	£60
64	Liberty LEP 4019	THAT'S ALL	£60
65	Liberty LEP 4028	I'M IN LOVE AGAIN	£60
65	Brunswick OE 9512	HAPPY GUY	£30

ALBUMS : LPS

57	London HA-P 2080	RICKY	£40
58	London HA-P 2119	RICKY NELSON	£40
59	London HA-P 2159	RICKY SINGS AGAIN	£30
59	London HA-P 2206	SONGS BY RICKY	£30
60	London HA-P 2290	MORE SONGS BY RICKY (gatefold sleeve, mono)	£25
60	London SAH-P 6102	MORE SONGS BY RICKY (gatefold sleeve, stereo)	£30
61	London HA-P 2379	RICK IS 21 (mono)	£25
61	London SAH-P 6179	RICK IS 21 (stereo)	£25

(Credited to Ricky Nelson)

62	London HA-P 2445	ALBUM SEVEN (mono)	£25
62	London SAH-P 6236	ALBUM SEVEN (stereo)	£25
63	London HA-P 8066	IT'S UP TO YOU	£25
63	Brunswick LAT 8545	FOR YOUR SWEET LOVE (mono)	£25
63	Brunswick STA 8545	FOR YOUR SWEET LOVE (stereo)	£30
64	Brunswick LAT 8562	RICKY SINGS "FOR YOU" (mono)	£25
64	Brunswick STA 8562	RICKY SINGS "FOR YOU" (stereo)	£40
64	Liberty LBY 3027	MILLION SELLERS	£20
64	Brunswick LAT/STA 8581	THE VERY THOUGHT OF YOU	£20
64	Brunswick LAT/STA 8596	SPOTLIGHT ON RICK	£20
65	Brunswick LAT 8615	BEST ALWAYS	£20
65	Brunswick LAT/STA 8630	LOVE AND KISSES	£20
66	Brunswick LAT/STA 8657	BRIGHT LIGHTS, COUNTRY MUSIC	£20
67	Brunswick LAT/STA 8680	COUNTRY FEVER	£20

SANDY NELSON

59	London HLP 9015	Drum Party/The Big Noise From Winnetka (78)	£25
60	Top Rank JKP 2060	RUSHING FOR PERCUSSION (EP, 2 tracks by Preston Epps)	£20
65	Liberty LEP 4033	SANDY NELSON PLAYS (EP)	£15
60	London HA-P 2260	TEEN BEAT (LP, mono)	£20
60	London SAH-P 6082	TEEN BEAT (LP, stereo)	£25
61	London HA-P 2425	LET THERE BE DRUMS (LP, mono)	£20
61	London SAH-P 6221	LET THERE BE DRUMS (LP, stereo)	£25
62	London HA-P 2446	DRUMS ARE MY BEAT! (LP, mono)	£20
62	London SAH-P 6237	DRUMS ARE MY BEAT! (LP, stereo)	£25
62	London HA-P 8009	DRUMMIN' UP A STORM (LP, mono)	£20
62	London SH-P 8009	DRUMMIN' UP A STORM (LP, stereo)	£25
63	London HA-P/SH-P 8029	COMPELLING PERCUSSION (LP)	£20
63	London HA-P/SH-P 8051	TEENAGE HOUSE PARTY (LP)	£20
65	Liberty LBY 3007	SANDY NELSON PLAYS (LP)	£20
65	Liberty LBY 3035	LIVE IN LAS VEGAS (LP)	£20
66	Liberty LBY 3061	DRUMS A GO-GO (LP)	£20
66	Liberty (S)LBY 3080	SUPERDRUMS (LP)	£20

(see also Preston Epps)

TERRY NELSON (& FIREBALLS)

65	Blue Beat BB 326	Help/PRINCE BUSTER: Johnny Dollar	£25
69	Rude Boy RBH 002	Woman Whine And Grine/Dem City Girls (actually the FIRE-BALLS)	£20

WILLIE NELSON

66	RCA Victor RD 7749	COUNTRY WILLIE (LP)	£15
66	Liberty (S)LBY 1240	AND THEN I WROTE (LP)	£15
69	RCA RD 7997	TEXAS IN MY SOUL (LP)	£15

NELSON TRIO (U.S.)

60	London HLL 9019	All In Good Time/The Town Crier	£15

NEMESIS

89	Intrigue IGE 5T	Heartbreaker/After The Storm (12")	£20
89	Intrigue IGE 5T	After The Storm/Oh Baby Now/Heartbreaker/Give Me An Intro (12")	£15

MINT VALUE £

89	Intrigue IGE 7T	The Way Love Is/(Instrumental Version) (12")	£30
90	Intrigue IGE 8T	I Need You So Bad/SHADES OF BLACK: Just A Little Bit (12")	£15

NEO MAYA

67	Pye 7N 17371	I Won't Hurt You/U.F.O.	£75

(see also Episode Six)

CHIITRA NEOGY

68	Morgan Bluetown MI003L	THE PERFUMED GARDEN (LP)	£30
68	Gemini GMX 5030	THE PERFUMED GARDEN (LP, reissue)	£25

NEON BOYS

90	Overground OVER 11	TIME (12" EP, 20 test pressings only)	£20

(see also Richard Hell, Television)

NEON HEARTS

77	Neon Hearts NEON 1	Venus Eccentric/Regulations (8" p/s)	£40
78	Satril SAT 133	Answers/Armchair Thriller (p/s)	£15
79	Satril SATL 4012	POPULAR MUSIC (LP)	£15

NEON (2)

80	3D 3D1	Making Waves/Me I See In You (p/s)	£20

NEON TETRA

82	Deeda DD 01	Tightrope/Night Boat To Amsterdam	£20

NEPTUNE'S EMPIRE

71	Polymax PXX 01	NEPTUNE'S EMPIRE (LP)	£200

NERO & GLADIATORS

61	Decca F 11329	Entry Of The Gladiators/Boots	£15
61	Decca F 11367	In The Hall Of The Mountain King/The Trek To Rome	£15
61	Decca F 11413	Czardas/That's A Long Time Ago	£20

(see also Laurie Jay, Gladiators, Screaming Lord Sutch & Savages, State Of Mickey & Tommy)

PAUL NERO (SOUNDS)

68	Liberty LBL 83100	NERO'S SOUL PARTY (LP)	£25

NERVE (1)

68	Page One POF 055	Magic Spectacles/Come The Day	£20
68	Page One POF 081	It Is/Mystery Lady	£18
68	Page One POF 097	Piece By Piece/Satisfying Kind	£15

(see also Lovin')

NERVES (1)

78	Lightning GIL 520	TV Adverts/Sex Education (p/s)	£35

NERVES (2)

81	Good Vibrations BIG 3	NOTRE DEMO (LP, official bootleg, foldover sleeve with booklet)	£20

NERVE SENTA

81	Tense Raven FRM 041	You Turn Me On/Secret Admirer	£25

NERVOUS NORVUS

56	London HLD 8338	Ape Call/Wild Dog Of Kentucky (gold label print)	£50
56	London HLD 8338	Ape Call/Wild Dog Of Kentucky (silver label print)	£20
57	London HLD 8383	Dig/Bullfrog Hop (gold label print)	£60
57	London HLD 8383	Dig/Bullfrog Hop (silver label print)	£30
62	Salvo SLO 1812	Does A Chinese Chicken Have A Pigtail/ROD BARTON: Dear Old San Francisco	£20
85	Big Beat NED 12	NERVOUS NORVUS (mini-LP)	£15

NERVOUS WRECKS

72	No label or cat. no	NERVE ENDING (LP)	£300

JIM NESBIT

65	Vocalion V 9241	Tiger In My Tank/I Can't Stand This Living Alone	£25

MICHAEL NESMITH (& FIRST/SECOND NATIONAL BAND)

70	RCA SF 8136	MAGNETIC SOUTH (LP, with First National Band)	£25
71	RCA SF 8209	NEVADA FIGHTER (LP, with First National Band)	£25
72	RCA SF 8276	TANTAMOUNT TO TREASON VOLUME ONE (LP, with Second National Band)	£20
73	RCA APL1 0164	PRETTY MUCH YOUR STANDARD RANCH STASH (LP, solo)	£15
75	Island ILPS 9428	THE PRISON (LP, boxed with book, unreleased in U.K.)	£0
76	RCA RS 1064	THE BEST OF MICHAEL NESMITH (LP)	£15

(see also Monkees, Wichita Train Whistle)

NEU!

73	United Artists UP 35485	Super/Neuschnee (p/s)	£25
73	United Artists UP 35485	Super/Neuschnee	£20
75	United Artists UP 35874	Isi/After Eight	£20
72	United Artists UAS 29396	NEU (LP, laminated cover)	£100
73	United Artists UAS 29500	NEU II (LP, gatefold sleeve)	£100
75	United Artists UAS 29782	NEU '75 (LP, gatefold sleeve)	£80
82	Cherry Red BRED 37	BLACK FOREST GATEAU (LP, compilation)	£30
10	Gronland LPGRONI	NEU (LP, gatefold, reissue, white vinyl)	£18
10	Gronland LPGRONII	NEU 2 (LP, gatefold, reissue, white vinyl)	£18
10	Gronland LPGRONIII	NEU '75 (LP, reissue)	£18
10	Gronland LPGRONIV	NEU! '86 (LP, yellow vinyl)	£15
10	Gronland LPGRONV5065001040981	NEU! (4-LP box set with 12", inserts)	£100

(see also Kraftwerk, La Dusseldorf)

NEU ELEKTRIKK
79 Synthethesia SGS 107   Lust Of Berlin/Distractions (p/s, stamped white labels) £20
NEUROSIS
04 Neurot NR 033   THE EYE OF EVERY STORM (LP, gatefold, inner, poster, grey marbled vinyl) £30
07 Neurot NR 050   GIVEN TO THE RISING (LP, gatefold, inner, black/white splattered vinyl) £20
NEUTRAL MILK HOTEL
95 Fire BLAZE 79   Everything Is/Snow Song Part 1...£20
98 Blue Rose BRRC 10237   Holland, 1945/Engine (picture disc, numbered fold-out poster in polythene bag..........£30
NEUTRONS
74 United Artists UAG 29652   BLACK HOLE STAR (LP, with inner sleeve) £25
75 United Artists UAG 29726   TALES FROM THE BLUE COCOONS (LP, laminated gatefold sleeve) £20
(see also Clive John, Gentle Giant, Man)
AARON NEVILLE
67 Stateside SS 584   Tell It Like It Is/Why Worry..£20
67 Stateside SS 584   Tell It Like It Is/Why Worry (DJ Copy)..£40
91 A&M AMY 835   Voodoo/Close Your Eyes/Hercules (12")..£15
67 Liberty LBY 3089   LIKE IT 'TIS (LP)...£50
86 Charly CRB 1111   MAKE ME STRONG (LP) £15
NEW YOUNG PONY CLUB
07 Modular Recordings MODVL FANTASTIC PLAYROOM (LP, printed inner) £45
     062
NEW AGE
82 Dining Out TUX 18   LIVIN FOR NOW (12" EP, p/s)..£15
82 Dining Out TUX 25   ALL THE MONKEYS AREN'T IN THE ZOO, MARYLOO (LP)...£20
NEW AGE STEPPERS
80 On-U Sound ONU 1   Fade Away/LONDON UNDERGROUND: Learn A Language (p/s)................................£15
81 Statik 612   My Love/Love Forever (12")...£20
80 On-U Sound ONULP 1   NEW AGE STEPPERS (LP) £30
81 Statik/On U Sound STATLP 2 ACTION BATTLEFIELD (LP)..£30
82 On-U Sound ONULP 21   FOUNDATION STEPPERS (LP)..£30
NEWBAN
11 BBE BBE223ALP   NEWBAN & NEWBAN 2 (2-LP, reissue) £20
NEWBEATS
65 Hickory 45-1320   I Can't Hear You No More/Little Child £15
65 Hickory 45-1332   Run Baby Run/Mean Woolly Willie £30
65 Hickory 45-1332   Run Baby Run/Mean Woolly Willie (DJ copy)..£70
66 Hickory 45-1366   Shake Hands (And Come Out Crying)/Too Sweet To Be Forgotten £20
66 Hickory 45-1387   Crying My Heart Out/Short Of Love £40
66 Hickory 45-1387   Crying My Heart Out/Short Of Love (DJ copy) £70
65 Hickory LPE 1503   NEWBEATS (EP)..£30
65 Hickory LPE 1506   AIN'T THAT LOVIN' YOU BABY (EP)...£30
66 Hickory LPE 1510   OH! GIRLS GIRLS (EP)..£30
65 Hickory LPM 120   BREAD AND BUTTER (LP)..£35
72 London SHE 8428   RUN BABY RUN (LP)..£15
NEW BLOCKADERS
82 Private Pressing   CHANGEZ LES BLOCKEURS (LP, 100 only, white label A4 sheet as cover) £300
91 Hypnagogia GOG 01   SYMPHONIE IN X MAJOR (LP, 500 only, numbered)...£20
NEWBOY
73 Count Shelly CS007   Sweet Talk/J ENGLISH: One And Only...£20
NEW BREED
65 Decca F 12295   Friends And Lovers Forever/Unto Us...£75
NEWBY & JOHNSON
70 Mercury 6052 027   I Want To Give You My Everything/Sweet Happiness £25
NEWCASTLE BIG BAND
72 Impulse ISS NBB 106   NEWCASTLE BIG BAND (LP, white labels, 2,000 only) £150
(see also Last Exit, Police, Sting, Radio Actors)
NEWCLEUS
84 Sunnyview SVLP 6600   JAM ON REVENGE (LP) £18
NEW COLONY SIX
66 London HLZ 10033   I Confess/Dawn Is Breaking £75
66 Stateside SS 522   At The River's Edge/I Lie Awake...£50
NEW CULTURE
72 Priory PRY 002   Seek Out The Sun/Strange £100
NEW CUOREY
73 Taurus TR 101   Vietnam/The Girl I Had £25
NEW DAWN
69 private pressing   MAINLINE (LP) £80
NEW DEAL STRING BAND
69 Argo ZDA 104   DOWN IN THE WILLOW (LP, with insert) £30
NEW DECADE
94 Out Of Romford OOR 011   NARROW MINDS (2-LP)...£18

MINT VALUE £

NEW DEPARTURES QUARTET
60s Transatlantic TRA 134   THE NEW DEPARTURES QUARTET (LP, with Stan Tracey) £40
(see also Stan Tracey)

MARTIN NEWELL
80 Off Street OSR 001   Young Jobless/Sylvie In Toytown (p/s)...£30
(see also Gypp, Cleaners From Venus)

NEW FACES
66 Pye 7N 17029   Like A Man/Shake Up The Party (Myra)...£15

NEW FORESTERS
65 Lyntone LYN 932/933   Travel/LIZARDS: My Love Goes On (Sheffield Students Rag record)...........................£30

NEW FORMULA
67 Piccadilly 7N 35381   Do It Again A Little Bit Slower/I'm On The Outside Looking In.................................£18
67 Piccadilly 7N 35401   I Want To Go Back There Again/Can't You See That She Loves Me.........................£18
68 Pye 7N 17552   My Baby's Coming Home/Burning In The Background Of My Mind £20
69 Pye 7N 17818   Stay Indoors/Hare Krishna (in export p/s) £40
69 Pye 7N 17818   Stay Indoors/Hare Krishna £25

NEW GENERATION (1)
69 Spark SRL 1000   Sadie And Her Magic Mister Garland/Digger £15
70 Spark SRL 1019   Police Is Here/Mister C..£15

NEW GENERATION (2)
80 Fight FT DD 4454   Long And Winding Road/BLACK STALLIONS: New Experience (12")...........................£50

NEW HERITAGE
73 Westwood WRS 028   ALL MANNER OF THINGS (LP) £50

NEW HOPE
69 London HL 10296   Won't Find Better Than Me/They Call It Love £18
(see also Kit Kats)

NEW INSPIRATION
67 Major Minor MM 539   You Made A Fool of Me/M.T. £25

NEW JACK PIMPS
94 Steppaz STEP 001   Water Jelly (Amen Lick)/Water Jelly (Copter Lick) (12") £25

NEW JAZZ GROUP
56 Tempo EXA 39   MODERN JAZZ SCENE (EP)...£50

NEW JAZZ ORCHESTRA
65 Decca LK 4690   WESTERN REUNION LONDON 1965 (LP, mono) £80
65 Decca SKL 4690   WESTERN REUNION LONDON 1965 (LP, stereo) £150
69 Verve SVLP 9236   DEJEUNER SUR L'HERBE (LP) £250
(see also Neil Ardley, Nucleus)

NEW JERSEY CONNECTION
82 Nitelife LIFE 1   Love Don't Come Easy/Love Don't Come Easy (Instrumental) (12") £16

NEW JERSEY KINGS
92 Acid Jazz JAZIDLP 33   PARTY TO THE BUS STOP (LP) £15
95 Acid Jazz JAZID123LP   STRATOSPHERE BREAKDOWN (LP)...£15
(see also James Taylor Quartet)

NEW JUMP BAND
68 Domain D 1   The Only Kind Of Girl/Seven Kinds Of Sweet Lovin'...£25

NEW KINGDOM
93 Gee Street 518 362 1   HEAVY LOAD (LP) £40

NEW LEAF
80 LEAF 101   Warning Take Warning/Roots Rock Reggae (no p/s) £30

ANDY NEWMAN
72 Track 2406 103   RAINBOW (LP, gatefold sleeve, black/silver label) £25
(see also Thunderclap Newman)

BRAD NEWMAN
62 Fontana H 357   Somebody To Love/This Time It's Love...£15

CARLTON NEWMAN
85 Roots Pool RP 003   Front Line/EDI FITZROY: Pressure £30

COLIN NEWMAN
80 Beggars Banquet BEGA 20   A-Z (LP, inner)...£30
81 4AD CAD 108   PROVISIONALLY ENTITLED THE SINGING FISH (LP) £20
82 4AD CAD 201   NOT TO (LP) £20
(see also Wire)

DEL NEWMAN SOUND
67 Columbia SCX 6181   FLOWER GARDEN (LP) £20

JIMMY (C.) NEWMAN
57 London HLD 8460   A Fallen Star/I Can't Go On This Way...£30
59 MGM MGM 1009   What'cha Gonna Do/So Soon £15
59 MGM MGM-EP 706   GRIN AND BEAR IT - COUNTRY AND WESTERN STYLE (EP)......................................£30

MARK NEWMAN
69 Lestar 712   MARK NEWMAN (EP)...£30

PAUL NEWMAN
66 Mercury MF 969   Ain't You Got A Heart/Tears On My Pillow..£50

RANDY NEWMAN
68	Reprise R(S)LP 6286	**RANDY NEWMAN CREATES SOMETHING NEW UNDER THE SUN** (LP)	£15
70	Reprise RSLP 6373	**12 SONGS** (LP)	£15
85	Warner Bros. K56404	**LITTLE CRIMINALS** (LP, Hi Fi News, Nimbus supercut)	£70

(see also Harry Nilsson, Tom Petty & Heartbreakers)

TOM NEWMAN
75	Virgin V 2022	**FINE OLD TOM** (LP, features Mike Oldfield)	£20
75	Virgin V 2042	**LIVE AT THE ARGONAUT** (LP, unreleased, test pressings only)	£80
77	Decca TXS 123	**FAERIE SYMPHONY** (LP, gatefold sleeve)	£30
88	Oceandisc	**OZYMANDIAS** (LP, unissued, 20 test pressings only in proof sleeve)	£30

(see also Jade Warrior, July, Mike Oldfield)

TONY NEWMAN
68	Decca F 12795	**Soul Thing/Let The Good Times Roll**	£30

(see also Sounds Incorporated, Flying Machine, Pinkerton['s Assorted Colours], May Blitz, Three Man Army)

THE NEW MASTERSOUNDS
00	Blow It Hard BIH 017	**One Note Brown/Burnt Black**	£20
01	Deep Funk DFLP 001	**KEB DARGE PRESENTS** (LP)	£40

NEW MATH
79	Reliable Gum 002	**Die Trying/Angela** (original issue, p/s)	£20

NEW MODEL ARMY
83	Shout QS 002/QF 001	**Bittersweet/Betcha/Tension** (p/s, with flexi "Fashion"/"The Cause")	£15
93	Epic 473562 1	**THE LOVE OF HOPELESS CAUSES** (LP)	£40

NEW MODEL SOLDIER
81	Bunny Rabbit BUN 001	**DANCE THE DEATH OF A THOUSAND CUTS EP**	£200

NEW MONITORS
72	Buddah 2011 118	**Fence Around Your Heart/Have You Seen Her**	£30

PETER NEWNHAM
77	B & C BCS 011	**Rudi/Outside My Window** (100 only)	£150

THE NEW ORDER
81	Come Org WDC 883011	**BRADFORD RED LIGHT DISTRICT** (cassette)	£50
81	Come Org. CARA12	**BRADFORD RED LIGHT DISTRICT** (LP)	£150

(see also Come)

NEW ORDER
SINGLES
81	Factory FAC 33	**Ceremony/In A Lonely Place** (embossed metallic p/s)	£15
81	Factory FAC 33T	**Ceremony/In A Lonely Place** (12", British racing green, with bronze type)	£20
81	Factory Benelux FBNL 8	**Everything's Gone Green/Mesh/Cries & Whispers** (12", yellow sleeve)	£20
82	Factory FAC 51B	**Rocking Carol/Ode To Joy** (flexidisc, given away at Hacienda, 4,000 only)	£30
82	Factory FAC 63	**Temptation/Hurt** (12", p/s)	£20
83	Factory FAC 7312	**Blue Monday/The Beach** (12", first pressing, die-cut sleeve, silver insert)	£30
85	Factory FAC 123	**The Perfect Kiss/The Kiss Of Death/Perfect Pit** (12", embossed silver p/s, pink	£15
86	Strange Fruit SFPS001	**PEEL SESSIONS** (12")	£15
88	Factory FACDV 73R	**Blue Monday 1988** (12 Inch)/**Blue Monday 1988** (7 Inch)/**Beach Buggy/Blue Monday 1988** (Video) (CD Video)	£50
88	Factory FACDV 183	**True Faith** (Remix 12 Inch)/**Evil Dust/True Faith** (7 Inch) (CD Video)/**True Faith** (CD Video)	£40
11	Rhino FAC 33	**Ceremony** (Original Version)/**In A Lonely Place** (12" Version)//**Ceremony** (Heart & Soul Rehearsal Version)/**In A Lonely Place** (Unreleased Rehearsal Version) (12")	£25
16	Mute MUTE 553	**People On The High Line** (Richard X Video Mix)/(Claptone Radio Edit) (uncut picture disc)	£100

SINGLES : PROMOS
83	Factory FAC 93	**Confusion** (Edit)/**Confusion** (Edit) (p/s, DJ promo only)	£20
84	Factory FAC 103	**Thieves Like Us** (Edit)/**Lonesome Tonight** (Edit) (p/s, DJ promo only)	£15
88	Factory FAC 223	**Fine Time/Don't Do It/Fine Line** (12" promo, pink p/s)	£25
89	Factory FAC 273/7	**Run 2** (Edit)/**MTO** (Edit) (DJ promo only, 500 pressed)	£20

ALBUMS
81	Factory FACT 50	**MOVEMENT** (LP, blue cardboard sleeve)	£40
83	Factory FACT 75	**POWER CORRUPTION & LIES** (LP, 1st pressing, die cut sleeve, A1/B1 Matrix numbers	£40
83	Factory FACT 75	**POWER CORRUPTION & LIES** (LP, repressing, A2/B2 Matrixes)	£20
85	Factory FACT 100	**LOW-LIFE** (LP, onion paper outer sleeve)	£40
86	Factory FACT 150SP	**BROTHERHOOD** (LP, limited metallic sleeve)	£40
86	Factory FACT 150	**BROTHERHOOD** (LP)	£20
87	Factory FACT 200	**THE GATEFOLD SUBSTANCE** (LP, numbered gatefold sleeve, 1,000 only)	£100
87	Factory FACT 200	**SUBSTANCE** (LP, 1st pressing, embossed sleeve, 2 inners)	£40
87	Factory FACT 200	**SUBSTANCE** (LP, non-embossed sleeve, 2 inners)	£30
87	Factory FACT 200c	**SUBSTANCE** (cassette, 200 only in box set with insert)	£20
89	Factory FACT 275	**TECHNIQUE** (LP, inner)	£20
90	Strange Fruit SFRLP 110	**PEEL SESSIONS** (LP)	£15
93	London 8284131	**REPUBLIC** (LP)	£40
94	London 8285801	(**THE BEST OF**) **NEW ORDER** (2LP, printed inners)	£150
95	London 8286571	(**THE REST OF**) **NEW ORDER** (2-LP)	£40
01	London 8573896211	**GET READY** (LP)	£40
05	London 2564622021	**WAITING FOR THE SIREN'S CALL** (2-LP)	£30
13	Rhino 2564662715	**LOST SIRENS** (LP, CD)	£15
13	London 2564 68879-7	**MOVEMENT** (LP, reissue, clear vinyl)	£40

			MINT VALUE £

15 Mute STUMM 390   **MUSIC COMPLETE** (2-LP, booklet) **£18**
15 Mute BXSTUMM 390   **MUSIC COMPLETE** (8 x 12", coloured vinyl, boxed set, signed) **£100**
15 Mute BXSTUMM 390   **MUSIC COMPLETE** (8 x 12", coloured vinyl, boxed set, unsigned) **£60**
17 Live Here Now LHN018LP   **NOMC15** (3-LP, clear vinyl) **£40**
(see also Joy Division, Electronic, Other Two, Revenge, Monaco, Bad Lieutenant)

NEW RACE
83 Statik STAT LP 16   **THE FIRST & THE LAST** (LP) **£25**

NEW RECRUITS
82 Dischord DIS 1   **Over The Pillow/The Aufrau Principle/All In An Hour** (no p/s) **£20**

NEW RELIGION
72 Bamboo BAM 70   **In The Beautiful Caribbean/Black Is Black** **£175**

NEWS FROM BABEL
84 Recommended RE 6116   **NEWS FROM BABEL - WORK RESUMED ON THE TOWER** (LP, hand-screened sleeve) **£30**
86 Re RE 1 14   **LETTERS HOME** (LP) **£25**

NEWS (1)
66 Decca F 12356   **The Entertainer/I Count The Tears** **£18**
(see also Patto, Glenn Hughes, Finders Keepers, Miller, Big Boy Pete)

NEWSFLASH
89 Newsflash NF 002   **Touch Me/Finding Out The Hard Way/White Beat** (12" p/s) **£40**
90 Newsflash 001   **Nobodies Home/Mundane Me And You** (p/s) **£50**

JOANNA NEWSOM
05 Drag City DC 303   **YS** (2-LP, gatefold, booklet) **£20**

OLIVIA NEWTON-JOHN
66 Decca F 12396   **Till You Say You'll Be Mine/For Ever** **£500**
80 Jet JET 10-185   **Xanadu/Fool Country** (10" pink vinyl, die-cut p/s, with ELO) **£30**
78 EMI EMAP 789   **TOTALLY HOT** (LP, picture disc, printed inner) **£60**
(see also Toomorrow, Marvin & Farrar)

NEWTOWN NEUROTICS
79 No Wonder A 45   **Hypocrite/You Said No** (no p/s, with insert & sticker) **£80**
79 No Wonder A 45   **Hypocrite/You Said No** **£20**
80 No Wonder NOW 4   **When The Oil Runs Out/Oh No** (p/s) **£40**
82 CNT 4/No Wonder NOW 56   **Kick Out The Tories!/Mindless Violence!** (p/s) **£15**
82 CNT CNT 010   **Licensing Hours/No Sanctuary** (p/s) **£18**
83 Razor RAZ 6   **BEGGARS CAN BE CHOOSERS** (LP) **£25**

NEW TRENDS
67 Columbia SX 6245   **THE NEW TRENDS** (LP) **£20**

NEW VICTORY BAND
78 Topic 12TS 382   **ONE MORE DANCE AND THEN** (LP) **£15**

NEW WANDERERS
79 Grapevine GRP 144   **This Man In Love/Adam And Eve** **£15**
79 Grapevine GRP 144   **This Man In Love/Adam And Eve** (DJ Copy) **£30**

NEW WORLD
83 Slipped Discs HD 106   **I Talk To My Car** (Some copies have New crossed out) **£60**

NEW YORK NEW YORK
85 Beach Culture 2 BC   **I WANNA BE LIKE YOU** (12" EP) **£15**
85 Izuma IZUMA LP 1   **NEW YORK NEW YORK** (LP) **£18**
(see also Higsons. Terry Edwards, Serious Drinking)

NEW YORK DOLLS
73 Mercury 6052 402   **Jet Boy/Vietnamese Baby** **£20**
73 Mercury 6338 270   **NEW YORK DOLLS** (LP, laminated front and black sleeve) **£60**
74 Mercury 6338 498   **TOO MUCH TOO SOON** (LP) **£40**
77 Mercury 9286.996/7   **NEW YORK DOLLS** (LP) **£20**
(see also Johnny Thunders, Heartbreakers, Idols)

NEW YORK PUBLIC LIBRARY
66 Columbia DB 7948   **I Ain't Gonna Eat Out My Heart Anymore/Rejected** **£25**
68 MCA MU 1025   **Gotta Get Away/Time Wastin'** **£15**

NEW YORK ROCK ENSEMBLE
71 CBS 5292   **Running Down The Highway/Law And Order** **£15**

NEW YORK PORT AUTHORITY
77 Invictus S INV 81951   **THREE THOUSAND MILES FROM HOME** (LP) **£15**

NEXT BAND
78 Gannet SRTS/79/CUS 159   **FOUR BY THREE EP** (p/s) **£60**
(see also Red Alert (3))

NEXUS 21
90 Network NWKT 15   **PROGRESSIVE LOGIC EP** (12", p/s) **£35**
89 Blue Chip BLUE TEC. 2   **THE RHYTHM OF LIFE** (LP) **£15**
(see also Altern 8)

NIADEM'S GHOST
86 Hibination HIDE 001   **IN SHELTERED WINDS** (LP) **£25**
(see also IQ)

NIANATTY
81 S&G SG 13   **One Love Stylee/DESMOND RHYTHM SECTION: One Love** (12") **£60**

NERMIN NIAZI
84	Sirrocco LPMDY 001	DISCO SE AAGAY (LP)	£100

NICE
67	Immediate IM 059	The Thoughts Of Emerlist Davjack/Angel Of Death	£15
68	Immediate IM 068	America/The Diamond Hard Blue Apples Of The Moon (pink label, in p/s)	£20
69	Immediate AS 4	She Belongs To Me/She Belongs To Me ('single sampler', promo)	£20
67	Immediate AS 2	ALBUM SAMPLER - THE THOUGHTS OF EMERLIST DAVJACK (1-sided LP, promo only)	£60
67	Immediate IMLP 016	THE THOUGHTS OF EMERLIST DAVJACK (LP, mono)	£70
67	Immediate IMSP 016	THE THOUGHTS OF EMERLIST DAVJACK (LP, stereo)	£50
68	Immediate IMSP 020	ARS LONGA VITA BREVIS (LP, laminated front, flipbacks, pink label, "Sold in U.K..." text)	£40
69	Immediate IMSP 026	THE NICE (LP, gatefold sleeve)	£30
70	Charisma CAS 1014	FIVE BRIDGES (LP, pink label, gatefold sleeve)	£20
71	Charisma CAS 1030	ELEGY (LP, gatefold sleeve pink 'scroll' label)	£20
72	Charisma CS1	AUTUMN '67 AND SPRING '68 (LP)	£30

(see also Keith Emerson, Emerson Lake & Palmer, Jackson Heights, Habits, Brian Davison, Refugee, Attack, Jet, P.P. Arnold)

NICK NICELY
80	Voxette VOX 1001	D.C.T. Dreams/Treeline (p/s, reissue copies £4)	£20
81	EMI EMI 5256	Hilly Fields (1892)/49 Cigars (p/s)	£15
04	Tenth Planet TP 059	PSYCHOTROPIA (LP, 1000 copies only)	£20

PAUL NICHOLAS
70	Polydor 56374	Freedom City/Run Shaker Life (with p/s)	£100
70	Polydor 56374	Freedom City/Run Shaker Life	£70
71	Polydor 2058 086	The World Is Beautiful/Lamplighter	£45

(see also Oscar, Paul Dean)

BILLY NICHOLLS
68	Immediate IM 063	Would You Believe/Daytime Girl (features Small Faces)	£70
73	Track 2094 109	Forever's No Time At All/This Song Is Green (with Pete Townshend)	£20
74	GM GMS 018	White Lightning/Daytime Girl	£20
68	Immediate IMCP 009	WOULD YOU BELIEVE (LP, withdrawn)	£5000
74	GM GML 1011	LOVE SONGS (LP)	£80
98	Tenth Planet TP 042	WOULD YOU BELIEVE (LP, reissue, with insert)	£45
99	South West SELP 003	SNAPSHOT (LP)	£25
07	Castle CMQLP 1523	WOULD YOU BELIEVE (2-LP, reissue, black or green vinyl)	£40

PENNY NICHOLS
68	Pye int 7N 2451	Look Around Rock/Farina	£35

HAL NICHOLSON
76	Concrete Jungle CJ 755	Blackman In A Babylon/Part 2	£15

LEA NICHOLSON
72	Trailer LER 3010	HORSEMUSIC (LP)	£20
72	Transatlantic TRA 254	GOD BLESS THE UNEMPLOYED (LP, with Stan Ellison)	£18

ROGER NICHOLSON
72	Trailer LER 3034	NONESUCH FOR DULCIMER (LP, red label)	£20

VIVIAN NICHOLSON
79	SRTS 79414	Spend Spend Spend/You're Number One	£50

NICKY AND THE DOTS
78	Small Wonder SMALL 12	Never Been So Stuck/Linoleum Walk (p/s)	£15

NICO
65	Immediate IM 003	I'm Not Sayin'/The Last Mile (early copies in blue/white "immediate" sleeves)	£90
65	Immediate IM 003	I'm Not Sayin'/The Last Mile (in standard black/white "immediate" sleeves)	£80
82	Immediate IMS 003	I'm Not Saying/The Last Mile (p/s, reissue)	£25
83	Aura AUS 137	Heroes/One More Chance (p/s)	£20
88	Strange Fruit SFPS 064	PEEL SESSIONS (12", p/s)	£15
18	Immediate IM003	I'm Not Sayin'/The Last Mile (p/s, reissue, white vinyl)	£15
68	Elektra EKL 4029	THE MARBLE INDEX (LP, orange label, mono)	£100
68	Elektra EKS 74029	THE MARBLE INDEX (LP, orange label, stereo)	£80
71	Reprise RSLP 6424	DESERT SHORE (LP, with John Cale)	£60
71	Reprise K 44102	DESERT SHORE (LP, with John Cale, 2nd pressing)	£30
71	MGM Select 2353 025	CHELSEA GIRL (LP)	£50
74	Island ILPS 9311	THE END (LP)	£40
81	Aura AUL 715	DRAMA OF EXILE (LP, colour cover)	£19
85	Island ILPS 9311	THE END (LP, reissue, blue label)	£18
86	Polydor 2353 025	CHELSEA GIRL (LP, reissue)	£15
86	Dojo DOJOLP 27	BEHIND THE IRON CURTAIN (2-LP)	£20

(see also John Cale, Velvet Underground, Ayers Cale Nico & Eno)

NICODEMUS
81	Cha Cha CHAD 44	Gunman Connection/It Have To Ram (12")	£30
81	Greensleeves GRED 75	BONE CONNECTION/LEROY SMART: All My Love (12")	£15
82	Cha Cha CHALP 011	GUNMAN CONNECTION (LP)	£40
82	Black Joy DHLP 2003	DANCE HALL STYLE (LP)	£50

JIMMY NICOL (& SHUBDUBS)
64	Pye 7N 15623	Humpty Dumpty/Night Train	£25
64	Pye 7N 15666	Husky/Don't Come Back (solo)	£18
64	Pye 7N 15699	Baby Please Don't Go/Shub Dubbery (possibly unissued)	£20

(see also Sound Of Jimmy Nicol, Georgie Fame)

NICOLETTE
92   Shut Up & Dance SUAD 004 **NOW IS EARLY** (LP) £20

WATT NICOLL
71   Xtra XTRA 1122   **NICE TO BE NICE** (LP, laminated front cover) £15

NICRA
77   Ogun OG 010   **LISTEN/HEAR** (LP) £18
(see also Keith Tippett)

LENNIE NIEHAUS OCTET
62   Contemporary LAC 1222   **ZOUNDS!** (LP) £40

NIEMEN
72   CBS 564896   **STRANGE IS THIS WORLD** (LP, orange/black label) £25

STEVE NIEVE
80   Comb 1   **OUTLINE ON A HAIRDO** (EP) £20

NIGGER KOJAK
83   Nigger Kojak NKLP 002   **ROCK JACK KOJAK** (LP) £15

NIGHT DOCTOR
81   Race Records RB DIS 001   Romancin'/Menelik (12") £35

NIGHTAIR
76   SRTY 79 CUS 410   **NIGHTAIR** (LP) £15

NIGHTCRAWLERS
67   London HLR 10109   **The Little Black Egg/You're Running Wild** £60

NIGHTIME FLYER (2)
81   Red Eye EYE 2   **Out With A Vengeance/Heavy Metal Rules** (p/s) £20

TUNDE NIGHTINGALE & HIS HIGHLIFE BOYS
68   Melodisc MLPAS 12-142   **THE BIRDS THAT SINGS ALL THE NIGHT** (LP) £15

NIGHTINGALES
82   Cherry Red BRED 39   **PIGS ON PURPOSE** (LP) £15
84   Vindaloo VILP 1   **1983-4 JUST THE JOB** (LP) £15

NIGHTMARES IN WAX
79   Inevitable INEV 0002   **BIRTH OF A NATION** (EP, with wraparound p/s) £20
84   KY KY 9   **Black Leather/Shangri-La** (12", 'horror' p/s) £18
85   KY KY 9 1/2   **Black Leather/Shangri-La/Girls Song** (12", different p/s, 3,000 only) £20
(see also Dead Or Alive)

NIGHTMARES ON WAX
91   Warp WARPLP 4   **A WORD OF SCIENCE** (THE 1st & FINAL CHAPTER) (LP) £20
95   Warp WARPLP 36   **SMOKERS DELIGHT** (2-LP, gatefold, inners) £40
99   Warp WARPLP 61   **CARBOOT SOUL** (2-LP, gatefold, inners) £30
02   Warp WARPLP 95   **MIND ELEVATION** (2-LP, gatefold, inners) £20
06   Warp WARPLP 133   **IN A SPACE OUTTA SOUND** (2-LP) £35
08   Warp WARPLP 159   **THOUGHT SO** (2-LP, gatefold, inners) £20
13   Warp WARPLP 241   **FEELIN GOOD** (2-LP) £20

NIGHT MOVES
83   GC GCT 2   **Transdance** (New York Disco Mix)**/Transdance** (UK Disco Mix)**/Nightdrive** (12") £30
84   GC/MCA GCT 1001   **Transdance** (Robot Rock) (UK Club Mix)**/You Can Take My Love/Beat This/Nightdrive** (12", p/s) £20

NIGHTRIDER
79   Wessex WEX 272   **DIGITAL TECHNIQUES EP: Gruesome Girls/Stay Clean/Happy Day** (p/s) £35

NIGHTRIDERS (1)
66   Polydor BM 56066   **Love Me Right Now/Your Friend** (withdrawn) £120
66   Polydor BM 56066   **Love Me Right Now/Your Friend** (promo copy) £85
66   Polydor BM 56116   **It's Only The Dog/Your Friend** £100
79   Stardust STR 1001   **I Saw Her With Another Guy/London Town** (picture insert) £25
(see also Mike Sheridan & Nightriders, Mike Sheridan's Lot, Idle Race)

NIGHTRIDERS (2)
79   Stardust STR 1001   **I Saw Her With Another Guy/London Town** (picture insert) £25

NIGHT RUN
81   RUN 001   **Forever/Crime Of Passion** (no ps) £80

NIGHTSHIFT (1)
65   Piccadilly 7N 35243   **Corrine Corrina/Lavender Tree** £15
65   Piccadilly 7N 35264   **That's My Story/Stormy Monday Blues** £18

NIGHT-TIMERS
65   Parlophone R 5355   **The Music Played On/Yield Not To Temptation** (featuring Herbie Goins) £70
(see also Herbie Goins & Night-Timers, Ronnie Jones)

NIGHTWING
83   Gull PGULP 1038   **STAND UP AND BE COUNTED** (LP, picture disc) £15
(see also Alec Johnson Band, Nutz)

NIGHTWISH
04   Back On Black BOBV 003 DPD   **ANGELS FALL FIRST** (2-LP picture discs, stickered bag) £20
04   Back On Black BOBV 004 DPD   **OCEANBORN** (2-LP picture discs, stickered bag) £20
04   Back On Black BOBV 006 DPD   **WISHMASTER** (2-LP picture discs, stickered bag) £20

04	Back On Black BOBV 007 DPD	OVER THE HILLS AND FAR AWAY (2-LP picture discs, stickered bag)	£20
04	Back On Black BOBV 008 DPD	CENTURY CHILD (2-LP picture discs, stickered bag)	£20
05	Back On Black BOBV 035 DPD	ONCE (2-LP picture discs, stickered bag)	£20

NIGHTWRITERS

88	Jack Trax JTX 19	Let The Music Use You (Club Mix)/(Radio Mix)/(Dub Mix) (12")	£20

NIHILIST SPASM BAND

85	United Dairies UD 016	1X - X = X (LP)	£20

BILL NILES

67	Decca F 12661	Pashionella Grundy/Bric-A-Bric Man	£15

WILLY NILLY

84	Ad Hoc AH 1	On The Spur Of The Moment/Half A Job (p/s, with 'time-table' insert)	£45

(see also Randy Newman, Ringo Starr, Cher)

(HARRY) NILSSON

68	RCA Victor RD/SF 7928	PANDEMONIUM SHADOW SHOW (LP, mono)	£25
68	RCA Victor RD/SF 7928	PANDEMONIUM SHADOW SHOW (LP, stereo)	£20
68	RCA RD/SF 7973	AERIAL BALLET (LP, mono)	£25
68	RCA RD/SF 7973	AERIAL BALLET (LP, stereo)	£20
69	RCA SF 8010	SKIDOO (LP, soundtrack)	£20
69	RCA SF 8046	HARRY (LP)	£20
74	Rapple/RCA APL1-0220	SON OF DRACULA (LP, soundtrack, with Ringo Starr, fold-out sleeve)	£15
80	RCA 6302 022	FLASH HARRY (LP, first pressing, those with 'barcode' are repressings)	£30

NIMBO

72	Pye 7N 45174	When The Swallows Fly/Noticeingly By	£15

LEONARD NIMOY

68	Dot (S)LPD 511	MR. SPOCK PRESENTS MUSIC FROM OUTER SPACE (LP)	£25
72	Rediffusion ZS 156	MUSIC FROM OUTER SPACE (LP, reissue of DOT (S) LPD 511)	£20

NINE DAYS WONDER

71	Harvest SHSP 4014	NINE DAYS WONDER (LP, textured sleeve, EMI logo on label)	£100

(see also Gnidralog)

NINE INCH NAILS

90	Island 12IS 482	Down On It (Skin)/Terrible Lie (Sympathetic Mix)/Down On It (Shred)/Down On It (Singe)/Terrible Lie (Empathetic Mix)/Down On It (Demo) (12", numbered limited edition)	£20
91	Island ISDJ 484	Head Like A Hole (Radio Edit) (promo, stickered p/s, same track both sides)	£20
92	Island IS 552	Physical (You're So)/Suck	£15
91	Island ILPS 9973	PRETTY HATE MACHINE (LP)	£20
92	Interscope ILPM 8004	BROKEN (1-sided 6 track mini LP with free 7" 'Physical'/'Suck')	£30
92	Island ILPM 8005	FIXED (remix mini LP)	£20
94	Island ILPSD 8012	THE DOWNWARD SPIRAL (double LP, gatefold sleeve, insert)	£70
99	Island ILPST 8091	THE FRAGILE (3-LP, inners booklet, white stickered sleeve)	£125
17	Nothing B002568201	THE FRAGILE (3-LP reissue, stickers sleeve)	£35

999

77	Labritain LAB 999	I'm Alive/Quite Disappointing (p/s)	£20
77	United Artists UP 36299	Nasty Nasty/No Pity (p/s, green vinyl)	£15
77	United Artists FREE 7	Nasty Nasty/No Pity (78rpm promo, 50 copies only)	£400
78	United Artists UAG 30199	999 (LP, with inner sleeve)	£25
78	United Artists UAG 30209	SEPARATES (LP, with inner sleeve)	£18
80	United Artists POLS 1013	BIGGEST PRIZE IN SPORT (LP)	£15
80	United Artists UA SOS 999	THE 999 SINGLES ALBUM (LP)	£15
90	Link LINK LP 125	CELLBLOCK TAPES (LP)	£15
15	Let Them Eat Vinyl LETV 216LP	THE BIGGEST PRIZE IN SPORT/THE BIGGEST TOUR IN SPORT (2-LP, green vinyl, reissue)	£18

(see also Kilburn & High Roads)

9.30 FLY

72	Ember NR 5062	9.30 FLY (LP, textured gatefold sleeve)	£250

9LAZY9

94	Ninja Tune ZEN 9	PARADISE BLOWN (2-LP)	£18

NINESENSE

76	Ogun OG 900	OH! FOR THE EDGE (LP)	£30
77	Ogun OG 910	HAPPY DAZE (LP)	£30

(see also Elton Dean, Julie Tippetts, Keith Tippett, Mark Charig, Harold Beckett, Alan Skidmore)

1984 (2)

79	LaVista	Music Press/She's A Razor (stamped plain die cut sleeve)	£60

1919

82	Red Rhino RED 22	Repulsion/Tear Down These Walls (white hand-written labels, 500 only)	£25
83	Abstract 12 ABS 017	Cry Wolf/Dream/Storm (12", p/s)	£18
83	Red Rhino REDLP 25	MACHINE (LP, inner)	£35

1910 FRUITGUM CO.

68	Pye Intl. N(S)PL 28115	SIMON SAYS (LP)	£15
69	Buddah 203 014	GOODY GOODY GUMDROPS (LP)	£15
70	Buddah 2359 006	HARD RIDE (LP)	£20

1991
13	Astro Dynamics ADLP 01	1991 (LP, blue vinyl, clear plastic sleeve)	£20

90 DEGREES
76	Vertigo 6059 155	Little Wing/Slave Trade	£15
76	Vertigo 6060 139	90 DEGREES INCLUSIVE (LP)	£20

NINEY (& DESTROYERS/OBSERVERS)
70	Amalgamated AMG 856	Niney Special/Danger Zone	£40
70	Pressure Beat PR 5501	Honey No Money (with SLIM SMITH)/INSPIRATIONS: This Message To You	£45
71	Big BG 317	You Must Believe/You Must Believe Version	£15
71	Big Shot BI 568	Blood And Fire/Mud And Water	£20
71	Big Shot BI 586	Message To The Ungodly/Message To The Ungodly - Version	£15
71	Gas GAS 167	Blood And Fire/ROLAND ALPHONSO: 33 66	£25
88	Trojan TRLS 263	BLOOD & FIRE (LP)	£15
05	Auralux LUXXLP 009	SUFFERATION (2-LP)	£25
12	Kingston KSLP039	SING IT WICKED STYLE (LP)	£15

(see also Observers)

NING
71	Decca F 23114	Machine/More Ning	£30

NINO & EBBTIDES
61	Top Rank JAR 572	Those Oldies But Goodies/Don't Run Away	£25

9TH CREATION
75	Pye 12138	FALLING IN LOVE (LP)	£20

NIPPLE ERECTORS
78	Soho SH 1/2	King Of The Bop/Nervous Wreck (with glossy p/s)	£40
78	Soho SH 1/2	King Of The Bop/Nervous Wreck (later matt p/s)	£20

(see also Nips, Pogues)

NIPS
78	Soho SH 4	All The Time In The World/Private Eyes (foldover p/s)	£40
80	Soho SH 9	Gabrielle/Vengeance	£30
80	Soho SH 9	Gabrielle/Vengeance (tour copy with 'licensed to cool' stamp)	£30
80	Chiswick CHIS 119	Gabrielle/Vengeance (reissue, p/s)	£15
81	Test Pressing TP 5	Happy Song/Nobody To Love (p/s)	£50
80	Soho HOHO 1	ONLY AT THE END OF THE BEGINNING (LP, with insert, white labels)	£35
87	Soho WIKM 66	BOPS, BABES, BOOZE & BOVVER (LP)	£20

(see also Nipple Erectors, Pogues)

NIRVANA (U.K.)
67	Island WIP 6016	Tiny Goddess/I Believe In Magic	£30
67	Island WIP 6020	Pentecost Hotel/Feelin' Shattered	£25
68	Island WIP 6029	Rainbow Chaser/Flashbulb	£25
68	Island WIP 6038	Girl In The Park/C Side In Ocho Rios	£25
68	Island WIP 6045	All Of Us (The Touchables)/Trapeze	£15
69	Island WIP 6052	Wings Of Love/Requiem To John Coltrane	£25
69	Island WIP 6057	Oh! What A Performance/Darling Darlene	£30
70	Pye International 7N 25525	The World Is Cold Without You/Christopher Lucifer	£20
71	Vertigo 6059 035	The Saddest Day Of My Life/(I Wanna Go) Home	£25
67	Island ILP 959	THE STORY OF SIMON SIMOPATH (LP, mono, pink label, black/orange circle logo)	£300
67	Island ILPS 9059	THE STORY OF SIMON SIMOPATH (LP, stereo, pink label, black/orange circle logo)	£400
68	Island ILPS 9087	ALL OF US (LP, pink label, black/orange circle logo)	£250
70	Pye Intl. NSPL 28132	DEDICATED TO MARKOS III (LP)	£250
71	Vertigo 6360 031	LOCAL ANAESTHETIC (LP, gatefold sleeve, swirl label)	£300
72	Philips 6308 089	SONGS OF LOVE AND PRAISE (LP)	£150
87	Bam-Caruso KIRI 061	BLACK FLOWER (LP)	£20

(see also Patrick Campbell-Lyons, Ray Singer, Pica, Hat & Tie)

NIRVANA (U.S.)
SINGLES
89	Tupelo TUP EP8	Blew/Love Buzz/Been A Son/Stain (12", p/s)	£40
89	Tupelo TUP CD8	Blew/Love Buzz/Been A Son/Stain (CD)	£30
90	Tupelo TUP 25	Sliver/Dive (gatefold p/s, green vinyl only, 2,000 pressed)	£25
91	Tupelo TUP EP25	Sliver/Dive/About A Girl (live)/Dive (12", p/s)	£15
91	Tupelo TUP EP25	Sliver/Dive/About A Girl (live)/Dive (12", repressing, blue vinyl, p/s)	£20
91	Geffen DGCT 5	Smells Like Teen Spirit (Edit)/Even In His Youth/Even In His Youth (12", p/s)	£15
91	Geffen DGCTP 5	Smells Like Teen Spirit (Edit)/Drain You (LP Version)/Aneurysm (12", picture disc, die-cut p/s)	£15
92	Geffen DGCS 7	Come As You Are/Endless Nameless (silver labels)	£20
92	Geffen DGCTP 7	Come As You Are/Endless Nameless/School (Live)	£35
92	Geffen DGCTP 7	Come As You Are/Endless, Nameless/School (live) (12", picture disc, die-cut p/s)	£20
92	Geffen DGCTP 9	Lithium/Been A Son (live)/Curmudgeon (12", picture disc, die-cut p/s)	£20
92	Geffen GFS 34	In Bloom/Sliver (live)/Polly (live) (p/s)	£15
92	Geffen DGCTP 34	In Bloom/Sliver (live)/Polly (live) (12", picture disc, die-cut p/s)	£20
93	Touch & Go TG 83	Oh, The Guilt/JESUS LIZARD: Puss (p/s, blue vinyl, with poster)	£40
93	Touch & Go TG 83	Oh, The Guilt/JESUS LIZARD: Puss (p/s, blue vinyl, without poster)	£15
93	Geffen GFST 54	Heart Shaped Box/Milk It/Marigold (12" p/s)	£15
94	Geffen (no cat. no.)	Penny Royal Tea (Scott Litt Mix)/Where Did You Sleep Last Night (live) (unreleased, 10 test pressings only)	£600
94	Geffen NIRPRO (no cat. no.)	Penny Royal Tea (Scott Litt Mix) (CD, 1-track, no inlay, promo only)	£600
95	Geffen GED 24901	SINGLES (6 x CD box set)	£25

| 11 | DGC B0015411-01 | HOARMOANING (12", brown vinyl) | £25 |

ALBUMS

89	Tupelo TUP LP 6	BLEACH (LP, 300 on white vinyl)	£175
89	Tupelo TUP LP 6	BLEACH (LP, 2,000 on green vinyl)	£50
89	Tupelo TUP LP 6	BLEACH (LP, black vinyl)	£30
89	Tupelo TUPLP 6	BLEACH (LP, mispressing with A side labels on both sides)	£25
91	Geffen DGC 24425	NEVERMIND (LP, with inner sleeve)	£45
92	Geffen GEF 24504	INCESTICIDE (LP, inner)	£15
93	Geffen GEF 24536	IN UTERO (LP, inner)	£40
94	Geffen GED 24727	UNPLUGGED IN NEW YORK (LP, white vinyl with inner sleeve)	£35
96	Geffen GEF 25105	FROM THE MUDDY BANKS OF THE WISHKAH (2-LP)	£25
98	Simply Vinyl SVLP 0048	IN UTERO (LP)	£20
98	Simply Vinyl SVLP 053	UNPLUGGED IN NEW YORK (LP, reissue)	£40
02	Sub Pop 9878700341	BLEACH (LP, reissue, 13 tracks, white marbled vinyl)	£20
02	Sub Pop 9878400341	BLEACH (LP, reissue, 11 tracks, white vinyl)	£15
09	DGC B0013538-01	LIVE AT READING (2-LP)	£20
09	Simply Vinyl SVLP 0038	NEVERMIND (LP, reissue)	£15
11	Geffen/Back To Black 602527779041	NEVERMIND (4 x LP, gatefold sleeve)	£50
11	Geffen/Back To Black 602527779041	NEVERMIND (4 x picture disc, gatefold sleeve)	£80

(see also Foo Fighters, Probot)

NISHI STREAK

90	Wink WR 001	1999/Hypnotise (p/s)	£40
90	Wink WR 001	1999/Hypnotise (12")	£80
91	Wink WR 002	In Love With You/Hypnotise (12")	£40

NITE-LITERS

| 72 | RCA SF 8282 | INSTRUMENTAL DIRECTIONS (LP) | £20 |

NITE PEOPLE

66	Fontana TF 747	Sweet Tasting Wine/Nobody But You	£25
67	Fontana TF 808	Trying To Find Another Man/Stay As Sweet As You Are	£20
67	Fontana TF 885	Summertime Blues/In The Springtime	£60
68	Fontana TF 919	Morning Sun/Where You There	£50
69	Page One POF 149	Love, Love, Love/Hot Smoke And Sassafras (with insert)	£25
69	Page One POF 149	Love, Love, Love/Hot Smoke And Sassafras	£15
69	Page One POF 159	Is This A Dream/Cream Tea	£25
70	Page One POF 174	Season Of The Rain/P.M.	£20
69	Page One POLS 025	P.M. (LP)	£600

(see also Banana Bunch)

NITE ROCKERS

| 58 | RCA RCA 1079 | Nite Rock (Lonely Train)/Oh! Baby | £50 |
| 58 | RCA RCA 1079 | Nite Rock (Lonely Train)/Oh! Baby (78) | £30 |

NITESHADES

| 65 | CBS 201763 | Be My Guest/I Must Reveal | £18 |

NITTY GRITTY

| 86 | Greensleeves GRED 195 | Man In A House/Version/False Alarm/Version (12") | £15 |
| 86 | Greensleeves GREL 93 | TURBO CHARGED (LP) | £18 |

NITTY GRITTY DIRT BAND

68	Liberty LBL/LBS 83122	PURE DIRT (LP)	£30
69	Liberty LBL/LBS 83286	DEAD AND ALIVE (LP)	£25
71	Liberty LBG 83345	UNCLE CHARLIE AND HIS DOG TEDDY (LP, gatefold sleeve)	£20
72	United Artists UAS 29284	ALL THE GOOD TIMES (LP)	£15
74	United Artists USD 307/8	STARS AND STRIPES FOREVER (2-LP)	£18

(see also Kaleidescope, Chris Darlow)

NITZER EBB

| 85 | Own label | BASIC PAIN PROCEDURE (EP, cassette, given away at gig) | £20 |

JACK NITZSCHE

63	Reprise R 20202	The Lonely Surfer/Song For A Summer Night	£30
63	Reprise R 20337	Night Walker/Green Grass Of Texas	£15
78	MCA MCA 366	Hard Workin' Man (featuring Captain Beefheart)/Coke Machine	£15
74	Warner Bros K 41211	ST GILES CRIPPLEGATE (LP)	£20

(see also Date With Soul, Mick Jagger, Captain Beefheart, Randy Newman, Crazy Horse)

NIX

| 82 | Electric Bubblegum EB 102 | Requiem For Mr. Spock/Hoots Mon (no p/s) | £40 |

NIX-NOMADS

| 64 | HMV POP 1354 | You're Nobody (Till Somebody Loves You)/She'll Be Sweeter Than You (demos miscredited to Nix-Nomands) | £60 |

NKENGAS

| 73 | Orbitone OT 005 | DESTRUCTION (LP) | £100 |
| 73 | Orbitone OT 006 | NKENGAS IN LONDON (LP) | £30 |

KWAME NKRUMAH

| 74 | Elegance BB 1011 | THE VOICE OF KWAME NKUMAH OF AFRICA (LP) | £60 |

NMONIC

| 00 | YNR YNR002 | REQUIEM (EP) | £20 |

NO DEPOSIT
| 79 | None | NO RETURN (LP, die cut white sleeve, hand stamped, hand numbered, lyric insert).......**£100** |

NO SUPPORT/LIMPS
79	Matchbox Classics MC 1	OPPOSITE SIDES EP (Split 7" with 2 tracks by Limps and 2 tracks by No Support, p/s) **£20**
79	Matchbox Classics MC 2	ANOTHER MATCHBOX CLASSIC? (Split EP, 2 tracks by Limps and 2 by No Support, with folded p/s).................**£40**
79	Matchbox Classics MC 2	ANOTHER MATCHBOX CLASSIC? (Split EP, 2 tracks by Limps and 2 by No Support, without folded p/s, just die-cut stamped sleeve) **£15**

NOAH HOUSE OF DREAD
82	On U Sound DP6	Murder/Stand Firm (10" p/s).................**£40**
82	On U Sound ON UP LP 20	HEART (LP).................**£40**
86	Noah HEART 2	HEART 2 (LP).................**£18**

RAB NOAKES
78	Ring O' 2017 115	Waiting Here For You/Restless (in p/s).................**£18**
78	Ring O' 2017 117	I Won't Let You Down/Long After Dark (unreleased) **£0**
70	Decca SKL 5061	DO YOU SEE THE LIGHTS (LP).................**£40**
72	A&M AMLS 68119	RAB NOAKES (LP, with Stealers Wheel).................**£25**
75	Warner Bros. K56114	NEVER TOO LATE (LP).................**£15**

NOBELMEN
| 59 | Top Rank JAR 155 | Thunder Wagon/Dragon Walk.................**£20** |
| 59 | Top Rank JAR 155 | Thunder Wagon/Dragon Walk (78).................**£15** |

IKE NOBLE
| 87 | Timeless TRPL 100 | IKE NOBLE (LP).................**£18** |

KEITH NOBLE & RADO KLOSE
| 70 | Eden EDEN LP 14 | MR COMPROMISE (LP,, private pressing, handmade sleeve, white labels).................**£750** |

PATSY ANN NOBLE
61	HMV POP 980	Good Looking Boy/The Guy Who Can Mend A Broken Heart.................**£25**
63	Columbia DB 4956	Don't You Ever Change Your Mind/Sour Grapes.................**£15**
63	Columbia DB 7008	Heartbreak Avenue/I'm Nobody's Baby.................**£15**
63	Columbia DB 7088	Accidents Will Happen/He Tells Me With His Eyes.................**£15**
65	Polydor BM 56054	He Who Rides A Tiger/City Of Night.................**£30**
(see also Trisha Noble)

TRISHA NOBLE
| 67 | MGM MGM 1371 | Live For Life/The New Is Rarely Patchka.................**£20** |
(see also Patsy Ann Noble)

WOODROW NOBLE
| 79 | Baby Mother HIT DD10 | Reggae A The Best (Feat. Prince Hammer)/Strike The Hammer Wild (12").................**£30** |

NOBLE KIND
| 86 | TNK 001 | Back In The Race/Where's Christopher?.................**£15** |

CLIFF NOBLES (& CO.)
| 68 | Direction 8-63477 | THE HORSE (LP).................**£25** |

NO COVER
| 82 | Guardian GRC 136 | 200 Voices/Seen Too Much (some with p/s).................**£200** |

NOCTURNAL EMISSIONS
81	Sterile ION 2	FRUITING BODY (LP).................**£50**
84	CFC LP 2	CHAOS - LIVE AT THE RITZY (LP).................**£20**
84	Illuminated JAMS LP 33	VIRAL SHEDDING (LP).................**£20**
84	Sterile EMISS 001	TISSUE OF LIES (LP, 1st batch numbered, some with 2 inserts).................**£75**
84	Sterile EMISS 001	TISSUE OF LIES (LP, later pressing in blue sleeve).................**£30**
84	Sterile SR 4	DROWNING IN A SEA OF BLISS (LP).................**£50**
84	Sterile SR 5	BEFEHLSNOTSTAND (LP).................**£25**
85	Sterile SRC 003	DEATHDAY (cassette).................**£15**
85	Sterile SR 7	SONGS OF LOVE AND REVOLUTION (LP).................**£15**
86	Sterile SR 9	SHAKE THOSE CHAINS, RATTLE THOSE CAGES (LP).................**£15**
87	Earhtly Delights EARTH 02	THE WORLD IS MY WOMB (LP).................**£20**
88	Earhtly Delights EARTH 04	SPIRITFLESH (LP).................**£20**
89	Earthly Delights EARTH 03	STONEFACE (LP).................**£15**
89	Earthly Delights EARTH 05	BEYOND LOGIC (LP, 250 signed).................**£25**
89	Earthly Delights EARTH 05	BEYOND LOGIC (LP).................**£18**
90	Earthly Delights EARTH 06	MOUTH OF THE BABES (LP).................**£30**
93	Earthly Delights EARTH 08	THE QUICKENING (LP, 250 signed).................**£25**
93	Earthly Delights EARTH 08	THE QUICKENING (LP).................**£18**
(see also Caroline K)

NOCTURNES (2)
| 64 | Solar SRP 102 | Trioka/Rawhide.................**£15** |

NOCTURNES (3)
68	Columbia DB 8453	Carpet Man/Look At Me.................**£15**
68	Columbia DB 8493	Montage/Fairground Man.................**£40**
68	Columbia S(C)X 6223	THE NOCTURNES (LP).................**£30**
68	Columbia S(C)X 6315	WANTED LIVE (LP).................**£30**
(see also Lyn Paul)

NOCTURNUS
| 92 | Earache MOSH 55 | THRESHOLDS (LP).................**£20** |

NODENS ICTUS
87 (No cat no) THE GROVE OF SELVES (Cassette LP) £50
(see also Ozric Tentacles)

DICK NOEL
56 London HLH 8295 (The Same Thing Happens With) **The Birds And The Bees/Birth Of The Blues**...............£20
(see also Nick Nobel)

NOEL & THE FIREBALLS
70 Pama PM 807 **Confussion** (sic)**/We Got To Have Loving** £15
70 Pama PM 808 **Can't Turn You Loose/Skinny Legs** £18

NO FAITH
81 No Faith NF 001 **Double Trouble/Only The Good Die Young** (p/s, private pressing)...............£120

NOIR
71 Dawn DNLS 3029 **WE HAD TO LET YOU HAVE IT** (LP, with insert).......................................£150

NOISE
79 Rok ROK IX/X **Criminal/BLUE MOVIES: Mary Jane** £15

NOISE ANNOYS
80 Adult Entertainment ADD 1 **Tomorrow/BATTERY BOYS: Cheap Local Talent** (p/s, stamped white labels)...................£20

NOISE FACTORY
92 3rd Party 3RD#01 **MY MIND EP** (12")..£20
92 3rd Party 3RD#02 **THE FIRE EP** (12")..£75
92 3rd Party 3RD#03 **ALIENATION EP** (12")..£25
92 3rd Party 3RD#04 **THE CAPSULE EP** (12")...£50
93 3rd Party 3RD#05 **YEAR OF THE LADIES EP** (12")..£18
93 Ibiza IR 026 **Can You Feel The Rush/Run Come Follow Me** (12")..£30
93 3rd Party 3RD#07 **A NEW SOMETHING EP** (12")...£25

NOIZ BOIZ
81 Caveman CMR 03 **Noiz Boiz/Flashback** (p/s)..£30

NO KIDDING
74 Wave **NO KIDDING** (LP) £15

DENNIS NOLAN
90 Blakamix BLKM 003 **Pillow Talk/Killer Thriller** (12")...£15

JOE NOLAN & HIS BAND
69 Jolly JY 013 **Cool It With Reggae/Reggae With Me** £150
69 Jolly JY 016 **Confidential/Poison Reggae** £40
(see also Bonnie Frankson)

TERRY NOLAND
58 Coral Q 72311 **Oh Baby! Look At Me/Puppy Love** £80
58 Coral Q 72311 **Oh Baby! Look At Me/Puppy Love** (78) £25

NAZ NOMAD & NIGHTMARES
84 Big Beat WIK 21 **GIVE DADDY THE KNIFE CINDY** (LP, purple vinyl) £20
(see also Damned)

NOMADS (1)
65 Grampian NAN 1008 **I'm Coming Home/Hey Little Girl** £70

NO-MAN
90s Hidden Art HA4 **Colours/Colours Remodelled** (7", promo, fold-out cover, 8 page press sheet).................£30
90 Probe Plus PP27T **COLOURS** (EP) (12") £35
91 One Little Indian 57TP12 **DAYS IN THE TREES EP** (12") £20
92 One Little Indian 63TP12 **OCEAN SONG EP** (12") £20
93 One Little Indian 83TP12 **ONLY BABY EP** (12") £20
93 Hidden Arts **SPEAK 1988-1989** (cassette) £60
91 One Little Indian TPLP 47M **LOVESIGHS - AN ENTERTAINMENT** (LP)..£20
93 One Little Indian TPLP 057 **LOVEBLOWS & LOVECRIES - A CONFESSION** (LP) £50
94 One Little Indian TPLP 067 **FLOWERMOUTH** (2-LP)...£70
06 Tonefloat TF 24 **((SPEAK))** (LP, 12" blue vinyl, 500 only) £30
06 Tonefloat TF 24 **((SPEAK))** (LP) £15
06 Tonefloat TF 26 **RETURNING JESUS - THE COMPLETE SESSIONS** (3-LP, purple vinyl)................£60
06 Tonefloat TF 26 **RETURNING JESUS - THE COMPLETE SESSIONS** (3-LP) £40
08 Tonefloat TF 48 **SCHOOLYARD GHOSTS** (2-LP, 7" marbled vinyl) £30
08 Tonefloat TF 48 **SCHOOLYARD GHOSTS** (2-LP)...£20
12 Burning Shed BSHED 1201V **LOVE AND ENDINGS** (2-LP, 300 only) £70
15 Kscope KSCOPE 864 **SCHOOLYARD GHOSTS** (2-LP, reissue)..£20
19 Caroline Int. CAROL 020LP **LOVE YOU TO BITS** (LP, blue vinyl) £40
(see also Porcupine Tree, Japan, Blackfield, Steven Wilson, Continuum (2))

NO MAN IS AN ISLAND
89 Plastic Head **The Girl From Missouri/Forest Almost Burning/Night Sky Sweet Earth/The Ballet Beast** (uncedited) (12")...£60
(see also No-Man, Porcupine Tree, Japan)

BILLY NOMATES
20 Invada INV024LP **BILLY NOMATES** (LP, red vinyl, 150 copies) £40
20 Invada INV024LP **BILLY NOMATES** (LP, gold vinyl, 200 copies)..£30

NOMEANSNO
89 Alternative Tentacles VIRUS 77 **WRONG** (LP, insert) £15
93 Alternative Tentacles VIRUS **WHY DO THEY CALL ME MR. HAPPY** (LP)..£40

KLAUS NOMI
81	RCA RCALP 6026	KLAUS NOMI (LP)	£15
82	RCA PL 70229	SIMPLE MAN (LP)	£15

NON
80	Mute MUTE 7	I Can't Look Straight/SMEGMA: Flash Cards (p/s, with 2 centre holes)	£20
81	Mute MUTE 015	NON EP (Rise/Out Out Out/Romance Fatal Dentro Deun Auto) (12", p/s)	£15
87	Mute STUMM 32	BLOOD AND FLAME (LP)	£20

(see also Boyd Rice)

NO NAMES
65	Polydor NH 59080	All Because Of You/She Is Mine	£40

NOOKIE
92	Reflective REFLECT 003	ACCOUSTIC ASSAULT SQUAD EP (12")	£40
93	Reinforced RIVET 1239	RETURN OF NOOKIE EP (12", p/s)	£25
94	Reinforced RIVET 1255	Give A Little Love/Give A Little Love (Manix Mix)/Livin' Inside A Dream/T-Three (12")	£15
95	Reinforced RIVET LP 05	THE SOUND OF MUSIC (2xLP)	£40

NOONDAY UNDERGROUND
00	Guided Missile GUIDE 45LP	SELF-ASSEMBLY (LP, ltd ed., insert, 180 gm)	£30

PETER NOONE
71	RAK 114	Oh You Pretty Thing/Together Forever (first pressing with incorrect song title)	£15
71	RAK 121	Walnut Whirl/Right On Mother	£15

NO OTHER NAME
79	Daylight LD 500	DEATH INTO LIFE (LP, with insert)	£25

NO QUARTER
83	Reel REEL 1	Survivors/Time And Space/Racing For Home (12", foldout p/s)	£40
83	Bonzo Bear	BIRDS OF PREY EP (12")	£30

NORBITON SURFERS
80	Hut S/80/CUS 700	Ivor The Engine/My Ego Dies (DIY p/s)	£30

KEN NORDINE
59	London Jazz EZ-D 19040	WORD JAZZ (EP)	£15
67	Philips BL 7785	COLOURS (LP)	£70

(see also Billy Vaughn & His Orchestra)

NORFOLK & JOY
79	Dara MPA 031	SCOTSOUNDS (LP)	£30

NO RIGHT TURN
83	Chelful CHL 001	NO (LP)	£25

NORMA & TONY
69	(No Cat. No.)	YOU ARE ALWAYS WELCOME AT OUR HOUSE (LP, private pressing, 100 only)	£80

NORMAL
78	Mute MUTE 001	Warm Leatherette/T.V.O.D (p/s)	£15

(see also Robert Rental)

NORMAL DAY
81	BRS 007 ND1	Somebody Said/Angelina, Angelina (no p/s)	£20

NORMAN CONQUEST
67	MGM MGM 1376	Two People/Upside Down	£120

(see also Factory, Peter & Wolves, John Pantry)

NORMAN & HOOLIGANS
77	President PT 461	I'm A Punk/Re-Entry	£20

LARRY NORMAN
76	Solid Rock ROCKY 1	IN ANOTHER LAND (LP, gatefold sleeve)	£15

MONTY NORMAN
63	United Artists UEP 1010	EXCERPTS FROM DR.NO - FILM SOUNDTRACK (EP)	£20
63	United Artists ULP 1097	DOCTOR NO (LP, soundtrack, mono)	£50
63	United Artists (S)ULP 1097	DOCTOR NO (LP, soundtrack, stereo)	£100

OLIVER NORMAN
67	Polydor 56176	Down In The Basement/Drowning In My Own Despair	£150

NORMIL HAWAIIANS
82	Illuminated JAMS 23	MORE WEALTH THAN MONEY (2-LP)	£30
84	Illuminated JAMS 28	WHAT'S GOING ON? (LP)	£30

ROY NORTH
63	Oak RGJ 107	Blues In Three/Blues In Five	£50

NORTHERN LIGHT
75	CBS 3370	Minnesota/Minnesota (DJ Version)	£25

NORTHERN LIGHTS (1)
66	United Artists UP 1123	No Time/Time To Move Along	£50
66	United Artists UP 1161	Through Darkness, Light/Baby Those Are The Rules	£50

(see also Hooten[anny] Singers, Abba)

NORTHERN LIGHTS (2)
79	MPA SMP 077	Bad Girl/Exodus (no p/s)	£25

NORTHERN PICTURE LIBRARY
93	Vinyl Japan TASK 6	Love Song For The Dead Che/The Way That Stars Die (12", p/s)	£18

94	Vinyl Japan TASK 25	**BLUE DISSOLVE EP** (12", p/s) £18
94	Sarah SARAH 94	**Paris/Norfolk Windmills** (p/s, insert) £35
94	Sarah SARAH 95	**Last September's Farewell Kiss/Signs** (p/s, insert) £35
93	Vinyl Japan ASKLP 23	**ALASKA** (LP) £50

(see also the Field Mice)

NORTHERN JAZZ ORCHESTRA
| 79 | SRTY 79 CUS 410 | **THAT'S THE ONE** (LP) ....£15 |

NORTHSIDE
| 91 | Factory FACT 310 | **CHICKEN RHYHMS** (LP) ....£25 |

NORTH STARS
| 66 | Fontana TF 726 | **She's So Far Out She's In/Eeenie Meenie Minee Mo** ....£30 |

NORTHWIND
| 71 | Regal Zono. SLRZ 1020 | **SISTER, BROTHER, LOVER** (LP) ....£350 |

(see also Elastic Band)

NOSEBLEEDS
| 77 | Rabid TOSH 12 | **Ain't Bin To No Music School/Fascist Pigs** (p/s) ....£30 |

(see also Durutti Column, Ed Banger, Blue Orchids)

NO SECURITY
| 89 | Peaceville VILE 11 | **BURY THE DEBT NOT THE DEAD** (split LP with DOOM) ....£18 |

NO SMOKE
| 89 | Warriors Beat WAFT 11 | **Koro Koro/Black Is Black/Koro Koro** (Dub Dance)/(Dub Dance II) (12") ....£15 |
| 90 | Warriors Dance WAFT 17 | **International Smoke Signals** (Dancin Mix)/(Chantin Mix)/**Ra Ra...East Of Eden** (Addis Mix)/(Original Version) (12") ....£20 |

NO SPORTS
| 87 | Unicorn PHZ 49 | **KING SKA** (LP) ....£15 |

NOSTROMO
| 79 | Bronze BRO 12BRO80 | **Alien/Around The World In 60 Seconds** (12", 'Alien' p/s) ....£15 |

NO SWEAT (1)
| 79 | Rip Off RIP 4 | **Start All Over Again/You Should Be So Lucky** (p/s) ....£30 |

(see also Clive Culbertson)

NOTATIONS (U.K.)
| 72 | Chapter One SCH 174 | **Need Your Love/Just Nothing Left To Give** ....£25 |

NOTATIONS (U.S.)
| 76 | Curtom K 56212 | **NOTATIONS** (LP) ....£30 |

FREDDIE NOTES & RUDIES
69	Downtown DT 427	**I Don't Wanna Lose That Girl/Train From Vietnam** £20
69	Grape GR 3010	**Guns Of Navarone/Yester-Me, Yester-You** £50
69	Grape GR 3011	**Babylon/Girl I've Got A Date** £20
69	Trojan TR 7713	**Shanghai/Rome Wasn't Built In A Day** £15
70	Trojan TMX 531	**Rocco/The Bull** (white labels only) £150
70	Trojan TR 7724	**Rocco/Don't Tell Your Mama** £60
70	Trojan TR 7734	**Down On The Farm/Easy Street** £30
70	Duke DU 63	**The Bull/River Ben Come Up** £75
70	Duke DU 68	**Chicken Inn/Chicken Scratch** £15
70	Trojan TBL 109	**UNITY** (LP) £25
70	Trojan TBL 152	**MONTEGO BAY** (LP) £20

NOTHINGS
| 65 | CBS 201779 | **At Times Like This/Love So Sweet** ....£15 |
| 65 | CBS 201779 | **At Times Like This/Love So Sweet** (promo) ....£150 |

NOTSENSIBLES
79	Redball RR 02	**(I'm In Love With) Margaret Thatcher/Little Boxes/Gary Bushell's Band Of The Week** (p/s) £30
80	Bent SMALL BENT 5	**Death To Disco/Coronation Street Hustle/Lying On The Sofa** (p/s) £25
80	Bent BIGBENT 6	**INSTANT CLASSICS** (LP) £50
80	Snotty Snail SSLP 1	**INSTANT CLASSICS** (LP, reissue) £30

NOTTINGHAM JAZZ ORCHESTRA
| 71 | Swift SP 55 | **FESITVAL SUITE** (LP) ....£50 |

NOTTS ALLIANCE
| 72 | Tradition TSR 011 | **THE CHEERFUL 'ORN** (LP, with Roy Harris) ....£15 |

NOUVELLE VAGUE
| 95 | Peacefrog PFG 051 | **NOUVELLE VAGUE** (LP, inner) ....£35 |
| 06 | Peacefrog PFG 079 | **BANDE A PART** (LP, poster) ....£20 |

HEATHER NOVA
| 93 | Big Life BFL LP2 | **GLOW STARS** (LP) ....£80 |

NOVA LOCAL
| 69 | MCA MUPS 377 | **NOVA 1** (LP) ....£40 |

PAUL NOVA
82	Exhibit 1 EX 001	**Julie Ann/Video Age** £60
83	Exhibit 1 EX 002	**Famous Boys/Home Sweet Home** £60
85	Exhibit 1 EX 004	**FANTASY AND FEELING EP** £60
84	Exhibit 1 EX 003	**TREES WITHOUT LEAVES** (LP) £300

NOVAK
| 97 | Enraptured WORM 2 | **Silver Seas/Schmaltz** (p/s in outer hand-sewn cloth sleeve with embroidered "Hand- | £15 |

knitted by Novak" label, 200 only, each different) ....

NOVAS (1)
63   RCA RCA 1360   **Push A Little Harder/Oh, Gee Baby!** **£30**

NOVAS (2)
65   London HLU 9940   **The Crusher/Take 7** **£35**

NOVEAU RICHE
81   Long Vehicle CND 1   **Modern Disease/Soul Boy** (no p/s) **£50**

NOW (1)
69   NEMS 56-4125   **Marcia/The Hands On My Clock Stand Still** **£35**

NOW (2)
77   Ultimate ULT 401   **Development Corporations/Why** (p/s) **£20**
77   Ultimate ULT 401   **Development Corporations/Why** (p/s, blue vinyl) **£40**
79   Raw RAW 31   **Into The 80s/Nine O'Clock** (no p/s, 800 only) **£200**

NO WAY
78   Our Own IS/NW/1035   **Breaking Point/TV Pox/30 Seconds** (p/s) **£200**

NOW GENERATION
74   Trojan TRLS 78   **FOR THE GOOD TIMES** (LP) **£25**
(see also I Roy, B.B. Seaton)

NOYES BROTHERS
80   Object Music OBJ 009/010   **SHEEP FROM GOATS** (2-LP) **£25**
(see also Steve Miro & Eyes, Spherical Objects)

NOYS OF US
60s   KPS KPS 502   **He's Alright Jill/What Can I Do** **£30**

N.R.B.Q. (NEW RHYTHM & BLUES QUINTET)
69   CBS 63653   **N.R.B.Q.** (LP) **£20**
(see also Carl Perkins)

N.S.U.
69   Stable SLE 8002   **TURN ON OR TURN ME DOWN** (LP) **£200**

NU-BIRTH
98   Locked On LOX 97T   **Anytime** (Rhythm Masters Mix)/(Dem 2 Nice 'N' Sleazy Mix)/(Tuff & Jam's Kick
      Dub)/**Original Mix** (12", p/s) **£20**

GUITAR NUBBIT
64   Bootleg 501   **Georgia Chain Gang/Hard Road** (99 copies only) **£45**
60s   XX MIN 705   **GUITAR NUBBIT** (EP) **£20**

NUCLEAR ASSAULT
88   Under One Flag FLAG 21P   **SURVIVE** (LP, picture disc) **£15**
88   Under One Flag FLAG 21   **SURVIVE** (LP) **£20**
89   Under One Flag FLAG 35   **HANDLE WITH CARE** (LP) **£20**

NUCLEAR SOCKETTS
81   Subversive SUB 001   **HONOUR BEFORE GLORY** (EP, folded p/s, 33rpm) **£25**
81   Subversive SUB 002   **Play Loud/Shadow On The Map** **£25**
82   None   **Riot Squad** (magazine flexi-disc with fold out picture insert) **£20**

(IAN CARR'S) NUCLEUS
70   Vertigo 6360 008   **ELASTIC ROCK** (LP, die cut gatefold sleeve, large swirl label) **£200**
70   Vertigo 6360 008   **ELASTIC ROCK** (LP, die cut gatefold sleeve, later 'spaceship' label) **£60**
71   Vertigo 6360 027   **WE'LL TALK ABOUT IT LATER** (LP, die cut gatefold sleeve, large swirl label) **£200**
71   Vertigo 6360 027   **WE'LL TALK ABOUT IT LATER** (LP, die cut gatefold sleeve, 'spaceship' label) **£60**
71   Vertigo 6360 039   **SOLAR PLEXUS** (LP, as Ian Carr's Nucleus, 1st pressing, gatefold sleeve, large swirl
      label) **£250**
72   Vertigo 6360 076   **BELLADONNA** (LP, as Ian Carr, 1st pressing, Matrix side 1, 6360076 1Y//1 1 1 3 Side 2,
      6360076 2Y//1 1 1 3, gatefold sleeve, swirl label) **£250**
73   Vertigo 6360 039   **SOLAR PLEXUS** (LP, as Ian Carr's Nucleus, 2nd pressing, gatefold sleeve, small swirl
      label) **£100**
74   Vertigo 6360 076   **BELLADONNA** (LP, as Ian Carr, 2nd pressing, Matrix side 1, 6360076 1Y//1 1 1 4 Side 2,
      6360076 2Y//1 1 1 5, gatefold sleeve, swirl label) **£100**
73   Vertigo 6360 091   **LABYRINTH** (LP, 'spaceship' label, any with swirl are Italian pressings!) **£60**
73   Vertigo 6360 100   **ROOTS** (LP, 'spaceship' label) **£150**
74   Vertigo 6360 110   **UNDER THE SUN** (LP, 'spaceship' label) **£70**
75   Vertigo 6360 076   **BELLADONNA** (LP, as Ian Carr, gatefold sleeve, 'spaceship' label) **£60**
75   Vertigo 6360 119   **SNAKE HIPS ETCETERA** (LP, laminated sleeve, 'spaceship' label) **£50**
75   Vertigo 6360 124   **ALLEY CAT** (LP, 'spaceship' label) **£100**
76   Vertigo 6360 039   **SOLAR PLEXUS** (LP, as Ian Carr's Nucleus, 3rd pressing gatefold sleeve, 'spaceship'
      label) **£30**
76   Vertigo 9286 019   **DIRECT HITS** (LP, 'spaceship' label) **£40**
77   Capitol EST 11771   **IN FLAGRANTI DELICTO** (LP) **£40**
79   Capitol E-ST 11916   **OUT OF THE LONG DARK** (LP) **£30**
89   BGO LP 47   **ELASTIC ROCK** (LP, reissue) **£15**
14   Timeless TIME 733   **SOLAR PLEXUS** (LP, reissue) **£18**
14   Gearbox GB 1529   **LIVE 1970** (2-LP) **£20**
21   Be With BEWITH102LP   **ROOTS** (LP, reissue) **£20**
(see also Don Rendell & Ian Carr Quintet, Neil Ardley, Centipede, Michael Garrick, New Jazz Orchestra, Linda Hoyle)

TED NUGENT (& AMBOY DUKES)
75   Discreet K 59203   **CALL OF THE WILD** (LP) **£15**
(see also [American] Amboy Dukes)

GARY NUMAN
SINGLES

79	Beggars Banquet BEG 29	**Complex/Bombers** (live) (p/s, 'mispressed' on dark red vinyl)	£18
80	Beggars Banquet BEG 35	**We Are Glass/Trois Gymnopedies** (First Movement) (p/s, custom factory pressings on green and yellow vinyl)	£500
80	Beggars Banquet BEG 46	**I Die, You Die/Down In The Park** (Piano Version) (p/s, mispressing, plays Remember I Was Vapour & "On Broadway" [SAM 126])	£22
81	Beggars Banquet BEG 62	**She's Got Claws/I Sing Rain** (p/s, mispressing, plays Dollar's Hand Held In Black And White)	£60
82	Beggars Banquet BEG 77	**We Take Mystery** (To Bed)/**The Image Is** (mispressed sleeve, no writing)	£35
83	Beggars Banquet BEG 95P	**Warriors/My Car Slides** (Uncut, aeroplane-shaped picture disc)	£400
84	Beggars Banquet TUB 1	**This Is My Life** (unissued promo for "THE PLAN LP", 300 white label test pressings only)	£100
85	Numa NUP 9	**Your Fascination/We Need It** (mispressed picture disc with pictures on the wrong side)	£18
85	Numa NU PROMO 1002	**WHITE NOISE** (12" 4-track sampler Beserker/We Are Glass/Cars/Are "Friends" Electric?)	£30
85	Numa NUM 7	**THE LIVE EP** (12", p/s, custom factory pressing on multicoloured vinyl)	£200
85	Numa NUM 13	**Miracles** (Extended)/**The Fear** (Extended) (12" mispressed sleeve: no red writing)	£30
86	Numa NUP 17	**I Can't Stop/Faces** (Uncut, aeroplane-shaped picture disc)	£100
87	Beggars Banquet BEG 199T	**Cars Extended E Reg Model/Are Friends Electric?/Cars** (E Reg Model)/**Cars** (Motorway Mix) (12" yellow/green/silver labels, export copies p/s)	£25
88	I.R.S. ILSPD 1004	**America/Respect** (live) (mispressed picture disc, 'Gary' picture both sides)	£45
93	Beggars Banquet BEG 246L	**Cars** ('93 Sprint)/**Cars** (Endurance) (Uncut McLaren F1-shaped picture disc)	£175
93	Beggars Banquet	**Cars** ('93 Sprint)/(Multivalve)/(Classic)/(Endurance)/(Top Gear)/(Motorway Mix)/ ('E' Reg Version) (CD, withdrawn, Extended 'E' Reg Model replaces Motorway Mix)	£30
93	Beggars Banquet BEG 264CD	**Cars '93 Sprint)/**(Multivalve)/(Classic)/(Endurance)/(Top Gear)/(Motorway Mix)/**'E' Reg Model)** (CD, Autosports Awards issue, 300 only)	£40
94	Numa NUM 26	**A Question Of Faith** (12", withdrawn, black labels with blue print)	£25
94	Numa NU 26	**A Question Of Faith/Whisper Of Truth** (fan club issue, white label, mail-order only)	£25
96	The Record Label SPIND 6	**Radio** (with N.R.G.)/**Radio** (extended mix) (CD, withdrawn)	£150
17	Electronic Sound 107481	**My Name Is Ruin** (Meat Beat Manifesto Poison Remix) Part One/**Part Two** (p/s)	£20

ALBUMS

80	Beggars Banquet BEGA 19	**TELEKON** (LP, dark red vinyl 'mispressing', with stickered sleeve.; with bonus single SAM 126 "Remember I Was Vapour [live]"/"On Broadway" [Live])	£20
80	Beggars Banquet BEGA 19	**TELEKON** (LP, dark red vinyl 'mispressing', with stickered sleeve)	£15
84	B. Banquet BEGA 55P	**THE PLAN** (LP, picture disc)	£15
84	Numa NUP 4	**BESERKER** (Uncut picture disc)	£375
84	Numa NUMA 1001	**BESERKER** (LP, mispressing, plays Imagination's GOLD on side 2)	£80
86	Numa NUMAP 1003	**THE FURY** (LP, mispress picture disc, "Your Fascination" 12" photo on A-side with lyric insert)	£25
86	Numa GNFCDA 1	**IMAGES 1 & 2** (2-LP, fan club issue with photo inserts, mail-order only, initial signed copies)	£20
87	Numa GNFCDA 2	**IMAGES 3 & 4** (2-LP, fan club issue with photo inserts, mail-order only, initial signed copies)	£20
87	Numa GNFCDA 3	**IMAGES 5 & 6** (2-LP, fan club issue with photo inserts, mail-order only, initial signed copies)	£20
87	Numa GNF CDA 4	**IMAGES 7 & 8** (2-LP, fan club issue with photo inserts, mail-order only, initial signed copies)	£20
87	Numa GNFCDA 4	**IMAGES 7 & 8** (2-LP, fan club issue with photo inserts, mail-order only)	£15
89	Numa GNF CDA 5	**IMAGES 9 & 10** (2-LP, fan club issue with photo inserts, mail-order only, initial signed copies)	£20
89	Numa GNFCDA 5	**IMAGES 9 & 10** (2-LP, fan club issue with photo inserts, mail-order only)	£15
88	Beggars Banquet BBL 47	**WARRIORS** (LP, 'Lowdown' reissue, white lettering on sleeve)	£35
94	Numa NUMA 1010	**DREAM CORROSION** (3-LP, autographed gatefold sleeve; copies bought at HMV with signed 10" x 8" photo)	£20
94	Numa NUMA 1011	**SACRIFICE** (LP, with lyric sheet, stickered sleeve & bonus single: The Seed Of A Lie [5.26]/"The Seed Of A Lie [7.07]")	£40
96	Polygram TV 531 149-2	**PREMIER HITS** (CD, mispressing, plays Mark Knogfler's Golden Heart)	£40
98	Eagle EAGBX025	**THE NUMA YEARS** (5-CD set of Beserker, The Fury, Strange Charm, Machine and Soul Sacrifice.)	£40
03	Jagged Halo JHLP 5	**HYBRID** (2-LP, numbered gatefold sleeve)	£30
06	Mortal Records LP001	**JAGGED** (1,000 only, white vinyl, first 250 copies hand signed, numbered and sold via offical Gary Numan website)	£45
06	Mortal Records LP001	**JAGGED** (LP, 1,000 only, white vinyl)	£25
08	OTB LP1	**PURE** (LP, 300 pressed in purple/red/clear vinyl (100 of each). **Final 2 tracks pressed on separate yellow vinyl 7)**	£35
08	OTB LP2	**EXILE** (LP, 300 copies, turquoise/white/orange vinyl (100 of each))	£30
08	VIN 180 LP 001	**THE PLEASURE PRINCIPLE** (LP, reissue)	£15
10	Vinyl 180 VIN180LP027	**1978/79** (4-LP box set, 500 copies comprising of Tubeway Army/Replicas/The Pleasure Principle and The Plan only for those who had bought earlier reissues of Replicas and The Pleasure Principle)	£90
11	Vinyl 180 VIN180LP038	**1980/81** (5-LP box set, Telekon 2-LPs, and Living Ornaments 3-LPs))	£60
11	Vinyl 180 VIN180LP037	**TELEKON** (2-LP reissue in gatefold sleeve)	£25
12	Let Them Eat Vinyl LETV044LP	**EXILE** (2-LP, grey vinyl)	£80
13	Mortal MORTAL LP 14	**SPLINTER** (2-LP, first issue with limited edition 12" x 12" signed print sold via official Gary Numan website)	£30
15	Beggars Banquet BBQLP 10	**THE PLEASURE PRINCIPLE** (LP, reissue, grey vinyl, 600 copies, gig only)	£40
15	Beggars Banquet BBQLP 19	**TELEKON** (2-LP, reissue, red vinyl, 600 copies, gig only)	£45
21	Ear Music 0216425EMX	**EXILE** (LP, reissue, obi, silver vinyl)	£50

(see also Tubeway Army, Paul Gardiner, Dramatis, Claire Hamill, Radio Heart, Nicky Robson, Paper Toys, Caroline Munro, Generator, Bauhaus, Bill Sharpe, Battles)

NUMBER NINE BREAD STREET
67	Holy Ground HG 112/1109	**NUMBER NINE BREAD STREET** (LP, 250 copies only)	**£400**

NUMBERS
79	Blasto SRTS 79/CUS/358	**ROCK STARS** (EP, with insert)	**£50**

NUMSKULLZ
00	Hombre MEX 018	**AD INFINITUM** (LP)	**£15**

NU NOTES
63	HMV POP 1232	**Hall Of Mirrors/Fury**	**£20**
64	HMV POP 1311	**Kathy/Sunset**	**£20**

(see also Russ Sainty & Nu Notes)

NUNS
81	Butt FUN 2	**Wild/Suicide Child** (p/s)	**£15**
81	Butt ALSO 001	**THE NUNS** (LP)	**£15**

NURON
93	Likemind LM 02	**Likemind 02** (12", 2 tracks by Nuron and 2 by Fugue) (12")	**£60**

(see also Stasis)

NURSE WITH WOUND
83	L.A.Y.L.A.H. LAY 3	**GYLLENSKÖLD, GEIJERSTAM AND I AT RYDBERG'S** (12" EP)	**£40**
87	Crystal/Wisewound WW 01	**Crank/TERMITE QUEEN: Wisecrack** (numbered plain black sleeve with printed band, 500 only)	**£20**
88	Yangki 002	**FAITH'S FAVOURITES EP: Swamp Rat** (with Current 93)**/Ballad Of The Pale Girl** (12", laminated p/s)	**£30**
88	Idle Hole MIRROR 003	**Cooloorta Moon/Great Empty Space** (12", p/s)	**£20**
90	Harbinger 001	**The Burial Of The Stoned Sardine/CURRENT 93: No Hiding From The Blackbird**	**£15**
90	United Dairies UD 031	**SORESUCKER EP: I Am The Poison/Journey Through Cheese** (12", p/s, 2,000 only)	**£20**
90	Shock SX 004	**Sinister Senile: Human Human Human/Psychedelic Underground** (45/33rpm, 1,000 only)	**£25**
92	Clawfist 12	**Steel Dream March Of The Metal Men/The Dadda's Intoxication** ('singles club' release, 33rpm, foldover p/s in poly bag, 1,400 only)	**£15**
93	Clawfist 20	**CRUMB DUCK** (10" EP, shared with Stereolab, 37 with handmade p/s (Gain/Sadier only)	**£100**
93	Clawfist 20	**CRUMB DUCK** (10" EP, shared with Stereolab, 1450 regular without handmade p/s)	**£20**
93	World Serpent WS 7003	**Alien** (1-sided, company sleeve 1,000 only)	**£25**
95	WN 001	**ALICE THE GOON** (1-sided 12", p/s, 500 only)	**£75**
04	United Durtro – UNITED DURTRO/JNANA 1974	**HAVING FUN WITH THE PRINCE OF DARKNESS** (7", p/s, insert, signed by Stapleton, also 'stamped' with image of Stapleton, UK edition of 40 copies)	**£70**
79	United Dairies UD 01	**CHANCE MEETING ON A DISSECTING TABLE OF A SEWING MACHINE AND AN UMBRELLA** (LP, 500 only, originals have hand-painted numbers; beware of bootlegs with printed numbers)	**£200**
80	United Dairies UD 03	**TO THE QUIET MEN FROM A TINY GIRL** (LP, numbered, 500 only, originals have hand-painted numbers; beware of bootlegs with printed numbers)	**£150**
80	United Dairies UD 04	**MERZBILD SCHWET** (LP, numbered, 500 only, originals have hand-painted numbers; beware of bootlegs with printed numbers)	**£150**
81	United Dairies UD 08	**INSECT AND INDIVIDUAL SILENCED** (LP, 1,000 only)	**£80**
83	Mi Mort MI MORT iii	**GYLLENSKÖLD, GEIJERSTAM & FRIENDS, LIVE AT BAR MALDOROR** (LP, some with insert)	**£40**
83	Third Mind TMR 03	**OSTRANENIE 1913** (LP, 3,000 only)	**£60**
85	L.A.Y.L.A.H. LAY 15	**THE SYLVIE AND BABS HI-FI COMPANION** (LP, gatefold sleeve)	**£25**
85	United Dairies UD 110	**DRUNK WITH THE OLD MAN OF THE MOUNTAINS** (LP)	**£25**
85	United Dairies UD 012	**HOMOTOPY TO MARIE** (LP, 5,000 only)	**£35**
86	United Dairies UD 019	**AUTOMATING VOL. 1** (LP, 3,000 only)	**£30**
86	United Dairies UD 020	**A MISSING SENSE** (LP, 1 side only; other side by Organum; 2,000 only)	**£30**
87	United Dairies UD 025	**DRUNK WITH THE OLD MAN OF THE MOUNTAINS** (LP, reissue, handmade custom sleeve, with insert, signed, 100 only)	**£150**
88	United Dairies UD 027	**ALAS THE MADONNA DOES NOT FUNCTION** (mini-LP, 45/33rpm, 3,000 only)	**£25**
88	Idle Hole MIRROR ONE	**SOLILOQUY FOR LILITH** (3-LP box set, 1,000 only)	**£80**
88	Idle Hole MIRROR 1C	**SOLILOQUY FOR LILITH PTS 5/6** (LP, with insert)	**£25**
89	Idle Hole MIRROR TWO	**PRESENTS THE SISTERS OF PATAPHYSICS** (LP, 1,000 only)	**£25**
89	United Dairies UD 030	**AUTOMATING VOL. II** (LP)	**£20**
89	United Dairies UD 032	**A SUCKED ORANGE** (LP, with full colour insert)	**£35**
89	United Dairies UD 032	**A SUCKED ORANGE** (LP)	**£30**
89	Yangki 003	**LUMBS SISTER** (LP)	**£30**
90	United Dairies UD 134	**PSILOTRIPITAKA** (3-LP [UD 01, 03 & 04], with bonus LP "Registered Nurse" [UD 00], 1,000 only, in leather bag)	**£400**
90	United Dairies UD 134	**PSILOTRIPITAKA** (3-LP [UD 01, 03 & 04], with bonus LP "Registered Nurse" [UD 00], 1,000 only)	**£150**
90	United Dairies UD 134CD	**PSILOTRIPITAKA** (3-CD [UD 01, 03 & 04], with bonus CD "Registered Nurse" [UD 00CD], 1,000 only, 30 in 'leather bondage bag')	**£400**
90	United Dairies UD 134CD	**PSILOTRIPITAKA** (3-CD [UD 01, 03 & 04], with bonus CD "Registered Nurse" [UD 00CD], 1,000 only))	**£60**
90	L.A.Y.L.A.H. LAY 30	**BRAINED/GYLLENSKÖLD** (LP, withdrawn)	**£35**
90	United Dairies UD 01	**CHANCE MEETING ON A DISSECTING TABLE OF A SEWING MACHINE AND AN UMBRELLA** (LP, reissue)	**£50**
90	United Dairies UD 04	**MERZBILD SCHWET** (LP, reissue)	**£40**
91	United Dairies UD 038	**CREAKINESS** (LP, with Spasm)	**£20**
91	United Dairies UD 09	**THE 150 MURDEROUS PASSIONS** (LP)	**£30**
91	United Dairies UD 09CD	**THE 150 MURDEROUS PASSIONS** (CD, sealed in black plastic, 500 only)	**£30**
93	United Dairies UD 059	**CRUMB DUCK** (LP, shared with Stereolab, reissue of Clawfist EP, 50 copies on pink vinyl)	**£50**
93	United Dairies UD 059	**CRUMB DUCK** (LP, shared with Stereolab, reissue of Clawfist EP, 500 on fluorescent yellow vinyl)	**£25**

94	United Dairies UD 043	SECOND PIRATE SESSION - ROCK'N'ROLL STATION - SPECIAL EDITION (LP, red vinyl, 500 only) £40
99	United Dairies UD 056	AN AWKWARD PAUSE (2-LP, translucent grey vinyl, 500 only, 1 side not available on CD) £40
00	United Dairies UD 081	ALICE THE GOON (1-sided reissue, 800 copies) £50
02	United Durtro UD 102	MAN WITH THE WOMAN FACE (LP, ltd. edition clear vinyl, poly sleeve, 2 inserts)........... £15
03	United Dairies UD 110	DRUNK WITH THE OLD MAN OF THE MOUNTAINS (LP, reissue) £25
00s	United Dairies UDX 092	SOLILOQUY FOR LILITH (3-CD box set) £30
07	United Dairies UD 08.C	INSECT AND INDIVIDUAL SILENCED (CD, 120 copies numbered with "insect") £90
09	United Dirter DPROMOCD 72	THE SURVEILLANCE LOUNGE/THE MEMORY SURFACE (3-CD) £30
09	United Dirter DPROMDLP71	CHANCE MEETING ON A DISSECTING TABLE OF A SEWING MACHINE AND AN UMBRELLA (2-LP, reissue, box set, T-shirt, badge, numbered, 250 only) £60
09	United Dirter DPROMDLP71	CHANCE MEETING ON A DISSECTING TABLE OF A SEWING MACHINE AND AN UMBRELLA (2-LP, reissue) £35
16	Dirtier DPROMBX119	SOLILOQUY FOR LILITH (4-LP box set reissue) £50

(see also Current 93, Organum/New Blockaders, Diana Rogerson, Sol Invictus, Steven Stapleton & David Tibet, Tibet & Stapleton, Whitehouse)

NU-SOUND EXPRESS LTD.
| 72 | Pye Int'l 7N 25580 | One More Time Y'all/A Rose For A Lady .... £20 |

NUTHIN' FANCY
| 80 | Dynamic Cat DC 1001 | Looking For A Good Time/Too Much Rock'n'Roll (p/s)...................................... £250 |

(see also Terraplane, Thunder)

NUTRONS
| 60s | Melodisc M 1593 | The Very Best Things/Stop For The Music .... £15 |

NUTSHELL
| 77 | Myrrh MYR 1056 | FLYAWAY (LP, inner).. £18 |
| 75 | Myrrh MYR 1029 | IN YOUR EYES (LP, lyric inner sleeve) .... £20 |

MAY'F NUTTER
| 66 | Vocalion VL 9282 | Head Shrinker/Don't Know What To Do .... £15 |

NUTZ
| 75 | A&M AMLS 68306 | NUTZ TOO (LP) .... £15 |

(see also Rage, Nightwing)

NUYORICAN SOUL
| 97 | Talkin Loud 534 451-1 | NUYORICAN SOUL (2-LP) .... £30 |
| 96 | Talkin Loud 578 795-1 | NUYORICAN SOUL (6 x 12" box set) .... £40 |

NYAH FEARTIES
| 86 | Nya DOPLP 001 | A TASTY HEIDFUL (LP) .... £25 |

NYAH SHUFFLE
| 70 | Grape GR 3021 | Sting Ray/Paradise .... £60 |
| 70 | Grape GR 3019 | Boot Lace/Honey Won't You Stay? .... £35 |

ADOMAKO NYAMEKYE
| 82 | YEB YEB 002 | ANO PLAN (LP).. £40 |
| 83 | YEB OLB 506 | KA NEA MAYE (LP) .... £60 |

JUDY NYLON
| 82 | On-U-Sound LP 16 | PAL JUDY (LP) .... £40 |

(see also John Cale, Snatch)

MICHAEL NYMAN
76	Obscure OBS 6	DECAY MUSIC (LP) £40
82	Piano SHEET 1	UNTITLED (LP).. £40
89	VRL VEBN55	THE NYMAN GREENAWAY SOUNDTRACKS (4-LP box set, booklet) £40

NYMONIC
| 00 | Y N R YNR02 | REQIEM (EP).. £18 |

LAURA NYRO
67	Verve Forecast VS 1502	Wedding Bell Blues/Stoney End £15
68	CBS 63346	ELI AND THE THIRTEENTH CONFESSION (LP, gatefold sleeve, orange label) £40
69	CBS 63510	NEW YORK TENDABERRY (LP, orange label) £20
69	Verve Forecast SVLP 6022	THE FIRST SONGS (LP) £15
70	CBS 64157	CHRISTMAS AND THE BEADS OF SWEAT (LP, orange label) £15
71	CBS S 64770	GONNA TAKE A MIRACLE (LP, with Labelle) £20

O

OAK
| 71 | Topic 12TS 212 | WELCOME TO OUR FAIR (LP).. £55 |

(see also Peta Webb)

OAKENSHIELD
| 82 | Acorn OAK 001 | ACROSS THE NARROW SEAS (LP) .... £18 |
| 85 | Acorn OAK 002 | AGAINST THE GRAIN (LP, with insert).. £18 |

OASIS

SINGLES

94	Creation CRE 176	Supersonic/Take Me Away (p/s)	£100
94	Creation CRE 176T	Supersonic/Take Me Away/I Will Believe (Live) (12", p/s)	£80
94	Creation CRE 182	Shakermaker/D'Yer Wanna Be A Spaceman?	£60
94	Creation CRE 182T	Shakermaker/D'Yer Wanna Be A Spaceman?/Alive (8 Track Demo) (12", p/s)	£75
94	Creation CRE 185	Live Forever/Up In The Sky (Acoustic) (jukebox issue, large centre hole)	£25
94	Creation CRE 185	Live Forever/Up In The Sky (Acoustic) (numbered foldover p/s in stickered poly bag)	£70
94	Creation CRE 185T	Live Forever/Up In The Sky (Acoustic)/Cloudburst (12", p/s, postcard)	£100
94	Creation CRE 190	Cigarettes & Alcohol/I Am The Walrus (live at Glasgow Cathouse June '94) (p/s, numbered)	£45
94	Creation CRE 190T	Cigarettes & Alcohol/I Am The Walrus (live at Glasgow Cathouse June '94)/Fade Away (12", p/s)	£70
94	Creation CRE 190	Cigarettes & Alcohol/I Am The Walrus (live at Glasgow Cathouse June '94) (numbered foldover p/s in poly bag)	£45
94	Creation CRECS 190	Cigarettes & Alcohol/I Am The Walrus (live at Glasgow Cathouse June '94) (cassette, flip-top 'cigarette' pack)	£40
94	Creation CRE 195T	Whatever/(It's Good) To Be Free/Slide Away (12", p/s)	£70
94	Creation CRE 195	Whatever/(It's Good) To Be Free (7", numbered foldover p/s in stickered poly bag)	£50
95	Creation CRE 204T	Some Might Say/Talk Tonight/Acquiesce (12", p/s)	£60
95	Creation CRE 212T	Roll With It/It's Better People/Rockin' Chair (12", p/s)	£45
95	Creation CRE 215	Wonderwall/Round Are Way (wraparound p/s)	£40
95	Creation CRE 215T	Wonderwall/Round Are Way/The Swamp Song (12", p/s)	£65
95	Creation CRE 204	Some Might Say/Talk Tonight (7", p/s)	£25
96	Creation CRE 221T	Don't Look Back In Anger/Step Out/Underneath The Sky (12", p/s)	£60
96	Creation CRE 221	Don't Look Back In Anger/Step Out (p/s, with poly outer)	£30
97	Creation CRE 256	D'You Know What I Mean/Stay Young	£20
97	Creation CRE 256T	D'You Know What I Mean?/Heroes/Angel Child (Demo) (12", p/s)	£60
97	Creation CRE 278T	Stand By Me/I Got The Fever/My Sister Lover (12", p/s)	£60
97	Creation CRE 278	Stand By Me/I Got The Fever (gatefold p/s)	£35
97	Creation CRE 282	All Around The World/The Fame (numbered p/s)	£40
97	Creation CRE 282T	All Around The World/The Fame/Flashbax (12", p/s)	£80
00	Big Brother RKID 001	Go Let It Out/Let's All Make Believe (p/s, postcard)	£25
00	Creation RKID 001T	Go Let It Out/Let's All Make Believe/(As Long As They've Got) Cigarettes In Hell (12", p/s)	£40
00	Creation RKID 003	Who Feels Love/One Way Road (p/s)	£25
00	Big Brother RKID 003T	Who Feels Love/One Way Road/Helter Skelter (12", p/s)	£50
00	Creation RKID 004	Sunday Morning Call/Carry Us All (p/s)	£30
00	Big Brother RKID 004T	Sunday Morning Call/Carry Us All/Full On (12", p/s)	£15
02	Big Brother RKID 24T	Stop Crying Your Heart Out/Thank You For The Good Times/Shout It Out Loud (12", p/s)	£40
02	Big Brother RKID 23	The Hindu Times/Just Getting Older (p/s, limited edition)	£40
02	Big Brother RKID 23T	The Hindu Times/Just Getting Older/Idler's Dream (12", p/s)	£60
02	Big Brother RKID 26	Little By Little/She Is Love (p/s, ltd. ed.)	£35
02	Big Brother RKID 26T	Little By Little/She Is Love/My Generation (12", p/s)	£60
03	Big Brother RKID 27	Songbird/(You've Got) The Heart Of A Star	£35
03	Big Brother RKID 27T	Songbird/(You've Got) The Heart Of A Star/Columbia (Live) (12", p/s)	£60
05	Big Brother RKID 32	Let There Be Love/Sittin' Here In Silence (On My Own) (10" p/s)	£40
05	Big Brother RKID 31	The Importance Of Being Idle/Pass Me Down The Wine	£35
06	Big Brother RKID 37	Stop The Clocks EP (2x7", p/s, stickers, numbered)	£50
08	Big Brother RKID 52	The Shock Of The Lightning/Falling Down (The Chemical Brothers Remix) (12", p/s)	£15
08	Big Brother RKID 52/SCD52	The Shock Of The Lightning/Falling Down (The Chemical Brothers Remix) (7" and CD set in 7" x 7" box sold via fan club/mail order, p/s)	£25
08	Big Brother RKID 55	I'm Outta Time/To Be Where There's Life (Neon Neon Remix) (p/s, glossy inner)	£20
08	Big Brother RKID 55X	I'm Outta Time (remix)/The Shock Of The Lightning (The Jagz Kooner Remix)	£15
09	Big Brother RKID 56	Falling Down/Those Swollen Hand Blues (p/s)	£20
09	Big Brother RKID 56T	Falling Down (A Monstrous Psychedelic Bubble Exploding In Your Mind) (5 mixes) (12", p/s)	£30
14	Big Brother RKID 70BOXX	Whatever/(It's Good) To Be Free/Side Away (12", p/s, reissue, mail-order or given away by band website with copies of Definitely Maybe boxed set)	£40
14	Big Brother RKID74T	Acquiesce (1-sided 12" sold by HMV shops)	£35
24	Big Brother RKID 010C	Supersonic/Take Me Away (7", Ltd Edition pearl vinyl, 30th anniversary issue, numbered, p/s)	£20

ALBUMS

94	Creation CRELP 169	DEFINITELY MAYBE (2LP, gatefold, postcard)	£350
95	Creation CRELP 189	(WHAT'S THE STORY) MORNING GLORY? (2LP, trifold sleeve, black inners, postcard)	£230
97	Creation (no cat. no.)	BE HERE NOW (LP, mail-order 12" box set, with The Making Of Be Here Now booklet, 1,000 only)	£200
97	Creation (no cat. no.)	BE HERE NOW (CD, mail-order 12" box set, with The Making Of Be Here Now booklet, 1,000 only)	£50
97	Creation CRELP 219	BE HERE NOW (2LP, gatefold)	£180
98	Creation CRELP 241	THE MASTERPLAN (3LP, gatefold, printed inners)	£200
98	Creation CRELX 241	THE MASTERPLAN (mail-order 7 x 10" single box set, slipcase)	£190
00	Big Brother RKID LP005	FAMILIAR TO MILLIONS (3LP, Limited Edition, trifold sleeve, 1000 only)	£550
00	Big Brother RKID LP002	STANDING ON THE SHOULDER OF GIANTS (LP, insert, gatefold)	£80
02	Big Brother RKID LP25	HEATHEN CHEMISTRY (2LP, booklet, gatefold)	£150
05	Big Brother RKID LP30X	DON'T BELIEVE THE TRUTH (LP, numbered art print, gatefold)	£150
06	Big Brother RKID LP36	STOP THE CLOCKS (3LP box set, booklet, hype sticker)	£200
08	Big Brother RKIDLP51	DIG OUT YOUR SOUL (2LP Limited Edition, gatefold)	£75
08	Big Brother RKIDBOX 51	DIG OUT YOUR SOUL (LP as 4 x 12"/CD/DVD box set)	£100

09	Big Brother RKIDBOX 58	OASIS (8LP box set, numbered, 1,500 only)	£800
10	Big Brother RKIDLP 66	TIME FLIES 1994-2009 (5-LP box set, compilation, 12" x 12" booklet)	£250
21	Big Brother RKIDLP 98	KNEBWORTH 1996 (3LP, tri-fold sleeve)	£30
21	Big Brother RKID 98BOX	KNEBWORTH 1996 (Super Deluxe Box set, 3LP, 2CD 2 Cassette, 3DVD, ephemera)	£150

ALBUMS : PROMOS

94	Creation CRECD 169P	DEFINITELY MAYBE (CD)	£50
95	Creation CRECD 189P	(WHAT'S THE STORY) MORNING GLORY? (CD, with "Step Out", black card p/s, withdrawn, beware of counterfeits)	£45
95	Creation CRECD 189P	(WHAT'S THE STORY) MORNING GLORY? (CD, without "Step Out", black card p/s)	£30
95	Creation C-CRE 189P	(WHAT'S THE STORY) MORNING GLORY? (cassette, with "Step Out", card p/s, withdrawn)	£25
97	Creation CCD 219	BE HERE NOW (CD, black card sleeve, in custom picture sleeve)	£30
98		THE MASTERPLAN (CD, slimline case, p/s)	£35
14	Big Brother OASCTRK1DMC69XXX	OASIS (replica of 1993 cassette demo tape)	£20

ALBUMS : LP REISSUES

09	Big Brother RKIDLP006X	DEFINITELY MAYBE (2LP, reissue, gatefold)	£80
09	Big Brother RKIDLP 007X	(WHAT'S THE STORY) MORNING GLORY? (2LP, reissue, trifold sleeve)	£120
09	Big Brother RKIDLP 008X	BE HERE NOW (2LP, reissue)	£75
09	Big Brother RKIDLP009X	THE MASTERPLAN (2LP, reissue, gatefold)	£40
09	Big Brother RKIDLP 002X	STANDING ON THE SHOULDER OF GIANTS (LP, reissue, gatefold)	£30
09	Big Brother RKIDLP 25X	HEATHEN CHEMISTRY (2LP, reissue, gatefold, 45rpm)	£30
09	Big Brother RKIDLP 51X	DIG OUT YOUR SOUL (2LP, reissue, gatefold)	£25
09	Big Brother RKIDLP30XX	DON'T BELIEVE THE TRUTH (LP, double-sided insert, reissue)	£20
14	Big Brother RKIDLP 70BOX	DEFINITELY MAYBE (2LP/3CD, 7" box set, booklet)	£230
16	Big Brother RKIDLP 85BOX	BE HERE NOW (2LP/3CD/12" white label/7" box set, booklet, postcards)	£300
16	Big Brother KIDLP 009	THE MASTERPLAN (2LP, reissue of 2009 version, 180g vinyl)	£30
18	Big Brother RKIDLP 30XX	DON'T BELIEVE THE TRUTH (LP, 180g vinyl)	£18
19	Big Brother RKIDLP 70PD	DEFINITELY MAYBE (2LP, reissue, Ltd Edition, picture discs with obi strip)	£60
19	Big Brother RKIDLP 70C	DEFINITELY MAYBE (2LP, reissue, Ltd Edition, silver vinyl, gatefold, 25th Anniversary Edition)	£50
20	Big Brother RKIDLP 73C	(WHAT'S THE STORY) MORNING GLORY? (2LP, trifold sleeve, silver vinyl, 25th Anniversary Edition)	£50
20	Big Brother RKIDLP 25X	HEATHEN CHEMISTRY (2LP, reissue)	£25
20	Big Brother RKIDLP 73PD	(WHAT'S THE STORY) MORNING GLORY? (2LP, picture discs with obi strip)	£60
23	Big Brother BLOOD 239	THE MASTERPLAN (2LP, numbered Zoetrope picture discs with obi strip)	£40
23	Big Brother RKIDLP 109C	THE MASTERPLAN (2LP, reissue. silver vinyl, 25th Anniversary Edition))	£30
23	RKIDLP 109CM	THE MASTERPLAN (2LP, reissue. green/black vinyl, Oasis store exclusive)	£40
23	Big Brother RKIDLP 85PD	BE HERE NOW (2LP, reissue, picture disc, 25th Anniversary Edition)	£25

PROMOS : SINGLES

93	Creation CTP 8	Columbia (Demo) (12", 1-sided, white label, 510 pressed)	£1200
94	Creation CRE 176TP	Supersonic/Take Me Away/I Will Believe (Live) (12", company sleeve)	£150
94	Creation CRE 182TP	Shakermaker/D'Yer Wanna Be A Spaceman?/Alive (8 Track Demo) (12")	£120
94	Creation CRE 185TP	Live Forever/Up In The Sky (Acoustic)/Cloudburst (12")	£135
94	Creation CTP 190	I Am The Walrus (Live At Glasgow Cathouse June '94) (12", 250 only, co. sl.)	£750
94	Creation CTP 190CL	Cigarettes & Alcohol (12", 1-sided)	£180
94	Creation CTP 190CL	Cigarettes & Alcohol/I Am The Walrus (live Glasgow Cathouse June '94)/ Fade Away (12", 300 only)	£150
94	Creation CRESCD 190P	Cigarettes & Alcohol/I Am The Walrus (live Glasgow Cathouse June '94)/ Listen Up/ Fade Away (CD)	£30
94	Creation CRE 195TP	Whatever (12", 1-sided, 560 only)	£180
94	Creation CTP 195	(It's Good) To Be Free (12", 1-sided, 360 only)	£150
94	Creation CREDM 001	DEFINITELY MAYBE (4 x 7" box set, in silver cigarette-pack-shaped plastic box, with booklet & interview CD)	£40
95	Creation CCD 169	Slide Away (CD, 1-track Brits Awards issue, 1,000 only; beware of counterfeits)	£30
95	Creation CCD 204	Some Might Say (CD, 1-track, 350 only)	£60
95	Creation CREMG 001	(WHAT'S THE STORY) MORNING GLORY? (4 x 7" box set, in gold cigarette-pack-shaped plastic box, with booklet & interview CD)	£60
95	Creation CTP 204	Acquiesce (12", 1-sided, 570 only)	£80
95	Creation CCD 204P	Acquiesce (CD, 1-track, 300 only)	£60
95	Creation CTP 212	Roll With It (12", 1-sided)	£120
95	Creation CTP 215	Round Are Way (12", 1-sided, 843 only)	£120
96	Creation CTP 221X	Cum On Feel The Noize/Champagne Supernova (Lynchmob Beats Mix) (12", 1,203 pressed, plain die-cut sleeve; beware of counterfeits)	£100
96	Creation CCD 221	Cum On Feel The Noize (CD, picture disc with football motif, no inlay, 500 only)	£250
97	Creation CTP 256	D'You Know What I Mean?/Heroes (12")	£45
97	Creation CTP 278	Stand By Me/I Got The Fever (12")	£50
97	Creation CTP 282	All Around The World/Street Fighting Man (12", black die-cut sleeve)	£100
97	Creation (no cat. no.)	VOX AMPLIFIER BOX (9CD, wooden guitar-amp-shaped box set in outer box, with booklets from "Silver" & "Gold" CD box sets; contains commerical issues of "Supersonic" through to "Don't Look Back In Anger"; in-house giveaway only)	£1200
98	Creation CRELP 241P	THE MASTERPLAN SAMPLER (Acquiesce/Underneath The Sky/I Am The Walrus/The Masterplan) (12" sampler)	£60
00	Creation CTP 327	Go Let It Out (12", 1-track, 1-sided, p/s)	£75
00	Big Brother FITB 001	Fuckin' In The Bushes (12", 1-sided, white label)	£60
00	Big Brother RKID 004TP	Sunday Morning Call (12", 1-sided, flipback laminated p/s)	£50
00	Big Brother RKID 03TP	Who Feels Love? (12", 1-sided, laminated p/s)	£75
01	Own label OASIS 10	10 YEARS OF NOISE & CONFUSION (Columbia/Rock & Roll Star (Live)/ Acquiesce/ Fuckin' In The Bushes) (10", promo-only, custom labels, die-cut sleeve, 200 only, with press release)	£60
01	Own label OASIS 10	10 YEARS OF NOISE & CONFUSION (Columbia/Rock & Roll Star (Live)/ Acquiesce/	£40

		Fuckin' In The Bushes (10", promo-only, custom labels, die-cut sleeve, 200 only, without press release)	
02	Big Brother RKID23TP	**The Hindu Times** (Spike Mix) (12", promo-only, custom logo sleeve, 250 only)	**£50**
02	Big Brother RKID24TP	**Stop Crying Your Heart Out** (Spike Mix) (12", custom sleeve, 250 only)	**£70**
02	Big Brother RKID25TPX	**Hung In A Bad Place** (12", 1-track, 1-sided, custom mauve/pink or brown sleeve)	**£70**
02	Big Brother RKID26TPX	**My Generation** (12" 1-sided promo with union flag sleeve, 800 only).............................	**£75**
02	Big Brother RKID27TP	**Columbia** (Live)/(You've Got) **The Heart Of A Star** (12", custom sleeve)	**£70**
02	Big Brother (No cat. no)	**Songbird** (Demo) (CD-R promo, 25 only)	**£200**
05	Big Brother RKID28TPX	**Can You See It Now? I Can See It Now** (12" 1-sided white label promo, 50 only)	**£500**
05	Big Brother RKID29TP	**Lyla** (12" 1-sided promo, 770 only)	**£60**
05	Big Brother RKID31TP	**Turn Up The Sun** (12" 1-sided promo in card sleeve and inner sleeve. 1,120 only)	**£120**
05	Big Brother RKID32TP	**Mucky Fingers** (12" 1-sided promo in double p/s, 950 copies)	**£160**
05	Big Brother RKID1 NIL	**Meaning Of Soul** (CDR promo)	**£160**
05	Big Brother (No cat. no)	**Cast No Shadow** (UNKLE Beachhead Mix) (C-R promo)	**£30**
06	Big Brother RKIDSCD35TP	**Champagne Supernova** (Lynchmob Beats Mix) (12", promo-only)	**£20**
06	Big Brother RKIDSCD35P	**Champagne Supernova** (Lynchmob Beats Mix) (CD-R, promo-only)	**£200**
07	Big Brother RKID39TP	**Lord Don't Slow Me Down** (12", promo-only)	**£175**
07	Big Brother RKIDSCD39P	**Lord Don't Slow Me Down** (CD-R, promo)	**£40**
14	Big Brother RKID72T	**Columbia** (1-sided 12", reissue sold at HMV shops)	**£15**
14	Big Brother RKID73BOXX	**Cum On Feel The Noize/Champagne Supernova** (Lynchmob Beats Mix) (12" reissue)	**£15**
14	Big Brother RKID73BOX	**Hello** (Demo)/**She's Electric** (Demo) (part of box set, but this price alone)	**£15**

(see also Beady Eye, Liam Gallagher, Noel Gallagher's High Flying Birds, Liam Gallagher John Squire)

OBERON
71	Acorn OBE LPS 1	**A MIDSUMMER NIGHT'S DREAM** (LP, private pressing)......................................	**£1000**

OBITUARY
89	Roadracer RO 9489	**SLOWLY WE ROT** (LP)	**£18**
90	Roadracer RO 9370	**CAUSE OF DEATH** (LP)	**£15**

HUGH O'BRIAN
58	HMV DLP 1189	**TV'S WYATT EARP SINGS** (10" LP)...	**£15**

JIMMY O'BRYANT
60	Heritage RE-101	**FAMOUS ORIGINAL WASHBOARD BAND, VOL. 1** (99 copies only) (EP).................	**£20**
60	Heritage RE-106	**FAMOUS ORIGINAL WASHBOARD BAND, VOL. 2** (99 copies only) (EP).................	**£20**

OBSCURE BY DEGREES
81	Ka KA 10	**I'm Dying/A Woman Like You** (p/s)	**£40**

OBSERVERS ALL STARS & KING TUBBY
75	Attack ATLP 017	**DUBBING WITH THE OBSERVER** (LP)	**£50**

OBSERVERS (1)
71	Big Shot BI 575	**Brimstone And Fire/Lightning And Thunder**	**£20**

(see also Niney)

OBSESSION
82	Wilde Bros SRTS 82 CUS 1344	**Clockwork Man/Hava Naglia**	**£50**

OBTAINERS
79	Dance Fools Dance (No cat. no.)	**Yeh Yeh Yeh/Pussy Wussy/MAG-SPYS: Lifeblood/Bombs** (stickered plain sleeve, 100 only)	**£400**

(see also Cure)

OBX
81	Cara CARA 002	**Sailplane/Breakdown And Cry**	**£20**

OCCASIONALLY DAVID
79	Oven Ready OD 77901	**TWIST AND SHOUT** (EP)	**£20**
80	Oven Ready OD 1/98002	**I Can't Get Used To Losing You** (So I'm Coming Back)/**Will You Miss Me Tonight?** (foldout p/s)	**£20**

OCCASIONAL WORD ENSEMBLE
69	Dandelion 63753	**THE YEAR OF THE GREAT LEAP SIDEWAYS** (LP)	**£50**

OCCULT CHEMISTRY
80	Bikini Girl (no. cat. no.)	**Water Earth Fire Air** (Rough Version) (5" clear flexidisc in stamped envelope with Bikini Girl magazine)	**£15**
81	Dining Out TUX 4	**Water Earth Fire Air/Fire Air Water Earth** (handmade p/s)	**£15**

(see also Twilight Zonerz)

OCCULT PUNK BAND
78	Gaslight GAS 001	**Happy With My Life/Black Mass** (no p/s, 200 only)..	**£15**

OCEAN COLOUR SCENE
90	!Phffft WAVE 1P	**One Of These Days/Talk On** (p/s, promo only)	**£15**
90	!Phffft WAVE 1	**One Of These Days/Talk On** (12", p/s, promo only)	**£20**
95	MCA OCS 1	**You've Got It Bad/You've Got It Bad** (p/s, promo only)	**£20**
96	MCA MCS 40021	**The Riverboat Song/So Bad** (p/s)	**£20**
92	Fontana 512 2692	**OCEAN COLOUR SCENE** (LP)	**£20**
96	MCA MCA 60008	**MOSELEY SHOALS** (2-LP, inners, stickered sleeve)	**£100**
97	MCA MCD 60034	**B-SIDES, SEASIDES AND FREE RIDES** (2-LP, with lyric booklet)	**£80**
97	MCA MCA 60048	**MARCHIN' ALREADY** (2-LP, with booklet)	**£80**
99	Island 546 671-1	**ONE FROM THE MODERN** (2-LP)	**£80**
01	Island 548 686-1	**MECHANICAL WONDER** (LP)...	**£50**
03	Sanctuary SANLP 160	**NORTH ATLANTIC DRIFT** (LP)	**£50**
05	Sanctuary SANLP 332	**A HYPERACTIVE WORKOUT FOR THE FLYING SQUAD** (LP).................................	**£50**
07	Moseley Shoals SANLP 332	**ON THE LEYLINE** (LP)	**£30**
15	Moseley Shoals OCSV3	**LIVE AT THE BRIDGEWATER HALL** (2-LP)	**£50**

17 Moseley Shoals OCSV4RSD **LIVE AT THE HYDRO** (LP, picture disc) **£25**
(see also Boys, Fanatics, Echo Base)

FRANK OCEAN
16 88395801421 9 **BOYS DON'T CRY** (book/magazine in foil wrapper, 2-track CD Mitsubishi Sony and Easy, 500 only) **£150**

OCEAN (2)
89 Baseline BASL 005 **You Are** (To Be Mine)/**Midnight Traveller** (12")...**£40**

OCEANLAB
09 Anjunabeats ANJ-124 **ON A GOOD DAY** (12", p/s) **£80**
(see also Above & Beyond)

OCEANS
80 Record Shack SHACK 129 **Bad Guy, Good Guy/Synth Good Guy** (12" white label)......................................**£40**
82 Record Shack SHACK 129 **Pacific Dreams/Pacific Dreams** (Instrumental) (12", white label, stickered or stamped label)...**£150**

OCEAN WISDOM
15 High Focus HFRT 1002 **SPLITTIN' THE RACKET EP** (12", p/s) **£35**
17 High Focus HFRLP 048 **CHAOS '93** (LP, gold vinyl) **£25**
18 High Focus HFRLP 068 **WIZVILLE** (LP) **£20**

PHIL OCHS
66 Elektra EKSN 45002 **I Ain't Marching Any More/That Was The President** **£15**
65 Elektra EKL 269 **ALL THE NEWS THAT'S FIT TO SING** (LP, 'guitar player' label, UK record in US sleeve).......**£30**
65 Elektra EKL 287 **I AIN'T MARCHIN' ANYMORE** (LP)...**£30**
66 Elektra EKL 310 **PHIL OCHS IN CONCERT** (LP, gold label)...**£30**
67 A&M AML(S) 913 **PLEASURES OF THE HARBOR** (LP)...**£25**
68 A&M AMLS 919 **TAPE FROM CALIFORNIA** (LP) **£25**
69 A&M AMLS 934 **REHEARSALS FOR RETIREMENT** (LP)...**£25**
70 A&M AMLS 973 **GREATEST HITS** (LP) **£18**

OCTAGON MAN
95 Electron TRONLP5X **THE EXCITING WORLD OF...** (3-LP) **£20**

JOHNNY OCTOBER
59 Capitol CL 15070 **Growin' Prettier/Young And In Love** **£15**
60 Capitol CL 15121 **So Mean/There'll Always Be A Feeling** **£15**

OCTODRED
95 Acid Fever MDMA 9501 **BIG FOOT EP** (12")...**£40**
95 Acid Fever MDMA 9502 **DOUBLE DIPPED EP** (12")...**£15**
96 Acid Fever MDMA 9601 **TECHNOLOGICAL ILLUSIONS VOL. 1 EP** (12") **£30**
96 Acid Fever MDMA 9603 **TECHNOLOGICAL ILLUSIONS VOL. 2 EP** (12") **£25**
96 Acid Fever MDMA 9606 **UNTITLED EP** (12")...**£40**
96 Acid Fever MDMA 9608 **PSYCHIK MONK EP** (12")...**£30**

OCTOPUS
69 Penny Farthing PEN 705 **Laugh At The Poor Man/Girl Friend** **£20**
70 Penny Farthing PEN 716 **The River/Thief** **£20**
70 Penny Farthing PELS 508 **RESTLESS NIGHT** (LP, gatefold sleeve, red/black label) **£700**
96 Essex ESSEX 1013LP **RESTLESS NIGHT** (LP, reissue, gatefold sleeve)...................................**£20**
(see also Cortinas)

MARTIN O'CUTHBERT
78 SRTS/78/CUS-114 Esoteric EEE 1 **B.E.M.S** (Bug Eyed Monsters)/**Fragments Of A Possessed Ego** (1st pressing, 1000 copies, push-out centre, folded b/w sleeve with SRTS cat no) **£20**
83 Martoc 001 **FOR ALIEN EARS** (LP)...**£30**

ANITA O'DAY
56 HMV CLP 1085 **ANITA** (LP)...**£15**
56 Columbia Clef 33C 9020 **ANITA O'DAY COLLATES** (10" LP)..**£15**
57 Columbia Clef 33CX 10068 **AN EVENING WITH ANITA O'DAY** (LP) **£15**
58 Columbia Clef 33CX 10125 **ANITA SINGS THE MOST** (LP) **£15**

PAT O'DAY
55 MGM SP 1129 **Earth Angel** (Will You Be Mine?)/**A Rusty Old Halo**.............................**£25**
55 MGM SP 1142 **Soldier Boy/Annie Oakley** **£15**

ODD
84 OK OK 007 **Last Time I Saw You/Look Into My Eyes** (p/s) **£15**

BILL ODDIE
66 Parlophone R 5433 **I Can't Get Through/Because She Is My Love** **£15**
(see also Ricky Livid)

ODDS
80 Double R RED 001 **Saturday Night/Not Another Love Song** (p/s).............................**£15**
81 JSO EAT 1 **Yesterday Man/So You Think** (p/s)...**£25**

ODDSOCKS
75 Sweet Folk & C. SFA 030 **MEN OF THE MOMENT** (LP) **£20**
(see also Bevis Frond)

ODDWORX
98 Sessions SES 002 **BODY LANGUAGE EP** (12")...**£20**

ANN ODELL
73 DJM DJLPS 434 **A LITTLE TASTE** (LP, gatefold) **£30**
(see also Chopyn, Blue Mink, CMU)

ODEONS
80   Ellie Jay EJSP 9480   Maybe Today/5.30 Anthem (p/s) £25
JOE ODOM
69   Capitol CL 15600   Big Love/It's In Your Power £15
AL O'DONNELL
72   Trailer LER 2073   AL O'DONNELL (LP, red label) £20
ALISON O' DONNELL
08   Fruits De Mer CRUSTACIAN
     03   Day Is Done/Frozen Warnings (p/s. coloured vinyl 300 only) £25
(see also Mellow Candle)
JOE O'DONNELL
77   Polydor 2383 465   GAODHAL'S VISION (LP) £22
(see also East of Eden, Mushroom, Rory Gallagher, Jade Warrior)
ODYSSEY (U.K.)
66   Strike JH 312   How Long Is Time/Beware £35
(see also Sons Of Fred)
ODYSSEY (U.S.)
73   Mowest MWS 7002   ODYSSEY (LP) £75
OEDIPUS COMPLEX
69   Phillips BF 1771   Up Down Round & Round/Empty Highways £40
OF MONTREAL
02   Track & Field HEAT 10 LP   ALDHILS ARBORETURN (LP) £20
OFFICERS & GENTLEMEN
84   Gap GAP 001   That's Life And Love/Noise (no p/s) £50
OFFICIAL SECRETS
81   Round RR1   Fooling My Heart/Paradise Time (p/s) £40
OFFSIDE
70   Pye Intl. 25534   Match Of The Day/Small Deal (p/s) £15
OFFSPRING (1)
72   RCA Victor 2198   Windfall/She Lives In A Big House £50
OFFSPRING (2)
84   Offspring Records OP001/
     SRT4K5169   One More Night/Nota Sad Song (this is how it is typed on B-side label)....£30
OFO THE BLACK COMPANY
72   London FL12261   Allah Wakbarr/Beautiful Daddy £75
O'HARA'S PLAYBOYS
67   Fontana TF 872   Ballad Of The Soon Departed/Tell Me Why....................................£50
68   Fontana (S)TL 5461   GET READY (LP) £50
OHIO EXPRESS
69   Pye Intl. NSPL 28117   OHIO EXPRESS (LP) £20
69   Buddah 203 015   CHEWY CHEWY (LP) £15
(see also Joey Vine)
OHIO KNOX
71   Reprise RSLP 6435   OHIO KNOX (LP, gatefold sleeve) £20
(see also Fifth Avenue Band)
OHIO PLAYERS
74   Mercury 6338 497   SKIN TIGHT (LP) £18
74   Mercury 9100 009   FIRE (LP) £18
75   DJM DJSLM 2015   FIRST IMPRESSIONS (LP)..£15
75   Mercury 9100 014   HONEY (LP) £15
89   Westbound SEW 014   PLEASURE (LP, reissue)..£20
89   Westbound SEW 004   PAIN (LP, reissue) £18
BOB OHIRI
77   Ashiko 001   UHURU AIYE (LP) £300
OHR MUSIK
97   Prescription DRUG 2   OHR MUSIK (LP, 99 copies only) £50
(see also Spiral Sky)
OH SEES
17   Castle Face CF-99   Dead Medic/A Few Days Of Reflection (12", blue vinyl)....................£20
16   Castle Face CF-080   A WEIRD EXITS (2-LP, green vinyl) £30
16   Castle Face CF-085   AN ODD ENTRANCES (2-LP, green vinyl and yellow flexi) £25
17   Castle Face CF-093   ORC (2-LP, bone coloured vinyl) £30
OI POLLOI
87   Oi! OIR 011   UNITE AND WIN (LP, with lyric sheet) £15
O'JAYS
65   Liberty LIB 66102   Lipstick Traces/Think It Over Baby £50
65   Liberty LIB 66102   Lipstick Traces/Think It Over Baby (DJ copy) £90
66   Liberty LIB 66197   Stand In For Love/Friday Night £30
67   Stateside SS 2073   I'll Be Sweeter Tomorrow/I Dig Your Act £60
67   Stateside SS 2073   I'll Be Sweeter Tomorrow/I Dig Your Act (DJ copy)......................£100
68   Bell BLL 1020   Look Over Your Shoulder/I'm So Glad I Found You £30
68   Bell BLL 1020   Look Over Your Shoulder/I'm So Glad I Found You (DJ copy)....£50

68	Bell BLL 1033	The Choice/Going Going Gone	£15
72	United Artists UP 35337	Working On Your Case/Hold On	£15
72	Philadelphia Intl. PIR 65932	BACK STABBERS (LP)	£18
73	EPIC EPC 65469	IN PHILADELPHIA (LP)	£15

O'KAYSIONS
| 68 | Stateside SS 2126 | Girl Watcher/Deal Me In | £25 |
| 68 | Stateside SS 2126 | Girl Watcher/Deal Me In (DJ copy) | £50 |

JOHNNY O'KEEFE (& DEE JAYS)
| 58 | Coral Q 72330 | Shake Baby Shake/Real Wild Child (as Johnny O'Keefe & Dee Jays) | £150 |
| 58 | Coral Q 72330 | Shake Baby Shake/Real Wild Child (as Johnny O'Keefe & Dee Jays) (78) | £60 |

(ROGER) EARL OKIN
| 69 | CBS 4495 | Stop And You'll Become Aware/You're Not There At All (as Earl Okin) | £22 |

OLA (& JANGLERS)
| 67 | Decca F 12646 | I Can Wait/Eeny Meeny Miney Moe | £15 |
| 68 | Big T BIG 108 | What A Way To Die/That's Why I Cry (solo) | £15 |

BABATUNDE OLATUNJI
| 73 | Paramount SPFL 289 | SOUL MAKOSSA (LP) | £15 |

O.L.D.
| 88 | Earache MOSH 7 | OLD LADY DRIVERS (LP) | £40 |
| 91 | Earache MOSH 41 | LO FLUX TUBE (LP) | £35 |

OLDEST PROFESSION
| 72 | Midas Private Pressing | THE OLDEST PROFESSION (LP) | £150 |

MIKE OLDFIELD
SINGLES
| 86 | Virgin VSS 863 | Shine (with Jon Anderson)/The Path (uncut picture disc) | £200 |
| 12 | Decca/Universal/UMC 00602537159628 | Music For The Opening Ceremony Of The London 2012 Olympic Games (12", 500 only, numbered, half pink/half blue coloured vinyl) | £150 |

ALBUMS
73	Virgin V 2001	TUBULAR BELLS (LP, gloss laminate sleeve with "130 Notting Hill Gate" address, White/black 'Twin' label)	£40
74	Virgin QV 2001	TUBULAR BELLS (LP, quadrophonic, with model plane noise at the end of side 2, stickered sleeve)	£20
74	Virgin V2013	HERGEST RIDGE (LP, A-1U/B-1U matrixes, poor pressing and many returned, most other "girl/dragon" pressings £5)	£15
75	Virgin QVQS 2043	OMMADAWN (LP, quadrophonic, stickered sleeve)	£18
75	Virgin VD 2502	V (2-LP, compilation, includes long version of 'Don Alfonso')	£20
76	Virgin QV 2043	OMMADAWN (LP, different quadrophonic mix, stickered sleeve)	£18
76	Virgin VBOX 1	BOXED (4-LP box set, with booklet)	£20
78	Virgin VDT 101	INCANTATIONS (2-LP, some with 7" red vinyl of Julie Covington, & poster)	£30
78	Virgin VDT 101	INCANTATIONS (2-LP)	£15
78	Virgin VP 2001	TUBULAR BELLS (LP, picture disc, die-cut sleeve, stereo remix of 1976 Boxed quadrophonic mix; with or without model plane noise)	£15
79	Virgin V 2141	PLATINUM (LP, with inner sleeve & "Sally"; matrix reads "V 2141 B1" or B2, 30,000 copies, withdrawn)	£20
79	Tellydisc TELLY 4	IMPRESSIONS (LP, mail-order only)	£20
84	Virgin V 2328	THE KILLING FIELDS (LP, with 20 page film booklet)	£15
97	Virgin LPCENT 18	TUBULAR BELLS (LP, coloured Dean label, audiophile pressing)	£20
01	Simply Vinyl SVLP 322	OMMADAWN (LP, Audiophile pressing on 180g vinyl, with 2 stickers)	£15
13	Mercury/UMC 374 045-1	CRISES (LP, reissue, Ltd ed. green transparent vinyl, printed inner)	£100
13	Mercury/UMC 374 044-8	CRISES (3-CD, 2-DVD box, 32-page hardback book)	£150
14	Virgin EMI Records 376 069-8	MAN ON THE ROCKS (2LP, g/f, printed inners)	£60
14	Virgin EMI RecordsVirgin EMI Records – 376 069-8	MAN ON THE ROCKS (3-CD box set, art cards, certificate of authenticity)	£30
16	Mercury 474 777-1	THE KILLING FIELDS (LP, printed inner)	£15
16	Mercury 474 779-1	THE 1984 SUITE (LP, printed inner, first 250 with embossed art print if purchased in bundle)	£20
16	Mercury 474 777-3	DISCOVERY (LP, reissue, printed inner)	£15
16	Mercury 570 580-9	COLLABORATIONS (LP, reissue of album only available in Boxed)	£15
17	Virgin EMI Records V 3166,	RETURN TO OMMADAWN (LP, 180g, g/f, printed inner. 24"x24" poster))	£60
23	EMI/Mercury/UMR V 2001RSDLP	OPUS ONE (LP, RSD 23, black poly-lined inners)	£20
23	EMI/Mercury/UMR V 200150LP	TUBULAR BELLS (2-LP, g/f, insert, 50th Anniversary Edition)	£30
23	Mercury/UMR V 200150BD	TUBULAR BELLS (Blu ray, ATMOS, 5.1, quad mixes, insert, Super Deluxe Edition exclusive)	£80
24	Mercury/UMR V2013-50 RSD	HERGEST RIDGE (THE 1974 DEMO) (LP, RSD, hype sticker to left top of shrink)	£25

PROMOS
74	Virgin VS 112	Hergest Ridge (1-sided white label)	£100
75	Virgin VDJ 1	Extract from The Orchestral Tubular Bells/Extract from The Orchestral Tubular Bells	£40
75	Virgin VS 117	Don Alfonso ('A' label)	£15
75	Virgin VDJ 9	An Extract From Ommadawn Part 1/An Extract From Ommadawn Part 2 (On Horseback) (12")	£50
79	Virgin VSDJ 317	Blue Peter (1-sided)	£20
85	Virgin SWALLOW 1	Etude/Moonlight Shadow/Portsmouth/In Dulci Jubilo (p/s, promo-only for "The Complete Mike Oldfield")	£30
87	Virgin CDEP 6	Islands/When The Night's On Fire/The Wind Chimes(Part One)/ Islands (Extended Version) (white gatefold stickered card p/s)	£20

MINT VALUE £

92	WEA SAM 1094	**OLDFIELD V THE ORB: Sentinel** (Total Overhaul/Sentinel Nobel Prize Mix/ Sentinel Orbular Bells/Sentinel 7" Mix (12"))	**£15**
92	WEA SAM 1150	**SENTINEL RESTRUCTURE MIXES: Satoshi Tomii Interpretation/ Global Lust Mix/ TranceMix/Tubular Beats** (12", title stickered red sleeve)	**£15**
76	Virgin QVQS 2043	**OMMADAWN** (LP, unreleased different quadrophonic mix, promo stickered sleeve)	**£30**
76	Virgin V BOX 1	**COLLABORATIONS** (LP, green/yellow label in stamped white sleeve)	**£20**
79	(no cat. no.)	**THE SPACE MOVIE** (4 x 1-sided acetates of unreleased LP containing music from soundtrack to the 'Space Movie' video; includes Orchestral Hergest Ridge, Orchestral Tubular Bells, Incantations, Ommadawn and Portsmouth, some extracts otherwise released)	**£400**
92	WEA WX 2002	**TUBULAR BELLS 2** (LP, stickered sleeve)	**£15**
94	WEA SAM 1477	**THE SONGS OF DISTANT EARTH** (CD in film can, with 2 inserts)	**£100**

(see also Sallyangie, David Bedford, Kevin Ayers & Whole World, Pekka, Lea Nicholson, Tom Newman)

OLD GOLD
70	Trend TNT 56	**It's Goodbye/Teachers Of Electricity**	**£30**

ANDREW OLDHAM (ORCHESTRA)
64	Decca F 11878	**365 Rolling Stones/Oh I Do Like To See Me On The 'B' Side**	**£30**
64	Decca F 11987	**We Don't All Wear D'Same Size Boots/Right Of Way**	**£30**
64	Ace Of Clubs ACL 1180	**16 HIP HITS** (LP)	**£40**
64	Decca LK 4636	**LIONEL BART'S MAGGIE MAY** (LP)	**£40**
66	Decca LK/SKL 4796	**THE ROLLING STONES SONGBOOK** (LP)	**£100**

(see also Aranbee Pop Symphony, Rolling Stones, Cleo, Bo & Peep, Jeannie & Her Redheads, Gulliver's Travels, Mighty Avengers, John Paul Jones)

WILL OLDHAM
97	Domino WIGLP 39	**JOYA** (LP, insert)	**£15**
00	Domino WIGLP 74	**GUARAPERO** (LOST BLUES 2) (2-LP)	**£20**

(see also Bonnie 'Prince' Billy, Palace Brothers)

OL DIRTY BASTARD
99	Elektra 7559624141	**N***A PLEASE** (2-LP)	**£40**

(see also Wu Tang Clan)

OLD SKOOL FLAVA
97	HMB OFF 397P	**VOLUME 3** (12")	**£30**

JOHNNY OLENN & HIS BAND
57	London HLU 8388	**I Ain't Gonna Cry No More/My Idea Of Love**	**£250**
57	London HLU 8388	**I Ain't Gonna Cry No More/My Idea Of Love** (78)	**£60**
59	Mercury AMT 1050	**Born Reckless/You Lovable You** (as Johnny Olenn & Blockbusters)	**£150**

O-LEVEL
78	Kings Road KR002	**THE MALCOLM EP** (red sleeve p/s)	**£750**
78	Psycho PSYCHO 2	**East Sheen/Pseudo Punk** ('map' p/s)	**£175**
78	Psycho PSYCHO 2	**East Sheen/Pseudo Punk** ('schoolboy' p/s)	**£150**
78	Psycho PSYCHO 1	**East Sheen/Pseudo Punk** ('collage' p/s)	**£175**
78	Kings Road KR 002	**THE MALCOLM EP** (photocopied wraparound p/s)	**£150**
78	Kings Road KR 002	**THE MALCOLM EP** (printed p/s)	**£40**

(see also Teenage Filmstars, Times, Television Personalities)

OLIVE BRANCH
68	Wren WRE 1044	**WREN** (EP)	**£15**

JOHNNY OLIVER
56	MGM SP 1165	**Chain Gang/These Hands**	**£25**

OLIVER (2)
74	Olive OL 1	**STANDING STONE** (LP, private pressing, withdrawn blue sleeve)	**£1000**
74	Olive OL 1	**STANDING STONE** (LP, private pressing, withdrawn, later green sleeve)	**£800**
92	Tenth Planet TP 001	**STANDING STONE** (LP, reissue, numbered, 500 only)	**£30**

NIGEL OLSSONS DRUM ORCHESTRA & CHORUS
71	DJM DJLP 5	**NIGEL OLSSON'S DRUM ORCHESTRA AND CHORUS** (LP, with poster)	**£25**

(see also Elton John, Hookfoot, Plastic Penny)

OLYMPICS
58	HMV POP 528	**Western Movies/Well!** (78)	**£15**
58	HMV POP 564	**(I Wanna) Dance With The Teacher/Everybody Needs Love**	**£20**
59	Columbia DB 4346	**Private Eye/**(Baby) **Hully Gully**	**£25**
60	Vogue Pop V 9174	**I Wish I Could Shimmy Like My Sister Kate/Workin' Hard**	**£15**
61	Vogue Pop V 9181	**Dance With A Dolly/Dodge City**	**£25**
61	Vogue Pop V 9184	**Little Pedro/CAPPY LEWIS: Bullfight**	**£20**
62	Vogue Pop V 9196	**The Twist/Everybody Likes To Cha Cha Cha**	**£15**
62	Vogue Pop V 9198	**The Stomp/Mash Them 'Taters**	**£20**
62	Vogue Pop V 9204	**Baby It's Hot/The Scotch**	**£25**
64	Sue WI 348	**The Bounce/Fireworks**	**£40**
65	Warner Bros WB 157	**Good Lovin'/Olympic Shuffle**	**£15**
66	Fontana TF 678	**We Go Together** (Pretty Baby)**/Secret Agents**	**£20**
66	Fontana TF 778	**Baby, Do The Philly Dog/Western Movies**	**£20**
69	Action ACT 4539	**Baby, Do The Philly Dog/Mine Exclusively**	**£20**
70	Action ACT 4556	**I'll Do A Little Bit More/Same Old Thing**	**£40**
61	Vocalion VAH 8059	**DANCE BY THE LIGHT OF THE MOON** (LP)	**£100**
67	London HA-M 8327	**SOMETHING OLD, SOMETHING NEW** (LP, unissued)	**£0**
67	Fontana TL 5407	**SOMETHING OLD, SOMETHING NEW** (LP)	**£60**
72	Jay Boy JSX 2008	**THE OLYMPICS** (LP)	**£20**

(see also Cappy Lewis)

OMEGA RED STAR
69 Decca LK/SKL 4974 **OMEGA RED STAR** (LP, unboxed Decca on label) £250

OMEGA TRIBE
82 Crass 221984/10 **ANGRY SONGS** (EP)..£15
83 Corpus Christi CHRIST O5 **NO LOVE LOST** (LP, inner)...£30
00 Rugger Bugger SEEP 018LP **MAKE TEA NOT WAR** (LP, printed inner sleeve)..............................£15
(see also Pete Fender)

OMEGA (1)
75 Decca SKL-R 5219 **HALL OF FLOATERS IN THE SKY** (LP)......................................£20
76 Decca SKL-R 5243 **TIME ROBBER** (LP) £20

OMEGA (2)
85 Rock Machine MACH 1 **THE PROPHET** (LP) £35

OMEN
69 Ackee ACK 102 **Don't Leave Me Never/No More** £20

OMEN SEARCHER
82 OCS 001 **Too Much/Teacher Of Sin** (p/s).......................................£50
82 OCS 002 **Teacher Of Sin/Too Much** (p/s).......................................£50

OMENKA BROTHERS
77 Ashiko **MR CROOKED CHIAUOTU** (LP)....................................£35

OMERTA
05 Northern Ambition NAM 007 **Everyone Is Frozen/Learn To Love The System** (p/s) £70
05 Northern Ambition NAM 008 **One Chance/Synchronise Your Smiles** (p/s)........................£50
06 Northern Ambition NAM 0011 **One More Minute/Follow Me Down** (p/s)......................£40
(see also Slow Readers Club)

OMNI TRIO
93 Moving Shadow SHADOW 32 **MYSTIC STEPPERS VOL 2** (12" EP)........................£15
93 Moving Shadow SHADOW 36 **RENEGADE SNARES VOL 3** (EP)..........................£25
95 Moving Shadow ASHADOWLP 1 **THE DEEPEST CUT VOL. 1** (2-LP) £30
96 Moving Shadow ASHADOWLP 6 **HAUNTED SCIENCE** (2-LP) £30
99 Moving Shadow ASHADOW 20LP **BYTE SIZED LIFE** (4-LP) £25
01 Moving Shadow ASHADOW 25 LP **EVEN ANGELS CAST SHADOWS** (2-LP)..............£25

OMNIA OPERA
93 Delerium DELEC LP 011 **OMNIA OPERA** (LP)...£30
97 Delerium DELECLP 044 **RED SHIFT** (LP) £20

ON A FRIDAY
86 OAF (no cat no) **ON A FRIDAY** (11-track demo cassette) £300
88 (No label or cat no) **Happy Song/To Be A Brilliant Light/Sinking Ship** (cassette) ...£250
90 (No label or cat no) **THE GREAT SHINDIG** (Cassette, 15 tracks, as SHINDIG) £250
91 (No label or cat no) **What Is That You Say?/Stop Whispering** (Demo)/**Give It Up** (Cassette, 3 known different cover inlays) £250
91 (No label or cat no) **I Can't** (Demo)/**Nothing Touches Me/Thinking About You** (EP Version)/**Phillipa Chicken/You** (Demo) (Cassette, known as "Manic hedgehog" demos) £250
(see also Radiohead)

ONDATROPICA
12 Soundway SNDWLP 045 **ONDATROPICA** (3LP, 7", gatefold, booklet)................£30
17 Soundway SNDWLP 092 **BAILE BUCANERO** (2LP, gatefold, printed inners) £20

ONE
69 Fontana STL 5539 **ONE** (LP, gatefold sleeve, black/silver label) £300

ONE & ONE
64 Decca F 11948 **I'll Give You Lovin'/It's Me** £15
(see also Ivy League)

ONE EYED JACKS (2)
78 Pennine PSS 154 **TAKE AWAY** (LP, in "One Eyed Jacks" brown paper carrier bag)....£25
78 Pennine PSS 154 **TAKE AWAY** (LP)..£20

ONE GANG LOGIC
79 Stark 1 **Alienate/Queue Here/Repeat Action/Who Killed Sex** (numbered p/s) £15

ONE HIT WONDERS
72 CBS 7760 **Hey Hey Jump Now/Goodbye**.......................£18

101'ERS
76 Chiswick (N)S 3 **Keys To Your Heart/5 Star Rock & Rock Petrol** (with p/s)....£50
79 Big Beat NS 3 **Keys To Your Heart/5 Star Rock & Rock Petrol** (reissue, with p/s)....£20
79 Big Beat NS 3 **Keys To Your Heart/5 Star Rock & Rock Petrol** £15
80 Big Beat NS 63 **Sweet Revenge/Rabies** (From The Dogs Of Love) (p/s)....£15
81 Andalucia AND 101 **ELGIN AVENUE BREAKDOWN** (LP, gatefold flip back sleeve with booklet)....£40
81 Andalucia AND 101 **ELGIN AVENUE BREAKDOWN** (LP, without booklet)........£25
05 Andalucia 0825646170035 **ELGIN AVENUE BREAKDOWN REVISITED** (2-LP, red vinyl)....£30
(see also Clash, Alvaro, Aquila)

100% PROOF
80	Smile SR 929	NEW WAY OF LIVIN' (EP) £25
81	Myrrh MYR 1107	100% PROOF (LP, with insert) £50

100% PURE POISON
74	EMI Untl. 501	You Keep Coming Back/(And When I Said) I Love You £20
77	EMI Intl. INS 3001	COMING RIGHT AT YOU (LP) £150

ONE IN A MILLION
67	CBS 202513	Use Your Imagination/Hold On £250
67	MGM MGM 1370	Fredereek Hernando/Double Sight £1000

(see also Thunderclap Newman)

1 SYNTAX 1
84	Proteus PRT 101	Negatives/Feel No Touch (p/s) £25

ONE BLOOD
81	One Blood NKRLP 001	IN LOVE (LP) £18
82	One Blood NKRLP 002	SUPER SHOWCASE (LP) £15

ONE CUT
98	Hombre MEX 006	CUT COMMANDER (12" EP, Banksy artwork) £400
00	Hombre MEX 016	UNDERGROUND TERROR TACTICS (12" EP Banksy artwork).............. £300
00	Hombre MEX 029	MR X/RHYTHM GEOMETARY (12" EP, Banksy artwork) £400
00	Hombre MEX 024	GRAND THEFT AUTO (2-LP, Banksy artwork) £200

MATTY O'NEIL
54	London L 1037	Don't Sell Daddy Any More Whiskey/Little Rusty (gold label, tri-centre) £30
54	London L 1037	Don't Sell Daddy Any More Whiskey/Little Rusty (silver label, tri-centre)......£15

ONE LOVE
77	Lightning TRO 9025	The Slave Trade/Roots £25

ONE TAKES
80	No Choice NC 001	Accident/Street Kid/Backdoor Dump/Eviction Orders (p/s) £20

1,000 VIOLINS
85	Dreamworld DREAM 2	Halcyon Days/I Remember When Everybody Used To Ride Bikes ... Now We All Drive Cars (12", p/s, 1,000 only) £20
87	Dreamworld DREAM 14	Locked Out Of The Love-In (p/s) £15
89	Immaculate 12 IMMAC 9	If Only Words (Would Let Me Conquer You)/Orange Sunshine Ride/I Left My Mind In San Francisco (12", p/s) £20
88	Immaculate IMMACLP 1	HEY MAN, THAT'S BEAUTIFUL (LP) £20
00	Vinyl Japan ASKLP 119	LIKE ONE THOUSAND VIOLINS (LP) £20

(see also Page Boys)

ONE TIME SYNCOPATED CODPIECE
71	Jon Hassell HASLP 1195	ONCE MORE WITH FEELING (LP, insert).. £100

ONE TWO & THREE
65	Decca F 12093	Black Pearl/Bahama Lullaby £15
65	Decca LK 4682	BLACK PEARLS AND GREEN DIAMONDS (LP) £200

ONE WAY SYSTEM
83	Anagram GRAM 003	ALL SYSTEMS GO (LP, with lyric inner) £15
83	Anagram GRAM 008	WRITING ON THE WALL (LP, with lyric inner) £15

ONE WAY TICKET
78	President PTLS 1069	TIME IS RIGHT (LP).. £200

(see also Five Day Rain)

ONLOOKERS
82	Demon D 1012	You And I/Understand/Julia (p/s) £18

ONLY ONES
78	CBS S CBS 6228	Another Girl, Another Planet/Special View (p/s, paper labels).............. £60
78	CBS S CBS 6228	Another Girl, Another Planet/Special View (p/s, injection moulded labels)...... £40
78	CBS S CBS 12-6576	Another Girl, Another Planet/As My Wife Says (12", p/s) £20
79	CBS S CBS 7963	Trouble In The World/Your Chosen Life (withdrawn 'group' black & red p/s) £350
78	CBS 82830	THE ONLY ONES (LP, orange label, with insert) £30
79	CBS 83451	EVEN SERPENTS SHINE (LP, gold embossed sleeve, orange label) £20
80	CBS 84089	BABY'S GOT A GUN (LP, with insert, orange label) £20
89	Strange Fruit SFRLP 102	PEEL SESSIONS ALBUM (LP)... £15
07	Pure Pleasure PPAN 82830	THE ONLY ONES (LP, reissue 180gm vinyl) £15

(see also England's Glory)

SEIGEN ONO
88	Venture VE10	CHINESE GREEN TABLE (LP) £15
88	Venture VE 51	COMMES DES GARCONS VOLUME 1 (LP) £40
89	Venture VE 52	COMMES DES GARCONS VOLUME 2 (LP) £40

YOKO ONO
81	Geffen K 99164	SEASON OF GLASS £15
16	Manimal Vinyl Records MANI-LP-066	YES, I'M A WITCH TOO £30
71	Apple APPLE 38	Mrs. Lennon/Midsummer New York £20
72	Apple APPLE 41	Mind Train/Listen, The Snow Is Falling (p/s)...................................... £25
73	Apple APPLE 47	Death Of Samantha/Yang Yang £20
73	Apple APPLE 48	Run Run Run/Men Men Men £20
70	Apple SAPCOR 17	YOKO ONO/PLASTIC ONO BAND (LP, with inner sleeve)...................... £60
71	Apple SAPTU 101/2	FLY (2-LP, laminated gatefold, inner sleeves, poster & postcard)........£100

73	Apple SAPDO 1001	APPROXIMATELY INFINITE UNIVERSE (2-LP, with lyric inner sleeves)	£40
73	Apple SAPCOR 26	FEELING THE SPACE (LP)	£40

(see also John Lennon, Bill Elliott & Elastic Oz Band)

ON 1 CREW
93	Bump BUST 3	LET EM AVE IT EP (12")	£40
93	Bump BUST 4	SINISTER BY DESIGN EP (12")	£30

ONSLAUGHT (1)
85	Children Of The Revolution GURT 2	POWER FROM HELL (LP, with inner)	£20

ONSLAUGHT (2)
85	69 Records SRTSK 5375	My Generation/Angel Of Mercy	£15

ON THE CARDS
84	OTC 001	This Is My Home Town/All In Vain	£18

ON THE WATERFRONT
86	Wizz	The Kids Are Allright/Never Surrender/Far From The Madding Crowd/Mrs. Harrington (12", p/s)	£60

ONYX
68	Pye 7N 17477	You've Gotta Be With Me/It's All Put On	£30
68	Pye 7N 17622	My Son John/Step By Step	£30
69	Pye 7N 17768	Tamaris Khan/So Sad Inside	£70
69	CBS 4635	Time Off/Movin' In	£20

OO BANG JIGGLY JANG
71	President PT 356	Hanging Tree/1000 Leagues	£15

OPAL
85	One Big Guitar OBG 002T	Northern Line/Empty Bottles/Soul Giver (12")	£15
87	Rough Trade RTT 129	Fell From The Sun/Freight Train/Grains Of Sand (12")	£15
87	Rough Trade ROUGH 116	HAPPY NIGHTMARE BABY (LP)	£30
89	Rough Trade ROUGH 128	EARLY RECORDINGS (LP)	£30

(see also Mazzy Star)

OPAL BUTTERFLY
68	CBS 3576	Beautiful Beige/Speak Up	£60
69	CBS 3921	Mary Anne With The Shakey Hand/My Gration Or?	£75
70	Polydor 2058 041	You're A Groupie Girl/Gigging Song	£75

(see also Hawkwind, Motorhead, Mott The Hoople)

JACKIE OPEL
63	Jump Up JU 512	TV In Jamaica/Worrell's Captaincy	£25
64	Black Swan WI 421	You're No Good/King Liges	£40
64	R&B JB 138	Stand By Me (as Jackie Opel & Hortense Ellis)/Solid Rock	£50
65	King KG 1011	Cry Me A River/Eternal Love	£30
64	R&B JB 160	Pity The Fool/The Day Will Come	£50
65	Island WI 203	Wipe Those Tears/Don't Take Your Love	£30
65	Island WI 209	Go Whey/Shelter The Storm	£250
65	Island WI 227	Old Rockin' Chair/SKATALITES: Song Of Love (B-side is actually "Ska In Vienna Woods")	£250
65	Ska Beat JB 190	Done With A Friend/More Wood In The Fire	£40
65	Ska Beat JB 227	The Lord Is With/A Little More (beware of counterfeits)	£150
66	Island WI 264	A Love To Share/ROLAND ALPHONSO: Devoted To You	£25
66	Rio R 117	I Am What I Am/JACKIE MITTOO & SKATALITES: Devil's Bug	£60
66	Rio R120	I Don't Want Her/SOUL BOYS: Rudie Get Wise	£60

(see also Jackie & Doreen, Doreen & Jackie, Hortense & Jackie)

OPEN CASKET
73	Royal RY1	Turning To The Sun/She Can Leave Now	£30

OPEN HOUSE
72	Nest NRS 102A	Mr Sparky/My Song	£40

OPEN MIND
69	Philips BF 1805	Magic Potion/Cast A Spell (Demo copy)	£500
69	Philips BF 1790	Horses And Chariots/Before My Time	£100
69	Philips BF 1805	Magic Potion/Cast A Spell	£600
69	Philips SBL 7893	OPEN MIND (LP, laminated sleeve, black/silver label)	£1000
86	Antar ANTAR 2	OPEN MIND (LP, reissue)	£20

(see also Drag Set)

OPEN ROAD
71	Greenwich GSLP 1001	WINDY DAZE (LP, gatefold sleeve)	£60

(see also Warm Sounds, Denny Gerrard, Donovan)

OPERA
79	Bead records BEAD 13	OPERA (LP)	£25

OPETH
01	Music For Nations MFSN 264	BLACKWATER PARK (2-LP)	£90
02	Peaceville DLPVILE 78	STILL LIFE (2-LP, 1000 only)	£60
03	Music For Nations MFSN 294	DAMNATION (LP)	£100
10	Peaceville VILLELP 78	STILL LIFE (2-LP, reissue, 2000 only)	£50

OPPRESSED
83	Oppressed OPPO 1	Work Together/Victims (p/s)	£20

MINT VALUE £

83	Firm NICK 1	NEVER SAY DIE (EP)	£18
84	Oppressed OPLP 1	OI! OI! MUSIC (LP)	£20
85	Skinhead CREW 1	FATAL BLOW (LP)	£20
88	OIR 12	DEAD AND BURIED (LP)	£15

(see also Rude Boys (2))

OPTIMISTS
81	Armageddon AS 018	Mull Of Kintyre/The Plumbers Song (p/s)	£18

OPUS
70	Columbia DB 8675	Baby, Come On/Angela Grey	£15

ORA
69	Tangerine OPLOP 0025	ORA (LP)	£350

(see also Byzantium, Movies)

ORAL
82	Conquest Quest 6	SEX (LP)	£20

ORAL EXCITERS
79	Three Elms TE 001	It's A Holiday/Tonight (p/s, 500 only)	£60

DAPHNE ORAM
62	HMV 7EG8762	LISTEN, MOVE AND DANCE 3 - ELECTRONIC SOUND PATTERNS (EP)	£30
62	HMV CLP 3531	LISTEN MOVE AND DANCE 1-3 (LP)	£40
72	HMS CLP 3762	LISTEN MOVE AND DANCE 1-3 (LP, reissue)	£30
10	Young Americans YOUNGAM 001	ORAMICS (4-LP)	£30
11	Young Americans YOUNGAM 003	THE ORAM TAPES VOLUME ONE (4-LP)	£35
13	Young Americans YOUNGAM 001	ORAMICS (4-LP, repressing, clear vinyl)	£40
14	Ecstatic ELP 005	SOUND HOUSES (LP)	£15
19	Young Americans YOUNGAM 001	ORAMICS (4-LP, repressing, clear vinyl, '2019 Edition' sticker on front)	£30

.O. RANG
94	Echo ECSY 6	SPOOR (12", p/s)	£15
94	Echo ECHLP 2	HEARD OF INSTINCT (LP, booklet)	£70
97	Echo ECHLP 10	FIELDS AND WAVES (2LP, gatefold)	£80

(see also Talk Talk, Rustin Man, Beth Gibbons & Rustin Man)

ORANGE BICYCLE
67	Columbia DB 8259	Hyacinth Threads/Amy Peate	£35
67	Columbia DB 8311	Laura's Garden/Lavender Girl	£25
68	Columbia DB 8352	Early Pearly Morning/Go With Goldie	£20
68	Columbia DB 8413	Jenskadajka/Nicely	£18
68	Columbia DB 8483	Sing This All Together/Trip On An Orange Bicycle	£25
69	Parlophone R 5789	Tonight I'll Be Staying Here With You/Last Cloud Home	£15
69	Parlophone R 5811	Carry That Weight/You Never Give Me Your Money/Want To B Side	£18
70	Parlophone R 5827	Take Me To The Pilot/It's Not My World	£20
70	Parlophone R 5854	Jelly On The Bread/Make It Rain	£20
71	Regal Zonophone RZ 3029	Goodbye Stranger/Country Comforts	£15
70	Parlophone PCS 7108	ORANGE BICYCLE (LP, laminated front sleeve, black/silver label)	£250
88	Morgan Bluetown MBT 5003	LET'S TAKE A TRIP ON AN ORANGE BICYCLE (LP)	£15
11	Morgan Bluetown BT 5007	ORANGE BICYCLE (LP, reissue, 500 only, orange vinyl, with numbered certificate)	£20

(see also Motherlight)

ORANGE BLOSSOM
74	Westwood WRS 038	KEEP ON PUSHING (LP)	£30

ORANGE DISASTER
80s	Neuter OD 1	Something's Got To Give/Out Of The Room/Hiding From Frank	£20

(see also Varicose Veins)

ORANGE GOBLIN
00	The Music Cartel TMC 036LP	THE BIG BLACK (LP)	£20
04	Rise Above RISELP 46	THIEVING FROM THE HOUSE OF GOD (LP, orange vinyl, 1000 only)	£25
07	Mayan MYNLP 058	HEALING THROUGH FIRE (LP)	£18
12	Back On Black BOBV 289LP	A EULOGY FOR THE DAMNED (LP, gatefold, merchandise insert, clear vinyl)	£20

ORANGE JUICE
80	Postcard 80-1	Falling And Laughing/Moscow Olympics/Moscow (foldover p/s in poly bag, with postcard; and with flexidisc "Felicity (live)" [I Wish I Was A Postcard 1], 963 only)	£400
80	Postcard 80-1	Falling And Laughing/Moscow Olympics/Moscow (foldover p/s in poly bag, without postcard and without flexidisc)	£100
80	I Wish I Was A Postcard 1	Felicity (live) (freebie flexidisc, also given away with fanzines)	£15
80	Postcard 80-2	Blue Boy/Lovesick (hand-coloured p/s in poly bag, blue labels)	£60
80	Postcard 80-2	Blue Boy/Love Sick (b/w and yellow labels/cream company sleeve)	£18
80	Postcard 80-2	Blue Boy/Love Sick (3rd issue, brown labels in brown company sleeve)	£15
80	Postcard 80-6	Simply Thrilled Honey/Breakfast Time (p/s with picture insert in poly bag)	£65
81	Postcard 81-2	Poor Old Soul/Poor Old Soul Pt. 2 (die-cut co. sleeve, with postcard)	£30
82	Polydor OJ 1	A Million Pleading Faces/Breakfast Time (12" promo in title sleeve)	£15
82	Polydor POLS 1057	YOU CAN'T HIDE YOUR LOVE FOREVER (LP, inner)	£25
82	Polydor POLS 1076	RIP IT UP (LP)	£25
84	Polydor 8237961	THE ORANGE JUICE (LP)	£15
92	Postcard DUBH 922	OSTRICH CHURCHYARD (LP, 1,000 with inner sleeve, bonus 10" "Irritation Disc" [922TEN])	£40

| 93 | Postcard DUBH 932 | THE HEATHER'S ON FIRE (LP)..£60 |
| 10 | Domino REWIGCD38X | ...COALS TO NEWCASTLE (7-CD box set)..£30 |

(see also Edwyn Collins, Fun Four, Josef K)

ORANGE MACHINE
| 68 | Pye 7N 17559 | Three Jolly Little Dwarfs/Real Life Permanent Dream ....£200 |
| 69 | Pye 7N 17680 | You Can All Join In/Dr. Crippen's Waiting Room..£175 |

(see also Danny Hughes)

ORANGE PEEL
| 71 | Reflection HRS 5 | I Got No Time/Searching For A Place To Hide...£25 |

ORANGE SEAWEED
| 68 | Pye 7N 17515 | Stay Awhile/Pictures In The Sky ....£70 |

(see also Fadin' Colours)

THE ORB
| 20 | Cooking Vinyl COOKLP757X | ABOLITION OF THE ROYAL FAMILIA (2LP, gatefold, clear vinyl, bonus Dub LP).................£60 |

SINGLES
89	Wau! Mr Modo MWS 010T	KISS (12" EP, 949 only, die-cut company sleeve)...£15
90	Wau! Mr Modo MWS 017T	A Huge Ever Growing Pulsating Brain That Rules From The Centre Of The Ultraworld: Loving You (Orbital Mix)/(Bucket And Spade Mix)/Why Is 6 Scared of 7? (12" p/s, B-side matrix states 'MWS 016T')...£15
92	Big Life BLRT 75	Blue Room Part 1/Blue Room Part 2 (12", p/s)..£15

ALBUMS
91	Big Life BLRDLP 5	THE ORB'S ADVENTURES BEYOND THE UNDERWORLD (2LP, printed inners, 'classical pressing' sticker on sleeve)...£50
91	Big Life BLRLP 14	THE ORB AUBREY MIXES: THE ULTRAWORLD EXCURSIONS (LP, with silver inners, deleted on day of release)..£30
91	Strange Fruit SFRLP 118	PEEL SESSIONS (LP, states Peel Sessions on slleve, The Peel Sessions on label))............£30
92	Big Life BLRLA 18	U.F.ORB (2LP, 12" and 2 art prints in unopened blue plastic cover) £60
92	Big Life BLRLA 18	U.F.ORB (2LP, 12" and 2 art prints in opened blue plastic cover) £30
93	Island ILPSQ 8022	LIVE 93 (4LP, gatefold, printed inners)...£60
94	Island ORBLP 1	POMME FRITZ (LP, printed inner) £30
95	Island ILPSD 8037	ORBUS TERRARUM (2LP, 'map pack', printed PVC with printed inners).................£80
97	Island ILPSD 8055	OBLIVION (2LP, printed inners, tour insert) £35
01	Island ILPSD 8100	CYDONIA (2LP, printed inners)..£40
04	Simply Vinyl S160026	BICYCLES AND TRICYCLES (2LP, PVC outer, printed inners)..................................£40
09	Malicious Damage MDV 646	BAGHDAD BATTERIES (ORBSESSIONS VOLUME III) (2LP, gatefold)..........................£40
09	Malicious Damage MDV646	BAGHDAD BATTERIES (ORBSESSIONS VOLUME III) (2LP, CD, box set, paraphernalia & documents)...£80
10	Sony 88697760441	METALLIC SPHERES (featuring David Gilmour) (2LP)..£40
16	Wau! Mr Modo/Island 0600753592861	THE ORB'S ADVENTURES BEYOND THE UNDERWORLD (4LP, gatefold,180g, RSD, reissue)...£120
17	Island/UMC 0602557753264	THE ORB'S ADVENTURES BEYOND THE UNDERWORLD (2LP, printed inners, reissue,180g, hype sticker) £30
17	Island/UMC 00602557797831	U.F.ORB (2LP, reissue, download voucher) £40
22	Island/UMC 483 800-0	U.F.ORB (2LP,30th Anniversary reissue, printed inners, ultra blue translucent vinyl).........£40
23	Sony DGORB001LP	METALLIC SPHERES IN COLOUR (with David Gilmour) (LP) £25

PROMOS
90	Wau! Mr Modo MWS 017T	A Huge Ever-Growing Pulsating Remix/From One Ear To Another/Why Is 6 Scared Of 7? (12", white label, 100 only)..£20
90	Wau! Mr Modo MWS 017R	A Huge Ever-Growing Pulsating Brain That Rules From The Centre Of The Ultraworld (Orbital Dance Mix)/(Orbital Radio Mix)/(Aubrey Mix Mk II) (12", stamped white label, 1,000 only)..£15
91	Big Life ORB PICTURE 3	Perpetual Dawn: Ultrabass II (12", 1-sided picture disc, mispressing, plays "Towers Of Dub (Ambient)", 400 pressed but 300 allegedly destroyed) £15

(see also System 7, KLF, Jah Wobble, Space, David Gilmour)

ORBIDÖIG
| 81 | Situation 2 SIT 15 | Nocturnal Operation/Down Periscope (p/s)..£25 |

(see also Sensational Creed)

ROY ORBISON

SINGLES
61	London HLU 7108	I'm Hurtin'/I Can't Stop Loving You (export issue)..£15
64	Ember EMB S 197	Rock House/You're My Baby..£20
64	Ember EMB S 200	This Kind Of Love/I Never Knew (in p/s)...£20
65	Ember EMB S 209	Sweet And Easy To Love/You're Gonna Cry (in p/s)..£15

EPs
57	London RE-S 1089	HILLBILLY ROCK (orange p/s, mauve/silver label, triangular centre) £150
57	London RE-S 1089	HILLBILLY ROCK (orange p/s, mauve/silver label, round centre).........................£100
60	London RE-U 1274	ONLY THE LONELY £25
63	London RE-S 1089	HILLBILLY ROCK (re-pressing, yellow p/s, silver-top, round centre).....................£80
63	London RE-U 1354	ROY ORBISON £20

(Later pressings are on London Monument label as were later pressings of RE-U 1274 and RE-U 1354)
64	Ember EP 4546	SWEET AND EASY TO LOVE...£40
64	Ember EP 4563	TRYIN' TO GET TO YOU £40
65	London RE-U 1439	ROY ORBISON'S STAGE SHOW HITS £15
65	Ember EP 4570	DEVIL DOLL £40
65	London RE-U 1440	LOVE HURTS...£15

ALBUMS : LONDON LPS
| 61 | London HA-U 2342 | LONELY AND BLUE ....£20 |

62	London HA-U 2437	CRYIN' (mono)	£20
62	London SAH-U 6229	CRYIN' (stereo)	£25
63	London HA-U 8108	IN DREAMS (mono)	£15
63	London SH-U 8108	IN DREAMS (stereo)	£25
64	London HA-U 8207	OH, PRETTY WOMAN	£15
65	London HA-U 8252	THERE IS ONLY ONE ROY ORBISON (mono)	£15
65	London SH-U 8252	THERE IS ONLY ONE ROY ORBISON (stereo)	£20
66	London HA-U 8279	THE ORBISON WAY (mono)	£15
66	London SH-U 8279	THE ORBISON WAY (stereo)	£20
66	London HA-U 8297	THE CLASSIC ROY ORBISON (mono)	£15

(The London LPs listed above were originally issued with plum labels [mono] or blue labels [stereo]. Later copies were re-pressed with black labels [mono] or plum labels [stereo] with a boxed London logo.)

66	London HA-U 8297	THE CLASSIC ROY ORBISON (black label mono)	£15
66	London SH-U 8297	THE CLASSIC ROY ORBISON (blue label stereo)	£15
67	London HA-U 8318	SINGS DON GIBSON (black label mono)	£15
67	London SH-U 8318	SINGS DON GIBSON (blue label stereo)	£15
68	London HA-U/SH-U 8357	CRY SOFTLY, LONELY ONE	£15
70	London HA-U 8406	THE BIG "O" (mono)	£15

ALBUMS : OTHER ALBUMS
64	Ember NR 5013	THE EXCITING SOUNDS OF ROY ORBISON (original copies list 'Great Newport Street' address on cover; reissued 1972)	£25
64	Ember NR 5013	THE EXCITING SOUNDS OF ROY ORBISON (reissued 1972)	£15
65	Ember FA 2005	ROY ORBISON AND OTHERS (with 4 tracks by Orbison)	£15

(see also Traveling Wilburys)

ORBIT FIVE
68	Decca F 12799	I Wanna Go To Heaven/Walking (in p/s)	£25
68	Decca F 12799	I Wanna Go To Heaven/Walking	£15

ORBITAL
18	ACP ACPV1806	MONSTERS EXIST (2-LP)	£18

SINGLES
89	Oh Zone ZONE 1	Chime/Deeper (12", p/s)	£20

ALBUMS
91	FFRR 828248-1	ORBITAL (2-LP)	£50
93	Internal TRULP 2	ORBITAL 2 (2-LP)	£50
94	Internal TRULP 5	SNIVILISATION (2-LP, gatefold sleeve, poster)	£50
96	Internal TRULP 10	IN SIDES (3-LP)	£100
99	FFRR 556 076-1	THE MIDDLE OF NOWHERE (2-LP)	£60
02	FFRR 092746190	WORK 1989-2002 (2-LP)	£50
03	EMI 7243 5 93784 11	OCTANE (LP, soundtrack)	£20
04	Orbital Music Orbital V001	BLUE ALBUM (2-LP)	£50
12	ACP ACPV1203	WONKY (2-LP)	£40
15	Vinyl Collector 0825646128747	ORBITAL (2-LP, 1st album, reissue 180gm)	£30
15	Warner Bros. TRULP 2-1	ORBITAL (2-LP, 2nd album, reissue 180gm)	£35

ORCA
92	Micro Genetic 001	9 Lives/Shining Bright (12")	£20
92	Lucky Spin LSR-ORC 1	DANCES WITH DOLPHINS EP NO. 1 (12", stickered, black die-cut sleeve)	£40
93	Lucky Spin LRS 006	DANCES WITH DOLPHINS EP NO. 2 (12")	£25
93	Lucky Spin LSR 011	4AM/Pure Bliss/Jungle Vibes/Pure Bliss (Remix) (100 on red vinyl)	£40
93	Lucky Spin LSR 011	4AM/Pure Bliss/Jungle Vibes/Pure Bliss (Remix) (black vinyl)	£30
93	Lucky Spin ORCA 6	BACK TO THE JUNGLE EP (12")	£20
94	Lucky Spin STU 06	4AM (Remix 1)/4AM (Remix 2) (12")	£20
94	Lucky Spin LSR 016	Intalect/Tranquility To Earth (12")	£100
95	Lucky Spin LSR 023	My Eyes/Liar (12")	£30
95	Lucky Spin LSR 026	Intalect (Remix)/Sample And Hold (12")	£18

ORCHESTRA BAOBAB
89	World Circuit WCB 014	PIRATES CHOICE - LEGENDARY 1982 SESSION (LP)	£50

ORCHESTRAL MANOEUVRES IN THE DARK (O.M.D.)
79	Factory FAC 6	Electricity/Almost (black 'braille' p/s)	£100
84	Virgin VSS 660	Locomotion/Her Body In My Soul (uncut train-shaped picture disc)	£35
85	Virgin VSY 766-14	So In Love (Extended)/Concrete Hands (Extended)/Maria Gallant (12" picture disc)	£15
13	100%100RSD27	THE FUTURE WILL BE SILENT (10", p/s)	£30
15	Pledge Music WN2PICDISC	DAZZLE SHIPS AT THE MUSEUM OF LIVERPOOL (12", picture disc)	£30
17	100%100T65	Isotope/Skin (12", p/s)	£20
17	100% 100T67	The Punishment Of Luxury (Extended)/Lampe Licht/The Punishment Of Luxury (12", p/s)	£18
80	Din Disc DID 2	ORCHESTRAL MANOEUVRES IN THE DARK (LP, 12" x 12" grid sleeve, black, blue or grey outer sleeves with orange, pink or red inner)	£25
80	Din Disc DID 6	ORGANISATION (LP, stickered sleeve, with insert & 7": "Introducing Radios"/ Distance Fades Between Us"/"Progress"/"Once When I Was Six" [DEP 2])	£15
91	Virgin V 2648	SUGAR TAX (LP, mispressing with extra track "All She Wants Is Everything" instead of "Neon Lights")	£15
84	Virgin V 2310	JUNK CULTURE (LP, stickered sleeve, with free 7": "[Angels Keep Turning] The Wheels Of The Universe" [JUNK 1])	£15
93	Virgin V2715	LIBERATOR (LP)	£40
96	Virgin V2807	UNIVERSAL (LP)	£80
10	100% BNLP001LP	HISTORY OF MODERN (2-LP, CD)	£50
13	100% 100LP26	ENGLISH ELECTRIC (LP, with CD)	£50

14	OTB OMD 1	**LIVE** (2-LP, blue or white vinyl, 100 only of each) **£75**
16	Live Here Now LHN004LP	**ORCHESTRAL MANOEUVRES IN THE DARK/ARCHITECTURE AND MORALITY/DAZZLE SHIPS** (3-LP, reissue, 1000 only) **£50**
17	100% 100LP66	**THE PUNISHMENT OF LUXURY** (LP)..............**£20**
17	100%100LP66Y	**THE PUNISHMENT OF LUXURY** (LP, yellow vinyl)..............**£25**
18	100% 100LP7C	**HISTORY OF MODERN** (2-LP, reissue, orange vinyl) **£40**

ORCHIDS (1)

63	Decca F 11743	**Gonna Make Him Mine/Stay At Home** **£25**
63	Decca F 11785	**Love Hit Me/Don't Make Me Mad**..............**£20**
64	Decca F 11861	**I've Got That Feeling/Larry** **£25**

(see also Exceptions)

ORCHIDS (2)

88	Sarah SARAH 002	**I've Got A Habit/Give Me Some Peppermint Freedom/Apologies** (foldover p/s with poster, 1,000 only) **£100**
88	Sarah SARAH 011	**UNDERNEATH THE WINDOW, UNDERNEATH THE SINK EP** (p/s) **£30**
88	Sha La La BaBaBaBaBa 5	**From This Day/SEA URCHINS: Summertime** (flexi, 2,500 only, 1,000 in p/s)..............**£15**
89	Sarah SARAH 023	**WHAT WILL WE DO NEXT? EP** (p/s) **£20**
90	Sarah SARAH 029	**Something For The Longing/Farewell Dear Bonnie/On A Sunday** (p/s, with inserts)..............**£15**
90	Caff CAFF 11	**An Ill Wind That Blows/All Those Things** (p/s, with insert) **£20**
91	Sarah SARAH 042	**PENETRATION EP** (12", p/s with insert) **£18**
92	Sarah SARAH 66	**Thaumaturgy/I Was Just Dreaming/Between Sleeping And Waking** (p/s, insert)..............**£15**
91	Sarah SARAH 605	**UNHOLY SOUL** (LP)..............**£35**
94	Sarah SARAH 617	**STRIVING FOR THE LAZY PERFECTION** (LP) **£50**
95	Sarah SARAH 401	**LYCEUM** (10" mini-LP) **£25**
95	Sarah SARAH 611 LP	**EPICUREAN: A SOUNDTRACK** (2-LP) **£40**

ORDINARY PEOPLE

97	Social Circles SC 001	**Keep Your Love/Milton Blues/Bonus Beatz** (12")..............**£50**
97	Social Circles JKSC 001	**Baby You Make My Heart Sing/I Need/I'll Take You There** (12") **£80**
98	Social Circles JKSC 002	**Baby You Make My Heart Sing/I'll Take You There** (12", reissue) **£60**
98	Social Circles JKSC 003	**I'M MISSING EP** (12", featuring Jude Mansi) **£20**

ORE

82	Bandit BR 003	**Your Time Will Come/Yellow River** (p/s)..............**£100**

ORGAN

06	Too Pure PURE 195LP	**GRAB THAT GUN** (LP, reissue of 2004 LP) **£75**

CHARLES ORGANAIRE

64	Blue Beat BB 241	**The Red Sea/You May Not Believe** (as Big Charlie) **£18**
64	R&B JB 149	**Little Village/It Happens On A Holiday** **£35**
64	Rio R 28	**Little Village/It Happens On A Holiday** (reissue) **£20**

ORGANIC STNTHETIC

97	Bang In Tunes BIT 012	**Organic/Transmissions** (12") **£15**

ORGANISATION

70	RCA SF 8111	**TONE FLOAT** (LP) **£400**

(see also Kraftwerk)

ORGANISERS

66	Pye 7N 17022	**Lonesome Road/The Organiser** **£75**

ORGANUM

94	Aeroplane AR 15	**Gloria** (1-sided, numbered p/s, 113 only)..............**£50**
95	Aeroplane AR 16	**Lysis** (1-sided, 72 only)..............**£50**
95	Aeroplane AR 17	**Kanroku** (1-sided 12", black outer sleeve, illustrated, stamped, signed and no'd inner sleeve, 111 only) **£60**
95	Aeroplane AR 19	**Rotor** (1-sided, signed, no'd, 83 only, p/s)..............**£60**
95	Aeroplane AR 20	**Arc** (1-sided, signed, no'd, 85 only, p/s)..............**£50**
96	Aeroplane AR 23	**Shovels** (1-sided, signed, no'd, 91 only, p/s)..............**£50**
96	Aeroplane AR 24	**Raw** (1-sided, signed, no'd, 83 only, p/s)..............**£50**
88	United Dairies UN 023	**SUBMISSION** (LP, 1000 only)..............**£40**
94	Aeroplane AR 14	**SPHYX** (LP, black picture label, 546 only)..............**£20**
94	Aeroplane AR 14	**SPHYX** (LP, blue picture label, 509 only, reissue) **£20**

(see also David Jackman)

ORGANUM/NEW BLOCKADERS

84	Aeroplane AR 7	**Pulp Parts 1 & 2** (gatefold p/s, 279 only) **£60**
85	Laylah/Antirecords LAY 19	**IN EXTREMIS** (LP)..............**£20**
88	Laylah LAY 012	**TOWER OF SILENCE** (LP) **£20**

(see also Current 93, Nurse With Wound, Eddie Prevost Band, David Jackman, New Blockaders)

ORIGINAL CHECKMATES

62	Pye 7N 15442	**Begin The Beguine** (Stomp)**/Begin The Beguine** **£15**
63	Decca F 11688	**Union Pacific/The Spy** **£30**

(see also Checkmates)

ORIGINAL DOWNTOWN SYNCOPATORS

63	J.R.T. Davies DAVLP 301/2	**THE ORIGINAL DOWNTOWN SYNCOPATORS** (10" LP, white labels only) **£20**

(see also Ron Geesin)

ORIGINAL ROCKERS

93	Different Drummer LP GOO 1	**ROCKERS TO ROCKERS** (LP) **£15**

ORIGINAL SIN

84	Sin S1N	**The Shadow/Salvation** (12", p/s, private pressing)..............**£25**

MINT VALUE £

ORIGINALS (1)
62	Top Rank JAR 600	Gimme A Little Kiss, Will Ya, Huh/At Times Like This	£35

ORIGINALS (2)
67	Tamla Motown TMG 592	Goodnight Irene/Need Your Lovin', Want You Back	£80
67	Tamla Motown TMG 592	Goodnight Irene/Need Your Lovin', Want You Back (DJ copy)	£150
70	Tamla Motown TMG 733	Baby I'm For Real/The Moment Of Truth	£18
69	Tamla Motown TMG 702	Green Grow The Lilacs/You're The One	£20
76	Tamla Motown TMG 1066	Six Million Dollar Man/Mother Nature's Best (unreleased)	£0
69	Tamla Motown TML 11116	GREEN GROW THE LILACS (LP, mono)	£60
69	Tamla Motow STML 11116	GREEN GROW THE LILACS (LP, stereo)	£55

ORIGINATION
92	Rudeboy RUDE 001	Break Down/Bass/R.E.S.P.E.C.T. (12")	£15
94	Rudeboy RUDE 007	Shine on '94/Shine On (Unreleased '92 Remix)/ Shine On '94 (Dub Version)/Shine On (Original '92 Mix) (12")	£30

ORIGINELLS 4
64	Columbia DB 7259	My Girl/Kathy (as Origenells)	£20
64	Columbia DB 7388	Nights/I Can Make You Mine	£18

ORIGIN UNKNOWN
92	Ram RAMM 002	Untitled (6.03)/Untitled (5.01)/Untitled (5.22)/Untitled (6.12) (12", stamped white labels, promo only, not released)	£20
90s	Ram RAMM 002	EASTERN PROMISE EP (12", stamped white label, 4 untitled tracks, promo only)	£120

ORIOLES
53	London L 1180	Hold Me, Thrill Me, Kiss Me/Teardrops On My Pillow (78)	£15
53	London L 1201	Crying In The Chapel/Don't You Think I Ought To Know (78)	£15
54	London HL 8001	In The Mission Of St. Augustine/Write And Tell Me Why (78)	£15

ORION (1)
84	Lost Moment LM 02	Insane In Another World/Storm (p/s)	£15

ORION (2)
87	Gypsy GYP 001	JACK ORION (LP)	£30

ORIOR
79	Crystal Groove 7E 2	Elevation/Tutankhamen/Quiet Sky (wraparound p/s, insert)	£35

ORKIDEA
99	Steel Fish Blue SFB 001	Unity (12", white label)	£45
05	Sential SE 002	BEAUTIFUL EP (12", p/s)	£60

TONY ORLANDO
61	Fontana H 308	Halfway To Paradise/Lonely Tomorrows	£20
62	Columbia DB 4871	Chills/At The Edge Of Tears	£20
63	Columbia DB 4954	Beautiful Dreamer/The Loneliest	£25
63	Columbia SEG 8238	BLESS YOU (EP)	£40
63	Fontana TFL 5167	BLESS YOU (LP, mono)	£50
63	Fontana STFL 582	BLESS YOU (LP, stereo)	£60

ORLANDO (1)
69	NEMS 56-4159	Am I The Same Guy/Poor Little Me	£100

ORLONS
62	Columbia DB 4865	The Wah Watusi/Holiday Hill	£35
62	Cameo Parkway C 231	Don't Hang Up/The Conservative	£25
63	Cameo Parkway C 243	South Street/Them Terrible Boots	£20
63	Cameo Parkway C 257	Not Me/My Best Friend	£15
63	Cameo Parkway C 273	Crossfire/It's No Big Thing	£15
63	Cameo Parkway C 287	Bon Doo Wah/Don't Throw Your Love Away	£20
63	Cameo Parkway C 295	Shimmy Shimmy/Everything Nice	£15
64	Cameo Parkway C 319	Rules Of Love/Heartbreak Hotel	£15
64	Cameo Parkway C 332	Knock Knock (Who's There)/Goin' Places	£15
66	Planet PLF 117	Spinnin' Top/Anyone Who Had A Heart	£150
72	Mojo 2092 029	Spinnin' Top/Anyone Who Had A Heart (reissue)	£15
62	Cameo Parkway C 1033	ALL THE HITS (LP)	£60
63	Cameo Parkway C 1061	BIGGEST HITS (LP)	£60
78	London HA-U 8504	CAMEO PARKWAY SESSIONS (LP)	£30

(see also Rosetta Hightower)

OROONIES
91	Demi Monde DMLP 1027	OF HOOF AND HORN (LP)	£18

JIM O'ROURKE
99	Domino WIGLP 62	EUREKA (LP)	£40
01	Domino WIGLP 104	INSIGNIFICANCE (LP)	£30
03	Three Poplars 3P08	SCEND (LP, reissue, clear vinyl)	£20

ORPHAN (1)
80	Orphan Records ORP-1	Little Mother/I Don't Want To Go (To Work Tomorrow), stamped inner sleeve and insert p/s)	£20

ORPHAN (2)
85	Swoop RTLS 013	Nervous/Little England (p/s)	£15

ORPHEUS
66	Red Bird RB 10-041	My Life/Music Minus Orpheus	£40
68	MGM MGM C(S) 8072	ORPHEUS (LP)	£25

BETH ORTON
96	Heavenly HVN 56	I Wish I Never Saw The Sunshine (p/s, 1-sided limited edition, 500 only)	£20
96	Heavenly HVNLP 17	TRAILER PARK (LP, 100 copies only)	£100
99	Heavenly HVNLP 22	CENTRAL RESERVATION (2-LP, gatefold sleeve, 1000 copies only)	£100
02	Heavenly HVNLP 37	DAYBREAKER (LP)	£40
12	Anti 7118-1	SUGARING SEASON (LP & CD)	£15

(see also Spill)

PAUL ORWELL
14	Heavy Soul ROR 059	Tell Me Tell Me/Little Reason (250 only, all signed)	£70
15	Heavy Soul ROR 064	You're Nothing Special/Like I Did Before (p/s, 250 only)	£25
16	Heavy Soul ROR 068	Attack/Let You Go (p/s, 200 only)	£15
16	Heavy Soul ROR 075	Don't Do As I Do Do As I Say/Pleasure Pill (300 only, die cut sleeve)	£15
16	Heavy Soul ROR 079	Too Young To Die (1-sided, p/s, 50 only in different coloured sleeves blue, yellow, green, pink and white)	£30
17	Heavy Soul ROR	Needles And Sins (1-sided white flexidisc)	£40
15	Heavy Soul ROR 065	BLOWING YOUR MIND AWAY (LP)	£45

EILEEN OSBORNE
75	Seagull SG1	SINGING SHORES (LP)	£15

MIKE OSBORNE
71	Turtle TUR 300	OUTBACK (LP)	£60
73	Cadillac SGC 1002	ORIGINAL (LP, as Mike Osborne & Stan Tracey)	£20
75	Ogun OG 300	BORDER CROSSING (LP)	£15
76	Ogun OG 700	ALL NIGHT LONG (LP)	£20
77	Ogun OG 210	TANDEM - LIVE AT BRACKNELL FESTIVAL (LP, with Stan Tracey)	£18
77	Ogun OG 810	MARCEL'S MUSE (LP)	£25

(see also Stan Tracey)

OZZY OSBOURNE
80	Jet JETP 12003	Mr. Crowley (live)/You Said It All (live)/Suicide Solution (live) (12", picture disc)	£15
82	Jet JETP 7030	Symptom Of The Universe/N.I.B. (picture disc)	£20
83	Epic TA 3915	Bark At The Moon/One Up The B-Side (12", p/s, silver vinyl)	£15
83	Epic WA 3915	Bark At The Moon/One Up The B-Side (12", picture disc, unreleased)	£0
86	Epic A 6859	Shot In The Dark/Rock'n'Roll Rebel (p/s, with autographed signature card)	£40
88	Epic 653 063-9	Miracle Man/Crazy Babies (head-shaped picture disc)	£25
88	Epic 652875 6	BACK TO OZ (12" EP, p/s, with poster)	£15
93	Epic 659 3406	Changes/Changes (extended version)/No More Tears (live)/ Desire (12" picture disc, with insert)	£15
96	Epic 663570 6	I Just Want You/Aimee/Voodoo Dancer (12", one side etched)	£20
81	Jet LP 234	BLIZZARD OF OZ (LP, with poster)	£40
81	Jet LP 234	BLIZZARD OF OZ (LP, without poster)	£20
81	Jet LP 237	DIARY OF A MADMAN (LP)	£20
82	Jet JETDP 401	TALK OF THE DEVIL (2-LP)	£20
83	Epic EPC 25739	BARK AT THE MOON (LP, 1st pressing with blue lettering)	£20
86	Epic EPC 26404	THE ULTIMATE SIN (LP)	£15
86	Epic EPC 11-26404	THE ULTIMATE SIN (LP, picture disc)	£20
87	Epic EPC 450475 1	RANDY RHOADS TRIBUTE (2-LP)	£20
88	Epic EPC 462581 1	NO REST FOR THE WICKED (LP)	£20
93	Epic 4737961	LIVE & LOUD (2-LP)	£80

(see also Black Sabbath, Lita Ford & Ozzy Osbourne)

JOHNNY OSBOURNE (& SENSATIONS)
70	Big Shot BI 549	See And Blind (solo)/THE TECHNIQUES: Scar Face	£30
72	Techniques TE 916	See And Blind/TECHNIQUES ALL STARS: Rema Skank	£30
75	Torpedo TOR 37	Put Away Your Gun/Version Gun	£60
80	Jammys JM 002	Long Long Life/HIGH MUNDELL: Walk With Jah (12")	£25
80	Cha Cha CHAD 27	Kiss Somebody/Version (12")	£35
80	Black Joy DH 810	Purify Your Heart/Politician (blue vinyl)	£40
80	Greensleeves GRED 34	Fally Ranking/Trench Town School (12")	£40
80	Unity UN 003	Original Rewind/LEROY SMART: Back Off (12")	£15
81	Greensleeves GRED 50	Back Off (with PAPA TULLO).Dub (12")	£35
81	Cha Cha CHAD 31	Nightfall/Dub Fall (12")	£20
81	Greensleeves GRED 60	Trying To Turn Me On/Turn On Dub (12")	£15
81	Simba LION 1	13 Dead (Nothing Said)/Black Lion Band Murder (12")	£25
81	Simba SIM 002	Don't Bite The Hand (with ASWAD)/Dub (10")	£25
82	Oak Sounds OSD 006	Yo Yo/ECHO MINOTT : Man In Love (12")	£15
82	Greensleeves GRE 884	Never Stop Fighting/ROOTS RADICS: Never Stop Dub	£20
86	Greensleeves GRED 208	Dub Plate Playing/COCOA TEA: Cocoa Tea Medley (12")	£40
89	Live & Love LLD 119	Chain Grabber/Watch Them A Watch (12", with PAPPA SAN)	£18
70	Trojan TTL29	COME BACK DARLING (LP)	£40
73	Big Shot BILP 103	READY OR NOT (LP)	£100
80	Greensleeves GREL 12	FALLY LOVER (LP, red vinyl)	£30
80	Jammy's JAM 1000	FOLLY RANKING (LP, orange vinyl)	£50
81	Cha Cha CHALP 010	IN NAH DISCO STYLE (LP)	£50
81	Black Joy DHLP 2001	WARRIOR (LP)	£35
82	Arrival ALP 002	YO YO (LP)	£15
82	Greensleeves GREL 38	NEVER STOP FIGHTING (LP)	£30
84	Selection SELP 01	REALITY (LP)	£25

BOB OSBURN
64	London HLD 9869	Bound To Happen/Think Of Me	£15

OSCAR BICYCLE
68   CBS 3237   On A Quiet Night/The Room Revolves Around Me £60

OSCAR (1)
66   Reaction 591 003   Club Of Lights/Waking Up £60
66   Reaction 591 006   Join My Gang/Days Gone By £40
67   Reaction 591 012   Over The Wall We Go/Every Day Of My Life £40
67   Reaction 591 016   Holiday/Give Her All She Wants £30
68   Polydor 56257   Open Up The Skies/Wild Ones £30
(see also Paul Dean, Paul Nicholas)

OSCAR (2)
74   Buk BULP 2001   OSCAR (LP)...£15

OSCILLATORS
79   Warren Records WAR-   Leonard Cheshire/Fast Breeder Reactor (fold-out p/s, with or without 'group' drawing,
     SEP-465   1000 only) £60
80   Yawn SRTS/80/CUS693   Marilyn Brown/E-Boat (fold out p/s) £20

OSHAMA
82   Smokey SMJD 007   Highway/Come The Time (12") £70

OSIBISA
71   Smoke SS 1001   Black Ant/Kotoko £20
71   MCA MDKS 8001   OSIBISA (LP, gatefold, purple/red 'dogbone' label)....................................£50
71   MCA MDKS 8005   WOYAYA (LP, gatefold, black/blue/white hexagon label) £35
72   MCA MDKS 8007   HEADS (LP, gatefold, black/blue/white label) £20
73   Warner Bros. WB 56022   HAPPY CHILDREN (LP) £15
73   Buddah 2318 087   SUPER FLY T.N.T. (LP, soundtrack) £15
74   MCA MCG 3508   OSIBISA (LP, reissue, rainbow label) £15
74   MCA MCG 3506   WOYAWA (LP, reissue, rainbow label) £15
74   Warner Bros. K 56048   OSIBIROCK (LP) £15
75   Bronze ILPS 9355   WELCOME HOME (LP) £30
76   Bronze ILPS 9411   OJAH AWAKE (LP) £15
77   Bronze BRSP 3   BLACK MAGIC NIGHT (2-LP) £20
80   Calibre CAB LP 1002   MYSTIC ENERGY (LP) £15
82   Magnet MAGL 5053   UNLEASHED (2-LP) £25
84   Premier CBR 1035   LIVE AT THE MARQUEE (LP)...£15
(see also Del Richardson, Sundae Times, Bessa Simons, Kiki Gyan, Spartacus R)

OSMOSIS
70   RCA VICTOR LPS 4369   OSMOSIS (LP) £20

OSMOND BROTHERS
63   MGM MGM 1208   Be My Little Baby Bumble Bee/I Wouldn't Know £15
63   MGM MGM-C 1011   NEW SOUND OF THE BROTHERS (LP)...£30

OSSIE & SWEET BOYS
67   Polydor 56167   Nothing Takes The Place Of You/Brixton Boo-Ga-Loo £15

OSSIE & UPSETTERS
66   Doctor Bird DB 1018   Turn Me On/True Love £40
(see also Upsetters)

AL OSTER
60s Dominion LP 1321   ECHO OF THE YUKON (LP) £20

OSU
83   Shaka XAKA 2   Light Up My Fire/Merry Go Round (p/s) £80

PETER O'SULLIVAN
76   Charisma CAS 1160   PETER O'SULLIVAN TALKS TURF (LP) £15

OSUNLADE
08   Strictly Rhythm SR12653 MOMMAS GROOVE (THE REMIXES) (12" p/s) £40
13   Yoruba YSD 56   Dionne/What Gets You High? (p/s, 250 only) £70
17   BBE/Yoruba BBE380ALP   PYROGRAPHY (3-LP. reissue with booklet) £35

OTHER BROTHERS
69   Pama PM 785   Let's Get Together/Little Girl £25

OTHER SIDE
87   Casual Sax SRT 8KS 1432 Is It Any Wonder/Let's Be Perfect (p/s) £40

OTHER TWO (2)
93   London 520028.1   THE OTHER TWO AND YOU (LP) £50
(see also Joy Division, New Order, Bad Lieutenant)

OTHERS (1)
64   Fontana TF 501   Oh Yeah/I'm Taking Her Home..£60
(see also Sands, Sundragon)

JOHNNY OTIS SHOW
58   Capitol CL 14817   Bye Bye Baby (as Johnny Otis Show with Marie Adams)/Good Golly £15
58   Capitol CL 14837   The Light Still Shines In My Window/All I Want Is Your Love (with Marie Adams)...........£25
58   Capitol CL 14854   Well, Well, Well, Well!/You Just Kissed Me Goodbye (with Mel Williams) £25
58   Capitol CL 14875   Ring-A-Ling/The Johnny Otis Hand Jive £25
58   Capitol CL 14875   Ring-A-Ling/The Johnny Otis Hand Jive (78) £20
58   Capitol CL 14941   Crazy Country Hop/Willie Did The Cha Cha £25
59   Capitol CL 15008   You/My Dear (as Johnny Otis Show with Mel Williams) £18
59   Capitol CL 15018   Castin' My Spell/Telephone Baby (as Johnny Otis Show with Marci Lee).....£25

59	Capitol CL 15057	Three Girls Named Molly Doin' The Hully Gully/I'll Do The Same Thing For You	£20
60	Capitol CL 15112	Mumblin' Mosie/Hey Baby, Don't You Know?	£15
59	Capitol EAP1 1134	THE JOHNNY OTIS SHOW (EP)	£25
65	Vocalion VEP 170162	JOHNNY OTIS (EP)	£50
58	Capitol T 940	THE JOHNNY OTIS SHOW (LP)	£100
69	Sonet SNTF 613	COLD SHOT (LP)	£15
72	Ember SPE 6604	FORMIDABLE (LP)	£15

(see also Marie Adams)

SHUGGIE OTIS
70	CBS 63996	HERE COMES SHUGGIE OTIS (LP)	£35

(see also Al Kooper & Shuggie Otis)

NOIT OTNI & PITS
79	Automotive AERS 107	A Heart Can Only Be Broken Once/Moving Target (in p/s)	£35
79	Automotive AERS 107	A Heart Can Only Be Broken Once/Moving Target	£25

JOHN OTWAY
72	County COUN 215	Gypsy/Misty Mountain (private pressing, County Recording Service, Bracknell on label, with duplicated lyric sheet)	£25
76	Viking YRS CF 01	Louisa On A Horse/Beware Of The Flowers (private pressing)	£15
79	Polydor 2059 105	Frightened And Scared (instrumental)/Are You On My Side? (p/s, only 3 copies pressed!)	£50
86	'Warner Bros' OTWEAY 1	The New Jerusalem/The Tyger (private pressing)	£20

JOHN OTWAY & WILD WILLY BARRETT
82	Empire HAM 5T	12 STITCH EP (12" EP in polythene bag with jay-card)	£15
77	Extracted EXLP 1	JOHN OTWAY AND WILD WILLY BARRETT (LP, handmade stickered sleeve)	£20
77	White label OBL 1	OTWAY AND BARRETT LIVE AT THE ROUNDHOUSE (private pressing LP, freebie, handwritten labels, plain sleeve, 250 numbered copies only)	£35

(see also Wild Willy Barrett)

OUR PLASTIC DREAM
67	Go AJ 11411	A Little Bit Of Shangrila/Encapsulated Marigold	£200

OUT OF THE SHADE
05	Roc Solid Records RSR 1	What You Want/What You Want (Version) (12")	£100

(see also Gold In The Shade)

OUTCASTS
78	It IT 4	Frustration/Don't Want To Be No Adult/You're A Disease (p/s)	£30
78	Good Vibrations GOT 3	Just Another Teenage Rebel/Love Is For Sops (poster p/s, various colours; 'band' p/s)	£50
78	Good Vibrations GOT 3	Just Another Teenage Rebel/Love Is For Sops (poster p/s, various colours; 'type' p/s)	£50
79	Good Vibrations GOT 17	Self Conscious Over You/Love You For Never (p/s)	£15
81	GBH GBH 001	Magnum Force/Gangland Warfare (p/s)	£20
79	Good Vibrations BIG 1	SELF CONSCIOUS OVER YOU (LP)	£25
82	Abstract ABT 004	BLOOD & THUNDER (LP)	£20

OUT DARE
94	Gash T5	OUT DARE EP (12", white label, with press sheet)	£150

OUTER LIMITS (3)
85	Dog Rock SD 106	Chase/Tell Me (p/s)	£20
85	Dog Rock SD 107	Edge Of Time/The Car/Lago/The Quest (12", p/s)	£20

OUTER LIMITS (1)
67	Elephant LUR 100	When The Work Is Thru'/5 MAN CARGO: What A Wonderful Feeling (Leeds Students Charity Rag record)	£55
67	Deram DM 125	Just One Me Chance/Help Me Please	£80
68	Immediate IM 067	Great Train Robbery/Sweet Freedom (demo only)	£70
68	Instant IN 001	Great Train Robbery/Sweet Freedom	£80

(see also Christie, Acid Gallery)

OUTER LIMITS (2)
71	Decca F 13176	The Dark Side Of The Moon/Black Boots	£15
74	Snow/Deroy 1049	(I'm Not) Your Stepping Stone/Great Balls Of Fire	£500

OUTLAW BLUES BAND
69	Stateside SSL 10290	BREAKING IN (LP)	£30

OUTLAW POSSE
91	Outlaw OP1	Sonz Of The Devil (12")	£15

OUTLAWS
61	HMV POP 844	Swingin' Low/Spring Is Near	£15
61	HMV POP 877	Ambush/Indian Brave	£15
61	HMV POP 927	Valley Of The Sioux/Crazy Drums	£20
62	HMV POP 990	Ku-pow!/Last Stage West	£20
62	HMV POP 1074	Sioux Serenade/Fort Knox	£20
63	HMV POP 1124	The Return Of The Outlaws/Texan Spiritual	£20
63	HMV POP 1195	That Set The Wild West Free/Hobo	£20
63	HMV POP 1241	Law And Order/Do-Da-Day	£20
64	HMV POP 1277	Keep-A-Knockin'/Shake With Me	£40
61	HMV CLP 1489	DREAM OF THE WEST (LP, mauve label, gold print)	£80
61	HMV CLP 1489	DREAM OF THE WEST (LP, later black label)	£60

(see also Mike Berry, Bobbie Graham, Rally Rounders, Houston Wells [& Marksmen])

OUT OF DARKNESS
70	Key KL 006	OUT OF DARKNESS (LP, laminated front sleeve)	£200

OUT OF ORDER (1)
81	Daviton SPEP 120	OUT OF CONTROL (EP, export copy, 500 only)	£40

OUT OF ORDER (2)
93	P19J20	Dark Sheep/Right Guard/Tears (12", white label)	£60
93	XYZ 123	Stung/Emotions (12", white label)	£60

OUTPATIENTS
80	KIK 1	Life On Earth/Home Is Where The Heart Is (with p/s)	£50
80	KIK 1	Life On Earth/Home Is Where The Heart Is (without p/s)	£30

OUTRAGEOUS
92	Kinetix KX2	THE TECHKORE EP (12")	£20

OUTSIDERS (U.K.)
78	Xciting Plastic	Vital Hours/Take Up (unissued)	£0

(see also Second Layer, Sound)

OUTSIDERS (U.K. 1)
65	Decca F 12213	Keep On Doing It/Songs We Sang Last Summer	£35

(see also Bunch Of Fives, Junior's Eyes, Tickle)

OUTSIDERS (U.K. 2)
77	Raw Edge RER 002	ONE TO INFINITY (EP)	£50
77	Raw Edge RER 001	CALLING ON YOUTH (LP, laminated sleeve)	£60
78	Raw Edge RER 003	CLOSE UP (LP, with insert)	£50

OUTSIDERS (U.S.)
66	Capitol CL 15435	Time Won't Let Me/Was It Really Real?	£35
66	Capitol CL 15435	Time Won't Let Me/Was It Really Real? (DJ copy)	£50
66	Capitol CL 15450	Girl In Love/What Makes You So Bad, You Weren't Brought Up That Way	£15
66	Capitol CL 15468	Respectable/Lost In My World	£20
67	Capitol CL 15495	I'll Give You Time/I'm Not Tryin' To Hurt You	£20

OUTSKIRTS OF INFINITY
87	Woronzow WOO 7	LORD OF THE DARK SKIES (LP)	£15
94	Dark Skies DSKLP 2	INCIDENT AT PILATUS (2-LP)	£18

OVALTINEES
83	BAA 021	BRITISH JUSTICE EP (p/s)	£80

OVARY LODGE
73	RCA SF 8372	OVARY LODGE (LP)	£100
76	Ogun OG 600	OVARY LODGE (LP)	£30

(see also Keith Tippett)

OVATIONZ
81	Dread At The Controls DCD 005	Forever Love/Forever Dub (12")	£15

OVERCOMERS
68	Bamboo BAM 64	Stop And Let Me Tell You/Take Courage Soul (unissued: white labels only)	£50

OVERDRIVE
81	Boring Grantham BGR 1	ON THE RUN (EP)	£80

OVERKILL
80	Killer EJSP 9357	Elemental/On My Own	£75

OVERLANDERS
66	Pye NEP 24245	MICHELLE (EP)	£25
66	Pye NPL 18138	MICHELLE (LP, laminated front sleeve with flipbacks)	£35

(see also Cuppa T)

OVERLORD
78	Airebeat ABT 3	Lucy/Guardsman/Johnny (p/s)	£30

OVERNIGHT PLAYERS
80	Cha Cha CHALP 008	BABYLON DESTRUCTION (LP, black, orange, yellow or red vinyl)	£80

OVERTAKERS
68	Amalgamated AMG 803	That's The Way You Like It/The Big Take-Over	£50
68	Amalgamated AMG 809	Girl You Ruff/KEITH BLAKE: Woo Oh Oh	£50

OWEN (SILVERA) & LEON
64	Island WI 146	Nextdoor Neighbour/ROLAND ALPHONSO: Feeling Fine	£35
64	Island WI 163	My Love For You/How Many Times	£25
64	Island WI 165	Running Around/SKATALITES: Around The World	£35
65	Island WI 170	I Want My Cock/BABA BROOKS & DON DRUMMOND: Dr Decker	£50
65	Ska Beat JB 189	Woman/BABA BROOKS with DON DRUMMOND: Doctor Decker	£30

(see also Leon & Owen, Tommy McCook)

OWEN (GRAY) & MILLIE
62	Island WI 014	Sugar Plum/OWEN GRAY: Jezebel	£15

(see also Owen Gray, Millie, Owen & Leon, Leon & Owen)

RAY OWEN('S MOON)
71	Polydor 2066-119	Try My Love/Talk To Me	£25
71	Polydor 2325 061	RAY OWEN'S MOON (LP, textured sleeve)	£80

(see also Juicy Lucy)

REG OWEN & HIS ORCHESTRA
56	Parlophone PMD 1045	SWING ME HIGH (10" LP)	£20

DONNIE OWENS
58	London HLU 8747	Need You/If I'm Wrong	£25
58	London HLU 8747	Need You/If I'm Wrong (78)	£15
59	London HLW 8897	Ask Me Anything/Between Midnight And Dawn (unissued)	£0

JAMIE OWENS
| 73 | Light LS 7012 | LAUGHTER IN YOUR SOUL (LP) | £15 |

OWL
| 68 | United Artists UP 2240 | Run To The Sun/Shades Of Blue And Green Water Flies | £20 |

TONY OXLEY (QUARTET)
69	CBS 52664	THE BAPTISED TRAVELLER (LP)	£125
70	CBS 64071	4 COMPOSITIONS FOR SEXTET (LP, with Derek Bailey)	£125
71	RCA SF 8215	ICHNOS (LP)	£100
70s	Incus INCUS 8	TONY OXLEY (LP, with Derek Bailey, et al.)	£100
70s	Incus INCUS 18	FEBRUARY PAPERS (LP)	£40
80s	Bead BEAD 25	THE GLIDER & THE GRINDER (LP)	£30

(see also Derek Bailey, Howard Riley)

TONY OXLEY, WOLFGANG FUCHS, PHILIPP WACHSMANN & HUGH METCALFE
| 87 | Bead Records BEAD 25 | THE GLIDER AND THE GRINDER (LP) | £20 |

TONY OXLEY ALAN DAVIE DUO
| 74 | ADMW 005 | THE TONY OXLEY ALAN DAVIE DUO (LP) | £60 |

OXYM
| 80 | Cargo CRS 003 | Music Power/Mind Key (p/s) | £40 |

OYSTER BAND
82	Pukka YOP 01	ENGLISH ROCK 'N' ROLL, 1800-1850 (LP)	£30
85	Pukka YOP 04	LIE BACK AND THINK OF ENGLAND (LP)	£30
85	Pukka YOP 07	LIBERTY HALL (LP)	£30

OYSTER CEILIDH BAND
| 80 | Dingles DIN 309 | JACK'S ALIVE (LP) | £20 |

OZARKS
| 63 | Vocalion V 9210 | Who Stole My Bird Dog/Any Waltz | £30 |

OZO
77	DJM DJT 10764	Anambra (Edited Version)/Anambra (12")	£40
82	Sphinx SPS 1201	Anambra River (Tranquil Rivers From The Floating Crystal City Of Budatan Shire Of Western Heaven)/Skintight (No Room To Move Up) (12")	£15
76	DJM DJF 20488	LISTEN TO THE BUDDHA (LP)	£40
78	DJM DJF 20517	MUSEUM OF MANKIND (LP)	£18

OZOMATLI
| 98 | Almo ALM LP61 | OZOMATLI (LP) | £40 |

OZRIC TENTACLES
89	Demi-Monde DMLP 1017	PUNGENT EFFULGENT (LP)	£20
90	Dovetail Records DOVE LP1	ERPLAND (2-LP)	£30
91	Dovetail DOVE LP 3	STRANGETUDE (LP)	£20
92	Black Adder OZT 01	MUCK KICKER (LP)	£20
93	Dovetail DOVELP6	JURASSIC SHIFT (LP)	£20
94	Dovetail DOVE LP7	ARBORESCENE (2-LP)	£30
98	Snapper SMALP 410	CURIOUS CORN (LP)	£40

(see also Oroonies)

AUGUSTUS PABLO
71	Big Shot BI 578	The Mood/HERMAN CHIN-LOY: New Love	£40
71	Big Shot BI 579	East Of The River Nile/HERMAN CHIN-LOY: East Of River Nile Version (B-side actually by Aquarians)	£45
71	Creole CR 1004	405 (actually "The Mood" by Tommy McCook)/Duck It Up (actually "Confidential Version" by Charmers)	£25
71	Ackee ACK 134	Still Yet/AQUARIANS: Version	£20
71	Ackee ACK 138	Snowball And Pudding/AQUARIANS: Version	£25
71	Duke DU 122	Reggae In The Fields/TOMMY McCOOK: Love Brother	£50
73	Randy's RAN 536	Bedroom Mazurka (as Augustus Pablo & Fay)/Melodica Version	£30
73	Atra ATRA 011	Lover's Mood/Lover's Rock	£25
74	Tropical AL 025	Too Late/Dub Organiser	£15
74	Tropical AL 035	Tales Of Pablo/BOOTHE STARS: Tales Dub	£18
74	Sydna DL1276	Pablo's Mercy/Version	£20
75	Fay Music FM 603	Fort Augustus Rock/Augustus In Kingston	£25
75	Island WIP 6226	King Tubby Meets The Rockers Uptown/Baby I Love You So	£25
75	Island 12 WIP 6226	King Tubby Meets The Rockers Uptown/JACOB MILLER: Baby I Love You So (12")	£30
75	Treble C CCC06	Liberation/Dubbing Pablo	£15
75	Treble C CCC014	Don Drummond/Thunderbolt Lady	£15
77	Hawkeye HE 005	East Of The River Nile/East Africa	£15
77	EJI 011	No Entry/BIG YOUTH: Strictly Rockers (12")	£40

79	Rockers APD 5	Power Of The Trinity/West Abyssinia Dub (12")..........................£30
79	Rockers APD 6	Twin Seal/Dub/NORRIS REID: Entrance To Jah World (12")..................£25
79	Rockers AP 1023	Crucial Burial/ROCKERS ALL STARS: Pope Paul Feel It/Sound Of Redemption - Scientist In Dub (12")................£30
79	Rockers AB1	Israel In Harmony/HUGH MUNDELL: Feeling Alright/Dub (12").............£35
79	Dub Vendor DVD 002	Oregan Style/Classical Illusion (12")...................£20
80	Greensleeves GRED 29	Presents El Rockers Chapters I - IV (12").................£20
80	Rockers APD 7	Hot Milk/Dub/Robin Bay Step/Dub (12").....................£25
74	Tropical TROPS 101	THIS IS AUGUSTO PABLO (LP)..............................£60
75	Trojan TRLS 115	ITAL DUB (LP, original issue with "12 Neasden Lane" address on sleeve and rough orange/white paper labels)................£35
75	Nationwide NW 03	THRILLER (LP)..£35
78	Greensleeves GREL 98	AFRICA MUST BE FREE BY 83 DUB (LP)....................£20
79	Greensleeves GREL 8	ORIGINAL ROCKERS (LP)..................................£25
79	Atra ATRALP 1003	LEGENDS (LP)..£20
80	Echo STLP 1002	THRILLER (LP, reissue)..................................£20
86	Greensleeves GREL 90	RISING SUN (LP)......................................£18
86	Trojan TRLS 115	ITAL DUB (LP, reissue, blue/white label).................£15
89	Yard RLP 001	KING TUBBYS MEETS THE ROCKERS UPTOWN (LP, reissue).......£25
91	Greensleeves GREL 145	ROCKERS INTERNATIONAL (LP)..........................£25
92	Greensleeves GREL 168	ROCKERS INTERNATIONAL II (LP).......................£15

(see also I Roy)

PACESETTERS
| 70 | Escort ERT 829 | Bits And Pieces/Nimrod Leap.....................................£20 |
| 74 | Saga SAGA 8154 | REGGAE MEETS POP (LP)..£25 |

PACIFIC DRIFT
70	Deram DM 304	Water Woman/Yes You Do...£20
70	Deram Nova DN 13	FEELIN' FREE (LP, mono, blue/silver labels).....................£250
70	Deram Nova SDN 13	FEELIN' FREE (LP, stereo, red/silver labels).................£175

(see also Wimple Winch, Just Four Men)

PACIFIC EARDRUM
| 78 | Charisma CAS 1136 | BEYOND PANIC (LP)..£20 |

PACIFIC GAS & ELECTRIC (P.G. & E.)
69	B&C CAS 1003	GET IT ON (LP)..£75
69	CBS 63822	PACIFIC GAS & ELECTRIC (LP, orange label)............................£30
70	CBS 64026	ARE YOU READY (LP, orange label).....................................£30
71	CBS 64295	HARD BURN (LP, orange label)...£30

PACIFIC SOUND
| 71 | M&M FMSS 10012 | Tribute To Jimi/Thick Fog.......................................£30 |

PACK (1)
| 65 | Columbia DB 7702 | Do You Believe In Magic?/Things Bring Me Down...................£40 |

PACK (2)
| 79 | SS PAK 1 | Brave New Soldiers/Heathen (p/s, 2,500 only)...........................£20 |

(see also Theatre Of Hate, Spear Of Destiny, Senate)

PACKABEATS
61	Parlophone R 4729	Gypsy Beat/Big Man..£15
62	Pye 7N 15480	Evening In Paris/The Traitors......................................£20
63	Pye 7N 15549	Dream Lover/Packabeat...£20

PACKERS
66	Pye International 7N 25343	Hole In The Wall/Go 'Head On.............................£20
69	Soul City SC 111	Hole In The Wall/Go 'Head On (reissue)..........................£15
70	Soul City SCM 003	HOLE IN THE WALL (LP)..£25

PAC-KEYS
| 68 | Speciality SPE 1003 | Stone Fox/Diggin'...£20 |

PAD ANTHONY
86	Live & Love LLDIS 0027	Dangerous System/Version (12")...........................£20
86	Witty MUMD 2	Turn Me Loose/Version (12")...£20
87	Jammys JAM 7	Gotta Be Strong/Version//You Gonna Be Late/Version (12").............£25

BERNARD PADDEN
| 83 | Dancing Sideways DS6X6 | Mass Movement/Career Advice (p/s)........................£15 |

PADDY, KLAUS & GIBSON
65	Pye 7N 15906	I Wanna Know/I Tried...£20
66	Pye 7N 17060	No Good Without You Baby/Rejected..................................£50
66	Pye 7N 17112	Teresa/Quick Before They Catch Us..................................£40

(see also Manfred Mann, Big Three, Rory Storm & Hurricanes, Kingsize Taylor)

BETTY PADGETT
| 76 | Dynamic DYN 125 | My Eyes Adore You/Love Forever..................................£30 |

PAGAN BEAU
| 82 | RVNIC Records AMO 24 | Odd Man Out/Natures Daughter (p/s).....................£15 |

PAGAN BO
| 78 | Planet ICLP 01 | TRADITIONAL BARD AND THE FUTURE INEVITABLE (LP)..................£175 |

CLEO PAGE
| 79 | JSP 4502 | I Love To Eat It - Hamburger/Goodie Train..............................£15 |
| 79 | JSP JSP 1003 | LEAVING MISSISSIPPI (LP)...£15 |

HOT LIPS PAGE & HIS ORCHESTRA
55	Parlophone MSP 6172	Ain't Nothing Wrong With That Boy/The Cadillac Song	£20

JIMMY PAGE
65	Fontana TF 533	She Just Satisfies/Keep Moving (promo sticker on label)	£750
65	Fontana TF 533	She Just Satisfies/Keep Moving	£650
91	Fontana TF 533	She Just Satisfies/Keep Moving (reissue as part of Fontana box set)	£15
12	Jimmypage.com JPRLP0002	LUCIFER RISING (AND OTHER SOUNDTRACKS) (LP, 93 signed)	£100
12	Jimmypage.com JPRLP0002	LUCIFER RISING (AND OTHER SOUNDTRACKS) (LP, 418 copies, these unsigned)	£60

(see also Led Zeppelin, Page & Plant, Firm, Yardbirds, Paul, Carter-Lewis & Southerners, Neil Christian & Crusaders, Bobby Graham, Robert Plant, Brian Auger, Cartoone, Maureeny Wishfull, Coverdale-Page)

PAGE ONE & THE OBSERVERS
76	Carib Gems CGLP 004	OBSERVATION OF LIFE DUB (LP)	£60

PATTI PAGE

ALBUMS
54	Mercury MG 25101	FOLK SONG FAVOURITES (10")	£20
55	Mercury MG 25197	PATTI'S SONGS (10")	£20
56	Mercury MPT 7510	CHRISTMAS WITH PATTI PAGE (10")	£20
57	Mercury MPT 7531	I'M GETTING SENTIMENTAL OVER YOU (10")	£20

PAGE BOYS (U.K.)
83	Whaam! WHAAM 10	You're My Kind Of Girl/In Love With You (p/s, 1,000 only)	£20

(see also 1,000 Violins)

PAGE FIVE
66	Parlophone R 5426	Let Sleeping Dogs Lie/I Know All About Her	£35

LARRY PAGE (ORCHESTRA)
57	Columbia DB 3965	Cool Shake/Start Movin' (In My Direction)	£25
58	Columbia DB 4012	That'll Be The Day/Please Don't Blame Me	£20
58	Columbia DB 4080	Under Control/This Is My Life	£20
59	Saga SAG 45-2902	Big Blon' Baby/I Vibrate	£25
65	Decca LK 4692	KINKY MUSIC (LP, as Larry Page Orchestra)	£50
68	Page One POL(S) 002	EXECUTIVE SUITE (LP, as Larry Page Orchestra)	£20

PAGE & PLANT
95	Fontana PPCDJ 3	Kashmir (CD promo, withdrawn)	£30
98	Mercury ADV 1998	Walking Into Clarksdale (CD promo, card sleeve)	£40
94	Fontana PP ID 1	NO QUARTER UNLEDDED (CD, radio-promo only, with 'question' booklet)	£50
94	Fontana 526 3621	NO QUARTER UNLEDDED (2-LP, gatefold, inners)	£75
98	Mercury ADV 982	TBA (CD, advance promo for WALKING INTO CLARKSDALE)	£30
98	Mercury PPTIC 1	WALKING INTO CLARKSDALE AN INTERVIEW (CD radio promo)	£30
98	Mercury 558 025 1	WALKING INTO CLARKSDALE (LP)	£100

(see also Jimmy Page, Robert Plant)

PAGE TEN
65	Decca F 12248	Boutique/Colour Talk	£18

(see also Niney)

PAICE, ASHTON & LORD
77	Polydor/Oyster 2391 269	MALICE IN WONDERLAND (LP, with inner sleeve)	£15

(see also Deep Purple, Jon Lord, Ashton & Lord, Ashton Gardner & Dyke, Elf)

MARTY PAICH
57	London LZ-U 14040	MARTY PAICH QUARTET (LP, with Art Pepper)	£45

HAL PAIGE & WHALERS
60	Melodisc MEL 1553	Going Back To My Home Town/After Hours Blues	£40

JOEY PAIGE
65	Fontana TF 554	Cause I'm In Love With You/Yeah Yeah Yeah	£20

ROSALIND PAIGE
55	London HL 8120	When The Saints Go Marching In/Nobody's Sweetheart Now	£30

PAIN KILLER
91	Earache MOSH 45	GUTS OF A VIRGIN (LP)	£20

PAINS OF BEING PURE AT HEART
08	Atomic Beat ABR 003	Kurt Cobain's Cardigan/PARALLELOGRAMS: 1 2 3 Go/Pop The Bubbles (p/s)	£45
09	Fortuna Pop! FPOP83LP	THE PAINS OF BEING PURE AT HEART (LP)	£15
09	Fortuna Pop! FPOP83LP	THE PAINS OF BEING PURE AT HEART (LP, white/black splatter vinyl)	£20
11	Fortuna Pop! PIASR 500 LP	BELONG (LP, blue vinyl)	£15

PAINTED SHIP
67	Mercury MF 988	Frustration/I Told Those Little White Lies	£130

PAISLEYS
83	Psycho PSYCHO 7	COSMIC MIND AT PLAY (LP, reissue)	£20

PALACE BROTHERS
94	Domino RUG 21T	AN ARROW THROUGH THE BITCH (12" EP, p/s)	£15
95	Domino RUG 35T	The Mountain/Gulf Shores/(End Of) Travelling/West Palm Beach (12", stickered p/s as Palace)	£18
93	Big Cat ABB 50	THERE IS NO ONE WHAT WILL TAKE CARE OF YOU (LP)	£15
94	Domino WIG 14	PALACE BROTHERS (LP)	£15
95	Domino WIGLP 21X	VIVA LAST BLUES (LP with 7" (RUG 39) stickered sleeve, as Palace Music)	£40
95	Domino WIGLP 21	VIVA LAST BLUES (LP, as Palace Music, without 7")	£25
96	Domino WIGLP 24	ARISE THEREFORE (LP)	£20

MINT VALUE £

98	Domino WIGLP 33	LOST BLUES AND OTHER SONGS (2-LP, gatefold, poster)	£25

(see also Bonnie 'Prince' Billy, Will Oldham)

PALADIN
71	Bronze ILPS 9150	PALADIN (LP, textured sleeve, Island credit on label)	£75
72	Bronze ILPS 9190	CHARGE (LP, gatefold sleeve, Island credit on label)	£75

(see also Arthur Brown, Glass Menagerie, McGuinness Flint)

PALE FOUNTAINS
82	Operation Twilight OPT 09	(There's Always) Something On My Mind/Just A Girl (p/s)	£25
84	Virgin V 2274	PACIFIC STREET (LP)	£20
85	Virgin V 2333	FROM ACROSS THE KITCHEN TABLE (LP, with inner sleeve)	£20

(see also Shack, Michael Head & Strands)

PALE SAINTS
90	4AD CAD 0002	THE COMFORTS OF MADNESS (LP, with 3 postcards)	£35
90	4AD CAD 0002	THE COMFORTS OF MADNESS (LP, without postcards)	£25
92	4AD CAD 2004	IN RIBBONS (LP, with free 7" "A Thousand Stars Burst Open"/A Revelation [RIB 1])	£35
92	4AD CAD 2004	IN RIBBONS (LP, with no free 7")	£25
94	4AD CAD 4014	SLOW BUILDINGS (LP)	£40

TOM PALEY
76	Kicking Mule SNKF 119	HARD LUCK PAPA (LP)	£18

(see also Peggy Seeger)

PALI GAP
82	Sinister SYN 001	Under The Sun/The Knives Are Out (p/s, with insert)	£20

PALLAS
82	Granite Wax GWS 1	Arrive Alive/Stranger (On The Edge Of Time) (two different p/s, with insert)	£50
82	Granite Wax GWS 1	Arrive Alive/Stranger (On The Edge Of Time) (two different p/s, without insert)	£40
78	Sue-i-cide PAL/101	THE PALLAS EP (stamped plain die-cut sleeve)	£50
85	Harvest 12PLS3D	THE KNIGHT MOVES EP (12" + free 7" Mad Machine / Stitch In Time, sealed in plastic sleeve)	£15
83	Cool King CKLP002	ARRIVE ALIVE (LP)	£15
84	Harvest SHSP2400 121	THE SENTINAL (LP, gatefold sleeve, with poster and sticker)	£18
86	Harvest SHVL 850	THE WEDGE (LP + inner sleeve)	£15

PALMA VIOLETS
13	Rough Trade TRADS 702	Invasion Of The Tribbles (1-sided other side etched, 2 badges in fold-out sleeve)	£35
13	Rough Trade RTRADELP700	180 (LP)	£15

JERRY PALMER
66	London 10026	Walking The Dog/Don't Leave Me Baby	£25

MICHAEL PALMER
84	Tonos 001	Modelling Girl/Soca Rumble (12")	£20
84	Greensleeves GRED 144	I'm Still Dancing/ROBERT FRENCH: No War (12")	£50
84	Greensleeves GREL 155	Done With It/Can't Take The Fuss (12")	£15
84	Simba SM 08	Me Nah Run/JACKIE PARRIS: When Your Are Young (12", with Aswad)	£25
84	Tonos TONLP 001	STAR PERFORMER (LP)	£25

MICHAEL PALMER AND JIM BROWN
83	Greensleeves GRED 131	Ghetto Dance/JAH THOMAS & ROOTS RADICS: Ghetto Dub (12")	£25

RICK PALMER
59	London HLL 8900	You Threw A Heart/My Greatest Wish (unreleased)	£0

ROY PALMER & STATE STREET RAMBLERS
54	London AL 3518	A CHICAGO SKIFFLE SESSION (10" LP)	£30

TONY PALMER
77	Eji E00009	Jah Shall Conquer/Commissioner (instrumental) (12")	£20

TRISTAN PALMER/PALMA
81	Orbit ORB 801	Caly Man/Ungrateful Girl (12")	£20
81	Greensleeves GRED 66	Entertainment/JAH THOMAS & TOYAN: Jah Guide (12")	£15
81	Art & Craft ACS 011	Fussing And Fighting (with Ranking Joe)/Version (12")	£20
82	Greensleeves GRED 93	Joker Smoker/PAPA BRUCE: Loafter Smoker (12")	£25
83	Greensleeves GRED 126	No Shot No Fire/BARRY BROWN: Jukes And Watches (12")	£20
83	Trojan TROT 9068	Settle Down Girl/Version (12")	£15
82	Vista STLP 1017	TOUCH ME TAKE ME (LP)	£15
82	Greensleeves GREL 43	JOKER SMOKER (LP)	£20
83	Trojan TRLS 215	SETTLE DOWN GIRL (LP)	£20

VIC PALMER COMBO
73	Ra RA EP 7009	ON HOLIDAY! (EP, p/s)	£15

PALMETTO KINGS
60	Starlite ST45 021	Ten Rum Bottles/Home Cookin' Mama	£15

CHARLIE PALMIERI
68	Atlantic 588157	LATIN BUGALU (LP)	£40

PAN
93	Big Cat ABB 49	HANGIN' OUT FOR JUNE (LP)	£15

PANAMA FRANCIS BLUES BAND
64	Stateside SL 10070	TOUGH TALK!! (LP)	£35

PANAMA LIMITED (JUG BAND)
69	Harvest HAR 5010	Lady Of Shallot/Future Blues	£30
70	Harvest HAR 5022	Round And Round/Rotting Wooden In A White Collar's Grave	£30

69	Harvest SHVL 753	**PANAMA LIMITED JUG BAND** (LP, laminated gatefold, "Sold in U.K..." text on 5 lines), no EMI on label)..£250
70	Harvest SHVL 753	**PANAMA LIMITED JUG BAND** (LP, laminated gatefold sleeve, 2nd pressing, no "Sold in U.K..." no EMI on label)..£60
70	Harvest SHVL 779	**INDIAN SUMMER** (LP, as Panama Limited, textured gatefold, no EMI on label) £300
08	Timeless TIME 713	**INDIAN SUMMER** (LP, reissue)...£18

(see also Ian (A) Anderson)

ALPHONSO PANCHO
| 79 | Attack TACK 3 | Love Is A Pleasure/Never Give Up In A Babylon...£20 |

(see also Pancho Alphonso)

GENE PANCHO
| 68 | Giant GN 21 | I Like Sweet Music/Seven Days (with Sandy & Superboys)....................................£40 |

(see also Gene Rondo)

PANDEMONIUM
67	CBS 202462	Season Of The Witch/Today I'm Happy £60
67	CBS 2664	No Presents For Me/The Sun Shines From His Eyes £300
68	CBS 3451	Chocolate Buster Dan/Fly With Me Forever...£70

PANDIT PRAN NATH
| 69 | Transatlantic TRA 193 | **EARTH GROOVE** (LP) ....£40 |

PANDORAS
| 67 | Liberty LIB 55954 | (I Could Write A Book) About My Baby/New Day...£18 |

PANHANDLE
| 72 | Decca SKL 5105 | **PANHANDLE** (LP, laminated cover, blue/silver label with boxed logo)....................£30 |

(see also Chris Spedding)

PANIC IN THE YEAR ZERO
| 81 | Vada ABER 4128 | Liberty Caps/Sometimes I Don't Know ....£20 |

PANIK
| 77 | Rainy City SHOT 1 | **IT WON'T SELL** (EP) ....£15 |

PAN PIPERS
| 69 | Pye 7N 17699 | Stop/Money Or Love ....£125 |

PAN SONIC
95	Blast First VBFFP 118	**VAKIO** (2-LP, reissue)...£25
97	Blast First BFFP 132	**KULMA** (LP, 2 x 12")...£20
00	Blast First BFFP 166	**AALTOPIIRI** (2-LP, print)..£20
04	Blast First BFFP 180BX	**KESTO** (4-CD box set)...£30
10	Blast First Petite PTYT 043	**HAINIO KEIJI - IN THE STUDIO** (2-LP)..£20

PANT
| 79 | Redball RR019X | Mother Fo/Modern/No Possessions/Mummy Told You ....£25 |

GARY PANTER & JAY COTTON
| 90 | Blast First FU 7 | **ONE HELL SOUNDWICH** (LP, picture disc) ....£20 |

JAN PANTER
65	Oriole CB 1938	My Two Arms Minus You Equals Tears/Does My Heart Show £25
65	CBS 201810	Let It Be Now/Stand By And Cry £20
66	Pye 7N 17097	Scratch My Back/Put Yourself In My Place £250

PANTERA
90	Atco 7567-91372-1	**COWBOYS FROM HELL** (LP) £40
92	Atco 756791758-1	**VULGAR DISPLAY OF POWER** (LP) £60
93	East West 92302	**FAR BEYOND DRIVEN** (2-LP, gatefold)..£60
96	East West 7559-61908-1	**GREAT SOUTHERN TRENDKILL** (LP) £50

PANTHER BURNS
| 81 | Rough Trade ROUGH 32 | **BEHIND THE MAGNOLIA CURTAIN** (LP, inner) ....£25 |

ROY PANTON
63	Blue Beat BB 182	Mighty Ruler/Run Old Man...£30
64	Blue Beat BB 219	Good From The Bad/Hell Gate...£30
64	Rio R 19	Cherita/Seek And You Shall Find...£20
64	Rio R 33	You Don't Know Me/KING EDWARD'S ALLSTARS: Doctor No................................£40
64	Island WI 137	Goodbye Peggy Darling (actually "Goodbye Peggy" by Stranger Cole)/ BABA BROOKS: Portrait Of My Love..£25

(see also Roy & Annette, Roy & Millie, Roy & Paulette, Roy & Yvonne, Roy & Duke Allstars, Roy & Patsy, Derrick Harriot, Leon & Owen, Charmers, Roy Patin)

JOHN PANTRY
72	Philips 6308 129	**JOHN PANTRY** (LP) £40
73	Philips 6308 138	**LONG WHITE TRAIL** (LP)..£20
80	Kingsway KMR 323	**TO STRANGERS AND FRIENDS** (LP)...£15
99	Tenth Planet TP 040	**THE UPSIDE DOWN WORLD OF JOHN PANTRY** (LP, limited edition, 1,000 only) £30

(see also Factory, Peter & Wolves, Norman Conquest, Sounds Around)

PAPA CHARJAN
| 82 | CF CF 006 | DJ Pumping/COURTNEY BARKELY: I Am Alright (12")..£20 |

PAPA TULLO
| 81 | Negus Roots NERT 006 | Church And State/Righteous Rock (12")..£15 |
| 82 | Negus Roots NERLP 004 | **TULLO AT HOME** (LP) ....£40 |

PAPADOCTRINE
| 95 | Alphaphone ALPHA 001 | Flesh Hunter/Hybrid Energy/Dreamreader (12")...£15 |

(see also Cabaret Voltaire, Richard H. Kirk)

NIKKI PAPAS
59	Parlophone R 4590	49 State Rock/Try Again	£40

PAPER BLITZ TISSUE
67	RCA Victor RCA 1652	Boy Meets Girl/Grey Man	£500

(see also Cupid's Inspiration)

PAPER BUBBLE
70	Deram DML 1059	SCENERY (LP, white/red label, Mono)	£350
70	Deram SML 1059	SCENERY (LP, white/red label, Stereo)	£200

(see also Dave Cousins)

PAPER DOLLS
68	Pye N(S)PL 18226	PAPER DOLLS HOUSE (LP)	£60

PAPER TISSUE
72	Dresden DR2	Wild Fire/Visions In The NIght	£50

PAPERHOUSE
91	Mystic Stones RUNE LP 11	SPONGY COMESTIBLES (LP)	£20

PARADE
67	A&M AMS 701	Sunshine Girl/This Old Melody	£18
67	A&M AMS 720	Radio Song/I Can See Love	£15

PARADISE HAMMER
70	Polydor 2058048	She Is Love/You Got Me In	£25
71	Polydor 2058084	1+1=2/To Live	£15

PARADISE LOST
90	Peaceville VILE 17	LOST PARADISE (LP)	£15
91	Peaceville VILE26L	GOTHIC (LP, gatefold, red vinyl)	£25
91	Peaceville VILE26L	GOTHIC (LP, gatefold)	£18
92	Music For Nations MFN 135	SHADES OF GOD (LP)	£20
93	Music For Nations MFN 152	ICON (2-LP)	£25
95	Music For Nations MFN 184	DRACONIAN TIMES (2-LP)	£35
97	Music For Nations MFN 222	LOST (2-LP)	£25

PARADISE SQUARE
74	None	NEVER THOUGHT I'D SEE THE DAY (LP, 100 only, hand-drawn covers)	£800

PARADISE (1)
77	Clubland SJP 775	One Of These Days/You're The One I Need (no p/s, 500 only)	£15

PARADISE (2)
80	Ebony EB 701	PARADISE (LP)	£125
82	Ebony EB 702	WORLD'S MIDNIGHT (LP)	£100
83	Priority PLP 1	LOVE IS THE ANSWER (LP)	£100

PARADONS
60	Top Rank JAR 514	Diamonds And Pearls/I Want Love	£60

PARADOX VOYEUR
80	Brigade BRIG 001	Deceit/E.D./Choosy (p/s)	£15

PARADOX (1)
68	Polydor 56275	The Wednesday Theme/Ring The Changes	£125

(see also David Walker)

PARAFFIN JACK FLASH LTD
68	Pye NSPL 18252	MOVERS AND GROOVERS (LP)	£18

PARAGONS
66	Doctor Bird DB 1060	Happy-Go-Lucky Girl/Love Brings Pain	£45
67	Island WI 3045	On The Beach/CAROL & TOMMY McCOOK: Sweet And Gentle (B-side actually by Tommy McCook & Supersonics)	£40
67	Island WI 3067	Talking Love/If I Were You	£40
67	Island WI 3093	So Depressed/We Were Meant To Be	£80
67	Treasure Isle TI 7009	Only A Smile/The Tide Is High	£25
67	Treasure Isle TI 7011	Mercy, Mercy, Mercy/Riding On A High And Windy Day	£25
67	Treasure Isle TI 7013	The Same Song/TOMMY McCOOK & SUPERSONICS: Soul Serenade	£30
67	Treasure Isle TI 7025	Wear You To The Ball/You Mean The World To Me	£40
68	Treasure Isle TI 7034	Silver Bird/My Best Girl	£25
68	Island WI 3138	Memories By The Score/The Number One For Me	£30
69	Studio One SO 2081	Have You Ever Been In Love/Change Your Style	£50
69	Duke DU 7	Left With A Broken Heart/I've Got To Get Away	£80
69	Crab 13	Take Your Hand From My Neck/Equality And Justice (actually by VICEROYS)	£40
77	Wildflower WF 523	Do The Best Thing/Best Thing	£15
80	Virgin VS 389	The Tide Is High/U ROY: Tide Is High	£15
12	Treasure Isle THB 7020	Joy In My Soul/THE TECHNIQUES: Travelling Man	£15
67	Treasure Isle DLM 5010	ON THE BEACH (LP)	£250
81	Starlight Records SLDLP 909	NOW (LP)	£20
81	Island ILPS 9631	THE PARAGONS (LP)	£15
74	Horse HRLP 703	THE PARAGONS WITH ROSALYN SWEAT (LP)	£40
92	Trojan TRLS 299	MY BEST GIRL WEARS MY CROWN (ROCK STEADY 1966-1968)	£18

(see also John Holt, Lester Sterling)

PARALEX
80	Reddingtons R.R. DAN 4	White Lightning/Travelling Man/Black Widow, (12", p/s, green vinyl)	£50

PARALLELOGRAMS
08   Atomic Beat ABR 003   1 2 3 Go/Pop The Bubbles/PAINS OF BEING PURE AT HEART: Kurt Cobain's Cardigan (p/s) £45

PARAMEDIC SQUAD
81   Gargoyle GRGL 2   Movement In Time/For You/Thinking Psychedelia (p/s) £25

PARAMETER
70   Deroy   GALACTIC RAMBLE (LP, 450 only, 4 page inner) £300

NORRIE PARAMOR & HIS ORCHESTRA
70   Polydor 56375   Randall And Hopkirk (Deceased)/A Summer Palace £65
(see also Harry Gold)

PARAMORE
06   Fueled By Ramen ATUK 037   Emergency/O'Star (poster sleeve) £20

PARAMOUNT ALL-STARS
50   Tempo R 20   Hometown Skiffle (Parts 1 & 2) (78) £20
(see also Blind Blake, Georgia Tom, Alex Hill, Papa Charlie Jackson, Blind Lemon Jefferson, Charlie Spand)

PARAMOUNT FOUR
09   Kent 6T 26   Sorry Ain't The Word/GENE & GARY: Baby Without You £20

PARAMOUNTS
64   Parlophone R 5107   Little Bitty Pretty One/A Certain Girl £20
64   Parlophone R 5155   I'm The One Who Loves You/It Won't Be Long £25
64   Parlophone R 5187   Bad Blood/Do I £25
65   Parlophone R 5272   Blue Ribbons/Cuttin' In £20
65   Parlophone R 5351   You Never Had It So Good/Don't Ya Like My Love £50
64   Parlophone GEP 8908   THE PARAMOUNTS (EP) £300
(see also Procol Harum)

PARANOIA
84   Rot ASS 11   SHATTERED GLASS (LP) £25

PARANOID LONDON
12   Paranoid London PDON 003   EATING GLUE EP (12", with Mutado Pintado) £30
12   Paranoid London PDON 004   PARIS DUB 1 EP (12" with Paris Brightledge) £20

PARCHMENT
72   Pye NSPL 18388   LIGHT UP THE FIRE (LP, textured sleeve with poster insert) £20
73   Pye NSPL 18409   HOLLYWOOD SUNSET (LP, gatefold) £15
75   Myrrh MYR 1028   SHAMBLEJAM (LP) £18
77   Pilgrim GRAPEVINE 106   REHEARSAL FOR A REUNION (LP) £15

WALTER PARDON
75   Leader LED 2063   A PROPER SORT (LP) £20

PAULA PARFITT
69   Beacon BEA 135   I'm Gonna Give You Back Your Ring/Love Is Wonderful (Beware of bootlegs! - originals have anti-slip grips around the label) £150

TINY PARHAM
50s   Audubon AAC   TINY PARHAM (10" LP) £25

BOBBY PARIS
68   Polydor 56747   Per So Nal Ly/Tragedy £80
69   Polydor 56762   Let The Sun Shine In/You £25
79   Capitol CL 16067   I Walked Away/H.B. BARNUM: Heartbreaker £15

PARIS CONNECTION
73   Explosion EX 2085   That Lady/Sonia £30

MICA PARIS
91   4th & Broadway 12BRWDJ207   A STAND FOR LOVE EP (12" promo p/s. Mispress, plays Prince's vocal version of 'A Stand For Love') £125

PARIS SISTERS
61   Top Rank JAR 588   I Love How You Love Me/I'll Be Crying Tomorrow £50
64   MGM MGM 1240   Dream Lover/Lonely Girl £50
(see also Date With Soul)

JOHN PARISH & POLLY JEAN HARVEY
96   Island ILPS 8051   DANCE HALL AT LOUSE POINT (LP) £60
09   Island 1797426   A WOMAN A MAN WALKED BY (LP) £25

PARISH HALL
70   Liberty LBS 83374   PARISH HALL (LP) £200

SIMON PARK
74   EMI EMC 3059   SOMETHING IN THE AIR (LP) £20

PARKE
71   Folk Heritage FHR 018S   PARKE (LP) £350
72   Folk Heritage FHR 028   JOY HEALTH LOVE AND PEACE (LP) £200

ALAN PARKER
70   Aristocrat AR 1022   GUITAR FANTASY (LP) £20
73   MCA MUPS 471   BAND OF ANGELS (LP) £20
(see also Hungry Wolf, Ugly Custard)

BENNY PARKER & DYNAMICS
64   Decca F 11944   Boys And Girls/You'll Be On Your Way £45

BOBBY PARKER
61	London HLU 9393	Watch Your Step/Steal Your Heart Away	£60
64	Sue WI 340	Watch Your Step/Steal Your Heart Away (reissue)	£55
69	Blue Horizon 57-3151	It's Hard But It's Fair/I Couldn't Quit My Baby	£45

CHARLIE PARKER
ALBUMS
52	Vogue LDE 004	CHARLIE PARKER VOLUME ONE (10")	£75
53	Vogue LDE 016	CHARLIE PARKER VOLUME TWO (10")	£75
56	Vogue LAE 12002	CHARLIE PARKER MEMORIAL ALBUM (gatefold sleeve w/ 2 inserts)	£25
55	Melodisc MLP 12-105	BIRD AT ST. NICK'S	£30
55	Columbia Clef 33CX 10004	CHARLIE PARKER BIG BAND	£40
56	Columbia Clef 33C 9026	BIRD AND DIZ (10", with Dizzy Gillespie)	£40
57	Columbia Clef 33CX 10081	APRIL IN PARIS (as Charlie Parker With Strings)	£35
57	Columbia Clef 33CX 10090	CHARLIE PARKER PLAYS COLE PORTER	£25
58	Columbia Clef 33CX 10117	CHARLIE PARKER JAZZ PERENNIAL	£15
58	London Jazz LTZ-C 15104	THE IMMORTAL CHARLIE PARKER VOL. 1	£15
58	London Jazz LTZ-C 15105	THE IMMORTAL CHARLIE PARKER VOL. 2	£15
58	London Jazz LTZ-C 15106	THE IMMORTAL CHARLIE PARKER VOL. 3	£15
58	London Jazz LTZ-C 15107	THE IMMORTAL CHARLIE PARKER VOL. 4	£15
58	Mercury MPL 12-105	BIRD AT NICK'S	£15
60	Collector JGN 1002	CHARLIE PARKER IN SWEDEN	£30

(see also Dizzy Gillespie & Charlie Parker, Sir Charles Thompson)

DAVID PARKER
71	Polydor 2460 101	DAVID PARKER (LP)	£50

(see also Andwella's Dream)

DEAN PARKER & REDCAPS
62	Decca F 11555	Stormy Evening/Blue Eyes And Golden Hair	£45

DYON PARKER
69	Marble Arch MAL 787	OUT ON THE HIGHWAY (LP)	£20

EDDIE PARKER (U.S.)
79	Grapevine GRP 119	Love You Baby (Parts 1 & 2) (in p/s) (DJ copy)	£20

EULA PARKER
58	Oriole CB 1411	Silhouettes/Hedgehopper	£20

(see also Frank Weir)

EVAN PARKER
75	Incus INCUS 19	SAXOPHONE SOLOS (LP)	£40
78	Incus INCUS 27	MONOCEROS (LP)	£30
80	Incus INCUS 39	SIX OF ONE (LP)	£30
86	Incus INCUS 49	THE SNAKE DECIDES (LP)	£50
89	Cadillac (no cat no)	COLLECTED SOLOS (4 x LP and cassette hand numbered to 200)	£175

EVAN PARKER, DEREK BAILEY, HAN BENNINK
70	Incus INCUS 1	THE TOPOGRAPHY OF THE LUNGS (LP)	£150
77	Incus INCUS 1	THE TOPOGRAPHY OF THE LUNGS (LP, reissue)	£40

EVAN PARKER, BARRY GUY & PAUL LYTTON
83	Incus INCUS 42	TRACKS (LP)	£40

EVAN PARKER & GEORGE LEWIS
80	Incus INCUS 35	FROM SAXOPHONE & TROMBONE (LP)	£40

EVAN PARKER, GEORGE LEWIS, BARRY GUY & PAUL LYTTON
83	Incus INCUS 45	HOOK, DRIFT & SHUFFLE (LP)	£50

EVAN PARKER & PAUL LYTTON
72	Incus INCUS 5	COLLECTIVE CALLS (URBAN) (TWO MICROPHONES) (LP)	£40
75	Incus INCUS 14	AT THE UNITY THEATRE (LP)	£40

(see also Derek Bailey & Evan Parker, Derek Bailey Evan Parker & Han Bennink)

(LITTLE) JUNIOR PARKER
61	Vogue V 9179	Stand By Me/I'll Forget About You (as Little Junior Parker)	£30
62	Vogue V 9193	Mary Jo/Annie Get Your Yo-Yo (as Little Junior Parker)	£30
66	Vocalion VP 9256	These Kind Of Blues (Parts 1 & 2)	£40
66	Vocalion VP 9256	These Kind Of Blues (Parts 1 & 2) (DJ copy)	£60
66	Vocalion VP 9275	Goodbye Little Girl/Walking The Floor Over You	£30
67	Mercury SMCL 20097	LIKE IT IS (LP)	£50
72	Groove Merchant GM 502	BLUE SHADOWS FALLING (LP)	£15
73	Groove Merchant GM 2205	GOOD THINGS DON'T HAPPEN EVERY DAY (LP, with Jimmy McGriff)	£15
73	Vogue LDM 30163	MEMORIAL (LP)	£15
73	People PLEO 4	YOU DON'T HAVE TO BE BLACK TO LOVE THE BLUES (LP)	£20

KEN PARKER
67	Island WI 3082	How Could I/SONNY BURKE: Choo Choo Train	£60
67	Studio One SO 2001	Have A Good Time/MR FOUNDATION: See Them A Come	£50
68	Island WI 3096	Down Low/Sad Mood	£50
68	Island WI 3105	Lonely Man/ERROL DUNKLEY: I Am Going Home	£100
68	Giant GN 34	Change Is Gonna Come/VAL BENNETT: Jumping With Val	£175
69	Bamboo BAM 1	My Whole World Is Falling Down/The Chokin' Kind	£30
69	Amalgamated AMG 847	It's Alright/COBBS: One One	£100
69	Amalgamated AMG 853	Only Yesterday/COBBS: Joe Gibbs Mood	£40
70	Duke DU 79	I Can't Hide/TOMMY McCOOK: Kansas City	£35

MINT VALUE £

70	Unity UN 553	When You Were Mine/CLAREDONIANS: The Angels (song actually "The Angels Listened In")	£15
71	Duke Reid DR 2504	Sugar Pantie (as Ken Parker & Tommy McCook; actually by Andy Capp)/ TOMMY McCOOK: All Afire	£15
71	Duke Reid DR 2521	Jimmy Brown/Version	£15
72	Melodisc SMLP 12-190	KEEP YOUR EYES ON JESUS (LP)	£85
74	Trojan TRLS 80	JIMMY BROWN (LP)	£25
75	Pisces PS 5002	A TOUCH OF INSPIRATION (LP)	£40

(see also Lyrics)

LARRY PARKER

80	Brightheath BRH 1	Perfect Dreams/Light	£20

LEWIS PARKER

95	White JED1	B BOY ANTICS (EP, different recording to Bite It! version - first batch with a black and white sticker, later batch has coloured sticker)	£70
96	Bite It! BITEDJ10	B BOY ANTICS (EP)	£45
96	Bite It! BITE11	Rise/Visions Of Splendour/Sea Freestyle (12")	£25
95	White LEWIS1	Wonderwall (7", 100 only)	£30
00	M'lic LEWISTDJ1LC03098	THE OPTIONS (EP)	£25
01	White SADTDJ13	It's All Happening Now/Schemes/What The Ancients Say (remixes) (EP, 50 copies only)	£20
03	Dusty Vinyl DV1JEDI	Mr Parker's Siesta/Blood (12")	£18
13	King Underground KU/WODV008	Fragments Of Glass (10" that came with a small number of THE PUZZLE: EPISODE 2)	£15
98	Melankolic SADT4	MASQUERADES AND SILHOUETTES (LP)	£75
02	Melankolic LPSAD14	IT'S ALL HAPPENING NOW (LP)	£70
06	Dusty Vinyl DVJEDI008	MASQUERADES AND SILHOUETTES INSTRUMENTALS (LP, 200 only with unreleased track)	£75
10	Project Moon Circle PMC 065	INTERNATIONAL SUMMERS (LP, with John Robinson)	£25
13	King Underground KU/WODV007	THE PUZZLE EPISODE 2 - THE GLASS CEILING (LP)	£45

MACEO PARKER

90	Verve 843 751-1	ROOTS REVISITED (LP)	£30

(see also Maceo & The Macks, Maceo & All The Kings Men)

RAYMOND PARKER

66	Sue WI 4024	Ring Around The Roses/She's Coming Home	£50

ROBERT PARKER

66	Island WI 286	Barefootin'/Let's Go Baby (Where The Action Is)	£30
66	Island WI 3008	Happy Feet/The Scratch	£20
74	Contemporaries CS 9010	Barefootin'/I Caught You In A Lie	£15
66	Island ILP 942	BAREFOOTIN' (LP)	£80

(see also Huey 'Piano' Smith & Clowns)

SONNY PARKER

56	Vogue V 2392	My Soul's On Fire/Disgusted Blues	£300
56	Vogue V 2392	My Soul's On Fire/Disgusted Blues (78)	£50

(see also Lionel Hampton)

PARKING LOT

69	Parlophone R 5779	Carpet Man/World Spinning Sadly	£45

JIMMY PARKINSON

56	Columbia SCM 5236	The Great Pretender/Hand In Hand	£30
57	Columbia 33S 1109	SOLO (10" LP)	£20

BERNICE PARKS

55	Coral Q 72056	Lovin' Machine/Only Love Me	£15

LLOYD PARKS

70	Harry J. HJ 6603	Feel A Little Better/I'll Be Your Man	£60
71	Upsetter US 379	Mighty Cloud Of Joy/UPSETTERS: Version	£25
72	Randy's RAN 524	Stars/Stars - Version	£20
74	Fab FAB 273	Schooldays/Version	£15
75	Cactus CT 75	Mafia/Mafia Version (Dub)	£25
74	Attack – ATLP 1009	OFFICIALLY (LP)	£40
75	Trojan Records TRLS 109	GIRL IN THE MORNING (LP)	£25
76	Trojan TRLS 126	LOVING YOU (LP)	£40

VAN DYKE PARKS

69	Warner Bros W(S) 1727	SONG CYCLE (LP)	£35
75	Warner Bros. K56161	CLANG OF THE YANKEE REAPER (LP)	£15
86	Edsel ED 210	DISCOVER AMERICA (LP. reissue)	£15
13	Bella Union BELLAV 396	SONGS CYCLED (2-LP, CD)	£20

PARLET

79	Casablanca CAL 2052	INVASION OF THE BOOTY SNATCHERS (LP)	£15

(see also Parliament)

PARLIAMENT

72	Invictus INV 522	Come In Out Of The Rain/Little Ole Country Boy	£15
71	Invictus SVT 1004	OSMIUM (LP)	£100
74	Casablanca NBLP 7002	UP FOR THE DOWN STROKE (LP)	£50
75	Casablanca CBC 4009	MOTHERSHIP CONNECTION (LP)	£40
75	Casablanca CAL 2012	CHOCOLATE CITY (LP)	£40
77	Casablanca CALD 5002	PARLIAMENT LIVE (2-LP)	£30

MINT VALUE £

77	Casablanca CALH 2021	**FUNKENTELECHY VS THE PLACEBO SYNDROME** (LP, with booklet and poster, some on red vinyl)	£35
90	Demon HDH LP 008	**RHENIUM** (LP)	£20
99	Sequel NEMLP 997	**OSMIUM** (LP, reissue)	£15

(see also Parliaments, Funkadelic, Parlet, Bootsy's Rubber Band, P-Funk Allstars)

PARLIAMENTS
67	Track 604 013	**I Wanna Testify/I Can Feel The Ice Melting**	£30
69	Track 604 032	**I Wanna Testify/I Can Feel The Ice Melting** (reissue)	£20

(see also Parliament, Funkadelic)

PARLOPHONE POPS ORCHESTRA
56	Parlophone R 4250	**Giddy Up A Ding Dong/**(We're Gonna) **Rock Around The Clock**	£15

(see also Ron Goodwin)

PARLOUR
10	Parlour PARLOUR NO2	**NO 2** (12', p/s)	£35
13	Parlour PARLOUR NO3	**NO 3** (12", p/s)	£35

PARLOUR BAND
72	Deram SDL 10	**IS A FRIEND?** (LP, laminated gatefold sleeve, white/red label)	£500

CHRIS PARMENTER ORCHESTRA
66	Polydor 56107	**Cul De Sac/Donkey**	£20

JACK PARNELL (ORCHESTRA)
54	Parlophone MSP 6078	**Skin Deep/Devil's Eyes** (B-side with Dennis Hale)	£20
54	Parlophone MSP 6102	**The Bandit** (with Dennis Hale)**/Annie's Blues** (with Annie Ross)	£18
52	Decca LF 1065	**THE JACK PARNELL QUARTET** (10" LP)	£25
58	Parlophone PMD 1053	**TRIP TO MARS** (10" LP)	£80

PAROT
73	Royal Blue RB 001	**Wake Up/I've Dreamed Of The Sun** (p/s)	£25

JACKIE PARRIS AND BIG YOUTH
79	Book Of Psalms BP 001	**Let Him Try/Really Together** (12")	£15

DEAN PARRISH
66	Stateside SS 531	**Tell Her/Fall On Me**	£80
66	Stateside SS 531	**Tell Her/Fall On Me** (DJ copy)	£125
66	Stateside SS 550	**Turn On Your Lovelight/Determination**	£150
66	Stateside SS 550	**Turn On Your Lovelight/Determination** (DJ copy)	£200
67	Stateside SS 580	**Skate** (Parts 1 & 2)	£60
67	Stateside SS 580	**Skate** (Parts 1 & 2) (DJ copy)	£100
75	UK USA 2	**I'm On My Way/Watch Out** (DJ copy)	£15

PARRISH & GURVITZ
71	Regal Zono. SRZA 8506	**PARRISH & GURVITZ** (LP, textured gatefold sleeve)	£35

(see also Baker Gurvitz Army, Three Man Army)

SAM PARRY
73	Argo ZDA 155	**IF SADNESS COULD SING** (LP)	£400

PARSON & SMITH
72	Polydor 2058229	**The Letter/When It Rains**	£30

ALAN PARSONS PROJECT
77	Arista AL 7002	**I ROBOT** (LP)	£15

(see also Andrew Powell & Philharmonic Orchestra))

BILL PARSONS & HIS ORCHESTRA
59	London HL 8798	**The All American Boy/Rubber Dolly** (78)	£15

GENE PARSONS
74	Warner Bros K 46257	**KINDLING** (LP)	£18

(see also Byrds, Flying Burrito Brothers)

GRAM PARSONS
73	Reprise K 44228	**GP** (LP, gatefold sleeve)	£40
74	Reprise K 54018	**GRIEVOUS ANGEL** (LP, with Emmylou Harris)	£40
76	A&M AMLH 65478	**SLEEPLESS NIGHTS** (LP, with Flying Burrito Brothers & Emmylou Harris)	£35
82	Sundown SDLP 003	**GRAM PARSONS AND THE FALLEN ANGELS** (LP, featuring Emmylou Harris)	£15

(see also Byrds, Flying Burrito Brothers)

PARTISANS (1)
82	No Future OI 2	**Police Story/Killing Machine** (p/s, with lyric insert)	£15
82	No Future OI 12	**17 Years Of Hell/The Power And The Greed/Bastards In Blue** (p/s)	£15
83	Cloak & Dagger PART 1	**Blind Ambition/Come Clean** (p/s)	£15
83	No Future PUNK 4	**PARTISANS** (LP)	£22
84	Cloak & Dagger PARTLP 1	**THE TIME WAS RIGHT** (LP, with inner)	£40

DON PARTRIDGE
68	Columbia S(C)X 6280	**DON PARTRIDGE** (LP)	£15

(see also Accolades)

PARTY DAY
83	Party Day FX 301	**Row The Boat Ashore/Poison** (p/s, insert)	£15
85	Rouska COME 1T	**Glasshouse/My Heroine/Let Us Shine/Smile** (12", p/s)	£20
85	Party Day FXLP 401	**GLASSHOUSE** (LP)	£30
86	Party Day PDLP 501	**SIMPLICITY** (LP)	£30

PASADENA ROOF ORCHESTRA
78	CBS CBS 12-637	**Pennies From Heaven/Back In Your Own Back Yard/Pennies From Heaven** (10" p/s, 2nd side plays at 78 rpm)	£15

PASHA
69   Liberty LBF 15199   Someone Shot The Lollipop Man/Pussy Willow Dragon £120
(see also Searchers)

JOE PASS
60s   Fontana 688 137 ZL   CATCH ME (LP) £20

PASSENGERS (1)
79   No label or cat. no   Something About You (I Don't Like)/Two Lovers (1st press, hand-written labels) £15

PASSENGERS (2)
96   Island OST 3   Your Blue Room (CD, 1-track promo, card sleeve, export issue) £30
95   Island OST 2   ORIGINAL SOUNDCHAT 1 (2-CD, music & interview disc, fold-out digipaks, with cue sheet, promo only) £60
95   Island ILPS8043   ORIGINAL SOUNDTRACKS (LP) £100
(see also U2, Brian Eno)

PASSION POLKA
82   Kinetic KR 01   Obsessions/Juliet (no p/s) £40

PASSION PIT
09   Frenchkiss 88697438861   MANNERS (LP) £40
12   Columbia 88725 41651 1   GOSSAMER (2-LP, with CD) £40

PASSIONS (1)
58   Capitol CL 14874   My Aching Heart/Jackie Brown £75

PASSIONS (2)
59   Top Rank JAR 224   Just To Be With You/Oh Melancholy Me £60
60   Top Rank JAR 313   I Only Want You/This Is My Love £70

PAST AND PRESENT
79   Rook CUS 423   FIRST TIME OUT (LP, private pressing) £30

PAST SEVEN DAYS
86   4AD AD 102   Raindance/So Many Others/Nothing (p/s) £15

PASTEL
21   Spirit Of Spike Island   DEEPER THAN HOLY (12", pink or orange neon vinyl, p/s) £40

PASTELS
82   Whaam! WHAAM 005   Songs For Children: Heavens Above!/Tea Time Tales (p/s) £80
83   Rough Trade RT 137   I Wonder Why/Supposed To Understand (p/s) £40
84   Creation CRE 005   Something Going On/Stay With Me Till Morning (foldaround p/s in poly bag) £35
84   Creation CRE 011T   A Million Tears/Baby Honey/Surprise Me (12", p/s) £15
85   Villa 21 VILLA 3   Heavens Above!/Tea Time Tales/I Wonder Why (live)/Tea Time Tales (live) (p/s) £25
95   Domino RUG 36T   Worlds Of Possibility/Photogram/Love, It's Getting Better/Ever Far (12", p/s) £15
87   Glass GLAL P021   UP FOR A BIT WITH THE PASTELS (LP, with inner) £20
88   Creation CRELP 031   SUCK ON (LP) £20
89   Chapter 22 CHAPLP 43   SITTIN' PRETTY (LP) £20
93   Paperhouse PAPLP 008   TRUCKROAD OF TROUBLE (2-LP) £40
94   Domino WIGLP 17   MOBILE SAFARI (LP, with free 7") £45
98   Domino WIGLP46   ILLUMINATI (2-LP) £40
97   Domino WIGLP 34   ILLUMINATION (LP) £50
03   Geographic GEOG18LP   LAST GREAT WILDERNESS (LP) £35
09   Geographic GEOG37LP   TWO SUNSETS (LP, with Tenniscoats) £20
13   Domino WIGLP 185   SLOW SUMMITS (LP) £15
(see also Buba & Shop Assistants, Vaselines)

PASTEL SIX
63   London HLU 9651   The Cinnamon Cinder/Bandido £20

PASTORAL SYMPHONY
68   President PT 202   Love Machine/Spread A Little Love Around £20

PAT
71   Gas GAS 158   Teach Me (actually "Words Of Temptation" by Earl Lawrence)/RHYTHM RULERS: Sea Breeze (actually by Im & David) £30

PAT & MARIE
66   Ska Beat JB 234   I Try Not To Tell You/PAT RHODEN: Don't Blame It On Me £15
66   Ska Beat JB 235   You're Really Leaving/PAT RHODEN: Broken Heart £15
(see also Pat Rhoden)

PATCHWORK (1)
72   Decca FR 13346   Laughing Sam (On The Phone)/Afrodisiac £40

JOHNNY PATE ORCHESTRA
73   Probe SPB 1077   SHAFT IN AFRICA (LP, soundtrack, with Four Tops) £40
74   ABC ABCL 5035   SHAFT IN AFRICA (LP, soundtrack, reissue) £15

PAMELA PATERSON
72   Polydor 2001 278   Finally (Theme From 'Gumshoe')/OLYMPIC STUDIO CONCERT ORCHESTRA: Music From 'Gumshoe' (p/s) £20

PATHETIX
78   No Records NO 001   Aleister Crowley/Don't Touch My Machine/Snuffed It (p/s, with insert) £35
79   TJM TJM 9   Love In Decay/Nil Carborundum/What Do You Expect? (with p/s) £200
79   TJM TJM 9   Love In Decay/Nil Carborundum/What Do You Expect? (without p/s) £40

PATHFINDERS (1)
64   Decca F 12038   I Love You Caroline/Something I Can Always Do £18

PATHFINDERS (2)
| 64 | Hayton SP 138/139 | What Do You Do/What'd I Say (private pressing) | £20 |

PATHFINDERS (3)
| 65 | Parlophone R 5372 | Don't You Believe It/Castle Of Love | £20 |

(see also [White] Trash, Poets)

PATHWAY TO YOUR MIND
| 68 | Major Minor SMLP 19 | PREPARING THE MIND AND BODY FOR MEDITATION (LP, spoken word) | £25 |

PATIENCE & PRUDENCE
56	London HLU 8321	Tonight You Belong To Me/A Smile And A Ribbon (Gold label)	£30
56	London HLU 8321	Tonight You Belong To Me/A Smile And A Ribbon (Silver label)	£15
57	London HLU 8369	Gonna Get Along Without Ya Now/The Money Tree (Gold label)	£30
57	London HLU 8369	Gonna Get Along Without Ya Now/The Money Tree (Silver label)	£15
57	London HL 7017	Gonna Get Along Without Ya Now/The Money Tree (export issue)	£20
57	London HLU 8425	Dreamer's Bay/We Can't Sing Rhythm And Blues	£15
57	London HLU 8493	You Tattletale/Very Nice Is Bali Bali	£15
57	London REU 1087	A SMILE AND A SONG (EP)	£40

SALLY PATIENCE
| 84 | Disc DEL 1 | The Triangle Man/Buried In My Boots (p/s) | £35 |

LEON PATILLO
| 70s | Maranatha MM 0049 | DANCE CHILDREN, DANCE (LP) | £18 |
| 70s | Myrrh MYR 1136 | LIVE EXPERIENCE (LP) | £18 |

BOBBY PATRICK BIG SIX
64	Decca F 11898	Shake It Easy Baby/Wildwood Days	£40
64	Decca F 12030	Monkey Time/Sweet Talk Me Baby	£30
64	Decca DFE 8570	TEENBEAT 3 (FROM STAR CLUB, HAMBURG) (EP)	£120

KENTRICK PATRICK
63	Island WI 066	Man To Man/ROLAND ALFONSO: Blockade (B-side actually "Hit And Run")	£40
63	Island WI 079	Don't Stay Out Late/Forever And Ever	£30
63	Island WI 104	The End Of The World/Little Princess	£35
63	Island WI 119	Golden Love/Beyond	£40
64	Island WI 132	Take Me To The Party/I'm Sorry	£25
64	Island WI 140	I Am Wasting Time/RANDY'S GROUP: Royal Charley	£120

(see also Lord Creator, Pridigal Creator. Fitz Vaughan Bryan's Orchestra)

PATRICK & LLOYD
| 70 | Big Shot BI 550 | Return Of The Pollock/PROPHETS: Concorde | £30 |

(see also Lloyd & Prophets)

PATRIOTS
| 66 | Fontana TF 650 | Prophet/I'll Be There | £20 |

PATRON OF THE ARTS
| 66 | Page One POF 012 | The True Patron Of The Arts/Eleanor Rigby (USA release credits it as Queen City Show Band) | £50 |

PATSY
68	Doctor Bird DB 1113	A Man Is Two Faced/LENNIE HIBBERT & COUNT OSSIE: Pure Soul	£200
68	Doctor Bird DB 1122	Little Flea/The Retreat Song	£60
68	High Note HS012	We Were Lovers/DELANO STEWART : Give Me A Chance	£75

(see also Patsy Todd, Derrick & Patsy, Stranger & Patsy, Emotions)

PATSY & PEGGY
| 70 | Hot Rod HR 107 | Dog Your Woman/Strictly Invitation | £100 |

BRIAN PATTEN
| 70 | Caedmon TC 1300 | BRIAN PATTEN (LP) | £20 |
| 76 | Tangent TGS 116 | VANISHING TRICK (LP) | £20 |

(see also Liverpool Scene, Roger McGough & Brian Patten)

DEE PATTEN
| 92 | Hard Hands HAND 003 T | WHO'S THE BAD MAN EP (12") | £30 |

PATTERN PEOPLE
| 68 | MGM MGM 1429 | Love Is A Lover Loving To Be Loved/Take A Walk In The Sunshine | £20 |

PATTERNS IN PERU
| 86 | Vernon YZ 60 | This Is The Night/Playing Games | £25 |
| 86 | Vernon YZ60T | This Is The Night (Extended)/Playing Games/This Is The Night (12" p/s) | £40 |

BOBBY PATTERSON (& MUSTANGS)
68	Pama PM 735	Broadway Ain't Funky No More/I Met My Match (with Mustangs)	£15
68	Pama PM 743	The Good Ol' Days/Don't Be So Mean	£20
68	Pama PM 754	Busy Busy Bee/Sweet Taste Of Love (with Mustangs)	£20
69	Pama PM 763	T.C.B. Or T.Y.A./What A Wonderful Night For Love (with Mustangs)	£20
69	Pama PM 773	My Thing Is Your Thing/Keep It In The Family	£20
72	Action ACT 4604	I'm In Love With You/Married Lady	£90
77	Contempo 2115	I Got To Get Over/If He Hadn't Slipped And Got Caught	£20

KELLEE PATTERSON
| 76 | Mint CHEW 10 | I'm Gonna Love You Just A Little More Baby/You Are So Beautiful | £60 |
| 95 | Hubbub HUBLP03 | KELLEE (LP, reissue) | £40 |

MARY-ANNE PATTERSON
| 70 | Joy JOYS 162 | ME (LP) | £300 |

OTTILIE PATTERSON

63	Columbia DB 7208	Baby Please Don't Go/I Feel So Good (with Sonny Boy Williamson)	£50
69	Marmalade 598 016	Spring Song/Sound Of The Door As It Closes	£25
69	Marmalade 598 020	Bitterness Of Death/Spring Song	£25
59	Pye NPL 18028	OTTILIE'S IRISH NIGHT (LP)	£15
69	Marmalade 608 011	3000 YEARS WITH OTTILIE (LP)	£125
69	Polydor 2384 031	SPRING SONG (LP)	£35

(see also Chris Barber)

ROBERT PATTERSON SINGERS

60s	United Artists UAS 29003	THE SOUL OF GOSPEL (LP)	£25
65	Fontana 688 516 ZL	I'M SAVED (LP)	£18

PATTERSONS

70	CBS 5083	I Can Fly/An Cailin Deas	£15
69	CBS M 63532	AGAIN (LP, mono)	£18
69	CBS 63522	AGAIN (LP, stereo)	£15

PATTERSON'S PEOPLE

66	Mercury MF 913	Shake Hands With The Devil/Deadly Nightshade	£40

(MIKE) PATTO

66	Columbia DB 8091	Can't Stop Talking About My Baby/Love (as Mike Patto)	£100
70	Vertigo 6360 016	PATTO (LP, textured gatefold sleeve, large swirl label)	£400
71	Vertigo 6360 032	HOLD YOUR FIRE (LP, 3-flap gatefold, small swirl label)	£600
72	Island ILPS 9210	ROLL 'EM SMOKE 'EM PUT ANOTHER LINE OUT (LP, pink rim/palm tree label)	£100

(see also Bo Street Runners, Breakaways, Boxer, News, Chicago Line, Timebox, Felder's Orioles, Steve York, Centipede, Grimms, Spooky Tooth, V.I.P.s)

ALEXANDER PATTON

66	Capitol CL 15461	A Lil Lovin' Sometimes/No More Dreams	£250
66	Capitol CL 15461	A Lil Lovin' Sometimes/No More Dreams (DJ copy)	£350

CHARLIE PATTON

50s	Heritage REU 4	CHARLIE PATTON (EP, 99 only)	£60

PATTY & EMBLEMS

64	Stateside SS 322	Mixed Up Shook Up Girl/Ordinary Guy	£50
64	Stateside SS 322	Mixed Up Shook Up Girl/Ordinary Guy (DJ copy)	£100

PAUL

65	Polydor BM 56045	Will You Follow Me/Head Death	£80

(see also Jimmy Page)

ANDREW PAUL

85	Fashion FAD 038	Hustle Them A Hustle/Bad Boys (12")	£25
85	Y&D YDD 0126	Under Me Sensima/Can't Take It No Longer (12", with the Offbeat Posse)	£30
87	Digikal DIG 004	Too Stush/Gunshot A Flow (12", p/s)	£30

BILLY PAUL

73	Epic EPC 65456	EBONY WOMAN (LP)	£15
74	Phil. Intl. PIR 65861	WAR OF THE GODS (LP, gatefold sleeve)	£15

BUNNY PAUL

54	Columbia SCM 5112	Such A Night/I'm Gonna Have Some Fun	£20
54	Columbia SCM 5131	Lovey Dovey/Answer The Call	£20

CHRIS PAUL

87	CBL 1	City Nights/City Nights (12")	£15
93	Kikman KIK 009	DANCE THE DESTINY EP (12")	£70

DARLENE PAUL

64	Capitol CL 15344	Act Like Nothing Happened/Little Bit Of Heaven	£30

EUGENE PAUL & PILOTS

70	Torpedo TOR 17	Sugar Dumpling/I May Dwell	£40

FRANKIE PAUL

85	Tonos TON 007	Shining Star/If I Am Wrong (12")	£30

JAI PAUL

12	XL XLD 5574	Jasmine (Demo)/Jasmine (Demo) Instrumental (12", p/s, 100 only, numbered)	£80

JASON PAUL

69	Pye 7N 17710	Shine A Little Light Into My Room/Paradise Pudding	£20

(see also Svensk)

JOHN E. PAUL

67	Decca F 12685	Prince Of Players/I Wanna Know (DJ copy with curved Decca logo inverted matrix)	£200
67	Decca F 12685	Prince Of Players/I Wanna Know (Boxed Decca logo, inverted matrix)	£100
67	Decca F 12685	Prince Of Players/I Wanna Know (Matrix number 41387 correct way up)	£20

LES PAUL (& MARY FORD)

55	Capitol CL 14212	Mister Sandman/That's What I Like	£15

LYN PAUL

75	Polydor 2383 340	GIVE ME LOVE (LP)	£15

(see also Nocturnes)

PAULA & JETLINERS

66	Rainbow RAI 102	The Great Pretender/The Legend Of The Man From U.N.C.L.E.	£15

PAUL & PAULA

63	Philips BBE 12639	YOUNG LOVERS (EP)	£20
63	Philips 652 026BL	SING FOR YOUNG LOVERS (LP)	£25

MINT VALUE £

63	Philips BL 7573	WE GO TOGETHER (LP)	£25
63	Philips BL 7587	HOLIDAY FOR TEENS (LP)	£25

PAUL AND RITCHIE & CRYING SHAMES
66	Decca F 12483	September In The Rain/Come On Back (more common demos are worth, £80)	£120

(see also Cryin' Shames, Gary Walker & Rain)

PAULETTE & DELROY
63	Island WI 120	Little Lover/Lovin' Baby	£30

(see also Paulette)

PAULINE (& BROWN SUGAR)
80	Studio WE 706	I Am So Proud/NATTY LOCKS: Studio 16 Workshop (12")	£25
80	Isis 1	Lion, Me And My Dread/Revelation Side (12")	£40

(see also Brown Sugar)

PAUL'S DISCIPLES
65	Decca F 12081	See That My Grave Is Kept Clean/Sixteen Tons	£35

PAUL'S TROUBLES
67	Ember EMB S 233	You'll Find Out/You've Got Something	£25

PAUPERS
68	Verve Forecast VS 1514	Think I Care/White Song	£15
69	Verve Forecast VS 1520	Southdown Road/Numbers	£15
68	Verve Forecast (S)VLP 6017	ELLIS ISLAND (LP, mono/stereo)	£30

(see also Lighthouse)

PAVEMENT (1)
69	Crystal CRY 3000	PAVEMENT (LP)	£40

PAVEMENT (2)
91	Big Cat ABB 34	SLANTED AND ENCHANTED (LP, with lyric sheet)	£30
93	Big Cat ABB 40	WESTING (BY MUSKET AND SEXTANT) (LP)	£45
94	Big Cat ABB 56L	CROOKED RAIN CROOKED RAIN (LP, with inner sleeve, some with free 7": "Haunt You Down"/"Jam Kids")	£50
95	Big Cat LC 5661	WOWEE ZOWEE (2-LP, 3-sided, 1 side etched gatefold cover)	£50
97	Domino WIGLP 31	BRIGHTEN THE CORNERS (LP)	£50
99	Domino WIGLP 66	TERROR TWILIGHT (LP)	£50
10	Domino WIGLP 250	QUARENTINE THE PAST (2-LP)	£20

(see also Stephen Malkmus)

RITA PAVONE
64	RCA RD 7657	RITA PAVONE (mono)	£20
64	RCA SF 7657	RITA PAVONE (stereo)	£20

GARY PAXTON
62	Liberty LIB 55485	Stop Twistin' Baby/Alley Oop Was A Two Dab Man	£15

(see also Skip & Flip)

TOM PAXTON
66	Elektra EKSN 45001	The Last Thing On My Mind/Goin' To The Zoo	£20
67	Elektra EPK 802	TOM PAXTON (EP)	£20
66	Elektra EKL 298/EKS 7298	AIN'T THAT NEWS (LP, U.K. pressing in U.S. sleeve)	£20

DAVEY PAYNE & MEDIUM WAVE
69	Ember EMB S 265	Walk In The Sunshine/Looking Towards The Sky (p/s)	£30

FREDA PAYNE
62	HMV POP 1091	He Who Laughs Last (Desafinado)/Slightly Out Of Tune	£15
73	Invictus INV 533	Band Of Gold/The Easiest Way To Fall (reissue, withdrawn)	£30
70	Invictus SVT 1001	BAND OF GOLD (LP)	£20
71	Invictus SVT 1005	CONTACT (LP)	£20

JACKIE PAYNE
77	Barak 4	I Found Myself/Instrumental	£15

JOHN PAYNTER
70	Universal Editions LYN 2351	HEAR AND NOW (EP)	£50

LOLA PAYOLA
81	Epic EPC 1499	Schoolgirl Song/I Got Married To A Man From Space (p/s)	£25

LAWRENCE PAYTON
74	ABC 4021	Tell Me You Love Me/Instrumental (DJ Copy)	£40
74	ABC 4021	Tell Me You Love Me/Instrumental	£25

(see also the Four Tops)

PAZ
79	Magnus 2	PAZ AT CHICHESTER (LP)	£25
82	Spotlite SPH 518	PAZ ARE BACK (LP)	£100
83	Spotlite SPJ 507	KANDEEN LOVE SONG (LP)	£40
83	Coda CODA 18	LOOK INSIDE (LP)	£15

(see also Lol Coxhill)

P BROTHERS
01	White (Heavy Bronx) PBHB 01	HEAVY BRONX EXPERIENCE VOL. 1 (EP)	£30
01	White (Heavy Bronx) PBHB 002	HEAVY BRONX EXPERIENCE VOL. 2 (EP)	£15

DAVE PEABODY
73	Village Thing VTS 22	PEABODY HOTEL (LP, with insert)	£50

PEACE

12	Deadly People	**Follow Baby/Li'l Echo** (picture disc, 500 only, 20 signed by band)	£20
12	Deadly People 88725473021	**DELICIOUS EP** (12" p/s, white vinyl, 300 only)	£80
13	Sony 88765473021	**IN LOVE** (LP, with red 12", booklet signed by band)	£50
14	Columbia 88875001541	**HAPPY PEOPLE** (2-LP, yellow/blue vinyl)	£35

DAVE PEACE QUARTET

69	Saga FID 2155	**GOOD MORNING MR. BLUES** (LP)	£15

(see also Birmingham)

PEACEMAKERS

65	Herald ELR 1070	**PEACEMAKERS EP**	£15
65	Herald ELR 1079	**PEACEMAKERS EP** (repressing)	£15
66	Cathedral CL 755	**PEACEMAKERS** (LP)	£50

PEACH PALF

97	Mighty Force MF 005	**Hardbody/Off You Girl** (12")	£20

PEACHES

02	Kitty Yo XLLP 163	**TEACHES OF PEACHES** (LP as 5x12")	£50
03	Kitty Yo XLLP 171	**FATHERFUCKER** (2-LP, pink vinyl)	£35
06	XL XLLP 201	**IMPEACH MY BUSH** (LP, pink vinyl)	£35
09	XL XLLP 415	**I FEEL CREAM** (2-LP, inners)	£30
11	XL Recordings XLLP 163	**TEACHES OF PEACHES** (2-LP, reissue, pink vinyl)	£20

PEACHES & HERB

67	CBS 202509	**Let's Fall In Love/We're In This Thing Together**	£30
67	CBS 202509	**Let's Fall In Love/We're In This Thing Together** (DJ copy)	£40
67	CBS 2866	**For Your Love/I Need Your Love So Desperately**	£25
67	CBS 2866	**For Your Love/I Need Your Love So Desperately** (DJ copy)	£40

PEACOCK

71	Famous FAM 109	**Sun Was In Your Eyes/Just A Lonely Man**	£20

ANNETTE PEACOCK

72	RCA SF 8255	**I'M THE ONE** (LP)	£50
79	Aura AUL 707	**THE PERFECT RELEASE** (LP)	£20

ANNETTE PEACOCK & PAUL BLEY

73	Freedom 2383 105	**DUAL UNITY** (LP)	£50

(see also Paul Bley, Bley-Peacock Synthesiser Show, Annette Peacock)

ROGER PEACOCK

65	Columbia DB7764	**Everybody's Talking About My Baby/Times Have Changed**	£20

TREVOR PEACOCK

61	Decca F 11414	**I Didn't Figure On Him To Come Back/Can I Walk You Home**	£22

PEAK FOLK

76	Folk Heritage FHR 082	**THE PEAK FOLK** (LP)	£40

PEANUT

65	Pye 7N 15963	**Home Of The Brave/I Wanna Hear It Again**	£30
66	Columbia DB 8032	**I'm Waiting For The Day/Someone's Gonna Be Sorry**	£22
67	Columbia DB 8104	**I Didn't Love Him Anyway/Come Tomorrow**	£20

(see also Ragdolls U.K.)

PEANUT BUTTER CONSPIRACY

67	CBS 2981	**It's A Happening Thing/Twice Is Life**	£15
68	CBS 63277	**THE GREAT CONSPIRACY** (LP)	£40

BOB PEARCE BLUES BAND

74	Westwood WRS 040	**LET'S GET DRUNK AGAIN** (LP)	£18

(see also Brother Bung)

MARY PEARCE

92	Baseline BASL 010T	**Love Away/Over** (12")	£20
92	Intrigue IGE 29T	**Don't Worry/(Midnite Remix)/Over** (12")	£15

PEARL JAM

92	Epic 657 857-8	**Even Flow/Dirty Frank/Oceans** (12", white vinyl, p/s)	£15
92	Epic 658 258-6	**Jeremy/Alive** (live)/**Footsteps** (12", picture disc, with card insert)	£25
92	Epic 658 258-2	**Jeremy/Yellow Ledbetter/Alive** (live) (CD, picture disc)	£15
93	Epic 660 020-6	**Daughter/Blood** (Live)/**Yellow Ledbetter** (Live) (12", ltd. ed. poster sleeve)	£15
99	Epic 6674797	**Last Kiss/Soldier Of Love** (red vinyl, p/s)	£35
91	Epic 468884	**TEN** (LP)	£80
92	Epic 468 884-0	**TEN** (LP, printed plastic sleeve, insert, picture disc)	£40
93	Epic 4745491	**VS** (LP, gatefold)	£60
94	Epic 477861-1	**VITALOGY** (LP, embossed gatefold sleeve, booklet)	£45
96	Epic 484448-1	**NO CODE** (LP, multi fold gatefold sleeve, inners, 9 photo cards)	£70
98	Epic 489365-1	**YIELD** (LP, die-cut sleeve, inner sleeve)	£50
98	Epic 429859-1	**LIVE ON TWO LEGS** (2-LP, stickered gatefold sleeve with inner sleeves)	£80
00	Sony E263665	**BINAURAL** (2 x LP, 3-part fold out sleeve with booklet)	£50
02	Epic 510000-1	**RIOT ACT** (2-LP, gatefold sleeve, inner sleeves)	£80

(see also Temple Of The Dog, Mad Season)

PEARLS BEFORE SWINE

68	Fontana STL 5503	**BALAKLAVA** (LP)	£45
68	Fontana STL 5505	**ONE NATION UNDERGROUND** (LP)	£40
69	Reprise RSLP 6364	**THESE THINGS TOO** (LP)	£20

70	Reprise RSLP 6405	THE USE OF ASHES (LP)...£30
71	Reprise RSLP 6442	CITY OF GOLD (LP)..£20
71	Reprise RSLP 6467	BEAUTIFUL LIES YOU COULD LIVE (LP) £15

BUSTER PEARSON BAND

73	Action ACT 4612	Big Funky/Pretty Woman...£15

DUKE PEARSON

68	Polydor 583 723	ANGEL EYES (LP) £100

JOHNNY PEARSON

66	Columbia DB 7851	Rat Catcher's Theme/Weaver's Green Theme........................£20
70	Aristocrat AR 103	SOUNDS EXTRAVAGANZA (LP)...£20

(see also John Barry Seven)

KEITH PEARSON'S RIGHT HAND BAND

76	Eron ER 014	KEITH PEARSON'S RIGHT HAND BAND (LP) £20

RONNIE PEARSON

58	HMV POP 489	Flippin' Over You/Teen-Age Fancy £700
58	HMV POP 489	Flippin' Over You/Teen-Age Fancy (78).................................£150

PEAS & BEANS OF CONSCIOUSNESS

92	Tribe SAM 16	Stomper (1-sided 12", 200 only)..£50

PEASANTS (1)

65	Columbia DB 7642	Got Some Lovin' For You Baby/Let's Get Together................£160

PEASANTS (2)

81	Homestead HRSS 009	Here She Comes/I Care For You/When I Close My Eyes/I Can Help £250

PEBBLE

74	Great Western DMHP 005	A GIFT WITH LOVE (LP)..£30

PEBBLES (1)

68	Major Minor MM 574	40 Miles Inside Your Heart/Get Around £15
69	Decca F 22944	Incredible George/Playing Chess £15

PEBBLES (2)

77	Arakwak AR01	Positive Vibrations/Cosmic Idrens £20

PEDDLERS

68	CBS 3734	Comin' Home Baby/Empty Club Blues.....................................£25
70	Phillips 6006034	Tell The World We're Not In/Rainy Day In London £20
73	Philips 6006 283	Sing Me An Old Song/It's So Easy £30
66	Philips BE 12954	SWINGING SCENE (EP)..£15
67	Philips (S)BL 7768	LIVE AT THE PICKWICK (LP, flipback sleeve) £15
67	CBS (S)BPG 63183	FREEWHEELERS (LP)..£15
68	CBS 63411	THREE IN A CELL (LP) £15
68	Fontana SFL 13016	THE FANTASTIC PEDDLERS (LP)..£15
70	CBS 63682	BIRTHDAY (LP) £15
70	Philips 6308 028	THREE FOR ALL (LP, flip top 'matchbox' cover) £15
71	Philips 6386 066	GEORGIA ON MY MIND (LP)..£15
72	Philips 6308 102	SUITE LONDON (LP)...£40

MIKE PEDICIN QUINTET

62	HMV POP 1001	When Cats Come Twistin' In/Gotta Twist £15

BOBBY PEDRICK

58	London HLX 8740	White Bucks And Saddle Shoes/Stranded £25
58	London HLX 8740	White Bucks And Saddle Shoes/Stranded (78).......................£18

ANN PEEBLES

72	London SHU 8434	STRAIGHT FROM THE HEART (LP) £20
74	London SHU 8468	I CAN'T STAND THE RAIN (LP) £30
76	London SHU 8490	TELLIN' IT (LP) £18

PEECH BOYS

83	Island ILPS 9761	LIFE IS SOMETHING SPECIAL (LP) £40

PAUL PEEK

61	Pye International 7N 25102	Brother In Law/Through The Teenage Years.................£20

(see also Gene Vincent & Blue Caps)

DAVID PEEL (& LOWER EAST SIDE)

68	Elektra EKL 4032	HAVE A MARIJUANA (LP, red label, mono)...............................£40
68	Elektra EKS 74032	HAVE A MARIJUANA (LP, red label, stereo).............................£25
70	Elektra 2401 001	AMERICAN REVOLUTION (LP) £20

PEELERS

72	Polydor Folk Mill 2460 165	BANISHED MISFORTUNE (LP) £150

PEELS

66	Audio Fidelity AFSP 527	Scrooey Mooey/Time Marches On £30

PEENUTS

67	Ember EMB S 242	The Theme For "The Monkees"/The World's Been Good To Me Tonight (in p/s) £20

PEEPERS

72	Bumble GE102	Ayeo/A Heavy Drinking Ego Shrinking £20

PEEPS

65	Philips BF 1421	Now Is The Time/Got Plenty Of Love £15
65	Philips BF 1443	What Can I Say?/Don't Talk About Love £15
66	Philips BF 1478	Gotta Get A Move On/I Told You Before..................................£60

(see also Martin Cure & Peeps, Sabres, Rainbows)

PEEP SHOW
67	Polydor 56196	Your Servant, Stephen/Mazy	£90
68	Polydor 52226	Esprit De Corps/Mino In A Mix Up	£15

BEV PEGG (AND FRIENDS)
75	Beaujangle DB 0006	AWAY FROM THE SAND (LP, 50 copies only)	£200

(see also Bev Pegg, Dave Cartwright, Brindley Brae)

BEV PEGG (& HIS GOIN' NOWHERE BAND)
78	Beaujangle DB 0007	NOSTALGIA IS A THING OF THE PAST (LP, private pressing, with booklet, 50 only; as Bev Pegg & His Goin' Nowhere Band)	£150
80	Beaujangle DB 0008	THE FOUNDRY DITTY AND THE INDUSTRIAL AIR (LP, private pressing, 500 only, 150 destroyed so only 350 out there...)	£45

(see also David Cartwright, Brindley Brae)

BOB PEGG
74	Transatlantic TRA 280	THE SHIPBUILDER (LP, with Nick Strutt, credited to Bob Pegg)	£18
75	Transatlantic TRA 299	ANCIENT MAPS (LP, with lyric insert)	£20

BOB & CAROL PEGG
71	Trailer LER 3016	HE CAME FROM THE MOUNTAIN (LP, red label, as Carole Pegg)	£35
72	Galliard GAL 4017	AND NOW IT IS SO EARLY - THE SONGS OF SYDNEY CARTER (LP)	£25

(see also Carol Pegg, Carolanne Pegg, Mr. Fox)

BOB PEGG & NICK STRUTT
73	Transatlantic TRA 265	BOB PEGG & NICK STRUTT (LP)	£25

CAROL(ANNE) PEGG
73	Transatlantic TRA 226	CAROLANNE PEGG (LP, gatefold sleeve)	£80

(see also Bob & Carol Pegg)

PEGGY
70	Hot Rod HR 103	I Shall Follow The Star/CARL LEVEY: Gifted At The Top	£20

PEGGY'S LEG
73	Bunch BAN 2001	GRINILLA (LP, with insert)	£400

(see also Skid Row, Jimi Slevin)

PEG LEG SAM
74	Flyright LP 507/8	THE LAST MEDICINE SHOW (2-LP)	£15

PEKKA
75	Virgin V 2036	B THE MAGPIE (LP as Pekka Pohjolo)	£20
77	Virgin V 2084	THE MATHEMATICIANS AIR DISPLAY (LP, features Mike Oldfield)	£15

DAVE PELL OCTET
54	London H-APB 1034	RODGERS AND HART GALLERY (10" LP)	£15

PELOTON
00	Chemikal Underground CHEM 040	THE GREAT EASTERN (LP)	£20

TRACY PENDARVIS
60	London HLS 9059	A Thousand Guitars/Is It Too Late	£30
60	London HLS 9213	Is It Me/South Bound Line	£25

PENDLEFOLK
70	Folk Heritage FHR 007	PENDLEFOLK (LP)	£18

PENELOPES FRIEND
87	MTG MTG 1	THE GAP EP (12")	£40

PENETRATION
77	Virgin VS 192	Don't Dictate/Money Talks (p/s, blue label)	£15
78	Virgin V 2109	MOVING TARGETS (LP, 15,000 on luminous vinyl)	£20
78	Virgin V 2109	MOVING TARGETS (LP, black vinyl)	£15
79	Virgin V2131	COMING UP FOR AIR (LP)	£15

PENETRATIONS
80	Kik KIK 5	Coming To You/Cheap Thrills	£100

JIM PENFOLD & THE HOLLYWOOD KILLERS
76	Rollerball ROLL 1	Hot Hazy Days/Unknown Person (no p/s)	£15

(see also Hollywood Killers)

EDWARD PENFOLD
16	Stolen Body SBR 012	CAULKHEAD (LP, 1st pressing, 100 only in hand-made hessian sleeve)	£20

PENGUINS
55	London HL 8114	Earth Angel/Hey Senorita (gold label print, triangular centre)	£1500
55	London HL 8114	Earth Angel/Hey Senorita (large centre hole, export issue)	£350
55	London HL 8114	Earth Angel/Hey Senorita (78)	£60

DAWN PENN
66	Rio R 113	Long Days Short Night/Are You There (label lists 'Dawn Tenn')	£125
67	Studio One SO 2030	You Don't Love Me/SOUL VENDORS: Portobello Road	£70
68	Island WI 3097	I'll Never Let You Go/MARK BROWN: Brown Low Special	£50
94	Big Beat 9417 14255-1	NO NO NO (2-LP)	£30

(see also Max Romeo, Viceroys)

TONY PENN
62	Starlite ST45 083	That's What I Like/I Won't Cry Anymore	£30

PENNY CANDLES
89	Red Eye RED 04	THE TAJ MAHAL EP (12" p/s)	£20

GEORGE A. PENNY
68　Trojan TR 625　　　　Win Your Love/VAL BENNETT: All In The Game £60

HANK PENNY
56　Parlophone MSP 6202　Bloodshot Eyes/Wham! Bam! Thank You Ma'am £100
56　Parlophone R 4120　Bloodshot Eyes/Wham! Bam! Thank You Ma'am (78) £18

PENNY PEEPS
68　Liberty LBF 15053　Little Man With A Stick/Model Village £300
68　Liberty LBF 15114　I See The Morning/Curly, The Knight Of The Road.............£40

PENNY WAGER
72　Folk Heritage FHR 0256　LIGHT OF OTHER DAYS (LP)..£75

PENNY ARCADE
70　Pye 7N.17943　The Two Of Us/Don't Need You Anymore £20

PENNYLANDERS
72　Ra RAEP 7005　SONGS OF LOOE £15

PENTAD
65　Parlophone R 5288　Silver Dagger/Nothing But Love £25
65　Parlophone R 5368　Don't Throw It All Away/Too Many Ways.........................£20
66　Parlophone R 5424　Something Other People Call Love/It Better Be Me £25

PENTAGONS
61　London HLU 9333　To Be Loved Forever/Down At The Beach £100

PENTAGRAM
87　Napalm FLAME 006　DAY OF RECKONING (LP)...£45
93　Peaceville VILE 38　RELENTLESS (LP, reissue of US self-titled debut)..............£50
93　Peaceville VILE 40　DAY OF RECKONING (LP, reissue)...................................£50
94　Peaceville VILE 42　BE FOREWARNED (2-LP, insert) £80

PENTANGLE
68　Big T BIG 109　Travellin' Song/Mirage (in title die-cut sleeve) £15
69　Big T BIG 124　Once I Had A Sweetheart/I Saw An Angel £20
68　Transatlantic TRA 162　THE PENTANGLE (LP, laminated sleeve, 1st pressing with no 'A Shel Talmy Production' beneath band name) £100
68　Transatlantic TRA 162　THE PENTANGLE (LP, 2nd pressing, with 'A Shel Talmy Production' beneath band name on labels) £50
68　Transatlantic TRA 178　SWEET CHILD (2-LP, gatefold, 1st pressing, internal flipback sleeve)............£80
68　Transatlantic TRA 178　SWEET CHILD (2-LP, gatefold, 2nd pressing with no internal flapjack sleeve and MacNeil Press Limited printer credit) £50
69　Transatlantic TRA 205　BASKET OF LIGHT (LP, gatefold sleeve) £60
70　Transatlantic TRA 228　CRUEL SISTER (LP, gatefold sleeve) £40
71　Transatlantic TRA 240　REFLECTION (LP, gatefold sleeve with inner sleeve) £35
72　Reprise K 44197　SOLOMON'S SEAL (LP, with lyric insert)...................£70
72　Transatlantic TRASAM 23　HISTORY BOOK (LP) £20
73　Transatlantic TRASAM 29　PENTANGLING (LP) £20
85　Spindrift SPIN 111　OPEN THE DOOR (LP) £25
(see also Bert Jansch, John Renbourn, Duffy's Nucleus)

PENWYKE
70　Cannon CN 11　Time To Let Go/No One Cares (p/s) £20

PENYA
17　On The Corner OTCLP003　SUPER LIMINAL (LP)..£15

PEOPLE BAND
70　Transatlantic TRA 214　THE PEOPLE BAND (LP, with Charlie Watts) £100
(see also Charlie Watts, Battered Ornaments)

PEOPLE (1)
69　Capitol CL 15553　I Love You/Somebody Tell Me My Name £22
69　Capitol CL 15599　Ulla/Turnin' Me In £22
71　Deram DM 346　In Ancient Times/Glastonbury..............................£125
69　Paramount SPFL 261　THERE ARE PEOPLE AND THERE ARE PEOPLE (LP) £25

PEOPLE'S STAR
76　Emerge EMLP 001　FESTAC EXPLOSION - THE PEOPLE STAR IN LONDON (LP) ...£25

PEPPELKADE 14
88　Top Shelf CAV 031　TIME FLIES EP (12")......................................£40

ART PEPPER
54　Vogue LDE 067　ART PEPPER QUARTET (10" LP) £200
57　London HLZ V 14038　ART PEPPER QUARTET (10" LP) £100
60　Contemporary LAC 12229　MODERN JAZZ CLASSICS (LP, as Art Pepper Eleven) ...£25
(see also Chet Baker)

JIM PEPPER
71　Atlantic 2400 149　PEPPER'S POW WOW (LP) £25

RED PEPPER
73　Phoenix SN1X 145　I'm Gonna Sit Right Down And Write Myself A Letter/I See A Land ...£20

DANNY PEPPERMINT (& JUMPING JACKS)
62　London HA-L 2438　TWIST WITH DANNY PEPPERMINT (LP) £30

PEPPERMINT RAINBOW
69　MCA MU 1076　Will You Be Staying After Sunday/And I'll Be There £20

ARMANDO PERAZA
68   Fontana STL 5525   WILD THING (LP) £25
PERCELLS
63   HMV POP 1154   What Are Boys Made Of?/Cheek To Cheek £20
PEREGRINE
72   Westwood WRS 016   SONGS OF MINE (LP) £150
RAY PEREIRA
70   Baf BAF 6   On Broadway/Hey Chick £30
PERERIN
80   Gwerin SYWM 215   HAUL AR YR EIRA (LP, with insert) £180
81   SYWM 230   TEITHGAN (LP) £120
PERE UBU
78   Radar RDR 1   DATAPANIK IN THE YEAR ZERO (12" EP) £18
78   Blank BLANK 001   THE MODERN DANCE (LP) £40
78   Chrysalis CHR 1207   DUB HOUSING (LP) £30
79   Rough Trade ROUGHUS 20   NEW PICNIC TIME (LP) £20
80   Rough Trade ROUGH 14   THE ART OF WALKING (LP, original with "Miles" & "Arabia") £18
81   Rough Trade ROUGH 22   THE MODERN DANCE (LP, reissue) £20
81   Rough Trade ROUGH 23   390° OF SIMULATED STEREO - UBU LIVE: VOLUME 1 (LP) £15
85   Rough Trade ROUGHUS 14   DUB HOUSING (LP, reissue) £15
85   Rough Trade ROUGH 83   TERMINAL TOWER (LP, gatefold sleeve) £15
88   Fontana SFLP 5   THE TENEMENT YEAR (LP) £15
88   Fontana SFLP 3   THE MODERN DANCE (LP, reissue, 1000 only) £15
15   Fire FIRELP 406   ELITISM FOR THE PEOPLE (2-LP, 12" with poster) £60
16   Fire FIRELP 422   ARCHITECTURE OF LANGUAGE 1979 - 1982 (4-LP box set) £50
17   Fire FIRELP 469   DRIVE, HE SAID 1994 - 2002 (4-LP box set, poster, download card) £45
(see also David Thomas)
CHRISTINE PERFECT
69   Blue Horizon 57-3165   When You Say/No Road Is The Right Road £35
70   Blue Horizon 57-3172   I'm Too Far Gone (To Turn Around)/Close To Me £35
70   Blue Horizon 7-63860   CHRISTINE PERFECT (LP) £200
82   CBS 32198   CHRISTINE PERFECT (LP, reissue) £15
(see also Fleetwood Mac, Illusive Dream, Chicken Shack, Rick Hayward)
PERFECT DISASTER
87   Glass GLALP 027   PERFECT DISASTER (LP) £30
PERFECT END
81   Hellfire HELL 1   Sweet Dreams/Natural Causes/Puppets £15
PERFECT PEOPLE
69   MCA MU 1079   House In The Country/Polyanna £15
PERFECTION
70   Stem ST 001   Ride High/Magic Meadow (p/s) £80
PERFECTORS
80   Active ACT 4   YT50295ID/Tiny Radios (p/s) £100
PERFORMERS
69   Action ACT 4552   I Can't Stop You/L.A. Stomp £25
PERFORMING FERRET BAND
80   Dead Hippy DHR3   Brow Beaton/Hoo-Shar/Disco One (EP, p/s) £20
81   Pig PIG 1   PERFORMING FERRET BAND (LP) £35
PERIDOTS
81   Optional Goods OG 1   Open Season/Calm (p/s) £20
PERISHERS
68   Fontana TF 965   How Does It Feel/Bye Bye Baby £40
(see also Seftones)
CARL PERKINS
78s
56   London HLU 8271   Blue Suede Shoes/Honey Don't £30
57   London HLS 8408   Matchbox/Your True Love £40
57   London HLS 8527   Glad All Over/Forever Yours £50
58   London HLS 8608   Lend Me Your Comb/That's Right £60
59   Philips PB 983   I Don't See Me In Your Eyes Anymore/One Ticket To Loneliness £70
SINGLES
56   London HLU 8271   Blue Suede Shoes/Honey Don't £175
57   London HLS 8408   Matchbox/Your True Love £175
57   London HLS8527   Glad All Over/Forever Yours £70
58   London HLS 8608   Lend Me Your Comb/That's Right £70
59   Philips PB 983   I Don't See Me In Your Eyes Anymore/One Ticket To Loneliness £20
61   Philips PB 1179   Anyway The Wind Blows/The Unhappy Girls £15
64   Brunswick 05905   Help Me Find My Baby/I Wouldn't Have You £15
64   Brunswick 05909   Big Bad Blues/Lonely Heart (with Nashville Teens) £15
64   Brunswick 05923   The Monkey Shine/Let My Baby Be £15
67   Stateside SS 599   A Country Boy's Dream/If I Could Come Back £15
68   London HLP 7125   A Country Boy's Dream/Shine Shine Shine (export issue) £15

MINT VALUE £

ALBUMS

59	London HA-S 2202	THE DANCE ALBUM OF CARL PERKINS (plum label, flipback sleeve)	£150
59	London HA-S 2202	THE DANCE ALBUM OF CARL PERKINS (plum label, non-flipback sleeve)	£50
66	Ember NR 5038	SUNSTROKE (shared with Jerry Lee Lewis)	£20
66	CBS Realm 52305	WHOLE LOTTA CARL PERKINS (original pressing with boxed square logo)	£50
66	CBS Realm 52305	WHOLE LOTTA CARL PERKINS	£25
68	CBS 63309	KING OF ROCK	£15
68	London HA-P/SH-P 8366	COUNTRY BOY'S DREAM	£20
82	Sun BOX 101	THE SUN YEARS (3-LP, box set with booklet)	£20

(see also N.R.B.Q.)

LASCELLES PERKINS

61	Blue Beat BB 41	Creation/Lonely Robin	£20
63	Island WI 038	Tango Lips (with Yvonne)/DENNIS SINDREY: Rub Up (B-side actually plays "Jamaica's Song")	£25
64	R&B JB 175	I Am So Grateful/When I Survey	£20
70	Escort ES 814	Please Stay/MATADORS: Voyage From The Moon	£35
71	Banana BA 317	Tell It All Brothers/SOUND DIMENSION: Polkadots	£15

(see also Tommy McCook)

POLLY PERKINS

63	Decca F 11583	I Reckon You (as Polly Perkins & Bill)/The Girls Are At It Again	£20
63	Oriole CB 1869	Sweet As Honey/I've Gotta Tell You	£20
63	Oriole CB 1929	Young Lover/You Too Can Be A Beatle	£20
63	Oriole CB 1979	Faling In Love Again/I Went By Your House Today	£20
73	Chapter One CMS 1018	LIBERATED WOMAN (LP)	£25

(see also Academy)

JEAN-JACQUES PERREY

71	Vanguard VSD 6525	KALEIDOSCOPIC VIBRATIONS - SPOTLIGHT ON THE MOOG (LP, 'kaleidoscope' sleeve, with Gershon Kingsley)	£18
72	Vanguard VSD 6549	MOOG INDIGO (LP, title sleeve)	£25
73	Vanguard VSD 79222	THE IN SOUND FROM WAY OUT! (LP, green/black 'starburst' sleeve, with Gershon Kingsley)	£20
73	Vanguard VSD 79286	THE AMAZING NEW ELECTRONIC POP SOUND OF... (LP)	£15
74	Vanguard DPS 2051	THE BEST OF THE MOOG (2-LP)	£18

PAT PERRIN

68	Island WI 3115	Over You/LLOYD TERRELL: Lost Without You	£25

PERRI'S

59	Oriole CB 1481	Jerri-Lee/Ballad Of A Happy Heart	£15
59	Oriole CB 1481	Jerri-Lee/Ballad Of A Happy Heart (78)	£15

BARBARA PERRY

70	Pama PM 795	Say You Need Me/Unloved	£15

BRENDAN PERRY

99	4AD CAD 9015	EYE OF THE HUNTER (LP, inner)	£100

JEFF PERRY

76	Arista ARIST 51	Love Don't Come No Stronger/I've Got To See You Right Away	£40

LEE 'SCRATCH' PERRY (& UPSETTERS)

63	R&B JB 102	Prince In The Back/Don't Copy	£50
63	R&B JB 104	Old For New/Prince And Duke	£50
63	R&B JB 106	Mad Head/Man And Wife	£50
63	R&B JB 135	Royalty/Can't Be Wrong	£50
64	R&B PJ 40001	Help The Weak/TOMMY MCCOOK: Exodus (promo copies only)	£120
63	Island WI 118	Never Get Weary/TOMMY McCOOK: Below Zero	£40
64	Port-O-Jam PJ 4001	Help The Weak/TOMMY McCOOK: Exodus	£60
64	Port-O-Jam PJ 4003	Bad Minded People/TOMMY McCOOK & HIS GROUP: Jam Rock	£50
64	Port-O-Jam PJ 4010	Chatty Chatty Woman/TOMMY McCOOK & HIS GROUP: Road Block	£70
65	Island WI 210	Please Don't Go/Bye, St. Peter (both sides with Soulettes)	£40
65	Island WI 223	Country Girl/Strange Country (as Upsetters; both act. by Ossie & Upsetters)	£30
65	Ska Beat JB 201	Roast Duck/Hand To Hand, Man To Man	£60
65	Ska Beat JB 203	Trail And Crosses/Jon Tom	£50
65	Ska Beat JB 212	Wishes Of The Wicked/Hold Down	£60
65	Ska Beat JB 215	Open Up/ROLAND ALPHONSO: Twin Double	£50
66	Ska Beat JB 251	The Woodman/Give Me Justice	£60
66	Island WI 259	Just Keep It Up/ROLAND ALPHONSO: James Bond	£350
66	Island WI 292	Doctor Dick (as King Perry)/SOUL BROTHERS: Magic Star	£40
66	Island WI 298	Rub And Squeeze (as King Perry & Soulettes)/SOUL BROTHERS: Here Comes The Minx	£40
67	Doctor Bird DB 1073	Run For Cover/Something You've Got (as Lee 'King' Perry & Sensations)	£45
67	Doctor Bird DB 1098	Whop Whop Man/Wind-Up Doll (with Dynamites)	£50
68	Amalgamated AMG 808	The Upsetter/Thank You Baby	£50
68	Doctor Bird DB 1146	People Funny Boy/BURT WALTERS: Blowing In The Wind	£35
68	Trojan TR 629	Sentence (as Danny & Lee)/LEE PERRY: You Crummy	£40
68	Trojan TR 644	Uncle Desmond/Bronco (with Upsetters)	£25
69	Upsetter US 303	People Funny Fi True/UPSETTERS: Ten To Twelve	£50
69	Upsetter US 324	Yakety Yak/Tackio (with Upsetters)	£35
70	Upsetter US 325	Kill Them All/Soul Walk (with Upsetters)	£35
71	Bullet BU 461	All Combine Pts 1& 2 (as Lee Perry & Upsetters)	£25
72	Upsetter US 385	French Connection (with Upsetters)/UPSETTERS: Version	£20
72	Upsetter US 389	Back Biter (with Dennis Alcapone)/UPSETTERS: Version	£25

73	Upsetter US 397	Jungle Lion/Freakout Skank	£200
73	Upsetter US 398	Cow Thief Skank (actually by Lee Perry & Charlie Ace)/Seven And Three Quarters Skank	£45
73	Bread BR 1111	Station Underground News/CARLTON & SHOES: Better Days	£100
73	Downtown DT 513	Bucky Skank/Lucky Skank	£70
73	Jackpot JP 812	Justice To The People/UPSETTERS: Version	£65
74	Dip DL 5060	Dreader Locks (& Junior Byles)/Militant Rock	£20
79	Black Art BH 001	Reggae Music (actually by Hugo Blackwood)/DOC ALIMANTADO: Rastaman Train (12")	£40
03	Trojan/Sanctuary TJITV005	Disco Devil/BOB MARLEY & WU CHU: Keep On Moving (12" reissue)	£40
71	Trojan Records TBL 166	AFRICA'S BLOOD (LP, orange/white labels)	£100
71	Trojan TBL 167	BATTLE AXE (LP)	£60
73	RHINO 8002	CLOAK & DAGGER (LP, as Scratch The Upsetter)	£200
75	Cactus CTLP 112	REVOLUTION DUB (LP)	£150
75	DIP DLPD 6002	KUNG FU MEETS THE DRAGON (LP, as The Mighty Upsetter)	£150
79	Island ILPS 9583	SCRATCH ON THE WIRE (LP)	£18
79	Jet Star PTLP 1023	THE BEST OF (LP)	£30
80	Black Ark Intl. BALP 4001	BLACK ARK VOLUME 2 (LP)	£35
83	Seven Leaves SLLP5	MEGATON DUB 2 (LP)	£20
83	Pama PTLP 1026	BEST OF LEE PERRY & THE UPSETTERS VOL. 2 (LP)	£50
83	Seven Leaves SLLP3	HEART OF THE ARK (LP)	£35
85	Trojan PERRY 1	UPSETTER BOX SET (3-LP)	£40
88	Trojan TRLS 254	GIVE ME POWER (LP, as Lee Perry & Friends)	£15
89	Trojan PERRY 2	OPEN THE GATE (3-LP as Lee Perry & Friends)	£60
90	Anachron TSLP 9006	REVOLUTION DUB (LP, reissue)	£35
95	Trojan Records TBL 166	AFRICA'S BLOOD (LP, reissue, blue/white labels)	£18
95	Justice League JJLP5000	KUNG FU MEETS THE DRAGON (LP, reissue, various coloured vinyl)	£20
98	Pressure Sounds PSLP19	PRODUCED & DIRECTED BY UPSETTER (2-LP)	£20
99	Pressure Sounds PSLP32	DIVINE MADNESS DEFINITELY (2-LP)	£25
05	Trojan TJBX 244	I AM THE UPSETTER (8 x 7" box set)	£35
11	Honest Jons HJRLP 109	THE RETURN OF PIPECOCK JACKXON (LP, reissue)	£15

(see also Upsetters, Defenders, Roland Alphonso, Bob Marley/Wailers, King Scratch, Punchers, Roy Shirley, Pioneers, Desmond Dekker)

MARK PERRY
80	Deptford Fun City DLP 06	SNAPPY TURNS (LP)	£25

(see also Alternative TV)

STEVE PERRY
60	HMV POP 745	Step By Step/Because They're Young	£15

PERRY SISTERS
59	Brunswick 05802	Fabian/Willie Boy	£25

PERSIAN RISK
81	SRT SRTS/81/CUS/1146	Calling For You/Chasing The Dragon (p/s)	£140
83	Neat NEAT 24	Ridin' High/Hurt You (p/s)	£25
86	Metal Masters METALLP 2	RISE UP (LP)	£18

(see also Motorhead)

PERSIMMON'S PECULIAR SHADES
68	Major Minor MM 554	Watchmaker/Coplington	£40

PERSONALITIES
65	Dice CC 30	I Remember/Suffering	£15
65	Ska Beat JB 222	Hey Little Girl/Teardrops	£30
66	Blue Beat BB 354	Push It Down/BUSTER'S ALL STARS: Blues Market	£50

PERSONS UNKNOWN
81	Po 1	Addiction/Addiction (p/s)	£25

PERSPICO ACUMINE (HOLDINGS)
86	él ACME 4	A PERFECT ACTION (LP)	£20

PERSUADERS
70	Nazarene ZR 1970	THE END IS NOT YET (LP)	£35

PERSUADERS!
93	Detour DR 001	Finished Forever/In The Night (p/s, 300 only)	£20

PERSUADERS (U.S.)
72	Atlantic K 40370	THE THIN LINE BETWEEN LOVE AND HATE (LP)	£20
73	Atlantic K 40476	THE PERSUADERS (LP)	£15

PERSUASIONS
65	Columbia DB 7560	I'll Go Crazy/Try Me	£30
65	Columbia DB 7700	Big Brother/Deep Down Love	£30
66	Columbia DB 7859	La, La, La, La, La/Opportunity	£30

PERSUASIONS (U.S.)
69	Minit MLF 11017	Party In The Woods/It's Better To Have Loved And Lost	£20
70	Straight STS 1062	A CAPPELLA (LP)	£40
72	Island ILPS 9201	STREET CORNER SYMPHONY (LP)	£20

MORRIS PERT
75	Chantry ABM 21	LUMINOS/CHROMOSPHERE/4 JAPANESE VERSES (LP)	£40
80	Chantry CHT 001	LUMINOS/CHROMOSPHERE/4 JAPANESE VERSES (LP, reissue)	£30
82	Chantry CHT 007	BOOK OF LOVE/FRAGMENTI I/ULTIMATE DECAY (LP)	£30

JON PERTWEE
72	Purple PUR 111	Who Is The Doctor/Pure Mystery	£20

MINT VALUE £

62	Phillips BBL 7558	SONGS FOR VULGAR BOATMEN (LP)	£20
80	Decca CROW 1	WORZEL GUMMIDGE SINGS (LP)	£15

(see also Rupert Hine, Derek Roy, BBC Radiophonic Workshop)o

PERUVIAN HIPSTERS
88	Hip HIP 001	Tony Hadley/It Doesn't Happen Everyday (p/s)	£35

PESHAY
95	Good Looking GLR 011	Piano Tune/Vocal Tune (12")	£60
93	Reinforced RIVET 1248	PROTÉGÉ EP (12")	£20

PESKY GEE!
69	Pye 7N 17708	Where Is My Mind/A Place Of Heart Break	£50
69	Pye N(S)PL 18293	EXCLAMATION MARK (LP, textured sleeve)	£250

(see also Black Widow)

PEST
03	Ninja Tune ZEN 74	NECESSARY MEASURES (2-LP)	£20

PETARDS
69	Liberty LBF 15206	Misty Island/Tartarex	£60

PETER
70	Sonet SON 2012	Peace/Values	£15

PETER & GORDON
68	Columbia DB 8398	I Feel Like Going Out/The Quest For The Holy Grail	£20
64	Columbia SEG 8348	NOBODY I KNOW (EP)	£15
64	Columbia 33SX 1630	PETER AND GORDON (LP, mono)	£20
64	Columbia SCX 3518	PETER AND GORDON (LP, stereo)	£25
64	Columbia 33SX 1660	IN TOUCH WITH PETER AND GORDON (LP, mono)	£25
64	Columbia SCN 3532	IN TOUCH WITH PETER AND GORDON (LP, stereo)	£25
65	Columbia 33SX 1761	HURTIN 'N' LOVIN' (LP, mono)	£25
65	Columbia SCX 3565	HURTIN 'N' LOVIN' (LP, stereo)	£30
66	Columbia SX 6045	PETER AND GORDON (LP, mono)	£25
66	Columbia SCX 6045	PETER AND GORDON (LP, stereo)	£30
66	Columbia SX 6097	SOMEWHERE... (LP, mono)	£25
66	Columbia SCX 6097	SOMEWHERE... (LP, stereo)	£30
65	Columbia SCXC 25	I GO TO PIECES (LP, export issue)	£20
66	Columbia SCXC 29	WOMAN (LP, export issue)	£20
66	Columbia SCXC 33	LADY GODIVA (LP, export issue)	£25

(see also Gordon Waller)

PETER & HEADLINES
64	Decca F 11980	Don't Cry Little Girl/It Was Love	£15
64	Decca F 12035	Tears And Kisses/I've Got My Reasons	£15

(see also Count Downe & Zeros)

PETER & PAUL
66	Blue Beat BB 364	Hosana/Schoolgirl	£20

PETER & PERSUADERS
65	Oak RGJ 197	The Wanderer/Wine Glass Rock/Oh My Soul/Cross My Heart (EP)	£50

PETER & TEST TUBE BABIES
81	No Future OI 4	Banned From The Pubs/Moped Lads/Peacehaven Wild Lads (p/s)	£18
82	No Future Punk 3	PISSED AND PROUD (LP, green vinyl)	£25
83	Trapper THIN 1	MATING SOUNDS OF SOUTH AMERICAN FROGS (LP, with lyric inner)	£20
85	Hairy Pie HP 1	THE LOUD BLARING PUNK ROCK LP (LP)	£15
87	Dojo LP 49	SOBERPHOBIA (LP)	£15

PETER & WOLVES
67	MGM MGM 1352	Little Girl Lost And Found/Is Me	£35
68	MGM MGM 1374	Lanternlight/Break Up-Break Down	£30
68	MGM MGM 1397	Julie/Birthday	£20
68	MGM MGM 1452	Woman On My Mind/Old & The New	£35

(see also Factory, Norman Conquest, John Pantry, Sounds Around)

PETER B'S
66	Columbia DB 7862	If You Wanna Be Happy/Jodrell Blues	£100

(see also Tony Colton, Peter Bardens, Peter Green, Cheynes, Shotgun Express)

PETER'S FACES
64	Piccadilly 7N 35205	Just Like Romeo And Juliet/Wait	£25

(see also White Plains)

JANICE PETERS & PLAYBOYS
58	Columbia DB 4222	This Little Girl's Gone Rockin'/Kiss Cha Cha	£30
58	Columbia DB 4222	This Little Girl's Gone Rockin'/Kiss Cha Cha (78)	£15
59	Columbia DB 4276	A Girl Likes/You're The One	£30

JOHNNY PETERS
65	Decca F 12172	When You Ask About Love/People Say	£25

LINDA PETERS
70	Warlock Music WMM 101/2	WARLOCK MUSIC SAMPLER (LP, sampler, 7 tracks by Elton John)	£1000

(see also Richard & Linda Thompson)

MARK PETERS & SILHOUETTES
63	Oriole CB 1836	Fragile (Handle With Care)/Janie	£30
64	Oriole CB 1909	Cindy's Gonna Cry/Show Her	£30
64	Piccadilly 7N 35207	Don't Cry For Me/I Told You So	£15

WENDY PETERS
68 Saga OPP 1   Morning Dew/I Don't Understand £18

CLIVE PETERSEN
61 Columbia DB 4687   For Every Boy/If No One Tells You £15

PAUL PETERSEN
68 Tamla Motown TMG 670   A Little Bit For Sandy/Your Love's Got Me Burnin' Alive £35

BOBBY PETERSON (QUINTET)
59 Top Rank JAR 232   The Hunch/Love You Pretty Baby (as Bobby Peterson Quintet) £15
64 Sue WI 342   Rockin' Charlie (Parts 1 & 2) (solo) £30
65 Sue WI 346   Piano Rock/One Day (solo) £30

RAY PETERSON
59 RCA RCA 1154   Shirley Purley/Come And Get It £15
60 RCA RCA 1175   Answer Me/Goodnight My Love, Pleasant Dreams £15
60 London HLX 9246   Corrine, Corrina/Be My Girl £15
62 London HLX 9489   I Could Have Loved You So Well/Why Don't You Write Me £15
61 London REX 1293   CORRINE CORRINA (EP) £30

PETS
58 London HL 8652   Cha-Hua-Hua/Cha-Kow-Ski £15

PET SHOP BOYS
SINGLES
84 Epic A 4292   West End Girls/Pet Shop Boys (p/s) £75
84 Epic TA 4292   West End Girls (Extended)/Pet Shop Boys (12", p/s) £50
85 Parlophone 12R 6097   Opportunities (Let's Make Lots of Money) (Dance Mix)/In The Night (Extended) (12", white p/s) £20
85 Parlophone 12RA 6097   Opportunities (Let's Make Lots of Money) (Version Latina)/(Dub For Money Remix)/In The Night (Extended Mix) (12", large picture labels, die-cut p/s) £40
85 Parlophone 12R 6097   Opportunities (Let's Make Lots of Money) (Dance Mix)/ In The Night (Extended) (12", p/s, mispressing, B-side plays "Opportunities [Dub For Money] Remix") £30
85 Parlophone 12R 6097   Opportunities (Let's Make Lots of Money) (Dance Mix)/In The Night (Extended) (12", p/s, 2nd mispressing, A-side plays "Opportunities [Version Latina]") £30
85 Parlophone 10R 6115   West End Girls (Untitled Mix)/A Man Could Get Arrested (4.09 Mix)/ West End Girls (7" Mix) (10", round foldout p/s; sealed with sticker) £60
86 Parlophone 10R 6116   Love Comes Quickly (Dance Mix)/That's My Impression (Disco Mix) (10", PVC sleeve with poster) £100
93 Parlophone R 6348   Can You Forgive Her? (7" Version)/Hey Headmaster (red or blue vinyl, factory custom pressing, p/s) £600
97 Parlophone Fan Club   It Doesn't Often Snow At Christmas (CD, fan club issue, in sealed silver bubble wrap) .. £125
12 Parlophone R6879   Leaving/Leaving (Demo) (signed p/s) £20
12 Parlophone 12R 6879   Leaving (Lost Her Remix)/(Happy Sad Remix)/(Happy Hour Remix) (12" signed p/s) £20

ALBUMS
86 Parlophone PCS 7303   PLEASE (LP, inner) £25
90 Parlophone PCSD 113   BEHAVIOUR (LP, red inner) £20
87 Parlophone PCSDX 104   ACTUALLY (LP, with U.S. import "Always On My Mind" 12", stickered sleeve) £25
88 Parlophone PCSX 7325   INTROSPECTIVE (LP, 3 x clear vinyl 12" factory custom pressing, with wraparound paper strip, 10 copies only) £1500
88 Parlophone PCSX 7325   INTROSPECTIVE (LP, 3 x black vinyl 12", with picture labels & wraparound paper obi strip) £50
91 Parlophone PMTV3   DISCOGRAPHY (2-LP) £50
93 Parlophone PCSD 143   VERY (LP) £40
96 Parlophone PCSD 170   BILINGUAL (LP) £50
00 Parlophone 724352185719   NIGHTLIFE (LP) £35
02 Parlophone 0 724358146   DISCO 3 (3-LP) £25
03 Parlophone 5938841   POPART - THE HITS (3-LP, printed inners) £200
07 Parlophone 506 0461   DISCO FOUR (REMIXED BY PET SHOP BOYS) (2LP, printed inners) £100
09 Vinyl Factory VF 003   YES (11 x 12" in smoked perspex box with gold-plated 'tick' on cover, with art print, signed and numbered by both band members, 300 only) £1500
13 Vinyl Factory VF 090   ELECTRIC (Box set 5 x 12", coloured vinyl in acrylic box, 12 page booklet)) £800
16 X2 008 VL1   SUPER (LP, gatefold, printed inner, white vinyl) £25
24 Parlophone 5054197903564   NONETHELESS (LP/12", white vinyl, deluxe edition, webstore exclusive, print)............. £70

PROMOS
84 Epic A4292   West End Girls/Pet Shop Boys (p/s, 'A' label promo) £30
85 Parlophone R 12R 6097   Opportunities (Let's Make Lots of Money)/In The Night (12", "photocopy" sl.) £30
86 Parlophone R 6116   Love Comes Quickly (1-sided, p/s) £40
86 Parlophone 12R 6129   Opportunities (Let's Make Lots of Money) (7.18 Shep Pettibone Mastermix)/Opportunities (4.27 Reprise)/Opportunities (6.44 Original Dance Mix)/Was That What It Was (12", autographed black die-cut sleeve, with press release) £35
86 Parlophone 12R 6129   Opportunities (Let's Make Lots of Money) (7.18 Shep Pettibone Mastermix)/Opportunities (4.27 Reprise)/Opportunities (6.44 Original Dance Mix)/Was That What It Was (12", autographed black die-cut sleeve, without press release) £35
90 Parlophone CDPCSD 113   BEHAVIOUR (CD, commercial issue, different inlay, in white monogrammed pouch, with full-album cassette & chronology) £75
91 Parlophone MFB 1   Music For Boys (12", 3 untitled mixes, hand-stamped white label) £25
92 Parlophone CDRX 6332   Go West (7" Version)/West End Girls (Sacha Mix)/Forever/Go West (Extended Dance Mix) (cassette, title sleeve) £150
93 Abbey Road   COMPILED EP (CD-R, Abbey Road title sleeve; autographed by The Boys, 20 only)......... £800
94 Parlophone 12RDJ 6386   Yesterday When I Was Mad (Jam & Spoon Mix)/(Junior Vasquez Factory Dub)/(Junior Vasquez Fabulous Dub)/(Junior Vasquez Body Dub)/(Coconut 12" Mix)/(RAF Zone Mix)/(RAF Dub Zone)/Euroboy/Some Speculation (12", double pack unique p/s) £15
96 Parlophone 12RDJD 6431   Before (Classic Paradise Mix)/(Afrodisiac Mix)/(Hedboys Mix)/ (Dub)/(Extended Mix) (2 x 12", blue 'penis' p/s) £25

MINT VALUE £

96	Parlophone 12RJD 6431	Before (Underground Mix)/(Bonus Dub)/(Underground Instrumental)/(Bonus Beats) (12", red 'penis' p/s)..£25
97	Parlophone 12 BARDJ 2	The Truck Driver & His Mate/Before (Love To Infinity Classic Paradise Mix) (12", 'two knobs' p/s, 150 copies)..£150
97	Parlophone 12BOYDJ 101	The Boy Who Couldn't Keep His Clothes On (Main Vocal)/(INT... Club Mix)/(Banji Girlfriend Beats)/(On Stage At Twilo)/(Radio Edit) (12", die-cut sleeve) £60
99	Parlophone (no cat. no.)	NIGHTLIFE (10" x 10" box in PVC slip case, contains interview CD, music CD, book, EPK & 3 photographs)..£50
01	10th Planet/PSBP/RUG	FIVE TITLES FROM CLOSER TO HEAVEN: Positive Role Model/Friendly Fire/ Shameless/K-Hole/For All Of Us (CD-R, title sleeve, all sung by Neil Tennant)...............£150
93	Parlophone DF 118	RELENTLESS (3 x 12", on pink/yellow/blue vinyl) £60
96	Parlophone BILING 1	BILINGUAL (A4 yellow box set, including "A Taste Of Bilingual" CD: (Discoteca/ Electricity/A Red Letter Day/It Always Comes As A Surprise/Se A Vida E) (with 2 photos & inset in transparent PVC box)...............................£50
96	Parlophone PSBCDDJ 1	BILINGUAL (A4 pale blue launch party promo box set including "A Taste Of Bilingual" CD [Before/Se A Vida E], & album cassette, unique inlay)...........................£200
01	Really Useful Group	CLOSER TO HEAVEN (CD-R, title sleeve; 19 tracks, all sung by Neil Tennant) £250
07	Parlophone DISCO004	DISCO 4 ALBUM SAMPLER (12" 4-tracks)..£20
07	Parlophone (no cat. No.)	DISCO FOUR (Promo CD-R, 5-track album sampler and press sheet, 30 copies)...............£40
06	Parlophone FUNDA001	Fundamentalism Part 1 (12", promo) £15
06	Parlophone FUNDA002	Fundamentalism Part 2 (12", promo) £15
06	Parlophone PSB002	Psychological (1-sided 12" promo no Pet Shop Boys credit on label) £25
06	Parlophone REMIXES01	Psychological (Ewan Pearson Mixes) (12" promo)...............................£25
06	Parlophone STUPID002	I'm With Stupid Remixes 1 (12" promo) £15
06	Parlophone STUPID001	I'm With Stupid Remixes 2 (12" promo) £15
06	Parlophone STUPID003	I'm With Stupid Remixes 3 (12" promo) £15
06	Parlophone PRIVATE001	In Private (Tomcraft Mixes) (12" promo) £20

(see also Eighth Wonder, Dusty Springfield, Electronic, Ian Wright)

MARY PETTI
61	RCA RCA 1239	Hey! Lawdy Lawdy/Gee, But It Hurts.................................£40

PETTICOATS
80	Bla Bla Bla 01	Normal/Allergy/I'm Free (with insert) £20

FRANK PETTY TRIO
53	MGM SP 1010	St. Louis Blues (Boogie Woogie)/Somebody Stole My Girl.................£20

TOM PETTY (& HEARTBREAKERS)
77	Shelter ISA 5014	TOM PETTY AND THE HEARTBREAKERS (LP)...........................£20
76	Shelter 1DJ 24A	OFFICIAL LIVE BOOTLEG (LP, with Heartbreakers, 1-sided 5-track, promo only)...........£20
78	Shelter ISA 5017	YOU'RE GONNA GET IT! (LP)......................................£20
79	MCA MCF 3044	DAMN THE TORPEDOS (LP)..£20
89	MCA Records MCG 6034	FULL MOON FEVER (LP)...£25
96	MCS 10964	GREATEST HITS (2-LP)..£80
94	Warner Bros. 9362 45759-1	WILDFLOWERS (2-LP) £200
99	Warner Bros. 9362-47294-1	ECHO (2-LP) £100

(see also Randy Newman, Traveling Wilburys, k.d. lang & Roy Orbison)

JOHN PFEIFFER
68	RCA VICS 1371	ELECTRONOMUSIC - 9 IMAGES (LP) £15

PFM
95	Good Looking GLR 012	One & Only/Dreams (12") £20
95	Good Looking GLR 012	The Western Tune/Hypnotizing (12")............................£35

P.F.M.
73	Manticore K 43502	PHOTOS OF GHOSTS (LP, laminated gatefold sleeve) £25
74	Manticore K 53502	THE WORLD BECAME THE WORLD (LP, die-cut sleeve with inner) £20
74	Manticore K 53506	COOK (LP) £15

P45
80	Jet 190	Right Direction/B.I.N.Y.C. £15

PHANTOM BAND
71	Polydor 2058-176	Loop-Di-Love/Funkin' About £30
72	Polydor 2058-290	Silhouettes/Drummitt £15

PHANTOM SLASHER
01	Noid NOIDLP 003	PUDDLE AND SPOUT (LP, as 2 x 12") £20

PHANTOMS
61	Palette PG 9014	Phantom Guitar/Cachina £20
60s	Arc ARC	GREAT GUITAR HITS (LP)..£20

PHARAOHS
58	Decca DFE 6522	THE PHARAOHS (EP)..£500

PHARCYDE
92	East West 7567-92222-1	BIZARRE RIDE II THE PHARCYDE (LP, European edition, 2-LP set is USA) £30
95	Go! Beat 828 736-1	LABCABINCALIFORNIA (2-LP, red and blue vinyl, free 12") £25
00	Four Music FOR 3003 1	BIZARRE RIDE II THE PHARCYDE (2-LP, reissue)......................£20

PHASE 4
66	Decca F 12327	What Do You Say About That/Think I'll Sit Down And Cry (1st issue)...........£25
66	Fab FAB 1	What Do You Say About That/I'm Gonna Sit Down And Cry (2nd issue) £20
67	Fab FAB 6	Man Am I Worried?/Listen To The Blues £50

PHASE 5
70	Polydor 2058 063	Star Trek/Enterprise £30

PHATES
79 Personal Propaganda PROP 4 ..... MODACOM: Cool Jerk/Tears Of A Dog (hand-made labels and p/s, 500 only)................£20

PHEETUS
78 Ric Rac RRS 002 ..... Nomads/Blind Man (no p/s, 200 only)...£35

PHENOMYNA
94 Applied Rhythmic Technology ART 6 ..... ART 5.1 EP (12")..£25
95 Applied Rhythmic Telecnology ART 7.1 ..... ART 5.2 EP (12")..£25

PHEON BEAR
73 Pye 7N 45232 ..... War Against War/87th Precinct £25

PHIL & FLINTSTONES
64 Bedrock PR 5371 ..... Love Potion No. 9/Honey Don't (private pressing) £80

PHI LIFE CYPHER
98 Compressed Knowledge CK001 ..... Baddest Man/Da Shinn/Rap 'N' Bullshit/Forever (12") £20
02 Jazz Fudge JFR 030 ..... THE CHOSEN FEW EP (with Taskforce)...£25
00 Jazz Fudge JFR 022 ..... MILLENNIAL METAPHORS (2-LP) £25

PHILIP & HIS FOETUS VIBRATIONS
82 Self Immol. WOMB KX 07 ..... Tell Me, What Is The Bane Of Your Life/Mother I've Killed The Cat (p/s) £25
(see also You've Got Foetus On Your Breath, Foetus Äœber Frisco, Foetus Under Glass, Scraping Foetus Off The Wheel)

LOUIS PHILIPPE
88 él ACME 15 ..... IVORY TOWER (LP) £20
86 el ACME 23 ..... AN APPOINTMENT WITH VENUS (LP) £30
89 él ACME 36 ..... YURI GAGARIN (LP)..£20

BRENDAN PHILIPS
66 Mercury MF 896 ..... Is It Worth A Try/When She's Kissing Me £25

PHILL MOST CHILL
06 Diggers With Gratitude DWG 001 ..... BE INTELLEGENT (EP, 100 only)......................................£300
11 Diggers With Gratitude DWG 008 ..... ALL CUTS RECORDED RAW (LP) £35
11 Diggers With Gratitude DWG 008 ..... ALL CUTS RECORDED RAW (LP, 25 copies only, alternative pressing, white stickered cover)................£350
11 Diggers With Gratitude DWG 008 ..... ALL CUTS RECORDED RAW (LP, coloured vinyl, alternative pressing EP and 7") £100

ANTHONY PHILLIPS
79 Arista SPART 1085/AFLP 1 ..... SIDES (LP, 1st 500 copies sealed with free LP "Private Parts & Pieces") £20
(see also Genesis)

BARRE PHILLIPS
69 Music Man SMLS 601 ..... UNACCOMPANIED BARRE (LP) £100

CONFREY PHILLIPS (TRIO)
57 Decca F 10866 ..... Shotgun Rock 'n' Roll/Hokey-Kokey Rock 'n' Roll (as Confrey Phillips Trio)........£20

(LITTLE) ESTHER (PHILLIPS)
62 Stateside SS 140 ..... Release Me/Don't Feel Rained On..£25
63 Ember EMB S 174 ..... Am I That Easy To Forget/I Really Don't Want To Know (as Little Esther Phillips)........£15
65 Sue WI 395 ..... The Chains/Feel Like I Wanna Cry (as Esther Philips)........£40
65 Atlantic AT 4028 ..... And I Love Him/Shangri-La £18
65 Atlantic AT 4048 ..... Let Me Know When It's Over/I Saw Me £15
66 Atlantic AT 4077 ..... I Could Have Told You/Just Say Goodbye........................£80
66 Atlantic AT 4077 ..... I Could Have Told You/Just Say Goodbye (DJ Copy)........£100
66 Atlantic 584 013 ..... When A Woman Loves A Man/Ups And Downs........£15
67 Atlantic 584 126 ..... I'm Sorry/Cheater Man £15
72 Atlantic K 10168 ..... Catch Me I'm Falling/Release Me £18
72 Kudu KUS 4000 ..... Home Is Where The Hatred Is/Til My Back Ain't Got No Bone........£20
73 Kudu KUS 4002 ..... I've Never Found A Man/Cherry Red..............................£15
63 Ember CW 103 ..... REFLECTIONS OF GREAT COUNTRY AND WESTERN STANDARDS (LP)........£50
65 Atlantic ATL 5030 ..... AND I LOVE HIM (LP) £50
67 Atlantic 587/588 010 ..... ESTHER PHILLIPS SINGS (LP) £30
72 Kudu KUL 2 ..... FROM A WHISPER TO A SCREAM (LP) £25
73 Kudu KUL 6 ..... ALONE AGAIN, NATURALLY (LP) £18
75 Kudu KUL 12 ..... PERFORMANCE (LP)..£15

FLIP PHILLIPS
56 Columbia/Clef 33C 9003 ..... FLIP PHILLIPS QUARTET (10" LP) £15

GLENN PHILLIPS
75 Caroline C 1519 ..... LOST AT SEA (LP) £20

GREGORY PHILLIPS
65 Immediate IM 004 ..... Down In The Boondocks/That's The One £30
(see also Remo Four)

JOHN PHILLIPS
70 Stateside-Dunhill SSL 5027 ..... JOHN PHILLIPS: THE WOLFKING OF L.A. (LP) £35
(see also Mamas & Papas)

MICHELLE PHILLIPS
77 A&M AMS 7340 ..... Victim Of Romance/Lady Of Fantasy £15

77 A&M AMLS 64651   VICTIM OF ROMANCE (LP) £30
(see also Mamas & Papas)

NOEL PHILLIPS
80 Jammys JM001   Youth Man/Living In The Ghetto (12") £25

PHIL PHILLIPS & TWILIGHTS
59 Mercury AMT 1059   Sea Of Love/Juella...£35
60 Mercury AMT 1072   Take This Heart/Verdi Mae £30
60 Mercury AMT 1093   Your True Love Once More/What Will I Tell My Heart £30
61 Mercury AMT 1139   I Love To Love You/No One Else But You £30

SHAWN PHILLIPS
67 Parlophone R 5606   Stargazer/Woman Mine...£80
65 Columbia 33SX 1748   I'M A LONER (LP) £120
66 Columbia S(C)X 6006   SHAWN (LP)..£250
70 A&M AMLS 978   CONTRIBUTION (LP) £18
71 A&M AMLS 2006   SECOND CONTRIBUTION (LP, with insert) £18
72 A&M AMLS 64324   COLLABORATION (LP) £18

TOM PHILLIPS/GAVIN BRYERS/FRED ORTON
78 Obscure OBS 9   IRMA - AN OPERA (LP)..£20

WARREN PHILLIPS & THE ROCKETS
69 Decca (S)PA 43   THE WORLD OF ROCK 'N' ROLL (LP) £15
(see also Foghat)

PHILOSOPHERS
69 Pye 7N 17740   The Lovedene Girls/I Believe Forever.................................£25

VINCE PHILPOTT & DRAGS
64 Decca F 11997   The Cramp/Eenie Meenie Miny Mo....................................£15

PHILWIT & PEGASUS
70 Chapter One CHR 137   The Elephant Song/Pseudo Phoney Mixed Up Croney £40
70 Chapter One CHSR 805 PHILWIT AND PEGASUS (LP) £40
(see also Mark Wirtz)

PHOENIX (2)
81 Rising PR 433032   PHOENIX RISING EP (Lonely Attack/The Minstrel/Understanding/Phoenix Rising 'Av An 'Am) (12" EP) £35

PHOENIX (3)
00 Source 7243 8 488531 1 UNITED (LP) £40
04 Source SOUR LP 095   ALPHABETICAL (LP)..£35
09 V2 VVR703394   WOLFGANG AMEDUES PHOENIX (LP, white vinyl) £20

PHONADS
81 SRT S81 CUS 1024   Talk To Me/You And Me (plain stickered sleeve).................£50

PHOTEK
95 Photek PTK 04   Water Margin/Fusion (12")...£20
95 Photex PTK 05   Seven Samurai/Complex (12") £18
95 Photek PTK 06   U.F.O./Rings Around Saturn (12", p/s) £20
96 Op ART OP 1   T-Raenon/(Version)/Kanei (12").......................................£20
97 Science QEDT2   Ni-Ten-Ichi-Ryu/The Fifth Column (12").............................£20
97 Science QEDT2   MODUS OPERANDI (3-LP) £40
98 Virgin QEDLP2   FORM AND FUNCTION (3-LP) £40
00 Science QEDLP6   SOLARIS (2-LP)...£20

PHOTOGRAPHED BY LIGHTNING
86 Fierce FRIGHT 008   Sleep's Terminator/Winter Trees (foldaround p/s, hand-coloured labels) £30

PHOTOGRAPHS
79 Do Not Bend AERS 106 Second Best/Seas/Here I Go Again (no p/s) £20

PHUTURE PHANTASY
88 Low Fat Vinyl LFV 1   SLAM (12")..£15

PHUTURE PRIMITIVE
93 Knifeforce KF 006   Full Metal Jacket/Twinkle (12") £30
94 Knifeforce KF 026   Lift Me Up/Infect Me (12")..£15

PHYSICS HOUSE BAND
13 Blood and Biscuits BSCTS024LP Horizons/Rapture (12") £45

PAUL PIACENTINI
85 Acting School Again ASA 01 OUT OF MY BOX (mini-LP) £40

PIANO RED
53 HMV 7M 108   Rockin' With Red/Red's Boogie £100
64 RCA RCX 7138   RHYTHM AND BLUES VOL. 2 (EP) £15
(see also Dr. Feelgood [U.S.])

PICA
71 Philips 6006 129   Rainbow Chaser/Ad Lib..£100
(see also Nirvana [UK])

PICADILLY LINE
67 CBS 2785   At The Third Stroke/How Could You Say You're Leaving Me £30
67 CBS 2958   Emily Small (The Huge World Thereof)/Gone Gone Gone........£25
68 CBS 3595   Yellow Rainbow/Evenings With Corrina £30
68 CBS 3595   Yellow Rainbow/I Know, She Believes (reissue with different B-side)........£25

MINT VALUE £

68	CBS 3743	Evenings With Corrina/My Best Friend	£20
67	CBS (S)BPG 63129	THE HUGE WORLD OF EMILY SMALL (LP, laminated front sleeve)	£350
67	CBS (S)BPG 63129	THE HUGE WORLD OF EMILY SMALL (LP, laminated front sleeve, promo insert)	£400

(see also Edwards Hand)

PICK A POW
| 93 | Sunjam SR 0014 | Time Hard/RICK WAYNE: Our Younger Years (12") | £40 |
| 94 | Sunjam SR 0015 | Wicked People/Only You (12") | £25 |

BUSTER PICKENS
| 60s | Heritage HLP 1008 | TEXAS PIANO (LP, 99 only) | £60 |

J.B. PICKERS
| 71 | London HLU 10334 | Super Soul Sounds/KIM & DAVE: Nobody Knows | £15 |

BOBBY (BORIS) PICKETT & CRYPT-KICKERS
| 73 | London ZGU 133 | MONSTER MASH (LP) | £20 |

DAN PICKETT
| 60s | XX MIN 710 | DAN PICKETT (EP) | £15 |

KENNY PICKETT
| 80 | F Beat PRO 2 | Got A Gun/Same | £15 |

(see also The Creation)

NICK PICKETT
| 72 | Reprise K 44172 | SILVERSLEEVES (LP) | £30 |

(see also John Dummer Blues Band)

WILSON PICKETT
63	Liberty LIB 10115	It's Too Late/I'm Gonna Love You	£30
65	Atlantic AT 4036	In The Midnight Hour/I'm Not Tired	£20
65	MGM MGM 1286	Let Me Be Your Boy/My Heart Belongs To You	£50
65	MGM MGM 1286	Let Me Be Your Boy/My Heart Belongs To You (DJ copy)	£100
65	Atlantic ATL 5037	IN THE MIDNIGHT HOUR (LP)	£50
66	Atlantic 587/588 029	THE EXCITING WILSON PICKETT (LP)	£30
66	Atlantic 587 032	IN THE MIDNIGHT HOUR (LP, reissue)	£25
67	Atlantic 587/588 057	THE WICKED PICKETT (LP)	£30
67	Atlantic 587/588 080	THE SOUND OF WILSON PICKETT (LP)	£30
68	Atlantic 587/588 092	THE BEST OF WILSON PICKETT (LP)	£20
68	Atlantic 587/588 107	I'M IN LOVE (LP)	£20
68	Atlantic 587/588 111	MIDNIGHT MOVER (LP)	£20
69	Atlantic 588 170	HEY JUDE (LP)	£20
70	Atlantic 2465 002	RIGHT ON (LP)	£20
70	Joy JOYS 181	IF YOU NEED ME (LP)	£20
71	Atlantic 2400 026	ENGINE NO. 9 - IN PHILADELPHIA (LP)	£20

(see also Falcons)

PICKWICKS
64	Decca F 11901	Apple Blossom Time/I Don't Wanna Tell You Again	£18
64	Decca F 11957	You're Old Enough/Hello Lady	£15
65	Warner Bros WB 151	Little By Little/I Took My Baby Home	£100

PICNIC BOYS
| 82 | Challet BEAN 001 | White Hotel/Dawn Patrol (p/s) | £20 |

PICTURE BOOK
| 84 | Crystal 2 | Laughing In My Hand/Reflex Action (with insert) | £70 |

PICTURE FRAME SEDUCTION
84	SOSO 33	I'm Good Enough For Me/Sabotage The Classes/Fur Queue	£40
87	PFS 2	Try With A Little Help From My Friends/And Entertainment USA	£40
85	Rot PFS 1	HAND OF THE RIDER (LP)	£40

PICTURES LIKE THIS
| 83 | TW HIT 112 | A Night's Vendetta/Defeat (p/s) | £251 |

PIED PIPERS (1)
| 54 | Parlophone CMSP 21 | Kissin' Drive Rock/Please Understand (export issue) | £15 |

PIED PIPERS (2)
| 66 | Columbia DB 7883 | Ragamuffin/Fat Marie | £30 |

JEFFREY LEE PIERCE
| 85 | Statik STATLP 25 | WILDWEED (LP, with free 7" PROMO 2) | £20 |
| 85 | Statik STATLP 25 | WILDWEED (LP) | £15 |

(see also Gun Club)

WEBB PIERCE
50s	Decca BM 311368	We'll Find A Way/Any Old Time (export issue)	£30
55	Decca BM 31172	Teen Age Boogie/I'm Really Glad You Hurt Me (export)	£150
56	Brunswick 05630	Teenage Boogie/Any Old Time	£150
56	Brunswick 05630	Teenage Boogie/Any Old Time (78)	£15
57	Brunswick 05682	Bye, Bye Love/Honky Tonk Song	£40
57	Brunswick 05682	Bye, Bye Love/Honky Tonk Song (78)	£15
59	Brunswick 05809	I Ain't Never/Shanghaied	£20
59	Brunswick 05809	I Ain't Never/Shanghaied (78)	£15
59	Parlophone GEP 8792	COUNTRY ROUND UP (EP)	£20
55	Brunswick LA 8716	THE WONDERING BOY (10" LP)	£30
60	Brunswick LAT 8324	WEBB! (LP)	£15
65	Brunswick LAT 8540	HIDEAWAY HEART (LP)	£15

MINT VALUE £

65	Brunswick LAT 8551	CROSS COUNTRY (LP)	£15

(see also Red Sovine & Webb Pierce)

PIERCES
07	Lizard King 102X	Sticks And Stones/Turn On Billie	£15
11	Polydor 2770932	YOU AND I (LP, insert)	£45

PIG
91	Concrete CPRODLP 017	PRAISE THE LARD (LP)	£70
17	Armalyte Industries ARMVNL 044	WRECKED (2-LP, reissue)	£40

MARTIN PIG
83	Rough Trade RT 092	Lovely Rita/Somebody Loves You	£15

PIG RIDER
74	Deroy	BLOODY TURKEY SANDWICHES (LP, 6 acetates only)	£200
75	Deroy	HETEROPHONIES (LP, acetate only)	£200

PIGSTY HILL LIGHT ORCHESTRA
71	Village Thing VTS 8	PIGGERY JOKERY (LP)	£20

DAVE PIKE
66	Atlantic 584 052	Sunny/HERBIE MANN: Philly Dog	£15
66	Atlantic 588 005	JAZZ FOR THE JET SET (LP)	£25
62	Esquire32-150	BOSA NOVA CARNIVAL (LP)	£15

RAY PILGRIM (& BEATMEN)
60	Oriole CB 1557	Baby Doll/Gambler's Guitar (solo)	£15

(see also Bud Ashton, Jaybirds, Typhoons)

TONY PILLEY
79	Barclay Towers BT2	Off The Hook/Mummy & Daddy (p/s, with poster)	£15

PILTDOWN MEN
62	Capitol CL 15245	A Pretty Girl Is Like A Melody/Big Lizzard	£20
61	Capitol EAP1 20155	GOODNIGHT MRS. FLINTSTONE (EP)	£25

SIR HUBERT PIMM
55	London HL 8155	Goodnight And Cheerio/Honky Tonk Train Blues	£50
55	London RE-U 1032	PIMM'S PARTY (EP, with Ellen Sutton)	£20

(see also Duke & Duchess)

PINCHERS
86	Blue Trac BTRP 001	CAN'T TAKE THE PRESSURE (LP)	£40

MICHAEL PINDER
76	Threshold TH 23	Carry On/I only Want To Be With You	£25

PINEAPPLE CHUNKS
65	Mercury MF 922	Drive My Car/Dream About	£15

PINEAPPLE THIEF
00	Obtuse OBT 001	Sherbert Gods/Perpetual Flying Objects (wraparound p/s in poly bag)	£25

PINEWOOD TOM/TOM TALL
59	Jazz Collector JEL 5	THE MALE BLUES VOLUME 4 (EP)	£18

PINK ELEPHANT
72	Pye 7N 45143	Down In The Valley/I'm Living In This World Just For You	£15

PINK FAIRIES
71	Polydor 2058 089	The Snake/Do It	£25
72	Polydor 2059 302	Well Well Well/Hold On	£25
76	Stiff BUY 2	Between The Lines/Spoiling For A Fight (promo 'plug' copy)	£15
71	Polydor 2383 045	NEVER-NEVERLAND (LP, printed PVC outer & gatefold card inner, in yellow bag with photos & notes)	£200
71	Polydor 2383 045	NEVER-NEVERLAND (LP, printed PVC outer & gatefold card inner, pink vinyl & "pink plastic" in text on rear sleeve, around 100 pressed)	£800
71	Polydor 2383 045	NEVER-NEVERLAND (LP, black vinyl, standard sleeve)	£50
72	Polydor 2383 132	WHAT A BUNCH OF SWEETIES (LP)	£30
73	Polydor 2383 212	KINGS OF OBLIVION (LP, with poster)	£50
75	Polydor 2384 071	FLASHBACK (LP)	£18
87	Demon FIEND 105	KILL EM AND EAT EM (LP)	£15

(see also Twink, Deviants, Lightning Raiders)

PINK FLOYD
SINGLES
67	Columbia DB 8156	Arnold Layne/Candy And A Currant Bun (solid centre)	£100
67	Columbia DB 8156	Arnold Layne/Candy And A Currant Bun (push-out centre)	£90
67	Columbia DB 8214	See Emily Play/Scarecrow (solid centre)	£80
67	Columbia DB 8214	See Emily Play/Scarecrow (push-out centre)	£65
67	Columbia DB 8310	Apples And Oranges/Paint Box (solid or push-out centre)	£150
68	Columbia DB 8401	It Would Be So Nice/Julia Dream (solid centre)	£150
68	Columbia DB 8401	It Would Be So Nice/Julia Dream (push-out centre)	£100
68	Columbia DB 8511	Point Me At The Sky/Careful With That Axe Eugene (push-out centre)	£100
81	Harvest HAR 5217	Money (Edit)/Let There Be More Light (unreleased, die-cut sleeve)	£0
81	Harvest 12HAR 5217	Money (Full Length)/Let There Be More Light (12", unreleased)	£0
87	EMI EMDJ 26	Learning To Fly (Edited Version)/One Slip (Edited Version)/Terminal Frost (no p/s, mispressing without "One Slip", 50 on black vinyl)	£20
87	EMI EMDJ 26	Learning To Fly (Edited Version)/One Slip (Edited Version)/Terminal Frost (no p/s, mispressing without "One Slip", 1,000 only on pink vinyl)	£15

MINT VALUE £

94	EMI 12EM 342	**High Hopes** (Album Version)/**Keep Talking** (Album Version)/**One Of These Days** (live) (12", 1-sided, laser-etched blue vinyl, p/s in outer gtefold p/s with 7 postcards) **£40**
13	Columbia DB 8214	**See Emily Play/Scarecrow** (p/s, reissue, pink vinyl, poster) **£15**
15	Parlophone 0825646018611	**PINK FLOYD 1965 - THEIR FIRST RECORDINGS** (2x7", gatefold p/s,1050 only, sticker to shrink) **£140**
17	Pink Floyd PFR12S6	**Interstellar Overdrive** (1966 Recording) (12", single-sided, printed inner, poster, postcard, RSD) **£30**
22	Pink Floyd PFRS 40/7	**Hey Hey Rise Up** (Pink Floyd ft. Andriy Khlyvnyuk)/**A Great Day For Freedom 2022** (p/s, die-cut inner) **£15**

ALBUMS

67	Columbia SX 6157	**THE PIPER AT THE GATES OF DAWN** (LP, 1st pressing, mono, blue/black labels, with "Sold in U.K..."and "Gramophone Co" text, first known matrixes XAX 3419 - 2 G1/XAX 3420 - 1 G1, flipback laminated sleeve, grey back, Ernest J. Day printing credit) **£800**
67	Columbia SCX 6157	**THE PIPER AT THE GATES OF DAWN** (LP, 1st pressing, stereo, blue/black labels, with "Sold in the U.K..." and "Gramophone Co." text, first known matrixes YAX 3419 - 1G1/YAX 3420 - 1-G1, flipback laminated sleeve, grey back, Ernest J. Day printing credit)......**£600**

(Second pressings have "File Under Pop" on half of the flipback; first pressings do not have this. Second pressing worth half to a third less)

69	Columbia SX 6157	**THE PIPER AT THE GATES OF DAWN** (2nd pressing, mono, black/silver labels with "sold in UK..." text, 1 EMI box, flipback laminated sleeve, grey back, Ernest J. Day printing credit)...**£500**
68	Columbia SX 6258	**A SAUCERFUL OF SECRETS** (LP, 1st pressing, mono, blue/black label, "Sold in U.K..." text, front laminated flipback sleeve.Gilmour spelt 'Gilmore' on label and sleeve, some early labels misspell first track as 'Let There Me More Light' and all songs are credited to Magdalene Music. Other early labels spell song titles correctly but all songs are still credited to Magdalene Music.Earliest matrixes XAX 3633-1 G1/XAX 3634-1 G1) **£600**
68	Columbia SCX 6258	**A SAUCERFUL OF SECRETS** (LP, 1st pressing, stereo, blue/black label, "Sold in U.K..." text, front laminated flipback sleeve. Gilmour spelt 'Gilmore' on label and sleeve, early label credit all songs to Magdalene Music. Earliest matrixes YAX 3633-1 G1/YAX 3634-1 R1)...**£400**
69	Columbia SCX 6157	**THE PIPER AT THE GATES OF DAWN** (3rd stereo pressing, black/silver labels without "Sold in the UK" but with "Gramophone Co." text, 1 EMI box, flipback laminated sleeve, grey back, Ernest J. Day printing credit)...**£125**
69	Columbia SCX 6346	**SOUNDTRACK FROM THE FILM 'MORE'** (LP, 1st pressing, laminated flipback sleeve, 'couple facing west' photo on green-tinted rear sleeve, with black/silver label, boxed logo and "Sold in UK..." text)...**£100**
69	Harvest SHDW 1/2	**UMMAGUMMA** (2-LP, 1st pressing, without EMI logo, laminated gatefold sleeve with 'London' spelt as 'Londen' with Ernest J Day & Co' printing credit)....................................**£100**
69	Harvest SHDW 1/2	**UMMAGUMMA** (2-LP, 2nd pressing with EMI logo and 'The Gramophone Co Ltd' label text, laminated gatefold sleeve)..**£40**
69	Harvest SHDW 1/2	**UMMAGUMMA** (2-LP, 3rd pressing, with EMI logo and 'EMI Records' label text, laminated gatefold sleeve)..**£30**
69	Columbia SCX 6157	**THE PIPER AT THE GATES OF DAWN** (2nd stereo pressing, black/silver labels with "Sold in the UK" and "Gramophone Co." text, 1 EMI box, flipback laminated sleeve, grey back, Ernest J. Day printing credit)...**£150**
69	Columbia SX 6258	**A SAUCERFUL OF SECRETS** (LP, 2nd pressing, mono, silver/black label, one EMI box at bottom of label. "Made in GT Britain. Sold in U.K..." text around bottom edge of label, front laminated flipback sleeve. Gilmour spelt 'Gilmore' on label and sleeve)...............**£200**
70	Columbia SCX 6258	**A SAUCERFUL OF SECRETS** (LP, 2nd pressing, stereo, silver/black label, one EMI box at bottom of label. "Made in GT Britain. Sold in U.K..." text around the bottom edge of label, front laminated flipback sleeve. Gilmour spelt 'Gilmore' on label and sleeve) **£150**
70	Columbia SCX 6258	**A SAUCERFUL OF SECRETS** (LP, 3rd pressing, stereo, silver/black label, one EMI box at bottom of label. "Made in GT Britain" text around bottom of label but no "Sold in U.K...". Front laminated flipback sleeve. Gilmour spelt 'Gilmore' on label and sleeve) **£100**
69	Columbia SCX 6346	**SOUNDTRACK FROM THE FILM 'MORE'** (LP, laminated non-flipback sleeve, 'couple facing west' photo on black-tinted rear sleeve)..**£80**
70s	Columbia SCX 6346	**SOUNDTRACK FROM THE FILM 'MORE'** (LP, laminated non-flipback sleeve, 'couple facing east' photo on black-tinted rear sleeve)...**£70**
70	MGM 2315 002	**ZABRISKIE POINT** (LP, soundtrack, with Jerry Garcia/Kaleidoscope, et al.) **£30**
70	Harvest SHVL 781	**ATOM HEART MOTHER** (LP, 1st pressing, gatefold sleeve, no EMI logo) **£150**

(First pressing Harvest LPs of UMMAGUMMA and ATOM HEART MOTHER have "The Gramophone..." text on label rim and "Harvest" on the left side of the label; second pressings have "The Gramophone..." text with a boxed EMI logo above "Harvest")

71	Columbia SCX 6167	**THE PIPER AT THE GATES OF DAWN** (4th stereo pressing, black/silver labels without "Sold in the UK..." text, 2 EMI boxes, "EMI records Ltd" text, Non-flipback laminated sleeve, white back, Garrod & Lofthouse printing credit)...**£100**
71	Harvest SHVL 795	**MEDDLE** (LP, textured inside/outside gatefold sleeve, 'The Gramophone Co Ltd' label text and 'Patent No 1224339' on rear of sleeve)...**£100**
71	Harvest SHVL 795	**ATOM HEART MOTHER** (LP, 2nd pressing with EMI logo, 'The Gramophone Co' label text, gatefold sleeve, matrixes SHVL 781 A-4 RD 2/SHVL 781 B-3 AO 1)............................**£50**
71	Harvest SHVL 795	**MEDDLE** (LP, textured outside gatefold sleeve, with 'The Gramophone Co Ltd' label text but no 'Patent no' on sleeve) **£40**
71	Columbia SCX 6258	**A SAUCERFUL OF SECRETS** (LP, 4th pressing, stereo, silver/black label, two EMI boxes at top and bottom of label. "Made in Gt Britain" text around the bottom edge of label but no "Sold in U.K..." Front laminated flipback sleeve. Gilmour spelt 'Gilmore' on label and sleeve) **with 2 EMI box logos**)...**£80**
71	Starline SRS 5071	**RELICS** (LP, white textured sleeve) **£15**
72	Harvest SHSP 4020	**OBSCURED BY CLOUDS** (LP, rounded sleeve, EMI logo on label) **£75**
73	Harvest SHVL 804	**THE DARK SIDE OF THE MOON** (LP, first pressing, solid light blue triangle label, black inner, 2 posters & 2 stickers, gatefold sleeve, only one side opening)........................**£1000**
73	Harvest SHVL 804	**THE DARK SIDE OF THE MOON** (LP, blue & black label, gatefold sleeve with black inner, 2 posters & 2 stickers, with stickered sleeve)..**£60**
73	Harvest SHVL 804	**THE DARK SIDE OF THE MOON** (LP, blue & black label, gatefold sleeve with black inner, 2 posters & 2 stickers, without stickered sleeve)...**£35**
73	Harvest Q4 SHVL 804	**THE DARK SIDE OF THE MOON** (LP, quadrophonic, gatefold sleeve, no inserts)...............**£60**
73	Columbia SCX 6258	**A SAUCERFUL OF SECRETS** (LP, 5th pressing, stereo, silver/black label, two EMI boxes at top and bottom of label. "EMI Records Ltd" replaces "Gramophone Company" in label rim text. Front laminated non-flipback sleeve. Gilmour spelt 'Gilmore' on label and sleeve)..**£60**
74	Harvest SHVL 781	**ATOM HEART MOTHER** (LP, 3rd pressing with EMI logo, 'EMI Records Ltd' label text, gatefold sleeve)..**£40**
73	Harvest Q4 SHVL 781	**ATOM HEART MOTHER** (LP, quadrophonic, gatefold sleeve, with 'quadrophonic' logo on front sleeve)..**£80**

Year	Label & Cat No	Description	Value
73	Harvest Q4 SHVL 781	**ATOM HEART MOTHER** (LP, quadrophonic, gatefold sleeve, without 'quadrophonic' logo on front sleeve, logo is inside)	**£50**
74	Harvest SHDW 403	**A NICE PAIR** (2LP, gatefold, printed inners; early copies with 'Mr Phang' dentist cover)	**£40**
74	Harvest SHDW 403	**A NICE PAIR** (2LP, gatefold, printed inners, later pressing with 'Monk' cover)	**£35**
75	Harvest SHVL 814	**WISH YOU WERE HERE** (LP, with inner sleeve, postcard & black cellophane wraparound with sticker, sealed)	**£500**
75	Harvest SHVL 814	**WISH YOU WERE HERE** (LP, with inner sleeve, postcard & black cellophane wraparound with sticker, unsealed)	**£150**
76	Harvest Q4 SHVL 814	**WISH YOU WERE HERE** (LP, quadrophonic, with inner sleeve)	**£75**
77	Harvest SHVL 815	**ANIMALS** (LP, 1st pressing, picture labels, non-barcode gatefold sleeve printed by 'Garrod & Lofthouse', with card inner with rounded edges, large thumb notch at top and catalogue number on bottom right of inner, Matrix numbers: SHVL 815 A-2U/B-2U)	**£100**
77	Harvest SHVL 815	**ANIMALS** (LP, contract pressing, no EMI stamper at 3 0 clock)	**£150**
77	Harvest SHVL 815	**ANIMALS** (LP, gatefold, later pressing, gloss or matt sleeve, inner)	**£30**
78	Harvest SHVLP 804	**THE DARK SIDE OF THE MOON** (LP, reissue, picture disc, 1000 only)	**£150**
78	Columbia SCX 6157	**THE PIPER AT THE GATES DAWN** (LP, 5th stereo pressing, black/silver labels without "Sold in UK..." text, 2 EMI boxes, "EMI Records Ltd" text. Non-flipback laminated sleeve, white back, Garrod & Lofthouse printing credit)	**£50**
79	Harvest SHDW 4111/4112	**THE WALL** (2LP, First press, MATRIXES: SHSP 4111 A-2U/B-3U/SHSP 4112 A-1U/B-5U: TML-M/TML-X/TML-M/TML-M stamped into dead wax. Creamy coloured sleeve, bricks do not align right to bottom of sleeve, inner surface of sleeve is heavyweight card and creamy in colour, 8th brick states "produced by David Gilmour" then "written by Roger Waters". 9th brick "words and music Roger Waters except "Young Lust", "Comfortably Numb"" etc. Inner sleeve has rounded edges and thumb notch along top edge. "SHDW 4111/1" in bottom right corner. Gatefold with 'static' transparent "title" sticker)	**£120**
79	Harvest SHDW 4111/4112	**THE WALL** (2LP, later pressing, lighter inner card browner in colour. Inside gatefold on right hand side 9th brick "Bob Ezrin, Roger Waters", 10th brick: no text, then Pink Floyd, names of the band. Square inner sleeve - usually - with OC-15863411/SHSP4111/2 catalogue numbers, gatefold)	**£40**
79	Harvest PF 11	**THE FIRST XI** (11LP box set, original sleeves, exclusive "The Dark Side Of The Moon" & "Wish You Were Here" picture discs, 1,000 only)	**£800**
81	Harvest SHVL 822	**A COLLECTION OF GREAT DANCE SONGS** (LP, printed inner)	**£20**
83	Columbia SCX 6258	**A SAUCERFUL OF SECRETS** (LP, 6th pressing, stereo, tan label)	**£30**
83	Fame FA 3065	**THE PIPER AT THE GATES OF DAWN** (7th stereo pressing, yellow or tan labels, non-laminated, non-flipback sleeve)	**£25**
83	Harvest SHPF 1983	**THE FINAL CUT** (LP, gatefold, title sticker)	**£30**
84	Columbia SCX 6157	**THE PIPER AT THE GATES OF DAWN** (6th stereo pressing, tan labels, non-flipback laminated sleeve, white back, Garrod & Lofthouse printing credit)	**£35**
84	Harvest/Numbus SHVL 814	**WISH YOU WERE HERE (LP, audiophile edition, Nimbus supercut sold through Hi-Fi Today magazine**	**£1250**
85	Harvest SHVL 804	**DARK SIDE OF THE MOON** (LP, reissue, gatefold sleeve, 2 posters and stickers 'barcode' on sleeve)	**£20**
85	Harvest SHVL 815	**ANIMALS** (LP, repressing, 'barcode' on sleeve)	**£15**
86	Fame 3163	**A SAUCERFUL OF SECRETS** (LP, 7th pressing, stereo, yellow Fame label)	**£25**
86	Harvest SHVL 795	**MEDDLE** (LP, repressing, black label)	**£25**
87	EMI EMD 1003	**A MOMENTARY LAPSE OF REASON** (LP, gatefold sleeve with inner)	**£25**
87	EMI EMD 1003	**A MOMENTARY LAPSE OF REASON** (LP, gatefold sleeve with inner, 2 posters, 'guaranteed' concert ticket application and stickered sleeve)	**£50**
88	EMI EQ 5009	**DELICATE SOUND OF THUNDER** (2-LP, gatefold, 2 inners)	**£35**
91	Fame 3163	**A SAUCERFUL OF SECRETS** (LP, 8th pressing, beige, tan label)	**£20**
92	EMI CDS 7805572	**SHINE ON** (9CD box set, with book and postcards)	**£150**
94	EMI EMD 1055	**THE DIVISION BELL** (LP, gatefold sleeve, with inner)	**£75**
95	EMI EMD 1078	**PULSE** (4LP slipcase box set, hardback book)	**£300**
97	EMI 859 857-1	**THE PIPER AT THE GATES OF DAWN** (LP, reissue, mono, gatefold sleeve with inner and 'art', inser)	**£65**
97	EMI LPCENT 11	**THE DARK SIDE OF THE MOON** (LP, reissue, EMI 100 Centenary, stickered sleeve)	**£50**
97	EMI EMD 1115	**WISH YOU WERE HERE** (LP, reissue, 'magnifying glass' cover)	**£35**
97	EMI SIGMA 630	**'97 VINYL COLLECTION** (7LP die-cut box set, includes "The Piper At The Gates Of Dawn" [EMD 1110], "The Wall" [EMD 1111], "Atom Heart Mother" [EMD 1112], "Relics" [EMD 1113], "The Dark Side Of The Moon" [EMD 1114], "Wish You Were Here" [EMD 1115])	**£400**
97	EMI EMD 1113	**RELICS** (LP, gatefold, poster)	**£50**
01	EMI 724353611118	**ECHOES** (THE BEST OF PINK FLOYD) (4LP box set, printed inners)	**£250**
03	EMI 5821361	**THE DARK SIDE OF THE MOON** (LP, gatefold, 30th anniversary edition, 'third' exclusive poster, 180g)	**£125**
11	EMI 029 8801	**WISH YOU WERE HERE** (LP, reissue, poster and postcard)	**£18**
11	EMI 50999 0 29431 2 1	**THE DARK SIDE OF THE MOON** (IMMERSION EDITON BOX SET) (3CD, 2DVD, 1BD, booklets, ephemera, scarf, marbles etc)	**£100**
11	50999 029435 2 7	**WISH YOU WERE HERE** (IMMERSION EDITION BOX SET) (2CD,2DVD, 1BD box, booklets, ephemera, scarf, marbles etc)	**£60**
12	EMI 5099902943923	**THE WALL** (IMMERSION EDITION BOX SET) (6CD, DVD, booklets, ephemera, scarf, marbles etc)	**£80**
13	Harvest 50999 029876 1 3	**THE DARK SIDE OF THE MOON** (LP, remastered, 40th Anniversary Edition, 180 gm, exclusive 'third poster')	**£60**
14	Parlophone 825646215478	**THE ENDLESS RIVER** (2LP, gatefold, printed inners, booklet)	**£35**
16	Pink Floyd PFRLP 8	**THE DARK SIDE OF THE MOON** (LP, gatefold, cover sticker, 180g, 2 posters & 2-stickers)	**£20**
18	Pink Floyd PFRLP 26	**THE PIPER AT THE GATES OF DAWN** (LP, mono, remaster, poster, envelope outer, RSD)	**£40**
22	Pink Floyd PFR28D	**ANIMALS 2018 REMIX** (LP/CD/DVD/BD box set, booklet, sticker, onsert)	**£60**
22	Pink Floyd PFRLP 28	**ANIMALS 2018 REMIX** (LP, gatefold, booklet)	**£30**
23	Pink Floyd Records PFR50	**THE DARK SIDE OF THE MOON** (50TH ANNIVERSARY BOX SET) (2LP, 2 7", 2CD, 2 BD, DVD, book, music book, ephemera)	**£160**
24	Pink Floyd PFR 42BD	**ANIMALS 2018 REMIX** (BD, ATMOS mix, booklet, stickers)	**£20**

ALBUMS : EXPORT LPS

Year	Label & Cat No	Description	Value
67	Odeon PSCX 6157	**THE PIPER AT THE GATES OF DAWN** (LP, stereo, UK sleeve with gold 'Odeon' sticker	**£2000**

over Columbia logo on rear, 'The Gramophone Co Ltd' label text on rim and 'Made in Gt. Britain' on black/silver label) ....

| 68 | Odeon PSCX 6258 | **A SAUCERFUL OF SECRETS** (LP, Stereo, UK sleeve with gold 'Odeon' sticker over 'Columbia logo on rear of sleeve, black/silver Odeon label) ....**£1000** |
| 69 | Odeon PSCX 6346 | **MORE** (LP, UK sleeve with gold 'Odeon' sticker over Columbia logo on rear of sleeve, black/silver Odeon label) ....**£800** |

PROMOS

67	Columbia DB 8156	**Arnold Layne/Candy And A Currant Bun** (demo copy in promo-only p/s, push-out centre) **£1500**
67	Columbia DB 8156	**Arnold Layne/Candy And A Currant Bun** (demo copy without p/s, push-out centre) **£500**
67	Columbia DB 8214	**See Emily Play/Scarecrow** (demo copy in promo-only p/s, push-out centre) **£1500**
67	Columbia DB 8214	**See Emily Play/Scarecrow** (demo copy without p/s, push-out centre) **£500**
67	Columbia DB 8310	**Apples And Oranges/Paintbox** (demo copy in promo-only p/s, push-out centre) **£1500**
67	Columbia DB 8310	**Apples And Oranges/Paintbox** (demo copy without p/s, push-out centre) **£500**
68	Columbia DB 8401	**It Would Be So Nice** (1-sided demo, push-out centre) **£1000**
68	Columbia DB 8511	**Point Me To The Sky/Careful With That Axe Eugene** (demo, with newsletter, push-out centre) **£900**
68	Columbia DB 8511	**Point Me To The Sky/Careful With That Axe, Eugene** (demo, with postcard, push-out centre) **£800**
69	Emidisc no cat. no.	**The Narrow Way** (acetate, different version, 1 copy only) **£2000**
81	Harvest HAR 5217	**Money** (1-sided pink vinyl promo in p/s, 200 only) **£100**
81	Harvest HAR 5217	**Money** (Edited Version) (1-sided, pink vinyl, 200 only) **£40**
81	Harvest HAR 5217	**Money** (Edited Version) (1-sided, pink vinyl, mispressing with "Let There Be More Light" label on B-side) **£50**
83	Harvest HARDJ 5224	**Not Now John/The Hero's Return** (I & II) **£30**
88	EMI 12PF 1	**Delicate Sound Of Thunder Sampler: Another Brick In The Wall Part 2/ One Of These Days/Run Like Hell** (12", black & pink sleeve) **£20**
88	EMI PSLP 1026	**Pink Floyd In Europe '88: Money/Shine On/Another Brick In The Wall Part 2/ One Slip/On The Turning Away/Learning To Fly** (12", with "Another Brick...Part 1" miscredit on rear p/s) **£20**

(see also Syd Barrett, Roger Waters, David Gilmour, Richard Wright, Nick Mason, Nick Mason's Saucerful of Secrets, Joker's Wild, Ron Geesin, Zee, Adam, Mike & Tim)

PINK INDUSTRY

85	Zulu ZULU RA 8	**What I Wouldn't Give/Bound By Silence** (p/s) **£15**
87	Cathexis CRL 16	**Don't Let Go/Ticket To Heaven/Empty Beach** (Remix) (12", p/s) **£15**
83	Zulu ZULU 2	**LOW TECHNOLOGY** (LP) **£15**
83	Zulu ZULU 4	**WHO TOLD YOU - YOU WERE NAKED** (LP) **£15**
85	Zulu ZULU 7	**NEW BEGINNINGS** (LP) **£25**
88	Cathexis CRL 18	**PINK INDUSTRY** (LP) **£25**

(see also Pink Military, Big In Japan)

PINK MILITARY

| 80 | Virgin/Eric's ERIC'S 004 | **DO ANIMALS BELIEVE IN GOD?** (LP) ....**£15** |

(see also Pink Industry, Big In Japan)

PINK PEOPLE

| 64 | Philips BF 1355 | **Psychologically Unsound/Cow Catcher** ....**£50** |
| 64 | Philips BF 1356 | **Indian Hate Call/I Dreamt I Dwelt In Marble Halls** ....**£20** |

(see also Four Squares)

PINK RHYTHM

85	Beggars Banquet BEG 126	**Melodies Of Love/Walking In The Rain** (p/s) **£20**
85	Beggars Banquet BEG 126T	**Memories Of Love/Walking In The Rain** (12", p/s) **£20**
85	Beggars Banquet BEG 136T	**Can't Get Enough Of Your Love/Can't Get Enough Of Your Dub** (12", p/s) **£15**
85	Beggars Banquet BEG 149T	**India/Trust Me/More And More/India** (Instrumental) (12", p/s) **£15**

(see also Freeez, Gamer 3, Midi Rain)

PINKERTON'S ('ASSORTED' COLOURS)

66	Decca F 12377	**Don't Stop Loving Me Baby/Will Ya?** (as Pinkerton's 'Assorted' Colours) **£15**
66	Decca F 12493	**Magic Rocking Horse/It Ain't Right** (as Pinkerton's Colours) **£35**
67	Pye 7N 17327	**Mum And Dad/On A Street Car** (as Pinkerton's Colours) **£18**
67	Pye 7N 17414	**There's Nobody I'd Sooner Love/Look At Me** (as Pinkerton's) **£40**
68	Pye 7N 17574	**Kentucky Woman/Behind The Mirror** (as Pinkerton's) **£18**

(see also Flying Machine, Liberators, Tony Newman)

FAYETTE PINKNEY

| 79 | Chopper CHOP E 3 | **ONE DEGREE** (LP) ....**£15** |

PINKY & PERKY

| 63 | Columbia 33SX 1550 | **PINKY & PERKY'S MELODYMASTER** (LP) ....**£20** |

PINNACLE

| 74 | Stag HP 125 | **ASSASSIN** (LP, laminated sleeve, black/silver label) ....**£150** |

DELROY PINNOCK

| 81 | SG 5 | **Babylon Walls/MIKEY RANKS : I Want To Be** ....**£70** |

GERALDO PINO

| 05 | Soundway SNDWLP005 | **AFRO SOCO SOUL LIVE** (LP, reissue, 1000 only) ....**£20** |
| 05 | Soundway SNDWLP006 | **LET'S HAVE A PARTY** (LP, reissue, 1000 only) ....**£20** |

BOB PINODO

| 78 | Bonzark INLS 6128 | **THE SHOW MASTER** (LP) ....**£30** |

PINPOINT

| 79 | Albion CEL 8 | **Richmond/Love Substiture** (p/s) ....**£80** |
| 80 | Albion ALB103 | **THIRD STATE** (LP, with free 12") ....**£20** |

PIO BO
93	Nucleus NUKE 010	The Best Time To Go Swimming: Disco Swim/Funky Swim (12")	£50

PIONEERS
66	Rio R 102	Good Nannie/Doreen Girl	£40
66	Rio R 106	Too Late/Give Up	£50
68	Blue Cat BS 100	Shake It Up/Goodies Are The Greatest	£120
68	Blue Cat BS 103	Give It To Me/LEADERS: Someday Someway	£120
68	Blue Cat BS 105	Whip Them/Some Having A Bawl	£60
68	Blue Cat BS 139	Reggae Beat/Miss Eve	£280
68	Caltone TONE 119	I Love No Other Girl/MILTON BOOTHE: I Used To Be A Fool	£140
68	Amalgamated AMG 811	Give Me Little Loving/This Is Soul (B-side actually by Lyn Tait & Jets)	£25
68	Amalgamated AMG 814	Long Shot/Dip And Fall Back	£30
68	Amalgamated AMG 821	Jackpot/CREATORS: Kimble (B-side actually by Lee Perry)	£30
68	Amalgamated AMG 823	No Dope Me Pony/LORD SALMONS: Great - Great In '68	£45
68	Amalgamated AMG 826	Tickle Me For Days/VERSATILES: The Time Has Come	£85
68	Amalgamated AMG 828	Catch The Beat/SIR GIBB'S ALLSTARS: Jana (B-side actually Immortals' "Jane Anne")	£40
68	Amalgamated AMG 830	Sweet Dreams/DAN D JR: Caterpillar Rock	£40
68	Pyramid PYR 6062	Easy Come, Easy Go/BEVERLEY'S ALLSTARS: Only A Smile (B-side actually by Lyn Tait & Jets) (some copies on JJ label)	£55
69	JJ PYR 6065	Pee Pee Cluck Cluck/BEVERLEY'S ALLSTARS: Exclusively	£125
69	Amalgamated AMG 833	Don't You Know/Me Naw Go A Believe	£120
69	Amalgamated AMG 835	Mama Look Deh/BLENDERS: Decimal Currency	£40
69	Amalgamated AMG 840	Who The Cap Fits/I'm Moving On	£60
69	Amalgamated AMG 850	Alli Button/HIPPY BOYS: Death Rides	£170
69	Trojan TR 672	Long Shot Kick The Bucket/RICO: Jumping The Gun	£25
69	Trojan TR 685	Black Bud/Too Late	£25
69	Trojan TR 698	Poor Rameses/BEVERLEY'S ALLSTARS: In Orbit (some in Hot Shot sleeve)	£30
70	Trojan TR 7781	Money Day/BEVERLEY ALL STARS: Ska Ba Do	£20
70	Trojan TR 7795	I Need Your Sweet Inspiration/Everything Nice	£15
71	Summit SUM 8511	Starvation/BEVERLEY'S ALLSTARS: Version	£20
72	Summit SUM 8535	Story Book Children/SIDNEY, GEORGE AND JACKIE: Gorgeous, Marvellous	£15
74	Trojan TR 7923	Honey Bee/Hot Blooded Man	£15
77	Mercury 6007147	My Good Friend James/Secrets Of You	£150
78	Ice GUY 14	My Good Friend James/Secrets Of You (reissue)	£150
11	Doctor Bird THB 7007	Easy Come Easy Go/DERRICK MORGAN AND DESMOND DEKKER: Mercy Mercy	£40
13	Trojan THB 7026	Mettle/BEVERLY'S ALL STARS: Hook, Line And Sinker	£25
68	Amalgam. AMGLP 2003	GREETINGS FROM THE PIONEERS (LP)	£150
70	Trojan TBL 103	LONGSHOT (LP)	£45
70	Trojan TBL 139	BATTLE OF THE GIANTS (LP)	£35
71	Trojan TRL 24	YEAH! (LP)	£15
74	Trojan TRLS 64	FREEDOM FEELING (LP)	£15
74	Trojan TRLS 98	I'M GONNA KNOCK ON YOUR DOOR (LP)	£18
76	Mercury 9286172	FEEL THE RHYTHM (LP)	£35
78	Trojan TRLS 156	PUSHER MAN (LP)	£25
79	Trojan TRLS 172	GREATEST HITS (LP)	£30

(see also Sir Gibbs, Rebels [Jamaica], Jackey Robinson, Moonboys, Sidney George & Jackie)

PIPES OF PAN (1)
67	Page One POF 038	Monday Morning Rain/Monday Morning Rain (Instrumental Mix)	£20

PIPES OF PAN (2)
71	Rolling Stones COC 49100	BRIAN JONES PLAYS WITH THE PIPES OF PAN AT JOUJOUKA (LP, gatefold sleeve with foldout insert; front cover with misprinted title)	£100
71	Rolling Stones COC 49100	BRIAN JONES PRESENTS THE PIPES OF PAN AT JOUJOUKA (LP, gatefold sleeve with foldout insert; "Presents" sticker on misprinted cover)	£90
71	Rolling Stones COC 49100	BRIAN JONES PRESENTS THE PIPES OF PAN AT JOUJOUKA (LP, gatefold sleeve with foldout insert; corrected title on front cover)	£80

(see also Rolling Stones)

PIPETTES
05	Unpopular UNPOP 6	I Like A Boy In Uniform/It Hurts To See You Dance So Well (hand-numbered p/s, insert, 500 only)	£25
06	Memphis Industries MIO 71S1	COLLECTORS BOX (4 x 7", coloured vinyl, HMV exclusive)	£25
06	Memphis Industries MII041111	WE ARE THE PIPETTES (LP)	£25

(see also Gwenno)

PIPS
61	Top Rank JAR 574	Every Beat Of My Heart/Room In Your Heart	£45

(see also Gladys Knight & Pips)

PIRATES
64	HMV POP 1250	My Babe/Casting My Spell	£40
66	Polydor BM 56712	Shades Of Blue/Can't Understand	£30
77	Warner Bros K 17002	Sweet Love On My Mind/You Don't Own Me/Don't Munchen It (p/s)	£15

(see also Johnny Kidd & Pirates, [Billy J. Kramer &] Dakotas)

PISCES
71	Trailer LER 2025	PISCES (LP)	£30

PISTONS
81	Humdrum ZIT 1	Solitary Reality/Hyper Active (p/s and insert)	£70

HARRY PITCH
68	MOR MR 101P	HARMONICA JEWEL BOX (LP)	£20

(see also Mr. Bloe)

GENE PITNEY
SINGLES
61	HMV POP 933	Every Breath I Take/Mr Moon, Mr Cupid & I	£30
67	Stateside SS 2060	Something's Gotten Hold Of My Heart/Building Up My Dream World (withdrawn)	£20
68	Stateside SS 2131	Yours Until Tomorrow/She's A Heartbreaker	£15
68	Stateside SS 2131	Yours Until Tomorrow/She's A Heartbreaker (DJ copy)	£30

EPs
63	HMV 7EG 8832	TOWN WITHOUT PITY	£20

ALBUMS : LPS
62	HMV CLP 1566	THE MANY SIDES OF GENE PITNEY	£30
63	United Artists ULP 1028	ONLY LOVE CAN BREAK A HEART (mono)	£20
63	United Artists (S)ULP 1028	ONLY LOVE CAN BREAK A HEART (stereo)	£30
63	United Artists ULP 1043	GENE PITNEY SINGS JUST FOR YOU	£20
64	United Artists ULP 1061	BLUE GENE	£20
64	United Artists ULP 1064	GENE PITNEY MEETS THE FAIR YOUNG LADIES OF FOLKLAND	£20
64	United Artists ULP 1073	GENE PITNEY'S BIG SIXTEEN	£15
65	Stateside SL 10120	I'M GONNA BE STRONG	£15
65	Stateside SL 10132	GENE PITNEY'S MORE BIG SIXTEEN (VOL. 2)	£15
65	Stateside SL 10147	GEORGE JONES AND GENE PITNEY (with George Jones)	£15
65	Stateside SL 10148	LOOKING THRU THE EYES OF LOVE	£15
65	Stateside SL 10156	SINGS THE GREAT SONGS OF OUR TIME	£15
66	Stateside SL 10173	IT'S COUNTRY TIME AGAIN (with George Jones)	£15

(see also Marc Almond & Gene Pitney, George Jones)

PIXIES
89	4AD BAD 909	HERE COMES YOUR MAN EP (12", p/s)	£15
89	4AD PIX ONE	DOOLITTLE SAMPLER: Debaser/Wave Of Mutilation/I Bleed/Gouge Away (12", 1-sided, title sleeve, promo only)	£15
90	4AD BAD 009	VELOURIA EP (12" p/s)	£15
90	4AD BAD 0014	DIG FOR FIRE EP (12", p/s)	£15
90	4AD PIX 3	EXTRACTS FROM BOSSANOVA: Allison/Rock Music/Down To The Well/The Happening (12", 1-sided, promo only)	£15
91	4AD PIX 4	EXTRACTS FROM TROMPE LE MONDE: U-Mass/Letter To Memphis/Subbacultcha (10", same track both sides, promo only)	£15
87	4AD MAD 709	COME ON PILGRIM (mini-LP)	£25
88	4AD CAD 803	SURFER ROSA (LP, with inner)	£50
89	4AD CAD 905	DOOLITTLE (LP, with lyric booklet & postcard, in carrier bag)	£50
89	4AD CAD 905	DOOLITTLE (LP, with lyric booklet & postcard)	£40
90	4AD CAD 0010	BOSSANOVA (LP, with booklet, inner)	£40
91	4AD CAD 1014	TROMPE LE MONDE (LP)	£45
97	4AD DADD 7011	DEATH TO THE PIXIES (4-10" LP, box set)	£100
02	Cooking Vinyl COOK 234	PIXIES - THE PURPLE TAPE (LP, inner, purple, green or orange vinyl)	£45
11	4AD CAD 2406	WAVE OF MUTILATION: THE BEST OF (2-LP, orange vinyl)	£20
14	Pixies PM006DLPR	INDIE CINDY (2x12", free 7" and download card)	£18

(see also Breeders, Frank Black)

PIXIES THREE
63	Mercury AMT 1214	Birthday Party/Our Love	£25

PLACEBO
95	Fierce Panda NING 13	Bruise Pristine/SOUP: M.E.L.T.D.O.W.N. (foldover p/s, 1500 only)	£35
99	Hut FLOOR TP 10	Without You I'm Nothing (with David Bowie) (UNKLE Remix)/(Flexirol Mix)/(Brothers In Rhythm Club Mix) (12" promo, 500 only, stickered die-cut sleeve)	£15
96	Hut LPFLOORY 2	PLACEBO (LP, gatefold, inner)	£100
98	Elevator FLOORLP 8	WITHOUT YOU I'M NOTHING (LP, gatefold)	£100
00	Elevator FLOORLP 13	BLACK MARKET MUSIC (LP, gatefold)	£60
03	Elevator FLOORLP 17	SLEEPING WITH GHOSTS (LP, triple gatefold sleeve)	£60
10	Elevator FLOORLP 17	COVERS (LP, reissue, 1000 only)	£100
04	Elevator FLOORLP 23	ONCE MORE WITH FEELING (2-LP)	£80
06	Elevator LPFLOOR 26	MEDS (LP, gatefold)	£50
09	Dreambrother BATTLE01BS	BATTLE FOR THE SUN (2-LP, 2-DVD box set)	£40

PLAGUE (1)
68	Decca F 12730	Looking For The Sun/Here Today, Gone Tomorrow	£250

PLAGUE (2)
79	Psycho P2615	In Love/Wimpey Bar Song (silk screened fold-out cover)	£50
79	Psycho P 2615	In Love/Wimpey Bar Song (2nd pressing, printed sleeve, pink vinyl)	£25
80	Evolution EV 4	Out With Me All Night/Er/Don't Want To Be Like Jimmy	£50

PLAID
92	GPR GENP(X) 7	Scoobs In Columbia (remixes) (12", custom sleeve)	£30
94	Clear CLR 409	ANDROID (12" EP, p/s, clear vinyl)	£20
94	Clear CLR 409	ANDROID (12" EP, p/s, black vinyl)	£15
95	Rumble RUMBLE 01	MIND OVER RHYTHM MEET THE MEN FROM PLAID (3 x 10" in p/s)	£15
92	Black Dog Prods. LP 1	MBUKI MVUKI (LP)	£80
97	Warp WARPLP54	NOT FOR THREES (2-LP)	£25
99	Warp WARPLP63	REST PROOF CLOCKWORK (2-LP, gatefold)	£40
00	Warp WARPLP74	TRAINER (3-LP, with poster)	£30
01	Warp WARPLP84	DOUBLE FIGURE (2-LP)	£30
03	Warp WARPLP114	SPOKES (LP)	£20

(see also Black Dog)

MINT VALUE £

PLAINSONG
72	Elektra K 42120	IN SEARCH OF AMELIA EARHART (LP, gatefold sleeve with lyric insert)	£25
73	Elektra K 42136	PLAINSONG II (LP, white label, promo only)	£120

(see also Andy Roberts, Ian Matthews)

PLAN B
06	679 679L134	WHO NEEDS ACTION WHEN YOU GOT WORDS (2-LP)	£50
10	679 5051865899303	THE DEFAMATION OF STRICKLAND BANKS (2-LP)	£150

PLANET EARTH
78	Pye NSPL 18556	PLANET EARTH (LP)	£25

PLANET GONG
78	Charly CYX 202	Opium For The People/Stoned Innocent Frankenstein (10", p/s)	£18
78	Charly CRM 2000	FLOATING ANARCHY - LIVE 1977 (LP)	£18

(see also Daevid Allen, Gong)

PLANETARY ASSAULT SYSTEMS
97	Peacefrog PF 063	ELECTRIC FUNK MACHINE (2-LP)	£20
97	Peacefrog PF 079	THE DRONE SECTOR (2-LP)	£20

PLANET P PROJECT
85	MCA MCSP311	PINK WORLD (2LP, gatefold sleeve)	£18

(see also Rainbow)

PLANETS (1)
60	Palette PG 9008	Like Party/Ippy Yippy Beatnik (only this value if in p/s)	£25

PLANETS (2)
60	HMV POP 818	Chunky/Screwball	£20
61	HMV POP 832	Jam Roll/Delaney's Theme	£25
61	HMV POP 895	Jungle Street/The Grasshopper	£25

PLANETS (3)
73	Bullet BU 528	People Get Funny/DOCBIRD ALL STARS : Funny Version	£15

ROBERT PLANT
67	CBS 202656	Our Song/Laughin' Cryin' Laughin' ('A' label demo)	£300
67	CBS 202656	Our Song/Laughin', Cryin', Laughin'	£350
67	CBS 202858	Long Time Coming/I've Got A Secret ('A' label demo)	£250
67	CBS 202858	Long Time Coming/I've Got A Secret	£300
82	Swan Song SAM154	PICTURES AT ELEVEN (LP, promo interview disc with cue sheet)	£20
82	Es Paranza SAM 169	THE PRINCIPLE OF MOVEMENTS (LP, promo interview disc with cue sheet)	£20
88	Es Paranza PR 2244	NON STOP GO! (LP, two disc set interview promo for NOW AND ZEN album)	£15
90	Es Paranza WX 339X	MANIC NIRVANA (LP, gatefold, numbered, picture inner bag)	£18
93	Fontana 514 867-1	FATE OF NATIONS (LP, inner)	£100
02	Mercury 063094-1	DREAMLAND (2-LP, numbered)	£100
05	Sanctuary SANLP 356	MIGHTY REARRANGER (LP)	£100
10	Decca/Universal 2748338	BAND OF JOY (2LP, fourth side etched, gatefold, printed inners)	£60

(see also Led Zeppelin, Listen, Jimmy Page, Robert Plant & The Strange Sensation, Page & Plant)

PLASMATICS
80	Stiff SEEZ 24	NEW HOPE FOR THE WRETCHED (LP, splatter vinyl)	£20

PLASTIC BERTRAND
78	Sire 9103258	AN 1 (LP, gatefold)	£20

PLASTIC GANGSTERS
83	Secret SHH 144	Plastic Gangster/Sretsgnag Citsalp (7", 12", no p/s on 12" stamped p/s on 7", unissued, 10 DJ copies only)	£250

(see also 4 Skins)

PLASTIC PENNY
68	Page One POF 079	Your Way To Tell Me Go/Baby You're Not To Blame	£20
69	Page One POF 107	Hound Dog/Currency	£20
69	Page One POF 146	She Does/Genevieve	£20
68	Page One POL(S) 005	TWO SIDES OF THE PENNY (LP, laminated front sleeve, flipbacks)	£100
69	Page One POLS 014	CURRENCY (LP, laminated front sleeve, flipbacks)	£150
70	Page One POLS 611	HEADS YOU WIN, TAILS I LOSE (LP)	£75

(see also Universals, Circles, Mick Grabham)

PLASTIC PEOPLE
79	Rising Son RS1	Demolition/XTRAVERTS: Police State (multi coloured vinyl)	£60

PLASTIC SANDWICHES
81	Ellie Jay EJSP 9746	Bayonets And Colours/Parties At War (p/s is two separate 7" pieces of paper)	£20

PLASTICLAND
84	Bam Caruso KIRI 034	PLASTICLAND (LP)	£15

PLASTIKMAN
93	Nova Mute NOMU22LP	SHEET ONE (2-LP)	£30
94	Nova Mute NOMU 37LP	MUSIK (2-LP, with bonus 1-sided etched 12")	£20
98	Nova Mute NOMU 65LP	CONSUMED (LP as 3 x 12")	£50
03	Nova Mute NOMULP 100LP	CLOSER (3-LP)	£80
11	M_nus MINUS 100 Analog	ARKIVES 1993 - 2010 (Box set, 6 x 12")	£100

PLATFORM SIX
65	Piccadilly 7N 35255	Money Will Not Mean A Thing/Girl Down Town	£70

EDDIE PLATT
58	Columbia DB 4101	Tequila/Pop Corn	£25

PLATTERS

78s

58	Mercury AMT 1016	Smoke Gets In Your Eyes/No Matter What You Are	£15
59	Mercury AMT 1039	Enchanted/The Sound And The Fury	£20
59	Mercury AMT 1053	Remember When/Love Of A Lifetime (featuring Tony Williams)	£30
60	Mercury AMT 1081	Harbour Lights/(By The) Sleepy Lagoon	£40

SINGLES

56	Mercury MT 117	The Great Pretender/Only You (And You Alone) (export issue)	£40
58	Mercury 7MT 197	Helpless/Indiff'rent	£30
58	Mercury 7MT 205	Don't Let Go/Are You Sincere?	£30
58	Mercury 7MT 227	You're Making A Mistake (featuring Tony Williams)/My Old Flame	£20
58	Mercury AMT 1001	I Wish/It's Raining Outside	£18
62	Ember JBS 701	Only You/Tell The World	£80
66	Stateside SS 511	I Love You 1000 Times/Hear No Evil, Speak No Evil, See No Evil	£25
67	Stateside SS 2007	With This Ring/If I Had A Love	£25
67	Stateside SS 2042	Washed Ashore (On A Lonely Island In The Sea)/What Name Shall I Give You My Love	£25
67	Stateside SS 2042	Washed Ashore (On A Lonely Island In The Sea)/What Name Shall I Give You My Love (DJ copy)	£60
67	Stateside SS 2067	Sweet Sweet Lovin'/Sonata	£20
67	Stateside SS 2067	Sweet Sweet Lovin'/Sonata (DJ copy)	£60
71	Pye Intl. 7N 25559	Sweet Sweet Lovin'/Going Back To Detroit	£15
87	Kent 6T3	SAMMY AMBROSE: Welcome To Dreamsville/PLATTERS: Not My Girl	£25

EPs

58	Mercury MEP 9526	THE FLYING PLATTERS VOL. I	£15
58	Mercury MEP 9528	THE FLYING PLATTERS VOL. II	£15
58	Mercury MEP 9537	THE PLATTERS	£15
62	Mercury ZEP 10126	THE PLATTERS ON A PLATTER	£15

ALBUMS : LPS

57	Mercury MPL 6504	THE PLATTERS	£35
57	Mercury MPL 6511	THE PLATTERS VOL. 2	£30
58	Mercury MPL 6528	THE FLYING PLATTERS	£30
58	Parlophone PMD 1058	THE PLATTERS (10")	£200
59	Mercury MMC 14009	AROUND THE WORLD WITH THE FLYING PLATTERS	£15
59	Mercury MMC 14010	THE PLATTERS ON PARADE	£15
59	Mercury MMC 14014	REMEMBER WHEN?	£15
60	Mercury MMC 14045	REFLECTIONS	£15
61	Mercury MMC 14072	LIFE IS JUST A BOWL OF CHERRIES	£15
67	Stateside S(S)L 10208	GOING BACK TO DETROIT	£15

(see also Buck Ram's Ramrocks, Linda Hayes)

PLAY

85	Survival SUR B1	RED MOVIES (LP)	£20

PLAYBOYS (U.S.)

58	London HLU 8681	Over The Weekend/Double Talk	£40
58	London HLU 8681	Over The Weekend/Double Talk (78)	£15

PLAYERS

63	Oriole CB 1861	Mockingbird/Bizet As It May	£25

PLAYGIRLS (JAMAICA)

65	Black Swan WI 456	Looks Are Deceiving/BABA BROOKS: Dreadnaught	£65

PLAYGIRLS (U.S.)

59	RCA RCA 1133	Hey Sport/Young Love Swings The World	£15
59	RCA RCA 1133	Hey Sport/Young Love Swings The World (78)	£15

PLAYGROUND

67	MGM MGM 1351	At The Zoo/Yellow Balloon	£20

PLAYGROUP

82	On U Sound BRED 28	EPIC SOUND BATTLES CHAPTER ONE (LP)	£15

PLAYING AT TRAINS

87	Idea IDT 001	A World Without Love/Just Around The Mountain/Playing At Trains/A Japanese Intervention (12" p/s)	£85
89	Octopus OCT 5	Walk On Water/Where The Buffalo Roam (p/s)	£250

(see also Waving At Trains)

PLAYN JANE

84	A&M JAYN13	FRIDAY THE 13TH (LIVE AT THE MARQUEE) (LP)	£15

BOBBY PLEASE

57	London HLB 8507	Your Driver's Licence, Please/Heartache Street (unissued, 2x 1-sided demos - price is for BOTH demos together)	£100
57	London HLB 8507	Your Driver's Licence, Please/Heartache Street (78)	£40

PLEASURE CELL

86	(No label) ANG 1	New Age/Common Ground	£25

PLEASURE FAIR

67	Uni UNL(S) 100	PLEASURE FAIR (LP)	£25

(see also Bread)

PLEASURE GARDEN

68	Sound For Industry SFI 31H/32H	Permissive Paradise/EMPEROR ROSKO & JONATHAN KING: Young London (flexidisc, art sleeve with small booklet)	£100

(see also Iveys)

PLEASURES
65   Sue WI 357   Music City/If I Had A Little Money £45

PLEBS
64   Decca F 12006   Bad Blood/Babe I'm Gonna Leave You £80
60s Oak   THE PLEBS (LP, 1-sided, private pressing) £1000

PLEIADIANS
95   Symbiosis SYB009   Pleiadians/Baording Pass To Balangan (12") £18
97   Dragonfly BFLL 24   IDENTIFIED FLYING OBJECT (2-LP) £50

PLEXUS
78   Look LKLP 6175   PLEXUS (LP) £65
79   Hill & Dale HD004   LIFE UP THE CREEK (LP) £55

PLINTH
13   Clay Pipe 08   MUSIC FOR SMALLS LIGHTHOUSE (LP, numbered, 500 only) £15
14   Kit (No cat no)   WINTERSONGS (LP, lino cut sleeve, vinyl repressing, 200 only) £15

PLONE
99   Warp WARPLP64   FOR BEGINNER PIANO (LP) £20

PLUGS
79   Cathedral CATH 1   Too Late/UFO/Sally (gatefold p/s) £20

JON PLUM
69   SNB 55-3971   Alice/Sunshine £20
69   SNB 55-4317   You Keep Changing Your Mind/An Apple Falls £15

PLUM & YOUTH
80s Checkmount CHK 1   I Got You Babe/Got To Be Moving On (p/s, withdrawn) £15
(see also Cozy Powell, Rainbow, Big Bertha)

PLUMMERS
64   Blue Beat BB 260   Johnny/Little Stars (actually by Plamers) £22

PLUS
70   Probe SPB 1009   SEVEN DEADLY SINS (LP, laminated front sleeve, flipbacks) £120

PLUTO
71   Dawn DNS 1017   Rag A Bone Joe/Stealing My Thunder £20
72   Dawn DNS 1026   I Really Want It/Something That You Loved £30
71   Dawn DNLS 3030   PLUTO (LP, laminated sleeve, lilac label) £250
89   See For Miles SEE 265   PLUTO...PLUS (LP, reissue) £25
(see also Dry Ice, Foundations)

PLUTOS PEOPLE
78   Jay Lee JL 6   Little Lady/It's Up To You (no p/s) £15

PNEUMONIA (1)
68   Oak RGJ 625   I Can See Your Face £500

PNEUMONIA (2)
79   Plastic PLAS 001   Exhibition/Coming Attack/U.K. DECAY: U.K. Decay/Carcrash (folded p/s) £25

P'O
83   Court COURT 1   WHILST CLIMBING THIEVES VIE FOR ATTENTION (LP) £50
(see also Wire, Cupol, Dome, Gilbert & Lewis, Bruce Gilbert, A.C. Marias)

POEME ELECTRONIQUE
82   Carrere CAR 228   The Echoes Fade/V.O.I.C.E. (p/s) £200

POET & ONE MAN BAND
69   Verve Forecast SVLP 6012   THE POET AND THE ONE MAN BAND (LP, laminated front sleeve, flipbacks) £100
(see also Tony Colton, Nicky Hopkins, Heads Hands & Feet)

POETS
64   Decca F 11995   Now We're Thru/There Are Some £20
65   Decca F 12074   That's The Way It's Got To Be/I'll Cry With The Moon £200
65   Decca F 12195   I Am So Blue/I Love Her Still £60
65   Immediate IM 006   Call Again/Some Things I Can't Forget £100
66   Immediate IM 024   Baby Don't You Do It/I'll Come Home £100
67   Decca F 12569   Wooden Spoon/In Your Tower £450
71   Strike Cola SC 1   Heyla Hola/Fun Buggy £50
(see also Pathfinders, [White] Trash, Blue)

POETS (IRELAND)
68   Pye 7N 17668   Locked In A Room/Alone Am I £240
68   Target 7N 17668   Locked In A Room/Alone Am I (Irish issue, different label) £240

POGUE MAHONE
84   Pogue Mahone PM 1   Dark Streets Of London/The Band Played Waltzing Mathilda (white label tour copy
                                   with 'harp' stamp, 237 only) £50

(see also Pogues)

POGUES
84   Stiff BUY DJ 212   The Irish Rover/DUBLINERS: Rare Old Mountain Dew (promo, dirty verse taken out for
                                   airplay) £15
84   Stiff BUY 212   Boys From The County Hell/Repeal Of The Licensing Laws (A-label promos in blue-
                                   tinted p/s) £15
84   Stiff BUY 207/BUY 212   Dark Streets Of London/The Band Played Waltzing Mathilda//Boys From The County
                                   Hell/Repeal Of The Licensing Laws (shrinkwrapped double pack) £20
85   Stiff BUY220   A Pair Of Brown Eyes/Whiskey You're The Devil (sealed and stickered with free copy of
                                   Boys From The County Hell 7") £30

85	Stiff DBUY 220	**A Pair Of Brown Eyes/Whiskey You're The Devil** (picture disc) **£15**
85	Stiff BUYIT 220	**A Pair Of Brown Eyes/Whiskey You're The Devil/Muirshin Durkin** (12", p/s)..................**£15**
85	Stiff BUY 212/BUY 220	**Boys From The County Hell/Repeal Of The Licensing Laws//A Pair Of Brown Eyes/ Whiskey You're The Devil** (shrinkwrapped double pack) **£15**
85	Stiff BUYIT 229	**Dirty Old Town/A Pistol For Paddy Garcia/The Parting Glass** (12", with poster & stickered p/s) **£20**
85	Stiff BUYIT 229	**Dirty Old Town/A Pistol For Paddy Garcia/The Parting Glass** (12", without poster & stickered p/s) **£15**
87	Stiff/Hell BLOOD 1	**The Good, The Bad & The Ugly/Rake At The Gates Of Hell** (unreleased) **£0**
87	Stiff/Hell BLOODY 1	**The Good, The Bad & The Ugly/Rake At The Gates Of Hell** (12", unreleased) **£0**
85	Stiff SEEZ 58	**RUM SODOMY & THE LASH** (LP) **£15**

(see also Pogue Mahone, Nips, Nipple Erectors, Radiators From Space, Shane MacGowan & the Popes)

POINDEXTER BROTHERS
| 66 | Verve VS 550 | **(Git Your) Backfield In Motion/(Grandma) Give That Girl Some Slack** ....**£20** |

POINT BLANK
| 96 | Phono PHONO 8 | **A Game Of Two Halves/Rog** (12") ....**£25** |

POISON GIRLS
79	Small Wonder WEENY 4	**HEX** (12" EP, with lyric insert) **£18**
80	Crass/Xntrix 421984/1	**Persons Unknown/CRASS: Bloody Revolutions** (folded 21" x 14" poster p/s) **£20**
80	Crass 421984/2	**CHAPPAQUIDICK** (LP, thin stapled gatefold sleeve with free flexidisc "Statement" [421984/7]) **£30**
81	XENTRIX XN2003	**TOTAL EXPOSURE** (LP, clear or black vinyl with outer poly bag) **£20**
81	XENTRIX XN2006	**WHERE'S THE PLEASURE?** (LP, lyric insert) **£20**
84	XENTRIX RM 101	**7 YEAR SCRATCH** (2-LP) **£20**
85	XENTRIX XN 2208	**SONGS OF PRAISE** (LP) **£15**

(see also Crass, Fatal Microbes/Poison Girls)

POISON IDEA
89	In Your Face FACE 06	**IAN MACKAYE** (EP) **£15**
90	Vinyl Solution SOL 025	**FEEL THE DARNESS** (LP, inner) **£15**
92	Vinyl Solution SOL 033	**BLANK BLACKOUT VACANT** (LP, inner, poster and free 7" [FART 4]) **£20**

POISON IVY
| 64 | Granta GR 7EP 1011 | **CLINGING MEMORIES** (EP) ....**£100** |

ROLO POLEY
| 69 | Jackpot JP 704 | **Zapatoo The Tiger/Music House** (both sides actually by Lester Sterling) ....**£45** |

POLICE
77	Illegal IL 001	**Fall Out/Nothing Achieving** (black & white p/s, red & black label, various designs) **£25**
78	A&M AMS 7348	**Roxanne/Peanuts** (2.52) ('telephone' p/s, typed matrix no., 'All Rights ...' on top half of label) **£15**
78	A&M AMS 7348	**Roxanne/Peanuts** (12", 'telephone' p/s) **£15**
79	A&M AMS 7381	**Can't Stand Losing You/Dead End Job** (p/s, mispressed B-side, plays "No Time This Time") **£20**
79	AMSP 7474	**Message In A Bottle** (Test pressing of unreleased 12") **£700**
79	Illegal IL 001	**Fall Out/Nothing Achieving** (reissue, various label designs, purple/blue p/s) **£15**
79	Illegal IL 001	**Fall Out/Nothing Achieving** (reissue, various label designs, black & orange p/s) **£30**
80	A&M AMPP 6001	**POLICE PACK** (6 x 7" printed foldout PVC pack [AMS 7348, 7381, 7402, 7474 & 7494] & "The Bed's Too Big Without You"/"Truth Hits Everybody" [AMPP 6001/E]; on blue vinyl with 6 inserts) **£25**
80	A&M SAMP 5	**SIX-TRACK RADIO SAMPLER** (custom p/s, promo radio sampler) **£15**
83	A&M AM 117/AM 01	**Every Breath You Take/Murder By Numbers//Truth Hits Everybody/ Man In A Suitcase** (double pack, gatefold p/s) **£30**
95	A&M 581 036 7	**Can't Stand Losing You** (live in Boston)/**Roxanne** (Live In Boston) (Police badge picture disc) **£15**
78	A&M AMLH 68502	**OUTLANDOS D'AMOUR** (LP, blue vinyl) **£25**
79	A&M AMLH 64792	**REGGATTA DE BLANC** (LP) **£15**
80	A&M AMLH 64831	**ZENYATTA MONDATTA** (LP) **£15**
81	A&M AMLK 63730	**GHOST IN THE MACHINE** (LP) **£15**
83	A&M AMLX 63735	**SYNCHRONICITY** (LP) **£15**

(see also Sting, Radio Actors, Zoot Money's Big Roll Band, Last Exit, Newcastle Big Band, Eberhard Schoener)

POLIPHONY
| 73 | Zella JHLPS 136 | **POLIPHONY** (LP, private pressing) ....**£150** |

POLITICIANS (1)
| 72 | Hot Wax HWX 114 | **Love Machine/Free Your Mind** ....**£15** |
| 72 | Hot Wax SHW 5007 | **THE POLITICIANS FEATURING MCKINLEY JACKSON** (LP) ....**£80** |

POLITICIANS (2)
| 79 | Political PEP 1 | **EP: Street Signs/Time Is Tight/Go Away/Fly With Me** (p/s, 500 only) ....**£150** |

FRANK POLK
| 65 | Capitol CL 15389 | **Trying To Keep Up With The Joneses/Welcome Home, Baby** ....**£60** |
| 65 | Capitol CL 15389 | **Trying To Keep Up With The Joneses/Welcome Home, Baby** (DJ copy) ....**£125** |

RAY POLLARD
65	United Artists UP 1111	**The Drifter/Let Him Go** (And Let Me Love You) **£500**
65	United Artists UP 1111	**The Drifter/Let Him Go** (And Let Me Love You) (DJ Copy) **£600**
66	United Artists UP 1133	**It's A Sad Thing/All The Things You Are** **£100**
66	United Artists UP 1133	**It's A Sad Thing/All The Things You Are** (DJ Copy) **£200**

(see also Wanderers)

POLYGON WINDOW
| 93 | Warp WARP 33 | **QUOTH** (12" EP, clear vinyl) ....**£18** |
| 92 | Warp WARP LP 7 | **SURFING ON SINE WAVES** (2-LP) ....**£45** |

MINT VALUE £

92	Warp WARP LP 7LTD	**SURFING ON SINE WAVES** (LP, clear vinyl)	£75

(see also Aphex Twin)

POLYPHEMUS
95	Acme AC 8010LP	**SCRAPBOOK OF MADNESS** (LP, reissue with insert, 500 only)	£18
95	Acme AC 8016LP	**STONEHOUSE** (LP, gatefold sleeve, 700 only)	£18

POLYPHONIC SPREE
02	Good Records 679L011TLP	**BEGINNING STAGES OF** (2-LP)	£40

PONI-TAILS
59	HMV POP 644	Moody/Oom Pah Polka	£15
59	HMV POP 663	I'll Be Seeing You/I'll Keep Tryin'	£15
58	HMV 7EG 8427	**THE PONI-TAILS** (EP)	£100

JEAN-LUC PONTY
69	Liberty LBL/LBS 83262	**ELECTRIC CONNECTION** (LP)	£20
70	Liberty LBL/LBS 83375	**KING KONG** (LP)	£20

(see also Frank Zappa)

PONY
73	Pye 7N 25663	It's Gonna Be So Easy/Til I Met You	£25

POOH
72	CBS 7930	I'll Close The Door Behind Me/The Suitcase	£20

POOH STICKS
88	Fierce FRIGHT 011	**On Tape** (p/s, 1-sided, etched)	£40
88	Fierce FRIGHT 011	**On Tape** (p/s, with unetched B-side)	£35
88	Fierce FRIGHT 021	**1-2-3 Red Light** (p/s, 1-sided)	£20
88	Fierce FRIGHT 023	**Heartbreak** (1-sided, etched B-side, hand-coloured promo p/s, with insert)	£40
88	Fierce FRIGHT 021-025	**FIERCE BOX SET** (5 x 1-sided etched discs, hand-coloured labels, with insert)	£50
88	Fierce FRIGHT 028	**HEROES AND VILLAINS** (LP, with inner)	£18
89	Fierce FRIGHT 034	**Dying For It** (p/s, sold at U.L.U. gig, 300 only, signed)	£25
89	Fierce FRIGHT 034	**Dying For It** (p/s, sold at U.L.U. gig, 300 only, unsigned)	£15
89	Fierce FRIGHT 034	**Dying For It** (1-sided, different p/s to above)	£15
89	53rd & 3rd AGAMC 5	**ORGASM** (LP, pink vinyl with insert for export)	£25
89	Fierce FRIGHT 025	**THE POOH STICKS** (mini-LP, with inner, black & white sleeve, 1-sided, side 2 etched)	£20
89	Fierce FRIGHT 035	**TRADE MARK OF QUALITY** (LP, mail-order only, plain stickered sleeve with insert, numbered)	£18

(see also Dumb Angels)

BRIAN POOLE
66	CBS 202349	**Everything I Touch Turns To Tears/I Need Her Tonight**	£22
67	CBS 3005	**Just How Loud/The Other Side Of The Sky**	£20

(see also Brian Poole & Tremeloes)

BRIAN POOLE & TREMELOES
62	Decca F 11455	**Twist Little Sister/Lost Love** (some with 'Trimiloes' on label)	£15
64	Decca DFE 8566	**BRIAN POOLE AND THE TREMELOES** (EP)	£15
65	Decca DFE 8610	**BRIAN POOLE AND THE TREMELOES** (EP)	£20
63	Ace of Clubs ACL 1146	**BIG BIG HITS OF '62** (LP)	£15
63	Decca LK 4550	**TWIST AND SHOUT WITH BRIAN POOLE AND THE TREMELOES** (LP)	£25
65	Decca LK 4685	**IT'S ABOUT TIME** (LP)	£30

(see also Brian Poole, Tremeloes)

LOU & LAURA POOLE
72	Jay Boy BOY 63	**Only You And I Know/Look At Me**	£15

POOR SOULS
65	Decca F 12183	**When My Baby Cries/My Baby She's Not There**	£25
66	Alp ALP 595 004	**Love Me/Please Don't Change Your Mind**	£50

POOR THINGS
66	CBS 202431	**We Trust In A Better Way Of Life/Danny Boy**	£50

GROOVY JOE POOVEY
70	Injun 100	**Ten Long Fingers On The 88 Keys/Thrill Of Love**	£15
71	Injun 101	**Move Around/BILL REEDER: Till I Waltz Again With You**	£15

IGGY POP
82	RCA Golden Groove GOLD 549	**The Passenger/Nightclubbing** (7", p/s)	£20
77	RCA PB 9093	**China Girl/Baby**	£15
77	RCA PB 9160	**Success/The Passenger**	£15
96	Virgin VUS116	**Lust For Life/**(Get Up I Feel Like Being A) **Sex Machine** (7", p/s, pink vinyl)	£20
73	CBS 65586	**RAW POWER** (LP, with inner, orange label, as Iggy & Stooges)	£100
78	Radar RAD 2	**KILL CITY** (LP, as Iggy Pop & James Williamson)	£20
77	RCA PL12275	**THE IDIOT** (LP, 1st pressing, orange labels)	£40
77	RCA PL12488	**LUST FOR LIFE** (LP, 1st pressing, orange labels)	£50
77	RCA PL 12796	**TV EYE - 1977 LIVE** (LP)	£15
79	Arista SPART 1092	**NEW VALUES** (LP)	£25
80	Arista SPART 1117	**SOLDIER** (LP, insert)	£25
81	Arista SPART 1158	**PARTY** (LP)	£15
81	RCA Int. INTS 5172	**THE IDIOT** (LP, reissue, green labels)	£30
81	RCA Int. INTS 5114	**LUST FOR LIFE** (LP, reissue, green labels)	£30
82	Chrysalis CHR 1399	**ZOMBIE BIRDHOUSE** (LP)	£15
84	RCA NL82488	**LUST FOR LIFE** (LP, reissue, black labels)	£30
87	Revenge MIG 2W	**I GOT A RIGHT** (LP, picture disc)	£18

MINT VALUE £

88	A&M AMA 5145	BLAH BLAH BLAH (LP)	£18
90	Virgin America VUSLP 19	BRICK BY BRICK (LP)	£20
93	Virgin VUSLP 64	AMERICAN CAESAR (2-LP)	£60
96	Virgin VUSLP 102	NAUGHTY LITTLE DOGGIE (LP)	£50
96	Virgin VUSLP 115	NUDE & RUDE: THE BEST OF IGGY POP (2-LP)	£100
97	EMI LPCENT 40	LUST FOR LIFE (LP, reissue)	£35
16	Caroline International CAROL011LPY	POST POP DEPRESSION	£40
19	CAROL019LPC	FREE (LP, sea blue vinyl)	£20
20	UMC 5771560	THE BOWIE YEARS (7CD cox set, booklet)	£50

(see also Stooges)

POP WILL EAT ITSELF
| 86 | Desperate SRT 1 | THE POPPIES SAY GRRrrr! (EP in stamped brown paper bag, stamped white labels) | £40 |

POPCORNS
| 63 | Columbia DB 4968 | Zero Zero/Chinese Twist | £15 |

TIM POPE
| 84 | Fiction FICS 21 | I Want To Be A Tree/The Double Crossing Of Two Faced Fred (p/s) | £15 |
| 84 | Fiction FICSX 21 | I Want To Be A Tree/(Elephant) Song/The Double Crossing Of Two Faced Fred (12", p/s) | £25 |

(see also Cure)

POP GROUP
79	Radar ADAT 1229	She Is Beyond Good And Evil/3.38 (12", p/s)	£25
79	Rough Trade RT 023	We Are All Prostitutes/Amnesty International Report On British Army Torture Of Irish Prisoners (p/s)	£18
80	Rough Trade RT 039/ Y Y1	Where There's A Will There's A Way/SLITS: In The Beginning There Was Rhythm (p/s)	£18
79	Radar RAD 20	Y (LP, with foldout colour poster)	£70
80	Rough Trade ROUGH 9	FOR HOW MUCH LONGER DO WE TOLERATE MASS MURDER? (LP, with 4 black-and-white posters)	£50
80	Y/Rough Trade ROUGH 12	WE ARE TIME (LP, plain black sleeve)	£20
96	Radar SCAN LP14	Y (LP, reissue)	£30

(see also Slits, Mark Stewart)

ANDRE POPP
| 74 | Polydor 2383 278 | MY MOVIE DREAMS (LP) | £15 |

FRANK POPP ENSEMBLE
| 01 | Blow Up BU026 | Hip Teens Don't Wear Blue Jeans/The Catwalk | £30 |

POPPIES
| 66 | Columbia DB 7879 | Lullaby Of Love/I Wonder Why | £30 |

KEITH POPPIN
| 75 | Sunshot SS001 | Envious/Fed Up | £15 |
| 79 | JB Music JBD 006 | Hold Not Thy Peace/Birdie (12") | £50 |

POPPYHEADS
| 88 | Sarah SARAH 006 | Cremation Town/Pictures You Weave/Dreamboat (foldaround p/s with large poster in poly bag) | £50 |

POP RIVETS
79	M.T. Sounds HEP 001	BACK FROM NOWHERE (EP, no p/s)	£30
79	M.T. Sounds HEP 002	BACK FROM NOWHERE (EP, split single with SULPHATE, no p/s)	£30
79	Hypocrite JIM 1	FUN IN THE U.K. (EP, no p/s, double pack)	£30
02	(No label) HAD 1	Kray Twins/BUFFS: All My Feelings Denied (no p/s, 450 free with Chatham's Burning fanzine)	£25
79	Hypocrite HIP 007	THE POP RIVETS GREATEST HITS (LP, silk-screened sleeve, 50 only)	£150
79	Hypocrite HIP 007	THE POP RIVETS GREATEST HITS (LP, title sleeve with Pop Rivets printed repeatedly across white sleeve, stamped white labels, 50 only)	£150
79	Hypocrite HIP 007	THE POP RIVETS GREATEST HITS (LP, printed sleeve, stamped white labels)	£50
79	Hypocrite HIP-O	EMPTY SOUNDS FROM ANARCHY RANCH (LP, coloured back, stamped labels)	£25
80	Hypocrite HIP 007	THE POP RIVETS GREATEST HITS (LP, screen printed sleeve, insert, 50 only)	£150
89	Hangman HANG 27 UP	ORIGINAL FIRST ALBUM!!! (LP)	£20
90	Hangman HANG 35 UP	LIVE IN GERMANY '79 (LP)	£15
90s	Damaged Goods DAMGOOD 142	CHATHAM'S BURNING (LP, brown vinyl)	£20

(see also Milkshakes)

POP ROCK
| 97 | Acid UKN 010 | PURPLE JELLY EP (2 x 12") | £60 |

POPSICLES
| 65 | Vocalion VH 9243 | I Don't Want To Be Your Baby Anymore/Baby I Miss You | £50 |

(see also Ellie Greenwich, Raindrops)

POP TOPS
| 72 | A&M AMS 7001 | Suzanne Suzanne/Oh Lord Why Lord | £15 |

POPULAR 5
| 68 | Minit MLF 11011 | I'm A Lovemaker/Little Bitty Pretty One | £15 |

POPULAR MECHANICS
| 87 | Ark DOVE 5 | INSECT CULTURE (LP) | £50 |

POP WORKSHOP
| 68 | Page One POF 091 | Fairyland/When My Little Girl Is Happy | £30 |

PORCUPINE TREE
SINGLES : SINGLES AND EPS
| 90 | Private (No Cat. No.) | LOVE, DEATH AND MUSSOLINI (EP, 10 copies, plain black cassette with 3 page | £400 |

		booklet)	£
92	Delerium DELEC EP 010	VOYAGE 34 (12" EP)	£50
92	Delerium DELEC EP 007	VOYAGE 34 (Astralasia Remix) (12" EP)	£25
92	Delerium DELECD EP 010	VOYAGE 34 (CD EP, first 100 with blue not green artwork)	£60
94	Delerium DELEC EP 032	Stars Die/Moonloop (12", p/s)	£15
96	Delerium DELEC EP 049	WAITING (EP 12")	£25
98	Chromatic CHR 003	METANOIA (EP, 2 x 10", 1,000 only)	£60
99	K-Scope/Snapper SMAS 103	Piano Lessons/Oceans Have No Memory (p/s, 1,000 copies)	£18
99	K-Scope/Snapper SMAS 107	Stranger By The Minute/Hallogallo (p/s, 1,000 only)	£18
99	K-Scope/Snapper SMAS 110	Pure Narcotic/Nine Cats - Acoustic (p/s)	£15
00	K-Scope/Snapper SMAS 7111	4 Chords That Made A Million/Orchidia (p/s, 1,000 only)	£15
01	Delerium (No Cat. No.)	TRANSMISSION IV - MOONLOOP EP (Free to Transmission Subscribers, 500 only)	£80

ALBUMS : ORIGINAL ALBUMS

89	Delerium DELC 0002	TARQUIN'S SEAWEED FARM (cassette, 1st issue, around 50 only)	£300
91	Delerium DELC 0002	TARQUIN'S SEAWEED FARM (cassette, 2nd issue, silver print, with A5 booklet, red/black text, 300 only)	£100
91	Delerium DELC 0002	TARQUIN'S SEAWEED FARM (cassette, silver print, with photocopied A5 booklet, label on Side 1, 200 only)	£50
91	Delerium DELC 0003	THE NOSTALGIA FACTORY (cassette, silver print, with A4 booklet, red/black text, 200 only)	£200
91	Delerium DELC 0003	THE NOSTALGIA FACTORY (cassette, with photocopied A5 booklet, label on Side 1, 200 only)	£60
92	Delerium DELEC 008	ON THE SUNDAY OF LIFE (2-LP, gatefold sleeve, 1,000 only)	£100
93	Delerium DELEC 020	UP THE DOWNSTAIR (LP)	£120
94	Magic Gnome MG 4299325	YELLOW HEADGROW DREAMSCAPE (CD, 2,500 only)	£100
95	Delerium DELECLP 028	THE SKY MOVES SIDEWAYS (LP, 2,000 on blue vinyl with poster)	£100
95	Delerium DELECLP 028	THE SKY MOVES SIDEWAYS (LP, black vinyl with poster)	£120
96	Delerium DELECLP 045	SIGNIFY (double LP, gatefold sleeve)	£100
97	Chromatic CHR 002	SPIRAL CIRCUS (LP, 500 only)	£150
01	K-Scope SMACD840	RECORDINGS (CD, numbered slipcase, 20,000 only)	£50
03	Lava 7567 931781	IN ABSENTIA (2-LP)	£100
05	Gates Of Dawn GOD 009	DEADWING (2-LP, black vinyl with poster)	£70
06	Delerium DELECLP 999	MOONLOOP (LP, 500 black vinyl in screen printed blue vinyl bag)	£35
06	Delerium DELECLP 999	MOONLOOP (LP, 99 clear vinyl in screen printed blue vinyl bag)	£70
06	Delerium DELECLP 999	MOONLOOP (LP, 500 white vinyl in screen printed blue vinyl bag)	£40
06	Gates Of Dawn GOD 011	STUPID DREAM (2-LP, black/grey 'marbled' vinyl)	£70
07	Tonefloat TF 40	FEAR OF A BLANK PLANET (2-LP, gatefold)	£80
07	Tonefloat TF 40	FEAR OF A BLANK PLANET (2-LP, 1000 only special edition with poster, booklet and slipcase)	£150
08	Tonefloat TF 46	WE LOST THE SKYLINE (LP, orange marbled vinyl)	£80
08	Tonefloat TF 46	WE LOST THE SKYLINE (LP, black vinyl)	£50
09	Tonefloat TF 82	THE INCIDENT (2-LP, with booklet in PVC slipcase, 2000 only)	£100
09	Tonefloat TF 82	THE INCIDENT (2-LP, standard issue)	£40
16	Kscope KSCOPE 894	THE DELERIUM YEARS 1994-1997 (Box set, 9-LP, booklet)	£100
17	Kscope KSCOPE 893	THE DELERIUM YEARS 1991-1993 (Box set, 9-LP, booklet)	£100

ALBUMS : ALBUM REISSUES

08	Kscope KSCOPE 801	ON THE SUNDAY OF LIFE (2-LP, reissue, orange vinyl)	£35
08	Kscope KSCOPE 801	ON THE SUNDAY OF LIFE (2-LP, reissue, black vinyl)	£25
08	Kscope KSCOPE 802	UP THE DOWNSTAIR (2-LP, reissue, red vinyl)	£25
08	Kscope KSCOPE 802	UP THE DOWNSTAIR (2-LP, reissue, black vinyl)	£30
10	Tonefloat TF 102	IN ABSENTIA (2-LP, reissue coloured vinyl, 1500 only)	£100
10	Tonefloat TF 102	IN ABSENTIA (2-LP, reissue black vinyl)	£40
10	Kscope KSCOPE 803	VOYAGE 34 (2-LP, white vinyl, 2000 only)	£40
11	Kscope KSCOPE 805	SIGNIFY (2-LP, reissue)	£30
11	Kscope KSCOPE 813	RECORDINGS (2-LP, gatefold, reissue)	£20
12	Kscope KSCOPE 834	COMA DIVINE (3-LP box set, reissue)	£35
12	Kscope KSCOPE 825	THE SKY MOVES SIDEWAYS (2-LP, reissue)	£25
13	Kscope KSCOPE 845	STUPID DREAM (2-LP, reissue)	£20
15	Tonefloat TF 40	FEAR OF A BLANK PLANET (2-LP, reissue, black inner sleeves)	£20

ALBUMS : PROMOS

93	Delerium DELEC PROMO CD 1	RADIO ACTIVE (CD, promo, 500 only)	£40
94	Delerium DELEC PROMO CASS 5	SPIRAL CIRCUS (cassette give away free with Transmission newsletter)	£175
97	None	PORCUPINE TREE DEMO (cassette-only, promo)	£100
97	Delerium DELEC PROMO CASS 10	INSIGNIFICANCE (promo cassette, demos and out-takes from SIGNIFY)	£60

(see also No Man, Steven Wilson, Blackfield, Continuum (2))

PORK DUKES

78	Wood PORK 001	THE PORK DUKES (LP, pink vinyl with warning sticker & postcard)	£25
80	Wood PORK 002	PIG OUT OF HELL (LP)	£25

PORNO CASSETTES

82	Heresy Records DOC 1	You're Face, A Fucking Disgrace/Dead End Yobs	£150

PORNO FOR PYROS

93	Warner Bros. 9362 45228-1	PORNO FOR PYROS (LP)	£50

DAVID PORTER

70	Stax SXATS 1034	GRITTY, GROOVY AND GETTIN' IT (LP)	£15
71	Stax STX 1030	VICTIM OF THE JOKE (LP)	£35

| 71 | Stax 2362 006 | INTO A REAL THING (LP) | £15 |

NOLAN PORTER

72	Probe PRO 580	If I Could Only Be Sure/Work It Out In The Morning	£100
72	Probe PRO 580	If I Could Only Be Sure/Work It Out In The Morning (DJ copy)	£175
72	Probe SPB 1067	NOLAN (LP)	£25

ROBIE PORTER

| 66 | MGM 1313 | Either Way I Lose/That's The Way Love Goes | £20 |

PORTER CUNNINGHAM

| 72 | Folk Heritage FHR 027 | OBSERVATIONS (LP) | £100 |

PORTION CONTROL

82	In Phaze POR CON 006	Surface And Be Seen/Spinola (Blotch)/Terror Leads To Better Days/Simple As ABC/Monstrous Bulk/He Is A Barbarian (12" p/s, with plastic outer sleeve)	£40
81	In Phaze PORCON 002	DINING ON THE FLESH (cassette box set with free flexi 7")	£70
81	In Phaze PORCON 002	GAINING MOMENTUM (cassette)	£40
82	In Phaze CP 007	I STAGGERED MENTALLY (LP)	£50
82	In Phase NCN	WITH MIXED EMOTION (cassette)	£40
82	Third Mind TMT 07	SHOT IN THE BELLY (cassette)	£40
83	In Phaze EZ 2	HIT THE PULSE (mini-LP, 45/33rpm)	£18
85	In Phaze PHA 5	SIMULATE SENSUAL (LP, clear vinyl, PVC sleeve with insert)	£20

PORTISHEAD

94	Go! Beat GODX 116	Sour Times/Sour Sour Times/Lot More/Sheared Times (12")	£20
94	Go! Beat GODX 114	Numb/Numbed In Moscow/Revenge Of The Number/Earth - Linger Remix/A Tribute To Monk & Canatella (12")	£20
94	Go! Beat GODX 120	Glory Box/Toy Box/Scorn/Sheared Box (12", p/s)	£20
97	Go! Beat 571 597-1	All Mine/Cowboys/Cowboys (Instrumental) (12", p/s)	£15
11	XL XLT 557	Chase The Tear/Doldrums Reimagine (12", signed)	£30
94	Go Beat! 828 522	DUMMY (LP, 1st pressing, with incorrect sample credits on inner sleeve)	£120
94	Go! Beat 828 522-1	DUMMY (LP, 2nd pressing, with correct sample credits on inner sleeve)	£80
97	Go! Beat PORT LP PRO	PORTISHEAD (2-LP, numbered promo)	£70
97	Go! Beat 314 539189-1	PORTISHEAD (2-LP)	£50
97	Go! Beat 539189-1	PORTISHEAD (LP, gloss sleeve)	£60
98	Go! Beat 559 424-1	ROSELAND NYC LIVE (2-LP, with poster)	£50
99	Simply Vinyl SVLP 115	PORTISHEAD (2-LP, reissue)	£40
00	Simply Vinyl SVLP 162	DUMMY (LP, reissue)	£35
08	Island 1766390	THIRD (2-LP, etched 12", print, with USB stick, numbered)	£60

(see also Jimi Entley Sound, Beak>, Beth Gibbons and Rustin Man, Beth Gibbons)

PORTOBELLO EXPLOSION

| 69 | Carnaby CNS 4001 | We Can Fly/Hot Smoke And Sasafrass (label credits Portebello Explosion) | £30 |

(see also Mirage, Jawbone, Spencer Davis Group)

PORTSMOUTH SINFONIA

73	Transatlantic TRA 275	PLAY THE POPULAR CLASSICS (LP)	£40
74	Transatlantic TRA 285	HALLELUJAH (LP)	£25
79	Philips 9109 231	20 CLASSIC ROCK CLASSICS (LP)	£30

PORTWAY PEDLARS

| 84 | Greenwich Village GVR 229 | IN GREENWOOD SHADES (LP) | £15 |

SANDY POSEY

67	MGM MGM-C(S) 8035	BORN A WOMAN (LP)	£30
67	MGM MGM-C(S) 8042	SINGLE GIRL (LP)	£25
68	MGM MGM-C(S) 8051	SANDY POSEY (LP)	£25
68	MGM MGM-C 8060	THE BEST OF SANDY POSEY (LP, original with blue label)	£20
68	MGM MGM-C(S) 8073	LOOKING AT YOU (LP)	£25

POSITIVE SIGNALS

| 80 | Yob YOB 001 | Media Man/Only For A Day/STRAND: Here Today Gone Tomorrow/Changing World (split EP, p/s) | £15 |

POSSESSED (1)

07	Rise Above Relics RARLP 002	EXPLORATION (LP, black vinyl and black vinyl 7")	£40
07	Rise Above Relics RARLP 002	EXPLORATION (LP, purple vinyl and purple vinyl 7")	£35
07	Rise Above Relics RARLP 002	EXPLORATION (LP, clear vinyl and clear vinyl 7", 100 only)	£50

POSSESSED (2)

| 86 | Under One Flag FLAG 3 | BEYOND THE GATES (LP) | £15 |
| 87 | Under One Flag M FLAG 16 | THE EYES OF HORROR EP (12", p/s) | £15 |

POST MORTEM

| 83 | Regime FM 006 | BETER OFF DEAD (EP) | £25 |

ADRIENNE POSTER/POSTA

63	Oriole CB 1890	Only Fifteen/There's Nothing You Can Do About That	£40
63	Decca F 11797	Only Fifteen/There's Nothing You Can Do About That (reissue)	£20
64	Decca F 11864	Shang A Doo Lang/When A Girl Really Loves You	£40
65	Decca F 12079	He Doesn't Love Me/The Way You Do The Things You Do	£25
65	Decca F 12181	The Winds That Blow/Back Street Girl	£25
66	Decca F 12329	Something Beautiful/So Glad You're Mine	£35
66	Decca F 12455	They Long To Be Close To You/How Can I Hurt You (as Adrienne Posta)	£20

POSTHUMAN

16	I Love Acid ILA 013	I LOVE ACID 013 (12", hand-stamped and numbered, 303 only)	£15
16	Balkan BV 20	IT'S A HOUSE THING EP (12")	£20
10	Balkan BV 07P	SYN EMERGENCE (2 x 12" different picture discs, with CD)	£20

POTENTIAL BAD BOY

93	Limited E Edition CW010	WORK THE BOX EP (12")	£30
95	Redskin/Third Eye TE001	Guns Out (Remix)/Murder Jumppan Sound/In Between The Beats/Unknown (12" with Bad Vibes)	£40
06	Sublogic/Ninety-Two Retro SLVR 001/9T2RX	Everyday Child (1-sided 12", 100 only, stamped and hand-numbered labels)	£40

POTENTIAL THREAT

82	Out Of Town HOOT 7	WHAT'S SO GREAT BRITAIN! (EP, 1st pressing, red sleeve with insert)	£30
80	XX MIN 709	WHAT'S SO GREAT BRITAIN! (EP, 2nd pressing, blue sleeve with insert)	£20
84	Children Of The Revolution COR 6	Brainwashed/Turn A Blind Eye/A Cry For Help/Conflict (p/s)	£15
86	Mortarhate MORT 24	DEMAND AN ALTERNATIVE (LP)	£30

POTION

81	Slapps & Sticks SAS 6	Catch The Feeling (Showstopper)/Showstopper (Instrumental) (12")	£50
81	UK Champagne FUNKY 5	Catch The Feeling/Showstopper (12")	£25

POT LIQUOR

70	Dawn DNLS 3016	FIRST TASTE (LP, withdrawn)	£90
72	Janus 6310 202	LEVEE BLUES (LP)	£30

PHIL POTTER

76	Genesis GEN 10	MY SONG IS LOVE UNKNOWN (LP)	£20
79	Dove DOVE 61	THE RESTORER (LP)	£15

POTTERS

72	Trent JT 100	We'll Be With You/Theme For A Team	£20

POTTING SHEDS

90	Mad Cat BSE 002	Second Best/Shape Out	£15
92	Mad Cat BSE 005	GOLDFISH MEMORY EP (12")	£15

ALLEN POUND'S GET RICH

66	Parlophone R 5532	Searchin' In The Wilderness/Hey You (rare stock copy)	£1000
66	Parlophone R 5532	Searchin' In The Wilderness/Hey You (more common demo)	£600

POUNDS X BUCKWILD

20	Daupe! DM SP 055	TRAFFICANTE (LP, 200 copies)	£40
20	Daupe! DM SP 055	TRAFFICANTE (LP, green vinyl, 100 copies)	£40
20	Daupe! DM SP 055	TRAFFICANTE (LP, splatter vinyl, 100 copies)	£50
20	Daupe! DM SP 055	TRAFFICANTE (LP, silver vinyl, 100 copies)	£40
20	Daupe! DM SP 055	TRAFFICANTE (LP, with obi strip, 20 copies)	£100

BUD POWELL (TRIO)

55	Vogue EPV 1030	BUD POWELL TRIO (EP)	£15
55	Vogue EPV 1033	BUD POWELL'S MODERNISTS (EP)	£15
55	Vogue EPV 1036	BUD POWELL TRIO (EP)	£15
55	Columbia Clef SEB 10013	BUD POWELL (EP)	£15
57	Columbia Clef SEB 10074	GENIUS OF BUD POWELL (EP)	£15
58	Columbia Clef SEB 10094	GENIUS OF BUD POWELL NO. 2 (EP)	£15
52	Vogue LDE 010	THE BUD POWELL TRIO (10" LP)	£20
54	Vogue LDE 053	JAZZ AT THE MASSEY HALL VOL. 2 (10" LP)	£20
56	Columbia Clef 33C 9016	BUD POWELL TRIO (10" LP)	£25
57	Columbia Clef 33CX 10069	JAZZ ORIGINAL (LP)	£30
58	Columbia Clef 33CX 10123	BLUES FOR BUD (LP)	£30
59	HMV CLP 1294	THE LONELY ONE (LP)	£30
63	Vogue LAE 558	THE BUD POWELL TRIO (LP)	£15
63	Columbia 33SX 1575	THE BUD POWELL TRIO FEATURING MAX ROACH (LP)	£25
64	Fontana FJL 903	HOT HOUSE (LP)	£25
68	Fontana SFJL 901	BLUES FOR BOUFFEMONT (LP)	£25

COZY POWELL

73	Rak 4C 006 94962	Dance With The Devil/And Then There Was Skin (export issue, p/s, RAK 164 in run out groove, blue or yellow vinyl)	£20

(see also Rainbow, Young Blood, Big Bertha, Ace Kefford Stand, Bedlam,, Black Sabbath, Jeff Beck, Whitesnake, Michael Schenker Group, Donovan, Gary Moore, Young & Moody, Brian May, Chick Churchill, Graham Bonnet, Emerson Lake & Powell, Jack Bruce, Plum & Youth, Suzi Quatro)

JANE POWELL

54	Capitol LC 6665	THREE SAILORS AND A GIRL (10" LP)	£20
57	HMV CLP 1131	JANE POWELL (LP)	£20

(see also Marilyn Monroe)

JIMMY POWELL (& DIMENSIONS)

62	Decca F 11447	Sugar Babe (Parts 1 & 2) (solo)	£15
64	Pye 7N 15663	That's Alright/I'm Looking For A Woman	£60
64	Pye 7N 15735	Sugar Babe/I've Been Watching You (as Jimmy Powell & 5 Dimensions)	£20
66	Strike JH 309	I Can Go Down/Love Me Right	£15
68	Decca F 12751	I Just Can't Get Over You/Real Cool (with Dimensions)	£20

KEITH POWELL (& VALETS)

63	Columbia DB 7116	The Answer Is No!/Come On And Join The Party (with Valets)	£15
64	Columbia DB 7229	Tore Up/You Better Let Him Go (with Valets)	£25
64	Columbia DB 7366	I Should Know Better (But I Don't)/Too Much Monkey Business (with Valets)	£35
65	Piccadilly 7N 35235	People Get Ready/Paradise	£15
65	Piccadilly 7N 35249	Come Home Baby/Beyond The Hill	£15
66	Piccadilly 7N 35275	Goodbye Girl/It Was Easier To Hurt Her	£15
66	Piccadilly 7N 35300	Victory/Some People Only	£15

| 66 | Piccadilly 7N 35353 | It Keeps Rainin'/Song of The Moon | £20 |

(see also Move, Carl Wayne & Vikings)

KEITH (POWELL) & BILLIE (DAVIES)

66	Piccadilly 7N 35288	When You Move, You Lose/Tastes Sour, Don't It? (as Keith & Billie)	£15
66	Piccadilly 7N 35321	You Don't Know Like I Know/Two Little People	£15
66	Piccadilly 7N 35340	Swingin' Tight/That's Really Some Good	£15

(see also Keith Powell, Billie Davis)

MARILYN POWELL

| 65 | Fontana TF 526 | Please Go Away/Where Did I Go Wrong | £40 |

POWER CUT/CASH CREW

| 88 | Vinyl Lab VL 004T | Mission Impossible/Microphone Maniac (12") | £15 |

DUFFY POWER

59	Fontana H.194	Dream Lover/That's My Little Suzie	£30
59	Fontana H.214	Kissin' Time/Ain't She Sweet	£20
59	Fontana H.230	Starry-Eyed/Prettier Than You	£15
60	Fontana H.279	Whole Lotta Shakin' Goin' On/If I Can Dream	£30
61	Fontana H.302	I've Got Nobody/When We're Walking Close	£15
61	Fontana H.344	No Other Love/What Now	£50
63	Parlophone R 4992	It Ain't Necessarily So/If I Get Lucky Someday	£30
63	Parlophone R 5024	I Saw Her Standing There (with Graham Bond Quartet)/Farewell Baby	£50
63	Parlophone R 5059	Hey Girl/Woman Made Trouble	£50
64	Parlophone R 5111	Parchman Farm/Tired, Broke And Busted (with Paramounts)	£50
64	Parlophone R 5169	Where Am I?/I Don't Care	£40
67	Parlophone R 5631	Davy O'Brien (Leave That Baby Alone)/July Tree	£40
70	CBS 5176	Hell Hound/Hummingbird	£15
71	Transatlantic TRA 229	INNOVATIONS (LP)	£60
73	GSF GS 502	DUFFY POWER (LP)	£30
73	Spark (Replay Series) SRLM 2005	DUFFY POWER (LP)	£20
76	Buk BULP 2010	POWERHOUSE (LP, revised reissue of GSF GS 502)	£15

(see also Alexis Korner, John McLaughlin, Jack Bruce, Graham Bond, Duffy's Nucleus)

POWER CUT CREW

| 88 | PowerCut PC001 | Power Cut 1/African Beats (12") | £15 |

POWER GLOVE

| 14 | Invada IVD132LP | FAR CRY 3 BLOOD DRAGON (2-LP, pink vinyl) | £60 |

POWERHOUSE

| 66 | Decca F 12471 | Chain Gang/Can You Hear Me? | £20 |

POWERLINE

81	Elite DAZZ 9	Step One/POWERLINE: Watching You (12")	£80
81	Elite DAZZ 7	Journey (6.54)/Double Journey (13.05) (12", stickered die cut sleeve)	£25
83	PLR PLR 1-7	Watching You (Vocal)/Watching You (Instrumental)	£30
83	PLR 1-12	Watching You (Vocal)/Watching You (Instrumental) (12")	£80
83	PLR 2-7	You The Girl (Vocal)/You The Girl (Instrumental)	£30
83	PLR 2-12	You The Girl (Vocal)/You The Girl (Instrumental) (12")	£75

POWERMAD

| 89 | Reprise 925 937-1 | ABSOLUTE POWER (LP) | £30 |

POWERPACK

66	CBS 202335	It Hurts Me So/What You Gonna Do	£50
67	CBS 202551	I'll Be Anything For You/The Lost Summer	£20
70	Polydor 2001 077	Oh Calcutta/Soul Searchin'	£20
69	Polydor 583 057	SOUL CURE (LP)	£60

(see also Procol Harum)

POWERPILL

92	ffrreedom TAB 110	Pac-Man (Original Edit)/Pac-Man (Mickey Finn's Yum Yum Edit)	£25
92	ffrreedom TABX 110	PAC MAN EP: Powerpill Mix/Ghost Mix/Choci's Hi Score Mix/Mickey Finn's Yum Yum Mix (12", limited edition yellow vinyl)	£30
92	ffrreedom TABX 110	PAC MAN EP: Powerpill Mix/Ghost Mix/Choci's Hi Score Mix/Mickey Finn's Yum Yum Mix (12")	£20

(see also Aphex Twin)

JETT POWERS

| 70 | Liberty LBS 83320 | CALIFORNIA LICENCE (LP) | £40 |

(see also P.J. Proby)

POWERS OF BLUE

| 67 | CBS 62953 | FLIP OUT! (LP) | £20 |

MIK POYNTER

| 96 | Ugly FF 001 | FAT FILTERS VOL. 1 (12") | £45 |
| 96 | Ugly FF 002 | FAT FILTERS VOL. 2 (12") | £40 |

P.P. & PRIMES

| 96 | Nice (no cat. no.) | Understanding/STEVIE'S BUZZ (i.e. Buzzcocks): Autumn Stone (promo only) | £25 |

(see also Primal Scream, P.P. Arnold)

PEREZ 'PREZ' PRADO & HIS ORCHESTRA

58	RCA RD 27102	DILO (LP)	£15
60	RCA RD 27046	LATIN SATIN (LP)	£15
64	Parlophone PMC 1226	A CAT IN LATIN (LP)	£15
74	Contour 2870 385	NOW (LP)	£15

PRAG VEC
81	Spec RESPECT 1	NO COWBOYS (LP, with insert)	£22

(see also Foetus etc.)

PRAISE
76	No Seven 001	BLESSED QUIETNESS (LP)	£40

PRAISE SPACE ELECTRIC
91	Pop God PGTT 005	PRAISE SPACE ELECTRIC (LP)	£15
94	Delerium DELEC LP 015	LEAVING DEMONS (LP)	£20

PRAM
92	Howl WAIL 001	GASH (LP)	£20
93	Too Pure PURE 26	THE STARS ARE SO BIG THE EARTH IS SO SMALL...STAY AS YOU ARE (LP, lyric inner)	£40
95	Too Pure PURE 46	SARGASSO SEA (LP, lyric inner)	£40
98	Domino WIGLP 49	NORTH POLE RADIO STATION (LP)	£30
00	Domino WIGLP 80	THE MUSEUM OF IMAGINARY ANIMALS (LP, lyric inner)	£40
01	Too Pure PURE 41	HELIUM (LP)	£35
03	Domino WIGLP 120	DARK ISLAND (LP)	£35

PRAMS (1)
81	Product/Ltd. Edition TAKE 2/4	Me/Modern Men/TV PRODUCT: Nowhere's Safe/Jumping Off Walls (foldout p/s)	£30

ANDY PRATT
69	Polydor 2489 003	RECORDS ARE LIKE LIFE (LP)	£25

GRAHAM & EILEEN PRATT
77	Cottage Records COT 811	CLEAR AIR OF THE DAY (LP)	£20
80	Dingle's DIN 308	TO FRIEND & FOE (LP)	£20
81	Dingle's DIN	BANDSTAND (LP)	£18
85	Plant Life PLR 068	HEIROGLYPHICS (LP, insert)	£15

PHIL PRATT
69	Jolly JY 008	Sweet Song For My Baby/THRILLERS: I'm Restless	£550
76	Student STU LP 1004	THE BEST DUB ALBUM IN THE WORLD (LP)	£150
78	Burning Sounds BS 1019	STAR WARS DUB (LP)	£100

(see also Charlie Ace, Larry Marshall, Don Drummond)

PHIL PRATT ALL STARS
70	Jackpot JP 748	Cut Throat/KEN BOOTHE: You Left The Water Running	£30
71	Punch PH 94	Winey Winey (actually "Kingstonians Medley" by Kingstonians)/There Is A Place (actually by Barrington Spence)	£30

(see also Dennis Alcapone, Horace Andy, Dennis Brown, Ken Boothe, Erroll Dunkley, John Holt, Delroy Wilson)

PATTY PRAVO
74	RCA 2483	Crazy Idea/Don't Be Sad	£20

PRAYING MANTIS
79	Ripper/Harvest HAR 5201	THE SOUNDHOUSE TAPES PART 2: Captured City/Johnny Cool (p/s)	£75
79	Ripper/Harvest 12HAR 5201	THE SOUNDHOUSE TAPES PART 2 (12")	£15
80	Gem GEMS 36	Praying Mantis/High Roller (p/s, with transfer)	£20
80	Gem GEMS 36	Praying Mantis/High Roller (p/s)	£18
82	Jet JET 7026	Tell Me The Nightmare's Wrong/A Question Of Time/Turn The Tables (p/s)	£20
81	Arista SPART 1153	TIME TELLS NO LIES (LP, with inner sleeve)	£25

(see also Stratus, Grand Prix, Uriah Heep)

PREACHERS
65	Columbia DB 7680	Hole In My Soul/Too Old In The Head	£100

(see also Herd, Denny Mitchel & Soundsations, Moon's Train)

PRECIOUS LITTLE
80	Rock On ROR 2	Give It To Me Now/Clean Living Boy (p/s)	£20

PRECISIONS
67	Track 604 014	If This Is Love (I'd Rather Be Lonely)/You'll Soon Be Gone	£40

PREDATOR (1)
78	Bust! SOL 2	Punk Man/Paperboy Song (with insert)	£60

PREDATOR (2)
85	CTM C 001	Don't Stop/Shotdown (in p/s)	£80
85	CTM C 001	Don't Stop/Shotdown	£30

PREDATORS
83	Ears And Eyes EER 012	SOCIAL DECAY (LP)	£40

PREDATUR
82	Quicksilver QUICK 5	Take A Walk/Seen You Here (p/s)	£75

PREFAB SPROUT
82	Candle CANDLE 1	Lions In My Own Garden (Exit Someone)/Radio Love	£25
85	Kitchenware KWLP 3	STEVE MCQUEEN (LP, inner)	£18
92	Columbia 4718861	THE BEST OF PREFAB SPROUT: A LIFE OF SURPRISES (LP)	£18

PREFECTS (1)
79	Rough Trade TR 040	Going Through The Motions/Things In General (no p/s)	£20

PREFUSE 73
03	Warp WARPLP 105	ONE WORD EXTINGUISHER (2-LP)	£30
03	Warp WARPLP 164	EXTINGUISHED: OUTTAKES (LP)	£20

PREGNANT INSOMNIA
67	Direction 58-3132	Wallpaper/You Intrigue Me	£50

PRELUDE (1)

72	Crotchet CME 18A/B	PRELUDE (LP, private pressing)	£70
73	Dawn DNLS 3052	HOW LONG IS FOREVER (LP, textured gatefold sleeve)	£20

PREMIERS (U.K.)

64	Silver Phoenix 1002	Tears, Tears/Bye Bye Johnny	£45

PREMIERS (U.S.)

64	Warner Bros WB 134	Farmer John/Duffy's Blues	£15
64	Warner Bros W 1565	FARMER JOHN "LIVE" (LP)	£60

PREMO & HOPETON

67	Rio R 139	Your Safekeep/Loving And Kind	£40
68	Pama PM 753	Peace On Earth/SCHOOL BOYS: Love Is A Message (as Premo & Joesph)	£300

THE PRE NEW

15	3 Loop Music 3range 37LP	THE MALE EUNUCH (LP, box set, print, stencil, badges)	£40

(see also Earl Brutus)

YVONNE PRENOSILOVA

65	Pye 7N 15775	When My Baby Cries/Come On Home	£35

PRESENCE(1)

79	SRTS.79/CUS 296	No Reason/I Care For You (no p/s)	£20

PRESENCE (2)

76	NC SLCW 1031	PRESENCE (LP)	£35

PRESIDENTS (1)

64	Decca F 11826	Candy Man/Let The Sunshine In	£50

ELVIS PRESLEY

78S : HMV 78S

56	HMV POP 182	Heartbreak Hotel/I Was The One	£20
56	HMV POP 213	Blue Suede Shoes/Tutti Frutti	£25
56	HMV POP 235	I Want You, I Need You, I Love You/My Baby Left Me	£25
56	HMV POP 249	Hound Dog/Don't Be Cruel	£15
56	HMV POP 253	Love Me Tender/Anyway You Want Me (That's How I Will Be)	£20
56	HMV POP 272	Blue Moon/I Don't Care If The Sun Don't Shine	£30
57	HMV POP 295	Mystery Train/Love Me	£40
57	HMV POP 305	Rip It Up/Baby, Let's Play House	£40
57	HMV POP 330	Too Much/Playing For Keeps	£30
57	HMV POP 359	All Shook Up/That's When Your Heartaches Begin	£15
57	HMV POP 378	Paralyzed/When My Blue Moon Turns To Gold Again	£30
57	HMV POP 408	Tryin' To Get To You/Lawdy, Miss Clawdy	£40
58	HMV POP 428	I'm Left, You're Right, She's Gone/How Do You Think I Feel?	£40

78S : RCA 78S

57	RCA RCA 1013	(Let Me Be Your) Teddy Bear/Loving You	£15
57	RCA RCA 1020	Party/Got A Lot O' Livin' To Do	£15
57	RCA RCA 1025	Santa Bring My Baby Back (To Me)/Santa Claus Is Back In Town	£25
58	RCA RCA 1028	Jailhouse Rock/Treat Me Nice	£15
58	RCA RCA 1043	Don't/I Beg Of You	£25
58	RCA RCA 1058	Wear My Ring Around Your Neck/Doncha' Think It's Time	£30
58	RCA RCA 1070	Hard Headed Woman/Don't Ask Me Why	£30
58	RCA RCA 1081	King Creole/Dixieland Rock	£30
58	RCA RCA 1088	All Shook Up/Heartbreak Hotel	£100
58	RCA RCA 1095	Hound Dog/Blue Suede Shoes	£100
59	RCA RCA 1100	One Night/I Got Stung	£60
59	RCA RCA 1113	(Now And Then There's) A Fool Such As I/I Need Your Love Tonight	£60
59	RCA RCA 1136	A Big Hunk O' Love/My Wish Came True	£100
60	RCA RCA 1187	Stuck On You/Fame And Fortune	£500
60	RCA RCA 1194	A Mess Of Blues/The Girl Of My Best Friend	£750

SINGLES : HMV 45S :PURPLE LABEL/SILVER PRINT

56	HMV 7M 385	Heartbreak Hotel/I Was The One	£175
56	HMV 7M 405	Blue Suede Shoes/Tutti Frutti	£250
56	HMV 7M 424	I Want You, I Need You, I Love You/My Baby Left Me	£150
56	HMV POP 253	Hound Dog/Don't Be Cruel	£100
56	HMV POP 253	Love Me Tender/Anyway You Want Me (That's How I Will Be)	£100
56	HMV POP 272	Blue Moon/I Don't Care If The Sun Don't Shine	£100
57	HMV POP 295	Mystery Train/Love Me	£150
57	HMV POP 305	Rip It Up/Baby, Let's Play House	£150
57	HMV POP 330	Too Much/Playing For Keeps	£150
57	HMV POP 359	All Shook Up/That's When Your Heartaches Begin ('removable/replaceable' centre)	£125
57	HMV POP 359	All Shook Up/That's When Your Heartaches Begin (solid centre)	£50
57	HMV POP 378	Paralyzed/When My Blue Moon Turns To Gold Again	£50
57	HMV POP 408	Tryin' To Get To You/Lawdy, Miss Clawdy	£50
58	HMV POP 428	I'm Left, You're Right, She's Gone/How Do You Think I Feel?	£50

SINGLES : HMV 45S: PURPLE LABEL/GOLD PRINT

56	HMV 7M 385	Heartbreak Hotel/I Was The One ('removable/replaceable' centre)	£300
56	HMV 7M 385	Heartbreak Hotel/I Was The One (solid centre)	£200
56	HMV 7M 405	Blue Suede Shoes/Tutti Frutti	£300
56	HMV 7M 424	I Want You, I Need You, I Love You/My Baby Left Me ('removable/replaceable centre)	£300

MINT VALUE £

56	HMV 7M 424	I Want You, I Need You, I Love You/My Baby Left Me ('solid centre)	£200
56	HMV POP 249	Hound Dog/Don't Be Cruel	£150
56	HMV POP 253	Love Me Tender/Anyway You Want Me (That's How I Will Be)	£150
56	HMV POP 272	Blue Moon/I Don't Care If The Sun Don't Shine ('removable/replaceable' centre)	£200
56	HMV POP 272	Blue Moon/I Don't Care If The Sun Don't Shine (solid centre)	£150
57	HMV POP 295	Mystery Train/Love Me ('removable/replaceable' centre)	£350
57	HMV POP 295	Mystery Train/Love Me (solid centre)	£200
57	HMV 7MC 42	Mystery Train/I Forgot To Remember To Forget (U.K. issue of export single, gold label print only, smooth edge to labels)	£300
57	HMV POP 305	Rip It Up/Baby, Let's Play House ('removable/replaceable' centre)	£300
57	HMV POP 305	Rip It Up/Baby, Let's Play House (solid centre)	£200
57	HMV POP 330	Too Much/Playing For Keeps	£120
57	HMV POP 359	All Shook Up/That's When Your Heartaches Begin (push-out centre)	£150
57	HMV POP 359	All Shook Up/That's When Your Heartaches Begin (solid centre)	£100
57	HMV POP 378	Paralyzed/When My Blue Moon Turns To Gold Again	£100

SINGLES : ORIGINAL RCA 45S: BLACK LABELS

57	RCA RCA 1013	(Let Me Be Your) Teddy Bear/Loving You	£20
57	RCA RCA 1020	Party/Got A Lot O' Livin' To Do	£20
57	RCA RCA 1025	Santa Bring My Baby Back (To Me)/Santa Claus Is Back In Town	£20
58	RCA RCA 1028	Jailhouse Rock/Treat Me Nice	£15
58	RCA RCA 1043	Don't/I Beg Of You	£15
58	RCA RCA 1058	Wear My Ring Around Your Neck/Doncha' Think It's Time	£15
58	RCA RCA 1070	Hard Headed Woman/Don't Ask Me Why	£15
58	RCA RCA 1081	King Creole/Dixieland Rock	£15
58	RCA RCA 1088	All Shook Up/Heartbreak Hotel	£50
58	RCA RCA 1095	Hound Dog/Blue Suede Shoes	£50
59	RCA RCA 1100	One Night/I Got Stung	£15
59	RCA RCA 1113	(Now And Then There's) A Fool Such As I/I Need Your Love Tonight	£15
59	RCA RCA 1136	A Big Hunk O' Love/My Wish Came True	£15

SINGLES : ORIGINAL RCA VICTOR 45S: BLACK LABELS

66	RCA Victor RCA 1509	Frankie And Johnny/Please Don't Stop Loving Me	£15
67	RCA Victor RCA 1565	Indescribably Blue/Fools Fall In Love	£20
67	RCA Victor RCA 1593	The Love Machine/You Gotta Stop	£15
67	RCA Victor RCA 1616	Long-Legged Girl (With The Short Dress On)/That's Someone You Never Forget	£20
67	RCA Victor RCA 1628	Judy/There's Always Me	£40
67	RCA Victor RCA 1642	Big Boss Man/You Don't Know Me	£20
68	RCA Victor RCA 1688	U.S. Male/Stay Away	£15
68	RCA Victor RCA 1714	Your Time Hasn't Come Yet Baby/Let Yourself Go	£15
68	RCA Victor RCA 1747	You'll Never Walk Alone/We Call On Him	£30
68	RCA Victor RCA 1768	A Little Less Conversation/Almost In Love	£25

SINGLES : ORIGINAL RCA VICTOR ORANGE LABEL 45S

70	RCA Victor RCA 1916	Don't Cry Daddy/Rubberneckin' (p/s)	£15
74	RCA Victor APBO 0196	Take Good Care Of Her/I've Got A Thing About You Baby (solid centre; most copies as U.S. imports with large centre hole in U.S. p/s)	£200
74	RCA Victor PB 10074	Promised Land/It's Midnight And I Miss You (2nd pressing with correct B-side title)	£15

SINGLES : OTHER RCA 45S

83	RCA RCAP 1028	Jailhouse Rock/The Elvis Medley (with "Hound Dog" credit on B-side) (reissue, picture disc)	£15
83	RCA RCAP 369	I Can Help/If Every Day Was Like Christmas/The Lady Loves Me (10", picture disc in clear plastic sleeve)	£15
84	RCA RCA 405	Green Green Grass Of Home/Release Me (And Let Me Love Again)/ Solitaire (p/s, with poster)	£20
87	RCA ARONT 1	Bossa Nova Baby/Ain't That Loving You Baby (12", p/s)	£15
88	RCA PT 49474	Mean Woman Blues/I Beg Of Of You (12", p/s)	£20
04	BMG 82876 619211	That's All Right/Blue Moon Of Kentucky (10", brown die-cut sleeve, with 'Sun' labels)	£15

SINGLES : OTHER SINGLES AND FLEXIDISCS

57	Weekend Mail (no cat. no.)	THE TRUTH ABOUT ME (1-sided 6" 78 rpm, mail-order only, in mailer)	£40
57	Weekend Mail (no cat. no.)	THE TRUTH ABOUT ME (1-sided 6" 78 rpm, mail-order only, not in mailer)	£25
77	RCA Victor 2694-2709	GOLD 16 SERIES (16 x p/s 7" in foldout cardboard carrier)	£30
79	RCA LB 1	The Wonder Of You/Noel Edmonds Introduces Record Year (Lever Brothers premium)	£20

SINGLES : RCA VICTOR 45S: BLACK LABEL REISSUES

64	RCA Victor RCA 1025	Santa Bring My Baby Back (To Me)/Santa Claus Is Back In Town	£15
64	RCA Victor RCA 1028	Jailhouse Rock/Treat Me Nice	£15
64	RCA Victor RCA 1043	Don't/I Beg Of You	£15
64	RCA Victor RCA 1070	Hard Headed Woman/Don't Ask Me Why	£15
64	RCA Victor RCA 1081	King Creole/Dixieland Rock	£15
64	RCA Victor RCA 1088	All Shook Up/Heartbreak Hotel	£15
64	RCA Victor RCA 1095	Hound Dog/Blue Suede Shoes	£15
64	RCA Victor RCA 1207	It's Now Or Never (O Sole Mio)/Make Me Know It	£15
64	RCA Victor RCA 1216	Are You Lonesome Tonight?/I Gotta Know	£15

SINGLES : RCA VICTOR 45S: ORANGE LABEL REISSUES

69	RCA Victor RCA 1088	All Shook Up/Heartbreak Hotel	£15
69	RCA Victor RCA 1095	Hound Dog/Blue Suede Shoes	£15
69	RCA Victor RCA 1207	It's Now Or Never (O Sole Mio)/Make Me Know It	£15
69	RCA Victor RCA 1216	Are You Lonesome Tonight?/I Gotta Know	£15
69	RCA Victor RCA 1226	Wooden Heart/Tonight Is So Right For Love	£30
69	RCA Victor RCA 1688	U.S. Male/Stay Away	£100

75	RCA MAXI 2601	Blue Moon/You're A Heartbreaker/I'm Left, You're Right, She's Gone ('Maximillion' sleeve) £20

SINGLES : RETROSPECTIVE RCA BLUE LABEL 45S
81	RCA RCA 43	Guitar Man/Faded Love (with matt U.K. p/s [cat. no. RCA 43]) £50

SINGLES : SINGLES BOX SET
77	RCA (no cat. no.)	PRESLEY GOLD - 16 NUMBER ONES (16 x 7", each in p/s, black box set)..........£40

EXPORT SINGLES : HMV EXPORT 45S
57	HMV 7MC 42	Mystery Train/I Forgot To Remember To Forget (gold label print, serrated edge to labels)..........£300
57	HMV 7MC 45	I Want You, I Need You, I Love You/My Baby Left Me (gold label print) £200
57	HMV 7MC 50	Hound Dog/Don't Be Cruel (gold label print)....................£150
57	HMV JO 465	Love Me Tender/Anyway You Want Me (That's How I'll Be) (gold label print)...........£150
57	HMV JO 466	Too Much/Playing For Keeps (gold label print) £200
57	HMV JO 473	All Shook Up/That's When Your Heartaches Begin (gold label print) £150

EPS : EP BOXED SETS
82	RCA EP 1	THE EP COLLECTION (11-EP box set, reissues, with booklet)....................£35
83	RCA EP 2	THE EP COLLECTION VOL. 2 (11-EP box set, reissues, with booklet) £50

EPS : HMV EPS
57	HMV 7EG 8199	LOVE ME TENDER (soundtrack, round centre) £70
57	HMV 7EG 8199	LOVE ME TENDER (soundtrack, removeable centre) £100
57	HMV 7EG 8256	GOOD ROCKIN' TONIGHT (round centre only) £200

EPS : ORIGINAL RCA EPS : ROUND CENTRES
60	RCA RCX 190	SUCH A NIGHT £25
62	RCA RCX 211	FOLLOW THAT DREAM (mispressing, 2nd side features Jim Reeves) £100
64	RCA Victor RCX 7141	LOVE IN LAS VEGAS (soundtrack) £20
64	RCA Victor RCX 7142	ELVIS FOR YOU VOL. 1 ....£50
64	RCA Victor RCX 7143	ELVIS FOR YOU VOL. 2 ....£50
64	RCA Victor RCX 135	ELVIS IN TENDER MOOD £20
65	RCA Victor RCX 7173	TICKLE ME (soundtrack) £35
65	RCA Victor RCX 7174	TICKLE ME VOL. 2 (soundtrack) £35
67	RCA Victor RCX 7187	EASY COME, EASY GO (soundtrack)....................£40

EPS : RCA EPS : ROUND CENTRE REPRESSINGS
60s	RCA RCX 101	PEACE IN THE VALLEY £20
60s	RCA RCX 104	ELVIS PRESLEY £15
60s	RCA RCX 106	JAILHOUSE ROCK (soundtrack) £15
60s	RCA RCX 117	KING CREOLE VOL. 1 (soundtrack) £15
60s	RCA RCX 121	ELVIS SINGS CHRISTMAS SONGS (gatefold p/s) £60
60s	RCA RCX 131	ELVIS SAILS (interview record) £25
60s	RCA RCX 135	ELVIS IN TENDER MOOD £20
60s	RCA RCX 1045	A TOUCH OF GOLD £25
60s	RCA RCX 175	STRICTLY ELVIS £20
60s	RCA RCX 1048	A TOUCH OF GOLD VOL. 2 ....£35

EPS : RCA EPS: TRIANGULAR CENTRES
57	RCA RCX 101	PEACE IN THE VALLEY £30
57	RCA RCX 104	ELVIS PRESLEY....................£40
58	RCA RCX 106	JAILHOUSE ROCK (soundtrack) £40
58	RCA RCX 117	KING CREOLE VOL. 1 (soundtrack, black label, cream or white rear p/s) £30
58	RCA RCX 118	KING CREOLE VOL. 2 (soundtrack, cream or white rear sleeve) £30
58	RCA RCX 121	ELVIS SINGS CHRISTMAS SONGS (1st issue, single sleeve)....................£60
58	RCA RCX 131	ELVIS SAILS (interview record, sleeve laminated front & back) £40
59	RCA RCX 135	ELVIS IN TENDER MOOD (with red print on rear sleeve) £40

(Originally issued with laminated front and back sleeves; later copies with front-only laminate are worth three quarters of these values.)

59	RCA RCX 1045	A TOUCH OF GOLD (laminated front sleeve only) £50
59	RCA RCX 175	STRICTLY ELVIS £40
60	RCA RCX 1048	A TOUCH OF GOLD VOL. 2 ....£80

EPS : RCA VICTOR EPS: BLACK LABEL RE-PRESSINGS
64	RCA Victor RCX 101	PEACE IN THE VALLEY £15
64	RCA Victor RCX 104	ELVIS PRESLEY £15
64	RCA Victor RCX 106	JAILHOUSE ROCK (soundtrack) £15
64	RCA Victor RCX 117	KING CREOLE VOL. 1 (soundtrack) £15
64	RCA Victor RCX 118	KING CREOLE VOL. 2 (soundtrack)....................£15
64	RCA Victor RCX 121	ELVIS SINGS CHRISTMAS SONGS (single p/s) £30
64	RCA Victor RCX 131	ELVIS SAILS (interview record) £15
64	RCA Victor RCX 1045	A TOUCH OF GOLD £15
64	RCA Victor RCX 175	STRICTLY ELVIS £15
64	RCA Victor RCX 1048	A TOUCH OF GOLD VOL. 2 ....£25

EPS : RCA VICTOR EPS: ORANGE LABEL RE-PRESSINGS
69	RCA Victor RCX 117	KING CREOLE VOL. 1 (soundtrack, push-out centre) £15
69	RCA Victor RCX 1045	A TOUCH OF GOLD (push-out centre) £15
69	RCA Victor RCX 1048	A TOUCH OF GOLD VOL. 2 (push-out centre) £15

ALBUMS : CDS
84	RCA PD 89061/2/3	THE LEGEND (3-CD, gold box set, with booklet, numbered, 5,000 only) £40
84	RCA PD 89061/2/3	THE LEGEND (3-CD, silver box set, 5,000 only, with booklet, numbered)..........£40

ALBUMS : LPS: 'LARGE' ORANGE RCA VICTOR STEREO RE-PRESSINGS
72	RCA Victor SF 8232	ELVIS FOR EVERYONE ('blue shirt'/'TV Special' sleeve)....................£40

MINT VALUE £

ALBUMS : LPS: 'SMALL' ORANGE RCA VICTOR MONO RE-PRESSINGS

69	RCA Victor RD 27052	ELVIS' CHRISTMAS ALBUM	£40
69	RCA Victor RD 27088	KING CREOLE (soundtrack)	£30
69	RCA Victor RD 27120	ELVIS	£30
69	RCA Victor RD 27128	A DATE WITH ELVIS	£30
69	RCA Victor RD 27159	ELVIS' GOLDEN RECORDS VOL. 2	£30
69	RCA Victor RD 27171	ELVIS IS BACK! (gatefold sleeve)	£30
69	RCA Victor RD 27192	G.I. BLUES (soundtrack)	£30
69	RCA Victor RD 27211	HIS HAND IN MINE	£15
69	RCA Victor RD 27224	SOMETHING FOR EVERYBODY	£30
69	RCA Victor RD 27238	BLUE HAWAII (soundtrack)	£30
69	RCA Victor RD 7528	ROCK 'N' ROLL NO. 2	£30
69	RCA Victor RD 7630	ELVIS' GOLDEN RECORDS VOL. 3	£30
69	RCA Victor RD 7723	FLAMING STAR AND SUMMER KISSES (soundtrack, orange label)	£300
69	RCA Victor RD 7810	PARADISE, HAWAIIAN STYLE (soundtrack)	£20
69	RCA Victor RD 7867	HOW GREAT THOU ART	£20
69	RCA Victor RD 7917	CLAMBAKE (soundtrack)	£30
69	RCA Victor RD 7924	ELVIS' GOLD RECORDS VOLUME 4	£15
69	RCA Victor RD 7957	SPEEDWAY (soundtrack, with Nancy Sinatra)	£20

ALBUMS : LPS: BLACK/RED SPOT RCA VICTOR RE-PRESSINGS

64	RCA Victor RD 7528	ROCK 'N' ROLL NO. 2 (reissue of HMV LP, mono)	£18
64	RCA Victor SF 7528	ROCK 'N' ROLL NO. 2 (reissue of HMV LP, stereo)	£25

ALBUMS : LPS: BLACK/SILVER SPOT RCA VICTOR RE-PRESSINGS

64	RCA Victor RC 24001	LOVING YOU (10" LP, mono only)	£60
64	RCA Victor RD 27052	ELVIS' CHRISTMAS ALBUM (laminated front & back covers, no pictures on back cover, mono only)	£60
64	RCA Victor RD 7528	ROCK 'N' ROLL NO. 2 (reissue of HMV LP, mono)	£18
64	RCA Victor SF 7528	ROCK 'N' ROLL NO. 2 (reissue of HMV LP, stereo)	£25
64	RCA Victor RD 27088	KING CREOLE (soundtrack, mono only)	£30
64	RCA Victor RD 27120	ELVIS (mono only)	£35
64	RCA Victor RD 27128	A DATE WITH ELVIS (mono only)	£20
64	RCA Victor RD 27159	ELVIS' GOLDEN RECORDS VOL. 2 (mono only)	£15
64	RCA Victor RD 27171	ELVIS IS BACK! (gatefold sleeve, mono)	£30
64	RCA Victor SF 5060	ELVIS IS BACK! (gatefold sleeve, stereo)	£40
64	RCA Victor RD 27192	G.I. BLUES (soundtrack, mono)	£15
64	RCA Victor SF 5078	G.I. BLUES (soundtrack, stereo)	£30
64	RCA Victor RD 27211	HIS HAND IN MINE (mono)	£25
64	RCA Victor SF 5094	HIS HAND IN MINE (stereo)	£30
64	RCA Victor RD 27224	SOMETHING FOR EVERYBODY (mono)	£18
64	RCA Victor SF 5106	SOMETHING FOR EVERYBODY (stereo)	£30
64	RCA Victor RD 27238	BLUE HAWAII (soundtrack, mono)	£18
64	RCA Victor SF 5115	BLUE HAWAII (soundtrack, stereo)	£25
64	RCA Victor RD 27265	POT LUCK (mono)	£15
64	RCA Victor SF 5135	POT LUCK (stereo)	£30

ALBUMS : LPS: GREEN RCA INTERNATIONAL ISSUES

72	RCA Intl. INTS 1414	BURNING LOVE AND HITS FROM HIS MOVIES (U.K. disc in U.K. sleeve)	£30

ALBUMS : LPS: HMV ISSUES

56	HMV CLP 1093	ROCK 'N' ROLL	£500
57	HMV CLP 1105	ROCK 'N' ROLL NO. 2	£700
57	HMV DLP 1159	THE BEST OF ELVIS (10")	£200

ALBUMS : LPS: ORIGINAL BLACK/RED SPOT RCA VICTOR ISSUES

64	RCA Victor RD 7630	ELVIS' GOLDEN RECORDS VOL. 3 (mono)	£20
64	RCA Victor SF 7630	ELVIS' GOLDEN RECORDS VOL. 3 (stereo)	£30
64	RCA Victor RD 7645	KISSIN' COUSINS (soundtrack, mono)	£18
64	RCA Victor SF 7645	KISSIN' COUSINS (soundtrack, stereo)	£30
64	RCA Victor RD 7678	ROUSTABOUT (soundtrack, mono)	£15
64	RCA Victor SF 7678	ROUSTABOUT (soundtrack, stereo)	£25
65	RCA Victor RD 7714	GIRL HAPPY (soundtrack, mono)	£20
65	RCA Victor SF 7714	GIRL HAPPY (soundtrack, stereo)	£30
65	RCA Victor RD 7723	FLAMING STAR AND SUMMER KISSES (soundtrack, mono only, black label)	£50
65	RCA Victor RD/SF 7752	ELVIS FOR EVERYONE (mono, 'orange shirt' sleeve)	£35
65	RCA Victor SF 7752	ELVIS FOR EVERYONE (stereo, 'orange shirt' sleeve)	£45
65	RCA Victor RD 7767	HAREM HOLIDAY (soundtrack, mono)	£20
65	RCA Victor SF 7767	HAREM HOLIDAY (soundtrack, stereo)	£25
66	RCA Victor RD 7793	FRANKIE AND JOHNNY (soundtrack, mono)	£20
66	RCA Victor SF 7793	FRANKIE AND JOHNNY (soundtrack, stereo)	£30
66	RCA Victor RD 7810	PARADISE, HAWAIIAN STYLE (soundtrack, mono)	£20
66	RCA Victor SF 7810	PARADISE, HAWAIIAN STYLE (soundtrack, stereo)	£30
66	RCA Victor RD 7820	CALIFORNIA HOLIDAY (soundtrack, mono)	£20
66	RCA Victor SF 7820	CALIFORNIA HOLIDAY (soundtrack, stereo)	£30
67	RCA Victor RD 7867	HOW GREAT THOU ART (mono)	£25
67	RCA Victor SF 7867	HOW GREAT THOU ART (stereo)	£35
67	RCA Victor RD 7892	DOUBLE TROUBLE (soundtrack, mono)	£15
67	RCA Victor SF 7892	DOUBLE TROUBLE (soundtrack, stereo)	£20
68	RCA Victor RD 7917	CLAMBAKE (soundtrack, black/red dot labels, mono)	£20
68	RCA Victor SF 7917	CLAMBAKE (soundtrack, black/red dot labels, stereo)	£25
68	RCA Victor RD 7924	ELVIS' GOLD RECORDS VOLUME 4 (with "Never Ending" listed on sleeve instead of	£30

		"Love Letters"; mono)	
68	RCA Victor SF 7924	ELVIS' GOLD RECORDS VOLUME 4 (with "Never Ending" listed on sleeve instead of "Love Letters"; stereo)	£30
68	RCA Victor RD 7924	ELVIS' GOLD RECORDS VOLUME 4 (corrected sleeve, mono)	£25
68	RCA Victor SF 7924	ELVIS' GOLD RECORDS VOLUME 4 (corrected sleeve, stereo)	£25
68	RCA Victor RD 7957	SPEEDWAY (soundtrack, with Nancy Sinatra, mono)	£30
68	RCA Victor SF 7957	SPEEDWAY (soundtrack, with Nancy Sinatra, stereo)	£25

ALBUMS : LPS: ORIGINAL BLACK/SILVER SPOT RCA ISSUES

57	RCA RC 24001	LOVING YOU (10", soundtrack)	£75
57	RCA RD 27052	ELVIS' CHRISTMAS ALBUM (laminated front & back covers with 4 pictures on back cover)	£100
58	RCA RD 27088	KING CREOLE (soundtrack)	£40
59	RCA RD 27120	ELVIS	£75
59	RCA RD 27128	A DATE WITH ELVIS	£60
60	RCA RD 27159	ELVIS' GOLDEN RECORDS VOL. 2	£30
60	RCA RD 27171	ELVIS IS BACK! (gatefold sleeve, mono)	£40
60	RCA SF 5060	ELVIS IS BACK! (gatefold sleeve, stereo)	£60
60	RCA RD 27192	G.I. BLUES (soundtrack, mono)	£18
60	RCA SF 5078	G.I. BLUES (soundtrack, stereo)	£25
61	RCA RD 27211	HIS HAND IN MINE (mono)	£25
61	RCA SF 5094	HIS HAND IN MINE (stereo)	£45
61	RCA RD 27224	SOMETHING FOR EVERYBODY (mono)	£20
61	RCA SF 5106	SOMETHING FOR EVERYBODY (stereo)	£35
61	RCA RD 27238	BLUE HAWAII (soundtrack, mono)	£15
61	RCA SF 5115	BLUE HAWAII (soundtrack, stereo)	£20
62	RCA RD 27265	POT LUCK (mono)	£20
62	RCA SF 5135	POT LUCK (stereo)	£30

ALBUMS : LPS: ORIGINAL BLACK/SILVER SPOT RCA VICTOR ISSUES

63	RCA Victor RD 7534	GIRLS! GIRLS! GIRLS! (soundtrack, mono)	£15
63	RCA Victor SF 7534	GIRLS! GIRLS! GIRLS! (soundtrack, stereo)	£35
63	RCA Victor RD 7565	IT HAPPENED AT THE WORLD'S FAIR (soundtrack, mono)	£18
63	RCA Victor SF 7565	IT HAPPENED AT THE WORLD'S FAIR (soundtrack, stereo)	£35
63	RCA Victor RD 7609	FUN IN ACAPULCO (soundtrack, mono)	£20
63	RCA Victor SF 7609	FUN IN ACAPULCO (soundtrack, stereo)	£35

ALBUMS : LPS: ORIGINAL ORANGE RCA VICTOR ISSUES

69	RCA Victor RD 8011	ELVIS ("TV Special" Soundtrack)	£15
69	RCA Victor RD 8029	FROM ELVIS IN MEMPHIS (mono)	£35
69	RCA Victor SF 8029	FROM ELVIS IN MEMPHIS (stereo)	£20
70	RCA Victor SF 8080/1	FROM MEMPHIS TO VEGAS - FROM VEGAS TO MEMPHIS (2LP, with 2 x 10" x 8" photos, glossy cover)	£30
70	RCA Victor SF 8080/1	FROM MEMPHIS TO VEGAS - FROM VEGAS TO MEMPHIS (2-LP, with 2 x 10" x 8" photos, matt cover)	£25
70	RCA SF 8128	ON STAGE, FEBRUARY 1970 (with 30" x 20" colour poster; glossy cover)	£15
70	RCA LPM 6401	WORLDWIDE 50 GOLD AWARD HITS VOL. 1 - A TOUCH OF GOLD (4-LP, box set with 20-page photo book)	£15
71	RCA LPM 6402	THE OTHER SIDES - WORLDWIDE 50 GOLD AWARD HITS VOL. 2 (4-LP, box with material patch & colour portrait)	£30
71	RCA Victor SF 8162	THAT'S THE WAY IT IS (glossy cover)	£15
71	RCA Victor SF 8172	I'M 10,000 YEARS OLD - ELVIS COUNTRY (with colour print, glossy cover)	£15
71	RCA Victor SF 8221	ELVIS SINGS THE WONDERFUL WORLD OF CHRISTMAS	£15
72	RCA Victor SF 8266	ELVIS NOW	£15
72	RCA Victor SF 8275	HE TOUCHED ME	£15
73	RCA Victor SF 8378	ELVIS (with "Fool" sticker, must be UK disc and UK cover!)	£40
73	RCA DPS 2040	ALOHA FROM HAWAII VIA SATELLITE (2-LP)	£20
73	RCA APL1 0388	RAISED ON ROCK/FOR OL' TIMES SAKE (U.K. disc in U.K. sleeve)	£150
74	RCA APL1 0475	GOOD TIMES (back cover credits "Loving Arms" or "Lovin' Arms")	£18
74	RCA APL1 0606	ELVIS AS RECORDED ON STAGE IN MEMPHIS	£15
74	RCA LPL1 7527	HITS OF THE 70s	£15
75	RCA APL1 0873	PROMISED LAND	£15
75	RCA APM1 0818	HAVING FUN WITH ELVIS ON STAGE	£20
75	RCA RS 1011	TODAY	£18
76	RCA RS 1060	FROM ELVIS PRESLEY BOULEVARD, MEMPHIS, TENNESSEE	£15
77	RCA PL 12274	WELCOME TO MY WORLD	£15
80	RCA CPL8 3699	ELVIS ARON PRESLEY (8-LP, box set)	£50
84	RCA PL 85172	A GOLDEN CELEBRATION (6-LP box set with inserts)	£30

ALBUMS : LPS: SILVER SPOT/'RED SEAL' RCA ISSUES

58	RCA RB 16069	ELVIS' GOLDEN RECORDS (maroon 'silver spot' label, gatefold sleeve with stapled-in 4-page photo booklet)	£100
60	RCA RB 16069	ELVIS' GOLDEN RECORDS ('Red Seal'/'silver spot' label, gatefold sleeve with stapled-in 2-page photo booklet)	£30
63	RCA RB 16069	ELVIS' GOLDEN RECORDS ('Red Seal'/'black spot' label, no booklet, gatefold sleeve)	£20
67	RCA RB 16069	ELVIS' GOLDEN RECORDS ('Red Seal'/'black spot' label, no booklet, single sleeve)	£18

ALBUMS : OTHER LPS

71	Camden CDS 1088	YOU'LL NEVER WALK ALONE (LP, withdrawn)	£150
78	St. Michael IMP 113	ELVIS (exclusive to Marks & Spencer)	£60
78	St. Michael IMPD 204	THE WONDERFUL WORLD OF ELVIS PRESLEY (2-LP, via Marks & Spencer)	£30
79	Hammer HMR 6002	THE KING SPEAKS (green sleeve)	£30
84	Imperial Records DR 1124	AMERICAN TRILOGY (3-LP, box set)	£25
85	Sunday 1	ELVIS: THE GOLDEN ALBUM (LP, available via Sunday Times magazine)	£20

MINT VALUE £

86	RCA AREP 1	ACUFF-ROSE PRESENTS ELVIS (promo-only, 300 copies)	£150

ALBUMS : REISSUES, RETROSPECTIVES & BOX SETS

00	Castle Music/BMG ELVIS 102	THAT'S THE WAY IT IS (5-LP)	£45
99	Castle Music/BMG ELVIS 100P	ARTIST OF THE CENTURY (box set, 5 x picture disc LPs & booklet, numbered)	£40
99	Castle Music/BMG ELVIS 100	ARTIST OF THE CENTUY (5-LP box set & booklet, numbered)	£40
99	Castle Music/BMG ELVIS 100R	ARTIST OF THE CENTURY (box set, 5-LP red vinyl & booklet, numbered)	£50
99	Castle Music/BMG ELVIS 100X	ARTIST OF THE CENTURY (box set, 5-LP, blue vinyl & booklet, numbered, HMV exclusive)	£50
99	Castle Music/BMG ELVIS 101X	THE SUN SINGLES COLLECTION (6 x 7" box set, yellow vinyl, numbered HMV exclusive)	£35
99	Castle Music/BMG ELVIS 101	THE SUN SINGLES COLLECTION (6 x 7" box set with poster, numbered)	£35
00	Castle Music/BMG ELVIS 103	THE UK NO. 1 SINGLES COLLECTION (17 x 7" box set with booklet)	£50
00	Castle Music/BMG ELVIS 103X	THE UK NO. 1 SINGLES COLLECTION (17 x 7" box set with booklet, coloured vinyl)	£75
00	Castle Music/BMG ELVIS 104X	PEACE IN THE VALLEY (5-LP box set, with bonus 10" EP)	£40
00	Castle Music/BMG ELVIS 104	PEACE IN THE VALLEY (5-LP box set)	£30
01	Castle Music/BMG ELVIS 105	THE INTERNATIONAL EP COLLECTION (11 x 7" EP box set with insert)	£30
01	Castle Music/BMG ELVIS 106	G.I. BLUES (LP, with bonus EP)	£15
01	Castle Music/BMG ELVIS 108	LIVE IN LAS VEGAS (5LP box set, 180g)	£120
01	Castle Music/BMG ELVIS 107	BLUE HAWAII (LP, with bonus EP)	£15
02	Castle Music/BMG ELVIS 111	JAILHOUSE ROCK (LP, with bonus EP)	£15
02	Castle Music/BMG ELVIS 112	KING CREOLE (LP, with bonus EP)	£15
02	Castle Music/BMG ELVIS 113	TICKLE ME (LP, with bonus EP)	£25
02	Castle Music/BMG ELVIS 110	LOVING YOU (LP, with bonus EP)	£15
18	RCA 19075809741	THE SEARCHER - THE ORIGINAL SOUNDTRACK (2LP, gatefold, printed inners)	£25
21	RCA 19439883881	ELVIS BACK IN NASHVILLE (2LP, gatefold, printed inners)	£30

(see also Jordanaires, Scotty Moore, Bill Black's Combo)

PRESSGANG
89	Vox Pop VOX 022	ROGUES (LP)	£15

RAY PRESSLEY
62	Longhorn BLH 0002	Living, Learning, Trying To Forget/Half A Love (estimated that around 1000 pressed)	£15

PRESSURE GROUP
87	Poltroon POL 001	ONLY GOD IS PERFECT (EP, 300 only)	£60

PRESSURE POINT
82	Pressure Point PP 001	Big Deal/Straight To The Point (p/s)	£15

PRESTIGE BLUES SWINGERS
59	Esquire 32-082	BLUES GROOVE (Tiny Grimes & Coleman Hawkins as Prestige Blues Swingers (LP)	£20
60	Esquire 32-110	OUTSKIRTS OF TOWN (LP)	£20

BILLY PRESTON
66	Sue WI 4012	Billy's Bag/Don't Let The Sun Catch You Cryin'	£25
66	Capitol CL 15458	In The Midnight Hour/Advice	£40
66	Capitol CL 15458	In The Midnight Hour/Advice (DJ copy)	£50
66	Capitol CL 15471	Sunny/Let The Music Play	£15
69	President PT 263	Billy's Bag/Goldfinger (different B-side)	£15
69	Apple APPLE 19	Everything's Alright/I Want To Thank You	£20
70	Apple APPLE 21	All That I've Got/As I Get Older (some in p/s)	£25
70	Soul City SC 107	Greazee (Parts 1 & 2)	£20
70	Soul City SC 107	Greazee (Parts 1 & 2) (DJ Copy)	£100
67	Capitol (S)T 2532	WILDEST ORGAN IN TOWN (LP)	£25
67	Sue ILP 935	THE MOST EXCITING ORGAN EVER (LP)	£60
69	President PTLS 1034	APPLE OF THEIR EYE (LP)	£20
69	Apple SAPCOR 9	THAT'S THE WAY GOD PLANNED IT (LP)	£40
70	Apple SAPCOR 14	ENCOURAGING WORDS (LP)	£70
70	Soul City SCM 002	GREAZEE SOUL (LP)	£30
70	Joy JOYS 174	GOSPEL IN MY SOUL (LP)	£20
91	Apple SAPCOR 9	THAT'S THE WAY GOD PLANNED IT (LP, gatefold sleeve, with bonus 12" [SAPCOR 92])	£30
93	Apple SAPCOR 14	ENCOURAGING WORDS (LP, gatefold sleeve with bonus 12" [SAPCOR 142])	£30

(see also Beatles)

EARL PRESTON
63	Fontana TF 406	I Know Something/Watch Your Step (as Earl Preston & T.T.'s)	£20
64	Fontana TF 481	Raindrops/That's For Sure (as Earl Preston & Realms)	£20

(see also Realm)

JOHNNY PRESTON
60	Mercury AMT 1092	Cradle Of Love/City Of Tears (some in p/s)	£20
61	Mercury AMT 1129	Leave My Kitten Alone/Do What You Did	£20

61	Mercury AMT 1145	Big Chief Heartbreak/Madre De Dios (Mother Of God)	£20
61	Mercury AMT 1164	New Baby For Christmas/Rock And Roll Guitar	£25
61	Mercury AMT 1167	Free Me/Kissing Tree	£25
60	Mercury ZEP 10078	RUNNING BEAR (EP)	£35
60	Mercury ZEP 10098	RING TAIL TOOTER (EP)	£35
61	Mercury ZEP 10116	TOKEN OF LOVE (EP)	£45
60	Mercury MMC 14051	JOHNNY PRESTON - RUNNING BEAR (LP)	£80

PRETENDERS

| 94 | WEA 4509-95822-1 | LAST OF THE INDEPENDENTS (LP) | £50 |

(see also Jimmy Edwards)

PRETTY BOY FLOYD & GEMS

| 79 | Rip Off RIP OFF 1 | Spread The Word Around/Hold Tight (p/s) | £15 |
| 79 | Rip Off RIP 10 | Sharon/The Instigator (p/s) | £20 |

PRETTY THINGS

64	Fontana TF 469	Rosalyn/Big Boss Man	£15
65	Fontana TF 585	Cry To Me/Get A Buzz	£20
65	Fontana TF 647	Midnight To Six Man/Can't Stand The Pain	£22
66	Fontana TF 688	Come See Me/£.s.d.	£35
66	Fontana TF 722	A House In The Country/Me Needing You	£25
66	Fontana TF 773	Progress/Buzz The Jerk	£30
67	Fontana TF 829	Children/My Time	£20
67	Columbia DB 8300	Defecting Grey/Mr. Evasion	£100
68	Columbia DB 8353	Talkin' About The Good Times/Walking Through My Dreams	£80
68	Columbia DB 8494	Private Sorrow/Balloon Burning	£40
69	Fontana TF 1024	Rosalyn/Don't Bring Me Down (p/s)	£15
64	Fontana TE 17434	THE PRETTY THINGS (EP)	£60
65	Fontana TE 17442	RAININ' IN MY HEART (EP)	£70
66	Fontana TE 17472	ON FILM (EP)	£150
65	Fontana TL 5239	THE PRETTY THINGS (LP)	£150
65	Fontana TL 5280	GET THE PICTURE (LP)	£200
67	Wing WL 1164	BEST OF THE PRETTY THINGS (LP)	£35
67	Fontana (S)TL 5425	EMOTIONS (LP, mono/stereo)	£150
67	Wing WL 1167	THE PRETTY THINGS (LP, reissue)	£40
68	Columbia SX 6306	S.F. SORROW (LP, gatefold sleeve, blue/black label, mono)	£700
68	Columbia SCX 6306	S.F. SORROW (LP, gatefold sleeve, blue/black label, stereo)	£400
70	Columbia SCX 6306	S.F. SORROW (LP, gatefold sleeve; silver/black label re-pressing, stereo)	£50
70	Harvest SHVL 774	PARACHUTE (LP, gatefold sleeve)	£125
70	Fontana Special SFL 13140	EMOTIONS (LP, reissue)	£20
72	Warner Bros K 46190	FREEWAY MADNESS (LP, gatefold sleeve)	£18
74	Swan Song SSK 59400	SILK TORPEDO (LP, gatefold sleeve with insert)	£15
75	Harvest SHDW 406	S.F. SORROW/PARACHUTE (2-LP)	£40
78	Butt Nott DO1	ELECTRIC BANANA THE SEVEN TIES (LP)	£15
77	Harvest SHSM 2022	SINGLES A'S & B'S (LP)	£20
89	Edsel XED236	S.F. SORROW (LP, reissue, gatefold)	£20

(see also Electric Banana, Twink, Viv Prince, Sunshine, Fenmen, Kate)

EDDIE PREVOST BAND

78	Matchless MR 1	LIVE VOLUME 1 (LP)	£30
78	Matchless MR 2	LIVE VOLUME 2 (LP)	£20
77	Spotlite SPJ 505	NOW HERE THIS THEN... (LP)	£20
85	Matchless MR 7	CONTINUUM (LP)	£15

(see also Amm, Organum)

ALAN PRICE (SET)

68	Decca F 12774	When I Was A Cowboy/Tappy Turquoise (export issue)	£20
67	Decca DFE 8677	THE AMAZING ALAN PRICE (EP)	£30
66	Decca LK 4839	THE PRICE TO PLAY (LP, laminate front cover, flipbacks)	£30
67	Decca LK/SKL 4907	A PRICE ON HIS HEAD (LP, laminated front cover)	£25

(see also Animals, Paul Williams Set, Johnny Almond Music Machine, Dave Greenslade)

LLOYD PRICE

57	London HL 8438	Just Because/Why (triangular centre)	£150
57	London HL 8438	Just Because/Why (round centre)	£80
57	London HL 8438	Just Because/Why (78)	£20
59	HMV POP 580	Stagger Lee/You Need Love	£15
59	HMV POP 580	Stagger Lee/You Need Love (78)	£25
59	HMV POP 598	Where Were You (On Our Wedding Day)?/Is It Really Love? (78)	£25
59	HMV POP 626	Personality/Have You Ever Had The Blues? (78)	£25
59	HMV POP 650	I'm Gonna Get Married/Three Little Pigs (78)	£60
60	HMV POP 712	Lady Luck/Never Let Me Go	£15
60	HMV POP 712	Lady Luck/Never Let Me Go (78)	£30
60	HMV POP 772	Question/If I Look A Little Blue (as Lloyd Price Orchestra) (78)	£40
59	HMV 7EG 8538	THE EXCITING LLOYD PRICE (EP, mono)	£50
59	HMV GES 5784	THE EXCITING LLOYD PRICE (EP, stereo)	£70
59	HMV CLP 1285	THE EXCITING LLOYD PRICE (LP)	£60
59	HMV CLP 1314	MR. PERSONALITY (LP)	£60
60	London HA-U 2213	LLOYD PRICE (LP)	£60
60	HMV CLP 1361	MR. PERSONALITY SINGS THE BLUES (LP)	£50
60	HMV CLP 1393	THE FANTASTIC LLOYD PRICE (LP, mono)	£40
60	HMV CSD 1323	THE FANTASTIC LLOYD PRICE (LP, stereo)	£50

MINT VALUE £

62	HMV CLP 1519	**COOKIN'** (LP, mono)	**£25**
62	HMV CSD 1413	**COOKIN'** (LP, stereo)	**£30**
63	Encore ENC 2004	**PRICE SINGS THE MILLION DOLLAR SELLERS** (LP)	**£15**
69	Major Minor SMLP 57	**LLOYD PRICE NOW** (LP)	**£20**

RAY PRICE
57	Philips BBE 12137	**RAY PRICE** (EP)	**£25**

(see also Cherry Wainer)

(ROCKIN') RED PRICE
56	Decca F 10822	**Rocky Mountain Gal/Rock O' The North** (as Red Price & His Rockin' Rhythm)	**£15**
57	Woodbine	**Woodbine Rock** (78, with picture on label, promo only)	**£40**
57	Woodbine	**Woodbine Rock** (78, without picture on label, promo only)	**£15**
58	Pye 7N 15169	**Weekend/The Sneeze**	**£20**
58	Pye 7N 15169	**Weekend/The Sneeze** (78)	**£25**
61	Parlophone R 4789	**Theme From "Danger Man"/Blackjack** (as Red Price Combo)	**£30**

RICK PRICE
71	Gemini GME 1017	**TALKING TO THE FLOWERS** (LP, laminated front sleeve)	**£50**

(see also Move, Sheridan-Price, Sight & Sound)

RIKKI PRICE
58	Fontana TFE 17100	**RIKKI PRICE** (EP)	**£20**

(see also Sheridan-Price)

SAMMY PRICE
63	Storyville A 45 068	**Boogieing With Big Sid/133 Street Boogie** (with p/s)	**£30**
63	Storyville A 45 068	**Boogieing With Big Sid/133 Street Boogie**	**£20**
57	Columbia SEG 7679	**ORIGINAL SAMMY BLUES** (EP)	**£20**
58	Vogue EPV 1146	**SAMMY PRICE** (EP)	**£60**
58	Vogue EPV 1151	**SAMMY PRICE'S BLUESICIANS** (EP)	**£60**
58	Vogue LAE 12027	**SWINGIN' PARIS STYLE** (LP)	**£40**
62	London Jazz LTZ-R 15240	**THE BLUES AIN'T NOTHIN'** (LP, mono)	**£30**
62	London Jazz SAH-R 6234	**THE BLUES AIN'T NOTHIN'** (LP, stereo)	**£40**

(see also Sister Rosetta Tharpe)

VINCENT PRICE
59	Columbia 33SX 1141	**VINCENT PRICE** (LP)	**£45**

PRIDE
85	Pride P.R.T. 001	**What's Love/No Emotion** (p/s)	**£25**

DICKIE PRIDE
59	Columbia DB 4283	**Slippin' 'N' Slidin'/Don't Make Me Love You**	**£40**
59	Columbia DB 4296	**Fabulous Cure/Midnight Oil**	**£30**
59	Columbia DB 4340	**Frantic/Primrose Lane**	**£20**
60	Columbia DB 4403	**Betty, Betty** (Go Steady With Me)**/No John**	**£20**
59	Columbia SEG 7937	**SHEIK OF SHAKE** (EP)	**£250**
61	Columbia 33SX 1307	**PRIDE WITHOUT PREJUDICE** (LP, mono)	**£60**
61	Columbia SCX 3369	**PRIDE WITHOUT PREJUDICE** (LP, stereo)	**£70**

(see also Guvners)

LOUIS PRIMA (& HIS ORCHESTRA)
56	Capitol CL 14669	**5 Months, 2 Weeks, 2 Days/Banana Split For My Baby**	**£20**
58	Capitol CL 14821	**Buona Sera/Beep! Beep!**	**£15**
58	Capitol T 908	**THE WILDEST SHOW AT TAHOE** (LP)	**£20**
57	Capitol T 755	**THE WILDEST** (LP)	**£30**
58	Capitol T 836	**THE CALL OF THE WILDEST** (LP)	**£20**

(see also Sam Butera's Witnesses)

LOUIS PRIMA & KEELY SMITH
59	Capitol T 1160	**HEY BOY! HEY GIRL!** (LP)	**£25**

(see also Keely Smith)

PRIMAL SCREAM
85	Creation CRE 017	**All Fall Down/It Happens** (foldaround p/s in poly bag)	**£25**
86	Creation CRE 026	**Crystal Crescent/Velocity Girl** (p/s)	**£18**
86	Creation CRE 026T	**Crystal Crescent/Velocity Girl/Spirea X** (12", p/s)	**£15**
87	Elevation ELV 2	**SONIC FLOWER GROOVE** (LP)	**£20**
89	Creation CRELP 054	**PRIMAL SCREAM** (LP, with bonus 45 "Split Wide Open 1"/ Lone Star Girl 1 [CREFRE 6, no p/s])	**£20**
91	Creation CRELP 076	**SCREAMADELICA** (2-LP)	**£80**
94	Creation CRELP 146	**GIVE OUT BUT DON'T GIVE UP** (2-LP, inners)	**£50**
97	Creation CRELP 224P	**ECHO DEK** (LP, promo, die-cut sleeve)	**£25**
97	Creation CREL 7224	**ECHO DEK** (5 x 7", box set)	**£30**
98	Creation CRELP 178	**VANISHING POINT** (2-LP, gatefold)	**£75**
99	Sony/Creation 88697811063	**SCREAMADELICA** (2-LP, reissue, red vinyl, numbered)	**£35**
00	Creation CRELP 239	**EXTERMINATOR** (EXTMNTR) (2-LP)	**£60**
02	Columbia 508923	**EVIL HEAT** (2-LP)	**£50**
03	Columbia 5136031	**DIRTY HITS** (3-LP)	**£40**
06	Columbia 82876831651	**RIOT CITY BLUES** (2-LP)	**£40**
08	B-Unique BUN 142 LP	**BEAUTIFUL FUTURE** (Box set, LP, poster, booklet)	**£60**
12	Sony 88697867991	**SCREAMADELICA** (2-LP reissue with free 12")	**£30**

(see also Jesus & Mary Chain, Revolving Paint Dream, P.P. & Primes, Death In Vegas)

PRIMARY SOURCE
93	Reinforced RIVET 1234	**Smile/The Och/Lovin You/Mic Check** (12")	**£45**

PRIME-MATES
69 Action ACT 4530 — Hot Tamales (Versions 1 & 2) £30

PRIME MOVERS
89 Cyanide CND 001 — SINS OF THE FOURFATHERS (LP) £25

PRIME RHYME MASTERS
91 Kold Sweat KS115 — You Need Discipline/To Kill A Mockingbird (12") £15

PRIMETTES
68 Ember EMBS 3398 — LOOKING BACK WITH THE PRIMETTES AND EDDIE FLOYD (LP, 1 side each) £40
73 Windmill WMD 192 — THE ROOTS OF DIANA ROSS AND EDDIE FLOYD (LP, reissue) £15
(see also Supremes, Eddie Floyd)

PRIMITIVE MAN
71 Decca F13188 — Animal Love/Major Barmy From The Army £30

PRIMITIVES
86 Head HEAD 010 — Thru The Flowers/Across My Shoulder/Lazy/She Don't Need You (12", unreleased, white label test pressings only) £30

PRIMITIVES (1)
64 Pye 7N 15721 — Help Me/Let Them Tell £220
65 Pye 7N 15755 — You Said/How Do You Feel £250
(see also Mal & Primitives)

PRIMITIVES (2)
91 RCA PL 75086 — GALORE (LP) £20

PRIMROSE
69 NEMS 56-4129 — Just For You/Nine Till Five £25

PRIMUS
90 Caroline CAROLLP 10 — FRIZZLE FRY (LP) £40
91 Interscope 7567916591 — SAILING THE SEAS OF CHEESE (LP) £25

PRINCE
SINGLES
79 Warner Bros K 17537T — I Wanna Be Your Lover/Just As Long As We're Together (12", company sleeve) £35
80 Warner Bros K 17590 — Sexy Dancer/Bambi (die-cut company sleeve) £30
80 Warner Bros K 17590T — Sexy Dancer (Remix)/Bambi (12", die-cut company sleeve) £100
81 Warner Bros K 17768 — Do It All Night/Head (die-cut company sleeve) £25
81 Warner Bros K 17768T — Do It All Night/Head (12", die-cut company sleeve) £60
81 Warner Bros K 17819 — Gotta Stop (Messin' About)/Uptown (p/s) £60
81 Warner Bros K 17819 — Gotta Stop (Messin' About)/I Wanna Be Your Lover (p/s) £60
81 Warner Bros LV 47 — Gotta Stop (Messin' About)/Uptown/Head (12", stickered p/s) £60
81 Warner Bros LV 47 — Gotta Stop (Messin' About)/I Wanna Be Your Lover/Head (12", stickered, colour p/s) ..£130
81 Warner Bros K 17866 — Controversy/When You Were Mine (p/s) £20
81 Warner Bros K 17866T — Controversy/When You Were Mine (12", p/s) £30
82 Warner Bros K 17922 — Let's Work/Ronnie, Talk To Russia (p/s) £40
82 Warner Bros K 17922T — Let's Work (Extended)/Ronnie, Talk To Russia (12", p/s) £40
83 Warner Bros W 9896 — 1999/How Come U Don't Call Me Anymore (paper labels, p/s, with free cassette mini-album in card p/s: "1999 (Edit)"/"Uptown"/"Controvesy"/"Dirty Minds"/"Sexuality") ..£40
83 Warner Bros W 9688T — Little Red Corvette (Full Length Version)/Automatic/International Lover (12", stickered p/s, with poster insert) £40
83 Warner Bros W 9688T — Little Red Corvette (Full Length Version)/Automatic/International Lover (12", 'negative image' p/s) £20
83 Warner Bros W 9436 — Little Red Corvette/Horny Toad (poster calendar p/s) £55
83 Warner Bros W 9436 — Little Red Corvette/Horny Toad (standard p/s) £40
83 Warner Bros W 9436T — Little Red Corvette (Full Length Version)/Horny Toad/D.M.S.R. (12", p/s) £15
83 Warner Bros W 9436T — Little Red Corvette (Full Length Version)/Horny Toad/D.M.S.R. (12", p/s, with spiral-bound calendar) £80
83 Warner Bros W 9436T — Little Red Corvette (Full Length Version)/Horny Toad/D.M.S.R. (12", p/s, with poster) ..£75
84 Warner Bros W 9286T — When Doves Cry/17 Days//1999/D.M.S.R. (12", stickered shrinkwrapped double pack) £20
84 Warner Bros W 9174P — Purple Rain/God (motorbike-shaped picture disc) £100
84 Warner Bros W 9174T — Purple Rain/God (instrumental) (12", p/s, initial pressing with poster) £15
84 Warner Bros W 9121TE — I Would Die 4 U (U.S. Remix)/Another Lonely Christmas (U.S. Remix) (12") £20
85 Paisley Park W 9052P — Paisley Park/She's Always In My Hair (shaped picture disc) £50
85 Paisley Park W 9052T — Paisley Park/She's Always In My Hair/Paisley Park (Remix) (12", mispressing with repeated 2nd track "She's Always In My Hair") £25
86 Paisley Park W 8751P — Kiss/Love Or Money (shaped picture disc with plinth) £30
86 Paisley Park W 8751T — Kiss (Extended)/Love Or Money (12", p/s, with poster) £15
86 Paisley Park W 8711P — Mountains (Ext.)/Alexa De Paris (Extended) (10", white vinyl in PVC sleeve) £20
86 Paisley Park W 8711T — Mountains (Extended 9.56)/Alexa De Paris (12", p/s, with poster) £20
86 Paisley Park W 8586F — Girls And Boys (Edit)/Under The Cherry Moon//She's Always In My Hair/ 17 Days (double pack, gatefold p/s) £15
86 Paisley Park W 8586P — Girls And Boys (Edit)/Under The Cherry Moon (shaped picture disc) £40
86 Paisley Park W 8586T — Girls And Boys/Under The Cherry Moon/Erotic City (12", p/s, with poster advertising London gigs) £18
87 Paisley Park W 8334P — If I Was Your Girlfriend/Shockadelica (peach vinyl, PVC cover, with postcards & stickers) £15
87 Paisley Park W 8288TP — I Could Never Take The Place Of Your Man/Hot Thing (Remixed Edit)/ Hot Thing (Extended) (12", picture disc) £15
88 Paisley Park 921 074-0 — I Wish U Heaven (Parts 1/2/3)/CAMILLE: Scarlet Pussy (Edit) (12", blue or purple vinyl) £1000

ALBUMS
79 Warner Bros. K56772 — PRINCE (LP, inner) £50

MINT VALUE £

80	Warner Bros. K 56862	**DIRTY MIND** (LP)	£40
81	Warner Bros. K 56950	**CONTROVERSY** (LP)	£40
83	Warner Bros. 923 809-1	**1999** (LP, original issue, single disc)	£20
83	Warner Bros. 92 3720-1	**1999** (2-LP)	£20
84	Warner Bros. 925 110-1	**PURPLE RAIN - MUSIC FROM THE MOTION PICTURE** (LP, purple vinyl with poster)	£80
84	Warner Bros. 925110-1	**PURPLE RAIN - MUSIC FROM THE MOTION PICTURE** (LP, with poster)	£20
86	Paisley Park 925 395-1	**PARADE** (LP, gatefold)	£20
86	Paisley Park WX 39P	**PARADE - MUSIC FROM "UNDER THE CHERRY MOON"** (LP, pic. disc, die-cut sleeve)	£200
87	Paisley Park WX 88	**SIGN O THE TIMES** (2-LP, inners)	£40
88	Paisley Park 925 720	**LOVESEXY** (LP, inner)	£25
89	Warner Bros. 925 936-1	**BATMAN** (MOTION PICTURE SOUNDTRACK) (LP, printed inner)	£20
91	Paisley Park 7599 25379-1	**DIAMONDS AND PEARLS** (2-LP, inners)	£25
92	Warner Bros. 9362-45037-1	**LOVE SYMBOL** (2-LP)	£100
94	Warners 936245793-1	**BLACK ALBUM** (LP, title sticker)	£35
94	Warner Bros. 9362 45700-1	**COME** (LP)	£50
95	NPG 6103-1	**EXODUS** (LP, as NPG)	£15
95	Warner Bros. 9362-45999-1	**THE GOLD EXPERIENCE** (2-LP)	£50
98	NPG BCT 9871	**CRYSTAL BALL** (4-CD, import only, as ß)	£40
99	Arista 07822 14624 1	**RAVE UN2 THE JOY FANTASTIC** (2-LP)	£40

PROMOS

81	Warner Bros SAM 172	**Dance Music Sex Romance/Dance Music Sex Romance** (12", p/s, promo only)	£100
84	Warner Bros	**Purple Rain** (promo only p/s, purple vinyl)	£60
84	Warner Bros SAM 230	**I Would Die 4 U/I would Die 4 U**	£30
91	Warner Brothers SAM 888	**Gett Off** (Urge Single Edit) (1-sided promo)	£15
92	Paisley Park W 0113	**Thunder** (DJ Edit) (1-sided promo only white label, stickered company sleeve)	£15
95	NPG 61225	**Get Wild** (Money Maker Radio Mix) (CD, as NPG, radio programmer's picture disc)	£45
96	NPG 60600	**Lovesign** (Radio Edit Mix)/(1-800 New Funk Version)/(The Storyboard Video Mix) (12", as ß, most with title sticker)	£35
96	NPG 60605	**Lovesign** (Radio Edit Mix)/(1-800 New Funk Version)/(The Storyboard Video Mix) (CD, as ß)	£30
04	Urban CK92560LP	**MUSICOLOGY** (2-LP, promo)	£50

PRINCE ALLAH/ALLABA

75	Cactus CT79	**Born A Fighter/TRADITION ALL STARS: Born A Fighter** (Dub) (as Prince Allaba)	£40
78	Freedom Sounds FSD 020	**Bucket Bottom/FULL WOOD: Stop And Think Me Over** (12")	£20
92	Xamayca Music XA002	**Jah Give I Love/Jerusalem** (12")	£40
02	Guiding Star GS 010	**Their Reward/Version**	£18
04	Stars TJITW018	**Daniel/TAPPA ZUKIE: Blackman** (12")	£15
96	Blood & Fire BAFLP 014	**ONLY LOVE AN CONQUER 1976-1979** (LP)	£40

(see also Rasalla, Keith Blake, The Leaders)

PRINCE BUSTER (& ALL STARS)

61	Starlite ST45 052	**Buster's Shack** (as Buster's Group)/**ERIC MORRIS: Search The World**	£30
62	Blue Beat BB 101	**My Sound That Goes Around/They Got To Go** (with Torchlighters)	£22
62	Blue Beat BB 116	**Independence Song** (with Bluebeats)/**RICO & BLUEBEATS: August 1962**	£25
62	Blue Beat BB 133	**Time Longer Than Rope/Fake King** (with Voice Of The People)	£25
62	Blue Beat BB 138	**One Hand Washes The Other/Cowboy Comes To Town**	£30
63	Blue Beat BB 150	**Run Man Run/Danny, Dane And Lorraine**	£25
63	Blue Beat BB 169	**Praise Without Raise/Three Against One** (unreleased, white labels only)	£100
63	Blue Beat BB 158	**Open Up, Bartender/Enjoy It** (B-side actually "Enjoy Yourself")	£35
63	Blue Beat BB 162	**Money/SCHOOL BOYS: Little Boy Blue**	£40
63	Blue Beat BB 163	**King, Duke, Sir/I See Them In My Sight**	£30
63	Blue Beat BB 167	**The Ten Commandments** (with All Stars)/**Buster's Welcome**	£20
63	Blue Beat BB 170	**Madness/PRINCE BUSTER ALL STARS: Toothache**	£40
63	Blue Beat BB 173	**Burning Creation/PRINCE BUSTER ALL STARS: Boop**	£30
63	Blue Beat BB 180	**Three More Rivers To Cross/RAYMOND HARPER & PRINCE BUSTER ALL STARS: African Blood**	£30
63	Blue Beat BB 186	**Fowl Thief/Remember Me**	£60
63	Blue Beat BB 189	**Watch It Blackhead/Hello My Dear**	£35
63	Blue Beat BB 192	**Rollin' Stone** (with Charmers)/**RICO & HIS BLUES BAND: This Day**	£30
63	Blue Beat BB 197	**Window Shopping/Sodom And Gomorrah**	£35
63	Blue Beat BB 199	**Spider And Fly/Three Blind Mice**	£30
63	Blue Beat BB 200	**Wash All Your Troubles Away/RICO & BLUE BEATS: Soul Of Africa**	£20
63	Dice CC 6	**They Got To Come/These Are The Times** (with Voice Of The People)	£15
63	Dice CC 11	**Blackhead Chinaman/You Ask** (I Had A Girl)	£18
63	Dice CC 18	**World Peace/The Lion Roars** (as Prince Buster & Hazel)	£15
64	Stateside SS 335	**30 Pieces Of Silver/Everybody Ska**	£25
64	Blue Beat BB 210	**Wash All Your Troubles Away/RICO & BLUE BEATS: Soul Of Africa** (p/s reissue)	£90
64	Blue Beat BB 211	**Bluebeat Spirit/Beggars Are No Choosers**	£35
64	Blue Beat BB 216	**You're Mine/Tongue Will Tell**	£35
64	Blue Beat BB 225	**Three Blind Mice/I Know**	£35
64	Blue Beat BB 232	**Sheep On Top** (song actually titled "She Pon Top")/**Midnight**	£45
64	Blue Beat BB 234	**She Loves You/Healing**	£70
64	Blue Beat BB 243	**Jealous/Buster's Ska**	£35
64	Blue Beat BB 248	**Thirty Pieces Of Silver/The National Dance**	£35
64	Blue Beat BB 254	**Wings Of A Dove/MAYTALLS: Sweet Love**	£35
64	Blue Beat BB 262	**Old Lady/Dayo Ska**	£40
64	Blue Beat BB 271	**No Knowledge In College/In The Middle Of The Night**	£45
64	Blue Beat BB 274	**I May Never Love You Again/Hey Little Girl**	£35
65	Blue Beat BB 278	**Blood Pressure/Islam**	£250

65	Blue Beat BB 281	Blues Market/MAYTALS: Looking Down The Street	£50
65	Blue Beat BB 282	Big Fight/Red Dress	£45
65	Blue Beat BB 293	Agua Fumar/Long Winter (with Charmers)	£40
65	Blue Beat BB 302	Ling Ting Tong/Walk Along	£100
65	Blue Beat BB 307	Bonanza/Wonderful Life	£35
65	Blue Beat BB 309	Here Comes The Bride (with Patsy Todd, as Jamaica's Greatest)/ BUSTER'S ALLSTARS: Burkes' Law	£40
65	Blue Beat BB 313	Everybody Yeah Yeah (as Jamaica's Greatest)/ BUSTER'S ALLSTARS: Gun The Man Down	£50
65	Blue Beat BB 314	Float Like A Butterfly/Haunted Room	£50
65	Blue Beat BB 316	Sugar Pop/Feel Up (as Prince & Jamaica's Greatest)	£40
65	Blue Beat BB 317	Come Home/I Thank You (as Jamaica's Greatest)	£45
65	Blue Beat BB 321	My Girl/BUSTER'S ALL STARS: The Fugitive	£60
65	Blue Beat BB 324	Al Capone/One Step Beyond (as Prince Buster's Allstars) (blue label)	£15
65	Blue Beat BB 324	Al Capone/One Step Beyond (as Prince Buster's Allstars) (other label colours)	£15
65	Blue Beat BB 328	Ambition/BUSTER'S ALL STARS: Ryging	£40
65	Blue Beat BB 330	Rum And Coca Cola/I Love Her	£100
65	Blue Beat BB 334	The Ten Commandments/BUSTER'S ALL STARS: Sting Like A Bee (reissue)	£15
65	Blue Beat BB 335	Respect/BUSTER'S ALL STARS: Virginia (B-side actually Dance Jamaica by Val Bennett & Prince Buster's All Stars)	£55
66	Blue Beat BB 338	Big Fight (Prince Buster Versus Duke Reid)/Adios, Senorita	£40
66	Blue Beat BB 339	Under Arrest (But Officer)/PRINCE BUSTER'S ALLSTARS: Say Boss Man	£40
66	Blue Beat BB 343	Prince Of Peace/Don't Throw Stones	£130
66	Blue Beat BB 352	Day Of Light (song actually "Dayo")/It's Too Late	£25
66	Blue Beat BB 355	Sunshine With My Girl/Girl Answer Your Name	£120
66	Blue Beat BB 357	I Won't Let You Cry/Hard Man Fe Dead	£80
66	Blue Beat BB 359	The Prophet (actually "Feel The Spirit" with Slim Smith)/ BUSTER'S ALL STARS: Lion Of Judah	£125
66	Blue Beat BB 362	To Be Loved/BUSTER'S ALLSTARS: Set Me Free	£30
66	Rainbow RAI 107	Your Turn (Sad Song)/If You Leave Me (with Allstars)	£40
67	Blue Beat BB 370	Shanty Town (Get Scanty)/BUSTER'S ALL STARS: Duppy	£45
67	Blue Beat BB 373	Knock On Wood/And I Love Her	£65
67	Blue Beat BB 377	Dark End Of The Street/Love Oh Love	£45
67	Blue Beat BB 378	Drunkard's Psalm (Wise Man)/7 Wonders Of The World (as Prince Buster All Stars)	£175
67	Blue Beat BB 382	Sit And Wonder (with His All Stars)/ROLAND ALFONSO: Sunrise In Kingston	£60
67	Blue Beat BB 383	Sharing You/You'll Be Lonely On The Blue Train (as Prince Buster's Allstars; A-side actually by Prince Buster, B-side actually by Rico's Band)	£30
67	Blue Beat BB 384	Take It Easy/Why Must I Cry (2nd issue, B-side actually by Hopeton Lewis)	£30
67	Blue Beat BB 387	Judge Dread (Judge Four Hundred Years)/FITZROY CAMPBELL & PRINCE BUSTER ALL STARS: Waiting For My Rude Girl	£20
67	Blue Beat BB 388	Dance Cleopatra/All In My Mind	£120
67	Blue Beat BB 390	Soul Serenade/Too Hot	£60
67	Blue Beat BB 391	Land Of Imagination/The Appeal (B-side actually "The Barrister Appeal")	£35
67	Blue Beat BB 393	Johnny Dollar/Rude Boys Rude	£50
67	Blue Beat BB 395	This Gun's For Hire/Yes, Daddy	£45
67	Blue Beat BB 397	Quit Place/Rude Boys Rude	£60
67	Blue Beat BB 400	All In My Mind/Judge Dread Dance (The Pardon)	£30
67	Blue Beat BB 402	Vagabond/PRINCE BUSTER ALL STARS: Come Get Me	£30
67	Philips BF 1552	The Ten Commandments/Don't Make Me Cry	£20
67	Fab FAB 10	Shakin' Up Orange Street/Black Girl (with Allstars)	£45
67	Fab FAB 11	Johnny Cool (Parts 1 & 2) (with Allstars)	£50
67	Fab FAB 16	Bye Bye Baby/Human (with Allstars)	£30
67	Fab FAB 25	Train To Girls Town/Give Love A Try (with Allstars)	£40
67	Fab FAB 26	Going To The River (as Prince Buster & Allstars)/ PRINCE BUSTER'S ALLSTARS: Julie On My Mind	£30
68	Fab FAB 31	Kings Of Old (My Ancestors)/Sweet Inspiration (with Allstars)	£65
68	Fab FAB 35	Try A Little Tenderness/All My Loving (with Allstars)	£600
68	Fab FAB 36	The Glory Of Love/Another Sad Nite	£30
68	Fab FAB 37	This Is A Hold Up/Julie On My Mind (with Allstars)	£40
68	Fab FAB 38	Free Love (with Allstars)/DALTONS: All Over The World	£50
68	Fab FAB 40	Rough Rider (with Allstars)/PRINCE BUSTER: 127 Orange Street (B-side actually by Prince Buster Allstars)	£30
68	Fab FAB 41	Shepperd Beng Beng (with Teddy King)/TENNORS: Ride Your Donkey	£30
68	Fab FAB 47	Going To Ethiopia (as Prince Buster & Allstars)/ PRINCE BUSTER ALLSTARS: Shakin' Up Orange Street	£35
68	Fab FAB 49	Glory Of Love/WAILERS: Mellow Mood (possibly white labels only)	£100
68	Fab FAB 56	Intensified Dirt/Don't You Know I Love You So (with Allstars)	£85
68	Fab FAB 57	Green Green Grass Of Home (as Prince Buster's Allstars; actually by Prince Buster & Allstars)/SOUL MAKERS: Girls Like You	£25
68	Fab FAB 58	We Shall Overcome/Keep The Faith (as Prince Buster's Allstars; actually by Prince Buster & Allstars)	£30
68	Fab FAB 64	Cool, Stroker/It's You I Love (B-side actually by Little Roy)	£60
68	Fab FAB 80	Hypocrite/New Dance (B-side actually by Little Roy)	£120
68	Fab FAB 81	Wine And Grine/The Scorcher (with Allstars)	£110
69	Unity UN 522	30 Pieces Of Silver/Everybody Ska (reissue)	£20
69	Fab FAB 82	Dr. Rodney (Black Power)/Taxation	£120
69	Fab FAB 92	Pharaoh House Crash/Ob-La-Di, Ob-La-Da	£30
69	Fab FAB 93	Ob-La-Di, Ob-La-Da/Wreck A Pum Pum	£15
69	Fab FAB 94	Hey Jude/Django Fever	£50
69	Fab FAB 102	Black Soul/CALEDONIANS: Oh Baby (B-side actually by Claredonians)	£45
69	Fab FAB 108	Whine And Grind/The Scorcher (with Allstars) (reissue)	£20

69	Fab FAB 118	Bull Buck/ROLAND ALPHONSO: One Heart	£25
69	Fab FAB 119	Let Her Go/Tie The Donkey's Tail	£15
69	Fab FAB 122	Stand Up/Happy Reggae (with Allstars)	£20
70	Fab FAB 127	Young Gifted And Black/PRINCE BUSTER'S ALLSTARS: The Rebel	£20
70	Fab FAB 131	That's All/The Preachin (B-side actually titled "The Preacher")	£50
70	Fab FAB 132	Ganja Plant/Creation	£25
70	Fab FAB 140	Hit Me Back/Give Peace A Chance	£30
70	Fab FAB 150	Big Five/Musical College	£15
70	Prince Buster PB 2	Rat Trap/Black Organ (B-side with Allstars but actually by Ansell Collins & Prince Buster's Allstars)	£15
71	Fab FAB 162	Baby Version (with Jan Fender)/Holly	£15
71	Fab FAB 176	Police Trim Rasta (with Allstars)/Smooth (B-side actually by Ansell Collins & Prince Buster Allstars)	£20
72	Prince Buster PB 14	Big Sister Stuff/Satta Massagana (with Allstars) (white label)	£20
72	Prince Buster PB20	They Got To Come/Time Longer Than Rope	£20
72	Prince Buster PB24	Giant/Science	£25
63	Blue Beat BBLP 802	I FEEL THE SPIRIT (LP)	£150
65	Blue Beat BBLP 805	SKA-LIP-SOUL (LP, with His All Stars)	£150
65	Blue Beat BBLP 806	IT'S BURKE'S LAW - JAMAICA SKA EXPLOSION! (LP, as Prince Buster All Stars; 2 different sleeves, laminated plain and unlaminated 'explosion')	£300
67	Blue Beat BBLP 807	WHAT A HARD MAN FE DEAD - PRINCE BUSTER SINGS FOR THE PEOPLE (LP, with Baba Brooks)	£300
67	Blue Beat BBLP 808	ON TOUR (LP)	£150
67	Blue Beat BBLP 809	JUDGE DREAD (LP)	£125
67	Blue Beat BBLP 820	SHE WAS A ROUGH RIDER (LP)	£100
68	Fab BBLP 820	SHE WAS A ROUGH RIDER (LP, reissue on Fab label)	£65
68	Fab BBLP 821	WRECK A PUM PUM (LP)	£65
69	Fab BBLP 822	THE OUTLAW (LP, title listed as "Queen Of The Outlaws" on disc)	£120
70	Fab MS 1	FABULOUS GREATEST HITS (LP, original issue with 'West Brothers Printers' credit on rear of sleeve)	£40
70	Fab MS 2	I FEEL THE SPIRIT (LP, copies in blue ink sleeve are worth £100)	£60
70	Fab MS 6	TUTTI FRUTTI (LP)	£65
72	Melodisc MLP 12-156	SISTER BIG STUFF (LP)	£50
72	Melodisc MLP 12-157	BIG FIVE (LP)	£35
73	Prince Buster PB 9	ORIGINAL GOLDEN OLDIES VOLUME 1 (LP)	£20
78	Fab MS 7	THE MESSAGE DUB WISE (LP)	£150
80	Fab MS1	FABULOUS GREATEST HITS (LP, reissue)	£15

(see also Buster's Allstars, Buster's Group, Dennis Alcapone, Jim Dakota, Hortense Ellis, Heptones, Eric Morris, Schoolboys, Protegue, Vietnam All Stars)

PRINCE CHARLIE

69	Coxsone CS 7101	Hit And Run/MEDIATORS: Darling, There I Stand	£100

PRINCE FAR I

76	Morpheus MOR 19	Zion Call/Version	£20
77	Lightning TRO 9000	Under Heavy Manners/Version	£15
82	On-U Sound DP 1	Virgin/Danger (10")	£20
83	Pre PRE 11-12	83 Struggle (with ASHANTIE ROY)/KONGO ASHANTIE ROY/Weeping Waiing (12")	£35
75	Carib Gems CGLP 1002	PSALMS FOR I (LP)	£45
78	Virgin Front Line FL 1013	MESSAGE FROM THE KING (LP)	£35
78	Virgin Front Line FL 1021	LONG LIFE (LP)	£20
79	Trojan TRLS 175	FREE FROM SIN (LP)	£20
79	Virgin Front Line FLX 4002	CRY TUFF DUB ENCOUNTER PART 2 (LP)	£50
79	Hit Run APLP 9006	DUB TO AFRICA (LP, as Prince Far I & The Arabs)	£65
79	Trojan Records TRLS 175	FREE FROM SIN (LP)	£15
80	Daddy Kool DKLP 15	CRY TUFF DUB ENCOUNTER CHAPTER III (LP, as Prince Far I & the Arabs)	£60
80	Trojan TRLS 205	CRY TUFF DUB ENCOUNTER CHAPTER IV (LP)	£25
80	Trojan TRLS 190	JAMAICAN HEROES (LP)	£30
80	Pre PRE XF 3	SHOWCASE IN A SUITCASE (LP)	£50
80	Pre PRE X 7	LIVITY (LP)	£35
81	Trojan TRLS 204	VOICE OF THUNDER (LP)	£20
84	Kingdom KVL 9016	UMKHONTO WE SIZWE (LP)	£15
95	Trojan TRLS 175	FREE FROM SIN (LP)	£18

(see also Arabs, Prince Cry Cry, King CC)

PRINCE FATTY

09	Mr. Bongo MRB 7060	Shimmy Shimmy Ya/Gin N Juice	£40
10	Mr. Bongo MB7061	Insane In The Brain/Insane In The Brain (dub mix)	£40

PRINCE HAMMER

77	Baby Mother HIT DD 11	Them Must Fall/Ball Of Fire (12")	£55
78	Hit Run HIT DP 15	Ten Thousand Lions/North London Thing (Carry The Swing) (12")	£60
83	Saab (No catalogue number)	Warika Hill/Africa Dance Hall (12")	£60
78	Virgin Frontline FL1004	BIBLE (LP)	£25
79	Hit Run APLP 9007	WORLD WAR DUB PART 1 (LP)	£120
79	Miss Pat Walker PW1	ROOTS ME ROOTS (LP)	£60

(see also Gen Brown)

PRINCE HAROLD

66	Mercury MF 952	Forget About Me/Baby You've Got Me	£15

PRINCE HERON

79	Jah Lion JBDC 806	Wip The Wicked Man/Kingston Rock (12", with Jah Brokie)	£15

PRINCE JAMMY

79	Trojan TRLS 174	KAMIKAZI DUB (LP)	£35

82	Greensleeves GREL 29	DESTROYS THE INVADERS (LP)	£25
83	CSA Records – CSLP 10	OSBOURNE IN DUB (LP)	£25
86	Greensleeves Records GREL 92	COMPUTERISED DUB (LP)	£25
96	Trojan TRLS 174	KAMAKAZI DUB (LP, reissue)	£15

(see also Crucial Bunny, Johnny Osborne)

PRINCE JAZZBO

73	Grape GR 3047	Free From Chains/LLOYD & PATSY: Papa Do It Sweet	£18
73	Techniques TE 921	Mr. Harry Skank/GLEN BROWN: Telavid Drums	£25
75	Jamatel JAL 04	Freedom/Free Dub	£15
77	Ujama UJA 0012	Learn Some More/I Am Roots/JOHNNY KOOL: Obidah/JA TONY: Run Bag-A-Wire (12")	£45
76	Third World TWLP 109	KICK BOY FACE (LP)	£40
76	Black Wax WAXLP 1	NATTY PASSING THRU' (LP)	£150

(see also Earl George)

PRINCE JAZZBO & I ROY

| 78 | Live & Love LAP 003 | STEP FORWARD YOUTH (LP) | £25 |

PRINCE LASHA ENSEMBLE

| 66 | CBS SBPG 62409 | INSIGHT (LP) | £30 |

PRINCE OF DARKNESS

69	Downtown DT 441	Burial Of Long Shot/MUSIC DOCTORS: Burial Of Long Shot	£25
69	Downtown DT 448	Meeting Over Yonder/MUSIC DOCTORS: Ghost Rider	£125
71	Downtown DT 467	Sound Of Today/MUSIC DOCTORS: Red Red Wine Version	£50

PRINCE PATO EXPEDITION

| 76 | Beacon BEAS 18 | FIREBIRD (LP) | £60 |

PRINCE & PRINCESS

| 65 | Aladdin WI 609 | Ready Steady Go/Take Me Serious | £25 |

PRINCE TALLIS & THE CHALLIS

| 72 | Upsetter US 383 | Who Feels It/THE UPSETTERS: He Who Feels It (Chapter 2) | £25 |

VIV PRINCE

| 66 | Columbia DB 7960 | Light Of The Charge Brigade/Minuet For Ringo | £30 |

(see also Pretty Things, Bunch Of Fives, Kate, Vamp, Chicago Line)

PRINCE WILLIAMS

| 74 | TKA ZA/B | Rasta Train/Good Old Days | £22 |

PRINCESS

| 86 | Supreme SU 1 | PRINCESS (LP, with poster) | £15 |

PRINCESS BALOU

| 81 | PB YYS 11 | Making Love To You/Making Love To You (Part II) (p/s) | £200 |

PRINCESS & SWINEHERD

| 68 | Oak RGJ 633 | PRINCESS AND THE SWINEHERD (LP, plain black sleeve) | £100 |

PRINCESS TINYMEAT

| 84 | Rough Trade RTT 160 | Sloblands/The Fairest Of Them All (12", some with sticker) | £15 |
| 87 | Rough Trade ROUGH 108 | HERSTORY (LP) | £20 |

(see laso Virgin Prunes, Daniel Figgis)

PRINCIPAL EDWARDS MAGIC THEATRE

73	Deram DM 398	Weekdaze/Whizzmore Kid	£15
69	Dandelion 63752	SOUNDTRACK (LP, gatefold sleeve)	£60
71	Dandelion DAN 8002	THE ASMOTO RUNNING BAND (LP, gatefold sleeve)	£40
74	Deram SML 1108	ROUND ONE (LP, white/red label with small logo)	£35

JOHN PRINE

| 72 | Atlantic K40357 | JOHN PRINE (LP) | £25 |

PRIORITY

| 79 | Brimstone BRS 1 | Visions Of Miranda Grey/Escape (p/s) | £30 |

PRIORY PARK

| 78 | Wild Dog DOGLP 16 | TRY FOR THE SUN (LP) | £40 |

PRISONERS

84	Big Beat SW 98	ELECTRIC FIT (EP)	£18
82	Own Up OWN UP U2	A TASTE OF PINK (LP)	£30
83	Big Beat WIK 19	THE WISERMISERDEMELZA (LP)	£20
85	Own Up OWN UP U2	A TASTE OF PINK (LP, reissue in pink sleeve on pink vinyl)	£35
85	Own Up OWN UP U3	THE LAST FOURFATHERS (LP)	£50
86	Countdown DOWN 2	IN FROM THE COLD (LP)	£20
89	Hangman HANG 23 UP	RARE AND UNISSUED (LP)	£35
91	Cyanide CND 2	RARE AND UNISSUED (LP, reissue)	£20

(see also James Taylor Quartet)

PRISONERS/MILKSHAKES

| 86 | Empire MIC 001 | THE LAST NIGHT AT THE MIC CLUB (LP, live, 1 side each) | £18 |
| 86 | Media Burn MB 17 | THEE MILKSHAKES VS. THE PRISONERS (LP, live, 1 side each) | £18 |

(see also Milkshakes)

MARK PRITCHARD

| 09 | Ho Hum HOHUM 003 | ?/The Hologram (10") | £30 |
| 10 | Deep Medi Muisc MEDI 25 | Elephant Dub/Heavy As Stone (12") | £25 |

PRIVATE DICKS
79 Heartbeat PULSE 6   She Said So/Private Dicks (p/s) £20

PRIVATE EYE
83 Spider SPY 001   Water Under The Bridge/I Cry For You (no p/s) £35

PRIVATE FUNK-SHUN
86 Private Funk-Shun KMJ 1 All That I Wanted Was You/Fantasy (12") £125

PRIVATE I'S
79 Cruise CR 001   Love Won't Let Me Wait/I'll Be Around..............................£20

PRIVATE LIFE
72 Realm RM 3   Put Her Down/Chasing Dragons £400

PRIVATE SECTOR
78 TJM TJM 8   Just Just (Wanna) Stay Free/Things Get Worse (p/s) £20

PRIVATE VIEW
84 New 7NL 100   Fashion Changeling/Walls (p/s) £25

PROBOT
04 Southern Lord SUNN 30LP PROBOT (2-LP) £60
(see also Foo Fighters, Nirvana)

P.J. PROBY
66   Fab FAB 2   You've Got Me Cryin'/I Need Love (in die-cut p/s) £20
67   Liberty LIB 55936   Nicki Hoeky/Good Things Are Coming My Way £15
67   Liberty LIB 55974   You Can't Come Home Again/Work With Me Annie £15
67   Liberty LIB 55974   You Can't Come Home Again/Work With Me Annie (DJ Copy) ...£30
68   Liberty LBF 15046   It's Your Day Today/I Apologise Baby (DJ Copy) £30
68   Liberty LBF 15152   The Day That Lorraine Came Down/Mery Hoppkins Never Had Days Like These (B-side features Led Zeppelin) ...£40
69   Liberty LBF 15245   Hanging From Your Loving Tree/Empty Bottles................£15
70s Rooster ROO 101   You've Got It All (with Polly Brown)/Starting All Over Again......£20
64   Liberty LEP 2192   P. J. PROBY (EP)..£15
65   Liberty LEP 2229   SOMEWHERE (EP) £15
65   Liberty LEP 2239   CHRISTMAS WITH P. J. (EP)..£15
66   Liberty LEP 2251   P. J.'s HITS (EP) £15
67   Liberty LEP 2267   PROBY AGAIN (EP) £20
65   Liberty LBY 1235   I AM P. J. PROBY (LP)..£15
65   Liberty LBY 1264   P. J. PROBY (LP)..£15
66   Liberty LBY 1291   P. J. PROBY IN TOWN (LP) £20
67   Liberty LBY 1361   ENIGMA (LP) £15
67   Liberty LBL/LBS 83045 PHENOMENON (LP)..£15
68   Liberty LBL/LBS 83087 BELIEVE IT OR NOT (LP) £15
69   Liberty LBS 83219E   THREE WEEK HERO (LP, featuring Led Zeppelin on "Jim's Blues") ...£45
(see also Jett Powers, Marc Almond)

PROCESSION
69 Mercury SMCL 20132   PROCESSION (LP) £30

PROCOL HARUM
67 Regal Zono. LRZ 1001   PROCOL HARUM (LP, laminated front sleeve, flipbacks, blue/silver label)......£200
68 Regal Zono. LRZ 1004   SHINE ON BRIGHTLY (LP, mono), laminated front sleeve, blue/silver label)......£200
67 Regal Zono. SLRZ 1004   SHINE ON BRIGHTLY (LP, stereo), laminated front sleeve, red/silver label)......£125
69 Regal Zono. SLRZ 1009   A SALTY DOG (LP, laminated sleeve, red/silver label) £150
70 Regal Zono. SLRZ 1014   HOME (LP, with lyric sheet)..£150
71 Chrysalis ILPS 9158   BROKEN BARRICADES (LP, gatefold sleeve, first pressing with a small white "i" at the top of the label)......£50
71 Chrysalis ILPS 9158   BROKEN BARRICADES (LP, gatefold sleeve) £25
72 Fly TOOFA 7/8   A WHITER SHADE OF PALE/A SALTY DOG (2-LP, reissue) £20
73 Chrysalis CHR 1037   GRAND HOTEL (LP, gatefold sleeve, booklet, green label) £30
74 Chrysalis CHR 1058   EXOTIC BIRDS AND FRUIT (LP)......................................£25
91 BMG PL 90589   THE PRODIGAL STRANGER (LP) £25
(see also Paramounts, Legend, Matthew Fisher, Robin Trower, Matthew Ellis, Freedom, Mick Grabham, Power Pack)

JUDD PROCTOR
64   Parlophone R 5126   Better Late/Boots £15
68   Morgan MR 103P   GUITARS GALORE (LP)..£40
70s Gemini GMX 5004   GUITARS GALORE (LP, reissue)......................................£25
see also Ray Ellington

MIKE PROCTOR
67 Columbia DB 8254   Mr. Commuter/Sunday, Sunday, Sunday £225

PRODIGY
91 XL XLT 17   WHAT EVIL LURKS EP (What Evil Lurks/We Gonna Rock/Android/ Everybody In The Place) (12", company sleeve)......£40
91 XL XLT 21   Charly (Alley Cat Mix)/Pandemonium/Your Love/Charly (Original Mix) (12", p/s) £18
91 XL XLS 26   Everybody In The Place (Fairground Edit)/G-Force (Energy Flow) ...£15
92 XL XLT 30   Fire (Burning Version)/(Sunrise Version)/(Original Version)/(Genaside II Remix) (12", p/s) ...£18
92 XL XLS 35   Out Of Space/Ruff In The Jungle Bizness (Uplifting Vibes Remix) ...£18
92 XL XLT 35   Out Of Space (Original Mix)/(Techno Underworld Remix)/Ruff In The Jungle Bizness (Uplifting Vibes Remix)/Music Reach 1,2,3,4 (Live) (12", p/s)......£20
93 XL EB 1   EARTHBOUND 1 : One Love (original Mix)/Full Throttle (original Mix) (12") ...£60
95 XL SC 1   SCIENIDE (12", white label, 500 hand-stamped promos only) ...£60
96 XL XLT 70   Firestarter/(Instrumental)/(Empirion Mix)/Molotov Bitch (12", p/s)...............£20

97	XL XLT 90	**Smack My Bitch Up** (LP Version)/**No Man Army/Smack My Bitch Up** (DJ Hype Remix)/**Mindfields** (Headrock Dub) (12", p/s)	£18
98	XL XLT90DJ	**Smack My Bitch Up/**(DJ Hype Remix)/**No Man Army/Minefields** (Headrock Dub) (12" promo)	£15
05	XL XLT 213	**Spitfire** (05 Version)**Spitfire** (Future Funk Squad's "Dogfight" Remix/Spitfire (Nightbreed Remix) (12" stickered p/s, with 2 stickers, 2000 only)	£25
05	XL XLS 213 CDE	**Spitfire** (05 Version)/**Spitfire** (Nightbreed Remix)/**Spitfire** (Future Funk Squad's "Dogfight" Remix) (CD stickered digipak 500 only)	£30
92	XL XLLP 110	THE PRODIGY EXPERIENCE (2-LP)	£60
94	XL XLLP 114	MUSIC FOR THE JILTED GENERATION (LP)	£60
97	XL XLLP 121	THE FAT OF THE LAND (2-LP)	£80
04	XL XLLP 183	ALWAYS OUTNUMBERED, NEVER OUTGUNNED (3-LP)	£100
09	Take Me To The Hospital HOSPLP001	INVADERS MUST DIE (2-LP)	£30
09	Take Me To The Hospital HOSPBOX001	INVADERS MUST DIE (Box set, CD/DVD/5x7")	£30
15	Take Me To The Hospital HOSPLP005	THE DAY IS MY ENEMY (2-LP)	£30
15	Take Me To The Hospital HOSPLP005	THE DAY IS MY ENEMY (2-LP as x 3 12", poster, print and download card)	£35
18	Take Me To The Hospital HOSPLP 538426301	NO TOURISTS (2-LP, clear or clear violet)	£20
18	Take Me To The Hospital 538426291	NO TOURISTS (2-LP)	£20
21	XL Recordings – XL121LPE2	THE FAT OF THE LAND 2-LP, reissue, obi, orange vinyl)	£50

(see also Leeroy Thornhill)

PRODUCERS
80	Magic Moon MACH 4	Walk Right Back/All The Rage	£15
80	Magic Moon MACH 1.S	On The Beach/Goin' Steady (die cut sleeve)	£20
80	Edge EDGE 2	On The Shelf/Talking About My Baby (no p/s)	£15

PRODUCT OF REASON
83	Tenuous Lynx LYNX 1	Man Of Your Dreams/These Days	£15

PROFESSIONALS
80	Virgin VS 376	1-2-3/White Light White Heat/Baby I Don't Care (p/s, signed by Cook & Jones)	£15
81	Virgin V 2220	I DIDN'T SEE IT COMING (LP)	£15

(see also Sex Pistols, Lightning Raiders, Steve Jones)

PROFESSIONAL UHURU DANCE BAND
71	Decca WAPS31	UHURU SPECIAL HI FI NUMBERS (LP)	£35

PROFESSOR LONGHAIR
65	Sue WI 397	Baby Let Me Hold Your Hand/Looka' No Hair	£40
78	Harvest HAR 5154	Mess Around/Tipitina	£15
72	Speakeasy 10-78	NEW ORLEANS 88 (10" LP)	£45
72	Atlantic K 40402	NEW ORLEANS PIANO (LP)	£30
78	Harvest SHSP 4086	LIVE ON THE QUEEN MARY (LP)	£30
80	Sonet SNTF 830	CRAWFISH SIESTA (LP)	£15
83	Stateside SSL 6004	LIVE ON THE QUEEN MARY (LP, reissue)	£18
81	JSP 1025	THE LONDON CONCERT (LP)	£15

FRANK PROFFITT
66	Topic 12T 162	NORTH CAROLINA SONGS AND BALLADS (LP)	£20

PROJECTIVE VISION
94	Holistic AB 06	Close Encounter/Equilibrium (12")	£40
94	Holistic AB 11	Apocalypse/Change (12")	£90

PROJECT FEATURING JASMIN
91	Unyque UNQ 113T	Soul (Vocal)/(Club Remix)/No Pain No Gain (12")	£15

PROLES
79	Rock Against Racism RAR 1	Stereo Love/Thought Crime/CONDEMNED: Soldier Boys/ Endless Revolution (p/s)	£45

PROMISE
69	NEMS 56-4129	Just For You/Nine To Five	£100

PROPAGANDA
85	ZTT 12 ZTAS 2	Das Testaments Des Mabuse/Femme Fatale/The 9th Life (Of Dr. Mabuse) (12", white p/s, title sticker reads "13th Life New Mix")	£15

(see also Act, Ralph Dorper, Claudia Brucken)

PROPERTY
70	Staple ST01	My Mind Sleeps/Calling You (some with p/s)	£150

PROPHECY OF DOOM
90	Deaf DEAF 02	ACKNOWLEDGE THE CONFUSION MASTER (LP, insert)	£20
90	Strange Fruit SFPS 079	PEEL SESSIONS EP (12", p/s)	£15

PROPHET
74	UK UK 64	Have Love Will Travel/Blues In B Sharp	£30

MICHAEL PROPHET
79	Grove GMDM 17	Turn Me Loose/Praise You Jah Jah (12")	£30
79	Grove GMDM 25	Warn Them Jah/Don't Interfere (12")	£45
80	Greensleeves GRED 44	Help Them Please/WAILING SOULS : See Baba Joe (12", green vinyl)	£30
80	Island/Grove Music 12WIP 6583	Fight to The Top (Discomix)/Love And Unity/Mash Down Rome (12")	£35
80	Black Roots BR 004	My Lady/Lady Dub (12")	£20
80	Love Linch LL 002	True Born African (with Soul Syndicate)/RANKING TOYAN: What A Bam Bam (12")	£30

MINT VALUE £

PROPHETS

80	Love Linch LL 012	Struggle/80s Struggle (12", some on blue vinyl)	£40
80s	WLN WLN 003	Rock Me Baby/Don't Throw Stone (12")	£20
81	Greensleeves GRED 59	Gunman/Cassandra (12")	£15
82	Greensleeves GRED 72	Here Comes The Bride/MYSTIC EYES: Bring The Kuchie Come	£20
82	Greensleeves GRED 87	Boom Him Up Now/Trouble Nobody (12")	£15
82	Greensleeves GRED 104	Just Talking/Thru Me (with Papa Dimes) (12")	£15
90	Passion PE 6	Your Love (Michael Prophet Version)/Your Love (Ricky Tuff Version)/Acapella Version (12")	£15
99	Blakamix BLK 030	Judgements/Dubments	£15
80	Greensleeves GREL 18	RIGHTEOUS ARE THE CONQUEROR (LP)	£25
80	Island ILPS 9606	SERIOUS REASONING (LP)	£25
81	Greensleeves GRED 104	MICHAEL PROPHET (LP)	£28

PROPHETS

78	Grove Music GMDM 12	Give Thanks And Praise/Till I Kiss You (12")	£40
79	Grove Music GMDM 4	Blessed Are The Meak (feat Trinity)/TOMMY MCCOOK: Stepping High (12", p/s)	£25

(see also Yabby U)

PROPHETS (JAMAICA)

70	Big Shot BI 554	Crystal Blue Persuasion (Parts 1 & 2)	£30
70	Big Shot BI 555	Tumble Time (Parts 1 & 2)	£35
70	Big Shot BI 557	Revenge Of Eastwood Version One/Version Two	£75
70	Jackpot JP 712	Let's Fall In Love/Purple Moon	£45

(see also Lloyd & Prophets, Claudette, Lloyd & Claudette, Patrick & Lloyd)

PROPHETS (U.S.)

69	Mercury MF 1097	I Got The Fever/Soul Control	£30
69	Mercury MF 1097	I Got The Fever/Soul Control (DJ copy)	£50

(see also Creation [U.S.])

PROTECTORS

73	Live Wire SON 4004	Loretta/Jump The Sidewalk	£15

PROTEGUE (& PRINCE BUSTER'S ALL STARS)

67	Blue Beat BB 398	Foul Dance/PRINCE BUSTER'S ALL STARS: This Is It	£30

PROTEX

78	Good Vibrations GOT 6	Don't Ring Me Up/(Just Want) Your Attention/Listening In (wraparound p/s)	£30
79	Polydor 2059 124	I Can't Cope/Popularity (p/s)	£25
79	Polydor 2059 167	I Can Only Dream/Heartache (p/s)	£15
80	Polydor 2059 245	A Place In Your Heart/Jeepster (p/s)	£15
01	Good Vibrations BIG 4	LISTENING IN (LP)	£18

PROTON

80	Ballistic 12BP 264	We're Funkin'/Make Your Move (Instrumental Version)	£40
81	Image IMA 1	Pay Up/Remixed Rhythm Track (12" as Proton Plus)	£20

PROTOS

82	Airship AP 391	ONE DAY A NEW HORIZON (LP)	£150

PROVIDENCE

72	Threshold THS 9	EVER SENSE THE DAWN (LP, gatefold sleeve with insert)	£40

PROWLER (1)

73	Parlophone R 5986	Pale Green (Hnmmmm) Driving Man/Jaywick Cowboy	£30

PROWLER (2)

83	Pirate SS 226 S8	Forgotten Angels/Don't Let Go (p/s)	£80
85	SRT SRT5KS/368	Alcatraz/So Lonely (p/s)	£70

PRUNES

70	Songbird SB 1023	Come A Little Closer/Come A Little Closer Version II	£30

(see also Eric Donaldson, West Indians)

SNOOKY PRYOR

70	Flyright LP 100	SNOOKY PRYOR (LP)	£15

RED PRYSOCK

59	Mercury AMT 1028	Chop Suey/Margie	£20
58	Mercury MPL 6535	THE BEAT (LP)	£50
58	Mercury MPL 6550	FRUIT BOOTS (LP)	£40
56	Mercury MPT 7517	JUMP RED JUMP (10" LP)	£40

PSEUDO EXISTORS

80	Dead Good DEAD 2	Pseudo Existence/Coming Up For Air/New Modern Warfare (rubber-stamped folded p/s, pink/white label)	£60
80	Dead Good DEAD 2	Pseudo Existence/Coming Up For Air/New Modern Warfare (rubber-stamped folded p/s, later red/black label & stamped white sleeve)	£35

PSEUDO 3

92	Music Madness MM001	Renk & Dirty/B-Line Stepper (12")	£40

P.S. PERSONAL

83	New World NEW 1	Shoot Me Down/Shoot Me Down (no p/s)	£25

PSYCHEDELIC FURS

80	CBS 84084	THE PSYCHEDELIC FURS (LP, pink sleeve)	£15
81	CBS SCBS 84892	TALK TALK TALK (LP)	£15
82	CBS CBS85909	FOREVER NOW (LP)	£15

(see also Unwanted)

PSYCHEOUT

00	Discord DISCORD 002	BOOM EP (12")	£15

MINT VALUE £

| 00 | Discord DISCORD 003 | **WARP EP** (12")..£60 |
| 00 | Discord DISCORD 004 | **TRAIN TRAX EP** (12")...£15 |

PSYCHIC PHENOMENA

| 97 | Lowlife LOW05 | **THE WHOLE CIRCUMFERENCE** (12", EP)...£15 |

PSYCHIC TV

82	Some Bizzare PTV 1	**Just Drifting/Breakthrough** (p/s)...£15
82	Some Bizzare PTV 1T	**Just Drifting/Just Drifting** (Midnight) (12", p/s)...£15
84	Temple TOPY 001	**Unclean/Mirrors** (12", p/s)..£15
86	Temple TOPIC 009	**Godstar/Godstar** (California Mix) (12", picture disc).......................................£15
88	DC DC 23	**Superman/Jack The Tab** (12", p/s, no artist credit on label).........................£15
82	Some Bizzare PSY 1	**FORCE THE HAND OF CHANCE** (LP, with bonus LP & double-sided poster, featuring Marc Almond)..£80
82	Some Bizzare PSY 1	**FORCE THE HAND OF CHANCE** (LP, with poster)...£35
83	CBS 25737	**DREAMS LESS SWEET** (LP, with inner sleeve, some with free 12" EP [XPR 1251])......£35
83	CBS 25737	**DREAMS LESS SWEET** (LP, with inner sleeve)...£25
84	Temple TOPY 003	**PAGAN DAY** (LP, picture disc, 999 copies)..£40
84	Gramm GRAMM 23	**THOSE WHO DO NOT** (2-LP, 5000 copies)...£30
85	Temple TOPY 004	**THEMES 2** (LP)..£25
85	Temple TOPY 008	**THEMES 3** (LP)..£25
85	Temple TOPY 010	**MOUTH OF THE NIGHT** (LP)..£20
85	Temple TOPIC 010	**MOUTH OF THE NIGHT** (LP, picture disc)..£25
86	Temple TOPIC 009	**GODSTAR** (LP, with picture disc)..£15
86	Temple TOPY 014	**LIVE IN PARIS** (LP)...£15
86	Temple TOPY 015	**LIVE IN TOKYO**...£15
87	Temple TOPY 016	**LIVE IN GLASGOW**...£15
87	Temple TOPY 018	**LIVE IN HEAVEN** (LP)...£15
87	Temple TOPY 026	**LIVE IN REYKJAUIK** (LP)..£15
87	Temple TOPY 027	**LIVE EN SUISSE** (LP)..£15
87	Temple TOPY 028	**LIVE IN TORONTO** (LP)...£15
87	Temple TOPY 029	**LIVE IN GOTTINGEN** (LP)..£15
88	Temple TOPY 031	**PSYCHIC TV** (LP, picture disc)..£15
88	Temple TOPY 032	**ALBUM 10** (LP, picture disc)..£15
88	Temple TOPY 038	**ALLEGORY AND SELF** (LP, blue vinyl)..£15
	(see also Throbbing Gristle)	

PSYCHO'S MUM

| 89 | Woronzow W 011 | **A SIBILANT SIN** (LP, with insert)...£15 |

PSYKIS

| 95 | Dee Jay DJX 025 | **Pretend** (12" 1-sided promo)...£20 |

PSYKYK VOLTS

| 79 | Ellie Jay EJPS 9262 | **Totally Useless/Horror Story No. 5** (p/s)...£20 |
| 79 | MHG GHM 109 | **Totally Useless/Horror Story No. 5**...£35 |

PSYLONS

| 87 | Iron Lung IL 001 | **All The Things We Need** (12", p/s)..£15 |

PTOLOMY PSYCON

| 71 | Hollick and Taylor HT/IPS 1306 | **LOOSE CAPACITOR** (10" LP, 235 only, silkscreened front sleeve, printed back)........£800 |

PUBLIC ENEMY

13	Vinyl Factory S714	**Harder Than You Think** (1-sided, Secret Seven, 100 only).............................£50
87	Def Jam 450482-1	**YO BUM RUSH THE SHOW** (LP, with lyric sheet)...£20
88	Def Jam 462415-1	**IT TAKES A NATION OF MILLIONS TO HOLD US BACK** (LP, inner)......................£25
90	Def Jam 466281	**FEAR OF A BLACK PLANET** (LP, inner)...£20
91	Def Jam 468751	**APOCALYPSE 91** (2LP, gatefold, printed inners)...£20
94	Def Jam 523 362-1	**MUSE SICK-N-HOUR MESS AGE** (2-LP, gatefold, printed inners)......................£25
05	Mercury 983 2545	**POWER TO THE PEOPLE AND THE BEATS** (5x12" box set, insert)......................£70

PUBLIC FOOT THE ROMAN

| 73 | Sovereign SVNA 7259 | **PUBLIC FOOT THE ROMAN** (LP, gatefold sleeve)..£100 |
| | (see also Movies) | |

PUBLIC IMAGE LTD (PIL)

78	Virgin VS 228	**Public Image/The Cowboy Song** (foldout 'newspaper' p/s)............................£30
79	Virgin VS 274-12	**Death Disco/And No Bird Do Sing** (1/2 Mix)/**Death Disco Megamix** (12", p/s, 5,000 only)...£15
78	Virgin V2114	**FIRST ISSUE** (LP, 1st pressing, printed inner, PiL on both labels, yellow sticker with SPOTS 007 and poster)..£150
78	Virgin V2114	**FIRST ISSUE** (LP. 1st pressing, with colour inner sleeve and PiL on both labels)......£30
79	Virgin V2114	**FIRST ISSUE** (LP, repressing with plain white inner sleeve)..........................£15
79	Virgin METAL 1	**METAL BOX** (LP, 3x12" with circular paper dividers & inner sheet in round tin)......£250
79	Virgin VD 2512	**SECOND EDITION** (standard issue, of Metal Box, 2LP, gatefold)......................£40
80	Virgin V 2183	**PARIS AU PRINTEMPS** (LP as 'IMAGE PUBLIQUE S.A)...£15
82	Virgin V 2189	**THE FLOWERS OF ROMANCE** (LP, insert)...£25
83	Virgin VGD 3508	**LIVE IN TOKYO** (2LP, fold-out insert)...£20
84	Virgin V 2309	**THIS IS WHAT YOU WANT...THIS IS WHAT YOU GET** (LP)....................................£25
86	Virgin V 2366	**ALBUM** (LP)..£25
87	Virgin V 2455	**HAPPY?** (LP, printed inner)..£20
89	Virgin V 2588	**9** (LP, printed inner)...£20
90	Virgin V 2644	**THE GREATEST HITS SO FAR (2LP, printed inners**...£40
90	Virgin MTLCD 1	**METAL BOX** (CD, in round tin with insert)..£35

MINT VALUE £

| 92 | Virgin V 2681 | THAT WHAT IS NOT (LP, printed inner) | £45 |
| 12 | PIL PIL 002 LP | THIS IS PIL (2LP, gatefold) | £30 |

(see also Sex Pistols, Jah Wobble, Vivien Goldman, Cowboys International)

PUBLIC SERVICE BROADCASTING

SINGLES

13	Test Card Recordings TCRVS 01	Signal 30/New Dimensions In Sound (7", p/s, orange vinyl, postcard, RSD)	£40
13	Test Card Recordings TCRVS 02	Theme From PSB/Everest [Live] (7", p/s, red or pink vinyl editions)	£15
13	Test Card Recordings TCR VS03	Night Mail (Ben Gomori's 12" Version)/(Baltic Fleet Remix)/(Radio Edit) (12", p/s, limited edition, download card)	£30
14	Test Card Recordings TCR VS04	Elfstedentocht Part 1/Elfstedentocht Part 2 (7", p/s, white vinyl, RSD)	£25
15	Test Card Recordings TCRVS	Go! (Radio Edit)/Go! (Errors Remix) (7". p/s, green vinyl, limited)	£15
16	Test Card Recordings TCR VS07	The Other Side (Radio Edit)/(Datassette Remix) (7", p/s, picture disc, RSD)	£15
18	Pias PIAS R991T	People Will Always Need Coal/(Flamingods Remix)/(Vessels Remix)/(Dark Sky Remix)/They Gave Me A Lamp (Plaid Remix)/(Nabihah Iqbal Remix) (12", p/s, 180g, RSD)	£15
24	Test Card Recordings TCRV S08	Gagarin/Gagarin (Instrumental) (7", p/s, red vinyl, RSD)	£20

EPs

10	Vanity Fare Recordings 001	EP ONE (10" EP, 250 Only, sold at gigs, some with handwritten note)	£200
12	Test Card Recordings TCR002	THE WAR ROOM (12" EP, limited edition, without barcode)	£40
15	Test Card Recordings TCR VS06	SPUTNIK/KOROLEV (12" EP, p/s)	£15
18	PIAS PIASR 1039T	WHITE STAR LINER (12" EP, p/s,180g)	£18

ALBUMS

13	Test Card Recordings VA01	INFORM-EDUCATE-ENTERTAIN (LP, gatefold, printed inner)	£20
15	Test Card Recordings TCR VA02X	THE RACE FOR SPACE (LP, gatefold, printed inner, booklet, clear vinyl)	£40
16	Test Card Recordings TCR VAR03X	THE RACE FOR SPACE/REMIXES (LP, orange vinyl)	£40
16	Test Card Recordings TCR VAL04X	LIVE AT BRIXTON (2LP/DVD, gatefold, printed inners, blue vinyl)	£30
17	PIAS PIASR 970LPX	EVERY VALLEY (LP, gatefold, printed inner, booklet, 180g, clear vinyl)	£20
21	PIAS PIASR 1230LPX	BRIGHT MAGIC (LP, gatefold, orange/black marbled vinyl)	£20
21	PIAS PIASR 1230LPX	BRIGHT MAGIC (LP, 2CD, folder gatefold, booklet, photographs, white vinyl)	£40
23	Test Card Recordings TCR VA05	THIS NEW NOISE (with Jules Buckley & BBC Symphony Orchestra) (2LP, gatefold, printed inners, white vinyl)	£30

GARY PUCKETT (& UNION GAP)

68	CBS (S) 63342	YOUNG GIRL (LP)	£20
68	CBS (S) 63429	INCREDIBLE (LP)	£20
70	CBS 63794	THE NEW GARY PUCKETT AND THE UNION GAP ALBUM (LP)	£20

PUDDING

| 67 | Decca F 12603 | The Magic Bus/It's Too Late | £70 |

TITO PUENTE

| 57 | RCA RD 27002 | LET'S CHA-CHA WITH PUENTE (LP) | £15 |
| 58 | RCA SF 5008 | MUCHO PUENTE (LP) | £15 |

PUFFIN CLUB

| 81 | Big Nob NOB 001 | Great Western Revival/Feel So Low/Anhedonia/Set A Table (no p/s, 50 only) | £15 |

DUDU PUKWANA

74	Caroline C1504	IN THE TOWNSHIPS (LP, as Dudu Pukwana & Spear)	£20
75	Caroline CA2005	FLUTE MUSIC (LP with Spear)	£40
81	Jika ZL 1	SOUNDS ZILA (LP)	£15
83	Jika ZL 2	LIFE IN BRACKNELL & WILLISAU (LP, featuring Dinise Saul)	£25
86	Jika ZL 3	ZILA 86 (LP)	£15

PULLED APART BY HORSES

| 10 | Transgressive TRANS117X | PULLED APART BY HORSES (LP) | £30 |

VERN PULLENS

| 72 | Injun 107 | Mama Don't Allow No Boppin'/Bop Crazy Baby | £15 |
| 72 | Injun 111 | Bop Crazy Baby/Would You Be Happy | £15 |

PULLOVERS

| 80 | Supermusic SUP 24/LYN 8613/4 | Peter Pan Pill/Spare Part Surgery (p/s, some with kidney donor card) | £20 |

PULP

SINGLES

83	Red Rhino RED 32	My Lighthouse (Remix)/Looking For Life (p/s)	£100
83	Red Rhino RED 37	Everybody's Problem/There Was (p/s)	£50
85	Fire BLAZE 5	Little Girl (With Blue Eyes)/Simultaneous/Blue Glow/The Will To Power (12", p/s)	£25
85	Fire BLAZE 5	Little Girl (With Blue Eyes)/Simultaneous/Blue GLow/The Will To Power, 12" promo)	£40
86	Fire BLAZE 10	Dogs Are Everywhere/The Mark Of The Devil/97 Lovers/Aborigine/ Goodnight (12", p/s)	£25
87	Fire BLAZE 17T	They Suffocate At Night (Uncut Version)/Tunnel (Full Length Version) (12", p/s)	£15
87	Fire BLAZE 21T	Masters Of The Universe (Sanitised Version)/Manon/Silence (12", promo)	£25
87	Fire BLAZE 21T	Masters Of The Universe (Sanitised Version)/Manon/Silence (12", p/s)	£25
90	Fire BLAZE 44T	Is This House?/This House Is Condemned (12" promo, 1-sided)	£25
92	Gift GIF 1	O.U. (Gone Gone)/Space/O.U. (Gone Gone) (Radio Edit) 12" promo & press sheet)	£20

92	Caff CAFF 17	My Legendary Girlfriend/Sickly Grin/Back In L.A. (foldover p/s with insert in poly bag, 500 only) £100
92	Gift GIF 3	Babies/Styloroc (Nites Of Suburbia)/Sheffield : Sex City (12" promo with press sheet) ...£40
92	Gift GIF 3	Babies/Styloroc (Nites Of Suburbia)/Sheffield: Sex City (12", p/s) £30
93	Gift 7GIF6	Razzmatazz/Inside Susan/59 Lyndhurst Grove (p/s) £15
93	Gift GIF 6	Razzmatazz/Inside Susan : A Story In 3 Songs (Stacks/Inside Susan/59 Lyndhurst Grove) (12" promo with press sheet) £35
94	Island IS 595	THE SISTERS EP (gatefold, numbered) £18
94	Island IS 674	Do You Remember The First Time?/Street Lites (p/s) £15
94	Island 12 IS 574	Do You Remember The First Time?/Street Lites/The Babysitter (12", p/s) £20
96	Island ISC 567	Lipgloss/You're A Nightmare (p/s, reissue, red vinyl) £20
96	Island ISC 574	Do You Remember The First Time/Street Lites (p/s, reissue, brown vinyl, p/s) £15
96	Island ISC 613	Common People/Underwear (p/s, reissue, yellow vinyl) £60
96	Island ISC 620	Sorted For E's And Whizz/Miss-Shapes (p/s, reissue, blue vinyl) £30
96	Island ISC 623	Disco 2000/Ansaphone (p/s, reissue, orange vinyl) £40
96	Island 12 IS 623	Disco 2000 (7" Mix)/Ansaphone/Disco 2000 (Motiv & Gimp Dub)/Disco 2000 (Motiv & Discoid Mix) (12" p/s) £15
96	Island ISC 632	Something Changed/Mile End (p/s, reissue pink vinyl) £30
96	Island (No Cat. No.)	SINGLES COLLECTION (7 x 7" boxed set, coloured vinyl) £150
98	Island 12 ISX 695 DJ	This Is Hardcore/Ladies Man/The Professional/This Is Hardcore (End Of The Line Remix) (12", p/s. promo) £20

ALBUMS

84	Red Rhino REDLP 29	IT (mini-LP) £40
87	Fire FIRELP 5	FREAKS (LP) £25
92	Fire FIRE 11026	SEPARATIONS (LP) £40
93	Island ILPM 2076	INTRO - THE GIFT RECORDINGS (LP, printed inner) £50
93	Fire FIRELP 5	FREAKS (LP, reissue, barcode on rear of sleeve) £15
94	Island ILPS 8025	HIS 'N' HERS (LP) £150
94	Fire FIRE LP 36	MASTERS OF THE UNIVERSE (PULP ON FIRE 1985-86) £35
95	Island ILPS 8041	DIFFERENT CLASS (LP, die-cut sleeve with 12 images on six 12 x 12 inserts) £300
95	Island ILPS 8041	DIFFERENT CLASS (LP, with 1 insert) £150
96	Nectar NTMLP 521	COUNTDOWN 1992-1983 (LP) £40
98	Island ILPSD 8066	THIS IS HARDCORE (2LP, gatefold, with insert) £150
99	Cooking Vinyl COOK CD 178	PULPED 93-92 (4-CD box set with booklet) £30
00	Simply Vinyl SVLP 166	DIFFERENT CLASS (LP, reissue 180gm vinyl) £35
01	Island ILPS 8110	WE LOVE LIFE (LP) £70
12	Fire FV223E	IT (mini-LP, reissue) £20

(see also Jarvis Cocker, Relaxed Muscle)

PULP MUSIC

| 79 | Pulp Music PB 1 | Low Flying Aircraft/Something Just Behind My Back/So Lo (blank labels, some numbered up to 2,000 & signed, with handmade sleeve) ....£25 |
| 79 | Pulp Music PB 1 | Low Flying Aircraft/Something Just Behind My Back/So Lo (blank labels, some numbered up to 2,000 & signed) ....£20 |

PULSAR

| 76 | Decca SKL-R 5228 | POLLEN (LP) ....£20 |
| 77 | Decca TXS 119 | STRANDS OF THE FUTURE (LP, gatefold sleeve) ....£25 |

PULSE (1)

| 70 | Major Minor SMLP 64 | PULSE (LP) ....£60 |

PULSE (2)

| 82 | Tomato OK 1 | Trouble With John/Red Day In Dallas ....£40 |

PUMPHOUSE GANG

| 79 | Splash SP 001 | Spotlight/Lights Out (no p/s) ....£15 |

(see also Slush)

PUNCHERS

| 70 | Punch PH 46 | Sons Of Thunder (actually by Lee Perry & The Upsetters)/ Only If You Understand ....£25 |

(see also Upsetters, Chuck Jr)

PUNCHIN' JUDY

| 73 | Transatlantic TRA 272 | PUNCHIN' JUDY (LP, laminated front sleeve) ....£20 |

(see also Downliner Sect)

PUNCTURE

| 77 | Small Wonder SMALL 1 | Mucky Pup/Can't Rock'n'Roll (p/s) ....£50 |

PUNCTURED TOUGH GUY

| 85 | Xcentric Noise NINIH 1 | ACID RAINS EP ....£18 |

PUNISHMENT OF LUXURY

| 79 | United Artists UAG 30258 | LAUGHING ACADEMY (LP, with inner sleeve) ....£20 |

PUPILS

| 66 | Wing WL 1150 | A TRIBUTE TO THE ROLLING STONES (LP) ....£40 |
| 69 | Fontana SFL 13087 | A TRIBUTE TO THE ROLLING STONES (LP, reissue) ....£15 |

(see also Eyes)

PUPPETS

63	Pye 7N 15556	Poison Ivy/Everybody's Talking £50
64	Pye 7N 15625	Shake With Me/Three Boys Looking For Love (existence unconfirmed) £0
64	Pye 7N 15634	Baby Don't Cry/Shake With Me £60

(BERNARD) PRETTY PURDIE

| 68 | Direction 8-63290 | SOUL DRUMS (LP) ....£40 |
| 71 | Philips 6369 421 | SOUL IS ... (LP) ....£25 |

PURE EVIL
73 Hybrid HB20 — Never Trust A Woman/I See You Now £30

PURE GENIUS
95 Peer Pressure PEER 001 — Undercover/Unbelievable (12") £20
96 Peer Pressure PEER 002 — LAW OF THE LAND (12" EP) £20

PURE HELL
78 Golden Sphinx GSX 002 — These Boots Are Made For Walking/No Rules (p/s) £20

PURE LOVE & PLEASURE
70 Stateside SSL 5026 — A RECORD OF PURE LOVE AND PLEASURE (LP) £30

PURESSENCE
92 Damn Loud 2DM01 — PETROL SKIN (EP, 1,000 only) £30
93 Damn Loud 2DM02 — OFFSHORE (EP, 1,000 only) £35
96 Island ILPS 8946 — PURESSENCE (LP) £30
98 Island ILPS 8064 — ONLY FOREVER (LP) £25

PURE VIBES
98 PV 001 — Murder Tune/Shake The Pressure/Got To Work (12") £30
98 PV 002 — Shake The Pressure (Remix 1)/(Remix 2)/(Remix 3) (12", white label) £50

PURGE
69 Corn CP 101 — The Mayor Of Simpleton Hall/The Knave (p/s) £200
69 Corn CP 101 — The Mayor Of Simpleton Hall/The Knave (without p/s) £90

JAMES & BOBBY PURIFY
66 Stateside SS 547 — I'm Your Puppet/So Many Reasons £20
67 Stateside SS 595 — Wish You Didn't Have To Go/You Can't Keep A Good Man Down £15
67 Stateside SS 2016 — Shake A Tail Feather/Goodness Gracious £25
67 Stateside SS 2049 — Let Love Come Between Us/I Don't Want To Have To Wait £25
68 Stateside SS 2093 — Do Unto Me/Everybody Needs Somebody £20
67 Stateside SL 10206 — JAMES AND BOBBY PURIFY (LP) £60
67 Bell MBLL/SBLL 101 — THE PURE SOUND OF THE PURIFYS (LP) £40

PURITAN GUITARS
80 Riverside Records — £100 In 15 MInutes/Making It (p/s, stamped white labels) £20

PURITY RING
11 Transparent TP 027 — Ungirthed/Lofticries (p/s, 300 only) £15
12 4AD CAD 3218 — SHRINES (LP, gatefold, teal-coloured vinyl) £18

ALTON PURNELL
70 Dixie DIX 4 — TRAVELLING LIGHT (LP) £30

PURPLE ALGAE
95 Poor Person Prod. PPPR 7 — ADRIFT ON A SEA OF SOUND (LP, handmade sleeve & 2 inserts, no'd, 500 only) £15

PURPLE DISCO MACHINE
17 Sweat It Out! SWEATA016V — SOULMATIC (2-LP) £70
21 Sweat It Out! SWEATSV020 — EXOTICA (2-LP) £25

PURPLE GANG
67 Big T BIG 101 — Granny Takes A Trip/Bootleg Whisky £15
68 Transatlantic TRA 174 — THE PURPLE GANG STRIKES (LP) £60

PURPLE HAZE
85 S.R.S. SRS 6 — Hear It On The Radio (p/s) £55

PURPLE HEARTS
80 Fiction FIX 002/2383 568 — BEAT THAT! (LP) £20
(see also Rage)

PURPLE WINE
71 The Mental Health Council — It's My Mind/I'm Lonely/Friends (p/s) £100
71 NBR (No cat no) — PURPLE WINE (LP, plain white cover) £300

PURPLEMAN & PAPPA TULLO
83 Vista Sounds VSLP 4024 — PURPLEMAN SAVES PAPPA TOLLO IN A DANCEHALL (LP) £40

PURSON
13 Rise Above RISE7/173 — The Contract/Blueprints Of The Dream (p/s, 100 on black vinyl) £15
13 Rise Above RISELP 152 — THE CIRCLE & THE BLUE DOOR (LP. 'die hard' edition, 180 gram vinyl, A2 poster, patch and die-cut gatefold sleeve, 100 only) £50

PURSUIT OF COLOUR
84 Colour — LOVE PLAYS EGO: Can't Let You Go/Radomontade (b/w, p/s allegedly 50 copies only) £200

PUSSY (1)
69 Morgan Bluetown BT 5002 — PUSSY PLAYS (LP) £1500
09 Morgan Bluetown BT 5002 — PUSSY PLAYS (LP, reissue by Secret Records/Record Collector, 350 only with signed and numbered laminated insert) £40
(see also Angel Pavement, Fortes Mentum)

PUSSY (2)
72 Deram DM 368 — Feline Woman/Ska Child £35
(see also Jerusalem. Gillan, Deep Purple)

PUSSYFOOT
66 Decca F 12474 — Freeloader/Things That Still Remind Me £25
67 Decca F 12561 — Mr Hyde/Hasty Words £30
67 Pye 7N 17395 — Dee Dee Do Your Dance/Big Brown Eyes £30
68 Pye 7N 17520 — Good Times/Till You Don't Want Me Anymore £25

(see also Rare Breed)

PUSSY GALORE
87	Vinyl Drip SUK 001	GROOVY HATE FUCK (LP)	£25
87	Product Inc. 33PROD 19	RIGHT NOW (LP)	£18
89	Product INCLP 1	DIAL M FOR MOTHERFUCKER (LP)	£18
90	Rough Trade ROUGH 149	HISTORIA DE LA MUSICA ROCK (LP)	£18

(see also Jon Spencer Blues Explosion)

ASHA PUTHLI
73	CBS 65804	ASHA PUTHLI (LP)	£20
75	CBS 80978	SHE LOVES TO HEAR THE MUSIC (LP)	£15
76	CBS 81443	THE DEVIL IS LOOSE (LP)	£30

PUZZLE
69	Stateside SS 2146	Hey Medusa/Make The Children Happy	£25
72	Jam JAM 1	Houla/Do You Feel The Pain	£40
69	Stateside SSL 10285	PUZZLE (LP)	£50

PVRIS
16	(No label or cat. no.)	ACOUSTIC (10", p/s, white vinyl)	£50

PYLON
80	Armageddon ARM 1	Cool/Dub/Driving School/Danger!! (10")	£15

PYLONS
80	Hi Voltage HVVS 701	Marvel World/Spoof (p/s)	£50

NATASHA PYNE
66	Polydor 56713	It's All In Your Head/I'm A Dreamer	£15

PYRAMID
67	Deram DM 111	Summer Of Last Year/Summer Evening	£50

(see also Fairport Convention, Ian Matthews)

PYRAMIDS (U.K.)
67	President PT 161	Train Tour To Rainbow City/John Chewey	£20
69	JJ DB 1307	Stay With Him/Chicken Mary	£150
70	Trojan TR 7770	To Sir With Love/Reggae Shuffle	£15
71	Trojan TR 7803	All For You/All For You Version	£15
71	Creole CR 1003	Mosquito Bite/Mother's Bath	£20
71	Creole 1006	Can't Leave Now/Teardrops	£25
68	President PTL 1021	THE PYRAMIDS (LP)	£100

(see also Equals, Little Grants & Eddie, Seven Letters, Bruce Ruffin)

PYRAMIDS (U.S.)
64	London HLU 9847	Penetration/Here Comes Marsha	£50

Q

Q
82	Cocteau COC 6	Playback/Music's Gone (p/s)	£15

Q.A.X.
82	Vinyl Beat VB 001	Heart Alone/Does Me Good (p/s)	£15
82	Vinyl Beat VB 002	Lightning Touch/Unconfirmed (p/s)	£15

Q-CHASTIC
92	Rephlex 002EP	Q-CHASTIC EP (double pack, existence unconfirmed)	£200

(see also Aphex Twin)

Q.LAZZARUS
91	All Nations ANRS 001	Goodby Horses/White Lines (p/s)	£100
91	All Nations 12ANRS 001	Goodby Horses/Goodby Horses (7" version)/White Lines (12", p/s)	£150

QPR
67	Eyemark EMS 1008	QPR The Greatest/Supporters Support Us	£45

Q-PROJECT
92	QTIP 001	FREESTYLE FANATIC EP (12", stamped white label, 4 untitled tracks)	£39
93	Legend LEG 001	Return Of Q Project/Champion Sound/Night Moves (12")	£20

QRUUX ADU XA
82	Shooting Star STAR 007	Shakin' All Over/Robotics (p/s, as K.A.D.)	£15

QT'S
79	SRT SRTS/79/CUS 429	SAVAGE IN THE CITY EP	£35

QUAD (1)
92	Kinetix KNT 008	INSTELLABRIATION TRILOGY PART II: UR Her Egg/Spirit Of Laurel Way (12")	£15
93	Kinetix KNT 11	QUADRAVILLE EP (12")	£15
94	Kinetix KNT 12	AQUAVILLE REMIXES (12")	£15

QUAD (2)
97	Acme AC 8020LP	QUAD (LP, clear vinyl in printed clear PVC cover)	£30
97	Prescription DRUG 3	Q (LP, hand-made sleeve, 99 copies only)	£100

(see also Sun Dial)

CHRISTINE QUAITE
62	Oriole CB 1739	Guilty Eyes/Oh My!	£20
62	Oriole CB 1772	Your Nose Is Gonna Grow/Our Last Chance	£15
63	Oriole CB 1845	Mister Heartache/Whisper Wonderful Words	£15
63	Oriole CB 1876	In The Middle Of The Floor/Tell Me Mama	£60
63	Oriole CB 1921	I Believe In Love/Here She Comes	£20
64	Oriole CB 1945	Mister Stuck Up/Will You Be The Same Tomorrow	£15
65	Stateside SS 435	If You've Got A Heart/So Near So Far	£20
66	Stateside SS 482	Long After Tonight Is All Over/I'm Hoping	£50
66	Stateside SS 482	Long After Tonight Is All Over/I'm Hoping (DJ copy)	£100

QUAKER CITY BOYS
59	London HLU 8796	Teasin'/Won't Y' Come Out, Mary Ann	£15

QUAKERMAN
95	U Star US 005	QUAKERMAN EP (12")	£20

QUAKERS
65	Oriole CB 1992	I'm Ready/Down The Road A Piece	£150
65	Studio 36 KSP 109/110	She's Alright/Talk To Me (only 50 pressed)	£600

QUALITY DRIVEL
81	No Cure WHOOP 1	SUBLIMINAL CUTS EP (p/s)	£35

QUANDO QUANGO
85	Factory FACT 110	PIGS & BATTLESHIPS (LP)	£18
85	Factory FACT 110c	PIGS & BATTLESHIPS (cassette, with postcards)	£18

QUANTIC
00	Breakin' Bread BNB 002	We Got Soul/Fresh Rhythm	£25
01	Tru Thoughts TRU 014	Life In The Rain/Common Knowledge/Time Is The Enemy (12")	£15
04	Tru Thoughts TRU 064	Don't Joke With A Hungry Man/(Instrumental Version)/Furthest Moment/Don't Joke With A Hungry Man (Acapella) (12", featuring Spanky Wilson)	£35
01	Tru Thoughts TRU LP 016	THE 5TH EXOTIC (2-LP)	£40
02	Tru Thoughts TRU LP 034	APRICOT MORNING (2-LP)	£30
04	Tru Thoughts TRU LP 062	MISHAPS HAPPENING (2-LP)	£15
06	Tru Thoughts TRU LP 100	AN ANNOUNCEMENT TO MAKE (2xLP)	£20

QUANTIC SOUL ORCHESTRA
03	Tru Thoughts TRU LP 029	STAMPEDE (LP)	£30
05	Tru Thoughts TRU LP 074	PUSHIN' ON (LP)	£30
07	Tru Thoughts TRU LP 139	TROPIDELICO (LP)	£25

QUARRY
87	QP QP 001	Just Another Day/Promised Land	£20

QUARRY MEN
58	'P.F. Phillips Kensington'	That'll Be The Day/In Spite Of All The Danger (78 rpm shellac acetate, handwritten labels, 1 copy only, owned by Paul McCartney)	£200000
81	'Percy Philips, Kensington'	That'll Be The Day/In Spite Of All The Danger (78rpm, private pressing reproduction of 1958 demo disc, repro Parlophone co. sleeve, 25 only)	£5000
81	'Percy Philips, Kensington'	That'll Be The Day/In Spite Of All The Danger (45rpm, private pressing reproduction of 1958 demo disc, repro Parlophone co. sleeve, 25 only)	£5000

(see also Beatles, Trad Grads)

QUARTER NOTES
57	Parlophone R 4365	My Fantasy/Ten Minutes To Midnight	£15

JOE QUARTERMAN & FREE SOUL
73	GSF GS 504	JOE QUARTERMAN & FREE SOUL (LP)	£50

QUARTZ (2)
77	Jet UP 36290	Sugar Rain/Street Fighting Lady/Mainline Riders	£15
80	Logo GOT 387	Satan's Serenade/Bloody Fool/Roll Over Beethoven (live) (12", p/s, blue vinyl)	£20
80	Logo GOT 387	Satan's Serenade/Bloody Fool/Roll Over Beethoven (live) (12", p/s, red vinyl)	£15
77	Jet UAG 30081	QUARTZ (LP, with inner sleeve)	£50
79	Jet JETLP 233	DELETED (LP, in sealed brown paper bag with insert. Reissue of 1st LP)	£18
80	Reddingtons R.R. REDD 001	QUARTZ LIVE - COUNT DRACULA (LP, in b&w 'live' sleeve)	£15
80	MCA MCF 3080	STAND UP AND FIGHT (LP, with lyric insert)	£15
83	Heavy Metal HMRPD 9	AGAINST ALL ODDS (LP, picture disc)	£20

(see also Black Sabbath, Copperfield, Bandy Legs)

QUASAR
82	Q QUA 1	FIRE IN THE SKY (LP, with insert)	£20

(see also Solstice)

QUASI
98	Domino WIGLP 55	FEATURING "BIRDS" (LP)	£20
99	Domino WIGLP 69	FIELD STUDIES (LP)	£20
01	Domino WIGLP 97	THE SWORD OF GOD (2-LP)	£18

QUATERMASS (1)
70	Harvest SVHL 775	QUATERMASS (LP, gatefold sleeve, no EMI logo on label)	£300
75	Harvest SHSM 2002	QUATERMASS (LP, reissue, different sleeve)	£40

(see also Ian Gillan Band, Episode Six, Hard Stuff)

QUATERMASS (2)
97	Metropolitan MM 027	The Judgement (12", no p/s)	£15

QUATOR
72	BBC RESL 6	Spy Trap/Playgirl	£30

QUATRAIN
69	Polydor 583 743	QUATRAIN (LP)	£60

SUZI QUATRO
72	Rak RAK 134	Rolling Stone/Brain Confusion (For All The Lonely People)	£30
73	Rak PSR 355	Primitive Love/Shakin' All Over (promo only)	£30
73	SRAK 505	SUZI QUATRO (LP)	£20
74	RAK SRAK 509	QUATRO (LP)	£15

FINLAY QUAYE
97	Epic 488758	MAVERICK A STRIKE (LP, insert)	£25

QUBISM
94	em:t 2294	QUBISM (CD, digipak)	£50

QUE BONO
81	Naked BARE 1	Making Noise/Emelia	£15

QUEEN

SINGLES
73	EMI EMI 2036	Keep Yourself Alive/Son And Daughter	£40
74	EMI EMI 2121	Seven Seas Of Rhye/See What A Fool I've Been (later solid centre pressing)	£40
75	EMI EMI 2256	Now I'm Here/Lily Of The Valley (later solid centre pressing)	£35
75	EMI EMI 2375	Bohemian Rhapsody/I'm In Love With My Car (p/s; beware counterfeits with 'computer-scanned' logo)	£35
76	EMI EMI 2494	You're My Best Friend/'39 (solid centre)	£30
76	EMI EMI 2565	Somebody To Love/White Man (p/s, push out centre, beware of counterfeit sleeves)	£25
76	EMI EMI 2565	Somebody To Love/White Man (solid centre)	£30
78	EMI EMI 2757	Spread Your Wings/Sheer Heart Attack (p/s, solid centre)	£15
78	EMI EMI 2870	Bicycle Race/Fat Bottomed Girls (different p/s for export to Belgium)	£200
79	EMI EMI 2910	Don't Stop Me Now/In Only Seven Days (p/s, solid centre)	£30
79	EMI EMI 2959	Love Of My Life (live)/Now I'm Here (live)	£20
82	EMI EMI 5293	Body Language/Life Is Real (Song For Lennon) (p/s, with Queen in red type on front of sleeve)	£80
82	EMI 12EMI 5325	Backchat (Extended)/Staying Power (12", p/s)	£20
84	EMI QUEEN 2	I Want To Break Free (Remix)/Machines (Back To Humans) ('Roger' p/s, with gold lettering)	£15
84	EMI QUEEN 2	I Want To Break Free (Remix)/Machines (Back To Humans) ('John' p/s, with gold lettering)	£18
84	EMI 12QUEEN 2	I Want To Break Free (Extended Remix)/Machines (Back To Humans) (12", p/s, with red background with gold lettering)	£20
84	EMI QUEEN 3	It's A Hard Life/Is This The World We Created...? ('Roger Taylor' overprinted photo p/s)	£20
84	EMI 12QUEEN 3	It's A Hard Life (Extended)/It's A Hard Life/ Is This The World We Created...? (12")	£25
84	EMI 12QUEENP 3	It's A Hard Life/Is This The World We Created...? (12", picture disc)	£20
84	EMI QUEEN 4	Hammer To Fall (Edit)/Tear It Up ('live' p/s, withdrawn)	£100
84	EMI 12 QUEEN 4	Hammer To Fall (The Headbangers Mix)/Tear It Up (12", 'live' p/s, withdrawn)	£150
84	EMI QUEEN 5	Man On The Prowl/Keep Passing The Open Windows (unreleased, white label test pressings only)	£150
84	EMI G 45 1	You're My Best Friend/Killer Queen (re-issue, Golden 45's series)	£20
85	EMI 12QUEEN 6	One Vision (Extended Vision)/Blurred Vision (12", printed PVC sleeve & red inner)	£30
86	EMI 12QUEENP7	A Kind Of Magic (Extended Version)/Don't Lose Your Head (Instrumental Version) (12", picture disc)	£35
86	EMI QUEEN P8	Friends Will Be Friends/Seven Seas Of Rhye (picture disc)	£40
86	EMI 12QUEEN 9	Who Wants To Live Forever (7" Version)/(Album Version)/Killer Queen/ Who Wants To Live Forever (Piano Version) (12", p/s)	£18
89	Parlophone CDQUEEN 10	I Want It All (Album Version)/Hang On In There/I Want It All (Single Version) (CD, picture disc)	£20
89	Parlophone QUEEN PD 11	Breakthru' (7" Mix)/Stealin' (shaped picture disc, 12" PVC sleeve with insert)	£20
89	Parlophone QUEEN PD 11	Breakthru' (7" Mix)/Stealin' (uncut picture disc, 12" PVC sleeve with insert)	£350
89	Parlophone 12QUEENX12	The Invisible Man (12" Version)/The Invisible Man (7" Version)/ Hijack My Heart (12", clear vinyl, PVC sleeve with insert)	£20
89	Parlophone CD QUEEN 12	The Invisible Man (12" Version)/Hijack My Heart/ The Invisible Man (Single Version) (CD)	£30
89	Parlophone QUEEN P14	Scandal/My Life Has Been Saved (poster p/s)	£20
89	Parlophone 12QUEENS 14	Scandal (12" Version)/My Life Has Been Saved/Scandal (7" Version)/ (12", p/s, 1-sided, B-side etched with group's signatures)	£25
89	Parlophone QUEEN H15	The Miracle/Stone Cold Crazy (live) (orange hologram p/s)	£15
89	Parlophone QUEEN H15	The Miracle/Stone Cold Crazy (live) (proof sleeve with negative hologram p/s)	£300
89	Parlophone 12QUEEN 15	The Miracle/Stone Cold Crazy (live)/My Melancholy Blues (live) (12", yellow p/s)	£15
89	Parlophone 12QUEENP 15	The Miracle/Stone Cold Crazy (live)/My Melancholy Blues (live) (12", turquoise p/s with print)	£20
89	Parlophone QUEENCD 15	The Miracle/Stone Cold Crazy (live)/My Melancholy Blues (live) (CD)	£30
91	Parlophone 12QUEEN 16	Innuendo (Explosive Version)/Under Pressure/Bijou (12", p/s)	£18
91	Parlophone 12QUEEN PD16	Innuendo (Explosive Version)/Under Pressure/Bijou (12", picture disc, PVC sleeve with insert)	£35
91	Parlophone QUEEN PD 17	I'm Going Slightly Mad/The Hitman (shaped picture disc with insert)	£25
91	Parlophone QUEEN PD 17	I'm Going Slightly Mad/The Hitman (uncut picture disc with insert)	£450
91	Parlophone 12QUEENG 17	I'm Going Slightly Mad/The Hitman/Lost Opportunity (12", gatefold p/s)	£25
91	Parlophone 12QUEEN PD18	Headlong/All God's People/Mad The Swine (12", clear vinyl picture disc, with insert in PVC sleeve)	£20
91	Parlophone QUEEN C19	The Show Must Go On/Keep Yourself Alive (cassette)	£15
91	Parlophone 12QUEENSG 19	The Show Must Go On/Keep Yourself Alive/Queen Talks (12", 1-sided, B-side etched with group's signatures, gatefold p/s)	£20
91	Parlophone QUEEN 19/20	The Show Must Go On/Bohemian Rhapsody (unissued, no p/s)	£500
95	Parlophone QUEENLH 24	Let Me Live/Fat Bottomed Girls (Jukebox 45, black vinyl no p/s)	£15

MINT VALUE £

96	Parlophone QUEENPD 24	**Let Me Live/Fat Bottomed Girls/Bicycle Race** (picture disc with poster)	£15
97	Parlophone QUEENLH 26	**No-One But You/We Will Rock You** (Original 1977 version) (unreleased)	£20
97	Parlophone QUEEN 26	**No-One But You** (Only The Good Die Young)**/Princes Of The Universe/ We Will Rock You** (Rick Rubin 'Ruined' Remix)**/Gimme The Prize** (Instrumental 'Eye' Remix) (Unissued 7")	£175
08	Parlophone 2370097	**C-Lebrity/Fire And Water** (picture disc, with Paul Rodgers)	£15
11	Island 2765780	**Stormtroopers In Stilettos/Stone Cold Crazy/Keep Yourself Alive** (numbered picture disc in PVC sleeve, 2000 only)	£15
15	Virgin/EMI 0602547500809	**Bohemian Rhapsody/I'm In Love With My Car** (12", p/s)	£25
17	Virgin 0602557907667	**We Are The Champions/We Will Rock You** (12", p/s)	£15
19	EMI 7735248	**Bohemian Rhapsody/I'm In Love With My Car** (reissue, purple/yellow vinyl, p/s)	£20
21	EMI 0602435763033	**Radio Ga Ga/I'm In Love With My Car** (blue vinyl, Roger Taylor p/s, numbered)	£100
21	EMI 0602435763040	**We Will Rock You/Sail Away Sweet Sister** (red vinyl, Brian May p/s, numbered)	£250
21	EMI 602435763026	**Spread Your Wings/One Year Of Love** (green vinyl, John Deacon p/s, numbered)	£100
21	EMI 602435763057	**Somebody To Love/You Take My Breath Away** (yellow vinyl, Freddie Mercury p/s, numbered)	£125

ALBUMS

73	EMI EMC 3006	**QUEEN** (LP, 1st pressing with "KIP-HUGGYPOO KISSY" hand-etched into side 1 run out groove, laminated cover)	£100
74	EMI EMA 767	**QUEEN II** (LP, laminated gatefold sleeve, lyric inner sleeve)	£50
74	EMI EMA 767	**QUEEN II** (laminated gatefold sleeve, 2nd pressing, (P) **1974 below Trident logo on both sides**)	£15
74	EMI EMC 3061	**SHEER HEART ATTACK** (LP, laminated sleeve, inner lyric sleeve)	£50
75	EMI EMTC 103	**A NIGHT AT THE OPERA** (LP, 1st pressing, embossed gatefold sleeve with cut corner inner, YAX 5063/4-2 "BLAIRS" in run-off)	£70
75	EMI EMTC 103	**A NIGHT AT THE OPERA** (LP, later pressings, embossed gatefold sleeve with 'shaped' inner sleeve)	£35
76	EMI EMTC 104	**A DAY AT THE RACES** (LP, gatefold, inner sleeve)	£40
77	EMI EMA 784	**NEWS OF THE WORLD** (LP, gatefold with lyric inner sleeve)	£40
78	EMI EMA 788	**JAZZ** (LP, gatefold sleeve with attached poster, inner sleeve has band shot on one side and track listing on the other)	£40
79	EMI EMSP 330	**LIVE KILLERS** (2-LP)	£25
80	EMI EMA 795	**THE GAME** (LP, inner sleeve)	£20
81	EMI EMTV30	**GREATEST HITS** (LP)	£30
81	EMI EMTV 30	**GREATEST HITS** (LP, mispress, side 2 plays "Anne Murray's Greatest Hits")	£50
82	EMI EMA 797	**HOT SPACE** (LP, inner)	£20
82	EMI FA 3040	**QUEEN** (LP, 'fame' reissue)	£15
84	Fame FA 4130991	**QUEEN II** (reissue, 'Fame' series)	£15
85	EMI QB 1	**THE COMPLETE WORKS** (14-LP box set including "Complete Vision" LP of non-LP tracks, 2 booklets & map, numbered; 600 autographed)	£1000
85	EMI QB 1	**THE COMPLETE WORKS** (14-LP box set including "Complete Vision" LP of non-LP tracks, 2 booklets & map, numbered)	£300
86	EMI EU 3509	**A KIND OF MAGIC** (LP, gatefold)	£20
86	EMI EU 3509	**A KIND OF MAGIC** ('Princes Of The Universe' proof sleeve; unreleased)	£500
86	EMI EMC 3519	**LIVE MAGIC** (LP, gatefold)	£15
89	Band Of Joy BOJLP 001	**QUEEN AT THE BEEB** (LP)	£30
89	EMI PCSD 107	**THE MIRACLE** (LP, inner)	£20
91	Parlophone PCSD 115	**INNUENDO** (LP, inner)	£50
91	Parlophone PMTV 2	**GREATEST HITS 2** (2-LP, embossed gatefold sleeve)	£25
92	Parlophone PCSP 725	**LIVE AT WEMBLEY** (2-LP, gatefold sleeve)	£150
92	Parlophone CDQTEL 0001	**BOX OF TRIX** (CD, box set, with video, book, poster, T-shirt, patch & badge)	£60
92	Parlophone CQTEL 0001	**BOX OF TRIX** (cassette, box set, with video, book, poster, T-shirt, patch & badge)	£50
95	Parlophone 724383608812	**MADE IN HEAVEN** (LP, stickered gatefold sleeve with inserts, ivory vinyl)	£100
95	Parlophone 724383608812	**MADE IN HEAVEN** (LP, gatefold sleeve, black vinyl)	£60
95	Parlophone QUEEN BOX 20	**ULTIMATE QUEEN** (20 x CD set, in numbered glazed box and numbered cardboard outer box, with Freddie hologram and 2 booklets)	£450
97	EMI LPCENT 25	**A NIGHT AT THE OPERA** (LP, reissue, EMI 100 Centenary, stickered sleeve)	£40
99	Parlophone 724352345211	**GREATEST HITS III** (2-LP with inners)	£100
99	Parlophone 724333994621	**A DAY AT THE RACES** (LP, remaster, reissue, 180gm)	£50
05	Parlophone 338 4781	**A NIGHT AT THE OPERA** (LP, reissue, half-speed remaster)	£20
05	Parlophone 724386321114	**QUEEN ON FIRE** (3-LP box set)	£75
09	EMI QUEENLP 1	**QUEEN** (LP, remastered)	£18
09	EMI QUEENLP 2	**QUEEN II** (LP, remastered)	£18
09	EMI QUEENLP 3	**SHEER HEART ATTACK** (LP, remastered)	£18
09	EMI QUEEN 4	**A NIGHT AT THE OPERA** (LP, reissue)	£20
09	EMI QUEEN 5	**A DAY AT THE RACES** (LP, reissue)	£18
09	EMI QUEEN 6	**NEWS OF THE WORLD** (LP, reissue, remastered)	£20
09	EMI QUEEN 10	**HOT SPACE** (LP, reissue, remastered)	£20
09	EMI QUEEN 12	**A KIND OF MAGIC** (LP, reissue, remastered)	£20
09	EMI 686644-1	**ABSOLUTE GREATEST** (3-LP box set)	£90
10	EMI QUEEN 7	**JAZZ** (LP, reissue, remastered, poster)	£25
14	Virgin EMI 0602537910748	**LIVE AT THE RAINBOW 74** (4LP, box set, inner sleeves, hype sticker)	£150
15	Virgin EMI 0602547500748	**A NIGHT AT THE ODEON** (2LP, gatefold, printed inners, 180g, download card)	£100
15	Virgin EMI 0602547500748	**A NIGHT AT THE ODEON** (CD/DVD/BD/12" box set, book, sticker, poster, replica programme)	£80
15	EMI 00602547202642	**QUEEN** (LP, remastered, 180gm)	£15
15	EMI 00602547288240	**QUEEN II** (LP, remastered, 180gm)	£15
15	EMI 00602547202680	**SHEER HEART ATTACK** (LP, remastered, 180gm)	£15
15	EMI 00602547202727	**NEWS OF THE WORLD** (LP, reissue, 180gm)	£20
15	EMI 00602547202758	**THE GAME** (LP, reissue, remastered, 180gm)	£20
16	Virgin EMI 0602557082227	**ON AIR** (3LP, box set, 180g, printed inners)	£60

16	Virgin EMI 0602557082227	**ON AIR** (6CD box set, card wallets, booklet)..£60
17	EMI 0602567090441	**NEWS OF THE WORLD** (LP, Marvel X-Men edition, with alternative cover, art print, stickers sleeve, numbered, sold at 2017 London Comic Con and Queen online store, around 250 copies, 180gm)...£1000
18	EMI 6781164	**JAZZ** (LP, reissue, picture disc, 1978 copies) £80
19	EMI 00602577626302	**THE WORKS** (LP, reissue, clear vinyl, HMV exclusive, stickered sleeve)....................£40
19	Virgin EMI 0602567988724	**BOHEMIAN RHAPSODY** (THE ORIGINAL SOUNDTRACK) (2LP, gatefold, printed inners).....£30
19	Virgin EMI 0602567988762	**BOHEMIAN RHAPSODY** (THE ORIGINAL SOUNDTRACK) (2LP, picture disc, die-cut gatefold,)..£60
21	EMI 00602507489465	**FLASH GORDON** (LP, reissue, remastered, picture disc, 1980 copies) £60
21	EMI 00602438852925	**QUEEN - THE GREATEST** (2LP, reissue of Greatest Hits, in slipcase, pop-up store/online exclusive) £100
22	EMI 00602508911330	**THE MIRACLE** (COLLECTOR'S EDITION) (LP/5CD/DVD/BD, book, memorabilia, without 'Teaser Tape') £100
22	EMI 00602508911330	**THE MIRACLE** (COLLECTOR'S EDITION) (LP/6CD/DVD/BD, book, ,memorabilia, contains 'Teaser Tape') £350
22	EMI 00602445904884	**THE MIRACLE** (LP, picture disc, die-cut sleeve, numbered limited edition, webstore exclusive) £40

PROMOS

73	EMI 2036	**Keep Yourself Alive/Son And Daughter** (demo copy, release date of (15.6.73) **on label, different mix of A side to that later released)**..£500
73	EMI 2036	**Keep Yourself Alive/Son And Daughter** (second demo copy, release date of (6.7.73) **on label)**..£250
73	EMI (no cat. no.)	**QUEEN** (LP, white label, EMI conference custom issue, die-cut sleeve, with outer envelope) £500
73	EMI (no cat. no.)	**QUEEN** (LP, white label, EMI conference custom issue, die-cut sleeve, without outer envelope) £400
74	EMI 2121	**Seven Seas Of Rhye/See What A Fool I've Been** (demo, with release date of (25.2.74) **on label)**..£80
75	EMI 2256	**Now I'm Here/Lily Of The Valley** (demo, with release date (17.1.75) **on label)** £80
77	EMI 2593	**Tie Your Mother Down/You And I** (demo) £45
77	EMI SP SLP 241 A1U	**We Will Rock You/We Are The Champions/Spread Your Wings** (12", 1-sided)............£1000
77	EMI 2623	**QUEEN'S FIRST EP: Good Old Fashioned Lover Boy/Death On Two Legs/ Tenement Funster/White Queen** (As It Began) (demo copy, p/s) £45
77	EMI 2708	**We Will Rock You/We Will Rock You** (demo, mispressing, We Are The Champions label on A side) £75
77	EMI 2708	**We Are The Champions/We Will Rock You** (demo) £40
77	EMI (no cat. no.)	**NEWS OF THE WORLD** (LP, box set, with factory sample sticker, 5 photos, bio, badge & demo copy of "We Are The Champions"/"We Will Rock You", 50 only).................£1000
78	EMI EMI 2375	**Bohemian Rhapsody/I'm In Love With My Car** (EMI 'Queen's Award For Export' in-house edition, blue vinyl, Queen crest label, hand-numbered, purple p/s., with invites, matches, pen, ticket, menu, outer card sleeve, scarf & EMI goblets in card box) £5000
78	EMI EMI 2375	**Bohemian Rhapsody/I'm In Love With My Car** (EMI 'Queen's Award For Export' in-house edition, blue vinyl, Queen crest label, hand-numbered, purple p/s., with outer 'EMI International' carrying envelope) £4000
78	EMI EMI 2375	**Bohemian Rhapsody/I'm In Love With My Car** (EMI 'Queen's Award For Export' in-house edition, blue vinyl, Queen crest label, hand-numbered, purple p/s...£3500
	(The blue vinyl 'Bohemian Rhapsody' was limited to 200 numbered copies)	
78	EMI 2757	**Spread Your Wings/Sheer Heart Attack** (demo) £45
78	EMI 2870	**Bicycle Race/Fat Bottomed Girls** (demo) £45
79	EMI EMI 2910	**Don't Stop Me Now/In Only Seven Days** (demo in p/s) £35
79	EMI 2959	**Love Of My Life** (live)**/Now I'm Here** (live) (demo) £60
79	EMI 5001	**Crazy Little Thing Called Love/We Will Rock You** (live) (demo) £35
80	EMI 5022	**Save Me/Let Me Entertain You** (live) (demo) £35
80	EMI 5076	**Play The Game/A Human Body** (demo) £35
80	EMI 5102	**Another One Bites The Dust/Dragon Attack** (demo) £35
84	EMI QUEEN 1	**Radio Ga Ga** (Edit)**/I Go Crazy** ('video shoot' p/s, unreleased, proofs only).............£750
84	EMI QUEENDJ 5	**Man On The Prowl/Thank God It's Christmas** £150
84	Flexi Ltd. (no cat. no.)	**Excerpts From Their New Album 'The Works'** (flexidisc sampler, p/s) £15
86	(no label or cat. no.)	**A Message From Queen** (cassette, 1st Fan Club Convention issue) £20
86	EMI 12 QUEEN 7	**A Kind Of Magic/A Dozen Red Roses For My Darling** (12" promo, white label with sticker) £40
86	EMI 12 QUEEN 7	**A Kind Of Magic/A Kind Of Magic** (12" promo, white label with sticker) £30
86	Parlophone EMCDV 2	**THE HIGHLANDER SELECTION** (CD Video, 50 only)..£400
86	EMI/Channel 4 QUEEN 7	**NETWORK QUEEN** ('A Kind Of Magic' 7" housed in promotional fold-out sleeve that opens up to depict illustrated band playing to audience. 50 made to promote TV advertising for July 1986 Wembley Stadium concerts)...£1000
89	Flexi Ltd. (no cat. no.)	**A Message From Queen** (flexidisc, 4th Fan Club Convention issue)..............................£25
89	Parlophone TEASER 1	**THE TEASER TAPE** (cassette, edits sampler for "The Miracle") £15
89	Parlophone CDPROMOQU 1	**I Want It All** (1-track CD promo)..£30
89	Parlophone QUEEN 10	**I Want It All/Hang On In There** (p/s in promo gatefold p/s, press release, B&W photo)...£80
89	Parlophone 12 QUEENX 12	**The Invisible Man** (12" Version)**/The Invisible Man** (7" Version)**/ Hijack My Heart** (12", clear vinyl test pressing with Queen logos within vinyl) £500
91	Parlophone (no cat. no.)	**A SAMPLE OF MAGIC** (CD, segued excerpts from "Greatest Hits 2").............................£60
91	EMI QUEEN DJ 16	**Innuendo/Innuendo** (12" promo, p/s) £30
91	Parlophone 12 QUEENDJ 18	**Headlong/All God's People/Mad The Swine** (12" promo) £25
91	Parlophone (no cat. no.)	**HINTS OF INNUENDO** (cassette, edits/out-takes sampler for "Innuendo").....................£30
91	EMI	**INNUENDO** (Promo boxed set with CD, cassette, calendar, folder, bio & photos).........£60
91	Parlophone (no cat. no.)	**EIGHT GOOD REASONS TO BUY GREATEST HITS 2** (cassette, segued excerpts)...............£30
94	EMI CD DIG 1	**DIGITAL MASTER SAMPLER** (CD, picture disc)..£45
95	EMI QUEEN DJ95	**Bohemian Rhapsody/I'm In Love With My Car** (purple vinyl, hand numbered, p/s, Fan Club Convention issue, 2,000 only)...£250
95	Parlophone QUEENLHDJ 21	**Heaven For Everyone** (Album Version)**/Heaven For Everyone** (Single Version) (jukebox issue, plain white sleeve, with poster, fold-out card & jukebox strip)......................£20

MINT VALUE £

96	Parlophone VIRGIN 1	**Heaven For Everyone/Heaven For Everyone** (12", white label, Virgin Radio 'Queen Day' competition prize, black 'Queen crest' p/s with handwritten details; mispressing with same tracks both sides, unreleased)	£0
96	Parlophone VIRGIN 2	**Heaven For Everyone** (12", 1-sided, white labels, Virgin Radio 'Queen Day' competition prize, 'Queen crest' p/s w/ handwritten details, 15 copies only)	£750
96	Parlophone VIRGIN 3	**A Winter's Tale** (12", 1-sided, white labels, Virgin Radio 'Queen Day' competition prize, 'Queen crest' p/s with handwritten details, 15 only)	£750
96	Parlophone VIRGIN 4	**Mother Love** (12", 1-sided, white labels, Virgin Radio 'Queen Day' competition prize, 'Queen crest' p/s with handwritten details, 15 only)	£750
96	Parlophone VIRGIN 5	**Let Me Live** (12", 1-sided, white labels, Virgin Radio 'Queen Day' competition prize, 'Queen crest' p/s with handwritten details, 15 only)	£750
96	Parlophone VIRGIN 6	**You Don't Fool Me** (12", 1-sided, white labels, Virgin Radio 'Queen Day' competition prize, 'Queen crest' p/s with handwritten details, 15 only)	£750
96	Parlophone VIRGIN 7	**It's A Beautiful Day** (12", 1-sided, white labels, Virgin Radio 'Queen Day' competition prize, 'Queen crest' p/s with handwritten details, 15 only)	£750
96	Parlophone VIRGIN 8	**I Was Born To Love You** (12", 1-sided, white labels, Virgin Radio 'Queen Day' competition prize, 'Queen crest' p/s with handwritten details, 15 only)	£750
96	Parlophone 12 RDJ 6446	**You Don't Fool Me** (Remixes) (12" promo, orange vinyl)	£50
97	Parlophone CDQT 1	**QUEEN ROCKS** (CD, Brian May interview)	£75
99	EMI QUEENWL 28	**Under Pressure** (Remixes) (with David Bowie) (12", white label, unreleased mix, promo only)	£30

MISPRESSINGS

78	EMI EMI 2870	**Bicycle Race/Fat Bottomed Girls** (p/s, B-side plays Crystal Gayle's 3 O'Clock In The Morning or Dollar track)	£50
79	EMI EMI 5001	**Crazy Little Thing Called Love/We Will Rock You** (live) (p/s, both sides play "We Will Rock You")	£40
80	EMI EMI 5076	**Play The Game/A Human Body** (p/s, both sides play "A Human Body")	£30
86	Parlophone RP 5452	**BEATLES: Paperback Writer/Rain** (picture disc, A-side plays Friends Will Be Friends)	£75

(see also Freddie Mercury, Brian May, Roger Taylor, Larry Lurex, Cross, Immortals, Hilary Hilary, Man Friday & Jive Junior)

QUEEN LATIFAH
93	Motown 530 272 1	**BLACK REIGN** (LP)	£45

QUEENS OF THE STONE AGE
00	Interscope 497 387-7	**The Lost Art Of Keeping A Secret/Ode To Clarrisa** (p/s)	£30
02	Interscope 497 812-7	**No One Knows/Tension Head** (Live From The Mean Fiddler) (p/s, grey vinyl)	£30
05	No label FUNMACHINE1	**The Fun Machine Took A Shit And Died/Commentary** (white label, signed)	£20
98	Roadrunner RR 8674-2	**QUEENS OF THE STONE AGE** (2-LP)	£150
00	Interscope 490 683-1	**X** (LP, gatefold sleeve)	£100
02	Interscope 493435-1	**SONGS FOR THE DEAF** (2-LP, gatefold)	£150
05	Interscope 490 864-1	**RATED R** (LP reissue)	£40
11	Music On Vinyl MOVLP 250	**LULLABIES TO PARALYZE** (2-LP, one side etched)	£30
11	Music On Vinyl MOVLP 250	**LULLABIES TO PARALYZE** (2-LP, red vinyl, one side etched)	£30
11	Rekords REK 001LP	**QUEENS OF THE STONE AGE** (2-LP reissue)	£100
13	Matador OLE 1048-1	**...LIKE CLOCKWORK** (2-LP, blue sleeve)	£30
13	Matador OLE 1048-1	**...LIKE CLOCKWORK** (2-LP, black artwork, 800 only)	£40
13	Matador OLE 1040-0	**...LIKE CLOCKWORK** (2-LP, red sleeve, 180 gram edition, booklet)	£35
17	Matador OLE 11251	**VILLAINS** (2-LP, 1 side etched)	£25

QUEENSRYCHE
94	EMI MTL 1081	**PROMISED LAND** (LP, clear vinyl)	£20

QUEERS
90	Shakin Street YEAH HUP 010	**GROW UP** (LP)	£30

QUEST
15	System SYSTM 011	**Belly Of The Beast/EGOLESS: Dub Liberation** (12")	£30

? & THE MYSTERIANS
66	Cameo Parkway C 428	**96 Tears/Midnight Hour**	£40
66	Cameo Parkway C 441	**I Need Somebody/'8' Teen**	£45
67	Cameo Parkway C 467	**Can't Get Enough Of You, Baby/Smokes**	£30
67	Cameo Parkway C 479	**Girl** (You Captivate Me)**/Got To**	£25
67	Cameo Parkway C 496	**Do Something To Me/Love Me Baby**	£25

QUESTIONS (1)
68	Decca F 22740	**We Got Love/Something Wonderful**	£35

TOMMY QUICKLY (& REMO FOUR)
63	Piccadilly 7N 35137	**Tip Of My Tongue/Heaven Only Knows** (solo)	£30

(see also Remo Four)

QUICKSAND
70	Carnaby CNS 4015	**Passing By/Cobblestones**	£15
73	Dawn DNLS 3056	**HOME IS WHERE I BELONG** (LP, gatefold sleeve, pink 'sun' label)	£150

(see also Man)

QUICKSILVER MESSENGER SERVICE
68	Capitol (S)T 2904	**QUICKSILVER MESSENGER SERVICE** (LP, black label with rainbow rim)	£80
69	Capitol E-(S)T 120	**HAPPY TRAILS** (LP)	£35
70	Capitol E-ST 391	**SHADY GROVE** (LP)	£20
70	Capitol EA-ST 498	**JUST FOR LOVE** (LP)	£20
71	Capitol EA-ST 630	**WHAT ABOUT ME?** (LP)	£15
72	Capitol E-SW 819	**QUICKSILVER** (LP)	£15
83	Psycho PSYCHO 10	**MAIDEN OF THE CANCER MOON** (2-LP)	£40

(see also Dino Valenti, Nicky Hopkins)

QUIET FIVE
65	Parlophone R 5273	**When The Morning Sun Dries The Dew/Tomorrow I'll Be Gone** (in p/s)	£20

66	Parlophone R 5421	Homeward Bound/Ain't It Funny What Some Lovin' Can Do	£18

(see also Kris Ife, Richard Barnes)

QUIET SUN

75	Island HELP 19	MAINSTREAM (LP, black label with pink 'i' label, printed 'sun' inner)	£40
77	Polydor 2343 093	MAINSTREAM (LP, reissue)	£20
12	Vinyl 180/Expression VIN180LP 043	MAINSTREAM (2LP, reissue, gatefold, printed inners, 180 g)	£35
12	Expression EXPCD 2R	MAINSTREAM (CD, hardback digipak)	£40

(see also Phil Manzanera, Roxy Music, Matching Mole)

QUIET WORLD

69	Dawn DNS 1001	Miss Whittington/There Is A Mountain (as Quiet World Of Lea & John)	£40
70	Dawn DNS 1005	Children Of The World/Love Is Walking	£40
70	Dawn DNLS 3007	THE ROAD (LP)	£200

(see also Genesis)

QUIK

67	Deram DM 121	Love Is A Beautiful Thing/Bert's Apple Crumble	£250
67	Deram DM 139	King Of The World/My Girl	£60
67	Deram DM 155	I Can't Sleep/Soul Full Of Sorrow	£80
98	Klooks Kleek 007	Bert's Apple Crumble/THE SONICS: The Witch (reissue)	£15

(see also Meddy Evils)

QUILL (1)

79	Kite KR 10	LIVE (LP)	£15

QUILL (2)

80	Kite KRS 10A	Love In A Jar/Time (no p/s)	£18

QUINCEHARMON

71	Columbia DB 8772	Suddenly The Whole World Is Mine/Strange Feeling	£15

PAUL QUINCHETTE

57	Esquire 32-057	ON THE SUNNY SIDE (LP)	£40

QUINCICASM

73	Saydisc SDL 249	QUINCICASM (LP)	£50

PAUL QUINN

92	Postcard DUBH 921	THE PHANTOMS AND THE ARCHETYPES (LP)	£50

QUINTESSENCE

71	Neon NE 1003	Sweet Jesus/You Never Stay The Same (in p/s)	£15
69	Island ILPS 9110	IN BLISSFUL COMPANY (LP, gatefold, pink label with white 'i' logo, booklet)	£100
70	Island ILPS 9128	QUINTESSENCE (LP, tri-fold sleeve, pink label with white 'i' logo)	£80
71	Island ILPS 9143	DIVE DEEP (LP, inner sleeve, pink rim palm tree label)	£60
72	RCA SF 8273	SELF (LP)	£20
72	RCA SF 8317	INDWELLER (LP)	£15

(see also Kala)

QUINTET MODERNE

87	Bead Records BEAD 26	IKKUNAN TAKANA (LP)	£20

QUINTET OF HOT CLUB OF FRANCE

53	Decca LF 1139	SWING FROM PARIS (10" LP)	£15

QUINTET OF THE YEAR

54	Vogue L.D.E. 087	JAZZ AT THE MASSAY HALL VOL. 3 (10" LP)	£18

QUIVER

71	Warner Bros K 46089	QUIVER (LP)	£30

(see also Bridget St. John, Natural Gas, Sutherland Brothers, Village)

QUODLING'S DELIGHT

76	Fanfare FR 2179	AMONG THE LEAVES SO GREEN (LP)	£25

QUOTATIONS (U.K.)

64	Decca F 11907	Alright Baby/Love You All Over Again	£25
68	CBS 3716	Cool It/Mark Of Her Head	£35

(see also Fleur De Lys, Johnny B. Great, Johnny Gustafson, Merseybeats, Johnny Goodison)

QUOTATIONS (U.S.)

61	HMV POP 975	Imagination/Ala-Men-Sy	£80

R

RAAW

78	Tempus TEM 111	Lili Twil/Just A Little Different (p/s)	£15

RABBIT

73	Island ILPS 9238	BROKEN ARROWS (LP, gatefold sleeve, pink rim palm tree label)	£18
74	Island ILPS 9289	DARK SALOON (LP)	£15

(see also Free; Kossoff, Kirke, Tetsu & Rabbit)

RABBITS

79	Stortbeat BEAT 4	Kitchen Parties/Tonight (numbered p/s, 1000 only)	£15

MICHAEL RABIN
58	Columbia 33CX 1597	MENDELSSOHN VIOLIN CONCERTO (LP)	£300
59	Capitol SP 8506	MOSAICS (LP, stereo)	£700
60	Capitol SP 8510	THE MAGIC BOW (LP, stereo)	£450
60	Capitol SP 8534	PAGANINI: CONCERTO NO 1 IN D MAJOR/WIENIAWSKI: CONCERTO NO.2 IN D MAJOR (LP, stereo)	£300

MIKE RABIN (& DEMONS)
64	Columbia DB 7350	Head Over Heels/Leaving You (as Mike Rabin & Demons)	£70
65	Polydor BM 56007	If I Were You/What Do You Do	£25

RAC
92	Nucleus NUKE 001	Monsoon/Yogomotion (12")	£30
92	Nucleus NUKE 004	Neo Rio/555/Choobes/Heaven (12")	£40
93	Nucleus NUKE 005	Hula Hoops/ESP/Microtropics/Wavelength (12")	£50

RACE FANS
68	Trojan TR 610	Bookie Man/UNIQUES: More Love	£60
68	Trojan TR 637	Time Marches On/SILVERTONES: Party Night	£80

YANK RACHELL TENNESSEE JUG BUSTERS
64	'77' LA 12-23	MANDOLIN BLUES (LP)	£30

RACONTEURS
06	XL XLLP 196X	BROKEN BOY SOLDIERS (LP)	£40
08	XL XLLP 359	CONSOLERS OF THE LONELY (2-LP)	£50

(see also White Stripes)

BOGDAN RACZYNSKI
02	Rephlex BRCOM 2	Fnick You DJ (Flashulb Remix)/Kimi Mix 2 (Nautillis Remix)	£25
99	Rephlex CAT 082 LP	BOKU MO WAKARAN (3-LP)	£40
99	Rephlex CAT 085 LP	SAMURAI MATH BEATS (2-LP)	£40
99	Rephlex CAT 089 LP	THINKING OF YOU (2-LP)	£25
01	Rephlex CAT 115 CD	MYLOVEILOVE (LP, cherry red vinyl)	£18
02	Rephlex CAT 120 LP	96 DRUM N BASS CLASSIXXX (2-LP)	£20
07	Rephlex CAT 193 LP	ALRIGHT! (2-LP)	£25

JIMMY RADCLIFFE
65	Stateside SS 374	Long After Tonight Is Over/What I Want I Can Never Have	£35
65	Stateside SS 374	Long After Tonight Is Over/What I Want I Can Never Have (DJ copy)	£150

RADHA KRISHNA
71	Columbia SCX 6462	RADHA KRISHNA (LP, composed & directed by John Mayer)	£45

(see also John Mayer)

RADHA KRISHNA TEMPLE (LONDON)
69	Apple APPLE 15	Hare Krishna Mantra/Prayer To The Spiritual Masters (p/s, as Radha Krishna Temple [London], with insert)	£30
69	Apple APPLE 15	Hare Krishna Mantra/Prayer To The Spiritual Masters (p/s, as Radha Krishna Temple [London], without insert)	£20
70	Apple APPLE 25	Govinda/Govinda Jai Jai (p/s)	£30
71	Apple SAPCOR 18	THE RADHA KRISHNA TEMPLE (LP, gatefold sleeve, with insert)	£50
71	Apple SAPCOR 18	THE RADHA KRISHNA TEMPLE (LP, gatefold sleeve, without insert)	£40
93	Apple SAPCOR 18	THE RADHA KRISHNA TEMPLE (LP, reissue, gatefold sleeve with inner)	£15

RADIANTS
64	Chess CRS 8002	Voice Your Choice/If I Only Had You	£40
64	Chess CRS 8002	Voice Your Choice/If I Only Had You (DJ copy)	£60
68	Chess CRS 8073	Hold On/I'm Glad I'm The Loser	£20
68	Chess CRS 8073	Hold On/I'm Glad I'm The Loser (DJ copy)	£50

(see also Caston & Majors)

RADIATION
80	Martin's Mart 1X	Johnny/Last Day (no p/s)	£15

RADIATORS (FROM SPACE)
78	Chiswick NS 24	Prison Bars/(Why Can't I Be A) Teenager In Love (unreleased, promo only white label in stamped white sleeve & loose printed labels)	£40
79	Chiswick NS 45	Walkin' Home Alone Again/Try And Stop Me/The Hucklebuck (unreleased; white label test pressings exist with loose labels; as Radiators)	£40
77	Chiswick WIK 4	TV TUBE HEART (LP)	£20

(see also Pogues)

RADICAL DANCE FACTION
80	Earth Zone EZ 001	BORDERLAND CASES (LP, 1st pressing with white picture sleeve)	£20
80	Earth Zone EZ 001	BORDERLAND CASES (LP, 2nd pressing with black picture sleeve)	£15
81	Earth Zone EZ 003	WATERLAND (LP)	£15
91	Zone EZ3V	WASTELAND EARTH (LP)	£15
95	Inna State 004DS4A	RAGAMUFFIN STATEMENT (LP)	£35

RADICAL FACE
12	Bear Machine	THE FAMILY TREE: THE ROOTS (LP, insert, some with art print)	£100

RADICAL SOUND
95	Jungle Mania JM 6	Trigger 1/Trigger 2 (12")	£40

RADICALS
84	Bluetrac BTR 003	Rum Tree/Racids In Dub (12")	£50

MARK RADICE
72	Paramount SPFA 7004	MARK RADICE (LP)	£20

RADIO GEMINI
74	Deroy DEROY 1064	THE RADIO GEMINI LP (LP)	£40

RADIOACTIVE
77	Beeb BEEB 021	Ten Years After/All Time Needletime Loser (no p/s)	£30

RADIO ACTORS
79	Charly CYS 1058	Nuclear Waste/Digital Love (p/s, reissue of Fast Breeder & Radio Actors single, 2 slightly different label designs)	£20

(see also Fast Breeder & Radio Actors, Sting, Newcastle Big Band, Police, Gilli Smyth, Inner City Unit, Steve Hillage, Sphynx)

RADIO BIRDMAN
78	Sire 6078 617	What Gives/Anglo Girl Desire	£20
78	Sire 9103 332	RADIOS APPEAR (LP, with inner sleeve)	£35

RADIO CITY
80	Media Wave MW 001	Love And A Picture/She's A Radio (p/s)	£200

RADIO DEPT
02	Rex REKD 30S	Liebling/We Would Fall Against The Tide (die-cut Rex sleeve)	£15
04	Rex REKD 41S	Why Don't You Talk About It?/I Don't Need Love, I've Got My Band (p/s)	£15
04	XL XLLP 177	LESSER MATTERS (LP)	£50

RADIO DOOM
79	Private Pressing	RADIO DOOM (LP, white sleeve 250 only)	£50

RADIOHEAD
SINGLES
92	Parlophone TCR 6312	DRILL EP (Prove Yourself/Stupid Car/You/Thinking About You) (cassette, 3,000 only)	£40
92	Parlophone 12R 6312	DRILL EP (Prove Yourself/Stupid Car/You/Thinking About You) (12", p/s, 3,000 only)	£300
92	Parlophone CDR 6312	DRILL EP (Prove Yourself/Stupid Car/You/Thinking About You) (CD, 3,000 only)	£80
92	Parlophone 12R 6078	Creep/Lurgee/Inside My Head/Million $ Question (12", p/s, 6,000 only)	£40
93	Parlophone 12R 6333	Anyone Can Play Guitar/Faithless, The Wonder Boy/Coke Babies (12", p/s)	£30
93	Parlophone 12R 6345	Pop Is Dead/Banana Co. (Acoustic)/Creep (live)/Ripcord (live) (12", g/fold p/s)	£35
93	Parlophone RS 6359	Creep/Yes I Am/Blow Out (Remix)/Inside My Head (live) (p/s, clear vinyl)	£20
93	Parlophone 12RG 6359	U.S. LIVE EP (Creep [Acoustic KROQ]/You [live]/Vegetable [live]/Killer Cars [live]) (12", numbered gatefold p/s)	£15
94	Parlophone 12R 6394	My Iron Lung/Punchdrunk Lovesick Singalong/The Trickster/ Lewis (Mistreated) (12", numbered p/s)	£25
95	Parlophone 8 83115 2	The Bends/My Iron Lung (Live At Forum)/Bones (Live At Forum) (CD, for export to Ireland, slimline jewel case)	£35
95	Parlophone 8 83115 2	The Bends/My Iron Lung (Live At Forum)/Bones (Live At Forum) (CD, for export to Ireland, mispressed with "Planet Telex" instead of "The Bends" slimline jewel case)	£40
96	Parlophone R 6419	Street Spirit (Fade Out)/Bishop's Robes (die-cut p/s, white vinyl)	£20
97	Parlophone NODATA 01	Paranoid Android/Polyethelene (Parts 1 & 2) (blue vinyl, die-cut p/s)	£20
97	Parlophone NODATALH 03	Karma Police (Album Version)/Lull (jukebox issue, black vinyl)	£15
97	Parlophone 12NODATA 03	Karma Police/Meeting Up The Aisle/Climbing Up The Walls (Zero 7 Mix) (12", p/s)	£30
98	Parlophone 12NODATA 04	No Surprises/Palo Alto (12", p/s)	£25
11	XL TICK 02	Supercollider/The Butcher (12" p/s, 2000 only, some with reversed labels)	£18
12	Young Turks YT 077	Bloom (Jamie XX Rework Pt. 3) (1-sided 12")	£40
16	XL XLS791	Burn The Witch/Spectre (p/s, 2500 only)	£30

ALBUMS
93	Parlophone PCS 7360	PABLO HONEY (LP, inner)	£100
95	Parlophone PCS 7372	THE BENDS (LP, 1st pressing without pixelated 0% on black and white side of inner sleeve)	£250
95	Parlophone PCS 7372	THE BENDS (LP, later pressings with pixelated 0% on black and white side of inner sleeve)	£150
97	Parlophone NODATA 02	OK COMPUTER (2-LP, 1st pressing)	£150
97	Parlophone NODATA 02	OK COMPUTER (2-LP, repressing on 180gm vinyl)	£60
00	Parlophone LPKIDA	KID A (2-LP 10")	£50
01	Parlophone LPFHEIT 45101	AMNESIAC (2-LP, 10")	£80
01	Parlophone 12FHEIT 45104	I MIGHT BE WRONG (mini-LP)	£35
03	Parlophone 5848052	HAIL TO THE THIEF (CD, limited issue, with foldout map)	£30
03	Parlophone 724358454314	HAIL TO THE THIEF (2-LP)	£60
07	Parlophone 5.09995E+12	RADIOHEAD (Mail-order 4GB shaped USB stick, bespoke box, 7 albums as WAV files)	£95
07	Xurbia Xendless Ltd X X001	IN RAINBOWS (box set, 2 x CD, 2-LP, 2 booklets in presentation case)	£100
07	XL Recordings XLLP 324	IN RAINBOWS (LP)	£35
08	Parlophone 724385522918	OK COMPUTER (2-LP, reissue)	£20
08	Parlophone 5099921b 210716	THE BEST OF (4-LP)	£80
09	Parlophone 584 5431	HAIL TO THE THIEF (2-LP, reissue, 180gm vinyl)	£20
11	Ticker Tape/XL TICK 001S	THE KING OF LIMBS (2-10" clear vinyl LPs, with CD, newspaper, acid tab sheet, mail order only in sealed plastic bag)	£60
11	Ticker Tape TICK001LP	THE KING OF LIMBS (LP, reissue)	£18
11	Ticker Tape TICK 010	TKOL RMX 1234567 (Box set, 7 x 12")	£80
17	XL XLLP790	A MOON SHAPED POOL (2-LP)	£20
17	XL XLLP790X	A MOON SHAPED POOL (2-LP, white vinyl)	£20
17	XL LLLPLLPLP 01	A MOON SHAPED POOL (2-LP, 2-CD with splice of original tape in hard case)	£60
17	XL XLLP 868	OK COMPUTER - OKNOTOK (3-LP, blue vinyl)	£25

PROMOS
92	EMI (no cat no)	Nothing Touches Me/Prove Yourself/I Can't (3-track internal EMI cassette)	£300
92	Parlophone 12 R 6312	DRILL EP (White label promo in die cut sleeve)	£80
92	Parlophone 12RDJ 6078	Creep/Lurgee/Inside My Head/Million Dollar Question (12", die-cut sleeve)	£40
92	Parlophone CDRDJ 6078	Creep (Radio Version)/Lurgee/Inside My Head/Million Dollar Question (CD)	£30

MINT VALUE £

93	Parlophone CDRDJ 6345	Pop Is Dead/Banana Co. (live)/**Creep** (live)/**Ripcord** (live) (CD)	**£40**
93	Parlophone CDRDJ 6359	**Creep** (CD, picture disc)	**£25**
93	Parlophone 12RDJ 6369	**Ripcord/Prove Yourself/Faithless, The Wonderboy/Stop Whispering** (Album Version) (12", p/s)	**£40**
93	Parlophone 12RDJ 6333	**Anyone Can Play Guitar/Faithless, The Wonder Boy/Coke Babies** (12", die-cut sleeve)	**£20**
93	Parlophone (no cat. No.)	**Stop Whispering** (U.S. Version - Chris Sheldon Remix)/**Creep** (Acoustic)/**Pop Is Dead/Inside My Head** (Live) (CD)	**£30**
94	Parlophone 12RSDJ 6394	**My Iron Lung/Lozenge Of Love/The Trickster/Punchdrunk Lovesick Singalong** (12", die-cut red sleeve)	**£18**
94	Parlophone 12RSDJ 6394	**My Iron Lung/Lozenge Of Love/The Trickster/Punchdrunk Lovesick Singalong** (12", die-cut blue sleeve)	**£18**
94	Parlophone 12RSDJ 6394	**My Iron Lung/Lewis** (Mistreated)/**Permanent Daylight/You Never Wash Up After Yourself** (12" die-cut red sleeve)	**£15**
94	Parlophone 12RSDJ 6394	**My Iron Lung/Lewis** (Mistreated)/**Permanent Daylight/You Never Wash Up After Yourself** (12" die-cut blue sleeve)	**£15**
95	Parlophone 12RDJ 6411	**Fake Plastic Trees/India Rubber/How Can You Be Sure?** (12", die-cut sleeve)	**£18**
95	Parlophone 12RDJ 6145	**Just/Planet Telex** (Karma Sun Ra Mix)**Killer Cars** (Mogadon Version) (12")	**£15**
95	Parlophone RHEAD US 1	**JUST FOR COLLEGE: India Rubber/Maquiladora/How Can I Be Sure?/Just** (CD)	**£70**
96	Parlophone 12RDJ 6419	**Street Spirit** (Fade Out)/**Talk Show Host/Bishop's Robes** (12", promo-only)	**£18**
97	EMI (no cat. no.)	**Airbag** (1-track Abbey Road CD-R with mini bio and title sleeve)	**£15**
97	Parlophone 724385522925	**OK COMPUTER** (Stickered jewel case, printed disc, mispressing plays Deep Purple's 'The Collection')	**£40**
97	Parlophone (no cat. no.)	**OK COMPUTER** (Cassette, in customized jiffy bag)	**£35**
97	Parlophone (no cat. no.)	**OK COMPUTER** (promo Aiwa personal stereo, glued-in cassette, two stickers)	**£120**
97	Parlophone CDPP 005	**OK COMPUTER** (CD, numbered title sleeve)	**£35**
97	Parlophone NODATA 02	**OK COMPUTER** (EPK, with CD & video in polystyrene case in jiffy bag)	**£70**
98	Parlophone 12DATADJO3	**Climbing Up The Walls** (Zero 7 Mix)/(Fila Brazilia Mix) (1-sided 12", 200 only)	**£40**
00	Parlophone 12KIDA 6	**Idioteque** (12", white label test pressing, p/s)	**£18**
01	Parlophone AMNESIAC 01	**4 SONGS FROM AMNESIAC: Pyramid Song/I Might Be Wrong/Packt Like Sardines In A Crushed Tin Box/Dollars & Cents** (CD, card sleeve)	**£30**
03	Parlophone 12RDJWL 6623	**SKTTERBRAIN** (Four Tet Mix)/**REMYXOMOTOSIS** (Super Collider Mix) (12", 100 only)	**£35**

(see also Headless Chickens, On A Friday, Thom Yorke, Jonny Greenwood, Atoms For Peace)

RADIO HEART

87	GFM GFMG 109	**Radio Heart/Radio Heart** (Instrumental) (Uncut picture disc)	**£150**
87	GFM GFMX 112	**London Times/Rumous** (Uncut picture disc)	**£150**
87	NBR NBRL 1	**RADIO HEART** (LP, withdrawn)	**£15**

(see also Gary Numan)

RADIO MOSCOW

91	Status RMLP 103	**WORLD SERVICE** (LP)	**£15**
92	Status RMLP 104	**GET A NEW LIFE** (LP)	**£15**

RADIO 9

90s	Enraptured RAPT 1031	**Motorik/Fluid/Moving In Two Directions/Pianosong** (10", 9 only)	**£15**

RADIOPHONIC WORKSHOP

73	BBC RESL 13	**Moonbase 3/World Of Dr. Who**	**£20**

(see also BBC Radiophonic Workshop)

RADIO RADIO

83	Radio RAD 101	**Calling/Signed With A Star**	**£20**

RADIO STARS

78	Chiswick CWK 3001	**HOLIDAY ALBUM** (LP, with inner sleeve)	**£15**

(see also John's Children, Andy Ellison, Trevor White)

RADIUM

81	Isotope 731	**THROUGH THE SMOKE** (EP)	**£125**

RAELET(T)S

67	HMV POP 1591	**One Hurt Deserves Another/One Room Paradise** (as Raelets)	**£30**

(see also Ray Charles, Merry Clayton)

GERRY RAFFERTY

71	Transatlantic TRA 241	**CAN I HAVE MY MONEY BACK?** (LP)	**£15**

(see also Humblebums, Fifth Column)

RAG DOLLS (U.S.)

64	Cameo Parkway P 921	**Society Girl/Ragen** (with Caliente Combo)	**£35**
65	Stateside SS 398	**Dusty/Hey Hoagy**	**£40**

RAG RUBY RED

84	Rag RAG 001	**Phantoms Of Fame/Sweet Banana**	**£60**

(see also Level 42)

RAGE (1)

81	Carrere CAR 182CT	**Out Of Control** (Extended Version)/**Double Dealer** (12", yellow vinyl, PVC sleeve)	**£15**

(see also Nutz)

RAGE (2)

86	Diamond RAGE 1	**Looking For You/Come On Now** (p/s)	**£20**
86	Diamond RAGE 112	**Looking For You/Come On Now/Great Balls Of Fire/Hallelujah I Love Her So** (12", unissued, test pressings only)	**£25**

(see also Case, Long Tall Shorty, Purple Hearts, Chords)

RAGE AGAINST THE MACHINE

93	Epic 658 492-6	**Killing In The Name/Clear The Lane/Darkness Of Greed** (12" white vinyl, p/s)	**£25**
93	Epic 659 258-6	**Bullet In The Head** (Remix)/**Bullet In The Head**/(Album Version) **Settle For Nothing** (live) (12" picture disc, p/s)	**£30**
92	Epic EPC 72224	**RAGE AGAINST THE MACHINE** (LP)	**£100**
92	Epic 47 22240	**RAGE AGAINST THE MACHINE** (LP, red vinyl, 12", tour edition)	**£200**

96	Epic 481026	EVIL EMPIRE (LP, inner)...	£75
99	Simply Vinyl SVLP 069	RAGE AGAINST THE MACHINE (LP, reissue)	£40
99	Epic 4919931000	THE BATTLE OF LOS ANGELES (LP)...	£70
00	Epic EPC 499921 1	RENEGADES (LP)	£50

RAGGA TWINS

99	Shut Up And Dance SUADLP 0025	REGGAE OWES ME MONEY - 3 TRACK SAMPLER (12", stamped white labels)................	£40
91	Shut Up And Dance SUADLP 002	REGGAE OWES ME MONEY (LP)...	£20

RAGGAMUFFINS

67	London HLU 10134	Four Days Of Rain/It Wasn't Happening At All	£15

RAGGED HEROES

83	Celtic CM 013	ANNUAL (LP)	£25

RAGGED TROUSERS

75	EMI 2300	Mountain Child/Maybe I'm In Love	£15

RAGING STORMS

62	London HLU 9556	The Dribble/Hound Dog	£30

LOU RAGLAND

73	Warner Bros. K 16312	Since You Said You'd Be Mine/I Didn't Mean To Love You (DJ Copy)	£80
73	Warner Bros K 16312	Since You Said You'd Be Mine/I Didn't Mean To Love You	£50

BUNNY RAGS

80	Black Ark International BA 601	Let Love Touch Us Now/I Am I Said/THE FIGHTER: Freedom Fighter (12")	£70

(see also Bunny & Ricky, Bunny Clarke)

RAH BAND

83	TMT TMTT 5	Messages From The Stars (Long Wave Mix)/(Astro Mix)/(Short Wave MIx) (12", blue vinyl)	£40
78	Ebony EBY 1001	THE CRUNCH AND BEYOND (LP)...	£15
81	DJM DJF 20573	RAH BAND (LP)	£15
83	TMT RAH-1	GOING UP (LP)	£20
84	S.O.U.N.D. SNDLP 60	UPPER CUTS (mini-LP)	£15

(see also Richard Hewson Orchestra)

RAIDER OF THE LOST DUB

81	Island ILPS 9705	RAIDERS OF THE LOST DUB (LP) (withdrawn due to legal action)	£40

RAIME

10	Blackest Ever Black BLACKEST001	RAIME EP (12")..	£20
10	Blackest Ever Black BLACKEST002	If Anywhere Was Here He Would Know Where We Are/This Foundry (Regis Version) (12")...	£20
12	Blackest Ever Black BLACKESTLP001	QUARTER TURNS OVER A LIVING LINE (2-LP)	£25

RAINBEAUS

60	Vogue V 9161	That's All I'm Asking Of You/Maybe It's Wrong................................	£150

(RITCHIE BLACKMORE'S) RAINBOW

83	Polydor POSPP 631	Street Of Dreams/Anybody There? (picture disc, 2000 only)................	£20
83	Polydor POSPP 654	Can't Let You Go/All Night Long (live) (guitar-shaped picture disc)	£15
75	Oyster OYA 2001	RITCHIE BLACKMORE'S RAINBOW (LP, gatefold sleeve, as Ritchie Blackmore's Rainbow)...	£80
76	Polydor 2490 137	RAINBOW RISING (LP, gatefold)...	£30
77	Polydor 2808 010 010	RAINBOW ON STAGE (LP, music & interview disc, with insert, promo only)	£100
79	Polydor POLD 5023	DOWN TO EARTH (LP, clear vinyl, with inner sleeve).......................	£18
78	Polydor POLD 5002	LONG LIVE ROCK 'N' ROLL (LP, gatefold sleeve, insert).......................	£15
83	Polydor POLD 5116	BENT OUT OF SHAPE (LP)	£15

(see also Deep Purple, Elf, Dio, Graham Bonnet, Cozy Powell, Roger Glover, Wild Horses)

CHRIS RAINBOW

81	EMI 12EMI 5215	Body Music/Girl In Collision (12", p/s)..	£15

RAINBOW FAMILY

72	President PT 375	Travellin' Lady/My Father	£60

RAINBOW FFOLLY

68	Parlophone R 5701	Go Girl/Drive My Car...	£70
67	Parlophone PMC/PCS 7050	SALLIES FFORTH (LP, laminated front, flipbacks, black/yellow label, "Sold in U.K..." text)...	£800

(see also Love Affair)

RAINBOW PEOPLE

68	Pye 7N 17582	Walk'll Do You Good/Dream Time	£15
68	Pye 7N 17624	The Sailing Song/Rainbows..	£15
69	Pye 7N 17759	Living In A Dream World/Happy To See You Again.........................	£40

RAINBOWS

69	CBS 3995	Rainbows/Nobody But You	£20
69	CBS 4568	New Day Dawning/Days And Nights	£40

(see also Peeps, Martin Cure & Peeps)

RAINCHECKS

64	Solar SRP 104	Something About You/You're My Angel	£20
65	R&B MRB 5002	How Are You Boy/Bye Bye Baby	£40

RAINCOATS

79	Rough Trade RT 013	Adventures Close to Home/In Love/Fairytale In The Supermarket	£25

MINT VALUE £

82	Rough Trade RT 093	Running Away/No Ones Little Girl	£25
83	Rough Trade RTT 153	Animal Rhapsody/Honey Mad Woman/No-Ones Little Girl (12")	£18
79	Rough Trade ROUGH 3	THE RAINCOATS (LP, with lyric booklet)	£60
81	Rough Trade ROUGH 13	ODYSHAPE (LP)	£40
83	Rough Trade ROUGH 66	MOVING (LP)	£25
87	Femme FELP 4.00287J	THE RAINCOATS (LP, reissue, white vinyl)	£15
95	Rough Trade R4031	LOOKING IN THE SHODOWS (LP)	£30

(see also Slits)

RAINDANCE
87	Raindance X1S 121	RAINDANCE (LP)	£40

RAINDROPS (U.S.)
63	London HL 9718	What A Guy/It's So Wonderful	£25
63	London HL 9769	The Kind Of Boy You Can't Forget/Even Though You Can't Dance	£30
64	London HL 9825	That Boy John/Hanky Panky	£20
64	Fontana TF 463	The Book Of Love/I Won't Cry	£25
64	London RE 1415	WHAT A GUY (EP)	£125
64	London HA 8140	THE RAINDROPS (LP)	£125

(see also Ellie Greenwich, Popsicles)

CLAIRE RAINE
68	Jolly JY 010	La-La-La/I Want You	£20

LORRY RAINE
54	London HL 8043	You Broke My Broken Heart/I'm In Love With A Guy	£25
55	London HL 8132	Love Me Tonight/What Would I Do	£40

MA RAINEY
53	London AL 3502	MA RAINEY VOLUME 1 (10" LP)	£25
55	London AL 3538	MA RAINEY VOLUME 2 (10" LP)	£25
56	London AL 3558	MA RAINEY VOLUME 3 (10" LP)	£25
50s	Ristic LP 13	MA RAINEY (10" LP)	£25
50s	Ristic LP 19	MA RAINEY (10" LP)	£25
62	Riverside RL 12-108	MA RAINEY SINGS THE BLUES (LP)	£20
64	Riverside RLP 8807	MOTHER OF THE BLUES (LP, gatefold sleeve with booklet)	£20

MA RAINEY & PAPA CHARLIE JACKSON
50s	Poydras 11	Ma And Papa Poorhouse Blues/Big Feeling Blues	£15

RAIN PARADE
83	Zippo ZING 001	EMERGENCY THIRD RAIL POWER TRIP (LP, gatefold)	£18

RAIN TREE CROW
91	Virgin V2659	RAIN TREE CROW (LP, glossy printed inner)	£50
19	Virgin/UMC 679 534-1	RAIN TREE CROW (LP, printed inner, reissue)	£40

(see also Japan)

MARVIN RAINWATER
55	MGM SP 1150	Tennessee Houn' Dog Yodel/Albino (Pink-Eyed) Stallion	£50
56	MGM MGM 929	What Am I Supposed To Do/Why Did You Have To Go And Leave Me	£25
57	MGM MGM 961	Gonna Find Me A Bluebird/So You Think You've Got	£15
61	London HLU 9447	Boo Hoo/I Can't Forget	£80
58	MGM MGM-EP 647	MEET MARVIN RAINWATER (EP)	£20
58	MGM MGM-EP 662	WHOLE LOTTA MARVIN (EP)	£20
59	MGM MGM-EP 685	MARVIN RAINWATER SINGS (EP)	£15
63	Ember EMB 4521	COUNTRY AND WESTERN FAVOURITES VOL. 2 (EP)	£15
58	MGM MGM-D 152	SONGS BY MARVIN RAINWATER (10" LP)	£60

(see also Connie Francis & Marvin Rainwater)

RAINY DAY
84	Rough Trade ROUGH 70	RAINY DAY (LP)	£25

RAINY DAZE
67	CBS 3200	What Do You Think/Autumn Leaves	£18
67	Polydor 56731	That Acapulco Gold/In My Mind Lives A Forest	£20
68	Polydor 56737	Blood Of Oblivion/Stop Sign	£20
68	CBS 56731	THAT ACAPULCO GOLD (LP, unissued in U.K.)	£0

RAINY DAYS
76	Seville SEV 1009	Party/Anything I Would Do For You	£40

RAISINS
68	Major Major MM 540	Ain't That Lovin' You Baby/Stranger Things Have Happened	£15
68	Major Minor MMLP 20	THE RAISINS (LP, also stereo SMLP 20)	£30

(see also Coloured Raisins)

RAKES
04	Trash Aesthetics TA 702	22 Grand Job/Something Clicked And I Fell Off The Edge (Pink vinyl, insert and Fold-out sleeve. 480 only)	£15
05	V2 VVR1032761	CAPTURE/RELEASE (LP)	£30
07	V2 VVR1041851	TEN NEW MESSAGES (LP)	£30

RALFI
75	Island USA 005	Wonderful Things/The Gambler	£15

DON RALKE ORCHESTRA
60	Warner Bros. WM 4007/ WS8007	BUT YOU NEVER HEARD GERSHWIN WITH BONGOS (LP)	£15

RALLY ROUNDERS
64 Lyntone LYN 573/574   Bike Beat Part 1/Bike Beat Part 2 (actually by the Outlaws) (p/s, flexidisc) £50
(see also Outlaws)

RALPHAEL
84 Diddy Doll RM 04   Disco Lady/Dance To The Late Night Groove (12")..........................£50
85 Simoon TC124   Disco Lady/Night Time Groove (p/s)..........................£40
85 Simoon RM001   MIXED RHYTHM (LP) £80

BUCK RAM'S RAMROCKS
63 London HLU 9677   Benfica/Odd Man Theme..........................£15
(see also Little Richard, Platters)

RAMASES
71 Philips 6113 001   Ballroom/Muddy Water..........................£25
71 Philips 6113 003   Jesus Come Back/Hello Mister..........................£25
71 Vertigo 6360 046   SPACE HYMNS (LP, foldout poster sleeve, small swirl label)..........................£350
71 Vertigo 6360 046   SPACE HYMNS (LP, foldout sleeve, later 'spaceship' label)..........................£70
75 Vertigo 6360 115   GLASS TOP COFFIN (LP, die-cut gatefold sleeve, 'spaceship' label)..........................£45
(see also 10cc, Ramases & Seleka, Ramases & Selket)

RAMASES & SELEKA
70 Major Minor MM 704   Love You/Gold Is The Ring..........................£50
(see also Ramases)

RAMASES & SELKET
68 CBS 3717   Crazy One/Mind's Eye £80
(see also Ramases)

RAMATAM
72 Atlantic K 40415   RAMATAM (LP) £15
(see also Iron Butterfly)

RAMBLERS
63 Decca F 11775   Dodge City/Just For Chicks..........................£40

RAMBLETTES
65 Brunswick 05932   Thinking Of You/On Back Street (DJ Copy) £35
65 Brunswick 05932   Thinking Of You/On Back Street £20

RAMBLIN' JIMMY DOLAN
51 Capitol CL 13600   Wine, Women And Pink Elephants/GENE O'QUIN: Boogie Woogie Fever (78)..........................£17

RAMBLING SYD RUMPO
70 Starline SRS 5034   THE BEST OF RAMBLING SYD RUMPO (LP) £15
(see also Kenneth Williams)

SID RAMIN
70 CBS 4813   Stiletto/Sugar In The Rain £20
69 CBS 70062   STILETTO (LP, soundtrack)..........................£30

LOUIE RAMIREZ
67 Mercury 20113   IN THE HEART OF SPANISH HARLEM (LP)..........................£25

RAM JAM BAND
65 Columbia DB 7621   Shake Shake Senora/Akinla £25
(see also Geno Washington & Ram Jam Band, Ram John Holder, Ram Holder Brothers)

RAMLEH
83 Broken Flag BF V4   THE HAND OF GLORY (EP, p/s)..........................£30
92 Dying Earth DE 003   Loser Patrol/Tracers (p/s, numbered, 500 only, 1st 30 in red sleeve)..........................£15
82 Broken Flag BF 01   31/5/1962 - 1982 (cassette)..........................£70
83 Broken Flag BF V2   A RETURN TO SLAVERY (LP, with Libertarian Recordings) £30
83 Broken Flag BF 07   LIVE McCARTHY (cassette)..........................£50
83 Broken Flag BF 20   LIVE NEW FORCE (cassette) £50
83 Broken Flag BF 24   LIVE PHENOL (cassette) £50
83 Broken Flag BF 25   LIVE PROSSNECK (cassette) £50
83 Broken Flag BF 28   LIVE AT MORDEN TOWER (cassette) £50
84 Broken Flag BF 37   104 WEEKS (cassette) £40
84 Broken Flag BF 38   AS I HAVE WON (cassette) £40
85 Broken Flag BF 40   AWAKE! (6 cassettes in lockable steel box with booklet) £400
87 Broken Flag BF 59   HOLE IN THE HEART (cassette) £40
94 Broken Flag BF 75   SOUNDCHECK CHANGLING (cassette) £20
95 Broken Flag BF 77   AIRBORNE BABEL (cassette) £20
95 Broken Flag BF 80   ELITE GYMNASTICS/LIVE 1983 (cassette) £20
(see also Skullflower)

RAMMSTEIN
04 Universal 9868673   Amerika/Wilder Wein (p/s)..........................£50
05 Universal 9870291   Keine Lust/Du Hast (Live) (p/s, clear vinyl)..........................£40
09 Spinefarm 2718498   Pussy (p/s,1-sided, limited edition blue vinyl) £30
11 Spinefarm SPINE768392   Waidmanns Heil/Leibe Ist Fur Alle da (300 only) £80
01 Motor 549 639-1   MUTTER (LP, gatefold) £60
09 Universal 2721463   LIEBE IST FUR ALLE DA (2-LP, pink vinyl, gatefold)..........................£80

RAMON & CRYSTALITES
71 Songbird SB 1053   Golden Chickens/Stranger Version £80

DEE DEE RAMONE & ICLC
94 World Service/Rough Trade RTD 157.1757.1   I HATE FREAKS LIKE YOU (LP, with inner)..........................£30

(see also Ramones)
RAMONES
SINGLES

76	Sire 6078 601	Blitzkrieg Bop/Havana Affair (in rare p/s)	£200
76	Sire 6078 601	Blitzkrieg Bop/Havana Affair	£25
77	Sire 6078 603	I Remember You/California Sun (live)/I Don't Wanna Walk Around With You (live) (p/s)	£50
77	Sire RAM 001 (6078 606)	Sheena Is A Punk Rocker/Commando/I Don't Care (12", with T-shirt offer on perforated centre of numbered p/s, 12,000 only)	£30
77	Sire RAM 001 (6078 606)	Sheena Is A Punk Rocker/Commando/I Don't Care (12", without T-shirt offer on perforated centre of numbered p/s, 12,000 only)	£15
77	Sire 6078 607	Swallow My Pride/Pinhead/Let's Dance (live) (p/s)	£20
77	Sire 6078 611	Rockaway Beach/Teenage Lobotomy/Beat On The Brat (p/s)	£20
77	Sire 6078 611	Rockaway Beach/Teenage Lobotomy/Beat On The Brat (12", p/s, with poster)	£30
78	Sire 6078 615	Do You Wanna Dance?/It's A Long Way Back To Germany/Cretin Hop (p/s)	£18
78	Sire (no cat. no.)	Questioningly/Don't Come Close/Sedated/I Just Want To Have Something To Do (with p/s, promo only, with spoken intros by Joey Ramone)	£45
78	Sire (no cat. no.)	Questioningly/Don't Come Close/Sedated/I Just Want To Have Something To Do (without p/s, promo only, with spoken intros by Joey Ramone)	£15
78	Sire SRE 1031	Don't Come Close/I Don't Want You (p/s, yellow vinyl)	£15
79	Sire SIR 4009	She's The One/I Wanna Be Sedated (p/s)	£15
80	RSO RSO 70 (2090 512)	I Wanna Be Sedated/The Return Of Jackie And Judy (p/s)	£18
80	Sire SREP 1	MELTDOWN WITH THE RAMONES: I Just Want To Have Something To Do/ Here Today Gone Tomorrow/I Wanna Be Your Boyfriend/Questioningly (EP)	£15
83	Sire W 9606	Time Has Come Today/Psycho Therapy (p/s)	£15
83	Sire W 9606T	Time Has Come Today/Sheena Is A Punk Rocker/Teenage Lobotomy/ Rock'n'Roll Radio (12", p/s)	£20
86	Beggars Banquet BEG 157T	Somebody Put Something In My Drink/(You) Can't Say Anything Nice/ Something To Believe In (12", p/s, with promo poster)	£15

ALBUMS

76	Sire 9103 253	RAMONES (LP, with insert)	£100
77	Sire 9103 254	RAMONES LEAVE HOME (LP, with "Carbona Not Glue" with inner sleeve)	£40
77	Sire 9103 254	RAMONES LEAVE HOME (LP, repressing without "Carbona Not Glue")	£35
77	Sire 9103 255	ROCKET TO RUSSIA (LP, with inner sleeve)	£50
78	Sire SRK 6063	ROAD TO RUIN (LP, yellow vinyl, inner)	£50
78	Sire SRK 6063	ROAD TO RUIN (LP)	£30
79	Sire SRK 6077	END OF THE CENTURY (LP, inner)	£30
79	Sire SRK2 6074	IT'S ALIVE (2-LP)	£30
81	Sire SRK 3571	PLEASANT DREAMS (LP)	£30
85	Beggars Banquet BEGA 59	TOO TOUGH TO DIE (LP)	£25
86	Beggars Banquet BEGA 70	ANIMAL BOY (LP, picture inner sleeve and poster)	£20
87	Beggars Banquet BEGA 89	HALFWAY TO SANITY (LP, inner)	£35
89	Chrysalis CHR 1725	BRAIN DRAIN (LP, inner)	£20
90	Beggar's Banquet	END OF THE DECADE (6 x 12" singles, box set with t-shirt, postcards & poster, 2,500 copies only)	£50
91	Chysalis CHR 1901	LOCO LIVE (LP, inner)	£40
92	Chrysalis 094632196019	MONDO BIZARRO (LP)	£70
93	Chrysalis CHR 6052	ACID EATERS (LP)	£100
95	Chrysalis 724383413614	ADIOS AMIGOS (LP)	£80
04	Earmark 40033 1 P	LIVE : JANUARY 7 1978 PART ONE (LP, picture disc)	£30

(see also Paley Brothers & Ramones)
MICHEL RAMOS

55	London DEP 95013	PLAYING THE CLASSICS (EP, export)	£20

RAMPENT

80	FMR 030 S80 CUS 804	Back Street Walker/Livin In The Past/Fight Back/No Friend Of Mine	£100

RAM RAM GO GO SOUND

69	Halagala HG 26	Pep 77/USA Outcry	£15

RAMRODS

65	United Artists UP 1113	Overdrive/Stalker	£15

RAMRODS (U.S.)

61	London HLU 9355	Loch Lomond Rock/Take Me Back To My Boots And Saddle	£20
61	London RE-U 1292	RIDERS IN THE SKY (EP)	£70

LEE RAMSEY

96	Real Deal RD 002	RD STYLE (EP)	£15

RANCHERS

65	Cavern Sound IMSTL 2	An American Sailor At The Cavern/Sidetracked	£25

RANDALL AND ANDY C.

94	Ram RAMM 11	Sound Control/Feel It (12")	£15

(see also Andy C)
ELLIOTT RANDALL

71	Polydor 2489 004	RANDALL'S ISLAND (LP)	£20

FREDDY RANDALL & HIS BAND

58	Parlophone PMD 1046	DR JAZZ (LP)	£20

TONY RANDALL & JACK KLUGMAN

72	Decca Phase Four PFS 4277	THE ODD COUPLE SINGS (LP)	£15

ALAN RANDALL
68 Electratone S1002   The Meditating Hindoo Man/Why Don't Women Like Me £15

TEDDY RANDAZZO (& DAZZLERS)
62 HMV POP 1067   Dance To The Locomotion/Cottonfields (as Teddy Randazzo & Dazzlers) £15
62 HMV CLP 1527   JOURNEY TO LOVE (LP, mono) £35
62 HMV CSD 1421   JOURNEY TO LOVE (LP, stereo) £40
63 HMV CLP 1601   TEDDY RANDAZZO TWISTS (LP, with Dazzlers) £90
(see also Three Chuckles)

LYNNE RANDELL
67 CBS 2847   Ciao Baby/Stranger In My Arms (DJ Copy)...............................£250
67 CBS 2847   Ciao Baby/Stranger In My Arms £200
67 CBS 2927   That's A Hoe Down/I Need You Boy £30

RAN-DELLS
63 London HLU 9760   The Martian Hop/Forgive Me Darling (I Have Lied) £25

BARBARA RANDOLPH
67 Tamla Motown TMG 628   I Got A Feelin'/You Got Me Hurtin' All Over (DJ copy) £100
67 Tamla Motown TMG 628   I Got A Feelin'/You Got Me Hurtin' All Over £65
79 Tamla Motown TMG 1133   Can I Get A Witness/You Got Me Hurtin' All Over/I Got A Feeling (reissue) £50

BOOTS RANDOLPH
63 London RE-U 1365   THE YAKETY SAX OF BOOTS RANDOLPH (EP) £15
63 London HA-U 8106   YAKETY SAX (LP)...£25
66 London HA-U 8280   MORE YAKETY SAX (LP, as Boots Randolph & His Combo) £20

RANDY
96 Rugger Bugger SEEP 20   THE REST IS SILENCE (LP, printed inner sleeve)............................£25
99 Rugger Bugger SEEP 026   YOU CAN'T KEEP A GOOD BAND DOWN (LP, gatefold) £25

RANDY & RAINBOWS
63 Stateside SS 214   Denise/Come Back £50

RANDY'S ALLSTARS
70 Randy's RAN 500   I'm The One, You're The One/End Us £35
70 Randy's RAN 501   Pepper Pot (act. with Count Machuki)/The Same Things (B-side actually by Gaylads) £70
70 Randy's RAN 505   Emperor Waltz/War £25
70 Randy's RAN 506   Blue Danube Waltz/Together (B-side actually by Delroy Wilson) £40
(see also Impact Allstars, Lyrics, Dave Barker, Ethiopians, Jimmy London)

RANEE & RAJ
68 Fontana TF 920   Feel Like A Clown/Rainbow Land £20
68 Fontana TF 941   Don't Tell Me I Must Go/Razor Edge £20

SUE RANEY
58 Capitol T 964   WHEN YOUR LOVER HAS GONE (LP) £15

WAYNE RANEY (STRING BAND)
54 Parlophone CSMP 20   Adam/The Roosters Are Crowing (export issue)...........................£25
58 Parlophone GEP 8746   COUNTRY AND WESTERN (EP) £30

RANGLERS
68 Trend TRE 1007   You Never Said Goodbye/Step Down £60

ERNEST RANGLIN
62 Island WI 015   Harmonica Twist/Mitty Gritty (as Ernest Ranglin Orchestra) £40
63 Island WI 128   Exodus/ROBERT MARLEY: One Cup Of Coffee............................£300
66 Black Swan IEP 704   ERNEST RANGLIN & THE G.B.'s (EP, with p/s).............................£280
66 Black Swan IEP 704   ERNEST RANGLIN & THE G.B.'s (EP) £80
64 Island ILP 909   WRANGLIN' (LP) £180
64 Island ILP 915   REFLECTIONS (LP) £200
83 Vista Sounds   FROM KINGSTON J.A. TO MIAMI U.S.A. (LP) £80
96 Island Jamaica Jazz IJLP 4002   BELOW THE BASSLINE (LP) £150
97 Island Jamaica Jazz IJLP4004 MEMORIES OF BARBER MACK (LP) £35
(see also Owen Gray, Graham Bond)

KENNY RANKIN
70 Mercury MF1128   Peaceful/The Dolphin £15

ROY RANKIN AND RAYMOND NAPTALI
81 KG Imperial KG 004   Go Deh In A Late Night Blues/Late Night Session/Babylon Policy/Peaceful Something (12", green vinyl)...£25
81 KG Imperial KG 007   African Daughter/Disc Jockey In A 81 Style (12") £15
82 CF CFLP 001   LATE NIGHT SESSION (LP) £50

RANKING ANN
83 Rough Justice RJ 001   Kill The Police Bill/Rough Justice Dub (12") £20
85 Ariwa ARL SL 003   Something Fishy Going On/SANE INMATES: Whisper To A Roar £20
86 Ariwa ARI 7 55   Feminine Gender/Right To Fight £20
82 Ariwa ARILP 002   A SLICE OF ENGLISH TOAST (LP) £50
82 Ariwa ARILP 010   SOMETHING FISHY GOING ON (LP) £50

RANKING DREAD
78 Greensleeves GRE10   Dub Sister Dub It/Nine Months Belly £15
80 Art & Craft ACD 005   DISCO EP SHOWCASE: Honda Accord/Joe Grine Girl/Baby Mother/Nice Up The Lawn (12", miscredited, artist actually Ranking Joe))..................................£15
80 Art & Craft AC006   DISCO EP SHOWCASE: My Liza/Same Thing/Hard Times Leave My Life/Jah Walk Through Galilee (12" green vinyl)...£30

MINT VALUE £

82	Greensleeves GRED 82	Shut Me Mouth/Shut Up Shut Up (Dub Version)	£30
82	Greensleeves GRED 96	My Mammy/Mammy Mammy (12")	£15
76	Burning Sounds BS 1025	GIRLS FIESTA (LP)	£25
79	Burning Sounds BS 1037	KUNTA KINTE ROOTS (LP)	£35
80	Freedom Sounds FSLP 001	LOTS OF LOVING (LP)	£25
82	Silver Camel SCLP 002	RANKING DREAD IN DUB (LP)	£40

RANKING JOE
80	Art & Craft ACD 005	DISCO EP SHOWCASE (12", rd, green or gold vinyl, some copies miscredited to Ranking Dread))	£15
78	Greensleeves GREL 2	WEAKHEART FADEAWAY (LP)	£30
79	Student NWLP 009	ROUND THE WORLD (LP)	£60
80	Greensleeves GREL 16	SATURDAY NIGHT JAMDOWN STYLE (LP)	£25
81	Copasetic COPLPS 003	DISCO SKATE (LP, blue or black vinyl)	£40

RANKING MANDEY
| 84 | Hibiscus ED 006 | Hard Times/Conflict & War (12", p/s) | £50 |

PETER RANKING AND GENERAL LUCKY
| 82 | Greensleeves GRED 98 | Beverly Black/Walk And Talk (12") | £18 |

RANKING ROCKER
| 80 | Disco Mix DM 01 | Give Jah The Glory/JAH I: Words Of Wisdom/RANKING ROCKER:Out Of The Ghetto/ Songs Of Jah (Disco Mix) (12") | £40 |

RANKING TREVOR
| 78 | Virgin Frontline FL1015 | IN FINE STYLE (LP) | £20 |

RANKING TREVOR AND TRINITY
| 78 | Cha Cha CHALP 001 | THREE PIECE CHICKEN AND CHIPS (LP, some copies on blue vinyl) | £35 |

RANKING SUPERSTAR
| 80 | Lord Koos KLP 1 | REPATRIATION TIME (LP) | £45 |

RANSOME HEAD
| 71 | York SYK 506 | Sing/Wide Wide River | £30 |

PETER RANSOME
| 72 | York FYK 402 | PETER RANSOME (LP, blue/silver label) | £25 |

RAOUL & RUINED
| 84 | Gutter Hearts GH 1 | BITE BACK + BLUES (LP, fan-club only issue) | £50 |
(see also Marc Almond)

RAPED
78	Parole KNIT 1	PRETTY PAEDOPHILES (EP)	£20
78	Parole PURL 1	Cheap Night Out/Foreplay Playground (p/s, with ad sheet)	£20
84	Iguana PILLAGED 1	PHILES AND SMILES (LP, official bootleg, with booklet)	£50
(see also Cuddly Toys)

RAPEMAN
| 88 | Fierce FRIGHT 031 | Hated Chinee/Marmoset (p/s) | £15 |
(see also Big Black)

JOHNNY RAPHAEL
| 58 | Vogue V 9104 | We're Only Young Once/The Lonely Road To Nowhere | £50 |
| 58 | Vogue V 9104 | We're Only Young Once/The Lonely Road To Nowhere (78) | £25 |

RAPID DANCE
| 82 | Resolute RO 1 | Fragments Of Youth/Hidden So Well (p/s) | £15 |

RAPIERS (1)
| 60s | Ilford Sound ILF 272 | The Phantom Stage/Valencia | £20 |

RAPIERS (2)
83	Red Door RA 001	THE RAPIERS VOL. 1 (EP)	£18
85	Off Beat WIK 40	STRAIGHT TO THE POINT (LP)	£18
87	Off Beat WIK 67	1961 (LP)	£18

BRIAN RAPKIN & KELVIN JONES
| 69 | MSR MID 1352 | DREAMS OF THE BEAST (LP) | £30 |

RARE AMBER
| 69 | Polydor BM 56309 | Malfunction Of The Engine/Blind Love | £30 |
| 69 | Polydor 583 046 | RARE AMBER (LP) | £250 |

RARE BIRD
70	Charisma CB 120	Sympathy/Devil's High Concern (in p/s)	£15
69	Charisma CAS 1005	RARE BIRD (LP, laminated front sleeve, pink 'scroll label)	£100
70	Charisma CAS 1011	AS YOUR MIND FLIES BY (LP, textured gatefold, pink 'scroll' label)	£75
72	Polydor 2442 101	EPIC FOREST (LP & poster, with bonus EP "Roadside Welcome"/Four Grey Walls/"You're Lost" [2814 011], p/s)	£150
72	Polydor 2442 101	EPIC FOREST (LP, gatefold with free EP but no poster)	£60
72	Polydor 2442 101	EPIC FOREST (LP with no poster or free EP)	£20
73	Polydor 2383 211	SOMEBODY'S WATCHING (LP, gatefold sleeve)	£20
(see also Fruit Machine)

RARE BREED
| 66 | Strike JH 316 | Beg, Borrow And Steal/Jeri's Theme | £30 |
(see also Ohio Express)

RARE EARTH
| 70 | Tamla Motown TMG 742 | Get Ready/Magic Key | £20 |
| 70 | Tamla Motown STML 11165 | GET READY (LP) | £20 |

MINT VALUE £

71	Tamla Motown STML 11180	**ECOLOGY** (LP)	£20
71	Rare Earth SREA 4001	**ONE WORLD** (LP, textured gatefold sleeve)	£18
72	Rare Earth SRESP 301	**IN CONCERT** (2-LP satchel sleeve)	£15

RARE MOODS
| 86 | AGR AGR 5 | **I've Got Love/Closer To Your Love** (p/s) | £20 |
| 86 | AGR AGR T5 | **I've Got Love/Closer To Your Love** (12") | £50 |

RASALLA
| 76 | Kiss KISS 17 | **Bosrah/Version** (with The Spear) | £30 |

(see also Prince Alla, Yabby U)

RASCALS (1)
| 68 | Atlantic 587/588 098 | **ONCE UPON A DREAM** (LP) | £18 |
| 71 | CBS S 64406 | **PEACEFUL WORLD** (2xLP) | £18 |

(see also Young Rascals)

RASCALS (2)
| 81 | Flexible FR 001 | **UP TO MISCHIEF** (sleeve back to front, no spine) | £80 |

RASCALS (3)
| 08 | Deltasonic DLTLP079 | **RASCALIZE** (LP) | £50 |

(EMPRESS) RASHEDA
87	Jah Shaka 862	**Psalms 61** (Hear My Cry)/**BLACK STEEL AND JAH SHAKA: Hear My Dub** (12")	£25
92	Rasheda Lioness RLM 001	**Only Jah Worthy/Give Jah Praise** (12")	£30
95	Roots Music RRLP 011	**HAIL H.I.M** (LP)	£30

RASI
| 83 | Yard Beat TB 001 | **Jah Spoke To I/You Wan Tan Style** | £25 |

RAS IMRU
| 80 | Jah Shaka KMD001 | **Marshall/SHAKA RYDIM SECTION : Warrior Style** (12") | £60 |
| 85 | House Of Asha HA1LP | **TRIBUTE TO SELASSE I** (LP) | £25 |

RAS MIDAS
| 79 | Tribesman TM 24 | **Natty Dread Surprise/Good Old Days Original** (with I-Roy) (12") | £60 |
| 79 | Warrior WAR 138 | **Can't Stop Rasta Now/Rain And Fire** (12") | £20 |

RAS NATURAL
| 03 | Unity Sound US006 | **Roar Like A Lion/Lion Chant/Version** (10") | £20 |

RASTAFARI
| 73 | Satril SAT8 | **Funky City/In The Garden** | £50 |

RATCHELL
| 72 | MCA MUPS 455 | **RATCHELL** (LP) | £15 |

RATIONAL ANTHEM
| 86 | Radio Humberside/HLS 001 | **THE NORTHERN TRAWL** (LP) | £50 |

ARMAN RATIP
| 70 | Columbia SCX 6532 | **INTRODUCING THE ARMAN RATIP TRIO** (LP) | £100 |
| 73 | Regal Zono. SLRZ 1038 | **THE SPY FROM ISTANBUL** (LP, gatefold sleeve) | £120 |

RATS (1)
64	Oak RGJ 145	**Spoonful** (1-sided, with foldout p/s)	£400
64	Oak RGJ 145	**Spoonful** (1-sided)	£250
65	Columbia DB 7483	**Spoonful/I've Got My Eyes On You Baby**	£120
65	Columbia DB 7607	**I Gotta See My Baby Everyday/Headin' Back** (To New Orleans)	£90
95	Tenth Planet TP 012	**THE RISE AND FALL OF BERNIE GRIPPLESTONE & THE SPIDERS FROM HULL** (LP, gatefold sleeve, 1,000 only)	£20

(see also Beat Boys, Mark Peters)

RATS (2)
| 64 | Oriole CB 1967 | **Parchman Farm/Every Day I Have The Blues** | £100 |
| 65 | CBS 201740 | **Sack Of Woe/Gimme That Wine** | £100 |

RATS (3)
74	Goodear EAR. 101	**Turtle Dove/Oxford Donna** (with p/s)	£40
74	Goodear EAR 101	**Turtle Dove/Oxford Donna** (without p/s)	£15
74	Goodear EARLH 5003	**FIRST** (LP)	£18

(see also World of Oz)

RATTLES
63	Philips BF 1277	**The Stomp/Zip A Dee Doo Dah**	£20
64	Decca F 11873	**Bye Bye Johnny/Roll Over Beethoven**	£25
64	Decca F 11936	**Tell Me What I Can Do/Sunbeam At The Sky**	£25
65	Fontana TF 618	**Come On And Sing/Candy To Me**	£25
66	Fontana TF 724	**Say All Right/Love Of My Life**	£25
71	Decca F 23119	**You Can't Have Sunshine Everyday/Where Is The Friend**	£15
71	Decca FR 13243	**The Devil's On The Loose/I Know You Don't Know**	£15
73	Decca FR 13390	**Devils Son/What Do I Care**	£20
64	Decca DFE 8568	**TEENBEAT FROM THE STAR CLUB HAMBURG** (EP)	£125
64	Philips BL 7614	**TWIST AT THE STAR CLUB HAMBURG** (LP)	£100
67	Mercury MG 1127	**GREATEST HITS** (LP)	£30
71	Decca SKL-R 5088	**THE RATTLES** (LP)	£30

(see also Wonderland)

RATTLING THRONTONS
| 80 | Beat Street BEAT 1 | **RATTLING THRONTONS EP** | £15 |

RAVE ONS
60s Sounds Good MT 103   She's A Spoon/Keep Wrong £120

CHRIS RAVEL & RAVERS
63 Decca F 11696   I Do/Don't You Dig This Kind Of Beat.. £20
(see also Chris Andrews)

RAVEN
82	Neat NEAT 1512	CRASH BANG WALLOP (Crash Bang Wallop/Firepower/Run Them Down/Rock Hard) (12" EP, mauve splattered vinyl) £15
81	Neat NEAT1001	ROCK UNTIL YOU DROP (LP + lyric insert) £20
83	Neat NEATP1001	ROCK UNTIL YOU DROP (reissue picture disc LP) £15

JON RAVEN
70s	Broadside	HARVEST (LP, with book) £15
71	Argo ZFB 29	KATE OF COALBROOKDALE (LP, as Jon & Mike Raven with Jean Ward) £100
73	Trailer LER 2083	SONGS OF A CHANGING WORLD (LP, with Nic Jones & Tony Rose, red label with insert)... £30
73	Broadside BRO 115	THE NAILMAKERS (LP, with Michael Totten)..................................... £15
75	Trailer LER 2083	SONGS OF A CHANGING WORLD (LP, 2nd pressing, with Nic Jones & Tony Rose, yellow label with insert)... £20
75	Broadside BOR 116	BALLAD OF THE BLACK COUNTRY (LP) £15
76	Broadside BRO 117	HARVEST (LP).. £50
81	Dingles DIN 319	REGAL SLIP (LP)... £30
(see also Halliard, Black Country Three, John Kirkpatrick)

JON AND MICHAEL RAVEN
68 Broadside BOR 100   SONGS OF THE BLACK COUNTRY (LP) £40

MICHAEL RAVEN AND JOAN MILLS
70	Roman Head RH 021	A COLLECTION OF FOLKSONGS AND GUITAR MUSIC (LP, 99 copies only) £80
72	Folk Heritage FHR 047	DEATH AND THE LADY (LP) £400
74	Folk Heritage FHR 053	THE JOLLY MACHINE (LP)... £50
74	Folk Heritage FHR 054	HYMN TO CHE GUEVARA (LP, 100 only) £500

MIKE RAVEN
66 Xtra 1046   GUITAR MAGIC (LP) £30

PAUL RAVEN (2)
68 MCA MU 1024   Musical Man/Wait For Me £15

SIMON RAVEN
66 Piccadilly 7N 35301   I Wonder If She Remembers Me/Sea Of Love £60

RAVENS ROCK GROUP
61 Pye International 7N 25077 The Ghoul Friend/Career Girl £20

RAVENS (1)
53	Oriole CB 1148	Rock Me All Night Long/Write Me One Sweet Letter (78) £15
53	Oriole CB 1149	Begin The Beguine/Looking For My Baby (78) £15
53	Oriole CB 1258	Who'll Be The Fool?/Rough Ridin' (78) £15

RAVENS (2)
63 Oriole CB 1910   I Just Wanna Hear You Say/Send Me A Letter £30

RAVERS
69 Upsetter US 312   Babam Bam/UPSETTERS: Medical Operation £140

RAW DEAL (2)
81 White Witch WIT 701   Out Of My Head/In The Mood (no p/s) £50

LOU RAWLS
67	Capitol CL 15488	You Can Bring Me All Your Heartaches/A Woman Who's A Woman £15
67	Capitol CL 15499	Dead End Street/Yes It Hurts Doesn't It... £20
67	Capitol CL 15507	Show Business/When Loves Goes Wrong £25
63	Capitol EAP-1 20646	LOST AND LOOKIN' (EP) £50
65	Capitol T 1824	BLACK AND BLUE (LP) £25
66	Capitol (S)T 2459	LIVE (LP) £20
67	Capitol (S)T 2566	SOULIN' (LP) £25
67	Capitol (S)T 2632	CARRYIN' ON! (LP) £20
68	Capitol (S)T 2864	FEELIN' GOOD (LP) £30
69	Capitol ST 2927	YOU'RE GOOD FOR ME (LP).. £20
69	Capitol E-ST 215	THE WAY IT WAS THE WAY IT IS (LP) £20

RAW MATERIAL
69	Evolution E 2441	Time And Illusion/Bobo's Party £60
70	Evolution E 2445	Hi There Hallelujah/Days Of The Fighting Cock £50
70	Evolution E 24495	Traveller Man (Part 1)/Part 2 .... £50
71	RCA Neon NE 1002	Ride On Pony/Religion £50
70	Evolution Z 1006	RAW MATERIAL (LP) £1000
71	RCA Neon NE 8	TIME IS (LP, gatefold sleeve) £1000
(see also Deep Feelings, Shoot)

DANNY RAY
76 Doctor DR 01   Revolution Rock/Version.. £30

DIANE RAY
63 Mercury AMT 1209   Please Don't Talk To The Lifeguard/That's All I Want From You............... £22

DON RAY
78 Polydor 2310610   THE GARDEN OF LOVE (LP)... £20

FROGGIE RAY
| 71 | Big BG 313 | Uncle Charlie/Party Version | £30 |
| 71 | Big BG 314 | Half Moon/RUPIE EDWARDS ALL STARS: Full Moon | £20 |

(see also Hugh Roy Jr. U Roy Jr.)

JAMES RAY
| 62 | Pye International 7N 25126 | If You Gotta Make A Fool Of Somebody/It's Been A Drag | £25 |
| 62 | Pye International 7N 25147 | Itty Bitty Pieces/You Remember The Face | £20 |

JOHNNIE RAY
53	Columbia SCM 5015	Walkin' My Baby Back Home/The Lady Drinks Champagne (B-side with the Four Lads)	£20
53	Columbia SCM 5033	Ma Says, Pa Says/A Full Time Job (with Doris Day)	£20
53	Columbia SCM 5041	Whiskey And Gin/Tell The Lady I Said Goodbye	£20
57	Philips JK 1016	Yes, Tonight, Josephine/No Wedding Today (jukebox issue)	£20
57	Philips JK 1033	Pink Sweater Angel/Texas Tambourine (jukebox issue)	£30
59	Philips PB 952	You're All That I Live For/I'll Never Fall In Love Again (78)	£20
62	London HLG 9484	I Believe (with Timi Yuro)/TIMI YURO: Smile	£15

(see also Timi Yuro)

RICARDO RAY
| 68 | Roulette RO 501 | Nitty Gritty/Mony Mony | £20 |

RAY & COLLUNEY
| 71 | Westwood WRS 001 | TYRANTS OF ENGLAND (LP) | £40 |

CHRIS(TINE) RAYBURN
| 68 | Music Factory CUB 2 | One Way Ticket/Photograph Of Love | £20 |
| 66 | Parlophone PCS7001 | CHRIS RAYBURN (LP) | £25 |

MARGIE RAYBURN
| 57 | London HLU 8515 | I'm Available/If You Were | £25 |
| 58 | London HLU 8648 | I Would/Alright, But It Won't Be Easy | £18 |

RAYKO
| 11 | Autodiscotheque 7 | Inside Out/Sexy Lady (12") | £40 |

DANNY RAYMOND
| 71 | Big Shot BI 587 | Sister Big Stuff/BOY FRIDAY: Free Man | £20 |

MARK RAYMOND & CROWD
| 64 | Columbia DB 7308 | Girls/Remember Me To Julie | £15 |

MARTIN RAYNOR & SECRETS
| 65 | Columbia DB 7563 | Candy To Me/You're A Wonderful One | £60 |

(see also Secrets, Simon's Secrets, Clifford T. Ward)

MIKE RAYNOR & THE CONDORS
| 67 | Decca F22690 | Is She A Woman NOw/My Shy Serenade (export p/s) | £40 |

RAYS
| 57 | London HLU 8505 | Silhouettes/Daddy Cool | £25 |

RAZAR
| 78 | Polydor 2058 983 | Ascension Day/Ain't No Mystery (company sleeve) | £35 |

(see also Third World War, Soho Jets)

RAZBERRY HOLIDAY BAND
| 89 | Caleche LIS 001 | Hangover Square/Promise | £20 |

RAZORCUTS
86	Subway Org. SUBWAY 5	Big Pink Cake/I'll Still Be There (foldover p/s with insert, poly bag, 2,000 only)	£20
86	Subway Org. SUBWAY 8	Sorry To Embarrass You/Summer In Your Heart (p/s, with insert, 2,000 only)	£20
80s	Caff CAFF 10	Sometimes I Worry About You/For Always/Sorry To Embarrass You/Music From The Big Pink (foldaround p/s with insert, 500 only)	£20
88	Creation CRELP 026	STORYTELLER (LP)	£25
89	Creation CRELP 045	THE WORLD KEEPS TURNING (LP)	£25

(see also Cinematics, Red Chair Fadeaway)

RAZORLIGHT
04	Vertigo 986 710-1	UP ALL NIGHT (LP, with free 7")	£40
06	Vertigo 17010901	RAZORLIGHT (LP)	£40
09	Vertigo 17050004	SLIPWAY FIRES (LP)	£18

RAZOR'S EDGE
| 66 | Stateside SS 532 | Let's Call It A Day, Girl/April | £15 |

CHRIS REA
| 74 | Magnet MAG 10 | So Much Love/Born To Lose (no p/s) | £25 |

REACTA
| 79 | Battery Operated WAC 1 | Stop The World/SUS (p/s) | £100 |

(see also Television Personalities)

REACTION (2)
| 70 | Columbia Blue Beat DB 119 | Oh Me, Oh My/RECO: It's Love | £20 |
| 70 | Attack ATT 8022 | You Yes You/CIMARONS: Be There | £15 |

(see also Ezz Reco, Joe Higgs)

REACTION (3)
| 78 | Island WIP 6437 | I Can't Resist/I Am A Case (p/s) | £20 |

(see also Talk Talk, Mark Hollis)

REACTION (4)
| 87 | Waterloo Sunset RUSS 105 | Make Up Your Mind/Four By Four | £18 |

REACTORS
81   Slam! SSM 018   Travel Broadens The Mind/Dreams Without Sleep......................£30

PAT READER
60   Triumph RGM 1024   Ricky/Dear Daddy £60
62   Piccadilly 7N 35077   Cha Cha On The Moon/May Your Heart Stay Young Forever £40
63   Oriole CB 1903   Helpless/Lover's Lane £30

BERTICE READING
57   Decca F 10965   No Flowers By Request/September In The Rain.....................£15
58   Parlophone R 4462   Rock Baby Rock/It's A Boy £60
58   Parlophone R 4462   Rock Baby Rock/It's A Boy (78)..................................£15

REALISTICS
77   Epic 5439   Love Vibrations/The Magic That You Do £15
79   Bronze BRO 81   Pure Magic/Right From The Start £20

REALITY FROM DREAM
75   (no label) CP 109   REALITY FROM DREAM (LP, private pressing).......................£150

REALITY (1)
67   Birchwood BW 01   Simple Skies/Ran Into The Forest £150

REAL KIDS
78   Bronze BRON 509   REAL KIDS (LP) £22

REALLY 3RDS
81   EJSP 9610   Everyday Everywhere/Daptapper (no p/s) £35

REALM
66   CBS 202044   Hard Time Loving You/Certain Kind Of Girl £35
(see also Earl Preston & Realms)

REAL MCCOY
68   Target 7N 17669   Quick Joey Small/Happiness Is Love £20
70   Marble Arch MAL 1251   THIS IS THE REAL McCOY (LP) £20
(see also Tony Colton)

REAL THING
75   Pye 7N 25681   Stone Cold Love Affair/A Love That's Real (solid and push out centres)......£25
81   Calibre CAB 109   I Believe In You/You're My Number One £30
81   Calibre CABL 109   I Believe In You (Extended Version)/You're My Number One (12")..£30
77   Aye NSPH 20   4 FROM 8 (LP) £25
78   Pye NSPL 18587   STEP INTO OUR WORLD (LP) £15
79   Calibre CAB LP 1001   SAINTS OR SINNERS (LP)..£15
(see also Chants)

REASONS
78   Island WIP 6467   Hard Day At The Office/Baby Bright Eyes (p/s)...................£30

REBEL REGULARS
81   Greensleeves GRED 48   Jah Love (with General Saint)/Irregular Dubs Part 1 and 2 (12")......£35

REBEL ROUSERS
68   Fontana TF 973   Should I?/As I Look..£200
(see also Cliff Bennett & Rebel Rousers, Soul Sounds)

REBELS
78   Rigid IS REB 1029   Suicide/The Leader Of The Rebellion £800

REBELS & ALLIES
79   Brixton Sound BS01234 BROKEN HEART (LP) £60

REBELS (JAMAICA)
70   Trojan TR 7779   It's All In The Game (lead vocal Jimmy Riley)/Easy Come £15
76   Black Wax WAX 16   Rhodesia/Version £20
(see also The Pioneers)

REBELS (U.K.)
67   Page One POF 017   Hard To Love You/Call Me £40

REBOUNDS
64   Fontana TF 461   Help Me/The World Is Mine £25

REBS
58   Capitol CL 14932   Bunky/Renegade £15

RECKLESS
92   Pulse-8 12LOSE 24   Time To Make The Floor Burn (The Reckless Hypermix)/Take Me (Ruff Mix)/Take Me
                            (Uplifting Piano Mix) (12", p/s)................................£25

RECO
69   Downtown DT 417   Quando Quando/Reg 'A' Jeg (as Reco & Rudies) £25
69   Jackpot JP 710   Memory Of Don Drummond/THE TOBIES: Resting £25
69   Treasure Isle TI 7052 The Lion Speaks/ANDY CAPP: Pop A Top £25
69   Pama ECO 14   RECO IN REGGAE LAND (LP)..£120
(see also Reaction, Don Reco, Rico Rodriguez, Joe Monsano, Slim Smith, Laurel Aitken)

DON RECO
71   Big Shot BI 597   Waterloo Rock/LLOYD'S ALL STARS: Walls Soul.....................£20
(see also Reco)

EZZ RECO & LAUNCHERS
64   Columbia SEG 8326   JAMAICA BLUE BEAT (EP) £25
(see also Reaction)

RECORDS
88   Waterfront WF 042   A SUNNY AFTERNOON IN WATERLOO (LP) £25
RECRUITS
83   RE1   THREE SQUEEZES EP (12", p/s) £30
89   SRT 9KS 1994 RE 2   See My Face/Dream Heaven Scene (p/s) £20
RED ALLIGATOR
69   Youngblood YB1004   Real Cool/Slow Down...£18
(see Jimmy Powell)
DANNY RED
93   Abba Jahnoi AJ 001   Jah Is Here/Version (12")...£18
95   Columbia 662157 6   BE GRATEFUL EP (12", p/s) £40
RED (2)
83   Jigsaw SAW 2   RED (LP, private pressing)..£25
RED ALERT (1)
69   Total TL3   Witch Woman/Sabra..£50
RED ALERT (2)
80   Guardian GM-RA/B 61   BORDER GUARDS (EP) £1000
83   No Future OI 27   THERE'S A GUITAR BURNING (12" EP)...£15
83   No Future PUNK 5   WE'VE GOT THE POWER (LP)..£15
RED ALERT (3)
82   Steel City AJS7R   Run To Ground/Wild You (no p/s, some with hand-made 'Wildfire' stickers over band
                                name)..£20
(see also Next Band)
RED BEANS & RICE
80   Chiswick CHIS 124   That Driving Beat/Throw It In The Grass £15
REDBONE
70   CBS 64069   REDBONE (LP) £15
70   CBS 64198   POTLATCH (LP) £15
72   Epic EQ 30815   MESSAGE FROM A DRUM (LP, quadraphonic)...£20
REDBRASS
76   Riverside RR 2   SILENCE IS CONSENT (LP, insert)..£20
REDCAPS
63   Decca F 11716   Shout/Little Things You Do..£20
63   Decca F 11789   Talkin' 'Bout You/Come On Girl £15
64   Decca F 11903   Mighty Fine Girl/Funny Things...£15
REDCELL
92   B12 B1205   REDCELL EP (12")..£25
92   B12 B1205   REDCELL EP (12", purple vinyl)...£80
92   B12 B1207   RETREAT FROM UNPLEASANT REALITIES EP (12")...£40
92   B12 B1207   RETREAT FROM UNPLEASANT REALITIES EP (12", blue vinyl).....................£60
92   B12 B1207   RETREAT FROM UNPLEASANT REALITIES EP (12", red vinyl)......................£60
93   B12 B1208   INTERIM OUTERIM EP(12")...£15
93   B12 B1208   INTERIM OUTERIM EP (12", white vinyl)...£60
96   B12 B1215   Untitled (12", White label promo)...£60
RED CHAIR FADEAWAY
89   Cosmic Eng. M. CTA 103   Let It Happen/Myra/Dragonfly/Grasshopper (12", p/s, 500 only) £15
90   Cosmic Eng. M. CTA 105   Mr Jones/Chimney Pots/Faraway Lights/Out Of The Grey (12", p/s, 450 only) £15
91   Tangerine MM 10   CURIOUSER AND CURIOUSER (LP, foldaround sleeve with booklet, no'd)........£20
(see also Razorcuts)
RED CLOUD
82   Echo STLP 1009   RED CLOUD IN DUB (LP) £30
RED CRAYOLA
78   Radar SAM 88   Pink Stainless Tail/13TH FLOOR ELEVATORS She Lives (In A Time Of Her Own) (promo)..£15
78   Radar RAD 12   THE PARABLES OF ARABLE LAND (LP, stickered sleeve) £20
79   Radar RAD 18   SOLDIER TALK (LP) £15
FREDDIE REDD
58   Nixa NJL 19   GET HAPPY (LP)...£200
GENE REDD & GLOBETROTTERS
59   Parlophone R 4584   Red River Valley Rock/Kentucky Home Rock..£15
OTIS REDDING

SINGLES : SINGLES AND LPS
64   London HLK 9833   Pain In My Heart/Something Is Worrying Me £25
64   London HLK 9876   Come To Me/Don't Leave Me This Way...£25
65   Atlantic AT 4024   Mr Pitiful/That's How Strong My Love Is...£25
65   Sue WI 362   Shout Bamalama/Fat Girl...£30
65   Atlantic AT 4029   I've Been Loving You Too Long/Winter Wonderland (unissued, demos only)................£75
65   Atlantic AT 4039   Respect/I've Been Loving You Too Long..£18
65   Atlantic AT 4050   My Girl/Down In The Valley...£15
69   Evolution E 2442   She's All Right/Tuff Enuff £15
66   Sue IEP 710   EARLY OTIS REDDING (EP) £100
65   Atlantic ATL 5029   THE GREAT OTIS REDDING SINGS SOUL BALLADS (LP) £50
66   Atlantic ATL 5041   OTIS BLUE: OTIS REDDING SINGS SOUL (LP) £60
66   Atlantic 587 011   THE SOUL ALBUM (LP)...£30

66	Atlantic 587 035	THE GREAT OTIS REDDING SINGS SOUL BALLADS (LP, reissue)	£20
66	Atlantic 587/588 036	OTIS BLUE: OTIS REDDING SINGS SOUL (LP, reissue, mono/stereo)	£35
67	Atlantic 587/588 050	COMPLETE AND UNBELIEVABLE: THE OTIS REDDING DICTIONARY OF SOUL (LP)	£25
67	Atlantic 587 042	PAIN IN MY HEART (LP)	£25
67	Stax VOLT 418	THE HISTORY OF OTIS REDDING (LP)	£30
68	Stax 589 016	OTIS REDDING IN EUROPE (LP)	£30
68	Stax 230 001/231 001	THE DOCK OF THE BAY (LP)	£20
68	Atlantic 587/588 113	THE IMMORTAL OTIS REDDING (LP)	£30
68	Atlantic 587/588 148	OTIS REDDING AT THE WHISKEY A GO GO, LOS ANGELES (LP)	£25
69	Atco 228 001	THE HISTORY OF OTIS REDDING (LP, reissue)	£15
69	Atco 228 025	LOVE MAN (LP)	£30
70	Atlantic 2464 003	REMEMBERING (LP)	£18
71	Atco 2400 018	TELL THE TRUTH (LP)	£18
71	Reprise K 40430	LIVE AT THE MONTEREY INTERNATIONAL POP FESTIVAL (LP, shared with Jimi Hendrix)	£30

OTIS REDDING & CARLA THOMAS
| 67 | Stax 589 007 | THE KING AND QUEEN OF SOUL | £30 |

(see also Carla Thomas)

RED DIRT
| 70 | Fontana STL 5540 | RED DIRT (LP) | £1750 |
| 10 | Morgan Bluetown BT 5004 | RED DIRT (LP, reissue, 500 only, with signed and numbered certificate) | £25 |

RED DRAGON
| 86 | Redman Intl. RED 4 | Ease Off/ADMIRAL TIBET: New Tactics (12") | £20 |

EMMA REDE
| 67 | Columbia DB 8136 | Just Like A Man/I Gotta Be With You (DJ copy) | £40 |
| 67 | Columbia DB 8136 | Just Like A Man/I Gotta Be With You | £20 |

(see also Jacky, Jackie Lee, Raindrops)

TEDDY REDELL
| 60 | London HLK 9140 | Judy/Can't You See | £60 |

RED FLY
| 70 | Red Fly RF 01 | Colour It Black/Scream It Out | £30 |

REDGEE SEEBOE
| 74 | Bug 38 | Please Don't Bring Your Sister/Daphnies Brains | £15 |

RED HARVEST
| 87 | Quiet QS 019 | Murder/Fifty Years/Burning Party (p/s) | £20 |

RED HAWKES
| 66 | ALP 595001 | Friday Night/Lonely Boy | £50 |

(see also Mark Five, Nazareth)

RED HERRING
| 87 | Crystal 717 | Albert Road/Harbour Lights | £30 |

RED HOT
| 91 | Robin Hood RH 005 | Letter To My Baby/Version (12") | £15 |

RED HOT & BLUE
| 85 | Northwood NOR 1 | RED HOT & BLUE (LP) | £25 |

RED HOT CHILI PEPPERS
89	EMI 12MT 70	KNOCK ME DOWN EP (12", p/s)	£15
90	EMI 12MTG 88	Higher Ground/Catholic Schoolgirls Rule/None As Weird As Me (12", gatefold sleeve)	£15
84	EMI USA MTL 1056	RED HOT CHILLI PEPPERS (LP)	£30
87	EMI America AML 2125	UPLIFT MOFO PARTY PLAN (LP)	£20
89	EMI America MTL 1046	MOTHERS MILK (LP)	£20
91	Warner Bros. 7599 26681-1	BLOOD SUGAR SEX MAGIK (2-LP, printed inners)	£60
95	Warner Bros. 9362 457331	ONE HOT MINUTE (2-LP)	£75
99	Warner Bros. 9362 47386-1	CALIFORNICATION (2-LP, 1st pressing with one small 'pressing' ring around centre hole)	£100
01	Warner Bros. 9362-47386-1	CALIFORNICATION (2-LP 2nd pressing with two 'pressing' rings around centre hole)	£50
02	Warner Bros. 9362-48140-1	BY THE WAY (2-LP)	£40
02	Warner Bros. 93624854-1	GREATEST HITS (2-LP)	£100
06	Warner Bros. 9362499961	STADIUM ARCADIUM (4xLP box set with foil outer & 2 booklets)	£100
06	Warner Bros. 9362443911	STADIUM ARCADIUM (4xLP, standard edition)	£50
11	Warner Bros. 9362-49564-6	I'M WITH YOU (2-LP)	£45

(see also Atoms For Peace)

RED HOUSE PAINTERS
94	4AD BAD 4004	Shock Me/Sundays And Holidays/Three-Legged Cat/Shock Me (12", p/s)	£40
92	4AD CAD 2014	DOWN COLOURFUL HILL (LP)	£80
93	4AD DAD 3008	RED HOUSE PAINTERS (2-LP, inner sleeves)	£80
93	4AD CAD 3016	RED HOUSE PAINTERS (LP, different release from DAD 3008)	£80
95	4A DADD 5005	OCEAN BEACH (LP, 2 x 10" with inner sleeves)	£80
16	4AD RHP BOX 1	RED HOUSE PAINTERS (6-LP bronze vinyl box set)	£150

RED LETTERS
| 79 | Burning Bing CPS 025 | Sacred Voices/Shot In The Dark/Science Has The Answer (folded p/s) | £120 |

RED LIGHT
94	Black Tracks BT 001	Skylarking/Liquidator (12")	£30
94	Red Light RL001	Coca Cola/Murder Tonight/Look Good (12")	£25
94	Red Light RL003	Wow Yeh/The Burial (12")	£25

94	Red Light RL003	Roots Rock/Fire (12")	£15
95	Red Light RL005	Get Up/Sensi (12")	£20
95	Red Light RL006	The Remix/Killer Sound Boy Nitty (12")	£20
95	Red Light RL009	Hunt And Seek/Selekta (12")	£30

RED LIGHTS

| 78 | Free Range PF 5 | Never Wanna Leave/Seventeen (p/s) | £70 |

RED LONDON

| 84 | Razor RAZ 10 | THIS IS ENGLAND (LP) | £30 |

RED LORRY, YELLOW LORRY

| 82 | Red Rhino RED 20 | Beating My Head/I'm Still Waiting (p/s) | £15 |

RED MEAT

| 72 | Worsley WR 1 | She/My Mind Sleeps On (p/s) | £50 |

RED MONEY

| 90 | PF&G PFG 001 | MY ERSTWHILE COMPANION EP | £15 |

JEAN REDPATH

| 66 | Bounty BY 6004 | LOVE LILT AND LAUGHTER (LP) | £20 |

RED RAGE

| 80 | Flicknife FLS 203 | Total Control/I Give You This (p/s) | £40 |

REDSKINS

| 82 | CNT CNT 007 | Lev Bronstein/The Peasant Army (p/s) | £25 |

RED SNAPPER

96	Warp WARLP45	PRINCE BLIMEY (2-LP)	£25
98	Warp WARLP56	MAKING BONES (2-LP)	£25
00	Warp WARLP78	OUR AIM IS TO SATISFY RED SNAPPER (2-LP)	£20

RED SQUARES

| 67 | Columbia DB 8160 | Mountain's High/Pity Me | £20 |

RED STRIPE

| 80 | Snotty Snail NELCOL 4 | Inside Of Pain/Wogs Go Home/Trois Vielles Sacs Assises Lisant (hand stamped sleeve and insert) | £100 |

RED TELEVISION

| 71 | Brecht Times | RED TELEVISION (LP, private pressing with insert) | £200 |

REDUCERS

| 78 | Vibes XP 1/VR 001 | Things Go Wrong/We Are Normal (p/s) | £50 |
| 79 | Vibes VR 003 | Man With A Gun/Vengeance/Can't Stop Now (p/s) | £50 |

REDWOOD

| 79 | SRT SRTS/79/CUS 582 | Give The Indian Back His Land/Rock Of Ages (500 only, this price for 300 in p/s and insert) | £35 |
| 79 | SRT SRTS/79/CUS 582 | Give The Indian Back His Land/Rock Of Ages (500 only, this price for 200 with no p/s) | £15 |

REDWOODS

| 62 | Columbia DB 4859 | Please Mr Scientist/Where You Used To Be | £25 |

DIZZY REECE QUINTET

58	Tempo EXA 84	A VARIATION ON MONK (EP)	£200
59	Tempo EXA 86	NOWHERE TO GO (EP, featuring Tubby Hayes)	£200
59	Tempo EXA 89	ON THE SCENE (EP)	£100
55	Tempo LAP 3	A NEW STAR... (10" LP)	£250
57	Tempo TAP 9	PROGRESS REPORT (LP)	£600
58	Esquire 32 185	ASIA MINOR (LP)	£100
84	Jasmine JASM 2013	PROGRESS REPORT (LP, reissue)	£20

(see also Victor Feldman, Ronnie Scott)

CHUCK REED

57	Brunswick 05646	Whispering Heart/Another Love Has Ended	£15
58	Columbia DB 4113	No School Tomorrow/Let's Put Our Hearts Together	£30
62	Stateside SS 108	Just Plain Hurt/Talking No Trash	£15

DENNY REED

| 61 | London HLK 9274 | A Teenager Feels It Too/Hot Water | £18 |

J REED

| 96 | Ugly UGM 005 | VIBE NATIONS EP (12") | £20 |

JERRY REED

58	Capitol CL 14851	Bessie Baby/Too Young To Be Blue	£300
58	Capitol CL 14851	Bessie Baby/Too Young To Be Blue (78)	£50
69	RCA SF 8006	ALABAMA WILD MAN (LP)	£18

JIMMY REED

60	Top Rank JAR 333	Baby What You Want Me To Do/Caress Me Baby	£20
60	Top Rank JAR 394	Found Love/Where Can You Be	£20
60	Top Rank JAR 533	Hush-Hush/Going By The River	£20
63	Stateside SS 205	Shame Shame Shame/Let's Get Together	£22
66	Sue WI 4004	Odds And Ends/Going By The River Pt. II (B-side actually Pt. I)	£40
67	HMV POP 1579	Two Ways To Skin A Cat/Got Nowhere To Go	£40
64	Stateside SE 1016	BLUES OF JIMMY REED (EP)	£30
64	Stateside SE 1026	I'M JIMMY REED (EP)	£30
62	Stateside SL 10012	JIMMY REED AT CARNEGIE HALL (LP)	£20
64	Stateside SL 10055	JUST JIMMY REED (LP)	£30
64	Stateside SL 10069	SINGS THE BEST OF THE BLUES (LP)	£20

MINT VALUE £

64	Stateside SL 10086	PLAYS 12-STRING GUITAR BLUES (LP)	£20
64	Stateside SL 10091	THE BOSS MAN OF THE BLUES (LP)	£30
65	Fontana 688 514 ZL	THINGS AIN'T WHAT THEY USED TO BE (LP)	£20
67	HMV CLP/CSD 3611	THE NEW JIMMY REED (LP)	£20
68	Stateside S(S)L 10221	SOULIN' (LP)	£35
69	Action ACLP 6011	DOWN IN VIRGINIA (LP)	£60

LOU REED

72	RCA RCA 2240	Walk And Talk It/Wild Child	£15
72	RCA SF 8281	LOU REED (LP, laminated sleeve, orange label)	£50
72	RCA LSP 4807	TRANSFORMER (LP, 1st pressing, laminated sleeve, orange labels)	£100
73	RCA LSP 4807	TRANSFORMER (LP, 2nd pressing, non-laminated sleeve, orange labels)	£40
73	RCA RS 1002	BERLIN (LP, orange labels with insert)	£30
74	RCA APL1 0472	ROCK N ROLL ANIMAL (LP, gatefold)	£20
74	RCA APL1 0611	SALLY CAN'T DANCE (LP, insert)	£15
75	RCA CPL 2 1101	METAL MACHINE MUSIC (2-LP, U.S. import with U.K. sticker)	£35
76	RCA RS 1035	CONEY ISLAND BABY (LP)	£15
78	Arista SPART 1045	STREET HASSLE (LP, insert)	£15
79	Arista SPART 1093	THE BELLS (LP)	£15
80	Arista SPART 1131	GROWING UP IN PUBLIC (LP)	£15
81	RCA Intl.INTS 5061	TRANSFORMER (LP, reissue, green labels)	£20
82	RCA NL84780	THE BLUE MASK (LP)	£15
89	Sire 925 829 1	NEW YORK (LP)	£20
96	Warner Bros. 9362 46159-1	SET THE TWILIGHT REELING (LP, inner)	£40

(see also Velvet Underground)

LULA REED

55	Parlophone CMSP 34	Troubles On Your Mind/Bump On A Log (export issue)	£60
55	Parlophone DP 408	Troubles On Your Mind/Bump On A Log (78, export issue)	£15

LULA REED & SYL JOHNSON

63	Ember EMB EP 4535	RHYTHM & BLUES BLUE BEAT STYLE (EP)	£70

LULA REED & FREDDIE KING

63	Ember EMB 4536	LULA REED AND FREDDIE KING (EP)	£60

(see also Freddie King)

OLIVER REED

61	Decca F 11390	The Wild One/Lonely For A Girl	£15
62	Piccadilly 7N 35037	Sometimes/Ecstasy	£15

(see also Joyce Blair)

TAWNY REED

65	Pye 7N 15935	Needle In A Haystack/I've Got A Feeling	£50
66	Pye 7N 17078	You Can't Take It Away/My Heart Cries	£30

WINSTON REEDY

80	Music Scene MKS 6255	That Girl/GEORGE FAITH: Eternal Love (12")	£18
82	SG SG 17	Daughter Of Zion/Zion Dub (12")	£30
83	Carousel 12CAR 48	Dim The Light/Shower Of Rain (12")	£20
84	Dep DEP 21	Ambition/Romantic Girl (12")	£15

REEF

95	Sony Soho Square 480698 1	REPLENISH (LP, gatefold)	£70
97	Sony 4869401	GLOW (LP)	£25

VALA REEGAN & VALARONS

66	Atlantic 584 009	Fireman/Living In The Past	£250
66	Atlantic 584 009	Fireman/Living In The Past (DJ copy)	£300

JUSTYN REES

70	Breakthrough HP 102	DOWN MY ROAD (LP)	£35

DELLA REESE

66	HMV POP 1553	It Was A Very Good Year/Solitary Woman	£30
68	Stateside SS 2128	It Was A Very Good Year/I Had To Know My Way Around	£20
59	London LTZ-J 15163	THE HISTORY OF THE BLUES (LP)	£30
60	RCA RD 27167/SF 5057	DELLA (LP)	£15
61	RCA RD 27208/SF 5091	DELLA DELLA CHA-CHA-CHA (LP)	£18
62	RCA RD 27234/SF 5112	SPECIAL DELIVERY (LP)	£20
63	RCA Victor RD/SF 7508	ON STAGE (LP)	£15
68	Stateside SL 10261	I GOTTA BE ME...THIS TRIP OUT (LP)	£35
74	People PLEO 7	LET ME IN YOUR LIFE (LP)	£30

TONY REESE

59	London HLJ 8987	Just About This Time Tomorrow/Lesson In Love	£20

EDDIE REEVES

62	London HL 9548	Cry Baby/Talk Talk	£20

JIM REEVES

78s

56	London HLU 8351	The Wilder Your Heart Beats, The Sweeter You Love/ Where Does A Broken Heart Go	£15
57	RCA RCA 1005	Four Walls/I Know And You Know	£15
58	RCA RCA 1074	Blue Boy/Theme Of Love	£15
59	RCA RCA 1144	Partners/I'm Beginning To Forget You	£30
60	RCA RCA 1168	He'll Have To Go/In A Mansion Stands My Love	£40

SINGLES

54	London HL 8014	Bimbo/Gipsy Heart	£100
54	London HL 8030	Mexican Joe/I Could Cry (with Circle O Ranch Boys)	£100
54	London HL 8055	Butterfly Love/It's Hard To Love Just One (with String Band)	£100
54	London HL 8064	Echo Bonita/Then I'll Stop Loving You (with Louisiana Hayride Band)	£100
54	London HL 8105	Padre Of Old San Antone/Mother Went A-Walkin'	£60
55	London HL 8118	Penny Candy/I'll Follow You (with Louisiana Hayride Band)	£60
55	London HLU 8185	Tahiti/Give Me One More Kiss	£60
55	London HL 8159	Drinking Tequila/Red-Eyed And Rowdy	£100

(The 45s listed above were Issued with gold label print on black labels.)

56	London HLU 8351	The Wilder Your Heart Beats, The Sweeter You Love/ Where Does A Broken Heart Go	£50

EPs

54	London RE-P 1015	THE BIMBO BOY (EP)	£40
55	London RE-P 1033	THE BIMBO BOY VOL. 2 (EP)	£40

REFARENDUM

70	RCA 1973	Lost and Found/Please Help Somebody	£20

REFLECTION

68	Reflection RS 6001	Brave New Day/Lord I Believe (p/s)	£60
68	Reflection RL 3015	THE PRESENT TENSE: SONGS OF SYDNEY CARTER (LP)	£18

(see also Sounds Of Salvation)

REFLECTIONS A.O.B.

86	Keep KEEP 1 12	ONLY IN MY DREAMS EP (12")	£40

REFLECTIONS (U.S.) (1)

64	Stateside SS 294	(Just Like) Romeo & Juliet/Can't You Tell By The Look In My Eyes	£60
64	Stateside SS 294	(Just Like) Romeo & Juliet/Can't You Tell By The Look In My Eyes (DJ copy)	£100
65	Stateside SS 406	Poor Man's Son/Comin' At You	£30
74	Tamla Motown TMG 907	(Just Like) Romeo & Juliet/Can't You Tell By The Look In My Eyes (reissue)	£15
77	ABC ABC 4181	Like Adam And Eve/AUGUST & DENEEN: We Go Together	£15
65	Stateside SE 1034	POOR MAN'S SON (EP)	£125

(see also The High and Mighty)

REFLECTIONS (U.S.) (2)

75	Capitol E-ST 11460	LOVE ON DELIVERY (LP)	£15

REFLEX ACTION

80	Shock Rock SS 506	Spies/Recession	£300

REFUGEE

74	Charisma CAS 1087	REFUGEE (LP, with lyric inner sleeve, large 'Mad Hatter' label)	£20

(see also Nice, Yes)

NORRIS REGAL

83	Sirion SRN 001	Struggle/Version (12")	£40

JOAN REGAN

54	Decca F 10362	Wait For Me, Darling (with Johnston Brothers)/Two Kinds Of Tears (gold lettering)	£20
60	Pye 7N 15310	One Of The Lucky Ones/My Thanks to You	£15
66	CBS 202100	Don't Talk To Me About Love/I'm No Toy	£20
66	CBS 202100	Don't Talk To Me About Love/I'm No Toy (DJ copy)	£30
67	CBS 2657	No-One Beside Me/A Love So Fine	£20
54	Decca LF 1182	THE GIRL NEXT DOOR (10" LP)	£40
56	Decca LK 4153	JUST JOAN (LP)	£100

TOMMY REGAN

64	Colpix PX 725	I'll Never Stop Loving You/This Time I'm Losing You (DJ Copy)	£125
64	Colpix PX 725	I'll Never Stop Loving You/This Time I'm Losing You	£100

(see also Marcels)

REGENTS (U.K.) (1)

63	Oriole CB 1912	Bye Bye Johnny/Come Along	£40

(see also Buddy Britten)

REGENTS (U.K.) (2)

66	CBS 202247	Words/Worryin' Kind	£45

REGENTS (U.S.)

61	Columbia DB 4666	Barbara Ann/I'm So Lonely	£30
61	Columbia DB 4694	Runaround/Laura My Darling	£30

REGGAE BOYS

69	Amalgamated AMG 841	Me No Born Ya/The Wicked Must Survive	£60
69	Amalgamated AMG 843	The Reggae Train/Dolly House On Fire	£60
69	Gas GAS 135	Ba Ba/GLEN ADAMS: Power Cut	£70
69	Unity UN 530	What You Gonna Do/HEDLEY BENNETT: Hot Coffee	£110
70	Bullet BU 431	Pupa Live On Eye Top/Give Me Faith	£40
70	Gas GAS 122	Phrases/Give Me Faith	£50
70	Pressure Beat PR 5503	Walk By Day, Fly By Night/JOE GIBBS & DESTROYERS: Unknown Tongue	£75

(see also Glen Adams, Alva Lewis, Upsetters)

REGGAE GEORGE

83	Greensleeves GRED 114	You'll Never Know/We Still Survive (12")	£15

REGGAE GIRLS

69	Nu Beat NB024	Rescue Me/SOULMATES: Unity Is Strength	£100

REGGAE REGULAR
84   Greensleeves GREL 64   GHETTO ROCK (LP)..£30

REGGAE STRINGS
73   Trojan TRLS 54   REGGAE STRINGS (LP)..£20
(see also Horace Faith)

ELIS REGINA
69   Philis BF 1812   Zazueiro/Corrioa De Jangada..£50
69   Philips SBL 7905   ELIS REGINA IN LONDON (LP)...£100

REGULARS
81   Soundoff SOFFLP 001   I & I (LP, with band name on gold sticker on front of sleeve) £30

LOU REICHNER BAND
80   ESR Records S/80/CUS 733   Photograph/I Sit And Stare/The End Of The World/Out On The Streets (also listed as
                                   ESR 4, 300 only, with insert)..£50
80   ESR Records S/80/CUS 733   Photograph/I Sit And Stare/The End Of The World/Out On The Streets (also listed as
                                   ESR 4, 300 only, without insert) £20

AL REID
69   Blue Cat BS 161   Vietcong/MAX ROMEO: Me Want Man £60
69   Blue Cat BS 163   Darling/MAX ROMEO: It's Not The Way...£120

CARLTON REID
66   Ska Beat JB 254   Funny/Turn On The Lights...£25
69   Blue Cat BS 162   Leave Me To Cry/Warning...£125

DENNIS REID
79   Discotheque PFL 2102   Living In The Slum/Prophet Shall Be Born (12")...£60

DUKE REID (& HIS GROUP)
60   Blue Beat BB 24   Duke's Cookies (with His Group)/JIVING JUNIORS: I Wanna Love £25
62   Blue Beat BB 119   Twelve Minutes To Go (actually by Don Drummond)/ HORTENSE ELLIS: Midnight
                                   Train..£30
63   Duke DK 1002   Pink Lane Shuffle (with His Group)/LAUREL AITKEN: Low Down Dirty Girl £20
67   Master's Time MT 003   Religious Service At Bond Street Gospel Hall/Religious Service At Bond Street Gospel
                                   Hall (Continued)...£15
67   Trojan TR 001   Judge Sympathy (actually by Freedom Singers & Duke Reid All Stars)/ROLAND
                                   ALPHONSO: Never To Be Mine...£50
60s Doctor Bird DB 1028   True Confessions (actually by the Silvertones)/TOMMY McCCOOK : More Love............£60
72   Duke Reid DR 2522   Hurt Parts 1 & 2 (actually by Eagles [Jamaica]) £20
69   Trojan TTL 8   GOLDEN HITS (LP)...£35
(see also Chuck & Darby, Derrick Morris, Stranger)

LEYROY REID
68   Blue Cat BS 125   The Fiddler/LOVELETTES: Shook £150
68   Blue Cat BS 127   Great Surprise/TEN(N)ORS: Khaki £65
(see also Nehemiah Reed)

MARC REID
66   CBS 202244   For No One/Lonely City Blues £15
67   CBS 202581   Magic Book/My World Turns Around £18
67   CBS 2950   We Should Live Together/Sale By Auction...£15

NEHEMIAH REID('S ALL STARS)
68   Island WI 3102   Family War/Give Me That Love £40
70   Hot Shot HS 03   Hot Pepper/Seawave (as Nehemiah Reid's All Stars).......................................£80
70   Torpedo TOR 23   Mafia/H.E.L.L. 5 (as Nehemiah Reid's All Stars)...£150
(see also Leyroy Reid, Cynthia Richards)

P. REID
65   Ska Beat JB 197   Redeemed/Goodbye World £18

SANDRA REID
83   Sir George SG 004   Don't Tell Me Tell Her/Kaleidoscope (12")..£75
83   Sir George SG 004   Don't Tell Me Tell Her/Kaleidoscope..£25
83   Sir George SGLP 001   IF DREAMS WERE REAL (LP) £20
84   Sir George SGLP 004   FEEL SO GOOD (LP) £25

TERRY REID (& JAYWALKERS)
68   Columbia DB 8409   Better By Far/Fires Alive...£20
69   Columbia PSRS 323   Superlungs (promo only, as "Terry Reid Is Superlungs").................................£25
69   Columbia SCX 6370   TERRY REID (LP, laminated front, flipbacks)...£50
69   M. For Pleasure MFP 5220   THE MOST OF TERRY REID (LP, reissue of Terry Reid).....................................£15
73   Atlantic K 40340   RIVER (LP, gatefold sleeve)..£50
76   ABC ABCL 5162   SEED OF MEMORY (LP)..£50
79   Capitol E-ST 11857   ROGUE WAVES (LP)..£15
91   WEA 9031 74905 1   THE DRIVER (LP) £25
(see also Peter Jay & Jaywalkers)

REIGN
70   Regal Zonophone RZ 3028   Line Of Least Resistance/Natural Lovin' Man £90
(see also Yardbirds, Keith Relf, Renaissance, Armageddon, Illusion)

REINCARNATE
82   Zipp REIN 001   Take It Or Leave It/Metal In Disguise...£70

REINDEER SECTION
01   Bright Star BSR 14V   Y'ALL GET SCARED NOW, YA HEAR! (LP) £30
02   Bright Star BSR 19V   SON OF EVIL REINDEER (LP) £30
(see also Arab Strap, Belle & Sebastian, Snow Patrol, Mogwai, Teenage Fanclub, Idlewild)

LOU REIZNER
69 Phillips   On Days Like This/Get A Bloomin' Move On £15
REJECTS
84 Heavy Metal HMR 22   QUIET STORM (LP)... £15
(see also Cockney Rejects)
REJOICE!
69 Stateside S(S)L 5009   REJOICE! (LP)... £20
RELATIVES
80 Smile SR 018   As A Child/Say Goodbye To Your Body £20
JANE RELF
71 Decca F 13231   Without A Song From You/Make My Time Pass By... £30
(see also Renaissance, Gordon Jackson)
KEITH RELF
66 Columbia DB 7920   Mr. Zero/Knowing £70
66 Columbia DB 8084   Shapes In My Mind/Blue Sands £100
(see also Yardbirds, Jim McCarty, Renaissance, Reign, Together, Armageddon)
RELOAD
92 Evolution EVO 01   RELOAD EP (12", plain sleeve) £20
92 Evolution EVO 02   AUTO RELOAD EP (12", with E 621) £35
92 Evolution EVO 03   RELOAD EP (12", 1-side credited to E 621) £40
93 Infonet INF 04LP   A COLLECTION OF SHORT STORIES (2-LP, with colour booklet)................................ £50
93 Infonet INF 04LP   A COLLECTION OF SHORT STORIES (2-LP) £40
(see also Global Communications, Link, Mystic Institute)
R.E.M.
SINGLES
83 I.R.S. PFSX 1026   Talk About The Passion/Shaking Through/Carnival Of Sorts (Box Cars)/1,000,000 (12",
                               p/s).. £15
84 I.R.S. IRSX 105   So. Central Rain (I'm Sorry)/Voice Of Harold/Pale Blue Eyes (12", p/s) £15
84 I.R.S. IRSX 107   (Don't Go Back To) Rockville/Wolves/9 - 9 (Live Version)/Gardening At Night (live) (12",
                               p/s).. £15
86 I.R.S. DIRM 128   Superman/White Tornado/Femme Fatale (CD, unissued)... £0
88 I.R.S. DIRM 161   Finest Worksong (LP Version)/Time After Time, Etc. (live)/ It's The End Of The World
                               As We Know It (And I Feel Fine) (CD, numbered stencilled 7" box, 5,000 only) £15
ALBUMS
83 IRS SP70604   MURMUR (LP, 1st pressing, with 'Original Sound recording made by IRS Inc') £30
84 IRS IRSA 7045   RECKONING (LP) £20
85 IRS MIRF 1003   FABLES OF THE RECONSTRUCTION/RECONSTRUCTION OF THE FABLES (LP) £20
86 IRS ILP 4653811   LIFE'S RICH PAGEANT (LP)... £20
87 IRS SP70054   DEAD LETTER OFFICE (LP) £15
90 IRS 46588-2   THE COLLECTION (5-CD box set) £40
91 Warner Bros. WX404   OUT OF TIME (LP, with free 7")... £40
91 Warner Bros. WX404   OUT OF TIME (LP, inner).. £30
92 Warner Bros. 9362-45055-1
    WX488   AUTOMATIC FOR THE PEOPLE (LP, 1st pressing with WMME in run out groove, inner) £60
92 Warner Bros. 9362-45055-1 AUTOMATIC FOR THE PEOPLE (LP, 2nd pressing without WMME and B922353 in run
    WX488   out groove, inner) £40
94 Warner Bros. 9362-45740-1 MONSTER (LP) £80
96 Warner Bros.   NEW ADVENTURES IN HI-FI (2-LP, gatefold) £150
    9362-463210-1
98 Warner Bros. 9362-47112-1 UP (2-LP) £150
01 Warner Bros. 9362 479461   REVEAL (LP)... £100
03 Warners 9362 48381-1   IN TIME: THE BEST OF REM 1988-2003 (2-LP)... £150
04 Warner Bros. 9362 48894-1 AROUND THE SUN (2-LP)... £150
11 Warner Bros. 9362-49626-9 COLLAPSE INTO NOW (LP)... £75
18 Craft 00888072067721   BEST OF REM AT THE BBC (2-LP, gatefold) £25
19 Craft 00888072067721   BINGO HAND JOB LIVE 1991 (2-LP)... £30
PROMOS
83 I.R.S. PFP 1017   Radio Free Europe/There She Goes Again (p/s, large 'A' on label)............................ £50
88 I.R.S. WIRM(T) 161 DL   Finest Worksong (Lengthy Club Mix)/Finest Worksong (Other Mix)/Time After Time
                               Etc. (12" in 'media' p/s)... £15
92 I.R.S. CDREM 92   THE ALTERNATIVE RADIO SAMPLER (CD, 7-track promo, includes unreleased version of
                               'Gardening At Night')... £50
03 Warners PR 04359   THE BEST OF REM - IN TIME 1980-2003 (promo box set containing 18 1-track CDs each
                               housed in individual card sleeve in flip top box)... £40
FLEXIDISCS : FLEXIDISCS & OTHER RELEASES
85 Bucketfull Of Brains BOB 5 Tighten Up (hard vinyl test pressing, 50 only) £50
92 Lyntone BOB 32   Academy Fight Song (live)/COAL PORTERS: Watching Blue Grass Burn (white label test
                               pressing)... £20
(see also Syd Straw)
REMARC
93 Dollar DOL 001   HELP ME (12", as Remarc!) £70
94 Dollar DOL 002   RICKY (12" with Lewi Cifer).. £50
94 Dollar DOL 003   RICKY REMIXES (12")... £30
REMA-REMA
80 4AD BAD 5   WHEEL IN THE ROSES: Feedback Song/Rema-Ream/Instrumental/Fond Affections
                               (12" EP, original pressing with blue labels) £40
80 4AD BAD 5   WHEEL IN THE ROSES: Feedback Song/Rema-Ream/Instrumental/Fond Affections
                               (12" EP) £25

(see also Adam & The Ants, Mass, Models, Wolfgang Press)

REMO FOUR
64	Piccadilly 7N 35175	I Wish I Could Shimmy Like My Sister Kate/Peter Gunn	£25
64	Piccadilly 7N 35186	Sally Go Round The Roses/I Know A Girl	£25
67	Fontana TF 787	Live Like A Lady/Sing Hallelujah	£70

(see also Tommy Quickly, Johnny Sandon, Gregory Phillips, Ashton Gardner & Dyke, Mike Hurst, George Harrison)

RENAISSANCE (U.K.)
70	Island WIP 6079	Island/The Sea	£15
78	Sire SRE 1022	Northern Lights/Opening Out (picture disc, export issue)	£15
79	Sire SIR 4019	Jekyll And Hyde/Forever Changing (withdrawn)	£15
69	Island ILPS 9114	RENAISSANCE (LP, gatefold, pink label with white 'i' logo)	£30
71	Island HELP 27	ILLUSION (LP, withdrawn, export only, black labeil with pink 'i' logo)	£50

(see also Keith Relf, Jane Relf, Yardbirds, Rupert's People, Reign)

RENAISSANCE (U.S.)
68	Polydor BM 56736	Mary Jane (Get Off The Devil's Merry-Go-Round)/Daytime Lovers	£35

DIANE RENAY
64	Stateside SS 270	Navy Blue/Unbelievable Guy	£15
64	Stateside SS 290	Kiss Me Sailor/Soft Spoken Guy	£15
64	MGM MGM 1262	Watch Out Sally/Billy Blue Eyes	£25
65	MGM MGM 1274	Troublemaker/I Had A Dream	£25

JOHN RENBOURN
65	Transatlantic TRA 135	JOHN RENBOURN (LP, 1st pressing, purple/white label with 'Transatlantic' on top of label)	£70
66	Transatlantic TRA 135	JOHN RENBOURN (LP, 2nd pressing, purple/white label with 'Transatlantic' on centre of label)	£50
66	Transatlantic TRA 149	ANOTHER MONDAY (LP, 1st pressing without title and catalogue number on spine)	£40
67	Transatlantic TRA 149	ANOTHER MONDAY (LP, 2nd pressing with title and catalogue number on spine)	£30
68	Transatlantic TRA 167	SIR JOHN ALOT OF MERRIE ENGLANDE'S MUSICK THYNGE AND YE GREENE KNIGHT (LP)	£30
70	Transatlantic TRA 224	THE LADY AND THE UNICORN (LP)	£25
72	Transatlantic TRA 135	JOHN RENBOURN (LP, reissue, 'World globe' label)	£15
72	Transatlantic TRA 149	ANOTHER MONDAY (LP, reissue, 'World globe' label)	£15
72	Transatlantic TRA 167	SIR JOHN ALOT OF MERRIE ENGLANDE'S MUSICK THYNGE AND YE GREENE KNIGHT (LP, reissue. 'World globe' label)	£15
72	Transatlantic TRA 247	FARO ANNIE (LP)	£30
76	Transatlantic TRA 336	THE HERMIT (LP)	£15
73	Transatlantic TRASAM 28	SO CLEAR - THE JOHN RENBOURN SAMPLER VOL. 2 (LP)	£15
77	KPM KPM 1203	THE GUITAR OF JOHN RENBOURN (LP, plain generic green KPM sleeve)	£35

(see also Pentangle, Bert Jansch & John Renbourn, Steve Tilston, Dorris Henderson)

JOHN RENBOURN'S SHIP OF FOOLS
88	Run River 009	SHIP OF FOOLS (LP)	£20

DON RENDELL
55	Tempo A 108	Muskrat Ramble/Thames Walk	£30
54	Vogue EPV 1009	MUSIC IN THE MAKING VOL 1. (EP)	£25
54	Vogue EPV 1034	MUSIC IN THE MAKING VOL 2 (EP)	£25
55	Tempo EXA 11	DON RENDELL QUARTET (EP)	£100
55	Tempo EXA 12	DON RENDELL SEXTET (EP)	£100
55	Tempo EXA 16	DON RENDELL SEXTET/DAMIAN ROBINSON TRIO (EP, 2 tracks each)	£50
55	Tempo EXA 20	DON RENDELL QUINTET (EP)	£60
57	Pye Jazz NJE 1044	DOGGIN AROUND - DON RENDELL JAZZ SIX (EP)	£50
58	Decca DFE 6501	PACKET OF BLUES (EP, as Don Rendell Jazz Six)	£30
59	Decca DFE 6587	THE JAZZ COMMITTEE (EP, featuring Don Rendell)	£100
54	Decca LK 4087	MODERN JAZZ AT THE FESTIVAL HALL (LP, also features Ken Moule Seven and Tony Crombie Orchestra)	£70
54	Vogue LDE 050	MUSIC IN THE MAKING (10" LP)	£100
55	Vogue LDE 144	DON RENDELL MEETS BOBBY JASPAR (10" LP)	£125
55	Tempo LAP 1	MEET DON RENDELL (10" LP)	£1000
56	Vogue LAE 12028	KENTON'S SIDEMEN (LP, featuring Don Rendell and Martial Solal)	£150
56	Nixa NJL 4	TENORAMA (LP)	£300
57	Nixa Jazz Today NJL 7	DON RENDELL PRESENTS THE JAZZ SIX (LP)	£200
58	Decca LK 4265	PLAYTIME (LP, as Don Rendell Jazz 6)	£200
62	Jazzland JLP 51	ROARIN' (LP, as Don Rendell New Jazz Quintet [with Graham Bond])	£250
72	Columbia SCX 6491	SPACEWALK (LP, as Don Rendell Quintet)	£150
75	Spotlite SPJ 501	LIVE AT THE AVGARDE GALLERY (LP, with the Joe Palin Trio)	£20
76	Spotlite SPJ 502	JUST MUSIC (LP, as Don Rendell 5)	£20
80	Spotlite SPJ 6315	EARTH MUSIC (LP, as Don Rendell 9)	£30
80	Spotlite SPJ 516	SET 2 (LP)	£20

(see also Frank Horrox)

DON RENDELL & IAN CARR QUINTET
65	Columbia 33SX 1733	SHADES OF BLUE (LP, flipback laminated sleeve)	£1500
66	Columbia S(C)X 6064	DUSK FIRE (LP, first pressing with blue label)	£800
68	Columbia S(C)X 6064	DUSK FIRE (LP, reissue, silver/black Columbia label with EMI box logo)	£350
68	Columbia SX 6214	PHASE III (LP, Mono)	£400
68	Columbia SCX 6214	PHASE III (LP, Stereo)	£400
69	Columbia SX 6316	LIVE (LP, Mono)	£300
69	Columbia SCX 6315	LIVE (LP, Stereo)	£300
69	Columbia SCX 6368	CHANGE IS (LP)	£400
10	Stamford STAMLP1006	LIVE AT THE UNION (2-LP)	£20

18	Jazzman JMANLP 106	THE COMPLETE LANSDOWNE RECORDINGS 1965 - 1969 (5-LP box set)	£200
19	Jazzman JMANLP 107X	SHADES OF BLUE (LP, reissue, inner)	£20
19	Jazzman JMANLP 108X	DUSK FIRE (LP, reissue, inner)	£20
19	Jazzman JMANLP 109X	PHASE III (LP, reissue, inner)	£20
19	Jazzman JMANLP 110X	LIVE (LP, reissue, inner)	£20
19	Jazzman JMANLP 111X	CHANGE IS (LP, reissue, inner)	£20

(see also Neil Ardley, Nucleus)

DON RENDELL QUARTET/JOE HARRIOT QUARTET
57	MGM MGM-EP 615	JAZZ BRITANNIA (EP, 2 tracks each)	£60

(see also Joe Harriott)

RENDESVIEW
71	Philron SP0019	It Shouldn't Have Happened/I'll Give You Love	£100

RENE & HIS ALLIGATORS
66	Decca F 22324	She Broke My Heart/I Can Wait	£18

GOOGIE RENE COMBO
60	London HLY 9056	Forever/Ez-zee	£20
66	Atlantic AT 4076	Smokey Joe's La La/Needing You	£30

RENE & ANGELA
80	Capitol E-ST 12077	RENE & ANGELA (LP)	£30
81	Capitol EMS 1118	WALL TO WALL (LP)	£25

RENEGADE (1)
73	Parlophone R 5981	Loving And Forgiving/Never Let Me Go	£20
74	Dawn DNS 1067	A Little Rock 'N' Roll/My Revolution	£25

RENEGADE (2)
80	White Witch WIT 1	LONELY ROAD (12" EP, with insert)	£100

RENEGADES
66	Polydor BM 56508	Cadillac/Every Minute Of The Day	£30
66	President PT 106	Thirteen Women/Walking Down The Street	£200
67	Parlophone R 5592	Take A Message/Second Thoughts	£25
68	Columbia DB 8383	No Man's Land/Sugar Loaf Mountain	£25

RENIA
73	Transatlantic TRA 261	FIRST OFFENDERS (LP)	£30

DON RENO & RED SMILEY
58	Parlophone GEP 8777	COUNTRY AND WESTERN (EP)	£30

GERRY RENO
63	Decca F 11774	It Only Happens In The Movies/One Lonely Guy	£15

ROBERT RENTAL
78	Regular ER 102	Paralysis/A.C.C. (photocopied black & white foldover p/s)	£30
78	Company/Regular RECO 2	Paralysis/A.C.C. (reissue, card gatefold p/s)	£20
80	Mute MUTE 010	On Location/Double Heart (p/s)	£15
79	Industrial IR 0007	THE BRIDGE (LP, with Thomas Leer)	£40
80	Rough Trade ROUGH 17	ROBERT RENTAL AND THE NORMAL (LP, 1-sided, plain red sleeve)	£25

(see also Thomas Leer)

REPARATA & DELRONS
65	Stateside SS 382	Whenever A Teenager Cries/He's My Guy	£30
65	Stateside SS 414	Tommy/Momma Don't Allow	£25
68	Bell BLL 1002	Captain Of Your Ship/Toom Toom (Is A Little Boy)	£15
68	RCA Victor RCA 1691	I Can Hear The Rain/Always Waitin'	£30
68	Bell BLL 1014	Saturday Night Didn't Happen/Panic	£50
68	Bell BLL 1014	Saturday Night Didn't Happen/Panic (DJ copy)	£60
68	Bell BLL 1021	Weather Forecast/You Can't Change A Young Boy's Mind	£20
72	Avco 6467 250	ROCK AND ROLL REVOLUTION (LP)	£40

REPLACEMENTS
87	Sire W 8297	Alex Chilton/Election day (p/s)	£20
87	Sire W8297	THE REPLACEMENTS EP	£15
84	Zippo ZONG 002	LET IT BE (LP)	£50
85	Sire 925330	TIM (LP)	£15
87	Sire 925557	PLEASED TO MEET ME (LP)	£20
89	What Goes On GOES ON 17	SORRY MA, FORGOT TO TAKE OUT THE TRASH (LP, reissue)	£30
88	What Goes On GOES ON 21	HOOTENANNY (LP, reissue)	£25
89	Sire 925831	DON'T TELL A SOUL (LP)	£15
89	What Goes On ON 20	STINK (mini-LP)	£18

REPORTERS (1)
81	GW1	Scoop/NBZ (p/s)	£40

REPORTERS (2)
81	Cloggtown CLOGGTOWN 1	Office Staff/Cinema/Lady Luck (p/s)	£20

REPULSION
89	Necrosis NECRO 0002	HORRIFIED (LP)	£30

REQUIEM
80	Sacrificial SAC 001	Angel Of Sin/Sacrificial Wanderer (no p/s)	£80

RESCUE COMPANY NO 1
72	Jam JAM 14	I Want To Save You/Amanda	£15
72	Jam JAM 27	I Stand Alone/You Shouldn't Have Been So Nice	£15

			MINT VALUE £

RESIDENTS

73 Jam JAM 45 — It's Only Words/Look Out £25

RESIDENTS

79 Virgin VR 3 — NIBBLES (LP, stickered sleeve, 5,000 only) £15
80 Pre PRE X2 — THE COMMERCIAL ALBUM (LP, 5,000 only, with incorrect song order) £15

RESISTANCE 77

82 Riot City RIOT 18 — NOWHERE TO PLAY (EP) £18
84 Rot ASS 6 — Vive The Resistance £20
84 Rot ASS 14 — THOROUGHBRED MEN (LP) £80

RESISTORS

80 Break SMASH 1 — For Jeanie/Takeaway Love/End Of The Line (p/s) £35
83 DT 027 — That's It/Steal My Love £25

RESTFULL ONES

70 Grade One GR 1 — Turn To The Sun/She's MIne £50

JOHNNY RESTIVO

59 RCA RCA 1143 — The Shape I'm In/Ya Ya (with triangular centre) £30
59 RCA RCA 1143 — The Shape I'm In/Ya Ya (later round centre pressing) £15
59 RCA RCA 1143 — The Shape I'm In/Ya Ya (78) £15
59 RCA RCA 1159 — I Like Girls/Dear Someone £15
59 RCA RCA 1159 — I Like Girls/Dear Someone (78) £20
60 Ember EMB S 135 — Look Here Now/Sweet Sweet Lovin' £15

RETREADS

81 Eddi Osmo EO 101 — Would You Listen Girl/One After 909/You Said You Knew (p/s, with mini-poster insert) £60

RETREAT FROM MOSCOW

80 Wicker Monkey WM 001/ — To The Night/Perception (p/s) £15
    MHMS 169/EJSP 9328

REUBEN

04 Extra Mile XMR001LP — RACECAR IS RACECAR BACKWARDS (LP) £150
05 Extra Mile XMR003LP — VERY FAST VERY DANGEROUS (LP) £50

REVELATION (1)

78 Write Sounds WTS 1003 — Jah Feelings/With You Boy (12") £20
78 Write Sounds WTS 1004 — Jah Feelings/Dub Feelings £22
78 Burning Sounds BS 1030 — BOOK OF REVELATION (LP) £30
79 Burning Vibrations BV 1007 — VARIATION ON A THEME (LP) £20

REVELATION (3)

91 Rise Above RISE 6 — SALVATIONS ANSWER (LP, stickered sleeve) £30

REVELLERS

67 Spin LP 1703 — REVELLERS AGAIN (LP) £35

REVELLS

71 CBS 7050 — Mind Party/Indian Ropeman £50

DIGGER REVELL'S DENVERMEN

63 Decca F 11657 — Surfside/Lisa Marie £20

REVELS

59 Top Rank JAR 235 — Midnight Stroll/Talking To My Heart £50

REVENGE (1)

78 Loony LOO 2 — We're Not Gonna Take It/Pornography (glossy p/s, counterfeits have matt sleeve, and lack ridge around label) £200
78 Loony LOO 1 — Our Generation/I Love Her Way (counterfeits lack ridge around label) £450

REVENGE (3)

89 Factyory FAC 247/7 — 7 Reasons/Jesus I Love You (white labels only) £30
90 Factory FACT 230 — ONE TRUE PASSION (LP) £15

(see also Joy Division, New Order, Monaco)

PAUL REVERE & THE RAIDERS (FEATURING MARK LINDSAY)

61 Top Rank JAR 557 — Like Long Hair/Sharon £20
65 Sue WI 344 — Like Long Hair/Sharon (reissue) £30
66 CBS 202027 — Just Like Me/B F D R F Blues £20
66 CBS 202205 — Kicks/Shake It Up £15
68 CBS 3310 — Too Much Talk/Happening '68 (featuring Mark Lindsay) £20
66 CBS (S)BPG 62406 — JUST LIKE US (LP) £25
66 CBS (S)BPG 62797 — MIDNIGHT RIDE (LP) £25
67 CBS (S)BPG 62963 — GOOD THING (LP) £20
68 CBS (S)BPG 63095 — REVOLUTION (LP) £20
69 CBS 63265 — GOIN' TO MEMPHIS (LP, mono/stereo) £20
69 CBS 63649 — HARD 'N' HEAVY (LP) £20

REVEREND W AWDRY

67 Chiltern C1000 — Edwards Day Out/Edward And John (in printed picture company sleeve) ... £20

REVILLOS

80 Snatzo/Dindisc DID X 3 — REV UP (LP, green or pink titles) £25
82 Superville SV 4001 — ATTACK! (LP, withdrawn) £40

(see also Rezillos)

REVOLUTION

66 Piccadilly 7N 35289 — Hallelujah/Shades Of Blue £65

(see also Hellions, Luther Grosvenor, Traffic, Dave Mason & Cass Elliot, Spirit)

(THE) REVOLUTIONARIES

77	Sky Note SKY DD 002	Afro Rock Part 1/Afro Rock Part 2 (12")	£85
77	Sky Note SKY 1002	El Bamba/Bamba In Dub	£15
78	Island IPR 2024	Headache/Bellyache/Toothache/Headache (12")	£30
78	Ballistic FORCE 2003	FATAL DUB (12" EP)	£20
76	Trenchtown TRELP 001	REVOLUTIONARY DUB (LP, with the We The People Band)	£60
78	Cha Cha CHALP 002	REACTION IN DUB (LP)	£40
78	Cha Cha CHALP 005	JONKANOO DUB (LP)	£30
79	Burning Vibrations BV 1002	DUTCH MAN DUB (LP)	£30
79	Burning Vibrations BV 1004	GREEN BAY DUB (LP)	£50
79	Burning Vibrations BV 1010	BURNING DUB (LP)	£35
79	Trojan TRLS 169	OUTLAW DUB (LP)	£25
82	Cha Cha CHALP 014	REVIVAL (LP)	£40
07	Pressure Sounds PSLP 55	DRUM SOUND: MORE GEMS FROM THE CHANNEL ONE DUB ROOM 1974-1980 (2-LP)	£20

REVOLUTIONARY ARMY OF INFANT JESUS

87	Probe Plus PROBE 12	THE GIFT OF TEARS (LP)	£100

REVOLUTIONARY BLUES BAND

70	MCA MUP(S) 402	REVOLUTIONARY BLUES BAND (LP)	£20

REVOLVER (1)

69	Young BLood YB 1006	Frisco Annie/Imaginations	£20

REVOLVER (2)

78	Rockburgh ROCS 203	Silently Screaming/On The Run (p/s)	£15

REVOLVING PAINT DREAM

84	Creation CRE 002	Flowers In The Sky/In The Afternoon (foldaround p/s in poly bag)	£20

(see also Laughing Apple, Primal Scream)

REVULSION

85	Radical Change RC 7	Ever Get The Feeling Of Utter... (12")	£20

REX (MORRIS) & MINORS

60	Triumph RGM 1023	Chicken Sax/Snake Eyes	£50

REXY

80	Alien ALIEN 12	(Don't) Turn Me Away/Rexy's Russian Blues	£40
81	Alien ALIEN 19	Running Out Of Time/Alien/Funky Butt (12", p/s)	£60
81	Alien ALIEN 17	In The Force/Johnny B. Goode (p/s)	£25
81	Alien BEALIEN2	RUNNING OUT OF TIME (LP)	£100
16	Lucky Number LUCKY090LP	RUNNING OUT OF TIME (LP, reissue)	£35

ALVINO REY

62	London HA-D 2414	ALVINO REY'S GREATEST HITS (LP)	£20

CHICO REY & JET BAND

70	Pye 7N 17899	Stiletto/Midnight In Mexico	£40

REYNARD

76	Pilgrim/Grapevine GRA 102	FRESH FROM THE EARTH (LP)	£40

DEBBIE REYNOLDS

58	MGM MGM-EP 670	DEBBIE REYNOLDS (EP)	£15
59	London HA-D 2200	DEBBIE (LP, mono)	£20
59	London SAH-D 6051	DEBBIE (LP, stereo)	£25
60	London HA-D 2294	AM I THAT EASY TO FORGET? (LP, mono)	£20
60	London SAH-D 6106	AM I THAT EASY TO FORGET? (LP, stereo)	£25
61	London HA-D 2326	FINE AND DANDY (LP)	£20
63	London HA-D 8075	GREAT FOLK HITS (LP, mono)	£20
63	London HA-D/SH-D 8075	GREAT FOLK HITS (LP, stereo)	£25

(see also Naturals [U.S.])

ELI REYNOLDS

70	Punch PH 37	Mr Car Man/Chiney Man	£20

JODY REYNOLDS

58	London HL 8651	Endless Sleep/Tight Capris	£25

L J REYNOLDS

82	Capitol 260	Special Effects/Key To The World	£20

TIMMY REYNOLDS

62	Ember EMB S 133	Lullaby Of Love/JEFF MILLS: Daddy's Home	£70

REZILLOS

77	Sensible FAB 1	I Can't Stand My Baby/I Wanna Be Your Man (p/s, 15,000, 5,000 numbered)	£35
77	Sensible FAB 1	I Can't Stand My Baby/I Wanna Be Your Man (p/s, 15,000, 10,000 unnumbered)	£15
77	Sensible FAB 2	Flying Saucer Attack/William Mysterious Overture (p/s, unissued)	£0
78	Sire 6198 215	Cold Wars/William Mysterious Overture (unissued, picture sleeve only)	£150
78	Sire K 56530	CAN'T STAND THE REZILLOS (LP, with inner sleeve & postcard insert)	£30
78	Sire SRK 6069	MISSION ACCOMPLISHED ... BUT THE BEAT GOES ON (LP, inner)	£20

(see also Revillos, Shake)

RHABSTALLION

81	Rhab RHAB 001	Day To Day/Breadline (p/s, with badge)	£30
81	Rhab RHAB 001	Day To Day/Breadline (p/s)	£20

RH FACTOR

03	Verve VERR01292-1	Poetry (DJ Spinna Remix)/(Album Version)/Forget Regret (Quantic Remix)/(Album Version) (12")	£20

MINT VALUE £

03	Verve 065 192-1	HARD GROOVE (2-LP)	£150

(see also Roy Hargrove)

RHINOCEROS
69	Elektra EKL 4030	RHINOCEROS (LP, orange label, also stereo EKS 74030)	£20
69	Elektra EKL 4056	SATIN CHICKENS (LP, also stereo EKS 74056)	£20
70	Elektra 2469 006	BETTER TIMES ARE COMING (LP, gatefold sleeve)	£15

RHODA WITH THE SPECIAL A.K.A.
82	2-Tone CHS TT 1218	The Boiler/Theme From The Boiler (12", p/s existence unconfirmed)	£20

(see also Special A.K.A.)

PAT RHODEN
65	Ska Beat JB 195	Jezebel/You Can Hold My Hand	£20
66	Blue Beat BB 360	Send Your Love/Make Believe	£15
70	Mary Lyn ML 101	Time Is Tight/MILTON & DENZIL: I Like It Like That	£20

(see also Pat Riden, Pat & Marie, Denzil & Pat)

EMITT RHODES
71	Probe SPBA 6256	EMITT RHODES (LP, gatefold sleeve)	£15
71	A&M AMLS 64254	AMERICAN DREAM (LP)	£15

TODD RHODES ORCHESTRA
55	Parlophone MSP 6171	Specks/Silver Sunset	£30

RHODESIANS
80	Period PER 001	Clock!!!/Postmortem (p/s)	£15

RHUBARB RHUBARB
68	President PT 229	Rainmaker/Moneylender	£160

GRUFF RHYS
11	Ovni OVNI 008	ATHEIST XMAS EP (12")	£15
04	Placid Casual PLC10LP	YR ATAL GENHEDLAETH (LP)	£25
11	Ovni OVNI 003	HOTEL SHAMPOO (LP)	£20
14	Turnstile TS008LP	AMERICAN INTERIOR (LP, 12", CD, print, box set)	£40

(see also Super Furry Animals)

RHYTHM HAWKS
79	Redball RR 011	ZODIAC EP	£25
81	Hot Rock HR45 009	No Chance/Clap Your Hands And Dance	£30

RHYTHM ACES
61	Starlite ST45 061	A Thousand Teardrops/Wherever You May Go	£20
61	Starlite ST45 066	Please Don't Go Away/Oh My Darling	£25
62	Blue Beat BB 134	I'll Be There/DON DRUMMOND: Dewdrops	£25
62	Island WI 032	C-H-R-I-S-T-M-A-S/TOP GRANT: A Christmas Drink	£18

RHYTHM & BLUES INC.
65	Fontana TF 524	Louie Louie/Honey Don't	£75

RHYTHM INVENTION
92	Nucleus NUKE 002	Crunch (Original)/(Thank Goodness It's Saturday Mix)/Luvvly/Jubbly (12")	£30

RHYTHM KINGS
63	Vocalion POP V 9212	Blue Soul/Exotic	£30

RHYTHM OF LIFE
82	Rational RATE 7	Uncle Sam/Portrait Of The Heart (p/s; label also lists Rhythm RHYTHM 2)	£15

(see also Josef K, Paul Haig)

RHYTHM RULERS
70	Bullet BU 447	Second Pressure/Sammy Dead	£35
70	Trojan TBL 132	MUDIES MOOD (LP)	£50

(see also Lloyd Jones, U Roy Junior, Matadors, Winston Groovy, Pat, Winston Wright)

RHYZE
80	EPIC S EPC 13 8794	JUST HOW SWEET IS YOUR LOVE (LP)	£20

RIBS
78	Aerco AERS 101	Man With No Brain/Long Time Coming (p/s)	£25

BOYD RICE & FRIENDS
81	Mute STUMM 4	BOYD RICE (LP)	£30
90	New European BADVC 1969	MUSIC, MARTINIS AND MISANTHROPY (LP, with inner sleeve)	£25

(see also Non, Death In June, Current 93)

MANDY RICE-DAVIES
64	Ember EMB 4537	MANDY (EP)	£40

BUDDY RICH
67	Fontana TF836	Norwegian Wood (This Bird Has Flown)/Monitor Theme	£20

CHARLIE RICH
60	London HLU 9107	Lonely Weekends/Everything I Do Is Wrong	£50
62	London HLS 9482	Just A Little Bit Sweet/It's Too Late	£40
67	London HLU 10104	Love Is After Me/Pass On By (silver-top label)	£15
67	London HLU 10104	Love Is After Me/Pass On By (DJ copy)	£70
65	RCA RD 7719	THAT'S RICH (LP)	£40
66	Philips BL 7695	THE MANY NEW SIDES OF CHARLIE RICH (LP)	£25

DAVE RICH
58	RCA RCA 1092	Burn On Love Fire/City Lights	£15

LEWIS RICH

66	Parlophone R 5434	I Don't Want To Hear It Anymore/Shedding Tears	£15

TONY RICH

66	Piccadilly 7N 35323	It's All Up To You Now/See Saw	£15

(see also Tony Sheveton)

RICHARD

69	Parlophone R 5754	A Little Bit/Take Me	£15

RICHARD BROTHERS

63	Island WI 060	I Need A Girl/Desperate Lover	£15
63	Island WI 109	I Shall Wear A Crown/BABA BROOKS: Robin Hood	£20

(see also Joe White)

CLIFF RICHARD (& DRIFTERS/SHADOWS)

78s

58	Columbia DB 4178	Move It!/Schoolboy Crush	£35
58	Columbia DB 4203	High Class Baby/My Feet Hit The Ground	£30
59	Columbia DB 4249	Livin' Lovin' Doll/Steady With You	£80
59	Columbia DB 4290	Mean Streak/Never Mind	£80
59	Columbia DB 4306	Living Doll/Apron Strings	£40

(The above 78s were credited to Cliff Richard & Drifters)

59	Columbia DB 4351	Travellin' Light/Dynamite (as Cliff Richard & Shadows)	£45
60	Columbia DB 4398	A Voice In The Wilderness/Don't Be Mad At Me (credited to Cliff Richard & Shadows)	£100

SINGLES : COLUMBIA

58	Columbia DB 4178	Move It!/Schoolboy Crush (green label)	£20
58	Columbia DB 4203	High Class Baby/My Feet Hit The Ground (green label)	£20
59	Columbia DB 4249	Livin' Lovin' Doll/Steady With You (green label)	£30
59	Columbia DB 4290	Mean Streak/Never Mind (green label)	£15
64	Columbia DB 7435	This Was My Special Day/I'm Feeling Oh So Lovely (withdrawn, credited to Cliff Richard, Audrey Bayley, Joan Palethorpe & Faye Fisher)	£25
66	Columbia PSRS 304	Finders Keepers (promo only, 1-sided, with spoken intro by Simon Dee)	£30

SINGLES : EMI SINGLES

74	EMI PSR 368	Nothing To Remind Me/The Learning (promo only)	£40
75	EMI EMI 2344	Honky Tonk Angel/(Wouldn't You Know It) Got Myself A Girl (withdrawn)	£15
84	EMI 5457	Ocean Deep/Baby You're Dynamite (p/s)	£20

EXPORT SINGLES

63	Columbia DC 758	What'd I Say/Blue Moon	£150
65	Columbia DC 762	Angel/Razzle Dazzle	£50

EPs

59	Columbia SEG 7895	SERIOUS CHARGE (soundtrack)	£30
59	Columbia SEG 7903	CLIFF NO. 1 (mono)	£25
59	Columbia ESG 7754	CLIFF NO. 1 (stereo)	£30
59	Columbia SEG 7910	CLIFF NO. 2 (mono)	£20
59	Columbia ESG 7769	CLIFF NO. 2 (stereo)	£25
59	Columbia SEG 7971	EXPRESSO BONGO (soundtrack, mono)	£15
59	Columbia ESG 7783	EXPRESSO BONGO (soundtrack, stereo)	£30
60	Columbia SEG 7979	CLIFF SINGS NO. 1 (mono)	£25
60	Columbia ESG 7788	CLIFF SINGS NO. 1 (stereo)	£30
60	Columbia SEG 7987	CLIFF SINGS NO. 2 (mono)	£25
60	Columbia ESG 7794	CLIFF SINGS NO. 2 (stereo)	£30
60	Columbia SEG 8005	CLIFF SINGS NO. 3 (mono)	£25
60	Columbia ESG 7808	CLIFF SINGS NO. 3 (stereo)	£30
60	Columbia SEG 8021	CLIFF SINGS NO. 4 (mono)	£25
60	Columbia ESG 7816	CLIFF SINGS NO. 4 (stereo)	£30
60	Columbia SEG 8050	CLIFF'S SILVER DISCS	£20
60	Columbia SEG 8065	ME AND MY SHADOWS NO. 1 (mono)	£25
60	Columbia ESG 7837	ME AND MY SHADOWS NO. 1 (stereo)	£30
61	Columbia SEG 8071	ME AND MY SHADOWS NO. 2 (mono)	£25
61	Columbia ESG 7481	ME AND MY SHADOWS NO. 2 (stereo)	£30
61	Columbia SEG 8078	ME AND MY SHADOWS NO. 3 (mono)	£25
61	Columbia ESG 7843	ME AND MY SHADOWS NO. 3 (stereo)	£30
61	Columbia SEG 8105	LISTEN TO CLIFF NO. 1 (mono)	£25
61	Columbia ESG 7858	LISTEN TO CLIFF NO. 1 (stereo)	£30
61	Columbia SEG 8119	DREAM (mono)	£15
61	Columbia ESG 7867	DREAM (stereo)	£20
61	Columbia SEG 8126	LISTEN TO CLIFF NO. 2 (mono)	£15
61	Columbia ESG 7870	LISTEN TO CLIFF NO. 2 (stereo)	£20
62	Columbia SEG 8133	CLIFF'S HIT PARADE	£20
62	Columbia SEG 8151	CLIFF RICHARD	£20
62	Columbia SEG 8159	HITS FROM 'THE YOUNG ONES'	£20
62	Columbia SEG 8168	CLIFF RICHARD NO. 2	£20

(The above EPs were originally issued with turquoise labels, later blue/black label copies are worth two-thirds these values.)

62	Columbia SEG 8203	CLIFF'S HITS	£20
63	Columbia SEG 8228	TIME FOR CLIFF AND THE SHADOWS (mono)	£20
63	Columbia ESG 7887	TIME FOR CLIFF AND THE SHADOWS (stereo, turquoise label)	£20
63	Columbia ESG 7887	TIME FOR CLIFF AND THE SHADOWS (stereo, blue/black label)	£20
63	Columbia SEG 8246	HOLIDAY CARNIVAL (mono)	£15

MINT VALUE £

63	Columbia ESG 7892	**HOLIDAY CARNIVAL** (stereo)	£20
63	Columbia SEG 8250	**HITS FROM 'SUMMER HOLIDAY'** (mono)	£15
63	Columbia SEG 7896	**HITS FROM 'SUMMER HOLIDAY'** (stereo)	£20
63	Columbia SEG 8263	**MORE HITS FROM 'SUMMER HOLIDAY'** (mono)	£15
63	Columbia ESG 7898	**MORE HITS FROM 'SUMMER HOLIDAY'** (stereo)	£20
63	Columbia SEG 8269	**CLIFF'S LUCKY LIPS**	£20
63	Columbia SEG 8272	**LOVE SONGS** (mono)	£20
63	Columbia ESG 7900	**LOVE SONGS** (stereo)	£20
64	Columbia SEG 8290	**WHEN IN FRANCE**	£20
64	Columbia SEG 8299	**CLIFF SINGS 'DON'T TALK TO HIM'**	£15
64	Columbia SEG 8320	**CLIFF'S PALLADIUM SUCCESSES**	£15
64	Columbia ESG 7902	**WONDERFUL LIFE** (stereo)	£15
64	Columbia SEG 8347	**A FOREVER KIND OF LOVE**	£15
64	Columbia ESG 7903	**WONDERFUL LIFE NO. 2** (stereo)	£15
64	Columbia ESG 7906	**HITS FROM 'WONDERFUL LIFE'** (stereo)	£15
65	Columbia SEG 8384	**WHY DON'T THEY UNDERSTAND?**	£15
65	Columbia SEG 8405	**LOOK IN MY EYES, MARIA**	£15
65	Columbia SEG 8444	**ANGEL**	£15
65	Columbia SEG 8450	**TAKE FOUR**	£15
66	Columbia SEG 8474	**WIND ME UP**	£15
66	Columbia SEG 8478	**HITS FROM 'WHEN IN ROME'**	£15
66	Columbia SEG 8488	**LOVE IS FOREVER**	£15
66	Columbia SEG 8510	**THUNDERBIRDS ARE GO!** (3 tracks by Cliff & Shadows, 1 solo)	£50
66	Columbia SEG 8517	**LA LA LA LA LA** (1 track by Bruce Welch & Hank Marvin)	£20
67	Columbia SEG 8527	**CINDERELLA**	£40

ALBUMS : COLUMBIA LPS

59	Columbia 33SX 1147	**CLIFF** (green labels)	£50
59	Columbia 33SX 1147	**CLIFF** (later blue/black labels)	£20
59	Columbia 33SX 1192	**CLIFF SINGS** (green labels)	£50
59	Columbia 33SX 1192	**CLIFF SINGS** (later blue/black labels)	£20
60	Columbia 33SX 1261	**ME AND MY SHADOWS** (mono)	£15
60	Columbia SCX 3330	**ME AND MY SHADOWS** (stereo)	£25
61	Columbia SCX 3375	**LISTEN TO CLIFF!** (stereo)	£15
61	Columbia 33SX 1368	**21 TODAY** (mono)	£15
61	Columbia SCX 3409	**21 TODAY** (stereo)	£15
62	Columbia 33SX 1431	**32 MINUTES AND 17 SECONDS WITH...** (mono)	£15
62	Columbia SCX 3436	**32 MINUTES AND 17 SECONDS WITH...**	£15
66	Columbia SX 6079	**FINDERS KEEPERS** (soundtrack, with inner sleeve, mono)	£15
66	Columbia SCX 6079	**FINDERS KEEPERS** (soundtrack, with inner sleeve, stereo)	£20
67	Columbia S(C)X 6133	**DON'T STOP ME NOW**	£15
67	Columbia JSX 6167	**GOOD NEWS** (export issue)	£20

ALBUMS : OTHER LPS

63	Elstree Extra Range	**SUMMER HOLIDAY** (2-LP, full soundtrack recording, 80 copies only)	£400
64	Elstree Extra Range	**WONDERFUL LIFE** (2-LP, full soundtrack recording, 150 copies only)	£250
64	EMI Regal SREG 1120	**ME AND MY SHADOWS** (export issue)	£20

FLEXIDISCS : FLEXIDISCS & OTHER RELEASES

98	Cruisin' The 50's CASB 007	**Breathless/Lawdy Miss Clawdy** (10" 78, p/s, with 6 inserts)	£30

(see also Drifters [U.K.], Shadows, Olivia Newton-John, Sheila Walsh, Janet Jackson, Elton John, Grazina)

WENDY RICHARD & DIANA BERRY

63	Decca F 11680	**We Had A Dream/Keep 'Em Looking Around**	£15

(see also Mike Sarne)

RICHARD & GLEN

72	Duke DU 141	**Boat To Progress** (Parts 1 & 2)	£20

RICHARD & YOUNG LIONS

66	Philips BF 1520	**Open Up Your Door/Once Upon Your Smile**	£50

CYNTHIA RICHARDS

69	Clandisc CLA 203	**Foolish Fool/KING STITT: On The Street**	£25
70	Clandisc CLA 210	**Conversation/DYNAMITES: Conversation Version II**	£20
71	Escort ERT 861	**Love & Unity/MAYTONES: Wah Noh Dead**	£18
71	G.G. GG 4528	**Place In My Heart/You've Got A Friend** (act. Irving [Brown] & Cynthia Richards)	£20
70	Trojan TBL 123	**FOOLISH FOOL** (LP, actually Clancy Eccles productions compilation)	£50

(see also Bobby Aitken, Lord Comic, Sir Lord Comic)

JOHNNY RICHARDS

59	Esquire 32-076	**THE RITES OF DIABLO** (LP)	£25

KEITH RICHARDS

79	Rolling Stones RSR 102	**Run Rudolph Run/The Harder They Come** (p/s)	£15
88	Virgin KEITH 1234	**Make No Mistake/Locked Away/Struggle/Big Enough** (4 x 1-sided 7", "Talk Is Cheap" sampler box set, promo only)	£90
88	Virgin 2-91047 A/B/C	**TALK IS CHEAP** (3 x 3" CDs in tin)	£40
92	Virgin VUSLP 59	**MAIN OFFENDER** (LP, inner)	£75

(see also Rolling Stones, Aranbee Pop Symphony Orchestra, Screamin' Jay Hawkins)

LISA RICHARDS

65	Vocalion VP 9244	**Mean Old World/Take A Chance**	£55
65	Vocalion VP 9244	**Mean Old World/Take A Chance** (DJ copy)	£70

LLOYD RICHARDS

64	Port-O-Jam PJ 4004	**Be Good/I Need You**	£25

ROY RICHARDS

66	Doctor Bird DB 1012	Contact/Maureen	£20
66	Island WI 297	Green Collie/MARCIA GRIFFITHS: You No Good	£40
66	Island WI 283	Double Trouble/FITSY & FREDDY: Why Did You Do It	£25
66	Island WI 299	Western Standard Time/(JA) EAGLES: What An Agony	£35
66	Island WI 3000	South Viet Nam/You Must Be Sorry (Vocal)	£25
67	Island WI 3027	Rub-A-Dub/SHARKS: Baby Come Home	£35
67	Tabernacle TS 1000	When I see Jesus/My Savior Come	£25
67	Island WI 3037	Hopeful Village Ska/DELROY WILSON: Ungrateful Baby	£45
67	Island WI 3050	Port-O-Jam/DELROY WILSON: Get Ready	£60
67	Studio One SO 2020	Hanky Panky/ALTON ELLIS: I Am Still In Love	£50
71	Fab FAB 17	Dirty People/D MAY: Where Have You Been (black label, promo only)	£50
72	Fab 33	Vodoo/STRANGER COLE: Black Is Black (white label, no artist credits)	£150

(see also Roland Alphonso, Lord Comic, Soul Vendors, Jackie Mittoo, Derrick Morgan, Righteous Flames)

TRUDY RICHARDS

57	Capitol T 838	CRAZY IN LOVE (LP)	£15

VIC RICHARDS

67	Polydor 56163	Jonathan Whatsit/Goodbye	£70

WINSTON RICHARDS

67	Rio R 124	Studio Blitz/Don't Up	£20

DEL RICHARDSON

73	MCA MUPS 491	PIECES OF A JIGSAW (LP, black/silver label)	£200

(see also Osibisa, Sundae Times)

JOE 'GROUNDHOG' RICHARDSON

69	Major Minor MM 632	Take It Off/Blues To Take It Off	£15

RICH FEVER

70	Parlophone R5869	Everything's Moving/King Of All The Kingdoms	£15

RICH GYPSY

80	Splash SP 016	What Hit Me (no p/s)	£25

TONY RICHIE

68	Beacon BEA 114	Anybody At The Party Seen Jenny/You Can't Win	£40

RICH KIDS

78	EMI EMC 3263	GHOSTS OF PRINCES IN TOWERS (LP)	£18

(see also Sex Pistols, Ultravox, Spectres, Visage)

JONATHAN RICHMAN & MODERN LOVERS

77	Beserkley BSERK 9	ROCK 'N' ROLL WITH THE MODERN LOVERS (LP)	£25
77	Beserkley BSERK 2	JONATHAN RICHMAN AND THE MODERN LOVERS (LP)	£25
77	Beserkley BSERK 12	MODERN LOVERS LIVE (LP)	£15
77	Beserkley BSERK 17	BACK IN YOUR LIFE (LP)	£18
81	Mohawk LBOM 1	ORIGINAL (LP)	£20
84	Rough Trade ROUGH 52	JONATHAN SINGS (LP)	£15
85	Rough Trade ROUGH 72	ROCKIN' & ROMANCE (LP)	£15
86	Rough Trade ROUGH 92	IT'S TIME FOR (LP)	£20
88	Demon FIEND 106	MODERN LOVERS 88 (LP)	£15
89	Special Delivery SPD 1024	JONATHAN RICHMAN (LP)	£15
90	Special Delivery SPD 1037	JONATHAN GOES COUNTRY (LP)	£15
90	Castle ESDLP 128	23 GREAT RECORDINGS BY (2-LP)	£18

RICH MIX

83	Satril 12 SAT 509	I Got The Love/Version (12")	£15

RICHMOND

73	Dart ARTS 65371	FRIGHTENED (LP, textured sleeve, lyric insert)	£30

FIONA RICHMOND

73	Raymond PR 112	FRANKLY FIONA (LP)	£50

RICH PICKINGS

69	Cresta CR 1	Time To Leave/Mind In Motion	£200
73	Taylor Made TM 11	Jump To It/My Heroes Back (not sure if this is same group as above)	£20

RICHUS FLAMES

67	Fab FAB 17	Need To Be Loved/I Am Going Home	£75

(see also Righteous Flames, Winston Jarrett)

RICK & KEENS

61	Mercury AMT 1150	Peanuts/I'll Be Home	£50

RICK & SANDY

65	Decca F 12196	Lost My Girl/I Can't Help It	£40
65	Decca F 12311	Creation/In A 100 Years From Now	£25

BERESFORD RICKETTS

60	Starlite ST45 025	Cherry Baby/I Want To Know	£30
60	Starlite ST45 029	Baby Baby/When I Woke Up	£30
61	Starlite ST45 048	Hold Me Tight/Dream Girl (as Ricketts & Rowe)	£30
62	Starlite ST45 079	I'm Going To Cry/Waiting For Me	£30
62	Blue Beat BB 107	You Better Be Going/I've Been Walking (as Beresford Ricketts & Blue Beats)	£22
63	Dice CC 12	Oh Jean/Rivers Of Tears (as Lauren Aitken's Group)	£20
66	Blue Beat BB 350	Jailer Bring Me Water/Careless Love	£22

RICKY & THE MUTATIONS
83	Cool Ghoul COOL 003	Thatcher Rap (12") £15

RICO (RODRIGUEZ)
61	Blue Beat BB 56	Luke Lane Shuffle (as Rico Rodrigues & Buster's All Stars)/ BUSTER'S GROUP: Little Honey £25
62	Island WI 022	Rico Special (as Emanuel Rodrigues Orchestra; some copies may credit Reco & His Happy Orchestra)/BUNNY & SKITTER: A Little Mashin'... £35
62	Planetone RC 1	London Here I Come/Midnight In Ethiopia £35
62	Planetone RC 4	Planet Rock/You Win.. £20
62	Planetone PT 35	Mighty As A Rose/MARVELLES: Tell All Those Girls... £50
62	Planetone RC 5	Youth Boogie/Western Serenade (as Rico's Combo) £20
67	Fab FAB 12	Jingle Bells/Silent Night (with His Boys) £25
68	Pama PM 706	Soul Man/It's Not Unusual (as Reco Rodriguez) £45
68	Pama PM 715	Tender Foot Ska/Memories (as Reco Rodriguez) £25
69	Blue Cat BS 160	The Bullet/Rhythm In (as Reco Rodriguez & His Rhythm Aces) £35
69	Bullet BU 407	Tribute To Don Drummond/Japanese Invasion (as Rico Rodriquez) £100
71	Duke DU 96	Surprise Package (as Rico & Satch)/PETE JOHNSON: I'm Sorry £50
72	Count Shelly CS 013	Jungle Fever/UNKNOWN: River Jordan (white labels only).. £60
77	Island WIP 6399	Africa/Afro-Dub... £20
77	Island IPR 2006	Ska-Wars/Ramble (12")... £20
78	Island IPR 2002	Dial Africa/Dub (12").. £25
79	Island IPR 2016	Take 5/Sound Check (12") £20
80	Island IPR 2030	Children Of Sanchez/You Really Got Me/Midnight In Ethiopia (12") £45
80	2-Tone CHS TT 15	Sea Cruise/Carolina £25
82	2-Tone CHS TT 19	Jungle Music/Rasta Call You (paper label, 2-Tone sleeve, with Special A.K.A.) £25
82	2-Tone CHS TT 1219	Jungle Music/Rasta Call You/Easter Island (12", p/s, with Special A.K.A.) £20
69	Trojan TTL 12	BLOW YOUR HORN (LP, as Rico & Rudies) £50
78	Island ILPS 9485	MAN FROM WARREIKA (LP) £50
78	Ghetto Rockers PRE 1	WARREIKA DUB (LP, white label, white sleeve, beware of bootlegs) £80
81	2 Tone CHR TT 5005	THAT MAN IS FORWARD (LP) £50
82	2 Tone CHR TT5006	JAMA RICO (LP) £50
00	Simply Vinyl SVLP 187	MAN FROM WAREIKA (LP, reissue) £18

(see also Special A.K.A., Reco, Andy Capp, Don Reco, Prince Buster, Pioneers, Stranger, Marvels)

RICOCHET
80	Heavy Rock HER 1	Midas Light/Off The Rails (p/s) £150

RICOTTI & ALBUQUERQUE
71	Pegasus PEG 2	FIRST WIND (LP).. £50

(see also Frank Ricotti, Henry Lowther)

FRANK RICOTTI QUARTET
69	CBS 52668	OUR POINT OF VIEW (LP) £50

(see also Ricotti & Albuquerque, Chris Spedding)

NELSON RIDDLE ORCHESTRA
62	MGM MGM-C 896	LOLITA (LP, soundtrack).. £30
64	Reprise R 2021	ROBIN AND THE SEVEN HOODS (LP, soundtrack)... £20
66	Stateside S(S)L 10179	BATMAN (LP, TV soundtrack) £50

RIDDLERS
66	Polydor BM 56716	Batman Theme/Weegie Walk £30

RIDE
89	Creation CRE 072T	RIDE EP (12")... £25
90	Creation CRE 075T	PLAY EP (12").. £25
90	Creation CRE 087T	FALL EP (12")... £25
91	No Label	Like A Snowflake (7" sold at London ULU gig 19/12/91) £20
91	Creation CRE 100T	TODAY FOREVER EP (12" p/s)... £20
92	Creation CRE 123T	Leave Them All Behind/Chrome Waves/Grasshopper (12", p/s) £20
92	Creation CRE 150P	Twisterella/Going Blank Again (promo).. £15
94	Creation CRE 184T	HOW DOES IT FEEL TO FEEL EP (12", p/s).. £15
94	Creation CRE 189T	I DON'T KNOW WHERE IT COMES FROM EP (12", p/s).. £15
94	Creation CRE 199T	BLACK NITE CRASH EP (12", p/s) £15
90	Creation CRELP 074	NOWHERE (LP, inner)... £100
92	Creation CRELP 124	GOING BLANK AGAIN (LP as 2 x 45rpm 12", gatefold sleeve, lyric inner) £100
94	Creation CRELP 147	CARNIVAL OF LIGHT (2-LP, gatefold sleeve, lyric insert) £100
96	Creation CRELP 180	TARANTULA (LP) £100
01	Ignition IGN LP 14	OX4: THE BEST OF (2-LP)... £40
12	Obscure Alternatives OAR 11081	GOING BLANK AGAIN (2-LP, reissue) £30
15	Ride RIDEMSC02LPX	NOWHERE (2-LP, reissue, gatefold, white/marbled vinyl, numbered, stickered sleeve) ..£100
15	Ride Music RIDEMSC06LP	OX4: THE BEST OF (2-LP, reissue, red vinyl) £25
17	Wichita WEBB510LP	WEATHER DIARIES (2-LP, purple vinyl, numbered).. £25
17	Wichita WEBB510LP	WEATHER DIARIES (2-LP, black or clear vinyl copies) £20

(see also Andy Bell)

RIDJ XYLON
95	Roots Man Pro RMP 001	Black Consciousness/War Rumour Of War//NAPHTALI: Satan Disciples/Conscious Dub/Satan War Dub (12") £50

RIFF
64	Blue Beat BB 242	Oh What A Feeling/Primitive Man £70

RIFF-RAFF
73	RCA SF 8351	RIFF-RAFF (LP, with booklet)	£45
73	RCA SF 8351	RIFF-RAFF (LP, without booklet)	£25
74	RCA LPL1 5023	ORIGINAL MAN (LP)	£30

RIFF RAFF
78	Chiswick SW 34	I WANNA BE A COSMONAUT (EP)	£25
79	Albion DEL 6	Barking Park Lane/RUAN O' LOCHLAINN: Sweet Narcissis	£15

RIFKIN
68	Page One POF 071	Continental Hesitation/We're Not Those People Any More	£60

THE RIFLES
06	Red Ink 82876 85972 1	NO LOVE LOST (LP)	£25
09	679 TRT 001	GREAT ESCAPE (2-LP)	£40
15	Cooking Vinyl COOKLP 595	NONE THE WISER (LP)	£20

ELEANOR RIGBY
85	Waterloo Sunset RUSS 101	I Want To Sleep With You/Till The End Of The Day (p/s with free condom and sticker)	£15
85	Waterloo Sunset RUSS 102	Take Another Shot Of My Heart/1995 (p/s, with story)	£20
87	Waterloo Sunset RUSS 103	Over And Over/Last Night In Soho (p/s)	£15
87	Waterloo Sunset RUSS 103T	Over And Over/Last Night In Soho (12", p/s)	£20
87	Waterloo Sunset WSR 001	CENSORSHIP (LP)	£60
87	Waterloo Sunset WSR 001	CENSORSHIP (LP, with poster)	£80
94	Future Legend FLEG 3	THE BEST OF ELEANOR RIGBY (LP, numbered)	£25

JOHN L RIGBY & THE ALWOODLEY JETS
77	Petal PTL 020	Sleepwalkin/4/12 (500 only, no p/s)	£15
77	Petal PTL 020	Sleepwalkin/4/12 (500 only, only a small number in this p/s)	£50

BRAM RIGG SET
67	Stateside SS 2020	Take The Time Be Yourself/I Can Only Give You Everything	£60

DIANA RIGG
72	RCA RCA 2178	Forget Yesterday/Sentimental Journey	£20
02	Harkit HRKLP	DIANA RIGG SINGS (LP, test pressings only)	£50

JACKIE RIGGS
56	London HLF 8244	The Great Pretender/His Gold Will Melt	£40

RIGHT IDEA
70	Wastelands WL003	Memories/Strike Back	£25

RIGHTEOUS BROTHERS
65	London HL 9962	Just Once In My Life/The Blues (withdrawn)	£25
66	Sue WI 4018	You Can Have Her/Justine	£20
65	Pye Intl. NEP 44043	THE RIGHTEOUS BROTHERS (EP)	£15
66	Verve VEP 5024	SOUL AND INSPIRATION (EP)	£15
65	Pye Intl. NPL 28056	SOME BLUE-EYED SOUL (LP)	£20
65	London HA 8226	YOU'VE LOST THAT LOVIN' FEELIN' (LP)	£20
65	Pye Intl. NPL 28059	RIGHT NOW! (LP)	£18
65	London HA 8245	JUST ONCE IN MY LIFE (LP)	£15
66	London HA 8278	BACK TO BACK (LP)	£15
66	Verve (S)VLP 9131	SOUL AND INSPIRATION (LP)	£15
66	Sue ILP 937	IN ACTION! (LP)	£40
68	Verve (S)VLP 9190	SOULED OUT (LP)	£15
67	Verve VLP 9168	SAYIN SOMETHIN' (LP)	£15

(see also Bill Medley)

RIGHTEOUS FLAMES
67	Fab FAB 18	Gimme Some Sign Girl/Let's Go To The Dance (B-side act. by Prince Buster)	£250
67	Fab FAB 30	When A Girl Loves A Boy/DALTONS: Never Kiss You Again (gold & blue labels)	£150
68	Coxsone CS 7061	You Don't Know/ROY RICHARDS & SOUL VENDORS: Summertime	£500
71	High Note HS 052	Run To The Rock/GAYTONES: Run To The Rock Version	£30
71	Nu Beat NB 083	Love And Emotion/Version	£25
73	RCA Victor RCA 2353	Let The Music Play/True Born African	£18
75	Grounation GRO 2026	Revolution/Version	£25

(see also Richus Flames, Alton Ellis, Flames, Soul Vendors)

RIGHTEOUS HOMES (FLAMES)
68	Coxsone CS 7049	I Was Born To Be Loved(as Righteous Homes)/NORMA FRAZER: Heartaches	£120
68	Blue Cat BS 112	Seven Letters (actually by Winston Jarrett)/SOUL VENDORS: To Sir With Love	£100

RIGHTEOUS TWINS
69	Blue Cat BS 174	If I Could Hear My Master/Satan Can't Prevail	£60

RIGOR MORTIS
73	Track 2406 106	RIGOR MORTIS SETS IN (LP, gatefold, inner sleeve)	£20

(see John Entwistle, Who)

RIKKI & THE LAST DAYS OF EARTH
77	(own label)	Oundle 29/5/77 (1-sided) (Tracks are City Of The Damned/Dorian Grey)	£60

J RILEY
68	Coxsone CS 7051	Great 68 Train/You Should Have Known	£250

(see also Jimmy Riley)

RILEY ALL STARS/KING TUBBY
76	Concrete Jungle CJDPLP	CONCRETE JUNGLE DUB (LP, 300 pressed)	£400

BOB RILEY

58	MGM MGM 977	The Midnight Line/Wanda Jean	£50

DESMOND RILEY

69	Downtown DT 432	Tear Them/GEORGE LEE & RUDIES: Chaka Ground	£50
69	Downtown DT 435	Tears On My Pillow/RUDIES: Man Pon Spot	£20
69	Downtown DT 436	If I Had Wings/AUDREY: You'll Lose A Good Thing	£100
69	Downtown DT 438	Out Your Fire/No Return	£40
69	Downtown DT 450	Skinhead, A Message To You/MUSIC DOCTORS: Going Strong	£125
69	Downtown DT 454	If I Had Wings/AUDREY: You'll Lose A Good Thing (reissue)	£20

HOWARD RILEY (TRIO)

68	Opportunity CP 2499	DISCUSSIONS (LP with insert, as Howard Riley Trio)	£800
69	CBS 52669	ANGLE (LP)	£50
70	CBS 64077	THE DAY WILL COME (LP)	£60
71	Turtle TUR 301	FLIGHT (LP, gatefold sleeve)	£150
75	Mosaic GCM 771	INTERTWINE (LP, solo)	£15
76	Incus INCUS 13	SYNOPSIS (LP, as Howard Riley Trio with Tony Oxley & Barry Guy)	£100
76	Mosaic GCM 781	SHAPED (LP, solo)	£15
76	Cannon CNN 5967	SINGLENESS (LP, solo)	£15
79	Spotlite	THE OTHER SIDE (LP)	£15
81	View VS 020	DUALITY (LP, solo)	£15
81	Impetus 38002	FACETS (box set, 3-LP with Barry Guy, John Stevens, Keith Tippett)	£50
89	Falcon 1	SOLO 74 (cassette LP)	£40

(see also Colosseum)

JEANNIE C. RILEY

69	Polydor 583 716	HARPER VALLEY P.T.A. (LP)	£15

JIMI/JIMMY RILEY

71	Supreme SUP 217	Mount Zion (actually by Jimi Riley & Stranger Cole)/ ECCLE & NEVIL: All Over	£20
75	Dip DL 5067	Ram Goat Liver/OMAR & MARSHA PERRY: Ram Goat Dub	£20
76	Upsetter UP 101	Give Me A Love/UPSETTERS: Give Me A Dub	£25
79	Attack TACK 1	Give Thanks And Praise/Feeling Is Believing (12")	£30
78	Burning Sounds BS 1011	SHOWCASE (LP)	£25
78	Burning Sounds BS 1029	MAJORITY RULE (LP)	£35
79	Trojan TRLS 167	TELL THE YOUTHS THE TRUTH (LP)	£20

(see also Martin Riley, Sensations, Uniques)

MARTIN RILEY

69	Gas GAS 114	Walking Proud/LLOYD CHARMERS: Why Baby	£100
69	Punch PH 7	Trying To Be Free/I've Got It Bad	£15
70	Camel CA 53	Catch This Sound/Suspense	£15
70	Escort ES 823	It Grows (actually "It's Growing")/We Had A Good Thing Going	£40

(see also Jimmy Riley, Slim Smith, Slickers)

TERRY RILEY

71	CBS 64259	CHURCH OF ANTHRAX (LP, with John Cale, dark orange label)	£35
71	CBS 64564	A RAINBOW IN CURVED AIR (LP)	£20
71	CBS 64665	IN "C" (LP)	£20
72	Shandar 83501/2	PERSIAN SURGERY DERVISHES (2-LP)	£40
80	CBS 73929	SHRI CAMEL (LP, insert)	£25
89	Edsel ED 314	IN C (LP, reissue)	£20

(see also John Cale)

WINSTON RILEY

73	Techniques TE 922	Woman Don't You Go Astray/Travelling Man	£15

(see also Techniques)

RILEY'S ALLSTARS

71	Banana BA 343	Glory Of Love (actually "Mystic Blue" by Hugh Hendricks & Buccaneers)/We'll Cry Together - Version	£15

(see also Bobby Davis, Techniques)

RIMBARA

85	Cordelia	ON DRY LAND (LP, with free 7", 400 copies only)	£30

RIMINGTON

73	Man MAM 95	In The Grip Of The Mullah/Dragon Child	£20

RIMSHOTS

00	Sequel NEM LP 507	SOUL TRAIN (LP, reissue)	£20

RIMSHOTS (1)

81	Spectro SPEC 101	At Night/Little Boys And Little Girls	£15

RINGS

77	Chiswick S 14	I Wanna Be Free/Automobile (1st pressing in laminated p/s)	£35
77	Chiswick S 14	I Wanna Be Free/Automobile (2nd pressing in non-laminated p/s)	£20

(see also Maniacs, Twink)

RINGS & THINGS

68	Fontana TF 987	Strange Things Are Happening/To Me: To Me: To Me	£200

RINKY DINKS

58	London HLE 8679	Early In The Morning/Now We're One (as Rinky-Dinks featuring Bobby Darin)	£25
59	London HLE 8793	Mighty Mighty Man/You're Mine (as Bobby Darin with Rinky Dinks)	£30

(see also Bobby Darin)

BOBBY RIO (U.S.)
63 Stateside SS 211 | Don Diddley/I Got You £25

BOBBY RIO (& REVELLES)
65 Pye 7N 15790 | Boy Meets Girl/Don't Break My Heart And Run Away £60
65 Pye 7N 15897 | Everything In The Garden/When Love Was Young..........................£50
65 Pye 7N 15958 | Value For Love/I'm Not Made Of Clay £50
66 Piccadilly 7N 35303 | Ask The Lonely/Be Lonely Little Girl (solo) £25

RIO GRANDE
71 RCA SF 8208 | RIO GRANDE (LP) £15

RIO GRANDES
66 Pyramid PYR 6001 | Soldiers Take Over/Moses...£30

RIOT CLONE
82 Riot Clone RC 001 | THERE'S NO GOVERNMENT LIKE NO GOVERNMENT (EP) £15

RIOTOUS BROTHERS
80 Riotous RI 001 | Vicki's Dancing/Operation Zero/Emotional Cripple (p/s) £25

RIOT ROCKERS
76 Box BOX 23A | Cast Iron Arm/Be Bop A Lula/Mystery Train/Mess Of Blues (no p/s)...........£60
78 Raw RAW 11 | Tennessee Saturday Night/Some Kinda Earthquake (with 'fast' version of A side)..........£20
78 Raw RAW 11 | Tennessee Saturday Night/Some Kinda Earthquake (with 'slow' version of A side) £15

RIOTS
65 Island WI 176 | Telling Lies/Don't Leave Me (actually by Techniques)..................£60
65 Island WI 195 | You Don't Know (actually by Techniques)/DON DRUMMOND & DRUMBAGO: Treasure Island £60
65 Island WI 197 | I Am In Love/When You're Wrong (actually by Techniques) £55
65 Island WI 247 | Yeah Yeah/BABA BROOKS: Virginia Ska £50
(see also Techniques)

RIOT SQUAD & MATUMBI
82 Extinguish EXT 004 | Why Do You Make Me Wait/Paraphrase (12") £20

RIOT SQUAD (1)
65 Pye 7N 15752 | Any Time/Jump £50
65 Pye 7N 15817 | I Wanna Talk About My Baby/Gonna Make You Mine.....................£60
65 Pye 7N 15869 | Nevertheless/Not A Great Talker...£60
66 Pye 7N 17041 | Cry Cry Cry/How Is It Done £50
66 Pye 7N 17092 | I Take It We're Through/Working Man £175
66 Pye 7N 17130 | It's Never Too Late To Forgive/Try To Realise £50
67 Pye 7N 17237 | Gotta Be A First Time/Bitter Sweet Love £60
(see also Graham Bonney, Jimi Hendrix Experience, Blue Aces)

RIOT SQUAD (2)
83 Rot ASS 1 | DON'T BE DENIED (EP)...£20
83 Rot ASS 2 | I'm OK Fuck You/In The Future/Friday Night (p/s) £15
84 Rot ASS 13 | NO POTENTIAL THREAT (LP, with free single [ASS3], stickered sleeve) £18

RIP CHORDS
78 Cells SELL 1 | Ringing In The Streets/Music Is Peace/Artist/Television Television (p/s)......................£18

RIP CHORDS (U.S.)
63 CBS AAG 143 | Here I Stand/Karen..£25
63 CBS AAG 162 | Gone/She Thinks I Still Care £20
64 CBS AAG 181 | Hey Little Cobra/The Queen £30
64 CBS AAG 202 | Three Window Coupe/Hot Rod USA £35
64 CBS BPG 62228 | HEY LITTLE COBRA (LP) £100
(see also Terry Day, Terry Melcher)

RIPCORD
89 Raging Records RAGE 2 | HARVEST HARDCORE (EP, foldout sleeve) £15
87 Manic Ears ACHE 005 | DEFIANCE OF POWER (LP, with insert) £20
88 Raging RAGE 001 | POETIC JUSTICE (LP, with inner)..£15

MINNIE RIPERTON
74 Epic SEPC 80426 | PERFECT ANGEL (LP, some with hype sticker) £30
75 Epic EPC 69142 | ADVENTURES IN PARADISE (LP) £30
02 Castle CMHLP 550 | COME INTO MY GARDEN (LP, reissue, gatefold).....................£18
01 Stateside 7243 5 35127 1 2 | LES FLEURS: THE MINNIE RIPERTON ANTHOLOGY (2LP, 180g) £80

RIPLEY WAYFARERS
71 Tradition TSR 006 | CHIPS AND BROWN SAUCE (LP, 500 only with front-laminated dark green and white flipback sleeve, title in blue) £30
73 Tradition TSR 006 | CHIPS AND BROWN SAUCE (LP, reissue, plain green sleeve, title in black) £15

RIP 'N' LAN
71 Crab CRAB 64 | In The Ghetto/Something Sweet £30

RIPPERS
68 Saga FID 21 42 | HONESTLY (LP) £35

RIPPLE
95 Charly CPLP 8093 | RIPPLE (LP, reissue) £15

RIP RIG & PANIC
81 Virgin VZZ13 | GOD (2 x 12") £15
82 Virgin V 2228 | I AM COLD (2 x 12") £15
83 Virgin V 2268 | ATTITUDE (LP) £15

MINT VALUE £

RISAN
82	Saffron	Eastern Palace/Part 2 .... £30

RISING FIRE
81	Cha Cha CHAD 45	You Lied/Free Blackman (12") £25

RISING HEAT
73	Firestone FS 02	My Magic Thimble/Evolution £25
75	Newbury N32	Drop The Act/Follow Me Home £40

RISING MOON
74	Theatre Projects 07691	RISING MOON (LP) £100

RISING SONS (U.S.)
65	Stateside SS 426	You're My Girl/Try To Be A Man £35

RITA
69	Major Minor MM 653	Erotica/Sexologie £15

RITA (ALSTON)
69	Jackpot JP 718	Love Making/NAT COLE: My Love £20

(see also Rita Alston)

RITA & TIARAS
79	Destiny DS 1002	Gone With The Wind Is My Love/Wild Times (DJ copy with p/s) £18

TEX RITTER
52	Capitol LC 6552	COWBOY FAVOURITES (10" LP) £20

RITUAL (1)
80	Mojo Funk MOD 1	Sore Lip/Non-Stop Boogie (p/s) £40

RITZ
74	Dawn DNS 1070	Jenny Gentle/Why Love £20

(see also Paul Ryder & The Time Machine)

RIVAL SCHOOLS
02	Island 548936	UNITED BY FATE (LP) £20
13	Shop Radio Cast 022	FOUND (LP, green vinyl, UK pressing sold via band website) £20

RIVALS (2)
78	Sound On Sound SOS 100	Skateboarding In The UK/Top Of The Pops... £35

RIVALS (3)
80	Ace ACE 007	Future Rights/Flowers (p/s) £100
80	Oakwood/Ace ACE 011	Here Comes The Night/Both Sides (p/s) £40

RIVAL SAVAGES
80	Savage VC 1968	Get Some/Garden Of The Damned (fold-out p/s, dust sleeve stapled) £20

HECTOR RIVERA
67	Polydor 65728	At The Party/Do It To Me £60
89	Horace's HRH 003	Playing It Cool/I Want A Chance For Romance (reissue) £35

BLUE RIVERS & MAROONS
67	Columbia Blue Beat DB 103	Witchcraft Man/Searching For You Baby £30
68	Columbia S(C)X 6192	BLUE BEAT IN MY SOUL (LP) £65

CLIFF RIVERS
63	London HLU 9739	True Lips/Marsha £40

DANNY RIVERS
60	Top Rank JAR 408	Hawk/I Got £40
60	Decca F 11294	Can't You Hear My Heart/I'm Waiting For Tomorrow £25
61	Decca F 11357	Once Upon A Time/My Baby's Gone Away (with Alexander Combo) £40
64	Decca F 11865	There Will Never Be Anyone Else/I Don't Think You Know How I Feel £25
62	HMV POP 1000	We're Gonna Dance/Movin' In (as Danny Rivers & River Men) £50

DEEK RIVERS
62	Oriole CB 1735	One Kiss/Outsider £25

JOHNNY RIVERS
66	Liberty LIB 12023	Secret Agent Man/Tom Dooley £15
66	Liberty LIB 66175	I Washed My Hands In Muddy Water/Roogalator £15
66	Liberty LEP 4049	MORE JOHNNY RIVERS (EP) £15
64	Liberty LBY 3031	AT THE WHISKY A GO-GO (LP) £20
65	Liberty LBY 3036	HERE WE A GO-GO AGAIN (LP) £15
65	Liberty LBY 3064	RIVERS ROCKS THE FOLK (LP) £20
68	Liberty LBS 83040	REWIND (LP) £15

MAVIS RIVERS
63	Reprise RS 20115	Slightly Out Of Tune/Footsteps Of A Fool £30

ROYD RIVERS & CLIFF AUNGIER
65	Decca LK 4696	WANDERIN' (LP) £35

(see also Cliff Aungier)

TONY RIVERS & THE CASTAWAYS
63	Columbia DB 7135	Shake Shake Shake/Row Row Row £20
64	Columbia DB 7224	I Love The Way You Walk/I Love You £15
64	Columbia DB 7336	Life's Too Short/Tell On Me £15
65	Columbia DB 7448	She/Till We Get Home £15
65	Columbia DB 7536	Come Back/What To Do £15
66	Columbia DB 7971	God Only Knows/Charade £20

66	Parlophone R 5400	Nowhere Man/The Girl From New York City	£25
66	Immediate IM 027	Girl Don't Tell Me/The Girl From Salt Lake City	£50

(see also Capability Brown, Grapefruit, Harmony Grass, Senators, Sugarbeats)

RIVIERAS
60	HMV POP 773	Blessing Of Love/Moonlight Cocktails	£120

RIVIERAS (U.S.)
64	Pye International 7N 25237	California Sun/H B Goose Step	£45

RIVINGTONS
62	Liberty LIB 55427	Papa Oom Mow Mow/Deep Water	£50
63	Liberty LIB 55553	The Bird's The Word/I'm Losing My Grip	£60
66	CBS 202088	Rose Growing In The Ruins/Tend To Business	£75

FREDDIE ROACH
67	Transatlantic PR 7490	THE SOUL BOOK (LP)	£40

MAX ROACH
60	Mercury MMC 14054	QUIET AS IT'S KEPT (LP)	£20
62	HMV CLP 1522	PERC 'N' BITTER SUITE (LP)	£15

MAX ROACH (& CLIFFORD BROWN GROUP)
55	Vogue LDE 117	MAX ROACH & CLIFFORD BROWN IN CONCERT VOL. 1 (10" LP)	£15
55	Vogue LDE 128	MAX ROACH & CLIFFORD BROWN IN CONCERT VOL. 2 (10" LP)	£15
58	Emarcy EJL 1282	JAZZ IN THREE-QUARTER TIME (LP)	£15
59	Emarcy MMB 12005	MAX ROACH, NEWPORT (LP, by Max Roach)	£15
59	Emarcy MMB 12009	THE MAX ROACH FOUR PLUS FOUR (LP, by Max Roach)	£15

(see also Clifford Brown)

ROAD
73	Rare Earth SRE 3006	ROAD (LP)	£50

(see also Noel Redding)

ROADRUNNERS
65	Cavern Sound 2BSNL 7	PANTOMANIA (EP, with tracks by Chris Edwards & Clive Wood)	£35

ROADSTER
81	Mayhem SRTS 81	Fantasy/45 MPH (p/s)	£30

ROADSTERS
64	Stateside SS 293	Joy Ride/Drag	£40

ROAMING DOG
72	Perfect PF 01	Sign Your Name/Eclipse	£50

ROARING SIXTIES
66	Marmalade 598 001	We Love The Pirates/I'm Leaving Town	£40

(see also Ivy League)

ROBAN'S SKIFFLE GROUP
61	Storyville A45 062	Careless Love/Frankie And Johnny (with p/s)	£35
61	Storyville A45 062	Careless Love/Frankie And Johnny	£18

E.G. ROBB
63	Columbia DB 7100	Stage To Cimarron/Jezebel	£15

MARTY ROBBINS
SINGLES
57	Philips JK 1019	A White Sport Coat (And A Pink Carnation)/Grown-Up Tears (jukebox issue)	£25

(see also Jordanaires)

MEL ROBBINS
59	London HLM 8966	Save It/To Know You (initially pressing with triangular centre)	£300
59	London HLM 8966	Save It/To Know You (later round centre)	£100
59	London HLM 8966	Save It/To Know You (78)	£40

SYLVIA ROBBINS
60	London HLJ 9118	Frankie And Johnny/Come Home	£35

(see also Mickey & Sylvia)

ROBERT & REMOULDS
79	Black & White BW 1	X No. 1/Do Eyes Ever Meet? (p/s)	£60

ANDY ROBERTS
70	RCA SF 8086	HOME GROWN (LP, laminated front sleeve, lyric insert)	£100
71	Charisma CAS 1034	HOME GROWN (LP, reissue, different sleeve)	£15
71	B&C	HOME GROWN (LP, reissue)	£20
71	Pegasus PEG 5	NINA AND THE DREAM TREE (LP)	£80
73	Elektra K 42139	URBAN COWBOY (LP, with insert, 'butterfly' label)	£20
73	Elektra K 42151	ANDY ROBERTS AND THE GREAT STAMPEDE (LP, gatefold sleeve)	£15

(see also Clayton Squares, Liverpool Scene, Everyone, Plainsong, Mighty Baby)

BOB ROBERTS (U.K.)
81	Solent SS 054	BREEZE FOR A BARGEMAN (LP)	£15

J. ROBERTS
70	Bamboo BAM 30	Someday We'll Be Together/SOUND DIMENSION: Everyday People	£20

JOHN ROBERTS
68	Sue WI 4042	Sockin' 1, 2, 3, 4/Sophisticated Funk	£50
68	Action ACT 4511	I'll Forget You/Be My Baby	£40

KEITH ROBERTS
72	Trailer LER 3031	PIER OF THE REALM (LP, red label)	£15

KENNY ROBERTS (2)
66	Pye 7N 17054	Run Like The Devil/Where Goes My Heart	£50
66	Pye 7N 17054	Run Like The Devil/Where Goes My Heart (DJ copy)	£75
65	Pye 7N 15882	Say, Do You Mean It/Since My Love Has Gone	£15

KIM ROBERTS
64	Decca F 11813	I'll Prove It/For Loving Me This Way	£65

ROCKY ROBERTS
67	Durium DRL 50026	SABATO SERA (LP)	£30

STEVE ROBERTS
80s	EXPLP 2002	DO YOU KNOW WHO I AM (LP)	£15

(see also U.K.Subs)

DALE ROBERTSON
60	RCA SF 5064	PRESENTS HIS ALBUM OF WESTERN CLASSICS (LP)	£20

JIM ROBERTSON
55	MGM SPC 7	Pride Of My Heart/Walkin' And Talkin' With The Lord (export issue)	£15

RICHIE ROBIN
60	Top Rank JAR 262	Strange Dream/GERRY GRANAHAN: It Hurts	£15

TINA ROBIN
58	Coral Q 72309	Everyday/Believe Me)	£20
58	Coral Q 72323	No School Tomorrow/Sugar Blues	£20
58	Coral Q 72323	No School Tomorrow/Sugar Blues (78)	£15

ROGER ROBIN
95	Saxon SHF 004	Do Right/Tell Me (12")	£20
98	Saxon SAX 065	Unity/Mix 2//My Medication/Version (12")	£15

ROBINS
60	Vogue V 9168	Cherry Lips/Out Of The Picture	£100
60	Vogue V 9173	Just Like That/Whole Lot Imagination	£100

(see also H.B. Barnum)

JIMMY ROBINS
68	President PT 118	I Can't Please You/I Made It Over	£150

ALVIN ROBINSON
64	Pye International 7N 25248	Something You Got/Searchin'	£25
64	Red Bird RB 10010	Down Home Girl/Fever	£30
66	Strike JH 307	You Brought My Heart Right Down To My Knees/Whatever You Had	£20

ANDY ROBINSON
68	Philips SBL 7887	PATTERNS OF REALITY (LP, laminated sleeve, black/silver label)	£30

BROTHER CLEOPHUS ROBINSON
57	Vogue EPV 1196	BROTHER CLEOPHUS ROBINSON (EP)	£25

DAVE ROBINSON
79	Bushays BFM 124	Ruby & Diamond (feat. Jah Thomas/Dub (12")	£25

EDDIE ROBINSON
74	Myrrh MYR 1013	REFLECTIONS OF THE MAN INSIDE (LP)	£15

FLOYD ROBINSON
60	RCA RD 27166	FLOYD ROBINSON (LP)	£40

FREDDY ROBINSON
72	Stax 2325 085	AT THE DRIVE-IN (LP)	£18

JACKEY ROBINSON
70	Punch PH 50	Heart Made Of Stone (actually by Jackie Bernard)/BOB TAYLOR: I May Never See My Baby Anymore	£20

(see also Jackie Robinson, Pioneers)

JACKIE ROBINSON
68	Amalgamated AMG 819	Over And Over/Woman Of Samaria	£45
68	Amalgamated AMG 824	Let The Little Girl Dance/DERRICK MORGAN: I Want To Go Home	£40

(see also Pioneers)

JIM ROBINSON NEW ORLEANS BAND
61	Riverside RLP 369	NEW ORLEANS: THE LIVING LEGENDS (LP)	£15
64	Riverside RLP 393	PLAYS SPIRITUAL AND BLUES (LP)	£15

J.P. ROBINSON
72	Atlantic K 10209	What Can I Tell Her/Please Accept My Call	£15

LLOYD ROBINSON
62	Blue Beat BB 122	Give Me A Chance/When You Walk	£20
63	Blue Beat BB 159	I Need Your Love/You Told Me	£30
69	Duke DU 5	Cuss Cuss/Lavender Blue	£200
70	Camel CA 41	The Worm/NEVILLE HYNES: Afro (actually by Neville Hinds)	£40
77	Cactus CT 109	Rocky Road/Version	£20
04	Trojan TJGSE014	Cuss Cuss/KING CANNON: Soul Special (reissue)	£15

(see also Lloyd Clarke, Lloyd Charmers, Lloyd & Devon, Lloyd & Glen, Harry J. Allstars, Matadors, Melodians)

M. ROBINSON
64	Port-O-Jam PJ 4114	Who Are You/Follow You	£15

MARTEL ROBINSON
75	Arrow AR 006	Sunny Soil/Sunny	£15
78	Ray RALP 33	COOL SHADY TREE (LP)	£20

PAUL ROBINSON
83 King City KCD 006   Come On Sister/Instrumental (12") £80

ROSCO ROBINSON
66 Pye International 7N 25385 That's Enough/One More Time £50
66 Pye International 7N 25385 That's Enough/One More Time (DJ copy) £100

SANDRA ROBINSON
85 Trojan TROT 9079   Sensi For Sale (Part 1)/TUFF TONES: Boogie Mix (Part 2)/SANDRA ROBINSON & TUFF
                               TONES: Depression/DAN AMBRASSA: Life's Riddle/TUFF TONES: Boogie Mix (12") £20

SUGAR CHILE ROBINSON
53 Capitol LC 6586   CAPITOL PRESENTS SUGAR CHILE ROBINSON (10" LP) £40

TOM ROBINSON (BAND)
75 Chebel SRT/CUS 015   GLAD TO BE GAY (EP, as Bradford Gay Liberation Front, no p/s) £250
79 Deviant Wrecords DEVIATE 1A Dyke's Gotta Do (What A Dyke's Gotta Do)/NOEL GREIG: Stand Together (All You Gay
                               Women All You Gay Men) (die cut sleeve with sticker)..............................£20
(see also Cafe Society, Billy Karloff [& Extremes])

ROBIN WANTS REVENGE
90 Jungle Jam JJR 102   ROBIN WANTS REVENGE EP (12") £40

CARSON ROBISON (& HIS PLEASANT VALLEY BOYS)
53 MGM SP 1024   Square Dance Jitterbug/Keep On Circlin' 'Round £18

RALPH ROBLES
69 London HA/SH 8385   TAKING OVER (LP)...£20

ALEXANDER ROBOTNICK
84 Sire SAM 258   Problemes D'Amour (Aah Ooh Ah Mix)/Problemes D'Amour (Edit) (12" promo only) £40

ROBOTS AND HUMANOIDS
96 Alphaphone ALPHA 004   Indigo Octagon/Moment Of Truth/Inner Landscape/Paranoia (12") £20
(see also Cabaret Voltaire, Richard H. Kirk)

JEREMY ROBSON
63 Columbia SEG 8244   BLUES FOR THE LONELY (EP, with Michael Garrick and Shake Keane) £100

NICKY ROBSON
80 Scratch SCR 006   Stars/Eye To Eye (p/s) £20
80 Scratch SCRT 006   Stars (Extended)/Eye To Eye (12") £45
(see also Gary Numan)

ROCAMARS
65 King KG 1031   All In Black Woman/Give Me Time £20

TONY ROCCO
62 Parlophone R 4886   Stalemate/Keep A Walking £15
62 Parlophone R 4946   Competition/Torture £15

HARRY ROCHE CONSTELLATION
67 CBS SBPG 63013   CASINO ROYALE (LP) £35
71 Studio Two TWO 340   SPINDRIFT (LP) £20
73 Pye Intl. NSPL 41024   SPIRAL (LP, laminated sleeve) £30
73 Pye QUAD 1022   SOMETIMES (LP, quadrophonic) £20

JOHNNY ROCK
55 Vogue VE170112   JOHNNY ROCK (EP) £40

PETE ROCK
98 RCA 74321619781   SOUL SURVIVOR (2-LP, inners) £25
01 BBE BBEBGLP 002   PETESTRUMENTALS (2-LP, gatefold) £20

PETE ROCK & C.L. SMOOTH
92 Elektra EKT 105   MECCA AND THE SOUL BROTHER (2-LP) £30
94 Elektra 7559-61661-1   THE MAIN INGREDIENT (2-LP) £20

ROCKABILLY REBS
79 SRTS 79 CUS 524   ROCKABILLY REBS (EP, no p/s) £100

ROCK-A-TEENS
59 Columbia DB 4361   Woo-Hoo/Untrue £40

ROCK BROTHERS
56 Parlophone MSP 6201   Dungaree Doll/Livin' It Up...£90
56 Parlophone R 4119   Dungaree Doll/Livin' It Up (78) £30

ROCKERS HI-FI
95 4th & Broadway BRLPD 615   ROCKERS TO ROCKERS (2-LP) £30
96 Different Drummer LP   MISH MASH (3-LP)...£25
    60016

ROCKET 88
81 Atlantic K 50776   ROCKET 88 (LP) £20
(see also Charlie Watts, Alexis Korner, Jack Bruce, Dick Heckstall-Smith)

ROCKET FROM THE CRYPT
93 Southern Studios PUS 007   Glazed/Pressures/Cut It Loose (white label test pressing, 5-10 copies only) £30
96 Dinked 1   Used/Lose Your Clown (in-store giveaway)...£20
95 Elemental ELM 27LP   HOT CHARITY (LP)...£15
08 One Little Indian ELM   ROCKET FROM THE CRYPT (LP, 1000 only) £18
    50DMM
08 One Little indian   SCREAM DRACULA SCREAM! (LP) £20
    ELM34DMM

ROCKETS
60	Philips PB 982	Gibraltar Rock/Walkin' Home	£20
60	Philips PB 982	Gibraltar Rock/Walkin' Home (78)	£40
61	Zodiac ZR 0010	Warrior/Countdown	£22

ROCKIN' BERRIES
63	Decca F 11698	Wah Wah Wah Woo/Rockin' Berry Stomp	£25
63	Decca F 11760	Itty Bitty Pieces/The Twitch	£20
65	Piccadilly NEP 34039	I DIDN'T MEAN TO HURT YOU (EP)	£35
65	Piccadilly NEP 34043	NEW FROM THE BERRIES (EP)	£35
65	Piccadilly NEP 34045	HAPPY TO BE BLUE (EP)	£50
78	Hollick & Taylor HT EPS 15615	FROM THE BERRIES (EP)	£15
64	Piccadilly NPL 38013	IN TOWN (LP)	£40
65	Piccadilly NPL 38022	LIFE IS JUST A BOWL OF BERRIES (LP)	£40

(see also Jefferson)

ROCKIN' DEVILS
79	Hit Stuff HS 004	Apache/Bony Moronie/Give Me Muddy Water/Rumplestiltskin (no p/s)	£30
79	HOT ROCK HS 007	GOT THEM BLUES (EP, red vinyl)	£40
75	Hot Stuff HSL 001	BRING BACK ROCK'N' ROLL (LP)	£50
75	Hot Stuff HSL 002	THAT OLD ROCK MUSIC'S HERE TO STAY (LP)	£60
75	Hot Stuff HSL 003	WITH A LITTLE HELP FROM OUR FRIEND (LP)	£20
76	Hot Stuff HSL 004	REMEMBER (LP)	£70
77	HOT ROCK HSL 005	OFF MY ROCKER (LP)	£40

ROCKIN' FOO
70	Stateside SSL 10303	ROCKIN' FOO (LP)	£22

ROCKIN' HORSE
71	Philips 6308 075	YES IT IS (LP, laminated sleve, black/silver label)	£150

(see also Jimmy Campbell, 23rd Turnoff, Kirkbys, Merseys)

ROCKIN' RAMRODS
66	Polydor BM 56512	Don't Fool With Fu Manchu/Tears Melt The Stone	£25

ROCKIN' REBELS
63	Stateside SS 162	Wild Weekend/Wild Weekend Cha Cha	£22
63	Stateside SS 187	Rockin' Crickets/Hully Gully Rock (both sides actually by Hot-Toddys)	£20

(see also Hot-Toddys)

ROCKIN' R'S
59	London HL 8872	The Beat/Crazy Baby	£40
59	London HL 8872	The Beat/Crazy Baby (78)	£30

ROCKIN' SAINTS
60	Brunswick 05843	Cheat On Me, Baby/Half And Half	£100

ROCKIN' SHADES
79	SRTS 79 CUS 404	LIVE AT CAISTER EP	£20

ROCKIN' VICKERS
64	Decca F 11993	I Go Ape/Someone Like You (as Rocking Vickers)	£40
66	CBS 202051	It's Alright/Stay By Me	£55
66	CBS 202241	Dandy/I Don't Need Your Kind	£40

(see also Motorhead)

ROCKING HORSE
71	Camel CA 75	Running Back Home/SOUL SYNDICATE BAND: Running Back - Version	£15
74	Sydna SYD 5026	Be Thankful/Thankful Dub	£15

ROCKING RICHARD AND WHISTLING VIC TEMPLAR
87	Hangman HANG 14 UP	PRESENT: TEA AND BACCY (LP)	£15

ROCK MACHINE
73	T.I.M.	THEMES (LP)	£60

(see also Ugly Custard)

ROCKS
88	GOTELOAN GLP A1 88 TR	Human Music/Freedom	£15

ROCKSTAR
76	MCA MCA 265	Mummy/Over The Hill	£15

ROCKSTEADYS
67	Giant GN 2	Squeeze And Freeze/JUNIOR SMITH: I'm A Good Boy	£35

ROCKSTONES
70	Trojan TR 7762	A.B.C. Reggae/BEVERLEY'S ALLSTARS: Be Yours	£30

(see also Gaylads)

ROCK TONE BAND
77	Militant ML 004	Burne Me Out/Version 1977	£150

ROCK WORKSHOP
70	CBS 64075	ROCK WORKSHOP (LP, orange label)	£35
71	CBS 64394	THE VERY LAST TIME (LP, gatefold sleeve, orange label)	£35

(see also Bob Downes, Alex Harvey)

ROCKY FELLERS
63	Stateside SS 175	Killer Joe/Lonely Treardrops	£20
63	Stateside SS 212	Like The Big Guys Do/Great Big World	£18
63	Pye International 7N 25225	Ching A Ling Baby/Hey Little Donkey	£22

ROCKY HORROR SHOW
87	Ode RHVX 1	ROCKY HORROR BOX SET (4-LP box, with inserts, numbered)	£20
87	Ode RHBXLP 1	ROCKY HORROR BOX SET (4-LP box, with different inserts to above)	£20
90	Ode RHBXCD 1	THE ROCKY HORROR PICTURE ALBUMS (15th ANNIVERSARY) (4-CD, with booklet)	£40

(see also Meat Loaf, Original Soundtracks)

RODD-KEN & CAVALIERS
60	Triumph RGM 1001	Magic Wheel/Happy Valley	£40

(see also Blue Men)

RODDY RADIATION & THE TEARJERKERS
80	Dodgy Demo Co	NOTHING LASTS FOREVER EP	£25

(see also Specials)

CLODA(GH) RODGERS
68	RCA 1684	Room Full Of Roses/Play The Drame To The End	£20
69	RCA SF 8033 / RD 8033	CLODAGH RODGERS (LP)	£20
69	RCA SF 8071	MIDNIGHT CLODAGH (LP)	£20
71	RCA SF 8180	RODGERS AND HEART (LP)	£20
72	RCA SF 8271	IT'S DIFFERENT NOW (LP, gatefold)	£15
73	RCA SF 8394	YOU ARE MY MUSIC (LP)	£15
77	Polydor 2383473	SAVE ME (LP)	£15

EILEEN RODGERS
61	London HLR 9271	Sailor (Your Home Is The Sea)/Wait Till Tomorrow	£15

JIMMIE RODGERS (THE BLUE YODELLER)
58	HMV 7EG 8163	JIMMIE RODGERS (EP)	£19
59	RCA RD 27110	TRAIN WHISTLE BLUES (LP)	£15
59	RCA RD 27138	NEVER NO MO' BLUES (JIMMIE RODGERS MEMORIAL ALBUM) (LP)	£15
61	RCA RD 27203	MY ROUGH AND ROWDY WAYS (LP)	£15
61	RCA RD 27241	JIMMIE THE KID (LP)	£15
62	RCA RD 7505	COUNTRY MUSIC HALL OF FAME (LP)	£15
63	RCA RD 7562	THE SHORT BUT BRILLIANT LIFE OF JIMMIE RODGERS (LP)	£15
64	RCA RD 7644	MY TIME AIN'T LONG (LP)	£15

JIMMIE RODGERS
58	Columbia 33SX 1082	JIMMIE RODGERS (LP)	£25
58	Columbia 33SX 1097	THE NUMBER ONE BALLADS (LP)	£25

RODNEY P (AKA RODDIE ROK)
13	Tru Thoughts TRU 7274	Success/Live Up	£25
02	Riddim Killah RKP04LP	THE FUTURE (LP, test pressing, version unreleased)	£80
04	Riddim Killah RKP04LP	THE FUTURE (LP- Limited White Vinyl)	£35

(see also London Posse)

TOMMY ROE (& ROEMANS)
63	HMV 7EG 8806	THE FOLK SINGER (EP)	£15
63	HMV CLP 1614	SHEILA (LP)	£40
64	HMV CLP 1704	EVERYBODY LIKES TOMMY ROE (LP)	£20
65	HMV CLP 1860	BALLADS AND BEAT (LP)	£20
69	Stateside S(S)L 10282	DIZZY (LP)	£15

CE CE ROGERS
87	Atlantic SAM 502	Someday (Club Mix)/(Some Dub)/)Accainsttrumental) (12" promo)	£25
89	Atlantic A 8852	Forever/Someday (p/s)	£20

DEAN ROGERS
61	Parlophone R 4835	Timber/High In A Misty Sky	£20

(see also Sydney James)

JULIE ROGERS
65	Mercury 20048 (S)MCL	THE SOUND OF JULIE (LP, mono/stereo)	£20
66	Mercury 20086 (S)MCL	CONTRASTS (LP, mono/stereo)	£20
67	Mercury 20100 (S)MCL	SONGS OF INSPIRATION (LP, mono/stereo)	£15

LINCOLN ROGERS
73	Phoenix NIX 137	Let Love Come Between Us/She Looked At Me With Love	£15

MARK ROGERS & MARKSMEN
63	Parlophone R 5045	Bubble Pop/Hold It!	£25

(see also Marksmen, Mark Wirtz)

PAULINE ROGERS
54	Columbia SCM 5106	Spinnin' The Blues/But Good	£20

SHORTY ROGERS & HIS ORCHESTRA
52	Capitol LC 6549	MODERN SOUNDS (10" LP, as Shorty Rogers & His Giants)	£15
54	HMV DLP 1030	COOL AND CRAZY (10" LP, featuring Giants)	£15
54	HMV DLP 1058	EIGHT SHORTY ROGERS' NUMBERS (10" LP)	£15
56	Contemporary LDC 190	SHELLY MANNE, SHORTY ROGERS AND JIMMY GIUFFRE - THE THREE (10" LP, with Shelly Manne & Jimmy Giuffre)	£18

(see also Boots Brown, Bud Shank, Shelly Manne, Jimmy Giuffre)

SIDNEY ROGERS
78	Ethnic Fight FTDD 4448	I Don't Want To End Up In Slavery/Mary And Bobby (12")	£60
74	Ethnic Fight ETH 2214S	MIRACLE WORKER (LP)	£30
75	Ethnic Fight EF 2222S	TIPPIN' IN (LP)	£60

TIMMIE ROGERS
57	London HLU 8510	Back To School Again/I've Got A Dog Who Loves Me	£60

57	London HLU 8510	Back To School Again/I've Got A Dog Who Loves Me (78)	£20
58	London HLU 8601	Take Me To Your Leader/Fla-Ga-La-Pa	£60
58	London HLU 8601	Take Me To Your Leader/Fla-Ga-La-Pa (78)	£20

TRACY ROGERS
66	Polydor 56077	Baby/Through Thick And Thin	£25

VERN ROGERS & HI-FI'S
62	Oriole CB 1785	That Ain't Right/Be Everything To Anyone You Love	£20
63	Oriole CB 1826	He's New To You/Can't Complain	£15
63	Oriole CB 1885	I Will/One Way Love Affair	£20
63	Oriole CB 1923	Anna/Pride	£15

DIANA ROGERSON
85	United Dairies UD 017	THE INEVITABLE CHRYSTAL BELLE SCRODD RECORD (LP)	£25
86	United Dairies UD 021	CHRYSTAL BELLE SCRODD: BELLE DE JOUR (LP)	£25

(see also Nurse With Wound)

ROG & PIP
14	Rise Above Relics RARLP 013	OUR REVOLUTION (LP)	£25

ROGUES (U.K.)
67	Decca F 12718	Memories Of Missy/And You Let Her Pass By	£30

ROGUES (U.S.)
65	CBS 201731	Everyday/Rogers Reef	£20

(see also Terry Day, Terry Melcher)

CHRIS ROHMANN
73	RCA Victor SF 8364	THE MAN I AM TODAY (LP)	£22

ROKES
67	RCA RCA 1587	Let's Live For Today/Ride On	£30
67	RCA RCA 1646	Hold My Hand/Regency Sue	£50
68	RCA RCA 1694	When The Wind Arises/The Works Of Bartholemew	£70

PAUL ROLAND
80	Ace ACE 013	THE WEREWOLF OF LONDON (LP)	£18

(see also Beau Brummel)

WALTER ROLAND/GEORGIA SLIM
59	Jazz Collector JEL 2	THE MALE BLUES VOL. 1 (EP)	£22

BARRY ROLFE
73	Philips 6006 331	Look The Business/Molly Molly	£30

PETER ROLFE
66	Strike JH 314	London/In The Middle Of Town	£20

ROLLERS (1)
61	London HLG 9340	Continental Walk/I Want You So	£18

ROLLING STONES
23	Rolling Stones 5546460	HACKNEY DIAMONDS (LP, gatefold, printed inner, clear diamond vinyl, indie exclusive)	£30

SINGLES : DECCA SINGLES
63	Decca F 11675	Come On/I Want To Be Loved (demo copies £350)	£50
63	Decca F 11742	Fortune Teller/Poison Ivy (solid centre, withdrawn)	£1500
63	Decca F 11764	I Wanna Be Your Man/Stones (B-side mis-spelled)	£35
63	Decca F 11764	I Wanna Be Your Man/Stoned	£20
64	No Cat. No.	We Were Falling In Love (EMI disc acetate, unreleased single)	£1000
65	Decca F 12104	The Last Time/Play With Fire	£15
65	Decca F 12220	(I Can't Get No) Satisfaction/The Spider And The Fly	£15
65	Decca F 12263	Get Off Of My Cloud/The Singer Not The Song	£15
66	Decca F 12395	Paint It, Black/Long Long While	£15

(The above singles were originally issued with a round Decca logo; later boxed-logo pressings are worth £4 each.)
66	Decca F 12497	Have You Seen Your Mother, Baby, Standing In The Shadow?/ Who's Driving Your Plane	£15
67	Decca F 12654	We Love You/Dandelion	£15
68	Decca F 12782	Jumping Jack Flash/Child Of The Moon	£15
69	Decca F 12952	Honky Tonk Women/You Can't Always Get What You Want (in demo-only p/s)	£70
69	Decca F 12952	Honky Tonk Women/You Can't Always Get What You Want	£15
71	Decca F 13203	Street Fighting Man/Surprise Surprise (jukebox edition)	£30
73	Decca F 13404	Sad Day/You Can't Always Get What You Want	£20
74	Decca F 13517	Paint It Black/It's All Over Now (release cancelled, demo-only)	£220
75	Decca F 13584	I Don't Know Why I Love You (credited to either 'Jagger/Richard/Taylor'/Try A Little Harder	£20
75	Decca F 13584	I Don't Know Why I Love You (credited Stevie Wonder')/Try A Little Harder	£15
87	Decca FX 102	Jumping Jack Flash/Child Of The Moon/Sympathy For The Devil (12", p/s, reissue)	£20

SINGLES : ROLLING STONES LABEL SINGLES
71	Rolling Stones RS 19100	Brown Sugar/Bitch/Let It Rock (in p/s)	£50
81	Rolling Stones	Beast Of Burden/Everything Is Turning Gold (unreleased)	£0
84	Rolling Stones SUGARP 1	Brown Sugar/Bitch (shaped picture disc)	£30
93	Rolling Stone RS LH 1	Brown Sugar/Start Me Up (jukebox issue, no p/s)	£15
93	Rolling Stone ORDER LH 1	Gimme Shelter (Live Version)/NEW MODEL ARMY FEATURING TOM JONES: Gimme Shelter (jukebox issue, no p/s)	£15
20	Rolling Stones 0714833	LIVING IN A GHOST TOWN (10", single-sided, purple vinyl, p/s)	£20
20	Rolling Stones 0714833	LIVING IN A GHOST TOWN (10", single-sided, orange vinyl, p/s)	£15
23	Rolling Stones 5812248	ANGRY (7", single-sided, etched, p/s, red vinyl)	£15
23	Rolling Stones 5546464	ANGRY (10", single-sided, etched, p/s)	£15

SINGLES : CBS SINGLES

89	CBS 655 193-5	Mixed Emotions (7" Version)/Fancyman Blues/Tumbling Dice/Miss You (CD, picture disc, in circular tin with 'tongue' logo sticker)	£35
89	CBS 655 214-2	Mixed Emotions (7" Version)/Fancyman Blues/Shattered/Waiting On A Friend (CD, picture disc, in circular tin with 'tongue' logo sticker)	£35
89	CBS 655 422-2	Rock And A Hard Place (7" Version)/(Dance Mix)/(Bonus Beats Mix)/ Cook Cook Blues (CD, picture disc, card sleeve)	£15
89	CBS 655 448-2	Rock And A Hard Place (7" Version)/Cook Cook Blues/It's Only Rock'n'Roll (But I Like It)/Rocks Off (3rd CD, picture disc, 7" box set with poster)	£25
90	CBS 656 065-5	Almost Hear You Sigh/Miss You/Waiting On A Friend/Wish I'd Never Met You (CD, in tin with 'Urban Jungle' sticker)	£30

SINGLES : VIRGIN SINGLES

94	Virgin VSCDG 1524	Out Of Tears (Don Was Edit)/I'm Gonna Drive/So Young/The Storm/ Jump On Top Of Me (CD, digipak, numbered, 4,000 only, withdrawn)	£250
94	Virgin VSP 1539	I Go Wild/I Go Wild (live) (numbered picture disc)	£20
96	Virgin VS 1578	Wild Horses/Tumbling Dice/Gimme Shelter (unreleased)	£0
96	Virgin VSCDT 1578	Wild Horses/Tumbling Dice/Gimme Shelter (CD, unreleased)	£0
97	Virgin VST 1653	Anybody Seen My Baby? (LP Edit)/(Soul Solution Remix)/(Bonus Roll) (12", p/s)	£15
97	Virgin VS 1653	Anybody Seen My Baby? (LP Edit)/(Soul Solution Remix Edit) (numbered picture disc, p/s, 7,500 only)	£15
98	Virgin VSTTDT 1667	Saint Of Me (remixes)/Anybody Seen My Baby? (remixes) (12", double pack, stickered p/s)	£15
98	Virgin VSTX 1667	Saint Of Me (remixes)/Anybody Seen My Baby? (remixes) (12", double pack, stickered p/s)	£15

SINGLES : OTHER SINGLES

72	Sound For Industry 107	Mick Jagger Introduces 'Exile On Main Street' (flexidisc free with NME, tracks by Curved Air and Fanny on other side)	£15
74	Atlantic K 19107	Brown Sugar/Happy/Rocks Off (unissued)	£300
15	Secret 7" S726	Dead Flowers (100 only, each with unique art sleeve)	£200

SINGLES : SINGLES BOX SETS

80	Decca STONE 1-12	SINGLE STONES (12-single box set)	£60
80	Decca BROWSE 1	SINGLE STONES (in-store, 3 x 12-single box set [STONE 1-12], with poster & badge, also available via mail-order)	£150

EXPORT SINGLES

63	Decca AT 15005	I Wanna Be Your Man/Stoned	£150
64	Decca AT 15006	Not Fade Away/Little By Little	£150
64	Decca AT 15032	Come On/Tell Me (You're Coming Back)	£150
64	Decca AT 15035	Empty Heart/Around And Around	£175
65	Decca AT 15039	Time Is On My Side/Congratulations	£175
65	Decca AT 15040	Little Red Rooster/Off The Hook	£110
65	Decca AT 15043	(I Can't Get No) Satisfaction/The Under Assistant West Coast Promotional Man (p/s)	£150
65	Decca F 12104	The Last Time/Play With Fire (with Dutch or Scandinavian p/s)	£85
65	Decca F 12220	(I Can't Get No) Satisfaction/The Under Assistant West Coast Promotional Man (with p/s)	£75
65	Decca F 12220	(I Can't Get No) Satisfaction/The Under Assistant West Coast Promotional Man	£30
65	Decca F 22180	Heart Of Stone/What A Shame (in p/s)	£140
65	Decca F 22180	Heart Of Stone/What A Shame	£100
65	Decca F 22265	Get Off My Cloud/I'm Free	£30
65	Decca F 22265	Get Off My Cloud/I'm Free (in p/s)	£75
66	Decca F 12395	Paint It, Black/Long Long While (p/s)	£50
66	Decca F 12331	19th Nervous Breakdown/As Tears Go By (with Dutch p/s)	£50
67	Decca F 12546	Let's Spend The Night Together/Ruby Tuesday (p/s)	£50
67	Decca F 12654	We Love You/Dandelion (p/s)	£50
67	Decca F 22706	2,000 Light Years From Home/She's A Rainbow	£50
68	Decca F 22825	Street Fighting Man (remix)/No Expectations (in p/s)	£50
68	Decca F 22825	Street Fighting Man (remix)/No Expectations	£30
69	Decca F 12952	Honky Tonk Women/You Can't Always Get What You Want (p/s)	£50
71	Decca F 13195	Street Fighting Man/Surprise Surprise/Everybody Needs Somebody To Love (33rpm maxi-single, p/s)	£40
71	Decca F 13126	Little Queenie/Love In Vain (in p/s)	£55
71	Decca F 13126	Little Queenie/Love In Vain	£20
71	Decca F 13204	Street Fighting Man/Everybody Needs Somebody To Love	£20
71	Decca F 13204	Street Fighting Man/Everybody Needs Somebody To Love (in p/s)	£40

EPs

64	Decca DFE 8560	THE ROLLING STONES (with unboxed Decca logo)	£40
64	Decca DFE 8590	FIVE BY FIVE (with unboxed Decca logo)	£40
65	Decca DFE 8620	GOT LIVE IF YOU WANT IT! (with unboxed Decca logo)	£40

EPS : EXPORT EPS

64	Decca SDE 7260	ROLLING STONES	£125
64	Decca SDE 7501	THE ROLLING STONES VOLUME 2	£125
65	Decca DFE 8620	GOT LIVE IF YOU WANT IT! (red label, some with yellow titles on p/s)	£125
65	Decca SDE 7502	GOT LIVE IF YOU WANT IT!	£125
65	Decca SDE 7503	ROLLING STONES (with "Out Of Our Heads [U.K. version]" sleeve)	£125

ALBUMS : DECCA ALBUMS

64	Decca LK 4605	ROLLING STONES (1st pressing, plays 2.52 version of "Tell Me"; Side 2 matrix: XARL 6272-1A)	£1000
64	Decca LK 4605	ROLLING STONES (2nd pressing, plays 4.06 version of "Tell Me"; sleeves list "Mona")	£350
64	Decca LK 4605	ROLLING STONES (2nd pressing, plays 4.06 version of "Tell Me"; more common, with sleeves that list "I Need You, Baby")	£200

MINT VALUE £

65	Decca LK 4661	**ROLLING STONES NO. 2**	**£200**
65	Decca LK 4661	**ROLLING STONES NO. 2** (with 'blind man' text pasted over on rear sleeve)	**£250**
65	Decca LK 4733	**OUT OF OUR HEADS** (mono)	**£120**
65	Decca SKL 4733	**OUT OF OUR HEADS** (stereo)	**£150**

(The above LPs were simultaneously pressed with both flipback and non-flipback sleeves. Values are the same.)

66	Decca LK 4786	**AFTERMATH** (mono)	**£125**
66	Decca SKL 4786	**AFTERMATH** (stereo)	**£150**
66	Decca LK 4786	**AFTERMATH** (mono, front cover title has purple shadow)	**£250**
66	Decca SKL 4786	**AFTERMATH** (stereo, front cover title is shadowed)	**£200**
66	Decca TXL 101	**BIG HITS** (HIGH TIDE AND GREEN GRASS) (1st pressing, gatefold sleeve, with stapled 12" x 12" picture booklet, mono)	**£100**
66	Decca TXS 101	**BIG HITS** (HIGH TIDE AND GREEN GRASS) (1st pressing, gatefold sleeve, with stapled 12" x 12" picture booklet, stereo)	**£100**
66	Decca TXL/TXS 101	**COULD YOU WALK ON THE WATER** (unreleased, proof sleeves exist)	**£0**
67	Decca TXS 101	**BIG HITS** (HIGH TIDE AND GREEN GRASS) (2nd pressing, gatefold sleeve, without booklet, stereo)	**£50**
67	Decca TXL 101	**BIG HITS** (HIGH TIDE AND GREEN GRASS) (2nd pressing, gatefold sleeve, without booklet, mono)	**£30**
67	Decca LK 4852	**BETWEEN THE BUTTONS** (mono)	**£175**
67	Decca SKL 4852	**BETWEEN THE BUTTONS** (stereo)	**£150**
67	Decca TXL 103	**THEIR SATANIC MAJESTIES REQUEST** (3-D gatefold sleeve with red inner, mono)	**£200**
67	Decca TXS 103	**THEIR SATANIC MAJESTIES REQUEST** (3-D gatefold sleeve with red inner, stereo)	**£150**
68	Decca LK 4955	**BEGGARS BANQUET** (gatefold sleeve, unboxed red label, with Stones Decca label insert, mono)	**£200**
68	Decca SKL 4955	**BEGGARS BANQUET** (gatefold sleeve, unboxed blue Decca label, with Stones Decca label insert, stereo)	**£150**
69	Decca LK 5019	**THROUGH THE PAST, DARKLY** (BIG HITS VOL. 2) (octagonal gatefold sleeve, mono)	**£80**
69	Decca SKL 5019	**THROUGH THE PAST, DARKLY** (BIG HITS VOL. 2) (octagonal gatefold sleeve, stereo)	**£65**
69	Decca LK 5025	**LET IT BLEED** (mono, red inner, with poster, with stickered sleeve)	**£400**
69	Decca LK 5025	**LET IT BLEED** (mono, red inner, with poster, without stickered sleeve)	**£100**
69	Decca SKL 5025	**LET IT BLEED** (stereo, blue inner, with poster, with stickered sleeve)	**£200**
69	Decca SKL 5025	**LET IT BLEED** (stereo, blue inner, with poster, without stickered sleeve)	**£60**
69	Decca TXL/TXS 103	**THEIR SATANIC MAJESTIES REQUEST** (2nd pressing, gatefold sleeve with red inner, stereo, stereo disc in stickered mono sleeve)	**£60**

All of the above LPs were originally issued with Decca labels with a large-print logo without a box surrounding it; later pressings with smaller print & boxed logo are worth around two-thirds the value.)

69	Decca TXL/TXS 103	**THEIR SATANIC MAJESTIES REQUEST** (2nd pressing, gatefold sleeve with red inner, mono)	**£50**
70	Decca SKL 5065	**GET YER YA-YA'S OUT!** (1st pressing with fully laminated sleeve front and back, with "sleeve printed in England" XZAL 10076 1W/XZAL 10077 1W. stereo)	**£80**
70	Decca SKL 5065	**GET YER YA-YA'S OUT!** (2nd pressing with laminated front sleeve front and un-laminated rear sleeve with "sleeve printed in England by Clout & Baker Ltd.")	**£20**
70	Decca TXS 101	**BIG HITS** (HIGH TIDE AND GREEN GRASS) (LP, reissue, green boxed Decca label, gatefold sleeve, with foldout insert, stereo only)	**£25**
70s	Decca SKL 4733	**OUT OF OUR HEADS** (2nd pressing, light green label, box Decca logo)	**£30**
70	Decca SKL 5025	**LET IT BLEED** (LP, reissue, stereo only, no mono/stereo indicator hole on rear sleeve, poster and inner sleeve, boxed logo on label)	**£50**
70	Decca SKL 4786	**BEGGARS BANQUET** (LP, reissue, laminated gatefold sleeve. small blue boxed Decca label, stereo)	**£30**
70	Decca SKL 4852	**BETWEEN THE BUTTONS** (LP, reissue, blue boxed label, laminated sleeve)	**£25**
71	Decca SKL 5084	**STONE AGE**	**£20**
71	Decca SKL 5101	**GIMME SHELTER**	**£18**
71	Decca NPS2	**THEIR SATANIC MAJESTIES REQUEST** (LP, gatefold, stereo reissue, boxed Decca logo)	**£25**
73	Decca SKL 5165	**GOLDEN B-SIDES** (unreleased, test pressings only)	**£1000**
73	Decca SKL 5173	**NO STONE UNTURNED**	**£20**

(Except where noted, the above Decca LPs were originally issued with dark blue labels & laminated sleeves; later copies are worth two-thirds the value.)

75	Decca (no cat. no.)	**THE HISTORY OF THE ROLLING STONES** (3-LP box set; 3x12" pink label test pressings exist, no sleeves, matrices read: ZAL 12996/7, ZAL 12998/9 & ZAL 13000/1; release cancelled in favour of "Rolled Gold" 2-LP set)	**£1000**
75	Decca SKL 5212	**METAMORPHOSIS** (dark blue label, matt sleeve)	**£20**
75	Decca TXS 103	**THEIR SATANIC MAJESTIES REQUEST** (3rd pressing, 3-D matt gatefold sleeve, stereo only)	**£25**
75	Decca ROST 3/4	**LIVE STONES** (2-LP compilation, pink label test pressings only, follow-up to "Rolled Gold", unreleased)	**£500**
75	Decca 6 28556	**ROLLED GOLD** (2-LP)	**£15**
79	Rolling Stones COC 69100	**EXILE ON MAIN STREET** (2-LP reissue, gatefold sleeve, inners)	**£40**
80	Decca TAB 1	**SOLID ROCK** (LP)	**£20**
83	Decca ROLL 1	**THE FIRST EIGHT STUDIO ALBUMS** (8-LP set, with 192-page book; wraparound card box, each LP has star printed on rear sleeve)	**£250**

ALBUMS : EXPORT LPS

64	London LL 3402	**12 X 5** (LP, for export with 'Congratulations' mis-print on rear of sleeve)	**£300**
65	Decca SKL 4725	**OUT OF OUR HEADS** (with U.S. track listing & cover design, unboxed Decca label logo, stereo, withdrawn)	**£250**
65	Decca LK 4725	**OUT OF OUR HEADS** (export, LP, with U.S. track listing & cover design, unboxed Decca label logo, mono, withdrawn)	**£200**
66	Decca LK 4838	**HAVE YOU SEEN YOUR MOTHER, LIVE** (export LP, laminated sleeve & unboxed Decca label logo, mono)	**£200**
66	Decca SKL 4838	**HAVE YOU SEEN YOUR MOTHER, LIVE** (export LP, laminated sleeve & unboxed Decca label logo, stereo)	**£250**
67	Decca LK 4888	**FLOWERS** (export LP, mono, laminated sleeve, unboxed Decca label logo)	**£400**
67	Decca SKL 4888	**FLOWERS** (export LP, stereo, laminated sleeve, unboxed Decca label logo)	**£250**
70	Decca SKL 4786	**AFTERMATH** (export LP, white label, black print, supposedly for export)	**£25**
70	Decca SKL 5065	**GET YER YA-YA'S OUT!** (export LP, white label, black print, supposedly for export)	**£20**
70	Decca TXS 103	**THEIR SATANIC MAJESTIES REQUEST** (export LP, gatefold sleeve, white label, black	**£25**

		print, supposedly for export)	
72	Decca LK/SKL 4838	**HAVE YOU SEEN YOUR MOTHER, LIVE** (export LP, later pressing, boxed logo, laminated sleeve)	**£80**
72	Decca LK/SKL 4888	**FLOWERS** (export LP, later pressing, laminated sleeve, boxed Decca label logo)	**£100**

ALBUMS : ROLLING STONES LABEL LPS

71	Rolling Stones COC 59100	**STICKY FINGERS** ('big' zip sleeve with insert)..	**£150**
71	Rolling Stones COC 59100	**STICKY FINGERS** (zip sleeve with insert)...	**£80**
72	Rolling Stones COC 69100	**EXILE ON MAIN STREET** (2-LP, gatefold, with inners, postcard inserts)	**£200**
72	Rolling Stones COC 69100	**EXILE ON MAIN STREET** (2-LP, with inners, TM next to Stones logo, without postcard inserts)	**£50**
73	Rolling Stones COC 59101	**GOAT'S HEAD SOUP** (gatefold sleeve, with 2 inserts)	**£60**
74	Rolling Stones COC 59103	**IT'S ONLY ROCK 'N' ROLL** (LP)	**£20**
76	Rolling Stones COC 59106	**BLACK AND BLUE** (LP, gatefold)	**£20**
78	Rolling Stones CUN 39108	**SOME GIRLS** (LP, die cut sleeve with uncensored inner sleeve, featuring Farrah Fawcett, Raquel Welch, Judy Garland and Marilyn Monroe)	**£35**
78	Rolling Stones CUN 39108	**SOME GIRLS** (LP, die cut sleeve with censored inner cover, it is believed that those with the red 'Some Girls' title is the rarest with blue, green and yellow being more common)..	**£20**
80	Rolling Stones CUN 39111	**EMOTIONAL RESCUE** (LP with poster)	**£20**
81	Rolling Stones CUN 39114	**TATTOO YOU** (LP)	**£20**
82	Rolling Stones CUN 39115	**STILL LIFE** (AMERICAN CONCERT 1981) (LP)	**£15**
82	Rolling Stones CUNP 39115	**STILL LIFE** (AMERICAN CONCERT 1981) (LP, picture disc, mispressed with wrong tracks)..	**£150**
82	Rolling Stones CUNP 39115	**STILL LIFE** (AMERICAN CONCERT 1981) (LP, picture disc)	**£25**
83	Rolling Stones 1A 0641654361	**UNDERCOVER** (LP)	**£18**
84	Rolling Stones 450196	**EXILE ON MAIN STREET** (2-LP, reissue in single sleeve)	**£20**
91	Rolling Stones 4681351	**FLASHPOINT** (LP, stickered sleeve. 12 page booklet)	**£20**
15	Rolling Stones ERDVLP 086	**THE MARQUEE CLUB LIVE IN 1971** (2LP, gatefold, printed inners)	**£40**
20	Rolling Stones 074 249-8	**GOATS HEAD SOUP** (LP, reissue, stickered sleeve, RS No.9 Carnaby Edition, red vinyl) ...**£150**
20	Rolling Stones 3523970	**STICKY FINGERS** (LP, reissue, stickered sleeve, RS No.9 Carnaby Edition, red vinyl)........**£150**
21	Rolling Stones COC 59106	**BLACK AND BLUE** (LP, reissue, stickered sleeve, RS No.9 Carnaby Edition, red vinyl) **£50**
21	Rolling Stones CUNS 39108	**SOME GIRLS** (LP, reissue, stickered sleeve, RS No. 9 Carnaby edition, red vinyl) **£50**
21	Rolling Stones CUNS 39114	**TATTOO YOU** (LP, reissue, stickered sleeve, RS No.9 Carnaby Edition, red vinyl)...........**£60**
21	Rolling Stones 355 867-4	**BLUE & LONESOME** (2LP, stickered sleeve, RS No.9 Carnaby Edition, red vinyl) **£50**
21	Rolling Stones 352 731-1	**HONK** (3LP, stickered trifold sleeve, printed inners, RS No.9 Carnaby Edition, red vinyl) ...**£60**
21	Rolling Stones 3594372	**A BIGGER BANG - LIVE ON COPACABANA BEACH** (3LP, stickered sleeve, RS No.9 Carnaby Edition, splatter vinyl, plastic sleeve, printed inners)..**£100**
23	Rolling Stones 558 083-9	**HACKNEY DIAMONDS** (LP, plastic outer, gatefold, printed inner, red vinyl, RS No. 9 Carnaby Edition)..	**£50**
23	Rolling Stones 5824805	**HACKNEY DIAMONDS** (LP, Zoetrope picture disc edition, PVC, sticker)	**£100**
23	Rolling Stones 5843905	**HACKNEY DIAMONDS** (LP, limited Paul Smith alternate cover, 2000 only, sold at Paul Smith stores in London, printed inner)	**£100**
23	Rolling Stones 5546462	**HACKNEY DIAMONDS** (LP, gatefold, printed inner, green vinyl, alternate artwork, Amazon exclusive)..	**£40**
23	Rolling Stones 5546459	**HACKNEY DIAMONDS** (LP, gatefold, printed inner, blue vinyl, alternate artwork, RS website exclusive)..	**£45**
23	Rolling Stones 5546461	**HACKNEY DIAMONDS** (LP, gatefold, printed inner, purple vinyl, HMV exclusive)	**£20**
23	Rolling Stones 5546463	**HACKNEY DIAMONDS** (LP, picture disc, PVC, sticker)	**£45**

ALBUMS : OTHER ALBUMS

77	CBS 450 208	**LOVE YOU LIVE** (2-LP)	**£25**
83	R. Digest GROLA 119	**THE GREAT YEARS** (4-LP, box set)	**£25**
86	CBS 86321	**DIRTY WORK** (LP, with inner)	**£25**
89	CBS 465752	**STEEL WHEELS** (LP)	**£15**
89	ABKCO 820900-1	**ROLLING STONES SINGLES COLLECTION/LONDON YEARS** (4-LP set).........................	**£45**
89	CBS 466 918 2	**COLLECTION 1971-1989** (15-CD box set, with bonus CD, 'Collector's Edition')	**£130**
91	Sony 468 135-9/468 135-2	**FLASHPOINT/INTERVIEW 1990** (2-CD pack, shrinkwrapped with tongue logo sticker, numbered)..	**£40**
94	Virgin V 2750	**VOODOO LOUNGE** (2-LP)	**£50**
95	Virgin V 2801	**STRIPPED** (2-LP with inner sleeves)	**£80**
97	Virgin V 2840	**BRIDGES TO BABYLON** (2-LP, with inner sleeves)	**£100**
97	Virgin LPCENT 38	**STICKY FINGERS** (LP, reissue, 180gm vinyl, metal zipper)	**£60**
02	Virgin CDVDXX2964	**FORTY LICKS** (Ltd edition CD box set)	**£35**
10	Polydor 0602527147277	**EMOTIONAL RESCUE** (LP, reissue, 180gm)...	**£20**
10	Polydor 0602527147284	**TATTOO YOU** (LP, reissue, 180gm)...	**£20**
10	Eagle Rock ERELP 815	**LADIES AND GENTLEMEN** (2-LP)...	**£20**
10	Polydor 0602527147291	**UNDERCOVER** (LP, reissue 180gm)	**£18**
10	Polydor 0602527147314	**STEEL WHEELS** (LP, reissue, 180gm)..	**£20**
10	Polydor 1602527147307	**DIRTY WORK** (LP, reissue, 180gm)...	**£15**
13	Eagle Vision ERDVLP 079	**SWEET SUMMER SUN** (3LP/DVD, foldout sleeve, printed inners)	**£40**

PROMOS : PROMO SINGLES

72	Rolling Stones SAM 3	**Excerpts From Exile On Main Street: All Down The Line/Rocks Off**..............................	**£400**
72	Rolling Stones SAM 4	**Excerpts From Exile On Main Street: Happy/Shine A Light**...	**£400**
76	Rolling Stones RS 19121 DJ	**Fool To Cry/Crazy Mama** (7" promo, mono mix, edited down to 3.59, no 'phased' electric piano intro)..	**£100**
83	R. Stones RSR 112 (DJ)	**Let's Spend The Night Together** (live)/**Start Me Up** (live)	**£20**
91	CBS A 026/B 027	**Highwire/Sympathy For The Devil** (live) (12")	**£15**
93	EMI ORDERLH 1	**Gimme Shelter** (live) (1-sided jukebox issue)	**£20**
93	Virgin STONES 1	**JUMP BACK** (EP)..	**£25**
98	Virgin VSTDJ 1667	**Saint Of Me** (Deep Dish Grunge Garage Remix) (Part 1)/(Part 2)/ (Grunge Garage Dub)/(Rolling Dub)/**Anyone Seen My Baby?** (Armand's Rolling Steelo Mix)/**Anyone**	**£20**

MINT VALUE £

		Seen My Baby? (Bonus Roll) (12" double pack, stickered sleeve)	
98	Virgin VSP 1700	**Out Of Control** (Bi-Polar At The Controls)/(Bi-Polar Outer Version) (withdrawn brown label)	£30
98	Virgin VSP 1700	**Out Of Control** (Bi-Polar At The Controls)/(Bi-Polar Outer Version) (withdrawn silver label)	£15
00s	Virgin DEVIL 666	**Sympathy For The Devil** (Fatboy Slim Remix)/(Neptunes Remix)//(Full Phat Remix)/ (Original Version) (2x12", with press sheet)	£20

PROMOS : PROMO LPS
69	Decca RSM. 1	**PROMOTIONAL ALBUM** (LP, U.K. disc in U.S. sleeve [lists RSD-1], 200 copies pressed [100 each for U.K. & U.S.], U.K. issues include a letter from Decca)	£2000
86	CBS SAMP 1103	**STONES ON CD - A RADIO SAMPLER** (CD, poly sleeve)	£200
89	CBS (no catalogue no.)	**STEEL WHEELS - THE ALBUM OF THE TOUR** (box set, with LP, CD, cassette and "Terrifying" 12", European tour dates & sticker)	£150
89	CBS SAMPC 1347	**SAY AHHH!** (LP, promo-only compilation)	£200
95	Virgin IVDG 2801	**STRIPPED** (2-CD, interview disc & album, fold-out digipak)	£40
97	Virgin (no catalogue no.)	**BRIDGES TO BABYLON** (CD in promo press box, with "Anybody Seen My Baby?" promo CD, press release, bottle opener, notebook and sheet of stamps, 200 only)	£150
97	Virgin IVDG 2840	**BRIDGES TO BABYLON INTERVIEW** (2-CD, interview disc & album, fold-out digipak)	£30
97	Virgin CDVDJ 2840	**BRIDGES TO BABYLON** (CD, with spoken word intros, 200 only)	£70
99	Virgin CDIDJ 2880	**NO SECURITY** (3-CD [2 interview discs], foldout digipak)	£45
90s	Virgin CDVDY 2964	**FORTY LICKS** (CD)	£45

(see also Mick Jagger, Keith Richards, Pipes of Pan at Joujouka, Bill Wyman, Charlie Watts, Andrew Oldham, Bobbie Miller)

(HENRY) ROLLINS BAND
91	Vinyl Solution VS 30	**Let There Be Rock/Carry Me Down** (12", p/s, as Henry Rollins & Hard-Ons)	£25
92	Imago PL 90641	**THE END OF SILENCE** (2-LP)	£15
94	Imago 72787 21034-1	**WEIGHT** (LP, clear vinyl)	£100

SONNY ROLLINS
56	Esquire 20-050	**SONNY ROLLINS QUARTET** (10" LP)	£65
57	Esquire 20-080	**SONNY ROLLINS QUINTET** (10" LP)	£50
57	Esquire 32-025	**SONNY ROLLINS PLUS FOUR** (LP)	£50
57	Esquire 32-035	**PERSPECTIVES** (LP, with Modern Jazz Quartet)	£50
58	Esquire 32-038	**WORKTIME** (LP)	£150
58	Esquire 32-045	**SAXOPHONE COLOSSUS** (LP, as Sonny Rollins Four)	£200
58	Contemporary LAC 12118	**WAY OUT WEST** (LP)	£70
58	Esquire 32-058	**TENOR MADNESS** (LP)	£100
59	Esquire 32-075	**ROLLINS PLAYS FOR BIRD** (LP)	£70
59	Esquire 32-085	**TOUR-DE-FORCE** (LP)	£70
59	MGM MGM-C 776	**SONNY ROLLINS AND THE BIG BRASS** (LP)	£20
60	Contemporary SCA 5013	**SONNY ROLLINS AND THE CONTEMPORARY LEADERS** (LP, stereo only)	£20
61	Esquire 32-175	**SONNY BOY** (LP)	£100
61	Riverside RLP 12-241	**THE SOUND OF SONNY** (LP)	£25
62	Riverside RLP 12-258	**FREEDOM SUITE** (LP)	£25
62	Esquire 32-155	**MOVIN' OUT** (LP)	£50
62	RCA RD/SF 7504	**THE BRIDGE** (LP)	£15
63	RCA RD/SF 7524	**WHAT'S NEW** (LP)	£20
63	RCA RD/SF 7546	**OUR MAN IN JAZZ** (LP)	£20
64	RCA RD/SF 7593	**SONNY MEETS HAWK** (LP, with Coleman Hawkins)	£20
64	RCA RD/SF 7626	**SONNY ROLLINS & CO.** (LP)	£20
65	RCA RD 7670	**NOW'S THE TIME** (LP)	£20
65	Fontana FJL 124	**BLOW!** (LP)	£25
66	HMV CLP 1915	**ROLLINS ON IMPULSE** (LP)	£25
66	Stateside SL 10164	**SAXOPHONE COLOSSUS** (LP, reissue)	£15
67	RCA RD/SF 7736	**STANDARD SONNY ROLLINS** (LP)	£15
67	HMV CLP/CSD 3529	**SONNY PLAYS ALFIE** (LP)	£15
67	HMV CLP/CSD 3610	**EAST BROADWAY RUNDOWN** (LP)	£15

(see also Modern Jazz Quartet, Thelonious Monk, Clifford Brown, Coleman Hawkins)

ROLL MOVEMENT
67	Go AJ 11410	**I'm Out On My Own/Just One Thing**	£35

ROLL-UPS
80	Bridgehouse BHS 6	**Blackmail/Hold On** (p/s)	£15
79	Bridgehouse BHLP 004	**LOW DIVES FOR HIGHBALLS** (LP)	£25

ROMAN INDEX
81	123 Se 15V	**Revolution/Burn Those Books** (p/s)	£20

MURRAY ROMAN
69	Track 613 007	**YOU CAN'T BEAT PEOPLE UP AND HAVE THEM SAY I LOVE YOU** (LP)	£20
69	Track 613 015	**A BLIND MAN'S MOVIE** (LP)	£20

ROMANY
71	BEV SLP 1323	**THE ROMANY** (LP)	£300

ROME STREETZ
20	Daupe! DM SP 057	**JOYERIA** (LP, as Rome Streetz x The Artivist, clear red vinyl, 100 only)	£40
20	Daupe! DM SP 057	**JOYERIA** (LP, as Rome Streetz x The Artivist, splatter vinyl, 100 only)	£40
20	Daupe! DM SP 057	**JOYERIA** (LP, as Rome Streetz x The Artivist, gold vinyl, 100 only)	£60
20	Daupe! DM SP 057	**JOYERIA** (LP, as Rome Streetz x The Artivist, frosted clear vinyl, 80 only)	£50
20	Daupe! DM SP 057	**JOYERIA** (LP, as Rome Streetz x The Artivist, black vinyl, 80 only)	£40
20	Daupe! DM SP 057	**JOYERIA** (LP, as Rome Streetz x The Artivist, black vinyl, 20 only, with OBI strip)	£100
20	Daupe! DM SP 064	**NOISE KANDY 4** (LP, splatter vinyl, 100 only)	£60
20	Daupe! DM SP 064	**NOISE KANDY 4** (LP, silver vinyl, 150 only)	£40

MINT VALUE £

| 20 | Daupe! DM SP 064 | **NOISE KANDY 4** (LP, black vinyl, 480 only) | £40 |
| 20 | Daupe! DM SP 064 | **NOISE KANDY 4** (LP, black vinyl, with OBI strip, 20 only) | £100 |

MAX ROMEO
67	Caltone TONE 106	**Don't Want To Let You Go/I Can't Do No More** (as Romeo & the Emotions with Tommy McCook and the Supersonics)	£70
68	Island WI 3104	**Put Me In The Mood/My One Girl**	£100
68	Island WI 3111	**Walk Into The Dawn/DAWN PENN: I'll Get You**	£200
69	Blue Cat BS 161	**We Want Man/AL REID: Vietcong**	£40
69	Blue Cat BS 163	**It's Not The Way** (as Maxie Romeo)/**AL REID: Darling**	£120
69	Nu Beat NB 022	**Blowing In The Wind/LARRY MARSHALL: Money Girl**	£60
69	Trojan TR 656	**Sweet Chariot/Far Far Away** (with Hippy Boys)	£20
69	Unity UN 511	**Twelfth Of Never** (actually by Pat Kelly)/**TARTONS: Solid As A Rock** (actually by Tartans)	£15
69	Unity UN 516	**Wine Her Goosie/KING CANNON: Fireball**	£30
69	Unity UN 532	**Mini-Skirt Vision/Far Far Away**	£25
70	Unity UN 544	**Melting Pot/HIPPY BOYS: Death Rides A Horse**	£45
70	Unity UN 545	**Clap Clap** (with Hippy Boys)/**You've Got Your Troubles**	£45
70	Unity UN 547	**What A Cute Man/Buy You A Rainbow**	£35
70	Unity UN 560	**Fish In The Pot/Feel It**	£30
71	Pama Supreme PS 328	**Ginal Ship/UPSETTERS: Version 2**	£30
71	Camel CA 66	**Black Equality/Suffering**	£20
71	Prince Buster PB 11	**Words Sounds And Power/Version**	£18
72	Camel CA 86	**Public Enemy Number One/How Long Must We Wait**	£30
75	Soul Food SF	**Copie Duppy/DYNAMITES: Love Forever** (white label only, as Tammie Lee, B-side actually by BIM SHERMAN)	£70
76	Island WIP 6330	**Chase The Devil/UPSETTERS FEAT. PRINCE JAZZBO: Croaking Lizard**	£40
92	Jah Shaka SHAKA 930	**Melt Away/Version**	£50
69	Pama PMLP 11	**A DREAM** (LP)	£60
71	Pama PMP 2010	**LET THE POWER FALL** (LP)	£50
75	Count Shelly CSLP 06	**EVERY MAN OUGHT TO KNOW** (LP)	£60
76	Island ILPS 9392	**WAR INA BABYLON** (LP)	£30
76	Tropical TSL 1000	**REVELATION TIME** (LP)	£60
78	Mango MLPS 9503	**RECONSTRUCTION** (LP, blue rim)	£30
92	Jah Shaka SHAKA 921	**FAR I - CAPTAIN OF MY SHIP** (LP)	£30
95	Jah Shaka SHAKA 951	**OUR RIGHTS** (LP)	£20
00	Simply Vinyl SVLP 250	**OPEN THE IRON GATE 1973-77** (2-LP)	£40

(see also Maxie & Glen, Henry & Lisa, Dennis Alcapone, David Isaacs)

VICTOR ROMEO
| 80 | Special Request LR 4 | **At The Club/DETONATORS: Lift Off** (12") | £15 |

(see also Detonators)

ROMEO Z
| 66 | CBS 202645 | **Come Back Baby/Since My Baby Said Goodbye** | £30 |

ROMEO & EMOTIONS
| 67 | Caltone TONE 106 | **Don't Want To Let You Go/I Can't Do No More** | £80 |

(see also Max Romeo)

CHAN ROMERO
| 59 | Columbia DB 4341 | **The Hippy Hippy Shake/If I Had A Way** | £100 |
| 60 | Columbia DB 4405 | **My Little Ruby/I Don't Care Now** | £200 |

ROMFORD STOMPERS
| 81 | Rott ROTT 1 | **Dead Girls/MARY & KEN: Happy** (stamped labels in stamped paper die-cut sleeve) | £20 |

RONALD & LLOYD
| 74 | Magnet MG 042 | **Back In My Arms/HEPTONES: Drifting Away** | £18 |

RONDELLS
| 58 | London HLU 8716 | **Good Good/Dreamy** (with Ned Jr.) | £60 |
| 58 | London HLU 8716 | **Good Good/Dreamy** (with Ned Jr.) (78) | £40 |

RONDELS
| 61 | London HLU 9404 | **Back Beat No. 1/Shades Of Green** | £20 |

GENE RONDO
68	Giant GN 39	**Ben Nevis/Grey Lies**	£28
68	Jolly JY 004	**Mary, Mary/Baby, Baby**	£25
69	Downtown DT 422	**A Lover's Question/HERBIE GRAY & RUDIES: Blue Moon**	£20
69	Downtown DT 431	**Sentimental Reasons/Then You Can Tell Me Goodbye**	£25
70	Downtown DT 459	**Spreading Peace/MUSIC DOCTORS: Guitar Riff**	£20
72	Count Shelly CS 005	**Happy Birthday Sweet Sixteen/Meditation**	£25
73	Sir Collins SCMW 003	**When I Give My Love/Overcome**	£20
73	Magnet MA 028	**Oh Sweet Africa/This Is Love**	£18
73	Magnet MA 035	**Valley Of Tears/He'll Break Your Heart**	£15
74	Queen Bee QB4	**Rebel Woman/Version**	£45
77	Third World TW 52	**Domestic Affair/Version**	£20
78	Burning Sounds BSD 007	**Jah Jah Worker/MILITANT BARRY: Natty Dredd Supreme/Africa Is My Home/MILITANT BARRY: Sound Call Africa** (12")	£20
85	Roots Pool RP002	**No One But You/SUGAR MINOTT: Children Of Africa**	£15
70	Trojan TBL 149	**ON MY WAY** (LP)	£40
77	Venture VNLP 8862	**MEMORIES** (LP)	£80

(see also Gene Pancho)

RONETTES

64	London HLU 9905	(The Best Part Of) **Breakin' Up/Big Red**	£20
64	London HLU 9922	**Do I Love You?/When I Saw You**	£20
64	London HLU 9931	(Walking) **In The Rain/How Does It Feel?**	£18
65	London HLU 9952	**Born To Be Together/Blues For Baby**	£20
65	London HLU 9976	**Is This What I Get For Loving You?/You Baby**	£30
66	London HLU 10087	**I Can Hear Music/When I Saw You** (withdrawn)	£100
64	London HA-U 8212	**PRESENTING THE FABULOUS RONETTES FEATURING VERONICA** (LP, original pressing on plum label)	£100
64	London HA-U 8212	**PRESENTING THE FABULOUS RONETTES FEATURING VERONICA** (LP, later pressing on black label)	£50
65	Colpix PXL 486	**THE RONETTES** (LP)	£80

(see also Ronnie Spector, Joey Dee & Starlighters)

RONNIE & DEL AIRES

64	Coral Q 72473	**Drag/Wigglin' 'N' Wobblin'**	£35

RONNIE & HI-LITES

62	Pye International 7N 25140	**I Wish That We Were Married/Twistin' And Kissin'**	£30

RONNIE & RAINBOWS

61	London HL 9345	**Loose Ends/Sombrero**	£25

RONNIE & ROY

59	Capitol CL 15028	**Big Fat Sally/Here I Am**	£150

RONNO

71	Vertigo 6059 029	**Fourth Hour Of My Sleep/Powers Of Darkness**	£65

(see also Mick Ronson)

RONNY & THE DAYTONAS

64	Stateside SS 333	**G.T.O./Hot Rod Baby**	£25
64	Stateside SS 367	**California Bound/Hey Little Girl**	£25
65	Stateside SS 391	**Bucket T/Little Rail Job**	£30
65	Stateside SS 432	**Beach Boy/No Wheels**	£30
66	Stateside SS 484	**Sandy/Sandy** (Instrumental)	£20

(see also Buzz & Bucky)

MICK RONSON

74	RCA 11474 XSP	**Love Me Tender/Slaughter On 10th Avenue** (1-sided red or black interview flexidisc, included in press kits)	£15
74	RCA Victor APL1-0353	**SLAUGHTER ON 10th AVENUE** (LP)	£20
74	RCA APL1-0681	**PLAY DON'T WORRY** (LP, laminated gatefold sleeve)	£20
94	Epic EPC 474742 1	**HEAVEN AND HULL** (LP, picture disc)	£50

(see also Ronno, David Bowie, Mott The Hoople, Slaughter & The Dogs, Ian Hunter)

ROOFTOP SINGERS

63	Fontana 680 999 TL	**WALK RIGHT IN** (LP)	£15
66	Fontana TFL 6065	**RAINY RIVER** (LP)	£15

(see also Tarriers)

ROOM FOR HUMANS

81	Bandit BR 001	**Telephone Telephone/Girl Friend**	£35

ROOM 10

65	Decca F 12249	**I Love My Love/Going Back**	£15

ROOM 13

82	Woronzow W 002	**Murder Mystery/Need Some Dub** (12", p/s)	£25

(see also Bevis Frond)

ROOM (1)

70	Deram SML 1073	**PRE-FLIGHT** (LP, non-laminated sleeve, white/red label)	£1200

ROOSEVELT SINGERS

73	Sioux SI 025	**Heavy Reggae/HONG GANG: Smoking Wild**	£20

ROOT & JENNY JACKSON

70	Beacon BEA 164	**Save Me/If I Didn't Love You**	£40

(see also (Root and) Jenny Jackson)

ROOTS MANUVA

95	Sound Of Money SNM006	**Next Typa Motion/Raw Uncut** (12")	£25
01	Big Dada BD022/7	**Witness** (1 Hope)/(Walworth Rockers Dub)	£20
02	Ultimate Dilemma UDR050	**Yellow Submarine** (12" 1-sided p/s, Banksy artwork)	£100
99	Big Dada BD010	**BRAND NEW SECOND HAND** (LP)	£25
01	Big Dada BDLP032	**RUN COME SAVE ME** (LP)	£20
02	Ultimate Dilemma UDR LP 019	**BADMEANINGOOD VOL 2** (2-LP, Banksy artwork)	£300
02	Big Dada BDLP040	**DUB COME SAVE ME** (LP)	£20
05	Big Dada BD 072	**AWFULLY DEEP** (LP)	£15

(see also IQ Procedure)

ROOTS RADICS

79	Form BB1004	**OUTERNATIONAL RIDDIM** (LP, with Revolutionaries)	£30
82	Cha Cha CHALP 012	**RADICFATION** (LP)	£50
82	Solid Groove SGL 102	**RADICAL DUB SESSION** (LP)	£60

ROOTS (1)

78	Greensleeves GRE 7	**Mash Down/Solja Man Skank**	£20

ROOTS (2)
93	Remedy RRLP 001	ORGANIX (2-LP)	£40
94	Geffen GEF 24708	DO YOU WANT MORE?!!!??! (2-LP)	£40
99	MCA MCA 11948	THINGS FALL APART (2-LP)	£50
02	MCA MCA 112 996-1	PHRENOLOGY (2-LP)	£50
04	Geffen 0602498624166	THE TIPPING POINT (2-LP)	£60

ROOTS ROCKERS
83	Vista Sounds VSLP 4056	FE ME DUB AND DUBWISE SHOWER (2-LP)	£25
83	Vista Sounds VSLP 4056	REGGAE MASTERPIECES IN DUB VOLUME 2 (LP)	£25

RO RO
70	Parlophone R 5920	Here I Go Again/What You Gonna Do	£20
72	Regal Zono. SRZA 8510	MEET AT THE WATER (LP, textured gatefold sleeve, red/silver label)	£300

ROSARIES
92	Sarah SARAH 623	FOREVER EP (p/s, insert)	£25

ANDY ROSE
58	London HLU 8761	Lov-A Lov-A Love/Just Young	£25

DUSTY ROSE
55	London HLU 8162	The Birds And The Bees/It Makes Me So Mad	£50
57	London RE-U 1078	COUNTRY SONGS (EP)	£40

JOHNNY ROSE
60	Capitol CL 15166	Linda Lee/The Last One To Know	£18

MICHAEL ROSE
76	Morpheus MOR 1008	Guess Who's Coming For Dinner/MORPHEUS PLAYERS: Straight To Rod's Head	£15
77	Carib Gems CG 002	Observe Life/SKIN, FLESH & BONES: Version	£40
79	Attack TACK 7	Born Free (with JAMMY)/DAD BROWN: Stand & Look (B-side actually by FANTELLS) (12")	£70

(see also Black Uhuru)

SAMANTHA ROSE
79	Empire EMPLP 902	IN PERSON (LP)	£15
82	World International WRLP 701	TOGETHER IN LOVE (LP)	£15

TIM ROSE
68	CBS 3277	I Got A Loneliness/Long Time Man	£30
67	CBS (S)BPG 63168	TIM ROSE (LP)	£30
69	CBS 63636	THROUGH ROSE COLOURED GLASSES (LP)	£30
71	Capitol ST 22673	LOVE - A KIND OF HATE STORY (LP)	£30
74	Dawn DNLS 3062	TIM ROSE (LP)	£18

TONY ROSE
70	Trailer LER 2013	YOUNG HUNTING (LP)	£15
72	Trailer LER 2024	UNDER THE GREENWOOD TREE (LP)	£15

ROSE COLOURED GLASS
71	President PT 338	Can't Find The Time/Mystic Touch	£15

LEONARD ROSENMAN ORCHESTRA
57	London HA-P 2040	A TRIBUTE TO JAMES DEAN (LP)	£20

ROSE OF AVALANCHE
89	Avalanche AVE4T	A PEACE INSIDE (LP)	£20

ROSES ARE RED
79	Posthumous Petal PET 1	Can't Understand/Your Love Is Like A Ballistic Missile (p/s)	£60

ROSE TATTOO
80	Repeal PRS 2724	Release Legalise/COL PATERSON: Bong On Aussie (500 only)	£40

ROSEWATER
71	Lost Dog L 001	Sally Anne/Mind Your Head	£15

ROSIE (& ORIGINALS)
61	London HLU 9266	Angel Baby/Give Me Love (as Rosie & Originals)	£30
61	Coral Q 72426	Lonely Blue Nights/We'll Have A Chance	£40

ROSKO
70	Philips 6009 070	Grab The Rabbit/Mohammed Ben Ali	£15

ANNIE ROSS
57	Pye Jazz NJE 1035	NOCTURNE FOR VOCALIST (EP)	£60
54	Esquire EP 1	WITH THE TEACHO WILTSHIRE GROUP (EP)	£40
64	Transatlantic TRAEP 112	GO TO THE WALL (EP)	£15
57	Nixa Jazz NJT 504	ANNIE BY CANDLELIGHT (10" LP)	£125
59	Vogue LAE 12203	ANNIE ROSS (LP, with Gerry Mulligan Quintet)	£60
60	Vogue LAE 12233	A GASSER (LP, with Zoot Sims)	£60
63	Ember NR 5008	A HANDFULL OF SONGS (LP)	£75
63	Transatlantic TRA 107	LOGUERRHYTHMS (LP)	£60
65	Golden Guinea GGL 0316	ANNIE BY CANDLELIGHT (LP, reissue)	£50
66	Xtra XTRA 1049	ANNIE ROSS WITH THE TONY KINSEY QUINTET (LP)	£60
71	Decca SKL 5099	YOU AND ME BABY (LP)	£20

(see also Tony Crombie, Dave Lambert, Gerry Mulligan, Zoot Sims, Jack Parnell, Art Blakey, Quincy Jones)

DIANA ROSS
71	Tamla Motown TMG 792	Surrender/I'm A Winner (green/white demo, stereo, has YTMG on label and etched into dead wax))	£25

MINT VALUE £

79	Tamla Motown PSLP 304	Love Hangover/Touch Me In The Morning/Remember Me (12", promo)	£30
70	Tamla Motown STML 11159	DIANA ROSS (LP)	£15
91	EMI EMP 1023	THE FORCE BEHIND THE POWER (LP)	£15
93	EMI ONE 1	ONE WOMAN (2-LP)	£40

(see also Supremes)

DOCTOR (ISAIAH) ROSS

66	Blue Horizon LP 1	THE FLYING EAGLE (LP, 99 copies only)	£1500
66	Xtra XTRA 1038	DOCTOR ROSS (LP, reissue of "The Flying Eagle")	£40
66	Bounty BY 6020	CALL THE DOCTOR (LP)	£60
72	Polydor 2460 169	LIVE AT MONTREUX (LP)	£30
75	Big Bear BEAR 2	THE HARMONICA BOSS (LP)	£25

GENE ROSS

| 58 | Parlophone R 4434 | Endless Sleep/The Only One | £25 |

JACKIE ROSS

64	Pye International 7N 25259	Selfish One/Everything But Love	£60
64	Pye International 7N 25259	Selfish One/Everything But Love (DJ copy)	£100
64	Chess CRS 8003	Jerk And Twine/New Lover	£40
64	Chess CRS 8003	Jerk And Twine/New Lover (DJ copy)	£70

JOAN ROSS

| 70 | Crab CRAB 61 | Band Of Gold/HAMMERS: Midnight Sunshine | £50 |

(see also T.T. Ross, Silkie Davis)

JOE E. ROSS

| 64 | Columbia 335X1710 | LOVE SONGS FROM A COP (LP) | £18 |

RONNIE ROSS

58	Parlophone PMC 1079	DOUBLE EVENT (LP)	£125
61	Ember EMB 3323	STOMPIN' WITH (LP)	£100
65	Ember FA 2023	THE SWINGIN' SOUNDS OF THE JAZZ MAKERS (LP, with Allan Ganley)	£70
69	Fontana SFJL 915	CLEOPATRA'S NEEDLE (LP)	£250

(see also Bill Le Sage)

T.T. ROSS (JOAN ROSS)

| 76 | Third World TWLP 201 | T.T. ROSS AND FRIENDS (LP) | £30 |
| 77 | Lovers Rock LP 005 | T.T. ROSS SHOWCASE (LP, no sleeve) | £40 |

LEON ROSSELSON

62	Topic TOP 77	SONGS FOR CITY SQUARES (EP)	£15
66	BOUNTY BY 6029	SONGS FOR SCEPTICAL CIRCLES (LP)	£60
70	Acorn CF 206	SONGS FOR SCEPTICAL CIRCLES (LP, reissue)	£20
71	Trailer LER 3015	THE WORD IS HUGGA MUGGA CHUGGA HUMBUGGA BOOM CHIT (LP, with Roy Bailey & Martin Carthy)	£20
75	Acorn CF 249	PALACES OF GOLD (LP)	£18
75	Acorn CF 251	THAT'S NOT THE WAY IT'S GOT TO BE (LP, with Roy Bailey)	£18

(see also Three City Four, Roy Bailey)

NITA ROSSI

65	Piccadilly 7N 35258	Every Little Day Now/Untrue Unfaithful	£40
66	Piccadilly 7N 35307	Here I Go Again/Something To Give	£40
66	Piccadilly 7N 35307	Here I Go Again/Something To Give (DJ copy)	£70

(see also Status Quo, Bernie Frost, Boz Frost, Mitchell/Coe Mysteries)

JOHN HENRY ROSTILL

| 71 | Columbia DB 8794 | Funny Old World/Green Apples | £30 |

(see also Shadows)

STEVE ROSTRON

| 74 | Sweet Folk & Country SFA 009 | NO STRANGER'S FACE (LP) | £30 |

VINCENT ROSWELL

| 82 | Water Mount MW 001 | Apple Of My Eye/Going To A Dance (12") | £100 |

ROTARY CONNECTION

68	Chess CRS 8072	Soul Man/Ruby Tuesday	£20
69	Chess CRS 8103	The Weight/Respect	£20
70	Chess CRS 8106	Want You To Know/Memory Band	£20
68	Chess CRL 4538	ROTARY CONNECTION (LP)	£30
69	Chess CRL(S) 4547	ALADDIN (LP)	£30
69	Chess CRLS 4551	SONGS (LP)	£30
71	Chess 6310 105	HEY, LOVE (LP, as New Rotary Connection)	£100

ROTATION

| 70 | Polydor 2041-037 | Ra-Ta-Ta/Rotation | £15 |

ROTEN ROSEN

| 87 | Virgin VS 1031 | Itsy Bitsy Teenie Weenie Honolulu-Strand Bikini (German Version) Itsy Bitsy Teenie Weenie Honolulu-Strand Bikini (English Version) (p/s) | £100 |
| 87 | Virgin VST 1031 | Itsy Bitsy Teenie Weenie Honolulu-Strand Bikini (German Version) Itsy Bitsy Teenie Weenie Honolulu-Strand Bikini (English Version)/Agent X (12", p/s) | £150 |

ROTHCHILDS

| 66 | Decca F 12488 | Artificial City/I Let Her Go | £15 |

ROOTS TRUNKS AND BRANCHES

| 79 | Splendor Heights WJWX 1945/2 | Just The Way You Are/Chicken Disco (12") | £20 |

ROUGE
78	SRT SRTSCUS 78104	Have You Seen Gene/Hard To Rock N Roll (no p/s)	£75

ROUGH ELEMENT
92	UAR UAR120020	The Elements/Breaking The Silence/Unbound Rage (remix) (EP)	£35
94	UAR 003	Reflex Reaction/Criminal Behaviour (12")	£15

ROUGH JUSTICE (1)
79	Croft TTS 7912	Black Knight (A Gothic Legend)/White Dove (200 only no p/s but all come with insert)	£50

ROUGH JUSTICE (2)
82	Rough Justice RJ 001	MILLION TO ONE (EP, p/s)	£200

ROUGH RIDERS
69	Jay Boy BOY 13	Boss/President House	£30
74	Rare Earth RES 118	Hot California Beach/Do You See Me	£20

ROULETTES
62	Pye 7N 15467	Hully Gully Slip 'N' Slide/La Bamba	£15
63	Parlophone R 5072	Soon You'll Be Leaving Me/Tell Tale Tit	£15
64	Parlophone R 5110	Bad Time/Can You Go	£20
64	Parlophone R 5148	I'll Remember Tonight/You Don't Love Me	£15
64	Parlophone R 5218	Stubborn Kind Of Fellow/Somebody	£25
65	Parlophone R 5278	I Hope He Breaks Your Heart/Find Out The Truth	£15
65	Parlophone R 5382	The Long Cigarette/Junk	£25
66	Parlophone R 5419	The Tracks Of My Tears/Jackpot	£20
66	Oak RGJ 205	I Can't Stop (1-sided, with p/s)	£250
66	Oak RGJ 206	I Can't Stop (1-sided)	£150
66	Parlophone R 5461	I Can't Stop/Yesterday, Today And Tomorrow	£20
67	Fontana TF 822	Rhyme Boy, Rhyme/Airport People	£40
67	Fontana TF 876	Help Me To Help Myself/To A Taxi Driver	£20
65	Parlophone PMC 1257	STAKES AND CHIPS (LP, laminated front cover, flipbacks, black/yellow label with "Sold in the U.K..." text)	£500

(see also Adam Faith, Unit 4 + 2, Argent)

ROUND ROBIN
64	London HLU 9908	Kick That Little Foot Sally Ann/Slauson Party	£20
64	London HLU 9908	Kick That Little Foot Sally Ann/Slauson Party (DJ copy)	£50

ROUNDHOUSE JUG BAND
61	Vintage Jazz Music VEP 10	ROUNDHOUSE JUG BAND EP (p/s)	£150

(see also Cyril Davis)

ROUNDTABLE
69	Jay Boy BOY 18	Saturday Gigue/Scarborough Fair	£20
69	Jay Boy JSL 2	SPINNING WHEEL (LP)	£40

ROUNDTREE
79	Island ILPS 9527	ROLLER DISCO (LP)	£20

CHARLIE ROUSE QUINTET
60	Riverside/Jazzland JLP19	TAKIN' CARE OF BUSINESS (LP)	£15

ROUTERS
63	Warner Bros WM/WS 8126	LET'S GO! WITH THE ROUTERS (LP, features Scott Walker)	£40
64	Warner Bros WM/WS 8144	PLAY 1963'S GREAT INSTRUMENTALS (LP)	£30
65	Warner Bros WM/WS 8162	CHARGE! (LP)	£30

(see also Scott Walker)

ROVERS
55	Capitol CL 14283	Ichi-Bon Tami, Dachi/Why Oh-h (Why Do You Lie To Me?)	£500
55	Capitol CL 14283	Ichi-Bon Tami, Dachi/Why Oh-h (Why Do You Lie To Me?) (78)	£90

ROWAN BROTHERS
72	CBS 1125	All Together/Lady Of Laughter	£20

ROWDIES
78	Birds Nest BN 109	A.C.A.B. (All Coppers Are Bastards)/Negative Malfunction/Free Zone	£50

(see also Boys, Lurkers, Steve Sharp & Cleancuts)

KEITH ROWE
77	Black Swan BS6	Groovy Situation/Groovy Dub (12")	£40
77	Black Swan WIP 6405	Groovy Situation/Groovy Dub	£20
81	Seven Leaves SLD 002	Groovy Situation/Groovy Dub (12")	£40

(see also Keith & Tex)

NORMIE ROWE
66	Polydor 56132	It's Not Easy/Mary Mary	£15

MAJOR ROWELY
65	Stateside SS 438	There's A Riot Going On/Do It The Right Way	£15

JACKIE ROWLAND
72	Sioux SI 015	Indian Reservation/JUNIOR SMITH: I'm In A Dancing Mood	£15
72	Sioux SI 022	Lonely Man/JOE MANSANO: The Trial Of Pama Dice	£20

(see also Joe Higgs)

PAUL ROWLAND
84	Master Discs MD 01	Paradise/The Force (p/s)	£80
84	Master Discs MDT 01	Paradise/The Force (12")	£100

STEVE ROWLAND
67	Fontana TF 844	So Sad/I See Red	£40

Rare Record Price Guide 2026

(see also Family Dogg)
JOHN ROWLES
| 68 | MCA MUP 335 | **JOHN ROWLES** (LP) | £15 |

ROX
| 82 | Teenteeze ROX 100 | **HOT LOVE IN THE CITY** (Hot Love In The City/Do Ya Feel Like Lovin'/Love Ya Like A Diamond (EP) | £25 |
| 83 | Music For Nations MFN 11 | **VIOLENT BREED** (LP, with innersleeve) | £15 |

ROXY MUSIC
14	Secret 7" S720	**Virginia Plain** (100 only, each with unique art sleeve)	£50
15	Universal 472 181 0	**Ladytron** (unreleased and unedited version)/**The Numberer** (Stereo remix by Steven Wilson) (10", p/s)	£15
72	Island ILPS 9200	**ROXY MUSIC** (LP, 1st pressing, Matrixes ILPS 9200 A-1U GM 1/ILPS 9200 B-1U GR 1, matt gatefold sleeve with Basing Street London W11 address, pink rim palm tree label)	£40
72	Island ILPS 9200	**ROXY MUSIC** (LP, 2nd pressing, Matrixes ILPS 9200 A-2U MR 1/ILPS 9200 B-3U GM 1, laminated gatefold sleeve with Basing Street London W11 address, pink rim palm tree label)	£20
73	Island ILPS 9232	**FOR YOUR PLEASURE** (LP, 1st pressing, Matrixes ILPS 9232 A-1 LA 1/ILPS 9232 B-1 GDG 1, laminated gatefold sleeve with Basing Street London W11 address , pink rim/palm tree label)	£40
73	Island ILPS 9252	**STRANDED** (LP, gatefold, pink rim, palm tree label)	£20
74	Island ILPS 9303	**COUNTRY LIFE** (LP, inner, pink rim palm tree label)	£20
75	Island ILPS 9344	**SIREN** (LP)	£15
81	Polydor/E.G. EGBS 001	**THE FIRST SEVEN ALBUMS** (7-LP box set plus insert)	£100
90	EG EGLP 77	**HEART STILL BEATING** (2-LP)	£50
95	VirginV 2791	**MORE THAN THIS - THE BEST OF BRYAN FERRY AND ROXY MUSIC** (2-LP)	£100
97	Virgin LPCENT 37	**ROXY MUSIC** (LP, reissue)	£25
20	Virgin 00602508553660	**ROXY MUSIC** (LP, reissue, clear vinyl, Steven Wilson remix)	£20

(see also Brian Eno, Bryan Ferry, Phil Manzanera,, Fripp & Eno)
HUGH ROY/U ROY
70	Supreme SUP 211	**Double Attack/Puzzle**	£20
70	Explosion EX 2040	**Whisper A Little Prayer** (actually by Audley Rollins)/ **Rain A Fall** (actually by Melanie)	£15
70	Punch PH 34	**Scandal/Son Of The Wise**	£15
70	Duke Reid DR 2509	**Wake The Town/Big Boy And Teacher**	£20
70	Duke Reid DR 2510	**Rule The Nation/NORA DEAN: Ay Ay Ay Ay**	£30
70	Duke Reid DR 2513	**Wear You To The Ball** (with John Holt)/**EARL LINDO: The Ball**	£25
70	Duke Reid DR 2514	**You'll Never Get Away/TOMMY McCOOK QUINTET: Rock Away**	£25
70	Duke Reid DR 2515	**Version Galore/TOMMY McCOOK: Nehru**	£30
71	Duke Reid DR 2516	**Testify/TOMMY McCOOK: Super Soul**	£35
71	Duke Reid DR 2517	**Tom Drunk** (with Hopeton Lewis)/**TOMMY McCOOK: Wailing**	£40
71	Duke Reid DR 2518	**True True/On The Beach**	£25
71	Duke Reid DR 2519	**Flashing My Whip/Do It Right**	£18
71	Treasure Isle TI 7059	**Drive Her Home** (Parts 1 & 2) (with Hopeton Lewis)	£15
71	Treasure Isle TI 7062	**Behold/Way Back Home** (with Tommy McCook)	£18
71	Treasure Isle TI 7064	**Everybody Bawlin'/Ain't That Loving You**	£18
71	Upsetter US 375	**Earthquake/Suspicious Minds**	£30
71	Not On Label P001	**Rhythim Land/Mr. Warner** (with Upsetters)	£45
71	Duke DU 105	**Love I Tender/JOYA LANDIS: When The Lights Are Low**	£20
72	G.G. GG 4532	**Way Down South/BILLY DYCE: Be My Guest**	£15
72	Dynamic DYN 448	**Festival Wise/Festival Wise Part 2**	£15
72	Banana BA 367	**Keep On Running/LARRY'S ALL STARS: Version**	£20
72	Grape GR 3026	**On Top The Peak/TYPHOON ALLSTARS: Race Attack**	£15
72	Pama PM 835	**Way Down South/BILLY DYCE: Be My Guest**	£15
72	Punch PH 104	**Nannyscrank** (title actually "Nanny Skank")/**PITTSBURG ALLSTARS: Scank Version**	£15
72	Green Door GD 4034	**Hudson Affair/KEITH HUDSON: Hot Stick - Version**	£40
73	Gayfeet GS 210	**Hard Feeling/Regular Style**	£15
73	Harry J. HJ 6651	**Treasure Isle Skank/Words Of Wisdom**	£15
73	Black Ark BAR 101	**006/Get Togther**	£70
76	Soulfood SF 001	**High Priest/London City Rock**	£25
71	Trojan TBL 161	**VERSION GALORE** (LP, as U Roy)	£35
74	Attack ATLP 1006	**U ROY** (LP, as U Roy)	£30
75	Virgin V2048	**DREAD IN A BABYLON** (LP, twin Virgin label)	£30
76	Carib Gems CGLP 107	**THE ORIGINATOR** (LP, with Nuroy)	£25
76	Virgin V2059	**NATTY REBEL** (LP)	£20
77	Virgin V2092	**RASTA AMBASSADOR** (LP)	£20
78	Virgin Frontline FL1018	**VERSION GALORE** (LP, reissue)	£15
78	Virgin Frontline FL 1023	**JAH SON OF AFRICA** (LP, red vinyl)	£20
78	Virgin Frontline FL 1023	**JAH SON OF AFRICA** (LP)	£15
79	Virgin Frontline FLX 4004	**WITH WORDS OF WISDOM** (LP)	£20
82	Trojan Records TRLS 211	**RAVER'S PARTY** (LP)	£20
83	Virgin 1007	**DREAD IN A BABYLON** (LP, reissue, red/green labels)	£20
02	Trojan TJALP 056	**VERSION GALORE** (LP, reissue, with barcode on rear)	£15
07	Ariwa ARILP 207	**OLD SCHOOL/NEW RULES** (LP)	£18

(see also Jeff Barnes, Melodians, Delroy Wilson)
I ROY
71	Moodisc MU 3509	**Musical Pleasure/JO JO BENNETT: Hot Pop**	£20
71	Moodisc MU 3510	**Heart Don't Leap** (as I. Roy & Dennis Walks)/ **DENNIS WALKS & MUDIE'S ALLSTARS: Snow Bird**	£15
71	Moodisc MU 3512	**Let Me Tell You Boy** (with Ebony Sisters)/**MUDIE'S ALLSTARS: Version**	£20
71	Moodisc HM 104	**The Drifter** (with Dennis Walks)/**JO JO BENNETT: Snowbird**	£22

MINT VALUE £

73	Pyramid PYR 7001	Tip From The Prince/Fat Beef Skank	£22
73	Attack ATT 8050	Space Flight/JERRY LEWIS: Burning Wire	£28
73	Downtown DT 503	Blackman's Time/High Jacking	£30
73	Downtown DT 519	Clapper's Tail/Live And Learn	£25
73	Duke DU 156	Buck And The Preacher/PETE WESTON ALLSTARS: Preacher - Version	£15
73	Smash SMA 2337	The Magnificent Seven/Leggo Beast	£15
73	Smash SMA 2338	Rose Of Sheron/Slip Out	£15
73	Techniques TE 926	Pauper And The King/GREGORY ISAACS: Loving Pauper	£20
73	Ackee ACK 503	Great Great Great (with Ken Parker)/RUPIE EDWARDS ALLSTARS: Version	£22
73	Ackee ACK 510	Sound Education/AUGUSTUS PABLO: Cinderella In Black	£25
73	Harry J HJ-6655	Musical Drum Sound/NOW GENERATION: Musical Drum - Version	£20
73	Pama PM 854	Cowtown Skank/AUGUSTUS PABLO: Cowtown Skank Version	£20
73	Dip DL73 5006	Don't Get Weary Joe Frazier/Don't Get Weary	£15
74	Atra ATRA 017	Yah Ma Ride/SWEET HARMONY: Mexican Rockin'	£20
77	Observer OB 002	Jamaican Girl/River Jordan/ OBSERVER IN FINE STYLE: First Cut/Second Cut (12", p/s)	£40
78	Jungle Beat JBDC 805	Troubles/I Man (12" with CLARKIE BURNS/FREDDY CLARK)	£100
79	Virgin Front Line FLS 124 12	Fire In A Wire/Hill And Gully (12")	£15
73	Trojan TRLS 63	PRESENTING I ROY (LP, original issue with "12 Neasden Lane" address and rough orange/white paper labels)	£45
74	Trojan TRLS 71	HELL AND SORROW (LP, original issue with "12 Neasden Lane" address and rough orange/white paper labels)	£35
74	Trojan TRLS 91	THE MANY MOODS OF I ROY (LP, original issue with "12 Neasden Lane" address and rough orange/white paper labels)	£35
75	Grounation GROL 504	TRUTH & RIGHTS (LP)	£25
76	Caroline CA 2011	CRISIS TIME (LP)	£25
76	Klik 9020	DREAD BALDHEAD (LP)	£45
77	Justice JUS LP 08	CAN'T CONQUER RASTA (LP)	£30
77	Virgin V 2075	MUSICAL SHARK ATTACK (LP)	£30
77	Virgin Frontline VF 1001	HEART OF A LION (LP)	£20
78	Virgin Frontline FL 1028	TEN COMANDMENTS (LP)	£15
78	Third World TWS 930	THE GODFATHER (LP)	£25
79	Virgin Frontline FLD 6002	THE GENERAL (LP, with free dub LP SPIDER'S WEB)	£30
79	Virgin Frontline FL 1033	WORLD ON FIRE (LP)	£15
79	Virgin Frontline FLS 4001	CANCER (LP)	£20
79	Virgin Frontline FLX 4001	CANCER DUB (LP)	£20
97	Blood & Fire BAFLP 016	DON'T CHECK WITH ME NO LIGHTWEIGHT STUFF (1972-75) (LP)	£20

(see also Keith Hudson & I Roy)

LEE ROY
65	Island WI 251	Oh Ee Baby/My Loving Baby Come Back	£20

MAD ROY
70	Banana BA 324	Nanny Version (actually by Dennis Alcapone)/BIGGER D: Freedom Version	£25
71	Banana BA 326	Home Version (actually by Dennis Alcapone)/SOUND DIMENSION: One Time	£20
71	Banana BA 327	Universal Love/ROLAND ALPHONSO: Shelly Belly	£20
71	Banana BA 328	Duppy Serenade/Sunshine Version (both sides actually by Dennis Alcapone)	£20

(see also Horse Mouth)

ROY REDMOND
67	Warner Bros WB 2075	Good Day Sunshine/That Old Time Feeling	£20

U ROY JUNIOR
72	Big BG 313	Uncle Charlie/Socialise	£20

(see also Hugh Roy, Dennis Alcapone, Sir Harry, Shorty Perry, Heptones, Herman Chin-Loy)

BILLY JOE ROYAL
62	Oriole CB 1751	Never In A Hundred Years/We Haven't A Moment To Lose	£20
65	CBS 201802	Down In The Boondocks/Oh! What A Night	£15
66	CBS 202087	Heart's Desire/Everbody's Gotta Cry	£40
66	CBS 202087	Heart's Desire/Everbody's Gotta Cry (DJ copy)	£75
66	CBS BPG 62590	INTRODUCING BILLY JOE ROYAL (LP)	£20

ROYAL BLOOD (1)
94	Phase One PRFLP001	ROYAL BLOOD (LP)	£40

(see also Exiles Intact)

ROYAL BLOOD (2)
13	Black Mammoth BMR 001	Out Of The Black/Come One Over (p/s, 500 only)	£40
14	Black Mammoth/Warner Bros. WEA 494	Figure It Out/Love & Leave It Alone	£15
14	Warner Bros. 8256462785541	ROYAL BLOOD (LP, white vinyl, 800 only sold via Rough Trade)	£50
14	Black Mammoth 8256462785541	ROYAL BLOOD (LP, signed, 500 copies)	£50
14	Black Mammoth 8256462785541	ROYAL BLOOD (LP, repressing, 100 only, numbered)	£20

ROYALETTES
65	MGM MGM 1272	Poor Boy/Watch What Happens	£15
65	MGM MGM 1279	It's Gonna Take A Miracle/Out Of Sight Out Of Mind	£25
65	MGM MGM 1279	It's Gonna Take A Miracle/Out Of Sight Out Of Mind (DJ copy)	£55
65	MGM MGM 1292	I Want To Meet Him/Never Again	£18
66	MGM MGM 1302	You Bring Me Down/Only When You're Lonely	£20
66	MGM MGM 1324	It's A Big Mistake/I Want To Meet Him	£15
68	Big T BIG 106	River Of Tears/Something Wonderful	£15
66	MGM MGM-C 8028	THE ELEGANT SOUND OF THE ROYALETTES (LP)	£100

ROYAL FAMILY & THE POOR
82	Factory FAC 43	ART-DREAM DOMINATION EP (12", p/s)	£15
84	Factory FACT 95	THE PROJECT - PHASE 1 OF THE TEMPLE OF THE 13TH TRIBE (LP, with booklet)	£20
87	Gaia PHASE 3	IN THE SEA OF E (LP)	£15

ROYAL GUARDSMEN
67	Stateside S(S)L 10202	SNOOPY VS THE RED BARON (LP)	£20
68	London HA-P/SH-P 8351	THE RETURN OF THE RED BARON (LP)	£15

ROYAL HOLIDAYS
58	London HLU 8722	Margaret/I'm Sorry (I Did You Wrong)	£70
58	London HLU 8722	Margaret/I'm Sorry (I Did You Wrong) (78)	£20

JAMES ROYAL (& HAWKS)
65	Parlophone R 5290	She's About A Mover/Black Cloud (as James Royal & Hawks)	£25
65	Parlophone R 5383	Work Song/I Can't Stand It	£35
67	CBS 202525	Call My Name/When It Comes To My Baby	£20
68	CBS 3232	I Can't Stand It/Little Bit Of Rain (DJ copy)	£125
68	CBS 3232	I Can't Stand It/Little Bit Of Rain	£60
68	CBS 3450	Hey Little Boy/Thru' The Love (DJ Copy)	£60
68	CBS 3450	Hey Little Boy/Thru' The Love	£30
68	CBS 3624	A Woman Called Sorrow/Fire	£20
69	CBS 3915	House Of Jack/Which Way To Nowhere	£30
69	CBS 4463	Send Out Love/I've Lost You	£30
69	CBS 63780	CALL MY NAME (LP)	£30
70	Carnaby CNLS 6008	ONE WAY (LP)	£50
72	Carnaby 6302 011	THE LIGHT AND SHADE OF JAMES ROYAL (LP)	£40

ROYAL RASSES
79	Warrior BP 327	Ain't Nobody Here But Me/Kingston II (Ghetto Rock) (12")	£80
79	Ballistic PRE 1	GOD SENT DUB (white label/plain sleeve) (LP)	£130
79	Warrior WARLP 2002	HARDER NA RASS! (LP)	£40
80	Ballistic LBR 1031	HARDER NA RASS! (LP)	£20

ROYAL ROCKERS
60	Top Rank JAR 326	Jet II/Swinging Mambo	£20

ROYALS
64	Blue Beat BB 259	Save Mama/Out De Fire	£30
68	Amalgamated AMG 831	Never See Come See/CANNONBALL BRYAN TRIO: Jumping Jack	£60
69	Trojan TR 662	Pick Out Me Eye/Think You Too Bad	£60
69	Duke DU 29	Never Gonna Give You Up/Don't Mix Me Up	£20
75	Mango MAN 1007	Peace And Love (Blacker Black)/Wigwam	£15
79	Warrior WAR 143	Rising Sun/It's Real (Gone Sweet)	£15
80	Warrior WAR 123	If You Want Good/When You Are Wrong (12")	£20
77	Magnum DEAD 1004	PICK UP THE PIECES (LP)	£25
78	Balistic UAS 30189	TEN YEARS AFTER (LP)	£30
78	Ballistic UAG 30206	ISRAEL BE WISE (LP)	£30
81	Kingdom KVLP 9006	MOVING ON (LP)	£20

ROYAL TEENS
58	HMV POP 454	Short Shorts/Planet Rock	£35
58	HMV POP 454	Short Shorts/Planet Rock (78)	£20
59	Capitol CL 15068	Little Cricket/Believe Me	£30

ROYALTONES
58	London HLJ 8744	Poor Boy/Wail!	£15
58	London HLJ 8744	Poor Boy/Wail! (78)	£20
61	London HLU 9296	Flamingo Express/Tacos	£15

ROYAL TRUX
93	Domino WIGLP 6	CATS & DOGS (LP)	£15
95	Hut HUTLP 23	THANK YOU (LP, purple vinyl)	£15
97	Domino WIGLP 40	SINGLES, LIVES, UNRELEASED (3-LP box set)	£18
98	Domino WIGLP 45	ACCELERATOR (LP)	£18
99	Domino WIGLP 68	VETERANS OF DISORDER (LP)	£15

ROYALTY
69	CBS 4181	That Kind Of Girl/Will You Be Staying After Sunday	£50
69	CBS 4498	Let's Ride/I Need Your Love	£60

ROY & ANNETTE
63	R&B JB 107	My Baby/Go Your Ways	£20

(see also Tommy McCook, Lester Sterling)

ROY & DUKE ALL STARS
68	Blue Cat BS 113	Pretty Blue Eyes Parts 1 & 2	£110
68	Blue Cat BS 117	The Train (vocal)/Instrumental Version	£80

(see also Roy Panton)

ROY & ENID
68	Coxsone CS 7063	Rocking Time/RALPH BLAKE: High Blood Pressure	£100
68	Coxsone CS 7069	He'll Have To Go/CARLTON & SHOES: Love Is A Treasure	£120
69	Coxsone CS 7088	Reggae For Days/SOUND DIMENSION: Holy Moses	£50

(see also Little Roys)

ROY (PANTON) & MILLIE
62	Island WI 005	We'll Meet/ROLAND ALPHONSO: Back Beat (B-side act. with City Slickers)	£25

63	Island WI 050	This World/Never Say Goodbye	£20
63	Island WI 090	There'll Come A Day/I Don't Want You	£20
63	Blue Beat BB 154	Over And Over/I'll Go (with Prince Buster All Stars)	£20
64	Black Swan WI 409	Cherry I Love You/You're The Only One	£30
64	Black Swan WI 410	Oh Merna/DON DRUMMOND: Dog War Bossa Nova	£30
64	Black Swan WI 427	Oh Shirley/Marie	£25

(see also Roy Panton, Millie [Small])

ROY (RICHARDS) & PAULETTE
63	Island WI 067	Have You Seen My Baby/Since You're Gone	£25

ROY (PANTON) & YVONNE (HARRISON)
64	Blue Beat BB 258	Little Girl/No More	£20
64	Black Swan WI 436	Two Roads/Join Together	£20

(see also Roy Panton)

ROY (PANTON) & PATSY
62	Blue Beat BB 118	My Happy Home/In Your Arms Dear (with Hersang & His Combo)	£25

(see also Roy Panton)

EARL ROYCE & OLYMPICS
64	Columbia DB 7433	Que Sera Sera/I Really Do	£25
65	Parlophone R 5261	Guess Things Happen That Way/Sure To Fall (In Love With You)	£25

ROYKSOPP
02	Wall Of Sound WALLLP 027	MELODY A.M. (2-LP, promo edition, 100 only - artwork by Banksy)	£4000
02	Wall Of Sound WALLLP 027	MELODY A.M. (2-LP)	£35
05	Wall Of Sound WALLLP035	THE UNDERSTANDING (2-LP)	£30

ROYKSOPP & ROBYN
14	Dog Triumph DOG007V	DO IT AGAIN (LP, white vinyl)	£35

ROY OF THE RAVERS
16	Acid Waxa ACIWAX 06	2 LATE 4 LOVE (12" EP, hand-stamped white sleeve with 'Roy of the Rovers' image, hand-stamped stamped white labels)	£60

ROYSTON
79	Tuzmadoner TUZMADONER 001	Snake's Song/Gerald's Eyes//DIFFERENT EYES: Uncomfortable/Snake's Song (stapled photocopied cover, rubber-stamped labels)	£100

LITA ROZA
53	Decca F 75082	(How Much Is) That Doggie In The Window/Tell Me We'll Meet Again (export issue)	£20
63	Ember EMB S 168	Mama (He Treats Your Daughter Mean)/(He's My) Dreamboat (as Lisa Rosa)	£30
65	Columbia DB 7689	Keep Watch Over Him/Stranger Things Have Happened	£30
57	Decca DFE 6386	LITA ROZA SELECTION (EP)	£30
57	Decca DFE 6399	LITA ROZA (EP)	£20
58	Decca DFE 6443	BETWEEN THE DEVIL AND THE DEEP BLUE SEA NO. 1 (EP)	£20
54	Decca LF 1187	PRESENTING LITA ROZA (10" LP)	£80
56	Decca LF 1243	LISTENING IN THE AFTER HOURS (10" LP)	£100
57	Decca LK 4171	LOVE IS THE ANSWER (LP)	£100
57	Decca LK 4218	BETWEEN THE DEVIL AND THE DEEP BLUE SEA (LP)	£90
58	Pye Nixa NPL 18020	ME ON A CAROUSEL (LP, mono)	£60
58	Pye Nixa NSPL 83003	ME ON A CAROUSEL (LP, stereo)	£80
60	Pye NPL 18047	DRINKA LITA ROZA DAY (LP)	£50
64	Ember NR 5009	LOVE SONGS FOR NIGHT PEOPLE (LP)	£25

(see also Stargazers, Johnston Brothers)

ROZAA & WINE
76	Right On! 104	Disco Boogie Woman/Disco Boogie Woman Part 2	£20

(see also David & Rozaa)

RT & B
79	Splendor Heights SH 1	Forward/Join Them (12")	£20

RUB-A-DUBS WITH DANDY
65	Blue Beat BB 304	Without Love/I Know	£25

(see also Dandy)

RUBAIYATS
68	Action ACT 4516	Omar Khayam/Tomorrow	£125

RUBBER BAND
69	Major Minor SMCP 5045	CREAM SONGBOOK (LP)	£20
69	Major Minor SMCP 5048	HENDRIX SONGBOOK (LP)	£20

RUBBER BOOTZ
67	Deram DM 134	Joy Ride/Chicano	£30

RUBIN
75	MCA MU 196	You've Been Away/Baby, You're My Everything (DJ copy)	£20

RUBY
74	Chrysalis CHR 1061	RED CRYSTAL FANTASIES (LP, textured sleeve, green label)	£20

(see also Procol Harum)

RUBY & ROMANTICS
64	London HLR 9881	Our Everlasting Love/Much Better Off Than I've Ever Been	£15
64	London HLR 9916	Baby Come Home/Every Day's A Holiday	£15
64	London HLR 9935	When You're Young And In Love/I Cry Alone	£15
65	London HLR 9972	Your Baby Doesn't Love You Anymore/We'll Meet Again	£15
69	A&M AMS 750	Hurting Each Other/Baby I Could Be So Good At Loving You	£15
63	London RE-R 1389	OUR DAY WILL COME (EP)	£35

64	London RE-R 1427	**HEY THERE LONELY BOY** (EP)	£40
63	London HA-R 8078	**OUR DAY WILL COME** (LP)	£40
66	London HA-R 8282	**GREATEST HITS** (LP)	£30

(see also Danny Davis Orchestra)

RUBY RUSHTON

15	22a 006	**TWO FOR JOY** (LP)	£30
17	22a 015	**TRUDI'S SONGBOOK VOLUME 1** (LP)	£30
17	22a 019	**TRUDI'S SONGBOOK VOLUME 2** (LP)	£20

(see also Tenderlonious)

RUD(D)Y (GRANT) & SKETTO (RICH)

62	Dice CC 5	**Summer Is Just Around The Corner/Nothing Like Time** (as Ruddy & Sketto & Reco's All Stars)	£25
62	Dice CC 7	**Little Schoolgirl/Hush Baby** (as Ruddy & Sketto & Baron Twist & His Knights)	£25
62	Dice CC 10	**Mr Postman/Christmas Blues** (as Rudy & Sketto with Laurel's Group)	£25
63	Dice CC 16	**Hold The Fire/Good Morning Mr Jones**	£25
63	Dice CC 19	**Never Set You Free/Brothers And Sisters**	£20
63	Blue Beat BB 198	**Was It Me/Minna Don't Deceive Me**	£20
64	Blue Beat BB 208	**Show Me The Way To Go Home/Let Me Dream**	£20
64	Blue Beat BB 230	**Ten Thousand Miles From Home/I Need Someone** (as Ruddy & Sketto)	£25
64	Blue Beat BB 252	**I Love You/If Only Tomorrow**	£25
65	Blue Beat BB 297	**See What You Done/Heart's Desire** (as Ruddy & Sketto)	£20
65	Blue Beat BB 310	**Oh Dolly/You're Mine** (as Ruddy & Sketto)	£20

RUDE AND DEADLY

95	Unity UNITY 002	**Lightnin' and Tundra/Mash Dem Down** (12")	£40
95	No Smoking SMOKE 7	**Give Me A Dub/Murder De Boy** (12", as Rude And Deadly Vs. The Dogz)	£25
97	Smokers Inc SINC 1200	**Give Me A Dubplate** (97 Remix) (12", 1-sided, stamped white labels)	£25
97	Smokers Inc SINC 1200	**Give Me A Dubplate** (97 Remix)/**Give Me A Dubplate** (Original Mix) (12")	£25

RUDE ASS TINKER

90s	Deathchant DEATH 30	**Imperial Break/Silk Ties** (12", limited issue)	£18

(see also Mu-Ziq, U-Ziq)

RUDE BOYS (1)

67	Island WI 3088	**Rock Steady Massachusetts/Going Home**	£30

RUDE BOYS (2)

89	Ska SKAT 002	**RUDE BOY SHUFFLE EP** (12")	£15

(see also Oppressed)

RUDI

78	Good Vibrations GOT 1	**Big Time/Number 1** (folded p/s, 3,000 only, push-put centre)	£30
79	Good Vibrations GOT 12	**I Spy/Genuine Reply/Sometimes/Ripped In Two** (p/s)	£30

RUDIES (FANATICS)

68	Blue Cat BS 107	**7-11** (Parts 1 & 2)	£180
68	Blue Cat BS 109	**Cupid/RECO'S ALLSTARS: Wise Message**	£80
68	Nu Beat NB 001	**Train To Vietnam/Skaville To Rainbow City**	£35
68	Nu Beat NB 005	**Engine 59/My Girl**	£70
68	Fab FAB 46	**I Wanna Go Home/La Mer**	£60
68	Fab FAB 70	**Give Me The Rights/I Do Love You** (as Rudies Fanatics)	£25
68	Fab FAB 71	**Mighty Meaty/Go** (as Rudies Fanatics)	£40
69	Doctor Bird DB 1302	**Baby Face/News**	£35
69	JJ DB 1301	**Sin Thing/What's Your Name**	£25
69	JJ DB 1302	**Boss Sound/RECO & RUDIES: Peace**	£200
69	Fab FAB 104	**Brixton Rocket/Rudie's Joy**	£500
70	Pama PM 789	**Give Peace A Chance/She**	£15
70	Trojan TR 7798	**Patches/The Split**	£40
71	Spinning Wheel SW 106	**My Sweet Lord/Devil's Lead Soup**	£90

(see also Freddie Notes, Sonny, Binns & Rudies, Rico, Dandy, Owen & Dandy, Downtown All Stars, Desmond Riley)

RUDIMENTAL

13	The Vinyl Factory VF 084	**HOME** (3-LP)	£60

RUDIMENTARY PENI

81	Outer Himalayan SRTS 81 CUS 1097	**RUDIMENTARY PENI** (EP, A4 foldout p/s with booklet)	£30
81	Outer Himalayan BOOBOO 1	**RUDIMENTARY PENI** (EP, later 14" x 7" sleeve)	£20
82	Crass 221984/2T	**FARCE EP** (Test pressing mispressed on 12" vinyl)	£200
82	Crass 211984/2	**FARCE** (EP, initial pressing in 21" x 14" foldout black & white p/s)	£20
00	Outer Himalayan BOOB007	**THE UNDERCLASS** (EP, p/s)	£30
04	Outer Himalayan BOOB008V	**ARCHAIC EP** (12")	£40
04	Outer Himalayan BOOB008V	**ARCHAIC EP** (12", white vinyl)	£25
08	Outer Himalayan BOOB009V	**NO MORE PAIN EP** (12", clear vinyl)	£40
08	Outer Himalayan BOOB009V	**NO MORE PAIN EP** (12", grey/white vinyl)	£20
83	Corpus Christi CHRIST ITS 6	**DEATH CHURCH** (LP, fold put poster sleeve)	£40
87	Corpus Christi CHRIST IT'S 15	**THE EPS OF RP** (LP)	£25
89	Corpus Christi BOOBOO 2	**CACOPHONY** (LP, with booklet)	£40
95	Outer Himalayan BOOB005V	**POPE ADRIAN 37th PSYCHRISTIC** (LP, unreleased test pressing)	£200

(see also Magits)

RUEFREX

80	Good Vibrations GOT 8	**One By One/Cross The Line/Don't Panic** (foldover p/s, 2 different designs)	£15

RAY RUFF & CHECKMATES
64 London HLU 9889 — **I Took A Liking To You/A Fool Again** £15

RUFF WITH THE SMOOTH
93 Basement BRSS 023 — **Art Of Intelligence/Sounds Superior** (12") £15

(see also Jack Smooth)

RUFFIANS
71 Banana BA 359 — **Room Full Of Tears** (actually by Sensations)**/Black Soul** (actually "Black And White - Version" by Riley's Allstars) £20

(see also Al Brown, Sensations)

BRUCE RUFFIN
69 Songbird SB 1002 — **Long About Now/Come See About Me** (as Bruce Ruffin & Temptations)....................... £30
69 Trojan TR 7704 — **Dry Up Your Tears/BEVERLEY'S ALLSTARS: One Way Street** £30
70 Summit SUM 8509 — **O-o-h Child/Bitterness Of Life** £18
71 Summit SUM 8516 — **Candida/Are You Ready** £15
71 Trojan TRL 23 — **RAIN** (LP) £30

DAVID RUFFIN
69 Tamla Motown TMG 689 — **My Whole World Ended** (The Moment You Left Me)**/ I've Got To Find Myself A Brand New Baby** (DJ Copy).. £80
69 Tamla Motown TMG 689 — **My Whole World Ended** (The Moment You Left Me)**/ I've Got To Find Myself A Brand New Baby** £20
69 Tamla Motown TMG 711 — **I've Lost Everything I've Ever Loved/We'll Have A Good Thing Going On** (DJ Copy).........£40
69 Tamla Motown TMG 711 — **I've Lost Everything I've Ever Loved/We'll Have A Good Thing Going On**...................... £15
77 Tamla Motown TMG 1093 — **You're My Peace Of Mind/Rode By The Place** (Where We Used To Stay) £15
77 Tamla Motown TMG 1078 — **I Can't Stop The Rain/My Whole World Ended** (The Moment You Left Me) £15
69 T. Motown (S)TML 11118 — **MY WHOLE WORLD ENDED** (LP, mono/stereo) £20
70 T. Motown (S)TML 11139 — **FEELIN' GOOD** (LP) £30
73 Tamla Motown STML 11228 — **DAVID RUFFIN** (LP) £20
75 Tamla Motown STML 11283 — **ME N ROCK AND ROLL ARE HERE TO STAY** (LP) £15
77 Motown STML 12064 — **IN MY STRIDE** (LP) £15

(see also Temptations)

JIMMY RUFFIN
66 Tamla Motown TMG 577 — **What Becomes Of The Broken-Hearted?/Baby I've Got It** £18
66 Tamla Motown TMG 577 — **What Becomes Of The Broken-Hearted?/Baby I've Got It** (DJ copy) £85
67 Tamla Motown TMG 593 — **I've Passed This Way Before/Tomorrow's Tears** £20
67 Tamla Motown TMG 593 — **I've Passed This Way Before/Tomorrow's Tears** (DJ copy) £20
67 Tamla Motown TMG 603 — **Gonna Give Her All The Love I Got/World So Wide, Nowhere To Hide** (DJ copy)............ £60
67 Tamla Motown TMG 603 — **Gonna Give Her All The Love I Got/World So Wide, Nowhere To Hide** £50
67 Tamla Motown TMG 617 — **Don't You Miss Me A Little Bit Baby/I Want Her Love**................................ £15
67 Tamla Motown TMG 617 — **Don't You Miss Me A Little Bit Baby/I Want Her Love** (DJ copy) £40
68 Tamla Motown TMG 649 — **I'll Say Forever My Love/Everybody Needs Love**................................... £15
68 Tamla Motown TMG 649 — **I'll Say Forever My Love/Everybody Needs Love** (DJ copy) £45
68 Tamla Motown TMG 664 — **Don't Let Him Take Your Love From Me/Lonely Lonely Man Am I** £18
68 Tamla Motown TMG 664 — **Don't Let Him Take Your Love From Me/Lonely Lonely Man Am I** (DJ copy) £30
67 Tamla Motown TML 11048 — **THE JIMMY RUFFIN WAY** (LP, mono) £40
67 Tamla Motown STML 11048 — **THE JIMMY RUFFIN WAY** (LP, stereo) £45
69 Tamla Motown TML 11106 — **RUFF 'N' READY** (LP, mono) £35
69 Tamla Motown STML 11106 — **RUFF 'N' READY** (LP, stereo) £30
70 Tamla Motown STML 11161 — **JIMMY RUFFIN ... FOREVER** (LP) £20
73 Polydor 2383 240 — **JIMMY RUFFIN** (LP) £20

JIMMY & DAVID RUFFIN
71 Tamla Motown STML 11176 — **I AM NOT MY BROTHER'S KEEPER** (LP) £25

(see also David Ruffin, Temptations)

RUFFNECK
93 Represent REPREC 1 — **Radford**(You Get Me)**/You And Me** (12") £25

RUFF SQWAD
03 Ruff Sqwad RUFF 1 — **Pied Piper/Stinging/Untitled** (12" white label).................................... £35
03 Ruff Sqwad RSQ 01 — **Tings In Boots/Instrumental/Raw To The Core** (12" white label)...................... £18
03 Ruff Sqwad RSQ 003 — **Misty Cold/Roots/Raw To The Core** (Vocal) (12" white label) £35
04 Ruff Sqwad RSQ 004 — **Lethal Injection/Pied Piper** (Slicks Vocal)/(Riko Vocal)/(Eskbar Vocal) (12" white label)...£30
04 Ruff Sqwad RSQ 005 — **Pied Piper** (Skepta Remix)/(Tinchy Stryda Vocal)/(Scratchy Vocal)/(Godsgift Vocal) (12" white label) £20
04 Ruff Sqwad RSQ 006 — **Misty Cold Remix/Pied Piper** (Shifty Vocal)**/Pied Piper** (Stamina Vocal)**/Pied Piper** (All In One Vocal) (12" white label) £25
04 Ruff Sqwad RQ 007 — **Anna** (Vocal)**/Anna** (Instrumental) (12" white label).............................. £20
04 Ruff Sqwad RQ 007A — **Love You Feel/Pied Piper** (Instrumental)**/Blaze** (12" white label).................... £20

RUFFWOOD ARTS
72 Liverpool LS 1529 — **KNIGHTS AND VILLEINS** (LP, with insert) £400

RUFIGE CRU
92 Reinforced RIVET 1220 — **Krisp Biscuit** (Power)**/Killa Muffin** (The Band Dog Mix) (12", die-cut title sleeve with tracks and artist mispelt) £15
92 Reinforced RIVET 1224 — **Darkrider/Believe/Menace/Jim Skreech** (12", p/s) £30
93 Reinforced RIVET 1244 — **Terminator II Remix/Fabio's Ghost** (The Edit)**/ Ghosts Of My Life/High Rollerz Ghostin' Out** (12", promo only) £25

RUFIGE KRU
07 Exit EXIT 010 — **Is This Real/Is This Real** (I'm Not Sure Remix) (12", p/s, yellow vinyl, poster) £25

RUFSTUFF
92 Lucky Spin LSR 01 — **Burn To The Spliff/Losing Control** (12") £25

RUGBYS
69	Polydor 56781	You And I/Stay With Me	£45
70	Polydor 56789	Wendegahl The Warlock/Light	£20

PETE RUGOLO (& DIAMONDS)
60	Warner Bros WM 4001	BEHIND BRIGITTE BARDOT - COOL SOUNDS FROM HER HOT SCENES (LP, gatefold, also stereo WS 8001)	£25

(see also Diamonds, Patti Page)

RULERS
66	Rio R 105	Don't Be A Rude Boy/Be Good	£25
66	Rio R 107	Copasetic/Too Late	£30
67	Rio R 132	Wrong 'em Boyo/Why Don't You Change	£70
67	Rio R 135	Well Covered/CARL DAWKINS: Help Time	£50
67	Rio R 138	Be Mine/CARL DAWKINS: Hot And Sticky	£50
69	Trojan TR 696	Got To Be Free/Situation	£50

RUMBLE
70	Warner Bros WB 8011	Rich Man, Poor Man/Let Me Down	£30

RUMBLERS
63	London HLD 9684	Boss/I Don't Need You No More	£20
65	King KG 1021	Soulful Jerk/Hey Did A Da Da	£60
63	London RE-D 1396	BOSSOUNDS (EP)	£100
63	London HA-D 8081	BOSSOUNDS (LP, mono)	£90
63	London SH-D 8081	BOSSOUNDS (LP, stereo)	£100

RUMPLESTILTSKIN
70	Bell BLL 1101	Squadron Leader Johnson/Rumplestiltskin	£20
70	Bell SBLL 130	RUMPLESTILTSKIN (LP, gatefold sleeve)	£60

(see also Clem Cattini)

RUN 229
80	MM JR 7040S	Soho/Dance/In This Day And Age	£40

RUNAWAYS
76	Mercury 6167 392	Cherry Bomb/Blackmail	£15
76	Mercury 9100 029	THE RUNAWAYS (LP, with gatefold sleeve & lyric sheet; U.S. pressing; with cat. no. SRM 1 1090, in U.K. sleeve)	£20
77	Mercury 9100 032	QUEENS OF NOISE (LP, with lyric sheet)	£18
77	Mercury 9100 046	LIVE IN JAPAN (LP)	£15
77	Mercury 9100 047	WAITIN' FOR THE NIGHT (LP)	£15
79	Cherry Red ARED 38	AND NOW ... THE RUNAWAYS (LP, 1,000 copies each in yellow, red, blue & orange vinyl, numbered)	£25

(see also Joan Jett, Lita Ford & Ozzy Osbourne)o

TODD RUNDGREN
72	Bearsville K 65501	SOMETHING/ANYTHING (2-LP)	£20
73	Bearsville K 45513	A WIZARD, A TRUE STAR (LP, gatefold)	£15

(see also Utopia)

RUN DMC
86	London Records LON 1	My Adidas/Peter Piper (p/s)	£15
84	4th & Broadway BRLP 506	RUN DMC (LP)	£25

RUNESTAFF
85	Heavy Metal HMRLP 26	RUNESTAFF (LP)	£15

RUNNER
79	Acrobat ACRO1	RUNNER (LP, with inner)	£15

RUNNERS
74	Ariel AR 11	Choose Me/Come Out Fighting	£15

RUNNING MAN
72	RCA Neon NE 11	THE RUNNING MAN (LP)	£750

(see also Ray Russell Quartet, Rock Workshop)

RUNRIG
83	Ridge RRS 003	Loch Lomond/Tuireadh Iain Ruaida (p/s)	£15
84	Simple SIM 4	Dance Called America/Na H Uain A's T-Earrach (p/s)	£30
84	Simple 12 SIM 4	Dance Called America/Na H Uain A's T-Earrach/Ribhinn (12", p/s)	£20
84	Simple SIM 8	Skye/Hey Mandu (p/s)	£15
89	Chrysalis CHS 12T 3404	News From Heaven/Chi Mi'n Tir/The Times They Are A'Changing (12", picture disc)	£20
90	Chrysalis CHSCD 1235941	CAPTURE THE HEART EP: Stepping Down The Glory Road/Satellite Flood/Harvest Moon/The Apple Came Down (12", p/s)	£15
78	Neptune NA 105	RUNRIG PLAY GAELIC (LP)	£20
79	Ridge RR 001	THE HIGHLAND CONNECTION (LP)	£15
81	Ridge RR 002	RECOVERY (LP, with inner)	£20

RUNS
80	Carrere CAR 139	Bun In The Oven/(Censored)(no p/s)	£20

RUNT
71	Bearsville K 44505	RUNT (LP)	£15
71	Bearsville K 44506	RUNT - THE BALLAD OF TODD RUNDGREN (LP)	£15

(see also Todd Rundgren, Utopia, Nazz)

RUPERT'S PEOPLE
67	Columbia DB 8226	Reflections Of Charles Brown/Hold On	£75

(this is the Fleur-De-Lys, they do not appear on the other 2 singles)
67	Columbia DB 8278	A Prologue To A Magic World/Dream In My Mind	£100

MINT VALUE £

68	Columbia DB 8362	I Can Show You/I've Got The Love	£120
01	Circle CPW L103	THE MAGIC WORLD OF RUPERT'S PEOPLE (LP, with free 7")	£30

(see also Renaissance, Fleur-De-Lys, Gun, Sweet Feeling)

RUPIE AND SIDY
70	Success RE 910	Return Of Herbert Spliffington/RUPIE EDWARDS ALL STARS: Young, Gifted And Black	£40

RUSH (AUSTRALIA)
67	Decca F 12614	Happy/Once Again	£20
67	Decca F 12635	Make Mine Music/Enjoy It	£20

RUSH (CANADA)
77	Mercury RUSH 7	Closer To The Heart/Bastille Day/Temples Of Syrinx (metallic blue label)	£18
82	Mercury RUSH 812	New World Man/Vital Signs (live)/Freewill (live) (12", p/s)	£15
82	Mercury RUSH 10 PD	Countdown/New World Man (shaped picture disc)	£15
84	Vertigo RUSH 1112	The Body Electric/The Analog Kid/Distant Early Warning (12", p/s)	£50
74	Mercury 9100 011	RUSH (LP, gatefold)	£30
75	Mercury 9100 013	FLY BY NIGHT (LP, gatefold)	£30
75	Mercury 9100 018	CARESS OF STEEL (LP, gatefold)	£30
76	Mercury 9100 039	2112 (LP)	£30
78	Mercury 9100 059	HEMISPHERES (LP, gatefold sleeve)	£30
78	Mercury 9100 059	HEMISPHERES (LP, mispressing, both sides play Side 1)	£60
80	Mercury 9100 071	PERMANENT WAVES (LP, with newspaper and lyric inner)	£20
81	Mercury 6337 160	MOVING PICTURES (LP)	£30
85	Vertigo VERHP 31	POWER WINDOWS (LP, picture disc, with discography on sleeve)	£20
91	Atlantic 756782293-1	ROLL THE BONES (LP)	£40
93	Atlantic 7567 82528-1	COUNTERPARTS (LP)	£75
02	Atlantic 83531-1	VAPOR TRAILS (2-LP)	£100
04	Atlantic 7567 83728 1	FEEDBACK (LP)	£30

(see also McKenzie Doug & Bob, Max Webster Band)

ED RUSH
92	Primavera PRIM 001	Edrush/Fat Girl (12", as Edrush)	£20
92	ER 007	I Wanna Stay In The Jungle/5AM/Touch Me/Keep On (12")	£20
92	PSY 001	Look What They've Done/What If My Heart Stops?/Look What They've Done (Dub Mix) (12")	£20
93	No U-Turn NUT 002	Bludclot Artattack/Bludclot Artattack (Dark Mix) (12")	£20
94	Jet Star XCT 001	Selecta/Selecta (Remix) (12")	£30
95	No U-Turn NUT 012	Guncheck/The Force Is Electric (Remix) (12")	£20
98	Virus VRS 001LP	WORMHOLE (5-LP, with Optical)	£40

MERRILEE RUSH & TURNABOUTS
68	Bell MBLL/SBLL 109	MERRILEE RUSH (LP)	£25

OTIS RUSH
66	Vocalion V-P 9260	Homework/I Have To Laugh	£100
66	Vocalion V-P 9260	Homework/I Have To Laugh (DJ copy)	£150
69	Blue Horizon 57-3159	All Your Love/Double Trouble	£25
68	Blue Horizon 7-63222	THIS ONE'S A GOOD UN (LP)	£90
69	Atlantic 588 188	MOURNING IN THE MORNING (LP)	£40
70s	Atlantic K 40495	MOURNING IN THE MORNING (LP, reissue)	£15
70	Python KM 3	GROANING THE BLUES (LP)	£50
76	Delmark DS 63?	COLD DAY IN HELL (LP)	£25

TOM RUSH
66	Xtra XTRA 5024	BLUES, SONGS & BALLADS (LP)	£30
66	Xtra XTRA 5053	I GOT A MIND TO RAMBLE (LP)	£30
67	Elektra EKL 308	TAKE A LITTLE WALK WITH ME (LP, also stereo EKS 7308)	£30
68	Elektra EKL 4018	THE CIRCLE GAME (also stereo EKS 74018) (LP, 1st issue black 'Elektra' on red label)	£25
69	Elektra EKL 4062	CLASSIC RUSH (LP, red label, also stereo EKS 74062)	£20

PATRICE RUSHEN
80	Elektra K 12414	Haven't You Heard/Keepin' Faith In Love (12")	£20
82	Elektra K 13173T	Forget Me Nots/Haven't You Heard/Never Gonna Give You Up (Won't Let You Be) (12")	£15
84	Elektra E 9702 (T)	Get Off (You Fascinate Me) (Dance Mix)/(Instrumental) (12")	£20
77	Prestige PR 10101	SHOUT IT OUT (LP, printed inner)	£25
78	Elektra K52104	PATRICE (LP, printed inner)	£15
79	Elektra K 52190	PIZZAZZ (LP, printed inner)	£20
80	Elektra K52260	POSH (LP, printed inner)	£15
82	Elektra K 52352	STRAIGHT FROM THE HEART (LP)	£20
84	Elektra 960 360-1	NOW (LP)	£15
18	Strut STRUT 205LP	REMIND ME (THE CLASSIC ELEKTRA RECORDINGS 1978-1984) (3LP, booklet)	£25

JIMMY RUSHING (WITH ADA MOORE & BUCK CLAYTON)
55	Vanguard PPT 12002	SINGS THE BLUES (10" LP)	£30
57	Vanguard PPT 12016	SHOWCASE (10" LP)	£30
57	Philips BBL 7105	CAT MEETS CHICK (LP, with Ada Moore & Buck Clayton)	£15
57	Philips BBL 7166	THE JAZZ ODYSSEY OF JAMES RUSHING ESQ (LP, with Buck Clayton)	£15
58	Vanguard PPL 11008	IF THIS AIN'T THE BLUES (LP)	£15

(see also Count Basie, Dave Brubeck)

JIMMY RUSHING/CHAMPION JACK DUPREE
64	Ember CJS 800	TWO SHADES OF BLUE (LP, 1 side each)	£30

(see also Champion Jack Dupree)

BARBARA RUSKIN
66	Piccadilly 7N 35274	Well How Does It Feel/Wishing Your Life Away £40
68	President PT 217	Pawnbroker Pawnbroker/Almost £25

ROGER RUSKIN SPEAR
74	United Artists UP 35721	I Love To Bumpity Bump/When Yuba Plays The Rhumba On The Tuba Down In Cuba....£20
71	United Artists UP 35221	REBEL TROUSER: Trouser Freak/Trouser Press/Release Me/Drop Out (EP, with p/s) £20
74	United Artists UAS 29508	UNUSUAL (LP) £20

(see also Bonzo Dog Doo-Dah Band, Topo D. Bill)

EDDIE RUSS
76	Impact IMP 5	Zauis/See The Light/Tea Leaves (12") £150

THANE RUSSAL (& THREE)
66	CBS 202049	Security/Your Love Is Burning Me (in p/s) £300
66	CBS 202049	Security/Your Love Is Burning Me...£150
66	CBS 202403	Drop Everything And Run/I Need You (solo) £150

CHARLOTTE RUSSE
68	Fontana BF1683	Anyway The Wind Blows/High On A Roof Top £25

ROLAND RUSSEL
68	Nu Beat NB 019	Rhythm Hips/RHYTHM FLAMES: Deltone Special £50

ARTHUR RUSSELL
86	Rough Trade RT RTT184	Let's Go Swimming (Coastal Dub)/(Gulf Stream Dub)/(Puppy Surf Dub) (12" p/s)...........£30
96	Talkin Loud TLDJ 49	In The Light Of The Miracle (Untitled Mix 1)/In The Light Of The Miracle (Ponytail Club Mix Part 1 & 2) (12" white label) £120
11	Eclectic Avenue BEAR 006	JUSTIN HARRIS PRESENTS ARTHUR RUSSELL - MOON (12") £15
87	Rough Trade ROUGH 114	WORLD OF ECHO (LP) £20
04	Soul Jazz SJRLP 083	THE WORLD OF ARTHUR RUSSELL (3-LP, original 2004 pressing) £30
10	Rough Trade RTRADLP 161	CALLING OUT OF CONTEXT (2-LP)...£18

(see also Dinosaur L, Necessaries)

CONNIE RUSSELL
55	Capitol CL 14236	Ayuh, Ayuh/I'm Making Believe £15

DEVON RUSSELL
75	Third World TW 06	Race Track Riot/Rat And Bat (as D. Russell with A (Alphonse) Bailey)............£40
75	Third World TW 07	Famine Time/Part 2 (as D. Russell)...£15
82	Ethnic ETH 2237	Come A Me Girl/Gully Banking £20
91	CS Sweetest CSLP 2	DARKER THAN BLUE (LP) £18

DOROTHY RUSSELL
71	Duke Reid DR 2524	You're The One I Love/Version £20

GEORGE RUSSELL
61	Riverside RLP 375	EZZ-THETICS (LP) £40
65	Polydor 583 705	AT BEETHOVEN HALL (PART 1) (LP) £18
65	Fontana 688 705 ZL	THE OUTER VIEW (LP. Stereo/mono)..£50
71	Flying Dutchman FD10124	ELECTRONIC SONATA FOR SOULS (LP)...£20

JANE RUSSELL
53	Columbia SCM 5043	Please Do It Again/Two Sleepy People (B-side with Bob Lowery) £15
59	MGM MGM-EP 702	JANE RUSSELL (EP) £40

JANET RUSSELL
88	Harbourtown HAR 003	GATHERING THE FRAGMENTS (LP) £20

JOHN RUSSELL/RICHARD COLDMAN
79	Incus INCUS 31	HOME COOKING/GUITAR SOLOS (LP, 1 side each)..£35

KIT RUSSELL
73	Deram DM 399	Peppers Last Stand/Shuffle Back £15

RAY RUSSELL QUARTET
68	CBS Realm 52586	TURN CIRCLE (LP) £80
69	CBS Realm 52663	DRAGON HILL (LP) £60
71	RCA SF 8214	JUNE 11TH 1971 (LP) £50
71	CBS 64271	RITES AND RITUALS (LP) £45
73	Black Lion BLP 12100	SECRET ASYLUM (LP, gatefold) £30
77	DJM DJF 20506	READY OR NOT (LP) £15

(see also Running Man, Chopyn)

WILLIAM RUSSO
63	Columbia 33SX 1508	RUSSO IN LONDON (LP)..£20
66	Columbia 33SX 1758	STONEHENGE (LP, with the London Jazz Orchestra) £35

RUSTIN MAN
19	Domino WIGLP 414XM	DRIFT CODE (LP, insert, signed print) £25
20	Domino WIGLP 468XM	CLOCKDUST (LP, gatefold insert, signed print)..£25

(see also Talk Talk, .O.Rang, Beth Gibbons & Rustin Man)

RUSTY & DOUG (KERSHAW)
59	Oriole CB 1510	Hey Mae!/Why Don't You Love Me £100
59	Oriole CB 1510	Hey Mae!/Why Don't You Love Me (78) £30
59	London HL 8972	I Like You (Like This)/Dancing Shoes £30
59	London HL 8972	I Like You (Like This)/Dancing Shoes (78) £30
62	Polydor NH 66970	Hey Mae!/Sweet Thing £20
62	Fontana 267 238 TF	Cajun Joe (The Ballad Of The Bayou)/Sweet Sweet Girl To Me £15

RUSTY NAIL
60s	Hi-Fi MEP 3093	RUSTY NAIL (EP, in p/s)	£100
60s	Hi-Fi MEP 3093	RUSTY NAIL (EP, no p/s)	£40

RUTH & BEAUTY
72	Montagu MONT 3000	29 Days To Doomsday/Cutting The Traces	£18

RUTHLESS RAP ASSASINS
87	White (Murdertone) AMC001	We Don't Care/Kiss AMC (12", 500 pressed)	£20

RUTLES
78	Warner Bros WB K56459	THE RUTLES (LP, gatefold, booklet and inner sleeve)	£20
96	Virgin VUSLP 119	ARCHAEOLOGY (LP, inner)	£20

(see also Dirk & Stig, Neil Innes, Monty Python, Beach Boys, Patto)

RUTS (D.C.)
79	People Unite SJP 795	In A Rut/H-Eyes (1,000 only, black-ringed label)	£150
83	Virgin VS 583-12	4-TRACK EP (12", p/s)	£15
83	Bohemian BO 3	Weak Heart/Militant (white label, with paper insert; as Ruts D.C., promo only)	£15
83	Bohemian BO 4	Stepping Bondage/Lobotomy/Rich Bitch (p/s)	£15
79	Virgin V 2132	THE CRACK (LP, stickered sleeve with "Pay no more than £3.99")	£20
80	Virgin V 2188	GRIN AND BEAR IT (LP, insert)	£20
81	Virgin V 2193	ANIMAL NOW (LP)	£15
82	Bohemian BOLP 4	RHYTHM COLLISION VOL 1 (LP)	£22
87	Link LP 013	LIVE AND LOUD (LP)	£15

(see also Laurel Aitken, Typhoons)

RU12
78	SRTS/78/CUS 131	SHE'S GONE EP (no p/s, 500 only)	£100

RYAN EXPRESS
74	Thor 1005 S	RYAN EXPRESS (LP, 200 only)	£50

BARRY RYAN (& MAJORITY)
69	MGM MGM-C(S) 8106	SINGS PAUL RYAN (LP)	£30
69	Polydor 583 067	BARRY RYAN (LP)	£25

(see also Paul & Barry Ryan)

KRIS RYAN (& QUESTIONS)
65	Mercury 10024 MCE	ON THE RIGHT TRACK (EP, as Kris Ryan & Questions)	£40

MARION RYAN
68	Philips BF 1721	Better Use Your Head/The Seasons Change	£30
57	Pye Nixa NEP 24041	THAT RYAN GIRL! (EP)	£20
58	Pye NEP 24079	MARION RYAN HIT PARADE (EP)	£20
59	Pye NPL 18030	A LADY LOVES! (LP, mono)	£25
59	Pye NSPL 18030	A LADY LOVES! (LP, stereo)	£30

(see also Ray Ellington, Gary Miller)

PAT RYAN
77	Folk Heritage FHR 094	LEABOY'S LASSIE (LP)	£25

PAUL & BARRY RYAN
67	Decca LK 4878	THE RYANS - TWO OF A KIND (LP)	£40
68	MGM MGM-C(S) 8081	PAUL AND BARRY RYAN (LP)	£25

(see also Barry Ryan)

PETE RYAN BAND
82	Ebony EBON 4	Dolly Parton's Tits/Eva On My Mind	£40

PHIL RYAN & CRESCENTS
65	Columbia DB 7574	Gypsy Woman/Be Honest With Yourself	£20

BOBBY RYDELL
59	Top Rank JAR 181	Kissin' Time/You'll Never Tame Me (78)	£25
60	Top Rank JKP 2059	LOVINGEST (EP)	£25
63	Cameo Parkway CPE 551	SWAY WITH BOBBY RYDELL (EP)	£15
63	Cameo Parkway CPE 553	BOBBY RYDELL (EP)	£15
60	Columbia 33SX 1243	WILD ONE (LP)	£40
61	Columbia 33SX 1308	SINGS AND SWINGS (LP)	£20
61	Columbia 33SX 1352	SALUTES "THE GREAT ONES" (LP)	£20
62	Columbia 33SX 1425	RYDELL AT THE COPA (LP)	£25
62	Cameo Parkway C 1019	ALL THE HITS (LP)	£15
63	Cameo Parkway C 1040	ALL THE HITS VOL. 2 (LP)	£15
63	Cameo Parkway C 1055	WILD (WOOD) DAYS (LP)	£15
65	Capitol T 2281	SOMEBODY LOVES YOU (LP)	£20

MAL RYDER (& SPIRITS)
63	Decca F 11669	Cry Baby/Take Over (as Mal Ryder & Spirits)	£20
64	Vocalion V 9219	See The Funny Little Clown/Slow Down	£70
64	Piccadilly 7N 35209	Your Friend/Forget It (as Mal Ryder & Spirits)	£40
65	Piccadilly 7N 35234	Lonely Room/Tell Your Friend	£22

(see also Mal & Primitives)

MITCH RYDER (& DETROIT WHEELS)
66	Stateside SS 481	Jenny Take A Ride/Baby Jane	£20
66	Stateside SS 498	Little Latin Lupe Lu/I Hope	£20
66	Stateside SS 521	Breakout/I Need Help	£50
66	Stateside SS 521	Breakout/I Need Help (DJ copy)	£100

MINT VALUE £

66	Stateside SS 549	Devil With A Blue Dress On (Medley)/I Had It Made	£20
67	Stateside SS 596	Sock It To Me Baby/I Never Had It Better	£20
67	Stateside SS 2023	Too Many Fish In The Sea/Three Little Fishes/One Grain Of Sand	£25
67	Stateside SS 2063	What Now My Love/Blessing In Disguise (solo)	£25
66	Stateside SE 1039	RIDIN' (EP)	£40
66	Stateside S(S)L 10178	TAKE A RIDE ... (LP)	£40
67	Stateside S(S)L 10189	BREAKOUT. . . !! (LP)	£30
67	Stateside S(S)L 10204	SOCK IT TO ME (LP)	£25
68	Stateside S(S)L 10229	WHAT NOW MY LOVE (LP, solo)	£30
69	Bell MBLL/SBLL 114	ALL MITCH RYDER HITS (LP)	£25

(see also Detroit)

STEVE RYDER
| 78 | Jammy JRUJ 1 | Ain't It Nice/Remember Me | £50 |

SABANOH 75
| 77 | Sabanoh Sound SB75 104 | Arata (Part 1)/Atata (Part 2) | £30 |

SABICAS
| 70 | Polyor 2482 023 | ROCK ENCOUNTER (LP, with Joe Beck) | £30 |

PARK SABLE & JUNGLE 'N' BEATS
| 64 | Fontana TF 457 | Never Be Blue/Rave On | £40 |

SABOTAGE
| 80 | Optimistic OPT 001 | WHEN THE WAR IS OVER (EP) | £18 |

SABRES
| 66 | Decca F 12528 | Roly Poly/Will You Always Love Me? | £30 |

(see also Peeps)

SABRES OF PARADISE
93	Sabres Of Paradise PT 001	United (Andrew Weatherall Mix) (12", p/s, actually remix of Throbbing Gristle's "United", 800 only)	£25
94	Warp WAP 50	Wilmot/Rumble Summons (12")	£15
93	Warp WARPLP 16	SABRESONIC (2-LP, with unreleased 7", 5,000 only)	£30
94	Warp WARPLP 26	HAUNTED DANCEHALL (2-LP, inners)	£18

SACRED
| 93 | Twilight 7R5010A | You're The Only One/Lost In Time | £20 |

SACRED ALIEN
| 81 | Greenwood GW 001 | Spiritual Planet/Energy (stickered labels, in p/s) | £30 |
| 83 | Heighway Robbery SAD 001 | Legends/VIRGIN: Sittin' In Front Row (gatefold p/s) | £30 |

SACRILEGE
85	C.O.T.R. GURT 4	BEHIND THE REALMS OF MADNESS (6-track mini LP)	£50
87	Under One Flag FLAG 15	WITHIN THE PROPHECY (LP)	£15
90	Metalcore CORE 8	BEHIND THE REALMS OF MADNESS (Mini-LP, reissue)	£20

SAD AFFAIR
| 71 | Lifelong LF 1 | Coloured Rice/Strange Sky | £30 |

SADDAR BAZAAR
| 95 | Delerium DELEC LP 034 | THE CONFERENCE OF THE BIRDS (LP) | £20 |

SADIE'S EXPRESSION
| 70 | Plexium PXM 13 | Old Whitrehall Number/Annie Wagon | £25 |

SADISTIC MIKA BAND
74	Harvest SHSP 4029	SADISTIC MIKA BAND (LP)	£20
75	Harvest SHSP 4043	BLACK SHIP (LP)	£15
75	Harvest SHSP 4049	HOT MENU (LP)	£20

BARRINGTON SADLER
| 69 | Clandisc CLA 204 | Soul Power/Rub It Down | £25 |

SAD LOVERS & GIANTS
81	Last Movement LM 003	CLE (EP)	£35
83	Last Movement LM 005	Colourless Dream/Things We Never DId	£20
82	Midnight CHIME 01	EPIC GARDEN MUSIC (LP)	£20
83	Midnight CHIME 03	FEEDING THE FLAME (LP)	£15
84	Midnight CHIME 07	IN THE BREEZE (LP)	£15
86	Midnight CHIME 22	TOTAL SOUND (LP)	£15
87	Midnight CHIME 30	THE MIRROR TEST (LP)	£15
90	Midnight CHIME 01.20 S	HEADLAND (LP)	£15

SAD PEOPLE
| 69 | Chapter One CH113 | Lonely Man/Turn Around | £15 |

SAFARI SOUNDS
| 94 | Droppin Science DS 004 | DROPPIN SCIENCE VOLUME 04 (12") | £15 |

SAFARIS (& PHANTOM BAND)
| 60 | Top Rank JAR 424 | Image Of A Girl/Four Steps To Love | £50 |

60	Top Rank JAR 528	The Girl With The Story In Her Eyes/Summer Nights (with Phantom Band)....................£40	

SAFFRON SUMMERFIELD
74	Mother Earth MUM 1001	SALISBURY PLAIN (LP)..£60	
76	Mother Earth MUM 1202	FANCY MEETING YOU HERE (LP)..£50	
76	Spectator	FANCY MEETING YOU HERE (LP, reissue)...£20	

SA55
86	1966 EJSP 9868	Compromised/Love Is Blind (p/s)...£80	

SAFRON
71	RA 5005	Tune For A Vagabond/Ladies In Waiting...£40	

SAGA
72	Westwood WRS 017	SAGA (LP)...£50	
73	Westwood WRS 036	SWEET PEG O'DERBY (LP)..£100	

MIKE SAGAR (& CRESTERS)
60	HMV POP 819	Deep Feeling/You Know (as Mike Sagar & Cresters)..............................£20	

(see also Cresters, Richard Harding)

SAGE
80	Redball RR 032	GOING STRONG (LP)...£45	

SAGITTARIUS
67	CBS 2867	My World Fell Down/Libra..£25	
68	CBS 3276	Another Time/Virgo...£25	

SAHARA (1)
75	Dawn DNLS 3068	SUNRISE (LP)..£35	

SAHARA (2)
85	Elite DAZZ 38	Love So Fine/(Club Mix) (12")...£15	

DOUG SAHM
73	Atlantic K 40466	DOUG SAHM AND BAND (LP, includes Bob Dylan and Dr. John)...............£18	

(see also Sir Douglas Quintet)

ST. CHRISTOPHER
89	Sarah SARAH 015	You Deserve More Than A Maybe/The Kind Of Girl/The Summer Of Love (foldaround p/s with poster in poly bag)....................£20	
89	Sarah SARAH 20	All Of A Tremble/My Fortune/The Hummingbird £18	
90	Sarah SARAH 34	Antoinette/Salvation (p/s, insert)...£20	
91	Sarah SARAH 46	Say Yes To Everything/It's Snowing On The Moon (p/s, insert)..............£20	
90	Sarah SARAH 403	BACHARACH (10" LP)..£20	

CHERYL ST. CLAIR
66	CBS 202041	My Heart Is Not In It/We Want Love £15	

JERRY ST. CLAIR
69	Philips BF 1796	Summer Exodus/Mrs. Jensen Sits Alone £15	

SAINT DAVIDS ROAD
69	Tangerine DP003	Let The Sun Come In/Mama Ain't Gonna Like What She Sees £15	

SAINT ETIENNE
92	Heavenly HVN 22	Live - Paris '92 (clear flexidisc, gig freebie, 1,000 only) £20	
93	Heavenly HVN 2912	Hobart Paving/Who Do You Think You Are (12", p/s, mispressed with Hobart Paving & "Your Head My Voice" on both sides).........................£15	
95	Heavenly HVN 41	XMAS '95: A Christmas Gift To You/Driving Home For Christmas/A Message In A Bottle (CD, signed fan club edition)..........£90	
91	Heavenly HVN LP1	FOXBASE ALPHA (LP)...£25	
93	Heavenly HVN 41	SO TOUGH (LP)..£30	
93	Heavenly HVNLP 6	YOU NEED A MESS OF HELP TO STAND ALONE (LP) £15	
94	Heavenly HVMLP 8	TIGER BAY (LP) £30	
95	Heavenly HVN 9CD	I LOVE TO PAINT (CD, fan club edition, 600 only) £40	
95	Heavenly HVNCD 10	TOO YOUNG TO DIE (CD, with bonus CD "Too Young To Die - The Remix Album" [HVN LP 10CDR])..........£30	
97	Heavenly HVN41-2	VALENTINES DAY (CD, EP fan club edition)..£50	
98	Fan Club SPCD 463	XMAS '98: I Don't Intend To Spend Christmas Without You/Kofi Annan (CD, fan club edition, in card sleeve)..........£40	
98	Creation CRELP 225	GOOD HUMOR (LP, with free 10")..£50	
00	Mantra MNTLP 1018	SOUND OF WATER (LP)...£40	
00	Mantra MNSTET 1	BUILT ON SAND: RARITIES 1994-1999 (CD, fan club edition) £40	
02	Mantra MNTLP 1033	FINISTERRE (LP) £30	
03	Heavenly HVN136CD	XMAS 2003 (CD, EP fan club issue)...£30	
05	Sanctuary SANLP 271	TALES FROM TURNPIKE HOUSE (LP)...£25	
08	Heavenly HVNLP 69	LONDON CONVERSATIONS - THE BEST OF ST. ETIENNE (2-LP) £20	
08	Foreign Office FOREIGN OFFICE 004	BOXETTE (4-CD, 3000 only)..£50	
12	Heavenly HVMLP 92	WORDS AND MUSIC BY SAINT ETIENNE (LP) £35	
17	Heavenly HVNLP 139	HOME COUNTIES (2-LP, hand-stickered sleeve)......................................£30	
17	Heavenly HVNLP 139 BUN	HOME COUNTIES (2-LP, CD and cassette)..£30	

(see also 50 Year Void, Sarah Cracknell, Mike Vickers)

KIRK ST. JAMES
70	Pye 7N 25518	My Love Oh Linda/Tears I Cry £60	

BARRY ST. JOHN
64	Decca F 11933	A Little Bit Of Soap/Thing Of The Past £20	
64	Decca F 11975	Bread And Butter/Cry To Me..£20	
65	Decca F 12111	Mind How You Go/Don't You Feel Proud £20	

MINT VALUE £

65	Decca F 12145	Hey Boy/I've Been Crying	£20
65	Columbia DB 7783	Come Away Melinda/Gotta Brand New Man	£15
66	Columbia DB 7868	Everything I Touch Turns To Tears/Sounds Like My Baby	£65
66	Columbia DB 7868	Everything I Touch Turns To Tears/Sounds Like My Baby (DJ copy)	£80
68	Major Minor MM 587	Cry Like A Baby/Long And Lonely Night	£15
69	Major Minor MM 604	By The Time I Get To Phoenix/Turn On Your Light	£15
69	M. Minor MMLP/SMLP 43	ACCORDING TO ST. JOHN (LP)	£50

BRIDGET ST. JOHN

69	Dandelion K 4404	To B Without A Hitch/Autumn Lullaby	£15
69	Dandelion 63750	ASK ME NO QUESTIONS (LP, gatefold sleeve)	£80
71	Dandelion DAN 8007	SONGS FOR THE GENTLE MAN (LP, gatefold sleeve)	£100
71	Dandelion K 49007	SONGS FOR THE GENTLE MAN (LP, gatefold sleeve, with cat no K 49007)	£30
72	Dandelion 2310 193	THANK YOU FOR... (LP, gatefold sleeve)	£100
74	Chrysalis CHR 1062	JUMBLE QUEEN (LP)	£40

(see also Kevin Ayers, Ron Geesin, Mike Oldfield, Quiver)

PAUL ST. JOHN

| 70 | Pye 7N 45190 | Flying Saucers Have Landed/Spaceship Love | £150 |

TAMMY ST. JOHN

64	Pye 7N 15682	Boys/Hey Hey Hey Hey	£15
65	Pye 7N 15762	He's The One For Me/I'm Tired Of Just Looking At You	£15
65	Pye 7N 15948	Dark Shadows And Empty Hallways/I Mustn't Cry	£15
66	Pye 7N 17042	Nobody Knows What's Goin' On (In My Mind But Me)/ Stay Together Young Lovers	£50
66	Pye 7N 17042	Nobody Knows What's Goin' On (In My Mind But Me)/ Stay Together Young Lovers (DJ copy)	£100
69	Tangerine DP 0007	Concerning Love/Sound Of Love	£300

(see also Trends)

ST. LOUIS JIMMY

| 53 | Esquire 10-319 | Holiday For Boogie/MEMPHIS SLIM: Harlem Bound (78) | £15 |

ST. LOUIS UNION

66	Decca F 12318	Girl/Respect	£15
66	Decca F 12386	Behind The Door/English Tea	£70
66	Decca F 12508	East Side Story/Think About Me	£150

(see also Medicine Head)

OLIVER ST. PATRICK & DIAMONDS

| 67 | Trojan TR 005 | I Want To Be Loved By You/Tulips | £60 |

CRISPIAN ST. PETERS

65	Decca F 12080	At This Moment/Goodbye, You'll Forget Me	£15
65	Decca F 12207	No No No/Three Goodbyes	£15
66	Decca F 12480	Changes/My Little Brown Eyes	£15
67	Decca DFE 8678	ALMOST PERSUADED (EP)	£55
66	Decca LK 4805	FOLLOW ME... (LP)	£60
70	Square SQA 102	SIMPLY... CRISPIAN ST. PETERS (LP)	£40

SAINT STEVEN

| 69 | Probe SPB 1005 | OVER THE HILLS/THE BASTICH (LP) | £75 |

ST. VALENTINE'S DAY MASSACRE

| 67 | Fontana TF 883 | Brother Can You Spare A Dime/Al's Party (with p/s) | £150 |
| 67 | Fontana TF 883 | Brother Can You Spare A Dime/Al's Party | £60 |

(see also Artwoods)

SAINTS (AUSTRALIA)

76	Power Exchange PX 242	I'm Stranded/No Time (p/s)	£20
77	Harvest HAR 5123	Erotic Neurotic/One Way Street (with p/s)	£150
77	Harvest HAR 5137	1, 2, 3, 4 (River Deep, Mountain High/Lipstick On Your Collar/One Way Street/ Demolition Girl) (EP, double pack, gatefold p/s)	£15
77	Harvest SHSP 4065	I'M STRANDED (LP)	£40
78	Harvest SHSP 4078	ETERNALLY YOURS (LP, with inner sleeve)	£30
78	Harvest SHSP 4094	PREHISTORIC SOUNDS (LP)	£25

SAINTS (JAMAICA)

66	Doctor Bird DB 1009	Brown Eyes/BABA BROOKS & HIS BAND: King Size	£30
69	Big Shot BI 522	Windy Part One/Windy Part Two	£25
73	Count Shelley CS 043	How Long/Feeling Good	£20

SAINTS (U.K.)

| 63 | Pye 7N 15548 | Wipe Out/Midgets | £25 |
| 63 | Pye 7N 15582 | Husky Team/Pigtails | £25 |

(see also Tornados, Heinz)

SAINTS (U.K.)

| 64 | MJB BEV 73/4 | SAINTS (10" LP, private pressing) | £300 |
| 64 | MJB BEVLP 127/8 | SAINTS ALIVE! (LP, private pressing) | £300 |

RUSS SAINTY (& NU NOTES)

| 60 | Decca F 11270 | Race With The Devil/Too Shy (solo) | £20 |

(see also Nu Notes)

KYU SAKAMOTO

| 62 | HMV CLP 1674 | SUKIYAKI (LP) | £40 |

(BOB) SAKER

| 68 | Polydor BM 56231 | Still Got You/Imagination (as Bob Saker) | £30 |
| 68 | Parlophone R 5740 | Foggy Tuesday/Ooh Nana Na (as Bob Saker) | £50 |

MINT VALUE £

| 69 | Parlophone R 5752 | Hey Joe!/Christianity | £15 |

SAL SALVADOR

| 55 | KPL 105 | SAL SALVADOR QUARTET (10" LP) | £15 |

SALAMANDER

| 70 | CBS 5102 | Crystal Ball/Billy | £15 |
| 71 | Youngblood SSYB 14 | THE TEN COMMANDMENTS (LP, gatefold poster sleeve) | £400 |

(see also Onyx)

SALEM

| 82 | Hilton FMR 056 | Cold As Steel/Reach To Eternity | £45 |

SALFORD JETS

| 78 | WEA K 18008 | Lookin' At The Squares/Dancing School (no p/s) | £15 |
| 79 | EMI INT 590 | Manchester Boys/Last Bus (p/s) | £20 |

SALIX ALBA

| 73 | Columbiab R5990 | I Can't Resist/Blue Sky | £30 |

SALLY AND THE ALLEY CATS

| 64 | Parlophone R 5183 | Is It Something That I Said/You Forgot To Remember | £15 |

SALLYANGIE

69	Big T BIG 126	Two Ships/Colours Of The World	£100
72	Philips 6006 259	Child Of Allah/Lady Go Lightly	£100
68	Transatlantic TRA 176	CHILDREN OF THE SUN (LP, gatefold sleeve, purple/white textured label)	£80
78	Transatlantic TRA 176	CHILDREN OF THE SUN (LP, reissue, different single sleeve)	£20

(see also Mike Oldfield, Sally Oldfield)

SALMONTAILS

| 80 | Oblivion OBL 001 | SALMONTAILS (LP, with Dave Pegg) | £20 |

SALT

| 78 | Grapevine GRA 111 | BEYOND A SONG (LP, with insert) | £18 |

SALT & PEPPER

| 61 | London HLU 9338 | High Noon/Come Softly To Me | £15 |

SALVATION (1)

| 69 | United Artists UP 35048 | Cinderella/The Village Shuck | £15 |
| 69 | United Artists UAS 29062 | SALVATION (LP) | £30 |

SALVATION (2)

| 83 | Merciful Release MRX 025 | Girlsoul/Evelyn/Dust Up (12", p/s) | £15 |

SAMMY SALVO

| 58 | RCA RCA 1032 | Oh Julie/Say Yeah | £25 |

SAM APPLE PIE

69	Decca F 22932	Tiger Man (King Of The Jungle)/Sometime Girl	£20
69	Decca LK-R 5005	SAM APPLE PIE (LP, mono, laminated front sleeve, unboxed logo label)	£300
69	Decca SKL-R 5005	SAM APPLE PIE (LP, stereo, laminated sleeve, unboxed logo label)	£250
73	DJM DJLPS 429	EAST 17 (LP)	£30

SAM & BILL

66	Pye International 7N 25355	Fly Me To The Moon/Treat Me Right	£15
67	Brunswick 05973	I Feel Like Cryin'/I'll Try	£50
67	Brunswick 05973	I Feel Like Cryin'/I'll Try (DJ copy)	£80

SAM & DAVE

66	King KG 1041	No More Pain/You Ain't No Big Thing Baby	£50
66	Atlantic AT 4066	You Don't Know Like I Know/Blame Me, Don't Blame My Heart	£20
67	Stax 601 004	Soothe Me/Sweet Pains (initial dark blue label)	£25
67	Stax 601 004	Soothe Me/Sweet Pains (later light blue label)	£20
66	King KGL 4001	SAM AND DAVE (LP)	£75
66	Atlantic 587/588 045	HOLD ON, I'M A COMIN' (LP)	£50
67	Stax 589 003	DOUBLE DYNAMITE (LP)	£50
68	Stax 589 015	SOUL MEN (LP)	£40
68	Major Minor MCP 5000	SAM AND DAVE (LP)	£22
69	Atlantic 588 154	I THANK YOU (LP)	£25
69	Atlantic 588 155	THE BEST OF SAM AND DAVE (LP)	£18
69	Atlantic 587/588 181	DOUBLE TROUBLE (LP)	£22
69	Atlantic 588 185	SOUL MEN (LP, reissue)	£15

SAM & KITTY

| 80 | Grapevine GRP 132 | I've Got Something Good/Love Is The Greatest (DJ Copy) | £20 |

SAMBA

| 17 | System SYSTM 019 | Kami/Hooves (with Sepia) (10") | £30 |

SAME

79	Wessex WEX 267	Wild About You/Movements (p/s)	£70
80	Blueprint BLU 2008	Movements/Wild About You (reissue with reversed sides & blue print on p/s)	£30
80	Blueprint BLU 2008	Movements/Wild About You (reissue with reversed sides no p/s)	£20

MIKE SAMMES SINGERS

| 68 | Davjon DJ 1006 | HYMNS A SWINGING (LP, with Ted Taylor Organisation) | £30 |
| 06 | Trunk JBH 109 LP | MUSIC FOR BISCUITS (LP, 750 only) | £35 |

SAMMY

| 72 | Philips 6308 136 | SAMMY (LP, laminated sleeve, black/silver label) | £40 |

(see also Ian Gillan, Audience, Episode Six, Quatermass, Roy Young Band, Stackridge, Ginhouse)

SAMPLES
80	Sample	**VENDETTA** (EP) (A4 fold-out sleeve, white labels, some stamped 'The Samples Cherry Red Records')	£125
84	No Future OI 14	**Dead Hero/Fire Around Round/Suspicion** (p/s)	£20

DAVE SAMPSON & HUNTERS
60	Columbia DB 4449	**Sweet Dreams/It's Lonesome**	£20
60	Columbia DB 4502	**If You Need Me/See You Around**	£15
61	Columbia SEG 8095	**DAVE** (EP, mono)	£40
61	Columbia ESG 7853	**DAVE** (EP, stereo)	£30

(see also Hunters [U.K.])

TOMMY SAMPSON
58	Melodisc MEL 1411	**Rockin'/Rock'n'Roll Those Big Brown Eyes** (with His Strongmen)	£22
58	Melodisc MEL 1411	**Rockin'/Rock'n'Roll Those Big Brown Eyes** (with His Strongmen) (78)	£20

SAMSON (1)
69	Instant INSP 004	**ARE YOU SAMSON** (LP)	£100

(see also Strider)

SAMSON (3)
78	Lightning GIL 547	**Telephone/Leavin' You** (p/s)	£35
79	Lightning GIL 553	**Mr. Rock'n'Roll/Drivin' Music** (p/s)	£35
80	EMI EMI 5061	**Vice Versa** (Edit)/**Hammerhead** (p/s, withdrawn, 1,000 demos only)	£40
82	Polydor SAM 2	**Red Skies/Young Idea** (unissued, promo only)	£18
86	Capitol 12CLP 395	**Vice Versa** (Remix)/**Losing My Grip** (Remix) (12", picture disc)	£15
79	Laser LAP 1	**SURVIVORS** (LP)	£18
80	Gem GEMLP 108	**HEAD ON** (LP, 2 different mixes, A1/B1 or A2/B2 in matrix; each with insert)	£15
80	Gem GEMLP 108	**HEAD ON** (LP, mispress with A1/B2 matrix)	£15
81	Gem GEMLP 113	**SHOCK TACTICS** (LP, release cancelled)	£0
81	RCA LP 5031	**SHOCK TACTICS** (LP, with insert)	£18
82	Polydor POLS 1077	**BEFORE THE STORM** (LP, with poster, stickered sleeve)	£20
84	Polydor POLD 5132	**DON'T GET MAD, GET EVEN** (LP, with insert)	£15
84	Polydor POLD 5132	**DON'T GET MAD, GET EVEN** (2-LP, white labels, 2 different mixes of same album, promo only)	£60

(see also Bruce Dickinson, Iron Maiden, John McCoy, Tiger, Colin Towns, Nicky Moore, Mammoth, Egypt)

SAM THE SHAM & THE PHARAOHS
65	MGM MGM 1269	**Woolly Bully/Ain't Gonna Move** (DJ Copy)	£50
66	MGM MGM 1298	**Red Hot/Long Long Way**	£15
67	MGM MGM 1343	**Black Sheep/My Day's Gonna Come**	£15
66	MGM MGM-EP 794	**RED HOT** (EP)	£60
65	MGM MGM-C 1007	**WOOLY BULLY** (LP)	£40
66	MGM MGM-C(S) 8032	**LI'L RED RIDING HOOD** (LP)	£30

JERRY SAMUELS
56	HMV 7M 411	**Puppy Love/The Chosen Few**	£15

(see also Napoleon XIV)

WINSTON SAMUELS
64	Black Swan WI 419	**Luck Will Come My Way/LLOYD BREVITT: One More Time**	£25
64	Black Swan WI 426	**You Are The One/Gloria Love** (B-side actually by Beltones)	£15
65	Ska Beat JB 196	**Be Prepared/Jericho Wall**	£18
65	Ska Beat JB 213	**My Bride To Be/LLOYD PREVITT: Wayward Ska**	£25
65	Ska Beat JB 214	**Never Again/My Angel**	£20
66	Ska Beat JB 238	**What Have I Done/Broken Hearted**	£20
66	Ska Beat JB 241	**Ups And Downs/Come What May**	£20
66	Ska Beat JB 244	**Time Will Tell/I'm Sorry**	£20
67	Island WI 3051	**The Greatest/FREDDIE & FITZY: Truth Hurts**	£50
67	Island WI 3053	**I Won't Be Discouraged/FREDDIE & FITZIE: Why Did My Little Girl Cry**	£50
67	Fab FAB 21	**Peace Of Mind/Shepherd Beng Beng** (by Prince Buster & Teddy King, white labels only)	£350
67	Fab FAB 14	**Holding Out/To The Other Man**	£50
67	Fab FAB 28	**Peace Of Mind/I'm Still Here**	£60
10	Randys THB 7002	**Lick It Back/COUNT MACHUKI: Pepper Pot**	£30

SAMURAI (1)
68	United Artists UP 2242	**Good Morning Starshine/Temple Of Gold**	£35
71	Greenwich GSLP 1003	**SAMURAI** (LP, gatefold sleeve, white/brown label)	£250

SAMURAI (2)
84	Ebony EBON 24	**SACRED BLADE** (LP)	£15

SAN FRANCISCO TKO'S
98	Kent 6T 14	**Make Up Your Mind/PEGGY GAINES: When The Boy That You Love**	£25

SANCTUARY
87	Epic 460811	**REFUGE DENIED** (LP)	£25

SAND
71	Philips 6006157	**Soft Lady/Babylon**	£20

SANDALWOOD
76	Canon CNNS 33	**Don't Let It Rain Today/In Dreams**	£25
71	S.R.T. 71136	**CHANGELING** (LP), hand pasted sleeve)	£3000
20	Seelie Court SCLP 002	**CHANGELING** (LP, reissue)	£20

ALEX SANDERS
70	A&M AMLS 984	**A WITCH IS BORN** (LP, foldout sleeve with warning sticker, withdrawn)	£100

PHARAOH SANDERS
66	ESP Disk/Fontana SFJL 931	PHARAOH SANDERS QUINTET (LP)	£35
70	Impulse AS 9138	TAUHID (LP)	£20
71	Probe SPB 1019	DEAF, DUMB AND BLIND (LP)	£35
72	Impulse AS 9219	BLACK UNITY (LP)	£35
72	Impulse AS 9227	LIVE AT THE EAST (LP)	£35
73	Impulse 9233	WISDOM THROUGH MUSIC (LP)	£30
74	Impulse 9254	VILLAGE OF PHARAOHS (LP)	£30
74	Impulse 9261	ELEVATION (LP)	£30
73	Impulse 9280	LOVE IN US ALL (LP)	£35
78	Arista SPART 1051	LOVE WILL FIND A WAY (LP)	£15
82	Jasmine JAS 53	THEMBI (LP)	£18
13	Universal Sounds USLP 55	ELEVATION (2-LP, reissue)	£35
15	Impulse AS 9181	KARMA (LP, reissue 180gm)	£25

JOHNNY SANDON (& REMO FOUR)
63	Pye 7N 15542	Lies/On The Horizon (as Johnny Sandon & Remo Four)	£15
63	Pye 7N 15559	Magic Potion/Yes (as Johnny Sandon & Remo Four)	£15

(see also Remo Four)

HOPE SANDOVAL & WARM INTENTIONS
00	Rough Trade RTRADE S008	AT THE DOORWAY AGAIN EP (12")	£25
01	Rough Trade RTRADELP 031	BAVARIAN FRUIT BREAD (LP)	£100

(see also Mazzy Star)

SANDOZ
93	Touch TONE 4	DARK CONTINENT (12" EP)	£30
94	Touch TO 23 12	INTENSELY RADIOACTIVE (LP as 2 x 12")	£25
95	Touch TO 28 12	EVERY MAN GOT DREAMING (LP as 2 x 12")	£25
02	Soul Jazz SJR LP 59	CHANT TO JAH: SANDOZ IN DUB (2-LP, reissue)	£25
06	Soul Jazz SRR LP 130	LIVE IN THE EARTH: SANDOZ IN DUB (CHAPTER 2) (2-LP)	£20
16	Mute SANDOZBX1	COLLECTED WORKS 1992-1994 (5-CD box set)	£30

(see also Cabaret Voltaire, Electronic Eye, Richard H. Kirk, Sweet Exorcist)

SAND PEBBLES
67	Track 604 015	Love Power/Because Of Love	£20
69	Track 604 028	Love Power/Because Of Love (reissue)	£15

SANDRA
86	10 TENY 78-12	(I'll Never Be) Maria Magdalena/Party Games/Little Girl (12", picture disc)	£15
86	10 TEN 113-12/TENY 78-12	In The Heat Of The Night/Heatwave (Instrumental)//(I'll Never Be) Maria Magdalena/Party Games/Little Girl (12", double pack, including picture disc, gatefold PVC sleeve)	£20
89	Siren SRNCD 85	Everlasting Love/Stop For A Minute/Everlasting Love (Remix)/ (I'll Never Be) Maria Magdalena (CD)	£50

SANDROSE
73	Polydor 2480 137	SANDROSE (LP)	£275

SANDS (IRELAND)
69	Tribune TRS 122	Dance Dance Dance/The Cheater	£20
69	Tribune TRS 129	Bubble Gum Music/Sherry	£15
69	Tribune	SAND DOIN'S (LP)	£50
70s	Plough PLX 501	TIME OUT WITH THE SANDS (LP)	£15

(see also Tony Kenny & Sands)

SANDS (U.K.)
67	Reaction 591 017	Mrs. Gillespie's Refrigerator/Listen To The Sky	£400

(see also Sundragon)

DAVEY SANDS & ESSEX
65	Decca F 12170	Please Me Mine/All The Time	£20
67	CBS 202620	Advertising Girl/Without You I'm Nothing	£25

EVIE SANDS
65	Red Bird BC 118	Take Me For A Little While/Run Home To Mama	£50
65	Red Bird BC 118	Take Me For A Little While/Run Home To Mama (DJ copy)	£85
66	Cameo Parkway C 413	Picture Me Gone/It Makes Me Laugh	£125
66	Cameo Parkway C 413	Picture Me Gone/It Makes Me Laugh (DJ copy)	£200

JODI(E) SANDS
57	London HL 8456	With All My Heart/More Than Only Friends (as Jodi Sands)	£15

TOMMY SANDS
57	Capitol CL 14695	Teen-Age Crush/Hep Dee Hootie (Cutie Wootie)	£25
57	Capitol CL 14724	Ring-A-Ding-A-Ding/My Love Song	£25
57	Capitol CL 14745	Goin' Steady/Ring My 'Phone	£25
57	Capitol CL 14811	Man, Like Wow!/A Swingin' Romance	£20
58	Capitol CL 14834	Sing, Boy, Sing/Crazy 'Cause I Love You	£15
58	Capitol CL 14872	Hawaiian Rock/Teen-Age Doll	£25
58	Capitol CL 14889	After The Senior Prom/Big Date	£20
58	Capitol CL 14925	Blue Ribbon Baby/I Love You Because (as Tommy Sands & Raiders)	£30
59	Capitol CL 14971	The Worryin' Kind/Bigger Than Texas	£35
59	Capitol CL 15013	Is It Ever Gonna Happen/I Ain't Gettin' Rid Of You	£30
66	Liberty LIB 55842	The Statue/Lolita	£45
66	Liberty LIB 55842	The Statue/Lolita (DJ copy)	£85
57	Capitol EAP1 848	STEADY DATE WITH TOMMY SANDS PT. 1 (EP)	£20
57	Capitol EAP2 848	STEADY DATE WITH TOMMY SANDS PT. 2 (EP)	£20

MINT VALUE £

57	Capitol EAP3 848	STEADY DATE WITH TOMMY SANDS PT. 3 (EP)	£20
57	Capitol EAP1 851	TEENAGE CRUSH (EP)	£20
59	Capitol EAP1 1081	SANDS STORM PART 1 (EP)	£20
59	Capitol EAP2 1081	SANDS STORM PART 2 (EP)	£20
59	Capitol EAP3 1081	SANDS STORM PART 3 (EP)	£20
59	Capitol EAP1 1123	THIS THING CALLED LOVE (EP)	£15
57	Capitol T 848	STEADY DATE WITH TOMMY SANDS (LP)	£40
58	Capitol T 929	SING, BOY, SING (soundtrack) (LP)	£40
59	Capitol T 1081	SANDS STORM! (LP)	£80
59	Capitol T 1123	THIS THING CALLED LOVE (LP)	£20
60	Capitol (S)T 1239	WHEN I'M THINKING OF YOU (LP, mono)	£15
60	Capitol (S)T 1239	WHEN I'M THINKING OF YOU (LP, stereo)	£15
61	Capitol T 1426	A DREAM WITH TOMMY SANDS (LP)	£15

TONY SANDS & DRUMBEATS

60s	Studio 36 NSRS EP 1/22	Shame Shame Shame/I Got A Feeling	£250

WES SANDS

63	Columbia DB 4996	There's Lots More Where This Came From/Three Cups	£45

(see also Brothers Kane, Sarstedt Brothers)

PAT SANDY

69	Attack ATT 8000	Gentle On My Mind/BIG L: Soulful	£30

SANDY COAST

69	Page One POLS 020	FROM THE STEREO WORKSHOP (LP)	£350
69	Page One MORS 201	SHIPWRECK (LP)	£300
73	Polydor 2310 277	STONEWALL (LP)	£20

SANG HUGH

75	Ethnic Fight EF 018	Last Call To Blackman/Black Track	£15

SAN REMO STRINGS

71	Tamla Motown TMG 795	Festival Time/All Turned On (DJ copy)	£30
72	Tamla Motown TMG 807	Reach Out, I'll Be There/Hungry For Love (DJ copy)	£30
73	Tamla Motown STML 11216	SAN REMO STRINGS SWING (LP)	£20

BOBBY SANSOM (& GIANTS)

63	Oriole CB 1837	There's A Place/Lucille (as Bobby Sansom & Giants)	£20
63	Oriole CB 1888	Where Have You Been/Do You Promise (as Bobby Sansom & Giants)	£18

MONGO SANTAMARIA

63	Riverside RIF 106909	Watermelon Man/Don't Bother Me No More	£20
65	CBS 201766	El Pussycat/Black Eyed Peas And Rice	£20
69	Direction 58-4086	Cloud Nine/Son Of A Preacher Man	£18
69	Direction 58-4430	Twenty Five Miles/El Tres	£15
66	CBS SS 62123	HEY! LET'S PARTY (LP)	£20
69	CBS S 233811	ALL STRUNG OUT (LP)	£20
71	CBS 63904	WORKING ON A GROOVY THING (LP)	£20
71	Atlantic 2400 140	MONGO'S WAY (LP)	£20

SANTANA

69	CBS 63815	SANTANA (LP, laminated sleeve original, orange label)	£30
70	CBS 64087	ABRAXAS (LP, orange label)	£25
71	CBS 69015	SANTANA (III) (LP, gatefold sleeve, some stickered, orange label)	£25
72	CBS CQ 30595	SANTANA (III) (LP, gatefold sleeve, quadrophonic)	£40
72	CBS 65299	CARAVANSERAI (LP, gatefold sleeve, orange label)	£20
73	CBS CQ 31610	CARAVANSERAI (LP, gatefold sleeve, quadrophonic)	£25
74	CBS CQ 32445	WELCOME (LP, embossed gatefold sleeve, quadrophonic)	£20
75	CBS CQ 30130	ABRAXAS (LP, gatefold sleeve, quadrophonic)	£20
75	CBS Q 69081	GREATEST HITS (LP, quadrophonic)	£15
75	CBS Q 69084	BORBOLETTA (LP, quadrophonic)	£15
76	CBS Q 86005	AMIGOS (LP, quadrophonic)	£15
85	CBS 69084	BORBOLETTA (LP, Nimbus Supercut, mail order only through Hi Fi Today magazine)	£80
90	Thunderbolt THBL 079	LATIN TROPICAL (LP)	£18
92	Polydor 513 197-1	MILAGRO (LP)	£20
00	Arista 07822 19080-1	SUPERNATURAL (2-LP)	£200
02	Arista 74321 97961-1	SHAMAN (2-LP)	£100

CARLOS SANTANA & BUDDY MILES

73	CBS CQ 31308	CARLOS SANTANA & BUDDY MILES LIVE (LP, quadrophonic)	£15

(see also Santana, Buddy Miles, Mahavishnu Orchestra, John McLaughlin, John Lee Hooker)

SANTELLS

66	Sue WI 4020	So Fine/These Are Love	£25

GRANT SANTINO & THE FAMILY

79	Polydor 2059 168	L.O.V.E./Try Love	£20
79	Polydor GS1	L.O.V.E./Try Love (12", promo only)	£100

SANTO & JOHNNY

59	Pye International 7N 25037	Sleep Walk/All Night Diner	£15
59	Pye International N 25037	Sleep Walk/All Night Diner (78 rpm)	£15
60	Parlophone R 4619	Tear Drop/The Long Walk Home	£15
60	Parlophone GEP 8806	SANTO AND JOHNNY NO. 1 (EP)	£30
60	Parlophone GEP 8813	SANTO AND JOHNNY NO. 2 (EP)	£30
64	Stateside S(S)L 1008	HAWAII (LP)	£20

SAPODILLA PUNCH
69   Mercury MF 112   Hold On I'm Coming/Back To Minor (DJ copy) £20

SAPPHIRE
82   Sapphire Rocks SRR 001   Jealousy (p/s)...£200
72   SRT SRT 72226   SAPPHIRE (LP) £200

SAPPHIRES
63   Stateside SS 223   Where Is Johnny Now/Your True Love...£40
64   Stateside SS 267   Who Do You Love/Oh So Soon £65
65   HMV POP 1441   Gotta Have Your Love/Gee Baby I'm Sorry £180
65   HMV POP 1441   Gotta Have Your Love/Gee Baby I'm Sorry (DJ copy).............£350
65   HMV POP 1461   Evil One/How Could I Say Goodbye £180
65   HMV POP 1461   Evil One/How Could I Say Goodbye (DJ copy) £300

SARABAND
73   Folk Heritage FHR 050   CLOSE TO IT ALL (LP)..£22

SARACEN
82   Nucleus MPGR 492   HEROES, SAINTS AND FOOLS (LP) £15

SARASOTA
96   BIT Productions MIKE 004   We're Gettin' Hot (1-sided 12") £40
97   BIT Productions MIKE 009   Pleasure/We're Gettin' Hot (the Maximum Project Pumped Up Remix) (stickered white label 12")...£40

SARDONICUS
73   Country Recording Service COUN 240   Nymph/Evaporated Brain £350

DON SARGENT
60   Vogue Pop V 9160   St. James' Infirmary/Gypsy Boots (triangular centre)...............£300

SARI & SHALIMARS
68   United Artists UP 2235   It's So Lonely (Being Together)/You Walked Out On Me Before £30

DEREK SARJEANT
61   Oak RGJ 101   FOLK SONGS SUNG BY DEREK SARJEANT (EP) £20
61   Oak RGJ 103   SONGS WE LIKE TO SING (EP, with tracks by Lisa Turner & Mick Wells)............£15
61   Oak RGJ 105   FOLK SONGS SUNG BY DEREK SARJEANT VOL. 2 (EP).............£15
63   Oak RGJ 117   MAN OF KENT (EP) £18
61   Oak RGJ 7444   ENGLISH FOLK SONGS (EP)..£20
61   Oak RGJ 7450   A SAILOR'S LIFE: SONGS OF THE SEA AND THE SHORE (EP) £20

MIKE SARNE
63   Parlophone DP 558   Just Like Eddie/Slow Twistin' Round The Totem Pole (export issue)..........£50
63   Parlophone GEP 8879   MIKE SARNE HIT PARADE (EP)...£15
62   Parlophone PMC 1187   COME OUTSIDE (LP) £25
(see also Wendy Richards, Le Roys, Billie Davis, Rod McKuen)

SAROFEEN & SMOKE
71   Pye International 7N 25556   Susan Jane/Tomorrow £15
71   Pye Intl. NSPL 28153   DO IT (LP) £40

SAROLTA
68   Island WIP 6035   Open Your Hands/L.O.V.E. £15

SARR BAND
78   Calendar LDAY 115   Double Action/Magic Mandrake (12")......................................£20
78   Calendar LDAY 115   Magic Mandrake/Double Action (12")......................................£25

PETER SARSTEDT
68   Island WIP 6028   I Must Go On/Mary Jane...£30
69   United Artists UP 35021   Frozen Orange Juice/Arethusa Loser £15
(see also Sarstedt Brothers, Brothers Kane, Peter Lincoln)

SARSTEDT BROTHERS
73   Regal Zono. SRZA 8516   WORLDS APART TOGETHER (LP, gatefold sleeve with booklet)............£20
(see also Brothers Kane, Peter Sarstedt, Eden Kane, Wes Sands)

DAN SARTAIN
09   Third Man TMR 011   Bohemian Grove/Atheist Funeral (100 only, luminous vinyl) £60

SAS
85   No Label SAS4   SUAVE AND SOPHISTICATED? (7" EP, fold-out sleeve) £25

SASPARELLA
69   Decca F 12892   Spooky/Come Inside £40

SASSAFRAS
73   Polydor 2383 245   EXPECTING COMPANY (LP)...£15

SASSENACHS
64   Fontana TF 518   That Don't Worry Me/All Over You £30

SATAN
82   Guardian GRC 145   Kiss Of Death/Heads Will Roll (with p/s) £200
82   Guardian GRC 145   Kiss Of Death/Heads Will Roll...£50
83   Roadrunner RR 9894   COURT IN THE ACT (LP, inner)..£40
85   Neat NEAT 1012   COURT IN THE ACT (LP, reissue).....................................£30

SATANIC MALFUNCTIONS
86   Teacore TEACORE 1   WHO WANTS THE WORLD EP (wraparound p/s) £15
88   Teacore TEA 2   HELLBOUND (LP, insert)..£20

MINT VALUE £

90	Teacore TEA 5	DISGRACE TO HUMANITY (LP, insert)	£20

SATANIC RITES
85	Chub CHUBLP 001	WHICH WAY THE WIND BLOWS (LP)	£25
87	Chub CHUBLP 002	NO USE CRYING (LP)	£30

SATAN'S RATS
77	DJM DJS 10819	In My Love For You/Façade (p/s)	£30
77	DJM DJS 10821	Year Of The Rats/Louise (p/s)	£25
78	DJM DJS 10840	You Make Me Sick/Façade (p/s)	£25
89	Overground OVER 01	Year Of The Rats/Louise (p/s, 25 gold vinyl, numbered test pressings)	£15
89	Overground OVER 02	In My Love For You/Facade (p/s, 25 gold vinyl, numbered test pressings)	£15

YOUNG SATCH
70	Black Swan BW 1401	Bonga Bonga Bonga/HI-TALS: Ram Buck (4-prong centre)	£45

(see also Rico & Satch, The Undivided)

GIRL SATCHMO
61	Blue Beat BB 45	Satchmo's Mash Potato/Darling	£20
62	Blue Beat BB 79	Twist Around Town/My New Honey (with Karl Rowe & Bluebeats)	£20
63	Blue Beat BB 156	Don't Be Sad/Brother Joe (with Les Dawson Combo)	£25
64	Blue Beat BB 227	Rhythm Of The New Beat/Blue Beat Chariot	£30
69	Fab FAB 111	Take You For A Ride/I'm Coming Home	£35
69	Trojan TR 676	Taken For A Ride/I'm Coming Home	£20

(see also Pat Satchmo, Sugar & Dandy)

PAT SATCHMO
69	Punch PH 9	Hello Dolly/ERIC DONALSON: Never Get Away	£200
69	Upsetter US 316	Hello Dolly/King Of The Trombone	£120
70	Punch PH 24	Wonderful World/MEDITATORS: Purple Mast	£50
70	Songbird SB 1039	A Handful Of Friends/CRYSTALITES: Handful - Version	£25
72	Attack ATT 8024	What's Going On/LLOYD & CAREY: Tubby's In Full Swing	£50

SATELLITES
84	Brickyard	HERE IS TODAY'S NEWS (LP)	£15

SATIN BELLS
69	Decca F 22937	I Stand Accused (Of Loving You)/Sweet Darlin'	£20

(see also Three Bells)

SATIN STORM
91	Satin Storm SSP 201	Satin Storm 1999/Pleasurezone (inst)/Buzz/Feel The Spirit (12")	£30
91	Satin Storm SSHC 1	See The Light/Call In The Hardcore/Kick Up A Sound Boy/Chill Out (12". As Satin Storm Dancers)	£15
92	Satin Storm DJT DAPSS 1	Let's Get Together/Free Your Mind (12". Artist not credited on labels)	£40
92	Satin Storm ST 01	Sweat/Can't Wait/Can't Take No More/Tekno/Satin Storm/EBGB (12")	£20
92	Satin Storm SSHC 2	What About What I Need /Drop That Bass/House Of My Dreams/Ram It (12" Artist not credited on labels)	£15
92	Satin Storm SSHC 3	Think I'm Going Out Of My Head/Unknown/What Do You Do? (12")	£15

SATISFACTION (1)
71	Decca SKL 5075	SATISFACTION (LP, laminated front sleeve, blue/silver boxed label)	£50

(see also Mike Cotton Sound)

SATISFACTION (2)
79	Live & Love LAP 005	SATISFACTION IN DUB (LP)	£40

SATISFIERS
57	Vogue Coral LVA 9068	THE SATISFIERS (LP)	£20

LIZZARD SATTAI
76	Trojan TRLS 138	LIZZARD (LP)	£30

SATURNALIA
71	Matrix TRIX 1	MAGICAL LOVE (LP, picture disc with 3D labels, with booklet & ticket)	£150
71	Matrix TRIX 1	MAGICAL LOVE (LP, allegedly some copies in laminated sleeve, picture disc with 3D labels, with booklet & ticket)	£500
73	Matrix TRIX 1	MAGICAL LOVE (LP, picture disc, reissue)	£25

(see also Horse)

SAUCERMAN
89	Fierce FRIGHT 035	I Will Be King/Sid James Rules (withdrawn)	£25

(see also Kray Cherubs)

KEN SAUL
70	City Music	Warm Summer Rain/Pictures Framed in My Mind	£80
71	Seashell SSLP 01	SONGS FOR A RAINY DAY (LP, 25 only, hand-made sleeve, hand-written labels)	£750
73	SSLP 002	SEASHELLS (LP, hand-made sleeve, insert, 100 only)	£750

(see also Stone Angel)

SAULT
19	Forever Living Originals FLO0002	5 (LP, 1st pressing, no 'FOREVER LIVING' in run out groove)	£25
20	Forever Living Originals FLO0003	7 (LP)	£20
20	Forever Living Originals FLO0003	7 (LP, repressing, blue vinyl)	£30
20	Forever Living Originals FLO0005	UNTITLED (BLACK IS) (LP, red vinyl 300 only)	£60
20	Forever Living Originals FLO0005	UNTITLED (BLACK IS) (LP, blue vinyl)	£35
20	Forever Living Originals FLO0005	UNTITLED (BLACK IS) (LP, white vinyl 300 only)	£60

20 Forever Living Originals
    FLO0006   UNTITLED (RISE) (LP)...£50
(see also Cleo Sol)

SAUNA YOUTH
12 Faux Disex FAUX 016   DREAMLAND (LP) £18
15 Upset! The Rhythm UTR 017 DISTRACTIONS (LP)..£15

LARRY SAUNDERS
74 London HLU 10469   On The Real Side/Let Me Be The Special One £20
74 London HLU 10469   On The Real Side/Let Me Be The Special One (DJ copy)...............£40

MAHALIA SAUNDERS
71 Moodisc HME 112   Down The Aisle/IAN ROBINSON: Three For One................£18
71 Upsetter US 374   Pieces Of My Heart/UPSETTERS: Version £25
71 Pama Supreme PS 331   Peace Of My Heart/Right On The Tip Of My Tongue.........£20

KEVIN SAUNDERSON
88 Kool Kat DJ 5   Bounce Your Body To The Box (Mike 'Hitman' Wilson Acid Remix)/(Original Detroit
                               Mix)/The Groove That Won't Stop (Detroit Special Mix)/Force Field (12")......................£15

TUPPER SAUSSY
63 London HAU 8127   DISCOVER TUPPER SAUSSY (LP) £15

LES SAUTERELLES
68 Decca F 22824   Heavenly Club/Dream Machine....................................£45

SAVAGE
83 Ebony EBON 12   LOOSE 'N' LETHAL (LP) £25

JOAN SAVAGE
57 Columbia DB 4039   Shake Me, I Rattle/Lula Rock-A-Hula £20

SAVAGE PENCIL
88 Blast First FU 3LP   PRESENTS ANGEL DUST: MUSIC FOR MOVIE BIKERS (LP, picture disc, 1,000 only) £15
(see also Art Attacks, Kray Cherubs)

SAVAGE RESURRECTION
68 Mercury MF 1027   Thing In E/Fox Is Sick £60
68 Mercury SMCL 20123   SAVAGE RESURRECTION (LP)......................................£175

SAVAGE ROSE
68 Polydor 184206   IN THE PLAIN (LP, red label).......................................£40
69 Polydor 184316   TRAVELLIN' (LP, red label)..£30
72 RCA Victor SF 8250   REFUGEE (LP, laminated front sleeve, orange label)........£30
71 RCA Victor SF 8169   YOUR DAILY GIFT (LP, laminated front sleeve, orange label) £30

SAVAGES
63 Decca DFE 8546   EVERYBODY SURF! WITH THE SURFIN' SAVAGES (EP) £200
(see also Soul Sounds, Screaming Lord Sutch, Circles, Tony Dangerfield & Thrills)

JULIAN JAY SAVARIN
73 Lyntone LYN 3426   I Am You/Kizeesh (Corgi Books sampler).......................£50
73 Birth RAB 2   WAITERS ON THE DANCE (LP, textured sleeve with insert) £500
73 Birth RAB 2   WAITERS ON THE DANCE (LP, textured sleeve without insert)...............£300
87 Five Hours Back TOCK 002   WAITERS ON THE DANCE (LP, reissue).........................£40
(see also Julian's Treatment)

RONNIE SAVOY
61 MGM MGM 1122   And The Heavens Cried/Big Chain £15

SAVOY BROWN (BLUES BAND)
66 Purdah 45-3503   I Tried/Can't Quit You Baby (as Savoy Brown's Blues Band) £300
67 Decca F 12702   Taste And Try, Before You Buy/Someday People (as Savoy Brown Blues Band)...............£20
69 Decca F 12843   Train To Nowhere/Tolling Bells £15
69 Decca F 12978   I'm Tired/Stay With Me Baby....................................£25
70 Decca F 13019   A Hard Way To Go/Waiting In The Bamboo Grove............£15
67 Decca LK 4883   SHAKE DOWN (LP, mono, unboxed logo label) £200
67 Decca SKL 4883   SHAKE DOWN (LP, stereo, unboxed logo label) £150
68 Decca LK 4935   GETTING TO THE POINT (LP, mono, unboxed logo label) £150
68 Decca SKL 4935   GETTING TO THE POINT (LP, stereo, unboxed logo label)...........£100
69 Decca SKL 4935   GETTING TO THE POINT (LP, second pressing, stereo, boxed logo) £25
69 Decca LK 4994   BLUE MATTER (LP, mono, unboxed logo label) £150
69 Decca SKL 4994   BLUE MATTER (LP, stereo, unboxed logo label)............£75
69 Decca LK 5013   A STEP FURTHER (LP, mono, unboxed logo label)..........£150
69 Decca SKL 5013   A STEP FURTHER (LP, stereo, unboxed logo label) £70
70 Decca LK 5043   RAW SIENNA (LP, mono, laminated gatefold sleeve, boxed logo label)..........£150
70 Decca SKL 5043   RAW SIENNA (LP, stereo, laminated gatefold sleeve, boxed logo label) £75
70 Decca SKL 5066   LOOKING IN (LP, 1st pressing, dull laminated gatefold sleeve).........£125
70 Decca SKL 5066   LOOKING IN (LP, 2nd pressing, glossy laminated gatefold sleeve)...........£50
71 Decca TXS 104   STREET CORNER TALKING (LP, gatefold sleeve)............£60
72 Decca TXS 107   HELLBOUND TRAIN (LP, gatefold sleeve) £35
73 Decca SKL 5152   LION'S SHARE (LP)..£15
73 Decca TXS 112   JACK THE TOAD (LP)..£18
(see also Warren Philips & The Rockets, Chris Youlden, Stone's Masonry, Jackie Lynton, Foghat)

SAVWINKLE AND TURNERHOPPER
70 Pye 7N 17913   Your Mother Thinks I'm A Hoodlum/Dirtyin' My Thing £20

'ACE' DINNING SAX
59 Top Rank JAR 184   Mulholland Drive/My Love £15

SAX MANIAX
82 Penthouse PENT 1201   OVERSAXED (LP) £15

AL SAXON
62 Piccadilly 7N 35036   Evil Eye/What More Can I Say £25
72 Phoenix NIX 125   Beautiful/Count To Ten £15
(see also Lana Sisters)

SKY 'SUNLIGHT' SAXON
87 Fierce FRIGHT 009   Dog=God (p/s, with badge, piece of shirt, sugar 'skycubes' & inserts) £20
84 Psycho PSYCHO 29   STARRY EYED (LP, clear vinyl) £20
(see also Seeds)

SAXON (1)
63 Ace Of Clubs ACL 1173   MEET THE SAXONS (LP) £80

SAXON (2)
79 Carrere CAL 110   SAXON (LP) £15
80 Carrere CAL 115   WHEELS OF STEEL (LP) £15
80 Carrere CAL 120   STRONG ARM OF THE LAW (LP) £15
82 Carrere CAL 137   THE EAGLE HAS LANDED (LP) £15
82 Carrere CAL 137   THE EAGLE HAS LANDED (LP, picture disc) £15
83 Carrere CAL 147   THE POWER AND THE GLORY (LP, picture disc) ...£15
84 Carrere CAL 200   CRUSADER (LP, gatefold) £15
84 Carrere CALP 200   CRUSADER (LP, picture disc) £18
85 Parlophone SAXONP 2   INNOCENCE IS NO EXCUSE (LP, picture disc) ...£20
87 EMI EMS 1163   DENIM AND LEATHER (LP, blue vinyl reissue) ...£18
93 Warhammer WARLP 10   FOREVER FREE (LP) £80

SAXONS
65 Decca F 12179   Saxon War Cry/Click-Ete-Clack £60
(see also Tornados)

ALEXEI SAYLE
84 Island ISP 162   'Ullo John! Gotta New Motor? (Part I)/(Part II) (7" shaped picture disc) ...£15
82 Springtime CAK 1   CAK! (LP) £15
(see also Alexei's Midnight Runners)

JOHNNY SAYLES
66 Liberty LIB 12042   Deep Down In Your Heart/Anything For You ...£40

SAY SHE SHE
23 Karma Chief KCR 12024   SILVER (2LP, transparent green vinyl, Rough Trade exclusive) ...£40
23 Karma Chief KCR-12021   PRISM (LP, fire red vinyl, Rough Trade exclusive) ...£20

SCABS
79 Clubland Records SJP 799 Amory Building/Leave Me Alone/Don't Just Sit There/U.R.E. (blue/black or red/black fold out 'envelope' p/s, 2 inserts) ...£40

SCAFFOLD
68 Parlophone PMC/PCS 7051 SCAFFOLD ... - LIVE AT QUEEN ELIZABETH HALL (LP, black/yellow label with "Sold in U.K..." text) ...£40
69 Parlophone PMC/PCS 7077 L THE P (LP, black/yellow label with "Sold in U.K..." text) ...£30
73 Island ILPS 9234   FRESH LIVER (LP, gatefold sleeve, pink rim palm tree label) ...£20
(see also McGough-McGear, Roger McGough, Mike McGear, Liverpool Scene, Grimms, John Gorman)

BOZ SCAGGS
69 Atlantic 588 205   BOZ SCAGGS (LP) £30
(see also Steve Miller Band, Steve York's Camelo Pardalis)

JOHNNY SCAR
85 Solomonic SM12 025   United Africa/Dub It In Africa (12") £200

SCARAB
80 Inferno HEADBANGER 1   Rock Night/Wicked Woman £30
84 Pharaoh PR-001   Poltergeist/Hell On Wheels (p/s) £50
03 Phoenix NWOBHM 7013   Rock Night/Wicked Woman (reissue, p/s, red vinyl 250 only, numbered) ...£15

SCARECROW
78 Spilt Milk SMFM 11278   SCARECROW (LP, numbered foldout sleeve with insert; beware of watermarked unnumbered copies) ...£150

SCARED OF THE DARK
86 Cottage Industry CIR 003 Give Me That Feeling/Summer Soul £20

SCARFACE (1)
75 DJM DJS 616   Dance To The Band/Tootsie Roll Baby £25

SCARFACE (2)
76 Concrete Jungle CJ 754 Blast Off/Blast Off 2 ....£20

SCARLET ALIVE
82 Jive Alive JA001   THE TERMINAL JIVE AND SCARLET ALIVE EP (2 tracks on one side, p/s, insert) ...£15
82 S.R.R. SRR011   On Earth And In Heaven/Always (p/s) £15

SCARLET TRAIN
87 Nightshift NISHI 202   FIMBRIA (Mini-LP) £20

SCARS
80 Pre PRE 005   Love Song/psychomodo (p/s) £15
81 Pre PREX 5   AUTHOR! AUTHOR! (LP) £15

SCATTEROCK
80 Rite Sound 010   Wonder Woman/Time £40

SCAVENGERZ DAUGHTER
91 SRT 91S2995   Eyes Of A Dead Man/Victim (no p/s) £15

SCENE (1)
80 Inferno BEAT 2   I've Had Enough/Show 'Em Now (p/s)... £20

SCENE (2)
80 Hole In The Wall HS 1   Hey Girl/Reach The Top (p/s) £50

SCENE (3)
85 Diamond DIA 007   Good Lovin'/2 Plus 2 (with p/s) £15
(see also Diplomats)

SCEPTRES
69 Spark SRL 1006   What's The Matter With Juliet/Something's Coming Along £30

SCHADEL
68 Pye 7N 17528   With The Sun In My Eyes/Goodbye Thimble Mill Lane £30
70 United Artists UAS 29114   SCHADEL NO.1 (LP, gatefold) £20

SCHEER
93 Son BUACD 293   Wish You Were Dead/Green Room Sex Kitten/Don't Know Why (p/s) £20
96 4AD CAD 6006   INFLICTION (LP) £15

SCHEME
82 No Label SS001   SCHEME SONGS (EP, 500 only, 2 inserts) £30
86 Scheme LP1   BLACK & WHITES (LP) £25

HANK SCHIFNER
69 Liberty LBF15244   Long John/How Or When £15

LALO SCHIFRIN
68 Dot DOT 103   Mission: Impossible/Jim On The Move £25
74 20th Century BTC 2150   Ape Shuffle (Theme From 'Planet Of The Apes')/Escape From Tomorrow £25
68 Dot (S)LPD 503   'MISSION: IMPOSSIBLE' - MUSIC FROM THE TV SERIES (LP, TV soundtrack) £40
69 Paramount SPFL 252   MORE 'MISSION: IMPOSSIBLE' (LP, TV soundtrack) £40

SCHIZO FUN ADDICT
08 Fruits De Mer CRUSTACIAN 01   Theme One/Ogden's Nut Gone Flake (p/s, coloured vinyl, 300 only)....... £40

SCHLEIMER K
81 Omega OMR 001   SCHLEIMER K (LP) £20
82 Glass GLASS 028   FUGUTIVE KIND (12" EP, p/s)... £18
83 Lone WOlf LW 101   WOUNDED WOOD (LP) £40

TOBIAS SCHMIDT
96 Mosquito MSQ 06   THE FINGERPRINT EP (12", p/s)... £15

ZAPPATTA SCHMIDT
70 President PT 318   You Got The Love/Someone In The Crowd £40
70 Torpedo TOR 28   Let's Do It Together/Hey Man. Why £25
71 President PTLS 1041   IT'S GONNA GET YOU (LP) £100
(see also Equals, Eddy Grant)

OLIVER LINDSEY SCHMITT
72 Private pressing   GRAFFENSTADDEN (LP) £30

EBERHARD SCHOENER
79 Harvest SHSM 2030   VIDEO-FLASHBACK (LP) £20
(see also Police)

JOHN SCHOFIELD
84 Arista/Nimbus AN 3022   BAR TALK (LP, Nimbus Supercut, mail order only from Practical Hi-Fi magazine).............. £30

SCHOLARS
64 Stagesound SDE 29370/1   THE SCHOLARS (EP, no p/s).. £15

SCHOOL TIES
81 School Ties SCF 01   No Future/Screw You £45
82 Quest S/82/Cus 1591   House Of The Rising Sun/Insanity (no p/s) £40

SCHOOLBOYS
69 Junior JR 113   Do It Now/Blame It On The Children £15

SCHOOL BOYS
63 Blue Beat BB 162   Little Boy Blue/PRINCE BUSTER: Money.............................. £40
63 Blue Beat BB 174   Little Dilly/The Joker (B-side actually by Prince Buster's Allstars)............. £40
64 Port-O-Jam PJ 4000   Dream Lover/I Want To Know £40
(see also Bill Gentles)

SCHOOLERS
69 Doctor Bird DB 1170   Ugly Man (actually by Scorchers)/Whip Cracker (actually by Vincent Gordon) £40

SCHOOLGIRL BITCH
78 Garage!/Aerco AERS 102   Abusing The Rules/Thinking For Yourself (spray-painted p/s)......................£200
78 Garage!/Aerco AERS 102   Abusing The Rules/Thinking For Yourself ('gasmask' p/s) £150
78 Garage!/Aerco AERS 102   Abusing The Rules/Thinking For Yourself ('queen' p/s)................£100
78 Garage!/Aerco AERS 102   Abusing The Rules/Thinking For Yourself (no p/s).....................£40

SCHOOL GIRLS
63 Blue Beat BB 168   Love Another Love/Little Keithie £20
63 Blue Beat BB 185   Live Up To Justice/Keith My Darling £20
64 Blue Beat BB 214   Sing And Shout/Last Time £20
64 Blue Beat BB 263   Never Let You Go/BUSTER'S ALL STARS: Supercharge £80

SCHOOL MEALS
78	Edible EAT 001	Headmaster (with insert, re-labelled Defendents)	£25

SCHOOL OF CULTURE
91	White CS12 01	Detonate To Activate/Come On 33	£30

JOHN SCHROEDER ORCHESTRA
65	Piccadilly 7N 35240	The Fugitive Theme/Don't Break The Heart Of Kimble (in p/s)	£15
65	Piccadilly 7N 35271	Agent 00 Soul/Night Rider	£30
66	Piccadilly 7N 35285	Hungry For Love/Soul Destroyer	£30
67	Piccadilly 7N 35362	Soul For Sale/Loving You Girl	£30
71	Pye 7N 45108	One Way Glass/The Bird Has Flown	£15
66	Piccadilly N(S)PL 38025	JOHN SCHROEDER'S WORKING IN THE SOULMINE (LP)	£50
67	Piccadilly N(S)PL 38036	THE DOLLY CATCHER! (LP)	£40
68	Marble Arch MAL 839	WORKING IN THE SOULMINE (LP, reissue)	£20
71	Pye NSPL 18362	WITCHI-TAI-TO (LP, textured gatefold sleeve)	£20
72	Polydor 2460 149	TV VIBRATIONS (LP)	£15
71	Polydor 2460 134	DYLAN VIBRATIONS (LP)	£15
71	Polydor 2460 135	PIANO VIBRATIONS (LP, with Rick Wakeman)	£40
71	Marble Arch MAL 1381	YOU'VE MADE ME SO VERY HAPPY (LP)	£30

IVY SCHULMAN & BOWTIES
57	London HLN 8372	Rock, Pretty Baby/BOWTIES: Ever Since I Can Remember	£50
57	London HLN 8372	Rock, Pretty Baby/BOWTIES: Ever Since I Can Remember (78)	£15

KLAUS SCHULZE
74	Caroline CA 2003	BLACK DANCE (LP, gatefold, black/white/red 'twin' label)	£20
75	Caroline CA 2006	TIMEWIND (LP, gatefold)	£20
76	Virgin V2064	MOONDAWN (LP, unissued)	£0
77	Island ISPS 9461	MIRAGE (LP)	£20
(see also Tangerine Dream) (Voices Of)			

SCHUNGE
72	Regal Zono. SLRZ 1033	BALLAD OF A SIMPLE LOVE (LP, unlaminated front sleeve)	£30
72	Regal Zono. SLRZ 1033	BALLAD OF A SIMPLE LOVE (LP, laminated front sleeve)	£25

SCHWARTZENEGGER
94	Rugger Bugger SEEP 009	THE WAY THINGS ARE AND OTHER STORIES (LP)	£20

SCIENCE POPTION
67	Columbia DB 8106	You've Got Me High/Back In Town	£100

SCIENTIST
80	JB JBLP 004	INTRODUCING (LP)	£75
80	Greensleeves GREL 13	HEAVYWEIGHT DUB CHAMPION (LP)	£60
81	Starlight SLD 901	DUB LANDING (LP)	£45
81	Greensleeves GREL 19	MEETS THE SPACE INVADERS (LP)	£40
81	Kingdom KVL 9001	IN THE KINGDOM OF DUB (LP)	£30
81	Greensleeves GREL 25	RIDS THE WORLD OF THE EVIL CURSE OF THE VAMPIRE (LP)	£50
82	Greensleeves GREL 37	WINS THE WORLD CUP (LP)	£40
82	Selena SLP 001	SCIENTIST MEETS THE ROOTS RADICS (LP)	£50
82	Greensleeves GREL 46	ENCOUNTERS PAC MAN (LP)	£50
82	Kingdom KVL 9011	HIGH PRIEST OF DUB (LP)	£30
86	Kingdom KVC 6005	CRUCIAL CUTS VOLUME 2 (LP)	£25
89	Tamoki Wambesi TWP 1022	INTERNATIONAL HEROES DUB (LP, with The Forces Of Music)	£25
96	Blood & Fire BAFLP 007	DUB IN THE (ROOTS TRADITION) (LP)	£15
08	Auralux LUXXLP 021	WORLD AT WAR (LP, reissue)	£18

SCIENTIST & PRINCE JAMMY
82	Trojan TRLS 210	SCIENTIST & PRINCE JAMMY STRIKE BACK (LP)	£40
97	Trojan TRLS 210	SCIENTIST & PRINCE JAMMY STRIKE BACK (LP, reissue)	£15

SCIENTIST VERSUS PRINCE JAMMY
80	Greensleeves GRED 10	THE BIG SHOWDOWN 1980 (LP)	£30
82	Starlight SLDLP 903	DUB LANDING VOLUME 2 (LP)	£25

SCIENTIST V THE PROFESSOR
83	Kingdom KVL 9015	DUB DUEL AT KING TUBBY'S (LP)	£35

SCIENTISTS (JAMAICA)
69	Amalgamated AMG 848	Professor In Action/SUPERSONICS: Reflections Of Don D	£60

SCIENTISTS
85	Karbon KAR 007	You Only Live Twice/If It's The Last Thing I Do (p/s)	£25
85	Karbon KAR 101 L	YOU GET WHAT YOU DESERVE (LP)	£20
86	Karbon KAR 103 L	WEIRD LOVE (LP)	£20
87	Karbon KAR 105 L	THE HUMAN JUKEBOX (LP)	£20

SCONEHEADS
81	Linden Sound LS 01	GO BUCKSKIN (EP, 700 pressed)	£30

SCOOP
80	Sharp POINT 1	You Can Do It/Disco/My Friend Tony/Anonymity (p/s)	£75

SCORCHED EARTH (1)
74	Youngblood YB1503	On The Run/Can You Feel It	£15

SCORCHED EARTH (2)
85	Carrere CAR 342	Tomorrow Never Comes/Questions (promo only)	£35
85	Carrere CART 342	Tomorrow Never Comes/Questions/So Long/Where Do We Go From Here (12", initial	£70

black sleeve)..

85	Carrere CART 342	Tomorrow Never Comes/Questions/So Long/Where Do We Go From Here (12", later red sleeve with insert)	£35

ERROL SCORCHER

78	Ballistic UAS 30198	RASTAFIRE (LP, with the Revolutionaries)	£25

SCORCHERS

69	Camel CA 17	Hold On Tight/THE ROYALS: 100 Lbs Of Clay	£80
69	Duke DU 26	Hear Ya/VIBRATORS: Live Life	£70

(see also Neville Hinds)

SCORE (1)

66	Decca F 12527	Please Please Me/Beg Me	£200

SCORN

92	Earache MOSH 54	VAE SOLIS (2-LP)	£20
95	Earache SCORN 001	ELLIPSIS (5 x 12" box set)	£18

SCORPIONS (GERMANY)

75	RCA RS 1039	IN TRANCE (LP, 'breast' sleeve)	£20
76	RCA RS 1023	FLY TO THE RAINBOW (LP)	£20
76	RCA PPL 1-4225	VIRGIN KILLER (LP, please note that 'banned; cover is German pressing not U.K.)	£15
79	Harvest LP SHSP 4097	LOVEDRIVE (LP)	£20
80	Harvest SHSP 4113	ANIMAL MAGNETISM (LP, inner sleeve)	£15
82	H.M. Worldwide HMILP 2	LONESOME CROW (LP, "castle" cover, clear vinyl)	£20
82	H.M. Worldwide HMILP 2	LONESOME CROW (LP, "castle" cover, black vinyl)	£15
82	H.M. Worldwide HMIPD 2	LONESOME CROW (LP, picture disc, re-issue)	£15
82	Harvest SHVL 823	BLACKOUT (LP, black or green print on label, inner sleeve)	£15
88	Harvest SHSPP 4125	SAVAGE AMUSEMENT (LP, picture disc, with lyric sheet)	£15
93	Mercury 518 280-1	FACE THE HEAT (LP)	£25

(see also Group, UFO)

SCORPIONS (U.K.)

61	Parlophone R 4740	(Ghost) Riders In The Sky/Torquay	£20
61	Parlophone R 4768	Rockin' At The Phil/Scorpio	£20

COLIN SCOT

71	United Artists UAG 29154	COLIN SCOT WITH FRIENDS (LP, laminated gatefold, friends include Peter Hammill & Peter Gabriel)	£30

(see also Peter Hammill, Peter Gabriel)

JOCK SCOT

80	Stiff MAX 1	A Souvenir To Commemorate The Wedding Of Dave (Robinson) And Rosemary. Featuring the dulcet tones Of Jock Scot (Promo Only)	£150

WINSTON SCOTLAND

72	Punch PH 100	Butter Cup/RONALD WILSON: I Care	£15

(see also Bunny Flip, Big Youth, Bongo Les, Dennis Alcapone)

SCOTS OF ST. JAMES

66	Go AJ 111404	Gypsy/Tic Toc	£200
67	Spot JW 1	Timothy/Eiderdown Clown	£350

(see also Hopscotch, Forever More, Five Day Rain)

ANITA SCOTT

61	Columbia DB 4623	A Million And One Tears/Come On And Dance With Me	£15

BILLY SCOTT

58	London HLU 8565	You're The Greatest/That's Why I Was Born	£20

BOBBY SCOTT (1)

56	London HL 8254	Chain Gang/Shadrack	£40
55	London Jazz LZ-N 14001	BOBBY SCOTT TRIO (10" LP)	£15

BRUCE SCOTT

65	Mercury MF 857	I Made An Angel Cry/Don't Say Goodbye To Me	£25

BUNNY SCOTT

75	2nd Tracs SK3	Come On Party/Azul Party	£15
75	Upsetter UP 100	I Am I Said/Let Love Us Now (as Bunny Ruggs)	£45
82	Seven Leaves SLD 01	What's The Use/I Never Had It So Good (12")	£22
75	KLIK KLP 9004	TO LOVE SOMEBODY (LP)	£60

(see also Bunny Clarke)

FREDDIE SCOTT

63	Colpix PX 692	Hey Girl/The Slide	£35
63	Colpix PX 709	I Got A Woman/Brand New World	£35
67	London HLZ 10103	Are You Lonely For Me/Where Were You	£15
67	London HLZ 10123	Cry To Me/No One Could Ever Love You	£15
71	Joy JOYS 215	ARE YOU LONELY FOR ME (LP)	£25

GARRETT SCOTT

70	Mercury 6052 024	I'm Gonna Give You All My Love/Now That I Love You	£15

HAZEL SCOTT

53	Capitol LC 6607	LATE SHOW (10" LP)	£20

JACK SCOTT (& CHANTONES)

58	London HLU 8626	My True Love/Leroy (78)	£15
58	London HLL 8765	With Your Love/Geraldine (as Jack Scott with Chantones)	£15
58	London HLL 8765	With Your Love/Geraldine (as Jack Scott with Chantones) (78)	£15
59	London HLL 8804	Goodbye Baby/Save My Soul (as Jack Scott with Chantones)	£15

MINT VALUE £

59	London HLL 8804	Goodbye Baby/Save My Soul (as Jack Scott with Chantones) (78)	£15
59	London HL 7069	Goodbye Baby/Save My Soul (export issue)	£20
59	London HLL 8851	I Never Felt Like This/Bella	£20
59	London HLL 8851	I Never Felt Like This/Bella (78)	£15
59	London HLL 8912	The Way I Walk/Midgie (triangular or round centre)	£25
59	London HLL 8912	The Way I Walk/Midgie (triangular or round centre) (78)	£15
59	London HLL 8970	There Comes A Time/Baby Marie (triangular or round centre)	£25
59	London HLL 8970	There Comes A Time/Baby Marie (78)	£15
59	London RE-I 1205	MY TRUE LOVE (EP, initial triangular centre)	£50
59	London RE-I 1205	MY TRUE LOVE (EP, later round centre)	£25
61	Top Rank JKP 3002	WHAT IN THE WORLD'S COME OVER YOU (EP)	£25
61	Top Rank JKP 3011	I REMEMBER HANK WILLIAMS (EP)	£25
58	London HA-L 2156	JACK SCOTT (LP)	£70
60	Top Rank BUY 034	I REMEMBER HANK WILLIAMS (LP)	£40
60	Top Rank 25-024	WHAT IN THE WORLD'S COME OVER YOU (LP)	£35
61	Top Rank 35-109	THE SPIRIT MOVES ME (LP)	£30
64	Capitol T 2035	BURNING BRIDGES (LP, mono)	£25
64	Capitol ST 2035	BURNING BRIDGES (LP, stereo)	£30

JANET SCOTT & JACKIE RAE

60	Fontana TFL 5102	WE LOVE LIFE! (LP, also stereo STFL 533)	£15

JILL SCOTT

00	Hidden Beach EPC 498625 1	WHO IS JILL SCOTT? - WORDS AND SOUNDS VOL. 1 (2-LP)	£40
04	Hidden Beach EPC 517652 1	BEAUTIFULLY HUMAN - WORDS AND SOUND VOL. 2 (2-LP)	£35

JIMMY SCOTT

68	Revolution REV 002	Ob-La-Di, Ob-La-Da/Story Part 2 - Allulo & Doh	£40
70	Revolution Soul REVS 505	Doh (Ob-La-Di-Ob-Lh-Da Story Part 2/Allulo (Part 1) Note: "lh" is how it is on the label	£40

JOHN SCOTT

67	Polydor 56184	Rocket To The Moon Theme/The Long Duel Theme	£15
66	Columbia SX 6026	LONDON SWINGS (LP)	£15
67	Columbia S(C)X 6149	COMMUNICATION (LP)	£30

JOHNNY SCOTT

67	Columbia S(C)X 6149	COMMUNICATION (LP)	£60
70	Fontana 6383 002	PURCELL VARIATIONS FOR FIVE (LP)	£25
73	JSD JSD 100	JOHN SCOTT DEMONSTRATION RECORD (LP, beware, many warped)	£80

JUDI SCOTT

68	Page One POF 066	Billy Sunshine/Happy Song	£25

LINDA SCOTT (1)

62	Pye International 7N 25146	Never In A Million Years/Through The Summer	£15
63	London HLR 9802	Let's Fall In Love/I Know It, You Know It	£20
61	Columbia 33SX 1386	STARLIGHT, STARBRIGHT (LP)	£60

LINDA SCOTT (2)

69	CBS 4528	The Composer/You Made A Fool Out Of Me (DJ copy)	£25
69	CBS 4528	The Composer/You Made A Fool Out Of Me	£15

MCBEAN SCOTT & CHAMPIONS

70	Jackpot JP 744	Top Of The World/LARRY LAWRENCE & CHAMPIONS: Everybody Reggae	£15

MIKE SCOTT (2)

95	Chrysalis CHR 6108	BRING 'EM ALL IN (LP, gatefold with inner)	£60

(see also Waterboys)

NICKY SCOTT

67	Immediate IM 044	Big City/Everything's Gonna Be Alright	£60
67	Immediate IM 045	Backstreet Girl/Chain Reaction	£50

PEGGY SCOTT & JO JO BENSON

69	Polydor 583 731	SOULSHAKE (LP)	£25
70	Polydor 583 756	LOVER'S HEAVEN (LP)	£25

ROBIN SCOTT

69	Head HDS 4003	The Sailor/Sound Of The Rain	£40
69	Head HDLS 6003	WOMAN FROM THE WARM GRASS (LP, textured sleeve with insert, yellow/black label)	£400
07	Sunbeam SBBLP 5009	WOMAN FROM THE WARM GRASS (LP, reissue)	£15

(see also Mighty Baby, M)

RONNIE SCOTT

57	Tempo A 153	I'll Take Romance/Speak Low (as Ronnie Scott New Quintet)	£35
55	Esquire EP 31	RONNIE SCOTT ORCHESTRA (EP)	£20
55	Esquire EP 51	RONNIE SCOTT QUARTET (EP)	£25
55	Esquire EP 61	RONNIE SCOTT ORCHESTRA (EP)	£20
55	Esquire EP 65	RONNIE SCOTT QUINTET (EP)	£25
56	Esquire EP 81	RONNIE SCOTT ORCHESTRA (EP)	£25
56	Esquire EP 85	RONNIE SCOTT ORCHESTRA (EP)	£30
56	Esquire EP 95	RONNIE SCOTT ORCHESTRA (EP)	£25
56	Tempo EXA 45	RONNIE SCOTT BLOWS WITH THE DIZZY REECE QUARTET (EP)	£100
52	Esquire 20-006	RONNIE SCOTT QUINTET (10" LP)	£100
54	Esquire 32-001	THE RONNIE SCOTT JAZZ CLUB VOLUME 1 (LP)	£50
54	Esquire 32-002	THE RONNIE SCOTT JAZZ CLUB VOLUME 2 (LP)	£50
54	Esquire 32-003	THE RONNIE SCOTT JAZZ CLUB VOLUME 3 (LP)	£50
54	Esquire 32-006	THE RONNIE SCOTT JAZZ CLUB VOLUME 4 (LP)	£50

MINT VALUE £

56	Decca LF 1261	AT THE ROYAL FESTIVAL HALL (10" LP)	£50
57	Philips BBL 7153	PRESENTING THE RONNIE SCOTT SEXTET (LP)	£100
66	Fontana TL 5332	THE NIGHT IS SCOTT AND YOU'RE SO SWINGABLE (LP)	£45
69	CBS Realm Jazz 523661	LIVE AT RONNIE SCOTT'S (LP)	£30
74	RCA Victor LPL1	SCOTT AT RONNIE'S (LP)	£20
77	Pye NSPL 18542	SERIOUS GOLD (LP)	£15

(see also Jazz Couriers, Tubby Hayes, Dizzy Reece)

SHARON SCOTT
| 96 | Kent 6T 12 | (Putting My Heart) Under Lock And Key/DEAN COURTNEY: Today Is My Day | £35 |

SHIRLEY SCOTT
62	Esquire 32-186	HIP TWIST (LP)	£25
66	Transatlantic PR 7205	HIP SOUL (LP)	£18
67	Transatlantic PR 7338	BLUE FLAMES (LP, with Stanley Turrentine)	£20
69	Atlantic 588 175	SOUL SONG (LP)	£15
71	Chess 6310 109	MYSTICAL LADY (LP)	£15

SIMON SCOTT (& LE ROYS)
64	Parlophone R 5164	Move It Baby/What Kind Of Woman (with Le Roys)	£15
65	Parlophone R 5298	Tell Him I'm Not Home (as Simon Scott & All Nite Workers)/Heart Cry	£18
69	Polydor 56355	Brave New World/I'm The Universe	£100

(see also Le Roys)

RAMBLIN' TOMMY SCOTT
| 54 | Parlophone CMSP 15 | Ain't Love Grand/What Do You Know - I Love Her (export issue) | £20 |

TONY SCOTT
| 69 | Escort ES 805 | What Am I To Do/Bring Back That Smile | £60 |

GIL SCOTT-HERON (& BRIAN JACKSON)
73	Philips 6073 705	Lady Day And John Coltrane/When You Are Who You Are (with Pretty Purdie & The Playboys)	£20
78	Arista ARIST 169	The Bottle (live)/Hello Sunday, Hello Road (12")	£20
73	Philips 6369 415	PIECES OF A MAN (LP)	£100
74	RCA SF 8428	THE REVOLUTION WILL NOT BE TELEVISED (LP)	£25
75	Arista ARTY 106	FIRST MINUTES OF A NEW DAY (LP)	£15
76	Arista DARTY 1	IT'S YOUR WORLD (LP, with Brian Jackson)	£30

SCOTTY (DAVID SCOTT)
70	Songbird SB 1044	Sesame Street/CRYSTALITES: Version	£30
71	Songbird SB 1049	Riddle I This/Musical Chariot	£25
71	Songbird SB 1056	Penny For Your Song/CRYSTALITES: Version	£15
72	Songbird SB 1080	Clean Race/CRYSTALITES: Version Train	£30
73	Count Shelley CS 036	Salvation Train/KEN PARKER: Message To Mary	£20
71	Trojan TRL 33	SCHOOL DAYS (LP)	£60
88	Trojan TRLS 264	UNBELIEVABLE SOUNDS (LP)	£20

(see also Lloyd Charmers, Joe White, Federals)

SCRAPING FOETUS OFF THE WHEEL
| 81 | Womb WOMB-OYBL-2 | HOLE (LP, gatefold sleeve with lyrics, also listed as FDL 3) | £15 |

(see also Foetus,You've Got Foetus On Your Breath, Philip & His Foetus Vibrations, Foetus Inc, Foetus Uber Frisco)

SCRAPYARD
| 58 | Abbey APR 168 | RECIPRICAL RHUMBAS (LP, private press, 250 copies, with insert) | £200 |

SCRATCH ACID
| 86 | Fundamental HOLY 1 | SCRATCH ACID (Mini-LP) | £20 |
| 86 | Fundamental SAVE 12 | JUST KEEP EATING (LP) | £15 |

(see also Jesus Lizard)

SCRATCH PERVERTS
| 03 | Ultimate Dilemma UDR LP 021 | BADMEANINGOOD VOL 4 (2-LP, Banksy artwork) | £400 |

SCREAMING DEAD
82	Skull DEAD 1	Valley Of The Dead/Schoolgirl Junkie (p/s)	£15
83	Skull DEAD 2	Paint It Black/Warriors (p/s)	£18
83	No Future OI 25	NIGHT CREATURES EP (12")	£20

DELTON SCREECHIE
80	Kim KIM 18	My Black Girl/Diamond & Pearl/B DONALDSON & U BLACK : You Are Mine (12")	£15
80	Moa Anbessa MA004	She Is My Woman/Woman Version (12")	£15
81	Moa Anbessa Intl MALP 001	LIVING IN THE GHETTO (LP)	£30
81	Moa Anbessa Intl MALP 002	SUFFERING IN THE GHETTO (LP)	£50

SCREECHING WEASEL
| 88 | Wet Spots WETLP 005 | BOOGADA BOOGADA BOOGADA (LP) | £25 |
| 88 | What Goes On GOES ON 18 | SCREECHING WEASEL (LP, with insert) | £20 |

SCREEMER
| 76 | Bell Bell 1483 | Interplanetary Twist/Billy | £15 |

SCREEN
| 95 | Muzic W'out Control MWC 021 | I Wait For You (Sweep Sweep Mix)/I Wait For You (Radio Sweep Mix)/I Wait For You (Pink Noise Mix)/I Wait For You (T Rex Mix) (12', p/s) | £60 |

SCREEN GEMZ
| 79 | Inflatable IN 001 | I Just Can't Stand Cars/Teenage Teenage | £200 |

SCRITTI POLITTI
| 78 | St. Pancras SCRIT 1 | Skank Bloc Bologna/Is And Ought Of The Western World/28.8.78 (photocopied | £20 |

stapled foldout p/s, hand-stamped white labels) ....

79	Rough Trade RT 034/St Pancras SCRIT 2	**WORK IN PROGRESS : 2ND PEEL SESSION** (7" EP p/s)................................	**£18**
06	Rough Trade RTRADLP 270	**WHITE BREAD BLACK BEER** (LP)	**£35**

SCROTUM POLES

79	Scrotum Poles ERECT 1	**Revelation: Why Don't You Come Out Tonight?/Night Train/Pick The Cat's Eyes Out/ Helicopter Honeymoon/Radio Tay** (handwritten labels, 2 p/s designs, with insert)	**£120**
79	Scrotum Poles ERECT 1	**Revelation: Why Don't You Come Out Tonight?/Night Train/Pick The Cat's Eyes Out/ Helicopter Honeymoon/Radio Tay** (handwritten labels, 2 p/s designs, without insert) ..	**£100**

SCRUBS

86	Anubis ANU 003	**Battle** (p/s)	**£15**

SCRUGG

68	Pye 7N 17451	**I Wish I Was Five/Everyone Can See**	**£90**
68	Pye 7N 17551	**Lavender Popcorn/Sandwichboard Man**	**£60**
69	Pye 7N 17656	**Will The Real Geraldine Please Stand Up/Only George**	**£90**

(see also Floribunda Rose, John T. Kongos)

MR. JOHNNY SEA

60s	Fontana FJL 315	**EVERYBODY'S FAVOURITE** (LP)	**£15**

SEA & CAKE

94	Rough Trade THRILL 021	**SEA & CAKE** (LP)	**£20**
97	Thrill Jockey THRILL LP 039UK	**THE FAWN** (LP, gatefold)	**£18**

(see also Tortoise)

SEA-DERS

67	Decca F 22576	**Thanks A Lot/Undecidedly**	**£80**
67	Decca DFE-R 8674	**THE SEA-DERS** (EP, export issue)	**£250**

(see also Cedars)

SEAHORSES

97	Geffen GEF 25134	**DO IT YOURSELF** (LP, printed inner)	**£150**
22	Music On Vinyl/Geffen MOVLP3040	**DO IT YOURSELF** (LP, reissue, Music On Vinyl sleeve/sticker, printed inner)	**£25**

(see also Stone Roses)

PHIL SEAMEN

68	Verve (S)VLP 9220	**PHIL SEAMEN NOW ... LIVE** (LP)	**£200**
68	Saga OPP 102	**MEETS EDDIE GOMEZ** (LP)	**£100**
72	Decibel BSN 103	**PHIL SEAMEN STORY** (LP)	**£50**
74	77 Records 77 SEU 12/53	**PHIL ON DRUMS** (LP)	**£50**

SEARCH PARTY

70	Red Bull RB1	**What Do You See Up There/Hidden Truth**	**£35**

SEARCHERS

SINGLES

65	Pye 7N 15992	**Take Me For What I'm Worth/Too Many Miles** (in export p/s)	**£25**
67	Pye 7N 17225	**Popcorn, Double Feature/Lovers**	**£20**
67	Pye 7N 17308	**Western Union/I'll Cry Tomorrow**	**£15**
67	Pye 7N 17424	**Secondhand Dealer/Crazy Dreams**	**£80**
68	Liberty LBF 15159	**Umbrella Man/Over The Weekend**	**£50**
69	Liberty LBF 15340	**Kinky Kathy Abernathy/Suzanna**	**£50**
71	RCA RCA 2057	**Desdemona/The World Is Waiting For Tomorrow**	**£15**
72	RCA RCA 2288	**Vahevala/Madman**	**£15**

EPs

63	Pye NEP 24183	**SWEETS FOR MY SWEET** (some copies with white & maroon label)	**£15**
64	Pye NEP 24184	**HUNGRY FOR LOVE**	**£20**
64	Pye NEP 24201	**THE SEARCHERS PLAY THE SYSTEM**	**£15**
64	Pye NEP 24204	**WHEN YOU WALK IN THE ROOM**	**£20**
65	Pye NEP 24218	**BUMBLE BEE**	**£20**
65	Pye NEP 24222	**SEARCHERS '65**	**£30**
65	Pye NEP 24228	**FOUR BY FOUR**	**£35**
66	Pye NEP 24263	**TAKE ME FOR WHAT I'M WORTH**	**£100**

ALBUMS

63	Pye NPL 18086	**MEET THE SEARCHERS**	**£50**
63	Pye NPL 18089	**SUGAR AND SPICE**	**£25**
64	Pye NPL 18092	**IT'S THE SEARCHERS**	**£25**
65	Pye NPL 18111	**SOUNDS LIKE SEARCHERS**	**£40**
65	Pye NPL 18120	**TAKE ME FOR WHAT I'M WORTH**	**£50**

(see also Chris Curtis, Pasha)

SEARS

84	Bluurg FISH 9	**IF ONLY...** (LP)	**£15**

SEA STONE

82	Plankton 02	**AGAINST THE TIDE** (EP, foldout sleeve)	**£40**
78	Plankton PKN 101	**MIRRORED DREAMS** (LP, with insert)	**£80**

SEATHROUGH

79	private pressing	**LALA LAPLA** (LP)	**£40**

B.B. SEATON (HORACE SEATON)

63	Island WI 123	**I'm So Glad/Tell Me**	**£30**
64	R&B JB 143	**Hold On/LESTER STERLING: Peace And Love**	**£40**

72	Bullet BU 514	I Miss My Schooldays/CONSCIOUS MINDS: School Days - Version	£20
72	Pama PM 864	I Want Justice/RUPIE EDWARD'S ALL STARS: Justice - Version	£20
73	Trojan TRLS 59	THIN LINE BETWEEN LOVE AND HATE (LP)	£20
74	Caroline CA 2002	DANCING SHOES (LP)	£20
75	Love LOV 01	GUN COURT DUB (LP, name not on sleeve or labels)	£50

(see also Bibby, Winston & Bibby, Gaylads)

SEA TRAIN

69	A&M AMLS 941	SEA TRAIN (LP)	£30
71	Capitol EA-ST 659	SEA TRAIN (LP, gatefold)	£20
72	Capitol EA-ST 829	MARBLEHEAD MESSENGER (LP, gatefold sleeve)	£20
73	Warner Bros K 46222	WATCH (LP, gatefold)	£20

(see also Blues Project, Old & In The Way)

SEA URCHINS

87	Kvatch KVATCH 001/	Clingfilm/GROOVE FARM: Baby Blue Marine (flexidisc, 1,000 only, 500 in p/s)	£25
87	Sha La La Ba Ba Ba Ba 5	Summershine/ORCHIDS: From This Day (flexidisc, 2,500 only, 1,000 with p/s)	£15
87	Sarah SARAH 001	Pristine Christine/Sullen Eyes/Everglades (foldaround p/s with 14" x 10" poster in poly bag, 1,600 only)	£300
88	Sarah SARAH 008	Solace/Please Rain Fall (foldaround p/s in poly bag)	£35
92	Sarah SARAH 609	STARDUST (LP)	£70

SEBASTIAN

11	BEC 5772823	TOTAL (2-LP/CD, gatefold)	£30

stylised as SebastiAn

JOHN SEBASTIAN

54	London HL 8029	Inca Dance/Foolish Waltz	£20
55	London HL 8131	Stranger In Paradise/Autumn Leaves	£15

JOHN (B.) SEBASTIAN

70	Reprise RSLP 6379	JOHN B. SEBASTIAN (LP, gatefold sleeve)	£20
71	Reprise K 44127	REAL LIVE JOHN SEBASTIAN (LP)	£15

(see also Lovin' Spoonful, Even Dozen Jug Band)

SECESSION

83	Garden GAR 1	Betrayal/Reflections (p/s)	£100
88	Siren SRNLP 11	A DARK ENCHANTMENT (LP, with inner)	£40

SECOND COMING

71	Mercury 6338 030	SECOND COMING (LP)	£50

SECOND HAND

72	Mushroom 50 MR 19	Funeral/Hangin' On An Eyelid	£100
68	Polydor 583 045	REALITY (LP, early copies crediting band as Moving Finger)	£300
68	Polydor 583 045	REALITY (LP, later copies not crediting band as Moving Finger)	£200
71	Mushroom MR 2006	DEATH MAY BE YOUR SANTA CLAUS (LP, 1st pressing, without "Funeral")	£300
72	Mushroom MR 2006	DEATH MAY BE YOUR SANTA CLAUS (LP, 2nd pressing, with "Funeral")	£150
07	Sunbeam SBRLP 5031	REALITY (LP, reissue)	£20

(see also Andreas Thomopoulos, Fungus, Chillum, Vulcans)

SECOND IMAGE

85	MCA MCF 3255	STRANGE REFLECTIONS (LP)	£18
83	Polydor POLS 1081	SECOND IMAGE (LP)	£18

SECOND LAYER

79	Tortch TOR 001	FLESH AS PROPERTY (EP, white p/s, black printed labels)	£30
80	Tortch TOR 006	State Of Emergency/I Need Noise/The Cutting Motion (p/s)	£30
81	Tortch/Fresh FRESH 5	FLESH AS PROPERTY (EP, reissue, yellow p/s & white labels)	£20
81	Cherry Red CHERRY 21	FLESH AS PROPERTY (EP, 2nd reissue, unreleased)	£0
82	Cherry Red BRED 14	WORLD OF RUBBER (LP, with inner)	£50

(see also Outsiders, Sound)

SECOND THOUGHTS

65	Recorded Sound Studios RSL 1596	Let's Stick Together/I'm Possessed	£300

(see also July, Nirvana)

SECONDARY MODERN

83	Sorthern Sounds DJG 1	Lucinda Dream/Boys Cry Too (p/s)	£60

SECOND OPINION

78	Tash TASH 0035	King Of The Raceway/Stormbird	£20

SECRET

78	Arista ARIST 173	Do You Really Care?/I Wanna Car Like That	£15

SECRET AFFAIR

79	I-Spy I SPY 1	GLORY BOYS (LP, with 2 inserts)	£15
80	I-Spy I SPY 2	BEHIND CLOSED DOORS (LP, with inner sleeve)	£15
82	I-Spy I SPY 3	BUSINESS AS USUAL (LP, stickered sleeve)	£15

(see also Advertising, Innocents [U.K.])

SECRET OYSTER

74	CBS 80489	SEA SON (LP)	£15

SECRET SHINE

91	Sarah SARAH 53	After Years/Snowfall Sorrow/Grey Skies (p/s)	£20
92	Sarah SARAH 61	Honey Sweet/Secret Shine (p/s)	£20
93	Sarah SARAH 71	Loveblind/Way Too High (p/s)	£20
94	Sarah SARAH 89	GREATER THAN GOD EP (10" p/s)	£60
93	Sarah SARAH 615	UNTOUCHED (LP)	£70

SECRET SQUIRREL
92	Bogwoppa BOGWOPPA 05	**E Drop/Come Rudeboy** (12", handwritten white label, with AJ Flex)	£60
92	Dance Bass DANCE BASS 01	**Mu-Venom/DDT** (12", stamped white label)	£50
92	Dance Bass DANCE BASS 02	**VOLUME 2 EP** (12")	£30
92	Dance Bass DANCE BASS 06	**THE MAGIC FLUTE EP** (12")	£30

(See also Undercover Elephant and DJ Secret Squirrel)

SECRETS (U.K.)
66	CBS 202466	**I Suppose/Such A Pity**	£40
67	CBS 202585	**Infatuation/She's Dangerous**	£40
67	CBS 2818	**I Intend To Please/I Think I Need The Cash**	£40

(see also Simon's Secrets, Clifford T. Ward, Martin Raynor & Secrets)

SECRETS (U.S)
64	Philips BF 1298	**The Boy Next Door/Learnin' To Forget**	£30
64	Philips BF 1318	**Hey Big Boy/Other Side Of Town**	£30

SECT (2)
86	Insect NASTY 1	**A Free England/Never Go** (p/s)	£20
89	Damaged Goods YUBB 2	**SUMMER GIRL EP**, blue vinyl)	£20
90	Damaged Goods YUBB 5	**REMEMBERING EP** (12")	£15
90	Combat CR 001	**PLAYING WITH FIRE EP** (12")	£20
87	Razor RAZ 27	**THE VOICE OF REASON** (LP)	£15

SECTION A
82	Subversive SUB	**TIME STANDS STILL EP**	£15

SECTION 5
85	Oi OIR 002	**WE WON'T CHANGE** (LP)	£20
87	Link LP 08	**FOR THE LOVE OF OI!** (LP)	£20
88	Link LINK LP 031	**STREET ROCK 'N' ROLL** (LP)	£15

SECTION 25
80	Factory FAC 18	**Girls Don't Count/New Noise/Up To You** (tracing paper p/s, produced by Ian Curtis and Rob Gretton)	£35
80	Factory FAC 18	**Girls Don't Count/New Noise Up To You** (12", 3 different p/s depicting band members girlfriends, produced by Ian Curtis and Rob Gretton)	£20
81	Factory FACT 45	**ALWAYS NOW** (LP, in envelope/folder with poster)	£60
81	Factory FACT 45	**ALWAYS NOW** (LP, in envelope/folder without poster)	£40
84	Factory FACT 90	**FROM THE HIP** (LP, with inner)	£35
86	Factory FACT 45c	**ALWAYS NOW** (reissue, cassette in box with insert)	£100
86	Factory FACT 90c	**FROM THE HIP** (reissue, cassette in box with insert)	£80
88	Factory FACT 160	**LOVE & HATE** (LP)	£30
12	Factory FACT 90	**FROM THE HIP** (2-LP, reissue)	£20

NEIL SEDAKA
59	RCA RCA 1099	**The Diary/No Vacancy**	£20
59	RCA RCA 1099	**The Diary/No Vacancy** (78)	£15
59	RCA RCA 1115	**I Go Ape/Moon Of Gold**	£15
59	RCA RCA 1115	**I Go Ape/Moon Of Gold** (78)	£15
59	RCA RCA 1130	**You've Got To Learn Your Rhythm And Blues/Crying My Heart Out For You**	£15
59	London HLW 8961	**Ring A Rockin'/Fly Don't Fly On Me**	£40

(The above 45s were originally issued with triangular centres; later round-centres are worth two-thirds these values.)

59	London HLW 8961	**Ring A Rockin'/Fly Don't Fly On Me** (78)	£20
59	RCA RCA 1152	**Oh! Carol/One Way Ticket** (78)	£40
60	RCA RCA 1178	**Stairway To Heaven/Forty Winks Away** (78)	£40
60	RCA RCA 1198	**Run Samson Run/You Mean Everything To Me** (78)	£40
63	RCA RCA 1368	**Bad Girl/Wait 'Til You See My Baby**	£15
59	RCA RCX 166	**NEIL SEDAKA** (EP)	£20
60	RCA RCX 186	**NEIL SEDAKA VOL. 2** (EP)	£20
62	RCA RCX 212	**NEIL SEDAKA VOL. 3** (EP)	£15
59	RCA RD 27140	**NEIL SEDAKA** (LP)	£40
60	RCA RD 27207	**CIRCULATE** (LP, mono)	£20
60	RCA SF 5090	**CIRCULATE** (LP, stereo)	£30

(see also Sam Cooke, Paul Anka, 10cc)

SEDITION 81
81	S81	**Royal Command/Prat Music** (p/s)	£100

SEDUCER
83	Sticky SSR 0017	**Call Your Name/Survivor** (small number in p/s)	£60
83	Sticky SSR 0017	**Call Your Name/Survivor** (no p/s)	£20
84	Thunderbolt THBE 1007	**Indecent Exposure/Down Down/No No Baby/DTs/Wild Joker** (12", p/s)	£25
85	Thunderbolt THBL 016	**CAUGHT IN THE ACT** (LP)	£25
86	Stud STUDLP 2	**'EADS DOWN - SEE YOU AT THE END** (LP)	£25

SEE SEE
10	Great Pop Supplement GPS 64	**LATE MORNING LIGHT** (LP, 250 only, black vinyl)	£15
10	Great Pop Supplement GPS 64	**LATE MORNING LIGHT** (LP, 300 only, milk chocolate vinyl)	£15

RUDY SEEDORF
65	Island WI 189	**One Million Stars/Mr. Blue**	£18

SEEDS
66	Vocalion VN 9277	**Pushin' Too Hard/Try To Understand**	£60
66	Vocalion VN 9277	**Pushin' Too Hard/Try To Understand** (DJ copy)	£100

67	Vocalion VN 9287	Can't Seem To Make You Mine/Daisy Mae	£40
88	Bam Caruso OPRA 091	Pushin' Too Hard/Greener Day	£15
67	Vocalion VAN 8062	A WEB OF SOUND (LP)	£120
67	Vocalion VAN 8070	FUTURE (LP, mono)	£50
67	Vocalion SAVN 8070	FUTURE (LP, stereo)	£60
78	Sonet SNTF 746	THE SEEDS (LEGENDARY MASTER RECORDINGS) (LP)	£15
88	Strange Things STRANGEP 1	EVIL HOODOO (LP, picture disc)	£15

(see also Sky Saxon, Ya Ho Wa 13)

SEEDS OF THE EARTH
| 75 | Contempo CS 2052 | Planting Seeds/Brother Bad | £20 |
| 75 | Contempo CS 2073 | Zion Plus/Phire | £20 |

SEEDY GEES
| 77 | Fairview SRTS FMR 006 | Redancer/Peggy Sue/Drinking Their Lives Away/I'll Meet You At Midnight | £30 |
| 80 | SRTS/80/CUS 646 | We Will Rock And Roll/Those Lonely Days/We Will Remember/We Will Dance Tonight | £30 |

MIKE SEEGER
| 65 | Fontana TFL 6039 | MIKE SEEGER (LP) | £15 |

(see also Peggy & Mike Seeger)

PEGGY SEEGER
57	Pye Jazz NJE 1043	ORIGINS OF SKIFFLE (EP)	£20
57	Topic 7T 18	COME ALONG JOHN (EP, 33 rpm with 2 inserts, one hand-typed insert)	£20
58	Topic TOP 18	COME ALONG JOHN (EP, 45 rpm reissue, with insert)	£15
60	Topic TOP 38	SHINE LIKE A STAR (EP)	£20
50s	Topic 10T 9	PEGGY SEEGER (10" LP)	£20
61	PRE 13005	THE BEST OF PEGGY SEEGER (LP)	£15

(see also Al Lloyd)

PEGGY SEEGER & GUY CARAWAN
| 58 | Nixa NPT 19029 | WE SING AMERICA (10" LP) | £30 |
| 58 | HMV CLP 1174 | AMERICA AT PLAY (LP) | £20 |

(see also Guy Carawan)

PEGGY & MIKE SEEGER
| 68 | Argo (Z)DA 80 | PEGGY 'N' MIKE (LP) | £15 |

(see also Ewan MacColl & Peggy Seeger, Mike Seeger)

PETE SEEGER
| 59 | Topic TOP 37 | HOOTENANNY NEW YORK CITY (EP, with Sonny Terry) | £15 |

(see also Big Bill Broonzy, Sonny Terry [& Brownie McGhee])

PETE SEEGER & BIG BILL BROONZY
| 64 | Xtra XTRA 1006 | IN CONCERT - PETE SEEGER & BIG BILL BROONZY (LP) | £20 |
| 66 | Verve Folkways ST SVLP 506 | IN CONCERT (LP, stereo, reissue) | £15 |

(see also Big Bill Broonzy)

SEEMON & MARIJKE
| 71 | A&M AMLS 64309 | SON OF AMERICA (LP) | £30 |

SEFTONS
| 66 | CBS 202491 | I Can See Through You/Here Today | £25 |

(see also Perishers)

TY SEGALL
| 12 | Drag City DC530 | TWINS (LP, gatefold) | £18 |

BOB SEGER (SYSTEM)
68	Capitol CL 15574	Ramblin' Gamblin' Man/Tales Of Lucy Blue (as Bob Seger System)	£15
70	Capitol CL 15642	Lucifer/Big River (as Bob Seger System)	£20
72	Reprise K 44214	SMOKIN' O.P.'s (LP)	£20

FLOYD LLOYD SEIVRIGHT
| 82 | Vista Sounds STLP 1016 | BETTER TO LAUGH THAN CRY (LP) | £15 |
| 83 | Tropic TLPS 0023 | SWEET LADY (LP) | £15 |

SEIZE
| 81 | Why Not? NOT 001 | Grovelands Road/Why? (p/s) | £18 |
| 82 | Why Not? NOT 002 | EVERYBODY DIES EP (p/s) | £30 |

RICHARD SELANO
| 69 | Jolly JY 019 | All Of The Time/Broken Romance | £40 |

SELECTED FOUR
| 71 | Banana BA 351 | Selection Train/SOUND DIMENSION: Version Train | £25 |

SELECTER
79	2-Tone CHS TT 4	On My Radio/Too Much Pressure (paper label, company sleeve)	£18
80	2-Tone CHS TT 8	Three Minute Hero/James Bond (paper label, company sleeve)	£20
80	2-Tone CHS TT 10	Missing Words/Carry Go Bring Home (paper label, company sleeve)	£20
89	2-Tone TTP1	THE SPECIALS: Rudi, A Message To You/Ghost Town//SELECTER: On My Radio/ MADNESS: One Step Beyond (promo, 40 only)	£200
80	2-Tone CDLTT 5002	TOO MUCH PRESSURE (LP)	£25
81	Chrysalis CHR 1306	CELEBRATE THE BULLET (LP)	£20

(see also Special A.K.A.)

RONNIE SELF
| 58 | Philips PB 810 | Bop-A-Lena/Ain't I A Dog (78) | £200 |

SELF ABUSE
| 83 | Radical Change RC 5 | (I DON'T WANT TO BE A) SOLDIERS (EP) | £18 |

BING SELFISH
83	El Frenzy NM008	SELFISH WORKS EP (12", p/s)	£40

BROTHER JOHN SELLERS
56	Vanguard EPP 14002	BLUES AND SPIRITUALS (EP)	£15
57	Columbia SEG 7740	BLUES AND SPIRITUALS (EP)	£15
57	Decca DFE 6457	BROTHER JOHN SELLERS IN LONDON (EP)	£15
56	Vanguard PPT 12008	BROTHER JOHN SELLERS SINGS BLUES AND FOLK SONGS (10" LP)	£25
57	Vanguard PPT 12017	JACK OF DIAMONDS AND OTHER FOLK SONGS AND BLUES (10" LP)	£25

PETER SELLERS (& SOPHIA LOREN)
66	United Artists UP 1152	After The Fox (as Peter Sellers & Hollies)/BURT BACHARACH: The Fox-Trot	£35
60	Parlophone PCS 3012	PETER AND SOPHIA (LP, with Sophia Loren, stereo)	£15

SELOFANE
68	CBS 3413	Girl Called Fantasy/Happiness Is Love	£15
68	CBS 3700	Shingle I.A.O./Chase The Face	£30

SELWYN & JOHN
67	CBS 2708	Bogey Man/When God Gave Us Names	£90

SEMA
82	Le Rey LR 06	THEME FROM HUNGER (EP)	£60
82	Le Rey LR 04	NOTES FROM UNDERGROUND (LP)	£150
83	Le Rey LR 101	EXTRACTS FROM ROSA SILBER (LP)	£80
84	Le Rey LR 102	THREE SEASONS ONLY (LP)	£60

SEMA 4
79	Pollen PBM 022	4 FROM SEMA 4 (EP, 2 different coloured sleeves, 500 only, numbered)	£100
79	Pollen PBM 024	UP DOWN AROUND (EP, 1,000 only)	£75

ARCHIE SEMPLE
60	Columbia 33SX 1240	JAZZ FOR YOUNG LOVERS (LP)	£25
62	77 LP/10	THE ARCHIE SEMPLE QUARTET (10" LP, 100 only)	£40
62	Columbia 33SX 1450	EASY LIVING (LP)	£20
63	Columbia 33SX 1580	THE TWILIGHT COMETH (LP)	£20
64	77 LEU 12/6	THE CLARINET OF ARCHIE SEMPLE (LP)	£20

SENATE
67	Columbia DB 8110	I Can't Stop/Ain't As Sweet As You	£60
68	United Artists (S)ULP 1180	THE SENATE SOCK IT TO YOU ONE MORE TIME (LP)	£40

(see also Garnet Mimms)

SENATORS
64	Dial DSP 7001	She's A Mod/Lot About You	£100
64	Oriole CB 1957	When Day Is Done/Breakdown	£50
65	CBS 201768	The Tables Are Turning/Stop Wasting Time	£30

(see also Tony Rivers & Castaways)

SENAY
15	Turkola TR-03	SENAY (LP, reissue)	£20

SENDELICA
10	Fruits De Mer CRUSTACIAN 13	A NICE PAIR (gatefold p/s, green vinyl)	£25

SEND/RETURN
95	Emote MOTE 002	Alright/Not Bad/Reasonable/Fair (12")	£80
95	Emote MOTE 003	Hair Of The Dog/Liquid Lunch/Nightcap (12")	£80

(see also Mark Churcher)

SENSATION
73	Sticky STY 5	Black Eyed Woman/Baby	£15

SENSATIONAL CREED
84	Beggars Banquet BEG 125	Nocturnal Operation/Down Periscope (p/s, reissue of Orbidöig single)	£15
84	Beggars Banquet BEG 125T	Nocturnal Operation/Down Periscope/Voyage Of The Titanic (12", p/s, reissue of Orbidöig single)	£25

(see also Orbidoig)

SENSATIONAL SPARES
83	Spare KF 001	No Time At All/The Windmill (no p/s)	£40

SENSATIONS (JAMAICA)
67	Doctor Bird DB 1074	A Thing Called Soul/BOBBY LEE & SENSATIONS: I Was Born A Loser	£65
67	Doctor Bird DB 1100	Right On Time/Lonely Lover	£200
67	Doctor Bird DB 1102	Born To Love You/Your Sweet Love	£85
68	Duke DU 2	Those Guys/I'll Never Fall In Love	£80
68	Island WI 3110	Long Time Me No See You Girl/ROY SHIRLEY: Million Dollar Baby	£200
69	Camel CA 31	The Warrior (actually by Johnny Osbourne & Sensations)/ JOHNNY ORGAN: Don Juan	£60
70	Techniques TE 902	War Boat/Mr Blue	£80
71	Duke DU 120	Remember/LARRY'S ALLSTARS: Madhouse	£40
71	Duke DU 121	What Are You Doing Sunday/RUFFIANS: Sweet Dream	£15

(see also Roy Shirley, Baba Dise, Winston Wright)

SENSATIONS (U.K.)
66	Decca F 12392	Look At My Baby/What A Wonderful Feeling	£20
71	MCA MK 5078	Oh My Eli/Let's Get A Little Sentimental	£30

SENSATIONS (FEATURING YVONNE) (U.S.)
61	Pye International 7N 25110	Music, Music, Music/A Part Of Me (as Sensations featuring Yvonne)	£25
62	Pye International 7N 25128	Let Me In/Oh Yes I'll Be True	£25

SEONA DANCING
| 83 | London LON 22 | More To Lose/You're On My Side (p/s) | £18 |
| 83 | London LON 32 | Bitter Heart/Tell Her (p/s) | £18 |

SEPTIC DEATH
| 85 | Pusmort 0012-01D | NOW THAT I HAVE THE ATTENTION... (LP, with inner sleeve, 18 tracks) | £15 |

SEPTIMUS
| 77 | Pennine PSS 134 | Ferrets/Do You Wanna Touch My Safety Pin? (no p/s) | £100 |

SEPULTURA
91	Roadracer RO 93281	ARISE (LP)	£40
91	Roadracer RO 9328-8	ARISE (LP, picture disc)	£35
94	Roadrunner RR 90000 0	CHAOS A.D. (CD, limited edition tin box; CD has embossed cover & different sleeve, Brazilian flag & 2 bonus tracks, "Policia" & "Inhuman Nature")	£40

SEQUENCE
| 84 | CAMM CAMM 01 | Child In The City/Theme (12") | £35 |

SERENDIPITY
| 68 | CBS 3733 | Through With You/I'm Flying | £130 |
| 69 | CBS 4428 | If I Could/Castles | £60 |

SERFS
| 69 | Capitol E-ST 207 | THE EARLY BIRD CAFE (LP) | £18 |

SERGEANT PEPPER
| 83 | Ariwa ARILP 006 | JUDGEMENT DAY (LP) | £25 |

WILL SERGEANT
| 78 | (no label or cat. no.) | WEIRD AS FISH (cassette, 7 copies only, each with a different cover) | £150 |

(see also Echo & Bunnymen)

SERIES RED
| 85 | Horizon RED 001 | Don't Go/Hold Back Your Feelings (p/s) | £35 |

SERIOUS DRINKING
| 83 | Upright UPLP 3 | THE REVOLUTION STARTS AT CLOSING TIME (LP, with beer mat) | £18 |

SERPENTINE
| 70 | Decca F23001 | Powerful Jim/I've Only Got Myself | £20 |

BETTIE SERVEERT
| 92 | Guernica GU 3 LP | PALOMINE (LP, with free 7") | £20 |

SERVICEMEN
| 00 | Grapevine 116 | Are You Angry/I Need A Helping Hand | £15 |
| 01 | Grapevine 136 | I'll Stop Loving You/Sweet Magic | £25 |

SESSION BOYS
| 70 | Lynn L29 | Looking To The Sun/Strike Back | £20 |

SESSION MEN
| 80 | LKJ 001 | THE SESSION MEN : Solitude/ABU BAKE : Introducing Abu Baka/MICHAEL SMITH : Mi Cyaan Believe It/Roots (12") | £25 |

CAMILO SESTO
| 72 | Pye Intl. 7N 25589 | To Be A Man/Now Is My Time (Yo Soy Asi) | £40 |

BOLA SETE
| 76 | Sonet SNTF 695 | OCEAN (LP) | £15 |

SETTERS
| 70 | Duke DU 65 | Paint Your Wagon/Organ Man (both sides actually by Hot Rod All Stars) | £140 |
| 70 | Trojan TR 7738 | Virgin Soldier/Brixton Reggae Festival (both actually by Hot Rod All Stars) | £60 |

SETTING SUN
| 68 | Oak RGI 840 | Ob La De Ob La Da/Boy Who Was Only One/Homeward Bound/Fascinating Rhythm | £40 |

SETTLERS
| 64 | Decca LK 4645 | SING OUT (LP) | £15 |
| 72 | York FYK 405 | LIGHTNING TREE (LP) | £15 |

SEVEN AGES OF MAN
| 72 | Rediffusion ZS 115 | SEVEN AGES OF MAN (LP, yellow/black label) | £40 |

(see also Madeline Bell, Gordon Beck)

SEVEN LETTERS/SYMARIP
69	Doctor Bird DB 1189	People Get Ready/The Fit (as Seven Letters)	£65
69	Doctor Bird DB 1194	Please Stay/Special Beat (as Seven Letters)	£70
69	Doctor Bird DB 1195	Flour Dumpling/Equality (as Seven Letters [Symarip])	£130
69	JJ DB 1206	Mama Me Want Girl/Sentry (as Seven Letters)	£40
69	JJ DB 1207	Soul Crash/Throw Me Things (as Seven Letters)	£100
69	Doctor Bird DB 1208	There Goes My Heart/Wish (as Seven Letters)	£100
69	Doctor Bird DB 1209	Bam Bam Baji/Hold Joe (as Seven Letters [Symarip])	£90
69	Doctor Bird DB 1306	Fung Shore/Tomorrow At Sundown (as Symarip)	£150
69	Treasure Isle TI 7050	Skinhead Moonstomp/Must Catch A Train (as Symarip)	£30
70	Treasure Isle TI 7054	Parson Corner/Redeem (as Symarip)	£30
70	Treasure Isle TI 7055	La Bella Jig/Holidays By The Sea (as Symarip)	£25
70	Attack ATT 8013	I Am A Puppet/Vindication (as Symarip)	£45
70	Trojan TBL 102	SKINHEAD MOONSTOMP (LP, as Symarip)	£80
80	Trojan TRLS 187	SKINHEAD MOONSTOMP (LP, reissue, blue label)	£25
13	Sunspot SUNSPLP011	SKINHEAD MOONSTOMP (LP, reissue)	£18

(see also Pyramids, Equals, Laurel Aitken)

SEVENTEEN
80 Vendetta VD 001   **Don't Let Go/Bank Holiday Weekend** (p/s) £100
(see also Alarm)

SEVENTH ANGEL
90 Under One Flag FLAG 51   **THE TORMENT** (LP) £15
92 Under One Flag FLAG 65   **LAMENT FOR THE WEARY** (LP, inner) £20

7TH PLAIN
93 General Production GPR(X) 16   **TO BE SURREAL EP** (12") £70
94 General Production GPR(X) 19   **ASTRA-NAUT EP** (12") £30
94 General Prod. GPRLP03   **THE 4 CORNERED ROOM** (2-LP, poster) £30
94 General Prod. GPRLP08   **MY YELLOW WISE RUG** (2-LP, as Luke Slaters 7th Plain) £25
96 General Prod. GPRLP16   **PLAYING WITH FOOLS** (2-LP, test pressings only) £200
(see also Luke Slater)

SEVENTH SEAL
90 Mystic Red Corp MRC 8004   **Sound Iration/Dub Seal** (12") £50

SEVENTH SON
82 Rising Son FMR 067   **Man In The Street/Immortal Hours** (in original p/s with bass player obscured) £50
82 Rising Son FMR 067   **Man In The Street/Immortal Hours** (revised p/s with 'clearer' band photograph) £35
84 Rising Son SRT4KS 282   **Metal To The Moon/Sound And Fury** (in gatefold p/s) £60
84 Rising Son SRT4KS 282   **Metal To The Moon/Sound And Fury** £30
87 Music Factory MF 0043   **Northern Boots/The Harder You Rock** (p/s) £18

SEVENTH WAVE
89 SRT SRT9KS 2018   **Tonight/Run** (p/s) £20
74 Gull GULP 1001   **THINGS TO COME** (LP) £15
75 Gull GULP 1010   **PSI-FI** (LP) £18
(see also Second Hand, Fungus, Ken Elliott)

SEVERE CARNAGE
90 White JC 002   **The Struggle Continues/Back To Basics** (12") £250

SEVERED HEAD
83 Plastic Canvas PC 002   **Heavy Metal/Killin' The Kidz** (p/s) £25

SEVERED HEADS
84 Ink INK 122   **DEAD EYES OPENED** (12" EP, p/s) £15
83 Ink INK 2   **SINCE THE ACCIDENT** (LP) £20
85 Ink INK 9   **CITY SLAB HORROR** (LP) £15
85 Ink INK 16D   **CLIFFORD DARLING PLEASE DON'T LIVE IN THE PAST** (2-LP) £20

DAVID SEVILLE & HIS ORCHESTRA (& THE CHIPMUNKS)
57 London HLU 8359   **Armen's Theme/Carousel In Rome** (initially gold label print) £20
(see also Alfi & Harry)

ALEC SEWARD
56 Vogue LDE 165   **CITY BLUES** (10" LP) £40

SEX
00 Grapevine 113   **It's You Baby** (It's You)/**It's You Baby** (Extended) £15

SEX AIDS
83 Riot City RIOT 23   **BACK ON THE PISS AGAIN** (EP) £20
(see also Vice Squad)

SEX GANG CHILDREN
82 Illuminated ILL 1112   **Beasts** (12", EP) £30

SEX PISTOLS
SINGLES
76 EMI 401   **Anarchy In The U.K** (4.01 longer version)/**No Fun** (Abbey Road 2-sided acetate, only 3 known to exist) £7000
76 EMI   **Anarchy In The U.K.** (3.36 version) (1-sided Abbey Road Acetate) £5000
76 EMI 2566   **Anarchy In The U.K./I Wanna Be Me** (2 x 1-sided white label test pressings, 4-pronge centre, MATRIXES EMI 2566 A1/EMI 2566B-2) £4000
76 EMI EMI 2566   **Anarchy In The U.K./I Wanna Be Me** (black p/s, with Chris Thomas production credit on B-side) £120
76 EMI EMI 2566   **Anarchy In The U.K./I Wanna Be Me** ('Demo, not for sale'. Black p/s, Chris Thomas credit on both sides and with information slip) £300
76 EMI EMI 2566   **Anarchy In The U.K./I Wanna Be Me** (Dave Goodman production credit on B-side) £60
76 EMI EMI 2566   **Anarchy In The U.K./I Wanna Be Me** (Anarchy label on both sides) £150
77 (no label or cat. no.)   **God Save The Queen/No Feeling** (double sided 7" acetate on LTS - few copies pressed and used by Malcolm McLaren to get gigs and record deal) £10000
77 A&M AMS 2784   **God Save The Queen/No Feeling** (white label test pressing, A2/B1 Matrixes) £7000
77 A&M AMS 7284   **God Save The Queen/No Feeling** (withdrawn, in brown envelope with press release) £12000
77 A&M AMS 7284   **God Save The Queen/No Feeling** (withdrawn, without brown envelope and press release) £10000
77 Virgin VS 181   **God Save The Queen/Did You No Wrong** (white label test pressing VS 181 A1/B1 Matrixes) £2500
77 Virgin VS 181   **God Save The Queen/Did You No Wrong** (Plain blue no Queen's head sample sleeve - two known copies, Jamie Reid autograph added later to one) £1500
77 Virgin VS 184 (not on acetate)   **Pretty Vacant** (1-sided acetate) £1000
77 Virgin VS 184   **Pretty Vacant/No Fun** (white label test pressing) £600
77 Virgin VS 184   **Pretty Vacant/No Fun** (p/s blue/white labels, with push-out centre) £30

77	Virgin VS 191	**Holidays In The Sun/Satellite** (withdrawn p/s) £40
77	Virgin/Lyntone LYN 3261	**Lentilmas - A Seasonal Offering To You From Virgin Records** (flexidisc, Xmas freebie to journalists; with Xmas card. It is believed that the Sex Pistols do not appear on this record) £1000
77	Virgin/Lyntone LYN 3261	**Lentilmas - A Seasonal Offering To You From Virgin Records** (flexidisc, Xmas freebie to journalists; without Xmas card. It is believed that the Sex Pistols do not appear on this record) £300
78	(No. Cat. No)	**SID VICIOUS: My Way** (1-sided Pye Studios Acetate) £700
78	Virgin VS 220	**No-One Is Innocent** (mispress, plays Motors track)**/SID VICIOUS: My Way** (p/s) £35
78	Virgin VS 22012	**The Biggest Blow** (A Punk Prayer By Ronald Biggs)**/**(Interview)**/SID VICIOUS: My Way** (12", p/s [matrix: VS 22012A3], without interview [VS 22012 A1]) £20
79	Virgin VS 290	**The Great Rock 'n' Roll Swindle** (mispressing with 'lawyers' telephone conversation' track)**/Rock Around The Clock** ('American Express' p/s) £30
80	Virgin VS 339	(I'm Not Your) **Stepping Stone/Pistols Propaganda** (p/s, mispressing, B-side plays "Substitute") £25
80	Virgin VS 339	(I'm Not Your) **Stepping Stone/Pistols Propaganda** (p/s, mispressing, B-side plays Gillan track "No Laughing In Heaven") £30
80	Virgin SEX 1	**PISTOLS PACK** (6 x 7" in p/s; all in plastic wallet) £80
85	Chaos DICK1	**Submission/No Feelings** (p/s, 5,000 only, pink vinyl) £15
85	Chaos SUB 1	**Submission** (12", 1-sided test pressing, die-cut sleeve, label has big red 'A') £30
85	Chaos	**Pretty Vacant** (unreleased, 20 copies only) £75
85	Chaos CARTEL 1	**Submission** (12" 1-track promo) £25
92	Virgin VS 1448	**Pretty Vacant/No Feelings** (p/s, Lady Di cover) £15

ALBUMS

77	Virgin V 2086	**NEVER MIND THE BOLLOCKS, HERE'S THE SEX PISTOLS** (LP, 1st pressing with poster and free 'Submission' 7", 11 tracks listed on rear sleeve (no 'Submission'). **Publishing credits '1977 Jones, Matlock, Cook & Rotten' except HOLIDAYS IN THE SUN** (side 1) **and BODIES** (side 2) **'Jones, Cook, Rotten & Vicious')**........................£100
77	Virgin V 2086	**NEVER MIND THE BOLLOCKS, HERE'S THE SEX PISTOLS** (LP, 1st pressing, poster and free 'Submission' 7", pink rear sleeve with no track listing, sources suggest as little as 1000 copies pressed with this sleeve, A1/B1 or A3/B2 matrixes. Publishing credits '1977 Jones, Matlock, Cook & Rotten' except HOLIDAYS IN THE SUN (side 1) **and BODIES** (side 2) **'Jones, Cook, Rotten & Vicious'))** £150
77	Virgin V 2086	**NEVER MIND THE BOLLOCKS, HERE'S THE SEX PISTOLS** (LP, 2nd pressing with 12 tracks (no track listing on pink rear sleeve, 'Bodies' moved to side 1 and 'Submission' added to side 2. Publishing credits, 'Copyright control 1977, Jones, Matlock. Cook, Rotten' except HOLIDAYS IN THE SUN, BODIES & EMI 'Copyright Control 1977 Jones, Cook, Rotten, Vicious') £40
77	Virgin V 2086	**NEVER MIND THE BOLLOCKS, HERE'S THE SEX PISTOLS** (LP, 3rd pressing with 12 tracks and 12 tracks listed on pink rear sleeve,Publishing credits on 'EMI' changed from 'Jones, Matlock, Cook, Rotten' to 'Jones, Cook, Rotten, Vicious') £30
77	Virgin V 2086	**NEVER MIND THE BOLLOCKS, HERE'S THE SEX PISTOLS** (LP, 3rd pressing with 12 tracks but 11 tracks listed on rear sleeve (no 'Submission'). **Publishing credits, 'Copyright control 1977, Jones, Matlock. Cook, Rotten' except HOLIDAYS IN THE SUN, BODIES & EMI 'Copyright Control 1977 Jones, Cook, Rotten, Vicious')** £25
77	Virgin V 2086/SPOTS 001	**NEVER MIND THE BOLLOCKS, HERE'S THE SEX PISTOLS** (LP, pink rear sleeve, with no track listing, with poster & 1-sided single, "Submission" [VDJ 24], shrinkwrapped, with orange or green-stickered versions extremely rare) £1500
78	Virgin VP 2086	**NEVER MIND THE BOLLOCKS, HERE'S THE SEX PISTOLS** (LP, picture disc) £40
78	Virgin V 2086	**NEVER MIND THE BOLLOCKS, HERE'S THE SEX PISTOLS** (LP, 1st reissue. Green label side 1, red label on side 2 - Matlock credit returns on 'EMI', rear sleeve has 11 or 12 track listing) £15
79	Virgin VD 2510	**THE GREAT ROCK 'N' ROLL SWINDLE** (2-LP, 1st pressing with 23 tracks including "Watcha Gonna Do About It", with paper insert) £250
79	Virgin VD 2510	**THE GREAT ROCK 'N' ROLL SWINDLE** (2-LP, 2nd pressing with 24 tracks. "I Wanna Be Me" and "Who Killed Bambi?" replace "Watcha Gonna Do About It", with spoken overdubs on "God Save The Queen Symphony" 2 stickers on front and 1 on rear) £40
79	Virgin VD 2510	**THE GREAT ROCK 'N' ROLL SWINDLE** (2-LP, 2nd pressing with 24 tracks. "I Wanna Be Me" and "Who Killed Bambi?" replace "Watcha Gonna Do About It", with spoken overdubs on "God Save The Queen Symphony" 1 sticker on front) £20
79	Virgin V 2142	**FLOGGING A DEAD HORSE** (LP) £15
80	Factory FACT 30	**THE HEYDAY** (gold interview cassette in satin pouch with Xmas card) £50
80	Factory FACT 30	**THE HEYDAY** (cassette, in vinyl pouch without Xmas card) £20
80	Virgin V 2168	**THE GREAT ROCK 'N' ROLL SWINDLE** (LP, compilation with 2 stickers on front and free poster) £350
84	Virgin OVED 136	**NEVER MIND THE BOLLOCKS, HERE'S THE SEX PISTOLS** (LP, reissue, misprinted with 'Belsen Was A Gas' on rear of sleeve and 'Liar' printed twice) £15
85	Virgin OVED 136	**NEVER MIND THE BOLLOCKS, HERE'S THE SEX PISTOLS** (LP, reissue, misprinted with 'Belsen Was A Gas' on rear of sleeve) £18
92	Virgin V2702	**KISS THIS** (2-LP) £25
97	EMI LPCENT20	**NEVER MIND THE BOLLOCKS, HERE'S THE SEX PISTOLS** (LP, reissue, EMI 100 Centenary edition, stickered sleeve) £25
98	Virgin VP 2087	**NEVER MIND THE BOLLOCKS, HERE'S THE SEX PISTOLS** (LP, pink vinyl reissue, numbered on rear sleeve) £20
06	Castle CMQLP 1395	**SPUNK** (LP, yellow vinyl) £15
12	Universal SEXPISYP 1977	**NEVER MIND THE BOLLOCKS, HERE'S THE SEX PISTOLS** (2-LP, reissue yellow/pink vinyl, 1977 copies only, numbered) £35

(see also Public Image Ltd, Professionals, Rich Kids, Steve Jones, Spectres (UK)

ANN SEXTON

| 87 | Charly CRB 1143 | **LOVE TRIALS** (LP, reissue) ....£15 |
| 03 | Soul Brother 1000001 | **ANTHOLOGY** (LP) ....£25 |

TONY SEXTON

69	Camel CA 35	**Nobody Knows/Somewhere** (with Jr. English) £20
78	Fight FTDD 4429	**My Heart Is Gone/VIN GORDON: Heartically/HIM & HER: Boneache/Pussy Galore** (12") £15
78	Horse HOSS 153	**Segregation/SUPER STAR: Segregation** (Version) £25
78	Burning Sounds BSD 005	**Desire** (with Jah Son)**/BOB DAVIS: World In My Arms** (12") £20

SEXWITCH
| 15 | Echo 538169301 | SEXWITCH (LP) | £40 |

(see also Bat For Lashes)

SEXY GIRLS
| 69 | Fab FAB 100 | Pon-Pon Song/LITTLE JOE & BUSTER'S ALLSTARS: Hy There (B-side actually by Melltones) | £15 |
| 69 | Dice CC 100 | Pon-Pon Song/LITTLE JOE & BUSTER'S ALLSTARS: Hy There (B-side actually by Melltones) (reissue) | £15 |

DENNY SEYTON & SABRES
64	Mercury MF 800	Tricky Dicky/Baby What You Want Me To Do	£20
64	Mercury MF 814	Short Fat Fanny/Give Me Back My Heart	£20
64	Mercury MF 824	The Way You Look Tonight/Hands Off	£20
65	Parlophone R 5363	Just A Kiss/In The Flowers By The Trees (as Denny Seyton Group)	£20
65	Wing WL 1032	IT'S THE GEAR (14 HITS) (LP)	£30

SFW
| 78 | Badarse SFW 1 | True Life/The March (no p/s) | £20 |

TONY SHABAZZ
| 79 | Ethnic Fight FT DD 4436 | Mr Fitzy/RUDDIE MOWATT: Public Enemy (12") | £60 |

SHABBY TIGER
| 76 | RCA Victor PL 25046 | SHABBY TIGER (LP) | £15 |

SHACK
88	Ghetto GHETT 1	ZILCH (LP, with free 12" distributed by Epic)	£20
88	Ghetto GHETT 1	ZILCH (LP, later independent issue)	£25
03	North Country NCLP 002	HERE'S TOM WITH THE WEATHER (LP)	£200
06	Sour Mash JDNCLP 006	THE CORNER OF MILES AND GIL (2-LP)	£150

(see also Pale Fountains, Michael Head & Strands)

SHADE JOEY & NIGHTOWLS
| 64 | Parlophone R 5180 | Bluebirds Over The Mountain/That's When I Need You Baby | £90 |

SHADER
| 81 | Piston Broke REDASH 1 | Bad News Blues (no p/s) | £100 |

SHADES
| 62 | Starlite ST45 074 | Weird Walk/Joe's Shuffle | £20 |

SHADES (JAMAICA)
| 69 | Gas GAS 119 | Never Gonna Give You Up/Let Me Remind You (both actually by Techniques) | £65 |

(see also Techniques)

SHADES OF BLUE (U.K.)
| 65 | Parlophone R 5270 | Voodoo Blues/Luceanne | £50 |
| 65 | Pye 7N 15988 | Where Did All The Good Times Go/I Ain't No Use | £15 |

SHADES OF BLUE (U.S.)
| 66 | Sue WI 4022 | Oh! How Happy/Little Orphan Boy | £35 |

SHADES OF JOY
| 69 | Fontana STL 5498 | SHADES OF JOY (LP) | £20 |

SHADES OF MACMURROUGH
| 73 | Polydor 2908 007 | CRAIG RIVER (LP, red label, Irish pressing) | £150 |

SHADES OF MORLEY BROWN
| 68 | Mercury MF1054 | Silly Girl/Pretty Bluebird | £120 |

SHADES (U.S.)
| 58 | London HLX 8713 | Sun Glasses (with Knott Sisters)/KNOTT SISTERS: Undivided Attention | £40 |

SHADES OF BLACK
| 90 | Intrigue IGE 12T | Play You A Song/Deeper Still/Shadows (12") | £15 |
| 92 | Intrigue IGE 25T | CLASSIC CUTS 2 (12" EP) | £15 |

SHADO
| 74 | Montrose MON 1001 | Evil City/Tell You I Know | £60 |

JOHNNY SHADOW (& DANNY GAVAN)
| 63 | Pye 7N 15506 | Golli Golli/I'm Coming Home To You (with Danny Gavan) (in p/s) | £15 |

(see also Ivy League)

SHADOWFAX
| 79 | BFD SFX 100 | Really Into You/Spare Wheel Driver (no p/s, band name spelt as Shaddowfax on label) | £50 |
| 80 | Risky Discs RISK 1 | The Russians Are Coming/Calling The Shots | £25 |

SHADOWLANDS
| 86 | Pharoah PR 002 | Cry From The Heart/Cold Nights (no p/s) | £15 |

SHADOW RING
96	Dry Leaf DF 006	Rats & Mice (lathe cut, 150 only)	£20
93	Dry Leaf DF 001	Don't Open The Window/The Heavy Foot Of The Lark	£20
93	Dry Leaf DF 002	CITY LIGHTS (LP)	£70

SHADOWS (U.K.)
SINGLES
59	Columbia DB 4387	Saturday Dance/Lonesome Fella	£40
59	Columbia DB 4387	Saturday Dance/Lonesome Fella (78)	£150
60	Columbia DB 4484	Apache/Quartermaster's Stores (later black label)	£15
65	Columbia DB 7588	Stingray/Alice In Sunderland (in export p/s)	£20
65	Columbia DB 7650	Don't Make My Baby Blue/My Grandfather's Clock (p/s)	£20

66	Columbia DB 8034	**The Dreams I Dream/Scotch On The Socks** ('B' label demos worth £50)	£35
67	Columbia PSR 305	**Thunderbirds Are Go** (1-sided advance promo)	£60
67	Columbia PSR 308	**Maroc 7** (1-sided demo with spoken-word intro)	£60
67	Columbia PSR 310	**Chelsea Boot/Jigsaw** (demo only)	£80
67	Columbia DB 8264	**Tomorrow's Cancelled/Somewhere**	£15
68	Columbia DB 8326	**Running Out Of World/HANK MARVIN: London's Not Too Far**	£15
68	Columbia DB 8372	**Dear Old Mrs. Bell/Trying To Forget The One You Love**	£15
69	Columbia DB 8628	**Slaughter On Tenth Avenue/HANK MARVIN: Midnight Cowboy**	£15

EPs

62	Columbia ESG 7881	**THE BOYS** (stereo, later black/blue labels)	£20
63	Columbia ESG 7883	**OUT OF THE SHADOWS** (stereo, turquoise labels)	£15
63	Columbia ESG 7883	**OUT OF THE SHADOWS** (stereo, black/blue labels)	£15
63	Columbia ESG 7895	**OUT OF THE SHADOWS NO. 2** (stereo ESG 7895)	£15
63	Columbia SEG 8286	**SHINDIG WITH THE SHADOWS**	£15
64	Columbia SEG 8321	**THOSE BRILLIANT SHADOWS**	£15
64	Columbia SEG 8342	**DANCE WITH THE SHADOWS**	£15
64	Columbia SEG 8362	**RHYTHM AND GREENS** (mono)	£15
64	Columbia ESG 7904	**RHYTHM AND GREENS** (stereo)	£20
64	Columbia SEG 8375	**DANCE WITH THE SHADOWS NO. 2**	£15
65	Columbia SEG 8396	**THEMES FROM "ALADDIN AND HIS WONDERFUL LAMP"**	£15
65	Columbia SEG 8408	**DANCE WITH THE SHADOWS NO. 3**	£15
65	Columbia SEG 8445	**ALICE IN SUNDERLAND**	£20
65	Columbia SEG 8459	**THE SOUND OF THE SHADOWS**	£25
66	Columbia SEG 8473	**THE SOUND OF THE SHADOWS NO. 2**	£25
66	Columbia SEG 8494	**THE SOUND OF THE SHADOWS NO. 3**	£25
66	Columbia SEG 8500	**THOSE TALENTED SHADOWS**	£22
66	Columbia SEG 8510	**THUNDERBIRDS ARE GO!** (with Cliff Richard)	£50
67	Columbia SEG 8528	**THE SHADOWS ON STAGE AND SCREEN**	£40

ALBUMS

61	Columbia 33SX 1374	**THE SHADOWS** (mono)	£20
61	Columbia SCX 3414	**THE SHADOWS** (stereo)	£30
62	Columbia 33SX 1458	**OUT OF THE SHADOWS** (mono)	£15
62	Columbia SCX 3449	**OUT OF THE SHADOWS** (stereo)	£20
63	Columbia 33SX 1522	**GREATEST HITS** (stereo SCX 1522)	£15
64	Columbia 33SX 1619	**DANCE WITH THE SHADOWS** (mono)	£15
64	Columbia SCX 3511	**DANCE WITH THE SHADOWS** (stereo)	£22
65	Columbia 33SX 1736	**THE SOUND OF THE SHADOWS** (mono)	£15
65	Columbia SCX 3554	**THE SOUND OF THE SHADOWS** (stereo)	£20
65	Columbia 33SX 1791	**MORE HITS!** (stereo SCX 3578)	£15
66	Columbia 33SX/SCX 6041	**SHADOW MUSIC**	£15
67	Columbia S(C)X 6148	**JIGSAW**	£15
67	Columbia S(C)X 6199	**FROM HANK, BRUCE, BRIAN AND JOHN**	£15
68	Columbia SX 6282	**ESTABLISHED 1958** (half by Cliff Richard, mono)	£15
70	Columbia SCX 6420	**SHADES OF ROCK**	£15
77	EMI EMTV 3	**TWENTY GOLDEN GREATS** (mispressing, side 2 plays Pink Floyd's "Animals")	£30

(see also Cliff Richard, Drifters, Five Chestnuts, Hank Marvin, Marvin Welch & Farrar, Bruce Welch, John Henry Rostill, Brian Bennett, Jet Harris, Vipers Skiffle Group, Marty Wilde, Krew Kats, Interns, Strangers, Wasp, Thunder Company, Alan Hawkshaw)

SHADOWS (U.S.)

58	HMV POP 563	**Jungle Fever/Under Stars Of Love**	£100
58	HMV POP 563	**Jungle Fever/Under Stars Of Love** (78)	£50

SHADOWS OF KNIGHT

66	Atlantic AT 4085	**Gloria/Dark Side**	£40
66	Atlantic 584 021	**Oh Yeah/Light Bulb Blues**	£35
66	Atlantic 584 045	**Bad Little Woman/Gospel Zone**	£30
67	Atlantic 584 136	**Someone Like Me/Three For Love**	£35
69	Buddah 201 024	**Shake/From Way Out To Way Under**	£30
79	Radar RAD 11	**GLORIA** (LP)	£15
98	Sundazed LP 5024	**GLORIA** (LP, 180gm vinyl, insert)	£18

DOREEN SHAFFER

70	Pama SECO 31	**FIRST LADY OF REGGAE** (LP)	£80

(see also Bob Marley/Wailers, Lloyd Clarke, Doreen & Jackie)

BOBBY SHAFTO

66	Parlophone R 5403	**Lonely Is As Lonely Does/The Same Old Room**	£15

SHAFTSBURY

80	O.K. OKA 001	**THE LULL BEFORE THE STORM** (LP, with insert)	£15

SHAG

95	No Label or cat no	**THE SHAG EP** (stamped white labels, 250 only)	£20

SHAG 'N' SKOOB

92	WINTER 3	**SKOOBY CHEWNZ VOL. 1 EP** (12")	£40

SHAG NASTY

79	Shag Nasty SN 1	**No Bullshit Just Rock 'n' Roll/Looking For A Love?** (p/s)	£40

NADINE SHAH

13	Apollo AMB1314LP	**LOVE YOUR MUM AND DAD** (LP, with CD)	£20
15	Apollo AMB1506LP	**FAST FOOD** (LP, red vinyl)	£18
17	1965 Recs OLIVE 1033V	**HOLIDAY DESTINATION** (2-LP)	£18

SHAKA FATMAN
80 Live And Love LAP 12   CONFRONTATION DUB - SHAKA (WARRIOR) VS. FATMAN (KILLER) (LP) £30

SHAKANE
70 UPC 110   Rhona/Find The Lady £15

SHAKE (2)
93 KMS UK8   CLUB SCAMS EP (12") £20

SHAKE APPEAL
88 Jericho JR 001   Amphetamine/ANYWAYS: Well Of Hurt (no p/s) £15

SHAKEOUTS
65 Columbia DB 7613   Every Little Once In A While/Well Who's That £60

SHAKER
94 Ugly Bird UBR 002   Mooncat (Spear Vocal Mix)/Mooncat (Boneseys Hand) (12") £20

SHAKERS (U.K.)
63 Polydor NH 52158   Money/Memphis Tennessee £25
63 Polydor NH 52213   Hippy Hippy Shake/Dr. Feelgood £25
63 Polydor NH 66991   Hippy Hippy Shake/Dr. Feelgood £25
63 Polydor NH 52258   Money/Hippy Hippy Shake £25
63 Polydor NH 52272   Whole Lotta Lovin'/I Can Tell £25
63 Polydor 237 139   LET'S DO THE SLOP, TWIST, MADISON, HULLY GULLY WITH THE SHAKERS (LP) £70
(see also Kingsize Taylor & Dominoes)

SHAKES
83 S 83 CUS 1982   Funeral Rites/I Kill God £30

CHRIS SHAKESPEARE GLOBE SHOW
69 Page One POF 113   Ob-La-Di, Ob-La-Da/Tin Soldier £25
(see also Globe Show)

JOHN SHAKESPEARE
69 Decca F 12896   Number One Theme/Fade Out (with p/s) £30

SHAKESPEARES
68 RCA Victor RCA 1695   Something To Believe In/Burning My Fingers £70
(see also Fynn McCool)

SHAKE THE TREE
88 Brickworks   SHAKE THE TREE (LP) £30

SHAKEY VICK
69 Pye NPL 18276   LITTLE WOMAN, YOU'RE SO SWEET (LP mono) £80
69 Pye NSPL 18276   LITTLE WOMAN, YOU'RE SO SWEET (LP stereo, in mono sleeve with 'STEREO NSPL'
        sticker on rear) £50

SAM SHAM
69 Blue Cat BS 157   Drumbago's Dead/SPARTERS: Song Of The Year £100

SHAM 69
77 Step Forward SF 4   I Don't Wanna/Ulster/Red London (black & white photo p/s) £40
77 Step Forward SF 412   I Don't Wanna/Ulster/Red London (12", black & white photo p/s)...............£20
77 Polydor (no cat. no.)   Song Of The Streets/Fanx (1-sided concert freebie, red brick-wall label; white label
        copies are counterfeits) £35
78 Polydor 2058 966   Borstal Breakout/Hey Little Rich Boy (p/s, most with 2058 966, cat no correction
        sticker on rear) £20
78 70s   What Have We Got? (1-sided gig only 45, 500 only) £30
79 Step Forward SF 412   I Don't Wanna/Red London/Ulster (12" reissue, yellow p/s) £15
79   Hersham Boys/Day Tripper (Original "Pye Studios" acetate for 'Hersham' single,
        release withdrawn as unable to clear copyright)...£250
87 Legacy LGY 70   Ban The Gun/Ban The Gun £15
78 Polydor 2383491   TELL US THE TRUTH (LP) £25
78 Polydor POLD 5010   THAT'S LIFE (LP, gatefold, with poster) £20
78 Polydor POLD 5010   THAT'S LIFE (LP, gatefold, without poster) £15
79 Polydor POLD 5025   THE ADVENTURES OF THE HERSHAM BOYS (LP, with 12" EP [2812 045], stickered
        sleeve) £20
79 Polydor POLD 5025   THE ADVENTURES OF THE HERSHAM BOYS (LP, gatefold) £15
80 Polydor POLD 5033   THE GAME (LP) £15
80 Polydor 2383 596   THE FIRST, THE BEST AND THE LAST (LP, with live EP [RIOT 1/2816 028]).........£18
86 Receiver RRLP 104   ANGELS WITH DIRTY FACES - THE BEST OF SHAM 69 (LP) £20
87 Link LINK LP 04   LIVE AND LOUD!! (LP, blue or black labels)..£15
88 Link LINK LP 025   LIVE AND LOUD!! VOLUME 2 (LP)...£15
91 Limited Edition LTD EDN LP   RARE AND UNRELEASED (LP) £15
     5
(see also Jimmy Edwards, Framed, Wanderers)

SHAMBLES
75 RCA RCA 2533   Hello Baby/Held Me Spellbound £50
(see also Mandrake Paddle Steramers, Prowler)

SHAME (1)
67 MGM MGM 1349   Don't Go 'Way Little Girl/Dreams Don't Bother Me (with picture insert) £150
67 MGM MGM 1349   Don't Go 'Way Little Girl/Dreams Don't Bother Me (without picture insert) £90
(see also Shy Limbs, King Crimson, Gods, Emerson Lake & Palmer)

SHAME (2)
16 Fnord FNORDSCR23   The Lick/Gold Hole (die-cut sleeve) £20
17 Fnord FNORDSCR13INS   Tasteless/Visa Vulture (die-cut sleeve) £20
17 Vinyl Me   Gone Fisting/Donk (p/s) £30

18	Dead Oceans DOC 187	ALL THE HITS (12" EP, p/s)	£15
20	Dead Oceans (none)	Tinsel Gate - Playable Christmas Card 500 only	£15
18	Dead Oceans DOC144	SONGS OF PRAISE (LP)	£20

SHAMEN
| 95 | One Little Indian TPLP 52L | AXIS MUTATIS/ARBOR BONA ARBOR MALA (4-LP) | £30 |
| 96 | One Little Indian TPLP 082 | HEMPTON MANOR (3-LP) | £30 |

(see also Stretchheads)

SHAMES
66	CBS 202344	Sugar And Spice/Ben Franklin's Almanac	£25
66	CBS 202450	I Wanna Meet You/We Could Be Happy	£18
67	CBS 2929	It Could Be We're In Love/I Was Lonely When	£22
68	CBS 3820	Greenburg, Glickstein, Charles, David, Smith And Jones/Warm	£15

(see also Isaac Guillory)

SHAMPOO
| 93 | Icerink DAV 06 | Blisters & Bruises/Paydirt/I Love Little Pussy (p/s, pink vinyl) | £20 |

SHAMROCKS
| 65 | Polydor BM 56503 | La La La La La/And I Need You | £20 |

WINSTON SHAN(D)
69	Bullet BU 399	Throw Me Corn/Darling Remember (B-side actually by Pat Edwards)	£35
69	Bullet BU 411	Matilda (as Wilston Shan)/HARMONIANS: Come To Me	£50
70	Moodisc MU 3505	I'll Run Away/Time Is The Master	£60
72	Camel CA 88	Audrey (as Winston Shan)/So Nice (as Winston Shan)	£20

SHANE & SHANE GANG
| 64 | Pye 7N 15662 | Whistle Stop/Who Wrote That Song | £35 |

SHANES
| 65 | Columbia DB 7601 | I Don't Want Your Love/New Orleans | £70 |

SHANGAANS
| 65 | Columbia DB 7551 | Genzene (What Have I Done)/Yeh Girl | £15 |
| 65 | Columbia Studio 2 TWO 109 | JUNGLE DRUMS (LP) | £25 |

SHANGAI
| 74 | Warner Bros K 56093 | SHANGHAI (LP) | £20 |
| 76 | Thunderbird THR 2000 | FALLEN HEROES (LP, lyric insert) | £30 |

(see also The Pirates, Cliff Bennett & The Rebel Rousers, Status Quo)

SHANGRI-LAS
65	Red Bird RB 10018	Give Him A Great Big Kiss/Twist And Shout	£15
65	Red Bird RB 10025	Out In The Streets/The Boy	£15
65	Red Bird RB 10030	Give Us Your Blessings/Heaven Only Knows	£15
65	Red Bird RB 10036	Right Now And Not Later/Train From Kansas City	£35
66	Red Bird RB 10043	I Can Never Go Home Anymore/Bulldog	£15
66	Red Bird RB 10048	Long Live Our Love/Sophisticated Boom Boom	£15
66	Red Bird RB 10053	He Cried/Dressed In Black	£15
66	Red Bird RB 10068	Past, Present, And Future/Paradise	£20
67	Mercury MF 962	The Sweet Sound Of Summer/I'll Never Learn	£15
67	Mercury MF 979	Take The Time/Footsteps On The Roof	£15
65	Red Bird RB 40 002	THE SHANGRI-LAS (EP)	£50
66	Red Bird RB 40 004	I CAN NEVER GO HOME ANYMORE (EP, unreleased)	£0
65	Red Bird RB 20 101	THE SHANGRI-LAS - LEADER OF THE PACK (LP)	£60
66	Mercury MCL 20096	GOLDEN HITS OF THE SHANGRI-LAS (LP)	£20

BUD SHANK
| 58 | Vogue LAE 12041 | THE BUD SHANK QUARTET FEATURING CLAUDE WILLIAMSON (LP) | £30 |
| 59 | Vogue LAE 12248 | LATIN CONTRASTS (LP) | £20 |

(see also Shorty Rogers)

ANANDA SHANKAR
| 69 | Reprise RSLP 6398 | ANANDA SHANKAR (JUMPING JACK FLASH) (LP) | £80 |
| 71 | Reprise K 44092 | ANANDA SHANKAR (LP, reissue) | £30 |

RAVI SHANKAR
72	Apple APPLE 37	Joi Bangla/Oh Bhaugowan/Raga Mishri-Jhinjhoti (p/s)	£40
71	Mushroom 300 MR 8	FOUR RAGA MOODS (2-LP)	£30
72	United Artists UAG 29379	AT THE WOODSTOCK FESTIVAL (LP, gatefold)	£15
73	Apple SAPDO 1002	IN CONCERT - 1972 (2-LP, with Ali Akbar Khan, gatefold sleeve)	£90

(see also Ali Akbar Khan, Will Sergeant)

BILL SHANKLY
| 70s | Technical TECLP 001A | SHANKS ON SOCCER (2-LP) | £20 |

DEAN SHANNON
| 60 | HMV POP 820 | Blinded With Love/Jezebel | £25 |
| 62 | HMV POP 1103 | Ubangi Stomp/Blowing Wild | £50 |

DEL SHANNON
SINGLES
61	London HLX 9317	Runaway/Jody (mispressed B-side, plays "The Snake" by Maximilian)	£30
65	Stateside SS 452	Move It On Over/She Still Remembers Tony	£15
66	Stateside SS 494	I Can't Believe My Ears/I Wish I Wasn't Me Tonight	£15
68	Liberty LBF 15079	Gemini/Magical Musical Box	£40

EPs

62	London RE-X 1332	RUNAWAY WITH DEL SHANNON	£20
63	London RE-X 1346	DEL SHANNON NO. 2	£20
63	London RE-X 1383	DEL'S OWN FAVOURITES	£20
63	London RE-X 1387	FROM DEL TO YOU	£20
67	Liberty LEP 2272	THE NEW DEL SHANNON	£40
65	Stateside SE 1029	DEL SHANNON HITS	£20

ALBUMS

61	London HA-X 2402	RUNAWAY WITH DEL SHANNON	£30
63	London HA-X 8071	HATS OFF TO DEL SHANNON	£30
63	London HA-X 8091	LITTLE TOWN FLIRT	£30
65	Stateside SL 10115	HANDY MAN	£40
65	Stateside SL 10130	DEL SHANNON SINGS HANK WILLIAMS	£30
65	Stateside SL 10140	ONE THOUSAND SIX HUNDRED AND SIXTY-ONE SECONDS WITH DEL SHANNON	£25
66	Liberty LBY 1320	THIS IS MY BAG (mono)	£25
66	Liberty SLBY 1320	THIS IS MY BAG (stereo)	£30
66	Liberty LBY 1335	TOTAL COMMITMENT (mono)	£25
66	Liberty SLBY 1335	TOTAL COMMITMENT (stereo)	£30
68	Liberty LBL/LBS 83114E	THE FURTHER ADVENTURES OF CHARLES WESTOVER	£80

(see also Maximilian)

SHAPE

| 71 | RCA RCA 2129 | My Friend John/Yes | £18 |

SHAPE OF THE RAIN

| 71 | RCA Neon NE 7 | RILEY, RILEY, WOOD & WAGGETT (LP, gatefold) | £250 |

SHAPES

| 79 | Sofa SEAT 1/FRR 004 | THE SHAPES (WOT'S FOR LUNCH, MUM?) (EP, no p/s, with insert) | £20 |
| 79 | Good Vibrations GOT 13 | Blast Off/Airline Disasters (p/s) | £15 |

HELEN SHAPIRO

SINGLES

64	Columbia DB 7190	Fever/Ole Father Time	£25
64	Columbia DB 7340	Shop Around/He Knows How To Love Me	£150
67	Columbia DB 8256	She Needs Company/Stop And You Will Become Aware	£250
67	Columbia DB 8256	She Needs Company/Stop And You Will Become Aware (DJ copy)	£300
69	Pye 7N 17785	You've Guessed/Take Me For A While	£20

EPs

| 61 | Columbia ESG 7872 | HELEN (stereo, 'smiling' or 'cross-armed' sleeve) | £15 |

ALBUMS

62	Columbia SCX 3438	TOPS' WITH ME (stereo)	£20
63	Columbia 33SX 1494	HELEN'S SIXTEEN (mono)	£20
63	Columbia SCX 3470	HELEN'S SIXTEEN (stereo)	£35
63	Columbia 33SX 1561	HELEN IN NASHVILLE	£20
64	Columbia 33SX 1661	HELEN HITS OUT (mono)	£20
64	Columbia SCX 3533	HELEN HITS OUT (stereo SCX 3533)	£35

SHAPIROS

| 79 | Now Records N 702 | Waitress/Isolde (no p/s, 1000 only) | £20 |

SHARADES

| 64 | Decca F 11811 | Dumb Head/Boy Trouble | £150 |

(see also Breakaways)

BILLY SHA RAE

| 71 | Action ACT 4602 | Do It/Crying Clown | £15 |

SHARK TABOO

| 82 | Risque SRTS 82 CUS 1374 | Crossfire/Dream Crumble | £20 |

SHARKS (1)

| 68 | RCA RCA 1776 | Goodbye Lorene/Funkology | £20 |

(see also Marcisa & Jeff, Roy Richards)

RALPH SHARON

| 53 | Decca LF 1138 | AUTUMN LEAVES (10" LP) | £20 |
| 53 | Lyragon AF 1 | COCKTAIL TIME (10" LP) | £15 |

SHARON AND MUSARRAT

| 81 | Multitone MUT 1003 | CHAL DISCO CHAL (LP) | £20 |

SHARON TATE EXPERIENCE

| 13 | Rise Above RISE7/175FREE | Christmas Killer/ADMIRAL SIR CLOUDESLEY SHOVEL: Blow Up The Xmas Tree 300 only: 100 white vinyl, 100 red vinyl and 100 green vinyl) | £80 |

(see also Uncle Acid and the Deadbeats)

BOBBY SHARP & OTHERS

| 65 | Stateside SS 404 | Blues For Mr. Charlie (Parts 1 & 2) (with Paul Sindap, Joe Lee Wilson & Little Butler) | £20 |

DEE DEE SHARP

62	Columbia DB 4818	Mashed Potato Time/Set My Heart At Ease	£25
62	Columbia DB 4874	Gravy (For My Mashed Potatoes)/Baby Cakes	£25
62	Cameo Parkway C 230	Ride/Night	£40
63	Cameo Parkway C 244	Do The Bird/Lover Boy	£25
63	Cameo Parkway C 260	Rock Me In The Cradle Of Love/You'll Never Be Mine	£20
63	Cameo Parkway C 274	Wild/Why Doncha Ask Me	£20

MINT VALUE £

65	Cameo Parkway C 375	I Really Love You/Standing In The Need Of Love	£80
65	Cameo Parkway C 375	I Really Love You/Standing In The Need Of Love (DJ copy)	£125
65	Cameo Parkway C 382	It's A Funny Situation/There Ain't Nothing I Wouldn't Do (demo-only)	£150
66	Atlantic 584 056	My Best Friend's Man/Bye Bye Baby	£20
69	Action ACT 4522	What Kind Of Lady/You're Gonna Miss Me	£80
79	London HA-U 8514	CAMEO PARKWAY SESSIONS (LP)	£25

(see also Chubby Checker & Dee Dee Sharp)

STEVE SHARP & THE CLEANCUTS
80	Happy Face MM 122	We Are The Mods/He Wants To Be A Mod	£125

(see also Rowdies)

BERNARD SHARPE
67	Parlophone R 5611	The Other Side Of The Sky/Where Do We Go	£15

RAY SHARPE
59	London HLW 8932	Linda Lu/Red Sails In The Sunset (triangular centre)	£50
59	London HLW 8932	Linda Lu/Red Sails In The Sunset (round centre)	£40
59	London HLW 8932	Linda Lu/Red Sails In The Sunset (78)	£30
63	United Artists UP 1032	Hey Little Girl/Day You Left Me	£15

SHARPEES
66	Stateside SS 495	Tired Of Being Lonely/Just To Please You	£75
66	Stateside SS 495	Tired Of Being Lonely/Just To Please You (DJ copy)	£150
73	President PT 389	Do The 45/Make Up Your Mind	£15

SHARPS
57	Vogue V 9086	Lock My Heart/Love Is Here To Stay	£500
57	Vogue V 9086	Lock My Heart/Love Is Here To Stay (78)	£100
58	Vogue V 9096	Shufflin'/What Will I Gain	£500
58	Vogue V 9096	Shufflin'/What Will I Gain (78)	£100

(see also Thurston Harris)

S-HATERS
81	Outer Himalayan OHR 02	Death Of A Vampire/Research (p/s)	£30
82	Outer Himalayan OHR 005	STORIES AS COLD AS THE IRISH SEA (7" EP)	£15

SHATTERED DOLLS
80	Rox ROX 1	Lipstick Killer/Talk To Me/Valley Of The Dolls 1 & 2	£20

MIKE SHAUN
63	Decca F 11733	So Lonely/Let's Fall In Love	£15

ADRIAN SHAW
96	Woronzow W0027	TEA FOR THE HYDRA (LP, 299 copies only, in hand-finished sleeves)	£15

(see also Hawkwind, Bevis Frond)

ALAN LEE SHAW
74	Alaska ALA 15	She Moans/Bolweevil	£120

MARLENA SHAW
76	Blue Note UAG 20006	JUST A MATTER OF TIME (LP)	£15
77	CBS S CBS 81844	SWEET BEGINNINGS (LP)	£15
79	CBS S CBS 83216	TAKE A BITE (LP)	£15
00	Soul Brother LP SBPJ 2	ANTHOLOGY (2-LP)	£20

NINA SHAW
68	CBS 3239	Woven In My Soul/Love So Fine (DJ copy)	£150
68	CBS 3239	Woven In My Soul/Love So Fine	£100

SANDIE SHAW
SINGLES
64	Pye 7N 15671	As Long As You're Happy Baby/Ya-Ya-Da-Da	£40
84	Rough Trade RT 130	Hand In Glove/I Don't Owe You Anything (white label test pressing)	£100

EPs
64	Pye NEP 24208	(THERE'S) ALWAYS SOMETHING THERE TO REMIND ME	£15
65	Pye NEP 24220	LONG LIVE LOVE	£15
65	Pye NEP 24232	TALK ABOUT LOVE	£15
65	Pye NEP 24234	SANDIE	£15
66	Pye NEP 24236	MESSAGE UNDERSTOOD	£15
66	Pye NEP 24247	TOMORROW	£20
66	Pye NEP 24254	NOTHING COMES EASY	£20
66	Pye NEP 24264	RUN WITH SANDIE SHAW	£25
67	Pye NEP 24271	SANDIE SHAW IN FRENCH	£25
67	Pye NEP 24273	SANDIE SHAW IN ITALIAN	£25
67	Pye NEP 24281	TELL THE BOYS	£25

ALBUMS
65	Pye NPL 18110	SANDIE	£15
65	Pye NPL 18121	ME	£15
69	Pye N(S)PL 18323	REVIEWING THE SITUATION	£50

THOMAS SHAW
72	Xtra XTRA 1132	THOMAS SHAW (LP)	£15

TIMMY SHAW & STERNPHONES
64	Pye International 7N 25239	Gonna Send You Back To Georgia/I'm A Lonely Guy	£30

TREVOR SHAW
81	CMS PR 26	WHEELS IN MOTION (LP)	£20

SHAZAM
| 83 | ADSR 001 | Let's Get Together/Memories | £150 |

SHED SEVEN
96	Polydor 575 929-2	Chasing Rainbows/In Command/The Skin I'm In (gatefold p/s)	£20
94	Polydor 523615-1	CHANGE GIVER (LP)	£70
96	Polydor 531039-1	A MAXIMUM HIGH (LP, with booklet)	£80
98	Polydor 557 359-1	LET IT RIDE (LP)	£80

BOBBY SHEEN
66	Capitol CL 15455	Dr. Love/Sweet, Sweet Love	£250
66	Capitol CL 15455	Dr. Love/Sweet, Sweet Love (DJ copies)	£300
72	Capitol CL 15713	Dr. Love/Sweet, Sweet Love (reissue)	£20
03	Atco 67855	Something New To Do/BEN E KING: I Can't Break The News To Myself	£15

(see also Bob B. Soxx & Blue Jeans)

SHEEP (U.K.)
| 73 | Myrrh MYR 1000 | SHEEP (LP, with insert) | £20 |

(see also Lonesome Stone)

SHEEP (U.S.)
| 66 | Stateside SS 493 | Hide And Seek/Twelve Months Later | £30 |

SHEEPHOUSE
| 71 | Decca 13229 | Juicy Lucy/Part 2 | £100 |

SHEER KHAN
| 84 | SRT 4KS 140 | Last Generation/Lady's Dance (p/s) | £70 |
| 85 | Mill | QUIET ENOUGH FOR LOVE (LP) | £30 |

SHEFFIELDS
64	Pye 7N 15600	It Must Be Love/Say Girl	£50
64	Pye 7N 15627	I Got My Mojo Working/Hey Hey Lover Boy	£70
65	Pye 7N 15767	Bag's Groove (Skat Walking)/Plenty Of Love	£75

SHEIKS (PORTUGAL)
| 66 | Parlophone R 5500 | Missing You/Tell Me Bird | £15 |

SHEIKS (U.S.)
| 59 | London HLW 9012 | Très Chic/Little French Doll (78) | £15 |

ALLEN SHELDON
| 70 | Plexium PXM 14 | Mirror Of My Mind/Old Windmill Tree | £50 |

DOUG SHELDON
62	Decca F 11529	Live Now Pay Later/Me	£15
65	Sue WI 332	Take It Like A Man/Lonely Boy	£40
63	Decca DFE 8527	HERE I STAND (EP)	£50

SANDI SHELDON
| 76 | Epic EPC 4186 | You're Gonna Make Me Love You/Baby You're Mine | £30 |

SHELL
| 66 | Columbia DB 8082 | Goodbye Little Girl/Little Bit Of Lovin' | £15 |

SHELLEY
| 64 | Pye 7N 15711 | I Will Be Wishing/Why Won't You Say (That You Love Me) | £15 |

PETE SHELLEY
| 82 | Lyntone 10952/53 | Qu'est-Ce Que C'est, Qu'est Que Ça (Dub)/ANIMAL MAGNET: More (hard vinyl test pressing, numbered, with info sheet/letter) | £15 |
| 80 | Groovy STP 2 | SKY YEN (mini-LP) | £18 |

(see also Buzzcocks, Free Agents)

SHELLS
| 61 | London HLU 9288 | Baby, Oh Baby/Angel Eyes | £30 |
| 62 | London HLU 9644 | It's A Happy Holiday/Deep In My Heart | £35 |

SHELLY
| 95 | Sarah SARAH 98 | Reproduction Is Pollution/Prejudice/Here (p/s) | £20 |

ANNE SHELTON
| 52 | Decca LF 1023 | FAVOURITES (10" LP) | £20 |

ROSCOE SHELTON
| 65 | Sue WI 354 | Strain On My Heart/Question (A- & B-side labels reversed) | £40 |

DEANNA SHENDEREY
| 65 | Decca F 12090 | Comin' Home Baby/I've Got That Feeling | £100 |

SHENLEY (DUFFAS) & ANNETTE
| 61 | Blue Beat BB 72 | Million Dollar Baby/The First Time I Met You | £20 |

SHENLEY (DUFFAS) & HYACINTH (BROWN)
| 66 | Rio R 80 | The World Is On A Wheel/ROY & CORNELL: Salvation | £20 |

(see also Baba Brooks)

SHENLEY (DUFFAS) & (LITTLE) LUNAN
| 65 | Rio R 52 | Something On Your Mind/The Rain Came Tumbling Down | £15 |

(see also Shenley Duffas)

SHEP & LIMELITES
| 61 | Pye International 7N 25090 | Daddy's Home/This I Know | £60 |
| 61 | Pye International 7N 25112 | Ready For Your Love/You'll Be Sorry | £100 |

DAVE SHEPHERD QUINTET
69	77 LEU 12/35	SHEPHERD'S DELIGHT (LP)	£20

ARCHIE SHEPP
66	HMV CLP/CSD 3524	FOUR FOR TRANE (LP)	£35
66	HMV CLP/CSD 3561	ON THIS NIGHT (LP)	£30
67	HMV CLP/CSD 3600	LIVE IN SAN FRANCISCO (LP)	£35
67	Polydor 623 235	ARCHIE SHEPP AND THE NEW YORK CONTEMPORARY FIVE (LP)	£30
67	Fontana 681 014 ZL	RUFUS (LP, with John Tchicai)	£35
68	Impulse MIPL/SIPL 508	MAMA TOO TIGHT (LP)	£35
68	Polydor 623 267	NEW YORK CONTEMPORARY FIVE VOL. 2 (LP)	£25
69	Impulse MILP/SIPL 512	THE MAGIC OF JU-JU (LP)	£30
69	Impulse MIPL/SIPL 516	THE WAY AHEAD (LP)	£40

(see also John Coltrane)

SHEPPARDS
71	Jay Boy BOY 30	How Do You Like It/Stubborn Heart	£40

SHEPHERD/SHEPPARD SISTERS
58	Mercury 7MT 196	Gettin' Ready For Freddy/Best Thing There Is (Is Love)(Sheppard Sisters	£15
63	London HLK 9681	Don't Mention My Name/What Makes Little Girls Cry	£20
63	London HLK 9758	Talk Is Cheap/Greatest Lover	£15

SHEPPERTON FLAMES
69	Deram DM 257	Take Me For What I Am/Goodbye	£20

(see also Mike Berry)

SHERE KHAN
69	Tepee TPR 1007	Little Louise/No Reason	£200
71	UPC 110	Rhone/Find The Lady	£60

SHERIDAN
70	Gemini GMS 001	Follow Me Follow/When Love Breaks Your Heart	£15

(see also Sheridan-Price, Mike Sheridan & Night Riders, Mike Sheridan's Lot)

DANI SHERIDAN
66	Planet PLF 106	Guess I'm Dumb/Songs Of Love	£50

MIKE SHERIDAN & NIGHT RIDERS
63	Columbia DB 7141	Tell Me What'cha Gonna Do/No Other Guy	£30
63	Columbia DB 7183	Please Mr. Postman/In Love	£30
64	Columbia DB 7302	What A Sweet Thing That Was/Fabulous	£25
65	Columbia DB 7462	Here I Stand/Lonely Weekends	£25

(see also Roy Wood, Idle Race, Mike Sheridan's Lot, Sheridan-Price, Sight & Sound)

MIKE SHERIDAN'S LOT
65	Columbia DB 7677	Take My Hand/Make Them Understand	£50
66	Columbia DB 7798	Don't Turn Your Back On Me, Babe/Stop, Look, Listen	£50

(see also Roy Wood, Idle Race, Mike Sheridan & Night Riders, Sheridan-Price, Sight & Sound)

SHERIDAN-PRICE
70	Gemini GMS 009	Sometimes I Wonder (as Sheridan & Rick Price)/SHERIDAN: Lightning Never Strikes Twice	£25
70	Gemini GME 1002	THIS IS TO CERTIFY THAT... (LP, gatefold sleeve)	£40

(see also Rick Price, Mike Sheridan & Nightriders, Mike Sheridan's Lot, Idle Race, Sight & Sound, Sheridan)

SHERMAN
72	Pye 7N45131	If You Could Read My Mind/Find My Way Back Home	£30

BIM SHERMAN
78	Yard International YI 1001	What Sweet You So/U BLACK: Pot A Bubble (12")	£15
79	Hit Run DD6/7	Down In Jamtown (with Jah Lion)/TEEM ALL STARS: Version (12")	£40
79	Hit Run HIT DD 11	Love Jah Only (with Jah Buzz)/CRYTUFF ALL STARS : Version (12")	£40
79	Attack TACK 9	Lightning And Thunder/Why Don't You Come On? (12")	£25
79	Savannah SUN 12-2	Golden Locks/Tribulation (12")	£40
83	On-U Sound DP 10	Keep You Dancing (with Dub Syndicate)/Can't Stop Jumping (with Dub Syndicate and Dr. Pablo) (10", p/s)	£60
77	Tribesman TM 007	LOVE FOREVER (LP)	£100
84	Century CENTURY 100	CENTURY (LP, with Voluntary)	£15
84	Century 200 C200	DANGER (LP)	£30
86	RDL RDL 600	HAUNTING GROUND (LP)	£20
87	RDL RDL 700	LOVER'S LEAP SHOWCASE (LP)	£18
88	On U Sound 17	ACROSS THE RED SEA (LP)	£20
88	RDL RDL 900	GHETTO DUB (LP)	£25
92	Century CENTURY 900	GHETTO DUB (LP, reissue)	£20

SHERRYS
62	London HLW 9625	Pop Pop Pop-Pie/Your Hand In Mine	£20
63	London HL 9686	Let's Stomp Again/Slop Time	£25
63	London RE 1363	DO THE POPEYE (EP)	£70

SHERWOOD
86	Sherwood SRT6KL 901	RIDING THE RAINBOW (12" EP)	£50

ADRIAN SHERWOOD
03	Real World LPRW 110	NEVER TRUST A HIPPY (2-LP)	£40

ROBERTA SHERWOOD
63	Stateside SL 10039	ON STAGE (LP)	£20

TONY SHERWOOD TRIO
60s Zodiac ZR 010   Piano Boogie Twist/Tom Dooley £15

SHE TRINITY
66   Columbia DB 7874   He Fought The Law/The Union Station Blues £20
66   Columbia DB 7992   Yellow Submarine/Promise Me You'll Never Cry £20
70   President PT 283   Hair/Climb That Tree £40
(see also Shotgun Express, Beryl Marsden, Gilded Cage)

SHEVELLES
63   Oriole CB 1915   Ooh Poo Pa Doo/Like I Love You £25

SHEVELLS
64   United Artists UP 1059 I Could Conquer The World/How Would You Like Me To Love You £30
65   United Artists UP 1076 Walking On The Edge Of The World/Not So Close £20
65   United Artists UP 1081 Watermelon Man/Taking Over Your Life £20
66   United Artists UP 1125 Come On Home/I Gotta Travel All Over...£45
68   Polydor 56239   Big City Lights/Coffee Song £15
(see also Mike Stevens & Shevells)

TONY SHEVETON
62   Oriole CB 1705   Lullaby Of Love/I Have A Feeling £20
62   Oriole CB 1726   Lonely Heart/Foolish Doubts £20
62   Oriole CB 1766   Hey Little Girl/Kissing Date £25
63   Oriole CB 1788   Runaround Sue Is Getting Married/I Love The Girl Next Door £25
63   Oriole CB 1895   A Million Drums/Dance With Me £20
64   Oriole CB 1975   Excuses/Is It Me, Is It You? £18
(see also Tony Rich)

SHIDE & ACORN
73   Private pressing   UNDER THE TREE (LP) £400
94   Acme AC 8006LP   UNDER THE TREE (LP, reissue, 500 only, numbered) £15
(see also Jeremy Cahill)

TREVOR SHIELD
69   Harry J TR 664   The Moon Is Playing Tricks On Me/KING CANNON: Soul Special £60
69   Trojan TR 665   Please/JAY BOYS: Splendour Splash £40
72   Ashanti ASH 407   Rough Road/JAY BOYS: Rough The Road £18
(see also Beltones, Trevor (Shield, Joe White with Glenn & Trevor)

SHIELDS
58   London HLD 8706   You Cheated/That's The Way It's Gonna Be £30

KEITH SHIELDS
67   Decca F 12572   Hey Gyp (Dig The Slowness)/Deep Inside Your Mind £70
67   Decca F 12609   The Wonder Of You/Run, Run, Run £30
67   Decca F 12666   So Hard Livin' Without You/Baby Do You Love Me £30
(see also Marty Wilde [& Wildcats])

ALLAN SHIERS
74   Profile GMOR 003   THE MAN IN ME (LP) £40

SUSAN SHIFRIN
71   Decca F13145   To Love/25 Miles £30

SAHIB SHIHAB QUARTET
70   Youngblood SSYB 12   SEEDS (LP) £100

SHILLELAGH SISTERS
84   CBS A 4684   Passion Fruit/These Boots Are Made For Walkin' (p/s) £15
84   CBS TA 4684   Passion Fruit/These Boots Are Made For Walkin'/Shout (12", p/s).........£30

SHINDIGS
65   Parlophone R 5316   One Little Letter/What You Gonna Do £35
65   Parlophone R 5377   A Little While Back/Why Say Goodbye £35

SHINDOGS
67   Fontana TF 790   Who Do You Think You Are/Yes, I'm Going Home £18
(see also Delaney & Bonnie, James Burton)

JOHNNY SHINES
69   Blue Horizon (S) 7-63212 LAST NIGHT'S DREAM (LP, with Otis Spann, mono or stereo) £90
74   Xtra XTRA 1142   COUNTRY BLUES (LP) £25

DON SHINN (& THE SOUL AGENTS)
66   Polydor BM 56075   A Minor Explosion/Pits Of Darkness (with The Soul Agents) £70
69   Columbia S(C)X 6319   TEMPLES WITH PROPHETS (LP) £125
69   Columbia SCX 6355   DEPARTURES (LP)..£150
(see also The Soul Agents)

SHINS
07   Sub Pop   Sea Legs/Strange Powers (p/s) £18

SHIP
72   Elektra K 42122   THE SHIP - A CONTEMPORARY FOLK JOURNEY (LP, gatefold sleeve)........£35

SHIRALEE
67   Fontana TF 855   I'll Stay By Your Side/Penny Wren...£20

SHIRELLES
58   Brunswick 05746   I Met Him On A Sunday/I Want You To Be My Boyfriend £70
58   Brunswick 05746   I Met Him On A Sunday/I Want You To Be My Boyfriend (78) £30
60   London HL 9233   Tonight's The Night/The Dance Is Over £20

MINT VALUE £

61	Top Rank JAR 549	Dedicated To The One I Love/Look-A-Here Baby	£18
61	Top Rank JAR 567	Mama Said/Blue Holiday	£15
62	Top Rank JAR 601	Baby It's You/The Things I Want To Hear	£20
62	Stateside SS 119	Welcome Home Baby/Mama Here Comes The Bride	£15
62	Stateside SS 129	Stop The Music/It's Love That Really Counts	£18
63	Stateside SS 181	Foolish Little Girl/Not For All The Money In The World	£15
63	Stateside SS 213	Don't Say Goodnight And Mean Goodbye/I Didn't Mean To Hurt You	£15
63	Stateside SS 232	What Does A Girl Do/Don't Let It Happen To Us	£15
63	Pye International 7N 25229	It's A Mad, Mad, Mad, Mad World/31 Flavours	£20
64	Pye International 7N 25233	Tonight You're Gonna Fall In Love With Me/20th Century Rock And Roll	£20
64	Pye International 7N 25240	Sha La La/His Lips Get In The Way	£15
64	Pye International 7N 25279	Maybe Tonight/Lost Love	£15
67	Pye International 7N 25425	Too Much Of A Good Thing/Bright Shiny Colours	£20
69	Mercury MF 1093	There's A Storm Going On In My Heart/Call Me (If You Want Me)	£22
75	Pye Disco Demand DDs 115	Last Minute Miracle/March	£15
61	Top Rank JKP 3012	THE SHIRELLES SOUND FEATURING "WILL YOU LOVE ME TOMORROW" (EP)	£100
61	Top Rank 35-115	THE SHIRELLES SING - TO TRUMPET AND STRINGS (LP)	£100
62	Stateside SL 10006	BABY IT'S YOU (LP)	£100
63	Stateside SL 10041	THE SHIRELLES' HITS (LP)	£50
70	Wand WNS 4	ETERNALLY SOUL (LP, with King Curtis)	£25
71	Wand WCS 1001	TONIGHT'S THE NIGHT (LP)	£15

(see also Shirley Alston)

DON SHIRLEY

56	London HA-A 2003	PIANO PERSPECTIVES (LP)	£15
56	London HA-A 2004	TONAL EXPRESSIONS (LP)	£15
57	London HAA 2046	IMPROVISATIONS (LP)	£15
62	London HAA 2448	DROWN IN MY OWN TEARS (LP, also stereo [SAHA 6238])	£15

ROY SHIRLEY

66	Ska Beat JB 253	Paradise/Calling (with Ken Boothe: uncredited)	£30
66	Doctor Bird DB 1068	Hold Them/Be Good	£30
67	Doctor Bird DB 1079	I'm The Winner/Sleeping Beauty	£45
67	Doctor Bird DB 1088	Prophet/What To Do	£40
67	Doctor Bird DB 1093	Music Field/LEE PERRY & DYNAMITES: Trial And Crosses	£50
67	Doctor Bird DB 1108	Thank You/Touch Them	£80
67	Caltone CAL 101	Get On The Ball/JOHNNY MOORE: Sound And Soul	£60
67	Island WI 3070	People Rock Steady/I'm Trying To Find A Home (actually by Uniques)	£90
67	Island WI 3071	Musical War/Soul Voice	£100
67	Island WI 3120	Girlie/GLEN ADAMS: She's So Fine	£80
68	Doctor Bird DB 1165	Hush A Bye/Musical Dinner	£35
68	JJ DB 1168	Dance The Reggay/The Agreement	£40
68	Giant GN 32	Dance Arena/The Musical Train	£40
68	Giant GN 33	Warming Up The Scene/GLEN ADAMS: Lonely Girl	£180
68	Island WI 3098	Thank You/Touch Them	£45
68	Island WI 3108	Move All Day/Rolling Rolling	£25
68	Island WI 3110	Million Dollar Baby/SENSATIONS: Long Time No See You Girl	£200
68	Island WI 3118	Good Is Better Than Bad/Fantastic Lover	£30
68	Island WI 3119	Facts Of Life/Lead Us Not Into Temptation (as Roy Shirley & Uniques; B-side actually by Roy Shirley & Slim Smith)	£60
68	Island WI 3125	If I Did Know/Good Ambition (solid orange label, later brown labels worth £20)	£40
68	Amalgamated AMG 815	The World Needs Love/Dance The Auna	£25
68	Fab FAB 54	Think About The Future/Golden Festival	£35
69	Duke DU 18	Life/I Like Your Smile	£20
72	Punch PH 103	Don't Be A Loser/Jamaican Girl	£15
74	Dip DL 5032	George Foreman Vs Muhammed Ali/DJ Race (white labels only)	£20
74	Florence F001	HOLD THEM (LP, with the Undivided Band, plain sleeve only)	£70
76	Trench Town TRELP 003	THE WINNER (LP)	£15

(see also Val Bennett, Glen Adams, Sensations, Denzil, Errol & His Group, Ronsig, Stranger & Glady)

SUSAN SHIRLEY

70	Philips 6006 037	Really Into Somethin'/My Friend The Clown	£30
71	Columbia DB 8787	True Love And Apple Pie/To Find Out (p/s)	£15

SHIRLEY & LEE

56	Vogue V 9059	Let The Good Times Roll/Do You Mean To Hurt Me So	£100
56	Vogue V 9059	Let The Good Times Roll/Do You Mean To Hurt Me So (78)	£20
57	Vogue V 9063	I Feel Good/Now That It's Over	£80
57	Vogue V 9063	I Feel Good/Now That It's Over (78)	£20
57	Vogue V 9067	That's What I Wanna Do/When I Saw You	£95
57	Vogue V 9067	That's What I Wanna Do/When I Saw You (78)	£20
57	Vogue V 9072	Rock All Nite/Don't You Know I Love You	£80
57	Vogue V 9072	Rock All Nite/Don't You Know I Love You (78)	£20
57	Vogue V 9084	Rockin' With The Clock/The Flirt	£80
57	Vogue V 9084	Rockin' With The Clock/The Flirt (78)	£20
57	Vogue V 9088	I Want To Dance/Marry Me	£60
57	Vogue V 9088	I Want To Dance/Marry Me (78)	£20
57	Vogue V 9094	Feel So Good/You'd Be Thinking Of Me	£60
57	Vogue V 9094	Feel So Good/You'd Be Thinking Of Me (78)	£20
58	Vogue V 9103	I'll Thrill You/Love No One But You	£85
58	Vogue V 9103	I'll Thrill You/Love No One But You (78)	£30

58	Vogue V 9118	Everybody's Rockin'/Don't Leave Me Here To Cry	£80
58	Vogue V 9118	Everybody's Rockin'/Don't Leave Me Here To Cry (78)	£25
59	Vogue V 9129	All I Want To Do Is Cry/Come On And Have Your Fun	£80
59	Vogue V 9129	All I Want To Do Is Cry/Come On And Have Your Fun (78)	£25
59	Vogue V 9135	A Little Word/That's What I'll Do	£60
59	Vogue V 9135	A Little Word/That's What I'll Do (78)	£30
59	Vogue V 9137	I'll Do It/Lee's Dream	£80

(The above 45s were originally issued with triangular centres; later round-centre issues are worth two-thirds of this value.)

59	Vogue V 9137	I'll Do It/Lee's Dream (78)	£30
59	Vogue V 9156	True Love/When Day Is Done	£60

(Later Vocalion pressings of the above 2 singles worth two-thirds of these values.)

59	Vogue V 9156	True Love/When Day Is Done (78)	£40
60	London HLI 9186	I've Been Loved Before/Like You Used To Do	£25
60	London HLI 9209	Let The Good Times Roll/Keep Loving Me	£20
65	Island WI 257	Let The Good Times Roll/I'm Gone	£20
57	Vogue VE 1-70101	ROCK 'N' ROLL (EP, triangular centre)	£200
57	Vogue VE 1-70101	ROCK 'N' ROLL (EP, later round centre)	£100
60	Vogue VE 1-70145	SHIRLEY AND LEE (EP)	£150
71	Jay Boy JSX 2005	LET THE GOOD TIMES ROLL (LP)	£20

SHIRLEY & RUDE BOYS
67	Blue Beat BB 375	Gently Set Me Free/BUSTER'S ALL STARS: Rock Steady	£200

SHIRTS
78	SHSP 4089	THE SHIRTS (LP, blue vinyl)	£15

SHITMAT
04	Planet Mu ZIQ 089	KILLABABYLONKUTZ (2-LP)	£18

SHIVA (2)
82	Heavy Metal HEAVY 13	Rock Lives On/Sympathy For The Devil (p/s)	£20
82	Heavy Metal HMRLP 6	FIREDANCE (LP)	£20

BUNNY SHIVEL
67	Capitol CL 15487	You'll Never Find A Love Like Mine/The Slide	£20

SHOC CORRIDOR
83	Shout LX 003	EXPERIMENTS IN INCEST (LP)	£45
84	Quiet QLP5	TRAIN OF EVENTS (LP)	£25

SHOCK
80	Sidewalk PC 5290	Angel Face/R.E.R.B (12")	£30
80	RCA DC 5290	Angel Face/R.E.R.B (12")	£15

SHOCKABILLY
84	Rough Trade ROUGH 68	COLOSSEUM (LP)	£15

SHOCK ABSORBERS
69	Major Minor SMCP 5028	GUITAR PARTY (LP)	£25

SHOCKING BLUE
69	Olga OLE 015	Send Me A Postcard/Harley Davidson (demo only)	£60
70	Penny Farthing PELS 500	SHOCKING BLUE AT HOME (LP)	£50
70	Penny Farthing PELS 510	SCORPIO'S DANCE (LP)	£40

SHOCK TREATMENT (1)
80	Skull SKR 2001	The Mugger/Nuclear Warfare (p/s)	£200

SHOES (2)
79	Sire SRK 6075	BLACK VINYL SHOES (LP)	£20

SHOES FOR INDUSTRY
80	Fried Egg FRY 1	TALK LIKE A WHELK (LP)	£20

SHOESTRING BAND
86	Attack ATA 913	High In The Sky/When The Lights Go Down (p/s)	£30
86	Attack ATA 006	SHOGUN (LP)	£40

SHOGUN MC
89	Blue Chip C22T	Ready For Action (12")	£15

TROY SHONDELL
62	Liberty LIB 55398	Island In The Sky/Tears From An Angel	£15
64	London HAY 8128	MANY SIDES OF TROY SHONDELL (LP)	£70

SHONDELLS
64	Ember EMB S 191	My Love/Don't Cry My Soldier Boy	£50

SHOO SHOO
77	Pilot PT 1	Clap Your Hands Louder/The Final Touch	£30

SHOOT
72	EMI EMA 73	ON THE FRONTIER (LP)	£25

(see also Manfred Mann Chapter 3, Yardbirds, Raw Material)

SHOP ASSISTANTS
86	Blue Guitar AZLP 2	SHOP ASSISTANTS (LP)	£20

(see also Buba & Shop assistants)

DINAH SHORE
58	RCA RD 27072	HOLDING HANDS AT MIDNIGHT (LP)	£15

BRIAN SHORT
71	Transatlantic TRA 245	ANYTHING FOR A LAUGH (LP, textured gatefold sleeve)	£30

(see also Black Cat Bones)
KEVIN SHORT
79 EMI INT 574   **Punk Strut/Short Cut** (no p/s, demos only)..£30

SHORT KUTS WITH EDDIE HARRISON
68 United Artists UP 2233   **Your Eyes May Shine/Letting The Tears Tumbling Down**...............................£40

WAYNE SHORTER
79 Blue Note LBR 1021   **THE SOOTHSAYER** (LP) £15

SHORT FUSE
72 Denby DB 316   **You Lied To Me/Circles** £50

SHORTWAVE (BAND)
77 Crescent/Avada ARS 111   **GREATEST HATS** (LP) £20

SHORTY (THE PRESIDENT)
73 Ackee ACK 509   **Aquarius Pressure/Halfway Tree Pressure** (as Shorty The President) £30
76 Cactus CTLP   **PRESENTING** (LP) £30
(see also Shorty Perry)

SHORTY & THEM
64 Fontana TF 460   **Pills Or Love's Labours Lost/Live Laugh And Love** £40

SHOT
86 Affair FAIR 2   **Main Thing** (Club Vocal)/(Dub Mix) (12") £20

SHOTGUN EXPRESS
66 Columbia DB 8025   **I Could Feel The Whole World Turn Round/Curtains** £80
67 Columbia DB 8178   **Funny 'Cos Neither Could I/Indian Thing**...£80
83 See For Miles CYM 2   **I Could Feel The Whole World Turn Round/Curtains/Funny 'Cos Neither Could I/
                                   Indian Thing** (10", p/s)...£15
(see also Rod Stewart, Peter Bardens, Spencer Davis, Brian Auger, She Trinity, Beryl Marsden, Fleetwood Mac)

SHOTS
65 Columbia DB 7713   **Keep A Hold Of What You've Got/She's A Liar** £70
(see also Smoke)

SHOUT (2)
92 Entity SHOUT   **Is It Ever Going To End** (Remix 1)/**Is It Ever Going To End** (Remix 2)/**Is It Ever Going To
                                   End**(Remix 3)/ **Is It Ever Going To End** (Radio Edit)/**Is It Ever Going To End** (Stiff Organ
                                   Mix)(12")...£60

SHOUTS
64 React EA 001   **She Was My Baby/That's The Way It's Gonna Be**...............................£50
(see also Gene Vincent)

THE SHOVE
81 Shove Off PBM033/S/81   **Raise The Roof Tonite/Violence/Pigs/Nutters Of York** (foldover p/s, 500 only) £40
81 Shove Off Records   **ROUGH AND READY EP** (with p/s)...£25
81 Shove Off Records   **ROUGH AND READY EP** £15

SHOW STOPPERS
68 Beacon 3-100   **Ain't Nothing But A House Party/What Can A Man Do** (red swirly label)......................£15
68 Beacon 3-106   **Shake Your Mini/Heartbreaker** £40
68 MGM MGM 1436   **Eeny Meeny/How Easy Your Heart Forgets Me** £15
69 Beacon BEA 130   **Just A Little Bit Of Lovin'/School Prom** £15
71 Beacon BEA 3-182   **Actions Speak Louder Than Words/ Pick Up Your Smile** £20

SHOWBIZ KIDS
80 Top Secret CON 1   **She Goes To Finos/I Don't Want To Discuss That** (p/s) £40
(see also Toy Dolls)

SHOW BOYS
69 Gas GAS 129   **People Are Wondering/Long Time** £45

SHOWMEN
62 London HLP 9481   **It Will Stand/Country Fool** £60
62 London HLP 9571   **The Wrong Girl/I Love You Can't You See** £175
69 Pama PM 767   **Action/What Would It Take** £15
(see also Norman Johnson, Chairmen Of The Board)

SHOWTIMERS
64 HMV POP 1328   **You Must Be Joking/Don't Say Goodbye** £15

SHOX
80 Axis AXIS 4   **No Turning Back/Lying Here** (p/s) £18

SHPONGLE
00 Twisted TWST   **DIVINE MOMENTS OF TRUTH** (12", p/s) £15
99 Twisted TWSLP 4   **ARE YOU SHPONGLED?** (2-LP, 1st 1000, numbered with gold/silver writing) £150
01 Twisted TWSLP 13   **TALES OF THE INEXPRESSABLE** (2-LP)...£125
03 Twisted TWSLP 23   **REMIXED** (2-LP)..£70
05 Twisted TWSLP 28   **NOTHING LASTS...BUT NOTHING IS LEFT** (2-LP)..............................£70
07 Twisted TWSLP 4   **ARE YOU SHPONGLED?** (2-LP reissue, clear sparkled vinyl) £40
08 Twisted TWSLP 13   **TALES OF THE INEXPRESSABLE** (2-LP, reissue clear sparkled vinyl) £40
10 Twisted TWSLP 36   **INEFFABLE MYSTERIES FROM SHPONGLAND** (2-LP)........................£35

MARK SHREEVE
83 Uniton U 021   **ASSASSIN** (LP) £15

DAVID SHRIGLEY
06 Contemporary Arts   **Ding/Dong** (p/s, 500 only) £20
06 Azuzi ALNLP16   **FORCED TO SPEAK WITH OTHERS** (LP) £20

SHRUG
95   Private Pressing   THE YOGURTS VS YOGURT DEBATE (Demo cassette, glued sleeve) £80
(see also Snow Patrol)

SHUBERT
68   Fontana TF 942   Until The Rains Come/Let Your Love Go £20

SALMAN SHUKUR
77   Decca Headline HEAD 16   OUD (LP) £18

MORT SHUMAN
59   Decca F 11184   Turn Me Loose/I'm A Man (tri-centre) £80
59   Decca F 11184   Turn Me Loose/I'm A Man £60
59   Decca F 11184   Turn Me Loose/I'm A Man (78) £25
67   Immediate IM 048   Monday Monday/Little Children £20

SHUSHA
71   Tangent TGS 108   PERSIAN LOVE SONGS AND MYSTIC CHANTS (LP) £15

SHUTDOWNS
63   Colpix PX 11016   Four In The Floor/Beach Buggy £50

SHY LIMBS
69   CBS 4190   Reputation/Love £70
69   CBS 4624   Lady In Black/Trick Or Two £150
(see also Shame)

SHY ONES
63   Oriole CB 1848   Nightcap/Carry Me Back £20
64   Oriole CB 1924   La Route/Susanna £18
(see also Spotnicks)

SHY (2)
83   Ebony EBON 15   ONCE BITTEN TWICE SHY (LP) £20

SHYSTER
68   Polydor 56202   Tick Tock/That's A Hoe Down £220
(see also Fleur-De-Lys)

SHY TOTS
82   ST EP 1   Gallery/Babble/English Industrial Estate (silk-screened cover)...........£25

SHYWOLF
82   MRS SW 001   Lucretia/California Jam (p/s)...£40

SIA
04   Go! Beat 986 610-1   COLOUR THE SMALL ONE (LP) £70

LEROY SIBBLES & ROCKY ELLIS
68   Studio One SO 2042   Love Me Girl/WRIGGLERS: Reel Up £80
79   Warrior Records WAR 133   Ras-Tafari/MYSTIC EYES: Forward With Love/Dub (12")...............£30
(see also John Holt, King Rocky)

DUDLEY SIBLEY
67   Coxsone CS 7010   Run Boy Run/Message Of Old (B-side actually by Joe Higgs & Ken Boothe) £70
67   Island WI 3034   Gun Man/Monkey Speaks His Mind (B-side actually by Dinsdell Thorpe)...................£50
(see also Delroy & Sporty, King Sporty, Mr. Foundation)

SICK THINGS
83   Chaos CHS 3   ANTI SOCIAL (EP) £25

SIDAN
72   Sain SAIN 27   LLIWIAU (EP)..£20
73   Sain SAIN 40   AI CYMRO WYT TI? (EP)...£20
75   Sain 1017   TEULU YNCL SAM (LP, laminated front cover) £50

SID & JOE & MOHAWKS
70   Pama PM 800   Down On The Corner/Who Is That Stranger..................................£20
(see also Mohawks)

SIDDELEYS
87   Medium Cool MC 005   What Went Wrong This Time?/No Names/My Favourite Wet Wednesday Afternoon (p/s)....................£40
88   Sombrero THREE   Sunshine Thuggery/Are You Still Evil When You're Sleeping/Falling Off My Feet Again (12", p/s) £35

FRANK SIDEBOTTOM
86   Regal Zonophone 12Z41   SCI-FI EP (12") £15
86   Regal Zonophone ZP41   SCI-FI EP (picture disc) £15
88   In Tape IT 058   5:9:88 (2-LP) £18
88   In Tape IT 060   13:9:88 (LP) £15
(see also Freshies, Chris Sievey, Billy & Barry Belly)

SIDEKICKS
66   RCA RCA 1538   Suspicions/Up On The Roof £20

SIDEWALK SOCIETY
10   Fruits De Mer Crustacean 14   In The First Place/(Tell Me) Have You Ever Seen Me/Lazy Old Sun/Dandelion (folded p/s)....................£30

SIDNEY, GEORGE & JACKIE
74   Attack ATT 8054   At The Club/Reggae Fever £275
(see also Pioneers)

PAUL SIEBEL
70   Elektra EKS 74064   WOODSMOKE AND ORANGES (LP) £20

| 71 | Elektra EKS 74081 | JACK-KNIFE GYPSY (LP) | £20 |

SIEGE
| 85 | Siege THM 1 | Goddess Of Fire (no p/s) | £18 |
| 90 | Revolution | Infest/Drop Dead (p/s) | £20 |

SIEGEL-SCHWALL BAND
| 68 | Vanguard SVRL 19044 | SHAKE (LP) | £20 |

CHRIS SIEVEY
79	Razz RAZZXEP 1	BAISER (33rpm EP, 2 tracks each by Sievey & Freshies, handwritten labels)	£40
80	Razz RAZZ 9	Last/Skip The Flight Jim (later promo edition, 50 copies only, hand-made sleeve, labels glued over original Rabid labels, please note that Skip The Flight Jim is actually Baiser)	£200
82	Razz RAZZ 8	RED INDIAN MUSIC (EP)	£18

(see also Freshies, Frank Sidebottom, Billy & Barry Belly)

LABI SIFFRE
03	Stateside SS 2228	I Got The . . ./ALL THE PEOPLE: Cramp Your Style (die-cut p/s)	£30
06	Stateside SS 2232	I Got The /The Vulture (die-cut p/s, no ellipsis after title)	£100
70	Pye Intl. NSPL 28135	LABI SIFFRE (LP)	£15
71	Pye Intl. NSPL 28147	THE SINGER AND THE SONG (LP, gatefold sleeve)	£15
72	Pye Intl. NSPL 28163	CRYING, LAUGHING, LOVING, LYING (LP, gatefold sleeve, lyric insert)	£35
75	EMI EMC 3065	REMEMBER MY SONG (LP, textured sleeve)	£200
98	EMI/Mr. Bongo MRBLP 011	REMEMBER MY SONG (LP, reissue)	£30
14	Mr Bongo MRBLP 120	REMEMBER MY SONG (LP, reissue, obi strip)	£25

RON SIG
| 71 | Camel CA 58 | 1970's/Version | £30 |

SIGHT & SOUND
| 68 | Fontana TF 927 | Ebenezer/Our Love (Is In The Pocket) | £50 |
| 68 | Fontana TF 982 | Alley Alley/Little Jack Monday | £15 |

(see also Jefferson, Sheridan & Price, Mike Sheridan)

BUNNY SIGLER
| 67 | Cameo Parkway P 153 | Let The Good Times Roll - Feel So Good/There's No Love Left | £30 |
| 67 | Cameo Parkway P 153 | Let The Good Times Roll - Feel So Good/There's No Love Left (DJ copy) | £60 |

SIGNIFICANT ZEROS
| 81 | Dingy Roons DINGE ONE | Jungle/Stiff Citizens | £20 |

SIGNS
| 66 | Decca F 12522 | Ain't You Got A Heart/My Baby Comes To Me | £40 |

SIGUE SIGUE SPUTNIK
| 86 | Parlophone PCSS 7305 | FLAUNT IT (LP, box set with insert) | £18 |

(see also Generation X, Sisters Of Mercy)

SIGUR RÓS
99	Fat Cat 12FAT 036	Svefn-G-Englar (12" EP, custom sleeve 2,000 only)	£20
00	Fat Cat 12FAT 039	NY BATTERI (mini-LP, 2,000 only)	£25
04	EMI 5496916	BA BA TI KI DI DO (12" EP)	£15
06	EMI 12EM 687	SAEGOPUR (12" p/s)	£15
00	Fat Cat FATLP 11	AGAETIS BYRJUN (2-LP)	£90
03	Fat Cat FATLP 22	() (LP)	£80
05	EMI 337 252 1	TAKK (2-LP, 10" special book edition)	£120
05	EMI 337252	SIGUR RÓS (2-LP, gatefold with inner sleeves and free 10")	£60
07	EMI 5099951041991	HEIMA (Box set, CD, DVD, 116 page book)	£50
09	Fat Cat FATLP 11X	AGAETIS BYRJUN (2-LP, reissue, 180 gm vinyl)	£30
09	Fat Cat FATLP 22X	() (2-LP, reissue, 180 gm vinyl)	£15
12	Krunk KRUNK7LP	INNI (3-LP, C-CD, DVD box set)	£30
12	Parlophone 5099962355513	VALTARI (2-LP, CD, gatefold)	£20
12	Parlophone 2564636943	VALTARI (2-LP, repressing)	£20
13	Parlophone P 958 4341	HVARF/HEIM (2-LP, one green and one blue)	£25
13	XL XLLP 606X	KVEIKUR (2-LP, 10" CD)	£20
13	XL XLB 606	KVEIKUR (8 x 12" and 1-sided 12" box set)	£100
13	XL XLLP 606X	KVEIKUR (2-LP, hand printed alternative sleeve, 50 only)	£120
18	XL XL918LP	ROUTE ONE (LP, reissue)	£35
18	XL XL920LP	LIMINAL REMIXES (LP, reissue)	£35

(see also Jonsi)

SILENT ECLIPSE
92	White (Mendoza) MEN018	How Many Miles Back To London/MCs (12")	£120
92	Mendoza MEN018	How Many Miles Back To London/MCs (12")	£80
92	Dope Jams DJAM1	Take The Stage (3 Mixes, promo 12" only)	£15

(see also Two Times Def)

SILENT MOVIES
| 79 | ESR Records ESR 1 | Ain't No Van Gough/What Did Ya Say? (p/s) | £40 |

SILENT NOISE
| 79 | Silent Noise/Easy ER 02 | I've Been Hurt (Too Many Times Before)/Heart To Heart | £75 |

SILENT ONES
| 70 | Pulse P1 | When It Rains/Lost Dreams (p/s) | £50 |

SILENT SCREAM
| 84 | Pure Motorised Instinct PMI 001 | Handstands/Jagged Path (p/s) | £25 |

SILENT WARRIORS
80   Catfish CT1   Ride Of Death/Firefly £50

SILENT NIGHT
83   Granny's Rockers S83/
     CVUS1847/UK   Cold Hearted Lady/Never Say It's Over (no p/s)..£40

SILHOUETTES (JAMAICA)
69   Sound System SSR 103   In Times Like These (act. by Lloyd Jackson & Groovers)/In Times Like These £70

SILHOUETTES (U.S.)
58   Parlophone R 4407   Get A Job/I Am Lonely £100
58   Parlophone R 4407   Get A Job/I Am Lonely (78) £50
58   Parlophone R 4425   Headin' For The Poorhouse/Miss Thing £150
58   Parlophone R 4425   Headin' For The Poorhouse/Miss Thing (78) £80

SILICON TEENS
80   Mute STUMM 2   MUSIC FOR PARTIES (LP) £20

SILKIE
65   Fontana TL 5256   THE SILKIE SING THE SONGS OF BOB DYLAN (LP)...£20

SILK TIE
73   Maple MP 004   Into The Night/Theresa £20

SILKY THREADS
75   Waverley WAV 1   Jump To It/She Runs £40

JUDEE SILL
72   Asylum SYLA 8751   JUDEE SILL (LP, gatefold sleeve) £40
73   Asylum SYL 9006   HEART FOOD (LP)..£25

JOHN SILVA
79   Jayesque (no Cat No)   MAKE UP YOUR MIND (LP, as John Silva Sextet) £150
78   Jayesque SRT/SRTX/78/CUS INN ATTENDANCE (LP)..£80
     134

SILVER EAGLE
67   MGM MGM 1345   Theodore/True As A Brand New Lie £30

SILVER (JAMAICA)
68   Jolly JY 006   Baby Oh Yeah/Rock Steady Is Here To Stay (as Silver & Magnets) £35
68   Jolly JY 012   Things/Sweet Lovin' £15
68   Jolly JY 017   I Need A Girl/Lost And Found £30
70   Columbia Blue Beat DB 117 Love Me Forever/Sugar, Sugar (B-side as Silver & Noreen) £70
71   Fab FAB 163   Change Has Got To Come/Magnet Stomp (as Silver & Magnets) £20

ANDEE SILVER
66   Fontana TF 666   Only Your Love Can Save Me/Window Shopping £25
69   Decca F 22872   Go Now/You're Just What I Was Looking For Today £20
69   Decca F 22953   With A Little Love/Te Quiero (unreleased) £0
70   Decca SKL-R 5059   A HANDFUL OF SILVER (LP)...£50

EDDIE SILVER
58   Parlophone R 4439   Seven Steps To Love/Put A Ring On Her Finger £15
58   Parlophone R 4439   Seven Steps To Love/Put A Ring On Her Finger (78) £15
58   Parlophone R 4483   Rockin' Robin/The Ways Of A Woman In Love £20
58   Parlophone R 4483   Rockin' Robin/The Ways Of A Woman In Love (78)...£20

HORACE SILVER QUINTET/TRIO
54   Vogue LDE 065   THE HORACE SILVER TRIO (10" LP) £20
69   Blue Note BST 84277   SERENADE TO A SOUL SISTER (LP) £25

LORRAINE SILVER
65   Pye 7N 15922   Lost Summer Love/I'll Know You'll Be There £100
65   Pye 7N 15922   Lost Summer Love/I'll Know You'll Be There (DJ copy)..£150
66   Pye 7N 17055   The Happy Faces/When The Love Light Starts Shining Thru His Eyes £40

MIKE SILVER & MIKE BEASON
69   Fontana STL 5506   THE APPLICANT (LP) £25

SILVER BIRCH
73   Brayford BRO 2   SILVER BIRCH (LP, private pressing) £150

SILVER BULLET
91   Parlophone R 6290   Ruff Karnage/Never Authorise Apocalypse (p/s) £35
91   Parlophone PCS 7350   BRING DOWN THE WALLS NO LIMIT SQUAD RETURNS (LP)...£15

SILVER BULLIT
72   Philips 6073808   Willpower Weak, Temptation Strong/Hittin' On You £15

SILVER BYKE
68   London HLZ 10200   I've Got Time/Who Needs Tomorrow £18

SILVER DOLLAR
74   Shire SH 003   Frightened/Oh You Devil £30

SILVERHEAD
73   Purple TPSA 7506   SILVERHEAD (LP, gatefold)...£40
73   Purple TPSA 7511   SIXTEEN AND SAVAGED (LP, gatefold sleeve) £45
(see also Blondie)

SILVER JEWS
96   Domino WIGLP 28   THE NATURAL BRIDGE (LP)..£35
98   Domino WIGLP 56   AMERICAN WATER (LP) £35

SILVER MACHINE
78   Hillside HIL SP 5004   Take Me In Your Arms/You'll Always Be The One (no p/s) £50

SILVER MOUNTAIN
83   Road Runner RR 9884   SHAKIN' BRAINS (LP) £15

PHIL SILVERS
57   Fontana Fortune Z 4040   BUGLE CALLS FOR BIG BAND (LP)..£15

SILVER SCREEN GIRLS
81   Siren SSG 1   Photographs/Silver Screen Girls (p/s)...£15

DOOLEY SILVERSPOON
75   Seville SEL 1   DOOLEY SILVERSPOON (LP) £15

SILVERSTARS
69   Trojan TR 646   Old Man Say/Promises...£120

SILVER STARS STEEL BAND
63   Island ILP 904   THE SILVER STARS STEEL BAND (LP) £20
(see also Clancy Eccles)

SILVERTONES
66   Doctor Bird DB 1028   True Confession (with Duke Reid)/TOMMY McCOOK & SUPERSONICS: More Love........£60
66   RYMSKA RA 105   True Confession/Honky Tonky Ska (with Granville Williams) £80
66   Doctor Bird DB 1041   It's Real (with Lynn Tait & Boys)/LYNN TAIT & BOYS: Storm Warning £50
67   Treasure Isle TI 7020   Cool Down/TOMMY McCOOK & SUPERSONICS: Shadow Of Your Smile...........£60
68   Treasure Isle TI 7027   In The Midnight Hour/TOMMY McCOOK & SUPERSONICS: Soul For Sale.........£25
68   Treasure Isle TI 7039   Old Man River/TOMMY McCOOK & SUPERSONICS: Our Man Flint £150
68   Treasure Isle TI 7042   Slow And Easy/TOMMY McCOOK & SUPERSONICS: Moving................£80
69   Trojan TR 7705   Intensified Change/Marie...£40
71   Clandisc CLA 234   Tear Drops Will Fall/DYNAMITES: Tear Drops - Version £15
77   Trojan TRO 9013   African Dub/Version..£35
77   Trojan TRO 9015   What A Situation/Version...£15
71   Trojan TRLS 69   SILVER BULLETS (LP) £100
(see also Valentines, Tommy McCook, Vincent Gordon, Alton Ellis, Carl Bryon, Charmers)

SILVERWING
83   Bullet BULP 1   ALIVE AND KICKING (LP) £15
(see also Big Amongst Sheep)

VICTOR SILVESTER & HIS ROCK 'N' ROLL RHYTHM
57   Columbia DB 3888   Rockin' Rhythm Roll/Society Rock £15
57   Columbia DB 3907   Alligator Roll/Off Beat Rock £15

TYRONE SIMEON
79   Burning Rockers BRD 010   Do Good In This Time/Do Good Dub (12") £15

SIMEONS
78   Freedom Sounds FSLP 002   DUB CONFERENCE IN LONDON (LP)...£25

LEO SIMMO
66   Big Beat BB351   I Love Her So/It's Good To Be Seen £25

BEVERLEY SIMMON(D)S
68   Pama PM 716   Mr. Pitiful/That's How Strong My Love Is £15
69   Pama PMLP 1   PAYS TRIBUTE TO OTIS REDDING (LP) £50
69   Pama PMLP/PMSP 9   REMEMBER OTIS (LP) £30
(see also Little Beverly)

DESMOND SIMMONS
81   Dome 33.1   ALONE ON PENGUIN ISLAND (LP) £15

(JUMPIN') GENE SIMMONS
64   London HLU 9913   Haunted House/Hey, Hey Little Girl £20
64   London HLU 9933   The Jump/The Dodo £20

GENE SIMMONS
79   Casablanca CAN 134   Radioactive/When You Wish Upon A Star (p/s, red vinyl with mask, picture label,
                                  mispressed with black/red vinyl) £50
79   Casablanca CAN 134   Radioactive/When You Wish Upon A Star (p/s, red vinyl with mask, picture label) £20
(see also Kiss)

JEFF SIMMONS
69   Straight STS 1057   LUCILLE HAS MESSED UP MY MIND (LP) £80
(see also Frank Zappa)

LITTLE MAC SIMMONS
66   Outasite OSEP 1   BLUES FROM CHICAGO (EP, 99 copies only) £200

TONY SIMMONS
83   Record Shack SOHOT 2   I Can't Let You Go/I Can't Let You Go (Instrumental) (12" promo only)..........£150

JAGO SIMMS
68   Fontana TF 901   In Too Deep/Conventional Fella..£45

JASON SIMMS & MUSIC THROUGH SIX
68   Domain D 5   It's Got To Be Mellow/MUSIC THROUGH SIX: Floppy Ears......................£20
(see also Music Through Six)

ZOOT SIMMS (JAMAICA)
63   Blue Beat BB 183   Press Along/PRINCE BUSTER ALLSTARS: 100 Ton Megaton (B-side actually "Mighty As A
                                  Rose" by Raymond Harper)..£40
63   Blue Beat BB 193   Golden Pen/ERIC MORRIS: So You Shot Reds....................................£45
64   Port-O-Jam PJ 4007   Please Don't Do It/Don't Do It (as Simms & [Lloyd] Robinson)..................£40

MINT VALUE £

68	Blue Cat BS 118	Bye Bye Baby/AL & THRILLERS: Heart For Sale	£150
69	Coxsone CS 7095	Tit For Tat/We Can Talk It Over (as Simms & Elmond)	£80

(see also Mr. Foundation, Alton Ellis)

SIMON
68	RCA Victor RCA 1668	Dream Seller/Sweet Reflections Of You	£15
69	Plum PLS 002	Mrs Lillyco/There's No More You	£40

JOE SIMON
66	London HLU 10057	Teenager's Prayer/Long Hot Summer	£30
68	Monument MON 1010	Nine Pound Steel/The Girl's Alright With Me	£20
70	Monument MON 1049	Yours Love/I Gotta Whole Lot Of Lovin'	£25
70	Monument MON 1051	That's The Way I Want Our Love/When	£15
67	Monument LMO/SMO 5005	SIMON PURE SOUL (LP)	£18
68	Monument LMO/SMO 5017	NO SAD SONGS (LP)	£18
69	Monument LMO/SMO 5026	SIMON SINGS (LP)	£18
70	Monument LMO/SMO 5030	THE CHOKIN' KIND (LP)	£18
70	Monument LMO/SMO 5033	BETTER THAN EVER (LP)	£18

PAUL SIMON
65	CBS 201797	I Am A Rock/Leaves That Are Green	£25
65	CBS (S) 62579	THE PAUL SIMON SONGBOOK (LP, mono, flipback sleeve)	£25
65	CBS (S) 62579	THE PAUL SIMON SONGBOOK (LP, stereo, flipback sleeve)	£30
72	CBS CQ 30750/Q 69007	PAUL SIMON (LP, quadrophonic)	£20
74	CBS CQ 32280/Q 69035	THERE GOES RHYMIN' SIMON (LP, quadrophonic)	£18
75	CBS Q 86001	STILL CRAZY AFTER ALL THESE YEARS (LP, quadrophonic)	£18
85	Warner Bros. WB WX52	GRACELAND (LP, embossed stickered sleeve)	£20

(see also Simon & Garfunkel, Jerry Landis, Tom & Jerry)

TONY SIMON
67	Track 604 012	Gimme A Little Sign/Never Too Much To Love	£40

SIMON & GARFUNKEL
66	CBS 202285	The Dangling Conversation/The Big Bright Green Pleasure Machine	£15
67	CBS 2911	Fakin' It/You Don't Know Where Your Interest Lies	£20
65	CBS EP 6053	WEDNESDAY MORNING 3AM (EP)	£20
66	CBS EP 6074	I AM A ROCK (EP)	£20
67	CBS EP 6360	FEELING GROOVY (EP)	£20
66	CBS (S)BPG 62690	THE SOUNDS OF SILENCE (LP, mono)	£20
66	CBS (S)BPG 62690	THE SOUNDS OF SILENCE (LP, stereo)	£35
66	CBS BPG 62860	PARSLEY, SAGE, ROSEMARY AND THYME (LP, mono, sleeve printed by 'Dawson Rossiter Limited')	£25
66	CBS (S)BPG 62860	PARSLEY, SAGE, ROSEMARY AND THYME (LP, stereo)	£35

(Originally issued with flipback sleeves & textured orange labels.)

67	Allegro ALL 836	SIMON AND GARFUNKEL (LP)	£20
68	CBS 63101	BOOKENDS (LP, mono)	£50
68	CBS 63101	BOOKENDS (LP, stereo, 1st issue, laminated front sleeve, textured orange labels, no 'stereo' on labels)	£50
68	CBS 56301	BOOKENDS (LP, stereo, 2nd issue, laminated front sleeve, textured or smooth orange labels, 'stereo' on labels)	£40
68	CBS (S) 70042	THE GRADUATE (LP, soundtrack, blue label, mono/stereo)	£15
68	CBS (S) 63370	WEDNESDAY MORNING 3AM (LP, flipback sleeve, textured orange label, mono/stereo)	£25
70	CBS S63699	BRIDGE OVER TROUBLED WATER (LP, 1st issue, laminated front sleeve, orange labels)	£20
70	CBS S63699	BRIDGE OVER TROUBLED WATER (LP, 1st issue, matt front sleeve, orange labels)	£15
72	CBS CQ 30995	BRIDGE OVER TROUBLED WATER (LP, quadrophonic)	£30
72	CBS S69003	SIMON & GARFUNKEL'S GREATEST HITS (LP)	£15

(see also Paul Simon, Art Garfunkel, Tom & Jerry)

NINA SIMONE
59	Parlophone R 4583	I Loves You Porgy/Love Me Or Leave Me	£20
66	Philips BF 1465	Either Way I Lose/Break Down And Let It Out	£15
69	RCA RCA 1903	Save Me/To Be Young Gifted And Black	£15
78	CTI CTSP 14	Baltimore/Forget	£30
94	Mercury MER 403	Feeling Good/My Baby Just Cares For Me (live) (VW p/s)	£40
02	Jazzman JM 023	Funkier Than A Mosquito/Save Me (jukebox centre)	£15
61	Parlophone GEP 8844	MY BABY JUST CARES FOR ME (EP)	£70
62	Parlophone GEP 8864	INTIMATE NINA SIMONE (EP)	£25
64	Colpix PXE 303	FINE AND MELLOW (EP)	£15
66	Colpix PXE 306	JUST SAY I LOVE HIM (EP)	£15
66	Colpix PXE 307	I LOVE TO LOVE (EP)	£15
61	Pye Intl. NPL 28014	AT THE TOWN HALL (LP)	£25
62	Pye Jazz NJL 36	FORBIDDEN FRUIT (LP)	£25
64	Colpix PXL 419	FORBIDDEN FRUIT (LP, reissue)	£15
64	Colpix PXL 421	NINA AT THE VILLAGE GATE (LP)	£25
65	Colpix PXL 465	FOLKSY NINA (LP)	£25
65	Fontana SFJL 954	TELL ME MORE (LP)	£20
65	Philips BL 7662	BROADWAY . . . BLUES . . . BALLADS (LP)	£20
65	Philips BL 7671	I PUT A SPELL ON YOU (LP)	£50
65	Philips BL 7678	IN CONCERT (LP)	£20
66	Philips BL 7683	PASTEL BLUES (LP)	£30
66	Philips (S)BL 7722	LET IT ALL OUT (LP)	£25
66	Philips (S)BL 7726	WILD IS THE WIND (LP)	£30
67	Philips (S)BL 7764	HIGH PRIESTESS OF SOUL (LP)	£25

67	RCA RD/SF 7883	SINGS THE BLUES (LP)	£50
68	RCA RD/SF 7967	SILK AND SOUL (LP)	£30
69	RCA Victor SF 7979	'NUFF SAID (LP)	£30
69	RCA SF 8018	TO LOVE SOMEBODY (LP)	£30
78	CTI 7084	BALTIMORE (LP, gatefold)	£25

SUGAR SIMONE
68	Fab FAB 33	I Love My Baby/I'll Keep You Satisfied	£18
66	Rainbow RAI 103	Is It Because/I Want To Know	£20
67	Sue WI 4029	Suddenly/King Without A Throne	£40
67	Go AJ 11409	It's Alright/Take It Easy	£30
68	CBS 3250	The Vow/Spinning Wheel	£18
69	Doctor Bird DB 1192	Black Is Gold/The Invitation	£20
69	Doctor Bird DB 1193	The Squeeze Is On/Tell Me	£25
70	Up Front SUPF 1	ALIVE AND WELL (LP)	£25

(see also Sugar & Dandy, Les Foster, Lance Hannibal)

BESSA SIMONS
| 90 | 3rd Eye (No cat no) | BESSA (LP) | £50 |

(see also Osibisa)

SIMON'S SECRETS
| 68 | CBS 3406 | Naughty Boy/Sympathy | £35 |
| 68 | CBS 3856 | I Know What Her Name Is/Keeping My Head Above Water | £40 |

(see also Secrets, Clifford T. Ward, Martin Raynor & Secrets)

SIMON SISTERS
| 64 | London HLR 9893 | Winkin', Blinkin' And Nod/So Glad I'm Here | £20 |
| 65 | London HLR 9984 | Cuddlebug/No One To Talk My Trouble To | £15 |

NIC SIMPER'S FANDANGO
| 79 | Gull GULP 1033 | SLIPSTREAMING (LP) | £20 |

(see also Deep Purple, Warhorse)

SIMPLE IMAGE
| 70 | Carnaby CNS 4013 | Spinning Spinning Spinning/Shy Boy | £15 |

SIMPLE MINDS
81	Virgin VS 451	Sweat In Bullet/20th Century Promised Land (original pressing, non-gatefold p/s)	£30
88	Virgin VS 860/VS 817	All The Things She Said/Don't You Forget About Me (Live)//Alive And Kicking/Alive And Kicking (Intrumental) double single pack in PVC sleeve sealed by sticker that states "double pack 2 for the price of 1")	£60
79	Zoom ZULP 1	LIFE IN A DAY (LP)	£15
79	Zoom SPART 1109	REAL TO REAL CACOPHONY (LP)	£15
80	Zoom SPART 1140	EMPIRES AND DANCE (LP)	£15
82	Virgin V2230	NEW GOLD DREAM (81-82-83-84) (LP, first pressing, printed gold inner)	£15
95	Virgin V2760	GOOD NEWS FROM THE NEXT WORLD (LP)	£80
16	Virgin ARHSLP 004	NEW GOLD DREAM (81-82-83-84) (LP, Abbey Road Half-Speed Master, obi strip, gold inner, Abbey Road certificate, 180 gm)	£40

(see also Johnny & Self Abusers)

SIMPLICITY PEOPLE
| 73 | Grape GR 3062 | Murderer/BIG YOUTH: The Killer | £15 |

DANNY SIMPSON
| 69 | Trojan TR 653 | Outa Sight/JOHN HOLT: I Want You Closer | £30 |

DUDLEY SIMPSON & BRIAN HODGSON
| 73 | Polydor 2383 210 | IN A COVENT GARDEN (LP) | £25 |

(See also BBC Radiophonic Workshop)

JEANETTE SIMPSON
67	Giant GN 16	Rain/Whatcha Gonna Do About It	£20
68	Giant GN 29	My Baby Just Cares For Me/Don't Let Me Cry No More (with Superboys)	£100
68	Giant GN 35	Through Loving You/Send Me Some Lovin' (with Missions)	£15

LEO SIMPSON
| 65 | Blue Beat BB 351 | I Love Her So/Good To Be Seen (as Leo Simmo) | £18 |

(see also Lionel Simpson)

LIONEL SIMPSON
65	Ska Beat JB 205	Tell Me What You Want/Love Is A Game	£20
65	Ska Beat JB 221	Red River Valley/Eight People	£15
66	Ska Beat JB 233	Give Over/Never Before	£15

(see also Leo Simpson)

MARTIN SIMPSON
| 76 | Trailer LER 2099 | GOLDEN VANITY (LP, yellow label) | £20 |
| 86 | Dambuster DAM 013 | NOBODY'S FAULT BUT MINE (LP) | £15 |

CHUCK SIMS
| 58 | London HLR 8577 | Little Pigeon/Life Isn't Long Enough | £150 |
| 58 | London HLR 8577 | Little Pigeon/Life Isn't Long Enough (78) | £60 |

FRANKIE LEE SIMS
| 71 | Specialty SNTF 5004 | LUCY MAE BLUES (LP) | £15 |

SIMS TWINS/VALENTINOS
| 68 | Soul City SCM 001 | THE VALENTINOS/THE SIMS TWINS (LP, 1 side each) | £60 |

ZOOT SIMS
| 57 | Esquire EP 183 | ZOOT! (EP) | £20 |

			MINT VALUE £
57	Esquire EP 204	ZOOT'S CASE (EP)	£20
52	Esquire 20-002	ZOOT SIMS QUARTET/QUINTET (10" LP)	£40
53	Esquire 20-010	ZOOT SIMS ALLSTARS (10" LP)	£40
53	Esquire 20-018	ZOOT SIMS QUARTET/QUINTET (10" LP)	£40
54	Vogue LDE 056	ZOOT SIMS GOES TO TOWN (10" LP)	£200
55	Esquire 20-040	ZOOT SIMS QUARTET/QUINTET (10" LP)	£60
56	Voge 12047	TONITE'S MUSIC TODAY (LP, with Bobby Brookmeyer)	£30
57	Esquire 32-040	ZOOT SIMS SEPTET (LP)	£60
58	HMV CLP 1165	GEORGE HANDY COMPOSITIONS (LP)	£30
58	HMV CLP 1188	PLAYS FOUR ALTOS (LP)	£40
61	Vogue LAE 12309	CHOICE (LP)	£40
61	Fontana TFL 5176	ZOOT AT RONNIE SCOTT'S (LP)	£200
61	Parlophone PMC 1169	DOWN HOME (LP)	£80
62	Fontana (S)TFL 588	ZOOT AT RONNIE SCOTT'S (LP, reissue)	£100
62	Fontana 886 151 TY	SOLO FOR ZOOT (LP, also mono [680 982 TL], £50)	£200
65	Fontana FJL 123	COOKIN'! (LP)	£150
60s	Xtra XTRA 5001	TROTTING! (LP)	£15

(see also Sims-Wheeler Vintage Jazz Band)

FRANK SINATRA

53	Columbia SCM 5052	Birth Of The Blues/Why Try To Change Me Now?	£20
53	Columbia SCM 5060	You Do Something To Me/Lover	£25
53	Columbia SCM 5076	Santa Claus Is Comin' To Town/My Girl	£25
54	Capitol CL 14064	Young-At-Heart/Take A Chance	£15
54	Capitol CL 14120	Three Coins In The Fountain/I Could Have Told You	£20
54	Capitol CL 14174	White Christmas/The Christmas Waltz	£15
54	Capitol CL 14188	When I Stop Loving You/It Worries Me	£15

(Originally issued with triangular centre; later round-centre copies are worth half this value.)

54	Capitol LC 6654	SONGS FOR YOUNG LOVERS (10")	£15
54	Capitol LC 6689	SWING EASY (10")	£15
54	Philips BBR 8003	SING AND DANCE WITH FRANK SINATRA (10")	£15
55	Capitol LC 6702	IN THE WEE SMALL HOURS VOL. 1 (10")	£15
55	Capitol LC 6705	IN THE WEE SMALL HOURS VOL. 2 (10")	£15
56	Capitol LCT 6106	SONGS FOR SWINGIN' LOVERS	£15
56	Capitol LCT 6111	FRANK SINATRA CONDUCTS TONE POEMS OF COLOUR	£15
59	Capitol T 581	IN THE WEE SMALL HOURS (LP, mono)	£25
62	Reprise R(9) 1006	SINATRA SINGS GREAT SONGS FROM GREAT BRITAIN (mono)	£15
62	Reprise R(9) 1006	SINATRA SINGS GREAT SONGS FROM GREAT BRITAIN (stereo)	£15
83	Mobile Fidelity SC 1	THE SINATRA COLLECTION (16-LPs in silver box, with Swing Easy LP unavailable elsewhere)	£40
85	Capitol SINATRA 20	FRANK SINATRA: THE CAPITOL YEARS (20-LP, box set)	£40

(see also Nancy Sinatra, Count Basie, Tommy Dorsey, Dean Martin)

NANCY SINATRA

61	Reprise RS 20017	Cuff Links And Tie Clips/Not Just Your Friend (with p/s)	£25
66	Reprise REP 30069	RUN FOR YOUR LIFE (EP)	£20
66	Reprise REP 30072	I MOVE AROUND (EP)	£15
67	Reprise REP 30080	SORRY 'BOUT THAT (EP)	£15
67	Reprise REP 30086	NASHVILLE NANCY (EP)	£15
66	Reprise R 6202	BOOTS (LP)	£25
66	Reprise R 6207	HOW DOES THAT GRAB YOU? (LP)	£25
66	Reprise R(S)LP 6221	NANCY IN LONDON (LP)	£25
67	Reprise RLP 6239	SUGAR (LP)	£25
67	Reprise R(S)LP 6251	COUNTRY, MY WAY (LP)	£20
68	Reprise R(S)LP 6277	MOVIN' WITH NANCY (LP)	£20
69	Reprise RSLP 6333	NANCY (LP, flipback sleeve, laminated front)	£20
73	RCA SF 8331	WOMAN (LP)	£15
72	RCA DPS 2037	THIS IS (2-LP)	£15

(see also Elvis Presley)

NANCY SINATRA & LEE HAZLEWOOD

67	Reprise REP 30083	JACKSON (EP)	£15
68	Reprise R(S)LP 6273	NANCY & LEE (LP)	£20
71	RCA Victor SF 8240	DID YOU EVER? (LP)	£18

(see also Lee Hazlewood, Frank Sinatra)

PAUL SINCLAIR

76	Third World TW 25	Naturalization/Version (as Paul Sinclaire)	£40
78	Lovers Rock DYS 68	Perfidia (vocal)/Perfidia (instrumental)//GLEN ADAMS: Can't Hide Love/Blue Moon (instrumental) (12")	£70

WINSTON SINCLAIR

69	Nu Beat NB 026	Another Heartache/Come On Little Girl	£20

(see also Harmonisers)

BETTY SINCLAIRE

70	Torpedo TOR 19	Why Why Why/HOT ROD ALL STARS: Fistful Of Dollars	£80

SINDELFINGEN

73	Deroy DER 035	ODGIPIG (LP, private pressing, with insert)	£1000
90	Cenotaph CEN 111	ODGIPIG/TRIANGLE (2-LP, reissue with live album, 300 only)	£40

TONY SINDEN

80	Piano PIANO 002	FUNCTIONAL ACTION PARTS 2 & 3 (LP)	£25

SINE
77   CBS 82870   HAPPY IS THE ONLY WAY (LP) £20
(see also Bumblebee Unlimited)

NALA SINEPHRO
21   NTS NTSM2V   LIVE AT REAL WORLD STUDIOS (1-sided 12", stamped, p/s, 250 only) £60

SINES
82   Rave PE 001   Wishing My Life/She Knows £30

PETE SINFIELD
73   Manticore K 43501   STILL (LP, textured gatefold pink sleeve) £25
73   Manticore K 43501   STILL (LP, textured gatefold blue sleeve) £20
(see also Emerson Lake & Palmer, King Crimson)

SINGAPORE
79   SRTS/79/CUS 274   Launching/A Bird With No Wings £200

RAY SINGER
65   Ember EMB S 215   I'm The Richest Man Alive/Pretty Little Rambling Rose (in p/s) £15
67   Ember EMB S 231   What's Done Has Been Done/Won't It Be Fine £60
66   Ember EMB 3364   RAY SINGER (LP) £40
(see also Nirvana [U.K.])

SUSAN SINGER
62   Oriole CB 1703   Gee It's Great To Be Young/Hello First Love £20
62   Oriole CB 1741   Bobby's Loving Touch/Johnny Summertime £150
62   Oriole CB 1778   Love Me With All Your Heart/Autumn Leaves.....................................£20
63   Oriole CB 1802   Lock Your Heart Away/Answer To A Prayer £20
63   Oriole CB 1882   I Know (You Don't Love Me No More)/That Old Feeling.....................£20
(see also Susan Holiday)

SINGER BLUE AND DUBATEERS
07   Dubateers DA 1007   Never Stop Praise Jah Jah/Jah Jah Dub/KENNY KNOTS & DUBATEERS: Show Dem/
                                    Rising Dub (10") £25

SINGERS & PLAYERS
82   On U Sound ON ULP5   WAR OF WORDS (LP) £25
82   On U Sound ON ULP11   REVENGE OF THE UNDERDOG (LP) £30
83   On U Sound ON ULP23   STAGGERING HEIGHTS (LP)..£20
84   Trance TCLP4   LEAPS & BOUNDS (LP, white vinyl) £30
88   On U Sound ON ULP39   VACUUM BUMPING (LP) £20

SINGING KETTLES
74   Hadley HS 20   A Satisfied Mind/Little Boy Lost..£15

SINGING LOINS
91   Hangman HANG 44 UP   SONGS FOR THE ORGAN (LP) £15
93   Hangman HANG 51 UP   STEAK AND GRAVY (LP) £15
(see also Billy Childish & Singing Loins)

SINGING POSTMAN
66   Parlophone PMC 7013   RECORDED DELIVERY (LP)...£15

SINGING PRINCIPAL
73   Action ACT 4608   Thank You Baby/Women's Lib £75

SINGLE FACTOR
84   SF Records SINFAX 001   Fresh Upon Her Lips/I Think I'm Falling In Love (p/s, 2 inserts) £50

SINGLES
78   Sing SING 1   Adolf Hitler/Mercy (no p/s)..£1000

MARGIE SINGLETON
60   Melodisc 45-1544   Angel Hands/The Eyes Of Love £15
62   Mercury AMT 1197   Magic Star/Only Your Shadow Knows £20
68   Fontana TL 5456   SINGS COUNTRY WITH SOUL (LP) £18

SINITTA
83   Midas 12MID 3   Never Too Late (Special Extended US Mix)/Never Too Late (Instrumental) (12", p/s).......£40

SINKING SHIPS
81   Recession REC S1   Dream/After The Rain (Live) £18

EARL SINK(S)
61   Warner Bros WB 38   Look For Me, I'll Be There/Super Market (as Earl Sink) £15
61   Warner Bros WB 51   Superstitious/Little Suzie Parker £20
63   Capitol CL 15310   Looking For Love/Raining On My Side Of Town (as Earl Sinks)...........£15
(see also Crickets, Sinx Mitchell)

SINNER
79   Whitetower AMC 705   Need Your Love/Beggar/God's In His Heaven (foldout p/s) £75

SINNERMAN & SARA
68   MGM MGM-C(S) 8099   SINNERMAN AND SARA (LP) £20

SIOUX
73   SRT SRT 73274   Prosmoe/Warlove/You're All I Need/Happiness In The Sky (EP).....................£75

SIOUXSIE AND THE BANSHEES
78   Polydor 2059 052   Hong Kong Garden/Voices (10,000 only in gatefold p/s; beige plastic, silver plastic, red
                                    plastic or red paper label)...£30
83   Fan Club FILE 1   Head Cut/Running Town (freebie, p/s) £30
87   Wonderland SHEPK 4   The Passenger/Hall Of Mirrors/You're Lost Little Girl/Sea Breezes/This Town Ain't Big
                                    Enough For Both Of Us/Gun (3 X promo 7" in plain black sleeves in foldout stickered   £20

and printed PVC wallet, single cat. no's SHESP 1/2/3)...

78	Polydor POLD 5009	**THE SCREAM** (LP, with inner sleeve)..	**£20**
79	Polydor POLD 5009	**THE SCREAM** (LP, second pressing, no inner sleeve and 'fully laminated limited edition' in gold on sleeve)	**£15**
79	Polydor POLD 5024	**JOIN HANDS** (LP, gatefold. with inner sleeve, stickered noting inclusion of 'Playground Twist'.)...	**£18**
81	Polydor POLD 5155	**JUJU** (LP, with inner)	**£15**
81	Polydor POLS 1056	**ONCE UPON A TIME : THE SINGLES** (LP, 1st pressing with Siouxsie art print)	**£18**
82	Polydor POLD 5064	**A KISS IN THE DREAMHOUSE** (LP, with inner sleeve).......................................	**£15**
83	Wonderland SHAH 1	**NOCTURNE** (2-LP, with pink/blue inner sleeves)	**£18**
84	SHE HP1	**HYAENA**..	**£25**
87	Wonderland SHELP 4	**THROUGH THE LOOKING GLASS** (LP, die-cut sleeve)..	**£15**
87	Wonderland SHELP 4	**THROUGH THE LOOKING GLASS** (LP, mispressing, 1 side plays Jimi Hendrix's "War Heroes")..	**£25**
91	Polydor 847731 7	**SUPERSTITION** (LP)	**£25**
92	Polydor 517160	**TWICE UPON A TIME - THE SINGLES** (2-LP)..	**£80**

(see also Cure, Glove)

SIR ALICK & PHRASER

82	Recommended/Black Noise 7 NO 5	**In Search Of The Perfect Baby/PROLIFIKURDS: Nursery Crymes** (printed p/s in PVC sleeve or standard p/s)...	**£20**

(see also Homosexuals)

SIR CHING I

70	Spark SRL 1041	**Hello Everyone/Hiawatha Mini Ha Ha Love**	**£300**

SIR (CLANCY) COLLINS (BAND)

68	Collins Downbeat CR 005	**Sock It Softly** (with Bob Stackie)**/LESTER STERLING, SIR COLLINS & BAND: Three Wise Men**	**£50**
68	Collins Downbeat CR 0011	**Collins And The Boys/Bob Stackie In Soho** (both with Bob Stackie).......................	**£40**
68	Collins Downbeat CR 0017	**Soul Feelings/SIR COLLINS: Hello Stella**	**£70**
69	Duke DU 46	**Black Panther/I Want To Be Loved**...	**£250**
69	Duke DU 47	**Black Diamonds** (with Diamonds)**/DIAMONDS: I Remember**	**£60**
69	Duke DU 55	**Brother Moses/Funny Familiar Feeling** (both with Earthquakes)...........................	**£70**
69	Duke DU 69	**Pair Of Wings/I Can't Stop Loving**	**£50**
73	Sir Collins Musical Wheel SC 06	**Gypsy Woman/I'm Free/Shakedown** (Sir Collins with the Versatiles)	**£45**
73	Sir Collins Musical Wheel SC 08	**Big Teacher/COLLINS & HONEY BOY: Once I Was Lonely**	**£30**
81	Sir Collins SC 001	**NEW CROSS FIRE PAGE ONE** (LP)..	**£40**

(see also Bob Stackie, Earthquakes, Collins Band, Owen Gray)

SIR COXSONE SOUND (LLOYD COXON)

75	Safari SFA 100	**KING OF THE DUB ROCK** (LP)...	**£50**
82	Regal RLP 001	**KING OF THE DUB ROCK PART 2** (LP)..	**£40**

SIR D'S GROUP

61	Blue Beat BB 66	**Hey Diddle Diddle** (with K. Brown)**/Pocket Money** (with Mossman & Zeddze)...............	**£25**

(see also Kent Brown & Rainbows)

SIR DOUGLAS QUINTET

65	London HA-U 8311	**THE SIR DOUGLAS QUINTET** (LP)..	**£40**
69	Mercury SMCL 20160	**MENDOCINO** (LP)	**£30**
69	Mercury SMCL 20186	**TOGETHER AFTER FIVE** (LP)	**£30**
75	Oval OVLM 5001	**MENDOCINO** (LP, with insert)..	**£15**

SIREN (1)

69	Dandelion 63755	**SIREN** (LP, laminated front sleeve, black/red/silver labels)...........................	**£60**
71	Dandelion DAN 8001	**STRANGE LOCOMOTION** (LP, gatefold sleeve)...	**£60**
71	Dandelion DAN 8001	**STRANGE LOCOMOTION** (LP, with later label listing K 49001).............................	**£25**

SIR GIBBS

68	Amalgamated AMG 822	**People Grudgeful/Pan Ya Machet** (both sides actually by Pioneers)	**£65**

SIR HARRY

71	Duke DU 127	**Last Call/ORGAN D: Hot Organ**	**£15**
72	Duke DU 136	**Apples To Apples/DRUM BEAT ALL STARS: Good Life**	**£15**
72	Bullet BU 519	**Mr. Parker's Daughter/U.ROY: On Top Of The Peak**	**£18**
72	Downtown DT 493	**Meet The Boss/Musical Fight**	**£40**
73	Downtown DT 504	**Apollo 17** (with Cables)**/Uptown Rock**	**£25**

(see also Barbara Jones)

SIR HORATIO

82	Rock Steady/666 Mix 1T	**Abracadubra/Sommadub** (12", plain sleeve)...	**£15**

(see also A Certain Ratio)

SIR LLOYD

71	Lion LEO 1	**Mosi/Nursery Rhyme Version**	**£20**

SIR LORD COMIC

67	Doctor Bird DB 1019	**Ska-ing West/MAYTALS: If You Act This Way**	**£40**
67	Doctor Bird DB 1070	**The Great Wuga Wuga** (with Cowboys)**/THREE TOPS: Feel So Lonesome**.....................	**£45**
70	Pressure Beat PR 5507	**Jack Of My Trade/CYNTHIA RICHARDS: United We Stand**	**£70**

(see also Lord Comic)

SIR LORD COMIXX

96	Ugly FF 004	**DANCETERIA** (12")...	**£30**

SIRUS

91	White 002	**THE ONE AND ONLY** (EP)...	**£75**
93	Go Boy GBR 001	**LYRICAL JUICE EP** (12")..	**£40**

SIR WASHINGTON
69	Star ST 1	Apollo 12/When You Kiss Me	£40
70	Saga BC 100	Apollo 13/Space	£40

SISTA MARY
07	Roots Injection RI 10 003	Blindeye/Version/Dem Lost/Version (10")	£25
08	Roots Injection RI 10 008	Hail Jah/RAS MUFFET: Version/Hail Jah/RAS MUFFET: Version (10")	£15
10	Cultivators 001	Can't Fool I/ITAL THUNDER MEETS ECHO ROOTS: Can't Dub/DANN I LOCKS: Steppin/Steppin Dub (12")	£35

SISTER
70	Camel CA 55	Feel It/MAYTONES: Serious	£15

SISTER BEVERLEY
76	Concrete Jungle CJ 605	Rasta Woman/Rasta Dub (white labels only)	£50
76	Rama (no cat no)	Rasta Woman/Rasta Woman Dub	£30

SISTER CANDY
83	Vista Sounds VSLP 4026	BLACK CULTURE (LP)	£20

SISTERS
73	Bell BELL 1307	Kick Your Boots Off/Driving Me Home	£15

SISTERS LOVE
73	Mowest MW 3009	I'm Learning To Trust My Man/Try It You'll Like It	£20
06	Soul Jazz SJR LP 133	GIVE ME YOUR LOVE (2-LP)	£18

SISTERS OF MERCY
80	Merciful Release MR 7	The Damage Done/Watch/Home Of The Hitmen (p/s, 1,000 only; beware of counterfeits without 'MR 7' matrix number)	£500
82	CNT CNT 002	Body Electric/Adrenochrome (p/s)	£200
82	Merciful Release MR 015	Alice/Floorshow (white background p/s)	£30
84	Merciful Release/WEA	ALICE/TEMPLE OF LOVE/REPTILE HOUSE/BODY AND SOUL (4 x 12" box set, promo only)	£750
84	Merciful Release MR 033	Walk Away/Poison Door (p/s, with flexidisc "Long Train" [SAM 218])	£15
84	Merciful Release MR 033T	Walk Away/Poison Door/On The Wire (12", p/s, with flexi "Long Train")	£15
88	Merciful Release MR 43TB	Dominion (Extended)/Untitled/Sandstorm/Emma (12", box set with poster)	£15
93	Merciful Release MR59T	Under The Gun (Metropolis)/Alice (1993)/Under The Gun (Jutland Mix) (12", poster p/s)	£15
85	Merciful Release MR337L	FIRST AND LAST AND ALWAYS (LP, gatefold)	£15
87	Merciful Release MR441L	FLOODLANDS (LP)	£15
90	Merciful Release MMR 449 L	VISION THING (LP)	£15
92	East West 9031 76476-`	SOME GIRLS WANDER BY MISTAKE (2-LP)	£25

(see also Mission, Ghost Dance, Dead Or Alive)

SITUATION
66	CBS 202392	Situation Now/Time	£30

SIVUCA
74	Vanguard VSD 79337	SIVUCA (LP)	£30

SIX TEASERS
89	Kent 6T 5	Doing The Hundred/WALLY COX: This Man Wants You	£15

SIX MINUTE WAR
80	(No label or cat no)	75P EP (7", fold-out p/s, 1st issue with 'soldier' sleeve)	£15

EARL SIXTEEN
79	Cha Cha CHAD 16	The World Has Begun (with the Heptones)/Make Up Your Mind (12")	£50
80	Sufferers Heights SUFF 007	African Tribesman/MIKEY DREAD: Butter Gainst Sun/Yoruba Dub (12")	£35
81	DATC DCD 004	MR D.J./GILLY BUCHANAN: Ghetto Youths/DATC MUSIC STABLE : Dub (12")	£25
81	Greensleeves GRED 64	Trials And Crosses/BARRY BROWN: Love Is What The World Wants (12")	£20
92	Riz RIZ 004	Natural Roots/Version/Part 2/Dub (12")	£40
81	Dread At The Controls DATCLP003	REGGAE SOUND (LP)	£30
83	Vista VSLP 4023	SHINING STAR (LP)	£30
93	Seven Leaves SLLP 08	PHOENIX OF PEACE (LP)	£35

16B
95	Stronghouse STR12 008	TRAIL OF DREAMS (12" EP, die-cut sleeve)	£20

SIX TEENS
56	London HLU 8345	A Casual Look/Teen Age Promise	£250
56	London HLU 8345	A Casual Look/Teen Age Promise (78)	£50

SIXTH COMM
87	Eyas Media EYAS 002	CONTENT WITH BLOOD/TURN OF THE WHEEL (LP, embossed, textured sleeve, 2,000 only)	£20
87	Eyas Media EYAS 005	TASTE FOR FLESH (LP, 1st 2,000 in laminated, full-cover sleeve)	£20
88	Eyas Media EYAS 006	FRUITS OF YGGDRASIL (LP, limited issue, 669 copies only)	£25
90	Eyas Media EYAS 013	ASYLUM (LP)	£15
90	Eyas Media EYAS 059	MORTHOGENISIS (LP)	£20

64 SPOONS
78	Bushbaby BBM 781	Ladies Don't Have Willies/Tails In The Sky (p/s)	£35

67 PARK LANE
69	Toast TT516	I'm So Happy To Be With You/I Got Love	£60

SIZE SEVEN GROUP
64	Rendevous HS 1/PR 5020	Crying My Heart Out/So How Come	£20

MINT VALUE £

SKA CHAMPIONS
65	Blue Beat BB 305	My Tears/Yesterday's Dreams	£25

SKA-DOWS
82	Cheapskate SKATE 3	SKA'D FOR LIFE (LP)	£15

SKA KINGS
64	Atlantic AT 4003	Jamaica Ska (actually by Keith Lynn & Ken Lazarus, & Byron Lee/Dragonaires)/Oil In My Lamp (actually by Eric Morris with Byron Lee & Dragonaires)	£20

SKANNA
92	White House WYHS 010	Intimidator/Jungle Rain/Cease Fire/Dreamin' (12")	£20
93	White House WYHS 013	The Future/Nightstalker/Intimidator (Technoid Mix)/Exit The Lights (12")	£50
93	Skanna 03	NIGHT STALKER EP (12")	£50
93	Skanna 04	Until The Night Is Morning/Untitled (12")	£50
93	Skanna 05	Heaven/Run To Me/This Way (12")	£30
94	Skanna 08	All You Wanted/The Greatest Thing (Criminal Minds Mix) (12")	£15
96	Skanna 09	Find Me/Find Me (Classic Skanna Mix) (12")	£20

(see also The Joker)

SKATALITES (JAMAICA)
65	Island WI 161	Trip To Mars/DOTTIE & BONNIE: Bunch Of Roses	£45
64	Island WI 164	Good News/OWEN & LEON: The Fits Is On Me	£25
65	Island WI 168	Guns Of Navarone (actually by Roland Alphonso & Studio One Orchestra)/Marcus Garvey (actually by Bongoman Byfield)	£25
65	Island WI 175	Dragon Weapon/DESMOND DEKKER & FOUR ACES: It Was Only A Dream	£80
65	Island WI 191	Dr. Kildare/Sucu Sucu	£70
65	Island WI 207	Ball O' Fire/LINVAL SPENCER: Can't Go On	£60
65	Island WI 226	Dick Tracy/RITA & SOULETTES: One More Chance	£110
65	Island WI 228	Beardman Ska/BONNIE & RITA: Bless You	£50
65	Island WI 244	Lucky Seven/JUSTIN HINDS & DOMINOES: Never Too Young	£25
66	Island WI 260	Independent Anniversary Ska (I Should Have Known Better)/WAILERS: Jumbie Jamboree	£100
65	Ska Beat JB 177	Latin Goes Ska/LORD TANAMO: Night Food Ska	£60
65	Ska Beat JB 178	Silver Dollar/My Business	£60
65	Ska Beat JB 182	Street Corner/DREAMLETS: Really Now	£85
65	Ska Beat JB 206	Timothy/KING SCRATCH & DYNAMITES: Gumma	£40
67	Studio One SOL 9006	SKA AUTHENTIC (LP)	£450
03	Motion FASTLP 009	THE LEGENDARY SKATALITES IN DUB (LP, red vinyl)	£25

(see also Justin Hinds, Deltas, Four Aces, Maytals, Jackie Opel, Joe White, Jackie Mittoo)

BOBBY SKEL
64	London HLU 9942	Kiss And Run/Say It Now	£15

SKELETAL FAMILY
83	Luggage RRP 00724	Trees/Just A Friend (foldout p/s)	£25
85	Red Rhino REDLP 57	FUTILE COMBAT (LP)	£15

(see also Ghost Dance)

SKELETON CREW
87	B BS 1	BOOGIE-WOOGIE, SKIFFLE & BLUES (12" EP, p/s)	£15
88	B BS 2	House Of The Rising Sun/Hurricane Janine (white label promo only)	£15

(see also King Earl Boogie Band, Manfred Mann's Earth Band)

SKELLATON
94	Viceroy GREEB028	Bangers 'n' Mash (12")	£30

SKEPTIX
82	Zenon SKEP 001	Routine Machine/Curfew (p/s)	£15
83	Zenon SKEP 002	Scarred For Life/Born To Lose/Peaceforce (p/s)	£15
83	Zenon SKEP 003	RETURN TO HELL (EP)	£15

SKERNE
81	Guardian GRC 81	BETTER LATE THAN NEVER (LP, private pressing)	£15

SKETTO
71	Big Shot BI 596	Know Your Friend/Three Sevens Version	£15

(, Ruddy and Sketto)

SKID
77	Galaxy GY 118	I Saw Her Standing There/Endless Sleep	£15

SKIDDY & DETROIT
72	Grape GR 3030	The Exile Song/BUNNY GALE: In The Burning Sun Joh-Ho	£35

ALAN SKIDMORE (QUINTET)
69	Deram Nova SDN 11	ONCE UPON A TIME (LP, Deram Nova on sleeve but has either Deram Nova or Decca Nova labels)	£250
71	Philips 6308 041	T.C.B. (LP)	£200

(see also John Mayall's Bluesbreakers, Brian Bennett, Centipede)

JIMMY SKIDMORE
72	DJM DJSL 026	SKID MARKS (LP)	£40

SKID ROW (IRELAND)
70	Song SO 002	New Places Old Faces/Misdemeanour Dream Felicity (Irish pressing)	£100
70	Song SO003	Saturday Morning Man (Irish pressing)	£25
70	CBS 4893	Sandie's Gone (Parts 1 & 2)	£15
71	CBS 7181	Night Of The Warm Witch/Mr. Deluxe	£15
70	CBS 63965	SKID (LP, orange label, red & blue sleeve)	£60
71	CBS 64411	34 HOURS (LP, gatefold sleeve, orange label)	£45

83 CBS 63964 **SKID ROW** (LP, different or alternative tracks) £15
(see also Gary Moore, Thin Lizzy, Peggy's Leg, UFO)

SKIDS
79 Virgin V 2116 **SCARED TO DANCE** (LP, blue vinyl, withdrawn) £1000
79 Virgin V2116 **SCARED TO DANCE** (LP, embossed sleeve black vinyl) £15
79 Virgin V 2138 **DAYS IN EUROPA** (LP, with insert, 1st pressing with withdrawn cover featuring German 'gothic' lettering & 1936 Olympics picture) £15
(see also Big Country)

SKILLETS
70 Pantonic PAN 6303 **BOTH SIDES NOW** (LP) £15

SKIN
88 Product Inc. 33 PROD 11 **SHAME, HUMILITY, REVENGE** (LP, with inner)...............................£20

SKIN ALLEY
70 CBS 5045 **Tell Me/Better Be Blind** £20
69 CBS 63847 **SKIN ALLEY** (LP, laminated front sleeve, orange label)...........................£150
70 CBS 64140 **TO PAGHAM AND BEYOND** (LP, gatefold sleeve, orange label) £60
72 Transatlantic TRA 260 **TWO QUID DEAL** (LP, laminated front with inner sleeve & poster) £50
73 Transatlantic TRA 273 **SKIN TIGHT** (LP) £25
75 Klik KLP 9007 **BAG-O-WIRE** (LP) £20

SKIN DEEP (1)
85 Enemy ENEMY 1 **FOOTBALL VIOLENCE** (EP) £500

SKIN DEEP (2)
88 Skank LP 103 **MORE THAN SKIN DEEP** (LP) £15

SKIN, FLESH & BONES
74 Opal PAL100 **Man Come, Man Go/Guitar Rhythm** £30
79 Love LPLV02 **FIGHTING DUB** (LP)...£80
(see also Vincent Gordon, Cynthia Richards)

J SCOTT SKINNER
75 Topic 12T 280 **STRATHSPEY KING** (LP, blue label) £15

JIMMIE SKINNER
59 Mercury AMT 1030 **Walkin' My Blues Away/Dark Hollow** £15

SKINNYMAN
04 Low Life LOW 36LP **COUNCIL ESTATE OF MIND** (LP) £60

SKIP BIFFERTY
67 RCA Victor RCA 1621 **On Love/Cover Girl** £30
67 RCA Victor RCA 1648 **Happy Land/Reason To Live** £40
68 RCA Victor RCA 1720 **Man In Black/Mr. Money Man** £55
68 RCA Victor RD/SF 7941 **SKIP BIFFERTY** (LP, black label) £400
68 RCA Victor RD/SF 7941 **SKIP BIFFERTY** (LP, later pressing with orange label) £200
(see also Chosen Few, Heavy Jelly, Griffin, Graham Bell, Arc, Bell & Arc, Loving Awareness)

SKIP & FLIP
59 Top Rank JAR 248 **Fancy Nancy/It Could Be** £15
(see also Gary Paxton, Skip Battin, Hollywood Argyles)

SKITZ
01 Ronin RDLP 2 **COUNTRYMAN** (LP) £15
02 Ultimate Dilemma UDR LP 018 **BADMEANINGOOD VOL 1** (2-LP, Banksy artwork)..................£300

SKITZOFRENIK
81 Guardian GRC 120 **USA/Lonely Road** (p/s) £100

SAM SKLAIR
69 Pye 7N 25488 **Zulu Warrior/Phata Phata** £15

YANI SKORDALIDIS
75 Pinnacle P8413 **Little Drummer Boy/Here Pussy Pussy** £15

SKREAM
06 Big Apple BAM 007 **Acid People/Get Mad/Who R Those Guys/Skunk Step** (12")................£25
06 Tempa TEMPALP 008 **SKREAM!** (3-LP)..£30
10 Tempa TEMPAL 016 **OUTSIDE THE BOX** (4-LP) £20

SKREWDRIVER
77 Chiswick S 11 **You're So Dumb/Better Off Crazy** (green p/s) £60
77 Chiswick S 11 **You're So Dumb/Better Off Crazy** (orange p/s) £50
77 Chiswick NS 11 **You're So Dumb/Better Off Crazy** (p/s, CBS repressing)...........£35
77 Chiswick NS 18 **Anti-Social/19th Nervous Breakdown** (p/s)..........................£40
78 Chiswick NS 28 **Streetfight/Unbeliever** (unissued, Trident label) £300
80 TJM TJM 4 **Built Up, Knocked Down/A Case Of Pride/Breakout** (p/s) £25
82 Skrewdriver SKREW 1T **BACK WITH A BANG** (12", p/s)..................................£40
83 White Noise WN 1 **White Power/Smash The I.R.A./Shove The Dove** (p/s)...........£70
83 White Noise WN 2 **Voice Of Britain/Sick Society** (p/s) £50
77 Chiswick CH 3 **ALL SKREWED UP** (mini-LP, 12-track, 45rpm, 3 different colour sleeves)........£100
77 Chiswick WIK 3 **ALL SKREWED UP** (LP, 15-track, 33rpm, unissued in U.K.; German-only) £100

SKROTEEZ
82 Skroteez SPILL 1 **OVERSPILL** (EP) £15

SKULLFLOWER
86 Broken Flag BF V9 **BIRTHDEATH** (12" EP) £80

MINT VALUE £

89	Shock SX 001	(I Live) **In The Bottomless Pit/Bo Diddley's Shitpump** (foldaround p/s in poly bag, 500 only, 75 copies in 'burns victim' sleeve)	£20
89	Shock SX 008	**XAMAN** (LP, 1000 only)	£20
89	Broken Flag BFV 10	**FORM DESTROYER** (LP)	£30
92	Headdirt HD 01	**IIIRD GATEKEEPER** (LP)	£30

(see also Ramleh)

SKULLHEAD

87	United SKULL 1	**WHITE WARRIOR** (LP)	£50
89	United SKULL 2	**ODIN'S LAW** (LP)	£20

SKULL SNAPS

73	GSF GS 27	**My Hang Up Is You/It's A New Day**	£200
95	Charly CPLP 8094	**SKULL SNAPS** (LP, first UK issue of 73 album, gatefold)	£30
18	Mr. Bongo MRBLP 184	**SKULL SNAPS** (LP, second UK issue, gatefold, insert)	£20

PATRICK SKY

65	Vanguard VSD 79179	**PATRICK SKY** (LP)	£20
70	Vanguard SVRL 19054	**A HARVEST OF GENTLE CLANG** (LP)	£20

SKYBIRD

74	Holyground HGS 118	**SUMMER OF '73** (LP, 250 copies only)	£60

SKYLINERS

59	London HLB 8829	**Since I Don't Have You/One Night, One Night**	£175
59	London HLB 8829	**Since I Don't Have You/One Night, One Night** (78)	£50
59	London HLU 8924	**This I Swear/Tomorrow**	£80
59	London HLU 8924	**This I Swear/Tomorrow** (78)	£50
59	London HLU 8971	**It Happened Today/Lonely Way**	£75
59	London HLU 8971	**It Happened Today/Lonely Way** (78)	£60
60	Polydor NH 66951	**Pennies From Heaven/I'll Be Seeing You**	£15
61	Pye International 7N 25091	**I'll Close My Eyes/The Door Is Still Open**	£20

SKYWHALE

77	Firebrand DM 013	**THE WORLD AT MINDS END** (LP)	£50

SKYY

79	Salsoul SSLP 1516	**SKYY** (LP)	£15
80	Salsoul SALP 231	**SKYYPORT** (LP)	£15

(see also New York Skyy)

SLACK ALICE

74	Philips 6308 214	**SLACK ALICE** (LP)	£20

(see also Sandra Alfred, Sandra Barry)

FREDDIE SLACK (& ORCHESTRA)

51	Capitol LC 6529	**FREDDIE SLACK'S BOOGIE WOOGIE** (10" LP)	£35

(see also Ella Mae Morse & Freddie Slack)

SLADE

SINGLES

69	Fontana TF 1056	**Wild Winds Are Blowing/One Way Hotel** (credited to The Slade)	£100
70	Fontana TF 1079	**Shape Of Things To Come/C'mon C'mon**	£80
70	Polydor 2058 054	**Know Who You Are/Dapple Rose**	£80
77	Barn 2014 106	**Burning In The Heat Of Love/Ready Steady Kids**	£18
78	Barn 2014 127	**Rock'n'Roll Bolero/It's Alright By Me**	£15
79	Barn BARN 010	**Sign Of The Times/Not Tonight Josephine**	£15
80	RSO RSO 051	**Okey Cokey/My Baby's Got It** (withdrawn reissue, existence unconfirmed)	£0
80	S.O.T.B. SUPER 45 3	**SIX OF THE BEST - NIGHT STARVATION** (12" EP, die-cut sleeve)	£15
85	RCA PB 40449/PB 40549	**Do You Believe In Miracles/My Oh My** (Swing Version)**//Santa Claus Is Coming To Town/Auld Lang Syne/You'll Never Walk Alone To Town/Auld Lang Syne/You'll Never Walk Alone**	£15
80s	Polydor 2058 422	**Merry Xmas Everybody/Don't Blame Me** (export p/s from various artist box set, green background, 4 individual photos)	£15

ALBUMS : LPS

70	Polydor 2383 026	**PLAY IT LOUD** (LP, sleeve printed by E.J. Day)	£40
70	Polydor 2383 026	**PLAY IT LOUD** (LP, later sleeve printed by Upton printers)	£25
72	Polydor 2383 101	**SLADE ALIVE!** (LP, gatefold)	£25
72	Polydor 2383 163	**SLAYED?** (LP, laminated sleeve)	£20
73	Polydor 2442 119	**SLADEST** (LP, gatefold, booklet)	£25
74	Polydor 2383 261	**OLD NEW BORROWED AND BLUE** (LP, gatefold)	£15
74	Polydor 2442 126	**SLADE IN FLAME** (LP, gatefold)	£20
76	Polydor 2383 377	**NOBODY'S FOOLS** (LP, printed inner)	£30
77	Barn 2314 103	**WHATEVER HAPPENED TO SLADE** (LP, lyric insert)	£40
78	Barn 2314 106	**SLADE ALIVE VOLUME 2** (LP)	£30
79	Barn NARB 003	**RETURN TO BASE** (LP)	£80
81	Cheapskate SKATE 1	**WE'LL BRING THE HOUSE DOWN** (LP, insert)	£15
81	RCA RCA LP 6021	**TILL DEAF DO US PART** (LP)	£20
82	RCA RCALP 3107	**SLADE ON STAGE** (LP)	£15
83	RCA PL 70116	**THE AMAZING KAMIKAZE SYNDROME** (LP, printed inner)	£15
85	RCA PL 70604	**ROGUES GALLERY** (LP, w/merch and Feel The Noize book insert)	£15
85	Telstar STAR 2271	**CRACKERS - THE SLADE CHRISTMAS PARTY ALBUM** (LP)	£15
87	RCA PL 71260	**YOU BOYZ MAKE BIG NOIZE** (LP)	£30
06	Salvo SALVOBX 401	**THE SLADE BOX - ANTHOLOGY 1969-1991** (4CD box set, booklet)	£40
09	Salvo SALVODCD 211	**LIVE AT THE BBC** (2CD, digipak, booklet)	£35
15	Salvo SALVOBX 412L	**WHEN SLADE ROCKED THE WORLD 1971-1975** (4LP/4CD/4x7"/7" flexidisc box set,	£200

coloured vinyl, 180g, books, Pledge edition with Flame lobby cards) ....
15	Salvo SALVOBX 412	**WHEN SLADE ROCKED THE WORLD 1971-1975** (4LP/4CD/4x7"/7" flexidisc box set, coloured vinyl, 180g, books) £100	
23	BMG BMGCAT 802LP	**KEEP YOUR HANDS OFF MY POWER SUPPLY** (LP, red vinyl, RSD)....................£20	
24	BMG BMGCAT 725LP	**LIVE AT THE NEW VICTORIA** (2LP, gatefold, transparent blue splatter vinyl)...................£30	

PROMOS
72	Polydor 2814 008	**Hear Me Calling/Get Down With It** (33rpm sampler for "Slade Alive", 500 only) £125
74	Polydor 2058 492	**The Bangin' Man/She Did It To Me** (export p/s) £25
75	Polydor 2058 585	**Thanks For The Memory** (with altered lyrics)/**Raining In My Champagne**.....................£25
77	Barn 2014 105	**Gypsy Roadhog/Forest Full Of Needles** (mono, DJ copy) £25
80	S.O.T.B. SUPER 3	**Night Starvation/When I'm Dancing I Ain't Fightin'** £45

FLEXIDISCS
72	Polydor/Sound For Industry SFI 122	**The Whole World's Going Crazee/MIKE HUGG: Bonnie Charlie** (33rpm with Music Scene magazine) £18
73	Lyntone LYN 2645	**Slade talk to Melanie readers** (with Melanie magazine) £15
74	Lyntone LYN 2797	**Slade exclusive to all 19 readers** (with 19 magazine)....................£15

(see also Ambrose Slade, Steve Brett, 'N Betweens, Vendors, Jimmy Lea, China Dolls,, Metal Gurus, Greenfields Of Tong)

SLADE BROTHERS
66	Pye 7N 17176	**What A Crazy Life/For A Rainy Day** £25
66	Pye 7N 17176	**Peace In My Mind/Life's Great Race** £60

SLAM CREEPERS
68	Olga OLE 009	**Saturday/Hold It Baby** £15

SLANES
65	Blue Beat BB 300	**It Takes Time/LIGES: Have Mercy Baby** (B-side actually by Frank Cosmo) £20

SLAPP HAPPY
74	Virgin VS 105	**Casablanca Moon/Slow Moon's Rose** £15
83	Half Cat HC 001	**Everybody's Slimmin'** (Even Men And Women!)/**Blue-Eyed William** (p/s).....................£15
72	Polydor 2310 204	**SORT OF** (LP, with German sleeve & insert).....................£500
74	Virgin V 2014	**SLAPP HAPPY** (LP, booklet insert) £40
75	Virgin V 2024	**DESPERATE STRAIGHTS** (LP, gatefold sleeve, with Henry Cow) £30
80	Recommended RR5	**ACNALBASAC NOOM** (LP, recorded 1973 with members of Faust) £40
81	Recommended RRS 5	**SORT OF** (LP, reissue) £40
98	V2 VVR1001661	**CA VA** (LP) £50

(see also Henry Cow, Peter Blegvad, Anthony Moore, Art Bears)

SLAUGHTER (& THE DOGS)
77	Rabid TOSH 101	**Cranked Up Really High/The Bitch** (p/s, blue, red and later cream plastic labels)...........£20
77	Rabid TOSH 101	**Cranked Up Really High/The Bitch** (p/s, repressings with b&w paper label)...................£15
78	Decca F 13758	**Quick Joey Small/Come On Back** (promo with self sealing 'spit proof' sticker on PVC sleeve).....................£75
88	Damaged Goods FNARR 1	**Where Have All The Boot Boys Gone/You're A Bore/Johnny T.** (p/s, 1,000 only: 500 on green vinyl, 500 on red vinyl) £15
78	Decca SKL 5292	**DO IT DOG STYLE** (LP) £30

(see also Studio Sweethearts, Ed Banger)

SLAVES
13	Fonthill F002	**Debbie Where's Your Car?/Okay/Not Ideal** £25
13	Fonthill F002	**Debbie Where's Your Car?/Okay/Not Ideal** (gold vinyl) £35
14	Fonthill (No cat no)	**Beauty Quest/Girl Fight x 15** (7" picture disc, tour issue).....................£20
13	Fonthill (No cat no)	**SUGAR COATED BITTER TRUTH** (LP, 300 only).....................£100
13	Fonthill (No cat no)	**SUGAR COATED BITTER TRUTH** (LP, 200 only, white vinyl).....................£110

SLAYER
84	Roadrunner RR 2444 2	**HAUNTING THE CHAPEL** (12" EP) £25
87	London LON 133	**Criminally Insane/Aggressive Perfector** (Remix) ('cross' p/s, on red vinyl with patch)......£35
87	London LONX 133	**Criminally Insane/Postmortem/Aggressive Perfector** (Remix) (12", red vinyl, no p/s)......£30
91	DEF DEFAP 912	**Seasons In The Abyss/Aggressive Perfector** (7" picture disc).....................£20
85	Roadrunner RR 9795	**HELL AWAITS** (LP) £20
87	Enigma 720151	**LIVE UNDEAD** (LP, picture disc) £25
86	London/Def Jam LONLP 34	**REIGN IN BLOOD** (LP, with inner).....................£25
87	London LONPP 34	**REIGN IN BLOOD** (LP, picture disc).....................£35
88	London/Def Jam LONLP 63	**SOUTH OF HEAVEN** (LP, stickered sleeve, inner).....................£30
90	Def American 846 871	**SEASONS IN THE ABYSS** (LP, with inner) £15
90	Metal Blade ZORRODM	**SHOW NO MERCY** (2-LP, reissue, poster) £30
91	Phonogram 510605-1	**DECADE OF AGGRESSION** (2-LP, booklet, 6,500 copies only) £25
98	American 491302 1	**DIABOLUS IN MUSICA** (2-LP, inners).....................£60
03	Universal B 00001519-02	**SOUNDTRACK TO THE APOCALYPSE** (4-CD set in 'ammo box' with backstage laminate, flag, bonus DVD in 'blood pack' and booklet).....................£35

SLEAFORD MODS
14	Fourth Dimension FDS 88	**Mr Jolly Fucker/Tweet Tweet Tweet** (p/s, 100 only, white vinyl, signed with badge) £75
14	Fourth Dimension FDS 88	**Mr Jolly Fucker/Tweet Tweet Tweet** (p/s, 100 only, red vinyl) £20
14	Fourth Dimension FDS 88	**Mr Jolly Fucker/Tweet Tweet Tweet** (p/s) £15
14	Fourth Dimension FDS 88	**Mr Jolly Fucker/Tweet Tweet Tweet** (p/s clear vinyl) £15
07	A52 Sounds A53CD001	**SLEAFORD MODS** (LP).....................£30
08	A52 Sounds A52CD002	**THE MEKON** (CD) £50
09	A52 Sounds A52CD003	**THE ORIGINATOR** (CD) £50
11	Deadly Beefburger A52CD004	**S.P.E.C.T.R.E.** (CD) £50
12	Deadly Beefburger DBRCD020	**WANK** (CD).....................£50

MINT VALUE £

14	Harbinger HARBINGER 106	**AUSTERITY DOGS** (LP)	£70
14	Harbinger HARBINGER 106	**AUSTERITY DOGS** (LP, repressing, clear vinyl)	£18
15	Harbinger HARBINGER 121	**DIVIDE AND EXIT** (LP, red vinyl)	£18
15	Harbinger HARBINGER 150	**KEY MARKETS** (LP)	£20
17	Rough Trade RTRADLPR 925	**ENGLISH TAPAS** (LP, red vinyl, insert, free 7" single)	£35

SLEATER-KINNEY
97	Matador OLE 269-1	**DIG ME OUT** (LP)	£25
00	Matador OLE 440-1	**LIVE IN PARIS** (LP,r	£20
00	Matador OLE 440-1	**ALL HANDS ON THE BAD ONE** (LP, printed inner)	£20
17	Sub Pop SP 1191	**LIVE IN PARIS** (LP, Ltd Ed, transparent green)	£20

SLEAZ BAND
74	Fontana 6007034	**All I Want Is You/Midnight Band**	£15

SLEAZE
75	No Cat no	**SLEAZE** (LP, white label private pressing, 50 only, insert)	£175

F. SLEDGE
67	Blue Beat BB 386	**Red Eye Girl/Try To Love Again** (actually by "Go On Girl"/"Giving You A Try Girl" by Freddie McKay & Buster's Group)	£40

PERCY SLEDGE
67	Atlantic 587/588 048	**WARM AND TENDER SOUL** (LP)	£20
67	Atlantic 587/588 081	**THE PERCY SLEDGE WAY** (LP)	£20
68	Atlantic 587/588 015	**WHEN A MAN LOVES A WOMAN** (LP)	£20
69	Atlantic 587/588 153	**THE BEST OF PERCY SLEDGE** (LP)	£15

SLEDGEHAMMER
79	Slammer SRTS79CUS 395	**Sledgehammer/Feel Good** (with p/s)	£20
85	Illuminated ILL 33	**In The Queue/Oxford City/1984** (shaped picture disc)	£25
83	Illuminated JAMS 32	**BLOOD ON THEIR HANDS** (LP)	£30
83	Illuminated JAMS 32	**BLOOD ON THEIR HANDS** (LP)	£25
84	Mausoleum LUST 834950	**SLEDGEHAMMER** (LP, with free 12")	£30

SLEEPER (2)
18	System SYSTM 022	**Oram Mode/Level Up** (12")	£30

SLEEPERS
80	Bat FMR 034	**Angel In A Raincoat/Endless/A Murder/TWBI**	£75

SLEEPWALKERS
59	Parlophone R 4580	**Sleep Walk/Golden Mile**	£15

SLEEPY
68	CBS 3592	**Love's Immortal Fire/Is It Really The Same**	£275
68	CBS 3838	**Rosie Can't Fly/Mrs. Bailey's Barbecue And Grill**	£60
68	No Cat No	**You'll See Me/Time Gone** (White label test pressing)	£250
(see also Grapefruit, Fynn McCool)			

SLENDER PLENTY
67	Polydor BM 56189	**Silver Tree Top School For Boys/I've Lost A Friend And Found A Lover**	£80

SLENDER THREAD
80	Rock MHMS 193	**I See The Light/Where Is The Beat**	£30

JIMI SLEVIN
82	Claddagh CCF 7	**FREEFLIGHT** (LP)	£45
(see also Peggy's Leg)			

GRACE SLICK
68	CBS 63476	**CONSPICUOUS ONLY IN IT'S ABSENCE** (LP, as Grace Slick And The Great Society)	£40

SLICKERS
68	Blue Cat BS 133	**Wala Wala/LESTER STERLING: Super Special**	£200
68	Blue Cat BS 134	**Nana** (actually by George Dekker)/**MARTIN RILEY: I May Never See My Baby Anymore**	£85
69	Blue Cat BS 154	**Frying Pan/RANFOLD WILLIAMS: Code It**	£140
69	Amalgamated AMG 852	**Man Beware/Matty Matty**	£50
69	Amalgamated AMG 866	**Money Raper/Man Beware**	£50
70	Bullet BU 449	**Coolie Gal/BIGGIE: Bawling Baby**	£50
70	Trojan TR 7718	**Run Fattie/Hoola Bulla** (song actually "Bulla Man")	£200
71	Punch PH 59	**Johnny Too Bad/Johnny Too Bad - Version**	£20
71	Dynamic DYN 406	**Johnny Too Bad/ROLAND ALFONSO: Saucy Horde** (act. by Roland Alphonso)	£30
71	Dynamic DYN 419	**You Can't Win/Don't Fight The Law**	£20
(see also G.G. Allstars, Clancy Eccles, Viceroys)			

SLIDE
80	Crash POW 4	**Superman's Shoes/Meet Your New Neighbour** (p/s)	£50

SLIM & FREEDOM SINGERS
70	Banana BA 304	**Do Dang Do** (actually by Leroy Sibbles)/**JACKIE MITTOO & SOUND DIMENSION: Hot Milk**	£60

SLINT
91	Touch & Go T&GLP64	**SPIDERLAND** (LP)	£18
93	Jennifer Hartman TG 138	**TWEEZ** (LP, reissue)	£25

SLIPKNOT
00	Roadrunner RR 8655-6	**SLIPKNOT** (LP, picture disc)	£15
01	Roadrunner 12 085641	**IOWA** (2-LP, gatefold, poster, mispressing on track 1 side 2)	£25

SLIPMASTER J
92	Lucky Spin LSR 005	**Symphonic** (1-sided 12")	£20

93	Dee Jay DJX 003	THE VISION EP (12")	£20
94	Lucky Spin STU-3	Groundhog Day (12" 1-sided white label)	£30
94	Lucky Spin STU 5	Groundhog Day Remix (12" 1-sided white label)	£20

SLIQUE
89	ChampionCHAMP 12 212	Never Give Up (Vocal)/(Instrumental)/Cheating (Vocal)/(Instrumental) (12")	£20

SLITS
79	Island WIP 6505	Typical Girls/I Heard It Through The Grapevine (p/s)	£25
79	Island 12 WIP 6505	Typical Girls/I Heard It Through The Grapevine/Typical Girls (Brink Style)/Liebe And Romanize (12", p/s)	£30
80	Rough Trade RT/Y 039	In The Beginning There Was Rhythm (1-sided promo)	£15
80	Rough Trade RT 039/Y Y 1	In The Beginning There Was Rhythm/POP GROUP: Where There's A Will There's A Way (p/s)	£18
80	Rough Trade/Y RT044/Y4	Man Next Door/Man Next Door (Version) (p/s)	£15
79	Island ILPS 9573	CUT (LP, laminated cover with inner sleeve)	£100
80	Rough Trade/Y Y 3	BOOTLEG RETROSPECTIVE (LP, plain sleeve)	£30
80	Basic 2	TYPICAL GIRLS LIVE IN CINCINNATI & SAN FRANCISCO USA (LP)	£30
81	CBS 85269	THE RETURN OF THE GIANT SLITS (LP, some with bonus 45 American Radio Interview/"Face Dub" [XPS 125])	£40
81	CBS 85269	THE RETURN OF THE GIANT SLITS (LP)	£20
88	Strange Fruit SFPS 021	THE PEEL SESSIONS (LP)	£20
89	Strange Fruit SFPMA 207	DOUBLE PEEL SESSIONS (LP)	£40
16	Island 4783700	CUT (LP, reissue, purple vinyl)	£20

(see also Raincoats)

P.F. SLOAN
72	Epic EPC 65179	RAISED ON RECORDS (LP, textured sleeve, lyric insert)	£25
80s	Big Beat WIK 73	SONGS OF OTHER TIMES (LP, some tracks as Grass Roots)	£25

(see also Grass Roots)

SAMMI SLOAN
68	Columbia DB 8480	Yes I Would/Be His Girl	£20

SLOANE SQUARE EAST
88	Hans Aid BMP 010	Hands Reach Out/Hand Reach Out (Remix) (p/s)	£15

SLOW CLUB
10	Moshi Moshi MOSHILP 29	YEAH SO (LP and CD, Record Store Day Release)	£18
12	Moshi Moshi MOSHILP 41	PARADISE (LP, blue vinyl)	£25

SLOWDIVE
17	Dead Oceans	Sugar For The Pill (Avalon Emerson's Gilden Escalation)/(Simon Scott Eurorack Remix) (12", p/s, signed, 20 only)	£250
90	Creation CRE 093T	Slowdive/Avalyn 1/Avalyn 2	£30
90	Creation CRE093T	SLOWDIVE EP	£30
91	Creation CRE 098T	Morningrise/She Calls/Losing Today (12")	£25
91	Creation CRE 112T	HOLDING OUR BREATH EP (12", p/s)	£20
91	Creation CRE 112	Catch The Breeze/Shine (p/s, numbered)	£15
93	Creation CRE 119T	OUTSIDE YOUR ROOM EP (12")	£50
93	Creation CRE 157T	5 EP (12")	£40
19	Sonic Cathedral SCR 117	Golden Hair (Live) Part 1/Part 2 (p/s, gold vinyl)	£80
91	Creation CRELP 094	JUST FOR A DAY (LP)	£60
92	Creation CRE X101	BLUE DAY (LP)	£80
93	Creation CRELP 139	SOUVLAKI (LP, picture inner sleeve)	£200
95	Creation CRELP 168	PYGMALION (LP)	£150
11	Music On Vinyl MOVLP354	JUST FOR A DAY (LP, reissue)	£25
11	Music On Vinyl MOVLP202	SOUVAKI (LP, reissue)	£25
12	Music On Vinyl MOVLP604	PYGMALION (LP, reissue)	£25
12	Music On Vinyl MOVLP604	PYGMALION (LP, white vinyl, 1000 only)	£25
15	Music On Vinyl MOVLP1380	BLUE DAY (LP, reissue)	£20

(see also Mojave 3, Rachel Goswell, Neil Halstead, Black Hearted Brother, Eternal)

SLOW DOG
72	Parlophone R5942	Walking Through The Blue Grass/Ain't Never Going Home	£30

SLOWGUNS
79	MPA SMP 088	TV Movie/American Heartbeat	£15

SLOWLOAD
71	MAM MAM 27	On The Road Again/Big Boobs Boogie	£35

(see also Fruit Eating Bears)

SLOW MOTION
79	RK RK 1024	Christmas Charade/Maybe	£40

SLOW READERS CLUB
13	(no label or cat. no.)	Forever In Your Debt/Days Like This Will Break Your Heart (p/s, 200 only)	£50
18	Modern Sky MODERN036LPX	BUILD A TOWER (LP, red vinyl)	£18
18	Modern Sky MODERN036LP	BUILD A TOWER (LP, different artwork, marigold and black swirl vinyl, insert signed by band)	£50
18	(No label or cat. no.)	CAVALCADE: LIVE AT THE MET (LP, white vinyl, with marbled effect, printed set list, 500 only)	£50

(see also Omerta)

SLOWTRAIN
80	Spirit SR 1	Ronnie/Just One Way	£30

MINT VALUE £

SLR CREW
88 SLR XPR1536   Bass Drum/Life's A Bitch (12") £50

SL TROOPERS
88 Global Rhythm GR001   Debut (Unarmed And Dangerous) (12", 500 pressed) £40

SLUSH
78 Ember EMB 5367   White Christmas/Rich Man (no p/s) £40
(See also Pumphouse Gang)

SLY ALICE
72 Sunday SUN 02   Drifting Away/The Games Over (p/s) £50

SLY & THE REVOLUTIONARIES
80 Trojan TRLS 186   BLACK ASH DUB (LP) £30

JOAN SMALL
57 Parlophone R 4269   Gonna Get Along Without You Now/You Can't Say I Love You To A Rock & Roll Tune £15

JOHN SMALL
70 G&W FAM 101   Let's Ride/A Woman Who Can Shake My Mind £15

KAREN SMALL
66 Vocalion V 9281   To Get You Back Again/That's Why I Cry £50

DENIS SMALLEY
81 University Of East Anglia   THE PULSE OF TIME (LP) £40
    UEA 81063

SMALL FACES

SINGLES
65 Decca F 12208   Whatcha Gonna Do About It?/What's A Matter, Baby? £20
65 Decca F 12276   I've Got Mine/It's Too Late £25
66 Decca F 12393   Hey Girl/Almost Grown £15
66 Decca F 12500   My Mind's Eye (alternate demo mix, matrix no. ends T1-1C)/I Can't Dance With You
                            (withdrawn) £30
67 Decca F 12565   I Can't Make It/Just Passing £25
67 Decca F 12565   I Can't Make It/Just Passing (in export p/s) £60
67 Decca F 12619   Patterns/E Too D (with export p/s) £140
67 Decca F 12619   Patterns/E Too D £70
67 Immediate AS 1   Small Faces (1-sided sampler for "Small Faces", promo only) £250
67 Immediate IM 062   Tin Soldier/I Feel Much Better (in p/s) £80
67 Immediate IM 062   Tin Soldier/I Feel Much Better £15
69 Immediate IM 077   Afterglow (Of Your Love)/Wham Bam, Thank You Mam (demos [perhaps some copies]
                            have demo version of B-side) £60
69 Immediate IM 077   Afterglow (Of Your Love)/Wham Bam, Thank You Mam (demos) £15

ALBUMS : LPS
66 Decca LK 4790   SMALL FACES (original red label) £250
67 Decca LK 4879   FROM THE BEGINNING (original red label) £280
67 Immediate IMLP 008   SMALL FACES (mono) £250
67 Immediate IMSP 008   SMALL FACES (stereo) £250
68 Immediate IMLP 012   OGDENS' NUT GONE FLAKE (lilac label, circular foldout sleeve, mono) ... £250
68 Immediate IMSP 012   OGDENS' NUT GONE FLAKE (lilac label, circular foldout sleeve, stereo) £150
68 Immediate IMLP 012   OGDENS' NUT GONE FLAKE (pink label, circular foldout sleeve, mono) ... £120
68 Immediate IMSP 012   OGDENS' NUT GONE FLAKE (pink label, circular foldout sleeve, stereo) £80
69 Decca LK 4790   SMALL FACES (boxed Decca label) £50
69 Decca LK 4879   FROM THE BEGINNING (boxed Decca label) £40
69 Immediate IMLP/IMSP 022   IN MEMORIAM (export issue [German copies more common, £60]) £150
69 Immediate IMAL 01/02   THE AUTUMN STONE (2-LP, gatefold sleeve) £80
75 Immediate/NEMS IML 1001 OGDENS' NUT GONE FLAKE (reissue, round sleeve, white label) £40
76 NEMS AML 1008   MAGIC MOMENTS £15
77 Immediate/NEMS IML 2001 OGDENS' NUT GONE FLAKE (reissue, square sleeve) £15
77 Decca ROOTS 5   ROCK ROOTS - THE DECCA SINGLES £15
78 Charly CR 300005   OGDENS' NUT GONE FLAKE (export release, square sleeve) £15
78 Charly CR 300025   THE SMALL FACES - LIVE U.K. 1969 (export release) £15
80 Virgin/Immediate V 2166 SMALL FACES: BIG HITS (gatefold sleeve) £15
80 Virgin/Immediate V 2178 FOR YOUR DELIGHT, THE DARLINGS OF WAPPING WHARF LAUNDERETTE £25
91 Castle CLACT 016   OGDENS' NUT GONE FLAKE (CD, in round tin box with beer mats & booklet) £60
96 Deram 844583   THE DECCA ANTHOLOGY 1965-1967 (2-LP) £25
97 Castle CLA 016   OGDENS' NUT GONE FLAKE (reissue, round sleeve with obi) £15
01 Strange Fruit SFRSLP 087 BBC SESSIONS (LP) £20
(see also Faces, Steve Marriott, Humble Pie, Jimmy Winston & His Reflections, Winston's Fumbs, Billy Nicholls)

SMALL FOUR
66 Pye 7N 17191   One Up On Me/I'll Find Him £20

SMALL HOURS
80 Automatic K 17708   The Kid/Business In Town/Midnight To Six/End Of The Night (p/s) £30
80 Automatic K 17708X   The Kid/Business In Town/Midnight To Six/End Of The Night (10", p/s) £20
81 Bridgehouse (No Cat No) Denis/Denis Dub (white label promo only) £70

SMALL WONDER
75 Dawn DNS 1094   Ordinary Boy/Ride A Black Sheep £18

GEORGE SMALLWOOD & MARSHMELLOW BAND
10 Jazzman JMANLP 031   JUST 4 YOU (2-LP) £18

SMALL WORLD
81	Whaam! WHAAM 003	Love Is Dead/Liberty (p/s)	£100
83	Valid VC 001	First Impressions/Stupidity Street/Tomorrow Never Comes (p/s)	£100

SMART
82	Complex CPX 001	This Time (p/s)	£35

SMART ALEC
79	B&C BCS 20	Scooter Boys/Soho (p/s)	£100

EVA SMART
76	Empire EMP 903	One Life to Live One Life To Love/One Life Version	£20
80	Empire EMPDC 310	Upside Down/In And Out	£25

LEROY SMART
75	Third world TW 022	Get Smart/KING TUBBY & THE AGGROVATORS: Version	£20
77	Conflict COND 2001	Jahovia/Dub (12")	£30
78	Andinet AT 001	Zion/Version	£25
78	Andinet AT 002	Faith/Version	£25
78	Write Sounds WTS 001	What I Will Do/ROY SINCLAIR: Rite Mix/LEROY SMART: Jah Almighty (12")	£25
79	Burning Sounds BDS 010	Find Your Destination/Jamaica In Peace (12")	£15
79	Burning Sounds BDS 011	No One Remember Me/Don't Be Late (12")	£15
70s	Aries ARI 002	Peace Is What We Want (with U. Brown)/Version (12", p/s)	£30
82	Time One TR 0016	Money Is Comfort/If I Give My Love (12", with Barry Brown)	£25
77	Conflict COLPD 2001	BALLISTIC AFFAIR (LP, gatefold, with free 12")	£40
77	Dread Hot DHLP 1001	DREAD HOT IN AFRICA (LP)	£40
77	Third World TWS 601	SUPER STAR (LP)	£30
78	Burning Sounds BS 1004	DREAD HOT IN AFRICA (LP, reissue)	£35
78	Burning Sounds BS 1005	IMPRESSIONS OF LEROY SMART (LP)	£15
78	Burning Sounds BS 1008	JAH LOVES EVERYONE (LP, green vinyl)	£35
78	Dread Hot DHLP 1004	IMPRESSIONS OF LEROY SMART (LP, reissue)	£30
78	Burning Sounds BS 1009	PROPAGANDA (LP, clear vinyl)	£25

LEROY SMART & BIG YOUTH
79	Dub Vendor DVD 01	Pride And Ambition (original style)/'79 Style (12")	£60

SMASHING PUMPKINS
91	Hut	I Am One (1-sided blue flexidisc)	£100
91	Caroline SMASH 1	Siva/Rhinoceros (no p/s, promo only)	£80
91	Hut HUTT 6	Siva/Window Paine (12", p/s, 5,000)	£30
92	Hut HUTT 10	LULL EP (Rhinoceros/Blue/Slunk/Bye June [Demo]) (12", p/s)	£20
92	Hut HUTEN 18	I Am One/Terrapin (live)/Bullet Train To Osaka (10", p/s, 6,000 only)	£20
93	Hut HUT 31	Cherub Rock/Purr Snickety (p/s, clear vinyl, numbered, 5,000 only)	£20
93	Sub Pop SP 90	Tristessa/La Dolly Vita/Honeyspider (12", 5,000 only)	£35
94	Hut SPBOX 1	SIAMESE SINGLES (Rocket/Never Let Me Down/Cherub Rock/Purr Snickety//Today/Apathy's Last Kiss/Smile [Disarm/Siamese Dream]) (4 x 7" box set, black vinyl, 6,000 only)	£50
94	Hut HUTL 48	Rocket/Never Let Me Down (box set, salmon pink vinyl, 1,500 only)	£40
91	Caroline CARLP 16	GISH (LP, 1st pressing, red label, inner)	£40
91	Hut HUT LP2	GISH (LP, inner)	£25
93	Hut HUTLP11	SIAMESE DREAM (2-LP)	£35
94	Hut HUTLPX 2	GISH (LP, reissue with inner)	£25
95	Hut HUTDLP 30	MELLON COLLIE AND THE INFINITE SADNESS (3 x LP, 12 page booklet, numbered)	£175
98	Hut HUTDLP 30	MELLON COLLIE AND THE INFINITE SADNESS (3 x LP, 12 page booklet, repressing and not numbered)	£60
96	Hut HUTLP 41	PISCES ISCARIOT (LP, compilation)	£30
96	Hut	THE AEROPLANE FLIES HIGH (5 x CD single box set with handle, lock & booklet)	£50
00	HUTDLP 59	MACHINA/THE MACHINES OF GOD (2-LP)	£35
12	Virgin 5099997855316	MELLON COLLIE AND THE INFINITE SADNESS (4 x LP, remastered repressing)	£50
14	Virgin 6 02537 89926-5	ADORE (2-LP, reissue of 1998 LP not issued on vinyl in UK)	£30

(see also Zwan)

ROY SMECK
54	Brunswick LA 8649	SONGS OF THE RANGE (10" LP)	£15

PHILIP LLOYD SMEE & DONATO CINICOLO III
71	Deroy PLS 1	DAS LUNE/SYNTHI-A (LP, private pressing, handmade sleeve, 2 copies only)	£500

SMILEY
72	Philips 6006 206	Penelope/I Know What I Want	£15

(see also Creation)

BRETT SMILEY
74	Anchor ANC 70	Va Va Va Voom/Space Age (with p/s)	£40
74	Anchor ANC 70	Va Va Va Voom/Space Age	£25

SMILEY CULTURE
86	Top Notch TOP LP 001	THE ORIGINAL (LP)	£15

SMILIN' JOE
54	London HL 8106	A.B.C.'s Parts 1 & 2 (78)	£40

SMITH
70	Probe PRO 508	Comin Back To Me/Minus Plus	£25
69	Stateside-Dunhill SSL 5016	A GROUP CALLED SMITH (LP)	£25
70	Stateside-Dunhill SSL 5031	MINUS PLUS (LP)	£25

SMITH (U.K.)
81	Rarn RARNS 1	Here Comes My Baby/Just Another Line/Too Late (p/s)	£25

MINT VALUE £

ADAM (ERIC) SMITH
62 Island WI 057 | I Wonder Why/My Prayer | £20

ALICE SMITH
06 BBE ASMITH 01 | LOVE ENDEAVOUR (12", die-cut sleeve) | £30

ARTHUR 'GUITAR BOOGIE' SMITH (& HIS CRACKERJACKS)
53 MGM SP 1008 | Guitar Boogie/Be Bop Rag | £25
53 MGM SP 1021 | Five String Banjo Boogie/South | £15
53 MGM SP 1039 | Express Train Boogie/River Rag | £15
54 MGM SP 1096 | Oh, Baby Mine, I Get So Lonely/Outboard | £15
54 MGM SP 1110 | Redheaded Stranger/Texas Hop | £20
54 MGM MGM-EP 510 | ARTHUR 'GUITAR BOOGIE' SMITH AND HIS CRACKERJACKS (EP) | £15
54 MGM MGM EPC 5 | ARTHUR 'GUITAR BOOGIE' SMITH (EP, export issue) | £15
59 MGM MGM-EP 695 | ARTHUR 'GUITAR BOOGIE' SMITH AND HIS CRACKERJACKS (EP) | £15
63 Stateside SE 1005 | MISTER GUITAR (EP) | £15
53 MGM MGM-D 111 | FINGERS ON FIRE (10" LP) | £20
54 MGM MGM-D 131 | FOOLISH QUESTIONS (10" LP) | £20

BEASLEY SMITH & HIS ORCHESTRA
56 London HLD 8235 | Goodnight, Sweet Dreams/Parisian Rag | £20
56 London HLD 8273 | My Foolish Heart/Old Spinning Wheel | £20

BETTY SMITH QUINTET
57 Tempo A 163 | Sweet Georgia Brown/Little White Lies | £20
57 Tempo EXA 74 | BETTY SMITH QUINTET (EP) | £30
57 Decca DFE 6446 | BETTY SMITH QUINTET (EP) | £30
58 Decca DFE 6547 | BETTY SMITH GROUP (EP) | £30

DAVE SMITH & ASTRONAUTS
67 Columbia Blue Beat DB 104 | A Lover Like You/Cup Of Love | £15
67 Amusicon SLE 10 | A Lover Like You/Cup Of Love | £15

DAVE SMITH & JUDY DINNING
83 Rubber RUB 043 | WAITING FOR THE CHANGE (LP) | £20

DEREK SMITH TRIO
56 Pye Nixa NJE 1036 | PIANO MOODS (EP) | £80

DICK SMITH BAND
79 Smile SR 012 | Body Heat/Motorway Madness (p/s) | £75
80 Hol-O-Gram HOL 001 | Way Of The World/Giving The Game Away (with p/s) | £45
80 Hol-O-Gram HOL 001 | Way Of The World/Giving The Game Away | £25

EDDIE SMITH
55 Parlophone MSP 6186 | Silver Star Stomp/Stumbling (as Eddie Smith & Chiefs) | £15
60 Top Rank JAR 285 | Upturn/Border Beat (as Eddie Smith & Hornets) | £25

EDGEWOOD SMITH & FABULOUS TAILFEATHERS
67 Sue WI 4037 | Ain't That Lovin'/Yeah | £50

EFFIE SMITH
66 Sue WI 4010 | Dial That Telephone Parts 1 & 2 | £30

ELLIOTT SMITH
99 Dreamworks DRMS 7 | Baby Britain/Waltz No. 1 (p/s) | £30
98 Domino REWIGLP 001 | ELLIOTT SMITH (LP) | £60
98 Domino REWIGLP 002 | ROMAN CANDLE (LP) | £60
98 Domino WIGLP 51 | EITHER/OR (LP) | £50
00 Geffen 533 867-8 | FIGURE 8 (2-LP, with lyric insert) | £30
04 Domino WIGLP 147 | FROM A BASEMENT ON THE HILL (2-LP) | £20
07 Domino WIGLP 198 | NEW MOON (2-LP) | £18
10 Domino WIGLP 265 | AN INTRODUCTION TO (LP) | £20
10 Domino REWIGLP1 | ELLIOTT SMITH (LP, reissue) | £20

ELSON SMITH
61 Fontana H 291 | Flip Flop/Are You Ready For That | £30

(LITTLE) GEORGE (HARMONICA) SMITH
65 Blue Horizon 45-1002 | Blues In The Dark/Telephone Blues (as Little George Smith) | £100
70 Blue Horizon 57-3170 | Someday You're Gonna Learn/Before You Do Your Thing (as George Smith) | £25
69 Liberty LBL/LBS 83218E | BLUES WITH FEELING - A TRIBUTE TO LITTLE WALTER (LP, with Chicago Blues Band) | £60
70 Blue Horizon 7-63856 | NO TIME TO JIVE (LP) | £100
71 Deram SML 1082 | ARKANSAS TRAP (LP) | £60
(see also Bacon Fat)

GLORIA SMITH
59 London HLU 8903 | Playmates/Don't Take Your Love From Me | £18

GORDON SMITH
69 Blue Horizon 57-3156 | Too Long/Funk Pedal | £30
69 Blue Horizon S7-63211 | LONG OVERDUE (LP, stereo) | £100
69 Blue Horizon M7-63211 | LONG OVERDUE (LP, mono) | £150
(see also Kevin Coyne)

HOBART SMITH
69 Topic 12T187 | THE OLD TIMEY RAP (LP) | £20

HUEY 'PIANO' SMITH & THE CLOWNS
58 Columbia DB 4138 | Don't You Just Know It/High Blood Pressure | £85
58 Columbia DB 4138 | Don't You Just Know It/High Blood Pressure (78) | £50

MINT VALUE £

60	Top Rank JAR 282	Don't You Just Know Kokomo/FRANKIE FORD: Cheatin' Woman	£20
65	Sue WI 364	If It Ain't One Thing It's Another/Tu-Ber-Cu-Lucas And The Sinus Blues	£25
65	Sue WI 380	Rockin' Pneumonia And The Boogie Woogie Flu (Parts 1 & 2)	£25
78	Chiswick NS 43	Rockin' Pneumonia And The Boogie Woogie Flu (unissued)	£0
65	Sue ILP 917	ROCKIN' PNEUMONIA AND THE BOOGIE WOOGIE FLU (LP, titled "Havin' A Good Time" on labels)	£40

(see also Frankie Ford, Lee Allen, Bobby Marchan, Robert Parker)

HURRICANE SMITH
| 72 | Columbia SCX 6510 | DON'T LET IT DIE (LP) | £15 |

JEFF SMITH
| 71 | RAK RAK 120 | Gypsy In My Blood/Going To A Party | £25 |

JIMMY SMITH
65	Verve VS 523	The Cat/Basin Street Blues	£20
62	Verve CLP 1596/CSD 1462	BASHIN' THE UNPREDICTABLE (Verve label with HMV number)	£25
63	Verve (S)VLP 9039	HOBO FLATS	£25
64	Verve VLP 9057	ANY NUMBER CAN WIN	£25
64	Verve VLP 9068	WHO'S AFRAID OF VIRGINIA WOOLF	£15
64	Verve (S)VLP 9079	THE CAT	£25
65	Verve (S)VLP 9093	MONSTER	£25
66	Verve (S)VLP 9108	ORGAN GRINDER SWING	£25
66	Verve (S)VLP 9123	GOT MY MOJO WORKING	£25
66	Verve (S)VLP 9142	HOOCHIE COOCHIE MAN	£25
67	Verve (S)VLP 9159	PETER & THE WOLF	£15
67	Verve (S)VLP 9160	THE DYNAMIC DUO (with Wes Montgomery)	£25
67	Verve (S)VLP 9182	RESPECT	£25
68	Verve (S)VLP 9218	STAY LOOSE	£25
68	Verve (S)VLP 9227	LIVIN' IT UP	£15
68	Verve (S)VLP 9231	CHRISTMAS COOKIN'	£15
69	Verve (S)VLP 9241	FURTHER ADVENTURES OF JIMMY AND WES (with Wes Montgomery)	£15
71	Verve 2304 020	I'M GON' GIT MYSELF TOGETHER	£15
74	Verve 2304 167	PORTUGUESE SOUL	£15

(see also Kenny Burrell)

JOEY SMITH & BABA BROOKS BAND
| 64 | R&B JB 131 | Maybe Once/Tell Me You're Mine | £25 |

JORJA SMITH
| 18 | FAMM JSLAFP01 | LOST & FOUND (LP) | £20 |

JUDI SMITH
| 65 | Decca F 12132 | Leaves Come Tumbling Down/Come My Way | £15 |

JUNIOR SMITH
67	Giant GN 1	Cool Down Your Temper/I'm Groovin'	£30
68	Giant GN 18	I'm Gonna Leave You Girl/I Love You, I Love You	£30
68	Giant GN 25	Come Cure Me/I Want Your Lovin'	£50
68	Gas GAS 132	Gimme Little/Trip To War Land	£20
72	Sioux SI 019	Saturday Child/JUMBO STERLING: Hot Dog	£20
72	Sioux SI 023	I Don't Know/JUMBO STERLING: My Sugar Ain't Sweet	£100

(see also Stranger Cole, Derrick Morgan, Rocksteadys)

KATHY SMITH
| 70 | Polydor 2310 081 | SOME SONGS I'VE SAVED (LP) | £60 |

KEELY SMITH (& LOUIS PRIMA)
61	London RE-D 1269	YOU LOVERS (EP)	£20
58	Capitol (S)T 914	I WISH YOU LOVE (LP, mono/stereo)	£15
59	Capitol T 1160	HEY BOY! HEY GIRL! (LP, soundtrack, with Louis Prima)	£25

(see also Louis Prima, Frank Sinatra)

KENDRA SMITH
| 95 | 4AD CAD 5006 | FIVE WAYS OF DISAPPEARING (LP) | £40 |

LONNIE SMITH
67	CBS 63146	FINGER LICKIN' GOOD (LP)	£25
69	Blue Note BST 84313	TURNING POINT (LP)	£25
69	Blue Note BST 84290	THINK (LP)	£25
70	Blue Note BST 84326	MOVE YOUR HAND (LP)	£30
70	Blue Note BST 84351	DRIVES (LP)	£25
96	Blue Note 724383124916	MOVE YOUR HAND (LP, reissue)	£20
97	Blue Note 724382996918	MOVE YOUR HAND (LP, reissue, repressing)	£20

LONNIE LISTON SMITH (& THE COSMIC ECHOES)
83	Doctor Jazz ASLP 1000	DREAMS OF TOMORROW	£20
75	RCA RCA 2568	Expansions (Parts 1 & 2) (& Cosmic Echoes)	£15
79	RCA PC 9450	Expansions/A Chance For Peace (12")	£35
83	Bluebird BRT 4	Expansions/Voodoo Woman (12")	£20
75	RCA SF 8434	EXPANSIONS (LP, with Cosmic Echoes)	£40
76	RCA SF 8461	VISIONS OF A NEW WORLD (LP, gatefold)	£60
76	RCA RS 1053	REFLECTIONS OF A GOLDEN DREAM (LP, with Cosmic Echoes)	£40
77	RCA PL 11822	RENAISSANCE (LP, with Cosmic Echoes)	£20
78	CBS 82837	LOVELAND (LP)	£20
79	CBS S CBS 83809	A SONG FOR THE CHILDREN (LP)	£15
80	CBS S CBS 84365	LOVE IS THE ANSWER (LP)	£20

LORENZO SMITH
66	Outasite 45-503	(Too Much) **Firewater/Count Down** (99 copies only)	£100

MARTHA SMITH
65	Pye 7N 15778	**As I Watch You Walk Away/It Always Seems Like Summer**	£20

MARVIN SMITH
66	Coral Q 72486	**Time Stopped/Have More Time**	£50
66	Coral Q 72486	**Time Stopped/Have More Time** (DJ copy)	£100

MEL SMITH
81	Mercury MEL 1	**Mel Smith's Greatest Hits/Richard & Joey** (p/s, with Roger Taylor)	£15

MICK SMITH
76	Midas MFHR 078	**SOMEBODY NOBODY KNOWS** (LP)	£30
77	Alida Star AS 771	**WORDS AND MUSIC** (LP)	£30
79	Repercussion RR 1000	**RAINDANCE** (LP, as Mike Smith)	£25

NR AND MRS SMITH AND MR DRAKE
84	Alphabet ALPH 005	t**MR AND MRS SMITH AND MR DRAKE** (cassette)	£50

(see also Cardiac Arrest 1, Cardiacs)

O.C. (OCIE) SMITH
57	London HLA 8480	**Lighthouse/Too Many** (as Ocie Smith)	£90
57	London HLA 8480	**Lighthouse/Too Many** (as Ocie Smith) (78)	£60
68	CBS (S) 63147	**THE DYNAMIC O.C. SMITH** (LP)	£20
68	CBS (S) 63362	**HICKORY HOLLER REVISITED** (LP)	£15
69	CBS 63805	**AT HOME** (LP)	£25

(see also Art Mooney)

OTELLO SMITH & TOBAGO BAD BOYS
68	Direction 8-63242	**THE BIG ONES GO SKA** (LP)	£40

PATTI SMITH (GROUP)
77	Arista ARIST 12135	**Gloria** (In Excelsis Deo)/**My Generation** (live) (12", Rough Trade copies in brown paper bag with titles in felt pen)	£15
78	Sire 6078 614	**Hey Joe** (Version)/**Piss Factory** (p/s)	£35
88	Fierce FRIGHT 017	**Brian Jones/Stockinged Feet/Jesus Christ** (1-sided, white label)	£15
75	Arista ARTY 122	**HORSES** (LP, 1st pressing, 'Horses' written in white, blue label)	£40
76	Arista SPARTY 1001	**RADIO ETHIOPIA** (LP, as Patti Smith Group, with lyric insert)	£25
78	Arista SPART 1043	**EASTER** (LP, lyric insert)	£25
79	Arista SPART 1086	**WAVE** (LP, insert)	£15
07	Columbia 88697094301	**TWELVE** (2-LP)	£60

PETER SMITH
70s	Pilgrim JLPS 148P	**FAITH, FOLK & CLARITY** (LP, with Kinfolk)	£18

RAY SMITH
60	London HL 9051	**Rockin' Little Angel/That's All Right**	£50

ROY SMITH (JAMAICA)
70	Grape GR 3013	**See Through Craze/TERRY CARL & DERRICK: I'm The One**	£30
70	Jackpot JP 723	**The Wedding/Air Balloon**	£20

(see also Carl & Derrick)

SLIM SMITH (& THE UNIQUES)
66	Island WI 3023	**I've Got Your Number/The New Boss**	£70
67	Coxsone CS 7016	**Hip Hug/FREEDOM SINGERS: I Want Money**	£140
67	Coxsone CS 7034	**Rougher Yet/I'll Never Let Go**	£150
67	Coxsone CS 7009	**Mercy Mercy/JACKIE MITTOO: Baba Boom**	£135
68	Trojan TR 619	**Watch This Sound/Out Of Love** (as Slim Smith & Uniques)	£45
69	Unity UN 504	**Everybody Needs Love/JUNIOR SMITH: Come Back Girl**	£25
69	Unity UN 508	**For Once In My Life/Burning Desire**	£25
69	Unity UN 510	**Zip-A-Di-Do-Da/On Broadway**	£25
69	Unity UN 513	**Let It Be Me/Love Makes Me Do Foolish Things** (both with Paulette)	£20
69	Unity UN 515	**Somebody To Love/Confusion**	£40
69	Unity UN 520	**Slipaway/Spanish Harlem**	£25
69	Unity UN 524	**Sunny Side Of The Sea/A Place In The Sun**	£40
69	Unity UN 527	**Blessed Are The Meek/Conversation**	£20
69	Unity UN 537	**Keep That Light Shining On Me/Build My World Around You**	£20
69	Unity UN 539	**Love Me Tender/This Feeling**	£30
69	Unity UN 542	**Honey/There's A Light**	£30
69	Gas GAS 132	**The Vow** (& Doreen Shaeffer)/**JAMES NEPHEW: Why Don't You Say**	£45
70	Gas GAS 150	**What Kind Of Life/MARTIN RILEY: It's All In The Game**	£20
70	Unity UN 570	**Jenny/The Race**	£30
70	S&S SC 001	**Strong Love/Strange World**	£40
71	Pama Supreme PS 334	**Send Me Some Loving/I'm Lost**	£18
71	Camel CA 81	**Spanish Harlem/Slip Away**	£25
71	Escort ERT 851	**My Love Come True/This Feeling**	£75
71	Escort ERT 852	**Life Keeps Turning/My Conversation**	£35
71	Escort ERT 859	**My Girl/RECO: Plus One**	£40
72	Jackpot JP 786	**I Need Your Loving/You've Got What It Takes**	£15
72	Jackpot JP 789	**Rain From The Sky/You're No Good**	£15
72	Jackpot JP 798	**Closer Together/Blinded By Love**	£20
72	Jackpot JP 799	**Turning Point/Money Lover**	£30
72	Dynamic DYN 428	**Just A Dream/Send Me Some Loving**	£20
72	Pama PM 850	**The Time Has Come/THE AGREVATORS: Version**	£15

MINT VALUE £

72	Pama Supreme PS 373	A Place In The Sun/Stranger On The Shore	£15
72	Camel CA 89	Take Me Back/Where Do I Turn	£20
72	Explosion EX 2074	The Time Has Come/Blessed Is The Man	£15
73	Green Door GD 4058	Let Me Love You/If It Don't Work Out	£15
73	Bullet BU 523	A Place In The Sun/Burning Fire	£35
69	Pama ECO 9	EVERYBODY NEEDS LOVE (LP)	£60
72	Trojan TBL 186	JUST A DREAM (LP)	£50
72	Trojan TBL 198	MEMORIAL (LP)	£30
70s	Lord Koos KLP 1	SLIM SMITH (LP)	£50
76	Angen ANGL 1	THE LATE AND GREAT (LP)	£40
76	Pama PMLP 3242	JUST A DREAM (LP, reissue)	£35
84	Pama PMLP 3240	TIME HAS COME (LP, actually a reissue of MEMORIAL)	£40

(see also Wonder Boy, Pioneers, Uniques, Roy Shirley, Ron Sig, Dakota Jim, Dennis Alcapone, David Isaacs, John Holt, (see also Wonder Boy, Pioneers, Uniques, Roy Shirley, Ron Sig, Dakota Jim, Dennis Alcapone, David Isaacs, John Holt,

SLIM SMITH & THE FREEDOM SINGERS
70	Banana BA 304	Do Dang Do/JACKIE MITTO: Hot Milk	£60

SOMETHIN' SMITH & THE REDHEADS
58	Fontana TFR 6005	PUT THE BLAME ON ME (10" LP)	£18

TAB SMITH & HIS ORCHESTRA
56	Vogue V 2410	Jump Time/Rock City	£15

TERRY SMITH
69	Philips (S)BL 7871	FALL OUT (LP, laminated sleeve, black/silver label)	£125
77	Lambert LAM 002	TERRY SMITH AND TONY LEE TRIO (LP)	£20

(see also If)

TONI SMITH
83	Malaco MAL 1213	Ooh...I Like The Way It Feels/(Instrumental)/Funk Beats (12", p/s)	£35

TRIXIE SMITH
50s	Poydras 101	TRIXIE SMITH (10" EP, 45 rpm)	£15
50s	Ristic 12	TRIXIE SMITH (10" EP, 45 rpm)	£15
50s	Audubon AAE	TRIXIE SMITH (10" LP)	£30

TRULY SMITH
66	Decca F 12373	My Smile Is Just A Frown Turned Upside Down/Love Is Me, Love Is You	£25
67	Decca F 12645	I Wanna Go Back There Again/Window Cleaner	£35
67	Decca F 12700	The Boy From Chelsea/Little Man With A Stick	£20
68	MGM MGM 1431	This Is The First Time/Taking Time Off	£20

VERDELLE SMITH
66	Capitol CL 15234	In My Room/Like A Man	£18

WARREN SMITH
60	London HL 7101	I Don't Believe I'll Fall In Love/Cave-In (export issue)	£25
61	London HLG 7110	Odds And Ends/A Whole Lot Of Nothin' (export issue)	£25

WAYNE SMITH
81	Black Joy DH 815	Life Is A Moment In Space/Ain't Me Without You (12")	£40
82	Black Joy DHB 17	Isim Skism/Rose Marie (12", with Yellowman)	£50
84	Greensleeves GRED 162	Come Along/Change Your Style (12")	£30
85	Greensleeves GRED 169	Under Me Sleng Teng/MICHAEL BUCKLEY: Dance Gate (12")	£30
85	Greensleeves GRED 183	Ickie All Over/TONTO IRIE: Life Story (12")	£30
85	Tonos TON 006	Dancing Machine/PATRICK ANDY: Leave The Door (12")	£30
85	Greensleeves GRED 177	Sleng Teng Mix Down Remix/PAD ANTHONY: Cry For Me (12")	£20
86	Ras RAST 7021	No Puppy Love/Teach Me To Dance (12")	£15
81	Black Joy BHLP 2005	YOUTHMAN SKANKING (LP)	£50

WHISPERING SMITH
72	Blue Horizon 2431 015	OVER EASY (LP)	£120

ORVILLE SMITH
91	Riz RIZ 001	Leaving Rome/BOMBASTIC CREW: Repatriation Dub	£15

SMITH & MIGHTY
95	More Rockers ZLPKR 002	BASS IS MATERNAL (2LP)	£40

SMITH & WESTON
73	Decca F 13441	A Shot Of Rhythm And Blues/Run Run Run	£15

SMITHFIELD MARKET
73	Gloucester GLS 0435	LONDON IN 1665 (LP, private pressing, gatefold sleeve, existence unconfirmed)	£0
74	Gloucester GLS 0443	AFTER SHAKESPEARE (LP, private pressing, die-cut sleeve, with insert, existence unconfirmed)	£0

THE SMITHS
SINGLES
83	Rough Trade RT 131	Hand In Glove/Handsome Devil (p/s, original pressing with Manchester address on rear sleeve)	£25
83	Rough Trade RT 131	Hand In Glove/Handsome Devil (p/s, second pressing with London address on rear label)	£15
83	Rough Trade RT 131	Hand In Glove/Handsome Devil (p/s, third pressing with no address)	£20
83	Rough Trade RT 131	Hand In Glove/Handsome Devil (later pressing with misprinted blue/negative p/s - beware of counterfeits!)	£2000
83	Rough Trade RT 136	This Charming Man/Jeane (unreleased first pressing with Rough Trade/Capitol logo and solid centre, p/s with Manchester address on rear)	£50
83	Rough Trade RT 136	This Charming Man/Jeane (Rough Trade/Capitol logo or reissued 'stamped' logo, p/s)	£15
83	Rough Trade RTT 136	This Charming Man (Manchester)/This Charming Man (London)/Accept Yourself/	£30

		Wonderful Woman (12", p/s; later pressing with band title on sleeve)	
83	Rough Trade RTT 136	**This Charming Man** (Manchester)/**This Charming Man** (London)/**Accept Yourself**/**Wonderful Woman** (12", p/s)	**£15**
83	Rough Trade RTT 136NY	**This Charming Man** (New York Vocal)/**This Charming Man** (New York Instrumental) (12", p/s)	**£15**
83	Rough Trade RTT 136NY	**This Charming Man** (New York Vocal)/**This Charming Man** (New York Instrumental) (12", p/s; later pressing with band title on sleeve)	**£50**
84	Rough Trade RTT 146	**What Difference Does It Make?/Back To The Old House/These Things Take Time** (Terence Stamp p/s, later pressing with band title on sleeve)	**£25**
84	Rough Trade RT 156	**Heaven Knows I'm Miserable Now/Suffer Little Children** (late solid centre pressing, p/s)	**£40**
84	Rough Trade RTT 156	**Heaven Knows I'm Miserable Now/Girl Afraid/Suffer Little Children** (mispressed 12" with extended version)	**£50**
85	Rough Trade RTT 181	**Shakespeare's Sister/What She Said/Stretch Out And Wait** (12", p/s, with misprinted red & green or magenta & green inner)	**£50**
86	Rough Trade RTT 193	**Panic/Vicar In A Tutu** (p/s, with square sheet of 'Hang The DJ' stickers)	**£25**
86	Rough Trade RT 193	**Panic/Vicar In A Tutu** (p/s, with round sheet of 'Hang The DJ' stickers)	**£20**
86	Rough Trade RTT 193	**Panic/Vicar In A Tutu/The Draize Train** (12", p/s, with 'Hang The DJ' stickers)	**£15**
87	Rough Trade RTT 195	**Shoplifters Of The World Unite/London/Half A Person** (12", p/s; in carrier bag)	**£30**
87	Rough Trade RTT 195	**Shoplifters Of The World Unite/London/Half A Person** (12", p/s, mispressing, A-side plays "You Just Haven't Earned It Yet Baby")	**£55**
87	Rough Trade RT 197	**Girlfriend In A Coma/Work Is A Four Letter Word** (misprinted green p/s, incorrectly shows additional 12" track 'I Keep Mine Hidden' on reverse of sleeve)	**£500**
87	Rough Trade RTT 197	**Girlfriend In A Coma/Work Is A Four Letter Word/I Keep Mine Hidden** (12", green p/s; some in grey p/s)	**£35**
87	Rough Trade RT 166	**William, It Was Really Nothing/How Soon Is Now?** (reissue, Billie Whitelaw p/s)	**£22**
87	Rough Trade RTT 166	**William, It Was Really Nothing/How Soon Is Now?/Please Please Please Let Me Get What I Want** (12", reissue, pale blue inner sleeve, cat no in top right hand corner in white, Billie Whitelaw p/s)	**£30**
92	WEA YZ0002	**How Soon Is Now?/Hand In Glove** (p/s, reissue)	**£15**
92	WEA YZ0003	**There Is A Light That Never Goes Out/Handsome Devil** (live) (p/s)	**£50**

SINGLES : CD REISSUE SINGLES

88	Rough Trade RTT 166CD	**William, It Was Really Nothing/How Soon Is Now?/Please Please Please Let Me Get What I Want**	**£30**
88	Rough Trade RTT 171CD	**Barbarism Begins At Home/Shakespeare's Sister/Stretch Out And Wait**	**£35**
88	Rough Trade RTT 215CD	**The Headmaster Ritual/Nowhere Fast** (live)/**Stretch Out And Wait** (live)/**Meat Is Murder** (live) (withdrawn Viv Nicholson cover)	**£45**

ALBUMS

84	Rough Trade ROUGH 61	**THE SMITHS** (LP, printed inner)	**£40**
84	Rough Trade ROUGH 76	**HATFUL OF HOLLOW** (LP, original gatefold issue, with incorrect sleeve - no black dot between 'Accept Yourself' and 'Girl Afraid' on rear sleeve, printed inner)	**£50**
85	Rough Trade ROUGH 81	**MEAT IS MURDER** (LP, printed inner)	**£40**
85	Rough Trade ROUGH CD 81	**MEAT IS MURDER** (CD, original issue)	**£30**
85	Rough Trade ROUGH CD 76	**HATFUL OF HOLLOW** (CD, original blue border sleeve)	**£50**
86	Rough Trade ROUGH 96	**THE QUEEN IS DEAD** (LP, gatefold, printed inner, MPO or EMI pressing)	**£55**
87	Rough Trade ROUGH 101	**THE WORLD WON'T LISTEN** (LP, printed inner)	**£40**
87	Rough Trade ROUGH 106	**STRANGEWAYS HERE WE COME** (LP, embossed sleeve, printed inner)	**£40**
88	Rough Trade ROUGH 126	**RANK** (LP, gatefold sleeve, with inner, ltd. edition with poster and cover sticker denoting amended catalogue number)	**£50**
88	Rough Trade ROUGH 126D	**RANK** (DAT)	**£50**
88	Rough Trade ROUGH 255	**LOUDER THAN BOMBS** (2LP, gatefold, UK version not US import, brown inners)	**£45**
93	WEA SMITHS 1	**THE SMITHS** (10" LP, reissue)	**£30**
93	WEA SMITHS 2	**HATFUL OF HOLLOW** (2-LP, 10" reissue)	**£30**
93	WEA SMITHS 3	**MEAT IS MURDER** (10" LP reissue)	**£30**
93	WEA SMITHS 4	**THE QUEEN IS DEAD** (10" LP reissue)	**£30**
93	WEA SMITHS 5	**THE WORLD WON'T LISTEN** (10" LP reissue)	**£30**
93	WEA SMITHS 6	**STRANGEWAYS, HERE WE COME** (10" LP)	**£30**
93	WEA SMITHS 7	**RANK** (10" 2-LP reissue)	**£35**
92	Warner Bros. 4509 90327-1	**BEST...1** (LP)	**£45**

ALBUMS : BOXED SETS

95	WEA 2564 69320-7	**SINGLES BOX** (12 x 7" numbered, with badges and poster)	**£80**
95	WEA 2564 69321-7	**SINGLES BOX** (12 x CD numbered)	**£45**
11	Rhino 2564665906	**COMPLETE** (17 LP, 8 CD, 25 7" DVD & booklet)	**£350**
11	Rhino 2564665908	**COMPLETE** (11 LP & booklet)	**£150**

PROMOS : PROMOS & TEST PRESSINGS

83	Rough Trade RT 131	**Hand In Glove** (white label 1983 test pressing - approx. 5 only)	**£1500**
83	N/A	**3-Pack** (Rough Trade promo cassette, promoting Hand In Glove and tracks by Zerra 1 and Influence)	**£100**
83	Rough Trade RT 136	**Reel Around The Fountain/Jeane** (unissued, white label test pressings only - beware of counterfeits!)	**£1200**
83	Rough Trade RT 136	**This Charming Man** (London Version) (rejected white label test pressing)	**£800**
83	Rough Trade RT 136	**This Charming Man** (Manchester) (one-sided white label test pressing)	**£300**
83	Rough Trade RTT 136NY	**This Charming Man** (New York vocal)/(New York Instrumental) (12" white label test pressing)	**£300**
84	Rough Trade RT 146	**What Difference Does It Make?/Back To The Old House** (white label test pressing)	**£50**
84	Rough Trade RTT 146	**What Difference Does It Make?/Back To The Old House/These Things Take Time** (12" white label test pressing)	**£100**
84	Rough Trade R 61 DJ	**Still Ill/You've Got Everything Now** (test pressing)	**£200**
84	Rough Trade RT 61 DJ	**Still Ill/You've Got Everything Now** (promo)	**£25**
84	Rough Trade ROUGH 61	**THE SMITHS** (white label test pressing)	**£30**
84	Rough Trade RT 131	**Hand In Glove** (one-sided white label 1984 test pressing)	**£100**
84	Rough Trade RT 131	**Hand In Glove/Handsome Devil** (white label test pressing for 1984 repressing)	**£100**

84	Rough Trade RT 156	**Heaven Knows I'm Miserable Now/Suffer Little Children** (one-sided test pressing) £200
84	Rough Trade RT 156	**Heaven Knows I'm Miserable Now/Suffer Little Children** (rejected white label test pressing with extended version) £800
84	Rough Trade RTT 156	**Heaven Knows I'm Miserable Now/Girl Afraid/Suffer Little Children** (rejected 12" white label test pressing with extended version) £800
84	Rough Trade RT 156	**Heaven Knows I'm Miserable Now/Suffer Little Children** (standard white label test pressing)...£20
84	Rough Trade RTT 156	**Heaven Knows I'm Miserable Now/Girl Afraid/Suffer Little Children** (standard 12" white label test pressing)...£200
84	Rough Trade RT 166	**William, It Was Really Nothing/Please Please Please Let Me Get What I Want** (white label test pressing)...£20
84	Rough Trade RTT 166	**William, It Was Really Nothing/How Soon Is Now?/Please Please Please Let Me Get What I Want** (12" white label test pressing)...£100
84	Rough Trade ROUGH 76	**HATFUL OF HOLLOW** (white label test pressing) £30
84	Copymasters	**HATFUL OF HOLLOW** (cassette, early version with unreleased tracks)...........................£100
85	Rough Trade RTT 171	**Barbarism Begins At Home** (12", 2 different 1-sided white label test pressings)............£500
85	Rough Trade RTT 171	**Barbarism Begins At Home** (12" one-sided, promo)..£85
85	Rough Trade RTT 171	**Barbarism Begins At Home** (edited version)/(long version)...£45
85	Rough Trade RTT 171	**Barbarism Begins At Home** (12", p/s, one-sided promo) £40
85	Rough Trade RT 176	**How Soon Is Now?/Oscillate Wildly** (white label test pressing with Oscillate Wildly instead of Well I Wonder on the B-side)..£400
85	Rough Trade RTT 176	**How Soon Is Now?/Well I Wonder/Oscillate Wildly** (12" white label test pressing) £200
85	Rough Trade ROUGH 81	**MEAT IS MURDER** (white label test pressing)..£300
85	Rough Trade RT 181	**Shakespeare's Sister/What She Said** (white label test pressing)......................................£200
85	Rough Trade RT 186	**Meat Is Murder/Nowhere Fast/Stretch Out And Wait** (live EP, unissued, test pressings only) £1000
85	Rough Trade RT 186	**Meat Is Murder/Nowhere Fast/Stretch Out And Wait** (live EP, unissued, Mayking test pressings - beware of counterfeits!) £500
85	Rough Trade RTT 186	**Meat Is Murder/William It Was Really Nothing/Nowhere Fast/Stretch Out And Wait /Miserable Lie** (live 12" EP, unissued, test pressings only-beware of counterfeits!) £1000
85	Rough Trade RT 186	**That Joke Isn't Funny Anymore/Meat Is Murder** (live) (white label test pressing) £100
85	RT 186	**That Joke Isn't Funny Anymore/Meat Is Murder** (live) (Mayking test pressing) £300
85	Rough Trade RTT 191	**The Boy With The Thorn In His Side/Rubber Ring/Asleep** (white label test pressing) £20
86	Rough Trade RT 192	**Bigmouth Strikes Again/Money Changes Everything** (white label test pressing)...........£200
86	Rough Trade RTT 192	**Bigmouth Strikes Again/Money Changes Everything/Unloveable** (12" white label test pressing)...£30
86	Rough Trade ROUGH 96	**THE QUEEN IS DEAD** (white label test pressing)...£150
86	Rough Trade ROUGH 96	**THE QUEEN IS DEAD** (Mayking test pressing) £300
86	Rough Trade RTT 193	**Panic/Vicar In A Tutu/The Draize Train** (12" white label test pressing with promo posters) £50
86	Rough Trade RT 194	**Ask/Cemetry Gates** (white label test pressing)...£250
87	Rough Trade RTT 195	**You Just Haven't Earned It Yet Baby/London/Half A Person** (12", white label test pressing) £800
87	Rough Trade ROUGH 101	**THE WORLD WON'T LISTEN** (white label test pressing) £20
87	Rough Trade RT 196	**Sheila Take A Bow/Is It Really So Strange?** (white label test pressing).........................£200
87	Rough Trade ROUGH 255	**LOUDER THAN BOMBS** (2-LP, white label test pressings)...£200
87	Rough Trade RT 197	**Girlfriend In A Coma/Work Is A Four Letter Word** (white label test pressing) £200
87	Rough Trade ROUGH 106	**STRANGEWAYS, HERE WE COME** (white label test pressing)...£20
87	Rough Trade RT 198	**I Started Something I Couldn't Finish/Pretty Girls Make Graves** (Troy Tate demo) (white label test pressing)...£200
87	Rough Trade RT 198	**I Started Something I Couldn't Finish/Pretty Girls Make Graves** (Mayking test pressing)...£500
87	Rough Trade RT 166-B	**How Soon Is Now?** (1-sided white label test pressing for B-side of re-issued William, It Was Really Nothing 7")..£200
88	Rough Trade ROUGH 126	**RANK** (white label test pressing; in misprinted sleeve, no cover star or title on sleeve, just states 'The Smiths') £200
88	Rough Trade ROUGH 126	**RANK** (white label test pressing) £20
06	Universal (No Cat. No)	**THE SMITHS** (2-CD Publishing sampler with 'The World Won't Listen' artwork on cover) £80

(see also Morrissey, Sandie Shaw, The The, Electronic)

SMITH SISTERS
| 80 | Union BB 1002 | **Sexy Eyes/Dub Version** (12")..£25 |

SMITHY ALL STARS
| 71 | Hillcrest HCT 3 | **Witchfinder General/Deserted** ....£80 |

SMOG
96	Domino RUG 45T	**KICKING A COUPLE AROUND EP** (12") £15
95	City Slang 049521	**WILD LOVE** (LP)...£20
97	Domino WIGLP 3	**RED APPLE FALLS** (LP)..£18
99	Domino WIGLP 60	**KNOCK KNOCK** (LP)..£25
00	Domino WIGLP 7	**DONGS OF SEVOTION** (2-LP)..£20
01	Domino WIGLP 99	**RAIN ON LENS** (LP)..£18
03	Domino WIGLP 127	**SUPPER** (LP)..£20
05	Domino WIGLP 158	**A RIVER AIN'T TOO MUCH TO LOVE** (LP)..£25

SMOKE DZA
19	Daupe! DM SP 051	**PRIME LOCATION VOLUMES 1 & 2** (12", p/s, 80 copies) £40
19	Daupe! DM SP 051	**PRIME LOCATION VOLUMES 1 & 2** (12", picture disc, 250 copies)....................................£40
19	Daupe! DM SP 051	**PRIME LOCATION VOLUMES 1 & 2** (12", p/s, red vinyl, 75 copies) £40
19	Daupe! DM SP 051	**PRIME LOCATION VOLUMES 1 & 2** (12", green vinyl, 80 copies)..£40
19	Daupe! DM SP 051	**PRIME LOCATION VOLUMES 1 & 2** (12",p/s, with obi strip, 20 copies)..............................£80

SMOKE (1)
| 67 | Columbia DB 8115 | **My Friend Jack/We Can Take It** ....£40 |

MINT VALUE £

67	Columbia DB 8252	If The Weather's Sunny/I Would If I Could, But I Can't	£35
67	Columbia DB 8252	If The Weather's Sunny/I Would If I Could, But I Can't (in export p/s)	£80
67	Island WIP 6023	It Could Be Wonderful/Have Some More Tea	£70
68	Island WIP 6031	Utterly Simple/Sydney Gill (unreleased)	£0
72	Regal Zonophone RZ 3071	Sugar Man/That's What I Want	£25
74	Decca FR 13514	My Lullaby/Looking High	£15
70s	Gull 128 301	IT'S SMOKE TIME (LP, reissue of German-only LP)	£20
88	M. Blue Town MBT 5001	MY FRIEND JACK (LP)	£15
12	M. Blue Town BT 5008	IT'S SMOKE TIME (LP, reissue with certificate)	£15

(see also Shots)

SMOKE (2)
70	Revolution Pop REVP 1002	Dreams Of Dreams/My Birth	£200

SMOKESTACK LIGHTNIN'
68	Bell BLL 1046	Light In My Window/Long Stemmed Eyes (John's Song)	£15
69	Bell MBLL/SBLL 116	OFF THE WALL (LP)	£40

SMOKEY BABE
62	77' LA 12-12	SMOKEY BABE AND HIS FRIENDS (LP)	£25

SMOKEY CIRCLES
70	Carnaby CNLS 6006	THE SMOKEY CIRCLES ALBUM (LP, union jack flag label)	£60

SMOKEY SMOTHERS
69	Polydor 623 239	THE DRIVING BLUES (LP)	£50

SMOKIE
75	RAK SRAK 510	PASS IT AROUND (LP, name spelt as SMOKEY on cover)	£15
75	RAK SRAK 517	CHANGING ALL THE TIME (LP)	£15
76	RAK SRAK 520	MIDNIGHT CAFE (LP)	£20
77	RAK SRAK 530	BRIGHT LIGHTS AND BACK ALLEYS (LP)	£20
79	RAK SRAK 6757	THE OTHER SIDE OF THE ROAD (LP)	£15
81	RAK SRAK 545	SOLID GROUND (LP)	£15
82	RAK SRAK 546	STRANGERS IN PARADISE (LP)	£18

THE SMOKIN' MOJO FILTERS
95	Go! Discs GOD 136	Come Together/THE BEAUTIFUL SOUTH: A Minute's Silence/DODGY: Is It Me/BLACK GRAPE: In The Name Of The Father (Crown Of Thorns Mix) (7")	£20

(See also Paul Weller, Oasis)

SMOKIN' ROADIE
83	Zone To Zone ZON 3	Midnight/Ripp Off (p/s)	£30

SMOOTH BUT HAZZARDOUS
92	Basement BRSS 007	Smooth But Hazzardous/Made U Dance/Violent Headrush (12")	£20
93	Sound Entity SENT 1200	We Are The Creator/Push Up The Levels (12")	£40
93	Sound Entity SENT 1205	Made You Dance (Carl Cox Remix)/Push Up The Levels (SBH Remix)/Push Up The Levels (Originla Mix) (12")	£15

JACK SMOOTH
91	Sound Entity SE 001	WAVEFORMS EP (12")	£15
91	Sound Entity SE 03	Untitled/Untitled/Untitled/Untitled (12", white label, hand-written labels, some in stamped sleeve)	£15
93	Sound Entity SENT 1201	Tell Me Something/Happy Nonsense (12", with Spencer T)	£20
93	Sound Entity SENT 120220	HURTS EP (12", with Alex Reece)	£40

(see also Ruff With The Smooth)

SMUDGE
94	Domino WIGLP 7	MANILOW (LP, with free 7")	£18

GILLI SMYTH & MOTHER GONG
78	Charly CRL 5007	MOTHER (LP, with insert)	£15

(see also Gong)

DONALD SMYTHE
71	Punch PH 83	Where Love Goes/HURRICANES: You Can Run	£380

SNAFU
74	WWA WWA 003	SNAFU (LP, gatefold sleeve)	£18

(see also Whitesnake, Freedom)

SNAKEBITE
83	Astor ASTOR 1	Blow You Away/Thin Ice (no p/s)	£25

SNAKEFINGER
80	Do It RIDE5	GREENER POSTURES (LP)	£15

(see also The Residents, Chilli Willi)

SNAKEHIPS
75	Eden EDENLP 75	SNAKEHIPS ARNOLD AND THE KING OF BOOGIE (LP)	£200

SNAPE
73	Transatlantic TRA 269	ACCIDENTALLY BORN IN NEW ORLEANS (LP)	£22

(see also Alexis Korner)

SNAPPED ANKLES
12	Ears Have Eyes EHE 001	True Ecology (Shit Everywhere)/Nowhere/True Ecology (10", p/s)	£20
15	Snapped Ankles (no Cat. No.)	I Want My Minutes Back/Instruminutel (p/s, white vinyl)	£20

SNAPPERS (1)
59	Top Rank JAR 167	Big Bill/If There Were	£18
59	Top Rank JAR 167	Big Bill/If There Were (78)	£25

SNAPPERS (2)
67 CBS 2719   Upside Down Inside Out/Memories £40

SNATCH (2)
80 Fetish FET 004   Shopping For Clothes/Joey/Red Army (12", die-cut p/s)....................................£20
(see also Johnny Thunders, Judy Nylon)

SNATCH BACK
79 CSS CS 002   Eastern Lady/Cryin' To The Night (no p/s) £80

SNEAKER PIMPS
96 Clean Up CUP020LP   BECOMING X (LP)...£50
99 Clean Up CUP040LP   SPLINTER (2-LP) £40
02 Tommy Boy TBV 1532   BLOODSPORT (2-LP, red vinyl) £30
08 Clean Up CUP020DMM   BECOMING X (2-LP, reissue, 1000 only, stickered sleeve)........................£25
08 Clean Up CUP040DMM   SPLINTER (2-LP, reissue, 1000 only, stickered sleeve)..........................£25

SNEAKERS
77 Petal PTL 010   Link Lady/Vapour Trails (no p/s, 500 only)......................................£150

SNEAKY PETES
60 Decca F 11199   Savage (Parts 1 & 2) £15

SNEEKERS
64 Columbia DB 7385   I Just Can't Get To Sleep/Bald Headed Woman £150

SNEEKY FEELINS
79 Warped W102   Private Mail/Only The Rain (p/s with insert) £50

DAVID SNELL
66 Decca SKL 4745   THE SUBTLE SOUND OF DAVID SNELL (LP)....................................£15

SNIFF 'N' THE TEARS
79 Chiswick NS 40   Driver's Seat (cancelled, test pressings only, picture sleeve) £15

SNIFTERS
78 Lightning GIL 534   I Like Boys/Baby Punker..£15

SNIVELLING SHITS
77 Ghetto Rockers PRE 2   Terminal Stupid/I Can't Come (p/s, 1st pressing of 500, paper labels/black print) £60
77 Ghetto Rockers PRE 2   Terminal Stupid/I Can't Come (p/s, 2nd pressing, plastic labels/juke box centre)............£25
89 Damaged Goods FNARR 4   Isgodaman?/Terminal Stupid/I Can't Come (p/s) £20
89 Damaged Goods FNARR4B   Isgodaman?/Terminal Stupid/I Can't Come (box set with badge & inserts, pink vinyl in stamped plain white sleeve) £25

SNOBS
64 Decca F 11867   Buckle Shoe Stomp/Stand And Deliver £15

SNOOKY & MOODY
66 Blue Horizon 45-1003   Snooky And Moody's Blues/Telephone Blues (99 copies only)....................£150

HANK SNOW (& RAINBOW RANCH BOYS)
54 HMV 7MC 7   Why Do You Punish Me (For Loving You)/When Mexican Joe Meets Jole Blon (with Rainbow Ranch Boys) (export issue)...£15
54 HMV 7MC 15   Spanish Fire Ball/Between Fire And Water (with Rainbow Ranch Boys)(export issue).....£15
54 HMV 7MC 24   My Arabian Baby/I Don't Hurt Anymore (with Rainbow Ranch Boys) (export issue).......£15
54 HMV 7MC 25   My Religion's Not Old-Fashioned (But It's Real Genuine)/The Alphabet (with Rainbow Ranch Boys) (export issue)..£15
54 HMV 7MC 31   Yellow Roses/Would You Mind (with Rainbow Ranch Boys) (export issue)......................£15
59 RCA RD 27115   WHEN TRAGEDY STRUCK (LP) £15

SNOW PATROL
98 Jeepster JPR7 004   Little Hide/Sticky Teenage Twin (1,000 only, p/s) £18
06 Fiction 0602517043985   Chasing Cars/Play Me Like You Own Hand (p/s, with inner p/s) £25
98 Jeepster JPRLP004   SONGS FOR POLAR BEARS (LP) £40
03 Polydor 9866073   FINAL STRAW (LP) £15
06 Polydor 985 362-2   EYES OPEN (2-LP) £15
08 Fiction 1785268   A HUNDRED MILLION SUNS (2 x 12" 45 rpm, gatefold) £20
09 Fiction 272201-1   UP TO NOW (box set, 3-LP, CD, DVD)..£50
(see also Shrug)

SNUFF
88 Deceptive   TWEET TWEET MY LOVELY (LP, with insert).....................................£15

SNUFF CREW
17 I Love Acid ILA 015   I LOVE ACID 015 (12", hand-stamped and numbered, 303 only) £15

SO WHAT!
86 No label or Cat. No.   It Is All Over/Now I Don't Want You Around (no p/s) £50

MIKE SOAR
72 Westwood WRS 014   OUR SIDE OF THE BRIDGE (LP) £400

SOCIALITES
64 Warner Bros WB 148   Jive Jimmy/You're Losing Your Touch £40

SOCIAL SECURITY
78 Heartbeat PULSE 1   I Don't Want My Heart To Rule My Head/Stella's Got A Fella/Cider/Choc Ice (p/s) £30

SOCIETIE
67 Deram DM 162   Bird Has Flown/Breaking Down £60

SO CONFUSING AND SO VERY CLEAR
76 CFC 19776   SO CONFUSING AND SO VERY CLEAR (LP) £70

SOCRATES
72	Deram DM 362	Eating Momma's Cookin'/Dearest Agnes	£15

SODS (1)
79	Tap TAP 1	Mopey Grape/Negative Positive (p/s)	£30
79	Stortbeat SB 5	No Pictures Of Us/Plaything (p/s)	£40

SODS (2)
79	Step Forward SFLP 3	MINUTES TO GO (LP)	£30

SOFERNO B
80	Soferno B SOLP 001	IN DUB (LP)	£70

SOFT BOYS
77	Raw RAW 5	GIVE IT TO THE SOFT BOYS (EP, acetate with withdrawn track, Vyrna Knowl Is A Headbanger in place of "Ventilator")	£200
77	Raw RAW 5	GIVE IT TO THE SOFT BOYS (EP)	£20
78	Radar ADA 8	(I Want To Be An) Anglepoise Lamp/Fat Man's Son (p/s)	£15
79	Raw RAW 37	GIVE IT TO THE SOFT BOYS (EP, unreleased reissue)	£0
79	Raw RAW 41	Where Are The Prawns (unreleased)	£0
82	Bucketfull Of Brains BOB 1	Love Poisoning/When I Was A Kid (p/s, with Bucketfull Of Brains magazine)	£15
89	Overground OVER 4	The Face Of Death/The Yodelling Hoover (p/s, 15 gold test pressings)	£15
79	Two Crabs CLAW 1001	A CAN OF BEES (LP, original issue, black & white labels)	£30
80	Aura AUL 709	A CAN OF BEES (LP, reissue)	£15
80	Armageddon ARM 1	UNDERWATER MOONLIGHT (LP)	£50
83	M. Music CHIME 0002	INVISIBLE HITS (LP)	£15
84	Two Crabs CLAW 1001	A CAN OF BEES (LP, 2nd reissue, black & red labels)	£15
86	Living Cream MOIST 1	UNDERWATER MOONLIGHT (LP, reissue, different cover)	£20
87	Glass Fish MOIST 4	LIVE AT THE PORTLAND ARMS (LP)	£20

(see also Robyn Hitchcock)

SOFT CELL
83	Some Bizzare BIZL 3	THE ART OF FALLING APART (LP/12", printed inners)	£15
80	Big Frock ABF 1	MUTANT MOMENTS (EP, plain p/s with postcard; beware of counterfeits without postcard & in wraparound p/s!)	£150
81	Some Bizzare HARD 12	Memorabilia (Extended)/Persuasion (Extended) (12", p/s)	£15
81	Some Bizzare No Cat. No.	Metro Mr. X/B-MOVIE: Remembrance Day (white label test pressing)	£60
82	Some Bizzare CELBX 1	THE 12" SINGLES (6 x 12" box set, with booklet)	£50
84	Some Bizzare BZSR 2212	Down In The Subway (Remix)/Disease And Desire/Born To Lose (12", p/s)	£18

(see also Marc Almond, Marc & Mambas, Anne Hogan)

SOFT ROCK
72	Philips 6308	INVENTION (LP)	£15

SOFT DRINKS
82	Outer Himalayan OH 4	Pepsi Cola/Pop Stars In Their Pyjames (with booklet and sticker)	£40

MICK SOFTLEY
65	Immediate IM 014	I'm So Confused/She's My Girl	£40
67	CBS 202469	Am I The Red One/That's Not My Kind Of Love	£200
65	Columbia 33SX 1781	SONGS FOR SWINGIN' SURVIVORS (LP)	£150
70	CBS 64098	SUNRISE (LP, gatefold sleeve)	£80
71	CBS 64395	STREET SINGER (LP)	£40
72	CBS 64841	ANY MOTHER DOESN'T GRUMBLE (LP)	£40

SOFT MACHINE
67	Polydor 56151	Love Makes Sweet Music/Reelin' Feelin' Squeelin'	£200
69	Probe SPB 1002	THE SOFT MACHINE VOLUME TWO (LP, 1st pressing, black/silver label, laminated flipback sleeve)	£80
69	Probe SPB 1002	THE SOFT MACHINE VOLUME TWO (LP, 2nd pressing, pink label, laminated flipback sleeve)	£70
70	CBS 66246	THIRD (2-LP, gatefold)	£50
71	CBS 64280	FOURTH (LP, embossed textured sleeve)	£35
72	Probe GTSP 204	VOLUMES ONE AND TWO (2-LP, yellow labels)	£25
72	CBS 64806	FIFTH (LP)	£25
73	CBS 68214	SIX (2-LP, gatefold sleeve)	£30
73	CBS 65799	SEVEN (LP, gatefold sleeve)	£30
75	Harvest SHSP 4044	BUNDLES (LP, with inner sleeve)	£30
76	Harvest SHSP 4056	SOFTS (LP)	£25
77	Harvest SHTW 800	TRIPLE ECHO (3LP, box set, booklet)	£60
78	Harvest SHSP 4083	ALIVE & WELL (LP)	£20
78	ABC ABCD 602	THE COLLECTION (2-LP, this is One and Two from same stampers as the 1972 2-LP set VOLUMES ONE AND TWO)	£20
81	EMI EMC 3348	LAND OF COCKAYNE (LP)	£15
87	Big Beat WIKA 57	SOFT MACHINE (LP, reissue)	£18
87	Big Beat WIKA 58	VOLUME TWO (LP, reissue)	£18
88	Reckless RECKLP5	LIVE AT THE PROMS (LP)	£15
88	Decal LIKD 35	THIRD (2-LP, reissue)	£20

(see also Robert Wyatt, Kevin Ayers, Hugh Hopper, Elton Dean, Daevid Allen, Matching Mole, 'Igginbottom, Lyn Dobson)

SOFTNESS
80	Remedy RM 119	You Ain't My Lover/Locked Doors	£30

SOFT SHOE
78	Aardvark AARD 1	FOR THOSE ALONE (LP, with insert)	£100

SOFT TOUCH (1)
67	W+G WG 001	A Silent Life/Ellusive Face (Private Pressing)	£300

SOFT TOUCH (2)
73 Acorn AC 04   Crazy Child/Down And Out £20

SOHO JETS
75 Polydor 2058 525   Hi Heel Tarzan/Night Flight £20
75 Polydor 2058 598   Denim Goddess/Smile...£20
(see also Razar)

SOHO SKIFFLE GROUP
57 Melodisc EMP 7 72   SOHO SKIFFLE GROUP (EP)..£75

CLEO SOL
20 Forever Living Originals   ROSE IN THE DARK (LP) £30
     FLO0004LP
(see also Sault)

SOL INVICTUS
90 Cerne 004   Abbatoirs Of Love/CURRENT 93: This Ain't The Summer Of Love (live in Japan, gig freebie, 93 with insert & gig ticket)...£50
90 Cerne 004   Abbatoirs Of Love/CURRENT 93: This Ain't The Summer Of Love (live in Japan, gig freebie, [200 without insert])..£25
91 Shock SX 016   See The Dove Fall/Somewhere In Europe (numbered foldover p/s in poly bag, 1,000 only)...£15
91 World Serpent WS7 002   Looking For Europe (1-sided, etched B-side, foldover sleeve in poly bag, 963 only) £15
89 SVL SVL 009   IN THE JAWS OF THE SERPENT (LP, with insert) £20
90 Tursa 001   TREES IN WINTER (LP) £30
90 Tursa 002   LEX TALIONIS (CD, special edit in leather wallet)...£30
91 Tursa 003   KILLING TIDE (LP) £25
00 Tursa 026   EVE (picture disc, 1,000 only) £20
01 Tursa 029   HILL OF CROSSES (LP, 1,000 only, signed) £20
(see also Current 93, Death In June, Nurse With Wound, Karl Blake)

SOLAR PLEXUS
73 Polydor 2383 222   SOLAR PLEXUS (LP) £35

SOLDIER
82 Heavy Metal HEAVY 12   Sheralee/Force (p/s, with postcard) £35
82 Heavy Metal HEAVY 12   Sheralee/Force (p/s, without postcard) £25

SOLDIER DOLLS
83 Scream 1   WHAT DO THEY KNOW? (EP)..£15
84 Scream 2   A TASTE OF BLOOD (EP, red vinyl)...£15

SOLID BRITISH HAT BAND
71 Longman LG 0 582 56421 2   MISTER MONDAY AND OTHER SONGS FOR THE TEACHING OF ENGLISH (LP, with insert)..£30
74 Longman LG 567   GOODBYE RAINBOW (LP, with insert) £30

SOLID GOLD CADILLAC
73 RCA SF 8311   SOLID GOLD CADILLAC (LP) £40
73 RCA SF 8365   BRAIN DAMAGE (LP)..£50
(see also Battered Ornaments, Chris Spedding, Mike Westbrook)

SOLID GROOVE
94 Clockwork CLOCK 1   Work That Groove (Original Mix)/(Groove MIx)/Deep State/Technohouse (12")............£15

SOLID N MIND
90 Liberty Grooves LIB001   An Original Break (12") £30
91 Liberty Grooves PPP001   Centre Stage/Woke With Nuthin' (Promo cassette) £50
91 Liberty Grooves LIB 002 1/2 Centre Stage/Woke With Nothin' (12")..£15
92 Liberty Grooves LIB 003   Battle Tipped Rhyme (12")..£18

SOLID ROCK BAND
78 Chapel Lane RWA 1   FOOTPRINTS ON THE WATER (LP, gatefold sleeve)...£15

SOLID SPACE
82 In Phaze IP 011   SPACE MUSEUM (cassette)..£150

SOLILOQUY
73 Lyntone LYN 2967   Father Moonshine/Asian Way/Lady Tarantula (50 only, no p/s).............................£300

SOLITAIRES
58 London HLM 8745   Walking Along/Please Kiss This Letter..£130
58 London HLM 8745   Walking Along/Please Kiss This Letter (78) £60

JAKE SOLLO
79 Pye N 102   JAKE SOLLO (LP) £30

NORMAN SOLOMAN
81 Black Joy DH 816   Joy Bells Ringing/JAYS: Unity Call (12") £25

SOLSTICE (1)
84 Equinox EQRLP 001   SILENT DANCE (LP, gatefold sleeve) £18

SOLSTICE (2)
08 Iron Kodex IK 003   ONLY THE STRONG SURVIVE (2-LP with free 7") £20

SOLUTION
72 Decca SKL-R 5124   SOLUTION (LP) £25

SOME CHICKEN
77 Raw RAW 7   New Religion/Blood On The Wall (p/s)..£20
78 Raw RAW 13   Arabian Daze/No. 7..£15
78 Raw RAW 13   Arabian Daze/No. 7 (purple vinyl)...£120

SOME OF MY BEST FRIENDS ARE CANADIAN
80   Bulge BLAST 4   Feeling Sheepish/Speaking Clock...£20

SOMEONE'S BAND
70   Deram DM 313   Story/Give It To You...£40
70   Deram SML 1068   SOMEONE'S BAND (LP)...£600

SOMERVILLE GENTLEMAN'S BAND
80   Somerville PLR 026   FAR FROM HOME (LP, gatefold insert with sticker over 'Plant Life' logo) £25

JOANIE SOMMERS
65   Warner Bros WB 150   If You Love Him/I Think I'm Gonna Cry £15
13   Harkit HRKS 8431   Don't Pity Me/Johnny Get Angry (p/s) £15
60   Warner Bros WEP 6013   POSITIVELY THE MOST (EP, also stereo WSEP 2013) £20
61   Warner Bros WEP 6047   THE VOICE OF THE SIXTIES (EP, also stereo WSEP 2047) £15
(see also Ed Byrnes)

SONGSTERS
54   London HL 8100   Bahama Buggy Ride/It Isn't Right £150

SON HOUSE
60s Saydisc Roots SL 504   THE VOCAL INTENSITY OF SON HOUSE (LP) £40
66   CBS (S)BPG 62604   THE LEGENDARY FATHER OF FOLK BLUES (LP) £35
70   Liberty LBS 83391   JOHN THE REVELATOR (LP) £30

SON HOUSE/J.D. SHORT
69   Xtra XTRA 1080   DELTA BLUES (LP) £20

SONIA
78   D Roy DRDD 006   Love Don't Live Here Any More/D ROY BAND: Version (12") £20
81   S & S FERGY 001   Checking It Out/Version (12", with Creation Rebel)..£20
80   Cha Cha CHAD 26   Easier To Love/That's The Way You Feel (12", with Earth & Stone) £15
79   D-Roy DRLP 1006   MAGIC LADY (LP) £60

SONIC BOOM
90   Silvertone SONIC 1   Octaves/Tremeloes (10", orange vinyl PVC sleeve, mail-order only) £18
90   Silvertone ORE ZLP 506   SPECTRUM (LP, gatefold rotatable plastic disc sleeve with inner) £40
(see also Spacemen 3, Spectrum)

SONIC YOUTH
86   Blast First BFFP 3   Flower/Halloween (12", p/s, some on yellow vinyl) £18
86   Blast First BFFP 3   Flower/Rewolf (12", p/s, censored version)...£15
86   Blast First BFFP 3(B)   (Savage Pencil etch)/Halloween II (12", p/s, A-side engraved, 1st 100 signed) £65
86   Blast First BFFP 3(B)   (Savage Pencil etch)/Halloween II (12", p/s, A-side engraved) £40
86   Blast First BFFP 3X   Flower/Halloween/Satan Supermix (12", unreleased) £0
86   Blast First BFFP 7   Starpower (edit)/Bubblegum (p/s, some with badge & poster) £20
88   Fierce FRIGHT 015/016   Stick Me Donna Magick Momma/Making The Nature Scene (live) (p/s, 2 x 1-sided 7"
                              with etched B-sides)...£30
88   Catalogue CAT 064   Teenage Riot (square flexidisc sewn into 'The Catalogue' magazine).............................£15
89   Blast First BFFP 46   Touch Me I'm Sick/MUDHONEY: Halloween (12", p/s) £15
91   DGC 21634   DIRTY BOOTS (12" EP) £15
92   Geffen DGCV 11   100% (10" EP, black vinyl promo)...£30
92   Geffen DGCT 11   100% (12" EP, promo only, white label) £40
00   Geffen SONIC 001   Free City Rhymes/Renegade Princess (7" promo p/s)...£40
85   Blast First BFFP 1   BAD MOON RISING (LP, with lyric insert) £30
86   Blast First BFFP 4   EVOL (LP)...£30
87   Blast First CHAT 1   SISTER INTERVIEW DISC (LP) £20
87   Blast First BFFP 20   SISTER (LP) £30
88   Blast First BFFP 34   DAYDREAM NATION (2-LP, 1st 1,000 with signed poster) £60
88   Blast First BFFP 34   DAYDREAM NATION (2-LP)...£25
90   WEA 7599 24297-1   GOO (LP, with free 7")...£25
90   WEA 7599 24297-1   GOO (LP)..£20
92   Geffen GEF24485[2]   DIRTY (2-LP) £35
93   Geffen GEF424515   DAYDREAM NATION (2-LP, reissue, poster) £20
94   Geffen GEF 24632   EXPERIMENTAL JET SET, TRASH & NO STAR (LP, blue vinyl) £25
95   Geffen GEF24825   WASHING MACHINE (2-LP)...£50
96   Blast First BFFP 113   CONFUSION IS SEX (LP, reissue) £15
98   Geffen GEF 25203   A THOUSAND LEAVES (2-LP)...£25
00   Geffen 069490650 1   NYC GHOSTS & FLOWERS (LP) £20
09   Matador OLE 8721   BATTERY PARK NYC, JULY 4th 2008 (LP) £18
09   Matador OLE 829-1   THE ETERNAL (2-LP)..£20
(see also Mudhoney)

SONNY
71   Ackee ACK 127   Love And Peace/LARRY & ALVIN: Throw Me Corn £20

SONNY & CHER
65   Vocalion VL 9247   The Letter/Spring Fever (B-side by 'Sonny & Cher (Instrumental)') £15
65   Reprise R 30056   CAESAR AND CLEO (EP, 2 tracks each by Sonny & Cher, Caesar & Cleo)..........................£25
(see also Caesar & Cleo, Cher, Sonny, Date With Soul)

SONNY & DAFFODILS
63   Ember EMB EP 4538   SONNY & DAFFODILS (EP) £50

SONNY (BURKE) & YVONNE
64   Island WI 134   Life Without Fun/SONNY BURKE GROUP: Mount Vesuvius...£25
(see also Sonny Burke)

SONNYJIM

18	Daupe! DM SP 034	**DEATH BY MISADVENTURE** (12", p/s, with Conway,red vinyl, 250 copies)	£40
18	Daupe! DM SP 034	**DEATH BY MISADVENTURE** (12", p/s, with Conway, picture disc, 250 copies)	£50
18	Daupe! DM SP 034	**DEATH BY MISADVENTURE** (12", p/s, with Conway, white vinyl, 250 copies)	£40
18	Daupe! DM SP 034	**DEATH BY MISADVENTURE** (12", p/s, with Conway, 250 copies)	£40
18	Daupe! DM SP 034	**DEATH BY MISADVENTURE** (12", p/s, with Conway, with obi strip, 20 copies)	£150
16	Daupe! DM SP 014	**MUD IN MY MALBEC** (LP, with OBI strip, 20 only)	£150
16	Daupe! DM SP 014	**MUD IN MY MALBEC** (LP, white vinyl, 100 only)	£100
16	Daupe! DM SP 014	**MUD IN MY MALBEC** (LP, 120 only)	£80

SON OF NOISE

91	Music Of Life NOTE53	**Son Of Noise/Ill Justice** (12")	£15
91	Kold Sweat KS117	**Master Of Menace/Milk In The Chocolate** (12")	£15
92	Kold Sweat KSLP03	**THE MIGHTY SON OF NOISE** (LP)	£20
95	Little Rascool MZE2711	**ACCESS DENIED** (LP)	£15

(see also Hardnoise)

SONS OF ALBATROSS

75	Decca FR 13605	**Africa/Ha-ri-ah**	£35

SONS OF DEMENTED CHILDREN

87	Hatter MAD 003	**Spoof Dealer/Busking** (p/s, with insert)	£18

SONS OF FRED

65	Columbia DB 7605	**Sweet Love/I'll Be There**	£200
65	Parlophone R 5391	**I, I, I** (Want Your Lovin')**/She Only Wants A Friend**	£100
66	Parlophone R 5415	**Baby What Do You Want Me To Do/You Told Me**	£200

(see also Odyssey)

SONS OF GLORY

62	Columbia 33SX 1474	**GOD GLORIFIES** (LP)	£25

SONS OF ISHMAEL

87	Manic Ears ACHE 10	**PARIAH MARTYR DEMANDS A SACRIFICE** (LP)	£15

SONS OF JAH

75	Bullet BU 557	**Nyah Chant/Rasta Waltz**	£20
78	Natty Congo NCDM 002	**Anthem/WIJA LINDO: His Majesty's Authority** (12")	£30
78	Natty Congo NC 001	**Save The Children/RANKING REUBEN: Psalm 72** (12")	£20
78	Natty Congo NC 002	**Israel/RANKING REUBEN: Dubsco** (12")	£20
79	Natty Congo PFUL 2301	**Home To Zion/Woman** (12")	£40
82	Natty Congo NCDM 013	**Breaking Down The Barriers/Barrier Dub** (12")	£20
78	Natty Congo PFULP 3501	**BANKRUPT MORALITY** (LP, with lyric sheet)	£20
79	Natty Congo PFULP 3502	**BURNING BLACK** (LP)	£30
80	Natty Congo PFULP 3505	**REGGAE HIT SHOWCASE** (LP)	£70
82	Natty Congo NCLP 001	**UNIVERSAL MESSAGE** (LP)	£25
82	Natty Congo NCLP 005	**URBAN GUERILLA** (LP, as Son Of Jah)	£50
83	Natty Congo NCLP 002	**WRITINGS ON THE WALL** (LP, as Son of Jah)	£30

SONS OF MAN

67	Oak RGJ 612	**SONS OF MAN** (EP, no p/s)	£400

SONS OF NUBIA

90	White SON1	**RAPS THE LAST MEANS** (EP)	£150

SONS OF PILTDOWN MEN

63	Pye International 7N 25206	**Mad Goose/Be A Party**	£20

SONS OF SOUL

66	Doctor Bird DB 1037	**Yeah Yeah Baby/So Ashamed**	£35

SONS OF MONKEYS

81	Slip 001	**Me & Mr. Suzuki/DECADES BY NIGHT: Life Spiral**	£50

SONS OF ROBIN STONE

74	Atlantic K 10441	**Got To Get You Back/Love Is Just Around The Corner**	£15

SONSONG

76	Zebra ZM 5761	**SONSONG** (LP)	£30

SOPHIE

12	Huntleys and Palmers HP006	**Nothing More To Say/Eeehhh** (12", p/s)	£60
13	Numbers NMBRS 26	**Bipp/Elle** (12", printed plastic sleeve)	£20
14	Numbers NMBRS 34	**Lemonade/Hard** (12")	£15
15	Numbers NMBRS 46	**Msmsmsm/Vyzee** (12")	£35
15	Numbers NMBRS 47	**L.O.V.E/Just Like We Never Said Goodbye** (12")	£30
18	Transgressive TRANS 368XX	**OIL OF EVERY PEARL'S UN-INSIDES** (LP, pink vinyl, 300 only)	£200
18	Transgressive TRANS 368X	**OIL OF EVERY PEARL'S UN-INSIDES** (LP, red vinyl, with poster)	£50

SOPHISTICATES

60s	Spectrum SPEEP 701	**AT THE WOODVILLE** (EP)	£15

SOPHOMORES

60s	Seeco CELP 451	**THE SOPHOMORES** (LP)	£30

SOPWITH CAMEL

86	Edsel ED 185	**FRANTIC DESOLATION** (LP, reissue)	£20

SORE POINTS

81	Pointless SRTS 81 CUS 1113	**Shop Born Sex/Never Gonna Go Outside At Any Point**	£25

SORE THROAT (2)
88	Acid Rain ARRGHHH001	DEATH TO CAPITALIST HARDCORE EP	£20
88	Meantime COX	UNHINDERED BY TALENT (LP, insert)	£15
89	Manic Ears ACHE	INDESTROY (LP, with lyric poster, as SAW THROAT)	£20
89	Earache MOSH 10	DISGRACE TO THE CORPSE OF SID (LP, insert)	£15
80s	Manic Ears ACHE	NEVER MIND THE NAPALM HERE'S SORE THROAT (LP)	£20

SORROWS
65	Piccadilly 7N 35219	I Don't Wanna Be Free/Come With Me	£40
65	Piccadilly 7N 35230	Baby/Teenage Letter	£50
65	Piccadilly 7N 35260	Take A Heart/We Should Get Along Fine	£25
66	Piccadilly 7N 35277	You've Got What I Want/No, No, No, No (export p/s)	£35
66	Piccadilly 7N 35277	You've Got What I Want/No, No, No, No	£20
66	Piccadilly 7N 35309	Let The Live Live/Don't Sing No Sad Songs For Me	£40
66	Piccadilly 7N 35336	Let Me In/How Love Used To Be	£40
67	Piccadilly 7N 35385	Pink, Purple, Yellow And Red/My Gal	£140
66	Piccadilly N(S)PL 38023	TAKE A HEART (LP, mono)	£250
66	Piccadilly N(S)PL 38023	TAKE A HEART (LP, stereo)	£350

(see also Don Fardon)

S.O.U.L. (SOUNDS OF UNITY & LOVE)
| 72 | Pye Intl. NSPL 28162 | CAN YOU FEEL IT (LP) | £80 |

JIMMY SOUL
| 63 | Stateside SS 178 | If You Wanna Be Happy/Don't Release Me | £20 |
| 64 | Stateside SE 1010 | IF YOU WANNA BE HAPPY (EP) | £50 |

SHARON SOUL
| 65 | Stateside SS 411 | How Can I Get To You/Don't Say Goodbye Love | £75 |
| 65 | Stateside SS 411 | How Can I Get To You/Don't Say Goodbye Love (DJ copy) | £120 |

SOUL AGENTS
64	Pye 7N 15660	I Just Wanna Make Love To You/Mean Woman Blues	£45
64	Pye 7N 15707	Seventh Son/Let's Make It Pretty Baby	£75
65	Pye 7N 15768	Don't Break It Up/Gospel Train	£70

(see also Loot, Don Shinn, Hoofoot)

SOUL AGENTS (JAMAICA)
67	Coxsone CS 7007	Get Ready It's Rocksteady/BOB & BELTONES: Smile Like An Angel (B-side actually by Bop & Beltones)	£30
67	Coxsone CS 7018	For Your Education/SUMMERTAIRES: Tell Me	£60
67	Coxsone CS 7027	Lecture/SOUL BOYS: Blood Pressure	£65

SOUL BOYS
| 66 | Rio R120 | Rudie Get Wise/JACKIE OPEL: I Don't Want Her | £60 |
| 67 | Island WI 3052 | Blood Pressure/RITA MARLEY: Come To Me | £150 |

(see also Soul Agents [Jamaica])

SOUL BROTHERS
| 65 | Decca F 12116 | I Keep Ringing My Baby/I Can't Take It | £18 |
| 65 | Parlophone R 5321 | I Can't Believe It/You Don't Want To Know | £15 |

SOUL BROTHERS (JAMAICA)
65	Ska Beat JB 226	Train To Skaville/WAILERS: I Made A Mistake	£200
66	Ska Beat JB 259	Bugaloo/I'll Come Back	£100
66	Rio R 118	Crawfish/RITA MARLEY: You Lied	£40
66	Rio R 121	Mr T.N.T./MARCIA GRIFFITHS: Mr Everything	£50
66	Island WI 282	Green Moon/E Gal OK	£30
66	Island WI 294	Ska-Bostello/DON DRUMMOND: Looking Through The Window	£30
66	Island WI 296	Sound One/MARTINE: Grandfather's Clock (B-side actually by Emille Straker & Merrymen or Martinis)	£50
66	Island WI 3013	More & More/DELROY WILSON: Dancing Mood	£40
66	Island WI 3016	Mr Flint/Too Young To Love (B-side actually by Freddie McGregor)	£40
67	Island WI 3038	Sound Pressure/ETHIOPIANS: For You	£30
67	Island WI 3039	Hi-Life/DELROY WILSON: Close To Me	£50
67	Coxsone CS 7001	Take Ten/HUGH GODFREY: Deh Pon Dem	£100
67	Coxsone CS 7020	Hey Windell/KEN BOOTHE: Home Home Home	£40
67	Coxsone CS 7024	One Stop/TENNORS: Pressure And Slide	£30
67	Studio One SO 2006	Hot And Cold/TERMITES: Mercy Mr. Percy	£150
67	Studio One SO 2034	Hot Rod/GAYLADS: Africa (We Want To Go)	£125
67	Island WI 3038	Sherry/SOUL JUNIOR : Out Of My Mind (Some list Bumps Oakley as the B-side)	£100
67	Studio One SO 2016	Honey Pot/VICEROYS: Lose And Gain	£60
70	Pressure Beat PR 5506	Pussy Catch A Fire (actually by Soul Twins)/DESTROYERS: Follow This Beat (B-side actually "Secret Weapon" by Ansell Collins)	£15
67	Coxsone CSL 8001	HOT SHOT SKA (LP)	£200
67	Coxsone CSL 8002	CARIB SOUL (LP)	£250

(see also Earl Van Dyke & Soul Brothers, Soul Twins, Lee Perry, Tony Gregory, Ethiopians, Itals, Hortense & Delroy, Gaylads, Jennors, Derrick Morgan, Summertaires, Delroy Wilson)

SOUL BROTHERS SIX
| 67 | Atlantic 584 118 | Some Kind Of Wonderful/I'll Be Loving You | £50 |
| 69 | Atlantic 584 256 | Some Kind Of Wonderful/Somebody Else Is Loving My Baby | £25 |

SOUL CAPSULE
| 01 | Aspect ASC3 | Law Of Grace/Meltdown/Meltdown (Dub) (12") | £150 |

SOUL CATS
| 69 | Camel CA 23 | Keep It Moving/Your Sweet Love | £30 |

69	Gas GAS 109	Choo Choo Train/The Load (actually "Swinging For Joy" by Count Ossie Band)	£30
70s	Junior JR 103	Reggay Got Soul (actually by Carl Bryan)/Land Of Love (reissue)	£15

SOUL CITY ORCHESTRA

77	Rouge RMS 109	MEAT TICKET (LP)	£40
78	De Wolfe DWS/LP 3387	RED LIGHT ZONE (LP)	£20

SOUL CITY

62	Cameo Parkway P 103	Everybody Dance Now/Who Knows	£100
62	Cameo Parkway P 103	Everybody Dance Now/Who Knows (DJ copy)	£125

SOUL CITY EXECUTIVES

69	Soul City SC 109	Happy Chatter/Falling In Love	£20

SOUL CLAN

68	Atlantic 584 202	Soul Meeting/That's How It Feels (in p/s)	£15
68	Atlantic 587 127	SOUL MEETING (LP)	£20

(see also Solomon Burke, Arthur Conley, Don Covay, Ben E. King, Joe Tex)

SOUL CONDOR

70	Polydor 2344002	CERTAIN LIONS & TIGERS (LP)	£25

SOUL CONNECTION

88	Intrigue IGE 001T	Oh Ivy!/In (and Out Of) Love/Find The Time (To Play) (12")	£15
88	Intrigue IGE SC1	ROUGH & READY (LP)	£30
90	Intrigue IGE SC2	RAW STREETSOUL (LP)	£50

SOUL DEFENDERS

71	Banana BA 354	Way Back Home/SOUL REBELS: Stand For Your Rights	£35
72	Ackee ACK 147	Sound Almighty/COUNT OSSIE: Meditation	£20

(see also Eric Donaldson, Carey Johnson)

SOUL DIRECTIONS

70	Attack ATT 8011	Su Su Su/Better Hearing	£200

SOUL DRIFTERS

07	Funk 45 FUNK45 037	Funky Soul Brother Part 1/Part 2 (reissue)	£15

SOULETTES

65	Ska Beat JB 204	Opportunity/DIZZY JOHNNY & STUDIO 1 ORCHESTRA: Sudden Destruction	£50
70	Upsetter US 337	Let It Be/UPSETTERS: Big Dog Bloxie	£30
71	Jackpot JP 766	My Desire/Bring It Up	£25
71	Jackpot JP 767	All Of Your Loving/LLOYD CLARKE: Love Me	£20

(see also Rita Marley, Ken Boothe, Roland Alphonso, Uniques)

SOUL FLAMES

68	Nu Beat NB 020	Mini Really Fit Dem/Soul Train	£200

(see also Alton Ellis)

SOULFUL STRINGS

67	Chess CRS 8068	Burning Spear/Within You, Without You	£30
67	Chess CRS 8068	Burning Spear/Within You, Without You (DJ Copy)	£50
69	Chess CRLS 4534	GROOVIN' WITH THE SOULFUL STRINGS (LP)	£20

SOUL GENERATION

73	Sticky SBL 135	BEYOND BODY AND SOUL (LP)	£25

SOUL KINGS

69	Blue Cat BS 169	The Magnificent Seven/RUPIE EDWARDS: Long Lost Love	£60

SOUL LEADERS

67	Rio R 134	Pour On The Sauce/Beauty Is Only Skin Deep	£40

SOULMATES (JAMAICA)

69	Amalgamated AMG 836	Them A Laugh And A Ki Ki/The Hippys Are Here (B-side actually by Hippy Boys)	£70
69	Amalgamated AMG 842	On The Move/Jump It Up (B-side actually by Viceroys)	£70
69	Camel CA 33	Beware Of Bad Dogs/Short Cut (actually by Glen Adams)	£50

SOULMATES (U.K.)

65	Parlophone R 5334	Too Late To Say You're Sorry/Your Love	£80
66	Parlophone R 5407	Bring Your Love Back Home (with Jet Set)/When Love Is Gone	£15

(see also Liza Strike)

SOUL OF THE CITY

77	Mandla MANDLA 002	CITY SOUL AND DIAGONAL STREET BLUES (LP)	£60

SOUL PARTNERS

69	Pama PM 766	Walk On Judge/Lose The One You Love	£20

SOUL PEOPLE

68	Island WIP 6040	Hummin'/Soul Drink	£35

SOUL PROPRIETORS

65	Concord CON STD 74	All/Lonely Separation (private pressing)	£300

SOUL REBELS

72	Banana BA 374	Listen And Observe/What's Love	£70
72	Count Shelly CS 001	Judgement Day Is Near/Solid As A Rock	£25
72	Count Shelly CS 003	I'm The One Who Loves You/I ROY: War Zone	£20

(see also Soul Defenders)

SOUL RHYTHMS

69	Bullet BU 404	Work Boy Work/CECIL THOMAS: Girl Lonesome Fever	£25
69	High Note HS 013	National Lottery/Round Seven	£30
69	Gas GAS 113	Soul Call/Musical Gate	£70

(see also Hippy Boys, Max Romeo)

SOULSAVERS
07	V2 VVR1045531	IT'S NOT HOW FAR YOU FALL IT'S HOW YOU LAND (LP)	£60

SOUL SEARCHERS
74	Sussex LPSX 4	SALT OF THE EARTH (LP)	£25
06	Soul Brother SBCS 24	WE THE PEOPLE (LP, reissue)	£15

SOUL SHACK
80	Record Shack GALD 003	Galactic Funk/(Instrumental) (12", white label only)	£40

SOUL SISTERS (JAMAICA)
69	Amalgamated AMG 839	Wreck A Buddy/VERSATILES: Push It In	£40

(see also Dennis Brown)

SOUL SISTERS (U.S.)
64	Sue WI 312	I Can't Stand It/Blueberry Hill	£40
64	Sue WI 336	Loop De Loop/Long Gone	£50
65	London HLC 9970	Foolish Dreamer/Good Time Tonight	£60
65	London HLC 9970	Foolish Dreamer/Good Time Tonight (DJ copy)	£100
64	Sue ILP 913	THE SOUL SISTERS (LP)	£150

SOUL SOUNDS
67	Columbia S(C)X 6158	SOUL SURVIVAL (LP)	£40

(see also Savages, Rebel Rousers)

SOUL STIRRERS
69	Duke DU 25	Come See About Me/LLOYD CHARMERS: 5 To 5	£60

(see also Sam Cooke)

SOUL SURVIVORS
67	Stateside SS 2057	Expressway To Your Heart/Hey Gyp	£30
68	Stateside SS 2094	Explosion (In Your Soul)/Dathon's Theme	£18
69	Atlantic 584 275	Mama Soul/Tell Daddy	£30

SOUL SYNDICATE
72	Green Door GD 4021	Riot (actually by Johnny Moore & Soul Syndicate)/Smoke Without Fire (actually by Keith Hudson)	£30

(see also Rockin' Horse)

SOUL TONES
70	Pama PM 790	Dancing Time/BUNNY BARRETT: Love Locked Out	£15

SOUL TOPS
67	Fab FAB 27	Baby I Got News/TEDDY KING & BUSTER'S ALL STARS: Mexican Divorce	£120
68	Nu Beat NB002	Rain And Thunder/Swing Baby	£60

SOUL TWINS (JAMAICA)
70	High Note HS 043	Little Suzie/Cherrie	£25
72	Clandisc CLA 238	Don't Call Me Nigga/DYNAMITES: Joe Louis	£35

SOUL II SOUL
89	10 DIX 82	CLUB CLASSICS VOL 1. (LP)	£15

SOUL VENDORS
67	Coxsone CS 07112	Honeypot/BUMPS OKALEY: Rag Doll (white label only)	£400
67	Coxsone CS 7028	You Troubled Me/BOP & BELTONES: Love	£80
67	Coxsone CS 7029	Fat Fish/MARCIA GRIFFITHS: Call To Me	£150
67	Studio One SO 2018	Rocking Sweet Pea/JOE HIGGS: Change Of Plans	£200
67	Studio One SO 2022	Cool Shade/RICHARD ACE: I Need You	£120
67	Studio One SO 2028	Just A Bit Of Soul/ALTON ELLIS: I Am Just A Guy	£120
67	Studio One SO 2031	Take Me/DELROY WILSON: I'm Not A King	£60
67	Studio One SO 2032	Pe Da Pa/ERNEST WILSON: Money Worries	£80
67	Studio One SO 2035	Pupa Lick/ETHIOPIANS: Leave My Business Alone	£40
68	Studio One SO 2038	Psychedelic Rock/GAYLADS: I'm Free	£500
68	Studio One SO 2043	Chinese Chicken/JACKIE MITTOO: Put It On	£250
68	Studio One SO 2044	Happy Ogan (actually titled "Happy Organ")/INVADERS: Soulful Music	£1200
68	Studio One SO 2048	Evening Time/RIGHTEOUS FLAMES: Ease Up	£120
68	Studio One SO 2058	Frozen Soul/ERNEST WILSON: If I Were A Carpenter	£200
68	Studio One SO 2066	Soul Joint/Soul Limbo	£200
68	Studio One SO 2070	Captain Cojoe/JACKIE MITTOO: Drum Song	£400
68	Coxsone CS 7037	Grooving Steady/ROY RICHARDS: Warm And Tender Ska	£120
68	Coxsone CS 7038	Whipping The Prince (actually by Ed Hangle & Alton Ellis)/HEPTONES: If You Knew	£100
68	Coxsone CS 7048	Last Waltz/HAMLINS: Sentimental Reasons	£100
68	Coxsone CS 7057	Real Rock/AL CAMPBELL: Don't Run Away	£220
68	Coxsone CS 7071	West Of The Sun/ALTON ELLIS: A Fool	£150
69	Coxsone CS 7084	Six Figure/DENZIL LAING: Man Payaba	£90
67	Coxsone CSL 8010	ON TOUR (LP)	£350

(see also Dobby Dobson, Norma Fraser)

SOULWAX
04	Pias B060DLP	ANY MINUTE NOW (2-LP, inners)	£20
05	PIAS PIASB 060	NITE VERSIONS (2-LP)	£40
07	Parlophone 509995092471	MOST OF THE REMIXES WE'VE MADE... (2-LP)	£20

SOUND
79	Torch TOR 003	PHYSICAL WORLD (EP)	£35
79	Torch TOR 008	THE SOUND (LP, possibly unissued)	£0
80	Korova KODE 2	JEOPARDY (LP, with inner)	£20

81	Korova KODE 5	**FROM THE LIONS MOUTH** (LP, gatefold)	£35
82	Warner Bros. 240019	**ALL FALL DOWN** (LP)	£20
85	Statik STAB 1	**SHOCK OF DAYLIGHT** (mini-LP)	£15
85	Statik STATLP 24	**HEAD & HEARTS** (LP)	£20
85	Statik STATDLP1	**IN THE HOTHOUSE** (2-LP, gatefold)	£25

(see also Outsiders, Second Layer)

SOUND BARRIER
68	Beacon BEA 109	**She Always Comes Back To Me/Groovin' Slow**	£100

SOUND CEREMONY
79	Celestial Sound RWG 001	**GUITAR STAR** (LP)	£20
79	Celestial Sound RWG 002	**RON WARREN GANDERTON & SOUND CEREMONY** (LP)	£40
81	Celestial Sound RWG 003	**PRECIOUS AS ENGLAND** (LP)	£20

SOUND DIMENSION
69	Coxsone CS 7083	**Scorcia/CECIL & JACKIE: Breaking Up** (B-side actually "Hold Me Baby" by Basil Daley)	£50
69	Coxsone CS 7085	**Soul Trombone** (Suffering Stink)/**LARRY & ALVIN: Your Cheating Heart**	£300
69	Coxsone CS 7090	**Soulful Strut/Breaking Up**	£300
69	Coxsone CS 7093	**More Scorchia** (dredited to Sound Dimensions)/**LENNIE HIBBERT: Village Soul**	£60
69	Coxsone CS 7097	**Time Is Tight/BARRY LLEWELLYN: Sad Song**	£60
69	Bamboo BAM 5	**Doctor Sappa Too/Soul Eruption** (B-side actually by Roy Richards & Sound Dimension)	£45
69	Bamboo BAM 7	**Baby Face/GLADIATORS: Any Where**	£30
69	Bamboo BAM 9	**Jamaica Rag/C. MARSHALL: I Need Your Loving**	£40
69	Bamboo BAM 13	**Whoopy/NORMA FRAZER: Working** (B-side actually by Marcia Griffiths)	£120
69	Bamboo BAM 14	**Black Onion/Bitter Blood**	£80
70	Bamboo BAM 18	**Poison Ivy/BOB ANDY: Bonopart** (actually by Al Senior)	£50
70	Bamboo BAM 50	**Soul Food/BURNING SPEAR: Door Peeper**	£80
70	Banana BA 313	**In The Summertime/In The Summertime - Version** (actually by Winston Francis)	£35
70	Supreme SUP 202	**More Games/MR. FOUNDATION: Maga Dog** (actually by Invaders)	£60

(see also Brentford Road Allstars, Jackie Mittoo, Bob Andy, Horace Andy, John Holt, Larry Marshall, Irving Brown, Heptones, Freedom Singers, Winston Francis, Jerry Jones, Ethiopians, Cables, Alton Ellis, Gladiators, Ken Boothe, Soul Vendors)

SOUNDCARRIERS
09	Melodic MELO 059	**HARMONIUM** (2-LP, print, download card)	£40
10	Melodic MELO 059	**CELESTE** (2-LP, gatefold)	£40
13	The Great Pop Supplement GPS 103	**THE OTHER WORLD OF THE SUONDCARRIERS** (LP)	£30
13	The Great Pop Supplement GPS 103	**THE OTHER WORLD OF THE SUONDCARRIERS** (LP, repressing, pink splatter vinyl)	£25
14	Ghost Box GBX 020LP	**ENTROPICALIA** (LP)	£20

SOUNDGARDEN
92	A&M AMY 723	**Rusty Cage/Touch Me/Show Me** (12", poster p/s, 5000 only)	£15
96	A&M 5818457	**Burden In My Hand/Karaoke** (p/s, white vinyl, numbered, 5000 only)	£15
89	A&M AMA 5252	**LOUDER THAN LOVE** (LP)	£15
91	A&M 395 374-1	**BADMOTORFINGER** (LP, blue vinyl)	£40
91	A&M 395 374 1	**BADMOTORFINGER** (LP)	£18
96	A&M 540 558-1	**DOWN ON THE UPSIDE** (2-LP)	£35
96	A&M 540 558-1	**DOWN ON THE UPSIDE** (2-LP, clear vinyl)	£45
94	A&M 540215-1	**SUPERUNKNOWN** (2 x LP, clear, orange or blue vinyl, stickered, 2 lyric sheets)	£60
11	A&M 80015268-01	**LIVE ON I-5** (2-LP)	£20
12	Vertigo 3719818	**KING ANIMAL** (2-LP)	£18

SOUND IRATION
89	Wau Mr. Modo MOWLP 001	**IN DUB** (LP)	£35
10	Year Zero YZLP 003	**IN DUB** (2-LP, reissue)	£18
89	Mystic Red Corp MRC 8888	**Seventh Seal/Dub Seal** (12")	£30
10	Year Zero YZD V003	**THE DUBZ** (2-LP)	£18

SOUNDLAB
93	Lucky Spin LSR 009	**VOLUME 1 EP** (12")	£20

SOUND NETWORK
65	Mercury MF 944	**Watching/How About Now**	£25

SOUND OF JIMMY NICOL
65	Decca F 12107	**Clementine/Bim Bam**	£25

(see also Jimmy Nicol)

SOUNDPROOF
71	Look LKSP511-301	**Friday Every Friday/Lonely Boy Lonely Girl**	£100

SOUNDS AROUND
66	Piccadilly 7N 35345	**What Does She Do?/Sad Subject**	£25
67	Piccadilly 7N 35396	**Red White And You/One Of Two**	£25

(see also Peter & Wolves, John Pantry, Norman Conquest, Factory)

SOUNDS INCORPORATED
61	Parlophone R 4815	**Mogambo/Emily**	£15
63	Decca F 11723	**Order Of The Keys/Keep Moving**	£25
65	Columbia DB 7737	**On The Brink/I'm Comin' Thru**	£40
67	Polydor 56209	**How Do You Feel/Dead As You Go**	£15
64	Columbia SEG 8360	**TOP GEAR** (EP)	£25
64	Columbia 33SX 1659	**SOUNDS INCORPORATED** (LP, mono)	£25
64	Columbia SCX 3531	**SOUNDS INCORPORATED** (LP, stereo)	£30
65	EMI Regal SREG 1071	**RINKY DINK** (LP, export issue)	£20
66	Studio Two TWO 144	**SOUNDS INCORPORATED** (LP)	£20

(see also Jeff Beck, May Blitz, Boxer, Tony Newman)

SOUNDS NICE
69 Parlophone PMC/PCS 7089 LOVE AT FIRST SIGHT (LP) £25

(see also Third Ear Band, Chris Spedding, Clem Cattini Ork)

SOUNDS OF BOB ROGERS
67 CBS 3018 Among My Souveneirs/Dream With Me £20

SOUNDS OF JOHNNY HAWKSWORTH
66 Columbia DB 8059 Goal/"Goal - World Cup 1966" Theme £15

SOUNDS OF MODIFICATION
68 Stateside SL/SSL 10262 SOUNDS OF MODIFICATION (LP)..£30

SOUNDS OF REFLECTION
68 Reflection RS6001SM Brave New Day/Lord Of Believe (p/s) £50

SOUNDS OF SALVATION
74 Reflection RL 310 SOUNDS OF SALVATION (LP, with booklet)...........................£90

(see also Reflection)

SOUNDS OF TIME
73 Columbia 9000 DANSE MACABRE (LP) £20

SOUNDS ORCHESTRAL
65 Pye NPL 38016 THUNDERBALL - SOUNDS ORCHESTRAL MEET JAMES BOND (LP, in gatefold sleeve) £20
65 Pye NPL 38016 THUNDERBALL - SOUNDS ORCHESTRAL MEET JAMES BOND (LP).................................£30

SOUNDS PROGRESSIVE
70 Eyemark EMCL 1009S KID JENSEN INTRODUCES SOUNDS PROGRESSIVE (LP) £40

SOUNDS SENSATIONAL
67 HMV POP 1584 Love In The Open Air/Night Cry £18

SOUND SCIENCE
91 Sound Entity SE 0002 HERT'Z SO GOOD EP (12") £15

SOUND STYLISTICS
02 Bruton BRO 209 Get Ya Some/Down Home Style/The Players Theme....................£40
07 Bruton FSR LP018 PLAY DEEP FUNK (LP)..£40

(see also James Taylor Quartet)

SOUND SYSTEM
65 Island WI 258 You Don't Know Like I Do/Take Me Serious................................£15

(see also Owen Gray)

SOUND VISION
70s Key KL 007 IN CONCERT (LP, featuring Judy MacKenzie)..............................£25

SOUP DRAGONS
86 Subway Organisation
     SUBWAY 4 THE SUN IS IN THE SKY (EP, unreleased, 1,000 only, foldaround p/s in poly bag) £15

(see also Future Pilot A.K.A.)

SOUP GREENS
65 Stateside SS 457 That's Too Bad/Like A Rolling Stone £70

SOUPHERBS
65 Oak RGJ 601 SOUPHERBS (LP) £350

SOURCE
86 Streetwave MKHAN 78 You Got The Love (featuring Candi Staton) (Extended)/(Radio Edit)/(Club Edit)/(House Acapella) (12") £15

SOURCE DIRECT
94 Odysee ODY 01 Future London/Shimmer (12")..£20
95 Metalheadz MET H 016 A Made Up Sound/The Cult (12") £15
95 Source Direct SD 001 Fabric Of Space/Bliss (12")..£20
95 Source Direct SD 002 Approach And Identity/Modem (12") £20
95 Source Direct SD 003 Snake Style/Exit 9 (12") £15

TIM SOUSTER
77 Transatlantic TRA 343 SW1T DR1MZ (LP)..£20

APRIL SOUTH
81 Rockelly RKR 10781 EJSP
     9730 Heroes Of The NIght/The Boys Are Out To Get Me (no p/s) £50
82 President PT 501 Heroes Of The NIght/The Boys Are Out To Get Me (p/s) £20

HARRY SOUTH ORCHESTRA
69 Philips BF 1770 Scarborough Fair/I'm Gonna Make You Love Me £25
75 EMI EMI 2252 The Sweeney (TV Theme) (Parts 1 & 2) £20
67 Mercury 20081 MCL PRESENTING HARRY SOUTH (LP)...£40

JOE SOUTH
62 Oriole CB 1752 Masquerade/I'm Sorry For You £20
69 Capitol CL 15608 Don't It Make You Want To Go Home/Heart's Desire £15

JERI SOUTHERN
55 Brunswick LA 8699 WARM (10" LP) £15
56 Brunswick LAT 8100 THE SOUTHERN STYLE (LP) £15

SOUTHERN SOUND
66 Columbia DB 7982 Just The Same As You/I Don't Wanna Go £300

SOUTHERN COMFORT
71 Harvest SHSP 4012 FROG CITY (LP, no EMI logo on label) £30

72	Harvest SHSP 799	SOUTHERN COMFORT (LP, gatefold, EMI logo on label)..£50
72	Harvest SHSP 4021	STIR DON'T SHAKE (LP, with EMI logo on label) £25

(see also Matthews Southern Comfort)

SOUTHERN DEATH CULT
83	Situation 2 SIT 19	Fatman/Moya (wraparound p/s)...£20

(see also Cult)

SOUTHLANDERS
58	Decca F 11032	I Wanna Jive Tonight/Torero £15
58	Decca F 11067	The Mole In A Hole/Choo-Choo-Choo-Choo Cha-Cha-Cha (tri-centre) £15

SOUTHSIDE JOHNNY & THE ASBURY JUKES
77	Epic EPC 5230	Little Girl So Fine/I Ain't Got The Fever (withdrawn)........................£20

SOUTHWEST F.O.B.
68	Stax STAX 107	Smell Of Incense/Green Skies £20

PHIL SOUTHWOOD
61	QRS 1-462	D's Dilemma/Sister Sadie (in p/s) £20

SOVEREIGNS
66	King KG 1050	Bring Me Home Love/That's The Way Love Is £15

RED SOVINE
56	Brunswick 05513	Why Baby Why? (with Webb Pierce)/Sixteen Tons £40

(see also Webb Pierce)

SOWELL RADICS
81	Attack TACK 24	Caution/Bali-Hi Special (12") £60
81	Attack TACK 27	Fight Fight Fight/Aces Rock (12").....................................£40
81	Dread At The Controls DATC 006	All Nite Jammin/All Night Dubbin (12")...............................£40
81	Big Youth Int. BYD 001	Love Is What She Wants/Love Dub (12") £35
82	SG SG 15	Wheel O' Matilda/Rub Dis Ya One Ya (12") £50

SOWERS WITH EILEEN GREAVES
69	Galliard GAL 4002	SEEDS (LP) £30

SO WHAT
70	CBS 5005	Flowers/Tell Me Now £20

BOB B. SOXX & THE BLUE JEANS
63	London HLU 9646	Zip-A-Dee-Doo-Dah/Flip And Nitty £20
63	London HLU 9694	Why Do Lovers Break Each Other's Heart?/Dr Kaplan's Office £25
63	London HLU 9754	Not Too Young To Get Married/Annette £20
63	London HA-U 8121	ZIP-A-DEE-DOO-DAH (LP) £100
75	Phil Spector Intl. 2307 004	BOB B. SOXX & THE BLUE JEANS (LP) £25

(see also Darlene Love, Bobby Sheen, Blossoms, Crystals, Phil Spector)

CATHERINE SPAAK
65	Fontana TL 5282	NOI SIAMO I GIOVANI (LP) £15

SPACE CADETS
96	Vinyl Japan JRLP 20	ASTROBILLY ROCKIN (LP) £20
00	Vinyl Japan JRLP 35	CADETS A GO GO (LP) £20

SPACE (1)
77	Pye NSLP 28232	MAGIC FLY (LP) £15
78	Pye NSPH 28505	DELIVERANCE (LP) £20
79	Pye NSPH 28725	JUST BLUE (LP) £15
79	Pye NSPH 28725	JUST BLUE (LP, picture disc) £20

(see also Madeline Bell)

SPACE (2)
90	Space LP 1	SPACE (LP) £60
90	Space CD 1	SPACE (CD, beware of counterfeits) £40

(see also J.A.M.S., KLF, Timelords, Angels One 5)

SPACE (3)
96	Gut GUT LP 1	SPIDERS (LP)..£30

SPACE ART
77	Arista AHAL 8001	SPACE ART (LP)..£20

SPACED
92	Incite INC 1/123	Deeper (Original Mix)/Deeper (Remix) (12", stickered white label)................£35
92	No Label PNI 001	Deeper (Mix 1)/(Mix 2)/Mix 3) (12", white label) £50

SPACEMEN 3
86	Glass GLAEP 105	Walkin' With Jesus (Sound Of Confusion)/Rollercoaster/Feel So Good (12" maxi-single, p/s, with numbered insert) £50
86	Glass GLAEP 105	Walkin' With Jesus (Sound Of Confusion)/Rollercoaster/Feel So Good (12" maxi-single, p/s, without numbered insert) £45
87	Glass GLAEP 108	Transparent Radiation/Ecstasy Symphony/Transparent Radiation (Flashback)/Things'll Never Be The Same/Starship (12" maxi-single, p/s) £40
88	Glass GLASS 12054	Take Me To The Other Side/Soul 1/That's Just Fine (12", p/s, yellow label) £30
89	Fire THREEBIE 3	THREEBIE 3: Starship/Revolution/Suicide/Repeater/Love Intro Theme (Xtacy) (12", mail-order only, numbered p/s).......................£20
89	Sniffin' Rock SR 008	When Tomorrow Hits (with Sniffin' Rock magazine) £15
89	Fire BLAZE 36T	Hypnotized/Just To See You Smile (Honey Pt 2)/The World Is Dying (12", with poster)...£18
90	Fierce FRIGHT 042	Dreamweapon/Ecstasy In Slow Motion (12")..............................£25
91	Fire BLAZE 41TR	Big City (Remix)/I Love You (Remix) (12", unissued, white label promo, 50 only) £60
13	Great Pop Supplement GPS	SPECTRUM: Bo's Web/SPACEMEN 3: Why Couldn't I See/MGMT: Something To Do £15

MINT VALUE £

	100	**WIth Prince** (withdrawn)	
86	Glass GLALP 018	**SOUND OF CONFUSION** (LP)	£50
87	Glass GLALP 026	**THE PERFECT PRESCRIPTION** (LP, gold/silver or bronze/silver sleeve)	£50
88	Glass GLALP 030	**PERFORMANCE** (LP)	£25
89	Fire FIRELP 16	**PLAYING WITH FIRE** (LP, embossed sleeve)	£40
89	Fire REFIRE 5	**SOUND OF CONFUSION** (LP, reissue)	£20
89	Fire REFIRE 6	**THE PERFECT PRESCRIPTION** (LP, reissue)	£20
91	Fire FIRE LP 23	**RECURRING** (LP)	£40
90	Fire REFIRE 11	**PERFORMANCE** (LP, reissue)	£18
95	Space Age ORBIT 001	**DREAMWEAPON** (2-LP)	£30
95	Space Age ORBIT 002LP	**LIVE IN EUROPE 1989** (2-LP)	£25
95	Fire FLIP DLP 003	**TRANSLUSCENT FLASHBACKS** (LP as 2 x 12")	£30
99	Space Age ORBIT 011LP	**PLAYING WITH FIRE** (2-LP, reissue)	£30
14	Fire FIRE 158	**TRANSLUSCENT FLASHBACKS** (3x12" box set)..	£40

(see also Sonic Boom, Spiritualized, Spectrum)

SPACEPIMP
95	Clear CLR 415	The Pimp/Spacechase/K9 Law (12", p/s, on clear vinyl)...	£25
95	Clear CLR 415	The Pimp/Spacechase/K9 Law (12", p/s)...	£20

SPACE TURKEYS
81	Tavern Sound	Fun With A Social Worker/Disco Not Disco (p/s)...	£15

SPAGHETTI HEAD
75	RCA RCA 2513	Big Noise From Winnetka/Funky Axe	£30

(see also Clem Cattini Ork, Tornados)

SPAGHETTI JUNCTION
72	Columbia DB 8935	Work's Nice - If You Can Get It/Step Right Up	£25

(see also Hank Marvin)

SPANIELS
71	Joy JOYS 197	THE SPANIELS (LP)..	£20

SPANISH BOYS
65	Blue Beat BB 331	I Am Alone/BUSTER'S ALL STARS: Vera Cruz...	£250

SPANISHTONIANS
67	Pyramid PYR 6009	Suffer Me Not/ROLAND ALPHONSO: Guantanamera Ska..	£30
67	Pyramid PYR 6018	Rudie Gets Plenty/ROLAND ALPHONSO: Sock It To Me	£100

SPANISH TOWN SKABEATS
65	Blue Beat BB 315	Oh My Baby (actually by Charmers)/Stop That Train..	£600
65	Blue Beat BB 320	King Solomon/BUSTER'S ALLSTARS: Devil's Daffodil	£60

SPANKY & OUR GANG
67	Mercury MF 982	Sunday Will Never Be The Same/Distance	£20
67	Mercury 20114 (S)MCL	SPANKY AND OUR GANG (LP)	£30
68	Mercury 20121 SCML	LIKE TO GET TO KNOW YOU (LP)	£30
69	Mercury 20150 SCML	ANYTHING YOU CHOOSE/WITHOUT RHYME OR REASON (LP)	£30

(see also Mama & Papas)

OTIS SPANN
64	Decca F 11972	Stirs Me Up/Keep Your Hand Out Of My Pocket	£25
68	Blue Horizon 57-3142	Bloody Murder/Can't Do Me No Good	£15
69	Blue Horizon 57-3155	Walkin'/Temperature Is Rising (with Fleetwood Mac)...	£25
64	Decca LK 4615	THE BLUES OF OTIS SPANN (LP)..	£70
64	Storyville SLP 157	GOOD MORNING MR. BLUES (LP)	£50
64	Storyville SLP 168	PIANO BLUES (LP, with Memphis Slim)...	£40
65	Decca LK 4661	BLUES NOW (LP)	£65
66	Stateside SL 10169	THE BLUES NEVER DIE (LP)	£35
67	HMV CLP/CSD 3609	BLUES ARE WHERE IT'S AT (LP)	£35
67	Storyville 670 157	PORTRAITS IN BLUES VOL. 3 (LP, reissue of SLP 157)	£15
67	Polydor 545 030	NOBODY KNOWS MY TROUBLES (LP)	£35
67	Bounty BY 6037	NOBODY KNOWS MY TROUBLES (LP)	£40
68	Stateside (S)SL 10255	BOTTOM OF THE BLUES (LP)..	£40
69	Chess CRLS 4556	FATHERS AND SONS (LP)..	£50
69	Blue Horizon S 7-63217	BIGGEST THING SINCE COLOSSUS (LP, with Fleetwood Mac)......................................	£100
69	Deram DML/SML 1036	CRACKED SPANNER HEAD (LP)	£45
69	Python KM 4	RAISED IN MISSISSIPPI (LP, 99 copies only, with Robert Jnr. Lockwood)	£90
70	Vanguard VSD 6514	CRYIN' TIME (LP)	£20

(see also Fleetwood Mac, Memphis Slim, Johnny Shines, Lonnie Johnson)

SPANNER THRU MA BEATBOX
87	Earthly Delights EARTH 3	SPANNER THRU MA BEATBOX (LP)...	£15

SPARE PARTS
79	Random SP 100	She's A New Kind Of Girl/Paint It Black (p/s)	£40

SPARKERS
69	Blue Cat BS 155	Dig It Up/DELROY WILSON: This Life Makes Me Wonder	£200

(see also Samuel Edwards)

LOU SPARKES
69	Gayfeet GS 203	By The Time I Get To Phoenix/Lover Boy	£30

KRISTINE SPARKLE
74	Decca SKL 5192	IMAGE (LP)	£15

SPARKLEHORSE

96	Parlophone 7243 8328 16 19	VIVADIXIESUBMARINETRANSMISSIONPILOT (LP)	£100
98	Parlophone 49 6014 1	GOOD MORNING SPIDER (LP)	£150

SPARKLES

74	Proteen PRO 1	THE SPARKLES EP (no ps)	£25

SPARKS

18	BMG 538362421	You Earned The Right Not To Be A Dick/Unaware (Shaped picture disc, RSD)	£15
74	Bezarsrville K45511	SPARKS (LP, reissue of original Halfnelson LP)	£20
19	BMG BMGCAT 406TLP	PAST TENSE (THE BEST OF SPARKS) (3LP, trifold sleeve)	£40

SINGLES

72	Bearsville K 15505	Wonder Girl/(No More) Mr. Nice Guy	£15
74	Island WIP 6193	This Town Ain't Big Enough For Both Of Us / Barbecutie (7", solid centre)	£15
75	Island WIP 6249	Looks, Looks, Looks/Pineapple (DJ copy in promo p/s)	£20
77	Island WIP 6282	I Want To Hold Your Hand/Under The Table With Her (promo only)	£40
76	Island WIP 6282	I Want To Hold Your Hand/England (withdrawn after 1 day)	£25
79	Virgin VS 244-12	The No. 1 Song In Heaven/The No. 1 Song In Heaven (Long Version) (12", p/s, blue or red vinyl)	£25
79	Virgin VS 270-12	Beat The Clock/Beat The Clock (Long Version) (12", black, blue, orange, yellow or pink vinyl, picture disc label, die-cut p/s)	£15
79	Virgin VS 289-12	Tryouts For The Human Race/Tryouts For The Human Race (Long Version) (12", die-cut p/s, orange, yellow, blue or green vinyl, picture disc label)	£15
93	Finiflex FF 1004	National Crime Awareness Week (13 Minutes In Heaven)/National Crime Awareness Week (Perkins Playtime) (12", p/s)	£20
93	Finiflex FFCD 1004	National Crime Awareness Week (Psycho Cut)/National Crime Awareness Week (Highly Strung Hoedown)/National Crime Awareness Week (Complete Psycho)/National Crime Awareness Week (13 Minutes In Heaven) (CD)	£30
97	Roadrunner RR 2262-6	The No. 1 Song In Heaven (Tin Tin Out Mix)/part 2/(Heavenly Dub) (with Jimmy Somerville) (12", die-cut sleeve)	£15
08	Lil' Beethoven LBRCDS102	Islington N1 (CD single, exclusive to 'Golden Ticket' purchases for 21 London shows)	£100
09	Lil' Beethoven LBRV 2	Lighten Up, Morrissey/Brenda's Always In The Way (7", p/s)	£15
12	Lil' Beethoven LBRV 6X	Two Hands, One Mouth/Mr. Hulot (10", picture disc, limited edition)	£30
17	BMG 538309831	Hippopotamus (7", p/s, single sided, etched, with pre-orders of Hippo album, 1000 only)	£50
19	BMG BMGCAT 423SV	Let's Go Surfing/She's Beautiful (So What) (7", p/s, ltd. ed., purple vinyl)	£15

ALBUMS : LPS

73	Bearsville K 45510	A WOOFER IN TWEETERS CLOTHING (LP)	£35
74	Island ILPS 9272	KIMONO MY HOUSE (LP, pink rim label, sleeve laminated both sides, A-2U/B-1U matrixes, inner)	£50
74	Island ILPS 9312	PROPAGANDA (LP, printed inner, sticker on top right hand corner)	£30
75	Island ILPS 9345	INDISCREET (LP, gatefold)	£30
76	Bearsville K 85505	2 ORIGINALS OF SPARKS (2LP, Sparks and A Woofer In Tweeter's Clothing, gatefold, booklet)	£40
76	Island ILPS 9445	BIG BEAT (LP, printed inner)	£25
77	CBS 82284	INTRODUCING SPARKS (LP, printed inner)	£35
79	Virgin V 2115	NO. 1 IN HEAVEN (LP, printed inner)	£40
79	Virgin V 2115	NO. 1 IN HEAVEN (LP, yellow vinyl, printed inner)	£45
80	Virgin V2137	TERMINAL JIVE (LP, printed inner)	£40
81	Why Fi WHO 1	WHOMP THAT SUCKER (LP, printed inner)	£30
86	Consolidated TOON LP 2	MUSIC THAT YOU CAN DANCE TO (LP)	£20
94	Logic 74321 24302-2	Excerpts From Gratuitous Sax & Senseless Violins (CD, picture disc, gatefold card p/s, promo only)	£30
04	Lil' Beethoven LBRV 001	LIL' BEETHOVEN (LP, black sleeve, printed inner)	£150
06	Gut GUTLP 53	HELLO YOUNG LOVERS (LP, printed inner)	£80
09	Lil Beethoven LBRV 4	THE SEDUCTION OF INGMAR BERGMAN (2LP, gatefold, booklet)	£80
09	Lil' Beethoven LBR V4X	THE SEDUCTION OF INGMAR BERGMAN (4LP, CD box set, booklet)	£150
13	Lil' Beethoven LBRBOX 6	NEW MUSIC FOR AMNESIACS - THE ULTIMATE COLLECTION (5CD box set, book, ephemera, badge, sticker, lanyard)	£300
14	Island/UMC 4707310	KIMONO MY HOUSE (2LP, 40th Anniversary, printed inners, download code)	£45
15	Island 0602547359117	THE ISLAND YEARS (5LP, box set, 100 copies with signed print)	£150
17	BMG 538279760	HIPPOPOTAMUS (2LP, gatefold, printed inners)	£25
17	BMG 538284620	HIPPOPOTAMUS (2LP, picture disc, gatefold, printed inners)	£35
17	Repertoire REP2357	ANGST IN MY PANTS (LP/CD, red vinyl, printed inner)	£40
18	Island/UMC 6702244	THE BEST AND THE REST OF THE ISLAND YEARS 74-78 (2LP, gatefold, red vinyl, RSD)	£25
18	Repertoire V282	STRETCHED (The 12" Mixes1979-1984) (2LP, gatefold, printed inners, clear vinyl)	£30
19	BMG BMGCAT 410CDX	GRATUITOUS SAX & SENSELESS VIOLINS (LP/2CD, yellow vinyl issue , gatefold, printed inner, booklet)	£40
20	BMG 538600810	A STEADY DRIP, DRIP, DRIP (2LP, gatefold, printed inners)	£20
20	BMG 538603240	A STEADY DRIP, DRIP, DRIP (2LP, gatefold, printed inners, blue/purple vinyl)	£25
20	BMG 538603250	A STEADY DRIP, DRIP, DRIP (2LP, gatefold, picture disc, inner)	£30
21	Milan 19439881911	ANNETTE (CANNES EDITION - SELECTIONS FROM THE MOTION PICTURE SOUNDTRACK) (LP, gatefold, printed inner, green vinyl)	£20
22	BMG BMGCAT 550DLP	BALLS (2LP, vinyl issue of 2000 CD, gatefold, printed inners)	£20
22	BMG BMGCAT 551LP	LIL' BEETHOVEN (LP, reissue, white sleeve, printed inner)	£20
22	BMG BMGCAT 552DLP	HELLO YOUNG LOVERS (2LP, reissue, gatefold, printed inners)	£25
22	BMG BMGCAT 553DLP	EXOTIC CREATURES OF THE DEEP (2LP, reissue of 2008 CD, gatefold, printed inners)	£20
22	BMG BMGCAT 572DLP	THE SEDUCTION OF INGMAR BERGMAN (2LP, gatefold, reissue, printed inners)	£30
23	Island 5504001	THE GIRL IS CRYING IN HER LATTE (LP, printed inner)	£25
23	Island 5504004	THE GIRL IS CRYING IN HER LATTE (LP, alternate sleeve, clear vinyl, printed inner, booklet)	£35
23	Island 5504002	THE GIRL IS CRYING IN HER LATTE (LP, picture disc)	£30

MINT VALUE £

| 24 | Lil' Beethoven LBRV 120X | NO. 1 IN HEAVEN/NOEL: IS THERE MORE TO LIFE THAN DANCING (2LP, white/green vinyl, obi strip, RSD) ....£40 |

(see also Trevor White, Radio Stars)

CANDY SPARLING
| 62 | Piccadilly 7N 35046 | When's He Gonna Kiss Me?/Lonely For You ....£15 |
| 63 | Piccadilly 7N 35096 | Can You Keep A Secret/Charm Bracelet ....£20 |

SPARROW (U.S.)
| 66 | CBS 202342 | Tomorrow's Ship/Isn't It Strange ....£75 |

(see also Steppenwolf)

JACK SPARROW
| 66 | Doctor Bird DB 1005 | Ice Water/ROLAND ALPHONSO: Ska-Culation ....£150 |
| 66 | Doctor Bird DB 1027 | More Ice Water/ROLAND ALPHONSO: Miss Ska-Culation ....£200 |

(see also Ethiopians)

SPARTA
80	Suspect SUS 1	Fast Lane/Fighting To Be Free (in p/s) £50
80	Suspect SUS 1	Fast Lane/Fighting To Be Free £18
81	Suspect SUS 2	Angel Of Death/Tonight (wraparound p/s) £25

(see also Ethiopians)

SPARTACUS R
79	Zara ZMRD 1	Mother Sucker/Stop Your Crying (12") £75
76	Zara ZMRL 101	WATCHING YOU GROW (LP, as Spartacus) £15
83	Zara ZMRLP 3	THIRD WORLD WAR (LP) £15
84	Zara ZMRLP 4	FREEDOM FIRST (LP) £15

(see also Osibisa)

SPARTAN WARRIOR
| 83 | Guardian GRC 2164 | STEEL 'N' CHAINS (LP) ....£20 |

SPASMS
| 80 | Ellie Jay SAP 001 | It Never Happens Like It Does On The Telly/Monday Morning (die cut p/s) ....£40 |

SPATTS
| 15 | B-Line Recordings BLN015 | Waiting For The Bomb/Chaos By Numbers (7" test pressing, never issued) ....£35 |

SPAZZTIC BLUR
| 87 | Earache MOSH 5 | BEFO DA AWBUM (LP) ....£15 |

ROGER RUSKIN SPEAR
| 72 | United Artists UAG 29381 | ELECTRIC SHOCKS (LP) ....£25 |

(see also Bonzo Dog [Doo Dah] Band)

SPECIAL DUTIES
81	Charnel H. SARCOPHAGI 2	Violent Society/Colchester Council (wraparound p/s) £30
82	Rondelet ROUND 15	VIOLENT SOCIETY (EP) £15
82	Rondelet ABOUT 9	77 IN 82 (LP) £25
97	Captain Oi! AHOY LP 75	77 IN 82 (LP, blue vinyl reissue) £15

SPECIALS (THE SPECIAL A.K.A.)
79	2-Tone TT 1/TT 2	Gangsters (as The Special A.K.A.)/THE SELECTER: The Selecter (paper label, in stamped plain white sleeve; matrix numbers TT1-3 & TT2-1) £45
79	2-Tone TT 1/TT 2	Gangsters (as The Special A.K.A.)/THE SELECTER: The Selecter (paper label) £15
81	2-Tone CHS TT 17	Ghost Town/Why/Friday Night Saturday Morning (paper labels p/s) £15
81	2-Tone CHS TT 1217	Ghost Town (6.02 Extended Version)/Why/Friday Night, Saturday Morning (12", p/s) ...£15
89	2-Tone TTP1	THE SPECIALS: Rudi, A Message To You/Ghost Town//SELECTER: On My Radio/MADNESS: One Step Beyond (promo, 40 only) £200
91	2-Tone CHSTT 30	Ghost Town/SPECIAL PRODUCTIONS: Ghost Dub '91 (p/s) £80
91	2-Tone CHSTT 12 30	Ghost Town/SPECIAL PRODUCTIONS: Ghost Dub '91 (12", p/s) £60
79	2-Tone CDLTT 5001	SPECIALS (LP) £30
80	2-Tone CDLTT 5003	MORE SPECIALS (LP, poster, bonus 7": Roddy Radiation & The Specials' "Braggin' And Tryin' Not To Lie"/Judge Roughneck's "Rude Buoys Outa Jail" [TT 999]) £50
80	2-Tone CDL TT5003	MORE SPECIALS (LP) £15
81	2-Tone CDLTT5001-P	SPECIALS (LP, picture disc) £150
84	2 Tone CHRTT 5008	IN THE STUDIO (LP, printed inner) £20
91	2 Tone CHRTT 5010	SINGLES (LP, printed inner) £30
92	2 Tone CHR TT 5011	THE SPECIALS - LIVE AT THE MOONLIGHT CLUB (LP) £70
92	Receiver RRLP 161	LIVE - TOO MUCH TOO YOUNG (LP) £30
99	Chrysalis/Two-Tone 499 4701	SPECIALS (LP, reissue, barcode on sleeve) £30

(see also Selecter, Rhoda, Rico, Desmond Dekkar, Vegas)

SPECIAL TOUCH
89	TSR TSCRT 1	That Special Touch/Instrumental Version (12") £20
90	TSR TSCRT 3	You're So Good/Instrumental Version (12") £20
90	TSR TSCRT 3/4	You're So Good/GOLD IN THE SHADE: Shining Through (12") £50
91	TSRTSRCT 6	Our Love Goes/FORVER MORE: Ain't Easy/CRUIZE: Get Your Loving (12") £40
92	TSR TSCRT 7	I Want You/Dance Mix/FOREVER MORE: Ain't Easy/LOLETA: Do You Really Love Me (12") £40
91	TSR TSCRLP 1	GARDEN OF LIFE (LP) £250

(see also Gold In The Shade)

SPECIFIK & PROJECT CEE
| 02 | Core Level CLM 001 | Where Your Mind Is ....£25 |

SPECIFIK
| 16 | B-Line Recordings BLN 021 | EIGHTY3 (LP, splatter vinyl) ....£20 |

SPECKLED RED

60s	Storyville SEP 384	STORYVILLE BLUES ANTHOLOGY VOL. 4 (EP)	£15
63	Esquire 32-190	THE DIRTY DOZENS (LP)	£30
71	VJM LC 11	OH RED (LP)	£20

PHIL SPECTOR

63	London HA-U 8141	A CHRISTMAS GIFT FOR YOU (LP, various artists, Spector as producer; plum label)	£80
63	London HA-U 8141	A CHRISTMAS GIFT FOR YOU (LP, various artists, Spector as producer; later black label)	£50
72	Apple APCOR 24	PHIL SPECTOR'S CHRISTMAS ALBUM (LP, reissue of London HA-U 8141)	£25
74	Warner Bros K 59010	PHIL SPECTOR'S CHRISTMAS ALBUM (LP, 2nd reissue, with poster)	£18
76	Phil Spector Intl. 2307 008	RARE MASTERS VOL. 1 (LP, various artists, Spector as producer)	£20
76	Phil Spector Intl. 2307 009	RARE MASTERS VOL. 2 (LP, various artists, Spector as producer)	£20
80	Phil Spector Intl. 2307 015	PHIL SPECTOR '74/'79 (LP, various artists, Spector as producer)	£25
81	Phil Spector Intl. WOS 001	WALL OF SOUND (9-LP box set, various artists, Spector as producer)	£60

(see also Ronettes, Crystals, Darlene Love, Bob B. Soxx & Blue Jeans, Teddy Bears)

RONNIE SPECTOR

71	Apple APPLE 33	Try Some, Buy Some/Tandoori Chicken (with p/s)	£30
81	Red Shadow LP 002	SIREN (LP)	£20

(see also Ronettes)

SPECTRES (IRELAND)

65	Lloyd Sound UED QU 1	The Facts Of Life/Whirlpool	£300

SPECTRES (1)

66	Piccadilly 7N 35339	I (Who Have Nothing)/Neighbour, Neighbour (A label demo)	£300
66	Piccadilly 7N 35339	I (Who Have Nothing)/Neighbour, Neighbour	£350
66	Piccadilly 7N 35352	Hurdy Gurdy Man/LAticia (A label demo)	£350
66	Piccadilly 7N 35352	Hurdy Gurdy Man/Laticia	£400
67	Piccadilly 7N 35368	We Ain't Got Nothin' Yet/I Want It (A label demo)	£400
67	Piccadilly 7N 35368	We Ain't Got Nothin' Yet/I Want It (beware bootlegs)	£400

(see also Traffic Jam, Status Quo)

SPECTRES (3)

13	Howling Owl HOWL 019	HUNGER EP (12", hand-made and numbered sleeve, 100 only)	£40
13	Howling Owl HOWL 019	HUNGER EP (12" 2nd pressing with printed sleeve, 100 copies)	£15
15	Howling Owl HOWL 043	Wonderful Christmas Time (lathe cut, 30 only)	£30
15	Sonic Cathedral SCR 086	Stealed Scene/LORELLE MEETS THE OBSOLETE: The Sky Of All Places (365 copies)	£15
15	Sonic Cathedral SCR 090LP	DYING (LP, grey vinyl)	£25

SPECTRUM (1)

69	RCA Intl. INTS 118	THE LIGHT IS DARK ENOUGH (LP)	£30
00	Subway TRUMP 1	THE LIGHT IS DARK ENOUGH (LP, reissue)	£20

SPECTRUM (2)

71	Parlophone R5908	I'll Be Gone/Launching Place	£15

SPECTRUM (3)

79	Ellie Jay EJSP 9287	Walk On City/Strangers From Me/Blonde On Blue/Ruvid	£40

SPECTRUM (5)

91	Silvertone SONIC 2	(I Love You)To The Moon And Back/Capo Waltz (Live) (p/s, with Outer Limits fanzine)	£25
92	Silvertone ORE 41	How You Satisfy Me/Don't Go (Instrumental 2) (clear vinyl, printed plastic sleeve)	£15
94	Silvertone ORE P56	Soul Kiss Glide Divine/STEREOLAB: Tone Burst (demo)/Tempter (demo) (unrel., with colour photocopied wraparound p/s, 25 test pressings only)	£150
94	Silvertone ORET 65	Undo The Taboo/In The Fullness Of Time/Turn The Tide (Sub Aqua)/Go To Sleep (12", p/s)	£15
13	Great Pop Supplement GSP100	Bo's Web/SPACEMEN 3: Why Couldn't I See/MGMT: Something To Do With Prince (withdrawn)	£20
92	Silvertone ORELP 518	SOUL KISS (GLIDE DIVINE) (LP, inner)	£50
92	Silvertone OREZLP 518	SOUL KISS (GLIDE DIVINE) (LP, clear vinyl, printed double walled PVC sleeve containing liquid)	£45
94	Silvertone ORELP 532	HIGHS, LOWS AND HEAVENLY BLOWS (LP)	£80
97	Space Age ORBIT 008LP	FOREVER ALIEN (2-LP)	£35
97	Space Age ORBIT 008LP	FOREVER ALIEN (2-LP, yellow vinyl)	£40

(see also Spacemen 3, Sonic Boom)

CHRIS SPEDDING

70	Harvest HAR 5013	Rock'n'Roll Band/BATTERED ORNAMENTS: Goodbye We Loved You (Madly)	£25
70	Harvest SHSP 4004	BACKWOOD PROGRESSION (LP, flipback sleeve no EMI logo on label)	£60
72	Harvest SHSP 4017	THE ONLY LICK I KNOW (LP, laminated sleeve, with EMI logo on label)	£40

(see also Sharks, Nucleus, Sounds Nice, Panhandle, Solid Gold Cadillac, Matthew Ellis, Vibrators, Battered Ornaments, IOFR)

SPEED (1)

78	It IT 1	Big City/All Day And All The Night (in p/s)	£40
78	It IT 1	Big City/All Day And All The Night	£15

(see also Cobra)

SPEED (2)

80	Speed GJS 001	Man In The Street/Down The Road (p/s)	£125

(see also Bruce Dickinson, Iron Maiden)

SPEEDBALL(S)

80	No Pap/Dirty Dick DD 1/2	No Survivors/Is Somebody There? (miscredited as 'Speedballs' on label, in withdrawn printed die-cut sleeve)	£60
80	No Pap/Dirty Dick DD 1/2	No Survivors/Is Somebody There? (miscredited as 'Speedballs' on label)	£25

SPELLBINDERS

66	CBS 202453	Help Me (Get Myself Back Together)/Danny Boy	£40
66	CBS 202453	Help Me (Get Myself Back Together)/Danny Boy (DJ copy)	£85

67	CBS 202622	Chain Reaction/For You	£40
67	CBS 202622	Chain Reaction/For You (DJ copy)	£75
69	Direction 58-3970	Help Me/Chain Reaction	£15

SPELLING MISSTEAKS
79	Stortbeat BEAT 7	POPSTAR (EP)	£50

BENNY SPELLMAN
62	London HLP 9570	Lipstick Traces/Fortune Teller	£50
62	London HLP 9570	Lipstick Traces/Fortune Teller (DJ Copy)	£100

BRUCE SPELMAN
70	Beacon BES 3	YOU DON'T KNOW WHAT YOU'RE PADDLING IN (LP)	£70
70	Montague MONS 1	YOU DON'T KNOW WHAT YOU'RE PADDLING IN (LP, different sleeve, blue/black label)	£40

BARRINGTON SPENCE
86	Camara CAM 002T	Hey Youthman/Version//K LEACOCK: Round And Round/Version (12")	£30
88	Camara CAM 004T	Sons Of Far I/Far I Dub (12")	£35
76	Trojan TRLS 117	SPEAK SOFTLY (LP)	£20
76	Klik KLP 9014	TEARS ON MY PILLOW (LP)	£25

DON SPENCER
67	Talus TP1010	Uproar In The House/On The G.P.O Tower	£20

(see also Le Roys)

DON SPENCER/XL5
63	HMV 7EG 8802	FIREBALL AND OTHER TITLES (EP, 2 tracks each)	£50

EDDIE SPENCER
76	Power Exchange PX 207	If This Is Love (I'd Rather Be Lonely)/Power Of Love	£25

JEREMY SPENCER (BAND)
70	Reprise RSLP 9002	JEREMY SPENCER (LP, label states K 44105 cat. no)	£40
71	Reprise K 44105	JEREMY SPENCER (LP, reissue)	£20

(see also Fleetwood Mac)

JON SPENCER BLUES EXPLOSION
91	Hut HUTLP 3	THE JON SPENCER BLUES EXPLOSION (LP)	£18
96	Mute STUMM 132	NOW I GOT WORRY (LP)	£20
98	Mute STUMM 156	ACME (LP, inner)	£20

(see also Pussy Galore)

SONNY SPENCER
59	Parlophone R 4611	Oh Boy/Gilee	£20

VIC SPENCER
17	Daupe! DM SP 022	THE GHOST OF LIVING (LP, 180 copies)	£70
17	Daupe! DM SP 022	THE GHOST OF LIVING (LP, purple vinyl, 100 copies)	£100
17	Daupe! DM SP 022	THE GHOST OF LIVING (LP, orange vinyl, 100 copies)	£100
17	Daupe! DM SP 022	THE GHOST OF LIVING (LP, with obi strip, 20 copies)	£100
17	Daupe! DM SP 030	WHO THE F*** IS VIC SPENCER (LP, with Chris Crack, pink vinyl, 130 copies)	£40
17	Daupe! DM SP 030	WHO THE F*** IS VIC SPENCER (LP, with Chris Crack, with OBI strip, 20 copies)	£150
17	Daupe! DM SP 025	WHO THE F*** IS VIC SPENCER (LP, with Chris Crack, 230 copies)	£40
18	Daupe! DM SP 030	SPENCER FOR HIGHER (LP, with SonnyJim, green vinyl, 125 copies)	£50
18	Daupe! DM SP 030	SPENCER FOR HIGHER (LP, with SonnyJim, black vinyl, 125 copies)	£50
18	Daupe! DM SP 030	SPENCER FOR HIGHER (LP, with SonnyJim, white vinyl, 125 copies)	£40
18	Daupe! DM SP 030	SPENCER FOR HIGHER (LP, with SonnyJim, red vinyl, 125 copies)	£40
18	Daupe! DM SP 030	SPENCER FOR HIGHER (LP, with SonnyJim, black vinyl, with OBI strip, 20 copies)	£150
18	Daupe! DM SP 038	DUFFLE OF GEMS (2-LP)	£40
18	Daupe! DM SP 038	DUFFLE OF GEMS (2-LP, picture disc)	£40
18	Daupe! DM SP 038	DUFFLE OF GEMS (2-LP, purple vinyl)	£30
18	Daupe! DM SP 038	DUFFLE OF GEMS (2-LP, with obi strip, 20 copies)	£100

SPENCERS WASHBOARD KINGS
69	Parlophone R 5782	Pimlico/Ordinary People	£15

SPERMICIDE
79	No Wonder NOW 3	Femme Prothèse/Belgique (p/s with lyrics)	£30

SPHERE
81	Cadillac SGE 1010	SPHERE (LP)	£25

SPHERES
78	Sphere	FESTIVAL AND SUNS (LP, with insert)	£25

(see also Jimmy Winston)

SPHERICAL OBJECTS
78	Object Music PBJ 001	PAST & PARCEL (LP)	£20
79	Object Music OBJ 004	ELLIPTICAL OPTIMISM (LP)	£20

(see also Noyes Brothers)

SPHYNKTA
83	Sultanic SUL 666	In The Shade Of The Gods/Jesus Bless My Upside-Down Cross (p/s, red vinyl, with 'devil' tattoo)	£60
83	Sultanic SUL 999	Death And Violence/Ritual Slaughter (Of Your Daughter) (p/s, red vinyl)	£40
84	Sultanic SUL 000	Spike Up My Sphynkta/No Pain No Gain (unissued)	£100

SPHYNX
78	Charisma CDS 4011	XITINTODAY (LP, with booklet)	£30
78	Charisma CDS 4011	XITINTODAY (LP, without booklet)	£20

(see also Inner City Unit, Gong, Radio Actors)

SPICE GIRLS
96	Virgin V 2812	SPICE (LP, with glossy picture/lyric insert)	£40
97	Virgin V 2850	SPICEWORLD (LP)	£40

SPICE (U.K.)
68	United Artists UP 2246	What About The Music?/In Love	£600

(see also Uriah Heep, Godz, Toe-Fat)

GEORGE SPICER
74	Topic 12T 235	BLACKBERRY FOLD (LP)	£15

SPIDELLS
66	Sue WI 4019	Find Out What's Happening/That'll Make My Heart Break	£50

SPIDER (1)
66	Decca F 12430	The Comedown Song/Blow Ya Mind	£50

SPIDER (2)
77	Pennine PSS 136	Back To The Wall/Down And Out (p/s, 500 only, these 300 with p/s)	£60
77	Pennine PSS 136	Back To The Wall/Down And Out (p/s, 500 only, these 200 without p/s)	£30

SPIDER (3)
80	Alien ALIEN 14	Children Of The Street/Down 'N' Out (in p/s)	£35
80	Alien ALIEN 16	College Luv/Born To Be Wild (in p/s)	£35

SPIDER & THE FLIES
07	Mute Irregulars IRREG 17	Metalurge/Desmond Leslie	£15

(see also Horrors)

SPIDERS
66	Philips BF 1531	Sad Sunset/Hey Boy	£40

SPIDERS (U.S.)
54	London HL 8086	I'm Slippin' In/I'm Searching (78)	£65

SPILL
92	Virgin VST 1141	Don't Wanna Know About Evil (Tumble Mix)/(Rumble Mix)/(Danny's Moto Mix)/(The Groovy Beats Mix) (12", p/s)	£15

(see also Beth Orton)

SPINNERS (U.S.)
61	Columbia DB 4693	That's What Girls Are Made For/Heebie Jeebies	£200
61	Columbia DB 4693	That's What Girls Are Made For/Heebie Jeebies (DJ copy)	£250
65	Tamla Motown TMG 514	Sweet Thing/How Can I? (demo with 'Spinners' credit)	£300
65	Tamla Motown TMG 514	Sweet Thing/How Can I? (demos with 'Detroit Spinners' credit)	£250
65	Tamla Motown TMG 514	Sweet Thing/How Can I? (stock copies credited to 'Spinners')	£400

(see also Detroit Spinners)

SPINNING JENNY
71	Midas MR004	SPINNING JENNY (LP)	£70

SPINNING WHEEL
79	Private pressing	JACOB'S FLEECE (LP)	£15

(see also Dragonsfire)

SPINNING WHEELS
75	Peter Dearden PD 205	SPINNING WHEELS (EP)	£15

SPIRALS
58	Capitol CL 14958	The Rockin' Cow/Everybody Knows	£15

SPIRAL SKY
93	Acme AC 8002LP	SPIRAL SKY (LP, numbered & sealed with insert, 500 only)	£30
94	Acme 8002LP	SPIRAL SKY (LP, 2nd pressing numbered & sealed with insert, 300 only)	£25

(see also Sun Dial, Ohr Musik)

SPIRAL STAIRCASE
68	CBS 3507	Baby What I Mean/Makin' Your Mind Up	£25
69	CBS 4187	More Today Than Yesterday/Broken Hearted Man	£50
69	CBS 4187	More Today Than Yesterday/Broken Hearted Man (DJ copy)	£80
69	CBS 4524	No One For Me To Turn To/Sweet Little Thing	£25

SPIRAL TRIBE
92	Big Life BLRT 79	Breach The Peace/Do ET/Seven/23 Minute Warning (12", p/s)	£25
92	Big Life BLRT 85	Forward The Revolution/World Traveller Adventurer/Ragga Boom/Track 13 (criminal drug)(12", p/s)	£25
92	Big Life BLRR 85	Forward The Revolution (the Youth remix) (1-sided, etched 12")	£15
93	Butterfly BFLT 04	Sirius 23/Earthworm/Going All The Way/Predator (12", p/s, as Spiral Tribe Sound System)	£20
93	Butterfly BFL LP 6	TECNO TERRA (2-LP)	£50

SPIRIT
68	CBS 3523	Uncle Jack/Mechanical World	£15
69	CBS 3880	I Got A Line On You/She Smiles	£25
68	CBS 63278	SPIRIT (LP, 1st pressing, stereo, laminated front cover, stereo sticker on rear, orange label)	£35
68	CBS 63278	SPIRIT (LP, 1st pressing, mono, laminated front cover, orange label)	£35
68	CBS 63523	THE FAMILY THAT PLAYS TOGETHER (LP, 1st pressing, mono, laminated front cover, orange label)	£40
68	CBS 63523	THE FAMILY THAT PLAYS TOGETHER (LP, 1st pressing, stereo, laminated front cover, stereo sticker on rear, orange label)	£25
69	CBS 63729	CLEAR (LP, laminated cover, orange label)	£30
70	Epic EPC 64191	THE TWELVE DREAMS OF DR. SARDONICUS (LP, g/fold sleeve, yellow label)	£20

MINT VALUE £

72	Epic EPC 64507	FEED-BACK (LP, gatefold sleeve, yellow label)	£15
75	Phonogram 6672 012	HIGHLIGHTS OF SPIRIT OF 76 (LP, promo)	£20
81	Beggars Banquet BEGA 23	POTATOLAND (LP, with cartoon book)	£15

(see also Kapt. Kopter & Fabulous Twirlybirds)

SPIRIT OF JOHN MORGAN

69	Carnaby CNLS 6002	THE SPIRIT OF JOHN MORGAN (LP, union jack flag label)	£200
70	Carnaby CNLS 6007	AGE MACHINE (LP, gatefold, union jack flag label)	£150
71	Carnaby GOLD 6437 503	THE SPIRIT OF JOHN MORGAN (LP, reissue, 'crab' label logo)	£50

(see also John Morgan)

SPIRIT OF MEMPHIS QUARTET

| 58 | Parlophone PMD 1070 | NEGRO SPIRITUALS (10" LP) | £25 |
| 65 | Vogue LAE 1033 | NEGRO SPIRITUALS (LP, reissue) | £15 |

SPIRIT OF PLAY

| 88 | Release KIDS 1988 | Children In Need/Children In Need (Instrumental) (with Paul McCartney) (in p/s) | £50 |

SPIRIT OF PROGRESS

| 71 | Philips 6006089 | Om Pa Pa/It's A Beautiful Day | £35 |

SPIRITBORN

| 84 | Spearhead | Pity The Unborn Child/Sing To The Lord | £20 |

SPIRITUALIZED

90	Dedicated ZB 43783	Anyway That You Want Me/Step Into The Breeze (p/s)	£15
90	Dedicated ZT 43784	Anyway That You Want Me (Extended)/Step Into The Breeze 1 & 2 (12", p/s)	£20
90	Dedicated ZT 43780	Anyway That You Want Me (Remix)/Step Into The Breeze 1 & 2 (12", p/s)	£20
91	Fierce FRIGHT 053	Feel So Sad/I Want You (gig freebie, no p/s, stamped plain white sleeve with date & venue details)	£15
91	Dedicated SPIRT 002	Run/I Want You (p/s, with luminous sleeve & clear luminous vinyl)	£15
91	Dedicated SPIRT 002T	Run/Luminescence (Stay With Me)/I Want You/Effervescent (Chimes) (12", with luminous sleeve)	£18
92	Dedicated SPIRT 005	Medication/Angel Sigh/Feel So Sad (white label test pressing, signed and inscribed by Jason Pierce in silver, limited availability through website)	£25
93	Dedicated SPIRT 006	Smiles (Live)/100 Bars (A Cappella) (7" flexidisc, fan-club only)	£20
93	Greenpeace GR'NP'CE 001	Good Dope, Good Fun/MERCURY REV: 'Boys Peel Out (Live)' (gig 7", with booklet)	£15
96	Dedicated SPIRT 101T	Pure Phase Tones For DJs (12")	£15
92	Dedicated DEDLP 004S	LAZER GUIDED MELODIES (2-LP, limited Edition, with bonus 7" single 'Anyway That You Want Me'/'Why Don't You Smile Now?' [CWNN 7001])	£60
92	Dedicated DEDLP 004S	LAZER GUIDED MELODIES (2-LP, limited. Edition, without bonus 7" single)	£40
93	Dedicated no cat. no.	SUMMER EUROPEAN 93 BOX (3-CD promo set, with ribbon and insert)	£80
93	Dedicated DEDLP 008	FUCKED UP INSIDE (LP, mail-order only)	£80
93	Dedicated DEDCD 008	FUCKED UP INSIDE (CD, mail-order only)	£35
93	Dedicated DEDLP 017	PURE PHASE (2-LP 45rpm)	£60
97	Dedicated DEDLP 034	LADIES AND GENTLEMEN WE ARE FLOATING IN SPACE (2-LP, limited issue)	£150
97	Dedicated DEDCD 034S	LADIES AND GENTLEMEN WE ARE FLOATING IN SPACE (12 x 3" CDs, in blister packs in card box with insert, 1000 only, 200 with clear plastic backs)	£80
97	Dedicated DEDCD 034S	LADIES AND GENTLEMEN WE ARE FLOATING IN SPACE (12 x 3" CDs, in blister packs in card box with insert, 1000)	£50
97	Dedicated DEDCD 034P	LADIES AND GENTLEMEN WE ARE FLOATING IN SPACE (CD, 'Elvis version', given to Mercury Music Prize personnel, 50 copies only)	£40
98	Deconstruction 74321662851	ROYAL ALBERT HALL (2-LP)	£50
01	Spaceman OPM001LP	LET IT COME DOWN (2-LP, postcard)	£40
03	Spaceman/Sanctuary OPM014LP/SANLP14	AMAZING GRACE (LP)	£20
08	Sanctuary 1768732	SONGS IN A&E (2-LP, green vinyl)	£25
08	Sanctuary 1768732	SONGS IN A&E (2-LP green vinyl, only availiable from Rough Trade)	£30
12	Double Six DSO 45LP	SWEET HEART/SWEET LIGHT (2-LP, white vinyl)	£18
12	Art Vinyl AVLP 11	LADIES AND GENTLEMEN WE ARE IN FLOATING IN SPACE (2-LP, reissue)	£25

(see also Spacemen 3)

SPIROGYRA

73	Polydor 2001-419	I Hear You're Going Nowhere/Old Boot Wine	£35
71	B&C CAS 1042	ST. RADIGUND'S (LP, with lyric inner)	£150
72	Pegasus PEG 13	OLD BOOT WINE (LP, textured sleeve)	£250
73	Polydor 2310 246	BELLS, BOOTS AND SHAMBLES (LP)	£800
14	Turning Round GYRALP5	SPIROGYRA 5 (LP)	£40

SPITEFUL CHILD

| 83 | Clubland SPJ 842 | Voices In The Night/Is It Love | £30 |
| 85 | SRT SKJ 648 | I Want To Hold You/Who's Crying Now | £20 |

SPITERI

| 73 | GM GML 1006 | SPITERI (LP) | £20 |

SPITFIRE (& BLACKFIRE BARMIES)

| 82 | Carrere CAR 253 | So You Want To Be A Rock'n'Roll Star/Spitfire Boogie | £50 |

SPITFIRE BOYS

77	RK RK 1001	British Refugee/Mein Kampf (push-out centre)	£75
77	RK RK 1001	British Refugee/Mein Kampf (reissue, solid centre, p/s)	£60
79	Impeccable SRTS/79/CUS481	Funtime/Transendental Changing	£35
83	RK RK 1001	British Refugee/Mein Kampf (2nd reissue to cash in on Frankie success p/s, no solid centre)	£75

(see also Frankie Goes To Hollywood)

SPITTIN IMAGE
79   Wessex WEX 270   Baby Goodbye/(Wish I Could See A) UFO (no p/s)......................................£15
SPITTIN MUSSELS
81   RAFOSM 1   Five Days A Week/Hold On Johnny (p/s)..£35
SPITZBROOK
79   Ace SPIT 1   Stranger/Looking At You (p/s)..£60
SPIV
73   Pye 7N 45293   Oh You Beautiful Child/Little Girl..£120
SPIZZ (OIL/ENERGI)
82   Rough Trade ROUGH501   SPIZZ HISTORY (LP)..£20
S.P.K. (SEPPUKU/SURGICAL PENIS KLINIK)
80   Industrial IR 0011   MEAT PROCESSING SECTION (Mekano/Slogun) (p/s, labels list "Slogan"/Factory, with
                                    insert, as Surgical Penis Klinik)..£30
83   Side Effekts SER 003   Dekompositiones (12", p/s, as Seppuku)...£20
81   Side Effekts SER 01   INFORMATION OVERLOAD UNIT (LP, 1st 1,000 with booklet).............................£70
81   Side Effekts SER 01   INFORMATION OVERLOAD UNIT (LP)..£50
83   Walter Ulbright WULP 002   AUTO-DA-FE (LP)...£20
86   Side Effekts SER 09   ZAMIA LEHMANNI (LP)...£15
80s Side Effekts SER 002   LEICHENSCHREI (LP)..£30
SPLASH
95   Dee Jay DJX 022R2   Babylon Remixes 2 (12")...£40
SPLINTER
76   Dark Horse DH 2   SPLINTER (LP, promo only, plain white sleeve).....................................£130
SPLIT BEAVER
81   Heavy Metal HEAVY 7   Savage/Hound Of Hell (with p/s)...£25
82   Heavy Metal HMRLP 3   WHEN HELL WON'T HAVE YOU (LP, silver label).......................................£18
82   Heavy Metal HMRLP 3   WHEN HELL WON'T HAVE YOU (LP, red label)..£15
SPLITCROW
84   Guardian GRC 21   ROCKSTORM (LP)..£15
SPLIT IMAGE
82   Heroes ER 01   Now That We've Parted...£25
SPLIT SCREENS
79   Rok ROK III/IV   Just Don't Try/JUST FRANK: You (die-cut company sleeve)...........................£35
SPLODGENESSABOUNDS
80   Deram ROLF 1   Two Little Boys/Horse/Sox/Butterfly (p/s, with 'Splodge' boomerang)..............£15
81   Deram SML 1121   SPLODGENESSABOUNDS (LP)...£15
SP MC
18   System SYSTM 020   Pondlife/R1 (10")..£25
SPOILERS
72   London HLU 10399   Turbo Rock/Sad Man's Land...£20
SPONOOCH
79   EMI EMI 2941   Crime Buster/Laserdance (12", p/s)..£50
SPONTANEOUS COMBUSTION
71   Harvest HAR 5046   Lonely Singer/200 Lives/Leaving...£15
72   Harvest HAR 5060   Gay Time Night/Spaceship..£30
73   Harvest HAR 5066   Sabre Dance/Sabre Dance...£15
72   Harvest SHVL 801   SPONTANEOUS COMBUSTION (LP, with EMI logo on label)..............................£125
72   Harvest SHVL 805   TRIAD (LP, with 3 inserts, with EMI logo on label)...............................£100
(see also Time)
SPONTANEOUS MUSIC ENSEMBLE
66   Eyemark EMP L1002   CHALLENGE (LP)..£450
68   Island ILP 979   KARYOBIN ... ARE THE IMAGINARY BIRDS SAID TO LIVE IN PARADISE (LP, pink label) ...£300
69   Marmalade 608 008   SPONTANEOUS MUSIC ENSEMBLE (LP)...£100
70   A A001   FOR YOU TO SHARE (LP)...£100
71   Tangent TNGS 107   SOURCE FROM AND TOWARDS (LP)..£35
72   Marmalade 2384 009   SPONTANEOUS MUSIC ENSEMBLE (LP, reissue)..£25
73   Emanem 303   FACE TO FACE (LP)...£30
73   Tangent TNGS 118   SO WHAT DO YOU THINK (LP)...£35
77   Incus INCUS 24   BIOSYSTEM (LP)..£50
82   Affinity AFF 81   1 2 ALBERT AYLER (LP)...£20
(see also Howard Riley Trio)
SPONTANEOUS MUSIC ORCHESTRA
75   A A003   + = (LP)..£75
81   Sweet Folk All SFA 112   SME + SMO IN CONCERT (LP)...£50
(see also Spontaneous Music Ensemble)
SPOOKEY
81   Satril HH 153   On The Rocks/Friends..£15
81   Satril 12 HH 153   Friends/On The Rocks (12")..£40
SPOOKY TOOTH
67   Island WIP 6022   Sunshine Help Me/Weird..£25
68   Island WIP 6037   Love Really Changed Me/Luger's Grove..£15
69   Island WIP 6048   Nobody There At All/ART: Room With A View (unissued, white labels only)..........£75
68   Island ILP 980/ILPS 9080   IT'S ALL ABOUT (LP, 1st pressing pink 'eye' label)...............................£150

MINT VALUE £

70	Island ILP 980/ILPS 9080	**IT'S ALL ABOUT** (LP, 2nd pressing, pink label white 'i' logo)	**£50**
69	Island ILPS 9098	**SPOOKY TWO** (LP, 1st pressing with pink 'eye' label, matrix numbers ILPS 9098 +A & +B stamped into dead wax. No 'Porky' or 'Pecko' in dead wax (unlike reissues), gatefold 'E.J.Day' sleeve)	**£100**
69	Island ILPS 9098	**SPOOKY TWO** (LP, 2nd pressing with white 'i' on pink label, with Jimmy Miller production credit around a centimetre beneath SPOOKY TOOTH on label)	**£70**
69	Island ILPS 9107	**CEREMONY** (LP, with Pierre Henry, pink label, gatefold sleeve)	**£100**
70	Island ILPS 9098	**SPOOKY TWO** (LP, 3rd pressing with white 'i' on pink label, with Jimmy Miller production credit directly beneath SPOOKY TOOTH on label)	**£50**
70	Island ILPS 9117	**THE LAST PUFF** (LP, pink label)	**£60**
73	Island ILPS 9227	**YOU BROKE MY HEART SO I BUSTED YOUR JAW** (LP, gatefold sleeve, lyric insert, pink rim label)	**£30**
73	Island ILPS 9255	**WITNESS** (LP, pink rim label)	**£30**
74	Good Ear EARL 2001	**THE MIRROR** (LP)	**£25**
74	Island ILPS 9292	**THE MIRROR** (LP, export issue)	**£25**
77	Island ILP 980/ILPS 9080	**IT'S ALL ABOUT** (LP, repressing, palm tree label)	**£50**

(see also Gary Wright, V.I.P.s, Art, Luther Grosvenor, Hellions, Revolution, State Of Mickey & Tommy, Mike Harrison)

SPOON FAZER

80	Project PROJECT 1	**MUSIC 2 DANCE 2** (EP, p/s)	**£20**
82	Illuminated ILL 912	**Sunset/Ballad Of The Insectman/Flying Bodies/Fly On The Wall** (12", p/s)	**£60**
21	OM Swagger OMSLP 002	**ALTERNATIVE REGRESSION THERAPY** (LP)	**£15**

SPOONFUL

77	Bunbury DCS 340	**Troubled Times/Country Blues** (2 known copies in p/s)	**£300**
77	Bunbury DCS 340	**Troubled Times/Country Blues** (no p/s)	**£50**

SPORTS

80	Sire SRUK 6001	**WHO LISTENS TO THE RADIO** (LP)	**£15**

SPORTS TEAM

18	Nice Swan NSWN 006	**WINTER NETS** (12" EP, p/s)	**£25**
18	Nice Swan/Holm Front NSWN10/HF001	**Margate/Kutcher** (p/s)	**£15**
18	(no label or cat. no.)	**Liberal Friends/Stanton** (p/s)	**£18**
18	Holm Fron HF002	**Get Along/Casper** (p/s)	**£20**

SPOTLIGHT

74	Globe GB 02	**Find The Light/Emily Cries** (p/s)	**£25**

SPOTLIGHTERS

59	Vogue Pop V 9130	**Please Be My Girlfriend/Whisper** (with Bob Thompson & His Band)	**£500**
59	Vogue Pop V 9130	**Please Be My Girlfriend/Whisper** (with Bob Thompson & His Band) (78)	**£100**

SPOTLIGHTS

66	Philips BF 1485	**Batman And Robin/Day Flower**	**£20**

SPOTNICKS

64	Oriole CB 1953	**Lovesick Blues/The Space Creatures**	**£15**
64	Oriole CB 1981	**Donner Wetter/Shamus O'Toole**	**£15**
63	Oriole EP 7075	**ON THE AIR** (EP)	**£20**
64	Oriole EP 7078	**SPOTNICKS IN PARIS** (EP)	**£20**
64	Oriole EP 7079	**SPOTNICKS AT THE OLYMPIA PARIS** (EP)	**£20**
63	Oriole PS 40036	**OUT-A SPACE: THE SPOTNICKS IN LONDON** (LP, mono)	**£25**
63	Oriole SPS 40037	**OUT-A SPACE: THE SPOTNICKS IN LONDON** (LP, stereo)	**£35**
64	Oriole PS 40054	**THE SPOTNICKS IN SPAIN** (LP)	**£30**
65	Oriole PS 40064	**THE SPOTNICKS IN BERLIN** (LP)	**£30**

(see also Bob Lander & Spotnicks, Shy Ones)

SPRATLEYS JAPS

18	(No label or cat no)	**Her/Hands** (lathe cut 7", clear vinyl, signed insert)	**£50**

JACK SPRATT

69	Coxsone CS 7100	**Give Me Your Love/LARRY & ALVIN: Magic Moments** (B-side actually by Leroy Sibbles and Heptones)	**£200**

SPREADEAGLE

72	Charisma CB 183	**How Can We Be Lost/Nightmare** (p/s, solid centre)	**£15**
72	Charisma CAS 1055	**THE PIECE OF PAPER** (LP, pink 'scroll' label)	**£20**

SPREDTHICK

78	An Actual ACT 003	**SPREDTHICK** (LP, with insert)	**£18**

SPRIGUNS (OF TOLGUS)

76	Decca F 13676	**Nothing Else To Do/Lord Lovell**	**£20**
77	Decca F 13739	**White Witch/Time Will Pass**	**£20**
75	Alida Star C'tage ASC7755	**JACK WITH A FEATHER** (LP, as Spriguns Of Tolgus)	**£1500**
76	Decca SKL 5262	**REVEL WEIRD & WILD** (LP, with lyric insert)	**£275**
77	Decca SKL 5286	**TIME WILL PASS** (LP, with lyric insert)	**£200**
92	Kissing Spell KSLP 002	**ROWDY DOWDY DAY** (LP, reissue)	**£15**

(see also Mandy Morton Band, Terra Cotta)

SPRING

71	RCA Neon NE 6	**SPRING** (LP, foldout sleeve, black inner sleeve)	**£1000**

SPRING OFFENSIVE

81	SO 1	**Cruising/Good To Be Back**	**£35**

SPRINGBOARD

69	Polydor 545007	**SPRINGBOARD** (LP)	**£100**

DUSTY SPRINGFIELD

67	Philips BF 1608	What's It Gonna Be/Small Town Girl	£25
68	Philips BF 1730	Son Of A Preacher Man/Just A Little Lovin' (Early In The Mornin')	£15
69	Philips BF 1811	Am I The Same Girl/Earthbound Gypsy	£20
70	Philips 6006 045	How Can I Be Sure/Spooky	£50
78	Mercury JUMBO 3	That'sThe Kind Of Love I've Got For You/That's The Kind Of Love I've Got For You (12", promo only)	£40
15	Mercury 4720263	What's It Gonna Be/Spooky (p/s)	£25
64	Philips BE 12560	I ONLY WANT TO BE WITH YOU (EP)	£15
64	Philips BE 12564	DUSTY (EP)	£15
65	Philips BE 12572	DUSTY IN NEW YORK (EP)	£18
65	Philips BE 12579	MADEMOISELLE DUSTY (EP)	£25
68	Philips BE 12605	IF YOU GO AWAY (EP)	£18
64	Philips BL 7594	A GIRL CALLED DUSTY (mono)	£20
64	Philips SBL 7594	A GIRL CALLED DUSTY (stereo)	£25
65	Philips RBL 1002	EVERYTHING'S COMING UP DUSTY (gatefold sleeve with booklet, mono)	£25
65	Philips SRBL 1002	EVERYTHING'S COMING UP DUSTY (gatefold sleeve with booklet, stereo)	£35
66	Philips BL 7737	GOLDEN HITS (LP, mono)	£15
66	Philips SBL 7737	GOLDEN HITS (LP, stereo)	£18
67	Philip BL 7820	WHERE AM I GOING? (LP, mono)	£25
67	Philip SBL 7820	WHERE AM I GOING? (LP, stereo)	£30
68	Philips (S)BL 7864	DUSTY... DEFINITELY (LP, stereo only)	£25
69	Philips SBL 7889	DUSTY IN MEMPHIS (LP, stereo only)	£60
70	Philips SBL 7927	FROM DUSTY... WITH LOVE (LP)	£20
80	Philips PRICE 83	IN MEMPHIS PLUS (LP)	£30
95	Columbia 478508 1	A VERY FINE LOVE (LP)	£15

(see also Lana Sisters, Springfields, Tom Springfield, Pet Shop Boys)

TOM SPRINGFIELD (& HIS) ORCHESTRA

68	Decca SKL 4967	SUN SONGS (LP)	£80
69	Decca LK/SKL 5003	LOVE'S PHILOSOPHY BY... (LP, featuring Dusty Springfield)	£30

(see also Springfields, Dusty Springfield)

SPRINGFIELDS (1)

63	Philips 433 643 BE	FOLK SONGS FROM THE HILLS (EP)	£15
62	Philips BBL 7551	KINDA FOLKSY (LP, mono)	£15
62	Philips SBBL 674	KINDA FOLKSY (LP, stereo)	£15
63	Philips 632 304 BL	FOLK SONGS FROM THE HILLS (LP)	£15

(see also Dusty Springfield, Lana Sisters, Tom Springfield, Mike Hurst)

SPRINGFIELDS (2)

88	Sarah SARAH 010	Sunflower/Clown/Are We Gonna Be Alright? (foldaround p/s with 14" x 10" poster in polyester bag; yellow p/s)	£30
88	Sarah SARAH 010	Sunflower/Clown/Are We Gonna Be Alright? (foldaround p/s with 14" x 10" poster in polyester bag; later orange p/s)	£18
91	Sarah SARAH 040	Wonder/Tomorrow Ends Today (p/s, with insert)	£15

SPRING HEEL JACK

80	Woodbine WSR 003	1960s Girl/How Many Colours (no p/s)	£20

BRUCE SPRINGSTEEN

75	CBS A 3661	Born To Run/Meeting Across The River	£15
76	CBS A 3940	Tenth Avenue Freeze-Out/She's The One	£25
78	CBS A 6424	Prove It All Night/Factory	£18
78	CBS A 6532	Badlands/Something In The Night	£15
78	CBS A 6720	Promised Land/Streets Of Fire	£65
80	CBS A 9309	Hungry Heart/Held Up Without A Gun (p/s, withdrawn first issue, black and white p/s, blue lettering)	£25
81	CBS A 9568	Sherry Darling/Independence Day (white label promo, 100 only 2 known copies with p/s listing 'Independence Day')	£2500
81	CBS A 9568	Sherry Darling/Independence Day (white label promo, 100 only)	£1500
81	CBS 9568	Sherry Darling/Be True (p/s)	£15
81	CBS A 1179	The River/Independence Day (p/s)	£15
81	CBS A 13-1179	The River/Born To Run/Rosalita (12", p/s, sleeves credit 'East Street Band')	£15
81	CBS A 1557	Cadillac Ranch/Wreck On The Highway (p/s)	£15
82	CBS A 2794	Atlantic City/Mansion On The Hill (p/s)	£20
82	CBS A 2969	Open All Night/The Big Pay Back (p/s)	£30
84	CBS WA 4436	Dancing In The Dark/Pink Cadillac (Cadillac-shaped picture disc)	£20
84	CBS WA 4662	Cover Me/Jersey Girl (live) (Bruce-shaped picture disc with plinth)	£25
85	CBS A 7077	Born To Run/Meeting Across The River (reissue, blue p/s, withdrawn)	£20
85	CBS WA 6342	I'm On Fire/Born In The U.S.A. (p/s, flag-shaped picture disc)	£20
85	CBS BRUCE 1	BORN IN THE U.S.A. - THE 12" COLLECTION (4 x 12" & 7", box with poster)	£20
87	CBS 651 295-0	Tunnel Of Love/Two For The Road (postcard-shaped picture disc)	£15
73	CBS 65480	GREETINGS FROM ASBURY PARK, N.J. (cutaway gatefold sleeve, orange label)	£20
74	CBS 65780	THE WILD, THE INNOCENT AND THE E STREET SHUFFLE (orange label, yellow lettering on sleeve; with "Ashbury" mis-spelling on label)	£20
75	CBS 69170	BORN TO RUN (with "John Landau" misprint on rear sleeve)	£30
78	CBS 86061	DARKNESS ON THE EDGE OF TOWN (LP)	£18
79	CBS 66353	BRUCE SPRINGSTEEN (3-LP, box set)	£18
80	CBS 88510	THE RIVER (2-LP)	£20
80	CBS 80959	BORN TO RUN (LP, reissue, half-speed master, 2 inserts)	£20
82	CBS 25100	NEBRASKA (LP, inner)	£20
84	CBS 86304	BORN IN THE U.S.A. (LP, inner, insert)	£20

MINT VALUE £

84	CBS 11-86304	BORN IN THE U.S.A. (picture disc)	£30
87	CBS 460 270-0	TUNNEL OF LOVE (picture disc)	£15
90	CBS LSP 980636 1	COLLECTED WORKS OF BRUCE SPRINGSTEEN (7 LP box set)	£200
92	Sony 471 423-0	HUMAN TOUCH (picture disc)	£15
92	Sony 471 424-0	LUCKY TOWN (picture disc, with side 1 on both sides)	£75
92	Sony 471 424-0	LUCKY TOWN (picture disc)	£15
92	Columbia 471423	LUCKY TOWN (LP)	£15
93	Columbia 473860-1	IN CONCERT (2-LP, stickered sleeve)	£40
95	Columbia 478555	GREATEST HITS (2-LP)	£40
96	Columbia C 67484	THE GHOST OF TOM JOAD (LP)	£100
02	Columbia COL 508000-1	THE RISING (2-LP)	£125
09	Columbia 88697453161	WORKING ON A DREAM (2-LP)	£18

(see also Roy Orbison)

SPRINGWELL
71	London HLU 10345	It's For You/Our Question	£15

SPRONG & NYAH SHUFFLE
69	Grape GR 3001	Moonwalk/Think	£30

BILLY SPROUD & ROCK 'N' ROLL SIX
57	Columbia DB 3893	Rock Mr. Piper/If You're So Smart (How Come You Ain't Rich)	£25
57	Columbia DB 3893	Rock Mr. Piper/If You're So Smart (How Come You Ain't Rich) (78)	£20

SPROUTS
58	RCA RCA 1031	Teen Billy Baby/Goodbye, She's Gone	£35
58	RCA RCA 1031	Teen Billy Baby/Goodbye, She's Gone (78)	£20

SPUD
75	Philips 9108 002	A SILK PURSE (LP)	£20

SPUD AND THE FABS
80	Whitetower AMC 706	Your Place Or Mine (p/s)	£25

THE SPUNKY SPIDER
73	Phoenix S-NIX 143	You Won't Come/Perchance	£80

SPUNKY ONIONS/GHETTOBETTIES
80	Temple Beat TR111	Split 7" (p/s)	£25

WILD JIMMY SPURRILL
60s	XX MIN 717	NOBLE 'THIN MAN' WATTS AND WILD JIMMY SPURRILL (EP)	£20

(see also Noble 'Thin Man' Watts, Guitar Crusher)

SPYROGYRA
79	Infinity (no cat. no.)	MORNING DANCE (LP, picture disc, in-house issue, top-flap poly sleeve, 50 copies)	£50

SQUAD
79	Squad SQS 1	Red Alert/£8 A Week (in die cut p/s)	£60
79	Squad SQS 1	Red Alert/£8 A Week	£20
79	Squad SQS 2	Millionaire/Brockhill Boys (p/s)	£40

SQUADRONAIRES
53	Decca LF 1141	CONTRASTS IN JAZZ (10" LP)	£15

SQUARE SET
71	Decca FR 13197	That's What I Want/Come On	£80

SQUAREPUSHER
96	Rephlex CATO37LP	FEED ME WEIRD THINGS (2-LP)	£30
97	Warp WARPLP50	HARD NORMAL DADDY (2-LP)	£20
98	Warp WARPLP57	MUSIC IS ROTTED ONE NOTE (LP)	£20
99	Warp WARPLP62	BUDAKHAN MINDPHONE (LP)	£20
99	Warp WARLP72	SELECTION SIXTEEN (2x12", with 10")	£20
99	Warp WARPLP85	GO PLASTIC (2-LP)	£20
02	Warp WARLPLP97	DO YOU KNOW SQUAREPUSHER? (LP)	£20
04	Warp WARPLP117	ULTRAVISITOR (2-LP)	£20
06	Warp WARPLP148X	HELLO EVERYTHING (3 x 12" plus bonus CD edition)	£20
08	Warp WARLP148	JUST A SOUVENEIR (LP)	£15

SQUARES (2)
91	Hangman HANG 45 UP	TRAPPED IN A SQUARE (LP)	£15
93	Hangman HANG 52 UP	CURSE OF THE SQUARES (LP)	£15

SQUEEK
72	Bronze BRO 130	Make Hay While The Sun Shines/L Amour D'un Apres Midi	£20

SQUEELER
79	Hit H.I.T. 101	Jennifer Broadhurst/Menace/I Just Want To Be Me/Framed (7" no p/s)	£100

SQUEEZE
77	BTM SBT 107	Take Me I'm Yours/No, Disco Kid, No (unreleased)	£0
78	A&M AMLH 68465	SQUEEZE (LP)	£15

SQUIBS
81	Oily SLICK 1	On The Line (plain sleeve, with insert)	£25
81	Oily SLICK 3	Parades/Out On The Town (p/s)	£20

BILLY SQUIER
86	Capitol 12CL 433	Love Is The Hero (extended version with Freddie Mercury intro)/Learn How To Live (live) (12", p/s)	£15

(see also Freddie Mercury, Roger Taylor)

SQUIRE
79	Rok ROK I/II	Get Ready To Go/COMING SHORTLY: Doing The Flail (company sleeve)	£35
83	Hi-Lo LO 01	HITS FROM 3,000 YEARS AGO (LP)	£18
83	Hi-Lo LO 02	GET SMART (LP, with poster)	£15
85	Hi-Lo LO 03	THE SINGLES ALBUM (LP)	£15

(see also Anthony Meynell)

CHRIS SQUIRE
75	Atlantic K 50203	FISH OUT OF WATER (LP, with inner sleeve & poster)	£20

(see also Yes)

JOHN SQUIRE
02	North Country NCLP 001	TIME CHANGES EVERYTHING (2LP, gatefold)	£60
04	North Country NCLP 003	MARSHALL'S HOUSE (LP,)	£60

(see also Stone Roses, Seahorses, Liam Gallagher John Squire)

SQUIRES
69	MCA MU 1060	Funky Bayswater/Games People Play	£20

ROSEMARY SQUIRES
56	MGM MGM-EP 640	MY LOVE IS A WANDERER (EP)	£40
60	HMV 7EG 8588	ROSEMARY (EP)	£40
63	HMV CLP 1669	EVERYTHINGS COMING UP ROSY (LP, mono)	£400
63	HMV CSD 1508	EVERYTHINGS COMING UP ROSY (LP, stereo)	£600
65	HMV CLP 1832	SOMETHING TO REMEMBER ME BY (LP, mono)	£80
65	HMV CSD 1586	SOMETHING TO REMEMBER ME BY (LP, stereo)	£120

S.R.C.
69	Capitol CL 15576	Black Sheep/Morning Mood	£35
69	Capitol (S)T 2991	S.R.C. (LP)	£80
69	Capitol E-(S)T 134	MILESTONES (LP)	£70
70	Capitol E-(S)T 273	TRAVELLER'S TALE (LP)	£70

(See also Streamliners with Joanne)

ROY ST. JOHN
76	Caroline CA 2008	DECLARE IMMIGRATION (LP)	£15

THOMAS ST. JOHN & WINSTON J
75	Sol-Fa International SAO 1	Funky Woman / Does It Have To Be This Way	£150

ASHBURY STABBINS DUO
76	Bead Records BEAD 4	FIRE WITHOUT STICKS (LP)	£50

STACCATOS
61	Parlophone R 4828	Main Line/Topaz	£15
68	NEMS 3003	Why Care About Today/Cry To Me	£25
68	Fontana TF 966	Butchers And Bakers/Imitations Of Love	£30

CLARENCE STACEY
59	Pye International 7N 25025	Just Your Love/Lonely Guy	£35
59	Pye International 7N 25025	Just Your Love/Lonely Guy (78)	£20

GWEN STACEY
65	RCA RCX 7166	INTRODUCING GWEN STACEY (EP)	£150

STACK OF HEARTS
86	SOH SOH 001	Danger Zone/Searching For A Spirit (no p/s)	£25

BOB STACKIE
68	Collins Downbeat CR 009	Grab It Hold It Feel It (with Sir Collins Band)/DAN SIMMONDS: Way Out Sound	£50

(see also Sir Collins [Band], Owen Gray)

STACKRIDGE
71	MCA MDKS 8002	STACKRIDGE (LP, gatefold sleeve, pink/orange 'dogbone' label)	£40
72	MCA MKPS 2025	FRIENDLINESS (LP, blue/black 'hexagon' label)	£20
74	MCA MCG 3501	THE MAN IN THE BOWLER HAT (LP, gatefold sleeve)	£15
74	Rocket PIGL 11	EXTRAVAGANZA (LP, gatefold label)	£15
76	MCA MCF 2747	DO THE STANLEY (LP)	£15
76	Rocket ROLL 3	MR. MICK (LP)	£15

STACKWADDY
71	Dandelion DAN 8003	STACKWADDY (LP, gatefold sleeve with lyric insert)	£175
71	Dandelion DAN 8003	STACKWADDY (LP, gatefold sleeve with lyric insert, as K 49003)	£40
72	Dandelion 2310 231	BUGGER OFF! (LP)	£175

JO STAFFORD
53	Columbia SCM 5012	It Is No Secret/He Bought My Soul At Calvary	£15
53	Columbia SCM 5013	You Belong To Me/Jambalaya (On The Bayou)	£50
53	Columbia SCM 5026	Keep It A Secret/Once To Every Heart	£15
53	Columbia SCM 5046	Something To Remember You By/Blue Moon	£15
53	Columbia SCM 5064	September In The Rain/JO STAFFORD & FRANKIE LAINE: Chow, Willy	£15
57	Philips JK 1003	On London Bridge/Perfect Love (jukebox issue)	£25
59	Philips PB 935	Pine Top's Boogie Woogie/All Yours (78)	£15
50	Capitol LC 6500	AMERICAN FOLK SONGS (10")	£20
51	Capitol LC 6515	KISS ME KATE (10", with Gordon MacRae)	£15
53	Capitol LC 6575	CAPITOL PRESENTS JO STAFFORD (10")	£15
54	Capitol LC 6635	CAPITOL PRESENTS JO STAFFORD, VOL. 2 (10")	£15
54	Columbia 33S 1024	AS YOU DESIRE ME (10")	£15
56	Philips BBR 8076	THE VOICE OF YOUR CHOICE (10")	£20
61	Philips BBL 7428	JO + JAZZ (also stereo SBBL 595)	£25

━━━━━━━━━━━━━━━━━━━━━━━━━━━━━━━━━━━━━ MINT VALUE £

(see also Tommy Dorsey)

JO STAFFORD & FRANKIE LAINE
| 53 | Columbia SCM 5014 | Settin' The Woods On Fire/Piece A-Puddin' | £20 |
| 55 | Philips BBR 8075 | FLOATIN' DOWN TO COTTON TOWN (10" LP) | £20 |

TERRY STAFFORD
63	Stateside SS 225	Heartache On The Way/You Left Me Here To Cry	£15
64	London RE-U 1436	SUSPICION (EP)	£40
64	London HA-U 8200	SUSPICION (LP)	£60

STAG MARKS BAND
| 81 | Double Image SRTS 81 CUS 1223 | Ain't No Fun On The Dole/Story Of My Life | £20 |

STAGEFRIGHT
| 85 | STN STN 1 | Strangers In The Night/Heartless/Rock City (no p/s) | £150 |

STAINED GLASS
| 74 | Sweet Folk & C. SFA 019 | OPEN ROAD (LP) | £200 |

GREG STAINER
| 97 | VIP 003 | ORIGINAL FLAVA EP (12") | £25 |

STAINS
| 79 | Redball RR 020 | Emotional Pills/Believer/Bored (p/s) | £100 |

STAIRS
| 92 | Imaginary MIRAGE 029 | Weed Bus (12", unissued, test pressings only, proof p/s) | £40 |

STAIRSTEPS
71	Buddah 2359 021	STEP BY STEP BY STEP (LP)	£20
71	Buddah 2365 015	STAY CLOSE TO ME (LP)	£20
72	Buddah 2365 016	THE STAIRSTEPS (LP)	£20
76	Dark Horse AMLH 22004	2ND RESSURECTION (LP)	£20

(see also Five Stairsteps)

STAKKA AND SKYNET
| 01 | Underfire UDFRLPS 04 | CLOCKWORK SAMPLER EP: Decoy/Side Effects (Kemal and Rob Data Remix)/9000 series/Side Effects (Teebee Remix) (2 x 12", stickered, die-cut sleeve) | £20 |
| 01 | Underfire UDRFRLP 04 | CLOCKWORK (LP, 5 discs) | £40 |

STALAG 17
| 85 | Mortarhate MORT 14 | THE TRUTH WILL BE HEARD (12", split EP with TOXIC WASTE) | £15 |

STALLION
| 75 | Flyright FLY 45 003 | Skinny Kid/Cobra | £45 |

STAMFORD BRIDGE
| 71 | Penny Farthing PELS 515 | FIRST DAY OF YOUR LIFE (LP) | £25 |

STAMINA
| 92 | Wax FLX 2052-1 | Onslaught (flexi, in card sleeve) | £20 |

TERRY STAMP
| 75 | A&M AMLH 68329 | FAT STICKS (LP, with lyric insert) | £100 |

(see also Third World War)

STAMPEDE
82	Polydor POSP 507	Photographs/Days Of Wine And Roses (A-side switched, no p/s)	£30
82	Polydor POSPX 507	Days Of Wine And Roses/Movin' On/Photographs/Missing You (12", p/s)	£20
82	Polydor ROCK 1	OFFICIAL BOOTLEG (LP)	£15
83	Polydor POLS 1083	HURRICANE TOWN (LP)	£15

STAMPEDERS
73	Regal Zonophone RZ3085	Ride In The Wind/Running Wild	£20
72	Regal Zono. SLRZ 1032	THE STAMPEDERS (LP)	£40
74	Regal Zono. SLRZ 1039	FROM THE FIRE (LP)	£50

JEAN STANBACK
| 69 | Deep Soul DS 9101 | I Still Love You/If I Ever Needed Love | £50 |

STANDELLS
64	Liberty LIB 55722	I'll Go Crazy/Help Yourself	£35
66	Capitol CL 15446	Dirty Water/Rari	£50
65	Liberty LBY 1243	THE STANDELLS IN PERSON AT P.J.'s (LP)	£60

STANDING OVATION
| 92 | Kold Sweat KS126 | Shadows Of Mayhem (12") | £15 |

STANDING FLAT
| 79 | MUN 001 | FASCINATION EP (p/s) | £15 |

STANDS
| 04 | Echo ECHLP 50 | ALL YEARS LEAVING (LP) | £30 |
| 05 | Echo ECHLP 60 | HORSE FABULOUS (LP) | £30 |

PAUL STANLEY
| 79 | Casablanca CAN 140 | Hold Me Touch Me/Goodbye (p/s, purple vinyl with mask & picture label, most with mispressed B-side: "Love In Chains") | £25 |

(see also Kiss)

PETE STANLEY & ROGER KNOWLES
| 75 | Xtra TRANS 1146 | PICKING AND SINGING (LP) | £25 |

PETE STANLEY & WIZZ JONES
| 65 | Columbia DB 7776 | The Ballad Of Hollis Brown/Riff Minor | £20 |

| 66 | Columbia SX 6083 | SIXTEEN TONS OF BLUEGRASS (LP) | £60 |

(see also Wizz Jones)

STANLEY AND THE TURBINES
| 83 | GG GGLP 0029 | BIG BAMBOO (LP) | £15 |

VIV(IAN) STANSHALL
70	Liberty LBF 15309	Labio-Dental Fricative/Paper Round (with Sean Head Show Band featuring Eric Clapton)	£40
71	Fly BUG 4	Suspicion (with Gargantuan Chums)/Blind Date (with biG GRunt)	£15
74	Warner Bros K 16424	Lakonga/Baba Tunde	£20
76	Harvest HAR 5114	Young Ones/Are You Havin' Any Fun/Question	£15
74	Warner Bros K 56052	MEN OPENING UMBRELLAS AHEAD (LP, with inner)	£70
78	Charisma CAS 1139	SIR HENRY AT RAWLINSON END (LP, soundtrack, with insert)	£25
81	Charisma CAS 1153	TEDDY BOYS DON'T KNIT (LP)	£25
84	Demon Verbals VERB 1	SIR HENRY AT NDIDDI'S KRAAL (LP)	£25

(see also Bonzo Dog [Doo Dah] Band, Grimms)

STAPLE SINGERS
67	Columbia DB 8292	For What It's Worth/Are You Sure?	£30
69	Soul City SC 117	For What It's Worth/Are You Sure? (reissue)	£18
62	Riverside REP 3220	THE SAVIOUR IS BORN (EP)	£15
63	Stateside SL 10015	SWING LOW (LP)	£30
63	Riverside RLP 3501	HAMMER AND NAILS (LP)	£25
65	Fontana 688 515 ZL	UNCLOUDY DAY (LP)	£20
66	Columbia SX 6023	FREEDOM HIGHWAY (LP)	£20
69	Stax (S)XATS 1004	SOUL FOLK IN ACTION (LP)	£15
69	Stax SXATS 1018	WE'LL GET OVER (LP)	£15
73	Stax 2325 103	BE WHAT YOU ARE (LP)	£20
80	Stax STM 7009	BRAND NEW DAY (LP)	£15

STUART A STAPLES
| 05 | Beggars Banquet BBQLP 242 | LUCKY DOG RECORDINGS (LP) | £40 |

(see also Asphalt RIbbons, Tindersticks)

JULIE STAPLETON
| 91 | V4Visions VIS 0612T | Wheres Your Love Gone (Remix)/(New York Mix)/Just Dreaming (12", p/s) | £15 |

STEVEN STAPLETON & DAVID TIBET
| 91 | United Dairies UD 037 | THE SADNESS OF THINGS/THE GRAVE AND BEAUTIFUL NAME OF SADNESS (LP, one side each) | £35 |

(see also Current 93, Nurse With Wound, Tibet & Stapleton)

STA-PREST
| 80 | Avatar AAA 103 | Schooldays/Tomorrow (p/s) | £75 |

STARBOUND
| 77 | Star Bound SB 01 | CHANGES (LP) | £20 |

STARBUCK
| 73 | Bradleys BRAD 312 | Do You Like Boys?/You Never Wanna Rock 'N' Roll | £15 |

(see also Mandrake Paddle Steamer, Shambles)

STARCROST
| 19 | Jazzman JMANLP 114 | STARCROST (LP) | £20 |

STARFIGHTERS
80	Motor City MCR 105	I'm Falling/Heaven And Hell (in p/s)	£40
81	Jive JIVET 003	Alley Cat Blues/Don't Touch Me (12", p/s)	£15
81	Jive HOP 200	STARFIGHTERS (LP, with inner)	£22

STARGAZERS
54	Decca F 10213	I See The Moon/Eh Cumpari	£25
54	Decca F 10259	The Happy Wanderer/Till We Two Are One	£15
55	Decca F 10626	Twenty Tiny Fingers/An Old Beer Bottle	£15
54	Decca LF 1186	PRESENTING THE STARGAZERS (10" LP)	£20
59	Decca LK 4309	SOUTH OF THE BORDER (LP)	£20

(see also Roy Smith & Stargazers, Lita Roza, Dickie Valentine)

STARJETS
| 79 | Epic S EPC 6968/7123 | It Really Doesn't Matter/Schooldays//Run With The Pack/Watch Out (double pack, die-cut sleeves, promo only) | £15 |
| 79 | Epic EPC 83534 | GOD BLESS STARJETS (LP) | £15 |

CHUKKI STARR
| 98 | Saxon SAX 064 | Mark A De Beast/(Version)//Youth Dem Anthem/Youth Dem Anthem (Mix 2) (12") | £25 |
| 98 | Ariwa ARI 147 | GHETTO YOUTHS (LP) | £20 |

CINDY STARR
| 68 | Columbia Blue Beat DB 107 | Pain Of Love/Hippy Ska (as Cindy Starr & Rude Boys) | £20 |
| 68 | Columbia Blue Beat DB 110 | The Way I Do/Sad Movies (Make Me Cry) (as Cindy Starr & Mopeds) | £15 |

(see also Teardrops)

EDWIN STARR
66	Polydor BM 56702	Stop Her On Sight (S.O.S.)/I Have Faith In You (demo)	£500
66	Polydor BM 56702	Stop Her On Sight (S.O.S.)/I Have Faith In You	£25
66	Polydor BM 56717	Headline News/Harlem	£20
67	Polydor BM 56726	It's My Turn Now/Girls Are Getting Prettier	£25
67	Tamla Motown TMG 630	I Want My Baby Back/Gonna Keep On Tryin' Till I Win	£30
67	Tamla Motown TMG 630	I Want My Baby Back/Gonna Keep On Tryin' Till I Win (DJ copy)	£50
68	Tamla Motown TMG 646	I Am The Man For You Baby/My Weakness Is You	£30

MINT VALUE £

68	Tamla Motown TMG 646	I Am The Man For You Baby/My Weakness Is You (DJ copy)	£90
68	Tamla Motown TMG 672	25 Miles/Mighty Good Lovin' (DJ copy)	£45
69	Tamla Motown TMG 692	Way Over There/If My Heart Could Tell The Story	£20
69	Tamla Motown TMG 692	Way Over There/If My Heart Could Tell The Story (DJ copy)	£50
69	Tamla Motown TMG 720	Oh How Happy/O, O, O, Baby (demos only, unissued, with Blinky)	£375
70	Tamla Motown TMG 725	Time/Running Back And Forth	£20
71	Tamla Motown TMG 790	Agent Double 0 Soul/Back Street (DJ copy)	£40
73	Tamla Motown TMG 875	You've Got My Soul On Fire/Love The Lonely People's Prayer	£20
75	Bradleys BRAD 7520	Stay With Me/I'll Never Forget You	£15
69	Tamla Motown STML 11094	SOUL MASTER (LP, mono)	£35
69	Tamla Motown STML 11094	SOUL MASTER (LP, stereo)	£40
69	Tamla Motown TML 11115	25 MILES (LP, mono)	£30
69	Tamla Motown STML 11115	25 MILES (LP, stereo)	£25
70	Tamla Motown (S)TML 11131	JUST WE TWO (LP, as Edwin Starr & Blinky)	£25
70	Tamla Motown STML 11171	WAR AND PEACE (LP)	£20
72	Tamla Motown STML 11199	INVOLVED (LP)	£20
72	Tamla Motown STML 11209	THE HITS OF EDWIN STARR (LP)	£15
74	Tamla Motown STML 11260	HELL UP IN HARLEM (LP, soundtrack)	£15

(see also Blinky & Edwin Starr, Holidays)

FREDDIE STARR & MIDNIGHTERS

63	Decca F 11663	Who Told You?/Peter Gunn Locomotion	£20
63	Decca F 11786	It's Shaking Time/Baby Blue	£20
64	Decca F 12009	Never Cry On Someone's Shoulder/Just Keep On Dreaming	£40

(see also Howie Casey & Seniors)

JIMMY STARR

58	London HL 8731	It's Only Make Believe/Ooh Crazy	£30
58	London HL 8731	It's Only Make Believe/Ooh Crazy (78)	£15

KAY STARR

54	Capitol CL 14151	Am I A Toy Or A Treasure?/Fortune In Dreams	£20
54	Capitol CL 14167	Fool, Fool, Fool/Allez-Vous En	£20
55	HMV 7M 300	If Anyone Finds This, I Love You/Turn Right	£15
56	HMV 7M 371	Rock And Roll Waltz/I've Changed My Mind 1,000 Times	£20
53	Capitol LC 6574	CAPITOL PRESENTS KAY STARR (10")	£25
54	Capitol LC 6630	THE KAY STARR STYLE (10")	£20
56	Capitol LC 6835	THE HITS OF KAY STARR (10")	£20
57	Capitol T 580	IN A BLUE MOOD	£20
57	London HA-U 2039	SWINGING WITH THE STARR	£20
58	RCA RD 27056	BLUE STARR	£20

RANDY STARR

57	London HL 8443	After School/Heaven High (Man So Low)	£30
58	Felsted AF 106	Pink Lemonade/Count On Me	£15

RINGO STARR

72	R.O.R. ROR 2001	Steel (1-sided promo-only interview disc for 'Ringo Or Robin' reception at Liberty's department store; available for 1 week only, p/s)	£1000
74	Parlophone PSR 374	Interview By Bob Mercer With Ringo For The Salesmen and Uxbridge Road/Only You (promo only)	£500
76	Apple R 6011	Oh My My/No No Song (not in die-cut apple sleeve)	£20
76	Polydor 2001 694	A Dose Of Rock 'N' Roll/Cryin'	£20
77	Polydor 2001 734	Drowning In The Sea Of Love/Just A Dream (credited to RINGO)	£50
78	Polydor 2001 795	Tonight/Heart On My Sleeve	£80
79	Apple R 5944	Back Off Boogaloo/Blindman (reissue, green apple label, 4-prong pushout centre)	£150
84	Apple G45 13	It Don't Come Easy/Back Off Boogaloo (P/s EMI Golden 45s series)	£20
08	Capitol LIV 8	Liverpool 8/For Love (p/s, red vinyl)	£20
70	Apple PCS 7101	SENTIMENTAL JOURNEY (LP)	£30
70	Apple TD-PCS 7101	SENTIMENTAL JOURNEY (reel-to-reel tape, jewel case)	£20
70	Parlophone PPCS 7101	SENTIMENTAL JOURNEY (LP, export edition, black/silver label, 'Parlophone' and 'EMI' boxed logos)	£250
70	Apple PAS 10002	BEAUCOUPS OF BLUES (LP, gatefold sleeve)	£40
73	Apple PCTC 252	RINGO (LP, gatefold with 12" x 12" booklet)	£15
74	Apple PCS 7168	GOODNIGHT VIENNA (LP, printed inner)	£15
75	Apple PCS 7170	BLAST FROM YOUR PAST (LP, printed inner)	£15
76	Polydor 2302-040	ROTOGRAVURE (LP, gatefold, printed inner, initial copies with free magnifying glass))	£20
77	Polydor 2310 556	RINGO THE 4TH (LP, printed inner, credited to RINGO)	£20
77	Polydor 2480 429	SCOUSE THE MOUSE (LP, with Adam Faith, Donald Pleasance etc.; with stickered sleeve & printed [not photocopied] competition insert)	£100
77	Polydor 2480 429	SCOUSE THE MOUSE (LP, with Adam Faith, Donald Pleasance etc.; without stickered sleeve & printed [not photocopied] competition insert)	£50
77	Polydor 3194 429	SCOUSE THE MOUSE (cassette)	£30
78	Polydor 2310-599B	BAD BOY (LP, printed inner)	£15
90	EMI EMS 1375	RINGO STARR AND HIS ALL STARR BAND (LP)	£30
92	Private Music 212 902	TIME TAKES TIME (LP, printed inner)	£20
13	Capitol/Apple 5099992877078	RINGO (3x7" box set, poster, customer plastic adapter hub, RSD)	£20
15	UMe 0602547237057	POSTCARDS FROM PARADISE (LP, 180g)	£30
19	UMe 00602508243752	WHAT'S MY NAME? (LP, printed inner, blue vinyl)	£30
21	UMe 3558580	ZOOM IN (5-track 12" EP, red vinyl)	£30
23	UMe 00602455866967	REWIND FORWARD (10" EP, p/s)	£20
24	UMe 00602465142549	CROOKED BOY (12" EP, black and white marbled vinyl, RSD)	£25

(see also Beatles, Harry Nilsson, Billy Connolly & Chris Tummings, Traveling Wilburys)

STELLA STARR
67	Piccadilly 7N 35366	Bring Him Back/Say It	£50
67	Piccadilly 7N 35366	Bring Him Back/Say It (DJ copy)	£80

TONY STARR
64	Decca F 11847	I'll Take A Rocket To The Moon/Next Train Leaving	£60

STARRY EYED & LAUGHING
74	CBS 80450	STARRY EYED & LAUGHING (LP)	£15

STARSAILOR
01	Chrysalis 7243 535350 1 8	LOVE IS HERE (LP)	£30

STARSHIP
77	Scratch SCH 01	Vampire For Your Love/You Can Dance/Hey Girl/Never Thought I'd See The Day	£15

STARSHIP ORCHESTRA
80	CBS 84558	CELESTIAL SKY (LP)	£20

STARVATION ARMY
83	Linden Sounds LS004	Stranger In My Room/Walrus Is Dead (no p/s)	£30

STASIS
92	B12 B1211	Point Of No Return (12", 300 only on silver vinyl)	£60
93	B12 B1211	Point Of No Return (12")	£40
93	Likemind 01	Likemind 01 (12", 3 Nuron tracks on B-side) (12")	£80
93	Peacefrog PF 013	Circuit Funk (12")	£35
93	Time Is Right TIT 005	Disco 4000 (Witness To The Future)/So-Lar/Vannannans Answer (Feat. Nuron) (12")	£60
94	Peacefrog PF 028	INSPIRATION (2-LP)	£50
96	Peacefrog PF 046	FROMTHEOLDTOTHENEW (2-LP)	£35

(see also Nuron)

STATEN ISLAND FERRY
69	Major Minor MM 643	Candy Bar/Charlie Chan	£20

STATE OF GRACE
83	PRT 12P266	Touching The Times/Instrumental Mix (12")	£60

STATE OF MICKEY & TOMMY
67	Mercury MF 996	With Love From One To Five/I Know What I Will Do	£150
67	Mercury MF 1009	Frisco Bay/Nobody Knows Where You've Been	£150

(see also Spooky Tooth, Nero & Gladiators)

STATESMEN
63	Studio Republic	FIVE PLUS ONE (LP, private pressing)	£100

STATIC (2)
81	Eeyo EEYO 1	Voice On The Line/Stealin' (no p/s, 1,000 only)	£15

(see also White Lightning)

(THE) STATICS
80	Mercury MER 41	Turn The Radio On/Over Now (as Static)	£20

STATION SKIFFLE GROUP
57	Esquire 10-503	Don't You Rock Me Daddy-O/Hugged My Honey (78)	£15
58	Esquire EP 161	STATION SKIFFLE GROUP (EP)	£50

(see also Jimmy Miller)

STATION 360
84	SRT STA 360	Optimist/Stars	£30

STATLER BROTHERS
66	CBS BPG 62713	FLOWERS ON THE WALL (LP)	£15

(see also Johnny Cash)

CANDI STATON
76	Warner Bros. SAM 60	Young Hearts Run Free/I Know (12" promo only)	£200
70	Capitol ST 21631	I'M JUST A PRISONER (LP)	£80
76	Warner Bros. K56259	YOUNG HEARTS RUN FREE (LP)	£15
99	React 149	OUTSIDE IN (2-LP)	£18

STATUES
60	London HLG 9192	Blue Velvet/Keep The Hall Burning	£45

STATUS QUO
SINGLES : PYE SINGLES
68	Pye 7N 17497	Black Veils Of Melancholy/To Be Free (1st pressing, plain black text on blue label, push-out centre)	£35
68	Pye 7N 17497	Black Veils Of Melancholy/To Be Free (1st pressing, plain black text on blue label, solid centre)	£50
68	Pye 7N 17497	Black Veils Of Melancholy/To Be Free (2nd pressing, blue label with black Pye banner, push-out centre)	£30
68	Pye 7N 17650	Technicolor Dreams/Paradise Flat	£800
69	Pye 7N 17665	Make Me Stay A Bit Longer/Aunt Nellie (blue label, push-out centre)	£25
69	Pye 7N 17665	Make Me Stay A Bit Longer/Aunt Nellie (blue label, solid centre)	£40
69	Pye 7N 17728	Are You Growing Tired Of My Love/So Ends Another Life (blue label, push-out centre)	£25
69	Pye 7N 17728	Are You Growing Tired Of My Love/So Ends Another Life (blue label, solid centre)	£35
69	Pye 7N 17825	The Price Of Love/Little Miss Nothing (blue label push-out centre)	£30
69	Pye 7N 17825	The Price Of Love/Little Miss Nothing (blue label solid centre)	£50
70	Pye 7N 17998	In My Chair/Gerdundula (blue label, push-out centre with p/s)	£50
70	Pye 7N 17998	In My Chair/Gerdundula (blue label solid centre, no p/s)	£20

Rare Record Price Guide 2026

MINT VALUE £

71	Pye 7N 45077	Tune To The Music/Good Thinking (blue label, push-out centre)	£20
71	Pye 7N 45077	Tune To The Music/Good Thinking (blue label, solid centre)	£50
73	Pye 7N 45253	Gerdundula/Lakky Lady (red/pink label, with black text, solid centre)	£15
73	Pye 7N 45253	Gerdundula/Lakky Lady (red/pink label, with silver text, solid centre)	£15

SINGLES : VERTIGO SINGLES

77	Vertigo 6059 184	Rockin' All Over The World/Ring Of A Change (p/s, with small poster)	£15
82	Vertigo QUO 9	Jealousy/Calling The Shots (unreleased in U.K.; Irish promos only)	£150
84	Vertigo QUO 15	Too Close To The Ground/I Wonder Why (release cancelled)	£0
85	Vertigo QUO 17	Naughty Girl (actually "Dreamin' ") (unreleased)	£0
86	Vertigo QUOPD 18	Rollin' Home/Lonely (uncut picture disc)	£175
86	Vertigo QUOPB 191	Red Sky/Don't Give It Up/The Milton Keynes Medley (12", 'Wembley Souvenir Pack', poster p/s)	£15
86	Vertigo QUOPD 20	In The Army Now/Heartburn (picture disc)	£15
89	Vertigo 080 630-2	Burning Bridges (On And Off And On Again) (Extended Version)/Whatever You Want (Extended Version)/Marguerita Time/Who Gets The Love?/Burning Bridges (Video) (CD Video)	£0
90	Vertigo QUO 2812	The Anniversary Waltz/The Power Of Rock/Perfect Remedy (12", p/s, mispress, B-side plays "Little Lady" (live) & exclusive "Paper Plane" re-recording)	£45
90	Vertigo QUO 2812	The Anniversary Waltz/The Power Of Rock/Perfect Remedy (12", p/s, mispress, A-side plays "The Power Of Rock [Full Version]")	£45
91	Vertigo QUO 31	Fakin' The Blues (Edit)/Heavy Daze (p/s, swirl label, release cancelled, approximately 25 copies only)	£1500
91	Vertigo QUO 3112	Fakin' The Blues (Edit)/Fakin' The Blues (Album Version)/Heavy Daze/Better Times (12", swirl label, p/s, cancelled, approx. 25 copies only)	£1500
91	Vertigo QUOCD 31	Fakin' The Blues (Edit)/Fakin' The Blues (Album Version)/Heavy Daze/Better Times (CD, unissued, 2,000 later sent out by fan club, no inlay)	£40
91	Vertigo STATUS 30	Can't Give You More/(Radio Edit)/Dead In The Water (swirl label, stickered stock p/s)	£80
92	Vertigo QUO 3212	Rock 'Til You Drop/Medley/Forty-Five Hundred Times (12", p/s, mispressing, omits "Forty-Five Hundred Times")	£15

SINGLES : OTHER SINGLES

75	Lyntone LYN 3154/5	Down Down/Break The Rules (Smiths Crisps flexidisc, with 'Smiths' p/s)	£15
80s	Lyntone QUO 1-4	Interview picture discs (4-single pack)	£20
99	From The Makers Of... FTMOCD1	FAKIN' THE BLUES (MILLENNIUM EDITION) (CD, fanclub mail order-only edition, hand-no'd exclusive p/s, contains unreleased Vertigo CD [QUOCD 31])	£50

ALBUMS : LPS

68	Pye NPL 18220	PICTURESQUE MATCHSTICKABLE MESSAGES (mono)	£200
68	Pye NSPL 18220	PICTURESQUE MATCHSTICKABLE MESSAGES (stereo)	£175
69	Pye NPL 18301	SPARE PARTS (blue label, mono)	£175
69	Pye NSPL 18301	SPARE PARTS (blue label, stereo)	£150
69	Marble Arch MAL 1193	STATUS QUO-TATIONS (mono)	£30
69	Marble Arch MAL(S) 1193	STATUS QUO-TATIONS (stereo, most copies exported)	£30
70	Pye NSPL 18344	MA KELLY'S GREASY SPOON (1st pressing, blue labels with poster)	£150
70	Pye NSPL 18344	MA KELLY'S GREASY SPOON (1st pressing, blue labels, no poster)	£30
70	Pye NSPL 18344	MA KELLY'S GREASY SPOON (2nd pressing, blue labels with black banner on top of label)	£25
71	Pye NSPL 18371	DOG OF TWO HEAD (gatefold sleeve, blue labels)	£40
71	Pye NSLP 18371	DOG OF TWO HEAD (gatefold sleeve, repressing, turquoise labels)	£20
71	Pye NSLP 18371	DOG OF TWO HEAD (gatefold sleeve, repressing, black & white labels)	£30
72	Vertigo 6360 082	PILEDRIVER (swirl label, gatefold sleeve)	£30
73	Vertigo 6360 098	HELLO! (spaceship label, with inner sleeve & poster)	£20
74	Vertigo 9102 001	QUO (with poster/lyric sheet)	£15
74	Record Club ACB 00217	QUO (Audio Club of Britain Record Club' issue ACB 00217 on labels, spine and rear sleeve)	£25
74	Vertigo ACB 00217/9102 001	QUO (hybrid issue with ACB 00217 on spine and 9102 001 on rear sleeve and labels)	£30
77	Vertigo 9286 686/7	STATUS QUO LIVE (2-LP, spaceship label)	£15
79	Pye NPSL18607	JUST FOR THE RECORD (red vinyl)	£15
79	Pye NSLP 18607	JUST FOR THE RECORD (repressing, black vinyl, black and white labels)	£20
82	Phonogram PRO BX 1	FROM THE MAKERS OF... (3-LP, with inserts in round metal tin, some numbered)	£20
83	Vertigo VERH 10	BACK TO BACK (in-store promo copies with poster insert)	£15
85	PRT Flashbacks FBLP 8082	NANANA	£15
87	PRT PYL 6020	PICTURESQUE MATCHSTICKABLE MESSAGES (LP, reissue)	£20
87	PRT PYL 6024	QUOTATIONS VOLUME ONE - THE EARLY YEARS	£15
87	PRT PYL 6025	QUOTATIONS VOLUME TWO - FLIPSIDES, ALTERNATIVES AND ODDITIES	£18
88	PRT PYX 4007	FROM THE BEGINNING (picture disc)	£25
90	Essential! ESBLP 136	THE EARLY WORKS (5-LP box set with book)	£30
91	Baktabak LINT 5003	INTROSPECTIVE (clear vinyl, 6 Pye-era tracks & interview)	£30
91	Vertigo 51 341-1	ROCK 'TILL YOU DROP (swirl label)	£40
92	Polydor 517 367-1	LIVE ALIVE QUO (with inner sleeve)	£40
94	Polydor 523 607-1	THIRSTY WORK (with inner sleeve)	£100
04	Earmark EAR 42032	SPARE PARTS (180gm reissue, stickered PVC wallet sleeve)	£40
04	Earmark EAR 42033	MA KELLY'S GREASY SPOON (180gm reissue stickered PVC wallet sleeve)	£40
04	Earmark EAR 42046	PICTURESQUE MATCHSTICKABLE MESSAGES (LP, reissue, in stickered PVC wallet)	£40
04	Earmark EAR 42035	DOG OF TWO HEADS (180gm reissue, stickered PVC wallet sleeve)	£40
07	Fourth Chord QUOLP 001	IN SEARCH OF THE FOURTH CHORD (LP, gatefold sleeve)	£25
11	Fourth Chord QUOBS002	QUID PRO QUO (2-LP, gatefold, mail order only)	£40
12	Music On Vinyl MOVLP 229	HELLO! (180gm reissue, lyrical insert, in stickered PVC sleeve)	£25
13	Fourth Chord QUOCD010	BULA QUO (box set, LP, 2-CD, 7-inch, poster, 5 postcards, flight ticket. Mail-order only)	£40
13	Demon DEMREC 17	IN SEARCH OF THE FOURTH CHORD (180gm picture disc, numbered stickered PVC sleeve. 500 only, mail-oder only)	£25
13	Demon DEMREC 18	QUID PRO QUO (180gm picture disc, numbered stickered PVC wallet sleeve, Mail-order	£25

only)...
| 14 | Mercury 3739863 | TOKYO QUO (gatefold, insert) ....£20 |

ALBUMS : CDS
| 01 | From The Makers Of ... FTMOCD2 | FTMO LIVE! NO.1 (fanclub mail-order only, soundchecks & interviews)...........................£30 |

PROMOS : PROMO ONLY SINGLES
68	Pye 7N 17449	Pictures Of Matchstick Men/Gentleman Joe's Sidewalk Café (75c Minimum) ('A' label)..£60
68	Pye 7N 17497	Black Veils Of Melancholy/To Be Free ('A' label) £70
68	Pye 7N 17581	Ice In The Sun/When My Mind Is Not Live ('A' label)..£60
68	Pye 7N 17650	Technicolor Dreams/Paradise Flat('A' label)...£700
69	Pye 7N 17665	Make Me Stay A Bit Longer/Aunt Nellie ('A' label)...£70
69	Pye 7N 17728	Are You Growing Tired Of My Love/So Ends Another Life ('A' label) £70
69	Pye 7N 17825	The Price Of Love/Little Miss Nothing ('A' label) £70
70	Pye 7N 17907	Down The Dustpipe/Face Without A Soul ('A' label) £60
70	Pye 7N 17998	In My Chair/Gerdundula ('A' label) £60
71	Pye 7N 45077	Tune To The Music/Good Thinking ('A' label) £60
72	Phonogram DJ 005	Roadhouse Blues/BLACK SABBATH: Children Of The Grave (100 copies only) £500
72	Vertigo 6059 071	Paper Plane/Softer Ride ('A' label) £45
73	Pye 7N 45229	Mean Girl/Everything ('A' label)..£50
73	Pye 7N 45253	Gerdundula/Lakky Lady ('A' label) £40
75	Lyntone LYN 3154	Down Down (Smiths Crisps 1-sided gold flexidisc test pressing, plays Bye Bye Baby by Bay City Rollers)...£25
75	Lyntone LYN 3155	Break The Rules (Smiths Crisps 1-sided gold flexidisc test pressing, plays Bye Bye Baby by Bay City Rollers)...£25
79	Pye 7P 103	In My Chair/Gerdundula ('A' label) £20
86	Vertigo QUODJ 2112	Dreamin' (Wet Mix)/Long-Legged Girls/The Quo Xmas Cake Mix (12") £15
88	Vertigo QUOLP 99	Ain't Complaining (12" promo, 1-sided)..£30
90	Vertigo (no cat. no.)	The Power Of Rock (Album Version)/(Single Edit)/Perfect Remedy (12" white label) £100
91	Vertigo QUO DJ 30	Can't Give You More/Dead In The Water (swirl label) £20

PROMOS : PROMO ONLY ALBUMS & ALBUM SAMPLERS
82	Phonogram PRO BX 1	FROM THE MAKERS OF... (3-LP, 20 copies in bronze tin for in-house use).......................£300
86	Vertigo MADDOX 18	IN THE ARMY NOW (LP, 4-track sampler, includes unreleased version of Dreamin') £50
88	Vertigo QUOLP 99	AIN'T COMPLAINING (LP, 4-track one-sided sampler)...£25
88	Vertigo	AIN'T COMPLAINING (box set containing LP sampler [QUOLP 99], cassette, 1-track video, photo & press sheet)..£70
88	Music & Media MM 1221	INTERVIEW (LP, uncut test pressing for unreleased saw-shaped picture disc) £50
89	Vertigo 842 077-9	LITTLE DREAMER (CD, card p/s, 4-track sampler for PERFECT REMEDY album)................£40
90	Phonogram (no cat. no.)	ROCKING ALL OVER THE YEARS SNIPPETS (cassette, titles inlay)................................£20
90	Vertigo 846 797-2	ROCKING ALL OVER THE YEARS (CD, in Butlin's party pack containing Kiss Me Quo baseball cap, stick of Status Quo rock, and selection of party poppers, streamers, whistle, trumpet, silver Quo balloons & pack of condoms, all with "Anniversary Waltz" stickers £75
02	Sanctuary CMRCD 490	SWEDISH RADIO SESSIONS (CD-R, titles insert, commercial release cancelled) £50

(see also Spectres, Traffic Jam, Rossi & Frost, Andy Bown,, Rockers, John Du Cann,, Stretch)

STAVERTON BRIDGE
| 76 | Saydisc SDL 266 | STAVERTON BRIDGE (LP, with lyrics)..£30 |

STEAK CATS
| 96 | April 10 Records TEN 4 | Last Night In A Porn Stars Bed I Became A Man/From Behind (12" 200 only).........£15 |
| 97 | April 10 LP1 | THE RISE OF ROSCOE (LP)..£15 |

STEAMHAMMER
69	CBS 4141	Junior's Wailing/Windmill...£25
69	CBS 4496	Autumn Song/Blues For Passing People £18
68	CBS (S) 63611	STEAMHAMMER (LP)...£100
70	CBS (S) 63694	STEAMHAMMER MK. II (LP) £100
70	B&C CAS 1024	MOUNTAINS (LP, stickered gatefold sleeve) £50
70	Reflection REFL 1	STEAMHAMMER (LP, reissue, different sleeve) £50
71	Reflection REFL 12	STEAMHAMMER MK. II (LP, reissue) £40

(see also Armageddon, Rod Stewart)

STEEL AN' SKIN
| 79 | Steel An Skin SS01 | Reggae Is Here Again/Fire In Soweto/Afro Punk Reggae (Dub) (12", p/s) ....£70 |
| 85 | Cougar (no cat. no.) | STEEL AN' SKIN (LP) ....£20 |

GARY STEEL SOUND
| 72 | Zel-La JHEPM 131 | Go Go Girl/I've Got A Feeling Coming On..£25 |

JAN STEELE & JOHN CAGE
| 76 | Obscure OBS 5 | VOICES AND INSTRUMENTS (LP) ....£20 |

TOMMY STEELE (& THE STEELMEN)
56	Decca F 10795	Rock With The Caveman/Rock Around The Town (with The Steelmen) £25
56	Decca F 10795	Rock With The Caveman/Rock Around The Town (with The Steelmen) (78) £15
56	Decca F 10808	Doomsday Rock/Elevator Rock £30
56	Decca F 10819	Singing The Blues/Rebel Rock (with The Steelmen) £20
57	Decca LF 1287	THE TOMMY STEELE STAGE SHOW (10")...£15
57	Decca LF 1288	THE TOMMY STEELE STORY (10")...£15

STEELEYE SPAN
70	RCA SF 8113	HARK! THE VILLAGE WAIT (LP, with lyric insert)..£40
71	B&C CAS 1029	PLEASE TO SEE THE KING (LP, in 'hessian' textured sleeve, insert)..........................£35
71	Pegasus PEG 9	TEN MAN MOP, OR MR. RESERVOIR BUTLER RIDES AGAIN (LP, gatefold sleeve, initially £50

MINT VALUE £

with 8-page booklet)...
72   Chrysalis CHR 1008   **BELOW THE SALT** (LP, gatefold, green label) **£18**
(see also Tim Hart & , Gay & Terry Woods, Ashley Hutchings, Fairport Convention, Martin Carthy, Bob Johnson & Pete Knight)

STEEL MILL
71   Penny Farthing PEN 770   **Green Eyed God/Zang Will**...**£15**
72   Penny Farthing PEN 783   **Get On The Line/Summer's Child**...**£20**
75   Penny Farthing PEN 894   **Green Eyed God/Zang Will** (reissue)..**£15**
75   Penny Farthing PELS 549   **GREEN EYED GOD** (LP, reissue, green sleeve. Original released in Germany in 1972 in black sleeve)..**£750**
11   Rise Above Relics RARLP 008   **JEWELS OF THE FOREST** (2-LP, 3 x 7" with booklet, 280 copies)..........................**£50**
11   Rise Above Relics RARLP 008   **JEWELS OF THE FOREST** (2-LP, green, clear or blue vinyl, booklet - 300 copies of each)....**£30**
11   Rise Above Relics RARLP 008   **JEWELS OF THE FOREST** (2-LP, with booklet)...**£20**

STEEL PULSE
76   Concrete Jungle CJ 602   **Kibudu Mansatta Abuku/Version** **£70**
80   PSLP 321   **STEEL PULSE DUB** (12", white labels only)...**£50**

STEELY DAN
74   Probe PRO 622   **Rikki Don't Lose That Number/Any Major Dude Will Tell You** (gatefold sleeve, 1974 'Spacemen' tour logo) **£50**
82   MCA MCAT 786   **FM EP** **£25**
85   MCA MCAT 852   **Reelin' In The Years/Rikki Don't Lose That Number/Do It Again/Haitian Divorce** (12", p/s)...**£20**
73   Probe SPB 1062   **CAN'T BUY A THRILL** (LP, original, with 'pink' label) **£25**
77   ABC ABCL5225   **AJA** (LP, gatefold, inner) **£15**
82   MCA MCF 3165   **GOLD** (LP, with free EP [MSAMT 21])...**£20**
03   Reprise 9362 48435 1   **EVERYTHING MUST GO** (LP) **£100**
(see also Donald Fagen)

WOUT STEENHUIS
70   Stereo2Stereo TWO 283   **BIRD IN THE PARK** (LP, features cover of Hum Dono) **£25**

STEEPLECHASE
71   Polydor 2489 001   **LADY BRIGHT** (LP) **£15**
(see also Dean Parrish)

STEERPIKE
68   (no label credit) ADM 417   **STEERPIKE** (LP, private pressing) **£550**

BILL STEGMEYER & HIS ORCHESTRA
54   London HL 8078   **On The Waterfront** (From The Film)/**We Just Couldn't Say Good-Bye** **£20**

LOU STEIN
57   London HLZ 8419   **Almost Paradise/Soft Sands**..**£20**

STEINWAYS
85   Kent TOWN 106   **You've Been Leading Me On/JOHNNY CASWELL: You Don't Love Me No More**...............**£20**

MIKE STEIPHENSON
73   Pye 7N 25577   **Rainbows/Dreams**...**£15**

STENCH
82   Sticky PEEL OFF 5   **MORAL DEBAUCHERY: Raspberry Cripple/Nonces/Adoption**..**£15**

MALCOLM STENT
70s   Starline SWL 2002   **GO AND PLAY UP YOUR OWN END** (LP) **£15**

STEPASIDE
80   Gale GALELP 01   **SIT DOWN AND RELAPSE** (LP)...**£20**

LEIGH STEPHENS
69   Philips SBL 7897   **RED WEATHER** (LP) **£70**
71   Charisma CAS 1040   **AND A CAST OF THOUSANDS** (LP) **£40**
(see also Blue Cheer)

STEPPENWOLF
68   RCA RCA 1679   **Sookie Sookie/Take What You Need**...**£15**
68   RCA RCA 1735   **Born To Be Wild/Everybody's Next One**..**£15**
68   Stateside-Dunhill SS 8003   **Magic Carpet Ride/Sookie Sookie**..**£15**
68   RCA RD/SF 7974   **STEPPENWOLF** (LP, 1st pressing, mono, band name in blue) **£150**
68   RCA RD/SF 7974   **STEPPENWOLF** (LP, repressing, stereo) **£80**
68   Stateside SL 5003   **STEPPENWOLF THE SECOND** (LP, mono) **£70**
69   Stateside (S)SL 5003   **STEPPENWOLF THE SECOND** (LP, stereo) **£40**
69   Stateside SL 5011   **AT YOUR BIRTHDAY PARTY** (LP, mono) **£40**
69   Stateside(S)SL 5011   **AT YOUR BIRTHDAY PARTY** (LP, stereo) **£35**
69   Stateside (S)SL 5015   **EARLY STEPPENWOLF** (LP) **£15**
69   Stateside (S)SL 10276   **CANDY** (LP, soundtrack, 2 tracks by Steppenwolf, 1 track by Byrds) **£30**
70   Stateside-Dunhill SSL 5020   **STEPPENWOLF** (reissue) **£15**
70   Stateside-Dunhill SSL 5021   **MONSTER** (LP, gatefold sleeve) **£18**
7)   Stateside-Dunhill SSL 5029   **STEPPENWOLF 'LIVE'** (LP, gatefold sleeve) **£20**
70   Probe SPBA 6254   **STEPPENWOLF 7** (LP) **£15**
71   Probe SPBA 6260   **FOR LADIES ONLY** (LP) **£15**
(see also John Kay)

STEPPING TALK
79   Eustone/Rough Trade TO1   **Alice In Sunderland/Health And Safety/Common Problems/John Turtles** (p/s, with stamped inner)..**£15**

STEREOLAB
91   Duophonic DS 45-01   **SUPER 45: The Light That Will Cease To Fail/Au Grand Jour/Brittle/Au Grand Jour!** (10" EP, with insert, mail-order, sold at gigs and some record shops 40 with hand-   **£175**

		painted p/s, in poly bag)	
91	Duophonic DS 45-01	**SUPER 45: The Light That Will Cease To Fail/Au Grand Jour/Brittle/Au Grand Jour!** (10" EP, with insert, mail-order, sold at gigs and some record shops)	£100
91	Duophonic DS 45-01	**SUPER 45: The Light That Will Cease To Fail/Au Grand Jour/Brittle/Au Grand Jour!** (25 test pressings, 10" cut into 12" discs)	£175
91	Duophonic DS 45-02	**STUNNING DEBUT ALBUM: Doubt/Clanger** (20 black test pressings withdrawn due to pressing fault/warping, different cut of both tracks)	£100
91	Duophonic DS 45-02	**STUNNING DEBUT ALBUM: Doubt/Clanger** (p/s, mail-order, sold at gigs and some Record shops gatefold p/s with insert in poly bag; mulit coloured vinyl, unknown quantity but probably over 200)	£150
91	Duophonic DS 45-02	**STUNNING DEBUT ALBUM: Doubt/Clanger** (p/s, mail-order, sold at gigs and some record Shops, gatefold p/s with insert in poly bag; 985 copies on clear vinyl)	£60
92	Duophonic DS 45-04	**Harmonium/Farfisa** (p/s, mail-order, gigs and some record shops 1,306 copies on transparent amber vinyl, with insert & fluorescent sticker)	£35
93	Duophonic DS45-05/06	**SHIMMIES IN SUPER 8** (2 x 7", green and white vinyl, foldout sleeve with inserts)	£25
92	Too Pure PURE 14	**Low Fi/Varoom!/Laissez-Faire/Elektro** (He Held The World In His Iron Grip) (10", p/s, clear vinyl, 2,000 only, numbered)	£25
93	Duophonic D-UHF-D 01	**Jenny Ondioline** (Part 1)/**Golden Ball** (Studio) (10", factory custom pressings; 3 on 'thick' clear vinyl, later endorsed & signed by band; no p/s)	£220
93	Duophonic D-UHF-D 01	**Jenny Ondioline** (Part 1)/**Golden Ball** (Studio) (10", factory custom pressings; 5 copies on multicoloured vinyl; 25 on 'thin' clear vinyl, no p/s)	£80
93	Clawfist 20	**CRUMB DUCK** (10" EP, shared with Nurse With Wound; 37 with hand-drawn p/s (Gain/Sadier only)	£120
93	Clawfist 20	**CRUMB DUCK** (10" EP, shared with Nurse With Wound; 1,450 regular p/s)	£20
93	Duophonic D-UHF-D 03	**French Disko/Jenny Ondioline** ('teaser' single, p/s, 1,500 only, with hand printed sleeves)	£50
93	Duophonic D-UHF-D 03	**French Disko/Jenny Ondioline** ('teaser' single, p/s, 1,500 only, regular printed sleeves)	£15
94	Silvertone	**Tone Burst** (demo)/**Tempter** (demo)/**SPECTRUM: Soul Kiss Glide Divine** (unreleased, with colour photocopied wraparound p/s, 25 test pressings only)	£150
94	Duophonic D-UHF-07	**Wow And Flutter/Heavy Denim** (3,000 only with hand-painted p/s)	£18
95	Wurlitzer Jukebox WJ 3	**The Eclipse/Yes Sir! I Can Moogie/CAT'S MIAOW: Shoot The Moon** (flexidisc, 1,000 only with insert and info sheet)	£18
95	Independent Project IP 060	**Blue Milk/One Thousand Miles An Hour/Aluminum Tune** (set of 4 singles all With same tracks in different coloured vinyl and different sets of gatefold sleeve. American Import. Singles worth £10 each)	£50
96	Duophonic D-UHF-D 10	**Cybele's Reverie/Les Yper Yper Sound/Brigitte/Young Lungs**(25 black vinyl test pressing and 102 cut into 12" disc)	£25
96	Lissy's LISS 15	**You Used To Call Me Sadness/FUXA: Skyhigh** (p/s, 400 on white vinyl)	£20
96	Duophonic D-UHF-D 12	**Speedy Car/TORTOISE: Yaus** (orange vinyl export issue, p/s, 3,000 only)	£15
97	Duophonic Super 45s DS 3311	**Simple Headphone Mind/NURSE WITH WOUND: Trippin' With The Birds** (12", 1,000 copies on yellow vinyl, in sealed foil sleeve)	£20
97	Duophonic Super 45s CD 3311	**Simple Headphone Mind/NURSE WITH WOUND: Trippin' With The Birds** (CD, sealed foil sleeve, 1,000 only)	£30
04	Duophonic D-UHF-D 30S	**Rose, My Pocket Brain!/Banana Monster Ne Repond Plus/University Microfilms International** (p/s, tour single, 500 only)	£15
92	Too Pure PURELP 11	**PENG!** (LP, inner sleeve, insert)	£20
93	Duophonic D-UHF-D 02	**TRANSIENT RANDOM NOISE-BURSTS WITH ANNOUNCEMENTS** (2-LP, with inner sleeves, poor playing-quality gold vinyl, with stickered sleeve, 1,500 only, numbered)	£70
93	Duophonic D-UHF-D 02	**TRANSIENT RANDOM NOISE-BURSTS WITH ANNOUNCEMENTS** (2-LP, inners, black vinyl)	£25
94	Duophonic D-UHF-D 05	**MARS AUDIAC QUINTET** (2-LP, without single)	£30
95	Duophonic D-UHF-D 05X	**MARS AUDIAC QUINTET** (2-LP, gatefold sleeve, 1st 1,000 copies with bonus coloured vinyl single "Klang Tone"/"Ulan Bator" [D-UHF-06])	£55
95	Duophonic D-UHF-D 08	**MUSIC FOR THE AMORPHOUS BODY STUDY CENTRE** (40 black vinyl test pressings 10" sides cut into 12" discs)	£80
95	Duophonic D-UHF-D 08	**MUSIC FOR THE AMORPHOUS BODY STUDY CENTRE** (10" LP, 3,000 only, insert)	£20
95	Duophonic D-UHF-CD 08	**MUSIC FOR THE AMORPHOUS BODY STUDY CENTRE** (CD, first issue with white cover & "1st edition" printed on disc available at Charles Long art exhibition; reissue has yellow sleeve)	£40
95	Duophonic D-UHF LP 09	**REFRIED ECTOPLASM - SWITCHED ON VOL 2 LP,** orange vinyl, card insert)	£30
96	United Dairies UD 059	**CRUMB DUCK** (LP, shared with Nurse With Wound (2 extra tracks, reissue of Clawfist EP, 50 copies on pink vinyl)	£70
96	United Dairies UD 059	**CRUMB DUCK** (LP, shared with Nurse With Wound (2 extra tracks, reissue of Clawfist EP, 500 on fluorescent green vinyl)	£40
96	Duophonic UHF D-UHF-D11	**EMPEROR TOMATO KETCHUP** (2-LP, yellow glitter vinyl, gatefold sleeve)	£80
96	Duophonic DUHFD11	**EMPEROR TOMATO KETCHUP** (2-LP, black vinyl)	£50
97	Duophonic D-UHF-D 17	**DOTS & LOOPS** (2-LP, one green, one white vinyl)	£50
98	Drag City CD 159	**ALUMINIUM TUNES - SWITCHED ON VOL. 3** (3 x LP)	£40
99	Duophonic D-UHF-D 23	**COBRA & PHASES GROUP PLAY VOLTAGE IN THE MILKY NIGHT** (2-LP)	£40
00	Duophonic D-UHF-D 25	**THE FIRST OF THE MICROBE HUNTERS** (2-LP)	£35
01	Duophonic D-UHF-D 27	**SOUND-DUST** (2-LP, hand-numbered, screenprinted heavy card sleeve, inners, 1200 only)	£50
01	Duophonic D-UHF-D 27	**SOUND-DUST** (2-LP, inners, 1800 only)	£40
04	Duophonic D-UHF-D 29	**MARGERINE ECLIPSE** (2-LP, 3500 only)	£35
06	(No Cat. No.)	**FAB FOUR SUTURE** (LP as 6 x 7" hand-stamped box)	£20
06	Duophonic D-UHF-D 31	**SERENE VELOCITY: A STEREOLAB ANTHOLOGY** (2-LP, numbered sticker on sleeve, inners)	£25
08	4AD CAD 2815	**CHEMICAL CHORDS** (2-LP)	£25
10	Duophonic D-UHF D32	**NOT MUSIC** (LP, clear vinyl)	£18

(see also McCarthy, Spectrum, Mouse On Mars, Cavern Of Anti Matter)

STEREO MC'S

89	4th & Broadway BRLP 532	**33 45 78** (LP)	£15
90	4th & Broadway 211 094	**SUPERNATURAL** (LP)	£15
92	4th & Broadway 512 743 1	**CONNECTED** (LP)	£20
01	Island ILPST 8106	**DEEP DOWN AND DIRTY** (3-LP)	£50

STEREOPHONICS

96	V2 SPH 1	Looks Like Chaplin/More Life In A Tramp's Vest (p/s, 500 only)	£40
96	V2 SPHD 1	Looks Like Chaplin/More Life In A Tramp's Vest/Raymond's Shops (CD)	£30
99	V2 no catalogue number	PERFORMANCE AND COCKTAILS (7 x 10" box set, with booklet and CD, promo mail order only)	£30
97	V2 VVR 1000 431	WORD GETS AROUND (LP, gatefold sleeve)	£60
97	V2 VVR 1000 431	WORD GETS AROUND (LP, with bonus 12")	£65
99	V2 VVR1004499	PERFORMANCE AND COCKTAILS (LP, gatefold)	£50
01	V2 VVR1015831	JUST ENOUGH EDUCATION TO PERFORM (2-LP, gatefold)	£40
03	V2 VVR 1021901	YOU GOTTA GO THERE TO COME BACK (2-LP)	£20
05	V2 VVR 1031051	LANGUAGE. SEX. VIOLENCE. OTHER? (LP)	£40
06	V2 VVR 1038091	LIVE FROM DAKOTA (2-LP)	£40
07	V2 VVR 1048561	PULL THE PIN (LP)	£40

STEREOS

61	MGM MGM 1143	I Really Love You/Please Come Back To Me	£50
61	MGM MGM 1149	The Big Knock/Sweet Water	£30

STEREOTYPES (1)

79	Hinterland/SRT no cat. no.	THE STEREOTYPES EP (no p/s)	£800
13	Hinterland (No Cat. No.)	THE STEREOTYPES EP (reissue, no p/s, signed insert, 350 only)	£15

FITZROY STERLING

68	Gas GAS 102	Got To Play It Cool/Jezebel	£20
70	Bullet BU 422	That's My Life/Queen Of Hearts	£15
70	Bullet BU 438	Freedom Street/FITZROY ALL STARS: Freedom Street Version	£15

LESTER STERLING (& HIS GROUP)

63	Island WI 121	Clean The City/Long Walk Home (B-side actually by Charmers)	£20
63	R&B JB 111	Air Raid Shelter/ROY & ANNETTE: I Mean It	£25
63	R&B JB 115	Gravy Cool/WINSTON & BIBBY: Lover Lover Man	£50
64	R&B JB 143	Peace And Love/HORACE SEATON: Hold On	£40
64	R&B JB 150	Hot Cargo/MAYTALS: Marching On	£45
64	R&B JB 155	Baskin' Hop (as Lester Sterling & His Group)/MAYTALS: Shining Light	£25
64	R&B JB 172	Indian Summer (as Lester Sterling & His Group)/STRANGER & PATSY: I'll Forgive You	£35
66	Doctor Bird DB 1057	Inez (with Tommy McCook & Supersonics)/GLORIA CRAWFORD: Sad Movies	£40
67	Doctor Bird DB 1107	Soul Voyage/ALVA LEWIS: Revelation	£60
67	Collins Downbeat CR 001	Sir Collins Special/Lester Sterling '67	£60
68	Coxsone CS 7080	Africkaan Beat/PARAGONS: My Satisfaction	£150
68	Blue Cat BS 116	Zigaloo/Wiser Than Solomon	£150
68	Unity UN 502	Bangarang (with Stranger Cole)/STRANGER COLE: If We Should Ever Meet	£25
69	Unity UN 505	Reggie On Broadway (this is what it states on label)/CLIQUE: Love Can Be Wonderful	£25
69	Unity UN 509	Spoogy/TOMMY McCOOK: Monkey Fiddle	£20
69	Unity UN 512	Regina/Bright As A Rose	£15
69	Unity UN 517	1,000 Tons Of Megaton/KING CANNON: Five Card Stud (white labels only)	£50
69	Unity UN 518	Man About Town/Man At The Door (white labels only)	£40
69	Unity UN 531	Lonesome Feeling/Bright As A Rose	£25
69	Big Shot BI 507	Forest Gate Rock/RAVING RAVERS: Rock Rock And Cry	£45
69	Gas GAS 103	Reggae In The Wind/SOUL SET: Try Me One More Time (B-side actually by Stranger & Gladdy)	£40
70	Unity UN 562	Slip Up/DAVE BARKER: On Broadway	£35
71	Nu Beat NB 095	Iron Side Part 1/COXSON'S ALL STARS: Iron Side Part 2	£25
71	Ocean CNBU 96	War Is Not The Answer Part 2/Iron Side Part 2 (promo only)	£15
72	Ashanti ASH 410	War Is Not The Answer/COXSON'S ALL STARS: Version	£18
69	Pama SECO 15	BANGARANG (LP)	£100

(see also Mister Versatile, Bobby Aitken, Eric Morris, Sir Collins Band, Slickers, Uniques)

STEROID KIDDIES

79	Steroid/Grundinga SK 001	THE KIDDIES EP	£55

STEROID MAXIMUS

90s	Big Cat ABB 28	QUILOMBO (LP)	£20

STEVE 'N' BONNIE

72	Young Blood SSYB 16	BRIEF ENCOUNTER (LP)	£18

STEVE & STEVIE

68	Toast TT510	Merry-Go-Round/Remains To Be Seen	£15
68	Toast TLP 2	STEVE AND STEVIE (LP)	£30

(see also Tin Tin, Fut)

APRIL STEVENS

67	MGM MGM 1366	Falling In Love Again/Wanting You	£100
67	MGM MGM 1366	Falling In Love Again/Wanting You (DJ copy)	£200

(see also Nino Tempo & April Stevens)

CAT STEVENS

67	Deram DML/SML 1004	MATTHEW AND SON (LP)	£25
67	Deram DML/SML 1018	NEW MASTERS (LP)	£25
67	Deram	CATS AND DOGS (LP, unreleased, test pressings only)	£30
70	Island ILPS 9118	MONA BONE JAKON (LP, inner, pink label with white 'i' logo)	£120
70	Island ILPS 9135	TEA FOR THE TILLERMAN (LP, gatefold, pink label, with white 'i' logo)	£70
71	Island ILPS 9135	TEA FOR THE TILLERMAN (LP, reissue, pink rim labels)	£20
73	Island ILPS 5924	FOREIGNER (LP, insert)	£15

CONNIE STEVENS
62	Warner Bros WM 4060	CONNIE (LP, mono)	£15
62	Warner Bros WS 8061	CONNIE (LP, stereo)	£25
63	Warner Bros WM/WS 8111	THE HANK WILLIAMS SONG BOOK (LP)	£15

(see also Edward Byrnes)

JOHN STEVENS AWAY
76	Vertigo 6360 131	JOHN STEVEN'S AWAY (LP)	£20
76	Vertigo 6360 135	SOMERWHERE IN BETWEEN (LP)	£20
78	Spotlite SPJ 508	NO FEAR! (LP)	£30
78	Spotlite SPJ 513	APPLICATION INTERACTION AND... (LP)	£30
82	Affinity AFF 101	FREEBOP (LP)	£20
84	Affinity AYF 130	THE LIFE OF RILEY (LP, as John Steven's Solkus)	£30

JOHNNY STEVENS & BLUE BEATS
64	Blue Beat BB 229	Shame/Ball And Chain	£20

MEIC STEVENS
65	Decca F 12174	Did I Dream/I Saw A Field (as Mike Stevens)	£40
70	Warner Bros WB 8007	Ballad Of Old Joe Blind/Blue Sleep	£15
70	Wren WSP 2005	Nid Oes Un Gwydr Ffenestr/Rhywbeth Gwell I Ddod	£40
78	YM SP 01	DIC PENDERYN EP (THEATR YR YMYLON Theatrical soundtrack)	£50
68	Wren WRE 1045	MIKE STEVENS (EP, p/s)	£50
68	Wren WRE 1053	RHIF 2 (EP, p/s)	£50
69	Wren WRE 1073	MWG (EP, p/s)	£50
70	Newyddion Da ND1	MEIC STEVENS (EP, p/s)	£100
70	Sain SAIN 004	Y BRAWN HOUDINI (EP, p/s)	£50
71	Wren WRE 1107	BYW YN Y WLAD (EP, p/s)	£50
71	Sain SAIN 13	DIONCH YN Y FAWR (EP, p/s)	£50
70	Warner Brothers WS 3005	OUTLANDER (LP, with insert)	£300
72	Wren WRL 536	GWYMON (LP)	£300
77	Sain SAIN 1065	GOG (LP)	£120
79	Tic Toc no cat. no.	CANAEON CYNNAR (LP, private pressing)	£220
82	Sain SAIN 1239	NOS DU NOS DA (LP)	£50
83	Sain SAIN 1312	LAPIS LAZULI (LP, lyric insert)	£50
86	Timeless TIME 705	TIMELESS (LP, reissue, 500 only)	£20

(see also Gary Farr)

MICK STEVENS
71	Deroy SC 024557351	SEE THE MORNING (LP, private pressing, handmade sleeve)	£2000
75	Deroy DER 1299	NO SAVAGE WORD (LP, private pressing, DER 1299 on run-out)	£3000
77	Spaceward Studios SRS 20	THE RIVER (LP, private pressing, lyric insert)	£100
79	Spaceward SRS 030	THE ENGLISHMAN (LP, lyric insert)	£80

MIKE STEVENS
66	Pye 7N 17243	Cathy's Clown/Go-Go Train	£60

(see also Shevells)

RICKY STEVENS
62	Columbia SEG 8172	I CRIED FOR YOU (EP)	£40

SHAKIN' STEVENS (& THE SUNSETS)
81	Magnum Force MFLP-004	AT THE ROCKHOUSE	£20
16	HEC Limited HEC102LP	ECHOES OF OUR TIMES (500 only red vinyl, lyric inner)	£50
70	Parlophone R 5860	Spirit Of Woodstock/Down On The Farm	£60
72	Polydor 2058 213	Sweet Little Rock'n'Roller/White Lightning	£50
74	Emerald MD 1176	Honey Honey/Holey Moley 2001	£25
79	Epic SEPC 7235	Spooky/I Don't Want No Other Baby	£20
80	Epic SEPC 8573	Hey Mae/I Guess I Was A Fool (in p/s)	£50
90	Epic SHAKY P13	Pink Champagne/Rockin' The Night Away (picture disc)	£40
70	Parlophone PCS 7112	A LEGEND (LP)	£80
71	CBS 52901	I'M NO J.D. (LP)	£40
72	Contour 2870 152	ROCKIN' AND SHAKIN' (LP)	£15
73	Emerald GES 1121	SHAKIN' STEVENS AND THE SUNSETS (LP)	£15
78	Track 2406 011	SHAKIN' STEVENS (LP, with insert)	£15
80	Epic EPC 84547	MARIE MARIE (LP, withdrawn)	£18

RICHARD STEVENSEN
70	Pye NSPL 18358	GATES OF ME (LP, textured sleeve)	£25

MICKEY STEVENSON
72	Ember NR 5063	HERE I AM (LP)	£20

AL STEWART
66	Decca F 12467	The Elf/Turn To Earth	£70
70	CBS 5351	The News From Spain/Elvaston Place	£15
67	CBS (S)BPG 63087	BEDSITTER IMAGES (LP)	£125
69	CBS (S) 63460	LOVE CHRONICLES (LP, gatefold sleeve)	£25
70	CBS 63848	ZERO SHE FLIES (LP, gatefold sleeve)	£22
70	CBS 64023	FIRST ALBUM (BEDSITTER IMAGES) (LP, remixed reissue, different track listing)	£25
72	CBS 64730	ORANGE (LP)	£20

(see also Jimmy Page)

BILLY STEWART
62	Pye International 7N 25164	Reap What You Sow/Fat Boy	£15
63	Pye International 7N 25222	Strange Feeling/Sugar And Spice	£15

MINT VALUE £

66	Chess CRS 8040	Summertime/To Love To Love	£15
69	Chess CRS 8092	Summertime/I Do Love You	£15
65	Chess CRE 6010	IN CROWD (EP, with Ramsey Lewis Trio, et al)	£30
67	Chess CRE 6024	I DO LOVE YOU (EP)	£30
66	Chess CRL 4523	UNBELIEVABLE (LP)	£30

BRIDIE STEWART

75	Affection AFF 1	Can't Let You Go/(Version)	£75
75	Affection AFF 003	Sugar Me Baby/Didn't Mean To Hurt You Baby	£80
82	SS SSMD 12	Keep An Eye On You/Aquastrumental (12")	£30

DELANO STEWART

68	Doctor Bird DB 1138	That's Life/Tell Me Baby	£50
68	High Note HS 004	Let's Have Some Fun/Dance With Me	£30
69	High Note HS 014	Rocking Sensation/GAYSTERS: One Look	£350
70	High Note HS 027	Got To Come Back/Don't Believe In Him	£20
70	High Hote HS 039	Wherever I Lay My Hat/Don't Believe Him (B-side actually by Gladstone Anderson & Gaytones)	£20
70	High Note HS 041	Stay A Little Bit Longer/Stay A Little Bit Longer (Version II) (B-side actually by Gladstone Anderson & Gaytones)	£20
70	Trojan TBL 138	STAY A LITTLE BIT LONGER (LP)	£75

(see also Winston Stewart, Gaylads, Patsy Todd)

(DAVE) STEWART & HARRISON

70	Multicord MULT SH 1	GIRL (EP)	£15

(see also Longdancer, Eurythmics)

PAUL STEWART (MOVEMENT)

67	Decca F12577	Saturday Mornin Man/Too Too Good (in export p/s)	£50
67	Decca F 12577	Saturday Morning Man/Too Too Good (as Paul Stewart Movement)	£15

(see also Hamilton & [Hamilton] Movement)

REX STEWART'S LONDON FIVE

55	Tempo EXA 8	REX STEWART'S LONDON FIVE (EP)	£15

ROD STEWART

64	Decca F 11996	Good Morning Little Schoolgirl/I'm Gonna Move To The Outskirts Of Town	£180
65	Columbia DB 7766	The Day Will Come/Why Does It Go On?	£150
66	Columbia DB 7892	Shake/I Just Got Some	£200
68	Immediate IM 060	Little Miss Understood/So Much To Say	£100
70	Vertigo 6086 002	It's All Over Now/Jo's Lament	£15
72	Phonogram DJ004	Twisting the Night Away (EP 1-track on 4 track promo 7" also featuring Chuck Berry, Diane Davidson and the Stylistics)	£20
77	Riva RIVA 1	You're Insane/You're Insane (DJ copy, 500 only)	£25
78	Riva RIVA 9	Sailing/Stone Cold Sober(HMS Ark Royal Commemorative issue, blue vinyl, p/s)	£150
70	Vertigo VO 4	AN OLD RAINCOAT WON'T EVER LET YOU DOWN (gatefold sleeve, large swirl label, original pressing with 'Philips' credit on label)	£125
70	Vertigo VO 4	AN OLD RAINCOAT WON'T EVER LET YOU DOWN (gatefold sleeve, 2nd pressing, large swirl label, later pressing without 'Philips' credit on label)	£45
70	Vertigo 6360 500	GASOLINE ALLEY (LP, 1st pressing, gatefold sleeve, large swirl label)	£100
71	Vertigo 6360 500	GASOLINE ALLEY (LP, 2nd pressing, gatefold sleeve, small swirl label)	£45
71	Mercury 6338 063	EVERY PICTURE TELLS A STORY (black label, with poster)	£30
71	Vertigo VO 4	AN OLD RAINCOAT WON'T EVER LET YOU DOWN (gatefold sleeve, 3rd pressing, with small 'swirl' and 'Vertigo' above centre hole, title all on one line)	£25
72	Vertigo VO 4	AN OLD RAINCOAT WON'T EVER LET YOU DOWN (gatefold sleeve, 4th pressing, small 'swirl' and 'Vertigo' above centre hole but title on two lines)	£25

(see also Jeff Beck, Shotgun Express, Faces, Long John Baldry, Steamhammer)

ROMAN STEWART

72	Songbird SB 1075	Changing Times (with Dave)/CRYSTALITES: Changing Times Version	£18
73	Downtown DT 518	Try Me/BIG YOUTH: Rhythm Style	£15
75	Morpheus MOR 1	In The Chapel/E MCLEAN: You Pick Me Up	£50
79	GGS 049	Don't Get Jumpy/GG ALL STARS: Dub Cut (12")	£25
78	Pirate PIR 002	Herbalist/Version (12", various coloured vinyl)	£35
78	Strong Like Sampson SLSD 06	Mr. Officer/Ain't Too Proud To Beg (12")	£40
79	Thompson & Koots TK002	Rice & Peas/Breaking Up (12", with Linval Thompson)	£40
80	D-Roy DRDD 25	What You Wanna Do/REVOLUTIONARIES: Rockers Delight (12")	£15

TINGA STEWART

74	Dragon DRA 1025	The Message/Dub	£25
84	Londisc LDLP 003	KEY TO YOUR HEART (LP)	£15

WINSTON STEWART

64	R&B JB 147	But I Do/MAYTALS: Four Seasons	£35
64	Port-O-Jam PJ 4002	All Of My Life/How Many Times	£30
65	Ska Beat JB 225	You Made Me Cry/CHECKMATES: Invisible Ska	£40

(see also Andy & Clyde, Gaylads, Delano Stewart, Winston & Tonettes)

WYNN STEWART

60	London HL 7087	Wishful Thinking/Uncle Tom Got Caught (export issue)	£20

STEWPOT & SAVE THE CHILDREN FUND CHOIR

68	MGM 1448	I Like My Toys/Myrtles Birthday	£20

J.E. STICK & DRUMBAGO

61	Blue Beat BB 64	Boss Gill/COUNT OSSIE : Cassavuba	£20

STICKLEBACKS

87	Dub House KS 1292	All You Get/It's For You	£20

STIFF LITTLE FINGERS

78	Rigid Digits SRD-1	Suspect Device/Wasted Life (hand-made p/s, 500 only, red label with catalogue number on right-hand side)	£200
78	Rigid Digits SRD-1	Suspect Device/Wasted Life (re-pressing, different machine-cut p/s, various colour labels/yellow labels)	£45
78	Rough Trade RT 004	78 R.P.M./Alternative Ulster (p/s, A & B-sides reversed)	£20
78	Rough Trade RT 004	Alternative Ulster/78 R.P.M. (p/s)	£15
79	Rough Trade ROUGH 1	INFLAMMABLE MATERIAL (LP, with inner)	£20
80	Chrysalis CHR 1270	NOBODY'S HEROES (LP, inner)	£18
80	Chrysalis CHR 1300	HANX! (LP)	£20
82	Chrysalis CHR 1400	NOW THEN... (LP, inner and poster)	£18
89	Limited Edition LTD EDT LP 3	LIVE IN SWEDEN (LP)	£15

(see also Billy Karloff & Extremes)

STIFFS

79	Dork UR 1	Standard English/S.C. Rip/Brookside Riot Squad (die-cut sleeve)	£25
79	Dork UR 2	Inside Out/Kids On the Street (die cut sleeve or later Zonophone Z3 p/s)	£20
80	Zonophone Z 14	Volume Control/Nothing To Lose (p/s)	£15

STILETTOS

80	Ariola ARO 200	This Is The Way/Who Can It Be (p/s)	£20

STILL COOL

79	Hit Run HITDD 22	Insane Love/Stereo Version '79 (12")	£25

STILL LIFE (1)

68	Columbia DB 8345	What Did We Miss/My Kingdom Cannot Lose	£100
71	Vertigo 6360 026	STILL LIFE (LP, gatefold sleeve, large swirl label)	£750

(see also Jon, Titus Groan)

STEPHEN STILLS

70	Atlantic 2401 004	STEPHEN STILLS (LP)	£35
71	Atlantic 2401 013	STEPHEN STILLS 2 (LP, gatefold sleeve)	£25
73	Atlantic K 40440	DOWN THE ROAD (LP)	£15
75	CBS 69146	STILLS LP, inner)	£15
08	Rhino 8122799297	JUST ROLL TAPE (LP, 180gm vinyl)	£15

(see also Buffalo Springfield, Al Kooper Mike Bloomfield & Stephen Stills, Crosby Stills Nash & Young, Manassas, Stills-Young Band)

STILLS-YOUNG BAND

76	Reprise K 54081	LONG MAY YOU RUN (LP)	£15

(see also Stephen Stills, Manassas, Neil Young, Buffalo Springfield, Crosby Stills Nash & Young)

STING

85	A&M DREAMP 1	THE DREAM OF THE BLUE TURTLES (LP, picture disc, die-cut sleeve, insert)	£15
93	A&M 540 075-1	TEN SUMMONERS TALES (LP, insert)	£50
94	A&M 540 307-1	FIELDS OF GOLD - THE BEST OF STING 1984 - 1994 (2LP, printed)	£150
96	A&M 540 486-1	MERCURY FALLING (LP, printed inner)	£80
09	Deutsche Grammophon 06025 271 3943	IF ON A WINTER'S NIGHT . . . (2LP, gatefold, printed inners)	£70
10	Deutsche Grammophon 06025 274 5321	SYMPHONICITIES (2LP)	£40
13	Cherrytree/A&M 3744812	THE LAST SHIP (LP, printed inner, 180g)	£20
16	Cherrytree/A&M 00602557117752	57TH AND 9TH (LP, blue vinyl, gatefold, printed inner)	£20
18	Cherrytree/A&M 00602567502890	44/876 (as STING & SHAGGY) (LP, gatefold, printed inner, red vinyl)	£20
19	Cherrytree/A&M 00602577587214	MY SONGS (2LP, gatefold, poster)	£30
19	Cherrytree/A&M 00602508335563	MY SONGS (LIVE) (2LP, printed inners, limited)	£25

(see also Police, Last Exit, [Fast Breeder &] Radio Actors, Newcastle Big Band)

STINGERS

72	Upsetter US 395	Preacher Man/UPSETTERS: Version	£40
72	Explosion EX 2075	Forward Up/UPSETTERS: Forward	£35

STING-RAYS

82	Big Beat SW 82	Dinosaurs/Math Of Trend/Another Cup Of Coffee/You're Gonna Miss Me (white label test pressing, 100 Club gig freebie, 80 only)	£20
87	Kaleidoscope Sound KSLP 1	CRYPTIC AND COFFEE TIME (LP)	£15
87	Big Beat WIK 61	THE ESSENTIAL EARLY STING-RAY RECORDINGS 1982 TO 1985 (LP)	£15
87	Raucous FASTBUCK 1	LIVE & RAW (10")	£15

STINGRAYS (1)

80	Earache SRTS./80/CUS 809	Still In Love WIth You/Wasting Your Time/Couldn't Get It Right/Walking Down London Street (EP)	£25

STINGRAYS (2)

80	Fried Egg EGG 006	Countdown/Exceptions Action	£40
81	Circus CIRC 0003	Never Do/Satellites	£20

STINKY TOYS

77	Polydor 2393 174	STINKY TOYS (LP)	£20

STIR

87	Spoonin SPOON 01	CHEEKY MONKEY (12", EP)	£20

(PETER) LEE STIRLING (& BRUISERS)

67	Decca F 12628	You Don't Live Twice/8.35 On The Dot	£25

(see also Hungry Wolf)

GARY STITES
59	London HLL 8881	Lonely For You/Shine That Ring	£25
59	London HLL 8881	Lonely For You/Shine That Ring (78)	£15
59	London HLL 9003	Starry Eyed/Without Your Love	£20
59	London HLL 9003	Starry Eyed/Without Your Love (78)	£15
60	London HLL 9082	Lawdy, Miss Clawdy/Don't Wanna Say Goodbye	£25

SONNY STITT
53	Esquire 20-013	SONNY STITT-BUD POWELL QUARTET (10" LP)	£20
58	Esquire 32-049	S.P.J. JAZZ (LP, with Bud Powell & J.J. Johnson)	£20
58	Columbia Clef 33CX 10114	NEW YORK JAZZ (LP)	£20
59	Esquire 32-078	STITT'S BITS (LP)	£20
59	HMV CLP 1280	ONLY THE BLUES (LP)	£20
60	HMV CLP 1384	SONNY STITT WITH THE OSCAR PETERSON TRIO (LP)	£20
61	HMV CLP 1420	BLOWS THE BLUES (LP, mono)	£20
61	HMV CSD 1341	BLOWS THE BLUES (LP, stereo)	£20
64	Chess CRL 4503	MY MAIN MAN (LP)	£15
67	Marble Arch MAL 753	SONNY STITT (LP)	£15

(see also J.J. Johnson)

CLIFF ST LEWIS
80	King Cliff KCLP 104	VERSATILITY 7 IN MANY MOODS (LP)	£30

STOCKER, GREENWOOD & FRIENDS
79	Changes CR1400	BILLY + NINE (LP)	£25

(see also Slack Alice)

KARLHEINZ STOCKHAUSEN
65	CBS S72647	MIKROPHONIE I/MIKROPHONIE II (LP)	£20
67	CBS 77209	COMPLETE PIANO MUSIC (2-LP, box set)	£40
67	Vox STABY 615	PROZESSION (LP)	£15
69	Vox VS 3184	STOCKHAUSEN (LP)	£15
70	Deutsche Grammophon 2543003	STIMMUNG (LP)	£20
74	Open University OP 15	TWENTIETH CENTURY MUSIC (LP)	£25
75	Deutsche Grammophon 2530 582	PROZESSION (LP, reissue)	£20

STOCK, HAUSEN & WALKMAN
97	Hot Air SPME 2	Buy Me/Sue Me (200 on light blue vinyl)	£15
99	Hot Air ALERT 01	Alert/Crash (500 only)	£20
91	Hot Air SHWCASS 001	WHAT'S UP? (Cassette in small cereal box, various inserts)	£20
98	Hot Air QRM LP 010	OH MY BAG! (LP, clear vinyl, 300 only)	£15
96	Hot Air QRM LP 101	ORGAN TRANSPLANTS VOL 1. (LP)	£15
00	Hot Air QRM LP 000	ORGAN TRANSPLANTS VOL 2. (LP)	£18

(see also Dummy Run)

STOCKHOLM MONSTERS
81	Factory FAC 41	Fairytales/Death Is Slowly (p/s)	£15
82	Factory FAC 58	Happy Ever After/Soft Babies (p/s)	£15
84	Factory FACT 80	ALMA MATER (LP)	£20

STOCKING TOPS
68	Toast TT 500	You're Never Gonna Get My Lovin'/You Don't Know What Love Is All About	£18
68	CBS 3407	I Don't Ever Wanna Be Kicked By You/The World We Live In Is A Lonely Place	£15

(see also Sue & Sunny, Myrtelles)

STOICS
68	RCA RCA 1745	Earth, Fire, Air And Water/Search Of The Sea	£30

STOKES
65	London HLU 9955	Whipped Cream/Pie Crust	£15

SIMON STOKES & NIGHTHAWKS
70	Elektra EKSN 45082	Voodoo Woman/Can't Stop Now	£20

JOOP STOKKERMANS
71	Gemini GM 2017	THE MAGIC OF THE ARP SYNTHESISER (LP)	£20

STOLEN POWER
81	Hornsey Rising POWER EP 1	The Wheel Is Turning/Family Snapshot/Sick And Tired/Little White Lies (p/s)	£30

STOLEN YOUTH
76	Sunday SUN 1	Wheels In Motion/Kick The Door Down	£30

RHET STOLLER (& HIS ECHOES)
64	Melodisc MEL 1595	Beat That/Treble Gold + One	£15
64	Windsor PS 119	Caravan/Short Cut	£20
64	Windsor PS 130	Ricochet/Knockout	£20
66	Columbia DB 8013	Uncrowned King/Surf Ride (unissued, demos only)	£20
67	Coronet EC 101	THE INCREDIBLE RHET STOLLER (LP)	£25

STOMPERS
62	Fontana H 385	Quarter To Four Stomp (Surf Stompin')/Foolish One	£50

ANGIE STONE
99	Arista 74321 72775	BLACK DIAMOND (2-LP)	£35

CLIFFIE STONE & HIS ORCHESTRA
55	Capitol CL 14330	Barracuda/The Popcorn Song (with Billy Strange & Speedy West)	£100
55	Capitol CL 14330	Barracuda/The Popcorn Song (with Billy Strange & Speedy West) (78)	£20

59	Capitol T 1080	THE PARTY'S ON ME (LP)	£15

(see also Jeanne Gayle, Billy Strange)

DAVID STONE

68	Reynold R 1	Trust Me/Evil Child	£20

DAVINA STONE

82	Ariwa ARI 1004	Love Power/Love On A Two Way Street (12")	£30

GEORGE STONE

65	Stateside SS 479	Hole In The Wall/My Beat	£20

KIRBY STONE QUARTET/FOUR

56	Vogue Coral Q 72129	Honey Hush/Lassus Trombone	£15

MARK STONE

58	London HLR 8543	Ever Since I Met Lucy/The Stroll	£70
58	London HLR 8543	Ever Since I Met Lucy/The Stroll (78)	£30

ROB STONE

68	Delta DT 3941	Sorry Suzanna/Peace Of Mind	£20

SLY (& FAMILY) STONE

68	Columbia DB 8369	Dance To The Music/Let Me Hear It From You	£100
68	Columbia DB 8369	Dance To The Music/Let Me Hear It From You (DJ copy)	£150
68	Direction 8-63412	DANCE TO THE MUSIC (LP)	£25
68	Direction 8-63461	M'LADY (LP)	£20
69	Direction 8-63655	STAND! (LP, CBS sleeve with Direction label)	£20
71	Epic S EPC 64613	THERE'S A RIOT GOING ON (LP, gatefold, yellow labels)	£30
70	Epic 462524	GREATEST HITS (LP)	£15
73	Epic EPC 69030	FRESH (LP, gatefold, inners, yellow labels)	£30
86	Edsel ZED 165	THERE'S A RIOT GOING ON (LP, reissue)	£18
87	Edsel XED 232	FRESH (LP, reissue)	£18
99	Epic SVLP 125	BEST OF SLY AND THE FAMILY STONE (LP)	£20

STONE ANGEL

75	SSLP 04	STONE ANGEL (LP, private pressing, blue/silver label)	£400
94	Acme AC 8008 LP	STONE ANGEL (LP, reissue, 500 only)	£15

(see also Ken Saul)

STONE CROSS

72	Access ACC 3	Light Up The Sun/At My Funeral	£35

STONEFIELD TRAMP

74	Acorn/Tramp CF 247	DREAMING (LP)	£300

(see also Terry Friend, Rob Van Spyk)

STONEGROUND

71	Warner Bros K 46087	STONEGROUND (LP)	£20
71	Warner Bros K 53999	FAMILY ALBUM (LP)	£20

STONEGROUND BAND

70s	Nut	SUNSTRUCK!! (LP, stickered sleeve)	£30

HARRY STONEHAM

76	One UP OU 2127	I FEEL GOOD, I FEEL FUNKY (LP)	£15

HARRY STONEHAM & JOHNNY EYDEN

67	Tepee TPRLP 100	TWO GUYS TO FOLLOW (LP, mono [70s reissues credited soley to Harry Stoneham £15])	£20

STONEHENGE MEN

62	HMV POP 981	Big Feet/Pinto	£30

STONEHOUSE

71	RCA SF 8197	STONEHOUSE CREEK (LP, laminated front sleeve, orange label)	£200

STONEPILLOW

69	Decca PFS 4163	ELEAZAR'S CIRCUS (LP, stereo, laminated front to sleeve)	£15

STONE ROSES

SINGLES

85	Thin Line THIN 001	So Young/Tell Me (12", p/s, 1,200 only; beware of counterfeits!)	£120
87	Black/Revolver 12 REV 36	Sally Cinnamon/Here It Comes/All Across The Sand (12", 'Printed In England' on rear p/s no barcode, "All Across The Sands" listed on label; different mixes of 2 tracks to later reissue - increasingly difficult to find original)	£30
88	Silvertone ORET 1	Elephant Stone (4.48)/Elephant Stone (7" Version) (3.00)/Full Fathom Five/The Hardest Thing In The World (12", p/s, cat. no. in black print on rear of p/s) (unique recording of Full Fathom Five on original pressing)	£25
89	Silvertone ORET 2	Made Of Stone/Going Down/Guernica (12", p/s, catalogue number in black print on rear of p/s)	£18
89	Silvertone OREZ 6	She Bangs The Drums/Mersey Paradise/Standing Here (12", p/s with colour print (I Wanna Be Adored cover), 5,000 only)	£15
89	Silvertone ORET 13	What The World Is Waiting For/Fools Gold 9.23 (12", stickered p/s credits What The World Is Waiting For, with print)	£15
90	Fierce FRIGHT 044	SPIKE ISLAND EP (fan interviews, P.A. announcements & fireworks, with cigarette, badge, bag of grass & banana sweet)	£18
91	Silvertone OREZ 31	I Wanna Be Adored (4.52)/Where Angels Play/Sally Cinnamon (live at the Hacienda) (12", stickered p/s with print)	£18
92	Silvertone ORET 40	I Am The Resurrection (Extended 19:9 Ratio Club Mix)/(Original LP Version)/Fools Gold (Bottom Won Mix) (12", with print)	£20
92	Silvertone SRBX 2	12" SINGLES COLLECTION (10 x 12" singles box set, numbered 1,000 only)	£150
92	Silvertone SRBX 1	COMPACT DISC SINGLES COLLECTION (8 x CD singles box set, 1,000 only)	£35
09	Silvertone 88697574727	THE 7" SINGLES COLLECTION (5 x 7" box set)	£30

MINT VALUE £

ALBUMS : LPS

89	Silvertone ORE LP 502	THE STONE ROSES (LP, original pressing, embossed sleeve with gold lettering)	£40
89	Silvertone ORE LP 502	THE STONE ROSES (LP, original pressing, not embossed gold lettering)	£25
91	Silvertone OREZ LP 502	THE STONE ROSES (2-LP, reissue, numbered gatefold sleeve with silver lettering)	£25
92	Silvertone ORE LP 521	TURNS INTO STONE (LP, original pressing)	£30
94	Geffen GEF 24503	SECOND COMING (2-LP, original pressing, gatefold)	£35
95	Silvertone ORE LP 535	THE COMPLETE STONE ROSES (2-LP)	£25
96	Garage Flower GARAGE LP 1	GARAGE FLOWER (LP, with print)	£40
96	Garage Flower GARAGE LP 1	GARAGE FLOWER (LP, without print)	£25
99	Geffen/Simply Vinyl SVLP 111	SECOND COMING (2-LP, limited edition, gatefold, heavy duty 180g vinyl)	£20
09	Silvertone 88697430302	THE STONES ROSES (Box set, 3-CD, LP, 2x12", DVD, memory stick)	£80
10	Silvertone Sony/BMG 88697694171	THE STONE ROSES (LP, 1000 only, numbered, 2010 Record Store day release with 6 art prints)	£30

PROMOS

85	Thin Line THIN 001	So Young/Tell Me (12" promo (pale) pink label test press) 100 pressed (in Cartel sleeve with press pack)	£400
85	Thin Line THIN 001	So Young/Tell Me (12" promo (pale) pink label test pressing, 100 pressed, this price without press pack)	£250
89	Silvertone ORE DJ T 13	Fools Gold 9.53/ What The World Is Waiting For (12" promo, b-side white label)	£20
92	Silvertone ORE T DJ 34	Waterfall (12" Version 5.23)/One Love (Adrian Sherwood 12" Version 7.10) (12" promo)	£15
90	Silvertone STONE ONE	Fools Gold (A Guy Called Gerald Remix)/Elephant Stone (DJ Mix) (12", white label) this is actually a bootleg recording by Hard Tymez Productions	£15

(see also Ian Brown, Seahorses)

STONE'S MASONRY

66	Purdah 45-3504	Flapjacks/Hot Rock (99 copies only)	£200

(see also Action, Mighty Baby)

STONE TEMPLE PILOTS

92	Atlantic 7567824	CORE (LP)	£40
94	Atlantic 82607	PURPLE - 12 GRACIOUS MELODIES (LP, purple vinyl)	£40

STONE THE CROWS

70	Polydor 2425 017	STONE THE CROWS (LP)	£80
70	Polydor 2425 042	ODE TO JOHN LAW (LP, gatefold sleeve)	£60
71	Polydor 2425 071	TEENAGE LICKS (LP, gatefold sleeve)	£60
72	Polydor 2391 043	ONTINUOUS PERFORMANCE (LP)	£20

(see also White Trash)

STONEY BROOK PEOPLE

69	CBS 4538	Easy To Be Hard/There's Tomorrow	£30

STONEY & MEAT LOAF

72	Rare Earth SRE 3005	STONEY AND MEAT LOAF (LP)	£25
79	Prodigal PDL 2010	MEAT LOAF (FEATURING STONEY & MEAT LOAF) (LP, revised reissue of "Stoney And Meat Loaf" with different tracks)	£15

(see also Meat Loaf)

STOOGES

05	Elektra 8122-74551-7	Down On The Street (Mono Single Mix)/T.V. Eye (Take 9)	£20
05	Elektra 8122732137	I Wanna Be Your Dog/Real Cool TIme (John Cale mix) (reissue)	£20
69	Elektra EKS 74051	THE STOOGES (LP, red label)	£250
70	Elektra 2410 009	FUN HOUSE (LP, red label)	£300
73	CBS 65586	RAW POWER (LP, as Iggy & Stooges, no name on front cover, plain orange label, with inner sleeve)	£100
77	Elektra K 42032	THE STOOGES (LP, reissue, 'butterfly' label)	£20
77	Elektra K 42051	FUN HOUSE (LP, reissue, 'butterfly' label)	£20
99	Elektra 7559624421	NO FUN (LP, as The Stooges featuring Iggy Pop)	£15
05	Elektra 8122 73237 1	THE STOOGES (2-LP, reissue, gatefold)	£25
05	Elektra 8122 73238 1	FUN HOUSE (2-LP, reissue, gatefold)	£25

(see also Iggy Pop)

STOPOUTS

78	Skeleton LYN 5912	Strange Thoughts/Just For You And Me (p/s)	£15

STOREY SISTERS

58	London HLU 8571	Bad Motorcycle/Sweet Daddy	£50
58	London HLU 8571	Bad Motorcycle/Sweet Daddy (78)	£25

STORM

85	Silent SILENT 1	Malice In Wonderland/Malice In Wonderland (Edit)/Doctor Storm (12", p/s)	£25

STORM/CUTMASTER SWIFT

91	White SOLID001	Playing The Field/Live In Spain (12")	£70

DANNY STORM (& STROLLERS)

63	Piccadilly 7N 35143	Say You Do/Let The Sunshine In (as Danny Storm & Strollers)	£15

GALE STORM

56	London HLD 8222	I Hear You Knocking/Never Leave Me	£50
56	London HLD 8232	Memories Are Made Of This/A Teen-Age Prayer	£30
56	London HLD 8283	Ivory Tower/I Ain't Gonna Worry	£25
56	London HLD 8286	Why Do Fools Fall In Love/I Walk Alone	£20
56	London HL 7008	Why Do Fools Fall In Love/I Walk Alone (export issue)	£20
56	London HLD 8311	Don't Be That Way (Please Listen To Me)/Tell Me Why	£25
56	London HLD 8329	A Heart Without A Sweetheart/Now Is The Hour	£15
57	London HLD 8393	Lucky Lips/On Treasure Island	£30

MINT VALUE £

57	London HLD 8413	Orange Blossoms/My Heart Belongs To You	£15
57	London HLD 8424	Dark Moon/A Little Too Late	£15
56	London HB-D 1056	PRESENTING GALE STORM (10" LP)	£40
58	London HA-D 2104	SENTIMENTAL ME (LP)	£30

RORY STORM & HURRICANES

| 63 | Oriole CB 1858 | Dr. Feelgood/I Can Tell | £45 |
| 64 | Parlophone R 5197 | America/Since You Broke My Heart | £25 |

(see also Keef Hartley, Paddy Klaus & Gibson)

STORMCHILD

| 82 | Serpent S001 | Rockin'Steady/Last Night (hand folded sleeve, white label, 50 only) | £1000 |

ROBB STORME (& WHISPERS)

| 66 | Columbia DB 7993 | Here Today/Don't Cry (as Robb Storme Group) | £20 |
| 62 | Decca DFE 6700 | WHEELS (EP) | £100 |

STORMER

| 78 | Ring O' 2017 113 | My Home Town/Shake It Baby (in promo p/s) | £70 |
| 78 | Ring O' 2017 113 | My Home Town/Shake It Baby | £40 |

STORM QUEEN

| 82 | Real Fire RF001 | Come Silent The Night/Raising The Roof (1st press, red labels no p/s) | £400 |
| 82 | Real Fire RF001 | Come Silent To The World/Raising The Roof (2nd press,black labels with correct spelling for A-side) | £275 |

STORMRIDER

| 77 | Crossover CS 7701 | Mr Supercool/Sister Bring Down (no p/s) | £30 |

STORMTROOPER (1)

| 78 | Solent SS 047 | I'm A Mess/It's Not Me (in stamped plain sleeve with insert) | £30 |

STORMTROOPER (2)

| 80 | Heartbeat BEAT 1 | Pride Before A Fall/Still Comin' Home (p/s) | £25 |

STORYTELLER (1)

| 70 | Transatlantic TRA 220 | STORYTELLER (LP, gatefold sleeve, white/lilav label, 't' logo) | £60 |
| 71 | Transatlantic TRA 232 | MORE PAGES (LP, textured sleeve) | £35 |

(see also Johnny Neal & Starliners, Terry Durham, Other Two, Andy Bown)

STORYTELLER (2)

| 79 | Alladin MDS 1002 | Just Another Cloud In The Sky/Weatherman | £20 |

STORYTELLER (3)

| 85 | Storyteller ZELSP 438 | Mystery Girl (p/s) | £50 |

LALLY STOTT

| 71 | Philips 6323 006 | CHIRPY CHIRPY CHEEP CHEEP (LP) | £15 |

DAVID STOUGHTON

| 68 | Elektra EKS 74034 | TRANSFORMER (LP) | £40 |

STOWAWAYS

| 79 | Supermusic SUP 27 | I Wanna Be Me/My Friends/You'll Tie Me Down (p/s) | £25 |

STRAFE FÜR REBELLION

| 80s | Touch TO 6 | SANTA MARIA (LP, with inner) | £15 |

STRAIGHT EIGHT

| 79 | Eel Pie EPRP 001 | NO NOISE FROM HERE (LP) | £15 |

STRAIGHT UP

| 80 | Rok XX/XIX | One Out All Out/JUSTIN CASE: T.V. (die-cut company sleeve) | £40 |

STRAIGHT CORNERS

| 80 | SRTS/80/CUS 809 | Legal Executive/Berlin Wall (p/s) | £25 |

STRAIGHT SHOOTER BAND

| 83 | Magic MR 001 | Blueman/Flag Of Freedom (p/s) | £20 |

STRAIGHTSHOOTER

| 79 | Strolling Bone S 79 CUS 398 | Straightshooter/She's So Fine (no p/s) | £120 |

NICK STRAKER

| 83 | Pinnacle PIN 100T | Turn Me Down/We Can Still Be Friends (12") | £15 |

STRAND

| 80 | Yob YOB 001 | Here Today Gone Tomorrow/Changing World/POSITIVE SIGNALS: Media Man/Only For A Day (split EP, p/s) | £15 |

PAULINE STRAND

| 68 | Carousel CR3 | Love Me Always/The End Of Me | £25 |

JOHN STRANG

| 68 | No label or cat no | THE MASTERPIECE (LP, 50 only, white labels in finished sleeve) | £400 |

BILLY STRANGE (& CHALLENGERS)

64	Vocalion V-N 9228	The James Bond Theme/007 Theme	£15
66	Vocalion V-N 9259	Get Smart/Run Spy, Run	£15
63	Vocalion VA/SVN 8022	12-STRING GUITAR (LP)	£15
64	Vocalion VAN 8026	MR GUITAR (LP)	£15
64	Vocalion VAN/SAVN 8032	THE JAMES BOND THEME (LP)	£20
65	Vocalion VAN/SAVN 8038	GOLDFINGER (LP)	£20
65	Vocalion VAN/SAVN 8042	ENGLISH HITS OF '65 (LP)	£15
65	Vocalion VAN/SAVN 8045	STRANGE PLAYS THE HITS (LP)	£15

(see also Cliffie Stone)

1015

STRANGE BROTHERS SHOW
70 Polydor 2001-116   Right On/Shakey Jakes £15

GILES STRANGE
66 Stateside SS 570   Watch The People Dance/You're Goin' Up To The Bottom (DJ Copy)...........£100
66 Stateside SS 570   Watch The People Dance/You're Goin' Up To The Bottom £80

STEVE STRANGE
82 Palace PALACE 1   In The Year 2525/Strange Connexions (white label, unreleased) £30
82 Palace PALACE 1   In The Year 2525/Strange Connexions (p/s, available separately)............£20
(see also Visage)

STRANGE CRUISE
86 EMI EMC 3513   STRANGE CRUISE (LP) £18

STRANGE DAYS (1)
75 Retreat RTL 6005   NINE PARTS TO THE WIND (LP, lyric inner sleeve, blue label) £25

STRANGE DAYS (2)
83 Powerstation OHM 1   Within These Walls/Swimming Into The Doctor £15

STRANGE FOX
70 Parlophone R5876   Bring It On HOme/Time And Tide..£30
73 Parlophone R5978   Rock 'N' Roll Band/Tamarin Girl...£15

STRANGE FRUIT
71 Village Thing VTSX 1001   Cut Across Shorty/Shake That Thing...£25

STRANGELOVE
94 Food FOODLP 11   TIME FOR THE REST OF YOUR LIFE (2-LP, numbered).................................£40
96 Food FOODLP 15   LOVE AND OTHER DEMONS (LP, with 12 page booklet)...............................£40
97 Food FOODLPD 24   STRANGELOVE (2-LP)...£40

STRANGELOVES
65 Stateside SS 446   I Want Candy/It's About My Baby £25
65 Immediate IM 007   Cara-Lin/Roll On Mississippi £30
66 London HLZ 10020   Night Time/Rhythm Of Love £50
69 London HLZ 10238   Honey Do/I Wanna Do It..£15
(see also Beach-Nuts)

STRANGE MOVEMENTS
79 Good Vibrations GOT 5   Dancing In The Ghetto/Amuse Yourself (foldout p/s) £25

STRANGER (COLE)
63 Blue Beat BB 165   Rough And Tough (with Duke Reid Band)/DUKE REID BAND: The Mood I Am In £40
63 Blue Beat BB 195   Miss Reamer/RICO & HIS BLUES BAND: Blues From The Hills £20
(see also Stranger Cole)

STRANGER (COLE) & GLADY (ANDERSON)
67 Island WI 3128   Love Me Today/Over Again..£100
68 Amalgamated AMG 806   Seeing Is Knowing/ROY SHIRLEY: Music Is The Key................................£40
71 Supreme SUP 227   My Application (as Stranger & Gladdy)/TADDY & DIAMONDS: Oh No, My Baby £25
73 Dragon DRA 1014   Conqueror/Conqueror (Instrumental Version)...£20
(see also Stranger Cole, Gladdy & Followers, Gladstone Anderson, Gladdy & Stranger, Charlie Kelly)

STRANGER (COLE) & KEN (BOOTHE)
63 R&B JB 120   Thick In Love/All Your Friends..£30
(see also Stranger Cole, Ken Boothe)

STRANGER (COLE) & PATSY (TODD)
63 Blue Beat BB 171   When I Call Your Name/Take My Heart (with Duke Reid All Stars).........£25
63 Island WI 113   Senor And Senorita/DON DRUMMOND: Snowboy..................................£35
64 Island WI 141   Oh Oh I Need You/DON DRUMMOND: J.F.K.'s Memory.........................£35
64 Island WI 144   Tom, Dick And Harry/We Two, Happy People £20
64 Island WI 152   Yeah Yeah Baby/BABA BROOKS: Boat Ride £25
64 Island WI 160   Miss B/Thing Come To Those Who Wait...£20
65 Black Swan WI 462   Hey Little Girl/CORNELL CAMBELL: Make Hay..£40
66 Rio R 81   Give Me One More Chance/Fire In Cornfield £18
66 Doctor Bird DB 1050   Give Me The Right/Tonight £30
67 Doctor Bird DB 1084   Tell It To Me/Your Photograph £120
67 Doctor Bird DB 1087   Down The Trainlines/Sing And Pray..£40
69 Escort ES 807   My Love/SWEET CONFUSION: Windsor Castle...£28
(see also Stranger Cole, Patsy)

STRANGERS (WITH MIKE SHANNON)
64 Philips BF 1335   One And One Is Two/Time And The River (as Strangers with Mike Shannon) £40
(see also Shadows)

STRANGERS
67 Pye 7N 17240   Look Out (Here Comes Tomorrow)/Mary Mary..£40
67 Pye 7N 17351   You Didn't Have To Be So Nice/Daytime Turns To Night £15
68 Pye 7N 17585   I'm On An Island/Step Inside £20

STRANGER THAN FICTION
79 Ellie Jay EJSP 9301   Into The Void/Darkness (p/s) £25
87 Constitution CON 3T   Prelude/Is She In Love With Love/The Realization (12", p/s) £25

STRANGE STONE
77 Own label DER 1399   STRANGE STONE (LP, private pressing, numbered sleeve with insert, 255 only) £400

STRANGE U
13 Eglo EGLP 025   SCARLET JUNGLE EP £50

14	White Label STRANGEU 01	**EP 2040** (EP)..£35
14	Y n R YNR 062	**Dolph Lundgren/Instrumental** (gig-only 7" with JEHST) £50
17	High Focus HFRLP 056	**#LP4080** (2-LP) £35

STRANGEWAYS
| 78 | Real ARE 2 | **Show Her you Care/You're On Your Own** (p/s)..........................£20 |
| 79 | Real ARE 7 | **Wasting Time/All The Sounds Of Fear** (p/s)...........................£30 |

STRANGLERS
SINGLES
| 77 | United Artists UP 36248 | **Peaches/Go Buddy Go** ('group' p/s with 'blackmail' lettering, withdrawn) ....£800 |
| 90 | Epic TEARS T1 | **96 Tears/Instead Of This/Poisonality** (12" p/s with 'paint set') ....£15 |

ALBUMS : LPS
77	United Artists UAG 30045	**STRANGLERS IV** (RATTUS NORVEGICUS) (LP, printed inner, 10,000 with 7" Choosey Susie/"Peasant In The Big Shitty" (Live At The Nashville, 12/76) **[FREE 3, orange p/s, "What Do You Expect..." in run-off groove], some with sticker)** £200
77	United Artists UAG 30045	**STRANGLERS IV** (RATTUS NORVEGICUS) (LP, printed inner) £40
77	United Artists UAG 30200	**NO MORE HEROES** (LP, printed inner) £30
78	United Artists UAK 30222	**BLACK AND WHITE** (LP, printed inner, 75,000 with white vinyl 7" "Walk On By"/"Tits"/Mean To Me **[FREE 9, black die-cut sleeve & card insert]**, mispressed on blue or beige vinyl) £80
78	United Artists UAK 30222	**BLACK AND WHITE** (LP, printed inner, 75,000 with white vinyl 7" "Walk On By"/"Tits"/Mean To Me **[FREE 9, black die-cut sleeve & card insert]**) £40
79	United Artists UAG 30224	**LIVE** (X-CERT) (LP, printed inner) £15
79	United Artists UAG 30262	**THE RAVEN** (LP, 20,000 with 3D cover, Australia cartoon on printed inner) £40
81	Liberty LBG 30313	**THE GOSPEL ACCORDING TO THE MENINBLACK** (LP, gatefold) £20
81	Liberty LBG 30342	**LA FOLIE** (LP, printed inner) £20
82	Liberty LBG 30353	**THE COLLECTION 1977- 1982** (LP, withdrawn plastic logo sleeve) £200
82	Liberty LBG 30353	**THE COLLECTION 1977- 1982** (LP) £15
83	Epic EPC 25237	**FELINE** (LP, printed inner, with bonus 1-sided 7" "Aural Sculpture" [XPS 167]) £40
84	EPC 26220	**AURAL SCULPTURE** (LP, lyric insert) £20
86	Epic EPC 26648	**DREAMTIME** (LP, picture disc) £30
86	Liberty SLK 5001	**OFF THE BEATEN TRACK** (LP) £15
88	Epic EPC 460259 1	**ALL LIVE AND ALL OF THE NIGHT** (LP, gatefold)......................£15
90	Epic 466483 1	**10** (LP, printed inner)...£15
90	Epic 466483 0	**10** (LP, picture disc) £15
92	Newspeak SPEAK DLP 101	**EARLY YEARS 74-75-76 RARE LIVE & UNRELEASED** (2LP, gatefold, orange/green vinyl) £50
92	China Records WOL 1030	**IN THE NIGHT** (LP, printed inner, SIS form) £40
93	Essential ESSLP 194	**SATURDAY NIGHT SUNDAY MORNING** (ALLY PALLY 1.8.90) (LP, gatefold sleeve, printed inner) £70
95	When! WEL LP 001	**ABOUT TIME** (LP, gatefold, numbered limited edition of 3000) £60
12	Absolute 12CG00 5V	**GIANTS** (LP, printed inner) £400
14	Let Them Eat Vinyl LETV332LP	**WRITTEN IN RED** (2LP, vinyl release of 97 CD, gatefold, printed inners, red vinyl).............£50
14	Let Them Eat Vinyl LETV331LP	**FRIDAY THE THIRTEENTH** (2LP, vinyl release of 97 CD, gatefold, grey vinyl).....................£50
14	Let Them Eat Vinyl LETV33LP	**COUP DE GRACE** (LP, vinyl issue of 98 CD, gatefold, red vinyl)...............£50
17	Coursegood CGLP5	**RATTUS RELIVED** (2LP, printed inners, print, orange vinyl, limited)............£100
21	Coursegood CGLP12L	**DARK MATTERS** (LP, printed inner, red/black smoke vinyl).........................£30
22	Coursegood Ltd. CGLP18	**SUITE XVI** (LP, vinyl issue of 2006 CD, printed inners, gold/black vinyl, numbered).........£40
22	Audio Platter PLATE 006LP	**IN THE BEGINNING: DEMOS AND LIVE RECORDINGS - '74-'76** (2LP, red vinyl, withdrawn)..........................£150
23	Absolute CGLP17	**NORFOLK COAST** (LP, vinyl issue of 2004 CD, printed inner, limited. numbered blue/white vinyl)..........................£100
23	Coursegood Ltd. CGLP13	**THEMENINBLACKINTOKYO** (2LP, gatefold) £100

PROMOS : FREEBIES, PROMOS & MISCELLANEA
75	(no cat no)	**My Young Dreams/Wasted** (existence unconfirmed) £150
77	United Artists FREE 4	**Peaches** (radio version)**/Go Buddy Go** (promo only, p/s)..................£750
77	United Artists FREE 4	**Peaches** (radio version)**/Go Buddy Go** (promo only, no p/s).................£150
77	United Artists UP 36211	**(Get A) Grip** (On Yourself)**/London Lady** (double A label demo) £25
77	United Artists UP 36277	**Something Better Change/Straighten Out**.........................£25
77	United Artists FREE 8	**No More Heroes** (1-sided radio edit, promo only) £150
77	United Artists UP 36300	**No More Heroes** (1-sided, misprinted "No More Stheroes") £25
77	United Artists UP 36300	**No More Heroes/In The Shadows** (p/s, stamped, misprinted "No More Stheroes").......£25
78	United Artists UP 36248	**Peaches/Go Buddy Go** (p/s, mispressing, B-side plays Buzzcocks' "Oh Shit")..............£75
78	United Artists UP 36429	**Walk On By** (Promo Edit)**/Old Codger/Tank**..........................£25
78	United Artists FREE 9	**Walk On By/Mean To Me/Tits** (EP [free with LP U.A. UAK 30222], mispressing, black die-cut sleeve & card insert, blue/clear vinyl)......................£30
78	United Artists FREE 9	**Walk On By/Mean To Me/Tits** (EP [free with LP U.A. UAK 30222], mispressing, black die-cut sleeve & card insert, pink/clear vinyl)...................£15
78	United Artists UP 36350	**5 Minutes/Rok It To Me Moon** (A label demo) £15
78	United Artists UP 36379	**Nice 'N' Sleazy/Shut Up** (p/s, mispressing, B-side plays tracks by other artist) £30
79	United Artists UA STR 1 DJ	**Don't Bring Harry/HUGH CORNWELL: Wired** (45rpm, promo only) £20
79	United Artists (no cat. no.)	**Two Sunspots** (unreleased) £30
79	United Artists UAG 30262	**THE RAVEN** (LP, mispressing, 2nd side plays country & western [B-side matrix: UAK 30263])..........................£25
80	Stranglers Info Service SIS 001	**Tomorrow Was The Hereafter/Bring On The Nubiles** (Cocktail Version) (numbered p/s, label has "Nublies")..........................£15
81	Liberty BP 393	**Just Like Nothing On Earth/Maninwhite** (p/s, mispressing, plays A-side both sides).......£20
82	United Artists BP 407	**Golden Brown/Love 30** (B-side plays "Everybody Salsa") £20

STRAPS
83 Cyclops CYC 2   THE STRAPS ALBUM (LP) £15
(see also Public Image Ltd.)

STRATEGY
82 Ebony EBON 7   Technical Overflow/Astral Planes (in p/s)...£60
82 Ebony EBON 7   Technical Overflow/Astral Planes £50

STRATE JACKET
80 Wessex WEX 269   You're A Hit/Too Soon Too Young (stamped plain sleeve) £15

STRATUS
85 Steel Trax STEEL 31001   THROWING SHAPES (LP) £18
(see also Grand Prix, Uriah Heep, Iron Maiden, Praying Mantis)

STRAWBERRY ALARM CLOCK
67 Pye International 7N 25436 Incense And Peppermints/The Birdman Of Alkatrash £30
68 Pye International 7N 25446 Tomorrow/Birds In My Tree £20
68 Pye International 7N 25456 Sit With The Guru/Pretty Song From Psych-Out £20
68 NPL 28106   INCENSE AND PEPPERMINTS (LP, mono) £200
68 Pye Intl. NSPL 28106   INCENSE AND PEPPERMINTS (LP, stereo) £150

STRAWBERRY CHILDREN
67 Liberty LBF 15012   Love Years Coming/One Stands Here £35
(see also Jim Webb)

STRAWBERRY SWITCHBLADE
85 Korova KODE 11   STRAWBERRY SWITCHBLADE (LP, with bonus 7" "Trees And Flowers", mispressed with some tracks playing twice & others out of order)...£15

(see also Poems)

STRAWBS
68 A&M AMS 725   Oh How She Changed/Or Am I Dreaming...£30
71 A&M AMS 837   Witchwood/Keep The Devil Outside/We'll Meet Again Sometime (live) (withdrawn) £30
69 Strawberry Music SAMPLER No. 1 STRAWBERRY MUSIC SAMPLER NO. 1 (LP, publisher's sampler, 100 only) £750
69 A&M AMLS 936   STRAWBS (LP; disc inserted in middle of sleeve)....................................£50
69 A&M AMLS 936   STRAWBS (LP; disc inserted at edge of sleeve)..£30
70 A&M AMLS 970   DRAGONFLY (LP, textured sleeve, lyric insert, mustard label) £40
70 A&M AMLS 994   JUST A COLLECTION OF ANTIQUES AND CURIOS (LP, laminated gatefold sleeve, mustard label; 2 different rear sleeves) £20
71 A&M AMLH 64304   FROM THE WITCHWOOD (LP, gatefold sleeve) £40
72 A&M AMLH 68078   GRAVE NEW WORLD (LP, triple gatefold sleeve, with 12-page booklet) £15
73 Hallmark SHM 813   ALL OUR OWN WORK (LP, with Sandy Denny) £20
74 A&M AMLH 63607   HERO AND HEROINE (LP, inner)..£15
74 A&M AMLH 68277   GHOSTS (LP, inner)...£15
(see also Dave Cousins, Sandy Denny, Fire, Foggy, Monks, Davey & Morris, Hudson-Ford, Yes, Rick Wakeman)

STRAW DOGS
81 (No label) DOG 001   Black Leather/Don't Need You/We Ain't Dead (Yet)/All The Lads (some with xeroxed sleeve)...£80

STRAY
70 Transatlantic PROMO 1   Only What You Make It/Time Machine £50
70 Transatlantic TRA 216   STRAY (LP, die-cut gatefold sleeve, white/lilac 't' logo label) £50
71 Transatlantic TRA 233   SUICIDE (LP, textured sleeve, white/lilac 't' logo label).........................£40
71 Transatlantic TRA 248   SATURDAY MORNING PICTURES (LP, gatefold sleeve).........................£25
73 Transatlantic TRA 268   MUDANZAS (LP, gatefold sleeve) £25
74 Transatlantic TRA 281   MOVE IT (LP, die-cut sleeve with inner) £15
75 Dawn DNLS 3066   STAND UP AND BE COUNTED (LP, lyric insert, pink 'sun' label) £15

STRAY DOG
73 Manticore K 43506   STRAY DOG (LP, textured sleeve, insert) £20
74 Manticore K 53504   WHILE YOU'RE DOWN THERE (LP) £20
(see also Emerson Lake & Palmer)

STREAK
72 A&M AME 602   Gonna Have A Good Time/Be Your Ryder/Hard Times (In New York City) (promo, b side plays at 33 rpm) £40
72 A&M AMS 7012   Gonna Have A Good Time/Be Your Ryder £15
73 Deram DM 376   Bang Bang Bullet/Black Jack Man...£15

STREAKERS
74 Dawn DNS 1066   Turn Me Down/Wake Up Sunshine £15

STREET BIZARRE
79 Monarch MON 05   Normal Life/Nervous Exhaustion...£150

GARY STREET & FAIRWAYS
68 Domain D 2   Flipperty Flop/Hold Me Closer...£20
(see also Fairways)

JUDY STREET
78 Grapevine GRP 106   What/You Turn Me On (DJ Copy) £15
82 Soul Stop SS 3003   What/HI-FLY: Theme For A Dream £15

STREET LEGAL
84 Weird Brothers SLW 1   Rollin' On/Mississippi Moonshine (p/s, initially with sticker over typo error in sleeve) .£150
84 Weird Brothers SLW 1   Rollin' On/Mississippi Moonshine (p/s, without sticker)............................£150

STREETFIGHTER
82 J.R. JR 7049S   CRAZY DREAM (EP)...£40

STREETFIGHTER (U.K.)
81 Streetfighter 749   STREETFIGHTER (12" EP) £25

STREET PEOPLE (2)
79 Ellie Jay EJSP 9276   PERSONAL VALUES EP (500 only, p/s) £75

STREETS
02 Locked On 679003TLP   ORIGINAL PIRATE MATERIAL (2-LP)....................................... £20
04 679 679LD70LP   A GRAND DON'T COME FOR FREE (2-LP) £25

STREET SERVICE
90 I Like It ILIT 01   JUST FOR YOU (LP)... £18

STREET SPIRITS
77 Storm SR 020   Street Strutting Punks/All Right/Excitement In The Air/Makin Me Sore (no p/s) £15

STREETWALKERS
76 Vertigo 9102 010   RED CARD (LP, red vinyl with inner sleeve, numbered, 'spaceship' label) £15
77 Vertigo 6641 703   LIVE (2-LP, gatefold sleeve) £15
(see also Hummingbird, Nicko McBrain)

STRESS (2)
85 Adventures In Reality ARR 14   THE BIG WHEEL (LP, with insert)...................................... £40

STRETCH
75 Anchor ANCL 2014   ELASTIQUE (LP) £15
76 Anchor ANCL 2016   YOU CAN'T BEAT YOUR BRAIN FOR ENTERTAINMENT (LP) £15
77 Anchor ANCL 2023   LIFE BLOOD (LP) £15
78 Hot Wax HW 1   FORGET THE PAST (LP)... £30
(see also Elmer Gantry, Kirby, Status Quo, Clifford Davis, Legs, Curved Air)

STRETCHHEADS
88 Moksha SOMALP2   FIVE FINGERS FOUR (LP) £20

DAVID STRETTON
68 Plum PL 4   Windmills/Haunted Staircase £20

WILLIAM R. STRICKLAND
69 Deram DML/SML 1041   WILLIAM R. STRICKLAND IS ONLY THE NAME (LP)............... £20

STRIDER
73 GM GML 1002   EXPOSED (LP, gatefold sleeve) £30
74 GM GML 1012   MISUNDERSTOOD (LP) £20
(see also Samson)

STRIFE
75 Chrysalis 1063   RUSH (LP).. £15
78 Gull GULP 1029   BACK TO THUNDER (LP, on green vinyl with poster) £18

STRIKE
80 Shock SRS 504   Teenage Rebel/Radio Songs (p/s, Irish issue but imported into U.K.)........... £150

LIZA STRIKE
68 Parlophone R 5725   All's Quiet On West 23rd/Mr Daddy-Man £15
(see also Liza & Jet Set, Soulmates, Vice Versa)

STRIKER BLUE
76 Bootlegger 596   Get On Down/Loyalty To The Board £75

STRING-A-LONGS
61 London RE-U 1322   THE STRING-A-LONGS (EP) £25
63 London RE-D 1350   THE STRING-A-LONGS (EP) £25
63 London RE-D 1398   STRINGALONG WITH THE STRING-A-LONGS (EP) £30
63 London HA-D 8054   THE STRING-A-LONGS (LP, mono).................................... £40
63 London SH-D 8054   THE STRING-A-LONGS (LP, stereo) £40
69 London HAU/SHU 8371   WIDE WORLD HITS (LP) £25

STRING CHEESE
72 RCA SF 8222   STRING CHEESE (LP)... £20

STRING DRIVEN THING
70 Concord CON 7   Another Night/Say What You Like £15
70 Concord CON 1001   STRING DRIVEN THING (LP, 100 only)................................ £300
72 Charisma CAS 1062   STRING DRIVEN THING (LP, gatefold, insert,large 'Mad Hatter' label)............ £40
73 Charisma CAS 1070   THE MACHINE THAT CRIED (LP, gatefold sleeve, large 'Mad Hatter' label)............ £40
74 Charisma CAS 1097   PLEASE MIND YOUR HEAD (LP, lyric sheet, small 'Mad Hatter' label) £15
76 Charisma CAS 1112   KEEP YOUR 'AND ON IT (LP, insert)................................... £15

STRIPES
82 Ellie Jay EJSP 9808/PINK01   One Step Ahead/Canteen Girls (no p/s) £100

STRIPES OF GLORY
62 Vogue V 9194   The Denial/O' Send The Fire £18

SYLVIA STRIPLIN
86 Music Of Love MOLS 8   Give Me Your Love/Will You Ever Pass This Way Again/Look Towards The Sky (12") £20
94 Expansion EXAPAND 47   You Can't Turn Me Away/INGRAM: Mi Sabrina Tecuana (12") £15
10 Universal Sounds US LP 34   GIVE ME YOUR LOVE (2-LP, reissue) £35

(THE) STROKES
01 Rough Trade RTRADES 010   The Modern Age/Last Nite (with barcode 2000 only)........... £25
01 Rough Trade RTRADES 041   Last Nite/When It Started (p/s)... £20
01 Rough Trade RTRADELP 030   IS THIS IT? (LP, 'STERLING' stamped in run-out groove)........... £80

03	Rough Trade RTRADELP 130	**ROOM ON FIRE** (LP)	£18
06	Rough Trade RTRADELP 330	**FIRST IMPRESSIONS OF EARTH** (LP)	£15

STROLLERS

61	London HLL 9336	Come On Over/There's No One But You	£40

BARRETT STRONG

60	London HLU 9088	**Money** (That's What I Want)/**Oh I Apologise**	£80
76	Capitol CL 15864	**Man Up In The Sky/Gonna Make It Right**	£40

STRUGGLE

80s	Regal RD 013	**No Stronger Love/Bad Boy** (12", with ENFORCER)	£20

JOE STRUMMER

03	Hellcat 1149-7	**Redemption Song/Arms Aloft/Junco Partner** (Live) (with the Mescaleros, picture disc, stickered polythene sleeve)	£18
87	Virgin V 2497	**WALKER** (LP, soundtrack)	£25
89	EPIC 465347	**EARTHQUAKE WEATHER** (LP, with inner)	£25
99	Mercury 546 654	**ROCK ART AND THE X-RAY STYLE** (LP, with the Mescaleros)	£100
01	Hellcat 0440-1	**GLOBAL A GO GO** (2-LP with the Mescaleros)	£80
03	Hellcat 0454-1	**STREETCORE** (LP, gatefold, with the Mescaleros)	£100
12	Hellcat 05251	**FRIDAY 15TH NOVEMBER 2002 ACTON TOWN HALL. LONDON** (2-LP, numbered)	£60
12	Hellcat HELL 20523	**STREETCORE** (LP, with CD, reissue, gatefold, with the Mescaleros)	£40
17	Hellcat 05251	**FRIDAY 15TH NOVEMBER 2002 ACTON TOWN HALL. LONDON** (2-LP, reissue, 500 copies)	£30
18	Ignition IGNLP 53X	**JOE STRUMMER 001** (3-LP and 12")	£50
18	Ignition IGNLP 53 BOX	**JOE STRUMMER 001** (3-LP, 12", 2-CD, cassette, screen print, 2 art prints, sticker, badge and replica driving license)	£100

(see also The Clash)

STRUTT

76	Brunswick BRLS 3021	**TIME MOVES ON** (LP)	£25

STRYDER

80	Quartz QS 010	**Forcin' Thru'/Settle Down**	£50

FRANKIE STUBBS

90s	Sounds Of Subterrania S09	**SECOND HAND SUIT** (10" EP)	£20
95	Rugger Bugger DUMP 025	**UNHINGED** (EP)	£15

(see also Leatherface)

STUD

70	Deram SML-R 1084	**STUD** (LP, laminated front sleeve, white/red label with small logo)	£175

(see also Taste, Blossom Toes, Eric Burdon & Animals)

STUDIO G'S

70	LPSG 100	**BETA GROUP** (LP, library edition)	£150
96	Tenth Planet TP 023	**BEAT GROUP** (LP, 600 only)	£20

STUDIO ONE ALLSTARS

67	Island WI 3038	**Sherry** (actually by Bumps Oakley)/**Out Of My Mind** (actually by Soul Junior)	£100

STUDIO PRESSURE

93	Certificate 18 CERT 1803	**Jump/Don't Worry/Know Yourself** (12")	£35
93	Certificate 18 CERT 1804	**Jump MK II/Presha/Test 1/Junglistics Pt 1** (12")	£40
94	Certificate 18 CERT 1808	**Relics/Presha III** (12")	£20

(see also System X (Ex))

STUDIO SIX

66	Polydor 56131	**When I See My Baby/Don't Tell Lies**	£15
67	Polydor 56219	**Strawberry Window/Falling Leaves**	£40

STUDIO SOUND

72	Downtown DT 489	**Give Me Some More/Some More Version**	£50

STUDIO SWEETHEARTS

79	DJM DJS 10915	**I Believe/It Isn't Me** (p/s)	£20

(see also Cult, Slaughter & Dogs)

STUDIO 2

95	Jet Star FJD 002	**Dirty Games/Who Bless Jah?** (12", stamped white labels)	£50

STUD LEATHER

73	Dart ART 2024	**Cut Loose/Emma Louise**	£100

STIKKI STUFF

81	Floppy Discs FLO 1	**School/The Wiggle** (12")	£15
81	Carrere CAR 206T	**School/The Wiggle** (12", reissue)	£18

STUPIDS

85	Children Of Rev. COR 3	**VIOLENT NUN** (EP, some mispressed)	£20
86	C.O.R. GURT 15	**RETARD PICNIC** (LP, 2 inserts)	£20
88	C.O.R. GURT 9	**PERUVIAN VACATION** (LP, blue cover, lyric sheet)	£15
88	Vinyl Solution SOL 2	**JESUS MEETS THE STUPIDS** (LP, insert with free 7")	£15

STURGEON ROW

79	RhopeySRTS 79 CUS 362	**FRICTION EP** (with insert)	£60

ST VINCENT

12	4AD AD 3211	**Krokodil/Grot** (die-cut sleeve, red vinyl)	£25
15	Secret 7& S727	**Digital Witness** (100 only, each with unique art sleeve)	£45
07	Beggars Banquet BBQLP 239	**MARRY ME** (LP)	£15
09	4AD CAD 2919	**ACTOR** (LP)	£18
11	4AD CAD 3123	**STRANGE MERCY** (LP)	£20

STYLE COUNCIL

89	Polydor TSCB 17	Promised Land (Juan Atkins Mix)/Can You Still Love Me? (7", stickered box set with numbered 7" in p/s & poster)	£20
89	Polydor TSC 18	Sure Is Sure/Love Of The World (unissued, acetates may exist)	£0
83	Polydor 815 277 1	INTRODUCING THE STYLE COUNCIL (LP)	£15
84	Polydor TSCLP 1	CAFÉ BLEU (LP)	£15
85	Polydor TSCLP 2	OUR FAVOURITE SHOP (LP, gatefold)	£20
86	Polydor TSCLP 3	HOME AND ABROAD (LP)	£20
87	Polydor TSCLP 4	THE COST OF LOVING (2-LP)	£35
87	Polydor TSCLP 4	THE COST OF LOVING (LP)	£15
88	Polydor TSCLP 5	CONFESSIONS OF A POP GROUP (LP)	£20
88	Polydor	CONFESSIONS OF A POP GROUP (box set, VHS & cassette;some with promo CD [CPGCD 1])	£50
88	Polydor	CONFESSIONS OF A POP GROUP (box set, VHS & cassette;some without promo CD [CPGCD 1])	£40
89	Polydor TSCTV 1	THE SINGULAR ADVENTURES OF (LP)	£15
89	polydor 557 789 2	THE COMPLETE ADVENTURES OF THE STYLE COUNCIL (Box set, 5-CD, booklet)	£60
98	Polydor TSCLP 6	MODERNISM: A NEW DECADE (LP, promo only)	£80
98	Polydor TSCLP 6	MODERNISM: A NEW DECADE (LP, 2 x 12" set, promo only)	£100
00	Polydor 549135-1	GREATEST HITS (2LP, gatefold, printed inners)	£50
17	Polydor/UMC TSCLP 6	MODERNISM: A NEW DECADE (2LP, reissue, yellow vinyl)	£60
20	Polydor 089 415 2	LONG HOT SUMMERS / THE STORY OF THE STYLE COUNCIL (3LP, pink, blue and orange vinyl)	£70

(see also Paul Weller, Jam, Merton Parkas, King Truman)

HARRY STYLES

17	Columbia 38-193244	Sign Of The Times/From The Dining Table (die-cut 'Columbia Presents' sleeve, ltd. ed)	£150
20	Erskine/Columbia 38-254898	Watermelon Sugar/Watermelon Sugar (Instrumental) (p/s, polaroids, via website)	£25
22	Erskine/Columbia 19658747257	Late Night Talking/Late Night Talking (Instrumental) (p/s)	£20
17	Erskine/Columbia 88985439031	HARRY STYLES (LP, gatefold)	£60
17	Columbia 88985 43678 2	HARRY STYLES (LP/CD, gatefold, white vinyl, booklet, prints, via website)	£60
19	Columbia 88985 439031	HARRY STYLES (LP, gatefold, 2 year anniversary edition, pink translucent vinyl, available for 24 hours only)	£400
19	Erskine/Columbia 194437051513	FINE LINE (2LP, gatefold, booklet, Coke bottle clear vinyl, website only)	£100
19	Erskine/Columbia 19439705141	FINE LINE (2LP, gatefold, booklet, black and white splatter vinyl)	£40
19	Erskine/Columbia19439723684	FINE LINE (3 Cassettes, slipcase, signed print, pop-up store exclusive)	£150
20	Erskine/Columbia 194398283111	FINE LINE (2LP, 1st anniversary box set, booklet, photos, ephemera, via website)	£70
22	Erskine/Columbia 19658708141	HARRY'S HOUSE (LP, gatefold, shrinkwrap with sticker, postcard, yellow translucent vinyl)	£40
22	Erskine/Columbia 19658700431	HARRY'S HOUSE (LP, gatefold, shrinkwrap with sticker, postcard, orange vinyl)	£30
22	Erskine/Columbia 19658700421	HARRY'S HOUSE (LP, gatefold, shrinkwrap with sticker, postcard, sea glass vinyl)	£30

STYLE X

81	Rygel RYGI 12	No Secret Affair (Instrumental)/No Secret Affair (Vocal) (12", no p/s)	£80

(see also Cloud (2))

STYLISTICS

71	Avco 6466 008	THE STYLISTICS (LP)	£15

STYLOS

64	Liberty LBS 10173	Head Over Heels/Bye Bye, Baby, Bye Bye	£100

POLY STYRENE

80	United Artists UAG 30320	TRANSLUCENCE (LP, with lyric inner)	£20
11	Future Noise FN 1	GENERATION INDIGO (LP)	£18

(see also X-Ray Spex, Mari Elliott)

STYVAR MANOR

70	Polydor 2058034	Just Dropped In/That's What I Need Most Of All	£40

DANNY SUAREZ

97	Groove Yard GYARD 15A	LIFE IN THE EAST VILLAGE EP (12")	£20

SUBCULTURE

83	Essential ESS 002	Loud & Clear/Rogue Trooper/University City (p/s)	£30

SUBDUED HUBBUB

70	Ra RALP 6005	SUBDUED HUBBUB (LP)	£15

SUBHUMANS

81	Spider Leg SDL 3	DEMOLITION WAR (EP, gatefold p/s with "Pay no more than 85p" rubber stamped on front cover)	£15
82	Spiderleg SDL9	THE DAY THE COUNTRY DIED (LP, gatefold, original pressing with "Pay no more than £3.25" on front cover)	£15
83	Bluurg FISH 5	TIME FLIES...BUT AEROPLANES CRASH (LP, insert)	£20
83	Bluurg Fish 8	FROM THE CRADLE TO THE GRAVE (LP, gatefold, original pressing with "Pay no more than £3.50" on front cover)	£15
85	Bluurg Fish VIG 1 T	20:20 SPLIT VISION (LP, with insert and has 'Pay no more than £3.50' on front sleeve)	£15
85	Bluurg FISH 12	WORDS APART (LP)	£15

SUBMARINER
93	Spacewatch FLX 2107	**Lyricist Downer/Seeming And The Meaning** (demo)**/STEREOLAB:Ronco Symphony** (demo) (clear vinyl flexi with paper strip insert) £25

SUB MURIS
83	Dog Rock SD 104	**Honesty/Open Doors** (p/s) £25

SUBSTITUTE
79	Ignition IR 2	**The One/Look Sharp** (in p/s) £35
79	Ignition IR 2	**The One/Look Sharp** £20

(see also Vibrators)

SUB SUB
90s	Ten TENX 373	**Space Face/Ecto-Jam-Sub** (12", die-cut sleeve) £35

(see also Doves)

SUBURBAN KNIGHTS
03	Peacefrog PFG025	**MY SOL DARK DIRECTION** (3-LP) £25

SUBURBAN STUDS
77	Pogo POG 001/LYN 44845	**No Faith/Questions** (no p/s, 'with horns' version) £35
78	Pogo POG 002	**I Hate School/Young Power** (p/s) £15
78	Pogo POW 001	**SLAM** (LP) £25

SUBWAYS
04	Private Pressing	**DEMO** (CD, sold at gigs, p/s) £30
05	Infectious 25646248	**YOUNG FOR ETERNITY** (LP, 2x10") £30
11	Cooking VInyl COOK 549	**MONEY & CELEBRITY** (LP, red vinyl) £25

SUBWAY SECT
78	Braik BRS 01	**Nobody's Scared/Don't Split It** (p/s) £30
78	Rough Trade RT 007	**Ambition/A Different Story** (initially in yellow text p/s) £15

(see also Vic Godard [& Subway Sect])

NIKKI SUDDEN
82	ABSTRACT ABT 003	**WAITING ON EGYPT** (LP) £25
83	Flicknife SHARP 110	**THE BIBLE BELT** (LP) £18
84	Glass GLALP 008	**JACOBITES** (LP, with Dave Kusworth) £15
91	UFO UFO 4	**THE JEWEL THIEF** (LP) £15

(see also Swell Maps, Jeremy Gluck)

(A) SUDDEN SWAY
80	Chant CHANT 1	**Jane's Third Party/Don't Go** (p/s, as A Sudden Sway) £15
81	Chant CHANT 2/EJSP 9692	**TO YOU, WITH REGARD** (12" EP, with insert) £20

SUDETEN CRECHE
83	Illuminated ILL 1712	**Kindergarten/Dance** (instrumental Version)**/Dance/Asylums in Beiruit** (12", p/s) £25

SUE & SUNNY
65	Columbia DB 7748	**Every Ounce Of Strength/So Remember** £15
67	Columbia DB 8099	**You Can't By-Pass Love/I Like Your Style** £25
68	CBS 3874	**The Show Must Go On/Little black Book** £20
68	Island WIP 6043	**Set Me Free/NIRVANA ORCHESTRA: City Of The South** £25
70	CBS 63740	**SUE AND SUNNY** (LP) £20
70	Reflection REFL 4	**SUE AND SUNNY** (LP, reissue) £20

(see also Myrtelles, Stockingtops, Brotherhood Of Man)

SUEDE
91	RML RML 001	**Be My God/Art** (12", unissued, white label copies only, MPO pressings,no p/s; counterfeits have off-white labels and no MPO etchings) £150
92	Nude NUD 1 S	**The Drowners** (Radio Edit)**/To The Birds** (p/s, 1,000 copies only) £30
92	Nude NUD 3S	**Metal MIckey/Where The Pigs Don't Fly** (p/s) £15
92	Nude NUD 3 T	**Metal Mickey/Where Pigs Don't Fly/He's Dead** (12", test pressing, plain sleeve) £30
93	Nude NUD 4S	**Animal Nitrate/The Big TIme** (p/s) £15
96	Nude NUD 21S	**Trash/Europe Is Our Playground** (p/s, mail order only) £15
04	S.I.S. SIS4CD	**SEE YOU IN THE NEXT LIFE** (CD, fan club farewell, 2000 copies) £50
11	Edsel DROWN 1	**The Drowners** (Demo)**/To The Birds** (Demo) (p/s, Record Store Day release) £18
93	Nude NUDE 1LP	**SUEDE** (LP, printed inner; with carrier bag from Chain With No Name stores) £100
93	Nude NUDE 1LP	**SUEDE** (LP, printed inner) £80
94	Nude NUDE 3	**DOG MAN STAR** (2LP, gatefold, printed inner, poster) £120
96	Nude NUDE 6LP	**COMING UP** (LP, printed inner) £80
99	Nude NUDE 14LP	**HEAD MUSIC** (2LP, printed inners) £60
13	Warner SUEDEBSX 001	**BLOODSPORTS** (LP/CD/7", booklet, hardback book) £50
13	Demon SUEDEBOX 1	**THE VINYL COLLECTION** (11LP box set, onset, original album packages) £180
14	Demon INSATIABLE 8	**ROYAL ALBERT HALL 24 MARCH 2010 (3LP,** £30
14	Demon SUEDEBOX 003	**7" SINGLES** (24x7" box set, booklet) £200
14	Demon INSATIABLE 1	**SUEDE** (LP, reissue, download card) £15
14	Demon INSATIABLE 3	**COMING UP** (LP, reissue, mispressing, side 1 plays side 2 of Avicci LP) £20
14	Demon INSATIABLE 3	**COMING UP** (LP, reissue, download card) £15
14	Demon INSATIABLE 4	**HEAD MUSIC** (2LP, reissue, download card) £18
14	Demon INSATIABLE 5	**A NEW MORNING** (LP, first vinyl release of 2002 CD, download card) £15
14	Demon INSATIABLE 7	**SCI-FI LULLABIES** (3LP, reissue, printed inners, download card) £25
15	Demon INSATIABLE 9	**DOG MAN STAR 20th ANNIVERSARY LIVE ROYAL ALBERT HALL** (2LP, gatefold, printed inners, RSD)) £25
15	Demon SUEDEBOX 006	**DOG MAN STAR 20th ANNIVERSARY LIVE ROYAL ALBERT HALL** (4LP/2CD, book, first 200 signed by Brett Anderson) £60
16	0825646032730	**NIGHT THOUGHTS** (2LP, 45rpm, gatefold, printed inners) £50
18	Warner 0190295642662	**THE BLUE HOUR** (2LP/2CD/DVD/7" box set, lyric sheets, art cards) £40

			MINT VALUE £
18	Warner 0190295625788	THE BLUE HOUR (2LP, gatefold, printed inners, blue vinyl)	£35
20	Demon DEMREC 630	SEE YOU IN THE NEXT LIFE (LP, printed inner, red vinyl, vinyl release of 2004 CD, RSD)	£35
20	Demon SUEDEBOX 012	THE BEST OF SUEDE - THE BEAUTIFUL ONES 1992-2018 (6LP box set, white vinyl, printed inners)	£70
20	Demon INSATIABLE10X	THE BEST OF SUEDE - THE BEAUTIFUL ONES 1992-2018 (2LP, printed inners, clear vinyl)	£20
22	BMG 538812651	AUTOFICTION (LP/CD, clear vinyl, cardboard envelope, stencil, signed art cards_	£60
22	BMG 538804791	AUTOFICTION (LP, printed inner, 'bricks & mortar' edition, grey vinyl)	£30
22	BMG 538804781	AUTOFICTION (LP/CD, alternate artwork, printed inner, clear vinyl)	£40
23	Demon DEMREC 1086	SUEDE DEMOS (LP, clear vinyl, RSD)	£30
24	BMG 964005521	AUTOFICTION: LIVE (LP, foldout envelope sleeve, grey vinyl	£25

(see also Elastica, Tears)

SUEDE CROCODILES
83	No Strings NOSP 2	Pleasant Dreams/Stop The Rain	£75

SUFJAN STEVENS
15	Asthmatic Kitty AKR 371	Exploding Whale/Fourth Of July (PPD Remix) (UK tour edition)	£25
05	Rough Trade RTRADLP 250	COME ON FEEL THE ILLINOISE (2-LP)	£30

SUGAR MINOTT
79	Sufferers Heights SUFF 002	Hard Time Pressure (with Captain Sinbad)/Dub On The Pressure (12")	£30
80	Strong Like Sampson SLSD 014	Half Of Love/AL CAMPBELL: Jah Shine On Me (12")	£25
81	SMP 101	Play Me Nah Play/Version (12", white label only)	£200
83	PCJ PCJ 001	Can't Stop Jah Music/PCJ: Nah Stop Jah Music (12")	£50
83	SMP SMP 003	Come Again/BERTIE AT THE CONTROLS: Dubbing A Storm At Omega Studio (12")	£150
84	Black Roots BR 181264	Now We Know/Row Fast (12")	£50
84	Black Roots LML 201284	Herbman Hustling/TAXI GANG: Hustling Dub (12")	£20
77	Studio One PSOL001	LIVE LOVING (LP)	£50
79	United Artists UAG 30310	GIVE THE PEOPLE (LP)	£20
79	Island ILPS 9591	BLACK ROOTS (LP)	£20
79	Trojan TRLS 173	GHETTO-OLOGY (LP)	£30
79	Warrior WARLP20	BITTER SWEET (LP)	£25
80	Black Roots BRLP 3000	AFRICAN GIRL (LP)	£25
70s	Uptempo UT 1	SHOWCASE (10" mini LP, no ps)	£40
82	Black Roots BRLP 001	MEET THE PEOPLE IN A LOVER DUBBER STYLE (LP)	£35

SUGAR SHACK
68	Tribune TRS 112	Sunshine Of Your Love/Morning Dew	£25

SUGAR (1)
69	CBS 4226	It Was Yesterday Today/11AM Tuesday Morning Taxi	£40

SUGAR (2)
92	Creation CRELP 129	COPPER BLUE (LP, lyric inner)	£25
93	Creation CRELP 153	BEASTER (mini-LP)	£15
94	Creation CRELP 172	FILE UNDER EASY LISTENING (LP)	£25

(see also Bob Mould, Husker Du)

SUGAR (SIMONE) & DANDY (LIVINGSTONE)
66	Blue Beat BB 367	Meditation (as Jetliners)/GIRL SATCHMO & JET LINERS: Nature Of Love	£15
64	Carnival CX 1000	THE SKA'S THE LIMIT (LP)	£40
67	Page One FOR 006	THE SKA'S THE LIMIT (LP, reissue)	£20

(see also Sugar Simone)

SUGAR & PEE WEE
58	Vogue Pop V 9112	One, Two, Let's Rock/Just A Few Little Words	£500
58	Vogue Pop V 9112	One, Two, Let's Rock/Just A Few Little Words (78)	£100

SUGARBEATS
66	Polydor BM 56069	I Just Stand Here/The Ballad Of Ole Betsy	£20
66	Polydor BM 56120	Alice Designs/Sunny Day Girl	£20

(see also Tony Rivers & Castaways)

SUGARCUBES
90	One Little Indian TP BOX 2	7.8 (8 x 7" box set)	£25
90	One Little Indian TP BOX 1	12.11 (11 x 12" box set)	£40
90	One Little Indian TP BOX 3	CD.6 (6 x CD box set)	£45
08	One Little Indian 950TP7BOX	BOX SET (8 x 7")	£25
88	One Little Indian TPLP 5	LIFE'S TOO GOOD (LP, green/blue/yellow/orange/pink sleeve)	£20
89	One Little Indian TPLP 15SP	HERE TODAY, TOMORROW NEXT WEEK! (LP, silver vinyl, gatefold sleeve with sticker & inner)	£20
89	One Little Indian TPLP 15L	SYKURMOLARNIR ILLUR ARFUR! (LP, as Sykurmolarnir, gatefold sleeve)	£15
92	One Little Indian TPLP40	IT'S IT (2-LP)	£30
92	One Little Indian TP LP 30	STICK AROUND FOR JOY (LP)	£25

(see also Bjork, Kukl)

SUGAR DEE & THE OFFBEAT POSSE
89	YND YDD 0137	Danger/Having A Party (12")	£25

SUGAR LOAF
70	RCA INTS 1113	SOUL STRUTTING (LP)	£30

SUGARLOAF
71	Liberty LBS 83415	SUGARLOAF (LP)	£15
75	Polydor 2310 394	DON'T CALL US, WE'LL CALL YOU (LP, with Jerry Corbetto)	£15

SUGAR LUMPS
69	Jay Boy BOY 16	Sugar Sugar/Can't We Be Friends	£20
70	Jay Boy BOY 20	Satan's People/Shame Shame	£20

SUGARPLUMS
70	Fab FAB 160	Red River Reggae/Too Much	£20

SUGAR SHOPPE
68	Capitol CL 15555	Skip-A-Long Sam/Let The Truth Come Out	£20

SUGARGLIDERS
92	Sarah SARAH 63	Letter From A Lifeboat/Strong/What We Had Hoped (p/s, insert)	£18
92	Sarah SARAH 67	Seventeen/Aloha Street/Fruitloopin' (p/s, insert)	£18
93	Sarah SARAH 72	Ahprahan/Corn Circles/Theme From Boxville (p/s, insert)	£25
93	Sarah SARAH 77	Trumpet Play/Unkind/Beloved (p/s, insert)	£25
93	Sarah SARAH 83	Will We Ever Learn?/Dolly/Reinventing Penicillin (p/s, insert)	£25
93	Sarah SARAH 86	Top 40 Sculpture/90 Days Of Moths And Rust/Yr. Jacket (p/s, insert)	£25
94	Sarah SARAH 619	WE'RE ALL TRYING TO GET THERE (LP)	£50

SUICIDAL TENDENCIES
87	Virgin VS 967-12	Possessed To Skate/Human Guinea Pig/Two Wrongs Don't Make A Right (12", picture disc)	£15
88	Virgin VST 1039	Institutionalised/War Inside My Head/Cyco (12", p/s)	£15
87	Virgin V 2495	SUICIDAL TENDENCIES (LP, with poster)	£18
88	Virgin V 2551	HOW WILL I LAUGH TOMORROW WHEN I CAN'T EVEN SMILE TODAY? (LP)	£15

SUICIDE
78	Bronze BRO 57	Cheree/I Remember (p/s, A label promo)	£70
78	Red Star/Bronze BRO 57	Cheree/I Remember (p/s)	£25
78	Red Star/Bronze 12 BRO 57	Cheree/I Remember (12", 'limited edition', p/s)	£20
79	IslandWIP 6543	Dream Baby Dream/Radiation (A label promo)	£40
79	Island WIP 6543	Dream Baby Dream/Radiation (p/s)	£40
79	Island 12 WIP 6543	Dream Baby Dream (Long Version)/Radiation (12", p/s)	£40
86	Demon D 1046	Cheree/I Remember (promo only)	£20
88	Chapter 22 12 CHAP 36	Surrender/Rain Of Ruin (12", die cut p/s)	£18
89	Chapter 22 12CHAP 42	SUICIDE (12", unissued)	£0
77	Red Star/Bronze BRON 508	SUICIDE (LP)	£60
78	Red Star FRANKIE 1	24 MINUTES OVER BRUSSELS (LP, official bootleg, 1,000 only, no p/s)	£100
80	Ze/Island ILPS 7007	SUICIDE: ALAN VEGA/MARTIN REV (LP, with printed inner sleeve)	£50
86	Demon FIEND 74	SUICIDE (LP, reissue, with incorrect Rocket U.S.A and Ghost Rider running order on side 1))	£40
86	Demon FIEND 74	SUICIDE (LP, reissue, tracks in correct order)	£25
88	Chapter 22 CHAP LP 35	A WAY OF LIFE (LP)	£40
98	Blast First BFFP 133 1/2	SUICIDE (2-LP, reissue)	£30
99	Blast First BFFP 162	THE SECOND ALBUM + FIRST REHEARSAL TAPES (2-LP, with insert)	£40
02	Blast First BFFP 168	AMERICAN SUPREME (2-LP)	£60
08	Blast First Petite PTYT 011	LIVE 1977 - 1978 (6-CD box set, booklet)	£40
19	Mute SUICIDELP01	SUICIDE (LP, reissue, with booklet, art print and com come with badge)	£15

(see also Alan Vega)

SUICIDE TWINS
86	Lick LICLP 9	SILVER MISSILES AND NIGHTINGALES (LP)	£15

BIG JIM SULLIVAN
65	Mercury MF 928	She Walks Through The Fair/Don't Know What I'm Doing (as Jim Sullivan Sound)	£25
67	Mercury SML 30001	SITAR BEAT (LP)	£40
74	Retreat RTA 4001	BIG JIM'S BACK (LP, gatefold sleeve, blue/green label)	£15

(see also Maureeny Wishfull, Brian Bennett, Tiger)

JOE SULLIVAN
56	London HA-U 2011	NEW SOLOS BY AN OLD MASTER (LP, thin card sleeve with no spine))	£15

MAXINE SULLIVAN
54	Parlophone MSP 6086	Boogie Woogie Maxine/Piper In The Glen (with Vic Ash)	£15

PETER SULLY
68	Polydor 56291	My Idea/Evil Woman (as Pete Sully And The Orchard)	£35

SULTANS OF PING (F.C.)
91	Divine ATHY 01	Where's Me Jumper/I Said I Am I Said (p/s)	£20
91	Divine ATHY 01T	Where's Me Jumper/I Said I Am I Said/Turnip Fish (12")	£25
93	Rhythm King 472495-1	CASUAL SEX IN THE CINEPLEX (LP, inner)	£25
94	Rhythm King 4747161	TEENAGE DRUG (LP)	£30
96	Rhythm King ATHY 05 LP	GOOD YEAR FOR TROUBLE (LP)	£30

YMA SUMAC
53	Capitol LC 6522	VOICE OF THE XTABAY (10" LP)	£15
54	Capitol LC 6609	LEGEND OF THE SUN VIRGIN (10" LP)	£15
59	Capitol T 1169	FUEGO DEL ANDE (LP)	£15
72	London HLU/SHU 8431	MIRACLES (LP)	£15

HUBERT SUMLIN
65	Blue Horizon 45-1000	Across The Board/Sumlin Boogie (99 copies only)	£150

(see also Howlin' Wolf)

DONNA SUMMER
82	Casablanca FEEL 12	I Feel Love (Mega Mix)/I Feel Love (Mega Edit) (12", reissue)	£15
75	GTO GTLP 008	LOVE TO LOVE YOU BABY (LP)	£15

(see also Donna Gaines, John Barry)

SUMMERHILL
69	Polydor 583 746	SUMMERHILL (LP)	£40

JOHN SUMMERS
65	Pye 15918	Don't Fool Yourself/Looking In Windows	£30

SUMMER SET
66	Columbia DB 8004	Farmer's Daughter/Papa-Oom-Mow-Mow	£40
66	Columbia DB 8004	Farmer's Daughter/What Are You Gonna Do (2nd issue with different B-side)	£40
67	Columbia DB 8215	Overnight Changes/It's A Dream	£120

(see also Candy Choir)

SUMMERTAIR GIRLS
66	Ska Beat JB 258	My Heart Cries Out/SOUL BROTHERS: James Bond Girl	£60

(see also Jackie Mittoo, Soul Agents)

SUMMIT UP
89	Soundworx SOX 101	Watch The Sun Light Up Your Face/I Don't Mind (The Nude Mix) p/s	£50

SUN ALSO RISES
70	Village Thing VTS 2	THE SUN ALSO RISES (LP, with insert)	£100

SUN DIAL
90	UFO 45 001T	Exploding In Your Mind/Otherside/Slow Motion (12", 1-sided, p/s)	£15
91	Tangerine TANGERINE 111	Exploding In Your Mind (Colour Mix)/Otherside/Slow Motion (12", unreleased, 80 white label test pressings only)	£30
90	Tangerine TAN 11145	Exploding In Your Mind/Other Side	£50
91	UFO PF 2	Fireball/Only A Northern Song ('Pre-Flight' 7", promo only)	£20
90	Tangerine MM 07	OTHER WAY OUT (LP, with insert, signed in silver ink)	£50
90	Tangerine MM 07	OTHER WAY OUT (LP, with insert)	£30
91	UFO UFO 1LP	OTHER WAY OUT (LP, reissue in gatefold sleeve)	£15
92	UFO UFO 8	REFLECTER (LP, with free 1-sided 7", Let It Go (live), TEX-4)	£20
92	UFO UFO 8	REFLECTER (LP, clear vinyl)	£20
93	Beggars Banquet BBQLP 138	LIBERTINE (LP, with poster)	£18
94	Acme AC 8001	RETURN JOURNEY (LP, official bootleg; 200 promos with inserts)	£40
94	Acme AC 8001	RETURN JOURNEY (LP, official bootleg; 500 numbered commercial copies)	£30
95	Acme AC 8011	ACID YANTRA (LP, gatefold sleeve, some purple vinyl)	£25
96	Acme AC 8015	LIVE DRUG (LP, red vinyl)	£15
02	Ace Of Discs ACE 001	WILD BUG (LP)	£15
05	Third Eye TESLP 1001	OTHER WAY IN (LP)	£15

(see also Modern Art, Spiral Sky, Quad)

SUNBIRD
70	Phillips 6011070	Brother Bird/Love Of The Free	£18

(see also Nirvana)

SUNCHARIOT
72	Decca F13317	Rosemarie/Do You Wanna Know	£15

SUNDAE TIMES
68	President PT 203	Baby Don't Cry/Aba-Aba	£25
68	President PT 219	Jack Boy/I Don't Want Nobody	£25
70	President PT 285	Live Today/Take Me Higher Baby	£25
70	Joy JOYS 159	US COLOURED KIDS (LP, laminated front sleeve, flipbacks)	£150

(see also Osibisa, Crosyby Stills Nash & Young, One)

SUNDANCE
73	Decca TXS 111	RAIN STEAM SPEED (LP, with insert)	£20
74	Decca SKL 5183	CHUFFER (LP)	£18

SUNDAY AFTERNOONS
70s	Longman	SUNDAY AFTERNOONS (LP)	£90

SUNDAYS
90	Rough Trade ROUGH 148	READING WRITING AND ARITHMATIC (LP)	£30
90	Rough Trade ROUGH 148P	READING, WRITING AND ARITHMETIC (LP, picture disc, stickered sleeve)	£25
92	Parlophone PCSD 121	BLIND (LP)	£70
97	Parlophone 724382121216	STATIC AND SILENCE (LP)	£70

SUNDOWNERS
68	Columbia DB 8339	Dr. J. Wallace-Brown/Love Is In The Air	£15

SUNDOWN PLAYBOYS
72	Apple APPLE 44	Saturday Nite Special/Valse De Soleil Couche (in p/s)	£35
72	Apple APPLE 44	Saturday Nite Special/Valse De Soleil Couche (10", 78rpm, pink-patterned die-cut sleeve)	£300

SUNDRAGON (1)
68	MGM MGM 1458	Five White Horses/Look At The Sun	£30
68	MGM MGM-C(S) 8090	GREEN TAMBOURINE (LP, yellow/black 'lion' label)	£175

(see also Sands)

SUNFIGHTER
76	EMI EMI 2493	Drag Race Queen/Riding On Your Star	£15

(see also Chris Rainbow)

SUNFLAYRE
70	Realm RM 1	The Passing Dream/Rich Woman (private pressing)	£300

SUNFOREST
70	Deram Nova DN 7	SOUND OF SUNFOREST (LP, mono, laminated front sleeve)	£400
70	Deram Nova SDN 7	SOUND OF SUNFOREST (LP, stereo, laminated front sleeve)	£300

SUNHOUSE
| 98 | Independiente ISOM 4LP | CRAZY ON THE WEEKEND (LP) | £70 |

SUNN 0)))
04	Anti-Mosh 444	Candlewolff Ov Thee Golden Chalice (12")	£35
03	Dirtier Promotions DPROMLP52	VOID (2-LP, 150 on green vinyl)	£45
03	Dirtier Promotions DPROMLP52	VOID (2-LP, 850 on black vinyl)	£25
13	Southern Lord SUNN 50	BLACK ONE (2-LP, reissue)	£20

SUNNY & THE SUNGLOWS/SUNLINERS
| 63 | London HL 9792 | Talk To Me (as Sunny & the Sunglows)/Every Week, Every Month, Every Year (as Sunny & the Sunliners) | £25 |

SUNNYLAND SLIM
65	77' LA 12-23	CHICAGO BLUES SESSION (LP, with Little Brother Montgomery)	£30
65	Storyville SLP 169	I DONE YOU WRONG (LP)	£20
69	Liberty LBS 83237	SLIM'S GOT THIS THING GOIN' ON (LP)	£30
69	Blue Horizon 7-63213	MIDNIGHT JUMP (LP, mono)	£100
69	Blue Horizon S7-63213	MIDNIGHT JUMP (LP, stereo)	£70

SUNNYSIDERS
55	London HL 8135	Hey! Mr. Banjo/Zoom, Zoom, Zoom	£50
55	London HL 8160	Oh Me Oh My Oh/(Let's Gather Round) The Parlour Piano	£30
55	London HLU 8180	Banjo Woogie/She Didn't Even Say Goodbye	£30
55	London HLU 8202	I Love You Fair Dinkum/Stay On The Sunny Side	£25
56	London HLU 8246	Doesn't He Love Me/Humdinger	£30

SUN PALACE
| 83 | Passion PASH 12 8 | Winning/Rude Movements (12", p/s) | £40 |

SUN RA
| 74 | Decca F 13542 | Can We Change/Don't Go (Demos only) | £30 |
(This artist has no link to the legendary Sun Ra)

SUN RA ARKESTRA
85	MT 1	Nuclear War/IAN DURY: Fuck Off Noddy (white label, 500 only)	£50
82	Y 1 RA	NUCLEAR WAR (12" EP)	£50
10	Jazzman JM 079	THE WORLD IS NOT MY HOME (3 x clear vinyl 7", numbered)	£35
69	Fontana STL 5514	HELIOCENTRIC WORLDS VOL. 1 (LP)	£100
69	Fontana STL 5499	HELIOCENTRIC WORLDS VOL. 2 (LP)	£100
68	Delmark DL 411	JAZZ BY SUN RA VOL 1. (LP, U.K. pressed record in American sleeve)	£40
71	Black Lion BLP 30103	PICTURES OF INFINITY - IN CONCERT (LP)	£40
71	Byg 529 341	THE SOLAR MYTH APPROACH VOL. 2 (LP)	£40
71	Polydor 2460 106	PICTURES OF INFINITY (LP)	£40
78	Affinity AFF 10	S-M APPROACH (LP, with Solar-Myth Ark)	£25
79	Cobra COB 37001	FATE IN A PLEASANT MOOD (LP)	£35
80	Y Y 19	STRANGE CELESTIAL ROAD (LP)	£40
81	Recommended RR 11	NUITS DE LA FOUNDATION MAEGHT VOL 1 (LP, plays at 45rpm, pasted front cover)	£30
81	Recommended RR 11	NUITS DE LA FOUNDATION MAEGHT VOL 1 (LP, plays at 45rpm, silk-screened sleeve)	£60
85	Saturn/Recommended SRRRD1	COSMO SUN CONNECTION (LP, pasted cover)	£300
88	Leo LR 154	LOVE IN OUTER SPACE (LP)	£25
89	Blast First BFFP 42	OUT THERE A MINUTE (LP)	£25
90	Blast First BFFP 60	SUN RA & MYTH SCIENCE ARKESTRA (3 x 10", box set, with insert)	£40
04	Art Yard ARTYARDLP 001	DISCO 3000 (LP, reissue)	£20
04	Art Yard ARTYARDLP 002	MEDIA DREAMS (LP, reissue)	£30
05	Art Yard ARTYARDLP 003	SLEEPING BEAUTY (LP, reissue)	£20
05	Art Yard ARTYARDLP 005	ON JUPITER (LP, reissue)	£25

SUNRAYS
| 65 | Capitol CL 15416 | I Live For The Sun/Bye, Baby, Bye | £15 |
| 66 | Capitol CL 15433 | Andrea/You Don't Phase Me | £15 |

SUNRISE
| 76 | Grapevine GRA 105 | BEFORE MY EYES (LP) | £30 |

SUN SET
| 67 | Polydor BM 56193 | East Baby/You Can Ride My Rainbow | £20 |

SUNSETS
| 61 | Ember EMB S 125 | Cry Of The Wild Goose/Manhunt | £15 |

SUNSHINE COMPANY
| 68 | Liberty LBL/LBS 83120 | THE SUNSHINE COMPANY (LP) | £35 |
| 69 | Liberty LBL/LBS 83159 | SUNSHINE AND SHADOWS (LP) | £35 |

SUNSHINE KID
| 73 | RCA RCA 2413 | My Linda/Get Your Rocks Off Baby | £25 |

SUNSHINE POWER
| 89 | Sing A Song SASM 1 | It's Too Late (Vocal)/It's Too Late (Instrumental)/It's Too Late (Accapella) (12" | £15 |

SUNSHINE (1)
| 72 | Warner Brothers K 46169 | SUNSHINE (LP, gatefold sleeve) | £15 |
(see also Pretty Things)

SUNSHINE THEATRE
| 71 | Harp SP1004 | Mountain/I Want | £400 |

SUNSTROKE
78 Hot Stuff HS 004 | **HERE COMES THE TRAIN EP** **£20**

SUNTREADER
73 Island HELP 13 | **ZIN ZIN** (LP, insert sleeve, black label, pink 'i' logo) **£15**

SUPER 8
95 García POUM 001 | **Billy The Kid/It Doesn't Matter/How Can I Understand The Flies?** ('hairloss' p/s, 500 only, 37 sold, 35 returned for refund, the rest believed burned) **£25**

SUPER TONES
70 Banana BA 312 | **Freedom Blues/First Time I Met You** **£50**

SUPERBOYS
68 Giant GN 22 | **Ain't That A Shame/Do It Right Now** **£30**
68 Giant GN 31 | **You're Hurtin' Me/Funky Soul** **£30**
(see also Dandy & Superboys, Little Sal)

SUPER CAT
88 Blue Trac BTRD 020 | **Nuff Man Dead Ya/ABC** (12") **£30**

SUPERCHUNK
95 City Slang EFA 049661 | **HERE'S WHERE THE STRINGS COME IN** (LP, insert) **£20**

SUPER COMBO
75 Rokel RKL 5001 | **Woko/Afro Funk** **£15**

SUPER FURRY ANIMALS
95 SFAP1 | **Frisbee** (12" promo, 1-sided, unreleased intended debut single. Not on a label) **£25**
96 Creation CRELP 190 | **FUZZY LOGIC** (LP, with insert) **£100**
97 Creation CRELP 214 | **RADIATOR** (2-LP) **£100**
98 Creation CRELP 228 | **OUT SPACED** (LP) **£100**
99 Creation CRELP 242 | **GUERRILLA** (2-LP, gatefold, pop up sleeve) **£100**
00 Placid Casual PLC03LP | **MWNG** (LP, ltd white vinyl, p/s PVC sleeve. 2000 copies) **£80**
01 Sony/Epic 5024131 | **RINGS AROUND THE WORLD** (2-LP, side 3 plays from inside out, with free 7" white label 7") **£200**
03 Epic 5123751 | **PHANTOM POWER** (2-LP etched vinyl with insert, 3000 copies) **£50**
04 Placid Casual PL07CD | **PHANTOM PHORCE** (2-LP ltd version with bonus 'Slow Life' EP disc, fold-out packaging. 3000 copies) **£25**
05 Epic 5176711 | **SONGBOOK - THE SINGLES VOLUME ONE** (2x12" pop up gatefold sleeve) **£35**
05 Sony 5205011 | **LOVE KRAFT** (2-LP, gatefold) **£50**
15 Domino REWIGLP98X | **MWNG** (3-LP, reissue, white vinyl) **£25**
(see also Gruff Rhys)

SUPERGRASS
94 Backbeat BEAT 4 | **Caught By The Fuzz/Strange Ones** (hand-stamped labels, 1,000 only, later re-pressed) ...**£30**
97 Parlophone GRASS 9497 | **THE SINGLES 1994-1997** (8 x 7" black vinyl, 'grass'-covered box set, with signed & numbered insert, promo only) **£30**
95 Parlophone PCSX 7373 | **I SHOULD COCO** (LP, with inner & bonus single "Stone Free"/"Odd?" [PCSS 7373]) **£70**
97 Parlophone 724385522819 | **IN IT FOR THE MONEY** (LP) **£60**
99 Parlophone 5220561 | **SUPERGRASS** (LP, with poster) **£70**
02 Parlophone 724354180019 | **LIFE ON OTHER PLANETS** (LP) **£40**
04 EMI 5789941 | **SUPERGRASS IS 10 : BEST OF 94-04** (2 x 10" LP, clear vinyl, gatefold) **£80**
05 Parlophone 333 334-1 | **ROAD TO ROUEN** (LP) **£35**
08 Parlophone 519 7341 | **DIAMOND HOO HA** (LP) **£20**
(see also Jennifers)

SUPERIMPOSERS
05 Little League LL 704 | **Seeing Is Believing/Shadows** **£75**

SUPERMATIX
81 MC 4 | **BAD TIMING EP** (p/s) **£20**

SUPER$HIT666
00 Infernal INFERNAL003LP | **SUPER$HIT666** (10" LP, with inner sleeve, purple vinyl) **£70**
00 Infernal INFERNAL 003LP | **SUPER$HIT666** (10" LP, with inner sleeve, black vinyl) **£50**
(see also Hellacopters, Wildhearts)

SUPERSISTER
71 Dandelion 2310 146 | **TO THE HIGHEST BIDDER** (LP, gatefold sleeve) **£125**
71 Polydor 2419 030 | **SUPER STARSHINE 3** (LP) **£40**
72 Polydor 2419 061 | **PRESENT FROM NANCY** (LP) **£40**
73 Polydor 2480 153 | **PUDDING & YESTERDAY** (LP) **£50**
73 Polydor 2925 021 | **ISKANDER** (LP, gatefold sleeve with lyric sheet) **£25**

SUPERTRAMP
70 A&M AMLS 981 | **SUPERTRAMP** (LP, laminated sleeve, brown label) **£50**
71 A&M AMLH 64306 | **INDELIBLY STAMPED** (LP, gatefold sleeve, brown label) **£50**
74 A&M AMLS 68258 | **CRIME OF THE CENTURY** (LP, lyric inner, 'McNeil Press Ltd' printing credit) **£15**
84 A&M AMLK63708 | **BREAKFAST IN AMERICA** (LP, Nimbus Supercut mail order only through Practical Hi Fi magazine **£80**

(DIANA ROSS &) SUPREMES
64 Stateside SS 257 | **When The Lovelight Starts Shining Thru' His Eyes/Standing At The Crossroads Of Love** **£50**
64 Stateside SS 257 | **When The Lovelight Starts Shining Thru' His Eyes/Standing At The Crossroads Of Love** (DJ copy) **£100**
(Credited to Supremes.)
64 Stateside SS 327 | **Where Did Our Love Go/He Means The World To Me** (DJ copy) **£100**
64 Stateside SS 350 | **Baby Love/Ask Any Girl** (DJ copy) **£100**
65 Stateside SS 376 | **Come See About Me/**(You're Gone But) **Always In My Heart** (DJ copy) **£100**

MINT VALUE £

65	Tamla Motown TMG 501	Stop! In The Name Of Love/I'm In Love Again (DJ copy)	£100
65	Tamla Motown TMG 516	Back In My Arms Again/Whisper You Love Me Boy	£25
65	Tamla Motown TMG 516	Back In My Arms Again/Whisper You Love Me Boy (DJ copy)	£85
65	Tamla Motown TMG 527	Nothing But Heartaches/He Holds His Own	£25
65	Tamla Motown TMG 527	Nothing But Heartaches/He Holds His Own (DJ copy)	£85
65	Tamla Motown TMG 543	I Hear A Symphony/Who Could Ever Doubt My Love	£20
65	Tamla Motown TMG 543	I Hear A Symphony/Who Could Ever Doubt My Love (DJ copy)	£75
66	Tamla Motown TMG 548	My World Is Empty Without You/Everything Is Good About You	£25
66	Tamla Motown TMG 548	My World Is Empty Without You/Everything Is Good About You (DJ copy)	£75
66	Tamla Motown TMG 560	Love Is Like An Itching In My Heart/He's All I Got	£50
66	Tamla Motown TMG 560	Love Is Like An Itching In My Heart/He's All I Got (DJ copy)	£150
66	Tamla Motown TMG 575	You Can't Hurry Love/Put Yourself In My Place	£15
66	Tamla Motown TMG 575	You Can't Hurry Love/Put Yourself In My Place (DJ copy)	£70
66	Tamla Motown TMG 585	You Keep Me Hangin' On/Remove This Doubt	£15
66	Tamla Motown TMG 585	You Keep Me Hangin' On/Remove This Doubt (DJ copy)	£60
67	Tamla Motown TMG 597	Love Is Here And Now You're Gone/There's No Stopping Us Now (DJ copy)	£70
67	Tamla Motown TMG 607	The Happening/All I Know About You (DJ copy)	£75

(The above 45s are credited to the Supremes.)

67	Tamla Motown TMG 616	Reflections/Going Down For The Third Time (DJ copy)	£60
67	Tamla Motown TMG 632	In And Out Of Love/I Guess I'll Always Love You (DJ copy)	£40
68	Tamla Motown TMG 650	Forever Came Today/Time Changes Things (DJ copy)	£40
68	Tamla Motown TMG 662	Some Things You Never Get Used To/You've Been So Wonderful To Me (DJ copy)	£40
68	Tamla Motown TMG 677	Love Child/Will This Be The Day? (DJ copy)	£40
68	Tamla Motown PSRS 317	Love Child (special Royal Command Performance promo sent to journalists with Ken East "talking invite" with Love Child playing in the background)	£70
69	Tamla Motown TMG 695	I'm Living In Shame/I'm So Glad I Got Somebody (Like You Around) (DJ copy)	£40
69	Tamla Motown TMG 704	No Matter What Sign You Are/The Young Folks (DJ copy)	£35
69	Tamla Motown TMG 721	Someday We'll Be Together/He's My Sunny Boy (DJ copy)	£35

(The above 45s are credited to Diana Ross & Supremes.)

70	Tamla Motown TMG 735	Up The Ladder To The Roof/Bill, When Are You Coming Back (DJ copy)	£30
70	Tamla Motown TMG 747	Everybody's Got The Right To Love/But I Love You More (DJ copy)	£25
71	Tamla Motown TMG 760	Stoned Love/Shine On Me (DJ copy)	£30
71	Tamla Motown TMG 782	Nathan Jones/Happy (Is A Bumpy Road) (DJ copy)	£30

(The above 45s are credited to the Supremes and do not feature Diana Ross)

65	Tamla Motown TME 2008	THE SUPREMES HITS (EP, with flipback sleeve & push-out centre)	£30
65	Tamla Motown TME 2008	THE SUPREMES HITS (EP)	£35
66	Tamla Motown TME 2011	SHAKE (EP)	£75
64	Stateside SL 10109	MEET THE SUPREMES (Stateside in green writing)	£50
65	Tamla Motown TML 11002	WITH LOVE - FROM US TO YOU (mono)	£60
65	Tamla Motown TML 11012	WE REMEMBER SAM COOKE	£50
65	Tamla Motown TML 11018	THE SUPREMES SING COUNTRY, WESTERN AND POP	£50
65	Tamla Motown TML 11020	MORE HITS BY THE SUPREMES	£35
66	T. Motown TML 11026	THE SUPREMES AT THE COPA (mono)	£25
66	T. Motown STML 11026	THE SUPREMES AT THE COPA (stereo)	£30
66	T. Motown TML 11028	I HEAR A SYMPHONY (mono)	£25
66	T. Motown TML 11028	I HEAR A SYMPHONY (stereo)	£30
66	T. Motown TML 11039	SUPREMES A-GO GO (mono)	£25
66	T. Motown STML 11039	SUPREMES A-GO GO (stereo)	£35
67	T. Motown TML 11047	THE SUPREMES SING MOTOWN (mono)	£25
67	T. Motown STML 11047	THE SUPREMES SING MOTOWN (stereo)	£30
67	T. Motown TML 11054	THE SUPREMES SING RODGERS AND HART (mono)	£20
67	T. Motown STML 11054	THE SUPREMES SING RODGERS AND HART (stereo)	£22

(The LPs listed above are credited to the Supremes, with flipback sleeves.)

68	T. Motown (S)TML 11063	GREATEST HITS (stereo/mono, original pressing with flipback laminated sleeve)	£15
68	T. Motown (S)TML 11070	'LIVE' AT LONDON'S TALK OF THE TOWN (mono/stereo)	£15
68	T. Motown (S)TML 11073	REFLECTIONS (mono/stereo)	£25
69	T. Motown TML 11088	SING & PERFORM FUNNY GIRL (mono)	£20
69	T. Motown STML 11088	SING & PERFORM FUNNY GIRL (stereo)	£18
69	T. Motown TML 11095	LOVE CHILD (mono)	£25
69	T. Motown STML 11095	LOVE CHILD (stereo)	£20
69	T. Motown TML 11114	LET THE SUNSHINE IN (mono)	£25
69	T. Motown STML 11114	LET THE SUNSHINE IN (stereo)	£22
70	T. Motown TML 11137	CREAM OF THE CROP (mono)	£20
70	T. Motown STML 11137	CREAM OF THE CROP (stereo)	£18

(The above LPs are credited to Diana Ross & Supremes. Originally issued with flipback sleeves; later pressings are worth two-third of these values.)

70	T. Motown STML 11157	RIGHT ON (as Supremes)	£20
70	T. Motown STML 11175	NEW WAYS BUT LOVE STAYS	£20
71	T. Motown STML 11189	TOUCH (LP, as Supremes)	£15
72	T. Motown STML 11210	FLOY JOY	£15
73	T. Motown STML 11222	PRODUCED AND ARRANGED BY JIMMY WEBB (LP, as Supremes)	£15
75	T. Motown STML 11293	THE SUPREMES	£15
76	T. Motown STML 12047	MARY, SCHERRIE & SUSAYE	£15

(see also Primettes, Diana Ross, Temptations, Four Tops, Florence Ballard)

SUPREMES & FOUR TOPS

71	T. Motown STML 11179	THE SUPREMES AND THE FOUR TOPS - MAGNIFICENT 7 (LP)	£15

DIANA ROSS & THE SUPREMES & THE TEMPTATIONS

69	T. Motown TML 11096	DIANA ROSS & THE SUPREMES JOIN THE TEMPTATIONS (LP, mono)	£20
69	T. Motown STML 11096	DIANA ROSS & THE SUPREMES JOIN THE TEMPTATIONS (LP, stereo)	£18

69	T. Motown (S)TML 11110	THE ORIGINAL SOUNDTRACK FROM TCB (LP, gatefold laminated sleeve)	£15
70	T. Motown TML 11122	TOGETHER (LP, flipback sleeve, mono)	£18
70	T. Motown STML 11122	TOGETHER (LP, flipback sleeve, stereo)	£15

SUPREME WARRIOR

| 83 | Supreme Warrior SW001 | Treading The Tightrope/Mad & Cynical | £50 |

SURFACE

83	Salsoul SAL 104	Falling In Love/Instrumental	£15
83	Salsoul SALT 104	Falling In Love/Instrumental (12")	£20
83	Salsoul SALT 104/XD 01291	Falling In Love (1-sided 12")	£15
15	Salsoul SALT 104	Falling In Love/Instrumental) (12", reissue)	£15

SURFACE TENSION

| 83 | Spiv 2TS | Rotation/Don't Let Them/Traffic Accident (p/s) | £15 |

SURFARIS

63	Brunswick 05894	Waikiki Run/Point Panic	£15
64	Brunswick 05902	Scatter Shield/Bat Man	£15
63	London RE-D 1405	WIPE OUT (EP)	£35
63	London HA-D 8110	WIPE OUT (LP)	£40
63	Brunswick LAT 8561	THE SURFARIS PLAY (LP, mono)	£30
63	Brunswick STA 8561	THE SURFARIS PLAY (LP, stereo)	£40
64	Brunswick LAT 8567	HIT CITY '64 (LP, mono)	£30
64	Brunswick STA 8567	HIT CITY '64 (LP, stereo)	£40
64	Brunswick LAT 8582	FUN CITY (LP)	£30
65	Brunswick LAT 8605	HIT CITY '65 (LP)	£40
65	Brunswick LAT 8631	IT AIN'T ME BABE (LP, mono)	£35
65	Brunswick STA 8631	IT AIN'T ME BABE (LP, stereo)	£40
66	Dot DLP 3535	WIPE OUT (LP, reissue)	£25
87	MCA MCL 1842	WIPE OUT - THE SINGLES ALBUM 1963-1967 (LP, withdrawn)	£20

SURGEON

| 96 | Downwards DNLP1 | COMMUNICATIONS (LP as 2 x 12") | £18 |
| 97 | Tresor 74321 47314 1 | BASICTONALVOCABULARY (LP as 2 x 12") | £18 |

SURGEONS

| 79 | Surgery S-100 | Sid Never Did It/Breaking Rocks On Riker's Island | £50 |

SURGICAL SUPPORTS

| 81 | Industrious Youth CONSTRUCT 2 | WITHDRAWN FOR DISPOSAL EP | £30 |

JOHN SURMAN (TRIO)

69	Deram DM 224	Obeah Wedding/Don't Stop The Carnival	£50
68	Deram DML/SML 1030	JOHN SURMAN (LP)	£100
69	Deram DML-R/SML-R 1045	HOW MANY CLOUDS CAN YOU SEE? (LP)	£100
70	Futura GER 12	ALORS! (LP)	£45
71	Dawn DNLS 3006	THE TRIO (LP, with Stu Martin, poster)	£70
71	Dawn DNLS 3018	WHERE FORTUNE SMILES (LP, with insert, with John McLaughlin, Karl Berger, Stu Martin & Dave Holland)	£40
71	Dawn DNLS 3022	CONFLAGRATION (LP)	£60
71	Deram SML 1094	TALES OF THE ALGONQUIN (LP, with John Warren)	£100
72	Island HELP 10	WESTERING HOME (LP)	£20
73	Island ILPS 9237	MORNING GLORY (LP)	£20
79	Ogun OG 259	BY CONTRACT (LP)	£18

(see also Morning Glory, Trio, Mike Westbook, John McLaughlin, Alan Skidmore/Mike Osborne/John Surman)

SURPRISES

| 79 | Dead Dog DEAD 01 | Jeremy Thorpe Is Innocent/Flying Attack/Little Sir Echo (p/s) | £35 |

SURVIVE

| 16 | HoloDeck HD015LP | HDO15 (LP. marbled grey vinyl) | £20 |
| 16 | Relapse RR7349 | RR7349 (LP. green vinyl) | £20 |

SURVIVORS (1)

| 65 | Rio R 55 | Take Charge/Ska-Ology | £25 |
| 65 | Rio R 70 | Rawhide Ska/OWEN GRAY: Girl I Want You | £35 |

SURVIVORS (3)

| 79 | Tribesman TM 22 | Angel Of Love/Fashion Rock (12") | £15 |

SUSHI

| 99 | Ariwa ARI 187 | Peace And Harmony/MAD PROFESSOR: Aahha (12") | £15 |

SUSIE (1)

| 71 | Decca F 13217 | I Feel The Earth Move/We Are All The Same | £20 |

SUSIE (2)

| 76 | King Cliff KC 001 | Love As Been Good/Version | £25 |

SUSPECT

| 71 | Decca FR 13218 | Mariooka/Belinda | £20 |

SUSSED (1)

| 79 | Shoestring LACE 002 | I Like You/Tango/The Perv (p/s) | £15 |

(SCREAMING) LORD SUTCH (& THE SAVAGES)

61	HMV POP 953	Till The Following Night/Good Golly Miss Molly	£30
63	Decca F 11598	Jack The Ripper/Don't You Just Know It	£15
63	Decca F 11747	I'm A Hog For You/Monster In Black Tights	£15
64	Oriole CB 1944	She's Fallen In Love With A Monster Man/Bye Bye Baby	£50

MINT VALUE £

64	Oriole CB 1962	Dracula's Daughter/Come Back Baby	£80
65	CBS 201767	The Train Kept A-Rollin'/Honey Hush (as Lord Sutch)	£50
66	CBS 202080	The Cheat/Black And Hairy	£50
70	Atlantic 584 321	Cause I Love You/Thumping Beat	£15
70	Atlantic 2400 008	LORD SUTCH AND HIS HEAVY FRIENDS (LP)	£25
72	Atlantic K 40313	HANDS OF JACK THE RIPPER (LP, as Lord Sutch & Heavy Friends)	£25
81	Ace MAD 1	THE METEORS MEET SCREAMING LORD SUTCH (mini-LP, 1 side each, stickered cartoon print on plain grey card sleeve, 1,000 only)	£100
82	Ace CHA 65	ROCK A HORROR (LP, gatefold)	£15

(see also Savages, Meteors, Led Zeppelin, Cliff Bennett & Rebel Rousers, Circles, Nero & Gladiators, Neil Christian & Crusaders)

SUTCLIFFE JUGEND
82	Come Org. WDC 883030	WE SPIT ON THEIR GRAVES (10 x cassette box)	£150
82	Come Org. WDC 883028	CAMPAIGN (cassette, beware of Japanese bootlegs)	£75

ROGER SUTCLIFFE
76	Look LKLP 6038RS	DEATH LETTER (LP)	£30

SUTHERLAND BROTHERS BAND
71	Island ILPS 9181	THE SUTHERLAND BROTHERS BAND (LP, blue inner)	£15

SUZANNE
77	Ring O' 2017 108	Born On Hallowe'en/Like No One Else (in promo p/s)	£25
78	Ring O' 2017 115	single (unreleased)	£0
78	Ring O' 2320 105	SUZANNE (LP, unreleased)	£0

SUZI & BIG DEE IRWIN
66	Polydor BM 65715	Ain't That Lovin' You Baby/I Can't Get Over You	£15

(see also Big Dee Irwin)

SUZY & THE RED STRIPES
79	A&M AMSP 7461	Seaside Woman/B-side To The Seaside (yellow vinyl, die-cut p/s, in box set with badge & 10 'saucy' mini-postcards)	£40

(see also Paul McCartney [& Wings])

SVENSK
67	Page One POF 036	Dream Magazine/Getting Old	£25
67	Page One POF 050	You/All I Have To Do Is Dream	£18

(see also Jason Paul)

SWALLOWS WITH SONNY THOMPSON
52	Vogue V 2136	Roll, Roll Pretty Baby/It Ain't The Meat (78)	£50

(see also Sonny Thompson & His Rhythm & Blues Band)

SWAMP DOGG
72	Mojo 2916 014	TOTAL DESTRUCTION TO YOUR MIND (LP)	£20
73	President PTLS 1	GAG A MAGGOT (LP)	£15

(see also Jerry Williams, Brooks & Jerry)

SWAMP CHILDREN
82	Factory FACT 70	SWAMP CHILDREN (LP)	£20

SWAN ARCADE
73	Trailer LER 2032	SWAN ARCADE (LP)	£20
84	Fellside FE 037	TOGETHER FOREVER (LP)	£18

SWANEE RIVER BOYS
54	Parlophone CMSP 7	Do You Believe/Gloryland Boogie (export issue)	£15

BETTYE SWANN
67	CBS 2942	Make Me Yours/I Will Not Cry	£70
67	CBS 2942	Make Me Yours/I Will Not Cry (DJ copy)	£100
67	CBS 2942	Make Me Yours/I Will Not Cry (DJ copy in p/s)	£150
69	Capitol CL 15586	Don't Touch Me/(My Heart Is) Closed For The Season	£30
04	Honest Jons HJRLP 8	BETTYE SWANN (2-LP)	£40

(see also Sam Dees & Bettye Swann)

SWANS (1)
63	Stateside SS 224	He's Mine/You Better Be A Good Girl Now	£40
64	Cameo Parkway C 302	The Boy With The Beatle Hair/Please Hurry Home	£40

SWANS (2)
84	K.422 KDE112	YOUNG GOD (12" EP)	£18
88	Product Inc. 12PROD 23	Love Will Tear Us Apart (Red Version)/Trust Me/Love Will Tear Us Apart (Black Version)/Our Love Lies (12", black vinyl, p/s)	£15
84	K. 422/Some Bizzare KCC 1	COP (LP, with inner)	£60
86	K. 422/Some Bizzare KCC 2	GREED (LP, with inner)	£25
86	K. 422/Some Bizzare KCC 3	HOLY MONEY (LP)	£18
87	Product Inc. 33PROD 17	CHILDREN OF GOD (2-LP)	£50
86	No label BURN ONE	PUBLIC CASTRATION IS A GOOD IDEA (2-LP)	£60
87	Young God LOVE 1	FEEL GOOD NOW (2-LP, with poster)	£35
89	MCA MCG 6047	THE BURNING WORLD (LP, with lyric inner)	£18
90	Young God	FILTH (LP, U.K. reissue, 500 only, numbered)	£30
91	Young God YGLP 3	WHITE LIGHT FROM THE MOUTH OF INFAMY (LP)	£75
92	Young God YGLP 5	LOVE OF LIFE (LP, insert)	£40
94	Young God YGLP 9	THE GREAT ANNIHILATOR (2-LP)	£125
95	Young God YGLP 004	BODY TO BODY, JOB TO JOB (LP)	£30
95	Young God YGLP 005B	LOVE OF LIFE (LP, in box)	£80

BENRICE SWANSON
65	Chess CRS 8008	Lying Awake/Baby I'm Yours	£30

65	Chess CRS 8008	Lying Awake/Baby I'm Yours (DJ copy)...	£50

DAVE SWARBRICK

67	Bounty BYI 6030	RAGS, REELS AND AIRS (LP, with Martin Carthy & Diz Disley)	£40
67	Polydor Special 236 514	RAGS, REELS AND AIRS (LP, reissue, with Martin Carthy & Diz Disley)...........	£25

(see also Martin Carthy & Dave Swarbrick, Fairport Convention,Young Tradition, Vashti Bunyan, Ian Campbell)

SWEAT

80	Double D DDLP	NO MORE RUNNING (LP, insert)..	£20

ROSALYN SWEAT & PARAGONS

73	Duke DU 160	Blackbird Singing/Always..	£25

(see also Paragons)

SWE-DANES

61	Warner Bros SWEP 2017	THE SWE-DANES (EP; stereo)..	£15

(see also Alice Babsi)

SWEDISH MODERN JAZZ GROUP

61	Tempo TAP 31	SAX APPEAL (LP)	£200

SWEENEY'S MEN

68	Transatlantic TRA 170	SWEENEY'S MEN (LP)	£90
69	Transatlantic TRA 200	THE TRACKS OF SWEENEY (LP)	£90
76	Transatlantic TRASAM 37	SWEENEY'S MEN (LP, reissue)...	£20
77	Transatlantic TRASAM 40	THE TRACKS OF SWEENEY (LP, reissue)	£18

(see also Gay & Terry Woods, Dr. Strangely Strange)

JIM SWEENY

58	Philips PB 811	The Midnight Hour/Till The Right One Comes Along	£20

SWEET

68	Fontana TF 958	Slow Motion/It's Lonely Out There	£400
69	Parlophone R 5803	The Lollipop Man/Time..	£100
70	Parlophone R 5826	All You'll Ever Get From Me/The Juicer	£40
70	Parlophone R 5848	Get On The Line/Mr. McGallagher...	£70
71	Parlophone R 5902	All You'll Ever Get From Me/The Juicer (reissue).................................	£15
73	RCA RCA 2403	Ballroom Blitz/Rock & Roll Disgrace (mispressed at wrong speed, 49rpm; matrix: 2403-A-1E)...	£15
78	Polydor POSP 5	California Nights/Show Me The Way (unreleased)................................	£0
79	Polydor POSP 73	Big Apple Waltz/Why Don't You	£20
80	RCA PE 5226	Fox On The Run/Hellraiser/Ballroom Blitz/Blockbuster (EP, p/s)	£15
80	Polydor POSP 160	Sixties Man/Oh Yeah	£15
80	Polydor POSP 160	Sixties Man/Oh Yeah (mispressing, B-side plays "Tall Girls")	£20
71	RCA SF 8288	FUNNY HOW SWEET CO-CO CAN BE (LP)..	£80
74	RCA LPL 15039	SWEET FANNY ADAMS (LP)	£80
74	RCA LPL 15080	DESOLATION BOULEVARD (LP, gatefold sleeve)	£60
75	RCA SPC 0001	STRUNG UP (2-LP)...	£50
76	RCA RS 1036	GIVE US A WINK (LP)..	£20
77	RCA PL 25072	OFF THE RECORD (LP, gatefold, with inner sleeve)	£18
78	Polydor POLD5001	LEVEL HEADED (LP)..	£20
79	Polydor POLD 5022	CUT ABOVE THE REST (LP, with inner sleeve)	£18
80	Polydor POLS 1021	WATER'S EDGE (LP)..	£25
82	Polydor 2311 1179	IDENTITY CRISIS (LP)..	£22
84	Anagram GRAM 16	SWEET SIXTEEN (LP)..	£15
84	Anagram P GRAM 16	SWEET SIXTEEN (LP, picture disc)	£25

(see also Brian Connolly, Mayfield's Mule, Elastic Band)

SWEET AIR

70	Chime CH 1	Pictures In A Puddle/Sally FInne	£200

SWEET AS CANDY

71	Stem ST 3	At The Bus Stop/The Missing Keys..	£20

SWEET BRIAR

70	Access ACC 314	The Liar/Choose Me/Sunworshipper (p/s)	£40

SWEET PEA

70	Tribual TR 1	Run To The Forest/I'm In My Bad Books......................................	£20

RACHEL SWEET

78	Stiff SEEZ 12	FOOL AROUND (LP, grey vinyl, printed inner)................................	£15

SWEET CHARIOT

72	De Wolfe DWLP 3230	SWEET CHARIOT & FRIENDS (LP, library issue only)	£40

SWEET CHARLES

88	Urban URB 15	Yes It's You/LYN COLLINS: Rock Me Again And Again And Again and Again..............	£25

SWEET CONFUSION

69	Escort ES 809	Elizabeth Serenade/Don At Rest..	£40
69	Escort ES 812	Hotter Scorcher/Conquer Lion	£30

(see also Stranger & Patsy)

SWEETCORN

71	Pye 7N45047	We Can Work Together/Carpet Ride..	£15

SWEETEST ACHE

90	Sarah SARAH 36	If I Could Shine/Here Comes The Ocean (p/s, insert)	£25
90	Sarah SARAH 39	Tell Me How It Feels/Heaven-Scented World (p/s, insert)	£25
91	Sarah SARAH 47	Everlasting/Sickening (p/s, insert)...	£25
91	Sarah SARAH 608	JAGUAR (LP)..	£50

SWEET FEELING
67   Columbia DB 8195   All So Long Ago/Charles Brown £200
(see also Rupert's People)

SWEETHEARTS
65   Blue Beat BB 389   Sit Down And Cry (actually with Clinton & Rufus)/PRINCE BUSTER: Ghost Dance............£80

HARRY SWEETING
68   Coxsone CSL 8012   FROM JAMAICA WITH LOVE (LP)...£100

SWEET INSPIRATIONS
68   Atlantic 587/588 090   THE SWEET INSPIRATIONS (LP) £25
69   Atlantic 587/588 137   WHAT THE WORLD NEEDS NOW IS LOVE (LP) £25
69   Atlantic 587/588 194   SWEETS FOR MY SWEET (LP)...£20
70   Atlantic 2465 003   SWEET SWEET SOUL (LP)..£20
79   RSO RSS 12   HOT BUTTERFLY (LP)..£15
20   Reel RMLP 6139LE   THE SWEET INSPIRATIONS (LP, reissue, 500 only, numbered)................................£20
(see also Cissy Houston)

SWEET PAIN
69   Mercury 20146 SMCL   SWEET PAIN (LP, laminated gatefold, black/silver label)......................................£175
(see also Dick Heckstall-Smith)

SWEET PLUM
69   Middle Earth MDS 103   Lazy Day/Let No Man Steal Your Thyme...£30
70   Middle Earth MDS 105   Set The Wheels In Motion/Catch A Cloud £30

SWEET REVENGE
80s SRS SRS 15   Feel The Bullets Bite/Inside Your Head...£125

SWEET SAVAGE
81   Park PRK 1001   Take No Prisoners/Killing Time (p/s, red and yellow label) £60
81   Park PRK 1001   Take No Prisoners/Killing Time (p/s, black and yellow label) £40
80s Crashed CAR 48   Straight Through The Heart/Teaser (no p/s)..£150
80s private pressing   The Raid/Prosecutors Of Greed (possibly unreleased) £50
(see also Dio, Whitesnake)

SWEETSHOP
68   Parlophone R 5707   Barefoot And Tiptoe/Lead The Way £30
(see also Mark Wirtz)

SWEET SLAG
71   President PTLS 1042   TRACKING WITH CLOSE-UPS (LP) £160

SWEET THURSDAY
69   Polydor 2310 051   SWEET THURSDAY (LP) £25
(see also Nicky Hopkins, Mark-Almond)

SWEGAS
71   Trend 6480 002   CHILD OF LIGHT (LP, gatefold sleeve)..£50

SWELL
92   Mean MEAN LP 002   ...WELL? (LP, marble vinyl) £15

SWELL MAPS
78   Rather GEAR ONE   Read About Seymour/Ripped And Torn/Black Velvet (p/s) £35
79   Rough Trade RT 010/Rather Read About Seymour/Ripped And Torn/Black Velvet (p/s, reissue, different back
     GEAR ONE MK. 2   sleeve)...£15
79   R. Trade RT 012/GEAR 3   Dresden Style/Mystery Track/Ammunition Train/Full Moon (Dub) (p/s)........£25
79   R. Trade RT 021/GEAR 6   Real Shocks/English Verse/Monlogues (p/s, 2 different colours)......................£25
79   R. Trade RT 036/GEAR 7   Let's Build A Car/Big Maz In The Country/...Then Poland (p/s) £15
79   Rough Trade ROUGH 2/   A TRIP TO MARINEVILLE (LP, with inner sleeve, with bonus EP in die-cut sleeve [Rather
     Rather TROY 1   GEAR FIVE])..£45
79   Rough Trade ROUGH 2/   A TRIP TO MARINEVILLE (LP, with inner sleeve, without bonus EP in die-cut sleeve
     Rather TROY 1   [Rather GEAR FIVE])..£30
80   Rough Trade ROUGH 15   SWELL MAPS IN 'JANE FROM OCCUPIED EUROPE' (LP)....................................£35
81   Rough Trade ROUGH 21   WHATEVER HAPPENS NEXT... (2-LP) £20
84   Rough Trade ROUGH 41   SWELL MAPS IN 'COLLISION TIME' (LP) £15
89   Mute MAPS 1   A TRIP TO MARINEVILLE (LP, reissue) £15
89   Mute MPAS 2   SWELL MAPS IN 'JANE FROM OCCUPIED EUROPE' (LP, reissue) £15
(see also Nikki Sudden, Steve Treatment,, Metrophase)

SWERVEDRIVER
91   Creation CRELP 093   RAISE (LP, with free 7")..£35
91   Creation CRELP 093   RAISE (LP, without free 7")..£20
93   Creation CRELP 143   MEZCAL HEAD (LP)..£70
95   Creation CRELP 157   EJECTOR SEAT RESERVATION (LP, with free 7") £70
95   Creation CRELP 157   EJECTOR SEAT RESERVATION (LP, without free 7") £60
98   Sonic Waves SWD 099LP   99TH DREAM (LP) £30

JONATHAN SWIFT
71   CBS 64412   INTROVERT (LP, side opening gatefold, nude cover)...£20
72   CBS 64751   SONGS (LP, with lyric insert) £15

TAYLOR SWIFT
19   Republic B0030483-21   Me!(featuring Brendon Urie of Panic! At The Disco) Same track both sides (7",black
                               vinyl, website exclusive, p/s, four cover variants with different cat nos.)............£80
19   Republic B0030509-11   Me!(Billboard Music Awards Live Rehearsal Audio) Same track both sides (12", picture
                               disc, website exclusive)...£180
19   Republic B0030508-21   Me!(Billboard Music Awards Live Rehearsal Audio) Same track both sides (7", black
                               vinyl, p/s, website exclusive)...£140

19	Republic B0030485-11	**Me!**(featuring Brendon Urie of Panic! At The Disco) **Same track both sides** (12", picture disc, website exclusive)	**£120**
20	Republic B0032764-21	**Cardigan** (Cabin In Candlelight Version)/**Cardigan** (7", white vinyl, available exclusively via Taylor Swift's website)	**£130**
20	Republic B0032765-11	**Cardigan** (Cabin In Candlelight Version)/**Cardigan** (12", white vinyl, available exclusively via Taylor Swift's website)	**£160**
20	Republic B0032733-21	**Cardigan/Cardigan** (Songwriting Voice Memo) (7", gold vinyl, available exclusively via Taylor Swift's website)	**£105**
20	Republic B0032734-01	**Cardigan/Cardigan** (Songwriting Voice Memo) (12", gold vinyl, available exclusively via Taylor Swift's website)	**£100**
20	Republic B0032760-11	**Cardigan/Cardigan** (Songwriting Voice Memo) (12" Picture Disc, available exclusively via Taylor Swift's website)	**£110**
20	Republic B0033165-11	**Christmas Tree Farm/Christmas Tree Farm** (Recorded Live at the 2019 iHeart Radio Jingle Ball) (12" Picture Disc, Available exclusively via Taylor Swift's website)	**£120**
22	Republic B 0035004-21	**The Lakes** (Album Version)/**The Lakes** (Original Version) (RSD 22, p/s, clear vinyl, 10,000 world-wide)	**£180**
14	Big Machine 0602547092687	**1989** (2LP, g/f)	**£25**
16	Big Machine Records 00843930021154	**TAYLOR SWIFT** (2LP, g/f, 2006 debut album made available on vinyl)	**£25**
16	Big Machine Records 00843930021147	**FEARLESS** (Platinum Edition) (2LP,g/f, reissue)	**£25**
16	Big Machine Records 00843930004003	**SPEAK NOW** (2LP, g/f, reissue)	**£25**
16	Big Machine Records 00843930007103	**RED** (2LP, g/f. reissue)	**£25**
17	Big Machine Records 00843930033119	**REPUTATION** (CD, A4 magazine Volume 1)	**£60**
17	Big Machine Records 00843930033126	**REPUTATION** (CD, A4 magazine Volume 2)	**£50**
17	Big Machine BMRCO 0600F	**REPUTATION** (2LP, picture disc, printed inners)	**£30**
18	Big Machine 00843930034659	**FEARLESS** (Platinum Edition) (2LP, g/f, RSD, crystal clear and metallic gold vinyl)	**£550**
18	Big Machine 00843930034673	**RED** (2LP, world-wide numbered reissue, g/f, Black Friday 2018, clear vinyl)	**£550**
18	Big Machine Records 00843930034666	**SPEAK NOW** (2LP, g/f, smoke vinyl, Black Friday)	**£450**
19	Republic Records 00602508148453	**LOVER** (2LP, pink and blue vinyl, printed inners)	**£30**
19	Republic 602508148453	**LOVER** (2LP, reissue, pink and blue translucent vinyl, hype sticker, gatefold sleeve)	**£30**
20	Republic 0602435034881	**FOLKLORE** (Deluxe Edition No. 1: 2LP, Brown vinyl, g/f, 'In The Trees' standard edition)	**£30**
20	Republic 602435034898	**FOLKLORE** (2LP, Deluxe edition No 2: 'In The Weeds', blue vinyl, gatefold sleeve)	**£190**
20	Republic 602435034904	**FOLKLORE** (2LP, Deluxe edition No 3: 'Meet Me Behind The Mall', grey vinyl, gatefold sleeve)	**£80**
20	Republic 602435034911	**FOLKLORE** (2LP, Deluxe edition No 4: 'Betty's Garden', lavender vinyl, gatefold sleeve)	**£160**
20	Republic 602435034928	**FOLKLORE** (2LP, Deluxe edition No 5: 'Stolen Lullabies', green vinyl, gatefold sleeve)	**£170**
20	Republic 602435034935	**FOLKLORE** (2LP, Deluxe edition No 6: 'Hide And Seek', blue vinyl, gatefold sleeve)	**£150**
20	Republic 602435034942	**FOLKLORE** (2LP, Deluxe edition No 7: 'Running Like Water', silver vinyl, gatefold sleeve)	**£150**
22	Republic 602435034959	**FOLKLORE** (2LP, Deluxe edition No 8: 'Clandestine Meetings', pink vinyl, gatefold sleeve)	**£150**
21	Republic B0033579-01	**FEARLESS** (TAYLOR'S VERSION) (3LP, Limited Edition, gold vinyl, gatefold sleeve, pressed in Germany)	**£45**
21	Republic B0033582-01	**FEARLESS** (TAYLOR'S VERSION) (3LP, Limited Edition, red opaque vinyl, hype sticker, 3 panel gatefold sleeve, Originally available from Target, pressed in Czech Republic)	**£45**
21	Republic Records B0033410-21	**EVERMORE** (2LP, g/f, printed inners, green vinyl)	**£25**
21	Republic B0034423-01	**RED** (TAYLOR'S VERSION) (4LP, Limited Edition, red vinyl, hype sticker. originally available from Target, pressed in Czech Republic)	**£70**
21	Republic B0034422-01	**RED** (TAYLOR'S VERSION) (4LP, Limited Edition, 45RPM black vinyl, hype sticker, gatefold sleeve, Worldwide release, pressed in Germany)	**£40**
21	Republic B0034572-02	**RED** (TAYLOR'S VERSION) (2CD, Signed edition, shrink-wrapped, booklet, available from Swift's UK online store)	**£150**
22	Republic 2448119230	**MIDNIGHTS** (LP, Lavender Marbled vinyl, g/f, 8-page booklet)	**£30**
22	Republic 2445790050	**MIDNIGHTS** (LP, Jade Green Marbled vinyl, g/f, 8-page booklet)	**£25**
22	Republic 2445790067	**MIDNIGHTS** (LP, Blood Moon Marbled vinyl, g/f, 8-page booklet)	**£25**
22	Republic 2445789825	**MIDNIGHTS** (LP, Moonstone Blue Marbled vinyl, g/f, 8-page booklet)	**£30**
22	Republic 2445832583	**MIDNIGHTS** (LP, Special Edition, mahogany marbled vinyl, hype sticker, gatefold sleeve)	**£25**
23	Republic 2445789825	**MIDNIGHTS** (LP, Special Edition: Repress, blue translucent marbled vinyl (Moonstone Blue), **hype sticker, gatefold sleeve, NB: slightly lighter colour than 2022 blue translucent version**)	**£20**
23	Big Machine B0033410-01	**EVERMORE** (2LP, Deluxe Edition, Repressing, opaque green vinyl, gatefold sleeve)	**£25**
23	Republic B0036425-0	**FOLKLORE: THE LONG POND STUDIO SESSIONS** (2LP, RSD, grey vinyl, hype sticker, gatefold sleeve)	**£260**
23	Republic 2448438096	**SPEAK NOW** (TAYLOR'S VERSION) (3LP, g/f, lilac marbled vinyl, printed inners)	**£30**
23	Republic 2448438034	**SPEAK NOW** (TAYLOR'S VERSION) (3LP, g/f, orchid marbled vinyl, printed inners)	**£35**
23	Republic 0245554214	**1989** (TAYLOR'S VERSION) (2LP, Special Edition ''Crystal Skies' blue vinyl, gatefold sleeve, pressed in Germany)	**£30**
23	Republic 0245554215	**1989** (TAYLOR'S VERSION) (2LP, Special Edition 'Rose Garden Pink' vinyl, gatefold sleeve, pressed in France)	**£35**
23	Republic 0245597657	**1989** (TAYLOR'S VERSION) (CD, 'Rose Garden Pink' edition, 16-page booklet, poster insert)	**£30**
24	Republic 602458933314	**THE TORTURED POETS DEPARTMENT** (2LP, clear vinyl edition with bonus track 'The Manuscript', inners, 24-page book-bound jacket gatefold. Some copies contain hand-written note by Taylor Swift)	**£30**
24	Republic 602458933321	**THE TORTURED POETS DEPARTMENT** (2LP, dark brown vinyl edition with bonus track 'The Manuscript', inners, 24-page book bound jacket, gatefold sleeve)	**£40**

MINT VALUE £

24	Republic 602458933345	THE TORTURED POETS DEPARTMENT (2LP, beige vinyl edition with bonus track 'The Bolter', inners, 24-page book bound jacket, gatefold sleeve)	£40
24	Republic 602465081350	THE TORTURED POETS DEPARTMENT (2LP, "smoke gray" colour vinyl edition with bonus track 'The Albatross', inners, 24-page book bound jacket, gatefold sleeve)	£40
24	Republic 602465081381	THE TORTURED POETS DEPARTMENT (2LP, 'Ghosted' white vinyl edition with bonus track 'The Manuscript', 24-page book bound jacket, booklet, gatefold sleeve)	£40
24	Republic 602465081411	THE TORTURED POETS DEPARTMENT (CD, Deluxe, "The Bolter" Collector's Edition, clear fatbox jewel case, with cloth patch, bookmark, magnet and four photo cards)	£30
24	Republic 602465081398	THE TORTURED POETS DEPARTMENT (CD, Deluxe, "The Albatross" Collector's Edition, clear fatbox jewel case, with cloth patch, bookmark, magnet and four photo cards)	£30
24	Republic 602465081404	THE TORTURED POETS DEPARTMENT (CD, Deluxe "The Black Dog" Collector's Edition, clear fatbox jewel case, with cloth patch, bookmark, magnet and four photo cards)	£30
24	Republic 602465081381	THE TORTURED POETS DEPARTMENT (CD, Deluxe, "The Manuscript" Collector's Edition, clear fatbox jewel case, with cloth patch, bookmark, magnet and four photocards)	£35
24	Republic 602458933314	THE TORTURED POETS DEPARTMENT (CD, UK and Ireland edition, inc. bonus track 'But Daddy I Love Him (Acoustic Version)' **jewel case, 20-page booklet, poster**)	£50
24	Republic 602465081343	THE TORTURED POETS DEPARTMENT (CD, Standard edition with Signed Insert, inc. bonus track 'The Manuscript' jewel case, 20-page booklet, poster)	£100

TUFTY SWIFT

77	Free Reed FRR 017	HOW TO MAKE A BAKEWELL TART (LP, with booklet)	£25
85	Shark SHARK 04	YOU'LL NEVER DIE FOR LOVE (LP, private pressing)	£15

SWIM DEEP

| 13 | Chess Club CCLP 02 | WHERE THE HEAVEN ARE WE (LP & 7" signed) | £40 |

SWINDLEFOLK

69	Deroy	SWINDLED (LP, private pressing)	£75
70	Deroy	A-ROVIN' (LP, private pressing)	£75
71	CAM 311	DUSK TO DAWN (LP, white label, hand-mae sleeves)	£150

RAY SWINFIELD

| 68 | Morgan MR 107P | ONE FOR RAY (LP) | £45 |

SWINGERS

60	Vogue V 9158	Love Makes The World Go Round/Jackie	£15
67	Blue Beat BB 379	Simpleton/FRANCIS: Warn The People	£75

SWINGING BLUE JEANS

63	HMV POP 1206	Do You Know/Angie	£15
66	HMV POP 1533	Sandy/I'm Gonna Have You	£15
66	HMV POP 1564	Rumours, Gossip, Words Untrue/Now The Summer's Gone	£15
67	HMV POP 1596	Tremblin'/Something's Coming Along	£18
67	HMV POP 1605	Don't Go Out Into The Rain/One Woman Man	£18
64	HMV 7EG 8850	SHAKE WITH THE SWINGING BLUE JEANS (EP)	£40
64	HMV 7EG 8868	YOU'RE NO GOOD MISS MOLLY (EP)	£40
64	HMV CLP 1802	BLUE JEANS A' SWINGING (LP, mono)	£60
64	HMV CSD 1570	BLUE JEANS A' SWINGING (LP, stereo)	£75
64	Regal SREG 1073	TUTTI FRUTTI (LP, export issue)	£50
67	MFP MFP 1163	SWINGING BLUE JEANS (LP, reissue of HMV CLP 1802)	£15
74	Dart BULL 1001	BRAND NEW AND FADED (LP)	£18

(see also Ray Ennis & Blue Jeans, Blue Jeans, Escorts)

SWINGING CATS

80	Two Tone CHS TT 14	Mantovani/Away (paper label, company sleeve)	£15
80	Two Tone CHS TT 14	Mantovani/Away (silver plastic label, company sleeve)	£25

SWINGING SAPERLIPOPETTE

| 79 | Kitty 7 | Little Claw/I'm Not A Teddy Bear | £30 |

SWINGING SOUL MACHINE

| 69 | Polydor 56760 | Spooky's Day Off/Nobody Wants You | £15 |

(see also Machine)

SWITCH 7

| 80 | Noisy HISS 1 | You Win/Credit Cards (no p/s) | £25 |

SWORDEDGE

| 80 | Swordedge 001 | SWORDEDGE (LP) | £250 |

SWORD OF JAH MOUTH

| 81 | Metro PBLP 001 | INVASION (LP) | £80 |

SWORN LORD

| 90 | Davy G DG003 | The Vengeance Is Mine (12") | £150 |

SWV

| 92 | RCA 07863 66074 1 | IT'S ABOUT TIME (LP) | £150 |

SYDNEY (CROOKS) ALL STARS

70	Bullet BU 436	The Return Of Batman/In Action	£30
70	Bullet BU 437	Outer Space/Full Moon	£40

(see also Pioneers, Junior English)

JOHN SYKES

| 82 | MCA MCA 792 | Please Don't Leave Me/(Instrumental) (with Phil Lynott, in p/s) | £35 |

(see also Thin Lizzy, Phil Lynott, Tygers Of Pan Tang, Whitesnake)

ROOSEVELT SYKES

56	Vogue V 2389	Fine And Brown/Too Hot To Hold	£75
56	Vogue V 2389	Fine And Brown/Too Hot To Hold (78)	£30
56	Vogue V 2393	Walkin' This Boogie/Security Blues	£75

MINT VALUE £

56	Vogue V 2393	Walkin' This Boogie/Security Blues (78) £30
66	Delmark DJB 2	BACK TO THE BLUES (EP) £30
62	Encore ENC 183	BIG MAN OF THE BLUES (LP) £25
61	Columbia 33SX 1343	FACE TO FACE WITH THE BLUES (LP) £30
62	Columbia 33SX 1422	THE HONEYDRIPPER (LP, with Alexis Korner) £60
65	Bluesville BVLP 1006	THE RETURN OF ROOSEVELT SYKES (LP) £25
67	77' 77LEU 12-50	BLUES FROM BAR ROOMS (LP) £30
67	Riverside RLP 8819	MR SYKES' BLUES 1929-1932 (LP) £22
67	Ember EMB 3391	ROOSEVELT SYKES SINGS THE BLUES (LP) £20
71	Barclay 920 294	THE HONEYDRIPPERS' DUKE'S MIXTURE (LP) £15
70s	Delmark DL 607	HARD DRIVIN' BLUES (LP, blue label) £15

(see also Robert Pete Williams)

SYKO & CARIBS
64	Blue Beat BB 213	Do The Dog/Jenny £20
64	Blue Beat BB 223	Big Boy/Sugar Baby £15

SYKO & MAK
92	PM PMT 004	HOMICIDE EP (12") £20

SYLTE SISTERS
63	London HLU 9753	Summer Magic/Well It's Summertime £15

SYLVAN
65	Columbia DB 7674	We Don't Belong/Life's Colours Have Gone £15

SYLVESTER'S JUKE BOX
73	CBS 8419	Juke Box/It's Because £50

SYLVIA
73	London SHU 8453	PILLOW TALK £20

SYLVIA (U.S.)
68	Soul City SC 103	I Can't Help It/It's A Good Life £20

DAVID SYLVIAN
84	Virgin V 2290	BRILLIANT TREES (LP, printed inner) £25
85	Virgin SYL 1	ALCHEMY: AN INDEX OF POSSIBILITIES (Cassette) £15
86	Virgin VDL 1	GONE TO EARTH (2LP, gatefold) £30
87	Virgin V 2471	SECRETS OF THE BEEHIVE (LP, 4-page insert) £50
89	Virgin DSCD 1	WEATHERBOX (5CD box set, poster, booklet) £120
04	Samadhisound SOUNDLP 1	BLEMISH (LP, gatefold, printed inner, 2000 only, extra track: Trauma) £200
10	Samadhisound SOUND LP 2	MANAFON (2LP, 180g, gatefold, printed inners, 1200 copies worldwide) £120
18	Virgin/UMC 671 524-6	DEAD BEES ON A CAKE (2LP, gatefold, printed inners, white vinyl, sticker to shrinkwrap, RSD, vinyl issue of 1999 CD) £70
18	Virgin/UMC 671 524-3	DEAD BEES ON A CAKE (2LP, reissue, gatefold, printed inners, sticker to shrink) £50
19	Virgin/UMC 679 533-3	ALCHEMY: AN INDEX OF POSSIBILITIES (LP, printed inner, vinyl release of 1985 cassette) £40
23	UMR 387 688-6	SAMADHISOUND 2003-2014 DO YOU KNOW ME NOW? (11CD box set, book) £180

(See also Japan, Virginia Astley)

DAVID SYLVIAN & ROBERT FRIPP
93	Virgin SYLLP 1	DARSHAN (12", silver inner) £30
93	Virgin V2712	THE FIRST DAY (2LP, printed inners) £150
94	Virgin DAMAGE 1	DAMAGE (gold CD, silver embossed box, booklet) £30

DAVID SYLVIAN AND HOLGER CZUKAY
88	Venture VE 11	PLIGHT & PREMONITION (LP) £40
89	Venture VE 49	FLUX + MUTABILITY (LP) £30

(see also David Sylvian, Can, Japan)

SYLVIN & GLENROY
70	Torpedo TOR 25	What You Gonna Do 'Bout It/KEN JONES: Sad Mood £40

SYMBOL
79	Art & Craft AC 001	Motherless Children/RANKING CARETAKER: Take It Away (12") £40
79	Kebra Nagast KH 04	Black Man's Word/Mr. Oppressor (12") £15

SYMBOLS
68	President PT 190	Lovely Way To Say Goodnight/Pretty City £18
68	President PT 216	Do I Love You/Schoolgirl £20
68	President PTL 1018	THE BEST PART OF THE SYMBOLS (LP) £25

SYMON & PI
68	Parlophone R 5662	Sha La La La Lee/Baby Baby £25

SYMPHONICS
73	Polydor 2058 341	Heaven Must Have Sent You/Using Me £15

SYMPHONIC SLAM
76	A&M AMLH 69023	SYMPHONIC SLAM (LP) £20

SYN
67	Deram DM 130	Created By Clive/Grounded £120
67	Deram DM 145	Flowerman/14-Hour Technicolour Dream £120

(see also Syndicats, Yes, Peter Banks)

SYNANTHESIA
69	RCA SF 8058	SYNANTHESIA (LP) £400

SYNCHROMESH
80	Rok ROK XI/XII	October Friday/E.F. BAND: Another Day Gone (company die-cut sleeve) £40

SYNDICATE OF SOUND
66	Stateside SS 523	Little Girl/You	£35
66	Stateside SS 538	Rumours/The Upper Hand	£18
66	Stateside S(S)L 10185	LITTLE GIRL (LP)	£50

SYNDICATE (2)
| 81 | EMI 12EMI 5182 | Dance You To The Ground/Step On The Gas (12") | £35 |

SYNDICATS
64	Columbia DB 7238	Maybellene/True To Me	£150
65	Columbia DB 7441	Howlin' For My Baby/What To Do	£250
65	Columbia DB 7686	On The Horizon/Crawdaddy Simone	£650
65	Columbia DB 7686	On The Horizon/Crawdaddy Simone (demos)	£450

(see also Peter Banks, Ray Fenwick, Syn, Tomorrow, Yes)

SYNTHETIC DREAMS
| 81 | Logical Step LOGIC 02 | Obsessions/U+500 (p/s) | £15 |

SYNYX
| 82 | Reality Attack RAF 1 | BLACK DEATH (EP, fold out sleeve,plain white labels) | £20 |

SYSTEM OF A DOWN
| 99 | Columbia/American | Sugar/War (live) | £30 |
| 01 | Columbia 5015341 | TOXICITY (LP) | £30 |

SYSTEM ROOTS
| 17 | System SYSTM 017 | Step On It/Step on It (Dub)/Sweet Harmony (12", p/s) | £15 |

SYSTEM (1)
| 77 | Tash | THE OTHER SIDE OF TIME (LP, 250 copies only) | £110 |

SYSTEM X (EX)
94	3rd Eye EYE 001	MINDGAMES EP (12")	£20
94	3rd Eye EYE 002	SOMETHING OF REAL EXISTENCE EP (12", white label, various coloured vinyl)	£20
94	3rd Eye EYE 004	SOMETHING OF INTELLEGENT EXISTENCE EP (12")	£25

(see also Studio Pressure)

SYZYGY
| 85 | Taptag TAP 3 | LADY IN GREY (mini-LP) | £20 |

(see also Blackthorn)

S/Z
| 83 | East Jazz Records 1 | S/Z (LP) | £25 |

GABOR SZABO
66	HMV CLP 3614	JAZZ RAGA (LP)	£25
67	Impulse MILP 506	THE SORCERER (LP, mono)	£30
69	Fontana STL 5489	BACCHANAL (LP)	£40

T

ANDY T
| 82 | 221984/05 | WEARY OF THE FLESH (EP) | £15 |

(see also Crass)

JAMIE T.
05	Pacemaker PANICSDJ 001	So Lonely Was The Ballad/Back In The Game (p/s, 500 only)	£15
07	Virgin 0094637885512	PANIC PREVENTION (LP)	£60
09	Virgin V3059	KINGS AND QUEENS (LP)	£40

PHILIP TABANE & MALOMBO
| 88 | Kijima BIG 002 | MALOMBO (LP) | £40 |

TABLE TOPPERS
| 62 | Starlite ST45 069 | Rocking Mountain Dew/My Wild Irish Rose Rock | £20 |

CHARLIE TABOR
| 63 | Island WI 061 | Blue Atlantic/Red Lion Madison | £20 |

JUNE TABOR
86	Strange Fruit SFPS 015	THE PEEL SESSIONS (12" EP)	£15
76	Topic 12TS 298	AIRS AND GRACES (LP)	£15
77	Topic 12TS 360	ASHES AND DIAMONDS (LP)	£15
05	Topic TSECD 4003	ALWAYS (4-CD box set, booklet)	£20

TAC-TIX
| 88 | R.E. Good GSM 188 | Whisper On The Street/R.E. Good (p/s) | £15 |

TAD & SMALL FRY
| 62 | London HLU 9542 | Checkered Continental Pants/Pretty Blue Jean Baby | £15 |

TADPOLE
| 73 | More MR2 | Follow The Rain/Suzy Jones | £15 |

TADPOLES
| 69 | High Note HS 032 | Rasta/Like Dirt | £25 |

TAFARI & PAUL FOX
| 90 | Cause N Effect CE 007 | Jah Jah Bless Mandela/Version | £20 |

90	Cause N Effect CE12 007	Jah Jah Bless Mandela/Version (12")	£25

TAG

75	Philips 6006 477	Off Down The Road/Guitar Love	£15

TAGES

66	Columbia DB 8019	Crazy 'Bout My Baby/In My Dreams	£15
66	HMV POP 1515	So Many Girls/I'm Mad	£50
67	Parlophone R 5640	Treat Me Like A Lady/Wanting	£15
68	Parlophone R 5702	There's A Blind Man Playin' Fiddle In The Street/Like A Woman	£15
68	MGM MGM 1443	Halcyon Days/I Read You Like An Open Book	£20

(see also Blond)

BLIND JOE TAGGART

52	Tempo R 55	Religion Is Something Within You/Mother's Love (78)	£20
55	Jazz Collector L 129	Religion Is Something Within You/Mother's Love (78, reissue)	£15

TAGMEMICS

80	Index INDEX 003	Chimneys/(Do The) Big Baby/Take Your Brain Out For A Walk (p/s, with insert)	£15

(see also Art Attacks)

TAICONDEROGA

69	Beacon BEA 143	Whichi Tai To/Speakin' My Mind	£70

JACQUELINE TAIEB

68	Fontana TF 952	Tonight I'm Going Home/7 A.M.	£150

LYN(N) TAIT(T) (& THE JETS)

66	Doctor Bird DB 1006	Vilma's Jump Up (as Lyn Taitt & The Comets)/GLEN MILLER & HONEYBOY MARTIN: Dad Is Home	£25
66	Doctor Bird DB 1047	Spanish Eyes (with Tommy McCook)/STRANGER & HORTENSE: Loving Wine	£50
67	Island WI 3066	Something Stupid/Blue Tuesday (as Lyn Tait & the Jets)	£35
67	Island WI 3075	I Don't Want To Make You Cry/Nice Time (as Lyn Tait & the Jets)	£250
68	Island WI 3139	Napoleon Solo/Pressure And Slide (as Lyn Taitt & the Jets)	£70
68	Amalgamated AMG 810	El Casino Royale/Dee's Special (as Lynn Taitt & the Jets)	£35
68	Pama PM 723	Soul Food/Music Flames (as Lyn Tait & the Jets)	£40
68	Island ILP 969	SOUNDS ROCK STEADY (LP, as Lyn Taitt & the Jets)	£250
68	Big Shot BBTL 4002	GLAD SOUNDS (LP, as Lynn Taitt & the Jets)	£150

(see also Mike Thompson Jnr, ALton Ellis, Ken Boothe, Baba Brooks)

PAULETTE TAJAH

93	Discotex DTLP 15	HAPPY MEMORIES VOL. 5 (LP)	£15

YUKIHIRIO TAKAHASHI

82	Alfa 86393	NEUROMANTIC (LP)	£15

(see also Yellow Magic Orchestra)

TAKE FIVE

60s	D.S.C.A (no cat. no.)	MY GIRL (EP, oversized p/s; Dundee Students Charity Appeal record)	£100

TAKE IT

79	Fresh Hold TRI	Man Made World/Taking Sides/How It Is (p/s)	£40
80	Fresh Hold FHR 1	Twenty Lines/Armchairs/Friends And Relations (foldout p/s with insert)	£20

TAKE THAT

91	Dance U.K. DUK 2	Do What U Like/Waiting Around (p/s)	£15
91	Dance U.K. 12DUK 2	Do What U Like (Club Mix)/Do What U Like (Radio Mix)/Waiting Around (12", p/s; most with wrong tracks listed on sleeve)	£25

(see also Robbie Williams)

TAKE 3

84	Elite DAZZ 32	Music & Time/Music & Time (extended version) (12")	£15

'TAKERS

64	Pye 7N 15690	If You Don't Come Back/Think	£25

(see also Undertakers, Jackie Lomax)

TAKO

08	Ambassador's Reception ABR 002	My Kind Of Woman/Flotation Dance/Space Fever/Data Transfer (12")	£15

TALAN

89	Talan SRT 9KS 2208	Spellbinder/Underground Madness (p/s)	£20

TALBOT BROTHERS

59	Melodisc MEL 1507	Bloodshot Eyes/She's Got Freckles	£15

TALES

73	MAM 93	Someone Like You/Rockin' Suzanna	£15

TALES OF JUSTINE

67	HMV POP 1614	Albert/Monday Morning (in p/s)	£180
67	HMV POP 1614	Albert/Monday Morning	£60
97	Tenth Planet TP 034	PETALS FROM A SUNFLOWER (LP, gatefold sleeve, numbered, 1,000 only)	£30

TALISKER

75	Caroline CA 1513	DREAMING OF GLENISLA (LP)	£25

TALISMAN (2)

84	Embryo CELA 1T	TAKIN THE STRAIN (LP)	£15

TALISMEN

65	Stateside SS 408	Masters Of War/Casting My Spell	£70

TALKIES

81	Hook HK1	I Fell In Love Last Night/Foreign Legion (p/s)	£20

TALKING HEADS

79	Sire SIR 4004/SAM 87	Take Me To The River/Found A Job//Love Goes To Building On Fire/ Psycho Killer (double pack, gatefold p/s)	£20
77	Sire 9103 328	TALKING HEADS:77 (LP, printed inner)	£25
78	Sire SR 6036	TALKING HEADS : 77 (LP, repressing with STRAWBERRY in run out groove, inner)	£15
78	Sire K 56531	MORE SONGS ABOUT BUILDING AND FOOD (LP, stickered sleeve, inner)	£20
79	Sire K 56707	FEAR OF MUSIC (LP, textured sleeve with free single "Psycho Killer"/"New Feeling" [SAM 108])	£30
79	Sire SRK6076	FEAR OF MUSIC (LP, textured sleeve, without free 7", inner)	£20
80	Sire SRK 6095	REMAIN IN LIGHT (LP, inner and insert)	£20
82	Sire SIR K 66112	THE NAME OF THIS BAND IS TALKING HEADS (2LP, printed inners))	£20
83	Sire 9237711	SPEAKING IN TONGUES (LP, clear vinyl in Robert Rauschenberg package)	£40
83	Sire 92 3883 1	SPEAKING IN TONGUES (LP)	£20
84	EMI 0642402431	STOP MAKING SENSE (LP, inner, booklet)	£15
85	EMI 2403521	LITTLE CREATURES (LP, inner)	£20
86	Sire EU3511	TRUE STORIES (LP, inner)	£20
88	Sire EMD 1005	NAKED (LP, inner and insert)	£20
99	EMI 4994711	STOP MAKING SENSE (2-LP, reissue)	£20

(see also Tom Tom Club, David Byrne & Brian Eno, Brian Eno & David Byrne, David Byrne)

TALK TALK

84	EMI EMI D 5433	Such A Shame/ Again, A Game . . . Again//THE TALK TALK DEMOS: Candy/Talk Talk/ Mirror Man (double pack, poster p/s)	£25
86	EMI 12EMID 5540	Life's What You Make It (Extended)/It's Getting Late In The Evening// It's My Life/ Does Caroline Know? (12", p/s, double pack)	£15
86	EMI EMIP 5551	Living In Another World/For What It's Worth (shaped picture disc)	£15
91	Verve TALKD1/2/3	After The Flood/Myrrhman//New Grass/Stump//Ascension Day/5.09 (3-CD, in die-cut box)	£40
82	EMI EMC 3413	THE PARTY'S OVER (LP, printed inner)	£20
84	EMI EMC 2400021	IT'S MY LIFE (LP, printed inner)	£25
86	EMI EMC 3506	THE COLOUR OF SPRING (LP, printed inners)	£25
88	Parlophone PCSD 105	SPIRIT OF EDEN (LP, printed inner)	£50
90	EMI PCSD 109	NATURAL HISTORY - THE BEST OF TALK TALK (LP, printed inner)	£25
91	Verve 847 717-1	LAUGHING STOCK (LP, printed inners)	£100
91	Parlophone PCS 7349	HISTORY REVISITED - THE REMIXES (LP)	£25
97	EMI LP CENT 14	THE COLOUR OF SPRING (LP, reissue, EMI 100 Centenary, stickered sleeve, virgin vinyl)	£40
99	Pond Life PLVP001 CD	LONDON 1986 (CD)	£30
00	Simply Vinyl SVLP 224	IT'S MY LIFE (LP, reissue, 180g, Simply Vinyl stickers and envelope PVC)	£40
12	EMI EMCX 3506	THE COLOUR OF SPRING (LP/DVD, printed inner, reissue, 180g)	£20
12	Parlophone PCSDX 105	SPIRIT OF EDEN (LP/DVD, reissue, 180g)	£20
12	Verve/Back To Black 533764	LAUGHING STOCK (LP, reissue, 180g, download card)	£40
16	Polydor 00600753655191	LAUGHING STOCK (LP, second reissue, 180g, download card)	£25
19	Parlophone PCSDX 105	SPIRIT OF EDEN (LP/DVD, second reissue, 180g, printed inner)	£25

(see also Reaction, Mark Hollis, .O.Rang, Rustin Man, Beth Gibbons & Rustin Man)

TOM TALL

55	London HL 8150	Are You Mine/Boom Boom Boomerang (as Ginny Wright & Tom Tall)	£20
55	London HLU 8216	Give Me A Chance/Remembering You	£40
56	London HLU 8231	Underway/Goldie Jo Malone	£40
56	London HLU 8231	Underway/Goldie Jo Malone (78)	£15
57	London HLU 8429	Don't You Know/If You Know What I Know (with Ruckus Taylor)	£40
57	London HLU 8429	Don't You Know/If You Know What I Know (with Ruckus Taylor) (78)	£15
55	London RE-U 1035	COUNTRY SONGS VOL. 2 (EP, as Tom Tall & Ginny Wright)	£25

(see also Ginny Wright)

TALULAH GOSH

86	53rd & 3rd AGARR 4/5T	Beatnik Boy/My Best Friend/Steaming Train/Just A Dream (12", p/s)	£15
87	53rd & 3rd AGAS 004	ROCK LEGENDS VOL. 69 (LP, clear vinyl)	£20
91	Sarah 064	THEY'VE SCOFFED THE LOT (LP)	£40

(see also Heavenly, Amelia Fletcher)

TAMANGOES
79	Grapevine GRP 122	I Really Love You/You've Been Gone So Long	£30

TAME DOLL
76	Hopscotch HP 7	I Don't Give A Damn/You	£20

TAMEN
72	Flake FL 1	Sweet Loretta, Make No Mistakes/Drifting (p/s)	£50

TAMINDAY
73	Dile DL3	Dear Lisa/Break The Chain	£30

TAMING THE OUTBACK
86	Black Sun BS 1	Blue Heart/Fire	£15

JAMES TAMLIN
65	Columbia DB 7438	Is There Time/Main Line Central Station	£20

TAMLINS
79	Deb Music DEB 007	Still Water/AUGUSTUS PABLO: Spirit Of Umoja (12")	£20
76	State ETAT 9	BLACK BEAUTY (LP)	£15

TAMPA RED
50	Jazz Collector L 58	Easy Rider Blues/Come On Mama Do That Dance (78)	£15
52	HMV JO 301	Pretty Baby Blues/Since Baby's Been Gone (78, export issue)	£15
50s	Square M 2	Moot It Boy/She Rocks Me (With One Steady Roll) (78)	£15

64	RCA RCX 7160	R & B VOL. 3 (EP) £25
60s	Memory TR 1	TAMPA RED (LP)..£35

TAMPA RED/GEORGIA TOM
59	Jazz Collector JEL 3	THE MALE BLUES VOLUME 2 (EP)..............................£20

TAMS
63	Stateside SS 146	Untie Me/Disillusioned £30
63	HMV POP 1254	What Kind Of Fool Do You Think I Am/Laugh It Off £20
64	HMV POP 1298	It's All Right, You're Just In Love/You Lied To Your Daddy...£18
64	HMV POP 1331	Hey Girl Don't Bother Me/Take Away £150
64	HMV POP 1331	Hey Girl Don't Bother Me/Take Away (DJ copy) £200
65	HMV POP 1464	Concrete Jungle/Till The End Of Time.......................£15
69	Stateside SS 2123	Be Young, Be Foolish, Be Happy/That Same Old Song ...£15
70	Capitol CL 15650	Too Much Foolin' Around/How Long Love £15
68	Stateside (S)SL 10258	A LITTLE MORE SOUL (LP)...£40
70	Stateside SSL 10304	BE YOUNG, BE FOOLISH, BE HAPPY (LP) £25

TANAMO
63	Island WI 108	Come Down/I Am Holding On (actually by Lord Tanamo)...£30

TANDOORI CASSETTE
83	IKA IKA 001	Angel Talk/Third World Brief Case (p/s, 5,000 only)......£20

(see also Nazareth, Alex Harvey, Tear Gas, Stone The Crows)

SHARON TANDY
65	Mercury MF 898	Love Makes The World Go Round/By My Side £30
65	Pye 7N 15806	Now That You've Gone/Hurtin' Me £40
65	Pye 7N 15939	I've Found Love/Perhaps Not Forever £15
67	Atlantic 584 098	Toe Hold/I Can't Get Over It.....................................£20
67	Atlantic 584 124	Stay With Me/Hold On...£60
67	Atlantic 584 137	Our Day Will Come/Look And Find £20
68	Atlantic 584 166	Fool On The Hill/For No One £20
68	Atlantic 584 181	Love Is Not A Simple Affair/Hurry Hurry Choo-Choo ...£40
68	Atlantic 584 194	You've Gotta Believe It/Border Town £20
68	Atlantic 584 214	The Way She Looks At You/He'll Hurt Me....................£30
68	Atlantic 584 219	Hold On/Daughter Of The Sun £100
69	Atlantic 584 242	Gotta Get Enough Time/Somebody Speaks Your Name ...£80

(see also Fleur-De-Lys, Tony & Tandy)

NORMA TANEGA
66	Stateside S(S)L 10182	WALKIN' MY CAT NAMED DOG (LP) £20

TANGENT
80	President PT483	Atlantica/Living In The City £15

TANGERINE DREAM
74	Virgin PR 214	Phaedra (Edit)/Mysterious Semblance At The Strand Of Nightmares (promo)...£30
76	Virgin VDJ 17	Stratosfear/The Big Sleep In Search Of Hades (promo only)...£25
77	MCA PSR 413	Betrayal (Sorceror Theme)/Search (promo only) £25
84	Jive Electro P 74	Warsaw In The Sun/Polish Dance (map-shaped picture disc)...£15
85	Jive JIVE 101	Streethawk/Tear Garden (p/s) £15
85	Jive Electro T 101	STREETHAWK (12" EP)...£20
74	Virgin V2010	PHAEDRA (LP, copies with A1U/B2U matrixes and catalogue number misprinted with catalogue number on top left hand of gatefold sleeve instead of rear)...£20
74	Polydor Super 2383 297	ATEM (LP)...£20
75	Virgin V2025	RUBYCON (LP, gatefold sleeve) £15
75	Polydor Super 2383 314	ALPHA CENTAURI (LP)...£20
76	Virgin V2503	ZEIT (2-LP, reissue) £25
76	Virgin V2068	STRATOSPHERE (LP, green "mirror" girl label, 'Robor Limited' sleeve) ...£15
76	Virgin V 2044	RICOCHET (LP, original copies with incorrect matrix numbers VS 2044 A1/B1 with "S" scratched out)...£15
78	Virgin V2111	FORCE MAJEURE (LP, clear vinyl, textured stickered sleeve) ...£15
80	Virgin VBOX 2	TANGERINE DREAM '70-80 (4-LP box set) £40
80	Virgin TCVX 2	TANGERINE DREAM '70-80 (4-cassette box set) £25
81	Virgin V 2212	EXIT (LP, 1st 1,000 with poster)...............................£15
84	MCA MCF 3233	FIRESTARTER (LP, soundtrack)..................................£15
84	Jive HIP 22	POLAND - THE WARSAW CONCERT (2-LP, gatefold sleeve, with inners) ...£15
84	Jive Electro HIPX 22	POLAND - THE WARSAW CONCERT (2-LP, picture disc)...£25
85	Heavy Metal HMXD 29	FLASHPOINT (CD, soundtrack; playable CD [most copies faulty])...£40
86	Jive Electro TANG 1	IN THE BEGINNING (6-LP box set, with booklet) £30
90	Virgin TD AK 11	TANGERINE DREAM (3-CD, 'Collector's Edition' box set)...£20
03	Virgin 724359612829	TANGENTS 1973 - 1983 (5-CD box set with booklet)...£20

(see also Edgar Froese, Klaus Schulze)

TANGERINE PEEL
67	United Artists UP 1193	Every Christian Lion-Hearted Man Will Show You/Trapped...£30
68	CBS 3402	Solid Gold Mountain/Light Across The River £130
68	CBS 3676	Talking To No One/Wishing Tree...............................£20
69	MGM MGM 1470	Never Say Never Again/A Thousand Miles Away £15
69	MGM MGM 1487	Play Me A Sad Song And I'll Dance/Wish You Could Be Here With Me ...£15
70	RCA LSA 3002	SOFT DELIGHTS (LP)..£40

TANGO
92	Formation FORM 12004	THE IMPACT EP (12", p/s) £25
93	F Project WHITE 024	Future Followers/Time Bomb (12")............................£20

TANGO & DOM
92 Double Vision DV 001   My Mind Is Going/Got To Release (12") £40

TANGO PROJECT
92 White 004   Project 1/Untitled (12", white label test pressing)..£100

TANK (1)
73 Polydor 2058391   Fast Train/The World's An Apple £20
72 Bumble GE 105   Heads I Win, Tails You Lose/Burgundy, Port And Red Wine.......................................£20

TANK (2)
82 Kamaflage KAM 3   Turn Your Head Around/Steppin' On A Landmine (p/s) £15
82 Kamaflage KAMLP 1   FILTH HOUNDS OF HADES (LP, 1st pressing, with black & yellow sleeve)..............£15
82 Kamaflage KAMLP 1   FILTH HOUNDS OF HADES (LP, 2nd pressing, with bonus p/s 7" Don't Walk Away (live)/"The Snake" [KAM F1])...£15
83 Music For Nations MFN 3P   THIS MEANS WAR (LP, picture disc)...£20
(see also Damned)

PHIL TANNER
68 EDF SSLP 1005   PHIL TANNER (LP, with lyric book) £25

TAN TAN
81 Maccabees MPCLP TT1   MUSICAL NOSTALGIA FOR TODAY (LP)...£40

TANTARA
86 President PT 543   I.D.O/Rumours £40
86 President PT 12-543   I.D.O/Rumours (12") £100

TANTARA BLADE
88 King Dice   Seven Shades Of Shame/This Car Has Crushed (p/s) £50

TANTONES
57 Vogue V 9085   So Afraid/Tell Me..£500
57 Vogue V 9085   So Afraid/Tell Me (78) £100

TAPESTRY (1)
67 London HLZ 10138   Carnaby Street/Taming Of The Shrew £30
68 NEMS 56-3679   Like The Sun/Florence £20
69 NEMS 5639-64   Heart & Soul/Who Wants Happiness £60

TAPESTRY (2)
73 Rosemount ROS EP 1   Oh Mountain/Till We Meet/Fire And Rain £30

TAPE WAVES
13 Box Bedroom BBR 3   DRIFTING EP (p/s, numbered, insert, 100 only)..£20

DEMETRISS TAPP
64 Coral Q 72470   Lipstick Paint A Smile On Me/If You Find Love £40

TARA
70 Polydor 2062009   Happy/The Love Of A Woman £15

TARANTULA
70 A&M AMLS 959   TARANTULA (LP) £15

TARHEEL SLIM & LITTLE ANN
65 Sue WI 390   You Make Me Feel So Good/Got To Keep On Lovin' You...£40

TARIKA BLUE
01 Soul Brother LP SCBS 11   ...THE VERY BEST OF (LP) £20

TARRIERS
56 London HLN 8340   Cindy, Oh Cindy/Only If You Praise The Lord (gold label lettering, as Vince Martin & Tarriers)..£15
57 Columbia 33S 1115   THE TARRIERS (10" LP) £15
62 London STA 8525   A LIVE PERFORMANCE AT THE BITTER END (LP) £15
(see also Rooftop Singers)

TARTAN HORDE
75 United Artists UP 35891   Bay City Rollers, We Love You/Rollers Theme £15
(see also Nick Lowe)

TARTANS
67 Island WI 3058   Dance All Night/What Can I Do...£50
68 Caltone TONE 115   Awake The Town (with Lynn Taitt's Band)/LYNN TAITT & JETS: The Brush.......................£70
68 Caltone TONE 117   Coming On Strong/It's Alright (with Tommy McCook's Band) £80
71 Escort ERT 843   A Day Will Come/ROBI'S All STARS: Version..£15
(see also Devon & Tartans, Kaddo Strings, Max Romeo, Derrick Morgan)

TARTS
81 If You Can't Take A Joke JOKE1   Tie Me Kangeroo Down/Gene Queenie...£100

TASAVALLAN PRESIDENTTI
73 Sonet SNTF 636   LAMBERTLAND (LP) £30
74 Sonet SNTF 658   MILKY WAY MOSES (LP, with insert) £30

TASKFORCE
00 White(Lowlife)grafpromo1   Graf Da Bus Up (12" - One sided, 500 pressed)..£15
00 White(Lowlife)no matrix   Wha Blow (12", 1-Sided white label, 200 only) £15
00 Lowlife LOW10   VOICE OF THE GREAT OUTDOORS (EP, 2000 only p/s) £40
01 Rehab RHB001   A LIFE WITHOUT INSTRUCTIONS (EP) £15
99 K'Boro KBR1005   NEW MIC ORDER (LP)..£40
03 MFTC MFTC 02   MUSIC FROM THE CORNER VOL 2 (2-LP) £50

TASSELS
59	London HL 8885	To A Soldier Boy/The Boy For Me	£100
59	London HL 8885	To A Soldier Boy/The Boy For Me (78)	£40
59	Top Rank JAR 229	To A Young Lover/My Guy And I	£30

TASSILLI PLAYERS
95	Universal Egg WWLP 011	WONDERFUL WORLD OF WEED IN DUB (LP)	£20

TASTE
68	Major Minor MM 560	Blister On The Moon/Born On The Wrong Side Of Time	£125
69	Polydor 56313	Born On The Wrong Side Of Time/Same Old Story	£40
70	Major Minor MM 718	Born On The Wrong Side Of Time/Blister On The Moon	£40
69	Polydor 583 042	TASTE (LP, laminated sleeve)	£100
70	Polydor 583 083	ON THE BOARDS (LP, textured sleeve)	£80
71	Polydor 2310 082	LIVE TASTE (LP)	£15
72	Polydor 2383 120	TASTE - LIVE AT THE ISLE OF WIGHT (LP)	£60

(see also Rory Gallagher, Stud)

BUDDY TATE
58	Felsted FAJ 7004	SWINGING LIKE TATE (LP)	£30

GRADY TATE
69	Fontana STL 5490	WINDMILLS OF MY MIND (LP)	£15

HOWARD TATE
66	Verve VS 541	Ain't Nobody Home/How Come My Bulldog Won't Bark	£15
67	Verve VS 549	Look At Granny Run Run/Half A Man	£20
67	Verve VS 552	Get It While You Can/Glad I Knew Better	£15
67	Verve VS 555	Baby I Love You/How Blue Can You Get	£25
67	Verve VS 556	I Learned It All The Hard Way/Part Time Love	£15
68	Verve VS 565	Stop/Shoot 'Em All Down	£15
68	Verve VS 571	Night Owl/Every Day I Have The Blues	£20
67	Verve (S)VLP 9179	GET IT WHILE YOU CAN (LP)	£70

TOMMY TATE
66	Columbia DB 8046	Big Blue Diamonds/A Lover's Reward	£75
66	Columbia DB 8046	Big Blue Diamonds/A Lover's Reward (DJ Copy)	£125

TATTY OLLITY
79	Tatty TR 101	Punktuation/Never Swat A Fly (p/s)	£30

ART TATUM
53	Capitol LC 6625	OUT OF NOWHERE (10" LP)	£15
54	Vogue LDE 081	ART TATUM "JUST JAZZ" (10" LP)	£15
55	Vogue Coral LRA 10011	THE ART TATUM TRIO (10" LP)	£15
55	Columbia Clef 33CX 10005	THE GENIUS OF ART TATUM (LP)	£15
55	Capitol LC 6638	ART TATUM ENCORES (10" LP)	£15
56	Columbia Clef 33CX 10053	THE GENIUS OF ART TATUM (NO. 2) (LP)	£15
57	Columbia Clef 33C 9033	THE GENIUS OF ART TATUM (NO. 3) (10" LP)	£15
57	Columbia Clef 33C 9039	PRESENTING THE ART TATUM TRIO (10" LP)	£15
57	Vogue Coral LVA 9047	HERE'S ART TATUM (LP)	£15
58	Columbia Clef 33CX 10115	ART TATUM (LP)	£15
59	Columbia Clef 33CX 10137	ART TATUM-BEN WEBSTER QUARTET (LP)	£20
60	Top Rank 35/067	ART TATUM DISCOVERIES (LP)	£15

BERNIE TAUPIN
71	DJM DJLPS 415	TAUPIN (LP, textured gatefold sleeve with booklet)	£50
71	DJM DJLPS 415	TAUPIN (LP, textured gatefold sleeve without booklet)	£20

JOHN TAVENER
70	Apple SAPCOR 15	THE WHALE (LP, gatefold sleeve)	£40
71	Apple SAPCOR 20	CELTIC REQUIEM (LP, gatefold sleeve, with insert & 'Apple' inner sleeve)	£80
77	Ring O' 2320 104	THE WHALE (LP, reissue, different single sleeve)	£45
92	Apple SAPCOR 15	THE WHALE (LP, 2nd reissue, gatefold sleeve with inner sleeve)	£25
93	Apple SAPCOR 20	CELTIC REQUIEM (LP, reissue, gatefold sleeve with inner sleeve)	£25

CYRIL TAWNEY
69	Polydor 236 577	THE OUTLANDISH KNIGHT (LP)	£20
70	Argo ZFB 4	SINGS CHILDREN'S SONGS FROM DEVON AND CORNWALL (LP)	£15
70	Argo ZFB 9	A MAYFLOWER GARLAND (LP)	£20

TAX DODGERS
93	TAX 2	Ragamuffin Bizness/Flying High (12", stamped white label)	£20
94	TAX IT	Hot Off D Press/Rebel Without Applause (Two Mixes) (12", stamped white labels)	£20

TAXMAN
84	Senator SEN 001	Bionic Tonic/Video Crazy (white label)	£35
88	Stush STU 002	Tina/Version/Vocal Version (12")	£30
93	Sir George SO 945	Well Armed And Dangerous/She Keeps Running Away (12")	£30

ALLAN TAYLOR
71	Liberty LBS 83483	SOMETIMES (LP, gatefold sleeve)	£50
72	United Artists UAS 29275	THE LADY (LP)	£50
73	United Artists UAG 29468	THE AMERICAN ALBUM (LP, gatefold sleeve)	£20

(see also Fairport Convention)

ARTHUR TAYLOR
59	Esquire 32149	TAYLOR'S TENNORS (LP)	£150

AUSTIN TAYLOR
60   Top Rank JAR 511 — Push Push/A Heart That's True £20

BARRY TAYLOR
70   Destiny DS 01 — Tiger Woman/I'll Shoot The Lights (p/s) £20

BILLY TAYLOR (TRIO)
57   Esquire EP 115 — MAMBO! (EP) £15
57   Esquire EP 169 — THE MOON IN CONCERT (EP) £20
54   Felsted EDL 87009 — JAZZ AT STORYVILLE (10" LP) £35
54   Esquire 20-053 — AT THE TOWN HALL 1954 (LP) £30
54   Esquire 32-010 — A TOUCH OF TAYLOR (LP) £30
57   HMV DLP 1181 — MY FAIR LADY LOVES JAZZ (10" LP) £20
60   Vogue LAE 12192 — TAYLOR MADE PIANO (LP) £20

BOBBY TAYLOR
64   Columbia DB 7282 — Temptation/Mod Bod £15

BOBBY TAYLOR (& VANCOUVERS)
68   Tamla Motown TMG 654 — Does Your Mama Know About Me/Fading Away (with Vancouvers) £50
69   Tamla Motown (S)TML 11093 — BOBBY TAYLOR AND THE VANCOUVERS (LP. mono/stereo)...................................£60
70   Tamla Motown (S)TML 11125 — TAYLOR MADE SOUL (LP, stereo, solo)...£140

BRYAN TAYLOR
61   Piccadilly 7N 35018 — The Donkey's Tale/Let It Snow On Christmas Day...£25

CECIL TAYLOR
60   Contemporary LAC12216 — LOOKING AHEAD! (LP) £35
77   Blue Note BNS 40023 — UNIT STRUCTURES (LP, reissue) £20
88   Leo LR 152 — CHINAMPAS (LP) £15
88   Leo LR 162 — TZOTZIL MUMMERS TZOTZIL (LP) £15
88   Leo LR 404/405 — LIVE IN BOLOGNA (2-LP) £25
88   Leo LR 408/409 — LIVE IN VIENNA (2-LP) £25

CECIL TAYLOR JAZZ UNIT
62   Fontana SFJL 926 — NEFERTITI, THE BEAUTIFUL ONE HAS COME (LP) £40

CHIP TAYLOR
73   Buddah 2318 074 — GASOLINE (LP) £25
74   Warner Bros K 56032 — CHIP TAYLOR'S LAST CHANCE (LP) £15
(see also Wes Voigt)

DEBBIE TAYLOR
76   Arista ARISTA 50 — I Don't Wanna Leave You/Just Don't Pay £30

ELIZABETH TAYLOR
63   Colpix PXL 459 — IN LONDON (LP, TV soundtrack, music by John Barry, mono)...............................£30
63   Colpix PXL 459 — IN LONDON (LP, TV soundtrack, music by John Barry, stereo)............................£35
(see also John Barry)

TED TAYLOR FOUR
62   Oriole CB 1713 — Jericho/Everytime We Say Goodbye...£15
62   Oriole CB 1767 — Surfrider/Spotlight £15

GEOFF TAYLOR
55   Esquire 20-060 — GEOFF TAYLOR ALL STARS (10" LP) £50

GLORIA TAYLOR
70   Polydor BM 56788 — You Gotta Pay The Price/Loving You And Being Loved By You £15

HOUND DOG TAYLOR
66   Outasite 45-504 — Christine/Alley Music (99 copies only)...£100

JAMES TAYLOR
70   Apple APPLE 32 — Carolina In My Mind/Something's Wrong £20
68   Apple APCOR 3 — JAMES TAYLOR (LP, gatefold sleeve, black inner, orange cover lettering, mono)...............£40
68   Apple SAPCOR 3 — JAMES TAYLOR (LP, gatefold sleeve, black inner, orange cover lettering, stereo).............£25
70   Apple SAPCOR 3 — JAMES TAYLOR (LP, 2nd issue, gatefold sleeve, 'Apple' inner sleeve, black cover lettering) £25
70   Warner Bros WS 1843 — SWEET BABY JAMES (LP, orange label, later green label) £20
71   Warner Bros WS 2561 — MUD SLIDE SLIM AND THE BLUE HORIZON (LP, g/fold sleeve, green label) £18
72   Warner Bros K 46043 — SWEET BABY JAMES (LP, reissue, green label) £15
91   Apple SAPCOR 3 — JAMES TAYLOR (LP, reissue, gatefold sleeve) £18

JAMES TAYLOR QUARTET
95   Acid Jazz JAZID 124S — Whole Lotta Love (white label, withdrawn) £50
96   Acid Jazz JAZID 139 — Creation (10", p/s, mispressed with Hungarian porn music on A-side) £35
87   Re-Elect Pres. REAGAN 2D — MISSION: IMPOSSIBLE (mini-LP, with film dialogue, 500 only) £30
(see also Prisoners, Daggermen, New Jersey Kings, Sound Stylistics)

JEREMY TAYLOR
66   Decca LK 4731 — ALWAYS SOMETHING NEW (LP) £30
68   Fontana (S)TL 5475 — HIS SONGS (LP) £20
69   Fontana (S)TL 5523 — MORE OF HIS SONGS (LP)...£20
72   Galliard GAL 4018 — PIECE OF GROUND (LP)..£15

JOHN TAYLOR
71   Turtle TUR 302 — PAUSE AND THINK AGAIN (LP) £400

JOHNNIE TAYLOR

67	Stax 601 003	Ain't That Lovin' You/Outside Love (dark blue label)	£50
67	Stax 601 003	Ain't That Lovin' You/Outside Love (light blue label)	£30
70	Stax STAX 150	Steal Away/Friday Night	£20
67	Stax 589 008	WANTED, ONE SOUL SINGER (LP)	£50
69	Stax (S)XATS 1006	WHO'S MAKING LOVE (LP)	£20
69	Stax 228 008	LOOKING FOR JOHNNIE TAYLOR (LP)	£25
69	Stax SXATS 1024	THE J.T. PHILOSOPHY CONTINUES (LP)	£25
70	Soul City SCB 2	ROOTS OF JOHNNIE TAYLOR (LP)	£75

(LITTLE) JOHNNY TAYLOR

65	Vocalion V 9234	Part Time Love/Somewhere Down The Line	£50
65	Vocalion V 9234	Part Time Love/Somewhere Down The Line (DJ copy)	£75
66	Vocalion VP 9264	One More Chance/Looking At The Future	£40
65	Vocalion VA-F 8031	LITTLE JOHNNY TAYLOR (LP)	£100
72	Mojo 2916 015	EVERYBODY KNOWS ABOUT MY GOOD THING (LP)	£30
73	Contempo COLP 1003	OPEN HOUSE AT MY HOUSE (LP)	£15
74	Contempo CLP 502	SUPER TAYLORS (LP, with Ted Taylor)	£15

JOSEPH TAYLOR

| 72 | Leader LEA 4050 | UNTO BRIGG FAIR (LP, gatefold sleeve with booklet) | £20 |

KAREN TAYLOR AND IAN SHAW

| 78 | Granny GRAN 001 | FRIENDS... (LP) | £40 |

KINGSIZE TAYLOR (& DOMINOS)

64	Polydor NH 66990	Memphis Tennessee/Money (reissue of Shakers single)	£30
64	Polydor NH 66991	Hippy Hippy Shake/Dr. Feelgood (reissue of Shakers single)	£30
64	Decca F 11874	Stupidity/Bad Boy	£50
64	Decca F 11935	Somebody's Always Trying/Looking For My Baby (solo)	£150
65	Polydor BM 56152	Thinkin'/Let Me Love You	£40
63	Polydor EPH21 628	TWIST AND SHAKE (EP, manufactured in Germany)	£110
64	Decca DFE 8569	TEENBEAT 2 - FROM THE STAR CLUB, HAMBURG (EP)	£130

(see also Shakers, Paddy Klaus & Gibson)

LINDA TAYLOR

| 82 | Groove Production GPLP 31 | TAYLOR MADE (LP) | £20 |

MICK TAYLOR

| 65 | CBS 201770 | London Town/Hoboin' | £40 |

MIKE TAYLOR

65	Columbia SX 6042	PENDULUM (LP)	£1500
67	Columbia SX 6137	TRIO (LP)	£1500
07	Trunk JBH 016 LP	MIKE TAYLOR REMEMBERED (LP)	£35

(see also Jack Bruce)

NEVILLE TAYLOR (& CUTTERS)

58	Parlophone R 4447	House Of Bamboo/Mercy, Mercy, Percy (solo)	£40
58	Parlophone R 4447	House Of Bamboo/Mercy, Mercy, Percy (solo) (78)	£20
58	Parlophone R 4476	Tears On My Pillow/I Don't Want To Set The World On Fire (solo)	£20
59	Parlophone R 4524	Crazy Little Daisy/The First Words Of Love (solo)	£20
60	Oriole CB 1546	Dance With Dolly/Free Passes	£20

(see also Bobbie Britton)

R. DEAN TAYLOR

71	Tamla Motown TMG 786	Ain't It A Sad Thing/Backstreet (unissued)	£0
71	Rare Earth RES 101	Ain't It A Sad Thing/Back Street (has TMG 786 matrix in run-out groove)	£15
74	Tamla Motown TMG 896	There's A Ghost In My House/Let's Go Somewhere (DJ Copy)	£25
71	Tamla Motown STML 11185	INDIANA WANTS ME (LP)	£18

ROD TAYLOR

78	Little Lute HITDD 311	If Jah Should Come Now/Africa Be Free/PRINCE HAMMER: Maccabee Bible (12")	£30
78	Freedom Sounds FS 004	Ethiopian King/Version	£20
78	Freedom Sounds FSD 004	Ethiopian King/PHILIP FRAZER: Come Ethiopians (12")	£40
79	Hit Run DD 16	No One Can Tell I About Jah/ERROL HOLT : Yes Yes Yes (12")	£60
79	Lovelinch LL05	True History (Disco Mix Version)/Scientist Vex Version (12")	£15
80	Strong Like Sampson SLSD 011	Jah Is Calling/Inside Right (12")	£20
81	Unity UP 003	Moving Out Ever/Version (12", with Ranking Dread)	£20
82	Dread At The Controls DATCD 015	Sun Moon and Stars/BLAKKA STAR: Rubber Dub Rock/ROOF RADICS: Hand Cuff Dub (12")	£15
78	Hit Run APLP 9031	IF JAH SHOULD COME NOW (LP)	£50
80	Greensleeves GREL 17	WHERE IS YOUR LOVE MANKIND? (LP, green vinyl)	£22

ROD TAYLOR & MIKEY DREAD & KING TUBBY

| 79 | Sufferers Heights SUFF 006 | Behold Him/Parrot Jungle/His Majesty/Dread All The Way (12") | £30 |

ROGER TAYLOR

77	EMI EMI 2679	I Wanna Testify/Turn On The TV (demo copies £40)	£30
81	EMI EMI 5200	My Country (Edit)/Fun In Space (p/s)	£20
84	EMI 12 EMI 5478	Man On Fire (Extended)/Killing Time (12", p/s)	£25
84	EMI EMI 5490	Strange Frontier/I Cry For You (Remix) (p/s)	£15
84	EMI 12 EMI 5490	Strange Frontier (Extended)/I Cry For You (Extended Remix)/ Two Sharp Pencils (Get Bad) (12", p/s)	£20
94	Parlophone NAZIS 1	Nazis 1994 (Radio Mix)/Nazis 1944 (Kick Mix) (12", black vinyl, p/s, promo only)	£15
94	Parlophone NAZIS 3	Nazis 1994 (Radio Mix)/(Kick Mix)/(Big Science Mix)/(Makita Mix) (12", black vinyl, p/s, promo only)	£15

MINT VALUE £

94	Parlophone 12RDJ 6379	**Nazis 1994** (Schindler's Mix)/(Big Science Mix)/(Makita Mix - Extended) (12", white label DJ promo)	£30
93	Parlophone PCSD 157	**HAPPINESS?** (LP, numbered)	£60
93	Parlophone PCSD 157	**HAPPINESS?** (LP, un-numbered)	£80
98	Parlophone 4967241	**ELECTRIC FIRE** (LP, orange vinyl)	£80

(see also Queen, Cross, Hilary Hilary, Ian Hunter, Fox,, Mel Smith, Billy Squier)

ROSEMARIE TAYLOR

75	JD 2009	**TAYLORMAID** (LP, private pressing with insert)	£200

SAM ('THE MAN') TAYLOR

54	MGM SP 1106	**Please Be Kind/This Can't Be Love** (as Sam 'The Man' Taylor & Cat Men)	£30
56	MGM MGM-EP 531	**SAM TAYLOR ORCHESTRA** (EP)	£35

(see also Claude Cloud)

TAYLOR SHARP & TAYLOR

70	CBS 5197	**The Look Of Love/Mr Snow**	£15

TYRONE TAYLOR

75	Torpedo TOR 48	**Move Up Blackman/Version**	£15
77	Observer OBMM 1000	**Soul On Fire** (Gregory Isaacs)**/Saturday Night** (Christine)**/Christine** (12")	£40

VERNON TAYLOR

59	London HLS 8905	**Today Is A Blue Day/Breeze** (unreleased)	£0
60	London HLS 9025	**Mystery Train/Sweet And Easy To Love**	£100

VIC TAYLOR

67	Treasure Isle TI 7021	**Heartaches/When It Comes To Loving You I'm Alright** (B-side actually "Loving Pauper" by Dobby Dobson)	£80
71	Trojan TRLS 38	**DOES IT HIS WAY** (LP)	£20

(see also Tommy McCook)

VINCE TAYLOR (& HIS PLAYBOYS)

58	Parlophone R 4505	**Right Behind You Baby/I Like Love** (solo)	£80
58	Parlophone R 4505	**Right Behind You Baby/I Like Love** (solo) (78)	£40
59	Parlophone R 4539	**Brand New Cadillac/Pledging My Love**	£70
60	Palette PG 9001	**I'll Be Your Hero/Jet Black Machine**	£25
61	Palette PG 9020	**Move Over Tiger/What'cha Gonna Do**	£25
97	Cruisin' 50 CASB 006	**Brand New Cadillac/Right Behind You Baby** (78, 300 only)	£30

VINCENT TAYLOR

80	Live & Love LLDIS 115	**Can't Seem To Forget You/Living A Lie** (12")	£50
80	Live & Love LLDIS 117	**Got To Have You/TAYLOR PLAYERS: Got You Version** (12")	£30

T-BONES

64	Columbia DB 7401	**How Many More Times/I'm A Lover Not A Fighter**	£60
65	Columbia DB 7489	**Won't You Give Him** (One More Chance)**/Hamish's Express Relief**	£35

(see also Gary Farr & T-Bones, Kevin Westlake)

T-BOYS

80	Nems BSS 104	**Bus Song/Mary Jane**	£30
81	Almost Animal AA001	**One Way Street/Factory Girl**	£20

JOHN TCHKAI

66	Fontana 881014/681 014ZL	**RUFUS** (LP, with ARCHIE SHEPP)	£20

TDS MOB

10	Diggers With Gratitude DWG 006	**THE DOPE COMMITTEE** (EP, 75 only, burgundy vinyl)	£45
10	Diggers With Gratitude DWG 006	**THE DOPE COMMITTEE** (EP, 275 only, black vinyl)	£25
10	Diggers With Gratitude DWG 007	**THE BOSTON CLASSICS** (EP, 75 only, white vinyl)	£35

TEA

75	Philips 6305 238	**TEA** (LP)	£15

TEA & SYMPHONY

69	Harvest HAR 5005	**Boredom/Armchair Theatre**	£20
69	Harvest SHVL 761	**AN ASYLUM FOR THE MUSICALLY INSANE** (LP, laminated gatefold sleeve. The name of the band appears above the "Harvest" logo. Those with "An Asylum For The Musically Insane" above the Harvest Logo are Dutch pressings from 1969)	£400
70	Harvest SHVL 785	**JO SAGO** (LP, gatefold sleeve no EMI logo on label)	£700

TEACH YOURSELF TURNTABLISM

04	Pedestrian	**TUTORITOOL - INTERACTIVE TURNTABLISM TUTORIAL** (LP, gatefold with inserts and inner sleeves, 1000 only)	£25

TEACHERS PET

80	TP 001	**Missing Person/Tug Of Love** (p/s)	£40

TEACHO & HIS STUDENTS

58	Felsted AF 104	**Rock-et/Stop**	£60
58	Felsted AF 104	**Rock-et/Stop** (78)	£30

TEA COMPANY

68	Mercury SMCL 20127	**COME AND HAVE SOME TEA WITH THE TEA COMPANY** (LP)	£50

TEAM DOKUS

94	Tenth Planet TP 007	**TEAM DOKUS** (LP, numbered, 500 only)	£25

TEAMWORKS

89	Wau! Mr. Modo WMS 014T	**Never Leave/Version/Rockfort Rock/Version** (12")	£15
89	Wau! Mr. Modo MOWLP 003	**TEAMWORKS PRESENTS RUDY LEE AND STEPPER** (LP)	£20

TEA PARTY
94	Chrysalis CHR 6072	**SPLENDOR SOILS** (LP)	£150
95	Chrysalis CHR 6108	**THE EDGES OF TWILIGHT** (LP)	£150

TEARDROP EXPLODES
79	Zoo CAGE 003	**Sleeping Gas/Camera Camera/Kirkby Workers' Dream Fades** (red p/s)	£20
79	Zoo CAGE 003	**Sleeping Gas/Camera Camera/Kirkby Workers' Dream Fades** (blue p/s)	£15
80	Zoo CAGE 008	**Treason** (It's Just A Story)/**Read It In Books** (in blue & green p/s)	£15
81	Mercury TEAR 4	**Ha Ha I'm Drowning/Poppies In The Field** (in withdrawn p/s, limited pressing with paper labels not moulded plastic)	£15
81	Mercury TEAR 44	**Ha Ha I'm Drowning/Poppies In The Field/Bouncing Babies/Read It In Books** (double pack, withdrawn gatefold p/s)	£40
80	Mercury 6359 035	**KILIMANJARO** (LP, 1st pressing, light blue labels, 'group photo' on cover & inner sleeve)	£20
80	Mercury 6359 035	**KILIMANJARO** (LP, 2nd pressing, dark blue labels)	£15
81	Mercury 6359056	**WILDER** (LP)	£15
90	Mercury 8424391	**EVERYBODY WANTS TO SHAG THE TEARDROP EXPLODES** (LP, with inner)	£15
90	Document DLP 4	**PIANO** (LP)	£15

(see also Julian Cope)

TEARDROPS (JAMAICA)
72	Fab FAB 187	**Let Me Be Free/Version** (white labels only)	£40
71	Ackee ACK 126	**Let Me Be Free/CINDY STARR: Sentimental Girl**	£15
71	Big Shot BI 582	**Two In One/LAURIE'S ALL STARS: Rock-A-Boogie**	£20

TEARDROPS (1)
78	Bent BIGB 3	**IN AND OUT OF FASHION** (12" EP, foldout p/s in poly bag)	£18
79	TJM TJM 9	**Seeing Double/Teardrops And Heartaches** (p/s)	£20
80s	Illuminated JAMS 2	**FINAL VINYL** (LP)	£15

TEAR GAS
70	Famous SFMA 5751	**PIGGY GO-GETTER** (LP, textured gtefold sleeve)	£100
71	Regal Zono. SLRZ 1021	**TEAR GAS** (LP)	£300

(see also Alex Harvey, Tandoori Cassette)

THE TEARS
05	Independiente ISOM49LP	**HERE COME THE TEARS** (LP, numbered)	£30

(see also Suede)

TEARS FOR FEARS
81	Mercury IDEA 12	**Suffer The Children** (Remix)/**Wino/Suffer The Children** (Instrumental) (12", p/s)	£15
82	Mercury IDEA 33	**Mad World/Mad World** (World Remix)//**Suffer The Children/ Ideas As Opiates** (double pack)	£20
82	Mercury IDEA 4	**Change/The Conflict** (withdrawn 'fishing net' sleeve)	£50
82	Mercury IDEA 412	**Change/The Conflict** (12" withdrawn 'fishing net' sleeve)	£100
83	Mercury IDEA R/B 5	**Pale Shelter/We Are Broken** (p/s, red or blue vinyl)	£15
84	Mercury IDEA 7	**Mother's Talk/Empire Building** (clear vinyl picture disc)	£20
15	Mercury 0600753579046	**Shout** (Extended Version)/**Everybody Wants To Rule The World** (Extended Version) (12", withdrawn)	£60
83	Mercury MERS 17	**THE HURTING** (LP, inner)	£15
89	Mercury MERH 58	**SONGS FROM THE BIG CHAIR** (LP)	£15
89	Fontana 838 730 1	**THE SEEDS OF LOVE** (LP)	£15
92	Fontana 510 939 1	**TEARS ROLL DOWN** (LP)	£40
93	Mercury 514875 1	**ELEMENTAL** (LP)	£150
14	Mercury 4700591	**SONGS FROM THE BIG CHAIR** (2014 STEREO MIX) (LP, reissue)	£80
17	Virgin EMI V 3197	**RULE THE WORLD** (2-LP)	£20

(see also Graduate)

TEARS ON THE CONSOLE
75	Holyground HG 120	**TEARS ON THE CONSOLE** (LP, with booklet, 120 demo copies only)	£150
90	Magic Mixture MM 3	**TEARS ON THE CONSOLE** (LP, reissue, 425 only, with insert)	£20

TEASER
89	LTW 9KS 2049	**Here Tonight** (p/s)	£20

TEA SET (1)
66	King KG 1048	**Join The Tea Set/Ready Steady Go!**	£25

TEA SET (2)
78	Waldo's Beat Series 003	**CUPS AND SAUCERS** (EP, with stapled lyric book sleeve)	£20

TECHNIQUES (JAMAICA)
65	Island WI 231	**Little Did You Know/DON DRUMMOND: Cool Smoke**	£60
67	Treasure Isle TI 7001	**You Don't Care** (with Tommy McCook & Supersonics Band)/ **TOMMY McCOOK & SUPERSONICS BAND: Down On Bond Street**	£50
67	Treasure Isle TI 7019	**Queen Majesty/Fighting For The Right**	£55
67	Treasure Isle TI 7026	**Love Is Not A Gamble/Bad-Minded People**	£40
68	Treasure Isle TI 7031	**My Girl/Drink Wine** (with Tommy McCook & Supersonics)	£30
68	Treasure Isle TI 7038	**Devoted/Bless You** (with Tommy McCook & Supersonics)	£35
68	Treasure Isle TI 7040	**It's You I Love/Travelling Man** (with Tommy McCook & Supersonics)	£60
68	Duke DU 1	**I Wish It Would Rain/There Comes A Time**	£60
69	Duke DU 6	**A Man Of My Word/The Time Has Come**	£70
69	Duke DU 22	**What Am I To Do/You're My Everything**	£60
69	Duke DU 60	**Where Were You/Just One Smile**	£25
69	Camel CA 10	**Who You Gonna Run To/Hi There** (B-side act. "Look Who's Back" by Carl Bryan)	£60
69	Camel CA 19	**Everywhere Everyone/Find Yourself Another Fool**	£35
70	Treasure Isle TI 7054	**He Who Keepeth His Mouth/One Day** (act. by Johnny Osborne & Sensations)	£25
70	Big Shot BI 536	**He Who Keepeth His Mouth/One Day** (act. by Johnny Osborne & Sensations)	£15

MINT VALUE £

71	Banana BA 350	Since I Lost You/RILEY'S ALLSTARS: Version	£15

(see also Techniques All Stars, Riots, Tommy McCook, Mighty Avengers, Gaylads, Rad Bryan)

TECHNIQUES (U.S.)
58	Columbia DB 4072	Hey! Little Girl/In A Round About Way	£45
58	Columbia DB 4072	Hey! Little Girl/In A Round About Way (78)	£15

TECHNIQUES ALL STARS
70	Big Shot BI 543	Come Back Darling/Move Over (actually by Johnny Osborne & Sensations)	£30
70	Big Shot BI 545	Elfrego Bacca (actually by Dave Barker)/TECHNIQUES: Iron Joe (B-side actually by Techniques All Stars)	£35
70	Techniques TE 900	Something Tender/CANNONBALL: Bewitch	£35
70	Trojan TR 7728	Eldora/TECHNIQUES: If It's Not True (B-side actually by Techniques All Stars)	£20

(see also Dennis Alcapone, Ansell Collins)

TECHNOSAURUS
93	Invention TBH 1	YOU GAVE ME NOTHING EP (12", stamped white labels)	£25

TEDDIE & THE TIGERS
67	Spin SP 2004	Hold On I'm Comin'/First Love Never Dies	£30

TEDDY
71	Upsetter US 353	Elusion/UPSETTERS: Big John Wayne	£25

TEDDY & THE TWILIGHTS
63	Stateside SS 167	I'm Just Your Clown/Bikini Bimbo	£22

TEDDY BEARS
59	London HLP 8836	I Don't Need You Anymore/Oh Why	£15
59	London HLP 8889	You Said Goodbye/If You Only Knew	£20
59	London HLP 8889	You Said Goodbye/If You Only Knew (78)	£15
59	London HA-P 2183	THE TEDDY BEARS SING! (LP)	£200

(see also Phil Spector, Carol Connors)

WILLIE TEE
67	Atlantic 584 116	Thank You John/Walking Up A One-Way Street	£35

TEEGARDEN & VAN WINKLE
69	Atco 228028	BUT ANYHOW (LP)	£15

TEENAGE FANCLUB
90	Paperhouse PAPER 003	Everything Flows/Primary Education/Speeeder (1,500 only, die-cut p/s)	£20
95	Creation CRE 216	TEENAGE FANCLUB HAVE LOST IT EP (7", p/s)	£20
90	Paperhouse PAPLP 004	A CATHOLIC EDUCATION (LP, gatefold sleeve)	£30
91	Creation CRELP 096	THE KING (LP, available for 1 week only, sprayed plain sleeve)	£40
91	Creation CRELP 106	BANDWAGONESQUE (LP, with inner)	£40
93	Creation CRELP 144	THIRTEEN (LP)	£40
95	Creation CRELP 137L	GRAND PRIX (LP, with free 7")	£80
95	Creation CRELP 137L	GRAND PRIX (LP, without free 7")	£60
97	Creation CRELP 196	SONGS FROM NORTHERN BRITAIN (LP)	£80
00	Columbia 5006221	HOWDY! (LP)	£50
03	Poolside POOLS 3LP	FOUR THOUSAND SEVEN HUNDRED AND SIXTY-SIX SECONDS - A SHORT CUT TO TEENAGE FANCLUB (2-LP)	£60
05	Pema PEMA 002LP	MAN-MADE (LP)	£25
10	Pema PEMA 007LP	SHADOWS (LP)	£20

(see also Boy Hairdressers, Clouds, Eugenius)

TEENAGE FILMSTARS
79	Clockwork COR 002	(There's A) Cloud Over Liverpool/Sometimes Good Guys Don't Follow Trends (1st 150 with foldout p/s)	£150
79	Clockwork COR 002	(There's A) Cloud Over Liverpool/Sometimes Good Guys Don't Follow Trends	£25
80	Wessex WEX 275	The Odd Man Out/I Apologise	£25
80	Blueprint BLU 2013	The Odd Man Out/I Apologise (reissue, p/s)	£20
80	Fab Listening FL 1	I Helped Patrick McGoohan Escape/We're Not Sorry (p/s)	£15

(see also Television Personalities, Times, O Level)

TEENAGERS
57	RCA RCX 102	THE TEENAGERS (EP)	£60

TEENBEATS
79	Safari SAFE 19	Strength Of The Nation/I'm Gone Tomorrow (in p/s)	£15

TEEN BEATS (U.S.)
60	Top Rank JAR 342	The Slop Beat/Califf Boogie (featuring Don Rivers & Califfs)	£25

TEEN QUEENS
65	R&B MRB 5000	Eddie My Love/Just Goofed	£30

TEE SET (1)
68	Pye 7N 25452	What Can I Do/Colours Of The Rainbow	£15

TEE SET (2)
70	Columbia SCX 6419	MA BELLE AMIE (LP)	£15

TEETH OF THE SEA
09	Rocket LAUNCH 031	ORPHANED BY THE OCEAN (LP, orange vinyl)	£18
10	Rocket LAUNCH 040	YOUR MERCY (LP)	£18
13	Rocket LAUNCH 059 LP	MASTER (LP, magenta vinyl)	£15
14	Rocket LAUNCH 064 LP	A FIELD IN ENGLAND RE-IMAGINED (LP, white vinyl, 200 only)	£20

TEK 9
92	Reinforced RIVET 1229	JUST A DREAM EP (12")	£20
93	Reinforced RIVET 1238	THE RETURN OF TEK 9 EP (12")	£15

| 93 | Reinforced RIVET 1253 | **BREAKIN' THE SOUND BARRIERS EP** (12") | £15 |
| 94 | Reinforced RIVET 1269 | **JUS' A LIKKLE SUMTIN' EP** (2x12") | £25 |

TELEGENTS
| 81 | Gent GEN 1 | **Get Out/Telephone Romance** (p/s) | £15 |
| 82 | Gent GEN 2 | **Seen It Before/TV Gents** (p/s) | £15 |

TELEMAN
| 15 | Speedy Wunderground SW011 | **Strange Combinations/**(Mr Dan's Strange Dubby Nations) | £25 |

TELESCOPES
89	What Goes On WHAT GOES ON 32	**TASTE** (LP, inner)	£18
90	Fierce FRIGHT 039	**TRADE MARK OF QUALITY** (LP)	£15
92	Creation CRELP 079	**TELESCOPES** (LP, with booklet)	£18

TELEVISION
79	Ork/WEA NYC 1T	**Little Johnny Jewel Parts 1 & 2/Little Johnny Jewel** (live) (12", p/s)	£15
77	Elektra K52046	**MARQUEE MOON** (LP, 1st pressing with quotation marks around title)	£50
77	Elektra K52046	**MARQUEE MOON** (LP, second pressing with no quotation marks around title)	£30
78	Elektra K52072	**ADVENTURE** (LP, red vinyl, insert)	£18
78	Elektra K52072	**ADVENTURE** (LP, black vinyl)	£15

(see also Neon Boys)

TELEVISION PERSONALITIES
78	Teen '78 SRTS/CUS/77/089	**14th Floor/Oxford Street W1** (1st issue as TEEN '78, 'Teen 78' p/s - (b&w, a few red or blue ones have surfaced) some with TELEVISION PERSONALITIES added later in pen, or on reversed sleeve)	£600
78	Teen '78 SRTS/CUS/77/089	**14th Floor/Oxford Street** (2nd issue, 'four pictures' p/s, TEEN '78 on labels)	£300
78	Teen '78 SRTS/CUS/77/089	**14th Floor/Oxford Street** (3rd issue, 'Santa p/s, TEEN '78 on labels)	£300
78	Teen '78 SRTS/CUS/77/089	**14th Floor/Oxford Street** (4th issue, no p/s, in brown die-cut sleeve handwritten by band members)	£75
78	Kings Road Records LYN 5976/5977	**WHERE'S BILL GRUNDY NOW?** (EP, 1st issue, 'Headless Man' p/s. Band name in upper case on front, no track list. Back of foldout features details of EP's pressing and printing. White labels, many hand stamped or handwritten. Matrix no's LYN-5976 and LYN-5977)	£75
78	Kings Road LYN 5976/7	**WHERE'S BILL GRUNDY NOW?** (EP, 2nd issue, 'Black Square' p/s with photo of Beatles on back. No track details. White labels, many hand stamped or handwritten. Matrix no's LYN-5976 and LYN-5977)	£60
78	Kings Road LYN 5976/7	**WHERE'S BILL GRUNDY NOW?** (EP, 3rd issue, 'Shane MacGowan' p/s, picture of Shane on front, reproduction of letter from Garry Bushell on back. White labels, many hand stamped or handwritten. Matrix no's LYN-5976 and LYN-5977)	£50
79	Rough Trade RT 033	**WHERE'S BILL GRUNDY NOW?** (EP, reissue, 2nd 'Headless Man' p/s, band name in upper/lower case, track titles on front cover. George & Ringo pics and 'Kings Road Records' address on back. RT 033 added to matrixes, printed labels (two variants) or rarer stamped labels)	£30
80	Rough Trade RT 051	**Smashing Time/King & Country** (test pressing, white label and sleeve with handwritten information)	£35
80	Rough Trade RT 051	**Smashing Time/King & Country** (p/s)	£25
81	Rough Trade RT 063	**I Know Where Syd Barrett Lives/Arthur The Gardener** (p/s)	£25
82	Whaam! WHAAM 4	**Three Wishes/Geoffrey Ingram/And Don't The Kids Just Love It** (p/s, 2 different sleeve designs with either a picture of Dan Treacy or picture of three children on back, White, red or green paper. 2,000 only)	£35
82	Creation Artefact 002/ Lyntone LYN 13546	**Biff Bang Pow!/A Picture Of Dorian Gray** (1-sided flexidisc, with Communication Blur fanzine)	£25
82	Creation Artefact 002/ Lyntone LYN 13546	**Biff Bang Pow!/A Picture Of Dorian Gray** (1-sided flexidisc, without Communication Blur fanzine)	£18
83	Rough Trade RT 109	**A Sense Of Belonging/Paradise Estate** (p/s)	£20
86	Dreamworld DREAM 4	**How I Learned To Love The Bomb/Then God Snaps His Fingers/Now You're Just Being Ridiculous** (12", p/s, 3,700 only)	£18
86	Dreamworld DREAM 007	**How I Learnt To Love The Bomb/Grocer's Daughter/Girl Called Charity** (Test pressings with handwritten labels)	£30
86	Dreamworld DREAM 10	**How I Learnt To Love The Bomb/Grocer's Daughter/Girl Called Charity** (7", reissue, p/s, 1,000 only)	£20
87	Dreamworld DREAM 13(T)	**Privilege/Me And My Desires** (unreleased)	£0
89	Caff CAFF 5	**I Still Believe In Magic/Respectable** (p/s, in poly bag, 500 only)	£35
89	Caff CAFF 5	**I Still Believe In Magic/Respectable** (p/s)	£25
90	Overground OVER 15	**The Prettiest Girl In The World/If That's What Love Is/Look Back In Anger** (Alternative Version)/**Silly Girl** (Alternative Version) (withdrawn,100 test pressings only)	£50
92	Overground OVER 25	**PART TIME PUNKS 4 Track EP** (reissue of WHERE'S BILL GRUNDY NOW? EP)	£18
81	Rough Trade ROUGH 24	**AND DON'T THE KIDS JUST LOVE IT** (LP, 1st 1,000 with insert)	£120
81	Rough Trade ROUGH 24	**AND DON'T THE KIDS JUST LOVE IT** (LP, no insert)	£80
81	Whaam! WHAAM 3	**MUMMY YOUR NOT WATCHING ME** (LP, 3,500 only, 1st 1,000 with insert)	£100
81	Whaam! WHAAM 3	**MUMMY YOUR NOT WATCHING ME** (LP, 3,500 only, 2,500 without insert)	£80
82	Whaam! BIG 5	**THEY COULD HAVE BEEN BIGGER THAN THE BEATLES** (LP, 2,500 only, hand-drawn or hand-painted sleeve, some with blue 'Wham' sticker)	£120
83	Whaam! BIG 10	**TURN ON ... TUNE IN** (LP, unreleased)	£0
85	Illuminated JAMS 37	**THE PAINTED WORD** (LP, with company inner sleeve)	£60
86	Dreamworld BIG DREAM 2	**THEY COULD HAVE BEEN BIGGER THAN THE BEATLES** (LP, reissue, new sleeve with insert)	£30
86	Dreamworld BIG DREAM 4	**MUMMY YOUR NOT WATCHING ME** (LP, reissue, new sleeve with insert)	£30
87	Dreamworld BIG DREAM 6	**PRIVILEGE** (LP, unreleased)	£0
90	Fire LP 21	**PRIVILEGE** (LP, insert)	£25
90	Fire REFIRE 7	**AND DON'T THE KIDS JUST LOVE IT** (LP, 2nd reissue, with inner)	£35
90	Fire REFIRE 8	**MUMMY YOUR NOT WATCHING ME** (LP, 2nd reissue, with inner)	£30
90	Fire REFIRE 9	**THEY COULD HAVE BEEN BIGGER THAN THE BEATLES** (LP, 2nd reissue, with inner)	£25
90	Fire REFIRE 10	**THE PAINTED WORD** (LP, reissue with inner)	£25
91	Overground OVER 21	**CAMPING IN FRANCE** (LP)	£18

			MINT VALUE £
92	Fire FIRE LP 32	CLOSER TO GOD (2-LP, gatefold sleeve)	£30
95	Overground OVER 41	I WAS A MOD BEFORE YOU WAS A MOD (LP, with inset)	£35
96	Overground OVER 52	PAISLEY SHIRTS AND MINI SKIRTS (LP, with insert)	£40

(see also Teenage Filmstars, Times, O Level, Missing Scientists, Reacta, Dry Rib, Slaughter, Gifted Children)

TELEX

79	Sire SRK 6072	LOOKING FOR ST. TROPEZ (LP, with lyric inner sleeve)	£15
80	Sire SRK 6090	NEUROVISION (LP)	£18
82	Interdisc INTO 1	BIRDS AND BEES (LP)	£15

SYLVIA TELLA

96	Saxon SAX 047	Brothers And Sisters/Version/Jamaica Land/Jamaica Land (mix II) (12")	£30
81	Sarge SRL 1005	SPELL (LP)	£20

TELSTARS

62	Oriole CB 1754	I Went A' Walkin'/A Rose And A Thorn	£20

TEMPEST (1)

85	Magnet PEST 1	Always The Same/Love In The Wintertime (p/s)	£50
85	Magnet 10PEST 1	Always The Same/The Physical Act (10")	£25
85	Magnet PEST 2	Bluebelle/I Want To Live (p/s)	£50
85	Magnet 10PEST 2	Bluebelle/I Want To Live (10")	£25
86	Magnet LAZY 1	Lazy Sunday/You've Always Got Something To Say (p/s)	£15
86	Magnet PEST 3	Didn't We Have A Nice Time?/The Physical Act	£50

TEMPEST (2)

73	Bronze ILPS 9220	TEMPEST (LP, foldover cover with lyric inner sleeve)	£80
74	Bronze ILPS 9267	LIVING IN FEAR (LP, die-cut cover with inner sleeve)	£70

(see also Colosseum, Patto)

KATE TEMPEST

13	Speedy Wunderground SW005	Hot Night Cold Spaceship/(Mr Dan's Monday Morning Remix)	£20
14	Speedy Wunderground SW009	Guts/(Mr Dan's Baloon Dub) (with Loyle Carner)	£40

BOB TEMPLE

57	Parlophone R 4264	Come Back, Come Back/Vim Vam Vamoose	£80

GERRY TEMPLE

61	HMV POP 823	No More Tomorrows/So Nice To Walk You Home	£40
61	HMV POP 939	Seventeen Come Sunday/Tell You What I'll Do	£30
63	HMV POP 1114	Angel Face/Since You Went Away	£45
68	RCA Victor RCA 1670	Lovin' Up A Storm/Everything I Do is Wrong	£20

RICHARD TEMPLE

70	Jay Boy BOY 31	That Beatin' Rhythm/Could It Be	£15
70	Jay Boy BOY 31	That Beatin' Rhythm/Could It Be (DJ copy)	£30
76	Contempo CS 9040	That Beatin' Rhythm/Could It Be (reissue)	£15

SHIRLEY TEMPLE

59	Top Rank JKR 8003	I REMEMBER (EP)	£20
63	Music For Pleasure MFP 1141	LITTLE MISS WONDERFUL (LP)	£15

TEMPLEAIRES

60s	Vogue V 2421	He Spoke/What Will Heaven Have In Store For Me	£20

TEMPLE OF LIFE

91	T Life 001	EDP/Relax Your Soul/Slayer/Trancetone (12", stamped white labels)	£50

TEMPLE OF THE DOG

92	A&M AM 0091	Hunger Strike/All Night Thing (picture disc)	£20
92	A&M AMY 0091	Hunger Strike/Your Saviour/All Night Thing (12", p/s, with poster)	£15
91	A&M 395350-1	TEMPLE OF THE DOG (LP)	£50

(see also Pearl Jam)

TEMPLE ROW

72	Polydor 2058254	King & Queen/One Of A Million Faces	£50

TEMPLES

13	Heavenly HVN 250	Shelter Song/Prisms (die-cut sleeve)	£50
13	Heavenly HVN 261	Colours To Life/Ankh (10" white vinyl, 300 only)	£15
14	Heavenly HVNLP 100	SUN STRUCTURES (LP, orange vinyl)	£60

TEMPLE SONGS

13	Box Bedroom BBR 4	ATONAL NOISE EP (p/s, insert, numbered, 100 only)	£20

NINO TEMPO

57	London HLU 8387	Tempo's Tempo/June's Blues (as Nino Tempo & His Band)	£200
57	London HLU 8387	Tempo's Tempo/June's Blues (as Nino Tempo & His Band) (78)	£50
58	London HB-U 1075	ROCK 'N' ROLL BEACH PARTY (10" LP)	£125

(see also Nino Tempo & April Stevens, April Stevenso)

NINO TEMPO & APRIL STEVENS

62	London HLK 9580	Sweet And Lovely/TOP NOTES: Twist And Shout	£15
64	London HA-K 8168	NINO TEMPO AND APRIL STEVENS - DEEP PURPLE (LP)	£20
64	Atlantic AL 5006	SING THE GREAT SONGS (LP, mono)	£15
64	Atlantic SAL 5006	SING THE GREAT SONGS (LP, stereo)	£18
66	Atlantic	HEY BABY (LP)	£15
67	London HA-U/SH-U 8314	ALL STRUNG OUT (LP)	£20

(see also Nino Tempo, April Stevens)

TEMPOS (1)
59	Pye International 7N 25026	See You In September/Bless You My Love	£100
59	Pye International 7N 25026	See You In September/Bless You My Love (78)	£40

TEMPREES
72	Stax 2325 083	LOVEMEN (LP)	£30
74	Stax STX 1040	3 (LP)	£15

TEMPTATIONS (1)
60	Top Rank JAR 384	Barbara/Someday	£30

TEMPTATIONS (2)
SINGLES
64	Stateside SS 278	The Way You Do The Things You Do/Just Let Me Know	£70
64	Stateside SS 278	The Way You Do The Things You Do/Just Let Me Know (DJ copy)	£120
64	Stateside SS 319	I'll Be In Trouble/The Girl's Alright With Me	£80
64	Stateside SS 319	I'll Be In Trouble/The Girl's Alright With Me (DJ copy)	£120
64	Stateside SS 348	Girl (Why You Wanna Make Me Blue)/Baby Baby I Need You	£80
64	Stateside SS 348	Girl (Why You Wanna Make Me Blue)/Baby Baby I Need You (DJ copy)	£240
65	Stateside SS 378	My Girl/(Talking 'Bout) Nobody But My Baby	£45
65	Stateside SS 378	My Girl/(Talking 'Bout) Nobody But My Baby (DJ copy)	£150
65	Tamla Motown TMG 504	It's Growing/What Love Has Joined Together	£40
65	Tamla Motown TMG 504	It's Growing/What Love Has Joined Together (DJ copy)	£100
65	Tamla Motown TMG 526	Since I Lost My Baby/You've Got To Earn It	£50
65	Tamla Motown TMG 526	Since I Lost My Baby/You've Got To Earn It (DJ copy)	£200
65	Tamla Motown TMG 541	My Baby/Don't Look Back	£45
65	Tamla Motown TMG 541	My Baby/Don't Look Back (DJ copy)	£100
66	Tamla Motown TMG 557	Get Ready/Fading Away	£30
66	Tamla Motown TMG 557	Get Ready/Fading Away (DJ copy)	£100
66	Tamla Motown TMG 565	Ain't Too Proud To Beg/You'll Lose A Precious Love (spelt "Previous")	£30
66	Tamla Motown TMG 565	Ain't Too Proud To Beg/You'll Lose A Precious Love (spelt "Previous") (DJ copy)	£130
66	Tamla Motown TMG 578	Beauty Is Only Skin Deep/You're Not An Ordinary Girl (DJ copy)	£140
66	Tamla Motown TMG 578	Beauty Is Only Skin Deep/You're Not An Ordinary Girl	£30
66	Tamla Motown TMG 587	(I Know) I'm Losing You/Little Miss Sweetness	£25
66	Tamla Motown TMG 587	(I Know) I'm Losing You/Little Miss Sweetness (DJ copy)	£80
67	Tamla Motown TMG 610	All I Need/Sorry Is A Sorry Word	£20
67	Tamla Motown TMG 610	All I Need/Sorry Is A Sorry Word (DJ copy)	£60
67	Tamla Motown TMG 620	You're My Everything/I've Been Good To You	£20
67	Tamla Motown TMG 620	You're My Everything/I've Been Good To You (DJ copy)	£50
67	Tamla Motown TMG 633	(Loneliness Made Me Realise) It's You That I Need/I Want A Love I Can See	£40
67	Tamla Motown TMG 633	(Loneliness Made Me Realise) It's You That I Need/I Want A Love I Can See (DJ copy)	£45
68	Tamla Motown TMG 641	I Wish It Would Rain/I Truly, Truly Believe	£20
68	Tamla Motown TMG 641	I Wish It Would Rain/I Truly, Truly Believe (DJ copy)	£30
68	Tamla Motown TMG 658	I Could Never Love Another (After Loving You)/Gonna Give Her All The Love I've Got	£15
68	Tamla Motown TMG 658	I Could Never Love Another (After Loving You)/Gonna Give Her All The Love I've Got (DJ copy)	£30
68	Tamla Motown TMG 671	Why Did You Leave Me Darling/How Can I Forget	£15
68	Tamla Motown TMG 671	Why Did You Leave Me Darling/How Can I Forget (DJ copy)	£30
69	Tamla Motown TMG 688	Get Ready/My Girl (DJ copy)	£30
69	Tamla Motown TMG 699	Ain't Too Proud To Beg/Fading Away (DJ copy)	£25
69	Tamla Motown TMG 707	Cloud Nine/Why Did She Have To Leave Me (Why Did She Have To Go) (DJ copy)	£25
83	Tamla Motown TMG 1320	Papa Was A Rolling Stone/FOUR TOPS: Medley	£35

EPs
65	Tamla Motown TME 2004	THE TEMPTATIONS (EP)	£50
66	Tamla Motown TME 2010	IT'S THE TEMPTATIONS	£40

ALBUMS : LPS
65	Tamla Motown TML 11009	MEET THE TEMPTATIONS	£200
65	Tamla Motown TML 11016	SING SMOKEY	£60
66	Tamla Motown TML 11023	THE TEMPTIN' TEMPTATIONS (mono)	£45
66	Tamla Motown STML 11023	THE TEMPTIN' TEMPTATIONS (stereo)	£55
66	Tamla Motown TML 11035	GETTIN' READY (mono)	£40
66	Tamla Motown STML 11035	GETTIN' READY (stereo)	£50
67	Tamla Motown STML 11057	WITH A LOT O'SOUL (stereo)	£40
67	Tamla Motown TML 11053	THE TEMPTATIONS LIVE! (stereo)	£25
67	Tamla Motown STML 11042	GREATEST HITS (stereo)	£25
67	Tamla Motown TML 11042	GREATEST HITS (mono)	£20
67	Tamla Motown TML 11053	TEMPTATIONS LIVE! (mono)	£20
67	Tamla Motown TML 11057	WITH A LOT O'SOUL (mono)	£35
68	Tamla Motown TML 11068	IN A MELLOW MOOD (mono)	£30
68	Tamla Motown STML 11068	IN A MELLOW MOOD (stereo)	£35
68	Tamla Motown TML 11079	WISH IT WOULD RAIN (LP, mono)	£30
68	Tamla Motown STML 11079	WISH IT WOULD RAIN (LP, stereo)	£35
68	Tamla Motown (S)TML 11079	THE TEMPTATIONS WISH IT COULD RAIN	£40
69	Tamla Motown TML 11104	THE TEMPTATIONS LIVE AT THE COPA (mono)	£30
69	Tamla Motown STML 11104	THE TEMPTATIONS LIVE AT THE COPA (stereo)	£25
69	Tamla Motown (S)TML 11109	CLOUD NINE (mono/stereo)	£30
70	Tamla Motown STML 11141	'LIVE' AT LONDON'S TALK OF THE TOWN (stereo, mono unconfirmed)	£20
70	Tamla Motown TML 11133	PUZZLE PEOPLE (mono)	£25

TEMPUS FUGIT

MINT VALUE £

70	Tamla Motown STML 11133	PUZZLE PEOPLE (stereo)	£22
70	Tamla Motown STML 11147	PSYCHEDELIC SHACK	£25
70	Tamla Motown STML 11170	GREATEST HITS Vol. 2	£15
71	Tamla Motown STML 11184	THE SKY'S THE LIMIT	£15
72	Tamla Motown STML 11202	SOLID ROCK	£15
72	Tamla Motown STML 11218	ALL DIRECTIONS	£15
73	Tamla Motown STML 11229	MASTERPIECE	£15

(see also David Ruffin, Diana Ross)

TEMPUS FUGIT
69	Philips BF 1802	Come Alive/Emphasis On Love	£60

10CC
73	UK UKAL 1005	10cc (LP)	£20
74	UK UKAL 1007	SHEET MUSIC (LP)	£20
75	Mercury 9102 501	HOW DARE YOU (LP, gatefold, printed inner)	£20
77	Mercury 9102 502	DECEPTIVE BENDS (LP)	£20
95	Avex AVEXLP	MIRROR MIRROR (LP)	£100
12	Mercury 5340276	TENOLOGY (4-CD box set)	£40

(see also Godley & Creme, Graham Gouldman, Lol, Mindbenders, Mockingbirds, Hotlegs, Whirlwinds, Yellow Bellow Room Boom, Nick Mason & Rick Fenn, Frabjoy & Runcible Spoon, Manchester Mob, Ramases, Festival)

TENASTELIN
86	Vibes Sounds VS 001	Commercial Bwoy/Burial Tonight (12")	£25
89	Wau! Mr. Modo MWS 011T	Jah Equity/Jah Equity (Version) (12")	£50
89	Wau! Mr. Modo MWS 015T	King Of Kings/Give Thanks And Praise (12")	£50
90	Black Legacy BL002	Urban Ghetto Youth/Run Away Mengistu (12")	£50
90	Conscious Sounds DPS 102	Can't Touch Jah/CENTRY: Version	£40
00	Jah Tubbys JT 7005	Look After Yourself/DISCIPLES RHYTHM SECTION: Dub Yourself	£20
89	Wai! Mr. Modo MOWLP 002	WICKED INVENTION (LP)	£50
92	Conscious Sounds DNC 001	SUN AND MOON (LP, as Tena Stelin Meets Centry)	£35

(see also Iration Steppas and Tena Stelin)

TENDER TONES
69	Crab CRAB 38	Devil Woman/Nobody Cares	£70

TENDERLONIOUS
13	22a 001	TENDERLONIOUS/AL DOBSON (12" split EP, 200 only, 1st pressing)	£15
14	Sounds Of The Universe SOTU 009	Caramel/Something Different (Vocal)/Something Different (Inst.) (12" with print)	£15
17	22a 014	SV Disco/Shakedown (p/s, 300 only some hand-coloured)	£20
16	22a 012	ON FLUTE (mini-LP)	£20
17	22a 017	8RICK CI7Y (LP, with Dennis Ayler)	£15
18	22a 022	THE SHAKEDOWN (2-LP, limited edition, hand-stamped labels, numbered with print)	£40

(see also Ruby Rushton)

TEN FEET
66	RCA RCA 1544	Got Everything But Love/Factory Worker	£100
67	CBS 3045	Shoot On Sight/Losing Game	£120

TEN FEET FIVE
65	Fontana TF 578	Baby's Back In Town/Send Me No More Lovin'	£45

(see also Troggs)

TENNENT & MORRISON
72	Polydor 2383 152	TENNENT & MORRISON (LP, with lyric insert)	£150

(see also Joe Soap)

TENNIS SHOES
78	Bonaparte BONE 3	(Do The) Medium Wave/Rolf Is Stranger Than Richard/So Large (p/s)	£15

TENNORS
68	JJ DB 1152	Massie Massa/CLIVE ALLSTARS: San Sebastian	£75
68	Doctor Bird DB 1175	Sufferer (Make It)/Little Things	£70
68	Island WI 3133	Ride Your Donkey/I've Got To Get You Off My Mind	£25
68	Island WI 3140	Copy Me Donkey (as Tenors)/The Stage (B-side actually by Ronnie Davis)	£40
68	Island WI 3156	Grampa/ROMEO STEWART: While I Was Walking	£40
68	Blue Cat BS 127	Khaki/LEYROY REID: Great Surprise (Pound Get A Blow)	£85
68	Big Shot BI 501	Reggae Girl/CLIVE ALLSTARS: Donkey Trot	£80
68	Fab FAB 41	Ride You Donkey/Cleopatra (as Tenners)	£25
68	Fab FAB 50	Let Go Yah Donkey/ROMEO STEWART: While I Was Walking	£40
69	Big Shot BI 514	You're No Good/Do The Reggae	£60
69	Big Shot BI 517	Another Scorcher/My Baby	£85
69	Duke Reid DR 2502	Hopeful Village/TOMMY McCOOK: The Village	£20
69	Bullet BU 406	Greatest Scorcher/Making Love (white labels only)	£100
69	Bullet BU 406	Festival Knocks/Making Love	£60
69	Crab CRAB 26	Baff Boom/Feel Bad	£50
69	Crab CRAB 29	True Brothers/Sign Of The Time	£50
69	Crab CRAB 36	I Want Everything/Cherry	£75
73	Explosion EX 2079	Weather Report/Weather Report - Version	£20
73	Pyramid PYR 7000	Money Never Built A Mountain/My World	£20

(see also Jennors, Prince Buster, Soul Brothers)

JIMI TENOR
97	Warp WARPLP 48	INTERVISION (2-LP)	£20
99	Warp WARLP 60	ORGANISM (LP)	£15

Rare Record Price Guide 2026   1050

TENOR SAW

84	SKD SKD 092	Bad Bwoy/Dub (12")...	£18
85	Kings & Lion KLJJ 003	Tidal Wave/Punkin Belly (12")..	£40
87	Blue Mountain BMD 034	Come Me Just A Come (Version)/SLY & ROBBIE: Version/Come Me Just A Come (Club Version)/SLY & ROBBIE: Version (12")..	£30
84	Hawkeye HLD 0012	CLASH (LP, with Coco Tea)..	£18
86	Uptempo UTLP 04	TENOR SAW MEETS DON ANGELO (LP)...	£25
94	Black Roots BR 002LP	WITH LOTS OF SIGNS (LP)..	£30

10,000 MANIACS

84	Reflex RE 1	My Mother The War (Remix)/Planned Obsolescence/National Education Week (12", p/s)...	£20
84	Press P 2010	HUMAN CONFLICT 5 (12" EP, gatefold p/s)..	£30
84	Press P 3001 LP	SECRETS OF THE I-CHING (LP, with insert)...	£25
84	Press P 3001 LP	SECRETS OF THE I-CHING (LP, with insert; later re-pressing in different 'Chinese Chicken' sleeve, some with insert)..	£15
87	Elektra EKT 41	IN MY TRIBE (LP, inner with free 7")..	£20
89	Elektra EKT57W	BLIND MAN'S ZOO (LP, with print)..	£15

10000 RUSSOS

15	Fuzz Club FC23V12	10000 RUSSOS (LP, white vinyl)...	£20
15	Fuzz Club FC23V12	10000 RUSSOS (LP, black & white vinyl, 100 only).....................................	£35

TEN WHEEL DRIVE (WITH GENYA RAVAN)

69	Polydor 583 577	CONSTRUCTION NO. 1 (LP)...	£20
70	Polydor 2425 002	BRIEF REPLIES (LP, with Genya Ravan)..	£20
71	Polydor 2425 065	PECULIAR FRIENDS (LP, with Genya Ravan)...	£20

(see also Goldie [& Gingerbreads])

TEN YEARS AFTER

68	Deram DM 176	Portable People/The Sounds	£20
71	Deram XDR 48532	She Lies In The Morning/Sweet Little Sixteen (demo only)........................	£15
67	Deram DML 1015	TEN YEARS AFTER (LP, mono)..	£100
67	Deram SML 1015	TEN YEARS AFTER (LP, stereo)...	£80
68	Deram DML 1023	UNDEAD (LP, mono)..	£80
68	Deram SML 1023	UNDEAD (LP, stereo)..	£60
69	Deram DML 1029	STONEDHENGE (LP, gatefold sleeve, mono)..	£70
69	Deram SML 1029	STONEDHENGE (LP, laminated gatefold sleeve, stereo)..............................	£50
69	Deram DML/SML 1052	SSSSH! (LP, gatefold sleeve, mono/stereo)...	£60
70	Deram DML 1065	CRICKLEWOOD GREEN (LP, gatefold sleeve, with 'Alvin Lee' poster, mono)	£100
70	Deram SML 1065	CRICKLEWOOD GREEN (LP, gatefold sleeve, with 'Alvin Lee' poster, stereo).....	£50
71	Deram SML 1078	WATT (LP, gatefold sleeve, with poster)...	£70
71	Chrysalis CHR 1001	A SPACE IN TIME (LP, 1st pressing with 'manufactures and distributed by Island Records Basing St' on top)..	£50
72	Deram SML 1096	ALVIN LEE AND COMPANY (LP)...	£15
72	Chrysalis CHR 1009	ROCK & ROLL MUSIC TO THE WORLD (gatefold sleeve)..............................	£18
78	Deram SML 1023	UNDEAD (LP, reissue)...	£15
74	Chrysalis CHR 1060	POSITIVE VIBRATIONS (LP)...	£15
80	Chrysalis CHR 1001	WATT (LP, reissue, single sleeve)..	£20

(see also Alvin Lee, Chick Churchill)

TEREA

11	Jazzman JMANLP 040	TEREA (LP, reissue)...	£40

TERMINAL

80	Cargo CRS 0081	Hold On/We're Only Human (in p/s)..	£100
82	Termite TERM 2	Am I Doing It Right/I Don't Mind/Turn Around And Don't Make Me Laugh (p/s)...........	£20

TERMINAL BEACH

82	TB SRTS 82	Love On Auto/Dark Words (p/s)	£50

TERMINAL CHEESECAKE

88	Wiiija WIIIJIT1	BLADDERSACK EP (12", p/s)..	£15
88	Wiiija WIIIJLP1	JOHNNY TOWN-MOUSE (LP)..	£20
89	Wiiija WIIIJLP3	V.C.L. (LP)...	£15
90	Pathological PATH 3	ANGELS IN PIGTAILS (LP)...	£25
92	World Serpent WSLP 001	PEARLESQUE KINGS OF THE JEWMOST (LP)...	£20
93	Jackass JAK 3	GATEAU D-ESPACE (mini-LP)...	£20
94	Jackass JAK 8	KING OF ALL SPACEHEADS (2-LP, golden vinyl, 1000 only, 500 with free live 12").........	£35
94	Jackass JAK 8	KING OF ALL SPACEHEADS (2-LP, golden vinyl, 1000 only, without 12")	£30

TERMINAL JIVE

82	Jive Alive JA001	THE TERMINAL JIVE AND SCARLET ALIVE EP (2 tracks on one side, p/s)	£15

TERMINAL SPECTATORS

82	Tiny Chariot CAT 002	Another Day Another Dream/Reach For The Sky......................................	£60

TERMITES

65	Oriole CB 1989	Tell Me/I Found My Place	£40
65	CBS 201761	Every Day Every Day/No-One In The Whole Wide World	£20

TERMITES (JAMAICA)

67	Coxsone CS01/02	Hold Down Rudie/JOE HIGGS AND THE WAILERS: Keep Cool (white label only)	£80
67	Studio One SO 2006	Mercy Mr. Percy/SOUL BROTHERS: Hot And Cold.......................................	£150
67	Studio One SO 2029	It Takes Two To Make Love/Beach Boy..	£100
67	Coxsone CS 7008	Sign Up/DELROY WILSON: Troubled Man...	£80
67	Coxsone CS 7025	Do It Right Now/SUMMERTAIRES: Stay (B-side actually by Gaylads)	£85
68	Studio One SO 2040	Mr D.J. (actually by Delroy Wilson)/Tripe Girl (actually by Heptones)...........	£110

MINT VALUE £

68	Coxsone CS 7039	Mama Didn't Know/I Made A Mistake	£375
68	Pama PM 729	Push It Up/Two Of A Kind (B-side act. by Clancy Eccles & Cynthia Richards)	£90
68	Pama PM 738	Show Me The Way/What Can I Do	£75
68	Trojan TR 634	Love You Kiss Up/TOMMY McCOOK : Regay	£120
69	Nu Beat NB 017	Push Push/Girls (actually by Hi Tones)	£60
67	Studio One SOL 9003	DO THE ROCK STEADY (LP)	£500

(see also Ken Boothe, Upsetters)

PETE TERRACE
67	Pye International 7N 25427	At The Party/No! No! No!	£30
67	Pye International 7N 25440	Shotgun Boo-Ga-Loo/I'm Gonna Make It	£40
67	Pye Intl. NPL 28102	BOOGALOO (LP)	£50

TERRA COTTA
78	Terra Cotta TC 001	To Be Near You (p/s, with insert)	£15

(see also Sprigguns)

TERRAIN
83	Terrain Musak TS 001	Who's To Blame?/Vacation (no p/s)	£150

TERRAPLANE (1)
70	Saturn R4	TERRAPLANE (LP, 2 inserts)	£200

TERRAPLANE (2)
85	Epic 26439	BLACK AND WHITE (LP)	£15

(see also Thunder, Nuthin' Fancy)

LLOYD TERRELL
68	Island WI 3158	My Argument (as Lloyd & Johnny Melody)/JOHNNY MELODY: Foey Man (B-side actually by George Dekker)	£300
68	Pama PM 740	How Come (actually by Lee Perry)/MRS MILLER: Oh My Lover	£15
69	Pama PM 752	Lulu Returns/MRS MILLER: I Feel The Music	£15
69	Nu Beat NB 023	Mr Rhya/After Dark	£18
70	Pama PM 792	Birth Control/VAL BENNET: Return To Peace	£18
70	Bullet BU 434	Exposure/Baby Huey	£18
70	Bullet BU 443	Oh Me Oh My/I Did It	£25
73	Pama PM 863	Big Eight/Lightning Stick (withdrawn)	£70

(see also Charmers, Lloyd Charmers, Lloyd & Johnny, Lloydie & Lowbites)

TAMMI TERRELL
66	Tamla Motown TMG 561	Come On And See Me/Baby Don'tcha Worry (DJ copy)	£200
66	Tamla Motown TMG 561	Come On And See Me/Baby Don'tcha Worry	£120
69	T. Motown (S)TML 11103	THE IRRESISTIBLE TAMMI TERRELL (LP, mono/stereo)	£100

(see also Marvin Gaye & Tammi Terrell)

TAMMI TERRELL/CHUCK JACKSON
69	Marble Arch MAL 1110	THE EARLY SHOW (LP)	£20

(see also Chuck Jackson)

PHIL TERRELL
94	Kent 6T 10	Love Has Passed Me By/VIC & JOHN: Why Did She Lie	£35

TERRORIZER
89	Earach MOSH 16	WORLD DOWNFALL (LP, with inner)	£30

TERRORVISION
92	Total Vegas ATVRLP 1	FORMALDEHYDE (LP, 14 tracks, green vinyl, 500 only, stickered sleeve)	£40
93	Total Vegas VEGASLPS 1	FORMALDEHYDE (reissue LP, 12 tracks, 1,000 copies with 12-page booklet, stickered sleeve & lyric inner)	£20
93	Total Vegas BOOT 1	LIVE AT THE DON VALLEY STADIUM (CD, picture disc, 250 promo copies only)	£30
94	Total Vegas VEGASLP 2	HOW TO MAKE FRIENDS AND INFLUENCE PEOPLE (LP, gatefold)	£15
96	Total Vegas VEGASLP 3	REGULAR URBAN SURVIVORS (LP)	£18

TERRY, CARL & DERRICK
69	Grape GR 3012	True Love/ROY SMITH: Another Saturday Night	£80

DEWEY TERRY
73	Tumbleweed TW 3502	CHIEF (LP)	£18

(see also Don & Dewey, Don Harris, Harvey Mandel)

GORDON TERRY
57	London REA 1098	COUNTRY CLAMBAKE (EP)	£20

PAT TERRY (GROUP)
70s	Myrrh MYR 1031	PAT TERRY GROUP (LP)	£18

SONNY TERRY (TRIO)
53	Parlophone MSP 6017	Hootin' Blues/TOMMY REILLY: Bop! Goes The Weasel	£35
56	Vogue EPV 1095	SONNY TERRY (EP)	£50
55	Vogue LDE 137	FOLK BLUES (10" LP)	£40
55	Vogue LDE 165	CITY BLUES (10" LP)	£40
58	Melodisc MLP 516	WHOOPIN' THE BLUES (10" LP)	£40
58	Topic 10T 30	HARMONICA BLUES (10" LP)	£40
65	Topic 12T 30	HARMONICA BLUES (12" LP, reissue)	£35
66	Xtra XTRA 5025	SONNY'S STORY (LP)	£25
69	Ember CW 136	BLIND SONNY TERRY & WOODY GUTHRIE (LP)	£15
69	Xtra XTRA 1064	SONNY TERRY (LP)	£15
60s	Mainstream MSL 1037	GOING DOWN SLOW (LP, with BROWNIE McGHEE & PEPPERMINT HARRIS)	£18
70	Xtra XTRA 1099	BLUES FROM EVERYWHERE (LP)	£15
71	Xtra XTRA 1110	ON THE ROAD (LP, with J.C. Burris)	£15

(see also Woody Guthrie)

SONNY TERRY & BROWNIE MCGHEE

60	Columbia DB 4433	Talking Harmonica Blues/Rockin' And Whoopin'	£35
64	Oriole CB 1946	Dissatisfied Woman/SONNY TERRY: Goin' Down Slow	£20
50s	Melodisc EPM7 83	ME AND SONNY (EP)	£25
59	Pye Jazz NJE 1074	TERRY AND McGHEE IN LONDON PT. 1 (EP)	£15
59	Topic TOP 37	HOOTENANNY NEW YORK CITY (EP, with Pete Seeger)	£15
61	Top Rank JKP 3007	WORK-PLAY-FAITH-FUN-SONGS (EP)	£15
64	Ember EP 4562	SONNY TERRY AND BROWNIE McGHEE (EP)	£20
64	Topic TOP 121	R AND B FROM S AND B (EP)	£15
64	Realm REP 4002	PAWNSHOP BLUES (EP)	£15
64	Vocalion EPV 1274	SONNY TERRY AND BROWNIE McGHEE (EP)	£20
65	Vocalion EPV 1279	I SHALL NOT BE MOVED (EP)	£20
58	Topic 12T 29	BROWNIE McGHEE AND SONNY TERRY (LP)	£30
58	Pye Nixa Jazz NJT 515	SONNY, BROWNIE AND CHRIS (10" LP, with Chris Barber)	£45
58	Pye Nixa Jazz NJL 18	SONNY TERRY AND BROWNIE McGHEE IN LONDON (LP)	£30
58	London Jazz LTZ-C 15144	BACK COUNTRY BLUES (LP)	£50
60	Columbia 33SX 1223	BLUES IS MY COMPANION (LP)	£50
61	World Record Club 7379	SONNY TERRY AND BROWNIE McGHEE (LP)	£20
61	Vogue LAE 12247	BLUES IS A STORY (LP, mono)	£30
61	Vogue SEA 5014	BLUES IS A STORY (LP, stereo)	£40
63	Vogue LAE 12266	DOWN SOUTH SUMMIT MEETIN' (LP)	£25
63	CBS 52165	BACK COUNTRY BLUES (LP)	£25
64	Xtra XTRA 1004	BIG BILL BROONZY/SONNY TERRY/BROWNIE McGHEE (LP)	£30
64	Vogue LAE 552	BROWNIE McGHEE AND SONNY TERRY (LP)	£30
64	Realm RM 165	BACK COUNTRY BLUES (LP)	£15
64	Stateside SL 10076	BLUES HOOT (LP, some tracks by Lightnin' Hopkins)	£40
64	Fontana 688 006ZL	LIVIN' WITH THE BLUES (LP)	£30
66	Philips BL 7675	AT THE BUNK HOUSE (LP)	£20
66	Verve VLP 5010	GUITAR HIGHWAY (LP, mono)	£20
66	Verve SVLP 5010	GUITAR HIGHWAY (LP, stereo)	£25
66	Fontana TL 5289	HOMETOWN BLUES (LP)	£20
69	Capitol T 20906	WHOOPIN' THE BLUES (LP)	£20
69	Stateside SSL 10291	LONG WAY FROM HOME (LP)	£15
70	Fontana SFJL 979	WHERE THE BLUES BEGAN (LP)	£20
73	Mainstream MSL 1019	HOMETOWN BLUES (LP, gatefold sleeve)	£15

(see also Brownie McGhee, Chris Barber, Pete Seeger, Big Bill Broonzy, Lightnin' Hopkins, Big Joe Turner)

SUSAN TERRY
62	Piccadilly 7N 35026	Along Came Love/Looking For A Boy	£15

TODD TERRY
95	Sound Of Ministry SOMLP2	A DAY IN THE LIFE (2-LP)	£15

TERRY & JERRY
65	R&B MRB 5009	People Are Doing It Every Day/Mama Julie	£22

TEST DEPARTMENT
82	Test TEST ONE	HISTORY (cassette, with booklet in plastic bag)	£15
85	Test TEST 33	BEATING THE RETREAT (LP, box set)	£18

TETRACK
77	Hawkeye HE 006	Let's Get Started/PABLO EXPERIENCE: Go it	£18
78	Greensleeves GRE 8	Only Jah Knows/ROCKERS ALL STARS: Jah Jah Dub	£20
78	Rockers APD 2	Love And Unity/JAH LEVI & JAH BULL: Two The Hard Way/JUNIOR DAN: Jah Foundation (12")	£45
89	Greensleeves GREL 121	LET'S GET STARTED (LP)	£20

ALAN TEW ORCHESTRA
76	Epic EPC 4676	The Sweeney/The Prowler	£15
67	Decca Phase 4 PFS 4120	THIS IS MY SCENE (LP)	£40
72	CBS 64665	LET'S FLY (LP)	£25

JOE TEX
65	Atlantic AT 4015	Hold What You've Got/Fresh Out Of Tears	£22
65	Atlantic AT 4021	You Better Get It/You Got What It Takes	£20
65	Sue WI 370	Yum Yum Yum/You Little Baby Face Thing	£40
65	Atlantic AT 4027	A Woman Can Change A Man/Don't Let Your Left Hand Know	£15
65	Atlantic AT 4045	I Want To (Do Everything For You)/Funny Bone	£15
65	Atlantic AT 4058	A Sweet Woman Like You/Close Your Door	£15
66	Atlantic AT 4081	The Love You Save/If Sugar Was As Sweet As You	£15
66	Atlantic 584 035	You Better Believe It/I Believe I'm Gonna Make It	£25
67	Atlantic 584 102	Show Me/Woman Sees A Hard Time (When Her Man Is Gone)	£15
65	Atlantic ATL 5043	THE NEW BOSS (LP)	£40
66	Atlantic ATL 587 009	THE LOVE YOU SAVE (LP)	£35
67	Atlantic 587 053	I'VE GOT TO DO A LITTLE BETTER (LP)	£25
67	Atlantic 587/588 059	THE NEW BOSS (LP, reissue)	£15
67	London HA-U 8334	THE BEST OF JOE TEX (LP)	£40
67	Atlantic 587/588 079	GREATEST HITS (LP)	£15
68	Atlantic 587/588 104	LIVE AND LIVELY (LP)	£25
68	Atlantic 587/588 118	SOUL COUNTRY (LP)	£20
69	Atlantic 587/588 130	YOU BETTER GET IT (LP)	£20
69	Atlantic 588 193	BUYING A BOOK (LP)	£15
77	EPIC EPC 81931	BUMPS AND BRUISES (LP)	£15

(see also Soul Clan)

TEXTONES
87   Enigma 3268-1   CEDAR CREEK (LP) £18

JAKE THACKRAY
67   Columbia SCX 6178   LAST WILL AND TESTAMENT (LP) £15

THAMESIDERS/DAVY GRAHAM
63   Decca DFE 8538   FROM A LONDON HOOTENANNY (EP, 2 tracks each)... £50
(see also Davy Graham)

THANES OF CAWDOR
87   DDT DISPLP11   THANES OF CAWDOR (LP) £18

SISTER ROSETTA THARPE
57   Mercury MPL 6529   GOSPEL TRAIN (LP) £25
59   Brunswick LAT 8290   GOSPEL TRAIN (LP) £20
61   Mercury MMC 14057   THE GOSPEL TRUTH (LP) £20
63   Society SOC 900   HOT HOT HOT (LP) £15
65   Ember NR 5023   SPIRITUALS IN RHYTHM (LP) £20
(see also Little Richard)

THAT CORPORATE FEELING
84   Platform SOUL XX1   The Rain Has Gone/Industrial Backlash (die-cut Corporate Feeling sleeve).............. £50

THATCHER ON ACID
88   Rugger Bugger SEEP 1   THATCHER ON ACID (LP) £15

T.H.C. ROLLER
94   Poor Person Prod. PPPR 4   CHAPTER IN THE LIFE OF T.H.C. ROLLER (LP, handmade sleeve with insert & king-size
                                rolling papers, numbered, 500 only) £20
94   Poor Person Prod.   THIS MUST BE THE JOINT (LP, 500 only) £70

THEATRE OF HATE
82   Burning Rome TOH 1   WESTWORLD (LP) £15
(see also Pack, Spear Of Destiny, Cult, Crisis)

THEE
65   Decca F 12163   Each And Every Day/There You Go! £40

THEE HEADCOATEES
97   Vinyl Japan ASKLP 65   BOSTIK HAZE (LP) £15

THEE HYPNOTICS
90   Situation 2 SITU 28   COME DOWN HEAVY (LP) £18

HANS THEESINK
80   Kettle KOP 7   LATE LAST NIGHT (LP) £25

THE FOR CARNATION
00   Domino WIGLP 77   THE FOR CARNATION (LP, insert) £80

BOB THEIL
82   Private (no cat. no.)   SO FAR (LP, private pressing).. £250

LLANS THELWELL & HIS CELESTIALS
66   Island WI 262   Choo Choo Ska/Lonely Night (B-side vocal: Busty Brown)................................... £60

THEM
64   Decca F 11973   Don't Start Crying Now/One Two Brown Eyes £80
65   Decca F 12281   Mystic Eyes/If You And I Could Be As Two.. £15
66   Decca F 12355   Call My Name/Bring 'Em On In £20
66   Decca F 12403   Richard Cory/Don't You Know?.. £20
67   Major Minor MM 509   Gloria/Friday's Child £20
67   Major Minor MM 513   The Story Of Them (Parts 1 & 2)... £25
65   Decca DFE 8612   THEM (EP, unboxed decca logo) £150
65   Decca DFE 8612   THEM (EP, export-only 'band-on-ladder' p/s) £500
65   Decca LK 4700   (THE ANGRY YOUNG) THEM (LP, original label, with flipback sleeve, 1st sleeve with
                                only Tommy Scott credited as producer) £200
65   Decca LK 4700   (THE ANGRY YOUNG) THEM (LP, original label, with flipback sleeve, 2nd sleeve with
                                Bert Berns and Dick Rowe added to production credits)....................................... £120
65   Parrot PA 61005   THEM (LP, mono, export only, UK pressed issue of 1st LP, in US sleeve).............. £150
66   Decca LK 4751   THEM AGAIN (LP, original label, with flipback sleeve).. £200
66   Decca LK 4751   THEM AGAIN (LP, unboxed Decca labels, flipback sleeve) £150
69   Decca LK 4700   (THE ANGRY YOUNG) THEM (LP, re-pressing, red label, boxed Decca logo) £50
70   Decca LK 4751   THEM AGAIN (LP, re-pressing, red label, boxed Decca logo) £60
70   Decca PA 86   THE WORLD OF THEM (LP, original issue, mono) £25
70   Decca (S) PA 86   THE WORLD OF THEM (LP, original issue, stereo) £15
73   Deram DPM 3001/2   THEM - FEATURING VAN MORRISON LEAD SINGER (2-LP, gatefold sleeve)......... £25
78   Sonet SNTF 738   BELFAST GYPSIES (LP, features Them without Van Morrison) £25
76   Decca ROOTS 3   ROCK ROOTS (LP).. £15
(see also Van Morrison, Trader Horne, Taste, Belfast Gypsies, Moses K. & Prophets, Peter Barden, Jackie McCauley)

THE PURIST
16   Daupe! DM SP 011   ROSES ARE RED...SO IS BLOOD (10", red vinyl, p/s, with Westside Gunn, 100 only).......£300
15   Daupe! DM SP 097   PYREX SCHOLAR (LP, clear vinyl)... £80

THERAPY
72   CBS 69017   ALMANAC (LP, gatefold sleeve with inside centre opening) £25
73   Indigo IRS 5124   ONE NIGHT STAND (LP, private pressing).. £15

THERAPY?
90   demo cassette   MEAT ABSTRACT (cassette sold at gigs, 150 only) £15

90	Multifuckingnational MFN 1	**Meat Abstract/Punishment Kisses** (p/s, labels on wrong sides, 1,000 only) **£30**
92	A&M (no cat. no.)	**TEETHGRINDER** (12", double pack, white labels in presentation pack)........................... **£30**
92	A&M THX 1	**Have A Merry Fucking Christmas: Teenage Kicks/With Or Without You** (Xmas gig freebie) **£18**
92	Wiiija WIJ 11	**PLEASURE DEATH** (mini-LP, 10 white labels).. **£35**
94	A&M 540196-1	**TROUBLEGUM** (LP, green vinyl) **£50**
95	A&M 540379-1	**INFERNAL LOVE** (LP, red vinyl) **£30**
98	A&M 582548-7	**SEMI-DETATCHED** (LP, as 6 x 7" box set) **£30**

THERMOMETERS
80	Fokker FEP 100	**20th Century Girl/Newtown Refugees/Stole Your Drugs** (in oversized p/s) **£30**
80	Fokker FEP 100	**20th Century Girl/Newtown Refugees/Stole Your Drugs** (p/s) **£20**

THESE IMMORTAL SOULS
87	Mute STUMM 48	**GET LOST (DON'T LIE)** (LP) **£20**
92	Mute STUMM 98	**I'M NEVER GONNA DIE AGAIN** (LP)... **£30**

(see also the Birthday Party)

THESE NEW PURITANS
13	PIAS INFECT 156LP	**FIELD OF REEDS** (2-LP, one side etched) **£18**

THE THE
80	4AD AD 10	**Controversial Subject/Black And White** (p/s).. **£30**
81	Some Bizzare BZS 4	**Cold Spell Ahead/Hot Ice** (p/s)... **£25**
86	Epic TRUTH Q3	**Infected/Infected** (Energy Mix)**/Disturbed** (12", uncensored 'wank' p/s) **£15**
82	private cassette	**PORNOGRAPHY OF DESPAIR** (LP, unreleased, cassettes exist).. **£0**
83	Epic EPC 25525	**SOUL MINING** (LP, with inner sleeve, initially with 12" single Perfect/"Soup Of Mixed Emotions"/"Fruit Of The Heart") **£75**
86	Epic EPC 26770	**INFECTED** (LP, with poster & inner, 1st 25,000 with 'torture' sleeve) **£20**
86	Epic EPC 26770	**INFECTED** (LP, with poster & inner)... **£15**
89	Epic 463319 1	**MIND BOMB** (LP) **£20**
93	Epic 472468-1	**DUSK** (LP)... **£150**
94	Epic 4781390	**HANKY PANKY** (LP as 2 x 10").. **£35**

(see also Matt Johnson, Gadgets)

THEY MUST BE RUSSIANS
79	Gramme/Lyntone LYN 6526/27	**Psycho Analysis/JOE 9T AND THE THUNDERBIRDS: Psycho Analysis** (p/s, stamped white label) **£15**
79	RVS 001	**THEY MUST BE RUSSIANS 4-TRACK EP** (p/s) **£15**
83	First Floor FF2	**THEY MUST BE RUSSIANS** (LP) **£15**

(see also Joe 9T & Thunderbirds)

MOR THIAM
16	Jazzman JMANLP 091	**DINI SAFARRAR** (DRUMS OF FIRE) (LP, reissue, numbered, download card)................... **£35**

THICK AS THIEVES
01	Noid NOIDLP 004	**THICK AS THIEVES** (2-LP) **£20**

THICK PIGEON
84	Factory FACT 85	**TOO CRAZY COWBOYS** (LP) **£40**

THIN END OF THE WEDGE
81	Jungle JR 051S	**Lights Are On Green/I'm Not Dead Yet** (in p/s)... **£30**

(see also Damascus)

FRODE THINGNAES QUINTET
78	BBC AIR 800037	**SOAPY CROW** (LP)... **£35**

THINGS FALL APART
72	President PT378	**Bye Bye My Rose/Manna**... **£20**

THIN ICE
88	Blag It SJP 858	**Freedom Road** (p/s).. **£40**

THIN LIZZY
SINGLES
70	Parlophone DIP 513	**The Farmer/I Need You** (Irish only, as Thin Lizzie).. **£1000**
71	Decca F 13208	**NEW DAY** (EP, 33rpm, gatefold p/s) **£300**
71	Decca F 13208	**NEW DAY** (EP, 33rpm, without p/s).. **£100**
72	Decca F 13355	**Whiskey In The Jar/Black Boys On The Corner** (demos in p/s)....................................... **£30**
73	Decca F 13402	**Randolph's Tango/Broken Dreams** (2 versions of A-side: matrices ZDR 53384 & ZCPDR 53312) **£15**
76	Vertigo 6059 150	**Jailbreak/Running Back** (p/s) **£25**
70s	Vertigo DJ 016	**It's Only Money/JANNE SCHAFFER: Dr Abraham** (promo only, no p/s)......................... **£200**
82	Vertigo LIZZY 10	**Hollywood** (Down On Your Luck) (10", p/s, 1-sided, existence unconfirmed).................... **£0**

ALBUMS
71	Decca SKL 5082	**THIN LIZZY** (dark blue/silver label, early copies with laminated sleeve) **£100**
71	Decca SKL 5082	**THIN LIZZY** (dark blue/silver label, later pressing with matt sleeve) **£35**
72	Decca TXS 108	**SHADES OF A BLUE ORPHANAGE** (1st pressing, gatefold sleeve, green label) **£75**
72	Decca TXLS 108	**SHADES OF A BLUE ORPHANAGE** (2nd pressing, gatefold sleeve, blue label)................... **£60**
73	Decca SKL 5170	**VAGABONDS OF THE WESTERN WORLD** (dark blue/silver label, with lyric insert)........... **£40**
73	Decca SKL 5170	**VAGABONDS OF THE WESTERN WORLD** (dark blue/silver label, without insert)............. **£20**
74	Vertigo 6360 116	**NIGHT LIFE** (LP, 'spaceship' label) **£15**
75	Vertigo 6360 121	**FIGHTING** (LP, 'spaceship' label) **£15**
76	Vertigo 9102 008	**JAILBREAK** (LP, die-cut sleeve, 'spaceship' label) **£30**
76	Vertigo 9102 012	**JOHNNY THE FOX** (LP, inner sleeve, 'spaceship' label)... **£15**
78	Vertigo 9199 645	**LIVE & DANGEROUS** (2-LP, inners)... **£25**
83	Vertigo VERL 3	**THUNDER AND LIGHTNING** (with free 12").. **£18**

MINT VALUE £

83	Vertigo VERD 6	**LIFE - LIVE** (2-LP, gatefold sleeve, with inners)	£15
92	Windsong WINLP024	**BBC RADIO 1 LIVE IN CONCERT** (2-LP emerald green vinyl)	£70

(see also Phil Lynott, Wild Horses, Eric Bell Band,, John Sykes, Gary Moore)

THIN YOGHURTS
80	Lowther Street Runner YOG 1	**Girl On The Bus/Drink Problem** (p/s)	£25

3RD ARMY
81	No 2	**March Of 10,000 Soldiers/All Set To Go** (no p/s)	£25
81	Elite DAZZ 10	**March Of 10,000 Soldiers** (All Set To Go)**/Step One** (12")	£50
81	Elite DAZZ 09	**Step One/POWERLINE: Watching You** (12")	£80

THIRD EAR BAND
69	Harvest SHVL 756	**ALCHEMY** (LP, with "Sold in U.K..." label text on 4 lines)	£125
69	Harvest SHVL 756	**ALCHEMY** (LP, later pressing without "Sold in U.K..." label text)	£50
70	Harvest SHVL 773	**THIRD EAR BAND: ELEMENTS** (LP, no EMI logo on label)	£60
72	Harvest SHSP 4019	**MUSIC FROM MACBETH** (LP, EMI logo on label)	£50
76	Harvest SHSM 2007	**EXPERIENCES** (LP)	£20
82	GI WAX 2	**ALCHEMY** (LP, reissue, single sleeve)	£18
88	Dropout DO 1999	**ALCHEMY** (LP, reissue)	£15
90	BGO BGOLP 89	**THIRD EAR BAND** (LP, reissue)	£18
90	Beat Goes On BGOLP 61	**MUSIC FROM MACBETH** (LP, reissue)	£15

(see also High Tide, Sounds Nice)

THIRD EYE BAND
82	Scarlet Quest 01	**Pass Myself/May The Circle Remain Unbroken** (p/s)	£80

THIRD MEN
79	SCHOOL 1	**You're So Fashionable/The Robot Age** (p/s)	£20

THIRD QUADRANT
82	Rock Cottage (no cat. no.)	**SEEING YOURSELF AS YOU REALLY ARE** (LP, private pressing, wraparound sleeve with handwritten insert, blank white label)	£40

3RD RAIL
92	Delirious DELIS 5	**Look No Further/123 Break/Stand By For Fast Beats/Drop** (KZ1 Remix) (12")	£40

THIRD RAIL
67	Columbia DB 8274	**Run, Run, Run/No Return**	£30

THIRD WORLD ALL STARS
75	Third World TWLP 103	**REBEL ROCK** (LP)	£25

THIRD WORLD WAR
71	Fly FLY 4	**THIRD WORLD WAR** (LP, with lyric insert)	£80
71	Fly FLY 4	**THIRD WORLD WAR** (LP, without lyric insert)	£50
72	Track 2406 108	**THIRD WORLD WAR II** (LP)	£80

(see also Terry Stamp)

THIRD GUITAR
05	Funk 45 FUNK45 025	**Baby Don't Cry/SOUL PLEASERS: Baby Don't Cry** (reissue)	£25

13 AMP
75	Power Exchange PX 114	**Need A Woman/Can You Feel The Music**	£15

THIRTEEN SENSES
02	Private Pressing	**NO OTHER LIFE IS ATTRACTIVE EP** (CD)	£35

13TH CHIME
81	Ellie Jay Records EJSP 9700	**Cuts Of Love/Coffin Maker** (foldout p/s)	£50
82	13th Chime THC 1	**Cursed/Dug Up** (p/s)	£40
82	13th Chime THC 2	**Fire/Hide And Seek/Sally Ditch** (p/s, 1,000 only)	£25

13TH FLOOR
17	Blue Candle BL 55056	**13TH FLOOR** (LP, reissue)	£15

13TH FLOOR ELEVATORS
78	Radar SAM 88	**She Lives** (In A Time Of Her Own)**/RED CRAYOLA: Pink Stainless Tail** (promo)	£15
78	Radar RAD 13	**THE PSYCHEDELIC SOUNDS OF ...** (LP)	£30
79	Radar RAD 15	**EASTER EVERYWHERE** (LP)	£30
89	Decal LIK 28	**EASTER EVERYWHERE** (LP, reissue)	£20
88	Decal LIK 19	**THE PSYCHEDELIC SOUNDS OF...** (LP, reissue)	£30
92	Xgarely/Decal LIKP 003	**THE PSYCHEDELIC SOUNDS OF...** (LP, picture disc)	£15
92	Decal LIKP002	**LIVE** (LP, picture disc with poster)	£15
01	Get Back GET 594	**EASTER EVERYWHERE** (LP, reissue)	£20
11	Charly 113L	**BULL OF THE WOODS** (2-LP, reissue, gatefold)	£20
11	International/Charly IA16	**MUSIC OF THE SPHERES** (Box set, 8-LP, 1 10" EP, booklet, 3-D prints)	£200

(see also Roky Erickson, Red Crayola)

13TH HOUR
81	Time And Motion SMT 2009	**Stereo Smiles/Inner Stu**	£20

38 SPESH
19	Daupe! DM SP 050	**A BULLET FOR EVERY HEATHEN** (LP, with Big Ghost Ltd, 230 copies)	£40
19	Daupe! DM SP 050	**A BULLET FOR EVERY HEATHEN** (LP, with Big Ghost Ltd, red vinyl, 200 copies)	£40
19	Daupe! DM SP 050	**A BULLET FOR EVERY HEATHEN** (LP, with Big Ghost Ltd, white vinyl, 200 copies)	£40
19	Daupe! DM SP 050	**A BULLET FOR EVERY HEATHEN** (LP, with Big Ghost Ltd, splatter vinyl, 100 copies)	£60
19	Daupe! DM SP 050	**A BULLET FOR EVERY HEATHEN** (LP, with Big Ghost Ltd, with obi strip, 20 copies)	£150

(see also El Camino)

31ST OF FEBRUARY
69	Vanguard (S)VRL 19045	**THE 31ST OF FEBRUARY** (LP)	£90

39 CLOCKS
83	Flicknife SHARP 109	BLADES IN YOUR MASQUERADE (LP)	£15

32ND TURN-OFF
69	Jay Boy JSL 1	32ND TURN OFF (LP, textured sleeve, brown/black label)	£300

(see also Equals)

30 SECONDS TO MARS
07	Virgin 00946354474 77	The Kill/Attack (live) (picture disc, PVC stickered sleeve)	£15
08	Virgin VUS 340	From Yesterday (red vinyl, 1-side etched)	£15
09	Virgin 509993/0943315	THIS IS WAR (gatefold, 2-LP with CD)	£18

THIS DRIFTIN'S GOTTA STOP
75	private pressing	THIS DRIFTIN'S GOTTA STOP (LP)	£30

THIS ETERNAL WAITING
86	I Live In Hell BURN 2	The Prize/Love And Live Tombs	£20

THIS HEAT
80	Piano THIS 1201	Health And Efficiency/Graphic/Varispeed (12", p/s with insert)	£25
79	Piano THIS 1	THIS HEAT (LP)	£60
81	Rough Trade ROUGH 26	DECEIT (LP, 1st pressing)	£45
88	These HEAT 1	THIS HEAT (reissue)	£30
88	These HEAT 1	DECEIT (reissue)	£30
98	These 12/6	REPEAT/HEALTH AND EFFICIENCY (2 x 12")	£20
99	These HEAT 10	MADE AVAILABLE: PEEL SESSIONS (LP)	£50
06	This Is LC 02677	OUT OF COLD STORAGE (6-CD box set)	£40

(see also Gareth Williams, Charles Hayward, Camberwell Now)

THIS KIND
67	MJB SP 112	Dirty City/I've Got It	£200

THIS MORTAL COIL
83	4AD BAD 310	16 Days/Gathering Dust/Song To The Siren/16 Days (reprise) (12", p/s)	£15
84	4AD CAD 411	IT'LL END IN TEARS (LP, inners)	£20
86	4AD DAD 609	FILIGREE AND SHADOW (2-LP, inners)	£25
91	4AD DAD 1005	BLOOD (2-LP, with inners)	£35

(see also Cocteau Twins, Modern English, Cindytalk)

THIS 'N' THAT
66	Mercury MF 938	Someday/Loving You	£20

(see also Cleo)

THIS PERFECT DAY
83	No Friction NFR 001	The Garden/The Time Of Your Life	£80

MABI THOBEJANE
97	M.E.L.T. 2000 BWLP096	MADIBA (LP)	£15

B.J. THOMAS
66	Hickory 45-1395	Never Tell/Billy & Sue	£15

CARLA THOMAS
61	London HLK 9310	Gee Whiz/For You	£20
61	London HLK 9359	A Love Of My Own/Promises	£15
62	London HLK 9618	I'll Bring It On Home To You/I Can't Take It	£15
64	Atlantic AT 4005	I've Got No Time To Lose/A Boy Named Tom	£18
67	Stax 601 008	When Tomorrow Comes/Unchanging Love (dark blue label)	£15
91	Kent 6T 7	I'll Never Stop Loving/Prophets Band/Peaches Baby	£60
91	Horace's HRH 007	I'll Never Stop Loving You/BARBARA LEWIS: The Stars	£40
67	Stax 589 004	CARLA THOMAS (LP)	£35
67	Stax 589 012	THE QUEEN ALONE (LP)	£20
69	Stax SXATS 1019	MEMPHIS QUEEN (LP)	£40
71	Stax 2362 023	LOVE MEANS ...(LP)	£20

(see also Otis Redding & Carla Thomas)

CLAUDETTE THOMAS
68	Caltone TONE 116	Roses Are Red My Love/YVONNE HARRISON: Near To You	£80

CREEPY JOHN THOMAS
69	RCA RCA 1912	Ride A Rainbow/Moon And Eyes Song	£15
69	RCA SF 8061	CREEPY JOHN THOMAS (LP, laminated front sleeve)	£300

(see also Paul Kossoff, Edgar Broughton Band)

DON THOMAS
76	DJM DJS 670	Come On Train Parts 1 & 2 (Promos in p/s)	£20

GENE THOMAS
64	United Artists UP 1047	Baby's Gone/Stand By Love	£20

HERSAL THOMAS
50	Parlophone R 3261	Suitcase Blues/Hersal Blues (78)	£35

IRMA THOMAS
64	Liberty LIB 66013	Breakaway/Wish Someone Would Care	£25
64	Liberty LIB 66041	Anyone Who Knows What Love Is (Will Understand)/Time Is On My Side	£20
65	Liberty LIB 66080	He's My Guy/True True Love	£20
65	Liberty LIB 66095	Some Things You Never Get Used To/You Don't Miss A Good Thing (Until It's Gone)	£20
65	Sue WI 372	Don't Mess With My Man/Set Me Free	£40
65	Liberty LIB 66106	I'm Gonna Cry Till My Tears Run Dry/ Nobody Wants To Hear Nobody's Troubles	£20
66	Liberty LIB 66137	Take A Look/What Are You Trying To Do	£75

MINT VALUE £

66	Liberty LIB 66137	Take A Look/What Are You Trying To Do (DJ copy)	£125
66	Liberty LIB 66178	It's A Man's-Woman's World	£20
65	Liberty LEP 4035	TIME IS ON MY SIDE (EP)	£100
68	Minit MLL/MLS 40004E	TAKE A LOOK (LP)	£75
76	Island HELP 29	LIVE (LP)	£15
81	Charly CRB 1020	IN BETWEEN TEARS (LP, reissue, different cover from US original)	£15
83	Kent 010	TIME IS ON MY SIDE (LP)	£15
19	Reel RMLP 4579LE	IN BETWEEN TEARS (LP, reissue, 500 only, white vinyl)	£15

JAMES 'CREOLE' THOMAS
18	22a 021	OMAS SEXTET (LP)	£40

JAMO THOMAS & HIS PARTY BROTHERS ORCHESTRA
66	Polydor BM 56709	I Spy (For The FBI)/Snake Hip Mama	£15
69	Chess CRS 8098	I'll Be Your Fool/Jamo Soul	£20

JIMMY THOMAS
69	Parlophone R 5773	The Beautiful Night/Above A Whisper (withdrawn)	£300
69	Parlophone R 5773	The Beautiful Night/Above A Whisper (withdrawn; DJ copy)	£250
69	Spark SRL1035	(We Ain't Looking For) No Trouble/Springtime	£200
81	Osceola OSC 1	Hang Right On In There Part 1/Driving Wheel (12. p/s)	£20
73	Contempo COLP 1002	ABYSS (LP)	£25

JOE THOMAS
72	People PLE 015	JOY OF COOKIN' (LP)	£15

KID THOMAS/EMANUEL BAND
64	'77' LA 12/26	VICTORY WALK (LP, with Barry Martyn's Band)	£30

LEON THOMAS
73	Philips 6369 417	BLUES & SOULFUL TRUTH (LP)	£30

NICKY THOMAS
70	Amalgamated AMG 863	Danzella/JOE GIBBS ALLSTARS: Kingstonians Reggae	£25
70	Trojan TR 7750	Love Of The Common People/DESTROYERS: Compass	£15
70	Trojan TBL 143	LOVE OF THE COMMON PEOPLE (LP)	£20
72	Trojan TRLS 25	TELL IT LIKE IT IS (LP)	£25

(see also Joe Gibbs)

PAT THOMAS (2)
80	Pan African PAR 003	1980 (LP)	£70
80	Pan African PAR 006	SWEETER THAN HONEY, CALYPSO MAHUNO AND HIGH LIFE CELEBRATION (LP, with Ebo Taylor)	£100
80	Nakasi NAK 004	MPAEBO (LP)	£100
84	Earthworks/Rough Trade ERT 1001	IN ACTION VOLUME 2 (LP, reissue)	£15
85	Jap JAP 0101	ASANTEMAN (LP)	£20

PETER THOMAS SOUND ORCHESTRA
68	Poydor 184171	ORGANIC (LP)	£35
70	Polydor 2418 074	CHARIOTS OF THE GODS (LP)	£35

RUDDY THOMAS
79	DEB DEB 015	Dry Up Your Tears/Rat Trap (12")	£25
80s	Shuttle SH 005	Bless You/The Right Time (12")	£15

RUDY THOMAS
83	Mobiliser MMLP 34	VERY BEST OF (LP)	£15

RUFUS THOMAS
63	London HLK 9799	Walking The Dog/Fine And Mellow	£25
64	London HLK 9850	Can Your Monkey Do The Dog/I Want To Get Married	£15
64	London HLK 9884	Somebody Stole My Dog/I Want To Be Loved	£15
64	Atlantic AT 4009	Jump Back/All Night Worker	£18
68	Stax 601 037	The Memphis Train/I Think I Made A Boo-Boo	£15
64	Atlantic AET 6001	DO THE DOG (EP)	£50
65	Atlantic AET 6011	JUMP BACK WITH RUFUS (EP)	£50
64	London HA-K 8183	WALKING THE DOG (LP)	£80
70	Stax SXATS 1033	FUNKY CHICKEN (LP)	£35
71	Stax 2363 001	FUNKY CHICKEN (LP, reissue)	£15
71	Stax 2362 010	DOING THE PUSH AND PULL LIVE AT P.J.'s (LP)	£25
72	Stax 2362 028	DID YOU HEAR ME? (LP)	£25
74	Stax STX 1004	CROWN PRINCE OF DANCE (LP)	£30
02	Stax SX2 135	THE FUNKIEST MAN (2-LP)	£20

TERRY-THOMAS ESQUIRE
61	Decca LK 4398	STRICTLY T-T (LP)	£40

TIMMY THOMAS
73	Mojo 2956 002	WHY CAN'T WE LIVE TOGETHER (LP)	£20

VAUGHAN THOMAS
71	DJM DJS 238	I Wanna Be Famous Like My Dad/Love	£15
72	Jam JAL 101	VAUGHAN THOMAS (LP, textured sleeve, white/red/black label)	£40

ANDREAS THOMOPOULOS
70	Mushroom 100 MR 1	SONGS OF THE STREET (LP)	£80
71	Mushroom 150 MR 4	BORN OUT OF THE TEARS OF THE SUN (LP)	£90

(see also Secondhand)

BOBBY THOMPSON

| 69 | Columbia Blue Beat DB 113 | That's How Strong My Love Is/Trouble In Town | £15 |
| 69 | Jolly JY 001 | That's How Strong My Love Is/Trouble In The Town | £50 |

(see also Dandy)

CARROLL THOMPSON

| 81 | Carib Gems CGLP 15 | HOPELESSLY IN LOVE (LP) | £25 |
| 93 | Ariwa ARILP 077 | THE OTHER SIDE OF LOVE (LP) | £15 |

CHERYLE THOMPSON

| 64 | Stateside SS 291 | Teardrops/Black Night | £30 |

CHRIS THOMPSON

| 73 | Village Thing VTS 21 | CHRIS THOMPSON (LP, allegedly 101 sold and 899 destroyed, 'Shorewood Packaging Ltd.' printer credit) | £250 |

COLIN THOMPSON

| 80 | Fellside FE 021 | THREE KNIGHTS (LP) | £15 |

DONNEY THOMPSON

| 79 | Third World TWDIS 20 | Rocking Time/PAGET KING: Close Encounter (12") | £60 |

EDDIE THOMPSON

55	Jazz Today JTE 101	THE FABULOUS EDDIE THOMPSON (EP)	£60
57	Nixa NJE 1030	PIANO MOODS VOLUME 6 (EP)	£60
60	Ember EMB 3303	PIANO MOODS (LP)	£100
60	Tempo TAP 24	HIS MASTER'S JAZZ (LP)	£250
69	77 LEU 12/39	BY MYSELF (LP)	£40

EVERAND THOMPSON

| 78 | Ultra PFU 1005 | Babylon Hustle Me/Babylon Version | £75 |

JOHNNY THOMPSON & ONE-EYED JACKS

| 65 | Ember EMB S 206 | For Us There'll Be No Tomorrow/Soul Chant (in p/s) | £20 |

KAY THOMPSON

| 56 | London HLA 8268 | Eloise/Just One Of Those Things | £40 |

LEROY THOMPSON

| 78 | Noel DN 005 | Hard Times Criminal Times/Since You Left Me & Gone (12") | £30 |

LINCOLN THOMPSON

| 80 | God Sent GDIS 1 | One Common Need/Food Clothing And Shelter (12", with the Rasses) | £60 |

LINVAL THOMPSON

78	Attack ATT 8135	I Love Marijuana/Jamaican Calley (Version)	£15
78	Star PTP 1007	If I Follow My Heart/THOMPSON ALL STARS: Rocking version (12")	£20
79	Burning Rockers BRD 003	Follow My Heart/THOMPSON ALL STARS: Rockers Version (12")	£20
79	Burning Sounds BSD 023	Rocking Vibration/Natty Dread (12')	£20
79	Burning Sounds BSD 031	Bound To Surrender/Dub Version (12")	£20
79	GG's GG 056	Mad Dog (with Ranking Trevor)/REVOLUTIONARIES: Kevin At The Controls (12")	£30
79	Greensleeves GRED 024	One More Chance/Long Time Me Na Rub You In A Dance (12", with Trinity)	£20
79	D-Roy DRDD 16	She Is Mad At Me/Stop Your War (12")	£30
80	Attack TACK 19	Here With Me/ROOTS RADICS BAND: Come On Baby Dub Style (12")	£15
80	Attack TACK 22	Pop No Style/SCIENTIST: Second Hand Girl (12")	£20
80	Black Joy DH 804	Brown Skin Girl/RANKING TREVOR: Brown Skin Girl Rub A Dub (12")	£15
80	Strong Like Sampson SLSD 04	Mr Boss Man (with Trevor Ranking)/BARNABOUS: Stop Push Me Around (12")	£20
80	Strong Like Sampson SLSD 016	Curfew/PAPPA TULLO: Morning Curfew (12")	£20
81	Cha Cha CHAD 29	Gambler/Everyday Rain (with WAYNE WADE, 12", blue vinyl)	£20
76	Third World TWLP 010	DON'T CUT OFF YOUR DREADLOCKS (LP)	£30
78	Trojan TRLS 151	I LOVE MARIJUANA (LP)	£35
78	Burning Sounds BSD 1014	LOVE IS THE QUESTION (LP)	£25
78	Burning Sounds BS 1027	ROCKING VIBRATION (LP)	£40
79	Burning Sounds BS 1035	I LOVE JAH (LP)	£35
79	Trojan TRLS 153	NEGREA LOVE DUB (LP)	£25
80	Burning Rockers BR 1006LP	FOLLOW MY HEART (LP)	£30
82	Greensleeves GREL 33	LOOK HOW ME SEXY (LP)	£18
83	Greensleeves GREL 51	BABY FATHER (LP)	£18
94	Trojan TRLS 153	NEGREA LOVE DUB (LP, reissue)	£18
96	Trojan TRLS 151	I LOVE MARIJUANA (LP, reissue)	£15
00	Blood & Fire SVLP 294	RIDE ON DREADLOCKS (2-LP)	£25

(see also Bunny Lion)

MIKE THOMPSON JNR.

| 67 | Island WI 3090 | Rocksteady Wedding/Flower Pot Bloomers (both with Lyn Taitt & Jets) | £25 |

MOLLIE THOMPSON

| 66 | Asteroid JH 101 | SONG NOTES SINGS FROM WORLDS AFAR (LP, private pressing) | £40 |

PETER THOMPSON & NTH DEGREE

| 65 | Fontana TF 656 | For Me It's All Over/The Way You Used To Do | £20 |

RICHARD THOMPSON

72	Island ILPS 9197	HENRY THE HUMAN FLY (LP, 'pink rim palm tree' label)	£25
83	Hannibal HNBL 1313	HAND OF KINDNESS (LP)	£15
84	Hannibal HNBL 1316	SMALL TOWN ROMANCE (LP)	£15
91	Capitol 0547957131	RUMOR AND SIGH (LP)	£40
93	Capitol 07777 81492 1 7	MIRROR BLUE (LP)	£80

MINT VALUE £

03	Diverse DIV 004DLP	THE OLD KIT BAG (2-LP)	£40
05	Diverse DIV009LP	FRONT PARLOUR BALLADS (LP)	£35
07	Diverse DIV011DLP	SWEET WARRIOR (2-LP)	£60
10	Proper PRPLP064	DREAM ATTIC (2-LP)	£25

RICHARD & LINDA THOMPSON

73	Island ILPS 9266	I WANT TO SEE THE BRIGHT LIGHTS TONIGHT (LP, palm tree pink rim label)	£35
74	Island ILPS 9305	HOKEY POKEY (LP, blue rim palm tree label with lyric inner sleeve)	£25
75	Island ILPS 9348	POUR DOWN LIKE SILVER (LP, 'palm tree' label with lyrics)	£20
75	Island	OFFICIAL LIVE TOUR 1975 (LP, unreleased, test pressings may exist)	£100
76	Island ILPS 9266	I WANT TO SEE THE BRIGHT LIGHTS TONIGHT (LP, repressing, blue rim)	£18
76	Island ICD 8	GUITAR/VOCAL (2-LP, gatefold sleeve, blue rim/palm tree label)	£25
78	Island ILPS 9266	I WANT TO SEE THE BRIGHT LIGHTS TONIGHT (LP, repressing, dark blue label)	£15

(see also Fairport Convention, Richard Thompson, Sandy Denny, Marc Ellington, Nick Drake, Gary Farr)

ROY THOMPSON

67	Columbia DB 8108	Sookie Sookie/Love You Say	£30

SIR CHARLES THOMPSON

53	Vogue LDE 032	SIR CHARLES THOMPSON'S ALL STARS WITH CHARLIE PARKER (10" LP)	£20
56	Vanguard PPT 12011	AND HIS BAND FEATURING COLEMAN HAWKINS (10" LP)	£15

SONNY THOMPSON & HIS RHYTHM & BLUES BAND

52	Vogue V 2143	Real, Real Fine (Parts 1 & 2) (78)	£15
53	Esquire 10-320	House Full Of Blues/Creepin' (78)	£15
53	Esquire 10-339	Screamin' Boogie/The Fish (78)	£15
60	Starlite ST45 008	Screamin' Boogie/The Fish	£250
56	Parlophone GEP 8562	SONNY THOMPSON INSTRUMENTALS (EP, as Sonny Thompson Orchestra)	£40

(see also Claude Cloud & Thunderclaps)

SUE THOMPSON

65	Hickory LPE 1507	INTRODUCING KRIS JENSEN AND SUE THOMPSON (EP, 2 tracks each)	£15
64	Hickory LPM 102	PAPER TIGER (LP)	£25

(see also Kris Jensen)

THOMPSON TWINS

80	Dirty Discs RANK 1	Squares And Triangles/Could Be Her...Could Be You (p/s, different colours)	£35
85	Arista TWINS 128	Roll Over (Again)/Fools In Paradise (Extended) (12", p/s, withdrawn)	£80
81	T Records TELP 1	A PRODUCT OF... (LP)	£15

GUNILLA THORN

63	HMV POP 1239	Merry-Go-Round/Go On Then	£90

TRACEY THORN

82	Cherry Red MRED 35	A DISTANT SHORE (LP)	£20
07	Virgin V 3030	OUT OF THE WOODS (LP)	£70

(see also Marine Girls, Everything But The Girl)

DAVID THORNE

64	Stateside SE 1020	WHAT WILL I TELL MY HEART (EP)	£25
63	Stateside SL 10036	THE ALLEY CAT SONGSTER (LP)	£35

KEN THORNE ORCHESTRA

68	United Artists ULP 1201	INSPECTOR CLOUSEAU (LP, soundtrack)	£30
69	Stateside S(S)L 10271	THE TOUCHABLES (LP, with Nirvana, Wynder K. Frog, et al.)	£50

WOODY THORNE

62	Vogue Pop V 9202	Sadie Lou/Teenagers In Love	£400

LEEROY THORNHILL

95	LP 001	LOWRISE (12" EP white label)	£30

(see also The Prodigy)

CLAUDE THORNHILL & HIS ORCHESTRA

54	London HL 8042	Pussy-Footin'/Adios	£40
54	London RE-P 1009	CLAUDE THORNHILL GOES MODERN (EP)	£20
54	London H-ABP 1019	CLAUDE THORNHILL GOES MODERN (10" LP)	£20
54	London H-ABP 1021	DREAM MUSIC (10" LP)	£20

WILLIE MAE 'BIG MAMA' THORNTON

54	Vogue V 2284	Hound Dog/Mischievous Boogie (78) (as Willie Mae 'Big Mama' Thornton)	£80
65	Sue WI 345	Tom Cat/Monkey In The Barn (as Willie Mae Thornton)	£250
69	Mercury SMCL 20176	STRONGER THAN DIRT (LP)	£40
78	Vanguard VPC 40001	MAMA'S PRIDE (LP)	£25

EDDIE THORNTON OUTFIT

69	Instant IN 003	Baby Be My Gal/SONNY BURKE OUTFIT: All You	£120

CLIFFORD THORNTON

76	JCOA/Virgin J2004	GARDENS OF HARLEM (LP, with Jazz Composers Orchestra)	£15

PETER THOROGOOD

68	Pye 7N 17597	Haunted/If No One Sang	£100

THOR'S HAMMER

66	Parlophone DP 565	Once/A Memory (export issue)	£200
66	Parlophone DP 567	If You Knew/Love Enough (export issue)	£185
66	Parlophone CGEP 62	THOR'S HAMMER (EP, export issue, gatefold p/s, with bonus 45 "If You Knew"/"Love Enough" [CGEP 62])	£1200

LINDA THORSON

68	Ember EMB S 257	Here I Am/Better Than Losing You (p/s)	£40

68	Ember EMB S 257	Here I Am/Better Than Losing You £15
70	Ember EMBS 284	Wishful Thinking/You Will Want Me £20
70	Ember LT 1	Bad Time To Stop Loving Me/Pick Up My Heart (promo) £25

THOSE ATTRACTIVE MAGNETS
83	Tavern AD MAG 10	Nightlife/Love Chimes (p/s) £70

THOSE DANCING DAYS
08	Wichita WEBB 184LP	IN OUR SPACE HERE SUITS (LP) £20

THOUGHT POLICE
79	Wessex WEX 263	Mr Sad/You Tell Me Lies/Pictures (p/s) £30

THOUGHTS
66	Planet PLF 118	All Night Stand/Memory Of Your Love £100

(see also Tiffany [& Thoughts], Paul Dean & Soul Savages)

THOUGHTS & WORDS
69	Liberty LBL 83224	THOUGHTS & WORDS (LP) £35

THREADBARE CONSORT
80s	private pressing	WEARING THIN (LP) £15

THREADS OF LIFE
72	Alco ALC 530	THREADS OF LIFE (LP, actually by Alco) £800

THREAT
80	One Web 001 WEB	Lullaby In C/High Cost Of Living £75

THREATS
82	Rondelet ROUND 22	GO TO HELL (EP) £15
82	Rondelet ROUND 29	Politicians & Ministers/Writing's On The Wall/Deep End Depression (p/s) £20
82	Rondelet ROUND 1229	POLITICIANS & MINISTERS (12" EP) £18

THREE BELLS
66	Columbia DB 7980	Cry No More/He Doesn't Want You £15

(see also Satin Bells)

THREE CAPS
66	Atlantic 584 004	Cool Jerk/Hello Stranger £15

(see also Capitols)

THREE CHUCKLES
55	HMV 7M 292	Runaround/At Last You Understand £40
55	HMV 7M 292	Runaround/At Last You Understand (78) £15
56	HMV 7M 333	Still Thinking Of You/Times Two I Love You £35
56	HMV 7M 333	Still Thinking Of You/Times Two I Love You (78) £15
57	HMV POP 292	We're Gonna Rock Tonight/Want You Give Me A Chance £80
57	HMV POP 292	We're Gonna Rock Tonight/Want You Give Me A Chance (78) £25

(see also Teddy Randazzo)

THREE CITY FOUR
65	Decca LK 4705	THREE CITY FOUR (LP) £150
67	CBS 63039	SMOKE AND DUST WHERE THE HEART SHOULD HAVE BEEN (LP) £100

(see also Martin Carthy, Leon Rosselson)

THREE COINS
70	Sugar SU 106	Come And Do The Right Thing/It's So Long £20

THREE DANCERS
87	Dilletante Disques 007	Seventeen/It Doesn't Matter (p/s) £40

3D PRODUCTION
80	Third Kind TKS 001	Riot/Riot (Rearrage) £40

THREE DEGREES
65	Stateside SS 413	Gee Baby I'm Sorry/Do What You're Supposed To Do £60
65	Stateside SS 459	Close Your Eyes/Gotta Draw The Line £70
65	Stateside SS 459	Close Your Eyes/Gotta Draw The Line (DJ copy) £100
71	Mojo 2916 002	THE THREE DEGREES (LP) £25

THREE DOG NIGHT
69	Stateside-Dun. (S)SL 5006	THREE DOG NIGHT (LP) £15

(see also Danny Hutton)

THREE GOOD REASONS
65	Mercury MF 899	Nowhere Man/Wire Wheels £18

THREE LITTLE PIGGIES
88	Mrs Slocombe	FRIVILOUS FROLICS (mini-LP) £50
89	Mrs Slocombe MSD2	Clarke's Commandos/Ain't He Happy/Uncle Chris (p/s) £80

THREE MAN ARMY
71	Pegasus PEG 3	A THIRD OF A LIFETIME (LP, gatefold) £80
74	Reprise K 54015	THREE MAN ARMY TWO (LP) £30

(see also Gun, Baker Gurvitz Army, Andy Newman, Spooky Tooth)

THREE PARTY SPLIT
79	B&C BCS 16	Dubious Parentage/Kandidate (p/s) £20
79	B&C BCS 19	Insane/Totally Insane (unissued, 1 known copy) £350

THREE PIECES
75	Fantasy FTC 116	I Need You Girl/Short'nin' Bread (Demo) £30
75	Fantasy FTC 116	I Need You Girl/Short'nin' Bread (unissued) £50
09	Fryers FRY 007	I Need You Girl/If Only I Could Prove To You (reissue) £25

MINT VALUE £

| 95 | BGP BDPD 1097 | **VIBES OF TRUTH** (LP, reissue) | £20 |

3 PM

91	Alma Vale ALMA 1	**Out Of Control** (12")	£15
91	Alma Vale ALMA 2	**ST.P/3PM/Lynx** (12")	£20
92	Busted Loop 3	**Better Late Than Never** (12")	£15

THREE QUARTERS

| 65 | Columbia DB 7467 | **People Will Talk/Love Come A-Tricklin' Down** | £15 |

3 THIEVES AND A LIAR

| 92 | 3 Thieves And A Liar 3TAL | **In The House/I Get A Chill/You Bring Me Joy/Tonight** (12") | £25 |

THREE TONES

| 70 | Bamboo BAM 32 | **Good Ways/Everything We Do** | £180 |

THREE TOPS

67	Doctor Bird DB 1101	**Miserable Friday/This World Has A Feeling**	£50
67	Studio One SO 2023	**Moving To Progress/Love And Inspiration**	£80
67	Trojan TR 003	**It's Raining/Sound Of Music** (Treetops on label)	£40
67	Treasure Isle TI 7008	**Do It Right/You Should Have Known**	£30
68	Coxsone CS 7033	**A Man Of Chances**(as Tree Tops)/**HORTENSE ELLIS: A Groovy Kind Of Love**	£300
71	Fab FAB 16	**Down At The Boneyard/ALF AND TEEP: Freedom, Justice And Equality** (promo only, black label)	£100
73	Bullet BU 527	**Take Time Out/Just Like A Log**	£20

(see also Dion Cameron & Three Tops, Sir Lord Comic, King Rocky)

THREE'S A CROWD

| 66 | Fontana TF 673 | **Look Around The Corner/Living In A Dream** | £20 |

(see also Embers, Writing On The Wall)

THRESHOLD OF PLEASURE

| 68 | Decca F12785 | **Rain Rain Rain/He Could Never Love You Like I Do** | £40 |

THRILLERS

| 68 | Blue Cat BS 128 | **The Last Dance/DELTA CATS: Unworthy Baby** | £500 |

(see also Phil Pratt)

PERCY 'THRILLS' THRILLINGTON

77	Regal Zono. EMI 2594	**Uncle Albert - Admiral Halsey/Eat At Home**	£100
77	Regal Zono. EMC 3175	**THRILLINGTON** (LP, with inner sleeve)	£200
77	Regal Zono. TC-EMC 3175	**THRILLINGTON** (cassette)	£25

(see also Paul McCartney)

THRILLS (1)

| 66 | Capitol CL 15469 | **No One/What Can Go Wrong** | £100 |
| 66 | Capitol CL 15469 | **No One/What Can Go Wrong** (DJ copy) | £200 |

THRILLS (2)

| 04 | V 2986 | **LET'S BOTTLE BOHEMIA** (LP, 7") | £70 |
| 03 | Virgin V 2975 | **SO MUCH FOR THE CITY** (LP) | £30 |

THROBBING GRISTLE

78	Industrial IR 0003	**United/Zyklon B Zombie** (p/s)	£20
78	Industrial IR 0003/U	**United/Zyklon B Zombie** (p/s, white or clear vinyl, 1,000 only of each)	£25
80	Industrial IR 0003	**United/Zyklon B Zombie** (longer version) (p/s, reissue, 'Memorial Issue' scratched in matrix)	£15
80	Industrial IR 0013	**Subhuman/Something Came Over Me** (in polythene camouflage bag)	£20
80	Industrial IR 0015	**Adrenalin/Distant Dreams** (Part Two) (in polythene camouflage bag)	£20
81	Fetish FET 006	**Discipline** (live, Berlin)/**Discipline** (live, Manchester) (12", p/s)	£20
77	Industrial IR 0002	**SECOND ANNUAL REPORT** (LP, 785 only, white hand-made sleeve, 'Nothing short of a total war' sticker on inner sleeve, xerox strip, 'technical note' strip & 2 or 3 TG stickers)	£250
78	Industrial IR 0004	**D.O.A. THE THIRD AND FINAL REPORT** (LP, 1st 1,000 with calendar & postcard)	£100
78	Industrial IR 0004	**D.O.A. THE THIRD AND FINAL REPORT** (LP)	£25
78	Fetish FET 2001	**SECOND ANNUAL REPORT** (LP, 2,000 only, T.G. 'lightning flash' sleeve, with questionnaire & insert, "Coom" mispelling)	£40
79	Fetish FET 2001	**SECOND ANNUAL REPORT** (LP, reissue, glossy sleeve with inserts, with correct "Coum" spelling)	£15
79	Industrial IR 0004	**D.O.A. THE THIRD AND FINAL REPORT** (LP, re-pressing, 1,000 only, banded as 16 equal length tracks)	£60
79	Industrial IR 0008	**20 JAZZ FUNK GREATS** (LP, 5,000 only, 1st 2,000 with b&w poster)	£80
79	Industrial IR 0008	**20 JAZZ FUNK GREATS** (LP, 5,000 only)	£40
80	Industrial IR 0009	**HEATHEN EARTH** (LP, gatefold sleeve, 785 on blue vinyl)	£100
80	Industrial IR 0009	**HEATHEN EARTH** (LP, gatefold sleeve)	£25
81	Fetish FET 2001	**SECOND ANNUAL REPORT** (LP, backwards version, 1st 2,000 in T.G. 'flash' sleeve)	£40
81	Fetish FET 2001	**SECOND ANNUAL REPORT** (LP, backwards version, later issue in black & white sleeve)	£15
81	Fetish FX 1	**A BOXED SET** (5-LP box set with 28-page booklet & badge, 5,000 only)	£150
82	Death 01	**MUSIC FROM THE DEATH FACTORY, MAY '79** (LP, 50 only)	£350
82	Power Focus 001	**ASSUME POWER FOCUS** (LP, 500 only, numbered)	£90
82	T.G. 33033	**LIVE AT THE DEATH FACTORY, MAY '79** (LP, reissue picture disc, 1,355 only)	£40
82	Karnage/Illuminated KILL 1	**THEE PSYCHICK SACRIFICE** (2-LP)	£30
83	Mute MIR 001	**THE SECOND ANNUAL REPORT** (LP, reissue)	£20
83	Mute MIR 002	**D.O.A. THE THIRD AND FINAL REPORT** (LP, reissue)	£20
83	Mute MIR 003	**20 JAZZ FUNK GREATS** (LP, reissue)	£20
83	Mute MIR004	**HEATHEN EARTH** (LP, reissue)	£20
84	Illuminated JAMS 35	**IN THE SHADOW OF THE SUN** (LP, soundtrack)	£20
84	Illuminated JAMS 39	**THE INDUSTRIAL RECORDS STORY 1976-1981** (LP)	£35
84	Casual Abandon CAS 1J	**ONCE UPON A TIME** (LP)	£15

84	Mental Decay 01-1	SPECIAL TREATMENT (LP)	£15
80s	Sprut 001	VERY FRIENDLY - THE FIRST ANNUAL REPORT OF T.G. (LP)	£25
80s	Industrial IRC 1-IRC 24	24 HOURS (box set of cassettes with total of 24 hours playing time; every set is unique)	£300
03	Grey Area	TG+ (10-CD box set with metal cards)	£70

(see also Psychic TV, Coil, Sabres Of Paradise)

THROWING MUSES

86	4AD CAD 607	THROWING MUSES (LP)	£15
87	4AD MAD 706	THE FAT SKIER (LP)	£15
88	4AD CAD 802	HOUSE TORNADO (LP)	£15
89	4AD CAD 901	HUNKPAPA (LP, lyric inner)	£15
91	4AD CAD 1002	THE REAL RAMONA (LP, inner)	£20
93	4AD CADD 2013	RED HEAVEN (LP, with free live Kristin Hersh LP)	£40
95	4AD CAD 5002	UNIVERSITY (LP)	£40
96	4AD CAD 6014	LIMBO (LP)	£40

(see also Belly, Kristin Hersh)

THE THRUST
| 80 | Ellie Jay EJSP 9341 | THE THRUST EP | £100 |

THUG LIFE
| 94 | Interscope 6544 92360-1 | VOLUME 1 (LP, inner) | £100 |

THUNDER
| 90 | EMI EMPD 126 | Dirty Love/Fired Up (uncut picture disc with insert in PVC sleeve) | £15 |

(see also Terraplane, Nuthin' Fancy)

JOHNNY THUNDER
63	Stateside SS 200	Jailer, Bring Me Water/Outlaw	£15
65	Stateside SS 370	Send Her To Me/Everybody Likes To Dance With Johnny	£20
63	Stateside SL 10029	LOOP DE LOOP (LP)	£75

JOHNNY THUNDER & RUBY WINTERS
| 67 | Stateside SS 2005 | Make Love To Me/Teach Me Tonight | £15 |

THUNDERBIRDS
| 66 | Polydor 56710 | Your Ma Said You Cried (In Your Sleep Last Night)/Before It's Too Late | £70 |

(see also Chris Farlowe & Thunderbirds)

THUNDERBIRDS (AUSTRALIA)
| 61 | Oriole CB 1610 | Wild Weekend/Rat Race | £20 |
| 61 | Oriole CB 1625 | New Orleans Beat/Delilah Jones | £20 |

THUNDERBIRDS (U.S.)
| 55 | London HL 8146 | Ayuh, Ayuh/Blueberries | £70 |
| 55 | London HL 8146 | Ayuh, Ayuh/Blueberries (78) | £15 |

(see also Bert Convy & Thunderbirds)

THUNDERBOLTS
| 62 | Decca F 11522 | Fugitive/Feelin' In A Mood | £15 |

THUNDERBOYS
| 80 | Recent EJSP 9339 | Fashion/Someone Like You (p/s) | £40 |

THUNDERCAT
| 17 | Brainfeeder BF064 | DRUNK (4-10"s, boxset, red vinyl) | £30 |

THUNDERCLAP NEWMAN
| 70 | Track 2406 003 | HOLLYWOOD DREAM (LP, gatefold sleeve, lyric insert) | £100 |
| 70 | Track 2406 003 | HOLLYWOOD DREAM (LP, gatefold sleeve, without lyric insert) | £30 |

(see also Stone The Crows, One In A Million, Paul McCartney & Wings, Speedy Keen, Andy Newman)

THUNDER COMPANY
| 70 | Columbia DB 8706 | Ridin' On The Gravy Train (5.03)/Bubble Drum | £40 |
| 70 | Columbia DB 8706 | Ridin' On The Gravy Train (2.35 Edit)/Bubble Drum (demo only) | £50 |

(see also Brian Bennett, Shadows)

THUNDERHEAD
| 93 | Thunderhead TH 01 | Lost In Time/Untitled (12") | £20 |

THUNDERMUG
| 72 | Axe AXS 502 | STRIKES (LP) | £15 |

JOHNNY THUNDERS (& THE HEARTBREAKERS)
78	Real ARE 1	Dead Or Alive/Downtown (p/s)	£20
78	Real ARE 3	You Can't Put Your Arms Around A Memory (Edit)/Hurtin' (p/s)	£15
78	Real ARE 3T	You Can't Put Your Arms Around A Memory/Hurtin' (12", p/s, blue or pink vinyl, die-cut company sleeve)	£15
14	Remarquable RBL 1	REAL TIMES EP (10", pink or blue vinyl, poster insert)	£20
77	Real RAL 1	SO ALONE (LP, with inner sleeve)	£30
86	Jungle JT BOX 1	ALBUM COLLECTION (3-LP & 12" box set with poster and badge)	£30

(see also New York Dolls, Heartbreakers)

SAM THUNDER
| 84 | Bullet BULP 5 | MANOUEVRES (LP, picture disc) | £18 |

THURSDAY'S CHILDREN
| 66 | Piccadilly 7N 35276 | Just You/You Don't Believe Me | £25 |
| 66 | Piccadilly 7N 35306 | Crawfish/Come Softly To Me | £15 |

(see also Phil Cordell)

BOBBY THURSTON
| 81 | Epic EPC A1301 | Very Last Drop/Life Is What You Make It | £20 |

81	Epic EPC A 13 1301	Very Last Drop/Life Is What You Make It (12")	£20
01	Expansion Special Reserve EXSR7-4	Just Ask Me/Treat Me The Same Way (reissue)	£20
80	Epic EPC 82257	YOU GOT WHAT IT TAKES (LP)	£15
81	Epic EPC 85070	MAIN ATTRACTION (LP)	£15
88	HI Hut HH 1135	SWEETEST PIECE OF THE PIE (LP)	£50
01	Expansion EXLM 8	SWEETEST PIECE OF THE PIE (LP, reissue)	£30

THYRDS

64	Oak RGJ 133	Hide 'N' Seek/I've Got My Mojo Working	£300
64	Decca F 12010	Hide 'N' Seek/No Time Like The Present	£60

TIAMAT

90	CMFT CMFT 6	SUMERIAN CRY (LP)	£40
90	Metalcore CORE 9	SUMERIAN CRY (LP, reissue)	£30

TIARAS

63	Warner Bros WB 92	You Told Me/I'm Gonna Forget You	£15

TIBET & STAPLETON

96	United Dairies UDOR 1	MUSICALISCHE KÜRBS HÜTTE (LP, clear vinyl, with insert)	£30

(see also Current 93, Steven Stapleton & David Tibet)o

TICKAWINDA

79	Pennine PSS 153	ROSEMARY LANE (LP)	£800

KATHRYN TICKELL

84	Saydisc SDL 343	ON KIELDER SIDE (LP)	£20

TICKLE

67	Regal Zonophone RZ 3004	Subway (Smokey Pokey World)/Good Evening	£500

(see also Junior's Eyes, Outsider, Bunch Of Fives)

TIC TAC TOE

92	Tic Tac Toe TTT 456	456/Ephemerol (12", stamped white label)	£30

PETER TIERNEY & NIGHTHAWKS

65	Fontana TF 547	Oh How I Need You/That's Too Bad (p/s)	£15

ROY TIERNEY

61	Philips BF 1159	Cupid/The Lonely One (in p/s)	£15

TIERNEY'S FUGITIVES

65	Decca F 12247	Did You Want To Run Away?/Morning Mist	£25

TIFFANIES

67	Chess CRS 8059	It's Got To Be A Great Song/He's Good For Me	£100
67	Chess CRS 8059	It's Got To Be A Great Song/He's Good For Me (DJ copy)	£150

TIFFANY (WITH THOUGHTS)

65	Parlophone R 5311	I Know/Am I Dreaming	£20
66	Parlophone R 5439	Find Out What's Happening/Baby Don't Look Down (as Tiffany with Thoughts)	£50

(see also Thoughts)

TIFFANY SHADE

68	Fontana (S)TL 5469	TIFFANY SHADE (LP)	£100

JIMMY & LOUISE TIG

69	Deep Soul DS 9105	A Love That Never Grows Cold/Who Can I Turn To	£40

TIGER

75	United Artists UP 35848	I Am An Animal/Stop That Machine	£20
76	Retreat RTL 6006	TIGER (LP, with lyric inner sleeve)	£15
76	EMI EMC3153	GOIN' DOWN LAUGHING (LP, lyric inner sleeve)	£15

(see also Hackensack, Samson, Brinsley Schwarz, Big Jim Sullivan)

TIGER ASHBY

80	T&A Records TA 1	Jet Free/Burning Cross (p/s)	£20

TIGER (JAMAICA)

70	New Beat NB 052	Soul Of Africa/Dallas Texas	£20
70	New Beat NB 064	Musical Scorcher/Three Dogs Night	£20
71	Camel CA 70	Guilty/United We Stand	£15
71	New Beat NB 075	African Beat/Black Man Land	£15

(see also Laurel Aitken)

TIGER LILY

77	Gull GULS 54	Monkey Jive/Ain't Misbehavin' (reissue, p/s)	£15

(see also Ultravox)

TIGERMOTH

84	Rogue FMSL 2006	TIGERMOTH (LP)	£15

TIGER TAILS

80	Snotty Snails NELCO 2	Words Without Conviction/Norman/Fashion Fool (p/s)	£20

TIGHT LIKE THAT

72	Village Thing VTS 12	HOKUM (LP)	£40

TIGHTS

78	Cherry Red CHERRY 1	Bad Hearts/It/Cracked (p/s)	£25
78	Cherry Red CHERRY 2	Howard Hughes/China's Eternal (p/s)	£15

TIKKI, TAKI, SUZI, LIES

70	UPC UPC 109	Ba-Da-Da-Dum/Dream Stealer	£25

JOHN TILBURY
75	Decca HEAD 9	MR JOHN CAGES PREPARED PIANO (LP)	£25

TILLERMEN
71	Duke DU 109	Be Loving To Me/Judgement Rock	£25

(see also Greyhound)

DEREK JOHN TILLEY
70	Decca F 13043	Sunny Day/Living For Love	£30

BERTHA TILLMAN
62	Oriole CB 1746	Oh, My Angel/Lovin' Time	£80

JOHNNY TILLOTSON
59	London HLA 8930	True True Happiness/Love Is Blind	£30
60	London HLA 9048	Why Do I Love You So/Never Let Me Go	£20
60	London HLA 9101	Earth Angel/Pledging My Love	£30
61	London HLA 9412	Without You/Cutie Pie	£15
62	London RE-A 1345	JOHNNY TILLOTSON (EP)	£35
63	London RE-A 1388	J.T. (EP)	£35
63	MGM MGM-EP 788	JOHNNY TILLOTSON (EP)	£20
64	MGM MGM-EP 790	JOHNNY TILLOTSON'S HIT PARADE (EP)	£20
61	London HA-A 2431	JOHNNY TILLOTSON'S BEST (LP)	£30
62	London HA-A 8019	IT KEEPS RIGHT ON A-HURTIN' (LP)	£25
64	MGM MGM-C 972	ALONE WITH YOU (LP)	£20
65	MGM C/CS 1002	SHE UNDERSTANDS ME (LP)	£20
65	MGM MGM-C(S) 8005	JOHNNY TILLOTSON SINGS OUR WORLD (LP)	£20
66	MGM MGM-C(S) 8025	NO LOVE AT ALL (LP)	£20

TILSLEY ORCHESTRA
66	Fontana TF 783	Thunderbirds Theme/Theme From "The Power Game"	£20
67	Fontana (S)TL 5411	TOP T.V. THEMES (LP)	£20

(see also Electric Banana)

STEVE TILSTON
71	Village Thing VTS 5	AN ACOUSTIC CONFUSION (LP)	£35
72	Transatlantic TRA 252	COLLECTION (LP, textured gatefold sleeve)	£18
77	Cornucopia CR 1	SONGS FROM THE DRESS REHEARSAL (LP, with Rupert Hine/John Renbourn)	£25
83	TM PROP 4	IN FOR A PENNY IN FOR A POUND (LP, with Peter Bardens)	£15

TIMBER TIMBRE
11	Full Time Hobby FTH 114LP	CREEP ON CREEPING ON (LP)	£18
14	Full Time Hobby FTH 189LP	HOT DREAMS (LP, white vinyl repressing)	£25

TIME
65	Pye 7N 17019	Take A Bit Of Notice/Every Now And Then	£60
66	Pye 7N 17146	The First Time I Saw The Sunshine/Annabel	£30

TIME
75	B.U.K. BULP 2005	TIME (LP)	£60

(see also Spontaneous Combustion)

T.I.M.E. (TRUST IN MEN EVERYWHERE)
68	Liberty LBL/LBS 83144	T.I.M.E. (LP)	£50
69	Liberty LBL/LBS 83232	SMOOTH BALL (LP)	£70

TIME MACHINE (2)
78	Rip Off RIP 6	NEVER MET SUZI EP	£40

TIMEBOX
67	Piccadilly 7N 35369	I'll Always Love You/Save Your Love	£100
67	Piccadilly 7N 35379	Soul Sauce/I Wish I Could Jerk Like My Uncle Cyril	£200
67	Deram DM 153	Walking Through The Streets Of My Mind/Don't Make Promises	£25
68	Deram DM 194	Beggin'/A Woman That's Waiting	£80
68	Deram DM 219	Girl Don't Make Me Wait/Gone Is The Sad Man	£35
69	Deram DM 246	Baked Jam Roll In Your Eye/Poor Little Heartbreaker	£30
69	Deram DM 271	Yellow Van/You've Got The Chance	£30

(see also Bo Street Runners, [Mike] Patto, V.I.Ps)

TIMECOP1983
19	Timeslave TSR58	JOURNEYS (2-LP, pink vinyl)	£40
18	Timeslave TSR45	NIGHT DRIVE (2-LP, purple vinyl, 500 only)	£70
19	Timeslave TSR45	NIGHT DRIVE (2-LP, repressing blue/black splatter, 500 only)	£50
20	Timeslave TSR45	NIGHT DRIVE (2-LP, repressing clear/purple splatter vinyl, 500 only)	£40
20	Timeslave TSR73	LOVERS PART 1 AND 2 (2-LP, blue/white and blue/pink splatter)	£60
21	Timeslave TSR73	LOVERS PART 1 AND 2 (2-LP, repressing, pink/blue split vinyl)	£30
21	Timeslave TSR71	REFLECTIONS (2-LP)	£50

TIMELORDS
88	KLF 003GG	Gary In The Tardis (Radio)/(Minimal) (white label promo, 500 only)	£15
88	KLF 003P	Doctorin' The Tardis (Radio)/(Minimal) (car-shaped picture disc)	£15
88	KLF 003R	Doctorin' The Tardis (Radio)/Doctorin' The Tardis (Minimal)/ Gary Glitter Joins The JAMs (12", 4,000 only, this price for those in full 'Gary Glitter' p/s)	£30

(see also KLF, JAMs, Bill Drummond, Orb, Space)

TIME MACHINE (1)
72	Play PLAY 41	Railroad/Going Down Down Down	£30

TIMES (1)
65	EMI 7ES 24	Ooh Wee/Shepherd Blues/Suzie/Running And Hiding (EP, demo only)	£70

| 66 | Columbia DB 7804 | Think About The Times/Tomorrow Night | £35 |
| 66 | Columbia DB 7904 | (She Can't Replace) The Love We Knew/Reconciled | £35 |

TIMES (2)

81	Whaam! WHAAM 2	Red With Purple Flashes/Biff! Bang! Pow! (p/s)	£100
82	Art Pop POP 49	I Helped Patrick McGoohan Escape/The Theme From "Danger Man" (p/s)	£20
82	Art Pop POP 50	Here Come The Holidays (Voici Les Vacances)/Three Cheers For The Sun (A-side as Joni Dee & Times, p/s, with 'Times' sticker)	£18
90	Caff CAFF 13	Extase/BIFF BANG POW!: Sleep (p/s, with insert)	£20
81	Whaam! BIG 1	POP GOES ART (LP, hand-sprayed sleeve)	£60
82	Art Pop ART 20	POP GOES ART! (LP, reissue, hand-sprayed sleeve, with magazine cuttings taped to plain white cover)	£35
82	Art Pop ART 20	POP GOES ART! (LP, reissue, hand-sprayed sleeve, without magazine cuttings taped to plain white cover)	£25
83	Art Pop ART 19	THIS IS LONDON (LP, white label with blue print)	£35
83	Art Pop ART 19	THIS IS LONDON (LP, black label with white print)	£18
83	Art Pop No. 1	I HELPED PATRICK McGOOHAN ESCAPE (mini-LP)	£18
86	Art Pop ART 16	UP AGAINST IT (LP)	£25
86	Art Pop ART 15	ENJOY! (LP, gatefold sleeve)	£15
90	Art Pop ART 20	POP GOES ART (LP, 'hand-painted' picture disc reissue, signed)	£15
91	Creation CRELP 091	PURE (LP)	£15
92	Creation CRELP 123	AT THE ASTRADOME LUNAVILLE (LP)	£15
93	Creation CRELP 137	ALTERNATIVE COMMERCIAL CROSSOVER (LP, with inner)	£15

(see also Television Personalities, Teenage Filmstars, O Level, Biff Bang Pow!, L'Orange Mechanik)

BOBBY TIMMONS

| 61 | Riverside RLP 334 | SOUL TIME (LP, with Art Blakey, also stereo [RLP 9334]) | £20 |
| 60 | Riverside 12-317 | THIS HERE IS (LP) | £20 |

TIMON

| 68 | Pye 7N 17451 | Bitter Thoughts Of Little Jane/Ramblin' Boy | £100 |

TIMONEERS

| 76 | WHM WHM 1919 | ROASTED LIVE (LP) | £20 |

TIM TAM & TURN ONS

| 67 | Island WIP 6007 | Wait A Minute/Ophelia | £50 |

TINARIWEN

| 08 | Independiente ISOM 65LP | AMAN IMAN (2-LP) | £50 |
| 09 | Independiente ISOM78LP | IMIDIWAN: COMPANIONS (LP) | £35 |

TINDERBOX (1)

| 68 | Polydor 56296 | Farewell Britannia/Rainsong | £60 |

TINDERBOX (2)

| 74 | Cannon CAN 2 | Inside A Dream/Sad N Lonely | £60 |

TINDERSTICKS

92	Tippy Toe 1	Patchwork/Milky Teeth (p/s, hand-coloured inner sleeve & insert; 1,000 only, numbered in positive or negative figures [from -500 to 500])	£60
93	Tippy Toe/Ché TIPPY-CHE 2	Marbles/Joe Stumble/For Those.../Benn (10", p/s, stickered PVC sleeve, inner sleeve & insert, 2,000 only)	£25
93	Tippy Toe 003	LIVE IN BERLIN: Raindrops/Tyed (in stamped brown paper bag, mail-order/tour release, 1,500 only)	£20
08	Lucky Dog LD 05	What Are You Fighting For? (one-sided 7", die cut sleeve, 200 only)	£15
93	This Way Up 518306	TINDERSTICKS (1st album) (2-LP, first 1000 with 4 postcards)	£100
93	This Way Up 518306	TINDERSTICKS (1st album) (2-LP, without postcards)	£60
93	This Way Up 518308-1	TINDERSTICKS (1st album) (2-LP reissue, green vinyl)	£50
95	This Way Up THIS 1.1	TINDERSTICKS (2nd album) (LP,with free 7")	£100
94	This Way Up WAY 3288	LIVE IN AMSTERDAM (10" LP, brown sleeve)	£40
95	This Way Up	THE BLOOMSBURY THEATRE 12/3/95 (LP, 2-10" LP)	£30
96	This Way Up 5243002	NENETTE ET BONI (LP)	£40
97	This Way Up 5243441	CURTAINS (2xLP)	£120
98	Island ILPS 8074	DONKEYS 92-97 (LP)	£80
99	Simply Vinyl SVLP 112	SIMPLE PLEASURE (LP)	£120
01	Beggars Banquet BBQLP 222	CAN OUR LOVE... (LP, gatefold)	£40
01	Beggars Banquet BBQLP 225	TROUBLE EVERY DAY (LP, soundtrack, with booklet)	£30
03	Beggars Banquet BBQLP 232	WAITING FOR THE MOON (LP)	£35
08	Beggars Banquet BBQLP 259	HUNGRY SAW (LP)	£35
10	4AD CAD 3X02	FALLING DOWN A MOUNTAIN (LP)	£15
10	This Way Up 518 306 1	TINDERSTICKS (2-LP, reissue of 1st LP)	£30
11	Moving Vinyl MOVLP 371	THE HUNGRY SAW (LP)	£20
13	Moving Vinyl MOVLP 712	TINDERSTICKS (2-LP, reissue of 2nd LP, blue vinyl)	£25

(see also Asphalt Ribbons, Stuart A. Staples)

TING TINGS

| 07 | No label or cat no | Fruit Machine/Impacilla Carpisung (4 x 100 7" given away at 4 live shows, customized blank sleeve) | £25 |
| 08 | Columbia – 88697318871 | WE STARTED NOTHING (LP, red vinyl) | £20 |

TINGA (STEWART) & ERNIE (WILSON)

| 69 | Explosion EX 2009 | She's Gone/Old Old Song | £100 |

TINKERBELL'S FAIRYDUST

67	Decca F 12705	Lazy Day/In My Magic Garden	£70
68	Decca F 12778	Twenty Ten/Walking My Baby	£80
69	Decca F 12865	Sheila's Back In Town/Follow Me Follow	£100
69	Decca LK/SKL 5028	TINKERBELL'S FAIRYDUST (LP, unreleased; finished copies in laminated front sleeve	£8000

with mono/stereo 'peephole' on rear, machine etched matrix number, blue/silver label with large unboxed Decca logo) ....

69   Decca LK/SKL 5028   TINKERBELL'S FAIRYDUST (LP, unreleased; test pressings in sleeve)...........................£2000

TIN MACHINE
89   EMI USA MTPD 76   Prisoner Of Love/Baby Can Dance (Live) (picture disc)...£15
89   EMI USA MTPD 73   Maggies Farm (Live)/Tin Machine (picture disc)...£15
89   EMI America MTLS 1044 TIN MACHINE (LP)...£20
91   Victory 828 272-1   TIN MACHINE II (LP)...£40
(see also David Bowie)

BABS TINO
62   London HLR 9589   Forgive Me/If I Didn't Love You So Much £30
63   London RE-R 1377   FORGIVE ME (EP) £100

TINOPENERS
79   Logo GO 375   Set Me Free/I'm Not Your Type..£150

TINS
79   Quest BR 001   There Is No Steel/Working For The Corporation £20

TINTERN ABBEY
67   Deram DM 164   Beeside/Vacuum Cleaner £1000

TIN TIN
69   Polydor 2384 011   TIN TIN (LP) £25
72   Polydor 2382 080   ASTRAL TAXI (LP) £20
(see also Steve & Stevie)

TINY TIM
68   Reprise RSLP 6292   GOD BLESS TINY TIM (LP) £20
69   Reprise RSLP 6323   TINY TIM'S SECOND ALBUM (LP) £20
69   Reprise RSLP 6351   FOR ALL MY LITTLE FRIENDS (LP) £20

TINY TOPSY (& CHARMS)
58   Parlophone R 4397   Come On, Come On, Come On/A Ring Around My Finger (with Charms)......................£80
58   Parlophone R 4397   Come On, Come On, Come On/A Ring Around My Finger (with Charms) (78) £25
58   Parlophone R 4427   You Shocked Me/Waterproof Eyes (solo)...£100
58   Parlophone R 4427   You Shocked Me/Waterproof Eyes (solo) (78) £25
61   Pye International 7N 25104 After Marriage Blues/Working On Me Baby (solo)...........................£30

DIMITRI TIOMKIN
54   Vogue Coral Q 2016   The High And The Mighty/Dial M For Murder.........................£15

KEITH TIPPETT
69   Polydor 2384 004   YOU ARE HERE, I AM THERE (LP)...£100
71   Vertigo 6360 024   DEDICATED TO YOU BUT YOU WEREN'T LISTENING (LP, gatefold sleeve, large swirl label) £175
72   RCA SF 8290   BLUEPRINT (LP)..£75
76   Steam SJ 104   TNT (LP, with Stan Tracey)..£15
77   Vinyl VS 101   WARM SPIRITS, COOL SPIRITS (LP) £15
78   Ogun OGD 003/4   FRAMES (2-LP) £30
78   Ogun OGUN 003/004   ARK (2-LP) £35
(see also Centipede, King Crimson, Ovary Lodge, Nicra)

JULIE TIPPETTS
76   Utopia UTS 601   SUNSET GLOW (LP) £22
(see also Julie Driscoll, Brian Auger, Centipede, Keith Tippett, Elton Dean, Ninesense, Mark Charig)

TIPPIE & THE CLOVERS
63   Stateside SS 160   My Heart Said/Bossa Nova Baby £25

LESTER TIPTON
80   Grapevine GRP 138   This Won't Change/MASQUERADERS: How £20

TIP TOPS
63   Cameo Parkway P 868   He's Braggin'/Oo-Kook-A-Boo...£35

TÍR NA NOG
71   Chrysalis ILPS 9153   TÍR NA NOG (LP, laminated gatefold sleeve)...........................£25
72   Chrysalis CHR 1006   A TEAR AND A SMILE (LP, gatefold sleeve) £20
73   Chrysalis CHR 1047   STRONG IN THE SUN (LP) £15

TITAN
80   Wild Dog DOG 26   East Wind West Wind/Losing The Fight....................................£200
83   After Hours AFT 09   Imaginary Lady/Tooty Flutey £30

TITANIC
72   CBS 8185   Rain 2,000/Blond...£20
71   CBS 64104   TITANIC (LP) £20
72   CBS 64791   SEA WOLF (LP, gatefold sleeve)...£20
73   CBS 65661   EAGLE ROCK (LP, gatefold sleeve) £15

TITANS
58   London HLU 8609   Don't You Just Know It/Can It Be £80
58   London HLU 8609   Don't You Just Know It/Can It Be (78)......................................£35

TITUS GROAN
70   Dawn DNX 2503   Open The Door Homer/Woman Of The World/Liverpool (p/s) £20
70   Dawn DNLS 3012   TITUS GROAN (LP, gatefold sleeve).......................................£350

CAL TJADER
65   Verve VS 529   Soul Sauce/Naked City Theme..£50

MINT VALUE £

65	Verve VS 529	Soul Sauce/Naked City Theme (DJ copy)	£80
58	Vocalion LAE 556	RITMO CALIENTE (LP, as Cal Tjader Quintet)	£20
60	Vocalion LAE 560	THE WEST SIDE STORY (LP)	£15
62	HMV/Verve CLP 1587	IN A LATIN BAG (LP, as Cal Tjader Sextet, also stereo [CSD 1454])	£15
65	Vocalion LAE-F 599	GREATEST HITS (LP)	£15
65	Verve (S)VLP 9136	SOUL BIRD: WHIFFENPOOF (LP)	£15
66	Verve (S)VLP 9155	SOUL BURST (LP)	£15
68	Verve (S)VLP 9192	THE BEST OF CAL TJADER (LP)	£15
68	Verve (S)VLP 9215	HIP VIBRATIONS (LP)	£20
61	Vogue SEA 568	CONCERT BY THE SEA (LP)	£15

TLC
94	La Face 73008 26009-1	CRAZYSEXYCOOL (LP)	£35

TMR
92	Pirate Club PCR 001	Pirate Toon (Moose Mix)/Pirate Toon (Pirate Excursion)/Pirate Toon (Pirate Dub) (12", white stamped label)	£60

T.N.T.
72	Jam JAM 4	Big Trouble (Part One)/Big Trouble (Part Two)	£40

TOAD
72	RCA Victor SF 8241	TOAD (LP)	£200

TOAD THE WET SPROCKET
79	Sprockets BRS 004	Pete's Punk Song/Feel It (fold out p/s)	£45
80	Sprockets BRS 008	Reaching For The Sky/One Glass Of Whiskey (foldout stapled p/s)	£70

TOASTERS
87	Unicorn PHZA-5	POOL SHARK (LP)	£18
90	Unicorn PHZA-60	FRANKENSKA (LP)	£15

TOBA
81	Connection CON 8101	Make Your Mind Up/Don't Take It (12")	£30
82	Connection CONT 8203	Moving Up/Moving Up (Instrumental) (12", red or blue vinyl)	£30

AMON TOBIN
97	Ninja Tune ZEN 29	BRICOLAGE (2-LP, gatefold sleeve)	£35
97	Ninja Tune ZEN 29	BRICOLAGE (2-LP, single sleeve)	£20
98	Ninja Tune ZEN 36	PERMUTATION (2-LP)	£35
00	Ninja Tune ZEN 48	SUPERMODIFIED (2-LP)	£40
02	Ninja Tune ZEN 70	OUT FROM OUT WHERE (2-LP)	£20
05	Ninja Tune ZEN 100	CHAOS THEORY (2-LP)	£50
11	Ninja Tune ZEN 171	CHAOS THEORY REMIXED (2-LP)	£100
15	Nina Tune ZEN 12387	DARK JOVIAN (2 x 12" etched on sides A and D, perspex box)	£40

TOBRUK
88	FM WKFMLP 105	PLEASURE AND PAIN (LP)	£15

TOBY JUG
69	Toby Toons TLP 01	GREASY QUIFF (LP, with insert, 50 only)	£15

TOBY TWIRL
68	Decca F 12728	Harry Faversham/Back In Time	£30
68	Decca F 12804	Toffee Apple Sunday/Romeo And Juliet 1968	£400
69	Decca F 12867	Movin' In/Utopia Daydream	£40
(see also Shades Of Blue)			

TODAY'S WITNESS
72	Emblem JDR 345	TODAY'S WITNESS (LP)	£35

ART & DOTTY TODD
58	London HLB 8620	Chanson D'Amour (Song Of Love)/Along The Trail With You	£18
59	London HLN 8838	Straight As An Arrow/Stand There, Mountain	£18

GARY TODD & ROGER TURNER
79	Incus INCUS 79	SUNDAY BEST (LP)	£50

NICK TODD
57	London HLD 8500	Plaything/The Honey Song	£40
58	London HLD 8537	At The Hop/I Do	£15
59	London HLD 8902	Tiger/Twice As Nice	£30

PATSY TODD
66	Doctor Bird DB 1086	Pata Pata Rocky Steady (with Count Ossie)/COUNT OSSIE: Nyah Bongo	£60
68	High Note HS 007	Fire In Your Wire/AL & VIBRATORS: Move Up Calypso	£15
69	High Note HS 012	We Were Lovers/Give Me A Chance (B-side with Delano Stewart)	£75
(see also Patsy, Stranger & Patsy, Derrick & Patsy)			

SHARKEY TODD & MONSTERS
59	Parlophone R 4536	Cool Gool/The Horror Show	£25
59	Parlophone R 4536	Cool Gool/The Horror Show (78)	£20
(see also Wally Whyton, Vipers [Skiffle Group])			

WILF TODD & HIS MUSIC
66	Oak WT 101	WILF TODD AND HIS MUSIC (LP)	£15

TOE-FAT
70	Parlophone R 5829	Working Nights/Bad Side Of The Moon	£15
70	Parlophone PCS 7097	TOE-FAT (LP, black/silver label with boxed logo)	£175
70	Regal Zono. SLRZ 1015	TOE-FAT TWO (LP, red/silver label)	£175
(see also Uriah Heep, Glass Menagerie)			

TOGETHER (1)
68	Columbia DB 8491	Henry's Coming Home/Love Mum And Dad	£70
69	Aurora 4278	Memories Of Melinda/Good Morning World	£50

(see also Keith Relf)

TOGETHER (2)
90	Thumbs Up Magic GH 001	Hardcore Uproar (12", white label)	£250
91	Thumbs Up Magic TUM002	The Luv Bug (12")	£70
92	Thumbs Up Magic GH003	The House Sound Vol 2/Coming On Strong (12", with CYBERTEC)	£60

TOGGERY FIVE
64	Parlophone R 5175	Bye Bye Bird/I'm Gonna Jump	£50
65	Parlophone R 5249	I'd Much Rather Be With The Boys/It's So Easy	£50

TOKENS
61	Parlophone R 4790	Tonight I Fell In Love/I Love My Baby	£30
62	RCA RD 27256	THE LION SLEEPS TONIGHT (LP, mono)	£30
62	RCA SF 5128	THE LION SLEEPS TONIGHT (LP, stereo)	£35
62	RCA RD 7535	WE THE TOKENS SING FOLK (LP)	£18

TOK-IO-ROSE
84	TOK 001	Bad Girls/Desperate Situation (p/s)	£40

TOKYO BLADE
85	Powerstation LEG 1T	THE CAVE SESSIONS (12" EP)	£15
85	Tokyo Blade TBR 1	BLACKHEARTS AND JADED SPADES (LP, gatefold sleeve)	£15

TOKYO ROSE
83	Guardian GRC 270	Dry Your Eyes/This Is Tokyo Rose (p/s)	£40

ISRAEL 'POPPER STOPPER' TOLBERT
71	Stax 2362 020	POPPER STOPPER (LP)	£18

TOLL
86	Broken Flag BF V7	CHRIST KNOWS (LP, featuring Tim Gane)	£20

(see also Ramleh, McCarthy)

GARY DALE TOLLETT & THE CRICKETS
01	Rollercoaster RRCT 1001	Go Boy Go/Gone (78 rpm, 250 only)	£15

JUKKA TOLONEN
74	Sonet STNF 652	TOLONOEN! (LP, laminated front cover)	£15

TOM & JERRIO
65	HMV POP 1435	Boo-Ga-Loo/Boomerang	£30

TOM & JERRY (CARTOON CHARACTERS)
58	MGM MGM-EP 688	JOHANN MOUSE (EP)	£15

TOM & JERRY (1)
59	Gala GSP 806	Baby Talk/PAUL SHELDON: Thank You Pretty Baby (picture labels)	£45
63	Pye International 7N 25202	I'm Lonesome/Looking At You	£95

(see also Simon & Garfunkel)

TOM AND JERRY
92	Tom And Jerry SHELL 001	The One Reason/The Second Reason (12")	£80
92	Tom And Jerry SHELL 002	We Can Be Free/For The Gold Teeth/Baby Don't Shout/Physics (12")	£90
93	Tom And Jerry SHELL 003	Papillon Love Song/A Patch Of Blue/B.O.S Realting/Cat Got Your Tongue (12")	£70
93	Tom And Jerry SHELL 004	Let Your Spirit Rise/Programme 205/Strings & Me/Mousetrap (Dangerous) (12")	£60
93	Tom And Jerry SHELL 005	Scooby's Dreaming/Neatly Dealt Wid/Nine Lives (Mind Out Tube Mice)/Yamming Snacks Like Shaggy (12")	£60
93	Tom And Jerry SHELL 006	All Alone Wid Dog Face/Laughing Like Muttley/Sun On My Head/Escape (12")	£60
93	Tom And Jerry SHELL 007	IT COMES A DIME A DOZEN EP (12")	£80
94	Tom And Jerry SHELL 008	Dancer/Thriller/Maxi(Mun) Style/I Wanna Say (Yeah) (12")	£40
94	Tom And Jerry SHELL 009	Still Lets Me Down/Luv & Run/Maxi(mun) Style Remix/Airfreshner/For Your Sampling Pleasure (12")	£60
94	Tom And Jerry SHELL 010	It's All Over/Who Kan Draw/Say Goodbye Broke My Heart/Max(imum) Booty Style Part III (12")	£40
94	Tom And Jerry SHELL 011	On & On/Follow Da Massive/Till The Morning/Tom & Jerry/Tom & Jerry (12")	£40
95	Tom And Jerry SHELL 012	Maxi(Mum) Style (Nasty Jungle Remix)/All Of My.../The Joker Played (12")	£30

TOM & MICK
69	Olga OLE 014	Somebody's Taken Maria Away/Pandemonium	£15

TOMANGOES
79	Grapevine GRP 122	I Really Love You/You've Been Gone So Long (reissue)	£25

ROLO TOMASSI
07	Danger! Laser! Phaser! Razor! DLPR 003	ROLO TOMASSI (EP, 1000 only, blue vinyl)	£20
08	Hassle HOFF055LP	HYSTERICS (LP)	£20
10	Holy Roar HRR046V	COSMOLOGY (LP, 100 on blue translucent or 100 on red translucent vinyl)	£25

TOM CATS
61	Starlite ST45 054	Tom Tom Cat/Big Brother	£25

TOMITA
77	RCA Red Seal RL1 1919	THE TOMITA PLANETS SUITE (LP, withdrawn after 1 day)	£15

LEE TOMLIN
66	CBS 202455	Sweet Sweet Lovin'/Save Me (DJ copy)	£150
66	CBS 202455	Sweet Sweet Lovin'/Save Me	£75

MINT VALUE £

ALAN TOMLINSON
81   Bead Records BEAD 17   STILL OUTSIDE (LP) £25

ALBERT TOMLINSON
68   Giant GN 28   Don't Wait For Me/LLOYD EVANS: Losing You...£300

LOUIS TOMLINSON
20   78 Productions   WALLS (LP, picture disc) £45
     19075814461

ROY TOMLINSON
68   Coxsone CS 7056   I Stand For I/MARTIN: I Second That Emotion (actually by Martin Riley) £150

TOMMY (MCCOOK) & UPSETTERS
69   Trojan TR 7717   Lock Jaw (vocal by Dave Barker)/YARDBROOMS: My Desire..............................£20
(see also Tommy McCook, Upsetters)

TOMORROW
67   Parlophone R 5597   My White Bicycle/Claramont Lake..£70
67   Parlophone R 5627   Revolution/Three Jolly Little Dwarfs...£70
69   Parlophone R 5813   My White Bicycle/Claramont Lake (reissue) £50
68   Parlophone PMC 7042   TOMORROW (LP, mono, yellow/black label with "Sold in U.K..." text)............£500
68   Parlophone PCS 7042   TOMORROW (LP, stereo, yellow/black label with "Sold in U.K..." text)..........£450
76   Harvest SHSM 2010   TOMORROW (LP, reissue)...£30
86   Decal LIK 2   TOMORROW (LP, reissue) £15
(see also Keith West, Steve Howe, Twink, Four + One, In Crowd, Syndicats, Aquarian Age, Fairies)

TOMORROW COME SOME DAY
69   SNB 97   TOMORROW COME SOME DAY (LP) £900
(see also Ithaca, Friends, Agincourt, Alice Through The Looking Glass, BBC Radiophonic Workshop/Peter Howell)

TOMORROW'S CHILDREN (JAMAICA)
67   Island WI 3073   Bang Bang Rock Steady/Rain Rock Steady (some w/same label on both sides) £600

TOMORROW'S PEOPLE
17   Melodies Int. MEL 005   OPEN SOUL (LP) £15

TOMPALL & GLASER BROTHERS
68   MGM MGM-C 8082   THROUGH THE EYES OF LOVE (LP) £25

TOM TOM CLUB
81   Island ILPS 9686   TOM TOM CLUB (LP) £25
(see also Talking Heads)

TONE DEAF & THE IDIOTS
79   Lyntone BLI 1/Angel BL 12   Why Does Politics Turn Men Into Toads/Repatriate The National Front (flexi) £15

ELEANOR TONER
65   Decca F 12192   Will You Still Love Me Tomorrow/Between The Window And The Phone £15

TONES ON TAIL
82   4AD BAD 203   A Bigger Splash/Means Of Escape/Copper/Instrumental (12", p/s)...................£20
84   Beggars Banquet BEGA 51   POP (LP) £20
(see also Bauhaus, Love & Rockets, Daniel Ash)

OSCAR TONEY JR.
67   Stateside SS 2033   For Your Precious Love/Ain't That True Love £20
67   Stateside SS 2033   For Your Precious Love/Ain't That True Love (DJ Copy).............................£50
67   Stateside SS 2046   Turn On Your Love Light/Any Day Now £20
67   Stateside SS 2061   You Can Lead Your Woman To The Altar/Unlucky Guy £20
73   Contempo CS2075   Chicken Heads/Everybody's Needed £15
67   Stateside (S)SL 10211   FOR YOUR PRECIOUS LOVE (LP) £40

TONGUE & GROOVE
69   Fontana STL 5528   TONGUE & GROOVE (LP) £45
(see also Charlatans)

TERRY TONIK
80   Posh TOFF 1   Just A Little Mod/Smashed And Blocked (with die-cut p/s) £150
80   Posh TOFF 1   Just A Little Mod/Smashed And Blocked (with promo A4 booklet) £70
80   Posh TOFF 1   Just A Little Mod/Smashed And Blocked £30

TONTO
74   Polydor 2383 308   IT'S ABOUT TIME (LP, insert, poster) £20
(see also Tonto's Expanding Head Band)

TONTON (MACOUTE)
72   RCA 2190   Summer Of Our Love/Greyhound Lady (as Tonton) £20
71   RCA Neon NE 4   TONTON MACOUTE (LP, gatefold sleeve, black inner).............................£300

TONTO'S EXPANDING HEAD BAND
71   Atlantic 2400 150   ZERO TIME (LP, gatefold sleeve) £25
(see also Tonto)

TONY & DENNIS
67   Trojan TR 002   Folk Song/TOMMY McCOOK & SUPERSONICS: Starry Night £35

TONY & GRADUATES
60s   Hit HIT 13   The Statue £50

TONY & HIPPY BOYS
69   Gas GAS 121   Janet/HARMONIANS: Believe Me (states 'Beleive' on label).......................£35

TONY & HOWARD WITH DICTATORS
65   Oriole CB 307   Just In Case/Walk Right Out Of The Blues £30

TONY & HOWIE
72   Banana BA 371   Fun It Up/Fun Version £100

TONY & JOE
58   London HLN 8694   The Freeze/Gonna Get A Little Kissin' Tonight £40
58   London HLN 8694   The Freeze/Gonna Get A Little Kissin' Tonight (78) £25

TONY & TANDY
69   Atlantic 584 262   Two Can Make It Together/The Bitter And The Sweet (with Fleur De Lys) £20
(see also Sharon Tandy, Fleur De Lys)

TONY, CARO & JOHN
72   private pressing   ALL ON THE FIRST DAY (LP, with insert) £300

TONY & CHAMPIONS
70   Duke DU 90   Eye For An Eye/CHAMPIONS: Broke My Heart - Version £20
(see also Errol & Champions, Domino Johnson)

TONY'S ALLSTARS
72   Green Door GD 4041   Rub Up A Daughter/DENNIS ALCAPONE: Daughter Version £15

TONY'S DEFENDERS
66   Columbia DB 7850   Yes I Do/It's Easy To Say Hello £35
66   Columbia DB 7996   Since I Lost You Baby/Waiting For A Call From You £35

TOO FUNK
95   Ferox FER 008   THE RETURN OF TOO FUNK (12" EP) £15

TOOL
94   Zoo-RCA 74321 19432-1   Prison Sex (LP Version)/Prison Sex (Edit Version)/Opiate (Live)/Undertow (Live) (12",
                                     grey vinyl)..£30

TOOMORROW
70   RCA RCA 1978   You're My Baby Now/Goin' Back (in custom RCA sleeve)......................................£60
70   Decca F 13070   I Could Never Live Without Your Love/Roll Like A River £60
70   RCA LSA 3008   TOOMORROW (LP, soundtrack, with insert)..£125
(see also Olivia Newton-John)

TOO MUCH
78   Lightning GIL 513   Who You Wanna Be/Another Time Another Place (in p/s) £35
78   Lightning GIL 552   Kick Me One More TIme//Be Mine/It's Only For Me (gatefold p/s) £30

DAVID TOOP
75   Obscure OBS 4   NEW AND REDISCOVERED MUSICAL INSTRUMENTS (LP, with Max Eastley & Brian
                                     Eno)..£25
79   Quartz 003   WOUNDS (LP, with Paul Burwell) £30
(see also Brian Eno)

TOOTS (ACTUALLY LEE PERRY)
70   Upsetter US 327   Do You Like It/UPSETTERS: Touch Of Fire £60

TOPO D. BILL
70   Charisma CB 116   Witchi Tai To/Jam (in p/s)..£20
(see also Bonzo Dog [Doo Dah] Band, Roger Ruskin Spear)

TOP TOPHAM
69   Blue Horizon 57-3167   Christmas Cracker/Cracking Up Over Christmas £25
70   Blue Horizon 7-63857   ASCENSION HEIGHTS (LP)..£120
(see also Fox, Yardbirds)

TORA TORA
80   Mancunian Metal TT 5000   Red Sun Setting/Highway (Shooting Like A Bullet) (p/s) £15
80   Tora TT 5001   Don't Want To Let You Go/Sorry I Broke Your Heart £40

TORCH
82   Ted TED 1   I Need Rock/Unknown (no p/s) £35

STEVE TORCH
79   Redball RR 005   Live In Fear/Fear/Smoke Your Own (p/s)...£20
(see also Dexys Midnight Runners, White & Torch)

MEL TORME (& MEL-TONES)
SINGLES
56   Vogue Coral Q 72150   Mountain Greenery/Jeepers Creepers £15
62   London HLK 9643   Comin' Home Baby/Right Now £30
62   London HLK 9643   Comin' Home Baby/Right Now (DJ copy)..£40
ALBUMS
57   Philips BBL 7205   TORME MEETS THE BRITISH...£20
63   London HA-K/SH-K 8021   MEL TORME AT THE RED HILL (with Jimmy Wisner Trio, mono/stereo)..........................£15
63   London HA-K 8065   COMIN' HOME BABY £25

TORNADOS
62   Decca F 11449   Love And Fury/Popeye Twist £15
64   Decca F 11889   Monte Carlo/Blue Blue Beat £20
64   Decca F 11946   Exodus/Blackpool Rock £20
65   Columbia DB 7455   Granada/Ragunboneman £25
65   Columbia DB 7589   Early Bird/Stompin' Through The Rye (as Tornados '65) £25
65   Columbia DB 7687   Stingray/Aqua Marina £40
66   Columbia DB 7856   Pop-Art Goes Mozart/Too Much In Love To Hear £30
66   Columbia DB 7984   Is That A Ship I Hear/Do You Come Here Often £40
62   Decca DFE 8510   THE SOUNDS OF THE TORNADOS (EP) £15
62   Decca DFE 8511   TELSTAR (EP) £15

MINT VALUE £

63	Decca DFE 8521	MORE SOUNDS FROM THE TORNADOS (EP)	£20
63	Decca DFE 8533	TORNADO ROCK (EP)	£25
63	Decca LK 4552	AWAY FROM IT ALL (LP)	£50
63	London LL 3279	TELSTAR - THE SOUND OF THE TORNADOS (LP, export copy, UK pressed LP in US sleeve)	£50

(see also Heinz, Billy Fury, Clem Cattini Ork, Saints, Roger LaVern & Microns, Saxons, George Bellamy, Gemini, Roger La Vern & Microns)

MITCHELL TOROK

54	London HL 8004	Caribbean/Weep Away (with Louisiana Hayride Band) (gold tri label)	£40
54	London HL 8004	Caribbean/Weep Away (with Louisiana Hayride Band) (round centre)	£20
54	London HL 8048	Hootchy Kootchy Henry (From Hawaii)/Gigolo	£50
54	London HL 8083	The Haunting Waterfall/Dancerette (with Louisiana Hayride Band)	£50
55	Brunswick 05423	The World Keeps Turning Around/A Peasant's Guitar	£15
56	Brunswick 05586	When Mexico Gave Up The Rhumba/I Wish I Was A Little Bit Younger	£25
56	Brunswick 05626	Red Light, Green Light (with Tulane Sisters)/Havana Huddle	£25
57	Brunswick 05642	Drink Up And Go Home/Take This Heart	£15
57	Brunswick 05657	Pledge Of Love/What's Behind That Strange Door	£15
54	London RE-P 1014	LOUISIANA HAYRIDE (EP, with Louisiana Hayride Band)	£20
60	London HA-W 2279	CARIBBEAN (LP)	£30

STEFANO TOROSSI

76	Conroy BMLP 143	FEELINGS (LP)	£500

MICHELLE TORR

66	Fontana TF 676	Only Tears Are Left For Me/I Love That Man	£15

DONALD TORR

69	CBS 4383	My Cherie Amour/Never Will I Be	£20

GEORGE TORRENCE & NATURALS

68	London HLZ 10181	Lickin' Stick/So Long Goodbye	£15

TORTOISE

96	Duophonic D-UHF-D 12	Yaus/STEREOLAB: Speedy Car (gig freebie, blue vinyl, p/s, 3,000 only)	£15
96	Duophonic D-UHF-D 12	Yaus/STEREOLAB: Speedy Car (orange vinyl export issue, p/s, 3,000 only)	£15
01	Duophonic Super 45s DS 33 09	Gamera/Cliff Dweller Society (12", 1500 on red vinyl, 1500 on clear vinyl, 1500 on black vinyl)	£15
01	Duophonic Super 45s DS 33 09	Gamera/Cliff Dweller Society (12", 1000 on fluorescent yellow vinyl)	£20
96	City Slang EFA 04971	RHYTHMS, RESOLUTIONS & CLUSTERS (LP, clear vinyl)	£30
98	City Slang EFA 08705-1	TNT (2-LP, gatefold sleeve)	£40
00	Warp WARPLP 81	STANDARDS (LP)	£20

(see also Sea & Cake)

TORTURE

81	Wildebeest WILD 1	Last Post/Lucky/Finding My Way Home	£50

TOSH

82	Bicycle MP 1003	ONE MORE FOR THE ROAD (LP)	£100

PETER TOSH

70	No label T 1023	No Sympathy (with The Wailers)/Boy Named Tom (actually Soulettes) (white label only)	£65
71	Bullet BU 486	Maga Dog/THIRD & FOURTH GENERATION: Bull Dog	£15
72	Pressure Beat PR 5509	Them A Fe Get A Beatin' (as Peter Touch)/ THIRD & FOURTH GENERATION: Version	£25
76	Virgin V 2061	LEGALIZE IT (LP)	£15
77	Virgin V 2081	EQUAL RIGHTS (LP, red "mirror" girl sleeve)	£15

(see also Peter Touch, Bob Marley & Wailers, Cat & Nicky Campbell, Glen Adams)

TOTAL CHAOS

81	Slam! SSM 026	There Are No Russians In Afghanistan/Primitive Feeling/Revolution Part 10 (p/s, lyric insert, original copies have "50p" on front)	£20
83	Volume VOLT 6	FIELDS AND BOMBS EP (12")	£15

TOTAL CONTRAST

84	Total Contrast TCR 2	Next Time I'll Know Better/Sunshine (12")	£35

TOTAL FIASCO

89	White TF001	See How They Run/Method To The Madness	£75

(see also Killa Instinct)

TOTNAMITES

61	Oriole CB 1615	Danny Boy/The Spurs Song	£15

TOTO

84	Polydor 422 8237-7	DUNE (LP, soundtrack, 1 track by Brian Eno)	£15

TINA TOTT

69	Pye 7N 17823	Take Away The Emptiness Too/Burning In The Background Of My Mind	£30

TOTTENHAM HOTSPUR F.C.

67	Columbia SEG 8532	THE SPURS GO MARCHING ON: SINGALONG SPURS (EP)	£20

(see also Terry Venables)

PETER TOUCH

65	Island WI 211	Hoot Nanny Hoot (actually by Peter Tosh & Wailers)/ BOB MARLEY: Do You Remember (actually Peter Tosh & Wailers)	£160
65	Island WI 215	Shame And Scandal (with Wailers)/WAILERS: The Jerk	£100
67	Island WI 3042	I Am The Toughest (actually by Peter Tosh & Wailers)/ MARCIA GRIFFITHS: No Faith	£75
67	Coxsone CS 7012	Dancing Time/Treat Me Good	£120
69	Jackpot JP 706	The Crimson Pirate/Moon Duck	£45
69	Unity UN 525	Return Of A Capone/LENEX BROWN : Q Club	£30

MINT VALUE £

69	Unity 529	Sun Valley/Headley Bennett - Drums Of Fu Man Chu	£40

(see also Peter Tosh, Bop & The Beltone, Glen Adams)

TOUCH (1)
69	Deram DML/SML 1033	THIS IS TOUCH (LP, with poster)	£200
69	Deram DML/SML 1033	THIS IS TOUCH (LP, without poster)	£100

(see also Kingsmen)

TOUCH (2)
80	Ariola ARO 243	Don't You Know What Love Is/My Life Depends On You (in p/s)	£20

TOUCH (3)
81	Record Corner EJSP 9750	Keep On/Keep On Remixin' (12")	£20
81	Elite DAZZ 11	Keep On/Keep On Remixin' (12")	£15
82	Elite DAZZ 14-7	Love Something Special/Keep On	£20
82	Elite DAZZ 14	Love Something Special/Love Speciality (12")	£15

TOUCHDOWN
83	Record Shack SHACK 12	Ease Your Mind (Remix)/Aquadance (12")	£20

TOUCH OF CLASS
76	GTO GTLP 024	I'M IN HEAVEN (LP, textured sleeve)	£15

TOUCHSTONE
72	MAS 9	MUSIC FROM PANDORAS BOX (LP, white label)	£2000

TOUGH CROWD
18	Tough Crowd TC001	TOUGH CROWD (LP)	£30

ALI FARKA TOURE
87	World Circuit WCB 007	ALI FARKA TOURE (LP)	£30
90	World Circuit WCB 017	THE RIVER (LP)	£80
94	World Circuit WCB 040	TALKING TIMBUKTU (LP, with Ry Cooder)	£50

TOURS
79	Tours T 1	Language School/Foreign Girls (paper p/s)	£20

ALLEN TOUSSAINT
69	Soul City SC 119	We The People/Tequila	£40
71	Wand WNS 14	TOUSSAINT (LP)	£25
72	Reprise K 44202	LIFE, LOVE AND FAITH (LP)	£40
75	Reprise K 54021	SOUTHERN NIGHTS (LP)	£35
85	Kent KENT 036	FROM A WHISPER TO A SCREAM (LP)	£15
85	Edsel ED 155	SOUTHERN NIGHTS (LP, reissue)	£25
06	Verve Forecast 0602498564547	THE RIVER IN REVERSE (2LP, with Elvis Costello, printed inners)	£50
16	Warner/Rhino R1 553408	LIVE IN PHILADELPHIA (LP, 180g, RSD)	£25

ROBERTA TOVEY
65	Polydor BM 56021	Who's Who/Not So Old (in p/s)	£45
65	Polydor BM 56021	Who's Who/Not So Old	£25

TOWER OF POWER
73	Warner. Bros. K 46223	TOWER OF POWER	£15
75	Warner Bros. K 56088	URBAN RENEWAL (LP)	£15

COLIN TOWNS
80	MCA MCA 643	Breakdown/Working Man (p/s)	£15

(see also Gillan, Samson)

ED TOWNSEND (& TOWNSMEN)
60	Warner Bros WB 21	Stay With Me (A Little While Longer)/I Love Everything About You	£40
59	Capitol EAP1 1091	ED TOWNSEND (EP)	£20
59	Capitol T 1140	NEW IN TOWN (LP)	£25
76	Curtom K 56180	NOW (LP)	£20

JOHN TOWNSEND
70s	Sweet Folk All SFA 002	NO MUCKING ABOUT (LP)	£18

PETE TOWNSHEND
82	Eva-Tone 623827XS	My Generation/Pinball Wizard (U.S. square flexidisc sewn into U.K. copies of Richard Barnes' Maximum R&B book; with book)	£20
72	Track 2408 201	WHO CAME FIRST (LP, gatefold sleeve with poster)	£25
72	Track 2408 201	WHO CAME FIRST (LP, laminated gatefold sleeve without poster)	£15
80	Atco SAM 121/122	THE PETE TOWNSHEND TAPES (2LP, promo)	£40
82	Atco SAM 150	PETE LISTENING TIME (LP, promo)	£40
17	UMC 5734718	PSYCHODERELICT (2LP, vinyl issue of 1993 CD, orange vinyl, printed inners)	£30

(see also The Who, Meher Baba, Billy Nicholls, Elton John)

PETE TOWNSHEND & RONNIE LANE
77	Polydor 2058 944	Street In The City/RONNIE LANE: Annie (limited issue)	£20

(see also Who, Ronnie Lane)

TOXIC
92	D-Zone DANCE 26	Simple Warnin' (Ruffneck Mix)/Simple Warnin' (Riffist Mix)/Simple Warnin' (Hi Power Version)Kik The Break (12", company sleeve)	£60

TOXIC REASONS
84	Alt. Tentacles VIRUS 42	KILL BY REMOTE CONTROL (LP)	£15

TOXIK EPHEX
89	One Up	THE ADVENTURES OF NOBBY PORTHOLE - THE COCK OF THE NORTH (LP)	£20

TOYAN
81	Greensleeves GREL 20	HOW THE WEST WAS WON (LP)	£25
83	Vista STLP 1023	MURDER (LP, as Toyan with Tippa Lee)	£45
83	Upfront UPFLP 11	DJ DADDY (LP)	£15

TOY DOLLS
81	GBH SSM 005	Tommy Kowey's Car/She Goes To Finos (500 only)	£200
81	GBH GRC 104	TOY DOLLS EP: Tommy Kowey's Car/She's A Working Ticket/Everybody Jitterbug/ Teenager In Love/I've Got Asthma (yellow paper p/s, with insert)	£60
82	Zonophone Z 31	Everybody Jitterbug/(She's A) Working Ticket (p/s)	£30
83	Volume VOL 3	Nellie The Elephant/Dig That Groove Baby (p/s)	£15
82	WOWLP 1	THE TOY DOLLS ALBUM (LP)	£20
84	Volume VOLP 1	DIG THAT GROOVE, BABY (LP)	£20
85	Volume VOLP 2	A FAR OUT DISC (LP)	£15
86	Volume VOLP 3	IDLE GOSSIP (LP)	£20
94	Toy Dolls NIT 2	TEN YEARS OF TOYS (LP, with inner)	£20

(see also Showbiz Kids)

TOY DOLLS (U.S.)
63	London HLN 9647	Little Tin Soldier/Fly Away	£30

TOYS
79	SRT SRTS/79/CUS 345	My Mind Wanders/The Girl On My Wall/Toytime/I'd Do Anything For You (p/s)	£20
79	Toy TOYS 2	STILL DANCING (EP, hand-stamped white label, foldaround p/s)	£100

TOYS
80	Red Bus RBUS 54	Go To The Police/Breakdown	£50

TOYS (U.S.)
66	Stateside SS 502	May My Heart Be Cast Into Stone/On Backstreet	£20
66	Stateside SS 519	Silver Spoon/Can't Get Enough Of You Baby	£22
66	Stateside SL 10175	THE TOYS SING "A LOVER'S CONCERTO" AND "ATTACK" (LP, mono)	£40
66	Stateside SSL 10175	THE TOYS SING "A LOVER'S CONCERTO" AND "ATTACK" (LP, stereo)	£50

T.P.I.
79	SRT SRTS 79 CUS 489	She's Too Clever For Me/You Rool Me (no p/s, 1000 only)	£90

TRACE (1)
74	Vertigo 6360 852	TRACE (LP)	£25
75	Vertigo 6413 080	BIRDS (LP)	£25

(see also Curved Air)

TRACE (2)
95	Lucky Spin LSR 019	Lost Entity Remix/Jazz Primitives (12")	£40

TRACER
83	Mouse Hole TRA 1	CHANNELLED AGGRESSION EP (p/s)	£125

STAN TRACEY
58	Vogue LA 160130	STAN TRACEY SHOWCASE (LP)	£70
59	Vogue LA 160155	LITTLE KLUNK (LP, as Stan Tracey Trio)	£130
65	Columbia 33SX 1774	JAZZ SUITE (LP, as Stan Tracey Quartet, also stereo SCX 3589)	£100
66	Columbia S(C)X 6051	ALICE IN JAZZLAND (LP, as Stan Tracey Big Band)	£40
67	Columbia S(C)X 6124	STAN TRACEY... IN PERSON (LP)	£40
68	Columbia S(C)X 6205	WITH LOVE FROM JAZZ (LP)	£50
69	Ace Of Clubs ACL 1259	LITTLE KLUNK (LP, reissue)	£30
69	Columbia S(C)X 6320	WE LOVE YOU MADLY (LP, as Stan Tracey Big Brass)	£50
69	Columbia SCX 6358	THE LATIN AMERICAN CAPER (LP, with Big Brass & Woodwind)	£40
70	Columbia SCX 6385	FREE AN' ONE (LP, as Stan Tracey Quartet)	£70
70	Columbia SCX 6413	SEVEN AGES OF MAN (LP, as Stan Tracey Big Band)	£35
72	Columbia SCX 6485	PERSPECTIVES (LP as Stan Tracey Trio)	£40
74	Cadillac SGC 1003	ALONE AT WIGMORE HALL (LP)	£15

(see also New Departures Quartet, Mike Osborne, Neil Ardley, Laurie Johnson)

TRACK
66	Columbia DB 7987	Why Do Fools Fall In Love?/Cry To Me	£18

TRACK 4
82	Track 4 TR4 001	Mr Charisma (p/s, with insert)	£100

TRACTOR (1)
72	Dandelion 2001 282	Stone Glory/Marie/As You Say	£15
72	Dandelion 2310 217	TRACTOR (LP)	£300
83	Thunderbolt THBL 002	TRACTOR (LP, reissue)	£20

(see also Way We Live)

TRACTOR (2)
77	Cargo CRS 002	No More Rock 'N' Roll/Northern City	£15

GRANT TRACY & SUNSETS
61	Ember EMB S 126	Say When/Please Baby Please	£20
61	Ember EMB S 130	Pretend/Love Me	£20
62	Ember EMB S 148	The Great Matchmaker/Tears Came Rolling Down	£20
62	Ember EMB S 155	Taming Tigers/The Painted Smile	£20
63	Decca F 11741	Everybody Shake/Turn The Lights Down, Jenny	£20
64	Ember EMB 3352	TEENBEAT (LP)	£80

(see also Pete Dello, Honeybus)

WENDALL TRACY
58	London HLM 8664	Who's To Know/Corrigidor Rock	£15

TRADER
| 79 | Bos | Back Street Trader/Love On The Run (p/s) | £15 |

TRADER HORNE
69	Pye 7N 17846	Morning Way/Sheena	£40
70	Dawn DNS 1003	Here Comes The Rain/Goodbye Mercy Kelly	£40
70	Dawn DNLS 3004	MORNING WAY (LP, gatefold, with photo & insert)	£300
70	Dawn DNLS 3004	MORNING WAY (LP, gatefold, without photo & insert)	£150

(see also Them, Fairport Convention, Jackie McAuley)

TRADEWINDS
| 59 | RCA RCA 1141 | Crossroads/Furry Murray | £20 |
| 59 | RCA RCA 1141 | Crossroads/Furry Murray (78) | £25 |

TRADE WINDS
| 65 | Red Bird RB 10020 | New York Is A Lonely Town/Club Seventeen | £22 |
| 66 | Kama Sutra KAS 202 | Mind Excursion/Little Susan's Dreaming | £20 |

TRADITION
77	Venture VNLP 8877	MOVIN' ON (LP)	£25
77	Venture CUT 6	IN DUB (LP)	£60
78	RCA PL 25169	TELL YOUR FRIENDS ABOUT DUB (LP)	£20
78	RAC PL 25186	ALTERNATIVE ROUTES (LP)	£30
80	Venture CUT 9	CAPTAIN GANJA AND THE SPACE PATROL (LP)	£200
80	Venture CUT 10	PARTY DISCO (LP, blue vinyl, no sleeve)	£250

TRAFFIC
67	Island WIP 6025	Here We Go Round The Mulberry Bush/Coloured Rain (1st 100,000 in p/s)	£15
68	Island WIP 6041	You Can All Join In/Withering Tree (unissued in U.K.)	£0
71	Island No Cat No	Welcome To The Canteen (promo 7" with blank labels in mini LP sleeve)	£40
71	Island TIM 1	Gimme Some Lovin Part One (live)/Gimme Some Lovin Part Two (live) (p/s, white label only)	£25
67	Island ILP 961	MR FANTASY (LP, gatefold sleeve internal flipbacks, 1st pressing pink label with black 'circle' logo, mono)	£300
67	Island ILPS 9061	MR FANTASY (LP, gatefold sleeve internal flipbacks, 1st pressing pink label with black 'circle' logo, stereo)	£250
68	Island ILPS 9081T	TRAFFIC (LP, gatefold sleeve with stapled-in booklet; pink label with black 'circle' logo)	£150
68	Island ILPS 9081T	TRAFFIC (LP, gatefold sleeve with stapled-in booklet; pink rim label with 'palm tree' logo)	£20
69	Island ILP(S) 9097	LAST EXIT (LP, pink label with black/red 'eyeball' logo)	£150
70	Island ILPS 9070	LAST EXIT (LP, 2nd pressing pink 'i' label)	£60
74	Island ILP(S) 9097	LAST EXIT (LP, pink rim label with 'palm tree' logo)	£20
69	Island ILP(S) 9112	THE BEST OF TRAFFIC (LP, 1st pressings with pink "I" label)	£30
69	Island ILPS 9061	MR. FANTASY (LP, 2nd pressing, stereo, pink 'i' label)	£150
70	Island ILPS 9081	MR. FANTASY (LP, 3rd pressing, pink rim label with 'palm tree' logo)	£20
70	Island ILPS 9116	JOHN BARLEYCORN MUST DIE (LP, gatefold sleeve, 1st pressings with pink "i" label)	£50
71	Island ILPS 9142	LIVE - NOVEMBER '70 (LP, unreleased, may exist as test pressing)	£0
71	Island ILPS 9166	WELCOME TO THE CANTEEN (LP, 'sniped' spine edges, pink rim palm tree label)	£40
71	Island ILPS 9180	THE LOW SPARK OF THE... (LP, laminated sleeve, pink rim/palm tree label)	£20
73	Island ILPS 9224	SHOOT OUT AT THE FANTASY FACTORY (LP, pink rim/palm tree label)	£15
73	Island ISLD 2	ON THE ROAD (2-LP, laminated gatefold sleeve)	£18
74	Island ILPS 9273	WHEN THE EAGLE FLIES (LP, 1st pressing. Hand etched MATRIXES: ILPS 9273 A-1U GT 1 STERLING/ILPS 9273 B-1U AM 2 STERLING)	£25

(see also Spencer Davis Group, Stevie Winwood, Revolution, Hellions, Dave Mason, Gordon Jackson)

TRAFFIC JAM
| 67 | Piccadilly 7N 35386 | Almost But Not Quite There/Wait Just A Minute (demo copy) | £400 |
| 67 | Piccadilly 7N 35386 | Almost But Not Quite There/Wait Just A Minute | £500 |

(see also Status Quo, Spectres)

TRAGEDY
| 10 | Diggers With Gratitude DWG 009 | THE BLACK RAGE DEMOS (EP, 75 only, red vinyl) | £60 |
| 10 | Diggers With Gratitude DWG 009 | THE BLACK RAGE DEMOS (EP, 175 only, black vinyl) | £30 |

TRAGICIAN
| 79 | Look LKSP 6411 | The Wild The Scared And The Timid/Traces Of Impact (numbered gatefold p/s) | £35 |

PHIL TRAINER
| 73 | BASF BAG 22 29107-3 | TRAINER (LP, gatefold) | £35 |

(see also Trees)

TRAIN SET
| 80s | Play Hard DEC 11 | She's Gone (12", p/s) | £35 |
| 89 | Play Hard DEC 17 | Hold On (12", p/s) | £35 |

TRAINSPOTTERS
| 79 | Arista ARIST 320 | Unfaithful/Hiring The Hall | £15 |

TRAITOR
| 81 | Airship APP 377 | That's Life/Stone Cold Sober | £100 |

TRAITS
| 67 | Pye International 7N 25404 | Harlem Shuffle/Strange Lips (Start Ole Memories) | £35 |

(see also Roy Head)

ALAN TRAJAN
| 69 | MCA MK 5002 | Speak To Me, Clarissa/This Might Be My Last Number | £50 |

MINT VALUE £

69	MCA MKPS 2000	FIRM ROOTS (LP, laminated front sleeve)	£120

TRAMLINE

68	Island ILPS 9088	SOMEWHERE DOWN THE LINE (LP, pink label black/orange circle)	£200
69	Island ILPS 9095	MOVES OF VEGETABLE CENTURIES (LP, pink label)	£200

(see also Whitesnake)

BOBBY LEE TRAMMELL

64	Sue WI 326	New Dance In France/Carolyn	£40

TRAMMPS

75	Phil. Int. PIR 80409	TRAMMPS (LP)	£15
75	Buddah BDLP 4036	THE LEGENDARY ZING ALBUM (LP)	£15

TRAMMY (RON WILSON)

72	Techniques TE 920	Horns Of Paradise/TECHNIQUES ALL STARS: Grass Root	£30

TRAMP

69	Music Man SMLS 603	TRAMP (LP, laminated front, flipbacks, white/black label)	£150
73	Spark Replay SRLM 2001	TRAMP (LP, reissue)	£30
74	Spark SRLP 112	PUT A RECORD ON (LP)	£30

(see also Dave Kelly, Jo-Ann Kelly, Brunning Hall Sunflower Blues Band, Fleetwood Mac)o

TRAMWAY

91	Sarah SARAH 52	Technical College/Balla (p/s, insert)	£20
91	Sarah SRH 43	Maritime City/Boathouse/Star (p/s, with insert)	£20

TRANE

71	BBC RESL 5	Wagoner's Walk/Jenny's Song/Ragged Bird/Mansion Of Cards (p/s)	£15

TRANQUILITY

72	Epic EPC 64729	TRANQUILITY (LP, yellow label)	£20
72	Epic EPC 65418	SILVER (LP, lyric insert, yellow label)	£15

TRANS AM

95	Thrill Jockey THRILL 024	TRANS AM (LP)	£15

TRANSATLANTICS

65	Fontana TF 593	Many Things From Your Window/I Tried To Forget	£35
65	Fontana TF 638	Stand Up And Fight Like A Man/But I Know	£20
65	Mercury MF 948	Don't Fight It/Look Before You Leap	£50
65	King KG 1033	Run For Your Life/It's All Over	£15
66	King KG 1040	Louie Go Home/Find Yourself Another Guy	£30

TRANSCRIPT CARRIERS

92	Transcript Carriers TC999	ALL FEAR IS BONDAGE (EP)	£40

TRANSISTORS

81	Open Circuit	RIOT SQUAD (EP)	£20

TRANSIT

09	Third Man TMR 012	Come On And Ride/After Party (100 only, luminous vinyl)	£40

TRANSMISSION

84	PMP PMP 001	Reaching Out/Bouncing Ball/Take It Easy/Mystery Lady (12", p/s)	£60

TRANSMITTERS

78	Ebony EYE 11	Party/0.5 Alive (p/s)	£15
78	Ebony EBY 1002	24 HOURS (LP)	£15

TRANSPARENT ILLUSION

81	Vortex VEX 001/002	Vortex/Nuclear Release (p/s)	£150
81	Vortex VEX 3	STILL HUMAN (LP)	£150
82	Vortex VEX 4	CHAGRIN RECEIVER (LP)	£20

TRANSVOLTA

79	Pinnacle PIN 3 12	Disco Computer/You're Disco (12")	£30

TERRY TRANZ & THE VESTITES

81	Go Round TOUCH 1	State Hand Out/We Had It Here (2 different white or yellow home-made sleeves)	£150

BOUBACAR TRAORE

90	Sterns 1032	MARIAMA (LP)	£40

TRAPEZE

79	Aura AUS 114	Don't Ask Me How I Know/Take Good Care (p/s)	£15
80	Aura AUS 116	Running Away/Don't Break My Heart (p/s)	£15
69	Threshold THS 2	TRAPEZE (LP, gatefold sleeve)	£90
70	Threshold THS 4	MEDUSA (LP)	£70
73	Threshold THS 8	YOU ARE THE MUSIC ... WE'RE JUST THE BAND (LP)	£20
74	Warner Bros K 56064	HOT WIRE (LP)	£15
81	Aura AUL 717	LIVE IN TEXAS ... DEAD ARMADILLOS (LP)	£15

(see also Finders Keepers, Montanas, Deep Purple, Glenn Hughes, Judas Priest, Whitesnake)

TRASH TOWN

85	Course CORS 1	Unlucky Numbers/Down	£18

TRASH (1)

69	Apple APPLE 6	Road To Nowhere/Illusions (initial copies as White Trash)	£200
69	Apple APPLE 6	Road To Nowhere/Illusions (later copies as Trash)	£70
69	Apple APPLE 17	Golden Slumbers - Carry That Weight/Trash Can	£30

(see also Poets, Pathfinders)

TRASHCAN SINATRAS

92	Go! Discs EXTCS1	Senses Working Overtime/For The Meantime (12", promo, numbered)	£25

90	Go! Discs 828 2011	CAKE (LP)	£35
93	Go! Discs 824 408-1	I'VE SEEN EVERYTHING (LP)	£150
96	Go! Discs 828 696-1	A HAPPY POCKET (LP)	£100

TRASHMEN

| 64 | Stateside SS 255 | Surfin' Bird/King Of The Surf | £35 |
| 64 | Stateside SS 276 | Bird Dance Beat/A-Bone | £35 |

TRAVELING WILBURYS

| 88 | Warner Bros WX 224W | VOLUME ONE (LP, some with stickered sleeve & sticker inserts) | £20 |

(see also George Harrison, Bob Dylan, Roy Orbison, Tom Petty)

TRAVELLERS

77	Paradise PDS 001	Jah Give Us The World (feat. U Brown)/Girl I Left Behind (12", p/s)	£15
77	Paradise PDL 002	BLACK BLACK MINDS (LP)	£80
05	Pressure Sounds PSLP 49	BLACK BLACK MINDS (2-LP, reissue)	£30

MERLE TRAVIS

| 53 | Capitol CL45 13985 | Gamblers Guitar/Shut Up And Drink Your Beer | £35 |

(see also Brown's Ferry Four)

PAUL TRAVIS

| 75 | A&M AMLS 68290 | RETURN OF THE NATIVE (LP, with lyric inner) | £15 |

(see also Travis)

TRAVIS (1)

| 73 | A&M AMLS 68120 | SHINE ON ME (LP) | £50 |

(see also Paul Travis)

TRAVIS (2)

96	Red Telephone Box PHONE 001	All I Want Do Is Rock/Line Is Fine/Funny Thing (10", numbered, stickered p/s, 750 only)	£30
97	Independiente ISOM 1LP	GOOD FEELING (LP, inner)	£50
99	Independiente ISOM 9 LP	THE MAN WHO (LP, with bonus remix 12")	£100
99	Independiente ISOM 9 LP	THE MAN WHO (LP)	£50
01	Independiente ISOM 25 LP	THE INVISIBLE BAND (LP, with free 7")	£40
03	Independiente ISOM 40LP	12 MEMORIES (LP)	£25
07	Epic ISOM 67LP	THE BOY WITH NO NAME (LP, and free 7")	£50
08	Red Telephone Box PHONE 004V	ODE TO J SMITH (LP)	£30

TRAVIS & BOB

| 59 | Pye International 7N 25018 | Tell Him No/We're Too Young | £15 |

TRAX

| 79 | Lonely LONESOME ONE | HOME EP | £20 |

TRAX FOUR

| 66 | Ace Of Clubs S/ACL 1216 | WINGDING PARTY!!! (LP, mono/stereo) | £55 |

JACK TRAYLOR & STEELWIND

| 73 | Grunt FTR 0194 | CHILD OF NATURE (LP) | £20 |

TREASURE BOY

| 67 | Trojan TR 010 | Love Is A Treasure (actually by Freddie McKay)/TOMMY McCOOK: Zazuka | £35 |

TREATMENT

81	Private Pressing	Stamp Out Mutants/Doncha Know (p/s)	£15
89	Number TAO 1	LIVE (LP)	£18
93	Delerium DELEC 026	CIPHER CAPUT (LP, insert)	£20

STEVE TREATMENT

78	Rather GEAR 2	A SIDED 45 EP (p/s)	£20
79	Backbone ZBHIT 1	Heaven Knows (Juvenile Wrecks)/Step Inside A Worn Out Shoe (fold-out p/s)	£20
79	Backbone ZBHIT 2	CHANGE OF PLAN EP (p/s)	£20

TREDEGAR

| 86 | Aries CEP 0001 | Duma/The Jester (p/s) | £75 |
| 86 | Aries CEP LP 001 | TREDEGAR (LP, gatefold sleeve, embossed) | £18 |

(see also Budgie)

HERBERT BEERBOHM TREE

| 65 | OMY 69 | KEEP THOSE DOGS AWAY (EP) | £25 |

TREES

70	CBS 5078	Nothing Special/Epitaph	£25
70	CBS 63837	THE GARDEN OF JANE DELAWNEY (LP)	£350
71	CBS 64168	ON THE SHORE (LP)	£400
87	Decal LIK 12	ON THE SHORE (LP, reissue)	£15
87	Decal LIK 15	THE GARDEN OF JANE DELAWNEY (LP, reissue)	£30
06	Sunbeam SBR2LP 5056	THE GARDEN OF JANE DELAWNEY (2-LP, reissue, 180gm vinyl, booklet)	£20
08	Sunbeam SBR2LP 5057	ON THE SHORE (2-LP, reissue, 180gm vinyl, booklet)	£30

(see also Casablanca, Juliet Lawson, Trainer)

TREETOPS

67	Parlophone R 5628	Don't Worry Baby/I Remember	£15
71	Columbia DB 8799	Without The One You Love/So Here I Go Again	£15
73	Columbia DB 9013	Gypsy/Life Is Getting Better	£15

TREKKAS

| 65 | Planet PLF 105 | Please Go/I Put A Spell On You | £150 |

TREM
83	AM 251	My Robotic Friend/Colour Vision (p/s, 1000 only)	£25

TREMELOES
66	Decca F 12423	Blessed/The Right Time	£20
66	CBS 202242	Good Day Sunshine/What A State I'm In	£15
68	CBS EP 6402	MY LITTLE LADY (EP)	£18
67	CBS (S)BPG 63017	HERE COME THE TREMELOES (LP)	£18
68	CBS (S)BPG 63138	THE TREMELOES: CHIP, RICK, ALAN AND DAVE (LP)	£18
69	CBS 63547	THE TREMELOES 'LIVE' IN CABARET (LP)	£15
70	CBS 64242	MASTER (LP)	£15

(see also Brian Poole & Tremeloes)

TREMORS
79	Redball RR 0002	Modern World/Smashed Reality (p/s)	£15

TREND (1)
67	Page One POF 004	Boyfriends And Girlfriends/Shoot On Sight	£80

TREND (2)
70	Trendy TREND 1	Teenage Crush/Cool Johnny (with press sheet)	£50
70	Trendy TREND 1	Teenage Crush/Cool Johnny	£40

TREND (3)
80	MCA MCA 583	Polly And Wendy/Family Way (p/s)	£20
80	MCA MCA 629	This Dance Hall Must Have A Back Way Out/Fiction, Love & Romance (p/s)	£15

TRENDS
63	Piccadilly 7N 35171	All My Loving/Sweet Little Miss Love	£15
64	Pye 7N 15644	You're A Wonderful One/The Way You Do The Things You Do	£20

(see also Tammy St. John)

TRENDSETTERS
64	Silver Phoenix 1001	You Don't Care/My Heart Goes	£65

TRENDSETTERS
60s	Oak RGJ 999	AT THE HOTEL DE FRANCE (EP)	£30

TRENDSETTERS LTD
64	Parlophone R 5118	In A Big Way/Lucky Date	£20
64	Parlophone R 5161	Hello Josephine/Move On Over	£20
64	Parlophone R 5191	Go Away/Lollipops And Roses	£15

(see also King Crimson, Giles Giles & Fripp, Brain)

TRENIERS
58	Coral Q 72319	Ooh-La-La/Pennies From Heaven	£25
58	Fontana H 137	Go! Go! Go!/Get Out Of The Car (featuring Don Hill, Alto Sax)	£100
59	London HLD 8858	When Your Hair Has Turned To Silver/Never, Never	£40
59	London HLD 8858	When Your Hair Has Turned To Silver/Never, Never (78)	£25

JACKIE TRENT
61	Oriole CB 1711	Pick Up The Pieces/In Your Heart	£15
62	Oriole CB 1749	The One Who Really Loves You/Your Conscience Or Your Heart	£40
63	Piccadilly 7N 35121	Melancholy Me/So Did I	£15
64	Piccadilly 7N 35165	If You Love Me/Only One Such As You	£40
66	Pye 7N 17047	You Baby/Send Her Away (DJ Copy)	£40
66	Pye 7N 17047	You Baby/Send Her Away	£30
67	Pye 7N 17249	Open Your Heart/Love Can Give	£15
65	Pye NEP 4225	WHERE ARE YOU NOW (EP)	£15
65	Pye NPL 18125	THE MAGIC OF JACKIE TRENT (LP)	£25
67	Pye NPL 18173	ONCE MORE WITH FEELING (LP)	£15
67	Pye NSPL 18201	STOP ME AND BUY ONE (LP)	£20
69	Pye NSPL 18315	THE LOOK OF LOVE (LP)	£20

JACKIE TRENT & TONY HATCH
68	Pye NPL 18214	THE TWO OF US (LP)	£20
68	Pye NSPL 18229	LIVE FOR LOVE (LP)	£20
68	Pye NSPL 18304	TOGETHER AGAIN (LP)	£15
74	Pye NSPL 18422	OPPOSITE YOUR SMILE (LP)	£15

TRESPASS
79	Trial CASE 1	One Of These Days/Bloody Moon (p/s)	£25
80	Trial CASE 2	Jealousy/Live It Up! (p/s)	£18
81	Trial CASE 3	Bright Lights/The Duel/Man And Machine (p/s)	£20

TREVER T
98	First Handed FHR 005	Loving You/On Me Mind Body And Soul Mix/Exclusive/On Me Mellow Mix (12")	£40

TREVOR (SHIELD)
64	Blue Beat BB 228	Down In Virginia/Hey Little Schoolgirl (with Caribs)	£25
68	Blue Cat BS 129	Tender Arms (with Joe White & Glen Brown)/DERMOTT LYNCH: Something Is Worrying Me	£100
68	Blue Cat BS 130	Pretty Girl (with Joe White & Glen Brown)/DERMOTT LYNCH: You Went Away	£500
69	Blue Cat BS 153	Everyday Is Like A Holiday/Have You Time (by Trevor & Maytones)	£200

ANDREYA TRIANA
10	Ninja Tune ZEN 155	LOST WHERE I BELONG (LP)	£30

TRIARCHY
79	SRT/79/CUS 599	Save The Khan/Juliet's Tomb (in p/s, 1,000 only)	£80

79	SRT/79/CUS 599	Save The Khan/Juliet's Tomb (1,000 only)	£30
79	Direct NEON 1	Save The Khan/Juliet's Tomb (reissue, p/s)	£35
80	Direct NEON 2	Metal Messiah/Sweet Alcohol/Hell Hound On My Trail (in p/s)	£70
80	Direct NEON 2	Metal Messiah/Sweet Alcohol/Hell Hound On My Trail	£30

TRIBAN
69	Cambrian MCT 592	TRIBAN (LP)	£15
72	Cambrian MCT 218	RAINMAKER (LP, laminated cover)	£18

TONY TRIBE
69	Downtown DT 419	Red Red Wine/RECO & RUDIES: Blues (some miscredited to Tony Tripe)	£30
69	Downtown DT 439	Gonna Give You All The Love/HERBIE GREY: Why Wait	£30

TRIBE (U.K.) (1)
66	Planet PLF 108	The Gamma Goochie/I'm Leavin'	£100
67	RCA RCA 1592	Love Is A Beautiful Thing/Steel Guitar	£25

TRIBE (U.K.) (2)
75	BB BB003	Africa (Part 1)/Africa (Part 2)	£30

TRIBE (U.S.)
66	Polydor 56510	Dancin' To The Beat Of My Heart/Woofin'	£70

TRIBESMAN
79	Boa BOA 102-12	Finsbury Park/The Tribe (12", p/s)	£30
80	Direct ROS001-12	Sunburst/Lion (Concrete Jungle) (12", p/s)	£20
12	Reggae Archive RARC001V	The Tribe/Dub/Finsbury Park/Dub (12", reissue)	£20
78	Promo 1	WONDER WOLF (mini-LP, promo only, white sleeve)	£25
79	Boa BOA 001	STREET LEVEL (LP)	£20

TRICKY
95	4th & Broadway BRLP 610	MAXINQUAYE (LP, gatefold, inner)	£50
96	4th & Broadway BRLP 623	PRE-MILLENIUM TENSION (LP)	£50
98	Island ILPSD 8071	ANGELS WITH DIRTY FACES (2-LP, numbered on rear)	£60
99	Island ILPS 8087	JUXTAPOSE (LP, with DJ Muggs and Grease)	£40
01	Anti 6596-1	BLOWBACK (LP)	£40
03	Anti 6648-1	VULNERABLE (LP, gatefold)	£20
08	Domino WIGLP 195	KNOWLE WEST BOY (LP)	£15
09	Domino WIGLP 230	TRICKY MEETS SOUTH RAKKAS CREW (2-LP)	£15
10	Domino WIGLP 256	MIXED RACE (LP)	£25

TRI-CORE
92	Underground UNR 001T	BELFAST SAYS EP (12")	£80

TRIDENT
84	SRT TRI 1	Destiny/Power Of The Trident	£50
(see also Filthy Rich)			

TRIFFIDS (2)
11	Domino REWIGCD 72X	COME RIDE WITH ME...WIDE OPEN ROAD (10-CD box set)	£70

TRIFLE
71	Dawn DNLS 3017	FIRST MEETING (LP, textured gatefold sleeve)	£150
(see also George Bean)			

TRILOGY
71	Mercury 6338 034	I'M BEGINNING TO FEEL IT (LP)	£20

TRINIDAD ALL STARS
59	Parlophone GEP 8625	TRINIDAD ALL STARS STEEL BAND (EP)	£50

TRINIDAD OIL COMPANY
77	Harvest SHSP 4070	THE CALENDAR SONG (LP)	£20

TRINITY
79	Attack TACK 2	Follow My Heart/Pope Paul Dead And Gone (12")	£30
70s	Burning Vibrations BVD 002	Roots Man Party/Healing The Nation (12", with Mystic EMP Group)	£20
80	Spectrum SP 01	Jamaican People A Nice People/Heaven And Hell/LLOYD CLARKE SPARROW: The Young Ones (12")	£35
79	Burning Sounds BDS 012	SHOWCASE EP (12")	£20
77	Magnum DERD 1003	UPTOWN GIRL (LP)	£20
79	Trojan TRLS 170	ROCK IN THE GHETTO (LP)	£20
81	JB JBLP 006	FULL HOUSE (LP)	£20
83	Vista Sounds VSLP 4009	SIDE KIKS (LP, reissue of Uptown Girl)	£15
00	Blood & Fire/Simply Vinyl SVLP 284	SHANTY TOWN DETERMINATION (2-LP)	£25

TRINITY HOUSE
77	Profile GMOR 146	FLASHBACK THROUGH HISTORY (LP, private pressing, with insert)	£40

TRIO
71	Dawn DNLS 3022	CONFLAGRATION (LP)	£60
76	Dawn DNLS 3072	LIVE AT WOODSTOCK TOWN HALL (LP, with Stu Martin)	£25
(see also John Surnam)			

TRIPPERS
66	Pye International 7N 25388	Dance With Me/Keep A-Knockin'	£20

TRIPTI DAS
67	Flowers FL 001	Kat Put Li {Puppet On A String)/Lagta Mahi Dil	£20

TRITONS
73	Bradley BAR 24	I Can't Get Not Satisfaction/Drifter	£50

TRIUMVIRAT
74	Harvest SHSP 4030	ILLUSION ON A DOUBLE DIMPLE (LP, 1st pressing normal green label)	£15
75	Harvest SHSP 4048	SPARTACUS (LP)	£15

TRIXIE'S BIG RED MOTORBIKE
82	Chew CH 9271	A Splash Of Red/Invisible Boyfriend (white label, stapled foldover p/s)	£15
95	Accident DENT 1	THE INTIMATE SOUND OF... (LP, handmade sleeve, numbered)	£40
95	Accident DENT 1	THE INTIMATE SOUND OF... (LP, green vinyl, 500 only)	£25

TRIXONS
69	Major Minor MM 665	Just Another Song/Sunny Side Sam	£15

MARCUS TRO
65	Ember EMB S 203	Tell Me/What's The Matter Little Girl (in p/s)	£18
65	Ember EMB 3365	INTRODUCING MARCUS TRO (LP)	£40

TROBWLL
79	Buwch Hapus MW 1	TAITH (EP)	£40

TROGGS
SINGLES
66	CBS 202038	Lost Girl/The Yella In Me	£50
67	Page One POF 022	My Lady/Girl In Black (withdrawn)	£50
73	Pye 7N 45295	Strange Movies/I'm On Fire	£15
67	Page One POE 001	TROGGS TOPS (EP)	£20
67	Page One POE 002	TROGGS TOPS VOLUME TWO (EP)	£40
67	Page One	TRACK A TROGG (EP, unreleased)	£0

ALBUMS
66	Fontana TL 5355	FROM NOWHERE - THE TROGGS (LP, mono)	£70
66	Fontana STL 5355	FROM NOWHERE - THE TROGGS (LP, stereo)	£80
66	Page One POL 001	TROGGLODYNAMITE (LP, mono)	£70
66	Page One POLS 001	TROGGLODYNAMITE (LP, stereo)	£90
67	Page One FOR 001	THE BEST OF THE TROGGS (LP)	£30
67	Page One POL 003	CELLOPHANE (LP, mono)	£80
67	Page One POLS 003	CELLOPHANE (LP, stereo)	£90
68	Page One POL 1	THE TROGGS ON TOUR (LP, export issue)	£150
68	Page One FOR 007	THE BEST OF THE TROGGS VOLUME TWO (LP)	£35
68	Page One POL(S) 012	MIXED BAG (LP)	£150
69	Page One POS 602	TROGGLOMANIA (LP)	£40
70	DJM Silverline DJML 009	CONTRASTS (LP, original issue)	£15
76	Penny Farthing PELS 551	THE TROGG TAPES (LP)	£20

(see also Chris Britton, Ronnie Bond, Ten Feet Five)

CHUCK TROIS & AMAZING MAZE
68	Action ACT 4517	Call On You/Woodsman	£25

TROJAN
88	GI GILP 444	THE MARCH IS ON (LP)	£18

TROJANS (1)
58	Decca F 11065	Man I'm Gonna Be/Make It Up	£15

TROJANS (2)
89	Gaz's LPGAZ 002	ALA-SKA (LP)	£15
95	Gaz's LPGAZ 012	STACK-A-DUB (2-LP)	£20

TRONICS (1)
61	Fontana H 348	Cantina/Pickin' & Stompin'	£18

TRONICS (2)
78	Tronics T 001	Suzie (actually "Suzie's Vibrator")/Favourite Girls (plain sleeve with inserts)	£25
81	Alien ALIEN 18	Shark Fucks/Time Off (p/s, with insert)	£25
81	Alien BALIEN 3	LOVE BACKED BY FORCE (LP)	£25

TROOPERS
57	Vogue V 9087	Get Out/My Resolution	£700
57	Vogue V 9087	Get Out/My Resolution (78)	£150

TROOPS FOR TOMORROW
82	Rhythmic RMNS 1	Songs Of Joy And Faith/Prisoner (p/s)	£15

TROPIC SHADOWS
72	Big Shot BI 603	Our Anniversary/Anniversary (Version)	£15

TROPICAL BREEZE
80	Silver Camel SC 001	So Naive/FORCE 7: Naivity (12")	£20
81	Daddy Kool DKR 126	You're The One/One + One Dub (12")	£30

ARCHIBALD TROTT
64	Black Swan WI 407	Get Together/Just Because	£40

(see also Baba Brooks)

TROUBLE
88	Justice JTT002	I Get Hype/I Guess It's Dope (12")	£20

BOBBY TROUP
54	Capitol LC 6660	BOBBY TROUP (10" LP)	£20

BOB TROW QUARTET
54	London HL 8082	Soft Squeeze Baby/I Went Along For The Ride	£40

ROBIN TROWER
| 73 | Chrysalis CHR 1039 | TWICE REMOVED FROM YESTERDAY (LP) | £15 |
| 74 | Chrysalis CHR 1057 | BRIDGE OF SIGHS (LP) | £15 |

(see also Paramounts, Procol Harum)

TROY
| 80s | Love Linch LL 022 | Love & Harmony/Land Of Love (12") | £20 |

DORIS TROY
63	London HLK 9749	Just One Look/Bossa Nova Blues	£35
64	Atlantic AT 4011	What'cha Gonna Do About It/Tomorrow Is Another Day	£25
65	Atlantic AT 4020	One More Chance/Please Little Angel	£18
65	Atlantic AT 4032	Heartaches/You'd Better Stop	£18
65	Cameo Parkway C 101	I'll Do Anything (He Wants Me To)/But I Love Him	£150
65	Cameo Parkway C 101	I'll Do Anything (He Wants Me To)/But I Love Him (DJ copy)	£200
68	Toast TT 507	I'll Do Anything (Anything He Wants Me To)/Heartaches	£15
70	Apple APPLE 24	Ain't That Cute/Vaya Con Dios (with p/s)	£22
70	Apple APPLE 28	Jacob's Ladder/Get Back	£15
71	Mojo 2092 011	I'll Do Anything (He Wants Me To)/But I Love Him (reissue)	£15
18	Super Disco Edits SDE 40	What'cha Gonna Do/You Got Me Baby (12")	£20
65	Atlantic AET 6007	WATCHA GONNA DO ABOUT IT (EP)	£100
70	Apple SAPCOR 13	DORIS TROY (LP)	£80
73	Mojo 2956 001	THE RAINBOW TESTAMENT (LP, with Gospel Truth)	£35
74	Polydor 2464 001	JUST ONE LOOK (LP)	£30
74	People PLEO 12	STRETCHIN' OUT (LP)	£20
92	Apple SAPCOR 13	DORIS TROY (LP, reissue, gatefold sleeve with bonus 12" [SAPCOR 132])	£35

TROY & THUNDERBIRDS
| 61 | London HL 9476 | Twistle/Take Ten | £15 |

WILLIAM TRUCKAWAY
| 69 | Reprise RS 20842 | Bluegreens On The Wing/Besides Yourself | £15 |
| 71 | Reprise K 44165 | BREAKAWAY (LP, with lyric insert) | £20 |

TRUE ADVENTURE
| 74 | Decca F 13528 | Where The Roxy Use To Be/Outlaw Love | £15 |

TRUE FEELINGS
| 81 | Amber EM001 | Love Me Love Me/Love Me Love Me Disco (12") | £200 |

TRUE IMAGE
| 02 | Grapevine G2K 45 105 | I'm Not Over You Yet/I'm Not Over You Yet (Extended) | £20 |

TRUE SPIRITED
| 70 | Wren WR 1 | Over And Over/Pollution | £30 |

TRUE STYLE
| 91 | Liberty Grooves LIB002 | CODES OF CONDUCT (EP) | £15 |

TRUFFLE
| 81 | Chesnut NUT 6 | Round Tower/If You Really Want (p/s) | £100 |

TRUK
| 71 | CBS 57201 | Winters Coming On/You | £15 |

JONNY TRUNK
01	Trunk TTT 001	The Snow It Melts/Scooby Don't (7", 300 only)	£25
01	Trunk TTT 002	Sister Woo/Mr Hand (300 only)	£20
03	Trunk TTT 004	Dead Soon/Dead Mouse Blues (7", 400 only)	£15
11	Ghost Box GBX 706	ANIMATION AND INTERPRETATION EP (p/s)	£25
04	Trunk JBH 008 LP	THE INSIDE OUTSIDE (LP, 500 only)	£35
09	Trunk JBH 033	JONNY TRUNK'S SCRAPBOOK (LP, 750 only)	£18

TRUTH (1)
65	Pye 7N 15923	Baby Don't You Know/Come On Home	£20
65	Pye 7N 15998	Who's Wrong/She's A Roller	£25
66	Pye 7N 17095	I Go To Sleep/Baby You've Got It	£30
66	Deram DM 105	Jingle Jangle/Hey Gyp (Dig The Slowness)	£100
67	Decca F 12582	Walk Away Renee/Fly Away Bird	£20
68	Decca F 22764	Seuno/Old Ma Brown	£60

TRUTH & BEAUTY
| 74 | Rak RAK 181 | Tuff Little Surfer Boy/Touch-a Touch-a Touch Me | £25 |

TRUTH CLUB
| 80 | Le Rey LR 01 | Sleight/FOTE: Looking For Lost Toy | £20 |

TRUTH OF TRUTHS
| 71 | Oak OR 1001 | TRUTH OF TRUTHS (LP) | £25 |

TRUTH (3)
| 92 | Funky Groove FUNKY 4 | The End/Calm Down/Newlands/Emotional/The Start (12") | £250 |

TRUTH, FACT & CORRECT
| 76 | Black Wax WAX 18 | Babylon Deh Pon Fire/Jungle Fever (with LYN 3754 etching in run-out groove) | £45 |

TRUX
| 82 | Trux TRX 01 | Bad Luck (no p/s) | £200 |

T.S.O.L.
| 81 | Frontier FLP 1004 | DANCE WITH ME (LP) | £18 |

T34
81	Spaceward DIV 1	Computer Dating/Mind Your Own Business	£20
83	Galaxy GAL 007	Rock On/Looking After Me (Looking After You) (p/s)	£20

T2
70	Decca SKL 5050	IT'LL ALL WORK OUT IN BOOMLAND (LP, blue/silver label/boxed logo)	£300

(see also Flies, Cross & Ross)

ERNEST TUBB (& HIS TEXAS TROUBADORS)
50	Decca BM 31206	The Blues/Half A Mind (Export Issue)	£15
56	Brunswick 05527	Thirty Days/Answer The Phone (triangular centre)	£30
56	Brunswick 05587	So Doggone Lonesome/If I Never Have Anything Else	£20
50s	Decca BM 31214	What Am I Living For/Goodbye Sunshine, Hello Blues (export issue)	£15
56	Brunswick LA 8736	JIMMIE RODGERS SONGS (10" LP)	£30

(see also Red Foley & Ernest Tubb)

JUSTIN TUBB
64	RCA RCX 7133	JUSTIN TUBB (EP)	£30

TUBES
79	A&M AMS 7423	Prime Time (promo box of 7 different coloured vinyl editions & picture disc)	£30

TUBEWAY ARMY
79	Beggars Banquet BEG 17T	Down In The Park/Do You Need The Service?/I Nearly Married A Human 2 (12", p/s)	£25
79	Beggars Banquet BEG 17T	Down In The Park/Do You Need The Service?/I Nearly Married A Human 2 (12", p/s, sleeve misprint with Leif Garrett's Feel The Need LP image overprinted on both sides)	£100
79	Beggars Banquet BEG 18	Are "Friends" Electric?/We Are So Fragile (p/s original semi-transparent sleeve)	£18
79	Banquet Banquet BEG 18P	Are "Friends" Electric?/We Are So Fragile (picture disc, with insert)	£20
79	Beggars Banquet BACK 2	That's Too Bad/Oh! Didn't I Say/Bombers/Blue Eyes/O.D. Receiver (double pack, gatefold p/s, mispressed 2nd disc omits "O.D. Receiver")	£15
78	Beggars Banquet BEGA 4	TUBEWAY ARMY (LP, blue vinyl, gatefold, hype sticker, some with badge)	£200
78	Beggars Banquet BEGA 4	TUBEWAY ARMY (LP, blue vinyl, gatefold stickered sleeve)	£80
79	Beggars Banquet BEGA 7	REPLICAS (LP, printed inner, black & white poster)	£25
79	Beggars Banquet BEGA 7	REPLICAS (LP, printed inner)	£18
79	Beggars Banquet BEGA 4	TUBEWAY ARMY (LP, reissue, 'head' sleeve, printed inner)	£25
79	Beggars Banquet BEGA 4	TUBEWAY ARMY (LP, reissue, mispressing, plays The Pleasure Principle on side 2)	£100
08	VIN 180 LP 002	REPLICAS (LP, (LP, pressed on 180 gram vinyl, numbered with 8" x 6" print)	£18
10	Vinyl 180 VIN180LP026	TUBEWAY ARMY (LP, blue vinyl reissue)	£18
15	Beggars Banquet BBQ LP 7	REPLICAS (LP, reissue, orange vinyl, 600 only, sold at gigs)	£40

(see also Gary Numan, Paul Gardiner)

TUBEWAY PATROL
81	Carrere CAR 218	Do Eyes Ever Meet/No Time (no p/s)	£18

TUBILAH DOG
96	S04	IN SEARCH OF PLAICE (LP, gatefold with poster)	£20

TUB-THUMPER
74	Alaska ALA 18	Kick Out The Jams/Kahoutec	£25

BESSIE TUCKER
55	HMV 7EG 8085	BLUES BY BESSIE (EP)	£20

BILLY JOE TUCKER
61	London HLD 9455	Boogie Woogie Bill/Mail Train	£60

TOMMY TUCKER
64	Pye International 7N 25238	Hi-Heel Sneakers/I Don't Want 'Cha	£20
64	Pye International 7N 25246	Long Tall Shorty/Mo' Shorty	£25
64	London HLU 9932	Oh! What A Feeling/Wine Bottles	£40
69	Chess CRS 8086	Hi-Heel Sneakers/I Don't Want 'Cha (reissue)	£15
64	Pye Intl. NEP 44027	HI HEEL SNEAKERS (EP)	£50

TUCKY BUZZARD
71	Capitol E-ST 864	WARM SLASH (LP, laminated front sleeve, flipbacks)	£60
73	Purple TPSA 7510	ALRIGHT ON THE NIGHT (LP, laminated gatefold sleeve)	£25
73	Purple TPSA 7512	BUZZARD (LP)	£20

HENRY TUDOR
67	Decca F12574	How Many Times/Another Name From Nowhere	£25

TUDOR LODGE
71	Vertigo 6059 044	The Lady's Changing Home/Back To The Good Times We Had	£75
71	Vertigo 6360 043	TUDOR LODGE (LP, foldout textured sleeve, swirl label)	£1750
88	Zap! ZAP 4	TUDOR LODGE (LP, reissue)	£25

TUDOR MINSTRELS
66	Decca F 12536	Love In The Open Air/A Theme From "The Family Way"	£22

TUESDAY
72	Pye 7N 45194	Big Mister Little Man/Sewing Machine	£20

TUESDAY'S CHILDREN
66	Columbia DB 7978	When You Walk In The Sand/High And Drifting	£20
66	Columbia DB 8018	High On A Hill/Summer Leaves Me With A Sigh	£22
67	King KG 1051	A Strange Light From The East/That'll Be The Day	£30
67	Pye 7N 17406	Baby's Gone/Guess I'm Losin' You	£15
68	Mercury MF 1063	She/Bright-Eyed Apples	£20

(see also Warm Sounds)

TUFF GONG ALLSTARS
72	Punch PH 114	You Should Have Known Better (actually by The Wailing Souls)/Known Better	£20

(see also Wailing Souls)
TUFF LITTLE UNIT
91 Warp WAP 12 — Join The Future/Master Plan (12")..£15

TONY TUFF
79 Niagra NIADD 101 — Ease Up Oppressor/JAH THOMAS: Answer The Phone (12")................£15
79 King Sounds GMDM 26 — You Wrong/TOMMY McCOOK: Sensimena (12")........................£25
80 Art & Craft 003 — Look Ya/TONY TUFF & JAH STITCH: Rumours Of War (12")................£35
80 Cha Cha CHAD 11 — Deliver Me/Africa We Want To Go (12")................................£20
80 Grove ILPS 9619 — TONY TUFF (LP)..£30

SHANE TUFF
82 Roots Man Pro RMP 002 — Can't Take No More/Yearning For Some Loving....................£40

NANA TUFFOUR
79 GAB 001 — HIGHLIFE ROMANCE (LP)..£80

LEE TULLY
57 London HL 8363 — Around The World With Elwood Pretzel (Parts 1 & 2) (gold print label).....£100
57 London HL 8363 — Around The World With Elwood Pretzel (Parts 1 & 2) (silver print label).....£60
57 London HL 8363 — Around The World With Elwood Pretzel (Parts 1 & 2) (78)................£25

TUMBLACK
79 Island 12XWIP 6500 — Caraiba (1-sided 12" promo)...£30
79 Island 12XWIP 6500 — Caraiba/Invocation (12", p/s).......................................£50

TUNDRA
70s Greenwich Village GVR 208 — THE KENTISH SONGSTER (LP)...................................£15
78 Sweet Folk & C. SFA 078 — A KENTISH GARLAND (LP, gatefold sleeve)........................£25
81 Greenwich Village GVR 218 — SONGS FROM GREENWICH (LP, gatefold sleeve)..................£15

TUNE ROCKERS
58 London HLT 8717 — The Green Mosquito/Warm Up..£20
58 London HLT 8717 — The Green Mosquito/Warm Up (78).......................................£15

TUNEWEAVERS
57 London HL 8503 — Happy Happy Birthday Baby/PAUL GAYTEN: Yo, Yo, Walk....................£80
(see also Paul Gayten)

TUNNEL RUNNERS
80 Sonic International SI 4282 — Plastic Land/Drug (numbered p/s)...........................£80

TUNNG
04 Static Caravan VAN 72 — Tales From Black/Pool Beneath The Pond (500 only)...............£15
05 Static Caravan VAN 73 — Maypole Song/Suprize Me 44 (100 lathe cut only, p/s)............£30
05 Static Caravan VAN 88 — MOTHER'S DAUGHTERS AND OTHER SONGS (LP, 300 only - withdrawn)...£50
06 Full Time Hobby FTH019LP — COMMENTS ON THE INNER CHORUS (LP, inner, poster).............£20
06 Static Caravan VAN 88V — MOTHER'S DAUGHTERS AND OTHER SONGS (LP, reissue, clear vinyl)..£20
07 Full Time Hobby FTH040LP — GOOD ARROWS (LP)...£15

K.T. TUNSTALL
05 Relentless LPREL06 — EYE TO THE TELESCOPE (LP)..£50

TURBO
80 Cargo CRS 004 — STALLION (EP, p/s)...£100

TURNBULL & ARKWRIGHT
72 Peacock PEA 501 — Smuggling Man/Misty Roses..£15

CHUCK TURNER
87 Stereo One STO 003 — Youthman Struggling/FUNNY WONDER: Jollification (12")..............£70
87 Live & Love LLD 44 — We Rule The Dance/We Rule The Dub (12")............................£30
88 Live & Love LALP 21 — ONE THE HARD WAY (LP)..£20

DENNIS TURNER
62 London HL 9537 — Lover Please/How Many Times...£25

FRANK TURNER
09 Xtra Mile — Reasons Not To Be An Idiot/Thunder Road (p/s, 300 only, each with hand-written reason not to be an idiot by Frank Turner).....£30

GORDON TURNER
70 Charisma CAS 1009 — MEDITATION (LP, 1st pressing laminated 'landscape' sleeve)..........£40
70 Charisma CAS 1009 — MEDITATION (LP, 2nd pressing non laminated 'blue room' sleeve)......£20

IKE TURNER
60s Ember EMB 3395 — IKE TURNER ROCKS THE BLUES (LP).......................................£50
72 United Artists UAG 29362 — BLUES ROOTS (LP)..£30
75 DJM DJSLM 2010 — FUNKY MULE (LP)...£15
(see also Ike & Tina Turner)

IKE & TINA TURNER
SINGLES
60 London HLU 9226 — A Fool In Love/The Way You Love Me...................................£20
61 London HLU 9451 — It's Gonna Work Out Fine/Won't You Forgive Me........................£20
64 Sue WI 306 — Gonna Work Out Fine/Won't You Forgive Me (reissue)........................£20
64 Sue WI 322 — The Argument/Poor Fool..£20
64 Sue WI 350 — I Can't Believe What You Say/My Baby Now..................................£40
65 Warner Bros WB 153 — Finger Poppin'/Ooh Poo Pah Doo....................................£25
65 Sue WI 376 — Please, Please, Please/Am I A Fool In Love................................£40
66 Warner Bros WB 5753 — Tell Her I'm Not Home/Finger Poppin'.............................£20
66 HMV POP 1544 — Anything You Wasn't Born With/Beauty Is Just Skin Deep..................£30

MINT VALUE £

66	London HLU 10083	A Love Like Yours (Don't Come Knockin' Every Day)/**Hold On Baby**	£18
66	Stateside SS 551	Goodbye, So Long/Hurt Is All You Gave Me	£18
66	Warner Bros WB 5766	Somebody (Somewhere) Needs You/(I'll Do Anything) Just To Be With You	£100
66	Warner Bros WB 5766	Somebody (Somewhere) Needs You/(I'll Do Anything) Just To Be With You (DJ copy)	£120
67	HMV POP 1583	I'm Hooked/Dust My Broom	£70
67	HMV POP 1583	I'm Hooked/Dust My Broom (DJ copy)	£120
67	London HLU 10155	I'll Never Need More Than This/Save The Last Dance For Me	£20
68	London HLU 10217	We Need An Understanding/It Sho' Ain't Me	£15
69	Minit MLF 11016	I'm Gonna Do All I Can/You've Got Too Many Ties That Bind	£15
71	Liberty LBF 15432	Proud Mary/Funkier Than A Mosquito's Tweeter	£15

EPs
64	Sue IEP 706	THE SOUL OF IKE AND TINA TURNER	£200
65	Warner Bros WEP 619	THE IKE AND TINA TURNER SHOW	£60
66	Warner Bros WEP 620	SOMEBODY NEEDS YOU	£70
83	Sue ENS 1	SUE SESSIONS	£15

ALBUMS
65	Warner Bros WM 8170	THE IKE AND TINA TURNER SHOW	£60
65	London HA-C 8248	THE GREATEST HITS OF IKE & TINA TURNER	£60
66	Ember EMB 3368	THE IKE AND TINA TURNER REVUE	£40
66	Warner Bros W 1579	THE IKE AND TINA TURNER SHOW	£40
66	London HA-U/SH-U 8298	RIVER DEEP MOUNTAIN HIGH	£40
67	Warner Bros WB 5904	THE IKE AND TINA TURNER SHOW VOL. 2	£35
69	London HA-U/SH-U 8370	SO FINE (with Fontella Bass)	£30
69	Liberty LBS 83241	OUTTA SEASON	£22
69	Minit MLS 40014	IN PERSON	£25
69	Warner Bros ES 1810	GREATEST HITS	£20
70	Liberty LBS 83350	COME TOGETHER	£20
70	Harvest SHSP 4001	THE HUNTER	£120
71	Liberty LBS 83455	WORKIN' TOGETHER	£20
71	Liberty LBS 83468/9	LIVE IN PARIS	£15
71	Capitol E-ST 571	HER MAN...HIS WOMAN	£15
71	United Artists UAD 60005/6	WHAT YOU HEAR IS WHAT YOU GET	£15
84	Kent KENT 014	THE SOUL OF IKE AND TINA (LP)	£20

(see also Ike Turner, Ikettes)

JESSE LEE TURNER
59	London HLL 8785	The Little Space Girl/Shake, Baby, Shake	£60
59	London HLL 8785	The Little Space Girl/Shake, Baby, Shake (78)	£30
60	London HLP 9108	I'm The Little Space Girl's Father/Valley Of Lost Soldiers	£20
60	Top Rank JAR 303	That's My Girl/Teenage Misery	£20

(see also Pete Johnson, Meade Lux Lewis, Pete Johnson, Albert Ammons, Sonny Terry & Brownie McGhee)

(BIG) JOE TURNER
51	Parlophone DP 265	Roll 'Em Pete/Goin' Away Blues (with Pete Johnson) (78, export only)	£60
56	London HLE 8301	Corrine Corrina/Morning, Noon And Night (triangular or centre)	£350
56	London HLE 8301	Corrine Corrina/Morning, Noon And Night (round centre)	£100
56	London HLE 8301	Corrine Corrina/Morning, Noon And Night (78)	£40
56	London HLE 8332	Boogie Woogie Country Girl/The Chicken And The Hawk	£600
56	London HLE 8332	Boogie Woogie Country Girl/The Chicken And The Hawk (78)	£45
57	London HLE 8357	Lipstick, Powder And Paint/Rock A While (gold label label print)	£350
57	London HLE 8357	Lipstick, Powder And Paint/Rock A While (silver label print)	£175
57	London HLE 8357	Lipstick, Powder And Paint/Rock A While (78)	£40
60	London HLE 9055	Honey Hush/Tomorrow Night	£60
60	London HLK 9119	My Little Honey Dripper/Chains Of Love	£50
65	Atlantic AT 4026	Midnight Cannonball/Baby I Still Want You	£20
57	London REE 1111	PRESENTING JOE TURNER (EP, initially tri-centre)	£250
57	London REE 1111	PRESENTING JOE TURNER (EP, later round centre)	£150
57	London Jazz LTZ-K 15053	BOSS OF THE BLUES (LP, mono)	£80
57	London Jazz SAH-K 6123	BOSS OF THE BLUES (LP, stereo)	£90
59	London HA-E 2173	ROCKIN' THE BLUES (LP)	£120
60	London Jazz LTZ-K 15205	BIG JOE RIDES AGAIN (LP, mono)	£75
60	London Jazz SAH-K 6123	BIG JOE RIDES AGAIN (LP, stereo)	£80
60	London HA-E 2231	BIG JOE IS HERE (LP)	£80
64	Realm RM 207	JOE TURNER SINGS THE BLUES VOL. 1 (LP)	£20
64	Realm RM 229	JOE TURNER SINGS THE BLUES VOL. 2 (LP)	£20
65	Fontana 688 802 ZL	JUMPIN' THE BLUES (LP)	£25
67	Atlantic Special 590 006	BOSS OF THE BLUES (LP)	£18
68	Stateside (S)SL 10226	SINGING THE BLUES (LP)	£18
70	Philips SBL 7911	THE REAL BOSS OF THE BLUES (LP)	£15

JOE TURNER/RUTH BROWN
56	London REE 1047	KING AND QUEEN OF R&B (EP, 2 tracks each)	£150

(see also Ruth Brown, Big Joe Turner)

JOE TURNER & PETE JOHNSON GROUP
56	Emarcy ERE 1500	JOE TURNER & PETE JOHNSON GROUP (EP)	£30

(see also Pete Johnson, Big Joe Turner)

MEL TURNER (& BANDITS)
61	Melodisc MEL 1580	Let Me Hold Your Hand/I'll Be With You In Apple Blossom Time (with Bandits)	£20
62	Columbia DB 4791	Daddy Cool/Swing Low Sweet Chariot (with Bandits)	£25

MINT VALUE £

63	Columbia DB 7076	I Can't Stand Up Alone/Doing The Ton (with Mohicans)	£15
66	Island WI 276	Welcome Home Little Darlin'/C'est L'Amour	£40

SAMMY TURNER

59	London HLX 8963	Always/Symphony	£15
59	London HLX 8963	Always/Symphony (78)	£20
60	London HLX 9062	Paradise/I'd Be A Fool Again	£15
62	London HLX 9488	Raincoat In The River/Falling	£25
60	London HA-X 2246	LAVENDER BLUE MOODS (LP)	£60

SPYDER TURNER

67	MGM MGM 1332	Stand By Me/You're Good Enough For Me	£20

TITUS TURNER

60	London HLU 9024	We Told You Not To Marry/Taking Care Of Business	£25
61	Oriole CB 1611	Pony Train/Bla Bla Cha Cha Cha	£20
61	Parlophone R 4746	Sound-Off/Me And My Lonely Telephone	£25
61	Blue Beat BB 32	Miss Rubberneck Jones/Way Down Yonder	£18

TURNING POINT

77	Gull GULP 1022	CREATURES OF THE NIGHT (LP)	£20
78	Gull GULP 1027	SILENT PROMISE (LP)	£15

TURNSTYLE

68	Pye 7N 17653	Riding A Wave/Trot	£325

TURQUOISE

68	Decca F 12756	53 Summer Street/Tales Of Flossie Fillett	£70
68	Decca F 12842	Woodstock/Saynia	£100

TURQUOISE DAYS

84	Disques Strategie STRAT XX1	Grey Skies/Blurred (p/s, 1000 only)	£80

STANLEY TURRENTINE

66	Fontana TL 5300	TIGER TAIL (LP)	£20
72	CTI CTL2	SUGAR (LP, gatefold)	£20
97	Blue Note 7243 8 29908 1 9	EASY WALKER (LP, reissue)	£18

(see also Milt Jackson & Stanley Turrentine)

HENRY TURTLE

72	Columbia DB 8859	Do You Believe/You Turned Your Back And Walked Away	£30

TURTLES

65	Pye International 7N 25320	It Ain't Me Babe/Almost There	£20
66	Pye International 7N 25341	Let Me Be/Your Ma Said You Cried (In Your Sleep Last Night)	£15
66	Immediate IM 031	You Baby/Wanderin' Kind	£25
67	Pye Intl. NEP 44089	IT AIN'T ME BABE (EP)	£45
67	London HA-U 8330	HAPPY TOGETHER (LP)	£20
68	London HA-U/SH-U 8376	THE TURTLES PRESENT THE BATTLE OF THE BANDS (LP)	£20

(see also Flo & Eddie, Frank Zappa)

TUSS

07	Rephlex CAT 190EP	CONFEDERATION TROUGH EP	£30
07	Rephlex CAT 189	RUSHUP EDGE (3-LP)	£60

(see also Aphex Twin, Polygon Window, Caustic Window)

TUTCH

80	Gargoyle GRGL 773	The Battle/You Don't Care/Round And Round	£60

TU-TONES

59	London HLW 8904	Still In Love WIth You/Saccharin Sally	£125
59	London HLW 8904	Still In Love WIth You/Saccharin Sally (78)	£30

TUXEDO

85	Rushmore RR/TX/238	Take It Easy/Set Me Free (p/s)	£35

TUXEDOMOON

80	PREX 4	DESIRE (LP, with art print insert)	£20
82	Operation Twilight OPT 1	DIVINE (LP)	£20
91	LTM LTM 2303	THE GHOST SONATA (LP)	£25

TV ON THE RADIO

06	4AD RTCM2	Province (with David Bowie, 200 only, green vinyl)	£40
09	Parlophone LCO 299	TV ON THE RADIO : Heroes/DAVID BOWIE : Heroes	£40
04	4AD CAD 2470	DESPERATE YOUTH, BLOODTHIRSTY BABES (LP, with free 12")	£20
04	4AD CAD 2470	DESPERATE YOUTH, BLOODTHIRSTY BABES (LP)	£15
06	4AD CAD 2607	RETURN TO COOKIE MOUNTAIN (LP)	£18
08	4AD CAD 2821	DEAR SCIENCE (2-LP, white vinyl)	£15

T.V. & TRIBESMEN

66	Pye International 7N 25375	Barefootin'/Fat Man	£20

TV 21

80	Powbeat AAARGH! 2	Ambition/Ticking Away/This Is Zero (foldout p/s)	£15

(see also DNV, Shake)

TWELFTH NIGHT (1)

73	Acorn CF 239	TWELFTH NIGHT (EP)	£70

TWELFTH NIGHT (2)

80	Twelfth Night TN 001	THE FIRST 7" ALBUM ("The Cunning Man"/"Für Helene") (p/s)	£30

TWELVE CUBIC FEET
82 Namedrop NR2   STRAIGHT OUT OF THE FRIDGE (10" EP, with Bumper Booklet).......................£40

20TH CENTURY FOX ORCHESTRA
65 Stateside SS422   Those Magnificent Men In Their Flying Machines/Arizona £15
(see also Ron Goodwin)

25 RIFLES
79 25 Rifles TFR 1   World War 3/Revolution Blues/Hey Little/Dance 'Bout Now (12")..................£20

23RD TURNOFF
67 Deram DM 150   Michael Angelo/Leave Me Here £90
(see also Kirkbys, Jimmy Campbell, Rockin' Horse)

23 JEWELS
79 Temporary TEMP 1   You Don't Know Me/Playing Bogart (white labels, plain sleeve with photocopied
     insert)..£20
81 Let's Call It Temporary TEMP I'll Pay For This/Down To Minimum (p/s) £15
     3

23 SKIDOO
81 Pineapple PULP 23   Ethics/Another Baby's Face (p/s) £15
81 Fetish FE 11   The Gospel Comes To New Guinea/Last Words (12", p/s) £15
82 Fetish FM 2008   SEVEN SONGS (mini-LP)..£20
83 Operation Twilight OPT 23   THE CULLING IS COMING (LP) £20
84 Illuminated JAM 40   URBAN GAMELAN (LP) £20
00 Virgin V2912   23 SKIDOO (2-LP)..£18
(see also Current 93)

24 CARAT BLACK
94 Stax SXD 090   GHETTO: MISFORTUNES WEALTH (LP, reissue) £20

24 HOUR EXPERIENCE
94 Nice N Ripe NNR 018   PART ONE: DUB ESSENTIALS (12") £15
94 Nice N Ripe NN R017   PART TWO: MORE DUB ESSENTIALS EP (12", 1st pressing red/black labels)...........£30
97 Nice N Ripe NNR 017   PART TWO: MORE DUB ESSENTIALS EP (12", 2nd pressing green labels)........£20

TWICE AS MUCH
66 Immediate IM 039   True Story/You're So Good..£18
67 Immediate IM 042   Crystal Ball/Why Don't They All Go Away And Leave Me Alone £18
66 Immediate IMLP 007   OWN UP (LP, mono) £90
66 Immediate IMSP 007   OWN UP (LP, stereo) £100
69 Immediate IMCP 013   THAT'S ALL (LP) £60

TWICE AS NICE
74 CAE TAN 1   Going Places/Follow Me Around/Have You Been Along Way...............£20
74 Tan 002   Thoughts Of You/Dan Dare Rides Again/Hometown £20

TWIGGY
67 Ember EMB S 239   Beautiful Dreams/I Need Your Hand In Mine (in p/s) £20
67 Ember EMB S 244   When I Think Of You/Over And Over (in p/s) £20
72 Ember SE 8012   TWIGGY & THE GIRLFRIENDS (LP) £20

CALVIN TWILIGHT
79 President PT 477   Harmony/Isabelle Blue £20
80 Norwood NR 2003 S 80 CUS Night Time In The City/Lovely Lady Smile £20
     803

TWILIGHT PASSION
88 Hard Records COMM 2   MEG 1 (12" EP p/s) £25

TWILIGHT ZONERS
79 ZIP/Dining Out ZEROZERO1 ZERO ZERO ONE (Hospital/The Wrap/Twister/The Film)(EP, various silk-screened in red
     & hand-coloured p/s, signed & numbered) £75
(see also Occult Chemistry)

TWILIGHTS (AUSTRALIA)
66 Columbia DB 8065   Needle In A Haystack/I Don't Know Where The Wind Will Blow Me £30
67 Columbia DB 8125   What's Wrong With The Way I Live/It's Dark £20
68 Columbia DB 8396   Cathy, Come Home/The Way They Play £30

TWILIGHTS (U.S.)
65 London HLU 9992   Take What I Got/She's There £25

TWIN FREAKS
05 Grazw GRAZ011   Rinse The Rain/What's That You're Doing? (12", promo, 200 only) £50
05 Parlophone 311 3001   TWIN FREAKS (2-LP, gatefold) £40
(see also Beatles, Paul McCartney/Wings, Fireman)

TWINK (& FAIRIES)
70 Polydor 2343 032   THINK PINK (LP, with pink lyric insert)...............................£500
70 Polydor 2343 032   THINK PINK (LP, without pink lyric insert) £200
70 Polydor 2343 032   THINK PINK (LP, red vinyl with pink lyric insert) £400
91 Twink LP 2   ODDS & BEGINNINGS (LP, with insert, numbered & signed, some on red vinyl, 1,500
     only)..£15
97 Twink LP4   THINK PINK (LP, reissue, 1000 only)..................................£25
(see also Pretty Things, Pink Fairies, Fairies, Tomorrow, Aquarian Age, Rings, Mick Farren, Magic Muscle)

TWINKLE (RIPLEY)
65 Decca F 12219   Poor Old Johnny/I Need Your Hand In Mine £15
65 Decca F 12305   The End Of The World/Take Me To The Dance £15
66 Decca F 12464   What Am I Doing Here With You?/Now I Have You £15
69 Instant IN 005   Micky/Darby And Joan...£15

74	Bradleys BRAD 7418	Days/Caroline (as Twinkle Ripley) (p/s) £15
82	EMI 5278	I'm A Believer/For Sale (p/s) £15
65	Decca DFE 8621	TWINKLE - A LONELY SINGING DOLL (EP)..£60

(see also Silkie Davis)

TWINKLE BROTHERS

70	Jackpot JP 740	Miss World/Take What You've Got £15
71	Big Shot BI 593	You Took Me By Suprise/You Took Me By Surprise - Version (both sides actually by Tony Brevitt) £15
79	Virgin Front Line FLS 123 12	Jahoviah/Free Africa (12")..£35
80	Virgin Front Line FLS 127 12	Never Get Burned/Jah Kingdom Come (12" white label) £30
81	Twinkle TW 1/12	Rasta Pon Top/It Gwine Dread (12")..£15
81	Twinkle A 621	Robot/Don't Turn Your Back On Jah (12")..£35
83	Twinkle NG 369	Let Jah In/Don't Jump The Fence (12")..£30
86	Jah Shaka SHAKA 855	Faith Can Move Mountain/Mob Fury (12")..£25
91	Twinkle NG 100	Ethiopia Is Calling/COLOUR RED: Ethiopia Here I Come (12") £18
92	Twinkle NG 106	The Reality Of Jah Kingdom/Twinkle Brothers....................................£20
92	Jah Shaka	Africa/Version (tracks not printed on labels) £20
92	Jah Shaka	Rasta Surface/Version (tracks not printed on labels)............................£20
92	Jah Shaka 855	Faith Can Move Mountains/Mob Fury (12") £15
75	Grounation GROL 506	RASTA PON TOP (LP)...£35
76	Carib Gems CGLP 1001	DO YOUR OWN THING (LP) £60
78	Front Line FCL 5001	LOVE (10" LP) £15
80	Virgin V2169	COUNTRYMEN (LP) £20
82	Twinkle NG 500	UNDERGROUND (LP) £15
82	Twinkle NNG 741	DUB MASSACRE (INNA MURDER STYLE) (LP) £15
83	Twinkle NG 502	DUB MASSACRE PART TWO (LP) £15
84	Twinkle NG 501	BURDEN BEARER (LP) £20
85	Twinkle NGLP 505	DUB MASSACRE PART THREE (LP) £15
89	Twinkle NG 515	DUB MASSACRE PART FOUR (LP) £15

(see also Busty Brown)

TWINN CONNEXION

16	Super Disco Edits SDE 17	Don't Fight The Love/Don't Fight The Love £20

TWINSET

67	Decca F 12629	Tremblin'/Sneakin' Up On You £25

TWIN-TONES

58	RCA RCA 1040	Jo Ann/Before You Go £50
58	RCA RCA 1040	Jo Ann/Before You Go (78) £15

TWIST & SHOUT

79	Wessex WEX 268	Bounce Back/As It Happens (p/s) £20

TWIST (1)

79	Polydor 2383 552	THIS IS YOUR LIFE (LP) £20

TWISTED NERVE

82	Playlist PLAY 3	CAUGHT IN SESSION EP (poster p/s) £15
83	Criminal Damage CRI 103	EYES YOU CAN DROWN IN EP £20
84	Nerve NERVE 1	SEANCE (Mini-LP)..£25

CONWAY TWITTY

78s

57	Mercury MT 173	Shake It Up/Maybe Baby £30
59	MGM MGM 1016	Hey Little Lucy! (Don'tcha Put No Lipstick On)/When I'm Not With You......£15
59	MGM MGM 1029	Mona Lisa/Heavenly £20
59	MGM MGM 1047	Rosaleena/Halfway To Heaven £30

SINGLES

60	MGM MGM 1082	Is A Blue Bird Blue/She's Mine...£15

EPs

58	MGM MGM-EP 684	IT'S ONLY MAKE BELIEVE £30
59	MGM MGM-EP 698	HEY LITTLE LUCY £50
60	MGM MGM-EP 719	SATURDAY NIGHT WITH CONWAY TWITTY £50
60	Mercury ZEP 10069	I NEED YOUR LOVIN' £100
60	MGM MGM-EP 738	IS A BLUEBIRD BLUE?..£40
61	MGM MGM-EP 752	THE ROCK 'N' ROLL STORY £50

ALBUMS

59	MGM MGM-C 781	CONWAY TWITTY SINGS £100
60	MGM MGM-C 801	SATURDAY NIGHT WITH CONWAY TWITTY £100
60	MGM MGM-C 829	LONELY BLUE BOY £100
63	MGM MGM-C 950	R AND B '63 ....£50
68	MCA MUP(S) 342	HERE'S CONWAY TWITTY (AND HIS LONELY BLUE BOYS) £18
68	MGM C/CS 8100	THE ROCK AND ROLL STORY £40
69	MCA MUPS 363	NEXT IN LINE £15

TWIZZLE & HOT ROD ALLSTARS

70	Torpedo TOR 3	Jook Jook/The Graduate £100

TWO

84	Reflex 12 RE 7	2 x 2 (12" EP)..£20
83	Future FL3	DREAMING SPIRES (LP) £25

MINT VALUE £

TWO & A HALF
67	Decca F 22672	Suburban Early Morning Station/Just Couldn't Believe My Ears	£15
67	Decca F 22715	I Don't Need To Tell You/Christmas Will Be Round Again	£18

TWO FINGERED APPROACH
82	Virus 026	World War Album/Society Hooked/Family Traditions (p/s. 500 only)	£60

TWO FOR THE ROAD
70s	Pastiche BJ 2929	TWO FOR THE ROAD (LP)	£20

TWO KINGS
65	Island WI 240	Rolling Stone/SUFFERER: Tomorrow Morning (B-side act. by Frank Cosmo)	£18
65	Island WI 249	Hit You Let You Feel It/Honey I Love You (both sides actually by Fugitives)	£18

TWO MAN SOUND
78	Miracle M12	Que Tal America/Brazil O Brazil (12")	£15

TWO-NINETEEN (2.19) SKIFFLE GROUP
57	Esquire 10-497	Freight Train Blues/Railroad Bill (78)	£15
57	Esquire 10-502	I'm A-Lookin' For A Home/When The Saints Go Marching In (78)	£15
57	Esquire 10-509	In The Valley/Tom Dooley (78)	£15
57	Esquire 10-512	Where Can I Go?/Roll The Union On (78)	£20
57	Esquire 10-515	This Little Light Of Mine/Union Maid (78)	£20
57	Esquire EP 126	TWO-NINETEEN SKIFFLE GROUP (EP)	£40
57	Esquire EP 146	TWO-NINETEEN SKIFFLE GROUP (EP)	£50
58	Esquire EP 176	TWO-NINETEEN SKIFFLE GROUP (EP)	£50
58	Esquire EP 196	TWO-NINETEEN SKIFFLE GROUP (EP)	£60

TWO OF CLUBS
64	Columbia DB 7371	The Angels Must Have Made You/True Love Is Here	£15

TWO PEOPLE (1)
76	Bright Spot BS 009	Time Is Precious/Jump Higher	£15

TWO PEOPLE (2)
86	Polydor POSP 818	Mouth Of An Angel/Let's Raise Murder (p/s)	£20

2 SLICES OF JAM
92	White Label	Pressing On Ya Mind/Beat Like This (12" white label)	£60

2 THE TOP
90	President PT12590	Score To Settle/The Matter At Hand (12")	£30

(see also Kinetic Effect)

2001
91	B12 B1202	SPACE AGE EP (12", white label promo)	£60
91	B12 B1202	SPACE AGE EP (12", orange marbled vinyl, 300 only)	£40
92	B12 B1202	SPACE AGE EP (12", black vinyl)	£35

2 3
78	Fast Products FAST 2	Where To Now?/All Time Low (p/s)	£15

TWO TIMES DEF
92	Mendoza MEN016	First And Last (Vocal)/First And Last (Instrumental)/First And Last (Alternative Mix) (12", stamped white labels)	£150

(see also Silent Eclipse)

TWO TONE COMMITTEE
91	Precinct PREC002	Beings From A Word Stuck Surface (12")	£35
98	Dope On Plastic 12 DOP 006	Submission (12" EP)	£15

2 BAD MICE
91	Moving Shadow SHADOW 3	2 Bad Mice/No Respect (12")	£20
92	Moving Shadow SHADOW 14	HOLD IT DOWN EP (12", p/s)	£20

TWO BANKS OF FOUR
03	Red Egyptian REJLP 001	THREE STREET WORLDS (2-LP)	£18

TWO DOOR CINEMA CLUB
12	Kitsume LP 046	BEACON (LP, red vinyl, CD)	£40

2-X-TREME
92	Empire E 001	X-TREMITY EP (12", white label stamped in red, beware of represses!)	£50

2562
08	Tectonic TEC 021	AERIAL (2-LP)	£25

2 KILOS ?
90	Radioactive Lamb (No Cat. No)	MOHAMED'S MIND (12" EP, later red/white labels)	£15
90	Radioactive Lamb (No Cat. No)	MOHAMED'S MIND (12", EP, 1st pressing, red/white labels, 150 only)	£30
91	Radioactive Lamb RAL 002	VISIONS OF PARADISE (12" EP, purple/white labels, blue vinyl 150 only)	£25
91	Radioactive Lamb RAL 002	VISIONS OF PARADISE (12" EP, purple/white labels)	£15
91	Radioactive Lamb RAL 003	UNTITLED EP (12")	£20
92	Radioactive Lamb RAL 005	THE NO SELL OUT EP (12", p/s)	£40

2 MEN AND A MAN
91	ZMAM XX1	Untitled/Untitled (12", white label only)	£25

2 PAC
95	Death Row DRWJB 3	California Love (Short Radio Edit)/(Short Remix Edit) (Jukebox pressing)	£40
95	Interscope 6544 92399-1	ME AGAINST THE WORLD (2-LP)	£100
97	Interscope HIP 195	R U STILL DOWN? (REMEMBER ME) (3-LP)	£50

98	Jive HIP 200	ME AGAINST THE WORLD (2-LP, reissue, stickers sleeve)	£100
01	Jive HIP 197	STRICTLY FOR MY N.I.G.G.A.Z.. (2-LP, reissue)	£50
02	Interscope 497 070 1	BETTER DAYZ (4-LP)	£40
02	Simply Vinyl S 12	ALL EYEZ ON ME (3-LP, reissue)	£30

TWO'S COMPANY
| 76 | Thor 1009 S | TWO'S COMPANY (LP, 200 only) | £50 |

ARLYNE TYE
| 59 | London HLL 8825 | The Universe/Who Is The One | £25 |
| 59 | London HLL 8825 | The Universe/Who Is The One (78) | £15 |

TYGERS OF PAN TANG
79	Neat NEAT 03	Don't Touch Me There/Burning Up/Bad Times (first pressing of around 1,000 in slightly oversized p/s giving it a 'home made' feel)	£25
81	MCA MCA 759	Do It Good/Slip Away (no p/s)	£30
80	MCA MCF 3075	WILD CAT (LP, with lyric insert)	£18
81	MCA MCF 3104	SPELLBOUND (LP, with poster)	£18
81	MCA MCF 3123	CRAZY NIGHTS (LP, stickered sleeve, insert, with bonus 12")	£22
81	MCA MCF 3123	CRAZY NIGHTS (LP, stickered sleeve, insert)	£15
85	MFN MFN 50	THE WRECK AGE (LP, lyric sleeve)	£15
86	Neat 1037	FIRST KILL (LP, with inner)	£15

(see also John Sykes)

BIG 'T' TYLER
| 57 | Vogue V 9079 | King Kong/Sadie Green | £200 |
| 57 | Vogue V 9079 | King Kong/Sadie Green (78) | £100 |

RED TYLER
| 56 | Parlophone MSP 6215 | Fool 'Em Devil/Stardust | £18 |

T. TEXAS TYLER
| 59 | Parlophone GEP 8788 | COUNTRY ROUND-UP (EP) | £30 |
| 67 | London HA-B 8322 | MAN WITH A MILLION FRIENDS (LP) | £25 |

TERRY TYLER
| 61 | Pye International 7N 25119 | A Thousand Feet Below/Answer Me | £15 |

TOBY TYLER
| 64 | Emidisc no cat. no. | The Road I'm On (Gloria)/Blowin' In The Wind (acetate, 1 copy only) | £3000 |
| 89 | Archive Jive TOBY 1 | The Road I'm On (Gloria) (mail-order issue, numbered p/s, 1-sided, 1,500 only) | £15 |

(see also Marc Bolan)

TYMES
63	Cameo Parkway P 884	Wonderful Wonderful/Come With Me To The Sea (in p/s)	£25
64	Cameo Parkway P 891	Somewhere/View From My Window	£15
64	Cameo Parkway P 908	To Each His Own/Wonderland Of Love	£15
64	Cameo Parkway P 919	The Magic Of Our Summer Love/With All My Heart	£15
64	Cameo Parkway P 924	Here She Comes/Malibu	£100
64	Cameo Parkway P 924	Here She Comes/Malibu (DJ copy)	£200
63	Cameo Parkway P 7032	SO MUCH IN LOVE (LP)	£70
69	Direction 8-63558	PEOPLE (LP, mono or stereo)	£25
78	London HAU 8516	CAMEO PARKWAY SESSIONS (LP)	£25

MCCOY TYNER
70s	Impulse IMPL 8043	INCEPTION (LP)	£15
76	Impulse IMPL 8010	LIVE AT NEWPORT (LP, reissue)	£15
77	Blue Note 84275	TENDER MOMENTS (LP, reissue)	£15

TYPE O NEGATIVE
92	Roadrunner RO 9174	THE ORIGIN OF THE FECES (NOT LIVE AT BRIGHTON BEACH) (LP)	£70
91	Roadrunner RO 9313-1	SLOW DEEP AND HARD (LP)	£40
93	Roadrunner RR 9100-1	BLOODY KISSES (2-LP)	£125
96	Roadrunner RR 8874-1	OCTOBER RUST (2-LP)	£100

TYPHOONS (1)
| 65 | Embassy WT 2006 | Ticket To Ride/Here Comes The Night/I'll Be There/I Can't Explain (EP) | £15 |

(see also Bud Ashton, Ray Pilgrim)

TYRANNOSAURUS REX
68	Regal Zonophone RZ 3008	Debora/Child Star (with promo only p/s)	£400
68	Regal Zonophone RZ 3008	Debora/Child Star (with promo only p/s, with insert)	£500
68	Regal Zonophone RZ 3008	Debora/Child Star (demo copy as above, but without promo only p/s)	£375
68	Regal Zonophone RZ 3008	Debora/Child Star	£35
68	Regal Zonophone RZ 3011	One Inch Rock/Salamanda Palaganda (promo only p/s)	£375
68	Regal Zonophone RZ 3011	One Inch Rock/Salamanda Palaganda (promo only p/s, with insert)	£425
68	Regal Zonophone RZ 3011	One Inch Rock/Salamanda Palaganda	£40
69	Regal Zonophone RZ 3016	Pewter Suitor/Warlord Of The Royal Crocodiles	£70
69	Regal Zonophone RZ 3022	King Of The Rumbling Spires/Do You Remember (with promo only p/s)	£450
69	Regal Zonophone RZ 3022	King Of The Rumbling Spires/Do You Remember (demo, without promo only p/s)	£400
69	Regal Zonophone RZ 3022	King Of The Rumbling Spires/Do You Remember	£40
70	Regal Zonophone RZ 3025	By The Light Of A Magical Moon/Find A Little Wood	£50
68	Regal Zonophone LRZ 1003	MY PEOPLE WERE FAIR AND HAD SKY IN THEIR HAIR BUT NOW THEY'RE CONTENT TO WEAR STARS ON THEIR BROWS (LP, mono, with lyric sheet & manuscript)	£100
68	Regal Zonophone LRZ 1003	MY PEOPLE WERE FAIR AND HAD SKY IN THEIR HAIR BUT NOW THEY'RE CONTENT TO WEAR STARS ON THEIR BROWS (LP, mono)	£50
68	Regal Zonophone SLRZ 1003	MY PEOPLE WERE FAIR AND HAD SKY IN THEIR HAIR BUT NOW THEY'RE CONTENT TO WEAR STARS ON THEIR BROWS (LP, stereo, with lyric sheet & manuscript)	£60
68	Regal Zonophone SLRZ 1003	MY PEOPLE WERE FAIR AND HAD SKY IN THEIR HAIR BUT NOW THEY'RE CONTENT TO	£20

			MINT VALUE £

		WEAR STARS ON THEIR BROWS (LP, stereo)	
68	Regal Zonophone TA-LRZ 1003	MY PEOPLE WERE FAIR AND HAD SKY IN THEIR HAIR BUT NOW THEY'RE CONTENT TO WEAR STARS ON THEIR BROWS (reel-to-reel tape, mono)	£35
68	Regal Zonophone LRZ 1005	PROPHETS, SEERS AND SAGES, THE ANGELS OF THE AGES (LP, with lyric sheet, textured sleeve, mono)	£100
68	Regal Zonophone SLRZ 1005	PROPHETS, SEERS AND SAGES, THE ANGELS OF THE AGES (LP, with lyric sheet, textured sleeve, stereo)	£80
69	R. Zonophone LRZ 1007	UNICORN (LP, gatefold sleeve, original with blue/silver label, mono)	£120
69	R. Zonophone LRZ 1007	UNICORN (LP, gatefold sleeve, later issue with red/silver label mono)	£60
70	R. Zonophone SLRZ 1007	UNICORN (LP, gatefold sleeve, original with blue/silver label, stereo)	£100
70	R. Zonophone SLRZ 1007	UNICORN (LP, gatefold sleeve, later issue with red/silver label, stereo)...............	£30
70	R. Zonophone SLRZ 1013	A BEARD OF STARS (LP, with lyric sheet)	£60
70	R. Zonophone SLRZ 1013	A BEARD OF STARS (LP, without lyric sheet)	£30

(see also Marc Bolan/T. Rex, John's Children, Dib Cochran & Earwigs)

TYRANT
83	SRTS 83 CUS 2046	Hold Back The Lightning/Eyes Of A Stranger	£400

TYRONE & CARR
73	Jam JAM 36	Love Me Love You/Take Me With You	£30
75	DJM DJS 349	Love Me Love You/Take Me With You	£30

GORDON TYRRALL
78	Hill & Dale HD 002	FAREWELL TO FOGGY HILLS (LP)	£18

TYSONDOG
85	Neat NEAT 4612	Shoot To Kill/Hammerhead/Changeling/Back To The Bullet (12", p/s)	£15
86	Neat NEAT 1031	CRIMES OF INSANITY (LP, with inner)	£18
84	Neat NEAT 1017	BEWARE OF THE DOG (LP, with insert)	£20

TYTAN
82	Kamaflage KAM 6	Blind Men And Fools/The Ballad Of Edward Case (p/s)	£18
82	Kamaflage KAMA 6	Blind Men And Fools/The Ballad Of Edward Case (12", p/s)........................	£20
85	Metal Masters METALP 105	ROUGH JUSTICE (LP)...	£22

(see also Angel Witch)

TZUKE & PAXO
76	Good Earth GD 12	These Are The Laws/It's Only Fantasies...	£15

U

U BLACK
78	Hit Run HIT 621	Wicked Are To Blame/Dub (12")	£20
77	Third World TWS 926	WESTBOUND THING A SWING (LP)	£40

U BROWN
77	Third World TWS 909	LONDON ROCK (LP)	£30
78	Live & Love LALP 002	REVELATION TIME (LP)	£30

UBIK
90	Zoom ZOOM 003	NON STOP TECHNO EP (12")	£20
92	Zoom ZOOM LP1	JUST ADD PEOPLE (LP)	£40

U.F.O.
70	Beacon BEA 161	Shake It About/Evil..	£40
70	Beacon BEA 165	Come Away Melinda/Unidentified Flying Object...................................	£30
70	Beacon BEA 172	Boogie For George/Treacle People (with postcard)	£35
70	Beacon BEA 172	Boogie For George/Treacle People	£25
71	Beacon BEA 181	Prince Kajuku/The Coming Of Prince Kajuku......................................	£25
73	Chrysalis CHS 2024	Give Her The Gun/Sweet Little Thing (unreleased in U.K.)	£0
75	Chrysalis CHS 2072	Shoot Shoot/Love Lost Love (unissued)	£0
77	Chrysalis CHS 2178	Gettin' Ready/Lights Out (unissued)	£0
70	Beacon BEAS 12	U.F.O. 1 (LP)	£150
72	Beacon BEAS 19	U.F.O. 2 - FLYING (ONE HOUR SPACE ROCK) (LP, 1st pressing, white label, with inner lyric sleeve)	£200
72	Beacon BEAS 19	U.F.O. 2 - FLYING (ONE HOUR SPACE ROCK) (LP, 2nd pressing, orange label)....	£80
74	Chrysalis CHS 1059	PHENOMENON (LP, misprinted green label, matt sleeve)	£15
76	Chrysalis CHR 1103	NO HEAVY PETTING (LP, 1st pressing, green labels, A1/B1 matrixes)	£20
77	Chrysalis CHR 1127	LIGHTS OUT (LP, 1st pressing, etched matrix numbers CHR1127 A/B, TML-S stamped into dead wax on both sides, green label wih red text on outer rim, 'Chrysalis Records Ltd, Printed in U.K.,' on spine)	£20

(see also Michael Schenker Group)

UGLY CUSTARD
70	Kaleidoscope KAL 100	UGLY CUSTARD (LP)	£150

(see also Hungry Wolf, Alan Parker, Rock Machine)

UGLYS
65	Pye 7N 15858	Wake Up My Mind/Ugly Blues...	£30
65	Pye 7N 15968	It's Alright/A Friend	£20
66	Pye 7N 17027	A Good Idea/A Quiet Explosion	£30
66	Pye 7N 17178	End Of The Season/Can't Recall Her Name	£40
67	CBS 2933	And The Squire Blew His Horn/Real Good Girl.....................................	£50

69   MGM MGM 1465   **I See The Light/Mary Cilento** (6 demo copies only, pink/silver labels) **£1500**
(see also Steve Gibbons, Balls, Lemon Tree, Move, Trevor Burton)

U.K. BONDS
66   Polydor BM 56112   **Anything You Do Is Alright/The Last Thing I Ever Do**..**£20**

U.K. DECAY
79   Plastic PLAS 001   **U.K. Decay/Car Crash/PNEUMONIA: Exhibition/Coming Attack** (folded p/s)..................**£25**
81   Fresh LP5   **FOR MADMEN ONLY** (LP)...**£18**
80s UK Decay DKLP1   **FOR MADMEN ONLY** (LP)...**£25**
13   Rainbow City LP 1606   **NEW HOPE FOR THE DEAD** (LP)..**£15**

UK PLAYERS
82   A&M AMLH 68544   **NO WAY OUT** (LP) **£30**

U.K. SUBS
78   City NIK 5   **C.I.D./Live In A Car/B.I.C.** (p/s, 1st pressing, red green or orange vinyl, "FOR STRONGER
                                    PAIN RELIEF" and "KEEP AWAY FROM CHILDREN" in run out grooves)............................**£40**
78   City NIK 5   **C.I.D./Live In A Car/B.I.C.** (p/s, 1st pressing, yellow vinyl, "FOR STRONGER PAIN
                                    RELIEF" and "KEEP AWAY FROM CHILDREN" in run out grooves) **£100**
78   City NIK 5   **C.I.D./Live In A Car/B.I.C.** (p/s, 2nd pressing, clear, blue orange and green vinyl, "A
                                    PORKY PRIME CUT" in side 1 run out groove)...**£25**
82   Ramkup CAC 2   **Party In Paris** (1-sided fan club single, no p/s, 500 only)...............................**£30**
11   Time & Matter T&M 005   **Product Supply/Rare Disease/Embryo** (p/s, 250 only, signed, white vinyl)....................**£40**
15   Time & Matter T&M 018   **AMOEBA SOUNDS EP** **£25**
15   Captain Oi! AHOY 704   **THE PEEL SESSIONS VOL 1** (7" EP 250 on white and 250 on yellow vinyl)......................**£25**
15   Captain Oi! AHOY 705   **THE PEEL SESSIONS VOL 2** (7" EP, 250 on green and 250 on white vinyl)......................**£25**
16   Captain Oi! AHOY 706   **THE PEEL SESSIONS VOL 3** (7" EP 250 on red and 250 on white vinyl).........................**£25**
16   Demon DEMRECBOX 09   **THE GEM SINGLES** (8 x 7" box set)...**£35**
18   Punkerama 2020 218   **Endangered Species/Lie Down And Die** (splatter pink and vinyl with silver flecks)..........**£15**
79   Gem GEMLP 100   **ANOTHER KIND OF BLUES** (LP, blue vinyl, with inner sleeve) **£25**
80   Gem GEMLP 106   **BRAND NEW AGE** (LP, clear vinyl, with insert)...**£20**
80   Gem GEMLP 111   **CRASH COURSE LIVE** (LP, purple vinyl, 15,000 with export 12" [GEMEP 1]).....................**£15**
80   Gem GEMLP 111   **CRASH COURSE LIVE** (LP)...**£15**
80   Stiff Records MAIL 1   **LIVE KICKS** (LP, brown card inner sleeve, mail order only).................................**£15**
81   Gem GEMLP 112   **DIMINISHED RESPONSIBILITY** (LP, red vinyl with inner sleeve)...............................**£15**
82   Abstract AABT 300   **RECORDED '79-'81** (LP, blue vinyl with free stencil).......................................**£15**
82   Abstract AABT 300   **RECORDED '79-'81** (LP, red vinyl)...**£15**
82   Abstract AABT 800   **THE SINGLES 78-82** (LP, blue vinyl)...**£15**
83   Scarlett FALLLP 018   **FLOOD OF LIES** (LP)..**£15**
85   RFB LP 1   **HUNTINGTON BEACH** (LP)...**£15**
97   Fallout LP 053   **PEEL SESSIONS 1978-79** (LP)...**£50**
11   Captain Oi! AHOYLP 310   **WORK IN PROGRESS** (LP, red vinyl)..**£40**
15   Captain Oi! AHOYLP 317   **YELLOW LEADER** (LP, yellow vinyl, clear yellow flexi and CD) **£150**
16   Demon DEMREC118   **THE GEM SINGLES** (LP, green vinyl)..**£15**
(see also Urban Dogs, Charlie Harper & Captain Sensible)

ANYAOGU UKONU & HIS AFRO-CALYPSOIANS
56   London HA-U 2019   **AFRO U.S.A** (LP) **£30**

U.K.S
64   HMV POP 1310   **Ever Faithful, Ever True/Your Love Is All I Want** **£25**
64   HMV POP 1357   **I Will Never Let You Go/I Know**...**£25**

TRACEY ULLMAN
83   Stiff BUY DJ 195   **Move Over Darling/Bobby's Girl** (pink promo, "A" label)...................................**£15**

JAMES 'BLOOD' ULMER
80   Rough Trade ROUGH 16   **ARE YOU GLAD TO BE IN AMERICA?** (LP) **£15**

ULTERIOR MOTIVES
79   Motive Music MMR 1   **Another Lover** (p/s) **£30**

ULTIMATE PAINTING
14   Trouble In Mind TIM 081LP   **ULTIMATE PAINTING** (LP, pink vinyl) **£25**
15   Trouble In Mind TIM 096LP   **GREEN LANES** (LP, marbled vinly) **£20**

ULTIMATE SPINACH
68   MGM MGM-C(S) 8071   **ULTIMATE SPINACH** (LP)..**£175**
68   MGM MGM-C(S) 8094   **BEHOLD AND SEE** (LP)...**£175**

ULTRAFUNK
75   Contempo CLP 509   **ULTRAFUNK** (LP)..**£50**
77   Contempo CLP 601   **MEAT HEAT** (LP)..**£40**

ULTRAMAGNETIC MCS
89   FFRR FFR 22   **Give The Drummer Some - Vocal Rermix/Moe Luv's Theme - Vocal Remix** (p/s)...........**£150**
92   FFRR FYHU 3458   **FUNK YOUR HEAD UP** (LP)..**£20**

ULTRAMARINE
91   Brainiak BRAINK 21LP   **EVERY MAN AND WOMAN IS A STAR** (2-LP) **£20**

ULTRA VIOLENT
83   Riot City RIOT 25   **CRIME FOR REVENGE** (EP) **£20**

ULTRA VIVID SCENE
89   4AD BAD 906   **Mercy Seat/Codeine/H Like In Heaven/Mercy Seat** (LP Version) (12", uncut p/s [most
                                    copies die-cut])..**£22**
88   4AD CAD 809   **ULTRA VIVID SCENE** (LP)...**£20**
90   4ad CAD 0005   **JOY 1967-1990** (LP)..**£15**
92   4AD CAD 2017   **REV** (LP)..**£20**

ULTRAVOX
77	Island IDJ-18	Dangerous Rhythm/My Sex/The Wild The Beautiful And The Damned (12" promo)	£15
20	Electronic Sound ES 768	Herr X/Alles Klar (p/s, clear vinyl)	£20
77	Island ILPS 9449	ULTRAVOX (LP, gatefold sleeve)	£25
77	Island ILPS 9505	HA! HA! HA! (LP, with 7" "Quirks"/"Modern Love" [WIP 6417] & inner sleeve)	£35
77	Island ILPS 9505	HA! HA! HA! (LP, without free single)	£20
78	Island ILPS 9555	SYSTEMS OF ROMANCE (LP, with inner sleeve)	£25
80	Chrysalis CHR 1296	VIENNA (LP)	£15
13	Chrysalis CHRS 1296	VIENNA (LP, reissue, white vinyl, lyric inner, stickered sleeve, 500 only)	£20

(see also Tiger Lily, John Foxx, Midge Ure, Helden)

UMPS & DUMPS
80	Topic 12TS 416	THE MOON'S IN A FIT (LP)	£15

UNANIMITY
69	Clementswood CC127	Loner/All Right	£50

UNAUTHORISED VERSION
69	CBS 4135	Hey Jude/Girl In A Bus Queue	£20

UNCLE DAVID
70	Westbrook WK2	Magic Mirror/You've Lost Me	£40

UNCLE DOG
72	Signpost SG 4253	OLD HAT (LP)	£200

(see also Carol Grimes)

UNCLE FUNKENSTEIN
08	Jazzman JMANLP 023	TOGETHER AGAIN (LP, reissue)	£35

UNCLE PO
78	Beeb BEEB 23	Use My Friends/15 Minutes	£25

UNCLE 22
93	Ram RAMM 008	SPICE OF LIFE EP: 6 Million Ways To Die (DJ Hype Remix)/6 Million Ways To Die (Uncle 22 Mix) (12")	£20
93	Pure Energy PE 004	Choose One (Part 1)/Choose One (Part 2)/Crazy Kid (12", with Navigator)	£15

UNCOMMUNITY
85	Black Dwarf BDBG 1	Brutality Of Fact/Wall Of Sleep (Soundtrack)/The Price Of Your Entry Is Sin (card sleeve, 525 only, numbered, hand-painted labels, with insert)	£25

(see also McCarthy)

UNCOOL DANCEBAND
79	Polydor PB 30	Let Me Be Your Boyfriend/Heads I Win (no p/s)	£100
81	Polydor POSP 253	Jacqueline/No. 17 (no p/s)	£20

UNDEAD
84	City 006	KILLING OF REALITY (LP, lyric insert)	£35

UNDERCOVER ELEPHANT & SECRET SQUIRREL
92	Dance Bass DANCE BASS 03	VOLUME 3 EP (12", stamped white label)	£30

(see also Secret Squirrel)

UNDERDOG
79	Dor Rock DRO1/01	Life At 21/Blue Water, White Death (no p/s)	£200

UNDERGROUND
69	Major Minor SMCP 5014	BEAT PARTY (LP)	£30

(see also Madeline Bell)

UNDERGROUND EVOLUTION
96	Ugly UGM 008	WALK ON WATER (12")	£18

UNDERGROUNDS
72	High Note HS 061	Skavito/Savito	£15

UNDERGROUND SET
70	Pantonic PAN 6302	UNDERGROUND SET (LP, laminated front sleeve, red/black label)	£70

UNDERGROUND WITH STYLE
92	UAR UAR001	Lyrics Of A Gangster/Unbound Rage/Words Of Reality (EP)	£40

UNDERGROUND ZERO
84	Underground UNDER 001	Seven Light Years/Canes Venatici (12")	£15

UNDERNEATH
86	él ACME 9	LUNATIC DAWN OF THE DISMANTLER (LP)	£20

(see also Karl Blake, Lemon Kittens)

UNDERTAKERS
63	Pye 7N 15543	Everybody Loves A Lover/Mashed Potatoes	£25
63	Pye 7N 15562	What About Us/Money	£25
64	Pye 7N 15607	Just A Little Bit/Stupidity	£30

(see also 'Takers, Jackie Lomax)

UNDER THE SUN
79	Redball RR 010	UNDER THE SUN (LP)	£50

UNDER THE GUN
85	Under The Gun UTG1	Dance Of The Samurai/Traitor (fold-out sleeve)	£25

UNDER THE SKIN
75	Scotty SC 01	Shake It Girl/Lose The Image	£20

UNDERTONES
78	Good Vibrations GOT 4	TEENAGE KICKS (EP, white poster p/s)	£100

MINT VALUE £

78	Good Vibrations GOT 4	**TEENAGE KICKS** (EP, pink/yellow/blue p/s) **£70**
79	Sire SIR 4022	**Here Comes The Summer/One Way Love/Top 20** (mispressing, A side plays Tubeway Army's Are Friends Electric?) **£60**
79	No label	**CRACKS 90 MANAGEMENT EP: Teenage Kicks/Get Over You/Jimmy Jimmy/ Here Comes The Summer** (promo-only, numbered with typed insert, 250 only) **£60**
80	Sire SAM 120	**HYPNOTIZED APPETIZER** (6-track promn 12" EP b/w custom sleeve) **£40**
16	Salvo SALVOSV 013	**My Perfect Cousin/Hard Luck** (Again)**/I Don't Wanna See You Again** (magnet p/s, red vinyl, reissue) **£20**
79	Sire SRK 6071	**UNDERTONES** (LP, black & white cover, without "Teenage Kicks" & "Get Over You" & different version of "Here Comes The Summer" to reissue, inner) **£30**
80	Sire SRK 6088	**HYPNOTISED** (LP, with cardboard mobile) **£15**
83	Ardeck ARD 104	**THE SIN OF PRIDE** (LP, mispressing with different tracks: Bittersweet & "Stand So Close") **£40**
83	Ardeck ARD 1654283	**ALL WRAPPED UP** (LP, with free LP) **£20**
94	Dojo DOJOLP 192	**HYPNOTISED** (10" LP, numbered, 500 only) **£15**
94	Dojo DOJOLP 193	**POSITIVE TOUCH** (10" LP, numbered, 500 only) **£15**
94	Dojo DOJOLP 194	**THE SIN OF PRIDE** (10" LP, numbered, 500 only) **£15**

(see also Feargal Sharkey)

UNDERWORLD

92	Tomato PLUM 2001	**Mother Earth/Mother Earth** (FM Mix)**/The Hump/The Hump** (Groove Without A Doubt Mix) (12", p/s) **£60**
93	Boys Own BOIX 13	**Mmm... Skyscraper I Love You/Mmm... Skyscraper I Love You** (Telegraph 6.11.92)**/Mmm... Skyscraper I Love You** (Jam Scraper) (12", p/s) **£20**
93	Boys Own Collect 002P	**Rez/Cowgirl** (12", glossy pink sleeve, pink vinyl, white label) **£20**
94	Junior Boys Own JBO 19	**Dark & Long** (Dark Train Mix)**/**(Burts Mix) (12", p/s) **£15**
14	Universal UMC COLLECT 020	**Rez/Cowgirl** (Alt Cowgirl C69 Mix From A1564) (12", yellow vinyl, die-cut sleeve, postcard, edition of 1000) **£30**
15	Secret 7" S728	**Something Slippy** (Nuxx) (100 only, each with unique art sleeve) **£25**
18	Electronic Sound ES 41	**Puppies/Twenty Three Blue** (p/s) **£15**
22	Underworldlive.com UWR 00095	**And I Will Kiss/Caliban's Dream** (12", 10th anniversary pressing) **£15**
23	Underworldlive.com UWR00096	**And The Colour Red** (Club Mix) (12", single sided, 1000 copies only) **£30**
23	Underworldlive.com UWR00097	**Denver Luna/Denver Luna**(Acapella)**/Denver Luna**(Instrumental) (12", pink vinyl, limited to 1000 copies) **£60**
93	Junior Boy's Own JBOLP1	**DUBNOBASSWITHMYHEADMAN** (2-LP) **£50**
96	Junior Boy's Own jbolp4	**SECOND TOUGHEST IN THE INFANTS** (2-LP, gatefold, printed inners) **£40**
98	Simply Vinyl S160017	**DUBNOBASSWITHMYHEADMAN** (2-LP, reissue) **£25**
99	Junior Boy's Own JBO1005431	**BEAUCOUP FISH** (2LP, gatefold) **£30**
99	JBO JBO1005439	**BEAUCOUP FISH** (Minidisc) **£30**
02	Junior Boy's Own JBO 1020102	**A HUNDRED DAYS OFF** (2-LP, gatefold, inners) **£25**
03	Back To Mine BACKLP13	**BACK TO MINE** (3LP V/A curated by Underworld) **£40**
03	JBO JBO 1024691	**1992-2002** (4LP, box set, printed inners, posters) **£120**
07	PIAS 451.1081.012	**OBLIVION WITH BELLS** (2-LP, printed inners) **£60**
09	Underworldlive.com UWR00032-1	**BARKING** (2-LP, printed inners) **£30**
14	Universal UMC 379 079 5	**DUBNOBASSWITHMYHEADMAN** (2LP, reissue) **£35**
14	Universal UMC 3790796	**DUBNOBASSWITHMYHEADMAN** (5CD, box set, booklet) **£50**
15	Universal UMC uwr00054	**SECOND TOUGHEST IN THE INFANTS** (2-LP, reissue, gatefold, printed inners) **£40**
15	Universal Music Catalogue uwr00051	**SECOND TOUGHEST IN THE INFANTS** (5CD, box set, booklet) **£40**
16	Caroline International UWR00062	**BARBARA, BARBARA WE FACE A SHINING FUTURE** (LP, printed inner) **£30**
17	UMC UWR 00073	**BEAUCOUP FISH** (2LP, reissue) **£40**
17	UMC UWR 00074	**BEAUCOUP FISH** (4CD box set, booklet) **£35**
19	Caroline International UWR00089	**DRIFT SERIES 1 SAMPLER** (2-LP. gatefold, printed inners, yellow) **£15**
19	Caroline International UWR 00087	**DRIFT SERIES 1** (7CD, 1 BD, box set, book) **£80**

(see also Lemon Interrupt, Underworld & Iggy Pop, Karl Hyde)

UNDERWORLD & IGGY POP

18	Caroline International UWIP002X	**TEATIME DUB ENCOUNTERS** (LP/EP, printed inners, clear vinyl) **£15**

(see also Underworld, Iggy Pop)

UNDISPUTED TRUTH

71	Parlophone TMG 776	**Save My Love For A Rainy Day/Since I Lost You** (mispress on Parlophone) **£60**
71	Tamla Motown TMG 789	**Smiling Faces Sometimes/You Got The Love I Need** **£18**
72	Tamla Motown STMA 8004	**FACE TO FACE WITH THE TRUTH** (LP) **£30**
72	Tamla Motown STML 11197	**THE UNDISPUTED TRUTH** (LP) **£30**
73	Tamla Motown STML 11240	**THE LAW OF THE LAND** (LP) **£30**
75	Tamla Motown STML 11277	**DOWN TO EARTH** (LP) **£20**
75	Tamla Motown STMA 8023	**COSMIC TRUTH** (LP) **£20**
75	Tamla Motown STML 12009	**HIGHER THAN HIGH** (LP) **£20**
76	Whitfield K 56289	**METHOD TO THE MADNESS** (LP) **£20**
79	Whitfield K 56497	**SMOKIN** (LP) **£20**

UNEXPLORED BEATS

95	Unexplored Beats UXB 001	**Skool Beats/Inner Life** (12") **£30**

(see also Black Dog)

CHARLIE UNGRY

80	Charlie Ungry CU 001	**House On Chester Road/Pleacher/Who Is My Killer** **£60**

UNICORN (1)
70	Hollick & Taylor HT 1258	Going Home/Another World	£300

UNICORN (2)
71	Transatlantic TRA 238	UPHILL ALL THE WAY (LP, gatefold, plastic inner)	£35
74	Charisma CAS 1092	BLUE PINE TREES (LP, small 'Mad Hatter' logo, Charisma house inner))	£20
76	Harvest SHSP 4054	TOO MANY CROOKS (LP, inner sleeve, EMI logo on label)	£15

UNIQUE (2)
08	Diggers With Gratitude DWG 003	THE DIE HARD (EP)	£120

UNIQUES (FEATURING JOE STAMPLEY) (U.S)
65	Pye International 7N 25303	Not Too Long Ago/Fast Way Of Living	£30
65	Pye International 7N 25303	Not Too Long Ago/Fast Way Of Living (DJ copy)	£50
66	Pye Intl. NPL 28094	UNIQUELY YOURS (LP)	£120

UNIQUES (JAMAICA)
67	Collins Downbeat CR 002	Dry The Water/I'm A Fool For You	£65
67	Island WI 3070	People Rock Steady/I'm Trying To Find A Home (credited to Roy Shirley)	£140
67	Island WI 3084	Gypsy Woman/KEN ROSS: Wall Flower	£130
67	Island WI 3086	Let Me Go Girl/SOULETTES: Dum Dum	£60
68	Island WI 3087	Never Let Me Go/DON LEE: Lee's Special	£40
68	Island WI 3106	Speak No Evil/GLEN ADAMS: That New Girl	£65
68	Island WI 3107	Lesson Of Love/DELROY WILSON: Til I Die	£80
68	Island WI 3114	Build My World Around You/LLOYD CLARKE: I'll Never Change	£70
68	Island WI 3117	Give Me Some More Of Your Loving/VAL BENNETT: Lovell's Special	£60
68	Island WI 3122	My Conversation/SLIM SMITH: Love One Another	£70
68	Island WI 3123	The Beatitude/KEITH BLAKE: Time On The River (actually "Time & The River")	£80
68	Island WI 3145	Girl Of My Dreams/LESTER STERLING: Tribute To King Scratch	£75
68	Trojan TR 619	Watch This Sound/Out Of Love	£40
68	Trojan TR 645	A-Yuh/Just A Mirage	£120
68	Blue Cat BS 126	Girls Like Dirt/ALVA LEWIS: She Is Leaving	£80
69	Gas GAS 117	Too Proud To Beg/Love And Devotion	£40
69	Nu Beat NB 034	Crimson And Clover/What A Situation	£75
69	Nu Beat NB 037	I'll Make You Love Me/Lover's Prayer	£50
69	Unity UN 527	The Beatitude/My Conversation	£45
69	Trojan TRL 15	ABSOLUTELY THE UNIQUES (LP)	£150
79	Plant PLAN 10002	GIVE THANKS (LP)	£30
78	Third World TWS 935	UNIQUE SHOWCASE VOLUME ONE (LP)	£35

(see also Slim Smith, Melodians, Lloyd Charmers, Tommy McCook)

UNIT 4 + 2
64	Decca F 11821	The Green Fields/Swing Down Chariot	£15
67	Fontana TF 834	Too Fast, Too Slow/Booby Trap	£20
67	Fontana TF 840	Butterfly/A Place To Go	£15
67	Fontana TF 891	Loving Takes A Little Understanding/Would You Believe What I Say? (as Unit)	£200
68	Fontana TF 931	You Ain't Goin' Nowhere/So You Want To Be A Blues Player	£15
69	Fontana TF 990	I Will/3.30	£50
65	Decca DFE 8619	UNIT 4 + 2 (EP)	£60
65	Decca LK 4697	UNIT 4 + 2 - 1st ALBUM (LP)	£60
69	Fontana SFL 13123	UNIT 4 + 2 (LP)	£50
76	Decca REM 6	REMEMBERING (LP)	£15

(see also Roulettes, Capability Brown, Argent)

UNIT 19
67	Unit 19 19 1006	GI Blues/Sleep Perchance To Dream	£15

UNIT 1
94	Creative Wax CW 102	Theme/Your Mind/Arden (12")	£15
94	Creative Wax CW 104	Atlantic Drama/Love Me (12")	£15

UNITED FUTURE ORGANISATION
94	Talkin Loud 518 166-1	UNITED FUTURE ORGANISATION (2-LP)	£20
96	Talkin Loud 534 587-1	3RD PERSPECTIVE (2-LP, with free 12")	£20
99	Brownswood PHJR-10003/4	BON VOYAGE (2-LP)	£20

UNITED SONS OF AMERICA
71	Mercury 6338 036	GREETINGS FROM THE U.S. OF A. (LP)	£18

UNITED SOUNDS OF LONDON
94	USL USL 6	Making Love/Making Dub (12")	£15

UNITED STATES DOUBLE QUARTET
67	Stateside SS 590	Life Is Groovy/Split	£20
67	BT Puppy BTS 45524	Life Is Groovy/Split (reissue)	£15

(see also Tokens, Kirby Stone 4)

UNITED STATES OF AMERICA
68	CBS 3745	Garden Of Earthly Delights/Love Song For The Dead Che	£15
68	CBS (S) 63340	UNITED STATES OF AMERICA (LP, laminated cover, mono/stereo)	£60
87	Edsel ED 233	UNITED STATES OF AMERICA (LP, reissue)	£15

UNITY ALL STARS
75	Nice N 001	Africa/BIG DREAD & UNITY ALL STARS: Africa Is Our Home	£25

UNITY AND FIRE
88	Delicious WGO 101	I Know A Girl/Nothing Brings You Nothing (p/s)	£100

UNIVERSAL ENERGY
77 Harvest SHSP 4075 — UNIVERSAL ENERGY (LP) £20

UNIVERSAL INDICATOR
92 Rephlex TB-303 — 1-BLUE (12") £35
92 Rephlex TR-606 — 2-RED (12") £35
93 Rephlex MC-202 — 3-YELLOW (12") £30
95 Rephlex SH-101 — 4-GREEN (7", 10" + 12" in bag, all green vinyl) £100
(see also Kosmik Kommando)

UNIVERSAL ROBOT BAND
84 Streetwave MKHAN 48 — Barely Breaking Even (85 Club MIx)/Barely Breaking Even (Edit)/Barely Breaking Even (Instrumental) (12") £30

UNIVERSALS (1)
67 Page One POF 032 — I Can't Find You/Hey You £200
67 Page One POF 049 — Green Veined Orchid/While The Cat's Away £35
(see also Chris Lamb & Universals, Gidian, Lace, Gary Walker & Rain, Plastic Penny)

UNIVERSALS (2)
06 Funk 45 FUNK45 031 — New Generation/The Way A Girl Should Be (reissue) £30

UNIVERSE
84 MBT U1107 — Every Single Night/(Instrumental) £15
84 MBT U1112 — Every Single Night/(Instrumental) (12") £20

U.N.K.L.E.
95 Mo Wax MW 028 — THE TIME HAS COME EP (2 x 12" EP, picture disc)................................£15
98 Mo Wax MW 085DJ — PSYENCE FICTION SURVIVAL KIT (promo, 12" in pop-up gatefold p/s, 5" vinyl single in envelope, bag of stickers, press release, all in box mailer, 700 only).....................£35
98 Mo Wax 085 — PSYENCE FICTION (2-LP) £25
98 Mo Wax 085 — PSYENCE FICTION (2-LP, hardcover gatefold sleeve with booklet) £40
03 Mo Wax MWU 001 — NEVER NEVER LAND (3-LP, gatefold sleeve) £18
03 Mo Wax MWU 001 — NEVER NEVER LAND (3-LP, picture discs, gatefold sleeve, foldout inserts) £20
07 Surrender ALL SURR LPXX — WAR STORIES (2-LP, gatefold sleeve) £15
07 Surrender ALL SURR LPXX — WAR STORIES (4x12", gatefold sleeve in slipcase with book)....£25
10 Surrender ALL SURR 017 LP — WHERE DID THE NIGHT FALL (3-LP box set with two books)....£250
11 Vinyl Factory VF 029 — THE HERETIC'S GATE SCORE (with Doug Foster) (1-sided LP, orange vinyl, sleeve signed and numbered by James Lavelle and Doug Foster, 100 only) £120
(see also DJ Shadow)

UNLEASHED
03 Century Media 77544-0 — AND WE SHALL TRIUMPH IN VICTORY (Numbered box set with 6 picture discs LPs and booklet, 2000 only) £60

UNLIMITED TOUCH
83 Prelude PRL 25294 — YES, WE'RE READY (LP) £15

UNLIMITED SOURCE
82 Source SM003 — Down In The Cellar/Lemonade/Nicola Nicola (12") £60

UN PROJET
81 Rygel RY2 — Ki-Ak/Un Projet (p/s) £15

UNREST
92 Guernica GU1 LP — IMPERIAL F.F.R.R. (LP, with free 7") £15
93 4AD CAD 3012 — PERFECT TEETH (LP) £15

UNSEEN TERROR
87 Earache MOSH 4 — HUMAN ERROR (LP, inner)..£15

UNTAMED YOUTH
79 Hardcore HAR 001 — Untamed Youth/Runnin' Wild (p/s, 1,000 only) £15

UNTAMED (1)
64 Decca F 12045 — So Long/Just Wait...£70
65 Parlophone R 5258 — Once Upon A Time/I'm Asking You £100
65 Stateside SS 431 — I'll Go Crazy/My Baby Is Gone £70
66 Planet PLF 103 — It's Not True/Gimme Gimme Some Shade £100
(see also Lindsay Muir's Untamed)

UNTOUCHABLES (JAMAICA)
68 Blue Cat BS 137 — Prisoner In Love/EDWARD RAPHAEL: True Love £70
68 Trojan TR 613 — Tighten Up/ROY SHIRLEY: Good Ambition...£40
70 Upsetter US 345 — Same Thing All Over/UPSETTERS: It's Over £40
70 Upsetter US 350 — Knock On Wood/UPSETTERS: Tight Spot (featured Dave Barker - uncredited) £200
71 Bullet BU 460 — Can't Reach You/CARL DAWKINS: Natural Woman £22
73 Bread BR 1113 — Pay For The Wicked/Pay For The Wicked - Version (actually titled "Pray For The Wicked') £30
79 Sagittarius SUS 10 — Help Us Jah/Sea Of Love (12") £20
03 Trojan TGSe 008 — Tighten Up/ROY SHIRLEY: Good Ambition (reissue).............................£18
(see also Inspirations, Dave Barker, Leroy Reid)

UNWANTED
77 Raw RAW 6 — Withdrawal/1978/Bleak Outlook (p/s)..£40
77 Raw RAWT 6 — Withdrawal/1978/Bleak Outlook (12", reissue) £20
78 Raw RAW 15 — Secret Police/These Boots Are Made For Walking (p/s)...............................£20
78 Raw RAW 30 — Memory Man/Guns Of Love (unissued)...£0
85 Delorian No One — SECRET PAST (LP) £15
(see also Psychedelic Furs)

UPBEATS
58	London HLU 8688	Just Like In The Movies/My Foolish Heart	£25
58	London HLU 8688	Just Like In The Movies/My Foolish Heart (78)	£15
59	Pye International 7N 25016	You're The One I Care For/Keep Cool Crazy Heart	£15
59	Pye International 7N 25028	Teenie Weenie Bikini/Satin Shoes	£15

PHIL UPCHURCH COMBO
61	HMV POP 899	You Can't Sit Down Parts 1 & 2	£35
66	Sue WI 4005	You Can't Sit Down Parts 1 & 2 (reissue)	£30
66	Sue WI 4017	Nothing But Soul/Evad	£40
72	Blue Thumb ILPS 9219	DARKNESS, DARKNESS (LP)	£20

UPCOMING WILLOWS
65	Island WI 182	Jonestown Special/SHENLEY DUFFAS: La La La	£40
65	Island WI 184	Red China/SHENLEY DUFFAS: You Are Mine	£50

(see also Shenley Duffas)

UPP
75	Epic EPC 80625	UPP (LP)	£15

(see also Clark-Hutchinson)

UPRISING
79	Tribesman TM 11	Come On Over/Try Me Girl (12")	£18

UPROAR
80s	Beat The System BTSLP 1	AND THE LORD SAID LET THERE BE UPROAR (LP)	£30

UPSETTERS (1)
65	Island WI 223	Country Girl/Strange Country (both sides actually by Ossie & Upsetters)	£35
65	Rio R 70	Walk Down The Aisle/So Bad	£40
66	Doctor Bird DB 1034	Wildcat/I Love You So	£40

(see also Ossie & Upsetters, Dave Barker)

UPSETTERS (2)
69	Duke DU 11	Eight For Eight/Stand By Me (B-side actually by Inspirations)	£55
69	Camel CA 13	Taste Of Killing/My Mob	£75
69	Punch PH 18	Return Of The Ugly/I've Caught You	£30
69	Punch PH 19	Dry Acid/REGGAE BOYS: Selassie	£60
69	Punch PH 21	Clint Eastwood/Lenox Mood	£20
69	Upsetter US 300	Eight For Eight/You Know What I Mean (B-side actually by Inspirations)	£40
69	Upsetter UP 301	Return Of Django/Dollar In The Teeth	£15
69	Upsetter US 303	Ten To Twelve/LEE PERRY: People Funny Fi True	£50
69	Upsetter US 305	Farmers In The Den/BUSTY BROWN : To Love Somebody	£65
69	Upsetter US 307	Night Doctor/TERMITES: I'll Be Waiting	£40
69	Upsetter US 309	Kiddyo/Endlessly (both sides actually by Silvertones)	£25
69	Upsetter US 310	Man From MI5/WEST INDIANS: Oh Lord	£55
69	Upsetter US 313	Live Injection/BLEECHERS: Everything For Fun	£40
70	Upsetter US 317	Vampire/BLEECHERS: Check Him Out (early copies with B-side listed as UPSETTERS worth £80)	£45
69	Upsetter US 315	Cold Sweat/Pound Get A Blow (B-side actually by Bleechers)	£60
70	Upsetter US 318	Soulful I/MILTON HENRY: Bread And Butter	£40
70	Upsetter US 321	Drugs And Poison/Stranger On The Shore	£30
70	Upsetter US 325	Kill Them All/Soul Walk	£45
70	Upsetter US 326	Bronco Ol' Man River/One Punch	£30
70	Upsetter US 331	Shocks A Mighty/DAVE BARKER: Set Me Free	£25
70	Upsetter US 332	Na Na Hey Hey/Pick Folk Kinkiest	£35
70	Upsetter US 333	Granny Show/Version	£30
70	Upsetter US 334	Fire Fire/Jumper	£75
70	Upsetter US 335	The Pillow/Grooving	£25
70	Upsetter US 336	Self Control/The Pill	£22
70	Upsetter US 338	Fresh Up/Toothaches	£60
70	Upsetter US 339	The Thanks We Get/Hurry Up	£40
70	Upsetter US 342	Dreamland/Version Of Cup (possibly unreleased)	£45
70	Upsetter US 343	Sipreano/Ferry Boat	£65
70	Upsetter US 346	Bigger Joke/Return Of The Vampire	£60
70	Upsetter US 349	Upsetting Station (actually plays "Did Your Grave" by Bob Marley & Wailers)/UPSETTERS: Justice (Instrumental)	£40
70	Upsetter US 352	Heart And Soul/Zig Zag	£70
70	Spinning Wheel SW 100	Haunted House/Double Wheel (beware of reissues with darker purple on labels)	£160
70	Spinning Wheel SW 101	The Miser/CHUCK JUNIOR: Do It Madly	£50
70	Spinning Wheel SW 102	The Chokin' Kind/CHUCK JUNIOR: Penny Wise	£150
70	Spinning Wheel SW 103	Land Of Kinks/O'NEIL HALL: This Man	£110
70	Trojan TR 7748	Family Man/Mellow Mood	£30
70	Trojan TR 7749	Capo/Mama Look	£45
70	Punch PH 27	The Result/Feel The Spirit	£80
71	Bullet BU 461	All Combine Parts 1 & 2	£18
71	Upsetter US 361	Capasetic (actually "Copasetic" by Lord Comic)/All Africans (actually "Don't Cross The Nation" by Little Roy)	£25
71	Upsetter US 365	Earthquake/JUNIOR BYLES: Palace Called Africa	£30
71	Upsetter US 370	Dark Moon/DAVID ISAACS: You'll Be Sorry	£25
72	Upsetter US 387	Festival Da-Da/JUNIOR BYLES: Version	£25
72	Upsetter US 393	Crummy People/BIG YOUTH: Moving - Version	£35
72	Upsetter US 394	Water Pump Parts 1 & 2	£15
73	Upsetter US 396	Puss See Hole/WINSTON GROOVY: Want To Be Loved	£15

73	Upsetter US 397	Jungle Lion/Freak Out Skank	£120
73	Upsetter US 398	Cow Thief Skank (with Charlie Ace)/7 3/4 Skank	£45
73	Downtown DT 499	Black Ipa/Ipa Skank	£35
73	Downtown DT 506	Sunshine Showdown/Sunshine Version	£40
73	Downtown DT 512	Tighten Up Skank/Mid-East Rock (vocals by Dillinger)	£125
73	Downtown DT 513	Bucky Skank/Yucky Skank	£70
74	Count Shelly CS 052	San-San/OSBOURNE GRAHAM: Baby Don't Go	£15
74	Dip DL 5031	Enter The Dragon/JOY WHITE: Lady Lady	£15
74	Dip DL 5032	Rebels Train/Rebels Dub	£25
75	Dip DL 5054	Cane River Rock/Riverside Rock	£35
75	Dip DL 5056	I Man Free/King Burnett: Version	£35
75	Dip DL 5073	Key Card/Domino Game	£20
75	Angen ANG 107	Stay Dread/Kingdom Of Dub	£25
75	Attack ATT 8090	Kiss Me Neck/Da Ba Day	£35
78	Island IPR 2010	Close Together/Dreadlocks In The Moonlight (12" as UPSETTER REVIEW featuring JUNIOR MURVIN)	£20
69	Pama Special PSP 1014	CLINT EASTWOOD (LP)	£100
69	Trojan TTL 13	THE UPSETTER (LP)	£50
69	Trojan TRL 19	THE RETURN OF DJANGO (LP, orange/white label)	£80
70	Trojan TTL 28	SCRATCH THE UPSETTER AGAIN (LP)	£55
70	Trojan TBL 119	THE GOOD, THE BAD AND THE UPSETTERS (LP)	£55
70	Trojan TBL 125	EASTWOOD RIDES AGAIN (LP)	£120
70	Pama SECO 24	THE MANY MOODS OF THE UPSETTERS (LP)	£100
74	Trojan TRLS 70	DOUBLE SEVEN (LP, black sticker on rear cover showing song titles and marketed by B & C Records	£75
75	DIP DLPD 6002	RETURN OF WAX (LP, label says "Upsetters" in red print, plain sleeve)	£300
76	Island ILPS 9417	SUPER APE (LP)	£65
90	Trojan PERRY 3	BUILD THE ARK (3-LP box set)	£40
99	Simply Vinyl SVLP 098	SUPER APE (LP, reissue, 180gm vinyl)	£20

(see also Lee Perry, Ossie & Upsetters, Hippy Boys, Bob Marley/Wailers, Family Man, Tommy McCook, Max Romeo, Melodians, Lord Creator, Dennis Alcapone)

UPTOWNERS
64	London HLU 9877	If'n/Search Is Over	£15

URBAN CLEARWAY (1)
70	Torpedo TOR 21	Open Up Wide Parts 1 & 2	£20

URBAN CLEARWAY (2)
82	Bandit X 82 CUS 1609	Lost Memories/You've Always Known (12", p/s)	£100

URBAN DISTURBANCE
79	Rok ROK V/VI	Wild Boys In Cortinas/V.I.P.s: Can't Let You Go (die-cut sleeve)	£25

URBAN DOGS
88	Fallout FALL LP 12	URBAN DOGS (LP)	£18

(see Hanoi Rocks, U.K. Subs, Vibrators)

URBAN MYTHS
98	Urban Myths MYTH 1	Lose You/Lose You (Dub)//Makin' Me Feel/No Man (12")	£20

URBAN TRIBE
92	Sub Assertive CUE 6	THE UNKNOWN EP (12", white label)	£20

URCHIN
77	DJM DJS 10776	Black Leather Fantasy/Rock & Roll Woman (in promo p/s)	£275
77	DJM DJS 10776	Black Leather Fantasy/Rock & Roll Woman (no p/s)	£100
78	DJM DJS 10850	She's A Roller/Long Time No Woman (in promo p/s)	£275
79	DJM DJS 10850	She's A Roller/Long Time No Woman (no p/s)	£100

(see also Iron Maiden)

URGENT CRUNCH
81	NYECK NECK 1	Listen To Silence/Trust (p/s)	£30

URIAH HEEP
76	Bronze BRODJ 1	One Way Or Another/Misty Eyes (promo only p/s, 750 copies)	£20
70	Vertigo 6360 006	VERY 'EAVY... VERY 'UMBLE (1st pressing, LP, gatefold sleeve, large swirl label. Matrixes: 1Y//1 420 113/2Y//1 420 111)	£400
71	Vertigo 6360 028	SALISBURY (LP, gatefold sleeve, large swirl label)	£400
71	Vertigo 6360 006	VERY 'EAVY... VERY 'UMBLE (2nd pressing, LP, reissue, Matrix 1Y//1 420 1 1 9/2Y//1 420 111)	£80
71	Bronze ILPS 9152	SALISBURY (LP, reissue, with 'Howards Printers (Slough) Ltd' printers credit)	£30
71	Bronze ILPS 9169	LOOK AT YOURSELF (LP, 'mirror' sleeve, inner sleeve)	£250
72	Bronze ILPS 9193	DEMONS AND WIZARDS (LP, gatefold, lyric inner)	£80
72	Island ILPS 9213	THE MAGICIAN'S BIRTHDAY (LP, gatefold with inner sleeve, abandoned Island pressing with pink rim palm tree label, with 'Bronze' records hand-written half-paste on label)	£200
72	Bronze ILPS 9213	MAGICIAN'S BIRTHDAY (LP, gatefold with inner sleeve)	£75
72	Vertigo 6360 006	VERY 'EAVY... VERY 'UMBLE (3rd pressing, LP, gatefold sleeve, small 'swirl' and 'Vertigo' above centre label)	£30
72	Bronze ILPS 9142	VERY 'EAVY... VERY 'UMBLE (LP, reissue, sleeve printed by 'Howards Printers (Slough) Ltd')	£25
73	Bronze ILPS 9245	SWEET FREEDOM (LP, gatefold with extra page)	£150
73	Bronze ISLD 1	LIVE (2-LP, laminated gatefold sleeve with booklet and inners)	£30
74	Island ILPS 9142	VERY 'EAVY... VERY 'UMBLE (LP, reissue, pink rim palm tree label)	£20
74	Bronze ILPS 9280	WONDERWORLD (LP, inner)	£20
75	Bronze ILPS 9335	RETURN TO FANTASY (LP, gatefold sleeve)	£50
76	Bronze ILPS 9384	HIGH AND MIGHTY (LP)	£50
77	Bronze ILPS 9193	DEMONS AND WIZARDS (LP, reissue, no insert)	£20

Rene URTREGER

77	Bronze BRON 504	**INNOCENT VICTIM** (LP)	£15
77	Bronze ILPS 9483	**FIREFLY** (LP)	£60
78	Bronze BRNA 512	**FALLEN ANGEL** (LP, gatefold)	£25
80	Bronze BRONX 524	**CONQUEST** (LP)	£30
91	Legacy LLP 37	**DIFFERENT WORLD** (LP)	£40
97	Castle ORR LP 003	**DEMONS AND WIZARDS** (LP, reissue, insert)	£18
95	HTD LP 33	**SEA OF LIGHT** (2-LP, with inner)	£35

(see also Gods, Head Machine, Natural Gas, Spice, King Crimson, John Lawton, Grand Prix, Stratus)

RENE URTREGER
56	Felsted ESD 3027	**SALUTE TO BUD POWELL** (EP)	£15
56	Felsted EDL 87020	**PLAYS BUD POWELL** (10" LP)	£30

U.S. T-BONES
66	Liberty LIB 55867	**Sippin'n'Chippin'/Moment Of Softness**	£15
66	Liberty LIB 55951	**The Proper Thing To Do/Tee-Hee-Hee**	£15

US & THEM
11	Fruits De Mer Crustacean 20	**Summerisle Songs From The Wicker Man** (1st press, white vinyl, folded white p/s, insert)	£20
11	Fruits De Mer Crustacean 20	**Summerisle Songs From The Wicker Man** (Repressing, orange/yellow vinyl, folded p/s, insert)	£15

USELESS UNICORN
74	Horny HORN 11	**RUBBER HORN** (LP, gatefold sleeve, with pop-up horn)	£15

USERS
77	Raw RAW 1	**Sick Of You/(I'm) In Love With Today** (p/s, numbered on rear, 2500 only)	£30
77	Raw RAW 1	**Sick Of You/(I'm) In Love With Today** (p/s, 2nd pressing, 5000 copies)	£15
77	Raw RAWT 1	**Sick Of You/(I'm) In Love With Today** (12", no p/s)	£15
78	Warped WARP 1	**Warped 45: Kicks In Style/Dead On Arrival** (p/s, 5,000 only, numbered sleeve, some un-numbered)	£30

UT
87	Blast First BFFP 12	**EARLY LIVE LIFE** (LP)	£15
87	Blast First BFFP 17	**IN GUT'S HOUSE** (LP, 2 x 12")	£15

UTOMICA
93	Pro-One PRONE 9T	**Rok A Bye/Rok A Bye** (12", stamped or hand-written white label)	£50
93	Pro-One PRONE 11T	**Pumpkin/Pumpkin** (12", white stamped label)	£15

UTOPIA (GERMANY)
73	United Artists UAG 29438	**UTOPIA** (LP)	£35

(see also Amon Duull)

UTOPIA (U.S.)
82	Epic EPC 25207	**UTOPIA** (LP, with free 5-track EP)	£20

(see also Todd Rundgren)

U-TURN
81	Epigram 001	**U-TURN EP** (detergent shaped sleeve)	£20

U2
SINGLES : SINGLES: IRISH PRESSINGS
79	CBS 7951	**U2: THREE** (Out Of Control/Stories For The Boys/Boy-Girl) (p/s, black vinyl) (CBS 'Sunburst Label' with UK TM NoB81 809) **on label** (1st Pressing)	£150
79	CBS 7951	**U2: THREE** (Out Of Control/Stories For The Boys/Boy-Girl) (p/s, black vinyl)	£50
80	CBS 7951	**U2: THREE** (Out Of Control/Stories For The Boys/Boy-Girl) (p/s, orange vinyl)	£150
80	CBS 7951	**U2: THREE** (Out Of Control/Stories For The Boys/Boy-Girl) (p/s, white vinyl)	£300
80	CBS 7951	**U2: THREE** (Out Of Control/Stories For The Boys/Boy-Girl) (p/s, yellow vinyl)	£100
80	CBS 7951	**U2: THREE** (Out Of Control/Stories For The Boys/Boy-Girl) (p/s, brown vinyl mispressing, fewer than 50 copies exist)	£1000
80	CBS 8306	**Another Day/Twilight** (Demo Version) (p/s, yellow vinyl)	£80
80	CBS 8306	**Another Day/Twilight** (Demo Version) (p/s, orange vinyl)	£150
80	CBS 8306	**Another Day/Twilight** (Demo Version) (p/s, white vinyl)	£350
80	CBS 8306	**Another Day/Twilight** (Demo Version) (p/s, black vinyl, with postcard designed by Bono)	£200
80	CBS 8306	**Another Day/Twilight** (Demo Version) (p/s, black vinyl, without postcard designed by Bono)	£40
80	CBS 8687	**11 O'Clock Tick Tock/Touch** (p/s, yellow vinyl)	£60
80	CBS 8687	**11 O'Clock Tick Tock/Touch** (p/s, orange vinyl)	£150
80	CBS 9065	**I Will Follow/Boy-Girl** (live) (p/s, yellow vinyl)	£50
80	CBS 9065	**I Will Follow/Boy-Girl** (live) (p/s, orange vinyl)	£100
80	CBS 9065	**I Will Follow/Boy-Girl** (live) (p/s, white vinyl)	£300
80	CBS 9065	**I Will Follow/Boy-Girl** (live) (p/s, brown vinyl, fewer than 50 copies)	£1500
81	CBS 12-7951	**U2: THREE** (12" EP, with numbered sticker, orange CBS sleeve, 1,000 only)	£2000
81	CBS 12-7951	**U2: THREE** (12" EP, reissue, die-cut CBS sleeve)	£60
81	CBS 12-7951	**U2: THREE** (12" EP, 2nd reissue, plain black sleeve, slightly different labels)	£40
82	CBS PAC 1	**4 U2 PLAY** (4 x 7", each in p/s, black vinyl)	£120
82	CBS PAC 1	**4 U2 PLAY** (4 x 7", each in p/s, yellow vinyl)	£300
82	CBS PAC 1	**4 U2 PLAY** (4 x 7", each in p/s, orange vinyl)	£600
82	CBS PAC 1	**4 U2 PLAY** (4 x 7", each in p/s, white vinyl)	£1000
85	CBS 40-7951	**U2: THREE** (cassette, reissue)	£50
80s	CBS PAC 2	**PAC 2** (4 x 7" with p/s in plastic wallet)	£60
80s	CBS PAC 3	**PAC 3** (4 x 7" with p/s in plastic wallet)	£50

SINGLES : SINGLES: UK PRESSINGS
80	Island WIP 6601	**11 O'Clock Tick Tock/Touch** (p/s)	£25

80	Island WIP 6630	A Day Without Me/Things To Make And Do (p/s)	£20
80	Island WIP 6656	I Will Follow/Boy-Girl (live) (p/s)	£15
84	Island ISP 202	Pride (In The Name Of Love)/Boomerang 2 (Vocal) (picture disc)	£20
85	Island ISP 220	The Unforgettable Fire/A Sort Of Homecoming (live) (Uncut, logo-shaped pic disc)	£600
85	Island ISP 220	The Unforgettable Fire/A Sort Of Homecoming (live) (logo-shaped pic disc)	£45
87	Island 12IS 340	Where The Streets Have No Name/Race Against Time/Silver And Gold/ The Sweetest Thing (12", p/s with "Silver And Gold" lyric insert)	£15
88	Island U2 PK 1	THE JOSHUA TREE SINGLES (4 x 7"s in PVC wallet with 'obi' band)	£40
89	Island CIDP 411	When Love Comes To Town/Dancing Barefoot/When Love Comes To Town (Live From The Kingdom Mix) (with BB King)/God Part II (The Hard Metal Dance Mix) (CD picture disc)	£15
89	Island ISB 422	All I Want Is You (Edit)/Unchained Melody (in numbered tin box)	£18
89	Island 12 ISB 422	All I Want Is You (Full Version)/Unchained Melody/Everlasting Love (12", p/s, box set with 4 prints)	£15
89	Island CIDP 422	All I Want Is You (4.14)/Unchained Melody/Everlasting Love/ All I Want Is You (Full Version) (CD, picture disc)	£15
91	Island 12IS 509	Mysterious Ways (4.04)/(Solar Plexus Extended Club Mix 7.01)/ (Apollo 440 Magic Hour Remix)/(Tabla Motown Remix)/(Solar Plexus Club Mix) (12" p/s, withdrawn)	£15
92	Island 12IS 525	Even Better Than The Real Thing/Salomé/Where Did It All Go Wrong/ Lady With The Spinning Head (UVI) (Extended Dance Mix) (12" with giant 'Zoo TV' poster)	£20
17	Third Man TMR 522	The Blackout/Jacknife Lee Remix (12", black and white vinyl, 750 worldwide, RSD)	£300
22	Island/UMC 3869295	A Celebration/A Celebration (Studio Out-Take)/Trash, Trampoline And The Party Girl/ Trash, Trampoline And The Party Girl (Live Köln 2015) (12", p/s, RSD)	£20
23	Island 5863778	Atomic City (single sided 7", p/s, luminous vinyl)	£15
24	Island 5892453	Atomic City (Live at Sphere, Las Vegas)/Atomic City (Mike Will Made-It Remix) (10", red vinyl, RSD)	£25

ALBUMS

80	Island ILPS 9646	BOY (LP)	£20
81	Island ILPS 9680	OCTOBER (LP)	£20
83	Island PILPS 9733	WAR (LP, picture disc, beware of counterfeits with ILPS cat. no.)	£100
85	Island CID 112	WAR (CD, pink cover lettering, no bar code)	£25
85	Island CID 102	THE UNFORGETTABLE FIRE (CD, no bar code)	£30
87	Island U2 6	THE JOSHUA TREE (LP, gatefold, insert)	£25
88	Island U27	RATTLE AND HUM (LP)	£18
91	Island U2-8	ACHTUNG BABY (LP, inner sleeve, lyric insert, 10 art prints)	£50
93	Island U2-9	ZOOROPA (LP, inner sleeve, lyric insert)	£80
97	Island U2 10	POP (2-LP, gatefold sleeve, insert, stickered sleeve)	£70
98	Island U2 11	THE BEST OF 1980-1990 (2-LP, gatefold sleeve)	£80
00	Island U2 12	ALL THAT YOU CAN'T LEAVE BEHIND (LP, with booklet)	£70
02	Island U2 13	THE BEST OF 1990-2000 (2-LP, gatefold)	£50
04	Island U2 14	HOW TO DISMANTLE AN ATOMIC BOMB (LP, with booklet)	£50
09	Island 1796038	NO LINE ON THE HORIZON (2-LP)	£30
06	Mercury U2 18	18 SINGLES (2-LP)	£40
11	Mercury 00602527788333	ACHTUNG BABY (2LP/ 6CD/4DVD, 5x7" 20th anniversary 'uber deluxe' box set, booklet, ephemera, magnetic tile cover)	£400
11	Mercury 602527788272	ACHTUNG BABY (2LP/2x blue vinyl 12" box set, 20th Anniversary Edition, booklet)	£150
14	Island 4704888	SONGS OF INNOCENCE (2LP, gatefold, printed inners, white vinyl)	£30
15	Island B0022855-01	SONGS OF INNOCENCE (2LP, 5000, numbered, RSD)	£150
17	Island 5797705	SONGS OF EXPERIENCE (2LP/CD box set, additional tracks, poster, newspaper)	£30
17	Island 5797704	SONGS OF EXPERIENCE (2LP, gatefold, insert, cyan vinyl, 180g)	£25
21	Island/UMC U28AB30	ACHTUNG BABY (2LP, 30th Anniversary edition, red/blue vinyl, alternate artwork, poster, ltd. ed., numbered, four cover variants)	£100
23	Island 00602445495580	SONGS OF SURRENDER (4LP box set, lyric booklets, limited edition)	£60
23	Island 5503418	SONGS OF SURRENDER (2LP, purple haze vinyl, gatefold, limited)	£50

PROMOS : PROMOS - SINGLES

80	Island WIP 6601	11 O'Clock Tick Tock/Touch (p/s, 'A' label)	£50
80	Island WIP 6630	A Day Without Me/Things To Make And Do (p/s, 'A' label)	£50
80	Island WIP 6656 DJ	I Will Follow (Special Edited DJ Version) (1-sided, company sleeve)	£80
81	WIP 6679	Fire (Radio Edit) (1-sided, p/s)	£70
81	WIP 6733	Gloria (Radio Edit) (1-sided, p/s)	£60
84	Island U2 2	Wire/Bad/The Unforgettable Fire (12", black die-cut sleeve)	£70
87	Island ISJ 328	I Still Haven't Found What I'm Looking For/Spanish Eyes (jukebox issue, solid centre)	£20
88	Island 12ISX 400	Desire (9.23 Hollywood Remix) (12", 1-sided, custom black p/s, 800 only)	£25
88	Island U2V 7	EXCERPTS FROM RATTLE AND HUM (In God's Country [live]/Hawkmoon 269/ Bad [live]/God Part II/With Or Without You [live]) (CD, card gatefold sleeve)	£70
88	Island IS 319	With Or Without You/Luminous Times (Hold Onto Love)/Walk To The Water/ With Or Without You (Video) (CD Video, withdrawn, less than 100 copies)	£350
89	Island 12 ISX 411	U2 3D DANCE MIXES: When Love Comes To Town (Live From The Kingdom Dance Mix)/God Part II (Hard Metal Dance Club Mix)/Desire (Hollywood Remix 5.23) (12" EP p/s)	£25
90	Island RHB 1	Night And Day (Twilight Remix)/Steel String Mix) (12", p/s, numbered, 4,000 copies only)	£50
91	Island U2-3	OCTOBER 1991: I Will Follow/Pride (In The Name Of Love)/God Part II/ Where The Streets Have No Name) (CD EP, 250 only)	£400
92	Island 12IS 550DJ	Salomé (Zooromancer Remix 8.02)/Can't Help Falling In Love (Mystery Train Dub 8.20) (12", black die-cut sleeve, 1,000 only)	£70
92	Island REAL 2DJ	Even Better Than The Real Thing (The Perfecto Mix-Radio Edit) (2-sided radio promo, some with p/s)	£40
92	Island REAL 2DJ	Even Better Than The Real Thing (The Perfecto Mix-Radio Edit) (2-sided radio promo, some with p/s)	£15
93	Island NUMCD 1	Numb (CD, 1-track, with lyric inner, 250 only)	£80
93	Island 12LEM DJ 1	Lemon (Bad Yard Club)/(Momo Beats)/(Version Dub)/(Serious Def Dub)// (Perfecto Mix)/(Trance Mix) (12", double pack, p/s, 1,000 only, numbered with press sheets)	£60

93	Island LEMCD 1	**Lemon** (Radio Edit) (CD, 1-track, with lyric inner)	**£30**
95	Island 12 MELON 1	**MELON** (Salomé [Zooromancer Remix]/Lemon [Bad Yard Club Mix]/ Numb [The Soul Assassins Mix]/Numb [Gimme Some More Dignity Mix]) (12" EP, 800 only)	**£20**
97	Island ISD(X) 649 D(J)	**Discothèque** (Howie B Hairy B Mix)/**Discothèque** (Hexidecimal Mix)// **Discothèque** (DM Deep Extended Club Mix)/**Discothèque** (DM Deep Beats Mix)/**Discotheque** (DM Tec Radio Mix)/**Discotheque** (DM Deep Instrumental Mix)/**Discotheque** (Single Version)/**Discotheque (David**	**£25**
97	Island 12IS 658DJ	**Staring At The Sun** (Monster Truck Mix)/**Staring At The Sun** (Lab Rat Mix)/ **Staring At The Sun** (Sad Bastard's Mix) (12", p/s)	**£20**
97	Island 12IS 664DJ	**Last Night On Earth** (First Night In Hell Remix)/**Happiness Is A Warm Gun** (The Gun Mix)/**Pop Muzik** (Pop Mart Mix)/**Happiness Is A Warm Gun** (The Danny Sabre Mix)/ (12" p/s)	**£20**
97	Island MUZIK 1	**Pop Muzik** (Pop Mart Mix - Radio Edit) (CD, 1-track, picture disc, jewel case, 250 only)	**£100**
97	Island MART 1	**Pop Muzik** (Pop Mart Mix)/**Last Night On Earth** (First Night In Hell Mix) (12", plain black die cut sleeve)	**£70**
97	Island ISJB 684	**If God Will Send His Angels** (Single Vesion)/**Sunday Bloody Sunday** (live from Sarajevo) (jukebox issue, large centre hole)	**£15**
97	Island 12MOFO 1	**Mofo** (Phunk Force Mix)/**Mofo** (Black Hole Dub)/**Mofo** (Romin Remix) (12", orange label, orange & silver die-cut title sleeve)	**£15**
97	Island 12MOFO 2	**Mofo** (Mother's Mix)/**Mofo** (House Flavor Mix)/**Mofo** (Romin Remix) (12", pink label, pink & silver die-cut title sleeve, 500 only)	**£15**
97	Island 12MOFO 3	**Mofo** (Explicit Mix) (12", 1-sided, stamped white label, plain black die-cut sleeve, 200 only)	**£50**
97	Island MOFOCD 1	**Mofo** (Album Version) (CD, 1-track, card sleeve, export issue [to Mexico])	**£80**
97	Island MOFOCD 2	**Mofo** (Phunk Force Mix) (CD, 1-track, jewel case, export issue [to Mexico])	**£60**
98	Island CIDDJ 727	**Sweetest Thing/Twilight** (Live)/**An Cat Dubh** (Live)/**Stories For Boys Out Of Control** (Live) (CD, die-cut sleeve)	**£50**
00	Island GROUND 1	**The Ground Beneath Her Feet** (1-sided promo)	**£100**
01	Island 12ISD 780	**Beautiful Day** (Quincy & Sonance Mix)/**Beautiful Day** (The Perfecto Mix)/(David Holmes Remix)/**Elevation** (The Vandit Club Mix)/(Influx Remix)/(Escalation Mix)/**Quincy & Sonance Remix**) (2x12", p/s, inners)	**£15**
00	Island 12 BEAUT 1	**Beautiful Day** (Quincey & Sonance Mix) (1-sided 12", in black die-cut title sleeve)	**£15**
01	Island 12 ELE 1	**Elevation** (Escalation Mix)/**Elevation** (Influx Mix) (12", red custom p/s, 250 only)	**£25**
02	Island 12REMIX U2 13	**U2 REMIXES FROM THE 1990S** (2 x 12" sampler, black inner sleeves, silver outer sleeve)	**£20**
02	Island CID 808	**Electrical Storm** (William Orbit Mix)/**New York** (Nice Mix)/**New York** (Nasty Mix)/ **Bad** (Live)/**Where The Streets Have No Name** (2-CD + DVD set in limited issue collectors' wallet, mail order only)	**£40**
03	Island 12 Sun U2	**Staring At The Sun** (Brothers In Rhythm Club Mix)/**Staring At The Sun** (Brothers In Rhythm Ambient Mix) (12", black die-cut custom sleeve)	**£15**
04	Island U2PRO2	**Vertigo** (Jacknife Lee 7" mix) (7" vinyl promo, picture sleeve. Matt/gloss finish)	**£50**
04	Island 10IS878DJ	**Vertigo** (Jacknife Lee 7" mix)/**Vertigo** (Jacknife Lee 10" mix) **10" vinyl p/s**	**£20**
04	Island CID878/X878/V878	**Vertigo** (CD1, CD2 & DVD set in wallet issued by U2.Com)	**£50**
05	Island CID886/X/V	**Sometimes You Can't Make It On Your Own** (CD1, CD2 & DVD set in wallet, issued by U2.com)	**£25**
05	Island CID890/X/V	**City Of Blinding Lights** (CD1, CD2 & DVD set in wallet via U2.com)	**£20**
05	Island CID906/X/V	**All Because Of You** (CD1, CD2 & DVD set in wallet in wallet via u2.com)	**£20**

PROMOS : PROMOS - ALBUMS

83	Island U2 1	**UNDER A BLOOD RED SKY - A DIALOGUE WITH U2 LIVE** (LP, custom sleeve, with cue sheet, numbered, 1,000 only)	**£75**
87	Island U2-6	**THE JOSHUA TREE** (CD, LP & cassette in black/gold 'pizza' box set)	**£250**
87	Island U2 6-1 - U2 6-5	**THE JOSHUA TREE COLLECTION** Red Hill Mining Town/Where The Streets Have No Name//Trip Through Your Wires/Running To Stand Still//I Still Haven't Found What I'm Looking For/One Tree Hill/Exit/Mothers Of The Disappeared/In God's Country/ Bullet The Blue Sky	**£500**
87	Island U2 6-1 - U2 6-5	**THE JOSHUA TREE COLLECTION** (5 x 7" black box set, with U2 6-1 mispressed with "Red Hill Mining Town" both sides, less than 50 copies)	**£1000**
87	Island U2CLP 1	**THE U2 TALKIE: A CONVERSATION WITH LARRY, BONO, ADAM & THE EDGE** (LP, music & interview with Dave Fanning for "The Joshua Tree")	**£30**
87	Island U2CC 1	**THE U2 TALKIE** (cassette)	**£20**
87	Island BOU2 1	**CASSETTE SAMPLER** (cassette, 17-track instore 'best of' compilation)	**£30**
88	Island U2-7	**RATTLE AND HUM** (CD, LP & cassette in flight case with leather tag, 250 only)	**£1000**
89	Island U2 2D1	**U2 2 DATE** (LP, 8-track hits compilation)	**£25**
91	Island U2-8	**ACHTUNG BABY** (CD, cassette in 'User's Kit', including map/poster, torch, key ring, spanner & screwdriver in printed green nylon kit bag)	**£500**
91	Island CIDDJ U2-8	**ACHTUNG** (graphics CD, in jewel case marked "promo only - not for sale")	**£100**
95	Island MELONCD 1	**MELON** (REMIXES FOR PROPAGANDA) (CD, 9-track compilation, card sleeve, fan club issue, 20,000 only; sealed with Propaganda No. 21)	**£50**
97	Island CID U2 10	**POP** (CD, in large cube-shaped picture box set, with prismatic pen & custom notepad)	**£200**
97	Island POP 1	**U2 TALK POP** (CD, interview with Dave Fanning, card sleeve)	**£50**
97	Island POP 2	**U2 TALK POP** (CD, interview with Dave Fanning, card sleeve, same tracks as POP 1)	**£50**
97	Island POP 3	**U2 TALK POP** (CD, interview with Dave Fanning, card sleeve, same as POP 1)	**£50**
98	Island CIDDU211	**THE BEST OF THE 'B' SIDES 1980-1990** (2-CD, discs marked 'A' and 'B', in card sleeves with gold slipcase)	**£50**
98	Island BXU2 11	**THE 'BEST OF' COLLECTION 1980-1990** (14 x 7" singles, 2-CDs, 16-page booklet, in gold box, 2000 copies only)	**£250**
00	Island CID U212	**ALL THAT YOU CAN'T LEAVE BEHIND** (promo pack, with 1-track CD Beautiful Day [BEAUT CD 1] in blue picture slipcase, booklet, window sticker, video tape, "playback" invitation in laminated picture bag with rope handles; with signed print)	**£600**
00	Island CID U212	**ALL THAT YOU CAN'T LEAVE BEHIND** (promo pack, with 1-track CD Beautiful Day [BEAUT CD 1] in blue picture slipcase, booklet, window sticker, video tape, "playback" invitation, in laminated picture bag with rope handles; without signed print)	**£200**
00	Island HASTACD 1	**HASTA LA VISTA BABY! LIVE FROM MEXICO CITY** (CD, fan-club only p/s)	**£50**
02	Island CIDDJ U2 13	**THE BEST OF THE B-SIDES OF 1990-2000** (2-CD set card sleeves in card wallet)	**£30**
02	Island BX U2 13	**THE BEST OF COLLECTION 1990-2000** (15 x 7", with 2 CDs & 16-page booklet in silver	**£200**

		fliptop card box)	
02	Island REMIXCD U2 13	**REMIXES FROM THE 90S** (2 x 12", promo p/s) **card wallet)**	**£20**
05	Island UCOMV1	**U2 COMMUNICATION** (CD & DVD fan club issue)	**£30**
06	Island U2.COM2	**U2 ZOO TV LIVE** (2xCD & poster in card sleeve & outer card slipcase Issued to U2.com subscribers only)	**£50**
07	Island U2.COM3	**U2 GO HOME - LIVE FROM SLANE CASTLE** (2xCD issued to u2.com subscribers only)	**£30**
08	Island	**U23D** (Promo CD, audio press kit, DVD box)	**£35**

(see also The Edge, Passengers)

U.V. POP

82	Pax PAX 9	**Just A Game/No Songs Tomorrow** (p/s)	**£30**
85	Flow Motion FM 007	**Anyone For Me/Hands To Me**	**£30**
85	Flow Motion FM 12/007	**ANYONE FOR ME** (12" EP)	**£35**
85	Native NTV4	**SERIOUS EP** (12")	**£20**
86	Extra EXTRA T001	**MUSIC TO YEAH TO EP** (12")	**£30**
83	Flow Motion FM 004	**NO SONGS TOMORROW** (LP)	**£40**
86	Extra EXTRA LP1	**BENDY BABY MAN** (LP)	**£50**

UWANDILE

87	Mother Africa MALP 01	**APARTHEID** (LP)	**£60**

UXB

80	Crazy Plane SP 002	**Crazy Today/Mister Fix It** (p/s)	**£100**

UZI

70	Beacon BEA 152	**Morning Train/Where Were You Last Night**	**£30**

U-ZIQ

93	Rephlex CAT 018	**Bluff Limbo** (remixes) (2 x 12", 800 only)	**£20**
17	Revoke REVOKE 003	**PTHAGONAL EP** (12") (100 only, white label)	**£40**
93	Rephlex CAT 013	**TANGO N VECTIF** (2-LP)	**£20**
95	Planet Mu FLATDLP 20	**IN PINE EFFECT** (2-LP)	**£15**
97	Planet Mu PULP 5	**LUNATIC HARNESS** (2-LP)	**£20**

(see also Mike & Rich)

DONNA V

96	Fashion FAD 153	**Prophecy Revealing** (Natural Mix)**/Mystic Mix/GENERALY LEVY : Inna We Culture/ Remember Yu Roots** (12")	**£35**

VACELS

65	Pye International 7N 25330	**Can You Please Crawl Out Your Window/I'm Just A Poor Boy**	**£35**

VAGABONDS

64	Island ILP 916	**PRESENTING THE FABULOUS VAGABONDS** (LP)	**£300**

(see also Jimmy James & Vagabonds, Jamaica's Own Vagabonds)

VAGINA DENTATA ORGAN

83	WSNS 001	**VAGINA DENTATA ORGAN PRESENTS: MUSIC FOR HASHASINS, IN MEMORIAM OF HASSAN-I-SABBAH** (LP, 500 copies)	**£50**
84	WSNS 002	**THE LAST SUPPER, THE REVEREND JIM JONES IN PERSON** (LP, picture disc, 912 numbered, with transcript)	**£90**
84	WSNS 002	**THE LAST SUPPER, THE REVEREND JIM JONES IN PERSON** (LP, picture disc, 912 numbered, without transcript)	**£80**
84	WSNS 003	**THE PAGAN DRUMS OF CALANDA** (LP, picture disc, 12 copies adorned with 'real' blood and handpainted)	**£300**
84	WSNS 003	**THE PAGAN DRUMS OF CALANDA** (LP, picture disc, 30 copies adorned with 'real' blood but not handpainted)	**£150**
84	WSNS 003	**THE PAGAN DRUMS OF CALANDA** (LP, picture disc, adorned with 'fake blood')	**£100**
84	WSNS 003	**THE PAGAN DRUMS OF CALANDA** (LP, 900 'bloodless' copies)	**£50**
86	WSNS 004	**COLD MEAT/EROS & THANATOS** (LP picture disc, 4 copies with 1 black side with Elvis image missing)	**£150**
86	WSNS 004	**COLD MEAT/EROS & THANATOS** (LP picture disc, 12 copies with hand drawings and personal dedications)	**£300**
86	WSNS 004	**COLD MEAT/EROS & THANATOS** (LP picture disc, no drawings or dedications)	**£50**
87	Temple TOPY 012	**MUSIC FOR THE HASHISHINS** (LP)	**£25**
87	Temple TPY 013	**THE LAST SUPPER** (LP)	**£25**

VAGRANTS

66	Fontana TF 703	**I Can't Make A Friend/Young Blues**	**£60**

VAIN AIMS

80	We Practice In a Gang WPG 1	**You/Count** (fold over stapled sleeves)	**£50**
80	We Practice In a Gang WPG 1	**You/Count** (with hand-made p/s)	**£100**

VALADIERS

63	Oriole CBA 1809	**I Found A Girl/You'll Be Sorry Someday**	**£1000**
63	Oriole CBA 1809	**I Found A Girl/You'll Be Sorry Someday** (DJ copy)	**£1000**

RICKY VALANCE

76	Valley VLY 001	**RICKY VALANCE** (EP, no p/s)	**£25**
78	Tank BBS 324	**RAINBOW** (LP)	**£40**

MINT VALUE £

JERRY VALE
59 Philips PB 963 Flame/The Moon Is My Pillow (78)..£15

RITCHIE VALENS
58 Pye International 7N 25000 Come On Let's Go/Dooby Dooby Wah £150
58 Pye International 7N 25000 Come On Let's Go/Dooby Dooby Wah (78) £80
59 London HL 8803 Donna/La Bamba..£30
59 London HL 8803 Donna/La Bamba (78) £80
59 London HL 7068 Donna/La Bamba (export issue)..£30
59 London HL 8886 That's My Little Suzie/Bluebirds Over The Mountains (tri centre)..£40
59 London HL 8886 That's My Little Suzie/Bluebirds Over The Mountains (round centre)..£20
59 London HL 8886 That's My Little Suzie/Bluebirds Over The Mountains (78) £80
62 London HL 9494 La Bamba/Ooh, My Head..£20
59 London RE 1232 RITCHIE VALENS (EP, initial pressing with triangular centre) £200
59 London RE 1232 RITCHIE VALENS (EP, later round centre) £150
61 London HA 2390 RITCHIE (LP) £150
64 London HA 8196 HIS GREATEST HITS (LP) £50
67 President PTL 1001 I REMEMBER RITCHIE VALENS (LP)..£20

DINO VALENTI
68 CBS 65715 DINO (LP) £45
(see also Quicksilver Messenger Service)

DICKIE VALENTINE (& STARGAZERS)
SINGLES
54 Decca F 10346 Endless/I Could Have Told You..£30
54 Decca F 10394 The Finger Of Suspicion (with Stargazers)/ Who's Afraid (Not I, Not I, Not I) £20
54 Decca F 10415 Mister Sandman/Runaround..£40
55 Decca F 10430 A Blossom Fell/I Want You All To Myself (Just You)..£15
55 Decca F 10628 Christmas Alphabet/Where Are You Tonight?..£20
55 Decca F 10645 The Old Pi-Anna Rag/First Love £15
56 Decca F 10798 Christmas Island/The Hand Of Friendship..£15

VALENTINE GUINNESS
80 RAK RAK 308 (Hey Hey) C.J.T./When Mandy Calls £35

VALENTINES (JAMAICA)
67 Doctor Bird DB 1065 Blam Blam Fever/BABA BROOKS: The Scratch £100

VALENTINES (U.S.)
60 Ember EMB S 123 Hey Ruby/That's How I Feel £90

ANNA VALENTINO
57 London HLD 8421 Calypso Joe/You're Mine..£30

DANNY VALENTINO
59 MGM MGM 1049 Stampede/(You Gotta Be A) Music Man £30
60 MGM MGM 1067 Biology/A Million Tears £20
60 MGM MGM 1109 Pictures From The Past/'Till The End Of Forever £15

MARK VALENTINO
63 Stateside SS 148 The Push And Kick/Walking Alone..£25
63 Stateside SS 186 Do It/Hey You're Looking Good £15
63 Stateside SS 233 Jivin' At The Drive In/Part Time Job..£25

VALENTINOS
68 Soul City SC 106 It's All Over Now/Tired Of Livin' In The Country £25
68 Stateside SS 2137 Tired Of Being Nobody/The Death Of Love £18
68 Soul City SCM 001 THE VALENTINOS/THE SIMS TWINS (LP, with Sims Twins)..£70
(see also Bobby Womack)

VALERIE (THE ROCK 'N' ROLL YOUNGSTER)
56 Columbia DB 3832 Tonight You Belong To Me/The Man Who Owns The Sunshine £20

VALERIE AND THE WEEK OF WONDERS
83 Soon Come VA 01 Too Late/Helpless (hand made p/s) £20

VALHALLA (1)
81 Asgard ASG 69151 Lightning In The Sky/These Sunday Nights..£300

JOE VALINO (& GOSPELAIRES)
57 HMV POP 283 The Garden Of Eden/Caravan £25
58 London HLT 8705 God's Little Acre/I'm Happy With What I've Got (with Gospelaires) £15

VALKYRIES
64 Parlophone R 5123 Rip It Up/What's Your Name?..£40

DIORIS VALLADARES ORCHESTRA
64 Island ILP 910 LET'S GO LATIN (LP, withdrawn)..£60

MARCOS VALLE
68 Verve VLP 9206 SAMBA '68 (LP)..£30
95 Mr. Bongo MRBLP003 THE ESSENTIAL MARCOS VALLE (LP) £20
95 Mr. Bongo MRBLP007 THE ESSENTIAL MARCOS VALLE VOL 2 (LP)..£20
97 Far Out FARO 022 NOVA BOSSA NOVA (LP)..£25

VALLEY FORGE
86 Revue REV 0312 FROM ACROSS THE SEE (12" EP, p/s)..£20

VALLEY OF ACHOR
75 Dovetail DOVE 18 A DOOR OF HOPE (LP, gatefold sleeve)..£15

(see also Wine Of Lebanon)

FRANKIE VALLI
67	Philips (S)BL 7814	SOLO (LP)	£25
69	Philips SBL 7856	TIMELESS (LP)	£20
77	Private Stock PVLP 1029	LADY PUT THE LIGHT OUT (LP, withdrawn)	£40

FRANKIE VALLI & THE FOUR SEASONS
71	Warner Bros K 16107	Whatever You Say/Sleeping Man (withdrawn, 300 only)	£45
72	Mowest MW 3002	The Night/When The Morning Comes	£75
72	Mowest MWSA 5501	CHAMELEON (LP)	£20

(see also Four Seasons, Wonder Who)

TONY VALOR SOUNDS
77	Brunswick BRBS 5003	GOTTA GET IT (LP)	£15

ANTON VALOTTI
75	Rouge RMS 106	BLACKOUT (LP)	£80

VALUES
66	Ember EMB S 211	Return To Me/That's The Way (with p/s)	£80
66	Ember EMB S 211	Return To Me/That's The Way	£50

HUBERT THOMAS VALVERDE & THE HTS
68	S n B 55 3922	Genevieve/We Don't Care	£25

VALVERDE BROTHERS
69	CBS 4519	River Of My Mind/I Wanna Love You	£20

VAL & V'S
67	CBS 2780	Do It Again A Little Bit Slower/For A Rainy Day	£20
67	CBS 2956	I Like The Way/With This Theme	£20
68	CBS 3316	This Little Girl/Dreamer	£15

VAMP
68	Atlantic 584 213	Floatin'/Thinkin' Too Much	£100
69	Atlantic 584 263	Green Pea/Wake Up And Tell Me (withdrawn)	£150

(see also Viv Prince, Clark-Hutchinson)

VAMPIRE WEEKEND
08	XL XLS 399	The Kids Don't Stand a Chance /(Chromeo Remix) (white vinyl)	£15
08	XL XLLP 318	VAMPIRE WEEKEND (LP)	£15
13	XL XLLP 556	MODERN VAMPIRES OF THE CITY (LP, hand-printed alternative sleeve, 50 only)	£70
13	XL XLLP 556	MODERN VAMPIRES OF THE CITY (LP, CD and poster)	£18

VAMPIRES (1)
59	Parlophone R 4599	Swinging Ghosts/Clap Trap	£20

VAMPIRES (2)
68	Pye 7N 17553	Do You Wanna Dance/My Girl	£20

VAMPS
79	Dental DK 001	She Exudes Sexuality/Love Letters/I Only Saw You (p/s, red vinyl, 1000 only, hand-made p/s)	£25

VAN DER GRAAF GENERATOR
SINGLES
69	Polydor 56758	People You Were Going To/Firebrand	£750
70	Charisma CB 122	Refugees/The Boat Of Millions Of Years (three prong centre)	£45
73	Charisma CB 175	Theme One/W (with p/s, "D.J. sample not for sale")	£50
72	Charisma CB 175	Theme One/W (with p/s, solid centre)	£30
76	Charisma PRO 002	Wondering (Song)/Wondering (Heroics) (promo only)	£25

ALBUMS
69	Mercury SMCL 20177	THE AEROSOL GREY MACHINE (LP, unreleased, finished gatefold sleeve only)	£750
70	Charisma CAS 1007	THE LEAST WE CAN DO IS WAVE TO EACH OTHER (LP, pink 'scroll' label, original mix, matrices read: CAS 1007 A/B, gatefold sleeve, with poster)	£400
70	Charisma CAS 1007	THE LEAST WE CAN DO IS WAVE TO EACH OTHER (LP, pink 'scroll' label, original mix, matrices read: CAS 1007 A/B, gatefold sleeve, without poster)	£60
70	Charisma CAS 1007	THE LEAST WE CAN DO IS WAVE TO EACH OTHER (LP, pink 'scroll' label, remix, matrices read: CAS 1007 A+G/B+G, gatefold sleeve; with poster)	£150
70	Charisma CAS 1007	THE LEAST WE CAN DO IS WAVE TO EACH OTHER (LP, pink 'scroll' label, remix, matrices read: CAS 1007 A+G/B+G, gatefold sleeve; without poster)	£50
70	Charisma CAS 1027	H TO HE, WHO AM THE ONLY ONE (LP, pink label, gatefold sleeve)	£150
70	Charisma CAS 1027	H TO HE, WHO AM THE ONLY ONE (LP, reissue 'Mad Hatter' label)	£30
71	Charisma CAS 1051	PAWN HEARTS (LP, gatefold, pink 'scroll' label, insert)	£100
71	Charisma CAS 1051	PAWN HEARTS (LP, gatefold, pink 'scroll' label, without insert)	£35
72	Charisma CS 2	1968-71 (LP, pink label)	£25
75	Charisma CAS 1109	GODBLUFF (LP, printed inner)	£30
76	Charisma CAS 1116	STILL LIFE (LP, small 'Mad Hatter' logo)	£30
76	Charisma CAS 1120	WORLD RECORD (LP)	£30
76	Charisma CAS 1007	THE LEAST WE CAN DO IS WAVE TO EACH OTHER (LP, gatefold reissue, 'Mad hatter' label)	£18
77	Charisma CAS 1131	THE QUIET ZONE/THE PLEASURE ZONE (LP, lyric insert, as Van Der Graaf, mispress 'Van Der Graff' on Side 2 label)	£30
78	Charisma CVLD 101	VITAL (2LP, gatefold, as Van Der Graaf)	£20
85	Demi Monde DM 003	TIME VAULTS (LP, reissue of 1981 cassette)	£20
00	Virgin VDGGBOX 1	THE BOX (4CD box set)	£35
11	Esoteric EVDGLP 1001	A GROUNDING IN NUMBERS (LP, die-cut sleeve, 2000 ltd, printed inner)	£30
12	Back On Black PCV004LP	THE LEAST WE CAN DO IS WAVE TO EACH OTHER (2LP, gatefold, reissue, 180g)	£30
12	Back On Black PCV 005LP	H TO HE, WHO AM THE ONLY ONE (2LP, gatefold, reissue, 180g)	£50

MINT VALUE £

12	Back On Black PCV006LP	**PAWN HEARTS** (2LP, gatefold, reissue, 180g)	£60
12	Back On Black PCV007LP	**GODBLUFF** (2LP, gatefold, reissue, 180g)	£40
12	E. Antenna EVDGLP 1003	**ALT** (LP, printed inner, 180g)	£25
14	Go Entertain GO2VIN 7339	**RECORDED LIVE IN CONCERT AT METROPOLIS STUDIOS LONDON** (2LP, gatefold)	£40
15	E. Antenna EANTLP 1044	**MERLIN ATMOS** (LP, gatefold)	£25
16	E. Antenna EANTLP 1062	**DO NOT DISTURB** (LP, gatefold, printed inner, 180g)	£20
19	Estoeric ECLEC 42661	**AEROSOL GREY MACHINE** (LP/2CD/7" box set, book, poster)	£50
21	Charisma/UMC 352 345 4	**THE CHARISMA YEARS 1970-1978** (17CD/3BD box set, book)	£150
22	Charisma/UMC 089 615-0	**THE LEAST WE CAN DO IS WAVE AT EACH OTHER** (LP, gatefold, poster, Abbey Road remaster)	£25
22	Charisma/UMC 089 607-2	**H TO HE WHO AM THE ONLY ONE** (LP, gatefold, Abbey Road remaster)	£20
22	Charisma/UMC 089 609-1	**PAWN HEARTS** (LP, gatefold, printed inner, Abbey Road remaster)	£25
22	Charisma/UMC 089 610-5	**GODBLUFF** (LP, printed inner, Abbey Road remaster)	£25
22	Esoteric ECLEC 142810	**INTERFERENCE PATTERNS** (13CD/1DVD box set, book, poster)	£60
23	E. Antenna EANTCD 41093	**THE BATH FORUM CONCERT** (2CD/DVD/BD)	£35

(see also Peter Hammill, Long Hello, Juicy Lucy, Misunderstood, David Jackson)

LEE VANDERBILT
74	Bell 1384	**It's Dawn Again/Pick Up Your Troubles**	£15

MAMIE VAN DOREN
58	Capitol CL 14850	**Something To Dream About/I Fell In Love** (promos in p/s)	£40
58	Capitol CL 14850	**Something To Dream About/I Fell In Love**	£25

LUTHER VANDROSS
83	Epic EPC A 3101	**Never Too Much/Don't You Know That?** (p/s, blue injection labels)	£15
81	Epic EPC 85275	**NEVER TOO MUCH** (LP)	£20
89	Epic 465801 1	**THE BEST OF LUTHER VANDROSS . . .THE BEST OF LOVE** (2LP, gatefold)	£20

(see also CHIC, Change, David Bowie)

VANDYKE & BAMBIS
64	Piccadilly 7N 35180	**Doin' The Mod/All I Want Is You**	£50

EARL VAN DYKE (& SOUL BROTHERS)
64	Stateside SS 357	**Soul Stomp/Hot 'N' Tot** (DJ copy)	£200
64	Stateside SS 357	**Soul Stomp/Hot 'N' Tot**	£125
65	Tamla Motown TMG 506	**All For You/Too Many Fish In The Sea** (as Earl Van Dyke & Soul Brothers)(DJ copy)	£175
65	Tamla Motown TMG 506	**All For You/Too Many Fish In The Sea** (as Earl Van Dyke & Soul Brothers)	£125
65	Tamla Motown TML 11014	**THAT MOTOWN SOUND** (LP)	£120

LEROY VAN DYKE
62	Mercury MMC 14101	**WALK ON BY** (LP)	£30
63	Mercury MMC 14118	**MOVIN' VAN DYKE** (LP)	£30

VAN DYKES
66	Stateside SS 504	**No Man Is An Island/I Won't Hold It Against You**	£25
66	Stateside SS 504	**No Man Is An Island/I Won't Hold It Against You** (DJ Copy)	£40
66	Stateside SS 530	**I've Gotta Go On Without You/What Will I Do**	£25

LON & DERREK VAN EATON
73	Apple APPLE 46	**Warm Woman/More Than Words** (in p/s)	£125
73	Apple APPLE 46	**Warm Woman/More Than Words**	£60
73	Apple SAPCOR 25	**BROTHER** (LP, gatefold sleeve, with insert)	£100
73	Apple SAPCOR 25	**BROTHER** (LP, gatefold sleeve, without insert)	£60

NICK VAN EEDE
79	Barn BARN 008	**I Only Want To Be Number One/Dicing**	£60

VANGELIS
75	RCA RS 1025	**HEAVEN AND HELL** (LP, gatefold sleeve)	£15
76	Polydor 2489 113	**L'APOCALYPSE DES ANIMAUX** (LP, TV soundtrack)	£18
15	Warner Bros. 0825646122110	**BLADE RUNNER** (LP, red or black vinyl)	£35

(see also Aphrodite's Child, Forminx, Cosmic Baby)

VAN HALEN
78	WARNER BROS K 56470	**VAN HALEN** (Burbank labels)	£15
84	92-3985-1	**1984** (MCMLXXXIV)	£15

CHERRY VANILLA
79	RCA PL 25217	**VENUS DE VINYL** (LP)	£15

VANILLA FUDGE
67	Atlantic 587/588 086	**VANILLA FUDGE** (LP, red & plum label)	£75
68	Atlantic 587 100	**THE BEAT GOES ON** (LP, mono)	£40
68	Atlantic 588 100	**THE BEAT GOES ON** (LP, stereo)	£40
68	Atlantic 587 110	**RENAISSANCE** (LP, mono)	£45
68	Atlantic 588 110	**RENAISSANCE** (LP, stereo)	£40
69	Atco 228 020	**NEAR THE BEGINNING** (LP)	£25
70	Atco 228 029	**ROCK 'N' ROLL** (LP)	£25

(see also Beck Bogert & Appice, Cactus)

VANITY FARE
69	Page One POLS 010	**THE SUN, THE WIND AND OTHER THINGS** (LP)	£45
70	DJM DJSL 001	**COMING HOME** (LP)	£20

(see also Avengers)

VANITY 6
82	Warner Bros. 57 023	**VANITY 6** (LP)	£15

TEDDY VANN (ORCHESTRA)
60   London HLU 9097   Cindy/I'm Waiting £25
DAVE VAN RONK
65   Stateside SL 10153   INSIDE (LP, laminated flipback sleeve) £30
ROB VAN SPYK
74   Acorn CF 241   FOLLOW THE SUN (LP)..£75
(see also Stonefield Tramp)
TOWNES VAN ZANDT
69   RCA SF 8040   OUR MOTHER THE MOUNTAIN (LP)..£30
73   United Artists UAS 29442 THE LATE GREAT TOWNES VAN ZANDT (LP, gatefold sleeve)............£30
87   Heartland HLD 003   AT MY WINDOW (LP)..£15
88   Decal LIK 32   TOWNES VAN ZANDT (LP, reissue)..£20
88   Decal LIK 25   DELTA MOMMA BLUES (LP, reissue)..£20
89   Decal LIK 59   FLYIN' SHOES (LP, reissue)..£15
VAPORS
80   United Artists UAG 30300 NEW CLEAR DAYS (LP)..£15
VARDI AND HIS ORCHESTRA
62   London 45 HLR 9518   Theme From Ballad Of A Soldier/Exodus - Main Theme..................£15
VARDIS
79   Redball RR 017   100 MPH (EP)..£150
VARIATIONS
65   Immediate IM 019   The Man With All The Toys/She'll Know I'm Sorry.........................£35
69   Major Minor MM 638   Crimson And Clover/She Couldn't Dance £20
VARICOSE VEINS
78   Warped WARP 1   INCREDIBLE (EP, mail-order only, 200 only, beware of counterfeits)...............£80
(see also Orange Disaster)
VARIOUSARTISTS
81   Not On Label – VA 1   SOLO ALBUM (LP)..£20
SYLVIE VARTAN
65   RCA Victor RCA 1490   One More Day/I Made My Choice £75
65   RCA Victor RCX 7165   SYLVIE VARTAN (EP)..£200
VARUKERS
83   Riot City RIOT 31   ANOTHER RELIGION ANOTHER WAR (12" EP)....................................£15
84   Rot ASS 16   MASSACRED MILLIONS (12" EP)..£20
83   Riot City RIOT 005   BLOODSUCKERS (LP, with inner)..£20
84   Attack ATTACK 001   PREPARE FOR THE ATTACK (LP, 1000 only).......................................£18
85   Liberate 1   ONE STRUGGLE ONE FIGHT (LP)..£15
87   Rot DUTCH 001   LIVE IN HOLLAND (LP)..£15
VASALINES
92   Avalanche ONLYLP 013   ALL THE STUFF AND MORE (LP)..£15
VASELINE TIGERS
80   Dance DANCE 513   I'm A Golliwog/Back In The Square (Again) £18
VASELINES
87   53rd & 3rd AGARR 10   Son Of A Gun/Rory Rides Away/You Think You're A Man (12", die-cut sleeve) £25
88   53rd & 3rd AGARR 17   Dying For It/Molly's Lips (p/s) £20
88   53rd & 3rd AGARR 17T   Dying For It/Molly's Lips/Teenage Superstars/Jesus Wants Me For A Sunbeam (12", p/s)........£15
90   53rd & 3rd AGAS 7   DUM DUM (LP) £30
98   Avalanche ONLY LP 013P   ALL THE STUFF AND MORE (LP, picture disc)....................................£15
14   Rosary RMUSIC1LPX   V FOR VASELINES (LP, red vinyl, 2-CD, signed, with poster)............£20
(see also Pastels)
VASHTI
65   Decca F 12157   Some Things Just Stick In Your Mind/I Want To Be Alone................£80
66   Columbia DB 7917   Train Song/Love Song..£60
(see also Vashti Bunyan)
FITZ VAUGHAN BRYAN ORCHESTRA
60   Melodisc 45/1560   Evening News/Hold Up Your Head And Smile £60
(see also Kendrick Patrick, Lord Creator)
FRANKIE VAUGHAN
53   HMV 7M 167   Istanbul (Not Constantinople)/Cloud Lucky Seven £20
57   Philips JK 1035   Kisses Sweeter Than Wine/Rock-A-Chicka (jukebox issue)..............£15
(see also Kaye Sisters, Marilyn Monroe)
MALCOLM VAUGHAN
56   HMV 7M 338   With Your Love/Small Talk £15
59   HMV CLP 1284   HELLO MALCOLM VAUGHAN (LP) £15
SARAH VAUGHAN
SINGLES
59   Mercury AMT 1057   Broken-Hearted Melody/Misty (78) £15
74   Mainstream MSS 355   I Need You Now (More Than Ever Before)/Do Away With April..............£15
ALBUMS
55   Oriole/Mercury MG 26005   IMAGES (10")..£20
55   Mercury MG 25188   THE DIVINE SARAH..£15
56   London HB-U 1049   SARAH VAUGHAN SINGS (10", with John Kirby & His Orchestra) £20

Billy VAUGHN (& HIS ORCHESTRA)

56	Emarcy EJL 100	IN THE LAND OF HI FI (10")	£20
56	Philips BBL 7082	SARAH VAUGHAN	£15
56	Mercury MPT 7503	MAKE YOURSELF COMFORTABLE (10")	£20
57	Mercury MPT 7518	IMAGES (10", reissue)	£15
57	Emarcy EJL 1258	SASSY	£15
57	Mercury MPL 6522	SINGS GREAT SONGS FROM HIT SHOWS PART 1	£15
57	Philips BBL 7165	LINGER AWHILE	£15
57	Mercury MPL 6523	SINGS GREAT SONGS FROM HIT SHOWS PART 2	£15
57	Mercury MPL 6525	SINGS GEORGE GERSHWIN VOL. 1	£15
57	Mercury MPL 6527	SINGS GEORGE GERSHWIN VOL. 2	£15
58	Mercury MPL 6532	WONDERFUL SARAH	£15
58	Emarcy EJL 1273	SWINGIN' EASY	£15
58	Mercury MPL 6540	IN ROMANTIC MOOD	£15
58	Mercury MPL 6542	AT MISTER KELLY'S	£15
59	Mercury MMC 14001	AFTER HOURS AT THE LONDON HOUSE	£15
59	Mercury MMC 14011	VAUGHAN AND VIOLINS (also stereo CMS 18003)	£15

BILLY VAUGHN (& HIS ORCHESTRA)

55	London HL 8112	Melody Of Love/Joy Ride (gold label print)	£15
55	London HLD 8205	The Shifting Whispering Sands (Parts 1 & 2) (with Ken Nordine) (gold print)	£15
56	London HLD 8238	Theme From 'The Threepenny Opera'/I'd Give A Million Tomorrows (gold label print, later with silver label print)	£20
56	London HLD 8319	When The Lilac Blooms Again/Autumn Concerto (gold label print)	£20
56	London HLD 8342	Petticoats From Portugal/La La Colette (gold label print)	£20
57	London HLD 8522	Raunchy/Sail Along Silvery Moon	£15

(see also Hilltoppers, Ken Nordine)

MORRIS VAUGHN

69	Fontana TF 1031	My Love Keeps Growing/Make It Look Good	£30

VBW

80	Heaven International	VBW EP (no p/s)	£40

V.D.U.'S

79	Thin Sliced	Don't Cry For Me/Little White Lie/Holiday Romances (p/s)	£30

VECO 19

90	Irdial Discs VCO 1	Eep!/Eep!/Hardhead (12")	£50

VED BUENS ENDE

95	Misanthropy AMAZON 006	WRITTEN IN WATERS (2-LP, marbled purple vinyl)	£60

CHUCK VEDDER

59	London HL 8951	Spanky Boy/Arriba	£30
59	London HL 8951	Spanky Boy/Arriba (78)	£20

BOBBY VEE

SINGLES

60	London HLG 9179	Devil Or Angel/Since I Met You, Baby	£20

EPs

61	London RE-G 1278	BOBBY VEE NO. 1	£15
61	London RE-G 1299	BOBBY VEE NO. 2	£15
61	London RE-G 1308	BOBBY VEE NO. 3	£15
61	London RE-G 1323	BOBBY VEE NO. 4	£20
61	London RE-G 1324	HITS OF THE ROCKIN' 50's	£30
62	Liberty LEP 2053	SINCERELY	£15
63	Liberty LEP 2084	JUST FOR FUN (2 tracks by Bobby Vee, 2 by Crickets)	£15
63	Liberty LEP 2089	A FOREVER KIND OF LOVE	£15
64	Liberty LEP 2181	NEW SOUNDS	£25
65	Liberty LEP 2212	BOBBY VEE MEETS THE VENTURES (with Ventures)	£25

ALBUMS

61	London HA-G 2320	BOBBY VEE SINGS YOUR FAVOURITES	£45
61	London HA-G 2352	BOBBY VEE (mono)	£20
61	London SAH-G 6152	BOBBY VEE (stereo)	£25
61	London HA-G 2374	WITH STRINGS AND THINGS (mono)	£15
61	London SAH-G 6174	WITH STRINGS AND THINGS (stereo)	£25
61	London HA-G 2406	SINGS HITS OF THE ROCKIN' 50s (mono)	£30
61	London SAH-G 6206	SINGS HITS OF THE ROCKIN' 50s (stereo)	£35
61	London HA-G 2428	TAKE GOOD CARE OF MY BABY (mono)	£20
61	London SAH-G 6224	TAKE GOOD CARE OF MY BABY (stereo)	£25
63	Liberty LBY 1147	BOBBY VEE MEETS THE VENTURES (with Ventures, mono)	£15
63	Liberty SLBY 1147	BOBBY VEE MEETS THE VENTURES (with Ventures, stereo)	£20

(see also Crickets, Ventures)

ALAN VEGA

81	Ze/Island ILPS 9692	COLLISION DRIVE (LP)	£15

(see also Suicide, Future Pilot AKA Alan Vega)

TATA VEGA

81	Motown STML 12138	GIVIN ALL MY LOVE (LP)	£20

VEGAS

92	RCA 743211104418	VEGAS (LP)	£30

(see also Eurythmics, Fun Boy Three, Specials)

VEINS
80   Redball RR 3 | Complete Control Rock 'n' Roll/Champagne £25

VEJTABLES
65   Pye International 7N 25339 | I Still Love You/Anything £50

VEKTORS
81   Little Black EJSP 9662 | Yesterday's Dream/Razor Smile/I Don't Know Why (300 only, no p/s) £35

RUTH VELDON
66   Decca F12436 | A Most Peculiar Man/Show Me The Way Back To My World £15

MARTHA VELEZ
69   London HLK 10280 | Tell Mama/Swamp Man £25
69   London HLK 10280 | Tell Mama/Swamp Man (DJ Copy) £40
72   Blue Horizon 2096 010 | Boogie Kitchen/Two Bridges £20
69   London HA-K/SH-K 8395 | FIENDS AND ANGELS (LP) £70
70   Blue Horizon 7-63867 | FIENDS AND ANGELS AGAIN (LP) £100
76   Sire 9103 252 | ESCAPE FROM BABYLON (LP) £20

VELLUM STAIRS
89   Marker JUNE 1002 | Jamie's Coming Back/Writing On The Wall (p/s) £25
90   Marker JUNE 1003 | You're Always Guilty/Karin Mist (p/s) £20

VELVELETTES
64   Stateside SS 361 | Needle In A Haystack/Should I Tell Them? (DJ Copy) £100
64   Stateside SS 361 | Needle In A Haystack/Should I Tell Them? £45
65   Stateside SS 387 | He Was Really Sayin' Something/Throw A Farewell Kiss (DJ Copy) £125
65   Stateside SS 387 | He Was Really Sayin' Something/Throw A Farewell Kiss £65
65   Tamla Motown TMG 521 | Lonely Lonely Girl Am I/I'm The Exception To The Rule (DJ Copy) £300
65   Tamla Motown TMG 521 | Lonely Lonely Girl Am I/I'm The Exception To The Rule £175
66   Tamla Motown TMG 580 | These Things Will Keep Me Loving You/Since You've Been Loving Me (DJ Copy) £100
66   Tamla Motown TMG 580 | These Things Will Keep Me Loving You/Since You've Been Loving Me £55
67   Tamla Motown TMG 595 | He Was Really Sayin' Something/Needle In A Haystack £30
90   Motorcity MOTCLP 43 | ONE DOOR CLOSES (LP) £15

VELVET CUSHION
71   Sky SKY 3 | Lost In The Maze/It's All Over Me £100

VELVET GLOVE
74   Fresh Air 6370 502 | SWEET WAS MY ROSE (LP, laminated sleeve, lyric insert) £15

VELVET HUSH
68   Oak RGJ 648 | Broken Heart/Lover Please £300
(see also Factory [Oak label])

VELVET MIST
70   Tank BSS 103 | Rock N Roll Band/Bye Bye Johnny (with booklet) £60

VELVET OPERA
69   CBS 63692 | RIDE A HUSTLER'S DREAM (LP) £100
(see also Elmer Gantry's Velvet Opera, Stretch, Hudson-Ford, Johnny Joyce)

VELVET SHADOWS
77   Horse HOSS 148 | Wailing Of Black People/Dubbin n Wailin £20

VELVETS
61   London HLU 9328 | That Lucky Old Sun/Time And Time Again £25
61   London HLU 9372 | Tonight (Could Be The Night)/Spring Fever £35
61   London HLU 9444 | Laugh/Lana £45
61   London RE-U 1297 | VELVETS (EP) £100

VELVETTES
64   Mercury MF 802 | He's The One I Want/That Little Boy Of Mine (in p/s) £25
64   Mercury MF 802 | He's The One I Want/That Little Boy Of Mine £20

VELVETT FOGG
69   Pye 7N 17673 | Telstar '69/Owed To The Dip £25
69   Pye NSPL 18272 | VELVETT FOGG (LP, laminated sleeve; beware of non-laminated counterfeits) £250
89   See For miles SEE 259 | VELVETT FOG (LP, reissue) £20
(see also Ghost)

VELVET UNDERGROUND
SINGLES
71   Atlantic 2091 088 | Who Loves The Sun/Sweet Jane £70
73   MGM 2006 283 | I'm Waiting For The Man/Run Run Run/Candy Says (as Lou Reed & Velvet Underground) £15
73   Atlantic K 10339 | Sweet Jane/Rock And Roll (as Velvet Underground featuring Lou Reed) £15
ALBUMS
67   Verve VLP 9184 | THE VELVET UNDERGROUND AND NICO (LP, single sleeve, 'non-banana' cover, mono) £300
67   Verve SVLP 9184 | THE VELVET UNDERGROUND AND NICO (LP, single sleeve, 'non-banana' cover, stereo) £200
68   Verve 2315 056 | THE VELVET UNDERGROUND AND NICO (LP, UK pressing in stickered US peelable banana gatefold censored sleeve, stereo) £250
68   Verve VLP 9201 | WHITE LIGHT WHITE HEAT (LP, 'skull' sleeve, mono) £250
68   Verve SVLP 9201 | WHITE LIGHT WHITE HEAT (LP, 'skull' sleeve, stereo) £150
69   MGM MGM-CS 8108 | THE VELVET UNDERGROUND (LP, 'Val Valentin mix', flapped laminated sleeve, with horizontal split of Lou Reed picture on rear sleeve) £200
71   MGM/Verve Super 2315 056 | THE VELVET UNDERGROUND AND NICO (LP, reissue stereo, UK LP in US Verve stereo V6 £80

MINT VALUE £

		5008 sleeve with peelable banana on front cover, UK sticker on back cover with 2315 056 covering US catalogue number, "Marketed by Polydor")	
71	Atlantic 2400 111	LOADED (LP)	£70
71	MGM 2315 056	THE VELVET UNDERGROUND AND NICO (LP, reissue, gatefold sleeve)	£25
71	MGM Select 2353 022	THE VELVET UNDERGROUND (LP, reissue, gatefold sleeve)	£35
71	MGM Select 2353 024	WHITE LIGHT WHITE HEAT (LP, reissue)	£25
72	MGM Select 2683 006	ANDY WARHOL'S VELVET UNDERGROUND (2-LP)	£30
72	Atlantic K 30022	LIVE AT MAX'S KANSAS CITY (LP)	£25
73	Polydor 2383 180	SQUEEZE (LP)	£40
77	Warner Bros. K40113	LOADED (LP, reissue)	£20
79	Mercury 6641 900	1969 VOL. 1 (2-LP)	£15
84	Polydor SPELP 73	WHITE LIGHT WHITE HEAT (LP, reissue, different sleeve)	£15
84	Polydor SPELP 20	THE VELVET UNDERGROUND AND NICO (LP, reissue)	£15
85	Polydor POLD 5167	VU (LP)	£18
86	Polydor VUBOX 1	THE VELVET UNDERGROUND BOX SET (5-LP box set, with booklet)	£60
86	Verve POLD 5208	ANOTHER VIEW (LP)	£15
95	Polydor 527887	PEEL SLOWLY AND SEE (5-CD box set, booklet)	£40
99	Simply Vinyl SVLP 090	THE VELVET UNDERGROUND AND NICO (LP, reissue)	£20
00	Simply Vinyl SVLP 200	WHITE LIGHT/WHITE HEAT (LP, reissue)	£15
12	Polydor B001764901	SCEPTER STUDIO SESSIONS (LP)	£20

(see also Lou Reed, Nico, John Cale)

VENDORS

64	Domino Studios (no cat. no.)	Don't Leave Me Now/Twilight Time/Take Your Time/Peace Pipe (acetate, private pressing, 12 copies only)	£500

(see also 'N Betweens, Slade)

VENGERS

63	Oriole CB 1879	Shake And Clap/Shakedown	£25

VENOM

81	Neat NEAT 08	In League With Satan/Live Like An Angel, Die Like An Devil (p/s)	£35
82	Neat NEAT 13	Bloodlust/In Nomine Satanas (p/s)	£30
82	Neat NEAT 13	Bloodlust/In Nomine Satanas (purple vinyl)	£80
83	Neat NEAT 27	Die Hard/Acid Queen (p/s, with poster)	£25
83	Neat NEAT 27	Die Hard/Acid Queen (p/s)	£15
83	Megaforce LOM 1/NEAT 27	Die Hard/Acid Queen (picture disc, export issue, 1,000 only)	£25
84	Neat NEATP 38	Warhead/Lady Lust (p/s, mauve vinyl)	£20
84	Neat NEAT 3812	Warhead/Lady Lust/Gates Of Hell (12", p/s)	£18
85	Neat NEATP 43	Manitou/Woman (picture disc)	£18
85	Neat NEATSHAPE 43	Manitou/Woman (shaped picture disc)	£20
85	Neat NEAT 4312	Manitou/Woman/Dead Of Night (12", p/s)	£18
85	Neat NEATS 47	Nightmare/Satanarchist (shaped picture disc)	£25
85	Neat NEAT 4712	Nightmare/Satanarchist/F.O.A.D./Warhead (live) (12", 'face' p/s)	£20
85	Neat NEAT 4712	Nightmare/Satanarchist/F.O.A.D./Warhead (live) (12", p/s, withdrawn)	£25
85	Neat NEATSP 4712	Nightmare/Satanarchist/F.O.A.D./Warhead (live) (12", picture disc, withdrawn)	£40
85	Neat 5312	HELL AT HAMMERSMITH EP (Witching Hour/Teacher's Pet/Poison) (12", 10,000 only)	£25
81	Neat 1002	WELCOME TO HELL (LP, 1st issue, with poster and lyric insert)	£30
82	Neat 1005	BLACK METAL (LP, 1st issue, textured sleeve, with poster, on coloured vinyl)	£35
82	Neat 1005	BLACK METAL (LP, 1st issue, textured sleeve, with poster, silver/red/green or blue labels)	£40
82	Neat NEAT 1005	BLACK METAL (LP, picture disc)	£30
82	Neat NEAT 1005	BLACK METAL (LP, green marbled vinyl)	£400
83	Neat NEATP 1002	WELCOME TO HELL (LP, reissue, purple vinyl)	£50
84	Neat NEAT 1015	AT WAR WITH SATAN (LP, textured sleeve, 1st 19,000 with poster)	£20
84	Neat NEAT 1015	AT WAR WITH SATAN (LP, textured sleeve)	£15
85	Neat NEATP 1005	BLACK METAL (LP, reissue, picture disc)	£40
85	Neat NEATP 1015	AT WAR WITH SATAN (LP, picture disc)	£40
85	Neat NEATP 1024	POSSESSED (LP, picture disc)	£20
85	Neat NEAT 1024	POSSESSED (LP, inner, blue vinyl)	£20
86	Demon APKPD 12	OBSCENE MATERIAL (LP, picture disc)	£20
86	Raw Power RAWLP 001	FROM HELL TO THE UNKNOWN (2-LP)	£25
86	A.P. APK 12	OFFICIAL BOOTLEG (LP, picture disc)	£15
89	Under One Flag FLAG 36P	PRIME EVIL (LP, numbered picture disc, stickered clear sleeve)	£20

CAROL VENTURA

65	Stateside SS 466	Please Somebody Help Me/The Old Lady Of Threadneedle Street	£20
65	Stateside SL 10146	CAROL! (LP)	£20
66	Stateside S(S)L 10180	I LOVE TO SING (LP)	£20

TOBY VENTURA

63	Decca F 11581	If My Heart Were A Storybook/Vagabond	£30

VENTURES

SINGLES

61	London HLG 9465	Blue Moon/Wailin'	£15
61	London HLG 7113	Lady Of Spain/Blue Moon (export issue)	£30
66	Liberty LIB 316	Secret Agent Man/007-11	£15
68	Liberty LBF 15075	Flights Of Fantasy/Pandora's Box	£15
70	Liberty LBF 15221	Hawaii Five-O - Theme/Higher Than Thou	£15

EPs

61	London REG 1279	THE VENTURES	£20
61	London REG 1283	THE VENTURES (export issue)	£20

61	London REG 1288	RAM-BUNK-SHUSH! £20
62	London REG 1326	ANOTHER SMASH £20
62	London REG 1328	COLOURFUL VENTURES £20
62	Liberty LEP 2058	TWIST WITH THE VENTURES £20
62	Liberty LEP 2131	SMASH HITS..£20
63	Liberty LEP 2104	THE VENTURES PLAY TELSTAR AND LONELY BULL £20
64	Liberty LEP 2174	THE VENTURES PLAY COUNTRY GREATS £20
65	Liberty LEP 2212	BOBBY VEE MEETS THE VENTURES (with Bobby Vee)........................£25
66	Liberty LEP 2250	SECRET AGENT MEN £25

ALBUMS

61	London HA-G 2340	THE VENTURES (mono)..£30
61	London SAH-G 6143	THE VENTURES (stereo) £40
61	London HA-G 2376	ANOTHER SMASH (mono) £20
61	London SAH-G 6209	ANOTHER SMASH (stereo) £30
61	London HA-G 2409	THE COLOURFUL VENTURES (mono) £20
61	London SAH-G 6209	THE COLOURFUL VENTURES (stereo) £30
62	Liberty LBY 1002	WALK DON'T RUN £25
62	London HA-G 2429	TWIST WITH THE VENTURES (mono) £20
62	London SAH-G 6225	TWIST WITH THE VENTURES (stereo) £30
62	Liberty LBY 1072	TWIST PARTY £20
63	Liberty (S)LBY 1110	GOING TO THE VENTURES DANCE PARTY! (mono) £20
63	Liberty (S)LBY 1110	GOING TO THE VENTURES DANCE PARTY! (stereo) £30
63	Liberty (S)LBY 1147	BOBBY VEE MEETS THE VENTURES (with Bobby Vee, mono) £20
63	Liberty (S)LBY 1147	BOBBY VEE MEETS THE VENTURES (with Bobby Vee, stereo) £25
63	Liberty (S)LBY 1150	SURFING (mono)..£22
63	Liberty (S)LBY 1150	SURFING (stereo) £30
64	Liberty (S)LBY 1169	LET'S GO! (mono)..£18
64	Liberty (S)LBY 1169	LET'S GO! (stereo) £25
64	Liberty (S)LBY 1189	THE VENTURES IN SPACE (mono) £22
64	Liberty (S)LBY 1189	THE VENTURES IN SPACE (stereo) £30
65	Liberty (S)LBY 1228	WALK DON'T RUN - VOL. 2 (mono) £22
65	Liberty (S)LBY 1228	WALK DON'T RUN - VOL. 2 (stereo)...£30
65	Liberty (S)LBY 1252	KNOCK ME OUT (mono) £20
65	Liberty (S)LBY 1252	KNOCK ME OUT (stereo) £20
65	Liberty (S)LBY 1270	ON STAGE (mono) £20
65	Liberty (S)LBY 1270	ON STAGE (stereo) £20
66	Liberty (S)LBY 1274	VENTURES A-GO GO (mono) £18
66	Liberty (S)LBY 1274	VENTURES A-GO GO (stereo) £20
66	Liberty (S)LBY 1285	THE VENTURES' CHRISTMAS ALBUM (mono) £20
66	Liberty (S)LBY 1285	THE VENTURES' CHRISTMAS ALBUM (stereo) £30
66	Liberty (S)LBY 1297	WHERE THE ACTION IS! (mono) £15
66	Liberty (S)LBY 1297	WHERE THE ACTION IS! (stereo) £18
66	Liberty (S)LBY 1323	GO WITH THE VENTURES (mono)...£15
66	Liberty (S)LBY 1323	GO WITH THE VENTURES (stereo)..£18
67	Liberty (S)LBY 1345	GUITAR FREAKOUT (mono) £15
67	Liberty (S)LBY 1345	GUITAR FREAKOUT (stereo)..£18
67	Liberty (S)LBY 1372	SUPER PSYCHEDELICS (mono) £15
67	Liberty (S)LBY 1372	SUPER PSYCHEDELICS (stereo)...£18

(see also New Ventures, Bobby Vee, Nokie Edwards)

VENUS IN FURS

83	Movement MOVEMENT 001	EXTENDED PLAY (p/s) £18
85	Backs 12CH 105	MOMENTO MORI EP (12", p/s)..£15
84	MOVEMENT 002LP	PLATONIC LOVE AND OTHER STORIES (LP)..£15
85	Backs NCH MLP 6	STRIP (LP) £15
89	Backs NCH LP 16	MEGALOMANIA (LP)..£20
90	Backs NCH LP 17	THE SPEED OF A PUN (LP)...£20

BILLY VERA & JUDY CLAY

68	Atlantic 588 158	THE STORYBOOK CHILDREN (LP) £20

JOHN VERITY BAND

74	Probe SPB 1087	JOHN VERITY BAND (LP) £35

(see also Argent)

TIM VERLANDER

72	Midas MR 007	TIM VERLANDER (LP, with booklet) £40

VERMILION

78	Illegal ILM 0010	Angry Young Women/Nymphomania/Wild Boys (p/s) £18

(see also Menace)

VERNON VERMONT

67	CBM CBM 02	Too Late/Come Back..£30

VERN & ALVIN

69	Blue Cat BS 167	Everybody Reggae/Another Fool £120
69	Big Shot BI 525	Old Man Dead/G.G. RHYTHM SECTION: Reggae Me £70

(see also Maytones)

MIKE VERNON

72	Blue Horizon 2096 007	Let's Try It Again/Little Southern Country Girl £25
71	Blue Horizon 2931 003	BRING IT BACK HOME (LP, textured sleeve with insert) £250
71	Blue Horizon 2931 003	BRING IT BACK HOME (LP, textured sleeve without insert)..............£175

VERNON & THE G.I.S

77	Creeper VGI 001	G.I. Bop/Jim Dandy (no p/s)	£25
77	Creeper VGI 002	Be-Boppin' Baby/Jungle Rock (no p/s)	£20
78	Creeper VGI 005/6	Follow Me/Better Get Rockin' (no p/s)	£20
78	Creeper VGI 007/008	Brand New Lover/All Night Long	£20

VERNONS GIRLS

58	Parlophone R 4497	Lost And Found/White Bucks And Saddle Shoes	£25
59	Parlophone R 4532	Jealous Heart/Now Is The Month Of Maying	£20
59	Parlophone R 4596	Don't Look Now But/Who Are They To Say?	£20
60	Parlophone R 4624	We Like Boys/Boy Meets Girl	£15
60	Parlophone R 4654	Madison Time (with Jimmy Saville)/The Oo-We	£15
63	Decca F 11781	Tomorrow Is Another Day/Why Why Why	£20
64	Decca F 11807	We Love The Beatles/Hey Lover Boy	£15
64	Decca F 11887	Only You Can Do It/Stupid Little Girl	£18
62	Decca DFE 8506	THE VERNONS GIRLS (EP)	£40
58	Parlophone PMC 1052	THE VERNONS GIRLS (LP)	£50

(see also Krimson Kake, Wilde Three, Lee Francis, Samantha Jones, Breakaways)

LILI VERONA

54	HMV 7MC 13	Massa Johnny/Hoggin' In The Cocoa (export issue)	£15
59	HMV DLP 1202	JAMAICA SINGS (10" LP)	£22

VERONICA FALLS

10	Trouble DUDE 016	Fell In Love In A Graveyard/Stephen (hand-printed sleeve, 300 only)	£20
11	Bella Union BELLAU 310	SIX COVERS (12" EP, 300 only)	£20
14	Beach Head VF 004	Nobody There/I Need You Around (numbered, 300 only)	£25
11	Bella Union BELLAV301W	VERONICA FALLS (LP, white vinyl, CD)	£30
13	Bella Union BELLACD383P	WAITING FOR SOMETHING TO HAPPEN (LP, CD)	£20

VERSA

06	Versa VER 01	Da VersAtile EP (12")	£30
12	Smokin' Sessions SMOKE 015	5AM (12")	£40
15	System SYSTM008	Rainfall in Dub/Road To Righteousness (10")	£40
16	System SYSTM 014	Dub Of Existence/Memories Of The East	£15

VERSA & ROWL

12	Smokin' Sessions SMOKE 020	JUPITER EP (12")	£25

VERSATILE NEWTS

80	Shanghai No. 2	Newtrition/Blimp (p/s, stamped white label)	£60

(see also Felt)

VERSATILES (JAMAICA)

68	Island WI 3142	Teardrops Falling/Someone To Love	£60
68	Amalgamated AMG 802	Just Can't Win/LEADERS: Sometimes I Sit Down Down And Cry	£60
68	Crab CRAB 1	Children Get Ready/Someone To Love	£70
69	Amalgamated AMG 854	Lu Lu Bell/Long Long Time	£100
69	Big Shot BI 520	Worries/VAL BENNETT: Hound Dog Special	£450
69	Crab CRAB 5	Spread Your Bed/Worries A Yard	£180
70	Nu Beat NB 060	Pick My Pocket/FREEDOM SINGERS: Freedom	£30
71	Nu Beat NB 076	Give It To Me/TIGER: With Hot	£30
74	Dip DL 5039	Cutting Rasor (as Versatiles)/UPSETTERS: Black Belt Jones	£45
74	No Label TSL EDT 1210/1211	Thanks We Get/Ungrateful Skank	£65

(see also Pioneers, Soul Sisters, Junior Byles)

VERTICAL HOLD

80	Vertical Hold VH 001	Rubber Cross/Injustice (p/s)	£40
84	Vertical Hold VH 002	Angel Dust/Four Years/Dub Years (p/s, insert)	£15
85	Vertical Hold VH 003	Bio-Hazard/The War That Time Won (p/s)	£15

VERVE

92	Hut HUTEN 21	GRAVITY GRAVE EP (Gravity Grave [Edit]/Endless Life/ She's A Superstar [Live at Clapham Grand]) (10", p/s)	£15
98	Hut HUTTX 100	SINGLES (Box set, 4 x 12")	£25
93	Hut HUTLP 3	A STORM IN HEAVEN (LP, gatefold)	£80
93	Jolly Roger JOLLY ROGER 2	VOYAGER 1 (LP, official bootleg, blue vinyl, 1,000 only)	£100
95	Hut HUTLP 27	A NORTHERN SOUL (2-LP, mirrored sleeve)	£100
97	Hut HUTLPX 45	URBAN HYMNS (2LP, with inner sleeves, printed outer mailer, 5,000 only)	£150
97	Hut HUTLPX 45	URBAN HYMNS (2-LP)	£80
08	Parlophone 82075 2355841	FORTH (LP)	£15
16	Virgin 00602547865380	A STORM IN HEAVEN (LP, reissue)	£15
16	Virgin 4786539	A NORTHERN SOUL (LP, reissue)	£15
16	Virgin EMI 4787014	URBAN HYMNS (2-LP, reissue)	£20

(see also Richard Ashcroft)

VERY THINGS

84	Reflex LEX 3	THE BUSHES SCREAM WHILE MY DADDY PRUNES (LP)	£15
93	Fire REFIRELP 13	IT'S A DRUG, IT'S A DRUG (LP)	£15

VETS

79	SRT SRTS 79 CUS 513	Flies/Contrix (wrap around p/s)	£50
80	Deckchair DECK 80/001	World In Action/GO ATTIC: Waiting For Fashion (fold-around p/s)	£25

VEX
84   Fight Back FIGHT 1   SANCTUARY (12" EP, with insert)..£50
ROD VEY
80   Rip Off RIP 13   Metal Love/Silicone City (die-cut sleeve)..£25
VHF (1)
80   Lion PAW 1   Heart Of Stone (no p/s) £40
VHF (2)
81   Distil DIST 81   First Impressions/First Impressions (no p/s, many labels signed) £35
81   Pennine   1st IMPRESSIONS (LP)..£90
LUKE VIBERT
98   Mo Wax MW 072 LP   BIG SOUP (2-LP, inners)..£20
DANNY VIBES
00   Jah Tubbys JT 006   Want No Wickedness/Want No Dub £20
VIBRASONIC
95   Yep! YEPLP 01   VIBRASONIC (LP)...£15
VIBRATIONS
61   Pye International 7N 25107 The Watusi/Wallflower £25
64   London HLK 9875   My Girl Sloopy/Daddy Woo Woo...£20
66   Columbia DB 7895   Canadian Sunset/The Story Of A Starry Night..£25
67   Columbia DB 8175   Pick Me/You Better Beware £30
67   Columbia DB 8318   Talkin' 'Bout Love/One Mint Julep £25
68   Direction 58-3511   Love In Them There Hills/Remember The Rain £15
67   Columbia SX 6106   NEW VIBRATIONS (LP) £75
69   Direction 8-63644   GREATEST HITS (LP) £30
72   RCA SF 8254   THE VIBRATIONS (LP)...£20
(see also Jayhawks)
VIBRATORS
76   RAK RAK 245   We Vibrate/Whips And Furs £15
77   RAK RAK 253   Bad Times/No Heart (unreleased, this price is for acetates, of which 2 copies exist)......£200
77   Epic EPC 82097   PURE MANIA (LP) £30
78   Epic EPC 82495   V2 (LP, with inner lyric sleeve) £30
82   Anagram GRAM 002   GUILTY (LP)..£15
(see also Chris Spedding, Substitute, Urban Dogs)
VIBRATORS (JAMAICA)
66   Doctor Bird DB 1036   Sloop John B/Amour £45
(see also Al & Vibrators, Wilbert Francis & Vibrators)
VIBRAVOID
09   Fruits De Mer Crustacean 07 KRAUT ROCK SENSATION EP (1st pressing, 300 copies on marbled blue vinyl) £45
09   Fruits De Mer Crustacean 07 KRAUT ROCK SENSATION EP (repressing, 300 copies on clear red vinyl) £35
10   Fruits De Mer Crustacean 10 WHAT COLOUR IS PINK EP (p/s, insert, 300 only, pink vinyl).......................................£30
VIBRONICS
98   Deep Root ROOT 002   Jah Light, Jah Love/Dub...£25
04   Jah Tubbys JT 10021   Terror/African Stone (10") £20
VIC & JOHN
94   Kent 6T 10   Why Did She Lie/PHIL TERRELL: Love Has Passed Me By £35
VICE CREEMS
78   Tiger GRRRR 1   Won't You Be My Girl?/01-01-212 (gatefold p/s)..£30
79   Zig Zag ZZ22 001   Danger Love/Like A Tiger (p/s) £25
VICE VERSA
80   Neutron NT 001/PX 1092   MUSIC 4 (EP, poster p/s) £30
(see also ABC, Liza Strike)
VICEROYS
67   Island WI 3095   Lip And Tongue/DAWN PENN: When I'm Gonna Be Free £125
67   Coxsone CS 7031   Magadown/RICHARD ACE: Don't Let The Sun Catch You Crying £150
67   Studio One SO 2016   Lose And Gain (as Voiceroys)/SOUL BROTHERS: Honey Pot................................£130
67   Studio One SO 2025   Shake Up/NORMA FRASER: Telling Me Lies £75
68   Studio One SO 2064   Last Night/Ya Ho...£250
68   Blue Cat BS 121   Fat Fish/OCTAVES: You're Gonna Lose £750
69   Punch PH 3   Jump In A Fire/Give To Get (as Voiceroys) £85
69   Crab CRAB 12   Work It/You Mean So Much To Me (B-side actually by Paragons)....................£60
79   Music Hawk MH 01   Can't Stop Us/ROD TAYLOR: Jah Jah Calling (12") £40
84   Greensleeves GRED 146   New Clothes/New Clothes Rhythm/Bubblers Version (12") £15
82   Trojan TRLS 206   WE MUST UNITE (LP) £45
83   Csa CSLP 5   BRETHEREN AND SISTREN (LP) £50
84   Greensleeves GREL 57   CHANCERY LANE (LP)..£15
(see also Richard Ace, Interns [Jamaica], Derrick Morgan, Vincent Gordon, Hub, Truth, Fact & Correct)
VICEROYS (U.K.)
70   Bullet BU 441   Chariot Coming/SYDNEY ALLSTARS: Stackata £25
70   Bullet BU 444   Power Control/SLICKERS: Dip Dip £25
70   Bullet BU 450   Come On Over/SYDNEY ALLSTARS: Version £20
70   Bullet BU 453   Fancy Clothes/BIGGIE: Jack And Jill £20
71   Bullet BU 470   Rebel Nyah/Feel The Spirit £20

VICE SQUAD
80	Riot City RIOT 1	Last Rockers/Living On Dreams/Latex Love (p/s, with poster)	£15
81	Riot City ZEM 103	NO CAUSE FOR CONCERN (LP)	£15
82	EMI ZEM 104	STAND STRONG STAND PROUD (LP, with inner)	£15
84	Anagram GRAM 14	SHOT AWAY (LP)	£15

(see also Sex Aids)

SID VICIOUS
79	Virgin V 2144	SID SINGS (LP, picture inner, with poster)	£45
79	Virgin V 2144	SID SINGS (LP, picture inner, without poster)	£15

(see also Sex Pistols)

MIKE VICKERS (ORCHESTRA)
65	Columbia DB 7657	On The Brink/The Puff Adder (as Mike Vickers & Orchestra)	£50
65	Columbia DB 7657	On The Brink/The Puff Adder (as Mike Vickers & Orchestra) (DJ Copy)	£100
66	Columbia DB 7825	Eleventy One/The Inkling	£20
66	Columbia DB 7906	Morgan - A Suitable Case For Treatment/Gorilla Of My Dreams (as Mike Vickers Orchestra)	£20
67	Columbia DB 8281	Captain Scarlet And The Mysterons/Kettle Of Fish	£30
68	Columbia S(C)X 6180	I WISH I WERE A GROUP AGAIN (LP)	£45

(see also Manfred Mann)

VICKY
67	Philips BF 1565	Colours Of Love (Love Is Blue)/Who Can Tell	£15

VICKY & JERRY
60	HMV POP 715	Don't Cry/A Year Ago Tonight	£20

VICTIM
78	Good Vibrations GOT 2	Strange Things By Night/Mixed Up World (wraparound p/s)	£15
79	TJM TJM 13	THE VICTIM (EP, unreleased)	£0
79	TJM TJM 14	Why Are Fire Engines Red/I Need You (p/s)	£30
80	TJM TJM 15	The Teen Age/Junior Criminals/Hung On To Yourself (p/s)	£25
80	Illuminated ILL 1	The Teen Age/Junior Criminals/Hung On To Yourself (p/s, reissue)	£15

VICTIMIZE
79	I.M.E. IME 1	Baby Buyer/Hi Rising Failure (folded p/s)	£70
80	I.M.E. IME 2	Where Did the Money Go/Innocence (p/s, some on white labels)	£80

VICTIMS OF CHANCE
70	Stable SLE 8004	VICTIMS OF CHANCE (LP)	£125

VICTIMS OF VICTIMISATION
87	Death DEAD 2	Kill Or Be Killed/As A Doornail (p/s)	£18

TONY VICTOR
62	Decca F 11459	Dear One/There Was A Time	£25

VICTORIA
71	Atlantic 2400 176	VICTORIA (LP)	£30
71	Atlantic 2466 008	SECRET OF THE BLOOM (LP)	£45

VICTORIANS
64	Liberty LIB 55693	Oh What A Night For Love/Happy Birthday Blue	£25

VICTORS (1)
65	Oriole CB 1984	Take This Old Hammer/Answer's No	£15

VICTORS (2)
69	High Note HS 019	Reggae Buddy/Easy Squeeze	£65
69	Studio One SO 2077	Things A-Come To Bump (A-side actually by BASES/LYRICS: Old Man Say	£70
71	Escort ERT 846	Me A Tell Yuh/LLOYD'S ALL-STARS: More Echoe	£45

VICTORY
82	Rods HOT 3	TAKING THE FIGHT (LP, with lyric insert)	£60

(see also Keith Howard)

VIDELS
60	London HLI 9153	Mister Lonely/I'll Forget You	£60

VIDEOS
81	Guardian GRC 85	Deo/Beautiful People/Him Or Me	£15

VIETNAM ALL STARS (ACTUALLY PRINCE BUSTER WITH UNKNOWN VOCALIST)
66	Rio R 109	The Toughest/ERROL DUNKLEY : Love Me Forever	£100

VIETNAMESE ROSE
82	aaron B ROSE 1	Curtains You/Tinker Tailor	£15

VIGILANTES
61	Pye International 7N 25082	Eclipse/Man In Space	£20

VIGRASS & OSBORNE
72	Uni UDLS 501	QUEUES (LP, gatefold)	£40

(PAUL) VIGRASS
69	RCA RCA 1857	Free Lorry Ride/Flying	£15

VIKINGS (JAMAICA)
63	Island WI 035	Maggie Don't Leave Me/Henchmen (both actually with Victor Wong)	£20
63	Island WI 075	Six And Seven Books Of Moses/Zacions (actually by Maytals)	£25
63	Island WI 101	Never Grow Old/Irene (actually by Maytals)	£30
63	Island WI 107	Just Got To Be/You Make Me Do (actually by Maytals)	£20
63	Island WI 117	Fever/Cheer Up (actually by Maytals)	£30

64	Island WI 167	Daddy/It's You (actually by Maytals)	£20
64	Black Swan WI 423	Down By The Riverside/This Way	£30
64	Black Swan WI 428	Treat Me Bad/Sitting On Top	£25
64	Black Swan WI 430	Come Into My Parlour/I Am In Love	£20

(see also Maytals, Flames [Jamaica], Bonnie & Skitto)

VIKINGS
66	Alp 595 011	Bad News Feeling/What Can I Do	£30

VIKINGS INTERNATIONAL
70s Penthouse	VOLUME 1 (LP)	£350

KURT VILE
13	Matador OLE 998-0	WALKIN ON A PRETTY DAZE (2-LP, blue vinyl with stickers)	£20
18	Matador OLE 1146-3	BOTTLE IT IN (2-LP, orange/yellow sunburst edition with stickers)	£40

VILLAGE
69	Head HDS 4002	Man In The Moon/Long Time Coming	£75

(see also Peter Bardens, Quiver)

VILLAGERS
88	Hole In One HOLEIN 1	Marie/Don't Try (p/s, 500 only)	£35

VILLAGERS/PARCEL OF ROGUES
73	Deroy (no cat. no.)	PARCEL OF FOLK (LP, private pressing, with insert)	£100

VILLIERS & GOLD
68	Polydor 56235	Of All The Young Girls/This East	£20

GENE VINCENT (& BLUE CAPS)

78s
56	Capitol CL 14599	Be-Bop-A-Lula/Woman Love	£15
56	Capitol CL 14628	Race With The Devil/Gonna Back Up, Baby	£25
56	Capitol CL 14637	Bluejean Bop/Who Slapped John?	£15
57	Capitol CL 14681	Jumps, Giggles And Shouts/Wedding Bells (Are Breaking Up That Old Gang Of Mine)	£30
57	Capitol CL 14693	Crazy Legs/Important Words	£30
57	Capitol CL 14722	Bi-I-Bickey-Bi, Bo-Bo-Go/Five Days, Five Days	£30
57	Capitol CL 14763	Lotta Lovin'/Wear My Ring	£25
57	Capitol CL 14808	Dance To The Bop/I Got It	£25
58	Capitol CL 14830	Walkin' Home From School/I Got A Baby	£35
59	Capitol CL 15053	Right Now/The Night Is So Lonely	£150

SINGLES
56	Capitol CL 14599	Be-Bop-A-Lula/Woman Love	£40
56	Capitol CL 14628	Race With The Devil/Gonna Back Up, Baby	£100
56	Capitol CL 14637	Bluejean Bop/Who Slapped John?	£60
57	Capitol CL 14681	Jumps, Giggles And Shouts/Wedding Bells (Are Breaking Up That Old Gang Of Mine) (promo copy in p/s)	£125
57	Capitol CL 14681	Jumps, Giggles And Shouts/Wedding Bells (Are Breaking Up That Old Gang Of Mine)	£100
57	Capitol CL 14693	Crazy Legs/Important Words (in p/s)	£75
57	Capitol CL 14693	Crazy Legs/Important Words	£50
57	Capitol CL 14722	Bi-I-Bickey-Bi, Bo-Bo-Go/Five Days, Five Days (in p/s)	£150
57	Capitol CL 14722	Bi-I-Bickey-Bi, Bo-Bo-Go/Five Days, Five Days	£75
57	Capitol CL 14763	Lotta Lovin'/Wear My Ring	£50
57	Capitol CL 14808	Dance To The Bop/I Got It	£50
58	Capitol CL 14830	Walkin' Home From School/I Got A Baby (in p/s)	£70
58	Capitol CL 14830	Walkin' Home From School/I Got A Baby	£50
58	Capitol CL 14868	Baby Blue/True To You	£40
58	Capitol CL 14908	Rocky Road Blues/Yes I Love You, Baby	£40
58	Capitol CL 14935	Git It/Little Lover	£40
59	Capitol CL 14974	Say Mama/Be Bop Boogie Boy	£30
59	Capitol CL 15000	Who's Pushin' Your Swing/Over The Rainbow	£20
59	Capitol CL 15035	Summertime/Frankie And Johnnie	£25
59	Capitol CL 15053	Right Now/The Night Is So Lonely	£20
59	Capitol CL 15099	Wild Cat/Right Here On Earth	£15
60	Capitol CL 15115	My Heart/I've Got To Get You Yet	£15

(Credited to Gene Vincent & Blue Caps.)
60	Capitol CL 15136	Pistol Packin' Mama (as Gene Vincent & Beat Boys)/Weeping Willow	£15
60	Capitol CL 15169	Anna-Annabelle/Ac-Cent-Tchu-Ate The Positive	£15
61	Capitol CL 15179	Maybe/Jezebel	£15
61	Capitol CL 15185	If You Want My Lovin'/Mister Loneliness	£15
61	Capitol CL 15202	She She Little Sheila/Hot Dollar	£15
61	Capitol CL 15215	I'm Going Home (To See My Baby)/Love Of A Man	£15
61	Capitol CL 15231	Unchained Melody/Brand New Beat (with The Blue Caps)	£15
62	Capitol CL 15243	Lucky Star/Baby Don't Believe Him (with Dave Burgess Band)	£18
62	Capitol CL 15264	Be-Bop-A-Lula/The King Of Fools (with Charles Blackwell Orchestra)	£15
63	Capitol CL 15290	Held For Questioning/You're Still In My Heart (with Charles Blackwell Orch.)	£15
63	Capitol CL 15307	Rip It Up/High Blood Pressure (unissued, demo copies only)	£250
63	Capitol CL 15307	Crazy Beat/High Blood Pressure	£40
63	Columbia DB 7174	Temptation Baby/Where Have You Been All My Life	£20
64	Columbia DB 7218	Humpity Dumpity/A Love 'Em And Leave 'Em Kinda Guy	£20
64	Columbia DB 7293	La-Den-Da Den-Da-Da/The Beginning Of The End	£20
64	Columbia DB 7343	Private Detective/You Are My Sunshine (as Gene Vincent & Shouts)	£20
66	London HLH 10079	Bird Doggin'/Ain't That Too Much	£30
66	London HLH 10099	Lonely Street/I've Got My Eyes On You	£30

68	Capitol CL 15546	Be-Bop-A-Lula/Say Mama	£15

EPs

58	Capitol EAP 1-985	HOT ROD GANG	£75
59	Capitol EAP 1-1059	A GENE VINCENT RECORD DATE	£75
60	Capitol EAP 3-1059	A GENE VINCENT RECORD DATE PART 3	£80
61	Capitol EAP 1-20173	IF YOU WANT MY LOVIN'	£80
62	Capitol EAP 1-20354	RACE WITH THE DEVIL	£80
63	Capitol EAP 1-20461	TRUE TO YOU	£80
64	Capitol EAP 1-20453	THE CRAZY BEAT OF GENE VINCENT NO. 1	£80
64	Capitol EAP 2-20453	THE CRAZY BEAT OF GENE VINCENT NO. 2	£80
64	Capitol EAP 3-20453	THE CRAZY BEAT OF GENE VINCENT NO. 3	£80
69	EMIdisc (no cat. no.)	LIVE & ROCKIN'! (fan club issue, mail-order, 99 only)	£250

ALBUMS : LPS

56	Capitol T 764	BLUEJEAN BOP! (original pressing with turquoise labels)	£130
56	Capitol T 764	BLUEJEAN BOP! (later pressing with rainbow labels)	£60
57	Capitol T 811	GENE VINCENT AND THE BLUECAPS (turquoise label)	£125
57	Capitol T 811	GENE VINCENT AND THE BLUECAPS (rainbow label)	£60
58	Capitol T 970	GENE VINCENT ROCKS! & THE BLUECAPS ROLL (turquoise label)	£130
58	Capitol T 970	GENE VINCENT ROCKS! & THE BLUECAPS ROLL (later rainbow label)	£60
59	Capitol T 1059	A GENE VINCENT RECORD DATE	£70
59	Capitol T 1207	SOUNDS LIKE GENE VINCENT	£70
60	Capitol T 1342	CRAZY TIMES! (mono)	£60
60	Capitol ST 1342	CRAZY TIMES! (stereo)	£70
63	Capitol T 20453	THE CRAZY BEAT OF GENE VINCENT	£65
64	Columbia 33SX 1646	SHAKIN' UP A STORM (as Gene Vincent & The Shouts)	£60
67	London HA-H 8333	GENE VINCENT	£50
67	Capitol T 20957	THE BEST OF GENE VINCENT ('rainbow' label; reissue with pink label £12)	£20
68	Capitol ST 21144	THE BEST OF GENE VINCENT VOL. 2 ('rainbow' label; reissue with pink label £12)	£20
70	Dandelion 63754	I'M BACK AND I'M PROUD (gatefold sleeve)	£30
71	Kama Sutra 2316 005	THE DAY THE WORLD TURNED BLUE	£20
71	Kama Sutra 2316 009	IF YOU COULD ONLY SEE ME TODAY	£20
87	Charly BOX 108	GENE VINCENT: THE CAPITOL YEARS '56-'63 (10-LP box set with 36-page booklet; later remastered and reissued with slimmer box, 1989)	£50
90	EMI CDGV 1	THE GENE VINCENT BOX SET (Complete Capitol & Columbia Recordings, 1956-64) (6-CD set)	£20

RORY VINCENT

73	Columbia SCXA 9254	SINGS THE MUSIC OF WLODEK GULGOWSKI (LP)	£20

JOEY VINE

65	Immediate IM 017	Down And Out/The Out Of Towner	£30

VINEGAR JOE

72	Island ILPS 9183	VINEGAR JOE (LP)	£30
72	Island ILPS 9214	ROCK 'N ROLL GYPSIES (LP, gatefold sleeve)	£25
73	Island ILPS 9262	SIX STAR GENERAL (LP, gatefold sleeve, inner)	£25

(see also Dada, Elkie Brooks)

VINES (1)

02	Heavenly HVNLP 36	HIGHLY EVOLVED (LP)	£25
04	Capitol 724358433814	WINNING DAYS (LP)	£20
06	Heavenly HVNLP 56	VISION VALLEY (LP)	£25

LEROY VINNEGAR

63	Contemporary LAC 570	LEROY WALKS AGAIN! (LP)	£30

EDDIE 'MR. CLEANHEAD' VINSON

51	Vogue V 2023	Queen Bee Blues/Jump And Grunt (78)	£15
64	Riverside RLP 3302	BACK DOOR BLUES (LP)	£40
72	Philips 6369 406	THE ORIGINAL CLEANHEAD (LP)	£18

(see also Wynonie Harris)

V. VINSTRICK & J.J. ALLSTARS

68	Doctor Bird DB 1167	Love Is Not A Game/CINDERELLA: The Way I See You	£65

IAN VINT

64	Columbia 33SX 1649	TELL ME WHY (LP)	£25

BOBBY VINTON

64	Columbia DB 7422	Mr Lonely/The Bell That Couldn't Jingle	£15
62	Columbia SEG 8212	YOUNG IN HEART (EP)	£20
64	Columbia SEG 8363	SONGS OF CHRISTMAS (EP)	£25
63	Columbia 33SX 1517	SINGS THE BIG ONES (LP)	£25
62	Columbia 33SX1465	ROSES ARE RED (LP)	£25
63	Columbia 33SX 1566	BLUE ON BLUE (LP)	£25
63	Columbia 33SX 1611	MY HEART BELONGS TO ONLY YOU (LP)	£25
65	Columbia 33SX1725	LAUGHING ON THE OUTSIDE (LP)	£25

VIOLATORS

82	No Future OI 9	Gangland/Fugitive (p/s, with insert)	£20
82	No Future OI 19	Summer Of '81/Live Fast Die Young (p/s)	£20
83	No Future OI 26	DIE WITH DIGNITY EP (12")	£50

VIOLENT FEMMES

83	Rough Trade ROUGH 55	VIOLENT FEMMES (LP)	£30
84	Slash SLAP 1	HALLOWED GROUND (LP)	£15

VIOLENTS
63   HMV POP 1130   Alpen Ros/Ghia £18

VIOLENT THIMBLE
67   Polydor 56217   Gentle People Parts 1 & 2 .... £15

VIPERS (SKIFFLE GROUP)
56   Parlophone R 4238   Ain't You Glad/Pick A Bale Of Cotton £20
57   Parlophone R 4261   Don't You Rock Me Daddy-O/10,000 Years Ago £20
57   Parlophone R 4286   Jim Dandy/Hi Liley, Liley Lo £15
57   Parlophone R 4289   The Cumberland Gap/Maggie May £15
57   Parlophone R 4308   Streamline Train/Railroad Steam Boat £15
57   Parlophone R 4351   Homing Bird/Pay Me My Money Down £15
57   Parlophone R 4371   Skiffle Party Medley Parts 1 & 2 .... £15
58   Parlophone R 4393   Baby Why?/No Other Baby (as Vipers) £15
58   Parlophone R 4435   Make Ready For Love/Nothing Will Ever Change (My Love For You)(as Vipers) £15
58   Parlophone R 4484   Summertime Blues/Liverpool Blues (as Vipers) £35
58   Parlophone R 4484   Summertime Blues/Liverpool Blues (as Vipers) (78) £20
57   Parlophone GEP 8615   SKIFFLE MUSIC VOL. 1 (EP) £20
57   Parlophone GEP 8626   SKIFFLE MUSIC VOL. 2 (EP) £20
57   Parlophone GEP 8655   SKIFFLING ALONG WITH THE VIPERS (EP) £20
57   Parlophone PMD 1050   COFFEE BAR SESSION (10" LP) £60
(see also Shadows, Wally Whyton, Sharkey Todd & Monsters)

VIPPS
66   CBS 202031   Wintertime/Anyone £80
(see also VIPS)

VIPS
64   RCA RCA 1427   Don't Keep Shouting At Me/She's So Good £100
66   Island WI 3003   I Wanna Be Free/Don't Let It Go £50
67   Island WIP 6005   Straight Down To The Bottom/In A Dream £80
(see also Vipps, Art, Spooky Tooth, Felder's Orioles, Timebox, Patto, Baron & His Pounding Piano, Keith Emerson)

V.I.P.S
78   Bust SOL 3   MUSIC FOR FUNSTERS (EP) £20
79   Rok ROK V/VI   Can't Let You Go/URBAN DISTURBANCE: Wild Boys In Cortinas £25
(see also Mood Six, Jed Dmochowski)

VIRGIL BROTHERS
69   Parlophone R 5787   Temptation 'Bout To Get Me/Look Away £15

VIRGINIA TREE
75   Minstrel 0001   FRESH OUT (LP) £50
(see also Shirley Kent, Ghost)

VIRGINIA WOLVES
66   Stateside SS 563   Stay/B.L.T. £50
66   Stateside SS 563   Stay/B.L.T. (DJ copy) £100

VIRGIN PRUNES
81   Baby BABY 001   TWENTY TENS (EP) £15
81   Rough Trade RT 072   Moments Of Mine (Despite Straight Lines)/In The Greylight/War/Moments Of Mine
                             (Despite Straight Lines) (1st issue in blue p/s with insert) £15
81   Rough Trade RT 89   A New Form Of Beauty 1; Sandpaper Lullaby/Sleep Fantasy Dreams (p/s) £15
82   Rough Trade TI COPY 007 A New Form Of Beauty 4:Din Glorious (cassette) £25
82   Rough Trade ROUGH 49   ...IF IF DIE, I DIE (LP) £15
87   Baby BABY 011   HERESIE (10", double pack, gatefold p/s, 1st 1,000 on clear vinyl)...... £15
(see also Gavin Friday)

VIRGIN SLEEP
67   Deram DM 146   Love/Halliford House £70
68   Deram DM 173   Secret/Comes A Time £80

VIRGO
89   Radical RADICAL 1   DO YOU KNOW WHO YOU ARE? (12" EP p/s) £20
89   Radical Records VIRG01 VIRGO (LP) £35

VIRTUE
85   Other OTH 1   We Stand To Fight/High Treason (p/s) £20

VIRTUES (JAMAICA)
65   Island WI 196   Your Wife And Mother/Amen (actually with Ambassadors) £40
68   Doctor Bird DB 1164   High Tide/RUPIE EDWARDS & VIRTUES: Burning Love £60
68   Doctor Bird DB 1166   Sweet Nanny/RUPIE EDWARDS : Falling In Love £70
(see also Lloyd & Devon)

VIRTUES (U.S.)
59   HMV POP 621   Guitar Boogie Shuffle/Guitar In Orbit £15
59   HMV POP 637   Flippin' In/Shufflin' Along £15

FRANK VIRTUOSO ROCKETS
56   Melodisc MEL 1393   Toodle-Oo Kangaroo/Hop-Skip-Jump Mambo (78) £15
58   Melodisc MEL 1386   Rollin' And A-Rockin'/Rock - Good Bye Mambo (red label, tri centre, export issue) £30
58   Melodisc MEL 1386   Rollin' And Rockin'/Toodle-Oo Kangaroo (green label, round centre) £15

VISAGE
79   Radar ADA 48   Tar/Frequency 7 (p/s) £15
81   Polydor POSPX 194   Fade To Grey/The Steps (12", p/s)... £15
(see also Rich Kids, Steve Strange, Strange Cruise, Midge Ure, Ultravox)

MINT VALUE £

TONY VISCONTI
74   Regal Zonophone RZ 3089   I Remember Brooklyn/Sitting In A Field Of Heather £20
(see also Dib Cochran & Earwigs)

VISCOUNTS
60   Pye NEP 24132   VISCOUNTS' HIT PARADE (EP) £20

VISCOUNTS (U.S.)
59   Top Rank JAR 254   Harlem Nocturne/Dig...£15
60   Top Rank JAR 388   The Touch (Le Grisbi)/Chug-A-Lug..£15
60   Top Rank JAR 502   Night Train/Summertime £18
61   Top Rank JKP 3005   VISCOUNTS ROCK (EP)...£35

VISIONS
69   Grape GR 3009   Captain Hook/The Girl £100
(see also King Horror)

VISITORS (1)
78   NRG SRTS/NRG 002   Take It Or Leave It/No Compromise...£25
79   Deep Heat DEEP ONE   Electric Heat/Moth/One Line (p/s)..£40
80   Departure RAPTURE 1   Empty Rooms/The Orcadian Visitors (foldover p/s) £15

VITAL DISORDERS
81   Lowther International VD 1   PRAMS EP: Snatcher/Tough TImes/'Prams (6 different p/s variations) £20
83   Vital Disorders VD3   Some People/Christmas Island Calypso (p/s) £15

VITAL DUB
77   Virgin V 2055   WELL CHARGED (LP, green two virgins label) £20

VITAL FORCE
87   Buce BUCE 1   Roll The Dice/Poor Little Rich Boy (no p/s) £25

VITAL ORGANS
82   Airship AP 594   Radio Active/Glastonbury (p/s) £15

VITAL REMAINS
92   Deaf DEAF 9   LET US PRAY (LP)...£25

VITAL SIGNS
83   Powerstation PS 1   Tradiing In Guilt/Miracles £80

VITAMIN B12
00   Private Press (No Cat. No.)   VITAMIN B12 (2-LP, 99 copies only)..£20

MIROSLAV VITOUS
79   Warner Bros. K 17448 T   New York CIty/Basic Laws (12") £40
76   Warner Bros. K56219   MAGIC SHEPHERD (LP)...£15

VIVEK
07   On The Edge OTE 001   Natural Mystic/Sunshine (12")...£18
13   System SYSTM 001   Asteroids/Over My Head/Over My Head (Om Unit Remix) (12")........................£40
13   System SYSTM 003   Mantra/Show Me/Soundman VIP/Asteroids VIP (2 x 12")..................................£30
15   System SYSTM 009   Square Up/Slippin' (12") £35
18   System SYSTM 010   94/Namaste (10")..£18

V-NECK
95   Emote MOTE 004   Auto/Quasi/Semi/Uni (12") £60
96   Emote MOTE 005   Woh Yeh/Burning The Toast/Woh Yeh (Version)/Dubbing The Toast (12") £20
97   Emote MOTE 006   At The Door (Remix)/(Original)/Red Eye Dub (12" as V Neck vs Zion Train) £40

CRISTIAN VOGEL
94   Ferox FER 004   NARCO SYNTHESIS EP (12", plain sleeve) £25
94   Mosquito MSQ 01   WE EQUATE MACHINES WITH FUNKINESS EP (12", custom sleeve) £25
95   Mosquito MSQ 03   ARTISTS IN CHARGE OF EXPERT SYSTEMS EP (12", custom sleeve)...............£20
95   Solid SOL 002   DEFUNKT EP (12". Three untitled tracks)...£20
96   Solid SOL 004   The Visit/Spoke/Small Dogs (12")...£30
(see also Blue Arsed Fly)

VOGUES (U.K.)
66   Columbia DB 7985   Younger Girl/Lies £18
(see also Llan)

VOGUES (U.S.)
65   London HLU 9996   You're The One/Some Words..£20
66   London HLU 10014   Five O'Clock World/Nothing To Offer You £20
66   King KG 1035   Magic Town/Humpty Dumpty £25
69   London HLG 10247   Five O'Clock World/You're The One..£15
66   King KGL 4003   MEET THE VOGUES (LP)..£45
66   King KGL 4006   FIVE O'CLOCK WORLD (LP) £40
69   Reprise RSLP 6314   TURN AROUND, LOOK AT ME (LP)..£20
69   Reprise RSLP 6326   TILL (LP)...£15

VOICE
66   Mercury MF 905   Train To Disaster/Truth...£250
(see also Karl Stuart & Profile, Profile, Miller Anderson)

VOICE OF PROGRESS
82   Negus Roots NERLP 003   MINI BUS DRIVER (LP) £30

VOICE OF THE PUPPETS
80   IS/VP/1044   I Don't Want To Know/You're All I Wanted (And A Car) (poster p/s)............................£300

VOICES
56	Beltona BL 2667	Rock And Roll Hit Parade Medley (Parts 1 & 2) £18

VOICES IN LATIN
68	Morgan MR 104P	VOICE IN LATIN (LP) £60

VOID
82	Hole In Space VOID 1	Into The Void/I Want You (no p/s) £40

STERLING VOID
89	DJ International/CBS 4661461	IT'S ALL RIGHT (LP) £18

VOIDS
66	Polydor BM 56073	Come On Out/I'm In A Fix £120

WES VOIGHT
59	Parlophone R 4586	I'm Movin' In/I'm Ready To Go Steady £80

(see also Chip Taylor)

VOIZ
77	Pilgrim/Grapevine GRA 110	BOANERGES (LP, with insert) £25

HOWARD VOKES COUNTRY BOYS
62	Starlite STEP 27	HOWARD VOKES COUNTRY BOYS (EP)... £15
63	Starlite STEP 37	MOUNTAIN GUITAR (EP) £15

VOLCANOS
61	Philips PB 1098	Ruby Duby Du/Redhead.. £20
61	Philips PB 1113	Tightrope/Great Imposter.. £20
62	Philips PB 1246	Polaris/Scotch Mist £20
60	Philips BBE 12432	THE VOLCANOS (EP) £100

VOLTZ
82	Airship PP 580	KNIGHT'S FALL (LP) £70

VOLUMES
62	Fontana 270 109TF	I Love You/Dreams £80
63	London HL 9733	Sandra/Teenage Paradise.. £75

VON TRAP FAMILY
80	Woronzow W 001	Brand New Thrill/Dreaming/No Reflexes (p/s, 500 only)................................. £40

(see also Bevis Frond)

ERIC VON SCHMIDT
68	Transatlantic PR 7384	ERIC SINGS VON SCHMIDT (LP) £80

VON SUDENFED
07	Domino WIGLP 190	TROMATIC REFLEXXIONS (2-LP) £25

(see also The Fall, Mouse On Mars)

VONTASTICS
66	Chess CRS 8043	Day Tripper/My Baby £25
67	Stateside SS 2002	Lady Love/When My Baby Comes Back Home.. £65
67	Stateside SS 2002	Lady Love/When My Baby Comes Back Home (DJ Copy)................................. £85

VOOMINS
65	Polydor 56001	If You Don't Come Back/March Of The Voomins... £35

VOXPOPPERS
58	Mercury 7MT 202	The Last Drag/Wishing For Your Love £30
58	Mercury 7MT 202	The Last Drag/Wishing For Your Love (78)... £25
58	Mercury MEP 9533	VOXPOPPERS (EP) £150

VOYAGER (1)
85	Fighting Cock	Run Away Heart/Don't Hold Back (p/s) £15

VOYAGER (2)
95	Lucky Spin LSR 018	PART 1: Knowledge/Haunted (12")... £25
95	Lucky Spin INT 002	PART 2: Eastern Promise/Voyager (12") £15

V2
78	Bent SMALL BENT 1	Speed Freak/Nothing To Do/That's It (800 only, later reissued on red vinyl) £40
78	Bent SMALL BENT 1	Speed Freak/Nothing To Do/That's It (red vinyl reissue)................................. £15
79	TJM TJM 1	Man In The Box/When The World Isn't There (12", p/s)................................... £20
79	TJM TJM 6	Is Anybody Out There? (unissued) £0
70s	Groove ZOE 1	Gee Whiz It's You/Face In The Crowd (p/s, stamped white labels)................. £30

VULCANS
72	Trojan TR 7863	Star Trek/Back A Yard... £20
72	Trojan TRLS 53	STAR TREK (LP)... £70

VULCAN'S HAMMER
73	Brown BVH 1	TRUE HEARTS AND SOUND BOTTOMS (LP, with insert)................................... £450

VULTURES
79	Rubber Connection SP 522	Time Let's Go/Is This A Man (p/s, with insert & sticker)................................... £15

VYLLIES
86	Fun After All AFTER 2	LILTH (LP) £25

PHIL WACHSMANN
85 Bead Records BEAD 23   **WRITING IN WATER** (LP) **£20**

PHILIPP WACHSMANN, RICHARD BESWICK & TONY WREN
77 Bead Records BEAD 7   **SPARKS OF THE DESIRE MAGNETO** (LP, with insert) **£30**

WACKERS (1)
63 Oriole CB 1902   **I Wonder Why/Why Can't It Happen To Me** **£25**
64 Piccadilly 7N 35195   **Love Or Money/Hooka Tooka** **£15**
64 Piccadilly 7N 35210   **The Girl Who Wanted Fame/You're Forgetting** **£15**

ADAM WADE
63 Columbia DB 4986   **Don't Let Me Cross Over/Rain From The Skies** **£70**
60 HMV 7EG 8620   **AND THEN CAME ADAM** (EP) **£15**
64 Columbia SEG 8316   **FOUR FILM SONGS** (EP) **£15**
61 HMV CLP 1451   **ADAM AND EVENING** (LP) **£30**

CLIFF WADE
69 Morgan Bluetown BT 1S   **You've Never Been To My House/Sister** **£30**

WAYNE WADE
75 Mango MAN 1005   **Black Is Our Colour/PROPHETS ALLSTARS: Upsetters Vengeance** **£20**
79 Cha Cha CHAD 34   **Tell Me What Going On/WAILING SOULS: Rudeboy Say Him Bad** (12") **£30**
80 Pirate PIR 003   **African Monica/Down In Iran** (12", yellow vinyl) **£35**
81 Greensleeves GRED 52   **Poor And Humble/BUNNY LIE LIE: Babylonian** (12") **£35**
78 Grove Music GMLP 3   **DANCING TIME** (LP) **£30**

WELLINGTON WADE
63 Oriole CB 1857   **Let's Turkey Trot/It Ain't Necessarily So** **£40**

(see also Ian & Zodiacs)

WAGADU
77 Rokel SD RK01   **Sweet Mother/Aki Special** (12", as Wagadu Gu) **£15**
79 Rokel ROK 12   **Freetown Calypso/Easy Dancin'** **£25**

ADRIAN WAGNER
74 Atlantic K 50082   **DISTANCES BETWEEN US** (LP, with Robert Calvert) **£22**

(see also Robert Calvert)

CHUCK WAGON
79 A&M AMS 7450   **Rock 'n' Roll Won't Go Away/The Spy In My Face** (p/s, purple vinyl) **£15**

(see also Dickies)

WAGON CHRIST
94 Rising High RSN LP 18   **PHAT LAB. NIGHTMARE** (2-LP) **£40**
95 Rising High RSN LP 30   **THROBBING POUCH** (2-LP) **£30**
98 Personal/Virgin V2863   **TALLY HO!** (2-LP) **£30**
01 Ninja Tune ZEN 54   **MUSIPAL** (2-LP) **£15**

WAHIB
82 Hits From Heaven HIT 1   **Brings On The Tears/Grey Blues** **£15**

BUNNY WAILER
76 Island BUNNY 1   **Blackheart Man/Amagideon** (12") **£28**
77 Island IPR 2003   **Get Up Stand Up/This Train** (12") **£20**
78 Island IPR 2015   **Love Fire/Love's Version** (12") **£15**
78 Island IPR 2025   **Roots, Radics, Rockers and Reggae/Fig Tree/Armagideon** (12") **£25**
81 Solomonic SM 01   **Rise & Shine/Riding** **£35**
81 Solomonic SM07   **Rise & Shine/Solomonic Dub** (12") **£50**
83 Solomonic SM 018   **Boderation/THE SOLOMONIC PLAYERS - Badder ridim** (12") **£25**
76 Island ILPS 9415   **BLACKHEART MAN** (LP, gatefold) **£30**
80 Island ISLP 9629   **SINGS THE WAILERS** (LP) **£18**
81 Solomic SMDUBLP 002   **DUB DISCO VOL. 2** (LP) **£18**

WAILERS (U.S.)
59 London HL 8958   **Tall Cool One/Road-Runner** **£25**
59 London HL 8958   **Tall Cool One/Road-Runner** (78) **£30**
59 London HL 8994   **Mau-Mau/Dirty Robber** **£150**
59 London HL 8994   **Mau-Mau/Dirty Robber** (78) **£70**

WAILING SOULS
70 Banana BA 305   **Row Fisherman Row/Thou Shalt Not Steal** **£60**
70 Banana BA 307   **Back Out/Pack Your Things** **£50**
71 Banana BA 335   **Walk Walk Walk/KING SPORTY: Love Me - Version** (B-side actually by Denis Alcapone)..**£60**
71 Green Door GD 4014   **Harbour Shark/Harbour Shark - Version** **£25**
78 Greensleeves GRED 1   **War/Jah Give Us Life** (12") **£20**
80 Greensleeves GRED 043   **Kingdom Rise Kingdom Fall/A Day Will Come** (12") **£35**
80 Taxi IPR 2044   **Old Broom/Bredda Gravilicious/Sweet Sugar Plum** (12") **£25**
81 Cha Cha CHAD 34   **Rudeboy Say Him Bad/WAYNE WADE: Tell Me What Going On** (12") **£30**
81 Greensleeves GRED 51   **Who No Waan Come/AL CAMPBELL: Unfaithful Children** (12") **£35**
81 Cha Cha CHAD 32   **Penny I Love You/EARL SIXTEEN: Black Man Time** (12") **£25**

81	Cha Cha CHAD 51	Grabbing And Running/Dub	£25
82	Greensleeves GRED 111	They Don't Know Jah/Sticky Stay (12")	£30
82	Upfront UPF 001	Take We Back (feat Ranking Trevor)/RANKING TREVOR: Yard Oh (12")	£15
82	Upfront UPF 004	Take A Taste/JOHNNY RINGO: Don't Know Much (12")	£15
83	Greensleeves GRED 115	Bounce Back/Sweetie (12")	£15
83	Greensleeves GRED 125	Water Pumpee/Shall Up (12")	£18
84	Greensleeves GRED 152	War Deh Round A Shop John/Peace And Love Shall Reign (12")	£30
79	Island ILPS 9523	WILD SUSPENSE (LP)	£20
81	Greensleeves GREL 21	FIRE HOUSE ROCK (LP)	£25
83	Greensleeves GREL 47	INCHPINCHERS (LP)	£20

(see also Denis Alcapone, Tuff Gong All Stars)

CHERRY WAINER

60	Columbia DB 4528	Happy Like A Bell (Ding Dong)/Money (That's What I Want)	£20
59	Pye NEP 24099	CHERRY WAINER (EP)	£15
60	Top Rank BUY 042	WALTZES IN SPRINGTIME (LP)	£15

(see also Red Price Combo)

PHIL WAINMAN

65	Columbia DB 7615	Hear Me A Drummer Man/Hear His Drums	£30
68	Fontana TF 978	Going Going Gone/Hey Paradiddle	£300

LOUDON WAINWRIGHT III

71	Atlantic 2400 103	ALBUM I (LP)	£22
72	Atlantic K 40272	ALBUM II (LP)	£15
79	Radar RAD 24	A LIVE ONE (LP)	£15

WAITING FOR THE SUN

78	Profile GMOR 167	WAITING FOR THE SUN (LP, private pressing)	£35

(see also After The Fire)

WAITRESSES

81	Ze Records WIP 6821	Christmas Wrapping/Hangover (stock copy promo, in bespoke Ze records paper wrapping)	£15

TOM WAITS

85	Island 12IS 260	In The Neighbourhood/Singapore//Tango Till They're Sore/Rain Dogs (12")	£15
73	Asylum SYM 9007	CLOSING TIME (LP, with insert)	£40
74	Asylum SYM 9012	THE HEART OF SATURDAY NIGHT (LP)	£30
75	Asylum SYSP 903	NIGHTHAWKS AT THE DINER (2-LP, gatefold sleeve)	£30
76	Asylum K 53030	CLOSING TIME (LP, reissue)	£20
76	Asylum K 53035	THE HEART OF SATURDAY NIGHT (LP, 'door' label)	£30
76	Asylum K 53050	SMALL CHANGE (LP, 'sky' label)	£40
77	Asylum K 53068	FOREIGN AFFAIRS (LP, with inner sleeve)	£20
79	Asylum K 53088	BLUE VALENTINE (LP, gatefold sleeve)	£20
80	Asylum K 52252	HEARTATTACK AND VINE (LP, with inner sleeve)	£25
81	Elektra K 52316	BOUNCED CHEQUES (LP)	£20
82	Island ILPS 9762	SWORDFISHTROMBONES (LP, inner 'blue' Island label)	£30
83	Island TW1	A CONVERSATION WITH TOM WAITS (LP promo interview disc)	£40
84	Asylum 960321-1	ASYLUM YEARS (2-LP)	£20
85	Island ILPS 9803	RAIN DOGS (LP)	£30
85	Island ILPM 9762	SWORDFISHTROMBONES (LP, repressing, white 'palm tree' label, generic Island inner)	£15
86	Island ITW 3	FRANK'S WILD YEARS (LP, gatefold)	£30
88	Island ITW4	BIG TIME (LP)	£25
91	Island 212370	NIGHT ON EARTH (LP)	£50
92	Island ILPS 9993	BONE MACHINE (LP)	£150
93	Island ILPS 8021	BLACK RIDER (LP, with inner)	£150

(see also Roy Orbison)

WAKE (1)

69	Pye 7N 17813	Angelina/So Happy	£15
70	Carnaby CNS 4010	Live Today Little Girl/Days Of Emptiness	£15
70	Carnaby CNLS 6005	23.59 (LP, union jack flag label)	£250

(see also Rubettes)

WAKE (2)

82	Scan SCN 01	On Our Honeymoon/Give Up (p/s in bag)	£25
87	Factory FAC12 178	Something No-one Else Can Bring/Gruesome Castle	£20
89	Sarah SARAH 21	Crush The Flowers/Carbrain (p/s, with postcard)	£20
93	Sarah SARAH 48	Major John/Lousy Pop Group (p/s)	£20
83	Factory FACT 60	HARMONY (LP)	£20
85	Factory FACT 130	HERE COMES EVERYBODY (LP)	£40
90	Sarah SARAH 602	MAKE IT LOUD (LP)	£40
94	Sarah SARAH 618	TIDAL WAVE OF HYPE (LP)	£60
12	Captured CT-152	HERE COMES EVERYBODY (2-LP box set, booklet and badge)	£40

JIMMY WAKELY

56	Vogue Coral Q 72125	Are You Mine? (with Ruth Ross)/Yellow Roses	£15
56	Brunswick 05542	Are You Satisfied? (with Gloria Wood)/Mississippi Dreamboat	£15
56	Brunswick 05563	Folsom Prison Blues/That's What The Lord Can Do	£20
57	Brunswick LAT 8179	SANTA FE TRAIL (LP)	£20

(see also Bob Hope, Margaret Whiting)

RICK WAKEMAN (BAND)

71	Polydor 2460 135	PIANO VIBRATIONS (LP, with John Schroeder Orchestra)	£100
74	A&M QU-84361	THE SIX WIVES OF HENRY VIII (LP, gatefold sleeve, quadrophonic mix)	£18

Conrad WALDRON

73	A&M AMLH 64361	THE SIX WIVES OF HENRY VIII (LP, gatefold sleeve)	£15
89	A&M RWCD 20	RICK WAKEMAN: 20TH ANNIVERSARY (4-CD box set, 1,000 only)	£40

(see also Strawbs, Yes, Dib Cochran & Earwigs, Steve Howe, Jon Anderson)

CONRAD WALDRON
81	Red Stripe SON 2233	you Love's A Voodoo/RED STRIPE BAND: The Heat Is On	£20

LARRINGTON WALKER
77	United Artists UP34210	Joy/Trust In Me	£25

WALHAM GREEN EAST WAPPING CARPET CLEANING RODENT & BOGGIT EXTERMINATING ASSOCIATION
68	Columbia DB 8426	Sorry Mr. Green/Death Of A Kind	£250

BOOTS WALKER
69	London HLP 10265	No One Knows/Geraldine	£15

CLINT WALKER
60	Warner Bros WSEP 2006	INSPIRATION (EP, stereo)	£15

DAVID WALKER
68	RCA RCA 1664	Ring The Changes/Keep A Little Love	£125

(see also Paradox)

GARY WALKER (& RAIN)
66	CBS 202036	You Don't Love Me/Get It Right	£20
68	Polydor 56237	Spooky/I Can't Stand To Lose You (as Gary Walker & Rain)	£20
69	Philips BF 1740	Come In You'll Get Pneumonia/Francis (as Gary Walker & Rain)	£60
66	CBS EPS 5742	HERE'S GARY (EP)	£45

(see also Walker Brothers, Paul & Ritchie & Cryin' Shames, Badfinger, Universals)

HOWARD WALKER & BEACHCOMBERS
70	Decca F12997	Eat Me/Love Will Find A Way	£15

JACKIE WALKER
58	London HLP 8588	Oh Lonesome Me/Only Teenagers Allowed	£250
58	London HLP 8588	Oh Lonesome Me/Only Teenagers Allowed (78)	£60

JERRY JEFF WALKER
68	Atco 228 006	MR BOJANGLES (LP)	£20
71	Atlantic 2466 007	BEIN' FREE (LP)	£18

JOHN WALKER
67	Philips (S)BL 7829	IF YOU GO AWAY (LP)	£25
69	Carnaby CNLS 6001	THIS IS JOHN WALKER (LP)	£25

(see also Walker Brothers, Johnny & Judy)

JUNIOR WALKER & ALL STARS
65	Tamla Motown TMG 509	Shotgun/Hot'Cha	£45
65	Tamla Motown TMG 509	Shotgun/Hot'Cha (DJ copy)	£100
65	Tamla Motown TMG 520	Do The Boomerang/Tune Up	£70
65	Tamla Motown TMG 520	Do The Boomerang/Tune Up (DJ copy)	£150
65	Tamla Motown TMG 529	Shake And Fingerpop/Cleo's Back	£50
65	Tamla Motown TMG 529	Shake And Fingerpop/Cleo's Back (DJ copy)	£80
66	Tamla Motown TMG 550	Cleo's Mood/Baby You Know It Ain't Right	£45
66	Tamla Motown TMG 550	Cleo's Mood/Baby You Know It Ain't Right (DJ copy)	£80
66	Tamla Motown TMG 559	Road Runner/Shoot Your Shot	£30
66	Tamla Motown TMG 559	Road Runner/Shoot Your Shot (DJ copy)	£100
66	Tamla Motown TMG 571	How Sweet It Is (To Be Loved By You)/Nothing But Soul	£25
66	Tamla Motown TMG 571	How Sweet It Is (To Be Loved By You)/Nothing But Soul (DJ copy)	£60
66	Tamla Motown TMG 586	Money (That's What I Want) Parts 1& 2	£30
66	Tamla Motown TMG 586	Money (That's What I Want) Parts 1& 2 (DJ copy)	£55
67	Tamla Motown TMG 596	Pucker Up Buttercup/Any Way You Wanna	£30
67	Tamla Motown TMG 596	Pucker Up Buttercup/Any Way You Wanna (DJ copy)	£60
68	Tamla Motown TMG 637	Come See About Me/Sweet Soul	£18
68	Tamla Motown TMG 637	Come See About Me/Sweet Soul (DJ copy)	£70
68	Tamla Motown TMG 667	Hip City Parts 1 & 2	£25
68	Tamla Motown TMG 667	Hip City Parts 1 & 2 (DJ copy)	£40
69	Tamla Motown TMG 682	Home Cookin'/Mutiny	£20
69	Tamla Motown TMG 682	Home Cookin'/Mutiny (DJ copy)	£30
69	Tamla Motown TMG 691	Road Runner/Shotgun (DJ copy)	£30
70	Tamla Motown TMG 727	These Eyes/I've Got To Find A Way To Win Maria Back (DJ copy)	£30
70	Tamla Motown TMG 750	Do You See My Love (For You Growing)/Groove And Move (DJ Copy)	£30
73	Tamla Motown UP MG 857	Way Back Home (Vocal)/Way Back Home (Instrumental)/Country Boy (reissue)	£20
74	Tamla Motown TMG 894	Gotta Hold On To This Feeling/I Ain't Going Nowhere (DJ copy)	£20
66	Tamla Motown TME 2013	SHAKE AND FINGERPOP (EP)	£55
65	Tamla Motown TML 11017	SHOTGUN (LP)	£55
66	T. Motown TML 11029	SOUL SESSION (LP, mono)	£50
66	T. Motown STML 11029	SOUL SESSION (LP, stereo)	£60
66	T. Motown TML 11038	ROAD RUNNER (LP, mono)	£35
66	T. Motown STML 11038	ROAD RUNNER (LP, stereo)	£45
69	T. Motown TML 11097	HOME COOKIN' (LP, mono)	£30
69	T. Motown STML 11097	HOME COOKIN' (LP, stereo)	£25
69	T. Motown (S)TML 11120	JUNIOR WALKER'S GREATEST HITS (LP, original with flipback sleeve)	£15
70	T. Motown (S)TML 11140	THESE EYES (LP)	£25
70	T. Motown STML 11152	LIVE (LP)	£20
70	T. Motown STML 11167	A GASSSSSSSSSSS! (LP)	£20
72	T. Motown STML 11198	RAINBOW FUNK (LP)	£20

| 72 | T. Motown STML 11211 | MOODY JR. (LP) | £18 |

KARL WALKER & ALLSTARS

| 66 | Rymska RA 103 | One Minute To Zero/Don't Come Back (both sides actually featuring Tommy McCook & Supersonics) | £45 |

(see also Ernel Braham)

ROB WALKER

| 71 | Upsetter US 366 | Run Up Your Mouth (actually by Stranger Cole)/UPSETTERS: Mouth Version | £20 |
| 71 | Jackpot JP 761 | Hear My Heart/Puppet On A String | £15 |

(see also Stranger Cole, Tommy McCook)

RONNIE WALKER

| 69 | Stateside SS 2151 | It's A Good Feeling/Precious | £30 |
| 69 | Stateside SS 2151 | It's A Good Feeling/Precious (DJ Copy) | £50 |

SCOTT WALKER

66	Liberty LEP 2261	SCOTT ENGEL (WALKER) (EP)	£35
67	Philips SBL 7816	SCOTT (LP, stereo)	£30
67	Philips BL 7816	SCOTT (LP, mono)	£40
68	Philips BL 7840	SCOTT 2 (LP, mono, with signed portrait)	£40
68	Philips BL 7840	SCOTT 2 (LP, mono, without signed portrait)	£20
68	Philips SBL 7840	SCOTT 2 (LP, stereo, with signed portrait)	£40
68	Philips SBL 7840	SCOTT 2 (LP, stereo, without signed portrait)	£20
68	Ember EMB LP 3393	LOOKING BACK WITH SCOTT WALKER (LP, mono or stereo)	£30
69	Philips SBL 7882	SCOTT 3 (LP, gatefold sleeve)	£50
69	Philips SBL 7900	SCOTT WALKER SINGS SONGS FROM HIS TV SERIES (LP)	£18
69	Philips SBL 7910	THE BEST OF SCOTT WALKER VOL. 1 (LP)	£18
69	Philips SBL 7913	SCOTT 4 (LP)	£60
70	Philips 6308 035	'TIL THE BAND COMES IN (LP)	£50
72	Philips 6308 127	THE MOVIEGOER (LP)	£25
73	Philips 6308 148	ANY DAY NOW (LP)	£30
73	CBS 65725	STRETCH (LP)	£20
73	Philips 6850 013	THE ROMANTIC SCOTT WALKER (LP, Audio Club issue)	£20
73	Philips 6856 022	TERRIFIC (LP, Audio Club issue, reissue of "Scott 2" with different tracks)	£40
74	CBS 80254	WE HAD IT ALL (LP)	£20
76	Philips 6625 017	SPOTLIGHT ON SCOTT WALKER (2-LP)	£18
81	Zoo ZOO 2	FIRE ESCAPE IN THE SKY - THE GODLIKE GENIUS OF SCOTT WALKER (LP)	£40
81	Philips 6359 090	SINGS JACQUES BREL (LP)	£15
84	Virgin V2303	CLIMATE OF HUNTER (LP, inner)	£25
90	Phonogram 824832	BOY CHILD - BEST OF 1967 - 1970 (LP)	£18
95	Fontana 526859-1	TILT (LP, limited edition)	£70
06	4AD DRIFT 1	THE DRIFT (2-LP, 500 promo copies with 24 page booklet)	£60
12	4AD CAD 3220	BISH BOSCH (2-LP, CD)	£20
14	4AD CAD 3428	SOUSED (2-LP with SUNN O))))	£30

(see also Scott Engel, Scott Engel & John Stewart, Walker Brothers, Routers)

STEWART WALKER

| 98 | Mosquito MSQ 012 | ARTIFICIAL MUSIC FOR ARTIFICIAL PEOPLE (12" EP) | £15 |

SYLFORD WALKER

75	Locks LOX 9	Burn Babylon/Burn Version	£40
79	Art & Craft AC 002	Book Of The Old Testament/JAH STITCH: Jah Speak Unto Moses (12")	£30
80	Art & Craft ACD002	I Love You (feat. Jah Stitch)/Version (12")	£20
88	Greensleeves GREL 119	LAMBS BREAD (LP)	£40

(see also Glen Brown)

T-BONE WALKER

54	London HL 8087	The Hustle Is On/Baby Broke My Heart (78)	£40
65	Liberty LIB 12018	Party Girl/Here In The Dark	£25
63	London REP 1404	TRAVELLIN' BLUES (EP)	£40
54	Capitol LC 6681	CLASSICS IN JAZZ (10" LP)	£40
63	Capitol T 1958	T-BONE WALKER (LP)	£50
65	Liberty LBY 3047	SINGS THE BLUES (LP)	£50
66	Liberty LBY 3057	SINGING THE BLUES (LP)	£40
68	MCA MUPS 331	THE TRUTH (LP)	£20
68	Stateside S(S)L 10223	STORMY MONDAY BLUES (LP)	£25
69	Stateside S(S)L 10265	FUNKY TOWN (LP)	£25
73	Reprise K 94001	VERY RARE (2-LP)	£15
74	Atlantic K 40131	T-BONE BLUES (LP)	£15

DEE WALKER

| 82 | Arts Network DEE 1 | DIAL 'L' FOR LOVE (mini-LP) | £30 |

WALKER BROTHERS

65	Philips BF 1401	Pretty Girls Everywhere/Doin' The Jerk	£15
66	Philips BE 12596	I NEED YOU (EP)	£15
67	Philips BE 12603	THE WALKER BROTHERS (EP, probably unreleased)	£0
65	Philips BL 7691	TAKE IT EASY WITH THE WALKER BROTHERS (LP)	£18
66	Philips BL 7732	PORTRAIT (LP, with photo insert, mono)	£20
66	Philips SBL 7732	PORTRAIT (LP, with photo insert, stereo)	£30
67	Philips (S)BL 7770	IMAGES (LP)	£20
67	Philips DBL 002	THE WALKER BROTHERS STORY (2-LP)	£18
78	GTO GTLP 033	NITE FLIGHTS (LP, gatefold sleeve)	£80
06	Universal Music Catalogue	EVERYTHING UNDER THE SUN (THE COMPLETE RECORDINGS) (5-CD box set, booklet)	£30

MINT VALUE £

983 984-4
16 Music On Vinyl MOVLP1356 **NITE FLIGHTS** (LP, reissue, g/f) **£30**
(see also Scott Walker, Scott Engel, John Walker, Gary Walker [& Rain], Routers)

TREVOR WALKERS
82 Mutual Life MU 002   **They'll Never Get Away/Version** (12", blue vinyl)..................... **£20**

DENNIS WALKS
68 Amalgamated AMG 816   **Having A Party/GROOVERS: Day By Day**... **£85**
68 Blue Cat BS 144   **Belly Lick/DRUMBAGO & BLENDERS: The Game Song**......................... **£400**
69 Bullet BU 402   **Heart Don't Leap/CLARENDONIANS: I Am Sorry**.............................. **£350**
69 Bullet BU 408   **Love Of My Life/Under The Shady Tree**... **£38**
69 Crab CRAB 10   **The Drifter/G.G. GROSSETT: Run Girl Run**..................................... **£100**
71 Moodisc HM 101   **Time Will Tell/Under The Shady Tree**.. **£20**
82 Greensleeves GREL 77   **Roast Fish And Cornbread/Wicked She WIcked** (12", with Billy Boyo) **£20**
(see also I Roy)

SHELTON WALKS
74 Dip DL 5026   **One Of Us Will Weep/KING EDWARDS ALL STARS: Version** **£22**

WALL
80 Fresh FRESHLP 2   **PERSONAL TROUBLES AND PUBLIC ISSUES** (LP)................................ **£15**
80 Fresh FRESHLP 2   **PERSONAL TROUBLES AND PUBLIC ISSUES LP, with insert, withdrawn "Crass style"
                              stencil lettered sleeve)** **£30**

ERROL WALLACE
69 Escort ES 817   **Bandit/ASTON BORROT: Family Man Mood** (actually by Aston "Family Man" Barrett) **£40**

JERRY WALLACE
58 London HL 8719   **With This Ring/How The Time Flies**.. **£40**
58 London HL 8719   **With This Ring/How The Time Flies** (78) **£15**
58 London HL 7062   **With This Ring/How The Time Flies** (export issue) **£30**
59 London HLH 8943   **Primrose Lane/By Your Side** (78) **£15**

MIKE WALLACE
70 Polydor 2058065   **Natural High/Mandrin**.. **£50**

SIPPIE WALLACE
67 Storyville 671 198   **SIPPIE WALLACE SINGS THE BLUES** (LP) **£15**

WALLACE BROTHERS
64 Sue WI 334   **Precious Words/You're Mine**... **£40**
65 Sue WI 355   **Lover's Prayer/Love Me Like I Love You**.. **£40**
67 Sue WI 4036   **I'll Step Aside/Hold My Heart For A While**...................................... **£40**
67 Sue ILP 950   **SOUL CONNECTION** (LP) **£250**

WALLACE COLLECTION
69 Parlophone R 5793   **Fly Me To The Earth/Love** **£25**

GORDON (WALLER)
68 Columbia DB 8337   **Rosecrans Boulevard/Red, Cream And Velvet**................................. **£20**
72 Vertigo 6360 069   **GORDON** (LP, as Gordon, single sleeve, small swirl label) **£1000**
(see also Peter & Gordon)

GEORGE WALLINGTON
56 Columbia Clef 33C9035   **THE WORK SHOP OF GEORGE WALLINGTON TRIO** (10" LP) **£60**
57 Esquire 32-132   **NEW YORK SCENE** (LP)... **£150**

BOB WALLIS & HIS STORYVILLE JAZZMEN
57 77 EP 10   **NEW ORLEANS JAM SESSION VOLUME 1** (EP) **£15**
59 77 Records 77LE 12/2   **THE RAVING SOUNDS OF BOB WALLIS** (LP) **£20**

SHANI WALLIS
63 Decca F11632   **My Heart Cries For You/All Over Again**... **£20**

WALL STREET DIVERSION
68 Concord CON 006   **She's Mine/Joey The Lipstick Collector**... **£25**

WALLY BROTHERS
74 Explosion EX 2090   **The Man Who Sold The World/Version** **£40**

WALRUS
70 Deram DM 308   **Who Can I Trust?/Tomorrow Never Comes** **£20**
71 Deram DM 323   **Never Let My Body Touch Ground/Why?** **£20**
71 Deram SML 1072   **WALRUS** (LP)... **£300**

JAMES WALSH GYPSY BAND
79 RCA PB 11403   **Cuz It's You Girl/Bring Yourself Together** **£50**
79 RCA PB 11403   **Cuz It's You Girl/Bring Yourself Together** (DJ copy)............................ **£100**

BURT WALTERS
68 Trojan TR 636   **Honey Love/KING CANNONBALL BRYAN: Thunderstorm**....................... **£65**
(see also Lee 'Scratch' Perry)

DAVE WALTON
66 CBS 202098   **Every Window In The City/I've Left The Troubled Ground**...................... **£15**
67 CBS 202508   **After You There Can Be Nothing/Can I Get It From You** **£30**
(see also The First Gear)

TRAVIS WAMMACK
65 Atlantic AT 4017   **Scratchy/Fire Fly** **£50**
65 Atlantic AT 4017   **Scratchy/Fire Fly** (DJ copy).. **£100**

WANDERERS
81 Polydor POSP 239   **Ready To Snap/Beyond The Law** **£25**

81	Polydor POSP 284	The Times They Are A'Changin'/Little Bit Frightening...£15
81	Polydor POLS 1028	ONLY LOVERS LEFT (LP)...£30

(see also Lords Of The New Church, Stiv Bators, Dead Boys, Sham 69)

WANDERERS (JAMAICA)
69	Trojan TR 7721	Wiggle Waggle/Jaga Jaga War £300

WANDERERS (U.S.)
60	MGM MGM 1102	I Could Make You Mine/I Need You More £50
61	MGM MGM 1169	As Time Goes By/There Is No Greater Love..£20
64	United Artists UP 1020	Run Run Senorita/After He Breaks Your Heart...£30

(see also Ray Pollard)

HANK WANGFORD
80	Cow Pie PIE 02	Cowboys Stay On Longer/Whiskey On £15

WANNADIES
95	Indolent DIELP 002	BE A GIRL (LP) £30
96	Indolent DIELP 008S	BAGSY ME (LP with free 7")...£30

DEXTER WANSEL
85	Streetwave SWAVE 9	Life On Mars/WILLIE BOBO: Always There (12") £25

WAR
80	MCA MCAT 557	The World Is A Ghetto (Special Disco Mix)/I'll Take Care Of You (12". p/s) £25
71	Liberty LBG 83478	WAR (LP)..£20
71	United Artists UAS 29269	ALL DAY MUSIC (LP)..£20
72	United Artists UAS 29400	THE WORLD IS A GHETTO (LP)..£20
73	United Artists UAG 29521	DELIVER THE WORD (LP)...£15
75	United Artists ILPS 9378	WHY CAN'T WE BE FRIENDS (LP, with poster)...£15
76	Island ISLD 8	LIVE (2-LP, Island reissue)..£15
77	MCA MCF 2822	GALAXY (LP, printed inner) £15

(see also Eric Burdon & War)

BILLY WARD & HIS DOMINOES
53	Parlophone R 3789	Don't Thank Me/Rags To Riches (78) £40
54	Parlophone MSP 6112	Three Coins In The Fountain/Lonesome Road...£150
54	Parlophone MSP 6112	Three Coins In The Fountain/Lonesome Road (78) £25
56	Brunswick 05599	St. Therese Of The Roses/Home Is Where You Hang Your Heart £40
57	Brunswick 05656	Evermore/Half A Love (Is Better Than None)...£30
57	London HLU 8465	Stardust/Lucinda...£20
57	London HLU 8502	Deep Purple/Do It Again £20
58	London HLU 8634	Jennie Lee/Music, Maestro, Please £20
59	London HLU 8883	Please Don't Say 'No'/Behave, Hula Girl..£20
58	London REU 1114	BILLY WARD & HIS DOMINOES (EP)...£100
58	Parlophone PMD 1061	BILLY WARD & HIS DOMINOES FEATURING CLYDE McPHATTER (10" LP) £600
58	London HA-U 2116	YOURS FOREVER (LP)..£60

(see also Dominoes, Clyde McPhatter, Jackie Wilson)

CHRISTIAN WARD
66	Decca F 12339	The Face Of Empty Me/Girl I Used To Know..£35

CLIFFORD T. WARD
72	Dandelion 2310 216	SINGER SONGWRITER (LP) £25
75	Charisma CAS 1098	ESCALATOR (LP) £15

(see also Secrets, Simon's Secrets, Martin Raynor & Secrets)

DALE WARD
64	London HLD 9835	Oh Julie/Letter From Sherry...£20

DOUGLAS WARD
71	Forward FS1001	FROM AN ELEVATED PLATFORM (LP) £20

JONATHAN WARD
67	Eyemark EMS 1009	Fools Paradise/One Step At A Time £30

ROBIN WARD
63	London HLD 9821	Wonderful Summer/Dream Boy £25

WARDENS
79	SNU PEAS TIC 001	Last Like This/Do So Well (with insert)...£50

WARDS OF COURT
67	Deram DM 127	All Night Girl/How Could Say One Thing £70

WARD SINGERS
56	London Jazz EZ-C 19024	THE FAMOUS WARD SINGERS (EP)..£20
56	London Jazz LZ-C 14013	THE FAMOUS WARD SINGERS (10" LP) £25

WARD 34
79	Woof Woof WOOF 1	Religion For The 70s/Disco Limbo (p/s) £20

LEON WARE
77	Motown STML 12050	MUSICAL MASSAGE (LP)..£25
99	Expansion EXLPM 5	INSIDE OF LOVE (LP, reissue)..£15
01	Elektra 7559-62728-1	LEON WARE (LP, reissue)...£15

WARFARE
83	Neat (No. cat. no.)	This Machine Kills/Burn Down The Kings Road (white label)..£20
84	Neat NEAT 49-12	TOTAL DEATH (12", EP) £15
84	Neat NEAT 1021	PURE FILTH (LP)...£15

WARHOLS
87	Zoot WAR 001	Fear Of Falling/Other Side	£20

WARHORSE
71	Vertigo 6059 027	St. Louis/No Chance	£20
70	Vertigo 6360 015	WARHORSE (LP, large swirl label, gatefold sleeve)	£300
72	Vertigo 6360 066	RED SEA (LP, small swirl label, gatefold sleeve)	£400
84	Thunderbolt THBL 010	RED SEA (LP, reissue, red vinyl)	£18
84	Thunderbolt THBL 010	RED SEA (LP, reissue)	£15
14	Repertoire V110	WARHORSE (LP, reissue)	£15
14	Repertoire V111	RED SEA (LP, reissue)	£15

(see also Deep Purple, Nic Simper's Fandango)

RAY WARLEIGH
69	Philips (S)BL 7881	RAY WARLEIGH'S FIRST ALBUM (LP)	£40

(see also John Mayall's Blues Breakers, Alexis Korner)

WARM HANDS
72	Access ACC 2	Disappear/My God I Love You	£25

JOHNNY WARMAN
78	Ring O' 2017 112	Head On Collision/London's Burning/Mind Games (in p/s)	£20
78	Ring O' 2017 112	Head On Collision/London's Burning/Mind Games	£15

WARM DUST
71	Trend 6099 002	It's A Beautiful Day/Worm Dance	£15
70	Trend TNLS 700	AND IT CAME TO PASS (2-LP, gatefold sleeve, grey label)	£200
71	Trend 6480 001	PEACE FOR OUR TIME (LP, gatefold sleeve, grey label)	£70

WARM GOLD
60s	Hurls 008	A TASTE OF CORNWALL (EP)	£25

WARM JETS (2)
96	Island 524 354-1	FUTURE SIGNS (LP)	£25

WARM SENSATION
69	Columbia DB 8568	I'll Be Proud Of You/The Clown	£25

(see also Ivy League)

WARM SOUNDS
67	Immediate IM 058	Sticks And Stones/Angeline	£20
67	Deram DM 120	The Birds And Bees/Doo-Dah	£15
68	Deram DM 174	Nite Is A-Comin'/Smeta Mergaty	£50

(see also Denny Gerrard, Tuesday's Children, Open Road)

FLORENCE WARNER
74	Epic EPC 80077	FLORENCE WARNER (LP)	£18

JACK WARNER
71	President PT 360	You Have Got The Gear/ Somebody Asked Me	£15
68	MFP MFP 1278	YER CAN'T 'ELP LAUGHIN' (LP)	£15

GUY WARREN OF GHANA
57	Brunswick LAJ 8237	AFRICA SPEAKS - AMERICA ANSWERS (LP)	£35
64	Columbia 33SX 1584	EMERGENT DRUMS (LP)	£100
69	Columbia SCX 6340	AFRO-JAZZ (LP, as Guy Warren Of Ghana)	£150
72	Regal Zono. SLRZ 1031	THE AFRICAN SOUNDS OF GUY WARREN OF GHANA (LP)	£100

WARREN G
94	Violator 314 523 335-1	REGULATE...G FUNK ERA (LP)	£25

WARRINGTON-RUNCORN NEW TOWN DEVELOPMENT PLAN
21	Castles In Space CiS 067	INTERIM REPORT, MARCH 1979 (repress, white vinyl)	£40
21	Castles In Space CiS 067	INTERIM REPORT, MARCH 1979 (repress, yellow vinyl)	£50
21	Castles In Space CiS 067	INTERIM REPORT, MARCH 1979 (repress, yellow/black splatter vinyl)	£40
21	Castles In Space Cis 088	PEOPLE & INDUSTRY (blue & white marble vinyl)	£30
21	Castles In Space CiS 088	PEOPLE & INDUSTRY (red & white marble vinyl)	£40
22	Castles In Space CiS 101	DISTRICTS ROADS OPEN SPACE (green vinyl)	£25
22	Castles In Space CiS 101	DISTRICTS ROADS OPEN SPACE (camouflage vinyl)	£30
23	Castles In Space CiS 101	DISTRICTS ROADS OPEN SPACE (repress, black clouds vinyl)	£15
23	Castles In Space CiS 101	DISTRICTS ROADS OPEN SPACE (repress, Rough Trade exclusive toxic sludge vinyl)	£20

WARRIÖR
80	Rambert RAM ONE	Don't Let It Show/The Lord's Prayer/Silver Lady (10", p/s)	£120
80	Goodwood GM 12326	TROUBLE MAKER (LP)	£150

WARRIOR (1)
72	Eden LP 27	INVASION! (LP, private pressing, plain white sleeve & label, some handwritten, 100 only)	£160
80	Rainbow RSL 132	LET BATTLE COMMENCE (LP, private pressing, 500 only)	£100

WARRIOR (2)
84	Warrior WOO 2	Breakout/Dragon Slayer/Take Your Chance (paper sleeve)	£55
83	Warrior WOO 1	FOR EUROPE ONLY (mini-LP)	£20

WARRIORS (1)
64	Decca F 11926	Don't Make Me Blue/You Came Along	£40

(see also Hans Christian, Jon Anderson)

WARRIORS (2)
79	Object OM 07	Martial Time/Martial Law (p/s)	£15

WARRIORS (3)
82	Ensign ENVY 6001	BEHIND THE MASK (LP)	£25

WARSAW PAKT
78	Island PAKT 1	Safe And Warm/Sick And Tired (with stamped sleeve)	£30
78	Island PAKT 1	Safe And Warm/Sick And Tired	£18
77	Island ILPS 9515	NEEDLE TIME (LP, numbered stamped mailer p/s, with insert)	£30

WARWICK
75	RAK RAK 211	Let's Get The Party Going/How Does It Feel	£15

DEE DEE WARWICK
65	Mercury MF 860	Do It With All Your Heart/Happiness	£20
65	Mercury MF 867	We're Doin' Fine/You Don't Know	£20
65	Mercury MF 890	Gotta Get Hold Of Myself/Another Lonely Saturday	£20
66	Mercury MF 909	A Lover's Chant/Worth Every Tear I Cry	£150
65	Mercury MF 937	I Want To Be With You/Alfie	£18
65	Mercury MF 953	Yours Till Tomorrow/I'm Gonna Make You Love Me	£15
67	Mercury MF 974	When Love Slips Away/House Of Gold	£40
68	Mercury MF 1061	I'll Be Better Off (Without You)/Monday, Monday	£20
71	Atlantic 2091 092	Suspicious Minds/I'm Glad I'm A Woman	£15
75	Private Stock PVT 13	Get Out Of My Life/Funny How We Change Places	£30
66	Mercury 10036 MCE	WE'RE DOING FINE (EP)	£80
71	Atco	TURNIN' AROUND (LP)	£30

DIONNE WARWICK
SINGLES
63	Stateside SS 157	Don't Make Me Over/I Smiled Yesterday	£22
63	Stateside SS 157	Don't Make Me Over/I Smiled Yesterday (DJ Copy)	£50
63	Stateside SS 191	This Empty Place/Wishin' And Hopin'	£22
76	Warner Bros SAM 61	Track Of The Cat/LIVERPOOL EXPRESS: You Are My Love (12", promo only)	£15

ALBUMS
64	Pye Intl. NPL 28037	PRESENTING DIONNE WARWICK	£20
64	Pye Intl. NPL 28046	MAKE WAY FOR DIONNE WARWICK	£15
65	Pye Intl. NPL 28055	THE SENSITIVE SOUND OF DIONNE WARWICK	£15
66	Pye Intl. NPL 28071	HERE I AM	£15
68	Pye Intl. N(S)PL 28114	VALLEY OF THE DOLLS (LP)	£15
73	Warner Bros. K46186	JUST BEING MYSELF (LP, credited to Dionne Warwicke)	£18

WASHBOARD RHYTHM KINGS
56	HMV 7EG 8101	WASHBOARD RHYTHM KINGS (EP)	£15

WASHBOARD SAM
72	RCA RD 8274	FEELING LOWDOWN (LP, with Big Bill Broonzy & Memphis Slim)	£15

(see also Big Bill Broonzy, Memphis Slim)

LALOMIE WASHBURN
77	Parachute RRL 2002	MY MUSIC IS HOT (LP)	£20

ALBERT WASHINGTON & KINGS
68	President PT 182	I'm The Man/These Arms Of Mine	£50

BABY WASHINGTON
64	Sue WI 302	That's How Heartaches Are Made/Doodlin'	£50
64	Sue WI 321	I Can't Wait Until I See My Baby/Who's Gonna Take Care Of Me	£50
65	London HLC 9987	Only Those In Love/Ballad Of Bobby Dawn	£25
68	United Artists UP 2247	Get A Hold Of Yourself/Hurt So Bad	£70
69	Atlantic 584 299	I Don't Know/I Can't Afford To Lose Him	£15
70	Atlantic 584 316	Breakfast In Bed/What Becomes Of A Broken Heart	£15
66	London HA-C 8260	THAT'S HOW HEARTACHES ARE MADE (LP)	£50
66	London HA-C 8292	ONLY THOSE IN LOVE (LP)	£50
68	United Artists SULP 1217	WITH YOU IN MIND (LP)	£40

BABY WASHINGTON & DON GARDNER
74	People PLEO 13	LAY A LITTLE LOVIN' ON ME (LP)	£20

(see also Don Gardner & Dee Dee Ford)

DELROY WASHINGTON
73	Sir Christopher KOO 022	Papa Was A Rolling Stone (as D. Washington)/KEITH HUDSON: Fight Fight	£60
77	Virgin VDJ 22	Give All The Praise To Jah/Stand Up And Be Happy (12")	£15
78	Burning Sounds BSD 006	Memories (with Jah Son)/EVERARD THOMPSON & SUPERSTAR: Rasta Roots (12")	£15
76	Virgin V 2060	I-SUS (LP, with insert)	£20
77	Virgin V 2088	RASTA (LP)	£20

(see also Carl Dawkins)

DINAH WASHINGTON
63	Columbia DB 7049	Soulville/Let Me Be The First To Know	£25
56	Emarcy EJT 501	AFTER HOURS WITH MISS D. (10" LP)	£30
57	Emarcy EJL 1255	DINAH (LP)	£25
57	Mercury MPL 6519	SINGS THE BEST IN BLUES (LP)	£15
59	Top Rank RX 3006	THE BLUES (LP, with Betty Roche)	£15
60	Mercury MMC 14030	WHAT A DIFF'RENCE A DAY MADE (LP)	£15
60	Mercury MMC 14048	THE UNFORGETTABLE DINAH WASHINGTON (LP)	£15
61	Mercury MMC 14063	I CONCENTRATE ON YOU (LP, mono)	£18
61	Mercury CMS 18043	I CONCENTRATE ON YOU (LP, stereo)	£20

(see also Brook Benton & Dinah Washington)

MINT VALUE £

ELLA WASHINGTON
69 Monument MON 1030   He Called Me Baby/You're Gonna Cry, Cry, Cry £20

GENO WASHINGTON & RAM JAM BAND
66 Piccadilly 7N 35359   Michael/Hold On To My Love £15
67 Piccadilly 7N 35392   She Shot A Hole In My Soul/I've Been Hurt By Love £15
66 Piccadilly NEP 34054   HI (EP) £25
68 Pye NEP 24293   DIFFERENT STROKES (EP) £20
68 Pye NEP 24302   SMALL PACKAGE OF HIPSTERS (EP) £20
66 Piccadilly NPL 38026   HAND CLAPPIN', FOOT STOMPIN', FUNKY-BUTT . . . LIVE! (LP) £20
67 Piccadilly N(S)PL 38032 HIPSTERS, FLIPSTERS, FINGER-POPPIN' DADDIES! (LP) £20
68 Piccadilly N(S)PL 38029 SHAKE A TAIL FEATHER! (LP) £15
68 Pye N(S)PL 18219   LIVE! - RUNNING WILD (LP) £15
(see also Ram Jam Band, Ram John Holder, Ram Holder Brothers, Dave Greenslade)

JERRY WASHINGTON
06 Jazzman JM 12 007   STONY ISLAND BAND: Stony Island Band/Don't Waste My Time (12" reissue) £20
75 Contempo CLP 517   RIGHT HERE IS WHERE YOU BELONG (LP) £35

GROVER WASHINGTON JR
71 Kid KU 03   INNER CITY BLUES (LP) £18
75 Kudu KU 20   MR MAGIC (LP) £18

KAMASI WASHINGTON
15 Brainfeeder BF 050   THE EPIC (3-LP, box set) £35
18 Young Turks YT176LP   HEAVEN AND EARTH (5-LP, tri-fold sleeve) £30

NORMAN T. WASHINGTON
68 Pama PM 741   Tip Toe/Don't Hang Around £25
69 Pama PM 749   Jumping Jack Flash/Spinning £30

SHERI WASHINGTON & BAND
57 Vogue V 9070   I Got Plenty/Ain't I Talkin' To You Baby £500
57 Vogue V 9070   I Got Plenty/Ain't I Talkin' To You Baby (78) £100

SISTER ERNESTINE B. WASHINGTON
55 Melodisc EPM 7-52   SISTER ERNESTINE WASHINGTON (EP) £20

TONY WASHINGTON (& HIS D.C.S)
63 React EA 002   Crying Man/Please Mr. DJ £20
63 Island WI 068   Something Gotta Be Done/TONY & LOUISE: I Have Said £20
64 Sue WI 327   Show Me How (To Milk A Cow)/Boof Ska £50
64 Fontana TF 478   Surely You Love Me/Man To Man £15
65 Black Swan WI 459   But I Do/Night Train (as Tony Washington & His D.C.s) £25
65 Black Swan WI 460   Dilly Dilly/Night Train (as Tony Washington & His D.C.s) £25
(see also Tony & Louise)

WASHINGTON D.C.S
64 Ember EMB S 190   Kisses Sweeter Than Wine/Where Did You Go £15
66 CBS 202226   32nd Floor/Whole Lot More £15
67 CBS 202464   Seek And Find/I Love Gerald Chevin The Great (in p/s) £70
67 CBS 202464   Seek and Find/I Love Gerald Chevin The Great (no p/s) £50
69 Domain D 9   I've Done It All Wrong/Anytime £30
(see also Dave Clark Five, Freedom)

WASHINGTON FLYER
79 EMI 2926   Bufflao Bill/Star Dance £15

WASP
75 EMI EMI 2253   Melissa/Little Miss Bristol £20
(see also Brian Bennett, Shadows)

W.A.S.P.
84 Music For Nations PKUT 109 Animal (Fuck Like A Beast)/Show No Mercy (shaped picture disc, pig's head or codpiece designs) £20
84 Music For Nations 12KUT 109 Animal (Fuck Like A Beast)/Show No Mercy (12", gold vinyl, U.K. issue pressed in France) £35
84 Music For Nations 12KUT 109 Animal (Fuck Like A Beast)/Show No Mercy (12", white, vinyl, U.K. issue pressed in France) £15
84 Music For Nations 12KUT 109 Animal (Fuck Like A Beast)/Show No Mercy (12", clear vinyl, U.K. issue pressed in France) £20
84 Music For Nations 12KUT 109 Animal (Fuck Like A Beast)/Show No Mercy (12", red vinyl, U.K. issue pressed in France) £15
89 Capitol ESTPD 2087   THE HEADLESS CHILDREN (LP, picture disc) £15
92 Parlophone PCSDS 118   CRIMSON IDOL (LP, red vinyl, inner) £50
95 RAW LP 103   STILL NOT BLACK ENOUGH (LP, 3000 only) £80

WASPS
77 4-Play FOUR 001   Teenage Treats/She Made More Magic (p/s) £25
77 NEMS NES 115   Can't Wait 'Til '78/MEAN STREET: Bunch Of Stiffs (p/s) £18

WASTE
86 Morterhate MORT 21   NOT JUST SOMETHING TO BE SUNG (EP, foldout p/s) £25

WASTED YOUTH
80 Bridge House BHLP006   WILD AND WANDERING (LP) £15
82 Bridge House BHLP007   THE BEGINNING OF THE END (LP, with free 'Caveman 7", 5000 only) £15

WASTELAND
79 Ellie Jay/Disaster EJSP 9261 WANT NOT EP (p/s, 2,000 only) £30
80 Invicta INV 014   Friends, Romans, Countrymen/Leave Me Alone (p/s, 1,000 only) £30

WATCHMAKERS
14 Box Bedroom Rebels BBR13 **WATCHMAKERS** (p/s, inserts, 150 only, numbered) £20

WATERBOYS
85 Ensign ENGL 5 **THIS IS THE SEA** (LP)...£15
11 Proper PRPLP 081 **AN APPOINTMENT WITH MR YEATS** (2-LP)...£25

WATERFALL
76 Bob FRR 001 **FLIGHT OF THE DAY** (LP, private pressing)...£100
79 Avada AVA 104 **THREE BIRDS** (LP, with insert) £22
81 Gun Dog GUN 003LP **BENEATH THE STARS** (LP, private pressing) £22

WATER FOR A THIRSTY LAND
74 MRA P 100 **WATER FOR A THIRSTY LAND** (LP, with insert) £22

SHEILA WATERHOUSE
71 Canvas CV 037 **Let Go Of The Chain/Love Me**...£20

WATER INTO WINE BAND
73 Myrrh MYR 1004 **HILL CLIMBING FOR BEGINNERS** (LP, brown cover, with insert) £150
73 Myrrh MYR 1004 **HILL CLIMBING FOR BEGINNERS** (LP, white cover, with insert) £100
76 CJT 002 **HARVEST TIME** (LP, private pressing, 500 copies).........................£100

WATERPROOF CANDLE
68 RCA RCA 1717 **Electrically Heated Child/Saturday Morning Repentance** £15

FREDDIE WATERS
75 Mint CHEW 2 **Groovin On My Baby's Love/Kung Fu & You Too** £20

MUDDY WATERS
53 Vogue V 2101 **Walkin' Blues/Rollin' Stone Blues** (78).....................................£80
54 Vogue V 2273 **Hello Little Girl/Long Distance Call** (78) £80
55 Vogue V 2372 **Honey Bee/Too Young To Know** (78).......................................£80
65 Chess CRS 8001 **My John The Conquer Root/Short Dress Woman** £20
65 Chess CRS 8019 **I Got A Rich Man's Woman/My Dog Can't Bark** £20
69 Chess CRS 8083 **Let's Spend The Night Together/I'm A Man**................................£25
69 Python PKM 04 **Country Boy/All Night Long** (99 copies only) £85
55 Vogue EPV 1046 **MUDDY WATERS WITH LITTLE WALTER** (EP)..........................£150
56 London RU-E 1060 **MISSISSIPPI BLUES** (EP) £175
63 Pye Intl. NEP 44010 **MUDDY WATERS** (EP) £40
65 Chess CRE 6006 **I'M READY** (EP)...£50
66 Chess CRE 6022 **THE REAL FOLK BLUES VOL. 4** (EP).....................................£45
59 London Jazz LJZ-M 15152 **THE BEST OF MUDDY WATERS** (LP) £100
61 Pye Jazz NJL 34 **AT NEWPORT** (LP)...£75
64 Pye Intl. NPL 28038 **MUDDY WATERS - FOLK SINGER** (LP) £60
64 Pye Intl. NPL 28040 **THE BEST OF MUDDY WATERS** (LP) £60
64 Pye Intl. NPL 28048 **MUDDY SINGS BIG BILL** (LP) £35
65 Chess CRL 4513 **AT NEWPORT** (LP, reissue) £40
66 Chess CRL 4515 **THE REAL FOLK BLUES** (LP) £35
67 Chess CRL 4525 **MUDDY, BRASS AND THE BLUES** (LP) £35
67 Chess CRL 4529 **SUPER BLUES** (LP, with Little Walter & Bo Diddley) £40
68 Chess CRL 4537 **THE SUPER SUPER BLUES BAND** (LP, with Howlin' Wolf & Bo Diddley) £50
68 Bounty BY 6031 **DOWN ON STOVALL'S PLANTATION** (LP) £30
69 Chess CRL 4542 **ELECTRIC MUD** (LP)..£40
69 Chess CRL 4553 **AFTER THE RAIN** (LP) £20
69 Chess CRL 4556 **FATHERS AND SONS** (LP) £30
69 Polydor 236 574 **BLUES MAN** (LP) £25
69 Python PLP 12 **MUDDY WATERS** (LP, 99 copies only) £80
69 Python PLP 18 **MUDDY WATERS VOLUME 2** (LP, 99 copies only) £80
69 Python PLP 19 **MUDDY WATERS VOLUME 3** (LP, 99 copies only) £80
70 Syndicate Chapter SC 001/2 **BACK IN THE EARLY DAYS** (2-LP) £15
70 Syndicate Chapter SC 002 **GOOD NEWS** (LP)...£15
70 Sunnyland KS 100 **VINTAGE MUDDY WATERS** (LP, gatefold sleeve with inserts, 99 copies only) £30
71 Chess 6671 001 **McKINLEY MORGANFIELD AKA MUDDY WATERS** (LP)...................£20
72 Black Bear LP 901 **RARE LIVE RECORDINGS VOL. 1** (LP) £15
72 Black Bear LP 902 **RARE LIVE RECORDINGS VOL. 2** (LP) £15
72 Black Bear LP 903 **RARE LIVE RECORDINGS VOL. 3** (LP) £15
72 Chess 6310 121 **THE LONDON SESSIONS** (LP) £15
77 Blue Sky SKY 81853 **HARD AGAIN** (LP)...£15
(see also Little Walter, Howlin' Wolf, Bo Diddley, Luther 'Georgia Boy Snake' Johnson)

ROGER WATERS
84 Harvest HAR 5230 **5.06 AM** (Every Stranger's Eyes)/**4.39 AM** (For The First Time Today) (p/s) £15
87 EMI EM 20 **Sunset Strip/Money** (live) (withdrawn).................................£200
70 Harvest SHSP 4008 **MUSIC FROM THE FILM "THE BODY"** (LP, with Ron Geesin, green labels, with Waters/Geesin photos)...£50
70 Harvest SHSP 4008 **MUSIC FROM THE FILM "THE BODY"** (LP, with Ron Geesin, black labels)............£20
84 Harvest SHVL 240105 **THE PROS AND CONS OF HITCH HIKING** (LP, gatefold) £30
87 EMI KAOS DJ 1 **RADIO KAOS** (LP, 'banded' radio promo, custom sleeve, printed inner)..........£120
87 EMI KAOS 1 **RADIO KAOS** (LP, printed inner, poster, stickered sleeve) £35
90 Mercury 846 611-1 **THE WALL** (LIVE IN BERLIN) (2LP, gatefold, printed inners) £30
92 Columbia 468761 **AMUSED TO DEATH** (2LP, booklet, sticker on shrinkwrap) £200
15 Columbia/Legacy 88875155411 **THE WALL** (OST) (3LP, trifold sleeve, printed inners) £40
15 Columbia/Legacy **AMUSED TO DEATH** (2LP, reissue, remixed, booklet, gatefold, 200g)............£50

15	Columbia/Legacy 88875075471 88875065801	AMUSED TO DEATH (2LP, reissue, remixed, picture discs, PVC gatefold, obi-strip)	£50
17	Columbia/Sony 88985 43649 1	IS THIS THE LIFE WE REALLY WANT? (2LP, gatefold, printed inners)	£25
20	Mercury/UMC 0602508538506	THE WALL (LIVE IN BERLIN) (2LP, clear vinyl, reissue, RSD, gatefold, printed inners)	£30
20	Columbia/Legacy 19439707691	US + THEM (OST) (3LP, trifold sleeve, printed inners, insert)	£30
23	Analogue Productions AAPP 468761-45	AMUSED TO DEATH (4LP, box set, 45rpm, 2015 remix)	£100
23	Columbia/Legacy 19658788891	THE LOCKDOWN SESSIONS (LP, gatefold, printed inner)	£20
23	SGB/Cooking Vinyl SGB50LP	THE DARK SIDE OF THE MOON REDUX (2LP, third side etched, gatefold, printed inners, triangular hype sticker, various coloured vinyl)	£30

(see also Pink Floyd, Ron Geesin)

LAL WATERSON & OLIVER KNIGHT
10	Three Black Feathers TBFLP 004	ONCE IN A BLUE MOON (LP, reissue)	£18

LAL & MIKE WATERSON
72	Trailer LES 2076	BRIGHT PHOEBUS (LP, original pressing, red/black label)	£100
73	Trailer LER 2076	BRIGHT PHOEBUS (LP, second pressing, yellow label)	£35
82	Highway	BRIGHT PHOEBUS (LP, reissue)	£20

LAL AND NORMA WATERSON
77	Topic 12T5331	A TRUE HEARTED GIRL (LP)	£20

(see also Watersons)

MIKE WATERSON
77	Topic 12TS 332	MIKE WATERSON (LP)	£20

(see also Waterson, Lal & Mike Waterson)

WATERSONS
65	Topic 12T 125	NEW VOICES (LP, blue label, with Harry Boardman & Maureen Craik)	£18
65	Topic 12T 136	FROST AND FIRE (LP, blue label)	£20
66	Topic 12T 142	WATERSONS (LP, blue label)	£20
66	Topic 12T 167	A YORKSHIRE GARLAND (LP, blue label)	£18
60s	Topic TS 346	THE WATERSONS SOUND (LP)	£15

LOVELACE WATKINS
67	Fontana TF 879	I Apologise Baby/You Can't Stop Love	£350

DOC WATSON
64	Fontana TFL 6045	DOC WATSON (LP)	£22
65	Fontana TFL 6055	DOC WATSON & SON (LP)	£20
72	Vanguard VSD 9/10	ON STAGE (2-LP)	£20

JOHN L. WATSON (& HUMMELFLUGS)
70	Deram SML 1061	WHITE HOT BLUE BLACK (LP)	£40

(see also Web)

JOHNNY WATSON & KAMPAI KINGS
60	Oriole CB 1532	Moshi, Moshi, Anone!/ABDULLA & HIS LITTLE BAND: Fatima's Theme (78)	£30

PAULA WATSON
63	Oriole 45-CV1785	Love Me Forever/Tell All The World About You	£20

BEN WATT
83	Cherry Red BRED 40	NORTH MARINE DRIVE (LP)	£20

(see also Everything But The Girl)

ANDY WATTS & COBRA
77	Nebula PSS 008	Anna/I Don't Wanna Fight (no p/s)	£35

BARI WATTS
80	Banazz BANAZZ 1	Move On Down/Rock 'N' Roll Romance (stamped die-cut sleeve, 500 only)	£20

CHARLIE WATTS
86	CBS 450 253-1	LIVE AT FULHAM TOWN HALL (LP, as Charlie Watts & His Orchestra, with insert)	£15
91	UFO UFO CD	FROM ONE CHARLIE (CD box set with book & Charlie Parker photo, signed)	£40
91	UFO UFO 2 LP	FROM ONE CHARLIE (10" LP, box set with book & Charlie Parker photo, signed)	£50
91	UFO UFO 2 LP	FROM ONE CHARLIE (10" LP, box set with book & Charlie Parker photo, unsigned)	£20

(see also Rolling Stones, People Band, Rocket 88)

NOBLE 'THIN MAN' WATTS (& HIS BAND)
57	London HLU 8627	Hard Times (The Slop)/Midnight Flight (with His Rhythm Sparks)	£75
57	London HLU 8627	Hard Times (The Slop)/Midnight Flight (with His Rhythm Sparks) (78)	£20
64	Sue WI 347	Noble's Theme/JUNE BATEMAN: I Don't Wanna	£70
79	Flyright 547	BLAST OFF (LP, mono)	£20

(see also Wild Jimmy Spurrill)

QUEENIE WATTS
66	Columbia SX 6047	QUEEN HIGH (LP, tip-on gloss sleeve)	£300

TREVOR WATTS
78	Ogun OG 526	CYNOSURE (LP)	£20

WATUSI WARRIORS
59	London HL 8866	Wa-Chi-Bam-Ba/Kalahari	£15

ASHANTI WAUGH
80	Attack TACK 20	Babylon Wrong/BARRY BROWN: Cool Pun Yu Corner (12")	£25

WAVEMAKER
75 Polydor 2383 331 15   WHERE ARE WE CAPTAIN? (LP) £15

WAVES
75 Stretch STR5   You Lose Out Girl/Hide Away £20

WAVING AT TRAINS
88 Gash 111   WAVING AT TRAINS (EP) £60
(see also Playing At Trains)

WAX DOCTOR
92 Basement BRSS 011   A New Direction/Herbal Tekno/Protplasm (12") £15
93 Basement BRSS 027   New Direction (93 Remix)/What's Goin' On (12", with Jack Smooth) £15
(see also Kev Bird)

WAX DOLL
76 Homer HM 009   Shout Loud/My Oh My £30

NANCY WAYBURN
65 Warner Bros WB 5646   The World Goes On Without Me/Listen To My Heart £15

OTIS WAYGOOD BAND
77 Decca 13688   Get It Started/Red Hot Passion £30

WAYGOOD ELLIS
67 Polydor 56729   I Like What I'm Trying To Do/Hey Lover £50
(see also Fleur-De-Lys)

ALVIS WAYNE
63 Starlite ST45 104   Don't Mean Maybe, Baby/I'd Rather Be With You £400

CARL WAYNE (& VIKINGS)
64 Pye 7N 15702   What's A Matter Baby/Your Loving Ways (as Carl Wayne & Vikings) £50
65 Pye 7N 15824   This Is Love/You Could Be Fun (as Carl Wayne & Vikings) £40
72 RCA SF 8239   CARL WAYNE (LP) £20
(see also Move, Ace Kefford Stand, Cheetahs, Acid Gallery, Keith Powell [& Valets])

CHRIS WAYNE & ECHOES
60 Decca F 11231   Lonely/Counting Girls £15

JEFF WAYNE
69 Columbia S(C)X 6330   TWO CITIES (LP, soundtrack) £35
(see also Ran-Dells)

JERRY WAYNE
60 Vogue V 9169   Half-Hearted Love/Ten Thousand Miles £25

JOHN WAYNE
73 RCA PL 13484   AMERICA, WHY I LOVE HER (LP) £15

PAT WAYNE (& BEACHCOMBERS)
63 Columbia DB 7121   Go Back To Daddy/Jambalaya £20
63 Columbia DB 7182   Roll Over Beethoven/Is It Love? £25
64 Columbia DB 7262   Bye Bye Johnny/Strictly For The Birds £25
64 Columbia DB 7417   Brand New Man/Nobody's Child £20

RICK WAYNE
93 Sunjam SR 0014   Our Younger Years/PICK A POW: TIme Hard (12") £30
94 Pathway To Freedom R+R 002   Almighty Father/Bad Behaviour (12") £80
02 One Studio OS4   Magnify/Version £20
02 One Studio OS5   If It Weren't For Jah/Version £20

RICK(Y) WAYNE (& OFF-BEATS)
60 Triumph RGM 1009   Chick A'Roo/Don't Pick On Me (with Fabulous Flee-Rakkers) £50
60 Pye 7N 15289   Make Way Baby/Goodness Knows (as Ricky Wayne & Off-Beats) £45
65 Oriole CB 306   Say You're Gonna Be My Own/It's A Crying Shame (as Rick Wayne) £20
65 CBS 201764   In My Imagination/Don't Ever Share Your Love (as Rick Wayne) £15
(see also [Fabulous] Flee-Rekkers)

TERRY WAYNE
57 Columbia DB 4002   Matchbox/Your True Love £25
57 Columbia DB 4035   Plaything/Slim Jim Tie £25
58 Columbia DB 4067   All Mama's Children/Forgive Me £25
58 Columbia DB 4112   Oh! Lonesome Me/There's Only One You £20
58 Columbia DB 4205   Little Brother/Where My Baby Goes £18
59 Columbia DB 4312   Brooklyn Bridge/She's Mine £20
58 Columbia SEG 7758   TERRIFIC (EP) £80

THOMAS WAYNE
59 London HLU 8846   Tragedy/Saturday Date £20
59 London HLU 8846   Tragedy/Saturday Date (78) £25
59 London HL 7075   Tragedy/Saturday Date (export issue) £20

WAYS & MEANS
66 Columbia DB 7907   Little Deuce Coupe/The Little Old Lady From Pasadena £25
66 Pye 7N 17217   Sea Of Faces/Make The Radio A Little Louder £25
68 Trend TRE 1005   Breaking Up A Dream/She £60

WAY WE LIVE
71 Dandelion DAN 8004   A CANDLE FOR JUDITH (LP, gatefold sleeve, label and sleeve DAN 8004) £250
71 Dandelion DAN 8004   A CANDLE FOR JUDITH (LP, gatefold sleeve, as K 49004) £125
(see also Tractor, Beau)

WE'RE ONLY HUMAN
82 VC VC 002   I Wouldn't Treat A Dog/Hold Your Head Up High (no p/s, 500 only) £40

WEAPON
80 Weapon WEAP 1   It's A Mad Mad World/Set The Stage Alight (p/s) £30
81 Virgin WEAPONE   It's A Mad Mad World/Set The Stage Alight (12", p/s, reissue) £40
(see also Wildfire)

WEASELSNOUT
72 Cartoon King Enterprises   UNSUNG LIES (LP, insert, private pressing) £800
       WUS 140

WEATHER
69 Philips BF 1734   Look In My Eyes/Running Forward £35

WEATHER REPORT
85 Nimbus 80027   MYSTERIOUS TRAVELLER (LP, Nimbus Supercut, mail order only through Practical Hi Fi
       magazine)..£60

ALFIE WEATHERBY
58 Columbia DC 729   49 Juke Boxes/Why Am I Crying? (78, export issue) £20

OSCAR WEATHERS
72 Mojo 2092 006   The Spoiler/You Want To Play..£15

VIVIAN WEATHERS
78 Virgin Frontline FL 1025   BAD WEATHER (LP)..£15

WEB (1)
68 Deram DM 201   Hatton Mill Morning/Conscience £25
68 Deram DM 217   Baby Won't You Leave Me Alone/McVernon Street £25
69 Deram DM 253   Monday To Friday/Harold Dubbleyew..£25
68 Deram DML 1025   FULLY INTERLOCKING (LP, mono) £100
68 Deram SML 1025   FULLY INTERLOCKING (LP, stereo) £120
70 Deram DAL-R 1058   THERAPHOSA BLONDI (LP, mono) £200
70 Deram SML-R 1058   THERAPHOSA BLONDI (LP, stereo) £125
70 Polydor 2383 024   I SPIDER (LP, gatefold sleeve, red label)..£500
(see also John L. Watson [& Hummelflugs], Samurai, Greenslade)

WEB (2)
96 Fat Cat 12FAT 001   EVA EP (12", plain sleeve) £20

DEAN WEBB
59 Parlophone R 4549   Warm Your Heart/Hey Miss Fannie £50
59 Parlophone R 4587   The Rough And The Smooth/Streamline Baby...£50

DON WEBB
60 Coral Q 72385   Little Ditty Baby/I'll Be Back Home £100

JIMMY WEBB
68 CBS 3672   I Keep It Hid/I Need You (as Jim Webb) £25
68 CBS (S) 63335   JIM WEBB SINGS JIM WEBB (LP, as Jim Webb, laminated front cover)............£25
71 Reprise RSLP 6421   WORDS AND MUSIC (LP, with insert) £20
72 Reprise K 44134   AND SO ON (LP)...£15
72 Reprise K 44173   LETTERS (LP) £15
77 Atlantic K 50370   EL MIRAGE (LP, with inner sleeve) £15
(see also Strawberry Children)

PETA WEBB
73 Topic 12TS 223   I HAVE WANDERED IN EXILE (LP, blue label) £35
(see also Oak)

PETA WEBB & PETE COOPER
86 Heart   HEART IS TRUE (LP)..£15

ROGER WEBB (& HIS TRIO)
67 RCA 1599   A Man And His Woman/The Spiderman...£30
64 Parlophone PMC 1233   JOHN, PAUL AND ALL THAT JAZZ (LP) £18

SKEETER WEBB
55 Parlophone CMSP 32   Was It A Bad Dream/Your Secret's Not A Secret Anymore (export issue) £15

SONNY WEBB & CASCADES
64 Oriole CB 1873   You've Got Everything/Border Of The Blues £45
64 Polydor NH 52158   You've Got Everything/Border Of The Blues (reissue)...............................£15

A J WEBBER
80 Gundog GUN 002   OF THIS LAND (LP) £30

MARLENE WEBBER
70 Bamboo BAM 33   My Baby/BRENTFORD ALLSTARS: You Gonna Hold Me (Version) £40
71 Ackee ACK 120   Natengula/Natengula-Kera (as Merlin Webber) £18
71 Ackee ACK 122   Cumbaya/Hail-Hi Freedom (as Merlin Webber) £15
71 Smash SMA 2322   Hard Life/COLLINS ALL STARS: Version Life (as Merlene Webber)................£50
76 Jama JALP 004   ONCE YOU HIT THE ROAD LP) £30
(see also Webber Sisters)

WEBBER SISTERS
67 Island WI 3109   My World/ALVA LEWIS: Lonely Still £60
(see also Delroy Wilson)

WEBBY JAY
79 Awawak DD 008   In The Rain/Rain Unlimited (12")..£20

WEBS
68	London HLU 10188	This Thing Called Love/Tomorrow £25

BEN WEBSTER
55	Columbia CLEF 33CX 10014	MUSIC FOR LOVERS (LP) £20
57	Vogue Coral 10021	TENOR SAX STYLIST (10" LP) £40
59	Columbia 33CX 10122	SOULVILLE (LP) £25
59	HMV CLP 1336	BEN WEBSTER AND ASSOCIATES (LP) £30
60	HMV CLP 1412	BEN WEBSTER MEETS OSCAR PETERSON (LP) £30
60	HMV CLP 1437	THE SOUL OF BEN WEBSTER (LP) £25
64	HMV CLP 1896	SEE YOU AT THE FAIR (LP) £20
65	Fontana FJL 126	INTIMATE! (LP) £20
67	Fontana FJL 316	BIG BEN TIME! (LP) £20
69	Ember CJS 822	BEN WEBSTER AT EASE (LP) £15
69	EMI SCX 6389	FOR THE GUV'NOR (LP) £20

DEENA WEBSTER
68	Parlophone R 5699	You're Losing/Wish You Were Here £25
68	Parlophone R 5721	Your Heart Is Free Just Like The Wind/Queen Merka And Me £25
68	Parlophone R 5738	Scarborough Fair/The Water Is Wide £25
69	Parlophone R 5798	Joey/It's Alright With Me £25
68	Parlophone PMC/PCS 7052	TUESDAY'S CHILD (LP) £200
14	Record Collector RCLP011	TUESDAY'S CHILD (LP, reissue) £30

WEDDING PRESENT
85	Reception REC 001	Go Out And Get 'Em Boy/(The Moment Before) Everything's Spoiled Again (p/s, 500 only, with poster & badge) £40
85	Reception REC 001	Go Out And Get 'Em Boy/(The Moment Before) Everything's Spoiled Again (p/s, 500 only, without poster & badge) £30
85	City Slang CSL 001	Go Out And Get 'Em Boy/(The Moment Before) Everything's Spoiled Again (reissue, different foldout p/s, 1,000 only) £15
87	Reception	A Million Miles/What Did Your Last Servant Die Of? (DJ promo, 200 only) £25
89	M'night Music DONG 39 CD	Pourquoi Es Tu Devenue Si Raisonable? (CD, unreleased) £0
90	RCA PB 43403	Brassneck/Don't Talk, Just Kiss (custom hand-painted p/s, 3,000 only) £40
92	RCA No Cat. No.	HIT PARADE (12 x 7" in custom box) £40
87	Reception LEEDS 1	GEORGE BEST (LP, 2,000 only with white vinyl 7": My Favourite Dress/ Every Mother's Son/Never Said [REC 005] & inner sleeve; later with bonus black vinyl 7" or 12" edition, £10) £40
87	Reception LEEDS 1	GEORGE BEST (LP) £30
88	Reception LEEDS 2	TOMMY (LP, 1,000 signed by band, with poster & inner sleeve) £20
89	RCA PL74302	BIZARRO (LP) £15
91	RCA PL 75012	SEAMONSTERS (LP, inner) £20
92	BMG PL75343	HIT PARADE 1 (LP) £30
94	RCA 8014524-044-1	WATUSI (LP, inner) £40
96	Cooking Vinyl COOK 099	SATURNALIA (LP, 2 x 10") £30
08	Vibrant VIBLP01	EL REY (LP) £30
10	Cooking Vinyl 900915	GEORGE BEST (2-LP, reissue) £30
12	Vinyl 180 VIN180LP039	BIZARRO (LP, reissue) £30
11	Vinyl 180 VIN180LP044	SEAMONSTERS (LP, reissue) £30
12	Vinyl 180 VIN180LP035	BIZARRO (LP, reissue, as 3 x 10") £35
12	Vinyl 180 VIN180LP045	SEAMONSTERS (LP, reissue as 3 x 10") £40
14	Demon DEMREC40X	GEORGE BEST (LP, reissue, red vinyl) £30
15	Scopitones TONE 020	TAKE FOUNTAIN (2-LP) £20

WEDGE
69	Midas MD3904	Sleep Child/Fly Away £25

WEDGWOODS
68	Columbia DB 8459	Red Sky At Night/When Day Is Done £15

WEE CHERUBS
84	Bogaten	Dreaming /Waiting For My Man (p/s, 400 only) £175

BUDDY WEED & HIS ORCHESTRA
57	Vogue V 9075	The Kent Song/For Love £25

BERT WEEDON
56	Parlophone MSP 6242	The Boy With The Magic Guitar/Flannel-Foot £20
57	Parlophone R 4256	Theme From ITV's '$64,000 Question'/Twilight Time £20
57	Parlophone R 4315	The Jolly Gigolo/Soho Fair £20
56	Esquire EP 56	WAXING THE WINNERS (EP) £25
59	Selmer Amplifiers	DEMONSTRATION RECORD WITH DAVID GELL (EP, with mailer) £20
60	Top Rank BUY 026	KINGSIZE GUITAR (LP) £20
61	Top Rank 35/101	HONKY TONK GUITAR (LP) £20

(see also George Chisholm, Craig Douglas)

WEEKND
13	Republic 602537512935	KISS LAND (2-LP) £20
15	Republic 0602547264756	HOUSE OF BALLOONS (2-LP) £30
15	Republic 0602547264930	THURSDAY (2-LP) £50
15	Republic 0602547261472	ECHOES OF SILENCE (2-LP) £50
17	Republic 0602557227512	STARBOY (2-LP, red vinyl) £30
20	Republic 00602507395711	BEAUTY BEHIND THE MADNESS (2-LP, yellow/black splatter vinyl) £40

WEEN
93	August RUST 002 LP	PURE GUAVA (2LP) £200

94	Flying Nun FN 31	CHOCOLATE & CHEESE (2-LP with free 7")	£40
95	Flying Nun FN 322	THE POD (2-LP, reissue)	£30
96	Flying Nun FN 386	12 GOLDEN COUNTRY GREATS (LP)	£40
97	Mushroom MUSH 3LP	THE MOLLUSK (LP, inner)	£50
00	Mushroom MUSH 69LP	WHITE PEPPER (LP)	£25
03	Sanctuary 0607684591	QUEBEC (2-LP)	£35
06	Schnitzel SRLP 125525	LIVE IN TORONTO CANADA FEATURING THE SHIT CREEK BOYS (2-LP, reissue white vinyl)	£25
07	Schnitzel SRLP 1255211	LA CUCARACHA (LP)	£20

WEEPING MESSERSCHMITTS

86	Upright UPT 17	NOTHING YET (12" EP, p/s)	£15

WEEZER

94	Geffen GFS 85	Undone: The Sweater Song/Mykel And Carli/Susanne/Holiday (blue vinyl, p/s)	£20
95	Geffen GFS 88	Buddy Holly/Jamie (p/s)	£18
95	Geffen GEF 24629	WEEZER (LP)	£50
96	Geffen 425007-1	PINKERTON (LP)	£40
02	Geffen DGC 25007	PINKERTON (LP, reissue)	£20

WE FIVE

66	Pye International 7N 25346	Let's Get Together/Cast Your Fate To The Wind	£20
66	Pye Intl. NEP 44056	LET'S GET TOGETHER (EP)	£60
65	Pye Intl. NPL 28067	YOU WERE ON MY MIND (LP)	£60

FRANK WEIR & HIS ORCHESTRA

54	Decca F 10271	The Happy Wanderer/From Your Lips	£15

(see also Bill Darnell, Vera Lynn, Janie Marden)

KLAUS WEISS

17	Trunk JBH 063 LP	TIME SIGNALS (LP, reissue)	£18

BRUCE WELCH

74	EMI EMI 2141	Please Mr. Please/Song Of Yesterday	£35

(see also Marvin, Welch & Farrar; Shadows, Cliff Richard)

ED WELCH

71	United Artists UAS 29248	CLOWNS (LP, with inner)	£15

KEN & MITZIE WELCH

62	London RE-R 1275	A PIANO, ICE BOX AND BED (EP)	£15

LENNY WELCH

65	London HLR 9981	Darling Take Me Back/Time After Time	£15
65	London HLR 10010	Run To My Lovin' Arms/Coronet Blue	£20
66	London HA-R/SH-R 8267	TWO DIFFERENT WORLDS (LP)	£25
66	London HA-R 8290	RAGS TO RICHES (LP)	£30

WELFARE STATE

78	Look LKLP 6347	WELFARE STATE SONGS (LP, with insert)	£60

WELL WISHERS

73	Pendant PEN 1	Find Mister Jameson/Weird	£40

PAUL WELLER

SINGLES

09	Universal (No cat no)	7 & 3 Is The Striker's Name (one sided 7", screen printed sleeve, 1000 only)	£50
10	V2	Aim High (Aim Higher)/Pieces Of A Dream (Dreams In Pieces)/Aim High (The Higher Aim)/Aim High (Like Water Needs A Flower) All The Amorphous Androgymous remixes (10", p/s, 500 only for 2010 Record Store Day)	£25
14	Virgin RSD14PW	Brand New Toys/Landslide ('two Virgins' label, white vinyl, stickered die-cut sleeve)	£20
24	Polydor 5888442	66 (LP/10" Deluxe Edition, poster, art print)	£100

ALBUMS

92	Go! Discs 828 343-1	PAUL WELLER (LP, gatefold sleeve, stapled-in lyric booklet)	£60
93	Go! Discs 828 435-1	WILD WOOD (LP, gatefold sleeve with 'obi' band inner & poster)	£120
94	Go! Discs 828 513-1	WILD WOOD (LP, gatefold sleeve with 'obi' band inner & poster; reissue with extra track 'Hung Up', 'second edition' on label of side 2)	£75
94	Go! Discs 828 561-1	LIVE WOOD (2-LP, single sleeve with picture inners)	£150
95	Go! Discs 828 619-1	STANLEY ROAD (LP, gatefold sleeve with Excerpts booklet)	£80
95	Go! Discs 850 070-7	STANLEY ROAD (6 x 7" singles in 7" box)	£90
97	Island ILPS 8058	HEAVY SOUL (LP, gatefold sleeve with picture inner & insert)	£80
97	Island CID 8058	HEAVY SOUL ("unofficial" wooden box set, 1,000 only, incl.: hinged wooden box, numbered certificate, promo CD, 5 postcards, CD booklet, promo 7", 5 guitar plectrums & polo shirt)	£175
98	Island ILPSD 8080	MODERN CLASSICS - THE GREATEST HITS (2-LP, gatefold sleeve with picture inners & insert)	£50
98	Island IBX 8080	MODERN CLASSICS (box set, numbered 4 x 7" + 16-page photo book & colour print)	£60
00	Island ILPS 8093	HELIOCENTRIC (LP, with foldout poster)	£200
01	Independiente ISOM26LP	DAYS OF SPEED (2-LP, gatefold sleeve with pic inners)	£250
02	Independiente ISOM33LP	ILLUMINATION (LP, rounded corners, gatefold sleeve with picture inner & booklet)	£200
03	Universal 0635271	FLY ON THE WALL (3-LP, stickered sleeve)	£175
04	V2 VVR 1026902	STUDIO 150 (CD, autographed for competition)	£30
04	V2 VVR 1026901	STUDIO 150 (LP, 2,000 only, with inner sleeve)	£250
05	V2 VVR 1033201	AS IS NOW (2-LP, gatefold, inners, print)	£150
06	V2 VVR 1039391	CATCH FLAME (2-LP, gatefold, 2 inners, free 7")	£150
08	Island 176935	22 DREAMS (2-LP, gatefold, booklet, with Island 'pink eye' logo)	£150
08	Universal 5313274	AT THE BBC (3-LP)	£100
10	Island 2732868	WAKE UP THE NATION (LP, flipback sleeve, inserts)	£100

14	Virgin V 3127	**MORE MODERN CLASSICS** (2-LP) £35
15	Vinyl Factory VVR798608	**SONIK KICKS** (LP) £35
15	Parlophone 0825646030354	**SATURNS PATTERN** (LP, clear vinyl)...............................£30
17	Parlophone 0190295866020	**MUSIC FROM THE FILM JAWBONE** (LP) £20
17	Parlophone 0190295845261	**A KIND REVOLUTION** (LP) £25
17	Parlophone 0190295830588	**A KIND REVOLUTION** (LP as 5 x 10")...........................£30
18	Parlophone 0190295635947	**TRUE MEANINGS** (2LP, 'tip-on' sleeve, booklet) £30
19	Parlophone 0190295494018	**OTHER ASPECTS** (3-LP, DVD) £40
19	Parlophone 0190295845261	**A KIND REVOLUTION** (LP, reissue, blue vinyl, numbered, 50 only, stickered sleeve)........£400
20	Polydor 00602508598579	**ON SUNSET** (2LP, gloss gatefold, rounded corner printed inners, purple vinyl)...............£30
20	Polydor 0880415	**ON SUNSET** (LP, picture disc, gatefold PVC, website exclusive) £30
21	Polydor 3556636	**FAT POP** (3-LP, box set) £100
21	Polydor 3554122	**FAT POP** (LP, red, yellow or orange vinyl)...................£20
24	Polydor 5888439	**66** (LP, gatefold, booklet, poster, green vinyl) £40

PROMOS

91	Freedom High FHP 1	**Into Tomorrow/Here's A New Thing** (7", white label promo, 1991) £25
91	Freedom High FHPT 1	**Into Tomorrow/Here's A New Thing/That Spiritual Feeling/Into Tomorrow** (8-Track Demo) (12", white label promo, 1991) £35
92	Echantillon (no cat. no.)	**Uh Huh Oh Yeh/Arrival Time/Fly On The Wall/ Always There To Fool You** (12", yellow label test pressing)............£50
92	Go! Discs KOSX 1	**Kosmos** (12", 1-sided)...£25
92	Go! Discs GOXDJ 102	**Kosmos** (12", printed label)..£25
93	Go! Discs GOTDJ 104	**Wild Wood/Ends Of The Earth** (10")...........................£20
94	Go! Discs PNME 1	**Shadow Of The Sun** (Live at Wolverhampton Civic Hall 9.3.94)**/ Sunflower** (Lynch Mob Dub Edit)**/Wild Wood** (Sheared Wood - Remixed by Portishead with A. Utley) (white label promo for NME cover mount) £35
95	Go! Discs LYNCH 1	**Lynch Mob Beats** (12", stamped 1-sided white label, 500 only) £60
95	Go! Discs SPLINT 1	**Walk On Gilded Splinters** (12", white label test pressing, 1-sided, 1995) £70
95	Go! Discs (no cat. no.)	**CD SAMPLER** (CD, given away in queue for 100 Club gig, 200 only) £45
95	Disctronics matrix: WELLERSPEC 01	**OUR PRICE PAUL WELLER SPECIAL** (CD, in-store album, no inlay, PVC outer) £60
96	Go! Discs PWRT 1	**PEACOCK SUIT** (CD, 7-track, picture disc in cloth bag)................£25
97	Island HEAVY 1	**Heavy Soul** (Pt 1)**/Heavy Soul** (Pt 2) (7", Island sleeve)..............£50
97	Island PWICD 1	**HEAVY SOUL** (box set: interview CD, EPK, 5 cards & insert) £45
97	Southern Songs WELLER 1	**LIVE... FROM THE ROOF OF THE HAYWARD GALLERY** (LP, finished sleeve, white labels)..£30
97	Island KINGS 1	**KINGS ROAD** (CD sampler, 350 only) £45
98	Island 12IS 711DJ	**Brand New Start/Right Underneath It** (12")...........£40
99	Island 12IS 734DJ	**Wild Wood** (The Sheared Wood Remix)**/Science** (Lynch Mob Remix with Psychonauts) (12", white label, only 130 copies mailed out) £18
99	Island INTCD 3	**IN CONVERSATION** (interview CD, gatefold card p/s) £30
00	Island HELIO-1	**Heliocentric** (Two Lone Swordsmen 4UR Mix)**/Heliocentric** (Original Version)**/There's No Drinking After You're Dead** (Noonday Underground Mix) (12" white label) £30
01	Independiente DOSB 1	**DAYS OF SPEED SELECTIONS** (3-CD set, card outer sleeve with CDs in individual card inners)............£50
03	Universal CUFF 1	**BUTTON DOWNS** (LP, promo-only vinyl edition of third disc of cover versions from Fly On The Wall) £35
05	V2 VVR 5033488P	**From The Floorboards Up** (7", white label test pressing, stamped white sleeve)...........£25
05	V2 VVR 1033202P	**SINGLES BOX** (box set, mail-order only, houses all As Is Now 7"s; priced without singles)............£20

(see also Jam, Style Council, Smokin' Mojo Filters, Andy Lewis & Paul Weller, Noonday Underground)

PAUL WELLER & THE RAKES

05	V2 FP01	**Shine On/Ausland Mission** (Promo, given out at Fred Perry party) £45

BOBBY WELLINS

78	Vortex VS1	**LIVE JUBILATION** (LP) £40
78	Vortex VS2	**DREAMS ARE FREE** (LP) £40

BOBBY WELLS

68	Beacon 3-102	**Let's Copp A Groove/Recipe For Love** (yellow label) £30
68	Beacon 3-102	**Let's Copp A Groove/Recipe For Love** (white label)..............£20
68	Beacon 3-102	**Let's Copp A Groove/Recipe For Love** (green label)..............£15

HOUSTON WELLS (& MARKSMEN)

63	Parlophone GEP 8878	**JUST FOR YOU** (EP) £50
64	Parlophone GEP 8914	**RAMONA** (EP)...£60
64	Parlophone PMC 1215	**WESTERN STYLE** (LP)..£50

(see also Marksmen, Outlaws)

JEAN WELLS

71	Mojo 2092 023	**After Loving You/Puttin' The Best On The Outside** £20
70	Sonet SNTF 606	**WORLD! HERE COMES JEAN WELLS** (LP) £50

JOHNNY WELLS (1)

59	Columbia DB 4377	**Lonely Moon/The One And Only One** £50

JOHNNY WELLS (2)

67	Parlophone R 5559	**Guess I'm Dumb/Wondering Why** £40

JUNIOR WELLS

66	Delmark DS 628	**Southside Blues Jam** (blue label)................................£20
68	Mercury MF 1056	**Girl You Lit My Fire/It's A Man Down There**..............£15
66	Delmark DL 612	**HOODOO MAN BLUES** (LP, mono, blue label)..............£100
66	Delmark DJB 1	**BLUES WITH A BEAT** (EP) £35
68	Fontana (S)TFL 6084	**IT'S MY LIFE BABY** (LP) £40
68	Vanguard SVRL 19011	**COMING AT YOU** (LP, also stereo, VSD 79262).............£30

MINT VALUE £

68	Vanguard SVRL 19028	IT'S MY LIFE BABY (LP, reissue)	£25
68	Mercury SMCL 20130	YOU'RE TUFF ENOUGH (LP)	£45
71	Delmark DS 628	SOUTHSIDE BLUES JAM (LP)	£22
74	Delmark DL 612	HOODOO MAN BLUES (LP, reissue, mono, blue label, with white rim)	£50
75	Delmark DS 635	JUNIOR WELLS ON TAP (LP)	£15

(see also Buddy Guy)

MARY WELLS

62	Oriole CBA 1762	You Beat Me To The Punch/Old Love	£70
63	Oriole CBA 1796	Two Lovers/Operator	£50
63	Oriole CBA 1829	Laughing Boy/Two Wrongs Don't Make A Right	£50
63	Oriole CBA 1847	Your Old Standby/What Love Has Joined Together	£50
63	Stateside SS 242	You Lost The Sweetest Boy/What's Easy For Two Is So Hard For One	£25
63	Stateside SS 242	You Lost The Sweetest Boy/What's Easy For Two Is So Hard For One (DJ Copy)	£100
64	Stateside SS 288	My Guy/Oh Little Boy (DJ Copy)	£100
64	Stateside SS 316	Once Upon A Time (with Marvin Gaye)/What's The Matter With You, Baby	£40
64	Stateside SS 316	Once Upon A Time (with Marvin Gaye)/What's The Matter With You, Baby (DJ Copy	£85
65	Stateside SS 372	Ain't It The Truth/Stop Takin' Me For Granted	£30
65	Stateside SS 372	Ain't It The Truth/Stop Takin' Me For Granted (DJ Copy)	£50
65	Stateside SS 396	Use Your Head/Everlovin' Boy	£30
65	Stateside SS 396	Use Your Head/Everlovin' Boy (DJ Copy)	£50
65	Stateside SS 415	Never Never Leave Me/Why Don't You Let Yourself Go	£20
65	Stateside SS 415	Never Never Leave Me/Why Don't You Let Yourself Go (DJ Copy)	£50
65	Stateside SS 439	He's A Lover/I'm Learnin'	£25
65	Stateside SS 439	He's A Lover/I'm Learnin' (DJ Copy)	£50
65	Stateside SS 463	Me Without You/I'm Sorry	£25
65	Stateside SS 463	Me Without You/I'm Sorry (DJ Copy)	£50
68	Stateside SS 2111	The Doctor/Two Lovers' History	£20
66	Atlantic AT 4067	Dear Lover/Can't You See (You're Losing Me)	£50
66	Atlantic 584 054	Me And My Baby/Such A Sweet Thing	£20
67	Atlantic 584 104	(Hey You) Set My Soul On Fire/Coming Home	£18
70	Direction 58-4816	Dig The Way I Feel/Love Shooting Bandit	£15
65	Tamla Motown TME 2007	MARY WELLS (EP)	£100
63	Oriole PS 40045	TWO LOVERS (LP)	£80
63	Oriole PS 40051	BYE BYE BABY (LP)	£90
64	Stateside SL 10095	SINGS MY GUY (LP)	£70
65	Stateside SL 10133	MARY WELLS (LP)	£80
65	Tamla Motown TML 11006	MY BABY JUST CARES FOR ME (LP)	£55
66	Stateside S(S)L 10171	LOVE SONGS TO THE BEATLES (LP)	£50
66	Tamla Motown TML 11032	GREATEST HITS (LP)	£35
68	Stateside S(S)L 10266	SERVIN' UP SOME SOUL (LP)	£50
68	Atlantic 587 049	THE TWO SIDES OF MARY WELLS (LP)	£30
69	Tamla Motown (S)TML 11102	VINTAGE STOCK (LP, unissued)	£0

(see also Marvin Gaye)

WENDY & LEMMY

82	Bronze BRO 151	Stand By Your Man/No Class/Masterplan (p/s)	£15

(see also Motorhead)

WE'RE TIRED

77	Deadline DEADS 8	My Life's On The Line/Against All Odds (p/s)	£20
77	Deadline DEADS 11	Guide Me Through Hell/Time Is Against Me (p/s)	£25
77	Deadline DEADLP 2	FIND THE PRICE IN TIME (LP)	£50

WERE ONLY HUMAN

83	VC Records VC002	Hold Your Head Up High/I Wouldn't Treat A Dog Like Me (no p/s)	£200

WERLWINDS

61	Columbia DB 4650	Winding It Up/Dig Deep	£22

BRIAN WESKE

62	Oriole CB 1723	In The Midst Of The Crowd/All Mine Alone	£15
62	Oriole CB 1776	24 Hours In A Day/Where Does The Clown Go	£15

FRED WESLEY & J.B.S

74	Polydor 2391 125	DAMN RIGHT, I AM SOMEBODY (LP, with J.B.s)	£25
74	Polydor 2391 161	BREAKIN' BREAD (LP, with J.B.s)	£20

(see also James Brown, J.B.s)

WES MINSTER FIVE

64	Carnival CV 7017	Shakin' The Blues/Railroad Blues	£50
65	Carnival CV 7019	Sticks And Stones/Mickey's Monkey	£50

(see also Maynell Wilson, Dave Greenslade)

V/ESS

73	Pye 7N 25607	Harmony/There's Gonna Be A Revolution	£15
77	Pinnacle 8450	Good Time/Carrie	£15

FRANK WESS

54	Atlantic Golden Bell ATL LP1	FRANK WESS QUINTET (10" LP)	£30

DODIE WEST

64	Decca F 12046	Goin' Out Of My Head/Is He Feeling Blue	£15
65	Piccadilly 7N 35239	In The Deep Of The Night/Rovin' Boy (in p/s)	£30
65	Piccadilly 7N 35239	In The Deep Of The Night/Rovin' Boy	£20

HARRY & JEANIE WEST
60	Melodisc EPM 7-111	SOUTHERN MOUNTAIN FOLK SONGS (LP)	£15

HEDY WEST
65	Topic 12T 117	OLD TIMES AND HARD TIMES (LP)	£20
66	Topic 12T 146	PRETTY SARO (LP)	£20
67	Topic 12T 163	BALLADS (LP, with Bill Clifton)	£20
67	Fontana STL 5432	SERVES'EM FINE (LP)	£20

KEITH WEST
67	Parlophone R 5651	Sam (From "A Teenage Opera')/MARK WIRTZ'S MOOD MOSAIC: Thimble Full Of Puzzles (promos in art sleeve)	£30
68	Parlophone R 5713	On A Saturday/The Kid Was A Killer	£65

(see also Tomorrow, Four + One, In Crowd, Mark Wirtz)

LESLIE WEST('S MOUNTAIN)
69	Bell BLL 1078	Dreams Of Milk And Honey/Wheels On Fire (as Leslie West's Mountain)	£20
69	Bell SBLL 126	MOUNTAIN (LP, as Leslie West's Mountain)	£40
75	RCA RS 1009	THE GREAT FATSBY (LP)	£20

(see also Jolliver Arkansas, Mountain, West Bruce & Laing)

MAE WEST
67	Stateside SS 2021	Twist And Shout/Day Tripper	£15
73	MGM 2006 203	Great Balls Of Fire/Men	£15
56	Brunswick LAT 8082	THE FABULOUS MAE WEST (LP)	£40
67	Stateside (S)SL 10197	WAY OUT WEST (LP)	£20
73	Polydor 2315 207	GREAT BALLS OF FIRE (LP)	£15

MIKE WESTBROOK (CONCERT BAND)
69	Deram DM 234	A Life Of Its Own/Can't Get It Out Of My Mind	£20
70	Deram DM 286	Requiem/Hooray	£20
70	Deram DM 311	Original Peter/Magic Garden (with Norma Winstone)	£200
67	Deram DML 1013	CELEBRATION (LP, as Mike Westbrook Concert Band)	£100
68	Deram DML/SML 1031	RELEASE (LP)	£100
69	Deram SML 1047	MARCHING SONG VOL. 1 (LP)	£125
69	Deram SML 1048	MARCHING SONG VOL. 2 (LP)	£125
70	Deram SML 1069	LOVE SONGS (LP, as Mike Westbrook Concert Band with Norma Winstone)	£150
71	RCA SER 5612	TYGER: A CELEBRATION OF WILLIAM BLAKE (LP, with insert)	£100
72	RCA Neon NE 10	MIKE WESTBROOK'S METROPOLIS (LP, gatefold sleeve)	£100
72	Cadillac SGC 1001	LIVE (LP, private pressing)	£25
75	RCA SF 8433	CITADEL/ROOM 315 (2-LP, with John Surman)	£30
75	Transatlantic TRA 323	LOVE/DREAM & VARIATIONS (LP)	£20
76	Transatlantic TRA 312	PLAYS FOR THE RECORD (LP, as Mike Westwood's Brass Band)	£18
78	Original ORA 001	GOOSE SAUCE (LP)	£18
78	Original ORA 002	PIANO (LP)	£18
79	RCA PL 25252	MAMA CHICAGO (LP)	£18
80	Original ORA 203	WESTBROOK BLAKE (LP)	£25
82	Original ORA 309	THE CORTEGE (LP)	£25
83	Westbrook LWN 1	A LITTLE WESTBROOK MUSIC (LP)	£25

(see also Solid Gold Cadillac, John Surman, Norma Winstone)

WEST COAST CONSORTIUM
67	Pye 7N 17352	Some Other Someday/Looking Back	£20
68	Pye 7N 17482	Colour Sergeant Lillywhite/Lady From Baltimore	£45

(see also Consortium)

WEST COAST DELEGATION
67	Deram DM 113	Reach The Top/Mr. Personality Man	£20

WEST COAST KNACK
67	Capitol CL 15497	I'm Aware/Time Waits For No One	£20

WEST COAST POP ART EXPERIMENTAL BAND
68	Reprise RSLP 6298	A CHILD'S GUIDE TO GOOD AND EVIL (LP)	£250

WEST FIVE
65	HMV POP 1396	Congratulations/She Mine	£40
65	HMV POP 1428	Someone Ain't Right/Just Like Romeo And Juliet	£35
66	HMV POP 1513	If It Don't Work Out/Back To Square One	£20

(see also Ferris Wheel)

WEST INDIANS
68	Doctor Bird DB 1121	Right On Time/Hokey Pokey	£60
68	Doctor Bird DB 1127	Falling In Love/I Mean It	£140
69	Camel CA 16	Strange Whisperings/CARL DAWKINS: Hard To Handle	£55

(see also Eric Donaldson, Prunes, Kilowatts, Upsetters)

KEVIN WESTLAKE & GARY FARR
68	Marmalade 598 007	Everyday/Green	£20

(see also Gary Farr & T-Bones, T-Bones, Blossom Toes, B.B. Blunder)

MALCOLM WESTLEIGHS BAND
73	Coysti CT 11	High Again/Delta Lady (p/s)	£20

WESTMORELITES
71	Fab FAB 16	Longing To Hold You/JACKIE BERNARD: Torture And Flames (promo only, black label)	£70

(see also Minstrels)

GLEN WESTON
67	Columbia DB8253	Pattern People/In The Still Of The night	£20

KIM WESTON

64	Stateside SS 359	A Little More Love/Go Ahead And Laugh (DJ copy)	£150
64	Stateside SS 359	A Little More Love/Go Ahead And Laugh	£100
65	Tamla Motown TMG 511	I'm Still Loving You/Just Loving You (DJ copy)	£300
65	Tamla Motown TMG 511	I'm Still Loving You/Just Loving You	£180
65	Tamla Motown TMG 538	Take Me In Your Arms (Rock Me A Little While)/Don't Compare Me With Her (DJ copy)	£100
65	Tamla Motown TMG 538	Take Me In Your Arms (Rock Me A Little While)/Don't Compare Me With Her	£80
66	Tamla Motown TMG 554	Helpless/A Love Like Yours (DJ Copy)	£400
66	Tamla Motown TMG 554	Helpless/A Love Like Yours	£100
67	MGM MGM 1338	I Got What You Need/Someone Like You	£30
67	MGM MGM 1357	That's Groovy/Land Of Tomorrow	£30
68	MGM MGM 1382	Nobody/You're Just The Kind Of Guy (DJ copy)	£50
68	MGM MGM 1382	Nobody/You're Just The Kind Of Guy	£20
80	Tamla Motown TMG 1000	Do Like I Do/MARVELETTES: Finders Keepers, Losers Weepers	£100
65	Tamla Motown TME 2005	KIM WESTON (EP)	£110
66	Tamla Motown TME 2015	ROCK ME A LITTLE WHILE (EP)	£450
67	MGM MGM-C(S) 8055	FOR THE FIRST TIME (LP)	£50
71	Stax 2362 021	KIM KIM KIM (LP)	£30

(see also Marvin Gaye & Kim Weston)

MARK WESTON & THE TWO PART TARIFF

69	Tepee TPR 1006	Standing At The Bus Stop/Portrait On The Blackboard	£40

PETE WESTON

70	Punch PH 28	In The Mood (& His Band) (credited to Pete Western)/ASTON BARRETT: Slide Mongoose	£15

(see also I Roy)

RANDY WESTON TRIO

55	London H-APB1040	RANDY WESTON PLAYS COLE PORTER IN A MODERN MOOD (10" LP)	£20
55	London HB-U1046	THE RANDY WESTON TRIO (10" LP with Art Blakey)	£20
56	London HA-U 2018	GET HAPPY WITH THE RANDY WESTON TRIO (LP)	£20
73	CTI CTL 12	BLUE MOSES (LP)	£18

WEST POINT SUPERNATURAL

67	Reaction 591 013	Time Will Tell/Night Train	£20

WESTSIDE GUNN

16	Daupe! DM SP 011	ROSES ARE RED...SO IS BLOOD (10", red vinyl, p/s, with The Purist, 100 only)	£300
16	Daupe! DM SP 016	GRISELDA GHOST (12", p/s, 250 copies, with Conway)	£300
16	Daupe! DM SP 016	GRISELDA GHOST (12", p/s, aqua marine vinyl, 150 copies, with Conway)	£400
16	Daupe! DM SP 016	GRISELDA GHOST (12", p/s, with obi strip, 20 copies only)	£500
16	Daupe! DM SP 017	HALL & NASH (12", p/s, 230 only, with Conway)	£250
16	Daupe! DM SP 017	HALL & NASH (12", p/s, liquor coloured vinyl, 150 only, with Conway)	£300
16	Daupe! DM SP 017	HALL & NASH (12", p/s, 20 only, with Conway)	£500
17	Daupe! DM SP 019	THERE'S GOD AND THERE'S FLYGOD, PRAISE BOTH (12", p/s, 230 only)	£150
17	Daupe! DM SP 019	THERE'S GOD AND THERE'S FLYGOD, PRAISE BOTH (12", p/s, gold vinyl, 150 only)	£200
17	Daupe! DM SP 019	THERE'S GOD AND THERE'S FLYGOD, PRAISE BOTH (12", p/s, with obi strip, 150 only)	£250
17	Daupe! DM SP 028	HITLER WEARS HERMES I (12", p/s,187 copies)	£200
17	Daupe! DM SP 028	HITLER WEARS HERMES I (12", p/s,cherry red vinyl, 187 copies)	£200
17	Daupe! DM SP 028	HITLER WEARS HERMES I (12", p/s, orange vinyl, 187 copies)	£200
17	Daupe! DM SP 028	HITLER WEARS HERMES I (12", p/s, gold vinyl, 187 copies)	£150
17	Daupe! DM SP 028	HITLER WEARS HERMES I (12", p/s, with obi strip, 20 copies)	£250
17	Daupe! DM SP 029	WESTSIDE DOOM (12", p/s, with MF Doom, 300 copies)	£100
17	Daupe! DM SP 029	WESTSIDE DOOM (12", p/s, with MF Doom, purple vinyl, 300 copies)	£100
17	Daupe! DM SP 029	WESTSIDE DOOM (12", p/s, with MF Doom, yellow vinyl, 300 copies)	£100
17	Daupe! DM SP 029	WESTSIDE DOOM (12", p/s, with MF Doom, picture disc, 300 copies)	£200
17	Daupe! DM SP 029	WESTSIDE DOOM (12", p/s, with MF Doom, with obi strip, 20 copies)	£300
16	Daupe! DM SP 012	FLYGOD (2-LP, 230 copies)	£400
15	Daupe! DM SP 008	HITLER WEARS HERMES II (LP, numbered, 150 copies)	£300
15	Daupe! DM SP 008	HITLER WEARS HERMES II (LP, numbered, clear red vinyl 100 copies)	£500
15	Daupe! DM SP 008	HITLER WEARS HERMES II (LP, with obi strip, 20 copies)	£400
15	Daupe! DM SP 010	HITLER WEARS HERMES III (LP, numbered, white vinyl 100 copies)	£500
15	Daupe! DM SP 010	HITLER WEARS HERMES III (LP, numbered, black vinyl, 150 copies)	£250
15	Daupe! DM SP 010	HITLER WEARS HERMES III (LP, with obi strip, 20 copies)	£400
17	Daupe! DM SP 020	HITLER WEARS HERMES IV (LP, 230 copies)	£200
17	Daupe! DM SP 020	HITLER WEARS HERMES IV (LP, clear vinyl, 125 copies)	£300
17	Daupe! DM SP 020	HITLER WEARS HERMES IV (LP, red vinyl, 150 copies)	£300
17	Daupe! DM SP 020	HITLER WEARS HERMES IV (LP, with obi strip, 20 copies)	£300
17	Daupe! DM SP 024	HITLER ON STEROIDS (LP as 2 x 12", with Green Lantern, 250 copies	£300
17	Daupe! DM SP 024	HITLER ON STEROIDS (LP as 2 x 12", with Green Lantern, red vinyl, 125 copies)	£250
17	Daupe! DM SP 024	HITLER ON STEROIDS (LP as 2 x 12", with Green Lantern, green vinyl, 125 copies)	£250
17	Daupe! DM SP 024	HITLER ON STEROIDS (LP as 2 x 12", with Green Lantern, with obi strip, 20 copies)	£400
18	Daupe! DM SP 031	HITLER WEARS HERMES V (LP, 250 copies)	£150
18	Daupe! DM SP 031	HITLER WEARS HERMES V (LP, pink vinyl, 250 copies)	£150
18	Daupe! DM SP 031	HITLER WEARS HERMES V (LP, yellow vinyl, 250 copies)	£150
18	Daupe! DM SP 031	HITLER WEARS HERMES V (LP, picture disc, 250 copies)	£150
18	Daupe! DM SP 031	HITLER WEARS HERMES V (LP, with obi strip, 20 copies)	£250
18	Daupe! DM SP 036	CHRIS BENOIT (2-LP, splatter vinyl, 375 copies)	£150
18	Daupe! DM SP 036	CHRIS BENOIT (2-LP, clear vinyl, 375 copies)	£150
18	Daupe! DM SP 036	CHRIS BENOIT (2-LP, with obi strip, 20 copies)	£200

18	Daupe! DM SP 036	GOD IS THE GREATEST (2-LP, 375 copies)	£100
18	Daupe! DM SP 036	GOD IS THE GREATEST (2-LP, clear vinyl, 375 copies)	£100
18	Daupe! DM SP 036	GOD IS THE GREATEST (2-LP, ruby red vinyl, 375 copies)	£100
18	Daupe! DM SP 036	GOD IS THE GREATEST (2-LP, mustard vinyl, 375 copies)	£100
18	Daupe! DM SP 036	GOD IS THE GREATEST (2-LP, cream vinyl, 375 copies)	£100
18	Daupe! DM SP 036	GOD IS THE GREATEST (2-LP, with obi strip, 20 copies)	£200
18	Daupe! DM SP 036	SUPREME BLIENTELE (2-LP, clear vinyl, 375 copies)	£100
18	Daupe! DM SP 036	SUPREME BLIENTELE (2-LP, 375 copies)	£100
18	Daupe! DM SP 036	SUPREME BLIENTELE (2-LP, red vinyl, 375 copies)	£100
18	Daupe! DM SP 036	SUPREME BLIENTELE (2-LP, with obi strip, 20 copies)	£200
18	Daupe! DM SP 040	HITLER WEARS HERMES VI (LP, red vinyl, two different covers)	£100
18	Daupe! DM SP 040	HITLER WEARS HERMES VI (LP, two different covers)	£100
18	Daupe! DM SP 040	HITLER WEARS HERMES VI (LP, picture disc, two different covers)	£100
18	Daupe! DM SP 040	HITLER WEARS HERMES VI (LP, with obi strip, two different covers, 20 of each)	£250
19	Daupe! DM SP 047	FOURTH ROPE (2-LP, 250 copies)	£150
19	Daupe! DM SP 047	FOURTH ROPE (2-LP, yellow vinyl, 250 copies)	£150
19	Daupe! DM SP 047	FOURTH ROPE (2-LP, red vinyl, 250 copies)	£150
19	Daupe! DM SP 047	FOURTH ROPE (2-LP, with obi strip, 20 copies)	£200
19	Daupe! DM SP 053	HITLER WEARS HERMES VII (LP)	£100
19	Daupe! DM SP 053	HITLER WEARS HERMES VII (LP, yellow vinyl, 333 copies)	£100
19	Daupe! DM SP 053	HITLER WEARS HERMES VII (LP, blue vinyl, 333 copies)	£120
19	Daupe! DM SP 053	HITLER WEARS HERMES VII (LP, red vinyl, 300 copies)	£100
19	Daupe! DM SP 053	HITLER WEARS HERMES VII (LP, picture disc, 300 copies)	£150
19	Daupe! DM SP 053	HITLER WEARS HERMES VII (LP, splatter vinyl,100 copies)	£200
19	Daupe! DM SP 053	HITLER WEARS HERMES VII (LP, with obi strip, 20 copies)	£300
20	Daupe! DM SP 056	FLYEST NIG@@ IN CHARGE - MIXTAPE VOL 1 (2-LP, 380 copies)	£40
20	Daupe! DM SP 056	FLYEST NIG@@ IN CHARGE - MIXTAPE VOL 1 (2-LP, white vinyl, 333 copies)	£40
20	Daupe! DM SP 056	FLYEST NIG@@ IN CHARGE - MIXTAPE VOL 1 (2-LP, aquamarine vinyl, 333 copies)	£40
20	Daupe! DM SP 056	FLYEST NIG@@ IN CHARGE - MIXTAPE VOL 1 (2-LP, orange vinyl, 333 copies)	£40
20	Daupe! DM SP 056	FLYEST NIG@@ IN CHARGE - MIXTAPE VOL 1 (2-LP, splatter, 100 copies)	£50
20	Daupe! DM SP 056	FLYEST NIG@@ IN CHARGE - MIXTAPE VOL 1 (2-LP, with obi strip, 20 copies)	£100
20	Daupe! DM SP 060	PRAY FOR PARIS (LP)	£150
20	Daupe! DM SP 060	PRAY FOR PARIS (LP, gold vinyl)	£150
20	Daupe! DM SP 060	PRAY FOR PARIS (LP, white vinyl)	£150
20	Daupe! DM SP 060	PRAY FOR PARIS (LP, French tricolour vinyl, 200 copies)	£250
20	Daupe! DM SP 060	PRAY FOR PARIS (LP, splatter vinyl, 100 copies)	£250
20	Daupe! DM SP 060	PRAY FOR PARIS (LP, with obi strip, 20 copies)	£300

WESTVIEW
| 67 | Tenby TB1 | She's A Witch/Time Passes Slowly | £40 |

WESTWIND
| 70 | Penny Farthing PELS 505 | LOVE IS (LP) | £225 |

WE THE PEOPLE
| 66 | London HLH 10089 | He Doesn't Go About It Right/You Burn Me Up And Down | £125 |

WE THREE TRIO
| 67 | Fontana TL 5308 | THE WE THREE TRIO (LP) | £15 |

WET LEG
21	Domino RUG 1232	Chaise Lounge/Chaise Lounge (demo) (p/s, first pressing with IΛ etched runout)	£30
22	Domino RUG 1232	Chaise Lounge/Chaise Lounge (demo) (p/s, repress with =Λ etched runout)	£15
22	Domino WIGLP496XG	WET LEG (LP, Deluxe Edition, green vinyl, with 7", It's Not Fun/It's A Shame)	£100
22	Domino WIGLP496X	WET LEG (LP, yellow vinyl, limited edition)	£30

WET WILLIE
| 71 | Atlantic 2400162 | WET WILLIE (LP) | £20 |

WE WERE PROMISED JETPACKS
09	Fat Cat FATLP 72	THESE FOUR WALLS (LP)	£40
11	Fat Cat FATLP 97	IN THE PIT OF THE STOMACH (LP)	£20
14	Fat Cat FATLP 127	UNRAVELLING (LP)	£18

WHALE FEATHERS
| 71 | Blue Horizon 2431 009 | WHALE FEATHERS (LP) | £175 |

WHALES
| 68 | CBS 3766 | Come Down Little Bird/Beachcomber | £20 |
| 69 | CBS 4126 | Tell It To The Rain/Girl, Hey Girl | £15 |

WHAM!
| 86 | Epic WHAM 2 | THE FINAL (2LP box set, picture discs,T-shirt, calendar, pencil, notepad, numbered certificate) | £150 |
| 23 | Epic 19658720477 | THE SINGLES (ECHOES FROM THE EDGE OF HEAVEN) (12x7"/1 cassette metal singles case box set, book, ephemera) | £200 |

(see also George Michael, Pepsi & Shirley)

WHAT
| 79 | Humber HREP 45 | What Is The Cure?/Anything Goes/East Coast Kids | £40 |

WHAT IS OIL
| 83 | Oof Potato BEAT 1 | HUMAN SUFFERING EP (p/s) | £40 |

WHAT THE CURTAINS
| 84 | Rideaux WTC 0042 | Crime Of Passion/Words (Can't Tell) | £20 |

WHAT TO WEAR
| 80 | Basic And Typical BAT 1 | CASUAL BUT SMART (EP) | £25 |

PEETIE WHEATSTRAW
69	Matchbox SDR 191	THE DEVIL'S SON IN LAW (LP)	£25
69	Matchbox SDR 192	THE HIGH SHERIFF FROM HELL (LP)	£25
74	Flyright LP 111	1930-36 (LP)	£15

KENNY WHEELER
68	Fontana STL 5494	WINDMILL TILTER (LP)	£150
77	Incus 10	SONG FOR SOMEONE (LP)	£60

(see also Johnny Dankworth, Elton Dean)

WHEELER ST JAMES & JAMES
72	RCA 2233	My Impersonal Life/Lovely To See You	£20

WHEELS OF TIME
67	Spin SP 62008	1984/So Long (not in company sleeves)	£90
67	Spin SP 62008	1984/So Long (in company sleeve)	£100

WHEELS (1)
65	Columbia DB 7682	Gloria/Don't You Know	£120
66	Columbia DB 7827	Bad Little Woman/Road Block (mispressing, demos & a few issues play "Call My Name" on B-side)	£150
66	Columbia DB 7827	Bad Little Woman/Road Block	£375
66	Columbia DB 7981	Kicks/Call My Name	£120

(see also Demick & Armstrong)

WHEELS (2)
71	Decca F13268	Take Me Home Country Roads/She Don't Mean It	£30

WHICHWHAT
69	Beacon BEA 127	Gimme Gimme Good Lovin'/Wonderland Of Love	£25
69	Beacon BEA 133	In The Year 2525/Parting	£15
69	Beacon BEA 144	I Wanna Be Free/It's All Over Again	£25
70	Beacon BEAS 14	WHICHWHAT'S FIRST (LP)	£50

WHIRLWIND
78	Chiswick NS 42	I Only Wish (That I'd Been Told)/Ducktails (unissued)	£0
79	Chiswick CHIS 117	You Got Class/Losing To You (unissued in U.K.; France-only)	£0
79	Lyntone (No Cat. No)	On Wheels (flexi, originally promo for Isle Of Man TT races, repackaged in picture sleeve with 2 inserts for 1979 Earls Court Concert)	£50
80	Chiswick CHIS 127	Stayin' Out All Night/Running Wild (unissued; p/s only)	£0
78	Chiswick WIK 7	BLOWIN' UP A STORM (LP, with 2 extra tracks)	£15
80	Chiswick CWK 3012	MIDNIGHT BLUE (LP)	£15

WHIRLWIND D
14	Tru-Tone TTR 007	Gain My Perspective/Run Fast (with Phill Most Chill & Mr Fantastic 12" test pressings only)	£40
14	B-Line Recordings BLN 006	NOMANSLAND (LP)	£15
16	B-Line Recordings BLI 001	THE OTHER SIDE OF NOMANSLANDS (LP, 100 only)	£20

WHIRLWIND D/MR THING/AGENT FINC & SPECIFIK
14	Tru-Tone TTR 006	Broadway (12", test pressings only)	£35

WHIRLWINDS
64	HMV POP 1301	Look At Me/Baby Not Like You	£50

(see also Mockingbirds, Graham Gouldman, 10cc)

NANCY WHISKEY (& HER SKIFFLERS)
57	Oriole CB 1394	He's Solid Gone/Ella Speed (as Nancy Whiskey & Her Skifflers)	£20
57	Topic 7T 10	NANCY WHISKEY SINGS (7" LP)	£25
57	Oriole MG 10018	THE INTOXICATING MISS WHISKEY (10" LP, with Chas McDevitt Skiffle Group)	£30

(see also Chas McDevitt Skiffle Group)

WHISTLE
73	York YR 201	The Party Must Be Over/Hideaway	£20
74	York YR 209	When The Lights Go Out On Broadway/Lincoln Lullabies	£20

WHISTLER (1)
71	Deram SML 1083	HO-HUM (LP)	£250

WHISTLER (2)
74	Capricorn CAP 2	I'm Running Out Of Time/Dear Diary	£15

WHISTLING WILLIE
68	Duke DU 8	Penny Reel/Soul Tonic	£20

(see also Neville)

SHARON WHITBREAD & FRED
72	RA RALP 6011	SPICE OF LIFE (LP)	£25

IAN WHITCOMB
73	Ember NR 5065	YOU TURN ME ON (LP, with Jimmy Page & John Paul Jones)	£40

BARRY WHITE
67	President PT 139	All In The Run Of A Day/Don't Take Your Love From Me	£30

BRIAN WHITE & MAGNA JAZZ BAND
62	HMV CLP 1534	BRIAN WHITE AND THE MAGNA JAZZ BAND (LP)	£80

BUKKA WHITE
66	Fontana 688 804 ZL	SKY SONGS (LP, with Big Willie)	£40
66	CBS Realm 52629	BUKKA WHITE (LP)	£40
69	Blue Horizon 7-63229	MEMPHIS HOT SHOTS (LP)	£80

CHRIS WHITE
77	Charisma CB 303	Don't Worry Baby/Child Of The Sun	£15
76	Charisma CAS 1118	MOUTH MUSIC (LP)	£15

(see also Joyce's Angels)

CHRISTINE WHITE
77	Black Jack BJLP 001	PURE LOVE (LP)	£25

DANNY WHITE
67	Sue WI 4031	Keep My Woman Home/I'm Dedicating My Life	£75

DUKE WHITE
63	Island WI 084	It's Over/Forever	£15
64	Black Swan WI 442	Be Wise/BABA BROOKS: Musical Workshop	£40
65	Black Swan WI 444	Sow Good Seeds/BABA BROOKS BAND: Bus Strike	£40

ED WHITE (THE SOUNDS OF)
61	Pye 7N SR15320	Coral Reef/Tropical Blue (stereo)	£20

GEORGIA WHITE
54	Vocalion V 1038	Was I Drunk?/Moonshine Blues (78)	£20

IAN WHITE
70	private pressing	IAN WHITE (LP)	£20

JACK WHITE
09	Third Man TMR 013	Fly Farm Blues (luminous one-sided Halloween cover, 100-only)	£120
21	Third Man TMR 748	Taking Me Back/Taking Me Back (Gently) (p/s, tri-colour vinyl)	£100
14	Third Man TMR 271	LAZARETTO (LP, printed inner, ultra vinyl w/hologram)	£30
22	Third Man TMR 753	ENTERING HEAVEN ALIVE (LP, printed inners, insert, turquoise vinyl, limited)	£40
24	Third Man TMR 1000	NO NAME (LP, plain white die-cut sleeve, white label, randomly given away at Third Man stores/online)	£500
24	Third Man TMR 1000	NO NAME (LP, printed inner, blue/black vinyl, limited edition)	£50

(see also White Stripes, Raconteurs, Dead Weather)

JAMES WHITE
79	Ze ZE 3303	OFF WHITE (LP, as James White & The Blacks)	£20
82	Animal CHR 1401	SAX MANIAC (LP, as James White & The Blacks)	£20

JAY WHITE
56	London RE-F 1045	FAR-AWAY PLACES VOL. 1 (EP)	£15

JEANETTE WHITE
69	A&M AMS 761	Music/No Sunshine	£30
69	A&M AMS 761	Music/No Sunshine (Yellow DJ copy or brown label)	£75

JOE WHITE
64	R&B JB 137	Sinners (as Joe White & Maytals)/ROLAND ALPHONSO: King Solomon	£40
64	Ska Beat JB 180	Punch You Down (with Chuck)/TOMMY McCOOK: Cotton Tree	£45
64	Island WI 145	When Are You Young/Wanna Go Home	£25
64	Island WI 159	Hog In A Co Co/SKATALITES: Sandy Gully	£30
64	Island WI 166	Downtown Girl/RICHARD BROS.: You Are My Sunshine (B-side is actually "Cool Smoke" by Don Drummond)	£40
65	Island WI 201	Low-Minded People (as Chuck & Joe White)/Irene	£20
66	Doctor Bird DB 1001	Every Night (with Chuck)/BABA BROOKS & HIS BAND: First Session	£30
66	Doctor Bird DB 1024	My Love For You/SAMMY ISMAY & BABA BROOKS BAND: Cocktails For Two	£25
66	Doctor Bird DB 1043	So Close (as Joe White & Della)/BABA BROOKS & HIS BAND: Eighth Games	£25
67	Doctor Bird DB 1069	Rudies All Around/Bad Man	£100
67	Doctor Bird DB 1080	Lovely Nights/I Need You	£20
67	Doctor Bird DB 1090	I Need A Woman/Hot Hops	£50
68	Blue Cat BS 108	Way Of Life (with Glen Brown & Trevor Shield/I'm So Proud	£175
68	Blue Cat BS 119	Try A Little Tenderness/LYN TAITT & CARL BRYAN: Tender Arms	£250
68	Blue Cat BS 130	Pretty Girl (with Glen Brown & Trevor Shield)/DERMOTT LYNCH: You Went Away	£100
69	Sugar ESS 102	My Guiding Star/If I Needed Someone	£70
70	Sugar SU 103	Yesterday/I Am Free	£160
70	Trojan TR 7742	So Much Love/Maybe Now	£20
71	Big BG 309	Baby I Care/Ain't Misbehavin'	£20
72	Dynamic DYN 440	Kenyata/RECORDING BAND: Version	£35
73	Gayfeet GS 202	If It Don't Work Out/BABA BROOKS BAND: Ki Salaboca	£15
77	Ultra PFU 1002	Give And Take (On Both Sides)/Roots Dub	£60
79	Splendor Heights SH 2	Forward To Zion/Only The Strong/Join Them/Are You Leavine Me (12" as Joe White Band)	£60
77	Trench Town TRELP 002	LOVE FOR EVERY FAMILY (LP)	£140
70s	Magnet MGT 006	SINCE THE OTHER DAY (LP)	£50

(see also Chuck, Rue Lloyd)

JOHN WHITE
78	Obscure OBS 8	MACHINE MUSIC (split LP with Gavin Bryers)	£20

JOY WHITE
75	Attack ATT 8093	Dread Out De/Dread Dub	£25
79	Tribesman TM 25	Always Together (with Jerry Baxter)/Dubbing To Sir Coxsone Sound (12")	£20
79	Fight FDD 4438	The First Cut Is The Deepest/ITALS : Rougher Yet (12")	£20
78	Hawkeye HLP 002	SENTIMENTAL REASONS (LP)	£30

K.C. WHITE
73	Green Door GD 4056	First Cut Is The Deepest/No Good Girl	£20
73	Technique TE 929	Anywhere But Nowhere/Bush In Session	£20

KITTY WHITE
54	London HL 8102	Jesse James/Scratch My Back (B-side with Dave Howard)	£200
54	London HL 8102	Jesse James/Scratch My Back (78, B-side with Dave Howard)	£20

LENNY WHITE
75	Atlantic K 50213	VENUSIAN SUMMER (LP)	£15

LOUISA JANE WHITE
69	Philips BF 1810	When The Battle Is Over/Blue Ribbons	£30
70	Philips BF 1834	How Does It Feel/Truth In My Tears	£100

SHEILA WHITE
66	CBS 202465	Misfit/Switch Off The Night	£15

TAM WHITE
67	Decca F 12711	World Without You/Someone You Should Know (unreleased)	£0
68	Decca F 12849	Waiting Till The Night Comes Around/Girl Watcher	£15
69	Deram DM 261	That Old Sweet Roll/Don't Make Promises	£25
70	Middle Earth MDS 104	Lewis Carroll/Future Thoughts	£50
70	Middle Earth MDLS 304	TAM WHITE (LP)	£100

(see also Boston Dexters)

TERRY WHITE & TERRIERS
59	Decca F 11133	Rock Around The Mailbags/Blackout	£80
59	Decca F 11133	Rock Around The Mailbags/Blackout (78)	£20

THOMAS WHITE
79	Hit Run HD 12	Ivory Girl/KEITH FRANCIS: Prejudice Country (12")	£50

TONY JOE WHITE
69	Monument MON 1031	Polk Salad Annie/Aspen Colorado	£15
68	Monument LMO/SMO 5027	BLACK AND WHITE (LP)	£15
70	Monument LMO/SMO 5035	TONY JOE WHITE CONTINUED (LP)	£15
70	Monument SMO 5043	TONY JOE (LP)	£15
71	Warner Bros WS 1900	TONY JOE WHITE (LP)	£18
72	Warner Bros K 46147	THE TRAIN I'M ON (LP)	£15
73	Warner Bros K 46229	HOME-MADE ICE CREAM (LP)	£15

TREVOR WHITE
76	Island WIP 6291	Crazy Kids/Movin' In The Right Direction (with p/s)	£20

(see also Sparks, Radio Stars)

WHITE CAR
81	Friday FRI 13	Cinema Girl/Channel One (p/s)	£25

WHITE DUCK
72	Uni UNLS 123	WHITE DUCK (LP)	£22
73	Uni UNLS 129	IN SEASON (LP)	£22

WHITE FEATHER
83	No No N.N001	Summer Days/Golden Haze/Feathered Girl (no p/s)	£15

WHITEFIRE
78	Whitefire 98DB 001	SUZANNE (EP)	£40

WHITE HART
79	Tradition TSR 033	IN SEARCH OF REWARD (LP)	£50

WHITE HEAT (1)
79	Valium VAL 01	Nervous Breakdown/Sammy Sez (gatefold p/s)	£25
80	Valium VAL 02	Finished With The Fashions/Ordinary Joe (p/s, with insert)	£20
81	Valium VAL 03	City Beat/It's No Use (Young Ones) (p/s)	£15
81	Valium VALP 101	IN THE ZERO HOUR (LP)	£25

WHITE HEAT (2)
84	RSR 007	Soldier Of Fortune/Lovemaker	£75
84	Rock Shop RSR 007	WHITE HEAT (LP)	£25

WHITEHOUSE
90	Sue Lawley SLS 002	Still Going Strong/Ankles And Wrists	£15
01	SLA-003	Cruise (Force The Truth)/Instrumental Version (12")	£20
02	SLA-004	Wriggle Like A Fucking Eel/Instrumental Version (12")	£18
80	Come Org. WDC 881004	BIRTHDEATH EXPERIENCE (LP, first pressing pink labels, 850 copies)	£150
80	Come Org. WDC 881005	TOTAL SEX (LP, 400 on green vinyl)	£120
80	Come Org. WDC 881005	TOTAL SEX (LP, 800 on black vinyl)	£80
80	Come Org. WDC 883005	TOTAL SEX (cassette)	£75
80	Come Org. WDC 883003	ULTRASADISM (cassette)	£60
81	Come Org. WDC 881010	DEDICATED TO PETER KÜRTEN, SADIST AND MASS SLAYER (LP, some on coloured vinyl, some in custom sleeve)	£120
80	Come Org. WDC 881007	ERECTOR (LP, different coloured vinyls)	£100
81	Come Org. WDC 881013	BÜCHENWALD (LP, clear vinyl)	£120
81	WDC 883013	BUCHENWALD (cassette)	£60
81	Come Org. WDC 881017	NEW BRITAIN (LP, with insert)	£125
82	Come Org. WDC 881027	PSYCHOPATHIA SEXUALIS (LP, clear vinyl, black is bootleg)	£200
82	Come Org. WDC 883020	LIVE ACTION 1 (cassette)	£45
83	Come Org. WDC 883027	PSYCHOPATHIA SEXUALIS (cassette)	£70
83	Come Org. WDC 883033	RIGHT TO KILL - DEDICATED TO DENNIS ANDREW NEILSEN (LP, & inserts)	£120
83	Come Org. WDC 883044048	USA I - V (5 cassettes documenting 1983 US tour, pice for each)	£45
85	Come Org. WDC	GREAT WHITE DEATH (LP)	£80

(Many Whitehouse LP's were issued in customised white card sleeves & were later available in a generic 'Peter Kürten' sleeve, originally used for the 2nd pressing of the 'Peter Kürten' LP. This latter design was also used for counterfeits. There may also be coloured vinyl variations which are worth the same)

80s	Come Org. WDC	**150 MURDEROUS PASSIONS** (LP, with Nurse With Wound)	£75
80s	United Dairies UD 009	**150 MURDEROUS PASSIONS** (LP, with Nurse With Wound, reissue)	£40
80s	United Dairies UD 009	**150 MURDEROUS PASSIONS** (LP, with Nurse With Wound, export issue, sealed in black vinyl)	£125
80s	Susan Lawley 1	**CREAM OF THE SECOND COMING** (2-LP)	£45
91	Susan Lawley SL 002	**THANK YOUR LUCKY STARS** (LP)	£30
92	Susan Lawley SL 003	**TWICE IS NOT ENOUGH** (LP)	£30

(see also Come, Nurse With Wound, New Order, Skullflower, Konstruktivits)

WHITE LABEL
11	White Label WHO0001LP	**STOLEN VOICES** (LP. ltd. ed)	£50

WHITE LIES
08	Fiction 1795718	**To Lose My Life** (6 x 7" box set with signed print)	£40

WHITE LIGHT
74	Scotia SCO/LP 4791	**PARABLE** (LP)	£300

WHITE LIGHTNING
84	Wild Party PP 1000	**This Poison Fountain/Hypocrite** (no p/s, 1,000 only)	£50
90	Workshop JOB LP 2	**AS MIDNIGHT APPROACHES** (LP, with inner)	£18

(see also Static)

WHITE LINING
70	Parlophone R 5868	**Back In The Sun/Mon Amour**	£20

WHITE MULE
70	UNI UNS 523	**Looking Through Cat's Eyes/Hundred Franc Blues**	£15

WHITE NOISE
75	Virgin VDJ 2	**An Extract From White Noise 2** (promo only)	£20
69	Island ILPS 9099	**AN ELECTRIC STORM** (LP, pink label black/orange circle logo)	£150
69	Island ILPS 9099	**WHITE NOISE** (LP, repressing pink label with white 'i' logo)	£50
75	Virgin V 2032	**WHITE NOISE 2** (LP)	£15
08	Island 5313 125	**AN ELECTRIC STORM** (LP, reissue, pink rim palm tree label)	£18

(see also BBC Radiophonic Workshop)

WHITE ON BLACK
74	Saydisc SDL 251	**WHITE ON BLACK** (LP, fully laminated sleeve)	£30

WHITE PLAINS
70	Deram SML 1067	**WHITE PLAINS** (LP, laminated cover)	£30
71	Deram SML 1092	**WHEN YOU ARE A KING** (LP)	£25

(see also David & Jonathan, Kestrels, Brotherhood Of Man, Peter's Faces, Carter-Lewis & Southerners, Ivy League)

WHITE RUSSIA
80	Trivia TRIV 01	**Valentine/Clothes** (p/s)	£40

WHITESNAKE
78	EMI International INEP 751	**SNAKEBITE** (EP, white vinyl, p/s; later black vinyl with no p/s)	£15
82	Liberty BP 418	**Love An' Affection/Victim Of Love** (withdrawn)	£35
78	EMI Intl. INS 3022	**TROUBLE** (LP, grey or pink inner sleeve)	£20
82	Liberty LBGP 30354	**SAINTS AN' SINNERS** (LP, picture disc)	£18
84	Liberty LBGP 240 000 0	**SLIDE IT IN** (LP, picture disc, U.S. mixes)	£18
87	EMI EMCP 3528	**WHITESNAKE 1987** (LP, picture disc)	£18
89	EMI EMCDJ 1013	**SLIP OF THE TONGUE** (LP, with track by track interview, promo only)	£20

(see also David Coverdale, Deep Purple, Rainbow, Roger Glover, Jon Lord, Cozy Powell, Young & Moody Band, Company, Snafu, Bogdon, Gogmagog, Tramline, National Health)

WHITE SPIRIT
81	MCA MCA 638	**Midnight Chaser/Suffragettes** (p/s)	£30
81	MCA MCA 652	**High Upon High/No Reprieve/Arthur Guitar**	£15
80	MCA MCF 3079	**WHITE SPIRIT** (LP, with lyric insert)	£18

(see also Gillan, Iron Maiden)

WHITE SS
78	White SS CIA 72	**Mercy Killing/I'm Not One** (live) (p/s)	£25

WHITE STRIPES
02	XL/MOJO no cat. no.	**Red Death At 6:14** (1-sided, promo only, red vinyl, numbered label, 3000 only, mail order only via Mojo magazine, with letter)	£25
03	XL XLS 162	**Seven Nation Army/Good To Me** (p/s)	£15
03	XL no cat. no.	**Seven Nation Army** (1-sided 12" promo, stamped white label, no p/s)	£25
04	XL XLS 181	**There's No Home For You Here/I Fought Piranhas/Let's Build A Home** (die-cut sleeve)	£15
05	XL (no. cat. No.)	**DENIAL TWIST** (10 x printed/stickered CD's in different artwork card wallets. One given away at each night of UK autumn tour. Each CD blank - 10 downloads were availiable online only, this price for complete set)	£200
01	XL XLLP 150	**DE STIJL** (LP)	£25
01	XL XLLP151	**WHITE BLOOD CELLS** (LP, red vinyl, insert)	£60
01	XL XLLP 151	**WHITE BLOOD CELLS** (LP)	£30
01	XL XLLP 149	**WHITE STRIPES** (LP)	£25
01	XL XLPD149	**WHITE STRIPES** (LP, picture disc)	£18
03	XL XLLP 162	**ELEPHANT** (2-LP, promo, custom sleeve, 500 only)	£100
05	XL XLLP 191 P	**GET BEHIND ME SATAN** (300 copies pressed for U.K.2-LP promo, different p/s)	£200
07	XL XLLP271	**ICKY THUMP** (2-LP, red/white vinyl)	£30

(see also Raconteurs)

WHITE TRASH
69	Apple APPLE 6	**Road To Nowhere/Illusions** (early copies as White Trash)	£200
69	Apple APPLE 6	**Road To Nowhere/Illusions** (later copies as Trash)	£60

(see also Trash, Poets, Stone The Crows)

WHITE ZOMBIE
89	Caroline CAROL 1457	God Of Thunder/Love Razor/Disaster Blaster 2 (12", withdrawn)	£15

DAVID WHITFIELD
54	Decca F 10327	Carla Mia/Love, Tears And Kisses	£15

WILBUR WHITFIELD
57	Vogue V 9078	P.B. Baby/The One I Love	£600
57	Vogue V 9078	P.B. Baby/The One I Love (78)	£150

(see also Little Wilbur & Pleasers)

LEONARD WHITING
65	Pye 7N 15943	The Piper/That's What Mama Says	£40

MARGARET WHITING
53	Capitol LC 6585	CAPITOL PRESENTS MARGARET WHITING (10" LP)	£15
56	Capitol LC 6811	MARGARET WHITING (10" LP)	£15
58	London HA-D 2109	GOIN' PLACES (LP)	£15
61	London HA-D 2321	JUST A DREAM (LP)	£20

(see also Jimmy Wakely, Bob Hope, Dean Martin)

RAY WHITLEY
65	HMV POP 1473	I've Been Hurt/There Is One Boy	£150
65	HMV POP 1473	I've Been Hurt/There Is One Boy (DJ copy)	£250

BOBBY WHITLOCK
72	CBS 65109	BOBBY WHITLOCK (LP)	£30
73	CBS 65301	RAW VELVET (LP)	£20

(see also Derek & Dominoes)

SLIM WHITMAN

SINGLES
54	London L 1149	Indian Love Call/China Doll	£20
54	London HL 1149	Indian Love Call/China Doll (re-pressing with different prefix)	£15
54	London L 1214	There's A Rainbow In Every Teardrop/Danny Boy	£20
54	London HL 1214	There's A Rainbow In Every Teardrop/Danny Boy (re-pressing)	£15
54	London L 1226	North Wind/Darlin' Don't Cry	£30
54	London HL 1226	North Wind/Darlin' Don't Cry (re-pressing with different prefix)	£30
54	London HL 8018	Stairway To Heaven/Lord, Help Me To Be As Thou	£30
54	London HL 8039	Secret Love/Why	£30
54	London HL 8061	Rose Marie/We Stood At The Altar	£15
54	London HL 8080	Beautiful Dreamer/Ride Away	£15
54	London HL 8091	The Singing Hills/I Hate To See You Cry	£15
57	London HLP 8420	Gone/An Amateur In Love (gold label print)	£15
59	London HLP 8896	What Kind Of God (Do You Think You Are)/A Tree In The Meadow (unissued)	£0

ALBUMS
54	London H-APB 1015	SLIM WHITMAN & HIS SINGING GUITAR (10", gold label print)	£40
54	London H-APB 1015	SLIM WHITMAN & HIS SINGING GUITAR (10", silver label print)	£25
56	London HA-U 2015	SLIM WHITMAN & HIS SINGING GUITAR VOL. 2	£30
59	London HA-P 2139	SLIM WHITMAN SINGS	£20
59	London HA-P 2199	SLIM WHITMAN SINGS VOL. 2	£20
61	London HA-P 2392	JUST CALL ME LONESOME	£20
60	London HA-P 2343	SLIM WHITMAN	£18
62	London HA-P 2443	SLIM WHITMAN SINGS VOL. 3 (Mono)	£18
62	London HA-P 2443	SLIM WHITMAN SINGS VOL. 3 (also stereo SAH-P 6232)	£20

MARVA WHITNEY
69	Polydor 583 767	IT'S MY THING (LP)	£75

(see also James Brown)

JAKI WHITREN
83	Living LRS 111	International Times/Inner Fire (p/s)	£20
83	Living 12 LR1	International Times/Dub Version (12", p/s)	£40
73	Epic EPC 65645	RAW BUT TENDER (LP, with insert)	£45
83	Living LR1	INTERNATIONAL TIMES (LP, with John Cartwright)	£100

TIM WHITSETT
64	Sue WI 318	Macks By The Tracks/Shine	£45

TIM WHITSETT/STICKS HERMAN
60s	Range JRE 7002	RHYTHM & BLUES (EP)	£30

PAUL WHITSUN JONES & WALLAS EATON & HOLLAND
65	Oriole CB 1991	Shake It Baby/Instant Marriage	£20

WHITSUNTIDE EASTER
77	Pilgrim/Grapevine GRA 109	NEXT TIME YOU PLAY A WRONG NOTE...MAKE IT A SHORT ONE (LP, gatefold sleeve)	£100

TOMMY WHITTLE (& HIS QUARTET)
57	HMV 45 POP 379	The Finisher/Cabin In The Sky	£25
55	Esquire EP 37	TOMMY WHITTLE QUINTET (EP)	£40
56	Esquire EP 37	TOMMY WHITTLE QUINTET (EP)	£40
58	HMV 7EG 8325	TOMMY WHITTLE QUARTET (EP)	£100
54	Esquire 20-028	WAXING WITH WHITTLE (LP)	£50
55	Esquire 20-048	TOMMY WHITTLE QUINTET (LP)	£60
56	Esquire 20-061	SPOTLIGHTING TOMMY WHITTLE (LP)	£90
56	Esquire 20-068	LULLABY & RHYTHM (LP)	£100

60	Tempo TAP 27	NEW HORIZONS (LP)..£1000
60s	Ember EMB 3305	EASY LISTENING (LP)..£75
67	Masquerade MQ 2000	SAX FOR DREAMERS (LP)..£100
77	Jam 648	WHY NOT? (LP)..£20
82	Tee Jay 101	THE NEARNESS OF YOU (LP)...£20
88	Esquire 334	MORE WAXING WITH WHITTLE (LP, reissue) £20

WHIZZ KIDS

| 79 | Dead Good DEAD SIX | P.A.Y.E./99% Proof/National Assistance/Cheek To Cheek (p/s, with insert) ....£20 |

THE WHO
SINGLES

65	Brunswick 05926	I Can't Explain/Bald Headed Woman.......................................£40
65	Brunswick 05935	Anyway Anyhow Anywhere/Daddy Rolling Stone £35
65	Brunswick 05944	My Generation/Shout And Shimmy...£20
66	Brunswick 05951	Circles/Instant Party Mixture (unreleased)............................£0
66	Reaction 591 001	Substitute/Circles (temporarily withdrawn)...........................£40
66	Reaction 591 001	Substitute/Instant Party (temporarily withdrawn) £30
66	Brunswick 05956	The Kids Are Alright/The Ox (existence unconfirmed)...........£0
66	Brunswick 05956	A Legal Matter/Instant Party £50
66	Reaction 591 001	Substitute/WHO ORCHESTRA: Waltz For A Pig (B-side actually by Graham Bond Organisation) £25
66	Brunswick 05965	The Kids Are Alright/The Ox £60
66	Brunswick 05968	La-La-La-Lies/The Good's Gone...£70
67	Track 604 006	The Last Time/Under My Thumb £65
67	Track 604 011	I Can See For Miles/Someone's Coming £15
68	Track 604 023	Dogs/Call Me Lightning £25
69	Track 613 013/014	TOMMY (2LP, 1st issue fold-out laminated gatefold sleeve made by E.J. Day, A1/B1/ A1/B1 matrixes, "double album" on labels and must not have catalogue number under 'ST33' on the right side (as this is a later pressing) with numbered 12-page booklet) £150
70	Track 2094 004	See Me, Feel Me/Overture From 'Tommy' (withdrawn)...........£40
71	Track 2094 009	Won't Get Fooled Again/Don't Know Myself (p/s, large centre)................................£25
71	Track 2094 009	Won't Get Fooled Again/Don't Know Myself (p/s, with middle)................................£35
78	Polydor Who 1 DJ	Who Are You/Had Enough (DJ copy in brown paper bag with 'Who Promotional Copy' stamped on outside)...£30
82	Polydor WHOPX 6	Athena/A Man Is A Man/Won't Get Fooled Again (12", picture disc, mispressing, plays "Why Did I Fall For That")..£15
88	Polydor POSPX 917	Won't Get Fooled Again/Boney Moronie/Dancing In The Street/Mary-Anne With The Shaky Hand (12", p/s)...£15
04	Polydor 9866447	THE FIRST SINGLES BOX (12 x 7" box set with booklet)............................£75
13	Universal 3716687	MUSIC FOR THE CLOSING CEREMONY OF THE LONDON 2012 OLYMPIC GAMES (12", p/ s, numbered)...£50
15	Polydor 4713989	THE BRUNSWICK SINGLES 1965-1966 (8x7" box set, booklet).........................£60
15	Polydor 4724720	THE REACTION SINGLES 1966 (5x7" box set, booklet) £40
15	Polydor 4737108	THE TRACK SINGLES 1967-1973 (15x7" box set, booklet) £80
16	Polydor 4765358	THE POLYDOR SINGLES (15x7" box set, booklet)......................................£60

EXPORT SINGLES

66	Brunswick 05956	A Legal Matter/Instant Party (with Scandinavian p/s) £150
68	Decca AD 1001	My Generation/Shout And Shimmy...£100
68	Decca AD 1001	My Generation/Shout And Shimmy (in p/s) £200
68	Decca AD 1002	A Legal Matter/Instant Party £100
72	Track 2094 102	Join Together/Baby Don't You Do It (p/s, for Spain with 'special Londres import' on front and 'Imported by Polydor S.A.' on rear)...£25

EPs

66	Reaction 592 001	READY STEADY WHO £90
70	Track 2252 001	EXCERPTS FROM "TOMMY" (33rpm) £25
83	Reaction WHO 7	READY STEADY WHO (reissue) £20

ALBUMS

65	Brunswick LAT 8616	MY GENERATION (laminated front sleeve, black/silver label)................£600
66	Reaction 593 002	A QUICK ONE (laminated sleeve, blue/silver label)...................£200
67	Track 612 002	THE WHO SELL OUT (LP, mono)...£200
67	Track 613 002	THE WHO SELL OUT (LP, stereo)..£150
67	Track 612 002	THE WHO SELL OUT (mono, 500 with stickered sleeve & poster) £800
67	Track 613 002	THE WHO SELL OUT (stereo, 500 with stickered sleeve & poster) £800
68	Track 612 006	DIRECT HITS (mono) £40
68	Track 613 006	DIRECT HITS (stereo) £50
69	Track 613 013/014	TOMMY (2LP, 2nd issue fold-out matt gatefold sleeve, no "double album" on labels with 12-page booklet, un-numbered)..£40
70	Track 2406 001	LIVE AT LEEDS (1st issue with BLACK stamp on front, foldout sleeve with 12 inserts including poster) £250
70	Track 2406 001	LIVE AT LEEDS (with BLUE or RED stamp on front, foldout sleeve with 12 inserts including poster stating 'Tuesdays At The Marquee') £80
70	Track 2406 001	LIVE AT LEEDS (with BLUE or RED stamp on front, foldout sleeve with 12 inserts including poster stating 'Live At Leeds', A1/B1 matrix') £50
70	Track 2406 001	LIVE AT LEEDS (second pressing, BLUE or RED stamp on front, foldout sleeve with 12 inserts including poster stating 'Live At Leeds', A3/B3 matrix') £40
70	Track 2407 008	BACKTRACK 8: A QUICK ONE (mono budget reissue) £25
70	Track 2407 009	BACKTRACK 9: SELL OUT (stereo budget reissue) £30
70	Track 2407 014	BACKTRACK 14: THE OX...£20
70	Track 2856 001	WHO DID IT? (mail-order only, withdrawn).............................£600
71	Track 2408 102	WHO'S NEXT (1st pressing with poly-lined inner sleeve with black and white Polydor artist photos on front and "HEAD HUNTERS - GET A HEAD" on rear. MATRIX: 2408 102 £50

		A1/B2) **Pleated end spines)**	
71	Track 2408 102	**WHO'S NEXT** (later pressing, MATRIX: 2408 102 A4/B3)	**£25**
71	Track 2406 006	**MEATY, BEATY, BIG AND BOUNCY** (gatefold sleeve)	**£30**
71	Track 2406 006	**MEATY, BEATY, BIG AND BOUNCY** (gatefold sleeve, mispressed, plays "The Seeker" instead of "Magic Bus")	**£40**
72	Track 2406 007	**TOMMY PART ONE**	**£20**
72	Track 2406 008	**TOMMY PART TWO** (with lyric sheet)	**£20**
73	Track 2406 110	**QUADROPHENIA** (2-LP, original with 22-page photo booklet, matt labels).......	**£60**
73	Track 613013/613014	**TOMMY** (2-LP, reissue)...	**£20**
74	Track ACB 254	**ODDS AND SODS** (LP)	**£45**
74	Track 2406 116	**ODDS AND SODS** (cut-away braille sleeve, with poster & lyric sheet)..........	**£40**
74	Track 2409209/10	**A QUICK ONE/THE WHO SELL OUT** (2-LP, reissue, E.J. Day printing credit)	**£70**
75	Polydor 2490 129	**THE WHO BY NUMBERS** (LP, numbered)	**£20**
76	Polydor 2478091	**THE STORY OF THE WHO** (2-LP, booklet)	**£25**
78	Polydor WHOD 5004	**WHO ARE YOU** (LP)	**£20**
79	Polydor 2488 739	**THE KIDS ARE ALRIGHT** (2-LP, booklet and inner sleeves)......................	**£30**
80	Virgin V 2179	**MY GENERATION** (reissue)	**£25**
80	Polydor 2683 084	**LIVE AT LEEDS/WHO ARE YOU** (2-LP)	**£20**
81	Polydor 2675 216	**PHASES** (9-LP box set, stickered cover)......................................	**£150**
81	Polydor	**FACE DANCES** (Promo boxed set with poster and bio of artists, numbered Peter Blake print, 300 only)	**£200**
81	Polydor WHOD 5037	**FACE DANCES** (LP, inner, poster)	**£20**
82	Polydor De Luxe WHOD 5066	**IT'S HARD** (LP)	**£15**
83	Polydor Mid Price SPELP 60	**LIVE AT LEEDS** (2-LP, reissue)	**£20**
83	Polydor SPELT 49	**WHO'S NEXT LP, reissue)**	**£20**
83	Polydor SPLEP 9	**RARITIES VOL 1 1966-1968** (LP)	**£15**
83	Polydor SPLEP 10	**RARITIES VOL 2 1970-1973** (LP)	**£15**
84	MCA WHO 1	**WHO'S LAST** (2LP, gatefold, printed inners)	**£20**
84	Polydor WHOH 17	**THE SINGLES** (LP)	**£20**
85	Polydor Impression IMDP 4	**THE WHO COLLECTION** (2LP, gatefold)	**£20**
88	Polydor SPELT 114	**A QUICK ONE** (LP, reissue)	**£25**
88	Polydor SPELT 115	**THE WHO SELL OUT** (LP, reissue)	**£20**
88	Polydor SVLP 201	**TOMMY** (2-LP, reissue)...	**£20**
88	Polydor WTV 1	**WHO'S BETTER WHO'S BEST** (LP)	**£20**
88	Polydor 8375571	**WHO'S MISSING** (LP)	**£20**
88	Polydor 8375581	**TWO'S MISSING** (LP)	**£20**
90	Virgin VDT 201	**JOIN TOGETHER** (3-LP, inner sleeves)	**£40**
99	Simply Vinyl SVLP 088	**WHO'S NEXT** (LP, reissue, 180gm)	**£30**
00	Polydor 5477271	**BBC SESSIONS** (2-LP)...	**£25**
01	Sanctuary CMYTV 164	**LIVE AT THE ISLE OF WIGHT 1970** (3LP, gatefold, reissue).....................	**£40**
01	Polydor 8310741	**QUADROPHENIA** (2-LP, reissue, 22 page book, 180gm)...........................	**£20**
02	Polydor 11398111	**MY GENERATION** (2-LP, reissue, first stereo remix with bonus tracks).........	**£40**
03	Polydor 076 176-1	**WHO'S NEXT** (3-LP, reissue)	**£40**
03	Polydor 8117151	**THE WHO BY NUMBERS** (LP, reissue)	**£20**
04	Polydor 8357281	**A QUICK ONE** (LP, reissue)	**£20**
08	Polydor 0042281365119	**WHO'S NEXT** (LP, reissue)	**£25**
10	Polydor 0602527500720	**LIVE AT LEEDS** (4-CD/LP/7 box set, extra tracks, 40th Anniversary Edition) ...	**£130**
11	Polydor 2780405	**QUADROPHENIA** (2-LP, reissue, 22 page book, 180gm)...........................	**£20**
11	Back On Black RCV 065LP	**LIVE AT THE ISLE OF WIGHT FESTIVAL** (3-LP)...................................	**£40**
12	Polydor 3715573	**THE STUDIO ALBUMS** (13-LP box set)...	**£200**
12	Eagle VV 3 LP 006	**LIVE AT THE ISLE OF WIGHT FESTIVAL** (3-LP, blue or white vinyl)..............	**£30**
13	Polydor 3715751	**ENDLESS WIRE** (2-LP)...	**£25**
13	Universal 00600753271278	**WHO'S NEXT** (LP, reissue, picture disc).....................................	**£35**
15	Polydor 3715603	**MY GENERATION** (LP, reissue)	**£20**
15	Polydor 3715608	**A QUICK ONE** (LP, reissue)	**£15**
15	Polydor 3715609	**THE WHO SELL OUT** (LP, reissue)	**£20**
15	Polydor 3715749	**TOMMY** (2-LP, reissue, 180gm)	**£25**
15	Polydor 3715630	**WHO ARE YOU** (LP, reissue, 180gm)	**£20**
15	Polydor 3715627	**THE WHO BY NUMBERS** (LP, reissue)	**£20**
15	Polydor 5780504	**QUADROPHENIA** (2-LP, reissue,180gm)	**£25**
16	Polydor 0600753698075	**LIVE AT LEEDS** (3LP, trifold sleeve, entire concert, half speed mastered, obi strip)	**£50**
17	Polydor 5372747	**MY GENERATION** (3-LP reissue)	**£30**
17	Polydor 5774830	**LIVE AT LEEDS** (LP, reissue)	**£20**
17	Polydor 5774828	**MEATY, BEATY, BIG AND BOUNCY** (LP, reissue)	**£20**
17	Eagle ER 416812	**TOMMY LIVE AT THE ALBERT HALL** (3-LP).......................................	**£25**
18	Polydor 3715614	**WHO'S NEXT** (LP, reissue, blue vinyl).......................................	**£15**
18	Polydor 6713232	**THE KIDS ARE ALRIGHT** (2LP, reissue, red and blue vinyl)	**£40**
18	Polydor 6744480	**LIVE AT FILLMORE EAST 1968** (3LP, gatefold, printed inners).................	**£30**
19	Polydor WHO 7748605	**WHO** (2LP/10", 45rpm, gatefold, blue/white/red vinyl)	**£40**
19	Polydor WHO 08249751921	**WHO** (LP, with additional Bonus Hits LP on cream vinyl, HMV exclusive).......	**£20**
19	Polydor/UMC 7768744	**THE KIDS ARE ALRIGHT** (2LP, reissue)...	**£18**
20	Polydor 7712462	**ODDS AND SODS** (2LP, red/yellow vinyl, die-cut sleeve, printed inners, half-speed, obi-strip)..	**£40**
22	Polydor/UMC 3894476	**IT'S HARD** (2LP, printed inners, poster, orange/yellow vinyl, half-speed, obi-strip, RSD) ...	**£30**
23	Polydor/UMR 3587307	**WHO'S NEXT/LIFEHOUSE** (10CD/1BD box set, 2 hardback books, ephemera envelope)..	**£100**
23	Polydor/UMR 3585904	**WHO'S NEXT** (3LP, gatefold, printed inners)	**£60**
23	Polydor/UMC ARHSLP 019	**WHO'S NEXT** (LP, half-speed master, obi-strip, certificate).................	**£25**

| 24 | Polydor 5864519 | THE STORY OF THE WHO (2LP, pink/blue vinyl, gatefold, booklet, RSD) | £30 |

PROMOS : DEMO SINGLES

65	Brunswick 05926	I Can't Explain/Bald Headed Woman (demo, red label)	£500
65	Brunswick 05935	Anyway Anyhow Anywhere/Daddy Rolling Stone (demo, red label)	£400
65	Brunswick 05944	My Generation/Shout And Shimmy (demo, red label)	£450
66	Brunswick 05956	A Legal Matter/Instant Party (demo, red label)	£400
66	Brunswick 05965	The Kids Are Alright/The Ox (demo, red label)	£400
66	Brunswick 05968	La-La-La-Lies/The Good's Gone (demo, red label)	£400
69	Track PRO 1	The Acid Queen/We're Not Gonna Take It (existence unconfirmed)	£0
69	Track PRO 2	Go To The Mirror!/Sally Simpson	£80
69	Track PRO 3	I'm Free/1921	£80
69	Track PRO 4	Christmas/Overture	£80
78	Polydor WHO 1 DJ 3	Who Are You (Edited Version) (single sided promo)	£75
82	Polydor WHOX 6A2420	Eminence Front/Athena/Dangerous)12", promo, stamped white sleeve large 1 and 2 on labels)	£50
07	The Who Group Ltd thewho.com1	VIEW FROM A BACKSTAGE PASS (2CD, booklet, free to subscribers of thewho.com)	£75

(see also High Numbers, Pete Townshend, Roger Daltrey, John Entwistle, Keith Moon, Graham Bond Organisation, Rigor Mortis, McEnroe & Cash)

WHO THE HELL DOES JANE SMITH THINK SHE IS

| 87 | Influx FUX 1 | Use/Imagination (p/s) | £25 |
| 87 | Influx FUX 1T | Use/Imagination (12", p/s) | £60 |

WI & HDEA

| 93 | Hype! VEN 001 | VENTURE F.M. PRESENTS SUMMER RUSH EP (12", stamped white label) | £20 |

WICHITA FALL

| 69 | Liberty LBS 83208 | LIFE IS BUT A DREAM (LP) | £25 |

WICHITA TRAIN WHISTLE

| 68 | Dot DOT 111 | Don't Cry Now/Tapioca Tundra (unissued) | £0 |
| 68 | Dot (S)LPD 516 | MICHAEL NESMITH PRESENTS THE WICHITA TRAIN WHISTLE SINGS (LP) | £40 |

(see also Michael Nesmith)

WICKY WACKY

| 90 | EMI WACKY PROMO 1 | Let's Get Down (6 mixes, promo only, 300 copies) | £50 |

(see also Cabaret Voltaire)

WIDERVISION

| 80 | Widermusic 001 | People/Truant (p/s) | £25 |

WIDOWMAKER

| 77 | United Artists UAG 30038 | TOO LATE TO CRY (LP, gatefold sleeve) | £15 |

(see also Luther Grosvenor, Steve Ellis, Huw Lloyd Langton)

TREVOR WIGGAN

| 75 | Not on label | Beg You Not To Go/JAH MAN: Please Stay | £100 |

WIGGANS

| 61 | Blue Beat BB 29 | Rock Baby/Let's Sing The Blues | £25 |

SPENCER WIGGINS

| 67 | Stateside SS 2024 | Uptight Good Woman/Anything You Do Is Alright | £25 |
| 70 | Pama PM 794 | I'm A Poor Man's Son/That's How Much I Love You | £25 |

WIGWAM

| 76 | Virgin V2051 | LUCKY GOLDEN STRIPES AND STARPOSE (LP, "mirror" girl label, lyric insert, embossed sleeve) | £20 |
| 75 | Virgin V 2035 | NUCLEAR NIGHTCLUB (LP) | £25 |

LEO WIJNKAMP JR

| 75 | Kicking Mule SNKF 108 | RAGS TO RICHES (LP) | £25 |
| 79 | Kicking Mule SNKF 156 | RETURN OF DR. HACKENBUSH (LP) | £25 |

WIKKYD VIKKER

| 83 | Boogie FUR 0235 | Black Of The Night/Release (no p/s) | £120 |

WILCO

97	Reprise 9362 46236-1	BEING THERE (2-LP)	£40
99	Reprise 9362 47282-1	SUMMERTEETH (2-LP)	£40
04	Nonesuch 76492-1	A GHOST IS BORN (2-LP)	£25

WILD ANGELS

68	Major Minor MM 569	Nervous Breakdown/Watch The Wheels Go Round	£25
70	B&C BCM 101	LIVE AT THE REVOLUTION (LP)	£15
70	B&C BCM 102	RED HOT'N'ROCKIN' (LP)	£15

WILD BOYS

| 80 | Ring Piece CUS 886 | Last One Of The Boys/We're Only Monsters (p/s) | £400 |

WILD BUNCH

| 84 | Ariwa ARILP 15 | THE WILD BUNCH (LP) | £20 |

WILDCATS (1)

| 59 | London HLT 8787 | Gazachstahagen/Billy's Cha Cha | £25 |

WILD COUNTRY

| 70 | Trafalgar TRAF 01 | Silent Village/Too Bad | £65 |

MARTY WILDE (& WILDCATS)

78s

| 57 | Philips PB 750 | Honeycomb/Wild Cat (as Marty Wilde & Wildcats) | £15 |
| 58 | Philips PB 781 | Love Bug Crawl/Afraid Of Love | £30 |

MINT VALUE £

58	Philips PB 804	Sing, Boy, Sing/Oh-Oh, I'm Falling In Love Again (with Wildcats)	£25
58	Philips PB 875	No One Knows/The Fire Of Love	£15
59	Philips PB 902	Donna/Love-a, Love-a, Love-a	£25
59	Philips PB 926	A Teenager In Love/Danny	£30
59	Philips PB 959	Sea Of Love/Teenage Tears	£40
59	Philips PB 972	It's Been Nice/Bad Boy	£40
60	Philips PB 1002	Johnny Rocco/My Heart And I	£50

SINGLES

57	Philips JK 1028	Honeycomb/Wild Cat (as Marty Wilde & Wildcats) (jukebox issue)	£50
58	Philips PB 804	Sing, Boy, Sing/Oh-Oh, I'm Falling In Love Again (with Wildcats)	£40
58	Philips PB 835	Endless Sleep/Her Hair Was Yellow (as Marty Wilde & Wildcats)	£15
58	Philips PB 875	No One Knows/The Fire Of Love	£15
61	Philips PB 1161	Hide And Seek/Crazy Dream	£15

EPs

57	Philips BBE 12164	PRESENTING MARTY WILDE	£30
58	Philips BBE 12200	MORE OF MARTY	£30
59	Philips BBE 12327	SEA OF LOVE	£30
60	Philips BBE 12385	VERSATILE MR. WILDE	£25
60	Philips BBE 12422	MARTY WILDE FAVOURITES	£25
62	Philips BBE 12517	COME RUNNING	£25
63	Philips BE 433 638	MARTY	£25

ALBUMS

59	Philips BBL 7342	WILDE ABOUT MARTY	£50
60	Philips BBL 7380	MARTY WILDE SHOWCASE	£35
60	Philips BBL 7385	THE VERSATILE MR. WILDE (mono)	£30
60	Philips SBBL 570	THE VERSATILE MR. WILDE (stereo)	£35

(see also Wilde Three, Brian Bennett, Shadows, Keith Shields, Deke Leonard)

OLIVER WILDE

| 15 | Howling Owl HOWL 042 | Yuletide (with EBU, 1-sided lathe cut, 30 only) | £25 |
| 13 | Howling Owl HOWL 022 | AN INTRODUCTION TO UNNATURAL LIGHTYEARS (LP, 1st pressing, white vinyl, 250 only, insert) | £30 |

WILDER BROTHERS

| 57 | HMV POP 365 | I Want You/Teenage Angel | £250 |
| 57 | HMV POP 365 | I Want You/Teenage Angel (78) | £50 |

WILDERNESS ROAD

| 74 | Dawn DNLS 3057 | WILDERNESS ROAD (LP, unissued) | £0 |

WILDE THREE

| 65 | Decca F 12131 | Since You've Gone/Just As Long | £75 |
| 65 | Decca F 12232 | I Cried/Well Who's That? | £75 |

(see also Marty Wilde, Justin Hayward, Vernons Girls)

WILDFIRE (1)

| 83 | Mausoleum SKUL 8307 | BRUTE FORCE AND IGNORANCE (LP) | £25 |
| 83 | Mausoleum SKUL 8338 | SUMMER LIGHTNING (LP, with insert) | £15 |

(see also Weapon)

GINGER WILDHEART

12	(No label or Cat. No)	555% (3-LP, red, white and blue vinyl, tri-fold sleeve, inners. Pledge mail order only)	£50
14	(No label or Cat. No)	ALBION (2-LP, gatefold sleeve. Pledge mail order only)	£40
15	GASSLP 001	YEAR OF THE FANCLUB (2-LP, clear glitter vinyl, gatefold and innder. Pledge mail-order only)	£40

(see also Wildhearts, Super$hit666, Jason & the Scorchers)

WILDHEARTS

SINGLES

92	East West YZ 669T	MONDO AKIMBO A-GO-GO (12" EP, with inner sleeve)	£35
92	East West YZ 669TX	MONDO AKIMBO A-GO-GO (12" EP, white vinyl, with inner sleeve, advance copies with artwork postcard & press sheet)	£60
92	East West YZ 669TX	MONDO AKIMBO A-GO-GO (12" EP, white vinyl, with inner sleeve)	£50
92	East West YZ 669CD	MONDO AKIMBO A-GO-GO (CD EP)	£40
04	(no label or cat no)	Vanilla Radio/Stormy In The North, Karma In The South (CD-R, p/s in DVD case, sold at gigs)	£40

ALBUMS

92	East West 4509-91202-1	DON'T BE HAPPY... JUST WORRY (LP, as 2 x 12", with inner sleeves)	£40
93	East West 4509-93287-1	EARTH VS THE WILDHEARTS (LP, with exclusive uncredited track)	£100
94	East West 4509-99039-2	FISHING FOR LUCKIES (CD, 6-track mini-album, fan club/mail-order only)	£40
95	East West 0630-10404-1	P.H.U.Q. (LP, gatefold sleeve)	£80
95	East West 0630-12850-1	FISHING FOR MORE LUCKIES (LP, reissue, with 3 extra tracks, Underkill, Saddened & I Wanna Go Where The People Go [Early Version], unreleased, most copies destroyed)	£500
95	East West 0630-12850-2	FISHING FOR MORE LUCKIES (LP, reissue, with 3 extra tracks Underkill, "Saddened" & "I Wanna Go Where The People Go [Early Version]")	£35
96	Round 0630-14888-1	FISHING FOR LUCKIES (2LP, reissue, gatefold, Side 3 exclusive to vinyl)	£80
97	Mushroom MUSH13LP	ENDLESS, NAMELESS (LP, inner sleeve)	£50
98	Kuro Neko KNEKLP3	ANARCHIC AIRWAVES - THE WiLDHEARTS AT THE BBC (2-LP, 200 mail-order copies only - 1000 copies made but 800 destroyed)	£60
99	Kuro Neko KNEK3LTD	ANARCHIC AIRWAVES - THE WiLDHEARTS AT THE BBC (2-CD, with bonus disc "THE REST OF READING")	£30
98	Kuro Neko KNEK4LB	LANDMINES & PANTOMIMES - THE LAST OF THE WiLDHEARTS...? (CD in square stickered metal tin in card box with insert, 1000 copies only)	£45
03	Gut GUTLP25	THE WILDHEARTS MUST BE DESTROYED (LP, gatefold sleeve)	£40

04	Gut GUTLP 32	**THE WILDHEARTS STRIKE BACK** (2LP, gatefold)	£60
08	Round ROUND010LP	**THE WILDHEARTS** (2 x LP, white vinyl, photo insert, 1,000 only)	£40
16	Round RRRLP001	**NEVER OUTDRUNK, NEVER OUTSUNG - PHUQ LIVE** (2-LP, purple vinyl with bonus CD, gatefold sleeve/inners. Pledge mail-order only)	£50
16	Round RRRLP001	**NEVER OUTDRUNK, NEVER OUTSUNG - PHUQ LIVE** (2-LP, yellow vinyl vinyl, reissue with bonus CD, gatefold sleeve/inners. Pledge mail-order only)	£25

(see also Energetic Krusher, Honeycrack, Jellys,, Super$hit666, Yo-Yo's)

WILD HORSES

81	EMI EMC 3368	**STAND YOUR GROUND** (LP, with inner sleeve)	£15

(see also Thin Lizzy, Motorhead, Rainbow, Dio)

WILD MAGNOLIAS

75	Barclay 80 529	**THE WILD MAGNOLIAS 1** (LP, gatefold sleeve)	£20
75	Barclay 90 033	**THEY CALL US WILD** (LP, gatefold sleeve)	£20

WILD OATS

63	Oak RGJ 117	**WILD OATS** (EP)	£750
95	Tenth Planet TP 013	**LIVE AT LEISTON** (LP, numbered)	£20
16	Big Beat HIQLP 044	**THE WILD OATS** (10" LP, reissue of original EP)	£15

WILD ONES (U.K.)

64	Fontana TF 468	**Bowie Man/Purple Pill Eater**	£75

WILD ONES (U.S)

65	United Artsts ULP 1119	**THE ARTHUR SOUND** (LP)	£40

WILD ORKID

94	Lucky Spin LSR 014	**The Magic In You/Orkid** (12")	£30

WILD PUSSY

88	Metallion	**MECHANARCH** (12", EP, wih insert)	£100

WILD SILK

69	Columbia DB 8534	(Visions In A) **Plaster Sky/Toymaker**	£30
69	Columbia DB 8611	**Help Me/Crimson And Gold**	£20

WILD SWANS

82	Zoo CAGE 009	**The Revolutionary Spirit/God Forbid** (12", p/s, with 'The Lament Of Icarus' painting in top right of front sleeve, withdrawn)	£15

WILD THING

70	Elektra EKS 74059	**PARTYIN'** (LP)	£18

WILD TURKEY

72	Chrysalis CHR 1002	**BATTLE HYMN** (LP, gatefold sleeve)	£40
73	Chrysalis CHR 1010	**TURKEY** (LP, gatefold sleeve)	£20

(see also Babe Ruth, Jethro Tull, Man, Gary Pickford-Hopkins, Whitesnake)

WILD UNCERTAINTY

66	Planet PLF 120	**A Man With Money/Broken Truth**	£100

WILD & WANDERING

86	Iguana VYK 14	**2,000 LIGHT ALES FROM HOME** (12" EP, with insert)	£25

(see also Pop Will Eat Itself)

WILDWEEDS

67	Chess CRS 8065	**It Was Fun While It Lasted/Sorrow's Anthem**	£20

WILEY

03	XL Recordings XLLP 178	**TREDDIN ON THIN ICE** (2-LP)	£25
07	Big Dada BD 104	**PLAYTIME IS OVER** (2-LP)	£25

WILFRED

70	Parlophone R5836	**Candle In The Wind/Between The Lines**	£15

MIKE WILHELM

76	Zigzag/United Artists ZZ 1	**MIKE WILHELM** (LP, sold via Zigzag magazine)	£45

(see also Charlatans, Flamin' Groovies)

ROBERT WILKINS

60s	Piedmont PLP 13162	**REV ROBERT WILKINS** (LP)	£20
70	Spokane SPL 1002	**BEFORE THE REVERENCE** (LP)	£40

WILLARDS LEAP

77	Wren CW 71010	**ADIEU, JOHN BARLEYCORN**	£20

E WILLIAM

67	Polydor 56181	**Lazy Life/Crazy How love Slips Away**	£50

AL WILLIAMS

80	Grapevine GRP 136	**I Am Nothing/Brand New Love**	£35
05	Grapevine G2K 45-162	**Try Then/LPTs: Try Me** (Instrumental)	£20

ANDY WILLIAMS

56	London HLA 8284	**Walk Hand In Hand/Not Any More**	£30
56	London HLA 8315	**Canadian Sunset/High Upon A Mountain** (gold label print)	£40
56	London HLA 8315	**Canadian Sunset/High Upon A Mountain** (silver label print)	£15
56	London HL 7013	**Canadian Sunset/High Upon A Mountain** (export issue)	£20
56	London HLA 8360	**Baby Doll** (From The Film)**/Since I've Found My Baby** (gold print)	£35
56	London HLA 8360	**Baby Doll** (From The Film)**/Since I've Found My Baby** (silver print)	£15
57	London HLA 8399	**Butterfly/It Doesn't Take Very Long**	£15
57	London HA-A 2054	**ANDY WILLIAMS SINGS STEVE ALLEN** (LP)	£20
58	London HA-A 2113	**ANDY WILLIAMS SINGS RODGERS AND HAMMERSTEIN** (LP)	£20
59	London HA-A 2203	**TWO TIME WINNERS** (LP)	£20

MINT VALUE £

AUDREY WILLIAMS
| 56 | MGM SP 1179 | Ain't Nothing Gonna Be All Right No How/Livin' It Up And Havin' A Ball | £25 |

(see also Hank Williams)

BIG JOE WILLIAMS
67	Delmark DJB 4	ON THE HIGHWAY (EP)	£15
63	Esquire 32-191	BLUES ON HIGHWAY 51 (LP)	£40
63	'77' LA 12-19	PINEY WOODS BLUES (LP)	£30
64	CBS BPG 63813	CLASSIC DELTA BLUES (LP)	£20
64	Storyville SLP 158	PORTRAITS IN BLUES VOLUME 4 (LP)	£20
64	Storyville SLP 163	PORTRAITS IN BLUES VOLUME 7 (LP)	£20
65	Fontana 688 800 ZL	TOUGH TIMES (LP)	£25
66	Xtra XTRA 1033	BIG JOE WILLIAMS (LP)	£30
66	Bounty BY 6018	BACK TO THE COUNTRY (LP)	£40
66	Society SOC 1020	BIG JOE, SONNY, BROWNIE, LIGHTNIN' (LP, with Lightnin' Hopkins, Sonny Terry & Brownie McGhee)	£15
69	Storyville 618 011	DON'T YOU LEAVE ME HERE (LP)	£20
69	Liberty LBL/LBS 83207	HAND ME DOWN MY OLD WALKING STICK (LP)	£20
69	Xtra XTRA 5059	LIVE AT FOLK CITY (LP)	£15
70	RCA Intl. INTS 1087	CRAWLIN' KING SNAKE (LP)	£18
72	Delmark DS 627	NINE STRING GUITAR (LP)	£15

BILLY WILLIAMS (QUARTET)
54	Vogue Coral Q 2012	Sh'Boom/Whenever Wherever	£15
54	Vogue Coral Q 2039	The Honeydripper/Love Me (as Billy Williams Quartet)	£40
56	Vogue Coral Q 72149	A Crazy Little Palace/Cry Baby (as Billy Williams Quartet)	£40
56	Vogue Coral Q 72180	Pray/You'll Reach Your Star	£18
57	Vogue Coral Q 72222	Follow Me/Shame, Shame, Shame (as Billy Williams Quartet)	£20
57	Vogue Coral Q 72222	Follow Me/Shame, Shame, Shame (as Billy Williams Quartet) (78)	£15
57	Vogue Coral Q 72241	Butterfly/The Pied Piper	£20
57	Vogue Coral Q 72266	I'm Gonna Sit Right Down And Write A Letter/Date With The Blues	£20
57	Vogue Coral Q 72295	Got A Date With An Angel/The Lord Will Understand	£30
58	Coral Q 72303	Don't Let Go/Baby, Baby (as Billy Williams Quartet)	£30
58	Coral Q 72316	Steppin' Out Tonight/There I've Said It Again (as Billy Williams Quartet)	£30
58	Coral Q 72331	I'll Get By/It's Prayin' Time	£15
59	Coral Q 72369	Goodnight Irene/Red Hot Love	£20
59	Coral Q 72377	Telephone Conversation/Go To Sleep, Go To Sleep, Go To Sleep (with Barbara McNair)	£15
58	Coral LVA 9092	BILLY WILLIAMS	£90
60	Coral LVA 9120	HALF SWEET HALF BEAT	£20
61	Coral LVA 9139	THE BILLY WILLIAMS REVUE	£20

(see also Barbara McNair)

BOBBY WILLIAMS
| 68 | Action ACT 4509 | Baby I Need Your Love/Try It Again | £50 |

CAROL WILLIAMS
| 76 | Salsoul SZ 2021 | Love Is You/Just Feel | £20 |
| 76 | Salsoul SLS 5506 | LECTRIC LADY (LP) | £15 |

CHRIS WILLIAMS & HIS MONSTERS
| 59 | Columbia DB 4383 | The Monster/The Eton Boating Song | £25 |
| 60 | Triumph RGM 1003 | Kicking Around/Midnight Rocker (unissued; white label demo copies only) | £250 |

CLARENCE WILLIAMS (& HIS WASHBOARD BAND)
54	Columbia SCM 5134	High Society/Left All Alone With The Blues	£20
54	London AL 3526	CLARENCE WILLIAMS AND HIS ORCHESTRA (10" LP)	£20
55	Columbia 33S 1067	BACK ROOM SPECIAL (10" LP)	£20
57	London AL 3561	CLARENCE WILLIAMS AND HIS ORCHESTRA VOL. 2 (10" LP)	£20

CLIVE WILLIAMS
| 69 | Rock Steady Rev. REVR 6 | Take Good Care Of My Baby/RICO: In Loving Memory Of Don Drummond | £25 |

DANNY WILLIAMS
64	HMV POP 1372	Forget Her, Forget Her/Lollipops And Roses	£30
65	HMV POP 1410	Go Away/Masquerade	£30
66	HMV POP 1506	I've Got To Find That Girl Again/Throw A Little Lovin' My Way	£30
67	Deram DM 149	Never My Love/Whose Little Girl Are You (with inverted matrix)	£30
62	HMV 7EG 8748	HITS OF DANNY WILLIAMS (EP)	£15
61	HMV CLP 1458	DANNY (LP, mono)	£25
61	HMV CSD 1369	DANNY (LP, stereo)	£20
61	HMV CLP 1521	MOON RIVER AND OTHER TITLES (LP)	£20
62	HMV CSD 1471	SWINGING FOR YOU (LP, stereo)	£15
66	HMV CLP/CSD 3523	ONLY LOVE (LP)	£20
67	Deram DML 1017	DANNY WILLIAMS (LP)	£20

EDWARD WILLIAMS
| 09 | Trunk JBH 034 | LIFE ON EARTH (LP, 750 only) | £20 |

ESTHER WILLIAMS
| 81 | RCA RCAT LP 5039 | INSIDE OF ME (LP) | £20 |

GARETH WILLIAMS
| 12 | Blackest Ever Black BLACKEST009 | FLAMING TUNES (LP, inner, insert) | £50 |

(see also This Heat)

GEORGE WILLIAMS
69	Bullet BU 405	No Business Of Yours/Mast It Up (actually titled "Mash It Up")	£35
77	Lovers Rock LRD 01	Reggae Woman/No One Takes The Place Of You (12")	£20

GEORGE WILLIAMS & HIS ORCHESTRA
56	HMV DLP 1140	RHYTHM WAS HIS BUSINESS (10" LP)	£15

GINGER WILLIAMS
77	B&B BBLP 1001	STRANGE WORLD (LP, purple vinyl)	£30
80	B&B BBLP 1111	COOL LOVING (LP, lilac vinyl)	£25

GRANVILLE WILLIAMS ORCHESTRA
67	Island ILP 971	HI-LIFE (LP)	£60

(see also Silvertones)

HANK WILLIAMS (& HIS DRIFTING COWBOYS)

78s
56	MGM MGM 889	The First Fall Of Snow/Someday You'll Call My Name (withdrawn)	£0

SINGLES
53	MGM SP 1016	I'll Never Get Out Of This World Alive/I Could Never Be Ashamed Of You (as Hank Williams & His Drifting Cowboys)	£50
53	MGM SP 1034	Kaw-Liga/Take These Chains From My Heart (& His Drifting Cowboys)	£50
53	MGM SP 1049	Ramblin' Man/I Won't Be Home No More	£40
53	MGM SP 1048	My Bucket's Got A Hole In It/Let's Turn Back The Years	£40
54	MGM SP 1067	Weary Blues (From Waitin')/I Can't Escape From You	£40
54	MGM SP 1085	There'll Be No Teardrops Tonight/Crazy Heart	£40
54	MGM SP 1102	I'm Satisfied With You/I Ain't Got Nothin' But Time	£40
56	MGM SP 1163	The First Fall Of Snow/Someday You'll Call My Name (unreleased)	£0
56	MGM MGM 921	There's No Room In My Heart (For The Blues)/I Wish I Had A Nickel	£30
56	MGM MGM 931	Blue Love (In My Heart)/Singing Waterfall	£30
57	MGM MGM 942	Low Down Blues/My Sweet Love Ain't Around	£30
57	MGM MGM 957	Rootie Tootie/Lonesome Whistle	£30
57	MGM MGM 966	Leave Me Alone With The Blues/With Tears In My Eyes	£30

EPs
54	MGM MGM-EP 512	HANK WILLIAMS AND HIS DRIFTING COWBOYS (company sleeve)	£25
54	MGM EPC 7	HANK WILLIAMS (export issue)	£30
55	MGM MGM-EP 551	JUST WAITIN' (as Luke The Drifter, company sleeve)	£20
55	MGM MGM-EP 551	JUST WAITIN' (as Luke The Drifter, later issue with p/s)	£30
56	MGM MGM-EP 569	I SAW THE LIGHT (No. 1) (company sleeve)	£15
56	MGM MGM-EP 569	I SAW THE LIGHT (No. 1) (later issue with p/s)	£20
57	MGM MGM-EP 582	HONKY TONKIN'	£20
57	MGM MGM-EP 608	I SAW THE LIGHT (No. 2)	£20
57	MGM MGM-EP 614	HONKY TONK BLUES	£20
58	MGM MGM-EP 639	SONGS FOR A BROKEN HEART (No. 1)	£20
58	MGM MGM-EP 649	SONGS FOR A BROKEN HEART (No. 2)	£20
58	MGM MGM-EP 675	HANK'S LAMENTS	£20
60	MGM MGM-EP 710	THE UNFORGETTABLE HANK WILLIAMS	£20
60	MGM MGM-EP 726	THE UNFORGETTABLE HANK WILLIAMS (No. 2)	£20
60	MGM MGM-EP 732	THE UNFORGETTABLE HANK WILLIAMS (No. 3)	£20
61	MGM MGM-EP 757	HANK WILLIAMS FAVOURITES	£20
63	MGM MGM-EP 770	THE AUTHENTIC SOUND OF THE COUNTRY HITS	£20

ALBUMS
52	MGM MGM-D 105	HANK WILLIAMS SINGS (10" LP, company sleeve)	£40
53	MGM MGM-D 105	HANK WILLIAMS SINGS (10" LP, later issue in p/s)	£50
53	MGM MGM-D 119	HANK WILLIAMS AS LUKE THE DRIFTER (10" LP, company sleeve)	£30
53	MGM MGM-D 119	HANK WILLIAMS AS LUKE THE DRIFTER (10" LP, later issue in p/s)	£40
55	MGM MGM-D 137	HANK WILLIAMS MEMORIAL ALBUM (10")	£30
56	MGM MGM-D 144	MOANIN' THE BLUES (10")	£40
58	MGM MGM-D 150	SING ME A BLUE SONG (10")	£40
58	MGM MGM-D 154	THE IMMORTAL HANK WILLIAMS (10")	£30
59	MGM MGM-C 784	THE UNFORGETTABLE HANK WILLIAMS	£20
60	MGM MGM-C 811	THE LONESOME SOUND OF HANK WILLIAMS	£30
60	MGM MGM-C 834	WAIT FOR THE LIGHT TO SHINE	£20
62	MGM MGM-C 893	ON STAGE	£20
63	MGM MGM-C 956	THE SPIRIT OF HANK WILLIAMS	£20
66	MGM MGM-C 8019	MAY YOU NEVER BE ALONE	£15
66	MGM MGM-C 8020	IN MEMORY OF HANK WILLIAMS	£15
66	MGM MGM-C 8021	I'M BLUE INSIDE	£20
66	MGM MGM-C 8022	LUKE THE DRIFTER	£15
66	MGM MGM-C 8023	THE MANY MOODS OF HANK WILLIAMS	£15
67	MGM MGM-C(S) 8031	THE LEGEND LIVES ANEW	£15
67	MGM MGM-C(S) 8038	MORE HANK WILLIAMS AND STRINGS	£15
67	MGM MGM-C 8040	LOVE SONGS, COMEDY AND HYMNS	£15
79	World Records SM 551-556	THE LEGENDARY HANK WILLIAMS (6-LP box set)	£20

(see also Audrey Williams)

JEANETTE WILLIAMS
69	Action ACT 4534	Stuff/You Gotta Come Through	£15

(see also Swamp Dogg, Brooks & Jerry)

MINT VALUE £

(LITTLE) JERRY WILLIAMS
65	Cameo Parkway C 100	Baby You're My Everything/Just What Do You Plan To Do About It	£85
65	Cameo Parkway C 100	Baby You're My Everything/Just What Do You Plan To Do About It (DJ copy)	£120

JIMMY WILLIAMS
65	Atlantic AT 4042	Walking On Air/I'm So Lost	£25

JOE WILLIAMS
56	London HB-C 1065	JOE WILLIAMS SINGS (10" LP)	£20
57	HMV CLP 1109	THE GREATEST (LP)	£15
58	Columbia 33SX 1087	A MAN AIN'T SUPPOSED TO CRY (LP)	£20
60	Columbia SCX 3308	JOE WILLIAMS SINGS ABOUT YOU (LP, stereo)	£15
60	Columbia SCX 3325	THAT KIND OF WOMAN (LP, stereo)	£15
61	Columbia SX 1392	TOGETHER (LP, with Harry "Sweets" Edison, also stereo SCX 3421)	£15

(see also Count Basie)

JOHN WILLIAMS
67	Columbia DB 8128	She's That Kind Of Woman/My Ways Are Set	£15
67	Columbia SX 6169	JOHN WILLIAMS (LP)	£100

(see also Maureeny Wishfull)

JOHN WILLIAMS ORCHESTRA (U.S.)
66	Stateside S(S)L 10187	HOW TO STEAL A MILLION (LP, soundtrack)	£25
83	MCA MCA 70000	E.T. - THE EXTRA TERRESTRIAL (LP, soundtrack, box set with booklet & poster)	£30
83	MCA CAC 70000	E.T. - THE EXTRA TERRESTRIAL (cassette, soundtrack box set with booklet & poster)	£30

JOHNNY WILLIAMS
74	Polydor 2001 596	You're Something Kinda Mellow/You Make Me Want To Last Forever	£25

KENNETH WILLIAMS
67	Decca LK 4856	ON PLEASURE BENT (LP)	£15

(see also Rambling Syd Rumpo)

LARRY WILLIAMS
57	London HLN 8472	Short Fat Fannie/High School Dance	£40
58	London HLN 8532	Bony Moronie/You Bug Me Baby	£20
58	London HLU 8604	Dizzy Miss Lizzy/Slow Down	£25
58	London HLU 8604	Dizzy Miss Lizzy/Slow Down (78)	£25
59	London HLU 8844	She Said "Yeah"/Bad Boy (silver top label)	£30
59	London HLU 8844	She Said "Yeah"/Bad Boy (78)	£30
60	London HLU 8911	I Can't Stop Loving You/Steal A Little Kiss	£30
60	London HLU 8911	I Can't Stop Loving You/Steal A Little Kiss (78)	£50
60	London HLM 9053	Baby, Baby/Get Ready	£30
65	Sue WI 371	Strange/Call On Me	£40
65	Sue WI 381	Turn On Your Lovelight/Dizzy Miss Lizzy	£40
68	MGM MGM 1447	Shake Your Body Girl/Love, I Can't Seem To Find It	£20
59	London RE-U 1213	LARRY WILLIAMS (EP)	£100
65	Sue ILP 922	LARRY WILLIAMS ON STAGE (LP)	£80
70s	Specialty SNTF 5025	SLOW DOWN (LP)	£20
70s	Speciality SNTF 5008	ORIGINAL HITS (LP)	£20

LARRY WILLIAMS & JOHNNY 'GUITAR' WATSON
65	Decca F 12151	Sweet Little Baby/Slow Down	£20
67	Columbia DB 8140	Mercy, Mercy, Mercy/A Quitter Never Wins	£60
67	Columbia DB 8140	Mercy, Mercy, Mercy/A Quitter Never Wins (DJ copy)	£175
76	Epic EPC 4421	Too Late/Two For The Price Of One	£20
65	Decca LK 4691	THE LARRY WILLIAMS SHOW (LP, with Stormsville Shakers)	£80

(see also Philip Goodhand-Tait [& Stormville Shakers])

LENNY WILLIAMS
78	ABC 4239	Midnight Girl/Cause I Love You	£15

LEW WILLIAMS
50s	London (no cat. no.)	Cat Talk (1-sided, orange label demo-only)	£50

LLOYD WILLIAMS
66	Doctor Bird DB 1051	Sad World/TOMMY McCOOK'S BAND: A Little Bit Of Heaven	£30
68	Treasure Isle TI 7029	Funky Beat/Goodbye Baby	£22
68	Doctor Bird DB 1135	Wonderful World (with Tommy McCook)/TOMMY McCOOK SUPERSONICS: Mad Mad World	£35
70	Bamboo BAM 41	I'm In Love With You/Little Girl	£60

LORETTA WILLIAMS
66	Atlantic 584 032	Baby Cakes/I'm Missing You	£50

LUCINDA WILLIAMS
89	Rough Trade 130	LUCINDA WILLIAMS (LP, with inner lyric bag)	£20

LUTHER WILLIAMS ORCHESTRA
61	Melodisc MLP 12-125	TROPICAL RHYTHMS OF JAMAICA (LP)	£15

MARY LOU WILLIAMS
64	Sue WI 311	Chuck-a-Lunk Jug (Parts 1 & 2)	£25
53	Vogue LDE 022	PLAYS IN LONDON (10" LP)	£20
54	Esquire 20-026	PIANO PANORAMA (10" LP)	£20
55	Felsted EDL 87012	IN PARIS (10" LP)	£20

MAURICE WILLIAMS (& ZODIACS)
60	Top Rank JAR 526	Stay/Do You Believe (as Maurice Williams & Zodiacs)	£15
61	Top Rank JAR 550	I Remember/Always	£20

61	Top Rank JAR 563	Come Along/Do I	£20
61	Top Rank JKP 3006	STAY WITH MAURICE WILLIAMS & THE ZODIACS (EP)	£100

(see also Gladiolas)

MIKE WILLIAMS
66	Atlantic 584 027	Lonely Soldier/If This Isn't Love	£25

MOON WILLIAMS
73	DJM DJS10283	Forever Kind Of Love/All For You (DJ Copy)	£200
74	DJM DJS 299	Excuse Me (For The Strange Things I Do)/Can't Live Without You	£18

OTIS WILLIAMS & HIS CHARMS
55	Parlophone CMSP 36	Ivory Tower/In Paradise (export issue)	£300
56	Parlophone MSP 6239	Ivory Tower/In Paradise	£400
56	Parlophone R 4175	Ivory Tower/In Paradise (78)	£15
56	Parlophone R 4210	One Night Only/It's All Over	£300
56	Parlophone R 4210	One Night Only/It's All Over (78)	£25
57	Parlophone R 4293	Walkin' After Midnight/I'm Waiting Just For You	£300
57	Parlophone R 4293	Walkin' After Midnight/I'm Waiting Just For You (78)	£50
58	Parlophone R 4495	The Secret/Don't Wake Up The Kids	£100
58	Parlophone R 4495	The Secret/Don't Wake Up The Kids (78)	£70
62	Parlophone R 4860	The Secret/Two Hearts	£60

(see also Charms)

PAUL WILLIAMS
70s	Parry Music Library PML 168	AQUARIUS (LP)	£18

PAUL WILLIAMS BIG ROLL BAND/SET
64	Columbia DB 7421	Gin House/Rockin' Chair (as Paul Williams Big Roll Band)	£20
65	Columbia DB 7768	The Many Faces Of Love/Jumpback (as Paul Williams & Zoot Money Band)	£30
68	Decca F 12844	My Sly Sadie/Stop The Wedding (as Paul Williams Set)	£15

(see also Zoot Money's Big Roll Band, John Mayall's Bluesbreakers, Alan Price [Set], Juicy Lucy)

PAUL WILLIAMS (1)
73	Sonet SNTF 654	IN MEMORY OF ROBERT JOHNSON (LP)	£15

PAUL WILLIAMS (2)
74	A&M AMLS 63653	PHANTOM OF THE PARADISE (LP, soundtrack)	£20

RANNY/RONNY WILLIAMS
69	Bullet BU 426	Summer Place (with Hippy Boys)/Big Boy	£30
69	Gas GAS 120	Throw Me Corn (as Ronny Williams)/HIPPY BOYS: Temptation	£45
69	Unity UN 526	Pepper Seed/Ambitious Beggar	£40
70	Punch PH 32	Smile/Musical I.D.	£20

(see also Ranny Bop)

ROBBIE WILLIAMS
98	Chrysalis/HMV HMV 78	Millennium/ROYAL ALBERT HALL ORCHESTRA: Nimrod, Enigma Variations Op. 36 (78rpm, promo only, 1,000 only, numbered p/s)	£25
98	Chrysalis CDPP 080	I'VE BEEN EXPECTING YOU (metal case with album CD, interview disc in digipak, EPK video in p/s, gold press release and photos)	£70
01	Chrysalis 7243 536826 1 3	SWING WHEN YOU'RE WINNING (LP)	£20
02	Chrysalis 7243 54399 41-1	ESCAPOLOGY (2-LP)	£100
04	Chrysalis 7243 8668191	GREATEST HITS (2-LP)	£20
05	Chrysalis 3418235	INTENSIVE CARE (2-LP)	£15

(see also Take That)

ROBERT WILLIAMS
90	Blast First FU8	CHROME, FIRE AND SMOKE (2-LP, picture disc, 1000 only)	£25

ROBERT PETE WILLIAMS
63	'77' LA 12-17	THOSE PRISON BLUES (LP)	£35
70s	Blues Beacon 1932 101ST	SUGAR FARM (LP)	£25
72	Saydisc AMS 2002	ROBERT PETE WILLIAMS (LP)	£18

ROBERT PETE WILLIAMS/ROOSEVELT SYKES
67	'77' LEU 12-50	BLUES FROM THE BOTTOM (LP)	£25

(see also Roosevelt Sykes)

RODIGAN V WILLIAMS
79	Exclusive/Ethnic Fight EFLP 60-11-13	ROCKERS ARENA (LP)	£50

ROY WILLIAMS TRINITY
73	Hillside HIL LP 1013	A TOUCH OF CLASS (LP)	£15
79	Hillside HIL LP 1016	GOOD NEWS IN TOWN (LP)	£45

SAM WILLIAMS
78	Grapevine GRP 116	Love Slipped Thru' My Fingers/TOWANDA BARNES: You Don't Mean It	£35

SHINA WILLIAMS
84	Earthworks/Rough Trade ET 003	Agboju Logun/Gboro Mi Ro (12", die-cut sleeve)	£50

SONNY WILLIAMS
59	London HLD 8931	Bye Bye Baby Goodbye/Lucky Linda	£45
59	London HLD 8931	Bye Bye Baby Goodbye/Lucky Linda (78)	£20

SYLVAN WILLIAMS
69	Big Shot BI 532	Sweeter Than Honey/Son Of Reggae	£45
69	Big Shot BI 533	This Old Man/When Morning Comes	£50

TOMMY WILLIAMS
76   Free Reed FRR 008   **SPRINGTIME IN BATTERSEA** (LP, gatefold sleeve) **£18**

TONY WILLIAMS
63   Philips BF 1282   **How Come/When I Had You** **£100**
60   Mercury MMC 14027   **A GIRL IS A GIRL IS A GIRL** (LP) **£40**
61   Reprise R 6001   **SINGS HIS GREATEST HITS** (LP, mono) **£20**
61   Reprise ST R9 6006   **SINGS HIS GREATEST HITS** (LP, stereo) **£30**
(see also Platters, Linda Hayes)

TONY WILLIAMS' LIFETIME
69   Polydor 583 574   **EMERGENCY!** (2-LP, gatefold sleeve) **£50**
70   Polydor 2425 019   **TURN IT OVER** (LP) **£25**
71   Polydor 2425 065   **EGO** (LP, textured gatefold sleeve) **£35**
(see also Lifetime, John McLaughlin)

WILLIE WILLIAMS, JACKIE MITTOO & MARSHAL COUSINS
79   Ziggy FDP 001   **Rocking Universally/JACKIE MITTOO & BONGO GENE: Universal rock** (12") **£30**

WILLYWILLIE/WILLI WILLIAMS
81   Black Roots BR0017   **Come Make We Rally/YABBY YOU: Thirty Pieces Of Silver** (12") **£80**
83   WLN WLN 004   **Repatriation/Come Along/Armagideon Time/Justice Tonight** (12") **£25**
92   Jah Shaka No Cat No   **Stand Up/Version** **£50**
92   Jah Shaka SHAKA 922   **NATTY WITH A CAUSE** (LP) **£22**
05   Blood & Fire BAFLP 048   **MESSENGER MAN** (2-LP, reissue) **£35**

WINSTON WILLIAMS
70   Jackpot JP 733   **D.J.'s Choice/SLIM SMITH: Can't Do Without It** (B-side actually titled "Lesson/Story Of Love" by Uniques) **£30**
70   Jackpot JP 743   **The People's Choice/BOBBY JAMES: Let Me Go Girl** **£40**
71   Jackpot JP 757   **Love Version/SLIM SMITH: Ball Of Confusion** **£30**

HARVEY WILLIAMS
94   Sarah SARAH 406   **REBELLION** (10" LP) **£15**

BOBBY WILLIAMSON
54   HMV 7MC 26   **Sh-Boom/Love March** (export issue) **£20**

MARK WILLIAMSON
70s   Myrrh MYR 1154   **MISSING IN ACTION** (LP) **£15**

ROBIN WILLIAMSON
72   Island HELP 2   **MYRRH** (LP, textured sleeve, black label with pink 'i' logo, lyric inner sleeve) **£35**
(see also Incredible String Band, Vashti Bunyan)

SONNY BOY WILLIAMSON (I)
69   Matchbox SDR 169   **SONNY BOY AND HIS PALS** (LP) **£30**
70   RCA Intl. INTS 1088   **BLUEBIRD BLUES** (LP) **£15**

SONNY BOY WILLIAMSON (I)/BIG BILL BROONZY
65   RCA Victor RD 7685   **BIG BILL BROONZY/SONNY BOY WILLIAMSON** (LP) **£30**

SONNY BOY WILLIAMSON (II)
63   Pye International 7N 25191   **Help Me/Bye Bye Bird** **£25**
64   Pye International 7N 25268   **Lonesome Cabin/The Goat** **£20**
65   Sue WI 365   **No Nights By Myself/Boppin' With Sonny Boy** **£40**
66   Chess CRS 8030   **Bring It On Home/Down Child** **£20**
66   Blue Horizon 45-1008   **From The Bottom/Empty Bedroom** **£80**
64   Pye Intl. NEP 44037   **SONNY BOY WILLIAMSON** (EP) **£25**
65   Chess CRE 6001   **HELP ME** (EP) **£25**
66   Chess CRE 6013   **IN MEMORIAM** (EP) **£35**
66   Chess CRE 6018   **REAL FOLK BLUES VOL. 2** (EP) **£30**
64   Pye Intl. NPL 28036   **DOWN AND OUT BLUES** (LP) **£60**
64   Storyville SLP 158   **PORTRAITS IN BLUES, VOL. 4** (LP) **£40**
65   Chess CRL 4510   **IN MEMORIAM** (LP) **£50**
66   Storyville SLP 170   **THE BLUES OF SONNY BOY WILLIAMSON** (LP) **£22**
66   Fontana 670 158   **PORTRAITS IN BLUES, VOL. 4** (LP, reissue) **£30**
67   Storyville 671 170   **THE BLUES OF SONNY BOY WILLIAMSON** (LP, reissue) **£25**
68   Marmalade 607/608 004   **DON'T SEND ME NO FLOWERS** (LP, with Brian Auger & Jimmy Page) **£80**
74   Rarity RLP 1   **THE LAST SESSIONS - 1963** (LP) **£25**
(see also Ottilie Patterson)

SONNY BOY WILLIAMSON (II) & YARDBIRDS
65   Fontana TL 5277   **SONNY BOY WILLIAMSON & THE YARDBIRDS** (LP) **£175**
68   Fontana SFJL 960   **SONNY BOY WILLIAMSON & THE YARDBIRDS** (LP, reissue, different sleeve) **£30**
71   Philips 6435 011   **SONNY BOY WILLIAMSON & THE YARDBIRDS** (LP, 2nd reissue) **£18**
(see also Yardbirds, Brian Auger)

STU WILLIAMSON
56   London Jazz LZ-N 14030   **SAPPHIRE** (10" LP) **£20**

WILLIE (FRANCIS) & LLOYD (LINDSAY)
71   Camel CA 80   **Marcus Is Alive/GLADIATORS: Freedom Train** **£25**
(see also Willie Francis)

DORIS WILLINGHAM
69   Jay Boy BOY 1   **You Can't Do That/Lost Again** **£15**

CHUCK WILLIS
57   London HLE 8444   **C.C. Rider/Ease The Pain** **£80**
57   London HLE 8444   **C.C. Rider/Ease The Pain** (78) **£30**

57	London HLE 8489	That Train Has Gone/Love Me Cherry	£80
57	London HLE 8489	That Train Has Gone/Love Me Cherry (78)	£20
58	London HLE 8595	Betty And Dupree/My Crying Eyes	£80
58	London HLE 8595	Betty And Dupree/My Crying Eyes (78)	£20
58	London HLE 8635	What Am I Living For/Hang Up My Rock And Roll Shoes	£50
58	London HLE 8635	What Am I Living For/Hang Up My Rock And Roll Shoes (78)	£25
58	London HL 7039	What Am I Living For/Hang Up My Rock And Roll Shoes (export issue)	£30
59	London HLE 8818	My Life/Thunder And Lightning	£45
59	London HLE 8818	My Life/Thunder And Lightning (78)	£30
59	Fontana TFE 17138	CHUCK WILLIS WAILS (EP)	£300
65	Atlantic ATL 5003	I REMEMBER CHUCK WILLIS (LP)	£80
69	Atlantic 588 145	I REMEMBER CHUCK WILLIS (LP, reissue)	£20

LARRY WILLIS
74	People PLEO 2	INNER CRISIS (LP)	£20

LLOYD WILLIS
70	Pressure Beat PR 5502	Mad Rooster (Parts 1 & 2)/NINEY & THE DESTROYERS: As Far As I Can See	£15
(see also Dynamic Gang, Urie Aldridge)

RALPH WILLIS
61	Esquire EP 241	RALPH WILLIS (EP)	£40

SLIM WILLIS
65	R&B MRB 5004	Running Around/No Feeling For You	£30

WILL-O-BEES
67	CBS 3263	It's Not Easy/Looking Glass	£15

WILLOWS
56	London HLU 8290	Church Bells May Ring/Baby Tell Me	£600
56	London HLU 8290	Church Bells May Ring/Baby Tell Me (78)	£80
(see also Tony Middleton)

BOB WILLS WITH TOMMY DUNCAN
60	London HL 7102	Heart To Heart Talk/What's The Matter With The Mill (export issue)	£20

MICK WILLS
88	Woronzow WOO 9	FERN HILL (LP)	£15

VIOLA WILLS
68	President PT 108	Lost Without The Love Of My Guy/I Got Love	£15

FRANKIE WILMOTT
86	Musical Ambassador MAD 005	Give Me No Rock (Sensemilla)/ANDY TOSH: Lick A Shot (12")	£50
87	Music House MH1	I Won't Give Up/I Won't Give Up (version) (12")	£15

SUE WILSHAW
69	SNB 55-3957	Empty Sunday/My My My	£15

AL WILSON
68	Liberty LBF 15044	Do What You Gotta Do/Now I Know What Love Is	£20
68	Liberty LBF 15121	The Snake/Who Could Be Lovin' You	£20
69	Liberty LBS 83173	SEARCHING FOR THE DOLPHINS (LP)	£20

BRIAN WILSON
66	Capitol CL 15438	Caroline, No/Summer Means New Love	£50
88	Sire W 7814 B	LOVE AND MERCY (7" box set, with interview and postcards, limited edition)	£40
98	Giant/Mojo 74321 58760 2	INTERVIEW/IMAGINATION (promo CD, with Peter Buck)	£40
04	Nonesuch 7559-79869-7	Wonderful/Wind Chimes (three different coloured vinyl - blue, yellow,green)	£18
(see also Beach Boys, Date With Soul, American Spring)

BRIAN WILSON & MIKE LOVE
67	Capitol CL 15513	Gettin' Hungry/Devoted To You (as Brian Wilson & Mike Love)	£30

CASSANDRA WILSON
93	Blue Note F671007	BLUE LIGHT 'TIL DAWN (LP)	£40
96	Blue Note 72438 37183 1 3	NEW MOON DAUGHTER (2-LP)	£80
99	Blue Note 602537813735	TRAVELLING MILES (2-LP)	£30
03	Blue Note 7243 58186017	GLAMOURED (2-LP)	£20

CLIVE WILSON
64	R&B JB 144	Mango Tree/Midnight In Chicago	£20

COLIN WILSON
75	Tabitha TAB 101	CLOUDBURST (LP)	£30

DELROY WILSON
63	Island WI 097	Naughty People/I Shall Not Remove	£25
63	Island WI 103	One, Two, Three/Back Biter	£20
63	Island WI 116	You Bend My Love/Can't You See	£30
63	R&B JB 108	Lion Of Judah/Joe Liges	£30
63	R&B JB 128	Prince Pharoah/Don't Believe Him	£25
63	R&B JB 132	Squeeze Your Toe/Sugar Pie	£30
64	Black Swan WI 405	Spit In The Sky/Voodoo Man	£25
64	Black Swan WI 420	Goodbye/Treat Me Right	£40
64	R&B JB 148	Lover Mouth/Every Mouth Must Be Fed	£30
64	R&B JB 168	Sammy Dead/CYNTHIA & ARCHIE: Every Beat	£25
65	Island WI 205	Pick Up The Pieces/Oppression	£55
66	Doctor Bird DB 1022	Give Me A Chance/(It's) Impossible	£35

MINT VALUE £

66	Island WI 3013	Dancing Mood/SOUL BROTHERS: More And More	£40
67	Island WI 3033	Riding For A Fall/Got To Change Your Ways	£75
67	Island WI 3037	Ungrateful Baby/ROY RICHARDS: Hopeful Village Ska	£45
67	Island WI 3039	Close To Me/SOUL BROTHERS: Hi-Life	£50
67	Island WI 3050	Get Ready/ROY RICHARDS: Port-O-Jam	£60
67	Studio One SO 2009	Won't You Come Home Baby/PETER & HORTENSE: I've Been Lonely	£70
67	Studio One SO 2014	Mother Word/HEPTONES: Fatty Fatty	£30
67	Studio One SO 2019	Never Conquer/Run For Your Life	£80
67	Studio One SO 2031	I'm Not A King/HEPTONES: Take Me (B-side actually by Soul Vendors)	£60
68	Island WI 3099	This Old Heart Of Mine/GLEN ADAMS: Grab A Girl	£70
68	Island WI 3127	Once Upon A Time/I Want To Love You (B-side actually with Stranger Cole)	£80
68	Coxsone CS 7064	True Believer/MARSHALL WILLIAMS: College Girl	£100
68	Studio One SO 2040	Mr. D.J./HEPTONES: Tripe Girl(both sides credited to Termites)	£110
68	Studio One SO 2046	Rain From The Skies/How Can I Love Someone	£75
68	Studio One SO 2057	Feel Good All Over/I Like The Way You Walk	£85
69	Studio One SO 2074	Easy Snappin'/WEBBER SISTERS: Come On	£50
69	High Note HS 011	Put Yourself In My Place/It Hurts	£45
69	High Note HS 015	I'm The One Who Loves You/AFROTONES: If I'm In A Corner	£40
69	High Note HS 022	Your Number One/I've Tried My Best	£40
69	High Note HS 028	Good To Me/What Do You Want Me To Do	£25
69	Camel CA 15	Sad Mood (actually by Ken Parker)/STRANGER COLE: Give It To Me	£70
70	Trojan TR 7740	Show Me The Way/BEVERLEY'S ALLSTARS: Version	£45
70	Trojan TR 7769	Gave You My Love/BEVERLEY'S ALLSTARS: Version	£50
70	Summit SUM 8503	Got To Get Away/BEVERLEY'S ALLSTARS: Version	£25
70	Unity UN 559	Drink Wine, Everybody/Someone To Call My Own	£35
71	Smash SMA 2317	I Am Trying/COLLINS ALLSTARS: Version	£30
71	Smash SMA 2318	Satisfaction/Satisfaction Version (B-side with Alton Ellis)	£40
71	Smash SMA 2323	What It Was/LLOYD CLARKE: Chicken Thief	£50
71	Jackpot JP 769	Cool Operator/I'm Yours	£15
71	Jackpot JP 780	Keep Your Love Strong/Nice To Be Near	£15
71	Jackpot JP 781	Peace And Love/JEFF BARNES: Who's Your Brother	£15
71	Banana BA 333	Just Because Of You/I Love You Madly	£60
72	Banana BA 367	You Keep On Running (& U Roy)/LARRY'S ALL STARS: Running Version	£18
72	Bullet BU 520	Hear Come The Heartaches (actually "Here Come The Heartaches")/ You'll Be Sorry	£18
72	Jackpot JP 792	Who Cares/HUGH ROY JUNIOR: Who Cares - Version	£15
72	Jackpot JP 804	Cheer Up/Loving You	£15
72	Fab FAB 32A/FAB34A	Your Love Is Amazing/KING SPORTY: A Year Full Of Sunday	£35
72	Spur SP 2	Adis Ababa/KEITH HUDSON: Rudie Hot Stuff	£50
73	Green Door GD 4060	Ain't That Peculiar/What Is Man	£30
73	Smash SMA 2336	Trying To Wreck My Life/Live And Learn	£20
75	Fab FAB 266	Dancing Mood/Version	£20
76	Third World TW03	Chueky Rock/You're No Good	£25
77	Tribesman TM 002	What Is Man/Version	£40
78	Burning Sounds BSD 017	All In This Together/Because I Am Black (12")	£25
78	Burning Sounds BSD 018	Love Got Me Doing Things/Go Away Little Girl (12")	£25
79	Cha Cha CHAD 10	Money Love/I Want To Love You (12")	£20
88	Conqueror LD 045	I Have Been In Love/NAGGO MORRIS AND THE HEPTONES: You Want To Get I Out (12")	£50
64	R&B JBL 1112	I SHALL NOT REMOVE (LP, beware of Jamaican copies in U.K. sleeves)	£600
68	Coxsone CSL 8016	GOOD ALL OVER (LP)	£200
72	Trojan TRLS 44	BETTER MUST COME (LP)	£40
73	Big Shot BILP 102	CAPTIVITY (LP)	£40
73	Warwick WLP 01	LIVE AS ONE (LP, white label only, includes track by Alton Ellis)	£150
77	Eji EJI 1001	MR. COOL OPERATOR (LP)	£30
78	Third World TWD 001	20 GOLDEN HITS (2-LP)	£50
78	Charmers LP 1	SARGE (LP)	£18
78	Burning Sounds BS 1020	LOVERS ROCK (LP)	£20
79	Groundnation GROL 501	FOR I AND I (LP)	£30
82	Black Music BMLP 803	GO AWAY DREAM (LP)	£20

(see also Hortense & Delroy, Joe Liges, Roy Richards, Soul Brothers, Dennis Alcapone, Stranger Cole, Uniques, Soul Vendors)

DENNIS WILSON (& RUMBO)

70	Stateside SS 2184	Sound Of Free/Lady (as Dennis Wilson & Rumbo)	£70
77	Caribou CRB 5663	River Song/Farewell My Friend	£15
77	Caribou CRB 81672	PACIFIC OCEAN BLUE (LP, gatefold sleeve, lyric insert, on blue vinyl)	£50
77	Caribou CRB 81672	PACIFIC OCEAN BLUE (LP, gatefold sleeve, lyric insert)	£40

(see also Beach Boys)

DENNIS WILSON

| 57 | Donegall DON 1005 | TRANSATLANTIC (LP) | £20 |
| 67 | Envoy VOS 3111 | DENNIS PLUS 3 (10" LP) | £35 |

THE DIERDRE WILSON TABAC

| 69 | RCA RCA 1880 | Get Back/Angel Baby | £15 |

DOYLE WILSON WITH JIMMY LACEY & BAND

| 58 | Vogue Pop V 9117 | Hey-Hey/You're The One For Me | £600 |
| 58 | Vogue Pop V 9117 | Hey-Hey/You're The One For Me (7) | £150 |

EDDIE WILSON (2)

| 69 | Action ACT 4536 | Shing-A-Ling Stroll/Don't Kick The Teenager Around | £25 |
| 70 | Action ACT 4555 | Get Out On The Street/Must Be Love | £20 |

ERNEST ('SOUL') WILSON

67	Studio One SO 2032	Money Worries/SOUL VENDORS: Pe Da Pa	£80
68	Studio One SO 2058	If I Were A Carpenter/SOUL VENDORS: Frozen Soul	£200
68	Coxsone CS 7044	Storybook Children (as Ernest 'Soul' Wilson)/LITTLE FREDDIE: After Laughter (B-side actually by Freddie McGregor)	£80
68	Coxsone CS 7059	Undying Love/SOUL VENDORS: Tropic Isle	£100
69	Amalgamated AMG 837	Private Number (A-side miscredit to Ernest Jones/GLEN ADAMS: She's So Fine	£50
69	Crab CRAB 9	Private Number/Another Chance	£40
69	Crab CRAB 17	Freedom Train/STRANGER COLE: You Should Never Have To Come	£45
69	Crab CRAB 21	Just Once In My Life (with Freddy)/GLEN ADAMS: Mighty Organ	£75
70	Crab CRAB 45	Sentimental Man/It's A Lie	£30
70	Unity UN 564	Love Makes The World Go Round/Love (Instrumental Version)	£30
71	Gas GAS 168	What You Gonna Do About it/DOBBY DOBSON: Halfway To Paradise	£60
78	Cha Cha CC 001	I Know Myself/REVOLUTIONARIES: I Know Myself Dub	£25
86	Natty Congo NCLP 006	LOVE REVOLUTION (LP)	£20

(see also Tinga & Ernest, Clarendonians, Freddy & Fitzie)

FLICK WILSON

77	Ultra PFU 1003	Keep The Troubles Down/Saturday Night Shubin (12")	£20
80	Greensleeves/Cool Rockers GRED 37	Slavemaster/Pretty Blue Eyes (12")	£40

FRANK WILSON

79	Tamla Motown TMG 1170	Do I Love You (Indeed I Do)/Sweeter As The Days Go By	£100
79	Tamla Motown TMG 1170	Do I Love You (Indeed I Do)/Sweeter As The Days Go By (DJ copy, p/s)	£200
04	Tamla Motown 982 153 0	Do I Love You (Indeed I Do)/CHRIS CLARK: Do I Love You (Indeed I Do) (die-cut p/s)	£25
18	Outta Sight SEV 001	Do I Love You (Indeed I Do)/Sweeter As The Days Go By (reissue)	£15

JACK WILSON QUARTET

64	London HA-K/SH-K 8170	THE JACK WILSON QUARTET (LP, featuring Roy Ayers)	£20
66	Vocalion LAE-L 603	RAMBLIN' (LP)	£20

(see also Roy Ayers)

JACKIE WILSON

78s

58	Coral Q 72332	I'm Wanderin'/As Long As I Live	£15
58	Coral Q 72338	We Have Love/Singing A Song	£15
58	Coral Q 72347	Lonely Teardrops/In The Blue Of The Evening	£40
59	Coral Q 72366	That's Why/Love Is All	£40
59	Coral Q 72372	I'll Be Satisfied/Ask	£50
59	Coral Q 72380	You Better Know It/Never Go Away	£75
59	Coral Q 72384	Talk That Talk/Only You, Only Me	£80

SINGLES

57	Vogue Coral Q 72290	Reet Petite/By The Light Of The Silvery Moon	£25
57	Coral Q 72290	Reet Petite/By The Light Of The Silvery Moon (2nd pressing)	£15
58	Coral Q 72306	To Be Loved/Come Back To Me	£25
58	Coral Q 72332	I'm Wanderin'/As Long As I Live	£25
58	Coral Q 72338	We Have Love/Singing A Song	£22
58	Coral Q 72347	Lonely Teardrops/In The Blue Of The Evening	£25
59	Coral Q 72366	That's Why/Love Is All	£20
59	Coral Q 72366	That's Why/Love Is All (mispressing, B-side plays "You Better Know It")	£15
59	Coral Q 72372	I'll Be Satisfied/Ask	£15
59	Coral Q 72380	You Better Know It/Never Go Away	£15
59	Coral Q 72384	Talk That Talk/Only You, Only Me	£15
60	Coral Q 72393	Doggin' Around/The Magic Of Love	£15
60	Coral Q 72407	A Woman, A Lover, A Friend/(You Were Made For) All My Love	£15
60	Coral Q 72412	Alone At Last/Am I The Man	£25
61	Coral Q 72421	The Tear Of The Year/My Empty Arms (withdrawn B-side, demos only)	£65
61	Coral Q 72424	The Tear Of The Year/Your One And Only Love	£15
61	Coral Q 72430	Please Tell Me Why/(So Many) Cute Little Girls	£15
61	Coral Q 72434	I'm Comin' On Back To You/Lonely Life	£15
61	Coral Q 72439	You Don't Know What It Means/Years From Now	£15
61	Coral Q 72444	The Way I Am/My Heart Belongs To Only You	£15
62	Coral Q 72450	The Greatest Hurt/There'll Be No Next Time	£15
62	Coral Q 72453	Sing (And Tell The Blues So Long)/I Found Love (B-side with Linda Hopkins)	£15
62	Coral Q 72454	I Just Can't Help It/My Tale Of Woe	£15
63	Coral Q 72460	Baby Workout/What Good Am I Without You	£15
63	Coral Q 72464	Shake A Hand/Say I Do (as Jackie Wilson & Linda Hopkins)	£15
63	Coral Q 72465	Shake! Shake! Shake!/He's A Fool	£15
63	Coral Q 72467	Baby Get It/The New Breed	£15
64	Coral Q 72474	Big Boss Line/Be My Girl	£15
64	Coral Q 72476	Squeeze Her - Tease Her (But Love Her)/Give Me Back My Heart	£15
65	Coral Q 72480	Yes Indeed!/When The Saints Go Marching In (with Linda Hopkins)	£18
65	Coral Q 72481	No Pity (In The Naked City)/I'm So Lonely	£20
65	Coral Q 72481	No Pity (In The Naked City)/I'm So Lonely (DJ copy)	£45
65	Coral Q 72482	I Believe I'll Love On/Lonely Teardrops	£15
66	Coral Q 72484	To Make A Big Man Cry/Be My Love	£20
66	Coral Q 72484	To Make A Big Man Cry/Be My Love (DJ copy)	£45
66	Coral Q 72487	Whispers/The Fairest Of Them All	£40
66	Coral Q 72487	Whispers/The Fairest Of Them All (DJ copy)	£85
67	Coral Q 72493	(Your Love Keeps Lifting Me) Higher And Higher/I'm The One To Do It	£20

MINT VALUE £

67	Coral Q 72493	(Your Love Keeps Lifting Me) **Higher And Higher/I'm The One To Do It** (DJ copy)	£85
67	Coral Q 72496	**Since You Showed Me How To Be Happy/The Who-Who Song**	£30
67	Coral Q 72496	**Since You Showed Me How To Be Happy/The Who-Who Song (DJ copy**	£75
68	Decca AD 1008	**For Your Precious Love/Uptight** (Everything's Alright) (export issue)	£25
73	Brunswick BR 3	**Beautiful Day/What'cha Gonna Do About Love**	£20
77	Brunswick BR 43	**It Only Happens When I Look At You/Just As Soon As The Feeling's Over** (DJ Copy)	£150
77	Brunswick BR 43	**It Only Happens When I Look At You/Just As Soon As The Feeling's Over**	£100

EPs

59	Coral FEP 2016	**JACKIE WILSON** (triangular centre)	£100
59	Coral FEP 2016	**JACKIE WILSON** (round centre)	£70
60	Coral FEP 2043	**THE DYNAMIC JACKIE WILSON** (triangular centre)	£100
60	Coral FEP 2043	**THE DYNAMIC JACKIE WILSON** (round centre)	£70

ALBUMS

58	Coral LVA 9087	**HE'S SO FINE**	£150
59	Coral LVA 9108	**LONELY TEARDROPS**	£150
60	Coral LVA 9121	**SO MUCH**	£110
60	Coral LVA 9130	**JACKIE SINGS THE BLUES**	£125
60	Coral LVA 9135	**MY GOLDEN FAVOURITES**	£90
61	Coral LVA 9144	**A WOMAN, A LOVER, A FRIEND**	£100
61	Coral LVA 9148	**YOU AIN'T HEARD NOTHIN' YET**	£85
62	Coral LVA 9151	**BY SPECIAL REQUEST** (mono)	£75
62	Coral SVL 3018	**BY SPECIAL REQUEST** (stereo)	£90
62	Coral LVA 9202	**BODY AND SOUL**	£65
63	Coral LVA 9209	**JACKIE WILSON AT THE COPA** (mono)	£70
63	Coral SVL 9209	**JACKIE** (stereo)	£80
63	Coral LVA 9214	**THE WORLD'S GREATEST MELODIES** (mono)	£55
63	Coral SVL 9214	**THE WORLD'S GREATEST MELODIES** (stereo)	£65
66	Coral LVA 9231	**SPOTLIGHT ON JACKIE WILSON**	£70
66	Coral LVA 9232	**SOUL GALORE** (mono)	£70
66	Coral SVL 9232	**SOUL GALORE** (stereo)	£80
67	Coral LVA 9235	**WHISPERS**	£75
68	MCA MUP(S) 304	**HIGHER AND HIGHER**	£20
68	MCA MUP(S) 333	**TWO MUCH** (with Count Basie & His Orchestra)	£20
69	MCA MUPS 361	**I GET THE SWEETEST FEELING**	£20
70	MCA MUPS 405	**DO YOUR THING**	£25
73	Brunswick BRLS 3001	**YOU GOT ME WALKIN'**	£25

(see also Billy Ward & Dominoes, Clyde McPhatter, Count Basie, Chi-Lites, Linda Hopkins)

JACKIE WILSON/CLYDE MCPHATTER

| 62 | Ember JBS 705 | **Tenderly/CLYDE McPHATTER: Harbour Lights** | £250 |
| 62 | Ember NR 5001 | **MEET BILLY WARD & THE DOMINOES** (LP, 1 side each) | £200 |

(see also Clyde McPhatter)

JONATHAN WILSON

13	Bella Union 5051083074186	**FANFARE** (LP/CD, gatefold, blue vinyl)	£20
14	Bella Union BELLA 469V	**SLIDE BY EP** (12"/CD EP)	£25
18	Bella Union BELLA730VX	**RARE BIRDS** (2LP, gatefold, printed inners, booklet, poster, stickers, white vinyl)	£30
20	Bella Union BELLA995VX	**DIXIE BLUR** (2LP, die-cut sleeve, printed inners, orange/yellow vinyl, booklet (some signed), **download card)**	£30
20	Bella Union BELLA1124V	**RARE BLUR** (12" EP, RSD)	£20
23	BMG 538912830	**EAT THE WORM** (2LP, booklet, printed inners)	£25

JR. WILSON

| 89 | Blue Trac BTRD 035 | **Speak Softly** (with T. Sparks and Mystic Man)**/CONROY SMITH: Problems** (12") | £40 |

MARTY WILSON & STRAT-O-LITES

| 58 | Brunswick 05750 | **Hey! Eula/Hedge-Hopper** | £20 |

MAYNELL WILSON (ACTUALLY WILSON MAYNELL) & WESTMINSTER FIVE

| 67 | CBM CBM 001 | **Motown Feeling/Mean Ole World** (with p/s) | £20 |

(see also Wes[t]minster Five)

MURRY WILSON

| 67 | Capitol (S)T 2819 | **THE MANY MOODS OF MURRY WILSON** (LP) | £20 |

(see also Beach Boys)

NANCY WILSON

65	Capitol CL 15412	**Where Does That Leave Me/Gentle Is My Love**	£25
66	Capitol CL 15443	**Power Of Love/Rain Sometimes**	£15
66	Capitol CL 15466	**You've Got Your Troubles/Uptight** (Everything's Alright)	£20
67	Capitol CL 15508	**Don't Look Over Your Shoulder/Mercy, Mercy, Mercy**	£15
68	Capitol CL 15547	**Face It Girl It's Over/The End Of Our Love**	£40
68	Capitol CL 15547	**Face It Girl It's Over/The End Of Our Love** (DJ copy)	£80
62	Capitol (S)T 1767	**HELLO YOUNG LOVERS** (LP, mono/stereo)	£18
63	Capitol (S)T 1828	**BROADWAY - MY LOVE** (LP, mono/stereo)	£18
63	Capitol (S)T 1934	**HOLLYWOOD - MY WAY** (LP, mono/stereo)	£18
63	Capitol (S)T 2012	**YESTERDAY'S LOVE SONGS** (LP, mono/stereo)	£18
64	Capitol (S)T 2082	**TODAY, TOMORROW, FOREVER** (LP)	£18
65	Capitol (S)T 2136	**THE NANCY WILSON SHOW** (LP)	£18
65	Capitol (S)T 2155	**HOW GLAD I AM** (LP)	£18
65	Capitol (S)T 2321	**TODAY- MY WAY** (LP)	£18
65	Capitol (S)T 2351	**GENTLE IS MY LOVE** (LP)	£18
66	Capitol (S)T 2433	**FROM BROADWAY WITH LOVE** (LP)	£18

66	Capitol (S)T 2495	A TOUCH OF TODAY (LP)	£30
66	Capitol (S)T 2555	TENDER LOVING CARE (LP)	£20
67	Capitol (S)T 2634	NANCY - NATURALLY (LP)	£20

NANCY WILSON & CANNONBALL ADDERLEY
62	Capitol ST 1657	NANCY WILSON & CANNONBALL ADDERLEY (LP, stereo)	£15

(see also Cannonball Adderley)

PEANUTS WILSON
58	Coral Q 72302	Cast Iron Arm/You've Got Love	£500
58	Coral Q 72302	Cast Iron Arm/You've Got Love (78)	£150

REUBEN WILSON (1)
76	Chess 6078 700	Got To Get Your Own Parts 1 & 2	£60
97	Blue Note 7243 8 29906 1 1	BLUE MODE (LP, reissue)	£15

ROB WILSON BAND
90	Metro Music MMI 6	The Girl In the Polka-Dot Dress/The Greatest Crime/King Of The Blues (p/s)	£20

RON WILSON
68	Island WI 3112	Dred Saras/DAVID BROWN: All My Life	£70

(see also Winston Scotland, Douglas Brothers)

SHARK WILSON & BASEMENT HEATERS
71	Ashanti ASH 400	Make It Reggae/Version	£40

SMILEY WILSON
60	London HLG 9066	Running Bear/Long As Little Birds Fly	£50

TONY WILSON
67	Columbia DB 8153	Can't Waste A Good Thing/What Did I Do?	£30

(see also Hot Chocolate)

TREVOR WILSON
65	Ska Beat JB 207	You Couldn't Believe/You Told Me You Care	£50

STEVEN WILSON
13	Kscope KSCOPE 838	Luminol/The Watchmaker (12" picture disc)	£18
05	Tonefloat TF 22	UNRELEASED ELECTRONIC MUSIC (2-LP, white vinyl)	£45
05	Tonefloat TF 22	UNRELEASED ELECTRONIC MUSIC (2-LP)	£40
09	Tonefloat TF 50	INSURGENTES (Box set, 4 x 10", 1000 only)	£250
09	Kscope KSCOPE 808	INSURGENTES (2-LP, gatefold sleeve, 2000 only)	£40
10	Tonefloat TF 107	TAPE EXPERIMENTS 1985-6 (2-LP)	£35
11	Kscope KSCOPE 818	GRACE FOR DROWNING (2-LP)	£20
12	Kscope KSCOPE 827	CATALOGUE/PRESERVE/AMASS (LP)	£15
13	Kscope KSCOPE 240	THE RAVEN THAT REFUSED TO SING AND OTHER STORIES (2-LP)	£20
15	Kscope KSCOPE 875	HAND. CANNOT. ERASE (2-LP)	£20
15	Tonefloat TF 22	UNRELEASED ELECTRONIC MUSIC (2-LP, reissue)	£20
17	Caroline Int. CAROL. 016LPB	TO THE BONE (2-LP, white vinyl)	£25

(see also Porcupine Tree, No Man)

WIMPLE WINCH
66	Fontana TF 686	What's Been Done/I Really Love You	£350
66	Fontana TF 718	Save My Soul/Everybody's Worried 'Bout Tomorrow	£500
67	Fontana TF 781	Rumble On Mersey Square South/Typical British Workmanship	£300
67	Fontana TF 781	Rumble On Mersey Square South/Typical British Workmanship (mispressing, B-side plays "Atmospheres")	£600
91	Bam Caruso KIRI 108	THE PSYCHEDELIC YEARS VOLUME 2 (LP)	£20

(see also Just Four Men, Four Just Men, Pacific Drift, Tristar Airbus)o

WIN
87	Swamplands	UH! TEARS BABY (CD)	£30

LEM WINCHESTER & BENNY GOLSON
59	Esquire 32-142	WINCHESTER SPECIAL (LP)	£25
61	Esquire 32-172	ANOTHER OPUS (LP)	£15

KAI WINDING
65	Verve VS 512	Comin' Home Baby/More	£15
55	London LTZ-N 15003	K AND J.J. (LP, with J.J. Johnson Quintet)	£15
59	Philips SBBL 515	TROMBONES (LP)	£18
61	Parlophone PMC 1138	SLIDE RULE (LP, with J.J. Johnson Quintet)	£20
63	Verve VLP 9049	SOUL SURFIN' (LP)	£30

(see also Dizzy Gillespie, J.J. Johnson Quintet)

WIND IN THE WILLOWS
68	Capitol CL 15561	Moments Spent/Friendly Lion	£25
68	Capitol ST 2956	WIND IN THE WILLOWS (LP)	£30

(see also Debbie Harry, Blondie)

WINDMILLS
88	S.T.S. 2	The Day Dawned On Me/Dolphins (p/s)	£20
90	Wasteful SRT 90s 2734	Nothing At All/Secrets (p/s)	£20

BARRY WINDOW
69	BAF BAF 7	I Thank You/End Of Our Road	£50

WINDOWS (1)
72	Polydor 2058 206	How Do You Do/Nobody's Baby	£18

WINDOWS (2)
78	Skeleton SKL 008	Re-Arrange/Over Dub (p/s)	£15
81	Skeleton SKULP 2	UPPERS ON DOWNERS (LP, with inserts)	£40

(see also Mutants)

WINDY & CARL
96 Enraptured RAPT 4509   **Christmas Song/GRIMBLE GRUMBLE: Odyssey And Oracle** (no'd p/s, coloured vinyl, 350 only) **£20**

WINDY CORNER
73 Deroy DER 977   **THE HOUSE AT WINDY CORNER** (LP, private pressing) **£300**

AMY WINEHOUSE
03 Island 12 IS 830 DJ   **Stronger Than Me** (Curtis Lynch Jnr Vocal Remix)/(Curtis Lynch Jnr Dub Remix) (12" Promo) **£30**
03 Island 12 IS 830   **Stronger Than Me** (Album Version(Curtis Lynch Jnr Remix featuring Blackout Ja and Isha Sesay)/(Harmonic 33 Remix)/**Acapella Version)** (12") **£15**
03 Island 12 ISX 840 DJ   **Take The Box** (Seiji's Buggin' Mix)/(Seiji's Buggin' Rub)/(The Headquarters Mix) (Promo 12") **£18**
03 Island ISX 852 DJ   **In My Bed** (Bass Gangsta Mix)/(CJ Mix)/(Full Length Version) (Promo 12")...............**£18**
03 Island 12 IS 852 DJ   **In My Bed** (Bugz In The Attic Vocal Mix)/(Bugz In The Attic Dub)/(Full Length Version) (Promo 12") **£18**
03 Island 12 IS 865 DJ   **Pumps** (MJ Cole Remix)/**Pumps** (Mylo Remix)/**Pumps** (Promo 12").......................**£18**
06 Island AMY 12 PRO 1   **Rehab** (Hot Chip Remix)/(Hot Chip Instrumental)/(Desert Eagle Discs Remix)/(Desert Eagle Discs Instrumental)/(Original Version) (Promo 12") **£25**
06 AMY/AMX 12 PRO   **Love Is A Losing Game** (Moody Boyz Dubstep Remix)/(Moody Boyz Dubland Version) (Promo 12", 300 only)..**£25**
06 Island AMY 7 PRO 2   **Love Is A Losing Game/**(Moody Boys Dubstep Remix) **promo, 300 only** **£40**
06 Island AMYLPPRO 1   **Back To Black** (The Rumble Strips Remix)/**Back To Black** (p/s, clear vinyl promo) **£20**
07 Island 1744792   **Tears Dry On Their Own/Tears Dry On Their Own** (NYPC's Fucked Mix) (p/s, clear vinyl) **£15**
03 Iniversal Island FRANK LP 3   **FRANK** (ALBUM SAMPLER) **EP** (promo 12", p/s)...**£20**
03 Island 9812918   **FRANK** (LP)..**£20**
07 Island 1735948   **FRANK - REMIXES** (2 x 12", gatefold) **£15**
07 Island/Universal 1734128   **BACK TO BLACK** (LP, inner)..**£20**
08 Island ILPS 8148   **FRANK** (LP, reissue, 180gm includes free download, sealed, stickered) **£20**
11 Island 279 060 3,   **LIONESS:HIDDEN TREASURES** (2LP, 45rpm, gatefold, printed inners) **£20**
15 Island 4765739   **AMY** (THE ORIGINAL SOUNDTRACK) (with Antonio Pinto) (2LP, gatefold, printed inners, 180gm)...**£20**
18 Island 0600753691090   **BACK TO BLACK** (2-LP, half-speed master, gatefold, printed inners, 180gm).....................**£35**
20 Island UMC 0727248   **AMY 12 x 7** (12x7" in wide-spined sleeves with inners, box set, booklet, set of three artcards with pink belly-band) **£70**
21 UMC 3541560   **AT THE BBC** (3LP, fold-out sleeve, printed inners)..**£30**
22 UMC/Island 4555684   **LIVE AT GLASTONBURY 2007** (2-LP, ltd ed. clear vinyl, gatefold, printed inners) **£25**

WINE OF LEBANON
76 Dovetail DOVE 46   **WINE OF LEBANON** (LP)..**£20**

WINNERS (1)
73 Ensign EN 39   **Sing Your Song/Have We Finished?** **£45**

WINNERS (2)
79 Ariola ARPD 144   **Get Ready For The Future/Music** (12")...**£15**

PETE WINSLOW & KING SIZE BRASS
73 BBC 103S   **GIRL ON THE TESTCARD** (LP) **£20**

WINSTON
74 York YR 212   **I Wanna Let Anna Go/Brother Jim** **£15**
73 Bradley BRAD 306   **Mona/Rockerdile** (p/s) **£20**

WINSTON (RICHARDS) & BIBBIE (B.B. SEATON)
63 R&B JB 115   **Lover Man/LESTER STIRLING: Gravy Cool** **£50**

WINSTON (FRANCIS) & CECIL (LOCKE)
70 Banana BA 306   **United We Stand/SOUND DIMENSION: Sweet Message** **£25**

WINSTON & ERROL
71 Punch PH 74   **There Is A Land/Goodnight My Love** **£18**

WINSTON & FAY
64 Blue Beat BB 272   **Fay Is Gone** (Winston & Errol)/**MONARCHS: Sauce And Tea** **£22**

WINSTON & GEORGE
66 Pyramid PYR 6002   **Denham Town/Keep The Pressure On** **£35**
12 Pyramid THB 7021   **Denham Town/THE RIO GRANDES: Soldiers Take Over** **£20**

JIMMY WINSTON (& HIS REFLECTIONS)
66 Decca F 12410   **Sorry She's Mine/It's Not What You Do** (But The Way That You Do It) **£300**
(see also Small Faces, Winston's Fumbs, Spheres)

WINSTON (GROOVY) & PAT (RHODEN)
68 Trojan TR 605   **Pony Ride/Baby You Send Me**...**£15**

WINSTON (RICHARDS) & TONETTES
65 Ska Beat JB 225   **You Make Me Cry/CHECKMATES: Invisible Ska** **£40**

WINSTON & ROY
62 Blue Beat BB 80   **Babylon Gone/COUNT OSSIE ON AFRICAN DRUMS: First Gone** **£35**

WINSTON & RUPERT
70 Bullet BU 425   **Come By Here/Somebody** **£50**
70 Moodisc HM 106   **Musically Beat/Let Me Tell You Girl** **£85**
(see also Eternals)

ERIC WINSTONE (& HIS) ORCHESTRA
64 Pye 7N 15603   **Dr. Who Theme/Pony Express** **£18**

NORMA WINSTONE
72 Argo ZDA 148   EDGE OF TIME (LP) £300
(see also Mike Westbrook, Michael Garrick)

WINSTONS
69 Pye International 7N 25493 Colour In Father/Amen, Brother...£20

WINSTON'S FUMBS
67 RCA RCA 1612   Real Crazy Apartment/Snow White...£600
(see also Small Faces, Jimmy Winston & His Reflections, Yes, Spheres, Federals)

EDGAR WINTER (GROUP)
70 CBS 64083   ENTRANCE (LP, as Edgar Winter)..£15
71 CBS 64298   EDGAR WINTER'S WHITE TRASH (LP)...£15
72 CBS 67244   ROAD WORK (2-LP)..£15

JOHNNY WINTER
69 CBS 63619   JOHNNY WINTER (LP) £25
69 Liberty LBL/LBS 83240E   THE PROGRESSIVE BLUES EXPERIMENT (LP)..£25
70 Buddah 2359 011   FIRST WINTER (LP) £20
70 CBS 66231   SECOND WINTER (2-LP, 3-sided)...£18
70 CBS 64117   JOHNNY WINTER AND... (LP)..£15
74 CBS CQ 32188/Q 65484   STILL ALIVE AND WELL (LP, quadrophonic)...£15

DON WINTERS
60 Brunswick 05827   Someday Baby/That's All I Need..£15

LIZ WINTERS & BOB CORT SKIFFLE GROUP
57 Decca F 10878   Freight Train/Love Is Strange £20
57 Decca F 10899   Maggie May/Jessamine £20
57 Decca DFE 6409   LIZ WINTERS AND BOB CORT (EP)...£25
(see also Bob Cort Skiffle Group)

LOIS WINTERS
56 London HLD 8266   Japanese Farewell Song/JAN GARBER & HIS ORCHESTRA: My Dear £35

RON WINTERS
63 Colpix PX 11022   Snow Girl/In The Middle Of The Morning £20

RUBY WINTERS
68 Stateside SS 2090   I Want Action/Better £150
68 Stateside SS 2090   I Want Action/Better (DJ copy) £200

WINTER'S REIGN
87 Loop LOPL 501   THE BEGINNING . . . (LP, with free 7") £15

STEVIE WINWOOD
77 Island WIP 6394   Time Is Running Out/Penultimate Zone (12", pre-release sleeve) £20
87 Island SW 1/2/3   BACK IN THE HIGH LIFE (3 x 7" set, each in p/s, promo only)........................£20
87 Island   CHRONICLES (5 x 7" box set, promo, 500 only) £30
(see also Winwood Kabaka Amoa, Anglos, Spencer Davis Group, Traffic, Blind Faith.)

WINWOOD/KABAKA/AMAO
73 Island HELP 14   AIYE-KETA THIRD WORLD (LP)..£15
(see also Stevie WInwood)

WIPEOUT
82 M&L MNL 2/ACE 37   Baby Please Don't Go/Two-O-Five/Crawdaddy/Should A' Known Better (p/s) £15
83 Out OUT 1A/B1   NO SWEAT (LP)..£15

WIPERS
84 Psycho PSYCHO 22   IS THIS REAL? (LP, with lyric insert)..£20
84 Psycho PSYCHO 23   YOUTH OF AMERICA (LP)...£20

WIRE
77 Harvest HAR 5144   Mannequin/Feeling Called Love/12XU (p/s) £100
77 Harvest HAR 5144   Mannequin/Feeling Called Love/12XU (no p/s) £30
78 Harvest HAR 5151   I Am The Fly/Ex-Lion Tamer (p/s)..£80
78 Harvest HAR 5151   I Am The Fly/Ex-Lion Tamer (no p/s) £30
78 Harvest HAR 5161   Dot Dash/Options R (p/s)...£50
78 Harvest HAR 5161   Dot Dash/Options R (no p/s)...£20
79 Harvest HAR 5172   Outdoor Miner/Practice Makes Perfect (p/s, white vinyl)............................£50
79 Harvest HAR 5172   Outdoor Miner/Practice Makes Perfect (p/s)...£20
79 Harvest HAR 5187   A Question Of Degree/Former Airline (p/s)...£40
79 Harvest HAR 5192   Map Ref 41° N 93° W/Go Ahead (p/s)..£40
79 Harvest SPSLP 299   154 (12", p/s, white label sampler with insert & press release; beware of counterfeits)...£35
81 Rough Trade RT 079   Our Swimmer/Midnight Bahnhof Cafe (p/s) £25
83 Rough Trade RTT 123   Crazy About Love/Second Length (Our Swimmer)/Catapult 30 (12", p/s, 2 different
                             sleeve colours) £20
86 Mute 12 MUTE 53   SNAKEDRILL (12" EP, p/s)...£15
89 Mute MUTE 87   Eardrum Buzz/The Offer (p/s, clear vinyl, withdrawn) £30
95 Touch TONE 5   THE FIRST LAST NUMBER (12" EP. p/s as Wir30)...£15
77 Harvest SHSP 4076   PINK FLAG (LP, with lyric inner) £80
78 Harvest SHSP 4093   CHAIRS MISSING (LP, 1st 10,000 with lilac lyric inner sleeve) £80
79 Harvest SHSP 4105   154 (LP, with inner lyric sleeve & bonus 7" EP: "Song 2"/"Get Down [Parts I & II]"/"Let's
                             Panic"/"Later"/"Small Electric Piece" [PSR 444])..£100
79 Harvest SHSP 4105   154 (LP, without 7")...£50
84 Rough Trade ROUGH 29   DOCUMENT AND EYEWITNESS (LP, with free 12" EP [ROUGH 2912]) £30
86 Pin Label PINKY 7   WIRE PLAY POP (mini-LP) £15

MINT VALUE £

86	Dojo DOJOLP 36	IN THE PINK (LP)	£15
87	Mute STUMM 42	THE IDEAL COPY (LP)	£15
87	Harvest SHSP 4076	PINK FLAG (LP, reissue, black label)	£30
87	Harvest SHSP 4093	CHAIRS MISSING (LP, reissue)	£30
87	Harvest SHSP 4105	154 (LP, reissue, barcoded on rear sleeve)	£30
88	Mute STUMM 54	A BELL IS A CUP UNTIL IT IS STRUCK (LP)	£20
89	Mute STUMM 66	IBTABA (LP)	£20
89	Harvest SHSP 4127	ON RETURNING (LP)	£30
89	Strange Fruit SFRLP 108	PEEL SESSIONS (LP)	£15
90	Mute STUMM 80	MANSCAPE (LP)	£18
91	Mute STUMM 74	THE DRILL (LP)	£20
91	Mute 7 STUMM 74	THE DRILL (3-LP and 7" box set, numbered)	£50
91	Mute STUMM 87	WIR (LP, as Wir, die-cut sleeve)	£20
93	Mute STUMM 116	1985-1990 (2-LP)	£40
96	WMO 4LP	TURNS AND STROKES (LP)	£40
03	PF456REDUX	PF456 REDUX (LP)	£35
08	Pink Flag PF 17 LP	OBJECT 47 (LP, with free 12")	£50
11	Pink Flag PF 18 LP	RED BARKED TREE (LP)	£20
18	Pink Flag PFS 1-9	NINE SEVENS (box set with 9 x 7" singles)	£70

(see also Dome, Cupol, Colin Newman, P'O, Bruce Gilbert, Gilbert & Lewis, Duet Emmo)

WIRE DOLL
71	Milestone MS 2	To The Sun/Terry I Love You	£15

MARK WIRTZ (ORCHESTRA & CHORUS)
68	Parlophone R 5668	(He's Our Dear Old) Weatherman (From "A Teenage Opera")/Possum's Dance	£30
68	Parlophone R 5683	Mrs. Raven/Knickerbocker Glory	£25
69	CBS 4306	My Daddie Is A Baddie/I Love You Because	£15
69	CBS 4539	Caroline/Goody, Goody, Goody	£18
64	World Record Club T 452	TEN AGAIN (LP, by Belle Gonzalez & Russ Loader, Wirtz as producer)	£30

(see also Mood Mosaic, Keith West, Sweet Shop, Philwit & Pegasus, Mark Rogers & Marksmen, Belle Gonzalez, Zion De Gallier, Elmer Hockett's Hurdy Gurdy, Steve Flynn, Matchmaker)

WISE BLOOD
91	Wise 003	DISHDIRT (LP, with sticker)	£15

(see also Foetus)

MAC WISEMAN
55	London HLD 8174	The Kentuckian Song/Wabash Cannon Ball	£30
56	London HLD 8226	My Little Home In Tennessee/I Haven't Got The Right To Love You	£30
56	London HLD 8259	Fireball Mail/When The Roses Bloom Again	£40
56	London HLD 8259	Fireball Mail/When The Roses Bloom Again (78)	£15
57	London HLD 8412	Step It Up And Go/Sundown	£400
57	London HLD 8412	Step It Up And Go/Sundown (78)	£40
59	London HL 7084	Jimmy Brown The Newsboy/I've Got No Use For Woman (export issue)	£20
56	London RE-D 1056	SONGS FROM THE HILLS (EP)	£20
58	London RE-D 1147	SONGS FROM THE HILLS VOL. 2 (EP)	£20
60	London RE-D 1242	SONGS FROM THE HILLS VOL. 3 (EP)	£20
56	London HB-D 1052	SONGS FROM THE HILLS (10" LP)	£30
60	London HA-D 2217	GREAT FOLK BALLADS (LP)	£20

TREVOR WISHART
78	York YES 7	RED BIRD: A POLITICAL PRISONER'S DREAM (LP, with insert)	£40
79	private pressing	BEACH SINGULARITY AND MENAGERIE (LP, with insert)	£20

WISHBONE ASH
70	MCA MKPS 2014	WISHBONE ASH (LP, gatefold sleeve, red/pink 'dogbone' label)	£150
70	MCA MDKS 2014	WISHBONE ASH (LP, blue/black labels)	£60
71	MCA MDKS 8004	PILGRIMAGE (LP, gatefold sleeve, purple/red 'dogbone' label)	£150
71	MCA MDKS 8004	PILGRIMAGE (LP, blue/black labels)	£50
72	MCA MDKS 8006	ARGUS (LP, gatefold sleeve, black/blue 'hexagon' label)	£150
73	MCA MDKS 8011	WISHBONE FOUR (LP, gatefold sleeve, black label, with poster & lyrics)	£40
73	MCA MKPS 2014	WISHBONE ASH (LP, reissue, black labels)	£30
73	MCA MDKS 8005	ARGUS (LP reissue, black labels)	£30
73	MCA ULD 2	LIVE DATES (2-LP, gatefold sleeve, pink label)	£25
74	MCA MCF 2585	THERE'S THE RUB (LP)	£15
76	MCA MCG 3523	NEW ENGLAND (LP)	£15
78	MCA MCG 3528	NO SMOKE WITHOUT FIRE (LP, with stickered sleeve & inner, with bonus live single "Come In From The Rain"/"Lorelei" [PSR 431])	£15
80	MCA MCG 4012	LIVE DATES II (LP, textured gatefold sleeve, with live bonus LP)	£15
85	Neat NEAT 1027	RAW TO THE BONE (LP)	£18
18	Madfish SMABX1065	THE VINTAGE YEARS 1970 - 1991 (box set, 30 x CD, booklet, posters, signed photos and 7" flexi)	£200

(see also Home, Big Daisy)

WISHFUL THINKING
66	Decca F 12438	Turning Round/V.I.P.	£20
68	Decca F 12760	It's So Easy/I Want You Girl	£15
67	Decca SKL 4900	LIVE VOL. 1 (LP)	£50
71	Charisma CAS 1038	HIROSHIMA (LP)	£25

WITCHCRAFT
04	Rise Above RISELP 47	WITCHCRAFT (LP)	£25
04	Rise Above RISEPD 47	WITCHCRAFT (LP, picture disc)	£30
07	Rise Above RISELP 103	THE ALCHEMIST (LP, blue vinyl, 25 only)	£120

| 07 | Rise Above RISELP 103 | THE ALCHEMIST (LP, green, clear, purple or suitably gold vinyl) | £20 |

WITCHDOCTOR AND THE SPIRIT
| 85 | Zella ZEL SPS 427 | Carry On/Version (no p/s) | £25 |

WITCHES BREW
| 80s | Pussy PU 016 | Angeline (p/s) | £20 |

WITCHFINDER GENERAL
81	Heavy Metal HEAVY 6	Burning A Sinner/Satan's Children (p/s)	£60
82	Heavy Metal 12HM 17	Soviet Invasion/Rabies/R.I.P. (live) (12", p/s)	£35
82	Heavy Metal HMRLP 8	DEATH PENALTY (LP, red, blue or clear vinyl, with inner)	£30
82	Heavy Metal HMRPD 8	DEATH PENALTY (LP, picture disc)	£18
83	Heavy Metal HMRLP 13	FRIENDS OF HELL (LP, red, silver or clear vinyl)	£20
83	Heavy Metal HMRPD 13	FRIENDS OF HELL (LP, picture disc)	£18

WITCHFYNDE
83	Expulsion OUT 3	I'd Rather Go Wild/Cry Wolf (p/s)	£20
80	Rondelet ABOUT 1	GIVE 'EM HELL (LP)	£25
80	Rondelet ABOUT 2	STAGE FRIGHT (LP)	£15
83	Expulsion PEXIT 5	CLOAK AND DAGGER (LP, picture disc)	£18
84	Mausoleum SKULL 8352	LORDS OF SIN (LP, gatefold sleeve, with bonus 12" [Cloak & Dagger/ I'd Rather Go Wild/ Moon Magic/Give 'Em Hell])	£15

WITCHING HOUR
| 92 | Succubus WITCHEP1 | HOURGLASS EP (12") | £30 |

BILL WITHERS
87	CBS 650992 6	Lovely Day/Lean On Me/Lovely Night For Dancing (12", p/s)	£20
72	A&M AMLS 68107	STILL BILL (LP, gatefold)	£30
71	Sussex LPSX 3	JUST AS I AM (LP)	£40
81	CBS 85049	GREATEST HITS (LP)	£18
73	A&M AMLD 3001	LIVE AT CARNEGIE HALL (2-LP)	£30
77	CBS 82265	MENAGERIE (LP)	£15

JIMMY WITHERSPOON

78s
54	Parlophone R 3914	It/Highway To Happiness	£20
54	Parlophone R 3951	Oh Boy/I Done Told You	£20
54	Vogue V 2261	Failing By Degrees/New Orleans Woman	£20
54	Vogue V 2295	Who's Been Jivin' With You/Rain, Rain, Rain	£20
56	Vogue V 2060	Big Fine Girl/No Rollin' Blues	£20
56	Vogue V 2356	Jump, Children/Take Me Back Baby	£20

SINGLES
54	Parlophone MSP 6125	It/Highway To Happiness	£100
54	Parlophone MSP 6142	Oh Boy/I Done Told You	£100
56	Vogue V 2060	Big Fine Girl/No Rollin' Blues	£75
62	Vogue V 2420	When The Lights Go Out/All That's Good	£75
64	Stateside SS 304	Evenin'/Money Is Getting Cheaper	£15
64	Stateside SS 325	I Will Never Marry/I'm Coming Down With The Blues	£15
64	Stateside SS 362	You're Next/Happy Blues	£15
65	Stateside SS 429	Come Walk With Me/Oh How I Love You	£15
65	Stateside SS 461	Love Me Right/Make My Heart Smile Again	£15
66	Stateside SS 503	If There Wasn't Any You/I Never Thought I'd See The Day	£15

EPs
61	Vogue EPV 1269	JIMMY WITHERSPOON AT MONTEREY	£30
61	Vogue EPV 1270	JIMMY WITHERSPOON AT MONTEREY No. 2	£30
64	Vocalion EPVH 1278	JIMMY WITHERSPOON.	£20
65	Vocalion EPVH 1284	OUTSKIRTS OF TOWN	£20
66	Vocalion VEH 170158	FEELING THE SPIRIT VOL. 1	£20
66	Vocalion VEH 170159	FEELING THE SPIRIT VOL. 2	£20

ALBUMS
59	London Jazz LTZ-K 15150	NEW ORLEANS BLUES (with Wilbur de Paris)	£40
60	Vogue LAE 12218	SINGIN' THE BLUES	£40
61	Vogue LAE 12253	AT THE RENAISSANCE (with Gerry Mulligan)	£35
64	Stateside SL 10088	EVENIN' BLUES	£35
65	Stateside SL 10105	BLUES AROUND THE CLOCK	£40
65	Fontana 688 005 ZL	THERE'S GOOD ROCKIN' TONIGHT	£30
65	Stateside SL 10114	SOME OF MY BEST FRIENDS ARE BLUES	£25
65	Stateside SL 10139	BLUE SPOON	£22
65	Vogue VRL 3005	JIMMY WITHERSPOON IN PERSON	£22
66	Ember EMB 3369	JIMMY WITHERSPOON.	£20
67	Fontana (S)TL 5382	'SPOON SINGS AND SWINGS	£25
67	Verve (S)VLP 9156	BLUE POINT OF VIEW	£18
67	Transatlantic PR 7300	EVENIN' BLUES (reissue)	£15
68	Transatlantic PR 7356	SOME OF MY BEST FRIENDS ARE THE BLUES (reissue)	£15
68	Stateside (S)SL 10232	LIVE	£20
68	Verve (S)VLP 9181	BLUES IS NOW (with Brother Jack McDuff)	£15
68	Verve (S)VLP 9216	SPOONFUL OF SOUL	£18
68	Transatlantic PR 7418	SPOON IN LONDON	£15
68	Transatlantic PR 7475	BLUES FOR EASY LIVERS	£15
69	Stateside SSL 10289	THE BLUES SINGER	£18

MINT VALUE £

69	Polydor Intl. 623 256	BACK DOOR BLUES	£20
71	Probe SPB 1031	HANDBAGS AND GLADRAGS	£15

(see also Eric Burdon & Jimmy Witherspoon, Brother Jack McDuff)

JIMMY WITHERSPOON/HELEN HUMES

60	Vogue EPV 1198	RHYTHM AND BLUES CONCERT (EP, 2 tracks each)	£80

(see also Helen Humes)

BITTER WITHY

69	Nevis NEVIS R005	SAMPLER (LP)	£20

WITNESSES

60s	Herald ELR 1076	THE WITNESSES (EP)	£70

D WITTER

78	D-Roy DRLP 1001	MAWAMBA DUB (WARRIOR) (LP)	£70

(See also World Sound & Power Band)

WIZARD'S CONVENTION

76	RCA RS 1085	WIZARD'S CONVENTION (LP, with insert)	£15

(see also Deep Purple, Roger Glover, Jon Lord, David Coverdale, Ray Fenwick, Glenn Hughes, ELP, Hardin & York)

WIZZ

85	Jah Life	MR. SUNSHINE (LP)	£40

WIZZARD

73	Harvest SHSP 4025	WIZZARD BREW (LP, with lyric insert)	£15
74	Warner Bros. K 56029	INTRODUCING EDDY AND THE FALCONS (LP, gatefold with poster)	£25

(see also Roy Wood, Balls, Idle Race, Grunt Futtock)

WJW & ROOTS TRUNKS & BRANCHES

79	Splendour Heights WJWX 1945	THE WEAK WILL BE STRONG (LP)	£25

W.L.S.

77	Cancer CAND 001	Dub Punk/Simply Funky (12")	£15

JEZZ WODROFFE

80	Graduate GRAD LP 1	OPPOSITE DIRECTIONS (LP)	£50

CHARLES WOLCOTT

60	MGM 1115	Leatherjacket Cowboy/Ruby Duby Do	£15

DARRYL WAY'S WOLF

73	Deram SDL 14	CANIS LUPUS (LP, as Darryl Way's Wolf, gatefold sleeve)	£18
73	Deram SML 1104	SATURATION POINT (LP, laminated sleeve, as Darryl Way's Wolf)	£15
74	Deram SML 1116	NIGHT MUSIC (LP)	£18

(see also Curved Air, King Crimson, Marillion)

WOLF

81	Gremlin GREM 72	See Them Running/Creatures Of The Night (no p/s)	£75
84	Mausoleum 8323	EDGE OF THE WORLD (LP)	£18

WOLF

82	Chrysalis CHS 2592	Head Contact/Rock'n'Roll (p/s, clear vinyl, with sticker)	£15

PATRICK WOLF

02	Faith & Industry FAI 001	THE PATRICK WOLF EP: Bloodbeat/Empress/A Boy Like Me/Pumpkin Soup (12")	£50

HENRY WOLFF AND NANCY HENNINGS

72	Island HELP 3	TIBETAN BELLS (LP, black label with pink "i")	£15

WOLFGANG PRESS

83	4AD (no cat. no.)	Kings Of Soul (Crowned Mix)/(De-Throned Mix)/(7" Mix) (12", same both sides, promo only, 50 copies pressed)	£15
95	4AD CAD 4016	FUNKY LITTLE DEMONS (LP)	£20

(see also Mass, Models)

WOLVES

64	Pye 7N 15676	Journey Into Dreams/What Do You Mean	£20
64	Pye 7N 15733	Now/This Year Next Year	£30
65	Pye 7N 17013	At The Club/Distant Dreams	£35
66	Parlophone R 5511	Lust For Life/My Baby Loves Them	£70

BOBBY WOMACK

68	Minit MLF 11005	What Is This?/What You Gonna Do	£15
73	United Artists UP 35512	Across 110th Street/Hang On In There (as Bobby Womack & Peace)	£25
74	Jay Boy BOY 75	What Is This?/I Wonder	£20
77	CBS 4827	Home Is Where The Heart Is/We've Only Just Begun	£30
77	CBS 4827	Home Is Where The Heart Is/We've Only Just Begun (DJ Copy)	£75
79	Arista ARIST 284	How Could You Break My Heart/I Honestly Love You	£15
82	Tamla Motown TMG1267	So Many Sides of You/Just My Imagination (7", p/s)	£30
87	Arista RIS 17	How Could You Break My Heart/Give It Up (p/s)	£20
87	Arista RIST 17	How Could You Break My Heart/Give It Up/Mr. D.J. Don't Stop The Music (12", p/s)	£15
71	United Artists UAS 29306	COMMUNICATION (LP)	£15
72	United Artists UAS 29365	UNDERSTANDING (LP)	£15
72	United Artists UAS 29451	ACROSS 110TH STREET (LP, soundtrack, with J.J. Johnson)	£20
73	United Artists UAG 29456	FACTS OF LIFE (LP, gatefold)	£15
79	Arista ARTY 165	ROADS OF LIFE (LP)	£20

(see also Valentinos)

WOMB

69	Dot DLP 25933	WOMB (LP)	£25
70	Dot DLP 25959	OVERDUB (LP)	£30

WOMBATS
07 No Label   Moving To New York/Happily Screwed/The Barman's Fault/Ba Ba Song (EP) £15

WOMENFOLK
64 RCA LSP 2919/SF 7671   NEVER UNDERESTIMATE THE POWER OF WOMENFOLK (LP)....................................£15
65 RCA RD 7704   AT THE HUNGRY I (LP) £15

(LITTLE) STEVIE WONDER

63	Oriole CBA 1853	Fingertips (Parts 1 & 2)	£40
63	Oriole CBA 1853	Fingertips (Parts 1 & 2) (DJ copy)	£85
63	Stateside SS 238	Workout, Stevie, Workout/Monkey Talk	£50
63	Stateside SS 238	Workout, Stevie, Workout/Monkey Talk (DJ copy)	£100
64	Stateside SS 285	Castles In The Sand/Thank You (For Loving Me All The Way)	£80
64	Stateside SS 285	Castles In The Sand/Thank You (For Loving Me All The Way) (DJ copy)	£100
64	Stateside SS 323	Hey, Harmonica Man/This Little Girl	£55
64	Stateside SS 323	Hey, Harmonica Man/This Little Girl (DJ copy)	£85

(The above 45's are credited to Little Stevie Wonder.)

65	Tamla Motown TMG 505	Kiss Me Baby/Tears In Vain	£50
65	Tamla Motown TMG 505	Kiss Me Baby/Tears In Vain (DJ copy)	£100
65	Tamla Motown TMG 532	High-Heel Sneakers/Music Talk	£40
65	Tamla Motown TMG 532	High-Heel Sneakers/Music Talk (DJ copy)	£100
66	Tamla Motown TMG 545	Uptight (Everything's Alright)/Purple Raindrops	£25
66	Tamla Motown TMG 545	Uptight (Everything's Alright)/Purple Raindrops (DJ cop)	£200
66	Tamla Motown TMG 558	Nothing's Too Good For My Baby/With A Child's Heart	£45
66	Tamla Motown TMG 558	Nothing's Too Good For My Baby/With A Child's Heart (DJ copy)	£150
66	Tamla Motown TMG 570	Blowin' In The Wind/Ain't That Asking For Trouble	£25
66	Tamla Motown TMG 570	Blowin' In The Wind/Ain't That Asking For Trouble (DJ copy)	£75
66	Tamla Motown TMG 588	A Place In The Sun/Sylvia	£20
66	Tamla Motown TMG 588	A Place In The Sun/Sylvia (DJ copy)	£50
67	Tamla Motown TMG 602	Travelin' Man/Hey Love	£18
67	Tamla Motown TMG 602	Travelin' Man/Hey Love (DJ copy)	£50
67	Tamla Motown TMG 613	I Was Made To Love Her/Hold Me (DJ copy)	£40
67	Tamla Motown TMG 626	I'm Wondering/Every Time I See You I Go Wild (DJ copy)	£40
68	Tamla Motown TMG 653	Shoo-Be-Doo-Be-Doo-Da-Day/Why Don't You Lead Me To Love (DJ copy)	£30
68	Tamla Motown TMG 666	You Met Your Match/My Girl	£15
68	Tamla Motown TMG 666	You Met Your Match/My Girl (DJ copy)	£35
68	Tamla Motown TMG 679	For Once In My Life/Angie Girl (DJ Copy)	£30
69	Tamla Motown TMG 690	My Cherie Amour/I Don't Know Why I Love You (DJ copy)	£25
69	Tamla Motown TMG 717	Yester-Me, Yester-You, Yesterday/I'd Be A Fool Right Now (DJ copy)	£25
70	Tamla Motown TMG 731	Never Had A Dream Come True/Somebody Knows, Somebody Cares (DJ copy)	£25
70	Tamla Motown TMG 744	Signed, Sealed, Delivered, I'm Yours/I'm More Than Happy (I'm Satisfied) (DJ copy)	£25
70	Tamla Motown TMG 757	Heaven Help Us All/I Gotta Have A Song (DJ copy)	£20
71	Tamla Motown TMG 772	We Can Work It Out/Don't Wonder Why (in p/s)	£30
71	Tamla Motown TMG 772	We Can Work It Out/Don't Wonder Why (DJ copy)	£25
71	Tamla Motown TMG 779	Never Dreamed You'd Leave Me In Summer/If You Really Love Me (DJ copy)	£25
64	Stateside SE 1014	I CALL IT PRETTY MUSIC BUT THE OLD PEOPLE CALL IT THE BLUES (EP)	£120

(Credited to Little Stevie Wonder.)

65	Tamla Motown TME 2006	LITTLE STEVIE WONDER (EP)	£90
63	Oriole PS 40049	TRIBUTE TO UNCLE RAY (LP)	£340
63	Oriole PS 40050	THE TWELVE-YEAR-OLD GENIUS - LIVE (LP)	£110
64	Stateside SL 10078	THE JAZZ SOUL OF LITTLE STEVIE WONDER (LP)	£150

(The above LP's are Credited to Little Stevie Wonder.)

65	Stateside SL 10108	HEY, HARMONICA MAN (LP)	£150

(Originally came with flipback sleeves)

66	Tamla Motown TML 11036	UPTIGHT (EVERYTHING'S ALRIGHT) (LP, mono)	£35
66	T. Motown TMG STML 11036	UPTIGHT (EVERYTHING'S ALRIGHT) (LP, stereo)	£45
67	Tamla Motown TML 11045	DOWN TO EARTH (LP, mono)	£30
67	Tamla Motown STML 11045	DOWN TO EARTH (LP, stereo)	£40
68	Tamla Motown STML 11059	I WAS MADE TO LOVE HER (LP, stereo)	£25
68	Tamla Motown TML 11059	I WAS MADE TO LOVE HER (LP, mono)	£20
68	T. Motown (S)TML 11075	GREATEST HITS (LP, mono/stereo)	£15
68	Tamla Motown (S)TML 11085	SOMEDAY AT CHRISTMAS (LP, mono/stereo)	£35
69	Tamla Motown (S)TML 11098	FOR ONCE IN MY LIFE (LP, mono/stereo)	£20
69	Tamla Motown (S)TML 11128	MY CHERIE AMOUR (LP, mono/stereo)	£18

(The LP's listed above originally came with flipback sleeves.)

70	T. Motown STML 11150	STEVIE WONDER LIVE	£15
70	Tamla Motown STML 11169	SIGNED SEALED AND DELIVERED	£15
71	Tamla Motown STML 11183	WHERE I'M COMING FROM (LP)	£15
72	Tamla Motown STMA 8002	MUSIC OF MY MIND (LP)	£15
73	Tamla Motown STMA 8007	TALKING BOOK (LP, gatefold)	£15
73	Tamla Motown STMA 8011	INNERVISIONS (LP, gatefold)	£15
74	Tamla Motown STMA 8019	FULFILLINGNESS FIRST FINALE (LP, gatefold)	£15
76	Tamla Motown TMSP 6002	SONGS IN THE KEY OF LIFE (2-LP, with free 7")	£30
79	Tamla Motown TMSP 6009	THE SECRET LIFE OF PLANTS (2-LP)	£20
05	Tamla Motown 12 MOW 13	A TIME 2 LOVE (LP)	£15

WONDER WHO
65	Philips BF 1440	Don't Think Twice, It's Alright/Sassy	£20
67	Philips BF 1600	Lonesome Road/FOUR SEASONS: Around And Around	£20

(see also Four Seasons, Frankie Valli)

WONDER BOY
69	Jackpot JP 703	Sweeten My Coffee (actually by Slim Smith)/MISTER MILLER: Cherry Pink	£25
69	Jackpot JP 705	Love Power (actually by Slim Smith)/LITTLE BOY BLUE: Since You Are Gone	£35

(see also Slim Smith)

GIRL WONDER
66	Doctor Bird DB 1015	Mommy Out Of The Light/Cutting Wood	£25

WONDERLAND
68	Polydor 56539	Poochy/Moscow	£15

ALICE WONDERLAND
63	London HLU 9783	He's Mine/Cha Linde	£20

WONDERS OF YOUTH
71	Alert AL 2	Down And Out Man/Terry	£25
72	Fly FL2	Jump Over My Head/Say Hello	£40

WONDER STUFF
87	Far Out GONE ONE	It's Not True.../A Wonderful Day/Like A Merry-Go-Round/Down Here (EP, p/s)	£40
87	Polydor	A HANDFUL OF SONGS (cassette, promo only, different to above)	£20
93	Polydor 519 8941	CONSTRUCTION FOR THE MODERN IDIOT (LP)	£30

(see also Vic Reeves)

ROYCE WONG
65	Blue Beat BB 301	Everything's Gonna Be Alright/Hang Your Head And Cry	£20

WOOB
93	Woob	WOOB WOOB WOOB (Cassette demo tape)	£20
94	Em:t	WOOB 1194 (CD)	£40
95	Em:t	WOOB 4495 (CD)	£40

ANITA WOOD
62	London HLS 9585	I'll Wait Forever/I Can't Show You How I Feel	£25
64	Sue WI 328	Dream Baby/This Happened Before	£40

BOBBY WOOD
64	Pye International 7N 25264	I'm A Fool For Loving You/My Heart Went Boing! Boing! Boing!	£15

BRENTON WOOD
70	Pye International 7N 25522	Great Big Bundle Of Love/Can You Dig It	£15
67	Liberty LBL/LBS 83088E	GIMME A LITTLE SIGN (LP)	£20

CHUCK WOOD
67	Big T BIG 104	Seven Days Too Long/Soul Shing-A-Ling	£20
67	Big T BIG 104	Seven Days Too Long/Soul Shing-A-Ling (DJ Copy)	£50

DEL WOOD
54	London HL 8036	Ragtime Annie/Backroom Polka	£50
54	London RE-P 1007	RAGTIME PIANO (EP)	£15

RONNIE WOOD
92	Continuum 12210-2	Show Me/Breathe On Me (CD, with Ronnie Wood print, signed & numbered, in black card case tied with ribbon, 600 only)	£50

(see also Faces, Rolling Stones, Jeff Beck)

ROY WOOD
73	Harvest SHVL 803	BOULDERS (LP, textured sleeve with EMI logo on label)	£25
76	Harvest SHDW 408	THE ROY WOOD STORY (LP)	£15

(see also Wizzard, Gerry Levine & Avengers, Mike Sheridan, Danny King['s Mayfair Set], Move, ELO, Renaissance [UK], Rockers, Birds)

WOODEN HORSE
72	York SYK 526	Pick Up The Pieces/Wake Me In The Morning	£20
73	York SYK 543	Wooden Horses/Typewriter And Guitar	£20
72	York FYK 403	WOODEN HORSE (LP)	£350
73	York FYK 413	WOODEN HORSE II (LP, withdrawn, with sleeve, blue/silver label)	£900
73	York FYK 413	WOODEN HORSE II (LP, withdrawn, without sleeve, blue/silver label)	£500

(see also Fox)

WOODEN O & GUESTS
69	Middle Earth MDLS 301	A HANDFUL OF PLEASANT DELITES (LP)	£150

(see also 'Middle Earth Sampler' in Various Artists section)

WOODEN SHJIPS
09	Great Pop Supplement GPS 50	I Believe It/SPACEMEN 3: Big City (demo) (red marbled vinyl, insert & sticker)	£15

GEORGE WOODHOUSE
79	Milestone M 001	Thanks/HOPETON JURNER: Living In The Ghetto (12")	£150

KEN WOODMAN & HIS PICCADILLY BRASS
66	Strike JLH 101	THAT'S NICE (LP)	£40

WOODMARK
83	Ooze S83 CUS 1692	When You're Gone/Life Is Cruel	£20

WOODPECKERS
65	Oriole CB 311	Hey Little Girl/What's Your Name	£20

CAROL WOODS
72	Ember NR 5059	OUT OF THE WOODS (LP)	£40

DONALD WOODS & EARL PALMER BAND
58	Vogue V 9107	Memories Of An Angel/That Much Of Your Love	£650
58	Vogue V 9107	Memories Of An Angel/That Much Of Your Love (78)	£150

GAY & TERRY WOODS
75	Polydor 2383 322	BACKWOODS (LP)	£50
76	Polydor 2383 375	THE TIME IS RIGHT (LP, with lyric insert)	£60
76	Polydor 2383 406	RENOWNED (LP, with lyric insert)	£50
78	Rockburgh ROC 104	TENDER HOOKS (LP, with lyric insert)	£20

(see also Woods Band, Gay Woods, Steeleye Span, Sweeney's Men)

JIMMY WOODS
63	Contemporary LAC 571	CONFLICT (LP)	£20

PEGGY WOODS
88	Kent 6T 4	Love Is Gonna Get You/ZZ: You Just Cheat And Lie	£20

PHIL WOODS
55	Esquire 20-055	NEW JAZZ QUINTET (10" LP)	£50
57	Esquire 32-020	WOODLORE (LP)	£80

TERRY WOODS
81	Chiswick CHIS 142	Tennessee Stud/I Don't Know About Love	£30

WOODS BAND
71	Greenwich GSLP 1004	THE WOODS BAND (LP, gatefold sleeve)	£150
77	Rockburgh CREST 29	THE WOODS BAND (LP, reissue in different sleeve)	£20

(see also Gay & Terry Woods)

MAGGIE WOODWARD
59	Vogue V 9148	Ali Bama/Zulu Warrior	£15
59	Vogue V 9148	Ali Bama/Zulu Warrior (78)	£20

WOODY KERN
69	Pye 7N 17672	Biography/Tell You I'm Gone (demo)	£100
69	Pye NSPL 18273	THE AWFUL DISCLOSURES OF MARIA MONK (LP)	£150

WOOL
69	Stateside SS2153	Love Love Love Love Love/If They Left Us Alone Now	£25

SHEB WOOLEY
51	MGM MGM 439	Hoot Owl Boogie/Country Kisses (78)	£20
55	MGM SP 1130	38-24-35/I Flipped	£25
55	MGM SPC 5	Hill Billy Mambo/I Go Outa My Mind (export issue)	£30
58	MGM MGM 981	The Purple People Eater/I Can't Believe You're Mine	£15
56	MGM MGM-EP 540	JEST PLAIN, WILD AND WOOLEY (EP)	£40
61	MGM MGM-C 859	SONGS FROM THE DAY OF RAWHIDE (LP)	£20
62	MGM MGM-C 903	THAT'S MY MA AND THAT'S MY PA (LP)	£20

CHARLIE WOOLFE
68	NEMS 56-3675	Dance Dance Dance/Home	£35

(see also At Last The 1958 Rock & Roll Show)

WOOLIES
67	RCA RCA 1602	Who Do You Love?/Hey Girl	£50

WOOLLY
72	RCA 2297	Golden Golden/Sugar Daddy Song	£20

WOOLLY FISH
70	Plexium PXM 16	The Way You Like It/The Sound Of Thick	£25

BRENDA WOOTTON
68	Pipers VRC 1	JOHN THE FISH (LP)	£20

JIMMY WORK
56	London HLD 8270	When She Said "You All"/There's Only One You	£60
56	London HLD 8270	When She Said "You All"/There's Only One You (78)	£20
56	London HLD 8308	You've Gotta Heart Like A Merry-Go-Round/Blind Heart	£45
56	London HLD 8308	You've Gotta Heart Like A Merry-Go-Round/Blind Heart (78)	£20
55	London RE-D 1039	COUNTRY SONGS - WORK STYLE (EP)	£30

WORKING MEN'S CLUB
19	Melodic MELO 120	Bad Blood/Suburban Heights (p/s)	£15
19	Heavenly HVN 520	Teeth/Teeth (Instrumental) (p/s)	£15
20	Heavenly HVNLP199RAW	WORKING MEN'S CLUB (LP, 300 only, hand-sprayed sleeve, poster, patch, hand-stamped)	£70

WORLD
70	Liberty LBG 83419	LUCKY PLANET (LP, textured gatefold sleeve)	£50

(see also Neil Innes, Bonzo Dog [Doo-Dah] Band)

WORLD COLUMN
76	Capitol CL 15852	So Is The Sun/It's Not Right (DJ Copy)	£15

WORLD OF OZ
68	Deram DM 187	The Muffin Man/Peter's Birthday (Black And White Rainbows)	£15
68	Deram DM 205	King Croesus/Jack	£15
69	Deram DM 233	Willow's Harp/Like A Tear	£25
69	Deram DML/SML 1034	THE WORLD OF OZ (LP)	£120

(see also David Kubinec)

WORLD SOUND & POWER BAND
80	D Roy DRLP 1006	MAWAMBA DUB (WARRIOR) CHAPTER TWO (LP)	£55

(See also D Witter)

WORMS
78	Ice GUY 21	London Bus (I Can't Take My Eyes Off You/Okay At Christmas (500 only)	£50

WORRYING KYNDE
67	Piccadilly 7N 35370	Call Out The Name/Got The Blame	£80

JOHNNY WORTH
60	Oriole CB 1545	Nightmare/Hold Me, Thrill Me, Kiss Me	£75

MARION WORTH
60	London HL 7089	Are You Willing, Willie/This Heart Of Mine (export issue)	£25
60	London HL 7097	That's My Kind Of Love/I Lost Johnny (export issue)	£25

TONY WORTH
69	Cleo CL 3194	Why Not Love Me/Dream	£20

WOULD-BE-GOODS
88	El GPO 39	The Camera Loves Me/Cecil Beaton's Diary (p/s)	£15
88	El ACME 14	THE CAMERA LOVES ME (LP)	£20

WOVEN WEB
72	Shell SH2	High On Life/Lost Inside The Well	£40

WRANGLER
14	MemeTune MEME14VA01	LA SPARK (LP)	£15
16	MemeTune MEME14VA04	WHITE GLUE (LP)	£15
16	MemeTune MEME16VA02	SPARKED (MODULAR REMIX PROJECT) (2-LP)	£18

(see also Cabaret Voltaire, Stephen Mallinder)

WRANGLERS
64	Parlophone R 5163	Liza Jane/It Just Won't Work	£70

(see also Kenny Bernard, Kenny & Wranglers)

LINK WRAY (& HIS RAY MEN)
58	London HLA 8623	Rumble/The Swag (as Link Wray & His Ray Men)	£50
58	London HLA 8623	Rumble/The Swag (as Link Wray & His Ray Men) (78)	£30
63	Stateside SS 217	Jack The Ripper/The Black Widow	£30
64	Stateside SS 256	The Sweeper/Weekend	£20
65	Stateside SS 397	Good Rockin' Tonight/I'll Do Anything For You	£20
64	Stateside SE 1015	MR. GUITAR (EP, sleeve credits Link Ray)	£100
71	Polydor 2489 029	LINK WRAY (LP)	£40
71	Union Pacific UP 002	THERE'S GOOD ROCKIN' TONIGHT (LP)	£25
73	Virgin V 2006	BEANS & FATBACK (LP)	£20
73	Polydor 2391063	BE WHAT YOU WANT TO (LP)	£15
74	Polydor 2391 128	THE LINK WRAY RUMBLE (LP)	£15
88	Hangman HANG 31 UP	64 (THE SWAN DEMOS) (LP)	£30
88	Hangman HANG 33 UP	JACK THE RIPPER (LP)	£30

(see also Robert Gordon with Link Wray)

RAY WRAY QUARTET
62	Salvo SLO 1808	When Your Lover Has Gone/A Song Is Born	£20

WRECKERS
64	Granta GR 7EP 1010	THE WRECKERS' SOUND (EP)	£120

WRECKLESS ERIC
78	Stiff SEEZ 6	WRECKLESS ERIC (LP, printed inner)	£15
78	Stiff SEEZ 9	THE WONDERFUL WORLD OF... (LP, picture disc in LP sleeve)	£15
80	Stiff SEEZ 21	BIG SMASH (2-LP)	£15
93	Hangman HANG 50 UP	THE DONOVAN OF TRASH (LP)	£18

(see also Len Bright Combo)

JENNY WREN
66	Fontana TF 672	Chasing My Dreams All Over Town/A Thought Of You	£250
66	Fontana TF 772	The Merry-Go-Round (Is Slowing You Down)/Take A Walk Bobby	£15

WRENS
96	Grass GROW 10021	SECAUCUS (LP)	£150
06	BB 0031	THE MEADOWLANDS (2-LP, gatefold)	£100

WRETCHED
81	Wretched Music GRC 102	DNR/Souls In Torment (500 only)	£50

WRIGGLERS
68	Giant GN 26	The Cooler/You Cannot Know	£400
68	Blue Cat BS 106	Get Right/If I Did Look	£120

BETTY WRIGHT
68	Atlantic 584 216	Girls Can't Do What The Guys Do/Sweet Lovin' Daddy	£15
72	Atlantic K 10143	Clean Up Woman/I'll Love You Forever	£15
72	Atlantic K 40364	I LOVE THE WAY YOU LOVE (LP)	£20
74	RCA SF 8408	DANGER - HIGH VOLTAGE (LP)	£20
76	RCA RS 1063	EXPLOSION (LP)	£20
77	T.K. XL 14053	THIS TIME FOR REAL (LP)	£20

CHARLES WRIGHT & WATTS 103RD STREET RHYTHM BAND
70	Warner Bros WB 7417	Express Yourself/Living On Borrowed Time	£20
70	Warner Bros 1864	EXPRESS YOURSELF (LP)	£30

DALE WRIGHT
58	London HLD 8573	She's Neat/Say That You Care (as Dale Wright & Rock-Its)	£175
58	London HLD 8573	She's Neat/Say That You Care (as Dale Wright & Rock-Its) (78)	£40
59	Pye International 7N 25022	That's Show Biz/That's My Gal (as Dale Wright & Wright Guys)	£80
59	Pye International 7N 25022	That's Show Biz/That's My Gal (as Dale Wright & Wright Guys) (78)	£50

EARL WRIGHT
75	Capitol CL 15825	Thumb A Ride/Like A Rolling Stone (DJ Copy)	£15

GARY WRIGHT('S WONDERWHEEL)
71	A&M AMLS 2004	EXTRACTIONS (LP, poster sleeve)	£30
72	A&M AMLS 64296	FOOTPRINT (LP)	£18
72	A&M AMLH 64362	RING OF CHANGES (LP, as Wright's Wonderwheel; unissued, test pressings only)	£50

(see also Spooky Tooth, Magic Christians, Thomas F. Browne)

GEORGE WRIGHT/NEVILLE MITCHELL
82	Kingdom KV 8026	GEORGE WRIGHT - You Are The One I Love/ROOTS RADICS - I Done It Dub/NEVILL MITCHELL - Get Out Of Hand/ROOTS RADICS - Hand Made Dub	£25

GINNY WRIGHT (& TOM TALL)
55	London HL 8119	Indian Moon/Your Eyes Feasted Upon Her (solo)	£50
55	London HL 8150	Are You Mine?/Boom Boom Boomerang (with Tom Tall)	£30
55	London RE-U 1035	COUNTRY SONGS VOL. 2 (EP, with Tom Tall)	£30

(see also T. Tommy Cutrer & Ginny Wright, Tom Tall)

MILTON WRIGHT & TERRA SHIRMA STRINGS
07	Jazzman JM12.011	Keep It Up/The Silence That You Keep (12", p/s)	£15
08	Jazzman JMANLP 025	SPACED (LP, reissue)	£30

NAT WRIGHT
59	HMV POP 629	Anything/For You My Love	£75

OTIS WRIGHT
67	Doctor Bird DLM 5005	PEACE PERFECT PEACE (LP)	£50
67	Doctor Bird DLM 5006	IT WILL SOON BE DONE (LP)	£50
69	High Note BSL5003	SACRED SONGS (LP)	£30
60s	Coxsone TLP 1001	OVER IN GLORYLAND (LP)	£50
73	Tabernacle BSLP 5021	SOUL STIRRING GOSPEL SONGS (LP)	£40

O.V. WRIGHT
65	Vocalion VP 9249	You're Gonna Make Me Cry/Monkey Dog	£20
66	Vocalion VP 9255	Poor Boy/I'm In Your Corner	£20
66	Vocalion VP 9272	Gone For Good/How Long Baby	£20
67	London HLZ 10137	8 Men 4 Women/Fed Up With The Blues	£15
68	Sue WI 4043	What About You/What Did You Tell This Girl Of Mine	£50
68	Action ACT 4505	Oh Baby Mine/Working Your Game	£15
69	Action ACT 4527	I Want Everyone To Know/I'm Gonna Forget About You	£15
65	Vocalion VEP 170165	CAN'T FIND TRUE LOVE (EP)	£100
68	Island ILP 975	8 MEN, 4 WOMEN (LP)	£120

OWEN WRIGHT
70	Banana BA 310	Wala Wala (actually by Burning Spear)/JERRY & FREEDOM SINGERS: Got To Be Sure (B-side actually by Horace Andy)	£80

RICHARD WRIGHT
78	Harvest SHVL 818	WET DREAM (LP, gatefold, hype sticker)	£30
96	EMI UK 7243 8 53645 2 5	BROKEN CHINA (CD, booklet)	£30
23	Parlophone 5054197662348	WET DREAM (LP, remixed, remastered, gatefold, blue marbled vinyl)	£30

(see also Pink Floyd, Zee)

RITA WRIGHT
68	Tamla Motown TMG 643	I Can't Give Back The Love I Feel For You/Something On My Mind	£25
68	Tamla Motown TMG 643	I Can't Give Back The Love I Feel For You/Something On My Mind (DJ copy)	£40
78	Jet UP 36382	Love Is All You Need/Touch Me, Take Me	£100

RUBEN WRIGHT
66	Capitol CL 15460	Hey Girl/I'm Walking Out On You	£35
66	Capitol CL 15460	Hey Girl/I'm Walking Out On You (DJ copy)	£75

RUBY WRIGHT
53	Parlophone MSP 6025	Till I Waltz Again With You/When I Gave You My Love (with Charlie Gore)	£20
54	Parlophone MSP 6073	Bimbo/Boy, You Got Yourself A Gal	£25
55	Parlophone MSP 6150	What Have They Told You?/I Had The Funniest Feeling	£15
56	Parlophone MSP 6209	I Fall In Love With You Ev'ry Day/Do You Believe?	£15
59	Parlophone GEP 8785	THE THREE STARS GIRL (EP)	£30

SAMUEL E. WRIGHT
73	Paramount PARA 3035	There's Something Funny Going On/300 Pounds Of Hunger	£15

SANDRA WRIGHT
89	Demon FIEND 138	WOUNDED WOMAN (LP)	£150

SEAN WRIGHT
78	Ellie Jay EJSP 8624	Strange Situation/Silent Dreams (1st issue, 50 with folded p/s some with insert)	£30
81	Media PR 001	Strange Situation/Silent Dreams (2nd issue, p/s as Media but new labels are pasted over records from 1st pressing)	£15

STEVE WRIGHT
59	London HLW 8991	Wild, Wild, Woman/Love You	£200
59	London HLW 8991	Wild, Wild, Woman/Love You (78)	£100

MINT VALUE £

STEVEN WRIGHT
93	Reggae On Top ROT 001	Vision Of Jah/Dub Versions (12")	£25

STEVIE WRIGHT
74	Polydor 2480 249	HARD ROAD (LP)	£20

SYREETA WRIGHT
72	Mowest MWS 7001	SYREETA (LP)	£25

WINSTON WRIGHT
69	Camel CA 32	Power Pack/TWO SPARKS: Throwing Stones	£80
69	Explosion EX 2003	Barefoot Brigade/Slippery (with the Crystalites)	£75
69	Trojan TR 7701	Moonlight Groover/SENSATIONS: Everyday Is Just A Holiday	£60
69	Trojan TR 7715	Moon Invader (with Tommy McCook)/RADCLIFF RUFFIN: You Got To Love Me	£50
70	Trojan TR 7775	Meshwire (with Tommy McCook)/BARONS: Darling Please Return	£45
70	Explosion EX 2011	Flight 404/LLOYD & ROBIN: Gawling Come Down (B-side actually Higher Than The Highest Mountain by Monty Morris)	£35
70	Explosion EX 2015	Funny Girl/Funny Girl Version II	£25
70	Duke DU 62	Poppy Cock (with J.J. All Stars)/CARL DAWKINS: This World And Me (B-side actually "Satisfaction")	£30
70	Bamboo BAM 60	Reggae Feet/DON DRUMMOND: Royal Flush (B-side act. titled "The Rocket")	£35
70	High Note HS 040	Soul Pressure/Seed You Sow (with Gaytones)	£30
70	Moodisc MU 3501	Musically Red (with Maudie's Allstars; actually also with Count Sticky)/ RHYTHM RULERS: Bratah	£150
70	G.G. GG 4504	It's Been A Long Time/PAULETTE & GEE: Feel It More And More	£15
70	Techniques TE 907	Top Secret/Crazy Rhythm	£85
71	Upsetter US 378	Example (with 3rd & 4th Generation)/UPSETTER: Version	£25
71	Duke DU 111	Silhouettes/That Did It	£20
71	Camel CA 71	Silhouettes/That Did It	£20
77	Third World TWS 923	JUMP THE FENCE (LP)	£20

(see also Ethiopians, John Holt, J.J. Allstars, Slickers)

WRIGHTSOUND
75	Peacock AT 842	Dance Apache/Jelly	£18

WRIT
66	Decca F 12385	Did You Ever Have To Make Up Your Mind/Solid Golden Teardrops	£20

WRITING ON THE WALL
69	Middle Earth MDS 101	Child On A Crossing/Lucifer Corpus	£60
73	Pye 7N 45251	Man Of Renown/Buffalo	£20
69	Middle Earth MDLS 303	THE POWER OF THE PICTS (LP, textured sleeve)	£400
95	Pie & Mash PAM 003	RARITIES FROM THE MIDDLE EARTH (LP, 500 copies only)	£15
95	Tenth Planet TP 017	CRACKS IN THE ILLUSION OF LIFE (LP, gatefold sleeve)	£18
96	Tenth Planet TP 018	BURGHLEY ROAD (LP, 1,000 copies only)	£18

(see also 'Middle Earth Sampler' in Various Artists; Three's A Crowd)

HENRY WU/JEEN BASSA
14	22a 002	HENRY WU/JEAN BASSA (12" split EP, 1st pressing red stamped labels)	£15

WURZEL
87	GWR GWT 4	Bess/People Say I'm Crazy/Midnight In London/E.S.P. (12", p/s)	£15

(see also Motorhead)

JOHNNY WYATT
68	President PT 109	This Thing Called Love/To Whom It May Concern (DJ Copy)	£50
68	President PT 109	This Thing Called Love/To Whom It May Concern (horizontal)	£30

ROBERT WYATT
87	Strange Fruit SFPS 037	PEEL SESSIONS (12")	£15
70	CBS 64189	THE END OF AN EAR (LP)	£40
74	Virgin V 2017	ROCK BOTTOM (LP, 1st pressing, coloured "girl and dragon" labels)	£40
75	Virgin V 2034	RUTH IS STRANGER THAN RICHARD (LP)	£40
82	Rough Trade ROUGH 35	NOTHING CAN STOP US (LP, early pressing without "Shipbuilding", insert)	£20
81	Virgin VGD 3505	ROCK BOTTOM/RUTH IS STRANGER THAN RICHARD (2-LP reissue)	£35
85	Rough Trade ROUGH 69	OLD ROTTENHAT (LP, gatefold)	£20
91	Rough Trade R2741	DONDESTAN (LP)	£30
07	Domino WIGLP 202	COMICOPERA (2-LP)	£20
08	Domino REWIGLP 47	CUCKOOLAND (2-LP)	£20
08	Domino REWIGLP 45	SHLEEP (2-LP)	£20

(see also Soft Machine, Matching Mole, Centipede, Ben Watt)

RICHARD ('POPCORN') WYLIE
63	Columbia DB 7012	Brand New Man/So Much Love In My Heart (as Richard Wylie)	£40

BILL WYMAN
83	Ripple (no cat. no.)	DIGITAL DREAMS (LP, soundtrack, promo only)	£50

(see also Rolling Stones)

WYNDER K. FROG
66	Island WI 280	Turn On Your Lovelight/Zooming (red &white label, 4-prong push-out centre)	£50
66	Island WI 3011	Sunshine Superman/Blues For A Frog (red & white label, 4-prong push-out label)	£40
67	Island WIP 6006	Green Door/Dancing Frog (pink label, 4-prong push-out)	£50
67	Island WIP 6014	I Am A Man/Shook Shimmy & Shake (pink label, 4-prong push out)	£60
68	Island WIP 6044	Jumping Jack Flash/Baldy (pink label, 4-prong push out)	£40
67	Island ILP 944	SUNSHINE SUPERFROG (LP, white label, mono)	£100
67	Island ILPS 9044	SUNSHINE SUPERFROG (LP, white label, stereo)	£125
68	Island ILPS 9082	OUT OF THE FRYING PAN (LP, pink label, orange/black circle, laminated sleeve)	£75

(see also Keef Hartley Band, Miller Anderson, Fair Weather, Grease Band)

WYNDRUSH
72   Wealden WS 116   **LET IT SHINE** (LP)..**£300**

PETER WYNGARDE
70   RCA Victor RCA 1967   **La Ronde De L'Amour/The Way I Cry Over You** **£30**
70   RCA Victor PW 1   **Commits Rape/The Way I Cry Over You** (LP sampler, promo only)...................**£45**
70   RCA Victor SF 8087   **PETER WYNGARDE** (LP, gatefold sleeve)...**£50**
(see also Tyrannosaurus Rex)

SANDY WYNNS
65   Fontana TF 550   **Touch Of Venus/Lovers' Quarrel** **£300**

MARK WYNTER
61   Decca LK 4409   **THE WARMTH OF WYNTER** (LP) **£25**
65   Ace Of Clubs ACL 1141 **MARK WYNTER** (LP)..**£15**
(see also Joe Brown & Mark Wynter)

X
80   Slash Records UK SR-104   **LOS ANGELES** (LP, with insert) **£18**
81   Slash/Rough Trade SR 107 **WILD GIFT** (LP) **£15**

NATHALIE XAVIER
81   People Unite PU NAT 1   **Atomic Energy/Set Me Free** (12") **£40**

X-CELLS
81   Snotty Snail NEL COL 4   **Freedom Man/SCHIZOID: Nowhere To Go** (p/s)..................................**£20**

X-CERTS
78   Zama   **Feeling The Groove** (p/s) **£15**

XCLUSIV
82   Le Maitre KA 100 12   **Fools Are Friendly/Insrumental** (12") **£50**
82   Le Maitre KA 100   **Fools Are Friendly/Insrumental** (p/s)...**£30**
82   Le Maitre KA 101   **Cest La Vie/Instrumental** **£20**

X-COLLECTOR
83   So So SOSO 027   **T.V. Set/Christine** **£25**

X-DREAM
98   Blue Room BRO66LP   **RADIO** (2-LP) **£18**

X-DREAMYSTS
78   Good Vibrations GOT 5   **Right Way Home/Dance Away Love** (p/s)..**£15**
80   Polydor   **XDREAMYSTS** (LP) **£25**

X-E-CUTORS
79   Rok ROK 13/14   **Too Far To Look Inside My Head/X-FILMS: After My Blood** (die-cut co. sleeve) **£15**

XERO
83   Brickyard XERO 1   **Oh Baby/Hold On** (2-track issue, p/s, Moon Williams on vocals)...................**£15**
83   Brickyard XERO 1T   **Oh Baby/Hold On/Lone Wolf** (12", plain card sleeve with sticker, withdrawn) **£15**
(see also Bruce Dickinson, Iron Maiden)

X-FILMS
79   Rok ROK XIII/XIV   **After My Blood/X-E-CUTORS: Too Far To Look Inside My Head** (die-cut co. sleeve)........**£15**

XILES
64   Xiles 80-XIL-1   **THE XILES** (EP, home-made p/s)...**£40**
65   Xiles XIL 004   **Our Love Will Never End/The Only People In This World** **£25**

XIT
72   Rare Earth SREA 4002   **PLIGHT OF THE RED MAN** (LP)..**£15**

XL5
63   HMV POP 1148   **XL5** (Zero G)**/Caviare** **£20**
63   HMV 7EG 8802   **FIREBALL AND OTHER TITLES** (EP, 2 tracks by Don Spencer) **£50**

X-MAL DEUTSCHLAND
83   4AD CAD 302   **FETISCH** (LP, inner) **£20**
84   4AD CAD 197   **TOCSIN** (LP)..**£20**
87   Xile XMAL P1   **VIVA** (LP) **£20**

X-MEN (2)
91   Mutant 12 MUTATE 1   **Mutants** (By Wolverine)**/Mutants** (By Storm) (12") **£30**
91   Mutant 12 MUTATE 2   **Childs Play** (Mix 1)/(Mix 2)**/Read Your Mind** (12")..........................**£35**
91   Mutant 12 MUTATE 3   **Breakout/Phase 2** (12")...**£20**

X-O-DUS
79   Factory FAC 11   **English Black Boys/See Them A-Come** (12", dark-grey textured p/s, later light grey p/s) **£20**

XPERTS
80   XP001   **Race/Beat Me**...**£15**

XPOZEZ
81   Retaliation FIGHT 1   **SYSTEMS KILL EP** (photocopied sleeve with insert stating that if you want a proper   **£60**

sleeve to send the band a SAE) ....

X-PRESS
80	Express 1	Junked Up Judy/Stop Start (p/s)	£90

X PROJECT
92	X Project XPROJECT 1	Walking In The Air (Mix 1)/(Mix 2)/(Mix 3)/(Mix 4) (12", stamped white label) £40	
00	Congo Natty LION 5	Jah Sunshine/Dubplate Mix (12")	£15

XPUPILS
81	Skool SKREP 0001	MONTPELLIER NEWS EP	£50

X-RAY SPEX
77	Virgin VS 189	Oh Bondage, Up Yours/I Am A Cliche (p/s, with large 'A' to denote promo copy, blue labelsl, A-1 Matrix with 'original' mix) £75	
77	Virgin VS 189	Oh Bondage, Up Yours/I Am A Cliche (in p/s, A-1 matrix, 'original' mix) £60	
77	Virgin VS 189	Oh Bondage, Up Yours/I Am A Cliche (in p/s, A-2 matrix, 'second' mix)..........................£40	
77	Virgin VS 189-12	Oh Bondage, Up Yours/I Am A Cliche (12", company sleeve) £20	
78	EMI International INT 553	The Day The World Turned Day-Glo/Lama Poseur (p/s, 15,000 orange vinyl) £15	
78	EMI International INT 563	Identity/Let's Submerge (p/s, on pink vinyl) £15	
78	EMI International INS 3023	GERM FREE ADOLESCENTS (LP laminated sleeve, with lyric inner sleeve)..................£40	
91	Receiver RRLP 145	OBSESSED WITH YOU - THE EARLY YEARS (LP)...£30	
91	Receiver RRLP 140	LIVE AT THE ROXY CLUB (LP)..£18	
01	Earmark 640005	GERM FREE ADOLESCENTS (LP, reissue, clear vinyl) £15	
(see also Poly Styrene, Essential Logic)			

X-RAYS
59	London HLR 8805	Chinchilla/Out Of Control £35	
59	London HLR 8805	Chinchilla/Out Of Control (78) £20	

XS DISCHARGE
80	G. Marxist COMMINIQUE 3	Across The Border/Frustration (p/s) £15	
80	Groucho Marxist WH 3	Life's A Wank (p/s) £20	

XS ENERGY
78	World WRECK 1	Eighteen/Jenny's Alright/Horrorscope! (numbered foldover yellow or green p/s, stamped white labels)..£40	
79	Dead Good DEAD 3	Use You/Imaginary (p/s) £15	

XTC
77	Virgin VS 188	Science Friction/She's So Square (unreleased, in picture sleeve)...............................£3000	
77	Virgin VS 188	Science Friction/She's So Square (unreleased, no picture sleeve)...............................£150	
92	Virgin VS 1426	Wrapped In Grey (p/s, withdrawn, 2,000 only) £30	
92	Virgin VSCDT 1426	WRAPPED IN GREY (CD EP, withdrawn, 2,000 only) £40	
78	Virgin V 2095	WHITE MUSIC (LP, with black inner sleeve)..£20	
78	Virgin V 2108	GO 2 (LP, with insert, 1st 15,000 with bonus 12" EP: "Go +")................................£25	
79	Virgin V 2129	DRUMS AND WIRES (LP, with gatefold insert, 1st 15,000 with free 7": Chain Of Command/"Limelight" [VDJ 30])..£25	
80	Virgin V 2173	BLACK SEA (LP, with green paper outer sleeve & lyric insert)..................................£25	
82	Virgin V 2223	ENGLISH SETTLEMENT (2-LP) £30	
83	Virgin V 2264	MUMMER (LP)..£25	
84	Virgin V 2251	WAXWORKS (LP, with bonus LP, "Beeswax") £25	
84	Virgin V 2325	THE BIG EXPRESS (LP, circular sleeve & lyric inner) £25	
86	Virgin V 2399	SKYLARKING (LP)..£25	
89	Virgin V 2381	ORANGES & LEMONS (2-LP) £30	
92	Virgin V 2699	NONSUCH (2-LP)...£70	
99	Cooking Vinyl COOK 172	APPLE VENUS (LP, inner)..£100	
99	Cooking Vinyl COOK 188	HOMESPUN (LP) £40	
00	Cooking Vinyl COOK 194	WASP STAR (2-LP, gatefold, inners)..£60	
01	Idea IDEA 004	HOMEGROWN (2-LP) £80	
10	Ape House APELP044D	SKYLARKING (2-LP, reissue, hardbound book edition) £100	
10	Ape House APELP044D	SKYLARKING (2-LP, reissue) £40	
16	Ape House APELPD105	ENGLISH SETTLEMENT (2-LP, reissue, box set with CD and booklet)...................£45	
(see also Mr Partridge,, Dukes Of Stratosphere Colonel)			

XTRACT
83	Pax PAX 10	Blame It On The Youth/War Heroes/Iron Lady/Boys In Blue (p/s) £25	

XTRAVERTS
78	Spike SRTS SP 001	Blank Generation/A-Lad-In-Sane £90	
78	Rising Sun RS 1	Police State/PLASTIC PEOPLE: Demolition (p/s, multi-coloured vinyl) £60	
81	Xtraverts XTRA 001	Speed/1984 (white labels, 'photo' foldout poster p/s) £35	
81	Xtraverts XTRA 001	Speed/1984 (white labels, 'no photo' foldout poster p/s) £50	
97	Bin Liner RUBBISH LP 001	SO MUCH HATE (LP) £20	

XTREME
80	Xtreme IS/X/1045	The Tramp/The Latest Craze (For Alison) £40	

XX
10	Young Turks YT 041	Do You Mind?/Hot Like Fire/Teardrops/Blood Red Moon (die-cut p/s with 3 inner p/s, tour issue) £20	
09	Young Turks YT031LP	XX (LP, CD, poster) £25	
13	Young Turks YT104	XX (11 x 7", box set) £40	
10	Young Turks YT031LP	XX (LP, 12", etched, 3 prints, 500 only) £50	
13	Young Turks YT105	COEXIST (11 x 7", box set)...£35	

XY LOVE
84	Moonboule BOULE 1	Whistle And They'll Come/Cinnamon Girl...£20	

YABBY U/YABBY YOU/YABBY YOUTH

78	Prophets PHTS 2337	King Pharaoh Plague On The Land/Babylon Kingdom Fall (12")	£30
78	Grove Music GMDM 6	Jah Vengeance/Free Africa (12", as Vivian "Yabby U" Jackson with Trinity)	£50
79	Grove Music GMDM 18	Babylon A Fall/TONY TUFF - Falling Babylon (12")	£40
79	Grove Music GMDM 24	Lady Lady/Stop Your Quarelling (12", B-side with Tommy McCook)	£30
76	Lucky PD LPYU	RAM-A-DAM (LP, white sleeve with separate cover sheet)	£250
76	Prophets VJ 8124	KING TUBBY'SPROPHECY OF DUB (LP, green label, plain sleeve)	£300
77	Grove Music GMLP 001	DELIVER ME FROM MY ENEMIES (LP, credited to The Yabby You Vibration on sleeve)	£60
77	Grove Music GMLP 004	BEWARE DUB (LP)	£150
78	Nationwide PRO 001	CHANT DOWN BABYLON KINGDOM (LP)	£120
78	RAMA/EVE PD LP YU	RAM-A-DAM (LP, reissue of Lucky PD LPYU)	£200
80	Grove/Island ILPS 9615	JAH JAH WAY (LP)	£40
82	WLN WNLP001	YABBY YOU MEETS SLY 'N' ROBBIE (LP, with Tommy McCook)	£20
84	Greensleeves GREL 86	COLLECTION (LP)	£30
97	Blood & Fire BAFLP 021	JESUS DREAD 1972 - 1977 (4-LP)	£50

(see also Vivian Jackson & the Prophets)

YACHTS

80	Radar RAD 27	YACHTS WITHOUT RADAR (LP, die-cut sleeve)	£15

(see also Big In Japan)

YA HO WA 13

83	Psycho PSYCHO 2	GOLDEN SUNRISE (LP, 319 copies only, different coloured vinyl)	£60

(see also Seeds)

YAKS

65	Decca F 12115	Yakety Yak/Back In '57	£15

YAMASUKI

05	Finders Keepers FKR 002LP	LE MONDE FABULEUX DES (LP, insert)	£35

YAMASUKIS

71	Dandelion DAN 7004	Yamasuki/Aieada (p/s)	£15

YAMI BOLO

86	Greensleeves GREL 140	JAH JAH MADE THEM ALL (LP)	£25

YANA

56	HMV POP 252	Climb Up The Wall/If You Don't Love Me	£20

YANCEY

79	Octane WS 302	Standing Waiting/Woman (no p/s)	£20

JIMMY YANCEY

54	HMV 7EG 8062	JIMMY YANCEY (EP)	£20
55	HMV 7EG 8083	JIMMY YANCEY (EP)	£20
58	Vogue EPV 1203	YANCEY'S PIANO (EP)	£20
54	London AL 3525	JIMMY YANCEY - A LOST RECORDING DATE (10" LP)	£25
56	Vogue LDE 166	JAZZ IMMORTALS VOLUME 2 (10" LP)	£30
68	Atlantic 590 018	LOWDOWN DIRTY BLUES (LP)	£15

MAMA YANCEY/DON EWELL

57	Tempo LAP 7	MAMA YANCEY-DON EWELL (10" LP)	£30

ZALMAN YANOVSKY

67	Kama Sutra KAS 209	As Long As You're Here/Ereh Er'uoy Sa Gnol Sa (unreleased)	£0
71	Kama Sutra 2316 003	ALIVE AND WELL IN ARGENTINA (LP)	£18

(see also Mugwumps, Lovin' Spoonful)

YARD ACT

20	Zen FC FC 002S	The Trappers Pelts/Fixer Upper (p/s, numbered)	£30
20	Zen FC FC 002S	The Trappers Pelts/Fixer Upper (yellow print p/s, numbered)	£45
20	Zen FC FC 002S	The Trappers Pelts/Fixer Upper (red print p/s, numbered)	£45
21	Zen FC FC 004S	Peanuts/Dark Days (silver p/s)	£20
21	Zen FC FC 004S	Peanuts/Dark Days (peanut coloured p/s, peanut coloured vinyl, insert and sticker)	£35
21	Zen FC FC 004S	Peanuts/Dark Days (green p/s, peanut coloured vinyl, insert and sticker)	£40
21	Zen FC FC 004S	Peanuts/Dark Days (red p/s, peanut coloured vinyl, insert and sticker)	£40
21	Zen FC FC 004S	Peanuts/Dark Days (yellow p/s, peanut coloured vinyl, insert and sticker)	£40
22	Zen FC ZENFC009LP	THE OVERLOAD (yellow vinyl, with CD)	£20
22	Zen FC ZENFC007LP	THE OVERLOAD (green transparent 'ghetto lettuce' vinyl, 180gm)	£20
22	Zen FC ZENFC 005LP	THE OVERLOAD (Golden Rover tyreprint sleeve, limited to 100, signed)	£100
22	Zen FC ZENFC 006LP	THE OVERLOAD (red and black vinyl, Rough Trade exclusive)	£40
22	Zen FC ZENFC017LP	THE OVERDUB (as Yard Act Vs. Mad Professor) (Rough Trade Exclusive, purple vinyl)	£20

YARDBIRDS

64	Columbia DB 7283	I Wish You Would/A Certain Girl	£40
64	Columbia DB 7391	Good Morning Little Schoolgirl/I Ain't Got You	£40
66	Columbia DB 7848	Shapes Of Things/Still I'm Sad (mispressing)	£45
66	Columbia DB 7928	Over Under Sideways Down/Jeff's Boogie	£15
66	Columbia DB 8024	Happenings Ten Years Time Ago/Psycho Daisies (4-prong push out centre, two font	£35

		variants)	
67	Columbia DB 8165	**Little Games/Puzzles**	**£35**
64	Columbia SEG 8421	**FIVE YARDBIRDS** (EP, flipback p/s)	**£100**
67	Columbia SEG 8521	**OVER UNDER SIDEWAYS DOWN** (EP)	**£225**
64	Columbia 33SX 1677	**FIVE LIVE YARDBIRDS** (LP, 1st pressing, blue/black label, flipback sleeve)	**£250**
69	Columbia 33SX 1677	**FIVE LIVE YARDBIRDS** (LP, 2nd pressing, black/silver label, flipback sleeve)	**£25**
60s	Columbia TA SX 6063	**FIVE LIVE YARDBIRDS** (reel-to-reel tape)	**£20**
66	Columbia SCXC 28	**HAVING A RAVE UP WITH THE YARDBIRDS** (LP, export issue)	**£200**
66	Columbia SX 6063	**THE YARDBIRDS** (LP, 1st pressing, blue/black label, flipback sleeve, mono)	**£70**
66	Columbia SCX 6063	**THE YARDBIRDS** (LP, 1st pressing, blue/black label, flipback sleeve, stereo)	**£60**
69	Columbia S(C)X 6063	**THE YARDBIRDS** (LP, 2nd pressing, black/silver label, flipback sleeve)	**£25**
70	Columbia S(C)X 6063	**THE YARDBIRDS** (LP, 3rd pressing, black/silver label, non-flipback sleeve; misprinted without front cover illustration)	**£20**
70	Columbia S(C)X 6063	**THE YARDBIRDS** (LP, 3rd pressing, black/silver label, non-flipback sleeve)	**£20**
84	Charly BOX 104	**SHAPES OF THINGS** (LP, box set)	**£50**
91	EMI 038-7 96064,	**LITTLE GAMES** (LP, UK issue of 1967 UK album)	**£20**
14	Parlophone 825646335404	**LITTLE GAMES** (LP, RSD, multi-coloured vinyl)	**£25**
20	Demon DEMREC622	**THE YARDBIRDS - ROGER THE ENGINEER/1966 SESSIONS** (2LP, RSD. white vinyl, booklet, printed inners))	**£30**
'Roger The Engineer' acknowledged as title of the album			
21	Demon DEMRECBOX55	**THE YARDBIRDS** (ROGER THE ENGINEER) (2LP/7"/3CD, box set, booklet, black vinyl edition)	**£80**
21	Demon DEMRECBOX55IN	**THE YARDBIRDS** (ROGER THE ENGINEER) (2LP/7"/3CD, box set, booklet, red, white & blue vinyl edition, indie store exclusive)	**£90**
21	Demon DEMRECBOX55X	**THE YARDBIRDS** (ROGER THE ENGINEER) (2LP/7"/3CD, box set, booklet, black vinyl Amazon edition with signed print, 500 ltd)	**£100**
(see also Eric Clapton, Jeff Beck, Jimmy Page, Keith Relf, Reign, Sonny Boy Williamson & Yardbirds, Shoot)			

TOM YATES
67	CBS BPG 63094	**SECOND CITY SPIRITUAL** (LP, as Thomas Yates)	**£100**
72	President PTLS 1053	**LOVE COMES WELL ARMED** (LP, with booklet)	**£30**
77	Satril SATL 4007	**SONG OF THE SHIMMERING WAY** (LP, with insert)	**£20**

Y BLEW
67	Qualiton QSP 7001	**Maes 'B'/Beth Sy'n Dod Rhyngom Ni** (p/s)	**£80**

Y DILFOR
73	Westwood WSR 002	**Y DILFOR** (LP)	**£30**

YEAH YEAH YEAHS
07	Polydor 1741099	**IS IS EP** (2 x 7")	**£15**
03	Dress Up 0760611	**FEVER TO TELL** (LP picture disc with bonus track 'Poor Song')	**£60**
06	Polydor 985 295-6	**SHOW YOUR BONES** (LP)	**£15**
09	Polydor 2702576	**IT'S BLITZ!** (LP)	**£15**

YEARS
79	Tuff Going TGF 123	**TUFF GOING EP** (p/s, 500 only)	**£80**
(see also Chameleons, Sun And The Moon)			

SAM YEBOAH
88	Asona ARLP 016	**MEBA FIE** (LP)	**£15**

YEH YEH
85	Berlin BRS 001	**You Will Pay/7 Bells** (1st pressing in grey p/s)	**£15**

YELLO
86	Mercury MERDP 218	**Goldrush/She's Got A Gun** (live at Palladium N.Y.)**//I Love You/ Desire** (double pack, unreleased)	**£0**
81	Do It RIDE 4	**SOLID PLEASURE** (LP)	**£20**
81	Do It RIDE 8	**CLARO QUE SI!** (LP)	**£20**
83	Stiff SEEZ 48	**YOU GOTTA SAY YES TO ANOTHER EXCESS** (LP, with bonus white label 12": "I Love You"/"Lost Again"/"You Gotta Say To Another Excess [Remix]"Pumping Velvet")	**£15**
85	Vertigo 822 820-1	**STELLA** (LP)	**£20**
87	Mercury MERH 100	**ONE SECOND** (LP, with bonus 12" in p/s: "Call It Love (Trego Snare Version 2)"/"Santiago [live at Roxy New York]")	**£20**
87	Mercury MERH 100	**ONE SECOND** (LP)	**£18**
88	Mercury 836 778-1	**FLAG** (LP, HMV competition issue, 100 only)	**£40**
91	Mercury 848 791-1	**BABY** (LP)	**£50**
94	Mercury 522 496-1	**ZEBRA** (LP)	**£125**
95	Urban 527 603-1	**HANDS ON YELLO** (2-LP)	**£60**
97	Mercury 534 353-1	**POCKET UNIVERSE** (2-LP)	**£150**
(see also Associates)			

YELLOW
70	CBS 4869	**Roll It Down The Hill/Living A Lie**	**£50**

YELLOW BALLOON
67	Stateside SS 2008	**Yellow Balloon/Noollab Wolley**	**£20**
68	Stateside SS 2124	**Stained Glass Window/Can't Get Enough Of Your Love**	**£20**

YELLOW BELLOW ROOM BOOM
68	CBS 3205	**Seeing Things Green/Easy Life**	**£30**
(see also 10cc, Frabjoy & Runcible Spoon)			

YELLOW MAGIC ORCHESTRA
79	A&M AMLH68506	**YELLOW MAGIC ORCHESTRA** (LP)	**£20**
80	A&M AMSP 7502	**FIRECRACKER** (LP, clear plastic sleeve, yellow vinyl)	**£15**
81	A&M AMLH 64853	**BGM** (LP)	**£15**
82	Alfa ALF 85664	**SOLID STATE SURVIVOR** (LP)	**£15**

(see also Ruichi Sakamoto, Yukihiro Takahashi)
YELLOW PAGES
68   Page One POF 090   **Here Comes Jane/Ring-A-Ding** **£25**
(see also Mirage)
YELLOW 6
90s Enraptured RAPTLP 36   **OVERTONE** (2-LP, clear vinyl, numbered, handprinted sleeve, 300 only) **£20**
YELLOW TAXI
70   President PT 296   **Anna Laura Lee/Mary Ann** **£15**
YELLOWMAN
82   Greensleeves GREL 36   **MISTER YELLOWMAN** (LP)..**£15**
82   Arrival ALP 004   **FOR YOUR EYES ONLY** (LP, as Yellowman And Fathead) **£15**
82   Greensleeves GREL 44   **BAD BOY SKANKING** (LP, as Yellowman and Fathead)...**£18**
82   Greensleeves GREL 49   **THE YELLOW, THE PURPLE AND THE NANCY** (LP, with Fathead, Purpleman and Sister
                              Nancy)..**£15**
84   Pama PMLP 3215   **OPERATION RADICATION** (10" LP)..**£20**
84   Greensleeves GREL 57   **ZUNGGUZUNGGUGUZUNGGUNZENG!!!** (LP)...**£18**
84   Arrival ARLP 013   **UNDER ME FAT THING** (LP)...**£15**
YELLOWSTONE & VOICE
72   Regal Zono. SRZA 8511   **YELLOWSTONE & VOICE** (LP) **£20**
YEMM & YEMEN
66   Columbia DB 8022   **Black Is The Night/Do Blondes Really Have More Fun?** **£35**
YEOW
82   Patch YEOW 001   **Prepare Yourself/Energy** (12") **£25**
YES
69   Atlantic 584 280   **Sweetness/Something's Coming**..**£60**
69   Atlantic 584 298   **Looking Around/Everydays** (unreleased; demos may exist) **£175**
70   Atlantic 584 323   **Time And A Word/The Prophet** **£150**
70   Atlantic 2091 004   **Sweet Dreams/Dear Father** **£45**
71   Atlantic 2814 003   **I've Seen All Good People** (a) **Your Move/Starship Trooper** (a) **Life Seeker** (promo
                              only) **£75**
72   6-A1/-B1   **Siberian Khatru/And You And I** (white label promo) **£50**
77   Atlantic K 10985   **Going For The One/Parallels** (unreleased, copies may exist) **£60**
77   Atlantic K 10985T   **Going For The One** (Extended)**/Parallels** (12", unreleased, copies may exist) **£40**
70s Lyntone LYN 2535   **Interview/Five Songs** (flexidisc or vinyl, with 80-page Yes songbook) **£70**
70s Lyntone LYN 2535   **Interview/Five Songs** (flexidisc or vinyl)..**£35**
69   Atlantic 588 190   **YES** (LP, gatefold, red/plum label with lyric insert)......................................**£175**
70   Atlantic 2400 006   **TIME AND A WORD** (LP, red/plum label, with lyric insert) **£150**
71   Atlantic 2400 101   **THE YES ALBUM** (LP, red/plum label, gatefold sleeve).......................................**£150**
71   Atlantic 2401 019   **FRAGILE** (LP, red/plum label, gatefold sleeve with booklet) **£125**
72   Atlantic K 50012   **CLOSE TO THE EDGE** (LP, 1st pressing with A1/B1 matrix numbers, no "W" logo at 3
                              O'clock, textured sleeve inside and outside, green inner sleeve, darker with lyric
                              insert)...**£70**
73   Atlantic K 60045   **YESSONGS** (3-LP, wide spine, 'book opening' gatefold sleeve printed by 'Robor Ltd' , no
                              'W' logo on labels, outline 'Yes' on inner sleeves, all matrixes end in '1")...................**£25**
73   Atlantic K 80001   **TALES FROM TOPOGRAPHIC OCEANS** (2-LP)...**£25**
74   Atlantic K 50096   **RELAYER** (LP, gatefold sleeve) **£30**
77   Atlantic DSK 50379   **GOING FOR THE ONE** (LP, as 3 x 12" singles, promo only).....................................**£100**
77   Atlantic K 50379   **GOING FOR THE ONE** (LP)...**£18**
80   Atlantic K 50842   **CLASSIC YES** (LP, with bonus 7" "Roundabout"/"Your Move" [SAM 141]).........................**£15**
80   Atlantic K 50842   **CLASSIC YES** (LP, promo, with different sleeve) **£30**
15   Music On Vinyl MOVLP1364 **TALK** (2-LP, reissue, 180g, 4-page insert, ltd. ed.) **£100**
19   Rhino Records R1 590763 **YES 50 LIVE** (4-LP, blue, green, clear, gold vinyl - gold etched on one side, g/f) **£50**
(see also Jon Anderson, Hans Christian, Syn, Syndicats, Winston's Fumbs, Warriors, Federals, Peter Banks, Flash, Asia, Rick Wakeman, Steve Howe, Refugee,
Chris Squire)
Y KANT TORI READ
17   Atlantic 081227942410   **Y KANT TORI READ** (LP, UK vinyl issue of 1988 US LP, printed inner, orange vinyl, RSD) **£30**
(see also Tori Amos, Guns N'Roses)
JOHN YLVISAKER
68   Avantgarde AV 107   **COOL LIVIN'** (LP) **£75**
YOBS
77   NEMS NES 114   **Run Rudolph Run/The Worm Song** (p/s) **£15**
(see also Boys)
MAHARISHI MAHESH YOGI
67   Liberty LBS 83075E   **MAHARISHI MAHESH YOGI** (LP) **£25**
SUSUMU YOKOTA
99   Leaf BAY 9   **IMAGE 1983-1998** (LP)..**£15**
00   Leaf BAY 13   **SAKURA** (2-LP) **£25**
YO LA TENGO
95   Duophonic Super 45s DS   **Evanescent Psychic Pez Drop/STEREOLAB: Long Hair Of Death** (gig single, fluorescent
     45-10   yellow vinyl)...**£40**
87   What Goes On GOES ON13   **NEW WAVE HOT DOGS** (LP)..**£20**
87   Shigaku SHIGLP 2   **RIDE THE TIGER** (LP) **£30**
89   What Goes On GOES ON28   **PRESIDENT YO LA TENGO** (LP)...**£20**
YOLANDA
60   Triumph RGM 1007   **With This Kiss/Don't Tell Me Not To Love You**..**£40**
(see also Kenny Graham & His Satellites)

STEVE YORK'S CAMELO PARDALIS
73   Virgin V 2003   **MANOR LIVE** (LP) £20
(see also Elkie Brooks, Boz Scaggs, Lol Coxhill, Graham Bond, Mike Patto)
PETE YORK PERCUSSION BAND
73   Decca TXS 109   **PERCUSSION BAND** (LP, with Ian Paice, gatefold sleeve) £50
(see also Spencer Davis Group, Hardin & York, Deep Purple)
RUSTY YORK
58   Parlophone R 4398   **Peggy Sue/Shake 'Em Up Baby** (unissued, demos only) £1500
(see also Bonnie Lou & Rusty York)
YORK BROTHERS
54   Parlophone CMSP 5   **Why Don't You Open The Door?/You're My Every Dream Come True** (export issue).......£20
54   Parlophone CMSP 22   **Strange Town/Three O'Clock Blues** (export issue) £20
58   Parlophone GEP 8736   **COUNTRY AND WESTERN** (EP) £40
58   Parlophone GEP 8753   **COUNTRY AND WESTERN NO. 2** (EP) £40
THOM YORKE
08   XL XLT 335   **Eraser Rmxs 1** (12", 2000 only) £15
08   XL XLT 336   **Eraser Rmxs 2** (12", 2000 only) £15
08   XL XLT 337   **Eraser Rmxs 3** (12", 2000 only) £15
11   Text 10   **Ego/Mirror** (12", with Burial and Four Tet, black labels on both sides)...........£18
06   XL XLLP 200   **THE ERASER** (LP, 3D effect on embossed sleeve) £30
15   Landgrab GRAB 001   **TOMORROW'S MODERN BOXES** (LP, white vinyl in resealable printed bag)....£20
(see also Radiohead, Atoms for Peace)
YO3
94   General Production GENPX 22   **DEEP SLEEP** (12" EP) £30
94   General Production GPRLP 05   **BITTER SWEET** (2-LP) £30
YOU
80   Ram RAMYOU2   **THE NIGHT AND MUSIC** (EP) £20
YOU KNOW WHO GROUP
65   London HLR 9947   **Roses Are Red My Love/Playboy** £20
YOU BAND
84   Guardian GRC 84   **Jonathan Oracle/Disco Inferno** (p/s)...........................£20
CHRIS YOULDEN
73   Deram SML 1099   **NOWHERE ROAD** (LP, lyric insert)................................£60
74   Deram SML 1112   **CITY CHILD** (LP) £50
BILLY YOUNG/LIZZIE MILES
56   HMV 7EG 8178   **THE BLUES THEY SANG** (EP, with Jelly Roll Morton) £20
DARREN YOUNG
63   Parlophone R 4919   **My Tears Will Turn To Laughter/I've Just Fallen For Someone**......£20
(see also Johnny Gentle)
DESI YOUNG
70   Pressure Beat PB 5504   **News Flash/JOE GIBBS & DESTROYERS: News Flash - Version** £25
(see also Desi Roots)
FARON YOUNG
55   Capitol CL 14336   **Live Fast, Love Hard, Die Young/Forgive Me, Dear**...............£30
56   Capitol CL 14574   **If You Ain't Lovin'** (You Ain't Livin')**/All Right** £20
56   Capitol CL 14655   **I've Got 5 Dollars And It's Saturday Night/You're Still Mine** £30
59   Capitol CL 15050   **I Hear You Talkin'/Country Girl** £25
GEORGIE YOUNG & ROCKIN' BOCS
58   London HLU 8748   **Nine More Miles/The Sneak** £15
58   London HLU 8748   **Nine More Miles/The Sneak** (78) £15
YOUNG JESSIE
58   London HLE 8544   **Shuffle In The Gravel/Make Believe** £300
58   London HLE 8544   **Shuffle In The Gravel/Make Believe** (78) £50
JIMMY YOUNG
55   Decca F 10502   **Unchained Melody/Help Me Forget** £15
55   Decca F 10597   **The Man From Laramie/No Arms Can Ever Hold You** £15
55   Decca F 10640   **Someone On Your Mind/I Look At You** £15
JOE E. YOUNG & TONIKS
68   Toast TT 502   **Life Time Of Lovin'/Flower In My Hand** £20
69   Toast TT 514   **Good Day Sunshine/Life Time Of Lovin'** £20
68   Toast (S)TLP 1   **SOUL BUSTER!** (LP) £40
JOHNNIE YOUNG
67   Polydor 56199   **Every Christian/Epitath To Mr Simon Sir** £20
67   Polydor 56186   **Craise Finton Kirk/I Am The World** £20
JOHNNY YOUNG
67   Decca F 22548   **Step Back/Cara Lyn** (as Johnny Young & Kompany)...............£15
70   Blue Horizon 7-63852   **FAT MANDOLIN** (LP)..£90
KAREN YOUNG
68   Major Minor MM 584   **Too Much Of A Good Thing/You Better Sit Down** £50
69   M. Minor MMLP/SMLP 66   **SINGS NOBODY'S CHILD AND 13 OTHER GREAT SONGS** (LP)......£20

KATHY YOUNG & INNOCENTS
61	Top Rank JAR 534	A Thousand Stars/Eddie My Darling	£40
61	Top Rank JAR 554	Happy Birthday Blues/Someone To Love	£30

(see also Innocents)

K.G. YOUNG
69	CBS 4302	Spider/Spider Woogie 9th Movement	£30

LEON YOUNG STRINGS
64	Pye 7N 15646	This Boy/Glad All Over	£40

LESTER YOUNG (QUINTET)
53	Mercury MG 25015	KANSAS CITY 7/THE LESTER YOUNG QUARTET (LP, 1 side each)	£30
55	Felsted EDL 87014	BATTLE OF THE SAXES (10" LP)	£35
55	Columbia Clef 33C 9001	LESTER YOUNG WITH THE OSCAR PETERSON TRIO (10" LP)	£40
56	Columbia Clef 33C 9015	LESTER YOUNG (10" LP)	£40
56	Columbia Clef 33CX 10031	THE PRESIDENT, LESTER YOUNG (LP)	£40
56	Columbia Clef 33CX 10054	THE JAZZ GIANTS '56 (LP)	£40
57	Columbia Clef 33CX 10070	PRES (LP)	£40
58	London Jazz LTZ-C 15132	BLUE LESTER (LP)	£40
59	HMV CLP 1302	PRES AND TEDDY (LP, with Teddy Wilson)	£25

(see also Count Basie, Coleman Hawkins & Lester Young)

LLOYD YOUNG
72	Bullet BU 500	Bread And Butter/SHALIMAR ALLSTARS: Version	£15
72	Green Door GD 4037	Shalimar Special/G. MAHTANI ALLSTARS: Version	£25
72	Techniques TE 917	High Explosion/ANSELL COLLINS: Version	£25

(see also Carey & Lloyd)

YOUNG LOVE
80	Flair FLA 001	Doing It The English Way/Easy To Do It (p/s)	£40

YOUNG MARBLE GIANTS
81	Rough Trade RT 059	TESTCARD (EP)	£20
80	Rough Trade ROUGH 8	COLOSSAL YOUTH (LP)	£50
83	Rough Trade ROUGH 57	NIPPED IN THE BUD (LP, compilation LP with The Gist and Weekend but features 9 Young Marble Giants tracks)	£20
84	Rough Trade ROUGHL8	COLOSSAL YOUTH (LP, reissue)	£15
07	Domino REWIGLP 32	COLOSSAL YOUTH (LP, reissue)	£18

YOUNG MC
88	4th & Broadway BRW 120	Know How (Vocal)/The Fastest Rhyme - My Name Is Young (Vocal) (p/s)	£50
88	4t4th & Broadway/Delicious Vinyl 12 BRW 120	KNOW HOW (12", EP)	£20

MIGHTY JOE YOUNG
69	Parlophone 5794	Why Don't You Follow Me/By My Side	£25
72	Delmark DS 629	BLUES WITH A TOUCH OF SOUL (LP, blue label)	£22

NEIL YOUNG
69	Reprise RS 23405	The Loner/Everybody Knows This Is Nowhere	£25
70	Reprise RS 20861	Oh Lonesome Me (Long Version)/Sugar Mountain	£30
70	Reprise RS 20958	Only Love Can Break Your Heart/Birds	£15
73	Reprise SAM 15	Don't Be Denied/Love In Mind/Last Dance (p/s, 1-sided, promo only sampler for "Time Fades Away" LP)	£30
74	Reprise K 14350	Southern Man/Till The Morning Comes/After The Goldrush/Heart Of Gold (special sleeve)	£20
74	Reprise K 14360	Walk On/For The Turnstiles	£20
69	Reprise RSLP 6317	NEIL YOUNG (LP, with name on front of sleeve)	£80
69	Reprise RSLP 6317	NEIL YOUNG (LP, without name on front of sleeve)	£100
69	Reprise RSLP 6349	EVERYBODY KNOWS THIS IS NOWHERE (LP)	£100
70	Reprise RSLP 6383	AFTER THE GOLDRUSH (LP, gatefold sleeve with lyric insert)	£60
71	Reprise K 44059	NEIL YOUNG (LP, reissue)	£20
71	Reprise K 44073	EVERYBODY KNOWS THIS IS NOWHERE (LP, reissue)	£20
71	Reprise K 44088	AFTER THE GOLDRUSH (LP, reissue, gatefold sleeve with lyric insert)	£25
72	Reprise K 54005	HARVEST (LP, thick cardboard gatefold sleeve with insert)	£60
72	Reprise K 64015	JOURNEY THROUGH THE PAST (2-LP, soundtrack, fold-out sleeve & inners)	£40
73	Reprise K 54010	TIME FADES AWAY (LP, with lyric insert)	£40
74	Reprise K 54014	ON THE BEACH (LP, with inner sleeve)	£70
75	Reprise K 54040	TONIGHT'S THE NIGHT (LP, gatefold sleeve with inner sleeve & insert)	£25
75	Reprise K 54057	ZUMA (LP, with inner sleeve & lyric insert)	£35
77	Reprise K 54088	AMERICAN STARS AND BARS (LP, with inner sleeve)	£18
77	Reprise K 64037	DECADE (3-LP)	£40
78	Reprise K 54099	COMES A TIME (LP)	£18
79	Reprise K 54105	RUST NEVER SLEEPS (LP, with inner sleeve & lyric insert)	£20
79	Reprise K 64041	LIVE RUST (2-LP, with inner sleeves)	£30
80	Reprise K 54109	HAWKS & DOVES (LP, with inner sleeve)	£15
82	Geffen GEF 25019	TRANS (LP, inner)	£15
85	Geffen GEF 26377	OLD WAYS (LP, inner sleeve)	£15
89	Reprise WX257	FREEDOM (LP)	£18
90	Geffen WX 374	RAGGED GLORY (LP, inner, with Crazy Horse)	£50
92	Reprise 9362450571	HARVEST MOON (LP)	£80
92	Reprise 7599 26671-1	WELD (2-LP with Crazy Horse)	£60
93	Geffen GEF24452	LUCKY THIRTEEN (LP)	£80
93	Reprise 9362-45310-1	UNPLUGGED (LP)	£100
94	Reprise 9362-45749-1	SLEEPS WITH ANGELS (2-LP, with Crazy Horse)	£100

MINT VALUE £

95	Reprise 9362 45934-1	MIRROR BALL (2-LP, with PEARL JAM)	£80
96	Vapor 9362-46171-1	DEAD MAN (2-LP)	£150
96	Reprise 9362461711	BROKEN ARROW (2-LP, with Crazy Horse)	£100
97	Reprise 9362466521	YEAR OF THE HORSE (2-LP, with Crazy Horse)	£100
00	Reprise 9362480361	ROAD ROCK (2-LP, insert)	£100
00	Reprise 9362473051	SILVER & GOLD (LP)	£20
02	Vapor 9362481111	ARE YOU PASSIONATE? (2-LP)	£50
03	Vapor 486992	GREENDALE (3-LP box set with green 7", booklet)	£175
06	Reprise 444991	LIVE AT THE FILLMORE EAST (LP, 180gm vinyl)	£20
12	Reprise 9362457491	PSYCHEDELIC PILL (3-LP, as Neil Young and Crazy Horse)	£30
15	Reprise 9362492611	BLUENOTE CAFE (4-LP)	£40
16	Reprise 9362492045	OFFICIAL RELEASE SERIES 8.5-13 (5-LP box set)	£50

(see also Buffalo Springfield, Crosby Stills Nash & Young, Stills-Young Band, Crazy Horse)

ROGER YOUNG

| 66 | Columbia DB 7869 | Sweet, Sweet Morning/Whatcha Gonna Give Me? | £60 |
| 66 | Columbia DB 8092 | No Address/It's Been Nice | £250 |

ROY YOUNG (BAND)

59	Fontana H 200	Just Keep It Up/Big Fat Mama	£25
59	Fontana H 215	Hey Little Girl/Just Ask Your Heart	£20
59	Fontana H 215	Hey Little Girl/Just Ask Your Heart (78)	£15
60	Fontana H 237	I Hardly Know Me/Gilee	£20
60	Fontana H 247	Taboo/I'm In Love	£15
70	RCA SF 8161	ROY YOUNG BAND (LP)	£20

SUSANNAH YOUNG

| 67 | Philips BL 7728 | SWEETEST SOUNDS (LP) | £15 |

TOMMIE YOUNG

| 74 | Contempo CLP 501 | DO YOU STILL FEEL THE SAME WAY (LP) | £50 |

VICKI YOUNG

55	Capitol CL 14228	Hearts Of Stone/Tweedlee Dee (triangular centre)	£40
55	Capitol CL 14281	Live Fast, Love Hard, Die Young/Zoom, Zoom, Zoom(triangular centre)	£25
56	Capitol EAP1 593	VICKI YOUNG (EP)	£35

YOUNG AL CAPONE

| 71 | Green Door GD 4012 | Girl Called Clover/Girl Called Clover (Version) | £25 |

YOUNG BLOOD

68	Pye 7N 17495	Green Light/Don't Leave Me In The Dark	£25
68	Pye 7N 17588	Just How Loud/Masquerade	£20
68	Pye 7N 17627	Bang-Shang-A-Lang/I Can't Stop	£20
69	Pye 7N 17696	The Continuing Story Of Bungalow Bill/I Will	£20

(see also Cozy Powell, Ace Kefford Stand, Big Bertha)

YOUNG BLOOD

| 84 | Landslide LAND 1 | FIRST BLOOD (12" EP, p/s) | £18 |

YOUNGBLOODS

| 69 | RCA SF 8026 | ELEPHANT MOUNTAIN (LP) | £22 |
| 70 | Warner Bros WS 1878 | ROCK FESTIVAL (LP) | £15 |

YOUNG BROTHERS

| 68 | MCA MU 1042 | I've Always Wanted Love/Mirror Mirror | £15 |

YOUNG DISCIPLES

| 91 | Talkin Loud 510097 | ROAD TO FREEDOM (LP, inner) | £15 |

YOUNG EARTH

| 70 | Priory PR3 | Silent Eyes/Death To Eliza | £50 |

YOUNGFOLK

| 68 | President PT 136 | Lonely Girl/Joey | £20 |

YOUNG FOLK

| 72 | Midas MR 001 | RIBBLE VALLEY DREAM (LP) | £50 |

YOUNG FREDDIE

| 70 | Camel CA 38 | Drink And Gamble/LENNOX BROWN & HUE ROY: King Of The Road | £25 |

(see also Freddie McGregor)

YOUNG GENTS

| 67 | M&G 01 | Lift Up Your Body/Evening Star | £30 |

YOUNG-HOLT TRIO

| 67 | Coral Q 72489 | Wack Wack/This Little Light Of Mine | £15 |
| 67 | Coral Q 72489 | Wack Wack/This Little Light Of Mine (DJ copy) | £40 |

YOUNG-HOLT UNLIMITED

| 73 | Contempo COLP-R 1004 | PLAYS SUPERFLY (LP) | £15 |
| 69 | MCA MUP(S) 368 | SOULFUL STRUT (LP) | £20 |

(see also Ramsey Lewis Trio)

YOUNG IDEA

| 68 | Music For Pleasure MFP 1225 | WITH A LITTLE HELP FROM MY FRIENDS (LP) | £20 |

YOUNG LIONS

| 78 | Discovery D-DISC 001 | Take Five (12", p/s) | £30 |

YOUNG RASCALS

| 65 | Atlantic AT 4059 | I Ain't Gonna Eat My Heart Out Anymore/Slow Down | £15 |

MINT VALUE £

66	Atlantic AT 4082	**Good Lovin'/Mustang Sally**	£15
66	Atlantic 584 024	**You Better Run/Love Is A Beautiful Thing**	£18
66	Atlantic 584 050	**Come On Up/What Is The Reason**	£18
66	Atlantic 584 067	**Too Many Fish In The Sea/No Love To Give**	£15
67	Atlantic 584 081	**I've Been Lonely Too Long/If You Knew**	£15
66	Atlantic 587/588012	**THE YOUNG RASCALS** (LP, mono, stereo)	£30
67	Atlantic 587/588 060	**COLLECTIONS** (LP)	£20
67	Atlantic 587/588 074	**GROOVIN'** (LP)	£25

(see also Rascals, Joey Dee & Starlighters)

RICHARD YOUNGS
88	No Fans NFR01	**ADVENT** (LP)	£25
94	Chocolate Monk CHOC 052	**MOTORWAY** (cassette album)	£20

YOUNG SISTERS
62	London HLU 9610	**Casanova Brown/My Guy**	£25

YOUNG SOULS
69	Amalgamated AMG 844	**Why Did You Leave/Main A Wail**	£100

YOUNG TRADITION
68	Transatlantic TRAEP 164	**CHICKEN ON A RAFT** (EP)	£25
66	Transatlantic TRA 142	**THE YOUNG TRADITION** (LP)	£22
67	Transatlantic TRA 155	**SO CHEERFULLY ROUND** (LP)	£18
68	Transatlantic TRA 172	**GALLERIES** (LP, with Dave Swarbrick)	£18

(see also Dave Swarbrick, Peter Bellamy)

YOUR OLD DROOG
17	Daupe! DM SP 021	**LOOSEYS** (12", p/s, 200 only)	£35
17	Daupe! DM SP 021	**LOOSEYS** (12", p/s, smoked vinyl, 100 only)	£40
17	Daupe! DM SP 021	**LOOSEYS** (12", p/s, with obi strip, 20 only)	£100
14	Chopped Herring CHDR00GLP01	**YOUR OLD DROOG** (2-LP)	£35
14	Chopped Herring CHDR00GLP01	**YOUR OLD DROOG** (2-LP, clear, red or yellow vinyl, 75 copies of each)	£50

JOHNNY YOUTH
69	Grape GR 3002	**Darling It Won't/HIP CITY BOYS: Moon Train**	£50

YOUTH (1)
66	Polydor 56121	**As Long As There Is Your Love/Your One And Only Love**	£20

YOUTH (2)
69	Deram DM 226	**Meadow Of My Love/Love Me Or Leave Me**	£20

YOU'VE GOT FOETUS ON YOUR BREATH
81	Self Imm. WOMB OYBL-1	**DEAF** (LP)	£25
81	Self Imm. WOMB OYBL-2	**ACHE** (LP)	£25

(see also Foetus etc., Philip & His Foetus Vibrations, Scraping Foetus Off The Wheel)

LES YPER SOUND
67	Fontana TF 880	**Too Fortiche/Psyche Rock**	£60

(see also Pierre Henry)

YR HWNTWS
82	Loco LOCO 1001	**YR HWNTWS** (LP)	£80

Y TRWYNAU COCH
70s	Record. Sqwar RSROC 1	**WASTOD AR Y TU FAS** (BANANAS) (EP, around 1,000 only)	£50
78	Record. Sqwar RSROC 002	**Merched Dan 15** (I Often Think Of Girls Under 15)/**Byw Ar Arian Fy Rhieni**/ **Mynd I'r Capel Mewn Levis/Ail Ddechre** (around 1,000 only)	£50
80	Record. Coch RCTC 3	**Methu Dawnsio/CRACH: Putain Rhad** (multifold p/s)	£20
81	Sain SAIN 92	**Paqn Fo Cyrff Yn Cwrdd/Beth Am Take Away/Camera Yn Y Gornel** (p/s)	£50
80s	Record. Coch OCHR 2198	**RHEDEG RHAG Y TORPIDOS** (LP)	£30

TIMI YURO
61	London HLG 9403	**Hurt/I Apologise**	£20
62	London HLG 9484	**Smile/I Believe** (B-side with Johnnie Ray)	£15
62	Liberty LIB 55469	**What's A-Matter Baby** (Is It Hurting You)/**Thirteenth Hour**	£30
63	Liberty LIB 55519	**The Love Of A Boy/I Ain't Gonna Cry No More**	£30
63	Liberty LIB 55519	**The Love Of A Boy/I Ain't Gonna Cry No More** (DJ Copy)	£60
64	Mercury MF 826	**If/I'm Afraid The Masquerade Is Over**	£20
65	Mercury MF 859	**Get Out Of My Life/Can't Stop Running Away**	£60
68	Liberty LBF 15092	**Something Bad On My Mind/Wrong**	£30
68	Liberty LIB 15142	**I Must Have Been Out Of My Mind/Interlude**	£25
68	Liberty LIB 15182	**It'll Never Be Over For Me/As Long As There Is You**	£1500
65	Liberty LEP 2214	**TIMI YURO: SOUL!** (EP)	£30
66	Liberty LEP 2252	**MAKE THE WORLD GO AWAY** (EP)	£25
62	London HA-G 2415	**TIMI YURO** (LP)	£75
62	Liberty LBY 1042	**SOUL!** (LP)	£35
63	Liberty LBY 1154	**WHAT'S A-MATTER BABY** (LP, mono)	£25
63	Liberty SLBY 1154	**WHAT'S A-MATTER BABY** (LP, stereo)	£30
64	Liberty LBY 1192	**MAKE THE WORLD GO AWAY** (LP)	£25
64	Mercury 20032 MCL	**THE AMAZING TIMI YURO** (LP)	£22
65	Liberty LBY 1247	**HURT** (LP)	£30
66	Liberty LBY 1275	**LET ME CALL YOU SWEETHEART** (LP, mono)	£20
66	Liberty SLBY 1275	**LET ME CALL YOU SWEETHEART** (LP, stereo)	£30
66	Liberty (S)LBY 1290	**THE BEST OF TIMI YURO** (LP)	£20
68	Liberty LBL/LBS 83115	**GREAT PERFORMANCES** (LP)	£15

MINT VALUE £

68	Liberty LBL/LBS 83128	TIMI IN THE BEGINNING (LP)	£20
69	Liberty LBS 83198E	SOMETHING BAD ON MY MIND (LP)	£50
69	Mercury SMWL 21010	TALENTED TIMI (LP)	£15

(see also Johnnie Ray)

ZABANDIS
82	True Vision TRV 001	Jah Jah Say/Things Are Getting Harder (12")	£200

JOHN ZACHERLE
58	London HLU 8599	Dinner With Drac Part 1/Dinner With Drac - Conclusion	£20

(see also Dave Appell & Applejacks)

ZAGADA
79	AJ B ZA001	THE ZAGADA AND FANS EP (12", p/s)	£30
79	AJB AJB 1004	SPECIAL (LP)	£80

ZAGER & EVANS
69	RCA SF 8056	2525 (LP)	£20

ZAKARRIAS
71	Deram SML 1091	ZAKARRIAS (LP, white/red label, small logo)	£1000

IWO ZALUSKI
73	Hobbiton HOB 103	LEGEND OF THE SAFFRON SORCERESS (EP, insert)	£150
69	John Hassell Records HAS LP 2026	BRANDYBUCK AND THE ELECTRIC ZEON BAND (LP, as Iwo Zaluski and the Cardinal Newman School)	£500
69	John Hassell Records HAS LP MAS 701	THE WORLD OF MY DREAMS (LP)	£100
74	Hobbiton HOB 104	THE REMARKABLE EARTH MAKING MACHINE (LP)	£150
75	Hobbiton HOB 105	TALES OF TOLKIEN HIGHLIGHTS (LP)	£150
77	Hobbiton HOB 107	A LIFE IN THE WEEK OF A DAY (LP)	£150

TOMMY ZANG
62	Polydor NH 66957	Hey, Good Lookin'/With Love (For You)	£20

FRANK ZAPPA/MOTHERS OF INVENTION
SINGLES
66	Verve VS 545	It Can't Happen Here/How Could I Be Such A Fool (as Mothers Of Invention)	£60
67	Verve VS 557	Big Leg Emma/Why Don't You Do Me Right (as Mothers Of Invention)	£60
71	Reprise K 14100	Tears Began To Fall/Junier Mintz Boogie (as Mothers Of Invention)	£40
71	United Artists UP 35319	What Will This Evening Bring Me This Morning?/Daddy, Daddy, Daddy	£35
80	CBS 7950	Joe's Garage/BOB DYLAN: When You Gonna Wake Up (mispressing)	£30
81	CBS A 12-1622	You Are What You Is/Pink Napkins/Harder Than Your Husband/Soup 'N Old Clothes (12", picture disc)	£15

ALBUMS : VERVE ORIGINALS
66	Verve VLP 9154	FREAK OUT! (as Mothers Of Invention, mono, single disc)	£150
66	Verve SVLP 9154	FREAK OUT! (as Mothers Of Invention, stereo, single disc)	£100
67	Verve VLP 9174	ABSOLUTELY FREE (as Mothers Of Invention, mono)	£150
67	Verve SVLP 9174	ABSOLUTELY FREE (as Mothers Of Invention, stereo)	£100
68	Verve VLP 9199	WE'RE ONLY IN IT FOR THE MONEY (as Mothers Of Invention, gatefold sleeve, mono)	£150
68	Verve SVLP 9199	WE'RE ONLY IN IT FOR THE MONEY (as Mothers Of Invention, gatefold sleeve, stereo)	£100
68	Verve VLP 9223	LUMPY GRAVY (gatefold sleeve, mono)	£150
68	Verve SVLP 9223	LUMPY GRAVY (gatefold sleeve, stereo)	£100
69	Verve VLP 9237	CRUISING WITH RUBEN AND THE JETS (as Mothers Of Invention, mono)	£150
69	Verve SVLP 9237	CRUISING WITH RUBEN AND THE JETS (as Mothers Of Invention, stereo)	£100
69	Verve VLP 9239	MOTHERMANIA - THE BEST OF THE MOTHERS (as Mothers Of Invention, mono)	£70
69	Verve SVLP 9239	MOTHERMANIA - THE BEST OF THE MOTHERS (as Mothers Of Invention, stereo)	£30

ALBUMS : VERVE REISSUES
71	Verve/Polydor 2683 004	FREAK OUT (2-LP)	£30
72	Verve/Polydor 2317 034	WE'RE ONLY IN IT FOR THE MONEY (gatefold sleeve)	£30
72	Verve/Polydor 2317 035	ABSOLUTELY FREE (gatefold sleeve)	£25
72	Verve/Polydor 2317 046	LUMPY GRAVY (gatefold sleeve)	£30
72	Verve/Polydor 2317 047	MOTHERMANIA - THE BEST OF THE MOTHERS	£25
73	Verve/Polydor 2352 017	MOTHERMANIA - THE BEST OF THE MOTHERS (2nd reissue)	£25
73	Verve/Polydor 2317 069	CRUISIN' WITH RUBEN AND THE JETS (gatefold sleeve)	£25
75	Verve/Polydor 2352 057	ROCK FLASHBACKS (LP)	£15

ALBUMS : ORIGINAL REPRISE/WARNER/DISCREET ISSUES
70	Reprise RSLP 6356	HOT RATS (1st pressing, pink, gold & green 'riverboat' label, gatefold sleeve)	£75
70	Reprise RSLP 6356	HOT RATS (2nd pressing, tan 'riverboat' label, gatefold sleeve)	£35
70	Reprise RSLP 6370	BURNT WEENY SANDWICH (as Mothers Of Invention, 1st pressing, pink, gold & green 'riverboat' label, gatefold sleeve)	£80
70	Reprise RSLP 2028	WEASELS RIPPED MY FLESH (as Mothers Of Invention, tan 'riverboat' label)	£40
70	Reprise RSLP 2030	CHUNGA'S REVENGE (tan 'riverboat' label, green gatefold sleeve)	£45
70	Reprise RSLP 2030	CHUNGA'S REVENGE (tan 'riverboat' label, red gatefold sleeve)	£20
71	Reprise K 44150	FILLMORE EAST, JUNE 1971 (as Mothers Of Invention)	£15

(First pressings issued without Warner Bros logo on label or sleeve; copies with Warners logos are post-1975 pressings worth £6-£8 each.)

71	Reprise K 44078	**HOT RATS** (tan 'riverboat' label, gatefold sleeve)	£25
71	Reprise K 44083	**BURNT WEENY SANDWICH** (tan 'riverboat' label)	£20
71	Reprise K 44019	**WEASELS RIPPED MY FLESH** (tan 'riverboat' label)	£15
71	Reprise K 44020	**CHUNGA'S REVENGE** (tan 'riverboat' label, gatefold sleeve)	£15

(Issued without Warner Bros logo on label or sleeve; post-1975 pressings with logos are worth £6-£8 each.)

72	Reprise K 44179	**JUST ANOTHER BAND FROM L.A.** (as Mothers Of Invention, gatefold sleeve)	£20
72	Reprise K 44203	**WAKA/JAWAKA** (HOT RATS)	£15
72	Reprise K 44209	**THE GRAND WAZOO** (gatefold sleeve)	£20
73	DiscReet K 41000	**OVER-NITE SENSATION** (as Mothers Of Invention, gatefold sleeve)	£15
74	DiscReet K 69201	**ROXY AND ELSEWHERE** (2-LP, as Mothers Of Invention, gatefold sleeve)	£15
74	DiscReet K 59201	**APOSTROPHE** (') (no lyric insert)	£15

(First pressings issued without Warner Bros logo on label or sleeve; copies with Warners logos are post-1975 pressings worth £6-£8 each.)

75	DiscReet K 59207	**ONE SIZE FITS ALL** (as Mothers Of Invention, gatefold sleeve)	£15

(First pressings issued without Warner Bros logo on label or sleeve; copies with Warners logos are post-1975 pressings worth £8-£12 each.)

76	Warner Bros K 56298	**ZOOT ALLURES** (LP)	£15
77	DiscReet K 69204	**ZAPPA IN NEW YORK** (LIVE) (2-LP, with & without reference to Punky's Whips)	£20
77	DiscReet K 69204	**ZAPPA IN NEW YORK** (LIVE) (2-LP, "Punky's Whips" listed on sleeve but not on label or LP)	£20
77	DiscReet K 69204	**ZAPPA IN NEW YORK** (LIVE) (2-LP, 1st pressing plays "Punky's Whips", listed on sleeve and on label)	£150
78	DiscReet K 59210	**STUDIO TAN**	£15
78	DiscReet K 59211	**SLEEP DIRT**	£15
78	DiscReet K 59212	**ORCHESTRAL FAVORITES**	£15

ALBUMS : CBS/EMI/OTHER LABELS

69	Transatlantic TRA 197	**UNCLE MEAT** (2-LP, as Mothers Of Invention)	£80
71	United Artists UDF 50003	**200 MOTELS** (2-LP, with booklet & poster, as Frank Zappa & Mothers Of Invention)	£40
79	CBS 88339	**SHEIK YERBOUTI** (2-LP, gatefold sleeve printed with lyrics)	£15
79	CBS 86101	**JOE'S GARAGE ACT 1** (gatefold sleeve, lyric insert)	£15
79	CBS 88475	**JOE'S GARAGE ACTS 2 & 3** (2-LP, gatefold sleeve, lyric insert)	£15
81	CBS 88560	**YOU ARE WHAT YOU IS** (2-LP, gatefold sleeve, lyric insert)	£15
81	CBS 88516	**TINSELTOWN REBELLION** (2-LP, gatefold sleeve with lyrics)	£15
81	CBS 66368	**SHUT UP 'N' PLAY YER GUITAR** (3-LP set, with inner sleeves)	£25
82	CBS 85804	**SHIP ARRIVING TOO LATE TO SAVE A DROWNING WITCH** (LP, with bonus 7" Shut Up 'N' Play Yer Guitar/"Variation On The C. Santana Secret" [XPS 147])	£20
84	EMI EL 2701531	**BOULEZ CONDUCTS ZAPPA: 'THE PERFECT STRANGER'**	£15
84	EMI EJ2702561	**FRANCESCO ZAPPA** (with inner sleeve)	£15
84	EMI 2402943	**THING-FISH** (3-LP, box set, with libretto)	£20
84	EMI EMC 3500	**THE MAN FROM UTOPIA**	£15
84	EMI FZAP1	**JOE'S GARAGE ACTS 1, 2 & 3** (3-LP, box set, inner sleeves only, with libretti)	£25
84	EMI E5 0021	**TINSELTOWN REBELLION** (2-LP, gatefold sleeve, printed with lyrics)	£15
84	EMI no cat. no.	**SHEIK YERBOUTI** (2-LP, gatefold sleeve, printed with lyrics)	£15
84	EMI no cat. no.	**SHUT UP 'N' PLAY YER GUITAR** (3-LP box set, with inner sleeves)	£25
84	EMI EN 2402343	**THEM OR US** (2-LP, gatefold sleeve, printed with lyrics)	£15
86	EMI EN 3521	**JAZZ FROM HELL**	£15
86	EMI EC 3507	**FRANK ZAPPA MEETS THE MOTHERS OF PREVENTION** (European version)	£15
95	Simply Vinyl SLVP 0024	**WEASELS RIPPED MY FLESH** (180gm vinyl)	£20
95	Simply Vinyl SLVP 0025	**BURNT WEENY SANDWICH** (gatefold sleeve, 180gm vinyl)	£20

ALBUMS : ZAPPA LABEL

84	Zappa Records ZAPPA 1	**FREAK OUT** (2-LP, gatefold sleeve, some in single sleeve £35)	£18
80s	Zappa Records ZAPPA 5	**LONDON SYMPHONY ORCHESTRA VOLUME II**	£15
88	Zappa Records ZAPPA 6	**GUITAR** (2-LP, gatefold sleeve)	£18
88	Zappa Records ZAPPA 7	**YOU CAN'T DO THAT ON STAGE ANY MORE SAMPLER** (2-LP, gatefold sleeve)	£15
90	Zappa Records ZAPPA 30	**THEM OR US** (2-LP, gatefold sleeve, printed with lyrics)	£15
90	Zappa Records ZAPPA 20	**JOE'S GARAGE ACTS 1, 2 & 3** (3-LP, box set, original sleeves, with libretti)	£30
91	Zappa Records ZAPPA 28	**SHEIK YERBOUTI** (2-LP, gatefold sleeve without lyrics)	£15
91	Zappa Records ZAPPA 35	**BURNT WEENY SANDWICH** (gatefold sleeve)	£15
91	Zappa Records ZAPPA 37	**ZAPPA IN NEW YORK** (LIVE) (2-LP, plays "Punky's Whips", listed on label, but not on sleeve)	£15
91	Zappa Records ZAPPA 42	**SHIP ARRIVING TOO LATE TO SAVE A DROWNING WITCH**	£15
92	Zappa Records ZAPPA 39	**ROXY AND ELSEWHERE** (2-LP, as Mothers Of Invention, gatefold lyric sleeve)	£20

(see also Flo & Eddie, Jeff Simmons, Wild Man Fischer, Captain Beefheart, John Lennon, Geronimo Black)

ZAP POW

76	Vulcan VULP 004	**NOW** (LP)	£15

ZARACK

99	All Tone AT 020	**Look Into My Eyes/My Eyes**	£45

LENA ZAVARONI

80	Galaxy GY 177	**Will he Kiss Me Tonight/Dream Come True** (no p/s)	£100
77	Galaxy GAL 6012	**PRESENTING LENA ZAVARONI** (LP)	£30
82	BBC REB 443	**HOLD TIGHT, IT'S LENA** (LP)	£40

ZEBEDEE

71	Decca F13144	**So Long Marianne/She Couldn't Make Gravy**	£30

ZEE

84	Harvest SHSP 24 0101 1	**IDENTITY** (LP, printed inner)	£25
19	The Strictly Limited Edition Vinyl Record Company TSLEVC3LP	**ZEE IDENTITY 2019** (LP, pink vinyl, limited to 100, signed by Dave Harris)	£150

(see also Rick Wright)

ZEEBRA
79	Jungle JR 7038S	Anytime/Sign Your Name/Lux Gud/Night (no p/s)	£25

ZEN
68	Philips BF 1746	Hair/Aquarius	£20

ZENITH
86	ZENITH 5001	Heavy Heavy Heart (p/s)	£75

SI ZENTNER ORCHESTRA
63	Liberty LBY 1164	RHYTHM PLUS BLUES (LP)	£15

ZEPHYR
70	Probe SPB 1006	ZEPHYR (LP)	£60

(see also Tommy Bolin)

ZEPHYRS
63	Decca F 11647	What's All That About/Oriental Dream	£40
64	Columbia DB 7199	I Can Tell/Sweet Little Baby	£50
64	Columbia DB 7324	A Little Bit Of Soap/No Message	£35
64	Columbia DB 7410	Wonder What I'm Gonna Do/Let Me Love You Baby	£35
65	Columbia DB 7481	She's Lost You/There's Something About You	£35
65	Columbia DB 7571	I Just Can't Take It/She Laughed	£35

EARL ZERO
78	Studio 16 WE 401	Rough And Tough/PRINCE JAZZBO: Suffer Must Live (12")	£30
79	Sufferers Height SUF004	Please Officer/AUGUSTUS PABLO: In Moonlight City (12")	£50
79	Greensleeves GRED 23	City Of The Wicked/Rightous Works (12")	£40
79	Student STU 007	IN THE RIGHT WAY (LP)	£80

ZERO LE CRECHE
84	Flicknife FLS 029	Last Year's Wife/Women Say (p/s)	£15
84	Flicknife FLST 029	Last Year's Wife/Women Say/Fall To Dust (p/s)	£25
85	Cherry Red 12 CHERRY 87	Falling/Beyond Westworld/Terminal Tracks (12", p/s)	£15

ZERO 7
00	Self released ZERO 7001	EP 1 (12")	£18
00	Ultimate Dilemma UDR 040	EP 2 (12", p/s)	£15
01	Ultimate Dilemma UDRLP	SIMPLE THINGS (2LP, gatefold, printed inners)	£80
04	Ultimate Dilemma 5050467 0987 1 8	WHEN IT FALLS (2LP)	£60
06	Ultimate Dilemma 5015011 2857 1 4	THE GARDEN (2LP, gatefold, printed inners)	£80
15	Warner Bros. 0825646132751	SIMPLE THINGS (2LP, reissue, 180gm vinyl, download card)	£20
21	New State Music NEW 9253LPC	SIMPLE THINGS (2LP, HMV 1921 Anniversary Edition, obi-strip, gatefold)	£40
22	New State Music NEW 9275LP	YEAH GHOST (2LP, gatefold, printed inners, reissue of 2009)	£20

ZERO TWENTY ONE
81	UK UK 201	Pop Song (p/s)	£100

ZEROS
77	Small Wonder SMALL 2	Hungry/Radio Fun	£20
79	Rok ROK XV/XVI	What's Wrong With A Pop Group/ACTION REPLAY: Decisions (die-cut co. sleeve)	£20

021
82	UK POP 0201	The Pop Song/Aversion! (p/s)	£40

MONICA ZETTERLUND
58	Columbia DB 4246	There's No You/Don't Be That Way	£15
59	Columbia SEG 8015	SWEDISH SWEET (EP)	£60
58	Columbia 33CSX 20	SWEDISH SENSATION (LP, export only)	£200
64	Philips BL 7647	MAKE MINE SWEDISH STYLE (LP)	£100

Z'EV
88	Coercion COERCIONLP 001	THE INVISIBLE MAN (LP)	£25

TUCKER ZIMMERMAN
69	Regal Zonophone RZ 3020	The Red Wind/Moondog	£25
69	Regal Zono. (S)LRZ 1010	TEN SONGS BY TUCKER ZIMMERMAN (LP)	£120
72	Village Thing VTS 13	TUCKER ZIMMERMANN (LP)	£70

PETER ZINOVIEFF
70	3M/Lyntone LYN 2443	A Lollipop For Papa (1-sided with book)	£50
70	3M/Lyntone LYN 2443	A Lollipop For Papa (1-sided without book)	£30

ZION TRAIN
99	Universal Egg WWLP030	LOVE REVOLUTIONARIES (2-LP)	£25

ZIOR
71	Nepentha 6129 002	Za Za Za Zilda/She's A Bad Bad Woman	£25
71	Nepentha 6129 003	Cat's Eyes/I Really Do	£20
71	Nepentha 6437 005	ZIOR (LP, gatefold sleeve)	£500

(see also Monument)

ZIPPER (1)
74	Youngblood YB 170	Streak Up And Down/Funk 74	£30

ZIPPERS
64	Hickory 45-1252	My Sailor Boy/Pretend You're Still Mine	£15

ZIPPS
79	Rip Off RIP 12	Friends/Don't Tell The Detectives (die cut p/s)	£60

ZIPS
79	Black Gold ZIPS1	Take Me Down/Don't Be Pushed Around/I'm In Love Over and Over (500 only with A4 insert & 2 stickers)	£150
80	Tenement Tunes TEN 01	Radioactivity/I'm Not Impressed (p/s)	£30

ZNR
81	Recommended RR 7	BARRICADE 3 (LP)	£18

ZODIAC
68	Elektra EKL 4009	COSMIC SOUNDS (LP, also stereo EKS 74009)	£70

ZODIACS
57	Oriole CB 1383	Why Don't They Understand/The Game Of Love	£18

ZOMBIES
64	Decca F 11940	She's Not There/You Make Me Feel Good	£15
64	Decca F 12004	Leave Me Be/Woman	£15
65	Decca F 12072	Tell Her No/What More Can I Do	£15
65	Decca F 12125	She's Coming Home/I Must Move	£15
65	Decca F 12225	Whenever You're Ready/I Love You	£15
65	Decca F 12296	Is This The Dream/Don't Go Away	£25
66	Decca F 12322	Remember You/Just Out Of Reach	£25
66	Decca F 12426	Indication/How We Were Before	£35
66	Decca F 12495	Gotta Get A Hold Of Myself/The Way I Feel Inside	£40
67	Decca F 12584	Goin' Out Of My Head/She Does Everything For Me	£50
68	Decca F 12798	I Love You/The Way I Feel Inside	£15
67	CBS 2960	Friends Of Mine/Beechwood Park	£60
67	CBS 3087	Care Of Cell 44/Maybe After He's Gone	£50
68	CBS 3380	Time Of The Season/I'll Call You Mine	£60
65	Decca DFE 8598	THE ZOMBIES (EP)	£125
65	Decca LK 4679	BEGIN HERE (LP)	£500
65	RCA RD 7791	BUNNY LAKE IS MISSING (LP, soundtrack)	£65
68	CBS 63280	ODESSEY AND ORACLE (LP, mono, CBS 'Sound of Entertainment' inner)	£1000
68	CBS S 63280	ODESSEY AND ORACLE (LP, stereo, CBS 'Sound of Entertainment' inner)	£700
70	Decca SPA 95	THE WORLD OF THE ZOMBIES (LP)	£18
73	Epic EPC 65728	TIME OF THE ZOMBIES (2-LP)	£40
76	Decca ROOTS 2	ROCK ROOTS (LP)	£15
86	Decca DOA 4	BEGIN HERE (LP, reissue, silver labels)	£20
15	Repertoire V 102 M	ODESSEY AND ORACLE (LP, reissue, mono half-speed master)	£30

(see also Unit Four Plus Two, Argent, Neil MacArthur, Colin Blunstone)

ZOO
70	Major Minor SMLP 74	ZOO (LP)	£50
71	Barclay 521172	ZOO (LP)	£30

ZOOM CLUB
80	Happy Face MM 130	I Can't Compete/It's Not Fair (no p/s)	£100

ZOOM LENS
80	Negative NEG 1	Side To Side/Running In Mazes (blue vinyl, p/s)	£25
84	Negative NEG 2	Welcome To China/Waxworks (p/s)	£25

ZOOT ALORS
79	Decca FR 13874	Send Me A Postcard/It's A Crime	£40

ZORKIE TWINS
80	Skeleton SKL 006	Mr. Simpson/From Now On (p/s)	£15

JOHN ZORN
86	Nonesuch 979 139-1	THE BIG GUNDOWN (LP, gatefold)	£20
87	Nonesuch 979 172-1	SPILLANE (LP)	£20
89	Nonesuch 960844-1	SPY VS SPY (LP)	£20
89	Nonesuch 7559 792381	NAKED CITY (LP)	£40

ZORRO
79	Bridgehouse BHEP 1	Arrods Don't Sell 'Em/Soldier Boy/Starflight (p/s)	£30

ZOUNDS
81	Crass 4219844/3	Can't Cheat Karma/War/Subvert (gatefold paper p/s, with poster)	£15
82	Rough Trade ROUGH 31	THE CURSE OF ZOUNDS (LP, inner)	£20

ZOVIET-FRANCE
82	Red Rhino RED 12	ZOVIET-FRANCE (12" EP, printed hessian sleeve)	£60
12	Altvinyl AV040/ AV041.AV042	7.10/12 (box set of one clear vinyl 7", one clear vinyl 10" and one clear vinyl 12", 250 only)	£50
83	Red Rhino RED 23	NORSCHE (LP)	£35
84	Red Rhino RED 40	MOHNOMISCHE (LP, 1st pressing with silver/dark green labels)	£80
84	Red Rhino RED 40	MOHNOMISCHE (LP, 2nd pressing with light green/dark green labels)	£40
84	Red Rhino REDLP 45	EOSTRE (LP)	£50
85	Singing Ringing	POPULAR SOVIET SONGS AND YOUTH MUSIC (2-cassette)	£40
86	Red Rhino RED 67	MISFITS, LOONY TUNES AND SQUALID CRIMINALS (LP)	£35
87	Red Rhino RED 68	A FLOCK OF ROTATIONS (LP)	£40
88	Red Rhino RED 91	SHOUTING AT THE GROUND (2-LP)	£40
90	Charm CHARRMLP 14	LOOK INTO ME (LP, 45rpm)	£40

ZUGZWANG
95	Aphelion AHP 001	Euphonic/Arrest/Focussed/Bermuda (12") £40
96	Aphelion AHP 002	MiiA/The Ticket/Tastes Like A Peach/Brighton Terrace SW2/Wireless (12") £30

TAPPA ZUKIE
75	Locks LOX 8	Judge I O' Lord/LLOYDIE SLIM AND KING TUBBY: State Dub £20
77	New Star DNEW 1	What's Yours/Make Faith (12", as Tappa Zukie & Knowledge) £25
73	Count Shelly CSLP 04	MAN A WARRIOR (LP) £60
76	Stars (No. Cat. No.)	TAPPA ZUKIE IN DUB (LP) £100
76	KLIK 9022	M.P.L.A. (LP) £20
78	Virgin Frontline FL1006	M.P.L.A. (LP, reissue) £20
78	Virgin Frontline FL1009	PEACE IN THE GHETTO (LP) £20
79	Virgin Frontline FL1029	TAPPA ZUKIE IN DUB (LP) £20
79	Virgin Frontline FL1032	TAPPER ROOTS LP) £15

(see also Honey Boy. Alton Ellis & Dennis Alcapone)

ZULEMA
75	RCA SF 8419	ZULEMA (LP) £15

ZULU
77	Big Bear BB9	Red Red Libanon/Okavanga Swamp £15

ZULU WARRIORS
89	Wau! Mr. Modo MOWLP 004	WARRIOR DUB (LP) £20

ZUM ZEAUX
70s	Black Pig PUG1	WOLF AT THE DOOR (LP) £40

ZUTONS
04	Deltasonic DLTLP019	WHO KILLED...THE ZUTONS (LP, with 3D glasses) £40
06	Deltasonic DLTLP040	TIRED OF HANGING AROUND (LP) £20

ZWAN
03	Reprise 9362-48436-1	MARY STAR OF THE SEA (2-LP) £50

(see also Smashing Pumpkins)

ZYGOAT
74	Polydor 2383 270	ELECTROPHON (LP) £20

ZZ
88	Kent 6T3	PEGGY WOODS: Love Is Gonna Get You/ZZ: You Just Cheat And Lie £20

ZZEBRA
74	Polydor 2058 446	Zardoz/Amusofi £20
74	Polydor 2383 296	ZZEBRA (LP) £20
75	Polydor 2383 326	PANIC (LP, with insert) £18

(see also John McCoy, Gillan)

ZZ TOP
72	London HLU 10376	Francene/Down Brownie £15
86	Warner Bros W 2003FP	Rough Boy/Delirious (shaped pic-disc, part 3 of interlocking set, shrinkwrapped with bonus 12") £30
86	Warner Bros W 2003FP	Rough Boy/Delirious (shaped pic-disc, part 3 of interlocking set) £30
71	London PS 584	ZZ TOP (LP, with inner sleeve) £60
72	London SH-U 8433	RIO GRANDE MUD (LP, original issue) £75
73	London SH-U 8459	TRES HOMBRES (LP, original issue) £50
75	London SH-U 8482	FANDANGO! (LP, original issue) £40
76	London LDU 1	TEJAS (LP, original foldout sleeve)...£40
83	Warner Bros W 3774	ELIMINATOR (LP, with bonus stickered p/s 12" "Legs [Metal Mix]").......................£15
83	Warner Bros W3774P	ELIMINATOR (LP, picture disc)...£20

Various Artists

VARIOUS ARTISTS EPs 50s/60s
(alphabetical by title)

A
62	MGM MGMEP 768	A VERY PRIVATE AFFAIR (includes Brigitte Bardot: Sidonie)...............................£60

B
64	Fontana TFE 18010	BLOWIN' IN THE WIND (withdrawn; Bob Dylan/Joan Baez/Pete Seeger) £100
64	Pye Intl. NEP 44029	THE BLUES VOL. 1 PT. 1 (John Lee Hooker/Muddy Waters/Sonny Boy Williamson/Jimmy Witherspoon) £35
60	Pye Intl. NEP 44035	THE BLUES VOL. 1 PT. 2 (Howling Wolf/Buddy Guy/Little Walter/Muddy Waters) £25
66	Chess CRE 6011	THE BLUES VOL. 2 PT. 1 (Otis Rush/Chuck Berry/John Lee Hooker/ Little Walter) £25
64	Pye Intl. NEP 44038	BLUES FESTIVAL (Sugar Pie De Santo/Willie Dixon/Sonny Boy Williamson/ Howlin' Wolf) £30
63	Columbia SEG 8226	BLUES ON PARADE NO. 1 (Jimmy Cotton/Brownie McGhee/ Roosevelt Sykes/Sonny Terry) £25
56	HMV 7EG 8178	THE BLUES THEY SANG (Lizzie Miles/Billy Young & Jelly Roll Morton) £20

C

| 60s Heritage 105 | THE COUNTRY BLUES (99 only)..£80 |

D

60s XX MIN 706	DARK MUDDY BOTTOM (Jimmy Slim/Good Jelly Bess/Lightning Leon/ Little Red Walters/Willie B.)...£20
50s Poydras 102	DEPRESSION BLUES £25
63 Decca DFE 8520	DISCS-A-GO GO (Karl Denver/Billy Fury/Jet Harris/Vernons Girls) £50
60s Jan & Dil JR 450	DOWN HOME BLUES - SIXTIES STYLE (Lightning Leon/Jerry McCain/ Little Red Walters) .£30
59 Fontana TFE 17146	DRUMBEAT (Lana Sisters/Adam Faith/Bob Miller & Millermen/ Sylvia Sands/Roy Young) £40

E

| 65 Edinburgh S.C. ESC 02 | EDINBURGH STUDENTS CHARITIES APPEAL (33rpm, die-cut paper p/s; Athenians/ Avengers/Ray & Archie Fisher/Lynn & Kathy)..£50 |
| 66 Edinburgh S.C. ESC 03 | EDINBURGH STUDENTS CHARITIES APPEAL (33rpm, Athenians/Gear System/Old Bailey's Jazz Advocates) ....£60 |

F

| 64 Pye Intl. NEP 44030 | FESTIVAL OF THE BLUES NO. 1 (Willie Dixon/Buddy Guy/Muddy Waters/ Sonny Boy Williamson)...£20 |
| 63 Decca DFE 8538 | FROM A LONDON HOOTENANNY (Davy Graham/Thamesiders) ....£25 |

G

67 Down with the Game 202	GOD DON'T LIKE IT (99 only)...£40
67 Down with the Game 203	GOD DON'T LIKE IT VOLUME 2 (99 only)..£40
60s XX MIN 707	GOING TO CALIFORNIA (Little Sonny Willis/Eddie Williams)........................£15
66 Pye Intl. NEP 45054	THE GREATEST ON STAGE (Maxine Brown/Chuck Jackson/Shirelles/ Dionne Warwick) £25
63 London RE-U 1393	GROUP OF GOODIES (Marcie Blane/Kokomo/Bill Black's Combo/ Ernie Maresca)..........£50
59 Mercury ZEP 10010	GROUPS GALORE (Del Vikings/Mark IV/Diamonds/Hi-Liters) £70

H

66 Pye NEP 24242	THE HITMAKERS VOL. 2 (Chuck Berry/Kinks/Sue Thompson/Shangri-La's) £30
66 Pye Intl. NEP 44065	HITMAKERS INTERNATIONAL (Fontella Bass/James Brown/Petula Clark/ Lovin' Spoonful)..£25
62 Mercury ZEP 10133	HITSVILLE! (Brook Benton/Crew Cuts/Phil Philips/Diamonds) £30
59 Coral FEP 2034	HITSVILLE VOL. 1 (Buddy Holly/McGuire Sisters/Betty Madigan/Billy Williams)..........£60
59 Coral FEP 2035	HITSVILLE VOL. 2 (Lennon Sisters/Art Lund/Teresa Brewer/Jackie Wilson) £50
65 Tamla Motown TME 2001	HITSVILLE U.S.A. NO. 1 (Marvin Gaye/Brenda Holloway/Carolyn Crawford/ Eddie Holland)...£110
66 Post War Blues 100	HOBOS AND DRIFTERS £50

I

| 65 Chess CRE 6010 | IN CROWD (Radiants/Ramsey Lewis Trio/Little Milton/Billy Stewart) ....£30 |

J

| 59 Decca DFE 6587 | THE JAZZ COMMITTEE (featuring Don Rendell)..£100 |

K

63 Lyntone LYN 347/348	KEELE RAG RECORD (flexidisc; Rhythm Unlimited & Halettes/Keele Quintet) £18
64 Lyntone LYN 508/509	KEELE RAG RECORD NO. 2 (flexidisc; Escorts/Lance Harvey & Kingpins/ Keele Row; some in die-cut sleeve) £35
65 Lyntone LYN 765/766	KEELE RAG RECORD (flexidisc; Bob Wilson/Changing Times/ Lance Harvey & Kingpins/ Incas)..£40
61 RCA Victor RCX 203	KINGS OF THE BLUES VOL. 2 (Jazz Gillum/Big Maceo/Washboard Sam/ Sonny Boy Williamson)..£20
61 RCA Victor RCX 204	KINGS OF THE BLUES VOL. 3 (Arthur Big Boy Crudup/Furry Lewis/ Poor Joe Williams).....£25
66 Holyground HG 111	THE LAST THING ON MY MIND (EP, 99 copies only).................................£80
60 Philips BBE 12414/	LET'S MAKE LOVE - FILM SOUNDTRACK (Yves Montand/Marilyn Monroe/ Frankie Vaughan; stereo)...£25
57 London RE-P 1096	LONDON HIT PARADE NO. 2 (Fats Domino/Slim Whitman/Ken Copeland/ Roy Brown)....£40
58 London RE-P 1137	LONDON TOPPERS NO. 3 (export issue; Slim Whitman/Fats Domino/ Ricky Nelson/ Ernie Freeman) £20

M

59 Jazz Collector JEL 2	THE MALE BLUES VOL. 1 (Georgia Slim/Walter Roland)................................£25
59 Jazz Collector JEL 4	THE MALE BLUES VOL. 3 (Blind Blake/Ramblin' Thomas)............................£25
59 Jazz Collector JEL 5	THE MALE BLUES VOL. 4 (Tall Tom/Pinewood Tom) £25
59 Jazz Collector JEL 8	THE MALE BLUES VOL. 5 (Blind Lemon Jefferson/Buddy Boy Hawkins) £20
60 Jazz Collector JEL 10	THE MALE BLUES VOL. 6 (Hound Head Henry/Frankie Jaxon)......................£20
60 Jazz Collector JEL 13	THE MALE BLUES VOL. 7 (Blind Lemon Jefferson/Ed Bell)...........................£20
61 Jazz Collector JEL 24	THE MALE BLUES VOL. 8 (Blind Lemon Jefferson/Leadbelly).......................£20
69 Middle Earth MDE 201	MIDDLE EARTH SAMPLER (WRITING ON THE WALL: Aries/WOODEN O: Overture/ ARCADIUM: Poor Lady) (promo only, 33rpm, no p/s)..............................£80
60s Jan & Dil TR 451	MORE DOWN HOME BLUES (Good Jelly Boss/Juke Boy Bonner/ Papa Lightfoot/Snooky Prior) £30

N

56 Vogue EPV 1106	NEGRO SPIRITUALS (Original Five Blind Boys/Sensational Nightingales) £18
64 Vocalion EPVP 1271	NEGRO SPIRITUALS (Dixie Hummingbirds/Sensational Nightingales) £18
64 Vocalion EPVP 1276	NEGRO SPIRITUALS (Five Blind Boys/Spirits Of Memphis) £18
66 Tamla Motown TME 2014	NEW FACES FROM HITSVILLE (Jimmy Ruffin/Chris Clark & Lewis Sisters/ Tammi Terrell/£350

Monitors) ....

O

65	Columbia SEG 8413	**ON THE SCENE** (Downliners Sect/Animals/Cherokees/Cheynes/ Georgie Fame/ Yardbirds)	£150
63	MGM MGM-EP 787	**ORIGINAL HITS** (Tommy Edwards/Johnny Ferguson/Jimmy Jones/ Conway Twitty)	£30
63	London RE-K 1390	**THE ORIGINAL HITS** (Drifters/Ritchie Barrett/Coasters/Ben E. King)	£40
65	Atlantic AET 6006	**ORIGINAL HITS VOL. 2** (Barbara Lewis/Coasters/Solomon Burke/Drifters)	£40
62	Ember EMB 4522	**ORIGINAL RHYTHM AND BLUES HITS** (Jesse Belvin/Ray Charles/ Linda Hayes/Jimmy McCracklin/Johnny Moore Blazers)	£75
55	Pye Jazz NJE 1043	**ORIGINS OF SKIFFLE** (Isla Cameron/Guy Carawan/Peggy Seeger)	£20

R

67	Action ACT 002 EP	**RAG GOES MAD AT THE MOJO** (33rpm; Joe Cocker's Blues Band/ Tangerine Ayr Band/ Pitiful Souls/Delroy Good Good Band)	£50
56	Vogue EPV 1113	**RHYTHM AND BLUES** (Dominoes/Swallows)	£300
63	Stateside SE 1008	**RHYTHM AND BLUES** (Jimmy Reed/John Lee Hooker)	£40
64	Stateside SE 1009	**R&B CHARTMAKERS** (Martha/Vandellas/Miracles/Marvin Gaye/Marvelettes)	£100
64	Stateside SE 1018	**R&B CHARTMAKERS NO. 2** (Miracles/Kim Weston/Supremes/Marvelettes)	£125
64	Stateside SE 1022	**R&B CHARTMAKERS NO. 3** (Marvin Gaye/Darnells/Eddie Holland/ Martha & Vandellas)	£125
64	Stateside SE 1025	**R&B CHARTMAKERS NO. 4** (Supremes/Eddie Holland/Temptations/ Contours)	£120
60	Vogue EPV 1198	**RHYTHM AND BLUES CONCERT** (Helen Humes/Jimmy Witherspoon)	£80
64	Pye Intl. NEP 44021	**RHYTHM AND BLUES SHOWCASE VOL. 1** (Don & Bob/Dale Hawkins/ Clarence Henry/ Larry Williams)	£30
64	Pye Intl. NEP 44022	**RHYTHM AND BLUES SHOWCASE VOL. 2** (Jimmy McCracklin/ Muddy Waters/Little Walter/Howlin' Wolf)	£30
57	Vogue VE 170111	**ROCK AND ROLL** (Mister Google Eyes August/Louis Jones Rock & Roll Band/Walter Price Rock & Roll Band/Clarence Gatemouth Brown)	£80
60	Top Rank JKP 2060	**RUSHING FOR PERCUSSION** (Preston Epps/Sandy Nelson)	£20

S

60s	S.A.U.C.C. PR 5462	**ST. ANDREWS UNIVERSITY CHARITIES CAMPAIGN** (20th Century Sounds/ Steve Hall & Roosters/Black Ring; no p/s)	£35
64	Lyntone LYN 738/739	**SHEFFIELD UNIVERSITY RAG RECORD** (flexidisc; Vantennas/Dave Allen Band/ Addy Street Five/Los Caribos; die-cut sleeve)	£40
55	Columbia SEG 7528	**SHOUT FOR JOY** (Pete Johnson/Albert Ammons/Meade Lux Lewis)	£30
63	London RE-P 1403	**SINGING THE BLUES** (Ernie K-Doe/Showmen/Jesse Hill/Chris Kenner)	£60
65	Keele Rag/Lyntone	**SOUNDS OF SAVILE** (flexidisc; Hipster Image/London Apprentices/ Tom & Brennie; some in die-cut title sleeve)	£60
60	Mercury ZEP 10088	**SURPRISE PACKAGE** (Ben Hewitt/Diamonds)	£50
59	Top Rank JKR 8007	**SWEET BEAT** (Lee Allen Band/Fred Parris/Cindy Mann/Mellokings)	£30

T

63	Oriole EP 7080	**TAKE SIX** (Mark Peters' Silhouettes/Ian & Zodiacs/Faron's Flamingos/Earl Preston & T.T.s/Rory Storm & Hurricanes/Sonny Wade & Cascades)	£25
59	Mercury ZEP 10015	**TEAR IT UP** (Boyd Bennett Orchestra/Red Prysock/Hi-Liters)	£25
57	Mercury MEP 9522	**TEEN-AGE ROCK** (Red Prysock/Rusty Draper/Chuck Miller/Crew Cuts)	£25
58	RCA RCX 111	**TEENAGE TOPS** (Ray Peterson/Jimmy Dell/Marlin Greene/Barry De Vorzon)	£20
64	Ember EMB 4540	**TEEN SCENE '64** (Dave Clark Five/Ray Singer/Washington D.C.s)	£20
65	Century 21 MA 105	**T.V. CENTURY 21 THEMES** (David Graham/Sylvia Anderson/Peter Dyneley/ Barry Gray Orchestra/Gary Miller/Eric Winstone Orchestra)	£15
64	Decca DFE 8585	**T.V. THEMES** (Andrew Oldham Orchestra/Ted Heath Music/Ron Grainer Music/Cyril Stapleton Orchestra)	£25
62	Starlite STEP 31	**TWIST OFF** (Wayne Farmer/Medallions/Charles Perrywell/Piano Slim/ Teenbeats/ Dellos)	£30
62	Starlite STEP 29	**TWIST ON** (Mighty Trojans/Dee Dee Gaudet/Dixie Lee/ Percy & The Rocking Aces)	£20

W

69	Apple CT 1	**WALLS ICE CREAM PRESENTS** (Mary Hopkin/Iveys/Jackie Lomax/ James Taylor; with p/ s)	£50
65	Liberty LEP 4036	**WE SING THE BLUES** (Jesse Hill/Ernie K. Doe/Aaron Neville/Benny Spellman)	£65
64	Fontana TFE 18009	**WITH GOD ON OUR SIDE** (withdrawn; Bob Dylan/Joan Baez/Pete Seeger)	£100
66	Chess CRE 6009	**WITH THE BLUES** (Eddie Boyd Blues Combo/Buddy Guy)	£40

Y

64	Fontana TFE 18011	**YE PLAYBOYS AND PLAYGIRLS** (withdrawn; Bob Dylan/Joan Baez/ Pete Seeger)	£100
68	Chess CRE 6026	**YOUR CHESS REQUESTS** (Fontella Bass/Tony Clarke/Mitty Collier/ Billy Stewart)	£40

VARIOUS ARTISTS SINGLES & EPs 70s/80s/90s/00s

A

87	London SAM 4	**ADONIS: No Way Back** (Club Mix)**/ADONIS : No Way Back** (Mix)**/HERCULES: 7 Ways To Jack/MR. FINGERS: Can You Feel It** (12", Promo only)	£30
09	Anjunabeats ANJEP 002	**ANJUNABEATS EP 002** (12", p/s)	£35
91	ART 1	**APPLIED RHYTHMIC TECHNOLOGY** (12" EP)	£25
98	Twisted Nerve TN 003	**ALL OAR NOTHING** (10", p/s; Badly Drawn Boy/Mum & Dad/Dakota Oak/ Sirconical/ Andy Votel)	£15
80	Deleted DEP 002	**ANGST IN MY PANTS** (2x7", fold-out numbered sleeve, Instant Automatons/Door & The Window/Mic Woods/Midnight Circus/012/Digital Dinosaurs/Missing Persons, etc)	£50

B

87	Other OTH 6	**BATTLEAXE** (p/s; Black Riders/Holosade/Kes/Teacher's Pet)	£30
78	Good Vibrations GOT 7	**BATTLE OF THE BANDS** (double pack, no'd p/s; Idiots/Rudi/Outcasts/Spider)	£25

81	Secret SHH 126	**BOLLOCKS TO CHRISTMAS** (p/s; Business/4-Skins/Gonads/Max Splodge)	£30
80	Crass 421984/5	**BULLSHIT DETECTOR (12", p/s; A.P.F. Brigade/Alternative/Amebix/ Clockwork Criminals/Counter Attack/Crass/Frenzy Battalion/Fuck The CIA/**	£0

C

15	Universal 00600753574263	**CAPITOL NORTHERN SOUL 7S BOX** (7 x 7" box set)	£80
15	Universal 00600753592380	**CHESS NORTHERN SOUL** (7 x 7" box set)	£100
16	Universal 535 923-8	**CHESS NORTHERN SOUL VOLUME 2** (7 x 7" box set)	£60
98	Twisted Nerve TNXMS 1	**CHRISTMAS STOCKING FILLER** (Badly Drawn Boy/Dakota Oak/Sirconical/Mum & Dad/ Elbow) (green vinyl in green wraparound sleeve or red vinyl in red sl.)	£25
13	Universal Music Operations MOD 65-7	**CIRCLES: THE MOD 45s BOX** (6x7", box set)	£50
80s	No Future	**A COUNTRY FIT FOR HEROES VOL. 2** (12", p/s)	£20
15	Cherry Red CRCREBOX 18	**CREATION ARTIFACT - THE FIRST TEN SINGLES**	£25
80	Newtown NTP 1	**CRIME DECK: Arms Race/BASIC UNIT: Ladder//BEAT NECESSITY: Just FIne/STORY SO FAR: Radiated** (p/s)	£100
07	Cultivated Electronics CE 001	**CULTIVATED ELECTRONICS EP 001** (12:)	£30
08	Cultivated Electronics CE 002	**CULTIVATED ELECTRONICS EP 002** (12:)	£50
08	Cultivated Electronics CE 003	**CULTIVATED ELECTRONICS EP 003** (12:)	£20

D

71	Dandelion DS 7001	**DANDELION** (die-cut sleeve; Principal Edwards Magic Theatre/Stackwaddy/ Siren/The Way We Live)	£15
92	Delirious DELIS 6	**DELIRIOUS PRIME CUTS VOL. 1** (12"; The Moog/Hardcore Rhythm Team/Justice And Mercy)	£40
01	Trunk WWW 1	**DIRTY FAN MAIL** (7", white vinyl)	£20
15	Disco Haman DISCOHAMAN 02	**DISCO HAMAN 2** (12")	£35
17	Disco Haman DISCOHAMAN 03	**DISCO HAMAN 3** (12")	£15
18	Disco Haman DISCOHAMAN 04	**DISCO HAMAN 4** (12")	£15
19	Disco Haman DISCOHAMAN 05	**DISCO HAMAN 5** (12")	£15
12	Fruits De Mer Crustacean 22	**DO NOT ADJUST YOUR SET EP** (purple vinyl)	£15

E

79	Fast Products FAST 9B	**EARCOM 2** (12", p/s; Joy Division/Thursdays/Basczax)	£50
99	Lowlife LOW8	**EASTER ISLAND** (EP, 750 only)	£15
10	Fruits De Mer Crustacean 15	**EDDIE COCHRAN INSTRUMENTALS EP**	£25
80	Newtown Products NTP 1	**SIMPLE APPROACH TO NEWTOWN PRODUCTS** (p/s)	£200
96	Mo' Wax MWEX 001-010	**EXCURSIONS** (10 x 12", box set; the Prunes/IO/Olde Scottish/David Caron/DJ Solo & DJ Aura/Midnight Funk Assoc./Stasis/Solo feat. JT/Twig Bud/DJ Shadow)	£30
99	AI AI 001	**EXPERIMENTS IN COLOUR** (12"; Normal/Cell/Fil)	£20

F

19	Electronic Sound ES 754	**A FACTORY ASSEMBLY** (2 x 7", A Certain Ration/Durutti Column/Minny Pops/Section 25. p/s)	£25
78	Factory FAC 2	**A FACTORY SAMPLE** (double pack, p/s, in plastic bag, with 5 stickers; Joy Division/ Cabaret Voltaire/Durutti Column/John Dowie)	£400
04	Firecracker FIREC001	**FIRECRACKER EP 1** (10")	£40
05	Firecracker FIREC002	**FIRECRACKER EP 1** (10")	£20
95	555 5X555	**5x555** (5x7" box set; Boyracer/Mike Nichols And His Excellency/Amy Linton & Stewart Anderson/Father/Hood)	£30
91	Fontana FONT 1	**THE FONTANA SINGLES BOX SET VOLUME 1 - HITS AND RARITIES** (12-single box set, with 12 inserts)	£30
91	Fontana FONT 2	**THE FONTANA SINGLES BOX SET VOLUME 2 - HITS AND RARITIES** (12-single box set, with 12 inserts)	£30
79	Heartbeat PULSE 4	**4 ALTERNATIVES** (p/s; 48 Hours/Joe Public/Numbers/X-Certs)	£15
80	Con (no cat. no.)	**THE FOUR EPs** (cassette; Mark Perry et al.)	£15
96	Ché CHE 059	**4 TRACK 3 DAY TOUR EP** (p/s, Mogwai/Urusei Yatsura/Backwater, 500 only)	£25
96	Mosquito MSQ 05	**FRESH AS YOU FUCKIN' LIKE** (12"; Paul Hannah/Russ Gabriel/Steve Patton/ Cristian Vogel/Si Begg)	£15
11	Fruits De Mer Crustacean 16	**THE FRUITS DE MER ANNUAL 2011** (2x7")	£30
11	Fruits De Mer Crustacean 23	**THE FRUITS DE MER ANNUAL 2012** (2x7", p/s)	£30

G

83	Mouth MOUTH 1	**G-FORCE** (Shady Deal/Dead Loss/Blythe Rocket/Egypt)	£20
70	Ra 5002	**GOOD TIDINGS OF GREAT JOY** (Faraway Folk, Torbay Quartet and Indiana HIghway)	£15
81	Thin Face JIM 1	**GOT MY GOAT EP**	£35
70	Village Thing VTSX 1000	**THE GREAT WHITE DAP** (Wizz Jones/Sun Also Rises/Ian A. Anderson/Pigsty Hill Light Orchestra)	£20

H

15	Hamas House HAMANHOUSE 01	**HAMAN HOUSE 1** (12", p/s)	£40
17	Hamas House HAMANHOUSE 02	**HAMAN HOUSE 2** (12", p/s)	£15
17	Hamas House HAMANHOUSE 03	**HAMAN HOUSE 3** (12", p/s)	£15
19	Hamas House HAMANHOUSE 04	**HAMAN HOUSE 4** (12", p/s)	£30

20	Hamas House HAMANHOUSE 05	**HAMAN HOUSE 5** (12", p/s) £15
06	Trojan TJBX 330	**HAUNTED HOUSE - SKINHEAD SEVENS BOXSET** (8 x 7", box, booklet) £150
80	Groucho Marxist	**HA! HA! FUNNY POLIS** (PAISLEY ROCKS AGAINST RACISM) (p/s; Defiant Pose/Fegs/ Urban Enemies/XS Discharge) £20
71	Abreaction ABR 001	**HART ROCK** (Brass Alley/Yellow/Trilogy/Lucas Tyson) (no p/s) £20

I

| 78 | Radar SAM 88 | **INTERNATIONAL ARTISTS** (13th Floor Elevators/Red Crayola/ Lost & Found/Golden Dawn; Red Crayola Hope & Anchor gig freebie ....£0 |

L

| 11 | Sanctuary | **LUCKY SEVENS** (7 x 7" box set of Trojan reissues, insert) ....£40 |

M

71	Track 2094 011	**MAXI TRACK RECORD** (John's Children/Crazy World Of Arthur Brown/ Thunderclap Newman/Jimi Hendrix; withdrawn blue sleeve crediting.............£0
71	Track 2094 011	**MAXI TRACK RECORD** (John's Children/Crazy World Of Arthur Brown/ Thunderclap Newman/Jimi Hendrix; red & white sleeve with press pack,..........£0
80	Paul Panic PANIC 001	**MELL SQUARE MUSICK** (1000 only, white labels, p/s, 50 came with inserts) £50
19	Mighty Force MFACID001	**MF ACID 1** (12", limited to 123 copies)..............................£20
19	Mighty Force MFACID002	**MF ACID 2** (12", limited to 123 copies)..............................£20
90	Mickey Rourke's Fridge MRF2	**MICKEY ROURKE'S FRIDGE PRESENTS EP**...............................£50
97	V/VM VVMT4	**MISSINGTOE & WHINE** (EP, 500 only) £15
99	Twisted Nerve TN 009	**MODERN MUSIC FOR MOTORCYCLES** (10" EP, some on yellow vinyl; Dakota Oak/Alfie/ Sirconical & Andy Votel/Mum & Dad/Badly Drawn Boy) £15
13	Universal 534 542 5	**MOTOWN 7s BOX: RARE AND UNRELEASED VINYL** (7 x 7" box set)............£200
14	Universal 535 056-2	**MOTOWN 7s BOX: RARE AND UNRELEASED VINYL VOLUME 2** (7 x 7" box set)........£100
16	Universal 536 953-7	**MOTOWN 7s BOX: RARE AND UNRELEASED VINYL VOLUME 3** (7 x 7" box set)........£60
17	Universal 537 482-5	**MOTOWN 7s BOX: RARE AND UNRELEASED VINYL VOLUME 4** (7 x 7" box set)........£50
80	EMI 12EMI 5074	**MUTHA'S PRIDE** (12", p/s; Wildfire/Quartz/White Spirit/Baby Jane) £20

N

98	Lowlife LOW6	**98 Series Vol. 1** (EP) £15
98	Lowlife LOW7	**98 Series Vol. 2** (EP) £15
80	Neutron NT 003	**1980! THE FIRST FIFTEEN MINUTES EP** (gatefold p/s with inserts; Vice Versa/Clock DVA/ I'm So Hollow/Stunt Kites)......................................£25

P

92	Art 2.1	**THE PHILOSOPHY OF SOUND AND MACHINES EP 1** (12") £30
92	Art 2.1	**THE PHILOSOPHY OF SOUND AND MACHINES EP 2** (12") £30
80s	A&M A&M PARTY 1/2/3/4/ 5/6	**THE PARTY PARTY PACK** (6 x 7", with picture sleeves, in PVC outer sleeve; Sting/ Pauline Black/Dave Edmunds/Midge Ure/Modern Romance/Bad Manners) £20
80	L'Aventure SNS 001	**THE POTENT HUMAN EP** (p/s, different coloured sleeves) £30
97	V/VM VVMT4	**PRIVILEGED FRAMES FOR REFERENCE** (12" EP, p/s, 450 only) £15

R

93	Raptor RAP 1	**RAPTOR PRESENTS . . .** (12", p/s, 500 only; Ash/Buttlip/Marrow Bone/Fat)........£40
10	Rave Wars RW1	**RAVE WARS** (p/s, red vinyl with random Star Wars figure) £40
12	Rave Wars RW2	**RAVE WARS II - THE HARDCORE STRIKES BACK** (p/s, blue vinyl with Star Wars figure).....£50
14	Rave Wars RW3	**RAVE WARS III** (p/s, black or orange vinyl, with Star Wars figure)..........£40
91	Ptolemaic Terrascope POT 8	**RED FLIPPER** (no p/s, Nurse With Wound/The Underworlde/Caravan Of Dreams) £20
83	Consett Music Project RD 1	**ROCK AND DOLE** (Obnoxious Tartus/Decade Waltz/Task Force/Hot Banana)...........£25

S

80	Sonic Int. S14283	**SEX, VIOLENCE & ETERNAL TRUTH** (Lost Boys/What To Wear/The Venom/The Dodos, oversized poster sleeve, 4 A5 inserts, 250 only, stickered white labels, stamped plain white inner sleeve)......................................£125
95	Enraptured RAPT 4502	**SILVER APPLES TRIBUTE** (10", 12 in hand-drawn sleeve; Windy & Carl/Scaredycat/ Third Eye Foundation/Flowchart/Sabine............................£30
14	Stateside 535 414-5	**STATESIDE 7S** (7 x 7" box set) £40
70s	Stiff BUY 1-10	**STIFF BOX SET NO. 1** (10 x 7" box set) £35
70s	Stiff BUY 11-20	**STIFF BOX SET NO. 2** (10 x 7" box set) £35
01	Edel 0128655ERESA	**SUBSTITUTE EP : THE SONGS OF THE WHO** (white vinyl, promo)...........£60

T

83	White Noise WN 3	**THIS IS WHITE NOISE** (p/s; Skrewdriver/Brutal Attack/Die Hards/A.B.H.)...........£60
02	Warner Bros 50466 13441	**TOP-DECK SKA 45'S BOX** (8 x 7"s, coloured vinyl in cardboard box)............£40
19	2 Tone CHSTT 5014	**2 TONE 7" TREASURES** (12x7", cushioned slip-record pack, 7"slipmat, signed card).........£90

U

| 80s | Fierce FRIGHT/SFTRI 38 | **AN UNHOLY MONTAGE** (200 only [100 U.K./100 U.S.], coloured vinyl with numbered insert)..£25 |
| 96 | V/VM VVMT1 | **UPLINK DATA TRANSMISSIONS** (12" EP, with 'data sheets', 250 only)...........£20 |

V

| 79 | Pink BRS 002/INK 1000 | **THE VOXHALL TRACKS - LUTON** (Klips/Para-Noia/Tee Vees/Friction (multifold p/s, 1000 only) ....£50 |

W

| 98 | Goldmine GS1000X | **WIGAN CASINO 25th ANNIVERSARY BOX SET** (10 x 7") ....£60 |
| 77 | MPL MPL 1 | **WE'VE MOVED!** (Wings/Gene Vincent/Frank Sinatra et al., promo only excerpts £350 |

sampler, with press pack)..

Y

| 80s | Wonderful World Of WOW 1 | YOU ARE NOT ALONE (p/s, with insert; Oi Polloi/Hex/Stalag 17/Symbol Of Freedom) .....£15 |

UNTITLED EPs & SINGLES 50s-00s

60s	Coxsone SCE 1	(no p/s, 33rpm; Gaylads/Hugh Godfrey/Glen & Dave/Roy Richards/ Cables/Richard Ace)..£85
69	De Wolfe	(Lemon Dips, et al.)..£75
94	Kennel Club VTDOG 10	TINDERSTICKS: Girl On Death Row/STRANGELOVE: Wolf's Story/GOD MACHINE: The Devil Song/BREED: Diamonds Are Forever (10", numbered p/s, free with....................£15
96	SKAM MASK 1	UNTITLED (12", custom sleeve, 100 only; Freeform/Funkstorung/Boards Of Canada/ Jega)..£150
97	SKAM MASK 2	UNTITLED (12", custom sleeve, 350 only; Hellinterface/Funkstorung/Bola/ Jega/ Intron)..£75

VARIOUS ARTISTS LPs & COMPILATIONS
(alphabetical by title)

A

88	Woronzow WOO 6	ACID JAM (with insert)..£18
88	Serious DRUG 1	ACID TRAX £15
88	Serious DRUG 2	ACID TRAX VOL 2 ....£20
88	Needle DRUG 3	ACID TRAX VOL 3 ....£15
88	Warriors Dance WAF 006	ACID TRAX AND WARRIORS DANCE..£15
89	Popdy POPDY 101	(0222) A COMPILATION OF CARDIFF BANDS (LP) £80
02	Topic TSFCD4001	THE ACOUSTIC FOLK BOX (4-CD) £15
69	Action ACLP 6005	ACTION PACKED SOUL £50
70s	Jem JEM	A DEAL A DAY..£25
96	Ferox FERLP 1	ADVENTURES IN TECHNO SOUL (2-LP; Too Funk/Paul Hannah/Carl Craig et al.)............£30
85	United Dairies UD 012	AN AFFLICTED MAN'S MUSICAL BOX (3 different editions, 1st in gatefold sleeve) £75
75	Leader LEE 4056	A FINE HUNTING DAY - SONGS OF THE HOLME VALLEY BEAGLES (with book) £15
70	Pama PMP 2004	AFRICAN MELODY £90
71	Trojan TBL 166	AFRICA'S BLOOD (Lee Perry, et al.) (orange/white label) £40
98	Harmless HURTLP016	AFRICAKFUNK (2-LP)..£30
77	Tartone TTL 101	AFRO AND REGGAE HITS £35
64	Decca LK 4606	AFTER SUNSET £150
66	Stateside SL 10172	AN ALBUM FULL OF SOUL £50
69	Key KL 002	ALIVE! £20
70	Talisman STAL 5013	ALL FOLK TOGETHER £20
84	Whaam! BIG 8	ALL FOR ART... AND ART FOR ALL £30
83	Neat NEAT 102A/B	ALL HELL LET LOOSE..£20
76	Count Shelly CSLP 08	ALL STAR £30
61	Blue Beat BBLP 801	ALL STARS - JAMAICAN BLUES £300
70s	Rare Records 2	AMERICAN FOLK BLUES FESTIVAL 1962 ....£25
64	Fontana TL 5204	AMERICAN FOLK BLUES FESTIVAL 1963 ....£25
65	Fontana TL 5225	AMERICAN FOLK BLUES FESTIVAL 1964 ....£25
66	Fontana TL 5286	AMERICAN FOLK BLUES FESTIVAL 1965 ....£25
66	Fontana (S)TL 5389	AMERICAN FOLK BLUES FESTIVAL 1966 (mono/stereo) £22
70	CBS 63912	AMERICAN FOLK BLUES FESTIVAL 1969 ....£20
80s	Pleasantly Surprised PS 2	THE ANGELS ARE COMING (2-cassette, with booklet) £25
83	No Future MPUNK 8	ANGELS WITH DIRTY FACES £18
60s	77' 77LA 12/13	ANGOLA PRISON SPIRITUALS £18
69	Immediate IMAL 03/04	ANTHOLOGY OF BRITISH BLUES VOLUME 1 (2-LP, gatefold sleeve)..£30
69	Immediate IMAL 05/06	ANTHOLOGY OF BRITISH BLUES VOLUME 2 (2-LP, gatefold sleeve)..£30
10	Fruits De Mer Crustacean 11	A PHASE WE'RE GOING THROUGH (300-500 only, light/dark grey vinyl)....................£35
10	Fruits De Mer Crustacean 11	A PHASE WE'RE GOING THROUGH (scarce coloured vinyl pressings)...........................£150
64	London HA-K/SH-K 8174	APOLLO SATURDAY NIGHT (mono/stereo)..£60
91	Delerium DELP 005D	A PSYCHEDELIC PSAUNA (2-LP) £30
92	Warp WARP LP 6	ARTIFICIAL INTELLEGENCE I £60
94	Warp WARLP LP 23	ARTIFICIAL INTELLEGENCE II (with 12")..£60
94	Warp WARLP LP 23	ARTIFICIAL INTELLEGENCE II (without 12")..£50
69	Atlantic 587/588 180	ATLANTIC BLOCKBUSTERS £20
65	Atlantic ATL 5020	ATLANTIC DISCOTHEQUE £40
64	Decca LK 4597	AT THE CAVERN £80
70	Beacon SBEAB 9	AUTHENTIC CHICAGO BLUES..£20
57	London WB 91034	AUTHENTIC CARIBBEAN CALYPSOS (10" LP) £30
64	Stateside SL 10107	AUTHENTIC SKA £70
64	Stateside SL 10068	AUTHENTIC R & B £40
79	Heartbeat HB 1	AVON CALLING - THE BRISTOL COMPILATION (with poster)..£25
95	Ministry Of Sound/AWOL LP 1	A.W.O.L: A WAY OF LIFE (3-LP, stickered sleeve)..£40
80	K-Tel NE 1100	AXE ATTACK (early copies with demo of Iron Maiden's "Running Free") £15
74	Deroy DER 1052	AYRSHIRE FOLK (LP, private pressing) £70

B

90	Warriors Dance WAFLP 4	BACK TO PRISON £20
70	Track 2407 001	BACKTRACK ONE £20
70	Track 2407 003	BACKTRACK THREE (The Who/The Jimi Hendrix Experience) £15

70	Track 2407 004	BACKTRACK FOUR (The Who/The Jimi Hendrix Experience)	£15
70	Track 2407 005	BACKTRACK FIVE (The Who/The Jimi Hendrix Experience)	£15
70	Track 2407 006	BACKTRACK SIX (The Parliaments etc)	£20
70	Track 2407 007	BACKTRACK SEVEN - MIXED BAG	£15
54	London AL 3535	BACKWOODS BLUES (10")	£50
73	Incus INCUS 11	BALANCE (Ian Brighton, et al.)	£60
62	Fontana 688 200 ZL	BALLIN'.	£18
68	Pama PMLP 4	BANG BANG LULU	£45
69	Pama Economy ECO7	BANGARANG (LP)	£60
73	BBC/Roundabout 17	BANG ON A DRUM	£18
60	Melodisc 12-115	BANJO BREAKDOWN	£15
59	Fontana TFR 6018	BARRELHOUSE, BOOGIE WOOGIE AND BLUES (10")	£20
58	Vogue Coral LRA 10022	BARRELHOUSE PIANO (10" LP)	£20
59	Vogue Coral LRA 10023	BARRELHOUSE PIANO VOLUME 2 (10" LP)	£20
95	Sarah SARAH 359	BATTERY POINT (LP)	£100
98	Trunk BARKED 3	THE BATTLE OF BOSWORTH (LP)	£15
64	Melodisc MLP 12-192	BATTLE OF THE GIANTS	£20
53	MGM MGM-D 115	A BATTLE OF JAZZ: HOT VERSUS COOL (10").	£30
71	BBC REC 118	BBC's FOLK ON TWO PRESENTS NORTHUMBRIAN FOLK	£15
69	Beacon BEAB 1	BEACON BRINGS IT TO YOU	£18
84	Well Suspect SUSS 1	THE BEAT GENERATION AND THE ANGRY YOUNG MEN	£20
86	Mercury WILD 1	BEAT RUNS WILD (Wet Wet Wet et al.)	£25
20	Decca 085 431-1	THE BEAT SCENE (2LP, Decca 90 RSD edition, insert)	£20
84	Xcentric ODDUMPTEENTH	BEATING THE MEAT	£30
82	X-centric Noise 2	BEAT THE MEAT (cassette LP, insert)	£50
68	Elektra EUK 262	BEGIN HERE (also stereo EUKS 7262)	£20
78	Rip Off ROLP 1	BELFAST ROCKS	£35
68	Bell MBLL 102	BELL'S CELLAR OF SOUL VOLUME 1	£30
69	Bell MBLL 107	BELL'S CELLAR OF SOUL VOLUME 2	£30
69	Bell MBLL 117	BELL'S CELLAR OF SOUL VOLUME 3	£30
69	Bell MBLL/SBLL 111	THE BEST FROM BELL	£20
69	Bell MBLL/SBLL 124	THE BEST FROM BELL VOLUME 2	£20
78	Stiff ODD 2	BE STIFF (TOUR '78 OFFICIAL RELEASE) (promo only, Stiff artists performing Devo's Be Stiff - some sold by mail order)	£18
78	Stiff DEAL 1	BE STIFF ROUTE '78 (with 16-page booklet & biographies, etc.)	£15
01	Blue Note 7243 5 30859 1 9	THE BEST OF BLUE BREAKBEATS (2LP)	£25
12	BBE 173 CLP 1	BEST OF DISCO DEMANDS (2-LP)	£20
12	BBE 173 CLP 2	BEST OF DISCO DEMANDS 2 (2-LP)	£20
96	Universal Sounds US LP 2	BEST OF BLACK JAZZ RECORDS (2-LP)	£25
69	Pama SECO 18	THE BEST OF CAMEL - AN OASIS OF SOUND	£350
92	Chrysalis CHR TT 5012	THE BEST OF 2 TONE (LP)	£80
83	Statik STATLP 14	THE BEST OF YOUR SECRET'S SAFE WITH US (LP/ 7". Single tracks: 'Sub Dub' by Sun Ya and 'The Fools' by Anthony Lindo [STAT26A/26B])	£20
86	Plastic Head PLASLP 008	BEYOND THE FENCE BEGINS THE SKY (LP)	£40
82	Open Door OD 001	BEYOND THE RIVER (LP, some with booklet)	£15
73	Attack ATLP 1011	BIG BAMBOO	£30
60	Fontana TFL 5080	THE BIG BEAT!	£55
85	Big Beat WIKM39	BIG BEAT BEACH PARTY	£15
78	Giorno GPS	BIG EGO	£20
72	CBS 64844	THE BIG SUR FESTIVAL	£18
73	Rhino SRNN 7002	BIG 12 - REGGAE STEADY GO VOL. 2	£18
70	Pama SECO 32	BIRTH CONTROL	£40
70	Matchbox SDX 207/8	BLACK DIAMOND EXPRESS TO HELL (2-LP)	£25
80	Form BB 1003	BLACK MAGIC DUB (LP)	£100
58	HMV CLP 1167	BLACK SLACKS AND BOBBY SOCKS (LP)	£150
70	Ember SE 8009	BLACK SOUL EXPLOSION	£18
70	CBS 52796	BLACK WHITES AND BLUES	£20
83	Quiet QLP 3	BLOOD ON THE ROQ! (withdrawn)	£15
10	Balkan BV 03	BLUE (with free CD)	£30
68	Coxsone CSP 1	BLUE BEAT SPECIAL	£60
92	Blue Note B1-99106	BLUE BREAK BEATS (You Gotta Hear Blue Note To Dig Def Jam!!!) (2-LP)	£30
93	Blue Note B1-89907	BLUE BREAK BEATS VOLUME TWO (You Gotta Hear Blue Note To Dig Def Jam!!!) (2-LP)	£25
96	Blue Note B1-54360	BLUE BREAK BEATS VOLUME THREE (You Gotta Hear Blue Note to Dig Def Jam!!!) (2-LP)	£35
98	Blue Note 724349402713	BLUE BREAK BEATS VOLUME FOUR (2-LP)	£40
96	Blue Note B1 54357	BLUE JUICE (2-LP)	£20
62	Columbia 33SX 1417	THE BLUES	£60
66	London HA-S 8265	THE BLUES CAME DOWN FROM MEMPHIS	£80
73	Flyright LP 504	BLUES CAME TO CHAPEL HILL	£15
71	Python PLP-KM 17	BLUES - CHICAGO STYLE (LP)	£45
60	Philips BBL 7369	BLUES FELL THIS MORNING	£40
79	Look LK LP 6400	BLUES FOR SUZY	£30
69	Chess CRLS 4558	BLUES FROM BIG BILL'S COPACABANA	£35
69	Python PLP 6	BLUES FROM CHICAGO (99 copies only)	£80
70	Python PLP 9	BLUES FROM CHICAGO VOL. 2 (99 copies only)	£80
71	Python PLP 15	BLUES FROM CHICAGO VOL. 3 (99 copies only)	£80
60s	Heritage 1004	BLUES FROM MAXWELL STREET (with insert, 99 copies only)	£100
71	Python PLP 21	BLUES FROM THE WINDY CITY (99 copies only)	£80
63	Stateside SL 10076	BLUES HOOT (Lightning Hopkins)	£35

57	Pye Nixa NJL 8	(ALAN LOMAX PRESENTS) **BLUES IN THE MISSISSIPPI NIGHT** £35
60s	Sunflower (no cat. no.)	**BLUES IS MY COMPANION** (99 copies only) £34
60s	Sunflower (no cat. no.)	**BLUES KEEP FALLING** (99 copies only) £80
69	Blue Horizon 7-66227	**BLUES JAM AT CHESS** (2-LP)....................................£60
67	Saydisc Match. SDM 142	**BLUES LIKE SHOWERS OF RAIN** £70
68	Saydisc Match. SDM 167	**BLUES LIKE SHOWERS OF RAIN VOLUME 2**....................................£70
65	Decca LK 4681	**BLUES NOW** £60
72	Blues Obscurities BOV 1	**BLUES OBSCURITIES VOL. 1: SOUTHERN BLUES/DARK MUDDY BOTTOM** (plain cover with photocopied inserts)....................................£40
72	Blues Obscurities BOV 2	**BLUES OBSCURITIES VOL. 2: LONESOME HARMONICA** £25
72	Blues Obscurities BOV 3	**BLUES OBSCURITIES VOL. 3: WEST COAST BLUES** £25
72	Blues Obscurities BOV 4	**BLUES OBSCURITIES VOL. 4: ONE RAINY MORNING**....................................£25
72	Blues Obscurities BOV 5	**BLUES OBSCURITIES VOL. 5: SOMETHING'S GONE WRONG**....................................£25
72	Blues Obscurities BOV 6	**BLUES OBSCURITIES VOL. 6: COMING BACK HOME** £25
72	Blues Obscurities BOV 7	**BLUES OBSCURITIES VOL. 7**....................................£25
72	Blues Obscurities BOV 8	**BLUES OBSCURITIES VOL. 8**....................................£25
72	Blues Obscurities BOV 9	**BLUES OBSCURITIES VOL. 9**....................................£25
72	Blues Obscurities BOV 10	**BLUES OBSCURITIES VOL. 10**....................................£25
74	London HA-U 8454	**BLUES OBSCURITIES VOL. 1: DARK MUDDY BOTTOM** (reissue)....................................£15
74	London HA-U 8455	**BLUES OBSCURITIES VOL. 2: LONESOME HARMONICA** (reissue) £15
69	Highway 51 H 102	**BLUES PEOPLE**....................................£40
68	Kokomo K 1001	**A BLUES POTPOURRI** (99 copies only) £60
71	Rarities (Tony's Records)	**BLUES RARITIES VOL. 1** (2-LP)....................................£25
69	Atlantic Special 590 019	**THE BLUES ROLL ON** (reissue of "Southern Folk Heritage: The Blues Roll On")....................................£15
69	Poppy PYM 11001	**BLUES ROOTS VOLUME ONE** £25
20	Decca 085 434-6	**THE BLUES SCENE** (2LP, Decca 90 RSD edition, insert)....................................£20
66	Decca LK 4748	**BLUES SOUTHSIDE CHICAGO** £55
71	Python PLP 16	**BLUES TODAY - SOUTHERN STYLE** (99 copies only) £40
12	Belter 001	**BONEHEAD CRUNCHERS VOLUME 1** (300 only) £40
12	Belter 002	**BONEHEAD CRUNCHERS VOLUME 2** (300 only) £30
13	Belter 003	**BONEHEAD CRUNCHERS VOLUME 3** (300 only) £25
13	Belter 004	**BONEHEAD CRUNCHERS VOLUME 4** (300 only) £20
13	Belter 005	**BONEHEAD CRUNCHERS VOLUME 5** (300 only) £20
09	BBE 142CLP	**THE BOOGIE BACK** (2-LP)....................................£40
55	London AL 3544	**BOOGIE WOOGIE WITH THE BLUES** (10")....................................£25
69	Pama SECO 17	**BOSS REGGAE** £200
74	Eron 002	**BOTH SIDES OF THE DOWNS** (with insert) £25
80	Aardvark STEAL 2	**BOUQUET OF STEEL** (blue vinyl with 27-page booklet) £15
81	Bristol Recorder BR 002	**THE BRISTOL RECORDER VOL. 2** (with magazine booklet) £15
68	Island ILP 966/ILPS 9066	**BRITISH BLUE-EYED SOUL**....................................£75
67	T. Motown TML 11059	**BRITISH MOTOWN CHARTBUSTERS** (mono, flipback sleeve)....................................£20
69	T. Motown STML 11055	**BRITISH MOTOWN CHARTBUSTERS** (stereo reissue, flipback sleeve)....................................£20
68	T. Motown (S)TML 11082	**BRITISH MOTOWN CHARTBUSTERS VOL. 2** (mono/stereo, flipback sleeve)....................................£18
83	Royal Records JBLP 306	**BRITISH MUSIC SCENE** (LP)....................................£80
70	Trojan TBL 106	**BRIXTON CAT** £50
64	Decca LK 4598	**BRUM BEAT**....................................£85
64	Dial DLP 1	**BRUM BEAT** £50
79	Big Bear BRUM 1	**BRUM BEAT - LIVE AT THE BARREL ORGAN** (2-LP, with inserts) £20
80	MCA MCF 3074	**BRUTE FORCE**....................................£20
69	Pama Economy SECO 18	**BULLET : A WORLD OF REGGAE, SKA, ROCK STEADY, BLUE BEAT** (LP)....................................£200
81	Crass 421984/4	**BULLSHIT DETECTOR 1**....................................£20
82	Crass 221984/3	**BULLSHIT DETECTOR 2** (2-LP) £20
84	Crass 1984/3	**BULLSHIT DETECTOR THREE** (2-LP) £15
82	Crass 221984/3	**BULLSHIT DETECTIVE** (2-LP) £15
83	Crass	**BULLSHIT DETECTIVE 3** £15
66	Decca LK 4734	**BUMPER BUNDLE 16 HITS** £25
77	Stiff SEEZ 2	**A BUNCH OF STIFF RECORDS**....................................£15
79	Cherry Red ARED 2	**BUSINESS UNUSUAL** (with Zig Zag small labels catalogue)....................................£30
81	Autumn AU 2	**BUSTED AT OZ**....................................£20
84	Dambusters DAM 003	**BUTTONS AND BOWS VOLUME 1** (2-LP) £30
84	Dambusters DAM 006	**BUTTONS AND BOWS VOLUME 2** (2-LP) £30

C

50s	Melodisc MLP 507	**CALYPSO CARNIVAL** (10" LP)....................................£18
72	Topic 12TS 219	**CANNY NEWCASSEL** (with booklet, blue label) £20
91	Horace's HRH 102	**CAPITAL SOUL - THE SOUND OF D.C. 1965/66** £20
77	Carib Gems CGDD 301	**CARIB GEMS DISCO DISC** £25
50s	Parlophone CPMD 13	**CARIBBEAN CALYPSO** (10" LP, export issue) £25
07	Jazzman JMAN018LP	**CAROLINA FUNK** (2-LP)....................................£30
81	Secret SEC 2	**CARRY ON OI!** £15
73	Nottingham Festival FEST 2	**CASTLE ROCK** £50
78	Nice NICE 1	**CATCH A WAVE** (2 x 10", gatefold sleeve) £30
80	Island IRSP7	**CATCH THIS BEAT** £20
90	Cerne CERNE 001/002/003	**THE CERNE BOX SET** (3-LP box set; Nurse With Wound/ Current 93/Sol Invictus; with 3 inserts)....................................£125
60s	Columbia	**CHARTBUSTERS USA**....................................£45
64	Chess CRL 4004	**CHESS STORY VOL. 1** £25
65	Chess CRL 4516	**CHESS STORY VOL. 2** £25
68	Sunflower ET 1401	**THE CHICAGO HOUSE BANDS** (99 copies only) £40

69	Kokomo K 1005	CHICAGO SESSIONS VOLUME 1 (99 copies only)	£50
80	Relics LSD 1	CHOCOLATE SOUP FOR DIABETICS VOL. 1	£15
81	Relics ACID 1	CHOCOLATE SOUP FOR DIABETICS VOL. 2 (gatefold sleeve)	£15
84	MCA CHUNK 1	CHUNKS OF FUNK	£20
73	United Artists UDX 205/6	CHRISTMAS AT THE PATTI (2 x 10", gatefold sleeve)	£22
68	Chess CRLS 4541	CHRISTMAS DEDICATION	£25
63	London HA-U 8141	A CHRISTMAS GIFT FOR YOU (plum label)	£80
78	Incus INCUS 33	CIRCADIAN RHYTHM	£50
91	Mastercut CUTSLP 1	CLASSIC MIX MASTERCUTS VOLUME 1 (2LP, gatefold)	£20
91	Mastercuts CUTSLP 3	CLASSIC MELLOW MASTERCUTS VOLUME 1 (2LP, gatefold)	£20
91	Mastercuts CUTSLP 2	CLASSIC JAZZ-FUNK MASTERCUTS VOLUME 1 (2LP, gatefold)	£25
91	Mastercuts CUTSLP 4	CLASSIC JAZZ-FUNK MASTERCUTS VOLUME 2 (2LP, gatefold)	£25
92	Mastercuts CUTSLP 6	CLASSIC FUNK MASTERCUTS VOLUME 1 (2LP, gatefold)	£25
92	Mastercuts CUTSLP 8	CLASSIC MELLOW MASTERCUTS VOLUME 2 (2LP, gatefold)	£15
92	Mastercuts CUTSLP 7	CLASSIC JAZZ-FUNK MASTERCUTS VOLUME 3 (2LP, gatefold)	£25
92	Mastercut CUTSLP 5	CLASSIC NEW JACK SWING MASTERCUTS VOLUME 1 (2LP, gatefold)	£20
92	Mastercuts CUTSLP 9	CLASSIC NEW JACK SWING MASTERCUTS VOLUME 2 (2LP, gatefold)	£15
93	Mastercuts CUTSLP 15	CLASSIC 80s GROOVE MASTERCUTS VOLUME 1 (2LP, gatefold)	£20
93	Mastercuts CUTSLP 10	CLASSIC SALSOUL MASTERCUTS VOLUME 1 (2LP, gatefold)	£20
93	Mastercuts CUTSLP 13	CLASSIC SALSOUL MASTERCUTS VOLUME 2 (2LP, gatefold)	£20
93	Mastercuts CUTSLP 14	CLASSIC FUNK MASTERCUTS VOLUME 2 (2LP, gatefold)	£20
93	Mastercuts CUTSLP 12	CLASSIC P-FUNK MASTERCUTS VOLUME 1 (2LP, gatefold)	£15
93	Mastercuts CUTSLP 11	CLASSIC RARE GROOVE MASTERCUTS VOLUME 1 (2LP, gatefold)	£20
94	Mastercuts CUTSLP 21	CLASSIC RARE GROOVE MASTERCUTS VOLUME 2 (2LP, gatefold)	£30
94	Mastercuts CUTSLP 18	CLASSIC NEW JACK SWING MASTERCUTS VOLUME 3 (2LP, gatefold)	£15
94	Mastercuts CUTSLP 17	CLASSIC MELLOW MASTERCUTS VOLUME 3 (2LP, gatefold)	£20
94	Mastercut sCUTSLP 19	CLASSIC ELECTRO MASTERCUTS VOLUME 1 (2LP, gatefold)	£20
94	Mastercuts CUTSLP 16	CLASSIC JAZZ-FUNK MASTERCUTS VOLUME 4 (2LP, gatefold)	£20
94	Mastercuts CUTSLP 23	CLASSIC JAZZ-FUNK MASTERCUTS VOLUME 5 (2LP, gatefold)	£20
94	Mastercuts CUTSLP 20	CLASSIC HOUSE MASTERCUTS VOLUME 1 (2LP, gatefold)	£25
94	Mastercuts CUTSLP 22	CLASSIC HOUSE MASTERCUTS VOLUME 2 (2LP, gatefold)	£20
95	Mastercuts CUTSLP 28	CLASSIC HOUSE MASTERCUTS VOLUME 3 (2LP, gatefold)	£18
95	Mastercuts CUTSLP 30	CLASSIC REGGAE MASTERCUTS VOLUME 1 (LP, gatefold)	£35
95	Mastercuts CUTSLP 25	CLASSIC DISCO MASTERCUTS VOLUME 1 (2LP, gatefold, some silver vinyl)	£20
95	Mastercuts CUTSLP 27	CLASSIC NEW JACK SWING MASTERCUTS VOLUME 4 (2LP, gatefold)	£15
95	Mastercuts CUTSLP 26	CLASSIC 80s GROOVE MASTERCUTS VOLUME 2 (2LP, gatefold)	£25
95	Mastercuts CUTSLP 24	CLASSIC FUNK MASTERCUTS VOLUME 3 (2LP, gatefold)	£25
95	Mastercuts CUTSLP 29	CLASSIC HIP-HOP MASTERCUTS VOLUME 1 (LP, gatefold)	£25
96	Mastercuts CUTSLP 35	CLASSIC HIP-HOP MASTERCUTS VOLUME 2 (LP, gatefold)	£15
96	Mastercuts CUTSLP 33	CLASSIC MELLOW MASTERCUTS VOLUME 4 (2LP, gatefold)	£20
96	Mastercuts CUTSLP 31	CLASSIC JAZZ-FUNK MASTERCUTS VOLUME 6 (2LP, gatefold)	£40
96	Mastercuts CUTSLP 37	CLASSIC JAZZ-FUNK MASTERCUTS VOLUME 7 (2LP, gatefold)	£25
96	Mastercut CUTSLP 32	CLASSIC ACID MASTERCUTS VOLUME 1 (LP, gatefold)	£25
96	Mastercuts CUTSLP 34	CLASSIC BALEARIC MASTERCUTS VOLUME 1 (LP, gatefold)	£15
97	Mastercuts CUTSLP 39	CLASSIC G-FUNK MASTERCUTS VOLUME 1 (2LP, gatefold)	£20
97	Mastercuts CUTSLP 36	CLASSIC 80s GROOVE MASTERCUTS VOLUME 3 (2LP, gatefold)	£25
98	Mastercut CUTSLP 40	CLASSIC R&B MASTERCUTS VOLUME 1 (2LP, gatefold)	£15
99	Mastercuts CUTSLP41	CLASSIC GARAGE MASTERCUTS VOLUME 1 (2LP, gatefold)	£30
00	Mastercuts CUTSLP 42	CLASSIC R&B MASTERCUTS VOLUME 2 (2LP, gatefold)	£15
00	Mastercuts CUTSLP 43	CLASSIC RARE GROOVE MASTERCUTS VOLUME 3 (2LP, gatefold)	£30
13	Trunk JBH 049 LP	CLASSROOM PROJECTS (LP)	£20
85	Pusmort 0012-02	CLEANSE THE BACTERIA	£20
90s	Distronics ITCD 3	THE CLOSING PARTY - IN THE CITY LIVE UNSIGNED (CD)	£50
99	Strut STRUTLP 001	CLUB AFRICA (2-LP)	£20
72	Trojan TBL178	CLUB REGGAE 3	£25
70	Trojan TTL 54	CLUB ROCK STEADY	£25
68	W.I.R.L. ILP 965	CLUB ROCK STEADY '68	£70
67	W.I.R.L. ILP 948	CLUB SKA '67	£50
67	W.I.R.L. ILP 956	CLUB SKA '67 VOL. 2	£60
70	Trojan TTL 48	CLUB SKA VOLUME ONE	£30
70	Trojan TTL 51	CLUB SKA VOLUME TWO (Existence unconfirmed)	£30
68	Island ILP 964	CLUB SOUL	£50
84	Kent 022	CLUB SOUL	£15
67	Elektra EUK 253	A COLD WIND BLOWS	£15
65	T. Motown TML 11001	A COLLECTION OF 16 TAMLA MOTOWN HITS	£25
67	T. Motown TML 11043	A COLLECTION OF 16 ORIGINAL BIG HITS VOL. 4	£35
67	T. Motown TML 11050	A COLLECTION OF 16 ORIGINAL BIG HITS VOL. 5	£35
68	T. Motown (S)TML 11074	A COLLECTION OF 16 ORIGINAL BIG HITS VOL. 6 (mono/stereo)	£20
69	T. Motown (S)TML 11092	A COLLECTION OF 16 ORIGINAL BIG HITS VOL. 7 - THE MOTOWN SOUND	£25
70	T. Motown (S)TML 11130	A COLLECTION OF 16 ORIGINAL BIG HITS VOL. 8	£20
86	Color Disc COLORS 4	COLOR SUPPLEMENT (400 only)	£15
93	2-Tone CDCHRTT 5013	THE COMPACT 2-TONE STORY (4-CD, box set with book)	£40
81	Springtime HA HA 6001	THE COMIC STRIP (LP, gatefold sleeve)	£15
76	Incus INCUS 21	COMPANY 1	£40
77	Incus INCUS 29	COMPANY 5	£40
77	Incus INCUS 30	COMPANY 7	£40
82	Starforce COMP 1	COMPILATION 1	£20
72	Apple STCX 3385	THE CONCERT FOR BANGLA DESH (3-LP box set, orange inside with BMI/ASCAP label	£75

credits, with booklet, featuring Bob Dylan) ....

64	Decca LK 4664	**CONVERSATION WITH THE BLUES**	**£70**
57	Tempo TAP 10	**COOL MUSIC FOR A HOT NIGHT - MOOD MUSIC IN THE MODERN MANNER**	**£150**
72	Wicksteed WCKLP 02	**CORBY CATCHMENT AREA** (private pressing)	**£200**
81	No Future OI 3	**COUNTRY FIT FOR HEROES**	**£15**
82	No Future 12 OI 23	**COUNTRY FIT FOR HEROES 2**	**£18**
69	Pama ECO 2	**CRAB - BIGGEST HITS**	**£150**
80	Rabid/Absurd LAST 1	**THE CRAP STOPS HERE**	**£25**
74	Eron 005	**CRYPTADIA**	**£15**
79	Trojan TRLS 180	**CREATION ROCKERS 1**	**£18**
79	Trojan TRLS 181	**CREATION ROCKERS 2**	**£20**
79	Trojan TRLS 183	**CREATION ROCKERS 3**	**£18**
79	Trojan TRLS 183	**CREATION ROCKERS 4**	**£15**
79	Trojan TRLS 184	**CREATION ROCKERS 5**	**£15**

D

81	Two Tone CHRTT 5004	**DANCE CRAZE** (with foldout poster)	**£40**
68	H. Note/B. Shot BSLP 5002	**DANCING DOWN ORANGE STREET**	**£150**
84	Kent KENT 026	**DANCING 'TIL DAWN**	**£15**
76	Dark Horse DH 1 (DHSAM 1)	**DARK HORSE RECORDS '76** (promo only sampler, stickered sleeve & inner)	**£40**
86	EMI EQ 5003	**DAVE CLARK'S TIME** (2-LP, with brochure and lyric inner, some with hologram)	**£30**
00	Nuphonic NUX 136LP	**DAVID MANCUSO PRESENTS THE LOFT VOL. 1** (4 x 12" with booklet)	**£100**
00	Nuphonic NUX 154LP	**DAVID MANCUSO PRESENTS THE LOFT VOL. 2** (4 x 12")	**£100**
79	Dead Good DEAD 4	**DEAD GOOD'S DEAD GOODS** (unissued)	**£0**
78	Virgin VD 2508	**DEAD ON ARRIVAL** (glow-in-the-dark vinyl with poster, export copies to US have "EXPACK 001" sticker on sleeve))	**£20**
66	Highway 51 H 100	**DECADE OF THE BLUES - THE 1950's** (99 copies only)	**£75**
66	Highway 51 H 104	**DECADE OF THE BLUES - THE 1950's VOLUME 2** (99 copies only)	**£50**
70	Polydor 2673 001	**DEEP OVERGROUND POP**	**£20**
70	Stax SXATS 1037	**THE DEEP SOUL OF STAX**	**£22**
83	Insane 1001	**DEMOLITION BLUES** (featuring the Oppressed/Deceased and Epidemic)	**£25**
86	Decal LIK 9	**DERAM DAYZE**	**£15**
68	Deram SML 1027	**THE DERAM GOLDEN POPS SAMPLER**	**£80**
67	Island ILP 955	**DERRICK HARRIOTT'S ROCK** (SKA) **STEADY PARTY**	**£500**
72	Trojan TTL 54	**DERRICK HARRIOTT'S ROCKSTEADY PARTY** (reissue - existence unconfirmed)	**£50**
85	Yangki 01	**DEVASTATE TO LIBERATE**	**£15**
89	Blast First BFDJ 1	**DEVIL'S JUKEBOX** (10 x 7" in numbered box, with booklet, 3,000 only)	**£20**
87	Manic Ears ACHE 3	**DIGGING IN WATER** (LP, featuring Disorder/Chaos UK/Oi Polloi..)	**£15**
74	DIP DLP 5026	**D.I.P. PRESENTS THE UPSETTER** (Lee Perry et al.)	**£175**
69	Minit MLL/MLS 40005	**DIRT BLUES**	**£25**
01	Trunk DFM 001 LP	**DIRTY FAN MAIL** (LP)	**£20**
70	BBC REC 65M	**DISC A DAWN**	**£20**
11	BBE BB E 172 CLP	**DISCO LOVE 2** (2-LP)	**£20**
13	BBE 224 CLP	**DISCO LOVE 3** (2-LP)	**£20**
15	BBE 319 CLP	**DISCO LOVE 4** (2-LP)	**£20**
67	Island ILP 943	**DOCTOR SOUL**	**£90**
82	BBC 2-LP-22001	**DOCTOR WHO COLLECTOR'S EDITION** (2-LP, with poster)	**£30**
80s	Pleasantly Surprised PS 12	**DOCUMENT** (cassette)	**£18**
84	Hope Springs HOP 1	**DON'T LET THE HOPE CLOSE DOWN**	**£15**
70	Python PLP	**DOWNHOME BLUES** (99 copies only)	**£90**
94	React REACT LP 55	**DOPE ON PLASTIC!** (2-LP)	**£20**
94	React REACT LP 65	**DOPE ON PLASTIC 2** (2-LP)	**£20**
96	React REACT LP 073	**DOPE ON PLASTIC 3** (2-LP)	**£20**
96	React REACT LP 97	**DOPE ON PLASTIC 4** (3-LP)	**£20**
98	React REACT LP 118	**DOPE ON PLASTIC 5** (4-LP)	**£20**
99	React REACT LP 147	**DOPE ON PLASTIC 6** (4-LP)	**£20**
00	React REACT LP 169	**DOPE ON PLASTIC 7** (3-LP)	**£20**
01	React REACT LP 195	**DOPE ON PLASTIC 8** (3-LP)	**£20**
70	Python PLP 14	**DOWNHOME BLUES VOLUME 2** (99 copies only)	**£90**
71	Python PLP 22	**DOWNHOME BLUES VOLUME 3** (99 copies only)	**£90**
87	No label or cat no	**DOUBLE EXPOSURE** (2-LP)	**£50**
67	Down With The Game 200	**DOWN WITH THE GAME VOLUME 1** (99 copies only)	**£40**
67	Down With The Game 201	**DOWN WITH THE GAME VOLUME 2** (99 copies only)	**£40**
68	Down With The Game 203	**DOWN WITH THE GAME VOLUME 3** (99 copies only)	**£40**
68	Down With The Game 204	**DOWN WITH THE GAME VOLUME 4** (99 copies only)	**£40**
68	Down With The Game 205	**DOWN WITH THE GAME VOLUME 5** (99 copies only)	**£40**
68	Down With The Game 206	**DOWN WITH THE GAME VOLUME 6** (99 copies only)	**£40**
67	Island ILP 954	**DR. KITCH**	**£60**
76	Live and Love LALP 05	**DREAD LOCKS IN JAMAICA**	**£30**
85	Capitol EG 26 0573 1-4	**DREAM BABIES**	**£15**
83	International INTEL 4	**DREAM SEQUENCE 2** (LP)	**£100**
59	Parlophone PMC 1101	**DRUMBEAT** (Adam Faith et al.)	**£30**
68	Island ILP 976	**THE DUKE AND THE PEACOCK**	**£150**
69	Trojan TTL 8	**DUKE REID'S GOLDEN HITS**	**£50**
67	Island ILP 958	**DUKE REID'S ROCK STEADY**	**£400**
70	Trojan TTL 53	**DUKE REID'S ROCK STEADY** (reissue, existence unconfirmed)	**£30**

E

17	Ace XXQLP2 049	**Bob Stanley & Pete Wiggs Present ENGLISH WEATHER** (2LP, clear vinyl))	£30
79	Fast FAST 9A	**EARCOM 1**	£30
70	Middle Earth MDLS 20	**EARTHED**	£75
80	Dead Good GOOD 1	**EAST** (with inner & stickered sleeve)	£25
81	Nothing Shaking SHAK 1	**EAST OF CROYDON** (with booklet)	£25
73	Southern Sound SD 200	**EAST VERNON BLUES**	£30
63	Decca LK 4546	**EDINBURGH FOLK FESTIVAL VOLUME 1**	£30
63	Decca LK 4563	**EDINBURGH FOLK FESTIVAL VOLUME 2**	£30
75	Island/Transatlantic	**ELECTRIC MUSE - THE STORY OF FOLK INTO ROCK** (4-LP box set with booklet)	£40
64	Turnabout TV340465	**ELECTRONIC MUSIC**	£25
73	YES 2-4	**ELECTRONIC MUSIC FROM YORK** (3-LP, box set, with insert)	£250
85	Push PUSH 001	**ELEGANCE, CHARM AND DEADLY DANGER**	£25
10	Universal Sound USLP 38	**ELEKTRONISCHE MUSIK AUS KOLN** (2-LP)	£20
80s	Master BBSLP 007	**ELEMENTALS**	£20
83	Extract XX 001	**THE ELEPHANT TABLE ALBUM** (2-LP)	£18
71	Island IDLP 1	**EL PEA** (pink rim label)	£15
77	EMI PSPL 209	**EMI INTRODUCES THE NEW BRONZE AGE** (LP)	£20
92	Sarah SARAH 628	**ENGINE COMMON**	£70
23	Chrysalis BRVC 75	**THE ENDLESS COLOURED WAYS** (THE SONGS OF NICK DRAKE) **(2LP, various artists + 1-sided Nick Drake 7" 'Tomorrow Is A Long Time', grey vinyl**	£35
83	Psycho PSYCHO 1	**ENDLESS JOURNEY VOL. 1** (numbered)	£20
83	Psycho PSYCHO 3	**ENDLESS JOURNEY VOL. 2** (numbered)	£15
83	Psycho PSYCHO 19	**ENDLESS JOURNEY VOL. 3** (numbered)	£15
88	MEK MEK 006	**THE ENGLISH REBELS** (with insert)	£20
84	Street Sounds HBOX 1	**ESSENTIAL ELECTRO** (9 LP box set, 5000 only)	£100
72	Blue Horizon 2683 007	**THE EXCELLO STORY** (2-LP)	£120
68	Amal. AMGLP 2002	**EXPLOSIVE ROCKSTEADY**	£85
87	Rot ASS 100	**THE END OF AN ERA** (LP)	£15

F

80	Factory FACT 24	**A FACTORY QUARTET** (2-LP, featuring Durutti Column, Kevin Hewick, Blurt & Royal Family And The Poor)	£20
76	Lightning LIP 2	**FAREWELL TO THE ROXY** (LP)	£20
73	Count Shelly CSLP 03	**FEELING HIGH VOL 1**	£45
68	Zeus CF 201	**FESTIVAL AT TOWERSEY**	£50
63	Pye Intl. NPL 28033	**FESTIVAL OF THE BLUES**	£30
65	Sue ILP 920	**50 MINUTES & 24 SECONDS OF RECORDED DYNAMITE!**	£100
	(Each of the above 10 LPs came with blue labels and a booklet.)		
85	L.A.Y.L.A.H. LAY 10	**THE FIGHT IS ON** (Nurse With Wound, Organum, et al.)	£30
72	Warner Bros K 66013	**FILLMORE: THE LAST DAYS** (3-LP box set with poster & booklet)	£35
88	Re-Elect The President NIXON 4	**THE FINAL COUNTDOWN** (LP)	£25
60	HMV CLP 1358/CSD 1298	**FINGS AIN'T WOT THEY USED TO BE**	£20
	(Each of the above 10 LPs came with blue labels and a booklet.)		
69	Music Man	**FIREPOINT - A COLLECTION OF FOLK BLUES**	£100
73	Spark SRLM 2003	**FIREPOINT - A COLLECTION OF FOLK BLUES** (reissue)	£30
	(Each of the above 10 LPs came with blue labels and a booklet.)		
95	Dub Jockey DJLP 005	**FIRST BOOK OF DUB CHANTS** (no sleeve)	£50
71	CBS 66311	**THE FIRST GREAT ROCK FESTIVALS OF THE 70s: ISLE OF WIGHT AND ATLANTA** (3-LP)	£30
73	Spaceward EDENLP 53	**THE FIRST LAME BUNNY ALBUM** (LP, fold out sleeve)	£400
57	Esquire 20-089	**THE FIRST NATIONAL SKIFFLE CONTEST** (10")	£80
56	Mercury MPT 7512	**FIRST ROCK 'N' ROLL PARTY** (10")	£130
	(Each of the above 10 LPs came with blue labels and a booklet.)		
89	Confection LC 7871	**FLAIR: THE OTHER WORLD OF BRITISH FOOTBALL** (2-LP)	£20
84	Kent KENT 017	**FOOT STOMPERS**	£15
83	Kent KENT 007	**FOR DANCERS ONLY**	£15
78	Trailer LER 2015	**FLYDE ACOUSTIC**	£15
64	Blue Beat BBLP 803	**FLY FLYING SKA**	£400
69	Atlantic 588 184	**FLYING HIGH** (record club edition)	£15
76	Flams/Wounded WR 1068	**FOLK AT THE CHEQUERS** (private pressing)	£15
73	Counterpoint CPT 3994	**FOLK FROM McTAVISH'S KITCHENS**	£30
73	Windmill WMD	**FOLK HERITAGE**	£30
73	Nottingham Festival FEST 1	**FOLK NOTTINGHAM STYLE**	£200
65	Decca LK 4783	**FOLK NOW**	£25
	(Each of the above 10 LPs came with blue labels and a booklet.)		
66	Folkscene FSP 001	**FOLK SCENE** (LP, private pressing)	£100
73	Eron ERON 001	**FOLK IN SANDWICH** (LP)	£40
69	Topic	**THE FOLK SONGS OF BRITAIN VOLS. 1-10** (10 x LP box set)	£80
57	HMV DLP 1143	**FOLK SONG TODAY** (SONGS AND BALLADS OF ENGLAND AND SCOTLAND) (10")	£25
71	Nicro K 220971	**FOLK UPSTAIRS**	£80
83	Greensleeves GREL 60	**FORWARD**	£20
92	Sarah SARAH 583	**FOUNTAIN ISLAND**	£70
65	Decca LK 4695	**FOURTEEN - THE LORD'S TAVERNERS' ALBUM**	£25
19	Decca 772 467-6	**THE FREAKBEAT SCENE** (2LP, Decca 90 RSD issue)	£25
70	Bamboo BLP 205	**FREEDOM SOUNDS**	£60
72	Trojan TRL 51	**FROM BAM BAM TO CHERRY OH BABY**	£20
81	Alternative ALT 007A	**FROM BROMLEY WITH LOVE** (LP)	£120

70	Liberty LBS 83278	**FROM THE VAULTS**	£15
83	New European BADVC 666	**FROM TORTURE TO CONSCIENCE** (with insert)	£80
71	Cutty Wren	**FROST LANE**	£50
89	Sub Pop DAMP 104	**FUCK ME, I'M RICH!**	£15
89	Unrest UNREST 14	**FULL FORCE VOL. 3**	£15
70	Trojan TBL 137	**FUNKY CHICKEN**	£25
70	Bamboo BLP 206	**FUNKY REGGAE**	£75
76	Burning Sounds BS 1024	**FUNNY FEELING** (LP)	£30
82	Come Org. WDC 881021	**FÜR ILSE KOCH** (some on red vinyl)	£120
70	RCA Victor SF 8118	**49 GREEK STREET** (LP, featuring Synanthesia, Nadia Cattouse, Tin Angel & Keith Christmas)	£70
03	Trunk JBH 004 LP	**FLEXI SEX** (LP)	£30
06	Trunk JBH 018 LP	**FUZZY FELT FOLK** (LP)	£60
06	Trunk JBH 018 LP	**FUZZY FELT FOLK** (LP, 100 with fuzzy felt inserts)	£80

G

95	Sarah SARAH 530	**GAOL FERRY BRIDGE**	£80
69	Pama ECO 4	**GAS - GREATEST HITS**	£160
66	Doctor Bird DSL 5001	**GAYFEET** (Jamaican sleeve and UK pressed LP)	£400
84	Kent KENT 021	**GEMS**	£15
55	HMV DLP 1039	**GENE NORMAN PRESENTS JUST JAZZ** (10")	£20
72	Chess 6641 047	**GENESIS - THE BEGINNINGS OF ROCK** (4-LP box set with booklet)	£60
73	Chess 6641 125	**GENESIS - MEMPHIS TO CHICAGO** (4-LP box set with booklet)	£60
75	Chess 6641 174	**GENESIS - SWEET HOME CHICAGO** (4-LP box set with booklet)	£60
69	Kokomo K 1004	**GEORGIA GUITARS 1927-1938** (99 copies only)	£60
67	Coxsone CSL 8007	**GET READY ROCK STEADY**	£200
02	Soundway SNDWLP001	**GHANA SOUNDZ - AFRO-BEAT, FUNK AND FUSION IN THE 70s** (2-LP)	£25
69	Pama SECO 20	**A GIFT FROM PAMA**	£60
20	Decca 085 423-8	**THE GIRLS' SCENE** (2LP, Decca 90 RSD edition, insert)	£20
80s	Sarah	**GLASS ARCADE** (The Field Mice/The Sea Urchins, et al.)	£50
72	Revelation REV 1/2/3	**GLASTONBURY FAYRE REVELATIONS - A MUSICAL ANTHOLOGY** (3-LP, poster sleeve with booklets, pyramid & printed polythene bag)	£200
66	Columbia SX 6062	**GO!**	£70
95	Lissy's LISS 5	**GODZ IS NOT A PUT ON** (500 only, in hand-pressed sleeve; some with free 7")	£30
70	Python LP 1	**GOIN' BACK TO CHICAGO** (99 copies only)	£80
60s	Heritage 1003	**GOING TO CALIFORNIA** (99 copies only)	£80
69	Oliver & Boyd SBN 05 002118/9	**THE GOLDEN BIRD** (2-LP)	£30
64	Columbia 33SX 1664	**GOLDEN GOODIES VOL. 1**	£60
64	Columbia 33SX 1672	**GOLDEN GOODIES VOL. 2**	£60
69	Roulette RCP 1000	**GOLDEN GOODIES VOL. 1**	£20
69	Roulette RCP 1001	**GOLDEN GOODIES VOL. 2**	£20
68	Allegro ALL885	**GOLDEN HITS OF SOUL**	£20
03	Dust To Digital DTD 01	**GOODBYE BABYLON** (6-CD box set)	£60
75	Eron 004	**GOOD FOLK OF KENT** (with insert)	£40
65	Atlantic ATL 5004	**GOOD OLD FIFTIES**	£55
68	Elek. EUK 260/EUKS 7260	**GOOD TIME MUSIC** (U.K. version of "What's Shakin' ", gold or red label)	£40
72	CBS 67234	**GOSPEL SOUND** (2-LP)	£20
59	Brunswick LAT 8290	**GOSPEL TRAIN**	£20
73	Greasy Truckers GT 4997	**GREASY TRUCKERS - LIVE AT DINGWALLS DANCE HALL** (2-LP with insert)	£18
73	United Artists UDX 203/4	**GREASY TRUCKERS PARTY** (2-LP, gatefold sleeve)	£20
54	London AL 3530	**THE GREAT BLUES SINGERS** (10")	£45
70	Trojan TBL 111	**GREATER JAMAICA - MOONWALK REGGAE**	£60
64	Stateside SL 10075	**THE GREATEST GOSPEL SONGS OF OUR TIME**	£25
67	Doctor Bird DLM 5009	**GREATEST JAMAICAN BEAT**	£200
70	Transatlantic TRASAM 17	**GREAT SCOTS SAMPLER**	£20
70	Transatlantic TRASAM 21	**GREAT SCOTS SAMPLER VOL. 2**	£20
54	HMV DLP 1054	**GREAT TRUMPET SOLOISTS** (10")	£20
10	Balkan BV 02	**GREEN** (with free CD)	£20
85	Crashed METALPS 107	**GREEN METAL**	£30
83	Anagram KILO 1	**GRIME OF THE CENTURY** (6-LP, box set)	£50
71	Bamboo BDLP 215	**GROOVING WITH BAMBOO**	£70
69	Direction 8-63452	**GROOVY BABY**	£15
63	Realm RM 149	**GROUP BEAT '63**	£40
63	London HA-U 8086	**GROUP OF GOODIES**	£55
78	Virgin VCL 5001	**GUILLOTINE** (10" mini-LP, with inner sleeve)	£18
71	Sunnyland KS 102	**GULF COAST BLUES** (99 copies only)	£40
69	Trojan TTL 16	**GUNS OF NAVARONE**	£35
84	Fashion FAD LP 001	**GREAT BRITISH MCS**	£15
79	Bead Records BEAD 15	**GROUPS IN FRONT OF PEOPLE** (LP)	£25
79	Bead Records BEAD 15	**GROUPS IN FRONT OF PEOPLE 2** (LP)	£25
76	Cactus CTLP 115	**GUSSIE PRESENTS THE RIGHT TRACKS**	£20
69	Liberty LBX 3	**GUTBUCKET**	£25
68	Island ILP 977	**GUY STEVENS' TESTAMENT OF ROCK AND ROLL**	£60
71	Wand WCS 1002	**THE GUYS WITH SOUL**	£20

H

80	Hackney Music Coll LP1	**HACKNEY MUSIC COLLECTIVE**	£25
88	Hangman HANG 22-UP	**HANGMAN SAMPLER**	£20

88	HandMade (no cat. no.)	HANDMADE FILMS MUSIC - THE 10TH ANNIVERSARY (CD, promo only)	£100
85	Anagram GRAM 23	HANG 11 (MUTANT SURF PUNKS)	£20
78	Black Symbol BS 004	HANDSWORTH EXPLOSION VOL 1 (LP)	£80
68	Immediate IMLYIN 2	HAPPY TO BE PART OF THE INDUSTRY OF HUMAN HAPPINESS	£18
88	Strange Fruit SFRLP 101	HARDCORE HOLOCAUST	£15
90	Strange Fruit SFRLP 113	HARCORE HOLOCAUST 2	£20
88	BPM BPLP2	HARDCORE ONE (LP)	£25
87	Music Scene MKSLP 11416	HARDER THAN THE REST (LP)	£40
74	Decca DPA 3009/10	HARD UP HEROES 1963-68 (2-LP, gatefold sleeve)	£20
99	Harvest 724352119820	HARVEST FESTIVAL (5-CD box set)	£20
69	Harvest SPSLP 118	HARVEST SAMPLER OF THE INITIAL FOUR JUNE RELEASES (promo only)	£300
84	Rot ASS 18	HAVE A ROTTEN CHRISTMAS (LP)	£25
71	Sunnyland KS 101	HAVIN' A GOOD TIME - CHICAGO BLUES ANTHOLOGY (99 copies only)	£50
12	Fruits De Mer CRUSTACEAN 26	HEAD MUSIC (2-LP, 850 only, gatefold sleeve, 1 LP yellow and one LP purple vinyl)	£25
71	Vertigo 6360 045	HEADS TOGETHER, FIRST ROUND (gatefold sleeve, swirl label)	£18
94	Mo' Wax MWLP 026	HEADZ: A SOUNDTRACK OF EXPERIMENTAL BEATHEAD JAMS (3-LP)	£25
96	Mo' Wax MW 061LP	HEADZ VOLUME 2A (4-LP)	£40
08	Jonny JBH 025 LP	HEAR O ISRAEL (LP)	£20
81	Red Stripe SNTF 856	THE HEAT IS ON	£40
90	Imaginary ILLUSION 016	HEAVEN AND HELL VOLUME 1: A TRIBUTE TO THE VELVET UNDERGROUND	£70
81	Heavy Metal HMR LP 1	HEAVY METAL HEROES	£30
82	Heavy Metal HMR LP 7	HEAVY METAL HEROES VOLUME 2	£25
84	Heavy Metal HMR LP 24	HEAVY METAL RECORDS (blue, clear & white vinyl, round sleeve)	£15
68	Trojan TRL 6	HERE COMES THE DUKE	£40
85	Rock 'N' Dole RDR 2	HEROES	£15
80s	Temps Modernes LTMV:XI	HEURES SANS SOLEIL	£20
69	Pama PSP 1002	HEY BOY HEY GIRL	£60
59	Parlophone PMD 1085	HIGHWAY TO HEAVEN (10")	£20
88	Westside HOUSEBX 1	THE HOUSE OF HITS - THE HISTORY OF HOUSE RECORDS (box set, 14-LPs, numbered)	£120
52	Capitol LC 6508	THE HISTORY OF JAZZ - THE SOLID SOUTH	£20
69	Bamboo BDLP 203	HISTORY OF SKA VOLUME ONE	£200
87	Fanfare/PWL HFCD 4	HIT FACTORY - THE BEST OF STOCK, AITKEN & WATERMAN VOL. 2 (CD, with exclusive mix of Kylie Minogue's "I Should Be So Lucky", etc)	£30
64	Pye NPL 18108	THE HITMAKERS	£20
65	Tamla Motown TML 11019	HITSVILLE U.S.A.	£35
67	Stax 589 005	HIT THE ROAD STAX	£30
81	United Dairies UD 05	HOISTING THE BLACK FLAG	£35
74	Melodisc 12-216	HONEYS	£75
84	Kent KENT 023	HOT CHILLS AND COLD THRILLS	£15
71	Pama PMP 2006	HOT NUMBERS	£40
71	Pama PMP 2009	HOT NUMBERS VOLUME TWO	£40
77	WEA M 100	HOT PLATTER CORDON BLEU (available via Melody Maker)	£20
70	Trojan TBL 128	HOT SHOTS OF REGGAE	£40
72	Hot Wax SHW 5008	HOT WAX GREATEST HITS	£15
69	Track 613 016	THE HOUSE THAT TRACK BUILT (gatefold sleeve)	£30
80	Stark ST1	HOUSEHOLD SHOCKS	£40
69	Blue Horizon PR 45/46	HOW BLUE CAN WE GET (2-LP, gatefold sleeve with insert)	£40
82	Native NAT 001	HUNDREDS AND THOUSANDS	£45

I

69	Liberty LBL/LBS 83252	I ASKED FOR WATER ... AND SHE GAVE ME GASOLINE	£80
88	Idea IDEALP 003	IDEA COMPENDIUM (LP)	£35
81	TJM TJML 1	IDENTITY PARADE (LP)	£15
02	Universal 0647491	IMPRESSED (2-LP, Gilles Peterson compilation)	£35
02	Universal 982 197 0	IMPRESSED 2 (2-LP, Gilles Peterson compilation)	£25
88	Bam Caruso MARX 085	ILLUSIONS FROM THE CRACKLING VOID	£15
90s	Dig The Fuzz DIG 013	ILLUSIONS OF ALICE IN BLACK (650 only, with booklet)	£20
69	Immediate IMLYIN 1	IMMEDIATE LETS YOU IN	£20
70	Highway 51 H-104	I'M YOUR COUNTRY MAN (99 copies only)	£40
95	Dig The Fuzz DIG 001	INCREDIBLE SOUND SHOW STORIES VOL 1: THE TECHNICOLOUR MILKSHAKE (LP)	£20
96	Dig The Fuzz DIG 004	INCREDIBLE SOUND SHOW STORIES VOL 2: WHEN THE TANGERINE STRIKES TWELVE (LP, gatefold sleeve, orange vinyl)	£20
96	Dig The Fuzz DIG 007	INCREDIBLE SOUND SHOW STORIES VOL 3: 200 FEEL DEEP IN A PURPLE IDEA (LP)	£20
96	Dig The Fuzz DIG 008	INCREDIBLE SOUND SHOW STORIES VOL 4: A TRIP ON THE MAGIC FLYING MACHINE (LP)	£20
96	Dig The Fuzz DIG 009	INCREDIBLE SOUND SHOW STORIES VOL. 5: YELLOW STREET BOUTIQUE (LP)	£20
97	Dig The Fuzz DIG 010	INCREDIBLE SOUND SHOW STORIES VOL. 6: PLASTIC & OTHER RUBBERS OF LIFE (LP)	£20
97	Dig THe Fuzz DIG 013	INCREDIBLE SOUND SHOW STORIES VOL. 7: ILLUSIONS OF ALICE IN BLACK (LP, with booklet)	£20
99	Dig The Fuzz DIG 016	INCREDIBLE SOUND SHOW STORIES: VOL. 8: PROFESSOR POTTS PORNOGRAPHIC PROJECTOR (LP, with booklet)	£30
99	Dig The Fuzz DIG 036	INCREDIBLE SOUND SHOW STORIES VOL. 9: CLAP HANDS DADDY COME HOME! (LP, with booklet)	£20
99	Dig THe Fuzz DIG 039	INCREDIBLE SOUND SHOW STIRIES VOL. 10: A HIDDEN SECRET GARDEN FOUND (LP, with booklet)	£20
99	Dig The Fuzz DIG 033	INCREDIBLE SOUND SHOW STORIES: VOL. 11: CRIMSON VALLET CREATURES IN YOUR ZOO (LP, with booklet)	£20
01	Dig THe Fuzz DIG 043	INCREDIBLE SOUND SHOW STORIES VOL. 12: FUZZ PUDDING FACTORY (LP)	£15
01	Buzz With Fuzz FUZZLP 3301	INCREDIBLE SOUND SHOW STORIES VOL. 13: FAR AWAY ROUNDABOUT (LP, 500 only)	£15

00	Dig THe Fuzz DIG 042	INCREDIBLE SOUND SHOW SPORIES VOL. 14: CANDY COLOURED DAYDREAMS (LP, with gatefold insert)	£20
03	Dig THe Fuzz DIG 046	INCREDIBLE SOUND SHOW STORIES VOL. 16 : SECOND GLANCE THROUGH THE LOOKING GLANCE (LP)	£20
02	Dig THe Fuzz DIG 045	INCREDIBLE SOUND SHOW STORIES VOL. 17 CLAP HANDS DADDY COME HOME1 PART 2 (LP, with inner sleeve, 400 only)	£20
66	CBS/Denson Shoes	THE IN CROWD (shoe offer compilation)	£25
69	Trojan TTL 15	INDEPENDENT JAMAICA	£50
79	Object Music OBJ 002	INDISCRETE MUSIC - DUBIOUS COLLABORATION (500 only)	£15
84	Illuminated JAMS 39	THE INDUSTRIAL RECORDS STORY 1976-1981	£35
84	United Dairies UD 015	IN FRACTURED SILENCE	£35
69	T. Motown (S)TML 11124	IN LOVING MEMORY (TRIBUTE TO MRS LOUCYE G. WAKEFIELD)	£55
70	Blue Horizon PR 37	IN OUR OWN WAY (OLDIES BUT GOODIES)	£20
84	People Unite PU 104	IN PROGRESS	£150
70	Ember EMB 34111	IN REGGAE TIME	£15
90	Warriors Dance WAFLP 3	INTERNATIONAL SMOKE SIGNAL	£35
83	Future FUTURE 1	INVISIBLE FRAME	£18
66	Ember FA 2034	IRELAND'S GREATEST SOUNDS: FIVE TOP GROUPS FROM BELFAST'S MARITIME CLUB	£70
79	Rationale RATE 8	IRRATIONALE (cassette, in bag with booklet)	£20
79	K Block	IS THE WAR OVER?	£25
61	Oriole MG 20046	IT'S ALL HAPPENING HERE	£35
85	Kent KENT 046	IT'S TORTURE	£15
84	Sain 002	IT'S UNHEARD OF	£150

J

69	Amalgamated CSP 3	JACKPOT OF HITS	£50
74	Atra ALP 001	JAH GUIDE - JAMAICA'S GREATEST HITS	£45
71	Ashanti SHAN 102	JAMAICAN FOLK SINGERS	£20
07	Soul Jazzz SJR LP 171	JAMAICA FUNK (2-LP)	£30
68	Blue Cat BCL 1	JAMAICAN MEMORIES	£150
64	Atlantic 587 075	JAMAICA SKA (colour 'Dancers' sleeve)	£100
67	Atlantic 587 075	JAMAICA SKA (reissue, orange sleeve)	£40
60s	Wirl WHIRL 1	JAMAICA'S AMBASSADORS OF SONG	£100
60s	Melodisc MLP 12-158	JAMAICA'S GREATEST	£40
72	Utd. Artists UAD 60027/8	THE JAMES BOND COLLECTION (2LP, gatefold, booklet)	£15
56	Tempo TAP 5	JAZZ AT THE FLAMINGO	£250
68	Columbia SLJS 1	JAZZ EXPLOSION	£25
72	Decca ECS 2114	JAZZ IN BRITAIN 1968-1969	£50
84	Streetsounds MUSIC 1	JAZZ JUICE	£25
85	Streetsounds SOUND 1	JAZZ JUICE (reissue)	£20
98	JBO JNR1001781	JBO: A PERSPECTIVE (4LP, box set)	£40
85	Natalie LIE 1	JOBS FOR THE BOYS	£15
77	Decca DPA 3035/3036	THE JOE MEEK STORY (2-LP)	£30
69	BBC REC 52S	JOHN PEEL PRESENTS TOP GEAR	£40
70	BBC REC 68M	JOHN PEEL'S ARCHIVE THINGS	£35
60	HMV CLP 1327	A JUG OF PUNCH (also issued as XLP 50003)	£25
81	Eric's ERICS 008	JUKEBOX AT ERIC'S	£20
76	RCA RS 1066	JUMPING AT THE GO GO	£18
64	R&B/Ska Beat JBL 1111	JUMP JAMAICA WAY	£650
69	RCA Intl. INT 1014	JUST A LITTLE BIT OF SOUL	£22
75	Count Shelly CSLP 7	JUST BETWEEN (nude cover)	£100
79	Kick KK 1	JUST FOR KICKS	£35

K

11	Fruits De Mer Crustacian 21	KEEP OFF THE GRASS (2-LP)	£20
56	Vogue LAE 12028	KENTON'S SIDEMEN (Don Rendell, et al.)	£150
81	White Witch	KENT ROCKS (200 only, white cover)	£180
54	HMV DLP 1048	KEYBOARD KINGS OF JAZZ (10")	£20
72	Key	KEY COLLECTION (with insert)	£15
82	Kik KIKLP 01	KIKROCK VOLUME ONE	£35
70	Trojan TBL 140	KING SIZE REGGAE	£35
72	Sioux SLX 7502	KING OF THE ROAD	£30
85	Rot ASS 21	KICK UP THE ARSE (LP)	£15

L

79	Cherry Red A RED 4	LABELS UNLIMITED (LP with inner)	£15
83	Fetish FR 2011	THE LAST TESTAMENT (with inner, stickered sleeve)	£18
87	Other OTH 10	LAST WARRIOR	£18
68	Island ILP 986	LEAPING WITH MR LEE (by Bunny Lee All Stars)	£400
80	Atra ATRA LP 1003	THE LEGEND (Augustus Pablo et al.)	£30
03	Ai AILP 004	LEISURE (100 copies only)	£15
99	Jazzman 1	LE JAZZBEAT!	£20
66	Blue Horizon LP 2	LET ME TELL YOU ABOUT THE BLUES (99 copies only)	£1000
84	Cult 1	LET'S GET PISSED IT'S CHRISTMAS	£15
66	Neshoba N 11	LET'S GO DOWN SOUTH (99 copies only)	£50
58	Brunswick LAT 8271	LET'S HAVE A PARTY	£30
81	Alt. Tentacles VIRUS 4	LET THEM EAT JELLYBEANS (with lyric poster)	£20
80s	Third Mind/Abstract	LIFE AT THE TOP	£20
85	Riot City CITY 019	LIFE'S A RIOT WITH RIOT CITY RECORDS	£20

MINT VALUE £

80	BUN 01	LIVE AT BUNJIES (gatefold sleeve with insert)	£30
77	NEMS NEL 6013	LIVE AT THE VORTEX	£15
65	Fontana TL 5240	LIVE AT THE WHISKEY A-GO-GO	£40
68	Big Shot BBTL 4000	LIVE IT UP	£150
64	Embassy WLP 6065	LIVERPOOL BEAT	£15
65	Ember NR 5028	LIVERPOOL TODAY - LIVE AT THE CAVERN	£40
08	Honest Jons HJRLP 33	LIVING IS HARD - WEST AFRICAN MUSIC IN BRITAIN 1927-29 (2-LP)	£20
70	Trojan TBL 135	LOCH NESS MONSTER	£50
98	Simply Vinyl SVLP 089	LOCK, STOCK AND TWO SMOKING BARRELS (2-LP)	£100
87	4AD CAD 703D	LONELY IS AN EYESORE (cardboard pack with book)	£40
87	4AD CADX 703	LONELY IS AN EYESORE (CD, LP & cassette, in wooden box with etching, screen print & video, 100 only)	£1000
71	Count Shelly SSLP 03	LOOK BEFORE YOU LEAP	£60
91	Holyground HG 121	LOOSE ROUTES (2-LP, gatefold foldover sleeve)	£30
78	Love Bird LB 430	LOVE AFFAIR	£30
69	Pama PSP 1001	THE LOVELY DOZEN	£60
96	Earth EARTHLP 001	LTJ BUKEM PRESENTS EARTH VOLUME 1 (5 LP box set, stickered box, 5 picture sleeves,5000 only)	£35
97	Earth EARTHLP 002	LTJ BUKEM PRESENTS EARTH VOLUME 2 (5 LP box set, 5 picture sleeves)	£25
98	Good Looking EARTH LP 003	LTJ BUKEM PRESENTS EARTH VOLUME 3 (5 LP box set)	£25

M

76	Cornish Legend CLM 1	MADE IN CORNWALL (with insert)	£60
02	Honest Jons HJRLP1	MALI MUSIC (2-LP, poster)	£25
03	Peckings PTI 001	MAMA PECKINGS AND THE DUTCHESS	£30
79	Object Music OBJ 003	A MANCHESTER COLLECTION	£25
70	Trojan TBL 129	MAN FROM CAROLINA	£30
70	CBS 52798	MA RAINEY AND THE CLASSIC BLUES SINGERS	£20
69	Marmalade 643 314	MARMALADE - 100% PROOF	£15
72	Village Thing VTSAM 16	MATCHBOX DAYS	£25
68	President PTL 1002	MAR-V-LUS SOUND OF R&B AND SOUL MUSIC	£20
60s	Wudwink ISMF 107	MARY'S FOLK	£200
96	Skam MASK 100	MASK 100 (100 only)	£250
97	Skam MASK 200	MASK 200 (LP, 200 only)	£150
98	Skam MASK 300	MASK 300 (LP, 300 only)	£50
98	Skam MASK 400	MASK 400 (LP, 400 only)	£40
99	Skam MASK 500	MASK 500 (LP, 500 only, includes remix of Bowie's Ashes To Ashes)	£80
69	Liberty LBL/LBS 83190	ME AND THE DEVIL	£75
88	Hangman HANG 15-UP	THE MEDWAY POETS (LP)	£20
87	Hangman HANG 4 UP	MEDWAY POWER HOUSE 1	£20
87	Hangman HANG 8 UP	MEDWAY POWER HOUSE 2	£20
88	Hangman HANG 17 UP	MEDWAY POWER HOUSE 3	£25
69	T. Motown (S)TML 11126	MERRY CHRISTMAS FROM MOTOWN (mono/stereo)	£40
10	Universal Sounds USLP5	MESSAGE FROM THE TRIBE (2-LP, reissue)	£30
80	BBC REH 397	METAL EXPLOSION	£20
80	EMI EMC 3318	METAL FOR MUTHAS	£20
97	Metalheadz METBOX 001	METALHEADZ (5 discs in circular tin, booklet)	£30
87	Other OTH 9	METAL WARRIOR	£50
66	Atlantic 587 021	MIDNIGHT SOUL	£20
80	Pipe PIPE 2	MINIATURES (with poster insert, 500 only)	£18
80	Pipe PIPE 2	MINIATURES (cassette with mini-booklet insert, 100 only)	£30
71	Trojan TBL 174	MISS LABBA LABBA	£30
60s	Bounty BY 6025	MODERN CHICAGO BLUES	£30
56	Tempo TAP 2	MODERN JAZZ SCENE 1956	£100
19	Decca 772 467-4	THE MOD SCENE (2LP, Decca 90 RSD edition, insert)	£30
79	Bridge House BHLP 003	MODS MAYDAY '79 (original issue)	£20
01	EMI 5 35078 2	MOJO PRESENTS ACID DROPS, SPACEDUST AND FLYING SAUCERS (4-CD box set)	£40
70	Trojan TTL 31	MOONLIGHT GROOVER	£35
62	HMV CLP 1583	MORE OF YOUR FAVOURITE TV AND RADIO THEMES	£20
67	Atlantic 587088	MORE MIDNIGHT SOUL	£15
65	private pressing	MORE SINGING AT THE COUNT HOUSE	£150
72	Island HELP 5	MORRIS ON (black label with pink 'i')	£20
86	Iguana VYK LP 11	MOTOR CITY 9 (with booklet)	£15
65	Tamla Motown TML 11007	THE MOTORTOWN REVUE LIVE	£80
66	Tamla Motown TML 11027	THE MOTORTOWN REVUE IN PARIS	£70
70	Tamla Motown (S)TML 11127	THE MOTORTOWN REVUE LIVE (mono/stereo)	£20
74	Tamla Motown STML 11270	MOTOWN CHARTBUSTERS VOL. 9 (green vinyl)	£15
66	Tamla Motown TML 11030	MOTOWN MAGIC	£35
68	Tamla Motown TML 11064	MOTOWN MEMORIES (flipback sleeve)	£60
68	Tamla Motown TML 11077	MOTOWN MEMORIES VOL. 2	£60
70	Tamla Motown STML 11143	MOTOWN MEMORIES VOL. 3	£50
72	Tamla Motown TMSP 1130	THE MOTOWN STORY (5-LP box set)	£20
83	Tamla Motown TMSP 6019	THE MOTOWN STORY - THE FIRST 25 YEARS (box set)	£20
77	Mountain PSLP 200	MOUNTAIN ROCKS INTO '77 (Mountain label sampler, promo only)	£20
84	Kent 013	MOVING ON UP	£15
83	Showcase SHOWC 1	MUSIC BIZ SHOWCASE '83	£50
71	Mushroom 100 MR 16	THE MUSHROOM FOLK SAMPLER	£40
57	Brunswick LAT 8201	MUSIC FOR THE BOYFRIEND - HE REALLY DIGS ROCK'N'ROLL	£100

57	Brunswick LAT 8202	MUSIC FOR THE BOYFRIEND - HE REALLY DIGS JAZZ £30
57	Brunswick LAT 8205	MUSIC FOR THE BOYFRIEND - THE FEMININE TOUCH £35
67	Argo RG 533	MUSIC FROM THE FAR NORTH (with foldout inner) £15
15	Balkan BV 16	MUTANT CITY ACID £25
15	Balkan BV 17	MUTANT CITY ACID 2..£20
16	Balkan BV 19	MUTANT CITY ACID 3..£20
17	Balkan BV 22	MUTANT CITY ACID 4..£18
81	Ze ISSP 4001	MUTANT DISCO (3 x 12" box set, numbered, 2,000 only) £20
04	Ze ZEREC LP02-2	MUTANT DISCO VOLUME 2 (2-LP)...£20
05	Ze ZEREC LP 14	MUTANT DISCO VOLUME 3 (2-LP)...£20
77	EMI NUT 4	MY GENERATION £15
89	Hangman HANG 35 UP	MEDWAY POWERHOUSE (LP)...£30

N

71	Eden LP 43	NAPTON FOLK CLUB (private pressing, 100 only)...£35
69	Bamboo BLP 201	NATURAL REGGAE VOLUME ONE...£60
70	Bamboo BLP 204	NATURAL REGGAE VOLUME TWO...£100
81	4AD CAD 117	NATURES MORTES - STILL LIVES (export issue)..£60
85	Musique Brut BRV 002	NECROPOLIS, AMPHIBIANS AND REPTILES: THE MUSIC OF ADOLF WOLFLI..............£20
71	RCA NEON 1	NEON PROMOTIONAL ALBUM £150
83	Pax PAX 14	NEVER MIND THE GONADS - HERE'S THE TESTICLES £15
87	Broken Flag BF V8	NEVER SAY WHEN...£40
77	Vertigo 6300 902	NEW WAVE...£20
79	Planet PR 003	NEW WAVE FROM THE HEART £70
69	Blue Horizon 7-63210	THE 1968 MEMPHIS COUNTRY BLUES FESTIVAL...£25
81	NMX	NMX: LIVE AT SHEFFIELD (cassette)...£20
68	Spark SRLM 107	NO INTRODUCTION £30
69	Trojan TTL 14	NO MORE HEARTACHES £35
70	Polydor 545 017	NON STOP SOUL £30
69	Regal Starline SRS 5013	NO ONE'S GONNA CHANGE OUR WORLD £18
89	Manic Ears ACHE 017	NORTH ATLANTIC NOISE ATTACK (2-LP, insert) £20
14	Harmless HURTBOX 007	NORTHERN SOUL: THE SOUNDTRACK (box set 14 x 7")...£80
14	Harmless NTHSOULLP01	NORTHERN SOUL: THE SOUNDTRACK (2-LP) £30
19	Decca 772 467-3	THE NORTHERN SOUL SCENE (2LP, Decca 90 RSD edition, insert)...............................£25
60	Fontana TFL 5123	NOTHIN' BUT THE BLUES (gatefold sleeve) £60
71	CBS 66278	NOTHING BUT THE BLUES (2-LP, Blue Horizon pressings may also exist (£75))...............£60
79	Giorno GPS	THE NOVA CONVENTION £20
70	Decca Nova SPA 72	NOVA SAMPLER £20
70s	Warm PFLP 201	NOVA-VAGA..£15
92	EMI NOD 8	NOW DANCE '92 (2LP, gatefold, features Madonna version of Shake Your Head by Was (Not Was))...£50
84	Virgin/EMI CDP 26 0408 2	NOW THAT'S WHAT I CALL MUSIC 4 (CD)...£400
86	Virgin/EMI CDNOW 8	NOW THAT'S WHAT I CALL MUSIC 8 (CD)..£30
87	Virgin/EMI CDNOW 9	NOW THAT'S WHAT I CALL MUSIC 9 (CD)..£30
92	EMI NOW 21	NOW THAT'S WHAT I CALL MUSIC 21 (2LP, gatefold) £30
92	EMI NOW 22	NOW THAT'S WHAT I CALL MUSIC 22 (2LP, gatefold) £30
92	EMI NOW 23	NOW THAT'S WHAT I CALL MUSIC 23 (2LP, gatefold) £35
93	EMI NOW 24	NOW THAT'S WHAT I CALL MUSIC 24 (2LP, gatefold) £35
93	EMI NOW 25	NOW THAT'S WHAT I CALL MUSIC 25 (2LP, gatefold) £35
93	EMI NOW 26	NOW THAT'S WHAT I CALL MUSIC 26 (2LP, gatefold) £35
94	EMI NOW 27	NOW THAT'S WHAT I CALL MUSIC 27 (2LP, gatefold) £40
94	EMI NOW 28	NOW THAT'S WHAT I CALL MUSIC 28 (2LP, gatefold) £40
94	EMI NOW 29	NOW THAT'S WHAT I CALL MUSIC 29 (2LP, gatefold) £50
95	EMI NOW 30	NOW THAT'S WHAT I CALL MUSIC 30 (2LP, gatefold) £60
95	EMI NOW 31	NOW THAT'S WHAT I CALL MUSIC 31 (2LP, gatefold) £60
95	EMI NOW 32	NOW THAT'S WHAT I CALL MUSIC 32 (2LP, gatefold) £80
96	EMI NOW 33	NOW THAT'S WHAT I CALL MUSIC 33 (2LP, gatefold) £90
96	EMI NOW 34	NOW THAT'S WHAT I CALL MUSIC 34 (2LP, gatefold) £90
96	EMI NOW 35	NOW THAT'S WHAT I CALL MUSIC 35 (2LP, gatefold) £100
22	Sony/EMI LPYBNOW 79	NOW YEARBOOK '79 (3LP, orange vinyl, limited edition) £40
22	Sony/EMI LPYBNOW 80	NOW YEARBOOK '80 (3LP, clear vinyl, limited edition) £60
22	Sony/EMI LPYBNOW 81	NOW YEARBOOK '81 (3LP, red vinyl, limited edition) £50
22	Sony/EMI LPYBNOW 82	NOW YEARBOOK '82 (3LP, yellow vinyl, limited edition)...£70
21	Sony/EMI LPYBNOW 83	NOW YEARBOOK '83 (3LP, translucent red vinyl, limited edition).............................£100
21	Sony/EMI LPYBNOW 84	NOW YEARBOOK '84 (3LP, blue vinyl, limited edition) £100
69	Pama ECO 6	NU BEAT - GREATEST HITS £100
73	Elektra K 62012	NUGGETS (Original Artyfacts From The First Psychedelic Era 1965-1968) (2-LP, gatefold sleeve)..£45
86	Numa NUMA 1004	NUMA RECORDS YEAR 1 (with bonus Italian 12" "My Dying Machine")..........................£15
81	Guardian Records	N E 1 (LP)...£40

O

69	Liberty LBS 83234	OAKLAND BLUES...£30
79	Rok ROK LP 001	ODD BODS, MODS AND SODS..£75
85	Micro MIC 15001	OFFERING OF ISCA (LP, features 2 tracks by Circuit 7) £100
58	Parlophone PMC 1072	OH BOY!..£40
78	Raw RAWLP 2	OH NO IT'S MORE FROM RAW (Users/Killjoys et al.) £20
80	EMI ZIT 1	OI! - THE ALBUM (initially mail-order only from Sounds magazine) £30
87	Link LP 23	OI! GLORIOUS OI! £15

Rare Record Price Guide 2026

84	Syndicate SYNLP 4	OI! OF SEX	£15
83	Secret SEC 5	OI! OI! THAT'S YER LOT	£15
60s	Melodisc MS 4	OLDIES BUT GOODIES	£65
64	Stateside SL 10094	OLDIES R & B	£70
06	Peckings PTI LP 003	OLD SKOOL YOUNG BLOOD (2-LP)	£40
69	Transatlantic XTRA 1076	O LIVERPOOL WE LOVE YOU (Stan Kelly/Bill Shankley/Jimmy Tarbuck et al.)	£40
68	Big Shot BBTL 4001	ONCE MORE	£130
69	Marmalade 643 314	100% PROOF	£15
99	Universal MCD 60066	1-2-3-4 PUNK AND NEW WAVE 1976 - 1979 (5-CD box set)	£30
86	Stateside/EMI SSL 6002	ONE MINIT AT A TIME	£18
73	Charisma CLASS 3	ONE MORE CHANCE	£20
63	Columbia 33SX 1536	ONE NIGHT STAND	£40
63	Stateside SL 10065	ON STAGE LIVE!	£65
69	Atco 228 009/010	ON STAGE - LIVE (2-LP)	£25
84	Sane SANE 003	ON THE STREET (LP)	£35
83	Kent KENT 006	ON THE SOUL SIDE	£15
64	Columbia 33SX 1662	ON THE SCENE	£90
84	Kent KENT 20	ON THE UP BEAT	£15
10	Balkan BV 05	ORANGE (with free CD)	£20
95	Tip TIPLP 2	ORANGE COMPILATION (2-LP)	£20
64	Rio RLP 1	THE ORIGINAL COOL JAMAICAN SKA	£150
70	Mercury SMCL 20182	ORIGINAL GOLDEN HITS OF THE GREAT BLUES SINGERS	£20
60	London HA-G 2308	THE ORIGINAL HITS	£30
61	London HA-G 2339	THE ORIGINAL HITS VOL. 2	£30
64	Vocalion VA 8017	ORIGINAL SURFIN' HITS	£70
62	London HA-U 2404	OUR SIGNIFICANT HITS	£70
83	Peninsula	OUT OF THE UNKNOWN	£70
13	Z ZEDDLP 028	OVERDOSE OF THE HOLY GHOST (2-LP)	£60

P

70	Golden Guinea GGL 0451	PADDY IS DEAD AND THE KIDS KNOW IT (LP)	£150
65	Blue Beat BBLP 804	PAIN IN MY BELLY	£300
67	Island ILP 945	PAKISTANI SOUL SESSION	£75
90	Factory FACT 400	PALATINE - THE FACTORY STORY (4-LP)	£150
85	LIL LP2	PARKSIDE STEELWORKS	£60
73	Charisma CAS 1078	THE PARLOUR SONG BOOK (LP)	£15
68	Studio One SOL 9009	PARTY TIME IN JAMAICA	£300
88	On U Sound 37	PAY IT ALL BACK VOL 1	£15
88	On U Sound 42	PAY IT ALL BACK VOL 2 (with booklet)	£20
77	CollinsMusic CM001 BLP	PEACE AND LOVE	£50
66	Decca LK 4824	PENTHOUSE MAGAZINE PRESENTS THE BEDSIDE BOND	£40
83	Psycho PSYCHO 6	THE PERFUMED GARDEN	£20
84	Psycho PSYCHO 15	THE PERFUMED GARDEN II	£20
81	Cherry Red BRED 15	PERSPECTIVES AND DISTORTION (gatefold sleeve)	£15
86	Streetsounds PHST 1986	THE PHILADELPHIA YEARS (14-LP box set)	£80
92	Art ART2 CD	THE PHILOSOPHY OF SOUND AND MACHINE (CD compilation)	£60
72	Apple APCOR 24	PHIL SPECTOR'S CHRISTMAS ALBUM (reissue of "A Christmas Gift For You")	£30
75	Warner Bros K 59010	PHIL SPECTOR'S CHRISTMAS ALBUM (2nd reissue, some with poster)	£18
80	Phil Spector Intl. 2307 015	PHIL SPECTOR '74/'79	£25
67	Riverside RLP 8809	PIANO BLUES 1927-1933	£20
60	HMV CLP 1362/XLP 50004	A PINCH OF SALT - BRITISH SEA SONGS OLD AND NEW	£30
53	London AL 3506	PIONEERS OF BOOGIE WOOGIE (10")	£40
54	London AL 3537	PIONEERS OF BOOGIE WOOGIE VOLUME TWO (10")	£40
98	Just Say JUSTLP 001-3	THE PIONEERS OF HOUSE MUSIC - CHICAGO REUNION (2-LP)	£20
80	Incus INCUS 37	PISA 1980: IMPROVISOR'S SYMPOSIUM	£50
13	RCLP 009	PLANKTON - A FRUITS DE MER COMPILATION (LP, gatefold with free 7")	£20
81	P. Surprised KLARK 002	PLEASANTLY SURPRISED - AN HOUR OF ELOQUENT SOUNDS (cassette)	£20
71	Argo ZPR 264/5	POETRY AND JAZZ IN CONCERT 250	£15
89	Link LINK LP 095	POP OI!	£20
68	Polydor 236 517/8/9	POP PARTY! (3-LP in box)	£20
68	Post War Blues PWB 1	POST WAR BLUES: CHICAGO (99 copies only)	£45
66	Post War Blues PWB 2	POST WAR BLUES: MEMPHIS ON DOWN (99 copies only)	£45
67	Post War Blues PWB 3	POST WAR BLUES: EASTERN AND GULF COAST STATES (99 copies only)	£45
68	Post War Blues PWB 4	POST WAR BLUES: TEXAS (99 copies only)	£45
68	Post War Blues PWB 5	POST WAR BLUES: DETROIT (99 copies only)	£45
60s	Post War Blues PWB 6	POST WAR BLUES: WEST COAST (99 copies only)	£45
60s	Post War Blues PWB 7	POST WAR BLUES: THE DEEP SOUTH (99 copies only)	£45
69	Python PWBC 1	POST WAR COLLECTOR SERIES VOL. 1 (99 copies only)	£80
80	4AD BAD 11	PRESAGES (mini-LP, green/pink or brown sleeve)	£15
79	Preseli PRE 001	PRESELI FOLK (private pressing with insert)	£30
77	Uptempo UTLP 001	PRESENTING THE POSSE	£30
70	Kokomo K 1006	PRE-WAR TEXAS BLUES (99 copies only)	£45
87	A&M AMA 3906	PRINCE'S TRUST 10TH ANNIVERSARY BIRTHDAY PARTY (2-LP, some stickered, with Paul McCartney 7": "Long Tall Sally"/"I Saw Her Standing There")	£20
90	Intrigue IGE LP4	PRODUCED BY NEMESIS VOL III	£18
90	United Dairies UD 134	PSILOTRIPITAKA (3-LP [UD 01, 03 & 04], with bonus LP "Registered Nurse" [UD 00], 1,000 only, some possibly in leather bag)	£400
90	United Dairies UD 134CD	PSILOTRIPITAKA (3-CD [UD 01, 03 & 04], with bonus CD "Registered Nurse" [UD 00CD], 1,000 only, 30 in 'leather bondage bag')	£400

91	Delerium DELP 005	PSYCHEDELIC SAUNA (2-LP, 500 numbered on multi-coloured vinyl)	£18
19	Decca 772 467-8	THE PSYCHEDELIC SCENE (2LP, Decca 90 RSD edition, insert)	£25
97	Simply Vinyl SVLP 0027	PULP FICTION (2-LP, reissue)	£18
81	Abstract AABT 100	PUNK AND DISORDERLY (red vinyl)	£20
82	Anagram GRAM 001	PUNK AND DISORDERLY 2 (blue vinyl)	£20
82	Anagram GRAM 005	PUNK AND DISORDERLY 2 (Multi-coloured vinyl)	£20
82	Pax 7	PUNK DEAD?...NAH MATE	£20
91	Sink Below SINK 2	PUNK'S NOT DREAD (LP, with inner)	£15
65	Sue ILP 919	PURE BLUES VOLUME ONE	£60
83	Guardian GRC 2162	PURE OVERKILL	£18
85	Color Disc COLORS 2	PURPLE TWILIGHT (400 only)	£20
68	Island ILP 978	PUT IT ON, IT'S ROCK STEADY	£40
71	Pye PSA 6	PYE SALES SAMPLER (sampler for Pye & Dawn releases; 99 copies only, with release sheet)	£20

Q

68	Stateside S(S)L 10209	A QUARTET OF SOUL	£50
70	Trojan TBL 136	QUEEN OF THE WORLD	£120
82	Quest BRA 002	THE QUEST TAPES	£75

R

07	Mikili AFRO 1	RARE AFRO & CARIBBEAN FUNK	£20
07	Mikili AFRO 2	RARE AFRO & CARIBBEAN FUNK VOL 2	£20
76	Grounation GROL 509	RAS CLAAT DUB	£50
69	United Artists (S)UX 1214	RAVE	£25
73	Attack ATLP 1012	RAVE ON BROTHER	£35
77	Raw RAWLP 1	RAW DEAL (black & white sleeve & red/blue label)	£25
19	Decca 772 467-7	THE R&B SCENE (2LP, Decca 90 RSD edition, insert)	£20
64	Decca LK 4577	READY, STEADY, GO!	£45
68	Pama PMLP 3	READY STEADY GO ROCKSTEADY	£70
64	Decca LK 4634	READY, STEADY, WIN	£75
65	Stateside SL 10112	THE REAL R & B	£40
89	Intrigue IGE LP1	THE REBEL PRESENTS	£30
95	4th & Broadway BRLPD 617	THE REBIRTH OF COOL PHIVE (2-LP)	£40
82	Recommended 104	RECOMMENDED SAMPLER	£15
79	Destiny DS 10001	THE RECORD COLLECTOR	£20
81	Recorder BR 003	RECORDER THREE	£20
70	CBS 52797	RECORDING THE BLUES	£22
12	Balkan BV 01	RED (with CD)	£30
65	Red Bird RB 20-102	RED BIRD GOLDIES	£50
69	Trojan TTL 11	RED RED WINE	£30
70	Downtown TBL 116	RED RED WINE VOLUME 2	£35
69	Trojan TBLS 105	REGGAE CHARTBUSTERS	£20
70	Pama Economy ECO 34	REGGAE FOR DAYS (LP)	£150
68	Big Shot BIL 3000	REGGAE GIRL	£200
69	Pama ECO 3	REGGAE HITS '69 VOL. 1	£35
69	Pama ECO 11	REGGAE HITS '69 VOL. 2	£50
69	Pama PTP 1001	REGGAE HIT THE TOWN	£50
68	Studio One SOL 9007	REGGAE IN THE GRASS	£150
71	Trojan TBL 181	REGGAE JAMAICA	£20
71	Trojan TBL 193	REGGAE JAMAICA VOL. 2	£20
71	Bamboo BDLP 208	REGGAEMATIC SOUNDS	£100
70	Trojan TBL 144	REGGAE MOVEMENT	£20
72	Trojan TBL 189	REGGAE POWER VOL 2	£45
72	Trojan TBL176	REGGAE REGGAE VOL 2	£45
69	Coxsone CSP 2	REGGAE SPECIAL	£50
71	Pama 2001	REGGAE SPECTACULAR WITH STRINGS	£25
70	Trojan TBL 151	REGGAE STEADY GO VOL 1	£18
73	Rhino SRNN 7001	REGGAE STEADY GO	£18
73	Trojan TRLS 54	REGGAE STRINGS	£30
74	Trojan TRLS 92	REGGAE STRINGS VOL 2	£18
68	Coxsone CSL 8017	REGGAE TIME	£150
72	Ashanti ANB 201	REGGAE TIME	£25
71	Pama PMP 2012	REGGAE TO REGGAE	£50
69	Pama PSP 1004	REGGAE TO UK WITH LOVE	£225
76	Third World TWLP 107	REGGAE VARIOUS ARTISTS	£70
86	Rot HELL 36	RELIGION AS HELL (LP)	£20
80s	Ré 0101	RE RECORDS QUARTERLY VOL. No. 1 (with book)	£15
01	Trunk/Second Coming SEC 001	RESURRECTION: THE AMPLIFIED BIBLE OF HEAVENLY GROOVES (LP)	£20
72	Count Shelly CSLP 01	RETURN TO ME REGGAE	£30
73	Count Shelly CSLP 02	RETURN TO ME REGGAE 2	£40
64	Decca LK 4616	RHYTHM AND BLUES	£80
64	Mercury MCL 20019	RHYTHM AND BLUES PARTY	£40
73	Tamla Motown STML 11232	RIC TIC RELICS	£20
68	Coxsone CSL 8015	RIDE ME DONKEY	£150
69	Trojan TTL 18	RIDE YOUR DONKEY	£40
85	Kent KENT 039	RIGHT BACK WHERE WE STARTED FROM	£15
03	Dig The Fuzz DIG048	RIOT OF THE AMPHETAMINE GENERATION (400 copies only, with booklet)	£40

MINT VALUE £

82	Riot City ASSEMBLY 1	RIOTOUS ASSEMBLEY (red vinyl)	£18
61	London HA-A 2338	ROCK-A-HITS	£40
57	London HB-C 1067	ROCK 'N' ROLL (10")	£40
20	Decca 085 432-1	THE ROCK'N'ROLL SCENE (2LP,Decca 90 RSD edition, insert)	£20
59	London HA-E 2180	ROCK AND ROLL FOREVER	£40
58	Decca LF 1300	ROCKIN' AT THE '2 I'S' (10")	£30
69	Decca LK 5002	ROCK STEADY	£30
69	Pama PMLP 7	ROCK STEADY COOL	£100
68	Coxsone CSL 8013	ROCK STEADY COXSONE STYLE	£175
67	Studio One SOL 9000	ROCK STEADY SKA	£200
80	Guardian GRC 80	ROKSNAX	£50
83	Cha Cha CHALP 016	ROOTS AND CULTURE	£25
10	Fruits De Mer Crustacean 18	ROQUETING THROUGH SPACE (LP and free 7")	£40
84	Rot ASS 15	ROT IN HELL (LP)	£25
82	Guardian GRC 130	ROXCALIBUR	£70
77	Harvest SHSP 4069	THE ROXY LONDON W.C.2 (JAN - APR 77) (with inner bag)	£25
94	Mo' Wax MWLP 003	ROYALTIES OVERDUE (2-LP, coloured vinyl)	£60
84	Bam Caruso KIRI 024	RUBBLE 1: THE PSYCHEDELIC SNARL (with 8-page insert; first 2000 with inner sleeve and lightshow labels)	£20
86	Bam Caruso KIRI 025	RUBBLE 2: POP-SIKE PIPE DREAMS (with inner sleeve)	£20
86	Bam Caruso KIRI 026	RUBBLE 3: NIGHTMARES IN WONDERLAND (with inner sleeve)	£20
86	Bam Caruso KIRI 027	RUBBLE 4: THE 49 MINUTE TECHNICOLOUR DREAM (some with 4-page insert; first 2000 with inner sleeve and lightshow labels)	£20
86	Bam Caruso KIRI 044	RUBBLE 5: THE ELECTRIC CRAYON SET (with inner sleeve)	£15
86	Bam Caruso KIRI 049	RUBBLE 6: THE CLOUDS HAVE GROOVY FACES (with inner sleeve)	£15
87	Bam Caruso KIRI 050	RUBBLE 7: PICTURES IN THE SKY (with inner sleeve)	£15
88	Bam Caruso KIRI 051	RUBBLE 8: ALL THE COLOURS OF DARKNESS	£15
87	Bam Caruso KIRI 065	RUBBLE 9: FROM THE HOUSE OF LORDS (1000 copies only)	£18
87	Bam Caruso KIRI 079	RUBBLE 9: PLASTIC WILDERNESS	£15
88	Bam Caruso KIRI 098	RUBBLE 10: PROFESSOR JORDAN'S MAGIC SOUND SHOW (with inner sleeve)	£15
86	Bam Caruso KIRI 069	RUBBLE 11: ADVENTURES IN THE MIST (with inner sleeve)	£20
86	Bam Caruso KIRI 070	RUBBLE 12: STAIRCASE TO NOWHERE (with inner sleeve)	£20
86	Bam Caruso KIRI 102	RUBBLE 13: FREAK BEAT FANTOMS	£20
88	Bam Caruso KIRI 106	RUBBLE 14: THE MAGIC ROCKING HORSE (with inner sleeve)	£20
91	Bam Caruso KIRI 084	RUBBLE 15: 5000 SECONDS OVER TOYLAND	£20
91	Bam Caruso KIRI 096	RUBBLE 16: GLASS ORCHID AFTERMATH	£15
91	Bam Caruso KIRI 099	RUBBLE 17: A TRIP IN A PAINTED WORLD	£20
92	Bam Caruso KIRI 101	RUBBLE 18: RAINBOW THYME WINDERS (unreleased, 25 test pressings only)	£200
92	Bam Caruso KIRI 109	RUBBLE 19: EIDERDOWN MINDFOG (unreleased, 25 test pressings only)	£200
90s	Bam Caruso KIRI 110	RUBBLE 20: THRICE UPON A TIME - NOTHING IS REAL (unreleased)	£0
91	Ruff Kut RCLP001	RUFF KUT	£145
81	Naive 002	RUPERT PREACHING AT A PICNIC (LP)	£100
74	Cactus CTLP 104	RUPIE'S GEMS	£30
76	Cactus CTLP 119	RUPIES GEMS CHAPTER II	£40
69	Xtra XTRA 1035	RURAL BLUES (2-LP)	£25

S

81	Adult Entertainments ADD 1LP	SAD DAY WE LEFT THE CROFT	£50
70	Transworld SPLP 101	SAMANTHA PROMOTIONS (orange cover, private pressing, a few with poster)	£600
70	Transworld SPLP 102	SAMANTHA PROMOTIONS (purple cover, private pressing, a few with poster)	£600
78	Live And Love LAP 005	SATISFACTION IN DUB	£50
60	Parlophone PMC 1130	SATURDAY CLUB	£30
64	Decca LK 4583	SATURDAY CLUB	£25
67	Atlantic Special 590 007	SATURDAY NIGHT AT THE APOLLO (reissue of "Apollo Saturday Night")	£20
81	Suspect SU S3	SCENE OF THE CRIME	£60
81	Treble Chants ASN 1	SCALING TRIANGLES (Petticoats/Sole Sisters/Sub Versa)	£60
65	Columbia 33SX 1730	SCENE '65	£125
69	Bamboo BDLP 202	A SCORCHA FROM BAMBOO	£80
95	Blue Eyed Dog VTDOG 12	SEARCH AND DISOBEY (2-LP, 10")	£20
81	Airship AP 342	SEASIDE ROCK (2-LP, with insert)	£20
81	Come Org. WDC 881008	THE SECOND COMING (various coloured vinyls)	£50
87	Cherry Red BRED 74	SEEDS I: POP (TV Personalities/Marine Girls, et al.)	£20
68	Elektra EUK 261	SELECT ELEKTRA (also stereo EUKS 7261)	£30
73	Lord Koos KLP 3	SEND REQUEST	£60
80	Kathedral KATH 1	SENT FROM COVENTRY (with booklet)	£15
84	Glass GLALP7	SHADOW AND SUBSTANCE	£15
88	Sarah SARAH 587	SHADOW FACTORY (The Sea Urchins/14 Iced Bears, et al.)	£40
74	Eron 003	SHEPWAY FOLK (with insert)	£30
84	Kent KENT 015	SHOES	£15
81	9 Danke 9DANKE	SHOOT THE HOSTAGES (screenprint sleeve, stapled, multiple inserts)	£150
86	GI GILP 999	SHOOTING FROM THE HIP	£20
78	Virgin VCL 5003	SHORT CIRCUIT - LIVE AT THE ELECTRIC CIRCUS (10"; orange, yellow or blue vinyl)	£120
78	Virgin VCL 5003	SHORT CIRCUIT - LIVE AT THE ELECTRIC CIRCUS (10"; black vinyl with free John Dowie EP [VED 1004])	£20
90	Horaces HRH 101	SHRINE - THE RAREST SOUL LABEL	£20
12	Robot Elephant RER 013	SID CHIP SOUNDS - THE MUSIC OF THE COMMODORE 64 (2-LP)	£50
84	Only A Revolution ONLY 2	SIGNAL TO NOISE SET	£40
66	Chess CRL 4519	SING A SONG OF SOUL	£40

73	Sir Collins SCMW 001	SIR COLLINS MUSIC WHEEL CHAPTER 1	£50
57	Parlophone PMC 1047	SIX-FIVE SPECIAL	£50
72	Trojan TBL 191	16 DYNAMIC REGGAE HITS	£18
73	Trojan TBL 209	16 DYNAMIC HITS 2	£20
71	Pama PMP 2015	16 DYNAMIC REGGAE HITS	£40
66	Island ILP 930	SKA AT THE JAMAICA PLAYBOY CLUB (gatefold sleeve)	£250
67	Coxsone CSL 8003	SKA-A-GO-GO	£200
66	Doctor Bird DLM 5000	SKA-BOO-DA-BA	£400
60s	Page One FOR 006	SKA'S THE LIMIT (copies on Carnival label CX 1000, worth £80)	£50
68	Ace Of Clubs ACL 1250	SKIFFLE	£30
81	RSB 1	THE SNOOPIES ALBUM (THE LAST REMAINS OF A RICHMOND VENUE) (numbered, with booklet, 1,000 only)	£20
60s	Solar	THE SOLAR BOX SET	£40
71	Bamboo BDLP 212	SOLID GOLD	£50
66	Atlantic ATL 5048	SOLID GOLD SOUL	£20
67	Atlantic 587 058	SOLID GOLD SOUL VOL. 2	£20
75	Disco Demand DDLP 5002	SOLID SOUL SENSATIONS	£18
72	South. Preservation SPR 1	SOME COLD RAINY DAY	£15
65	Lestar LLP 101	SOME FOLK IN LEICESTER (private pressing)	£20
13	RCLP 010	SOMETHING IN THE WATER (LP, gatefold)	£30
13	RCLP 010	SOMETHING IN THE WATER (LP, gatefold, clear vinyl band edition, 100 only)	£50
84	Adventures In Reality ARR 017	SOMETHING STIRS	£15
70	Pama PMP 2003	SOMETHING SWEET THE LADY	£150
69	Liberty LBX 4	SON OF GUTBUCKET	£20
76	Harvest SHSM 2012	SON OF MORRIS ON	£18
83	Syndicate SYNLP 3	SON OF OI!	£15
12	Fruits De Mer Crustacean 25	SORROW'S CHILDREN	£25
84	Kent KENT 011	SOUL CLASS OF '66	£15
69	Direction (S)PR 28	SOUL DIRECTION	£25
69	Page One POS 608	SOULED AGAIN	£20
69	Polydor 584 163	SOUL FEVER	£20
60s	Minit MLL 40011E	SOUL FOOD	£40
69	Soul City SCB 1	SOUL FROM THE CITY	£45
70	Specialty SPE 6606	SOUL FROM THE VAULTS	£15
70	Polydor 583 757	SOUL GOLD	£18
68	Trojan TRL 3	SOUL OF JAMAICA	£50
86	None	SOUL OF HARINGAY	£100
68	Polydor Special 236 213	SOUL PARTY	£20
69	Pama PMLP 8	SOUL SAUCE	£70
69	Polydor 236 554	SOUL SELLER	£18
69	United Artists UAL 29018	SOUL SENSATION	£15
85	Kent KENT 041	SOUL SERENADE	£15
66	Stateside SL 10186	SOUL SIXTEEN	£45
66	Sue ILP 934	SOUL '66	£60
67	CBS BPG 62965	SOUL SOUNDS	£25
67	HMV CLP 3619	SOUL SOUNDS OF THE 60s	£45
98	BBE BBELP 013	SOUL SPECTRUM (2-LP)	£40
67	Stateside SL 10203	SOUL SUPPLY	£50
69	Atlantic 218005	SOUL TOGETHER	£15
73	Trojan TRLS 74	SOUL TO SOUL DJ CHOICE	£20
65	Pye Intl. NPL 28061	THE SOUND OF BACHARACH	£20
95	EMI EMI 8322 801	THE SOUND GALLERY	£25
15	DJ International DJISX1001	SOUND OF DJ INTERNATIONAL (3-LP)	£20
19	Pikes PIKESLP002	THE SOUND OF MERCURY RISING (2-LP, compiled by DJ Harvey)	£30
68	President PTL 1008	THE SOUND OF SOUL	£30
79	Grapevine GRAL 1001	SOUND OF THE GRAPEVINE	£20
69	Cambridge University Press	SOUNDS AND SILENCE	£75
64	Stateside SL 10077	THE SOUND OF THE R&B HITS	£65
70	Sentinel SENS 1001	SOUNDS LIKE WEST CORNWALL	£20
09	Finders Keepers FK023LLP	THE SOUNDS OF WONDER (2-LP)	£25
09	Finders Keepers FK023LLP	THE SOUNDS OF WONDER (2-LP, limited edition 100 only different sleeve)	£40
69	London HAK 8405	SOUTHERN COMFORT	£125
83	Spectrum ASPEC 001	SOUTHERN COMFORT	£75
80s	Spectrum ASPEC 003	SOUTHERN COMFORT 3	£50
70	Saydisc RL 328	SOUTHERN SANCTIFIED SINGERS (insert)	£20
71	Python PLP 10	SOUTHSIDE CHICAGO (99 copies only)	£80
58	Tempo TAP 17	SPEAK LOW - MORE MUSIC IN THE MODERN MANNER	£400
69	BAF BAF001	SPECIAL BAF SOUNDS VOL. 1	£30
18	Trunk JBH070LP	SPIDER-JAZZ (splatter vinyl)	£30
13	Rongorongo RORO LP1	SPIKY DREAD ISSUE ONE	£15
73	Tempo TMP 9001	SPIN A MAGIC TUNE	£20
82	WEA K 58415	A SPLASH OF COLOUR	£15
62	Liberty LBY 1001	THE STARS OF LIBERTY	£30
57	Decca LF 1299	STARS OF THE 6.5 SPECIAL (10")	£50
84	Broken Flag BF V5	STATEMENT	£40
85	Statik POL 274	STATIK COMPILATION ONE (2-LP)	£20
04	Ai AILP 006	STATION (2-LP, clear vinyl, 1000 copies only)	£15
69	Stax XATS 1007	STAX SOUL EXPLOSION	£18

MINT VALUE £

70s	Stax STXH 5004	THE STAX STORY (VOL. 1)	£20
70s	Stax STXH 5005	THE STAX STORY (VOL. 1)	£15
67	Stax 589 010	THE STAX/VOLT SHOW VOL. 1	£20
67	Stax 589 011	THE STAX/VOLT SHOW VOL. 2	£20
07	Step Forward CMXBX 1509	STEP FORWARD - I WANNA PUNK ROCK - SINGLES COLLECTION (10x7")	£25
94	Tenth Planet TP 010	THE STORY OF OAK RECORDS	£25
70	Pama PMP 2002	STRAIGHTEN UP	£70
71	Pama PMP 2007	STRAIGHTEN UP VOLUME TWO	£40
71	Pama PMP 2014	STRAIGHTEN UP VOLUME THREE	£40
72	Pama PMP 2017	STRAIGHTEN UP VOLUME FOUR	£30
00	BBE BBELP 031	STRANGE GAMES & FUNKY THINGS III (3 x 12")	£35
77	Beggars Banquet BEGA 1	STREETS	£15
80s	Streetsounds	STREETSOUND ELECTRO (box set)	£70
79	Open Eye OE LP 501	STREET TO STREET - A LIVERPOOL ALBUM	£20
81	Decca SKIN 1	STRENGTH THROUGH OI!	£50
85	Wonderful World WOWLP 3	STRENGTH THROUGH OI! (reissue)	£20
86	Sub Pop SP 0010	SUB POP 100	£20
83	Sane SANE 001	SUBTLE HINTS	£100
81	Chick CHR 001	SUBWAY (clear vinyl)	£15
73	Vertigo 6499 386	SUCK IT AND SEE (2-LP, spaceship label)	£20
98	Sorted SRLP 04	SUCTION PRINTS (handpainted or wraparound sleeve)	£35
65	Sue ILP 919	SUE SAMPLER RECORD FOR CLUBS (promo, no sleeve, typed labels with detail sheet)	£120
65	London HA-C 8239	THE SUE STORY	£60
65	Sue ILP 925	THE SUE STORY!	£55
69	United Artists UAS 29028	THE SUE STORY (reissue)	£18
66	Sue ILP 933	THE SUE STORY VOL. 2	£55
66	Sue ILP 938	THE SUE STORY VOL. 3	£55
76	Giorno GPS	SUGAR, ALCOHOL & MEAT	£20
82	CBS 22139	SUMMER MEANS FUN (2-LP)	£20
75	Island ISS 1	SUMMER '75 (promo-only sampler)	£15
66	Reprise R 5031	THE SUMMIT	£30
02	Sun FBUBX 002	SUN RECORD COMPANY 50 GOLDEN YEARS 1952-2002 (8-CD + 7")	£40
86	Sun/Charly BOX 105	SUN RECORDS: THE BLUES YEARS (9-LP box with booklet)	£40
81	Sunset Gun	SUNSET GUN (cassette with Sunset Gun fanzine)	£15
68	Ember NR 5038	SUNSTROKE	£20
73	Philips 6369 416	SUPER BLACK BLUES	£20
68	Pye Intl. NPL 28107	SUPER SOUL	£25
96	Trunk BARKED 1 LP	THE SUPER SOUNDS OF BOSWORTH (promo cassette, 50 only)	£50
68	Chess SRL 4537	SUPER SUPER BLUES BAND	£25
74	People PLEO 24	SUPER SWEET SOUL	£15
64	Vocalion VA 8018	SURF BATTLE	£60
86	Capitol EMS 1180	SURF CITY/DRAG CITY	£25
88	Decal LIK 39	SURFERS STOMP	£25
73	Pye/Disques Vogue HEN 1	SURPRISE PARTIE TOUS LES JEUNES	£18
71	Blue Horizon 7-66263	SWAMP BLUES (2-LP)	£75
68	Stateside S(S)L 10243	SWEET SOUL SOUNDS	£50
68	Coxsone CSL 8018	SWING EASY	£125
58	Tempo TAP 21	SWINGIN' THE BLUES (with Victor Fedman, Tubby Hayes, Don Rendell, Ronnie Scott & Dizzy Reece)	£250
93	Tenth Planet TP 002	SYDE TRYPS ONE (numbered, 500 only, with insert)	£40
93	Tenth Planet TP 004	SYDE TRYPS TWO ... FROM THERE TO UNCERTAINTY (numbered, 500 only, with insert)	£30
93	Tenth Planet TP 006	SYDE TRYPS THREE (numbered, 500 only, with insert)	£30
94	Tenth Planet TP 008	SYDE TRYPS FOUR (numbered, 500 only, with insert)	£60
95	Tenth Planet TP 020	SYDE TRYPS VOLUME 5 (numbered, 500 only, insert)	£25
96	Tenth Planet TP 024	SYDE TRYPS SIX (numbered, gatefold sleeve, 1,000 only)	£30
01	Tenth Planet TP 052	SYDE TRYPS VOLUME SEVEN (numbered, 1000 only, insert)	£20
82	EBONY 2 S82 CUS 1362	SYNTHETIC ROMANCE (LP)	£450
15	System SYSTM 004	SYSTEM SOUND EP (4 x 10" BOX SET)	£50
78	BBC REC 303	SCRAPBOOK OF 1977 (LP)	£15
96	Trunk BARKED 1	THE SUPER SOUNDS OF BOSWORTH (LP, 3000 copies)	£30
96	Trunk BARKED 2	THE SUPER SOUNDS OF BOSWORTH 2 (LP, 1000 only with track 1 missing on side 2 due to pressing fault)	£50

T

72	Rubber RUB 001	TAKE OFF YOUR HEAD AND LISTEN	£15
78	Grapevine GRAL 1000	TALK OF THE GRAPEVINE	£25
85	Kent KENT 045	TEAR IN MY EYES	£30
58	Capitol T 1009	TEENAGE ROCK (turquoise or 'rainbow' label)	£40
90	Sarah SARAH 37G	TEMPLE CLOUD - A SARAH COMPILATION (LP)	£45
56	Nixa Jazz Today NJL 4	TENORAMA	£300
02	Jazzman JMANLP 006	TEXAS FUNK (2-LP)	£30
69	Highway 51 H 103	TEXAS-LOUISIANA BLUES (99 copies only)	£60
82	No Future PUNK 9	THERE IS NO FUTURE	£18
72	Dandelion 2485 021	THERE IS SOME FUN GOING FORWARD (with poster)	£18
82	Big Beat NED 3	THESE CATS AIN'T NOTHING BUT TRASH	£20
69	Action ACLP 6009	THESE KIND OF BLUES VOL. 1	£80
81	TTFTC 001	THE THING FROM THE CRYPT (I NEARLY DIED LAUGHING)	£50
87	Kent KENT 066	THINK SMART SOUL STRINGS	£15

57	Tempo TAP 11	THIRD BRITISH FESTIVAL OF JAZZ	£50
80s	Come Org. WDC 881021	33 FÜR ILSE KOCH (some on red vinyl)	£70
68	Minit MLL/MLS 40002	THIRTY-THREE MINITS OF BLUES AND SOUL	£45
83	2-Tone CHR TT 5007	THIS ARE 2-TONE (with free poster, green or pink sleeve)	£30
64	Island ILP 910	THIS IS BLUE BEAT (unreleased, white labels may exist)	£250
76	Loma/Warners K 56265	THIS IS LOMA VOL. 1	£20
76	Loma/Warners K 56266	THIS IS LOMA VOL. 2	£20
76	Loma/Warners K 56267	THIS IS LOMA VOL. 3	£20
76	Loma/Warners K 56268	THIS IS LOMA VOL. 4	£20
76	Loma/Warners K 56269	THIS IS LOMA VOL. 5	£20
76	Loma/Warners K 56270	THIS IS LOMA VOL. 6	£20
63	Oriole PS 40047	THIS IS MERSEYBEAT VOL. 1	£50
63	Oriole PS 40048	THIS IS MERSEYBEAT VOL. 2	£50
80	Grapevine GRAL 1002	THIS IS NORTHERN SOUL	£30
86	OI OIR 004	THIS IS OI!	£15
69	Pama PSP 1003	THIS IS REGGAE	£30
71	Pama PMP 2005	THIS IS REGGAE VOLUME TWO	£30
71	Pama PMP 2008	THIS IS REGGAE VOLUME THREE	£40
72	Pama PMP 2016	THIS IS REGGAE VOLUME FOUR	£30
69	Island IWP 3	THIS IS SUE!	£25
63	RCA RD/SF 7608	THE THREE GREAT GUYS (Paul Anka, Sam Cooke & Neil Sedaka)	£15
70	Saydisc Matchbox SDR182	THOSE CAKEWALKIN' BABIES FROM HOME	£22
66	Allegro ALL 807	THUNDERBALL AND OTHER SECRET AGENT THEMES	£15
69	Trojan TTL 7	TIGHTEN UP VOLUME TWO (pink Island label with different track listing & sleeve)	£40
82	Mobile Suit SUIT 1	TOKYO MOBILE MUSIC 1 (LP)	£20
92	Too Pure SFRLP 119	TOO PURE - THE PEEL SESSIONS (LP, limited issue, custom sleeve)	£20
64	Golden Guinea GGL 0277	TOP 10 HITS, ORIGINAL ARTISTS	£15
72	Studio 2 TWO 391	TOP TV THEMES AND COMMERCIALS	£30
56	Tempo TAP 4	TOP TRUMPETS	£250
82	Zoo ZOO 4	TO THE SHORES OF LAKE PLACID (gatefold sleeve with 4-page booklet)	£18
92	Trojan TRLS 304	TOUGHER THAN TOUGH	£18
60s	Fishers Music	TRANSAFRICK MUSICMAKERS	£25
77	Free Reed FRRD 021/022	THE TRANSPORTS (2-LP, with book)	£60
76	Eron 006	TRAVELLING FOLK (with insert)	£25
61	77' LA 12-2	A TREASURY OF FIELD RECORDINGS VOLUME 1	£35
61	77' LA 12-3	A TREASURY OF FIELD RECORDINGS VOLUME 2	£35
84	Parlophone CAV 1	TRIBUTE TO THE CAVERN (LP)	£40
69	Key KL 003	A TRIBUTE TO YOUTH PRAISE	£20
80	Skeleton SKL LP 1	A TRIP TO THE DENTIST (with insert)	£15
61	Parlophone PMC 1139	TRIPLE TREAT	£25
03	Trojan TRBLP 003	TROJAN ROCKSTEADY BOX (3-LP)	£100
74	Trojan TDRLP1	THE TROJAN SOUND (LP)	£15
71	Trojan TALL 1	TROJAN STORY (3xLP in fold-over sleeve)	£40
80	Trojan TALL 100	TROJAN STORY (3-LP)	£30
82	Trojan TALL 200	TROJAN STORY VOLUME 2 (BOX SET)	£60
89	Warriors Dance WAFLP 2	THE TUFFEST OF THE TUFFEST	£30
74	Melodisc 12-193	12 BIG HITS- SOUNDS OF YOUNG JAMAICA	£60
74	Melodisc 12-217	12 CARAT GOLD	£35
76	Lucky LYLP 5004	TWELVE TRIBES OF ISRAEL (LP)	£200
73	Trojan TRLS 81	20 EXPLOSIVE REGGAE HITS	£18
65	Ember EMB 3359	25 YEARS OF RHYTHM & BLUES HITS	£30
89	WEA 241 690-1	TWIST & SHOUT - 12 ATLANTIC TRACKS PRODUCED BY PHIL SPECTOR (gatefold sleeve)	£35
63	Philips BL 7578	TWIST AT THE STAR-CLUB, HAMBURG	£50
82	Beat The System BTSLP 1	TOTAL ANARCHY (LP)	£15
89	2-TONE CHR TT 5009	THE 2 TONE STORY (2-LP)	£30

U

68	BBC REC 28M	ULSTER'S FLOWERY VALE	£15
69	Island ILP 993/ILPS 9093	THE UNFOLDING OF THE BOOK OF LIFE VOL. 1	£45
72	Nevis NEV R 007	UNITY CREATES STRENGTH	£25
69	Pama ECO 7	UNITY'S GREATEST HITS	£110
88	Unicorn PHZA 17	UNSUNG HEROES (red vinyl)	£15
80	Safari UPP 1	UPPERS ON THE SOUTH DOWNS (original issue without Purple Hearts)	£15
68	Atlantic 588 122	UPTOWN SOUL	£20
72	Village Thing VTSAM 15	US	£20

V

78	Attrix RB 03	VAULTAGE '78 (TWO SIDES OF BRIGHTON) (originally hand-screened sleeve, later with insert)	£20
80	Attrix RB 11LP	VAULTAGE 80	£15
71	Trojan TBL 175	VERSION GALORE VOLUME TWO	£15
73	Trojan TBL 200	VERSION GALORE VERSION THREE	£30
72	Trojan TBL 182	VERSION TO VERSION	£18
70	Vertigo 6499 407/8	VERTIGO ANNUAL 1970 (2-LP, set no.: 6657 001)	£30
10	Balkan BV 06	VIOLET (with free CD)	£20

W

| 70s | Object Music OBJ 007 | WAITING ROOM | £15 |

Rare Record Price Guide 2026

MINT VALUE £

85	Psycho PSYCHO 35	THE WAKING DREAM	£15
64	Pye Intl. NPL 28041	WALKING BY MYSELF	£40
64	Pye Intl. NPL 28044	WALKING THE BLUES	£35
81	Phil Spector Intl. WOS 001	WALL OF SOUND (9-LP box set)	£60
03	Soul Brother LP SBPJ 14	WANTS LIST (2-LP)	£30
05	Soul Brother LP SBPJ 27	WANTS LIST 2 (2-LP)	£30
09	Warp WARP 20	WARP 20 (5 x 10", 5-CD, booklet, box set)	£150
79	A&M AMLH 64761	THE WARRIORS	£20
98	Warp WAP 100	WE ARE REASONABLE PEOPLE (3-LP)	£30
78	Bridgehouse BHLP 001	A WEEKEND AT THE BRIDGEHOUSE E16 (with bonus 12" EP)	£30
81	Romans In Britain NERO 1	WELCOME TO NORWICH A FINE CITY (LP)	£70
87	Streetsounds WTND 1	WEST END STORY (2-LP)	£20
93	West End 110651	WEST END STORY VOL 1	£20
93	West End 110691	WEST END STORY VOL 2	£20
93	West End 110941	WEST END STORY VOL 3	£20
84	Rot ASS 4	WET DREAMS (LP)	£20
70	Harry J TTL 34	WHAT AM I TO DO	£40
80	S & T	WHERE THE HELL IS LEICESTER? (with bonus single & booklet)	£25
86	Sunrise A40 111M	WHERE WOULD YOU RATHER BE TONIGHT?	£25
83	Kamera KAM 14	THE WHIP (with insert)	£20
79	London Bomp DHS-Z 3	WHO PUT THE BOMP? (2-LP, gatefold sleeve)	£25
70	Trojan TBL 134	WHO YOU GONNA RUN TO	£50
72	private pressing	WHOLLY GRAIL	£25
98	Trunk BARKED 3CP	THE WICKER MAN (promo cassette, 50 only)	£30
81	Cherry Red BRED 24	WILD PAARTY SOUNDS VOLUME 1	£20
91	Cherry Red BRED 24	WILD PAARTY SOUNDS VOLUME 1 (reissue)	£25
66	Dot DLP 3535	WIPE OUT	£25
67	RCA Victor RD 7840	WOMEN OF THE BLUES	£20
81	Glass GLASS 010	THE WONDERFUL WORLD OF GLASS	£15
96	Magna Carta MA 9010/2	WORKING MAN	£15
63	London HA-P 8099	A WORLD OF BLUES	£25
85	Radical Change RCLP 4	WORDS WORTH SHOUTING (insert)	£15
78	Yuk NE 1023	THE WORLD'S WORST RECORD SHOW (multi-coloured vinyl)	£20
89	Woronzow WOO 10	WORONZOID (2-LP)	£20

Y

10	Balkan BV 04	YELLOW (with free CD)	£15
85	Cathexis/Pleasantly Surprised PS 014	YOU BET WE'VE GOT SOMETHING AGAINST YOU	£15
70	Trojan TBL 142	YOU CAN'T WINE	£65
69	Trojan TTL 9	YOU LEFT ME STANDING	£40
84	Peninsula PENCV 1002	YOUNG BLOOD (LP)	£50
69	Youngblood SBYB 1	YOUNGBLOOD VOL. 1	£15
71	Youngblood SBYB4	YOUNBLOOD VOL. 2	£18
70	Pama ECO 35	YOUNG GIFTED AND BLACK	£175
71	Bamboo BDLPS 211	YOUR JAMAICAN GIRL	£50
82	Statik STATLP 7	YOUR SECRET'S SAFE WITH US (2-LP)	£20

Z

91	Document ZBOX 1	ZOO: THE COMPLETE WORKS (Box set 3-LP, 12", 1,000 only)	£60
84	Zulu ZULU 6	THE ZULU COMPILATION	£20

FILM & TV SOUNDTRACK LPs

(alphabetical by title, composers/artists in brackets)

(Only the first issue of soundtracks by the Beatles and Elvis Presley are listed below: for later repressings see their entries)

A

73	United Artists UAS 29451	ACROSS 110TH STREET (J.J. Johnson & Bobby Womack)	£15
62	RCA RD 7512	ADVISE AND CONSENT (Jerry Fielding)	£15
13	Rook RFV 002	A FIELD IN ENGLAND (2-LP, white vinyl, poster, blade of grass)	£100
67	United Artists (S)ULP 1172	AFRICA ADDIO (Riz Ortolani/Jimmy Roselli)	£20
66	United Artists (S)ULP 1151	AFTER THE FOX (Burt Bacharach/Hollies)	£25
64	Parlophone PMC 1230	A HARD DAY'S NIGHT (Beatles) (LP, mono, 1st pressing, with The Parlophone Co. Ltd label rim copy & "Sold In The UK..." text)	£100
64	Parlophone PCS 3058	A HARD DAY'S NIGHT (Beatles) (LP, stereo, 1st pressing, with "The Parlophone Co. Ltd" label rim copy & "Sold In The UK..." text; stereo, with mid-sized "stereo")	£250
56	Nixa NPT 19010	ALEXANDER THE GREAT (Mario Nascimbene) (10"; beware of counterfeits)	£40
69	MGM CS 8112	ALFRED THE GREAT (Ray Leppard)	£100
61	Fontana TFL 591	ALL NIGHT LONG (LP, mono, Dave Brubeck, Tubby Hayes, Johnny Dankworth et al.)	£30
61	Fontana STFL 591	ALL NIGHT LONG (LP, stereo, Dave Brubeck, Tubby Hayes, Johnny Dankworth et al.)	£20
65	Reprise R 6151	AMERICANIZATION OF EMILY (Johnny Mandel)	£20
65	RCA RD 7732	THE AMOROUS ADVENTURES OF MOLL FLANDERS (John Addison)	£35
57	Brunswick LAT 8175	ANASTASIA (Alfred Newman)	£15
60	Philips SBBL 514	ANATOMY OF A MURDER (Duke Ellington)	£25
76	BBC REB 236	ANGELS AND 15 OTHER BBC TV THEMES (Alan Parker, et al.)	£15
72	Polydor 2383 109	ANTONY AND CLEOPATRA (John Scott) (foldout sleeve)	£20
60	London HA-T 2287	THE APARTMENT (Adolph Deutsch)	£18

79	Elektra K 62025	APOCALYPSE NOW (2-LP, music & dialogue)	£20
69	CBS 70054	APRIL FOOLS (Marvin Hamlisch)	£15
66	RCA Victor RD 7817	ARABESQUE (Henry Mancini)	£15
66	Fontana FJL 135	L'ASCENSEUR POUR L'ECHAFAUD/FEMME DISPARAISSANTE (Miles Davis/Art Blakey [1 side each])	£30
54	HMV DLPC 1	AS LONG AS THEY'RE HAPPY (Jack Buchanan) (10")	£50
67	Pye NPL 18198	AT LAST THE 1948 SHOW (TV soundtrack)	£25
67	Marble Arch MAL 695	THE AVENGERS AND OTHER FAVOURITES (Laurie Johnson)	£35

B

66	Fontana TL 5306	BABY, THE RAIN MUST FALL (Elmer Bernstein)	£15
62	Pye Intl. NPL 28020	BARABBAS (Mario Nascimbene)	£15
68	Stateside (S)SL 10260	BARBARELLA (Bob Crewe/Charles Fox)	£75
67	London HA-D 8337	BAREFOOT IN THE PARK (Neal Hefti)	£15
66	Stateside S(S)L 10179	BATMAN (Nelson Riddle) (TV show music)	£50
13	Silva SILLP 1316	BATMAN BEGINS (2-LP, 500 only)	£30
66	Warner Bros W 1617	BATTLE OF THE BULGE (Benjamin Frankel)	£25
60	Columbia 33SX 1225	BEAT GIRL (John Barry/Adam Faith)	£40
57	London HAP 2056	BEAU JAMES (Joseph Lilley)	£25
64	RCA Victor RD 7679	BECKET (dialogue only)	£15
68	Decca LK 4923	BEDAZZLED (LP, mono, Peter Cook/Dudley Moore)	£100
70	Island ILPS 9140	BE GLAD FOR THE SONG HAS NO ENDING (Incredible String Band)	£15
15	Finders Keepers FKR79L	BELLADONNA (leather sleeve)	£40
60	Capitol W/SW 1435	BELLS ARE RINGING (André Previn) (mono/stereo)	£15
60	MGM MGM-C(S) 8031	BEN HUR (Miklos Rozsa) (box set with hardback book; mono/stereo)	£15
70	Stateside SSL 10311	BEYOND THE VALLEY OF THE DOLLS (Stu Phillips/Strawberry Alarm Clock)	£70
68	MGM MGM-C(S) 8066	BIGGEST BUNDLE OF THEM ALL (Riz Ortolani/Eric Burdon)	£20
69	United Artists (S)ULP 1228	THE BIG GUNDOWN (Ennio Morricone)	£15
67	United Artists (S)ULP 1183	BILLION DOLLAR BRAIN (Richard Rodney Bennett)	£30
73	Polydor 2490 117	BLACK CAESAR (James Brown)	£35
	Cinephile CINLP004	THE BLACK WINDMILL	£30
72	Pye NSPL 18376	BLOOMFIELD	£15
66	MGM MGM-C(S) 8039	BLOW-UP (Herbie Hancock/Yardbirds)	£80
68	Dot (S)LPD 508	BLUE (Manos Hadjidakis)	£30
61	RCA RD 27238	BLUE HAWAII (Elvis Presley) (black/silver label, mono)	£15
61	RCA SF 5115	BLUE HAWAII (Elvis Presley) (black/silver label, stereo)	£20
87	Thats Entertainment TER 1127	BLUE VELVET (Angelo Badalamenti)	£20
62	RCA RD 7520	BONANZA (L.Greene, M. Langdon)	£20
69	MCA MUPS 360	BOOM! (John Barry/Georgie Fame)	£60
68	Warner Bros W 1742	BONNIE AND CLYDE (Charles Strouse)	£20
70	Paramount SPFL 263	BORSALINO (Claude Bolling)	£15
58	RCA RD 27054	BOTH ENDS OF THE CANDLE (Gogi Grant)	£15
57	Brunswick LAT 8193	BOY ON A DOLPHIN (Hugo Friedhoffer)	£30
71	Capitol E-SW 621	THE BUGALOOS (LP)	£30
72	Bell BELLS 209	THE BURGLARS (Ennio Morricone)	£30
66	RCA RD 7791	BUNNY LAKE IS MISSING (Paul Glass/Zombies)	£65
65	Liberty LBY 1246	BURKE'S LAW (Herschel/Burke/Gilbert) (TV series music)	£15
63	RCA Victor SF 7580	BYE BYE BIRDIE (musical) (Charles Strouse; stereo)	£15
80	Chrysalis CHR 1294	BABYLON (blue/white label)	£20
05	Trunk JBH 016LP/PD	BOD: WORDS & MUSIC (LP 1-sided picture disc)	£20
07	Trunk JBH 023 LP	BLOOD ON SATAN'S CLAW (LP, 500 only)	£40

C

66	RCA Victor RD 7820	CALIFORNIA HOLIDAY (Elvis Presley) (black/red dot labels, mono)	£20
66	RCA Victor SF 7820	CALIFORNIA HOLIDAY (Elvis Presley) (black/red dot labels, stereo)	£30
69	Stateside (S)SL 10276	CANDY (Dave Grusin/Steppenwolf, et al.)	£30
69	MCA MUPS 380	CAN HEIRONYMUS MERKIN EVER FORGET MERCY HUMPPE AND FIND TRUE HAPPINESS? (Anthony Newley)	£30
60	Delyse DL 3057/DLS 6057	CAPTAIN HORATIO HORNBLOWER (Robert Farnon) (mono)	£30
76	United Artists UA 30033	CARRIE (Pino Donaggio)	£40
67	RCA Victor RD/SF 7874	CASINO ROYALE (Burt Bacharach/Herb Alpert/Dusty Springfield) (mono/stereo	£30
66	United Artists (S)ULP 1140	CAST A GIANT SHADOW (Elmer Bernstein/Vince Hill)	£18
65	Columbia SX 1756	CATCH US IF YOU CAN (Dave Clark Five)	£30
62	Warner Bros WS 8177	THE CHAPMAN REPORT (Leonard Rosenman)	£15
63	RCA SF 7620	CHARADE (Henry Mancini)	£20
63	MGM MGM-C 969	THE CHARGE IS MURDER (John Green)	£20
68	United Artists SULP 1189	THE CHARGE OF THE LIGHT BRIGADE (John Addison/Manfred Mann)	£18
66	CBS (S)BPG 62665	THE CHASE (John Barry) (mono) (stereo copy is £30)	£20
69	Polydor 583 736	CHE! (Lalo Schifrin)	£15
67	Fontana TL 5417	CHIMES AT MIDNIGHT (Angelo Lavagnino)	£30
74	ABC ABCL 5068	CHINATOWN (Jerry Goldsmith)	£20
68	RCA Victor RD/SF 7917	CLAMBAKE (Elvis Presley) (black/red dot labels, mono/stereo)	£20
01	Trunk SOUP 001LP	THE CLANGERS (Vernon Elliot) (TV soundtrack, with knitted sleeve, 26 only)	£150
01	Trunk SOUP 001LP	THE CLANGERS (Vernon Elliot) (TV soundtrack, without knitted sleeve)	£30
18	Trunk JBH 078LP	THE CLANGERS (Vernon Elliot) (LP, reissue)	£18
63	Stateside S(S)L 10044	CLEOPATRA (Alex North)	£15
65	Fontana (S)TL 5259	THE COLLECTOR (Maurice Jarre)	£25
67	MGM MGM-C(S) 8058	THE COMEDIANS (Laurence Rosenthal)	£15

72	Pye NSPL 18389	CONCERTO FOR HARRY - SOMETHING TO HIDE (Roy Budd)..................................£25
75	Polydor 2383 350	CONFESSIONS OF A POP PERFORMER (Three's A Crowd/Ed Welch) £30
71	Philips 6332 033	CONTINENTAL CIRCUS (Gong) £20
62	Parlophone PMC 1194	THE COOL MIKADO (John Barry Seven/Frankie Howerd, et al.)............................£25
70	United Artists UAS 29119	COTTON COMES TO HARLEM (Galt McDermott) £30
67	Brunswick AXA 4544	COUNTESS FROM HONG KONG (Charles Chaplin) (with booklet)......................£15
70	Capitol E-ST 640	CROMWELL (Frank Cordell) £15
70	Word WST 5550	THE CROSS & THE SWITCHBLADE (Ralph Carmichael) £25
77	EMI EMA 782	CROSS OF IRON (Ernest Gold) (gatefold sleeve) £15
80	CBS 70182	CRUISING (John Hiatt/Willy DeVille/Germs) £25
73	Buddah 2318 091	CURTIS IN CHICAGO (Curtis Mayfield/Impressions/Jerry Butler, Gene Chandler, Leroy Hutson) (TV soundtrack, gatefold sleeve) £15
68	Stateside (S)SL 10222	CUSTER OF THE WEST (Bernardo Segall) £20

D

62	Fontana TFL 5184	DANGEROUS FRIENDSHIPS (Art Blakey, et. al.) £25
63	MGM MGM-C 952	DAVID AND LISA (Mark Lawrence/Victor Feldman All Stars)................................£15
04	Trunk JBH 011 LP	DAWN OF THE DEAD (LP, 500 only) £30
67	Stateside (S)SL 10217	THE DAY THE FISH CAME OUT (Mikis Theodorakis) £30
18	Laced LMLP 020	DEAD CELLS (2-LP, orange and violet vinyl) £80
68	Stateside (S)SL 10263	DEADFALL (John Barry/Shirley Bassey) £20
73	Columbia SCX 6550	DEAF SMITH AND JOHNNY EARS (Daniele Patucchi) £35
74	CBS 80546	DEATH WISH (Herbie Hancock)..£15
68	Stateside (S)SL 10259	DECLINE AND FALL... OF A BIRDWATCHER (Ron Goodwin) £125
55	MGM MGM-C 755	DEEP IN MY HEART (Howard Keel/Vic Damone, et al.) £15
00	Trunk/Bonk XXX 1 LP	DEEP THROAT (LP) £20
58	London HA-D 2111	DESIRE UNDER THE ELMS (Elmer Bernstein) £20
63	Colpix PXL 440	DIAMOND HEAD (John Williams) £15
76	Pye Intl. NSPL 28219	DIAMOND MERCENARIES (Georges Garvarentz) £15
76	Bradley BRADS 8002	DIAMONDS (Roy Budd) £50
71	United Artists UAS 29216	DIAMONDS ARE FOREVER (John Barry/Shirley Bassey) (LP) £25
59	Top Rank RX 3016	THE DIARY OF ANNE FRANK (Alfred Newman) £30
83	Ripple (no cat. no.)	DIGITAL DREAMS (Bill Wyman) (promo only) £50
68	MGM MGM-C(S) 8048	DIRTY DOZEN (Frank de Vol/Trini Lopez) (yellow label) £18
67	CBS S 63189	DR. FAUSTUS (Mario Nascimbene) £75
65	United Artists ULP 1097	DOCTOR NO (Monty Norman) (mono) £50
65	United Artists (S)ULP 1097	DOCTOR NO (Monty Norman) (stereo) £100
62	Columbia 33SX 1446	DON'T KNOCK THE TWIST (Chubby Checker/Gene Chandler, et al.)................£25
18	Laced (no Cat no)	DOOM (ORIGINAL GAME SOUNDTRACK) (2-LP, red vinyl) £40
67	RCA Victor SF 7892	DOUBLE TROUBLE (Elvis Presley) (black/red dot labels, stereo) (Mono version RD7892 = £15)..£20
12	Death Waltz DW 004	DONNIE DARKO (Michael Andrews: blue/black vinyl, lithograph, 100 only)....£50
12	Death Waltz DW 004	DONNIE DARKO (Michael Andrews: blue vinyl, lithograph, 300 only)................£30
12	Death Waltz DW 004	DONNIE DARKO (Michael Andrews: standard black vinyl, poster) £15
74	Enterprise ENTF 3003	DON'T LOOK NOW (Pino Donaggio) £40
69	Capitol EST 672	THE DOUBLE DECKERS (TV soundtrack) £30
87	Crammed MTM 14	DOWN BY LAW (John Lurie) £20
70	President PTLS 1068	DRAKE'S DREAM (Paul Jones)..£20
12	Invada INV106LP	DRIVE £40
59	Parlophone PMCL 1101	DRUMBEAT (Adam Faith/John Barry Seven, et al.)..£50
58	Decca LF 1308	THE DUKE WORE JEANS (Tommy Steele) (10")..£15

E

58	HMV DLP 1088	EDDIE FOY AND THE SEVEN LITTLE FOYS (10", Bob Hope/James Cagney)....£30
54	Brunswick LAT 8040	THE EGYPTIAN (Alfred Newman)..£25
67	Columbia S(C)X 6155	EL DORADO (Nelson Riddle) £25
63	Colpix PXL 459	ELIZABETH TAYLOR IN LONDON (John Barry) (mono/stereo) £20
69	RCA Victor RD 8011	ELVIS ("TV Special", mono) £15
74	Warner Bros K 56084	EMMANUELLE (Pierre Bachelet)..£15
57	Vogue Coral LVA 9063	END AS A MAN (Kenyon Hopkins) £30
74	Warner Bros K 46275	ENTER THE DRAGON (Lalo Schifrin) £40
84	Alt. Ten. VIRUS 30	ERASERHEAD (Fats Waller/Peter Ivers/et al.) (with insert) £40
81	That's Entertainment TER 1011	ESCAPE FROM NEW YORK (John Carpenter and Alan Howarth) £25
12	Death Waltz DW 0002	ESCAPE FROM NEW YORK (poster, inner, orange/green vinyl, 100 only)........£40
76	EMI EMC 3148	ESCAPE FROM THE DARK (Ron Goodwin) £15
63	Parlophone PMC 1198	THE ESTABLISHMENT (Peter Cook, et al.)..£20
83	MCA MCA 70000	E.T. - THE EXTRA TERRESTRIAL (John Williams) (box set, with booklet & poster)........£30
83	MCA CAC 70000	E.T. - THE EXTRA TERRESTRIAL (John Williams) (cassette, box set, with booklet & poster)..£15
67	Brunswick LAT 8678	AN EVENING WITH BORIS KARLOFF AND FRIENDS £30
97	London 828 939-1	EVENT HORIZON (featuring Orbital) £25
87	That's Entertainment TER 1142	EVIL DEAD II (Joseph Lo Duca) £45
74	Warner Bros K 56071	THE EXORCIST (Jack Nitzsche, et al.)..£20
72	Deram SML 1095	EXTREMES (Tony Klinger & Michael Lyons)..£100

F

| 57 | Capitol LCT 6139 | A FACE IN THE CROWD (Tom Glazer) (10") ....£20 |
| 64 | CBS (S)BPG 62277 | FALL OF THE ROMAN EMPIRE (Dimitri Tiomkin) ....£20 |

67	Decca LK 4847	THE FAMILY WAY (Paul McCartney/George Martin) (mono)	£70
67	Decca SKL 4847	THE FAMILY WAY (LP, stereo, soundtrack)	£90
60	Top Rank 30/003/4/5	FANTASIA (various classical pieces) (3-LP, with book)	£30
58	Capitol LCT 6162	A FAREWELL TO ARMS (Mario Nascimbene)	£15
67	MGM MGM-C(S) 8053	FAR FROM THE MADDING CROWD (Richard Rodney Bennett)	£20
68	London HA-U/SH-U 8358	THE FASTEST GUITAR ALIVE (Roy Orbison)	£20
67	Stateside S(S)L 10213	FATHOM (Johnny Dankworth)	£40
73	Pye NSPL 18398	FEAR IS THE KEY (Roy Budd)	£50
70	United Artists UAS 29118	FELLINI-SATYRICON (Nino Rota)	£20
65	Columbia 33SX 1693	FERRY CROSS THE MERSEY (Gerry & Pacemakers/Cilla Black/Fourmost) (also stereo SCX 3544 = £35)	£25
99	Restless Records 74321716431	FIGHT CLUB (2-LP)	£80
01	Simply Vinyl SLVP 161	FIGHT CLUB (2-LP, reissue)	£50
63	CBS SBPG 62148	55 DAYS AT PEKING (Dimitri Tiomkin/Andy Williams)	£18
66	Columbia SX 6079	FINDERS KEEPERS (Cliff Richard) (with inner sleeve, mono) (stereo SCX 6079 = £15)	£15
57	Brunswick LAT 8194	FIRE DOWN BELOW (Arthur Benjamin)	£25
67	RCA Victor RD/SF 7875	A FISTFUL OF DOLLARS (Ennio Morricone)	£30
72	United Artists UAS 29345	A FISTFUL OF DYNAMITE (Ennio Morricone)	£40
65	RCA Victor RD 7723	FLAMING STAR AND SUMMER KISSES (Elvis Presley) (mono only, black labels)	£50
85	Heavy Metal HMXD 29	FLASHPOINT (Tangerine Dream) (CD, playable [most copies faulty])	£50
61	Golden Guinea GGL 0092	THE FLINTSTONES (TV soundtrack)	£15
62	Brunswick LAT 8392	FLOWER DRUM SONG (Nancy Kwan, et al.) (also stereo STA 3054)	£15
64	Ace Of Clubs ACL 1166	FLYING CLIPPER (Riz Ortolani)	£15
13	Death Waltz DW03.5	THE FOG (black vinyl)	£40
13	Death Waltz DW03.5	THE FOG (splatter vinyl)	£30
73	York BYK 715	FOLLYFOOT (LP)	£20
65	Ember NR 5029	FOUR IN THE MORNING (John Barry) (mono)	£35
74	T. Motown STML 11269	FOXY BROWN (Willie Hutch)	£40
66	RCA Victor RD 7793	FRANKIE AND JOHNNY (Elvis Presley) (black/red dot labels, mono) (Stereo SF 7793 = £30)	£20
94	FREE LP FRE4	FREE D	£80
64	Fontana TL 5208	FREEDOM ROAD (Madeleine Bell, et al.) (TV production)	£15
10	Finders Keepers FKR 038LP	LE FRISSON DES VAMPIRES (OST) (ACANTHUS) (LP, insert)	£20
63	United Artists (S)ULP 1052	FROM RUSSIA WITH LOVE (John Barry/Matt Monro) (mono/stereo)	£30
60	London HA-T 2257	THE FUGITIVE KIND (Kenyon Hopkins)	£30
67	RCA RD 7860	FUNERAL IN BERLIN (Konrad Elfers/Puppets)	£20
63	RCA Victor RD/SF 7609	FUN IN ACAPULCO (Elvis Presley) (black/silver label, mono. (stereo = £35)	£20

G

70	Stateside SOSL 10091	THE GAMES (Francis Lai)	£200
65	Liberty (S)LBY 1261	GENGHIS KHAN (Dusan Radic) (mono/stereo)	£20
56	Vogue Coral LVA 9003	GENTLEMEN MARRY BRUNETTES (Robert Farnon)	£30
53	MGM MGM-D 116	GENTLEMEN PREFER BLONDES (Marilyn Monroe, et al.) (10")	£75
65	Mercury 20061 MCL	GENTLE RAIN (Luis Bonfa & Deodato)	£15
99	Cinephile CINLP001	GET CARTER (LP, gatefold)	£25
70	RCA SF 8137	GETTING STRAIGHT (Ronald Stein)	£20
57	Capitol LCT 6122	GIANT (Dimitri Tiomkin)	£15
60	RCA RD 27192	G.I. BLUES (Elvis Presley) (black/silver label, mono) (stereo SF 5078 = £25)	£15
66	MGM MGM-C(S) 8034	GIRL FROM U.N.C.L.E. (Jerry Goldsmith & Teddy Randazzo)	£40
65	RCA Victor RD 7714	GIRL HAPPY (Elvis Presley) (black/red dot labels, mono) (stereo SF 7714 = £30)	£20
68	Polydor 583 714	GIRL ON A MOTORCYCLE (Les Reed)	£40
63	RCA Victor RD 7534	GIRLS! GIRLS! GIRLS! (Elvis Presley) (black/silver labels, mono) (Stereo SF 7534 = £35)	£15
66	United Artists SULP 1120	THE GLORY GUYS (Riz Ortolani)	£30
72	Paramount SPFA 7003	THE GODFATHER (Nino Rota) (gatefold sleeve)	£15
75	ABC ABCL 5128	THE GODFATHER - PART 2 (Nino Rota) (gatefold sleeve)	£15
58	London HA-T 2125	GOD'S LITTLE ACRE (Elmer Bernstein)	£20
72	Mother MO 4001	GOLD (MC5/David McWilliams, et al.)	£35
73	United Artists UAS 29576	THE GOLDEN VOYAGE OF SINBAD (Miklos Rozsa)	£15
64	United Artists ULP 1076	GOLDFINGER (John Barry/Shirley Bassey) (mono) (Stereo, SULP 1076 = £30)	£15
64	Decca LK 4673	GONKS GO BEAT (Lulu/Nashville Teens/Graham Bond, et al.)	£100
68	United Artists (S)ULP 1197	THE GOOD, THE BAD AND THE UGLY (Ennio Morricone)	£15
69	Warner Bros W(S) 1786	GOODBYE COLUMBUS (Charles Fox/Association)	£18
70	DJM DJLPS 408	GOODBYE GEMINI (Christopher Gunning/Peddlers/Jackie Lee)	£50
63	United Artists (S)ULP 1041	THE GREAT ESCAPE (Elmer Bernstein) (mono/stereo)	£15
71	Pye NSPL 18373	GREAT SONGS AND THEMES FROM GREAT FILMS (Roy Budd)	£40
75	MCA MCF 2707	THE GREAT WALDO PEPPER (Henry Mancini)	£15
68	United Artists SULP 1220	GREAT WESTERN FILM THEMES (Various Artists)	£15
70	Polydor 2384 021	GROUPIE GIRL (Opal Butterfly/English Rose, et al.)	£40
09	Trunk JBH 032 LP	G SPOTS (LP)	£20
67	RCA RD/SF 7899	GUNN (Henry Mancini)	£18

H

20	Varese Sarabande VSD00026	HACKERS (2-LP, reissue, original release was CD-only)	£40
65	United Artists SULP 1106	THE HALLELUJAH TRAIL (Elmer Bernstein)	£15
75	Contour 2870 437	THE HANGED MAN (Bullet) (TV soundtrack)	£40
68	United Artists SULP 1204	HANG 'EM HIGH (Dominic Frontiere) (stereo/mono)	£15
69	United Artists SULP 1231	HANNIBAL BROOKS (Francis Lai)	£30

70	United Artists UAS 29084	THE HAPPY ENDING (Michel Legrand)	£20
56	Philips BBL 7100	HAPPY HOLIDAY (Jo Stafford)	£15
65	RCA Victor RD 7767	HAREM HOLIDAY (Elvis Presley) (black/red dot labels, mono) (stereo SF 7767 = £25)	£20
65	Warner Bros W 1599	HARLOW (Neal Hefti)	£15
80s	PRT/Chips CHILP 1	HAWK THE SLAYER (Harry Robertson) (gatefold sleeve)	£15
68	RCA RD/SF 8051	HEAD (Monkees) (mono) **Stereo = £60)**	£90
72	Reprise K 44168	THE HEIST (Quincy Jones/Little Richard)	£15
74	Tamla Motown STML 11260	HELL UP IN HARLEM (Edwin Starr)	£15
65	Parlophone PMC 1255	HELP! (Beatles) (1st pressing, with "The Gramophone Co. Ltd" & "Sold In The UK..." label text; mono, with "mono" in outline type on front cover)	£100
65	Parlophone PCS 3071	HELP! (Beatles) (1st pressing, with "The Gramophone Co. Ltd" & "Sold In The UK..." label text; stereo, with "stereo" in outline type on front cover)	£150
67	United Artists ULP 1186	HERE WE GO ROUND THE MULBERRY BUSH (Spencer Davis/Traffic/Andy Ellison) (mono) (stereo SULP 1186 = £35)	£40
59	Capitol T 1160	HEY BOY! HEY GIRL! (Louis Prima/Keely Smith, et al.)	£25
62	Columbia 33SX 1421	HEY, LET'S TWIST (Joey Dee, et al.)	£20
83	A&R FILM 001	HIGH ROAD TO CHINA (John Barry)	£15
70	Columbia SCX 6443	HIS LAND (Cliff Richard/Cliff Barrows)	£15
67	United Artists ULP 1161	THE HONEY POT (John Addison)	£15
59	London HA-T 2197	THE HORSE SOLDIERS (David Buttolph)	£15
16	Laced (no Cat no)	HOTLINE MIAMI (3-LP, red, black and yellow vinyl)	£200
59	Philips BBL 7292	HOUSEBOAT (George Duning)	£25
87	Silva Screen FILM 041	HOW TO GET AHEAD IN ADVERTISING/WITHNAIL & I	£20
65	United Artists (S)ULP 1098	HOW TO MURDER YOUR WIFE (Neal Hefti)	£15
72	Atlantic K 40371	HOW TO STEAL A DIAMOND IN FOUR UNEASY LESSONS (Quincy Jones)	£15
66	Stateside S(S)L 10187	HOW TO STEAL A MILLION (John Williams)	£25
67	RCA Victor RD/SF 7877	HURRY SUNDOWN (Hugo Montenegro)	£20

I

70	United Artists UAS 29044	IF IT'S TUESDAY THIS MUST BE BELGIUM (Walter Scharf)	£15
67	Brunswick LAT/STA 8689	I'LL NEVER FORGET WHAT'S 'ISNAME (Francis Lai)	£50
65	United Artists ULP 1105	I'LL TAKE SWEDEN (Bob Hope/Frankie Avalon, et al.)	£15
68	RCA Victor RD/SF 7931	IN COLD BLOOD (Quincy Jones)	£20
65	RCA RD 7707	IN HARM'S WAY (Jerry Goldsmith)	£25
67	Stateside S(S)L 10207	IN LIKE FLINT (Jerry Goldsmith)	£50
68	United Artists ULP 1201	INSPECTOR CLOUSEAU (Ken Thorne)	£20
69	RCA Victor RD/SF 7990	INTERLUDE (Georges Delarue/Timi Yuro)	£15
62	Colpix PXL 427	THE INTERNS (Leith Stevens)	£18
67	United Artists (S)ULP 1181	IN THE HEAT OF THE NIGHT (Quincy Jones/Ray Charles)	£25
65	CBS BPG 62530	THE IPCRESS FILE (John Barry) (mono only)	£150
84	Illuminated JAMS 35	IN THE SHADOW OF THE SUN (Throbbing Gristle)	£20
66	CBS (S)BPG 62843	IS PARIS BURNING? (Maurice Jarre)	£18
69	Paramount SPFL 256	THE ITALIAN JOB (Quincy Jones/Matt Monro)	£75
63	RCA Victor RD 7565	IT HAPPENED AT THE WORLD'S FAIR (Elvis Presley) (black/silver label, mono) (stereo SF 7565 = £35)	£18
63	Columbia 33SX 1537	IT'S ALL HAPPENING (Tommy Steele/Shane Fenton, et al.) (also stereo SCX 3486)	£15
63	United Artists (S)ULP 1053	IT'S A MAD MAD MAD MAD WORLD (Ernest Gold)	£15
65	Decca LK 4677	I'VE GOTTA HORSE (Billy Fury/Bachelors, et al.)	£40
71	CBS 70083	I WALK THE LINE (Johnny Cash)	£15
07	Trunk JBH 027 LP	IVOR THE ENGINE & POGLES WOOD (LP)	£15

J

57	Capitol LCT 6140	THE JAMES DEAN STORY (Leith Stevens)	£25
54	Brunswick LA 8671	JAZZ THEMES FROM "THE WILD ONE" (Leith Stevens) (10")	£30
62	HMV CLP 1582	JESSICA (Mario Nascimbene)	£15
77	Pye NSPH 28504	JESUS OF NAZARETH (Maurice Jarre) (gatefold sleeve)	£15
73	Reprise K 44017	JIMI HENDRIX - SOUNDTRACK RECORDINGS FROM THE FILM (2-LP)	£18
71	Mercury 6338 029	JOE (Bobby Scott/Jenny Butler)	£20
64	United Artists ULP 1060	JOHNNY COOL (Billy May/Sammy Davis Jr.)	£25
72	Reprise K 64015	JOURNEY THROUGH THE PAST (Neil Young) (2-LP, fold-out cover with inner sleeves)	£40
77	Polydor/EG 2302 079	JUBILEE (Adam & Ants/Brian Eno, et al.)	£20
61	HMV CLP 1545	JUDGEMENT AT NUREMBURG (Ernest Gold)	£15
67	Fontana (S)TL 5317	JULIET OF THE SPIRITS (Nino Rota)	£30
63	Decca LK 4524	JUST FOR FUN (Tornados/Karl Denver, et al.)	£25
64	Decca LK 4620	JUST FOR YOU (Applejacks/Merseybeats, et al.)	£40
70	Monument LMO/SMO 5031	JUSTINE (Jerry Goldsmith)	£20

K

71	MGM 2315 019	KELLY'S HEROES (Lalo Schifrin/Mike Curb)	£25
01	Trunk KES 001 LP	KES (LP - 1-sided)	£40
66	United Artists (S)ULP 1139	KHARTOUM (Frank Cordell)	£30
72	Polydor 2383 102	KIDNAPPED (Roy Budd/Mary Hopkin)	£25
58	RCA RD 27088	KING CREOLE (Elvis Presley) (black/silver labels)	£40
76	Reprise K 54090	KING KONG (John Barry) (with poster)	£15
61	MGM MGM-CS 6043	KING OF KINGS (Miklos Rozsa)	£20
58	Capitol LCT 6165	KINGS GO FORTH (Elmer Bernstein)	£18
66	Fontana (S)TL 5302	KING RAT (John Barry)	£18
64	RCA Victor RD 7645	KISSIN' COUSINS (Elvis Presley) (black/red dot labels, mono) (stereo SF 7645 = £30)	£18
54	MGM MGM-C 753	KISS ME KATE (Howard Keel, et al.)	£15

| 65 | United Artists ULP 1104 | THE KNACK (AND HOW TO GET IT) (John Barry) | £80 |
| 74 | Warner Bros K 46271 | KUNG FU (TV soundtrack) (with inner sleeve) (Jim Helms) | £20 |

L

61	RCA RD 27202	LA DOLCE VITA (Nino Rota) (gatefold sleeve)	£50
63	Ace Of Hearts AH 70	THE LADY AND THE TRAMP (Peggy Lee)	£20
69	Stateside S(S)L 10267	LADY IN CEMENT (Hugo Montenegro)	£40
71	United Artists UAS 29120	THE LANDLORD (Al Kooper)	£20
00	DC DC 33LP	LA PLANETE SAUVAGE (LP, reissue)	£30
72	MGM 2315 072	THE LAST RUN (Jerry Goldsmith/Steve Lawrence)	£25
73	United Artists UAS 29440	LAST TANGO IN PARIS (Gato Barbieri)	£15
71	Probe SPB 1027	THE LAST VALLEY (John Barry) (mono, with insert) (stereo = £20)	£15
85	United Artists 86002	LEGEND (Jerry Goldsmith)	£25
74	Warner Bros K 56085	THE LEGEND OF THE 7 GOLDEN VAMPIRES (James Bernard/Peter Cushing)	£18
64	Stateside S(S)L 10058	THE LEOPARD (Nino Rota)	£30
70	Apple PXS 1	LET IT BE (Beatles) (LP box set, 1st pressing, dark green label, red Apple logo on LP rear sleeve & white inner, with Get Back book housed in black card tray ['PXS1'] not listed on package)	£1000
70	Apple PCS 7096	LET IT BE (Beatles) (2nd pressing, green Apple logo on rear sleeve, plain white inner)	£40
60	Philips BBL 7414/SBBL 592	LET'S MAKE LOVE (Marilyn Monroe/Yves Montand/Frankie Vaughan)	£40
64	Columbia SX 1626	LILIES OF THE FIELD (Jerry Goldsmith)	£20
66	MGM MGM-CS 8029	THE LIQUIDATOR (Lalo Schifrin/Shirley Bassey)	£40
73	United Artists UAS 29475	LIVE AND LET DIE (George Martin/Wings) (LP)	£20
13	Capitol CAP 28415-1	LIVE AND LET DIE (George Martin/Wings) (LP, reissue, gatefold)	£25
76	MGM 2315 376	LOGAN'S RUN (Jerry Goldsmith)	£20
62	MGM MGM-C 896	LOLITA (Nelson Riddle)	£30
67	Polydor 583 014	LONG DUEL (Patrick John Scott/Vince Hill)	£20
63	Stateside S(S)L 10045	THE LONGEST DAY (dialogue only)	£20
83	CES CES 1001	THE LONG GOOD FRIDAY (Francis Monkman) (numbered sleeve with insert, black label print, 2,000 only)	£50
83	CES CES 1001	THE LONG GOOD FRIDAY (Francis Monkman) (re-pressing, with insert, blue label print, 500 only)	£40
84	CES CES 1001	THE LONG GOOD FRIDAY (Francis Monkman) (3rd pressing, with insert, blue label print, 5,000 only)	£40
89	Silva Screen FILM 020	THE LONG GOOD FRIDAY (Francis Monkman) (reissue)	£20
70	CBS 70073	LOOT (Keith Mansfield/Steve Ellis)	£40
65	Colpix PXL 521	LORD JIM (Bronislau Kaper)	£15
69	Uni UNLS 103	LOST MAN (Quincy Jones)	£25
70	CBS 70067	LOVE CIRCLE (Ennio Morricone)	£50
57	RCA RC 24001	LOVING YOU (Elvis Presley) (10", silver spot label)	£75

M

73	Tamla Motown STMA 8003	THE MACK (Willie Hutch)	£35
69	Warner Bros WS 1805	THE MADWOMAN OF CHAILLOT (Michael Lewis)	£15
70	Pye Intl. NSPL 28133	THE MAGIC CHRISTIAN (Ken Thorne/Badfinger, et al.)	£35
54	Brunswick LAT 8045	MAGNIFICENT OBSESSION (Frank Skinner)	£20
65	MGM MGM-C 995	THE MAGNIFICENT SHOWMAN (Dimitri Tiomkin)	£25
76	Atlantic K 50308	MAHONEY'S LAST STAND (Ronnie Lane & Ron Wood)	£15
63	Ace Of Clubs ACL 1135	MAIGRET (Ron Grainer) (TV series music)	£15
66	CBS SBPG 62525	MAJOR DUNDEE (Daniele Amfitheatrof/Mitch Miller)	£15
11	Finders Keepers FKRO40LP	MALA MORSKA (ZDENEK LISKA) (foil/red wax edition)	£30
67	RCA RB 6712/3	A MAN FOR ALL SEASONS (2-LP, dialogue only)	£15
59	Top Rank 35/043	MAN FROM INTERPOL (Tony Crombie) (TV series music)	£25
66	RCA Victor RD 7758	THE MAN FROM U.N.C.L.E. (Hugo Montenegro)	£40
13	Death Waltz DW 014	MANIAC (flesh coloured vinyl)	£20
13	Death Waltz DW 014	MANIAC (silver vinyl)	£30
64	Stateside S(S)L 10087	MAN IN THE MIDDLE (Lionel Bart & John Barry)	£30
56	Brunswick LAT 8101	THE MAN WITH THE GOLDEN ARM (Elmer Bernstein)	£20
74	United Artists UAS 29671	THE MAN WITH THE GOLDEN GUN (John Barry/Lulu)	£15
63	Stateside S(S)L 10048	MARILYN (Marilyn Monroe) (mono/stereo)	£40
72	MCA MUPS 441	MARY QUEEN OF SCOTS (John Barry)	£20
70	United Artists UAS 29122	MASTER OF THE ISLANDS (Henry Mancini)	£15
69	Philips SBL 7876	MAYERLING (Francis Lai)	£20
64	United Artists SULP 1059	McLINTOCK (Frank De Vol)	£35
80	Polydor POLD 5034	McVICAR (Roger Daltrey) (some on clear vinyl)	£15
71	Polydor 2383 043	MELODY (Bee Gees, Richard Hewson, et al.)	£15
57	London HA-P 2076	MEN IN WAR (Elmer Bernstein)	£15
69	Bell BELL 6053	MERRY CHRISTMAS (David Frost/Billy Taylor)	£20
65	MGM MGM-C 8001	MICKEY ONE (Stan Getz & Eddie Sauter) (with booklet, mono) (stereo MGM-CS 8001 = £25)	£20
66	Mercury 20072 (S)MCL	MIRAGE (Quincy Jones)	£25
61	HMV CLP 1481	THE MISFITS (Alex North)	£25
68	Dot (S)LPD 503	MISSION: IMPOSSIBLE - MUSIC FROM THE TV SERIES (Lalo Schifrin)	£40
54	Mercury 25181	MISS SADIE THOMPSON (George Duning) (10")	£30
66	Fontana TL 5347	MODESTY BLAISE (Johnny Dankworth)	£40
70	Paramount SPFL 259	THE MOLLY MAGUIRES (Henry Mancini)	£15
80	BBC REB 384	MONKEY (Godiego) (TV soundtrack)	£25
69	Paramount SPFL 255	MONTE CARLO OR BUST! (Ron Goodwin)	£25
79	United Artists UAG 30247	MOONRAKER (John Barry/Shirley Bassey)	£15
69	Columbia SCX 6346	MORE (Pink Floyd) (laminated flipback sleeve, 'couple facing west' photo on green-	£100

MINT VALUE £

		tinted rear sleeve)..........	
70s	Columbia SCX 6346	**MORE** (Pink Floyd) (laminated non-flipback sleeve, 'couple facing west' photo on black-tinted rear sleeve).............	£80
70s	Columbia SCX 6346	**MORE** (Pink Floyd) (laminated non-flipback sleeve, 'couple facing east' photo on black-tinted rear sleeve).............	£70
69	Paramount SPFL 252	**MORE 'MISSION: IMPOSSIBLE'** (Lalo Schifrin)...........	£40
60	MGM MGM-C(S) 857	**MORE MUSIC FROM BEN-HUR** (Miklos Rozsa)...........	£15
66	RCA Victor RD 7832	**MORE MUSIC FROM 'THE MAN FROM U.N.C.L.E.'** (Hugo Montenegro)	£45
62	MGM	**MORE MUSIC FROM 'MUTINY ON THE BOUNTY'** (Bronislau Kaper)	£20
68	MGM CS8063	**MORE THAN A MIRACLE** (Piero Piccioni)...........	£15
67	RCA RD 7847	**MURDERERS' ROW** (Lalo Schifrin)	£50
80	Unicorn Kachana KPM 7009	**MUSIC FROM THE AVENGERS, THE NEW AVENGERS AND THE PROFESSIONALS**............	£20
70	Harvest SHSP 4008	**MUSIC FROM THE BODY** (Ron Geesin & Roger Waters) (photos/green labels)	£50
90	Warner Bros. 7599 26316-1	**MUSIC FROM TWIN PEAKS**...........	£40
62	MGM MGM-CS 6060	**MUTINY ON THE BOUNTY** (Bronislau Kaper)	£20
85	Cloud Nine CN 4002	**MYSTERIOUS ISLAND** (Bernard Herrman)	£15

N

70	United Artists UAS 29108	**NED KELLY** (Shel Silverstein/Mick Jagger/Waylon Jennings)...........	£30
72	Bell BELLS 202	**NICHOLAS AND ALEXANDRA** (Richard Rodney Bennet)	£15
67	RCA RD 7848	**NIGHT OF THE GENERALS** (Maurice Jarre)	£30
65	MGM MGM-C 994	**NIGHT OF THE IGUANA** (Benjamin Frankel)	£15
69	United Artists (S)ULP 1235	**THE NIGHT THEY RAIDED MINSKY'S** (Charles Strouse)	£20
62	Decca LK 4527	**NINE HOURS TO RAMA** (Malcolm Arnold)	£50
68	Dot (S)LPD 507	**NO WAY TO TREAT A LADY** (American Breed)	£20

O

72	Harvest SHSP 4020	**OBSCURED BY CLOUDS** (Pink Floyd) (rounded sleeve)	£75
76	Phase 4 Stereo PF5 4381	**OBSESSION** (Bernard Herrman)...........	£15
83	A&M 394 967-2	**OCTOPUSSY** (John Barry) (CD, withdrawn)	£75
68	Dot (S)LPD 514	**THE ODD COUPLE** (Neal Hefti)	£15
60	London HA-T 2220	**ODDS AGAINST TOMORROW** (John Lewis)	£20
57	Brunswick LAT 8226	**OMAR KHAYYAM/THE MOUNTAIN** (Victor Young/Daniele Amfitheatrof)	£30
75	Fantasy FTA 3004	**ONE FLEW OVER THE CUCKOO'S NEST** (Jack Nitzsche) (gatefold sleeve)...........	£15
69	United Artists UAS 29020	**ON HER MAJESTY'S SECRET SERVICE** (John Barry) (foldout sleeve)	£25
70	Fontana SFJL 950	**ORFEU NEGRO (BLACK ORPHEUS)** (Luis Bonfa/Antonio Carlos Jobim)	£15
69	RCA SF 8014	**OTLEY** (Stanley Myers/Don Partridge)	£25
66	Stateside S(S)L 10174	**OUR MAN FLINT** (Jerry Goldsmith)...........	£30
76	Warner Bros K 56286	**THE OUTLAW JOSEY WALES** (Jerry Fielding)...........	£25

P

63	Warner Bros WM 8141	**PALM SPRINGS WEEKEND** (Frank Perkins)	£20
66	RCA Victor SF 7810	**PARADISE, HAWAIIAN STYLE** (Elvis Presley) (black/red dot labels, mono) (stereo SF 7810 = £30)	£20
61	HMV CLP 1499	**PARIS BLUES** (Duke Ellington)	£15
61	Warner Bros WS 8044	**PARRISH** (Max Steiner/George Greely)	£20
65	Mercury 20063 SML	**THE PAWNBROKER** (Quincy Jones)	£30
66	Philips (S)BL 7782	**THE PEKING MEDALLION** (Georges Garvarentz/Dusty Springfield)	£40
67	Ember NR 5040	**THE PENTHOUSE** (John Hawksworth)...........	£40
71	Pye NSPL 18365	**PERCY** (Kinks)	£50
70	Warner Bros WS 2554	**PERFORMANCE** (First pressing, orange label, Mick Jagger/Jack Nitzsche/Randy Newman, et al.)	£40
70	Warner Bros WS 2554	**PERFORMANCE** (Second pressing, green label, Mick Jagger/Jack Nitzsche/Randy Newman, et al.)	£35
59	RCA RD 27123/SF 5033	**PETER GUNN** (Henry Mancini)	£15
79	Gem GEM 102	**PHANTASM** (Fred Myrow & Malcolm Seagrave)	£60
56	Brunswick LAT 8120	**PICNIC** (George Duning)	£20
68	Philips SBL 7858	**PLAYTIME** (Jacques Tati, Yan Tatore, Leo Petit)	£35
70	Paramount SPFL 258	**POOKIE** (Fred Karlin/Sandpipers)...........	£15
57	Capitol LCT 6141	**THE PRIDE AND THE PASSION** (Georges Antheil)	£15
86	Bam Caruso WEBA 066	**THE PRISONER** (Ron Grainer, et al.) (fan club issue, gatefold sleeve with inner sleeve, booklet, membership form, map & poster)	£40
67	HMV CLP/CSD 3623	**PRIVILEGE** (Paul Jones & Mike Leander)	£40
69	RCA SF 8072	**THE PRODUCERS** (John Morris)	£15
69	United Artists UAS 29005	**A PROFESSIONAL GUN** (Ennio Morricone)	£25
67	RCA Victor RD/SF 7876	**THE PROFESSIONALS** (Maurice Jarre)	£50
60	Contemporary LAC 12293	**THE PROPER TIME** (Shelly Manne)	£15
68	Stateside S(S)L 10248	**PRUDENCE AND THE PILL** (Bernard Ebbinghouse)	£25
75	Unicorn RHS 336	**PSYCHO** (Bernard Herrmann)	£20
03	Trunk JBH002LP	**PSYCHOMANIA**	£60

Q

71	Sonet SNTF 622	**QUIET DAYS IN CLICHY** (Country Joe McDonald)	£15
66	CBS (S)BPG 62869	**THE QUILLER MEMORANDUM** (John Barry/Matt Monro) (mono/stereo)	£25

R

71	Reprise K 44159	**RAINBOW BRIDGE** (Jimi Hendrix) (matt gatefold sleeve, 'steamboat' label)...........	£20
13	Network 7959033	**RANDALL & HOPKIRK (DECEASED)** (Edwin Astley) (LP, gatefold, 180g)	£20
75	Dart ARTS 65376	**RANSOM** (Jerry Goldsmith)	£40
60	London HAD 2288	**THE RAT RACE** (Sam Butera & The Witnesses)	£25

67	United Artists (S)ULP 1184	RED AND BLUE (Vanessa Redgrave)..£40
72	Paramount SPFL 275	THE RED TENT (Ennio Morricone)..£15
75	RCA Red Seal RS 1010	THE RETURN OF THE PINK PANTHER (Henry Mancini)..................................£15
69	United Artists ULP 29069	REVOLUTION (Quicksilver Messenger Service/Steve Miller, et al.)................£20
70	United Artists UAS 29137	RIDER IN THE RAIN (Francis Lai)..£25
68	MGM MGM-C(S) 8079	THE RISE AND FALL OF THE THIRD REICH (Lalo Schifrin)...............................£20
53	Brunswick LA 8578	ROAD TO BALI (Bob Hope, Bing Crosby) (10")...£30
62	Decca LKR 4427	THE ROAD TO HONG KONG (Robert Farnon/Bob Hope & Bing Crosby)...........£20
54	Brunswick LAT 8031	THE ROBE...£15
67	Decca LK/SKL 4892	ROBBERY (Johnny Keating/Jackie Lee)..£30
64	Reprise R 2021	ROBIN AND THE SEVEN HOODS (Nelson Riddle)..£20
61	RCA RD 27233	ROCCO AND HIS BROTHERS (Nino Rota)..£20
57	Mercury MPT 7527	ROCK ALL NIGHT (Platters, Norah Hayes, et al.) (10")....................................£125
67	Polydor 583 013	JULES VERNE'S ROCKET TO THE MOON (John Scott).....................................£100
57	Brunswick LAT 8162	ROCK, PRETTY BABY (Henry Mancini/Rod McKuen)...£80
87	Ode RHVX 1	ROCKY HORROR BOX SET (Richard O'Brien) (4-LP box, with inserts, numbered).............£20
87	Ode RHBXLP 1	ROCKY HORROR BOX SET (Richard O'Brien) (4-LP box, with different inserts to above)...£20
83	Ode OSVP 78332	THE ROCKY HORROR PICTURE SHOW ALBUM (picture disc)...........................£15
90	Ode RHBXCD 1	THE ROCKY HORROR PICTURE SHOW - 15TH ANNIVERSARY (Richard O'Brien et al.) (4-CD box)...........£40
68	Dot (S)LPD 519	ROSEMARY'S BABY (Kryzstophe Komeda)..£50
65	Parlophone PMC 1262	ROTTEN TO THE CORE (New Jazz Voices)..£20
64	RCA Victor RD 7678	ROUSTABOUT (Elvis Presley) (black/red dot labels, mono) (stereo SF 7678 = £25).........£15
64	Capitol (S)T 1771	ROUTE 66 AND OTHER GREAT T.V. THEMES (Nelson Riddle) (TV show)........£15
18	Laced LMLP014	RUINER (2-LP, red and black vinyl)..£80
66	United Artists ULP 1147	THE RUSSIANS ARE COMING THE RUSSIANS ARE COMING (Johnny Mandel)...£15

S

72	RCA SF 8211	SACCO AND VANZETTI (Ennio Morricone/Joan Baez).......................................£20
53	Brunswick LA 8604	SALOMÉ (George Duning) (10")...£30
68	United Artists SULP 1202	SALT AND PEPPER (Johnny Dankworth/Sammy Davis Jr)..................................£15
65	Mercury MCL 20065	THE SANDPIPER (Johnny Mandel)...£15
78	Polydor 2480 429	SCOUSE THE MOUSE (Ringo Starr/Adam Faith, et al.) (some w/stickered sleeve & printed [not photocopied] competition insert)..........£100
78	Polydor 3194 429	SCOUSE THE MOUSE (Ringo Starr/Adam Faith, et al.) (cassette)....................£30
62	Reprise R 2013	SERGEANTS 3 (Billy May)..£20
73	Paramount SPFL 296	SERPICO (Mikis Theodorakis)..£26
64	United Artists ULP 1072	THE 7th DAWN (Riz Ortolani)..£15
74	United Artists UAS 29763	THE SEVENTH VOYAGE OF SINBAD (Bernard Hermann)................................£20
16	Laced LMLP007	SHADOW WARRIOR 2 (12", picture disc)...£35
71	Stax 2659 007	SHAFT - ORIGINAL SOUNDTRACK (Isaac Hayes) (2-LP, gatefold sleeve)..........£15
73	Probe SPB 1077	SHAFT IN AFRICA (Johnny Pate/Four Tops)..£40
72	MGM 2315 115	SHAFT'S BIG SCORE! (Gordon Parks/O.C. Smith/Isaac Hayes)........................£35
66	CBS BPG 62755	SHAKESPEARE WALLAH (Satyajit Ray)...£15
68	Philips SBL 7867	SHALAKO (Robert Farnon)...£15
80	Warner Bros K 56827	THE SHINING (Bela Bartok et al.)...£25
12	Trunk RSD 001	THE SHUTTERED ROOM (9 copies only, stamped white labels, inserts, stamped white sleeve)..........£300
12	Trunk RSD 001	THE SHUTTERED ROOM (25 copies only, stamped white labels, inserts, screenprinted brown sleeve)..........£400
70	Stateside SSL 10307	THE SICILIAN CLAN (Ennio Morricone)...£40
12	Rook RFV 001	SIGHTSEERS SESSIONS (45rpm red vinyl LP, poster, 150 only).....................£100
72	MCA MUPS 458	SILENT RUNNING (Pete Schikele/Joan Baez)...£20
66	RCA RD 7792	THE SILENCERS (Elmer Bernstein/Vikki Carr)...£30
58	Capitol T 929	SING, BOY, SING (Tommy Sands)..£50
78	Charisma CAS 1139	SIR HENRY AT RAWLINSON END (Vivian Stanshall) (with insert).....................£20
16	Laced 302 067 410 1	65DAYSOFSTATIC (2-LP)...£35
16	Laced LMLP004X	65DAYSOFSTATIC (4-LP)...£100
64	United Artists ULP 1071	633 SQUADRON (Ron Goodwin)...£20
69	RCA SF 8010	SKIDOO (Nilsson)...£20
73	Polydor 2391 084	SLAUGHTER'S BIG RIP-OFF (James Brown)..£30
66	Mercury MCL 20080	THE SLENDER THREAD (Quincy Jones)...£20
69	NEMS 6-70059	THE SMASHING BIRD I USED TO KNOW (Bobby Richards).................................£20
68	Stateside S(S)L 10224	SMASHING TIME (John Addison)..£30
73	PRT FBLP 8085	SMIKE..£15
56	Pye Disneyland DPL 39003	SNOW WHITE AND THE SEVEN DWARFS (Disney Orchestra)...........................£30
70	Pye NSPL 18348	SOLDIER BLUE AND OTHER THEMES (Roy Budd)..£40
60	London HA-T 2221	SOLOMON AND SHEBA (Mario Nascimbene)...£75
59	Capitol LCT 6180	SOME CAME RUNNING (Elmer Bernstein)...£15
59	London HA-T 2176	SOME LIKE IT HOT (Marilyn Monroe) (also stereo SAH-T 6040 = £60)...........£50
67	RCA RD 7845	SONGS FROM THE SWINGER (Marty Paich/Ann-Margret)................................£30
74	Rapple/RCA APL1-0220	SON OF DRACULA (Ringo Starr/Harry Nilsson, fold-out sleeve).......................£15
69	RCA Victor SF 8024	THE SOUTHERN STAR (Matt Monro/Georges Garvarentz)...............................£20
58	London HA-D 2079	SPANISH AFFAIR (Daniele Amfitheatrof)..£20
61	Brunswick LAT 8363	SPARTACUS (Alex North) (gatefold sleeve)..£20
68	RCA Victor SF 7957	SPEEDWAY (Elvis Presley/Nancy Sinatra) (black/red dot labels, mono) (stereo SF 7957 = £25)..........£30
53	Capitol CCL 7505	SPELLBOUND/THE RED HOUSE (Miklos Rozsa) (10").......................................£25
66	RCA RD 7787	THE SPY WHO CAME IN FROM THE COLD (Sol Kaplan)....................................£20

			MINT VALUE £
68	CBS 62919	THE SPY WITH THE COLD NOSE (Riz Ortolani)	£35
66	Fontana TL 5354	STAGECOACH (Jerry Goldsmith)	£25
77	20th C. BTD 541	STAR WARS (John Williams) (2-LP, with insert and poster)	£20
69	CBS 70062	STILETTO (Sid Ramin)	£30
52	Capitol LC 6542	A STREET CAR NAMED DESIRE (Alex North) (10")	£35
63	Elstree Extra Range	SUMMER HOLIDAY (2-LP, full soundtrack recording, 80 copies only)	£400
63	Columbia SCX 3462	SUMMER HOLIDAY (Cliff Richard) (first pressing, stereo, with inner sleeve, with green labels)	£25
57	London HA-R 2077	THE SUN ALSO RISES (Hugo Friedhofer)	£25
55	HMV DLP 1104	SUN VALLEY SERENADE (Glenn Miller)	£15
62	Golden Guinea GGL 0106	SUPERCAR - FLIGHT OF FANCY (Barry Gray/Edwin Astley)	£50
72	Buddah 2318 065	SUPERFLY (Curtis Mayfield) (gatefold sleeve)	£20
73	Buddah 2318 087	SUPER FLY T.N.T. (Osibisa)	£15
64	Stateside SL 10089	SURF PARTY (Astronauts, Routers, et al.)	£50
79	EMI EMC 3222	SUSPIRIA (Goblin)	£40
57	Brunswick LAT 8195	SWEET SMELL OF SUCCESS (Elmer Bernstein)	£20
68	Stateside S(S)L 10250	THE SWEET RIDE (Pete Rugolo/Dusty Springfield)	£15
68	CBS 70043	THE SWIMMER (Marvin Hamlisch)	£25
65	MGM MGM-C 8012	THE SWINGIN' SET (Dave Clark Five/Animals, et al.)	£30
66	Mercury 20057 SMCL	SYLVIA (David Raksin)	£15
16	Laced (no Cat no)	SYMPHONIC FANTASIES TOKYO: MUSIC FROM SQUARE ENIX (3-LP)	£60

T

70	Pye NSPL 18353	TAKE A GIRL LIKE YOU (Stanley Myers/Foundations)	£30
01	Simply Vinyl SVLP 358	THE TAKING OF PELHAM ONE TWO THREE	£40
57	Vogue Coral LVA 9070	TAMMY/INTERLUDE (Frank Skinner/Debbie Reynolds) (1 film per side)	£30
63	United Artists ULP 1025	TARAS BULBA (Franz Waxman)	£25
76	Arista ARTY 132	TAXI DRIVER (Bernard Herrman)	£30
58	London HA-D 2074-5	THE TEN COMMANDMENTS (Elmer Bernstein) (2-LP)	£15
71	RCA Victor SF 8162	THAT'S THE WAY IT IS (Elvis Presley) (glossy or matt sleeve)	£15
63	Parlophone PMC 1197	THAT WAS THE WEEK THAT WAS (Millicent Martin, et al.) (also stereo PCS 3040)	£15
59	Coral LVA 9102	THEMES FROM HORROR MOVIES (Dick Jacobs)	£15
73	Elektra K 46239	THE THIEF WHO CAME TO DINNER (Henry Mancini)	£15
82	MCA MCF 3148	THE THING (Ennio Morricone)	£30
70	United Artists UAS 29128	THEY CALL ME MISTER TIBBS (Quincy Jones)	£60
69	Philips SBL 7898	THEY CAME TO ROB LAS VEGAS (Georges Gavarentz)	£40
70	Stateside SSL 10305	THEY SHOOT HORSES, DON'T THEY? (John Green)	£15
66	Verve VLP 9147	THIS PROPERTY IS CONDEMNED (Kenyon Hopkins)	£35
68	United Artists SULP 1218	THE THOMAS CROWN AFFAIR (Michel Legrand/Noel Harrison)	£35
70	Sunset SLS 50519	THE THOMAS CROWN AFFAIR (Michel Legrand, reissue)	£20
65	Stateside SL 10136	THOSE MAGNIFICENT MEN IN THEIR FLYING MACHINES (Ron Goodwin)	£20
54	Capitol LC 6665	THREE SAILORS AND A GIRL (Gordon MacRae, et al.) (10")	£30
61	Golden Guinea GGL 0065	THREE WORLDS OF GULLIVER (Bernard Herrmann)	£20
85	Cloud Nine CN 4003	THREE WORLDS OF GULLIVER (Bernard Herrmann) (reissue)	£15
65	United Artists (S)ULP 1110	THUNDERBALL (John Barry) (mono/stereo)	£15
67	United Artists (S)ULP 1159	THUNDERBIRDS ARE GO! (Barry Gray/Cliff Richard & Shadows) (mono) (stereo = £120)	£100
66	NPL 18154	TILL DEATH US DO PART (Warren Mitchell et al.)	£15
69	Polydor 583 717	TILL DEATH DO US PART (Wilfred Burns)	£15
63	MGM MGM-C 934	TO KILL A MOCKINGBIRD (Elmer Bernstein)	£20
06	Trunk JBH 017 LP	THE TOMORROW PEOPLE (LP)	£40
59	MGM MGM-C 772	TOM THUMB (Russ Tamblyn)	£15
68	Instant INLP 002	TONITE LET'S ALL MAKE LOVE IN LONDON (Pink Floyd/Chris Farlowe, et al.)	£100
70	RCA LSA 3008	TOOMORROW (with insert)	£125
67	Fontana (S)TL 5446	TO SIR, WITH LOVE (Ron Grainer/ Lulu/Mindbenders)	£35
69	Stateside S(S)L 10271	THE TOUCHABLES (Ken Thorne/Nirvana/Wynder K. Frog, et al.)	£35
66	Polydor 582 004	THE TRAP (Ron Goodwin)	£40
96	EMI EMC 3789	TRAINSPOTTING (2-LP)	£80
67	United Artists ULP 1176	TRIPLE CROSS (Georges Garvarentz/Tony Allen)	£25
82	CBS 70223	TRON (Wendy Carlos/Journey)	£15
73	T. Motown STML 11225	TROUBLE MAN (Marvin Gaye)	£20
74	Stax STXD 4001/2	TRUCK TURNER (Isaac Hayes) (2-LP)	£15
03	XL XLLP 161	28 DAYS LATER	£100
01	Factory FAC 401	24 HOUR PARTY PEOPLE (12" promo, Joy Division/New Order/Happy Mondays)	£40
69	Polydor 583 728	TWISTED NERVE/LES BICYCLETTES DE BELSIZE (Les Reed/Barry Mason, Bernard Herrman)	£80
69	Columbia S(C)X 6330	TWO CITIES (Jeff Wayne)	£30
67	RCA RD/SF 7891	TWO FOR THE ROAD (Henry Mancini)	£15
63	United Artists ULP 1027	TWO FOR THE SEESAW (André Previn)	£15
71	United Artists UDF 50003	200 MOTELS (Frank Zappa) (2-LP, with booklet & poster)	£40
70	MCA MKPS 2013	TWO MULES FOR SISTER SARA (Ennio Morricone)	£30
62	Columbia 33SX 1482	TWO TICKETS TO PARIS (Joey Dee)	£20

U

04	Trunk JBHO10LP	UFO (500 black/500 clear vinyl)	£50
60	London HA-T 2258	THE UNFORGIVEN (Dimitri Tiomkin)	£18
68	Fontana (S)TL 5460	UP THE JUNCTION (Manfred Mann)	£25
70	Fontana 6852 005	UP THE JUNCTION (Manfred Mann) (reissue)	£15
69	Stax (S)XATS 1005	UPTIGHT (Booker T & MGs)	£15

V

73	Philips 6303 075	THE VALACHI PAPERS (Riz Ortolani)	£25
11	Finders Keepers FKRO48LP	VALERIE AND HER WEEK OF WONDERS (lubos Fiser)	£20
68	Stateside (S)SL 10228	VALLEY OF THE DOLLS (André Previn/John Williams)	£20
71	London SH-U 8420	VANISHING POINT (Delaney & Bonnie/Sam & Dave, et al.)	£20
82	MGM 2315 437	VICTOR, VICTORIA (Henry Mancini)	£15
63	Colpix PXL 516	THE VICTORS (Sol Kaplan/Frank Sinatra)	£15
58	London HAT 2118	THE VIKINGS (Mario Nascimbene)	£20
68	Dot (S)LPD 515	VILLA RIDES (Maurice Jarre)	£15
63	MGM MGM-C 951/CS 6074	THE VIPs (Miklos Rozsa)	£20
66	United Artists (S)ULP 1126	VIVA MARIA! (Georges Delerue) (mono/stereo)	£30

W

60	Mercury MMC 14033	WAGON TRAIN (Stanley Wilson, et al.)	£25
62	MGM MGM-C 891	WALK ON THE WILD SIDE (Elmer Bernstein)	£15
66	Brunswick STA 8636	THE WAR LORD (Jerome Moross)	£35
78	Satril SATL 4009	THE WATER MARGIN (Godiego) (TV soundtrack)	£20
67	Virtuoso TPLS 13010	WELLES RAISES KANE (Bernard Herrman)	£30
64	Piccadilly N(S)PL 38011	WHAT A CRAZY WORLD (Joe Brown/Susan Maughan/Marty Wilde; mono/stereo)	£22
66	RCA SF 7818	WHAT DID YOU DO IN THE WAR, DADDY? (Henry Mancini)	£15
65	United Artists ULP 1096	WHAT'S NEW PUSSYCAT? (Burt Bacharach/Tom Jones/Manfred Mann, et al.)	£20
66	MGM MGM-C(S) 8006	WHEN THE BOYS MEET THE GIRLS (Connie Francis/Herman's Hermits) (mono/stereo)	£15
69	MGM MGM-C(S) 8102	WHERE EAGLES DARE (Ron Goodwin)	£20
66	United Artists (S)ULP 1166	WHIPLASH WILLIE (André Previn)	£15
67	United Artists (S)ULP 1168	THE WHISPERERS (John Barry)	£40
67	Warner Bros W 1656	WHO'S AFRAID OF VIRGINIA WOOLF? (Alex North)	£25
83	Atlantic 78 00731	THE WICKED LADY (Tony Banks/Christopher Palmer) (LP)	£15
98	Trunk BARKED 4	THE WICKER MAN (Giovanni) (1st pressing, black vinyl)	£75
98	Trunk BARKED 4	THE WICKER MAN (Giovanni) (2nd pressing, red vinyl with inserts)	£90
02	Silva Screen/ Simply Vinyl SVLP389	THE WICKER MAN (Giovanni) (reissue, gatefold, printed inners, PVC sleeve	£30
10	Silva Screen/M.O.V. MOVLP 063	THE WICKER MAN (Giovanni) (LP, reissue, gatefold, printed inner, PVC outer)	£30
12	Silva Screen/M.O.V. MOVLP 063	THE WICKER MAN (Giovanni) (LP, repress, gatefold, printed inner, orange marbled vinyl, limited edition)	£35
13	Silva Screen SILLP 1440	THE WICKER MAN (Giovanni) (LP, 40th Anniversary Edition, new tracklisting and artwork, 500 only, certificate of authenticity)	£100
15	Silva Screen SILLP1440	THE WICKER MAN (Giovanni) (LP, repress of 2013 edition, white vinyl, 1000 only)	£40
21	Silva Screen SILLP1440	THE WICKER MAN (Giovanni) (LP, gatefold, printed inner, 'new edition', yellow vinyl)	£25
90	London 845128	WILD AT HEART	£20
57	London HA-N 2023	WILD BILL HICKOCK AND JINGLES ON THE SANTA FE TRAIL (TV s/track)	£18
69	Warner Bros WS 1814	THE WILD BUNCH (Jerry Fielding) (orange label original)	£25
71	Warner Bros K 46035	THE WILD BUNCH (Jerry Fielding) (reissue)	£15
78	A&M AMLH 64730	THE WILD GEESE (Roy Budd/Joan Armatrading)	£15
68	Capitol (S)T 5099	WILD IN THE STREETS (Les Baxter/Gurus) (original issue, black label, rainbow rim)	£25
71	MGM 2315 062	WILD ROVERS (Jerry Goldsmith)	£20
83	Chrysalis CHR 1453	WILD STYLE (various artists)	£25
71	Paramount SPFL 274	WILLY WONKA AND THE CHOCOLATE FACTORY (Leslie Bricusse)	£25
75	Arista ARTY 111	THE WIND AND THE LION (Jerry Goldsmith)	£15
87	Filmtrax MOMENT 110	WITHNAIL AND I (David Dundas)	£40
57	MGM MGM-C 757	THE WIZARD OF OZ (Judy Garland, et al.)	£40
67	Capitol (S)T 2800	WOMAN TIMES SEVEN (Riz Ortolani)	£18
64	Elstree Extra Range	WONDERFUL LIFE (2-LP, full soundtrack recording, 150 copies only)	£250
68	Apple APCOR 1	WONDERWALL MUSIC (George Harrison) (with insert & black inner sleeve, mono)	£250
68	Apple SAPCOR 1	WONDERWALL MUSIC (George Harrison) (with insert & black inner sleeve, stereo)	£100
70	Atlantic 2663 001	WOODSTOCK (Jimi Hendrix/Who/Joe Cocker, et al.) (3-LP in foldout sleeve with inners)	£18
60	RCA RD 27198	THE WORLD OF SUZIE WONG (George Duning)	£15
57	Brunswick LAT 8174	WRITTEN ON THE WIND/FOUR GIRLS IN TOWN (Frank Skinner)	£25

Y

69	Apple PMC 7070	YELLOW SUBMARINE (Beatles) (1st pressing, laminated flipback sleeve with red lines above & below rear liner note & black inner; with "Sold In The UK..." label text, mono	£300
69	Apple PCS 7070	YELLOW SUBMARINE (Beatles) (1st pressing, laminated flipback sleeve with red lines above & below rear liner note & black inner; with "Sold In The UK..." label text, stereo)	£150
17	Laced LMLP008	YOOKA LAYLEE (2-LP, green and purlple vinyl)	£60
69	CBS (S) 70045	YOU ARE WHAT YOU EAT (Tiny Tim/Electric Flag, et al.)	£18
79	MCA MCF 2804	YOUNGBLOOD (War)	£15
66	Philips (S)BL 7792	YOUNG GIRLS OF ROCHEFORT (Michel Legrand)	£25
57	Brunswick LAT 8252	THE YOUNG LIONS (Hugo Friedhofer)	£35
61	Columbia 33SX 1384	THE YOUNG ONES (Cliff Richard) (with inner sleeve, also stereo SCX 3397 = £30)	£15
67	United Artists (S)ULP 1171	YOU ONLY LIVE TWICE (John Barry/Nancy Sinatra)	£15
65	MGM MGM-CS 6081	YOUR CHEATIN' HEART (Hank Williams Jr.)	£15
67	Kama Sutra KLP 402	YOU'RE A BIG BOY NOW (Lovin' Spoonful)	£18

Z

| 70 | MGM MGM CS 8120 | ZABRISKIE POINT (Pink Floyd/Jerry Garcia/Kaleidoscope, et al.) | £30 |
| 69 | Philips 600-287 | ZITA | £40 |

MINT VALUE £

12	Death Waltz DW001	**ZOMBIE 2** (clear splatter vinyl)	£25
12	Death Waltz DW001	**ZOMBIE 2** (red vinyl)	£15
64	Ember NR 5012	**ZULU** (John Barry) (yellow/orange label, flipback sleeve)	£20

A-Z

70	Argo ZTA 501-2	**ALICE IN WONDERLAND** (2-LP, Jane Asher)	£15

MUSIC LIBRARY LPs

At one point in time little was known about the mysterious and often forgotten sub genre of music known as library, or rather non-commercial music

pressed just for use in film, TV and radio. Thankfully, the internet has allowed light to be shined into the darkest nooks and crannies of this genre and

labels like Trunk have reissued many wonderful examples of this music. Since the mid 1990s collecting interest has peaked, dropped away and is now

well on the rise again, as are prices for some of the rarer and more important pieces. Collectors either favour early recordings by famous artists such as

Jimmy Page or Tubby Hayes or those of a more funky persuasion that can be mined for breakbeats. Original pressing numbers and distribution still

remain mysterious, although most people guestimate that 500 to 1,000 copies for each library pressing is about the average, especially as we move

towards the mid 1970s. Older and larger music companies such as De Wolfe originally issued recordings on ten inch (throughout the late 1960s) in

incredibly short runs - maybe only 200 - 300 copies, and if these recordings proved commercially successful they were repressed later on twelve inch.

Obviously the original smaller pressings are more desirable. But still pressing numbers and habits remain shrouded in mystery. It has to be noted that

many international and desirable labels distributed their library recordings over here and these do turn up from time to time, however we only list

original UK pressings in this price guide. Also, it is worth noting that for libraries such as Chappell and Conroy, not all LPs have titles, they simply list the

artist names and track titles. In these cases we have just put own the LP catalogue numbers. One final note, all library records are still the property of

the libraries companies that issued them and they can, at any time, ask for them back. Like promos for pop and rock artists this is all a little unlikely, but

you have been warned.

AMPHONIC

71	AMPS LP 101	**BIG BAND SOUNDS OF TODAY** (OTTO KELLER BAND)	£15
72	AMPS LP 102	**THE ALL ELECTRIC STEAM RADIO BAND**	£30
72	AMPS LP 103	**HAVE BAND - WILL TRAVEL**	£20
72	AMPS LP 104	**MORTIMERS PEOPLE**	£15
72	AMPS LP 105	**THE OTTO KELLER ORCHESTRA**	£20
73	AMPSLP1001	**MOODSETTER/PACESETTER**	£30
73	AMPS 1001	**SMALL GROUP + SYNTHESISER** (JAMES CLARK SOUNDS)	£35
73	AMPS 1002	**SCENE SETTER**	£40
73	AMPS 1003	**DYNAMIC RHYTHMS**	£20
73	AMPS 1004	**MORTIMERS PEOPLE**	£20
73	AMPS 1005	**ACTION!**	£30
73	AMPS 1006	**SMOOTH THEMES/SWINGING PERCUSSION**	£20
74	AMPS 107	**THE HAPPY BEAT**	£15
74	AMPS 108	**SUPER SOUNDS UNLIMITED**	£60
74	AMPS 109	**START THE DAY RIGHT**	£18
74	AMPS 110	**IN A QUIET MOOD**	£18
74	AMPS 111	**THE LONDON LIFE**	£35
75	AMPS 112	**SPECIAL ASSIGNMENT**	£70
74	AMPS 113	**MELODY ALL THE WAY**	£20
75	AMPS 114	**SOUNDS 80**	£60
76	AMPS 115	**DIMENSIONS IN SOUND**	£25
76	AMPS 116	**SYD DALE SPECIAL** (MUNICH CONCERT POP ORCHESTRA)	£15
76	AMPS 117	**IT'S ALL IN THE BEAT** (MUNICH CONCERT POP ORCHESTRA)	£25
76	AMPS 118	**PICTURES IN SOUND**	£45
77	AMPS 119	**MELLOW MOODS**	£20
77	AMPS 120	**WHERE THE ACTION IS**	£30
78	AMPS 121	**MOOGERAMA** (PADDY KINGSLAND)	£35
78	AMPS 122	**KEYBOARD COLLECTION**	£18
79	AMPS 123	**NIGHT BIRD** (Keith Mansfield)	£125
79	AMPS 124	**ONCE MORE FROM THE TOP** (THE DOUBLE DOZEN ORCHESTRA)	£20
80	AMPS 125	**LET ME CALL YOU SWINGER** (THE DOUBLE DOZEN ORCHESTRA)	£20
80	AMPS 126	**JUMP TO IT** (NOAH'S PEOPLE)	£20
80	AMPS 009	**WOTTA LOTTA BRASS**	£20
80	AMPS 1010	**SHADES OF GRAY** (STEVE GRAY ORCHESTRA)	£40
80	AMPS 1011	**METROPOLIS NOW** (DICK WALTER)	£30
81	AMPS 127	**IT'S A COLOURFUL WORLD**	£20
81	AMPS 1012	**KEEPING IT LOOSE**	£20
81	AVF 1	**SOUND STAGE I**	£30
81	AVF 1	**MUSIC ACTION** (SOUND STAGE 1) (different sleeve)	£30
81	AVF 2	**SOUND STAGE 2**	£20
81	AVF 3	**SOUND STAGE 3**	£25
83	AMPS 129	**DANCE DATE** (THE DOUBLE DOZEN ORCHESTRA)	£20
83	AMPS 128	**SCENE IN MANHATTAN**	£20
81	AVF 4	**SOUND STAGE 4**	£20
81	AVF 5	**SOUND STAGE 5**	£18
81	AVF 6	**SOUND STAGE 6**	£20
82	AVF 7	**SOUND STAGE 7**	£30

MINT VALUE £

82	AVF 8	SOUND STAGE 8	£15
82	Sound Stage 9	SOUND STAGE 9	£20
83	AVF 10	SOUND STAGE 10	£15
83	AVF 11	SOUND STAGE 11	£18
83	AVF 12	SOUND STAGE 12	£20
83	AVF 13	SOUND STAGE 13	£20
83	AVF 14	SOUND STAGE 14	£18
83	AVF 15	SOUND STAGE 15	£15
83	AVF 16	SOUND STAGE 16	£15
87	AVF 57	SOUND STAGE 57: OFFICE HOURS	£40

APOLLO SOUND

67	APP APS 1001	MEDITATIONS FOR BRASS/SUITE FOR BRASS INSTRUMENTS (WESTMINISTER BRASS ENSEMBLE) (10")	£20
68	APP 5001	INSTRUMENTAL POPS NO. 1	£15
68	APP 5002	INSTRUMENTAL POPS NO. 2	£20
68	App 5003	INSTRUMENTAL POPS NO. 3	£20
69	App 5004	INSTRUMENTAL POPS NO. 4	£20
69	APP 5007	MELODY AND RHYTHM 1 (JOHN FOX ORCHESTRA/DAVID LINDUP SOUND)	£40
69	APP 5008	MELODY AND RHYTHM 2 (LEM ARCON AND HIS ORCHESTRA/DAVID LINDUP SOUND)	£25
70	APP 5009	MELODY AND RHYTHM 3	£25
71	APP 5010	MELODY AND RHYTHM 4 (BUXTON ORR SOUND/LEM ARCON AND HIS BAND)	£40
71	APP 5011	MELODY AND RHYTHM 5 (REG TILSLEY AND HIS MUSIC)	£20
71	APP 5012	DENGA (ROBIN JONES AND HIS QUINTET, blue label)	£40
71	APP 5012	DENGA (ROBIN JONES AND HIS QUINTET, yellow label)	£30
71	APP 5013	COLOURS IN RHYTHM VOLUME 1 (WILF TODD/PETER BALDING)	£40
71	APP 5014	MELODY AND RHYTHM 6 (JOSE PRIVSEK)	£40
71	APP 5015	JAZZ IN LANDSCAPE (JOHN PORTER TRIO)	£20
71	APP5016	EL MAJA (ROBIN JONES SEVEN, blue label)	£125
72	APP 5017	INSTRUMENTAL GROUPS 1 (MOJMIR SEPE)	£20
72	APP 5017	INSTRUMENTAL GROUPS 2 (SIMON GALE MUSIC)	£20
72	APP 5019	INSTRUMENTAL GROUPS 3 (JURE ROBEZNIK)	£25
72	APP 5020	SIMPLE MELODY 1 (BORIS KOVACIC)	£25
73	APP 5021	COLOURS IN RHYTHM 2 (KARL HEINZ LOGES MUSIC/MARTIN GOLDSTEIN PLAYERS)	£30
73	APP 5022	COLOURS IN RHYTHM 3 (SIMON GALE MUSIC/DICK HUNTER FIVE)	£20
73	APP 5023	MELODY AND RHYTHM 7 (DICK HUNTER FIVE/GORDON LANGFORD GROUP)	£50
74	APP 5024	COLOURS IN RHYTHM 4 (PETER HUGHES QUINTET/TED NORD SOUND)	£60
74	APP 5025	MELODY AND RHYTHM 8 (BUDAPEST RADIO ORCHESTRA/GORDON LANGFORD GROUP)	£20
75	APP 5026	COLOURS IN RHYTHM 5 (BUDAPEST RADIO ORCHESTRA/REG TILSLEY GROUP)	£60
75	APP 5027	MELODY AND RHYTHM 9 (JUDD PROCTER SEXTET/POLISH RADIO ORCHESTRA)	£30
75	APP 5028	COLOURS IN RHYTHM 6 (REG TILSLEY SOUND/POLISH RADIO ORCHESTRA)	£50
75	APP 5029	PERSPECTIVES (IAN HENRY TRIO)	£25
76	APP 5030	MELODY AND RHYTHM 10 (POLISH RADIO ORCHESTRA/PETER SANDER PLAYERS)	£80
77	APP 5031	COLOURS IN RHYTHM 7 (REG TILSLEY PLAYERS/POLISH RADIO ORCHESTRA)	£40
77	APP 5032	MELODY AND RHYTHM 11 (POLISH RADIO ORCHESTRA/PETER SANDER GROUP)	£20
77	APP 5033	MELODY AND RHYTHM 12 (BUDAPEST RADIO ORCHESTRA/POLISH RADIO ORCHESTRA)	£40
77	APP 5034	MELODY AND RHYTHM 13 (POLISH RADIO ORCHESTRA/PETER SANDER PLAYERS)	£30
78	APP 5035	MELODY AND RHYTHM 14 (BUDAPEST RADIO ORCHESTRA/POLISH RADIO ORCHESTRA)	£40
78	APP 5036	COLOURS IN RHYTHM 8 (BUDAPEST RADIO ORCHESTRA/POLISH RADIO ORCHESTRA)	£35
80	APP 5037	MELODY AND RHYTHM 15 (KENNETH B. JONES/POLISH RADIO ORCHESTRA)	£30
80	APP 5038	HIS AND HERS (PETER SANDERS/JACQUELINE BINNS ENSEMBLE)	£20

BACKGROUND MUSIC

68	Audio BMP 137	SCARLATTI SOUNDS	£15
71	Audio BMP 138	HORNS IN RHYTHM/ON THE CLASSICAL BEAT	£20
71	Audio BMP 139	STRINGS GO POP/BRASS & STRING BAG	£100

BOSWORTH

66	BLP 102	ELECTRONIC MUSIC (VACLAV NELHYBEL, 10" LP)	£80
69	BLP 103	THE MELODY MEN AND THE SWING MEN (HAROLD GELLAR SOUND) (10")	£20
69	BLP 104	TIJUANA SOUND/ATONAL JAZZ STRUCTURES (HEINZ HOTTER/JAZZ ARCHITECTS) (10")	£25
69	BLP 105	EBBINGHOUSE SOUND/IN A SWINGING MOOD (BERNARD EBBINGHOUSE/ERWIN LEHN ORCHESTRA) (10")	£20
69	BLP 106	A MODERN SOUND (ERWIN LEHN DANCE ORCHESTRA) (10")	£20
69	BLP 107	A MUSICAL MELANGE (EDWIN LEHN ORCHESTRA) (10")	£20
68	BLP 108	MODERN DRAMATICS (ERWIN LEHN ORCHESTRA/KENNY SALMON MODERN JAZZ GROUP (10")	£20
69	BLP 109	MODERN RHYTHM (10")	£20
69	BLP 110	MODERN INDUSTRIALS (CONTINENTAL THEATRE ORCHESTRA/CONTEMPORARY MUSIC GROUP) (10")	£20
69	BLP 116	INDUSTRIAL ROCK/SOUNDS OF THE METROPOLIS (10")	£20
69	BLP 111	ACHIEVEMENT/BRIGHT MOVEMENT (CONTINENTAL THEATRE ORCHESTRA) (10")	£20
69	BLP 112	ROUND THE WORLD/MELODY AND RHYTHM (10")	£20
69	BLP 117	ORCHESTRAL POTPOURRI (INTERNATIONAL ORCHESTRA)	£30
70	BLP 118	MODERN DRAMATICS/DRUMS AND PERCUSSION (SEVENTY SOUNDS GROUP/SPERIE KARAS) (10")	£25
70	BLP 119	JAZZ POTPOURRI/THE JOLLY JOKERS	£25
70	BLP 120	HARD AND FAST/MELLOW MOODS (SYDNEY DALE ORCHESTRA)	£25
71	BLP 121	MISCELLANEA (KURT EDELHAGEN ORCHESTRA) (10")	£25

MINT VALUE £

71	BLP 122	DRAMATIC MELODIES AND SIMPLE MELODIES (SYD DALE)	£25
71	BLP 123	FIVE INVENTIONS FOR FLUTE AND SIX PERSPECTIVES FOR STRINGS (DERRICK MASON)	£30
71	BLP 124	ROMANTIC STRINGS AND A PIANO AND DRAMATIC SOUNDS	£30
72	BLP 125	THE BIG BAND SOUND AND ORCHESTRAL SOUNDS (KURT EDELHAGEN ORCHESTRA)	£30
72	BLP 126	RHYTHMIC MOODS (KURT EDELHAGEN ORCHESTRA) (10")	£35
72	BLP 127	IN A QUIET MOOD/HAPPY BEAT (10")	£20
73	BLP 130	SOUNDS ELECTRIC AND FLUGAL SOUNDS/KEYBOARD PLUS AND MODERN MELODY	£25
73	BLP 131	HENRY'S HAPPY SOUND/LINKS ELECTRIC/EASY LISTENING/MODERN MOVEMENT	£20
73	BLP 132	VISIONS/CLASSICA A LA MODE/FOUR PERIOD PIECES	£25
73	BLP 133	DRAMATICS ELECTRONIC (FRANK GARTNER)	£35
73	BLP 134	DRAMATIC DIVERSIONS/ROMANTIC RELAXATION/GENTLE MOVEMENT	£35
74	BLP 135	MOVEMENT IN RHYTHM/RHYTHM AT RANDOM	£80
74	BLP 136	BRASSY AND RHYTHMIC	£30
74	BLP 137	FLUTES, GUITARS AND KEYBOARDS (ANTHONY MAWER)	£30
74	BLP 138	WALTZ, SHUFFLE AND SWING/LATIN AMERICA TIME/SWING TO A MELODY	£20
75	BLP 139	SEVEN SHADES OF SOUND (SEVEN SHADOWS)	£40
75	BLP 140	BIG AND BRASSY/LIGHT AND EASY	£20
75	BLP 141	AMERICA '76	£100
75	BLP 142	LET'S GO SOLO/ROCK BEAT/DRUMS & PERCUSSION	£60
75	BLP 143	MUSICAL COCKTAIL 1 & 2/MUSICAL FLASHES	£100
76	BLP 144	THE GENTLE TOUCH/BRIGHT AND BRASSY	£20
76	BLP 145	HARD AND FAST/MELLOW MOODS/MISCELLANEOUS MOODS	£20
76	BLP 146	ROMANTIC STRINGS/DRAMATIC SOUNDS/SIMPLE MELODIES/DRAMATIC MELODIES	£30
76	BLP 147	BIG BAND SOUNDS/ORCHESTRAL SOUNDS/RHYTHMIC MOODS/IN A QUIET MOOD	£20
77	BLP 148	SOFT SWEET AND SWING	£40
77	BLP 149	THE '77 SOUND/MUSICAL COCKTAILS (NO.3)	£30
77	BLP 150	MUSICAL CONCEPTIONS/MORE MUSICAL CONCEPTIONS	£40
77	BLP 151	MUSICAL COCKTAIL NO. 4	£100

BRUTON

78	BRN 1	HERITAGE/PARONAMA	£20
78	BRE 1	PLAYTIME	£15
78	BRL 1	AUTURBINE (1st pressing, white textured sleeve)	£40
78	BRF 1	COMEDY SITUATIONS/COMEDY SYNTHESIZER	£20
78	BRA 1	FANFARES, LINKS, BRIDGES, STINGS	£15
78	BRQ 1	CONFLICT/WAR OF NERVES	£20
78	BRM 1	MENACE	£40
78	BRR 1	FRANCE	£15
78	BRG 1	SPORTS STADIUM	£15
78	BRB 1	JINGLES VOL. 1	£15
78	BRK 1	DRIVING FORCE	£50
78	BRI 1	TERRESTRIAL JOURNEY	£40
78	BRS 1	PALAIS DE DANCE/DEAR OLD DIXIELAND	£15
78	BRC 1	HARP	£15
78	BRP 1	BAROQUE ENSEMBLE	£15
78	BRJ 1	GREAT EXPECTATIONS	£20
78	BRD 1	FOUR SEASONS/COUNTRY LIFE	£15
78	BRO 1	PALM COURT	£15
78	BRH 1	ROCK CITY	£40
78	BRC 2	HARPSICHORD	£15
78	BRH 2	HEAVY ROCK	£40
78	BRR 2	WESTERN MUSIC	£15
78	BRP 2	BAROQUE	£15
78	BRM 2	ABSTRACTIONS IN TIME	£40
78	BRR 2	WESTERN MUSIC	£15
78	BRJ 2	DRAMA MONTAGE	£80
78	BRD 2	GOLDEN PLAINS	£40
78	BRI 2	TEMPUS FUGIT	£60
78	BRK 2	HIGH ADVENTURE	£70
78	BRS 2	SWING WITH THE BIG BANDS	£15
78	BRL 2	INDUSTRIAL POWER	£25
78	BRG 2	CONTEMPORARY ORCHESTRAL	£15
78	BRN 2	IMPRESSIVE SCENES	£20
78	BRB 2	JINGLES VOL. 2	£15
78	BRC 3	CLASSICAL GUITAR	£15
78	BRH 3	ROCK 'N' ROLL	£15
78	BRR 3	GREECE/CENTRAL EUROPE	£15
78	BRD 3	LITTLE CREATURES	£20
78	BRI 3	CITY OF THE FUTURE SUITE/EQUINOX	£30
78	BRJ 3	IMPORTANT PROJECT/WONDERS OF THE WORLD/ENDEAVOUR	£20
78	BRN 3	PROGRESS	£20
78	BRG 3	COUNTRY BOUND	£15
78	BRI 10	FANTASIA	£80
78	BRP 3	MASTERWORKS/IMPRESSIONS	£15
78	BRM 3	DARKSIDE	£60
78	BRH 4	DISCO HAPPENING	£40
78	BRR 4	THE ORIENT	£15
78	BRG 4	GOOD TIMES	£15

78	BRM 4	FEAR	£40
78	BRR 5	IRELAND	£15
78	BRR 6	COUNTRY & WESTERN	£15
78	BRR 7	INDIA/ARABIA	£15
78	BRJ 8	DRAMA MONTAGE VOLUME 2	£75
78	BRN 8	EXPANDING HORIZONS	£20
78	BRJ 12	WILDLIFE	£50
78	BRD 8	TONE POEMS	£40
78	BRG 6	SUNNY SIDE	£100
79	BRI 6	FRONTIERS OF SCIENCE	£120
78	BRJ 9	WEB OF INTRIGUE	£40
79	BRJ 4	THRILLER/SUITE OF THE HURRICANE/SHARK OF THE SUITE	£25
79	BRJ 7	LIFE OF ADVENTURE/VIDEO TECHNIQUES	£20
79	BHR 5	LIGHT MY FIRE	£70
79	BRK 4	DRAMATIC ACTION	£30
79	BRI 4	ENERGISM	£40
79	BRK 5	CONTEMPORARY ACTION	£40
79	BRS 3	SMALL BAND JAZZ	£20
79	BRK 5	CONTEMPORARY MOTION	£40
79	BRD 10	RELAX	£40
79	BRK 3	SPEED FEVER	£35
79	BRL 4	FUTURAMA	£40
79	BRE 3	KIDS AND CARTOONS	£20
79	BRG 7	SPREAD YOUR WINGS	£30
80	BRI 8	KINETICS/VISION	£40
80	BRD 13	SERENITY	£40
80	BRM 5	HOUSE OF HORROR	£25
80	BRL 6	UNDERGROOVE	£40
80	BRH 10	BLOW OUT	£20
80	BRI 12	GYROSCOPE	£60
80	BRI 9	SUSPENSIONS/GALAXY	£50
80	BRI 11	THE VIDEO AGE	£50
81	BRM 6	BUILDING TENSION	£40
81	Bruton BRM 8	WATCHFUL EYE	£45
81	BRL 7	MUSIC MACHINE	£60
81	BRJ 22	INTERPOL	£100
81	BRJ 24	EARTH	£40
81	BRM 9	SURVIVAL	£40
82	BRI 21	TOMORROW'S WORLD	£70
82	BRI 22	MUSIC BEDS	£50
83	BRJ 25	ESPIONAGE	£30
83	BRM 11	STRANGE	£25
84	BRI 23	FORCEFIELD	£30
84	BRK 9	HIGH TENSION	£30
85	BRM 13	STRING TENSION	£30
84	BRR 18	EAST MEETS WEST	£70

(The first 50 Bruton LPs were issued simultaneously in April 1978)

CHAPPELL

66	LPC 712-717	VARIOUS ARTISTS	£25
66	LPC 781-885	VARIOUS ARTISTS	£20
66	LPC 861-866	VARIOUS ARTISTS	£30
68	LPC 1005-1009	VARIOUS ARTISTS	£20
70	CIS 5003	INDUSTRIAL SOUNDS VOL 2	£25
70	CIS 5007	LIGHT ATMOSPHERE VOL 2	£40
70	CIS 5008	MUSIC FOR DRAMA VOL 1	£30
70	CIS 5009	MUSIC FOR DRAMA VOL 2	£25
70	CIS 5013	DANCE MUSIC VOL 1 (NIGHT CLUB)	£20
70	CIS 5023	JAZZ (SMALL GROUP)	£30
70	CIS 5024	MUSIC FOR DRAMA VOL 3	£30
70	672-677	672-677	£25
70	678-682	678-682	£20
70	LPC 1032	THE EIFFEL TOWER	£50
70	LPC 1034	OLE JENSEN AND HIS MUSIC	£30
70	LPC 1036	PAUL DUPONT AND HIS ORCHESTRA	£50
70	LPC 1038	OLE JENSEN AND HIS MUSIC	£30
70	LPC 1039	OLE JENSEN AND HIS MUSIC	£30
71	LPC 1040	OLE JENSEN AND HIS MUSIC	£15
70	LPC 1042	JOHN CACAVAS/PAUL DUPONT	£20
70	LPC 1043	ROGER ROGER	£20
70	LPC 1044	OLE JENSEN AND HIS MUSIC	£25
70	LPC 1045	LEE MASON AND HIS ORCHESTRA	£200
70	LPC 1047	OLE JENSEN AND HIS MUSIC	£30
70	LPC 1049	OLE JENSEN AND HIS MUSIC	£20
72	LPC 1051	LEE MASON AND HIS ORCHESTRA	£75
72	LPC 1052	MARK DUVAL AND HIS MUSIC	£60
72	LPC 1053	POP SOUNDS	£40
73	LPC 1055	ELECTRONIC MUSIC	£35
73	LPC 1056	MARK DUVAL AND HIS MUSIC	£50

MINT VALUE £

73	LPC 1058	MARK DUVAL AND HIS MUSIC	£35
73	LPC 1059	LEE MASON AND HIS ORCHESTRA	£80
73	LPC 1060	ROBERT FARNON	£15
73	LPC 1062	PAUL DUPONT AND HIS ORCHESTRA	£30
73	LPC 1063	THE RED BRICKS	£50
73	LPC 1065	MARK DUVAL AND HIS ORCHESTRA - RHYTHM N BRASS	£100
73	LPC 1066	MUSIC BY ROGER ROGER	£30
73	LPC 1068	POP SOUNDS - MAD DOG	£40
73	LPC 1069	MARK DUVAL AND HIS MUSIC - LIGHT AND BRIGHT	£40
74	LPC 1070	MARK DUVAL AND HIS MUSIC - BRASS AND RHYTHMS	£100
74	LPC 1071	MARK DUVAL AND HIS MUSIC - SOFT AND SWEET	£40
74	LPC 1075	MARK DUVAL AND HIS MUSIC - LIGHT AND BRIGHT	£20
74	LPC 1076	MARK DUVAL AND HIS MUSIC - BRASS AND RHYTHMS	£100
74	LPC 1077	MARK DUVAL AND HIS MUSIC - SOFT AND SWEET	£30
75	LPC 1082	ELECTRONIC MUSIC/SYNTHESIZER EFFECTS	£25
77	LPC 1085	MARK DUVAL AND HIS ORCHESTRA	£30
77	LPC 1086	ZOUCHE ORCHESTRA - A HUNK OF FUNK	£25
77	LPC 1087	PAUL DUPONT AND HIS ORCHESTRA - TAPESTRY	£60
77	LPC 1088	PAUL REY - ZAP! KAPOW!!	£20
79	LPC 1090	BECKETT & HOWARD - NICE AND MEAN	£20
79	LPC 1091	SUGAR AND SPICE	£40
79	LPC 1092	REPERTOIRE EVOCATEUR	£15

CHAPPELL INTERNATIONAL

73	CAL 4001	HAPPY MUSIC/COMEDY MUSIC	£20
73	CAL 4002	MOOG SYNTHESISER MUSIC	£40
73	CAL 4004	SOUNDS ELECTRONIC	£50
73	CAL 4005	MUSIC FOR DRAMA	£40
74	CAL 4006	HAPPY AND SWEET MUSIC/GOLDEN OLDIES	£15
73	CAL 4007	SMALL GROUP SOUNDS	£25
73	CAL 4008	BAND MUSIC	£15
73	CAL 4009	THE SOUND OF STRINGS	£40
74	CAL 4010	MUSIC BY ROGER ROGER	£30
74	CAL 4012	NATIONAL FLAVOURS	£15
74	CAL 4011	ORCHESTRAL SOUNDS	£15
74	CAL 4013	SMALL GROUP SOUNDS	£200
74	CAL 4015	MUSIC FOR DRAMA (ORCHESTRAL)	£40
74	CAL 4015	MUSIC FOR DRAMA (SMALL GROUPS)	£45
74	CAL 4016	LIGHT AND SWEET	£15
74	CAL 4017	BAND MUSIC	£15

CONROY

70	BMLP 070	UNTITLED	£15
70	BMLP 071	UNTITLED	£20
70	BMLP 072	ELEKTRONIC PERCUSSION POINTS	£30
70	BMLP 073	UNTITLED	£15
70	BMLP 074	THEME SETS	£40
70	BMLP 075	THEME SETS	£20
70	BMLP 076	THEME SETS	£15
70	BMLP 077	THEME SETS	£15
70	BMLP 078	DOUBLE CROSS	£20
70	BMLP 079	CAPITAL CITIES	£15
70	BMLP 080	ELECTROSCOPE	£30
71	BMLP 085	MODERN MOVEMENTS	£35
72	BMLP 086	RHYTHMIC UNDERSCORES	£25
71	BMLP 089	LARRY ROBBIN'S PERCUSSION	£50
71	BMLP 090	LARRY ROBBIN'S PERCUSSION/UNDERDRAMA	£40
71	BMLP 090A	LARRY ROBBIN'S PERCUSSION/UNDERDRAMA (repressing with different - full orange - cover)	£40
71	BMLP 091	HARP QUARTET	£20
72	BMLP 092	LONDON'S UNDERGROUND	£75
72	BMLP 092	LONDON'S UNDERGROUND (repressing with full orange cover)	£50
72	BMLP 093	LARRY ROBBIN'S SPORTSTUDIO BAND	£50
72	BMLP 093A	LARRY ROBBIN'S SPORTSTUDIO BAND (repressing with full orange sleeve)	£80
72	BMLP 094	INDUSTRIAL OPENINGS AND ENDINGS	£20
72	BMLP 095	MOOD MOVEMENTS	£20
72	BMLP 097	MOOD MOVEMENTS - AFRO PATTERNS	£80
72	BMLP 098	MODERN MOVEMENT - PERCUSSIVE MOMENT	£30
72	BMLP 099	BRIGHT HAPPY BEAT/GENTLE LYRICAL BEAT	£30
73	BMLP 101	HAPPY MOOG	£25
73	BMLP 102	DYNAMIC DRUMS PLUS	£50
73	BMLP 103	LARRY ROBBIN'S CLAP TRAP DRUMS/DRUM BAND	£40
73	BMLP 104	MODERATE BEAT MOVEMENTS	£30
73	BMLP 107	MODERN MOVEMENT - ACTION TRACKS	£30
74	BMLP 112	WILDLIFE - THEME SETS	£15
74	BMLP 113	WAY IN WAY OUT	£25
74	BMLP 114	SOFT SOUNDS AND GENTLE MOVEMENTS	£40
75	BMLP 115	LONDON'S UNDERGROUND 2	£40
75	BMLP 117	KLAUS WEISS SOUNDS AND PERCUSSION	£100
75	BMLP 118	WALT ROCKMAN MOOG MOODS	£18

75	BMLP 121	BACKGROUND ACTION	£200
75	BMLP 122	MULTI TRACKS	£80
75	BMLP 123	ELECTRONIC SOUNDS - ORGAN SOUNDS	£30
75	BMLP 124	DRAMATIC TEMPI	£100
75	BMLP 125	ALL KINDS OF MACHINES	£60
75	BMLP 126	HANS EHRLINGER SWINGING BAROQUE BRASS	£20
75	BMLP 128	CHROMOZONES	£50
75	BMLP 129	PANORAMIC SRINGS - SOFT SOUNDS	£25
75	BMLP 131	ON THE ROAD	£40
75	BMLP 132	SOUNDS FUNKY	£60
75	BMLP 133	MODERN MIXTURE	£40
76	BMLP 133	PERCUSSION PLUS VOLS 3 AND 4	£18
75	BMLP 143	FEELINGS	£500
75	BMLP 144	LIGHT ACTIVITY/DRAMATIC	£25
75	BMLP 145	NEW DIMENSION	£80
75	BMLP 150	DRAMA TENSION	£40
76	BMLP 158	PSYCHOSES SUITE	£30
76	BMLP 162	ACTION AND ACTIVITY	£40
76	BMLP 163	SPAGE AGE	£30
76	BMLP 167	BRASSBOUND BACKGROUND	£35
76	BMLP 176	MOVING PERCUSSION	£40
77	BMLP 177	DRAMATIC ACTION - DRAMATIC SOUNDS	£40

CONROY EUROBEATS SERIES

73	EURO 1	SILLY SYNTHESISERS	£30
73	EURO 2	ETHNIC SONGS AND DANCES/INDIA - A THEME SET	£60
73	EURO 3	MODERN BAROQUE	£30
73	EURO 4	ROMANTIC BACKGROUNDS	£50
73	EURO 5	DRAMATIC BACKGROUNDS	£100
73	EURO 6	SOLO INSTRUMENTS	£20
73	EURO 7	GOING WEST - TWO GUITARS	£20
73	EURO 8	CLASSICAL VIEW/NEW TESTAMENT	£20
73	EURO 9	THEMES AND BACKGROUNDS/TWO MOODS	£20
73	EURO 10	WORLD AT WORK	£150
73	EURO 11	COLLA VOCE	£100

DE WOLFE

64	DW/LP 2824	YOUNG WORLD (10")	£30
64	DW/LP 2853	GUITARS IN MOTION (10")	£15
65	DW/LP 2890	ILLUSTRATIONS NO 4 (10")	£20
65	DEW/LP 2918	ILLUSTRATIONS NO 5 (10")	£30
65	DW/LP 2922	POWER PROJECT (10")	£30
66	DW/LP 2949	BAND 8 (10")	£60
66	DW/LP 2950	HIGH SPEED JAZZ (10")	£40
66	DW/LP 2966	MIND ON THE RUN (10")	£200
66	DW/LP 2968	JOURNEY INTO SOUND (10")	£40
66	DW/LP 2969	AN EYE FOR AN EYE (10")	£60
66	DW/LP 2973	ABSTRACTIONS OF THE INDUSTRIAL NORTH (10")	£250
66	DW/LP 2974	THE WILD ONE (10") - (features Jimmy Page)	£150
66	DW/LP 2975	TOWN BEAT (10")	£80
66	DW/LP 2981	ON THE TOWN (10")	£20
66	DW/LP 2987	CONTINENT SEVEN (10")	£25
66	DWLP 2990	YOUNG BEAT (10")	£20
67	DL/LP 3019	THE NEW BREED (10")	£80
67	DW/LP 3022	CHECKPOINT (10")	£20
67	DW/LP 3023	THE SWINGING CITY (10")	£25
67	DW/LP 3024	SILK ORGANDIE (10")	£20
67	DW/LP 3029	POLARIS (10")	£60
67	DW/LP 3030	LUNAR PROBE (10")	£80
67	DW/LP 3032	THE MUSIC OF REG TILSLEY (10")	£20
67	DW/LP 3033	CHAPTER TWO - BEAT GROUP (10")	£25
67	DW/LP 3036	ARCTIC LIFE (10")	£18
67	DW/LP 3040	ELECTRIC BANANA (10")	£150
67	DW/LP 3046	YOUNG FRIENDS (10" LP)	£20
67	DW/LP 3049	Z PATROL	£30
67	DW/LP 3063	ASSIGNEMENT LONDON	£50
67	DW/LP 3066	DON'T LOSE YOUR COOL (10")	£200
68	DW/LP 3069	MORE ELECTRIC BANANA (10")	£200
68	DW/LP 3070	BIG CITY STORY	£20
68	DW/LP 3084	ELECTROSHAKE (10" LP)	£70
68	DW/LP 3097	ON THE BUTTON (10")	£20
68	DW/LP 3088	QUIETLY WITH JOHAN (10")	£20
69	DW/LP 3108	QUINTET OF MODERN JAZZ	£25
69	DW/LP 3110	TIME OUT TO LISTEN	£50
69	DW/LP3114	WHO'S GONN BUY (THE LEMON DIPS) (10")	£150
69	DW/LP 3115	JOHNNY HAWKSWORTH'S CARIBBEAN SOUND	£35
69	DW/LP 3116	BEST OF JOHNNY HAWKSWORTH	£20
69	DW/LP 3119	TOOTH FOR A TOOTH	£40
69	DW/LP 3123	EVEN MORE ELECTRIC BANANA	£100
69	DW/LP 3127	AMBER TURNING MAUVE	£18

MINT VALUE £

69	DW/LP 3131	MOSAIC	£20
69	DW/LP 3135	ELECTROSHAKE No. 2	£40
69	DW/LP 3136	POP SOUNDS BY THE COOL	£100
69	DW/LP 3141	NEW DECADE	£20
69	DW/LP 3149	A DAY IN THE LIFE OF	£30
70	DW/LP 3154	HEAVY GRAVY	£25
70	DW/LP 3174	THEME AND VARIATION	£20
71	DW/LP 3182	VOCAL PATTERNS	£150
71	DW/LP 3185	BUMPER BUNDLE	£20
71	DW/LP 3193	ILLINOIS	£20
71	DW/LP 3199	ATOMIC BUTTERFLY	£35
71	DW/LP 3200	SING ME A SONG	£35
71	DW/LP 3201	ELECTROBEDS VOL. 1	£20
71	DW/LP 3205	PINK SAUCE	£25
71	DW/LP 3208	ELECTROBEDS VOL. 2	£20
71	DW/LP 3212	MOONSHADE	£80
71	DW/LP 3214	ANGLO AMERICAN JAZZ	£100
71	DW/LP 3215	CULT AND COLOUR	£20
71	DW/LP 3219	ALTERNATIVES	£40
71	DW/LP 3220	AFRO-ROCK	£250
71	DW/LP 3224	LITTLE BOSSA	£40
72	DW/LP 3225	FORMULA	£40
72	DW/LP 3227	VOCAL SHADES AND TONES	£200
72	DW/LP 3228	PROTOTYPE	£80
72	DW/LP 3229	FREE AS AIR	£50
72	DW/LP 3230	SWEET CHARIOT AND FRIEND	£30
72	DW/LP 3238	9-10-OUT	£35
72	DW/LP 3243	HOGAN, THE HAWK AND DORTY JOHN CROWN	£80
72	DW/LP 3247	THE ART OF THE SYNTHESISER	£50
72	DW/LP 3255	TILSLEY ORCHESTRAL NO. 10	£80
72	DW/LP 3258	GREAT DAY	£80
72	DW/LP 3259	HERE AND THERE	£20
73	DW/LP 3260	MUSIC FOR TUNED PERCUSSION	£25
73	DW/LP 3262	BLACK PEARL	£100
73	DW/LP 3263	OUTPUT	£40
73	DW/LP 3265	BRASS GAME	£30
73	DW/LP 3271	SYNTHESISER CONTACT	£40
73	DW/LP 3275	HEAVY TRUCKIN'	£50
73	DW/LP 3284	HOT LICKS	£60
73	DW/LP 3285	BIG BEAT	£300
74	DWS/LP 3276	METROPOLIS	£20
74	DW/LP 3278	HOT ICE	£100
74	DWS/LP 3291	ELECTRIC BIRD	£40
74	DWS/LP 3292	DARK MYSTERY	£30
75	DWS/LP 3298	SOUL SARABANDE	£25
75	DWS/LP 3300	SPINECHILLER	£25
75	DWS/LP 3302	AWAKENING	£30
75	DWS/LP 3304	SOUNDS UNUSUAL	£40
75	DWS/LP 3312	LIKE A FRIEND	£25
75	DWS/LP 3314	GO LIGHTLY	£25
75	DWS/LP 3315	DANGEROUS CONNECTION	£80
74	DW/LP 3318	HARD HITTER	£150
75	DW/LP 3319	METAL SUNRISE	£60
75	DWS/LP 3321	GOOD COMPANY	£35
75	DWS/LP 3322	DREAM KINGDOM	£60
75	DWS/LP 3323	SLICED ORANGE	£60
75	DWS/LP 3324	BITE HARD	£80
76	DWS/LP 3327	STRETCH	£25
76	DWS/LP 3328	RHYMES	£200
76	DW/LP 3331	RUBBER RIFF	£40
76	DWS/LP 3336	DISCO QUEEN	£30
76	DWS/LP 3338	WINGS	£40
77	DWS/LP 3340	THE WORLD OF PERCUSSION AND TUNED PERCUSSION	£25
77	DWS/LP 3351	8 DAYS A WEEK	£40
77	DWS/LP 3352	OPTIMUM	£40
77	DWS/LP 3358	CONNECTION	£35
77	DWS/LP 3363	NATURAL BREAK	£15
78	DWS/LP 3374	SCHIZO	£20
78	DWS/LP 3378	KALEIDOSCOPE	£40
78	DWS/LP 3380	GUN BARREL HIGHWAY	£15
78	DWS/LP 3381	THE RETURN OF ELECTRIC BANANA	£50
78	DW/LP 3385	FOREST OF EVIL	£60
78	DWS/LP 3387	RED LIGHT ZONE	£30
78	DW/LP 3392	MEAN AND DIRTY	£200
78	DWS/LP 3393	SLIPSTREAM	£20
78	DWS/LP 3394	BADLY BRUISED, SLIGHTLY STONED	£50
79	DWS/LP 3397	FURTHER EXPLORATION OF THE ART OF THE SYNTHESISER	£30
79	DWS/LP 3398	TUMBLING DICE	£25

79	DWS/LP 3399	HUBBLE BUBBLE	£30
79	DWS/LP 3405	MEETING POINT	£20
79	DWS/LP 3414	PUSH BUTTON	£70
79	DWS/LP 3416	GROOVE TUBE	£30
80	DWS/LP 3412	POWER SOURCE	£20
80	DWS/LP 3421	BACKING TRACKS	£20
80	DWSLP 3428	IN MOTION	£200
80	DWSLP 3429	GUN MAN	£30
80	DWSLP 3435	THE PROFESSIONALS	£35
80	DWSLP 3437	SUNNY JIM	£20
80	DWSLP 3438	MOVING ON THROUGH	£20
80	DWSLP 3445	SPACE DRIVE	£40
81	DWSLP 3457	SOUND WAVES PART 2	£30
81	DWSLP 3468	THE SHADOW	£35
81	DW/LP 3469	FOREST OF EVIL PART 2	£60
82	DW/LP 3465	FEELING ALAVE	£25
82	DWSLP 3481	HIGH CLIMBER	£30
82	DWSLP 3482	ELECTRA	£15
82	DWSLP 3483	DELTA	£40
82	DWSLP 3485	MELODIOUS THUNK	£25
82	DWSLP 3487	PIUSSYFOOTING	£30
82	DWSLP 3491	OXYGEN	£30
83	DWSLP 3502	FLASHPOINT	£30
83	DWSLP 3504	MILLENNIUM	£30
83	DWSLP 3509	BACKING TRACKS VOLUME 2	£30
84	DWSLP 3525	BACKING TRACK VOLUME 3	£30
86	DWSLP 3566	SILICON VALLEY	£15

DE WOLFE "IN EDITIONS" SERIES

76	Timing 14	CRADLE OF TIME	£50

DAY & HUNTER

68	FDH LP 1018	DIPLOMATIC IMMUNITY	£70
68	FDH LP 1019	SPECTRUM OF COLOUR	£20
68	FDH LP 1020	PROGRESSIONS	£20
68	FDH LP 1023	PROECTIONS	£20

HARMONIC

68	CBW 616	SHAKIN' AND SOULIN'	£40
68	CBW 617	NEAR DRAMATIC	£30
69	CBW 622	SUITE IN BEAT AND SUITE IN BLUES	£20
68	CBD 609	BEAT!	£25
68	CBO 613	INDUSTRIAL ESPIONAGE SUITE	£150
68	CBG 610	SWINGING SINGERS	£20
68	CBL 618	FONTEYNS FOLK JAZZ	£20
69	CBL 621	MORE BEAT	£40
69	CBW 598	RONNIE ROSS PLAYS (NO 1)	£200
70	CBW 628	BEAT DRAMA	£30
71	CBO 640	STUDIES IN DRAMA	£20
71	CBW 637	DRAMA IN RHYTHM	£50
72	CBO 654	CITY VISIT	£40
73	CBO 665	WEIGHTY AND SOLID	£40
71	CBW 639	PSYCHO SOUL AND DRAMATIC ORCHESTRAL SUITE	£100
72	CBW 659	STUDIES FOR GUITAR AND DRAMA BEAT	£40
72	CBW 660	THEMES IN BEAT	£100
72	CBJ 674	SYNTHETICS	£40
76	CBJ 670	SYNTHETRONICS	£70
76	CBD 671	A GOOD MUSIC	£25
76	CBG 672	MODERN DRAMATIC ACTIONS	£40
76	CBG 674	UNDERSCORES	£20

HUDSON

71	HMC LP 501	ROCKING TEMPO (PETER MERRICK)	£15
71	HMC LP 502	INVENTION (PAUL KASS)	£15
71	HMC LP 503	SIT BACK	£20
71	HMC LP 504	CLASSICAL COLOURS (REG TILSLEY)	£15
72	HMC LP 505	FRIENDLY FACE (P RENO)	£20
72	HMC LP 506	MINDBINDER (PETER MERRICK)	£50
72	HMC LP 507	DRAMATURGY/COSMOGONY (PAUL LEMEL)	£40
74	HMC LP 508	THIS IS BRASS (J. TROMBEY)	£15
74	HMC LP 509	EMPTY HORIZONS (PIERRE ARVAY)	£40
74	HMC LP 510	CHICKEN WIRE AND HEN'S NEXT	£20
74	HMC LP 511	HOT BREATH (PETER RENO/REG TILSLEY)	£40
74	HMC LP 512	PRESTIGE LINE (NICK INGMAN/GRAHAM PRESKETT)	£30
75	HMC LP 513	BLOOD ON THE FLOWERS (PRESTON JAMES)	£80
76	HMC LP 514	STEPPING QUICK (R WALE)	£15
76	HMC LP 516	CLASSICAL INTERLUDE (SIMON PARK)	£15
76	HMC LP 517	DECISIVE ACTION (KEITH PAPWORTH)	£50
79	HMC LP 518	DIMPLES (SOHO JAZZ GROUP)	£20
79	HMC LP 519	NETWORK (COMPLEX STUDIO GROUP)	£15
79	HMC LP 521	WORK IN - WALK OUT	£20

MINT VALUE £

79	HMC LP 523	BLUEPRINT (TAKE SIX)	£50
80	HMC LP 524	DAWN OF MAN	£15
80	HMC LP 525	BLACK SUN	£20
81	HMC LP 528	CHAMPAGNE COCKTAIL	£15
81	HMC LP 527	HEADLINE	£20
81	HMC LP 529	VIEWPOINT	£15
82	HMC LP 530	WHODUNNIT?	£15
82	HMC LP 531	AWAYDAY (PETER FENN)	£15
82	HMC LP 532	ACROSS THE BOARD (TREVOR BROWN)	£15
82	HMC LP 533	SUNNY SIDE UP (TAKE SIX)	£15
82	HMC LP 534	SLAVE DRIVER (BLUE STEEL)	£15
83	HMC LP 535	PRIDE OF THE TOWN (KEITH PAPWORTH)	£15
83	HMC LP 536	SWINGS AND ROUNDABOUTS	£15
83	HMC LP 537	MIXED SELLS (ASTRAL SOUNDS)	£15
83	HMC LP 538	PORTRAITS IN SOUND	£15
83	HMC LP 539	JONAH SYMPHONIA	£15

JW THEME MUSIC

70	JW 401	NEW SOUNDS FOR FLUTE, PERCUSSION AND SYNTHESISER (Bob Downes)	£125
72	JW 402	ELECTRONIA/HAIR RAISERS (W. Merrick Farran/Edgar M. Vetter/T. Elerth)	£60
73	JW 403	BE DAZZED/MAKE RHYTHM (Albert Mayer/Don Harper)	£40
74	JW 404	FACES OF FUNK (Chunky Junket)	£40
74	JW 405	TUNE IN - DROP OUT (Kelly's Eye)	£80
74	JW 406	STRINGS GO POP/BRASS & STRING BAG (Don Harper)	£100
74	JW 407	MILITARY BAND/BRASS BAND (The Band of the Scots Guards)	£15
74	JW 408	HORNS IN RHYTHM - ON THE CLASSICAL BEAT (Paul Lewis)	£15
76	JW 409	SOFT SELL (Reg Wale)	£15
76	JW 410	THE ELECTRIC STRINGMOBILE (Peter Thomas)	£30
76	JW 411	EASY COME, EASY GO (Sam Fonteyn)	£15
76	JW 412	RENT-A-MOOD! (Toni Campo)	£60
77	JW 413	EL PIANO (Ray Davies)	£30
77	JW 414	FLAVOUR OF THE MONTH (Geoff Bastow)	£60
77	JW 415	SWINGS AND ROUNDABOUTS (Vic Flick)	£20
78	JW 416	ALL THE ARABIAS (Ali Ishfahan/George Fraid)	£35
78	JW 417	IDENTI-KIT (John Leach & George Fenton)	£15
79	JW 418	WIDE REPERCUSSIONS (Johnny Dean/Eric Allen)	£15
79	JW 419	PHOTO-FIT (John Leach & George Fenton)	£20
79	JW 420	TRADEWINDS (Jim Parker)	£15
79	JW 421	RHYTHM AND BRASS (Ray Davies)	£20
80	JW 422	ELECTRIC LIGHT (John G. Tyssen & Daniele Prencipe)	£35
80	JW 423	KEYBOARD HARMONY (Anthony Mawer)	£20
80	JW 424	MIDAS TOUCH (Melting Pot)	£40
80	JW 425	TOOLS OF THE TRADE (Dave Richmond & Harold Fisher)	£25
80	JW 426	FURTHER REPERCUSSIONS (Johnny Dean)	£15
80	JW 427	SOUND WAVES (F.Brian)	£15

KPM

66	KPM 1001	THE MOOD MODERN	£20
66	KPM 1002	THE SOUNDS OF SYD DALE	£50
66	KPM 1003	THE BACKGROUNDS	£15
66	KPM 1004	COLOURED STRINGS	£30
66	KPM 1004	SACRED MUSIC	£35
66	KPM 1006	LIGHT INTIMATIONS 1	£20
66	KPM 1007	LIGHT INTIMATIONS 2	£25
66	KPM 1008	A DISTINCTIVE APPROACH	£20
66	KPM 1009	ACCENT ON PERCUSSION	£30
66	KPM 1010	HAPPY FAMILIES	£25
66	KPM 1011	ORIGINAL APPLICATION OF THE AUGMENTED STRING QUARTET	£15
66	KPM 1012	LIGHTWEIGHT BACKGROUNDS	£25
67	KPM 1013	HARP SOLOS	£15
67	KPM 1014	ALL THAT JAZZ	£40
67	KPM 1015	THE SOUND OF POP	£50
67	KPM 1016	PLEASURE SPECTACLE	£20
67	KPM 1017	IMPACT AND ACTION	£40
67	KPM 1018	TENSION AND SUSPENSE	£30
67	KPM 1019	COMEDY	£15
67	KPM 1020	TWENTIETH CENTURY PORTRAIT	£15
68	KPM 1021	LIGHT JAZZ FEELING	£30
68	KPM 1022	SUITE FOR HORN, WOODWIND AND STRINGS	£15
68	KPM 1024	SERIAL STRUCTURES	£15
68	KPM 1066	PROCESS AND PRESTIGE/FOURTH DIMENSION	£20
68	KPM 1024	IT'S ABOUT TIME	£20
68	KPM 1026	ORCHESTRAL KALEIDOSCOPE	£25
68	KPM 1027	SOUL ORGAN SHOWCASE	£75
68	KPM 1028	MINIATURE MOODS	£15
68	KPM 1029	COLOURS IN RHYTHM	£40
68	KPM 1030	BAR PIANO	£15
68	KPM 1031	MUSIC OF THE NATIONS - ARABIC/ASIAN/ORIENTAL	£40
68	KPM 1032	JAZZ ORCHESTRAL	£30
68	KPM 1033	MASQUERADE	£15

68	KPM 1035	UNDERSCORE	£80
68	KPM 1036	GENTLE SOUNDS	£15
68	KPM 1037	FLAMBOYANT THEMES	£60
68	KPM 1038	FLAMBOYANT THEMES VOL. 2	£60
68	KPM 1039	LIGHT INTIMATIONS 3	£15
68	KPM 1040	THEME SUITES VOL. 2	£18
69	KPM 1041	FLAMBOYANT THEMES VOL. 3	£30
69	KPM 1042	JAZZ GRAPHICS/SPY SET	£50
69	KPM 1043	BEAT INCIDENTAL	£80
69	KPM 1044	THE BIG BEAT (Mohawks & Alan Hawkshaw)	£200
69	KPM 1045	CHILDREN AND ANIMATION	£30
69	KPM 1046	SOUNDS IN PERCUSSION	£30
69	KPM 1043	SINGLE INSTRUMENTS VOL 1 - PERCUSSION	£40
69	KPM 1048	TWO HARPSICHORD/TWO ELIZABETHAN SUITES	£20
66	KPM/ACW1	MUSIC FOR YOUR MOVIES	£20
68	KPM INT 001	JAZZ CONVENTION VOLUME I	£80
68	KPM INT 002	JAZZ CONVENTION VOLUME II	£175
68	KPM INT 004	JAZZ CONVENTION VOLUME III	£200
69	KPM 1051	LIGHT INTIMATIONS VOL. IV	£20
69	KPM 1049	CHORUS AND ORCHESTRA (SYD DALE)	£100
69	KPM 1050	NATURE STUDY	£15
69	KPM 1052	CHRISTMAS PARTY	£15
69	KPM 1053	NATIVE AFRICA	£25
69	KPM 1054	NATIVE AFRICA	£30
70	KPM 1055	DRAMATIC BACKGROUND	£40
70	KPM 1056	UNDERSCORE VOL. 2	£50
70	KPM 1057	SCENE SETTERS - FANFARES AND PUNCTUATIONS	£20
70	KPM 1058	GENTLE SOUNDS VOL. 2	£30
70	KPM 1059	GENTLE SOUNDS VOL. 3	£30
70	KPM 1060	OPEN AIR	£20
69	KPM 1061	IMPACT AND ACTION VOL. 2	£50
70	KPM 1062	ON THE LIGHTER SIDE	£25
70	KPM 1063	CONTEMPORARY COLOUR	£40
70	KPM 1064	HAPPY NOVELTIES	£15
70	KPM 1065	FLAMBOYANT THEMES VOL. 4	£40
70	KPM 1067	THE BIG BEAT VOL. 2	£200
70	KPM 1068	THE HERITAGE OF MAN/TEXTURES FOR STRING QUINTET, KEYBOARD AND PERCUSSION	£18
70	KPM 1069	THE CONTEMPORARY ORCHESTRA/INTERFUSIONS	£15
70	KPM 1070	BUGALOO IN BRAZIL	£100
70	KPM 1071	THE BRAZILIAN SUITE	£150
70	KPM 1072	THE GUITAR FAMILY	£15
70	KPM 1073	CONTEMPORARY GUITAR	£15
70	KPM 19074	MARCHES FOR ANY OCCASION	£15
70	KPM 1075	MUSIC IN A SERIOUS VEIN/MUSIC IN A LIGHTER VEIN	£20
70	KPM 1076	SPEED AND EXCITEMENT	£80
70	KPM 1077	PROGRESSIVE POP	£80
70	KPM 1078	SWEET GROOVE	£30
71	KPM 1083	PIANO COCKTAIL	£15
71	KPM 1079	BEAT INDUSTRIAL	£50
71	KPM 1080	BEAT INCIDENTAL	£50
71	KPM 1080	FLUTE FOR MODERNS	£60
71	KPM 1081	CARTOON CAPERS	£20
71	KPM 1082	THE BRASS FAMILY	£15
71	KPM 1085	ELECTRONIC MUSIC	£50
72	KPM 1084	MEDITERRANEAN INTRIGUE/MARTENOT	£60
71	KPM 1086	MUSIC FOR A YOUNG GENERATION	£60
71	KPM 1087	TECHNICAL STANDPOINT/SPICE OF LIFE	£30
71	KPM 1088	BASS GUITAR AND PERCUSSION	£80
71	KPM 1089	BASS GUITAR AND PERCUSSION - VOLUME 2	£60
71	KPM 1090	BASS GUITAR AND PERCUSSION - VOLUME 3	£30
71	KPM 1091	VIBRAPHONE JAZZ QUARTET	£25
71	KPM 1092	TODAYS ACHIEVEMENTS/TOPICAL EVENTS	£20
71	KPM 1093	THE WORLD OF JOHNNY SCOTT	£15
71	KPM 1094	ACCENT ON PERCUSSION/CONSTRUCTION IN JAZZ	£50
71	KPM 1095	THEME SUITES/MUSTANG	£60
71	KPM 1097	JAZZROCK	£60
72	KPM 1098	PROGRESS AND PRESTIGE VOLUME 2	£18
72	KPM 1099	OPEN AIR - VOLUME 2	£15
72	KPM 1100	THE BIG SCREEN	£20
72	KPM 1101	A MOOG FOR ALL REASONS	£30
72	KPM 1102	ELECTROSOUND	£80
72	KPM 1103	ELECTROMUSIC	£30
72	KPM 1104	ELECTROSONIC	£75
72	KPM 1105	MEDIEVAL MUSIC	£15
72	KPM 1106	WOODWIND AND HARPSICHORD	£15
72	KPM 1107	HARPSICHORD OLD AND NEW	£15
72	KPM 1108	THE SOLO HARP	£15

			MINT VALUE £
72	KPM 1109	THE MAGIC OF BOUCHETY	£20
72	KPM 1110	LIFE IS FOR LIVING	£30
72	KPM 1111	BRASS PLUS MOOG	£50
72	KPM 1112	THE RHYTHM OF MODERN LIFE/VAUDEVILLE	£15
72	KPM 1113	PERCUSSION WORKSHOP	£20
73	KPM 1118	THE HUMAN TOUCH	£25
73	KPM 1119	LOOK ON THE BRIGHT SIDE	£20
73	KPM1120	DAYBREAK	£40
73	KPM 1121	FUSION - CONTEMPORARY STYLES IN ELECTRO-POP	£80
73	KPM 1122	MOVE WITH THE TIMES	£60
73	KPM 1123	FRIENDLY FACES	£40
73	KPM 1173	HAPPY RAINBOWS	£25
73	KPM 1124	BIG BUSINESS	£80
73	KPM 1125	VOICES IN HARMONY	£200
73	KPM 1126	SUMMER SONGBIRDS	£60
73	KPM 1128	COUNTERPOINT IN RHYTHM	£40
73	KPM 1129	THE CONTEMPORARY HARP	£20
73	KPM 1130	AFRO ROCK	£200
73	KPM 1131	TRENDSETTERS	£50
73	KPM 1132	SYNTHESIS	£100
73	KPM 1133	ANIMATION PLAYTIME	£15
74	KPM 1134	CHILDOOD	£15
74	KPM 1135	DISCOTHEQUE	£30
74	KPM 1136	INDUSTRIAL PANORAMA	£100
74	KPM 1137	GREAT EXPECTATIONS	£35
74	KPM 1138	GATHERING CROWDS	£20
74	KPM 1139	HAPPY HEARTS	£20
74	KPM 1140	SOFT HORIZONS	£18
74	KPM 1141	IMAGES	£125
74	KPM 1142	WOODWIND	£15
74	KPM 1143	SUSPENDED WOODWIND	£30
74	KPM 1151	COME DANCING	£15
74	KPM 1152	SOUND ODYSSEY	£20
74	KPM 1153	ELECTRONIC LIGHT ORCHESTRA	£20
74	KPM 1154	ELECTROSOUND VOLUME 2	£60
74	KPM 1155	A MOOG FOR MORE REASONS	£30
75	KPM 1156	METROPOLIS	£70
75	KPM 1157	THE HUNTER/ADVENTURE SUITE	£100
75	KPM 1158	FLAMBOYANT THEMES VOL. 5	£20
75	KPM 1159	THE PLEASURES OF LIFE	£60
75	KPM 1160	FRIENDS AND LOVERS	£50
75	KPM 1161	INDUSTRY VOL 1	£50
75	KPM 1162	INDUSTRY VOL 2	£40
75	KPM 1163	ROCK SPECTRUM	£50
75	KPM 1164	LOONY TUNES	£15
75	KPM 1165	A JAZZ INCLINATION	£40
75	KPM 1166	PIANO VIBERATIONS	£75
75	KPM 1167	OUTDOOR LIFE	£18
75	KPM 1168	DRAMATIC ACTION	£100
75	KPM 1169	ARP ODYSSEY	£30
75	KPM 1170	SOUNDS OF THE TIME	£75
75	KPM 1171	IMPACT AND ACTION	£60
76	KPM 1172	VISUAL IMPACT	£100
76	KPM 1173	SOLID GOLD	£40
76	KPM 1174	AMUSEMENT	£50
76	KPM 1175	LOVES THEMES	£40
76	KPM 1176	CHARTBUSTERS	£18
76	KPM 1177	HOT WAX	£80
76	KPM 1178	CARICATURE	£20
76	KPM 1179	ORCHESTRAL CONTRASTS	£25
76	KPM 1180	TENDER EMOTIONS	£30
76	KPM 1181	SILVER BAND	£15
76	KPM 1182	TRADITIONAL FOLK MUSIC OF GREAT BRITAIN AND FRANCE	£15
77	KPM 1183	MIDDLE EAST SUITE/INDIA	£40
77	KPM 1184	GEMINI SUITE	£20
77	KPM 1185	THE STRING FAMILY	£15
77	KPM 1187	THE NATURE OF WOODWIND	£15
77	KPM 1188	CONTEMPO	£100
77	KPM 1189	DISTINCTIVE THEMES/RACE TO ACHIEVEMENT	£150
77	KPM 1190	VIVID UNDERSCORES	£75
77	KPM 1191	LANDSCAPES/THINGS TO COME/NEW INNOVATIONS SUITE	£15
77	KPM 1192	THE ROAD FORWARD	£100
77	KPM 1193	CLASSICAL SYNTHESIZER/STAINED GLASS WINDOWS	£18
77	KPM 1194	BIG CITY SUITE/JINGLE JANGLE JINGLES	£60
77	KPM 1195	MUSIC SUITES VOL. 1	£20
77	KPM 1196	ROCK ON	£50
77	KPM 1197	INDUSTRY VOL 3	£20
77	KPM 1198	THE LIGHTER SIDE/LIFE OF LEISURE	£25

77	KPM 1199	THE CLASSICAL HARP	£20
77	KPM 1120	DAYBREAK	£40
77	KPM 1214	PULSE OF THE CITY	£15

PEER INTERNATIONAL

69	PIL 9001	THE GOOD WORD	£25
70	PIL 9002	PACE-SETTER	£20
70	PIL 9003	STRING SCENE	£20
70	PIL 9004	SOUL OF A CITY	£40
70	PIL 9005	INTER RELATION	£30
70	PIL 9006	MY THING (Sven Libaek And His Orchestra)	£250
70	PIL 9007	SOUND OF MEXICO	£18
71	PIL 9008	COMBUSTION	£30
71	PIL 9009	BIG HAMMER	£100
71	PIL 9010	DELMA	£15
71	PIL 9011	THE WORLD OVER	£15
71	PIL 9012	NO WAITING	£20
72	PIL 9013	MINDBENDER	£500
72	PIL 9014	ZENITH	£30
72	PIL 9015	SUN SEEKER	£20
72	PIL 9016	GEMINI	£35
73	PIL 9017	CONTRASTS IN JAZZ VOL 1	£15
73	PIL 9018	CONTRASTS IN JAZZ VOL 2	£25
73	PIL 9019	CONTRASTS IN JAZZ VOL 3	£35
73	PIL 9021	FLIP TOP	£30
73	PIL 9023	REGGAE FOR REAL	£250
74	PIL 9024	CONFRONTATION	£25
74	PIL 9025	SWEET SURPRISE	£20
74	PIL 9026	SOLAR FLARES	£350
74	PIL 9027	ELECTRIC BAZAAR	£150
75	PIL 9028	SCOOP!	£200
76	PIL 9029	FIVE PLUS FOUR	£200
76	PIL 9030	FREE DIMENSION	£20
76	PIL 9032	TRENDY	£15
76	PIL 9034	EARTH SHAKER	£70
76	PIL 9035	TIME OF YOUR LIFE	£20
76	PIL 9036	ROCK ALLEGRO	£20
77	PIL 9037	HIT MAN	£100
77	PIL 9038	HANGOVER	£100
78	PIL 9039	LOST STAR	£200
79	PIL 9040	POINT BLANK	£40
80	PIL 9042	PRETTY POSE	£20
80	PIL 9043	WORKFORCE	£60
80	PIL 9042	CENTRAL PARK	£15

PROGRAMME MUSIC

73	Programme PM 001	BEATS & BALLADS	£25
73	Programme PM 002	CONTRASTS	£30
74	Programme PM 003	SHADES OF ROCK	£25
74	Programme PM 004	FACES OF FUNK	£30
74	Programme PM 005	HARMONY GRASS/REGGAE	£25
74	Programme PM 006	DESIGN IN BRASS AND SILVER	£20
75	Programme PM 007	STRICTLY FOR THE BIRDS AND STRAIGHT DOWN THE MIDDLE	£25
75	Programme PM 008	ON THE SIDE OF THE ANGELS	£35
75	Programme PM 011	MUSIC TO VARNISH OWLS BY	£100
75	Programme PM 009	FURTHER FACES	£40
75	Programme PM 010	MORE THAN SOMEWHAT!	£25
75	Programme PM 012	LIGHT AND SHADE	£25
75	Programme PM 013	SHEER ENJOYMENT	£25
75	Programme PM 014	A HUNDRED AND ONE GUITARS	£20
76	Programme PM 015	DOUBLE EXPOSURE	£40
77	Programme PM 016	ROCK REFLECTIONS	£15
77	Programme PM 017	GUITAR BREAK	£18
77	Programme PM 019	MEDIUM - RARE	£40
78	Programme PM 020	HARD CORE...SOFT CENTRE	£18
78	Programme PM 022	CHOICE MORSELS	£25
78	Programme PM 023	TAKE YOUR PICK!	£15
79	Programme PM 024	LUCKY NUMBERS	£18
79	Programme PM 025	HEY DISCO!	£120
79	Programme PM 026	SUPERTRAX	£20

REGENCY LINE

75	RL 1001	LIGHT BACKGROUND VOL 1.	£20
75	RL 1002	THEMES	£30
75	RL 1003	ROCK	£30
75	RL 1004	BOLIVIAN CARNIVAL	£40
75	RL 1005	LATIN POP	£30
75	RL 1006	MUSIQUE MEDIEVALE	£15
75	RL 1007	HARPSICHORD	£20
75	RL1008	SYNTHESIZER SPOTS	£30

MINT VALUE £

75	RL 1009	HARMONICA	£18
75	RL 1010	HEAVY ROCK	£60
75	RL 1011	WESTERN MUSIC	£15
75	RL 1012	FESTIVAL OF BRASS	£15
75	RL 1013	DRAMATIC MOODS	£40
75	RL 1014	LIGHT BACKGROUND VOL II	£15
75	RL 1015	THEMES VOL II	£35
75	RL 1016	SAMPLER	£15
75	RL 1017	FLUTE AND SAX	£30
75	RL 1018	PLAYTIME	£20
76	RL1019	THE DETECTIVES	£40
76	RL 1020	BITS 'N' PIECES	£20
76	RL1021	ROCKIN IN RHYTHM	£50
76	RL1022	HAPPY HOLIDAY	£60
76	RL 1023	STRANGE!!!	£20
76	RL 1024	GRECIAN ADVENTURE/GYPSY	£15
76	RL 1025	ROCK 'N' ROLL	£15
76	RL 1026	SPORT	£15
76	RL1027	LATE NIGHT MUSIC	£30
76	RL1028	DISCO HAPPENING	£40
77	RL 1029	PALM COURT	£15
77	RL 1030	NEWS!!!	£15
77	RL 1031	CLASSICAL GUITAR	£15
77	RL 1033	HAPPY GUITAR	£15
77	RL 1034	CHINESE	£15
77	RL 1036	TENSION UNLIMITED	£80

ROUGE MUSIC

75	RMS LP 101	SKYBOAT	£25
75	RMS LP 102	SWEET SOUL	£30
75	RMS LP 103	INTERLACE	£30
75	RMS LP 104	THE KING AND THE CLOWN	£30
75	RMS 105	HI-FLY	£30
75	RMS LP 106	BLACKOUT	£150
76	RMS LP 107	RETURN TO BASE	£15
76	RMS LP 108	COBRA	£40
77	RMS LP 109	MEAL TICKET	£60
77	RMS LP 110	MUSIC REPORT	£60
77	RMS LP 111	KITES	£20
77	RMS LP 112	LET THE MUSIC PLAY	£20
78	RMS LP 113	HARD AS ROCK	£20
79	RMS LP 114	SOFT AND TENDER	£15
78	RMS LP 115	DO IT	£25
78	RMS LP 116	FADED JEANS	£15
78	RMS LP 117	ALL ABOUT THE SEA	£15
78	RMS LP 118	DISCOS LIKE THIS	£40
79	RMS LP 119	PULSES	£30
79	RMS LP 120	CANDOUR	£20
79	RMS LP 121	FRIDAY GIRL	£25
79	RMS LP 122	ROBOT DANCER	£40
80	RMS LP 124	COUNTRY GRASS	£15
81	RMS LP 125	MAKING TRACKS	£15
81	RMS LP 126	PATTERNS	£50
81	RMS LP 127	DANCING GRASS	£15
81	RMS LP 128	IMPETUS	£15
81	RMS LP 129	PLAY ON	£20
81	RMS LP 130	GLASS HEAD	£25
81	RMS LP 131	SPERDOUP	£35
81	RMS LP 132	SLICED APPLE	£30
81	RMS LP 133	PIPSQUEEK	£15
81	RMS LP 134	WHISPER TO THE MOON	£15
81	RMS LP 135	HISTORY OF JAZZ	£15
82	RMS LP 136	TELETEXT	£35
82	RMS LP 137	VOYAGE OF DISCOVERY	£15
82	RMS LP 138	MOVEMENT	£25
82	RMS LP 140	INSTANT REGGAE	£18
82	RMS LP 141	HERCULES	£15
82	RMS LP 142	RED KITE	£40
82	RMS LP 143	NEW AGE	£15
82	RMS LP 144	REMEMBER	£15
82	RMS LP 145	DRUMATICS	£20
83	RMS LP 147	CUTAWAY	£20
83	RMS LP 148	SOLARIUM	£20
83	RMS LP 149	SOME SHUFFLIN'	£15
83	RMS LP 150	BASS MOODS VOL 1	£20
83	RMS LP 151	BASS MOODS VOL 2	£20
83	RMS LP 152	UNDERCOVER	£30
84	RMS LP 153	TOMORROW, TODAY	£18
84	RMS LP 154	SNEAKING UP	£18

84	RMS LP 157	BREAKDANCE	£20
84	RMS LP 158	TOPSY TURVY	£15
85	RMS LP 159	AHEAD OF THE FIELD	£15
85	RMS LP 160	NEW OUTLOOK	£15
86	RMS LP 161	REFLEX	£15
86	RMS LP 162	REFLEX (REMIXES)	£15
85	RMS LP 165	SOUND ON SOUND	£15
86	RMS LP 168	AUDIOTRONICS	£15
86	RMS LP 170	REGGAE INVASION	£30
86	RMS LP 169	HIGHLIGHTS	£15
87	RMS LP 173	PACW AGE	£15
87	RMS LP 175	CHANGING SEASONS	£25
87	RMS LP 178	KINETICS	£20

SOUNDS OF NOW

71	Sounds Of Now 1	SOUNDS OF NOW (ERIC SIDAY)	£50
71	Sounds Of Now 2	SOUNDS OF NOW 2 (ERIC SIDAY)	£75
72	Sounds Of Now 3	SOUNDS OF NOW 2 (PAUL DUNLAP)	£100

SOUTHERN MUSIC

66	MQLP 19	ELECTRONIC MUSIC	£20
68	MQLP 27	THE SCOTTMEN	£20
70	MQLP 47	JAZZ BEAT/JAZZ BEAT BOSSA NOVA	£30
71	MQLP 32	JAZZ DRAMATIC	£30
72	MQLP 38	ELECTRONIC MUSIC	£75
72	MQLP 39	AFRO SPOOKY	£200
73	MQLP 40	ELECTRONIC MUSIC	£30
78	MQLP 48	Electronic Music	£75
78	MQLP 51	EXOTICA	£30

STANDARD

70	ESL 196	NATIONAL BALKAN ENSEMBLE	£20
74	ESL 127	ELECTRONIC MUSIC	£70
75	ESL 133	ENCORE ELECTRONIC	£40
69	ESL 103	SOLO GUITAR (Michael Chapman)	£60
00	ESL 104	ELECTRONIC MUSIC	£100

STUDIO G

70	LPSG 1001	BEAT GROUP	£80
70	LPSG 1002	BIG JAZZ AND BIG BEAT	£25
70	LPSG 1003	LIGHT JAZZ	£25
70	LPSG 1004	ANIMALS AND CHILDREN	£20
70	LPSG 1005	SCENIC AND ROMANCE	£20
70	LPSG 1006	DESCRIPTIVE SUITES VOLUME 1	£20
70	LPSG 1007	INDUSTRIAL AND WAR	£20
70	LPSG 1008	DRAMATIC AND HORROR VOLUME 1	£30
70	LPSG 1009	ELECTRONIC AGE	£70
70	LPSG 1010	LOCATIONS AND COMEDY VOLUME 1	£15
70	LPSG 1011	PERIOD MUSIC AND SOLO INSTRUMENTS	£15
70	LPSG 1012	NATIONAL	£15
74	LPSG 2001	DISCO BEAT	£40
74	LPSG 2002	COOL BEAT	£60
74	LPSG 2003	LIGHT MOVEMENT VOLUME 2	£15
74	LPSG 2004	ANIMALS AND CHILDREN VOLUME 2	£20
74	LPSG 2005	SCENIC AND ROMANCE VOLUME 2	£20
74	LPSG 2006	DESCRIPTIVE	£15
74	LPSG 2007	INDUSTRIAL AND WAR VOLUME 2	£15
74	LPSG 2008	DRAMA AND HORROR VOLUME 2	£20
74	LPSG 2009	AVANT GARDE	£75
74	LPSG 2010	LOCATIONS AND COMEDY VOLUME 2	£15
74	LPSG 2011	PERIOD MUSIC VOLUME 2	£15
74	LPSG 2012	NATIONAL - VOLUME 2	£15
76	LPSG 3001	POP SPECTRUM VOLUME 3	£40
76	LPSG 3002	BEAT UNDERSCORE	£80
76	LPSG 3003	THEMATIC MUSIC VOLUME 3	£15
76	LPSG 3004	ANIMALS AND CHILDREN VOLUME 3	£15
78	LPSG 3005	TRAVEL AND ROMANCE VOLUME 3	£15
78	LPSG 3006	MUSIC FOR STRINGS	£15
78	LPSG 3007	RHYTHM - INDUSTRIAL UNDERSCORE - VOLUME 3	£250
78	LPSG 3008	DRAMA AND HORROR VOLUME 3	£40
78	LPSG 3009	MUSIC FOR SYNTHESIZERS	£40
78	LPSG 3010	LOCATIONS AND COMEDY VOLUME 3	£15
78	LPSG 3012	MUSIC OF THE MIDDLE EAST	£25
79	LPSG 4001	ACTION DISCO	£60
81	LPSG 4002	IMAGES	£40
81	LPSG 4003	TITLE MUSIC	£15
80	LPSG 4004	ABSTRACTS	£40
82	LPSG 4005	NATURES WORLD	£40
82	LPSG 4008	JAZZ FUNK ROAD	£15

STUDIO ONE

71	SO7	MAURICE POP	£15

MINT VALUE £

| 73 | SO14 | PIERRE LAVIN POP BAND | £30 |

SYLVESTER MUSIC

67	SMC/LP501	JAZZ WAVES (10")	£25
67	SMC/LP502	VOICES IN THE WIND (10")	£30
67	SMC/LP503	STRIPTEASE (10")	£15
67	SMC/LP504	AQUAPLANE (10")	£20
67	SMC/LP505	ZENITH (10")	£30
67	SMC/LP506	TUTTI FLUTTI (10")	£20
67	SMC/LP507	GO (10")	£20
68	SMC/LP508	KIKI (10")	£20
68	SMC/LP509	CONTEMPORARY ARTS (10")	£15
68	SMC/LP510	EMBARGO (10")	£20
68	SMC/LP511	RHYTHM FOR URSULA (10")	£20
68	SMC/LP512	EXCHANGES (10")	£20
68	SMC/LP513	SILHOUETTES	£20
68	SMC/LP514	HEMISPHERE (10")	£15
68	SMC/LP515	AND SO ON... (10")	£20
68	SMC/LP516	RACING TEMPO (10")	£15
68	SMC/LP517	PHILOSOPHALE (10")	£20
68	SMC/LP518	IMAGES MUSICALES NO 1	£15
69	SMC/LP519	CHATEAU (10")	£15
69	SMX/LP520	PLAQUES TORNANTES (10")	£50
69	SMC/LP521	PRAELUDIUM (10")	£15
69	SMC/LP522	THE MUSIC OF ERIC TOWREN	£15
70	SMC/LP523	PICTURES OF CHILDREN	£20
70	SMC/LP524	ACTION	£20
70	SMC/LP525	JAZZ FOR ACTION	£35
71	SMC/LP526	POST COMBUSTION	£25
71	SMC/LP527	BLUE CYLINDER	£30
71	SMC/LP528	CHRONORADIAL	£20
71	SMC/LP529	ULTRA POP-UP	£60
71	SMC/LP530	MOODS AND MARCHES	£15
71	SMC/LP531	RAGGERS	£35
71	SMC/LP532	BEFORE OR AFTER	£40
71	SMC/LP533	FILIGREE	£15
72	SMC/LP534	LIFE STORY	£20
72	SMC/LP535	STROLL THROUGH BRAZIL	£15
72	SMC/LP536	PATCHWORK ORCHESTRA VOLUME ONE	£25
72	SMC/LP537	PATCHWORK ORCHESTRA VOLUME TWO	£25
72	SMC/LP538	PATCHWORK ORCHESTRA VOLUME THREE	£40
72	SMC/LP539	PATCHWORK ORCHESTRA VOLUME FOUR	£25
72	SMC/LP541	COMMERCIAL SOUNDS	£20
72	SMC/LP542	CITY IN TERROR	£20
74	SMCS/LP544	AQUASUN	£30
79	SMCS/LP555	CHARADE	£30
80	SMCS/LP556	TINTED GLASS	£30
81	SMCS/LP557	BRIGHT AND SHINING	£50

THEMES INTERNATIONAL

73	TIM 1001	THE LIGHTER TOUCH	£20
70	TIM 1002	NEW BLOOD	£80
70	TIM 1003	MAIN THEMES AND SIG TUNES	£30
73	TIM 1006	THE ROMANTIC MOOD	£20
73	TIM 1007	LIGHT ACTIVITY	£20
73	TIM 1008	DRAMATIC ACTION	£40
73	TIM 1009	HAPPY PASTIMES	£20
73	TIM 1011	THE ROCK MACHINE	£50
74	TIM 1012	SYNTHESIZER AND PERCUSSION	£100
74	TIM 1013	BREATH OF DANGER	£60
74	TIM 1014	FREEDOM ROAD	£35
74	TIM 1015	MYSTERY MOVIE	£100
76	TIM 1017	ROCK COMEDY	£30
75	TIM 1018	THE ALL AMERICAN POWERHOUSE	£100
76	TIM 1019	JE T'AIME	£70
76	TIM 1020	PAN AMERICAN TRAVELOGUE	£70
76	TIM 1021	THE VOICE OF SOUL	£175
76	TIM 1022	THE SOUND OF SOUL	£100
76	TIM 1023	PULSE OF EVENTS	£80
76	TIM 1024	DRAMA SUITE VOL 1	£100
76	TIM 1025	DRAMA SUITE PART II	£200
77	TIM 1026	THINGS TO COME	£35
77	TIM 1027	CONTEMPORARY CONTRASTS	£35
79	TIM 1029	PERCUSSION SPECTRUM	£40
78	TIM 1030	LISTEN TO L.A.	£35
78	TIM 1031	HAVE SOUND WILL TRAVEL	£30
78	TIM 1032	STREET PICTURES	£25
78	TIM 1033	KEYTRONICS	£30
78	TIM 1034	WISH YOU WERE HERE	£20
81	TIM 1037	STREET LEVEL	£30

82   TIM 1040   NIGHT SENSATIONS £20

TAX SCAM RECORDS

Back in the late 70s there was a legal loophole that was exploited in America where the potential sales of a record could be legally offset against costs.

This led to the formation of a number of 'tax scam' labels where albums were recorded and pressed up in small numbers with the sole intention of

avoiding tax. There was, as you might imagine, much more to the process than that but the key thing was to make it look as if the record had been

released in order to generate the tax loss that could lead to a profit for the company or investors concerned. As far as we know most of these labels

were confined to America but it appears that Ebonite Records was a label that licensed material to the U.K.. This label then pressed records up with a

view to selling them in the normal legal fashion. These records were, however, all released at once as an advert in Melody Maker in 1978 suggests. There

were over 80 titles. The advert stated "the most extensive collection of hit product to hit the world." This was somewhat far from the truth as many of

the records - that ranged from jazz standards to pop covers - were very poor as the musicians involved (all working under a number of made-up names)

recorded, in some instances, some awful cover versions that - for some reason - went on for several minutes or more in order that the record could be

classed as an LP - even though they were marketed as 12" singles. indeed. It is probably true to suggest that it was quantity rather than quality that was

the order of the day as some records have different artist titles but it is obvious from the playing - and in some cases awful singing - that they were

recorded by the same people at the same session and then spread over different releases. Of course, some of the musicians involved were very good

and turned out slabs of funk/disco/soul that is now sought after and collectable. There are some absolute killers out there and some of the excellent

records put out by Ebonite in the U.K. testify to this. The Returners 12" is a case in point whereas others are so bad that is is not even funny. This list is

not exhaustive as some records were named in that 1978 advert that have, as far as we know, not surfaced - as yet. These artists have mouth watering

names like Blind Faith, Midshipmen, The Bodybuilders, Cabaret, The Short People, The Astronomers, Wrecking Havok and The Earth City Rockers etc.. If

you find any of them or know of any other examples of tax related records pressed for the U.K. please let us know. Finally, although the ultra collectable

DISCO FOX LP was listed in that Melody Maker advert we have yet to see a UK pressing. Those that have surfaced so far have been US pressings.

78	Ebonite EE001	VOYAGE: Watermelon Man/Maiden Voyage (33rpm 12")	£20
78	Ebonite EE003	LOVE MAKERS: Gloria/What's Going On (33rpm 12")	£60
78	Ebonite EE004	AFTER TIME: Itchy Fingers/When Your Lovers Gone/Time After Time/Love For Sale (33rpm 12")	£25
78	Ebonite EE005	BLUESERS: All Blues/Blues In G (33rpm 12")	£20
78	Ebonite EE007	MISTY TIME: Laura/Now's The Time//Misty (33rpm 12")	£18
78	Ebonite EE009	ANYTIME: Do It Any Way You Want To Do It/The World Is A Ghetto (33rpm 12")	£40
78	Ebonite EE010	JOGGERS: Killer Joe/Milestones/The Nearness Of You (33rpm 12")	£20
78	Ebonite EE011	RELATIVITY: Bad Luck/Peace Song/Low Down (33rpm 12")	£30
78	Ebonite EE012	LUMBERJACKS: Lady Bird/Blue Train/Forest Flower (33rpm 12")	£20
78	Ebonite EE019	SOMEBODY: Meditations/There Will Never Be Another You/Everybody Loves Somebody (33rpm 12")	£15
78	Ebonite EE027	CLASS ACT: When The Lights Are Low/The Strut/Stairway To The Stars (33rpn 12").......	£15
78	Ebonite EE028	FINDERS: You'll Never Find/Blues In C/Breezin (33rpm 12")	£15
78	Ebonite EE030	SECRET SERVICE: Maiden Voyage/Secret Love/Bongo Bop (33rpm 12")	£15
78	Ebonite EE037	QUIZMASTERS: If You Want Me To Stay/Fever (33rpm 12")	£30
78	Ebonite EE038	LADY MAKERS: Ain't No Sunshine When She's Gone/East Of The Sun/Mr Luckt (33rpm 12")	£35
78	Ebonite EE043	BARTENDERS: I Love Everything About You/Love Hangover (33rpm 12")	£20
78	Ebonite EE044	STAR RIDERS: Stella By Starlight/Blooz/Cute/It's Yours/Take The A Train (33rpm 12") ...	£15
78	Ebonite EE050	ENGLISH MUSTARD: English Mustard/I Don't Know (33rpm 12")	£15
78	Ebonite EE055	PEPPER SHAKERS: Fever/Shake Your Booty (33rpm 12")	£30
78	Ebonite EE056	SENTIMENTALISTS: Getting Sentimental Over You/Poincianna/Love Walked In (33rpm 12")	£15
78	Ebonite EE065	MICRONIZERS: Tangerine/Mercy Mercy (33rpm 12")	£20
78	Ebonite EE067	G MEN: Somewhere In The Night/You'd Be So Nice To Come Home To/Godfathers Theme/Blues In G (33rpm 12")	£20
78	Ebonite EE069	AMOURIZERS: Our Love Is Here To Stay/Naima (33rpm 12")	£18
78	Ebonite EE072	BUTCHERMEN: Mack The Knife And Other Ditties/Jazzy Rock/Changing Moods (33rpm 12")	£20
78	Ebonite EE074	STOMPERS: Killing Me Softly/Stomping at The Savoy (33rpm 12")................................	£15
78	Ebonite EE077	THE RETURNERS: It Seems That Way/Long Road Back/Here We Go (33rpm 12")............	£50
78	Ebonite EE080	CITY OF ANGELS: Angel Eyes/Au Preavauve/Living For The City (33rpm 12").................	£15
78	Ebonite EE083	WINTER SUN: Baby It's Cold Outside/Sunny Moon For Two/Colors (33rpm 12")...........	£15
78	Ebonite EE086	AFFIRMATIVES: Getting The Prize/This Masquerade (33rpm 12").................................	£20
78	Ebonite EE088	LITTLE SUNFLOWER: Little Sunflower/Hang Up Your Hangups (33rpm 12")	£40
78	Ebonite EE089	WARLOCKS: Witchcraft/Impressions (33rpm 12")..	£30
78	Ebonite EE090	WINEMAKERS: I'm Gonna Love You A Little Bit More/Heard It Through The GrapevineGhetto (33rpm 12")	£25
78	Ebonite EE092	UMBRELLISTICS: Ease On Down The Road/Here's That Rainy Day/Sunny (33rpm 12")....£15	
78	Ebonite EE093	BEATFINDERS: Samba De Orpheo/Walking In Rhythm/Sway (33rpm 12").....................	£25
78	Ebonite EE096	MARKSMEN: Watermelon Man/Disco Queen (33rpm 12")..	£35
78	Ebonite EE104	PERSUASIVE JAZZ: Nicole/Polynesian/Pretty Elizabeth Jane (33rpm 12" in Persuasive Jazz sleeve)..	£40
78	Ebonite EE108	DESTRUCTORS: Sunshine/The Ghetto (33rpm 12")...	£15
78	Ebonite EE115	GROOVERS: Do You Like It/Groovin (33rpm, 12")	£40
78	Ebonite EE148	CHAMELEONS: Chameleon/Sure Is unky/Foot Stompin Music (33rpm 12")	£20
78	Ebonite EE166	LOVE MAGIC: Isn't She Lovely/Superstition (33rpm, 12")..	£40
78	Ebonite EE169	SKY LAW: That's The Way Of The World/Kalimba (33rpm 12")	£30

MINT VALUE £

78	Ebonite EE171	FORAGERS: What's Going On/Grapevine/You're All I Need (33rpm 12")..........................£18
78	Ebonite EE173	SONGSTERS: I'm Gonna Love You A Little Bit More/Sing A Song (33rpm 12") £25
78	Ebonite EE172	MOUNTAIN WOMAN: Ain't No Mountain High Enough/Super Woman (33rpm 12").......£15
78	Ebonite EE 177	SECRET RAINBOW: April In Paris/Secret Love/Somewhere Over The Rainbow (33rpm 12")...£15
78	Ebonite EE179	PSYCHOSIS: Amalgamation/I Mean You/Tenor Madness (33rpm 12")............................£15
78	Ebonite EE181	SEVEN COLOURS: Summertime/Canadian Sunset/Girl Talk (33rpm 12").........................£15
78	Ebonite EE524	INVERTERS: Colours/Nobody Loves You When You're Down And Out (33rpm 12") £15
78	Ebonite EE520	CALENDARS: Like A Rolling Stone/Taxman/Last TIme (33rpm 12") £15
78	Ebonite EE544	MEASURING STICK: I Love Music/How Long Has This Been Going On (33rpm 12").........£25
78	Ebonite EE595	JOG WALKERS: Walking To New Orleans/Life In The Jungle Boogie/California Dreaming (33rpm 12")...£15
78	Ebonite EE605	SANDSTORM: Season Of The Witch/All Along The Watch Tower/Take FIve (33rpm 12")..£15
78	Ebonite EE 1009	THE WORKING MAN: Coming Home/Georgia (33rpm 12")..£15
78	Ebonite EE1016	HEY MEN: Hey Joe/Crossroads (33rpm, 12")...£15
78	Ebonite EE 1001	ESCHALOT: Love Love You/Come On Up (33rpm 12") £15
78	Ebonite EE 5017	INSPECTOR GENERALS: (33rpm 12")..£15
78	Ebonite EE 5021	POLARIZATION: (LP, die cut sleeve) £15
78	Ebonite EE 7010	THE INVISIBLE CHASE: Red House Blues/Catch The Wind/I Want You (33rpm 12")........£18

ACKNOWLEDGEMENTS

MY SINCERE THANKS

Simon Ashley, Mark Burgess, Laurence Cane-Honeysett, John Coleman, Chas Chandler, Graham Hill, Dudley Jaynes, Iain McDermott, Paul & Lee Phelps, Dean & Chris Poole – the work goes on with the website and for next edition already. Thanks to Alan Woodburn. Next time.

FURTHER THANKS FOR SUGGESTIONS, COMMENTS AND VIBES

Mark Adams, Jo Adams, David Barraclough, Steve Burniston, John Chadwick, Johnny Chandler, Paul Despy, Niall Doherty, Charles Donovan, Lee Dorrian, Jules Easlea, Flora Easlea, Billy Edwards, Jerry Ewing, Paul & Karen Fairweather and all the team at Omega, Joe Geesin, Steve Hammonds, Stevie Horton, Alistair Johnson, Jo Kendall, Paul Lester, Dave Lewis, Holly Lippold, Elisabeth Matos, Theo Morgan, Pete Nash, Richard Noller, DJ Miss Twist, Neal Price, Richard Prout, John Reed, Dave Saunders, Dirk Serroels, Andy Spofforth, Stephan Van Zal, Jan Vollaard, Lois Wilson, and without doubt, the wonderful Tom & crew at Southend Record Fair. Marley Tha Dogg, Duncan, Mark & Ian, RIP.

CONSULTANTS, PAST AND PRESENT especially, Billy Albert, Keith Ashford, Keith Badman, Alan Barndale, John Barnjum, Rob Barrs, Mikael Billborn, Pete Bonner, Marco Bonacchi, Greg Brooks, Andy Brooksbank, Colin Carroll, Jeremy Collingwood, Nigel Cook, Augusto Croce, Peter Croxson, Mark Darby, Brian Davis, Nick Farmer, Les Hare, Herve Denoyelle, Frank Deserto, John Esplen, Mark Evetts, Sean Forbes, Douglas Galloway, Roger Gobell, Kevin Goulding, Tim Greenhall, Steve Guntrip, Marco Henning, Al Hine, Sam Hobden, Jason Hodgson, John Hodgson, Dizzy Holmes, Justin Huntley, Max Hooley, Gordon Johnson, Michael Johnson, Sid Johnson, Damien Jones, Mark Jones, Tim Jones, Chris Knight, Freek Kinkelaar, Jake Kennedy, Andrew Lee, Graeme McLagan, John Manship, Haaken Eric Mathiesen, Ian McCann, Joel McIver, Lee Medhurst, Mike at Elista, Howie Moxon, Pol O'Maoleoin, Lorne Murdoch, Andy 'Eau De' Neill, Roscoe Patrol, Chas Pearson, Derek Penny, Stephen Power, Andy Price, Jay Rathbone, Ian Roberts, Barry Smith, Phil Smith, Bob Stoat, Torbjorn Stuhre, Brian Strong, Mitchell Thompson, Jonny Trunk, John Tucker, Peter Vickers, J Walton, Jamie Ward, Ben Watkins, Garry Warren, Martin Webb, Alan Whitaker, Alan Woodburn, Eric White, Robin Wills, Conrad Zimmer. Thanks to users of the online site, readers of *Record Collector* and the electronic collecting community worldwide who also submitted corrections, amendments, or new additions too numerous to list here. **SPECIAL THANKS** to previous editors, contributors and the vast numbers of fanzines, websites, forums and fan clubs whose hard work and expertise has helped – and continues – to make *RCRRPG* what it is today. Finally, all love to Yura & Val and their teams. So greatly appreciated.

PAST MASTERS: THE FORMER EDITORS
HERE'S A LOOK AT THE PEOPLE WHO GOT US THIS FAR

Sean O'Mahony
Founding Editor 1986
Sean O'Mahony was old school. In fact, he was so old school, he was actually the pasture on which the foundation of the education establishment was built. He had an eccentric, maverick spirit and a strong sense of knowing what would sell. The first issue of *Record Collector* included a four-page article on "Collecting Rare Records", featuring everyone from Bowie and Bolan to Sex Pistols and Northern soul. *Record Collector* soon became the bible for vinyl aficionados and for lovers of rock, pop, soul, metal, jazz, folk, noise and blues, old and new. And we owe it all to the gentleman who appeared to have stepped out of the monochrome 60s...
Sean O'Mahony passed away in 2020 at the age of 88.

Peter Doggett
Editor 1987-1993
"I was involved with the *Rare Record Price Guide* from day one, until early this century. In those pre-internet days, you had to find information the hard way – lots of long phone calls to collectors, trying to establish whether a particular record really existed or not. Some of the rarest items were harder to capture than the Loch Ness monster."
Peter Doggett is the esteemed author of many different titles – read all about them here: www.peterdoggett.org/about.

John Reed
Editor 1995-1997
"Working on the original 1993 edition of the *Price Guide* was great fun. Felt like a blank canvas. There'd been the slim A5 orange version (which I'd bought at the time) but this was going to be an altogether heftier proposition. In some ways, pre-internet, we felt that the information itself was as vital as the values. So many records we'd never heard of! Hours were spent on the phone to trusted dealers who were expert in myriad genres. Mind-numbing days thumbing through old record catalogues, label listings, back issues and any other discographies we could lay our hands on. Think it took maybe 18 months but felt like we'd climbed Everest! Later editions seemed much more straightforward. So pleased, decades later, the *RRPG* still sails!"
John Reed is the Director Of Catalogue at Cherry Red Records.

Andy Davis
Editor 1999
"When I joined the company in 1991, I was a natural born list-maker and a callow youth. Half my time was spent on *RC* and the rest helping Research Editor John Reed create the first weighty edition of the *RRPG*. I was given the rear end of the panto horse, P to Z, from Pacific Gas & Electric through to ZZ Top (whose last entry status soon gave way to Zzebra). But it was no pantomime; it was a monumental

and meticulous task. Pre-internet, the research was paper-based and we mined every source available, from retail industry catalogues, to independently-published label listings all the way down to photocopied fanzines. There was no fieldwork but we had an ever expanding network of preferred – sometimes reluctant – record shops and dealers. Whole days were spent on the phone checking facts and debating whether a 7" was worth £4 and an LP £10 (the entry level values) or £5 and £12. Three-figure prices were relatively rare, and we found records worth over £1,000 both eye-popping and mind-boggling; collecting wasn't as dynamic as it is today. Later, I succeeded John and gained my own assistant – Jack Kane. When I was promoted to Editor of the magazine, Jack inherited the RRPG, and his particular and wonderfully peculiar mind lent itself to the task admirably. They were good old days... no, they were pioneering days. Oh yes, they were."

Andy Davis writes and collects, and researches for many Beatles-related projects.

Jack Kane
Editor 2001-2006

Tim Jones, news editor and staff writer for RC, who worked with dear Jack 1998-2005, writes: "Jack Kane was a one-off. Mostly off. Part of his anti-charm. The eccentrically attired Jason King of RC, beneath the bristly surface, he was in-house philosopher/cosmologist/theologian/pronk aficionado, with a wealth of pan-genre knowledge, and the ability to elaborate it with eloquence. Or punch your lights out if you said, "Near-Mint." The standard-setter. Much missed."

Jack died in May 2005.

Ian Shirley
Editor 2008-2024

"I took over the helm of the RRPG after the sad passing of Jack Kane. Back then, everything was done manually on Word documents with experts, dealers and shops submitting price updates and suggestions by marking up copies of previous guides, typed or handwritten lists. My stewardship of the Guide saw the rise of online dealing, sales and trades and the emergence of sites like Popsike, Discogs and eBay sales. Collectors old and young made the transition from shops to online trading as rare record dealing went global. There was then a vinyl revival which saw new shops open and many are now stocked with the latest albums, plus re-pressings and reissues of everything from the Sex Pistols *Never Mind The Bollocks* to Kate Bush's *The Red Shoes*. It's like going into a record shop in the 70s again. I greatly expanded the coverage of the Guide to incorporate more reggae, soul, funk, hip-hop, electronica, shoegaze, dance, disco, indie and collectable areas such as 90s and early 00s vinyl. The Guide got thicker even as I also decreased prices of some 50s and 60s music that had declined in value. I also oversaw the transition of the RRPG to online. Best of all, I set up and managed *Record Collector*'s own vinyl reissue label and some of those records are now rare and in the Guide! I'm proud to have edited the Guide. The aim was simple, to give dealers, experts and the naïve, prices for rare and collectable records pressed in the UK. That way if they were selling their own collection, genres they knew nothing about, or vinyl inherited from a relative, they had a window into the sweetshop of one of the greatest pursuits in the entire world – buying and selling rare records, whether they are worth £30 or £500."

Ian Shirley is production manager at ACE Records and the proprietor of OM Swagger Music.

THE HOME OF VINYL

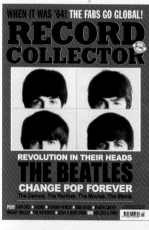

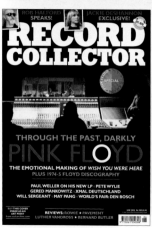

DIGITAL SUBSCRIPTIONS ARE ALSO NOW AVAILABLE

DIGITAL ONLY

- ✓ 13 Issues available on mobile/tablet
- ✓ Save on cover price and international postage price
- ✓ Keep digital copies on your device
- ✓ NEW: Access to the digital archive via the *Record Collector* app

PRINT & DIGITAL BUNDLE

- ✓ 13 Issues delivered to your door
- ✓ 13 Issues available on mobile/tablet
- ✓ Unlimited access to the *Rare Record Price Guide* Online
- ✓ NEW: Access to the digital archive via the *Record Collector* app

SUBSCRIBER BENEFITS INCLUDE

- ✓ Your magazine delivered to your door, or your device, before it hits the shops
- ✓ SAVE on the cover price – up to 30% off
- ✓ EXCLUSIVE offers and discounts on *Record Collector* products and our vinyl range
- ✓ EXCLUSIVE music calendar at Christmas**
- ✓ FREE gift for new subscribers***

SUBSCRIBE NOW

 020 8752 8193 quote code RRPGSA

 shop.recordcollectormag.com/rrpgsa

 subscriptions@metropolis.co.uk

*Based on current cover price and for UK Direct Debit only. Call for other rates.** Print and bundle only.
*** Free gift is for new UK subscribers only. Gift will be posted on receipt of payment. Limited number available.
To claim your free gift please contact us on the above number.

RECORD COLLECTOR BACK ISSUES

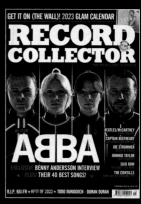

To purchase print copies and for the latest digital/bundle subscription offers visit: shop.recordcollectormag.com Access to the archive of back issues from no. 408 is now available via the *Record Collector* app.

THE HOME OF VINYL

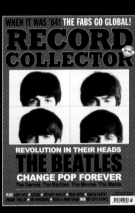

RECORD COLLECTOR'S SPECIAL EDITION

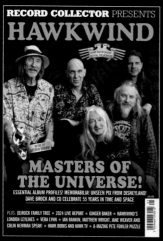

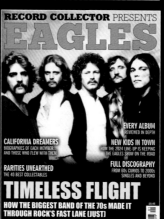